BARRON'S

PROFILES OF AMERICAN COLLEGES

25TH EDITION 2003

Compiled and Edited by the College Division of
Barron's Educational Series

BARRON'S

Opinions and details expressed in articles and profiles in this publication are those of the individual writers and the schools, and do not necessarily reflect those of the publisher.

All inquiries should be addressed to:
Barron's Educational Series, Inc.
250 Wireless Boulevard
Hauppauge, New York 11788
http://www.barronseduc.com

International Standard Book No. 0-7641-1796-3

International Standard Serial No. 1065-5026

PRINTED IN THE UNITED STATES OF AMERICA
9 8 7 6 5 4 3 2

CONTENTS

PREFACE

Barron's *Profiles of American Colleges* is the most all-encompassing, easy-to-use guide available. All four-year institutions that offer bachelor's degrees are described if they are fully accredited or are recognized candidates for accreditation. The comprehensive, concise capsule and detailed essay on each school give an easy-to-absorb, complete picture of the colleges that interest the reader. And the attractive graphic design provides added readability.

The capsule of each profile lists important information for quick reference: address and phone and fax numbers; enrollment; calendar; fall application deadline; size and salary level of the faculty; percentage of faculty members who hold doctorates; student/faculty ratio; tuition and fees; room-and-board costs; the number of students who applied to the freshman class, were accepted, and enrolled; the median SAT* I and/or ACT scores for 2000–2001; and finally, the College Admissions Selector Rating for the school. The information in the essay portion of each profile ranges from available housing and the financial aid climate to admissions requirements and the success of graduates. There are twenty-one categories of information under eight main headings: Student Life, Programs of Study, Admissions, Financial Aid, International Students, Computers, Graduates, and Admissions Contact. The Admissions Contact section also gives Internet addresses and video availability.

We are confident that the features we have added in recent years, along with those that have appeared in previous editions of Barron's *Profiles*, will make this twenty-fifth edition the most thorough guide available to the college-bound student.

A Word of Thanks

To all the college admissions officers, to participating high school advisers, to the students, parents, and other supporters of Barron's *Profiles of American Colleges*, we offer our sincere thanks.

Grateful acknowledgment is made to the late Gloria M. Barron, who inspired the editors and production personnel to create a book that would offer every possible assistance in selecting the best college.

We acknowledge with thanks the demanding editing tasks performed by Senior Editor Max Reed, College Division Coordinator Kathy Ammirati, and Assistants Eileen Seidler, Alison Kaminsky, and Barbara Fuller, along with the database designers and our hardworking editing and keyboarding staff.

CONTRIBUTORS

Steven R. Antonoff, Ph.D.
Educational Consultant
Antonoff Associates, Inc.
Denver, Colorado

Barbara J. Aronson
Career Center Coordinator
Miramonte High School
Orinda, California

Anthony F. Capraro, III, Ph.D.
President, Teach Inc.
College Counseling
Larchmont, New York

Marguerite J. Dennis
Vice President for Development and Enrollment
Suffolk University
Boston, Massachusetts

Benjamin W. Griffith
Former Dean of the Graduate School
West Georgia College
Carrolton, Georgia

Sheldon Halpern
Former Dean
Enrollment Management
Caldwell College
Caldwell, New Jersey

Ira Wolf, Ph.D.
President
PowerPrep, Inc.
Roslyn Heights, New York

*SAT is a registered trademark owned by the College Entrance Examination Board. No endorsement of this product is implied or given.

AN EXPLANATION OF THE BOOK

You have been thinking about going to college within the next couple of years, and now you're convinced that it's time to get somewhat serious about your plans, and take some steps that will lead to your ultimate college decisions, right?

But how do you go about taking these steps? How much does college cost? How can you and your parents afford it? What about entrance exams? How can you possibly know where you want to go and even if you decide *that,* how do you apply with any degree of assurance that you will be accepted? What if you decide, apply, and then get turned down? How can you ensure that *that* doesn't happen? And if you do get past all those hurdles, how can you determine your college major, when you don't have a clue as to what you want to do *after* college?

But right now—where do you begin? In addition to hundreds of two-year schools, there are more than 1600 accredited four-year colleges in the United States, and your options are almost unlimited. But Barron's *Profiles of American Colleges* can point you in the right direction, and help you through the coming months of decision making.

You will find articles that will guide you in evaluating your own needs and interests, selecting the college, filling out the application, writing the essay, having the interview, finding the money, and surviving the freshman year.

There is advice on selecting a major and a career, and the Index of College Majors—a helpful aid for students who want to know which colleges offer the major they have selected. More than 600 majors are listed, along with the in-state costs and the Admissions Selector Rating in easy-to-read columns.

There is advice for international students, as well as a list of schools' in-state costs from least to most expensive. There is also a geographic chart that gives students quick information about schools on a state-by-state basis.

The College Admissions Selector Ratings give applicants an idea of the competition they will encounter when applying to a particular school. And you will find a key to abbreviations and an explanation of the actual college entries.

The heart of the book, of course, is the detailed descriptions of the colleges, including a special section of religious schools that prepare students for careers in the clergy and related fields. The college Profiles are presented alphabetically by state, and the states are also arranged in alphabetical order. Maps of the states begin each chapter. Actually, Barron's *Profiles of American Colleges* covers more than the fifty states; it also describes colleges in the District of Columbia, Puerto Rico, and selected universities in Canada and abroad (along with advice for international students) as well as state and private systems of higher education, for a total of more than 1700 Profile entries.

This expanded and updated edition of *Profiles of American Colleges* will answer all of your questions as you embark on this most significant experience—college application, acceptance, and enrollment.

KEY TO ABBREVIATIONS

DEGREES

A.A.—Associate of Arts
A.A.S.—Associate of Applied Science
A.B. or B.A.—Bachelor of Arts
A.B.J.—Bachelor of Arts in Journalism
A.S.—Associate of Science

B.A.—Bachelor of Arts
B.A.A.—Bachelor of Applied Arts
B.A.A.S. or B.Applied A.S.—Bachelor of Applied Arts and Sciences
B.Ac. or B.Acc.—Bachelor of Accountancy
B.A.C.—Bachelor of Science in Air Commerce
B.A.C.V.I.—Bachelor of Arts in Computer and Video Imaging
B.A.E. or B.A.Ed.—Bachelor of Arts in Education
B.A.G.E.—Bachelor of Arts in General Education
B.Agri.—Bachelor of Agriculture
B.A.G.S.—Bachelor of Arts in General Studies
B.A.J.S.—Bachelor of Arts in Judaic Studies
B.A.M.—Bachelor of Arts in Music
B.Applied Sc.—Bachelor of Applied Science
B.A.R.—Bachelor of Religion
B.Arch.—Bachelor of Architecture
B.Arch.Hist.—Bachelor of Architectural History
B.Arch.Tech.—Bachelor of Architectural Technology
B.Ar.Sc.—Baccalaurium Artium et Scientiae (honors college degree) (Bachelor of Arts & Sciences)
B.Art.Ed.—Bachelor of Art Education
B.A.S.—Bachelor of Applied Science
B.A.S.—Bachelor of Arts and Sciences
B.A.Sec.Ed.—Bachelor of Arts in Secondary Ed.
B.A.S.W.—B.A. in Social Work
B.A.T.—Bachelor of Arts in Teaching
B.B. or B.Bus.—Bachelor of Business
B.B.A.—Bachelor of Business Administration
B.B.E.—Bachelor of Business Education
B.C. or B.Com. or B.Comm.—Bachelor of Commerce
B.C.A.—Bachelor of Creative Arts
B.C.E.—Bachelor of Civil Engineering
B.C.E.—Bachelor of Computer Engineering
B.Ch. or B.Chem.—Bachelor of Chemistry
B.Ch.E.—Bachelor of Chemical Engineering
B.C.J.—Bachelor of Criminal Justice
B.C.M.—Bachelor of Christian Ministries
B.Church Mus.—Bachelor of Church Music
B.C.S.—Bachelor of College Studies
B.E.—Bachelor of English
B.E. or B.Ed.—Bachelor of Education
B.E.—Bachelor of Engineering
B.E.D.—Bachelor of Environmental Design
B.E.E.—Bachelor of Electrical Engineering
B.En. or B.Eng.—Bachelor of Engineering
B.E.S. or B.Eng.Sc.—Bachelor of Engineering Science
B.E.T.—Bachelor of Engineering Technology
B.F.A.—Bachelor of Fine Arts
B.G.S.—Bachelor of General Studies
B.G.S.—Bachelor of Geological Sciences
B.H.E.—Bachelor of Health Education
B.H.P.E.—Bachelor of Health and Physical Education
B.H.S.—Bachelor of Health Science
B.I.D.—Bachelor of Industrial Design
B.I.M.—Bachelor of Industrial Management
B.Ind.Tech.—Bachelor of Industrial Technology
B.Int.Arch.—Bachelor of Interior Architecture
B.Int.Design—Bachelor of Interior Design
B.I.S.—Bachelor of Industrial Safety
B.I.S.—Bachelor of Interdisciplinary Studies
B.J.—Bachelor of Journalism
B.J.S.—Bachelor of Judaic Studies
B.L.A. or B.Lib.Arts—Bachelor of Liberal Arts
B.L.A. or B.Land.Arch.—Bachelor in Landscape Architecture
B.L.I.—Bachelor of Literary Interpretation
B.L.S.—Bachelor of Liberal Studies
B.M. or B.Mus. or Mus.Bac.—Bachelor of Music
B.M.E.—Bachelor of Mechanical Engineering
B.M.E. or B.M.Ed. or B.Mus.Ed.—Bachelor of Music Education
B.Med.Lab.Sc.—Bachelor of Medical Laboratory Science
B.Min—Bachelor of Ministry
B.M.P. or B.Mu.—Bachelor of Music in Performance
B.Mus.A.—Bachelor of Applied Music
B.M.T.—Bachelor of Music Therapy
B.O.T.—Bachelor of Occupational Therapy
B.P.A.—Bachelor of Public Administration
B.P.E.—Bachelor of Physical Education
B.Perf.Arts—Bachelor of Performing Arts
B.Ph.—Bachelor of Philosophy
B.Pharm.—Bachelor of Pharmacy
B.Phys.Hlth.Ed.—Bachelor of Physical Health Education
B.P.S.—Bachelor of Professional Studies
B.P.T.—Bachelor of Physical Therapy
B.R.E.—Bachelor of Religious Education
B.R.T.—Bachelor of Respiratory Therapy
B.S. or B.Sc. or S.B.—Bachelor of Science
B.S.A. or B.S.Ag. or B.S.Agr.—Bachelor of Science in Agriculture
B.Sacred Mus.—Bachelor of Sacred Music
B.Sacred Theol.—Bachelor of Sacred Theology
B.S.A.E.—Bachelor of Science in Agricultural Engineering
B.S.A.E. or B.S.Art Ed.—Bachelor of Science in Art Education
B.S.Ag.E.—Bachelor of Science in Agricultural Engineering
B.S.A.S.—Bachelor of Science in Administrative Sciences
B.S.A.T.—Bachelor of Science in Athletic Training
B.S.B.—Bachelor of Science (business)
B.S.B.A. or B.S.Bus. Adm.—Bachelor of Science in Business Administration
B.S.Bus.—Bachelor of Science in Business
B.S.Bus.Ed.—Bachelor of Science in Business Education
B.S.C.—Bachelor of Science in Commerce
B.S.C.E. or B.S.C.I.E.—Bachelor of Science in Civil Engineering
B.S.C.E.T—B.S. in Computer Engineering Technology
B.S.Ch. or B.S.Chem. or B.S. in Ch.—Bachelor of Science in Chemistry
B.S.C.H.—Bachelor of Science in Community Health
B.S.Ch.E.—Bachelor of Science in Chemical Engineering
B.S.C.I.S.—Bachelor of Science in Computer Information Sciences
B.S.C.J.—Bachelor of Science in Criminal Justice
B.S.C.L.S.—Bachelor of Science in Clinical Laboratory Science
B.S.Comp.Eng.—Bachelor of Science in Computer Engineering
B.S.Comp.Sci. or B.S.C.S.—Bachelor of Science in Computer Science
B.S.Comp.Soft—Bachelor of Science in Computer Software
B.S.Comp.Tech.—Bachelor of Science in Computer Technology
B.Sc.(P.T.)—Bachelor of Science in Physical Therapy
B.S.C.S.T.—Bachelor of Science in Computer Science Technology
B.S.D.H.—Bachelor of Science in Dental Hygiene
B.S.Die—Bachelor of Science in Dietetics
B.S.E. or B.S.Ed. or B.S.Educ.—Bachelor of Science in Education
B.S.E. or B.S in E. or B.S. in Eng.—Bachelor of Science in Engineering
B.S.E.E.—Bachelor of Science in Electrical Engineering
B.S.E.E.T.—Bachelor of Science in Electrical Engineering Technology
B.S.E.H.—Bachelor of Science in Environmental Health
B.S.Elect.T.—Bachelor of Science in Electronics Technology
B.S.El.Ed. or B.S. in Elem. Ed.—Bachelor of Science in Elementary Education
B.S.E.P.H.—Bachelor of Science in Environmental and Public Health
B.S.E.S.—Bachelor of Science in Engineering Science
B.S.E.S.—Bachelor of Science in Environmental Studies
B.S.E.T.—Bachelor of Science in Engineering Technology
B.S.F.—Bachelor of Science in Forestry
B.S.F.R.—Bachelor of Science in Forestry Resources
B.S.F.W.—Bachelor of Science in Fisheries and Wildlife
B.S.G.—Bachelor of Science in Geology

B.S.G.—Bachelor of Science in Gerontology
B.S.G.E.—Bachelor of Science in Geological Engineering
B.S.G.S.—Bachelor of Science in General Studies
B.S.H.C.A.—Bachelor of Science in Health Care Administration
B.S.H.E.—Bachelor of Science in Home Economics
B.S.H.F.—Bachelor of Science in Health Fitness
B.S.H.M.S.—Bachelor of Science in Health Management Systems
B.S.H.S.—Bachelor of Science in Health Sciences
B.S.H.S.—Bachelor of Science in Human Services
B.S.I.A.—Bachelor of Science in Industrial Arts
B.S.I.E.—Bachelor of Science in Industrial Engineering
B.S.I.M.—Bachelor of Science in Industrial Management
B.S. in Biomed.Eng.—Bachelor of Science in Biomedical Engineering
B.S. in C.D.—Bachelor of Science in Communication Disorders
B.S.Ind.Ed.—Bachelor of Science in Industrial Education
B.S.Ind.Tech.—Bachelor of Science in Industrial Technology
B.S. in Sec.Ed.—Bachelor of Science in Secondary Education
B.S.I.S.—Bachelor of Science in Interdisciplinary Studies
B.S.I.T.—Bachelor of Science in Industrial Technology
B.S.J.—Bachelor of Science in Journalism
B.S.L.E.—Bachelor of Science in Law Enforcement
B.S.M.—Bachelor of Science in Management
B.S.M.—Bachelor of Science in Music
B.S.M.E.—Bachelor of Science in Mechanical Engineering
B.S.Med.Tech. or B.S.M.T.—Bachelor of Science in Medical Technology
B.S.Met.E.—Bachelor of Science in Metallurgical Engineering
B.S.M.R.A.—Bachelor of Science in Medical Records Administration
B.S.M.T.—Bachelor of Science in Medical Technology
B.S.M.T.—Bachelor of Science in Music Therapy
B.S.Mt.E.—Bachelor of Science in Materials Engineering
B.S.Mus.Ed.—Bachelor of Science in Music Education
B.S.N.—Bachelor of Science in Nursing
B.S.Nuc.T.—Bachelor of Science in Nuclear Technology
B.S.O.A.—Bachelor of Science in Office Administration
B.S.O.E.—Bachelor of Science in Occupational Education
B.S.O.T.—Bachelor of Science in Occupational Therapy
B.S.P. or B.S.Pharm—Bachelor of Science in Pharmacy
B.S.P.A.—Bachelor of Science in Public Administration
B.S.Pcs.—Bachelor of Science in Physics
B.S.P.E.—Bachelor of Science in Physical Education
B.S.P.T.—Bachelor of Science in Physical Therapy
B.S.Rad.Tech.—Bachelor of Science in Radiation Technology
B.S.R.C.—Bachelor of Science in Respiratory Care
B.S.R.S.—Bachelor of Science in Radiological Science
B.S.R.T.T.—Bachelor of Science in Radiation Therapy Technology
B.S.S.—Bachelor of Science in Surveying
B.S.S.—Bachelor of Special Studies
B.S.S.A.—Bachelor of Science in Systems Analysis
B.S.Soc. Work or B.S.S.W.—Bachelor of Science in Social Work
B.S.Sp.—Bachelor of Science in Speech
B.S.S.T.—Bachelor of Science in Surveying and Topography
B.S.T. or B.S.Tech.—Bachelor of Science in Technology
B.S.S.W.E.—Bachelor of Science in Software Engineering
B.S.V.T.E.—Bachelor of Science in Vocational Technical Education
B.S.W.—Bachelor of Social Work
B.T. or B.Tech.—Bachelor of Technology
B.Th.—Bachelor of Theology
B.T.S.—Bachelor of Technical Studies
B.U.S.—Bachelor of Urban Studies
B.V.M.—Bachelor of Veterinarian Medicine
B.Voc.Arts or B.V.A.—Bachelor of Vocational Arts
B.V.E.D. or B.Voc.Ed.—Bachelor of Vocational Education

D.D.S.—Doctor of Dental Surgery

Ed.S.—Education Specialist

J.D.—Doctor of Jurisprudence

LL.B.—Bachelor of Laws

M.A.—Master of Arts
M.A.Ed.—Master of Arts in Education
M.A.T.—Master of Arts in Teaching
M.B.A.—Master of Business Administration
M.D.—Doctor of Medicine
M.F.A.—Master of Fine Arts
M.P.A.—Master of Public Administration
M.S.—Master of Science
Mus.B. or Mus.Bac.—Bachelor of Music

Ph.D.—Doctor of Philosophy

R.N.—Registered Nurse

S.B. or B.S. or B.Sc.—Bachelor of Science

OTHER ABBREVIATIONS

AABC—Accrediting Association of Bible Colleges
AACN—American Association of Colleges of Nursing
AACSB—American Assembly of Collegiate Schools of Business
AAFCS—American Association of Family and Consumer Sciences
AALE—American Academy for Liberal Education
AALS—Association of American Law Schools
AAMFT—American Association for Marriage and Family Therapy
ABA—American Bar Association
ABET—Accreditation Board for Engineering and Technology
ABFSE—American Board of Funeral Service Education
ABHES—Accrediting Bureau of Health Education Schools
ACBSP—Association of Collegiate Business Schools and Programs
ACCE—American Council for Construction Education
ACE HSA—Accrediting Commission on Education for Health Services Administration
ACE JMC—American Council on Education in Journalism and Mass Communication
ACOTE—American Council for Occupational Therapy Education
ACPE—Association for Clinical Pastoral Education, Inc.
ACPE—American Council on Pharmaceutical Education
ACS—American Chemical Society
ACT—American College Testing Program
ADA—American Dietetic Association
ADA—American Dental Association
ADDA—American Design Drafting Association
AFSA—Application for Federal Student Aid
AHEA—American Home Economics Association
AHIMA—American Health Information Management Association
ALA—American Library Association
ALIGU—American Language Institute of Georgetown University
AMAC AHEA—American Medical Association Committee on Allied Health Education and Accreditation
AOA—American Osteopathic Association
AOA—American Optometric Association
AOTA—American Occupational Therapy Association
AP—Advanced Placement
APA—American Podiatry Association
APA—American Psychological Association
APET—Asset Placement Evaluation Test
APIEL—Advance Placement International English Language Exam
APTA—American Physical Therapy Association
ASHA—American School Health Association

ASLA—American Society of Landscape Architects
ASLHA—American Speech-Language-Hearing Association
ATSUSC—Association of Theological Schools in the United States and Canada
AUCC—Association of Universities and Colleges of Canada
AVMA—American Veterinary Medical Association

BEOG—Basic Educational Opportunity Grant (now Pell Grant)

CAA—Council on Aviation Accreditation
CAADE—California Association for Alcohol/Drug Educators
CAAHEP—Commission on Accreditation of Allied Health Education Programs
CAAP—College Achievement Admission Program
CACREP—Council for Accreditation of Counseling and Related Educational Programs
CAPTE—Commission on Accreditation in Physical Therapy Education
CAS—Certificate of Advanced Study
CCE—Council on Chiropractic Education
CCNE—Commission on Collegiate Nursing Education
CCTE—California Commission on Teacher Credentialing
CDN—Canadian
CED—Council for Education of the Deaf
CEEB—College Entrance Examination Board
CELT—Comprehensive English Language Test
CEPH—Council on Education for Public Health
CLAST—College Level Academic Skills Test
CLEP—College-Level Examination Program
COE—Council on Occupational Education
CRDA—Candidates Reply Date Agreement
CRE—Council on Rehabilitation Education
CSAB—Computing Science Accreditation Board
CSS—College Scholarship Service
CSS/Profile—College Scholarship Service Financial Aid Profile
CSWE—Council on Social Work Education
CWS—College Work-Study

EESL—Examination of English as a Second Language
ELPT—English Language Proficiency Test (SAT II)
ELS/ALA—English Language Services/American Language Academy
EMH—Educable Mentally Handicapped
EOP—Equal Opportunity Program
ESL—English as a Second Language
ETS—Educational Testing Service

FAFSA—Free Application for Federal Student Aid
FET—Full-time equivalent
FFS—Family Financial Statement
FIDER—Foundation for Interior Design Education Research
FISL—Federally Insured Student Loan
FTE—Full-Time Equivalent

GED—General Educational Development (high school equivalency examination)
GPA—Grade Point Average
GRE—Graduate Record Examination
GSLP—Guaranteed Student Loan Program
G-STEP—Georgia State Test for English Proficiency

HEOP—Higher Equal Opportunity Program
HPER—Health, Physical Education, and Recreation

IACBE—International Assembly for Collegiate Business Education
IAME—International Association for Management Education
IB—International Baccalaureate
IELTS—International English Language Testing System

JRCERT—Joint Review Committee on Education in Radiologic Technology

LCME—Liaison Committee on Medical Education

MAPS—Multiple Assessment Program/Services
MELAB—Michigan English Language Assessment Battery
MUSIC—Multi User System for Interactive Computing

NAAB—National Architectural Accrediting Board
NAACLS—National Accrediting Agency for Clinical Laboratory Educators
NAIT—National Association of Industrial Technology
NAPNES—National Association for Practical Nurse Education and Service
NASAD—National Association of Schools of Art and Design
NASD—National Assocation of Schools of Dance
NASDTEC—National Association of State Development Teacher Education
NASM—National Association of Schools of Music
NASPAA—National Association of Schools of Public Affairs and Administration
NASPE—National Association of Sport and Physical Education
NAST—National Association of Schools of Theatre
NCATE—National Council for Accreditation of Teacher Education
NCCAA—National Christian College Athletic Association
NCOPE—National Commission on Orthotic and Prosthetic Education
NDEA—National Defense Education Act
NLN—National League for Nursing
NRPA—National Recreation and Park Association

PCS—Parents' Confidential Statement
PAIR—PHEAA Aid Information Request
PEP—Proficiency Examination Program
PHEAA—Pennsylvania Higher Education Assistance Agency
PSAT/NMSQT—Preliminary Scholastic Aptitude Test/National Merit Scholarship Qualifying Test

ROTC—Reserve Officers Training Corps
RSE—Regents Scholarship Examination (New York State)

SAAC—Student Aid Application for California
SACU—Service for Admission to College and University (Canada)
SAF—Society of American Foresters
SAM—Single Application Method
SAR—Student Aid Report
SAT—Scholastic Assessment Testing (formerly ATP–Admissions Testing Program)
SCAT—Scholastic College Aptitude Test
SCS—Students' Confidential Statement
SEOG—Supplementary Educational Opportunity Grant
SOA—Society of Actuaries

TAP—Tuition Assistance Program (New York State)
TDD—Telecommunication Device for the Deaf
TEAC—Teacher Education Accreditation Council
TOEFL—Test of English as a Foreign Language
TTY—Talking Typewriter

UAP—Undergraduate Assessment Program
UP—Undergraduate Program (area tests)

VFAF—Virginia Financial Assistance Form

WPCT—Washington Pre-College Test

FURTHER READING TO HELP PREPARE FOR COLLEGE

Two other Barron's books present more detailed information on selected schools. Barron's *Guide to the Most Competitive Colleges* features lengthy pieces written by recent graduates of some of the nation's most prestigious colleges. *Barron's Best Buys* by Lucia Solórzano features some 300 colleges and universities that are perceived to give the best bargains in higher education. These essays are written by the author, with input from deans and students from each of the schools.

College students considering application to a graduate professional school will find relevant information in *Barron's Guide to Medical and Dental Schools*, *Barron's Guide to Law Schools*, and *Barron's Guide to Graduate Business Schools*.

Further information on entrance examinations and other aspects of college can be found in the following Barron's publications, all of which are available from Barron's Educational Series, 250 Wireless Boulevard, Hauppauge, New York 11788 or at *www.barronseduc.com*.

College Reference

Barron's Guide to the Most Competitive Colleges
Barron's Best Buys in College Education
Complete College Financing Guide
Writing a Successful College Application Essay

Study Tips/Reference

Student Success Secrets
Study Tactics

Standardized Test Preparation

ACT—How to Prepare for the ACT
ACT—Pass Key to the ACT

PSAT-NMSQT—How to Prepare for the Preliminary SAT/National Merit Scholarship Qualifying Test
PSAT-NMSQT—Pass Key to the PSAT-NMSQT

SAT I—Hot Words for SAT I
SAT I—How to Prepare for the SAT I
SAT I—Math Workbook for the SAT I
SAT I—Pass Key to the SAT I
SAT I—Verbal Workbook

SAT II—How to Prepare for SAT II
- *American History and Social Studies*
- *Biology*
- *Chemistry*
- *French (audiocassette package)*
- *Literature*
- *Mathematics Level I + IC*
- *Mathematics Level IIC*
- *Physics*
- *Spanish (audiocassette package)*
- *World History*
- *Writing*

AP—How to Prepare for the Advanced Placement Examinations:
- *Biology*
- *Calculus*
- *Chemistry*
- *English*
- *European History*
- *Physics B*
- *Spanish (audiocassette package)*
- *Statistics*
- *U.S. Government and Politics*
- *United States History*

Other Test Preparation

How to Prepare for the Michigan Test Battery
CSUWP—How to Prepare for the California State University Writing Proficiency Exams

Pocket Guide Series

Pocket Guide Thesaurus
Pocket Guide to Correct English
Pocket Guide to Correct Grammar
Pocket Guide to Correct Punctuation
Pocket Guide to Correct Spelling
Pocket Guide to Study Tips
Pocket Guide to Synonyms
Pocket Guide to Vocabulary

Vocabulary and Language Arts

The Art of Styling Sentences
1100 Words You Need to Know
How to Write Themes and Term Papers
Ten Steps in Writing the Research Paper
WordPlay—600 Words You Need to Know (audiocassette package)

Software—Standardized Test Preparation

- *GMAT* Book with CD-ROM
- *GRE* Book with CD-ROM
- *LSAT* Book with CD-ROM
- *NCLEX-PN* Book with CD-ROM
- *NCLEX-RN* Book with CD-ROM
- *SAT I* Book with CD-ROM
- *SAT I* Safari Program on CD-ROM
- *TOEFL* Book with CD-ROM

PART I

AN INTRODUCTION TO COLLEGE

You'll soon be on your way to college—but how much thought have you given it so far? Have you started thinking about the career that's in your future?

- Which college will help you make the most of your natural abilities and interests, and get you ready for life?
- Which courses should you take?

This section will help you find answers to these questions. It will also give you advice on:

- how to apply to schools
- how to increase your chances of acceptance
- how to finance your education

And just as important, this introductory section will give you valuable tips on how to get through that critical freshman year.

KNOWING YOURSELF

You have in your hands a book that will give you answers to your questions about the qualities and features of more than 1680 colleges. But before you start reading the descriptions and getting the answers, you need to know what questions to ask about finding the college that is right for you. Although you need to ask questions about "getting in" i.e., exploring colleges in terms of ease of admission for you, most of your questions should focus on the more significant issue of "fitting in." Fitting in means finding a college where you will be comfortable; where you are compatible with your peers, and where the overall atmosphere encourages your growth as a student and as a person.

This article is designed to help you assess some values and attitudes that will help you determine where you will fit in. It will enable you to ask the right questions. Not all colleges are for everyone; careful thinking about your interests, ideals, and values will lead you to find the college that is right *for you*. Colleges are not "good" or "bad" in a generic sense; they are either good or bad matches for you.

The two tests that follow will be helpful in thinking about yourself as a future college student; they should help you make the right college choice.

THE COLLEGE PLANNING VALUES ASSESSMENT

Students have different reasons for going to college. Ten reasons or values are found to be most important to students as they think about college. Knowing about your values is important as the first step in identifying the colleges where you will fit in and be happy.

To complete the assessment, read through the list of ten values— A–J. Think about the outcomes you hope college will produce for you. Each student will rank them differently; hence, there are no "right" answers. Whereas several, or even most, of these values may be significant for you in one way or another, the goal is to decide the relative importance of each. With 10 being highest and 1 being lowest, *rank* them on the basis of:

What do you want college to do for you?

—— A. To provide me with an academic challenge.
—— B. To provide me with opportunities to exchange intellectual ideas with teachers and students.
—— C. To provide me with lots of fun experiences.
—— D. To prepare me to make a lot of money.
—— E. To provide me with recognition for accomplishments.
—— F To provide me with opportunities to contribute to others' welfare.
—— G. To help me prepare for a career.
—— H. To give me independence.
—— I. To provide opportunities for me to grow religiously or spiritually.
—— J. To provide me with a variety of new experiences.

Now go back and circle the values that you have marked with either a 10, 9, or 8. What do your college planning values say about you?

If ***A*** was among the top three priorities on your list, you will want to explore the academic character of the colleges you are considering. Although all colleges are, by definition, intellectual centers, some put more priority on challenging students and pushing them to their limits. Reading about the academic features of the colleges you are considering will be important. (In the college Profiles, pay attention to the *special* section to learn about these features.) Your high ranking of this value says that you will be able to take advantage of intellectual opportunities at college. You may want to select a college where your SAT I scores are similar to or slightly above the ranges of other admitted students: at those colleges you will be able to shine academically. You may desire to take an active part in classroom discussions and will want a college where the student faculty ratio is low. A word of caution here: some students select this value because they see the prestige of the college as all-important in their choice. Although it is appropriate to look for a strong faculty and a highly regarded college, you want a college that will give you the greatest chance of academic success. It is success in college, not just academic reputation or prestige, that will lead to admission into graduate school or a broad selection of jobs.

If ***B*** was among your top three priorities, you feel challenged and stimulated by academics and classroom learning. You will want to find a college where your mind will be stretched. You will want to choose a college where you can explore a range of new academic subjects. A liberal arts and sciences college may give you an enriching breadth of academic offerings. You will want to look for a college where academic clubs are popular and where you have a good chance of knowing professors and sharing ideas with them. Access to faculty is important to you and you will want to look at the student faculty ratio in colleges you consider. Also note the ratio of undergraduate students to graduate students. Primarily undergraduate institutions will be the colleges that may best be able to meet your needs, because you will be the focus of teachers' attention. Teachers at such colleges place their priority on teaching and are not distracted by the needs of graduate students or by pressure to balance teaching and student time with research and writing.

If ***C*** was circled, you derive satisfaction from social opportunities. You will want a college where the academic demands will not diminish your ability to socialize. You likely will want a good balance between the social and academic sides of campus life. You will want to explore the percentage of students who get involved in intramural sports, clubs, or fraternities and sororities. (This information is listed in each college profile.) Look at your college choices on the basis of school spirit and sporting events offered. The profiles list popular campus events: see if they sound exciting to you. Also look at the percentage of students who stay on campus over the weekend. You will also want a college where it is easy to make friends. Both small and larger colleges would be appropriate for you. Although a larger college would expose you to more students and a larger quantity of potential friends, studies show that students at smaller colleges become more involved in activities and build deep friendships more quickly. Look for supportiveness and camaraderie in the student body.

If ***D*** is circled, you will want to consider earning potential, advancement opportunities, and the future market for the careers you consider. You will want to consider this value in your career planning. Remember, however, that there is no sure road to riches! You not only must pick a career direction carefully, but must choose a college where the potential for academic success—good grades—is high. The name of a particular college is less important than good grades or contributions to campus life when securing a good job or being admitted to graduate school. Even if you find that a particular career has tremendous earning potential, those earnings may come to only those who are most successful in the profession. Look at average salaries, but also consider your interests, values, and personality before making your final career choice.

If ***E*** is high on your list, you take pleasure in being known for your success in an area of interest. For instance, you might feel good about being recognized or known in school as a good student, a top athlete, or a leader in a club. No doubt this type of recognition contributes to your confidence. You might look for colleges where you will be able to acquire or continue to receive this recognition. Often, recognition is easier to achieve at smaller colleges where you would not be competing against large numbers of students hoping to achieve the same recognition. You will also want to choose colleges where it is easy to get involved and where the activities offered are appealing to you. You may want to consider the benefits of being a "big fish in a small pond."

If ***F*** is important, that value will no doubt guide your vocational or avocational pursuits. You may find yourself choosing a career in which this value can be fulfilled, or you may seek opportunities on a college campus where you can be of service. You will want to choose a college where community service is valued. Look at the *activities* section and note whether community service-related involvements are available.

If ***G*** was circled, you may know what career you want to pursue or you may be concerned but uncertain about your career decision. If you have tentatively selected a career, you will want to choose a college where you can take courses leading to the attainment of a degree in your chosen field. Explore the *programs of study* section in the profiles to determine whether a college you are considering offers the course work you desire. You will want to make a note of the most popular majors and the strongest majors as they are listed. If you don't yet know what career would suit you, remember, that for most careers, a broad, solid liberal arts foundation is considered good preparation. You will want to look at opportunities for internships and take advantage of the career planning and placement office at your chosen college. Finding a career that will be fulfilling is one of the most important choices you will make in your life. Your selection of a college will be your first step toward achieving your career goal.

If ***H*** is circled, it suggests that personal autonomy is important to you. College is, in general, a time for independence, and students are often anxious to make their own decisions without parental involvement. If you feel you can handle lots of independence, you will want to look for colleges where there is some freedom in choosing courses and where students are given responsibility for their own lives. Colleges vary in terms of these factors. Note particularly the *required* section under *programs of study,* which tells you the courses that must be fulfilled by all students. Be certain that you will not be stifled by too many rules and regulations. You may also want to look for colleges where the personal development of students receives high priority. A priority on independence also suggests that you will be comfortable being away from home and on your own.

If ***I*** is one of your top three choices, you will want to look first at the religious affiliation of each of your college options. You may want a college that has a relationship with your particular religious group. Or you may desire a large number of students who belong to the same denomination as you do. The profiles will also give you the percentage of students who are members of the major religious denominations. As you explore colleges, you will also want to see if the college has a commitment to the values and ideals held by you or your family.

If ***J*** is appealing, you like newness and will likely be stimulated by new experiences and new activities. You may see college-going as an adventure and will want to pick colleges where you can meet your need for stimulation and excitement. Because you value newness, you should not hesitate to attend college in a different part of the country or to experience an environment or a climate that is quite different from your high school. You will also want to look for evidence of diversity in the student body. As you read the descriptions, look for colleges with lots of new opportunities for growth and for personal expansion.

Now that you've read about your top three values, answer the following question on a separate sheet of paper: In your own words, what do your top three values say about what you are looking for in a college? Then, share that information with your college adviser as he or she assists you in finding colleges that are right for you.

SELF-KNOWLEDGE QUESTIONNAIRE

The following seven items—A–G—will help you in thinking about yourself as a college student and the ease with which you will likely proceed through the college selection process. Read each statement and determine whether it is true or not true of you. After each question, you will see numbers ranging from 1 to 5. Circle 1 if the statement is very true of you. Circle 5 if the statement is not true of you. Use 2, 3, or 4 to reflect varying levels of preference. Be realistic and honest.

A. I am confident about my academic abilities for college (such as reading, writing, and note taking).

Very true of me 1 2 3 4 5 Not true of me

Academic abilities such as reading speed and comprehension, writing, note taking, calculating, speaking, and listening are important for college students. You will be called upon to use such skills in your college classes. If you are confident about your academic skills, you can approach picking a college with the ease of knowing that you will be able to master the academic rigors of college life. If you circled 3, 4, or 5 you will want to work on these skills in your remaining days in high school. You will want to choose colleges where you can work to strengthen these skills. Some colleges provide a learning skills center in which you are able to get help if you are having difficulty writing a paper or understanding the content of a class. If you are less than confident, you might look to colleges where you will not be intimidated by the skills of the other students.

B. My study skills and time management are good.

Very true of me 1 2 3 4 5 Not true of me

Study skills and time management are two of the most important qualities for an efficient and productive college student. Successful college students are average or above in organizing themselves for studying, scheduling, and using study time productively, and differentiating important content of a lecture or a book from supplementary information. In addition, they complete assignments on time and don't get flustered if they have several papers or a couple of tests due on the same day. If you circled 3, 4, or 5, it is important to work on improving these skills during your remaining high school days. You might consider the following:

- Seek help from your parents, a teacher, a counselor, or a learning specialist in becoming more organized.
- Try keeping a calendar. Anticipate each step necessary in preparing for every test and every paper.
- Be responsible for your own appointments.
- Check to see if a study skills course is offered at a local community college or university. Or consider reading a book on study skills.

C. I am motivated to succeed in college.

Very true of me 1 2 3 4 5 Not true of me

Motivation is definitely the most important skill you bring to college. Those students who want to succeed do succeed! Studies show that it is motivation, not your SAT scores, that determines academic success in college. And motivation means knowing not only that you want to go to college, but that you also want to be a student. Some students want to go to college for the fun aspects, but forget that college is primarily an academic experience. So if you circled 1 or 2, great, you're off to a good start. If you circled 3, 4, or 5, it may be an appropriate time to consider your wants and needs in a college. What sort of college would help motivate you? Would a college with a balance between academics and social life be appealing? Would you be more motivated if you were near a large and interesting city? Would nice weather be a distraction rather than an energizer? Is a trade or technical school best for you? Have you considered taking some time off between high school and college? Considering such questions is important, and the time to do that exploration is now.

D. I am a good decision maker.

Very true of me 1 2 3 4 5 Not true of me

Decisions, decisions, decisions. The college selection process is full of decisions! What colleges will I initially consider? To which colleges will I apply for admission? What college will I eventually attend? You will be facing these decisions in the upcoming months. If you circled 1 or 2, you are on your way. If you circled 3, 4, or 5, think about an important decision you made recently. Why didn't it go well? If you can analyze your decision-making weakness in that situation, it may help to avoid any potential pitfalls in your college decision making. The following suggestions will help you improve your ability to make the right college choice:

- Clearly articulate what you're looking for in a college. Write down those features that will make a college right for you.

- List and compare pros and cons of alternative colleges. Every college has both.
- Evaluate each college on the basis of the criteria you set for yourself. Remember, you're looking for a college where you will get in *and* fit in.

E. I'm a good information gatherer; for example, I am usually able to find books, articles, and so on to help me do a history research paper.

Very true of me 1 2 3 4 5 Not true of me

Finding a college requires you to be a good researcher. There is so much information about colleges to sort through and analyze. If you feel you can do good research, fine, you're on your way. If you circled 3, 4, or 5, the following ideas may be helpful:

- Start with this book and look for colleges that are consistent with what you want. Remember that your primary concern is where you will fit in. Use your college-going values and your responses in this questionnaire to guide your thinking about colleges that will match you.
- Work closely with your college counselor, and seek impressions from students and others with reliable and up-to-date information about colleges of interest. You will make a better decision with credible and extensive input.
- Look for differences in features that are important to you. Is ease of making friends important to you? What about balance between academics and social life? Do you want teachers to know you?

F. I feel I adapt to new situations easily.

Very true of me 1 2 3 4 5 Not true of me

Everyone goes through changes in life. Some move through transition periods with great ease, others find them more difficult. You may have experienced the changes that come after a change of schools (even from middle school to high school), the illness or death of a relative, or the divorce of your parents. If you circled 1 or 2, you are not likely to be intimidated by a college in another part of the country or a college very different from your high school. If you circled 3, 4, or 5, you may want to carefully look at colleges that are a bit closer to home or colleges where the same values, perceptions, and attitudes exist as were true in your high school. Almost everyone has fear and apprehension about leaving for college. But if that fear is significant, you will want to choose a college where you will feel comfortable. Visits to college campuses may be particularly significant in feeling good about potential choices.

G. It is easy for me to meet people and establish friendships.

Very true of me 1 2 3 4 5 Not true of me

Identifying and nurturing friendships is an important skill for college adjustment. If you circled 3, 4, or 5, you will want to look carefully at colleges where there are few cliques, where there is an atmosphere of sharing, and where students report that it is relatively easy to integrate into the campus environment. Your choice of a college is a quest for a good social fit. Your thorough review of the profiles and even visits to college campuses will be helpful in assuring your ability to fit in and be comfortable.

FINAL THOUGHTS

If you took time to carefully consider the issues raised in both the Values Assessment and the Self-Knowledge Questionnaire, you should have gained new insights and perspectives about yourself. You will want to share these results with your parents and with your guidance counselor. Elicit their help in getting more insight as to how they see you as a prospective college student. Finally, two suggestions:

- As you research colleges, consider what you have learned about yourself. You want a college that is a good match with your values and interests.
- Spend time on your college search. It will take many hours of organized planning and investigation. But the time spent will result in a better choice and a greater likelihood that you will spend four productive and exciting years in college.

Good luck. There are lots of colleges out there that want you. Let your knowledge of yourself and your objective analysis of potential college options guide you to college environments where you will be able to shine. Success in college is in your hands. Make the most of the opportunity.

Steven R. Antonoff, Ph.D.
Educational Consultant
Antonoff Associates, Inc.
Denver, Colorado

FINDING THE RIGHT COLLEGE

When you begin to think about college, you are embarking on a major research project. You have many choices available to you in order to get the best possible education for which you are qualified. Most readers of these Profiles are high school seniors or recent high school graduates planning to enroll full time in four-year colleges or universities.

Let us help make the book work for you!

THE BUYERS' MARKET

When your parents graduated from high school in the 1970s, colleges were crowded with the baby boom generation. Since then, the teenaged population has been decreasing, whereas the number and variety of colleges has continued to expand. The law of supply and demand is on your side.

Today there are about 1650 four-year colleges and universities, of which 130 are specialized institutions, such as music and art colleges or theological seminaries. Most existing institutions have grown larger, and many have expanded their programs, offering master's and doctoral degrees as well as bachelor's.

Total graduate and undergraduate students has also grown, from under 4 million in 1960 to more than 14.3 million today. Almost half are part-time students, including many working adults; their numbers have been increasing since the 1960s and 1970s. Part-time enrollments are mostly concentrated in the two-year colleges, which enroll about a third of all students.

You Are In Demand

Four-year colleges and universities doubled their enrollments in the 1960s and 1970s, and they still need to fill their classrooms and dormitories with full-time students between 18 and 22 years of age. Such students are getting harder to find. The number of high school seniors hit an all-time high of 3.1 million in 1977. Based on current projections, graduating classes will fall to 2.3 million in the 21st century. That's why institutions are recruiting so vigorously, sending you mailings, visiting your high schools, and setting up displays at college fairs. They need you as much as you need them.

MAKING A SHORT LIST

You have probably already started a list of colleges you know about from friends or relatives who have attended them, from recommendations by teachers, or by their academic or athletic reputations. This list will grow as you read the Profiles, receive college mailings, and attend college fairs. If you are interested in preparing for a very specific career, such as engineering, agriculture, health care, or architecture, you should add only institutions that offer that program. If you want to study business, teacher education, or the arts and sciences, almost every college can provide a suitable major. Either way, your list will soon include dozens of institutions. Most students apply to between two and five colleges. In order to narrow your list, you should follow a three-step process:

- **Check your realistic options,** eliminating colleges at which you would not qualify for admission and those that are beyond your family's financial means.
- **Screen the list** according to your preferences, such as institutional size, type, and location.
- **Evaluate the institutions,** using published information and campus visits to make judgments about which colleges can give you the best quality and value.

The following sections will guide you through each of these steps.

REALISTIC OPTIONS

Admissions Competitiveness

The first question most students ask about a college is, "How hard is it to get in?" It should certainly not be the last question. Admissions competitiveness is not the only, or even the most important, measurement of institutional quality. It makes sense to avoid wasting time, money, and useless disappointment applying to institutions for which you clearly are not qualified. Nevertheless, there are many colleges for which you are qualified, and you can make a good choice from among them. The buyer's market has not necessarily forced admission standards down everywhere. The most prestigious institutions are rarely affected by market conditions. Some of the better known public colleges and universities have raised their admission standards in recent years, as their lower prices have attracted larger numbers of applicants. But there remain hundreds of fine public and private colleges, with good local reputations, that will welcome your application.

Use the College Admissions Selector to compare your qualifications to the admissions competitiveness of the institutions of your list. Make sure you read the descriptions of standards very carefully. Even if you meet the stated qualifications for *Most Competitive* or *Highly Competitive* institutions, you cannot assume that you will be offered admission. These colleges receive applications from many more students than they can enroll and reject far more than they accept. When considering colleges rated *Very Competitive* or *Competitive*, remember that the median test scores identify the middle of the most recent freshman class; half of the admitted students had scores lower than the median, and half were above. If your high school grades and class rank are within the stated range, and your SAT I and ACT scores are even a little below the stated median, your chances of acceptance are very good. Students in the top quarter of their high school classes who score above 1200 on the SAT I or 26 on the ACT qualify for acceptance at the *Very Competitive* colleges and universities.

Students of average ability are admissible to most of the colleges and universities rated as *Competitive* and to virtually all of those rated as *Less Competitive*. They would need high school grades of C+ or better and SAT I total scores of about 1000 or ACT composite scores above 21.

Cost

The cost of the most expensive colleges and universities is approaching $30,000 a year. This is widely publicized and very frightening, especially to your parents. But you don't have to spend that much for a good education. Most private colleges charge between $15,000 and $19,000 a year for tuition and room and board. Public institutions generally cost between $7000 and $10,000 a year for in-state residents. Because many states have been cutting budgets in recent years, tuition at public institutions is now rising faster than at private ones. If you can commute to school from home, you can save about $3500 to $4500 in room and board, but should add the cost of transportation. The least expensive option is to attend a local community college for two years, at about $1000 a year, and then transfer to a four-year institution to complete your bachelor's degree. Depending on what you may qualify for in financial aid, and what your family is willing to sacrifice, you may have more choices than you think.

SCREEN BY PREFERENCE

The self-knowledge tests should indicate whether you are more likely to be comfortable far from or near to home, at an urban or rural campus, coed or single sex, or small or large college. It is best, however, not to eliminate any options without at least visiting a few campuses of different types to judge their feeling and style first hand. Choosing the proper institutional size and whether to live on campus or commute from home are more complicated questions.

Large Universities and Small Colleges

Only one-fifth of American colleges and universities have enrollments of 5000 or more, but they account for more than half the 7 million plus students who are pursuing bachelor's degrees. The rest are spread out among more than 1000 smaller schools. There are advantages and disadvantages that go with size.

At a college of 5000 or fewer students, you will get to know the campus quickly. You will not have to compete with many other students for the use of the library or when registering for courses. You can get to know your professors personally and become familiar with most of your fellow students. On the other hand, you may have little privacy and a limited choice of activities. Students at small schools often feel pressure to conform to prevailing customs.

As colleges and universities enroll more students, they offer a greater variety of courses, professors, facilities, and activities. Within a large campus community, you can probably find others who share your special interests and form a circle of good friends. But you may also find the libraries more crowded, many classes closed out, and competition very stiff for athletic teams or musical groups.

Many of the largest institutions are universities offering Ph.Ds., medicine, law, or other doctoral programs as well as bachelor's and master's degrees. Many colleges that do not offer these programs call themselves universities; and a few universities, Dartmouth among them, continue to call themselves colleges. Don't go by the name, but by the academic program. Universities emphasize research. University faculty need specialized laboratory equipment, computers, library material, and technical assistance for their research.

Because this is very expensive, universities usually charge higher tuition than colleges, even to their undergraduate students. Tuition at public universities can run 25 to 100 percent more than at public colleges in the same state. Private universities generally charge about 50 percent more than similarly located private colleges. In effect, undergraduates at universities subsidize the high cost of graduate programs. Freshmen and sophomores usually receive some instruction from graduate student assistants and fellows, who are paid to be apprentice faculty members.

However, most private universities and many public ones have extensive reputations. They have larger and more up-to-date libraries, laboratories, computers, and other special resources than colleges. They attract students from many states and countries and provide a rich social and cultural environment.

Living On and Off Campus

Deciding whether you will stay in a dormitory or at home is more than a matter of finances or how close to the college you live. You should be aware that students who live on campus, especially during the freshman year, are more likely to pass their courses and graduate than students who commute from home. Campus residents spend more time with faculty members, have more opportunity to use the library and laboratories, and are linked to other students who help one another with their studies. Residence hall life usually helps students mature faster as they participate in social and organizational activities.

About 25 percent of college freshmen live with their parents. If you commute to school, you can get maximum benefits from your college experience by spending time on campus between and after classes. If you need a part-time job, get employment in the college library, offices, or dining halls. Use the library to do homework in an environment that may be less distracting than at home. If possible, have some dinners on campus, to make friends with other students and participate in evening social and cultural events. Get involved in campus activities, participating in athletics, working on the newspaper, attending a meeting, or rehearsing a play.

If you will be living on campus, you may be able to choose among different types of residence buildings. Small dormitories are two to four stories high and house 250 or fewer students. They foster more quiet and privacy than larger buildings. High-rise units can house 1000 or more. They usually offer dining halls, snack bars, game rooms, and laundries all under one roof. Most older halls provide single or double rooms, with shared bathrooms on each floor. Newer halls frequently offer suites, in which a common living/study area and bathroom are shared by eight to twelve students occupying single or double bedrooms. Some students enjoy a larger "family" group; others prefer having only one roommate.

Campus food is usually wholesome, bland, and laden with carbohydrates to meet the high energy demands of active young people. You may have a choice of food plans between 10 and 21 meals a week. Other plans allow you to prepay a fixed dollar amount and purchase food by the item rather than by the meal. Food services make most of their profits on meals that are paid for but never eaten. Choose a meal plan that fits your own eating habits. Meal plans can usually be supplemented or increased, but they rarely can be reduced or refunded. Many colleges today offer a wide variety of food including vegetarian and kosher diets as well as more salads and pasta.

Many students live off campus after their freshman or sophomore year, either by choice or because the school does not have room for them on campus. Schools try to provide listings of available off-campus rooms and apartments that meet good standards for safety and cleanliness. Many colleges also offer health care and food services to students who live off campus.

It is usually more expensive to live in an apartment than in a dormitory, especially if you plan to prepare your own meals. Great care must be taken in choosing apartment mates. In addition to the usual problems that may arise through personality conflicts, others may develop because apartment mates share payments for rent and utilities and responsibilities for cleaning, shopping, and cooking. It is much harder to find new people to share an apartment in mid-lease than it is to change roommates on campus.

MAKING QUALITY JUDGMENTS

Once you have narrowed your list, you should decide where to apply on the basis of quality. It is not as difficult as you may think to make such judgments. You have to be willing to read the information in this book and the literature that the schools send out, to visit a few campuses, and to ask plenty of questions. You can usually ask questions of the admissions office, by mail or in person during a campus visit. Sometimes, as indicated in the following sections, it is better to ask questions at the offices most directly involved. Because colleges sincerely are interested in helping you make the right choice, they generally will welcome your questions and answer them politely and honestly.

The Faculty

The most important resources of any college or university are its professors. Admissions brochures usually point out the strengths of the faculty, but provide little detail. You should direct your questions about the faculty and other academic matters to the office of academic affairs. Find out what percentage of the faculty have the Ph.D. or other doctoral degrees. Although there is no fixed right number, it should be at least the majority. Schools start bragging in their brochures when 70 percent or more of the faculty have the Ph.D., so that seems to be a common benchmark of quality.

Recruiting brochures also emphasize faculty research, because the prestige of professors depends largely on the books and articles they have published. Good researchers may or may not make good teachers. Ask how often the best researchers teach undergraduate courses, and whether they instruct small as well as large classes. For example, a Nobel prize chemist may lecture to 500 students at a time but never show up in the laboratories where graduate assistants actually teach individual students.

Also ask about class size, because this determines the amount of individual attention students get from professors. Student/faculty ratios, which usually range from 10 to 20 students per professor, don't really tell you much. Every school offers a mixture of large and small classes. Here are some general standards:

- Science and technology courses should enroll only 25 to 30 students in each laboratory session, but may combine a number of laboratory classes for large weekly lectures.
- Skill development courses such as speech, foreign language, English composition, and fine and performing arts should have classes of 25 or fewer. Mathematics and computer science require considerable graded homework, and classes should be no larger than 35.
- Clinical courses in nursing and other health fields are partly based in hospitals or other health care facilities. In such courses, each 10 students should be supervised by a professor. Similarly, each student teacher should be placed with an experienced elementary or secondary school teacher and visited periodically by a member of the college faculty.
- Most other courses in humanities, social sciences, and professional areas are taught by classroom lectures and discussion. Classes should average 35 to 45 in introductory courses such as general psychology or American government. They should be smaller in advanced or specialized courses, such as Shakespeare or tax accounting.
- Many introductory courses, especially at universities, are taught in lecture classes of 100 or more. This is acceptable, if those courses also include small weekly discussion groups for individual instruction. Sometimes these discussion groups are taught by graduate student assistants rather than regular professors. Although graduate assistants lack teaching experience, they are very often highly capable. You should ask whether the teaching done by graduate assistants is closely supervised by regular faculty members.

Academic Programs

Even colleges and universities that boast fine and well qualified faculties can be short of professors in certain programs, particularly in business, computer science, and engineering. These continue to be popular majors although business, the most popular, has declined slightly since 1990. Some schools depend on instruction by part-time faculty members or fill in with available teachers from other specializations. Many international students are enrolled in technical doctoral programs, so you may find yourself being taught mathematics or engineering by a teaching assistant whose English you cannot understand. If you are interested in these subjects, check to see whether full-time faculty members teach at least 80 percent of the courses.

Other programs may have sufficient faculty but too few student majors. Physics, foreign languages, and philosophy usually have many students in required introductory courses but few taking the major. Because of small enrollments, these departments may not be able to offer their advanced and specialized courses on a regular basis. You should review the college catalog to see whether all of the courses required for majoring in the program are offered at least once every two years.

The academic department gives strength to the program by bringing together faculty members who share a common area of study and make sure their students get the instruction they need. Even at a small college, a department should have at least three full-time professors to offer a major program. Some programs, usually called interdisciplinary, are taught by groups of faculty members from several departments. These programs generally have the word *studies* in their titles; for example, Middle-Eastern Studies, Communication Studies, Women's Studies, or Ethnic Studies. Interdisciplinary committees are usually effective for a few years, after which the faculty members tend to pay more attention to their own departments. If you enroll in one of these programs, you may not have a regular faculty adviser or a good choice of courses for enrollment.

Sometimes highly specialized programs are offered within more general departments. Examples are semantics or linguistics (within the English department), social work or anthropology (within sociology), or broadcasting (within speech). Such a program may be taught by one faculty specialist, and you could be left stranded if that person leaves. On the other hand, that faculty member may hold tenure and teach the subject successfully for many years.

Internships are available at many colleges. They provide an opportunity to experience work in your major and learn from experienced people in your field. Many students have received job offers after participating in an internship program during the school year or during summer vacation.

Accreditation

General standards of academic quality are established by associations of colleges and universities through a process called voluntary accreditation. The criteria include: standards for admission of students; faculty qualifications; content of courses; grading standards; professional success of alumni; adequacy of libraries, laboratories, computers, and other support facilities; administrative systems and policy decision making; and financial support.

Six regional associations (New England, Middle States, Southern, North Central, Northwest, and Western) evaluate and accredit colleges as total institutions. Bible colleges have their own accrediting association. Other organizations evaluate and accredit specific programs, primarily in technical fields, like engineering and architecture; or those that require licensing, such as teaching and health care.

Accreditation must be periodically renewed, usually every five to ten years. Any school that is more than five years old and is not accredited probably has serious quality problems. One that was previously granted accreditation and then lost it is in deep trouble. On the other hand, accreditation means only that the school meets minimum standards. It is not a rating of school quality or a comparison to other schools. Accreditation information can be found in the college catalog.

Libraries

Most people judge libraries by the size of the collection, the bigger the better. Collection size is important, but only in relation to the variety and level of programs offered. A small liberal arts college can support its baccalaureate programs with a collection of 200,000 to 300,000 volumes. A university with many professional schools and doctoral programs may require over 2 million. Many books and journals are now available on computer, through the Internet, or on CD-ROM.

You may often find that the book or journal you need is owned by the library but unavailable. Frequently used material may be misplaced, lost, or out on loan. Many libraries are better at purchasing books than at getting them into the hands of their readers. You can look for some indications of the quality of a library's services.

The main stacks should be open to students, with the possible exception of rare books, bound journals, and other special items. Open stacks encourage browsing and save students from waiting on line while a library assistant fetches a few books at a time. Instead, assistants constantly should be picking up unused materials from reading desks or carts and putting them back on the shelves.

Good circulation policies encourage students to check materials out for short periods and to return them promptly. One week or less loans are appropriate for books regularly used in courses, and four week loans should be the maximum for other materials. A recall system should be available to get back borrowed material when it is needed. Journals, reference material, or books placed on reserve for assigned reading should be used within the library while it is open, and circulated overnight only at closing time.

Much information is now available on computer and access to library computers varies from campus to campus. A tour of these campus facilities would help to determine student access. The library should be open at night and on weekends, at least at those times when it is most likely to be used. Friday and Saturday nights and Sunday mornings are the times when libraries can usually be closed without serious loss of access to students. Professional librarians should be available to assist you whenever the library is open.

A modern academic library also should offer the following services.

- Interlibrary loans to get materials from other libraries.
- Online computerized searching of bibliographic databases. These databases automatically provide listings and summaries of books and articles by subject, author, and date.
- Tours and workshops to guide students in using the library.
- Reading lists for various subjects and courses.

Technology

Whatever your courses of study, you will use computers. You will learn to do mathematical and scientific problem solving; to classify, sort, and retrieve information; and to write, revise, and type manuscripts.

Many institutions require students to have personal computers. Colleges often offer the best price for new computers. You may want to check out the options before you purchase a computer from home.

During the busy times of the term, particularly around midterms and finals, computer laboratories are likely to be crowded. Today, many dorm rooms are wired for computers and direct connections are linked to the campus library.

GETTING THE MOST FROM YOUR CAMPUS VISIT

To learn everything important about a college, you need more than the standard presentation and tour given to visiting students and parents. Plan your visit for a weekday during the school term. This will let you see how classes are taught and how students live. It also is the best time to meet faculty and staff members, or to go to a dean's office for information. If the college does not schedule group presentations or tours at the time you want, call the office of admissions to arrange for an individual tour and interview. At the same time, ask the admissions office to make appointments with people you want to meet.

To find out about a specific academic program, ask to meet the department chairperson. If you are interested in athletics, religion, or music, meet the coach, the chaplain, or the conductor of the orchestra. Your parents will also want to talk to a financial aid counselor about scholarships, grants, and loans. The office of academic affairs can help with your questions about courses or the faculty. The office of student affairs is in charge of residence halls, health services, and extracurricular activities. Each of these areas has a dean or vice president and a number of assistants, so you should be able to get your questions answered even if you go in without an appointment.

Take advantage of a group presentation and tour if one is scheduled on the day of your visit. Much of what you learn may be familiar, but other students and parents will ask about some of the same things you want to know. Student tour guides are also good sources of information. They love to talk about their own courses, professors, and campus experiences.

Finally, explore the campus on your own. Visit the library and computer facilities, to see whether they are adequate for all the students using them. Check the condition of the buildings and the grounds. If they appear well maintained, the college probably has good overall management. If they look run down, the college may have financial problems that also make it scrimp on the book budget or laboratory supplies. Visit a service office, such as the registrar, career planning, or academic advising. Observe whether they treat students courteously and seem genuinely interested in helping them.

Talk to some of the students who are already enrolled at the college. They will usually speak frankly about weekend activities, whether they find it easy to talk to professors out of class, and how much drinking or drug abuse there is on campus. Most importantly, meeting other students will help you discover how friendly the campus is and whether the college will suit you socially and intellectually.

More than buildings and courses of study, a college is a community of people. Only during a campus visit can you experience the human environment in which you will live and work during four critical years.

CHECKLIST QUESTIONS

The following questions form a checklist to evaluate each college or university you are considering. Use the Profiles, literature from the colleges, and your own inquiries and observations to get the answers.

I. Identify good possibilities. Only colleges for which all five answers are "Yes" should go on your final list.

1. Is the college accredited by its regional association?
2. Does the college offer the program I want to study?
3. Do I have a good chance to be admitted?
4. Can my family manage the costs? (Read Finding the Money, page 15, before answering this question.)
5. Is the location at an acceptable distance from home?

II. Compare colleges for quality and value. The more questions you answer "Yes," the better that college is for you.

A. Academics

1. Does a majority of the faculty have doctoral degrees?
2. Do the best research professors teach undergraduate courses?
3. Do class sizes meet the standards described in this article?
4. Do regular faculty members teach at least 80 percent of courses?
5. Does the major program have enough full-time faculty members?
6. Does the major program offer its courses on a regular schedule?

B. Support Services

1. Is the library collection adequate for the college programs?
2. Does the library offer good services and accessible hours?
3. Are student computer facilities readily available?
4. Do the people in the admissions, financial aid, and other service offices seem attentive and genuinely interested in helping students?

C. Campus Environment

1. Will I be comfortable with the size and setting of the campus?
2. Will I find activities that meet my interests?
3. Will I find the other students compatible?
4. Will I find the housing and food services suitable?
5. Does the campus seem well maintained and managed?

Sheldon Halpern
Barbara Aronson

COLLEGE ENTRANCE EXAMINATIONS

By providing you with exactly the same information about each of the colleges in which you are interested, the book you are now reading, *Profiles of American Colleges*, will help you narrow down the list of colleges to which you will apply. Of course, your final decision will be influenced by many other factors, many of which are far more important: actual visits to the colleges; virtual visits on the Internet; viewings of videotapes; advice from guidance counselors, parents, teachers, and friends.

In much the same way, by providing college admissions officers with the same information about thousands of applicants, the results of college entrance exams can help them narrow down the list of students they are considering accepting. The results of these exams help admissions officers compare students with widely differing backgrounds. Students from different high schools in different states who earn the same grade in their biology classes, B+ say, have used different textbooks, have performed different labs, have taken different tests, and in general often exhibit great disparity in their level of mastery of the subject; indeed, even within the same school, a grade of B+ from one teacher might not represent the same level of accomplishment as a B+ from another teacher. However, a grade of 650 on the Biology SAT II, or a 4 on the Biology AP test means the same thing whether it was earned by a student from a rural community in Idaho, an inner-city school in New York, or a private prep school in Massachusetts. Because students all across the country take the same standardized test on the same day, colleges can give greater credence to the results, than they can to the results of final exams from different schools.

KINDS OF COLLEGE ENTRANCE EXAMINATIONS

Although some students who go from high school to two-year community colleges do not take any college entrance tests, most do, and virtually all students who are applying to four-year colleges will take some of the following exams:

- PSAT/NMSQT or the Preliminary SAT/National Merit Scholarship Qualifying Test.
- SAT I: Reasoning Tests.
- SAT II: Subject Tests.
- Advanced Placement (AP) Examinations.
- The ACT Assessment.

The PSAT/NMSQT

The PSAT/NMSQT measures verbal and mathematical reasoning necessary for success in college. It is a standardized test taken by students in high schools throughout the country, in October of their junior year. The test consists of five sections: two 25-minute verbal sections (52 questions total), two 25-minute math sections (40 questions), and one 30-minute writing skills section (39 questions).

This Preliminary SAT is also the qualifying test for the scholarship competition conducted by the National Merit Scholarship Corporation, an independent, nonprofit organization supported by grants from over 600 corporations, private foundations, colleges, and universities. All students whose scores are in the top 5% of students taking the exam that year receive National Merit Letters of Commendation. In addition, students whose scores are in the top 1.5% of those taking the exam that year become National Merit Semifinalists. Those who advance to finalist standing by meeting additional requirements compete for one-time National Merit $2000 Scholarships and renewable four-year Merit Scholarships, which may be worth as much as $8000 a year for four years.

In addition, this test is used by the National Achievement Scholarship Program for outstanding African American students. Top-scoring black students in each of the regional selection units established for the competition continue in the competition for nonrenewable National Achievement $2000 Scholarships and for four-year Achievement Scholarships sponsored by more than 175 organizations.

Test-Taking Strategies for the PSAT/NMSQT

1. Know what to expect. The first verbal section of the PSAT has 25 questions and the second verbal section has 27. In total, there will be 13 sentence completions, 13 verbal analogies, and 26 reading comprehension questions. The first math section has 20 multiple-choice questions; the second math section has 12 quantitative comparison questions and 8 questions for which no choices are provided and whose answers must be entered in a special grid. Calculators may be used on any question in the math sections. The writing skills section has 39 multiple-choice questions—19 questions in which you have to identify grammatical errors in sentences; 14 questions which require you to improve a given sentence; and 6 questions in which you have to make improvements in the structure of a paragraph.

2. On average, wild guessing has no effect on your score. Educated guessing, on the other hand, can improve your score dramatically. On all multiple-choice questions, try to eliminate as many obviously incorrect answer choices as possible, and then guess from among the choices still remaining.

3. Expect easy questions at the beginning of each set of the same question type. Within each set (except for the reading comprehension questions), the questions progress from easy to difficult. In other words, the first verbal analogy questions in a set will be easier than the last verbal analogy questions in that set; the first quantitative comparison questions will be easier than the last ones.

4. Take advantage of the easy questions to boost your score. Remember: each question is worth the same number of points. Whether it is easy or difficult, whether it takes you ten seconds or two minutes to answer, you get the same number of points for each question you answer correctly. Your job is to answer as many questions as you can without rushing so fast that you make careless errors. Take enough time to get those easy questions right!

The SAT I

The SAT I is a reasoning test consisting of two parts—Verbal Reasoning and Mathematical Reasoning. It is designed to measure your ability to do college work. Part of the test deals with verbal skills with an emphasis on critical reading including a double passage with different points of view. The verbal sections measure the extent of your vocabulary, your ability to interpret and create ideas, and your ability to reason logically and draw conclusions correctly. The mathematics part measures your ability to reason with numbers and mathematical concepts. It tests your ability to handle general number concepts rather than specific achievement in mathematics. Calculators are permitted on each math section.

The Verbal Reasoning sections are 30, 30, and 15 minutes in length and include 19 sentence completion, 19 analogy, and 40 reading comprehension questions. The Mathematics Reasoning sections are 30, 30, and 15 minutes in length and include 35 multiple choice, 15 quantitative comparison, and 10 student-produced response questions.

The SAT I is given on seven Saturdays during the year—once each in January, March (or April), May, June, October, November, and December. Applicants may request, for religious reasons, to take the test on the Sunday following the regularly scheduled date.

You can register by mail by using the registration form available at your school or online at www.collegeboard.org.

On each part of the SAT I—verbal and math—you earn a raw score and a scaled score. On each part, the raw score is calculated by giving you one point for each question that you answer correctly and deducting one quarter of a point for each question that you answer incorrectly. (On quantitative comparison questions, the deduction is one-third of a point and on student-produced response questions, there is no deduction.) This raw score is not reported to you or to the colleges. Instead, the raw score on each part is converted to a scaled score between 200 and 800, with 500 being the median score on each part. In discussing their SAT I scores, most students add their verbal and math scores. So a student whose scores were 550 on the verbal section and 600 on the math section would say, "I got an 1150."

Test-Taking Strategies for the SAT I

1. Know what to expect. For the critical reading part of the verbal section, be prepared to find 4 passages with content as follows: one in social science, one in natural science, and two in fiction or nonfiction. In the mathematical reasoning section be prepared to find 15 quantitative comparison questions, 35 multiple-choice questions, and 10 questions for which you will be required to produce a response.
2. Pace yourself properly. It is much better to slow down and avoid careless errors than it is to speed up in an effort to answer all the questions. You can earn an above-average score (over 1000) by correctly answering fewer than half of the questions on the test and omitting the rest. Even scores of 1300 can be achieved by omitting more than 20% of the questions.
3. Read carefully. Make sure you are answering the question asked, not a similar one you once encountered. Underline key words (e.g., NOT and EXCEPT) to make sure you do not answer the opposite of the question asked.
4. Learn the directions for each type of question before taking the test. During the test, do not waste even one second reading the directions or looking at the sample questions.
5. Always answer the easy questions first (the ones at the beginning of each section). Do not panic if you can't answer a question. Do not spend too much time on any one question. If you are truly stuck, make an educated guess if possible (see below), and move on. Remember that each question is worth the same one point, and the next few questions may be much easier for you.
6. On average, wild guessing does not affect your score—it is unlikely to help, but it is equally unlikely to hurt you. The choice is yours. However, educated guessing—when you can eliminate one or more of the answer choices—can significantly increase your score! In particular, don't omit critical reading questions if you have read the passage; you can always eliminate some of the choices. Most math questions contain at least one or two choices that are absurd (for example, negative choices when you know that the answer must be positive); eliminate them and guess.

SAT II: Subject Tests

These tests are one-hour, multiple-choice question tests. You may take one, two, or three tests on any one test date. Unlike the SAT I, these tests measure knowledge and application of knowledge. Some colleges require specific subject tests, whereas others allow applicants to choose the ones they wish to present with the admission application. Those colleges that do require these tests may use them to determine acceptance or placement in college courses. The tests in foreign language not only are used for placement, but also for possible exemption from a foreign language requirement. If the college of your choice does not require these tests, but you would like to demonstrate proficiency in a particular field, take the test anyway and have your scores sent.

Tests are given in writing, literature, history, mathematics, sciences, and several foreign languages.

Advanced Placement (AP) Examinations

The College Board also conducts Advanced Placement tests, given to high school students who have completed advanced or honors courses and wish to get college credit. Many secondary schools offer college-level courses in calculus, statistics, art, psychology, European history, American history, Latin, Spanish, French, German, biology, chemistry, and physics. As a result of scores obtained on these tests, colleges grant credit or use the results for placement in advanced college courses.

The ACT Assessment

The registration form for the ACT includes a detailed questionnaire that takes about one hour to complete. As a result of the answers to those questions about your high school courses, personal interests, and career plans, plus the scores on your ACT, an ACT Assessment Student Report is produced. This is made available to you, your high school, and to any college or scholarship source that you request. Decisions regarding college acceptance and award of scholarships are the result. This information is kept confidential and is released only according to your written instructions. To obtain an ACT application form, write or call ACT Registration, P.O. Box 414, Iowa City, Iowa 52243, telephone (319) 337-1270.

The ACT measures knowledge, understanding, and skills acquired in the educational process. The test is made up of four distinct sections: English, mathematics, reading, and science reasoning.

On the ACT, you should answer all questions, because your score is based on the number of questions you answer correctly. There is no penalty for wrong answers. For each of the four tests the total number of correct responses yields a raw score. A table is used to convert the raw scores to *scaled scores.* The highest possible scaled score for each test is 36. The average of the four scaled scores yields the *composite score.*

The ACT English Test is a 75-item, 45-minute test that measures punctuation, grammar, usage, sentence structure, spelling, and vocabulary. The test consists of five passages, each accompanied by multiple-choice test items. A total score is reported as well as a subscore for the 40 usage questions and a subscore for the 35 questions dealing with the rhetorical skills.

Test-Taking Strategies for the ACT English Test

1. Pace yourself. You have 45 minutes to complete 75 questions.
2. Skim through the whole passage quickly to get the author's view.
3. Read the sentences immediately before and after the one containing an underlined portion.

The ACT Mathematics Test has 60 questions to answer in 60 minutes. The test emphasizes quantitative reasoning rather than memorized formulas. Five content areas are included in the mathematics test. About 12 questions deal with pre-algebra topics, such as operations with whole numbers, decimals, fractions, and integers. About the same number of questions deal with elementary algebra. Usually 18 questions are based on intermediate algebra and coordinate geometry. About 14 questions are based on plane geometry and usually four items are based on right triangle trigonometry and basic trigonometric identities.

Test-Taking Strategies for the ACT Mathematics Test

1. Spend an average of one minute on each question, less on the easy questions, more on the difficult ones.
2. Be sure to answer each question even if you have to guess.
3. Make sure your answers are reasonable.

The ACT Reading Test is a 40-item, 35-minute test that measures reading comprehension. Three scores are reported for this test: a total score, a subscore based on the 20 items in the social studies and natural sciences sections, and a subscore on the 20 items in the prose fiction and humanities sections.

Test-Taking Strategies for the ACT Reading Test

1. Read each passage carefully. Underline important ideas in the passage.
2. Pace yourself. You have 40 questions to answer in 35 minutes.
3. Refer to the passage and in particular to your underlined sections when answering the questions.

The ACT Science Reasoning Test presents seven sets of scientific information in three different formats: graphs, tables, and other schematic forms (38 percent); description of experiments (45 percent); and expression of conflicting viewpoints (17 percent). The 40 items are to be answered in 35 minutes. The content of the test is drawn from biology, chemistry, physics, geology, astronomy, and meteorology. Background knowledge at the level of a high school general science course is all that is needed to answer these questions. The test emphasizes scientific reasoning skills rather than recall of scientific content, skill in mathematics, or reading ability.

Test-Taking Strategies for the ACT Science Reasoning Test

1. Read the scientific material before you begin answering a question. Read tables and text carefully, underlining important ideas.
2. Look for flaws in the experiments and devise ways of improving the experiments.
3. When you are asked to compare viewpoints, make notes in the margin of the printed material summarizing each viewpoint.

A FINAL WORD

Don't take any examination without preparation, even though you will find descriptions of these tests that say they test skills developed over years of study both in and out of school. Don't walk in cold, even though you believe that you meet all the qualities colleges are looking for.

Although the College Board suggests no special preparation, it does distribute to applicants the booklet, "Taking the SAT I Reasoning Test." It also makes available other publications containing former test questions along with advice on how to cope with the questions. Evidently, all candidates need some form of preparation.

The American College Testing Program furnishes the booklet, "Preparing for the ACT Assessment." This gives specific information about the test, test questions, and strategies for taking each of the four parts. It also describes what to expect on the test day and gives practice with typical questions.

Barron's Educational Series publishes books to help you prepare for these tests. They are available at all bookstores and in many libraries. You should be sure to use them before taking any of these tests.

Although no high school student takes all of the college-entrance exams described above, virtually all students planning to attend a four-year college take at least one of them—the SAT I or ACT. Prepare conscientiously for each exam that you take and you will provide the colleges to which you are applying with valuable information about your abilities. Good luck!

Ira K. Wolf
President
PowerPrep, Inc.

GETTING IN

The college admission process—getting in—begins the minute you start making your first choices in course selection and in cocurricular activities in junior high school, middle school, and high school. These initial and ongoing decisions are crucial to your future well-being. They lay the groundwork for the curriculum you will follow throughout your high school career: they are not easily reversed. These are the decisions that will allow you to market yourself to the colleges of your choice.

STUDENTS TAKE NOTE!

There is a myth prevalent among college-bound students throughout the country that the best way to gain entrance to the selective colleges is to be well rounded. This term usually refers to students who have earned good grades in high school (B+ or better) and participated in a wide range of cocurricular activities.

However, most admission officers at the selective colleges prefer applications from candidates they term angular—students who have demonstrated solid academic achievement in and out of school *and* who have developed one or two particularly strong cocurricular skills, interests, and activities. These angular students are very different in character from the well-rounded students who are very good at everything, yet excel at little, if anything.

William Fitzsimmons, Dean of Admission at Harvard, says that Harvard is looking for a well-rounded class, which means Harvard is most interested in admitting angular students—students who have excelled at something. He cautions, though, that "...It is a mistake to denigrate or underestimate that persuasive power of high grades, rank, double 800s on the SAT I, 36 on the ACT, and equally impressive SAT II scores. NOTE: As of the school year 2002–2003, the SAT II will no longer be offered with the option of score choice. The selective colleges take many of these academically high profile applicants. But the numbers game alone often won't get you in! It would be fairly simple for Harvard to enroll an entire freshman class with a superior academic profile and little depth of quality in areas that make up the personality of the class. We just would not do that!"

Dean Fitzsimmons is saying that the majority of the successful applicants to selective colleges must have some major commitment(s) combined with excellent academic qualities. A strong impact results from quality involvements rather than a proliferation of joinings and transient interests. Essentially, the angular applicant is a committed individual, while the well-rounded candidate is merely involved.

STUDENTS AND PARENTS TAKE AN EARLY, ACTIVE ROLE

Students and parents must make time to ensure an early, active role in the college admissions process. Each year, starting in the seventh grade, students and parents should take the time to sit down with the student's guidance counselor and talk meaningfully about the following:

- selection and level of courses, projecting through the senior year of high school;
- cocurricular activities available, such as drama, music, athletics, academic clubs, community activities, student government, and other special interest groups; and
- summer study, work, or recreation.

Why is this important to getting in? As sure as taxes and death, there is going to come a time in your senior year when you, the college-bound student, will be asked to choose colleges, complete the college application, write your college essay(s), and have an interview—either on the college campus, or in your hometown.

You must create the personal marketing, which will take place during the application process in your senior year, long before your senior year starts. By the time you reach that long-awaited dream of being a senior, you and you alone have created the person you must market to the colleges of your choice. You must understand that the person you have created is the only person you have to market. There is no Madison Avenue glitz involved in this marketing process! You don't create a pseudo marketing campaign that shows you jumping off a bridge with a bungee cord tied to your sneakers. Admission counselors can tell the difference between a real marketing effort and a pseudo marketing campaign.

THE APPLICATION FORM

Today colleges are offering their application on hard copy, computer disk, E-mail, or through on-line services of the Internet. Each application form differs from college to college, with the exception of those colleges that use the common application. When you start to work, be sure to note all deadlines, follow all directions, be complete, be neat, fill out the geographical data with accurate facts, and type it all (unless you print exceptionally well). Always review the entire application before you start to fill it out, and complete the entire application before you start the next one. Remember the application is *you* to the admissions committee member reading it. Even though "a book should not be judged by its cover," appearances do influence opinions.

It is best to work through a rough draft of the application before you actually work on the application copy to be submitted. Remember to make a copy of all parts of the finished application in the event that yours gets lost and a replacement must be sent.

You are responsible for giving the Secondary School Report, found in each application, directly to your high school guidance counselor. Your counselor is responsible for sending official copies of grades, rank in class (if any), the school's profile, and a written recommendation regarding you. It also is your responsibility to call or fill out the appropriate forms for either the SAT I and/or SAT II or the ACT, to send the appropriate test information directly to each college to which you have applied, even if your scores are on your high school transcript. Your college file will not be considered complete, and will not be sent to the admission committee for a decision, without these official scores. Additionally, many colleges want recommendations from one or two teachers. Choose wisely and allow each teacher plenty of time. Request letters from teachers who know you best. If English is your interest, be sure to choose an English teacher. If you are fluent in Spanish and have future interest in Spanish at college, ask the Spanish teacher. Remember, though you have many interests and have participated in many activities—you are developing an admissions package as part of your marketing of yourself. Emphasize your strengths and show how they are integrated into your activities and achievements.

Cocurricular activities usually are athletic or nonathletic. If you have won athletic awards, note them. If you have had the starring role in the spring musical for the last two years, say so. If you are an editor on the school newspaper, specify this. Admissions people view your activities with special interest. They realize how very time consuming these activities can be and how they sometimes bring very few accolades. List these activities in the order of importance to you. If you do not believe that the application allows you the opportunity to show your depth of commitment to one or two cocurricular areas, you may add an addendum. Use the KISS (Keep It Short and Simple) method. This is an addendum, not an essay, letter, or dissertation. Be honest!

Some applications have mini essays. When space is provided, be sure you are concise, clear, and grammatically correct. Here, less is more. Your ability to organize your thoughts and present them concisely is being tested. You will receive your chance to impress each college with your prose in the long essay segment of the application. Some colleges have as many as four long essays, whereas some require none. In addition to the short and long essay questions, some colleges ask the student for a graded paper signed by the teacher.

Some colleges encourage you to support your application with additional materials. If you are given this option, consider what will strengthen your application: musical tapes, art and/or photography portfolios, published writings, an exceptional graded term paper, all the additional opportunities for the college to get to know you better and for you to increase your image as an angular candidate. Such additions help the admissions committee to get a better handle on who you are in relation to other applicants. Be sure your presentation is clear and as professional as possible. These additions are not going to be evaluated by the admissions committee. Your material will be directed to the appropriate department for evaluation and an evaluative note will be sent back to the admissions committee. It is this note that will become part of your admissions package, the same way an athletic coach evaluates potential student/athletes.

Proofread all parts of the application. Be sure you, the student, place your signature where it is required. Then place everything, including the registration fee check, in a large manila envelope and give it to your college guidance counselor. After adding the completed Secondary School Report to the application, your guidance counselor will mail it. Your job is now finished and the waiting begins!

E-Mail, On-line Services through the College or the Internet

We have joined the 21st century with E-mail and on-line services of the Internet offering college applications. This movement promises to be the wave of the future. Certainly ecologically correct, by producing as close to a paperless process as possible, this method is still in cyberspace. Be sure you know what you are doing when you use any of these methods. It is seriously suggested that you take the time to call the college shortly after sending this type of application, to ensure that your application is on file. If you have an addendum or two, you may want to speak to an admission clerk to make sure each addendum has reached the office of admission in the format you desired. If it were my application and I chose any of these methods, I'd still send my musical tape, the slides for my art portfolio, and such, by certified or registered mail. Clarity is so important to the professionals who will be evaluating these addenda for your college admission process!

PC- and Mac-Based Computer Disk Applications

Since the emergence of on-line applications, fewer colleges have a computer disk application. If you wish to apply this way, make sure that your target college has authorized the disk: there are a number of organizations selling computer disk applications without the consent of the college. Make sure the service to which you have subscribed allows you to print a hard copy of the application, even if they want you to send the disk back to the service or to the college. Do yourself a favor and print an extra copy of the application for your personal college file—it is very easy for the post office or college to lose your information. It is also wise, if you have to send the disk with the application, to write, "DO NOT SCAN" on the envelope. It is highly probable that the information on the disk will be lost if it is passed through a scanning machine.

The Common Application

About 200 colleges in the United States have agreed that students may apply to their colleges by completing one common application. Some of the colleges using the common application also have their own application. Students applying to a college that allows an applicant a choice of using either the college's own application or the common application, obviously face a choice. The use of the common application substantially reduces the time spent composing different essay answers and neatly typing separate application forms. If you are one of those who must make a choice between the common application and the application of the college, you should understand that each college using the common application (either as its only application or as an alternative application) has the right to ask for a supplement. If you choose the common application, be very sure to read the pages surrounding the common application carefully. Each college has a paragraph in which they discuss their deadlines, requirements for admission, and specify if they require supplemental information. The supplemental information can range from an additional essay or two, to additional information about your cocurricular activities.

All the colleges participating in the common application have each member of their admission staff sign a statement that they will NOT discriminate in the admissions process among students who submit the common application versus students who submit the college's application. However, there are counselors who believe that when there is a choice, the applicant has a better chance of conveying information by using the college's application; there is a vast difference in format between the two applications, even if the college requires a supplement. Check with your guidance counselor if you are unsure regarding your choice of format. To access the common application online, go to:

www.commonapp.org

College Web Sites

Most colleges today have their own web site. Here you will find a wealth of information. Some colleges have even put their viewbook and course curriculum guide, as well as their application, on their site. Visit each college's web page—the addresses are in the Admissions Contact section of the college Profiles in this book. You'll be a much better informed consumer.

THE INTERVIEW

The interview is a contrived situation that few people enjoy, of which many people misunderstand the value, and about which everyone is apprehensive. However, no information from a college catalog, no friend's friend, no high school guidance counselor's comments, and no parental remembrances from bygone days can surpass the value of your college campus visit and interview. This first hand opportunity to assess your future alma mater will confirm or contradict other impressions and help you make a sound college acceptance.

Many colleges will recommend or request a personal interview. It is best to travel to the campus to meet with a member of the admissions staff if you can; however, if you can't, many colleges will arrange to have one of their representatives, usually an alumnus, interview you in your hometown.

Even though the thought of an interview might give you enough butterflies to lift you to the top of your high school's flagpole, here are some tips that might make it a little easier.

1. **Go prepared.** Read the college's catalog and this book's Profile ahead of time so you won't ask "How many books are in your library?" or "How many students do you have?" Ask intelligent questions that introduce a topic of conversation that you want the interviewer to know about you. The key is to distinguish yourself in a positive way from thousands of other applicants. Forge the final steps in the marketing process you have been building since your first choices in the college admission process back in junior high school. The interview is your chance to enhance those decisions.
2. **Nervousness** is absolutely and entirely normal. The best way to handle it is to admit it, out loud, to the interviewer. Richard Shaw, Dean of Admission at Yale University, sometimes relates this true story to his apprehensive applicants. One extremely agitated young applicant sat opposite him for her interview with her legs crossed, wearing loafers on her feet. She swung her top leg back and forth to some inaudible rhythm. The loafer on her top foot flew off her foot, hit him in the head, ricocheted to the desk lamp and broke it. She looked at him in terror, but when their glances met, they both dissolved in laughter. The moral of the story—the person on the

other side of the desk is also a human being and wants to put you at ease. So admit to your anxiety, and don't swing your foot if you're wearing loafers! (And by the way, she was admitted.)

3. **Be yourself.** Nobody's perfect, and everyone knows nobody's perfect, so admit to a flaw or two before the interviewer goes hunting for them. The truly impressive candidate will convey a thorough knowledge of self.
4. **Interview the interviewer.** Don't passively sit there and allow the interviewer to ask all the questions and direct the conversation. Participate in this responsibility by assuming an active role. A thoughtful questioner will accomplish three important tasks in a successful interview:

   demonstrate interest, initiative, and maturity for taking partial responsibility for the content of the conversation;
   guide the conversation to areas where he/she feels most secure and accomplished; and
   obtain answers. Use your genuine feelings to react to the answers you hear. If you are delighted to learn of a certain program or activity, show it. If you are curious, ask more questions. If you are disappointed by something you learn, try to find a path to a positive answer. Then consider yourself lucky that you discovered this particular inadequacy in time.
5. **Parents** do belong in your college decision process as your advisers! Often it is they who spend the megabucks for your next four years. They can provide psychological support and a stabilizing influence for sensible, rational decisions. However, they do NOT belong in your interview session. In essence, the sage senior will find constructive ways to include parents in the decision-making process as catalysts, without letting them take over (as many are apt to do) the interview process. You may want your parents to meet and speak briefly to your interviewer prior to your interview and that is fine, but parents may not accompany you into the interview session! Arrange with your parents to meet somewhere out of the interview building after your interview is over. You do not want the interviewer inviting your parents back to the interview room. As intelligent as parents may be, they do not perceive the answers to questions the same way you do. The worst scenario I can imagine is the interviewer asking your parents some of the same questions that were asked you, and that is highly likely. Parents just answer questions differently than teenagers. At best, the scenario creates a long, long ride home, and when you get home you can't punish your parents by taking the car keys away from them, or grounding them for a week. At worst, the scenario has caused a blight in your admissions file. This is your time! Keep it that way!
6. **Practice makes perfect.** Begin your interviews at colleges that are low on your list of preferred choices, and leave your first-choice colleges until last. If you are shy, you will have a chance to practice vocalizing what your usually silent inner voice tells you. Others will have the opportunity to commit their inevitable first blunders where they won't count as much.
7. **Departing impressions.** There is a remarkable tendency for the student to base final college preferences on the quality of the interview only, or on the personal reaction to the interviewer as the personification of the entire institution. Do not do yourself the disservice of letting it influence an otherwise rational selection, one based on institutional programs, students, services, and environment. After the last good-bye and thank you has been smiled, and you exhale deeply on your way out the door, go ahead and congratulate yourself. If you used the interview properly, you will know whether or not you wish to attend that college and why.
8. **Send a thank-you note** to your interviewer. A short and simple handwritten or typed note will do—and if you forgot to mention something important about yourself at the interview, here's your chance.

WRITING THE COLLEGE ESSAY

Do the colleges read the essays you write on their applications? You bet your diploma they do. Here is your chance to strut your stuff, stand up, be counted, and stylize your way into the hearts of the decision makers.

Write it, edit it, review it. Rewrite it. Try to show why you are unique and how the college will benefit having you in its student body. This is not a routine homework assignment, but a college level essay that will be carefully examined for spelling, grammar, content, and style of a high school senior. As strenuous an effort as it may be, completing the essay gives the admissions committee a chance to know the real you, a three-dimensional human being with passions, preferences, strengths, weaknesses, imagination, energy, and ambition. Your ability to market yourself will help the deans and directors of admission remember your application from among the sea of thousands that flood their offices each year.

First, maximize your strengths—use your essays to say what you want to say. The answer to a specific question on the college's part still provides an opening for you to furnish background information about yourself, your interests, ambitions, and insights. For example, the essay that asks you to name your favorite book and the reason for your selection could be answered with the title of a Dr. Seuss book because you are considering a career as an elementary school teacher. If you are interested in business, read about a famous businessman you admire and then discuss your interest in business.

Whatever the essay questions are, autobiographical or otherwise, select the person or issue that puts you in the position to discuss the subject in which you are the most well versed. In essence, all of your essay responses are autobiographical in the sense that they will illustrate something important about yourself, your values, and the kind of person you are (or hope to become). If personal values are important to you, and they should be, then here is your opportunity to stress their importance.

Because many colleges will ask for more than one essay, make sure that the *sum* of the essays in any one college application covers your best points. Do not repeat your answers, even if the questions sound alike. Cover the most important academic and cocurricular activities (most important meaning the one in which you excelled and/or in which you spent the most quality time).

If you are fortunate to have a cooperative English teacher, you might request a critique of your first draft, but be sure to allow enough time for a careful evaluation and your revision.

Write the essays yourself—no substitutes or stand-ins. College admission professionals can discern mature adult prose from student prose.

PARTING WORDS

You may wish to ask yourself the following questions to help you decide which is your Paradise College. Most of this information is in the individual college Profiles in this book.

1. **Caliber of School Programs** Is the college known for its English department or chemistry department? What are its strengths?
2. **Selectivity of Admissions** Is the college Most Competitive, Highly Competitive, Very Competitive, Competitive, Less Competitive or Noncompetitive? Check the Selector Ratings.
3. **Chances of Admission** Be realistic. What are your chances of getting in? How far can you reach? Listen when you are given advice!

4. **Location of the School** Is the school near home, one hour away, 300 miles away, or across the United States?
5. **Rural, Suburban, Urban Campus** Is the school in the city or in a rural area?
6. **Size of the School** Can you spend four years at a small liberal arts college of 800 undergraduates? Do you need the larger atmosphere of a university? Do not equate size with social life!
7. **State College vs. Private College** Is the college a large state university with most of the student population from the state where it's located? Is it one of the public "Ivies"? Will you be a minority in the state school?
8. **Geographical Diversity** Is the college a regional one attracting students from the same state or region? Or is it a college, regardless of its size, which attracts students from all over the United States, or the world at large?
9. **Cost of College** What is the tuition? What are the living costs? What travel costs are there from home to campus? Are there hidden costs?
10. **Financial Aid** With a great percentage of undergraduates at many private colleges on financial aid of some type, where do you fit? What monies are available for the students at the schools of your choice? Is the college need blind in its admission program?
11. **Living Conditions** Is housing on campus guaranteed for all four years? Are the dorms coed? Are there single-sex dorms? Are alternatives in housing available?
12. **Socialization** Is it a grind school—all work, work, work? Is it fraternity- and sorority-oriented? What are the on-campus facilities for socialization?
13. **Safety on Campus** Are the dorms secure and locked? What's the safety system on the campus?
14. **Core Curriculum—Distribution Credits** Does the college require (for graduation) a specific number of credits in different academic disciplines? For example, does the student have to take six credits in philosophy before graduating? Is a self-designed curriculum possible?
15. **Sophomore Standing** Does the college accept AP credits? Does it offer advanced standing for an AP course, or just a credit toward graduation?
16. **Junior Year Abroad** Are there opportunities to study in Italy, Japan, or Australia, for example, while you are an undergraduate?
17. **Internships** Are there opportunities for hands-on experience while in college? Which departments have formal internship opportunities?
18. **Graduate School After College** What percentage of its graduates go on to graduate school immediately upon graduation, or within five years? What is the record of those who successfully get into the law, medical, or business school of their choice?
19. **Placement After Graduation** Is there an office for job placement after college? Is there an alumni network that helps in job placement?
20. **Weekend College** Do the students remain on campus on weekends, or is it a suitcase college?
21. **Minorities** What percentage of the students are minorities? Reflect on the racial, ethnic, and religious minority roles in the college you are considering. How would you feel being Jewish at a Roman Catholic college for example—or Catholic at a Jewish college?
22. **Sports Facilities** Is there a swimming pool? Are there horse stables? Is there an ice hockey rink on campus?
23. **Library Facilities** How many books are in the library? Is it computerized? Is the campus library tied into a larger network?
24. **Athletic Programs** Is the ice hockey team a varsity sport? Does the lacrosse team play Division I or III? Is basketball strong? Do they have a women's squash team?
25. **Honors Programs** Are honors programs available? What are they? Who is eligible?
26. **Student Body** Are the students politically active? Are they professional in orientation?
27. **Faculty** Are all classes taught by full professors? Or are TAs (teaching assistants) the norm?
28. **Computer Labs** Are computers required of incoming freshmen? What are the facilities on campus? Can you have your own PC in your room?
29. **Campus Visits** If possible, make a visit to the campus. Spend some time talking to students for a feel of the campus.
30. **Special Talents** Recognize your special talents and discover where they fit best. Often, a special talent becomes a scale-tipper in the admissions process.
31. **Special Family Circumstances** Talk with your parents about their expectations. Discuss your needs as well as their thoughts.
32. **Legacy** Does your family have a history at a specific school? Are you interested in continuing the tradition?
33. **Note Well—Final List** Be sure the final list is a realistic one. It should include "reaches," "targets," and "safeties." No matter which one admits you—it must fit!

Finding and applying to the best colleges for you is not supposed to be easy, but it can be fun. Parents, guidance counselors, and teachers are there to help you, so don't struggle alone. Keep your sense of humor and a smile on your face as you go about researching, exploring, and discovering your ideal college.

Last but not least is The Parent Credo: The right college is the one where your child will fit in scholastically and socially. Be realistic in your aspirations and support the child's choice!

Anthony F. Capraro, III, Ph.D.
President, Teach Inc.
College Counseling
Purchase, New York

FINDING THE MONEY

Postsecondary education is a major American industry. A greater proportion of students pursue postsecondary education in the United States than in any other industrialized country. Annually, more than 13 million students study at over 8000 institutions of higher learning. The diversity of our system of higher education is admired by educators and students throughout the world. There is no reason to believe that this system will change in the future. However, college costs and the resources available to parents and students to meet those costs have changed.

Unfortunately, many high school students and their parents believe either that there is no financial aid available or that they will not qualify for any type of financial assistance from any source. Neither assumption is correct. College costs have increased and will continue to increase. Federal allocations, for some financial aid programs, have decreased. But this decline has been met with generous increases in financial aid from state and school sources.

American students and their parents should realize that they must assume the primary role in planning to meet their future college costs and that the family financial planning process must begin much earlier than has been the case.

COLLEGE COSTS

- Eighty-two percent of all parents believe college costs are too expensive.
- In the year 2000, the average cost of education, including tuition, fees, and room and board for one year at a public college would have been about $10,000 and for a private college and university, the total cost could have exceeded $20,000.
- While college costs will increase each year, it is important to remember that currently about 4 percent of all college students attend schools with tuition costs exceeding $10,000 and only 50 percent pay the full cost of attendance at these colleges and universities.

STUDENT FINANCIAL AID

- In 2002, the total amount of financial aid available from federal, state, and institutional sources to postsecondary students exceeded $50 billion.
- Approximately 60 percent of all students enrolled in higher education receive some type of financial assistance.
- Federal student aid remains the largest source of funding at 75 percent of total aid.
- Ten years ago the majority of federal financial assistance was grants. Today, an equal amount of grant and loan money is awarded from federal sources.

TIMETABLE FOR APPLYING FOR FINANCIAL AID

Sophomore Year of High School

Most families wait until a child has been accepted into a college or university to begin planning on how the family will meet those college costs. However, a family's college financial planning should begin much earlier.

Students, as early as the sophomore year of high school, should begin a systematic search for colleges that offer courses of study that are of interest. There are many computer programs that can be helpful in this process. These programs can match a student's interest with colleges fitting the profile. Considering that half of all students who enter college either drop out or transfer to another school, this type of early selection analysis can be invaluable.

After selecting certain schools for further consideration, you should write to the school and request a viewbook, catalog, and financial aid brochure. After receiving this information, you and your family should compare the schools. Your comparison should include academic considerations as well as financial. Don't rule out a school because you think you can't afford it. Remember the financial aid programs at that school may be more generous than at a lower-priced school. If possible, visit the college and speak with both an admission and financial aid counselor. If it is not possible to visit all the schools, call the schools and obtain answers to your questions about admission, financial aid, and placement after graduation.

Junior Year of High School

The comparative analysis of colleges and universities that you began in your sophomore year should continue in your junior year. By the completion of your junior year, you and your parents should have some idea of what it will cost to attend and the financial aid policies of each of the schools you are considering.

Some colleges and universities offer prospective applicants an early estimate of their financial aid award. This estimate is based upon information supplied by the family and can provide assistance in planning a family's budget. Remember that for most families, financial aid from federal, state, and school sources will probably not meet the total cost of attendance.

Families should remember that college costs can be met over the course of the academic year. It is not necessary to have all of the money needed to attend school available at the beginning of the academic year. Student and family savings, as well as student employment throughout the year, can be used to meet college costs.

Senior Year of High School

January

By January of your senior year of high school you should know which colleges and universities you want to receive your financial aid application forms. Be certain that you have completed not only the federal financial aid application form, but also any necessary state or school forms. Read carefully all of the instructions. Application methods and deadline dates may differ from one college to another. Submit an application clean of erasures or notations in the margins, and sign all of the application forms.

February

Approximately six weeks after you submit your application for financial aid, you will receive a report from the service agency you selected containing information on your family's expected contribution and your eligibility for financial aid. You and your parents should discuss the results of the financial aid application with regard to family contribution, educational costs, and how those costs can be met.

March

Beginning in March, most colleges begin to make financial aid decisions. If your application is complete, your chances of receiving an award letter early are greater than if additional information is required.

The financial aid award letter you receive from your school serves as your official document indicating the amount of financial aid you will receive for the year. You must sign and return a copy of the award letter to your school if you agree to accept their offer of financial aid.

If your family's financial circumstances change and you need additional funding, you should make an appointment to speak with your school's financial aid director or counselor. College financial aid personnel are permitted to exercise professional judgment and make adjustments to a student's financial need. Your letter of appeal should state explicitly how much money you need and why you need it.

TIPS ON APPLYING FOR FINANCIAL AID

1. Families can no longer wait until a child is accepted into college before deciding how they will finance that education. Earlier college financial planning is necessary.
2. Families should assume a much more active role in locating the resources necessary to fund future college costs.
3. Families should assume that college costs will continue to increase.
4. Families should assume that in the future the federal government will not substantially increase financial aid allocations.
5. Families should obtain information on a wide range of colleges including the many excellent low-cost schools.
6. Families should seek information about all of the funding sources available at each school they are considering.
7. Families should seek the advice and expertise of financial experts for college financing strategies. College financial planning should specify the amount of money a family should invest or save each month in order to meet future college bills.
8. Families should investigate all of the legitimate ways of reducing their income and assets before filing for financial aid.
9. Families should know how financial aid is awarded and the financial aid policies and programs of each school they are considering.
10. Families should realize that although the job of financing a college education rests primarily with them, they probably will not be able to save the entire cost of their child's college education. They probably will be eligible to receive some type of financial aid from some source and they will have to borrow a portion of their child's college education costs.
11. Families should be advised that the federal government frequently changes the rules and regulations governing financial aid eligibility. Check with your high school guidance counselor or college financial aid administrator for the latest program qualifications.

Marguerite J. Dennis
Vice President for Development
and Enrollment
Suffolk University
Boston, Massachusetts

SURVIVING THE FRESHMAN YEAR

COLLEGE: IT'S DIFFERENT

In college you are likely to hear fellow students say, "I don't know what that prof *wants*, and she won't *tell* me." "I wrote about three papers in high school, and now they want one every week." Though these students may be exaggerating a bit, college *is* different, both in the quality and the amount of work expected. Sometimes in high school the basic concepts of a course are reduced to a set of facts on a study sheet, handed to students to be reviewed and learned for a test.

In college, it is the concepts and ideas that are most important. These can only be grasped through a real understanding of the facts as they interrelate and form larger patterns. Writing papers and answering essay questions on tests can demonstrate a genuine understanding of the concepts, and this is why they are so important to college instructors. Learning to deal with ideas in this way can be a long-term asset, developing your independence, intellectual interests, and self-awareness.

Don't be discouraged; you are not alone. Most of your fellow students are having equally difficult times adjusting to a new learning method. Persist, and you will improve, leading to a lifetime habit of critical thinking and problem solving that can benefit you in many important ways.

College is also different outside of classes. Now that you have the freedom to choose how to spend time and what types of relationships to make, you have a bewildering number of possibilities.

MAKING A GOOD IMPRESSION

Here you are, plopped down in a strange place, feeling a bit like Dorothy transported to Oz. Your first goal is to make a good impression, showing your best self to those who will be important in your life for the next four years and even longer.

Impressing Faculty Members Favorably

Faculty members come in all ranks, from the graduate assistant, who teaches part-time while pursuing a degree, to a lofty full professor, who teaches primarily graduate students. Though different in rank and seniority, they respond to their students in roughly the same ways. They are, after all, people, with families and relationships much like your own. To have a good working relationship with them, try the following suggestions:

- **Make up your own mind about your instructors.** Listening to other students talk about teachers can be confusing. If you listen long enough, you will hear arguments for and against each of them. Don't allow hearsay to affect your own personal opinion.
- **Get to know your instructors firsthand.** Set up a meeting, during regular office hours. Don't try to settle important issues in the few moments before and after class.
- **Approach a discussion of grades carefully.** If you honestly believe that you have been graded too low, schedule a conference. Do not attack your instructor's integrity or judgment. Instead, say that you had expected your work to result in a better grade and would like to know ways to improve. Be serious about overcoming faults.
- **Don't make excuses.** Instructors have heard them all and can rarely be fooled. Accept responsibility for your mistakes, and learn from them.
- **Pay attention in class.** Conversing and daydreaming can insult your instructor and inhibit the learning process.
- **Arrive ahead of time for class.** You will be more relaxed, and you can use these moments to review notes or talk with classmates. You also demonstrate to your instructor a commitment to the class.
- **Participate in class discussions.** Ask questions and give answers to the instructor's questions. Nothing pleases an instructor more than an intelligent question that proves you are interested and prepared.
- **Learn from criticism.** It is an instructor's job to correct your errors in thinking. Don't take in-class criticism personally.

Impressing Fellow Students Favorably

Relationships with other students can be complex, but there are some basic suggestions that may make life easier in the residence halls and classrooms:

- **Don't get into the habit of bragging.** Frequent references to your wealth, your outstanding friends, your social status, or your family's successes are offensive to others.
- **Don't pry.** When your fellow students share their feelings and problems, listen carefully and avoid any tendency to intrude or ask embarrassing questions.
- **Don't borrow.** Borrowing a book, a basketball, or a few bucks may seem like a small thing to you, but some people who have trouble saying no may resent your request.
- **Divide chores.** Do your part; agree on a fair division of work in a lab project or a household task.
- **Support others.** Respect your friends' study time and the "Do not disturb" signs on their doors. Helping them to reach their goals will help you as well.
- **Allow others to be upset.** Sometimes, turning someone's anger into a joke, minimizing their difficulties, or belittling their frustration is your worst response. Support them by letting them release their emotions.
- **Don't preach.** Share your opinions when asked for, but don't try to reform the world around you.
- **Tell the truth.** Your reputation is your most important asset. When you make an agreement, keep it.

MANAGING YOUR TIME

Everyone, no matter how prominent or how insignificant, has 168 hours a week to spend. In this one asset we are all equal. There are students on every college campus, however, who seem to accomplish all their goals and still find time for play and socializing. There are others who seem to be alternating between frantic dashes and dull idleness, accomplishing very little. To the first group, college is a happy, fulfilling experience; to the latter, it is maddeningly frustrating. The first group has gained control of time, the second is controlled by that elusive and precious commodity.

- **Know where your time goes.** Unfortunately, we cannot store up time as we do money, to be used when the need is greatest. We use it as it comes, and it is amazing how it sometimes comes slowly (as in the last five minutes of a Friday afternoon class) or quickly (as in the last hour before a final exam). The first step in controlling time is to determine exactly how you use it. For a while, at least, you should carefully record how much time you spend in class, going to and from class, studying, sleeping, eating, listening to music, watching television, and running errands. You need to know what happens to your 168 hours. Only then can you make sensible decisions about managing them.
- **Make a weekly schedule.** You can schedule your routine for the week, using the time plan forms available at most college bookstores or by making your own forms.
- **First schedule the inflexible blocks of time.** Your class periods, transportation time, sleeping, and eating will form relatively routine patterns throughout the week. Trying to shave minutes off these important activities is often a mistake.

- **Plan your study time.** It is preferable, though not always possible, to set your study hours at the same time every weekday. Try to make your study time *prime time,* when your body and mind are ready for a peak performance.
- **Plan time for fun.** No one should plan to spend four years of college as a working robot. Fun and recreation are important, but they can be enjoyed in short periods just as well as long. For example, jogging with friends for 30 minutes can clear the mind, tone up the muscles, and give you those all-important social contacts. Parties and group activities can be scheduled for weekends.
- **Be reasonable in your time allotments.** As you progress through your freshman year, you will learn more precisely how much time is required to write a paper or complete a book report. Until then, schedule some extra minutes for these tasks. You are being unfair to yourself by planning one hour for a job that requires two.
- **Allow flexibility.** The unexpected is to be expected. There will be interruptions to your routine and errands that must be run at certain times. Allow for these unforeseen circumstances.

STUDYING EFFECTIVELY

Your most important activity in college is studying. Efficient study skills separate the inept student (who may spend just as many hours studying as an "A" student) from the excellent student, who thinks while studying and who uses common sense strategies to discover the important core of courses. The following suggested game plan for good study has worked in the past; it can work for you.

- **Make a commitment.** It is universally recommended that you spend two hours studying for every hour in class. At the beginning of your college career, be determined to do just that. It doesn't get easy until you make up your mind to do it.
- **Do the tough jobs first.** If certain courses are boring or particularly difficult, study them first. Don't read the interesting, enjoyable materials first, saving the toughies for the last sleepy twinges of your weary brain.
- **Study in short sessions.** Three two-hour sessions, separated from each other by a different activity, are much better than a long six-hour session.
- **Use your bits of time.** Use those minutes when you're waiting for a bus, a return call, laundry to wash, or a friend to arrive. Some of the best students I know carry 3 × 5 cards filled with definitions, formulas, or equations and learn during brief waiting periods. Most chief executives form the habit early of using bits of time wisely.

Digesting a Textbook

1. **Preview chapters.** Before you read a chapter in your textbook, preview it. Quickly examine the introductory paragraphs, headings, tables, illustrations, and other features of the chapter. The purpose is to discover the major topics. Then you can read with increased comprehension because you know where the author is leading.
2. **Underline the important points as you read.** Underlining should never be overdone; it can leave your textbook almost completely marked and less legible to read. Only the major ideas and concepts should be highlighted.
3. **Seven categories of information are commonly found in textbooks.** Be particularly alert when you see the following; get your marking pen ready.
   Definitions of terms.
   Types or *categories* of items.
   Methods of accomplishing certain tasks.
   Sequences of events or stages in a process.
   Reasons or *causes.*
   Results or *effects.*
   Contrasts or *comparisons* between items.
4. **Repeat information you need to learn.** When the object is to learn information, nothing is so effective as reciting the material, either silently or aloud.
5. **Don't read all material the same way.** Decide what you need to learn from the material and read accordingly. You read a work of fiction to learn the characters and the narrative; a poem, to learn an idea, an emotion, or a theme: a work of history, to learn the interrelationships of events. Do not read every sentence with the same speed and concentration; learn when to skim rapidly along. Remember, your study time is limited and the trick is to discriminate between the most important and the least important. No one can learn *everything* equally well.
6. **The five-minute golden secret.** As soon as possible after class is over—preferably at your desk in the classroom—skim through the chapter that has just been covered, marking the points primarily discussed. Copy what was written on the board. Now you know what the professor thinks is important!

TAKING TESTS SKILLFULLY

Try to predict the test questions. At some college libraries, copies of old examinations are made available to students. If you can legally find out your professor's previous test methods do so.

Ask your professor to describe the format of the upcoming test: multiple-choice? true-false? essay questions? problems? Adjust your study to the format described.

Listen for clues in the professor's lecture. Sometimes the questions posed in class have a way of reappearing on tests. If a statement is repeated several times or recurs in a subsequent lecture, note it as important.

As you review for the test, devise questions based on the material, and answer them. If you are part of a study group, have members ask questions of the others.

Common Sense Tactics

Arrive on the scene early; relax by breathing deeply. If the instructor gives instructions while distributing the test, listen very carefully.

- **Scan the whole test first.** Notice the point value for each section and budget your time accordingly.
- **Read the directions carefully** and then reread them. Don't lose points because you misread the directions.
- **Answer the short, easy questions first.** A bit of early success stimulates the mind and builds your confidence.
- **Leave space between answers.** You may think of a brilliant comment to add later.
- **Your first instinct is often the best** in answering true-false and multiple-choice questions. Look for qualifiers such as *never, all, often,* or *seldom* in true-false statements. Usually a qualifier that is absolute (*never, all,* or *none*) will indicate a false statement. Work fast on short-answer questions: they seldom count many points.
- **Open-book tests are no picnic.** Don't think that less study is required for an open-book test. They are often the most difficult of all examinations. If the material is unfamiliar, you won't have time to locate it and learn it during the test period.

Important Essay Strategies

- **Read the question carefully** and find out exactly what is asked for. If you are asked to contrast the French Revolution with the American Revolution and you spend your time describing each, without any contrasting references, your grade will be lowered.
- **Know the definitions of key words** used in essay questions:
  analyze: discuss the component parts.
  compare: examine for similarities.
  criticize: give a judgment or evaluation.
  define: state precise meaning of terms.

describe: give a detailed picture of qualities and characteristics.
discuss: give the pros and cons: debate them, and come to a conclusion.
enumerate: briefly mention a number of ideas, things, or events.
evaluate: give an opinion, with supporting evidence.
illustrate: give examples (illustrations) relating to a general statement.
interpret: usually means to state in other words, to explain, make clear.
outline: another way of asking for brief listings of principal ideas or characteristics. Normally the sentence or topic outline format is not required.
prove: give evidence and facts to support the premise stated in the test.
summarize: give an abbreviated account, with your conclusions.

- **Write a short outline** before you begin your essay. This organizes your thinking, making you less likely to leave out major topics.
- **Get to the point immediately.** Don't get bogged down in a lengthy introduction.
- **Read your essay over** before you hand it in. Words can be left out or misspelled. Remember that essay answers are graded somewhat subjectively, and papers that are correctly and neatly written make a better impression.
- **Learn from your test paper** when it is returned. Students who look at a test grade and discard the paper are throwing away a valuable tool. Analyze your mistakes honestly; look for clues for improvement in the professor's comments.

WRITING A TERM PAPER

Doing convincing library research and writing a term paper with correct footnotes and bibliography is a complicated procedure. Most first-year English composition courses include this process. Good students will work hard to master this skill because they know that research papers are integral parts of undergraduate and graduate courses.

Many students make the mistake of waiting until near the deadline to begin a term paper. At the busy end of the term, with final exams approaching, they embark on the uncertain time span of research and writing. Begin your term paper early, when the library staff is unhurried and ready to help and when you are under less pressure. It will pay dividends.

REGULATING YOUR RELATIONSHIPS

Find your special friends who believe in your definition of success. In a fast-paced environment like college, it is important to spend most of your time with people who share your ideas toward learning, where you can be yourself, without defensiveness. To find your kind of friends, first ask yourself: What is success? Is it a secure position and a comfortable home? A life of serving others? A position of power with a commodious executive suite? A challenging job that allows you to be creative? When you have answered honestly, you will have a set of long-range personal goals, and you can begin looking for kindred souls to walk with you on the road to success.

There will be, of course, some persons around you who are determined not to succeed, who for some reason program their lives for failure. Many college freshmen never receive a college degree; some may start college with no intention of passing courses. Their goal is to spend one hectic term as a party animal. If you intend to succeed at college, spending time among this type will be a considerable handicap. Consider making friends who will be around longer than the first year.

If possible, steer clear of highly emotional relationships during your first year of college. You don't have time for a broken heart, and relationships that begin with a rush often end that way.

MAINTAINING YOUR HEALTH

Poor health can threaten your success in the first year of college as nothing else can. No matter how busy you are, you must not forget your body and its needs: proper food, sufficient sleep, and healthy exercise. Many students, faced with the stress of college life, find themselves overmunching junk foods and gaining weight. Guard against this. Drugs and alcohol threaten the health and the success of many college students.

A FINAL WORD

So there it is. If you have read this far, you probably have a serious interest in succeeding in your first year of college. You probably have also realized that these suggestions, even if they sound a bit preachy, are practical and workable. They are based on many years of observing college students.

Benjamin W. Griffith
Former Dean, Graduate School
West Georgia College
Carrollton, Georgia

PART II

COLLEGE FACTS AND FINANCES

Now that you've read through Part I, you'll need specific information on the colleges that best match your needs and aptitudes. Here's where you'll find essential information in a nutshell.

Facts and figures on all schools are listed in chart form to help you make quick and easy comparisons. Thumbnail data include:

- campus environment
- degrees offered
- composition of the student body
- enrollment figures
- test scores of entering freshmen
- fall application deadlines

You'll also see at a glance how much it's going to cost you for tuition, room-and-board, and related expenses. In-state costs are broken down on a state-by-state basis, each range starting with colleges that don't charge tuition and going up the scale to the most expensive schools.

C[redacted]E[redacted]ES AT A G[redacted]AN[redacted]E

The charts on these pages present some of the basic data that initially concerns many students. All of the four-year accredited schools in the United States are listed here alphabetically by state. The type of college environment (from urban to rural) is given, followed by degrees offered and whether the institution is public or private. Information about whether the student body is coed or primarily men or women, and whether fraternities or sororities are on campus follows. The undergraduate enrollment for the fall of 2001 is given as well as the median test scores for freshmen who took the ACT or the SAT I. Finally, the fall admissions deadline is shown. "Open" usually indicates that admission applications will be accepted until a few weeks before classes begin.

NAME OF SCHOOL	TOWN	ENVIRONMENT U-Urban R-Rural SU-Suburban SM-Small Town	DEGREES AWARDED A-Associate B-Bachelor M-Master D-Doctorate	CONTROL Pri-Private, Pub-Public	FRATERNITIES AND SORORITIES F-Fraternities S-Sororities F, S-Both No-Neither	STUDENTS: C-Coed M-Men W-Women PM-Primarily Men PW-Primarily Women	UNDERGRADUATE ENROLLMENT FALL 2001	TEST SCORES: ACT Median	ACT Below 21	ACT 21-23	ACT 24-26	ACT 27-28	ACT Above 28	SAT I VERBAL REASONING Median	Below 500	500-599	600-700	Above 700	SAT I MATHEMATICAL REASONING Median	Below 500	500-599	600-700	Above 700	APPLICATION DEADLINE Month / Day
Alabama																								
Alabama Agricultural and Mechanical University	Normal	SU	A,M,D	Pub	F,S	C	4,320		40	35	10	10	5											7/15
Alabama State University	Montgomery	U	B,M	Pub	F,S	C	4,711	17	88	9	2	1		414	87	10	3		410	86	12	2		7/30
Auburn University	Auburn University	SM	B,M,D	Pub	F,S	C	18,798	23	23	30	26	11	10	540	26	49	22	3	560	19	48	28	4	8/1
Auburn University Montgomery	Montgomery	U	B,M,D		F,S	C	4,165		63	21	13	3	1											Open
Birmingham-Southern College	Birmingham	U	B,M	Pri	F,S	C	1,347		19		60		21		7	40	41	12		13	43	38	6	1/15
Concordia College	Selma	SM	A,B		No	C	758																	
Faulkner University	Montgomery	U	A,B,M,D	Pri	F,S	C	2,298	20																Open
Huntingdon College	Montgomery	SU	A	Pri	F,S	C	615	24	17	25	24	19	15	590	7	46	39	8	580	30	31	39		Open
Jacksonville State University	Jacksonville	SM	B,M,D	Pub	F,S	C	7,009	17	71	29														Open
Judson College	Marion	SM	B	Pri	No	W	345	23	33	29	22	4	12		25	50	25			75	25			Open
Miles College	Birmingham	U	A,B	Pri	F,S	C	1,400																	Open
Oakwood College	Huntsville	SU	A,B	Pri	No	C	1,778	18	68	19	10	2	1	484	57	31	11	1	454	64	29	6	1	Open
Samford University	Birmingham	SU	A,B,M,D	Pri	F,S	C	2,890	25	13	29	24	16	18	580	19	42	28	11	550	21	45	27	7	8/1
Southern Christian University	Montgomery		B,M,D	Pri	No	C	195																	Open
Spring Hill College	Mobile	SU	A,B,M	Pri	F,S	C	1,244	23	24	27	24	13	12	530	36	36	22	6	520	42	35	19	4	7/1
Stillman College	Tuscaloosa	SM	B	Pri	F,S	C	1,460																	
Talladega College	Talladega	SM	B	Pri	F,S	C	660																	Open
Troy State University	Troy	SM	A,B,M	Pub	F,S	C	4,607	21	51	21	13	9	6											Open
Troy State University/Dothan	Dothan	U	A,B,M	Pub	No	C	1,499	22	44	38	6	6	6											Open
Troy State University/Montgomery	Montgomery	U	A,B,M	Pub	No	C	2,705																	Open
Tuskegee University	Tuskegee	R	B,M,D	Pri	F,S	C	2,610		76	20	3	1			75	23	3			76	20	4		
University of Alabama	Tuscaloosa	SU	B,M,D	Pub	F,S	C	15,171	23	27	30	23	12	13	550	27	45	23	5	550	28	42	23	6	6/1
University of Alabama at Birmingham	Birmingham	U	B,M,D	Pub	F,S	C	9,954	21	44	26	15	7	8											8/1
University of Alabama at Huntsville	Huntsville	SU	B,M,D	Pub	F,S	C	5,466	24	18	25	30	14	13	550	26	42	24	8	570	25	36	30	9	8/15
University of Mobile	Mobile	SU	A,B,M	Pri	No	C	1,803		50	21	15	7	8											9/10
University of Montevallo	Montevallo	SM	B,M	Pub	F,S	C	2,559	22	39	28	9	9	5											8/1
University of North Alabama	Florence	U	B,M	Pub	F,S	C	4,852	21	48	24	19	5	4											7/1
University of South Alabama	Mobile	SU	B,M,D	Pub	F,S	C	9,572	23																8/10
University of West Alabama	Livingston	SM	A,B,M	Pub	F,S	C	1,595																	Open
Alaska																								
Alaska Pacific University	Anchorage	SU	A,B,M		No	C	433	20	50	20	15	15		520	30	55	15		470	63	33	4		2/1
Sheldon Jackson College	Sitka	SM	A,B	Pri	No	C	240																	Open
University of Alaska Anchorage	Anchorage	U	A,B,M	Pub	No	C	12,600																	
University of Alaska Fairbanks	Fairbanks	SM	A,B,M,D	Pub	F,S	C	6,310	21	48	22	17	5	8	510	40	37	20	3	510	46	36	17	2	8/1
University of Alaska Southeast	Juneau	SU	A,B,M	Pub	No	C	1,990																	Open
Arizona																								
American Indian College of the Assemblies of God	Phoenix	U	A,B	Pri	No	C	71	13	75	25				375	100				325	100				Open
Arizona State University-Main	Tempe	U	B,M,D	Pri	F,S	PW	35,191	23	26	28	25	11	11	542	30	45	20	5	555	24	44	27	6	Open
DeVry University/Phoenix	Phoenix	SU	A,B	Pri	No	C	3,050																	Open
Embry-Riddle Aeronautical University	Prescott	R	A,B,M	Pri	F,S	PW	1,724	24	21	23	27	17	10	540	26	49	23	2	560	19	46	30	5	Open
Grand Canyon University	Phoenix	SU	B,M	Pri	No	C	1,609																	Open
Northern Arizona University	Flagstaff	SM	B,M,D	Pub	F,S	C	13,740								33	45	19	3		33	43	21	3	3/1
Prescott College	Prescott	SM	B,M	Pri	No	C	827								30	49	21			14	49	33	4	Open
University of Arizona	Tucson	U	B,M,D		F,S	C	26,878																	4/1
University of Phoenix	Phoenix	U	A,B,M	Pri	No	C																		Open
Western International University	Phoenix	U	A,B,M	Pri	No	C	880																	Open
Arkansas																								
Arkansas Baptist College	Little Rock	U	A,B	Pri	No																			
Arkansas State University	State University	SM	A,B,M,D	Pub	F,S	C	9,426	22	41	22	24	8	5											
Arkansas Tech University	Russellville	SM	A,B,M	Pub	F,S	C	5,205	21	45	21	22	7	5											Open
Harding University	Searcy	SM	B,M	Pri	F,S	C	4,078	24	27	23	21	12	17	550	15	43	36	6	540	22	40	30	6	6/1
Henderson State University	Arkadelphia	SM	A,B,M	Pub	F,S	C	3,050	22	40	25	23	8	4	500	44	37	15	4	550	33	33	30	4	Open
Hendrix College	Conway	SU	B,M	Pri	No	C	1,079	27	4	9	27	19	41	628	5	28	47	20	604	10	34	46	10	Open
John Brown University	Siloam Springs	SM	A,B	Pri	No	C	1,545	25	20	22	28	12	18	575	18	47	24	11	555	17	51	26	6	
Lyon College	Batesville	SM	B	Pri	F,S	C	526	25	7	27	28	24	14	540	26	45	29		560	26	41	29	4	Open
Ouachita Baptist University	Arkadelphia	SM	A,B	Pri	F,S	C	1,657	24	23	27	25	10	15	550	27	40	29	7	550	30	39	27	4	Open
Philander Smith College	Little Rock	U	B	Pri	No		1,000	14																Open
Southern Arkansas University	Magnolia	SM	A,B,M	Pub	F,S	C	2,863		53	24	17	4	2											Open
University of Arkansas	Fayetteville	U	B,M,D	Pub	F,S	C	12,818	24	16	26	25	13	20	560					580	19	39	35	7	8/15
University of Arkansas at Little Rock	Little Rock	U	A,B,M,D	Pub	F,S	C	9,184	19	64	18	12	3	3											Open
University of Arkansas at Monticello	Monticello	SM	A,B,M	Pub	F,S	C	2,130		61	21	16	1	1		82	9	9			64	18	18		Open

NAME OF SCHOOL	TOWN	ENVIRONMENT U-Urban R-Rural SU-Suburban SM-Small Town	DEGREES AWARDED A-Associate B-Bachelor M-Master D-Doctorate	CONTROL Pri-Private, Pub-Public	FRATERNITIES AND SORORITIES F-Fraternities S-Sororities F,S-Both No-Neither	STUDENTS: C-Coed M-Men W-Women PM-Primarily Men PW-Primarily Women	UNDERGRADUATE ENROLLMENT FALL 2001	TEST SCORES: ACT Median	ACT Below 21	ACT 21-23	ACT 24-26	ACT 27-28	ACT Above 28	SAT I VERBAL REASONING Median	SAT I Verbal Below 500	SAT I Verbal 500-599	SAT I Verbal 600-700	SAT I Verbal Above 700	SAT I MATHEMATICAL REASONING Median	SAT I Math Below 500	SAT I Math 500-599	SAT I Math 600-700	SAT I Math Above 700	APPLICATION DEADLINE Month / Day
University of Arkansas at Pine Bluff	Pine Bluff	SM	A,B,M	Pub	F,S	C	3,052																	
University of Central Arkansas	Conway	SM	A,B,M,D	Pub	F,S	C	7,650		32	22	22	14	10											8/1
University of the Ozarks	Clarksville	SM	B	Pri	No	C	654	23	20	43	20	10	7	506	50	26	24		425	62	29	9		7/1
Williams Baptist College	Walnut Ridge	R	A,B	Pri	No	C	688	21	55	17	19	6	3											Open
California																								
Art Center College of Design	Pasadena	SU	B,M	Pri	No	C	1,377																	Open
Art Institute of Southern California	Laguna Beach	SM	B	Pri	No	C	210		3	90	6	1			6	88	4	2		17	80	3		
Azusa Pacific University	Azusa	SM	B,M,D	Pri	No	C	3,654		56		38		7		24	25	45	7		24	47	25	4	Open
Biola University	La Mirada	SU	B,M,D	Pri	No	C	2,950	24	23	20	23	16	16	600	23	39	32	7	610	23	41	32	4	6/1
California Baptist University	Riverside	SU	B,M	Pri	No	C	1,580	20	53	24	11	8	4	504	47	37	15	1	490	52	38	8	2	Open
California College of Arts and Crafts	San Francisco	U	B,M	Pri	No	C	1,164	22	14	50	27	9		547	26	50	19	5	507	45	37	18		2/15
California Institute of Technology	Pasadena	SU	B,M,D	Pri	No	C	942							740	1	1	19	80	790			2	98	1/1
California Institute of the Arts	Valencia	SU	B,M	Pri	No	C	823																	1/11
California Lutheran University	Thousand Oaks	U	B,M	Pri	No	C	1,830																	3/1
California Maritime Academy	Vallejo	SU	B	Pub	No	C	653	21						512					532					
California Polytechnic State University	San Luis Obispo	SU	B,M	Pub	F,S	C	17,066		38	55	8				19	48	30	4		9	34	45	11	11/30
California State Polytechnic University, Pomona	Pomona	SU	B,M	Pub	F,S	C	17,005	20	56	26	12	4	2	481	58	33	8	1	530	35	40	21	3	11/1
California State University, Bakersfield	Bakersfield	U	B,M	Pub	F,S	C	5,228							450	70	24	5		470	60	33	7		Open
California State University, Chico	Chico	SM	B,M	Pub	F,S	C	14,634	21						500					510					
California State University, Dominguez Hills	Carson	U	B,M	Pub	F,S	C	7,680																	
California State University, Fresno	Fresno	SU	B,M,D	Pub	F,S	C	16,088	18	68	17	10	3	2	460	65	27	7	1	470	59	30	10	1	5/15
California State University, Fullerton	Fullerton	SU	B,M	Pub	F,S	C	22,450								66	26	7	1		56	31	12	1	Open
California State University, Hayward	Hayward	SU	B,M	Pub	F,S	C	10,800																	7/12
California State University, Long Beach	Long Beach	SU	B,M	Pub	F,S	C	24,110								60	31	8	1		52	36	10	2	11/30
California State University, Los Angeles	Los Angeles	U	B,M,D	Pub	F,S	C	13,898																	6/15
California State University, Monterey Bay	Seaside	SU	B,M	Pub	No	C	1,991																	Open
California State University, Northridge	Northridge	SU	B,M	Pub	F,S	C	24,463							466	68	25	7		448	60	31	8	1	11/30
California State University, Sacramento	Sacramento	U	B,M	Pub	F,S	C	21,503	20	59	23	13	3	2	475	58	33	8	1	470	50	36	13	1	Open
California State University, San Bernardino	San Bernardino	SU	B,M	Pub	F,S	C	11,020	18	78	15	6			440	75	21	4		450	71	24	5		11/1
California State University, San Marcos	San Marcos	SU	B,M	Pub	F,S	C																		11/30
California State University, Stanislaus	Turlock	R	B,M	Pub	F,S	C	5,624	20	62	18	14	3	3	480	43	48	8	1	480	43	48	8	1	Open
Chapman University	Orange	SU	B,M,D		F,S	C	3,127	24	3	47	22	23	5	583	12	50	33	6	590	9	48	39	5	1/31
Christian Heritage College	El Cajon	SU	A,B	Pri	No	C	600																	
Claremont McKenna College	Claremont	SM	B	Pri	No	C	1,044	30						690					700					1/1
Cogswell Polytechnical College	Sunnyvale	SU	B	Pri	No	C	500																	
Concordia University	Irvine	SU	A,B,M	Pri	No	C	1,112	22	36	39	13	5	7	500	45	41	12	1	510	44	41	13	1	5/1
DeVry University/Fremont	Fremont	SU	A,B	Pri	No	C	2,278																	Open
DeVry University/Long Beach	Long Beach	U	A,B	Pri	No	C	2,853																	Open
DeVry University/Pomona	Pomona	U	A,B	Pri	No	C	3,669																	Open
DeVry University/West Hills	West Hills	SU	A,B	Pri	No	C	1,351																	Open
Dominican University of California	San Rafael	SU	B,M		No	C	946		31	38	22	6	3	508	42	35	20	2	480	45	41	13		3/2
Fresno Pacific University	Fresno	SU	A,B,M	Pri	No	C	1,056	22	40	25	15	15	5	512	49	35	15	1	517	49	36	15		7/31
Golden Gate University	San Francisco	U	B,M,D	Pri	No	C	1,301																	6/1
Harvey Mudd College	Claremont	SU	B		No	C	706							710		4	45	51	750			17	83	1/15
Holy Names College	Oakland	U	B,M	Pri	No	C	506							440	68	21	6		460	73	19	8		8/1
Hope International University	Fullerton	U	A,B,M	Pri	No	C	840																	5/1
Humboldt State University	Arcata	SM	B,M	Pub	F,S	C	7,114	22	38	27	23	7	5	530	37	41	20	2	520	41	41	18	1	Open
Humphreys College	Stockton	SU	A,B,D		No	C	760																	Open
La Sierra University	Riverside	SU	A,B,M,D	Pri	No	C	1,050																	8/15
Loyola Marymount University	Los Angeles	SU	B,M	Pri	F,S	C	4,959								14	51	31	4		12	47	36	5	2/1
Master's College	Santa Clarita	R	B,M	Pri	No	C	1,174	24	18	29	30	11	11	575	18	38	35	9	557	25	40	30	5	3/2
Menlo College	Atherton	SU	B	Pri	No	C	630																	Open
Mills College	Oakland	U	B,M	Pri	No	W	730								15	34	41	10		24	51	21	3	2/1
Mount Saint Mary's College	Los Angeles	U	A,B,M	Pri	S	PW	920								36	47	16	2		48	38	14	1	2/15
National University	La Jolla	U	A,B,M	Pri	No	C	5,360																	Open
New College of California	San Francisco	U	B,M	Pri	No	C	150																	
Notre Dame de Namur University	Belmont	SU	A,B,M	Pri	No	C	967	19	66	20	14			460	69	22	9		460	64	27	8	1	
Occidental College	Los Angeles	U	B,M	Pri	F,S	C	1,770							610					610					1/15
Otis College of Art and Design	Los Angeles	U	B,M	Pri	No	C	927	22	42	21	21	11	5	474	57	30	13	1	521	41	39	18	2	2/15
Pacific Union College	Angwin	SM	A,B,M	Pri	No	C	1,599																	Open
Pepperdine University	Malibu	SU	B,M,D	Pri	F,S	C	2,790																	1/15
Pitzer College	Claremont	SU	B	Pri	No	C	921	25	7	10	47	12	23	620	5	32	48	15	610	9	38	48	5	1/15
Point Loma Nazarene University	San Diego	SU	B,M	Pri	F,S	C	2,353	23	19	37	24	10	11	553	25	47	24	4	553	23	46	28	3	3/1
Pomona College	Claremont	SU	B		F	C	1,570	31		1	6	23	70	720		4	30	66	720		5	30	66	1/2
Saint Mary's College of California	Moraga	SU	B,M,D	Pri	No	C	2,487	22	33	30	22	6	10	540	26	50	22	2	550	23	53	21	3	2/1
Samuel Merritt College	Oakland	U	B,M	Pri	No	C	300																	
San Diego State University	San Diego	U	B,M,D	Pub	F,S	C	27,871	21	46	29	18	6	1	500	45	42	11	1	530	35	46	18	1	11/30
San Francisco Art Institute	San Francisco	U	B,M	Pri	No	C	500																	9/1
San Francisco Conservatory of Music	San Francisco	U	B,M	Pri	No	C	141							580	27	27	37	9	550	20	53	20	7	2/1
San Francisco State University	San Francisco	U	A,B,M,D	Pub	F,S	C	20,730																	
San Jose State University	San Jose	U	B,M	Pub	F,S	C	21,417																	Open
Santa Clara University	Santa Clara	SU	B,M,D	Pri	No	C	4,279	27						608	11	42	42	5	631	5	33	52	10	1/15
Scripps College	Claremont	SU	B	Pri	No	W	786	30				15	84	650	2	18	53	27	620	4	32	50	14	2/1
Simpson College	Redding	SU	A,B,M	Pri	No	C	986	21	50	22	18	8	3	530	44	40	15	1	510	55	30	13	1	Open
Sonoma State University	Rohnert Park	SU	B,M	Pub	F,S	C	6,278							514					507					11
Southern California Institute of Architecture	Los Angeles	U	B,M	Pri	No	C	210																	

NAME OF SCHOOL	TOWN	ENVIRONMENT U-Urban R-Rural SU-Suburban SM-Small Town	DEGREES AWARDED A-Associate B-Bachelor M-Master D-Doctorate	CONTROL Pri-Private, Pub-Public	FRATERNITIES AND SORORITIES F-Fraternities S-Sororities F,S-Both No-Neither	STUDENTS: C-Coed M-Men W-Women PM-Primarily Men PW-Primarily Women	UNDERGRADUATE ENROLLMENT FALL 2001	TEST SCORES ACT Median	ACT Below 21	ACT 21-23	ACT 24-26	ACT 27-28	ACT Above 28	SAT I VERBAL REASONING Median	Below 500	500-599	600-700	Above 700	SAT I MATHEMATICAL REASONING Median	Below 500	500-599	600-700	Above 700	APPLICATION DEADLINE Month / Day
Stanford University	Stanford	SU	B,M,D	Pri	F,S	C	6,443																	12/15
Thomas Aquinas College	Santa Paula	R	B	Pri	No	C	301	28		9	26	30	35	650		21	58	21	610	3	42	51	5	Open
United States International University	San Diego	SU	A,B,M,D	Pri	No	C	510																	Open
University of California at Berkeley	Berkeley	U	B,M,D	Pub	F,S	C	22,677							635	8	23	39	30	674	5	14	35	46	11/30
University of California at Davis	Davis	SU	B,M,D	Pub	F,S	C	21,293		21	22	29	15	13							8	34	45	13	
University of California at Irvine	Irvine	SU	B,M,D	Pub	F,S	C	15,390																	11/30
University of California at Los Angeles	Los Angeles	U	B,M,D	Pub	F,S	C	25,328	27	2	26	48	24		620	9	28	43	19	670	4	19	41	36	11/30
University of California at Riverside	Riverside	U	B,M,D	Pub	F,S	C	12,714	21	47	26	16	6	5	500	47	36	15	2	560	26	39	28	7	11/30
University of California at San Diego	La Jolla	SU	B,M,D	Pub	F,S	C	16,496																	11/30
University of California at Santa Barbara	Santa Barbara	SU	B,M,D	Pub	F,S	C	17,724	25						580	15	40	37	8	620	8	31	45	15	11/30
University of California at Santa Cruz	Santa Cruz	SM	B,M,D	Pub	F,S	C	12,034	23						572					577					11/30
University of Judaism College of Arts and Sciences	Bel Air	SU	B,M	Pri	No	C	106																	1/31
University of La Verne	La Verne	SU	A,B,M,D	Pri	F,S	C	1,422	22	48	29	12	7	4	490	50	40	8	2	500	49	39	11	1	2/1
University of Redlands	Redlands	SM	B,M	Pri	F,S	C	1,946	23	26	30	24	12	8	560	17	52	26	5	560	18	51	29	3	2/1
University of San Diego	San Diego	U	B,M,D	Pri	F,S	C	4,809	26		33	56	16	8	575	13	47	35	5	590	10	41	43	5	1/5
University of San Francisco	San Francisco	U	B,M,D	Pri	F,S	C	4,445	23	24	33	21	10	12	550	21	47	28	3	550	17	55	25	3	2/15
University of Southern California	Los Angeles	U	B,M,D	Pri	F,S	C	16,020	29		2	10	27	61	650	1	22	52	25	670	1	13	51	36	1/10
University of the Pacific	Stockton	SU	B,M,D	Pri	F,S	C	3,185	23	20	30	29	12	8	570	25	48	24	4	550	17	42	33	8	2/15
Vanguard University of Southern California	Costa Mesa	SU	B,M	Pri	No	C	1,578	22						501	45	43	11	1	491	54	35	10	1	Open
Westmont College	Santa Barbara	SU	B		No	C	1,381	26	2	21	30	24	23	610	4	43	40	13	600	5	39	48	8	2/15
Whittier College	Whittier	SU	B,M,D	Pri	F,S	C	1,270	23	47	21	17	7	8	539	34	42	21	3	541	34	40	20	6	2/1
Woodbury University	Burbank	SU	B,M	Pri	F,S	C	1,020																	Open

Colorado

NAME OF SCHOOL	TOWN	ENVIRONMENT	DEGREES AWARDED	CONTROL	FRATERNITIES AND SORORITIES	STUDENTS	UNDERGRADUATE ENROLLMENT FALL 2001	ACT Median	ACT Below 21	ACT 21-23	ACT 24-26	ACT 27-28	ACT Above 28	SAT I Verbal Median	Below 500	500-599	600-700	Above 700	SAT I Math Median	Below 500	500-599	600-700	Above 700	APPLICATION DEADLINE
Adams State College	Alamosa	SM	A,B,M	Pub	No	C	2,048	22	55	28	11	4	2											8/1
Colorado Christian University	Lakewood	SU	A,B,M	Pri	No	C	1,763	23	28	26	28	10	8	540	34	37	27	2	530	35	41	22	2	8/1
Colorado College	Colorado Springs	SU	B,M	Pri	F,S	C	1,934	28	1	14	63		23	640	7		48	19	640	5	28	51	16	1/15
Colorado School of Mines	Golden	SM	B,M,D	Pub	F,S	C	2,556	27		16	30	35	19	580	13	42	36	9	650	2	24	56	18	6/1
Colorado State University	Fort Collins	SU	B,M,D	Pub	F,S	C	19,899	23	13	34	30	12	12	540	26	48	23	4	550	22	47	27	4	7/1
Colorado Technical University	Colorado Springs	SU	A,B,M,D	Pri	No	C	1,200																	Open
DeVry University/Colorado Springs	Colorado Springs		A,B	Pri	No	C	128																	Open
DeVry University/Denver	Denver		A,B	Pri	No	C	269																	Open
Fort Lewis College	Durango	SM	A,B	Pub	No	C	4,441	20	60	24	11	4	1	500	54	35	10	1	490	50	38	11	1	8/1
Mesa State College	Grand Junction	SM	A,B,M	Pub	No	C	5,297	20	54	26	14	4	2		54	34	11			53	36	11	1	7/31
Metropolitan State College of Denver	Denver	U	B	Pub	No	C	18,445	19	65	21	10	2	2	470	57	32	10	1	460	65	25	10		8/12
Naropa University	Boulder	U	B,M	Pri	No	C	402																	2/15
Regis University	Denver	SU	B,M	Pri	No	C	1,098	24	28	24	24	13	11	535	31	46	20	3	528	34	42	20	4	Open
United States Air Force Academy	USAFA	SU	B	Pub	No	C	4,365																	1/31
University of Colorado at Boulder	Boulder	SU	B,M,D	Pub	F,S	C	23,998		10	25	33	16	16		13	49	32	5		10	42	39	8	2/15
University of Colorado at Colorado Springs	Colorado Springs	U	B,M,D	Pub	F,S	C	5,244	23	23	23	38	8	8	531	29	50	18	3	540	29	46	23	2	7/1
University of Colorado at Denver	Denver	U	B,M,D	Pub	No	C	8,350																	7/22
University of Denver	Denver	SU	B,M,D	Pri	F,S	C	3,992	24						554					563					2/1
University of Northern Colorado	Greeley	SU	B,M,D	Pub	F,S	C	10,213	22	36	30	23	7	5	520	39	42	17	2	520	38	44	16	2	8/1
University of Southern Colorado	Pueblo	U	B,M	Pub	F,S	C	5,324							504	49	37	12	2	507	48	37	14	1	7/28
Western State College of Colorado	Gunnison	R	B	Pub	F,S	C	2,302	20	55	28	14	3	1	500	48	40	12		490	52	38	10		Open

Connecticut

NAME OF SCHOOL	TOWN	ENVIRONMENT	DEGREES AWARDED	CONTROL	FRATERNITIES AND SORORITIES	STUDENTS	UNDERGRADUATE ENROLLMENT FALL 2001	ACT Median	ACT Below 21	ACT 21-23	ACT 24-26	ACT 27-28	ACT Above 28	SAT I Verbal Median	Below 500	500-599	600-700	Above 700	SAT I Math Median	Below 500	500-599	600-700	Above 700	APPLICATION DEADLINE
Albertus Magnus College	New Haven	SU	A,B,M	Pri	No	C	1,872							473	50	35	10	5	448	56	35	9		Open
Central Connecticut State University	New Britain	SU	B,M	Pub	F,S	C	9,551							488	55	38	6	1	492	54	39	6	1	5/1
Charter Oak State College	New Britain	SU	A,B	Pub	No	C	1,496																	Open
Connecticut College	New London	SM	B,M		No	C	1,835	27	3	5	28	36	28	660		13	55	32	650	1	16	66	18	1/1
Eastern Connecticut State University	Willimantic	SU	A,B,M	Pub	No	C	5,017							500	47	43	9	1	500	47	43	9	1	5/1
Fairfield University	Fairfield	SU	B,M		No	C	4,164							584	9	46	39	6	596	7	41	47	5	2/1
Mitchell College	New London	SU	A,B	Pri	No	C	708	18						470	78	19	3		430	78	20	2		8/30
Quinnipiac University	Hamden	SU	B,M	Pri	F,S	C	5,056		15	29	25	25	6		29	56	13	2		23	56	19	2	2/15
Sacred Heart University	Fairfield	SU	A,B,M	Pri	F,S	C	4,131							523	37	49	12	1	524	28	57	14	1	12/1
Saint Joseph College	West Hartford	SU	B,M	Pri	No	PW	1,287																	5/1
Southern Connecticut State University	New Haven	U	A,B,M	Pub	F,S	C	8,316							480	60	27	7	6	470	66	29	6		Open
Teikyo Post University	Waterbury	U	A,B	Pri	No	C	1,350																	
Trinity College	Hartford	U	B,M		F	C	2,074	27	4	17	26	19	33	630	3	23	57	16	640	3	22	60	15	1/15
United States Coast Guard Academy	New London	SU	B	Pub	No	C	897	27						620	2	35	51	12	640	1	22	57	20	12/15
University of Bridgeport	Bridgeport	U	A,B,M,D	Pri	F,S	C	1,181							430	67	24	7	2	460	65	20	11	4	4/1
University of Connecticut	Storrs	R	A,B,M,D	Pub	F,S	C	13,588							560	18	52	27	4	580	13	48	33	7	3/1
University of Hartford	West Hartford	SU	A,B,M,D	Pri	F,S	C	5,425	23	29	35	18	6	12	520	38	46	14	2	530	34	47	17	2	Open
University of New Haven	West Haven	SU	A,B,M	Pri	F,S	C	2,532							480	55	35	9	1	480	57	35	7	1	Open
Wesleyan University	Middletown	SU	B,M,D		F,S	C	2,792	29						690	2	13	37	48	690	2	9	45	44	1/1
Western Connecticut State University	Danbury	SU	A,B,M	Pub	F,S	C	5,080							480	60	34	6		480	60	32	7	1	Open
Yale University	New Haven	U	B,M,D	Pri	F,S	C	5,253																	12/31

Delaware

NAME OF SCHOOL	TOWN	ENVIRONMENT	DEGREES AWARDED	CONTROL	FRATERNITIES AND SORORITIES	STUDENTS	UNDERGRADUATE ENROLLMENT FALL 2001	ACT Median	ACT Below 21	ACT 21-23	ACT 24-26	ACT 27-28	ACT Above 28	SAT I Verbal Median	Below 500	500-599	600-700	Above 700	SAT I Math Median	Below 500	500-599	600-700	Above 700	APPLICATION DEADLINE
Delaware State University	Dover	SU	B,M	Pub	F,S	C	2,910																	6/1
Goldey-Beacom College	Wilmington	SU	A,B,M	Pri	F,S		1,310																	Open
University of Delaware	Newark	SM	A,B,M,D		F,S	C	17,431							570	13	53	30	4	590	10	43	40	7	2/15
Wesley College	Dover	SM	A,B,M	Pri	F,S	C	1,396							464	69	26	4	1	461	73	23	4		Open
Wilmington College	New Castle	U	A,B,M,D	Pri	F	C	3,472							450					400					Open

NAME OF SCHOOL	TOWN	ENVIRONMENT (U-Urban R-Rural SU-Suburban SM-Small Town)	DEGREES AWARDED (A-Associate B-Bachelor M-Master D-Doctorate)	CONTROL (Pri-Private, Pub-Public)	FRATERNITIES AND SORORITIES (F-Fraternities S-Sororities F, S-Both No-Neither)	STUDENTS (C-Coed M-Men W-Women PM-Primarily Men PW-Primarily Women)	UNDERGRADUATE ENROLLMENT FALL 2001	ACT: Median	ACT: Below 21	ACT: 21-23	ACT: 24-26	ACT: 27-28	ACT: Above 28	SAT I VERBAL REASONING: Median	SAT I VERBAL REASONING: Below 500	SAT I VERBAL REASONING: 500-599	SAT I VERBAL REASONING: 600-700	SAT I VERBAL REASONING: Above 700	SAT I MATHEMATICAL REASONING: Median	SAT I MATHEMATICAL REASONING: Below 500	SAT I MATHEMATICAL REASONING: 500-599	SAT I MATHEMATICAL REASONING: 600-700	SAT I MATHEMATICAL REASONING: Above 700	APPLICATION DEADLINE Month / Day
District of Columbia																								
American University	Washington	SU	A,B,M,D	Pri	F,S	C	5,474	26						609	4	37	46	13	597	6	43	43	8	2/1
Catholic University of America	Washington	U	B,M,D	Pri	F,S	C	2,587		18	29	20	19	14		15	42	34	9		16	47	32	5	2/15
Corcoran School of Art and Design	Washington	U	A,B	Pri	No	C	320																	Open
Gallaudet University	Washington	U	A,B,M,D	Pri	F,S	C	1,250																	Open
George Washington University	Washington	U	A,B,M,D	Pri	F,S	C	8,695	26	4	16	31	24	25	620	5	32	48	15	620	3	34	51	12	2/1
Georgetown University	Washington	U	B,M,D	Pri	No	C	6,422																	1/10
Howard University	Washington	U	B,M,D	Pri	F,S	C	6,570																	
Southeastern University	Washington	U	A,B,M	Pri	F		513																	Open
Strayer University	Washington	U	A,B,M	Pri	No	C	11,785																	Open
Trinity College	Washington	U	B,M	Pri	No	W	1,040																	Open
University of the District of Columbia	Washington	SU	A,B,M	Pub	F,S	C	9,250																	Open
Florida																								
Barry University	Miami Shores	SU	B,M,D	Pri	F,S	C	6,006								25	75				25	75			Open
Beacon College	Leesburg	SM	A,B	Pri	No	C																		Open
Bethune-Cookman College	Daytona Beach	U	B	Pri	F,S	C	2,724							410	86	11	3		410	88	9	3		7/30
Carlos Albizu University	Miami	U	B,M,D	Pri	No	C	144																	Open
Clearwater Christian College	Clearwater	SM	A,B	Pri	No	C	640																	
DeVry University/Orlando	Orlando		A,B	Pri	No	C	803																	
Eckerd College	St. Petersburg	SU	B	Pri	No	C	1,582	25	13	36	30	9	12	574	20	48	24	8	563	21	50	24	5	4/1
Edward Waters College	Jacksonville	U	B	Pri	F,S	C	480																	
Embry-Riddle Aeronautical University	Daytona Beach	U	A,B,M	Pri	F,S	C	4,641	23	20	33	26	9	12	530	31	46	20	3	560	19	46	29	6	7/1
Flagler College	St. Augustine	SM	B		No	C	1,852	23	11	46	23	15	5	560	13	60	23	4	550	18	56	25	1	3/1
Florida Agricultural and Mechanical University	Tallahassee	U	A,B,M,D	Pub	F,S	C	11,266		64	23	10	3					1	99						5/15
Florida Atlantic University	Boca Raton	SU	A,B,M,D	Pub	F,S	C	18,757	22	40	30	17	8	5	514	41	43	13	3	523	36	46	16	2	6/1
Florida Gulf Coast University	Fort Myers	R	B,M	Pub	F,S	C	3,403	21	30	48	9	12	1	510	43	42	14	1	500	42	44	13	1	Open
Florida Hospital College of Health Sciences	Orlando	U	A,B	Pri	No	C	746	19																
Florida Institute of Technology	Melbourne	SM	A,B,M,D	Pri	F,S	C	2,191	25	11	25	27	19	18	560	9	38	42	11	610	19	47	31	4	Open
Florida International University	Miami	U	A,B,M,D	Pub	F,S	C	25,971	24	1	16	57	17	9	560	12	57	24	4	560	10	62	25	3	Open
Florida Memorial College	Miami	U	B	Pri	No	C																		Open
Florida Southern College	Lakeland	SU	B,M	Pri	F,S	C	1,827	23	30	29	23	9	9	490	37	45	16	2	490	37	44	16	2	8/1
Florida State University	Tallahassee	SU	A,B,M,D	Pub	F,S	C	28,231	25	9	31	30	15	14	580	13	47	35	5	580	11	46	38	5	3/1
International College	Naples	SU	A,B,M	Pri	No	C	795																	Open
Jacksonville University	Jacksonville	SU	B,M		F,S	C	1,840																	Open
Lynn University	Boca Raton	SU	A,B,M	Pri	F	C	1,821	22							56	40	3	1		58	35	6	1	Open
New College of Florida	Sarasota	SU	B	Pub	No	C	634	28	2	5	19	25	50	702		7	33	60	636		27	54	19	5/1
Northwood University	West Palm Beach	SU	A,B	Pri	No	C	963	20	57	23	20			480	64	32	4		470	61	36	4		8/1
Nova Southeastern University	Fort Lauderdale	SU	A,B,M,D	Pri	F,S	C	4,014																	Open
Palm Beach Atlantic College	West Palm Beach	U	A,B,M	Pri	No	C	2,216		4	51	41		4		23	52	22	3		34	44	19	3	Open
Ringling School of Art and Design	Sarasota	U	B	Pri	F,S	C	969	27						510	41	39	15	4	500	49	34	16	2	Open
Rollins College	Winter Park	SU	B,M		F,S	C	1,676	26	15	25	25	20	15	595	12	48	35	5	595	13	47	35	5	2/15
Saint Leo University	Saint Leo	R	A,B,M	Pri	F,S	C	912	20	61	22	12	5		470	59	32	9		480	56	37	7		8/1
Saint Thomas University	Miami	SU	B,M	Pri	F,S	C	1,300																	Open
Southeastern College	Lakeland	SM	B	Pri	No	C	1,363																	8/1
Stetson University	Deland	SM	B,M		F,S	C	2,174	24	23	27	29	12	9	562	20	48	26	6	559	24	43	29	4	3/1
University of Central Florida	Orlando	U	A,B,M,D	Pub	F,S	C	30,036	25	9	26	36	17	12	572	11	54	32	3	580	10	49	36	5	5/15
University of Florida	Gainesville	SU	B,M,D	Pub	F,S	C		27	1	11	24	30	34	625	4	30	53	13	642	2	23	58	17	1/29
University of Miami	Coral Gables	SU	B,M,D	Pri	F,S	C	9,359								8	42	41	9		8	38	43	11	2/15
University of North Florida	Jacksonville	U	A,B,M,D	Pub	F,S	C	11,599	21	37	47	12	2	2	566	15	54	27	4	560	16	55	27	2	7/2
University of South Florida	Tampa	U	A,B,M,D	Pub	F,S	C	28,769	21						520	40	42	16	2	520	36	44	18	2	5/1
University of Tampa	Tampa	U	A,B,M	Pri	F,S	C	3,327	23	3	48		45	4	539					534	37	48	14	1	Open
University of West Florida	Pensacola	SU	A,B,M,D	Pub	F,S	C	7,422	23						540	25	50	25		530	25	50	25		6/30
Webber International University	Babson Park	SM	A,B,M	Pri	No	C	451	18	45	49	5	1		480	82	16	2		490	64	34		2	8/1
Georgia																								
Agnes Scott College	Atlanta/Decatur	U	B,M		No	W	853																	3/1
Albany State University	Albany	U	A,B,M	Pub	F,S	C	3,015	17	86	9	4	1		450	79	20	1		450	78	19	3		7/1
American InterContinental University	Atlanta	U	A,B	Pri	No	C	990																	Open
Armstrong Atlantic State University	Savannah	U	A,B,M	Pub	S	C	5,061							510	43	35	20	2	500	49	32	17	2	7/10
Art Institute of Atlanta	Atlanta	SU	A,B	Pri	No	C	2,438																	
Atlanta College of Art	Atlanta	U	B	Pri	No	C	440																	Open
Augusta State University	Augusta	U	A,B,M	Pub	F,S	C	4,680								53	35	11	1		59	34	7		7/21
Berry College	Mount Berry	R	B,M	Pri	No	C	1,846		19	28	21	14	17		15	42	33	10		17	48	30	5	2/1
Brenau University Women's College	Gainesville	SM	B,M	Pri	S	W	572							540	36	41	21	2	510	40	44	16		Open
Brewton-Parker College	Mt. Vernon	R	A,B	Pri	F,S	C	1,130																	
Clark Atlanta University	Atlanta	U	B,M,D	Pri	F,S		3,923	18	77	14	7	2		450	76	21	2		450	81	16	3		7/1
Clayton College and State University	Morrow	SU	A,B	Pub	No	C	4,675		86		14				49	41	11			50	42	8		7/1
Columbus State University	Columbus	SU	A,B,M	Pub	F,S	C	4,624	20						494					479					8/1
Covenant College	Lookout Mountain	SU	A,B,M	Pri	No	C	901	25	13	31	21	15	20	590	8	43	32	17	560	19	44	29	8	5/1
DeVry University/Alpharetta	Alpharetta	SU	A,B	Pri	No	C	1,548																	Open
DeVry University/Decatur	Decatur	SU	A,B	Pri	No	C	2,925																	Open
Emory University	Atlanta	SU	A,B,M,D	Pri	F,S	C	6,374			1	15	32	52			17	62	21			9	60	31	1/15
Fort Valley State University	Fort Valley	R	A,B,M		F,S	C	2,335																	
Georgia College and State University	Milledgeville	U	B,M	Pub	F,S	C	4,083	20	55	35	9	1		520	33	56	11		510	39	51	10		7/15
Georgia Institute of Technology	Atlanta	U	B,M,D	Pub	F,S	C	11,043							642	2	23	54	22	689	1	5	47	47	1/15
Georgia Southern University	Statesboro	SM	B,M,D	Pub	F,S	C	12,798							510	42	48	9	1	510	42	46	12		7/1
Georgia Southwestern State University	Americus	SM	A,B,M	Pub	F,S	C	1,947	21	42	50	8			519	37	48	13	2	499	48	39	12	1	8/1

NAME OF SCHOOL	TOWN	ENVIRONMENT U-Urban R-Rural SU-Suburban SM-Small Town	DEGREES AWARDED A-Associate B-Bachelor M-Master D-Doctorate	CONTROL Pri-Private, Pub-Public	FRATERNITIES AND SORORITIES F-Fraternities S-Sororities F, S-Both No-Neither	STUDENTS: C-Coed M-Men W-Women PM-Primarily Men PW-Primarily Women	UNDERGRADUATE ENROLLMENT FALL 2001	TEST SCORES: ACT						SAT I VERBAL REASONING					SAT I MATHEMATICAL REASONING					APPLICATION DEADLINE Month / Day
								Median	Below 21	21-23	24-26	27-28	Above 28	Median	Below 500	500-599	600-700	Above 700	Median	Below 500	500-599	600-700	Above 700	
Georgia State University	Atlanta	U	B,M,D	Pub	F,S	C	18,245	21	13		63	23	1	530	34	47	17	2	530	33	48	18	2	5/1
Kennesaw State University	Kennesaw	SU	B,M	Pub	F,S	C	12,432								29	51	19			35	48	15		
LaGrange College	LaGrange	SM	A,B,M	Pri	F,S	C	902	20	46	22	23	7	2	520	43	42	11	4	500	48	41	12		Open
Mercer University	Macon	SU	B,M,D	Pri	F,S	C	4,740	25						580	14	47	32	7	590	11	47	36	6	7/1
Morehouse College	Atlanta	U	B	Pri	F	M	2,729	22	48	28	15	6	3	525	39	40	18	3	535	44	36	19	2	2/15
Morris Brown College	Atlanta	U	B	Pri	F,S	C	2,175																	
North Georgia College and State University	Dahlonega	SM	A,B,M	Pub	F,S	C	3,434	21	39	39	20			530	27	56	15	2	510	38	45	15	1	7/1
Oglethorpe University	Atlanta	SU	B,M	Pri	F,S	C	1,060																	
Paine College	Augusta	U	B	Pri	F,S	C	860																	8/1
Piedmont College	Demorest	SM	B,M	Pri	No	C	990	19	58	19	15	8		500	45	39	14	2	500	48	39	11	2	Open
Reinhardt College	Waleska	SM	A,B		No	C	1,100																	Open
Savannah College of Art and Design	Savannah	U	B,M	Pri	No	C	4,707	23	24	29	22	14	11	550	28	43	24	5	524	39	40	18	3	Open
Savannah State University	Savannah	SU	B,M	Pub	F,S	C	2,050																	6/1
Shorter College	Rome	SM	B	Pri	F,S	C	970	22	35	34	20	10	1	530	35	43	19	3	520	37	47	14	2	Open
South College	Savannah	U	A,B	Pri	No	C	550																	Open
Southern Polytechnic State University	Marietta	SU	A,B,M	Pub	F,S	C	3,015		69		29		2		28	55	15	2		15	53	28	4	8/1
Spelman College	Atlanta	U	B	Pri	S	W																		2/1
State University of West Georgia	Carrollton	SU	B,M,D	Pub	F,S	C	7,254	20	63	23	10	2	2	505	50	39	10	1	500	52	39	9	1	7/3
Thomas University	Thomasville	R	A,B,M	Pri	No	C	561	18	80	10	10			475	67	23	10		455	77	20	4		Open
Toccoa Falls College	Toccoa Falls	SM	A,B	Pri	No	C	916	22	40	16	21	16	7	510					488					Open
University of Georgia	Athens	SM	A,B,M,D		F,S	C	24,829	25						597	6	44	41	9	601	5	42	45	8	1/15
Valdosta State University	Valdosta	U	A,B,M,D	Pub	F,S	C	7,939			16	70	13	1	515	46	42	11	1	508	46	43	10	1	8/1
Wesleyan College	Macon	SU	B,M	Pri	No	W	674		13	31	24	16	16		16	45	29	10		16	51	32	3	3/1
Hawaii																								
Brigham Young University/Hawaii	Laie	SM	A,B	Pri	No	C	2,278	22	38	27	23	9	3											2/15
Chaminade University of Honolulu	Honolulu	U	A,B,M	Pri	No	C	2,034	20	60	23	10	7		461	69	28	3		475	60	33	7		Open
Hawaii Pacific University	Honolulu	U	A,B,M	Pri	No	C	6,759	21	31	37	20	10	2	550	46	39	9	6	550	39	45	14	2	Open
University of Hawaii at Hilo	Hilo	SM	B,M	Pub	No	C	2,826	21	48	23	17	6	4	480	54	34	10	2	500	47	37	14	2	7/1
University of Hawaii at Manoa	Honolulu	U	B,M,D	Pub	F,S	C	12,054	22	29	35	25	7	4	520	35	47	16	2	560	19	49	27	5	6/1
Idaho																								
Albertson College of Idaho	Caldwell	SM	B	Pri	F,S	C	778	25	16	23	27	19	15	560	18	48	28	6	565	20	41	37	2	6/1
Boise State University	Boise	U	A,B,M,D	Pub	F,S	C	13,290																	7/18
Idaho State University	Pocatello	SM	A,B,M,D	Pub	F,S	C	11,167	20	52	24	16	5	3	525	35	43	21		530	36	33	27	4	8/1
Lewis-Clark State College	Lewiston	U	A,B	Pub	No	C	2,953	20	59	20	15	3	3	482	65	26	8	1	483	54	38	8		Open
Northwest Nazarene University	Nampa	SM	A,B,M	Pri	No	C	1,096	23	35	23	21	10	10											Open
University of Idaho	Moscow	SM	B,M,D	Pub	F,S	C	9,081	23	25	25	24	12	14	550	28	41	26	5	550	24	42	28	6	8/1
Illinois																								
Augustana College	Rock Island	SU	B	Pri	F,S	C	2,232	26	10	23	24	18	25											Open
Aurora University	Aurora	SU	B,M,D	Pri	F,S	C	1,323	20	54	25	11	8	2	485	33	66			500	66		33		Open
Benedictine University	Lisle	SU	A,B,M,D	Pri	No	C	1,986		4	49	30	10	5											Open
Blackburn College	Carlinville	R	B	Pri	No	C	571	22	35	27	32	6												Open
Bradley University	Peoria	U	B,M	Pri	F,S	C	5,167	25	8	20	32	18	22	590	11	39	40	10	610	10	36	42	12	Open
Chicago State University	Chicago	U	B,M	Pub	F,S	C	5,140	17	93	5	2													11/15
Columbia College Chicago	Chicago	U	B,M	Pri	No	C	8,911	19																8/15
Concordia University, River Forest	River Forest	SU	B,M	Pri	No	C	1,280																	Open
DePaul University	Chicago	U	B,M,D	Pri	F,S	C	13,020	23	24	30	26	24	3	560	22	45	29	4	550	27	46	24	3	2/1
DeVry University/Addison (DuPage County)	Addison	SU	A,B	Pri	No	C	3,543																	Open
DeVry University/Chicago	Chicago	U	A,B	Pri	No	C	4,011																	Open
DeVry University/Tinley Park	Tinley Park		A,B	Pri	No	C	1,662																	Open
Dominican University	River Forest	SU	B,M		No	C	1,189	22	33	31	20	11	5											Open
Eastern Illinois University	Charleston	SM	B,M	Pub	F,S	C	9,116	22	48	28	18	4	2											Open
East-West University	Chicago	U	A,B	Pri	No	C	590																	Open
Elmhurst College	Elmhurst	SU	B,M	Pri	F,S	C	2,410	22	32	34	19	7	5											4/1
Eureka College	Eureka	SM	B	Pri	F,S	C	510	21	48	21	17	8	6											Open
Greenville College	Greenville	SM	B,M		No	C	1,040																	Open
Illinois College	Jacksonville	SM	B	Pri	F,S	C	874	23	41	31	15	11	8	530	25	25	50		590	20	80			Open
Illinois Institute of Technology	Chicago	U	B,M,D	Pri	F,S	C	1,842	28		5	24	21	50	650	1	25	57	17	690		13	50	37	Open
Illinois State University	Normal	U	B,M,D	Pub	F,S	C	18,472	23	25	36	27	8	4											3/1
Illinois Wesleyan University	Bloomington	SU	B	Pri	F,S	C	2,064			4	29	27	40		3	30	46	21		2	26	53	19	3/1
Judson College	Elgin	SU	B	Pri	No	C	1,100																	Open
Kendall College	Evanston	SU	A,B	Pri	No	C	530																	Open
Knox College	Galesburg	SM	B	Pri	F,S	C	1,143	26	11	15	29	14	31	620	9	32	38	21	610	12	30	49	9	2/15
Lake Forest College	Lake Forest	SU	B,M	Pri	F,S	C	1,260	25	9	23	29	21	18	560	22	43	30	5	570	21	40	33	6	3/1
Lewis University	Romeoville	SU	A,B,M	Pri	F,S	C	3,383	22	42	32	16	6	4	530	36	43	21		570	36	36	29		Open
Loyola University of Chicago	Chicago	U	B,M,D	Pri	F,S	C	7,497	25	16	23	26	18	17	580	13	45	35	7	580	17	41	35	7	4/1
MacMurray College	Jacksonville	SM	A,B	Pri	F,S	C	655	22	49	31	12	4	3	500	48	39	12		510	53	37	8		Open
McKendree College	Lebanon	SM	B	Pri	F,S	C	2,107	24	26	29	25	12	8											Open
Millikin University	Decatur	SU	B,M	Pri	F,S	C	2,389	24	19	27	28	16	11	550	44	34	18	4	510	29	41	27	3	Open
Monmouth College	Monmouth	SM	B	Pri	F,S	C	1,072	22																Open
NAES College	Chicago	U	B	Pri	No	C	80																	Open
National-Louis University	Chicago	SU	B,M,D	Pri	S	C	3,345																	Open
North Central College	Naperville	SU	B,M	Pri	No	C	2,220	24	14	28	31	14	14	550	25	46	28	1	550	20	41	34		Open
North Park University	Chicago	U	B,M,D	Pri	No	C	1,573	23	33	26	22	11	8											Open
Northeastern Illinois University	Chicago	U	B,M	Pub	S	C	8,324																	7/1
Northern Illinois University	DeKalb	SM	B,M,D	Pub	F,S	C	17,468	22	30	32	22	9	7											8/1

NAME OF SCHOOL	TOWN	ENVIRONMENT (U-Urban R-Rural SU-Suburban SM-Small Town)	DEGREES AWARDED (A-Associate B-Bachelor M-Master D-Doctorate)	CONTROL (Pri-Private, Pub-Public)	FRATERNITIES AND SORORITIES (F-Fraternities S-Sororities F, S-Both No-Neither)	STUDENTS: C-Coed M-Men W-Women PM-Primarily Men PW-Primarily Women	UNDERGRADUATE ENROLLMENT FALL 2001	TEST SCORES: ACT Median	ACT Below 21	ACT 21-23	ACT 24-26	ACT 27-28	ACT Above 28	SAT I VERBAL REASONING Median	SAT I Verbal Below 500	SAT I Verbal 500-599	SAT I Verbal 600-700	SAT I Verbal Above 700	SAT I MATHEMATICAL REASONING Median	SAT I Math Below 500	SAT I Math 500-599	SAT I Math 600-700	SAT I Math Above 700	APPLICATION DEADLINE Month / Day
Northwestern University	Evanston	SU	B,M,D	Pri	F,S	C	7,816	31	1	3	9	13	75	690	1	9	46	44	710	1	6	36	58	1/1
Olivet Nazarene University	Bourbonnais	SM	A,B,M	Pri	No	C	2,061	23	31	34	13	12	10											8/1
Principia College	Elsah	R	B	Pri	No	C	554	25	27	25	22	6	20	577	21	41	26	13	564	19	46	32	4	3/1
Quincy University	Quincy	SM	A,B,M	Pri	F,S	C	1,147	22	35	31	21	7	6	500	50	30	20		520					Open
Rockford College	Rockford	SU	B,M	Pri	No	C	1,056	22	47	20	15	8	10	530					520					Open
Roosevelt University	Chicago	U	B,M,D	Pri	F,S	C	4,628																	Open
Saint Xavier University	Chicago	U	B,M	Pri	No	C	2,815	21	52	25	16	3	3											8/15
School of the Art Institute of Chicago	Chicago	U	B,M	Pri	No	C	1,802																	Open
Shimer College	Waukegan	SU	B	Pri	No	C	108																	3/1
Southern Illinois University at Carbondale	Carbondale	SM	A,B,M,D	Pub	F,S	M	16,802	22	27	35	22	9	7											Open
Southern Illinois University Edwardsville	Edwardsville	SU	B,M	Pub	F,S	C	9,799		42	26	19	7	5											5/31
Trinity Christian College	Palos Heights	SU	B	Pri	No	C	794	23	32	26	20	11	11	518					515					8/15
Trinity College of Nursing	Moline	U	A,B	Pri	No	C																		Open
Trinity International University	Deerfield	SU	B,M,D	Pri	No	C	1,200	24	32	31	25	8	4	565	20	43	29	8	535	33	47	20		Open
University of Chicago	Chicago	U	B,M,D	Pri	F,S	C	4,072																	1/1
University of Illinois at Chicago	Chicago	U	B,M,D	Pub	F,S	C	15,887																	2/1
University of Illinois at Urbana-Champaign	Urbana	SM	B,M,D	Pub	F,S	C	28,746																	1/1
University of Saint Francis	Joliet	SU	B,M	Pri	No	C	1,384																	Open
VanderCook College of Music	Chicago	U	B,M	Pri	F,S	C	83	23	33	20	27	7	13											6/1
West Suburban College of Nursing	Oak Park	SU	B	Pri	No	C																		Open
Western Illinois University	Macomb	R	B,M	Pub	F,S	C	10,755	23	40	32	19	5	4											
Wheaton College	Wheaton	SU	B,M,D	Pri	No	C	2,378			7	16	21	56		2	17	49	32		4	16	50	30	1/15

Indiana

NAME OF SCHOOL	TOWN	ENVIRONMENT	DEGREES AWARDED	CONTROL	FRATERNITIES AND SORORITIES	STUDENTS	UNDERGRADUATE ENROLLMENT FALL 2001	ACT Median	ACT Below 21	ACT 21-23	ACT 24-26	ACT 27-28	ACT Above 28	SAT I Verbal Median	SAT I Verbal Below 500	SAT I Verbal 500-599	SAT I Verbal 600-700	SAT I Verbal Above 700	SAT I Math Median	SAT I Math Below 500	SAT I Math 500-599	SAT I Math 600-700	SAT I Math Above 700	APPLICATION DEADLINE Month / Day
Anderson University	Anderson	SU	A,B,M,D	Pri	No	C	2,005																	Open
Ball State University	Muncie	SU	A,B,M,D	Pub	F,S	C	15,609	22	35	25	23	8	9	520	41	43	14	2	520	39	42	17	2	3/1
Bethel College	Mishawaka	SU	A,B,M	Pri	No	C	1,541	22						540	37	37	22	4	530	35	39	24	2	8/1
Butler University	Indianapolis	SU	B,M,D	Pri	F,S	C	3,573																	Open
Calumet College of St. Joseph	Whiting	U	A,B	Pri	No	C	1,020																	Open
DePauw University	Greencastle	SM	B	Pri	F,S	C	2,219		4	18	30	23	25		6	46	37	11		7	40	43	10	2/1
Earlham College	Richmond	SM	B,M	Pri	No	C	1,078	26	18	15	26	20	21	630	11	23	46	20	590	21	33	35	11	2/15
Franklin College of Indiana	Franklin	SM	B	Pri	F,S	C	1,028	23	27	41	27		4	525	37	42	16	2	527	31	49	16	1	Open
Goshen College	Goshen	SM	B	Pri	No	C	986	26	21	12	21	16	30	575	23	34	30	13	566	26	37	24	13	8/15
Grace College	Winona Lake	R	A,B,M	Pri	No	C	972	23	38	23	25	10	4	532	34	44	20	2	579	39	43	16	2	8/1
Hanover College	Hanover	R	B	Pri	F,S	C	1,111	25	24	18	21	14	23	560	24	43	29	4	560	22	41	33	4	3/1
Huntington College	Huntington	SM	A,B,M	Pri	No	C	830																	8/1
Indiana Institute of Technology	Fort Wayne	U	A,B,M	Pri	F,S	C	2,470	21						455					478					Open
Indiana State University	Terre Haute	U	A,B,M,D	Pub	F,S	C	9,734	19	63	21	10	3	2	460	65	27	7	1	460	63	29	7	1	8/1
Indiana University Bloomington	Bloomington	SM	A,B,M,D	Pub	F,S	C	30,157	24		4	36	51	9	542	29	45	22	4	554	25	42	27	5	2/1
Indiana University East	Richmond	SM	A,B	Pub	F,S	C	2,405	20	12	32	48	20		462	68	27	5		445	73	24	2	1	Open
Indiana University Kokomo	Kokomo	SM	A,B,M	Pub	No	C	2,519	19	31	58	10		1	479	59	34	6	1	465	67	27	6		8/3
Indiana University Northwest	Gary	U	A,B,M	Pub	F,S	C	4,027	20		29	46	24	2	451	70	25	5		429	77	19	5		8/1
Indiana University South Bend	South Bend	SU	A,B,M	Pub	S	C	6,070	20	2	30	45	20	4	486	56	33	11		475	61	30	9		Open
Indiana University Southeast	New Albany	SU	A,B,M	Pub	F,S	C	5,668	20		24	58	18		480	59	33	8		468	64	30	6		7/15
Indiana University-Purdue University Fort Wayne	Fort Wayne	SU	A,B,M	Pub	F,S	C	10,282	20	24	57	18		2	481	59	32	8	1	482	58	32	9	1	8/1
Indiana University-Purdue University Indianapolis	Indianapolis	U	A,B,M,D	Pub	F,S	C	20,695	21	12	25	53	21	1	492	56	34	9	1	489	58	32	9	1	Open
Indiana Wesleyan University	Marion	U	A,B,M	Pri	No	C	5,721	23						539	38	35	24	4	543	28	48	21	4	8/1
Manchester College	North Manchester	SM	A,B,M	Pri	No	C	1,135	23	14	48	30		5	510	46	40	12	2	520	42	39	17	2	Open
Marian College	Indianapolis	U	A,B		No	C	1,260	20	56	21	15	6	1	490	51	42	6	1	490	50	38	11	1	Open
Martin University	Indianapolis	U	B,M	Pri	No	C	565																	Open
Oakland City University	Oakland City	SM	A,B,M	Pri	No	C	1,070																	Open
Purdue University/Calumet	Hammond	U	A,B,M	Pub	F,S	C	8,120							460	67	28	5	1	450	69	24	6	1	Open
Purdue University/West Lafayette	West Lafayette	SU	A,B,M,D	Pub	F,S	C	30,987	25	1	32	54		13	550	25	48	23	4	584	18	39	34	9	Open
Rose-Hulman Institute of Technology	Terre Haute	SU	B,M	Pri	F,S	C	1,573	28			9	56	35	610					680	1	11	48	40	3/1
Saint Joseph's College	Rensselaer	SM	A,B,M	Pri	No	C	914	22	37	27	18	10	8	499	51	40	7	2	505	52	33	14	1	Open
Saint Mary-of-the-Woods College	St. Mary-of-the-Woods	R	A,B,M	Pri	No	W	1,384	23						506					475					7/15
Saint Mary's College	Notre Dame	SU	B	Pri	No	PW	1,523	25	12	23	36	16	12	560	18	48	30	4	550	20	46	30	4	3/1
Taylor University	Upland	R	A,B	Pri	No	C	1,858	27	6	16	25	28	25	600	13	31	47	9	610	10	35	44	11	1/15
Tri-State University-Main Campus	Angola	SM	A,B		F,S	C	1,268																	6/1
University of Evansville	Evansville	U	A,B,M	Pri	F,S	C	2,674	25	2	28	39	16	15	559	22	45	27	6	561	18	47	30	5	
University of Indianapolis	Indianapolis	SU	A,B,M,D	Pri	No	C	2,854																	Open
University of Notre Dame	Notre Dame	SU	B,M,D	Pri	No	C	8,208	31	1	1	6	7	85	670	3	13	48	37	690	1	9	42	48	1/7
University of Saint Francis	Fort Wayne	SU	A,B,M	Pri	No	C	1,555																	Open
University of Southern Indiana	Evansville	SU	A,B,M	Pub	F,S	C	8,783	19	62	22	11	3	2	472	63	29	8		474	61	30	8	1	8/15
Valparaiso University	Valparaiso	SM	A,B,M,D		F,S	C	2,873	27	5	19	27	20	29	580	13	41	36	10	580	11	45	31	13	8/15
Wabash College	Crawfordsville	SM	B	Pri	F	M	849	26	10	18	33	20	19	589	13	40	36	10	603	6	36	47	11	2/1

Iowa

NAME OF SCHOOL	TOWN	ENVIRONMENT	DEGREES AWARDED	CONTROL	FRATERNITIES AND SORORITIES	STUDENTS	UNDERGRADUATE ENROLLMENT FALL 2001	ACT Median	ACT Below 21	ACT 21-23	ACT 24-26	ACT 27-28	ACT Above 28	SAT I Verbal Median	SAT I Verbal Below 500	SAT I Verbal 500-599	SAT I Verbal 600-700	SAT I Verbal Above 700	SAT I Math Median	SAT I Math Below 500	SAT I Math 500-599	SAT I Math 600-700	SAT I Math Above 700	APPLICATION DEADLINE Month / Day
Allen College	Waterloo	SU	A,B,M	Pri	No	C	233	20	63	26	11													Open
Briar Cliff University	Sioux City	SU	A,B,M	Pri	No	C	969																	Open
Buena Vista University	Storm Lake	SM	B,M	Pri	No	C	1,292	22	45	19	22	8	7											Open
Central College	Pella	SU	B	Pri	F,S	C	1,623																	3/1
Clarke College	Dubuque	U	A,B,M	Pri	No	C	1,052	24	24	31	32	8	4	504	55	18	18	9	501	45	27	27		Open
Coe College	Cedar Rapids	U	B,M	Pri	F,S	C	1,280	24	16	24	32	15	13	570	15	49	29	6	570	18	41	37	4	3/1
Cornell College	Mount Vernon	SM	B		F,S	C	986	24	15	25	31	14	15	580	27	26	42	5	580	18	36	37	9	Open
Dordt College	Sioux Center	R	A,B,M	Pri	No	C	1,396	24	18	28	24	16	14	580	17	38	38	7	580	19	38	33	10	7/1
Drake University	Des Moines	SU	B,M,D	Pri	F,S	C	3,577	25	9	24	29	15	25	570	16	37	36	11	590	24	39	32	6	3/1
Graceland University	Lamoni	SM	B,M	Pri	No	C	1,372	22	46	22	20	5	7	511	48	28	15	9	503	52	21	24	3	5/1

NAME OF SCHOOL	TOWN	ENVIRONMENT U-Urban R-Rural SU-Suburban SM-Small Town	DEGREES AWARDED A-Associate B-Bachelor M-Master D-Doctorate	CONTROL Pri-Private, Pub-Public	FRATERNITIES AND SORORITIES F-Fraternities S-Sororities F, S-Both No-Neither	STUDENTS: C-Coed M-Men W-Women PM-Primarily Men PW-Primarily Women	UNDERGRADUATE ENROLLMENT FALL 2001	TEST SCORES: ACT Median	ACT Below 21	ACT 21-23	ACT 24-26	ACT 27-28	ACT Above 28	SAT I VERBAL REASONING Median	Below 500	500-599	600-700	Above 700	SAT I MATHEMATICAL REASONING Median	Below 500	500-599	600-700	Above 700	APPLICATION DEADLINE Month / Day
Grand View College	Des Moines	U	A,B	Pri	No	C	1,402	20	54	26	15	4	1											Open
Grinnell College	Grinnell	SM	B	Pri	No	C	1,338	30	5	3	11	14	67	680	1	9	43	47	660		15	52	33	1/20
Iowa State University	Ames	SU	B,M,D	Pub	F,S	C	23,060	24		3	40	45	12											8/21
Iowa Wesleyan College	Mount Pleasant	SM	B	Pri	F,S	C	812	17	80	11	9													Open
Loras College	Dubuque	SM	A,B,M	Pri	F,S	C	1,636																	Open
Luther College	Decorah	SM	B	Pri	F,S	C	2,575	25	10	25	26	17	22	616	7	31	47	15	603	10	32	47	11	3/1
Maharishi University of Management	Fairfield	SM	A,B,M,D	Pri	No	C	210	25						585	19	23	50	8	573	26	27	35	12	4/15
Mercy College of Health Sciences	Des Moines	U	A,B	Pri	No	C																		
Morningside College	Sioux City	SU	B,M	Pri	F,S	C	837	22	44	25	18	9	4											Open
Mount Mercy College	Cedar Rapids	U	B	Pri	No	C	1,387	23	24	24	28	24	4											
Mount Saint Clare College	Clinton	SM	A,B	Pri	No	C	479	20	56	21	19	1	3	445	83	17			435	83	17			8/15
Northwestern College of Iowa	Orange City	SM	A,B	Pri	No	C	1,294	24	21	21	28	14	16											Opcn
Saint Ambrose University	Davenport	U	B,M,D	Pri	No	C	2,271	21	46	29	16	5	4											Open
Simpson College	Indianola	SU	B	Pri	F,S	C	1,816	24	18	30	27	18	14	590	23	45	27	6	580	30	34	31	6	Open
University of Dubuque	Dubuque	SU	A,B,M	Pri	F,S	C	756	23	38	34	15	8	4	500					500					5/1
University of Iowa	Iowa City	SM	B,M,D	Pub	F,S	C	19,603	24	14	28	30	18	13	590	14	38	36	13	605	14	33	39	15	5/15
University of Northern Iowa	Cedar Falls	SM	B,M,D	Pub	F,S	C	12,474	23	27	32	24	9	8	529	37	35	24	4	531	39	31	24	7	8/15
Upper Iowa University	Fayette	R	A,B,M	Pri	F,S	C	703	21	40	20	20	15	5											Open
Wartburg College	Waverly	SM	B	Pri	No	C	1,649	24	22	21	25	18	14	580	21	42	18	18	610	18	30	36	15	8/1
William Penn University	Oskaloosa	R	A,B	Pri	F,S	C	1,547	21	49	36	12	2	1											Open
Kansas																								
Baker University	Baldwin City	R	B	Pri	F,S	C	765	24																Open
Benedictine College	Atchison	SM	A,B,M	Pri	No	C	1,297	22	34	28	19	10	9	517	49	34	12	5	511	46	32	20	2	Open
Bethany College	Lindsborg	R	B	Pri	F,S	C	622	26	50	13	24	6	7											8/1
Bethel College	North Newton	SU	B	Pri	No	C	525	24	28	24	20	10	18											Open
Emporia State University	Emporia	SM	B,M,D	Pub	F,S	C	4,287																	Open
Fort Hays State University	Hays	SM	A,B,M	Pub	F,S	C	4,565		47	24	18	6	5											Open
Friends University	Wichita	U	A,B,M	Pri	F,S	C	1,017	21																Open
Kansas State University	Manhattan	SU	A,B,M,D	Pub	F,S	C	18,770																	Open
Kansas Wesleyan University	Salina	U	A,B,M	Pri	F,S	C	710																	Open
McPherson College	McPherson	SM	A,B	Pri	No	C	397	20	60	22	12	4	1	490	54	40	3	3	480	63	27	10		Open
MidAmerica Nazarene University	Olathe	SU	A,B,M	Pri	No	C	1,290	23	31	37	14	9	9	550	17	52	27	4	490	26	48	26		8/1
Newman University	Wichita	U	A,B,M	Pri	No	C	1,520																	Open
Ottawa University	Ottawa	SM	B	Pri	No	C	475	20																Open
Pittsburg State University	Pittsburg	SM	A,B,M	Pub	F,S	C	5,470	21																Open
Saint Mary College	Leavenworth	SM	A,B,M	Pri	No	C	484	22	26	28	28	13	5											Open
Southwestern College	Winfield	SM	B,M	Pri	F,S	C	1,175	23	12	48	38		2	480	64	25	11		480					8/1
Sterling College	Sterling	SM	B	Pri	No	C	461	22	41	14	26	9	10	490	56	13	31		510	44	44	12		Open
Tabor College	Hillsboro	R	A,B	Pri	No	C	572	22																8/1
University of Kansas	Lawrence	SU	B,M,D	Pub	F,S	C	20,062	25	17	25	27	13	18											4/1
Washburn University of Topeka	Topeka	U	A,B,M,D	Pub	F,S	C	5,098	21	43	24	20	7	6											8/3
Wichita State University	Wichita	U	A,B,M,D	Pub	F,S	C	11,303	21	45	27	17	6	5											
Kentucky																								
Alice Lloyd College	Pippa Passes	R	B	Pri	No	C	565	20	45	34	10	9	2		15	30	55			15	30	45	5	8/1
Asbury College	Wilmore	R	B,M		No	C	1,328																	8/1
Bellarmine University	Louisville	SU	B,M	Pri	F,S	C	1,735	24	3	37	27	27	6	530	29	47	19	3	540	33	43	20	2	8/15
Berea College	Berea	SM	B	Pri	No	C	1,674	23	21	30	29	11	9	555	24	44	27	5	540	29	44	24	3	Open
Brescia University	Owensboro	U	A,B,M	Pri	No	C	802	22	36	30	16	11	7											Open
Campbellsville University	Campbellsville	SM	A,B,M	Pri	No	C	1,628	21	47	30	17	3	3											7/1
Centre College	Danville	SM	B	Pri	F,S	C	1,070	27		11	33	25	30	631	5	33	49	13	618	6	39	48	7	2/1
Cumberland College	Williamsburg	SM	B,M	Pri	No	C	1,569	21	40	35	13	7	5	491	53	42	5		509	47	38	14	1	Open
Eastern Kentucky University	Richmond	SM	A,B,M	Pub	F,S	C	12,804	21																8/1
Georgetown College	Georgetown	SU	B,M	Pri	F,S	C	1,362	25	13	31	26	16	14											
Kentucky Christian College	Grayson	SM	A,B,M	Pri	No	C	578		43	23	19	5	9		68	16	16			52	44	4		Open
Kentucky State University	Frankfort	SM	B		F,S	C	2,280																	Open
Kentucky Wesleyan College	Owensboro	U	B	Pri	F,S	C	671	22						480	57	30	13		495	65	17	17		Open
Lindsey Wilson College	Columbia	SM	A,B,M	Pri	No	C	1,370																	Open
Midway College	Midway	R	A,B	Pri	No	PW	874	19	53	29	8			520	42	29	29		471	57	43			Open
Morehead State University	Morehead	SM	A,B,M	Pub	F,S	C	7,199	20																Open
Murray State University	Murray	SM	A,B,M	Pub	F,S	C	7,775	23	20	30	30	12	8											8/1
Northern Kentucky University	Highland Heights	SU	A,B,M	Pub	F,S	C	10,838																	8/1
Pikeville College	Pikeville	SM	A,B,D	Pri	No	C	948	18	67	17	10	5	1	360	92	8			360	100				8/23
Spalding University	Louisville	U	A,B,M,D	Pri	No	C	786	21																8/1
Thomas More College	Crestview Hills	SU	A,B,M	Pri	No	C	1,412																	8/15
Transylvania University	Lexington	U	B	Pri	F,S	C	1,052	26	7	14	27	23	29	610	15	36	34	15	600	17	32	40	11	3/1
Union College	Barbourville	SM	A,B,M	Pri	No	C	576																	Open
University of Kentucky	Lexington	SU	B,M,D	Pub	F,S	C	6,845																	2/15
University of Louisville	Louisville	U	A,B,M,D	Pub	F,S	C	14,131		36	26	20	9	9											Open
Western Kentucky University	Bowling Green	SU	A,B,M	Pub	F,S	C	14,135																	8/1
Louisiana																								
Centenary College of Louisiana	Shreveport	SU	B,M	Pri	F,S	C	910	26	9	23	27	19	22	580	21	34	36	9	580	15	40	35	10	2/15
Dillard University	New Orleans	U	B	Pri	F,S	C	2,137	22																Open
Grambling State University	Grambling	SM	A,B,M,D	Pub	F,S	C	4,052	17	90	7	3													Open
Louisiana College	Pineville	SM	B	Pri	F,S	C	1,204	23	27	33	22	12	6											Open
Louisiana State University and Agricultural and Mechanical College	Baton Rouge	U	B,M,D	Pub	F,S	C	26,528	24	17	35	24	13	10											4/15
Louisiana State University in Shreveport	Shreveport	U	B,M	Pub	F,S	C	3,555																	

NAME OF SCHOOL	TOWN	ENVIRONMENT U-Urban R-Rural SU-Suburban SM-Small Town	DEGREES AWARDED A-Associate B-Bachelor M-Master D-Doctorate	CONTROL Pri-Private, Pub-Public	FRATERNITIES AND SORORITIES F-Fraternities S-Sororities F, S-Both No-Neither	STUDENTS: C-Coed M-Men W-Women PM-Primarily Men PW-Primarily Women	UNDERGRADUATE ENROLLMENT FALL 2001	TEST SCORES: ACT Median	ACT Below 21	ACT 21-23	ACT 24-26	ACT 27-28	ACT Above 28	SAT I VERBAL REASONING Median	Below 500	500-599	600-700	Above 700	SAT I MATHEMATICAL REASONING Median	Below 500	500-599	600-700	Above 700	APPLICATION DEADLINE Month / Day
Louisiana Tech University	Ruston	SM	A,B,M,D	Pub	F,S	C	9,060		36	28	21	9	6											8/4
Loyola University New Orleans	New Orleans	U	B,M,D	Pri	F,S	C	3,792																	2/15
McNeese State University	Lake Charles	SU	A,B,M	Pub	F,S	C	6,845																	Open
Nicholls State University	Thibodaux	SM	A,B,M	Pub	F,S	C	6,543	19	66	23	8	2	1	482	46	34	20		483	56	29	15		
Northwestern State University of Louisiana	Natchitoches	SM	A,B,M	Pub	F,S	C	8,373	21	61	21	11	4	3											8/15
Our Lady of Holy Cross College	New Orleans	U	A,B,M	Pri	No	C	1,250	20	60	22	5	1												7/20
Southeastern Louisiana University	Hammond	SM	A,B,M	Pub	F,S	C	12,821	20	62	26	8	2	1											7/15
Southern University and A&M College	Baton Rouge	U	A,B,M,D	Pub	F,S	C	7,472																	7/1
Southern University at New Orleans	New Orleans	SU	B	Pub	No	C																		7/1
Tulane University	New Orleans	U	A,B,M,D	Pri	F,S	C	7,522							659	3	12	52	33	644	3	18	55	24	1/15
University of Louisiana at Lafayette	Lafayette	U	A,B,M,D	Pub	F,S	C	13,913	21	49	31	13	5	3											Open
University of Louisiana at Monroe	Monroe	U	A,B,M,D	Pub	F,S	C	8,835																	Open
University of New Orleans	New Orleans	U	B,M,D	Pub	F,S	C	12,967	20	52	29	12	4	3	520	44	34	18	4	514	44	34	19	3	7/1
Xavier University of Louisiana	New Orleans	U	B,M,D	Pri	F,S	C	3,096		79		20		1		52	36	11	2		53	35	10	1	3/1

Maine

NAME OF SCHOOL	TOWN	ENVIRONMENT	DEGREES AWARDED	CONTROL	FRATERNITIES AND SORORITIES	STUDENTS	UNDERGRADUATE ENROLLMENT FALL 2001	ACT Median	ACT Below 21	ACT 21-23	ACT 24-26	ACT 27-28	ACT Above 28	SAT I Verbal Median	Below 500	500-599	600-700	Above 700	SAT I Math Median	Below 500	500-599	600-700	Above 700	APPLICATION DEADLINE
Bates College	Lewiston	SU	B	Pri	No	C	1,767							670	1	8	61	30	670		6	63	31	1/15
Bowdoin College	Brunswick	SM	B	Pri	No	C	1,635							690	2	8	43	47	680	2	8	52	38	1/1
Colby College	Waterville	SM	B	Pri	No	C	1,809	28		7	65	28		660	2	14	53	31	670		10	55	35	1/1
College of the Atlantic	Bar Harbor	SM	B,M	Pri	No	C	269	26			40		60	628		39	43	18	593	10	39	47	4	3/1
Husson College	Bangor	U	A,B,M	Pri	F,S	C	1,536	22	40	20	40			450	76	22	2	1	458	70	25	5		Open
Maine College of Art	Portland	U	B,M		No	C	410	21	50	17	17	17		530	38	41	19	2	480	61	33	6		Open
Maine Maritime Academy	Castine	SM	A,B,M	Pub	F	C	713							513					524	33	49	16	1	7/1
Saint Joseph's College of Maine	Standish	R	A,B,M	Pri	No	C	893																	Open
Thomas College	Waterville	R	A,B,M	Pri	F,S	C	760																	Open
Unity College	Unity	R	A,B	Pri	No	C	512							490	75	25			490	75	25			Open
University of Maine	Orono	SM	B,M,D	Pub	F,S	C	8,511	23	28	29	24	12	7	540	29	47	21	3	540	31	43	22	4	Open
University of Maine at Augusta	Augusta	SM	A,B	Pub	No	C	5,575																	6/15
University of Maine at Farmington	Farmington	SM	B	Pub	No	C	2,419							530	38	43	16	3	515	43	39	17	1	Open
University of Maine at Fort Kent	Fort Kent	SM	A,B	Pub	F,S	C	925																	Open
University of Maine at Machias	Machias	R	A,B	Pub	F,S	C	910																	Open
University of Maine at Presque Isle	Presque Isle	R	A,B	Pub	F,S	C	1,367																	Open
University of New England	Biddeford	R	A,B,M,D	Pri	No	C	1,389							530	34	48	16	1	540	35	46	19		
University of Southern Maine	Gorham	U	A,B,M	Pub	F,S	C	8,831		43	40	14		3	522	39	44	15	2	519	41	45	13	1	2/15

Maryland

NAME OF SCHOOL	TOWN	ENVIRONMENT	DEGREES AWARDED	CONTROL	FRATERNITIES AND SORORITIES	STUDENTS	UNDERGRADUATE ENROLLMENT FALL 2001	ACT Median	ACT Below 21	ACT 21-23	ACT 24-26	ACT 27-28	ACT Above 28	SAT I Verbal Median	Below 500	500-599	600-700	Above 700	SAT I Math Median	Below 500	500-599	600-700	Above 700	APPLICATION DEADLINE
Baltimore Hebrew University	Baltimore	U	A,B,M,D	Pri	No	C	210																	Open
Bowie State University	Bowie	SU	B,M,D	Pub	F,S	C	3,542							448	77	20	2	1	435	82	16	2		8/1
Capitol College	Laurel	R	A,B,M	Pri	No	C	830							475	67	31	1	1	505	44	43	12	1	Open
College of Notre Dame of Maryland	Baltimore	SU	B,M	Pri	No	PW	2,370																	Open
Columbia Union College	Takoma Park	SU	A,B,M	Pri	No	C	1,069	20	59	21	10	7	2	500	61	27	11	1	395	68	25	7		8/15
Coppin State College	Baltimore	U	B,M	Pub	F,S	C	3,239																	7/15
Frostburg State University	Frostburg	SM	B,M	Pub	F,S	C	4,354		66	27	5	2			50	39	10	1		46	41	12	1	Open
Goucher College	Baltimore	SU	B,M	Pri	No	C	1,232							620	8	32	50	10	570	13	48	37	2	2/1
Hood College	Frederick	SU	B,M	Pri	No	PW	784	23	22	33	22	17	6	577	17	41	35	7	557	20	49	25	7	2/15
Johns Hopkins University	Baltimore	U	B,M,D	Pri	F,S	C	3,961	31		3	9	14	75	690	1	8	44	47	720		3	30	67	1/1
Loyola College in Maryland	Baltimore	U	B,M,D	Pri	No	C	3,443							600	5	43	47	6	610	3	36	54	6	1/15
Maryland Institute College of Art	Baltimore	U	B,M	Pri	No	C	1,195							570	18	41	33	8	550	27	42	20	3	1/15
Morgan State University	Baltimore	SU	B,M,D	Pub	F,S	C	5,800																	
Mount Saint Mary's College	Emmitsburg	R	B,M		No	C	1,542							542	27	51	20	2	541	28	51	19	2	3/1
Saint John's College	Annapolis	SM	B,M	Pri	No	C	477																	Open
Saint Mary's College of Maryland	St. Marys City	R	B	Pub	No	C	1,688							620	6	29	47	18	610	7	39	48	6	1/15
Salisbury University	Salisbury	SM	B,M	Pub	F,S	C	6,060							550	23	54	21	2	570	16	53	29	2	1/15
Sojourner-Douglass College	Baltimore	U	B	Pri	No	C	240																	Open
Towson University	Towson	SU	B,M,D	Pub	F,S	C	13,959								25	55	19	2		20	57	22	2	5/1
United States Naval Academy	Annapolis	SM	B		No	C	4,100																	Open
University of Maryland/Baltimore County	Baltimore	SU	B,M,D	Pub	F,S	C	9,328	23	16	34	23	10	17	590	11	43	37	9	610	4	38	44	14	3/15
University of Maryland/College Park	College Park	SU	B,M,D	Pub	F,S	C	24,449								7	34	45	14		5	22	51	22	2/15
University of Maryland/Eastern Shore	Princess Anne	R	B,M,D	Pub	F,S	C	3,134																	
University of Maryland/University College	Adelphi	U	A,B,M	Pub	No	C	16,062																	Open
Villa Julie College	Stevenson	SU	A,B,M		S	C	2,376							518	39	45	15	1	517	40	43	16	1	3/1
Washington College	Chestertown	SM	B,M		F,S	C	1,223	23	27	19	35	5	14	578	16	44	33	7	567	16	51	30	4	2/15
Western Maryland College	Westminster	SM	B,M	Pri	F,S	C	1,641							563	18	53	23	6	560	19	51	27	3	3/15

Massachusetts

NAME OF SCHOOL	TOWN	ENVIRONMENT	DEGREES AWARDED	CONTROL	FRATERNITIES AND SORORITIES	STUDENTS	UNDERGRADUATE ENROLLMENT FALL 2001	ACT Median	ACT Below 21	ACT 21-23	ACT 24-26	ACT 27-28	ACT Above 28	SAT I Verbal Median	Below 500	500-599	600-700	Above 700	SAT I Math Median	Below 500	500-599	600-700	Above 700	APPLICATION DEADLINE
American International College	Springfield	U	A,B,M,D	Pri	F,S	C	1,068							476	59	32	7	2	484	54	34	9	3	Open
Amherst College	Amherst	SM	B	Pri	No	C	1,631	29	4	5	12	12	67	705		8	31	61	697		8	34	57	12/31
Anna Maria College	Paxton	R	A,B,M	Pri	No	C	832	18	71	29				480	59	34	6	1	470	64	29	7		3/1
Art Institute of Boston at Lesley University	Boston	U	B	Pri	No	C	791							513	29	49	20	2	489	49	44	6	1	
Assumption College	Worcester	U	A,B,M	Pri	No	C	2,066	22	35	35	23	6	2	530	27	54	18	1	540	29	52	18	1	3/1
Atlantic Union College	South Lancaster	SM	A,B,M	Pri	No	C	602	17	71	15	8	6		430	69	26	8		410	72	23	5		8/1
Babson College	Babson Park	SU	B,M	Pri	F,S	C	1,719							600	3	44	48	5	640		19	63	17	2/1
Bay Path College	Longmeadow	SU	A,B,M	Pri	No	W	918		33	67					53	36	10	1		62	35	4	1	Open
Becker College	Worcester	SU	A,B		No	C	1,298																	Open
Benjamin Franklin Institute of Technology	Boston	U	A,B	Pri	No	C	314																	8/15
Bentley College	Waltham	SU	A,B,M		F,S	C	4,256							560	12	62	24	1	600	4	45	46	5	2/1
Berklee College of Music	Boston	U	B,M	Pri	No	C	3,415																	Open

NAME OF SCHOOL	TOWN	ENVIRONMENT U-Urban R-Rural SU-Suburban SM-Small Town	DEGREES AWARDED A-Associate B-Bachelor M-Master D-Doctorate	CONTROL Pri-Private, Pub-Public	FRATERNITIES AND SORORITIES F-Fraternities S-Sororities F, S-Both No-Neither	STUDENTS: C-Coed M-Men W-Women PM-Primarily Men PW-Primarily Women	UNDERGRADUATE ENROLLMENT FALL 2001	TEST SCORES: ACT Median	ACT Below 21	ACT 21-23	ACT 24-26	ACT 27-28	ACT Above 28	SAT I VERBAL REASONING Median	Below 500	500-599	600-700	Above 700	SAT I MATHEMATICAL REASONING Median	Below 500	500-599	600-700	Above 700	APPLICATION DEADLINE Month / Day
Boston Architectural Center	Boston	U	B,M	Pri	No	C	490																	Open
Boston College	Chestnut Hill	SU	B,M,D		No	C	9,000								4	18	56	22		2	13	55	30	1/2
Boston Conservatory	Boston	U	B	Pri	F,S	C	365																	Open
Boston University	Boston	U	B,M,D	Pri	F,S	C	17,602	28			9	62	29	640		25	55	20	650		17	61	22	1/1
Brandeis University	Waltham	SU	B,M,D	Pri	No	C	3,081							660	1	12	55	32	670	1	14	48	37	1/31
Bridgewater State College	Bridgewater	SU	B,M	Pub	F,S	C	7,199	20						500					500					3/1
Cambridge College	Cambridge		B		No		397																	Open
Clark University	Worcester	U	B,M,D	Pri	No	C	2,138	25	14	21	30	16	19	500	10	39	41	10	580	11	48	36	5	2/1
College of Our Lady of the Elms	Chicopee	SU	A,B,M	Pri	No	C	630							491	51	41	8		475	56	37	5	2	Open
College of the Holy Cross	Worcester	SU	B	Pri	No	C	2,811							630	3	26	54	17	628	2	24	60	14	1/15
Curry College	Milton	SU	B,M	Pri	No	C	2,315																	
Eastern Nazarene College	Quincy	SU	A,B,M	Pri	No	C	640																	
Emerson College	Boston	U	B,M,D		F,S	C	3,412	26	6	20	31	31	12	617	3	36	47	14	584	8	50	36	5	2/1
Emmanuel College	Boston	U	B,M	Pri	No	PW	1,309	24	30	20	25	15	10	510	43	38	19		490	52	37	11		
Endicott College	Beverly	SU	A,B,M	Pri	No	C		21	38	58	4			514	40	51	9		508	42	52	5		Open
Fisher College	Boston	U	A,B		No	C	534																	Open
Fitchburg State College	Fitchburg	SM	B,M	Pub	F,S	C	3,219							510	43	44	12	1	500	46	44	10		4/1
Framingham State College	Framingham	SU	B,M	Pub	No	C	4,043							528	32	55	12	1	513	41	50	8	1	3/1
Gordon College	Wenham	SM	B,M	Pri	No	C	1,624	26	3	15	37	23	22	600	6	40	43	11	580	10	45	41	4	3/1
Hampshire College	Amherst	R	B	Pri	No	C		28	2	10	26	28	34	650	3	21	46	30	600	11	40	42	7	2/1
Harvard University/Harvard College	Cambridge	U	B,M,D	Pri	No	C	6,670																	1/1
Hellenic College/Holy Cross Greek Orthodox School of Theology	Brookline	U	B,M	Pri	No		58	17	50	50				501	34	33	33		507	55	25	20		8/15
Lasell College	Newton	SU	A,B	Pri	No	C	859							460	60	36	4		450	60	35	5		Open
Lesley College	Cambridge	U	A,B,M,D	Pri	No	PW	553								42	48	9	1		53	39	6	2	3/15
Massachusetts College of Art	Boston	U	B,M	Pub	No	C	1,458							567	15	50	28	8	535	30	47	21	2	3/1
Massachusetts College of Liberal Arts	North Adams	R	B,M	Pub	F,S	C	1,395																	Open
Massachusetts College of Pharmacy and Health Sciences	Boston	U	A,B,M,D	Pri	F,S	C	1,817							508	41	44	10	2	542	20	62	14	3	2/1
Massachusetts Institute of Technology	Cambridge	U	B,M,D	Pri	F,S	C	4,220	32			5	7	87	720		4	32	63	770		1	11	89	1/1
Massachusetts Maritime Academy	Buzzards Bay	SM	B	Pub	No	C	831							510	48	42	9	1	530	36	47	16	1	Open
Merrimack College	North Andover	SU	A,B,M	Pri	F,S	C	2,568	24	2	70	25	3		540	6	67	25	2	560	7	69	19	5	2/15
Montserrat College of Art	Beverly	SU	B	Pri	No	C	382							514	40	44	13	3	477	72	24	4		Open
Mount Holyoke College	South Hadley	SM	B,M	Pri	No	W	2,037	27	1	13	60	26		645	2	21	55	22	615	3	32	52	13	1/15
Mount Ida College	Newton Centre	SU	A,B	Pri	No	C	1,165																	Open
New England Conservatory of Music	Boston	U	B,M,D	Pri	F,S	C	381																	12/1
Newbury College	Brookline	SU	A,B		No	C	3,300	19	75			25		460	72	23	3	2	450	72	22	5	1	3/1
Nichols College	Dudley	R	A,B,M	Pri	No	C	1,297							450	70	26	4		460	68	29	4		Open
Northeastern University	Boston	U	A,B,M,D		F,S	C		25						570	16	49	31	5	590	9	45	39	8	Open
Pine Manor College	Chestnut Hill	SU	A,B	Pri	No	W	406	17	79	14	7			440	69	24	7		420	77	19	4		Open
Regis College	Weston	SU	A,B,M	Pri	No	W	851							510	43	37	16	4	490	52	40	8	1	
Salem State College	Salem	U	B,M	Pub	No	C	6,840																	Open
Simmons College	Boston	U	B,M,D	Pri	No	PW	1,167	23						566	16	48	31	5	539	29	47	23	1	2/1
Simon's Rock College of Bard	Great Barrington	SM	A,B	Pri	No	C	414	25		50	20	20	10	635	4	33	39	24	580	26	34	30	10	6/30
Smith College	Northampton	SM	B,M,D	Pri	No	PW	2,665	28	5	7	30	15	43	650	4	20	45	28	610	4	33	45	15	1/15
Springfield College	Springfield	SU	B,M,D	Pri	No	C	2,182							500	49	43	7		510	41	42	16	1	4/1
Stonehill College	Easton	SU	B,M	Pri	No	C	2,162	25						580	8	51	39	2	590	6	48	42	4	1/15
Suffolk University	Boston	U	A,B,M,D	Pri	F	C	3,437							500	47	42	11	1	490	52	39	9		Open
Tufts University	Medford	SU	B,M,D	Pri	F,S	C	4,755																	1/1
University of Massachusetts Amherst	Amherst	SM	A,B,M,D		F,S	C	19,368								24	45	26	5		19	45	29	7	2/1
University of Massachusetts Boston	Boston	U	B,M,D	Pub	No	C	10,565							523	54	30	14	2	535	48	34	17	2	1/11
University of Massachusetts Dartmouth	North Dartmouth	SU	B,M,D	Pub	F,S	C	6,638							520	35	45	17	2	530	32	47	19	2	Open
University of Massachusetts Lowell	Lowell	U	A,B,M,D	Pub	No	C	9,543							519	38	46	14	2	537	28	50	19	3	Open
Wellesley College	Wellesley	SU	B	Pri	No	W	2,273	29						679	1	11	42	46	666	2	13	52	33	1/15
Wentworth Institute of Technology	Boston	U	A,B	Pri	No	C	3,273							483	58	32	9	1	519	39	44	15	2	5/1
Western New England College	Springfield	SU	A,B,M,D	Pri	No	C	3,091							510	43	45	11	1	530	34	47	18	1	Open
Westfield State College	Westfield	R	B,M	Pub	No	C	4,062								40	48	12			41	48	11		3/1
Wheaton College	Norton	SU	B	Pri	No	C	1,551	25	4	19	69	8		610	5	34	51	10	590	6	45	45	4	1/15
Wheelock College	Boston	U	B,M	Pri	No	C	616							519	38	43	15	4	499	47	37	12	4	3/1
Williams College	Williamstown	SM	B,M	Pri	No	C	2,120																	
Worcester Polytechnic Institute	Worcester	SU	B,M,D	Pri	F,S	C	2,771	29						620	7	43	40	10	680	21	19	55	25	2/1
Worcester State College	Worcester	U	B,M	Pub	No	C	4,915	20	50	31	15	4		500	49	43	7	1	490	52	40	7	1	

Michigan

NAME OF SCHOOL	TOWN	ENVIRONMENT	DEGREES AWARDED	CONTROL	FRATERNITIES AND SORORITIES	STUDENTS	UNDERGRADUATE ENROLLMENT FALL 2001	ACT Median	ACT Below 21	ACT 21-23	ACT 24-26	ACT 27-28	ACT Above 28	SAT I Verbal Median	Below 500	500-599	600-700	Above 700	SAT I Math Median	Below 500	500-599	600-700	Above 700	APPLICATION DEADLINE Month / Day
Adrian College	Adrian	SM	A,B	Pri	F,S	C	1,055	22	39	27	21	8	5											3/15
Albion College	Albion	SM	B	Pri	F,S	C	1,548	25	13	22	29	17	19	580	13	44	37	6	580	15	43	35	7	
Alma College	Alma	SM	B	Pri	F,S	C	1,371	25	13	27	30	16	14											
Andrews University	Berrien Springs	R	A,B,M,D	Pri	F,S		1,785																	Open
Aquinas College	Grand Rapids	SU	A,B,M	Pri	No	C	2,016	24	31	25	25	9	9											Open
Baker College of Flint	Flint	U	A,B		No	C	4,399																	Open
Calvin College	Grand Rapids	SU	B,M	Pri	No	C	4,257	26	10	19	29	21	21	580	14	43	30	13	600					8/15
Central Michigan University	Mount Pleasant	SM	B,M,D	Pub	F,S	C	19,530	22	35	32	22	7	4	520	44	40	13	1	530	33	44	21	3	Open
Cleary College	Ann Arbor	SU	A,B	Pri	No	C	655																	Open
College For Creative Studies	Detroit	U	B	Pri	No	C	1,152	21						521					526					3/1
Concordia University	Ann Arbor	SU	A,B,M	Pri	No	C	533	23	37	23	20	9	11											9/1
Cornerstone University and Grand Rapids Baptist Seminary	Grand Rapids	SU	A,B,M		No	C	1,716	23	30	27	24	11	8											Open
Davenport University	Grand Rapids	SU	A,B,M	Pri	No	C	2,034																	Open
Eastern Michigan University	Ypsilanti	SU	B,M,D	Pub	F,S	C	18,502																	7/31
Ferris State University	Big Rapids	SM	A,B,M,D	Pub	F,S	C	10,092	19																Open
Grace Bible College	Grand Rapids	SU	A,B	Pri	No	C	149	21	48	32	14		6											Open

NAME OF SCHOOL	TOWN	ENVIRONMENT U-Urban R-Rural SU-Suburban SM-Small Town	DEGREES AWARDED A-Associate B-Bachelor M-Master D-Doctorate	CONTROL Pri-Private, Pub-Public	FRATERNITIES AND SORORITIES F-Fraternities S-Sororities F,S-Both No-Neither	STUDENTS: C-Coed M-Men W-Women PM-Primarily Men PW-Primarily Women	UNDERGRADUATE ENROLLMENT FALL 2001	TEST SCORES: ACT Median	ACT Below 21	ACT 21-23	ACT 24-26	ACT 27-28	ACT Above 28	SAT I VERBAL REASONING Median	Below 500	500-599	600-700	Above 700	SAT I MATHEMATICAL REASONING Median	Below 500	500-599	600-700	Above 700	APPLICATION DEADLINE Month / Day
Grand Valley State University	Allendale	SM	B,M	Pub	F,S	C	16,385	23	26	34	25	8	7											7/31
Hillsdale College	Hillsdale	SM	B	Pri	F,S	C	1,138	26	6	20	35	14	25	630	6	31	40	23	600	8	39	41	12	7/15
Hope College	Holland	SU	B	Pri	F,S	C	2,999	25		2	34	49	15	595	12	39	37	12	603	13	30	41	16	Open
Kalamazoo College	Kalamazoo	SU	B		No	C		28	1	5	33	22	39	637	1	27	52	20	624	1	31	52	16	2/15
Kendall College of Art and Design of Ferris State University	Grand Rapids	U	B	Pub	No	C	856																	Open
Kettering University	Flint	SU	B,M	Pri	F,S	C		26	3	15	44	19	19	590	9	48	36	7	640		20	62	19	Open
Lake Superior State University	Sault Sainte Marie	SM	A,B,M	Pub	F,S	C	3,200																	Open
Lawrence Technological University	Southfield	SU	A,B,M	Pri	F,S	C	2,926																	Open
Madonna University	Livonia	SU	A,B,M	Pri	No	C	3,043	23	23	42	30	5												Open
Marygrove College	Detroit	U	A,B,M	Pri	No	PW	879	19																8/15
Michigan State University	East Lansing	SU	B,M,D		F,S	C	34,874	24	17	28	30	12	13	560	25	42	26	7	580	19	38	33	10	7/25
Michigan Technological University	Houghton	SM	A,B,M,D	Pub	F,S	C	5,938	25	10	20	32	18	20	580	14	44	36	6	610	8	36	44	12	Open
Northern Michigan University	Marquette	U	A,B,M	Pub	F,S	C	7,673																	Open
Northwood University	Midland	SU	A,B,M	Pri	F,S	C	1,846	20	59	23	13	3	2	460	65	21	15		490	53	34	13		8/1
Oakland University	Rochester	SU	B,M,D	Pub	F,S	C	12,529	21	43	29	19	5	4											
Olivet College	Olivet	SM	B,M	Pri	F,S	C	893	20	25	40	15	15	5											Open
Rochester College	Rochester Hills	SU	A,B	Pri	No	C	927																	Open
Saginaw Valley State University	University Center	SU	B,M	Pub	F,S	C	6,900	21	51	25	15	6	3											Open
Saint Mary's College	Orchard Lake	SU	B		No	C	345																	
Siena Heights University	Adrian	SM	A,B,M	Pri	F,S	C	966	22	55	30	12	3												Open
Spring Arbor University	Spring Arbor	SM	A,B,M	Pri	No	C	1,139	22	31	30	22	11	6											Open
University of Detroit Mercy	Detroit	U	A,B,M,D	Pri	F,S	C	4,000																	
University of Michigan/Ann Arbor	Ann Arbor	SU	B,M,D	Pub	F,S	C	24,547	28	3	9	22	23	42	630	5	29	47	17	660	3	16	48	33	2/1
University of Michigan/Dearborn	Dearborn	SU	B,M	Pub	F,S	C	718	23																
University of Michigan/Flint	Flint	U	B,M	Pub	F,S	C	5,879	22																2/15
Wayne State University	Detroit	U	B,M,D	Pub	F,S	C	18,489	20																8/1
Western Michigan University	Kalamazoo	U	B,M,D	Pub	F,S	C	23,156	22	36	31	21	7	5											Open
William Tyndale College	Farmington Hills	SU	A,B	Pri	No	C	608	23	29	25	25	14	7											Open

Minnesota

NAME OF SCHOOL	TOWN	ENVIRONMENT	DEGREES AWARDED	CONTROL	FRATERNITIES AND SORORITIES	STUDENTS	UNDERGRADUATE ENROLLMENT FALL 2001	ACT Median	ACT Below 21	ACT 21-23	ACT 24-26	ACT 27-28	ACT Above 28	SAT I Verbal Median	Below 500	500-599	600-700	Above 700	SAT I Math Median	Below 500	500-599	600-700	Above 700	Application Deadline
Augsburg College	Minneapolis	U	B,M	Pri	No	C	2,780	23	29	28	26	8	9	541	32	34	30	4	542	24	52	20	4	8/15
Bemidji State University	Bemidji	SM	A,B,M	Pub	F,S	C	4,314	22	27	47	20	6												Open
Bethel College	St. Paul	SU	A,B,M	Pri	No	C	2,700	24						590	19	37	38	6	593	21	40	31	8	12/1
Carleton College	Northfield	SM	B	Pri	No	C	1,948		1	5			51		2	8	41	49		1	11	46	42	1/15
College of Saint Benedict	St. Joseph	SM	B	Pri	No	W	2,100	25	7	27	33	13	20	600	18	26	45	11	600	16	31	50	3	Open
College of Saint Catherine	St. Paul	U	A,B,M	Pri	S	W	3,600		27	26	28	10	8		30	30	34	6		18	36	37	9	Open
College of Saint Scholastica	Duluth	SU	B,M	Pri	No	C	1,700	23	19	32	27	19		560	14	57	22	7	580	14	50	29	7	Open
College of Visual Arts	St. Paul	U	B	Pri	No	C	269																	Open
Concordia College/Moorhead	Moorhead	U	B	Pri	No	C	2,920																	Open
Concordia University	St. Paul	U	A,B,M	Pri	No	C	1,511																	8/1
Gustavus Adolphus College	St. Peter	SM	B	Pri	F,S	C	2,592	26	8	22	31	16	23	600	14	34	34	18	620	10	34	41	15	5/1
Hamline University	St. Paul	U	B,M,D	Pri	S	C	1,873	24						585					564					5/1
Macalester College	St. Paul	U	B	Pri	No	C	1,822	29		2	13	23	62	690		8	52	40	660		17	58	25	1/15
Metropolitan State University	St. Paul	U	B,M	Pub	No	C	5,662																	Open
Minneapolis College of Art and Design	Minneapolis	U	B,M	Pri	No	C	580																	Open
Minnesota State University, Mankato	Mankato	R	A,B,M	Pub	F,S	C	11,640																	Open
Moorhead State University	Moorhead	SU	A,B,M	Pub	F,S	C	5,900																	
North Central University	Minneapolis	U	A,B	Pri	No	C	1,160																	6/1
Northwestern College	St. Paul	SU	A,B	Pri	No	C	1,602	24	25	25	26	14	10	591	19	28	41	12	568	25	40	16	19	8/1
Saint Cloud State University	St. Cloud	SU	A,B,M,D	Pub	F,S	C	14,714	21	46	29	18	4	2											Open
Saint John's University	Collegeville	R	B,M	Pri	No	M	1,888	25	6	26	33	17	18	580	14	44	33	9	620	8	36	47	9	Open
Saint Mary's University of Minnesota	Winona	SM	B,M,D	Pri	F,S	C	1,368	23	30	26	21	13	9											5/1
Saint Olaf College	Northfield	SM	B	Pri	No	C	3,011			10	28	26	36		3	29	52	16		3	31	51	15	2/1
Southwest State University	Marshall	R	A,B,M	Pub	No	C	2,850																	
University of Minnesota/Crookston	Crookston	R	B	Pub	No	C	2,170																	Open
University of Minnesota/Duluth	Duluth	SU	B,M	Pub	F,S	C	8,780	23	19	28	35	15	3											8/1
University of Minnesota/Morris	Morris	SM	B	Pub	No	C	1,927	24	15	26	30	14	15	584	17	39	32	12	572	22	44	26	8	3/15
University of Minnesota/Twin Cities	Minneapolis	U	B,M,D	Pub	F,S	C	30,136	25	17	22	28	16	17	590	14	36	38	12	620	11	28	42	20	12/15
University of Saint Thomas	St. Paul	U	B,M,D	Pri	No	C	5,416	25	11	25	29	19	16	570	20	41	33	6	600	16	34	46	4	Open
Winona State University	Winona	SM	A,B,M	Pub	F,S	C	7,114	23																Open

Mississippi

NAME OF SCHOOL	TOWN	ENVIRONMENT	DEGREES AWARDED	CONTROL	FRATERNITIES AND SORORITIES	STUDENTS	UNDERGRADUATE ENROLLMENT FALL 2001	ACT Median	ACT Below 21	ACT 21-23	ACT 24-26	ACT 27-28	ACT Above 28	SAT I Verbal Median	Below 500	500-599	600-700	Above 700	SAT I Math Median	Below 500	500-599	600-700	Above 700	Application Deadline
Alcorn State University	Alcorn State	R	A,B,M	Pub	F,S	C	2,543			87	12	1												Open
Belhaven College	Jackson	U	A,B,M	Pri	No	C	1,666	24	32	25	15	15	13	609	26	29	35	9	583	36	40	17	7	Open
Blue Mountain College	Blue Mountain	R	B	Pri	No	PW	404	19	64	20	11	4	1	470	50	50			435	50	50			Open
Delta State University	Cleveland	SM	B,M,D	Pub	F,S	C	3,292	21	58	22	12	4	3											8/1
Jackson State University	Jackson	U	B,M,D	Pub	F,S	C	5,200																	Open
Millsaps College	Jackson	U	B,M	Pri	F,S	C	1,221	26	4	23	25	17	31	600	8	39	41	12	590	12	39	39	10	2/1
Mississippi College	Clinton	SU	B,M	Pri	No	C	2,289	23	23	30	27	7	13											Open
Mississippi State University	Mississippi State	SM	B,M,D	Pub	F,S	C	13,604																	5/1
Mississippi University for Women	Columbus	SM	A,B,M	Pub	F,S	C	3,200																	Open
Mississippi Valley State University	Itta Bena	SM	B,M	Pub	F,S	C	2,636	18	91	7	1	1		480	55	44			428	89	11			8/10
Rust College	Holly Springs	SM	A,B	Pri	F,S	C	801	15	81	18	1													7/15
Tougaloo College	Tougaloo	SU	A,B	Pri	F,S	C	940																	Open
University of Mississippi	University	SM	B,M,D	Pub	F,S	C	9,891		27	26	21	11	15											4/1
University of Southern Mississippi	Hattiesburg	SU	B,M,D	Pub	F,S	C	10,607	22	43	25	17	6	9											
William Carey College	Hattiesburg	SM	B,M	Pri	F,S	C	1,850																	

Missouri

NAME OF SCHOOL	TOWN	ENVIRONMENT (U-Urban R-Rural SU-Suburban SM-Small Town)	DEGREES AWARDED (A-Associate B-Bachelor M-Master D-Doctorate)	CONTROL (Pri-Private, Pub-Public)	FRATERNITIES AND SORORITIES (F-Fraternities S-Sororities F,S-Both No-Neither)	STUDENTS (C-Coed M-Men W-Women PM-Primarily Men PW-Primarily Women)	UNDERGRADUATE ENROLLMENT FALL 2001	TEST SCORES: ACT Median	ACT Below 21	ACT 21-23	ACT 24-26	ACT 27-28	ACT Above 28	SAT I VERBAL REASONING Median	SAT I Verbal Below 500	SAT I Verbal 500-599	SAT I Verbal 600-700	SAT I Verbal Above 700	SAT I MATHEMATICAL REASONING Median	SAT I Math Below 500	SAT I Math 500-599	SAT I Math 600-700	SAT I Math Above 700	APPLICATION DEADLINE Month / Day
Avila College	Kansas City	SU	B,M	Pri	No	C	1,235	22	30	49	12	6	3	475					545					Open
Central Methodist College	Fayette	SM	A,B	Pri	F,S	C	831	20	51	25	13	8	3											Open
Central Missouri State University	Warrensburg	SM	A,B,M	Pub	F,S	C	9,068	22	39	33	16	7	5											
College of the Ozarks	Point Lookout	SM	B	Pri	No	C	1,395	21	10	65	22	3	3											2/1
Columbia College	Columbia	SM	A,B,M	Pri	No	C	855	22	42	26	22	6	4			50	50				50	50		Open
Culver-Stockton College	Canton	R	B	Pri	F,S	C	821	21	51	25	15	5	4	490	62	30	4	4	490	52	33	14		Open
Deaconess College of Nursing	St. Louis	U	A,B	Pri	No	C	246																	Open
DeVry University/Kansas City	Kansas City	U	A,B	Pri	No	C	2,620																	Open
Drury University	Springfield	U	B,M	Pri	F,S	C	1,450	25	10	25	27	14	23	543	30	49	19	2	556	14	61	16	9	8/1
Evangel University	Springfield	U	A,B,M	Pri	No	C	1,529	21	6	49	22	18	5											
Fontbonne University	St. Louis	SU	B,M	Pri	F	C	1,516	22	37	34	18	7	4											8/1
Hannibal-LaGrange College	Hannibal	SM	A,B	Pri	No	C	1,099	21	25	47	21		7	540					580					8/29
Harris-Stowe State College	St. Louis	U	B	Pub	F,S	C	1,306																	Open
Jewish Hospital College of Nursing and Allied Health	St. Louis	U	A,B,M	Pri	No	C	385																	Open
Kansas City Art Institute	Kansas City	U	B	Pri	No	C	537	23	28	33	25	12	2	552	26	39	29	6	522	39	37	20	4	
Lester L. Cox College of Nursing and Health Sciences	Springfield	U	A,B	Pri	No	C	312	22		94	5		1											2/1
Lincoln University	Jefferson City	SM	A,B,M		F,S	C	3,075		76	16	6	1	1											7/15
Lindenwood University	St. Charles	SU	B,M	Pri	F,S	C	3,853	22																Open
Maryville University of Saint Louis	St. Louis	SU	B,M		No	C	2,632																	
Missouri Baptist College	St. Louis	SU	A,B,M	Pri	No	C	2,734	21	48	25	7	5	5											Open
Missouri Southern State College	Joplin	SM	A,B	Pub	F,S	C	5,917	22	45	24	18	8	5											8/21
Missouri Valley College	Marshall	SM	A,B	Pri	F,S	C	1,565																	Open
Missouri Western State College	St. Joseph	SU	A,B	Pub	F,S	C	5,102	19	63	21	11	3	2											7/25
Northwest Missouri State University	Maryville	R	B,M	Pub	F,S	C	5,600		33	32	21	8	5											Open
Park University	Parkville	SU	A,B,M	Pri	No	C	9,262	19	73	13	10	2	1											8/15
Research College of Nursing	Kansas City	U	B,M		F,S	C	152	22	23	46	31													6/30
Rockhurst University	Kansas City	U	B,M	Pri	F,S	C	2,011		28	26	23	14	9		28	48	22	2		42	40	14	4	6/30
Saint Louis University	St. Louis	U	A,B,M,D	Pri	F,S	C	7,157		6	16	28	20	30		12	38	42	8		12	33	43	12	8/1
Southeast Missouri State University	Cape Girardeau	SM	A,B,M	Pub	F,S	C	8,098	22	39	28	18	8	7											Open
Southwest Baptist University	Bolivar	R	A,B,M	Pri	No	C	2,714	23	25	29	29	8	9	520	33	50	14	3	540	40	38	17	5	Open
Southwest Missouri State University	Springfield	SU	B,M	Pub	F,S	C	14,550																	
Stephens College	Columbia	U	A,B,M	Pri	S	W	618	23	26	29	28	10	7	560	11	51	38		500	27	62	9	2	Open
Truman State University	Kirksville	SM	B,M	Pub	F,S	C	5,685	27	2	15	30	21	33	610	8	37	39	17	590	10	40	40	10	3/1
University of Missouri/Columbia	Columbia	SM	B,M,D	Pub	F,S	C	18,431	26	7	23	29	17	24											5/1
University of Missouri/Kansas City	Kansas City	U	B,M,D	Pub	F,S	C	8,299	24	25	23	22	15	15											Open
University of Missouri/Rolla	Rolla	SM	B,M,D	Pub	F,S	C	3,731	27	5	15	25	16	39											7/1
University of Missouri/St. Louis	St. Louis	U	B,M,D	Pub	F,S	C	12,251		4	52	37		6		33	36	26	5		31	40	24	5	7/1
Washington University in St. Louis	St. Louis	SU	B,M,D	Pri	F,S	C	6,772			2	6	16	76		1	7	48	44			3	38	59	1/15
Webster University	St. Louis	SU	B,M,D	Pri	No	C	4,711	24	22	25	26	12	15	565	12	46	30	12	542	27	53	16	4	3/1
Westminster College	Fulton	SM	B	Pri	F,S		768	24																Open
William Jewell College	Liberty	SU	B	Pri	F,S	C	1,089		2	45	43		12		20	46	20	14		19	33	41	7	3/15
William Woods University	Fulton	SM	B,M		F,S	C	989	22						523					509					Open

Montana

NAME OF SCHOOL	TOWN	ENVIRONMENT	DEGREES AWARDED	CONTROL	FRATERNITIES AND SORORITIES	STUDENTS	UNDERGRADUATE ENROLLMENT FALL 2001	ACT Median	ACT Below 21	ACT 21-23	ACT 24-26	ACT 27-28	ACT Above 28	SAT I Verbal Median	SAT I Verbal Below 500	SAT I Verbal 500-599	SAT I Verbal 600-700	SAT I Verbal Above 700	SAT I Math Median	SAT I Math Below 500	SAT I Math 500-599	SAT I Math 600-700	SAT I Math Above 700	APPLICATION DEADLINE Month / Day
Carroll College	Helena	SM	A,B	Pri	No	C	1,347		2	43	46		9		22	49	25	5		24	50	22	4	6/1
Montana State University-Billings	Billings	U	A,B,M	Pub	No	C	3,872	20	56	27	11	5	1	477	60	32	7		490	49	41	9	1	Open
Montana State University-Bozeman	Bozeman	SM	B,M,D		F,S	C	10,537	23	27	30	23	11	9	540	31	45	22	2	550	25	44	26	5	Open
Montana State University-Northern	Havre	SM	A,B,M	Pub	No	C	1,490																	Open
Montana Tech of The University of Montana	Butte	SM	A,B,M	Pub	No	C	2,005	21	49	20	18	7	6	528	35	38	24	3	550	26	36	31	7	
Rocky Mountain College	Billings	SM	A,B	Pri	No	C	777	22	42	17	28	7	5	493	50	39	11		501	41	48	11		8/1
University of Great Falls	Great Falls	U	A,B,M	Pri	No	C	756		44	28	18	3	8		44	25	31			47	40	13		8/1
University of Montana	Missoula	U	A,B,M,D	Pub	F,S	C	10,454	23	27	33	23	10	7	546	26	46	22	5	538	30	45	22	3	7/1
University of Montana—Western	Dillon	SM	A,B	Pub	No	C	1,163																	7/1

Nebraska

NAME OF SCHOOL	TOWN	ENVIRONMENT	DEGREES AWARDED	CONTROL	FRATERNITIES AND SORORITIES	STUDENTS	UNDERGRADUATE ENROLLMENT FALL 2001	ACT Median	ACT Below 21	ACT 21-23	ACT 24-26	ACT 27-28	ACT Above 28	SAT I Verbal Median	SAT I Verbal Below 500	SAT I Verbal 500-599	SAT I Verbal 600-700	SAT I Verbal Above 700	SAT I Math Median	SAT I Math Below 500	SAT I Math 500-599	SAT I Math 600-700	SAT I Math Above 700	APPLICATION DEADLINE Month / Day
Bellevue University	Bellevue	SU	B,M	Pri	No	C	3,205																	Open
Chadron State College	Chadron	SM	B,M	Pub	No	C	2,394	22	45	21	19	9	5		67	33				50	33	17		Open
Clarkson College	Omaha	U	A,B,M	Pri	No	PW	362	22	5	90	5													Open
College of Saint Mary	Omaha	SU	A,B	Pri	No	PW	930	22																Open
Concordia University Nebraska	Seward	SM	B,M	Pri	No	C	1,191	23																8/1
Creighton University	Omaha	U	A,B,M,D	Pri	F,S	C	3,655	25	11	21	28	21	19	577	16	47	32	7	576	17	42	32	9	8/1
Dana College	Blair	SM	B	Pri	No	C	565	22	41	23	24	6	6	490	60	23	10	7	505	57	33	10		8/1
Doane College	Crete	SM	B,M	Pri	F,S	C	971	23																8/15
Hastings College	Hastings	R	B,M	Pri	F,S	C	1,067	24	15	31	24	16	14											8/1
Midland Lutheran College	Fremont	SM	A,B	Pri	F,S	C	991	22	9	64	15	10	2											7/15
Nebraska Methodist College of Nursing and Allied Health	Omaha	U	A,B,M	Pri	No	C	347	20	60	30	5		5											4/1
Nebraska Wesleyan University	Lincoln	SU	B,M	Pri	F,S	C	1,621	24	13	30	31	14	12											5/1
Peru State College	Peru	R	B,M	Pub	No	C	1,450		49	32	14	4	1											Open
Union College	Lincoln	SU	A,B	Pri	No	C	922																	Open
University of Nebraska at Kearney	Kearney	SM	B,M	Pub	F,S	C	5,840																	Open
University of Nebraska at Lincoln	Lincoln	U	A,B,M,D	Pub	F,S	C	17,985	24	19	44	25		12	567	23	39	28	10	583	19	35	33	13	6/30
University of Nebraska at Omaha	Omaha	SU	A,B,M,D	Pub	F,S	C	11,138	22	39	31	18	6	6											8/1
Wayne State College	Wayne	R	B,M	Pub	F,S	C	2,835	21	52	23	16	5	4											Open
York College	York	SM	A,B	Pri	F,S	C	455		48	22	14	11	5		25	50	25			25	37	38		

NAME OF SCHOOL	TOWN	ENVIRONMENT U-Urban R-Rural SU-Suburban SM-Small Town	DEGREES AWARDED A-Associate B-Bachelor M-Master D-Doctorate	CONTROL Pri-Private, Pub-Public	FRATERNITIES AND SORORITIES F-Fraternities S-Sororities F, S-Both No-Neither	STUDENTS: C-Coed M-Men W-Women PM-Primarily Men PW-Primarily Women	UNDERGRADUATE ENROLLMENT FALL 2001	TEST SCORES: ACT Median	ACT Below 21	ACT 21-23	ACT 24-26	ACT 27-28	ACT Above 28	SAT I VERBAL REASONING Median	Below 500	500-599	600-700	Above 700	SAT I MATHEMATICAL REASONING Median	Below 500	500-599	600-700	Above 700	APPLICATION DEADLINE Month / Day
Nevada																								
Sierra Nevada College-Lake Tahoe	Incline Village	R	B	Pri	No	C	320																	3/15
University of Nevada/Las Vegas	Las Vegas	U	B,M,D	Pub	F,S	C	18,606		15	55	27		2											8/15
University of Nevada/Reno	Reno	U	B,M,D	Pub	F,S	C	10,478	22	34	30	21	8	7	517	41	41	16	2	524	38	40	14	3	3/1
New Hampshire																								
Colby-Sawyer College	New London	SM	A,B		No	C	901	20						500					500					Open
College for Lifelong Learning	Concord	SM	A,B	Pub	No	C	2,200																	Open
Daniel Webster College	Nashua	SU	A,B	Pri	No	C	578							523	36	50	12	2	536					Open
Dartmouth College	Hanover	R	B,M,D	Pri	F,S	C	4,118							710		7	33	60	720	1	4	30	66	1/1
Franklin Pierce College	Rindge	R	B,M	Pri	No	C	1,548							500	57	32	10		483	63	30	6	1	Open
Hesser College	Manchester		A,B	Pri	No	C	466																	
Keene State College	Keene	SU	A,B,M	Pub	F,S	C	4,400	19	70	20	7	2		490	52	38	9	1	480	58	34	9	1	3/1
New England College	Henniker	SM	A,B,M		F,S	C	796							460	64	30	5	1	450	71	24	5		
Plymouth State College	Plymouth	SM	B,M	Pub	F,S	C	3,429																	4/1
Rivier College	Nashua	SU	A,B,M	Pri	No	C	1,468							480					470					Open
Saint Anselm College	Manchester	SU	B	Pri	No	C	1,964							560	18	54	26	2	560	17	57	24	2	3/1
Southern New Hampshire University	Manchester	SU	A,B,M,D	Pri	F,S	C	3,907							473	65	28	7		482	58	32	7		3/15
Thomas More College of Liberal Arts	Merrimack	SU	B	Pri	No	C																		Open
University of New Hampshire	Durham	R	A,B,M,D		F,S	C	10,400							550	24	50	23	3	550	19	48	29	4	2/1
New Jersey																								
Bloomfield College	Bloomfield	SU	B		F,S	C	1,762							430	82	15	2		430	84	15	1		Open
Caldwell College	Caldwell	SU	B,M	Pri	No	C	1,923							460	69	26	5		460	67	27	5	1	Open
Centenary College	Hackettstown	SU	A,B,M	Pri	F,S	C	1,453	22	29	43	14	14		496	56	33	11		493	53	40	6	1	Open
College of New Jersey, The	Ewing	SU	B,M	Pub	F,S	C	5,973							620	2	34	51	13	650	1	20	59	20	2/15
College of Saint Elizabeth	Morristown	SU	B,M	Pri	No	PW	1,251							450	56	34	8	2	460	56	33	7	4	8/15
DeVry College of Technology/ North Brunswick	North Brunswick	SM	A,B	Pri	No	C	3,912																	Open
Drew University/College of Liberal Arts	Madison	SM	B,M,D	Pri	No	C	1,536							610	8	32	44	16	600	10	39	39	12	2/15
Fairleigh Dickinson University/ Madison campus	Madison	SU	A,B,M		F,S	C	2,427								48	40	12			42	45	12	1	3/1
Fairleigh Dickinson University/ Teaneck Campus	Teaneck	SU	A,B,M,D		F,S	C	4,113								65	29	6			60	33	7	1	3/1
Felician College	Lodi	SU	A,B,M	Pri	No	C	1,618							450	78	20	2		455	75	23	2		Open
Georgian Court College	Lakewood	SU	B,M		No	PW	1,580																	8/1
Kean University	Union	SU	B,M	Pub	F,S	C	9,467							494	54	42	4		505	45	49	6		6/15
Monmouth University	West Long Branch	SU	A,B,M	Pri	F,S	C	4,179								34	52	13	1		28	54	17	1	3/1
Montclair State University	Upper Montclair	SU	B,M	Pub	F,S	C	9,720																	3/1
New Jersey City University	Jersey City	U	B,M	Pub	F,S	C	5,800																	4/1
New Jersey Institute of Technology	Newark	U	B,M,D	Pub	F,S	C	5,698							536	29	49	20	2	593	8	44	42	7	4/1
Princeton University	Princeton	SM	B,M,D	Pri	No	C	4,611	33						720		2	27	71	740		1	24	75	1/2
Ramapo College of New Jersey	Mahwah	SU	B,M	Pub	F,S	C	4,890							550	18	58	22	2	550	16	57	25	2	3/1
Richard Stockton College of New Jersey	Pomona	SU	B,M	Pub	F,S	C	6,138							550	32	50	16	2	570	30	50	18	2	5/1
Rider University	Lawrenceville	SU	A,B,M	Pri	F,S	C	4,306							510	41	46	12	1	520	37	48	13	2	Open
Rowan University	Glassboro	SM	B,M,D	Pub	F,S	C	8,325							559	13	60	25	2	574	10	55	32	3	3/15
Rutgers, The State University of New Jersey New Brunswick Campus	New Brunswick	SM	B,M,D	Pub	F,S	C	27,927																	Open
Rutgers, The State University of New Jersey/CamdenCampus	Camden	U	B,M	Pub	No	C	3,625																	Open
Rutgers, The State University of New Jersey/—Newark Campus	Newark	U	B,M,D	Pub	No	C	5,682																	12/1
Saint Peter's College	Jersey City	U	A,B,M	Pri	No	C	2,810																	Open
Seton Hall University	South Orange	SU	B,M,D	Pri	F,S	C	5,490																	3/1
Stevens Institute of Technology	Hoboken	U	B,M,D	Pri	F,S	C	1,649							630	8	36	44	12	710	2	11	55	34	2/15
Thomas Edison State College	Trenton	U	A,B,M	Pub	No	C																		Open
Westminster Choir College of Rider University	Princeton	SU	B,M	Pri	No	C	320																	Open
William Paterson University of New Jersey	Wayne	SU	B,M	Pub	F,S	C	8,295																	
New Mexico																								
College of Santa Fe	Santa Fe	SU	B,M	Pri	No	C	1,340																	Open
College of the Southwest	Hobbs	SM	B,M	Pri	No	C	613	20	56	22	9	9	4	450	64	22	14		450	64	22	14		Open
Eastern New Mexico University	Portales	SM	A,B,M	Pub	F,S	C	2,980																	Open
New Mexico Highlands University	Las Vegas	SM	A,B,M	Pub	F	C	1,886	18	81	17	1		1	360	77	23			415	65	34	1		Open
New Mexico Institute of Mining and Technology	Socorro	SM	A,B,M,D	Pub	No	C	1,256	26	6	22	27	15	30		12	36	40	12		14	26	43	17	8/1
New Mexico State University	Las Cruces	U	A,B,M,D		F,S	C	12,584		49	27	15	6	3											Open
Saint John's College	Santa Fe	SU	B,M	Pri	No	C	445	30						680	2	15	38	46	620	6	36	41	18	Open
University of New Mexico	Albuquerque	U	A,B,M,D	Pub	F,S	C	16,441	21	41	27	20	7	6	540	34	38	24	4	520	39	39	20	3	6/23
Western New Mexico University	Silver City	SM	A,B,M	Pub	No	C	620																	
New York																								
Adelphi University	Garden City	SU	A,B,M,D	Pri	F,S	C	3,391							530	32	47	20	1	530	31	45	22	2	Open
Albany College of Pharmacy	Albany	U	B,M,D	Pri	F,S	C	588							550					590					2/1
Albert A. List College of Jewish Studies	New York	U	B	Pri	No	C	177	28		10	20	40	30	661	2	20	52	26	650	4	22	70	4	2/15
Alfred University	Alfred	R	B,M,D	Pri	F,S	C	2,114	24						556	24	44	27	5	561	18	48	30	4	2/1

NAME OF SCHOOL	TOWN	ENVIRONMENT U-Urban R-Rural SU-Suburban SM-Small Town	DEGREES AWARDED A-Associate B-Bachelor M-Master D-Doctorate	CONTROL Pri-Private, Pub-Public	FRATERNITIES AND SORORITIES F-Fraternities S-Sororities F, S-Both No-Neither	STUDENTS: C-Coed M-Men W-Women PM-Primarily Men PW-Primarily Women	UNDERGRADUATE ENROLLMENT FALL 2001	TEST SCORES: ACT Median	ACT Below 21	ACT 21-23	ACT 24-26	ACT 27-28	ACT Above 28	SAT I VERBAL REASONING Median	SAT I Verbal Below 500	SAT I Verbal 500-599	SAT I Verbal 600-700	SAT I Verbal Above 700	SAT I MATHEMATICAL REASONING Median	SAT I Math Below 500	SAT I Math 500-599	SAT I Math 600-700	SAT I Math Above 700	APPLICATION DEADLINE Month / Day
Audrey Cohen College	New York	U	A,B,M	Pri	No	C																		8/1
Bard College	Annandale-on-Hudson	R	B,M,D		No	C	1,343							660		13	53	34	620		26	54	20	1/15
Berkeley College	White Plains	SU	A,B	Pri	No	C	690																	Open
Berkeley College of New York City	New York	U	A,B	Pri	No	C	1,720																	Open
Boricua College	New York	U	B	Pri	No	C	1,150																	Open
Canisius College	Buffalo	U	A,B,M	Pri	F,S	C	3,376	24	30	25	22	12	11	540	31	47	2	2	550	26	46	25	3	Open
Cazenovia College	Cazenovia	SM	A,B	Pri	No	C	910	19	75	18	4	3		455	72	21	7		446	74	24	2		Open
City University of New York/ Baruch College	New York	U	B,M,D	Pub	F,S	C	13,186							500	48	40	11	1	540	22	47	27	4	5/1
City University of New York/ Brooklyn College	Brooklyn	U	B,M	Pub	F,S	C	10,112																	Open
City University of New York/ City College	New York	U	B,M	Pub	No	C	8,067								62	25	11	2		48	31	15	5	12/1
City University of New York/ College of Staten Island	Staten Island	U	A,B,M,D	Pub	No	C	9,876							430	79	18	3		440	75	22	3		Open
City University of New York/ Herbert H. Lehman College	Bronx	U	B,M	Pub	S	C	7,200																	
City University of New York/ Hunter College	New York	U	B,M	Pub	F,S	C	15,703							500	52	38	9	1	500	48	41	10	1	Open
City University of New York/ John Jay College of Criminal Justice	New York	U	A,B,M	Pub	No	C	10,428							459	64	31	4	1	442	70	25	4	1	Open
City University of New York/ Medgar Evers College	Brooklyn	U	A,B	Pub	F,S	C	4,716																	Open
City University of New York/ New York City Technical College	Brooklyn	U	A,B	Pub	F,S	C	11,029																	Open
City University of New York/ Queens College	Flushing	U	B,M	Pub	F,S	C	11,213							504	47	38	13	2	537	31	45	21	3	
City University of New York/York College	Jamaica	U	B	Pub	No	C	5,253																	Open
Clarkson University	Potsdam	R	B,M,D	Pri	F,S	C	2,610							570	16	46	31	7	610	5	34	48	13	3/1
Colgate University	Hamilton	R	B,M	Pri	F,S	C	2,781	31		2	11	20	67	680	3	16	53	28	685	2	11	55	32	1/15
College of Aeronautics	Flushing	U	A,B	Pri	No	C	1,301							450					450					Open
College of Mount Saint Vincent	Riverdale	U	A,B,M	Pri	No	C	1,161							490	54	36	9	1	480	53	41	6		3/1
College of New Rochelle	New Rochelle	SU	B,M	Pri	No		908	18						480	60	30	9	1	460	68	25	6	1	8/15
College of New Rochelle - School of New Resources	New Rochelle	U	B	Pri	No	C	4,215																	8/15
College of Saint Rose	Albany	SU	B,M		No	C	2,856	22	30	36	24	6	4	580	31	52	16	1	520	35	51	13	1	2/1
Columbia University/Barnard College	New York	U	B	Pri	No	W	2,261	28		8	21	19	52	670	1	10	52	37	660	2	12	57	29	1/1
Columbia University/Columbia College	New York	U	B	Pri	F,S	C		30		4	38		58	720		7	29	64	710		6	34	60	1/2
Columbia University/Fu Foundation School of Engineering and Applied Science	New York	U	B,M,D	Pri	F,S	C		29				53	47	690	1	5	49	44	760			14	86	1/2
Columbia University/School of General Studies	New York	U	B,M,D	Pri	F,S	C	1,140																	
Concordia College	Bronxville	SU	A,B	Pri	No	C	662	23	19	30	20	15	20	465	41	41	16	2	457	44	45	10		3/15
Cooper Union for the Advancement of Science and Art	New York	U	B,M	Pri	F,S	C	880																	
Cornell University	Ithaca	R	B,M,D	Pri	F,S	C	13,801							660	2	13	48	37	700		8	36	56	1/1
Daemen College	Amherst	SU	B,M	Pri	F,S	C	1,875	21	47	28	18	5	2	490	54	38	8		480	56	35	9		
DeVry Institute of Technology/ New York	Long Island City	U	A,B	Pri	No	C	2,036																	Open
Dominican College	Orangeburg	SU	A,B,M		No	C	1,660																	Open
Dowling College	Oakdale	SU	B,M,D	Pri	No	C	2,863																	Open
D'Youville College	Buffalo	U	B,M	Pri	No	C	961	23	16	50	25		8	460	61	34	5		480	64	30	4	2	Open
Eastman School of Music	Rochester	U	B,M,D	Pri	F,S	C																		12/1
Elmira College	Elmira	SU	B	Pri	No	C	1,584	25	20	26	32	16	6	550	31	43	23	3	540	32	48	18	2	6/15
Eugene Lang College of New School University	New York	U	B,M,D	Pri	No	C	515																	
Excelsior College	Albany	SU	A,B,M		No	C																		Open
Fashion Institute of Technology/ State University of New York	New York	U	A,B,M	Pub	No	C	10,680																	1/1
Five Towns College	Dix Hills	SU	A,B	Pri	No	C	1,029	18	98	2				482	75	24	1		467	60	39	1		Open
Fordham University	Bronx	U	B,M,D	Pri	No	C	7,062	25						580					580					2/1
Friends World Program	Southampton	R	B	Pri	No	C	192																	Open
Hamilton College	Clinton	R	B	Pri	F,S	C	1,707							640	4	21	51	24	640	3	21	58	18	
Hartwick College	Oneonta	SM	B	Pri	F,S	C	1,446	24						555	23	48	26	4	556	19	52	26	2	2/15
Hilbert College	Hamburg	U	A,B	Pri	No	C	964	19	60	28	6	6		447	77	17	6		451	70	25	5		Open
Hobart and William Smith Colleges	Geneva	SM	B	Pri	F	C	1,892								13	50	33	4		12	52	33	3	2/1
Hofstra University	Hempstead	SU	B,M,D	Pri	F,S	C	9,645	22	26	38	22	10	4	540	21	58	19	2	550	18	57	23	2	
Houghton College	Houghton	R	A,B	Pri	No	C	1,427	26	16	21	25	15	23	592	15	39	31	15	576	18	42	32	8	Open
Iona College	New Rochelle	SU	B,M	Pri	F,S	C	3,417	19						500	47	41	11	1	500	47	40	12	1	3/15
Ithaca College	Ithaca	SM	B,M	Pri	F,S	C	6,209							580	10	48	37	5	580	8	49	40	4	3/1
Juilliard School	New York	U	B,M,D	Pri	No	C	506																	12/1
Keuka College	Keuka Park	R	B,M	Pri	No	C	1,063	21	21	60	10	9		486	60	30	9	1	488	53	41	6		
Laboratory Institute of Merchandising	New York	U	A,B	Pri	No	C	340							484	61	36	3		459	68	31	1		Open
Le Moyne College	Syracuse	SU	B,M	Pri	No	C	2,445	23	24	37	24	8	6	550	24	53	20	3	555	18	57	23	2	3/1
Long Island University/Brooklyn Campus	Brooklyn	U	A,B,M,D	Pri	F,S	C	5,509																	Open
Long Island University/ C.W. Post Campus	Brookville	SU	A,B,M,D	Pri	F,S	C	6,496							489	54	35	10	1	492	55	35	10		2/1
Long Island University/ Southampton College	Southampton	R	B,M	Pri	No	C	3,205	23	15	45	40			522	29	42	25	4	503	29	47	21	3	
Manhattan College	Riverdale	U	B,M	Pri	F,S	C	2,608							530	27	55	16	2	540	23	50	24	3	3/1
Manhattan School of Music	New York	U	B,M,D	Pri	F,S	C	395																	12/3
Manhattanville College	Purchase	SU	B,M	Pri	No	C	1,578	24						530					530					Open

NAME OF SCHOOL	TOWN	ENVIRONMENT U-Urban R-Rural SU-Suburban SM-Small Town	DEGREES AWARDED A-Associate B-Bachelor M-Master D-Doctorate	CONTROL Pri-Private, Pub-Public	FRATERNITIES AND SORORITIES F-Fraternities S-Sororities F, S-Both No-Neither	STUDENTS: C-Coed M-Men W-Women PM-Primarily Men PW-Primarily Women	UNDERGRADUATE ENROLLMENT FALL 2001	TEST SCORES: ACT						SAT I VERBAL REASONING					SAT I MATHEMATICAL REASONING					APPLICATION DEADLINE Month / Day
								Median	Below 21	21-23	24-26	27-28	Above 28	Median	Below 500	500-599	600-700	Above 700	Median	Below 500	500-599	600-700	Above 700	
Mannes College of Music	New York	U	B,M	Pri	No	C	124																	12/15
Marist College	Poughkeepsie	SU	B,M	Pri	F,S	C	4,713	25						567	9	59	29	3	580	8	54	36	2	2/15
Marymount College/Tarrytown	Tarrytown	SU	A,B	Pri	No	PW	1,001							485	57	32	10	1	465	64	31	5		8/1
Marymount Manhattan College	New York	U	B		S	C	2,707	25						534					500					
Medaille College	Buffalo	U	A,B,M	Pri	No	C	1,512							470	70	25	5		450	80	18	2		8/15
Mercy College	Dobbs Ferry	SU	A,B,M	Pri	No	C	38,565																	Open
Molloy College	Rockville Centre	SU	A,B,M	Pri	No	C	2,012							501	49	40	11		509	47	39	12	2	Open
Monroe College	Bronx		B		No																			8/15
Mount Saint Mary College	Newburgh	SU	B,M	Pri	No	C	1,816							516	41	46	9	1	502	47	42	9	1	Open
Nazareth College of Rochester	Rochester	SU	B,M	Pri	No	C	1,898	25	13	26	35	14	12	570	13	53	31	3	570	14	54	28	5	2/15
New York Institute of Technology	Old Westbury	SU	A,B,M	Pri	F,S	C	5,549	23	50	12	10	10	18	530	35	47	18	2	570	13	47	35	5	2/1
New York University	New York	U	A,B,M,D	Pri	F,S	C	19,028	29		4	9	28	59	670		12	53	35	670	1	12	50	37	1/15
Niagara University	Niagara University	SU	A,B,M	Pri	F	C	2,460	21						521	40	45	14	1	523	37	46	16	1	8/15
Nyack College	Nyack	SU	A,B,M	Pri	No	C	1,897		42	21	19	7	12											Open
Pace University	New York	U	A,B,M,D	Pri	F,S	C	8,913	22	35	41	12	12		514	38	49	12	1		29	48	22	1	Open
Parsons School of Design	New York	U	A,B,M	Pri	No	C	2,311								43	32	19	6		32	40	22	6	Open
Polytechnic University/Brooklyn	Brooklyn	U	B,M,D	Pri	F,S	C	1,465							590	4	57	35	3	660		13	62	25	Open
Pratt Institute	Brooklyn	U	A,B,M	Pri	F,S	C	2,765																	
Rensselaer Polytechnic Institute	Troy	SU	B,M,D	Pri	F,S	C	5,272	26	4	20	32	24	20	625	4	29	50	17	683		7	50	43	1/1
Roberts Wesleyan College	Rochester	SU	A,B,M	Pri	No	C	1,235	24	32	32	20	8	7	562	25	50	21	4	547	30	40	17	1	2/1
Rochester Institute of Technology	Rochester	SU	A,B,M,D	Pri	F,S	C	12,029		7	19	27	24	23		12	43	37	8		4	33	48	15	
Russell Sage College	Troy	U	B,M	Pri	No	W	797	24	15	31	31	8	15	516	31	53	15	1	510	39	42	18		8/1
Saint Bonaventure University	St. Bonaventure	SM	B,M	Pri	No	C	2,164	21	62	22	9	5	1	535	38	44	17	1	530					4/1
Saint Francis College	Brooklyn	U	A,B		F,S	C	2,222							480	56	32	11	1	490	51	34	14	1	Open
Saint John Fisher College	Rochester	SU	B,M	Pri	No	C	2,350	23	25	34	31	7	4	530	29	53	18	1	540	26	51	22	1	
Saint John's University	Jamaica	SU	A,B,M,D	Pri	F,S	C	14,485							510	39	46	14	1	530	30	46	22	2	Open
Saint Joseph's College, New York	Brooklyn	U	B,M		F,S	C	1,123							517	40	49	11		511	54	39	7		8/1
Saint Lawrence University	Canton	R	B,M	Pri	F,S	C	1,988							570	17	46	31	6	570	15	46	34	4	2/15
Saint Thomas Aquinas College	Sparkill	SU	A,B,M	Pri	No	C	2,010																	
Sarah Lawrence College	Bronxville	SU	B,M	Pri	No	C	1,214	27	3	14	31	20	32	670	3	18	48	31	590	8	43	43	7	1/15
School of Visual Arts	New York	U	B,M	Pri	No	C	4,840								35	44	16	4		42	41	15	1	3/15
Siena College	Loudonville	SU	B		No	C	3,377	24						545	21	57	21	1	561	17	54	27	2	3/1
Skidmore College	Saratoga Springs	SM	B,M	Pri	No	C	2,488	27		16	70		11	620	5	33	50	13	610	4	33	54	9	1/15
State University of New York/ College at Brockport	Brockport	SM	B,M	Pub	F,S	C	6,764	23	28	33	22	10	7	527	33	55	12	1	535	29	54	17	1	Open
State University of New York/ College at Buffalo	Buffalo	U	B,M	Pub	F,S	C	9,590	21	63	23	11	1	3	490	54	37	8	1	490	52	41	6	1	
State University of New York/ College at Cortland	Cortland	SM	B,M	Pub	F,S	C	5,850		2	58	39		1		39	52	8			28	60	12		
State University of New York/ College at Fredonia	Fredonia	SM	B,M	Pub	F,S	C	4,909																	
State University of New York/ College at Geneseo	Geneseo	SM	B,M	Pub	F,S	C	5,371	26	2	20	31	22	25	602	4	41	48	7	610	3	37	53	7	1/15
State University of New York/ College at Old Westbury	Old Westbury	SU	B	Pub	F,S	C	3,076																	Open
State University of New York/ College at Oneonta	Oneonta	R	B,M	Pub	S	C	5,458	22	10	60	27	3		527	31	56	12	1	532	26	60	13	1	5/1
State University of New York/ College at Oswego	Oswego	SM	B,M	Pub	F,S	C	7,062								25	57	17	1		24	56	19	1	1/15
State University of New York/ College at Plattsburgh	Plattsburgh	SU	B,M	Pub	F,S	C	5,382	21	40	36	16	6	3	530	33	50	15	2	520	31	52	16	1	2/15
State University of New York/ College at Potsdam	Potsdam	R	B,M	Pub	F,S	C	3,475	23	29	30	19	13	9	530	34	43	20	3	530	33	48	17	2	Open
State University of New York/ College at Purchase	Purchase	SU	B,M	Pub	No	C	3,866							559	22	45	28	5	528	32	48	17	2	8/15
State University of New York/ College of Agriculture and Technology at Cobleskill	Cobleskill	R	A,B	Pub	No	C	2,450	19	66	19	9	4	2	460	45	13	2		460	43	16	2		Open
State University of New York/ College of Environmental Science and Forestry	Syracuse	U	A,B,M,D	Pub	F,S	C	1,263	24						560	16	50	30	4	560	12	50	33	4	3/1
State University of New York/ College of Technology at Alfred	Alfred	R	A,B	Pub	F,S	C	3,041	20						464					488					Open
State University of New York/ College of Technology at Farmingdale	Farmingdale	SU	A,B	Pub	No	C	5,449																	Open
State University of New York/ Empire State College	Saratoga Springs		A,B,M	Pub	No	C	8,060																	Open
State University of New York/ Maritime College	Throggs Neck	SU	A,B,M	Pub	No	C	655																	Open
State University of New York/ University at Albany	Albany	SU	B,M,D	Pub	F,S	C	11,884								11	55	30	4		6	52	37	5	3/1
State University of New York/ University at Binghamton	Binghamton	SU	B,M,D	Pub	F,S	C	10,167	26	7	18	33	21	21	591	9	43	41	7	624	3	31	50	16	2/15
State University of New York/ University at Buffalo	Buffalo	SU	B,M,D	Pub	F,S	C	17,290	25	7	23	31	18	21	566	16	51	28	5	589	8	48	37	7	
State University of New York/ University at New Paltz	New Paltz	SM	B,M	Pub	F,S	C	6,082							560	16	56	25	3	560	13	59	26	2	5/1
State University of New York/ University at Stony Brook	Stony Brook	SU	B,M,D	Pub	F,S	C	13,646							550	22	50	24	4	590	7	46	36	11	7/10
Syracuse University	Syracuse	U	B,M,D	Pri	F,S	C	10,702								9	41	41	9		5	34	48	13	1/1
Touro College	New York	U	A,B,M,D	Pri	No	C	6,119	23	8	50	8	17	17	570	22	38	32	8	550	27	40	27	6	Open
Union College	Schenectady	U	B,M	Pri	F,S	C	2,118	26						600	5	43	45	7	630	2	30	53	15	1/15
United States Merchant Marine Academy	Kings Point	SU	B	Pub	No	C																		

NAME OF SCHOOL	TOWN	ENVIRONMENT U-Urban R-Rural SU-Suburban SM-Small Town	DEGREES AWARDED A-Associate B-Bachelor M-Master D-Doctorate	CONTROL Pri-Private, Pub-Public	FRATERNITIES AND SORORITIES F-Fraternities S-Sororities F, S-Both No-Neither	STUDENTS: C-Coed M-Men W-Women PM-Primarily Men PW-Primarily Women	UNDERGRADUATE ENROLLMENT FALL 2001	TEST SCORES: ACT Median	ACT Below 21	ACT 21-23	ACT 24-26	ACT 27-28	ACT Above 28	SAT I VERBAL REASONING Median	Below 500	500-599	600-700	Above 700	SAT I MATHEMATICAL REASONING Median	Below 500	500-599	600-700	Above 700	APPLICATION DEADLINE Month / Day
United States Military Academy	West Point	SM	B	Pub	No	C	4,165																	
University of Rochester	Rochester	SU	B,M,D	Pri	F,S	C	4,665		1	7	16	22	53		2	17	54	27		1	9	50	39	1/20
Utica College of Syracuse University	Utica	SU	B,M	Pri	F,S	C	2,143							500					578					Open
Vassar College	Poughkeepsie	SU	B,M	Pri	No	C	2,439	30						685		7	50	44	660		13	60	27	1/1
Wagner College	Staten Island	SU	B,M	Pri	F,S	C	1,620																	
Webb Institute	Glen Cove	SU	B	Pri	No	C								640		20	45	35	700			45	55	2/15
Wells College	Aurora	SM	B	Pri	No	W	448	25	17	23	23	27	10	580	15	49	31	5	540	27	50	23		3/1
Yeshiva University	New York	U	A,B	Pri	No	C	2,310																	
North Carolina																								
Appalachian State University	Boone	R	B,M,D	Pub	F,S	C	12,560							548	25	51	22	3	553	20	53	24	2	Open
Barber-Scotia College	Concord	SU	B	Pri	F,S	C	566		89	6	3		2	375	94	4	1		370	91	7	1		Open
Barton College	Wilson	SU	B,M	Pri	F,S	C	1,229							460	73	26	2		460	69	28	3		Open
Belmont Abbey College	Belmont	SU	B	Pri	F,S	C	1,055																	
Bennett College	Greensboro	U	A,B	Pri	S	W	520																	Open
Cabarrus College of Health Sciences	Concord		B		No		280																	Open
Campbell University	Buies Creek	R	A,B,M,D	Pri	No	C	2,453							530	43	41	13	4	528	41	38	17	3	Open
Catawba College	Salisbury	SM	B,M		No	C	1,435							490	51	39	10		490	52	39	8	1	Open
Davidson College	Davidson	SM	B	Pri	F	C	1,674	29	2	8	17	18	54	660	1	16	52	31	660	2	14	55	30	1/2
Duke University	Durham	SU	B,M,D	Pri	F,S	C	6,071			2		40	58	700	1	8	41	50	720		6	31	63	1/2
East Carolina University	Greenville	U	B,M,D	Pub	F,S	C	15,460	20	59	29	8	2	2	511	43	46	10	1	519	38	50	11	1	3/15
Elizabeth City State University	Elizabeth City	SM	B	Pub	F,S	C	1,965																	Open
Elon University	Elon	SU	B,M	Pri	F,S	C	4,160							560	15	57	26	2	560	13	57	27	3	2/1
Fayetteville State University	Fayetteville	U	B,M	Pub	F,S	C	3,807								82	17	1			83	16	1		
Gardner-Webb University	Boiling Springs	SM	A,B,M	Pri	No	C	2,578							510	49	36	13	19	510	49	38	12	1	Open
Greensboro College	Greensboro	U	B	Pri	No	C	1,139	18	69	11	15	2	3	470	64	27	7	2	470	60	30	8	2	
Guilford College	Greensboro	SU	B	Pri	No	C	1,490		19	22	23	9	27		17	38	37	8		23	47	26	4	2/15
High Point University	High Point	SU	B,M	Pri	F,S	C	2,590							503	48	39	11	2	504	46	38	14	2	Open
Johnson C. Smith University	Charlotte	U	B	Pri	F,S	C	1,595	17						483	88	11	1		486	88	11	1		8/1
Lees-McRae College	Banner Elk	R	B	Pri	No	C	792	20	64	19	13	3	1	490	56	38	6		470	65	25	10		Open
Lenoir-Rhyne College	Hickory	SU	B,M	Pri	F,S	C	1,316	21	54	24	17	2	3	511	50	34	14	2	517	42	46	11	1	Open
Livingstone College	Salisbury	SM	B	Pri	F,S	C	700																	
Mars Hill College	Mars Hill	R	B	Pri	F,S	C	1,242	19																Open
Meredith College	Raleigh	SU	B,M		No	W	2,307																	2/15
Methodist College	Fayetteville	SU	A,B,M	Pri	F,S	C	1,845	20	55	25	15	2	3	490	56	35	8	1	500	50	35	14	1	Open
Montreat College	Montreat	R	A,B	Pri	No	C	997							500	52	39	9		500	53	38	8	1	Open
Mount Olive College	Mount Olive	SM	A,B	Pri	No	C	1,775		81	16	2	1		450	71	25	3	1	460					Open
North Carolina Agricultural and Technical State University	Greensboro	U	B,M,D	Pub	F,S	C	6,610																	6/1
North Carolina Central University	Durham	U	B,M	Pub	F,S	C	4,232	17	94	3	2			431	83	15	2		430	85	14	1		7/1
North Carolina School of the Arts	Winston-Salem	U	B,M	Pub	No	C	708	24						570	17	44	30	8	540	25	47	24	3	3/1
North Carolina State University	Raleigh	U	A,B,M,D		F,S	C	21,773	22	4	7	65	10	14	520	12	50	35	3	550	2	35	50	13	2/1
North Carolina Wesleyan College	Rocky Mount	SU	B	Pri	F,S	C	795																	7/15
Pfeiffer University	Misenheimer	R	B,M	Pri	No	C	1,076	21	66	22	11			500	48	33	10	1	510	42	37	13	1	8/25
Queens College	Charlotte	SU	B,M	Pri	F,S	C	1,199		30	34	23	11	2		34	48	16	2		35	51	14		Open
Saint Andrews Presbyterian College	Laurinburg	SM	B	Pri	No	C	639								50	35	11	4		56	32	12		Open
Saint Augustine's College	Raleigh	U	B	Pri	F,S	C	1,360																	7/1
Salem College	Winston-Salem	U	B,M	Pri	No	PW	926	25	19	13	29	23	16	584	13	41	40	6	536	29	50	20	1	Open
Shaw University	Raleigh	U	A,B,M	Pri	F,S	C	2,102																	7/30
University of North Carolina at Asheville	Asheville	SU	B,M	Pub	F,S	C	3,211	24	15	34	24	12	15	570	11	48	33	8	570	12	49	34	5	3/15
University of North Carolina at Chapel Hill	Chapel Hill	SU	B,M,D	Pub	F,S	C	15,844	26	10	13	28	17	32	620	5	30	47	18	640	4	25	49	22	1/15
University of North Carolina at Charlotte	Charlotte	SU	B,M,D	Pub	F,S	C	15,135	21	45	31	15	5	3	520	39	46	14	1	530	33	47	19	1	7/1
University of North Carolina at Greensboro	Greensboro	U	B,M,D	Pub	F,S	C	10,376							520	41	41	15	3	510	44	40	14	1	8/1
University of North Carolina at Pembroke	Pembroke	SM	B,M	Pub	F,S	C	3,506							461	71	24	4	1	463	69	27	4		7/15
University of North Carolina at Wilmington	Wilmington	SU	B,M	Pub	F,S	C	9,792		6	31	32	29	2	543	30	53	16	1	548	24	58	17	1	2/7
Wake Forest University	Winston-Salem	SU	B,M,D	Pri	F,S	C	3,987																	1/15
Warren Wilson College	Asheville	SM	B,M	Pri	No	C	781																	3/15
Western Carolina University	Cullowhee	R	B,M,D	Pub	F,S	C	5,665							490	50	38	10	2	500	48	40	11	1	7/15
Wingate University	Wingate	SM	B,M	Pri	F,S	C	1,255	20	54	13	23		7	510	42	45	11	2	520	39	43	16	2	
Winston-Salem State University	Winston-Salem	SU	B,M	Pub	F	C	2,962							420					420					Open
North Dakota																								
Dickinson State University	Dickinson	R	A,B	Pub	No	C	2,101																	8/15
Jamestown College	Jamestown	SM	B	Pri	No	C	1,138	22	39	24	20	9	8											Open
Mayville State University	Mayville	R	A,B	Pub	No	C	755	20	63	18	13	2	2											Open
Minot State University	Minot	SM	A,B,M	Pub	No	C	3,326	21																Open
North Dakota State University	Fargo	U	B,M,D	Pub	F,S	C	9,429	23	28	29	24	10	9											8/15
University of Mary	Bismarck	SU	B,M	Pri	No	C	1,940	22																Open
University of North Dakota	Grand Forks	U	B,M,D	Pub	F,S	C	9,785		28	28	25	11	9											7/1
Valley City State University	Valley City	SM	B	Pub	F,S	C	1,005	21	49	27	17	5	3											Open
Ohio																								
Antioch College	Yellow Springs	SM	B		No	C	600																	2/1
Art Academy of Cincinnati	Cincinnati	U	A,B,M	Pri	No	C	218	22						580					582					6/30
Ashland University	Ashland	SM	A,B,M,D	Pri	F,S	C	2,040							510					512					Open
Baldwin-Wallace College	Berea	SU	B,M	Pri	F,S	C	3,993	24	20	30	30	11	9	565	16	45	33	6	570	17	40	35	8	5/1
Bluffton College	Bluffton	SM	B,M	Pri	No	C	976	23	29	30	25	9	7	541	37	41	16	6	530	29	51	18	2	5/31
Bowling Green State University	Bowling Green	SM	B,M,D	Pub	F,S	C	15,868	22	39	30	20	6	4											7/15

NAME OF SCHOOL	TOWN	ENVIRONMENT U-Urban R-Rural SU-Suburban SM-Small Town	DEGREES AWARDED A-Associate B-Bachelor M-Master D-Doctorate	CONTROL Pri-Private, Pub-Public	FRATERNITIES AND SORORITIES F-Fraternities S-Sororities F,S-Both No-Neither	STUDENTS: C-Coed M-Men W-Women PM-Primarily Men PW-Primarily Women	UNDERGRADUATE ENROLLMENT FALL 2001	TEST SCORES: ACT Median	ACT Below 21	ACT 21-23	ACT 24-26	ACT 27-28	ACT Above 28	SAT I VERBAL REASONING Median	SAT I Verbal Below 500	SAT I Verbal 500-599	SAT I Verbal 600-700	SAT I Verbal Above 700	SAT I MATHEMATICAL REASONING Median	SAT I Math Below 500	SAT I Math 500-599	SAT I Math 600-700	SAT I Math Above 700	APPLICATION DEADLINE Month / Day
Capital University	Columbus	SU	B,M	Pri	F,S	C	2,708	23	26	31	24	10	9	541					526	34	41	22	2	4/15
Case Western Reserve University	Cleveland	U	B,M,D	Pri	F,S	C	3,381		2	5	14	19	60		2	20	46	32		1	11	41	47	2/1
Cedarville University	Cedarville	SM	A,B,M	Pri	No	C	2,943	25	3	24	36	18	19	590	8	44	34	10	580	11	44	36	9	Open
Central State University	Wilberforce	R	B,M	Pub	F,S	C	1,320	15	89	10	1													3/31
Cincinnati College of Mortuary Science	Cincinnati	U	A,B	Pri	No	C	126																	10/1
Cleveland Institute of Art	Cleveland	U	B,M		F,S	C	614	21	39	22	26	8	5	551	19	48	33		525	36	43	21		7/1
Cleveland Institute of Music	Cleveland	U	B,M,D	Pri	No	C	225																	
Cleveland State University	Cleveland	U	B,M,D	Pub	F,S	C	10,433	19	63	20	13	3	1	480	59	30	10	1	480	57	33	9	1	7/15
College of Mount St. Joseph	Cincinnati	SU	A,B,M	Pri	No	C	2,071	22	18	40	27	12	3	490	55	34	10	1	490	51	39	8	2	8/15
College of Wooster	Wooster	SU	B		F,S	C	1,823	25	10	23	29	17	21	600	10	37	39	13	590	12	39	40	7	2/15
Columbus College of Art and Design	Columbus	U	B	Pri	No	C	1,700																	Open
David N. Myers College	Cleveland	U	A,B,M	Pri	No	C	1,096																	Open
Defiance College	Defiance	SM	A,B,M	Pri	F,S	C	830																	Open
Denison University	Granville	SU	B	Pri	F,S	C	2,107	27	5	13	27	23	32	600	5	44	39	12	610	4	41	45	10	2/1
DeVry University/Columbus	Columbus	U	A,B	Pri	No	C	3,793																	Open
Franciscan University of Steubenville	Steubenville	SM	A,B,M	Pri	F,S	C	1,733	24	23	27	24	14	12	570	16	44	33	3	550	22	51	24	3	6/30
Franklin University	Columbus	U	A,B,M		No	C	4,650																	Open
Heidelberg College	Tiffin	SM	B,M	Pri	F,S	C	1,320	22						515					520					5/1
Hiram College	Hiram	R	B	Pri	No	C	1,190	24	28	23	22	15	12	580	22	37	31	10	570	24	43	29	4	2/1
John Carroll University	University Heights	SU	B,M	Pri	F,S	C	3,508	24	22	29	25	14	10	570	16	52	26	6	580	12	45	39	4	2/1
Kent State University	Kent	SU	A,B,M,D	Pub	F,S	C	18,382	21	43	31	18	5	3	500	45	41	13	1	500	43	41	15	1	Open
Kenyon College	Gambier	R	B	Pri	F,S	C	1,587	29		5	53		42	650	1	20	50	30	630	2	27	54	17	1/15
Lake Erie College	Painesville	SM	B,M		No	C	607	21	46	27	18	8	1	580	52	28	15	5	510	55	35	10		Open
Lourdes College	Sylvania	SU	A,B	Pri	No	C	1,219	19							50	50				50	50			Open
Malone College	Canton	SU	B,M	Pri	No	C	1,900	23	28	29	23	9	11	550	21	55	21	3	550	29	40	26	5	7/1
Marietta College	Marietta	SM	A,B,M	Pri	F,S	C	1,148	23	31	26	25	11	7	550	31	41	26	2	550	28	41	28	3	4/15
Miami University	Oxford	SM	B,M,D	Pub	F,S	C	15,153																	1/31
Mount Union College	Alliance	SU	B	Pri	F,S	C	2,368	22	38	29	20	11	3											Open
Mount Vernon Nazarene College	Mt. Vernon	SM	A,B,M	Pri	No	C	2,106	22	38	27	20	8	8	530	38	33	25	5	540	21	54	18	7	5/31
Muskingum College	New Concord	SM	B,M	Pri	F,S	C	1,662	22	39	28	20	8	5	530	37	40	20	3	530	33	41	22	4	6/1
Notre Dame College	South Euclid	SU	A,B,M	Pri	No	C	800	21	30	50	19	1		495	50	25	25		470	65	15	20		Open
Oberlin College	Oberlin	SM	B,M		No	C	2,840	29	3	5	16	21	55	680	3	12	40	45	660	2	19	52	27	1/15
Ohio Dominican College	Columbus	U	A,B	Pri	No	C	2,197		56	26	15	3	1											Open
Ohio Northern University	Ada	SM	B,D	Pri	F,S	C	2,296	25	16	22	30	16	16	560	20	44	33	3	590	18	39	38	5	8/1
Ohio State University at Lima	Lima	SU	A,B,M	Pub	No	C	1,213																	7/1
Ohio State University at Mansfield	Mansfield	SU	A,B	Pub	No	C	1,230																	Open
Ohio State University at Marion	Marion	R	A,B,M	Pub	No	C																		Open
Ohio State University at Newark	Newark	SU	A,B,M	Pub	No	C	2,079	19	77	15	4	3	1	490					485					7/1
Ohio University	Athens	SM	A,B,M,D	Pub	F,S	C	17,178	23	17	34	29	10	10	540	24	51	22	3	550	34	49	25	2	2/1
Ohio Wesleyan University	Delaware	SM	B	Pri	F,S	C	1,886	27		27	23	27	23	605	10	33	45	12	615	9	32	45	14	3/1
Otterbein College	Westerville	SU	B,M	Pri	F,S	C	2,551	23	34	25	25	10	6	540	27	45	25	3	534	32	41	26	1	3/1
Shawnee State University	Portsmouth	SM	A,B	Pub	F,S	C	3,364	19	62	23	12	2												Open
The Ohio State University	Columbus	U	B,M,D	Pub	F,S	C	36,049	25	10	21	23	17	19	575	17	41	35	7	594	13	36	41	10	2/15
Tiffin University	Tiffin	SM	A,B,M	Pri	F,S	C	1,379	19	59	18	8	3		520	82	17	5		480	82	17	5		Open
Union Institute and University	Cincinnati	U	B,D	Pri	No	C	681																	10/1
University of Akron	Akron	U	A,B,M,D	Pub	F,S	C	20,180	20						503	50	35	11	4	511	48	33	18	1	8/15
University of Cincinnati	Cincinnati	U	A,B,M,D	Pub	F,S	C	19,876	22	37	23	19	10	9	518	38	39	20	4	533	35	35	25	5	7/31
University of Dayton	Dayton	SU	B,M,D	Pri	F,S	C	7,018						17											Open
University of Findlay	Findlay	SM	A,B,M	Pri	F,S	C	3,381	21	30	37	22	8	3	504	45	32	22	1	522	42	47	10	1	6/1
University of Rio Grande	Rio Grande	R	A,B,M	Pri	F,S	C	1,855																	
University of Toledo	Toledo	SU	A,B,M,D	Pub	F,S	C	16,754			17	49	30	3		45	39	14	2		39	37	21	4	Open
Urbana University	Urbana	SM	A,B,M	Pri	No	C	1,358																	Open
Ursuline College	Pepper Pike	SU	B,M	Pri	No	PW	1,019	21	44	30	18	2	6	507	53	34	13		481	56	41	3		Open
Walsh University	North Canton	SM	A,B,M	Pri	No	C	1,401	21	44	28	20	5	3											Open
Wilberforce University	Wilberforce	R	B	Pri	F,S	C	800																	Open
Wilmington College	Wilmington	SM	B,M	Pri	F,S	C	1,227	21																Open
Wittenberg University	Springfield	SU	B,M	Pri	F,S	C	2,163	25	12	24	32	21	12	580	13	45	35	7	585	12	46	36	6	3/15
Wright State University	Dayton	SU	B,M,D	Pub	F,S	C	12,220																	Open
Xavier University	Cincinnati	SU	A,B,M,D	Pri	No	C	4,006		8	24	32	17	20		13	41	39	8		16	42	34	8	2/1
Youngstown State University	Youngstown	U	A,B,M,D	Pub	F,S	C	11,036	20	54	22	15	5	4											8/15

Oklahoma

NAME OF SCHOOL	TOWN	ENVIRONMENT	DEGREES AWARDED	CONTROL	FRATERNITIES AND SORORITIES	STUDENTS	UNDERGRADUATE ENROLLMENT FALL 2001	ACT Median	ACT Below 21	ACT 21-23	ACT 24-26	ACT 27-28	ACT Above 28	SAT I Verbal Median	SAT I Verbal Below 500	SAT I Verbal 500-599	SAT I Verbal 600-700	SAT I Verbal Above 700	SAT I Math Median	SAT I Math Below 500	SAT I Math 500-599	SAT I Math 600-700	SAT I Math Above 700	APPLICATION DEADLINE Month / Day
Bartlesville Wesleyan College	Bartlesville	SU	A,B	Pri	F	C	540																	Open
Cameron University	Lawton	SM	A,B,M	Pub	F,S	C	4,736																	Open
East Central University	Ada	SM	B,M	Pub	F,S	C	3,423	21	52		36	10	2											Open
Langston University	Langston	R	A,B,M	Pub	F,S	C	4,020																	Open
Northeastern State University	Tahlequah	SM	B,M,D	Pub	F,S	C	7,611	24																Open
Northwestern Oklahoma State University	Alva	SM	B,M	Pub	F,S	C	1,622	21	53	25	12	7	3											Open
Oklahoma Baptist University	Shawnee	SM	A,B		F,S	C	2,011	25	10	30	25	16	19	590	16	36	36	12	560	21	41	29	9	8/1
Oklahoma Christian University	Oklahoma City	SU	B,M	Pri	No	C	1,710	23	30	20	21	12	17	560	25	39	3	1	570	28	32	32	8	Open
Oklahoma City University	Oklahoma City	U	B,M	Pri	F,S	C	1,861		57		41		2		26	48	23	3		22	52	21	5	8/22
Oklahoma Panhandle State University	Goodwell	R	A,B	Pub	No	C	1,232																	Open
Oklahoma State University	Stillwater	SM	B,M,D		F,S	C	17,211	23	21	29	25	11	14	550	25	43	26	5	570	23	37	32	8	Open
Oral Roberts University	Tulsa	SU	B,M,D	Pri	No	C	3,087		12	50	33	5			31	42	23	4		38	36	21	5	Open
Saint Gregory's University	Shawnee	SU	A,B	Pri	F,S	C	757	20	54	23	15	5	5											Open
Southeastern Oklahoma State University	Durant	R	B,M	Pub	F,S	C	3,638	20	58	23	12	4	3											Open
Southern Nazarene University	Bethany	SU	A,B,M	Pri	No	C	1,705																	
Southwestern Oklahoma State University	Weatherford	SM	A,B,M,D	Pub	F,S	C	3,858	21	49	26	14	7	4											8/5
University of Central Oklahoma	Edmond	SU	B,M	Pub	F,S	C	12,288	22	41	31	17	7	4											8/15
University of Oklahoma	Norman	SU	B,M,D	Pub	F,S	C	18,675	25	13	22	33	14	19	572					576					6/1

NAME OF SCHOOL	TOWN	ENVIRONMENT U-Urban R-Rural SU-Suburban SM-Small Town	DEGREES AWARDED A-Associate B-Bachelor M-Master D-Doctorate	CONTROL Pri-Private, Pub-Public	FRATERNITIES AND SORORITIES F-Fraternities S-Sororities F,S-Both No-Neither	STUDENTS: C-Coed M-Men W-Women PM-Primarily Men PW-Primarily Women	UNDERGRADUATE ENROLLMENT FALL 2001	TEST SCORES: ACT Median	ACT Below 21	ACT 21-23	ACT 24-26	ACT 27-28	ACT Above 28	SAT I VERBAL REASONING Median	SAT I Verbal Below 500	SAT I Verbal 500-599	SAT I Verbal 600-700	SAT I Verbal Above 700	SAT I MATHEMATICAL REASONING Median	SAT I Math Below 500	SAT I Math 500-599	SAT I Math 600-700	SAT I Math Above 700	APPLICATION DEADLINE Month / Day
University of Science and Arts of Oklahoma	Chickasha	SM	B	Pub	F,S	C	1,452	20	54	25	15	3	2											9/10
University of Tulsa	Tulsa	U	B,M,D	Pri	F,S	C	2,769	27		24	27	16	33	630	5	33	41	21	610	7	33	40	20	
Oregon																								
Art Institute of Portland	Portland	U	A,B	Pri	No	C	903																	Open
Cascade College	Portland	SU	B	Pri	No	C	330																	Open
Concordia University	Portland	U	A,B,M	Pri	No	C	889		37	34	18	5	6		40	45	10	6		51	34	14	1	Open
Eastern Oregon University	La Grande	R	A,B,M	Pub	No	C	2,820	22	19	58	22	2		485	56	34	10	1	484	54	40	6		9/15
George Fox University	Newberg	SM	B,M,D	Pri	No	C	1,665	23	22	30	22	12	14	570	17	45	30	8	550	23	44	28	5	6/1
Lewis and Clark College	Portland	SU	B,M		No	C	1,682			16	24	24	36		2	18	58	22		3	36	48	13	2/1
Linfield College	McMinnville	SM	B	Pri	F,S	C	1,602	23	28	23	24	15	10	534	26	48	22	4	540	23	51	24	2	2/15
Marylhurst University	Marylhurst	SU	B,M	Pri	No	C	577																	Open
Northwest Christian College	Eugene	U	A,B,M	Pri	No	C	385																	
Oregon Institute of Technology	Klamath Falls	SM	A,B,M	Pub	F,S	C	3,086	21	14	57	25	4		520	43	37	17	3	520	40	40	16	4	6/1
Oregon State University	Corvallis	SM	B,M,D	Pub	F,S	C	14,877	23	30	27	22	11	10	530	35	41	22	2	550	29	41	26	4	3/1
Pacific Northwest College of Art	Portland	U	B	Pri	No	C	291																	3/1
Pacific University	Forest Grove	SM	B,M,D	Pri	F,S	C	1,075																	2/15
Portland State University	Portland	U	B,M,D	Pub	F,S	C	13,601	22	37	28	24	5	6	504	44	37	16	3	509	46	31	19	4	Open
Reed College	Portland	U	B,M	Pri	No	C	1,396	29		2	12	17	69	690	1	8	42	49	650	1	17	59	24	1/15
Southern Oregon University	Ashland	SM	B,M	Pub	No	C	4,896	23						521	39	40	19	2	514	41	44	15	1	Open
University of Oregon	Eugene	SU	B,M,D	Pub	F,S	C	15,113							554	25	42	27	6	551	26	43	27	4	2/1
University of Portland	Portland	SU	B,M	Pri	No	C	2,509							574	11	49	40	6	570	12	46	38	4	2/1
Warner Pacific College	Portland	U	A,B,M	Pri	No	C	645																	Open
Western Baptist College	Salem	SU	A,B	Pri	No	C	725	22	31	23	31	15		540	23	49	26	2	543	31	42	23	4	8/1
Western Oregon University	Monmouth	R	A,B,M	Pub	No	C	4,339	21	23	31	25	19	2	495	55	33	11	1	485	52	38	9	1	Open
Willamette University	Salem	U	B,M,D		F,S	C	1,773	27	7	15	26	23	29	610	6	32	48	14	610	5	32	49	14	2/1
Pennsylvania																								
Albright College	Reading	SU	B	Pri	F,S	C	1,809							510	40	44	15	1	510	41	44	15		Open
Allegheny College	Meadville	SM	B	Pri	F,S	C	1,879	25	8	23	38	16	15	600	9	40	40	11	590	9	41	43	7	2/15
Alvernia College	Reading	SU	A,B,M	Pri	No	C	1,582		44	44	11			491	52	40	7	1	478	61	33	5		Open
Arcadia University	Glenside	SU	B,M,D	Pri	No	C	1,649							540	24	46	24	3	510	36	46	17	1	Open
Bloomsburg University of Pennsylvania	Bloomsburg	SM	A,B,M	Pub	F,S	C	7,222							500	45	45	9		510	42	46	12		
Bryn Athyn College of the New Church	Bryn Athyn	SU	A,B,M	Pri	No	C	140							580	13	44	31	13	570	33	28	38		3/1
Bryn Mawr College	Bryn Mawr	SU	B,M,D	Pri	No	W	1,333	29						660	2	17	50	31	630	3	26	57	14	1/15
Bucknell University	Lewisburg	SM	B,M	Pri	F,S	C	3,430								3	26	57	15		1	15	60	25	1/1
Cabrini College	Radnor	SU	B,M	Pri	No	C	1,639							470	59	34	7		470	65	28	7		Open
California University of Pennsylvania	California	SM	A,B,M	Pub	F,S	C	5,076							480	65	28	6	1	480	67	27	4	2	Open
Carlow College	Pittsburgh	U	B,M	Pri	No	PW	1,623	23	44	24	24	3	5	504	47	42	11		469	61	31	7	1	Open
Carnegie Mellon University	Pittsburgh	SU	B,M,D	Pri	F,S	C	5,135																	
Cedar Crest College	Allentown	SU	A,B	Pri	No	W	1,593	24	14	24	29	19	14	540	30	40	27	3	520	37	38	23	2	Open
Chatham College	Pittsburgh	U	B,M,D	Pri	No	PW	588	24	28	21	23	15	13	550	22	49	28		510	43	41	15		Open
Chestnut Hill College	Philadelphia	SU	A,B,M,D	Pri	No	C	922																	Open
Cheyney University of Pennsylvania	Cheyney	SU	B,M	Pub	F,S	C	1,198	15						379					368					5/30
Clarion University of Pennsylvania	Clarion	SM	A,B,M	Pub	F,S	C	5,812																	Open
College Misericordia	Dallas	SU	B,M	Pri	No	C	1,726							500					500					Open
Curtis Institute of Music	Philadelphia	U	B	Pri	No	C	120																	Open
De Sales University	Center Valley	SU	B,M	Pri	S	C	2,013							530	29	45	23	4	530	34	42	21	3	Open
Delaware Valley College	Doylestown	SU	A,B,M	Pri	F,S	C	1,920	19	80		20			490	52	36	10	1	500	48	40	12		Open
Dickinson College	Carlisle	SU	B	Pri	F,S	C	2,208	28						620	1	33	51	15	610	3	35	53	8	2/1
Drexel University	Philadelphia	U	B,M,D	Pri	F,S	C	11,019							560	17	50	29	4	595	9	41	42	8	3/1
Duquesne University	Pittsburgh	U	B,M,D	Pri	F,S	C	5,404	26	28	31	23	9	9	540	29	48	22	1	540	28	47	23	2	7/1
East Stroudsburg University of Pennsylvania	East Stroudsburg	SM	B,M	Pub	F,S	C	4,782							480	57	36	6	1	490	57	37	6		3/1
Eastern College	St. Davids	SM	A,B,M	Pri	No	C	1,902	23						562	22	46	24	8	537	30	44	24	2	Open
Edinboro University of Pennsylvania	Edinboro	SM	A,B,M	Pub	F,S	C	6,684	19	68	18	10	3	1	470	61	30	8	1	460	64	30	6		Open
Elizabethtown College	Elizabethtown	SM	A,B,M	Pri	No	C	1,888							560	20	52	25	3	560	26	41	30	3	
Franklin and Marshall College	Lancaster	SU	B	Pri	No	C	1,887	27						620	4	32	46	18	640	2	25	52	21	2/1
Gannon University	Erie	U	A,B,M,D	Pri	F,S	C	2,463	23						523	40	45	19	1	531	35	47	17	1	Open
Geneva College	Beaver Falls	SM	A,B,M	Pri	No	C	1,829	26	17	7	46	45	2	590	31	44	20	5	590	40	38	20	2	Open
Gettysburg College	Gettysburg	SM	B	Pri	F,S	C	2,258								5	47	42	5		3	45	46	6	2/15
Grove City College	Grove City	SM	B	Pri	F,S	C	2,312	27	2	10	26	24	38	634	4	25	49	22	635	3	24	53	20	2/15
Gwynedd-Mercy College	Gwynedd Valley	SU	A,B,M	Pri	No	C	1,900							490	62	32	6		490	64	29	4	1	8/1
Haverford College	Haverford	SU	B	Pri	No	C	1,138							720	3	10	36	51	710	3	10	43	44	1/15
Holy Family College	Philadelphia	SU	A,B,M	Pri	No	C	1,849							470	65	32	3		450	73	23	4		Open
Immaculata College	Immaculata	SU	A,B,M,D	Pri	No	PW	2,776							510					470	59	29	12		5/1
Indiana University of Pennsylvania	Indiana	SM	A,B,M,D	Pub	F,S	C	11,763								34	49	15	2		40	47	12	1	Open
Juniata College	Huntingdon	SM	B		No	C	1,302							577	13	46	35	6	583	11	44	39	5	3/15
Keystone College	La Plume	R	A,B	Pri	No	C	1,374							440	76	20	4		420	82	16	2		Open
King's College	Wilkes Barre	U	A,B,M	Pri	No	C	2,068																	5/1
Kutztown University of Pennsylvania	Kutztown	SM	B,M	Pub	F,S	C	7,293							490	55	37	7	1	490	56	36	8		Open
La Roche College	Pittsburgh	SU	A,B,M	Pri	No	C	1,661						1											Open
La Salle University	Philadelphia	U	A,B,M,D	Pri	F,S	C	3,905							550	27	46	24	3	550	30	46	20	4	4/1
Lafayette College	Easton	SU	B	Pri	F,S	C	2,330	28	1	3	14	66	16	610	3	28	58	11	650	2	23	54	21	1/1
Lebanon Valley College of Pennsylvania	Annville	SM	A,B,M	Pri	F,S	C	1,920	24	29	14	29	18	11	545	26	49	23	2	554	27	43	26	2	Open
Lehigh University	Bethlehem	SU	B,M,D	Pri	F,S	C	4,650							620	3	29	55	14	660	1	13	55	31	1/1
Lincoln University	Lincoln University	R	B,M	Pub	F,S	C	1,438							422					410					Open
Lock Haven University of Pennsylvania	Lock Haven	R	A,B,M	Pub	F,S	C	4,081	21	49	26	25	1		490	46	43	10		500	51	41	8		Open
Lycoming College	Williamsport	SM	B	Pri	F,S	C	1,429	23						550	32	45	21	2	530	35	45	18	2	4/1
Mansfield University	Mansfield	R	A,B,M	Pub	F,S	C	3,018							523	55	36	9	1	514	58	36	6		7/1

NAME OF SCHOOL	TOWN	ENVIRONMENT U-Urban R-Rural SU-Suburban SM-Small Town	DEGREES AWARDED A-Associate B-Bachelor M-Master D-Doctorate	CONTROL Pri-Private, Pub-Public	FRATERNITIES AND SORORITIES F-Fraternities S-Sororities F, S-Both No-Neither	STUDENTS: C-Coed M-Men W-Women PM-Primarily Men PW-Primarily Women	UNDERGRADUATE ENROLLMENT FALL 2001	TEST SCORES: ACT Median	ACT Below 21	ACT 21-23	ACT 24-26	ACT 27-28	ACT Above 28	SAT I VERBAL REASONING Median	SAT I Verbal Below 500	SAT I Verbal 500-599	SAT I Verbal 600-700	SAT I Verbal Above 700	SAT I MATHEMATICAL REASONING Median	SAT I Math Below 500	SAT I Math 500-599	SAT I Math 600-700	SAT I Math Above 700	APPLICATION DEADLINE Month / Day
Marywood University	Scranton	SU	A,B,M,D	Pri	F,S	C	1,668	22	40	30	25	5		510	39	45	13	3	500	49	38	10	3	Open
MCP Hahnemann University	Philadelphia	U	A,B,M,D	Pri	No	C	672																	6/1
Mercyhurst College	Erie	SU	A,B,M	Pri	No	C	3,200	22	33	37	18	7	5	550	33	47	19	2	530	34	47	17	2	Open
Messiah College	Grantham	SM	B	Pri	No	C	2,858	25	10	20	35	13	22	590	10	44	35	11	590	7	45	39	8	
Millersville University of Pennsylvania	Millersville	SM	A,B,M	Pub	F,S	C	6,597	21	40	34	23	2	2	530	33	49	17	2	540	27	50	21	2	Open
Moore College of Art and Design	Philadelphia	U	B	Pri	No	W	613							510	45	37	16	2	486	59	31	9		Open
Moravian College	Bethlehem	SU	B,M	Pri	F,S	C	1,324							562	19	51	24	6	560	19	54	22	5	3/1
Mount Aloysius College	Cresson	SM	A,B	Pri	No	C	1,153	19	92		8			450	73	24	3		460	80	18	2		Open
Muhlenberg College	Allentown	SU	B	Pri	F,S	C	2,555							602	5	47	40	8	612	4	46	41	9	2/15
Neumann College	Aston	SU	A,B,M	Pri	No	C	1,741							450	74	23	3		430	80	17	3		Open
Peirce College	Philadelphia	U	A,B	Pri	No	C	2,837																	Open
Penn State University at Erie/ Behrend College	Erie	SU	A,B,M	Pub	F,S	C	3,550								32	51	15	2		26	47	25	2	Open
Penn State University/Altoona	Altoona	SU	A,B		F,S	C	3,813							499	48	42	10		512	42	41	15	2	Open
Penn State University/ University Park Campus	University Park	SU	A,B,M,D		F,S	C	34,505							589	11	43	36	10	614	8	30	46	16	Open
Pennsylvania College of Technology	Williamsport	U	A,B	Pub	No	C	5,538							452					469					Open
Philadelphia Biblical University	Langhorne	SU	A,B,M	Pri	No	C	1,060	24	26	22	31	4	17	550	27	41	27	5	540	31	46	22	1	Open
Philadelphia University	Philadelphia	SU	A,B,M	Pri	F,S	C	2,756							520	35	49	14	2	530	30	50	19	1	Open
Point Park College	Pittsburgh	U	A,B,M	Pri	No	C	2,644	22	38	30	13	12	7	523	39	44	11	6	494	48	40	11	1	Open
Robert Morris University	Moon Township	SU	B,M,D	Pri	F,S	C	3,813							487	58	33	8	1	490	53	35	11	1	Open
Rosemont College	Rosemont	SU	B,M	Pri	No	PW	797							560	24	44	25	4	520	38	42	13	4	Open
Saint Francis University	Loretto	R	B,M	Pri	F,S	C	1,416																	7/1
Saint Joseph's University	Philadelphia	SU	A,B,M,D	Pri	F,S	C	4,589	30						605					612					Open
Saint Vincent College	Latrobe	SU	B	Pri	No	C	1,222	23	32	20	30	9	9	540	31	44	20	6	530	35	40	22	4	5/1
Seton Hill College	Greensburg	SM	B,M	Pri	No	C	1,128							520	40	49	9	3	490	55	35	12		Open
Shippensburg University of Pennsylvania	Shippensburg	R	B,M	Pub	F,S	C	6,238							534	28	56	15	2	542	26	52	21	1	Open
Slippery Rock University	Slippery Rock	SM	B,M,D	Pub	F,S	C	6,500	20	57	25	13	2	2	484	58	35	7	1	477	60	32	7		5/1
Susquehanna University	Selinsgrove	SM	A,B		F,S	C	1,854																	3/1
Swarthmore College	Swarthmore	SU	B,M	Pri	F	C	1,467							740	1	6	22	72	720		5	28	67	1/1
Temple University	Philadelphia	U	A,B,M,D	Pub	F,S	C	19,606							520	36	44	17	3	520	38	44	16	2	4/1
Thiel College	Greenville	R	A,B	Pri	F,S	C	1,189	19	63	18	12	4	3	480	60	28	12		470	58	35	7		
University of Pennsylvania	Philadelphia	U	A,B,M,D	Pri	F,S	C	9,730	30			7	12	81	690		8	45	47	710		4	37	59	1/1
University of Pittsburgh at Bradford	Bradford	SM	A,B	Pub	F,S	C	1,465							495	50	38	12		500	49	40	9	2	Open
University of Pittsburgh at Greensburg	Greensburg	SU	B	Pub	No	C	1,758							512	46	43	11		511	44	44	12		Open
University of Pittsburgh at Johnstown	Johnstown	SU	A,B	Pub	F,S	C	3,096																	Open
University of Pittsburgh at Pittsburgh	Pittsburgh	U	B,M,D	Pub	F,S	C	17,798	26	5	23	28	18	26	592	8	47	38	7	600	6	42	43	9	Open
University of Scranton	Scranton	U	A,B,M	Pri	No	C	4,060							566	14	55	26	4	565	17	47	32	3	3/1
University of the Arts	Philadelphia	U	B,M	Pri	No	C	1,918							539	32	42	23	3	511	44	40	16		Open
University of the Sciences in Philadelphia	Philadelphia	U	B,M,D	Pri	F,S	C	2,150	24	2	41	31	23	3	535	26	50	22	2	565	15	56	26	3	Open
Ursinus College	Collegeville	SU	B	Pri	F,S	C	1,324							600		41	40	13	600	9	34	50	7	2/15
Villanova University	Villanova	SU	A,B,M,D	Pri	F,S	C	7,315							610	6	38	49	7	630	3	24	59	14	1/7
Washington and Jefferson College	Washington	SM	A,B	Pri	F,S	C	1,240	24	7	17	45	20	11	550	24	51	24	1	560	22	45	31	2	3/1
Waynesburg College	Waynesburg	SM	A,B,M	Pri	No	C	1,453								61				480					Open
West Chester University of Pennsylvania	West Chester	SU	A,B,M	Pub	F,S	C	10,220								33	54	12	1		33	53	13	1	Open
Westminster College	New Wilmington	R	B,M	Pri	F,S	C	1,473	23	26	32	26	11	5	530	38	42	19	2	540	34	47	17	3	
Widener University	Chester	SU	A,B,M,D	Pri	F,S	C	3,105							530	46	42	11	1	540	44	39	14	3	2/15
Wilkes University	Wilkes Barre	U	B,M		No	C	2,023							510	40	43	15	2	520	39	37	20	4	Open
Wilson College	Chambersburg	SM	A,B	Pri	No	W	296	22	50	25	25			510	50	35	15		500	51	39	10		Open
York College of Pennsylvania	York	SU	A,B,M	Pri	F,S	C	5,119							548	17	56	23	4	541	19	59	20	2	Open

Puerto Rico

NAME OF SCHOOL	TOWN	ENVIRONMENT	DEGREES AWARDED	CONTROL	FRATERNITIES AND SORORITIES	STUDENTS	UNDERGRADUATE ENROLLMENT FALL 2001	ACT Median	ACT Below 21	ACT 21-23	ACT 24-26	ACT 27-28	ACT Above 28	SAT I Verbal Median	SAT I Verbal Below 500	SAT I Verbal 500-599	SAT I Verbal 600-700	SAT I Verbal Above 700	SAT I Math Median	SAT I Math Below 500	SAT I Math 500-599	SAT I Math 600-700	SAT I Math Above 700	APPLICATION DEADLINE Month / Day
American University in Puerto Rico	Bayamon	U	A,B	Pri	No	C																		Open
Caribbean University	Bayamon	U	B		No		3,100																	Open
Central University of Bayamon	Bayamon	U	A,B,M	Pri	No	C	2,872																	4/15
Conservatory of Music of Puerto Rico	San Juan	U	B	Pub	No	C																		
Escuela de Artes Plasticas de Puerto Rico	San Juan	U	B	Pub	No	C	313																	5/16
Inter-American University of Puerto Rico/Aguadilla Campus	Aguadilla	SU	A,B	Pri	No	C	3,800																	5/1
Inter-American University of Puerto Rico/Arecibo Campus	Arecibo	SU	A,B,M	Pri	F,S	C	4,125																	
Inter-American University of Puerto Rico/Barranquitas Regional College	Barranquitas	SM	A,B	Pri	No	C	1,700																	
Inter-American University of Puerto Rico/Bayamon University College	Bayamon	U	B	Pri	No	C																		
Inter-American University of Puerto Rico/Fajardo Campus	Fajardo	U	A,B,M,D	Pri	No	C																		8/15
Inter-American University of Puerto Rico/Metropolitan Campus	San Juan	U	A,B,M,D	Pri	No	C	7,284																	5/1
Inter-American University of Puerto Rico/ Ponce Regional College	Ponce	U	B	Pri	No	C																		
Inter-American University of Puerto Rico/San Germ·n	San Germ·n	R	A,B,M,D	Pri	No	C	4,556							455	68	27	4		468	63	28	8	1	5/15
Pontifical Catholic University of Puerto Rico/Ponce	Ponce	U	A,B,M,D	Pri	F,S	C	7,074							510	75	19	6		499	73	19	7	1	7/15
Turabo University	Gurabo	SU	A,B,M	Pri	No																			
Universidad Adventista de las Antillas	Mayaguez	SM	A,B	Pri	F,S	C	719																	Open
Universidad Metropolitana	Rio Piedras	U	A,B,M	Pri	No	C																		Open
Universidad Politecnica de Puerto Rico	Hato Rey	U	B,M	Pri	No	C	4,895																	7/30

NAME OF SCHOOL	TOWN	ENVIRONMENT U-Urban R-Rural SU-Suburban SM-Small Town	DEGREES AWARDED A-Associate B-Bachelor M-Master D-Doctorate	CONTROL Pri-Private, Pub-Public	FRATERNITIES AND SORORITIES F-Fraternities S-Sororities F,S-Both No-Neither	STUDENTS: C-Coed M-Men W-Women PM-Primarily Men PW-Primarily Women	UNDERGRADUATE ENROLLMENT FALL 2001	TEST SCORES: ACT						SAT I VERBAL REASONING					SAT I MATHEMATICAL REASONING					APPLICATION DEADLINE Month / Day
								Median	Below 21	21-23	24-26	27-28	Above 28	Median	Below 500	500-599	600-700	Above 700	Median	Below 500	500-599	600-700	Above 700	
University of Puerto Rico at Humacao	Humacao	SU	A,B	Pub	F	C	4,476							543					543					11/14
University of Puerto Rico/Arecibo	Arecibo	U	A,B	Pub	F,S	C	4,667																	11/17
University of Puerto Rico/Bayamon University College Campus	Bayamon	SU	A,B	Pub	No	C	5,860																	12/20
University of Puerto Rico/ Cayey University College	Cayey	U	A,B	Pub	F	C	4,089																	
University of Puerto Rico/Mayaguez	Mayaguez	U	A,B,M,D	Pub	F,S	C	11,351							576	14	49	35	2	634	8	27	48	17	11/15
University of Puerto Rico/Rio Piedras	San Juan	U	B,M,D	Pub	No	C	17,787								16	40	39	5		17	32	35	17	2/15
University of the Sacred Heart	Santurce	U	A,B,M	Pri	No	C	4,684																	
Rhode Island																								
Brown University	Providence	U	B,M,D	Pri	F,S	C	5,999	30		6	33		61	700	2	12	35	51	700	1	8	36	56	1/1
Bryant College	Smithfield	SU	B,M	Pri	F,S	C	3,007	22	22	39	25	10	4	520	35	52	13		560	16	53	28	3	3/15
Johnson and Wales University	Providence	U	A,B,M,D	Pri	F,S	C	8,566								67	27	5	1		66	29	5		Open
Providence College	Providence	SU	B,M	Pri	No	C	4,389	26	11	25	33	20	11	589	7	49	37	7	590	7	46	42	5	1/15
Rhode Island College	Providence	SU	B,M	Pub	F,S	C	6,750																	
Rhode Island School of Design	Providence	U	B,M	Pri	No	C	1,845							600	13	36	36	15	600	7	39	42	10	2/15
Roger Williams University	Bristol	SM	B,M	Pri	No	C	3,073							530	35	48	16	1	540	30	48	20	2	
Salve Regina University	Newport	SU	A,B,M,D	Pri	No	C	1,894							520	36	48	15	1	520	39	50	11		3/1
University of Rhode Island	Kingston	SM	B,M,D	Pub	F,S	C	10,579																	3/1
South Carolina																								
Allen University	Columbia	SM	A,B	Pri	F,S	C	340																	Open
Benedict College	Columbia	U	B	Pri	F,S	C	2,750							380					380					Open
Charleston Southern University	Charleston	SU	A,B,M	Pri	No	C	2,444	22						530	28	55	15	2	530	28	59	14		Open
Citadel, The	Charleston	SU	B,M	Pub	No	C	2,100	22	29	37	23	7	4	530	33	44	20	2	530	31	48	18	3	Open
Claflin University	Orangeburg	SU	B	Pri	F,S	C	1,460	19						500					425					Open
Clemson University	Clemson	SM	B,M,D	Pub	F,S	C	13,462	25	9	24	35	13	19	560	16	51	28	4	570	11	44	36	7	5/1
Coastal Carolina University	Conway	SU	B,M	Pub	F,S	C	4,771	21	42	35	16	4	3	510	42	46	11	1	520	40	43	16	1	8/15
Coker College	Hartsville	SM	B	Pri	No	C	449	19	60	15	1	10	10	495	49	39	10	1	490	56	35	9		Open
College of Charleston	Charleston	U	B,M	Pub	F,S	C	9,466								6	54	35	5		6	58	33	3	5/1
Columbia College	Columbia	U	B,M	Pri	No	W	1,243							524					489					Open
Converse College	Spartanburg	U	B,M	Pri	No	W	732	24	27	20	28	10	15	560	22	40	32	6	550	24	48	25	3	8/15
Erskine College	Due West	R	B,M,D	Pri	F,S	C	594	24	7	26	48	11	7	570	20	43	32	5	570	21	46	32	3	Open
Francis Marion University	Florence	R	B,M	Pub	F,S	C	2,822							506	49	37	13	1	505	46	41	12	1	Open
Furman University	Greenville	SU	B,M		F,S	C	2,745																	1/15
Lander University	Greenwood	SM	B,M	Pub	F,S	C	2,505	20	54	31	10	4		490	56	34	9	1	490	50	40	9	1	Open
Limestone College	Gaffney	SU	A,B	Pri	S	C	516	19	66	24	4	4	2	480	26	39	35		492	57	34	8	1	8/26
Morris College	Sumter	U	B	Pri	F,S	C	986							378	94	6			376	92	8			Open
Newberry College	Newberry	SM	B	Pri	F,S	C	759	20	89	12				482	54	38	7	1	492	53	39	6	2	Open
Presbyterian College	Clinton	SM	B	Pri	F,S		1,235							561	16	54	26	4	562	15	49	32	4	Open
South Carolina State University	Orangeburg	SM	B,M,D		F,S	C	3,951	17						434					432					7/31
Southern Wesleyan University	Central	R	A,B,M	Pri	No	C	1,996	20	58	22	14	6		510	39	50	11		510	47	40	12	1	8/10
University of South Carolina at Aiken	Aiken	SU	A,B,M	Pub	F,S	C	3,139																	Open
University of South Carolina at Columbia	Columbia	U	A,B,M,D	Pub	F,S	C	15,506	23	24	35	19	9	12	540	27	48	21	5	550	22	48	24	6	1/1
University of South Carolina at Spartanburg	Spartanburg	U	A,B,M	Pub	F,S	C	3,495																	Open
Voorhees College	Denmark	R	B	Pri	F,S	C	756	17						370					410					8/15
Winthrop University	Rock Hill	SM	B,M	Pub	F,S	C	4,838	22	30	38	20	7	5	530	37	44	16	3	525	35	49	14	2	6/1
Wofford College	Spartanburg	U	B	Pri	F,S	C	1,107	25	10	32	31	8	18	600	11	43	39	7	612	8	40	43	9	2/1
South Dakota																								
Augustana College	Sioux Falls	SU	B,M	Pri	No	C	1,774	25	16	27	24	15	18	590	19	42	32	7	590	16	36	42	6	Open
Black Hills State University	Spearfish	SM	A,B,M	Pub	F,S	C	3,474	21	50	28	15	4	2											Open
Dakota State University	Madison	SM	A,B,M	Pub	No	C	1,843	22																Open
Dakota Wesleyan University	Mitchell	SM	A,B,M	Pri	No	C	687																	8/25
Huron University	Huron	SM	A,B,M	Pri	No	C	544		35	53	10	3												8/1
Mount Marty College	Yankton	SM	A,B,M	Pri	No	C	1,069	21	49	25	15	5	5											Open
National American University	Rapid City	SM	A,B,M	Pri	No	C	852																	Open
Northern State University	Aberdeen	U	A,B,M	Pub	No	C	2,649	21	45	22	16	6	3											8/15
Oglala Lakota College	Kyle	R	B	Pri	No	C																		Open
Presentation College	Aberdeen	SM	A,B	Pri	No	C	615																	
Sinte Gleska University	Rosebud	R	A,B,M	Pri	No	C	336																	Open
South Dakota School of Mines and Technology	Rapid City	SU	A,B,M,D	Pub	F,S	C	2,075	24	21	24	28	12	14											8/15
South Dakota State University	Brookings	SM	A,B,M,D	Pub	F,S	C	7,793		42	28	19	7	4											Open
University of Sioux Falls	Sioux Falls	SU	A,B,M	Pri	No	C	1,122	23	43	29	19	5	4											Open
University of South Dakota	Vermillion	R	A,B,M,D	Pub	F,S	C	5,363		15	52	24	5	4											Open
Tennessee																								
Aquinas College	Nashville	U	A,B	Pri	No	C		19																Open
Austin Peay State University	Clarksville	U	A,B,M	Pub	F,S	C	6,985	20	52	30	12	4	2	480	50	42	7	1	470	59	32	9		8/10
Belmont University	Nashville	U	B,M	Pri	F,S	C	2,617	25	20	30	29	13	8	570	15	46	32	7	560	23	44	28	5	8/1
Bethel College	McKenzie	SM	B,M	Pri	F,S	C	840	20																8/30
Bryan College	Dayton	SM	A,B	Pri	No	C		24						570					540					Open
Carson-Newman College	Jefferson City	SM	A,B,M	Pri	F,S	C	1,991	23	34	26	22	9	8											8/15
Christian Brothers University	Memphis	U	B,M	Pri	F,S	C	1,659	24	26	28	22	9	14	553	27	46	19	8	562	28	30	29	13	7/15
Crichton College	Memphis	SU	B		No	C	1,043	19	59	20	15	7												Open
Cumberland University	Lebanon	SM	A,B,M	Pri	F,S	C	970																	Open

NAME OF SCHOOL	TOWN	ENVIRONMENT U-Urban R-Rural SU-Suburban SM-Small Town	DEGREES AWARDED A-Associate B-Bachelor M-Master D-Doctorate	CONTROL Pri-Private, Pub-Public	FRATERNITIES AND SORORITIES F-Fraternities S-Sororities F, S-Both No-Neither	STUDENTS: C-Coed M-Men W-Women PM-Primarily Men PW-Primarily Women	UNDERGRADUATE ENROLLMENT FALL 2001	TEST SCORES: ACT Median	ACT Below 21	ACT 21-23	ACT 24-26	ACT 27-28	ACT Above 28	SAT I VERBAL REASONING Median	Below 500	500-599	600-700	Above 700	SAT I MATHEMATICAL REASONING Median	Below 500	500-599	600-700	Above 700	APPLICATION DEADLINE Month / Day
David Lipscomb University	Nashville	SU	B,M	Pri	No	C	2,394																	Open
East Tennessee State University	Johnson City	SM	A,B,M,D	Pub	F,S	C	9,328	21	44	28	17	7	5	500	47	33	15	4	490	52	34	12	2	Open
Fisk University	Nashville	U	B,M	Pri	F,S	C	814	19	60	28	7	3	2	448					441	72	22	4	2	6/15
Freed-Hardeman University	Henderson	SM	B,M	Pri	No	C	1,414	23	28	22	25	13	12											Open
King College	Bristol	SU	B,M	Pri	No	C	655	23	5	47	20	22	6	550	27	43	23	7	540	33	37	24	3	Open
Knoxville College	Knoxville	U	A,B		No	C		16	95	5														Open
Lambuth University	Jackson	U	B	Pri	F,S	C	903		17	35	26	15	7											Open
Lane College	Jackson	SM	B	Pri	F,S	C	696	16	95	5														7/1
Lee University	Cleveland	SU	B,M	Pri	No	C	3,155	22						528	37	39	20	3	558	44	33	20	2	9/1
LeMoyne-Owen College	Memphis	U	B	Pri	F,S	C	735	16	92	7	1			390	100				365	100				4/1
Lincoln Memorial University	Harrogate	R	A,B,M	Pri	F,S	C	875																	Open
Maryville College	Maryville	SU	B	Pri	No	C	1,026	24						560	26	35	29	10	540	25	50	23	2	3/1
Memphis College of Art	Memphis	U	B,M	Pri	No	C	265	21	51	26	13	8	2											Open
Middle Tennessee State University	Murfreesboro	U	A,B,M,D	Pub	F,S	C	18,130	22	40	31	18	6	5	527					513					7/1
Milligan College	Milligan College	SU	B,M	Pri	No	C	789	23						530	29	46	22	3	530	35	44	20	1	8/15
Rhodes College	Memphis	U	B,M	Pri	F,S	C	1,535	28		5	26	23	46	655					650		21	62	17	2/1
Southern Adventist University	Collegedale	SM	A,B,M	Pri	No	C	2,098	22	11	49	34	6												Open
Tennessee State University	Nashville	U	A,B,M,D	Pub	F,S	C	7,060	21																8/1
Tennessee Technological University	Cookeville	SM	B,M,D	Pub	F,S	C	7,099	22	36	28	20	8	8											7/21
Tennessee Wesleyan College	Athens	SM	B	Pri	S	C	786	22																Open
Trevecca Nazarene University	Nashville	U	A,B,M,D	Pri	No	C	1,159	22	36	28	21	8	8	550					530					Open
Tusculum College	Greeneville	SM	B,M	Pri	No	C	1,557																	Open
Union University	Jackson	SU	A,B,M,D	Pri	F,S	C	1,965	24	4	43	39	14		575	20	38	32	10	550	26	39	22	13	Open
University of Memphis	Memphis	U	B,M,D	Pub	F,S	C	15,612	21	11	56	30	3		540	31	43	18	8	530	32	39	25	5	8/1
University of Tennessee at Chattanooga	Chattanooga	U	B,M	Pub	F,S	C	7,105	22	46	25	16	7	6	530	39	33	22	6	520	21	35	36	8	8/1
University of Tennessee at Knoxville	Knoxville	U	B,M,D	Pub	F,S	C	20,124	23	25	29	28	9	9	545	30	42	22	6	547	29	39	26	5	2/1
University of Tennessee at Martin	Martin	R	B,M	Pub	F,S	C	5,478																	Open
University of the South	Sewanee	SM	B,M,D		F,S	C	1,329				22	61	17		4	35	48	13		2	39	51	8	2/1
Vanderbilt University	Nashville	U	B,M,D	Pri	F,S	C	6,077		3	50	47				2	19	55	24		1	11	51	37	1/7

Texas

NAME OF SCHOOL	TOWN	ENVIRONMENT	DEGREES AWARDED	CONTROL	FRATERNITIES AND SORORITIES	STUDENTS	UNDERGRADUATE ENROLLMENT FALL 2001	ACT Median	ACT Below 21	ACT 21-23	ACT 24-26	ACT 27-28	ACT Above 28	SAT I Verbal Median	Below 500	500-599	600-700	Above 700	SAT I Math Median	Below 500	500-599	600-700	Above 700	APPLICATION DEADLINE Month / Day
Abilene Christian University	Abilene	SM	A,B,M,D	Pri	F,S	C	4,234	24	22	29	20	13	16	550	26	44	22	8	550	25	44	24	6	Open
Angelo State University	San Angelo	SM	A,B,M	Pub	F,S	C	5,829	21	50	29	14	5	2	550	55	32	12	1	490	49	39	10	2	8/9
Austin College	Sherman	SU	B,M	Pri	F,S	C	1,227	26	6	21	28	19	26	598	8	39	44	9	602	6	41	42	11	3/1
Baylor University	Waco	U	B,M,D	Pri	F,S	C	12,190	24	8	31	32	15	13	580	12	48	31	8	590	8	44	38	10	Open
Concordia University at Austin	Austin	U	A,B	Pri	No	C	740	20	58	20	13	4	5	493	51	39	10	1	497	52	36	11	1	
Dallas Baptist University	Dallas	U	A,B,M	Pri	No	C	3,340	20	46	32	15	5	2	520	36	45	18	1	527	35	52	10	3	Open
DeVry University/Dallas	Irving	SU	A,B	Pri	No	C	3,569																	Open
East Texas Baptist University	Marshall	SM	A,B	Pri	F,S	C	1,509		54	24	14	5	3											Open
Hardin-Simmons University	Abilene	U	B,M	Pri	F,S	C	1,902	22	44	25	21	6	4	505	43	42	15		510	45	41	14		Open
Houston Baptist University	Houston	U	A,B,M	Pri	F,S	C	1,953	22						527					525					Open
Howard Payne University	Brownwood	SM	A,B	Pri	F,S	C	1,526	22	29	31	22	10	8	525	32	45	21	3	530	31	50	18	1	8/1
Huston-Tillotson College	Austin	U	B	Pri	F,S	C	618	17						450					450					3/1
Jarvis Christian College	Hawkins	R	B	Pri	F,S	C	571	15	99	1				368	60	30	10		364	60	30	10		8/1
Lamar University	Beaumont	U	A,B,M,D	Pub	F,S	C	8,417	22						482					473					8/10
LeTourneau University	Longview	U	A,B,M	Pri	No	C	2,807	25	6	23	29	12	28	570	11	44	32	13	580	12	41	35	11	8/1
Lubbock Christian University	Lubbock	SU	A,B,M	Pri	No	C	1,701	20	53	23	16	5	3	490	51	33	14	2	500	48	41	8	3	Open
McMurry University	Abilene	U	B	Pri	F,S	C	1,378	21	47	22	18	9	4	500	46	40	14		500	46	40	14	1	Open
Midwestern State University	Wichita Falls	U	A,B,M	Pub	F,S	C	5,288	20	26	56	16		2	474					486					8/7
Northwood University	Cedar Hill	SU	A,B	Pri	No	C	1,114	18	78	15	4	2		470					460					8/1
Our Lady of the Lake University of San Antonio	San Antonio	U	B,M,D	Pri	No	C	2,196																	Open
Paul Quinn College	Dallas	U	B	Pri	F,S	C	770																	
Prairie View A&M University	Prairie View	SM	B,M,D		F,S	C	5,387	17	85	10	4	1		410	84	15	1		410	84	14	2		7/1
Rice University	Houston	U	B,M,D		No	C	2,890			3	27		70		2	10	31	57		1	7	29	63	1/2
Saint Edward's University	Austin	U	B,M	Pri	No	C	3,369	22	34	33	25	7	2	540	31	45	22	2	540	30	50	18	3	7/1
Saint Mary's University of San Antonio	San Antonio	SU	B,M,D	Pri	F,S	C	2,613	22	30	41	22	4	3	520	33	50	16	1	530	30	53	15	1	Open
Sam Houston State University	Huntsville	SM	B,M,D	Pub	F,S	C	11,273							490	54	36	9	1	490	56	35	8	1	Open
Schreiner University	Kerrville	SM	A,B,M		F	C	791	20	56	14	18	11	2	500	47	36	12	5	490	51	30	19		8/1
Southern Methodist University	Dallas	SU	B,M,D	Pri	F,S	C	5,721	25	8	23	35	16	17	580	13	47	33	7	590	9	43	38	9	1/15
Southwest Texas State University	San Marcos	SU	B,M,D	Pub	F,S	C	20,184	22	21	43	26	6	3	530	28	54	16	2	530	25	56	18	1	7/1
Southwestern Adventist University	Keene	R	A,B,M	Pri	No	C	1,163	21	46	33	15	1	5	490	52	29	18	1	460	68	26	5	1	9/5
Southwestern Christian College	Terrell	R	B	Pri	No	C																		
Southwestern University	Georgetown	SU	B	Pri	F,S	C	1,320	26	8	16	25	23	27	615	6	31	49	14	612	6	32	50	12	2/15
Stephen F. Austin State University	Nacogdoches	SM	B,M,D	Pub	F,S	C	10,283																	Open
Sul Ross State University	Alpine	R	A,B,M	Pub	No	C	1,488	17	81	13	5	1												Open
Tarleton State University	Stephenville	SM	B,M	Pub	F,S	C	6,715	20	59	24	11	3	1	476	60	32	8	1	487	54	37	8	1	8/1
Texas A&M University	College Station	U	B,M,D		F,S	C	36,603	25						576	20	40	33	7	602	10	40	37	13	2/15
Texas A&M University at Commerce	Commerce	SM	B,M,D	Pub	F,S	C	4,448	21						485					545					8/6
Texas A&M University at Galveston	Galveston	SU	B	Pub	No	C	1,366	24	15	24	45	8	8	550	36	43	19	2	560	33	48	18	1	Open
Texas A&M University at Kingsville	Kingsville	SM	B,M,D	Pub	F,S	C	5,008																	Open
Texas Christian University	Fort Worth	SU	B,M,D	Pri	F,S	C	6,885																	2/15
Texas Lutheran University	Seguin	SU	A,B	Pri	F,S	C	1,473	22	38	24	22	10	6	520	42	39	17	2	520	35	48	16	1	8/1
Texas Southern University	Houston	U	B,M,D	Pub	F,S	C	6,485																	7/31
Texas Tech University	Lubbock	U	B,M,D	Pub	F,S	C	21,269	23	22	31	27	10	10	540	28	50	19	2	557	3	26	50	21	Open
Texas Wesleyan University	Fort Worth	U	B,M	Pri	F,S	C	1,714	20	60	29	89	3		486	68	28	4		472	62	30	7	1	Open
Texas Woman's University	Denton	U	B,M,D	Pub	S	PW	4,730																	7/15
Trinity University	San Antonio	SU	B,M		F,S	C	2,345	28	1	8	28	24	39	630	2	29	52	17	640	1	25	61	13	2/1
University of Dallas	Irving	SU	B,M,D	Pri	No	C	1,255	26	7	23	22	21	27	615	8	34	41	17	593	12	37	42	9	2/15
University of Houston	Houston	U	B,M,D	Pub	F,S	C	25,230	21	48	28	13	6	5	500	47	37	14	2	520	37	40	20	3	5/1
University of Houston-Downtown	Houston	U	B	Pub	S	C	9,643																	Open
University of Mary Hardin-Baylor	Belton	SM	B,M	Pri	No	C	2,434	21	41	26	21	6	6	520	37	49	12	2	510	41	44	15		Open

NAME OF SCHOOL	TOWN	ENVIRONMENT U-Urban R-Rural SU-Suburban SM-Small Town	DEGREES AWARDED A-Associate B-Bachelor M-Master D-Doctorate	CONTROL Pri-Private, Pub-Public	FRATERNITIES AND SORORITIES F-Fraternities S-Sororities F,S-Both No-Neither	STUDENTS: C-Coed M-Men W-Women PM-Primarily Men PW-Primarily Women	UNDERGRADUATE ENROLLMENT FALL 2001	TEST SCORES: ACT Median	ACT Below 21	ACT 21-23	ACT 24-26	ACT 27-28	ACT Above 28	SAT I VERBAL REASONING Median	SAT I Verbal Below 500	SAT I Verbal 500-599	SAT I Verbal 600-700	SAT I Verbal Above 700	SAT I MATHEMATICAL REASONING Median	SAT I Math Below 500	SAT I Math 500-599	SAT I Math 600-700	SAT I Math Above 700	APPLICATION DEADLINE Month / Day
University of North Texas	Denton	U	B,M,D	Pub	F,S	C	21,675	22	38	30	21	7	4	530	34	43	20	3	530	36	40	21	5	6/15
University of Saint Thomas	Houston	U	B,M,D	Pri	No	C	1,851	25	6	29	27	24	14	560	13	56	30	2	560	14	50	31	5	Open
University of Texas at Arlington	Arlington	U	B,M,D	Pub	F,S	C	16,330	21	44	30	19	5	3	520	39	45	16	1	530	34	45	20	1	6/1
University of Texas at Austin	Austin	U	B,M,D	Pub	F,S	C	38,609	25	9	22	30	18	21	590	12	38	38	12	620	7	30	44	20	2/1
University of Texas at Dallas	Richardson	SU	B,M,D	Pub	F,S	C	7,480	24	13	30	26	12	19	560	19	43	32	6	600	12	36	40	12	8/1
University of Texas at El Paso	El Paso	U	B,M,D	Pub	F,S	C	13,642	19	31	57	12			464	69	27	5		464	65	30	5		7/31
University of Texas at San Antonio	San Antonio	SU	B,M,D	Pub	F,S	C	17,425	20	55	27	13	3	2	490	51	38	10	1	500	50	39	10	1	7/1
University of Texas-Pan American	Edinburg	SM	B,M,D	Pub	F,S	C	11,971	17	51	42	7				72	23	5			69	24	6	1	8/1
University of the Incarnate Word	San Antonio	U	B,M,D	Pri	F,S	C	3,519																	Open
Wayland Baptist University	Plainview	SM	A,B,M	Pri	F,S	C	932	19	60	15	15	5	5	470	60	22	17	1	480	58	27	13	2	Open
West Texas A&M University	Canyon	SM	B,M	Pub	F,S	C	5,316	21	51	25	17	4	3	514	47	39	13	1	519	53	34	12	1	Open
Wiley College	Marshall	SM	B		No																			Open

Utah

NAME OF SCHOOL	TOWN	ENVIRONMENT	DEGREES AWARDED	CONTROL	FRATERNITIES AND SORORITIES	STUDENTS	UNDERGRADUATE ENROLLMENT FALL 2001	ACT Median	ACT Below 21	ACT 21-23	ACT 24-26	ACT 27-28	ACT Above 28	SAT I Verbal Median	SAT I Verbal Below 500	SAT I Verbal 500-599	SAT I Verbal 600-700	SAT I Verbal Above 700	SAT I Math Median	SAT I Math Below 500	SAT I Math 500-599	SAT I Math 600-700	SAT I Math Above 700	APPLICATION DEADLINE
Brigham Young University	Provo	SU	B,M,D	Pri	No	C	29,815	27	3	11	30	23	34											2/15
Southern Utah University	Cedar City	SM	A,B,M	Pub	F,S	C	5,884	21		21	52	25	2	488	45	39	14	2	503	46	35	14	3	7/1
University of Utah	Salt Lake City	U	B,M,D	Pub	F,S	C	22,234	22	32	29	22	9	8											7/1
Utah State University	Logan	SM	A,B,M,D	Pub	F,S	C	19,295	22	36	28	18	9	9	510	42	38	16	4	520	39	38	19	4	7/1
Weber State University	Ogden	U	A,B,M	Pub	F,S	C	16,619	22	44	25	19	7	5											7/1
Westminster College	Salt Lake City	SU	B,M		No	C	1,782	23	21	27	31	13	8	563	29	38	23	10	533	29	48	17	6	Open

Vermont

NAME OF SCHOOL	TOWN	ENVIRONMENT	DEGREES AWARDED	CONTROL	FRATERNITIES AND SORORITIES	STUDENTS	UNDERGRADUATE ENROLLMENT FALL 2001	ACT Median	ACT Below 21	ACT 21-23	ACT 24-26	ACT 27-28	ACT Above 28	SAT I Verbal Median	SAT I Verbal Below 500	SAT I Verbal 500-599	SAT I Verbal 600-700	SAT I Verbal Above 700	SAT I Math Median	SAT I Math Below 500	SAT I Math 500-599	SAT I Math 600-700	SAT I Math Above 700	APPLICATION DEADLINE
Bennington College	Bennington	SM	B,M	Pri	No	C	537							620	5	31	45	19	571	19	40	33	8	1/1
Burlington College	Burlington	U	A,B	Pri	No	C	267																	Open
Castleton State College	Castleton	R	A,B,M	Pub	No	C	1,542							460	58	36	6	1	460	66	31	3		Open
Champlain College	Burlington	SU	A,B	Pri	No	C	2,523	20	17	60	15	7	1	470	25	60	14	1	490	25	58	15	2	Open
College of Saint Joseph	Rutland	R	A,B,M	Pri	No	C	385																	Open
Goddard College	Plainfield	R	B,M	Pri	No	C								609	8	32	43	16	541	27	48	19	5	Open
Green Mountain College	Poultney	SM	B	Pri	No	C	659																	Open
Johnson State College	Johnson	SM	A,B,M	Pub	No	C	1,387							480	58	37	5		460	71	27	2		3/1
Lyndon State College	Lyndonville	SM	A,B,M	Pub	No	C	1,134							470	58	34	8		480	61	32	7		Open
Marlboro College	Marlboro	R	B,M	Pri	No	C	331	28			25	37	38	640	6	25	45	24	570	14	55	26	5	3/1
Middlebury College	Middlebury	SM	B,M,D	Pri	No	C	2,307	32		2	6	52	40	740	2	4	37	57	730	1	4	39	56	12/15
Norwich University	Northfield	R	A,B	Pri	No	C	1,510																	Open
Saint Michael's College	Colchester	SU	B,M	Pri	No	C	2,021							560	17	53	26	4	560	17	54	26	2	2/1
Southern Vermont College	Bennington	SM	A,B	Pri	No	C	457	19	36	57			7	480	57	36	5	1	480	70	26	4		Open
Sterling College	Craftsbury Common	R	A,B	Pri	No	C	81	20	33	66				550					520					Open
University of Vermont	Burlington	SU	A,B,M,D	Pub	F,S	C	8,592	24	15	30	31	12	12	560	18	50	29	3	570	16	48	33	3	1/15
Vermont Technical College	Randolph Center	R	A,B	Pub	No	C	1,272	21		100				480	59	30	10	1	510	50	36	13	1	Open
Woodbury College	Montpelier	SM	A,B	Pri	No	C	157																	Open

Virginia

NAME OF SCHOOL	TOWN	ENVIRONMENT	DEGREES AWARDED	CONTROL	FRATERNITIES AND SORORITIES	STUDENTS	UNDERGRADUATE ENROLLMENT FALL 2001	ACT Median	ACT Below 21	ACT 21-23	ACT 24-26	ACT 27-28	ACT Above 28	SAT I Verbal Median	SAT I Verbal Below 500	SAT I Verbal 500-599	SAT I Verbal 600-700	SAT I Verbal Above 700	SAT I Math Median	SAT I Math Below 500	SAT I Math 500-599	SAT I Math 600-700	SAT I Math Above 700	APPLICATION DEADLINE
Averett University	Danville	SU	A,B,M	Pri	F,S	C	1,589	18	74	13	10	3		480	43	34	8	2	460	49	27	8		Open
Bluefield College	Bluefield	SM	A,B	Pri	F,S	C	848	19	64	20	9	7		470	63	32	3	2	450	66	29	5		Open
Bridgewater College	Bridgewater	SM	B	Pri	No	C	1,260	21	43	16	17	11	13	510	42	38	18	2	515	42	36	21	1	Open
Christendom College	Front Royal	R	A,B,M	Pri	No	C	331	25	10	24	34	17	14	650		32	35	33	580	16	38	38	8	2/15
Christopher Newport University	Newport News	SU	B,M	Pub	F,S	C	5,158	20	55	37	8				12	56	28	3		17	58	24	1	3/1
College of William and Mary	Williamsburg	SM	B,M,D	Pub	F,S	C	5,604	30		2	15	10	73	680					660	2	16	50	30	1/7
DeVry University/Crystal City	Arlington		A,B	Pri	No	C	243																	Open
Eastern Mennonite University	Harrisonburg	SM	A,B,M	Pri	No	C	1,020	23	33	20	13	20	15	530	38	30	24	8	530	41	31	23	5	Open
Emory & Henry College	Emory	R	B,M	Pri	F,S	C	989		32	33	22	10	3	530	34	46	20	2	520	40	48	12		4/15
Ferrum College	Ferrum	R	B	Pri	No	C	949							450	73	23	3	1	440	75	22	3		Open
George Mason University	Fairfax	SU	B,M,D	Pub	F,S	C	15,802		14	66	19		2	530	33	47	18	3	540	28	49	20	3	2/1
Hampden-Sydney College	Hampden-Sydney	R	B	Pri	F	M	1,026	22						561	25	41	28	6	562	18	47	31	4	3/1
Hampton University	Hampton	U	A,B,M	Pri	F,S	C	4,953																	3/15
Hollins University	Roanoke	SU	B,M	Pri	No	PW	818	25	6	33	30	20	11	590	15	37	35	13	550	28	47	23	2	2/15
James Madison University	Harrisonburg	SM	B,M,D	Pub	F,S	C	14,069							578	13	54	30	3	585	11	50	36	3	1/15
Liberty University	Lynchburg	SU	A,B,M,D	Pri	No	C	5,391																	6/30
Longwood College	Farmville	SM	B,M	Pub	F,S	C	3,560							530	26	55	17	2	550	30	55	14	1	3/1
Lynchburg College	Lynchburg	SU	B,M	Pri	F,S	C	1,733	20	63	17	13	1	5	518	39	45	15	1	508	44	44	11	2	
Mary Baldwin College	Staunton	SM	B,M	Pri	No	PW	1,489							530	29	48	20	3	500	48	40	12		4/15
Mary Washington College	Fredericksburg	SM	B,M	Pub	No	C	4,104	27						611	3	35	50	12	590	6	47	43	4	2/1
Marymount University	Arlington	SU	A,B,M		No	C	2,112	20	63	25	8	4		500	47	40	11	2	490	51	39	9	1	Open
Norfolk State University	Norfolk	U	A,B,M,D		F,S	C	5,963	17	89	9	2			425	83	16	1		420	87	12	1		Open
Old Dominion University	Norfolk	U	B,M,D	Pub	F,S	C	13,098	20	59	14	13	11	3	510	41	44	14	1	510	45	41	13	1	2/15
Radford University	Radford	SM	B,M	Pub	F,S	C	8,063	19	75	25				499	50	41	8	1	492	53	38	9		4/1
Randolph-Macon College	Ashland	SU	B	Pri	F,S	C	1,150							550	21	56	19	5	550	22	57	21		3/1
Randolph-Macon Woman's College	Lynchburg	SU	B	Pri	No	W	721	26	11	19	25	19	26	610	11	33	40	16	560	20	46	32	2	3/1
Roanoke College	Salem	SU	B	Pri	F,S	C	1,790							560	20	47	29	4	550	21	56	22	2	3/1
Saint Paul's College	Lawrenceville	SM	B	Pri	F,S	C	550																	Open
Shenandoah University	Winchester	SM	A,B,M,D	Pri	No	C	1,361	20	50	32	5	5	9	510	44	39	13	4	490	53	35	11	1	Open
Sweet Briar College	Sweet Briar	R	B	Pri	No	W	738	24	17	28	30	10	15	580	21	39	37	3	540	28	44	26	2	2/1
University of Richmond	University of Richmond	SU	A,B,M	Pri	F,S	C	3,021		1	10	57		32		4	22	56	18		3	14	64	20	2/1
University of Virginia	Charlottesville	SU	B,M,D	Pub	F,S	C	13,764	29						650	4	19	47	30	670	2	16	45	37	1/2
University of Virginia's College at Wise	Wise	SM	B	Pub	F,S	C	1,480	20	70		27	2	1	490	59	31	8	2	470	64	30	5	1	8/1
Virginia Commonwealth University	Richmond	U	B,M,D	Pub	F,S	C	17,148	20	54	27	13	3	3	520	38	41	19	2	510	44	40	14	2	2/1
Virginia Intermont College	Bristol	U	A,B	Pri	S	C	918	19	66	31	3			491	53	35	9	3	450	75	23	2		Open
Virginia Military Institute	Lexington	SM	B	Pub	No	C	1,311	23						570	15	56	24	5	564	12	52	34	3	4/1
Virginia Polytechnic Institute and State University	Blacksburg	R	A,B,M,D	Pub	F,S	C	21,584																	1/15

NAME OF SCHOOL	TOWN	ENVIRONMENT (U-Urban R-Rural SU-Suburban SM-Small Town)	DEGREES AWARDED (A-Associate B-Bachelor M-Master D-Doctorate)	CONTROL (Pri-Private, Pub-Public)	FRATERNITIES AND SORORITIES (F-Fraternities S-Sororities F, S-Both No-Neither)	STUDENTS: C-Coed M-Men W-Women PM-Primarily Men PW-Primarily Women	UNDERGRADUATE ENROLLMENT FALL 2001	TEST SCORES: ACT Median	ACT Below 21	ACT 21-23	ACT 24-26	ACT 27-28	ACT Above 28	SAT I VERBAL REASONING Median	SAT I Verbal Below 500	SAT I Verbal 500-599	SAT I Verbal 600-700	SAT I Verbal Above 700	SAT I MATHEMATICAL REASONING Median	SAT I Math Below 500	SAT I Math 500-599	SAT I Math 600-700	SAT I Math Above 700	APPLICATION DEADLINE Month / Day
Virginia State University	Petersburg	SU	B,M		F,S	C	3,499	17	71	17	9	3		410	85	13	2		390	89	9	1		5/1
Virginia Union University	Richmond	U	B,M,D	Pri	F,S	C	1,377																	
Virginia Wesleyan College	Norfolk/Virginia Beach	U	B	Pri	F,S	C	1,408																	Open
Washington and Lee University	Lexington	SM	B,D	Pri	F,S	C	1,767	30			51		49	670	1	10	53	36	675	1	9	54	36	1/15
Washington																								
Central Washington University	Ellensburg	R	B,M	Pub	No	C	8,306	20	50	27	14	5	3	490	52	35	12	1	500	48	39	12	1	Open
City University	Renton	SU	A,B,M	Pri	No	C	3,005																	Open
Cornish College of the Arts	Seattle	U	B		No	C	650																	8/15
DeVry University/Seattle	Federal Way		A,B	Pri	No	C	561																	Open
Eastern Washington University	Cheney	SM	B,M	Pub	F,S	C	2,958	20						499					499					3/1
Evergreen State College	Olympia	SM	B,M	Pub	No	C	4,040							586	15	37	38	10	536	30	49	19	2	3/1
Gonzaga University	Spokane	U	B,M,D	Pri	No	C	3,483	26	6	21	25	24	24	580	22	43	30	5	590	20	46	30	4	2/1
Henry Cogswell College	Everett	SU	B	Pri	No	C	258	26			100			540	30	42	24	4	550	31	41	21	9	Open
Heritage College	Toppenish	R	A,B,M	Pri	No	C	670																	Open
Northwest College	Kirkland	SU	A,B,M	Pri	No	C	1,046																	8/1
Pacific Lutheran University	Tacoma	SU	B,M		No	C	3,184	24	20	22	29	14	15	550	24	45	28	4	550	30	44	25	4	Open
Saint Martin's College	Lacey	SU	A,B,M	Pri	F,S	C	1,201	21	41	38	12	8		502	48	41	8	3	491	54	34	12		Open
Seattle Pacific University	Seattle	U	B,M,D	Pri	No	C	2,828	27		3	42	42	13	630	31	44	30	8	620	22	42	31	5	6/1
Seattle University	Seattle	U	B,M,D	Pri	No	C	3,352	25						560	20	40	34	6	560	17	47	32	4	2/1
University of Puget Sound	Tacoma	SU	B,M	Pri	F,S	C	2,590	27	3	14	28	27	28	630	2	28	59	11	620	4	31	56	9	2/1
University of Washington	Seattle	U	B,M,D	Pub	F,S	C	25,660	25	16	24	28	15	17	569	22	43	28	7	590	15	40	35	10	1/15
Walla Walla College	College Place	SM	A,B,M	Pri	No	C	1,577																	Open
Washington State University	Pullman	SM	B,M,D	Pub	F,S	C	17,476							513	41	39	18	2	518	41	39	18	2	Open
Western Washington University	Bellingham	SM	B,M	Pub	No	C	11,641	23	27	29	24	12	8	540	27	46	24	3	540	26	48	24	2	3/1
Whitman College	Walla Walla	SM	B		F,S	C	1,439		2	3	17	15	63	659		19	51	30	649	2	17	58	24	2/1
Whitworth College	Spokane	SU	B,M		No	C	1,878	26						572	18	44	31	7	575	15	45	34	6	3/1
West Virginia																								
Alderson-Broaddus College	Philippi	SM	A,B,M	Pri	F,S	C	741	20						510					476					8/1
Bethany College	Bethany	SM	B	Pri	F,S	C	771	23						511					510					Open
Bluefield State College	Bluefield	SM	A,B	Pub	F,S	C	2,339	18	80	18	2													Open
Concord College	Athens	SM	A,B	Pub	F,S	C	3,055	27		21	55	22	2	560	56	25	16	3	560	55	30	12	3	Open
Davis and Elkins College	Elkins	SM	A,B	Pri	F,S	C	668	21						480					480					Open
Fairmont State College	Fairmont	SM	A,B,M	Pub	F,S	C	6,724		71	18	7	3	1											6/15
Glenville State College	Glenville	R	A,B	Pub	F,S	C	2,144	18	73	19	6	2		472	66	24	10		471	69	21	10		Open
Marshall University	Huntington	U	A,B,M,D	Pub	F,S	C	9,653	21	48	27	15	5	5											9/1
Mountain State University	Beckley	SM	A,B,M	Pri	No	C	2,422	19	85	12	2	1		472	68	27	5		469	57	35	6	2	Open
Ohio Valley College	Vienna	SU	A,B	Pri	No	C	453	20	57	29	9	3	2	480	59	28	10	3	450	65	22	13		Open
Salem International University	Salem	R	A,B,M	Pri	F,S	C	455	18	70	12	14	4		480	56	32	10	2	460	62	26	10	2	Open
Shepherd College	Shepherdstown	SM	A,B	Pub	F,S	C	4,391	20	53	26	13	3	3	500	49	36	12	2	500	48	40	11		2/1
University of Charleston	Charleston	U	A,B,M	Pri	F,S	C	1,089	21	48	32	16	3	1	480	50	43	6	1	490					
West Liberty State College	West Liberty	R	A,B	Pub	F,S	C	2,633	19	68	20	8	3	1	467	65	28	6	1	467	66	26	8		8/1
West Virginia State College	Institute	SU	A,B	Pub	F,S	C	4,823																	8/10
West Virginia University	Morgantown	SM	B,M,D	Pub	F,S	C	16,121		35	27	22	9	7	512	43	44	12	1	521	38	46	15	1	8/1
West Virginia University Institute of Technology	Montgomery	SM	A,B,M	Pub	F,S	C	2,353	20	50	33	10	5	2	501	50	35	15		525	55	27	18		8/1
West Virginia Wesleyan College	Buckhannon	SM	B,M	Pri	F,S	C	1,537	22	36	29	19	7	9	500	43	41	15	1	510	45	40	13	2	8/1
Wheeling Jesuit University	Wheeling	SU	B,M	Pri	No	C	1,249	21	42	23	21	8	6	510	40	47	12	1	520					Open
Wisconsin																								
Alverno College	Milwaukee	U	A,B,M	Pri	No	W	1,779																	8/1
Beloit College	Beloit	SM	B	Pri	F,S	C	1,272	27	3	19	28	19	31	640	8	25	47	20	600	13	37	42	8	2/1
Cardinal Stritch University	Milwaukee	SU	A,B,M,D	Pri	No	C	3,123																	4/1
Carroll College	Waukesha	SU	B,M		F,S	C	2,680	23	28	25	27	13	7											Open
Carthage College	Kenosha	SU	B,M		F,S	C	2,259	23	38	26	18	10	8	530	39	41	17	3	510	44	31	20	5	Open
Concordia University Wisconsin	Mequon	SU	A,B,M	Pri	No	C	3,845	22	38	25	23	8	6											8/1
Edgewood College	Madison	SU	A,B,M	Pri	No	C	1,632	22	30	32	24	8	6											8/1
Lakeland College	Sheboygan	R	B,M	Pri	F,S	C	847	20	58	22	14	5	1	430	73	13	13		480	55	33	13		7/15
Lawrence University	Appleton	U	B		F,S	C	1,323		3	11	20	24	42		9	28	40	23		2	32	43	23	1/15
Marian College of Fond du Lac	Fond du Lac	SM	B,M	Pri	F,S	C	1,629	20	59	25	10	5	1											Open
Marquette University	Milwaukee	U	A,B,M,D	Pri	F,S	C	7,499	25		1	31	58	11	580	14	43	35	7	580	17	41	36	7	Open
Milwaukee Institute of Art and Design	Milwaukee	U	B	Pri	No	C	650																	4/1
Milwaukee School of Engineering	Milwaukee	U	B,M	Pri	F,S	C	2,246	26	5	24	27	20	24	555	24	43	28	5	635	4	22	60	14	Open
Mount Mary College	Milwaukee	SU	B,M	Pri	No	W	1,080	21	51	27	20	2												8
Mount Senario College	Ladysmith	R	A,B	Pri	No	C	672	20						380	100				470	88	13			Open
Northland College	Ashland	SM	B	Pri	F,S	C		24	22	30	20	16	12	576	22	33	36	9	561	20	45	31	4	
Ripon College	Ripon	SM	B	Pri	F,S	C	906	24	23	27	25	13	12	577	20	32	44	4	604	12	32	44	12	8/1
Saint Norbert College	De Pere	SU	B,M	Pri	F,S	C	2,059		14	30	31	14	10											Open
Silver Lake College of the Holy Family	Manitowoc	R	A,B,M	Pri	No	C	663																	Open
University of Wisconsin/Eau Claire	Eau Claire	U	A,B,M	Pub	F,S	C	10,218	23	13	38	31	11	7	600	25	21	45	9	610	11	32	49	8	Open
University of Wisconsin/Green Bay	Green Bay	SU	A,B,M	Pub	F,S	C	5,383	23	27	33	27	8	5											2/1
University of Wisconsin/La Crosse	La Crosse	SM	A,B,M	Pub	F,S	C	8,486	24	6	37	39	11	7											Open
University of Wisconsin/Madison	Madison	U	B,M,D	Pub	F,S	C	25,616	27	2	17	10	36	35	620	6	31	45	17	640	6	22	52	19	2/1
University of Wisconsin/Milwaukee	Milwaukee	U	B,M,D	Pub	F,S	C	19,959																	Open
University of Wisconsin/Oshkosh	Oshkosh	U	A,B,M	Pub	F,S	C	9,216	22	34	36	22	6	3											8/1
University of Wisconsin/Parkside	Kenosha	SU	B,M	Pub	No	C	4,370																	
University of Wisconsin/Platteville	Platteville	R	A,B,M	Pub	F,S	C	4,850	21	35	33	20	8	5											Open
University of Wisconsin/River Falls	River Falls	SM	A,B,M	Pub	F,S	C	5,314	23	26	36	25	8	5											
University of Wisconsin/Stevens Point	Stevens Point	SM	A,B,M	Pub	F,S	C	8,512	23	25	37	25	8	5	530	32	45	18	5	540	26	55	1		Open

NAME OF SCHOOL	TOWN	ENVIRONMENT U-Urban R-Rural SU-Suburban SM-Small Town	DEGREES AWARDED A-Associate B-Bachelor M-Master D-Doctorate	CONTROL Pri-Private, Pub-Public	FRATERNITIES AND SORORITIES F-Fraternities S-Sororities F, S-Both No-Neither	STUDENTS: C-Coed M-Men W-Women PM-Primarily Men PW-Primarily Women	UNDERGRADUATE ENROLLMENT FALL 2001	TEST SCORES: ACT Median	ACT Below 21	ACT 21-23	ACT 24-26	ACT 27-28	ACT Above 28	SAT I VERBAL REASONING Median	Verbal Below 500	Verbal 500-599	Verbal 600-700	Verbal Above 700	SAT I MATHEMATICAL REASONING Median	Math Below 500	Math 500-599	Math 600-700	Math Above 700	APPLICATION DEADLINE Month / Day
University of Wisconsin/Stout	Menomonie	R	B,M	Pub	F,S	C	7,258	22		9	64	26	2											Open
University of Wisconsin/Superior	Superior	U	A,B,M	Pub	No	C	2,434	24		7	63	29	1	660	25	25	50		670		75	25		4/1
University of Wisconsin/Whitewater	Whitewater	SM	A,B,M	Pub	F,S	C	9,351																	Open
Viterbo University	LaCrosse	U	B,M	Pri	No	C	1,714	21	44	33	13	6	4											8/1
Wisconsin Lutheran College	Milwaukee	SU	B	Pri	No	C	716	25	15	19	35	13	18											9/1
Wyoming																								
University of Wyoming	Laramie	SM	B,M,D	Pub	F,S	C	8,550	23	27	28	25	10	10	539	31	43	23	3	546	29	41	24	7	8/10

IN-STAT[redacted]ST RANGES DIRE[redacted]Y

The breakdown of in-state tuition, room, and board costs for the 2001-2002 academic year are arranged from least expensive to most expensive. Within each range are lists of schools that don't charge for tuition or room and board, and those that do.

Less Than $2000

Colleges without Tuition, Room, and Board

California State University, San Marcos, CA (no R & B)
Charter Oak State College, CT (no R & B)
Curtis Institute of Music, PA (no R & B)
Escuela de Artes Plasticas de Puerto Rico, PR (no R & B)
University of Puerto Rico/Arecibo, PR (no R & B)
University of Puerto Rico/Bayamon University College Campus, PR (no R & B)

Colleges with Tuition, Room, and Board

Alice Lloyd College, KY
Conservatory of Music of Puerto Rico, PR (no R & B)
Excelsior College, NY (no R & B)
Oglala Lakota College, SD (no R & B)
Southern University at New Orleans, LA (no R & B)
United States Air Force Academy, CO
United States Coast Guard Academy, CT (no R & B)
United States Military Academy, NY
United States Naval Academy, MD
University of Puerto Rico at Humacao, PR (no R & B)
University of Puerto Rico/Cayey University College, PR (no R & B)

$2000-$3999

Colleges without Tuition, Room, and Board

American University in Puerto Rico, PR
Augusta State University, GA (no R & B)
Bluefield State College, WV (no R & B)
Caribbean University, PR (no R & B)
Central University of Bayamon, PR (no R & B)
City University of New York/Brooklyn College, NY (no R & B)
City University of New York/City College, NY (no R & B)
City University of New York/Herbert H. Lehman College, NY (no R & B)
City University of New York/John Jay College of Criminal Justice, NY (no R & B)
City University of New York/Queens College, NY (no R & B)
City University of New York/York College, NY (no R & B)
Clayton College and State University, GA (no R & B)
Harris-Stowe State College, MO (no R & B)
Inter-American University of Puerto Rico/Aguadilla Campus, PR (no R & B)
Inter-American University of Puerto Rico/Arecibo Campus, PR (no R & B)
Inter-American University of Puerto Rico/Barranquitas Regional College, PR (no R & B)
Kennesaw State University, GA (no R & B)
Langston University, OK (no R & B)
Louisiana State University in Shreveport, LA (no R & B)
Metropolitan State College of Denver, CO (no R & B)
Metropolitan State University, MN (no R & B)
Ohio State University at Lima, OH (no R & B)
Ohio State University at Mansfield, OH (no R & B)
Ohio State University at Marion, OH (no R & B)
Prairie View A&M University, TX (no R & B)
Sinte Gleska University, SD (no R & B)
Thomas Edison State College, NJ (no R & B)
Troy State University/Dothan, AL (no R & B)
Troy State University/Montgomery, AL (no R & B)
University of Colorado at Denver, CO (no R & B)
University of Houston-Downtown, TX (no R & B)
University of Maine at Augusta, ME (no R & B)
University of the District of Columbia, DC (no R & B)
Valley City State University, ND (no R & B)

Colleges with Tuition, Room, and Board

City University of New York/Baruch College, NY (no R & B)
City University of New York/College of Staten Island, NY (no R & B)
City University of New York/Medgar Evers College, NY (no R & B)
City University of New York/New York City Technical College, NY (no R & B)
College of the Ozarks, MO
Indiana University East, IN (no R & B)
Indiana University Kokomo, IN (no R & B)
Indiana University Northwest, IN (no R & B)
Indiana University South Bend, IN (no R & B)
Indiana University Southeast, IN (no R & B)
Indiana University-Purdue University Fort Wayne, IN (no R & B)
Inter-American University of Puerto Rico/Bayamon University College, PR (no R & B)
Inter-American University of Puerto Rico/Ponce Regional College, PR (no R & B)
Northeastern Illinois University, IL (no R & B)
Oklahoma Panhandle State University, OK
Savannah State University, GA (no R & B)
State University of New York/Empire State College, NY (no R & B)
Universidad Metropolitana, PR (no R & B)
Wesleyan University, CT

$4000-$5999

Colleges without Tuition, Room, and Board

Bellevue University, NE (no R & B)
College for Lifelong Learning, NH (no R & B)
College of New Rochelle - School of New Resources, NY (no R & B)
Inter-American University of Puerto Rico/Fajardo Campus, PR (no R & B)
NAES College, IL (no R & B)
Sojourner-Douglass College, MD (no R & B)
United States Merchant Marine Academy, NY (no R & B)
Universidad Politecnica de Puerto Rico, PR (no R & B)
University of Maryland/University College, MD (no R & B)
University of Massachusetts Boston, MA (no R & B)
University of Michigan/Dearborn, MI (no R & B)
University of Michigan/Flint, MI (no R & B)
Western International University, AZ (no R & B)

Colleges with Tuition, Room, and Board

Alabama Agricultural and Mechanical University, AL
Albany State University, GA
Alcorn State University, MS
Arkansas Baptist College, AR
Auburn University, AL
Auburn University Montgomery, AL
Austin Peay State University, TN
Berea College, KY
California State University, Dominguez Hills, CA
California State University, Fullerton, CA
California State University, Los Angeles, CA
Cameron University, OK
City University of New York/Hunter College, NY
Delta State University, MS
Dickinson State University, ND
East Central University, OK
Eastern New Mexico University, NM
Elizabeth City State University, NC
Fayetteville State University, NC
Florida Hospital College of Health Sciences, FL
Grambling State University, LA
Inter-American University of Puerto Rico/Metropolitan Campus, PR (no R & B)
McNeese State University, LA
Minot State University, ND
Mississippi University for Women, MS
Nicholls State University, LA
Northeastern State University, OK
Northwestern Oklahoma State University, OK
Northwestern State University of Louisiana, LA
Our Lady of Holy Cross College, LA (no R & B)
Salem State College, MA
Southeastern Oklahoma State University, OK
Southern Arkansas University, AR
Southwestern Oklahoma State University, OK
Texas Woman's University, TX
Trinity College of Nursing, IL (no R & B)
Turabo University, PR (no R & B)
University of Arkansas at Little Rock, AR
University of Arkansas at Monticello, AR
University of Central Oklahoma, OK
University of Louisiana at Lafayette, LA
University of Louisiana at Monroe, LA
University of North Carolina at Pembroke, NC
University of Puerto Rico/Mayaguez, PR
University of Puerto Rico/Rio Piedras, PR
University of Science and Arts of Oklahoma, OK
University of Texas at El Paso, TX
University of Texas-Pan American, TX
University of the Sacred Heart, PR
Western Carolina University, NC
Western New Mexico University, NM
Winston-Salem State University, NC

$6000-$7999

Colleges without Tuition, Room, and Board

Boricua College, NY (no R & B)
Boston Architectural Center, MA (no R & B)
Calumet College of St. Joseph, IN (no R & B)
City University, WA (no R & B)
Franklin University, OH (no R & B)
Heritage College, WA (no R & B)
Humphreys College, CA (no R & B)
National University, CA (no R & B)
Rutgers, The State University of New Jersey/CamdenCampus, NJ (no R & B)
Rutgers, The State University of New Jersey/—Newark Campus, NJ (no R & B)
Union Institute and University, OH (no R & B)
University of Phoenix, AZ (no R & B)
Wilmington College, DE (no R & B)

Colleges with Tuition, Room, and Board

Adams State College, CO
Alabama State University, AL
American Indian College of the Assemblies of God, AZ
Angelo State University, TX
Appalachian State University, NC
Arizona State University-Main, AZ
Arkansas State University, AR
Arkansas Tech University, AR
Armstrong Atlantic State University, GA
Baker College of Flint, MI
Bemidji State University, MN
Black Hills State University, SD
Boise State University, ID
Bridgewater State College, MA
Brigham Young University, UT
Brigham Young University/Hawaii, HI
Cabarrus College of Health Sciences, NC (no R & B)
California State University, Bakersfield, CA
California State University, Fresno, CA
California State University, Hayward, CA
California State University, Long Beach, CA
California State University, Monterey Bay, CA
California State University, Northridge, CA
California State University, Sacramento, CA
California State University, San Bernardino, CA
Central Missouri State University, MO
Chadron State College, NE
Clemson University, SC
Columbus State University, GA
Concord College, WV
Cooper Union for the Advancement of Science and Art, NY
Dakota State University, SD
East Carolina University, NC
East Tennessee State University, TN
Eastern Kentucky University, KY
Eastern Washington University, WA
Emporia State University, KS
Fairmont State College, WV
Fitchburg State College, MA
Florida Agricultural and Mechanical University, FL
Florida Memorial College, FL (no R & B)
Florida State University, FL
Fort Hays State University, KS
Fort Lewis College, CO
Fort Valley State University, GA
Framingham State College, MA
Francis Marion University, SC
Georgia College and State University, GA

Georgia Southern University, GA
Georgia Southwestern State University, GA
Georgia State University, GA
Glenville State College, WV
Henderson State University, AR
Idaho State University, ID
Inter-American University of Puerto Rico/San Germ·n, PR
International College, FL (no R & B)
Jackson State University, MS
Jacksonville State University, AL
Kansas State University, KS
Kentucky State University, KY
Knoxville College, TN (no R & B)
Lamar University, TX
Lewis-Clark State College, ID
Lincoln University, MO
Louisiana Tech University, LA
Marshall University, WV
Mayville State University, ND
Middle Tennessee State University, TN
Midwestern State University, TX
Miles College, AL
Minnesota State University, Mankato, MN
Mississippi State University, MS
Mississippi Valley State University, MS
Missouri Southern State College, MO
Missouri Western State College, MO
Montana State University-Billings, MT
Montana Tech of The University of Montana, MT
Moorhead State University, MN
Morehead State University, KY
Murray State University, KY
New Mexico Highlands University, NM
New Mexico Institute of Mining and Technology, NM
New Mexico State University, NM
North Carolina Agricultural and Technical State University, NC
North Carolina Central University, NC
North Carolina School of the Arts, NC
North Dakota State University, ND
North Georgia College and State University, GA
Northern Arizona University, AZ
Northern Kentucky University, KY
Northern State University, SD
Northwest Missouri State University, MO
Oklahoma State University, OK
Peru State College, NE
Philander Smith College, AR
Pittsburg State University, KS
Pontifical Catholic University of Puerto Rico/Ponce, PR
Purdue University/Calumet, IN (no R & B)
Rust College, MS
Saint Cloud State University, MN
Sam Houston State University, TX
San Francisco State University, CA
Shepherd College, WV
South Carolina State University, SC
South Dakota School of Mines and Technology, SD
South Dakota State University, SD
Southeastern Louisiana University, LA
Southern Illinois University Edwardsville, IL
Southern Polytechnic State University, GA
Southern University and A&M College, LA
Southern Utah University, UT
Southwest Missouri State University, MO
Southwest State University, MN
Southwestern Christian College, TX
State University of West Georgia, GA
Stephen F. Austin State University, TX
Sul Ross State University, TX
Tarleton State University, TX
Tennessee State University, TN
Tennessee Technological University, TN
Texas A&M University at Commerce, TX
Texas A&M University at Galveston, TX
Texas A&M University at Kingsville, TX
Texas Southern University, TX
Troy State University, AL
Universidad Adventista de las Antillas, PR
University of Alabama, AL
University of Alabama at Huntsville, AL
University of Alaska Southeast, AK
University of Arkansas at Pine Bluff, AR
University of Central Arkansas, AR
University of Florida, FL
University of Hawaii at Hilo, HI
University of Hawaii at Manoa, HI
University of Idaho, ID
University of Kansas, KS
University of Kentucky, KY
University of Louisville, KY
University of Maine at Fort Kent, ME
University of Maine at Machias, ME
University of Maine at Presque Isle, ME
University of Memphis, TN
University of Mississippi, MS
University of Montana—Western, MT
University of Montevallo, AL
University of Nebraska at Kearney, NE
University of Nebraska at Omaha, NE
University of North Alabama, AL
University of North Carolina at Asheville, NC
University of North Carolina at Charlotte, NC
University of North Carolina at Greensboro, NC
University of North Carolina at Wilmington, NC
University of North Dakota, ND
University of North Texas, TX
University of Northern Iowa, IA
University of Oklahoma, OK
University of South Alabama, AL
University of South Carolina at Aiken, SC
University of South Carolina at Spartanburg, SC
University of South Dakota, SD
University of Southern Colorado, CO
University of Southern Mississippi, MS
University of Tennessee at Chattanooga, TN
University of Texas at Arlington, TX
University of Utah, UT
University of West Alabama, AL
University of West Florida, FL
University of Wisconsin/Eau Claire, WI
University of Wisconsin/Green Bay, WI
University of Wisconsin/La Crosse, WI
University of Wisconsin/Oshkosh, WI
University of Wisconsin/Parkside, WI
University of Wisconsin/Platteville, WI
University of Wisconsin/River Falls, WI
University of Wisconsin/Stevens Point, WI
University of Wisconsin/Stout, WI
University of Wisconsin/Superior, WI
University of Wisconsin/Whitewater, WI
University of Wyoming, WY
Utah State University, UT
Valdosta State University, GA
Virginia Polytechnic Institute and State University, VA
Washburn University of Topeka, KS
Wayne State College, NE
Wayne State University, MI
Webb Institute, NY
Weber State University, UT
West Liberty State College, WV
West Texas A&M University, TX
West Virginia State College, WV
West Virginia University Institute of Technology, WV
Western Kentucky University, KY
Western State College of Colorado, CO
Wichita State University, KS
Worcester State College, MA

$8000-$9999

Colleges without Tuition, Room, and Board

Baltimore Hebrew University, MD (no R & B)
Colorado Technical University, CO (no R & B)
DeVry College of Technology/North Brunswick, NJ (no R & B)
DeVry University/Chicago, IL (no R & B)
DeVry University/Columbus, OH (no R & B)
DeVry University/Dallas, TX (no R & B)
DeVry University/Decatur, GA (no R & B)
DeVry University/Fremont, CA (no R & B)
DeVry University/Long Beach, CA (no R & B)
DeVry University/Phoenix, AZ (no R & B)
DeVry University/Pomona, CA (no R & B)
East-West University, IL (no R & B)
Golden Gate University, CA (no R & B)
Kendall College of Art and Design of Ferris State University, MI (no R & B)
Martin University, IN (no R & B)
Mercy College of Health Sciences, IA (no R & B)
New College of California, CA (no R & B)
Saint Francis College, NY (no R & B)
Saint Joseph's College, New York, NY (no R & B)
South College, GA (no R & B)
Southeastern University, DC (no R & B)
Strayer University, DC (no R & B)

Colleges with Tuition, Room, and Board

Allen University, SC
Ball State University, IN
Bloomsburg University of Pennsylvania, PA
Blue Mountain College, MS
Bowie State University, MD
California Polytechnic State University, CA
California State Polytechnic University, Pomona, CA
California State University, Chico, CA
California State University, Stanislaus, CA
Carlos Albizu University, FL (no R & B)
Central Michigan University, MI
Central State University, OH
Central Washington University, WA
Cheyney University of Pennsylvania, PA
Chicago State University, IL
Christopher Newport University, VA
Citadel, The, SC
Coastal Carolina University, SC
College of Charleston, SC
College of the Southwest, NM
Colorado State University, CO
Concordia College, AL
Coppin State College, MD
David N. Myers College, OH (no R & B)
Delaware State University, DE
DeVry Institute of Technology/New York, NY (no R & B)
DeVry University/Addison (DuPage County), IL (no R & B)
DeVry University/Alpharetta, GA (no R & B)
DeVry University/Colorado Springs, CO (no R & B)
DeVry University/Denver, CO (no R & B)
DeVry University/Kansas City, MO (no R & B)
DeVry University/Orlando, FL (no R & B)
DeVry University/Tinley Park, IL (no R & B)
DeVry University/West Hills, CA (no R & B)
East Stroudsburg University of Pennsylvania, PA
Eastern Michigan University, MI
Eastern Oregon University, OR
Edinboro University of Pennsylvania, PA
Evergreen State College, WA
Fashion Institute of Technology/State University of New York, NY
Florida Atlantic University, FL
Florida Gulf Coast University, FL
Florida International University, FL
Frostburg State University, MD
George Mason University, VA
Georgia Institute of Technology, GA
Humboldt State University, CA
Illinois State University, IL
Indiana State University, IN
Indiana University of Pennsylvania, PA
Indiana University-Purdue University Indianapolis, IN
Iowa State University, IA
James Madison University, VA
Jarvis Christian College, TX
Kutztown University of Pennsylvania, PA
Lake Superior State University, MI
Lander University, SC
LeMoyne-Owen College, TN (no R & B)
Lester L. Cox College of Nursing and Health Sciences, MO
Lock Haven University of Pennsylvania, PA
Longwood College, VA
Louisiana State University and Agricultural and Mechanical College, LA
Mansfield University, PA
Mary Washington College, VA
Massachusetts College of Liberal Arts, MA
Massachusetts Maritime Academy, MA
Mesa State College, CO
Montana State University-Bozeman, MT
Montana State University-Northern, MT
Morris College, SC
Mountain State University, WV
New College of Florida, FL
New Jersey City University, NJ
Norfolk State University, VA
North Carolina State University, NC
Northern Illinois University, IL
Northern Michigan University, MI
Oakland University, MI
Ohio State University at Newark, OH
Old Dominion University, VA
Oregon Institute of Technology, OR
Oregon State University, OR
Park University, MO
Paul Quinn College, TX
Radford University, VA
Rhode Island College, RI
Saginaw Valley State University, MI
San Diego State University, CA
San Jose State University, CA
Shawnee State University, OH
Shippensburg University of Pennsylvania, PA
Slippery Rock University, PA
Sonoma State University, CA
Southeast Missouri State University, MO
Southern Christian University, AL (no R & B)
Southern Illinois University at Carbondale, IL
Southern Oregon University, OR
Southwest Texas State University, TX
State University of New York/College at Buffalo, NY
State University of New York/College at Geneseo, NY
State University of New York/College at Old Westbury, NY
State University of New York/College at Oneonta, NY
State University of New York/College at Plattsburgh, NY
State University of New York/College of Technology at Alfred, NY
State University of New York/University at New Paltz, NY
Texas A&M University, TX
Texas Tech University, TX
Thomas University, GA
Tougaloo College, MS
Truman State University, MO
University of Alaska Anchorage, AK
University of Alaska Fairbanks, AK
University of Arizona, AZ
University of Arkansas, AR
University of Central Florida, FL
University of Colorado at Boulder, CO
University of Colorado at Colorado Springs, CO
University of Georgia, GA
University of Houston, TX
University of Iowa, IA
University of Maine at Farmington, ME

University of Maryland/Eastern Shore, MD
University of Massachusetts Dartmouth, MA
University of Massachusetts Lowell, MA
University of Minnesota/Crookston, MN
University of Missouri/Columbia, MO
University of Missouri/Kansas City, MO
University of Missouri/St. Louis, MO
University of Montana, MT
University of Nebraska at Lincoln, NE
University of Nevada/Las Vegas, NV
University of Nevada/Reno, NV
University of New Mexico, NM
University of North Carolina at Chapel Hill, NC
University of North Florida, FL
University of Northern Colorado, CO
University of Oregon, OR
University of Rio Grande, OH
University of South Carolina at Columbia, SC
University of South Florida, FL
University of Southern Indiana, IN
University of Tennessee at Knoxville, TN
University of Tennessee at Martin, TN
University of Texas at Austin, TX
University of Texas at Dallas, TX
University of Texas at San Antonio, TX
University of Virginia, VA
University of Virginia's College at Wise, VA
University of Wisconsin/Madison, WI
University of Wisconsin/Milwaukee, WI
Virginia Commonwealth University, VA
Virginia Military Institute, VA
Virginia State University, VA
Voorhees College, SC
Washington State University, WA
West Chester University of Pennsylvania, PA
West Virginia University, WV
Western Illinois University, IL
Western Oregon University, OR
Western Washington University, WA
Westfield State College, MA
Wiley College, TX
Winona State University, MN
Winthrop University, SC
Wright State University, OH
Youngstown State University, OH

$10,000-$11,999

Colleges without Tuition, Room, and Board

Burlington College, VT (no R & B)
Cleary College, MI (no R & B)
Peirce College, PA (no R & B)

Colleges with Tuition, Room, and Board

Aquinas College, TN (no R & B)
Bennett College, NC
Bowling Green State University, OH
Brewton-Parker College, GA
Bryn Athyn College of the New Church, PA
California University of Pennsylvania, PA
Cambridge College, MA (no R & B)
Castleton State College, VT
Central Connecticut State University, CT
Cincinnati College of Mortuary Science, OH (no R & B)
Clarion University of Pennsylvania, PA
Cleveland State University, OH
College of Aeronautics, NY (no R & B)
College of William and Mary, VA
Colorado School of Mines, CO
Cumberland University, TN
Davenport University, MI
DeVry University/Crystal City, VA (no R & B)
DeVry University/Seattle, WA (no R & B)
Eastern Connecticut State University, CT
Eastern Illinois University, IL
Ferris State University, MI
Flagler College, FL
Goldey-Beacom College, DE
Grand Valley State University, MI
Huron University, SD
Indiana University Bloomington, IN
Jamestown College, ND
Jewish Hospital College of Nursing and Allied Health, MO
Johnson State College, VT
Kean University, NJ
Keene State College, NH
Kent State University, OH
Lane College, TN
Lawrence Technological University, MI
Lee University, TN
Lincoln University, PA
Louisiana College, LA
Lyndon State College, VT
Madonna University, MI
Maine Maritime Academy, ME
Michigan State University, MI
Michigan Technological University, MI
Millersville University of Pennsylvania, PA
Montclair State University, NJ
Morgan State University, MD
Nebraska Methodist College of Nursing and Allied Health, NE
Oakland City University, IN (no R & B)
Ohio University, OH
Ottawa University, KS (no R & B)
Paine College, GA
Penn State University/University Park Campus, PA
Plymouth State College, NH
Portland State University, OR
Purdue University/West Lafayette, IN
Salisbury University, MD
Southeastern College, FL
Southern Connecticut State University, CT
State University of New York/College at Brockport, NY
State University of New York/College at Cortland, NY
State University of New York/College at Fredonia, NY
State University of New York/College at Oswego, NY
State University of New York/College at Potsdam, NY
State University of New York/College at Purchase, NY
State University of New York/College of Agriculture and Technology at Cobleskill, NY
State University of New York/College of Technology at Farmingdale, NY
State University of New York/Maritime College, NY
State University of New York/University at Albany, NY
State University of New York/University at Binghamton, NY
State University of New York/University at Buffalo, NY
State University of New York/University at Stony Brook, NY
Stillman College, AL
Talladega College, AL
The Ohio State University, OH
Towson University, MD
University of Akron, OH
University of Alabama at Birmingham, AL
University of California at Irvine, CA
University of California at San Diego, CA
University of California at Santa Barbara, CA
University of Delaware, DE
University of Illinois at Chicago, IL
University of Illinois at Urbana-Champaign, IL
University of Maine, ME
University of Maryland/College Park, MD
University of Massachusetts Amherst, MA
University of Minnesota/Duluth, MN
University of Minnesota/Morris, MN
University of Minnesota/Twin Cities, MN
University of Missouri/Rolla, MO
University of New Orleans, LA
University of Southern Maine, ME
University of Toledo, OH
University of Washington, WA
Vermont Technical College, VT
Wayland Baptist University, TX
Western Connecticut State University, CT
Western Michigan University, MI
William Carey College, MS
William Paterson University of New Jersey, NJ
William Tyndale College, MI
Williams Baptist College, AR

$12,000-$13,999

Colleges without Tuition, Room, and Board

American InterContinental University, GA (no R & B)
Art Institute of Portland, OR (no R & B)
Henry Cogswell College, WA (no R & B)
Holy Family College, PA (no R & B)
Laboratory Institute of Merchandising, NY (no R & B)
Lourdes College, OH (no R & B)
Molloy College, NY (no R & B)
Prescott College, AZ (no R & B)

Colleges with Tuition, Room, and Board

Barber-Scotia College, NC
Benedict College, SC
Berkeley College of New York City, NY (no R & B)
Bethel College, TN
Blackburn College, IL
California Maritime Academy, CA
Claflin University, SC
Clarkson College, NE
Clearwater Christian College, FL
College of New Jersey, The, NJ
College of Visual Arts, MN (no R & B)
Crichton College, TN
Dallas Baptist University, TX
Deaconess College of Nursing, MO
East Texas Baptist University, TX
Edward Waters College, FL
Faulkner University, AL
Fisk University, TN
Grace Bible College, MI
Grove City College, PA
Hannibal-LaGrange College, MO
Harding University, AR
Howard Payne University, TX
Huston-Tillotson College, TX
Judson College, AL
Kentucky Christian College, KY
Lincoln Memorial University, TN
Livingstone College, NC
Massachusetts College of Art, MA
Miami University, OH
National American University, SD
National-Louis University, IL (no R & B)
North Central University, MN
Ohio Valley College, WV
Oklahoma Baptist University, OK
Penn State University at Erie/Behrend College, PA
Penn State University/Altoona, PA
Pennsylvania College of Technology, PA
Pikeville College, KY
Presentation College, SD
Ramapo College of New Jersey, NJ
Reinhardt College, GA
Richard Stockton College of New Jersey, NJ
Rowan University, NJ
Rutgers, The State University of New Jersey New Brunswick Campus, NJ
Saint Augustine's College, NC
Saint Gregory's University, OK
Saint Mary's College, MI
Saint Paul's College, VA
Shaw University, NC
Southwest Baptist University, MO
State University of New York/College of Environmental Science and Forestry, NY
Tennessee Wesleyan College, TN
University of California at Davis, CA
University of California at Los Angeles, CA
University of California at Riverside, CA
University of California at Santa Cruz, CA
University of Cincinnati, OH
University of Connecticut, CT
University of Mary, ND
University of Mary Hardin-Baylor, TX
University of Maryland/Baltimore County, MD
University of Michigan/Ann Arbor, MI
University of Mobile, AL
University of New Hampshire, NH
University of Pittsburgh at Bradford, PA
University of Pittsburgh at Greensburg, PA
University of Pittsburgh at Johnstown, PA
University of Pittsburgh at Pittsburgh, PA
University of Rhode Island, RI
University of the Ozarks, AR
Woodbury College, VT (no R & B)
York College, NE
York College of Pennsylvania, PA

$14,000-$15,999

Colleges without Tuition, Room, and Board

Cogswell Polytechnical College, CA (no R & B)

Colleges with Tuition, Room, and Board

Art Institute of Southern California, CA (no R & B)
Baker University, KS
Bartlesville Wesleyan College, OK
Bethune-Cookman College, FL
Bluefield College, VA
Brescia University, KY
Campbellsville University, KY
Cascade College, OR
Columbia College, MO
Culver-Stockton College, MO
Cumberland College, KY
Dakota Wesleyan University, SD
Drury University, MO
Evangel University, MO
Ferrum College, VA
Freed-Hardeman University, TN
Friends University, KS
Graceland University, IA
Hardin-Simmons University, TX
Houston Baptist University, TX
Howard University, DC
Huntington College, IN (no R & B)
Husson College, ME
John Brown University, AR
Kentucky Wesleyan College, KY
Lambuth University, TN
Liberty University, VA
Lubbock Christian University, TX
Marylhurst University, OR
McMurry University, TX
Mercy College, NY
Midway College, KY
Mississippi College, MS
Missouri Baptist College, MO
Monroe College, NY
Morris Brown College, GA
Mount Marty College, SD
Mount Olive College, NC
New Jersey Institute of Technology, NJ
Newman University, KS
North Carolina Wesleyan College, NC
Oakwood College, AL
Oklahoma City University, OK
Rochester College, MI
Saint Mary's College of Maryland, MD
Sheldon Jackson College, AK
Shorter College, GA
Silver Lake College of the Holy Family, WI
Southern Adventist University, TN
Southern Nazarene University, OK
Southwestern Adventist University, TX
Spalding University, KY
Temple University, PA
Texas Wesleyan University, TX
Toccoa Falls College, GA
Touro College, NY
Trevecca Nazarene University, TN
Tuskegee University, AL
Union College, KY
Union College, NE
University of California at Berkeley, CA

University of Great Falls, MT
University of Vermont, VT
Virginia Union University, VA
Webber International University, FL
Wilberforce University, OH

$16,000-$17,999

Colleges without Tuition, Room, and Board

Audrey Cohen College, NY (no R & B)
Southern California Institute of Architecture, CA (no R & B)

Colleges with Tuition, Room, and Board

Abilene Christian University, TX
Alaska Pacific University, AK
Allen College, IA
Alverno College, WI
Andrews University, MI
Art Academy of Cincinnati, OH (no R & B)
Averett University, VA
Avila College, MO
Barton College, NC
Belhaven College, MS
Bethany College, KS
Bethel College, IN
Bethel College, KS
Bloomfield College, NJ
Bryan College, TN
California Baptist University, CA
Campbell University, NC
Cardinal Stritch University, WI
Carson-Newman College, TN
Cedarville University, OH
Central Methodist College, MO
Chaminade University of Honolulu, HI
Charleston Southern University, SC
Christendom College, VA
Clark Atlanta University, GA
College of Saint Joseph, VT
Colorado Christian University, CO
Concordia University at Austin, TX
Concordia University Nebraska, NE
Concordia University Wisconsin, WI
Cornish College of the Arts, WA (no R & B)
David Lipscomb University, TN
Dillard University, LA
Doane College, NE
Gallaudet University, DC
Gardner-Webb University, NC
Grace College, IN
Grand View College, IA
Hampton University, VA
Hanover College, IN
Hastings College, NE
Hawaii Pacific University, HI
Hellenic College/Holy Cross Greek Orthodox School of Theology, MA
Hesser College, NH
Hilbert College, NY
Hope International University, CA
Illinois College, IL
Indiana Wesleyan University, IN
Johnson C. Smith University, NC
Kansas Wesleyan University, KS
King College, TN
LaGrange College, GA
Lakeland College, WI
Lees-McRae College, NC
Limestone College, SC
Lindenwood University, MO
Lindsey Wilson College, KY
Lyon College, AR
MacMurray College, IL
Marian College of Fond du Lac, WI
Marygrove College, MI
McPherson College, KS
Meredith College, NC
MidAmerica Nazarene University, KS
Milligan College, TN
Missouri Valley College, MO
Montreat College, NC
Mount Senario College, WI
Mount Vernon Nazarene College, OH
Northwest College, WA
Northwestern College of Iowa, IA
Oklahoma Christian University, OK
Olivet College, MI
Ouachita Baptist University, AR
Our Lady of the Lake University of San Antonio, TX
Pacific Northwest College of Art, OR
Philadelphia Biblical University, PA
Piedmont College, GA
Queens College, NC
Saint Edward's University, TX
Saint Mary College, KS
Salem International University, WV
Samford University, AL
Shimer College, IL
Siena Heights University, MI
Southern Vermont College, VT
Southern Wesleyan University, SC
Southwestern College, KS
Spring Arbor University, MI
Sterling College, KS
Tabor College, KS
Texas Lutheran University, TX
Thomas More College, KY
Thomas More College of Liberal Arts, NH
Tiffin University, OH
Tusculum College, TN
University of Saint Francis, IN
University of Sioux Falls, SD
Upper Iowa University, IA
Urbana University, OH
Villa Julie College, MD
Virginia Intermont College, VA
Walsh University, OH
Waynesburg College, PA
Wesley College, DE
Wesleyan College, GA
Westminster College, UT
William Jewell College, MO
William Penn University, IA
Xavier University of Louisiana, LA

Over $18,000

Colleges without Tuition, Room, and Board

Art Center College of Design, CA (no R & B)
Bates College, ME (no R & B)
Colby College, ME (no R & B)
Middlebury College, VT (no R & B)
Otis College of Art and Design, CA (no R & B)
San Francisco Art Institute, CA (no R & B)

Colleges with Tuition, Room, and Board

Adelphi University, NY
Adrian College, MI
Agnes Scott College, GA
Albany College of Pharmacy, NY
Albert A. List College of Jewish Studies, NY
Albertson College of Idaho, ID
Albertus Magnus College, CT
Albion College, MI
Albright College, PA
Alderson-Broaddus College, WV
Alfred University, NY
Allegheny College, PA
Alma College, MI
Alvernia College, PA
American International College, MA
American University, DC
Amherst College, MA
Anderson University, IN
Anna Maria College, MA
Antioch College, OH
Aquinas College, MI
Arcadia University, PA
Art Institute of Atlanta, GA
Art Institute of Boston at Lesley University, MA
Asbury College, KY
Ashland University, OH
Assumption College, MA
Atlanta College of Art, GA
Atlantic Union College, MA
Augsburg College, MN
Augustana College, IL
Augustana College, SD
Aurora University, IL
Austin College, TX
Azusa Pacific University, CA
Babson College, MA
Baldwin-Wallace College, OH
Bard College, NY
Barry University, FL
Bay Path College, MA
Baylor University, TX
Beacon College, FL
Becker College, MA
Bellarmine University, KY
Belmont Abbey College, NC
Belmont University, TN
Beloit College, WI
Benedictine College, KS
Benedictine University, IL
Benjamin Franklin Institute of Technology, MA
Bennington College, VT
Bentley College, MA
Berkeley College, NY
Berklee College of Music, MA
Berry College, GA
Bethany College, WV
Bethel College, MN
Biola University, CA
Birmingham-Southern College, AL
Bluffton College, OH
Boston College, MA
Boston Conservatory, MA
Boston University, MA
Bowdoin College, ME
Bradley University, IL
Brandeis University, MA
Brenau University Women's College, GA
Briar Cliff University, IA
Bridgewater College, VA
Brown University, RI
Bryant College, RI
Bryn Mawr College, PA
Bucknell University, PA
Buena Vista University, IA
Butler University, IN
Cabrini College, PA
Caldwell College, NJ
California College of Arts and Crafts, CA
California Institute of Technology, CA
California Institute of the Arts, CA
California Lutheran University, CA
Calvin College, MI
Canisius College, NY
Capital University, OH
Capitol College, MD
Carleton College, MN
Carlow College, PA
Carnegie Mellon University, PA
Carroll College, MT
Carroll College, WI
Carthage College, WI
Case Western Reserve University, OH
Catawba College, NC
Catholic University of America, DC
Cazenovia College, NY
Cedar Crest College, PA
Centenary College, NJ
Centenary College of Louisiana, LA
Central College, IA
Centre College, KY
Champlain College, VT
Chapman University, CA
Chatham College, PA
Chestnut Hill College, PA
Christian Brothers University, TN
Christian Heritage College, CA
Claremont McKenna College, CA
Clark University, MA
Clarke College, IA
Clarkson University, NY
Cleveland Institute of Art, OH
Cleveland Institute of Music, OH
Coe College, IA
Coker College, SC
Colby-Sawyer College, NH
Colgate University, NY
College For Creative Studies, MI
College Misericordia, PA
College of Mount Saint Vincent, NY
College of Mount St. Joseph, OH
College of New Rochelle, NY
College of Notre Dame of Maryland, MD
College of Our Lady of the Elms, MA
College of Saint Benedict, MN
College of Saint Catherine, MN
College of Saint Elizabeth, NJ
College of Saint Mary, NE
College of Saint Rose, NY
College of Saint Scholastica, MN
College of Santa Fe, NM
College of the Atlantic, ME
College of the Holy Cross, MA
College of Wooster, OH
Colorado College, CO
Columbia College, SC
Columbia College Chicago, IL
Columbia Union College, MD
Columbia University/Barnard College, NY
Columbia University/Columbia College, NY
Columbia University/Fu Foundation School of Engineering and Applied Science, NY
Columbia University/School of General Studies, NY
Columbus College of Art and Design, OH
Concordia College, NY
Concordia College/Moorhead, MN
Concordia University, CA
Concordia University, MI
Concordia University, MN
Concordia University, OR
Concordia University, River Forest, IL
Connecticut College, CT
Converse College, SC
Corcoran School of Art and Design, DC
Cornell College, IA
Cornell University, NY
Cornerstone University and Grand Rapids Baptist Seminary, MI
Covenant College, GA
Creighton University, NE
Curry College, MA
Daemen College, NY
Dana College, NE
Daniel Webster College, NH
Dartmouth College, NH
Davidson College, NC
Davis and Elkins College, WV
De Sales University, PA
Defiance College, OH
Delaware Valley College, PA
Denison University, OH
DePaul University, IL
DePauw University, IN
Dickinson College, PA
Dominican College, NY
Dominican University, IL
Dominican University of California, CA
Dordt College, IA
Dowling College, NY
Drake University, IA
Drew University/College of Liberal Arts, NJ
Drexel University, PA
Duke University, NC
Duquesne University, PA
D'Youville College, NY
Earlham College, IN
Eastern College, PA
Eastern Mennonite University, VA
Eastern Nazarene College, MA
Eastman School of Music, NY
Eckerd College, FL
Edgewood College, WI
Elizabethtown College, PA
Elmhurst College, IL
Elmira College, NY
Elon University, NC
Embry-Riddle Aeronautical University, AZ
Embry-Riddle Aeronautical University, FL
Emerson College, MA
Emmanuel College, MA
Emory & Henry College, VA
Emory University, GA
Endicott College, MA
Erskine College, SC
Eugene Lang College of New School University, NY
Eureka College, IL
Fairfield University, CT
Fairleigh Dickinson University/Madison campus, NJ
Fairleigh Dickinson University/Teaneck Campus, NJ
Felician College, NJ
Fisher College, MA
Five Towns College, NY
Florida Institute of Technology, FL
Florida Southern College, FL
Fontbonne University, MO
Fordham University, NY
Franciscan University of Steubenville, OH
Franklin and Marshall College, PA
Franklin College of Indiana, IN
Franklin Pierce College, NH
Fresno Pacific University, CA
Friends World Program, NY
Furman University, SC

Gannon University, PA
Geneva College, PA
George Fox University, OR
George Washington University, DC
Georgetown College, KY
Georgetown University, DC
Georgian Court College, NJ
Gettysburg College, PA
Goddard College, VT
Gonzaga University, WA
Gordon College, MA
Goshen College, IN
Goucher College, MD
Grand Canyon University, AZ
Green Mountain College, VT
Greensboro College, NC
Greenville College, IL
Grinnell College, IA
Guilford College, NC
Gustavus Adolphus College, MN
Gwynedd-Mercy College, PA
Hamilton College, NY
Hamline University, MN
Hampden-Sydney College, VA
Hampshire College, MA
Hartwick College, NY
Harvard University/Harvard College, MA
Harvey Mudd College, CA
Haverford College, PA
Heidelberg College, OH
Hendrix College, AR
High Point University, NC
Hillsdale College, MI
Hiram College, OH
Hobart and William Smith Colleges, NY
Hofstra University, NY
Hollins University, VA
Holy Names College, CA
Hood College, MD
Hope College, MI
Houghton College, NY
Huntingdon College, AL
Illinois Institute of Technology, IL
Illinois Wesleyan University, IL
Immaculata College, PA
Indiana Institute of Technology, IN
Iona College, NY
Iowa Wesleyan College, IA
Ithaca College, NY
Jacksonville University, FL
John Carroll University, OH
Johns Hopkins University, MD
Johnson and Wales University, RI
Judson College, IL
Juilliard School, NY
Juniata College, PA
Kalamazoo College, MI
Kansas City Art Institute, MO
Kendall College, IL
Kenyon College, OH
Kettering University, MI
Keuka College, NY
Keystone College, PA
King's College, PA
Knox College, IL
La Roche College, PA
La Salle University, PA
La Sierra University, CA
Lafayette College, PA
Lake Erie College, OH
Lake Forest College, IL
Lasell College, MA
Lawrence University, WI
Le Moyne College, NY
Lebanon Valley College of Pennsylvania, PA
Lehigh University, PA
Lenoir-Rhyne College, NC
Lesley College, MA
LeTourneau University, TX
Lewis and Clark College, OR
Lewis University, IL
Linfield College, OR
Long Island University/Brooklyn Campus, NY
Long Island University/C.W. Post Campus, NY
Long Island University/Southampton College, NY
Loras College, IA
Loyola College in Maryland, MD
Loyola Marymount University, CA
Loyola University New Orleans, LA
Loyola University of Chicago, IL
Luther College, IA
Lycoming College, PA
Lynchburg College, VA
Lynn University, FL
Macalester College, MN
Maharishi University of Management, IA
Maine College of Art, ME
Malone College, OH
Manchester College, IN
Manhattan College, NY
Manhattan School of Music, NY
Manhattanville College, NY
Mannes College of Music, NY
Marian College, IN
Marietta College, OH
Marist College, NY
Marlboro College, VT
Marquette University, WI
Mars Hill College, NC
Mary Baldwin College, VA
Maryland Institute College of Art, MD
Marymount College/Tarrytown, NY
Marymount Manhattan College, NY
Marymount University, VA
Maryville College, TN
Maryville University of Saint Louis, MO
Marywood University, PA
Massachusetts College of Pharmacy and Health Sciences, MA
Massachusetts Institute of Technology, MA
Master's College, CA
McKendree College, IL
MCP Hahnemann University, PA
Medaille College, NY
Memphis College of Art, TN
Menlo College, CA
Mercer University, GA
Mercyhurst College, PA
Merrimack College, MA
Messiah College, PA
Methodist College, NC
Midland Lutheran College, NE
Millikin University, IL
Mills College, CA
Millsaps College, MS
Milwaukee Institute of Art and Design, WI
Milwaukee School of Engineering, WI
Minneapolis College of Art and Design, MN
Mitchell College, CT
Monmouth College, IL
Monmouth University, NJ
Montserrat College of Art, MA
Moore College of Art and Design, PA
Moravian College, PA
Morehouse College, GA
Morningside College, IA
Mount Aloysius College, PA
Mount Holyoke College, MA
Mount Ida College, MA
Mount Mary College, WI
Mount Mercy College, IA
Mount Saint Clare College, IA
Mount Saint Mary College, NY
Mount Saint Mary's College, CA
Mount Saint Mary's College, MD
Mount Union College, OH
Muhlenberg College, PA
Muskingum College, OH
Naropa University, CO
Nazareth College of Rochester, NY
Nebraska Wesleyan University, NE
Neumann College, PA
New England College, NH
New England Conservatory of Music, MA
New York Institute of Technology, NY
New York University, NY
Newberry College, SC
Newbury College, MA
Niagara University, NY
Nichols College, MA
North Central College, IL
North Park University, IL
Northeastern University, MA
Northland College, WI
Northwest Christian College, OR
Northwest Nazarene University, ID
Northwestern College, MN
Northwestern University, IL
Northwood University, FL
Northwood University, MI
Northwood University, TX
Norwich University, VT
Notre Dame College, OH
Notre Dame de Namur University, CA
Nova Southeastern University, FL
Nyack College, NY
Oberlin College, OH
Occidental College, CA
Oglethorpe University, GA (no R & B)
Ohio Dominican College, OH
Ohio Northern University, OH
Ohio Wesleyan University, OH
Olivet Nazarene University, IL
Oral Roberts University, OK
Otterbein College, OH
Pace University, NY
Pacific Lutheran University, WA
Pacific Union College, CA
Pacific University, OR
Palm Beach Atlantic College, FL
Parsons School of Design, NY
Pepperdine University, CA
Pfeiffer University, NC
Philadelphia University, PA
Pine Manor College, MA
Pitzer College, CA
Point Loma Nazarene University, CA
Point Park College, PA
Polytechnic University/Brooklyn, NY
Pomona College, CA
Pratt Institute, NY
Presbyterian College, SC
Princeton University, NJ
Principia College, IL
Providence College, RI
Quincy University, IL
Quinnipiac University, CT
Randolph-Macon College, VA
Randolph-Macon Woman's College, VA
Reed College, OR
Regis College, MA
Regis University, CO
Rensselaer Polytechnic Institute, NY
Research College of Nursing, MO
Rhode Island School of Design, RI
Rhodes College, TN
Rice University, TX
Rider University, NJ
Ringling School of Art and Design, FL
Ripon College, WI
Rivier College, NH
Roanoke College, VA
Robert Morris University, PA
Roberts Wesleyan College, NY
Rochester Institute of Technology, NY
Rockford College, IL
Rockhurst University, MO
Rocky Mountain College, MT
Roger Williams University, RI
Rollins College, FL
Roosevelt University, IL
Rose-Hulman Institute of Technology, IN
Rosemont College, PA
Russell Sage College, NY
Sacred Heart University, CT
Saint Ambrose University, IA
Saint Andrews Presbyterian College, NC
Saint Anselm College, NH
Saint Bonaventure University, NY
Saint Francis University, PA
Saint John Fisher College, NY
Saint John's College, MD
Saint John's College, NM
Saint John's University, MN
Saint John's University, NY
Saint Joseph College, CT
Saint Joseph's College, IN
Saint Joseph's College of Maine, ME
Saint Joseph's University, PA
Saint Lawrence University, NY
Saint Leo University, FL
Saint Louis University, MO
Saint Martin's College, WA
Saint Mary-of-the-Woods College, IN
Saint Mary's College, IN
Saint Mary's College of California, CA
Saint Mary's University of Minnesota, MN
Saint Mary's University of San Antonio, TX
Saint Michael's College, VT
Saint Norbert College, WI
Saint Olaf College, MN
Saint Peter's College, NJ
Saint Thomas Aquinas College, NY
Saint Thomas University, FL
Saint Vincent College, PA
Saint Xavier University, IL
Salem College, NC
Salve Regina University, RI
Samuel Merritt College, CA
San Francisco Conservatory of Music, CA (no R & B)
Santa Clara University, CA
Sarah Lawrence College, NY
Savannah College of Art and Design, GA
School of the Art Institute of Chicago, IL
School of Visual Arts, NY
Schreiner University, TX
Scripps College, CA
Seattle Pacific University, WA
Seattle University, WA
Seton Hall University, NJ
Seton Hill College, PA
Shenandoah University, VA
Siena College, NY
Sierra Nevada College-Lake Tahoe, NV
Simmons College, MA
Simon's Rock College of Bard, MA
Simpson College, CA
Simpson College, IA
Skidmore College, NY
Smith College, MA
Southern Methodist University, TX
Southern New Hampshire University, NH
Southwestern University, TX
Spelman College, GA
Spring Hill College, AL
Springfield College, MA
Stanford University, CA
Stephens College, MO
Sterling College, VT
Stetson University, FL
Stevens Institute of Technology, NJ
Stonehill College, MA
Suffolk University, MA
Susquehanna University, PA
Swarthmore College, PA
Sweet Briar College, VA
Syracuse University, NY
Taylor University, IN
Teikyo Post University, CT
Texas Christian University, TX
Thiel College, PA
Thomas Aquinas College, CA
Thomas College, ME
Transylvania University, KY
Trinity Christian College, IL
Trinity College, CT
Trinity College, DC
Trinity International University, IL
Trinity University, TX
Tri-State University-Main Campus, IN
Tufts University, MA
Tulane University, LA
Union College, NY
Union University, TN
United States International University, CA
Unity College, ME
University of Bridgeport, CT
University of Charleston, WV
University of Chicago, IL
University of Dallas, TX
University of Dayton, OH
University of Denver, CO
University of Detroit Mercy, MI
University of Dubuque, IA
University of Evansville, IN
University of Findlay, OH
University of Hartford, CT
University of Indianapolis, IN
University of Judaism College of Arts and Sciences, CA
University of La Verne, CA
University of Miami, FL
University of New England, ME
University of New Haven, CT
University of Notre Dame, IN
University of Pennsylvania, PA
University of Portland, OR
University of Puget Sound, WA
University of Redlands, CA
University of Richmond, VA
University of Rochester, NY
University of Saint Francis, IL
University of Saint Thomas, MN
University of Saint Thomas, TX
University of San Diego, CA
University of San Francisco, CA
University of Scranton, PA
University of Southern California, CA
University of Tampa, FL
University of the Arts, PA
University of the Incarnate Word, TX
University of the Pacific, CA

University of the Sciences in Philadelphia, PA
University of the South, TN
University of Tulsa, OK
Ursinus College, PA
Ursuline College, OH
Utica College of Syracuse University, NY
Valparaiso University, IN
Vanderbilt University, TN
VanderCook College of Music, IL
Vanguard University of Southern California, CA
Vassar College, NY
Villanova University, PA
Virginia Wesleyan College, VA
Viterbo University, WI
Wabash College, IN
Wagner College, NY
Wake Forest University, NC
Walla Walla College, WA
Warner Pacific College, OR
Warren Wilson College, NC
Wartburg College, IA
Washington and Jefferson College, PA
Washington and Lee University, VA
Washington College, MD
Washington University in St. Louis, MO
Webster University, MO
Wellesley College, MA
Wells College, NY
Wentworth Institute of Technology, MA
West Suburban College of Nursing, IL
West Virginia Wesleyan College, WV
Western Baptist College, OR
Western Maryland College, MD
Western New England College, MA
Westminster Choir College of Rider University, NJ
Westminster College, MO
Westminster College, PA
Westmont College, CA
Wheaton College, IL
Wheaton College, MA
Wheeling Jesuit University, WV
Wheelock College, MA
Whitman College, WA
Whittier College, CA
Whitworth College, WA
Widener University, PA
Wilkes University, PA
Willamette University, OR
William Woods University, MO
Williams College, MA
Wilmington College, OH
Wilson College, PA
Wingate University, NC
Wisconsin Lutheran College, WI
Wittenberg University, OH
Wofford College, SC
Woodbury University, CA
Worcester Polytechnic Institute, MA
Xavier University, OH
Yale University, CT
Yeshiva University, NY

PART III

INDEX OF COLLEGE MAJORS

By now, you either have a clear idea about what your college major will be, or you are worrying about it. This section presents an overview of academic majors as well as information about some of the careers for which each major prepares you.

Majors are listed alphabetically in chart form. This lets you compare the various schools that offer the majors that interest you. You'll also be able to compare each school's Selector Rating and in-state costs.

After you've found a representative sampling of the schools that offer majors in the fields you may want to pursue, go on to the college Profiles that make up this book's main section.

DECIDING ON A MAJOR AND CAREER

What is a major? All four-year colleges require the satisfactory completion of a certain number of courses to graduate. A **major** consists of a concentration of courses in a specialized field of study. Most majors require about one third of your college time and the course work usually is done in the last two years of college. The other two thirds of your college time usually are occupied by general education courses that are required for college graduation and elective courses that you elect, or choose, to enhance and broaden your educational knowledge. After successful completion of the courses in your major, along with the general education and elective requirements, you may be eligible for graduation and receive the undergraduate baccalaureate (bachelor) degree. Your adviser, usually a member of the teaching faculty in your major, helps you to select required courses and plan all requirements for the completion of the major.

What is a minor? A minor usually consists of a number of courses in a field of study other than the major, however, the required units of study are fewer than those required of the major. Many colleges today do not require a formal minor for graduation. Your adviser will inform you if you have to complete one. The more practical reason for a minor is to supplement and strengthen your major. For example: A computer science major may be required to take a certain number of mathematics courses that, when totaled up, meet the definition of a minor, or perhaps a dual major.

Majors And Careers. Deciding upon a major is one of the most important decisions you will have to make. With its emphasis on a structured course of study, a major not only provides for intellectual growth, self-improvement, general knowledge, and a search for truth and understanding, but often provides the required technical training to enter and become successful in the work world. Personal enlightenment is a noble goal, but most students no longer can afford the monetary expenses and the time to pursue courses that do not lead to a major that ties into career goals.

Information on majors and careers is presented here to help you to make college and career decisions. Those decisions should take into consideration the clarification of occupational and personal values, life-style goals and work interests, and the education and training needed for long-range self-satisfaction and job success.

WHAT ARE SOME DIFFERENT APPROACHES TO MAJORS?

Job training. You may want to go to college for one main reason: to acquire specific job skills to qualify for direct job entry. The course work usually is work-related and technical and it is evident that the skills learned in class can be directly applied to a job. For example, if you want to become a professional engineer in one of the many engineering specialties, you will have to complete a four- to five-year engineering curriculum that is quite rigidly prescribed.

Examples of other four-year majors in which you learn technical skills that lead to direct job entry are: accounting, agronomy, architecture, computer science, dance, elementary education, forestry, geology, nursing, and social work.

The generalist approach. You may be the type of person who wants to pursue a more general major that may not directly tie into job entry, but will improve your general knowledge and prepare you as a generalist with intellectual and problem-solving skills rather than technical training. This kind of major is often referred to as liberal arts, humanities, or general studies. Many majors in the social sciences, biological sciences, communications, and the arts are looked at as liberal arts majors in which the bachelor degree will not guarantee direct job entry in a job associated with the major.

Many professional graduate schools (law, medicine, education, business, journalism) prefer candidates who have undergraduate degrees in the liberal arts. Also, many employers prefer to hire the liberal arts major because that person may possess superior analytical skills to apply to problem-solving and innovation.

Special talent/aptitude approach. You may want to select a certain major because you have a special talent and a strong interest in a certain field. It is always a good idea to know your strengths and build on them. Do you have a strong interest in writing? acting? music? art? mathematics? computers? leadership? The list could go on. You can select a major that helps you to further your talents. College life certainly will be more enjoyable if you take courses that will give you personal satisfaction, and in your career planning you might give thought to designing a career that will allow you to enjoy a life-style compatible with your special talents.

Dual major. Many colleges advise dual majors for career preparation. This is true especially in preparing to enter a scientific career, where it is essential to be well-grounded in both the physical and biological sciences.

Individually-designed major. You may have highly divergent interests that cut across traditional lines. Many colleges will allow you to design a major that will satisfy your goals. For example, you may have artistic talents and scientific interests. You might combine the two, and even though the college of your choice does not offer the major, you might design a scientific illustration major that meets faculty approval.

TYING COLLEGE MAJOR PLANNING TO CAREER PLANNING

In the next section we will present relevant educational and career information on nine broad fields of study from which you may choose a major. Relevant facts will be presented to help you to decide upon a major based upon career planning.

Each of the nine fields of study has specific information on majors and careers that you will want to consider carefully when making your decision. Before you begin to look at that information, here is a brief explanation of what you will find within each of the nine fields of study.

- **Representative majors.** The majors listed are the most popular ones in their field.
- **Interests.** Interests that you should have. You will be most successful and fulfilled if you carefully assess your interests and make your plans based upon your interests rather than upon how much money you will make.
- **Job requirements.** These are the most relevant general requirements for careers associated with the field of study.
- **Related jobs.** Consider the present and future job titles associated with the field of study. These job titles come from Occupational Employment Statistics (OES) compiled by the U.S. Department of Labor, Bureau of Labor Statistics.
- **Employment information.** This tells how many people work in the field of study, and, in general terms, where they work.
- **Employment outlook.** The generalized outlook prediction to the year 2005 comes from authoritative *Department of Labor* sources, and can vary greatly depending upon the state of the economy and rapidly changing technological demands. All college graduates should recognize the need to be prepared to meet the challenges of a dynamic and competitive labor market. Job outlook also varies a great deal from region to region.

REPRESENTATIVE MAJORS AND RELATED CAREER INFORMATION

1. AGRICULTURE

The work done by agricultural scientists has played an important part in making American agriculture the most productive in the world. Agricultural scientists study farm crops and animals and develop ways of improving their quantity and quality. They look for ways to increase yields with less labor, control pests and weeds more effectively, and conserve soil and water. Agricultural science is closely related to biological science in that both involve the study of living organisms; agricultural scientists then apply this knowledge to solving practical problems in agriculture.

A high proportion of all agricultural scientists manage or administer research and development projects or marketing or production operations in companies that produce agricultural chemicals or machinery. Many do research and development. Some spend most of their time in laboratories, but some in research and development spend much of their time working with plants and animals in the field. Some agricultural scientists work as consultants to business firms or to government agencies.

Agricultural scientists usually specialize in one area.

Representative majors: agricultural science, agricultural business, agronomy, animal science, dairy science, food science, forestry, horticultural science, ornamental horticulture, plant science, poultry science, range management, soil science.

Interests: interests in plants and animals. These interests can be satisfied in farming, forestry, fishing, and related fields.

Job requirements: leadership/persuasion, helping/instructing others, problem-solving/creativity, initiative, work as part of a team, frequent public contact, manual dexterity.

Related jobs: agronomist, animal scientist, apiculturist, dairy scientist, entomologist, food scientist, horticulturist, poultry scientist.

Employment: 54,000 agricultural, forest, and conservational scientists work in teaching, research, farm and forest management, service companies, seed companies, wholesale distribution, and food product companies.

Employment outlook: employment opportunities for agricultural, forest, and conservational scientists are expected to be good through the year 2005.

Animal Science

Here you will carry out investigations and experiments on breeding, feeding, management, and diseases of farm and domestic animals to improve their health and yield. Some are animal geneticists, breeders, physiologists, or scientists. You probably will do well in such courses as statistics, genetics, anatomy, entomology, ecology, quantitative analysis, botany, zoology, animal breeding, avian science, livestock evaluation. Animal scientists will find job opportunities with the federal government in the Department of Agriculture. Others will find jobs in colleges and universities doing research and teaching. Some jobs can be found in private industry in the pharmaceutical, chemical, food, and agricultural services industries.

Fish and Game Management

You will analyze fish eggs, larvae, fish parasites, and diseases. You will learn to operate fish cultures facilities, tag and mark fish, detect problems of water pollution, analyze, identify, collect, control, and preserve populations of fur and game animals. You probably will do well in such courses as biological sciences, botany, chemistry, mathematics, physics, zoology, ecology, wildlife management. Many jobs in this field can be found with governmental agencies. Some jobs can be found in private industry providing consultation and research. Others will find positions doing research and teaching in colleges and universities.

Forestry

In this major you will learn to manage, protect, and develop forest lands and their resources for economic and recreational purposes; plan and supervise the cutting and harvesting of timber; carry out forestation and reforestation activities; manage parks and camps. You probably will do well in such courses as forest management, botany, forestry, chemistry, ecology, silviculture, dendrology, surveying, aerial photogrammetry, mathematics, geology. Most foresters find employment with federal or state governmental agencies. Others find jobs in private industry. Many foresters are self-employed, running plant nurseries, or have their own large or small tree and plant farms.

Horticulture

In this field you will be concerned with orchards, garden plants, flowers, ornamental plants, and nursery stock. You will study problems of plant production, processing, and disease resistance. You will study soil and climatic conditions. You probably will do well in such courses as biology, botany, chemistry, ecology, zoology, horticulture, plant pathology, soil chemistry, statistics, landscape and design. Horticulturists may find employment with private horticulture service companies. Others will find employment with federal or state agencies. Many are self-employed, running a nursery or a large or small farm. Some will find positions with colleges or universities doing research and teaching.

Natural Resource Management

Deals with the conservation of our forests, our rangeland, and our wildlife; the management, improvement, and development of these great resources; everything from protecting forests from fires, to preserving wildlife native habitats. You probably will do well in such courses as geology, mineralogy, stratigraphy, geochemistry, mathematics, research methods, environmental science, physical science, range and wildlife management. Private industries, such as engineering, manufacturing, and construction provide jobs for graduates of this field. Governmental agencies and colleges and universities employ workers in research, inspection and teaching.

Poultry Science

In this area you will specialize in research, production, management, feeding, and processing of poultry. You will be concerned with egg production, fryer operations, breeder flock management, and hatcheries as well as feeding programs and marketing. You probably will do well in such courses as statistics, genetics, comparative anatomy, entomology, ecology, quantitative analysis, botany, zoology, avian science, mathematics, chemistry, research methods. Most jobs for poultry scientists are found in universities doing research and teaching. Others will find employment with private industries and governmental agencies.

Range Management

Here you will study agronomy, animal science, soil science, botany, geology, and engineering. You will learn about water-shed development and timber production as well as setting up recreational areas and support systems for wildlife. You probably will do well in such courses as range management, biological sciences, chemistry, physics, plant sciences, soil science, animal science, wildlife management, ecology, conservation, geology. Most range managers are employed by private ranch and farm owners. Others are employed by federal and state governmental agencies.

Soil Science

Study the physical, chemical, biological characteristics, and behavior of soils, investigate soils both in the field and in the lab, classify soils in terms of their capability of producing crops, grasses, and trees, make land appraisals. You probably will do well in such courses as biological sciences, chemistry, hydrology, physics, mathematics, geology, environmental science, ecology, soil conservation. Most soil scientists are employed by the federal government. Others find positions with colleges and universities doing research and teaching. Others are employed by private consultation firms providing technical assistance to farmers, ranchers, and others concerned with the conservation of soil, water, and related natural resources.

2. BIOLOGICAL SCIENCE

The biological sciences are concerned with the world of living things—men and microbes, wild and domestic animals, plants and insects, birds and fish. Some scientists in this field conduct research to expand our knowledge about living organisms; others teach in colleges and universities and also conduct research. Still others apply biological knowledge to the solution of practical problems, such as the development of new drugs and vaccines or new strains of plants. Among professional workers in applied fields are agriculturists, conservationists, foresters, and soil scientists.

Biological scientists, who may also be called life scientists, study the structure of living organisms, their life processes and evolutionary development.

Biological scientists may be classified into three broad groups characterized by the type of organism with which they work: botanists study plants, microbiologists work with microorganisms, and zoologists are concerned with animals. Some biological scientists whose work cuts across more than one of these major groupings, as is frequently the case with college teachers, may simply call themselves biologists.

Representative majors: biochemistry, biology, biophysics, biotechnology, cell biology, microbiology, molecular biology, bacteriology, botany, mycology, plant genetics, plant pathology, plant pharmacology, plant physiology, enfomology, genetics, pathology, pharmacology, physiology, zoology.

Interests: interests in plants and animals. These interests may be satisfied by doing research and conducting experiments to find out more about plants, animals, and other living things, or conducting research to improve medicine, health, and living conditions for human beings.

Job requirements: problem-solving/creativity, initiative.

Related jobs: aquatic biologist, biochemist, biologist, biophysicist, botanist, cytologist, geneticist, microbiologist, nematologist, physiologist, plant pathologist, zoologist.

Employment: 101,000 biological scientists work in teaching, research and development, management consulting, business and government, and sales and service.

Employment outlook: employment of biological scientists

is expected to increase faster than the average through the year 2005.

Biochemistry

Learn how chemical substances enter into or are created in living things; how drugs, foods, hormones, serums, and other substances can influence organisms. You will perform tests to identify, classify, and analyze various chemical reactions. You probably will enjoy courses in chemistry, quantitative analysis, statistics, biology, botany, computer science, foreign language, physics, mathematics, nutrition. About one half of biochemists are employed in colleges and universities doing research and teaching. Others work for the federal government. Many work for the Department of Agriculture, the National Institutes of Health, and the Defense Department. Many positions are available in private industry, mostly in the pharmaceutical, chemical, food, and agricultural services industries.

Biology

You will study the structure of living organisms, their life processes and evolutionary development and the relation between these organisms and their environment. You may specialize in research centering on plants, animals, or human organisms. You probably will enjoy courses in biological science, chemistry, physics, mathematics, zoology, anatomy, botany, microbiology, biometrics, computer science. Job opportunities are available in high schools, colleges, and universities. Employment opportunities can be found with governmental agencies. Many find jobs with the Department of Agriculture, the National Institutes of Health, the Department of Interior. Others find employment in private industry.

Cell and Molecular Biology

This is a challenging study of what cells are, how they are put together, what makes them work, what makes them differ from each other, how they associate and interact, what goes wrong in disease states, and eventually, how you can intervene in these processes in a beneficial way. You probably will enjoy courses in chemistry, physics, mathematics, biology, molecular biology, virology, cytology, genetics, biophysics, physiology, microbiology, immunology. Most molecular biologists are hired as lab technicians or research associates in universities, medical schools, or governmental research labs. Some are employed in large pharmaceutical companies, others operate privately as genetic counselors or teachers.

Ecology

This major is concerned with the interrelationships of organisms and their environments; encompasses many kinds of science. You will study the effect of environmental influences such as rainfall, temperature, altitude, and pollution on the survival of man. You probably will enjoy courses in ecology, biological sciences, chemistry, physics, mathematics, statistics, environmental studies, geology, computer science, public health. Ecologists will find job opportunities with federal and state governmental agencies. Most will find jobs with the Department of Agriculture. Many will find positions with colleges and universities doing research and teaching.

Genetics

Primarily concerned with the nature, transmission, and transplant of genes from one organism to another. You will study their effects on everything from the manufacture of hormones, proteins, and enzymes to curing hereditary diseases. You probably will enjoy courses in genetics, statistics, anatomy, entomology, ecology, quantitative analysis, botany, zoology, animal breeding, computer science, biological sciences. Geneticists may find jobs doing research and conducting experiments to find out more about plants, animals, and other living things for manufacturing plants, governmental agencies, universities, and hospitals.

Marine Biology

Here you will analyze and study plants, fish, and animal species living in the oceanic environment; search for new foods and drugs from the ocean. You will study the life cycles, ecologies, and migration of fish; experiment with underwater farms. You probably will enjoy courses in biology, quantitative analysis, statistics, botany, zoology, computer science, physics, underwater photography. Job opportunities may be found in manufacturing plants, governmental agencies, universities, and production industries doing research and conducting experiments to improve the quality of plants and animals living in water.

Microbiology

You will concentrate on microorganisms, bacteria, yeasts, fungi, protozoa, and one-celled algae; also the application of these organisms in the production of wine, beer, bread, and cheese, as well as antibiotics and industrial chemicals. Many work in clinical laboratories in medical research. You probably will enjoy courses in quantitative analysis, statistics, biology, botany, marine science, computer science, ecology, nutrition. Most microbiologists find employment positions with colleges and universities doing research and teaching. Some find employment with federal and state government agencies. Others work in private industry mostly in pharmaceutical, chemical, food, and agricultural service industries.

Physiology

In this major you will learn about cells, tissues, and organisms and the effects of environmental factors on life processes; as well as growth, respiration, excretion, reproduction, and other functions of plants and animals; what happens and why. You probably will enjoy courses in quantitative analysis, statistics, biology, botany, marine science, computer science, genetics, zoology, anatomy, physics. Most physiologists may find job positions with colleges and universities doing research and teaching. Some will find opportunities with federal and state government agencies. Others will find jobs in private industry mostly in nonprofit research organizations and foundations.

Zoology

The study encompasses the identification, description, and classification of animals, fish, reptiles, insects, protozoa, and so on; also the life histories, habits, diseases, life processes, and distribution of these species within the environment. You probably will do well in such courses as anatomy, chemistry, embryology, microbiology, zoology, genetics, animal systemics, marine biology, entomology, ornithology, ichthyology. Most job openings may be found with federal and state government agencies. Other opportunities may be found in private industry or nonprofit research organizations and foundations.

3. BUSINESS

Executives, administrators, managers, and their support staff are found in every organization. They establish goals, direct operations, and control major activities of their organizations. As a group, these workers are older, more experienced, more highly trained, and, consequently more highly paid than most other workers. The proportion of these workers with four or more years of college is more than twice that of the total work force; and on the average their salaries are more than 50 percent higher than that of the total work force.

Executives, administrators, and managers must rapidly assess large amounts of information prepared by their support staff. For example, the chief executive officer may base a policy decision upon economic reports developed by budget specialists. Financial managers analyze data meticulously summarized by accountants. Personnel managers monitor information on staffing patterns compiled by personnel specialists. Marketing and sales executives develop strategies to market their firms' products based upon information furnished by buyers.

Representative majors: accounting, banking and finance, business economics, hotel and restaurant management, international business management, marketing, personnel management.

Interests: interest in organized activities and attention to details. These interests may be satisfied in a variety of jobs in business operations. Interests may be satisfied in the fields of business administration, computer science, financial services, office management, or personnel supervision.

Job requirements: leadership/persuasion, helping/instructing others, problem-solving/creativity, initiative, work as part of a team, frequent public contact.

Related jobs: financial institution manager, personnel/labor relations manager, purchasing manager, account executive, advertising manager, marketing manager, department manager, office manager, education administrator, health services manager, property manager, restaurant/food service manager, government legislator, general manager underwriter, accountant, auditor, retail/wholesale buyer.

Employment: 16.1 million business executives, administrators, and management support personnel work in private industry, government agencies, and self-employment.

Employment outlook: employment of business executives, administrators, and management support personnel will be favorable through the year 2005.

Accounting

This major allows you to learn to keep track of expenditures, income, profit and loss, prepare financial reports, and calculate taxes. You may specialize in auditing, taxes, or consulting. Many accountants seek CPA certification after graduation. You probably will enjoy courses in statistical methods, management, accounting, finance, economics, computer science, auditing, taxation, business management, business law. Most accountants are engaged in public accounting as proprietors, partners, or employees of independent accounting firms. Some accountants are self-employed. Others work for the federal, state, or local government agencies, or teach accounting in schools, colleges, and universities.

Actuarial Science

You will learn to calculate the probability of death, illness, disability, retirement, unemployment, and property loss. You will work mainly for insurance or financial institutions. You may want to specialize in health, property, life, or liability insurance, or in pension plans. You probably will do well in such courses as statistics, finance, insurance, accounting, math analysis, differential equations, graph theory, banking. Most actuaries work for life insurance companies. Others work for property and liability companies. Others work for private organizations administering independent pension and welfare plans or for governmental agencies.

Banking and Finance

This is the study of the financial operations and transactions used by banks, other financial institutions, and businesses. The study is related to the fields of real estate, risk management, insurance, international finance, accounting and capital markets. You probably will do well in such courses as finance, business administration, accounting, economics, commercial law, political science, statistics, investment finance, computer science, marketing. The greatest percentage of the graduates in banking and finance will find employment as bank officers in commercial, mutual savings, or federal reserve banks. The remaining will find jobs in establishments, such as credit agencies, savings and loan association, mortgage banking, and agricultural credit agencies.

Business Administration

This study opens the door to many challenges in the world of business. It offers a variety of managerial opportunities in finance and accounting, marketing, information management, operations and production, general management, retailing, and consulting. You probably will enjoy courses in business administration, economics, mathematics, accounting, computer science, marketing, business law, organizational behavior, statistics. The majority of business administration graduates find employment within the manufacturing industries, such as automotive, aerospace, commercial and investment banking, consulting services, retailing, and communications. A smaller percent find jobs in the federal, state, and local government. Some find jobs in private foundations and professional organizations.

Business Economics

This field of study deals with a branch of economics that uses statistical and mathematical models to explain business cycles and the flow of goods and services. You probably will enjoy courses in business, economics, statistics, finance, marketing, business law, mathematics, computer science, business communications. Graduates in this field who are classified as economists will find employment in government agencies. Private industry, manufacturing firms, banks, insurance companies, security and investment companies, economic research firms, and consulting firms offer many job opportunities. Some will find jobs as teachers.

Hotel and Restaurant Management

In this field you will learn to manage the total or partial operation of a hotel or a restaurant; see to it that it is run efficiently and profitably. You will be concerned with personnel, services, supplies, business aspects, decision-making, accounting, and public relations. You probably will enjoy courses in hotel administration, accounting, economics, marketing, computer science, maintenance engineering, food service management, catering, tourism. The largest percentage of graduates will find employment in one of many thousands of hotels, motels, or restaurants throughout the nation in an organizing or reorganizing capacity. Some will find employment in convention or tourist centers.

International Business

For this field you should have an interest in travel or living in a foreign social, cultural, or business environment. Your work could involve the building of offices or plants in foreign countries. You might be sent as a technical specialist abroad to expand the distribution of a product internationally. You probably will enjoy courses in business administration, economics, accounting, business law, computer science, marketing, foreign language, political science, history, tourism. A large percentage of graduates will find employment in banks as an international officer advising customers with financial dealing in foreign trade. Some will find jobs in the international currency exchange. Others will find jobs with governmental agencies or with importing and exporting firms.

Labor Relations

You will learn to deal with various aspects of employer-employee relations, such as wage and salary negotiations, benefits and welfare, affirmative action, grievances, abuses and demands, labor laws, union organizations, and collective bargaining. You probably will do well in such courses as business administration, business law, personnel administration, psychology, sociology, counseling, political science. Most job opportunities will be with private industry, such as manufacturers, banks, insurance companies, airlines, department stores, labor unions, governmental agencies, and many other business concerns. Some will be self-employed, whereas others will find jobs teaching.

Marketing

The purpose of marketing is to increase sales of products or services. Here you will learn to analyze, compile data, research, and, hopefully, affect the purchasing power of the American public. You will learn about advertising and human relations. You probably will do well in such courses as marketing business management, economics, statistics, computer science, advertising, business law, accounting, finance, psychology, consumer relations. Most jobs for marketing research workers are found in manufacturing companies, advertising agencies, and independent research organizations. Many are employed by stores, radio and television firms, and newspapers. Others work for university research centers and governmental agencies.

Transportation Studies

You will study a variety of traffic management services from air and ocean to rail and truck. You will learn about other related fields, such as urban renewal, development of highways and mass transit systems, airports, communication networks, and sewage systems. You probably will do well in such courses as transportation studies, systems analysis, computer science, economics, engineering, drafting, ecology, mathematics, urban planning, marketing. The greatest percentage of jobs will be found in industries involved with moving people and material. Job opportunities can be found with airlines, bus lines, railroads, and trucking companies. A number of jobs can be found with federal, state, and local government agencies.

4. COMMUNICATIONS AND THE ARTS

The art of communications is as old as humanity. Its importance in modern society becomes apparent when you try to imagine the world without radio, television, newspapers, magazines, or books. From the earliest discoveries of papermaking techniques to today's use of computers and satellites that transmit information around the world instantaneously, people have sought ways of recording the events around them and conveying, the information to others. Communication is the process of transmitting information to an audience through a variety of media.

The visual arts occupations include both fine and applied artists. Fine artists create objects of beauty that are appreciated for purely aesthetic reasons. Applied artists create or design objects that are both practical and attractive.

The performing arts include acting, dancing, instrumental music, and singing. These fields have the common goals of entertaining, communicating with, and affecting the emotions of audiences.

Representative majors: advertising, communications, journalism, music, public relations, radio/television, telecommunications, motion picture technology, photographic technology, art conservation, art history, arts management, drawing, fine arts, painting, sculpture, studio art, cinematography, dance, dramatic arts, film arts, jazz, musical theater, visual and performing arts.

Interests: interests in creative expression of feelings or ideas. These interests can be satisfied in several of the creative or performing arts. Interests in communications may be satisfied with jobs on newspapers, in radio and television studios, and in the theater and motion picture industries. Interests in visual arts may be satisfied with jobs for advertising agencies, printing and publishing firms, television and motion picture studios, museums, and restoration laboratories.

Job requirements: persuasion, helping/instructing others, problem-solving/creativity, initiative, work as part of a team, frequent public contact, manual dexterity.

Related jobs: columnist, commentator, writer, playwright, editor, technical writer, lobbyist, public-relations representative, news analyst, announcer, disk jockey, photographer, photojournalist, art director, interior director, illustrator, music director, music composer, music arranger, musician, choreographer.

Employment: 1.5 million work in the communications, art, and entertainment fields.

Employment outlook: employment of workers in the communications and the arts field will have average growth through the year 2005.

Advertising

You will plan and prepare advertisements for newspapers, magazines, radio, TV, billboards, brochures. You may specialize in copywriting, layout, research. You will use creative talents to market a product to prospective clients. You probably will enjoy courses in English, creative writing, technical writing, speech, marketing, economics, public speaking, psychology, statistics, finance, management, sociology, computer science, art. Many workers in advertising are hired by advertising and public relations agencies. Others work for nonprofit organizations and various kinds of businesses. Some are self-employed.

Communications

Communications studies involve the understanding of the role of mass communication in society. You will study the nature, function, content, values, and effects of communication on public policy and opinion, covers the nature of language and communication media. You probably will enjoy courses in English, creative writing, technical writing, speech, marketing, economics, public speaking, psychology, statistics, sociology, foreign language, journalism, research methods, advertising. Many graduates in this field find work with advertising and public relations agencies. Others work for newspapers and radio/television companies. Some work for nonprofit organizations and various kinds of businesses.

Creative Writing

The emphasis here is upon the study and practice of writing as opposed to the traditional English and literature majors. You will learn to communicate experiences and awareness in the special language of fiction, drama, and poetry. You will have to dedicate yourself to developing the craft of creative expression using language as the artistic medium. You probably will do well in such courses as English, American literature, English literature, world literature, humanities, social sciences, short story writing, poetry, playwriting, philosophy, history, psychology. Most creative writers free-lance. That is, they produce articles or books for publication and offer them to publishers, often through an agent. Radio, television, and cinema companies provide employment for a limited number of talented script writers. Newspapers and magazines also employ columnists and feature writers to do creative writing. Perserverance is required of those who hope to earn a living in this field. However, it can be very personally and financially rewarding.

Design

You will learn to design products, articles, and materials in such a way that they are not only functional but visually pleasing; often set styles and fashion trends; usually specialize in one product or activity from industrial design to fashion design. You probably will enjoy courses in fine arts, arts and crafts, sketching, cinematography, photojournalism, painting process, printing process, drafting, rendering, silk screen process, graphics. Employment opportunities are best in wholesale and retail trade—in florist shops, furniture and home furnishing stores, and apparel stores. Others find jobs in manufacturing industries. Some job opportunities may be found with engineering, architectural, and construction firms. Government agencies employ some designers. Others are self-employed.

Dramatic Arts

You should possess such talents as an actor, dancer, or musician that you might contribute to the cultural enrichment and entertainment of our society. You will undergo long, tedious training and emotional strain in a very competitive field. You probably will do well in such courses as acting techniques, technical theater, dramatic literature, drama, speech, oral interpretation, radio and TV operations, pantomime, stagecraft, technical speaking. Full-time jobs are available at local radio and television stations, and in some community, school, and traveling theatrical companies. Artists are employed by motion picture, television, and radio studios, and by stock companies, theaters, and other places where plays or floor shows are presented.

English

This major deals with the linguistic and literary richness of the English language, as well as some of the cultural history of the English speaking world. You may concentrate on specific areas: creative writing, comparative and American literature, or semantics. You probably will enjoy courses in English, communications, literature, comparative literature, foreign language, writing, poetry, drama, semantics. Jobs are available in cities all over the country. Most are found in areas where motion picture and television studios are located or where large publishing companies have their headquarters. Others are found with newspapers and publishing companies. Many creative writers are self-employed. Teaching positions are found in schools, colleges, and universities.

Film Production

You will study the theory and practice of film production and the techniques used in this medium of communications. This major is for students who recognize the cinema to be an independent, powerful, and unique medium in today's world. You will be called upon to do creative work as well as learn the rapidly changing technology aspects. You probably will enjoy courses in history of films, film production, production laboratory, film aesthetics, film writing, humanities, literature, speech, dramatic arts, music, cinematography. Most filmmakers are employed by private cinema companies at movie capitals around the world. Many work for a time to gain experience and then seek the capital investment to go into business for themselves. Television studios employ a large number of camera technicians and directors to produce everything from soap operas to news documentaries.

Fine Arts

You will draw or design your interpretations of objects, people, and nature using a wide variety of substances, from water-colors and oils to stone and metal. Specialization may range from fashion illustrator or graphic artist to cartoonist. You probably will do well in such courses as art history, fine arts, anatomy, polymer chemistry, sculpturing, foundry, mechanical drawing, arts and crafts, design drafting, architectural rendering. Workers in this field may find jobs with advertising agencies, printing and publishing firms, television and motion picture studios, museums, and restoration laboratories. Some artists work for manufacturers in retail and wholesale trade. Others operate their own commercial art studio.

Journalism

This study embraces the writing, editing, managing, and production of newspapers and magazines; involved also are the fields of advertising, public relations, radio, TV, and motion pictures. You will learn to interview people, review records, observe events, and do journalistic research. You probably will enjoy courses in English, philosophy, economics, social sciences, political science, writing, editing, reporting, mass media, photojournalism. Many workers in this field are employed by newspapers, publishing companies, radio and television stations, networks, and news services. Some work for private industry or for the government.

Music

Deals with the art of sound that expresses ideas and emotions; either classical, jazz, or rock. You may set goals to appear as soloist, become a member of a quartet, a symphony, an opera orchestra, or a dance band. Many specialize in certain kinds of musical instruments. You probably will enjoy courses in music, band, orchestra, instrumental ensembles, choir, chorus, drama, voice, radio and television operation, foreign language, opera, arranging, directing techniques, history of music. Full-time work is found at local radio and television stations, nightclubs, restaurants, and public and private schools. Musicians are also employed by community bands and orchestras, and some work for music publishing firms. Music teachers give private lessons or work for schools.

Photography

Deals with the use of cameras and film to portray people, places, and events. This is both an artistic and technical field. You will be involved in everything from taking motion pictures and video/TV to still, portrait, aerial, and commercial photography. You probably will do well in such courses as photography techniques, photochemistry and processing, photojournalism, cinematography. Full-time jobs are found with photographic or commercial art studios. Other employers include newspapers, magazines, radio and television stations, motion picture companies, government agencies, and manufacturing firms. Teaching positions may be found in schools, colleges, and universities.

Radio and Television

Deals with a wide variety of activities concerning the planning, preparation, and production of radio and television programs; for some it is programming, engineering, or sales. You probably will enjoy courses in radio and television operations, audio visual techniques, film editing, speech, voice, grammar, foreign language, technical speaking, public relations. Workers in this field find employment with motion picture, television, and radio studios. Some find jobs teaching in schools, colleges, and universities.

5. COMPUTER AND PHYSICAL SCIENCE

Mathematics and statistics are sciences that, through the use of quantitative techniques, facilitate our understanding and expression of ideas in many kinds of work. Although mathematics, statistics, and computers are used extensively in many occupations, people in the occupations covered in this section use quantitative techniques to a much greater degree than others, and often devise new techniques to solve problems.

Physical scientists investigate the structure and composition of the earth and the universe. Many physical scientists perform research designed to increase basic scientific knowledge. Others employ the results of research to solve practical problems in developing new products, locating new sources of oil, or forecasting the weather.

Representative majors: computer graphics, computer and information sciences, computer mathematics, computer programming, data processing, information sciences and systems, microcomputer software, robotics, systems analysis, analytical chemistry, chemistry, inorganic chemistry, organic chemistry, pharmaceutical chemistry, physical chemistry, actuarial sciences, applied mathematics, mathematics statistics, atomic/molecular physics, electron physics, elementary particle physics, fluids and plasmas, nuclear physics, optics, physics, solid state physics.

Interests: interests in discovering, collecting, and analyzing information about the natural world, and in applying scientific research findings to problems. These interests may be satisfied by investigating, discovering, or testing new theories; by developing new or improved materials or processes for use in production and construction; or doing research in such fields as geology, astronomy, oceanography, and computer science.

Job requirements: leadership/persuasion, helping/instructing others, problem-solving/creativity, initiative, work as part of a team.

Related jobs: systems analyst, information scientist, computer programmer, statistician, actuary, financial analyst, mathematician, astronomer, physicist, chemist, meteorologist, geologist, geophysicist, hydrologist, oceanographer, seismologist, environmental analyst.

Employment: 771,000 computer and physical scientists work in research, teaching, government agencies, and private industry.

Employment outlook: Employment of computer and physical scientists is expected to have average growth through the year 2005.

Astronomy

In this major you will study the sizes, shapes, motion, and all other physical properties of the sun, moon, stars, and planets. You may use your knowledge of astronomy in space exploration and the development of space technology. You probably will do well in such courses as mathematics, physics, chemistry, earth science, computer science, biology, astrophysics, astronomical sciences. Most astronomers find jobs in research programs either with aerospace industries manufacturing spacecrafts, or with commercial spacecraft enterprises. A number are employed by governmental agencies, such as the departments of defense and commerce. Jobs may be found with NASA, observatories, and universities.

Chemistry

A study of the science of physical substances; the study of atoms, molecules, elements, and compounds. You will learn to perform chemical tests and develop new chemical products, monitor the air, food, and drugs for pollutions. There are many subfields to specialize in. You probably will do well in such courses as analytical chemistry, inorganic chemistry, organic chemistry, physical chemistry, mathematics, physics, nuclear science. About two thirds of all chemists work for manufacturing firms. Jobs may be found in federal, state, and local governments, such as the departments of defense, health, and human resources, and agriculture. Jobs may be found in research organizations and as teachers.

Computer Science

Here you will learn to design new computers, computer languages, related devices, and research into new ways to use computers effectively; or become involved in aspects of artificial intelligence from pattern recognition to problem-solving. You probably will enjoy courses in mathematics, accounting, physical science, engineering, computer science, logic, linguistics, statistics. Most computer scientists will find job opportunities with manufacturing firms. Others will find jobs as consultants or as teachers in training and college institutions.

Earth Science

This science touches base with geology, geophysics, geography, meteorology, oceanography, hydrology, and so on; everything from the movement of continents to the eruption of volcanoes and the science of earthquakes. There are many specialties. You probably will enjoy courses in mathematics, physical science, geology, meteorology, environmental science, oceanography, geography. Most earth scientists find jobs in the energy and mining industries. Many find teaching and research jobs in educational institutions. Some find careers with governmental agencies such as the U.S. Geological Survey, National Science Foundation, the departments of interior, agriculture, transportation, and NASA.

Geology

A study of the earth's structure, composition, and history. You will examine rocks, minerals, and fossils, record data, and prepare maps; conduct surveys and advise suitability of sites; living conditions can be primitive and physically trying while on field trips. You probably will enjoy courses in physical science, biological science, mathematics, computer science, geological sciences, hydrology, soil science. Forty percent of the geologists find work in oil and gas companies either in service or exploration. Some work for mining and quarrying companies. Some work as consultants or are self-employed. Governmental agencies offer jobs in the Bureau of Mines, U.S. Geological Survey, Bureau of Reclamation. Jobs as teachers may be offered by universities and colleges.

Information Science

You will learn to design information systems to provide management or clients with specific data from computer storage. You will use electronic data processing, mathematics, and computer sys-terms. You probably will do well in such courses as mathematics, computer science, information science, communications, library systems, English, linguistics. Information scientists are employed by electronic semiconductor firms to design microprocessor programs, computers, computer languages, and related devices. Some are employed to do research work in the field of artificial intelligence. Others work in governmental agencies, colleges, and universities, or are self-employed.

Mathematics

This major allows you to learn to solve both theoretical and practical problems that can be explained in mathematical terms. You will study all aspects of algebra, geometry, advanced mathematics, and computer languages. You probably will do well in such courses as advanced mathematics, probability, theory, statistics, mathematical analysis, computer science, physical science, economics, logistics. Most mathematicians find teaching jobs in high schools, colleges, and universities. The remainder work in high technology industries, such as research and development laboratories, engineering, architectural, and surveying services, business services, communications, aircraft and space, and for governmental agencies.

Meteorology

You will concentrate on the phenomena that take place in the Earth's blanket of air and atmosphere. You will study wind, clouds, temperature patterns, and precipitation. The primary concern is to understand and predict weather conditions on Earth and in space. You probably will do well in such courses as meteorology, physics, mathematics, chemistry, computer science, astronomy, geology, geography. Most meteorologists are employed by the National Weather Service. Others find employment working for a public or private television or radio station as a weather forecaster. Some private industries recognize the value of having their own weather meteorological services.

Oceanography

You will use the principles and techniques of natural science, engineering, and mathematics to study oceans, their movements, physical properties, and plant and marine life. You will use your knowledge to develop improved technologies to utilize the vast resources of oceans. You probably will do well in such courses as physics, chemistry, biological science, mathematics, geology, life support and diving technology, photography, engineering. About one half of oceanographers find employment with colleges and universities as teachers and researchers. One fourth find jobs in private industry dealing with research and underwater projects. Others find jobs in governmental agencies.

Physics

Here you will deal with problems relating to matter and energy or the basic laws of nature. You will study everything from the nature and behavior of atoms and their components and relativity theories to light in space. You probably will do well in such courses as physics, chemistry, mathematics, astronomy, mechanics, electromagnetism, electronics, optics, thermodynamics, atomic and molecular physics. Private industry employs about two thirds of all the nonacademic physicists in companies manufacturing electrical equipment, aircraft, and missiles, chemicals, and scientific equipment. A large percentage find positions in universities doing research and teaching. Others find jobs in hospitals and commercial research laboratories.

Systems Analysis

In this field you will learn to devise computerized systems to meet the needs of clients. The system may be in business, science, engineering, or medicine. Computer programming knowledge is essential. You probably will do well in such courses as computer science, mathematics, accounting, business management, physical science, engineering, informational science, statistics. Most systems analysts work for industries that manufacture durable computer goods, governmental agencies, banks, insurance, and data processing service. Some find jobs in research and teaching.

6. EDUCATION

Teaching and counseling are people-oriented fields that involve helping others learn, acquire information, or gain insight into themselves. These professionals usually require a bachelor's degree, although some require a master's or doctoral degree.

Teaching is one of the largest occupations in the United States. By 2005 kindergarten and elementary school teachers will hold about 2.2 million jobs, secondary school teachers will hold 1.7 million, and college and university teachers will hold about 800,000. Many others hold jobs as teachers in preschool programs and nursery schools; in public and private vocational education programs; in dance, music, and art studios; as librarians, counselors, and advisers.

Representative majors: adult education research, curriculum and instruction, education, educational statistics, educational testing, higher education research, comparative education, school psychology, social foundations, student counseling, administration of special education, adult education administration, community college education administration, elementary education, junior high education, early childhood education, secondary education, teacher's aide, teacher education in specific subjects.

Interests: interests in leading and influencing others. These interests may be satisfied by helping others to learn by doing general and specialized teaching; by teaching the skills for a specific trade, or by providing educational and career development counseling services.

Job requirements: leadership/persuasion, helping/instructing others, problem-solving/creativity, initiative, work as part of a team, frequent public contact, physical stamina.

Related jobs: preschool teacher, elementary teacher, secondary school teacher, special education teacher, vocational education teacher, adult education teacher, sports and physical training instructors, college/university faculty member, educational counselor, vocational counselor, educational administrator.

Employment: 5.7 million educators work in teaching, counseling, and library and informational services in public and private educational settings.

Employment outlook: employment of teachers and educational specialists is expected to grow faster than average through the year 2005.

Art Education

You will learn to instruct pupils in art, such as sketching, painting, designing, and sculpturing, or in an applied field: ceramics, weaving, textile design, jewelry making, and such. You will observe pupils work to make criticism and corrections; plan exhibits and art shows. You probably will enjoy courses in art history, fine arts, anatomy, commercial art, craft arts, educational psychology, sociology, adolescent behavior, teaching methods, survey of architecture. Most job opportunities are found in schools, colleges, and universities. Some jobs may be found in the area of health and recreation. Other employment opportunities are found in manufacturing and wholesale trades.

Developmental Psychology

You will concentrate on the developmental approach to human behavior to prepare yourself for graduate programs in basic research and the teaching of psychology or you may wish to enter a counseling field in education or social work. This is the undergraduate major that many educational psychologists take. A closely related major is child development. You probably will enjoy courses in psychology, behavioral sciences, social sciences, statistics, adolescent psychology, child psychology, theories of personality, abnormal psychology, psycholinguistics, English, biological sciences. Most developmental psychologists work in the field of education in public schools and colleges either as teachers or as counseling psychologists. Some are self-employed and work as consultants, especially in the field of special education.

Early Childhood Education

You will learn to teach preschool students through art, music, play, poetry, and stories to prepare for learning language, science, numbers, and social studies. You will design programs to develop students mental capacities, learning abilities and emotional growth. You probably will do well in such courses as child development, sociology, anthropology, speech, special education, teaching methods, education psychology, nonacademic tutoring, school health. Most job opportunities are found in private preschools and nurseries. Other teaching positions are found in public and private elementary schools. Some day-care and nursery jobs may be found with large business and industrial firms.

Elementary Education

You will learn to teach pupils the basic academic, social, and manipulative skills; you will also develop in students good study and work habits, as well as an appreciation for learning. You will learn to prepare lesson plans, tests, records, and reports, and how to confer with parents. You probably will enjoy courses in public speaking, educational psychology, child development, reading, mathematics, social studies, science, art, music, teaching methods, school health. Teaching positions are found in preschool and elementary schools. Other job opportunities are found in colleges and universities that train teachers.

Foreign Language

You will learn to teach students and adults to speak and translate a foreign language competently; to prepare them for the growing need for linguists. You may become a translator, journalist, research worker, diplomat, flight attendant, teacher, or a foreign travel consultant. You probably will do well in such subjects as foreign language, literature, area studies, history, writing, classics, public speaking, educational psychology, teaching methods, philology. Most job openings may be found in public schools and colleges. Some positions may be found in private schools. Some job opportunities may be found in government agencies. A few positions may be found in business.

Guidance

You will learn to help students develop in one or more areas of guidance: academic, social, personal, or career development. Your goal will be to assist students to achieve satisfying and satisfactory life adjustments to their problems. You will also work with parents and authorities. You probably will do well in such courses as psychology, sociology, biology, computer science, counseling techniques, statistics, education, tests and measurements—mental health, community relations, courses in drug and child abuse. Most counselors are employed by public and private schools, colleges, and universities. Other job opportunities may be found with state and local rehabilitation agencies. Veterans Administration rehabilitation programs, and V.A. hospitals. Others work for public and private community mental health and social service agencies and organizations.

Health Education

You will learn to implement strategies related to individual and community health education topics for children and adults. Emphasis is placed on specific health problems of the age group and how the educator can promote good health practices. You probably will enjoy courses in health, first aid procedures, psychology, sociology, anthropology, teaching methods, public health administration, child care, nutrition, drug use and abuse. Most of the workers in this field are hired by government institutions. Some work for schools. Others work for recreational agencies and nonprofit organizations. A few work in businesses.

Music Education

You will learn to teach private, group, or classroom instrumental music or singing lessons. You will learn to organize musicians into bands or orchestras. You may specialize in classical or popular. With an exceptional degree of talent, you may want to perform professionally, as well as teach. You probably will enjoy courses in band, instrumental ensembles, choir, chorus, drama, voice, composition, arranging, foreign language, educational psychology, sociology, teaching methods, history of music. Most musicians work in cities in which entertainment and recording activities are concentrated. Jobs are found with symphony groups, orchestras, churches, clubs, and restaurants. Teaching positions are found in schools, colleges, and universities.

Physical Education

Here you will learn to teach and supervise individual and team sports. You will demonstrate sports techniques, analyze physical capabilities and needs of students, and administer corrective exercises and physical conditioning. A major goal is to provide students with activities to maximize physical fitness. You probably will do well in such courses as sport skills, coaching methods, officiating, teaching methods, psychomotor learning, kinesiology, physiology of exercise, sport rules and regulations, tests and measurements, school health. Most jobs in this field are found in public and private schools, colleges, and universities. Other positions may be found with state and local recreational agencies. Some opportunities may be found in business or in private recreational facilities, such as ski resorts, tennis courts, and gymnasiums.

Secondary Education

You will learn to teach one or more high school subjects using various teaching methods. You will develop and plan teaching materials and assignments and learn to construct tests. You may teach science, math, social studies, English, music, art, physical education, or other subjects. You probably will do well in such courses as specialized subject matter, speech, educational psychology, child development, philosophy, sociology, anthropology, adolescent behavior, teaching methodologies. Most secondary school teachers are employed in public schools. Others are employed in private schools.

Special Education

You will prepare to work with handicapped children and adults in a variety of settings. You will learn to coordinate the services available to handicapped persons and provide appropriate educational experiences for the deaf, blind, aphasic, physically disabled. You probably will do well in such courses as psychology, philosophy, adolescent behavior, child development, educational methods, speech, nonacademic tutoring, assessment and teaching of educationally handicapped, resources and materials. Employment opportunities are found in public and private schools, colleges, and universities.

7. ENGINEERING AND ENVIRONMENTAL DESIGN

Engineers, surveyors, and architects do planning and design. Engineers design machines, processes, systems, and structures. Surveyors measure and lay out land and building boundaries. Architects design buildings and other structures, as well as outdoor areas.

Architects, engineers, and surveyors often work together on building projects. Architects design the building, concentrating on the visual appearance as well as the needs of owners and occupants; engineers design the building's mechanical, heating, and electric systems; and surveyors lay out the building boundaries and the boundaries of the land it occupies.

Engineers apply scientific and mathematical theories and principles to solve practical technical problems. Most work in one of the more than 25 specialties recognized by professional societies. Electrical, mechanical, civil, industrial, chemical, and aerospace engineering are the largest. Although many engineers work in design and development, others work in testing, production, operations, and maintenance.

Representative majors: architecture, aerospace engineering, agricultural engineering, architectural engineering, biomedical engineering, ceramic engineering, chemical engineering, civil engineering, computer engineering, electrical/electronics engineering, environmental engineering, geological engineering, industrial engineering, materials engineering, mechanical engineering, metallurgical engineering, mining engineering, nuclear engineering, petroleum engineering, surveying and mapping sciences, textile engineering.

Interests: interests in applying mechanical principles to practical situations by use of machines or tools. These interests can be satisfied by planning, designing, and directing the development and construction of buildings, bridges, roads, airports, dams, sewage systems, air conditioning systems, mining machinery, and other structures and equipment.

Job requirements: problem-solving/creativity, initiative, work as part of a team, manual dexterity.

Related jobs: architect, marine architect, landscape architect, surveyor, aeronautical engineer, ceramic engineer, civil engineer, marine engineer, metallurgical engineer, mining engineer, petroleum engineer, chemical engineer, nuclear engineer, waste management engineer, computer engineer, electrical engineer, electronics engineer, industrial engineer, mechanical engineer, design engineer, safety engineer.

Employment: 1.8 million architects, engineers, and surveyors provide developing, managing, and consulting services to business and industrial firms.

Employment outlook: employment of workers in engineering and related fields is expected to grow faster than average through the year 2005.

Aeronautical Engineering

In this field you will study the physics of propulsion, fluid mechanics, and aerodynamic structures, and flight and space mechanics. You will learn to design, test, and build aircraft, spacecraft, satellites, missiles, and jet and rocket engines. You probably will do well in such courses as higher mathematics, physics, biological science, computer science, general engineering, drafting, aerodynamics, aerothermochemistry. Most are employed in the aircraft and aircraft parts industry. Some work for federal government agencies, primarily for NASA and the Department of Defense. A few work for the commercial airlines, consulting firms, and for colleges and universities.

Architecture

You will learn to plan, design, and supervise the construction of buildings, houses, factories, skyscrapers, schools, and other structures. You will learn to make them attractive, usable, energy efficient, and economical. Eventually you must qualify for state license after graduation. You probably will do well in such courses as architectural theory, design, graphics, computer science, general engineering, urban planning, mathematics, physics, economics, history of art. Most architects work for architectural firms. The remainder work directly for builders, real estate developers, or large construction projects as well as government agencies responsible for housing and community planning, such as the departments of defense, interior, and housing and urban development.

Chemical Engineering

In this major you will learn to turn chemicals into products through research and development and devise economical and efficient production processes. You will learn to work in a number of fields: cosmetics, fertilizers, paints, dyes, pesticides, oil refining, pollution prevention, and others. You probably will do well in such courses as chemistry, physics, mathematics, computer science, general engineering, electrochemical processes, nuclear science. The greatest percent of the chemical engineers work for manufacturing industries, primarily in chemical, petroleum refining, and related industries. About one out of six work for engineering service or consulting firms and the balance work for government agencies.

Civil Engineering

This major teaches you to design and construct buildings, roads and highways, railroads, airports, tunnels and bridges, and sewage systems. Your studies will embrace soil mechanics, hydraulics, and structural engineering. You probably will do well in such courses as mathematics, physics, chemistry, general engineering, computer science, surveying, hydrology, soil mechanics. Most civil engineers work in federal, state, and local government agencies. A number work for firms that provide engineering, design, and architectural consulting services. The remainder work for one of a number of industries as well as public utility and railroad companies.

Computer Engineering

You will learn the fundamentals of electrical and electronic engineering with an emphasis on computer technology. You might major in a specialized branch, such as software engineering, computer design, systems design. You probably will do well in such courses as electronic circuits, data communication, computer structure and language, digital systems, higher mathematics, physics, control systems, solid state electronics, signal processing. Most jobs are in firms that manufacture and develop computers and ancillary hardware. Those who specialize in software will find employment in a growing number of firms that manufacture software. There is a great opportunity in this field to consult, or to start up a new business. Most engineers work in very specialized geographic areas where the electronics and computer industries have concentrated.

Electrical Engineering

This is the largest and fastest growing branch of engineering. It is a diverse field best described by the breadth of the technical societies within the field. Everything from communications and computers, nuclear and plasma science to ultrasonics can be included in the curriculum. You probably will do well in such courses as mathematics, physics, chemistry, general engineering, computer science, power and energy, systems engineering, bioelectronics. Most jobs are in firms that manufacture electrical and electronic equipment, business machines, communications equipment, scientific equipment, and aircraft equipment. Most of the remaining jobs are found in consulting firms, public utility companies, and government agencies.

Engineering Technology

The training is usually more limited in scope than that of general engineering; emphasis is more practical, whereas general engineering is more theoretical. Many serve as direct supporting personnel to engineers and scientists. You probably will do well in such courses as mathematics, physics, chemistry, computer science, engineering analysis, dynamic systems analysis, drafting. The greatest percent of the engineering technicians work in private industry, primarily in the manufacturing sector. Most jobs can be found in electrical or electronic equipment, machinery, and professional and scientific equipment industries. The balance work in a number of different areas, such as wholesale trades, public utilities, and for federal, state, and local government agencies.

General Engineering

You will study the principles of engineering, taking all core courses required of professional engineers. You may have an opportunity to design your major to meet specific career goals in engineering. You probably will do well in such courses as mathematics, physics, chemistry, computer science, energy and power, solar energy, environmental engineering. Most engineers work for manufacturing industries, such as chemical, electrical, and electronic equipment, aircraft, machinery, scientific instruments, and motor vehicle industries. A smaller percent work for federal, state, and local governments. The remainder hold faculty positions in colleges and universities.

Industrial Engineering

Here you will learn to coordinate people, machines, and materials; plan the layout of factories for efficiency, and engage in time, motion, and incentive studies. You will be involved in safety studies, cost and quality control measures, and long-range planning goals. You probably will do well in such courses as mathematics, physics, chemistry, computer science, human engineering, construction and mechanical engineering, operation research. Three out of four jobs are in manufacturing industries. Because of their skills, mechanical engineers can be found in almost any type of organization and are more widely distributed in industry than other engineers. As an example, some work for banks, hospitals, insurance companies, retail organizations, and consulting firms.

Mechanical Engineering

You will be primarily concerned with mechanical devices; everything from can openers to rocket fuel pumps and nuclear reactors. You will learn about heat, machines, and power. Many engineers specialize in various industries: auto, textile, marine, petroleum. You probably will do well in such courses as mathematics, physics, chemistry, computer science, design, manufacturing processes, thermodynamics, fluid mechanics. Three out of five jobs are in manufacturing. Most jobs are in the machinery, transportation equipment, electrical equipment, and fabricated metals industries. Business and engineering consulting services and governmental agencies provide most of the remaining jobs.

Metallurgical Engineering

You will learn about ores, the extraction of metals from them, and the refining, fabricating, alloying, casting, and the heat treatment of metals. You will also learn to design and operate fabricating plants. You probably will do well in such courses as mathematics, physics, chemistry, computer science, general engineering, thermodynamics, physical metallurgy, metallography, chemical metallurgy. Most metallurgical engineers work in one of the three main branches of metallurgy—extractive or chemical, physical, and mechanical or process. The metal producing industries provide over one fourth of all jobs. Some work in industries that manufacture machinery, aircraft and parts, and electrical equipment. Others work in engineering consulting firms and government agencies.

Nuclear Engineering

This is a field of study emphasizing the use of mathematics and science in the research, design, development, testing, and modification of nuclear energy systems and nuclear power plants. You probably will do well in such courses as mathematics, physics, chemistry, computer science, nuclear engineering, nuclear reactor theory, nuclear materials, neutron scattering theory. About 40 percent of the nuclear engineers work for the federal government, such as the navy department and the Nuclear Regulatory Commission. Other engineers work for the Department of Energy, public utilities, or as consultants. Some work for manufacturers of nuclear power equipment.

Petroleum Engineering

You will learn about the exploration and drilling for fossil fuel both on land and sea, and how to maximize the recovery of oil and gas through engineering processes. Many engineers are involved in looking for new sources of energy, such as geothermal and shale. You probably will do well in such courses as geology, recovery methods, reservoir engineering, stratigraphy and sedimentation, well logging, chemistry, physics, computer science, energy resource engineering. Most jobs are found with major oil companies and hundreds of smaller independent oil exploration, production, and service companies. A number of petroleum engineers work for engineering consulting firms, government agencies, and equipment suppliers. A few work as independent consultants.

8. HEALTH PROFESSIONS

Health practitioners diagnose, treat, and strive to prevent illness and disease. Although all of them practice the art of healing, they differ in methods of treatment and areas of specialization.

Training to become a health practitioner is much more rigorous than training for most other professional occupations, but practice also offers unusual rewards. Incomes of health practitioners greatly exceed the average and generally are higher than those of other professional workers with similar years of graduate education. Furthermore, health practitioners enjoy great prestige within the community, and most derive considerable satisfaction from knowing that their work contributes directly to the well-being of others.

All health practitioners must have the ability and perseverance to complete the years of study required.

They should be emotionally stable, able to make decisions in emergencies, and have a strong desire to help the sick and injured. Sincerity and an ability to gain the confidence of patients also are important qualities.

Representative majors: basic clinical health science, chiropractic, dental specialties, emergency/disaster science, gerontology, health care administration, health sciences, medical laboratory, medical records administration, nurse anesthetist, nursing, optometry, pharmacy, podiatry, family planning, predentistry, premedicine, prepharmacy, preveterinary, public health laboratory science, speech pathology, sports medicine, dental assistant, dental hygiene, geriatric aide, medical assistant, ophthalmic services, practical nursing, veterinarian's assistant.

Interests: interests in discovering, collecting, and analyzing information. These interests may be satisfied in applying scientific research findings to problems in medicine, examining teeth and treating dental problems, planning and carrying out medical care programs, diagnosing illness in animals, giving medical treatment to people, examining eyes and prescribing corrective procedures, or performing surgery to repair injuries or to remove diseased organs.

Job requirements: leadership/persuasion, helping/instructing others, problem-solving/creativity, initiative, work as a part of a team, frequent public contact, manual dexterity.

Related jobs: pathologist, anesthesiologist, cardiologist, dermatologist, gynecologist, internist, neurologist, obstetrician, ophthalmologist, pediatrician, physician, radiologist, surgeon, urologist, allergist, dentist, endodontist, optometrist, podiatrist, chiropractor, veterinarian, respiratory therapist, occupational therapist, audiologist, registered nurse, licensed practical nurse, physician assistant, optician, pharmacist, dietitian, dental hygienist.

Employment: 3.2 million health professionals work in hospitals, clinics, health facilities, industrial plants, and governmental agencies.

Employment outlook: employment opportunities are expected to grow much faster than average through the year 2005.

Dentistry

A field of study dealing with the prevention and treatment of diseases and malformations of the teeth and gums. You probably will do well in such courses as anatomy, physiology, biochemistry, microbiology, toxicology, genetics, pharmacology, chemistry, physics, nutrition, calculus, clinical pathology, dental sciences. Nine out of ten dentists are in private practice. Of the remainder, about half do research, teach, or hold positions in dental schools. Some work in hospitals and clinics.

Dietetics

You will learn to plan and supervise the preparation of nutritious meals to help people maintain or recover good health; plan menus and modify diets for special medical patients; manage personnel and budgets; advise patients on nutrition. You probably will do well in such courses as biology, organic chemistry, human physiology, nutrition, diet and therapy, bacteriology, public speaking, technical writing, food management, statistics, food science. Health care facilities, including hospitals, nursing homes, and clinics, are the major source of jobs in this field. Business firms that provide food services for hospital patients on a contract basis employ a small but growing number of dietitians and nutritionists. Others find jobs in schools, colleges, universities, prisons, and hotel and restaurant chains.

Hospital Administration

You will learn to direct the many activities of a hospital and coordinate the administrative duties with medical services; supervise personnel, budget preparation, accounting procedures, supplies, space needs, staffing, and the policies of the hospital. You probably will enjoy courses in health management, personnel management, gerontology, environmental health and safety, biology, psychology, business administration, computer science, accounting. Almost half of all jobs are in hospitals. Other health services managers find jobs in offices of physicians, nursing homes, offices of dentists, outpatient care facilities, and medical and dental laboratories.

Medical Technology

You will learn to perform complicated chemical, microscopic, and bacteriological tests to provide data for use in treatment and diagnosis of diseases; examine body fluids, make cultures or tissue samples, and check blood samples. You probably will do well in such courses as life science, chemistry, biology, mathematics, computer science, report writing, hematology, microserology, immunology. Most medical technologists and technicians find jobs in hospitals. Others work in independent laboratories, physician's offices, clinics, public health agencies, pharmaceutical firms, and research institutions.

Medicine

You will learn to diagnose and treat people who are ill or in poor health. You will be concerned with the prevention of disease and the rehabilitation of the injured or ill. You may specialize in one of over 30 fields. You probably will do well in such courses as anatomy, physiology, biochemistry, microbiology, toxicology, genetics, pharmacology, chemistry, physics, nutrition, calculus, clinical pathology, physiology, public health. About half of all physicians are in office-based practice. About one fourth of all physicians are residents or full-time staff members in hospitals. Others find a practice in clinics, urgent care centers, birthing centers, schools, and prisons.

Nursing

In nursing you will learn to give direct nursing care to patients or supervise others who offer care to patients, administer medications and treatments prescribed by the doctors, observe and record symptoms and behaviors of the patients, promote good health. You probably will do well in such courses as nursing (basic, medical-surgical, obstetrics, pediatrics, geriatrics, clinical practice), chemistry, nutrition, physiology, anatomy, psychology, pharmacology. Most nurses find employment in hospitals. Others find jobs in offices of physicians, governmental agencies, nursing and personal care facilities, educational services, personnel supply services, health and allied services, and outpatient care facilities.

Occupational Therapy

You will learn to determine the educational, recreational, vocational, and other activities needed to hasten a patient's recovery. You may also have to design special equipment to do certain tasks, to use artificial limbs, or to regain the use of muscles. You probably will enjoy courses in anatomy, chemistry, physiology, nutrition, biology, neurology, pathology, therapeutic exercises, physics, psychology, arts and crafts. The largest number of jobs are in hospitals, including a substantial number in rehabilitation and psychiatric hospitals. A large number of job opportunities are in school systems and schools for handicapped children. Other job opportunities are found in nursing homes, home health agencies, community mental health centers, adult day-care programs, outpatient clinics, and residential care facilities.

Optometry

You will learn to examine eyes to determine visual efficiency and performance, diseases or other abnormalities, use various instruments and prescribe corrective procedures; some treatments call for glasses, special lenses, vision therapy, or visual training. You probably will do well in such courses as calculus, statistics, geometrical optics, microbiology, ocular anatomy and pathology, neurophysiology, physics, biochemistry. The majority of optometrists are in private practice. Others seek partnership or group practices. Others find salaried jobs with health maintenance organizations and other types of health care clinics. Others work for the Veterans Administration, public and private health agencies, and insurance companies.

Pharmacy

This study emphasizes the science of drugs—their composition, chemical, and physical properties. You must understand the effects of drugs and test for purity and strength. You probably will do well in such courses as organic chemistry, quantitative analysis, calculus, biology, pharmacology, anatomy, physics, microbiology, biochemistry. Most pharmacists practice in community pharmacies independently owned or part of a chain. About one fifth of all pharmacists own their own businesses. Others find jobs in hospitals, pharmaceutical manufacturing companies, wholesaling companies, and government and educational institutions.

Physical Therapy

Physical therapists assist and help persons with muscle/nerve/joint problems, or with burns, bone diseases, or injuries to overcome their disabilities. Following doctors' orders you will use exercise, mechanical equipment, or application of massage/heat/light. You probably will do well in such courses as anatomy, physiology, neuroanatomy, neurophysiology, biomechanics of motion, human growth and development, disease and trauma, therapeutics procedures, and athletic injuries. Hospitals are the largest employer of physical therapists. Other jobs in this field are in rehabilitation facilities, home health agencies, and nursing homes. Other therapists work in residential facilities for handicapped children, school systems, clinics, health maintenance organizations, and physicians' offices.

Public Health

In this field you will learn to plan, organize, and direct health education programs for group and community needs. Sanitation, the prevention of communicable diseases, and how to accomplish it, will be emphasized. You probably will do well in such courses as anatomy, physiology, biochemistry, microbiology, toxicology, genetics, pharmacology, chemistry, physics, nutrition, calculus, clinical pathology, biomedical and environmental health. Many jobs in this field are with federal, state, and local government. Other positions are found with private industrial firms that deal with public sanitation, health, and safety.

Veterinary Medicine

You will learn to diagnose and treat diseases and disorders of animals. You will also give advice on the care and breeding of animals, poultry, and birds. You will learn to perform surgery or prescribe and administer drugs. There are only 18 schools with very demanding admission standards. You probably will do well in such courses as anatomy, physiology, biochemistry, microbiology, toxicology, genetics, pharmacology, chemistry, physics, nutrition, calculus, clinical pathology, zoology. Most veterinarians are in private practice. The federal government employs veterinarians in the Department of Agriculture. Other employers of veterinarians are state and local governments, international health agencies, colleges, research laboratories, and pharmaceutical companies.

9. SOCIAL SCIENCE

Many of the workers described in this section are concerned with the social needs of people. For example, clinical psychologists help the mentally or emotionally disturbed adjust to life through behavior modification programs and other techniques. Social workers in a wide range of settings address the needs of individuals, families, groups, and communities. Their work may involve anything from helping an elderly person adjust to life in a nursing home to organizing fund-raising for community social welfare activities.

Other workers described in this section conduct basic and applied research in the social sciences. They deal primarily with data and things rather than people. They use established methods to assemble a body of fact and theory that contributes to human knowledge. Social scientists investigate all aspects of human society—from an anthropologist studying the origins of the human race or a historian studying an ancient civilization to a political scientist analyzing the results of presidential elections or a market research analyst conducting a survey of consumers' preferences.

Representative majors: anthropology, archaeology, behavioral sciences, criminology, demography, economics, geography, history, international development, international relations, political science, rural sociology, sociology, urban studies, psychology, public affairs, social work, religion, law, legal assistant, prelaw.

Interests: interests in helping others with their mental, spiritual, social, physical, or vocational needs. These interest can be satisfied by conducting research into all aspects of human behavior, language, work, politics, life-style, and cultural expression. Social scientists are employed by museums, schools, and colleges, government agencies, and private research foundations.

Job requirements: leadership/persuasion, problem-solving/creativity, work as part of a team, frequent public contact.

Related jobs: economist, urban planner, psychologist, political scientist, genealogist, historian, sociologist, anthropologist, archaeologist, artifacts conservator, intelligence specialist, medical social worker, psychiatric social worker, probation officer, human service worker, recreation worker, clergy, director of religious activities, lawyer, paralegal.

Employment: 1.3 million social scientists work in education, public, and private agencies.

Employment outlook: employment opportunities for health professions are expected to grow much faster than average through the year 2005.

Anthropology

You will make comparative studies in relation to the distribution, origin, and evolution of man, cultures that man has created and their social and physical characteristics. Studies include primitive as well as modern man. You probably will enjoy courses in cultural anthropology, archeology, linguistics, physical anthropology, social sciences, sociology, foreign language, museology, and moral ritual institutions. Most anthropologists find employment with governmental agencies. Some work for private businesses and others for museums and other nonprofit institutions. Others find research and teaching positions with colleges and universities.

Economics

In economics you will learn to plan, design, and conduct research into activities devoted to satisfying human wants. You will analyze the relationship between supply and demand. You will also study the problems of inflation, unemployment, tariffs, taxation, and foreign trade. You probably will do well in such courses as economics, business history, banking, international economics, marketing, computer science, finance, business law, political science, econometrics, statistics. Opportunities for job placement should be best in business and industry, research organizations, and consulting firms. The need for economic analyses by lawyers, accountants, engineers, health service administrators, and urban planners will increase the number of job opportunities.

History

As a history major you will study the social, economic, and political developments of societies. You will learn to analyze historical happenings and report on their significance as a teacher, writer, or reporter. You probably will do well in such courses as history, research methods, computer science, statistical methods, anthropology, sociology, philosophy. Most historians are employed by colleges and universities in research or teaching. Some work for government agencies. Others work for private institutions, such as museums and other nonprofit institutions.

Humanities

You will explore human thought and expression through aesthetic, historical, philosophical, sociopolitical, psychological, and symbolic contexts. You will be concerned with the relationships among cultural communities and creators with them. The studies serve as a liberal and broad training for professional careers. You probably will enjoy courses in English, literature, history, classics, culture studies, history of art and music, philosophy, psychology, foreign language, social and natural sciences. Those who graduate with just a bachelor's degree will have to apply for those jobs that will accept a liberal arts education as entry-level training, such as management trainee positions in corporations, banks, and government agencies. Many use humanities as an undergraduate degree to become teachers. Some may become writers or communications specialists in humanistic endeavors.

International Relations

You will engage in activities that cross international boundaries. You will learn about alliances and interests all over the globe. You will study contemporary international problems, diplomatic techniques, trade, business, communications, and politics. You probably will do well in such courses as economics, business management, communications, psychology, political science, sociology, linguistics, international law. Most jobs are found with the governmental agencies. Others will find job openings in colleges and universities doing research and teaching. Some will find jobs in banking and consulting firms.

Law

You will learn the law and how to represent a client in court or before a government agency. In general practice you will learn to deal with many legal affairs, or specialize in a specific branch: tax, criminal, patent, labor, or corporation law. You probably will do well in such courses as legal procedures, political science, judicial systems, legal procedures, economic analysis, contract law, labor relations law, statistical methods, criminal procedure, civil procedure, accounting. People in this field either work for others, or set up private law practices. Many find work in private business or with government agencies. Many lawyers go into politics or take management jobs with businesses.

Philosophy

You will seek a balance between vision and self-criticism in the development of a philosophy. You will grope with the philosophical thinking of how the great minds of past and present have answered the most serious questions of the universe. Philosophy is a foundation for teaching, religion, wisdom, and logical thinking. You probably will enjoy courses in philosophy, psychology, sociology, perception, computer science, anthropology, foreign language, education, logic, philosophy of religion, ethics. Most jobs in this field are found in colleges and universities in research and teaching. Other jobs are found in churches and social service agencies.

Political Science

A study of government and the nature of politics. You will study government at every level, analyze the operations of every form of government, attempt to find theoretical and practical solutions to political problems. You probably will do well in such courses as political science, history, international law, statistics, public law, geography, public administration, psychology, economics, computer science, and urban affairs. Many people in this field work for governmental agencies. Many jobs can be found in colleges and universities in research and teaching. Some political scientists are self-employed doing research, or special studies for business, industry, or government.

Psychology

You will seek to understand people and explain their actions; help people to achieve satisfactory personal adjustments; interview patients; give diagnostic tests, and offer therapy. Some work with animal behavior. There are over 30 specialties. You probably will enjoy courses in psychology (developmental, abnormal, child, social, animal, and experimental), computer science, statistical methods, anthropology, sociology, psychobiology. Many people in this field find employment with governmental agencies. Some work for private businesses. Others are self-employed. Jobs may be found in colleges and universities in research and teaching.

Public Administration

The study of public administration deals with at least five areas of specialization: personnel, management, public relations, finance, and planning. Some studies touch base with all areas, along with administrative analysis, research, and engineering. The studies lead to jobs to manage public agencies. You probably will do well in such courses as public administration, psychology, management, finance, sociology, computer science, economics, urban affairs, administrative law, public policy. Most jobs in this field are found in federal, state, and local governmental agencies. Other jobs may be found in nonprofit institutions or organizations, such as museums, the Salvation Army, and the Boy Scouts.

Religious Studies

You must possess a strong religious faith and a desire to help and serve the spiritual needs of others. You will learn to coordinate religious activities and promote religious education. You may learn to provide counseling and guidance services. The studies demand considerable initiative and self-discipline. You probably will enjoy courses in foreign language, music, fine art, philosophy, psychology, sociology, comparative religion, religious history, education, public speaking, anthropology, origins of Christianity. Jobs in this field are found in schools, churches, hospitals, and social service agencies. Some of these establishments are run by nonprofit organizations and many are operated by federal, state, and local governmental agencies. Self-employment in this kind of work is possible.

Social Work

You must be concerned with many types of social problems and needs—among them poverty, unemployment, illness, broken homes, family maladjustment; also various handicaps, antisocial behavior, and inadequate housing. You will learn to offer a wide range of social services to people in need. You probably will enjoy courses in psychology, sociology, biology, anthropology, interviewing techniques, social legislation, urban studies, political science, counseling, ethnics, geriatrics. Most jobs in this field are found with federal, state and local governmental agencies. Some jobs are found with some nonprofit organizations, churches, and hospitals.

Sociology

In sociology you will study the many groups of human organizations: families, tribes, communities, villages, and states. You will study the behavior and interaction of these groups, and trace their origin and growth. You will analyze the influence of group activities on individual and group behavior. You probably will do well in such courses as sociology, anthropology, geography, political science, psychology, research methods, computer science, statistical methods, criminology, sociological analysis. Most jobs in this field are found in governmental agencies. Some jobs are available in private businesses and others in nonprofit institutions. Jobs in research and teaching are found in colleges and universities. Some sociologists are self-employed doing research or special studies for business, industry, or government.

Urban Studies

You will learn to develop programs to provide for future growth and revitalization of urban, suburban, and rural communities. You will help make decisions on social, economic, and environmental problems. You will deal with personnel, budgets, plans, and civic leaders. You probably will enjoy courses in urban studies (demography, ecology, complex organizations and institutions), regional planning, finance, engineering, architecture, sociology, economics, political science, public policy. Most jobs are found with federal, state, and local governmental agencies. Some urban planners are self-employed doing research or special studies for business, industry, or government.

LOCATING FURTHER JOB INFORMATION RELATED TO YOUR MAJOR

In the previous section you found careers in which you may have an interest within fields of study, and generalized information about those careers. You may now want to go further and find more specific information. Good sources of occupational information are public libraries, high school and college career centers, and standard reference sources. Here are some suggestions in using these sources.

Public libraries. Most public libraries have career/occupational information collections. The *ERIC Digest*, sponsored by the Office of Educational Research, U.S. Department of Education, recommends these topics for occupational research in libraries:

- printed resources including bibliographies, lists of local, state, and federal job opportunities, and descriptions of all types of jobs;
- information about professional associations—directories, joblines or hotlines, employment within professions, training requirements, and job opportunities;
- information on specific careers—salaries, qualifications, benefits, job market outlook, and job descriptions;
- information about potential employers—size of companies, location of offices, types of jobs, specific hiring policies toward women, minorities, the handicapped, mid-life career changers.

High school and college career centers. Many high schools and colleges maintain career centers that cover a variety of topics. Their services usually include:

- a resource room that contains standard occupational information references;
- computerized occupational information systems;
- guidance personnel especially trained to provide professional career guidance;
- specialized workshops and career-related programs;
- résumé writing, job search methods, and interviewing techniques;
- interest inventories that will help you to measure your interests in a valid and reliable way.

Take advantage of what career centers have to offer! They are specialists in career and college planning!

Standard reference sources. Although each library and career center will have its own collection of resources on occupational information, listed below are some standard references you may want to investigate.

The Career Guide. Parsippany, New Jersey: Dun's Employment Opportunities Directory. This guide contains up-to-date, comprehensive, accurate coverage on employers and career opportunities. It includes lists of U.S. companies with 1000 or more employees with the name and address of the company, an overview of the company, what opportunities are available, location of offices, benefits, and the name of a contact person.

U.S. Department of Labor, *Dictionary of Occupational Titles*, 1991. Washington, D.C.: U.S. Employment Service. The DOT gives comprehensive, standardized descriptions of duties of over 12,000 occupations. It is designed to match job requirements and worker skills.

U.S. Department of Labor, *Occupational Outlook Handbook*. Updated biennially. This handbook includes information about specific jobs, working conditions, training and education needed, projected earnings, and job prospects.

Interest inventories. Perhaps you have had the good fortune to take a career interest inventory. If so you may have a pretty good idea of what your career interests are. Interest inventories measure your interests and give you a good idea of what careers might be most satisfying to you. If you have not taken an inventory, or wish to retest your interests, see your counselor or career technician for advice. There are a large number of interest inventories to choose from. A career interest inventory that you can complete on your own and that ties college major decision-making to career planning is *The Major-Minor Finder.* Ask your counselor for it or write to CFKR Career Materials, 11860 Kemper Road, Unit 7, Auburn, California 95603 for information on how you may purchase this instrument.

CHOOSING A COLLEGE TO MATCH YOUR INTERESTS

Your first-choice major and your career plans will become important criteria in choosing a college. Your free choice may be limited by financial or other considerations. However, if at all possible, give high priority to your major and career planning and choose a college that best matches those plans. Your major will have a strong influence in choosing a college. The college major that you choose may influence your final college choice.

- **Some majors are rare and specialized.** Special attention must be given to those majors that are fairly rare and specialized. You will be limited in the number of colleges to choose from. Of the more than 2000 four-year colleges in the United States, only 73 have aeronautical engineering; 51 have agricultural engineering; 24 have architectural engineering majors; 55 have biomedical engineering; 43 have landscape engineering; 28 have petroleum engineering; 57 have business statistics; 71 have astronomy; 26 have oceanography (must be near the ocean); 75 have resource management; 76 have pharmacy; 73 have occupational therapy. This is just a partial listing. If you choose a fairly rare major, you may have to travel a distance to find a college that offers it. Check with your career center or public library for listings of colleges that offer your major.
- **Some majors are traditional and offered widely.** Most colleges offer a common core of traditional majors in business, science, social science, communications, and humanities that by their very title signify a general major. Many students take these general majors as preparation for the job market, or for preparation to a graduate or professional school. Examples of majors that are offered widely by four-year colleges are: business administration, chemistry, mathematics, physics, economics, history, philosophy, political science, psychology, sociology, general biology, art, communications, dramatic arts, music, English, and elementary education. Some colleges also offer majors that include courses in a broad area of studies, such as: liberal arts, humanities, social science, prelaw, environmental science, physical science, urban studies, ethnic studies, international relations.

If you should choose one of these more general, and commonly offered majors, you will have a much broader choice of colleges. However, an undergraduate degree (B.A. or B.S.) in one of these traditional majors, generally will not prepare you for direct job entry at a professional level. If your goal is to work as a recognized professional in your major field, you will want to make plans to go on to a graduate school to obtain an advanced degree. For example, a B.A. in psychology will not provide sufficient training to become a licensed psychologist; historians, political scientists, sociologists, biologists, and so on, must have advanced degrees to work as professionals. *This is why it is very important that you make your college plans to include your long-range career goals.*

- **Some majors are offered in schools within universities.** Majors in the engineering, business, agriculture, education, and health fields differ from the more traditional majors in that they usually are completed in separate schools within universities. Because these majors are quite specialized and require special labs and equipment and a specialized faculty, not all colleges and universities can afford to staff these majors. Also, there can be a great variance in academic reputation and course requirements from school to school. For example: some universities are noted for their School of Engineering, some for their School of Business Administration, some for their School of Agriculture, School of Medicine, School of Public Health, and so on. If you plan to complete a major in one of these fields you should study carefully the admissions requirements, the courses required to complete the major, and the reputation of the school. Most of the courses you will have to take in the major are technical in content where job skills are acquired for entry into a profession. *Your career opportunities may be enhanced by completing a strong program in a fully-accredited and prestigious school.*

In addition to the consideration of a major in choosing a four-year college, you should consider the size, location, cost, entrance requirements, social and academic reputations, private or public, accreditation, and scholarship/financial aid offerings.

It is strongly advised that you go through these steps in your college planning.

- **Read college catalogs and handbooks.** Catalogs are the best source for up-to-date, specific information. Catalogs can reveal the purposes and goals, the academic strengths, and philosophy of universities, as well as the specifics of college majors.
- **Visit college campuses.** At an early date, visit the campuses of preferred colleges to get a firsthand view of what the campuses are like. During the visit, talk to students to get their unbiased views of the college—academic and social. If possible visit the department that offers the major in which you are interested and talk to a faculty member about the major.
- **Explore financial aid.** If you have financial needs, consider that private colleges usually cost more than public colleges; community colleges offer excellent courses that can be transferred to four-year colleges; transportation costs to out-of-state colleges can be very expensive; out-of-state colleges usually charge additional fees for nonresidents; some colleges are much more

endowed and provide more financial aid than others; most colleges have a financial aid office—get as much information as you can; the Armed Forces offer financial aid programs, the ROTC, and the service academies; get all necessary financial aid forms, and file them on time!

- **Write to professional organizations for college and career advice.** Professional organizations may have pertinent information on lists of colleges that are accredited for professional training. You may obtain addresses of professional organizations from libraries and career centers.

MAKING THE FINAL DECISIONS

Making important decisions and setting long range goals is never an easy task. Making a decision on what you will study in college for four or more years, and how this will fit into your life-style and your career goals is very important and very personal. In this article, stress was placed upon getting sufficient information for decision-making. You now should have a good idea of what a college major is and the different approaches to majors. You also should have knowledge of the wide range of majors that are offered in nine major fields of study, and related career information.

In your final decision-making, first take a broad view of the nine fields. Look carefully at all career options within the nine fields. Don't just limit yourself to a major or a career that might have been recommended by your family or friends. The final decisions should be yours, and you will have to take responsibility to reach your goals. In the final analysis you will have to look into yourself. As Plato once said, "Know thyself, and to thine own self be true."

- **Assess your aptitudes and interests.** What can you do? What do you like to do? Use the services of your career center and guidance counselors to clarify aptitudes and interests.
- **Assess your career goals.** Tie your career goals to your college planning. Look at all options. Don't limit yourself.
- **Assess your values.** What do you want out of life? What is important to you? Material wealth? Family? The social good? Academic achievement? Advancement? Travel? Creativity? Power? Caring for people? Fame and prestige? Community service? Adventure? Beauty and art? Try to match your college and career planning with your values so that you can have the kind of life-style that will be satisfying and rewarding to you.

The more you know about your aptitudes, interests, career goals, and values the better your decisions will be. In the final analysis, good decision-making is based upon knowing the facts, and being flexible enough to alter decisions when they are not in your best interests.

We wish you well in your college major and the career path that you choose!

Robert Kauk and Francis Ferry

INDEX OF COLLEGE MAJORS

This section of *Profiles of American Colleges* will help you quickly determine which schools offer the major in which you are interested, the in-state tuition, room and board costs, and the Selector Rating. The colleges are listed alphabetically and the first column indicates the state where each is located. These data reflect the 2001-2002 academic year. You will be able to compare schools offering those majors that interest you the most and see what their in-state costs and Selector Ratings are, before reading the Profiles in the main section of the book (see page 227 for Selector Rating details). You may also discover some new schools or majors that interest you.

ACCOUNTING

School	ST	$IS	SR
Abilene Christian Univ	TX	16,300	VC
Adams State College	CO	7,468	C
Adelphi Univ	NY	23,320	VC
Adrian College	MI	19,670	C
Alabama A&M Univ	AL	5,100	LC
Alabama State Univ	AL	6,404	C
Alaska Pacific Univ	AK	16,450	C
Albany State Univ	GA	5,764	C+
Albertson College of Idaho	ID	23,900	VC
Albertus Magnus College	CT	22,154	C
Albright College	PA	27,642	C
Alcorn State Univ	MS	5,594	LC
Alderson-Broaddus College	WV	19,640	C
Alfred Univ	NY	27,212	C+
Alvernia College	PA	20,790	C
American International College	MA	22,268	LC
American Univ	DC	31,544	VC+
Anderson Univ	IN	19,430	LC
Andrews Univ	MI	17,696	LC
Angelo State Univ	TX	7,028	C
Appalachian State Univ	NC	6,353	C
Arcadia Univ	PA	26,650	C
Arizona State Univ-Main	AZ	7,726	C
Arkansas Baptist College	AR	5,530	LC
Arkansas State Univ	AR	7,480	C
Arkansas Tech Univ	AR	6,256	C
Asbury College	KY	18,540	VC
Ashland Univ	OH	22,182	LC
Assumption College	MA	26,320	C
Atlantic Union College	MA	34,034	LC
Auburn Univ	AL	5,510	C
Auburn Univ Montgomery	AL	5,330	NC
Augsburg College	MN	22,978	C
Augusta State Univ	GA	2,282	C
Augustana College	IL	24,117	VC+
Augustana College	SD	20,760	VC
Aurora Univ	IL	18,551	C
Austin Peay State Univ	TN	5,814	LC
Averett Univ	VA	17,980	LC
Avila College	MO	17,720	C
Azusa Pacific Univ	CA	22,422	VC
Baker College of Flint	MI	7,720	NC
Baker Univ	KS	14,780	C+
Baldwin-Wallace College	OH	22,010	VC+
Ball State Univ	IN	8,660	C
Barry Univ	FL	24,100	LC
Bartlesville Wesleyan College	OK	14,100	LC
Barton College	NC	16,834	LC
Baylor Univ	TX	18,298	VC+
Becker College	MA	21,230	LC
Belhaven College	MS	16,040	C+
Bellarmine Univ	KY	20,440	VC
Bellevue Univ	NE	4,125	NC
Belmont Abbey College	NC	19,630	LC
Belmont Univ	TN	19,066	VC
Bemidji State Univ	MN	7,957	C
Benedict College	SC	12,662	LC
Benedictine College	KS	18,485	LC
Benedictine Univ	IL	21,330	C
Bennett College	NC	11,200	C
Bentley College	MA	31,060	HC
Berkeley College	NY	21,545	LC
Berkeley College of New York City	NY	12,500	LC
Berry College	GA	18,850	C
Bethany College	KS	16,602	C+
Bethany College	WV	18,566	C
Bethel College	IN	17,650	LC
Bethel College	KS	17,355	C+
Bethel College	MN	22,740	VC
Bethune-Cookman College	FL	15,746	C
Birmingham-Southern College	AL	22,960	C
Black Hills State Univ	SD	6,652	LC
Blackburn College	IL	13,690	C
Bloomfield College	NJ	17,000	C
Bloomsburg Univ of Pennsylvania	PA	9,434	C
Bluefield State College	WV	2,178	LC
Bluffton College	OH	20,644	C
Boise State Univ	ID	6,531	LC
Boston College	MA	33,330	MC
Boston Univ	MA	34,358	MC
Bowling Green State Univ	OH	10,794	C
Bradley Univ	IL	20,970	VC
Brenau Univ Women's College	GA	20,100	C
Brescia Univ	KY	14,225	C
Briar Cliff Univ	IA	18,657	LC
Brigham Young Univ	UT	7,840	HC
Brigham Young Univ/Hawaii	HI	6,890	C
Bryant College	RI	25,980	VC
Bucknell Univ	PA	31,096	HC
Buena Vista Univ	IA	22,828	C
Butler Univ	IN	25,580	VC+
Cabrini College	PA	25,950	LC
Caldwell College	NJ	20,940	LC
Calif Lutheran Univ	CA	23,500	LC
Calif State Polytechnic Univ, Pomona	CA	8,615	C
Cal State, Fullerton	CA	5,440	LC
Cal State, Hayward	CA	7,400	LC
Cal State, Long Beach	CA	7,400	LC
Cal State, Los Angeles	CA	5,050	C
Cal State, Northridge	CA	7,781	C
Cal State, Sacramento	CA	7,488	C
Cal State, San Bernardino	CA	6,516	C
Calumet College of St. Joseph	IN	7,500	LC
Calvin College	MI	20,050	NC
Cameron Univ	OK	5,560	NC
Campbell Univ	NC	16,599	C
Campbellsville Univ	KY	14,340	C
Canisius College	NY	24,696	C+
Capital Univ	OH	23,630	C
Cardinal Stritch Univ	WI	17,620	C
Caribbean Univ	PR	3,000	
Carlow College	PA	19,366	C
Carroll College	MT	19,140	C
Carroll College	WI	21,170	C
Carson-Newman College	TN	16,490	C
Carthage College	WI	23,670	C
Case Western Reserve Univ	OH	27,418	C
Catholic Univ of America	DC	29,332	VC
Cedar Crest College	PA	25,145	C+
Cedarville Univ	OH	17,553	VC
Centenary College	NJ	22,430	C
Centenary College of Louisiana	LA	21,600	C+
Central College	IA	21,206	C
Central Conn State Univ	CT	10,404	C
Central Methodist College	MO	16,460	C
Central Mich Univ	MI	8,355	C
Central Missouri State Univ	MO	7,920	C
Central State Univ	OH	8,922	C+
Central Univ of Bayamon	PR	3,335	
Central Washington Univ	WA	8,985	LC
Chaminade Univ of Honolulu	HI	17,370	C
Champlain College	VT	19,680	C
Chapman Univ	CA	30,218	VC
Chatham College	PA	25,454	C+
Chestnut Hill College	PA	24,790	LC
Chicago State Univ	IL	8,851	C+
Christian Brothers Univ	TN	19,820	VC
Christopher Newport Univ	VA	8,862	VC
City Univ	WA	7,425	NC
CUNY/Baruch College	NY	3,275	VC+
CUNY/Brooklyn College	NY	3,403	LC
CUNY/College of Staten Island	NY	3,358	NC
CUNY/Herbert H. Lehman College	NY	3,320	LC
CUNY/Hunter College	NY	5,147	C+
CUNY/Medgar Evers College	NY	3,282	NC
CUNY/Queens College	NY	3,403	VC
CUNY/York College	NY	3,292	NC
Claremont McKenna College	CA	32,700	MC
Clarion Univ of Pennsylvania	PA	11,272	LC
Clark Atlanta Univ	GA	17,174	C
Clarke College	IA	20,625	C+
Clarkson Univ	NY	29,884	VC
Clayton College and State Univ	GA	2,322	C+
Clearwater Christian College	FL	13,160	LC
Cleary College	MI	10,350	LC
Clemson Univ	SC	7,600	C
Cleveland State Univ	OH	10,146	NC
Coastal Carolina Univ	SC	9,220	C
Coe College	IA	24,750	VC
College Misericordia	PA	23,380	LC
College of Charleston	SC	8,350	HC
College of Mount St. Joseph	OH	20,290	C
College of New Jersey	NJ	13,425	HC
College of Notre Dame of Maryland	MD	23,100	LC
College of Our Lady of the Elms	MA	20,644	C
College of St. Benedict	MN	23,921	VC
College of St. Catherine	MN	22,324	VC
College of St. Elizabeth	NJ	22,510	C
College of St. Joseph	VT	17,400	NC
College of St. Rose	NY	19,084	C
College of St. Scholastica	MN	22,378	C+
College of Santa Fe	NM	20,250	LC
College of the Ozarks	MO	2,650	C+
College of the Southwest	NM	8,456	NC
Colo Christian Univ	CO	17,714	C
Colo State Univ	CO	9,672	C
Columbia College	SC	19,050	LC
Columbia Union College	MD	19,027	C+
Columbus State Univ	GA	7,228	LC
Concord College	WV	7,122	C+
Concordia College/Moorhead	MN	18,835	C
Concordia Univ	MN	19,912	C
Concordia Univ at Austin	TX	16,740	LC
Concordia Univ Nebr	NE	17,770	C
Concordia Univ Wisc	WI	16,600	LC
Concordia Univ, River Forest	IL	20,000	LC
Converse College	SC	21,990	VC
Cornerstone Univ and Grand Rapids Baptist Seminary	MI	18,092	C
Creighton Univ	NE	23,476	VC
Culver-Stockton College	MO	15,400	LC
Cumberland College	KY	14,864	C
Daemen College	NY	20,620	C
Dakota Wesleyan Univ	SD	15,512	C
Dallas Baptist Univ	TX	13,682	LC
Dana College	NE	18,046	C
Davenport Univ	MI	10,057	NC
David Lipscomb Univ	TN	16,158	VC
David N. Myers College	OH	9,475	C
Davis and Elkins College	WV	19,270	LC
De Sales Univ	PA	22,610	VC
Defiance College	OH	19,580	LC
Delaware State Univ	DE	8,104	LC
Delaware Valley College	PA	24,213	LC
Delta State Univ	MS	5,416	C
DePaul Univ	IL	23,590	VC
Dickinson State Univ	ND	5,495	NC
Dillard Univ	LA	16,046	VC
Doane College	NE	17,600	LC
Dominican College	NY	20,400	LC
Dominican Univ	IL	20,800	C
Dordt College	IA	18,100	C+
Dowling College	NY	20,281	LC
Drake Univ	IA	22,830	VC
Drury Univ	MO	15,250	VC
Duquesne Univ	PA	24,242	C+
D'Youville College	NY	18,704	C
East Carolina Univ	NC	7,766	C
East Central Univ	OK	4,578	C
East Tenn State Univ	TN	7,127	C
East Texas Baptist Univ	TX	12,349	LC
Eastern College	PA	19,641	LC
Eastern Conn State Univ	CT	10,362	C
Eastern Illinois Univ	IL	10,101	C
Eastern Kentucky Univ	KY	6,552	C
Eastern Mennonite Univ	VA	20,700	VC
Eastern Mich Univ	MI	9,855	C
Eastern Nazarene College	MA	19,433	LC
Eastern New Mexico Univ	NM	4,113	LC
Eastern Oregon Univ	OR	8,772	C
Eastern Washington Univ	WA	7,972	LC
Edgewood College	WI	18,304	C
Edinboro Univ of Pennsylvania	PA	9,328	LC
Edward Waters College	FL	13,124	LC
Elizabeth City State Univ	NC	5,550	LC
Elizabethtown College	PA	26,000	VC
Elmhurst College	IL	21,750	C
Elmira College	NY	31,070	VC+
Elon Univ	NC	19,430	VC
Emory & Henry College	VA	19,462	C
Emory Univ	GA	33,792	MC
Emporia State Univ	KS	6,198	LC
Eureka College	IL	22,200	C
Evangel Univ	MO	14,050	C
Excelsior College	NY	915	SP
Fairfield Univ	CT	30,885	HC
Fairleigh Dickinson Univ/Madison campus	NJ	25,500	C
Fairleigh Dickinson Univ/Teaneck Campus	NJ	24,646	C
Fairmont State College	WV	7,010	NC
Fayetteville State Univ	NC	5,590	LC
Ferris State Univ	MI	10,816	C
Ferrum College	VA	15,990	LC
Flagler College	FL	10,550	VC+
Florida A&M Univ	FL	6,948	C
Florida Atlantic Univ	FL	8,832	C
Florida Gulf Coast Univ	FL	9,201	C
Florida International Univ	FL	9,486	VC
Florida Memorial College	FL	6,000	LC
Florida Southern College	FL	19,430	C
Florida State Univ	FL	7,835	HC
Fordham Univ	NY	30,710	VC
Fort Hays State Univ	KS	6,294	LC
Fort Lewis College	CO	7,659	LC
Fort Valley State Univ	GA	6,014	LC
Francis Marion Univ	SC	7,682	C
Franciscan Univ of Steubenville	OH	19,100	C+
Franklin and Marshall College	PA	32,410	HC
Franklin College of Indiana	IN	19,905	C
Franklin Pierce College	NH	26,125	LC
Franklin Univ	OH	6,324	SP
Freed-Hardeman Univ	TN	14,290	VC
Fresno Pacific Univ	CA	19,740	C
Friends Univ	KS	15,962	LC
Frostburg State Univ	MD	9,680	C
Furman Univ	SC	25,492	HC
Gallaudet Univ	DC	16,554	SP
Gannon Univ	PA	18,848	C
Gardner-Webb Univ	NC	17,400	C
Geneva College	PA	19,990	C+
George Mason Univ	VA	9,192	C
George Washington Univ	DC	32,170	HC
Georgetown College	KY	18,400	VC
Georgetown Univ	DC	34,847	MC
Georgia College and State Univ	GA	7,344	C
Georgia Southern Univ	GA	6,958	C
Georgia Southwestern State Univ	GA	6,013	C
Georgia State Univ	GA	7,792	LC
Georgian Court College	NJ	19,040	LC
Glenville State College	WV	6,588	NC
Golden Gate Univ	CA	8,592	NC
Goldey-Beacom College	DE	11,440	C
Gonzaga Univ	WA	24,276	HC+
Gordon College	MA	23,594	VC+
Goshen College	IN	18,950	VC+
Grace College	IN	16,768	C
Graceland Univ	IA	15,845	C
Grambling State Univ	LA	5,325	NC
Grand Canyon Univ	AZ	30,000	LC
Grand Valley State Univ	MI	10,040	C
Grand View College	IA	17,596	NC
Greensboro College	NC	19,080	LC
Greenville College	IL	19,226	LC
Grove City College	PA	12,280	MC
Guilford College	NC	23,255	C
Gustavus Adolphus College	MN	24,190	VC+
Gwynedd-Mercy College	PA	22,350	C
Hampton Univ	VA	17,112	C+
Hannibal-LaGrange College	MO	12,530	C
Harding Univ	AR	13,528	VC
Hardin-Simmons Univ	TX	14,165	C
Hartwick College	NY	33,090	C+
Hastings College	NE	17,854	C+
Hawaii Pacific Univ	HI	17,790	C
Heidelberg College	OH	23,879	C
Henderson State Univ	AR	6,269	C
Hesser College	NH	16,210	LC
High Point Univ	NC	20,220	LC
Hilbert College	NY	16,830	LC
Hillsdale College	MI	20,586	VC+
Hofstra Univ	NY	23,252	C
Holy Family College	PA	13,710	LC
Hope College	MI	22,922	C+
Houghton College	NY	21,810	VC+
Houston Baptist Univ	TX	15,300	LC
Howard Payne Univ	TX	13,834	C+
Howard Univ	DC	15,522	LC
Humphreys College	CA	6,900	NC
Huntingdon College	AL	18,400	VC
Husson College	ME	15,360	LC
Idaho State Univ	ID	7,030	C+
Illinois College	IL	16,234	C
Illinois State Univ	IL	9,235	C
Illinois Wesleyan Univ	IL	26,970	HC
Immaculata College	PA	22,400	LC
Indiana Inst of Technology	IN	18,806	C
Indiana State Univ	IN	8,461	LC
Indiana Univ Bloomington	IN	10,712	C+

ST = STATE **$IS** = IN-STATE COSTS **SR** = SELECTOR RATING

School	ST	$IS	SR
Indiana Univ Kokomo	IN	3,422	LC
Indiana Univ Northwest	IN	3,447	C
Indiana Univ of Pennsylvania	PA	9,133	C
Indiana Univ South Bend	IN	3,515	C
Indiana Univ Southeast	IN	3,459	C
Indiana Univ-Purdue Univ Fort Wayne	IN	3,166	LC
Indiana Univ-Purdue Univ Indianapolis	IN	9,473	C
Indiana Wesleyan Univ	IN	17,680	C
Inter-American Univ of PR/ Aguadilla Campus	PR	3,278	
Inter-American Univ of PR/ Arecibo Campus	PR	3,300	
Inter-American Univ of PR/ Barranquitas Regional College	PR	3,300	LC
Inter-American Univ of PR/ Bayamon Univ College	PR	3,700	
Inter-American Univ of PR/ Fajardo Campus	PR	4,000	
Inter-American Univ of PR/ Metropolitan Campus	PR	4,166	
Inter-American Univ of PR/ Ponce Regional College	PR	3,700	
Inter-American Univ of PR/ San GermÈn	PR	6,390	
International College	FL	7,230	NC
Iona College	NY	26,556	C
Iowa State Univ	IA	8,108	VC
Iowa Wesleyan College	IA	18,840	C
Ithaca College	NY	28,719	HC
Jackson State Univ	MS	6,776	LC
Jacksonville State Univ	AL	6,568	LC
Jacksonville Univ	FL	21,110	LC
James Madison Univ	VA	9,552	HC
Jamestown College	ND	11,310	NC
John Brown Univ	AR	15,080	VC
John Carroll Univ	OH	24,140	VC
Johnson and Wales Univ	RI	21,558	LC
Johnson State College	VT	10,776	C
Judson College	IL	18,980	LC
Juniata College	PA	26,080	VC
Kansas State Univ	KS	6,995	C
Kansas Wesleyan Univ	KS	17,400	C+
Kean Univ	NJ	11,159	C
Kennesaw State Univ	GA	2,306	LC
Kent State Univ	OH	11,104	C
Kentucky State Univ	KY	6,146	NC
Kentucky Wesleyan College	KY	15,800	C
Keuka College	NY	21,170	C
Keystone College	PA	19,066	LC
King's College	PA	24,680	C
Knoxville College	TN	6,200	LC
Kutztown Univ of Pennsylvania	PA	8,907	C
La Roche College	PA	18,854	LC
La Salle Univ	PA	27,890	C
La Sierra Univ	CA	19,260	LC
LaGrange College	GA	17,496	C
Lake Erie College	OH	21,350	LC
Lake Superior State Univ	MI	9,034	LC
Lakeland College	WI	17,950	C
Lamar Univ	TX	6,816	LC
Langston Univ	OK	2,308	LC
Lasell College	MA	24,100	C
Lawrence Tech Univ	MI	11,429	C
Le Moyne College	NY	23,840	C
Lebanon Valley College of Pennsylvania	PA	25,700	VC
Lee Univ	TN	10,198	LC
Lehigh Univ	PA	32,290	MC
LeMoyne-Owen College	TN	8,450	NC
Lenoir-Rhyne College	NC	19,186	C
LeTourneau Univ	TX	19,020	VC
Lewis Univ	IL	20,960	C
Liberty Univ	VA	14,500	C
Limestone College	SC	16,900	C
Lincoln Memorial Univ	TN	12,620	LC
Lincoln Univ	MO	7,158	NC
Lincoln Univ	PA	11,198	C+
Lindenwood Univ	MO	17,250	C
Lindsey Wilson College	KY	16,392	LC
Linfield College	OR	25,840	VC
Livingstone College	NC	13,360	LC
LIU/Brooklyn Campus	NY	22,290	C
LIU/C.W. Post Campus	NY	25,380	C
Loras College	IA	22,994	C+
Louisiana State Univ and A&M College	LA	8,014	VC
Louisiana State Univ in Shreveport	LA	2,480	NC
Louisiana Tech Univ	LA	6,506	C
Loyola College in Maryland	MD	30,900	HC
Loyola Marymount Univ	CA	28,754	HC
Loyola Univ New Orleans	LA	23,506	VC+
Loyola Univ of Chicago	IL	25,992	VC
Lubbock Christian Univ	TX	14,226	LC
Luther College	IA	23,300	VC+
Lycoming College	PA	24,780	C
Lynchburg College	VA	23,405	C
Lyndon State College	VT	11,313	LC
Lynn Univ	FL	24,550	C
Lyon College	AR	16,500	VC
MacMurray College	IL	17,790	LC
Madonna Univ	MI	11,504	VC
Malone College	OH	19,190	C
Manchester College	IN	22,010	C
Manhattan College	NY	25,500	VC
Mansfield Univ	PA	9,648	C
Marian College	IN	21,020	C
Marian College of Fond du Lac	WI	17,935	LC
Marietta College	OH	24,580	C
Marist College	NY	24,756	VC
Marquette Univ	WI	24,836	C+
Mars Hill College	NC	18,600	LC
Marshall Univ	WV	7,752	LC
Martin Univ	IN	8,370	SP
Marymount Manhattan College	NY	23,195	VC
Marymount Univ	VA	21,560	LC
Maryville Univ of St. Louis	MO	18,680	C
Marywood Univ	PA	24,639	C
McKendree College	IL	18,300	C+
McMurry Univ	TX	15,287	C
McNeese State Univ	LA	5,259	LC
McPherson College	KS	17,710	C
Mercer Univ	GA	24,130	VC
Mercy College	NY	15,875	LC
Mercyhurst College	PA	20,694	C
Meredith College	NC	17,500	C
Merrimack College	MA	25,725	VC
Mesa State College	CO	8,051	C
Messiah College	PA	23,180	VC
Methodist College	NC	19,526	C
Metropolitan State College of Denver	CO	2,338	LC
Metropolitan State Univ	MN	2,943	SP
Miami Univ	OH	12,885	VC+
Mich State Univ	MI	10,386	VC
MidAmerica Nazarene Univ	KS	16,960	C
Middle Tenn State Univ	TN	6,994	C
Midland Lutheran College	NE	18,600	C
Midwestern State Univ	TX	6,704	NC
Miles College	AL	7,870	NC
Milligan College	TN	17,550	C
Millikin Univ	IL	24,415	C+
Millsaps College	MS	22,608	VC+
Minn State Univ, Mankato	MN	7,296	LC
Minot State Univ	ND	5,466	LC
Miss College	MS	14,574	C
Miss State Univ	MS	7,853	C
Miss Univ for Women	MS	5,446	LC
Miss Valley State Univ	MS	6,345	C
Missouri Baptist College	MO	15,762	LC
Missouri Southern State College	MO	6,666	C
Missouri Valley College	MO	17,400	LC
Missouri Western State College	MO	6,662	NC
Molloy College	NY	13,940	C
Monmouth College	IL	21,550	C
Monmouth Univ	NJ	24,042	C
Montana State Univ-Billings	MT	7,653	NC
Moorhead State Univ	MN	7,000	LC
Moravian College	PA	27,065	VC
Morehead State Univ	KY	6,510	C
Morehouse College	GA	19,814	C
Morgan State Univ	MD	10,078	LC
Morningside College	IA	19,124	C
Morris Brown College	GA	15,993	LC
Mount Aloysius College	PA	18,186	LC
Mount Marty College	SD	15,656	LC
Mount Mary College	WI	18,024	C
Mount Mercy College	IA	19,390	VC
Mount Olive College	NC	14,410	LC
Mount St. Clare College	IA	19,050	LC
Mount St. Mary College	NY	18,825	C
Mount St. Mary's College	MD	25,740	C
Mount Senario College	WI	17,750	C
Mount Union College	OH	21,120	C
Mount Vernon Nazarene College	OH	17,027	C
Muhlenberg College	PA	28,170	HC
Murray State Univ	KY	6,672	C
Muskingum College	OH	18,760	C
National American Univ	SD	13,680	NC
National Univ	CA	7,755	SP
National-Louis Univ	IL	13,995	NC
Nazareth College of Rochester	NY	22,036	VC
Neumann College	PA	22,040	NC
New Jersey City Univ	NJ	9,100	LC
New Mexico Highlands Univ	NM	6,256	NC
New Mexico State Univ	NM	7,302	C
New York Inst of Technology	NY	21,756	C
New York Univ	NY	35,200	MC
Newberry College	SC	19,670	LC
Newbury College	MA	21,490	C
Newman Univ	KS	14,098	LC
Niagara Univ	NY	22,250	C+
Nicholls State Univ	LA	5,290	NC
Nichols College	MA	24,610	LC
Norfolk State Univ	VA	8,382	LC
N Car Agricultural and Technical State Univ	NC	6,659	LC
N Car Central Univ	NC	6,418	LC
N Car State Univ	NC	8,680	HC
N Car Wesleyan College	NC	15,650	LC
North Central College	IL	22,944	C+
N Dak State Univ	ND	7,004	VC
North Georgia College and State Univ	GA	6,322	C+
North Park Univ	IL	24,030	C
Northeastern Illinois Univ	IL	2,898	NC
Northeastern State Univ	OK	4,704	LC
Northeastern Univ	MA	30,078	VC
Northern Arizona Univ	AZ	7,398	C
Northern Illinois Univ	IL	9,545	C
Northern Kentucky Univ	KY	6,352	NC
Northern Mich Univ	MI	9,693	C
Northern State Univ	SD	6,279	LC
Northwest Missouri State Univ	MO	7,922	LC
Northwest Nazarene Univ	ID	18,380	C
Northwestern College	MN	19,816	C+
Northwestern College of Iowa	IA	17,630	C+
Northwestern Okla State Univ	OK	4,542	NC
Northwestern State Univ of Louisiana	LA	5,745	NC
Northwood Univ	FL	19,179	LC
Northwood Univ	MI	18,360	LC
Northwood Univ	TX	18,135	C
Norwich Univ	VT	21,064	LC
Notre Dame College	OH	20,425	C
Notre Dame de Namur Univ	CA	26,932	LC
Nova Southeastern Univ	FL	20,104	LC
Nyack College	NY	18,540	C
Oakland City Univ	IN	11,286	LC
Oakland Univ	MI	9,418	C
Oakwood College	AL	14,904	C
Oglethorpe Univ	GA	19,100	LC
Ohio Northern Univ	OH	27,765	VC
Ohio State Univ at Marion	OH	3,606	NC
Ohio Univ	OH	11,769	C
Ohio Valley College	WV	13,650	C+
Ohio Wesleyan Univ	OH	29,670	VC+
Okla Baptist Univ	OK	13,878	VC
Okla Christian Univ	OK	16,500	VC
Okla City Univ	OK	15,810	C
Okla Panhandle State Univ	OK	3,812	NC
Okla State Univ	OK	7,650	VC
Old Dominion Univ	VA	9,386	C
Olivet College	MI	17,410	C
Olivet Nazarene Univ	IL	18,444	C
Oral Roberts Univ	OK	18,490	C
Oregon State Univ	OR	9,612	VC
Ottawa Univ	KS	11,800	LC
Otterbein College	OH	23,439	C
Ouachita Baptist Univ	AR	16,460	VC
Our Lady of Holy Cross College	LA	5,140	NC
Our Lady of the Lake Univ of San Antonio	TX	17,336	C
Pace Univ	NY	24,200	C
Palm Beach Atlantic College	FL	23,310	C
Park Univ	MO	9,816	C
Paul Quinn College	TX	8,150	LC
Penn State Univ at Erie/ Behrend College	PA	12,326	C
Penn State Univ/Univ Park Campus	PA	11,126	VC
Pennsylvania College of Technology	PA	12,860	NC
Pepperdine Univ	CA	32,830	VC
Peru State College	NE	6,342	NC
Pfeiffer Univ	NC	18,580	C
Philadelphia Univ	PA	24,722	C
Philander Smith College	AR	7,380	NC
Pittsburg State Univ	KS	6,228	NC
Plymouth State College	NH	11,024	LC
Point Loma Nazarene Univ	CA	21,380	VC
Point Park College	PA	20,290	C
Pontifical Catholic Univ of PR/Ponce	PR	7,076	
Portland State Univ	OR	11,220	C
Prairie View A&M Univ	TX	3,172	LC
Presbyterian College	SC	23,356	VC
Providence College	RI	27,620	HC
Purdue Univ/Calumet	IN	6,630	NC
Purdue Univ/West Lafayette	IN	10,284	VC
Queens College	NC	17,250	C
Quincy Univ	IL	20,450	C
Quinnipiac Univ	CT	27,370	C
Radford Univ	VA	8,302	C
Ramapo College of New Jersey	NJ	13,550	VC
Randolph-Macon College	VA	24,395	C
Regis Univ	CO	25,740	C+
Rhode Island College	RI	8,700	LC
Richard Stockton College of New Jersey	NJ	12,165	VC
Rider Univ	NJ	27,400	C
Rivier College	NH	24,215	C
Robert Morris Univ	PA	18,730	C
Roberts Wesleyan College	NY	20,160	C+
Rochester College	MI	15,404	C+
Rochester Inst of Technology	NY	26,232	VC+
Rockford College	IL	23,930	C
Rockhurst Univ	MO	20,090	C
Rocky Mountain College	MT	18,113	C
Roger Williams Univ	RI	29,010	C
Roosevelt Univ	IL	20,240	LC
Rosemont College	PA	24,060	C
Rowan Univ	NJ	12,365	VC
Rutgers, The State Univ of New Jersey New Brunswick Campus	NJ	12,709	C
Rutgers, The State Univ of New Jersey/ CamdenCampus	NJ	6,484	C
Rutgers, The State Univ of New Jersey/Newark Campus	NJ	6,394	C
Sacred Heart Univ	CT	26,588	VC
Saginaw Valley State Univ	MI	9,465	C
St. Ambrose Univ	IA	19,994	C
St. Anselm College	NH	27,405	C
St. Augustine's College	NC	12,990	C+
St. Bonaventure Univ	NY	21,956	C
St. Cloud State Univ	MN	7,180	C
St. Edward's Univ	TX	17,846	C
St. Francis College	NY	9,610	C
St. Francis Univ	PA	24,486	LC
St. John Fisher College	NY	21,800	C
St. John's Univ	MN	23,640	VC
St. John's Univ	NY	26,660	C
St. Joseph's College	IN	21,640	C
St. Joseph's College, New York	NY	9,802	C
St. Joseph's Univ	PA	29,715	VC+
St. Leo Univ	FL	19,250	LC
St. Louis Univ	MO	26,590	VC+
St. Martin's College	WA	20,566	C
St. Mary College	KS	17,298	C
St. Mary-of-the-Woods College	IN	21,320	LC
St. Mary's College of Calif	CA	27,575	C
St. Mary's Univ of Minn	MN	19,975	C
St. Mary's Univ of San Antonio	TX	19,735	C
St. Michael's College	VT	26,935	VC
St. Norbert College	WI	23,169	VC
St. Peter's College	NJ	22,292	LC
St. Thomas Aquinas College	NY	20,590	LC
St. Thomas Univ	FL	19,500	LC
St. Vincent College	PA	22,942	VC
St. Xavier Univ	IL	21,104	C
Salem College	NC	23,065	VC
Salem State College	MA	4,481	LC
Salisbury Univ	MD	10,576	VC
Salve Regina Univ	RI	26,460	C
Sam Houston State Univ	TX	6,076	LC
Samford Univ	AL	16,340	VC
San Diego State Univ	CA	9,716	C+
San Francisco State Univ	CA	7,139	LC
San Jose State Univ	CA	8,187	C
Santa Clara Univ	CA	28,371	VC+
Savannah State Univ	GA	2,550	LC
Schreiner Univ	TX	19,254	C
Seattle Pacific Univ	WA	22,674	C+
Seattle Univ	WA	24,183	VC
Seton Hall Univ	NJ	26,910	LC
Seton Hill College	PA	21,875	C
Shaw Univ	NC	12,810	C
Shepherd College	WV	7,062	LC
Shippensburg Univ of Pennsylvania	PA	9,652	C
Shorter College	GA	15,185	C
Siena College	NY	22,685	VC
Siena Heights Univ	MI	16,140	LC
Silver Lake College of the Holy Family	WI	15,516	LC
Simmons College	MA	30,418	VC
Simpson College	CA	19,200	C
Simpson College	IA	21,200	C+
Slippery Rock Univ	PA	9,152	LC
S Car State Univ	SC	6,586	LC
Southeast Missouri State Univ	MO	8,367	C+
Southeastern College	FL	11,648	LC
Southeastern Louisiana Univ	LA	6,047	LC
Southeastern Okla State Univ	OK	4,917	C
Southeastern Univ	DC	8,505	LC
Southern Adventist Univ	TN	15,600	C
Southern Arkansas Univ	AR	5,740	LC
Southern Conn State Univ	CT	10,310	C
Southern Illinois Univ at Carbondale	IL	8,621	C
Southern Illinois Univ Edwardsville	IL	7,869	LC
Southern Methodist Univ	TX	28,349	VC
Southern Nazarene Univ	OK	14,634	NC
Southern New Hampshire Univ	NH	23,852	C
Southern Oregon Univ	OR	9,429	C
Southern Univ and A&M College	LA	6,365	C+
Southern Univ at New Orleans	LA	995	NC
Southern Utah Univ	UT	7,254	C
Southern Vermont College	VT	17,685	C
Southern Wesleyan Univ	SC	17,280	C
Southwest Baptist Univ	MO	13,426	LC

ST = STATE $IS = IN-STATE COSTS   SR = SELECTOR RATING

School	ST	$IS	SR
Southwest Missouri State Univ	MO	7,600	LC
Southwest State Univ	MN	7,117	LC
Southwest Texas State Univ	TX	8,730	VC
Southwestern Okla State Univ	OK	4,801	C
Southwestern Univ	TX	22,550	HC
Spalding Univ	KY	15,196	C
Spring Arbor Univ	MI	17,976	C
Spring Hill College	AL	23,250	C
SUNY/College at Brockport	NY	10,267	C
SUNY/College at Fredonia	NY	10,125	C
SUNY/College at Geneseo	NY	9,970	HC
SUNY/College at Old Westbury	NY	9,818	LC
SUNY/College at Oneonta	NY	9,981	C
SUNY/College at Oswego	NY	10,856	C
SUNY/College at Plattsburgh	NY	9,729	C
SUNY/Univ at Albany	NY	10,997	VC
SUNY/Univ at Binghamton	NY	10,653	HC
SUNY/Univ at New Paltz	NY	9,685	VC
State Univ of West Georgia	GA	7,101	C
Stephen F. Austin State Univ	TX	6,905	C
Stephens College	MO	22,295	C
Stetson Univ	FL	25,640	VC
Stonehill College	MA	26,852	HC
Strayer Univ	DC	8,789	SP
Suffolk Univ	MA	26,516	C
Sul Ross State Univ	TX	6,582	LC
Susquehanna Univ	PA	27,270	VC
Syracuse Univ	NY	30,710	HC
Tabor College	KS	17,600	LC
Talladega College	AL	10,110	LC
Tarleton State Univ	TX	7,160	C
Taylor Univ	IN	21,562	VC+
Teikyo Post Univ	CT	21,800	C
Temple Univ	PA	14,124	C
Tenn State Univ	TN	7,058	VC
Tenn Tech Univ	TN	6,968	C
Tenn Wesleyan College	TN	13,030	C
Texas A&M Univ	TX	8,988	VC
Texas A&M Univ at Commerce	TX	7,326	C
Texas A&M Univ at Kingsville	TX	6,446	LC
Texas Christian Univ	TX	19,910	C
Texas Southern Univ	TX	6,576	NC
Texas Tech Univ	TX	8,825	C
Texas Wesleyan Univ	TX	14,710	C
Texas Woman's Univ	TX	5,855	LC
Ohio State Univ	OH	10,819	VC
Thiel College	PA	18,419	LC
Thomas College	ME	18,915	LC
Thomas Edison State College	NJ	2,750	SP
Thomas More College	KY	17,700	LC
Tiffin Univ	OH	17,250	C
Touro College	NY	14,950	VC
Towson Univ	MD	11,088	VC
Transylvania Univ	KY	21,780	VC+
Trevecca Nazarene Univ	TN	15,752	C
Trinity Christian College	IL	19,415	C
Trinity International Univ	IL	20,640	C+
Tri-State Univ-Main Campus	IN	21,200	C
Troy State Univ	AL	7,696	C
Troy State Univ/Dothan	AL	3,296	C
Troy State Univ/ Montgomery	AL	3,080	NC
Truman State Univ	MO	8,568	VC+
Tulane Univ	LA	34,013	HC+
Turabo Univ	PR	4,110	
Tuskegee Univ	AL	14,600	LC
Union College	KY	15,920	C
Union College	NE	14,650	C
Union Univ	TN	18,930	C+
Universidad Metropolitana	PR	3,324	
Univ of Akron	OH	10,530	NC
Univ of Alabama	AL	7,402	C
Univ of Alabama at Birmingham	AL	10,110	C
Univ of Alabama at Huntsville	AL	7,916	VC
Univ of Alaska Anchorage	AK	9,100	NC
Univ of Alaska Fairbanks	AK	8,265	NC
Univ of Alaska Southeast	AK	7,900	LC
Univ of Arizona	AZ	8,614	C
Univ of Arkansas	AR	8,334	VC
Univ of Arkansas at Little Rock	AR	5,637	NC
Univ of Arkansas at Monticello	AR	5,940	NC
Univ of Arkansas at Pine Bluff	AR	7,925	C
Univ of Bridgeport	CT	23,020	C
Univ of Central Arkansas	AR	6,388	C
Univ of Central Florida	FL	8,251	VC
Univ of Central Okla	OK	5,205	C
Univ of Charleston	WV	20,640	C
Univ of Cincinnati	OH	12,491	LC
Univ of Colo at Boulder	CO	9,255	VC
Univ of Conn	CT	12,122	VC
Univ of Dayton	OH	20,400	VC
Univ of Delaware	DE	10,824	VC
Univ of Denver	CO	28,783	VC
Univ of Detroit Mercy	MI	21,620	LC
Univ of Dubuque	IA	19,990	C
Univ of Evansville	IN	22,865	VC+
Univ of Findlay	OH	23,962	NC
Univ of Florida	FL	7,874	HC
Univ of Georgia	GA	8,656	VC
Univ of Great Falls	MT	15,360	C
Univ of Hartford	CT	28,884	C
Univ of Hawaii at Manoa	HI	7,862	VC
Univ of Houston	TX	8,410	C
Univ of Houston-Downtown	TX	2,006	NC
Univ of Idaho	ID	7,026	C
Univ of Illinois at Chicago	IL	10,702	VC
Univ of Illinois at Urbana-Champaign	IL	11,316	HC+
Univ of Indianapolis	IN	20,840	C
Univ of Iowa	IA	8,607	C+
Univ of Kansas	KS	7,232	VC
Univ of Kentucky	KY	7,765	C
Univ of La Verne	CA	24,280	C
Univ of Louisiana at Lafayette	LA	5,200	C
Univ of Louisiana at Monroe	LA	5,207	NC
Univ of Louisville	KY	7,402	LC
Univ of Maine at Augusta	ME	3,928	C
Univ of Maine at Machias	ME	7,689	LC
Univ of Maine at Presque Isle	ME	7,964	LC
Univ of Mary	ND	12,900	LC
Univ of Mary Hardin-Baylor	TX	13,929	C
Univ of Maryland/College Park	MD	11,959	C
Univ of Maryland/Eastern Shore	MD	9,258	C
Univ of Maryland/Univ College	MD	5,910	SP
Univ of Mass Amherst	MA	10,995	VC
Univ of Mass Dartmouth	MA	9,852	C
Univ of Memphis	TN	7,271	C
Univ of Miami	FL	31,130	HC
Univ of Mich/Flint	MI	4,323	C
Univ of Minn/Crookston	MN	9,626	NC
Univ of Minn/Twin Cities	MN	11,123	VC
Univ of Miss	MS	7,666	C
Univ of Missouri/Columbia	MO	9,803	HC
Univ of Missouri/Kansas City	MO	9,685	VC
Univ of Missouri/St. Louis	MO	9,966	C
Univ of Mobile	AL	13,620	LC
Univ of Montana	MT	8,038	C
Univ of Montevallo	AL	7,266	C
Univ of Nebr at Kearney	NE	7,048	NC
Univ of Nebr at Lincoln	NE	8,325	C+
Univ of Nebr at Omaha	NE	6,867	C
Univ of Nevada/Las Vegas	NV	8,281	VC
Univ of Nevada/Reno	NV	8,737	C
Univ of New Haven	CT	23,860	LC
Univ of New Mexico	NM	8,026	C
Univ of New Orleans	LA	10,160	C
Univ of North Alabama	AL	7,016	NC
Univ of N Car at Asheville	NC	6,896	VC
Univ of N Car at Charlotte	NC	7,254	C
Univ of N Car at Greensboro	NC	6,858	C
Univ of N Car at Pembroke	NC	5,914	LC
Univ of N Car at Wilmington	NC	7,769	C
Univ of N Dak	ND	7,067	VC
Univ of North Florida	FL	8,089	VC
Univ of North Texas	TX	7,629	C
Univ of Northern Colo	CO	8,082	C+
Univ of Northern Iowa	IA	7,850	C
Univ of Notre Dame	IN	30,707	MC
Univ of Okla	OK	7,616	VC
Univ of Oregon	OR	9,969	C
Univ of Pennsylvania	PA	34,614	MC
Univ of Phoenix	AZ	7,000	SP
Univ of Pittsburgh at Greensburg	PA	12,842	C
Univ of Pittsburgh at Johnstown	PA	13,044	LC
Univ of Pittsburgh at Pittsburgh	PA	13,592	HC
Univ of Portland	OR	24,950	VC
Univ of PR at Humacao	PR	1,245	
Univ of PR/Bayamon Univ College Campus	PR	1,600	
Univ of PR/Cayey Univ College	PR	1,245	
Univ of PR/Mayaguez	PR	5,285	
Univ of PR/Rio Piedras	PR	5,510	
Univ of Redlands	CA	29,246	VC
Univ of Rhode Island	RI	12,414	C
Univ of Richmond	VA	27,300	HC
Univ of Rio Grande	OH	8,728	NC
Univ of St. Francis	IL	19,650	C
Univ of St. Francis	IN	17,790	LC
Univ of St. Thomas	MN	24,044	VC
Univ of St. Thomas	TX	18,752	VC
Univ of San Diego	CA	29,198	HC
Univ of San Francisco	CA	27,302	VC
Univ of Science and Arts of Okla	OK	5,245	C
Univ of Scranton	PA	27,964	C+
Univ of Sioux Falls	SD	16,390	C
Univ of S Car at Columbia	SC	8,748	VC
Univ of S Car at Spartanburg	SC	7,318	C+
Univ of S Dak	SD	7,036	C
Univ of South Florida	FL	8,154	C
Univ of Southern Calif	CA	33,647	MC
Univ of Southern Colo	CO	7,821	LC
Univ of Southern Indiana	IN	8,655	LC
Univ of Southern Maine	ME	10,569	C
Univ of Southern Miss	MS	6,155	LC
Univ of Tampa	FL	22,612	C
Univ of Tenn at Knoxville	TN	8,214	C
Univ of Tenn at Martin	TN	8,268	C
Univ of Texas at Arlington	TX	7,192	LC
Univ of Texas at Austin	TX	9,437	HC
Univ of Texas at Dallas	TX	9,305	VC
Univ of Texas at El Paso	TX	5,076	LC
Univ of Texas at San Antonio	TX	9,088	NC
Univ of Texas-Pan American	TX	4,823	C
Univ of the District of Columbia	DC	2,844	NC
Univ of the Incarnate Word	TX	18,478	C
Univ of the Ozarks	AR	13,904	C
Univ of the Sacred Heart	PR	5,375	
Univ of Toledo	OH	11,206	NC
Univ of Tulsa	OK	19,090	HC
Univ of Utah	UT	7,703	C
Univ of Vermont	VT	14,761	C+
Univ of Virginia's College at Wise	VA	8,302	C
Univ of Washington	WA	10,361	VC
Univ of West Alabama	AL	6,048	C
Univ of West Florida	FL	7,518	C
Univ of Wisc/Eau Claire	WI	7,032	VC
Univ of Wisc/Green Bay	WI	7,148	C
Univ of Wisc/La Crosse	WI	7,250	VC
Univ of Wisc/Madison	WI	8,262	VC
Univ of Wisc/Milwaukee	WI	8,907	LC
Univ of Wisc/Oshkosh	WI	6,130	LC
Univ of Wisc/Platteville	WI	7,282	C
Univ of Wisc/River Falls	WI	6,356	LC
Univ of Wisc/Stevens Point	WI	7,116	C
Univ of Wisc/Superior	WI	7,051	C+
Univ of Wisc/Whitewater	WI	6,937	C
Univ of Wyoming	WY	7,143	LC
Upper Iowa Univ	IA	17,438	C
Ursinus College	PA	31,350	VC
Ursuline College	OH	19,430	LC
Utah State Univ	UT	6,771	C
Utica College of Syracuse Univ	NY	24,400	LC
Valdosta State Univ	GA	6,908	C
Valparaiso Univ	IN	23,570	VC+
Vanguard Univ of Southern Calif	CA	20,212	C
Villanova Univ	PA	31,997	HC
Virginia Commonwealth Univ	VA	9,030	C
Virginia Polytechnic Inst and State Univ	VA	7,652	C
Virginia State Univ	VA	8,182	LC
Virginia Union Univ	VA	15,358	LC
Viterbo Univ	WI	18,043	C
Voorhees College	SC	9,976	C+
Wagner College	NY	27,000	C
Wake Forest Univ	NC	30,290	MC
Walsh Univ	OH	16,880	C
Wartburg College	IA	21,165	VC
Washburn Univ of Topeka	KS	6,766	NC
Washington and Jefferson College	PA	26,255	VC
Washington and Lee Univ	VA	25,095	MC
Washington State Univ	WA	9,388	C
Washington Univ in St. Louis	MO	34,593	MC
Wayne State Univ	MI	6,720	C
Waynesburg College	PA	17,610	LC
Webber International Univ	FL	14,695	LC
Weber State Univ	UT	6,897	NC
Webster Univ	MO	19,804	VC
Wesley College	DE	17,869	C
Wesleyan College	GA	17,050	VC
West Chester Univ of Pennsylvania	PA	9,792	VC
West Liberty State College	WV	6,056	LC
West Texas A&M Univ	TX	6,538	C
West Virginia State College	WV	6,264	NC
West Virginia Univ	WV	8,304	C
West Virginia Univ Inst of Technology	WV	7,518	NC
West Virginia Wesleyan College	WV	22,920	C
Western Baptist College	OR	19,700	C+
Western Carolina Univ	NC	5,667	C
Western Conn State Univ	CT	10,074	C
Western Illinois Univ	IL	9,571	C
Western International Univ	AZ	5,800	SP
Western Kentucky Univ	KY	6,834	C
Western Mich Univ	MI	10,016	C
Western New England College	MA	23,882	C
Western New Mexico Univ	NM	5,950	LC
Western State College of Colo	CO	7,585	LC
Western Washington Univ	WA	8,624	VC
Westminster College	MO	19,990	C+
Westminster College	PA	22,960	C
Westminster College	UT	17,226	C
Wheeling Jesuit Univ	WV	22,660	C
Whitworth College	WA	23,938	VC
Wichita State Univ	KS	6,879	C
Widener Univ	PA	26,920	C
Wilberforce Univ	OH	14,937	LC
Wilkes Univ	PA	25,800	C
William Jewell College	MO	17,150	VC
William Paterson Univ of New Jersey	NJ	11,000	LC
William Penn Univ	IA	17,575	C
William Woods Univ	MO	19,390	LC
Wilmington College	DE	6,530	NC
Wilmington College	OH	21,826	C
Wilson College	PA	21,337	LC
Wingate Univ	NC	19,140	C
Winona State Univ	MN	8,570	C
Winston-Salem State Univ	NC	5,927	LC
Wofford College	SC	23,995	VC
Woodbury Univ	CA	25,344	LC
Wright State Univ	OH	9,141	LC
Xavier Univ	OH	23,880	C
Xavier Univ of Louisiana	LA	17,000	LC
Yeshiva Univ	NY	21,400	C
York College	NE	13,500	C
York College of Pennsylvania	PA	12,550	VC
Youngstown State Univ	OH	9,318	NC

ACTUARIAL SCIENCE

School	ST	$IS	SR
Ball State Univ	IN	8,660	C
Bellarmine Univ	KY	20,440	VC
Bradley Univ	IL	20,970	VC
Bryant College	RI	25,980	VC
Butler Univ	IN	25,580	VC+
Carroll College	WI	21,170	C
Central Conn State Univ	CT	10,404	C
Central Mich Univ	MI	8,355	C
Central Missouri State Univ	MO	7,920	C
Central Washington Univ	WA	8,985	LC
CUNY/Baruch College	NY	3,275	VC+
Dominican College	NY	20,400	LC
Drake Univ	IA	22,830	VC
Eastern Mich Univ	MI	9,855	C
Florida A&M Univ	FL	6,948	C
Florida State Univ	FL	7,835	HC
Frostburg State Univ	MD	9,680	C
Georgia State Univ	GA	7,792	LC
Indiana Univ Northwest	IN	3,447	C
Lebanon Valley College of Pennsylvania	PA	25,700	VC
Lincoln Univ	PA	11,198	C+
Maryville Univ of St. Louis	MO	18,680	C
Missouri Valley College	MO	17,400	LC
New York Univ	NY	35,200	MC
N Dak State Univ	ND	7,004	VC
Northwestern College of Iowa	IA	17,630	C+
Ohio Univ	OH	11,769	C
Penn State Univ/Univ Park Campus	PA	11,126	VC
Purdue Univ/West Lafayette	IN	10,284	VC
Rider Univ	NJ	27,400	C
Roosevelt Univ	IL	20,240	LC
Seton Hill College	PA	21,875	C
Southern Adventist Univ	TN	15,600	C
SUNY/College at Brockport	NY	10,267	C
SUNY/Univ at Albany	NY	10,997	VC
Temple Univ	PA	14,124	C
Ohio State Univ	OH	10,819	VC
Thiel College	PA	18,419	LC
Univ of Central Okla	OK	5,205	C
Univ of Illinois at Urbana-Champaign	IL	11,316	HC+
Univ of Iowa	IA	8,607	C+
Univ of Minn/Twin Cities	MN	11,123	VC
Univ of Nebr at Lincoln	NE	8,325	C+
Univ of Northern Colo	CO	8,082	C+
Univ of Pennsylvania	PA	34,614	MC
Univ of St. Thomas	MN	24,044	VC
Univ of Wisc/Madison	WI	8,262	VC
Utica College of Syracuse Univ	NY	24,400	LC

ADDICTION STUDIES

School	ST	$IS	SR
Alvernia College	PA	20,790	C
Calumet College of St. Joseph	IN	7,500	LC
Graceland Univ	IA	15,845	C
Kansas Wesleyan Univ	KS	17,400	C+
Minot State Univ	ND	5,466	LC
Missouri Valley College	MO	17,400	LC
Newman Univ	KS	14,098	LC
Southern Univ at New Orleans	LA	995	NC
Univ of Central Okla	OK	5,205	C
Univ of Detroit Mercy	MI	21,620	LC
Univ of Mary	ND	12,900	LC
Univ of S Dak	SD	7,036	C

ADVERTISING

School	ST	$IS	SR
Abilene Christian Univ	TX	16,300	VC
Adams State College	CO	7,468	C
American International College	MA	22,268	LC
Appalachian State Univ	NC	6,353	C
Art Center College of Design	CA	21,110	SP
Atlanta College of Art	GA	18,600	SP
Barry Univ	FL	24,100	LC
Boston Univ	MA	34,358	MC
Brigham Young Univ	UT	7,840	HC
Cal State, Fullerton	CA	5,440	LC
Cal State, Hayward	CA	7,400	LC
Campbell Univ	NC	16,599	C
Central State Univ	OH	8,922	C+
CUNY/Baruch College	NY	3,275	VC+
Clarke College	IA	20,625	C+
Cleveland Inst of Art	OH	22,680	SP
College For Creative Studies	MI	20,938	SP
Columbia College Chicago	IL	22,063	LC
Columbus College of Art and Design	OH	22,210	SP
Concordia College/Moorhead	MN	18,835	C
Drake Univ	IA	22,830	VC
Drury Univ	MO	15,250	VC
East Central Univ	OK	4,578	C
Eastern Mich Univ	MI	9,855	C
Eastern Nazarene College	MA	19,433	LC
Edinboro Univ of Pennsylvania	PA	9,328	LC
Emerson College	MA	29,978	HC
Fashion Inst of Technology/SUNY	NY	9,504	C+
Ferris State Univ	MI	10,816	C
Florida Southern College	FL	19,430	C
Florida State Univ	FL	7,835	HC
Franklin Pierce College	NH	26,125	LC
Gannon Univ	PA	18,848	C
Grand Valley State Univ	MI	10,040	C
Harding Univ	AR	13,528	VC
Hawaii Pacific Univ	HI	17,790	C
Iona College	NY	26,556	C
Iowa State Univ	IA	8,108	VC
Johnson and Wales Univ	RI	21,558	LC
Kent State Univ	OH	11,104	C
Lamar Univ	TX	6,816	LC
Marietta College	OH	24,580	C
Marquette Univ	WI	24,836	C+
Marywood Univ	PA	24,639	C
Mercyhurst College	PA	20,694	C
Metropolitan State Univ	MN	2,943	SP
Mich State Univ	MI	10,386	VC
Midland Lutheran College	NE	18,600	C
Minneapolis College of Art and Design	MN	23,560	SP
Moorhead State Univ	MN	7,000	LC
Murray State Univ	KY	6,672	C
New York Inst of Technology	NY	21,756	C
Northeastern State Univ	OK	4,704	LC
Northeastern Univ	MA	30,078	VC
Northern Arizona Univ	AZ	7,398	C
Northwest Missouri State Univ	MO	7,922	LC
Northwood Univ	FL	19,179	LC
Northwood Univ	MI	18,360	LC
Ohio Univ	OH	11,769	C
Okla Christian Univ	OK	16,500	VC
Okla City Univ	OK	15,810	C
Parsons School of Design	NY	32,242	SP
Penn State Univ/Univ Park Campus	PA	11,126	VC
Pepperdine Univ	CA	32,830	VC
Point Park College	PA	20,290	C
Portland State Univ	OR	11,220	C
Quinnipiac Univ	CT	27,370	C
Rider Univ	NJ	27,400	C
Roosevelt Univ	IL	20,240	LC
St. Cloud State Univ	MN	7,180	C
Salem State College	MA	4,481	LC
San Jose State Univ	CA	8,187	C
School of Visual Arts	NY	26,000	SP
Simmons College	MA	30,418	VC
Southeast Missouri State Univ	MO	8,367	C+
Southern Methodist Univ	TX	28,349	VC
Southwest Texas State Univ	TX	8,730	VC
Spring Hill College	AL	23,250	C
Syracuse Univ	NY	30,710	HC
Texas A&M Univ at Commerce	TX	7,326	C
Texas Christian Univ	TX	19,910	C
Texas Tech Univ	TX	8,825	C
Texas Woman's Univ	TX	5,855	LC
Thomas Edison State College	NJ	2,750	SP
Union Univ	TN	18,930	C+
Univ of Akron	OH	10,530	NC
Univ of Alabama	AL	7,402	C
Univ of Arkansas at Little Rock	AR	5,637	NC
Univ of Central Florida	FL	8,251	VC
Univ of Central Okla	OK	5,205	C
Univ of Colo at Boulder	CO	9,255	VC
Univ of Florida	FL	7,874	HC
Univ of Georgia	GA	8,656	VC
Univ of Illinois at Urbana-Champaign	IL	11,316	HC+
Univ of Kansas	KS	7,232	VC
Univ of Kentucky	KY	7,765	C
Univ of Louisiana at Lafayette	LA	5,200	C
Univ of Miami	FL	31,130	HC
Univ of Miss	MS	7,666	C
Univ of Missouri/Columbia	MO	9,803	HC
Univ of Nebr at Kearney	NE	7,048	NC
Univ of Nebr at Lincoln	NE	8,325	C+
Univ of Northern Colo	CO	8,082	C+
Univ of Okla	OK	7,616	VC
Univ of Scranton	PA	27,964	C+
Univ of S Car at Columbia	SC	8,748	VC
Univ of Southern Miss	MS	6,155	LC
Univ of Tenn at Knoxville	TN	8,214	C
Univ of Texas at Austin	TX	9,437	HC
Univ of the Sacred Heart	PR	5,375	
Univ of Wisc/Eau Claire	WI	7,032	VC
Washington State Univ	WA	9,388	C
Washington Univ in St. Louis	MO	34,593	MC
Waynesburg College	PA	17,610	LC
Webster Univ	MO	19,804	VC
Wesleyan College	GA	17,050	VC
West Virginia Univ	WV	8,304	C
Western Kentucky Univ	KY	6,834	C
Western Mich Univ	MI	10,016	C
Western New England College	MA	23,882	C
Winona State Univ	MN	8,570	C
Xavier Univ	OH	23,880	C
Youngstown State Univ	OH	9,318	NC

AERONAUTICAL ENGINEERING

School	ST	$IS	SR
Arizona State Univ-Main	AZ	7,726	C
Auburn Univ	AL	5,510	C
Bethel College	IN	17,650	LC
Boston Univ	MA	34,358	MC
Calif Inst of Technology	CA	27,663	MC
Calif Polytechnic State Univ	CA	8,747	VC
Calif State Polytechnic Univ, Pomona	CA	8,615	C
Case Western Reserve Univ	OH	27,418	C
Clarkson Univ	NY	29,884	VC
Embry-Riddle Aeronautical Univ	AZ	23,470	C+
Embry-Riddle Aeronautical Univ	FL	24,790	C
Florida Inst of Technology	FL	25,250	VC
Georgia Inst of Technology	GA	9,028	HC+
Illinois Inst of Technology	IL	25,182	HC+
Iowa State Univ	IA	8,108	VC
Mass Inst of Technology	MA	35,228	MC
New York Inst of Technology	NY	21,756	C
N Car State Univ	NC	8,680	HC
Okla State Univ	OK	7,650	VC
Penn State Univ/Univ Park Campus	PA	11,126	VC
Princeton Univ	NJ	35,072	MC
Purdue Univ/West Lafayette	IN	10,284	VC
Rensselaer Polytechnic Inst	NY	33,863	HC+
St. Louis Univ	MO	26,590	VC+
San Diego State Univ	CA	9,716	C+
San Jose State Univ	CA	8,187	C
SUNY/Univ at Buffalo	NY	11,033	VC
Texas A&M Univ	TX	8,988	VC
Ohio State Univ	OH	10,819	VC
United States Air Force Academy	CO		MC
United States Naval Academy	MD		MC
Univ of Arizona	AZ	8,614	C
Univ of Calif at Davis	CA	12,796	VC
Univ of Calif at Irvine	CA	11,756	C
Univ of Calif at Los Angeles	CA	13,227	MC
Univ of Central Florida	FL	8,251	VC
Univ of Cincinnati	OH	12,491	LC
Univ of Colo at Boulder	CO	9,255	VC
Univ of Florida	FL	7,874	HC
Univ of Illinois at Urbana-Champaign	IL	11,316	HC+
Univ of Kansas	KS	7,232	VC
Univ of Maryland/College Park	MD	11,959	C
Univ of Miami	FL	31,130	HC
Univ of Mich/Ann Arbor	MI	13,003	HC+
Univ of Minn/Twin Cities	MN	11,123	VC
Univ of Missouri/Rolla	MO	10,034	C
Univ of Notre Dame	IN	30,707	MC
Univ of Okla	OK	7,616	VC
Univ of Southern Calif	CA	33,647	MC
Univ of Washington	WA	10,361	VC
West Virginia Univ	WV	8,304	C
Western Mich Univ	MI	10,016	C
Wichita State Univ	KS	6,879	C

AERONAUTICAL SCIENCE

School	ST	$IS	SR
Dowling College	NY	20,281	LC
Embry-Riddle Aeronautical Univ	AZ	23,470	C+
Embry-Riddle Aeronautical Univ	FL	24,790	C
Florida Inst of Technology	FL	25,250	VC
LeTourneau Univ	TX	19,020	VC
Rocky Mountain College	MT	18,113	C
Stanford Univ	CA	34,222	MC
SUNY/College of Technology at Farmingdale	NY	11,269	C
Univ of Maryland/Eastern Shore	MD	9,258	C
Western Mich Univ	MI	10,016	C

AERONAUTICAL TECHNOLOGY

School	ST	$IS	SR
Andrews Univ	MI	17,696	LC
Central Washington Univ	WA	8,985	LC
Dowling College	NY	20,281	LC
Embry-Riddle Aeronautical Univ	FL	24,790	C
Indiana State Univ	IN	8,461	LC
Kansas State Univ	KS	6,995	C
Kent State Univ	OH	11,104	C
LeTourneau Univ	TX	19,020	VC
Purdue Univ/West Lafayette	IN	10,284	VC
Tenn State Univ	TN	7,058	VC
Univ of Alaska Anchorage	AK	9,100	NC
Western Mich Univ	MI	10,016	C

AEROSPACE STUDIES

School	ST	$IS	SR
Cal State, Long Beach	CA	7,400	LC
Cornell Univ	NY	34,614	MC
Embry-Riddle Aeronautical Univ	AZ	23,470	C+
Embry-Riddle Aeronautical Univ	FL	24,790	C
Florida Inst of Technology	FL	25,250	VC
Indiana Univ Bloomington	IN	10,712	C+
Mass Inst of Technology	MA	35,228	MC
Middle Tenn State Univ	TN	6,994	C
Miss State Univ	MS	7,853	C
Rochester Inst of Technology	NY	26,232	VC+
Syracuse Univ	NY	30,710	HC
United States Air Force Academy	CO		MC
Univ of Alabama	AL	7,402	C
Univ of Arizona	AZ	8,614	C
Univ of Calif at San Diego	CA	11,372	HC
Univ of Central Florida	FL	8,251	VC
Univ of N Dak	ND	7,067	VC
Univ of Tenn at Knoxville	TN	8,214	C
Univ of Texas at Austin	TX	9,437	HC
Univ of Virginia	VA	9,391	HC+
West Virginia Univ	WV	8,304	C

AFRICAN AMERICAN STUDIES

School	ST	$IS	SR
Amherst College	MA	34,340	MC
Arizona State Univ-Main	AZ	7,726	C
Bates College	ME	34,100	MC
Brandeis Univ	MA	34,481	MC
Brown Univ	RI	34,973	MC
Cal State, Fresno	CA	7,762	C
Cal State, Fullerton	CA	5,440	LC
Cal State, Long Beach	CA	7,400	LC
Cal State, Los Angeles	CA	5,050	C
Cal State, Northridge	CA	7,781	C
Carleton College	MN	30,780	MC
Chicago State Univ	IL	8,851	C+
CUNY/College of Staten Island	NY	3,358	NC
CUNY/Herbert H. Lehman College	NY	3,320	LC
CUNY/Hunter College	NY	5,147	C+
CUNY/York College	NY	3,292	NC
Claremont McKenna College	CA	32,700	MC
Coe College	IA	24,750	VC
College of the Holy Cross	MA	32,780	MC
College of Wooster	OH	28,350	VC
Columbia Univ/Columbia College	NY	35,190	MC
Columbia Univ/School of General Studies	NY	35,000	C
Dartmouth College	NH	34,458	MC
Denison Univ	OH	29,640	HC
Duke Univ	NC	34,396	MC
Earlham College	IN	27,446	VC+
Eastern Illinois Univ	IL	10,101	C
Eastern Mich Univ	MI	9,855	C
Fordham Univ	NY	30,710	VC
Guilford College	NC	23,255	C
Hampshire College	MA	33,881	HC+
Harvard Univ/Harvard College	MA	34,269	MC
Howard Univ	DC	15,522	LC
Indiana State Univ	IN	8,461	LC
Indiana Univ Bloomington	IN	10,712	C+
Indiana Univ Northwest	IN	3,447	C
Knox College	IL	28,230	HC
Loyola Marymount Univ	CA	28,754	HC
Luther College	IA	23,300	VC+
Martin Univ	IN	8,370	SP
Metropolitan State College of Denver	CO	2,338	LC
Miami Univ	OH	12,885	VC+
Morehouse College	GA	19,814	C
Morgan State Univ	MD	10,078	LC
Mount Holyoke College	MA	34,128	HC
Norfolk State Univ	VA	8,382	LC
Northeastern Univ	MA	30,078	VC
Northwestern Univ	IL	33,615	MC
Oakland Univ	MI	9,418	C
Oberlin College	OH	33,140	HC+
Ohio Univ	OH	11,769	C
Ohio Wesleyan Univ	OH	29,670	VC+
Penn State Univ/Univ Park Campus	PA	11,126	VC
Pitzer College	CA	33,930	HC
Pomona College	CA	33,960	MC
Purdue Univ/West Lafayette	IN	10,284	VC
Rhode Island College	RI	8,700	LC
Roosevelt Univ	IL	20,240	LC
Rutgers, The State Univ of New Jersey New Brunswick Campus	NJ	12,709	C
Rutgers, The State Univ of New Jersey/CamdenCampus	NJ	6,484	C
St. Augustine's College	NC	12,990	C+
San Francisco State Univ	CA	7,139	LC
Scripps College	CA	30,400	HC+
Seton Hall Univ	NJ	26,910	LC
Simmons College	MA	30,418	VC
Simon's Rock College of Bard	MA	32,450	HC
Smith College	MA	33,302	HC+
Southern Methodist Univ	TX	28,349	VC
Stanford Univ	CA	34,222	MC
SUNY/College at Brockport	NY	10,267	C
SUNY/College at Cortland	NY	10,564	C
SUNY/College at Geneseo	NY	9,970	HC
SUNY/Univ at Albany	NY	10,997	VC
SUNY/Univ at Binghamton	NY	10,653	HC
SUNY/Univ at Buffalo	NY	11,033	VC
Syracuse Univ	NY	30,710	HC
Temple Univ	PA	14,124	C
Ohio State Univ	OH	10,819	VC
Univ of Calif at Berkeley	CA	14,134	MC
Univ of Calif at Los Angeles	CA	13,227	MC
Univ of Calif at Riverside	CA	12,479	C
Univ of Calif at Santa Barbara	CA	11,732	VC
Univ of Chicago	IL	35,087	MC
Univ of Cincinnati	OH	12,491	LC
Univ of Illinois at Chicago	IL	10,702	VC
Univ of Iowa	IA	8,607	C+
Univ of Kansas	KS	7,232	VC
Univ of Maryland/Baltimore County	MD	12,190	VC
Univ of Maryland/College Park	MD	11,959	C
Univ of Mass Amherst	MA	10,995	VC
Univ of Mass Boston	MA	4,227	C
Univ of Miami	FL	31,130	HC
Univ of Mich/Ann Arbor	MI	13,003	HC+
Univ of Minn/Twin Cities	MN	11,123	VC
Univ of New Mexico	NM	8,026	C
Univ of N Car at Chapel Hill	NC	8,789	HC
Univ of N Car at Charlotte	NC	7,254	C
Univ of Northern Colo	CO	8,082	C+
Univ of Okla	OK	7,616	VC
Univ of Pennsylvania	PA	34,614	MC
Univ of Pittsburgh at Pittsburgh	PA	13,592	HC
Univ of Puget Sound	WA	28,285	HC
Univ of S Car at Columbia	SC	8,748	VC
Univ of South Florida	FL	8,154	C
Univ of Southern Calif	CA	33,647	MC
Univ of Tenn at Knoxville	TN	8,214	C
Univ of Virginia	VA	9,391	HC+
Univ of Washington	WA	10,361	VC
Univ of Wisc/Madison	WI	8,262	VC
Univ of Wisc/Milwaukee	WI	8,907	LC
Vanderbilt Univ	TN	34,482	MC
Washington Univ in St. Louis	MO	34,593	MC
Wayne State Univ	MI	6,720	C
Wellesley College	MA	33,394	MC
Wesleyan Univ	CT	3,405	MC
William Paterson Univ of New Jersey	NJ	11,000	LC
Yale Univ	CT	34,030	MC

AFRICAN LANGUAGES

School	ST	$IS	SR
Duke Univ	NC	34,396	MC
Univ of Calif at Los Angeles	CA	13,227	MC
Univ of Wisc/Madison	WI	8,262	VC

AFRICAN STUDIES

School	ST	$IS	SR
Bard College	NY	33,912	HC
Bowdoin College	ME	32,650	MC
Bowling Green State Univ	OH	10,794	C
Brandeis Univ	MA	34,481	MC
Cal State, Dominguez Hills	CA	5,840	LC
Carleton College	MN	30,780	MC
CUNY/Brooklyn College	NY	3,403	LC
CUNY/Queens College	NY	3,403	VC
Colgate Univ	NY	33,480	MC
College of the Holy Cross	MA	32,780	MC
Conn College	CT	33,585	MC
Cornell Univ	NY	34,614	MC
Dartmouth College	NH	34,458	MC
Dillard Univ	LA	16,046	VC
Duke Univ	NC	34,396	MC
Emory Univ	GA	33,792	MC
Fordham Univ	NY	30,710	VC
Franklin and Marshall College	PA	32,410	HC
Hamilton College	NY	34,150	HC
Hampshire College	MA	33,881	HC+
Hofstra Univ	NY	23,252	C
Howard Univ	DC	15,522	LC
Kent State Univ	OH	11,104	C
Lafayette College	PA	32,655	MC
Lehigh Univ	PA	32,290	MC
Morris Brown College	GA	15,993	LC
New York Univ	NY	35,200	MC
Ohio Univ	OH	11,769	C
St. Lawrence Univ	NY	32,605	VC
San Diego State Univ	CA	9,716	C+
Shaw Univ	NC	12,810	C
SUNY/College at Brockport	NY	10,267	C
SUNY/College at Oneonta	NY	9,981	C
SUNY/Univ at Stony Brook	NY	10,998	VC
Tenn State Univ	TN	7,058	VC
Tulane Univ	LA	34,013	HC+
Univ of Calif at Davis	CA	12,796	VC
Univ of Kansas	KS	7,232	VC
Univ of Louisville	KY	7,402	LC
Univ of Mich/Ann Arbor	MI	13,003	HC+
Univ of Minn/Twin Cities	MN	11,123	VC
Univ of N Car at Chapel Hill	NC	8,789	HC
Univ of Pennsylvania	PA	34,614	MC
Vassar College	NY	33,450	MC
Washington Univ in St. Louis	MO	34,593	MC
Wayne State Univ	MI	6,720	C
Youngstown State Univ	OH	9,318	NC

AGRICULTURAL BUSINESS MANAGEMENT

School	ST	$IS	SR
Alabama A&M Univ	AL	5,100	LC
Arkansas State Univ	AR	7,480	C
Arkansas Tech Univ	AR	6,256	C
Auburn Univ	AL	5,510	C
Calif Polytechnic State Univ	CA	8,747	VC
Calif State Polytechnic Univ, Pomona	CA	8,615	C
Cal State, Chico	CA	8,598	LC
Cal State, Fresno	CA	7,762	C
Central Missouri State Univ	MO	7,920	C
College of the Ozarks	MO	2,650	C+
Colo State Univ	CO	9,672	C
Cornell Univ	NY	34,614	MC
Delaware State Univ	DE	8,104	LC
Dickinson State Univ	ND	5,495	NC
Eastern New Mexico Univ	NM	4,113	LC
Eastern Oregon Univ	OR	8,772	C
Fort Hays State Univ	KS	6,294	LC
Freed-Hardeman Univ	TN	14,290	VC
Iowa State Univ	IA	8,108	VC
Kansas State Univ	KS	6,995	C
Lindenwood Univ	MO	17,250	C
Louisiana State Univ and A&M College	LA	8,014	VC
Louisiana Tech Univ	LA	6,506	C
Lubbock Christian Univ	TX	14,226	LC
McNeese State Univ	LA	5,259	LC
Middle Tenn State Univ	TN	6,994	C
Miss State Univ	MS	7,853	C
Missouri Valley College	MO	17,400	LC
Montana State Univ-Bozeman	MT	8,431	C
New Mexico State Univ	NM	7,302	C
Nicholls State Univ	LA	5,290	NC
N Car Agricultural and Technical State Univ	NC	6,659	LC
N Car State Univ	NC	8,680	HC
N Dak State Univ	ND	7,004	VC
Northwest Missouri State Univ	MO	7,922	LC
Northwestern College of Iowa	IA	17,630	C+
Northwestern Okla State Univ	OK	4,542	NC
Okla Panhandle State Univ	OK	3,812	NC
Okla State Univ	OK	7,650	VC
Oregon State Univ	OR	9,612	VC
Penn State Univ/Univ Park Campus	PA	11,126	VC
Prairie View A&M Univ	TX	3,172	LC
Purdue Univ/West Lafayette	IN	10,284	VC
S Car State Univ	SC	6,586	LC
S Dak State Univ	SD	6,848	C
Southeast Missouri State Univ	MO	8,367	C+
Southern Arkansas Univ	AR	5,740	LC
Southwest State Univ	MN	7,117	LC
Southwest Texas State Univ	TX	8,730	VC
SUNY/College of Agriculture and Technology at Cobleskill	NY	11,200	C+
Stephen F. Austin State Univ	TX	6,905	C
Sul Ross State Univ	TX	6,582	LC
Tarleton State Univ	TX	7,160	C
Texas A&M Univ	TX	8,988	VC
Texas A&M Univ at Kingsville	TX	6,446	LC
Texas Tech Univ	TX	8,825	C
Univ of Arkansas	AR	8,334	VC
Univ of Calif at Davis	CA	12,796	VC
Univ of Delaware	DE	10,824	VC
Univ of Florida	FL	7,874	HC
Univ of Idaho	ID	7,026	C
Univ of Louisiana at Monroe	LA	5,207	NC
Univ of Maryland/College Park	MD	11,959	C
Univ of Minn/Crookston	MN	9,626	NC
Univ of Minn/Twin Cities	MN	11,123	VC
Univ of Nebr at Lincoln	NE	8,325	C+
Univ of Tenn at Martin	TN	8,268	C
Univ of Wisc/Madison	WI	8,262	VC
Univ of Wisc/Platteville	WI	7,282	C
Univ of Wisc/River Falls	WI	6,356	LC
Univ of Wyoming	WY	7,143	LC
Utah State Univ	UT	6,771	C
Washington State Univ	WA	9,388	C
West Texas A&M Univ	TX	6,538	C
West Virginia Univ	WV	8,304	C

AGRICULTURAL ECONOMICS

School	ST	$IS	SR
Alabama A&M Univ	AL	5,100	LC
Alcorn State Univ	MS	5,594	LC
Central Missouri State Univ	MO	7,920	C
Colo State Univ	CO	9,672	C
Cornell Univ	NY	34,614	MC
Eastern Oregon Univ	OR	8,772	C
Fort Valley State Univ	GA	6,014	LC
Kansas State Univ	KS	6,995	C
Langston Univ	OK	2,308	LC
McPherson College	KS	17,710	C
Miss State Univ	MS	7,853	C
N Car Agricultural and Technical State Univ	NC	6,659	LC
N Car State Univ	NC	8,680	HC
N Dak State Univ	ND	7,004	VC
Okla State Univ	OK	7,650	VC
Oregon State Univ	OR	9,612	VC
Prairie View A&M Univ	TX	3,172	LC
Purdue Univ/West Lafayette	IN	10,284	VC
S Dak State Univ	SD	6,848	C
Southern Illinois Univ at Carbondale	IL	8,621	C
Southern Univ and A&M College	LA	6,365	C+
Tarleton State Univ	TX	7,160	C
Tenn Tech Univ	TN	6,968	C
Texas A&M Univ	TX	8,988	VC
Texas A&M Univ at Commerce	TX	7,326	C
Ohio State Univ	OH	10,819	VC
Truman State Univ	MO	8,568	VC+
Univ of Arizona	AZ	8,614	C
Univ of Arkansas	AR	8,334	VC
Univ of Calif at Davis	CA	12,796	VC
Univ of Conn	CT	12,122	VC
Univ of Delaware	DE	10,824	VC
Univ of Georgia	GA	8,656	VC
Univ of Hawaii at Manoa	HI	7,862	VC
Univ of Idaho	ID	7,026	C
Univ of Illinois at Urbana-Champaign	IL	11,316	HC+
Univ of Kentucky	KY	7,765	C
Univ of Maryland/College Park	MD	11,959	C
Univ of Minn/Twin Cities	MN	11,123	VC
Univ of Missouri/Columbia	MO	9,803	HC
Univ of Nebr at Lincoln	NE	8,325	C+
Univ of Nevada/Reno	NV	8,737	C
Univ of Tenn at Knoxville	TN	8,214	C
Univ of Wisc/Madison	WI	8,262	VC
Univ of Wisc/Platteville	WI	7,282	C
Utah State Univ	UT	6,771	C
Virginia Polytechnic Inst and State Univ	VA	7,652	C
Washington State Univ	WA	9,388	C
West Texas A&M Univ	TX	6,538	C

AGRICULTURAL EDUCATION

School	ST	$IS	SR
Alabama A&M Univ	AL	5,100	LC
Arkansas State Univ	AR	7,480	C
Cal State, Fresno	CA	7,762	C
Central Missouri State Univ	MO	7,920	C
Clemson Univ	SC	7,600	C
College of the Ozarks	MO	2,650	C+
Colo State Univ	CO	9,672	C
Delaware State Univ	DE	8,104	LC
Eastern New Mexico Univ	NM	4,113	LC
Fort Valley State Univ	GA	6,014	LC
Iowa State Univ	IA	8,108	VC
Kansas State Univ	KS	6,995	C
Mich State Univ	MI	10,386	VC
Miss State Univ	MS	7,853	C
Montana State Univ-Bozeman	MT	8,431	C
Morehead State Univ	KY	6,510	C
Murray State Univ	KY	6,672	C
New Mexico State Univ	NM	7,302	C
N Car Agricultural and Technical State Univ	NC	6,659	LC
N Car State Univ	NC	8,680	HC
N Dak State Univ	ND	7,004	VC
Northwest Missouri State Univ	MO	7,922	LC
Okla Panhandle State Univ	OK	3,812	NC
Okla State Univ	OK	7,650	VC
Penn State Univ/Univ Park Campus	PA	11,126	VC
Purdue Univ/West Lafayette	IN	10,284	VC
S Dak State Univ	SD	6,848	C
Southern Arkansas Univ	AR	5,740	LC
Southwest Missouri State Univ	MO	7,600	LC
Stephen F. Austin State Univ	TX	6,905	C
Tarleton State Univ	TX	7,160	C
Tenn Tech Univ	TN	6,968	C
Texas A&M Univ at Commerce	TX	7,326	C
Texas A&M Univ at Kingsville	TX	6,446	LC
Ohio State Univ	OH	10,819	VC
Univ of Arizona	AZ	8,614	C
Univ of Arkansas	AR	8,334	VC
Univ of Arkansas at Pine Bluff	AR	7,925	C
Univ of Conn	CT	12,122	VC
Univ of Delaware	DE	10,824	VC
Univ of Florida	FL	7,874	HC
Univ of Georgia	GA	8,656	VC
Univ of Idaho	ID	7,026	C
Univ of Illinois at Urbana-Champaign	IL	11,316	HC+
Univ of Kentucky	KY	7,765	C
Univ of Louisiana at Lafayette	LA	5,200	C
Univ of Maryland/Eastern Shore	MD	9,258	C
Univ of Minn/Twin Cities	MN	11,123	VC
Univ of Nebr at Lincoln	NE	8,325	C+
Univ of Tenn at Knoxville	TN	8,214	C
Univ of Tenn at Martin	TN	8,268	C
Univ of Wisc/Madison	WI	8,262	VC
Univ of Wisc/Platteville	WI	7,282	C
Univ of Wisc/River Falls	WI	6,356	LC
Univ of Wyoming	WY	7,143	LC
Utah State Univ	UT	6,771	C
Virginia Polytechnic Inst and State Univ	VA	7,652	C
Washington State Univ	WA	9,388	C
West Virginia Univ	WV	8,304	C

AGRICULTURAL ENGINEERING

School	ST	$IS	SR
Auburn Univ	AL	5,510	C
Calif Polytechnic State Univ	CA	8,747	VC
Clemson Univ	SC	7,600	C
Colo State Univ	CO	9,672	C
Cornell Univ	NY	34,614	MC
Iowa State Univ	IA	8,108	VC
Kansas State Univ	KS	6,995	C
N Car State Univ	NC	8,680	HC
N Dak State Univ	ND	7,004	VC
Penn State Univ/Univ Park Campus	PA	11,126	VC
Purdue Univ/West Lafayette	IN	10,284	VC
S Dak State Univ	SD	6,848	C
Texas A&M Univ	TX	8,988	VC
Univ of Arizona	AZ	8,614	C
Univ of Arkansas	AR	8,334	VC
Univ of Calif at Davis	CA	12,796	VC
Univ of Florida	FL	7,874	HC
Univ of Georgia	GA	8,656	VC
Univ of Idaho	ID	7,026	C
Univ of Illinois at Urbana-Champaign	IL	11,316	HC+
Univ of Minn/Twin Cities	MN	11,123	VC
Univ of Nebr at Lincoln	NE	8,325	C+
Univ of Tenn at Knoxville	TN	8,214	C
Univ of Wisc/Madison	WI	8,262	VC
Univ of Wisc/River Falls	WI	6,356	LC
Utah State Univ	UT	6,771	C
Virginia Polytechnic Inst and State Univ	VA	7,652	C
Washington State Univ	WA	9,388	C

AGRICULTURAL ENGINEERING TECHNOLOGY

School	ST	$IS	SR
Central Missouri State Univ	MO	7,920	C
Fort Valley State Univ	GA	6,014	LC
Miss State Univ	MS	7,853	C
Montana State Univ-Bozeman	MT	8,431	C
S Dak State Univ	SD	6,848	C
Univ of Arizona	AZ	8,614	C
Univ of Wisc/Platteville	WI	7,282	C

AGRICULTURAL MECHANICS

School	ST	$IS	SR
Montana State Univ-Northern	MT	8,600	NC
Murray State Univ	KY	6,672	C
N Dak State Univ	ND	7,004	VC
Northwest Missouri State Univ	MO	7,922	LC
Purdue Univ/West Lafayette	IN	10,284	VC
SUNY/College of Agriculture and Technology at Cobleskill	NY	11,200	C+
Stephen F. Austin State Univ	TX	6,905	C
Tarleton State Univ	TX	7,160	C
Univ of Idaho	ID	7,026	C
Univ of Illinois at Urbana-Champaign	IL	11,316	HC+
Univ of Nebr at Lincoln	NE	8,325	C+
Univ of Wisc/Madison	WI	8,262	VC
Washington State Univ	WA	9,388	C

AGRICULTURE

School	ST	$IS	SR
Alcorn State Univ	MS	5,594	LC
Andrews Univ	MI	17,696	LC
Arkansas State Univ	AR	7,480	C
Auburn Univ	AL	5,510	C
Austin Peay State Univ	TN	5,814	LC
Berea College	KY	4,070	VC
Calif Polytechnic State Univ	CA	8,747	VC
Calif State Polytechnic Univ, Pomona	CA	8,615	C
Cal State, Chico	CA	8,598	LC
Clemson Univ	SC	7,600	C
College of the Ozarks	MO	2,650	C+
Cornell Univ	NY	34,614	MC
Delaware Valley College	PA	24,213	LC
Eastern Kentucky Univ	KY	6,552	C
Eastern New Mexico Univ	NM	4,113	LC
Ferrum College	VA	15,990	LC
Fort Hays State Univ	KS	6,294	LC
Hampshire College	MA	33,881	HC+
Illinois State Univ	IL	9,235	C
Iowa State Univ	IA	8,108	VC
Lincoln Univ	MO	7,158	NC
McNeese State Univ	LA	5,259	LC
Mich State Univ	MI	10,386	VC
Miss State Univ	MS	7,853	C
Morehead State Univ	KY	6,510	C
Murray State Univ	KY	6,672	C
New Mexico State Univ	NM	7,302	C
N Car State Univ	NC	8,680	HC
N Dak State Univ	ND	7,004	VC
Northwest Missouri State Univ	MO	7,922	LC
Northwestern Okla State Univ	OK	4,542	NC
Oregon State Univ	OR	9,612	VC
Penn State Univ/Univ Park Campus	PA	11,126	VC
Purdue Univ/West Lafayette	IN	10,284	VC
Rice Univ	TX	24,325	MC
Rutgers, The State Univ of New Jersey New Brunswick Campus	NJ	12,709	C
Sam Houston State Univ	TX	6,076	LC
S Dak State Univ	SD	6,848	C
Southeast Missouri State Univ	MO	8,367	C+
Southern Arkansas Univ	AR	5,740	LC
Southern Nazarene Univ	OK	14,634	NC
Southern Univ and A&M College	LA	6,365	C+
Southern Utah Univ	UT	7,254	C
Southwest Missouri State Univ	MO	7,600	LC
Southwest Texas State Univ	TX	8,730	VC
Stephen F. Austin State Univ	TX	6,905	C
Tarleton State Univ	TX	7,160	C
Tenn State Univ	TN	7,058	VC
Tenn Tech Univ	TN	6,968	C
Texas A&M Univ at Commerce	TX	7,326	C
Truman State Univ	MO	8,568	VC+
Univ of Arkansas at Monticello	AR	5,940	NC
Univ of Arkansas at Pine Bluff	AR	7,925	C
Univ of Conn	CT	12,122	VC

School	ST	$IS	SR
Univ of Delaware	DE	10,824	VC
Univ of Georgia	GA	8,656	VC
Univ of Hawaii at Hilo	HI	6,497	C
Univ of Hawaii at Manoa	HI	7,862	VC
Univ of Idaho	ID	7,026	C
Univ of Kentucky	KY	7,765	C
Univ of Maine	ME	10,798	C
Univ of Maryland/College Park	MD	11,959	C
Univ of Maryland/Eastern Shore	MD	9,258	C
Univ of Missouri/Columbia	MO	9,803	HC
Univ of Nebr at Lincoln	NE	8,325	C+
Univ of Tenn at Knoxville	TN	8,214	C
Univ of Tenn at Martin	TN	8,268	C
Univ of Vermont	VT	14,761	C+
Univ of Wyoming	WY	7,143	LC
Virginia State Univ	VA	8,182	LC
Washington State Univ	WA	9,388	C
West Texas A&M Univ	TX	6,538	C
West Virginia Univ	WV	8,304	C
Western Illinois Univ	IL	9,571	C
Western Kentucky Univ	KY	6,834	C
Wilmington College	OH	21,826	C

AGRONOMY

School	ST	$IS	SR
Alabama A&M Univ	AL	5,100	LC
Alcorn State Univ	MS	5,594	LC
Brigham Young Univ	UT	7,840	HC
Calif State Polytechnic Univ, Pomona	CA	8,615	C
College of the Ozarks	MO	2,650	C+
Colo State Univ	CO	9,672	C
Cornell Univ	NY	34,614	MC
Iowa State Univ	IA	8,108	VC
Kansas State Univ	KS	6,995	C
McPherson College	KS	17,710	C
Miss State Univ	MS	7,853	C
New Mexico State Univ	NM	7,302	C
N Car State Univ	NC	8,680	HC
Northwest Missouri State Univ	MO	7,922	LC
Okla Panhandle State Univ	OK	3,812	NC
Penn State Univ/Univ Park Campus	PA	11,126	VC
Prairie View A&M Univ	TX	3,172	LC
Purdue Univ/West Lafayette	IN	10,284	VC
S Dak State Univ	SD	6,848	C
Southeast Missouri State Univ	MO	8,367	C+
Southwest Missouri State Univ	MO	7,600	LC
Stephen F. Austin State Univ	TX	6,905	C
Texas Tech Univ	TX	8,825	C
Truman State Univ	MO	8,568	VC+
Univ of Conn	CT	12,122	VC
Univ of Florida	FL	7,874	HC
Univ of Hawaii at Manoa	HI	7,862	VC
Univ of Illinois at Urbana-Champaign	IL	11,316	HC+
Univ of Maryland/College Park	MD	11,959	C
Univ of Nebr at Lincoln	NE	8,325	C+
Univ of Wisc/River Falls	WI	6,356	LC
Washington State Univ	WA	9,388	C
West Virginia Univ	WV	8,304	C

AIR TRAFFIC CONTROL

School	ST	$IS	SR
Daniel Webster College	NH	24,870	C
Florida Memorial College	FL	6,000	LC
Thomas Edison State College	NJ	2,750	SP
Univ of N Dak	ND	7,067	VC

AIRCRAFT MECHANICS

School	ST	$IS	SR
Andrews Univ	MI	17,696	LC
College of Aeronautics	NY	10,730	SP
Concordia Univ	MI	20,500	C
Kent State Univ	OH	11,104	C
Lewis Univ	IL	20,960	C
Pennsylvania College of Technology	PA	12,860	NC
St. John's Univ	NY	26,660	C
St. Louis Univ	MO	26,590	VC+
Western Mich Univ	MI	10,016	C

AIRLINE PILOTING AND NAVIGATION

School	ST	$IS	SR
Baylor Univ	TX	18,298	VC+
College of Aeronautics	NY	10,730	SP
Daniel Webster College	NH	24,870	C
Eastern Kentucky Univ	KY	6,552	C
Indiana State Univ	IN	8,461	LC
Lewis Univ	IL	20,960	C
Louisiana Tech Univ	LA	6,506	C
Metropolitan State College of Denver	CO	2,338	LC
Ohio Univ	OH	11,769	C
Pacific Union College	CA	20,250	VC
St. Louis Univ	MO	26,590	VC+

School	ST	$IS	SR
Univ of Illinois at Urbana-Champaign	IL	11,316	HC+
Univ of Louisville	KY	7,402	LC

ALLIED HEALTH

School	ST	$IS	SR
Adams State College	CO	7,468	C
Albany State Univ	GA	5,764	C+
Andrews Univ	MI	17,696	LC
Bridgewater College	VA	22,950	C
Champlain College	VT	19,680	C
Clark Atlanta Univ	GA	17,174	C
Clayton College and State Univ	GA	2,322	C+
College of Mount St. Vincent	NY	24,230	C
Davenport Univ	MI	10,057	NC
East Stroudsburg Univ of Pennsylvania	PA	8,430	LC
East Tenn State Univ	TN	7,127	C
Eastern Mich Univ	MI	9,855	C
Fairleigh Dickinson Univ/Teaneck Campus	NJ	24,646	C
Ithaca College	NY	28,719	HC
Johnson State College	VT	10,776	C
Madonna Univ	MI	11,504	VC
Mars Hill College	NC	18,600	LC
Marygrove College	MI	16,075	C
Mass College of Pharmacy and Health Sciences	MA	27,131	SP
Merrimack College	MA	25,725	VC
Montclair State Univ	NJ	10,287	LC
National American Univ	SD	13,680	NC
Rochester Inst of Technology	NY	26,232	VC+
Roosevelt Univ	IL	20,240	LC
Saginaw Valley State Univ	MI	9,465	C
San Francisco State Univ	CA	7,139	LC
Univ of Alabama at Birmingham	AL	10,110	C
Univ of Florida	FL	7,874	HC
Univ of Northern Colo	CO	8,082	C+
Univ of St. Francis	IL	19,650	C
Univ of St. Francis	IN	17,790	LC
Univ of S Dak	SD	7,036	C
Univ of Texas at El Paso	TX	5,076	LC
Ursuline College	OH	19,430	LC
West Texas A&M Univ	TX	6,538	C
Youngstown State Univ	OH	9,318	NC

AMERICAN INDIAN STUDIES

School	ST	$IS	SR
Arizona State Univ-Main	AZ	7,726	C
Black Hills State Univ	SD	6,652	LC
Univ of Minn/Twin Cities	MN	11,123	VC
Univ of N Car at Pembroke	NC	5,914	LC
Univ of Science and Arts of Okla	OK	5,245	C
Univ of S Dak	SD	7,036	C
Univ of Wisc/Eau Claire	WI	7,032	VC

AMERICAN LITERATURE

School	ST	$IS	SR
Bard College	NY	33,912	HC
Blackburn College	IL	13,690	C
Brandeis Univ	MA	34,481	MC
Brown Univ	RI	34,973	MC
Eastern Mich Univ	MI	9,855	C
Florida State Univ	FL	7,835	HC
Middlebury College	VT	34,300	MC
New York Univ	NY	35,200	MC
Washington Univ in St. Louis	MO	34,593	MC

AMERICAN SIGN LANGUAGE

School	ST	$IS	SR
East Central Univ	OK	4,578	C
Gardner-Webb Univ	NC	17,400	C
Goshen College	IN	18,950	VC+
Indiana Univ-Purdue Univ Indianapolis	IN	9,473	C
Keuka College	NY	21,170	C
Maryville College	TN	23,210	VC
Univ of Rochester	NY	32,979	HC
Western Oregon Univ	OR	8,829	C

AMERICAN STUDIES

School	ST	$IS	SR
Albion College	MI	25,224	VC
Albright College	PA	27,642	C
American Univ	DC	31,544	VC+
Amherst College	MA	34,340	MC
Ashland Univ	OH	22,182	LC
Austin College	TX	22,150	VC+
Bard College	NY	33,912	HC
Bates College	ME	34,100	MC
Bay Path College	MA	22,308	C
Baylor Univ	TX	18,298	VC+
Boston Univ	MA	34,358	MC
Bowling Green State Univ	OH	10,794	C
Brandeis Univ	MA	34,481	MC
Brigham Young Univ	UT	7,840	HC
Cabrini College	PA	25,950	LC
Cal State, Chico	CA	8,598	LC
Cal State, Fullerton	CA	5,440	LC
Cal State, San Bernardino	CA	6,516	C
Carleton College	MN	30,780	MC
Case Western Reserve Univ	OH	27,418	C
Cedarville Univ	OH	17,553	VC
Chaminade Univ of Honolulu	HI	17,370	C
CUNY/Brooklyn College	NY	3,403	LC
CUNY/College of Staten Island	NY	3,358	NC
CUNY/Herbert H. Lehman College	NY	3,320	LC
CUNY/Queens College	NY	3,403	VC
Claremont McKenna College	CA	32,700	MC
Coe College	IA	24,750	VC
Colby College	ME	34,290	MC
College of Our Lady of the Elms	MA	20,644	C
College of St. Elizabeth	NJ	22,510	C
College of St. Joseph	VT	17,400	NC
College of St. Rose	NY	19,084	C
College of William and Mary	VA	10,002	MC
Columbia Univ/Barnard College	NY	33,694	MC
Columbia Univ/Columbia College	NY	35,190	MC
Conn College	CT	33,585	MC
Cornell Univ	NY	34,614	MC
Creighton Univ	NE	23,476	VC
David Lipscomb Univ	TN	16,158	VC
DePaul Univ	IL	23,590	VC
Dickinson College	PA	32,210	VC+
Dominican College	NY	20,400	LC
Dominican Univ	IL	20,800	C
Drew Univ/College of Liberal Arts	NJ	32,152	VC
Eastern Conn State Univ	CT	10,362	C
Eckerd College	FL	25,500	C+
Elmhurst College	IL	21,750	C
Elmira College	NY	31,070	VC+
Erskine College	SC	21,399	VC
Florida State Univ	FL	7,835	HC
Fordham Univ	NY	30,710	VC
Franklin and Marshall College	PA	32,410	HC
Franklin College of Indiana	IN	19,905	C
Franklin Pierce College	NH	26,125	LC
George Washington Univ	DC	32,170	HC
Georgetown College	KY	18,400	VC
Georgetown Univ	DC	34,847	MC
Goucher College	MD	30,650	VC+
Hamilton College	NY	34,150	HC
Hampshire College	MA	33,881	HC+
Harding Univ	AR	13,528	VC
Harvard Univ/Harvard College	MA	34,269	MC
High Point Univ	NC	20,220	LC
Hillsdale College	MI	20,586	VC+
Hobart and William Smith Colleges	NY	33,195	VC
Hofstra Univ	NY	23,252	C
Huntingdon College	AL	18,400	VC
Idaho State Univ	ID	7,030	C+
Johns Hopkins Univ	MD	35,226	MC
Keene State College	NH	11,280	C
Kent State Univ	OH	11,104	C
King College	TN	17,800	VC
Knox College	IL	28,230	HC
Lafayette College	PA	32,655	MC
Lake Forest College	IL	27,460	VC
Lebanon Valley College of Pennsylvania	PA	25,700	VC
Lehigh Univ	PA	32,290	MC
Lenoir-Rhyne College	NC	19,186	C
Lindsey Wilson College	KY	16,392	LC
Manhattanville College	NY	28,730	VC
Marist College	NY	24,756	VC
Mary Washington College	VA	9,032	VC+
Marymount College/Tarrytown	NY	23,850	C
Mass Inst of Technology	MA	35,228	MC
Meredith College	NC	17,500	C
Miami Univ	OH	12,885	VC+
Mich State Univ	MI	10,386	VC
Middlebury College	VT	34,300	MC
Millikin Univ	IL	24,415	C+
Mills College	CA	27,950	C
Miss College	MS	14,574	C
Montreat College	NC	17,164	C
Moorhead State Univ	MN	7,000	LC
Mount Holyoke College	MA	34,128	HC
Mount St. Mary's College	CA	24,430	C
Mount Union College	OH	21,120	C
Muhlenberg College	PA	28,170	HC
Muskingum College	OH	18,760	C
Nazareth College of Rochester	NY	22,036	VC
Northwestern Univ	IL	33,615	MC
Occidental College	CA	32,288	HC
Oglethorpe Univ	GA	19,100	LC
Okla State Univ	OK	7,650	VC
Oregon State Univ	OR	9,612	VC
Our Lady of the Lake Univ of San Antonio	TX	17,336	C
Penn State Univ/Univ Park Campus	PA	11,126	VC
Pfeiffer Univ	NC	18,580	C
Pitzer College	CA	33,930	HC
Pomona College	CA	33,960	MC
Providence College	RI	27,620	HC
Purdue Univ/West Lafayette	IN	10,284	VC
Queens College	NC	17,250	C
Ramapo College of New Jersey	NJ	13,550	VC
Randolph-Macon Woman's College	VA	25,820	VC+
Rider Univ	NJ	27,400	C
Roger Williams Univ	RI	29,010	C
Roosevelt Univ	IL	20,240	LC
Rutgers, The State Univ of New Jersey New Brunswick Campus	NJ	12,709	C
Rutgers, The State Univ of New Jersey/CamdenCampus	NJ	6,484	C
St. John Fisher College	NY	21,800	C
St. John's Univ	NY	26,660	C
St. Joseph College	CT	25,960	LC
St. Louis Univ	MO	26,590	VC+
St. Michael's College	VT	26,935	VC
St. Olaf College	MN	25,880	HC
St. Peter's College	NJ	22,292	LC
St. Thomas Univ	FL	19,500	LC
Salem College	NC	23,065	VC
Salve Regina Univ	RI	26,460	C
San Diego State Univ	CA	9,716	C+
San Francisco State Univ	CA	7,139	LC
Scripps College	CA	30,400	HC+
Shenandoah Univ	VA	22,550	NC
Siena College	NY	22,685	VC
Siena Heights Univ	MI	16,140	LC
Simon's Rock College of Bard	MA	32,450	HC
Skidmore College	NY	34,201	VC+
Smith College	MA	33,302	HC+
Southern New Hampshire Univ	NH	23,852	C
Southwest Texas State Univ	TX	8,730	VC
Southwestern Univ	TX	22,550	HC
Stanford Univ	CA	34,222	MC
SUNY/College at Geneseo	NY	9,970	HC
SUNY/College at Old Westbury	NY	9,818	LC
SUNY/College at Oswego	NY	10,856	C
SUNY/Univ at Buffalo	NY	11,033	VC
SUNY/Univ at Stony Brook	NY	10,998	VC
Stetson Univ	FL	25,640	VC
Stonehill College	MA	26,852	HC
Syracuse Univ	NY	30,710	HC
Temple Univ	PA	14,124	C
Trinity College	CT	34,300	HC
Trinity College	DC	21,370	LC
Tufts Univ	MA	34,874	MC
Tulane Univ	LA	34,013	HC+
Union College	NY	32,646	HC
Univ of Alabama	AL	7,402	C
Univ of Arkansas	AR	8,334	VC
Univ of Calif at Berkeley	CA	14,134	MC
Univ of Calif at Davis	CA	12,796	VC
Univ of Calif at Los Angeles	CA	13,227	MC
Univ of Calif at Santa Cruz	CA	13,655	VC
Univ of Colo at Boulder	CO	9,255	VC
Univ of Dayton	OH	20,400	VC
Univ of Florida	FL	7,874	HC
Univ of Hawaii at Manoa	HI	7,862	VC
Univ of Idaho	ID	7,026	C
Univ of Iowa	IA	8,607	C+
Univ of Kansas	KS	7,232	VC
Univ of Maryland/Baltimore County	MD	12,190	VC
Univ of Maryland/College Park	MD	11,959	C
Univ of Mass Boston	MA	4,227	C
Univ of Mass Lowell	MA	9,470	VC
Univ of Miami	FL	31,130	HC
Univ of Mich/Ann Arbor	MI	13,003	HC+
Univ of Mich/Dearborn	MI	4,677	VC
Univ of Minn/Twin Cities	MN	11,123	VC
Univ of Missouri/Kansas City	MO	9,685	VC
Univ of New England	ME	24,110	LC
Univ of New Mexico	NM	8,026	C
Univ of N Car at Chapel Hill	NC	8,789	HC
Univ of Northern Iowa	IA	7,850	C
Univ of Notre Dame	IN	30,707	MC
Univ of Pittsburgh at Bradford	PA	12,696	C
Univ of Pittsburgh at Greensburg	PA	12,842	C
Univ of Pittsburgh at Johnstown	PA	13,044	LC
Univ of Richmond	VA	27,300	HC
Univ of Rio Grande	OH	8,728	NC
Univ of St. Francis	IN	17,790	LC
Univ of South Florida	FL	8,154	C
Univ of Southern Calif	CA	33,647	MC
Univ of Texas at Austin	TX	9,437	HC
Univ of Texas at Dallas	TX	9,305	VC

School	ST	$IS	SR
Univ of Texas at San Antonio	TX	9,088	NC
Univ of the South	TN	27,290	HC
Univ of Wyoming	WY	7,143	LC
Upper Iowa Univ	IA	17,438	C
Ursuline College	OH	19,430	LC
Utah State Univ	UT	6,771	C
Valparaiso Univ	IN	23,570	VC+
Vanderbilt Univ	TN	34,482	MC
Vassar College	NY	33,450	MC
Virginia Wesleyan College	VA	22,350	LC
Warner Pacific College	OR	20,370	LC
Washington College	MD	28,040	VC
Washington State Univ	WA	9,388	C
Washington Univ in St. Louis	MO	34,593	MC
Wayne State Univ	MI	6,720	C
Wellesley College	MA	33,394	MC
Wells College	NY	19,350	VC
Wesley College	DE	17,869	C
Wesleyan Univ	CT	3,405	MC
West Chester Univ of Pennsylvania	PA	9,792	VC
Western Conn State Univ	CT	10,074	C
Western Mich Univ	MI	10,016	C
Wheaton College	MA	32,940	VC
Whitworth College	WA	23,938	VC
Willamette Univ	OR	29,422	VC+
Williams College	MA	32,270	MC
Wingate Univ	NC	19,140	C
Wittenberg Univ	OH	28,766	VC
Yale Univ	CT	34,030	MC
Youngstown State Univ	OH	9,318	NC

ANATOMY

School	ST	$IS	SR
Andrews Univ	MI	17,696	LC
Duke Univ	NC	34,396	MC

ANIMAL SCIENCE

School	ST	$IS	SR
Abilene Christian Univ	TX	16,300	VC
Alabama A&M Univ	AL	5,100	LC
Alcorn State Univ	MS	5,594	LC
Andrews Univ	MI	17,696	LC
Angelo State Univ	TX	7,028	C
Arkansas State Univ	AR	7,480	C
Auburn Univ	AL	5,510	C
Berry College	GA	18,850	C
Brigham Young Univ	UT	7,840	HC
Calif State Polytechnic Univ, Pomona	CA	8,615	C
Cal State, Fresno	CA	7,762	C
Clemson Univ	SC	7,600	C
College of the Ozarks	MO	2,650	C+
Colo State Univ	CO	9,672	C
Cornell Univ	NY	34,614	MC
Delaware Valley College	PA	24,213	LC
Florida A&M Univ	FL	6,948	C
Fort Valley State Univ	GA	6,014	LC
Hampshire College	MA	33,881	HC+
Iowa State Univ	IA	8,108	VC
Kansas State Univ	KS	6,995	C
Langston Univ	OK	2,308	LC
Louisiana State Univ and A&M College	LA	8,014	VC
Louisiana Tech Univ	LA	6,506	C
Lubbock Christian Univ	TX	14,226	LC
McNeese State Univ	LA	5,259	LC
McPherson College	KS	17,710	C
Mich State Univ	MI	10,386	VC
Middle Tenn State Univ	TN	6,994	C
Miss State Univ	MS	7,853	C
Montana State Univ-Bozeman	MT	8,431	C
Murray State Univ	KY	6,672	C
New Mexico State Univ	NM	7,302	C
N Car Agricultural and Technical State Univ	NC	6,659	LC
N Car State Univ	NC	8,680	HC
N Dak State Univ	ND	7,004	VC
Northwest Missouri State Univ	MO	7,922	LC
Okla Panhandle State Univ	OK	3,812	NC
Okla State Univ	OK	7,650	VC
Oregon State Univ	OR	9,612	VC
Penn State Univ/Univ Park Campus	PA	11,126	VC
Prairie View A&M Univ	TX	3,172	LC
Purdue Univ/West Lafayette	IN	10,284	VC
Rutgers, The State Univ of New Jersey New Brunswick Campus	NJ	12,709	C
Sam Houston State Univ	TX	6,076	LC
S Dak State Univ	SD	6,848	C
Southeast Missouri State Univ	MO	8,367	C+
Southern Illinois Univ at Carbondale	IL	8,621	C
Southwest Missouri State Univ	MO	7,600	LC
Southwest Texas State Univ	TX	8,730	VC
Southwestern Univ	TX	22,550	HC
SUNY/College of Agriculture and Technology at Cobleskill	NY	11,200	C+
SUNY/College of Environmental Science and Forestry	NY	12,446	VC
Stephen F. Austin State Univ	TX	6,905	C
Sul Ross State Univ	TX	6,582	LC
Tarleton State Univ	TX	7,160	C
Tenn Tech Univ	TN	6,968	C
Texas A&M Univ	TX	8,988	VC
Texas A&M Univ at Commerce	TX	7,326	C
Texas A&M Univ at Kingsville	TX	6,446	LC
Texas Tech Univ	TX	8,825	C
Ohio State Univ	OH	10,819	VC
Truman State Univ	MO	8,568	VC+
Tuskegee Univ	AL	14,600	LC
Univ of Arizona	AZ	8,614	C
Univ of Arkansas	AR	8,334	VC
Univ of Calif at Davis	CA	12,796	VC
Univ of Calif at San Diego	CA	11,372	HC
Univ of Conn	CT	12,122	VC
Univ of Delaware	DE	10,824	VC
Univ of Denver	CO	28,783	VC
Univ of Florida	FL	7,874	HC
Univ of Hawaii at Manoa	HI	7,862	VC
Univ of Idaho	ID	7,026	C
Univ of Illinois at Urbana-Champaign	IL	11,316	HC+
Univ of Kentucky	KY	7,765	C
Univ of Maine	ME	10,798	C
Univ of Maryland/College Park	MD	11,959	C
Univ of Mass Amherst	MA	10,995	VC
Univ of Missouri/Columbia	MO	9,803	HC
Univ of Nebr at Lincoln	NE	8,325	C+
Univ of Nevada/Reno	NV	8,737	C
Univ of New Hampshire	NH	13,207	C
Univ of PR/Mayaguez	PR	5,285	
Univ of Rhode Island	RI	12,414	C
Univ of Tenn at Knoxville	TN	8,214	C
Univ of Tenn at Martin	TN	8,268	C
Univ of Vermont	VT	14,761	C+
Univ of Wisc/Madison	WI	8,262	VC
Univ of Wisc/Platteville	WI	7,282	C
Univ of Wisc/River Falls	WI	6,356	LC
Univ of Wyoming	WY	7,143	LC
Utah State Univ	UT	6,771	C
Virginia Polytechnic Inst and State Univ	VA	7,652	C
Washington State Univ	WA	9,388	C
West Texas A&M Univ	TX	6,538	C
West Virginia Univ	WV	8,304	C

ANIMATION

School	ST	$IS	SR
Art Inst of Southern Calif	CA	14,500	SP
Cal State, Fullerton	CA	5,440	LC
Cogswell Polytechnical College	CA	14,400	LC
College For Creative Studies	MI	20,938	SP
School of Visual Arts	NY	26,000	SP
Southern Adventist Univ	TN	15,600	C

ANTHROPOLOGY

School	ST	$IS	SR
Adelphi Univ	NY	23,320	VC
Agnes Scott College	GA	24,950	VC
Albertson College of Idaho	ID	23,900	VC
Albion College	MI	25,224	VC
American Univ	DC	31,544	VC+
Amherst College	MA	34,340	MC
Andrews Univ	MI	17,696	LC
Appalachian State Univ	NC	6,353	C
Arizona State Univ-Main	AZ	7,726	C
Auburn Univ	AL	5,510	C
Ball State Univ	IN	8,660	C
Bard College	NY	33,912	HC
Bates College	ME	34,100	MC
Baylor Univ	TX	18,298	VC+
Beloit College	WI	27,482	HC
Bennington College	VT	31,350	VC
Biola Univ	CA	21,902	VC
Bloomsburg Univ of Pennsylvania	PA	9,434	C
Boise State Univ	ID	6,531	LC
Boston Univ	MA	34,358	MC
Bowdoin College	ME	32,650	MC
Brandeis Univ	MA	34,481	MC
Bridgewater State College	MA	7,589	C+
Brigham Young Univ	UT	7,840	HC
Brown Univ	RI	34,973	MC
Bryn Mawr College	PA	33,580	HC+
Bucknell Univ	PA	31,096	HC
Butler Univ	IN	25,580	VC+
Calif State Polytechnic Univ, Pomona	CA	8,615	C
Cal State, Bakersfield	CA	6,090	LC
Cal State, Chico	CA	8,598	LC
Cal State, Dominguez Hills	CA	5,840	LC
Cal State, Fresno	CA	7,762	C
Cal State, Fullerton	CA	5,440	LC
Cal State, Hayward	CA	7,400	LC
Cal State, Long Beach	CA	7,400	LC
Cal State, Los Angeles	CA	5,050	C
Cal State, Northridge	CA	7,781	C
Cal State, Sacramento	CA	7,488	C
Cal State, San Bernardino	CA	6,516	C
Cal State, Stanislaus	CA	8,895	C
Calif Univ of Pennsylvania	PA	10,388	C
Canisius College	NY	24,696	C+
Carleton College	MN	30,780	MC
Case Western Reserve Univ	OH	27,418	C
Catholic Univ of America	DC	29,332	VC
Central College	IA	21,206	C
Central Conn State Univ	CT	10,404	C
Central Mich Univ	MI	8,355	C
Central Washington Univ	WA	8,985	LC
Centre College	KY	24,000	HC
CUNY/Brooklyn College	NY	3,403	LC
CUNY/City College	NY	3,309	LC
CUNY/Herbert H. Lehman College	NY	3,320	LC
CUNY/Hunter College	NY	5,147	C+
CUNY/Queens College	NY	3,403	VC
CUNY/York College	NY	3,292	NC
Claremont McKenna College	CA	32,700	MC
Clarion Univ of Pennsylvania	PA	11,272	LC
Cleveland State Univ	OH	10,146	NC
Colby College	ME	34,290	MC
Colgate Univ	NY	33,480	MC
College of Charleston	SC	8,350	HC
College of the Holy Cross	MA	32,780	MC
College of William and Mary	VA	10,002	MC
College of Wooster	OH	28,350	VC
Colo College	CO	31,525	HC+
Colo State Univ	CO	9,672	C
Columbia Univ/Barnard College	NY	33,694	MC
Columbia Univ/Columbia College	NY	35,190	MC
Columbia Univ/School of General Studies	NY	35,000	C
Conn College	CT	33,585	MC
Cornell College	IA	24,980	VC
Cornell Univ	NY	34,614	MC
Dartmouth College	NH	34,458	MC
Davidson College	NC	30,823	MC
DePauw Univ	IN	28,000	HC
Dickinson College	PA	32,210	VC+
Dowling College	NY	20,281	LC
Drew Univ/College of Liberal Arts	NJ	32,152	VC
Duke Univ	NC	34,396	MC
Earlham College	IN	27,446	VC+
East Carolina Univ	NC	7,766	C
Eastern Kentucky Univ	KY	6,552	C
Eastern Mich Univ	MI	9,855	C
Eastern New Mexico Univ	NM	4,113	LC
Eastern Oregon Univ	OR	8,772	C
Eastern Washington Univ	WA	7,972	LC
Eckerd College	FL	25,500	C+
Edinboro Univ of Pennsylvania	PA	9,328	LC
Elmira College	NY	31,070	VC+
Emory Univ	GA	33,792	MC
Florida Atlantic Univ	FL	8,832	C
Florida State Univ	FL	7,835	HC
Fordham Univ	NY	30,710	VC
Fort Lewis College	CO	7,659	LC
Franciscan Univ of Steubenville	OH	19,100	C+
Franklin and Marshall College	PA	32,410	HC
Franklin Pierce College	NH	26,125	LC
George Mason Univ	VA	9,192	C
George Washington Univ	DC	32,170	HC
Georgia Southern Univ	GA	6,958	C
Georgia State Univ	GA	7,792	LC
Gettysburg College	PA	32,070	HC
Grand Valley State Univ	MI	10,040	C
Grinnell College	IA	28,300	HC+
Gustavus Adolphus College	MN	24,190	VC+
Hamilton College	NY	34,150	HC
Hamline Univ	MN	23,339	C+
Hampshire College	MA	33,881	HC+
Hanover College	IN	17,560	VC
Hartwick College	NY	33,090	C+
Harvard Univ/Harvard College	MA	34,269	MC
Haverford College	PA	34,300	MC
Hawaii Pacific Univ	HI	17,790	C
Heidelberg College	OH	23,879	C
Hendrix College	AR	18,463	HC
Hobart and William Smith Colleges	NY	33,195	VC
Hofstra Univ	NY	23,252	C
Howard Univ	DC	15,522	LC
Humboldt State Univ	CA	8,582	C
Idaho State Univ	ID	7,030	C+
Illinois State Univ	IL	9,235	C
Indiana State Univ	IN	8,461	LC
Indiana Univ Bloomington	IN	10,712	C+
Indiana Univ of Pennsylvania	PA	9,133	C
Indiana Univ-Purdue Univ Fort Wayne	IN	3,166	LC
Indiana Univ-Purdue Univ Indianapolis	IN	9,473	C
Iowa State Univ	IA	8,108	VC
Ithaca College	NY	28,719	HC
James Madison Univ	VA	9,552	HC
Johns Hopkins Univ	MD	35,226	MC
Johnson State College	VT	10,776	C
Judson College	IL	18,980	LC
Juniata College	PA	26,080	VC
Kalamazoo College	MI	26,955	HC+
Kansas State Univ	KS	6,995	C
Kent State Univ	OH	11,104	C
Kenyon College	OH	32,130	HC+
Knox College	IL	28,230	HC
Kutztown Univ of Pennsylvania	PA	8,907	C
Lafayette College	PA	32,655	MC
Lake Forest College	IL	27,460	VC
Lawrence Univ	WI	27,711	HC
Lehigh Univ	PA	32,290	MC
Lewis and Clark College	OR	29,010	VC
Lincoln Univ	PA	11,198	C+
Linfield College	OR	25,840	VC
LIU/Brooklyn Campus	NY	22,290	C
Longwood College	VA	8,950	C
Louisiana State Univ and A&M College	LA	8,014	VC
Loyola Univ of Chicago	IL	25,992	VC
Luther College	IA	23,300	VC+
Lycoming College	PA	24,780	C
Macalester College	MN	28,814	HC+
Manchester College	IN	22,010	C
Mansfield Univ	PA	9,648	C
Marlboro College	VT	26,410	VC+
Marquette Univ	WI	24,836	C+
Mass Inst of Technology	MA	35,228	MC
Mercyhurst College	PA	20,604	C
Metropolitan State College of Denver	CO	2,338	LC
Miami Univ	OH	12,885	VC+
Mich State Univ	MI	10,386	VC
Middle Tenn State Univ	TN	6,994	C
Middlebury College	VT	34,300	MC
Millersville Univ of Pennsylvania	PA	10,153	VC
Mills College	CA	27,950	C
Minn State Univ, Mankato	MN	7,296	LC
Miss State Univ	MS	7,853	C
Monmouth College	IL	21,550	C
Monmouth Univ	NJ	24,042	C
Montana State Univ-Bozeman	MT	8,431	C
Montclair State Univ	NJ	10,287	LC
Moorhead State Univ	MN	7,000	LC
Mount Holyoke College	MA	34,128	HC
National-Louis Univ	IL	13,995	NC
Nazareth College of Rochester	NY	22,036	VC
Nebr Wesleyan Univ	NE	18,767	VC
New College of Calif	CA	8,900	NC
New College of Florida	FL	8,130	HC+
New Mexico Highlands Univ	NM	6,256	NC
New Mexico State Univ	NM	7,302	C
New York Univ	NY	35,200	MC
North Central College	IL	22,944	C+
N Dak State Univ	ND	7,004	VC
North Park Univ	IL	24,030	C
Northeastern Illinois Univ	IL	2,898	NC
Northeastern Univ	MA	30,078	VC
Northern Arizona Univ	AZ	7,398	C
Northern Illinois Univ	IL	9,545	C
Northern Kentucky Univ	KY	6,352	NC
Northwestern State Univ of Louisiana	LA	5,745	NC
Northwestern Univ	IL	33,615	MC
Oakland Univ	MI	9,418	C
Oberlin College	OH	33,140	HC+
Occidental College	CA	32,288	HC
Ohio Univ	OH	11,769	C
Ohio Wesleyan Univ	OH	29,670	VC+
Old Dominion Univ	VA	9,386	C
Olivet College	MI	17,410	C
Oregon State Univ	OR	9,612	VC
Pace Univ	NY	24,200	C
Pacific Lutheran Univ	WA	23,318	VC
Penn State Univ/Univ Park Campus	PA	11,126	VC
Pitzer College	CA	33,930	HC
Plymouth State College	NH	11,024	LC
Pomona College	CA	33,960	MC
Portland State Univ	OR	11,220	C
Prescott College	AZ	13,430	C
Princeton Univ	NJ	35,072	MC
Purdue Univ/West Lafayette	IN	10,284	VC
Radford Univ	VA	8,302	C
Reed College	OR	33,350	HC+
Rhode Island College	RI	8,700	LC
Rhodes College	TN	26,466	HC+
Richard Stockton College of New Jersey	NJ	12,165	VC
Ripon College	WI	24,180	VC+
Rockford College	IL	23,930	C
Rocky Mountain College	MT	18,113	C
Rollins College	FL	31,223	HC

School	ST	$IS	SR
Rutgers, The State Univ of New Jersey New Brunswick Campus	NJ	12,709	C
St. Cloud State Univ	MN	7,180	C
St. John Fisher College	NY	21,800	C
St. John's Univ	NY	26,660	C
St. Lawrence Univ	NY	32,605	VC
St. Mary's College of Calif	CA	27,575	C
St. Mary's College of Maryland	MD	14,104	HC
St. Michael's College	VT	26,935	VC
St. Vincent College	PA	22,942	VC
Salve Regina Univ	RI	26,460	C
San Diego State Univ	CA	9,716	C+
San Francisco State Univ	CA	7,139	LC
San Jose State Univ	CA	8,187	C
Santa Clara Univ	CA	28,371	VC+
Sarah Lawrence College	NY	37,516	HC
Scripps College	CA	30,400	HC+
Seton Hall Univ	NJ	26,910	LC
Skidmore College	NY	34,201	VC+
Slippery Rock Univ	PA	9,152	LC
Smith College	MA	33,302	HC+
Sonoma State Univ	CA	8,953	C
Southeast Missouri State Univ	MO	8,367	C+
Southern Illinois Univ at Carbondale	IL	8,621	C
Southern Illinois Univ Edwardsville	IL	7,869	LC
Southern Methodist Univ	TX	28,349	VC
Southern Oregon Univ	OR	9,429	C
Southwest Missouri State Univ	MO	7,600	LC
Southwest Texas State Univ	TX	8,730	VC
Spelman College	GA	19,215	C+
Stanford Univ	CA	34,222	MC
SUNY/College at Brockport	NY	10,267	C
SUNY/College at Buffalo	NY	8,025	C
SUNY/College at Cortland	NY	10,564	C
SUNY/College at Geneseo	NY	9,970	HC
SUNY/College at Oneonta	NY	9,981	C
SUNY/College at Oswego	NY	10,856	C
SUNY/College at Plattsburgh	NY	9,729	C
SUNY/College at Potsdam	NY	10,519	C
SUNY/College at Purchase	NY	10,587	VC
SUNY/Univ at Albany	NY	10,997	VC
SUNY/Univ at Binghamton	NY	10,653	HC
SUNY/Univ at Buffalo	NY	11,033	VC
SUNY/Univ at New Paltz	NY	9,685	VC
SUNY/Univ at Stony Brook	NY	10,998	VC
State Univ of West Georgia	GA	7,101	C
Swarthmore College	PA	34,538	MC
Sweet Briar College	VA	25,310	VC
Syracuse Univ	NY	30,710	HC
Temple Univ	PA	14,124	C
Texas A&M Univ	TX	8,988	VC
Texas A&M Univ at Commerce	TX	7,326	C
Texas A&M Univ at Kingsville	TX	6,446	LC
Texas Tech Univ	TX	8,825	C
Ohio State Univ	OH	10,819	VC
Thomas Edison State College	NJ	2,750	SP
Towson Univ	MD	11,088	VC
Trinity College	CT	34,300	HC
Trinity Univ	TX	21,444	HC
Tufts Univ	MA	34,874	MC
Tulane Univ	LA	34,013	HC+
Union College	NY	32,646	HC
Univ of Akron	OH	10,530	NC
Univ of Alabama	AL	7,402	C
Univ of Alabama at Birmingham	AL	10,110	C
Univ of Alaska Anchorage	AK	9,100	NC
Univ of Alaska Fairbanks	AK	8,265	NC
Univ of Arizona	AZ	8,614	C
Univ of Arkansas	AR	8,334	VC
Univ of Calif at Berkeley	CA	14,134	MC
Univ of Calif at Davis	CA	12,796	VC
Univ of Calif at Irvine	CA	11,756	C
Univ of Calif at Los Angeles	CA	13,227	MC
Univ of Calif at Riverside	CA	12,479	C
Univ of Calif at San Diego	CA	11,372	HC
Univ of Calif at Santa Barbara	CA	11,732	VC
Univ of Calif at Santa Cruz	CA	13,655	VC
Univ of Central Florida	FL	8,251	VC
Univ of Chicago	IL	35,087	MC
Univ of Cincinnati	OH	12,491	LC
Univ of Colo at Boulder	CO	9,255	VC
Univ of Colo at Colo Springs	CO	9,403	C
Univ of Colo at Denver	CO	3,673	C
Univ of Conn	CT	12,122	VC
Univ of Delaware	DE	10,824	VC
Univ of Denver	CO	28,783	VC
Univ of Evansville	IN	22,865	VC+
Univ of Florida	FL	7,874	HC
Univ of Georgia	GA	8,656	VC
Univ of Hawaii at Hilo	HI	6,497	C
Univ of Hawaii at Manoa	HI	7,862	VC
Univ of Houston	TX	8,410	C
Univ of Idaho	ID	7,026	C
Univ of Illinois at Chicago	IL	10,702	VC
Univ of Illinois at Urbana-Champaign	IL	11,316	HC+
Univ of Indianapolis	IN	20,840	C
Univ of Iowa	IA	8,607	C+
Univ of Kansas	KS	7,232	VC
Univ of Kentucky	KY	7,765	C
Univ of La Verne	CA	24,280	C
Univ of Louisiana at Lafayette	LA	5,200	C
Univ of Louisville	KY	7,402	LC
Univ of Maine	ME	10,798	C
Univ of Maryland/Baltimore County	MD	12,190	VC
Univ of Maryland/College Park	MD	11,959	C
Univ of Mass Amherst	MA	10,995	VC
Univ of Mass Boston	MA	4,227	C
Univ of Mass Dartmouth	MA	9,852	C
Univ of Memphis	TN	7,271	C
Univ of Miami	FL	31,130	HC
Univ of Mich/Ann Arbor	MI	13,003	HC+
Univ of Mich/Dearborn	MI	4,677	VC
Univ of Mich/Flint	MI	4,323	C
Univ of Minn/Duluth	MN	10,436	C
Univ of Minn/Morris	MN	10,716	VC
Univ of Minn/Twin Cities	MN	11,123	VC
Univ of Miss	MS	7,666	C
Univ of Missouri/Columbia	MO	9,803	HC
Univ of Missouri/St. Louis	MO	9,966	C
Univ of Montana	MT	8,038	C
Univ of Nebr at Lincoln	NE	8,325	C+
Univ of Nevada/Las Vegas	NV	8,281	VC
Univ of Nevada/Reno	NV	8,737	C
Univ of New Hampshire	NH	13,207	C
Univ of New Mexico	NM	8,026	C
Univ of New Orleans	LA	10,160	C
Univ of N Car at Chapel Hill	NC	8,789	HC
Univ of N Car at Charlotte	NC	7,254	C
Univ of N Car at Greensboro	NC	6,858	C
Univ of N Car at Wilmington	NC	7,769	C
Univ of N Dak	ND	7,067	VC
Univ of North Florida	FL	8,089	VC
Univ of North Texas	TX	7,629	C
Univ of Northern Iowa	IA	7,850	C
Univ of Okla	OK	7,616	VC
Univ of Oregon	OR	9,969	C
Univ of Pennsylvania	PA	34,614	MC
Univ of Pittsburgh at Greensburg	PA	12,842	C
Univ of Pittsburgh at Pittsburgh	PA	13,592	HC
Univ of PR/Rio Piedras	PR	5,510	
Univ of Redlands	CA	29,246	VC
Univ of Rhode Island	RI	12,414	C
Univ of Rochester	NY	32,979	HC
Univ of San Diego	CA	29,198	HC
Univ of South Alabama	AL	6,976	LC
Univ of S Car at Columbia	SC	8,748	VC
Univ of S Dak	SD	7,036	C
Univ of South Florida	FL	8,154	C
Univ of Southern Calif	CA	33,647	MC
Univ of Southern Maine	ME	10,569	C
Univ of Southern Miss	MS	6,155	LC
Univ of Tenn at Knoxville	TN	8,214	C
Univ of Texas at Arlington	TX	7,192	LC
Univ of Texas at Austin	TX	9,437	HC
Univ of Texas at El Paso	TX	5,076	LC
Univ of Texas at San Antonio	TX	9,088	NC
Univ of Texas-Pan American	TX	4,823	C
Univ of the South	TN	27,290	HC
Univ of Toledo	OH	11,206	NC
Univ of Tulsa	OK	19,090	HC
Univ of Utah	UT	7,703	C
Univ of Vermont	VT	14,761	C+
Univ of Virginia	VA	9,391	HC+
Univ of Washington	WA	10,361	VC
Univ of Wisc/Madison	WI	8,262	VC
Univ of Wisc/Milwaukee	WI	8,907	LC
Univ of Wisc/Oshkosh	WI	6,130	LC
Univ of Wyoming	WY	7,143	LC
Ursinus College	PA	31,350	VC
Valdosta State Univ	GA	6,988	C
Vanderbilt Univ	TN	34,482	MC
Vanguard Univ of Southern Calif	CA	20,212	C
Vassar College	NY	33,450	MC
Wagner College	NY	27,000	C
Wake Forest Univ	NC	30,290	MC
Washburn Univ of Topeka	KS	6,766	NC
Washington College	MD	28,040	VC
Washington State Univ	WA	9,388	C
Washington Univ in St. Louis	MO	34,593	MC
Wayne State Univ	MI	6,720	C
Webster Univ	MO	19,804	VC
Wellesley College	MA	33,394	MC
Wells College	NY	19,350	VC
Wesleyan Univ	CT	3,405	MC
West Chester Univ of Pennsylvania	PA	9,792	VC
West Virginia Univ	WV	8,304	C
Western Carolina Univ	NC	5,667	C
Western Conn State Univ	CT	10,074	C
Western Kentucky Univ	KY	6,834	C
Western Mich Univ	MI	10,016	C
Western Oregon Univ	OR	8,829	C
Western State College of Colo	CO	7,585	LC
Western Washington Univ	WA	8,624	VC
Westminster College	MO	19,990	C+
Wheaton College	IL	21,934	HC
Wheaton College	MA	32,940	VC
Whitman College	WA	29,086	HC
Wichita State Univ	KS	6,879	C
Widener Univ	PA	26,920	C
Willamette Univ	OR	29,422	VC+
William Paterson Univ of New Jersey	NJ	11,000	LC
Williams College	MA	32,270	MC
Wright State Univ	OH	9,141	LC
Yale Univ	CT	34,030	MC
Youngstown State Univ	OH	9,318	NC

APPAREL AND ACCESSORIES MARKETING

School	ST	$IS	SR
Bluffton College	OH	20,644	C
Bowling Green State Univ	OH	10,794	C
Calif State Polytechnic Univ, Pomona	CA	8,615	C
Colo State Univ	CO	9,672	C
Fashion Inst of Technology/SUNY	NY	9,504	C+
Indiana Univ Bloomington	IN	10,712	C+
Kansas State Univ	KS	6,995	C
Kentucky State Univ	KY	6,146	NC
Northwood Univ	TX	18,135	C
S Dak State Univ	SD	6,848	C
Univ of Arkansas	AR	8,334	VC
Youngstown State Univ	OH	9,318	NC

APPAREL DESIGN

School	ST	$IS	SR
Art Inst of Portland	OR	13,725	SP
Concordia College/Moorhead	MN	18,835	C
Florida State Univ	FL	7,835	HC
Gallaudet Univ	DC	16,554	SP
Kansas State Univ	KS	6,995	C
Oregon State Univ	OR	9,612	VC
Purdue Univ/West Lafayette	IN	10,284	VC
Rhode Island School of Design	RI	30,227	SP
Univ of Wisc/Stout	WI	7,192	C

APPLIED ART

School	ST	$IS	SR
Centenary College	NJ	22,430	C
Cleveland Inst of Art	OH	22,680	SP
Daemen College	NY	20,620	C
Edinboro Univ of Pennsylvania	PA	9,328	LC
Minn State Univ, Mankato	MN	7,296	LC
Oral Roberts Univ	OK	18,490	C
Point Park College	PA	20,290	C
Rochester Inst of Technology	NY	26,232	VC+
Southwest Texas State Univ	TX	8,730	VC
Univ of North Texas	TX	7,629	C
West Texas A&M Univ	TX	6,538	C

APPLIED MATHEMATICS

School	ST	$IS	SR
American Univ	DC	31,544	VC+
Andrews Univ	MI	17,696	LC
Asbury College	KY	18,540	VC
Auburn Univ	AL	5,510	C
Baylor Univ	TX	18,298	VC+
Berry College	GA	18,850	C
Bloomfield College	NJ	17,000	C
Boston Univ	MA	34,358	MC
Brown Univ	RI	34,973	MC
Cal State, Long Beach	CA	7,400	LC
Cal State, Los Angeles	CA	5,050	C
Carroll College	WI	21,170	C
Case Western Reserve Univ	OH	27,418	C
CUNY/Brooklyn College	NY	3,403	LC
Clarkson Univ	NY	29,884	VC
Colby College	ME	34,290	MC
Columbia Univ/Fu Foundation School of Engineering and Applied Science	NY	35,190	MC
Columbia Univ/School of General Studies	NY	35,000	C
Dowling College	NY	20,281	LC
East Central Univ	OK	4,578	C
Eastern Mich Univ	MI	9,855	C
Ferris State Univ	MI	10,816	C
Florida Inst of Technology	FL	25,250	VC
Florida International Univ	FL	9,486	VC
Florida State Univ	FL	7,835	HC
Geneva College	PA	19,990	C+
George Washington Univ	DC	32,170	HC
Georgia Inst of Technology	GA	9,028	HC+
Grand View College	IA	17,596	NC
Hampden-Sydney College	VA	24,871	C
Harvard Univ/Harvard College	MA	34,269	MC
Hawaii Pacific Univ	HI	17,790	C
Illinois Inst of Technology	IL	25,182	HC+
Indiana Univ of Pennsylvania	PA	9,133	C
Johns Hopkins Univ	MD	35,226	MC
Johnson C. Smith Univ	NC	16,560	C+
Kent State Univ	OH	11,104	C
Kentucky State Univ	KY	6,146	NC
Kettering Univ	MI	23,256	HC
King College	TN	17,800	VC
La Roche College	PA	18,854	LC
Le Moyne College	NY	23,840	C
Limestone College	SC	16,900	C
Lincoln Univ	PA	11,198	C+
Mary Baldwin College	VA	23,440	C
Metropolitan State Univ	MN	2,943	SP
New Jersey Inst of Technology	NJ	14,690	VC
Norfolk State Univ	VA	8,382	LC
North Central College	IL	22,944	C+
Northwestern Univ	IL	33,615	MC
Ohio Univ	OH	11,769	C
Pacific Union College	CA	20,250	VC
Piedmont College	GA	16,900	C
Purdue Univ/West Lafayette	IN	10,284	VC
Rochester Inst of Technology	NY	26,232	VC+
St. Augustine's College	NC	12,990	C+
St. Louis Univ	MO	26,590	VC+
San Francisco State Univ	CA	7,139	LC
Simon's Rock College of Bard	MA	32,450	HC
SUNY/College at Oswego	NY	10,856	C
SUNY/Univ at Albany	NY	10,997	VC
SUNY/Univ at Stony Brook	NY	10,998	VC
Stevens Inst of Technology	NJ	31,510	HC+
Univ of Arkansas at Pine Bluff	AR	7,925	C
Univ of Calif at Berkeley	CA	14,134	MC
Univ of Calif at Los Angeles	CA	13,227	MC
Univ of Calif at San Diego	CA	11,372	HC
Univ of Colo at Boulder	CO	9,255	VC
Univ of Colo at Denver	CO	3,673	C
Univ of Houston-Downtown	TX	2,006	NC
Univ of Idaho	ID	7,026	C
Univ of Mass Boston	MA	4,227	C
Univ of Mass Lowell	MA	9,470	VC
Univ of Miami	FL	31,130	HC
Univ of Mich/Ann Arbor	MI	13,003	HC+
Univ of Missouri/Rolla	MO	10,034	C
Univ of Missouri/St. Louis	MO	9,966	C
Univ of New Haven	CT	23,860	LC
Univ of Pittsburgh at Greensburg	PA	12,842	C
Univ of Rochester	NY	32,979	HC
Univ of S Car at Aiken	SC	7,828	LC
Univ of Tenn at Chattanooga	TN	7,783	C
Univ of Texas at Dallas	TX	9,305	VC
Univ of Texas at El Paso	TX	5,076	LC
Univ of Virginia	VA	9,391	HC+
Univ of Wisc/Madison	WI	8,262	VC
Univ of Wisc/Milwaukee	WI	8,907	LC
Univ of Wisc/Stout	WI	7,192	C
Valdosta State Univ	GA	6,988	C
Washington Univ in St. Louis	MO	34,593	MC
West Virginia State College	WV	6,264	NC
Western Mich Univ	MI	10,016	C
Wingate Univ	NC	19,140	C
Yale Univ	CT	34,030	MC

APPLIED MUSIC

School	ST	$IS	SR
Baylor Univ	TX	18,298	VC+
Concordia College	NY	19,200	VC
Covenant College	GA	21,970	C+
Dallas Baptist Univ	TX	13,682	LC
DePaul Univ	IL	23,590	VC
Eastern Mich Univ	MI	9,855	C
Geneva College	PA	19,990	C+
Grand Canyon Univ	AZ	30,000	LC
Hardin-Simmons Univ	TX	14,165	C
Inter-American Univ of PR/Bayamon Univ College	PR	3,700	
Inter-American Univ of PR/Fajardo Campus	PR	4,000	
Inter-American Univ of PR/Ponce Regional College	PR	3,700	
Judson College	AL	13,790	C
Kansas State Univ	KS	6,995	C
Lenoir-Rhyne College	NC	19,186	C
Meredith College	NC	17,500	C
Mich State Univ	MI	10,386	VC
Miss College	MS	14,574	C
Nebr Wesleyan Univ	NE	18,767	VC
New England Conservatory of Music	MA	31,200	SP
Newberry College	SC	19,670	LC
Sul Ross State Univ	TX	6,582	LC
Texas Southern Univ	TX	6,576	NC

School	ST	$IS	SR
Texas Woman's Univ	TX	5,855	LC
Trinity Christian College	IL	19,415	C
Univ of Houston	TX	8,410	C
Univ of Idaho	ID	7,026	C
Univ of Mich/Ann Arbor	MI	13,003	HC+
Univ of Nevada/Reno	NV	8,737	C
Univ of Texas at Austin	TX	9,437	HC
Viterbo Univ	WI	18,043	C
Wartburg College	IA	21,165	VC
Western Mich Univ	MI	10,016	C

APPLIED PHYSICS

School	ST	$IS	SR
Angelo State Univ	TX	7,028	C
Armstrong Atlantic State Univ	GA	7,084	C
Beloit College	WI	27,482	HC
Bethel College	IN	17,650	LC
Columbia Univ/Fu Foundation School of Engineering and Applied Science	NY	35,190	MC
East Carolina Univ	NC	7,766	C
Goucher College	MD	30,650	VC+
Hiram College	OH	27,034	VC
Indiana Univ of Pennsylvania	PA	9,133	C
Kettering Univ	MI	23,256	HC
Linfield College	OR	25,840	VC
New Jersey Inst of Technology	NJ	14,690	VC
Northeastern Univ	MA	30,078	VC
Pacific Lutheran Univ	WA	23,318	VC
Providence College	RI	27,620	HC
Purdue Univ/West Lafayette	IN	10,284	VC
Saginaw Valley State Univ	MI	9,465	C
Shippensburg Univ of Pennsylvania	PA	9,652	C
SUNY/College at Geneseo	NY	9,970	HC
Stevens Inst of Technology	NJ	31,510	HC+
Texas Tech Univ	TX	8,825	C
Tufts Univ	MA	34,874	MC
Univ of Alaska Fairbanks	AK	8,265	NC
Univ of Calif at Los Angeles	CA	13,227	MC
Univ of Calif at San Diego	CA	11,372	HC
Univ of Nevada/Las Vegas	NV	8,281	VC
Univ of N Dak	ND	7,067	VC
Whitworth College	WA	23,938	VC
Xavier Univ	OH	23,880	C

APPLIED PSYCHOLOGY

School	ST	$IS	SR
Christian Brothers Univ	TN	19,820	VC

ARABIC

School	ST	$IS	SR
Dartmouth College	NH	34,458	MC
Georgetown Univ	DC	34,847	MC
Lincoln Univ	PA	11,198	C+
SUNY/Univ at Binghamton	NY	10,653	HC
Ohio State Univ	OH	10,819	VC
Univ of Calif at Los Angeles	CA	13,227	MC
Univ of Mich/Ann Arbor	MI	13,003	HC+
Univ of Texas at Austin	TX	9,437	HC
Washington Univ in St. Louis	MO	34,593	MC
Wayne State Univ	MI	0,720	C

ARCHEOLOGY

School	ST	$IS	SR
Bard College	NY	33,912	HC
Baylor Univ	TX	18,298	VC+
Boston Univ	MA	34,358	MC
Bowdoin College	ME	32,650	MC
Bryn Mawr College	PA	33,580	HC+
CUNY/Brooklyn College	NY	3,403	LC
CUNY/Hunter College	NY	5,147	C+
College of Wooster	OH	28,350	VC
Columbia Univ/Columbia College	NY	35,190	MC
Columbia Univ/School of General Studies	NY	35,000	C
Cornell Univ	NY	34,614	MC
George Washington Univ	DC	32,170	HC
Hamilton College	NY	34,150	HC
Haverford College	PA	34,300	MC
Mass Inst of Technology	MA	35,228	MC
Mercyhurst College	PA	20,694	C
Oberlin College	OH	33,140	HC+
Princeton Univ	NJ	35,072	MC
Stanford Univ	CA	34,222	MC
SUNY/College at Potsdam	NY	10,519	C
Tufts Univ	MA	34,874	MC
Univ of Calif at Berkeley	CA	14,134	MC
Univ of Evansville	IN	22,865	VC+
Univ of Indianapolis	IN	20,840	C
Univ of Kansas	KS	7,232	VC
Univ of Mich/Ann Arbor	MI	13,003	HC+
Univ of Missouri/Columbia	MO	9,803	HC
Univ of Texas at Austin	TX	9,437	HC
Univ of Wisc/La Crosse	WI	7,250	VC
Washington and Lee Univ	VA	25,095	MC
Washington Univ in St. Louis	MO	34,593	MC
Wesleyan Univ	CT	3,405	MC
Wheaton College	IL	21,934	HC
Yale Univ	CT	34,030	MC

ARCHITECTURAL ENGINEERING

School	ST	$IS	SR
Calif Polytechnic State Univ	CA	8,747	VC
Drexel Univ	PA	27,657	VC
Illinois Inst of Technology	IL	25,182	HC+
Kansas State Univ	KS	6,995	C
Milwaukee School of Engineering	WI	25,680	VC+
N Car Agricultural and Technical State Univ	NC	6,659	LC
Okla State Univ	OK	7,650	VC
Parsons School of Design	NY	32,242	SP
Penn State Univ/Univ Park Campus	PA	11,126	VC
Princeton Univ	NJ	35,072	MC
Purdue Univ/West Lafayette	IN	10,284	VC
Tenn State Univ	TN	7,058	VC
Univ of Cincinnati	OH	12,491	LC
Univ of Colo at Boulder	CO	9,255	VC
Univ of Hartford	CT	28,884	C
Univ of Houston	TX	8,410	C
Univ of Idaho	ID	7,026	C
Univ of Kansas	KS	7,232	VC
Univ of Miami	FL	31,130	HC
Univ of Missouri/Rolla	MO	10,034	C
Univ of Nebr at Lincoln	NE	8,325	C+
Univ of Nevada/Las Vegas	NV	8,281	VC
Univ of Texas at Austin	TX	9,437	HC
Univ of Wyoming	WY	7,143	LC
Vermont Technical College	VT	11,704	C

ARCHITECTURAL TECHNOLOGY

School	ST	$IS	SR
Brown Univ	RI	34,973	MC
Fairmont State College	WV	7,010	NC
Florida International Univ	FL	9,486	VC
SUNY/College of Technology at Alfred	NY	9,188	C
Univ of Cincinnati	OH	12,491	LC
Univ of Southern Miss	MS	6,155	LC
Wentworth Inst of Technology	MA	20,450	C

ARCHITECTURE

School	ST	$IS	SR
Andrews Univ	MI	17,696	LC
Arizona State Univ-Main	AZ	7,726	C
Auburn Univ	AL	5,510	C
Ball State Univ	IN	8,660	C
Baylor Univ	TX	18,298	VC+
Bennington College	VT	31,350	VC
Boston Architectural Center	MA	6,405	SP
Calif College of Arts and Crafts	CA	27,366	SP
Calif Polytechnic State Univ	CA	8,747	VC
Calif State Polytechnic Univ, Pomona	CA	8,615	C
Catholic Univ of America	DC	29,332	VC
Columbia Univ/Barnard College	NY	33,694	MC
Columbia Univ/Columbia College	NY	35,190	MC
Columbia Univ/School of General Studies	NY	35,000	C
Conn College	CT	33,585	MC
Cooper Union for the Advancement of Science and Art	NY	6,500	MC
Cornell Univ	NY	34,614	MC
Drexel Univ	PA	27,657	VC
Drury Univ	MO	15,250	VC
Florida Atlantic Univ	FL	8,832	C
Georgia Inst of Technology	GA	9,028	HC+
Hampshire College	MA	33,881	HC+
Hampton Univ	VA	17,112	C+
Hobart and William Smith Colleges	NY	33,195	VC
Howard Univ	DC	15,522	LC
Illinois Inst of Technology	IL	25,182	HC+
Iowa State Univ	IA	8,108	VC
Kansas State Univ	KS	6,995	C
Kent State Univ	OH	11,104	C
Lawrence Tech Univ	MI	11,429	C
Lehigh Univ	PA	32,290	MC
Louisiana State Univ and A&M College	LA	8,014	VC
Louisiana Tech Univ	LA	6,506	C
Mass College of Art	MA	13,703	SP
Miami Univ	OH	12,885	VC+
Miss State Univ	MS	7,853	C
New Jersey Inst of Technology	NJ	14,690	VC
New York Inst of Technology	NY	21,756	C
N Car State Univ	NC	8,680	HC
N Dak State Univ	ND	7,004	VC
Norwich Univ	VT	21,064	LC
Okla State Univ	OK	7,650	VC
Penn State Univ/Univ Park Campus	PA	11,126	VC
Philadelphia Univ	PA	24,722	C
Portland State Univ	OR	11,220	C
Prairie View A&M Univ	TX	3,172	LC
Pratt Inst	NY	27,550	SP
Princeton Univ	NJ	35,072	MC
Rensselaer Polytechnic Inst	NY	33,863	HC+
Rhode Island School of Design	RI	30,227	SP
Rice Univ	TX	24,325	MC
Roger Williams Univ	RI	29,010	C
Savannah College of Art and Design	GA	25,075	SP
Southern Calif Inst of Architecture	CA	16,740	SP
Southern Illinois Univ at Carbondale	IL	8,621	C
Southern Polytechnic State Univ	GA	6,662	C
Southern Univ and A&M College	LA	6,365	C+
SUNY/Univ at Buffalo	NY	11,033	VC
Syracuse Univ	NY	30,710	HC
Temple Univ	PA	14,124	C
Texas Tech Univ	TX	8,825	C
Ohio State Univ	OH	10,819	VC
Thomas Edison State College	NJ	2,750	SP
Tufts Univ	MA	34,874	MC
Tulane Univ	LA	34,013	HC+
Univ of Arizona	AZ	8,614	C
Univ of Arkansas	AR	8,334	VC
Univ of Calif at Berkeley	CA	14,134	MC
Univ of Detroit Mercy	MI	21,620	LC
Univ of Florida	FL	7,874	HC
Univ of Hawaii at Manoa	HI	7,862	VC
Univ of Houston	TX	8,410	C
Univ of Illinois at Chicago	IL	10,702	VC
Univ of Illinois at Urbana-Champaign	IL	11,316	HC+
Univ of Kansas	KS	7,232	VC
Univ of Maryland/College Park	MD	11,959	C
Univ of Memphis	TN	7,271	C
Univ of Miami	FL	31,130	HC
Univ of Mich/Ann Arbor	MI	13,003	HC+
Univ of Minn/Twin Cities	MN	11,123	VC
Univ of Nebr at Lincoln	NE	8,325	C+
Univ of New Mexico	NM	8,026	C
Univ of N Car at Charlotte	NC	7,254	C
Univ of Okla	OK	7,616	VC
Univ of Oregon	OR	9,969	C
Univ of Pennsylvania	PA	34,614	MC
Univ of San Francisco	CA	27,302	VC
Univ of Southern Calif	CA	33,647	MC
Univ of Tenn at Knoxville	TN	8,214	C
Univ of Texas at Arlington	TX	7,192	LC
Univ of Texas at Austin	TX	9,437	HC
Univ of Texas at San Antonio	TX	9,088	NC
Univ of the District of Columbia	DC	2,844	NC
Univ of Utah	UT	7,703	C
Univ of Virginia	VA	9,391	HC+
Univ of Wisc/Milwaukee	WI	8,907	LC
Virginia Polytechnic Inst and State Univ	VA	7,652	C
Washington State Univ	WA	9,388	C
Washington Univ in St. Louis	MO	34,593	MC
Wellesley College	MA	33,394	MC
Wentworth Inst of Technology	MA	20,450	C
Woodbury Univ	CA	25,344	LC
Yale Univ	CT	34,030	MC

AREA STUDIES

School	ST	$IS	SR
American Univ	DC	31,544	VC+
Bard College	NY	33,912	HC
College of Wooster	OH	28,350	VC
Columbia Univ/Columbia College	NY	35,190	MC
Duke Univ	NC	34,396	MC
Eastern Mich Univ	MI	9,855	C
Hofstra Univ	NY	23,252	C
Lake Forest College	IL	27,460	VC
Rice Univ	TX	24,325	MC
Univ of Alaska Fairbanks	AK	8,265	NC
Univ of Miss	MS	7,666	C
Univ of Okla	OK	7,616	VC
Univ of Virginia	VA	9,391	HC+
Washington State Univ	WA	9,388	C
Washington Univ in St. Louis	MO	34,593	MC

ART

School	ST	$IS	SR
Abilene Christian Univ	TX	16,300	VC
Adams State College	CO	7,468	C
Adrian College	MI	19,670	C
Albany State Univ	GA	5,764	C+
Albertson College of Idaho	ID	23,900	VC
Albion College	MI	25,224	VC
Albright College	PA	27,642	C
Alverno College	WI	16,930	LC
Andrews Univ	MI	17,696	LC
Angelo State Univ	TX	7,028	C
Anna Maria College	MA	22,800	LC
Appalachian State Univ	NC	6,353	C
Aquinas College	MI	20,052	C+
Arizona State Univ-Main	AZ	7,726	C
Arkansas Tech Univ	AR	6,256	C
Armstrong Atlantic State Univ	GA	7,084	C
Asbury College	KY	18,540	VC
Ashland Univ	OH	22,182	LC
Atlantic Union College	MA	34,034	LC
Augusta State Univ	GA	2,282	C
Augustana College	SD	20,760	VC
Austin College	TX	22,150	VC+
Austin Peay State Univ	TN	5,814	LC
Avila College	MO	17,720	C
Ball State Univ	IN	8,660	C
Barry Univ	FL	24,100	LC
Bates College	ME	34,100	MC
Baylor Univ	TX	18,298	VC+
Belhaven College	MS	16,040	C+
Bellarmine Univ	KY	20,440	VC
Bennington College	VT	31,350	VC
Berea College	KY	4,070	VC
Berry College	GA	18,850	C
Bethany College	KS	16,602	C+
Bethel College	IN	17,650	LC
Bethel College	KS	17,355	C+
Biola Univ	CA	21,902	VC
Black Hills State Univ	SD	6,652	LC
Blackburn College	IL	13,690	C
Bluffton College	OH	20,644	C
Boise State Univ	ID	6,531	LC
Bowling Green State Univ	OH	10,794	C
Brescia Univ	KY	14,225	C
Bridgewater College	VA	22,950	C
Bridgewater State College	MA	7,589	C+
Brigham Young Univ/Hawaii	HI	6,890	C
Bucknell Univ	PA	31,096	HC
Buena Vista Univ	IA	22,828	C
Caldwell College	NJ	20,940	LC
Calif Baptist Univ	CA	16,736	C
Calif Lutheran Univ	CA	23,500	LC
Calif State Polytechnic Univ, Pomona	CA	8,615	C
Cal State, Bakersfield	CA	6,090	LC
Cal State, Chico	CA	8,598	LC
Cal State, Dominguez Hills	CA	5,840	LC
Cal State, Fresno	CA	7,762	C
Cal State, Hayward	CA	7,400	LC
Cal State, Long Beach	CA	7,400	LC
Cal State, Northridge	CA	7,781	C
Cal State, San Bernardino	CA	6,516	C
Calif Univ of Pennsylvania	PA	10,388	C
Campbell Univ	NC	16,599	C
Campbellsville Univ	KY	14,340	C
Cardinal Stritch Univ	WI	17,620	C
Carlow College	PA	19,366	C
Carroll College	WI	21,170	C
Carthage College	WI	23,670	C
Castleton State College	VT	10,922	LC
Catholic Univ of America	DC	29,332	VC
Cedar Crest College	PA	25,145	C+
Centenary College of Louisiana	LA	21,600	C+
Central Conn State Univ	CT	10,404	C
Chadron State College	NE	6,211	NC
Chaminade Univ of Honolulu	HI	17,370	C
Chapman Univ	CA	30,218	VC
Chicago State Univ	IL	8,851	C+
CUNY/Brooklyn College	NY	3,403	LC
CUNY/College of Staten Island	NY	3,358	NC
CUNY/Queens College	NY	3,403	VC
Clarion Univ of Pennsylvania	PA	11,272	LC
Clark Atlanta Univ	GA	17,174	C
Clarke College	IA	20,625	C+
Cleveland State Univ	OH	10,146	NC
Coe College	IA	24,750	VC
Coker College	SC	20,120	C
Colby College	ME	34,290	MC
Colby-Sawyer College	NH	27,850	LC
College of Mount St. Joseph	OH	20,290	C
College of St. Benedict	MN	23,921	VC
College of St. Elizabeth	NJ	22,510	C
College of St. Mary	NE	18,726	C
College of the Ozarks	MO	2,650	C+
Colo Christian Univ	CO	17,714	C
Colo State Univ	CO	9,672	C
Columbia College	MO	15,082	C
Columbia College Chicago	IL	22,063	LC
Columbus State Univ	GA	7,228	LC
Concordia Univ	CA	22,290	C
Concordia Univ	MI	20,500	C
Concordia Univ	MN	19,912	C
Concordia Univ Wisc	WI	16,600	LC
Concordia Univ, River Forest	IL	20,000	LC
Conn College	CT	33,585	MC
Creighton Univ	NE	23,476	VC
Culver-Stockton College	MO	15,400	LC
Cumberland College	KY	14,864	C
Daemen College	NY	20,620	C

School	ST	$IS	SR
Dakota Wesleyan Univ	SD	15,512	C
Dana College	NE	18,046	C
Davidson College	NC	30,823	MC
Davis and Elkins College	WV	19,270	LC
Defiance College	OH	19,580	LC
Delta State Univ	MS	5,416	C
DePaul Univ	IL	23,590	VC
Dillard Univ	LA	16,046	VC
Doane College	NE	17,600	LC
Dominican Univ	IL	20,800	C
Dominican Univ of Calif	CA	27,948	C
Drew Univ/College of Liberal Arts	NJ	32,152	VC
Earlham College	IN	27,446	VC+
East Carolina Univ	NC	7,766	C
East Central Univ	OK	4,578	C
East Stroudsburg Univ of Pennsylvania	PA	8,430	LC
East Tenn State Univ	TN	7,127	C
Eastern Illinois Univ	IL	10,101	C
Eastern Kentucky Univ	KY	6,552	C
Eastern Mennonite Univ	VA	20,700	VC
Eastern Mich Univ	MI	9,855	C
Eastern New Mexico Univ	NM	4,113	LC
Eastern Oregon Univ	OR	8,772	C
Eastern Washington Univ	WA	7,972	LC
Edgewood College	WI	18,304	C
Edinboro Univ of Pennsylvania	PA	9,328	LC
Elizabeth City State Univ	NC	5,550	LC
Elizabethtown College	PA	26,000	VC
Elmhurst College	IL	21,750	C
Elmira College	NY	31,070	VC+
Elon Univ	NC	19,430	VC
Emory & Henry College	VA	19,462	C
Emporia State Univ	KS	6,198	LC
Evangel Univ	MO	14,050	C
Felician College	NJ	20,050	LC
Ferrum College	VA	15,990	LC
Flagler College	FL	10,550	VC+
Florida Atlantic Univ	FL	8,832	C
Florida International Univ	FL	9,486	VC
Fontbonne Univ	MO	18,046	C
Fort Hays State Univ	KS	6,294	LC
Fort Lewis College	CO	7,659	LC
Freed-Hardeman Univ	TN	14,290	VC
Friends Univ	KS	15,962	LC
Furman Univ	SC	25,492	HC
George Fox Univ	OR	24,095	VC
Georgetown College	KY	18,400	VC
Georgia College and State Univ	GA	7,344	C
Georgia Southern Univ	GA	6,958	C
Georgia State Univ	GA	7,792	LC
Georgian Court College	NJ	19,040	LC
Gonzaga Univ	WA	24,276	HC+
Gordon College	MA	23,594	VC+
Grace College	IN	16,768	C
Grambling State Univ	LA	5,325	NC
Green Mountain College	VT	24,130	C
Greensboro College	NC	19,080	LC
Greenville College	IL	19,226	LC
Grinnell College	IA	28,300	HC+
Hamilton College	NY	34,150	HC
Hamline Univ	MN	23,339	C+
Hampton Univ	VA	17,112	C+
Hannibal-LaGrange College	MO	12,530	C
Hanover College	IN	17,560	VC
Harding Univ	AR	13,528	VC
Hartwick College	NY	33,090	C+
Hendrix College	AR	18,463	HC
High Point Univ	NC	20,220	LC
Hiram College	OH	27,034	VC
Holy Family College	PA	13,710	LC
Hood College	MD	26,020	VC
Houghton College	NY	21,810	VC+
Howard Payne Univ	TX	13,834	C+
Humboldt State Univ	CA	8,582	C
Huntingdon College	AL	18,400	VC
Huntington College	IN	15,480	LC
Idaho State Univ	ID	7,030	C+
Illinois State Univ	IL	9,235	C
Indiana Univ of Pennsylvania	PA	9,133	C
Indiana Wesleyan Univ	IN	17,680	C
Ithaca College	NY	28,719	HC
Jackson State Univ	MS	6,776	LC
Jacksonville Univ	FL	21,110	LC
James Madison Univ	VA	9,552	HC
John Brown Univ	AR	15,080	VC
Johnson State College	VT	10,776	C
Judson College	AL	13,790	C
Kalamazoo College	MI	26,955	HC+
Kansas State Univ	KS	6,995	C
Keene State College	NH	11,280	C
Kennesaw State Univ	GA	2,306	LC
Kentucky Wesleyan College	KY	15,800	C
La Sierra Univ	CA	19,260	LC
Lafayette College	PA	32,655	MC
Lake Forest College	IL	27,460	VC
Lakeland College	WI	17,950	C
Lehigh Univ	PA	32,290	MC
LeMoyne-Owen College	TN	8,450	NC
Lincoln Univ	MO	7,158	NC
Lincoln Univ	PA	11,198	C+
Lindsey Wilson College	KY	16,392	LC
Linfield College	OR	25,840	VC
Longwood College	VA	8,950	C
Lourdes College	OH	13,100	LC
Luther College	IA	23,300	VC+
Lynchburg College	VA	23,405	C
Lyon College	AR	16,500	VC
Macalester College	MN	28,814	HC+
MacMurray College	IL	17,790	LC
Madonna Univ	MI	11,504	VC
Malone College	OH	19,190	C
Manchester College	IN	22,010	C
Manhattanville College	NY	28,730	VC
Marian College of Fond du Lac	WI	17,935	LC
Mary Baldwin College	VA	23,440	C
Marygrove College	MI	16,075	C
Marylhurst Univ	OR	15,343	NC
Maryville College	TN	23,210	VC
Mass Inst of Technology	MA	35,228	MC
McKendree College	IL	18,300	C+
McMurry Univ	TX	15,287	C
McPherson College	KS	17,710	C
Meredith College	NC	17,500	C
Methodist College	NC	19,526	C
Metropolitan State College of Denver	CO	2,338	LC
Miami Univ	OH	12,885	VC+
Middlebury College	VT	34,300	MC
Millersville Univ of Pennsylvania	PA	10,153	VC
Millikin Univ	IL	24,415	C+
Millsaps College	MS	22,608	VC+
Minn State Univ, Mankato	MN	7,296	LC
Minot State Univ	ND	5,466	LC
Miss College	MS	14,574	C
Miss State Univ	MS	7,853	C
Miss Valley State Univ	MS	6,345	C
Missouri Southern State College	MO	6,666	C
Missouri Valley College	MO	17,400	LC
Molloy College	NY	13,940	C
Monmouth College	IL	21,550	C
Monmouth Univ	NJ	24,042	C
Montana State Univ-Bozeman	MT	8,431	C
Morehouse College	GA	19,814	C
Morningside College	IA	19,124	C
Mount Mercy College	IA	19,390	VC
Mount Olive College	NC	14,410	LC
Mount St. Mary's College	CA	24,430	C
Mount Union College	OH	21,120	C
Mount Vernon Nazarene College	OH	17,027	C
Muhlenberg College	PA	28,170	HC
Muskingum College	OH	18,760	C
Nazareth College of Rochester	NY	22,036	VC
Nebr Wesleyan Univ	NE	18,767	VC
New Mexico Highlands Univ	NM	6,256	NC
New Mexico State Univ	NM	7,302	C
Newberry College	SC	19,670	LC
Newman Univ	KS	14,098	LC
Nicholls State Univ	LA	5,290	NC
N Car Central Univ	NC	6,418	LC
N Dak State Univ	ND	7,004	VC
North Georgia College and State Univ	GA	6,322	C+
Northeastern Univ	MA	30,078	VC
Northern Kentucky Univ	KY	6,352	NC
Northwest Missouri State Univ	MO	7,922	LC
Northwest Nazarene Univ	ID	18,380	C
Northwestern State Univ of Louisiana	LA	5,745	NC
Northwestern Univ	IL	33,615	MC
Notre Dame College	OH	20,425	C
Notre Dame de Namur Univ	CA	26,932	LC
Oberlin College	OH	33,140	HC+
Oglethorpe Univ	GA	19,100	LC
Ohio Dominican College	OH	18,100	LC
Ohio Univ	OH	11,769	C
Okla Christian Univ	OK	16,500	VC
Okla City Univ	OK	15,810	C
Okla State Univ	OK	7,650	VC
Olivet Nazarene Univ	IL	18,444	C
Oregon State Univ	OR	9,612	VC
Ottawa Univ	KS	11,800	LC
Otterbein College	OH	23,439	C
Our Lady of the Lake Univ of San Antonio	TX	17,336	C
Pacific Lutheran Univ	WA	23,318	VC
Palm Beach Atlantic College	FL	23,310	C
Penn State Univ/Univ Park Campus	PA	11,126	VC
Pepperdine Univ	CA	32,830	VC
Piedmont College	GA	16,900	C
Pikeville College	KY	12,000	NC
Pine Manor College	MA	19,344	LC
Pittsburg State Univ	KS	6,228	NC
Pitzer College	CA	33,930	HC
Plymouth State College	NH	11,024	LC
Point Loma Nazarene Univ	CA	21,380	VC
Prairie View A&M Univ	TX	3,172	LC
Quincy Univ	IL	20,450	C
Radford Univ	VA	8,302	C
Ramapo College of New Jersey	NJ	13,550	VC
Randolph-Macon Woman's College	VA	25,820	VC+
Regis College	MA	26,750	C
Rhodes College	TN	26,466	HC+
Roanoke College	VA	24,689	VC
Rockford College	IL	23,930	C
Rocky Mountain College	MT	18,113	C
Rutgers, The State Univ of New Jersey New Brunswick Campus	NJ	12,709	C
Rutgers, The State Univ of New Jersey/ CamdenCampus	NJ	6,484	C
Sacred Heart Univ	CT	26,588	VC
Saginaw Valley State Univ	MI	9,465	C
St. John's Univ	MN	23,640	VC
St. John's Univ	NY	26,660	C
St. Joseph's College	IN	21,640	C
St. Mary College	KS	17,298	C
St. Mary's College	IN	24,474	VC
St. Mary's College of Calif	CA	27,575	C
St. Norbert College	WI	23,169	VC
St. Vincent College	PA	22,942	VC
Salisbury Univ	MD	10,576	VC
Sam Houston State Univ	TX	6,076	LC
Samford Univ	AL	16,340	VC
Santa Clara Univ	CA	28,371	VC+
Savannah College of Art and Design	GA	25,075	SP
Seattle Pacific Univ	WA	22,674	C+
Seton Hall Univ	NJ	26,910	LC
Shenandoah Univ	VA	22,550	NC
Shepherd College	WV	7,062	LC
Shippensburg Univ of Pennsylvania	PA	9,652	C
Shorter College	GA	15,185	C
Simmons College	MA	30,418	VC
Simon's Rock College of Bard	MA	32,450	HC
Simpson College	IA	21,200	C+
Sinte Gleska Univ	SD	2,268	NC
Skidmore College	NY	34,201	VC+
Sonoma State Univ	CA	8,953	C
S Dak State Univ	SD	6,848	C
Southeast Missouri State Univ	MO	8,367	C+
Southeastern Louisiana Univ	LA	6,047	LC
Southern Adventist Univ	TN	15,600	C
Southern Arkansas Univ	AR	5,740	LC
Southern Illinois Univ at Carbondale	IL	8,621	C
Southern Illinois Univ Edwardsville	IL	7,869	LC
Southern Oregon Univ	OR	9,429	C
Southern Utah Univ	UT	7,254	C
Southwest Baptist Univ	MO	13,426	LC
Southwest Missouri State Univ	MO	7,600	LC
Southwest State Univ	MN	7,117	LC
Southwest Texas State Univ	TX	8,730	VC
Southwestern Univ	TX	22,550	HC
Spalding Univ	KY	15,196	C
Spelman College	GA	19,215	C+
Spring Arbor Univ	MI	17,976	C
Stanford Univ	CA	34,222	MC
SUNY/College at Buffalo	NY	8,025	C
SUNY/College at Cortland	NY	10,564	C
SUNY/College at Oneonta	NY	9,981	C
SUNY/College at Oswego	NY	10,856	C
SUNY/Univ at Binghamton	NY	10,653	HC
State Univ of West Georgia	GA	7,101	C
Stephen F. Austin State Univ	TX	6,905	C
Sterling College	KS	16,370	VC
Stetson Univ	FL	25,640	VC
Stillman College	AL	11,370	LC
Susquehanna Univ	PA	27,270	VC
Swarthmore College	PA	34,538	MC
Syracuse Univ	NY	30,710	HC
Tarleton State Univ	TX	7,160	C
Taylor Univ	IN	21,562	VC+
Temple Univ	PA	14,124	C
Tenn State Univ	TN	7,058	VC
Texas Lutheran Univ	TX	17,660	C
Texas Southern Univ	TX	6,576	NC
Texas Tech Univ	TX	8,825	C
Texas Wesleyan Univ	TX	14,710	C
Ohio State Univ	OH	10,819	VC
Thiel College	PA	18,419	LC
Thomas Edison State College	NJ	2,750	SP
Thomas More College	KY	17,700	LC
Tougaloo College	MS	9,200	NC
Towson Univ	MD	11,088	VC
Trinity Christian College	IL	19,415	C
Truman State Univ	MO	8,568	VC+
Union Univ	TN	18,930	C+
Univ of Akron	OH	10,530	NC
Univ of Alaska Anchorage	AK	9,100	NC
Univ of Alaska Fairbanks	AK	8,265	NC
Univ of Alaska Southeast	AK	7,900	LC
Univ of Arkansas	AR	8,334	VC
Univ of Arkansas at Little Rock	AR	5,637	NC
Univ of Arkansas at Monticello	AR	5,940	NC
Univ of Arkansas at Pine Bluff	AR	7,925	C
Univ of Calif at Los Angeles	CA	13,227	MC
Univ of Calif at Riverside	CA	12,479	C
Univ of Calif at Santa Barbara	CA	11,732	VC
Univ of Calif at Santa Cruz	CA	13,655	VC
Univ of Central Florida	FL	8,251	VC
Univ of Charleston	WV	20,640	C
Univ of Conn	CT	12,122	VC
Univ of Delaware	DE	10,824	VC
Univ of Denver	CO	28,783	VC
Univ of Evansville	IN	22,865	VC+
Univ of Florida	FL	7,874	HC
Univ of Georgia	GA	8,656	VC
Univ of Great Falls	MT	15,360	C
Univ of Hawaii at Hilo	HI	6,497	C
Univ of Hawaii at Manoa	HI	7,862	VC
Univ of Houston	TX	8,410	C
Univ of Idaho	ID	7,026	C
Univ of Iowa	IA	8,607	C+
Univ of Kansas	KS	7,232	VC
Univ of La Verne	CA	24,280	C
Univ of Louisiana at Monroe	LA	5,207	NC
Univ of Louisville	KY	7,402	LC
Univ of Maine	ME	10,798	C
Univ of Maine at Augusta	ME	3,928	C
Univ of Maine at Farmington	ME	9,163	C
Univ of Maine at Presque Isle	ME	7,964	LC
Univ of Mass Boston	MA	4,227	C
Univ of Memphis	TN	7,271	C
Univ of Miami	FL	31,130	HC
Univ of Minn/Duluth	MN	10,436	C
Univ of Miss	MS	7,666	C
Univ of Missouri/Kansas City	MO	9,685	VC
Univ of Montana--Western	MT	6,915	NC
Univ of Montevallo	AL	7,266	C
Univ of Nebr at Lincoln	NE	8,325	C+
Univ of Nevada/Reno	NV	8,737	C
Univ of New Haven	CT	23,860	LC
Univ of New Orleans	LA	10,160	C
Univ of North Alabama	AL	7,016	NC
Univ of N Car at Asheville	NC	6,896	VC
Univ of N Car at Pembroke	NC	5,914	LC
Univ of North Florida	FL	8,089	VC
Univ of North Texas	TX	7,629	C
Univ of Northern Colo	CO	8,082	C+
Univ of Okla	OK	7,616	VC
Univ of Puget Sound	WA	28,285	HC
Univ of Redlands	CA	29,246	VC
Univ of Rhode Island	RI	12,414	C
Univ of Rio Grande	OH	8,728	NC
Univ of Science and Arts of Okla	OK	5,245	C
Univ of South Alabama	AL	6,976	LC
Univ of S Dak	SD	7,036	C
Univ of South Florida	FL	8,154	C
Univ of Southern Colo	CO	7,821	LC
Univ of Tampa	FL	22,612	C
Univ of Texas at El Paso	TX	5,076	LC
Univ of Texas at San Antonio	TX	9,088	NC
Univ of Texas-Pan American	TX	4,823	C
Univ of the Incarnate Word	TX	18,478	C
Univ of the Ozarks	AR	13,904	C
Univ of the Pacific	CA	28,255	VC
Univ of the South	TN	27,290	HC
Univ of Tulsa	OK	19,090	HC
Univ of Utah	UT	7,703	C
Univ of Vermont	VT	14,761	C+
Univ of Virginia	VA	9,391	HC+
Univ of Virginia's College at Wise	VA	8,302	C
Univ of Wisc/Eau Claire	WI	7,032	VC
Univ of Wisc/La Crosse	WI	7,250	VC
Univ of Wisc/Oshkosh	WI	6,130	LC
Univ of Wisc/River Falls	WI	6,356	LC
Univ of Wyoming	WY	7,143	LC
Upper Iowa Univ	IA	17,438	C
Ursuline College	OH	19,430	LC
Valdosta State Univ	GA	6,988	C
Valley City State Univ	ND		LC
Valparaiso Univ	IN	23,570	VC+
Vassar College	NY	33,450	MC
Virginia Intermont College	VA	17,510	C
Virginia Wesleyan College	VA	22,350	LC
Wabash College	IN	25,335	HC
Wake Forest Univ	NC	30,290	MC
Walla Walla College	WA	20,925	C
Warren Wilson College	NC	19,968	C
Wartburg College	IA	21,165	VC
Washburn Univ of Topeka	KS	6,766	NC
Washington and Jefferson College	PA	26,255	VC
Washington College	MD	28,040	VC
Wayland Baptist Univ	TX	11,271	NC
Wayne State College	NE	6,255	NC
Wayne State Univ	MI	6,720	C

ST = STATE $IS = IN-STATE COSTS SR = SELECTOR RATING

School	ST	$IS	SR
Waynesburg College	PA	17,610	LC
Webster Univ	MO	19,804	VC
West Chester Univ of Pennsylvania	PA	9,792	VC
West Texas A&M Univ	TX	6,538	C
West Virginia Univ	WV	8,304	C
Western Carolina Univ	NC	5,667	C
Western Conn State Univ	CT	10,074	C
Western Illinois Univ	IL	9,571	C
Western Mich Univ	MI	10,016	C
Western Oregon Univ	OR	8,829	C
Western State College of Colo	CO	7,585	LC
Western Washington Univ	WA	8,624	VC
Westminster College	PA	22,960	C
Westmont College	CA	29,748	VC
Wheaton College	IL	21,934	HC
Whittier College	CA	29,108	C
Whitworth College	WA	23,938	VC
Wichita State Univ	KS	6,879	C
Wilkes Univ	PA	25,800	C
William Carey College	MS	10,150	LC
William Jewell College	MO	17,150	VC
William Woods Univ	MO	19,390	LC
Williams Baptist College	AR	10,750	C
Williams College	MA	32,270	MC
Wilmington College	OH	21,826	C
Wingate Univ	NC	19,140	C
Winston-Salem State Univ	NC	5,927	LC
Winthrop Univ	SC	9,106	C
Wisc Lutheran College	WI	19,216	VC
Xavier Univ	OH	23,880	C
Yale Univ	CT	34,030	MC
Youngstown State Univ	OH	9,318	NC

ART EDUCATION

School	ST	$IS	SR
Abilene Christian Univ	TX	16,300	VC
Adams State College	CO	7,468	C
Adelphi Univ	NY	23,320	VC
Alabama A&M Univ	AL	5,100	LC
Alabama State Univ	AL	6,404	C
Alfred Univ	NY	27,212	C+
Alverno College	WI	16,930	LC
Anderson Univ	IN	19,430	LC
Andrews Univ	MI	17,696	LC
Anna Maria College	MA	22,800	LC
Appalachian State Univ	NC	6,353	C
Arcadia Univ	PA	26,650	C
Arkansas State Univ	AR	7,480	C
Arkansas Tech Univ	AR	6,256	C
Armstrong Atlantic State Univ	GA	7,084	C
Asbury College	KY	18,540	VC
Ashland Univ	OH	22,182	LC
Augustana College	IL	24,117	VC+
Averett Univ	VA	17,980	LC
Azusa Pacific Univ	CA	22,422	VC
Baker Univ	KS	14,780	C+
Baldwin-Wallace College	OH	22,010	VC+
Ball State Univ	IN	8,660	C
Bartlesville Wesleyan College	OK	14,100	LC
Barton College	NC	16,834	LC
Baylor Univ	TX	18,298	VC+
Beloit College	WI	27,482	HC
Bemidji State Univ	MN	7,957	C
Berea College	KY	4,070	VC
Berry College	GA	18,850	C
Bethany College	KS	16,602	C+
Bethel College	MN	22,740	VC
Birmingham-Southern College	AL	22,960	C
Black Hills State Univ	SD	6,652	LC
Blackburn College	IL	13,690	C
Boise State Univ	ID	6,531	LC
Boston Univ	MA	34,358	MC
Bowling Green State Univ	OH	10,794	C
Brenau Univ Women's College	GA	20,100	C
Brescia Univ	KY	14,225	C
Brigham Young Univ	UT	7,840	HC
Brigham Young Univ/Hawaii	HI	6,890	C
Buena Vista Univ	IA	22,828	C
Cal State, Fullerton	CA	5,440	LC
Calumet College of St. Joseph	IN	7,500	LC
Calvin College	MI	20,050	NC
Carlow College	PA	19,366	C
Carroll College	WI	21,170	C
Carson-Newman College	TN	16,490	C
Case Western Reserve Univ	OH	27,418	C
Catholic Univ of America	DC	29,332	VC
Central Conn State Univ	CT	10,404	C
Central Mich Univ	MI	8,355	C
Central Missouri State Univ	MO	7,920	C
Central State Univ	OH	8,922	C+
Central Washington Univ	WA	8,985	LC
Chicago State Univ	IL	8,851	C+
CUNY/Brooklyn College	NY	3,403	LC
CUNY/City College	NY	3,309	LC
CUNY/Herbert H. Lehman College	NY	3,320	LC
CUNY/Hunter College	NY	5,147	C+
CUNY/Queens College	NY	3,403	VC
Claflin Univ	SC	12,735	C+
Clarke College	IA	20,625	C+
Coastal Carolina Univ	SC	9,220	C
Coker College	SC	20,120	C
Colby-Sawyer College	NH	27,850	LC
College of Mount St. Joseph	OH	20,290	C
College of New Jersey	NJ	13,425	HC
College of New Rochelle	NY	20,000	C
College of Notre Dame of Maryland	MD	23,100	LC
College of St. Catherine	MN	22,324	VC
College of St. Rose	NY	19,084	C
College of the Ozarks	MO	2,650	C+
Columbus State Univ	GA	7,228	LC
Concord College	WV	7,122	C+
Concordia College/Moorhead	MN	18,835	C
Converse College	SC	21,990	VC
Cornell College	IA	24,980	VC
Culver-Stockton College	MO	15,400	LC
Cumberland College	KY	14,864	C
Daemen College	NY	20,620	C
Dakota State Univ	SD	6,950	C
Dana College	NE	18,046	C
David Lipscomb Univ	TN	16,158	VC
Defiance College	OH	19,580	LC
Delaware State Univ	DE	8,104	LC
Dickinson State Univ	ND	5,495	NC
Dordt College	IA	18,100	C+
East Carolina Univ	NC	7,766	C
East Central Univ	OK	4,578	C
Eastern Kentucky Univ	KY	6,552	C
Eastern Mich Univ	MI	9,855	C
Eastern Washington Univ	WA	7,972	LC
Edinboro Univ of Pennsylvania	PA	9,328	LC
Elmhurst College	IL	21,750	C
Elmira College	NY	31,070	VC+
Emmanuel College	MA	23,802	C+
Emporia State Univ	KS	6,198	LC
Escuela de Artes Plasticas de PR	PR	1,874	
Fairmont State College	WV	7,010	NC
Fisk Univ	TN	13,700	LC
Flagler College	FL	10,550	VC+
Florida A&M Univ	FL	6,948	C
Florida International Univ	FL	9,486	VC
Florida Southern College	FL	19,430	C
Florida State Univ	FL	7,835	HC
Fontbonne Univ	MO	18,046	C
Fort Hays State Univ	KS	6,294	LC
Francis Marion Univ	SC	7,682	C
Freed-Hardeman Univ	TN	14,290	VC
Friends Univ	KS	15,962	LC
Gallaudet Univ	DC	10,554	SP
Georgia Southern Univ	GA	6,958	C
Georgia Southwestern State Univ	GA	6,013	C
Georgia State Univ	GA	7,792	LC
Goshen College	IN	18,950	VC+
Grace College	IN	16,768	C
Grambling State Univ	LA	5,325	NC
Grand Canyon Univ	AZ	30,000	LC
Grand Valley State Univ	MI	10,040	C
Green Mountain College	VT	24,130	C
Greensboro College	NC	19,080	LC
Greenville College	IL	19,226	LC
Gustavus Adolphus College	MN	24,190	VC+
Hardin-Simmons Univ	TX	14,165	C
Hastings College	NE	17,854	C+
High Point Univ	NC	20,220	LC
Hillsdale College	MI	20,586	VC+
Hofstra Univ	NY	23,252	C
Hope College	MI	22,922	C+
Houston Baptist Univ	TX	15,300	LC
Howard Univ	DC	15,522	LC
Huntingdon College	AL	18,400	VC
Huntington College	IN	15,480	LC
Indiana State Univ	IN	8,461	LC
Indiana Univ of Pennsylvania	PA	9,133	C
Indiana Univ-Purdue Univ Indianapolis	IN	9,473	C
Indiana Wesleyan Univ	IN	17,680	C
Inter-American Univ of PR/San GermÈn	PR	6,390	
Iowa Wesleyan College	IA	18,840	C
Jacksonville Univ	FL	21,110	LC
Johnson State College	VT	10,776	C
Kansas State Univ	KS	6,995	C
Kansas Wesleyan Univ	KS	17,400	C+
Kennesaw State Univ	GA	2,306	LC
Kent State Univ	OH	11,104	C
Kentucky State Univ	KY	6,146	NC
Kentucky Wesleyan College	KY	15,800	C
Kutztown Univ of Pennsylvania	PA	8,907	C
LaGrange College	GA	17,496	C
Lamar Univ	TX	6,816	LC
Lawrence Univ	WI	27,711	HC
Lenoir-Rhyne College	NC	19,186	C
Limestone College	SC	16,900	C
Lincoln Univ	MO	7,158	NC
Lindenwood Univ	MO	17,250	C
LIU/Brooklyn Campus	NY	22,290	C
LIU/C.W. Post Campus	NY	25,380	C
LIU/Southampton College	NY	26,270	C
Longwood College	VA	8,950	C
Loras College	IA	22,994	C+
Louisiana College	LA	11,516	C
Louisiana State Univ in Shreveport	LA	2,480	NC
Louisiana Tech Univ	LA	6,506	C
Lubbock Christian Univ	TX	14,226	LC
Malone College	OH	19,190	C
Manchester College	IN	22,010	C
Manhattanville College	NY	28,730	VC
Mansfield Univ	PA	9,648	C
Marian College of Fond du Lac	WI	17,935	LC
Mars Hill College	NC	18,600	LC
Mary Baldwin College	VA	23,440	C
Marymount College/Tarrytown	NY	23,850	C
Maryville College	TN	23,210	VC
Maryville Univ of St. Louis	MO	18,680	C
Marywood Univ	PA	24,639	C
Mass College of Art	MA	13,703	SP
McKendree College	IL	18,300	C+
Mercyhurst College	PA	20,694	C
Messiah College	PA	23,180	VC
Methodist College	NC	19,526	C
Miami Univ	OH	12,885	VC+
Mich State Univ	MI	10,386	VC
Middle Tenn State Univ	TN	6,994	C
Midland Lutheran College	NE	18,600	C
Millersville Univ of Pennsylvania	PA	10,153	VC
Millikin Univ	IL	24,415	C+
Minn State Univ, Mankato	MN	7,296	LC
Miss College	MS	14,574	C
Miss Univ for Women	MS	5,446	LC
Missouri Southern State College	MO	6,666	C
Missouri Western State College	MO	6,662	NC
Monmouth Univ	NJ	24,042	C
Montana State Univ-Billings	MT	7,653	NC
Montclair State Univ	NJ	10,287	LC
Montserrat College of Art	MA	20,335	SP
Moore College of Art and Design	PA	23,125	SP
Moorhead State Univ	MN	7,000	LC
Moravian College	PA	27,065	VC
Morningside College	IA	19,124	C
Mount Mary College	WI	18,024	C
Mount Senario College	WI	17,750	C
Mount Vernon Nazarene College	OH	17,027	C
Murray State Univ	KY	6,672	C
Nazareth College of Rochester	NY	22,036	VC
New Jersey City Univ	NJ	9,100	LC
New York Inst of Technology	NY	21,756	C
Norfolk State Univ	VA	8,382	LC
N Car Agricultural and Technical State Univ	NC	6,659	LC
North Georgia College and State Univ	GA	6,322	C+
Northeastern State Univ	OK	4,701	LC
Northern Arizona Univ	AZ	7,398	C
Northern Illinois Univ	IL	9,545	C
Northern Kentucky Univ	KY	6,352	NC
Northern Mich Univ	MI	9,693	C
Northern State Univ	SD	6,279	LC
Northwest Missouri State Univ	MO	7,922	LC
Northwest Nazarene Univ	ID	18,380	C
Northwestern College	MN	19,816	C+
Northwestern College of Iowa	IA	17,630	C+
Oakland City Univ	IN	11,286	LC
Ohio Univ	OH	11,769	C
Ohio Wesleyan Univ	OH	29,670	VC+
Okla Baptist Univ	OK	13,878	VC
Okla Christian Univ	OK	16,500	VC
Old Dominion Univ	VA	9,386	C
Oral Roberts Univ	OK	18,490	C
Ouachita Baptist Univ	AR	16,460	VC
Our Lady of the Lake Univ of San Antonio	TX	17,336	C
Palm Beach Atlantic College	FL	23,310	C
Penn State Univ/Univ Park Campus	PA	11,126	VC
Peru State College	NE	6,342	NC
Piedmont College	GA	16,900	C
Pittsburg State Univ	KS	6,228	NC
Plymouth State College	NH	11,024	LC
Pontifical Catholic Univ of PR/Ponce	PR	7,076	
Pratt Inst	NY	27,550	SP
Prescott College	AZ	13,430	C
Purdue Univ/West Lafayette	IN	10,284	VC
Quincy Univ	IL	20,450	C
Radford Univ	VA	8,302	C
Rhode Island College	RI	8,700	LC
Rivier College	NH	24,215	C
Roberts Wesleyan College	NY	20,160	C+
Rocky Mountain College	MT	18,113	C
Rosemont College	PA	24,060	C
Saginaw Valley State Univ	MI	9,465	C
St. Ambrose Univ	IA	19,994	C
St. Cloud State Univ	MN	7,180	C
St. John's Univ	NY	26,660	C
St. Mary-of-the-Woods College	IN	21,320	LC
St. Michael's College	VT	26,935	VC
St. Olaf College	MN	25,880	HC
St. Thomas Aquinas College	NY	20,590	LC
St. Vincent College	PA	22,942	VC
St. Xavier Univ	IL	21,104	C
Salem State College	MA	4,481	LC
School of the Art Inst of Chicago	IL	27,800	SP
Schreiner Univ	TX	19,254	C
Seattle Pacific Univ	WA	22,674	C+
Seton Hill College	PA	21,875	C
Shepherd College	WV	7,062	LC
Silver Lake College of the Holy Family	WI	15,516	LC
S Car State Univ	SC	6,586	LC
S Dak State Univ	SD	6,848	C
Southeast Missouri State Univ	MO	8,367	C+
Southeastern Louisiana Univ	LA	6,047	LC
Southeastern Okla State Univ	OK	4,917	C
Southern Arkansas Univ	AR	5,740	LC
Southern Conn State Univ	CT	10,310	C
Southern Univ at New Orleans	LA	995	NC
Southern Utah Univ	UT	7,254	C
Southwest Baptist Univ	MO	13,426	LC
Southwest Missouri State Univ	MO	7,600	LC
Southwest State Univ	MN	7,117	LC
Southwest Texas State Univ	TX	8,730	VC
Southwestern Okla State Univ	OK	4,801	C
Spelman College	GA	19,215	C+
SUNY/College at Buffalo	NY	8,025	C
SUNY/College at Potsdam	NY	10,519	C
SUNY/Univ at New Paltz	NY	9,685	VC
State Univ of West Georgia	GA	7,101	C
Stephen F. Austin State Univ	TX	6,905	C
Sul Ross State Univ	TX	6,582	LC
Syracuse Univ	NY	30,710	HC
Tarleton State Univ	TX	7,160	C
Taylor Univ	IN	21,562	VC+
Temple Univ	PA	14,124	C
Tenn Tech Univ	TN	6,968	C
Texas Christian Univ	TX	19,910	C
Texas Tech Univ	TX	8,825	C
Ohio State Univ	OH	10,819	VC
Towson Univ	MD	11,088	VC
Trinity Christian College	IL	19,415	C
Trinity Univ	TX	21,444	HC
Troy State Univ	AL	7,696	C
Union College	NE	14,650	C
Univ of Akron	OH	10,530	NC
Univ of Arizona	AZ	8,614	C
Univ of Arkansas at Pine Bluff	AR	7,925	C
Univ of Central Arkansas	AR	6,388	C
Univ of Central Florida	FL	8,251	VC
Univ of Central Okla	OK	5,205	C
Univ of Cincinnati	OH	12,491	LC
Univ of Dallas	TX	22,128	VC+
Univ of Dayton	OH	20,400	VC
Univ of Evansville	IN	22,865	VC+
Univ of Findlay	OH	23,962	NC
Univ of Florida	FL	7,874	HC
Univ of Georgia	GA	8,656	VC
Univ of Idaho	ID	7,026	C
Univ of Illinois at Chicago	IL	10,702	VC
Univ of Illinois at Urbana-Champaign	IL	11,316	HC+
Univ of Indianapolis	IN	20,840	C
Univ of Iowa	IA	8,607	C+
Univ of Kansas	KS	7,232	VC
Univ of Kentucky	KY	7,765	C
Univ of Louisiana at Lafayette	LA	5,200	C
Univ of Louisiana at Monroe	LA	5,207	NC
Univ of Louisville	KY	7,402	LC
Univ of Maine	ME	10,798	C
Univ of Mary Hardin-Baylor	TX	13,929	C
Univ of Maryland/College Park	MD	11,959	C
Univ of Maryland/Eastern Shore	MD	9,258	C
Univ of Mass Dartmouth	MA	9,852	C
Univ of Mich/Ann Arbor	MI	13,003	HC+
Univ of Minn/Duluth	MN	10,436	C
Univ of Minn/Twin Cities	MN	11,123	VC
Univ of Missouri/Columbia	MO	9,803	HC
Univ of Montana--Western	MT	6,915	NC
Univ of Montevallo	AL	7,266	C
Univ of Nebr at Kearney	NE	7,048	NC
Univ of Nebr at Lincoln	NE	8,325	C+
Univ of New Mexico	NM	8,026	C

School	ST	$IS	SR
Univ of North Alabama	AL	7,016	NC
Univ of N Car at Chapel Hill	NC	8,789	HC
Univ of N Car at Charlotte	NC	7,254	C
Univ of N Car at Greensboro	NC	6,858	C
Univ of N Car at Pembroke	NC	5,914	LC
Univ of North Florida	FL	8,089	VC
Univ of Northern Iowa	IA	7,850	C
Univ of Rio Grande	OH	8,728	NC
Univ of St. Francis	IN	17,790	LC
Univ of Sioux Falls	SD	16,390	C
Univ of S Car at Columbia	SC	8,748	VC
Univ of S Dak	SD	7,036	C
Univ of South Florida	FL	8,154	C
Univ of Southern Indiana	IN	8,655	LC
Univ of Southern Miss	MS	6,155	LC
Univ of Tenn at Chattanooga	TN	7,783	C
Univ of Tenn at Knoxville	TN	8,214	C
Univ of Tenn at Martin	TN	8,268	C
Univ of the Pacific	CA	28,255	VC
Univ of Toledo	OH	11,206	NC
Univ of Utah	UT	7,703	C
Univ of Vermont	VT	14,761	C+
Univ of West Florida	FL	7,518	C
Univ of Wisc/Eau Claire	WI	7,032	VC
Univ of Wisc/Madison	WI	8,262	VC
Univ of Wisc/Milwaukee	WI	8,907	LC
Univ of Wisc/Oshkosh	WI	6,130	LC
Univ of Wisc/Platteville	WI	7,282	C
Univ of Wisc/River Falls	WI	6,356	LC
Univ of Wisc/Stout	WI	7,192	C
Univ of Wisc/Superior	WI	7,051	C+
Univ of Wisc/Whitewater	WI	6,937	C
Utah State Univ	UT	6,771	C
Valdosta State Univ	GA	6,988	C
Valley City State Univ	ND		LC
Virginia Commonwealth Univ	VA	9,030	C
Virginia Union Univ	VA	15,358	LC
Virginia Wesleyan College	VA	22,350	LC
Viterbo Univ	WI	18,043	C
Wartburg College	IA	21,165	VC
Washburn Univ of Topeka	KS	6,766	NC
Washington and Jefferson College	PA	26,255	VC
Washington Univ in St. Louis	MO	34,593	MC
Wayne State Univ	MI	6,720	C
Weber State Univ	UT	6,897	NC
West Liberty State College	WV	6,056	LC
West Texas A&M Univ	TX	6,538	C
West Virginia State College	WV	6,264	NC
West Virginia Wesleyan College	WV	22,920	C
Western Carolina Univ	NC	5,667	C
Western Kentucky Univ	KY	6,834	C
Western Mich Univ	MI	10,016	C
Western New Mexico Univ	NM	5,950	LC
Western State College of Colo	CO	7,585	LC
Western Washington Univ	WA	8,624	VC
Westfield State College	MA	8,394	C
Westmont College	CA	29,748	VC
Wichita State Univ	KS	6,879	C
Wilkes Univ	PA	25,800	C
Wingate Univ	NC	19,140	C
Winona State Univ	MN	8,570	C
Wittenberg Univ	OH	28,766	VC
Wright State Univ	OH	9,141	LC
Xavier Univ of Louisiana	LA	17,000	LC
Youngstown State Univ	OH	9,318	NC

ART HISTORY AND APPRECIATION

School	ST	$IS	SR
Adelphi Univ	NY	23,320	VC
Albion College	MI	25,224	VC
Allegheny College	PA	27,780	VC
American Univ	DC	31,544	VC+
Aquinas College	MI	20,052	C+
Arizona State Univ-Main	AZ	7,726	C
Art Academy of Cincinnati	OH	16,550	SP
Augsburg College	MN	22,978	C
Augustana College	IL	24,117	VC+
Baker Univ	KS	14,780	C+
Bard College	NY	33,912	HC
Baylor Univ	TX	18,298	VC+
Beloit College	WI	27,482	HC
Birmingham-Southern College	AL	22,960	C
Bloomsburg Univ of Pennsylvania	PA	9,434	C
Boston College	MA	33,330	MC
Boston Univ	MA	34,358	MC
Bowdoin College	ME	32,650	MC
Bowling Green State Univ	OH	10,794	C
Bradley Univ	IL	20,970	VC
Brandeis Univ	MA	34,481	MC
Brigham Young Univ	UT	7,840	HC
Brown Univ	RI	34,973	MC
Bryn Mawr College	PA	33,580	HC+
Bucknell Univ	PA	31,096	HC
Cal State, Fullerton	CA	5,440	LC
Cal State, Los Angeles	CA	5,050	C
Calvin College	MI	20,050	NC
Canisius College	NY	24,696	C+
Carleton College	MN	30,780	MC
Carlow College	PA	19,366	C
Case Western Reserve Univ	OH	27,418	C
Catholic Univ of America	DC	29,332	VC
Chatham College	PA	25,454	C+
Chestnut Hill College	PA	24,790	LC
CUNY/Brooklyn College	NY	3,403	LC
CUNY/Queens College	NY	3,403	VC
CUNY/York College	NY	3,292	NC
Clark Univ	MA	29,170	HC
Clarke College	IA	20,625	C+
Colgate Univ	NY	33,480	MC
College of Charleston	SC	8,350	HC
College of New Rochelle	NY	20,000	C
College of Notre Dame of Maryland	MD	23,100	LC
College of Santa Fe	NM	20,250	LC
College of the Holy Cross	MA	32,780	MC
Colo College	CO	31,525	HC+
Columbia Univ/Barnard College	NY	33,694	MC
Columbia Univ/Columbia College	NY	35,190	MC
Columbia Univ/School of General Studies	NY	35,000	C
Concordia College/ Moorhead	MN	18,835	C
Concordia Univ	MN	19,912	C
Conn College	CT	33,585	MC
Cornell Univ	NY	34,614	MC
Dartmouth College	NH	34,458	MC
Denison Univ	OH	29,640	HC
DePauw Univ	IN	28,000	HC
Dominican Univ of Calif	CA	27,948	C
Drake Univ	IA	22,830	VC
Drury Univ	MO	15,250	VC
Duke Univ	NC	34,396	MC
Duquesne Univ	PA	24,242	C+
East Carolina Univ	NC	7,766	C
Eastern College	PA	19,641	LC
Eastern Washington Univ	WA	7,972	LC
Edinboro Univ of Pennsylvania	PA	9,328	LC
Emmanuel College	MA	23,802	C+
Emory Univ	GA	33,792	MC
Florida State Univ	FL	7,835	HC
Fordham Univ	NY	30,710	VC
Framingham State College	MA	7,259	C
Franklin and Marshall College	PA	32,410	HC
Gallaudet Univ	DC	16,554	SP
George Mason Univ	VA	9,192	C
George Washington Univ	DC	32,170	HC
Georgian Court College	NJ	19,040	LC
Gettysburg College	PA	32,070	HC
Goucher College	MD	30,650	VC+
Hamilton College	NY	34,150	HC
Hamline Univ	MN	23,339	C+
Hampshire College	MA	33,881	HC+
Hanover College	IN	17,560	VC
Hartwick College	NY	33,090	C+
Harvard Univ/Harvard College	MA	34,269	MC
Haverford College	PA	34,300	MC
Hiram College	OH	27,034	VC
Hofstra Univ	NY	23,252	C
Hollins Univ	VA	24,328	VC
Howard Univ	DC	15,522	LC
Indiana State Univ	IN	8,461	LC
Indiana Univ-Purdue Univ Indianapolis	IN	9,473	C
Ithaca College	NY	28,719	HC
Jacksonville Univ	FL	21,110	LC
James Madison Univ	VA	9,552	HC
John Carroll Univ	OH	24,140	VC
Johns Hopkins Univ	MD	35,226	MC
Juniata College	PA	26,080	VC
Kalamazoo College	MI	26,955	HC+
Kansas City Art Inst	MO	25,880	SP
Kean Univ	NJ	11,159	C
Kendall College of Art and Design of Ferris State Univ	MI	8,820	SP
Kent State Univ	OH	11,104	C
Kenyon College	OH	32,130	HC+
Knox College	IL	28,230	HC
Lawrence Univ	WI	27,711	HC
Lewis and Clark College	OR	29,010	VC
Lindenwood Univ	MO	17,250	C
Loras College	IA	22,994	C+
Lourdes College	OH	13,100	LC
Loyola Marymount Univ	CA	28,754	HC
Lycoming College	PA	24,780	C
Manhattanville College	NY	28,730	VC
Mansfield Univ	PA	9,648	C
Marian College	IN	21,020	C
Mars Hill College	NC	18,600	LC
Mary Washington College	VA	9,032	VC+
Marymount College/ Tarrytown	NY	23,850	C
Mass College of Art	MA	13,703	SP
Messiah College	PA	23,180	VC
Mich State Univ	MI	10,386	VC
Mills College	CA	27,950	C
Monmouth Univ	NJ	24,042	C
Montana State Univ-Billings	MT	7,653	NC
Moravian College	PA	27,065	VC
Mount Holyoke College	MA	34,128	HC
Nazareth College of Rochester	NY	22,036	VC
New England College	NH	20,706	LC
New York Univ	NY	35,200	MC
Northern Arizona Univ	AZ	7,398	C
Northwestern Univ	IL	33,615	MC
Oakland Univ	MI	9,418	C
Occidental College	CA	32,288	HC
Ohio Univ	OH	11,769	C
Old Dominion Univ	VA	9,386	C
Penn State Univ/Univ Park Campus	PA	11,126	VC
Pomona College	CA	33,960	MC
Portland State Univ	OR	11,220	C
Pratt Inst	NY	27,550	SP
Providence College	RI	27,620	HC
Purdue Univ/West Lafayette	IN	10,284	VC
Randolph-Macon College	VA	24,395	C
Ripon College	WI	24,180	VC+
Rockford College	IL	23,930	C
Roger Williams Univ	RI	29,010	C
Rollins College	FL	31,223	HC
Roosevelt Univ	IL	20,240	LC
Rutgers, The State Univ of New Jersey New Brunswick Campus	NJ	12,709	C
Rutgers, The State Univ of New Jersey/ CamdenCampus	NJ	6,484	C
St. Joseph College	CT	25,960	LC
St. Louis Univ	MO	26,590	VC+
St. Olaf College	MN	25,880	HC
St. Peter's College	NJ	22,292	LC
St. Vincent College	PA	22,942	VC
Salem College	NC	23,065	VC
Salve Regina Univ	RI	26,460	C
Santa Clara Univ	CA	28,371	VC+
Sarah Lawrence College	NY	37,516	HC
Savannah College of Art and Design	GA	25,075	SP
School of the Art Inst of Chicago	IL	27,800	SP
Scripps College	CA	30,400	HC+
Seton Hill College	PA	21,875	C
Siena Heights Univ	MI	16,140	LC
Simon's Rock College of Bard	MA	32,450	HC
Skidmore College	NY	34,201	VC+
Smith College	MA	33,302	HC+
Southern Conn State Univ	CT	10,310	C
Southern Methodist Univ	TX	28,349	VC
SUNY/College at Buffalo	NY	8,025	C
SUNY/College at Geneseo	NY	9,970	HC
SUNY/College at Potsdam	NY	10,519	C
SUNY/College at Purchase	NY	10,587	VC
SUNY/Univ at Albany	NY	10,997	VC
SUNY/Univ at Binghamton	NY	10,653	HC
SUNY/Univ at Buffalo	NY	11,033	VC
SUNY/Univ at New Paltz	NY	9,685	VC
SUNY/Univ at Stony Brook	NY	10,998	VC
Susquehanna Univ	PA	27,270	VC
Swarthmore College	PA	34,538	MC
Sweet Briar College	VA	25,310	VC
Syracuse Univ	NY	30,710	HC
Temple Univ	PA	14,124	C
Texas Christian Univ	TX	19,910	C
Texas Tech Univ	TX	8,825	C
Trinity College	CT	34,300	HC
Troy State Univ	AL	7,696	C
Truman State Univ	MO	8,568	VC+
Tufts Univ	MA	34,874	MC
Tulane Univ	LA	34,013	HC+
Union College	NY	32,646	HC
Univ of Alabama	AL	7,402	C
Univ of Arizona	AZ	8,614	C
Univ of Arkansas at Little Rock	AR	5,637	NC
Univ of Calif at Davis	CA	12,796	VC
Univ of Calif at Irvine	CA	11,756	C
Univ of Calif at Los Angeles	CA	13,227	MC
Univ of Calif at Riverside	CA	12,479	C
Univ of Calif at San Diego	CA	11,372	HC
Univ of Calif at Santa Barbara	CA	11,732	VC
Univ of Calif at Santa Cruz	CA	13,655	VC
Univ of Chicago	IL	35,087	MC
Univ of Colo at Boulder	CO	9,255	VC
Univ of Conn	CT	12,122	VC
Univ of Dallas	TX	22,128	VC+
Univ of Delaware	DE	10,824	VC
Univ of Denver	CO	28,783	VC
Univ of Evansville	IN	22,865	VC+
Univ of Florida	FL	7,874	HC
Univ of Hartford	CT	28,884	C
Univ of Houston	TX	8,410	C
Univ of Illinois at Chicago	IL	10,702	VC
Univ of Illinois at Urbana-Champaign	IL	11,316	HC+
Univ of Iowa	IA	8,607	C+
Univ of Kansas	KS	7,232	VC
Univ of Kentucky	KY	7,765	C
Univ of Louisville	KY	7,402	LC
Univ of Maryland/College Park	MD	11,959	C
Univ of Mass Amherst	MA	10,995	VC
Univ of Mass Dartmouth	MA	9,852	C
Univ of Memphis	TN	7,271	C
Univ of Miami	FL	31,130	HC
Univ of Mich/Ann Arbor	MI	13,003	HC+
Univ of Mich/Dearborn	MI	4,677	VC
Univ of Minn/Morris	MN	10,716	VC
Univ of Minn/Twin Cities	MN	11,123	VC
Univ of Miss	MS	7,666	C
Univ of Missouri/Columbia	MO	9,803	HC
Univ of Missouri/Kansas City	MO	9,685	VC
Univ of Missouri/St. Louis	MO	9,966	C
Univ of Nebr at Lincoln	NE	8,325	C+
Univ of Nevada/Las Vegas	NV	8,281	VC
Univ of New Hampshire	NH	13,207	C
Univ of New Mexico	NM	8,026	C
Univ of N Car at Chapel Hill	NC	8,789	HC
Univ of N Car at Wilmington	NC	7,769	C
Univ of North Texas	TX	7,629	C
Univ of Northern Iowa	IA	7,850	C
Univ of Notre Dame	IN	30,707	MC
Univ of Okla	OK	7,616	VC
Univ of Oregon	OR	9,969	C
Univ of PR/Rio Piedras	PR	5,510	
Univ of Richmond	VA	27,300	HC
Univ of Rochester	NY	32,979	HC
Univ of St. Thomas	MN	24,044	VC
Univ of South Alabama	AL	6,976	LC
Univ of S Car at Columbia	SC	8,748	VC
Univ of Southern Calif	CA	33,647	MC
Univ of Tenn at Knoxville	TN	8,214	C
Univ of Texas at Arlington	TX	7,192	LC
Univ of Texas at Austin	TX	9,437	HC
Univ of the Pacific	CA	28,255	VC
Univ of the South	TN	27,290	HC
Univ of Toledo	OH	11,206	NC
Univ of Utah	UT	7,703	C
Univ of Vermont	VT	14,761	C+
Univ of Washington	WA	10,361	VC
Univ of Wisc/Madison	WI	8,262	VC
Univ of Wisc/Milwaukee	WI	8,907	LC
Univ of Wisc/Superior	WI	7,051	C+
Univ of Wisc/Whitewater	WI	6,937	C
Villanova Univ	PA	31,997	HC
Washburn Univ of Topeka	KS	6,766	NC
Washington and Lee Univ	VA	25,095	MC
Washington Univ in St. Louis	MO	34,593	MC
Wayne State Univ	MI	6,720	C
Wellesley College	MA	33,394	MC
Wesleyan College	GA	17,050	VC
Wesleyan Univ	CT	3,405	MC
Western Mich Univ	MI	10,016	C
Wheaton College	MA	32,940	VC
Whitman College	WA	29,086	HC
Wichita State Univ	KS	6,879	C
Willamette Univ	OR	29,422	VC+
William Paterson Univ of New Jersey	NJ	11,000	LC
Williams College	MA	32,270	MC
Winthrop Univ	SC	9,106	C
Wofford College	SC	23,995	VC
Wright State Univ	OH	9,141	LC
Yale Univ	CT	34,030	MC
Youngstown State Univ	OH	9,318	NC

ART THERAPY

School	ST	$IS	SR
Albertus Magnus College	CT	22,154	C
Alverno College	WI	16,930	LC
Andrews Univ	MI	17,696	LC
Anna Maria College	MA	22,800	LC
Arcadia Univ	PA	26,650	C
Bowling Green State Univ	OH	10,794	C
Brescia Univ	KY	14,225	C
Capital Univ	OH	23,630	C
Carlow College	PA	19,366	C
College of New Rochelle	NY	20,000	C
Converse College	SC	21,990	VC
Edgewood College	WI	18,304	C
Emmanuel College	MA	23,802	C+
LIU/C.W. Post Campus	NY	25,380	C
Marygrove College	MI	16,075	C
Marywood Univ	PA	24,639	C
Mercyhurst College	PA	20,694	C
Millikin Univ	IL	24,415	C+
Mount Mary College	WI	18,024	C
Russell Sage College	NY	23,674	C+
Seton Hill College	PA	21,875	C
Spring Hill College	AL	23,250	C
Springfield College	MA	24,520	C
Univ of Indianapolis	IN	20,840	C
Univ of Wisc/Superior	WI	7,051	C+

ARTS ADMINISTRATION/ MANAGEMENT

School	ST	$IS	SR
Adrian College	MI	19,670	C
Appalachian State Univ	NC	6,353	C
Bellarmine Univ	KY	20,440	VC
Benedictine Univ	IL	21,330	C
Bennett College	NC	11,200	C

School	ST	$IS	SR
Brenau Univ Women's College	GA	20,100	C
Buena Vista Univ	IA	22,828	C
Butler Univ	IN	25,580	VC+
Cal State, Hayward	CA	7,400	LC
Chatham College	PA	25,454	C+
Concordia College	NY	19,200	VC
Culver-Stockton College	MO	15,400	LC
Drury Univ	MO	15,250	VC
Eastern Mich Univ	MI	9,855	C
Franklin Pierce College	NH	26,125	LC
Goucher College	MD	30,650	VC+
Green Mountain College	VT	24,130	C
Huntingdon College	AL	18,400	VC
Lees-McRae College	NC	17,106	LC
LIU/C.W. Post Campus	NY	25,380	C
Mary Baldwin College	VA	23,440	C
Marywood Univ	PA	24,639	C
Millikin Univ	IL	24,415	C+
Newberry College	SC	19,670	LC
North Georgia College and State Univ	GA	6,322	C+
Northern Arizona Univ	AZ	7,398	C
Ohio Univ	OH	11,769	C
Pfeiffer Univ	NC	18,580	C
Point Park College	PA	20,290	C
Quincy Univ	IL	20,450	C
Randolph-Macon College	VA	24,395	C
Salem College	NC	23,065	VC
Seton Hill College	PA	21,875	C
Shenandoah Univ	VA	22,550	NC
Simmons College	MA	30,418	VC
Spring Hill College	AL	23,250	C
Univ of Findlay	OH	23,962	NC
Univ of Hartford	CT	28,884	C
Univ of Kentucky	KY	7,765	C
Univ of Mich/Dearborn	MI	4,677	VC
Univ of the Pacific	CA	28,255	VC
Univ of Tulsa	OK	19,090	HC
Univ of Wisc/Stevens Point	WI	7,116	C
Upper Iowa Univ	IA	17,438	C
Viterbo Univ	WI	18,043	C
Wagner College	NY	27,000	C
Wartburg College	IA	21,165	VC
Waynesburg College	PA	17,610	LC
Wright State Univ	OH	9,141	LC

ASIAN/AMERICAN STUDIES

School	ST	$IS	SR
Cal State, Fullerton	CA	5,440	LC
Cal State, Northridge	CA	7,781	C
Columbia Univ/Columbia College	NY	35,190	MC
Pitzer College	CA	33,930	HC
Scripps College	CA	30,400	HC+
Univ of Calif at Berkeley	CA	14,134	MC
Univ of Calif at Los Angeles	CA	13,227	MC
Univ of Calif at Santa Barbara	CA	11,732	VC
Univ of Southern Calif	CA	33,647	MC
Univ of Washington	WA	10,361	VC

ASIAN/ORIENTAL STUDIES

School	ST	$IS	SR
Amherst College	MA	34,340	MC
Augustana College	IL	24,117	VC+
Bard College	NY	33,912	HC
Baylor Univ	TX	18,298	VC+
Bowdoin College	ME	32,650	MC
Bowling Green State Univ	OH	10,794	C
Brigham Young Univ	UT	7,840	HC
Cal State, Chico	CA	8,598	LC
Cal State, Long Beach	CA	7,400	LC
Carleton College	MN	30,780	MC
Case Western Reserve Univ	OH	27,418	C
CUNY/City College	NY	3,309	LC
Claremont McKenna College	CA	32,700	MC
Coe College	IA	24,750	VC
Colgate Univ	NY	33,480	MC
College of the Holy Cross	MA	32,780	MC
Colo College	CO	31,525	HC+
Columbia Univ/Columbia College	NY	35,190	MC
Cornell Univ	NY	34,614	MC
Dartmouth College	NH	34,458	MC
Duke Univ	NC	34,396	MC
Emory Univ	GA	33,792	MC
Florida State Univ	FL	7,835	HC
Furman Univ	SC	25,492	HC
Hamilton College	NY	34,150	HC
Hampshire College	MA	33,881	HC+
Harvard Univ/Harvard College	MA	34,269	MC
Hobart and William Smith Colleges	NY	33,195	VC
Hofstra Univ	NY	23,252	C
Lake Forest College	IL	27,460	VC
Lehigh Univ	PA	32,290	MC
Loyola Marymount Univ	CA	28,754	HC
Macalester College	MN	28,814	HC+
Manhattanville College	NY	28,730	VC
Mary Baldwin College	VA	23,440	C
Mount Holyoke College	MA	34,128	HC
Oakland Univ	MI	9,418	C
Occidental College	CA	32,288	HC
Pacific Lutheran Univ	WA	23,318	VC
Pitzer College	CA	33,930	HC
Pomona College	CA	33,960	MC
Rutgers, The State Univ of New Jersey New Brunswick Campus	NJ	12,709	C
St. Andrews Presbyterian College	NC	19,720	LC
St. John's Univ	NY	26,660	C
St. Lawrence Univ	NY	32,605	VC
St. Olaf College	MN	25,880	HC
Samford Univ	AL	16,340	VC
San Diego State Univ	CA	9,716	C+
Sarah Lawrence College	NY	37,516	HC
Scripps College	CA	30,400	HC+
Seton Hall Univ	NJ	26,910	LC
Simon's Rock College of Bard	MA	32,450	HC
Skidmore College	NY	34,201	VC+
Southwest Texas State Univ	TX	8,730	VC
SUNY/Univ at Albany	NY	10,997	VC
Swarthmore College	PA	34,538	MC
Temple Univ	PA	14,124	C
Tufts Univ	MA	34,874	MC
Tulane Univ	LA	34,013	HC+
Univ of Alabama	AL	7,402	C
Univ of Calif at Berkeley	CA	14,134	MC
Univ of Calif at Riverside	CA	12,479	C
Univ of Calif at Santa Barbara	CA	11,732	VC
Univ of Chicago	IL	35,087	MC
Univ of Cincinnati	OH	12,491	LC
Univ of Colo at Boulder	CO	9,255	VC
Univ of Denver	CO	28,783	VC
Univ of Florida	FL	7,874	HC
Univ of Hawaii at Manoa	HI	7,862	VC
Univ of Iowa	IA	8,607	C+
Univ of Mich/Ann Arbor	MI	13,003	HC+
Univ of New Mexico	NM	8,026	C
Univ of Northern Iowa	IA	7,850	C
Univ of Okla	OK	7,616	VC
Univ of Oregon	OR	9,969	C
Univ of Puget Sound	WA	28,285	HC
Univ of Redlands	CA	29,246	VC
Univ of Tenn at Knoxville	TN	8,214	C
Univ of Texas at Austin	TX	9,437	HC
Univ of the South	TN	27,290	HC
Univ of Utah	UT	7,703	C
Univ of Vermont	VT	14,761	C+
Univ of Washington	WA	10,361	VC
Univ of Wisc/Madison	WI	8,262	VC
Valparaiso Univ	IN	23,570	VC+
Vassar College	NY	33,450	MC
Washington State Univ	WA	9,388	C
Washington Univ in St. Louis	MO	34,593	MC
Wellesley College	MA	33,394	MC
Wesleyan Univ	CT	3,405	MC
Wheaton College	MA	32,940	VC
Whitman College	WA	29,086	HC
Williams College	MA	32,270	MC

ASTRONOMY

School	ST	$IS	SR
Amherst College	MA	34,340	MC
Benedictine College	KS	18,485	LC
Boston Univ	MA	34,358	MC
Bryn Mawr College	PA	33,580	HC+
Calif Inst of Technology	CA	27,663	MC
Case Western Reserve Univ	OH	27,418	C
Colgate Univ	NY	33,480	MC
Columbia Univ/Barnard College	NY	33,694	MC
Columbia Univ/Columbia College	NY	35,190	MC
Columbia Univ/School of General Studies	NY	35,000	C
Cornell Univ	NY	34,614	MC
Eastern College	PA	19,641	LC
Eastern Mich Univ	MI	9,855	C
Harvard Univ/Harvard College	MA	34,269	MC
Haverford College	PA	34,300	MC
Indiana Univ Bloomington	IN	10,712	C+
Lycoming College	PA	24,780	C
Minn State Univ, Mankato	MN	7,296	LC
Mount Holyoke College	MA	34,128	HC
Mount Union College	OH	21,120	C
Northwestern Univ	IL	33,615	MC
Oberlin College	OH	33,140	HC+
Penn State Univ/Univ Park Campus	PA	11,126	VC
San Diego State Univ	CA	9,716	C+
Smith College	MA	33,302	HC+
SUNY/Univ at Stony Brook	NY	10,998	VC
Swarthmore College	PA	34,538	MC
Ohio State Univ	OH	10,819	VC
Univ of Arizona	AZ	8,614	C
Univ of Colo at Boulder	CO	9,255	VC
Univ of Delaware	DE	10,824	VC
Univ of Denver	CO	28,783	VC
Univ of Florida	FL	7,874	HC
Univ of Georgia	GA	8,656	VC
Univ of Hawaii at Hilo	HI	6,497	C
Univ of Illinois at Urbana-Champaign	IL	11,316	HC+
Univ of Iowa	IA	8,607	C+
Univ of Kansas	KS	7,232	VC
Univ of Maryland/College Park	MD	11,959	C
Univ of Mass Amherst	MA	10,995	VC
Univ of Mich/Ann Arbor	MI	13,003	HC+
Univ of Minn/Twin Cities	MN	11,123	VC
Univ of N Car at Chapel Hill	NC	8,789	HC
Univ of Okla	OK	7,616	VC
Univ of Pittsburgh at Pittsburgh	PA	13,592	HC
Univ of Southern Calif	CA	33,647	MC
Univ of Texas at Austin	TX	9,437	HC
Univ of Virginia	VA	9,391	HC+
Univ of Washington	WA	10,361	VC
Univ of Wisc/Madison	WI	8,262	VC
Univ of Wyoming	WY	7,143	LC
Valdosta State Univ	GA	6,988	C
Vassar College	NY	33,450	MC
Villanova Univ	PA	31,997	HC
Wellesley College	MA	33,394	MC
Wesleyan Univ	CT	3,405	MC
Wheaton College	MA	32,940	VC
Williams College	MA	32,270	MC
Yale Univ	CT	34,030	MC
Youngstown State Univ	OH	9,318	NC

ASTROPHYSICS

School	ST	$IS	SR
Agnes Scott College	GA	24,950	VC
Boston Univ	MA	34,358	MC
Cal State, Northridge	CA	7,781	C
Columbia Univ/Columbia College	NY	35,190	MC
Conn College	CT	33,585	MC
Florida Inst of Technology	FL	25,250	VC
Howard Univ	DC	15,522	LC
Indiana Univ Bloomington	IN	10,712	C+
Mich State Univ	MI	10,386	VC
Princeton Univ	NJ	35,072	MC
Swarthmore College	PA	34,538	MC
Texas Christian Univ	TX	19,910	C
Tufts Univ	MA	34,874	MC
Univ of Calif at Berkeley	CA	14,134	MC
Univ of Calif at Los Angeles	CA	13,227	MC
Univ of Mich/Ann Arbor	MI	13,003	HC+
Univ of Minn/Twin Cities	MN	11,123	VC
Univ of New Mexico	NM	8,026	C
Univ of Okla	OK	7,616	VC
Villanova Univ	PA	31,997	HC
Williams College	MA	32,270	MC

ATHLETIC TRAINING

School	ST	$IS	SR
Adams State College	CO	7,468	C
Alderson-Broaddus College	WV	19,640	C
Alfred Univ	NY	27,212	C+
Alvernia College	PA	20,790	C
Asbury College	KY	18,540	VC
Ashland Univ	OH	22,182	LC
Augustana College	SD	20,760	VC
Averett Univ	VA	17,980	LC
Bartlesville Wesleyan College	OK	14,100	LC
Barton College	NC	16,834	LC
Belhaven College	MS	16,040	C+
Benedictine College	KS	18,485	LC
Berry College	GA	18,850	C
Bethany College	KS	16,602	C+
Bethel College	MN	22,740	VC
Boston Univ	MA	34,358	MC
Bridgewater College	VA	22,950	C
Bryan College	TN	16,400	VC
Calif Univ of Pennsylvania	PA	10,388	C
Campbell Univ	NC	16,599	C
Campbellsville Univ	KY	14,340	C
Canisius College	NY	24,696	C+
Carroll College	WI	21,170	C
Catawba College	NC	19,620	C
Cedarville Univ	OH	17,553	VC
Central Conn State Univ	CT	10,404	C
Central Methodist College	MO	16,460	C
Coe College	IA	24,750	VC
Colby-Sawyer College	NH	27,850	LC
College of Mount St. Joseph	OH	20,290	C
College of the Southwest	NM	8,456	NC
Concordia Univ Wisc	WI	16,600	LC
Culver-Stockton College	MO	15,400	LC
Dakota Wesleyan Univ	SD	15,512	C
Delta State Univ	MS	5,416	C
Dominican College	NY	20,400	LC
Duquesne Univ	PA	24,242	C+
East Carolina Univ	NC	7,766	C
East Central Univ	OK	4,578	C
East Texas Baptist Univ	TX	12,349	LC
Eastern Nazarene College	MA	19,433	LC
Elmhurst College	IL	21,750	C
Erskine College	SC	21,399	VC
Eureka College	IL	22,200	C
Florida Southern College	FL	19,430	C
Franklin College of Indiana	IN	19,905	C
Gardner-Webb Univ	NC	17,400	C
Georgia College and State Univ	GA	7,344	C
Graceland Univ	IA	15,845	C
Greensboro College	NC	19,080	LC
Hamline Univ	MN	23,339	C+
Henderson State Univ	AR	6,269	C
High Point Univ	NC	20,220	LC
Hofstra Univ	NY	23,252	C
Howard Payne Univ	TX	13,834	C+
Huntingdon College	AL	18,400	VC
Indiana Univ Bloomington	IN	10,712	C+
Ithaca College	NY	28,719	HC
Johnson State College	VT	10,776	C
Kent State Univ	OH	11,104	C
Lake Superior State Univ	MI	9,034	LC
Lasell College	MA	24,100	C
Lewis Univ	IL	20,960	C
Liberty Univ	VA	14,500	C
Lincoln Memorial Univ	TN	12,620	LC
Lindenwood Univ	MO	17,250	C
Linfield College	OR	25,840	VC
Louisiana College	LA	11,516	C
Lynchburg College	VA	23,405	C
Marist College	NY	24,756	VC
Mars Hill College	NC	18,600	LC
Marymount Univ	VA	21,560	LC
McKendree College	IL	18,300	C+
Mercyhurst College	PA	20,694	C
Meredith College	NC	17,500	C
Messiah College	PA	23,180	VC
Methodist College	NC	19,526	C
Miami Univ	OH	12,885	VC+
MidAmerica Nazarene Univ	KS	16,960	C
Middle Tenn State Univ	TN	6,994	C
Minn State Univ, Mankato	MN	7,296	LC
Missouri Baptist College	MO	15,762	LC
Mount Marty College	SD	15,656	LC
Mount Union College	OH	21,120	C
National American Univ	SD	13,680	NC
Nebr Wesleyan Univ	NE	18,767	VC
New Mexico State Univ	NM	7,302	C
Newman Univ	KS	14,098	LC
N Car Wesleyan College	NC	15,650	LC
N Dak State Univ	ND	7,004	VC
Northeastern Univ	MA	30,078	VC
Ohio Northern Univ	OH	27,765	VC
Ohio Univ	OH	11,769	C
Olivet College	MI	17,410	C
Otterbein College	OH	23,439	C
Park Univ	MO	9,816	C
Pfeiffer Univ	NC	18,580	C
Plymouth State College	NH	11,024	LC
Purdue Univ/West Lafayette	IN	10,284	VC
Quincy Univ	IL	20,450	C
Rivier College	NH	24,215	C
Roanoke College	VA	24,689	VC
Rockford College	IL	23,930	C
Russell Sage College	NY	23,674	C+
Salem International Univ	WV	17,263	LC
Salisbury Univ	MD	10,576	VC
Samford Univ	AL	16,340	VC
Shaw Univ	NC	12,810	C
Simpson College	IA	21,200	C+
S Dak State Univ	SD	6,848	C
Southeast Missouri State Univ	MO	8,367	C+
Southern Nazarene Univ	OK	14,634	NC
Southern Utah Univ	UT	7,254	C
Southwest Baptist Univ	MO	13,426	LC
Southwest Missouri State Univ	MO	7,600	LC
Southwest Texas State Univ	TX	8,730	VC
Southwestern Okla State Univ	OK	4,801	C
SUNY/College at Cortland	NY	10,564	C
Stetson Univ	FL	25,640	VC
Tabor College	KS	17,600	LC
Taylor Univ	IN	21,562	VC+
Towson Univ	MD	11,088	VC
Trinity International Univ	IL	20,640	C+
Univ of Akron	OH	10,530	NC
Univ of Alabama	AL	7,402	C
Univ of Central Arkansas	AR	6,388	C
Univ of Conn	CT	12,122	VC
Univ of Delaware	DE	10,824	VC
Univ of Evansville	IN	22,865	VC+
Univ of Findlay	OH	23,962	NC
Univ of Hawaii at Manoa	HI	7,862	VC
Univ of Indianapolis	IN	20,840	C
Univ of Kansas	KS	7,232	VC
Univ of Mary	ND	12,900	LC
Univ of Miami	FL	31,130	HC
Univ of Minn/Duluth	MN	10,436	C
Univ of Nebr at Lincoln	NE	8,325	C+
Univ of New Hampshire	NH	13,207	C
Univ of New Mexico	NM	8,026	C
Univ of N Car at Wilmington	NC	7,769	C
Univ of N Dak	ND	7,067	VC
Univ of North Florida	FL	8,089	VC
Univ of Northern Iowa	IA	7,850	C
Univ of San Francisco	CA	27,302	VC
Univ of the Pacific	CA	28,255	VC
Univ of Tulsa	OK	19,090	HC
Univ of Utah	UT	7,703	C
Univ of Vermont	VT	14,761	C+

School	ST	$IS	SR
Univ of West Alabama	AL	6,048	C
Univ of Wisc/La Crosse	WI	7,250	VC
Univ of Wisc/Stevens Point	WI	7,116	C
Upper Iowa Univ	IA	17,438	C
Valparaiso Univ	IN	23,570	VC+
Virginia State Univ	VA	8,182	LC
Washington State Univ	WA	9,388	C
Waynesburg College	PA	17,610	LC
Weber State Univ	UT	6,897	NC
West Chester Univ of Pennsylvania	PA	9,792	VC
West Virginia Univ	WV	8,304	C
Whitworth College	WA	23,938	VC
William Woods Univ	MO	19,390	LC
Wilmington College	OH	21,826	C
Wingate Univ	NC	19,140	C
Xavier Univ	OH	23,880	C

ATMOSPHERIC SCIENCES AND METEOROLOGY

School	ST	$IS	SR
Cornell Univ	NY	34,614	MC
Creighton Univ	NE	23,476	VC
Florida Inst of Technology	FL	25,250	VC
Florida State Univ	FL	7,835	HC
Iowa State Univ	IA	8,108	VC
Jackson State Univ	MS	6,776	LC
Lewis Univ	IL	20,960	C
Lyndon State College	VT	11,313	LC
Metropolitan State College of Denver	CO	2,338	LC
Millersville Univ of Pennsylvania	PA	10,153	VC
N Car State Univ	NC	8,680	HC
Northern Illinois Univ	IL	9,545	C
Northland College	WI	21,435	C+
Penn State Univ/Univ Park Campus	PA	11,126	VC
Plymouth State College	NH	11,024	LC
Purdue Univ/West Lafayette	IN	10,284	VC
St. Cloud State Univ	MN	7,180	C
St. Louis Univ	MO	26,590	VC+
SUNY/College at Brockport	NY	10,267	C
SUNY/College at Oneonta	NY	9,981	C
SUNY/College at Oswego	NY	10,856	C
SUNY/Maritime College	NY	10,025	LC
SUNY/Univ at Albany	NY	10,997	VC
SUNY/Univ at Stony Brook	NY	10,998	VC
Texas A&M Univ	TX	8,988	VC
United States Air Force Academy	CO		MC
Univ of Arizona	AZ	8,614	C
Univ of Calif at Davis	CA	12,796	VC
Univ of Calif at Los Angeles	CA	13,227	MC
Univ of Hawaii at Manoa	HI	7,862	VC
Univ of Kansas	KS	7,232	VC
Univ of Louisiana at Monroe	LA	5,207	NC
Univ of Mich/Ann Arbor	MI	13,003	HC+
Univ of Missouri/Columbia	MO	9,803	HC
Univ of Nebr at Lincoln	NE	8,325	C+
Univ of N Car at Asheville	NC	6,896	VC
Univ of N Dak	ND	7,067	VC
Univ of Northern Colo	CO	8,082	C+
Univ of Okla	OK	7,616	VC
Univ of South Alabama	AL	6,976	LC
Univ of Utah	UT	7,703	C
Univ of Washington	WA	10,361	VC
Univ of Wisc/Madison	WI	8,262	VC
Valparaiso Univ	IN	23,570	VC+
Western Conn State Univ	CT	10,074	C

AUDIO TECHNOLOGY

School	ST	$IS	SR
American Univ	DC	31,544	VC+
Berklee College of Music	MA	27,005	SP
Cogswell Polytechnical College	CA	14,400	LC
Columbia College Chicago	IL	22,063	LC
Five Towns College	NY	18,850	SP
Hofstra Univ	NY	23,252	C
Indiana Univ Bloomington	IN	10,712	C+
Lebanon Valley College of Pennsylvania	PA	25,700	VC
School of the Art Inst of Chicago	IL	27,800	SP
Southwest Texas State Univ	TX	8,730	VC
SUNY/College at Fredonia	NY	10,125	C
Univ of Hartford	CT	28,884	C
Univ of Miami	FL	31,130	HC
Univ of New Haven	CT	23,860	LC
Webster Univ	MO	19,804	VC

AUTOMOTIVE TECHNOLOGY

School	ST	$IS	SR
Andrews Univ	MI	17,696	LC
Benjamin Franklin Inst of Technology	MA	20,650	SP
Cal State, Los Angeles	CA	5,050	C
Central Missouri State Univ	MO	7,920	C
Minn State Univ, Mankato	MN	7,296	LC
Montana State Univ-Northern	MT	8,600	NC
Pennsylvania College of Technology	PA	12,860	NC
Rochester Inst of Technology	NY	26,232	VC+
SUNY/College of Technology at Farmingdale	NY	11,269	C
Univ of Southern Colo	CO	7,821	LC
Walla Walla College	WA	20,925	C
Weber State Univ	UT	6,897	NC
Western Mich Univ	MI	10,016	C

AVIAN SCIENCES

School	ST	$IS	SR
Bowling Green State Univ	OH	10,794	C
Minn State Univ, Mankato	MN	7,296	LC
Quincy Univ	IL	20,450	C
Southern Illinois Univ at Carbondale	IL	8,621	C
Univ of Calif at Davis	CA	12,796	VC
Univ of N Dak	ND	7,067	VC

AVIATION ADMINISTRATION/ MANAGEMENT

School	ST	$IS	SR
Andrews Univ	MI	17,696	LC
Auburn Univ	AL	5,510	C
Averett Univ	VA	17,980	LC
Baker College of Flint	MI	7,720	NC
Bridgewater State College	MA	7,589	C+
Cal State, Los Angeles	CA	5,050	C
Christian Heritage College	CA	18,000	LC
College of Aeronautics	NY	10,730	SP
Daniel Webster College	NH	24,870	C
Delta State Univ	MS	5,416	C
Eastern Mich Univ	MI	9,855	C
Embry-Riddle Aeronautical Univ	AZ	23,470	C+
Florida Inst of Technology	FL	25,250	VC
Florida Memorial College	FL	6,000	LC
Geneva College	PA	19,990	C+
Henderson State Univ	AR	6,269	C
Jacksonville Univ	FL	21,110	LC
Kent State Univ	OH	11,104	C
Lewis Univ	IL	20,960	C
Louisiana Tech Univ	LA	6,506	C
Lynn Univ	FL	24,550	C
Marywood Univ	PA	24,639	C
Metropolitan State College of Denver	CO	2,338	LC
Minn State Univ, Mankato	MN	7,296	LC
Ohio Univ	OH	11,769	C
Park Univ	MO	9,816	C
Quincy Univ	IL	20,450	C
Robert Morris Univ	PA	18,730	C
Rocky Mountain College	MT	18,113	C
St. Cloud State Univ	MN	7,180	C
St. Francis College	NY	9,610	C
St. Louis Univ	MO	26,590	VC+
Salem International Univ	WV	17,263	LC
Southern Illinois Univ at Carbondale	IL	8,621	C
Southern Nazarene Univ	OK	14,634	NC
SUNY/College of Technology at Farmingdale	NY	11,269	C
Univ of Dubuque	IA	19,990	C
Univ of Louisiana at Monroe	LA	5,207	NC
Univ of New Haven	CT	23,860	LC
Univ of N Dak	ND	7,067	VC
Univ of Okla	OK	7,616	VC
Univ of the District of Columbia	DC	2,844	NC
Western Mich Univ	MI	10,016	C
Westminster College	UT	17,226	C
Wilmington College	DE	6,530	NC

AVIATION COMPUTER TECHNOLOGY

School	ST	$IS	SR
Andrews Univ	MI	17,696	LC
Central Missouri State Univ	MO	7,920	C
College of the Ozarks	MO	2,650	C+
Florida Inst of Technology	FL	25,250	VC
Florida Memorial College	FL	6,000	LC
Kent State Univ	OH	11,104	C
Metropolitan State College of Denver	CO	2,338	LC
Okla State Univ	OK	7,650	VC
Thomas Edison State College	NJ	2,750	SP
Walla Walla College	WA	20,925	C

BACTERIOLOGY

School	ST	$IS	SR
Univ of Calif at Davis	CA	12,796	VC
Univ of Wisc/Madison	WI	8,262	VC

BALLET

School	ST	$IS	SR
Belhaven College	MS	16,040	C+
Friends Univ	KS	15,962	LC
Indiana Univ Bloomington	IN	10,712	C+
N Car School of the Arts	NC	7,797	SP
Texas Christian Univ	TX	19,910	C

BANKING AND FINANCE

School	ST	$IS	SR
Abilene Christian Univ	TX	16,300	VC
Adams State College	CO	7,468	C
Adelphi Univ	NY	23,320	VC
Alabama A&M Univ	AL	5,100	LC
Alabama State Univ	AL	6,404	C
Alfred Univ	NY	27,212	C+
Alvernia College	PA	20,790	C
American Univ	DC	31,544	VC+
Anderson Univ	IN	19,430	LC
Andrews Univ	MI	17,696	LC
Angelo State Univ	TX	7,028	C
Appalachian State Univ	NC	6,353	C
Arcadia Univ	PA	26,650	C
Arizona State Univ-Main	AZ	7,726	C
Arkansas State Univ	AR	7,480	C
Ashland Univ	OH	22,182	LC
Auburn Univ	AL	5,510	C
Auburn Univ Montgomery	AL	5,330	NC
Augusta State Univ	GA	2,282	C
Austin Peay State Univ	TN	5,814	LC
Avila College	MO	17,720	C
Baker Univ	KS	14,780	C+
Baldwin-Wallace College	OH	22,010	VC+
Ball State Univ	IN	8,660	C
Baylor Univ	TX	18,298	VC+
Becker College	MA	21,230	LC
Benedictine Univ	IL	21,330	C
Bentley College	MA	31,060	HC
Bethel College	MN	22,740	VC
Boise State Univ	ID	6,531	LC
Boston College	MA	33,330	MC
Boston Univ	MA	34,358	MC
Bowling Green State Univ	OH	10,794	C
Bradley Univ	IL	20,970	VC
Brescia Univ	KY	14,225	C
Bryant College	RI	25,980	VC
Buena Vista Univ	IA	22,828	C
Butler Univ	IN	25,580	VC+
Cabrini College	PA	25,950	LC
Calif State Polytechnic Univ, Pomona	CA	8,615	C
Cal State, Fullerton	CA	5,440	LC
Cal State, Long Beach	CA	7,400	LC
Cal State, Los Angeles	CA	5,050	C
Cal State, Northridge	CA	7,781	C
Cal State, Sacramento	CA	7,488	C
Cal State, San Bernardino	CA	6,516	C
Cameron Univ	OK	5,560	NC
Canisius College	NY	24,696	C+
Caribbean Univ	PR	3,000	
Catholic Univ of America	DC	29,332	VC
Cedarville Univ	OH	17,553	VC
Central Conn State Univ	CT	10,404	C
Central Mich Univ	MI	8,355	C
Central Missouri State Univ	MO	7,920	C
Central State Univ	OH	8,922	C+
Central Washington Univ	WA	8,985	LC
Chicago State Univ	IL	8,851	C+
Christopher Newport Univ	VA	8,862	VC
CUNY/Brooklyn College	NY	3,403	LC
Clarion Univ of Pennsylvania	PA	11,272	LC
Clarkson Univ	NY	29,884	VC
Cleary College	MI	10,350	LC
Clemson Univ	SC	7,600	C
Cleveland State Univ	OH	10,146	NC
Coastal Carolina Univ	SC	9,220	C
College of Notre Dame of Maryland	MD	23,100	LC
College of St. Joseph	VT	17,400	NC
Colo State Univ	CO	9,672	C
Columbus State Univ	GA	7,228	LC
Concord College	WV	7,122	C+
Concordia Univ	MN	19,912	C
Concordia Univ Wisc	WI	16,600	LC
Creighton Univ	NE	23,476	VC
Culver-Stockton College	MO	15,400	LC
Dallas Baptist Univ	TX	13,682	LC
David Lipscomb Univ	TN	16,158	VC
De Sales Univ	PA	22,610	VC
Defiance College	OH	19,580	LC
DePaul Univ	IL	23,590	VC
Dowling College	NY	20,281	LC
Drake Univ	IA	22,830	VC
Duquesne Univ	PA	24,242	C+
East Carolina Univ	NC	7,766	C
East Central Univ	OK	4,578	C
East Texas Baptist Univ	TX	12,349	LC
Eastern Illinois Univ	IL	10,101	C
Eastern Kentucky Univ	KY	6,552	C
Eastern Mich Univ	MI	9,855	C
Eastern New Mexico Univ	NM	4,113	LC
Eastern Washington Univ	WA	7,972	LC
Edinboro Univ of Pennsylvania	PA	9,328	LC
Elmhurst College	IL	21,750	C
Emory Univ	GA	33,792	MC
Excelsior College	NY	915	SP
Fairfield Univ	CT	30,885	HC
Fairmont State College	WV	7,010	NC
Fayetteville State Univ	NC	5,590	LC
Ferris State Univ	MI	10,816	LC
Ferrum College	VA	15,990	LC
Florida A&M Univ	FL	6,948	C
Florida Atlantic Univ	FL	8,832	C
Florida Gulf Coast Univ	FL	9,201	C
Florida International Univ	FL	9,486	VC
Florida Southern College	FL	19,430	C
Florida State Univ	FL	7,835	HC
Fort Hays State Univ	KS	6,294	LC
Francis Marion Univ	SC	7,682	C
Franklin Pierce College	NH	26,125	LC
Franklin Univ	OH	6,324	SP
Freed-Hardeman Univ	TN	14,290	VC
Gannon Univ	PA	18,848	C
George Mason Univ	VA	9,192	C
George Washington Univ	DC	32,170	HC
Georgetown College	KY	18,400	VC
Georgetown Univ	DC	34,847	MC
Georgia Southern Univ	GA	6,958	C
Georgia State Univ	GA	7,792	LC
Golden Gate Univ	CA	8,592	NC
Goldey-Beacom College	DE	11,440	C
Grand Canyon Univ	AZ	30,000	LC
Grand Valley State Univ	MI	10,040	C
Grove City College	PA	12,280	MC
Gwynedd-Mercy College	PA	22,350	C
Hampton Univ	VA	17,112	C+
Hardin-Simmons Univ	TX	14,165	C
Hillsdale College	MI	20,586	VC+
Hofstra Univ	NY	23,252	C
Houston Baptist Univ	TX	15,300	LC
Howard Univ	DC	15,522	LC
Huron Univ	SD	10,450	C
Husson College	ME	15,360	LC
Idaho State Univ	ID	7,030	C+
Illinois State Univ	IL	9,235	C
Illinois Wesleyan Univ	IL	26,970	HC
Indiana State Univ	IN	8,461	LC
Indiana Univ Bloomington	IN	10,712	C+
Indiana Univ of Pennsylvania	PA	9,133	C
Indiana Univ Southeast	IN	3,459	C
Indiana Univ-Purdue Univ Fort Wayne	IN	3,166	LC
Indiana Univ-Purdue Univ Indianapolis	IN	9,473	C
Inter-American Univ of PR/ Bayamon Univ College	PR	3,700	
Inter-American Univ of PR/ Fajardo Campus	PR	4,000	
Inter-American Univ of PR/ Metropolitan Campus	PR	4,166	
Inter-American Univ of PR/ Ponce Regional College	PR	3,700	
Inter-American Univ of PR/ San GermÈn	PR	6,390	
Iona College	NY	26,556	C
Iowa State Univ	IA	8,108	VC
Ithaca College	NY	28,719	HC
Jackson State Univ	MS	6,776	LC
Jacksonville State Univ	AL	6,568	LC
Jacksonville Univ	FL	21,110	LC
James Madison Univ	VA	9,552	HC
John Carroll Univ	OH	24,140	VC
Johns Hopkins Univ	MD	35,226	MC
Juniata College	PA	26,080	VC
Kansas State Univ	KS	6,995	C
Kean Univ	NJ	11,159	C
Kennesaw State Univ	GA	2,306	LC
Kent State Univ	OH	11,104	C
King's College	PA	24,680	C
Kutztown Univ of Pennsylvania	PA	8,907	C
La Roche College	PA	18,854	LC
La Salle Univ	PA	27,890	C
La Sierra Univ	CA	19,260	LC
Lasell College	MA	24,100	C
Lawrence Tech Univ	MI	11,429	C
Lehigh Univ	PA	32,290	MC
Lewis Univ	IL	20,960	C
Lincoln Univ	PA	11,198	C+
Lindenwood Univ	MO	17,250	C
Linfield College	OR	25,840	VC
LIU/Brooklyn Campus	NY	22,290	C
LIU/C.W. Post Campus	NY	25,380	C
Loras College	IA	22,994	C+
Louisiana State Univ and A&M College	LA	8,014	VC
Louisiana State Univ in Shreveport	LA	2,480	NC
Louisiana Tech Univ	LA	6,506	C
Loyola Univ New Orleans	LA	23,506	VC+
Loyola Univ of Chicago	IL	25,992	VC
Lubbock Christian Univ	TX	14,226	LC
Manchester College	IN	22,010	C
Manhattan College	NY	25,500	VC
Manhattanville College	NY	28,730	VC
Marian College	IN	21,020	C
Marquette Univ	WI	24,836	C+
Marymount Univ	VA	21,560	LC
Marywood Univ	PA	24,639	C
McKendree College	IL	18,300	C+
McMurry Univ	TX	15,287	C
McNeese State Univ	LA	5,259	LC
Medaille College	NY	18,320	C
Mercer Univ	GA	24,130	VC
Mercyhurst College	PA	20,694	C

ST = STATE $IS = IN-STATE COSTS SR = SELECTOR RATING

School	ST	$IS	SR
Metropolitan State College of Denver	CO	2,338	LC
Metropolitan State Univ	MN	2,943	SP
Miami Univ	OH	12,885	VC+
Middle Tenn State Univ	TN	6,994	C
Midwestern State Univ	TX	6,704	NC
Millikin Univ	IL	24,415	C+
Minn State Univ, Mankato	MN	7,296	LC
Minot State Univ	ND	5,466	LC
Miss State Univ	MS	7,853	C
Missouri Southern State College	MO	6,666	C
Monmouth Univ	NJ	24,042	C
Montana State Univ-Billings	MT	7,653	NC
Moorhead State Univ	MN	7,000	LC
Morehead State Univ	KY	6,510	C
Morehouse College	GA	19,814	C
Mountain State Univ	WV	8,180	NC
Murray State Univ	KY	6,672	C
National Univ	CA	7,755	SP
New Jersey City Univ	NJ	9,100	LC
New Mexico Highlands Univ	NM	6,256	NC
New Mexico State Univ	NM	7,302	C
New York Inst of Technology	NY	21,756	C
New York Univ	NY	35,200	MC
Nicholls State Univ	LA	5,290	NC
Nichols College	MA	24,610	LC
Norfolk State Univ	VA	8,382	LC
North Central College	IL	22,944	C+
North Georgia College and State Univ	GA	6,322	C+
North Park Univ	IL	24,030	C
Northeastern State Univ	OK	4,704	LC
Northern Arizona Univ	AZ	7,398	C
Northern Illinois Univ	IL	9,545	C
Northern Mich Univ	MI	9,693	C
Northern State Univ	SD	6,279	LC
Northwest Missouri State Univ	MO	7,922	LC
Northwestern College	MN	19,816	C+
Northwood Univ	FL	19,179	LC
Northwood Univ	MI	18,360	LC
Northwood Univ	TX	18,135	C
Notre Dame de Namur Univ	CA	26,932	LC
Oakland Univ	MI	9,418	C
Ohio Univ	OH	11,769	C
Okla Baptist Univ	OK	13,878	VC
Okla City Univ	OK	15,810	C
Okla State Univ	OK	7,650	VC
Old Dominion Univ	VA	9,386	C
Oral Roberts Univ	OK	18,490	C
Pace Univ	NY	24,200	C
Palm Beach Atlantic College	FL	23,310	C
Park Univ	MO	9,816	C
Penn State Univ at Erie/Behrend College	PA	12,326	C
Penn State Univ/Univ Park Campus	PA	11,126	VC
Philadelphia Univ	PA	24,722	C
Pittsburg State Univ	KS	6,228	NC
Pontifical Catholic Univ of PR/Ponce	PR	7,076	
Portland State Univ	OR	11,220	C
Prairie View A&M Univ	TX	3,172	LC
Providence College	RI	27,620	HC
Purdue Univ/Calumet	IN	0,030	NC
Quincy Univ	IL	20,450	C
Quinnipiac Univ	CT	27,370	C
Radford Univ	VA	8,302	C
Richard Stockton College of New Jersey	NJ	12,165	VC
Rider Univ	NJ	27,400	C
Robert Morris Univ	PA	18,730	C
Rochester Inst of Technology	NY	26,232	VC+
Rockhurst Univ	MO	20,090	C
Roger Williams Univ	RI	29,010	C
Roosevelt Univ	IL	20,240	LC
Rutgers, The State Univ of New Jersey New Brunswick Campus	NJ	12,709	C
Rutgers, The State Univ of New Jersey/CamdenCampus	NJ	6,484	C
Rutgers, The State Univ of New Jersey/Newark Campus	NJ	6,394	C
Sacred Heart Univ	CT	26,588	VC
Saginaw Valley State Univ	MI	9,465	C
St. Anselm College	NH	27,405	C
St. Bonaventure Univ	NY	21,956	C
St. Cloud State Univ	MN	7,180	C
St. Edward's Univ	TX	17,846	C
St. John's Univ	NY	26,660	C
St. Joseph's College	IN	21,640	C
St. Joseph's Univ	PA	29,715	VC+
St. Louis Univ	MO	26,590	VC+
St. Martin's College	WA	20,566	C
St. Mary's Univ of San Antonio	TX	19,735	C
St. Thomas Aquinas College	NY	20,590	LC
St. Thomas Univ	FL	19,500	LC
St. Vincent College	PA	22,942	VC
St. Xavier Univ	IL	21,104	C
Salem State College	MA	4,481	LC
Sam Houston State Univ	TX	6,076	LC
San Diego State Univ	CA	9,716	C+
San Francisco State Univ	CA	7,139	LC
San Jose State Univ	CA	8,187	C
Santa Clara Univ	CA	28,371	VC+
Schreiner Univ	TX	19,254	C
Seattle Univ	WA	24,183	VC
Seton Hall Univ	NJ	26,910	LC
Seton Hill College	PA	21,875	C
Shippensburg Univ of Pennsylvania	PA	9,652	C
Siena College	NY	22,685	VC
Simmons College	MA	30,418	VC
Southeast Missouri State Univ	MO	8,367	C+
Southeastern Louisiana Univ	LA	6,047	LC
Southeastern Univ	DC	8,505	LC
Southern Conn State Univ	CT	10,310	C
Southern Illinois Univ at Carbondale	IL	8,621	C
Southern Methodist Univ	TX	28,349	VC
Southern Nazarene Univ	OK	14,634	NC
Southern New Hampshire Univ	NH	23,852	C
Southern Utah Univ	UT	7,254	C
Southwest Missouri State Univ	MO	7,600	LC
Southwest Texas State Univ	TX	8,730	VC
Southwestern Okla State Univ	OK	4,801	C
Spring Hill College	AL	23,250	C
SUNY/College at Old Westbury	NY	9,818	LC
SUNY/College at Oswego	NY	10,856	C
SUNY/Univ at New Paltz	NY	9,685	VC
State Univ of West Georgia	GA	7,101	C
Stephen F. Austin State Univ	TX	6,905	C
Stetson Univ	FL	25,640	VC
Stonehill College	MA	26,852	HC
Suffolk Univ	MA	26,516	C
Syracuse Univ	NY	30,710	HC
Talladega College	AL	10,110	LC
Tarleton State Univ	TX	7,160	C
Taylor Univ	IN	21,562	VC+
Teikyo Post Univ	CT	21,800	C
Temple Univ	PA	14,124	C
Tenn Tech Univ	TN	6,968	C
Texas A&M Univ	TX	8,988	VC
Texas A&M Univ at Commerce	TX	7,326	C
Texas A&M Univ at Kingsville	TX	6,446	LC
Texas Christian Univ	TX	19,910	C
Texas Southern Univ	TX	6,576	NC
Texas Tech Univ	TX	8,825	C
Thomas Edison State College	NJ	2,750	SP
Tiffin Univ	OH	17,250	C
Touro College	NY	14,950	VC
Troy State Univ	AL	7,696	C
Troy State Univ/Dothan	AL	3,296	C
Troy State Univ/Montgomery	AL	3,080	NC
Tuskegee Univ	AL	14,600	LC
Union College	NE	14,650	C
Union Univ	TN	18,930	C+
Univ of Akron	OH	10,530	NC
Univ of Alabama	AL	7,402	C
Univ of Alabama at Birmingham	AL	10,110	C
Univ of Alabama at Huntsville	AL	7,916	VC
Univ of Alaska Anchorage	AK	9,100	NC
Univ of Arizona	AZ	8,614	C
Univ of Arkansas	AR	8,334	VC
Univ of Arkansas at Little Rock	AR	5,637	NC
Univ of Bridgeport	CT	23,020	C
Univ of Central Arkansas	AR	6,388	C
Univ of Central Florida	FL	8,251	VC
Univ of Central Okla	OK	5,205	C
Univ of Cincinnati	OH	12,491	LC
Univ of Colo at Boulder	CO	9,255	VC
Univ of Conn	CT	12,122	VC
Univ of Dayton	OH	20,400	VC
Univ of Delaware	DE	10,824	VC
Univ of Denver	CO	28,783	VC
Univ of Evansville	IN	22,865	VC+
Univ of Findlay	OH	23,962	NC
Univ of Florida	FL	7,874	HC
Univ of Hartford	CT	28,884	C
Univ of Hawaii at Manoa	HI	7,862	VC
Univ of Houston	TX	8,410	C
Univ of Houston-Downtown	TX	2,006	NC
Univ of Idaho	ID	7,026	C
Univ of Illinois at Chicago	IL	10,702	VC
Univ of Illinois at Urbana-Champaign	IL	11,316	HC+
Univ of Indianapolis	IN	20,840	C
Univ of Iowa	IA	8,607	C+
Univ of Kentucky	KY	7,765	C
Univ of Louisiana at Lafayette	LA	5,200	C
Univ of Louisiana at Monroe	LA	5,207	NC
Univ of Louisville	KY	7,402	LC
Univ of Maine at Augusta	ME	3,928	C
Univ of Mary Hardin-Baylor	TX	13,929	C
Univ of Maryland/College Park	MD	11,959	C
Univ of Mass Amherst	MA	10,995	VC
Univ of Mass Dartmouth	MA	9,852	C
Univ of Memphis	TN	7,271	C
Univ of Miami	FL	31,130	HC
Univ of Mich/Flint	MI	4,323	C
Univ of Miss	MS	7,666	C
Univ of Missouri/Columbia	MO	9,803	HC
Univ of Montana	MT	8,038	C
Univ of Montevallo	AL	7,266	C
Univ of Nebr at Kearney	NE	7,048	NC
Univ of Nebr at Lincoln	NE	8,325	C+
Univ of Nebr at Omaha	NE	6,867	C
Univ of Nevada/Las Vegas	NV	8,281	VC
Univ of Nevada/Reno	NV	8,737	C
Univ of New Haven	CT	23,860	LC
Univ of New Mexico	NM	8,026	C
Univ of New Orleans	LA	10,160	C
Univ of North Alabama	AL	7,016	NC
Univ of N Car at Charlotte	NC	7,254	C
Univ of N Car at Greensboro	NC	6,858	C
Univ of N Car at Wilmington	NC	7,769	C
Univ of N Dak	ND	7,067	VC
Univ of North Florida	FL	8,089	VC
Univ of North Texas	TX	7,629	C
Univ of Northern Iowa	IA	7,850	C
Univ of Notre Dame	IN	30,707	MC
Univ of Okla	OK	7,616	VC
Univ of Pennsylvania	PA	34,614	MC
Univ of Pittsburgh at Johnstown	PA	13,044	LC
Univ of Pittsburgh at Pittsburgh	PA	13,592	HC
Univ of Portland	OR	24,950	VC
Univ of PR/Bayamon Univ College Campus	PR	1,600	
Univ of PR/Mayaguez	PR	5,285	
Univ of PR/Rio Piedras	PR	5,510	
Univ of Rhode Island	RI	12,414	C
Univ of St. Francis	IL	19,650	C
Univ of St. Thomas	MN	24,044	VC
Univ of St. Thomas	TX	18,752	VC
Univ of San Francisco	CA	27,302	VC
Univ of Scranton	PA	27,964	C+
Univ of South Alabama	AL	6,976	LC
Univ of S Car at Columbia	SC	8,748	VC
Univ of South Florida	FL	8,154	C
Univ of Southern Indiana	IN	8,655	LC
Univ of Southern Miss	MS	6,155	LC
Univ of Tampa	FL	22,612	C
Univ of Tenn at Knoxville	TN	8,214	C
Univ of Tenn at Martin	TN	8,268	C
Univ of Texas at Arlington	TX	7,192	LC
Univ of Texas at Austin	TX	9,437	HC
Univ of Texas at El Paso	TX	5,076	LC
Univ of Texas at San Antonio	TX	9,088	NC
Univ of Texas-Pan American	TX	4,823	C
Univ of the District of Columbia	DC	2,844	NC
Univ of the Incarnate Word	TX	18,478	C
Univ of Toledo	OH	11,206	NC
Univ of Tulsa	OK	19,090	HC
Univ of Utah	UT	7,703	C
Univ of Washington	WA	10,361	VC
Univ of West Florida	FL	7,518	C
Univ of Wisc/Eau Claire	WI	7,032	VC
Univ of Wisc/La Crosse	WI	7,250	VC
Univ of Wisc/Madison	WI	8,262	VC
Univ of Wisc/Milwaukee	WI	8,907	LC
Univ of Wisc/Oshkosh	WI	6,130	LC
Univ of Wisc/Whitewater	WI	6,937	C
Univ of Wyoming	WY	7,143	LC
Upper Iowa Univ	IA	17,438	C
Utah State Univ	UT	6,771	C
Valdosta State Univ	GA	6,988	C
Valparaiso Univ	IN	23,570	VC+
Vanguard Univ of Southern Calif	CA	20,212	C
Villanova Univ	PA	31,997	HC
Virginia Polytechnic Inst and State Univ	VA	7,652	C
Virginia Union Univ	VA	15,358	LC
Walsh Univ	OH	16,880	C
Wartburg College	IA	21,165	VC
Washburn Univ of Topeka	KS	6,766	NC
Washington State Univ	WA	9,388	C
Washington Univ in St. Louis	MO	34,593	MC
Wayne State Univ	MI	6,720	C
Waynesburg College	PA	17,610	LC
Webber International Univ	FL	14,695	LC
Weber State Univ	UT	6,897	NC
West Chester Univ of Pennsylvania	PA	9,792	VC
West Liberty State College	WV	6,056	LC
West Texas A&M Univ	TX	6,538	C
West Virginia State College	WV	6,264	NC
West Virginia Univ	WV	8,304	C
Western Baptist College	OR	19,700	C+
Western Carolina Univ	NC	5,667	C
Western Conn State Univ	CT	10,074	C
Western Illinois Univ	IL	9,571	C
Western International Univ	AZ	5,800	SP
Western Kentucky Univ	KY	6,834	C
Western Mich Univ	MI	10,016	C
Western New England College	MA	23,882	C
Westminster College	PA	22,960	C
Wichita State Univ	KS	6,879	C
Widener Univ	PA	26,920	C
Wilberforce Univ	OH	14,937	LC
William Paterson Univ of New Jersey	NJ	11,000	LC
Wilmington College	DE	6,530	NC
Wingate Univ	NC	19,140	C
Winona State Univ	MN	8,570	C
Wofford College	SC	23,995	VC
Woodbury Univ	CA	25,344	LC
Wright State Univ	OH	9,141	LC
Xavier Univ	OH	23,880	C
Xavier Univ of Louisiana	LA	17,000	LC
York College	NE	13,500	C
York College of Pennsylvania	PA	12,550	VC
Youngstown State Univ	OH	9,318	NC

BEHAVIORAL SCIENCE

School	ST	$IS	SR
Andrews Univ	MI	17,696	LC
Bartlesville Wesleyan College	OK	14,100	LC
Calif Baptist Univ	CA	16,736	C
Calif State Polytechnic Univ, Pomona	CA	8,615	C
Cal State, Dominguez Hills	CA	5,840	LC
Cal State, Monterey Bay	CA	6,250	LC
Capital Univ	OH	23,630	C
Chaminade Univ of Honolulu	HI	17,370	C
College for Lifelong Learning	NH	4,100	SP
College of St. Scholastica	MN	22,378	C+
Concordia College	NY	19,200	VC
Concordia Univ	CA	22,290	C
Concordia Univ at Austin	TX	16,740	LC
Concordia Univ Nebr	NE	17,770	C
Dakota Wesleyan Univ	SD	15,512	C
Drew Univ/College of Liberal Arts	NJ	32,152	VC
East-West Univ	IL	9,140	LC
Erskine College	SC	21,399	VC
Green Mountain College	VT	24,130	C
Indiana Univ East	IN	3,415	C
Indiana Univ Kokomo	IN	3,422	LC
Johnson State College	VT	10,776	C
King College	TN	17,800	VC
Lakeland College	WI	17,950	C
Lehigh Univ	PA	32,290	MC
Manhattanville College	NY	28,730	VC
Martin Univ	IN	8,370	SP
Mercy College	NY	15,875	LC
Metropolitan State College of Denver	CO	2,338	LC
Missouri Baptist College	MO	15,762	LC
Mount Marty College	SD	15,656	LC
Mount Mary College	WI	18,024	C
National Univ	CA	7,755	SP
New York Inst of Technology	NY	21,756	C
North Central Univ	MN	12,744	LC
Northwest College	WA	17,471	C
Oglethorpe Univ	GA	19,100	LC
Our Lady of Holy Cross College	LA	5,140	NC
Our Lady of the Lake Univ of San Antonio	TX	17,336	C
Pacific Union College	CA	20,250	VC
Point Park College	PA	20,290	C
Rochester College	MI	15,404	C+
Southern Adventist Univ	TN	15,600	C
Sterling College	KS	16,370	VC
Tenn Wesleyan College	TN	13,030	C
Trevecca Nazarene Univ	TN	15,752	C
United States Air Force Academy	CO		MC
United States Military Academy	NY		MC
Univ of Calif at Davis	CA	12,796	VC
Univ of Evansville	IN	22,865	VC+
Univ of La Verne	CA	24,280	C
Univ of Maine at Fort Kent	ME	7,450	LC
Univ of Maine at Machias	ME	7,689	LC
Univ of Maine at Presque Isle	ME	7,964	LC
Univ of Mary	ND	12,900	LC
Univ of Mich/Dearborn	MI	4,677	VC
Univ of Rio Grande	OH	8,728	NC
Univ of Utah	UT	7,703	C
Univ of Wisc/Madison	WI	8,262	VC
Warren Wilson College	NC	19,968	C
Western International Univ	AZ	5,800	SP
Western Mich Univ	MI	10,016	C

School	ST	$IS	SR
Widener Univ	PA	26,920	C
Wilmington College	DE	6,530	NC
Wilson College	PA	21,337	LC
York College of Pennsylvania	PA	12,550	VC

BIBLICAL LANGUAGES

School	ST	$IS	SR
Abilene Christian Univ	TX	16,300	VC
Asbury College	KY	18,540	VC
Baylor Univ	TX	18,298	VC+
Concordia Univ	MI	20,500	C
Concordia Univ Wisc	WI	16,600	LC
Cornerstone Univ and Grand Rapids Baptist Seminary	MI	18,092	C
David Lipscomb Univ	TN	16,158	VC
Luther College	IA	23,300	VC+
North Central Univ	MN	12,744	LC
Southern Nazarene Univ	OK	14,634	NC
Toccoa Falls College	GA	14,220	C
Union Univ	TN	18,930	C+
Univ of Mich/Ann Arbor	MI	13,003	HC+
Walla Walla College	WA	20,925	C

BIBLICAL STUDIES

School	ST	$IS	SR
Abilene Christian Univ	TX	16,300	VC
Albert A. List College of Jewish Studies	NY	18,500	HC+
Asbury College	KY	18,540	VC
Azusa Pacific Univ	CA	22,422	VC
Belhaven College	MS	16,040	C+
Bethel College	IN	17,650	LC
Biola Univ	CA	21,902	VC
Cascade College	OR	14,800	NC
Cedarville Univ	OH	17,553	VC
Christian Heritage College	CA	18,000	LC
Clearwater Christian College	FL	13,160	LC
Colo Christian Univ	CO	17,714	C
Cornerstone Univ and Grand Rapids Baptist Seminary	MI	18,092	C
Covenant College	GA	21,970	C+
Crichton College	TN	12,680	LC
Dallas Baptist Univ	TX	13,682	LC
Eastern College	PA	19,641	LC
Eastern Mennonite Univ	VA	20,700	VC
Evangel Univ	MO	14,050	C
Faulkner Univ	AL	13,000	C
Freed-Hardeman Univ	TN	14,290	VC
Geneva College	PA	19,990	C+
George Fox Univ	OR	24,095	VC
Gordon College	MA	23,594	VC+
Goshen College	IN	18,950	VC+
Grace College	IN	16,768	C
Hannibal-LaGrange College	MO	12,530	C
Hope International Univ	CA	16,940	NC
Houghton College	NY	21,810	VC+
Huntington College	IN	15,480	LC
Indiana Wesleyan Univ	IN	17,680	C
John Brown Univ	AR	15,080	VC
Kentucky Christian College	KY	13,472	C
King College	TN	17,800	VC
LeTourneau Univ	TX	19,020	VC
Lubbock Christian Univ	TX	14,226	LC
Malone College	OH	19,190	C
Master's College	CA	21,500	C+
Messiah College	PA	23,180	VC
Milligan College	TN	17,550	C
Montreat College	NC	17,164	C
Northwest College	WA	17,471	C
Northwestern College	MN	19,816	C+
Nyack College	NY	18,540	C
Ohio Valley College	WV	13,650	C+
Okla Christian Univ	OK	16,500	VC
Oral Roberts Univ	OK	18,490	C
Ouachita Baptist Univ	AR	16,460	VC
Philadelphia Biblical Univ	PA	16,295	C+
Rochester College	MI	15,404	C+
Samford Univ	AL	16,340	VC
Simpson College	CA	19,200	C
Southeastern College	FL	11,648	LC
Southern Christian Univ	AL	8,480	LC
Southwest Baptist Univ	MO	13,426	LC
Southwestern Christian College	TX	7,500	NC
Tabor College	KS	17,600	LC
Taylor Univ	IN	21,562	VC+
Toccoa Falls College	GA	14,220	C
Trinity Bible College	ND		
Trinity Christian College	IL	19,415	C
Trinity International Univ	IL	20,640	C+
Union Univ	TN	18,930	C+
Univ of Evansville	IN	22,865	VC+
Univ of Mich/Ann Arbor	MI	13,003	HC+
Vanguard Univ of Southern Calif	CA	20,212	C
Western Baptist College	OR	19,700	C+
Wheaton College	IL	21,934	HC
William Tyndale College	MI	11,150	C
York College	NE	13,500	C

BILINGUAL/BICULTURAL EDUCATION

School	ST	$IS	SR
Boston Univ	MA	34,358	MC
Cal State, San Bernardino	CA	6,516	C
Central Mich Univ	MI	8,355	C
Chicago State Univ	IL	8,851	C+
CUNY/Brooklyn College	NY	3,403	LC
College of Our Lady of the Elms	MA	20,644	C
Eastern Mich Univ	MI	9,855	C
Hofstra Univ	NY	23,252	C
McMurry Univ	TX	15,287	C
Mount Mary College	WI	18,024	C
Northeastern Illinois Univ	IL	2,898	NC
St. Edward's Univ	TX	17,846	C
St. John's Univ	NY	26,660	C
St. Thomas Aquinas College	NY	20,590	LC
Southwest Texas State Univ	TX	8,730	VC
SUNY/College at Old Westbury	NY	9,818	LC
Stephen F. Austin State Univ	TX	6,905	C
Texas Christian Univ	TX	19,910	C
Texas Southern Univ	TX	6,576	NC
Univ of Findlay	OH	23,962	NC
Univ of Houston-Downtown	TX	2,006	NC
Univ of Minn/Twin Cities	MN	11,123	VC
Univ of New Mexico	NM	8,026	C
Western Illinois Univ	IL	9,571	C

BIOCHEMISTRY

School	ST	$IS	SR
Abilene Christian Univ	TX	16,300	VC
Adelphi Univ	NY	23,320	VC
Agnes Scott College	GA	24,950	VC
Albright College	PA	27,642	C
Alvernia College	PA	20,790	C
American International College	MA	22,268	LC
American Univ	DC	31,544	VC+
Andrews Univ	MI	17,696	LC
Angelo State Univ	TX	7,028	C
Arizona State Univ-Main	AZ	7,726	C
Asbury College	KY	18,540	VC
Atlantic Union College	MA	34,034	LC
Auburn Univ	AL	5,510	C
Austin College	TX	22,150	VC+
Averett Univ	VA	17,980	LC
Azusa Pacific Univ	CA	22,422	VC
Bard College	NY	33,912	HC
Bates College	ME	34,100	MC
Baylor Univ	TX	18,298	VC+
Beloit College	WI	27,482	HC
Benedictine College	KS	18,485	LC
Benedictine Univ	IL	21,330	C
Bennington College	VT	31,350	VC
Bethany College	WV	18,566	C
Bethel College	MN	22,740	VC
Biola Univ	CA	21,902	VC
Boston College	MA	33,330	MC
Boston Univ	MA	34,358	MC
Bowdoin College	ME	32,650	MC
Bowling Green State Univ	OH	10,794	C
Bradley Univ	IL	20,970	VC
Brandeis Univ	MA	34,481	MC
Brigham Young Univ	UT	7,840	HC
Brown Univ	RI	34,973	MC
Bucknell Univ	PA	31,096	HC
Calif Lutheran Univ	CA	23,500	LC
Calif Polytechnic State Univ	CA	8,747	VC
Cal State, Fullerton	CA	5,440	LC
Cal State, Hayward	CA	7,400	LC
Cal State, Long Beach	CA	7,400	LC
Cal State, Los Angeles	CA	5,050	C
Cal State, Northridge	CA	7,781	C
Cal State, San Bernardino	CA	6,516	C
Calvin College	MI	20,050	NC
Campbell Univ	NC	16,599	C
Canisius College	NY	24,696	C+
Capital Univ	OH	23,630	C
Carroll College	WI	21,170	C
Case Western Reserve Univ	OH	27,418	C
Catholic Univ of America	DC	29,332	VC
Cedar Crest College	PA	25,145	C+
Centenary College of Louisiana	LA	21,600	C+
Centre College	KY	24,000	HC
Charleston Southern Univ	SC	17,122	C
Chatham College	PA	25,454	C+
Chestnut Hill College	PA	24,790	LC
Chicago State Univ	IL	8,851	C+
CUNY/College of Staten Island	NY	3,358	NC
CUNY/Queens College	NY	3,403	VC
Claremont McKenna College	CA	32,700	MC
Clark Univ	MA	29,170	HC
Clemson Univ	SC	7,600	C
Coe College	IA	24,750	VC
Colgate Univ	NY	33,480	MC
College Misericordia	PA	23,380	LC
College of Charleston	SC	8,350	HC
College of Mount St. Vincent	NY	24,230	C
College of St. Benedict	MN	23,921	VC
College of St. Catherine	MN	22,324	VC
College of St. Elizabeth	NJ	22,510	C
College of St. Rose	NY	19,084	C
College of St. Scholastica	MN	22,378	C+
College of the Holy Cross	MA	32,780	MC
College of Wooster	OH	28,350	VC
Colo College	CO	31,525	HC+
Colo State Univ	CO	9,672	C
Columbia Union College	MD	19,027	C+
Columbia Univ/Barnard College	NY	33,694	MC
Columbia Univ/Columbia College	NY	35,190	MC
Conn College	CT	33,585	MC
Dartmouth College	NH	34,458	MC
David Lipscomb Univ	TN	16,158	VC
Denison Univ	OH	29,640	HC
Dickinson College	PA	32,210	VC+
Dominican Univ	IL	20,800	C
Duquesne Univ	PA	24,242	C+
East Carolina Univ	NC	7,766	C
East Stroudsburg Univ of Pennsylvania	PA	8,430	LC
Eastern College	PA	19,641	LC
Eastern Mennonite Univ	VA	20,700	VC
Eastern Mich Univ	MI	9,855	C
Eastern Washington Univ	WA	7,972	LC
Edinboro Univ of Pennsylvania	PA	9,328	LC
Elizabethtown College	PA	26,000	VC
Elmira College	NY	31,070	VC+
Emmanuel College	MA	23,802	C+
Fairleigh Dickinson Univ/ Teaneck Campus	NJ	24,646	C
Florida Inst of Technology	FL	25,250	VC
Florida State Univ	FL	7,835	HC
Franklin and Marshall College	PA	32,410	HC
Georgetown Univ	DC	34,847	MC
Georgian Court College	NJ	19,040	LC
Gettysburg College	PA	32,070	HC
Grinnell College	IA	28,300	HC+
Grove City College	PA	12,280	MC
Gustavus Adolphus College	MN	24,190	VC+
Hamilton College	NY	34,150	HC
Harding Univ	AR	13,528	VC
Hartwick College	NY	33,090	C+
Harvard Univ/Harvard College	MA	34,269	MC
Hofstra Univ	NY	23,252	C
Holy Family College	PA	13,710	LC
Hood College	MD	26,020	VC
Hope College	MI	22,922	C+
Idaho State Univ	ID	7,030	C+
Illinois Inst of Technology	IL	25,182	HC+
Illinois State Univ	IL	9,235	C
Immaculata College	PA	22,400	LC
Indiana Univ Bloomington	IN	10,712	C+
Indiana Univ of Pennsylvania	PA	9,133	C
Iowa State Univ	IA	8,108	VC
Ithaca College	NY	28,719	HC
Jamestown College	ND	11,310	NC
John Brown Univ	AR	15,080	VC
Juniata College	PA	26,080	VC
Kansas State Univ	KS	6,995	C
Kenyon College	OH	32,130	HC+
Keuka College	NY	21,170	C
King College	TN	17,800	VC
Knox College	IL	28,230	HC
La Salle Univ	PA	27,890	C
La Sierra Univ	CA	19,260	LC
Lafayette College	PA	32,655	MC
LaGrange College	GA	17,496	C
Le Moyne College	NY	23,840	C
Lebanon Valley College of Pennsylvania	PA	25,700	VC
Lehigh Univ	PA	32,290	MC
Lewis and Clark College	OR	29,010	VC
Lewis Univ	IL	20,960	C
Loras College	IA	22,994	C+
Louisiana State Univ and A&M College	LA	8,014	VC
Louisiana State Univ in Shreveport	LA	2,480	NC
Loyola Marymount Univ	CA	28,754	HC
Madonna Univ	MI	11,504	VC
Manchester College	IN	22,010	C
Manhattan College	NY	25,500	VC
Manhattanville College	NY	28,730	VC
Mansfield Univ	PA	9,648	C
Marietta College	OH	24,580	C
Marlboro College	VT	26,410	VC+
Marquette Univ	WI	24,836	C+
Mary Baldwin College	VA	23,440	C
Maryville College	TN	23,210	VC
McMurry Univ	TX	15,287	C
Mercyhurst College	PA	20,694	C
Merrimack College	MA	25,725	VC
Messiah College	PA	23,180	VC
Miami Univ	OH	12,885	VC+
Mich State Univ	MI	10,386	VC
Middlebury College	VT	34,300	MC
Mills College	CA	27,950	C
Minn State Univ, Mankato	MN	7,296	LC
Miss College	MS	14,574	C
Miss State Univ	MS	7,853	C
Montclair State Univ	NJ	10,287	LC
Mount Holyoke College	MA	34,128	HC
Mount St. Mary's College	CA	24,430	C
Mount St. Mary's College	MD	25,740	C
Muhlenberg College	PA	28,170	HC
Murray State Univ	KY	6,672	C
Nazareth College of Rochester	NY	22,036	VC
Nebr Wesleyan Univ	NE	18,767	VC
New Mexico State Univ	NM	7,302	C
New York Univ	NY	35,200	MC
Niagara Univ	NY	22,250	C+
N Car State Univ	NC	8,680	HC
North Central College	IL	22,944	C+
Northeastern Univ	MA	30,078	VC
Northern Mich Univ	MI	9,693	C
Northwest Nazarene Univ	ID	18,380	C
Norwich Univ	VT	21,064	LC
Notre Dame de Namur Univ	CA	26,932	LC
Oakland Univ	MI	9,418	C
Oakwood College	AL	14,904	C
Oberlin College	OH	33,140	HC+
Occidental College	CA	32,288	HC
Ohio Northern Univ	OH	27,765	VC
Ohio Univ	OH	11,769	C
Ohio Wesleyan Univ	OH	29,670	VC+
Okla Christian Univ	OK	16,500	VC
Okla City Univ	OK	15,810	C
Okla State Univ	OK	7,650	VC
Old Dominion Univ	VA	9,386	C
Olivet College	MI	17,410	C
Oregon State Univ	OR	9,612	VC
Otterbein College	OH	23,439	C
Penn State Univ/Univ Park Campus	PA	11,126	VC
Philadelphia Univ	PA	24,722	C
Pitzer College	CA	33,930	HC
Portland State Univ	OR	11,220	C
Providence College	RI	27,620	HC
Purdue Univ/West Lafayette	IN	10,284	VC
Queens College	NC	17,250	C
Quinnipiac Univ	CT	27,370	C
Ramapo College of New Jersey	NJ	13,550	VC
Regis College	MA	26,750	C
Regis Univ	CO	25,740	C+
Rensselaer Polytechnic Inst	NY	33,863	HC+
Richard Stockton College of New Jersey	NJ	12,165	VC
Rider Univ	NJ	27,400	C
Ripon College	WI	24,180	VC+
Roanoke College	VA	24,689	VC
Roberts Wesleyan College	NY	20,160	C+
Rochester Inst of Technology	NY	26,232	VC+
Rosemont College	PA	24,060	C
Russell Sage College	NY	23,674	C+
Rutgers, The State Univ of New Jersey New Brunswick Campus	NJ	12,709	C
Rutgers, The State Univ of New Jersey/ CamdenCampus	NJ	6,484	C
Saginaw Valley State Univ	MI	9,465	C
St. Anselm College	NH	27,405	C
St. Bonaventure Univ	NY	21,956	C
St. Edward's Univ	TX	17,846	C
St. John's Univ	MN	23,640	VC
St. Lawrence Univ	NY	32,605	VC
St. Mary's Univ of San Antonio	TX	19,735	C
St. Michael's College	VT	26,935	VC
St. Peter's College	NJ	22,292	LC
St. Vincent College	PA	22,942	VC
Samford Univ	AL	16,340	VC
San Francisco State Univ	CA	7,139	LC
San Jose State Univ	CA	8,187	C
Schreiner Univ	TX	19,254	C
Seattle Pacific Univ	WA	22,674	C+
Seattle Univ	WA	24,183	VC
Seton Hill College	PA	21,875	C
Siena College	NY	22,685	VC
Simmons College	MA	30,418	VC
Simpson College	IA	21,200	C+
Skidmore College	NY	34,201	VC+
Smith College	MA	33,302	HC+
S Dak State Univ	SD	6,848	C
Southern Conn State Univ	CT	10,310	C
Southern Methodist Univ	TX	28,349	VC
Southwest Texas State Univ	TX	8,730	VC
Southwestern College	KS	17,656	C
Spelman College	GA	19,215	C+
Spring Arbor Univ	MI	17,976	C
Spring Hill College	AL	23,250	C
Springfield College	MA	24,520	C
SUNY/College at Fredonia	NY	10,125	C
SUNY/College at Geneseo	NY	9,970	HC
SUNY/College at Plattsburgh	NY	9,729	C
SUNY/Univ at Albany	NY	10,997	VC

School	ST	$IS	SR
SUNY/Univ at Binghamton	NY	10,653	HC
SUNY/Univ at Buffalo	NY	11,033	VC
SUNY/Univ at Stony Brook	NY	10,998	VC
Stetson Univ	FL	25,640	VC
Stevens Inst of Technology	NJ	31,510	HC+
Stonehill College	MA	26,852	HC
Suffolk Univ	MA	26,516	C
Susquehanna Univ	PA	27,270	VC
Swarthmore College	PA	34,538	MC
Sweet Briar College	VA	25,310	VC
Temple Univ	PA	14,124	C
Tenn Tech Univ	TN	6,968	C
Texas A&M Univ	TX	8,988	VC
Texas Tech Univ	TX	8,825	C
Texas Wesleyan Univ	TX	14,710	C
Ohio State Univ	OH	10,819	VC
Trinity College	CT	34,300	HC
Trinity College	DC	21,370	LC
Trinity Univ	TX	21,444	HC
Tufts Univ	MA	34,874	MC
Tulane Univ	LA	34,013	HC+
Union College	NY	32,646	HC
Univ of Arizona	AZ	8,614	C
Univ of Calif at Davis	CA	12,796	VC
Univ of Calif at Los Angeles	CA	13,227	MC
Univ of Calif at Riverside	CA	12,479	C
Univ of Calif at San Diego	CA	11,372	HC
Univ of Calif at Santa Barbara	CA	11,732	VC
Univ of Calif at Santa Cruz	CA	13,655	VC
Univ of Chicago	IL	35,087	MC
Univ of Cincinnati	OH	12,491	LC
Univ of Colo at Boulder	CO	9,255	VC
Univ of Dallas	TX	22,128	VC+
Univ of Dayton	OH	20,400	VC
Univ of Delaware	DE	10,824	VC
Univ of Denver	CO	28,783	VC
Univ of Detroit Mercy	MI	21,620	LC
Univ of Georgia	GA	8,656	VC
Univ of Houston	TX	8,410	C
Univ of Illinois at Chicago	IL	10,702	VC
Univ of Illinois at Urbana-Champaign	IL	11,316	HC+
Univ of Iowa	IA	8,607	C+
Univ of Kansas	KS	7,232	VC
Univ of Maine	ME	10,798	C
Univ of Maryland/Baltimore County	MD	12,190	VC
Univ of Maryland/College Park	MD	11,959	C
Univ of Mass Amherst	MA	10,995	VC
Univ of Mass Boston	MA	4,227	C
Univ of Mass Dartmouth	MA	9,852	C
Univ of Miami	FL	31,130	HC
Univ of Mich/Ann Arbor	MI	13,003	HC+
Univ of Mich/Dearborn	MI	4,677	VC
Univ of Minn/Twin Cities	MN	11,123	VC
Univ of Missouri/Columbia	MO	9,803	HC
Univ of Nebr at Lincoln	NE	8,325	C+
Univ of Nevada/Reno	NV	8,737	C
Univ of New Hampshire	NH	13,207	C
Univ of New Mexico	NM	8,026	C
Univ of North Texas	TX	7,629	C
Univ of Northern Colo	CO	8,082	C+
Univ of Notre Dame	IN	30,707	MC
Univ of Oregon	OR	9,969	C
Univ of Pennsylvania	PA	34,614	MC
Univ of PR/Mayaguez	PR	5,285	
Univ of Redlands	CA	29,246	VC
Univ of Richmond	VA	27,300	HC
Univ of Rochester	NY	32,979	HC
Univ of Scranton	PA	27,964	C+
Univ of Southern Colo	CO	7,821	LC
Univ of Tampa	FL	22,612	C
Univ of Tenn at Knoxville	TN	8,214	C
Univ of Texas at Arlington	TX	7,192	LC
Univ of Texas at Austin	TX	9,437	HC
Univ of the Pacific	CA	28,255	VC
Univ of the Sciences in Philadelphia	PA	24,826	VC
Univ of Tulsa	OK	19,090	HC
Univ of Vermont	VT	14,761	C+
Univ of Washington	WA	10,361	VC
Univ of Wisc/Eau Claire	WI	7,032	VC
Univ of Wisc/Madison	WI	8,262	VC
Univ of Wisc/Milwaukee	WI	8,907	LC
Ursinus College	PA	31,350	VC
Utah State Univ	UT	6,771	C
Vassar College	NY	33,450	MC
Virginia Polytechnic Inst and State Univ	VA	7,652	C
Walla Walla College	WA	20,925	C
Wartburg College	IA	21,165	VC
Washington State Univ	WA	9,388	C
Washington Univ in St. Louis	MO	34,593	MC
Wellesley College	MA	33,394	MC
Wells College	NY	19,350	VC
Wesleyan Univ	CT	3,405	MC
West Chester Univ of Pennsylvania	PA	9,792	VC
Western Kentucky Univ	KY	6,834	C
Western Mich Univ	MI	10,016	C
Western Washington Univ	WA	8,624	VC
Wheaton College	MA	32,940	VC
Whittier College	CA	29,108	C
Widener Univ	PA	26,920	C
Wilkes Univ	PA	25,800	C
William Jewell College	MO	17,150	VC
Worcester Polytechnic Inst	MA	34,480	HC+
Xavier Univ of Louisiana	LA	17,000	LC
Yale Univ	CT	34,030	MC

BIOENGINEERING

School	ST	$IS	SR
Arizona State Univ-Main	AZ	7,726	C
Florida State Univ	FL	7,835	HC
Louisiana State Univ and A&M College	LA	8,014	VC
Miss State Univ	MS	7,853	C
Okla State Univ	OK	7,650	VC
Oral Roberts Univ	OK	18,490	C
Syracuse Univ	NY	30,710	HC
Texas A&M Univ	TX	8,988	VC
Univ of Arkansas	AR	8,334	VC
Univ of Calif at Berkeley	CA	14,134	MC
Univ of Calif at Davis	CA	12,796	VC
Univ of Calif at San Diego	CA	11,372	HC
Univ of Delaware	DE	10,824	VC
Univ of Georgia	GA	8,656	VC
Univ of Idaho	ID	7,026	C
Univ of Illinois at Chicago	IL	10,702	VC
Univ of Illinois at Urbana-Champaign	IL	11,316	HC+
Univ of Maine	ME	10,798	C
Univ of Maryland/College Park	MD	11,959	C
Univ of Nebr at Lincoln	NE	8,325	C+
Univ of Pennsylvania	PA	34,614	MC
Univ of Pittsburgh at Pittsburgh	PA	13,592	HC
Univ of Toledo	OH	11,206	NC
Univ of Utah	UT	7,703	C
Vanderbilt Univ	TN	34,482	MC
Walla Walla College	WA	20,925	C
Washington Univ in St. Louis	MO	34,593	MC
Western New England College	MA	23,882	C

BIOLOGY/BIOLOGICAL SCIENCE

School	ST	$IS	SR
Abilene Christian Univ	TX	16,300	VC
Adams State College	CO	7,468	C
Adelphi Univ	NY	23,320	VC
Adrian College	MI	19,670	C
Agnes Scott College	GA	24,950	VC
Alabama A&M Univ	AL	5,100	LC
Alabama State Univ	AL	6,404	C
Albany State Univ	GA	5,764	C+
Albertson College of Idaho	ID	23,900	VC
Albertus Magnus College	CT	22,154	C
Albion College	MI	25,224	VC
Albright College	PA	27,642	C
Alcorn State Univ	MS	5,594	LC
Alderson-Broaddus College	WV	19,640	C
Alfred Univ	NY	27,212	C+
Alice Lloyd College	KY	1,785	VC
Allegheny College	PA	27,780	VC
Allen Univ	SC	9,600	NC
Alma College	MI	22,586	VC
Alvernia College	PA	20,790	C
Alverno College	WI	16,930	LC
American International College	MA	22,268	LC
American Univ	DC	31,544	VC+
Amherst College	MA	34,340	MC
Anderson Univ	IN	19,430	LC
Andrews Univ	MI	17,696	LC
Angelo State Univ	TX	7,028	C
Anna Maria College	MA	22,800	LC
Appalachian State Univ	NC	6,353	C
Aquinas College	MI	20,052	C+
Arcadia Univ	PA	26,650	C
Arizona State Univ-Main	AZ	7,726	C
Arkansas State Univ	AR	7,480	C
Arkansas Tech Univ	AR	6,256	C
Armstrong Atlantic State Univ	GA	7,084	C
Asbury College	KY	18,540	VC
Ashland Univ	OH	22,182	LC
Assumption College	MA	26,320	C
Atlantic Union College	MA	34,034	LC
Auburn Univ	AL	5,510	C
Auburn Univ Montgomery	AL	5,330	NC
Augsburg College	MN	22,978	C
Augusta State Univ	GA	2,282	C
Augustana College	IL	24,117	VC+
Augustana College	SD	20,760	VC
Aurora Univ	IL	18,551	C
Austin College	TX	22,150	VC+
Austin Peay State Univ	TN	5,814	LC
Averett Univ	VA	17,980	LC
Avila College	MO	17,720	C
Azusa Pacific Univ	CA	22,422	VC
Baker Univ	KS	14,780	C+
Baldwin-Wallace College	OH	22,010	VC+
Ball State Univ	IN	8,660	C
Barber-Scotia College	NC	13,100	C
Bard College	NY	33,912	HC
Barry Univ	FL	24,100	LC
Bartlesville Wesleyan College	OK	14,100	LC
Barton College	NC	16,834	LC
Bates College	ME	34,100	MC
Bay Path College	MA	22,308	C
Baylor Univ	TX	18,298	VC+
Belhaven College	MS	16,040	C+
Bellarmine Univ	KY	20,440	VC
Belmont Abbey College	NC	19,630	LC
Belmont Univ	TN	19,066	VC
Beloit College	WI	27,482	HC
Bemidji State Univ	MN	7,957	C
Benedict College	SC	12,662	LC
Benedictine College	KS	18,485	LC
Benedictine Univ	IL	21,330	C
Bennett College	NC	11,200	C
Bennington College	VT	31,350	VC
Berea College	KY	4,070	VC
Berry College	GA	18,850	C
Bethany College	KS	16,602	C+
Bethany College	WV	18,566	C
Bethel College	IN	17,650	LC
Bethel College	KS	17,355	C+
Bethel College	MN	22,740	VC
Bethel College	TN	12,980	C
Bethune-Cookman College	FL	15,746	C
Biola Univ	CA	21,902	VC
Birmingham-Southern College	AL	22,960	C
Black Hills State Univ	SD	6,652	LC
Blackburn College	IL	13,690	C
Bloomfield College	NJ	17,000	C
Bloomsburg Univ of Pennsylvania	PA	9,434	C
Blue Mountain College	MS	9,100	LC
Bluefield College	VA	14,200	C
Bluefield State College	WV	2,178	LC
Bluffton College	OH	20,644	C
Boise State Univ	ID	6,531	LC
Boston College	MA	33,330	MC
Boston Univ	MA	34,358	MC
Bowdoin College	ME	32,650	MC
Bowie State Univ	MD	9,300	C+
Bowling Green State Univ	OH	10,794	C
Bradley Univ	IL	20,970	VC
Brandeis Univ	MA	34,481	MC
Brenau Univ Women's College	GA	20,100	C
Brescia Univ	KY	14,225	C
Brewton-Parker College	GA	10,810	LC
Briar Cliff Univ	IA	18,657	LC
Bridgewater College	VA	22,950	C
Bridgewater State College	MA	7,589	C+
Brigham Young Univ	UT	7,840	HC
Brigham Young Univ/Hawaii	HI	6,890	C
Brown Univ	RI	34,973	MC
Bryan College	TN	16,400	VC
Bryn Athyn College of the New Church	PA	10,590	NC
Bryn Mawr College	PA	33,580	HC+
Bucknell Univ	PA	31,096	HC
Buena Vista Univ	IA	22,828	C
Butler Univ	IN	25,580	VC+
Cabrini College	PA	25,950	LC
Caldwell College	NJ	20,940	LC
Calif Baptist Univ	CA	16,736	C
Calif Inst of Technology	CA	27,663	MC
Calif Lutheran Univ	CA	23,500	LC
Calif Polytechnic State Univ	CA	8,747	VC
Calif State Polytechnic Univ, Pomona	CA	8,615	C
Cal State, Bakersfield	CA	6,090	LC
Cal State, Chico	CA	8,598	LC
Cal State, Dominguez Hills	CA	5,840	LC
Cal State, Fresno	CA	7,762	C
Cal State, Fullerton	CA	5,440	LC
Cal State, Hayward	CA	7,400	LC
Cal State, Long Beach	CA	7,400	LC
Cal State, Los Angeles	CA	5,050	C
Cal State, Northridge	CA	7,781	C
Cal State, Sacramento	CA	7,488	C
Cal State, San Bernardino	CA	6,516	C
Cal State, San Marcos	CA	1,736	LC
Cal State, Stanislaus	CA	8,895	C
Calif Univ of Pennsylvania	PA	10,388	C
Calumet College of St. Joseph	IN	7,500	LC
Calvin College	MI	20,050	NC
Cameron Univ	OK	5,560	NC
Campbell Univ	NC	16,599	C
Campbellsville Univ	KY	14,340	C
Canisius College	NY	24,696	C+
Capital Univ	OH	23,630	C
Cardinal Stritch Univ	WI	17,620	C
Caribbean Univ	PR	3,000	
Carleton College	MN	30,780	MC
Carlow College	PA	19,366	C
Carnegie Mellon Univ	PA	32,682	MC
Carroll College	MT	19,140	C
Carroll College	WI	21,170	C
Carson-Newman College	TN	16,490	C
Carthage College	WI	23,670	C
Case Western Reserve Univ	OH	27,418	C
Castleton State College	VT	10,922	LC
Catawba College	NC	19,620	C
Catholic Univ of America	DC	29,332	VC
Cedar Crest College	PA	25,145	C+
Cedarville Univ	OH	17,553	VC
Centenary College	NJ	22,430	C
Centenary College of Louisiana	LA	21,600	C+
Central College	IA	21,206	C
Central Conn State Univ	CT	10,404	C
Central Methodist College	MO	16,460	C
Central Mich Univ	MI	8,355	C
Central Missouri State Univ	MO	7,920	C
Central State Univ	OH	8,922	C+
Central Univ of Bayamon	PR	3,335	
Central Washington Univ	WA	8,985	LC
Centre College	KY	24,000	HC
Chadron State College	NE	6,211	NC
Chaminade Univ of Honolulu	HI	17,370	C
Chapman Univ	CA	30,218	VC
Charleston Southern Univ	SC	17,122	C
Chatham College	PA	25,454	C+
Chestnut Hill College	PA	24,790	LC
Cheyney Univ of Pennsylvania	PA	9,993	C
Chicago State Univ	IL	8,851	C+
Christian Brothers Univ	TN	19,820	VC
Christian Heritage College	CA	18,000	LC
Christopher Newport Univ	VA	8,862	VC
Citadel, The	SC	9,126	C
CUNY/Brooklyn College	NY	3,403	LC
CUNY/City College	NY	3,309	LC
CUNY/College of Staten Island	NY	3,358	NC
CUNY/Herbert H. Lehman College	NY	3,320	LC
CUNY/Hunter College	NY	5,147	C+
CUNY/Medgar Evers College	NY	3,282	NC
CUNY/Queens College	NY	3,403	VC
CUNY/York College	NY	3,292	NC
Claflin Univ	SC	12,735	C+
Claremont McKenna College	CA	32,700	MC
Clarion Univ of Pennsylvania	PA	11,272	LC
Clark Atlanta Univ	GA	17,174	C
Clark Univ	MA	29,170	HC
Clarke College	IA	20,625	C+
Clarkson Univ	NY	29,884	VC
Clearwater Christian College	FL	13,160	LC
Clemson Univ	SC	7,600	C
Cleveland State Univ	OH	10,146	NC
Coastal Carolina Univ	SC	9,220	C
Coe College	IA	24,750	VC
Coker College	SC	20,120	C
Colby College	ME	34,290	MC
Colby-Sawyer College	NH	27,850	LC
Colgate Univ	NY	33,480	MC
College Misericordia	PA	23,380	LC
College of Charleston	SC	8,350	HC
College of Mount St. Vincent	NY	24,230	C
College of Mount St. Joseph	OH	20,290	C
College of New Jersey	NJ	13,425	HC
College of New Rochelle	NY	20,000	C
College of Notre Dame of Maryland	MD	23,100	LC
College of Our Lady of the Elms	MA	20,644	C
College of St. Benedict	MN	23,921	VC
College of St. Catherine	MN	22,324	VC
College of St. Elizabeth	NJ	22,510	C
College of St. Mary	NE	18,726	C
College of St. Rose	NY	19,084	C
College of St. Scholastica	MN	22,378	C+
College of Santa Fe	NM	20,250	LC
College of the Holy Cross	MA	32,780	MC
College of the Ozarks	MO	2,650	C+
College of the Southwest	NM	8,456	NC
College of William and Mary	VA	10,002	MC
College of Wooster	OH	28,350	VC
Colo Christian Univ	CO	17,714	C
Colo College	CO	31,525	HC+
Colo State Univ	CO	9,672	C
Columbia College	SC	19,050	LC
Columbia Univ/Barnard College	NY	33,694	MC
Columbia Univ/Columbia College	NY	35,190	MC
Columbia Univ/School of General Studies	NY	35,000	C
Columbus State Univ	GA	7,228	LC
Concord College	WV	7,122	C+
Concordia College	NY	19,200	VC
Concordia College/Moorhead	MN	18,835	C
Concordia Univ	CA	22,290	C
Concordia Univ	MI	20,500	C
Concordia Univ	MN	19,912	C
Concordia Univ	OR	20,500	LC
Concordia Univ Nebr	NE	17,770	C
Concordia Univ Wisc	WI	16,600	LC

School	ST	$IS	SR
Concordia Univ, River Forest	IL	20,000	LC
Conn College	CT	33,585	MC
Converse College	SC	21,990	VC
Coppin State College	MD	9,133	LC
Cornell College	IA	24,980	VC
Cornell Univ	NY	34,614	MC
Cornerstone Univ and Grand Rapids Baptist Seminary	MI	18,092	C
Covenant College	GA	21,970	C+
Creighton Univ	NE	23,476	VC
Crichton College	TN	12,680	LC
Culver-Stockton College	MO	15,400	LC
Cumberland College	KY	14,864	C
Curry College	MA	26,025	LC
Daemen College	NY	20,620	C
Dakota State Univ	SD	6,950	C
Dakota Wesleyan Univ	SD	15,512	C
Dallas Baptist Univ	TX	13,682	LC
Dana College	NE	18,046	C
Dartmouth College	NH	34,458	MC
David Lipscomb Univ	TN	16,158	VC
Davidson College	NC	30,823	MC
Davis and Elkins College	WV	19,270	LC
De Sales Univ	PA	22,610	VC
Defiance College	OH	19,580	LC
Delaware State Univ	DE	8,104	LC
Delaware Valley College	PA	24,213	LC
Delta State Univ	MS	5,416	C
Denison Univ	OH	29,640	HC
DePaul Univ	IL	23,590	VC
DePauw Univ	IN	28,000	HC
Dickinson College	PA	32,210	VC+
Dickinson State Univ	ND	5,495	NC
Dillard Univ	LA	16,046	VC
Doane College	NE	17,600	LC
Dominican College	NY	20,400	LC
Dominican Univ	IL	20,800	C
Dominican Univ of Calif	CA	27,948	C
Dordt College	IA	18,100	C+
Dowling College	NY	20,281	LC
Drake Univ	IA	22,830	VC
Drew Univ/College of Liberal Arts	NJ	32,152	VC
Drexel Univ	PA	27,657	VC
Drury Univ	MO	15,250	VC
Duke Univ	NC	34,396	MC
Duquesne Univ	PA	24,242	C+
D'Youville College	NY	18,704	C
Earlham College	IN	27,446	VC+
East Carolina Univ	NC	7,766	C
East Central Univ	OK	4,578	C
East Stroudsburg Univ of Pennsylvania	PA	8,430	LC
East Tenn State Univ	TN	7,127	C
East Texas Baptist Univ	TX	12,349	LC
Eastern College	PA	19,641	LC
Eastern Conn State Univ	CT	10,362	C
Eastern Illinois Univ	IL	10,101	C
Eastern Kentucky Univ	KY	6,552	C
Eastern Mennonite Univ	VA	20,700	VC
Eastern Mich Univ	MI	9,855	C
Eastern Nazarene College	MA	19,433	LC
Eastern New Mexico Univ	NM	4,113	LC
Eastern Oregon Univ	OR	8,772	C
Eastern Washington Univ	WA	7,972	LC
Eckerd College	FL	25,500	C+
Edgewood College	WI	18,304	C
Edinboro Univ of Pennsylvania	PA	9,328	LC
Edward Waters College	FL	13,124	LC
Elizabeth City State Univ	NC	5,550	LC
Elizabethtown College	PA	26,000	VC
Elmhurst College	IL	21,750	C
Elmira College	NY	31,070	VC+
Elon Univ	NC	19,430	VC
Emmanuel College	MA	23,802	C+
Emory & Henry College	VA	19,462	C
Emory Univ	GA	33,792	MC
Emporia State Univ	KS	6,198	LC
Erskine College	SC	21,399	VC
Eureka College	IL	22,200	C
Evangel Univ	MO	14,050	C
Fairfield Univ	CT	30,885	HC
Fairleigh Dickinson Univ/ Madison campus	NJ	25,500	C
Fairleigh Dickinson Univ/ Teaneck Campus	NJ	24,646	C
Fairmont State College	WV	7,010	NC
Faulkner Univ	AL	13,000	C
Fayetteville State Univ	NC	5,590	LC
Felician College	NJ	20,050	C
Ferris State Univ	MI	10,816	C
Ferrum College	VA	15,990	LC
Fisk Univ	TN	13,700	LC
Fitchburg State College	MA	7,836	C
Florida A&M Univ	FL	6,948	C
Florida Atlantic Univ	FL	8,832	C
Florida Inst of Technology	FL	25,250	VC
Florida International Univ	FL	9,486	VC
Florida Memorial College	FL	6,000	LC
Florida Southern College	FL	19,430	C
Florida State Univ	FL	7,835	HC
Fontbonne Univ	MO	18,046	C
Fordham Univ	NY	30,710	VC

School	ST	$IS	SR
Fort Hays State Univ	KS	6,294	LC
Fort Lewis College	CO	7,659	LC
Fort Valley State Univ	GA	6,014	LC
Framingham State College	MA	7,259	C
Francis Marion Univ	SC	7,682	C
Franciscan Univ of Steubenville	OH	19,100	C+
Franklin and Marshall College	PA	32,410	HC
Franklin College of Indiana	IN	19,905	C
Franklin Pierce College	NH	26,125	LC
Freed-Hardeman Univ	TN	14,290	VC
Fresno Pacific Univ	CA	19,740	C
Friends Univ	KS	15,962	LC
Frostburg State Univ	MD	9,680	C
Furman Univ	SC	25,492	HC
Gallaudet Univ	DC	16,554	SP
Gannon Univ	PA	18,848	C
Gardner-Webb Univ	NC	17,400	C
Geneva College	PA	19,990	C+
George Fox Univ	OR	24,095	VC
George Mason Univ	VA	9,192	C
George Washington Univ	DC	32,170	HC
Georgetown College	KY	18,400	VC
Georgetown Univ	DC	34,847	MC
Georgia College and State Univ	GA	7,344	C
Georgia Inst of Technology	GA	9,028	HC+
Georgia Southern Univ	GA	6,958	C
Georgia Southwestern State Univ	GA	6,013	C
Georgia State Univ	GA	7,792	LC
Georgian Court College	NJ	19,040	LC
Gettysburg College	PA	32,070	HC
Glenville State College	WV	6,588	NC
Gonzaga Univ	WA	24,276	HC+
Gordon College	MA	23,594	VC+
Goshen College	IN	18,950	VC+
Goucher College	MD	30,650	VC+
Grace College	IN	16,768	C
Graceland Univ	IA	15,845	C
Grambling State Univ	LA	5,325	NC
Grand Canyon Univ	AZ	30,000	LC
Grand Valley State Univ	MI	10,040	C
Grand View College	IA	17,596	NC
Green Mountain College	VT	24,130	C
Greensboro College	NC	19,080	LC
Greenville College	IL	19,226	LC
Grinnell College	IA	28,300	HC+
Grove City College	PA	12,280	MC
Guilford College	NC	23,255	C
Gustavus Adolphus College	MN	24,190	VC+
Gwynedd-Mercy College	PA	22,350	C
Hamilton College	NY	34,150	HC
Hamline Univ	MN	23,339	C+
Hampden-Sydney College	VA	24,871	C
Hampshire College	MA	33,881	HC+
Hampton Univ	VA	17,112	C+
Hannibal-LaGrange College	MO	12,530	C
Hanover College	IN	17,560	VC
Harding Univ	AR	13,528	VC
Hardin-Simmons Univ	TX	14,165	C
Hartwick College	NY	33,090	C+
Harvard Univ/Harvard College	MA	34,269	MC
Harvey Mudd College	CA	31,605	MC
Hastings College	NE	17,854	C+
Haverford College	PA	34,300	MC
Heidelberg College	OH	23,879	C
Henderson State Univ	AR	6,269	C
Hendrix College	AR	18,463	HC
High Point Univ	NC	20,220	LC
Hillsdale College	MI	20,586	VC+
Hiram College	OH	27,034	VC
Hobart and William Smith Colleges	NY	33,195	VC
Hofstra Univ	NY	23,252	C
Hollins Univ	VA	24,328	VC
Holy Family College	PA	13,710	LC
Holy Names College	CA	23,220	C
Hood College	MD	26,020	VC
Hope College	MI	22,922	C+
Houghton College	NY	21,810	VC+
Houston Baptist Univ	TX	15,300	LC
Howard Payne Univ	TX	13,834	C+
Howard Univ	DC	15,522	LC
Humboldt State Univ	CA	8,582	C
Huntingdon College	AL	18,400	VC
Huntington College	IN	15,480	LC
Husson College	ME	15,360	LC
Huston-Tillotson College	TX	12,977	LC
Idaho State Univ	ID	7,030	C+
Illinois College	IL	16,234	C
Illinois Inst of Technology	IL	25,182	HC+
Illinois State Univ	IL	9,235	C
Illinois Wesleyan Univ	IL	26,970	HC
Immaculata College	PA	22,400	LC
Indiana State Univ	IN	8,461	LC
Indiana Univ Bloomington	IN	10,712	C+
Indiana Univ East	IN	3,415	C
Indiana Univ Kokomo	IN	3,422	LC
Indiana Univ Northwest	IN	3,447	C
Indiana Univ of Pennsylvania	PA	9,133	C
Indiana Univ South Bend	IN	3,515	C
Indiana Univ Southeast	IN	3,459	C

School	ST	$IS	SR
Indiana Univ-Purdue Univ Fort Wayne	IN	3,166	LC
Indiana Univ-Purdue Univ Indianapolis	IN	9,473	C
Indiana Wesleyan Univ	IN	17,680	C
Inter-American Univ of PR/ Aguadilla Campus	PR	3,278	
Inter-American Univ of PR/ Arecibo Campus	PR	3,300	
Inter-American Univ of PR/ Bayamon Univ College	PR	3,700	
Inter-American Univ of PR/ Fajardo Campus	PR	4,000	
Inter-American Univ of PR/ Metropolitan Campus	PR	4,166	
Inter-American Univ of PR/ Ponce Regional College	PR	3,700	
Inter-American Univ of PR/ San GermÈn	PR	6,390	
Iona College	NY	26,556	C
Iowa State Univ	IA	8,108	VC
Iowa Wesleyan College	IA	18,840	C
Ithaca College	NY	28,719	HC
Jackson State Univ	MS	6,776	LC
Jacksonville State Univ	AL	6,568	LC
Jacksonville Univ	FL	21,110	LC
James Madison Univ	VA	9,552	HC
Jamestown College	ND	11,310	NC
Jarvis Christian College	TX	9,035	NC
John Brown Univ	AR	15,080	VC
John Carroll Univ	OH	24,140	VC
Johns Hopkins Univ	MD	35,226	MC
Johnson C. Smith Univ	NC	16,560	C+
Johnson State College	VT	10,776	C
Judson College	AL	13,790	C
Judson College	IL	18,980	LC
Juniata College	PA	26,080	VC
Kalamazoo College	MI	26,955	HC+
Kansas State Univ	KS	6,995	C
Kansas Wesleyan Univ	KS	17,400	C+
Kean Univ	NJ	11,159	C
Keene State College	NH	11,280	C
Kennesaw State Univ	GA	2,306	LC
Kent State Univ	OH	11,104	C
Kentucky State Univ	KY	6,146	NC
Kentucky Wesleyan College	KY	15,800	C
Kenyon College	OH	32,130	HC+
Keuka College	NY	21,170	C
King College	TN	17,800	VC
King's College	PA	24,680	C
Knox College	IL	28,230	HC
Knoxville College	TN	6,200	LC
Kutztown Univ of Pennsylvania	PA	8,907	C
La Roche College	PA	18,854	LC
La Salle Univ	PA	27,890	C
La Sierra Univ	CA	19,260	LC
Lafayette College	PA	32,655	MC
LaGrange College	GA	17,496	C
Lake Erie College	OH	21,350	LC
Lake Forest College	IL	27,460	VC
Lake Superior State Univ	MI	9,034	LC
Lakeland College	WI	17,950	C
Lamar Univ	TX	6,816	LC
Lambuth Univ	TN	14,254	C
Lander Univ	SC	8,618	LC
Lane College	TN	10,400	C+
Langston Univ	OK	2,308	LC
Lawrence Univ	WI	27,711	HC
Le Moyne College	NY	23,840	C
Lebanon Valley College of Pennsylvania	PA	25,700	VC
Lee Univ	TN	10,198	LC
Lees-McRae College	NC	17,106	LC
Lehigh Univ	PA	32,290	MC
LeMoyne-Owen College	TN	8,450	NC
Lenoir-Rhyne College	NC	19,186	C
LeTourneau Univ	TX	19,020	VC
Lewis and Clark College	OR	29,010	VC
Lewis Univ	IL	20,960	C
Lewis-Clark State College	ID	6,496	C
Liberty Univ	VA	14,500	C
Limestone College	SC	16,900	C
Lincoln Memorial Univ	TN	12,620	LC
Lincoln Univ	MO	7,158	NC
Lincoln Univ	PA	11,198	C+
Lindenwood Univ	MO	17,250	C
Lindsey Wilson College	KY	16,392	LC
Linfield College	OR	25,840	VC
Livingstone College	NC	13,360	LC
Lock Haven Univ of Pennsylvania	PA	9,534	C
LIU/Brooklyn Campus	NY	22,290	C
LIU/C.W. Post Campus	NY	25,380	C
LIU/Southampton College	NY	26,270	C
Longwood College	VA	8,950	C
Loras College	IA	22,994	C+
Louisiana College	LA	11,516	C
Louisiana State Univ and A&M College	LA	8,014	VC
Louisiana State Univ in Shreveport	LA	2,480	NC
Louisiana Tech Univ	LA	6,506	C
Lourdes College	OH	13,100	LC
Loyola College in Maryland	MD	30,900	HC
Loyola Marymount Univ	CA	28,754	HC

School	ST	$IS	SR
Loyola Univ New Orleans	LA	23,506	VC+
Loyola Univ of Chicago	IL	25,992	VC
Lubbock Christian Univ	TX	14,226	LC
Luther College	IA	23,300	VC+
Lycoming College	PA	24,780	C
Lynchburg College	VA	23,405	C
Lyon College	AR	16,500	VC
Macalester College	MN	28,814	HC+
MacMurray College	IL	17,790	LC
Madonna Univ	MI	11,504	VC
Maharishi Univ of Management	IA	20,660	VC
Malone College	OH	19,190	C
Manchester College	IN	22,010	C
Manhattan College	NY	25,500	VC
Manhattanville College	NY	28,730	VC
Mansfield Univ	PA	9,648	C
Marian College	IN	21,020	C
Marian College of Fond du Lac	WI	17,935	LC
Marietta College	OH	24,580	C
Marist College	NY	24,756	VC
Marlboro College	VT	26,410	VC+
Marquette Univ	WI	24,836	C+
Mars Hill College	NC	18,600	LC
Marshall Univ	WV	7,752	LC
Martin Univ	IN	8,370	SP
Mary Baldwin College	VA	23,440	C
Mary Washington College	VA	9,032	VC+
Marygrove College	MI	16,075	C
Marymount College/ Tarrytown	NY	23,850	C
Marymount Manhattan College	NY	23,195	VC
Marymount Univ	VA	21,560	LC
Maryville College	TN	23,210	VC
Maryville Univ of St. Louis	MO	18,680	C
Marywood Univ	PA	24,639	C
Mass College of Liberal Arts	MA	8,717	LC
Mass Inst of Technology	MA	35,228	MC
Master's College	CA	21,500	C+
Mayville State Univ	ND	6,440	NC
McKendree College	IL	18,300	C+
McMurry Univ	TX	15,287	C
McNeese State Univ	LA	5,259	LC
McPherson College	KS	17,710	C
Medaille College	NY	18,320	C
Mercer Univ	GA	24,130	VC
Mercy College	NY	15,875	LC
Mercyhurst College	PA	20,694	C
Meredith College	NC	17,500	C
Merrimack College	MA	25,725	VC
Mesa State College	CO	8,051	C
Messiah College	PA	23,180	VC
Methodist College	NC	19,526	C
Metropolitan State College of Denver	CO	2,338	LC
Metropolitan State Univ	MN	2,943	SP
Miami Univ	OH	12,885	VC+
Mich State Univ	MI	10,386	VC
Mich Tech Univ	MI	11,088	VC
MidAmerica Nazarene Univ	KS	16,960	C
Middle Tenn State Univ	TN	6,994	C
Middlebury College	VT	34,300	MC
Midland Lutheran College	NE	18,600	C
Midway College	KY	15,815	C
Midwestern State Univ	TX	6,704	NC
Miles College	AL	7,870	NC
Millersville Univ of Pennsylvania	PA	10,153	VC
Milligan College	TN	17,550	C
Millikin Univ	IL	24,415	C+
Mills College	CA	27,950	C
Millsaps College	MS	22,608	VC+
Minn State Univ, Mankato	MN	7,296	LC
Minot State Univ	ND	5,466	LC
Miss College	MS	14,574	C
Miss State Univ	MS	7,853	C
Miss Univ for Women	MS	5,446	LC
Miss Valley State Univ	MS	6,345	C
Missouri Baptist College	MO	15,762	LC
Missouri Southern State College	MO	6,666	C
Missouri Valley College	MO	17,400	LC
Missouri Western State College	MO	6,662	NC
Molloy College	NY	13,940	C
Monmouth College	IL	21,550	C
Monmouth Univ	NJ	24,042	C
Montana State Univ-Billings	MT	7,653	NC
Montana State Univ-Bozeman	MT	8,431	C
Montana State Univ-Northern	MT	8,600	NC
Montana Tech of The Univ of Montana	MT	7,845	C
Montclair State Univ	NJ	10,287	LC
Moorhead State Univ	MN	7,000	LC
Moravian College	PA	27,065	VC
Morehead State Univ	KY	6,510	C
Morehouse College	GA	19,814	C
Morgan State Univ	MD	10,078	LC
Morningside College	IA	19,124	C
Morris Brown College	GA	15,993	LC
Morris College	SC	9,995	LC

ST = STATE **$IS** = IN-STATE COSTS **SR** = SELECTOR RATING

School	ST	$IS	SR
Mount Holyoke College	MA	34,128	HC
Mount Marty College	SD	15,656	LC
Mount Mary College	WI	18,024	C
Mount Mercy College	IA	19,390	VC
Mount Olive College	NC	14,410	LC
Mount St. Clare College	IA	19,050	LC
Mount St. Mary College	NY	18,825	C
Mount St. Mary's College	CA	24,430	C
Mount St. Mary's College	MD	25,740	C
Mount Senario College	WI	17,750	C
Mount Union College	OH	21,120	C
Mount Vernon Nazarene College	OH	17,027	C
Muhlenberg College	PA	28,170	HC
Murray State Univ	KY	6,672	C
Muskingum College	OH	18,760	C
National-Louis Univ	IL	13,995	NC
Nazareth College of Rochester	NY	22,036	VC
Nebr Wesleyan Univ	NE	18,767	VC
Neumann College	PA	22,040	NC
New College of Florida	FL	8,130	HC+
New England College	NH	20,706	LC
New Jersey City Univ	NJ	9,100	LC
New Jersey Inst of Technology	NJ	14,690	VC
New Mexico Highlands Univ	NM	6,256	NC
New Mexico Inst of Mining and Technology	NM	7,152	VC+
New Mexico State Univ	NM	7,302	C
New York Inst of Technology	NY	21,756	C
New York Univ	NY	35,200	MC
Newberry College	SC	19,670	LC
Newman Univ	KS	14,098	LC
Niagara Univ	NY	22,250	C+
Nicholls State Univ	LA	5,290	NC
Norfolk State Univ	VA	8,382	LC
N Car Agricultural and Technical State Univ	NC	6,659	LC
N Car Central Univ	NC	6,418	LC
N Car State Univ	NC	8,680	HC
N Car Wesleyan College	NC	15,650	LC
North Central College	IL	22,944	C+
N Dak State Univ	ND	7,004	VC
North Georgia College and State Univ	GA	6,322	C+
North Park Univ	IL	24,030	C
Northeastern Illinois Univ	IL	2,898	NC
Northeastern State Univ	OK	4,704	LC
Northeastern Univ	MA	30,078	VC
Northern Arizona Univ	AZ	7,398	C
Northern Illinois Univ	IL	9,545	C
Northern Kentucky Univ	KY	6,352	NC
Northern Mich Univ	MI	9,693	C
Northern State Univ	SD	6,279	LC
Northland College	WI	21,435	C+
Northwest Missouri State Univ	MO	7,922	LC
Northwest Nazarene Univ	ID	18,380	C
Northwestern College	MN	19,816	C+
Northwestern College of Iowa	IA	17,630	C+
Northwestern Okla State Univ	OK	4,542	NC
Northwestern State Univ of Louisiana	LA	5,745	NC
Northwestern Univ	IL	33,615	MC
Norwich Univ	VT	21,064	LC
Notre Dame College	OH	20,425	C
Notre Dame de Namur Univ	CA	26,932	LC
Oakland City Univ	IN	11,286	LC
Oakland Univ	MI	9,418	C
Oakwood College	AL	14,904	C
Oberlin College	OH	33,140	HC+
Occidental College	CA	32,288	HC
Oglethorpe Univ	GA	19,100	LC
Ohio Dominican College	OH	18,100	LC
Ohio Northern Univ	OH	27,765	VC
Ohio Univ	OH	11,769	C
Ohio Wesleyan Univ	OH	29,670	VC+
Okla Baptist Univ	OK	13,878	VC
Okla Christian Univ	OK	16,500	VC
Okla City Univ	OK	15,810	C
Okla Panhandle State Univ	OK	3,812	NC
Okla State Univ	OK	7,650	VC
Old Dominion Univ	VA	9,386	C
Olivet College	MI	17,410	C
Olivet Nazarene Univ	IL	18,444	C
Oral Roberts Univ	OK	18,490	C
Oregon State Univ	OR	9,612	VC
Ottawa Univ	KS	11,800	LC
Ouachita Baptist Univ	AR	16,460	VC
Our Lady of Holy Cross College	LA	5,140	NC
Our Lady of the Lake Univ of San Antonio	TX	17,336	C
Pace Univ	NY	24,200	C
Pacific Lutheran Univ	WA	23,318	VC
Pacific Union College	CA	20,250	VC
Pacific Univ	OR	24,250	C
Paine College	GA	11,896	LC
Palm Beach Atlantic College	FL	23,310	C
Park Univ	MO	9,816	C
Paul Quinn College	TX	8,150	LC
Penn State Univ at Erie/ Behrend College	PA	12,326	C
Penn State Univ/Univ Park Campus	PA	11,126	VC
Pepperdine Univ	CA	32,830	VC
Peru State College	NE	6,342	NC
Pfeiffer Univ	NC	18,580	C
Philadelphia Univ	PA	24,722	C
Philander Smith College	AR	7,380	NC
Piedmont College	GA	16,900	C
Pikeville College	KY	12,000	NC
Pine Manor College	MA	19,344	LC
Pittsburg State Univ	KS	6,228	NC
Pitzer College	CA	33,930	HC
Plymouth State College	NH	11,024	LC
Point Loma Nazarene Univ	CA	21,380	VC
Point Park College	PA	20,290	C
Pomona College	CA	33,960	MC
Pontifical Catholic Univ of PR/Ponce	PR	7,076	
Portland State Univ	OR	11,220	C
Prairie View A&M Univ	TX	3,172	LC
Presbyterian College	SC	23,356	VC
Prescott College	AZ	13,430	C
Princeton Univ	NJ	35,072	MC
Principia College	IL	23,865	C+
Providence College	RI	27,620	HC
Purdue Univ/Calumet	IN	6,630	NC
Purdue Univ/West Lafayette	IN	10,284	VC
Queens College	NC	17,250	C
Quincy Univ	IL	20,450	C
Quinnipiac Univ	CT	27,370	C
Radford Univ	VA	8,302	C
Ramapo College of New Jersey	NJ	13,550	VC
Randolph-Macon College	VA	24,395	C
Randolph-Macon Woman's College	VA	25,820	VC+
Reed College	OR	33,350	HC+
Regis College	MA	26,750	C
Regis Univ	CO	25,740	C+
Reinhardt College	GA	13,300	C
Rensselaer Polytechnic Inst	NY	33,863	HC+
Rhode Island College	RI	8,700	LC
Rhodes College	TN	26,466	HC+
Rice Univ	TX	24,325	MC
Richard Stockton College of New Jersey	NJ	12,165	VC
Rider Univ	NJ	27,400	C
Ripon College	WI	24,180	VC+
Rivier College	NH	24,215	C
Roanoke College	VA	24,689	VC
Roberts Wesleyan College	NY	20,160	C+
Rochester Inst of Technology	NY	26,232	VC+
Rockford College	IL	23,930	C
Rockhurst Univ	MO	20,090	C
Rocky Mountain College	MT	18,113	C
Roger Williams Univ	RI	29,010	C
Rollins College	FL	31,223	HC
Roosevelt Univ	IL	20,240	LC
Rose-Hulman Inst of Technology	IN	27,707	HC+
Rosemont College	PA	24,060	C
Rowan Univ	NJ	12,365	VC
Russell Sage College	NY	23,674	C+
Rust College	MS	7,800	C+
Rutgers, The State Univ of New Jersey New Brunswick Campus	NJ	12,709	C
Rutgers, The State Univ of New Jersey/ CamdenCampus	NJ	6,484	C
Sacred Heart Univ	CT	26,588	VC
Saginaw Valley State Univ	MI	9,465	C
St. Ambrose Univ	IA	19,994	C
St. Andrews Presbyterian College	NC	19,720	LC
St. Anselm College	NH	27,405	C
St. Augustine's College	NC	12,990	C+
St. Bonaventure Univ	NY	21,956	C
St. Cloud State Univ	MN	7,180	C
St. Edward's Univ	TX	17,846	C
St. Francis College	NY	9,610	C
St. Francis Univ	PA	24,486	LC
St. John Fisher College	NY	21,800	C
St. John's Univ	MN	23,640	VC
St. John's Univ	NY	26,660	C
St. Joseph College	CT	25,960	LC
St. Joseph's College	IN	21,640	C
St. Joseph's College of Maine	ME	22,500	LC
St. Joseph's College, New York	NY	9,802	C
St. Joseph's Univ	PA	29,715	VC+
St. Lawrence Univ	NY	32,605	VC
St. Leo Univ	FL	19,250	LC
St. Louis Univ	MO	26,590	VC+
St. Martin's College	WA	20,566	C
St. Mary College	KS	17,298	C
St. Mary-of-the-Woods College	IN	21,320	LC
St. Mary's College	IN	24,474	VC
St. Mary's College	MI	13,314	LC
St. Mary's College of Calif	CA	27,575	C
St. Mary's College of Maryland	MD	14,104	HC
St. Mary's Univ of Minn	MN	19,975	C
St. Mary's Univ of San Antonio	TX	19,735	C
St. Michael's College	VT	26,935	VC
St. Norbert College	WI	23,169	VC
St. Olaf College	MN	25,880	HC
St. Paul's College	VA	13,340	C
St. Peter's College	NJ	22,292	LC
St. Thomas Univ	FL	19,500	LC
St. Vincent College	PA	22,942	VC
St. Xavier Univ	IL	21,104	C
Salem College	NC	23,065	VC
Salem International Univ	WV	17,263	LC
Salem State College	MA	4,481	LC
Salisbury Univ	MD	10,576	VC
Salve Regina Univ	RI	26,460	C
Sam Houston State Univ	TX	6,076	LC
Samford Univ	AL	16,340	VC
San Diego State Univ	CA	9,716	C+
San Francisco State Univ	CA	7,139	LC
San Jose State Univ	CA	8,187	C
Santa Clara Univ	CA	28,371	VC+
Sarah Lawrence College	NY	37,516	HC
Savannah State Univ	GA	2,550	LC
Schreiner Univ	TX	19,254	C
Scripps College	CA	30,400	HC+
Seattle Pacific Univ	WA	22,674	C+
Seattle Univ	WA	24,183	VC
Seton Hall Univ	NJ	26,910	LC
Seton Hill College	PA	21,875	C
Shaw Univ	NC	12,810	C
Shawnee State Univ	OH	8,634	NC
Shenandoah Univ	VA	22,550	NC
Shepherd College	WV	7,062	LC
Shippensburg Univ of Pennsylvania	PA	9,652	C
Shorter College	GA	15,185	C
Siena College	NY	22,685	VC
Siena Heights Univ	MI	16,140	LC
Silver Lake College of the Holy Family	WI	15,516	LC
Simmons College	MA	30,418	VC
Simon's Rock College of Bard	MA	32,450	HC
Simpson College	IA	21,200	C+
Skidmore College	NY	34,201	VC+
Slippery Rock Univ	PA	9,152	LC
Smith College	MA	33,302	HC+
Sonoma State Univ	CA	8,953	C
S Car State Univ	SC	6,586	LC
S Dak State Univ	SD	6,848	C
Southeast Missouri State Univ	MO	8,367	C+
Southeastern College	FL	11,648	LC
Southeastern Louisiana Univ	LA	6,047	LC
Southeastern Okla State Univ	OK	4,917	C
Southern Adventist Univ	TN	15,600	C
Southern Arkansas Univ	AR	5,740	LC
Southern Conn State Univ	CT	10,310	C
Southern Illinois Univ at Carbondale	IL	8,621	C
Southern Illinois Univ Edwardsville	IL	7,869	LC
Southern Methodist Univ	TX	28,349	VC
Southern Nazarene Univ	OK	14,634	NC
Southern Oregon Univ	OR	9,429	C
Southern Univ and A&M College	LA	6,365	C+
Southern Univ at New Orleans	LA	995	NC
Southern Utah Univ	UT	7,254	C
Southern Wesleyan Univ	SC	17,280	C
Southwest Baptist Univ	MO	13,426	LC
Southwest Missouri State Univ	MO	7,600	LC
Southwest State Univ	MN	7,117	LC
Southwest Texas State Univ	TX	8,730	VC
Southwestern Adventist Univ	TX	14,798	C
Southwestern College	KS	17,656	C
Southwestern Okla State Univ	OK	4,801	C
Southwestern Univ	TX	22,550	HC
Spalding Univ	KY	15,196	C
Spelman College	GA	19,215	C+
Spring Arbor Univ	MI	17,976	C
Spring Hill College	AL	23,250	C
Springfield College	MA	24,520	C
Stanford Univ	CA	34,222	MC
SUNY/College at Brockport	NY	10,267	C
SUNY/College at Buffalo	NY	8,025	C
SUNY/College at Cortland	NY	10,564	C
SUNY/College at Fredonia	NY	10,125	C
SUNY/College at Geneseo	NY	9,970	HC
SUNY/College at Old Westbury	NY	9,818	LC
SUNY/College at Oneonta	NY	9,981	C
SUNY/College at Oswego	NY	10,856	C
SUNY/College at Plattsburgh	NY	9,729	C
SUNY/College at Potsdam	NY	10,519	C
SUNY/College at Purchase	NY	10,587	VC
SUNY/College of Environmental Science and Forestry	NY	12,446	VC
SUNY/Univ at Albany	NY	10,997	VC
SUNY/Univ at Binghamton	NY	10,653	HC
SUNY/Univ at Buffalo	NY	11,033	VC
SUNY/Univ at New Paltz	NY	9,685	VC
SUNY/Univ at Stony Brook	NY	10,998	VC
State Univ of West Georgia	GA	7,101	C
Stephen F. Austin State Univ	TX	6,905	C
Stephens College	MO	22,295	C
Sterling College	KS	16,370	VC
Stetson Univ	FL	25,640	VC
Stillman College	AL	11,370	LC
Stonehill College	MA	26,852	HC
Suffolk Univ	MA	26,516	C
Sul Ross State Univ	TX	6,582	LC
Susquehanna Univ	PA	27,270	VC
Swarthmore College	PA	34,538	MC
Sweet Briar College	VA	25,310	VC
Syracuse Univ	NY	30,710	HC
Tabor College	KS	17,600	LC
Talladega College	AL	10,110	LC
Tarleton State Univ	TX	7,160	C
Taylor Univ	IN	21,562	VC+
Temple Univ	PA	14,124	C
Tenn State Univ	TN	7,058	VC
Tenn Tech Univ	TN	6,968	C
Tenn Wesleyan College	TN	13,030	C
Texas A&M Univ	TX	8,988	VC
Texas A&M Univ at Commerce	TX	7,326	C
Texas A&M Univ at Galveston	TX	7,269	C+
Texas A&M Univ at Kingsville	TX	6,446	LC
Texas Christian Univ	TX	19,910	C
Texas Lutheran Univ	TX	17,660	C
Texas Southern Univ	TX	6,576	NC
Texas Tech Univ	TX	8,825	C
Texas Wesleyan Univ	TX	14,710	C
Texas Woman's Univ	TX	5,855	LC
Ohio State Univ	OH	10,819	VC
Thiel College	PA	18,419	LC
Thomas Edison State College	NJ	2,750	SP
Thomas More College	KY	17,700	LC
Thomas More College of Liberal Arts	NH	17,700	C
Thomas Univ	GA	8,770	NC
Tougaloo College	MS	9,200	NC
Touro College	NY	14,950	VC
Towson Univ	MD	11,088	VC
Transylvania Univ	KY	21,780	VC+
Trevecca Nazarene Univ	TN	15,752	C
Trinity Christian College	IL	19,415	C
Trinity College	CT	34,300	HC
Trinity College	DC	21,370	LC
Trinity International Univ	IL	20,640	C+
Trinity Univ	TX	21,444	HC
Tri-State Univ-Main Campus	IN	21,200	C
Troy State Univ	AL	7,696	C
Troy State Univ/Dothan	AL	3,296	C
Truman State Univ	MO	8,568	VC+
Tufts Univ	MA	34,874	MC
Turabo Univ	PR	4,110	
Tusculum College	TN	17,900	LC
Tuskegee Univ	AL	14,600	LC
Union College	KY	15,920	C
Union College	NE	14,650	C
Union College	NY	32,646	HC
Union Univ	TN	18,930	C+
United States Air Force Academy	CO		MC
Universidad Adventista de las Antillas	PR	6,675	
Univ of Akron	OH	10,530	NC
Univ of Alabama	AL	7,402	C
Univ of Alabama at Birmingham	AL	10,110	C
Univ of Alabama at Huntsville	AL	7,916	VC
Univ of Alaska Anchorage	AK	9,100	NC
Univ of Alaska Fairbanks	AK	8,265	NC
Univ of Alaska Southeast	AK	7,900	LC
Univ of Arizona	AZ	8,614	C
Univ of Arkansas	AR	8,334	VC
Univ of Arkansas at Little Rock	AR	5,637	NC
Univ of Arkansas at Monticello	AR	5,940	NC
Univ of Arkansas at Pine Bluff	AR	7,925	C
Univ of Bridgeport	CT	23,020	C
Univ of Calif at Berkeley	CA	14,134	MC
Univ of Calif at Davis	CA	12,796	VC
Univ of Calif at Irvine	CA	11,756	C
Univ of Calif at Los Angeles	CA	13,227	MC
Univ of Calif at Riverside	CA	12,479	C
Univ of Calif at San Diego	CA	11,372	HC
Univ of Calif at Santa Barbara	CA	11,732	VC
Univ of Calif at Santa Cruz	CA	13,655	VC

School	ST	$IS	SR
Univ of Central Arkansas	AR	6,388	C
Univ of Central Florida	FL	8,251	VC
Univ of Central Okla	OK	5,205	C
Univ of Charleston	WV	20,640	C
Univ of Chicago	IL	35,087	MC
Univ of Cincinnati	OH	12,491	LC
Univ of Colo at Colo Springs	CO	9,403	C
Univ of Colo at Denver	CO	3,673	C
Univ of Conn	CT	12,122	VC
Univ of Dallas	TX	22,128	VC+
Univ of Dayton	OH	20,400	VC
Univ of Delaware	DE	10,824	VC
Univ of Denver	CO	28,783	VC
Univ of Detroit Mercy	MI	21,620	LC
Univ of Dubuque	IA	19,990	C
Univ of Evansville	IN	22,865	VC+
Univ of Findlay	OH	23,962	NC
Univ of Georgia	GA	8,656	VC
Univ of Great Falls	MT	15,360	C
Univ of Hartford	CT	28,884	C
Univ of Hawaii at Hilo	HI	6,497	C
Univ of Hawaii at Manoa	HI	7,862	VC
Univ of Houston	TX	8,410	C
Univ of Idaho	ID	7,026	C
Univ of Illinois at Chicago	IL	10,702	VC
Univ of Illinois at Urbana-Champaign	IL	11,316	HC+
Univ of Indianapolis	IN	20,840	C
Univ of Iowa	IA	8,607	C+
Univ of Kansas	KS	7,232	VC
Univ of Kentucky	KY	7,765	C
Univ of La Verne	CA	24,280	C
Univ of Louisiana at Monroe	LA	5,207	NC
Univ of Louisville	KY	7,402	LC
Univ of Maine	ME	10,798	C
Univ of Maine at Augusta	ME	3,928	C
Univ of Maine at Farmington	ME	9,163	C
Univ of Maine at Fort Kent	ME	7,450	LC
Univ of Maine at Machias	ME	7,689	LC
Univ of Maine at Presque Isle	ME	7,964	LC
Univ of Mary	ND	12,900	LC
Univ of Mary Hardin-Baylor	TX	13,929	C
Univ of Maryland/Baltimore County	MD	12,190	VC
Univ of Maryland/College Park	MD	11,959	C
Univ of Maryland/Eastern Shore	MD	9,258	C
Univ of Mass Amherst	MA	10,995	VC
Univ of Mass Boston	MA	4,227	C
Univ of Mass Dartmouth	MA	9,852	C
Univ of Mass Lowell	MA	9,470	VC
Univ of Memphis	TN	7,271	C
Univ of Miami	FL	31,130	HC
Univ of Mich/Ann Arbor	MI	13,003	HC+
Univ of Mich/Dearborn	MI	4,677	VC
Univ of Mich/Flint	MI	4,323	C
Univ of Minn/Duluth	MN	10,436	C
Univ of Minn/Morris	MN	10,716	VC
Univ of Minn/Twin Cities	MN	11,123	VC
Univ of Miss	MS	7,666	C
Univ of Missouri/Columbia	MO	9,803	HC
Univ of Missouri/Kansas City	MO	9,685	VC
Univ of Missouri/Rolla	MO	10,034	C
Univ of Missouri/St. Louis	MO	9,966	C
Univ of Mobile	AL	13,620	LC
Univ of Montana	MT	8,038	C
Univ of Montevallo	AL	7,266	C
Univ of Nebr at Kearney	NE	7,048	NC
Univ of Nebr at Lincoln	NE	8,325	C+
Univ of Nebr at Omaha	NE	6,867	C
Univ of Nevada/Las Vegas	NV	8,281	VC
Univ of Nevada/Reno	NV	8,737	C
Univ of New England	ME	24,110	LC
Univ of New Hampshire	NH	13,207	C
Univ of New Haven	CT	23,860	LC
Univ of New Mexico	NM	8,026	C
Univ of New Orleans	LA	10,160	C
Univ of North Alabama	AL	7,016	NC
Univ of N Car at Asheville	NC	6,896	VC
Univ of N Car at Chapel Hill	NC	8,789	HC
Univ of N Car at Charlotte	NC	7,254	C
Univ of N Car at Greensboro	NC	6,858	C
Univ of N Car at Pembroke	NC	5,914	LC
Univ of N Car at Wilmington	NC	7,769	C
Univ of N Dak	ND	7,067	VC
Univ of North Florida	FL	8,089	VC
Univ of North Texas	TX	7,629	C
Univ of Northern Colo	CO	8,082	C+
Univ of Northern Iowa	IA	7,850	C
Univ of Notre Dame	IN	30,707	MC
Univ of Oregon	OR	9,969	C
Univ of Pennsylvania	PA	34,614	MC
Univ of Pittsburgh at Bradford	PA	12,696	C
Univ of Pittsburgh at Greensburg	PA	12,842	C
Univ of Pittsburgh at Johnstown	PA	13,044	LC
Univ of Pittsburgh at Pittsburgh	PA	13,592	HC

School	ST	$IS	SR
Univ of Portland	OR	24,950	VC
Univ of PR at Humacao	PR	1,245	
Univ of PR/Cayey Univ College	PR	1,245	
Univ of PR/Mayaguez	PR	5,285	
Univ of PR/Rio Piedras	PR	5,510	
Univ of Puget Sound	WA	28,285	HC
Univ of Redlands	CA	29,246	VC
Univ of Rhode Island	RI	12,414	C
Univ of Richmond	VA	27,300	HC
Univ of Rio Grande	OH	8,728	NC
Univ of Rochester	NY	32,979	HC
Univ of St. Francis	IL	19,650	C
Univ of St. Francis	IN	17,790	LC
Univ of St. Thomas	MN	24,044	VC
Univ of St. Thomas	TX	18,752	VC
Univ of San Diego	CA	29,198	HC
Univ of San Francisco	CA	27,302	VC
Univ of Science and Arts of Okla	OK	5,245	C
Univ of Scranton	PA	27,964	C+
Univ of Sioux Falls	SD	16,390	C
Univ of South Alabama	AL	6,976	LC
Univ of S Car at Aiken	SC	7,828	LC
Univ of S Car at Columbia	SC	8,748	VC
Univ of S Car at Spartanburg	SC	7,318	C+
Univ of S Dak	SD	7,036	C
Univ of South Florida	FL	8,154	C
Univ of Southern Calif	CA	33,647	MC
Univ of Southern Colo	CO	7,821	LC
Univ of Southern Indiana	IN	8,655	LC
Univ of Southern Maine	ME	10,569	C
Univ of Southern Miss	MS	6,155	LC
Univ of Tampa	FL	22,612	C
Univ of Tenn at Chattanooga	TN	7,783	C
Univ of Tenn at Knoxville	TN	8,214	C
Univ of Tenn at Martin	TN	8,268	C
Univ of Texas at Arlington	TX	7,192	LC
Univ of Texas at Austin	TX	9,437	HC
Univ of Texas at Dallas	TX	9,305	VC
Univ of Texas at El Paso	TX	5,076	LC
Univ of Texas at San Antonio	TX	9,088	NC
Univ of Texas-Pan American	TX	4,823	C
Univ of the District of Columbia	DC	2,844	NC
Univ of the Incarnate Word	TX	18,478	C
Univ of the Ozarks	AR	13,904	C
Univ of the Pacific	CA	28,255	VC
Univ of the Sacred Heart	PR	5,375	
Univ of the Sciences in Philadelphia	PA	24,826	VC
Univ of the South	TN	27,290	HC
Univ of Toledo	OH	11,206	NC
Univ of Tulsa	OK	19,090	HC
Univ of Utah	UT	7,703	C
Univ of Vermont	VT	14,761	C+
Univ of Virginia	VA	9,391	HC+
Univ of Virginia's College at Wise	VA	8,302	C
Univ of Washington	WA	10,361	VC
Univ of West Alabama	AL	6,048	C
Univ of West Florida	FL	7,518	C
Univ of Wisc/Eau Claire	WI	7,032	VC
Univ of Wisc/Green Bay	WI	7,148	C
Univ of Wisc/La Crosse	WI	7,250	VC
Univ of Wisc/Milwaukee	WI	8,907	LC
Univ of Wisc/Oshkosh	WI	6,130	LC
Univ of Wisc/Parkside	WI	6,160	LC
Univ of Wisc/Platteville	WI	7,282	C
Univ of Wisc/River Falls	WI	6,356	LC
Univ of Wisc/Stevens Point	WI	7,116	C
Univ of Wisc/Superior	WI	7,051	C+
Univ of Wisc/Whitewater	WI	6,937	C
Univ of Wyoming	WY	7,143	LC
Upper Iowa Univ	IA	17,438	C
Ursinus College	PA	31,350	VC
Ursuline College	OH	19,430	LC
Utah State Univ	UT	6,771	C
Utica College of Syracuse Univ	NY	24,400	LC
Valdosta State Univ	GA	6,988	C
Valley City State Univ	ND		LC
Valparaiso Univ	IN	23,570	VC+
Vanderbilt Univ	TN	34,482	MC
Vanguard Univ of Southern Calif	CA	20,212	C
Vassar College	NY	33,450	MC
Villa Julie College	MD	16,026	C
Villanova Univ	PA	31,997	HC
Virginia Commonwealth Univ	VA	9,030	C
Virginia Intermont College	VA	17,510	C
Virginia Military Inst	VA	9,968	C+
Virginia Polytechnic Inst and State Univ	VA	7,652	C
Virginia State Univ	VA	8,182	LC
Virginia Union Univ	VA	15,358	LC
Virginia Wesleyan College	VA	22,350	LC
Viterbo Univ	WI	18,043	C
Voorhees College	SC	9,976	C+
Wabash College	IN	25,335	HC
Wagner College	NY	27,000	C

School	ST	$IS	SR
Wake Forest Univ	NC	30,290	MC
Walla Walla College	WA	20,925	C
Walsh Univ	OH	16,880	C
Warner Pacific College	OR	20,370	LC
Warren Wilson College	NC	19,968	C
Wartburg College	IA	21,165	VC
Washburn Univ of Topeka	KS	6,766	NC
Washington and Jefferson College	PA	26,255	VC
Washington and Lee Univ	VA	25,095	MC
Washington College	MD	28,040	VC
Washington State Univ	WA	9,388	C
Washington Univ in St. Louis	MO	34,593	MC
Wayland Baptist Univ	TX	11,271	NC
Wayne State Univ	MI	6,720	C
Waynesburg College	PA	17,610	LC
Weber State Univ	UT	6,897	NC
Webster Univ	MO	19,804	VC
Wellesley College	MA	33,394	MC
Wells College	NY	19,350	VC
Wesley College	DE	17,869	C
Wesleyan College	GA	17,050	VC
Wesleyan Univ	CT	3,405	MC
West Chester Univ of Pennsylvania	PA	9,792	VC
West Liberty State College	WV	6,056	LC
West Texas A&M Univ	TX	6,538	C
West Virginia State College	WV	6,264	NC
West Virginia Univ	WV	8,304	C
West Virginia Univ Inst of Technology	WV	7,518	NC
West Virginia Wesleyan College	WV	22,920	C
Western Carolina Univ	NC	5,667	C
Western Conn State Univ	CT	10,074	C
Western Illinois Univ	IL	9,571	C
Western Kentucky Univ	KY	6,834	C
Western Maryland College	MD	26,000	VC
Western Mich Univ	MI	10,016	C
Western New England College	MA	23,882	C
Western New Mexico Univ	NM	5,950	LC
Western Oregon Univ	OR	8,829	C
Western State College of Colo	CO	7,585	LC
Western Washington Univ	WA	8,624	VC
Westfield State College	MA	8,394	C
Westminster College	MO	19,990	C+
Westminster College	PA	22,960	C
Westminster College	UT	17,226	C
Westmont College	CA	29,748	VC
Wheaton College	IL	21,934	HC
Wheaton College	MA	32,940	VC
Wheeling Jesuit Univ	WV	22,660	C
Whitman College	WA	29,086	HC
Whittier College	CA	29,108	C
Whitworth College	WA	23,938	VC
Wichita State Univ	KS	6,879	C
Widener Univ	PA	26,920	C
Wilberforce Univ	OH	14,937	LC
Wiley College	TX	8,100	LC
Wilkes Univ	PA	25,800	LC
Willamette Univ	OR	29,422	VC+
William Carey College	MS	10,150	LC
William Jewell College	MO	17,150	VC
William Paterson Univ of New Jersey	NJ	11,000	LC
William Penn Univ	IA	17,575	C
William Woods Univ	MO	19,390	LC
Williams Baptist College	AR	10,750	C
Williams College	MA	32,270	MC
Wilmington College	OH	21,826	C
Wilson College	PA	21,337	LC
Wingate Univ	NC	19,140	C
Winona State Univ	MN	8,570	C
Winston-Salem State Univ	NC	5,927	LC
Winthrop Univ	SC	9,106	C
Wisc Lutheran College	WI	19,216	VC
Wittenberg Univ	OH	28,766	VC
Wofford College	SC	23,995	VC
Worcester Polytechnic Inst	MA	34,480	HC+
Worcester State College	MA	7,901	LC
Wright State Univ	OH	9,141	LC
Xavier Univ	OH	23,880	C
Xavier Univ of Louisiana	LA	17,000	LC
Yale Univ	CT	34,030	MC
Yeshiva Univ	NY	21,400	C
York College	NE	13,500	C
York College of Pennsylvania	PA	12,550	VC
Youngstown State Univ	OH	9,318	NC

BIOMEDICAL ENGINEERING

School	ST	$IS	SR
Boston Univ	MA	34,358	MC
Case Western Reserve Univ	OH	27,418	C
Catholic Univ of America	DC	29,332	VC
Columbia Univ/Fu Foundation School of Engineering and Applied Science	NY	35,190	MC
Drexel Univ	PA	27,657	VC
Duke Univ	NC	34,396	MC
Florida State Univ	FL	7,835	HC
Johns Hopkins Univ	MD	35,226	MC
Louisiana Tech Univ	LA	6,506	C
Marquette Univ	WI	24,836	C+
Mercer Univ	GA	24,130	VC
Mich Tech Univ	MI	11,088	VC
Milwaukee School of Engineering	WI	25,680	VC+
New York Inst of Technology	NY	21,756	C
Northwestern Univ	IL	33,615	MC
Purdue Univ/West Lafayette	IN	10,284	VC
Rensselaer Polytechnic Inst	NY	33,863	HC+
St. Louis Univ	MO	26,590	VC+
Tufts Univ	MA	34,874	MC
Tulane Univ	LA	34,013	HC+
Univ of Akron	OH	10,530	NC
Univ of Alabama at Birmingham	AL	10,110	C
Univ of Conn	CT	12,122	VC
Univ of Hartford	CT	28,884	C
Univ of Iowa	IA	8,607	C+
Univ of Miami	FL	31,130	HC
Univ of Rhode Island	RI	12,414	C
Univ of Rochester	NY	32,979	HC
Univ of Southern Calif	CA	33,647	MC
Univ of Utah	UT	7,703	C
Univ of Vermont	VT	14,761	C+
Univ of Wisc/Madison	WI	8,262	VC
Washington Univ in St. Louis	MO	34,593	MC
Worcester Polytechnic Inst	MA	34,480	HC+
Wright State Univ	OH	9,141	LC
Yale Univ	CT	34,030	MC

BIOMEDICAL EQUIPMENT TECHNOLOGY

School	ST	$IS	SR
Andrews Univ	MI	17,696	LC
Thomas Edison State College	NJ	2,750	SP
Univ of Houston	TX	8,410	C
Univ of Vermont	VT	14,761	C+

BIOMEDICAL SCIENCE

School	ST	$IS	SR
Andrews Univ	MI	17,696	LC
Brown Univ	RI	34,973	MC
Cal State, Northridge	CA	7,781	C
LIU/C.W. Post Campus	NY	25,380	C
Lynchburg College	VA	23,405	C
Marquette Univ	WI	24,836	C+
MCP Hahnemann Univ	PA	18,510	SP
Okla State Univ	OK	7,650	VC
Oral Roberts Univ	OK	18,490	C
Rutgers, The State Univ of New Jersey New Brunswick Campus	NJ	12,709	C
St. Francis College	NY	9,610	C
Texas A&M Univ	TX	8,988	VC
Univ of Mich/Ann Arbor	MI	13,003	HC+
Univ of Miss	MS	7,666	C
Univ of New England	ME	24,110	LC
Univ of South Alabama	AL	6,976	LC
Univ of Vermont	VT	14,761	C+

BIOMETRICS AND BIOSTATISTICS

School	ST	$IS	SR
Cornell Univ	NY	34,614	MC
La Sierra Univ	CA	19,260	LC
Southwestern Adventist Univ	TX	14,798	C

BIOPHYSICS

School	ST	$IS	SR
Andrews Univ	MI	17,696	LC
Brown Univ	RI	34,973	MC
Centenary College of Louisiana	LA	21,600	C+
Columbia Univ/Columbia College	NY	35,190	MC
Harvard Univ/Harvard College	MA	34,269	MC
Illinois Inst of Technology	IL	25,182	HC+
Iowa State Univ	IA	8,108	VC
Johns Hopkins Univ	MD	35,226	MC
La Sierra Univ	CA	19,260	LC
Okla City Univ	OK	15,810	C
Oregon State Univ	OR	9,612	VC
Pacific Union College	CA	20,250	VC
Rensselaer Polytechnic Inst	NY	33,863	HC+
St. Bonaventure Univ	NY	21,956	C
St. Mary's Univ of Minn	MN	19,975	C
Southwestern Okla State Univ	OK	4,801	C
SUNY/College at Geneseo	NY	9,970	HC
SUNY/Univ at Buffalo	NY	11,033	VC
Temple Univ	PA	14,124	C
Univ of Calif at San Diego	CA	11,372	HC
Univ of Conn	CT	12,122	VC
Univ of Houston	TX	8,410	C
Univ of Illinois at Urbana-Champaign	IL	11,316	HC+
Univ of Mich/Ann Arbor	MI	13,003	HC+
Univ of Pennsylvania	PA	34,614	MC

ST = STATE $IS = IN-STATE COSTS SR = SELECTOR RATING

School	ST	$IS	SR
Univ of Scranton	PA	27,964	C+
Univ of Southern Calif	CA	33,647	MC
Univ of Southern Indiana	IN	8,655	LC
Walla Walla College	WA	20,925	C
Washington Univ in St. Louis	MO	34,593	MC
Wellesley College	MA	33,394	MC
Yale Univ	CT	34,030	MC

BIOPSYCHOLOGY

School	ST	$IS	SR
Columbia Univ/Barnard College	NY	33,694	MC
Nebr Wesleyan Univ	NE	18,767	VC
Philadelphia Univ	PA	24,722	C
Rider Univ	NJ	27,400	C
Russell Sage College	NY	23,674	C+
Tufts Univ	MA	34,874	MC
Univ of Calif at Santa Barbara	CA	11,732	VC
Univ of Mich/Ann Arbor	MI	13,003	HC+
Vassar College	NY	33,450	MC
Washington Univ in St. Louis	MO	34,593	MC

BIOTECHNOLOGY

School	ST	$IS	SR
Cabrini College	PA	25,950	LC
Calif State Polytechnic Univ, Pomona	CA	8,615	C
Calvin College	MI	20,050	NC
CUNY/York College	NY	3,292	NC
Elizabethtown College	PA	26,000	VC
Marywood Univ	PA	24,639	C
Minn State Univ, Mankato	MN	7,296	LC
Missouri Southern State College	MO	6,666	C
Montana State Univ-Bozeman	MT	8,431	C
N Dak State Univ	ND	7,004	VC
Plymouth State College	NH	11,024	LC
Purdue Univ/Calumet	IN	6,630	NC
Quinnipiac Univ	CT	27,370	C
Rochester Inst of Technology	NY	26,232	VC+
Rutgers, The State Univ of New Jersey New Brunswick Campus	NJ	12,709	C
Springfield College	MA	24,520	C
SUNY/Univ at Buffalo	NY	11,033	VC
Tufts Univ	MA	34,874	MC
Univ of Delaware	DE	10,824	VC
Univ of Maine	ME	10,798	C
Univ of New Hampshire	NH	13,207	C
Univ of New Haven	CT	23,860	LC
Univ of Northern Iowa	IA	7,850	C
Univ of PR/Mayaguez	PR	5,285	
Univ of Southern Colo	CO	7,821	LC
Univ of Wisc/River Falls	WI	6,356	LC
Villa Julie College	MD	16,026	C
William Paterson Univ of New Jersey	NJ	11,000	LC
William Penn Univ	IA	17,575	C
Worcester Polytechnic Inst	MA	34,480	HC+
Worcester State College	MA	7,901	LC

BOTANY

School	ST	$IS	SR
Andrews Univ	MI	17,696	LC
Auburn Univ	AL	5,510	C
Ball State Univ	IN	8,660	C
Brigham Young Univ	UT	7,840	HC
Calif State Polytechnic Univ, Pomona	CA	8,615	C
Cal State, Long Beach	CA	7,400	LC
Colo State Univ	CO	9,672	C
Conn College	CT	33,585	MC
Cornell Univ	NY	34,614	MC
Delaware State Univ	DE	8,104	LC
Eastern Mich Univ	MI	9,855	C
Eastern Washington Univ	WA	7,972	LC
Hampshire College	MA	33,881	HC+
Howard Univ	DC	15,522	LC
Humboldt State Univ	CA	8,582	C
Idaho State Univ	ID	7,030	C+
Iowa State Univ	IA	8,108	VC
Juniata College	PA	26,080	VC
Kent State Univ	OH	11,104	C
Marlboro College	VT	26,410	VC+
Mars Hill College	NC	18,600	LC
Miami Univ	OH	12,885	VC+
Mich State Univ	MI	10,386	VC
N Car State Univ	NC	8,680	HC
N Dak State Univ	ND	7,004	VC
Northern Arizona Univ	AZ	7,398	C
Northern Mich Univ	MI	9,693	C
Northwest Missouri State Univ	MO	7,922	LC
Ohio Wesleyan Univ	OH	29,670	VC+
Okla State Univ	OK	7,650	VC
Oregon State Univ	OR	9,612	VC
Rutgers, The State Univ of New Jersey New Brunswick Campus	NJ	12,709	C
San Francisco State Univ	CA	7,139	LC
San Jose State Univ	CA	8,187	C
Southern Illinois Univ at Carbondale	IL	8,621	C
Southwest Texas State Univ	TX	8,730	VC
SUNY/College of Environmental Science and Forestry	NY	12,446	VC
Texas A&M Univ	TX	8,988	VC
Texas A&M Univ at Commerce	TX	7,326	C
Univ of Akron	OH	10,530	NC
Univ of Arkansas	AR	8,334	VC
Univ of Calif at Davis	CA	12,796	VC
Univ of Calif at Los Angeles	CA	13,227	MC
Univ of Calif at Riverside	CA	12,479	C
Univ of Florida	FL	7,874	HC
Univ of Georgia	GA	8,656	VC
Univ of Great Falls	MT	15,360	C
Univ of Hawaii at Manoa	HI	7,862	VC
Univ of Idaho	ID	7,026	C
Univ of Kentucky	KY	7,765	C
Univ of Maine	ME	10,798	C
Univ of Mich/Ann Arbor	MI	13,003	HC+
Univ of Minn/Twin Cities	MN	11,123	VC
Univ of Montana	MT	8,038	C
Univ of Okla	OK	7,616	VC
Univ of Tenn at Knoxville	TN	8,214	C
Univ of Texas at Austin	TX	9,437	HC
Univ of Vermont	VT	14,761	C+
Univ of Washington	WA	10,361	VC
Univ of Wisc/Madison	WI	8,262	VC
Univ of Wisc/Milwaukee	WI	8,907	LC
Univ of Wyoming	WY	7,143	LC
Weber State Univ	UT	6,897	NC
Western New Mexico Univ	NM	5,950	LC

BRITISH STUDIES

School	ST	$IS	SR
Bard College	NY	33,912	HC
Vassar College	NY	33,450	MC

BROADCASTING

School	ST	$IS	SR
Abilene Christian Univ	TX	16,300	VC
Alabama State Univ	AL	6,404	C
Arizona State Univ-Main	AZ	7,726	C
Asbury College	KY	18,540	VC
Ashland Univ	OH	22,182	LC
Baldwin-Wallace College	OH	22,010	VC+
Ball State Univ	IN	8,660	C
Barry Univ	FL	24,100	LC
Baylor Univ	TX	18,298	VC+
Bemidji State Univ	MN	7,957	C
Black Hills State Univ	SD	6,652	LC
Boston Univ	MA	34,358	MC
Bowie State Univ	MD	9,300	C+
Bowling Green State Univ	OH	10,794	C
Cal State, Fullerton	CA	5,440	LC
Cal State, Hayward	CA	7,400	LC
Cameron Univ	OK	5,560	NC
Campbell Univ	NC	16,599	C
Cedarville Univ	OH	17,553	VC
Central Methodist College	MO	16,460	C
Central Mich Univ	MI	8,355	C
Central Missouri State Univ	MO	7,920	C
Central State Univ	OH	8,922	C+
Central Washington Univ	WA	8,985	LC
Chicago State Univ	IL	8,851	C+
CUNY/Brooklyn College	NY	3,403	LC
College of the Ozarks	MO	2,650	C+
Concord College	WV	7,122	C+
Dordt College	IA	18,100	C+
Drake Univ	IA	22,830	VC
Drury Univ	MO	15,250	VC
Eastern Kentucky Univ	KY	6,552	C
Eastern Nazarene College	MA	19,433	LC
Eastern Washington Univ	WA	7,972	LC
Edinboro Univ of Pennsylvania	PA	9,328	LC
Elon Univ	NC	19,430	VC
Emerson College	MA	29,978	HC
Evangel Univ	MO	14,050	C
Florida State Univ	FL	7,835	HC
Fontbonne Univ	MO	18,046	C
Fordham Univ	NY	30,710	VC
Freed-Hardeman Univ	TN	14,290	VC
Geneva College	PA	19,990	C+
George Washington Univ	DC	32,170	HC
Georgia Southern Univ	GA	6,958	C
Gonzaga Univ	WA	24,276	HC+
Grand Valley State Univ	MI	10,040	C
Grand View College	IA	17,596	NC
Harding Univ	AR	13,528	VC
Hastings College	NE	17,854	C+
Hofstra Univ	NY	23,252	C
Howard Univ	DC	15,522	LC
Illinois College	IL	16,234	C
Indiana State Univ	IN	8,461	LC
Indiana Univ-Purdue Univ Fort Wayne	IN	3,166	LC
Ithaca College	NY	28,719	HC
John Brown Univ	AR	15,080	VC
Kent State Univ	OH	11,104	C
Lewis Univ	IL	20,960	C
Lincoln Memorial Univ	TN	12,620	LC
LIU/Brooklyn Campus	NY	22,290	C
LIU/C.W. Post Campus	NY	25,380	C
Loras College	IA	22,994	C+
Mansfield Univ	PA	9,648	C
Marietta College	OH	24,580	C
Marquette Univ	WI	24,836	C+
McNeese State Univ	LA	5,259	LC
Mercyhurst College	PA	20,694	C
Messiah College	PA	23,180	VC
Miami Univ	OH	12,885	VC+
Minot State Univ	ND	5,466	LC
Montclair State Univ	NJ	10,287	LC
Moorhead State Univ	MN	7,000	LC
Morris College	SC	9,995	LC
Murray State Univ	KY	6,672	C
North Central College	IL	22,944	C+
Northern Arizona Univ	AZ	7,398	C
Northern Mich Univ	MI	9,693	C
Northwest Missouri State Univ	MO	7,922	LC
Northwestern College	MN	19,816	C+
Northwestern Okla State Univ	OK	4,542	NC
Northwestern Univ	IL	33,615	MC
Ohio Northern Univ	OH	27,765	VC
Ohio Univ	OH	11,769	C
Ohio Wesleyan Univ	OH	29,670	VC+
Okla Baptist Univ	OK	13,878	VC
Okla Christian Univ	OK	16,500	VC
Okla City Univ	OK	15,810	C
Oral Roberts Univ	OK	18,490	C
Otterbein College	OH	23,439	C
Penn State Univ/Univ Park Campus	PA	11,126	VC
Point Park College	PA	20,290	C
Prairie View A&M Univ	TX	3,172	LC
Purdue Univ/Calumet	IN	6,630	NC
Radford Univ	VA	8,302	C
Roosevelt Univ	IL	20,240	LC
Rowan Univ	NJ	12,365	VC
St. Cloud State Univ	MN	7,180	C
San Diego State Univ	CA	9,716	C+
San Francisco State Univ	CA	7,139	LC
San Jose State Univ	CA	8,187	C
Savannah State Univ	GA	2,550	LC
Shaw Univ	NC	12,810	C
Sojourner-Douglass College	MD	4,170	LC
Southern Adventist Univ	TN	15,600	C
Southern Arkansas Univ	AR	5,740	LC
Southern Illinois Univ at Carbondale	IL	8,621	C
Southern Methodist Univ	TX	28,349	VC
Southwest Missouri State Univ	MO	7,600	LC
Southwest Texas State Univ	TX	8,730	VC
Southwestern Adventist Univ	TX	14,798	C
Spring Hill College	AL	23,250	C
SUNY/College at Buffalo	NY	8,025	C
SUNY/College at Oswego	NY	10,856	C
SUNY/Univ at New Paltz	NY	9,685	VC
Stephen F. Austin State Univ	TX	6,905	C
Suffolk Univ	MA	26,516	C
Syracuse Univ	NY	00,710	HC
Temple Univ	PA	14,124	C
Texas A&M Univ at Commerce	TX	7,326	C
Texas Christian Univ	TX	19,910	C
Texas Tech Univ	TX	8,825	C
Toccoa Falls College	GA	14,220	C
Trevecca Nazarene Univ	TN	15,752	C
Troy State Univ	AL	7,696	C
Union Univ	TN	18,930	C+
Univ of Akron	OH	10,530	NC
Univ of Central Florida	FL	8,251	VC
Univ of Central Okla	OK	5,205	C
Univ of Cincinnati	OH	12,491	LC
Univ of Colo at Boulder	CO	9,255	VC
Univ of Dayton	OH	20,400	VC
Univ of Findlay	OH	23,962	NC
Univ of Georgia	GA	8,656	VC
Univ of Illinois at Urbana-Champaign	IL	11,316	HC+
Univ of Indianapolis	IN	20,840	C
Univ of Iowa	IA	8,607	C+
Univ of Kansas	KS	7,232	VC
Univ of La Verne	CA	24,280	C
Univ of Louisiana at Lafayette	LA	5,200	C
Univ of Miami	FL	31,130	HC
Univ of Miss	MS	7,666	C
Univ of Missouri/Columbia	MO	9,803	HC
Univ of Nebr at Kearney	NE	7,048	NC
Univ of Nebr at Lincoln	NE	8,325	C+
Univ of Nebr at Omaha	NE	6,867	C
Univ of N Car at Greensboro	NC	6,858	C
Univ of N Car at Pembroke	NC	5,914	LC
Univ of Northern Iowa	IA	7,850	C
Univ of Okla	OK	7,616	VC
Univ of S Car at Columbia	SC	8,748	VC
Univ of Southern Calif	CA	33,647	MC
Univ of Southern Colo	CO	7,821	LC
Univ of Southern Indiana	IN	8,655	LC
Univ of Tenn at Knoxville	TN	8,214	C
Univ of Texas at Arlington	TX	7,192	LC
Univ of Wisc/Eau Claire	WI	7,032	VC
Valparaiso Univ	IN	23,570	VC+
Wartburg College	IA	21,165	VC
Washington State Univ	WA	9,388	C
Wayne State Univ	MI	6,720	C
Waynesburg College	PA	17,610	LC
Webster Univ	MO	19,804	VC
West Texas A&M Univ	TX	6,538	C
West Virginia Univ	WV	8,304	C
Western Kentucky Univ	KY	6,834	C
Western Mich Univ	MI	10,016	C
Westminster College	PA	22,960	C
Winona State Univ	MN	8,570	C
York College of Pennsylvania	PA	12,550	VC
Youngstown State Univ	OH	9,318	NC

BUSINESS ADMINISTRATION AND MANAGEMENT

School	ST	$IS	SR
Adams State College	CO	7,468	C
Adelphi Univ	NY	23,320	VC
Adrian College	MI	19,670	C
Alabama A&M Univ	AL	5,100	LC
Alabama State Univ	AL	6,404	C
Alaska Pacific Univ	AK	16,450	C
Albertson College of Idaho	ID	23,900	VC
Albright College	PA	27,642	C
Alcorn State Univ	MS	5,594	LC
Alderson-Broaddus College	WV	19,640	C
Alfred Univ	NY	27,212	C+
Alice Lloyd College	KY	1,785	VC
Allen Univ	SC	9,600	NC
Alma College	MI	22,586	VC
Alvernia College	PA	20,790	C
Alverno College	WI	16,930	LC
American InterContinental Univ	GA	12,000	NC
American International College	MA	22,268	LC
American Univ	DC	31,544	VC+
Anderson Univ	IN	19,430	LC
Andrews Univ	MI	17,696	LC
Angelo State Univ	TX	7,028	C
Anna Maria College	MA	22,800	LC
Aquinas College	MI	20,052	C+
Aquinas College	TN	10,050	LC
Arcadia Univ	PA	26,650	C
Arkansas Baptist College	AR	5,530	LC
Arkansas State Univ	AR	7,480	C
Arkansas Tech Univ	AR	6,256	C
Asbury College	KY	18,540	VC
Ashland Univ	OH	22,182	LC
Assumption College	MA	26,320	C
Atlantic Union College	MA	34,034	LC
Auburn Univ	AL	5,510	C
Auburn Univ Montgomery	AL	5,330	NC
Audrey Cohen College	NY	17,715	C
Augsburg College	MN	22,978	C
Augusta State Univ	GA	2,282	C
Augustana College	IL	24,117	VC+
Augustana College	SD	20,760	VC
Aurora Univ	IL	18,551	C
Austin College	TX	22,150	VC+
Austin Peay State Univ	TN	5,814	LC
Averett Univ	VA	17,980	LC
Avila College	MO	17,720	C
Azusa Pacific Univ	CA	22,422	VC
Babson College	MA	33,290	HC
Baker College of Flint	MI	7,720	NC
Baker Univ	KS	14,780	C+
Baldwin-Wallace College	OH	22,010	VC+
Ball State Univ	IN	8,660	C
Barber-Scotia College	NC	13,100	C
Bartlesville Wesleyan College	OK	14,100	LC
Barton College	NC	16,834	LC
Bay Path College	MA	22,308	C
Baylor Univ	TX	18,298	VC+
Becker College	MA	21,230	LC
Belhaven College	MS	16,040	C+
Bellarmine Univ	KY	20,440	VC
Bellevue Univ	NE	4,125	NC
Belmont Abbey College	NC	19,630	LC
Belmont Univ	TN	19,066	VC
Beloit College	WI	27,482	HC
Bemidji State Univ	MN	7,957	C
Benedict College	SC	12,662	LC
Benedictine College	KS	18,485	LC
Benedictine Univ	IL	21,330	C
Bennett College	NC	11,200	C
Bentley College	MA	31,060	HC
Berea College	KY	4,070	VC
Berkeley College	NY	21,545	LC
Berkeley College of New York City	NY	12,500	LC
Berry College	GA	18,850	C
Bethany College	KS	16,602	C+
Bethel College	IN	17,650	LC
Bethel College	KS	17,355	C+
Bethel College	MN	22,740	VC
Bethel College	TN	12,980	C
Bethune-Cookman College	FL	15,746	C
Biola Univ	CA	21,902	VC

School	ST	$IS	SR
Birmingham-Southern College	AL	22,960	C
Black Hills State Univ	SD	6,652	LC
Blackburn College	IL	13,690	C
Bloomfield College	NJ	17,000	C
Bloomsburg Univ of Pennsylvania	PA	9,434	C
Blue Mountain College	MS	9,100	LC
Bluefield College	VA	14,200	C
Bluefield State College	WV	2,178	LC
Bluffton College	OH	20,644	C
Boise State Univ	ID	6,531	LC
Boricua College	NY	7,375	C
Boston College	MA	33,330	MC
Boston Univ	MA	34,358	MC
Bowie State Univ	MD	9,300	C+
Bowling Green State Univ	OH	10,794	C
Bradley Univ	IL	20,970	VC
Brenau Univ Women's College	GA	20,100	C
Brescia Univ	KY	14,225	C
Brewton-Parker College	GA	10,810	LC
Briar Cliff Univ	IA	18,657	LC
Bridgewater College	VA	22,950	C
Brigham Young Univ	UT	7,840	HC
Bryan College	TN	16,400	VC
Bryant College	RI	25,980	VC
Bucknell Univ	PA	31,096	HC
Buena Vista Univ	IA	22,828	C
Cabrini College	PA	25,950	LC
Caldwell College	NJ	20,940	LC
Calif Baptist Univ	CA	16,736	C
Calif Lutheran Univ	CA	23,500	LC
Calif Maritime Academy	CA	12,256	C
Calif Polytechnic State Univ	CA	8,747	VC
Calif State Polytechnic Univ, Pomona	CA	8,615	C
Cal State, Bakersfield	CA	6,090	LC
Cal State, Chico	CA	8,598	LC
Cal State, Dominguez Hills	CA	5,840	LC
Cal State, Fresno	CA	7,762	C
Cal State, Fullerton	CA	5,440	LC
Cal State, Hayward	CA	7,400	LC
Cal State, Long Beach	CA	7,400	LC
Cal State, Los Angeles	CA	5,050	C
Cal State, Northridge	CA	7,781	C
Cal State, Sacramento	CA	7,488	C
Cal State, San Bernardino	CA	6,516	C
Cal State, San Marcos	CA	1,736	LC
Cal State, Stanislaus	CA	8,895	C
Calif Univ of Pennsylvania	PA	10,388	C
Calumet College of St. Joseph	IN	7,500	LC
Calvin College	MI	20,050	NC
Cameron Univ	OK	5,560	NC
Campbell Univ	NC	16,599	C
Campbellsville Univ	KY	14,340	C
Canisius College	NY	24,696	C+
Capital Univ	OH	23,630	C
Cardinal Stritch Univ	WI	17,620	C
Caribbean Univ	PR	3,000	
Carlos Albizu Univ	FL	9,309	C
Carlow College	PA	19,366	C
Carnegie Mellon Univ	PA	32,682	MC
Carroll College	MT	19,140	C
Carroll College	WI	21,170	C
Carson-Newman College	TN	16,490	C
Carthage College	WI	23,670	C
Cascade College	OR	14,800	NC
Case Western Reserve Univ	OH	27,418	C
Castleton State College	VT	10,922	LC
Catawba College	NC	19,620	C
Catholic Univ of America	DC	29,332	VC
Cedar Crest College	PA	25,145	C+
Cedarville Univ	OH	17,553	VC
Centenary College	NJ	22,430	C
Centenary College of Louisiana	LA	21,600	C+
Central College	IA	21,206	C
Central Conn State Univ	CT	10,404	C
Central Methodist College	MO	16,460	C
Central Mich Univ	MI	8,355	C
Central Missouri State Univ	MO	7,920	C
Central State Univ	OH	8,922	C+
Central Univ of Bayamon	PR	3,335	
Central Washington Univ	WA	8,985	LC
Chadron State College	NE	6,211	NC
Chaminade Univ of Honolulu	HI	17,370	C
Champlain College	VT	19,680	C
Chapman Univ	CA	30,218	VC
Charleston Southern Univ	SC	17,122	C
Chatham College	PA	25,454	C+
Chestnut Hill College	PA	24,790	LC
Cheyney Univ of Pennsylvania	PA	9,993	C
Chicago State Univ	IL	8,851	C+
Christian Brothers Univ	TN	19,820	VC
Christian Heritage College	CA	18,000	LC
Christopher Newport Univ	VA	8,862	VC
Citadel, The	SC	9,126	C
City Univ	WA	7,425	NC
CUNY/Brooklyn College	NY	3,403	LC
CUNY/City College	NY	3,309	LC
CUNY/College of Staten Island	NY	3,358	NC
CUNY/Herbert H. Lehman College	NY	3,320	LC
CUNY/Medgar Evers College	NY	3,282	NC
CUNY/York College	NY	3,292	NC
Claflin Univ	SC	12,735	C+
Clarion Univ of Pennsylvania	PA	11,272	LC
Clark Atlanta Univ	GA	17,174	C
Clark Univ	MA	29,170	HC
Clarke College	IA	20,625	C+
Clarkson College	NE	12,178	C
Clarkson Univ	NY	29,884	VC
Clayton College and State Univ	GA	2,322	C+
Clearwater Christian College	FL	13,160	LC
Cleary College	MI	10,350	LC
Clemson Univ	SC	7,600	C
Coastal Carolina Univ	SC	9,220	C
Coe College	IA	24,750	VC
Coker College	SC	20,120	C
Colby-Sawyer College	NH	27,850	LC
College Misericordia	PA	23,380	LC
College of Charleston	SC	8,350	HC
College of Mount St. Vincent	NY	24,230	C
College of Mount St. Joseph	OH	20,290	C
College of New Jersey	NJ	13,425	HC
College of New Rochelle	NY	20,000	C
College of Notre Dame of Maryland	MD	23,100	LC
College of Our Lady of the Elms	MA	20,644	C
College of St. Catherine	MN	22,324	VC
College of St. Elizabeth	NJ	22,510	C
College of St. Joseph	VT	17,400	NC
College of St. Mary	NE	18,726	C
College of St. Rose	NY	19,084	C
College of St. Scholastica	MN	22,378	C+
College of Santa Fe	NM	20,250	LC
College of the Ozarks	MO	2,650	C+
College of the Southwest	NM	8,456	NC
College of William and Mary	VA	10,002	MC
Colo Christian Univ	CO	17,714	C
Colo State Univ	CO	9,672	C
Colo Technical Univ	CO	9,425	LC
Columbia College	MO	15,082	C
Columbia College	SC	19,050	LC
Columbia Union College	MD	19,027	C+
Columbus State Univ	GA	7,228	LC
Concord College	WV	7,122	C+
Concordia College	AL	9,307	NC
Concordia College	NY	19,200	VC
Concordia College/Moorhead	MN	18,835	C
Concordia Univ	CA	22,290	C
Concordia Univ	MI	20,500	C
Concordia Univ	MN	19,912	C
Concordia Univ	OR	20,500	LC
Concordia Univ at Austin	TX	16,740	LC
Concordia Univ Nebr	NE	17,770	C
Concordia Univ Wisc	WI	16,600	LC
Concordia Univ, River Forest	IL	20,000	LC
Converse College	SC	21,990	VC
Coppin State College	MD	9,133	LC
Cornerstone Univ and Grand Rapids Baptist Seminary	MI	18,092	C
Covenant College	GA	21,970	C+
Creighton Univ	NE	23,476	VC
Crichton College	TN	12,680	LC
Culver-Stockton College	MO	15,400	LC
Cumberland College	KY	14,864	C
Cumberland Univ	TN	11,970	LC
Curry College	MA	26,025	LC
Daemen College	NY	20,620	C
Dakota State Univ	SD	6,950	C
Dakota Wesleyan Univ	SD	15,512	C
Dallas Baptist Univ	TX	13,682	LC
Dana College	NE	18,046	C
Daniel Webster College	NH	24,870	C
Davenport Univ	MI	10,057	NC
David Lipscomb Univ	TN	16,158	VC
David N. Myers College	OH	9,475	C
Davis and Elkins College	WV	19,270	LC
De Sales Univ	PA	22,610	VC
Defiance College	OH	19,580	LC
Delaware State Univ	DE	8,104	LC
Delaware Valley College	PA	24,213	LC
Delta State Univ	MS	5,416	C
DePaul Univ	IL	23,590	VC
DeVry/New York	NY	9,865	LC
DeVry Univ/Addison (DuPage County)	IL	8,805	LC
DeVry Univ/Alpharetta	GA	8,805	LC
DeVry Univ/Chicago	IL	8,805	LC
DeVry Univ/Colo Springs	CO	9,465	LC
DeVry Univ/Columbus	OH	8,805	LC
DeVry Univ/Crystal City	VA	10,065	C
DeVry Univ/Dallas	TX	8,805	LC
DeVry Univ/Decatur	GA	8,805	LC
DeVry Univ/Denver	CO	9,465	LC
DeVry Univ/Fremont	CA	9,865	C
DeVry Univ/Kansas City	MO	8,805	LC
DeVry Univ/Long Beach	CA	9,140	LC
DeVry Univ/Orlando	FL	9,865	LC
DeVry Univ/Phoenix	AZ	8,805	LC
DeVry Univ/Pomona	CA	9,205	LC
DeVry Univ/Seattle	WA	10,065	LC
DeVry Univ/Tinley Park	IL	8,805	LC
DeVry Univ/West Hills	CA	9,205	LC
Dickinson State Univ	ND	5,495	NC
Dillard Univ	LA	16,046	VC
Doane College	NE	17,600	LC
Dominican College	NY	20,400	LC
Dominican Univ	IL	20,800	C
Dordt College	IA	18,100	C+
Dowling College	NY	20,281	LC
Drake Univ	IA	22,830	VC
Drexel Univ	PA	27,657	VC
Drury Univ	MO	15,250	VC
Duquesne Univ	PA	24,242	C+
D'Youville College	NY	18,704	C
East Carolina Univ	NC	7,766	C
East Central Univ	OK	4,578	C
East Stroudsburg Univ of Pennsylvania	PA	8,430	LC
East Texas Baptist Univ	TX	12,349	LC
Eastern College	PA	19,641	LC
Eastern Conn State Univ	CT	10,362	C
Eastern Illinois Univ	IL	10,101	C
Eastern Kentucky Univ	KY	6,552	C
Eastern Mennonite Univ	VA	20,700	VC
Eastern Mich Univ	MI	9,855	C
Eastern Nazarene College	MA	19,433	LC
Eastern New Mexico Univ	NM	4,113	LC
Eastern Oregon Univ	OR	8,772	C
Eastern Washington Univ	WA	7,972	LC
East-West Univ	IL	9,140	LC
Eckerd College	FL	25,500	C+
Edgewood College	WI	18,304	C
Edinboro Univ of Pennsylvania	PA	9,328	LC
Edward Waters College	FL	13,124	LC
Elizabeth City State Univ	NC	5,550	LC
Elizabethtown College	PA	26,000	VC
Elmhurst College	IL	21,750	C
Elmira College	NY	31,070	VC+
Elon Univ	NC	19,430	VC
Embry-Riddle Aeronautical Univ	FL	24,790	C
Emmanuel College	MA	23,802	C+
Emory & Henry College	VA	19,462	C
Emory Univ	GA	33,792	MC
Emporia State Univ	KS	6,198	LC
Endicott College	MA	23,704	C
Erskine College	SC	21,399	VC
Eureka College	IL	22,200	C
Excelsior College	NY	915	SP
Fairfield Univ	CT	30,885	HC
Fairleigh Dickinson Univ/Madison campus	NJ	25,500	C
Fairleigh Dickinson Univ/Teaneck Campus	NJ	24,646	C
Fairmont State College	WV	7,010	NC
Faulkner Univ	AL	13,000	C
Fayetteville State Univ	NC	5,590	LC
Felician College	NJ	20,050	C
Ferris State Univ	MI	10,816	C
Ferrum College	VA	15,990	LC
Fisher College	MA	23,100	C
Fisk Univ	TN	13,700	LC
Fitchburg State College	MA	7,836	C
Flagler College	FL	10,550	VC+
Florida A&M Univ	FL	6,948	C
Florida Atlantic Univ	FL	8,832	C
Florida Inst of Technology	FL	25,250	VC
Florida International Univ	FL	9,486	VC
Florida Memorial College	FL	6,000	LC
Florida Southern College	FL	19,430	C
Florida State Univ	FL	7,835	HC
Fontbonne Univ	MO	18,046	C
Fordham Univ	NY	30,710	VC
Fort Hays State Univ	KS	6,294	LC
Fort Lewis College	CO	7,659	LC
Fort Valley State Univ	GA	6,014	LC
Framingham State College	MA	7,259	C
Francis Marion Univ	SC	7,682	C
Franciscan Univ of Steubenville	OH	19,100	C+
Franklin and Marshall College	PA	32,410	HC
Franklin College of Indiana	IN	19,905	C
Franklin Pierce College	NH	26,125	LC
Franklin Univ	OH	6,324	SP
Freed-Hardeman Univ	TN	14,290	VC
Fresno Pacific Univ	CA	19,740	C
Friends Univ	KS	15,962	LC
Frostburg State Univ	MD	9,680	C
Furman Univ	SC	25,492	HC
Gallaudet Univ	DC	16,554	SP
Gannon Univ	PA	18,848	C
Gardner-Webb Univ	NC	17,400	C
Geneva College	PA	19,990	C+
George Mason Univ	VA	9,192	C
George Washington Univ	DC	32,170	HC
Georgetown Univ	DC	34,847	MC
Georgia College and State Univ	GA	7,344	C
Georgia Inst of Technology	GA	9,028	HC+
Georgia Southern Univ	GA	6,958	C
Georgia Southwestern State Univ	GA	6,013	C
Georgia State Univ	GA	7,792	LC
Georgian Court College	NJ	19,040	LC
Gettysburg College	PA	32,070	HC
Glenville State College	WV	6,588	NC
Gonzaga Univ	WA	24,276	HC+
Gordon College	MA	23,594	VC+
Goshen College	IN	18,950	VC+
Grace Bible College	MI	12,600	C
Grace College	IN	16,768	C
Graceland Univ	IA	15,845	C
Grambling State Univ	LA	5,325	NC
Grand Canyon Univ	AZ	30,000	LC
Grand Valley State Univ	MI	10,040	C
Grand View College	IA	17,596	NC
Green Mountain College	VT	24,130	C
Greensboro College	NC	19,080	LC
Greenville College	IL	19,226	LC
Grove City College	PA	12,280	MC
Guilford College	NC	23,255	C
Gustavus Adolphus College	MN	24,190	VC+
Gwynedd-Mercy College	PA	22,350	C
Hamline Univ	MN	23,339	C+
Hampton Univ	VA	17,112	C+
Hannibal-LaGrange College	MO	12,530	C
Hanover College	IN	17,560	VC
Harding Univ	AR	13,528	VC
Hardin-Simmons Univ	TX	14,165	C
Hartwick College	NY	33,090	C+
Hastings College	NE	17,854	C+
Hawaii Pacific Univ	HI	17,790	C
Heidelberg College	OH	23,879	C
Henderson State Univ	AR	6,269	C
Henry Cogswell College	WA	13,080	SP
Heritage College	WA	6,450	NC
Hesser College	NH	16,210	LC
High Point Univ	NC	20,220	LC
Hilbert College	NY	16,830	LC
Hillsdale College	MI	20,586	VC+
Hofstra Univ	NY	23,252	C
Hollins Univ	VA	24,328	VC
Holy Family College	PA	13,710	LC
Holy Names College	CA	23,220	C
Hood College	MD	26,020	VC
Hope College	MI	22,922	C+
Hope International Univ	CA	16,940	NC
Houghton College	NY	21,810	VC+
Houston Baptist Univ	TX	15,300	LC
Howard Payne Univ	TX	13,834	C+
Howard Univ	DC	15,522	LC
Humboldt State Univ	CA	8,582	C
Humphreys College	CA	6,900	NC
Huntingdon College	AL	18,400	VC
Huntington College	IN	15,480	LC
Huron Univ	SD	10,450	C
Husson College	ME	15,360	LC
Huston-Tillotson College	TX	12,977	LC
Idaho State Univ	ID	7,030	C+
Illinois College	IL	16,234	C
Illinois State Univ	IL	9,235	C
Illinois Wesleyan Univ	IL	26,970	HC
Immaculata College	PA	22,400	LC
Indiana Inst of Technology	IN	18,806	C
Indiana State Univ	IN	8,461	LC
Indiana Univ Bloomington	IN	10,712	C+
Indiana Univ East	IN	3,415	C
Indiana Univ Kokomo	IN	3,422	LC
Indiana Univ Northwest	IN	3,447	C
Indiana Univ of Pennsylvania	PA	9,133	C
Indiana Univ South Bend	IN	3,515	C
Indiana Univ Southeast	IN	3,459	C
Indiana Univ-Purdue Univ Indianapolis	IN	9,473	C
Indiana Wesleyan Univ	IN	17,680	C
Inter-American Univ of PR/Aguadilla Campus	PR	3,278	
Inter-American Univ of PR/Arecibo Campus	PR	3,300	
Inter-American Univ of PR/Barranquitas Regional College	PR	3,300	LC
Inter-American Univ of PR/Bayamon Univ College	PR	3,700	
Inter-American Univ of PR/Fajardo Campus	PR	4,000	
Inter-American Univ of PR/Metropolitan Campus	PR	4,166	
Inter-American Univ of PR/Ponce Regional College	PR	3,700	
Inter-American Univ of PR/San GermÈn	PR	6,390	
International College	FL	7,230	NC
Iona College	NY	26,556	C
Iowa State Univ	IA	8,108	VC
Iowa Wesleyan College	IA	18,840	C
Ithaca College	NY	28,719	HC
Jackson State Univ	MS	6,776	LC
Jacksonville Univ	FL	21,110	LC
James Madison Univ	VA	9,552	HC
Jamestown College	ND	11,310	NC

School	ST	$IS	SR
John Brown Univ	AR	15,080	VC
John Carroll Univ	OH	24,140	VC
Johns Hopkins Univ	MD	35,226	MC
Johnson and Wales Univ	RI	21,558	LC
Johnson C. Smith Univ	NC	16,560	C+
Johnson State College	VT	10,776	C
Judson College	AL	13,790	C
Judson College	IL	18,980	LC
Juniata College	PA	26,080	VC
Kansas State Univ	KS	6,995	C
Kean Univ	NJ	11,159	C
Kendall College	IL	19,119	LC
Kent State Univ	OH	11,104	C
Kentucky Christian College	KY	13,472	C
Kentucky State Univ	KY	6,146	NC
Kentucky Wesleyan College	KY	15,800	C
Kettering Univ	MI	23,256	HC
Keuka College	NY	21,170	C
King College	TN	17,800	VC
King's College	PA	24,680	C
Knoxville College	TN	6,200	LC
Kutztown Univ of Pennsylvania	PA	8,907	C
La Roche College	PA	18,854	LC
La Salle Univ	PA	27,890	C
La Sierra Univ	CA	19,260	LC
LaGrange College	GA	17,496	C
Lake Erie College	OH	21,350	LC
Lake Superior State Univ	MI	9,034	LC
Lakeland College	WI	17,950	C
Lamar Univ	TX	6,816	LC
Lambuth Univ	TN	14,254	C
Lander Univ	SC	8,618	LC
Lane College	TN	10,400	C+
Langston Univ	OK	2,308	LC
Lasell College	MA	24,100	C
Lawrence Tech Univ	MI	11,429	C
Le Moyne College	NY	23,840	C
Lee Univ	TN	10,198	LC
Lees-McRae College	NC	17,106	LC
Lehigh Univ	PA	32,290	MC
LeMoyne-Owen College	TN	8,450	NC
Lenoir-Rhyne College	NC	19,186	C
LeTourneau Univ	TX	19,020	VC
Lewis Univ	IL	20,960	C
Lewis-Clark State College	ID	6,496	C
Liberty Univ	VA	14,500	C
Limestone College	SC	16,900	C
Lincoln Memorial Univ	TN	12,620	LC
Lincoln Univ	MO	7,158	NC
Lincoln Univ	PA	11,198	C+
Lindenwood Univ	MO	17,250	C
Lindsey Wilson College	KY	16,392	LC
Linfield College	OR	25,840	VC
Livingstone College	NC	13,360	LC
Lock Haven Univ of Pennsylvania	PA	9,534	C
LIU/Brooklyn Campus	NY	22,290	C
LIU/C.W. Post Campus	NY	25,380	C
Longwood College	VA	8,950	C
Loras College	IA	22,994	C+
Louisiana College	LA	11,516	C
Louisiana State Univ and A&M College	LA	8,014	VC
Louisiana State Univ in Shreveport	LA	2,480	NC
Louisiana Tech Univ	LA	6,506	C
Lourdes College	OH	13,100	LC
Loyola College in Maryland	MD	30,900	HC
Loyola Marymount Univ	CA	28,754	HC
Loyola Univ New Orleans	LA	23,506	VC+
Loyola Univ of Chicago	IL	25,992	VC
Lubbock Christian Univ	TX	14,226	LC
Lycoming College	PA	24,780	C
Lynchburg College	VA	23,405	C
Lyndon State College	VT	11,313	LC
Lynn Univ	FL	24,550	C
Lyon College	AR	16,500	VC
MacMurray College	IL	17,790	LC
Madonna Univ	MI	11,504	VC
Malone College	OH	19,190	C
Manchester College	IN	22,010	C
Mansfield Univ	PA	9,648	C
Marian College	IN	21,020	C
Marian College of Fond du Lac	WI	17,935	LC
Marist College	NY	24,756	VC
Marquette Univ	WI	24,836	C+
Mars Hill College	NC	18,600	LC
Martin Univ	IN	8,370	SP
Mary Baldwin College	VA	23,440	C
Mary Washington College	VA	9,032	VC+
Marygrove College	MI	16,075	C
Marymount College/Tarrytown	NY	23,850	C
Marymount Manhattan College	NY	23,195	VC
Marymount Univ	VA	21,560	LC
Maryville College	TN	23,210	VC
Maryville Univ of St. Louis	MO	18,680	C
Marywood Univ	PA	24,639	C
Mass College of Liberal Arts	MA	8,717	LC
Master's College	CA	21,500	C+
Mayville State Univ	ND	6,440	NC
McKendree College	IL	18,300	C+
McMurry Univ	TX	15,287	C
McNeese State Univ	LA	5,259	LC
McPherson College	KS	17,710	C
Medaille College	NY	18,320	C
Menlo College	CA	24,000	LC
Mercer Univ	GA	24,130	VC
Mercy College	NY	15,875	LC
Mercyhurst College	PA	20,694	C
Meredith College	NC	17,500	C
Merrimack College	MA	25,725	VC
Mesa State College	CO	8,051	C
Messiah College	PA	23,180	VC
Methodist College	NC	19,526	C
Metropolitan State Univ	MN	2,943	SP
Miami Univ	OH	12,885	VC+
Mich State Univ	MI	10,386	VC
Mich Tech Univ	MI	11,088	VC
MidAmerica Nazarene Univ	KS	16,960	C
Middle Tenn State Univ	TN	6,994	C
Midland Lutheran College	NE	18,600	C
Midway College	KY	15,815	C
Midwestern State Univ	TX	6,704	NC
Miles College	AL	7,870	NC
Millersville Univ of Pennsylvania	PA	10,153	VC
Milligan College	TN	17,550	C
Millikin Univ	IL	24,415	C+
Millsaps College	MS	22,608	VC+
Milwaukee School of Engineering	WI	25,680	VC+
Minn State Univ, Mankato	MN	7,296	LC
Miss College	MS	14,574	C
Miss State Univ	MS	7,853	C
Miss Univ for Women	MS	5,446	LC
Miss Valley State Univ	MS	6,345	C
Missouri Baptist College	MO	15,762	LC
Missouri Southern State College	MO	6,666	C
Missouri Valley College	MO	17,400	LC
Missouri Western State College	MO	6,662	NC
Molloy College	NY	13,940	C
Monmouth College	IL	21,550	C
Monmouth Univ	NJ	24,042	C
Montana State Univ-Billings	MT	7,653	NC
Montana State Univ-Bozeman	MT	8,431	C
Montclair State Univ	NJ	10,287	LC
Montreat College	NC	17,164	C
Moorhead State Univ	MN	7,000	LC
Morehouse College	GA	19,814	C
Morgan State Univ	MD	10,078	LC
Morningside College	IA	19,124	C
Morris Brown College	GA	15,993	LC
Morris College	SC	9,995	LC
Mount Aloysius College	PA	18,186	LC
Mount Ida College	MA	25,375	LC
Mount Marty College	SD	15,656	LC
Mount Mary College	WI	18,024	C
Mount Mercy College	IA	19,390	VC
Mount Olive College	NC	14,410	LC
Mount St. Clare College	IA	19,050	LC
Mount St. Mary College	NY	18,825	C
Mount St. Mary's College	CA	24,430	C
Mount St. Mary's College	MD	25,740	C
Mount Senario College	WI	17,750	C
Mount Union College	OH	21,120	C
Mount Vernon Nazarene College	OH	17,027	C
Mountain State Univ	WV	8,180	NC
Muhlenberg College	PA	28,170	HC
Murray State Univ	KY	6,672	C
Muskingum College	OH	18,760	C
National American Univ	SD	13,680	NC
National Univ	CA	7,755	SP
National-Louis Univ	IL	13,995	NC
Nazareth College of Rochester	NY	22,036	VC
Nebr Wesleyan Univ	NE	18,767	VC
Neumann College	PA	22,040	NC
New England College	NH	20,706	LC
New Jersey City Univ	NJ	9,100	LC
New Mexico Highlands Univ	NM	6,256	NC
New Mexico Inst of Mining and Technology	NM	7,152	VC+
New Mexico State Univ	NM	7,302	C
New York Inst of Technology	NY	21,756	C
New York Univ	NY	35,200	MC
Newberry College	SC	19,670	LC
Newbury College	MA	21,490	C
Newman Univ	KS	14,098	LC
Niagara Univ	NY	22,250	C+
Nicholls State Univ	LA	5,290	NC
Nichols College	MA	24,610	LC
N Car Agricultural and Technical State Univ	NC	6,659	LC
N Car Central Univ	NC	6,418	LC
N Car State Univ	NC	8,680	HC
N Car Wesleyan College	NC	15,650	LC
North Central College	IL	22,944	C+
N Dak State Univ	ND	7,004	VC
North Georgia College and State Univ	GA	6,322	C+
North Park Univ	IL	24,030	C
Northeastern Illinois Univ	IL	2,898	NC
Northeastern State Univ	OK	4,704	LC
Northeastern Univ	MA	30,078	VC
Northern Arizona Univ	AZ	7,398	C
Northern Illinois Univ	IL	9,545	C
Northern Mich Univ	MI	9,693	C
Northern State Univ	SD	6,279	LC
Northland College	WI	21,435	C+
Northwest Christian College	OR	19,680	LC
Northwest College	WA	17,471	C
Northwest Missouri State Univ	MO	7,922	LC
Northwest Nazarene Univ	ID	18,380	C
Northwestern College	MN	19,816	C+
Northwestern College of Iowa	IA	17,630	C+
Northwestern Okla State Univ	OK	4,542	NC
Northwestern State Univ of Louisiana	LA	5,745	NC
Northwood Univ	FL	19,179	LC
Northwood Univ	MI	18,360	LC
Northwood Univ	TX	18,135	C
Norwich Univ	VT	21,064	LC
Notre Dame de Namur Univ	CA	26,932	LC
Nova Southeastern Univ	FL	20,104	LC
Nyack College	NY	18,540	C
Oakland City Univ	IN	11,286	LC
Oakland Univ	MI	9,418	C
Oakwood College	AL	14,904	C
Oglala Lakota College	SD	1,950	NC
Oglethorpe Univ	GA	19,100	LC
Ohio Dominican College	OH	18,100	LC
Ohio Northern Univ	OH	27,765	VC
Ohio State Univ at Lima	OH	3,603	NC
Ohio State Univ at Newark	OH	8,103	NC
Ohio Univ	OH	11,769	C
Ohio Valley College	WV	13,650	C+
Ohio Wesleyan Univ	OH	29,670	VC+
Okla Baptist Univ	OK	13,878	VC
Okla Christian Univ	OK	16,500	VC
Okla City Univ	OK	15,810	C
Okla Panhandle State Univ	OK	3,812	NC
Okla State Univ	OK	7,650	VC
Old Dominion Univ	VA	9,386	C
Olivet College	MI	17,410	C
Olivet Nazarene Univ	IL	18,444	C
Oral Roberts Univ	OK	18,490	C
Oregon State Univ	OR	9,612	VC
Ottawa Univ	KS	11,800	LC
Otterbein College	OH	23,439	C
Ouachita Baptist Univ	AR	16,460	VC
Our Lady of Holy Cross College	LA	5,140	NC
Our Lady of the Lake Univ of San Antonio	TX	17,336	C
Pace Univ	NY	24,200	C
Pacific Lutheran Univ	WA	23,318	VC
Pacific Union College	CA	20,250	VC
Pacific Univ	OR	24,250	C
Paine College	GA	11,896	LC
Palm Beach Atlantic College	FL	23,310	C
Park Univ	MO	9,816	C
Paul Quinn College	TX	8,150	LC
Peirce College	PA	10,650	C
Penn State Univ at Erie/Behrend College	PA	12,326	C
Penn State Univ/Altoona	PA	12,578	C
Penn State Univ/Univ Park Campus	PA	11,126	VC
Pennsylvania College of Technology	PA	12,860	NC
Pepperdine Univ	CA	32,830	VC
Peru State College	NE	6,342	NC
Pfeiffer Univ	NC	18,580	C
Philadelphia Biblical Univ	PA	16,295	C+
Philander Smith College	AR	7,380	NC
Piedmont College	GA	16,900	C
Pikeville College	KY	12,000	NC
Pine Manor College	MA	19,344	LC
Pittsburg State Univ	KS	6,228	NC
Plymouth State College	NH	11,024	LC
Point Loma Nazarene Univ	CA	21,380	VC
Point Park College	PA	20,290	C
Pontifical Catholic Univ of PR/Ponce	PR	7,076	
Portland State Univ	OR	11,220	C
Prairie View A&M Univ	TX	3,172	LC
Presbyterian College	SC	23,356	VC
Presentation College	SD	13,508	NC
Principia College	IL	23,865	C+
Providence College	RI	27,620	HC
Queens College	NC	17,250	C
Quincy Univ	IL	20,450	C
Quinnipiac Univ	CT	27,370	C
Radford Univ	VA	8,302	C
Ramapo College of New Jersey	NJ	13,550	VC
Regis Univ	CO	25,740	C+
Reinhardt College	GA	13,300	C
Rhode Island College	RI	8,700	LC
Rhodes College	TN	26,466	HC+
Richard Stockton College of New Jersey	NJ	12,165	VC
Rider Univ	NJ	27,400	C
Ripon College	WI	24,180	VC+
Rivier College	NH	24,215	C
Roanoke College	VA	24,689	VC
Robert Morris Univ	PA	18,730	C
Roberts Wesleyan College	NY	20,160	C+
Rochester College	MI	15,404	C+
Rochester Inst of Technology	NY	26,232	VC+
Rockford College	IL	23,930	C
Rockhurst Univ	MO	20,090	C
Rocky Mountain College	MT	18,113	C
Roger Williams Univ	RI	29,010	C
Roosevelt Univ	IL	20,240	LC
Rosemont College	PA	24,060	C
Rowan Univ	NJ	12,365	VC
Russell Sage College	NY	23,674	C+
Rust College	MS	7,800	C+
Rutgers, The State Univ of New Jersey New Brunswick Campus	NJ	12,709	C
Rutgers, The State Univ of New Jersey/Newark Campus	NJ	6,394	C
Sacred Heart Univ	CT	26,588	VC
Saginaw Valley State Univ	MI	9,465	C
St. Ambrose Univ	IA	19,994	C
St. Andrews Presbyterian College	NC	19,720	LC
St. Anselm College	NH	27,405	C
St. Augustine's College	NC	12,990	C+
St. Cloud State Univ	MN	7,180	C
St. Edward's Univ	TX	17,846	C
St. John's Univ	NY	26,660	C
St. Joseph's College	IN	21,640	C
St. Joseph's College of Maine	ME	22,500	LC
St. Joseph's College, New York	NY	9,802	C
St. Joseph's Univ	PA	29,715	VC+
St. Leo Univ	FL	19,250	LC
St. Louis Univ	MO	26,590	VC+
St. Mary College	KS	17,298	C
St. Mary-of-the-Woods College	IN	21,320	LC
St. Mary's College	IN	24,474	VC
St. Mary's College	MI	13,314	LC
St. Mary's College of Calif	CA	27,575	C
St. Mary's Univ of Minn	MN	19,975	C
St. Mary's Univ of San Antonio	TX	19,735	C
St. Michael's College	VT	26,935	VC
St. Norbert College	WI	23,169	VC
St. Paul's College	VA	13,340	C
St. Peter's College	NJ	22,292	LC
St. Thomas Aquinas College	NY	20,590	LC
St. Thomas Univ	FL	19,500	LC
St. Vincent College	PA	22,942	VC
St. Xavier Univ	IL	21,104	C
Salem College	NC	23,065	VC
Salem International Univ	WV	17,263	LC
Salem State College	MA	4,481	LC
Salisbury Univ	MD	10,576	VC
Salve Regina Univ	RI	26,460	C
Sam Houston State Univ	TX	6,076	LC
Samford Univ	AL	16,340	VC
San Diego State Univ	CA	9,716	C+
San Francisco State Univ	CA	7,139	LC
San Jose State Univ	CA	8,187	C
Schreiner Univ	TX	19,254	C
Seattle Pacific Univ	WA	22,674	C+
Seattle Univ	WA	24,183	VC
Seton Hall Univ	NJ	26,910	LC
Seton Hill College	PA	21,875	C
Shaw Univ	NC	12,810	C
Shawnee State Univ	OH	8,634	NC
Shenandoah Univ	VA	22,550	NC
Shepherd College	WV	7,062	LC
Shippensburg Univ of Pennsylvania	PA	9,652	C
Shorter College	GA	15,185	C
Siena Heights Univ	MI	16,140	LC
Sierra Nevada College-Lake Tahoe	NV	21,060	LC
Silver Lake College of the Holy Family	WI	15,516	LC
Simpson College	CA	19,200	C
Skidmore College	NY	34,201	VC+
Slippery Rock Univ	PA	9,152	LC
Sojourner-Douglass College	MD	4,170	LC
Sonoma State Univ	CA	8,953	C
S Car State Univ	SC	6,586	LC
South College	GA	8,720	LC
Southeastern College	FL	11,648	LC
Southeastern Louisiana Univ	LA	6,047	LC
Southeastern Okla State Univ	OK	4,917	C
Southeastern Univ	DC	8,505	LC
Southern Adventist Univ	TN	15,600	LC
Southern Arkansas Univ	AR	5,740	LC
Southern Conn State Univ	CT	10,310	C
Southern Illinois Univ at Carbondale	IL	8,621	C
Southern Illinois Univ Edwardsville	IL	7,869	LC
Southern Methodist Univ	TX	28,349	VC

ST = STATE $IS = IN-STATE COSTS SR = SELECTOR RATING

School	ST	$IS	SR
Southern Nazarene Univ	OK	14,634	NC
Southern New Hampshire Univ	NH	23,852	C
Southern Oregon Univ	OR	9,429	C
Southern Polytechnic State Univ	GA	6,662	C
Southern Univ and A&M College	LA	6,365	C+
Southern Univ at New Orleans	LA	995	NC
Southern Utah Univ	UT	7,254	C
Southern Vermont College	VT	17,685	C
Southern Wesleyan Univ	SC	17,280	C
Southwest Baptist Univ	MO	13,426	LC
Southwest Missouri State Univ	MO	7,600	LC
Southwest State Univ	MN	7,117	LC
Southwest Texas State Univ	TX	8,730	VC
Southwestern Adventist Univ	TX	14,798	C
Southwestern College	KS	17,656	C
Southwestern Okla State Univ	OK	4,801	C
Southwestern Univ	TX	22,550	HC
Spalding Univ	KY	15,196	C
Spring Arbor Univ	MI	17,976	C
Spring Hill College	AL	23,250	C
Springfield College	MA	24,520	C
SUNY/College at Brockport	NY	10,267	C
SUNY/College at Buffalo	NY	8,025	C
SUNY/College at Fredonia	NY	10,125	C
SUNY/College at Geneseo	NY	9,970	HC
SUNY/College at Old Westbury	NY	9,818	LC
SUNY/College at Oswego	NY	10,856	C
SUNY/College at Plattsburgh	NY	9,729	C
SUNY/College at Potsdam	NY	10,519	C
SUNY/Empire State College	NY	3,545	SP
SUNY/Maritime College	NY	10,025	LC
SUNY/Univ at Albany	NY	10,997	VC
SUNY/Univ at Binghamton	NY	10,653	HC
SUNY/Univ at Buffalo	NY	11,033	VC
SUNY/Univ at New Paltz	NY	9,685	VC
SUNY/Univ at Stony Brook	NY	10,998	VC
Stephen F. Austin State Univ	TX	6,905	C
Stephens College	MO	22,295	C
Sterling College	KS	16,370	VC
Stetson Univ	FL	25,640	VC
Stillman College	AL	11,370	LC
Stonehill College	MA	26,852	HC
Strayer Univ	DC	8,789	SP
Sul Ross State Univ	TX	6,582	LC
Susquehanna Univ	PA	27,270	VC
Syracuse Univ	NY	30,710	HC
Tabor College	KS	17,600	LC
Talladega College	AL	10,110	LC
Tarleton State Univ	TX	7,160	C
Teikyo Post Univ	CT	21,800	C
Temple Univ	PA	14,124	C
Tenn State Univ	TN	7,058	VC
Tenn Tech Univ	TN	6,968	C
Tenn Wesleyan College	TN	13,030	C
Texas A&M Univ at Commerce	TX	7,326	C
Texas A&M Univ at Kingsville	TX	6,446	LC
Texas Christian Univ	TX	19,910	C
Texas Lutheran Univ	TX	17,660	C
Texas Southern Univ	TX	6,576	NC
Texas Tech Univ	TX	8,825	C
Texas Wesleyan Univ	TX	14,710	C
Texas Woman's Univ	TX	5,855	LC
Thiel College	PA	18,419	LC
Thomas College	ME	18,915	LC
Thomas Edison State College	NJ	2,750	SP
Thomas More College	KY	17,700	LC
Thomas Univ	GA	8,770	NC
Tiffin Univ	OH	17,250	C
Toccoa Falls College	GA	14,220	C
Touro College	NY	14,950	VC
Towson Univ	MD	11,088	VC
Transylvania Univ	KY	21,780	VC+
Trevecca Nazarene Univ	TN	15,752	C
Trinity Christian College	IL	19,415	C
Trinity College	DC	21,370	LC
Trinity International Univ	IL	20,640	C+
Trinity Univ	TX	21,444	HC
Tri-State Univ-Main Campus	IN	21,200	C
Troy State Univ	AL	7,696	C
Troy State Univ/Dothan	AL	3,296	C
Troy State Univ/ Montgomery	AL	3,080	NC
Truman State Univ	MO	8,568	VC+
Tulane Univ	LA	34,013	HC+
Turabo Univ	PR	4,110	
Tuskegee Univ	AL	14,600	LC
Union College	KY	15,920	C
Union College	NE	14,650	C
Union Univ	TN	18,930	C+
United States International Univ	CA	18,675	LC
Universidad Adventista de las Antillas	PR	6,675	
Universidad Metropolitana	PR	3,324	
Universidad Politecnica de PR	PR	4,695	
Univ of Akron	OH	10,530	NC
Univ of Alabama at Huntsville	AL	7,916	VC
Univ of Alaska Anchorage	AK	9,100	NC
Univ of Alaska Fairbanks	AK	8,265	NC
Univ of Alaska Southeast	AK	7,900	LC
Univ of Arizona	AZ	8,614	C
Univ of Arkansas	AR	8,334	VC
Univ of Arkansas at Little Rock	AR	5,637	NC
Univ of Arkansas at Monticello	AR	5,940	NC
Univ of Arkansas at Pine Bluff	AR	7,925	C
Univ of Bridgeport	CT	23,020	C
Univ of Calif at Berkeley	CA	14,134	MC
Univ of Calif at Riverside	CA	12,479	C
Univ of Central Arkansas	AR	6,388	C
Univ of Central Florida	FL	8,251	VC
Univ of Central Okla	OK	5,205	C
Univ of Charleston	WV	20,640	C
Univ of Cincinnati	OH	12,491	LC
Univ of Colo at Boulder	CO	9,255	VC
Univ of Colo at Colo Springs	CO	9,403	C
Univ of Colo at Denver	CO	3,673	C
Univ of Conn	CT	12,122	VC
Univ of Delaware	DE	10,824	VC
Univ of Denver	CO	28,783	VC
Univ of Detroit Mercy	MI	21,620	LC
Univ of Dubuque	IA	19,990	C
Univ of Evansville	IN	22,865	VC+
Univ of Findlay	OH	23,962	NC
Univ of Georgia	GA	8,656	VC
Univ of Great Falls	MT	15,360	C
Univ of Hawaii at Hilo	HI	6,497	C
Univ of Hawaii at Manoa	HI	7,862	VC
Univ of Houston	TX	8,410	C
Univ of Houston-Downtown	TX	2,006	NC
Univ of Illinois at Chicago	IL	10,702	VC
Univ of Illinois at Urbana-Champaign	IL	11,316	HC+
Univ of Indianapolis	IN	20,840	C
Univ of Iowa	IA	8,607	C+
Univ of Judaism College of A&S	CA	24,230	C
Univ of Kansas	KS	7,232	VC
Univ of La Verne	CA	24,280	C
Univ of Louisiana at Lafayette	LA	5,200	C
Univ of Louisiana at Monroe	LA	5,207	NC
Univ of Louisville	KY	7,402	LC
Univ of Maine	ME	10,798	C
Univ of Maine at Augusta	ME	3,928	C
Univ of Maine at Fort Kent	ME	7,450	LC
Univ of Maine at Machias	ME	7,689	LC
Univ of Maine at Presque Isle	ME	7,964	LC
Univ of Mary	ND	12,900	LC
Univ of Mary Hardin-Baylor	TX	13,929	C
Univ of Maryland/College Park	MD	11,959	C
Univ of Maryland/Eastern Shore	MD	9,258	C
Univ of Maryland/Univ College	MD	5,910	SP
Univ of Mass Amherst	MA	10,995	VC
Univ of Mass Dartmouth	MA	9,852	C
Univ of Mass Lowell	MA	9,470	VC
Univ of Memphis	TN	7,271	C
Univ of Miami	FL	31,130	HC
Univ of Mich/Ann Arbor	MI	13,003	HC+
Univ of Mich/Dearborn	MI	4,677	VC
Univ of Mich/Flint	MI	4,323	C
Univ of Minn/Crookston	MN	9,626	NC
Univ of Minn/Duluth	MN	10,436	C
Univ of Minn/Twin Cities	MN	11,123	VC
Univ of Miss	MS	7,666	C
Univ of Missouri/Columbia	MO	9,803	HC
Univ of Missouri/Kansas City	MO	9,685	VC
Univ of Missouri/Rolla	MO	10,034	C
Univ of Missouri/St. Louis	MO	9,966	C
Univ of Mobile	AL	13,620	LC
Univ of Montana	MT	8,038	C
Univ of Montevallo	AL	7,266	C
Univ of Nebr at Kearney	NE	7,048	NC
Univ of Nebr at Lincoln	NE	8,325	C+
Univ of Nebr at Omaha	NE	6,867	C
Univ of New England	ME	24,110	LC
Univ of New Hampshire	NH	13,207	C
Univ of New Haven	CT	23,860	LC
Univ of New Mexico	NM	8,026	C
Univ of New Orleans	LA	10,160	C
Univ of N Car at Asheville	NC	6,896	VC
Univ of N Car at Chapel Hill	NC	8,789	HC
Univ of N Car at Charlotte	NC	7,254	C
Univ of N Car at Greensboro	NC	6,858	C
Univ of N Car at Pembroke	NC	5,914	LC
Univ of N Car at Wilmington	NC	7,769	C
Univ of North Florida	FL	8,089	VC
Univ of North Texas	TX	7,629	C
Univ of Northern Colo	CO	8,082	C+
Univ of Okla	OK	7,616	VC
Univ of Oregon	OR	9,969	C
Univ of Phoenix	AZ	7,000	SP
Univ of Pittsburgh at Bradford	PA	12,696	C
Univ of Pittsburgh at Johnstown	PA	13,044	LC
Univ of Pittsburgh at Pittsburgh	PA	13,592	HC
Univ of PR at Humacao	PR	1,245	
Univ of PR/Arecibo	PR	1,095	
Univ of PR/Bayamon Univ College Campus	PR	1,600	
Univ of PR/Cayey Univ College	PR	1,245	
Univ of PR/Mayaguez	PR	5,285	
Univ of PR/Rio Piedras	PR	5,510	
Univ of Puget Sound	WA	28,285	HC
Univ of Redlands	CA	29,246	VC
Univ of Rhode Island	RI	12,414	C
Univ of Richmond	VA	27,300	HC
Univ of Rio Grande	OH	8,728	NC
Univ of St. Francis	IL	19,650	C
Univ of St. Francis	IN	17,790	LC
Univ of St. Thomas	MN	24,044	VC
Univ of St. Thomas	TX	18,752	VC
Univ of San Diego	CA	29,198	HC
Univ of San Francisco	CA	27,302	VC
Univ of Science and Arts of Okla	OK	5,245	C
Univ of Scranton	PA	27,964	C+
Univ of Sioux Falls	SD	16,390	C
Univ of South Alabama	AL	6,976	LC
Univ of S Car at Aiken	SC	7,828	LC
Univ of S Car at Columbia	SC	8,748	VC
Univ of S Car at Spartanburg	SC	7,318	C+
Univ of South Florida	FL	8,154	C
Univ of Southern Calif	CA	33,647	MC
Univ of Southern Colo	CO	7,821	LC
Univ of Southern Indiana	IN	8,655	LC
Univ of Southern Maine	ME	10,569	C
Univ of Southern Miss	MS	6,155	LC
Univ of Tampa	FL	22,612	C
Univ of Tenn at Chattanooga	TN	7,783	C
Univ of Tenn at Knoxville	TN	8,214	C
Univ of Tenn at Martin	TN	8,268	C
Univ of Texas at Arlington	TX	7,192	LC
Univ of Texas at Austin	TX	9,437	HC
Univ of Texas at Dallas	TX	9,305	VC
Univ of Texas at San Antonio	TX	9,088	NC
Univ of the District of Columbia	DC	2,844	NC
Univ of the Incarnate Word	TX	18,478	C
Univ of the Ozarks	AR	13,904	C
Univ of the Pacific	CA	28,255	VC
Univ of the Sacred Heart	PR	5,375	
Univ of Toledo	OH	11,206	NC
Univ of Utah	UT	7,703	C
Univ of Vermont	VT	14,761	C+
Univ of Virginia's College at Wise	VA	8,302	C
Univ of Washington	WA	10,361	VC
Univ of West Alabama	AL	6,048	C
Univ of West Florida	FL	7,518	C
Univ of Wisc/Eau Claire	WI	7,032	VC
Univ of Wisc/Green Bay	WI	7,148	C
Univ of Wisc/La Crosse	WI	7,250	VC
Univ of Wisc/Madison	WI	8,262	VC
Univ of Wisc/Milwaukee	WI	8,907	LC
Univ of Wisc/Oshkosh	WI	6,130	LC
Univ of Wisc/Parkside	WI	6,160	LC
Univ of Wisc/Platteville	WI	7,282	C
Univ of Wisc/River Falls	WI	6,356	LC
Univ of Wisc/Stevens Point	WI	7,116	C
Univ of Wisc/Stout	WI	7,192	C
Univ of Wisc/Superior	WI	7,051	C+
Univ of Wisc/Whitewater	WI	6,937	C
Univ of Wyoming	WY	7,143	LC
Upper Iowa Univ	IA	17,438	C
Urbana Univ	OH	17,004	C
Ursinus College	PA	31,350	VC
Ursuline College	OH	19,430	LC
Utah State Univ	UT	6,771	C
Utica College of Syracuse Univ	NY	24,400	LC
Valdosta State Univ	GA	6,988	C
Valley City State Univ	ND		LC
Valparaiso Univ	IN	23,570	VC+
Vanguard Univ of Southern Calif	CA	20,212	C
Villa Julie College	MD	16,026	C
Villanova Univ	PA	31,997	HC
Virginia Commonwealth Univ	VA	9,030	C
Virginia Intermont College	VA	17,510	C
Virginia State Univ	VA	8,182	LC
Virginia Union Univ	VA	15,358	LC
Virginia Wesleyan College	VA	22,350	LC
Viterbo Univ	WI	18,043	C
Voorhees College	SC	9,976	C+
Wagner College	NY	27,000	C
Wake Forest Univ	NC	30,290	MC
Walla Walla College	WA	20,925	C
Walsh Univ	OH	16,880	C
Warner Pacific College	OR	20,370	LC
Wartburg College	IA	21,165	VC
Washburn Univ of Topeka	KS	6,766	NC
Washington and Jefferson College	PA	26,255	VC
Washington and Lee Univ	VA	25,095	MC
Washington College	MD	28,040	VC
Washington State Univ	WA	9,388	C
Washington Univ in St. Louis	MO	34,593	MC
Wayland Baptist Univ	TX	11,271	NC
Wayne State College	NE	6,255	NC
Webber International Univ	FL	14,695	LC
Weber State Univ	UT	6,897	NC
Webster Univ	MO	19,804	VC
Wells College	NY	19,350	VC
Wesley College	DE	17,869	C
Wesleyan College	GA	17,050	VC
West Chester Univ of Pennsylvania	PA	9,792	VC
West Liberty State College	WV	6,056	LC
West Texas A&M Univ	TX	6,538	C
West Virginia State College	WV	6,264	NC
West Virginia Univ	WV	8,304	C
West Virginia Univ Inst of Technology	WV	7,518	NC
West Virginia Wesleyan College	WV	22,920	C
Western Baptist College	OR	19,700	C+
Western Conn State Univ	CT	10,074	C
Western Illinois Univ	IL	9,571	C
Western International Univ	AZ	5,800	SP
Western Kentucky Univ	KY	6,834	C
Western Maryland College	MD	26,000	VC
Western Mich Univ	MI	10,016	C
Western New England College	MA	23,882	C
Western New Mexico Univ	NM	5,950	LC
Western Oregon Univ	OR	8,829	C
Western State College of Colo	CO	7,585	LC
Western Washington Univ	WA	8,624	VC
Westfield State College	MA	8,394	C
Westminster College	MO	19,990	C+
Westminster College	PA	22,960	C
Westminster College	UT	17,226	C
Whittier College	CA	29,108	C
Whitworth College	WA	23,938	VC
Wichita State Univ	KS	6,879	C
Widener Univ	PA	26,920	C
Wilberforce Univ	OH	14,937	LC
Wiley College	TX	8,100	LC
Wilkes Univ	PA	25,800	C
William Carey College	MS	10,150	LC
William Jewell College	MO	17,150	VC
William Paterson Univ of New Jersey	NJ	11,000	LC
William Penn Univ	IA	17,575	C
William Tyndale College	MI	11,150	C
William Woods Univ	MO	19,390	LC
Williams Baptist College	AR	10,750	LC
Wilmington College	DE	6,530	NC
Wilmington College	OH	21,826	C
Wingate Univ	NC	19,140	C
Winona State Univ	MN	8,570	C
Winston-Salem State Univ	NC	5,927	LC
Winthrop Univ	SC	9,106	C
Wisc Lutheran College	WI	19,216	VC
Wittenberg Univ	OH	28,766	VC
Woodbury Univ	CA	25,344	LC
Worcester State College	MA	7,901	LC
Xavier Univ	OH	23,880	C
Xavier Univ of Louisiana	LA	17,000	LC
Yeshiva Univ	NY	21,400	C
York College	NE	13,500	C
York College of Pennsylvania	PA	12,550	VC
Youngstown State Univ	OH	9,318	NC

BUSINESS DATA PROCESSING

School	ST	$IS	SR
Eastern Mich Univ	MI	9,855	C
Faulkner Univ	AL	13,000	C
Montana State Univ-Billings	MT	7,653	NC

BUSINESS ECONOMICS

School	ST	$IS	SR
Adams State College	CO	7,468	C
Alabama State Univ	AL	6,404	C
Albertus Magnus College	CT	22,154	C
Alfred Univ	NY	27,212	C+
American International College	MA	22,268	LC
Andrews Univ	MI	17,696	LC
Arkansas State Univ	AR	7,480	C
Ashland Univ	OH	22,182	LC
Auburn Univ	AL	5,510	C
Auburn Univ Montgomery	AL	5,330	NC
Aurora Univ	IL	18,551	C
Baker Univ	KS	14,780	C+

ST = STATE **$IS** = IN-STATE COSTS **SR** = SELECTOR RATING

BUSINESS EDUCATION

ST = STATE $IS = IN-STATE COSTS SR = SELECTOR RATING

INDEX OF COLLEGE MAJORS

School	ST	$IS	SR
MidAmerica Nazarene Univ	KS	16,960	C
Middle Tenn State Univ	TN	6,994	C
Midland Lutheran College	NE	18,600	C
Minot State Univ	ND	5,466	LC
Miss College	MS	14,574	C
Miss State Univ	MS	7,853	C
Missouri Southern State College	MO	6,666	C
Montana State Univ-Northern	MT	8,600	NC
Montclair State Univ	NJ	10,287	LC
Morehead State Univ	KY	6,510	C
Morningside College	IA	19,124	C
Morris Brown College	GA	15,993	LC
Mount Mary College	WI	18,024	C
Mount St. Clare College	IA	19,050	LC
Mount Vernon Nazarene College	OH	17,027	C
Murray State Univ	KY	6,672	C
Nazareth College of Rochester	NY	22,036	VC
New York Inst of Technology	NY	21,756	C
Nicholls State Univ	LA	5,290	NC
Norfolk State Univ	VA	8,382	LC
N Car Agricultural and Technical State Univ	NC	6,659	LC
Northern Arizona Univ	AZ	7,398	C
Northern Kentucky Univ	KY	6,352	NC
Northern Mich Univ	MI	9,693	C
Northern State Univ	SD	6,279	LC
Northwest Missouri State Univ	MO	7,922	LC
Northwestern College of Iowa	IA	17,630	C+
Northwestern Okla State Univ	OK	4,542	NC
Oakland City Univ	IN	11,286	LC
Oakwood College	AL	14,904	C
Oglala Lakota College	SD	1,950	NC
Ohio Univ	OH	11,769	C
Okla Panhandle State Univ	OK	3,812	NC
Oral Roberts Univ	OK	18,490	C
Ouachita Baptist Univ	AR	16,460	VC
Pace Univ	NY	24,200	C
Pacific Union College	CA	20,250	VC
Philander Smith College	AR	7,380	NC
Pontifical Catholic Univ of PR/Ponce	PR	7,076	
Rider Univ	NJ	27,400	C
Robert Morris Univ	PA	18,730	C
St. Augustine's College	NC	12,990	C+
St. Mary's Univ of San Antonio	TX	19,735	C
St. Paul's College	VA	13,340	C
Salem State College	MA	4,481	LC
Shepherd College	WV	7,062	LC
Shippensburg Univ of Pennsylvania	PA	9,652	C
Siena Heights Univ	MI	16,140	LC
Simpson College	IA	21,200	C+
S Car State Univ	SC	6,586	LC
Southeast Missouri State Univ	MO	8,367	C+
Southeastern Okla State Univ	OK	4,917	C
Southern Arkansas Univ	AR	5,740	LC
Southern Illinois Univ at Carbondale	IL	8,621	C
Southern Nazarene Univ	OK	14,634	NC
Southern New Hampshire Univ	NH	23,852	C
Southern Univ at New Orleans	LA	995	NC
Southern Utah Univ	UT	7,254	C
Southwest Missouri State Univ	MO	7,600	LC
Southwest State Univ	MN	7,117	LC
Southwestern Adventist Univ	TX	14,798	C
SUNY/College at Buffalo	NY	8,025	C
SUNY/College at Oneonta	NY	9,981	C
SUNY/College at Oswego	NY	10,856	C
State Univ of West Georgia	GA	7,101	C
Stephen F. Austin State Univ	TX	6,905	C
Suffolk Univ	MA	26,516	C
Tabor College	KS	17,600	LC
Tarleton State Univ	TX	7,160	C
Temple Univ	PA	14,124	C
Texas A&M Univ at Commerce	TX	7,326	C
Texas Wesleyan Univ	TX	14,710	C
Thomas College	ME	18,915	LC
Union College	KY	15,920	C
Union College	NE	14,650	C
Univ of Akron	OH	10,530	NC
Univ of Arkansas at Monticello	AR	5,940	NC
Univ of Arkansas at Pine Bluff	AR	7,925	C
Univ of Central Florida	FL	8,251	VC
Univ of Central Okla	OK	5,205	C
Univ of Cincinnati	OH	12,491	LC
Univ of Dayton	OH	20,400	VC
Univ of Findlay	OH	23,962	NC
Univ of Georgia	GA	8,656	VC
Univ of Idaho	ID	7,026	C
Univ of Kentucky	KY	7,765	C
Univ of Louisville	KY	7,402	LC
Univ of Maine at Machias	ME	7,689	LC
Univ of Mary Hardin-Baylor	TX	13,929	C
Univ of Maryland/Eastern Shore	MD	9,258	C
Univ of Minn/Twin Cities	MN	11,123	VC
Univ of Montana--Western	MT	6,915	NC
Univ of Nebr at Kearney	NE	7,048	NC
Univ of Nebr at Lincoln	NE	8,325	C+
Univ of New Mexico	NM	8,026	C
Univ of New Orleans	LA	10,160	C
Univ of North Alabama	AL	7,016	NC
Univ of N Car at Greensboro	NC	6,858	C
Univ of N Dak	ND	7,067	VC
Univ of North Texas	TX	7,629	C
Univ of Northern Iowa	IA	7,850	C
Univ of Rio Grande	OH	8,728	NC
Univ of St. Francis	IN	17,790	LC
Univ of South Florida	FL	8,154	C
Univ of Southern Indiana	IN	8,655	LC
Univ of Southern Miss	MS	6,155	LC
Univ of Tenn at Martin	TN	8,268	C
Univ of the Incarnate Word	TX	18,478	C
Univ of the Ozarks	AR	13,904	C
Univ of Toledo	OH	11,206	NC
Univ of Wisc/Eau Claire	WI	7,032	VC
Univ of Wisc/Whitewater	WI	6,937	C
Utah State Univ	UT	6,771	C
Valdosta State Univ	GA	6,988	C
Valley City State Univ	ND		LC
Virginia Polytechnic Inst and State Univ	VA	7,652	C
Virginia State Univ	VA	8,182	LC
Virginia Union Univ	VA	15,358	LC
Viterbo Univ	WI	18,043	C
Walla Walla College	WA	20,925	C
Wayne State Univ	MI	6,720	C
Weber State Univ	UT	6,897	NC
West Texas A&M Univ	TX	6,538	C
Western Kentucky Univ	KY	6,834	C
Western Mich Univ	MI	10,016	C
Western New Mexico Univ	NM	5,950	LC
Westfield State College	MA	8,394	C
Wiley College	TX	8,100	LC
Winona State Univ	MN	8,570	C
Wittenberg Univ	OH	28,766	VC
Wright State Univ	OH	9,141	LC
York College of Pennsylvania	PA	12,550	VC
Youngstown State Univ	OH	9,318	NC

BUSINESS LAW

School	ST	$IS	SR
Bowling Green State Univ	OH	10,794	C
Iona College	NY	26,556	C
Lamar Univ	TX	6,816	LC
Marymount Univ	VA	21,560	LC
Ohio Univ	OH	11,769	C
Saginaw Valley State Univ	MI	9,465	C
Temple Univ	PA	14,124	C
Univ of Miami	FL	31,130	HC
Washington State Univ	WA	9,388	C
Western Carolina Univ	NC	5,667	C

BUSINESS STATISTICS

School	ST	$IS	SR
Baylor Univ	TX	18,298	VC+
Cal State, Los Angeles	CA	5,050	C
Univ of Illinois at Chicago	IL	10,702	VC
Univ of PR/Rio Piedras	PR	5,510	
Washington State Univ	WA	9,388	C
Western Mich Univ	MI	10,016	C

BUSINESS SYSTEMS ANALYSIS

School	ST	$IS	SR
Arkansas State Univ	AR	7,480	C
Baylor Univ	TX	18,298	VC+
Eastern Mich Univ	MI	9,855	C
Husson College	ME	15,360	LC
Johnson State College	VT	10,776	C
Louisiana Tech Univ	LA	6,506	C
Messiah College	PA	23,180	VC
Montana Tech of The Univ of Montana	MT	7,845	C
Rochester Inst of Technology	NY	26,232	VC+
Southern Illinois Univ at Carbondale	IL	8,621	C
Texas A&M Univ	TX	8,988	VC
Univ of Findlay	OH	23,962	NC
Univ of N Car at Wilmington	NC	7,769	C
Villa Julie College	MD	16,026	C

CANADIAN STUDIES

School	ST	$IS	SR
Brigham Young Univ	UT	7,840	HC
Duke Univ	NC	34,396	MC
Franklin College of Indiana	IN	19,905	C
St. Lawrence Univ	NY	32,605	VC
SUNY/College at Plattsburgh	NY	9,729	C
Univ of Vermont	VT	14,761	C+
Univ of Washington	WA	10,361	VC
Western Washington Univ	WA	8,624	VC

CARIBBEAN STUDIES

School	ST	$IS	SR
CUNY/Brooklyn College	NY	3,403	LC
Dartmouth College	NH	34,458	MC
Florida State Univ	FL	7,835	HC
Pitzer College	CA	33,930	HC
SUNY/Univ at Albany	NY	10,997	VC
SUNY/Univ at Binghamton	NY	10,653	HC
Union College	NY	32,646	HC
Univ of Miami	FL	31,130	HC

CARTOGRAPHY

School	ST	$IS	SR
East Central Univ	OK	4,578	C
Ohio Univ	OH	11,769	C
Salem State College	MA	4,481	LC
Southwest Missouri State Univ	MO	7,600	LC
Southwest Texas State Univ	TX	8,730	VC
Univ of Idaho	ID	7,026	C
Univ of Wisc/Madison	WI	8,262	VC

CELL BIOLOGY

School	ST	$IS	SR
Ball State Univ	IN	8,660	C
Bard College	NY	33,912	HC
Beloit College	WI	27,482	HC
Bucknell Univ	PA	31,096	HC
Cal State, Long Beach	CA	7,400	LC
Florida State Univ	FL	7,835	HC
Johns Hopkins Univ	MD	35,226	MC
Johnson State College	VT	10,776	C
Mansfield Univ	PA	9,648	C
Ohio Univ	OH	11,769	C
Okla State Univ	OK	7,650	VC
Rutgers, The State Univ of New Jersey New Brunswick Campus	NJ	12,709	C
San Francisco State Univ	CA	7,139	LC
Southwest Missouri State Univ	MO	7,600	LC
SUNY/College at Plattsburgh	NY	9,729	C
Texas Tech Univ	TX	8,825	C
Tulane Univ	LA	34,013	HC+
Univ of Calif at Santa Barbara	CA	11,732	VC
Univ of Colo at Boulder	CO	9,255	VC
Univ of Maine	ME	10,798	C
Univ of Maryland/College Park	MD	11,959	C
Univ of Mich/Ann Arbor	MI	13,003	HC+
Univ of Minn/Twin Cities	MN	11,123	VC
Univ of Rochester	NY	32,979	HC
Washington State Univ	WA	9,388	C

CELTIC STUDIES

School	ST	$IS	SR
Bard College	NY	33,912	HC
Univ of Calif at Berkeley	CA	14,134	MC

CERAMIC ART AND DESIGN

School	ST	$IS	SR
Alfred Univ	NY	27,212	C+
Andrews Univ	MI	17,696	LC
Arizona State Univ-Main	AZ	7,726	C
Barton College	NC	16,834	LC
Calif College of Arts and Crafts	CA	27,366	SP
Cal State, Fullerton	CA	5,440	LC
College For Creative Studies	MI	20,938	SP
Edinboro Univ of Pennsylvania	PA	9,328	LC
Howard Univ	DC	15,522	LC
Indiana Univ-Purdue Univ Indianapolis	IN	9,473	C
Kansas City Art Inst	MO	25,880	SP
Maryland Inst College of Art	MD	27,720	SP
Mass College of Art	MA	13,703	SP
McMurry Univ	TX	15,287	C
Northern Mich Univ	MI	9,693	C
Northwest Nazarene Univ	ID	18,380	C
Ohio Northern Univ	OH	27,765	VC
Ohio Univ	OH	11,769	C
Rhode Island School of Design	RI	30,227	SP
Rochester Inst of Technology	NY	26,232	VC+
School of the Art Inst of Chicago	IL	27,800	SP
Syracuse Univ	NY	30,710	HC
Univ of Dallas	TX	22,128	VC+
Univ of Mass Dartmouth	MA	9,852	C
Univ of Miami	FL	31,130	HC
Univ of Mich/Ann Arbor	MI	13,003	HC+
Univ of North Texas	TX	7,629	C
Univ of Oregon	OR	9,969	C
Univ of the Arts	PA	24,230	SP
Washington Univ in St. Louis	MO	34,593	MC
Western Mich Univ	MI	10,016	C

CERAMIC ENGINEERING

School	ST	$IS	SR
Alfred Univ	NY	27,212	C+
Clemson Univ	SC	7,600	C
Rutgers, The State Univ of New Jersey New Brunswick Campus	NJ	12,709	C
Ohio State Univ	OH	10,819	VC
Univ of Illinois at Urbana-Champaign	IL	11,316	HC+
Univ of Missouri/Rolla	MO	10,034	C
Univ of Washington	WA	10,361	VC

CERAMIC SCIENCE

School	ST	$IS	SR
Maine College of Art	ME	26,367	SP
Univ of Hartford	CT	28,884	C

CHEMICAL ENGINEERING

School	ST	$IS	SR
Arizona State Univ-Main	AZ	7,726	C
Auburn Univ	AL	5,510	C
Bethel College	IN	17,650	LC
Brigham Young Univ	UT	7,840	HC
Bucknell Univ	PA	31,096	HC
Calif Inst of Technology	CA	27,663	MC
Calif State Polytechnic Univ, Pomona	CA	8,615	C
Cal State, Long Beach	CA	7,400	LC
Carnegie Mellon Univ	PA	32,682	MC
Case Western Reserve Univ	OH	27,418	C
Christian Brothers Univ	TN	19,820	VC
CUNY/City College	NY	3,309	LC
Clarkson Univ	NY	29,884	VC
Clemson Univ	SC	7,600	C
Cleveland State Univ	OH	10,146	NC
Colo School of Mines	CO	11,578	HC
Colo State Univ	CO	9,672	C
Columbia Univ/Fu Foundation School of Engineering and Applied Science	NY	35,190	MC
Cooper Union for the Advancement of Science and Art	NY	6,500	MC
Cornell Univ	NY	34,614	MC
Delaware State Univ	DE	8,104	LC
Dordt College	IA	18,100	C+
Drexel Univ	PA	27,657	VC
Florida A&M Univ	FL	6,948	C
Florida Inst of Technology	FL	25,250	VC
Florida International Univ	FL	9,486	VC
Florida State Univ	FL	7,835	HC
Geneva College	PA	19,990	C+
Georgia Inst of Technology	GA	9,028	HC+
Hampton Univ	VA	17,112	C+
Howard Univ	DC	15,522	LC
Illinois Inst of Technology	IL	25,182	HC+
Iowa State Univ	IA	8,108	VC
Johns Hopkins Univ	MD	35,226	MC
Kansas State Univ	KS	6,995	C
Lafayette College	PA	32,655	MC
Lamar Univ	TX	6,816	LC
Lehigh Univ	PA	32,290	MC
Louisiana State Univ and A&M College	LA	8,014	VC
Louisiana Tech Univ	LA	6,506	C
Manhattan College	NY	25,500	VC
Mass Inst of Technology	MA	35,228	MC
McNeese State Univ	LA	5,259	LC
Mich State Univ	MI	10,386	VC
Mich Tech Univ	MI	11,088	VC
Miss State Univ	MS	7,853	C
Montana State Univ-Bozeman	MT	8,431	C
New Jersey Inst of Technology	NJ	14,690	VC
New Mexico Inst of Mining and Technology	NM	7,152	VC+
New Mexico State Univ	NM	7,302	C
New York Univ	NY	35,200	MC
Norfolk State Univ	VA	8,382	LC
N Car Agricultural and Technical State Univ	NC	6,659	LC
N Car State Univ	NC	8,680	HC
Northeastern Univ	MA	30,078	VC
Northwestern Univ	IL	33,615	MC
Ohio Univ	OH	11,769	C
Okla State Univ	OK	7,650	VC
Oregon State Univ	OR	9,612	VC
Penn State Univ/Univ Park Campus	PA	11,126	VC
Polytechnic Univ/Brooklyn	NY	33,090	HC
Prairie View A&M Univ	TX	3,172	LC
Princeton Univ	NJ	35,072	MC
Purdue Univ/West Lafayette	IN	10,284	VC
Rensselaer Polytechnic Inst	NY	33,863	HC+
Rose-Hulman Inst of Technology	IN	27,707	HC+

ST = STATE **$IS** = IN-STATE COSTS **SR** = SELECTOR RATING

School	ST	$IS	SR
Rutgers, The State Univ of New Jersey New Brunswick Campus	NJ	12,709	C
San Jose State Univ	CA	8,187	C
Savannah State Univ	GA	2,550	LC
S Dak School of Mines and Technology	SD	7,438	C+
Stanford Univ	CA	34,222	MC
SUNY/College of Environmental Science and Forestry	NY	12,446	VC
SUNY/Univ at Buffalo	NY	11,033	VC
SUNY/Univ at Stony Brook	NY	10,998	VC
Stevens Inst of Technology	NJ	31,510	HC+
Syracuse Univ	NY	30,710	HC
Tenn Tech Univ	TN	6,968	C
Texas A&M Univ	TX	8,988	VC
Texas A&M Univ at Kingsville	TX	6,446	LC
Texas Tech Univ	TX	8,825	C
Ohio State Univ	OH	10,819	VC
Tri-State Univ-Main Campus	IN	21,200	C
Tufts Univ	MA	34,874	MC
Tulane Univ	LA	34,013	HC+
Tuskegee Univ	AL	14,600	LC
Universidad Politecnica de PR	PR	4,695	
Univ of Akron	OH	10,530	NC
Univ of Alabama	AL	7,402	C
Univ of Alabama at Huntsville	AL	7,916	VC
Univ of Arizona	AZ	8,614	C
Univ of Arkansas	AR	8,334	VC
Univ of Calif at Berkeley	CA	14,134	MC
Univ of Calif at Davis	CA	12,796	VC
Univ of Calif at Irvine	CA	11,756	C
Univ of Calif at Los Angeles	CA	13,227	MC
Univ of Calif at Riverside	CA	12,479	C
Univ of Calif at San Diego	CA	11,372	HC
Univ of Calif at Santa Barbara	CA	11,732	VC
Univ of Cincinnati	OH	12,491	LC
Univ of Colo at Boulder	CO	9,255	VC
Univ of Conn	CT	12,122	VC
Univ of Dayton	OH	20,400	VC
Univ of Delaware	DE	10,824	VC
Univ of Detroit Mercy	MI	21,620	LC
Univ of Florida	FL	7,874	HC
Univ of Houston	TX	8,410	C
Univ of Idaho	ID	7,026	C
Univ of Illinois at Chicago	IL	10,702	VC
Univ of Illinois at Urbana-Champaign	IL	11,316	HC+
Univ of Iowa	IA	8,607	C+
Univ of Kansas	KS	7,232	VC
Univ of Kentucky	KY	7,765	C
Univ of Louisiana at Lafayette	LA	5,200	C
Univ of Louisville	KY	7,402	LC
Univ of Maine	ME	10,798	C
Univ of Maryland/Baltimore County	MD	12,190	VC
Univ of Maryland/College Park	MD	11,959	C
Univ of Mass Amherst	MA	10,995	VC
Univ of Mass Lowell	MA	9,470	VC
Univ of Mich/Ann Arbor	MI	13,003	HC+
Univ of Minn/Duluth	MN	10,436	C
Univ of Minn/Twin Cities	MN	11,123	VC
Univ of Miss	MS	7,666	C
Univ of Missouri/Columbia	MO	9,803	HC
Univ of Missouri/Rolla	MO	10,034	C
Univ of Nebr at Lincoln	NE	8,325	C+
Univ of Nevada/Reno	NV	8,737	C
Univ of New Hampshire	NH	13,207	C
Univ of New Haven	CT	23,860	LC
Univ of New Mexico	NM	8,026	C
Univ of N Dak	ND	7,067	VC
Univ of Notre Dame	IN	30,707	MC
Univ of Okla	OK	7,616	VC
Univ of Pennsylvania	PA	34,614	MC
Univ of Pittsburgh at Pittsburgh	PA	13,592	HC
Univ of PR/Mayaguez	PR	5,285	
Univ of Rhode Island	RI	12,414	C
Univ of Rochester	NY	32,979	HC
Univ of South Alabama	AL	6,976	LC
Univ of S Car at Columbia	SC	8,748	VC
Univ of South Florida	FL	8,154	C
Univ of Southern Calif	CA	33,647	MC
Univ of Tenn at Knoxville	TN	8,214	C
Univ of Texas at Austin	TX	9,437	HC
Univ of Toledo	OH	11,206	NC
Univ of Tulsa	OK	19,090	HC
Univ of Utah	UT	7,703	C
Univ of Virginia	VA	9,391	HC+
Univ of Washington	WA	10,361	VC
Univ of Wisc/Madison	WI	8,262	VC
Univ of Wyoming	WY	7,143	LC
Vanderbilt Univ	TN	34,482	MC
Villanova Univ	PA	31,997	HC
Virginia Commonwealth Univ	VA	9,030	C
Virginia Polytechnic Inst and State Univ	VA	7,652	C
Washington and Lee Univ	VA	25,005	MC
Washington State Univ	WA	9,388	C
Washington Univ in St. Louis	MO	34,593	MC
Wayne State Univ	MI	6,720	C
West Virginia Univ	WV	8,304	C
West Virginia Univ Inst of Technology	WV	7,518	NC
Western Mich Univ	MI	10,016	C
Widener Univ	PA	26,920	C
Worcester Polytechnic Inst	MA	34,480	HC+
Xavier Univ	OH	23,880	C
Yale Univ	CT	34,030	MC
Youngstown State Univ	OH	9,318	NC

CHEMICAL ENGINEERING TECHNOLOGY

School	ST	$IS	SR
Univ of Hartford	CT	28,884	C
Univ of PR/Arecibo	PR	1,095	

CHEMICAL TECHNOLOGY

School	ST	$IS	SR
Florida State Univ	FL	7,835	HC
Gallaudet Univ	DC	16,554	SP
Inter-American Univ of PR/ Arecibo Campus	PR	3,300	
Inter-American Univ of PR/ Bayamon Univ College	PR	3,700	
Inter-American Univ of PR/ Fajardo Campus	PR	4,000	
Inter-American Univ of PR/ Ponce Regional College	PR	3,700	
Midwestern State Univ	TX	6,704	NC
Univ of Cincinnati	OH	12,491	LC

CHEMISTRY

School	ST	$IS	SR
Abilene Christian Univ	TX	16,300	VC
Adams State College	CO	7,468	C
Adelphi Univ	NY	23,320	VC
Adrian College	MI	19,670	C
Agnes Scott College	GA	24,950	VC
Alabama A&M Univ	AL	5,100	LC
Alabama State Univ	AL	6,404	C
Albany State Univ	GA	5,764	C+
Albertson College of Idaho	ID	23,900	VC
Albion College	MI	25,224	VC
Albright College	PA	27,642	C
Alcorn State Univ	MS	5,594	LC
Alderson-Broaddus College	WV	19,640	C
Alfred Univ	NY	27,212	C+
Allegheny College	PA	27,780	VC
Alma College	MI	22,586	VC
Alvernia College	PA	20,790	C
Alverno College	WI	16,930	LC
American International College	MA	22,268	LC
American Univ	DC	31,544	VC+
Amherst College	MA	34,340	MC
Anderson Univ	IN	19,430	LC
Andrews Univ	MI	17,696	LC
Angelo State Univ	TX	7,028	C
Appalachian State Univ	NC	6,353	C
Aquinas College	MI	20,052	C+
Arcadia Univ	PA	26,650	C
Arizona State Univ-Main	AZ	7,726	C
Arkansas State Univ	AR	7,480	C
Arkansas Tech Univ	AR	6,256	C
Armstrong Atlantic State Univ	GA	7,084	C
Asbury College	KY	18,540	VC
Ashland Univ	OH	22,182	LC
Assumption College	MA	26,320	C
Auburn Univ	AL	5,510	C
Augsburg College	MN	22,978	C
Augusta State Univ	GA	2,282	C
Augustana College	IL	24,117	VC+
Augustana College	SD	20,760	VC
Austin College	TX	22,150	VC+
Austin Peay State Univ	TN	5,814	LC
Averett Univ	VA	17,980	LC
Avila College	MO	17,720	C
Azusa Pacific Univ	CA	22,422	VC
Baker Univ	KS	14,780	C+
Baldwin-Wallace College	OH	22,010	VC+
Ball State Univ	IN	8,660	C
Bard College	NY	33,912	HC
Barry Univ	FL	24,100	LC
Bartlesville Wesleyan College	OK	14,100	LC
Barton College	NC	16,834	LC
Bates College	ME	34,100	MC
Baylor Univ	TX	18,298	VC+
Belhaven College	MS	16,040	C+
Bellarmine Univ	KY	20,440	VC
Belmont Univ	TN	19,066	VC
Beloit College	WI	27,482	HC
Bemidji State Univ	MN	7,957	C
Benedict College	SC	12,662	LC
Benedictine College	KS	18,485	LC
Benedictine Univ	IL	21,330	C
Bennett College	NC	11,200	C
Bennington College	VT	31,350	VC
Berea College	KY	4,070	VC
Berry College	GA	18,850	C
Bethany College	KS	16,602	C+
Bethany College	WV	18,566	C
Bethel College	IN	17,650	LC
Bethel College	KS	17,355	C+
Bethel College	MN	22,740	VC
Bethel College	TN	12,980	C
Bethune-Cookman College	FL	15,746	C
Birmingham-Southern College	AL	22,960	C
Black Hills State Univ	SD	6,652	LC
Blackburn College	IL	13,690	C
Bloomfield College	NJ	17,000	C
Bloomsburg Univ of Pennsylvania	PA	9,434	C
Blue Mountain College	MS	9,100	LC
Bluefield College	VA	14,200	C
Bluffton College	OH	20,644	C
Boise State Univ	ID	6,531	LC
Boston College	MA	33,330	MC
Boston Univ	MA	34,358	MC
Bowdoin College	ME	32,650	MC
Bowling Green State Univ	OH	10,794	C
Bradley Univ	IL	20,970	VC
Brandeis Univ	MA	34,481	MC
Brescia Univ	KY	14,225	C
Briar Cliff Univ	IA	18,657	LC
Bridgewater College	VA	22,950	C
Bridgewater State College	MA	7,589	C+
Brigham Young Univ	UT	7,840	HC
Brown Univ	RI	34,973	MC
Bryn Mawr College	PA	33,580	HC+
Bucknell Univ	PA	31,096	HC
Buena Vista Univ	IA	22,828	C
Butler Univ	IN	25,580	VC+
Cabrini College	PA	25,950	LC
Caldwell College	NJ	20,940	LC
Calif Inst of Technology	CA	27,663	MC
Calif Lutheran Univ	CA	23,500	LC
Calif Polytechnic State Univ	CA	8,747	VC
Calif State Polytechnic Univ, Pomona	CA	8,615	C
Cal State, Bakersfield	CA	6,090	LC
Cal State, Chico	CA	8,598	LC
Cal State, Dominguez Hills	CA	5,840	LC
Cal State, Fresno	CA	7,762	C
Cal State, Fullerton	CA	5,440	LC
Cal State, Hayward	CA	7,400	LC
Cal State, Long Beach	CA	7,400	LC
Cal State, Los Angeles	CA	5,050	C
Cal State, Northridge	CA	7,781	C
Cal State, Sacramento	CA	7,488	C
Cal State, San Bernardino	CA	6,516	C
Cal State, San Marcos	CA	1,736	LC
Cal State, Stanislaus	CA	8,895	C
Calif Univ of Pennsylvania	PA	10,388	C
Calvin College	MI	20,050	NC
Cameron Univ	OK	5,560	NC
Campbell Univ	NC	16,599	C
Campbellsville Univ	KY	14,340	C
Canisius College	NY	24,696	C+
Capital Univ	OH	23,630	C
Cardinal Stritch Univ	WI	17,620	C
Carleton College	MN	30,780	MC
Carlow College	PA	19,366	C
Carnegie Mellon Univ	PA	32,682	MC
Carroll College	MT	19,140	C
Carroll College	WI	21,170	C
Carthage College	WI	23,670	C
Case Western Reserve Univ	OH	27,418	C
Catawba College	NC	19,620	C
Catholic Univ of America	DC	29,332	VC
Cedar Crest College	PA	25,145	C+
Cedarville Univ	OH	17,553	VC
Centenary College of Louisiana	LA	21,600	C+
Central College	IA	21,206	C
Central Conn State Univ	CT	10,404	C
Central Methodist College	MO	16,460	C
Central Mich Univ	MI	8,355	C
Central Missouri State Univ	MO	7,920	C
Central State Univ	OH	8,922	C+
Central Univ of Bayamon	PR	3,335	
Central Washington Univ	WA	8,985	LC
Centre College	KY	24,000	HC
Chadron State College	NE	6,211	NC
Chaminade Univ of Honolulu	HI	17,370	C
Chapman Univ	CA	30,218	VC
Charleston Southern Univ	SC	17,122	C
Chatham College	PA	25,454	C+
Chestnut Hill College	PA	24,790	LC
Cheyney Univ of Pennsylvania	PA	9,993	C
Chicago State Univ	IL	8,851	C+
Christian Brothers Univ	TN	19,820	VC
Citadel, The	SC	9,126	C
CUNY/Brooklyn College	NY	3,403	LC
CUNY/City College	NY	3,309	LC
CUNY/College of Staten Island	NY	3,358	NC
CUNY/Herbert H. Lehman College	NY	3,320	LC
CUNY/Hunter College	NY	5,147	C+
CUNY/Queens College	NY	3,403	VC
CUNY/York College	NY	3,292	NC
Claflin Univ	SC	12,735	C+
Claremont McKenna College	CA	32,700	MC
Clarion Univ of Pennsylvania	PA	11,272	LC
Clark Atlanta Univ	GA	17,174	C
Clark Univ	MA	29,170	HC
Clarke College	IA	20,625	C+
Clarkson Univ	NY	29,884	VC
Clemson Univ	SC	7,600	C
Cleveland State Univ	OH	10,146	NC
Coastal Carolina Univ	SC	9,220	C
Coe College	IA	24,750	VC
Coker College	SC	20,120	C
Colby College	ME	34,290	MC
Colgate Univ	NY	33,480	MC
College Misericordia	PA	23,380	LC
College of Charleston	SC	8,350	HC
College of Mount St. Vincent	NY	24,230	C
College of Mount St. Joseph	OH	20,290	C
College of New Jersey	NJ	13,425	HC
College of New Rochelle	NY	20,000	C
College of Notre Dame of Maryland	MD	23,100	LC
College of Our Lady of the Elms	MA	20,644	C
College of St. Benedict	MN	23,921	VC
College of St. Catherine	MN	22,324	VC
College of St. Elizabeth	NJ	22,510	C
College of St. Mary	NE	18,726	C
College of St. Rose	NY	19,084	C
College of St. Scholastica	MN	22,378	C+
College of Santa Fe	NM	20,250	LC
College of the Holy Cross	MA	32,780	MC
College of the Ozarks	MO	2,650	C+
College of William and Mary	VA	10,002	MC
College of Wooster	OH	28,350	VC
Colo College	CO	31,525	HC+
Colo School of Mines	CO	11,578	HC
Colo State Univ	CO	9,672	C
Columbia College	SC	19,050	LC
Columbia Union College	MD	19,027	C+
Columbia Univ/Barnard College	NY	33,694	MC
Columbia Univ/Columbia College	NY	35,190	MC
Columbia Univ/School of General Studies	NY	35,000	C
Columbus State Univ	GA	7,228	LC
Concord College	WV	7,122	C+
Concordia College/ Moorhead	MN	18,835	C
Concordia Univ	OR	20,500	LC
Concordia Univ Nebr	NE	17,770	C
Concordia Univ, River Forest	IL	20,000	LC
Conn College	CT	33,585	MC
Converse College	SC	21,990	VC
Coppin State College	MD	9,133	LC
Cornell College	IA	24,980	VC
Cornell Univ	NY	34,614	MC
Covenant College	GA	21,970	C+
Creighton Univ	NE	23,476	VC
Crichton College	TN	12,680	LC
Culver-Stockton College	MO	15,400	LC
Cumberland College	KY	14,864	C
Curry College	MA	26,025	LC
Daemen College	NY	20,620	C
Dakota State Univ	SD	6,950	C
Dana College	NE	18,046	C
Dartmouth College	NH	34,458	MC
David Lipscomb Univ	TN	16,158	VC
Davidson College	NC	30,823	MC
Davis and Elkins College	WV	19,270	LC
De Sales Univ	PA	22,610	VC
Delaware State Univ	DE	8,104	LC
Delaware Valley College	PA	24,213	LC
Delta State Univ	MS	5,416	C
Denison Univ	OH	29,640	HC
DePaul Univ	IL	23,590	VC
DePauw Univ	IN	28,000	HC
Dickinson College	PA	32,210	VC+
Dickinson State Univ	ND	5,495	NC
Dillard Univ	LA	16,046	VC
Doane College	NE	17,600	LC
Dominican Univ	IL	20,800	C
Dordt College	IA	18,100	C+
Drake Univ	IA	22,830	VC
Drew Univ/College of Liberal Arts	NJ	32,152	VC
Drexel Univ	PA	27,657	VC
Drury Univ	MO	15,250	VC
Duke Univ	NC	34,396	MC
Duquesne Univ	PA	24,242	C+
Earlham College	IN	27,446	VC+
East Carolina Univ	NC	7,766	C
East Central Univ	OK	4,578	C
East Stroudsburg Univ of Pennsylvania	PA	8,430	LC
East Tenn State Univ	TN	7,127	C
East Texas Baptist Univ	TX	12,349	LC
Eastern College	PA	19,641	LC
Eastern Illinois Univ	IL	10,101	C

ST = STATE $IS = IN-STATE COSTS SR = SELECTOR RATING

School	ST	$IS	SR
Eastern Kentucky Univ	KY	6,552	C
Eastern Mennonite Univ	VA	20,700	VC
Eastern Mich Univ	MI	9,855	C
Eastern Nazarene College	MA	19,433	LC
Eastern New Mexico Univ	NM	4,113	LC
Eastern Oregon Univ	OR	8,772	C
Eastern Washington Univ	WA	7,972	LC
Eckerd College	FL	25,500	C+
Edgewood College	WI	18,304	C
Edinboro Univ of Pennsylvania	PA	9,328	LC
Elizabeth City State Univ	NC	5,550	LC
Elizabethtown College	PA	26,000	VC
Elmhurst College	IL	21,750	C
Elmira College	NY	31,070	VC+
Elon Univ	NC	19,430	VC
Emmanuel College	MA	23,802	C+
Emory & Henry College	VA	19,462	C
Emory Univ	GA	33,792	MC
Emporia State Univ	KS	6,198	LC
Erskine College	SC	21,399	VC
Eureka College	IL	22,200	C
Evangel Univ	MO	14,050	C
Fairfield Univ	CT	30,885	HC
Fairleigh Dickinson Univ/ Madison campus	NJ	25,500	C
Fairleigh Dickinson Univ/ Teaneck Campus	NJ	24,646	C
Fairmont State College	WV	7,010	NC
Fayetteville State Univ	NC	5,590	LC
Ferrum College	VA	15,990	LC
Fisk Univ	TN	13,700	LC
Florida A&M Univ	FL	6,948	C
Florida Atlantic Univ	FL	8,832	C
Florida Inst of Technology	FL	25,250	VC
Florida International Univ	FL	9,486	VC
Florida Memorial College	FL	6,000	LC
Florida Southern College	FL	19,430	C
Florida State Univ	FL	7,835	HC
Fordham Univ	NY	30,710	VC
Fort Hays State Univ	KS	6,294	LC
Fort Lewis College	CO	7,659	LC
Fort Valley State Univ	GA	6,014	LC
Framingham State College	MA	7,259	C
Francis Marion Univ	SC	7,682	C
Franciscan Univ of Steubenville	OH	19,100	C+
Franklin and Marshall College	PA	32,410	HC
Franklin College of Indiana	IN	19,905	C
Freed-Hardeman Univ	TN	14,290	VC
Fresno Pacific Univ	CA	19,740	C
Friends Univ	KS	15,962	LC
Frostburg State Univ	MD	9,680	C
Furman Univ	SC	25,492	HC
Gallaudet Univ	DC	16,554	SP
Gannon Univ	PA	18,848	C
Gardner-Webb Univ	NC	17,400	C
Geneva College	PA	19,990	C+
George Fox Univ	OR	24,095	VC
George Mason Univ	VA	9,192	C
George Washington Univ	DC	32,170	HC
Georgetown College	KY	18,400	VC
Georgetown Univ	DC	34,847	MC
Georgia College and State Univ	GA	7,344	C
Georgia Inst of Technology	GA	9,028	HC+
Georgia Southern Univ	GA	6,958	C
Georgia Southwestern State Univ	GA	6,013	C
Georgia State Univ	GA	7,792	LC
Georgian Court College	NJ	19,040	LC
Gettysburg College	PA	32,070	HC
Glenville State College	WV	6,588	NC
Gonzaga Univ	WA	24,276	HC+
Gordon College	MA	23,594	VC+
Goshen College	IN	18,950	VC+
Goucher College	MD	30,650	VC+
Graceland Univ	IA	15,845	C
Grambling State Univ	LA	5,325	NC
Grand Canyon Univ	AZ	30,000	LC
Grand Valley State Univ	MI	10,040	C
Greensboro College	NC	19,080	LC
Greenville College	IL	19,226	LC
Grinnell College	IA	28,300	HC+
Grove City College	PA	12,280	MC
Guilford College	NC	23,255	C
Gustavus Adolphus College	MN	24,190	VC+
Hamilton College	NY	34,150	HC
Hamline Univ	MN	23,339	C+
Hampden-Sydney College	VA	24,871	C
Hampshire College	MA	33,881	HC+
Hampton Univ	VA	17,112	C+
Hanover College	IN	17,560	VC
Harding Univ	AR	13,528	VC
Hardin-Simmons Univ	TX	14,165	C
Hartwick College	NY	33,090	C+
Harvard Univ/Harvard College	MA	34,269	MC
Harvey Mudd College	CA	31,605	MC
Hastings College	NE	17,854	C+
Haverford College	PA	34,300	MC
Heidelberg College	OH	23,879	C
Henderson State Univ	AR	6,269	C
Hendrix College	AR	18,463	HC
High Point Univ	NC	20,220	LC

School	ST	$IS	SR
Hillsdale College	MI	20,586	VC+
Hiram College	OH	27,034	VC
Hobart and William Smith Colleges	NY	33,195	VC
Hofstra Univ	NY	23,252	C
Hollins Univ	VA	24,328	VC
Holy Family College	PA	13,710	LC
Hood College	MD	26,020	VC
Hope College	MI	22,922	C+
Houghton College	NY	21,810	VC+
Houston Baptist Univ	TX	15,300	LC
Howard Payne Univ	TX	13,834	C+
Howard Univ	DC	15,522	LC
Humboldt State Univ	CA	8,582	C
Huntingdon College	AL	18,400	VC
Huntington College	IN	15,480	LC
Huston-Tillotson College	TX	12,977	LC
Idaho State Univ	ID	7,030	C+
Illinois College	IL	16,234	C
Illinois Inst of Technology	IL	25,182	HC+
Illinois State Univ	IL	9,235	C
Illinois Wesleyan Univ	IL	26,970	HC
Immaculata College	PA	22,400	LC
Indiana State Univ	IN	8,461	LC
Indiana Univ Bloomington	IN	10,712	C+
Indiana Univ Northwest	IN	3,447	C
Indiana Univ of Pennsylvania	PA	9,133	C
Indiana Univ South Bend	IN	3,515	C
Indiana Univ Southeast	IN	3,459	C
Indiana Univ-Purdue Univ Fort Wayne	IN	3,166	LC
Indiana Univ-Purdue Univ Indianapolis	IN	9,473	C
Indiana Wesleyan Univ	IN	17,680	C
Inter-American Univ of PR/ Arecibo Campus	PR	3,300	
Inter-American Univ of PR/ Bayamon Univ College	PR	3,700	
Inter-American Univ of PR/ Fajardo Campus	PR	4,000	
Inter-American Univ of PR/ Metropolitan Campus	PR	4,166	
Inter-American Univ of PR/ Ponce Regional College	PR	3,700	
Inter-American Univ of PR/ San GermÈn	PR	6,390	
Iowa State Univ	IA	8,108	VC
Iowa Wesleyan College	IA	18,840	C
Ithaca College	NY	28,719	HC
Jackson State Univ	MS	6,776	LC
Jacksonville State Univ	AL	6,568	LC
Jacksonville Univ	FL	21,110	LC
James Madison Univ	VA	9,552	HC
Jamestown College	ND	11,310	NC
Jarvis Christian College	TX	9,035	NC
John Brown Univ	AR	15,080	VC
John Carroll Univ	OH	24,140	VC
Johns Hopkins Univ	MD	35,226	MC
Johnson C. Smith Univ	NC	16,560	C+
Judson College	AL	13,790	C
Judson College	IL	18,980	LC
Juniata College	PA	26,080	VC
Kalamazoo College	MI	26,955	HC+
Kansas State Univ	KS	6,995	C
Kansas Wesleyan Univ	KS	17,400	C+
Kean Univ	NJ	11,159	C
Keene State College	NH	11,280	C
Kennesaw State Univ	GA	2,306	LC
Kent State Univ	OH	11,104	C
Kentucky State Univ	KY	6,146	NC
Kentucky Wesleyan College	KY	15,800	C
Kenyon College	OH	32,130	HC+
King College	TN	17,800	VC
King's College	PA	24,680	C
Knox College	IL	28,230	HC
Knoxville College	TN	6,200	LC
Kutztown Univ of Pennsylvania	PA	8,907	C
La Roche College	PA	18,854	LC
La Salle Univ	PA	27,890	C
La Sierra Univ	CA	19,260	LC
Lafayette College	PA	32,655	MC
LaGrange College	GA	17,496	C
Lake Erie College	OH	21,350	LC
Lake Forest College	IL	27,460	VC
Lakeland College	WI	17,950	C
Lamar Univ	TX	6,816	LC
Lambuth Univ	TN	14,254	C
Lander Univ	SC	8,618	LC
Lane College	TN	10,400	C+
Langston Univ	OK	2,308	LC
Lawrence Tech Univ	MI	11,429	C
Lawrence Univ	WI	27,711	HC
Le Moyne College	NY	23,840	C
Lebanon Valley College of Pennsylvania	PA	25,700	VC
Lee Univ	TN	10,198	LC
Lehigh Univ	PA	32,290	MC
LeMoyne-Owen College	TN	8,450	NC
Lenoir-Rhyne College	NC	19,186	C
LeTourneau Univ	TX	19,020	VC
Lewis and Clark College	OR	29,010	VC
Lewis Univ	IL	20,960	C
Lewis-Clark State College	ID	6,496	C
Limestone College	SC	16,900	C

School	ST	$IS	SR
Lincoln Memorial Univ	TN	12,620	LC
Lincoln Univ	MO	7,158	NC
Lincoln Univ	PA	11,198	C+
Lindenwood Univ	MO	17,250	C
Linfield College	OR	25,840	VC
Livingstone College	NC	13,360	LC
Lock Haven Univ of Pennsylvania	PA	9,534	C
LIU/Brooklyn Campus	NY	22,290	C
LIU/C.W. Post Campus	NY	25,380	C
LIU/Southampton College	NY	26,270	C
Longwood College	VA	8,950	C
Loras College	IA	22,994	C+
Louisiana College	LA	11,516	C
Louisiana State Univ and A&M College	LA	8,014	VC
Louisiana State Univ in Shreveport	LA	2,480	NC
Louisiana Tech Univ	LA	6,506	C
Lourdes College	OH	13,100	LC
Loyola College in Maryland	MD	30,900	HC
Loyola Marymount Univ	CA	28,754	HC
Loyola Univ New Orleans	LA	23,506	VC+
Loyola Univ of Chicago	IL	25,992	VC
Lubbock Christian Univ	TX	14,226	LC
Luther College	IA	23,300	VC+
Lycoming College	PA	24,780	C
Lynchburg College	VA	23,405	C
Lyon College	AR	16,500	VC
Macalester College	MN	28,814	HC+
MacMurray College	IL	17,790	LC
Madonna Univ	MI	11,504	VC
Maharishi Univ of Management	IA	20,660	VC
Malone College	OH	19,190	C
Manchester College	IN	22,010	C
Manhattan College	NY	25,500	VC
Manhattanville College	NY	28,730	VC
Mansfield Univ	PA	9,648	C
Marian College	IN	21,020	C
Marian College of Fond du Lac	WI	17,935	LC
Marietta College	OH	24,580	C
Marist College	NY	24,756	VC
Marlboro College	VT	26,410	VC+
Marquette Univ	WI	24,836	C+
Mars Hill College	NC	18,600	LC
Marshall Univ	WV	7,752	LC
Martin Univ	IN	8,370	SP
Mary Baldwin College	VA	23,440	C
Mary Washington College	VA	9,032	VC+
Marygrove College	MI	16,075	C
Marymount College/ Tarrytown	NY	23,850	C
Maryville College	TN	23,210	VC
Maryville Univ of St. Louis	MO	18,680	C
Mass College of Pharmacy and Health Sciences	MA	27,131	SP
Mass Inst of Technology	MA	35,228	MC
Mayville State Univ	ND	6,440	NC
McKendree College	IL	18,300	C+
McMurry Univ	TX	15,287	C
McNeese State Univ	LA	5,259	LC
McPherson College	KS	17,710	C
Mercer Univ	GA	24,130	VC
Mercyhurst College	PA	20,694	C
Meredith College	NC	17,500	C
Merrimack College	MA	25,725	VC
Messiah College	PA	23,180	VC
Methodist College	NC	19,526	C
Metropolitan State College of Denver	CO	2,338	LC
Miami Univ	OH	12,885	VC+
Mich State Univ	MI	10,386	VC
Mich Tech Univ	MI	11,088	VC
MidAmerica Nazarene Univ	KS	16,960	C
Middle Tenn State Univ	TN	6,994	C
Middlebury College	VT	34,300	MC
Midland Lutheran College	NE	18,600	C
Midway College	KY	15,815	C
Midwestern State Univ	TX	6,704	NC
Miles College	AL	7,870	NC
Millersville Univ of Pennsylvania	PA	10,153	VC
Milligan College	TN	17,550	C
Millikin Univ	IL	24,415	C+
Mills College	CA	27,950	C
Millsaps College	MS	22,608	VC+
Minn State Univ, Mankato	MN	7,296	LC
Minot State Univ	ND	5,466	LC
Miss College	MS	14,574	C
Miss State Univ	MS	7,853	C
Miss Univ for Women	MS	5,446	LC
Miss Valley State Univ	MS	6,345	C
Missouri Baptist College	MO	15,762	LC
Missouri Southern State College	MO	6,666	C
Missouri Western State College	MO	6,662	NC
Monmouth College	IL	21,550	C
Monmouth Univ	NJ	24,042	C
Montana State Univ-Billings	MT	7,653	NC
Montana State Univ- Bozeman	MT	8,431	C
Montana State Univ- Northern	MT	8,600	NC

School	ST	$IS	SR
Montana Tech of The Univ of Montana	MT	7,845	C
Montclair State Univ	NJ	10,287	LC
Moorhead State Univ	MN	7,000	LC
Moravian College	PA	27,065	VC
Morehead State Univ	KY	6,510	C
Morehouse College	GA	19,814	C
Morgan State Univ	MD	10,078	LC
Morningside College	IA	19,124	C
Morris Brown College	GA	15,993	LC
Mount Holyoke College	MA	34,128	HC
Mount Marty College	SD	15,656	LC
Mount Mary College	WI	18,024	C
Mount St. Mary College	NY	18,825	C
Mount St. Mary's College	CA	24,430	C
Mount St. Mary's College	MD	25,740	C
Mount Union College	OH	21,120	C
Mount Vernon Nazarene College	OH	17,027	C
Muhlenberg College	PA	28,170	HC
Murray State Univ	KY	6,672	C
Muskingum College	OH	18,760	C
Nazareth College of Rochester	NY	22,036	VC
Nebr Wesleyan Univ	NE	18,767	VC
New College of Florida	FL	8,130	HC+
New Jersey City Univ	NJ	9,100	LC
New Jersey Inst of Technology	NJ	14,690	VC
New Mexico Highlands Univ	NM	6,256	NC
New Mexico Inst of Mining and Technology	NM	7,152	VC+
New Mexico State Univ	NM	7,302	C
New York Inst of Technology	NY	21,756	C
New York Univ	NY	35,200	MC
Newberry College	SC	19,670	LC
Newman Univ	KS	14,098	LC
Niagara Univ	NY	22,250	C+
Nicholls State Univ	LA	5,290	NC
Norfolk State Univ	VA	8,382	LC
N Car Agricultural and Technical State Univ	NC	6,659	LC
N Car Central Univ	NC	6,418	LC
N Car State Univ	NC	8,680	HC
N Car Wesleyan College	NC	15,650	LC
North Central College	IL	22,944	C+
N Dak State Univ	ND	7,004	VC
North Georgia College and State Univ	GA	6,322	C+
North Park Univ	IL	24,030	C
Northeastern Illinois Univ	IL	2,898	NC
Northeastern State Univ	OK	4,704	LC
Northeastern Univ	MA	30,078	VC
Northern Arizona Univ	AZ	7,398	C
Northern Illinois Univ	IL	9,545	C
Northern Kentucky Univ	KY	6,352	NC
Northern Mich Univ	MI	9,693	C
Northern State Univ	SD	6,279	LC
Northland College	WI	21,435	C+
Northwest Missouri State Univ	MO	7,922	LC
Northwest Nazarene Univ	ID	18,380	C
Northwestern College of Iowa	IA	17,630	C+
Northwestern Okla State Univ	OK	4,542	NC
Northwestern State Univ of Louisiana	LA	5,745	NC
Northwestern Univ	IL	33,615	MC
Norwich Univ	VT	21,064	LC
Notre Dame College	OH	20,425	C
Oakland City Univ	IN	11,286	LC
Oakland Univ	MI	9,418	C
Oakwood College	AL	14,904	C
Oberlin College	OH	33,140	HC+
Occidental College	CA	32,288	HC
Oglethorpe Univ	GA	19,100	LC
Ohio Dominican College	OH	18,100	LC
Ohio Northern Univ	OH	27,765	VC
Ohio Univ	OH	11,769	C
Ohio Wesleyan Univ	OH	29,670	VC+
Okla Baptist Univ	OK	13,878	VC
Okla Christian Univ	OK	16,500	VC
Okla City Univ	OK	15,810	C
Okla Panhandle State Univ	OK	3,812	NC
Okla State Univ	OK	7,650	VC
Old Dominion Univ	VA	9,386	C
Olivet College	MI	17,410	C
Olivet Nazarene Univ	IL	18,444	C
Oral Roberts Univ	OK	18,490	C
Oregon State Univ	OR	9,612	VC
Ottawa Univ	KS	11,800	LC
Otterbein College	OH	23,439	C
Ouachita Baptist Univ	AR	16,460	VC
Our Lady of the Lake Univ of San Antonio	TX	17,336	C
Pace Univ	NY	24,200	C
Pacific Lutheran Univ	WA	23,318	VC
Pacific Union College	CA	20,250	VC
Pacific Univ	OR	24,250	C
Paine College	GA	11,896	LC
Park Univ	MO	9,816	C
Penn State Univ at Erie/ Behrend College	PA	12,326	C

ST = STATE **$IS** = IN-STATE COSTS **SR** = SELECTOR RATING

School	ST	$IS	SR
Penn State Univ/Univ Park Campus	PA	11,120	VC
Pepperdine Univ	CA	32,830	VC
Pfeiffer Univ	NC	18,580	C
Philadelphia Univ	PA	24,722	C
Philander Smith College	AR	7,380	NC
Piedmont College	GA	16,900	C
Pikeville College	KY	12,000	NC
Pittsburg State Univ	KS	6,228	NC
Pitzer College	CA	33,930	HC
Plymouth State College	NH	11,024	LC
Point Loma Nazarene Univ	CA	21,380	VC
Polytechnic Univ/Brooklyn	NY	33,090	HC
Pomona College	CA	33,960	MC
Pontifical Catholic Univ of PR/Ponce	PR	7,076	
Portland State Univ	OR	11,220	C
Prairie View A&M Univ	TX	3,172	LC
Presbyterian College	SC	23,356	VC
Princeton Univ	NJ	35,072	MC
Principia College	IL	23,865	C+
Providence College	RI	27,620	HC
Purdue Univ/Calumet	IN	6,630	NC
Purdue Univ/West Lafayette	IN	10,284	VC
Quincy Univ	IL	20,450	C
Quinnipiac Univ	CT	27,370	C
Radford Univ	VA	8,302	C
Ramapo College of New Jersey	NJ	13,550	VC
Randolph-Macon College	VA	24,395	C
Randolph-Macon Woman's College	VA	25,820	VC+
Reed College	OR	33,350	HC+
Regis College	MA	26,750	C
Regis Univ	CO	25,740	C+
Rensselaer Polytechnic Inst	NY	33,863	HC+
Rhode Island College	RI	8,700	LC
Rhodes College	TN	26,466	HC+
Richard Stockton College of New Jersey	NJ	12,165	VC
Rider Univ	NJ	27,400	C
Ripon College	WI	24,180	VC+
Rivier College	NH	24,215	C
Roanoke College	VA	24,689	VC
Roberts Wesleyan College	NY	20,160	C+
Rochester Inst of Technology	NY	26,232	VC+
Rockford College	IL	23,930	C
Rockhurst Univ	MO	20,090	C
Rocky Mountain College	MT	18,113	C
Roger Williams Univ	RI	29,010	C
Rollins College	FL	31,223	HC
Roosevelt Univ	IL	20,240	LC
Rose-Hulman Inst of Technology	IN	27,707	HC+
Rosemont College	PA	24,060	C
Rowan Univ	NJ	12,365	VC
Russell Sage College	NY	23,674	C+
Rust College	MS	7,800	C+
Rutgers, The State Univ of New Jersey New Brunswick Campus	NJ	12,709	C
Rutgers, The State Univ of New Jersey/ CamdenCampus	NJ	6,484	C
Sacred Heart Univ	CT	26,588	VC
Saginaw Valley State Univ	MI	9,465	C
St. Ambrose Univ	IA	19,994	C
St. Andrews Presbyterian College	NC	19,720	LC
St. Anselm College	NH	27,405	C
St. Augustine's College	NC	12,990	C+
St. Bonaventure Univ	NY	21,956	C
St. Cloud State Univ	MN	7,180	C
St. Edward's Univ	TX	17,846	C
St. Francis Univ	PA	24,486	LC
St. John Fisher College	NY	21,800	C
St. John's Univ	MN	23,640	VC
St. John's Univ	NY	26,660	C
St. Joseph College	CT	25,960	LC
St. Joseph's College	IN	21,640	C
St. Joseph's College of Maine	ME	22,500	LC
St. Joseph's College, New York	NY	9,802	C
St. Joseph's Univ	PA	29,715	VC+
St. Lawrence Univ	NY	32,605	VC
St. Louis Univ	MO	26,590	VC+
St. Martin's College	WA	20,566	C
St. Mary College	KS	17,298	C
St. Mary's College	IN	24,474	VC
St. Mary's College	MI	13,314	LC
St. Mary's College of Calif	CA	27,575	C
St. Mary's College of Maryland	MD	14,104	HC
St. Mary's Univ of Minn	MN	19,975	C
St. Mary's Univ of San Antonio	TX	19,735	C
St. Michael's College	VT	26,935	VC
St. Norbert College	WI	23,169	VC
St. Olaf College	MN	25,880	HC
St. Peter's College	NJ	22,292	LC
St. Thomas Univ	FL	19,500	LC
St. Vincent College	PA	22,942	VC
St. Xavier Univ	IL	21,104	C
Salem College	NC	23,065	VC
Salem State College	MA	4,481	LC
Salisbury Univ	MD	10,576	VC
Salve Regina Univ	RI	26,460	C
Sam Houston State Univ	TX	6,076	LC
Samford Univ	AL	16,340	VC
San Diego State Univ	CA	9,716	C+
San Francisco State Univ	CA	7,139	LC
San Jose State Univ	CA	8,187	C
Santa Clara Univ	CA	28,371	VC+
Sarah Lawrence College	NY	37,516	HC
Savannah State Univ	GA	2,550	LC
Schreiner Univ	TX	19,254	C
Scripps College	CA	30,400	HC+
Seattle Pacific Univ	WA	22,674	C+
Seattle Univ	WA	24,183	VC
Seton Hall Univ	NJ	26,910	LC
Seton Hill College	PA	21,875	C
Shaw Univ	NC	12,810	C
Shawnee State Univ	OH	8,634	NC
Shenandoah Univ	VA	22,550	NC
Shepherd College	WV	7,062	LC
Shippensburg Univ of Pennsylvania	PA	9,652	C
Shorter College	GA	15,185	C
Siena College	NY	22,685	VC
Siena Heights Univ	MI	16,140	LC
Simmons College	MA	30,418	VC
Simon's Rock College of Bard	MA	32,450	HC
Simpson College	IA	21,200	C+
Skidmore College	NY	34,201	VC+
Slippery Rock Univ	PA	9,152	LC
Smith College	MA	33,302	HC+
Sonoma State Univ	CA	8,953	C
S Car State Univ	SC	6,586	LC
S Dak School of Mines and Technology	SD	7,438	C+
S Dak State Univ	SD	6,848	C
Southeast Missouri State Univ	MO	8,367	C+
Southeastern Louisiana Univ	LA	6,047	LC
Southeastern Okla State Univ	OK	4,917	C
Southern Adventist Univ	TN	15,600	C
Southern Arkansas Univ	AR	5,740	LC
Southern Conn State Univ	CT	10,310	C
Southern Illinois Univ at Carbondale	IL	8,621	C
Southern Illinois Univ Edwardsville	IL	7,869	LC
Southern Methodist Univ	TX	28,349	VC
Southern Nazarene Univ	OK	14,634	NC
Southern Oregon Univ	OR	9,429	C
Southern Univ and A&M College	LA	6,365	C+
Southern Univ at New Orleans	LA	995	NC
Southern Utah Univ	UT	7,254	C
Southern Wesleyan Univ	SC	17,280	C
Southwest Baptist Univ	MO	13,426	LC
Southwest Missouri State Univ	MO	7,600	LC
Southwest State Univ	MN	7,117	LC
Southwest Texas State Univ	TX	8,730	VC
Southwestern Adventist Univ	TX	14,798	C
Southwestern College	KS	17,656	C
Southwestern Okla State Univ	OK	4,801	C
Southwestern Univ	TX	22,550	HC
Spalding Univ	KY	15,196	C
Spelman College	GA	19,215	C+
Spring Arbor Univ	MI	17,976	C
Spring Hill College	AL	23,250	C
Springfield College	MA	24,520	C
Stanford Univ	CA	34,222	MC
SUNY/College at Brockport	NY	10,267	C
SUNY/College at Buffalo	NY	8,025	C
SUNY/College at Cortland	NY	10,564	C
SUNY/College at Fredonia	NY	10,125	C
SUNY/College at Geneseo	NY	9,970	HC
SUNY/College at Old Westbury	NY	9,818	LC
SUNY/College at Oneonta	NY	9,981	C
SUNY/College at Oswego	NY	10,856	C
SUNY/College at Plattsburgh	NY	9,729	C
SUNY/College at Potsdam	NY	10,519	C
SUNY/College at Purchase	NY	10,587	VC
SUNY/College of Environmental Science and Forestry	NY	12,446	VC
SUNY/Univ at Albany	NY	10,997	VC
SUNY/Univ at Binghamton	NY	10,653	HC
SUNY/Univ at Buffalo	NY	11,033	VC
SUNY/Univ at New Paltz	NY	9,685	VC
SUNY/Univ at Stony Brook	NY	10,998	VC
State Univ of West Georgia	GA	7,101	C
Stephen F. Austin State Univ	TX	6,905	C
Stetson Univ	FL	25,640	VC
Stevens Inst of Technology	NJ	31,510	HC+
Stonehill College	MA	26,852	HC
Suffolk Univ	MA	26,516	C
Sul Ross State Univ	TX	6,582	LC
Susquehanna Univ	PA	27,270	VC
Swarthmore College	PA	34,538	MC
Sweet Briar College	VA	25,310	VC
Syracuse Univ	NY	30,710	HC
Tabor College	KS	17,600	LC
Talladega College	AL	10,110	LC
Tarleton State Univ	TX	7,160	C
Taylor Univ	IN	21,562	VC+
Temple Univ	PA	14,124	C
Tenn State Univ	TN	7,058	VC
Tenn Tech Univ	TN	6,968	C
Tenn Wesleyan College	TN	13,030	C
Texas A&M Univ	TX	8,988	VC
Texas A&M Univ at Commerce	TX	7,326	C
Texas A&M Univ at Kingsville	TX	6,446	LC
Texas Christian Univ	TX	19,910	C
Texas Lutheran Univ	TX	17,660	C
Texas Southern Univ	TX	6,576	NC
Texas Tech Univ	TX	8,825	C
Texas Wesleyan Univ	TX	14,710	C
Texas Woman's Univ	TX	5,855	LC
Ohio State Univ	OH	10,819	VC
Thiel College	PA	18,419	LC
Thomas Edison State College	NJ	2,750	SP
Thomas More College	KY	17,700	LC
Tougaloo College	MS	9,200	NC
Touro College	NY	14,950	VC
Towson Univ	MD	11,088	VC
Transylvania Univ	KY	21,780	VC+
Trevecca Nazarene Univ	TN	15,752	C
Trinity Christian College	IL	19,415	C
Trinity College	CT	34,300	HC
Trinity College	DC	21,370	LC
Trinity International Univ	IL	20,640	C+
Trinity Univ	TX	21,444	HC
Tri-State Univ-Main Campus	IN	21,200	C
Troy State Univ	AL	7,696	C
Truman State Univ	MO	8,568	VC+
Tufts Univ	MA	34,874	MC
Tulane Univ	LA	34,013	HC+
Turabo Univ	PR	4,110	
Tuskegee Univ	AL	14,600	LC
Union College	NE	14,650	C
Union College	NY	32,646	HC
Union Univ	TN	18,930	C+
United States Air Force Academy	CO		MC
United States Military Academy	NY		MC
United States Naval Academy	MD		MC
Univ of Akron	OH	10,530	NC
Univ of Alabama	AL	7,402	C
Univ of Alabama at Birmingham	AL	10,110	C
Univ of Alabama at Huntsville	AL	7,916	VC
Univ of Alaska Anchorage	AK	9,100	NC
Univ of Alaska Fairbanks	AK	8,265	NC
Univ of Arizona	AZ	8,614	C
Univ of Arkansas	AR	8,334	VC
Univ of Arkansas at Little Rock	AR	5,637	NC
Univ of Arkansas at Monticello	AR	5,940	NC
Univ of Arkansas at Pine Bluff	AR	7,925	C
Univ of Calif at Berkeley	CA	14,134	MC
Univ of Calif at Davis	CA	12,796	VC
Univ of Calif at Irvine	CA	11,756	C
Univ of Calif at Los Angeles	CA	13,227	MC
Univ of Calif at Riverside	CA	12,479	C
Univ of Calif at San Diego	CA	11,372	HC
Univ of Calif at Santa Barbara	CA	11,732	VC
Univ of Calif at Santa Cruz	CA	13,655	VC
Univ of Central Arkansas	AR	6,388	C
Univ of Central Florida	FL	8,251	VC
Univ of Central Okla	OK	5,205	C
Univ of Charleston	WV	20,640	C
Univ of Chicago	IL	35,087	MC
Univ of Cincinnati	OH	12,491	LC
Univ of Colo at Boulder	CO	9,255	VC
Univ of Colo at Colo Springs	CO	9,403	C
Univ of Colo at Denver	CO	3,673	C
Univ of Conn	CT	12,122	VC
Univ of Dallas	TX	22,128	VC+
Univ of Dayton	OH	20,400	VC
Univ of Delaware	DE	10,824	VC
Univ of Denver	CO	28,783	VC
Univ of Detroit Mercy	MI	21,620	LC
Univ of Evansville	IN	22,865	VC+
Univ of Florida	FL	7,874	HC
Univ of Georgia	GA	8,656	VC
Univ of Hartford	CT	28,884	C
Univ of Hawaii at Hilo	HI	6,497	C
Univ of Hawaii at Manoa	HI	7,862	VC
Univ of Houston	TX	8,410	C
Univ of Idaho	ID	7,026	C
Univ of Illinois at Chicago	IL	10,702	VC
Univ of Illinois at Urbana Champaign	IL	11,316	HC+
Univ of Indianapolis	IN	20,840	C
Univ of Iowa	IA	8,607	C+
Univ of Kansas	KS	7,232	VC
Univ of Kentucky	KY	7,765	C
Univ of La Verne	CA	24,280	C
Univ of Louisiana at Lafayette	LA	5,200	C
Univ of Louisiana at Monroe	LA	5,207	NC
Univ of Louisville	KY	7,402	LC
Univ of Maine	ME	10,798	C
Univ of Mary Hardin-Baylor	TX	13,929	C
Univ of Maryland/Baltimore County	MD	12,190	VC
Univ of Maryland/College Park	MD	11,959	C
Univ of Maryland/Eastern Shore	MD	9,258	C
Univ of Mass Amherst	MA	10,995	VC
Univ of Mass Boston	MA	4,227	C
Univ of Mass Dartmouth	MA	9,852	C
Univ of Mass Lowell	MA	9,470	VC
Univ of Memphis	TN	7,271	C
Univ of Miami	FL	31,130	HC
Univ of Mich/Ann Arbor	MI	13,003	HC+
Univ of Mich/Dearborn	MI	4,677	VC
Univ of Mich/Flint	MI	4,323	C
Univ of Minn/Duluth	MN	10,436	C
Univ of Minn/Morris	MN	10,716	VC
Univ of Minn/Twin Cities	MN	11,123	VC
Univ of Miss	MS	7,666	C
Univ of Missouri/Columbia	MO	9,803	HC
Univ of Missouri/Kansas City	MO	9,685	VC
Univ of Missouri/Rolla	MO	10,034	C
Univ of Missouri/St. Louis	MO	9,966	C
Univ of Mobile	AL	13,620	LC
Univ of Montana	MT	8,038	C
Univ of Montevallo	AL	7,266	C
Univ of Nebr at Kearney	NE	7,048	NC
Univ of Nebr at Lincoln	NE	8,325	C+
Univ of Nebr at Omaha	NE	6,867	C
Univ of Nevada/Las Vegas	NV	8,281	VC
Univ of Nevada/Reno	NV	8,737	C
Univ of New Hampshire	NH	13,207	C
Univ of New Haven	CT	23,860	LC
Univ of New Mexico	NM	8,026	C
Univ of New Orleans	LA	10,160	C
Univ of North Alabama	AL	7,016	NC
Univ of N Car at Asheville	NC	6,896	VC
Univ of N Car at Chapel Hill	NC	8,789	HC
Univ of N Car at Charlotte	NC	7,254	C
Univ of N Car at Greensboro	NC	6,858	C
Univ of N Car at Pembroke	NC	5,914	LC
Univ of N Car at Wilmington	NC	7,769	C
Univ of N Dak	ND	7,067	VC
Univ of North Florida	FL	8,089	VC
Univ of North Texas	TX	7,629	C
Univ of Northern Colo	CO	8,082	C+
Univ of Northern Iowa	IA	7,850	C
Univ of Notre Dame	IN	30,707	MC
Univ of Okla	OK	7,616	VC
Univ of Oregon	OR	9,969	C
Univ of Pennsylvania	PA	34,614	MC
Univ of Pittsburgh at Bradford	PA	12,696	C
Univ of Pittsburgh at Johnstown	PA	13,044	LC
Univ of Pittsburgh at Pittsburgh	PA	13,592	HC
Univ of Portland	OR	24,950	VC
Univ of PR at Humacao	PR	1,245	
Univ of PR/Cayey Univ College	PR	1,245	
Univ of PR/Mayaguez	PR	5,285	
Univ of PR/Rio Piedras	PR	5,510	
Univ of Puget Sound	WA	28,285	HC
Univ of Redlands	CA	29,246	VC
Univ of Rhode Island	RI	12,414	C
Univ of Richmond	VA	27,300	HC
Univ of Rio Grande	OH	8,728	NC
Univ of Rochester	NY	32,979	HC
Univ of St. Francis	IN	17,790	LC
Univ of St. Thomas	MN	24,044	VC
Univ of St. Thomas	TX	18,752	VC
Univ of San Diego	CA	29,198	HC
Univ of San Francisco	CA	27,302	VC
Univ of Science and Arts of Okla	OK	5,245	C
Univ of Scranton	PA	27,964	C+
Univ of Sioux Falls	SD	16,390	C
Univ of South Alabama	AL	6,976	LC
Univ of S Car at Aiken	SC	7,828	LC
Univ of S Car at Columbia	SC	8,748	VC
Univ of S Car at Spartanburg	SC	7,318	C+
Univ of S Dak	SD	7,036	C
Univ of South Florida	FL	8,154	C
Univ of Southern Calif	CA	33,647	MC
Univ of Southern Colo	CO	7,821	LC
Univ of Southern Indiana	IN	8,655	LC
Univ of Southern Maine	ME	10,569	C
Univ of Southern Miss	MS	6,155	LC
Univ of Tampa	FL	22,612	C

School	ST	$IS	SR
Univ of Tenn at Chattanooga	TN	7,783	C
Univ of Tenn at Knoxville	TN	8,214	C
Univ of Tenn at Martin	TN	8,268	C
Univ of Texas at Arlington	TX	7,192	LC
Univ of Texas at Austin	TX	9,437	HC
Univ of Texas at Dallas	TX	9,305	VC
Univ of Texas at El Paso	TX	5,076	LC
Univ of Texas at San Antonio	TX	9,088	NC
Univ of Texas-Pan American	TX	4,823	C
Univ of the District of Columbia	DC	2,844	NC
Univ of the Incarnate Word	TX	18,478	C
Univ of the Ozarks	AR	13,904	C
Univ of the Pacific	CA	28,255	VC
Univ of the Sacred Heart	PR	5,375	
Univ of the Sciences in Philadelphia	PA	24,826	VC
Univ of the South	TN	27,290	HC
Univ of Toledo	OH	11,206	NC
Univ of Tulsa	OK	19,090	HC
Univ of Utah	UT	7,703	C
Univ of Vermont	VT	14,761	C+
Univ of Virginia	VA	9,391	HC+
Univ of Virginia's College at Wise	VA	8,302	C
Univ of West Alabama	AL	6,048	C
Univ of West Florida	FL	7,518	C
Univ of Wisc/Eau Claire	WI	7,032	VC
Univ of Wisc/Green Bay	WI	7,148	C
Univ of Wisc/La Crosse	WI	7,250	VC
Univ of Wisc/Madison	WI	8,262	VC
Univ of Wisc/Milwaukee	WI	8,907	LC
Univ of Wisc/Oshkosh	WI	6,130	LC
Univ of Wisc/Parkside	WI	6,160	LC
Univ of Wisc/Platteville	WI	7,282	C
Univ of Wisc/River Falls	WI	6,356	LC
Univ of Wisc/Stevens Point	WI	7,116	C
Univ of Wisc/Superior	WI	7,051	C+
Univ of Wisc/Whitewater	WI	6,937	C
Univ of Wyoming	WY	7,143	LC
Upper Iowa Univ	IA	17,438	C
Ursinus College	PA	31,350	VC
Utah State Univ	UT	6,771	C
Utica College of Syracuse Univ	NY	24,400	LC
Valdosta State Univ	GA	6,988	C
Valley City State Univ	ND		LC
Valparaiso Univ	IN	23,570	VC+
Vanderbilt Univ	TN	34,482	MC
Vanguard Univ of Southern Calif	CA	20,212	C
Vassar College	NY	33,450	MC
Villa Julie College	MD	16,026	C
Villanova Univ	PA	31,997	HC
Virginia Commonwealth Univ	VA	9,030	C
Virginia Military Inst	VA	9,968	C+
Virginia Polytechnic Inst and State Univ	VA	7,652	C
Virginia State Univ	VA	8,182	LC
Virginia Union Univ	VA	15,358	LC
Virginia Wesleyan College	VA	22,350	LC
Viterbo Univ	WI	18,043	C
Wabash College	IN	25,335	HC
Wagner College	NY	27,000	C
Wake Forest Univ	NC	30,290	MC
Walla Walla College	WA	20,925	C
Walsh Univ	OH	16,880	C
Warren Wilson College	NC	19,968	C
Wartburg College	IA	21,165	VC
Washburn Univ of Topeka	KS	6,766	NC
Washington and Jefferson College	PA	26,255	VC
Washington and Lee Univ	VA	25,095	MC
Washington College	MD	28,040	VC
Washington State Univ	WA	9,388	C
Washington Univ in St. Louis	MO	34,593	MC
Wayland Baptist Univ	TX	11,271	NC
Wayne State College	NE	6,255	NC
Wayne State Univ	MI	6,720	C
Waynesburg College	PA	17,610	LC
Weber State Univ	UT	6,897	NC
Wellesley College	MA	33,394	MC
Wells College	NY	19,350	VC
Wesleyan College	GA	17,050	VC
Wesleyan Univ	CT	3,405	MC
West Chester Univ of Pennsylvania	PA	9,792	VC
West Liberty State College	WV	6,056	LC
West Texas A&M Univ	TX	6,538	C
West Virginia State College	WV	6,264	NC
West Virginia Univ	WV	8,304	C
West Virginia Univ Inst of Technology	WV	7,518	NC
West Virginia Wesleyan College	WV	22,920	C
Western Carolina Univ	NC	5,667	C
Western Conn State Univ	CT	10,074	C
Western Illinois Univ	IL	9,571	C
Western Kentucky Univ	KY	6,834	C
Western Maryland College	MD	26,000	VC
Western Mich Univ	MI	10,016	C
Western New England College	MA	23,882	C
Western New Mexico Univ	NM	5,950	LC
Western Oregon Univ	OR	8,829	C
Western State College of Colo	CO	7,585	LC
Western Washington Univ	WA	8,624	VC
Westminster College	MO	19,990	C+
Westminster College	PA	22,960	C
Westminster College	UT	17,226	C
Westmont College	CA	29,748	VC
Wheaton College	IL	21,934	HC
Wheaton College	MA	32,940	VC
Wheeling Jesuit Univ	WV	22,660	C
Whitman College	WA	29,086	HC
Whittier College	CA	29,108	C
Whitworth College	WA	23,938	VC
Wichita State Univ	KS	6,879	C
Widener Univ	PA	26,920	C
Wilberforce Univ	OH	14,937	LC
Wiley College	TX	8,100	LC
Wilkes Univ	PA	25,800	C
Willamette Univ	OR	29,422	VC+
William Carey College	MS	10,150	LC
William Jewell College	MO	17,150	VC
William Paterson Univ of New Jersey	NJ	11,000	LC
Williams College	MA	32,270	MC
Wilmington College	OH	21,826	C
Wilson College	PA	21,337	LC
Wingate Univ	NC	19,140	C
Winona State Univ	MN	8,570	C
Winston-Salem State Univ	NC	5,927	LC
Winthrop Univ	SC	9,106	C
Wisc Lutheran College	WI	19,216	VC
Wittenberg Univ	OH	28,766	VC
Wofford College	SC	23,995	VC
Worcester Polytechnic Inst	MA	34,480	HC+
Worcester State College	MA	7,901	LC
Wright State Univ	OH	9,141	LC
Xavier Univ	OH	23,880	C
Xavier Univ of Louisiana	LA	17,000	LC
Yale Univ	CT	34,030	MC
Yeshiva Univ	NY	21,400	C
York College of Pennsylvania	PA	12,550	VC
Youngstown State Univ	OH	9,318	NC

CHILD CARE/CHILD AND FAMILY STUDIES

School	ST	$IS	SR
Albright College	PA	27,642	C
Ashland Univ	OH	22,182	LC
Audrey Cohen College	NY	17,715	C
Baylor Univ	TX	18,298	VC+
Becker College	MA	21,230	LC
Bennington College	VT	31,350	VC
Berea College	KY	4,070	VC
Bowling Green State Univ	OH	10,794	C
Central Missouri State Univ	MO	7,920	C
Concordia Univ	MN	19,912	C
East Carolina Univ	NC	7,766	C
Eastern Kentucky Univ	KY	6,552	C
Edgewood College	WI	18,304	C
Eureka College	IL	22,200	C
Florida State Univ	FL	7,835	HC
Freed-Hardeman Univ	TN	14,290	VC
Gallaudet Univ	DC	16,554	SP
Georgetown College	KY	18,400	VC
Georgia Southern Univ	GA	6,958	C
Indiana State Univ	IN	8,461	LC
Indiana Univ of Pennsylvania	PA	9,133	C
Iowa State Univ	IA	8,108	VC
Jackson State Univ	MS	6,776	LC
Lasell College	MA	24,100	C
Medaille College	NY	18,320	C
N Car Central Univ	NC	6,418	LC
N Dak State Univ	ND	7,004	VC
Northern Illinois Univ	IL	9,545	C
Northwest Missouri State Univ	MO	7,922	LC
Ohio Univ	OH	11,769	C
Okla Christian Univ	OK	16,500	VC
Okla State Univ	OK	7,650	VC
Park Univ	MO	9,816	C
Plymouth State College	NH	11,024	LC
Portland State Univ	OR	11,220	C
Purdue Univ/West Lafayette	IN	10,284	VC
Seton Hill College	PA	21,875	C
Southwest Missouri State Univ	MO	7,600	LC
Southwest Texas State Univ	TX	8,730	VC
SUNY/College at Oneonta	NY	9,981	C
SUNY/College at Plattsburgh	NY	9,729	C
Syracuse Univ	NY	30,710	HC
Tenn Tech Univ	TN	6,968	C
Texas A&M Univ at Kingsville	TX	6,446	LC
Univ of Arizona	AZ	8,614	C
Univ of Georgia	GA	8,656	VC
Univ of Louisiana at Monroe	LA	5,207	NC
Univ of Maine	ME	10,798	C
Univ of Nevada/Reno	NV	8,737	C
Univ of New Mexico	NM	8,026	C
Univ of N Car at Charlotte	NC	7,254	C
Univ of N Car at Greensboro	NC	6,858	C
Univ of Tenn at Knoxville	TN	8,214	C
Univ of Tenn at Martin	TN	8,268	C
Univ of Texas at Austin	TX	9,437	HC
Univ of Wisc/Madison	WI	8,262	VC
Univ of Wisc/Stout	WI	7,192	C
Ursuline College	OH	19,430	LC
Utah State Univ	UT	6,771	C
Virginia Polytechnic Inst and State Univ	VA	7,652	C
West Virginia Univ	WV	8,304	C
Western Carolina Univ	NC	5,667	C
Wheelock College	MA	25,520	C
Youngstown State Univ	OH	9,318	NC

CHILD PSYCHOLOGY/ DEVELOPMENT

School	ST	$IS	SR
Alverno College	WI	16,930	LC
Appalachian State Univ	NC	6,353	C
Bay Path College	MA	22,308	C
Bethel College	TN	12,980	C
Bluffton College	OH	20,644	C
Cal State, Bakersfield	CA	6,090	LC
Cal State, Chico	CA	8,598	LC
Cal State, Fresno	CA	7,762	C
Cal State, Fullerton	CA	5,440	LC
Cal State, Los Angeles	CA	5,050	C
Cal State, Northridge	CA	7,781	C
Cal State, Stanislaus	CA	8,895	C
Colby-Sawyer College	NH	27,850	LC
College of the Ozarks	MO	2,650	C+
East Tenn State Univ	TN	7,127	C
Eastern Nazarene College	MA	19,433	LC
Fort Valley State Univ	GA	6,014	LC
Hope International Univ	CA	16,940	NC
Humboldt State Univ	CA	8,582	C
Iowa State Univ	IA	8,108	VC
Kentucky State Univ	KY	6,146	NC
Madonna Univ	MI	11,504	VC
Marist College	NY	24,756	VC
Marygrove College	MI	16,075	C
Meredith College	NC	17,500	C
Metropolitan State Univ	MN	2,943	SP
Middle Tenn State Univ	TN	6,994	C
Mills College	CA	27,950	C
Missouri Baptist College	MO	15,762	LC
Mount Ida College	MA	25,375	LC
Mount St. Mary's College	CA	24,430	C
New Mexico State Univ	NM	7,302	C
N Car Agricultural and Technical State Univ	NC	6,659	LC
N Car Central Univ	NC	6,418	LC
Point Loma Nazarene Univ	CA	21,380	VC
St. Joseph College	CT	25,960	LC
San Diego State Univ	CA	9,716	C+
Siena Heights Univ	MI	16,140	LC
Southern Vermont College	VT	17,685	C
Spelman College	GA	19,215	C+
Stephen F. Austin State Univ	TX	6,905	C
Texas Woman's Univ	TX	5,855	LC
Thomas Edison State College	NJ	2,750	SP
Tufts Univ	MA	34,874	MC
Univ of Minn/Twin Cities	MN	11,123	VC
Univ of North Texas	TX	7,629	C
Univ of Pittsburgh at Pittsburgh	PA	13,592	HC
Utica College of Syracuse Univ	NY	24,400	LC
Vanderbilt Univ	TN	34,482	MC
Whittier College	CA	29,108	C

CHINESE

School	ST	$IS	SR
Arizona State Univ-Main	AZ	7,726	C
Bard College	NY	33,912	HC
Bates College	ME	34,100	MC
Bennington College	VT	31,350	VC
Brigham Young Univ	UT	7,840	HC
CUNY/Hunter College	NY	5,147	C+
Claremont McKenna College	CA	32,700	MC
Conn College	CT	33,585	MC
Dartmouth College	NH	34,458	MC
George Washington Univ	DC	32,170	HC
Georgetown Univ	DC	34,847	MC
Grinnell College	IA	28,300	HC+
Harvard Univ/Harvard College	MA	34,269	MC
Hobart and William Smith Colleges	NY	33,195	VC
Lincoln Univ	PA	11,198	C+
Middlebury College	VT	34,300	MC
Oakland Univ	MI	9,418	C
Pomona College	CA	33,960	MC
Portland State Univ	OR	11,220	C
Reed College	OR	33,350	HC+
Rutgers, The State Univ of New Jersey New Brunswick Campus	NJ	12,709	C
San Francisco State Univ	CA	7,139	LC
Stanford Univ	CA	34,222	MC
SUNY/Univ at Albany	NY	10,997	VC
Ohio State Univ	OH	10,819	VC
Tufts Univ	MA	34,874	MC
Univ of Calif at Berkeley	CA	14,134	MC
Univ of Calif at Davis	CA	12,796	VC
Univ of Calif at Irvine	CA	11,756	C
Univ of Calif at Los Angeles	CA	13,227	MC
Univ of Calif at Riverside	CA	12,479	C
Univ of Calif at San Diego	CA	11,372	HC
Univ of Calif at Santa Barbara	CA	11,732	VC
Univ of Colo at Boulder	CO	9,255	VC
Univ of Hawaii at Manoa	HI	7,862	VC
Univ of Maryland/College Park	MD	11,959	C
Univ of Mass Amherst	MA	10,995	VC
Univ of Mich/Ann Arbor	MI	13,003	HC+
Univ of Minn/Twin Cities	MN	11,123	VC
Univ of Notre Dame	IN	30,707	MC
Univ of Oregon	OR	9,969	C
Univ of Pittsburgh at Pittsburgh	PA	13,592	HC
Univ of Utah	UT	7,703	C
Univ of Wisc/Madison	WI	8,262	VC
Washington Univ in St. Louis	MO	34,593	MC
Wellesley College	MA	33,394	MC
Yale Univ	CT	34,030	MC

CHIROPRACTIC

School	ST	$IS	SR
Univ of Hartford	CT	28,884	C
Univ of Southern Colo	CO	7,821	LC
Valley City State Univ	ND		LC

CHRISTIAN EDUCATION

School	ST	$IS	SR
Anderson Univ	IN	19,430	LC
Biola Univ	CA	21,902	VC
Cedarville Univ	OH	17,553	VC
Columbia College	SC	19,050	LC
Concordia Univ	CA	22,290	C
Concordia Univ Nebr	NE	17,770	C
Defiance College	OH	19,580	LC
Erskine College	SC	21,399	VC
Hannibal-LaGrange College	MO	12,530	C
Malone College	OH	19,190	C
MidAmerica Nazarene Univ	KS	16,960	C
Milligan College	TN	17,550	C
Mount Vernon Nazarene College	OH	17,027	C
Muskingum College	OH	18,760	C
Northwestern College	MN	19,816	C+
Olivet Nazarene Univ	IL	18,444	C
Pfeiffer Univ	NC	18,580	C
Seattle Pacific Univ	WA	22,674	C+
Southeastern College	FL	11,648	LC
Taylor Univ	IN	21,562	VC+
Toccoa Falls College	GA	14,220	C
Westminster College	PA	22,960	C

CHRISTIAN STUDIES

School	ST	$IS	SR
Alderson-Broaddus College	WV	19,640	C
Bluefield College	VA	14,200	C
Brewton-Parker College	GA	10,810	LC
Bryan College	TN	16,400	VC
Calif Baptist Univ	CA	16,736	C
Campbellsville Univ	KY	14,340	C
Eastern Nazarene College	MA	19,433	LC
Grand Canyon Univ	AZ	30,000	LC
Hillsdale College	MI	20,586	VC+
Houston Baptist Univ	TX	15,300	LC
Howard Payne Univ	TX	13,834	C+
Lewis Univ	IL	20,960	C
Miss College	MS	14,574	C
Rochester College	MI	15,404	C+
Shorter College	GA	15,185	C
Texas Wesleyan Univ	TX	14,710	C
Trinity International Univ	IL	20,640	C+
Union Univ	TN	18,930	C+
Univ of Chicago	IL	35,087	MC
Univ of St. Thomas	MN	24,044	VC
William Tyndale College	MI	11,150	C

CITY/COMMUNITY/REGIONAL PLANNING

School	ST	$IS	SR
Alabama A&M Univ	AL	5,100	LC
Calif Polytechnic State Univ	CA	8,747	VC
Cornell Univ	NY	34,614	MC
East Carolina Univ	NC	7,766	C
Eastern College	PA	19,641	LC
Eastern Mich Univ	MI	9,855	C
Indiana Univ of Pennsylvania	PA	9,133	C
Iowa State Univ	IA	8,108	VC
Mansfield Univ	PA	9,648	C
Mich State Univ	MI	10,386	VC
New Mexico State Univ	NM	7,302	C
Plymouth State College	NH	11,024	LC
Southwest Texas State Univ	TX	8,730	VC

School	ST	$IS	SR
Univ of Arizona	AZ	8,614	C
Univ of Cincinnati	OH	12,491	LC
Univ of Illinois at Urbana-Champaign	IL	11,316	HC+
Univ of New Hampshire	NH	13,207	C
Univ of Virginia	VA	9,391	HC+

CIVIL ENGINEERING

School	ST	$IS	SR
Alabama A&M Univ	AL	5,100	LC
Arizona State Univ-Main	AZ	7,726	C
Auburn Univ	AL	5,510	C
Bethel College	IN	17,650	LC
Bradley Univ	IL	20,970	VC
Brigham Young Univ	UT	7,840	HC
Bucknell Univ	PA	31,096	HC
Calif Inst of Technology	CA	27,663	MC
Calif Polytechnic State Univ	CA	8,747	VC
Calif State Polytechnic Univ, Pomona	CA	8,615	C
Cal State, Chico	CA	8,598	LC
Cal State, Fresno	CA	7,762	C
Cal State, Fullerton	CA	5,440	LC
Cal State, Long Beach	CA	7,400	LC
Cal State, Los Angeles	CA	5,050	C
Cal State, Sacramento	CA	7,488	C
Calvin College	MI	20,050	NC
Caribbean Univ	PR	3,000	
Carnegie Mellon Univ	PA	32,682	MC
Carroll College	MT	19,140	C
Case Western Reserve Univ	OH	27,418	C
Catholic Univ of America	DC	29,332	VC
Christian Brothers Univ	TN	19,820	VC
Citadel, The	SC	9,126	C
CUNY/City College	NY	3,309	LC
Clarkson Univ	NY	29,884	VC
Clemson Univ	SC	7,600	C
Cleveland State Univ	OH	10,146	NC
Colo State Univ	CO	9,672	C
Columbia Univ/Fu Foundation School of Engineering and Applied Science	NY	35,190	MC
Cooper Union for the Advancement of Science and Art	NY	6,500	MC
Cornell Univ	NY	34,614	MC
Delaware State Univ	DE	8,104	LC
Drexel Univ	PA	27,657	VC
Duke Univ	NC	34,396	MC
Florida A&M Univ	FL	6,948	C
Florida Inst of Technology	FL	25,250	VC
Florida International Univ	FL	9,486	VC
Florida State Univ	FL	7,835	HC
George Mason Univ	VA	9,192	C
George Washington Univ	DC	32,170	HC
Georgia Inst of Technology	GA	9,028	HC+
Gonzaga Univ	WA	24,276	HC+
Howard Univ	DC	15,522	LC
Illinois Inst of Technology	IL	25,182	HC+
Indiana Inst of Technology	IN	18,806	C
Iowa State Univ	IA	8,108	VC
Johns Hopkins Univ	MD	35,226	MC
Kansas State Univ	KS	6,995	C
Lafayette College	PA	32,655	MC
Lamar Univ	TX	6,816	LC
Lawrence Tech Univ	MI	11,429	C
Lehigh Univ	PA	32,290	MC
Louisiana State Univ and A&M College	LA	8,014	VC
Louisiana Tech Univ	LA	6,506	C
Loyola Marymount Univ	CA	28,754	HC
Manhattan College	NY	25,500	VC
Marquette Univ	WI	24,836	C+
Mass Inst of Technology	MA	35,228	MC
McNeese State Univ	LA	5,259	LC
Merrimack College	MA	25,725	VC
Messiah College	PA	23,180	VC
Mich State Univ	MI	10,386	VC
Mich Tech Univ	MI	11,088	VC
Miss State Univ	MS	7,853	C
Montana State Univ-Bozeman	MT	8,431	C
Morgan State Univ	MD	10,078	LC
New Jersey Inst of Technology	NJ	14,690	VC
New Mexico State Univ	NM	7,302	C
New York Univ	NY	35,200	MC
N Car Agricultural and Technical State Univ	NC	6,659	LC
N Car State Univ	NC	8,680	HC
N Dak State Univ	ND	7,004	VC
Northeastern Univ	MA	30,078	VC
Northern Arizona Univ	AZ	7,398	C
Northwestern Univ	IL	33,615	MC
Norwich Univ	VT	21,064	LC
Ohio Northern Univ	OH	27,765	VC
Ohio Univ	OH	11,769	C
Okla State Univ	OK	7,650	VC
Old Dominion Univ	VA	9,386	C
Oregon Inst of Technology	OR	8,718	C
Oregon State Univ	OR	9,612	VC
Penn State Univ/Univ Park Campus	PA	11,126	VC
Polytechnic Univ/Brooklyn	NY	33,090	HC
Portland State Univ	OR	11,220	C
Prairie View A&M Univ	TX	3,172	LC
Princeton Univ	NJ	35,072	MC
Purdue Univ/West Lafayette	IN	10,284	VC
Rensselaer Polytechnic Inst	NY	33,863	HC+
Rose-Hulman Inst of Technology	IN	27,707	HC+
Rutgers, The State Univ of New Jersey New Brunswick Campus	NJ	12,709	C
St. Martin's College	WA	20,566	C
San Diego State Univ	CA	9,716	C+
San Francisco State Univ	CA	7,139	LC
San Jose State Univ	CA	8,187	C
Santa Clara Univ	CA	28,371	VC+
Savannah State Univ	GA	2,550	LC
Seattle Univ	WA	24,183	VC
S Dak School of Mines and Technology	SD	7,438	C+
S Dak State Univ	SD	6,848	C
Southern Illinois Univ at Carbondale	IL	8,621	C
Southern Illinois Univ Edwardsville	IL	7,869	LC
Southern Univ and A&M College	LA	6,365	C+
Stanford Univ	CA	34,222	MC
SUNY/Univ at Buffalo	NY	11,033	VC
Stevens Inst of Technology	NJ	31,510	HC+
Syracuse Univ	NY	30,710	HC
Temple Univ	PA	14,124	C
Tenn State Univ	TN	7,058	VC
Tenn Tech Univ	TN	6,968	C
Texas A&M Univ	TX	8,988	VC
Texas A&M Univ at Kingsville	TX	6,446	LC
Texas Tech Univ	TX	8,825	C
Ohio State Univ	OH	10,819	VC
Tri-State Univ-Main Campus	IN	21,200	C
Tufts Univ	MA	34,874	MC
Tulane Univ	LA	34,013	HC+
Union College	NY	32,646	HC
United States Air Force Academy	CO		MC
United States Coast Guard Academy	CT		MC
United States Military Academy	NY		MC
Universidad Politecnica de PR	PR	4,695	
Univ of Akron	OH	10,530	NC
Univ of Alabama	AL	7,402	C
Univ of Alabama at Birmingham	AL	10,110	C
Univ of Alabama at Huntsville	AL	7,916	VC
Univ of Alaska Anchorage	AK	9,100	NC
Univ of Alaska Fairbanks	AK	8,265	NC
Univ of Arizona	AZ	8,614	C
Univ of Arkansas	AR	8,334	VC
Univ of Calif at Berkeley	CA	14,134	MC
Univ of Calif at Davis	CA	12,796	VC
Univ of Calif at Irvine	CA	11,756	C
Univ of Calif at Los Angeles	CA	13,227	MC
Univ of Central Florida	FL	8,251	VC
Univ of Cincinnati	OH	12,491	LC
Univ of Colo at Boulder	CO	9,255	VC
Univ of Colo at Denver	CO	3,673	C
Univ of Conn	CT	12,122	VC
Univ of Dayton	OH	20,400	VC
Univ of Delaware	DE	10,824	VC
Univ of Detroit Mercy	MI	21,620	LC
Univ of Evansville	IN	22,865	VC+
Univ of Florida	FL	7,874	HC
Univ of Hartford	CT	28,884	C
Univ of Hawaii at Manoa	HI	7,862	VC
Univ of Houston	TX	8,410	C
Univ of Idaho	ID	7,026	C
Univ of Illinois at Chicago	IL	10,702	VC
Univ of Illinois at Urbana-Champaign	IL	11,316	HC+
Univ of Iowa	IA	8,607	C+
Univ of Kansas	KS	7,232	VC
Univ of Kentucky	KY	7,765	C
Univ of Louisiana at Lafayette	LA	5,200	C
Univ of Louisville	KY	7,402	LC
Univ of Maine	ME	10,798	C
Univ of Maryland/College Park	MD	11,959	C
Univ of Mass Amherst	MA	10,995	VC
Univ of Mass Dartmouth	MA	9,852	C
Univ of Mass Lowell	MA	9,470	VC
Univ of Memphis	TN	7,271	C
Univ of Miami	FL	31,130	HC
Univ of Mich/Ann Arbor	MI	13,003	HC+
Univ of Minn/Twin Cities	MN	11,123	VC
Univ of Miss	MS	7,666	C
Univ of Missouri/Columbia	MO	9,803	HC
Univ of Missouri/Kansas City	MO	9,685	VC
Univ of Missouri/Rolla	MO	10,034	C
Univ of Missouri/St. Louis	MO	9,966	C
Univ of Nebr at Lincoln	NE	8,325	C+
Univ of Nevada/Las Vegas	NV	8,281	VC
Univ of Nevada/Reno	NV	8,737	C
Univ of New Hampshire	NH	13,207	C
Univ of New Haven	CT	23,860	LC
Univ of New Mexico	NM	8,026	C
Univ of New Orleans	LA	10,160	C
Univ of N Car at Charlotte	NC	7,254	C
Univ of N Dak	ND	7,067	VC
Univ of North Florida	FL	8,089	VC
Univ of Notre Dame	IN	30,707	MC
Univ of Okla	OK	7,616	VC
Univ of Pennsylvania	PA	34,614	MC
Univ of Pittsburgh at Pittsburgh	PA	13,592	HC
Univ of Portland	OR	24,950	VC
Univ of PR/Mayaguez	PR	5,285	
Univ of Rhode Island	RI	12,414	C
Univ of South Alabama	AL	6,976	LC
Univ of S Car at Columbia	SC	8,748	VC
Univ of South Florida	FL	8,154	C
Univ of Southern Calif	CA	33,647	MC
Univ of Tenn at Knoxville	TN	8,214	C
Univ of Tenn at Martin	TN	8,268	C
Univ of Texas at Arlington	TX	7,192	LC
Univ of Texas at Austin	TX	9,437	HC
Univ of Texas at El Paso	TX	5,076	LC
Univ of Texas at San Antonio	TX	9,088	NC
Univ of the District of Columbia	DC	2,844	NC
Univ of the Pacific	CA	28,255	VC
Univ of Toledo	OH	11,206	NC
Univ of Utah	UT	7,703	C
Univ of Vermont	VT	14,761	C+
Univ of Virginia	VA	9,391	HC+
Univ of Washington	WA	10,361	VC
Univ of Wisc/Madison	WI	8,262	VC
Univ of Wisc/Milwaukee	WI	8,907	LC
Univ of Wisc/Platteville	WI	7,282	C
Univ of Wyoming	WY	7,143	LC
Utah State Univ	UT	6,771	C
Valparaiso Univ	IN	23,570	VC+
Vanderbilt Univ	TN	34,482	MC
Villanova Univ	PA	31,997	HC
Virginia Military Inst	VA	9,968	C+
Virginia Polytechnic Inst and State Univ	VA	7,652	C
Washington State Univ	WA	9,388	C
Washington Univ in St. Louis	MO	34,593	MC
Wayne State Univ	MI	6,720	C
West Virginia Univ	WV	8,304	C
West Virginia Univ Inst of Technology	WV	7,518	NC
Western Kentucky Univ	KY	6,834	C
Widener Univ	PA	26,920	C
Worcester Polytechnic Inst	MA	34,480	HC+
Youngstown State Univ	OH	9,318	NC

CIVIL ENGINEERING TECHNOLOGY

School	ST	$IS	SR
Alabama A&M Univ	AL	5,100	LC
Central Conn State Univ	CT	10,404	C
Fairleigh Dickinson Univ/Teaneck Campus	NJ	24,646	C
Fairmont State College	WV	7,010	NC
Lincoln Univ	MO	7,158	NC
Metropolitan State College of Denver	CO	2,338	LC
Montana State Univ-Northern	MT	8,600	NC
Murray State Univ	KY	6,672	C
Old Dominion Univ	VA	9,386	C
Pennsylvania College of Technology	PA	12,860	NC
Point Park College	PA	20,290	C
Rochester Inst of Technology	NY	26,232	VC+
S Car State Univ	SC	6,586	LC
Southern Polytechnic State Univ	GA	6,662	C
Texas Southern Univ	TX	6,576	NC
Thomas Edison State College	NJ	2,750	SP
Univ of Houston	TX	8,410	C
Univ of N Car at Charlotte	NC	7,254	C
Univ of Pittsburgh at Johnstown	PA	13,044	LC
Univ of Southern Colo	CO	7,821	LC
Wentworth Inst of Technology	MA	20,450	C
Western Kentucky Univ	KY	6,834	C
Youngstown State Univ	OH	9,318	NC

CLASSICAL LANGUAGES

School	ST	$IS	SR
Agnes Scott College	GA	24,950	VC
Asbury College	KY	18,540	VC
Ball State Univ	IN	8,660	C
Bard College	NY	33,912	HC
Beloit College	WI	27,482	HC
Berea College	KY	4,070	VC
Bryn Mawr College	PA	33,580	HC+
Calvin College	MI	20,050	NC
Carroll College	MT	19,140	C
Concordia College/Moorhead	MN	18,835	C
DePauw Univ	IN	28,000	HC
Dickinson College	PA	32,210	VC+
Duke Univ	NC	34,396	MC
Duquesne Univ	PA	24,242	C+
Eastern Mich Univ	MI	9,855	C
Fordham Univ	NY	30,710	VC
La Salle Univ	PA	27,890	C
Loras College	IA	22,994	C+
Marquette Univ	WI	24,836	C+
Mount Holyoke College	MA	34,128	HC
Ohio Univ	OH	11,769	C
Rockford College	IL	23,930	C
St. Bonaventure Univ	NY	21,956	C
St. Mary's College of Calif	CA	27,575	C
St. Peter's College	NJ	22,292	LC
Scripps College	CA	30,400	HC+
Siena College	NY	22,685	VC
Texas Tech Univ	TX	8,825	C
Univ of Calif at Berkeley	CA	14,134	MC
Univ of Calif at Santa Cruz	CA	13,655	VC
Univ of Houston	TX	8,410	C
Univ of Kansas	KS	7,232	VC
Univ of Mass Boston	MA	4,227	C
Univ of Mich/Ann Arbor	MI	13,003	HC+
Univ of Minn/Twin Cities	MN	11,123	VC
Univ of N Car at Chapel Hill	NC	8,789	HC
Univ of N Dak	ND	7,067	VC
Univ of St. Thomas	MN	24,044	VC
Vanderbilt Univ	TN	34,482	MC
Wright State Univ	OH	9,141	LC
Yeshiva Univ	NY	21,400	C

CLASSICAL/ANCIENT CIVILIZATION

School	ST	$IS	SR
Agnes Scott College	GA	24,950	VC
Bates College	ME	34,100	MC
Beloit College	WI	27,482	HC
Boston College	MA	33,330	MC
Boston Univ	MA	34,358	MC
Bowdoin College	ME	32,650	MC
Bowling Green State Univ	OH	10,794	C
Carleton College	MN	30,780	MC
Centre College	KY	24,000	HC
Christendom College	VA	16,700	VC+
CUNY/Queens College	NY	3,403	VC
Clark Univ	MA	29,170	HC
Cleveland State Univ	OH	10,146	NC
Coe College	IA	24,750	VC
Colby College	ME	34,290	MC
Columbia Univ/Barnard College	NY	33,694	MC
Columbia Univ/Columbia College	NY	35,190	MC
Columbia Univ/School of General Studies	NY	35,000	C
Cornell College	IA	24,980	VC
Cornell Univ	NY	34,614	MC
Creighton Univ	NE	23,476	VC
Dartmouth College	NH	34,458	MC
Denison Univ	OH	29,640	HC
DePauw Univ	IN	28,000	HC
Dickinson College	PA	32,210	VC+
Duke Univ	NC	34,396	MC
Earlham College	IN	27,446	VC+
Emory Univ	GA	33,792	MC
Florida State Univ	FL	7,835	HC
Fordham Univ	NY	30,710	VC
Gonzaga Univ	WA	24,276	HC+
Hamilton College	NY	34,150	HC
Hollins Univ	VA	24,328	VC
Kalamazoo College	MI	26,955	HC+
Lehigh Univ	PA	32,290	MC
Loras College	IA	22,994	C+
Loyola College in Maryland	MD	30,900	HC
Loyola Marymount Univ	CA	28,754	HC
Loyola Univ New Orleans	LA	23,506	VC+
Loyola Univ of Chicago	IL	25,992	VC
Miami Univ	OH	12,885	VC+
Mich State Univ	MI	10,386	VC
Middlebury College	VT	34,300	MC
Mount Holyoke College	MA	34,128	HC
New York Univ	NY	35,200	MC
Rhodes College	TN	26,466	HC+
Rollins College	FL	31,223	HC
St. Louis Univ	MO	26,590	VC+
St. Olaf College	MN	25,880	HC
St. Peter's College	NJ	22,292	LC
Scripps College	CA	30,400	HC+
Seton Hall Univ	NJ	26,910	LC
Smith College	MA	33,302	HC+
SUNY/Univ at Albany	NY	10,997	VC
SUNY/Univ at Binghamton	NY	10,653	HC
Swarthmore College	PA	34,538	MC
Sweet Briar College	VA	25,310	VC
Syracuse Univ	NY	30,710	HC
Trinity College	CT	34,300	HC
Univ of Calif at Berkeley	CA	14,134	MC
Univ of Calif at Davis	CA	12,796	VC
Univ of Calif at Irvine	CA	11,756	C
Univ of Calif at Los Angeles	CA	13,227	MC
Univ of Calif at Riverside	CA	12,479	C
Univ of Chicago	IL	35,087	MC
Univ of Cincinnati	OH	12,491	LC

School	ST	$IS	SR
Univ of Evansville	IN	22,865	VC+
Univ of Florida	FL	7,874	HC
Univ of Georgia	GA	8,656	VC
Univ of Idaho	ID	7,026	C
Univ of Illinois at Chicago	IL	10,702	VC
Univ of Iowa	IA	8,607	C+
Univ of Maryland/Baltimore County	MD	12,190	VC
Univ of Mich/Ann Arbor	MI	13,003	HC+
Univ of Miss	MS	7,666	C
Univ of N Dak	ND	7,067	VC
Univ of Notre Dame	IN	30,707	MC
Univ of Oregon	OR	9,969	C
Univ of Richmond	VA	27,300	HC
Univ of St. Thomas	MN	24,044	VC
Univ of Tenn at Knoxville	TN	8,214	C
Univ of Texas at Arlington	TX	7,192	LC
Univ of Texas at Austin	TX	9,437	HC
Wellesley College	MA	33,394	MC
Wesleyan Univ	CT	3,405	MC
Wheaton College	MA	32,940	VC
Willamette Univ	OR	29,422	VC+
Xavier Univ	OH	23,880	C
Yale Univ	CT	34,030	MC

CLASSICS

School	ST	$IS	SR
Agnes Scott College	GA	24,950	VC
Albertus Magnus College	CT	22,154	C
Amherst College	MA	34,340	MC
Assumption College	MA	26,320	C
Augustana College	IL	24,117	VC+
Austin College	TX	22,150	VC+
Ball State Univ	IN	8,660	C
Bard College	NY	33,912	HC
Baylor Univ	TX	18,298	VC+
Boston College	MA	33,330	MC
Boston Univ	MA	34,358	MC
Bowdoin College	ME	32,650	MC
Brandeis Univ	MA	34,481	MC
Brown Univ	RI	34,973	MC
Bryn Mawr College	PA	33,580	HC+
Bucknell Univ	PA	31,096	HC
Calvin College	MI	20,050	NC
Carleton College	MN	30,780	MC
Case Western Reserve Univ	OH	27,418	C
Catholic Univ of America	DC	29,332	VC
CUNY/Brooklyn College	NY	3,403	LC
CUNY/Hunter College	NY	5,147	C+
Claremont McKenna College	CA	32,700	MC
Colby College	ME	34,290	MC
Colgate Univ	NY	33,480	HC
College of Charleston	SC	8,350	HC
College of New Rochelle	NY	20,000	C
College of Notre Dame of Maryland	MD	23,100	LC
College of St. Benedict	MN	23,921	VC
College of the Holy Cross	MA	32,780	MC
College of William and Mary	VA	10,002	MC
Colo College	CO	31,525	HC+
Columbia Univ/Barnard College	NY	33,694	MC
Columbia Univ/Columbia College	NY	35,190	MC
Columbia Univ/School of General Studies	NY	35,000	C
Conn College	CT	33,585	MC
Cornell Univ	NY	34,614	MC
Dartmouth College	NH	34,458	MC
Davidson College	NC	30,823	MC
Drew Univ/College of Liberal Arts	NJ	32,152	VC
Duquesne Univ	PA	24,242	C+
Elmira College	NY	31,070	VC+
Emory & Henry College	VA	19,462	C
Emory Univ	GA	33,792	MC
Florida State Univ	FL	7,835	HC
Franciscan Univ of Steubenville	OH	19,100	C+
Franklin and Marshall College	PA	32,410	HC
George Washington Univ	DC	32,170	HC
Georgetown Univ	DC	34,847	MC
Georgia State Univ	GA	7,792	LC
Gettysburg College	PA	32,070	HC
Grinnell College	IA	28,300	HC+
Gustavus Adolphus College	MN	24,190	VC+
Hamilton College	NY	34,150	HC
Hampden-Sydney College	VA	24,871	C
Hanover College	IN	17,560	VC
Harvard Univ/Harvard College	MA	34,269	MC
Haverford College	PA	34,300	MC
Hellenic College/Holy Cross Greek Orthodox School of Theology	MA	17,215	C
Hillsdale College	MI	20,586	VC+
Hiram College	OH	27,034	VC
Hobart and William Smith Colleges	NY	33,195	VC
Hofstra Univ	NY	23,252	C
Howard Univ	DC	15,522	LC
Indiana Univ Bloomington	IN	10,712	C+
Johns Hopkins Univ	MD	35,226	MC
Kent State Univ	OH	11,104	C
Kenyon College	OH	32,130	HC+
Knox College	IL	28,230	HC
Lawrence Univ	WI	27,711	HC
Lehigh Univ	PA	32,290	MC
Lenoir-Rhyne College	NC	19,186	C
Loyola Marymount Univ	CA	28,754	HC
Macalester College	MN	28,814	HC+
Manhattanville College	NY	28,730	VC
Marquette Univ	WI	24,836	C+
Mary Washington College	VA	9,032	VC+
Middlebury College	VT	34,300	MC
Millsaps College	MS	22,608	VC+
Monmouth College	IL	21,550	C
Montclair State Univ	NJ	10,287	LC
New College of Florida	FL	8,130	HC+
New York Univ	NY	35,200	MC
North Central College	IL	22,944	C+
Northwestern Univ	IL	33,615	MC
Oberlin College	OH	33,140	HC+
Pacific Lutheran Univ	WA	23,318	VC
Penn State Univ/Univ Park Campus	PA	11,126	VC
Pitzer College	CA	33,930	HC
Pomona College	CA	33,960	MC
Princeton Univ	NJ	35,072	MC
Purdue Univ/West Lafayette	IN	10,284	VC
Randolph-Macon College	VA	24,395	C
Randolph-Macon Woman's College	VA	25,820	VC+
Reed College	OR	33,350	HC+
Rutgers, The State Univ of New Jersey New Brunswick Campus	NJ	12,709	C
St. Anselm College	NH	27,405	C
St. John's Univ	MN	23,640	VC
St. Peter's College	NJ	22,292	LC
Samford Univ	AL	16,340	VC
San Diego State Univ	CA	9,716	C+
San Francisco State Univ	CA	7,139	LC
Santa Clara Univ	CA	28,371	VC+
Sarah Lawrence College	NY	37,516	HC
Seattle Pacific Univ	WA	22,674	C+
Skidmore College	NY	34,201	VC+
Smith College	MA	33,302	HC+
Southern Illinois Univ at Carbondale	IL	8,621	C
Southwestern Univ	TX	22,550	HC
Stanford Univ	CA	34,222	MC
SUNY/Univ at Binghamton	NY	10,653	HC
SUNY/Univ at Buffalo	NY	11,033	VC
Swarthmore College	PA	34,538	MC
Syracuse Univ	NY	30,710	HC
Temple Univ	PA	14,124	C
Ohio State Univ	OH	10,819	VC
Trinity College	CT	34,300	HC
Truman State Univ	MO	8,568	VC+
Tufts Univ	MA	34,874	MC
Tulane Univ	LA	34,013	HC+
Union College	NY	32,646	HC
Univ of Akron	OH	10,530	NC
Univ of Alabama	AL	7,402	C
Univ of Arizona	AZ	8,614	C
Univ of Arkansas	AR	8,334	VC
Univ of Calif at Irvine	CA	11,756	C
Univ of Calif at Riverside	CA	12,479	C
Univ of Calif at San Diego	CA	11,372	HC
Univ of Calif at Santa Barbara	CA	11,732	VC
Univ of Chicago	IL	35,087	MC
Univ of Colo at Boulder	CO	9,255	VC
Univ of Conn	CT	12,122	VC
Univ of Dallas	TX	22,128	VC+
Univ of Hawaii at Manoa	HI	7,862	VC
Univ of Houston	TX	8,410	C
Univ of Illinois at Chicago	IL	10,702	VC
Univ of Illinois at Urbana-Champaign	IL	11,316	HC+
Univ of Iowa	IA	8,607	C+
Univ of Maryland/College Park	MD	11,959	C
Univ of Mass Amherst	MA	10,995	VC
Univ of Mass Boston	MA	4,227	C
Univ of Missouri/Columbia	MO	9,803	HC
Univ of Montana	MT	8,038	C
Univ of Nebr at Lincoln	NE	8,325	C+
Univ of New Hampshire	NH	13,207	C
Univ of New Mexico	NM	8,026	C
Univ of N Car at Asheville	NC	6,896	VC
Univ of N Car at Chapel Hill	NC	8,789	HC
Univ of Okla	OK	7,616	VC
Univ of Oregon	OR	9,969	C
Univ of Pennsylvania	PA	34,614	MC
Univ of Pittsburgh at Pittsburgh	PA	13,592	HC
Univ of Puget Sound	WA	28,285	HC
Univ of Rhode Island	RI	12,414	C
Univ of Rochester	NY	32,979	HC
Univ of S Car at Columbia	SC	8,748	VC
Univ of South Florida	FL	8,154	C
Univ of Southern Calif	CA	33,647	MC
Univ of Tenn at Knoxville	TN	8,214	C
Univ of Texas at Austin	TX	9,437	HC
Univ of Texas at San Antonio	TX	9,088	NC
Univ of the Pacific	CA	28,255	VC
Univ of Utah	UT	7,703	C
Univ of Vermont	VT	14,761	C+
Univ of Virginia	VA	9,391	HC+
Univ of Washington	WA	10,361	VC
Univ of Wisc/Madison	WI	8,262	VC
Univ of Wisc/Milwaukee	WI	8,907	LC
Valparaiso Univ	IN	23,570	VC+
Vanderbilt Univ	TN	34,482	MC
Villanova Univ	PA	31,997	HC
Wabash College	IN	25,335	HC
Wake Forest Univ	NC	30,290	MC
Washington and Lee Univ	VA	25,095	MC
Washington State Univ	WA	9,388	C
Washington Univ in St. Louis	MO	34,593	MC
Wayne State Univ	MI	6,720	C
Wesleyan Univ	CT	3,405	MC
Wheaton College	MA	32,940	VC
Whitman College	WA	29,086	HC
Williams College	MA	32,270	MC
Xavier Univ	OH	23,880	C
Yale Univ	CT	34,030	MC

CLINICAL PSYCHOLOGY

School	ST	$IS	SR
Averett Univ	VA	17,980	LC
Bard College	NY	33,912	HC
Drake Univ	IA	22,830	VC
Eastern Nazarene College	MA	19,433	LC
Marywood Univ	PA	24,639	C
Tufts Univ	MA	34,874	MC
Univ of New Haven	CT	23,860	LC

CLINICAL SCIENCE

School	ST	$IS	SR
Appalachian State Univ	NC	6,353	C
Arizona State Univ-Main	AZ	7,726	C
Benedictine Univ	IL	21,330	C
Bloomfield College	NJ	17,000	C
Cal State, Bakersfield	CA	6,090	LC
Cal State, Dominguez Hills	CA	5,840	LC
Campbell Univ	NC	16,599	C
Canisius College	NY	24,696	C+
Carroll College	MT	19,140	C
Elizabethtown College	PA	26,000	VC
Fairleigh Dickinson Univ/ Teaneck Campus	NJ	24,646	C
Felician College	NJ	20,050	C
Florida Gulf Coast Univ	FL	9,201	C
George Washington Univ	DC	32,170	HC
Gwynedd-Mercy College	PA	22,350	C
Ithaca College	NY	28,719	HC
Jamestown College	ND	11,310	NC
Jewish Hospital College of Nursing and Allied Health	MO	11,200	SP
Marquette Univ	WI	24,836	C+
Maryville Univ of St. Louis	MO	18,680	C
MCP Hahnemann Univ	PA	18,510	SP
Mich State Univ	MI	10,386	VC
Monmouth Univ	NJ	24,042	C
Neumann College	PA	22,040	NC
New York Inst of Technology	NY	21,756	C
N Dak State Univ	ND	7,004	VC
Northern Illinois Univ	IL	9,545	C
Northern Mich Univ	MI	9,693	C
Ohio Univ	OH	11,769	C
Olivet Nazarene Univ	IL	18,444	C
Ramapo College of New Jersey	NJ	13,550	VC
Rockhurst Univ	MO	20,090	C
St. Louis Univ	MO	26,590	VC+
San Francisco State Univ	CA	7,139	LC
S Dak State Univ	SD	6,848	C
Southwest Texas State Univ	TX	8,730	VC
Spalding Univ	KY	15,196	C
SUNY/Univ at Stony Brook	NY	10,998	VC
Thomas Edison State College	NJ	2,750	SP
Univ of Kansas	KS	7,232	VC
Univ of Louisiana at Monroe	LA	5,207	NC
Univ of Maine	ME	10,798	C
Univ of Mass Lowell	MA	9,470	VC
Univ of Nevada/Las Vegas	NV	8,281	VC
Univ of N Dak	ND	7,067	VC
Univ of Rhode Island	RI	12,414	C
Univ of South Alabama	AL	6,976	LC
Univ of Texas at El Paso	TX	5,076	LC
Univ of Texas at San Antonio	TX	9,088	NC
Univ of Wisc/Milwaukee	WI	8,907	LC
Univ of Wisc/Stevens Point	WI	7,116	C
Walsh Univ	OH	16,880	C
Weber State Univ	UT	6,897	NC
West Liberty State College	WV	6,056	LC
Western Carolina Univ	NC	5,667	C

CLOTHING AND TEXTILES MANAGEMENT/ PRODUCTION/SERVICES

School	ST	$IS	SR
Appalachian State Univ	NC	6,353	C
Cheyney Univ of Pennsylvania	PA	9,993	C
College of the Ozarks	MO	2,650	C+
East Carolina Univ	NC	7,766	C
Eastern Mich Univ	MI	9,855	C
Florida State Univ	FL	7,835	HC
Framingham State College	MA	7,259	C
Johnson and Wales Univ	RI	21,558	LC
Miss Univ for Women	MS	5,446	LC
N Car Agricultural and Technical State Univ	NC	6,659	LC
N Car State Univ	NC	8,680	HC
Northwest Missouri State Univ	MO	7,922	LC
San Francisco State Univ	CA	7,139	LC
Seattle Pacific Univ	WA	22,674	C+
Southern Illinois Univ at Carbondale	IL	8,621	C
Southwest Missouri State Univ	MO	7,600	LC
Texas Southern Univ	TX	6,576	NC
Texas Tech Univ	TX	8,825	C
Ohio State Univ	OH	10,819	VC
Univ of Alabama	AL	7,402	C
Univ of Georgia	GA	8,656	VC
Univ of North Texas	TX	7,629	C
Univ of Northern Iowa	IA	7,850	C

COGNITIVE SCIENCE

School	ST	$IS	SR
Brown Univ	RI	34,973	MC
Cal State, Stanislaus	CA	8,895	C
Dartmouth College	NH	34,458	MC
George Fox Univ	OR	24,095	VC
Hampshire College	MA	33,881	HC+
Indiana Univ Bloomington	IN	10,712	C+
Johns Hopkins Univ	MD	35,226	MC
Lehigh Univ	PA	32,290	MC
Mass Inst of Technology	MA	35,228	MC
Northwestern Univ	IL	33,615	MC
Occidental College	CA	32,288	HC
SUNY/College at Oswego	NY	10,856	C
Tulane Univ	LA	34,013	HC+
Univ of Calif at Berkeley	CA	14,134	MC
Univ of Calif at Los Angeles	CA	13,227	MC
Univ of Calif at San Diego	CA	11,372	HC
Univ of Denver	CO	28,783	VC
Univ of Georgia	GA	8,656	VC
Univ of Kansas	KS	7,232	VC
Univ of Pennsylvania	PA	34,614	MC
Univ of Rochester	NY	32,979	HC
Univ of Texas at Dallas	TX	9,305	VC
Vanderbilt Univ	TN	34,482	MC
Vassar College	NY	33,450	MC
Villanova Univ	PA	31,997	HC
Washington and Lee Univ	VA	25,095	MC
Wellesley College	MA	33,394	MC

COMMERCIAL ART

School	ST	$IS	SR
American InterContinental Univ	GA	12,000	NC
Ashland Univ	OH	22,182	LC
Brenau Univ Women's College	GA	20,100	C
Cazenovia College	NY	19,885	LC
Central Missouri State Univ	MO	7,920	C
Fort Valley State Univ	GA	6,014	LC
Graceland Univ	IA	15,845	C
Madonna Univ	MI	11,504	VC
Millikin Univ	IL	24,415	C+
Missouri Western State College	MO	6,662	NC
Oral Roberts Univ	OK	18,490	C
St. Thomas Aquinas College	NY	20,590	LC
Southwest Baptist Univ	MO	13,426	LC
Union College	NE	14,650	C
Univ of Indianapolis	IN	20,840	C
Univ of North Texas	TX	7,629	C
Univ of St. Francis	IN	17,790	LC
Washington Univ in St. Louis	MO	34,593	MC

COMMUNICATIONS

School	ST	$IS	SR
Abilene Christian Univ	TX	16,300	VC
Adelphi Univ	NY	23,320	VC
Adrian College	MI	19,670	C
Alabama State Univ	AL	6,404	C
Albertus Magnus College	CT	22,154	C
Albright College	PA	27,642	C
Alcorn State Univ	MS	5,594	LC
Alderson-Broaddus College	WV	19,640	C
Alfred Univ	NY	27,212	C+
Allegheny College	PA	27,780	VC
Alma College	MI	22,586	VC
Alvernia College	PA	20,790	C
Alverno College	WI	16,930	LC
American International College	MA	22,268	LC
American Univ	DC	31,544	VC+
Anderson Univ	IN	19,430	LC
Andrews Univ	MI	17,696	LC
Angelo State Univ	TX	7,028	C
Antioch College	OH	25,072	LC
Appalachian State Univ	NC	6,353	C

School	ST	$IS	SR
Miami Univ	OH	12,885	VC+
Mich State Univ	MI	10,386	VC
MidAmerica Nazarene Univ	KS	16,960	C
Middle Tenn State Univ	TN	6,994	C
Midland Lutheran College	NE	18,600	C
Midwestern State Univ	TX	6,704	NC
Miles College	AL	7,870	NC
Millersville Univ of Pennsylvania	PA	10,153	VC
Milligan College	TN	17,550	C
Millikin Univ	IL	24,415	C+
Minn State Univ, Mankato	MN	7,296	LC
Minot State Univ	ND	5,466	LC
Miss College	MS	14,574	C
Miss State Univ	MS	7,853	C
Miss Univ for Women	MS	5,446	LC
Miss Valley State Univ	MS	6,345	C
Missouri Baptist College	MO	15,762	LC
Missouri Southern State College	MO	6,666	C
Missouri Valley College	MO	17,400	LC
Missouri Western State College	MO	6,662	NC
Molloy College	NY	13,940	C
Monmouth College	IL	21,550	C
Monmouth Univ	NJ	24,042	C
Montana State Univ-Billings	MT	7,653	NC
Montana State Univ-Northern	MT	8,600	NC
Montana Tech of The Univ of Montana	MT	7,845	C
Moorhead State Univ	MN	7,000	LC
Morehead State Univ	KY	6,510	C
Morningside College	IA	19,124	C
Morris Brown College	GA	15,993	LC
Mount Ida College	MA	25,375	LC
Mount Mary College	WI	18,024	C
Mount Olive College	NC	14,410	LC
Mount St. Clare College	IA	19,050	LC
Mount St. Mary College	NY	18,825	C
Mount St. Mary's College	MD	25,740	C
Mount Union College	OH	21,120	C
Mount Vernon Nazarene College	OH	17,027	C
Muhlenberg College	PA	28,170	HC
Murray State Univ	KY	6,672	C
Muskingum College	OH	18,760	C
National Univ	CA	7,755	SP
Nebr Wesleyan Univ	NE	18,767	VC
Neumann College	PA	22,040	NC
New England College	NH	20,706	LC
New Mexico Highlands Univ	NM	6,256	NC
New Mexico State Univ	NM	7,302	C
New York Inst of Technology	NY	21,756	C
New York Univ	NY	35,200	MC
Newberry College	SC	19,670	LC
Newbury College	MA	21,490	C
Newman Univ	KS	14,098	LC
Niagara Univ	NY	22,250	C+
Nicholls State Univ	LA	5,290	NC
Norfolk State Univ	VA	8,382	LC
N Car Agricultural and Technical State Univ	NC	6,659	LC
N Car State Univ	NC	8,680	HC
North Central College	IL	22,944	C+
North Central Univ	MN	12,744	LC
N Dak State Univ	ND	7,004	VC
North Park Univ	IL	24,030	C
Northeastern State Univ	OK	4,704	LC
Northeastern Univ	MA	30,078	VC
Northern Arizona Univ	AZ	7,398	C
Northern Illinois Univ	IL	9,545	C
Northern Mich Univ	MI	9,693	C
Northwest Christian College	OR	19,680	LC
Northwest Missouri State Univ	MO	7,922	LC
Northwest Nazarene Univ	ID	18,380	C
Northwestern College	MN	19,816	C+
Northwestern College of Iowa	IA	17,630	C+
Northwestern Okla State Univ	OK	4,542	NC
Northwestern Univ	IL	33,615	MC
Norwich Univ	VT	21,064	LC
Notre Dame College	OH	20,425	C
Notre Dame de Namur Univ	CA	26,932	LC
Nyack College	NY	18,540	C
Oakland Univ	MI	9,418	C
Oakwood College	AL	14,904	C
Oglethorpe Univ	GA	19,100	LC
Ohio Dominican College	OH	18,100	LC
Ohio Northern Univ	OH	27,765	VC
Ohio Univ	OH	11,769	C
Okla Baptist Univ	OK	13,878	VC
Okla Christian Univ	OK	16,500	VC
Okla City Univ	OK	15,810	C
Okla State Univ	OK	7,650	VC
Old Dominion Univ	VA	9,386	C
Olivet College	MI	17,410	C
Oral Roberts Univ	OK	18,490	C
Ottawa Univ	KS	11,800	LC
Otterbein College	OH	23,439	C
Ouachita Baptist Univ	AR	16,460	VC
Our Lady of the Lake Univ of San Antonio	TX	17,336	C
Pace Univ	NY	24,200	C
Pacific Lutheran Univ	WA	23,318	VC
Pacific Union College	CA	20,250	VC
Paine College	GA	11,896	LC
Palm Beach Atlantic College	FL	23,310	C
Park Univ	MO	9,816	C
Penn State Univ at Erie/Behrend College	PA	12,326	C
Penn State Univ/Univ Park Campus	PA	11,126	VC
Pepperdine Univ	CA	32,830	VC
Pfeiffer Univ	NC	18,580	C
Pine Manor College	MA	19,344	LC
Pittsburg State Univ	KS	6,228	NC
Plymouth State College	NH	11,024	LC
Point Loma Nazarene Univ	CA	21,380	VC
Point Park College	PA	20,290	C
Pontifical Catholic Univ of PR/Ponce	PR	7,076	
Prairie View A&M Univ	TX	3,172	LC
Pratt Inst	NY	27,550	SP
Prescott College	AZ	13,430	C
Principia College	IL	23,865	C+
Purdue Univ/Calumet	IN	6,630	NC
Purdue Univ/West Lafayette	IN	10,284	VC
Queens College	NC	17,250	C
Quincy Univ	IL	20,450	C
Quinnipiac Univ	CT	27,370	C
Radford Univ	VA	8,302	C
Ramapo College of New Jersey	NJ	13,550	VC
Randolph-Macon Woman's College	VA	25,820	VC+
Regis College	MA	26,750	C
Regis Univ	CO	25,740	C+
Reinhardt College	GA	13,300	C
Rensselaer Polytechnic Inst	NY	33,863	HC+
Rhode Island College	RI	8,700	LC
Rice Univ	TX	24,325	MC
Rider Univ	NJ	27,400	C
Rivier College	NH	24,215	C
Robert Morris Univ	PA	18,730	C
Roberts Wesleyan College	NY	20,160	C+
Rochester College	MI	15,404	C+
Rochester Inst of Technology	NY	26,232	VC+
Rockhurst Univ	MO	20,090	C
Rocky Mountain College	MT	18,113	C
Roger Williams Univ	RI	29,010	C
Roosevelt Univ	IL	20,240	LC
Rosemont College	PA	24,060	C
Rowan Univ	NJ	12,365	VC
Russell Sage College	NY	23,674	C+
Rust College	MS	7,800	C+
Rutgers, The State Univ of New Jersey New Brunswick Campus	NJ	12,709	C
Saginaw Valley State Univ	MI	9,465	C
St. Ambrose Univ	IA	19,994	C
St. Andrews Presbyterian College	NC	19,720	LC
St. Augustine's College	NC	12,990	C+
St. Cloud State Univ	MN	7,180	C
St. Edward's Univ	TX	17,846	C
St. Francis College	NY	9,610	C
St. Francis Univ	PA	24,486	LC
St. John Fisher College	NY	21,800	C
St. John's Univ	MN	23,640	VC
St. John's Univ	NY	26,660	C
St. Joseph's College	IN	21,640	C
St. Joseph's College of Maine	ME	22,500	LC
St. Louis Univ	MO	26,590	VC+
St. Mary's College	IN	24,474	VC
St. Mary's College	MI	13,314	LC
St. Mary's College of Calif	CA	27,575	C
St. Mary's Univ of San Antonio	TX	19,735	C
St. Norbert College	WI	23,169	VC
St. Olaf College	MN	25,880	HC
St. Thomas Aquinas College	NY	20,590	LC
St. Thomas Univ	FL	19,500	LC
St. Vincent College	PA	22,942	VC
St. Xavier Univ	IL	21,104	C
Salem College	NC	23,065	VC
Salem International Univ	WV	17,263	LC
Salem State College	MA	4,481	LC
Salisbury Univ	MD	10,576	VC
Salve Regina Univ	RI	26,460	C
San Diego State Univ	CA	9,716	C+
Santa Clara Univ	CA	28,371	VC+
Savannah State Univ	GA	2,550	LC
Seattle Pacific Univ	WA	22,674	C+
Seattle Univ	WA	24,183	VC
Seton Hall Univ	NJ	26,910	LC
Seton Hill College	PA	21,875	C
Shenandoah Univ	VA	22,550	NC
Shepherd College	WV	7,062	LC
Shippensburg Univ of Pennsylvania	PA	9,652	C
Shorter College	GA	15,185	C
Siena Heights Univ	MI	16,140	LC
Simmons College	MA	30,418	VC
Simpson College	CA	19,200	C
Simpson College	IA	21,200	C+
Slippery Rock Univ	PA	9,152	LC
Sonoma State Univ	CA	8,953	C
S Dak State Univ	SD	6,848	C
Southeast Missouri State Univ	MO	8,367	C+
Southeastern College	FL	11,648	LC
Southeastern Louisiana Univ	LA	6,047	LC
Southern Adventist Univ	TN	15,600	C
Southern Arkansas Univ	AR	5,740	LC
Southern Conn State Univ	CT	10,310	C
Southern Illinois Univ Edwardsville	IL	7,869	LC
Southern Nazarene Univ	OK	14,634	NC
Southern New Hampshire Univ	NH	23,852	C
Southern Oregon Univ	OR	9,429	C
Southern Univ and A&M College	LA	6,365	C+
Southern Utah Univ	UT	7,254	C
Southern Vermont College	VT	17,685	C
Southwest Baptist Univ	MO	13,426	LC
Southwest Missouri State Univ	MO	7,600	LC
Southwest State Univ	MN	7,117	LC
Southwest Texas State Univ	TX	8,730	VC
Southwestern Adventist Univ	TX	14,798	C
Southwestern College	KS	17,656	C
Southwestern Okla State Univ	OK	4,801	C
Southwestern Univ	TX	22,550	HC
Spalding Univ	KY	15,196	C
Spring Arbor Univ	MI	17,976	C
Stanford Univ	CA	34,222	MC
SUNY/College at Brockport	NY	10,267	C
SUNY/College at Buffalo	NY	8,025	C
SUNY/College at Cortland	NY	10,564	C
SUNY/College at Fredonia	NY	10,125	C
SUNY/College at Geneseo	NY	9,970	HC
SUNY/College at Oneonta	NY	9,981	C
SUNY/College at Oswego	NY	10,856	C
SUNY/College at Plattsburgh	NY	9,729	C
SUNY/Univ at Albany	NY	10,997	VC
SUNY/Univ at Buffalo	NY	11,033	VC
SUNY/Univ at New Paltz	NY	9,685	VC
State Univ of West Georgia	GA	7,101	C
Stephen F. Austin State Univ	TX	6,905	C
Stetson Univ	FL	25,640	VC
Stonehill College	MA	26,852	HC
Suffolk Univ	MA	26,516	C
Sul Ross State Univ	TX	6,582	LC
Susquehanna Univ	PA	27,270	VC
Syracuse Univ	NY	30,710	HC
Tabor College	KS	17,600	LC
Taylor Univ	IN	21,562	VC+
Temple Univ	PA	14,124	C
Texas A&M Univ at Kingsville	TX	6,446	LC
Texas Christian Univ	TX	19,910	C
Texas Lutheran Univ	TX	17,660	C
Texas Southern Univ	TX	6,576	NC
Texas Tech Univ	TX	8,825	C
Texas Wesleyan Univ	TX	14,710	C
Texas Woman's Univ	TX	5,855	LC
Ohio State Univ	OH	10,819	VC
Thiel College	PA	18,419	LC
Thomas Edison State College	NJ	2,750	SP
Thomas More College	KY	17,700	LC
Toccoa Falls College	GA	14,220	C
Towson Univ	MD	11,088	VC
Trevecca Nazarene Univ	TN	15,752	C
Trinity Christian College	IL	19,415	C
Trinity College	DC	21,370	LC
Trinity International Univ	IL	20,640	C+
Trinity Univ	TX	21,444	HC
Tri-State Univ-Main Campus	IN	21,200	C
Troy State Univ	AL	7,696	C
Truman State Univ	MO	8,568	VC+
Tulane Univ	LA	34,013	HC+
Union College	NE	14,650	C
Union Univ	TN	18,930	C+
Univ of Akron	OH	10,530	NC
Univ of Alabama at Birmingham	AL	10,110	C
Univ of Alabama at Huntsville	AL	7,916	VC
Univ of Alaska Anchorage	AK	9,100	NC
Univ of Alaska Fairbanks	AK	8,265	NC
Univ of Alaska Southeast	AK	7,900	LC
Univ of Arizona	AZ	8,614	C
Univ of Arkansas	AR	8,334	VC
Univ of Bridgeport	CT	23,020	C
Univ of Calif at Berkeley	CA	14,134	MC
Univ of Calif at Davis	CA	12,796	VC
Univ of Calif at Los Angeles	CA	13,227	MC
Univ of Calif at San Diego	CA	11,372	HC
Univ of Calif at Santa Barbara	CA	11,732	VC
Univ of Central Arkansas	AR	6,388	C
Univ of Central Florida	FL	8,251	VC
Univ of Central Okla	OK	5,205	C
Univ of Charleston	WV	20,640	C
Univ of Cincinnati	OH	12,491	LC
Univ of Colo at Boulder	CO	9,255	VC
Univ of Colo at Colo Springs	CO	9,403	C
Univ of Colo at Denver	CO	3,673	C
Univ of Conn	CT	12,122	VC
Univ of Dayton	OH	20,400	VC
Univ of Delaware	DE	10,824	VC
Univ of Denver	CO	28,783	VC
Univ of Detroit Mercy	MI	21,620	LC
Univ of Evansville	IN	22,865	VC+
Univ of Findlay	OH	23,962	NC
Univ of Georgia	GA	8,656	VC
Univ of Hartford	CT	28,884	C
Univ of Hawaii at Hilo	HI	6,497	C
Univ of Hawaii at Manoa	HI	7,862	VC
Univ of Houston	TX	8,410	C
Univ of Idaho	ID	7,026	C
Univ of Indianapolis	IN	20,840	C
Univ of Iowa	IA	8,607	C+
Univ of Kentucky	KY	7,765	C
Univ of La Verne	CA	24,280	C
Univ of Louisiana at Lafayette	LA	5,200	C
Univ of Louisville	KY	7,402	LC
Univ of Maine	ME	10,798	C
Univ of Maine at Presque Isle	ME	7,964	LC
Univ of Mary	ND	12,900	LC
Univ of Mary Hardin-Baylor	TX	13,929	C
Univ of Maryland/College Park	MD	11,959	C
Univ of Maryland/Univ College	MD	5,910	SP
Univ of Mass Amherst	MA	10,995	VC
Univ of Memphis	TN	7,271	C
Univ of Miami	FL	31,130	HC
Univ of Mich/Ann Arbor	MI	13,003	HC+
Univ of Mich/Flint	MI	4,323	C
Univ of Minn/Duluth	MN	10,436	C
Univ of Missouri/Columbia	MO	9,803	HC
Univ of Missouri/Kansas City	MO	9,685	VC
Univ of Missouri/St. Louis	MO	9,966	C
Univ of Mobile	AL	13,620	LC
Univ of Montana	MT	8,038	C
Univ of Montana--Western	MT	6,915	NC
Univ of Montevallo	AL	7,266	C
Univ of Nebr at Kearney	NE	7,048	NC
Univ of Nebr at Lincoln	NE	8,325	C+
Univ of Nebr at Omaha	NE	6,867	C
Univ of Nevada/Las Vegas	NV	8,281	VC
Univ of New Hampshire	NH	13,207	C
Univ of New Haven	CT	23,860	LC
Univ of New Mexico	NM	8,026	C
Univ of New Orleans	LA	10,160	C
Univ of North Alabama	AL	7,016	NC
Univ of N Car at Asheville	NC	6,896	VC
Univ of N Car at Charlotte	NC	7,254	C
Univ of N Car at Greensboro	NC	6,858	C
Univ of N Car at Pembroke	NC	5,914	LC
Univ of N Dak	ND	7,067	VC
Univ of North Florida	FL	8,089	VC
Univ of North Texas	TX	7,629	C
Univ of Northern Colo	CO	8,082	C+
Univ of Northern Iowa	IA	7,850	C
Univ of Okla	OK	7,616	VC
Univ of Pennsylvania	PA	34,614	MC
Univ of Pittsburgh at Bradford	PA	12,696	C
Univ of Pittsburgh at Greensburg	PA	12,842	C
Univ of Pittsburgh at Johnstown	PA	13,044	LC
Univ of Pittsburgh at Pittsburgh	PA	13,592	HC
Univ of Portland	OR	24,950	VC
Univ of PR/Rio Piedras	PR	5,510	
Univ of Puget Sound	WA	28,285	HC
Univ of Rhode Island	RI	12,414	C
Univ of Rio Grande	OH	8,728	NC
Univ of St. Francis	IL	19,650	C
Univ of St. Francis	IN	17,790	LC
Univ of St. Thomas	MN	24,044	VC
Univ of St. Thomas	TX	18,752	VC
Univ of San Diego	CA	29,198	HC
Univ of San Francisco	CA	27,302	VC
Univ of Science and Arts of Okla	OK	5,245	C
Univ of Scranton	PA	27,964	C+
Univ of Sioux Falls	SD	16,390	C
Univ of South Alabama	AL	6,976	LC
Univ of S Car at Aiken	SC	7,828	LC
Univ of S Car at Columbia	SC	8,748	VC
Univ of S Car at Spartanburg	SC	7,318	C+
Univ of South Florida	FL	8,154	C
Univ of Southern Calif	CA	33,647	MC
Univ of Southern Colo	CO	7,821	LC
Univ of Southern Indiana	IN	8,655	LC
Univ of Southern Maine	ME	10,569	C
Univ of Southern Miss	MS	6,155	LC

School	ST	$IS	SR
Univ of Tampa	FL	22,012	C
Univ of Tenn at Chattanooga	TN	7,783	C
Univ of Tenn at Martin	TN	8,268	C
Univ of Texas at Arlington	TX	7,192	LC
Univ of Texas at El Paso	TX	5,076	LC
Univ of Texas at San Antonio	TX	9,088	NC
Univ of Texas-Pan American	TX	4,823	C
Univ of the Arts	PA	24,230	SP
Univ of the Incarnate Word	TX	18,478	C
Univ of the Ozarks	AR	13,904	C
Univ of the Pacific	CA	28,255	VC
Univ of the Sacred Heart	PR	5,375	
Univ of Toledo	OH	11,206	NC
Univ of Tulsa	OK	19,090	HC
Univ of Utah	UT	7,703	C
Univ of Virginia's College at Wise	VA	8,302	C
Univ of Washington	WA	10,361	VC
Univ of West Florida	FL	7,518	C
Univ of Wisc/Eau Claire	WI	7,032	VC
Univ of Wisc/Green Bay	WI	7,148	C
Univ of Wisc/La Crosse	WI	7,250	VC
Univ of Wisc/Madison	WI	8,262	VC
Univ of Wisc/Milwaukee	WI	8,907	LC
Univ of Wisc/Parkside	WI	6,160	LC
Univ of Wisc/River Falls	WI	6,356	LC
Univ of Wisc/Stevens Point	WI	7,116	C
Univ of Wisc/Stout	WI	7,192	C
Univ of Wisc/Superior	WI	7,051	C+
Univ of Wisc/Whitewater	WI	6,937	C
Univ of Wyoming	WY	7,143	LC
Upper Iowa Univ	IA	17,438	C
Urbana Univ	OH	17,004	C
Ursinus College	PA	31,350	VC
Utica College of Syracuse Univ	NY	24,400	LC
Valparaiso Univ	IN	23,570	VC+
Vanderbilt Univ	TN	34,482	MC
Vanguard Univ of Southern Calif	CA	20,212	C
Villanova Univ	PA	31,997	HC
Virginia Commonwealth Univ	VA	9,030	C
Virginia Polytechnic Inst and State Univ	VA	7,652	C
Virginia Wesleyan College	VA	22,350	LC
Wake Forest Univ	NC	30,290	MC
Walla Walla College	WA	20,925	C
Walsh Univ	OH	16,880	C
Wartburg College	IA	21,165	VC
Washburn Univ of Topeka	KS	6,766	NC
Washington State Univ	WA	9,388	C
Wayland Baptist Univ	TX	11,271	NC
Wayne State College	NE	6,255	NC
Wayne State Univ	MI	6,720	C
Waynesburg College	PA	17,610	LC
Weber State Univ	UT	6,897	NC
Webster Univ	MO	19,804	VC
Wesley College	DE	17,869	C
Wesleyan College	GA	17,050	VC
West Chester Univ of Pennsylvania	PA	9,792	VC
West Liberty State College	WV	6,056	LC
West Virginia State College	WV	6,264	NC
West Virginia Univ	WV	8,304	C
Western Baptist College	OR	19,700	C+
Western Carolina Univ	NC	5,667	C
Western Conn State Univ	CT	10,074	C
Western Illinois Univ	IL	9,571	C
Western Kentucky Univ	KY	6,834	C
Western Maryland College	MD	26,000	VC
Western Mich Univ	MI	10,016	C
Western State College of Colo	CO	7,585	LC
Western Washington Univ	WA	8,624	VC
Westfield State College	MA	8,394	C
Westminster College	PA	22,960	C
Westminster College	UT	17,226	C
Westmont College	CA	29,748	VC
Wheaton College	IL	21,934	HC
Whitworth College	WA	23,938	VC
Wichita State Univ	KS	6,879	C
Widener Univ	PA	26,920	C
Wilberforce Univ	OH	14,937	LC
Wiley College	TX	8,100	LC
Wilkes Univ	PA	25,800	C
William Carey College	MS	10,150	LC
William Jewell College	MO	17,150	VC
William Paterson Univ of New Jersey	NJ	11,000	LC
William Penn Univ	IA	17,575	C
William Woods Univ	MO	19,390	LC
Wilmington College	OH	21,826	C
Wilson College	PA	21,337	LC
Wingate Univ	NC	19,140	C
Winona State Univ	MN	8,570	C
Winston-Salem State Univ	NC	5,927	LC
Winthrop Univ	SC	9,106	C
Wisc Lutheran College	WI	19,216	VC
Wittenberg Univ	OH	28,766	VC
Worcester State College	MA	7,901	LC
Wright State Univ	OH	9,141	LC
Xavier Univ	OH	23,880	C
Xavier Univ of Louisiana	LA	17,000	LC
Yeshiva Univ	NY	21,400	C
York College	NE	13,500	C
York College of Pennsylvania	PA	12,550	VC
Youngstown State Univ	OH	9,318	NC

COMMUNICATIONS TECHNOLOGY

School	ST	$IS	SR
Alverno College	WI	16,930	LC
Cal State, Monterey Bay	CA	6,250	LC
Champlain College	VT	19,680	C
Chestnut Hill College	PA	24,790	LC
Eastern Mich Univ	MI	9,855	C
Hofstra Univ	NY	23,252	C
James Madison Univ	VA	9,552	HC
Lewis Univ	IL	20,960	C
Loyola Univ New Orleans	LA	23,506	VC+
Montana Tech of The Univ of Montana	MT	7,845	C
Rice Univ	TX	24,325	MC
Salve Regina Univ	RI	26,460	C
Southern Polytechnic State Univ	GA	6,662	C
Trevecca Nazarene Univ	TN	15,752	C

COMMUNITY HEALTH WORK

School	ST	$IS	SR
Baylor Univ	TX	18,298	VC+
Cal State, Los Angeles	CA	5,050	C
CUNY/York College	NY	3,292	NC
Delaware State Univ	DE	8,104	LC
Florida State Univ	FL	7,835	HC
Georgia Southern Univ	GA	6,958	C
Hofstra Univ	NY	23,252	C
Ithaca College	NY	28,719	HC
John Brown Univ	AR	15,080	VC
Kent State Univ	OH	11,104	C
Lewis Univ	IL	20,960	C
Liberty Univ	VA	14,500	C
Malone College	OH	19,190	C
Morris College	SC	9,995	LC
New Mexico State Univ	NM	7,302	C
Ohio Univ	OH	11,769	C
Purdue Univ/West Lafayette	IN	10,284	VC
St. Joseph's College, New York	NY	9,802	C
Simmons College	MA	30,418	VC
Slippery Rock Univ	PA	9,152	LC
Southwest Texas State Univ	TX	8,730	VC
SUNY/College at Old Westbury	NY	9,818	LC
SUNY/College at Potsdam	NY	10,519	C
Univ of Calif at Davis	CA	12,796	VC
Univ of Central Okla	OK	5,205	C
Univ of Maine at Farmington	ME	9,163	C
Univ of Mass Lowell	MA	9,470	VC
Univ of N Car at Pembroke	NC	5,914	LC
Univ of Northern Colo	CO	8,082	C+
Univ of St. Thomas	MN	24,044	VC
Univ of Tenn at Knoxville	TN	8,214	C
Univ of Wisc/La Crosse	WI	7,250	VC
Univ of Wisc/Superior	WI	7,051	C+
Western Conn State Univ	CT	10,074	C
Western Mich Univ	MI	10,016	C
William Paterson Univ of New Jersey	NJ	11,000	LC
Youngstown State Univ	OH	9,318	NC

COMMUNITY PSYCHOLOGY

School	ST	$IS	SR
East Texas Baptist Univ	TX	12,349	LC
Southwestern Okla State Univ	OK	4,801	C
Univ of Mich/Flint	MI	4,323	C
Univ of New Haven	CT	23,860	LC
Univ of PR/Rio Piedras	PR	5,510	

COMMUNITY SERVICES

School	ST	$IS	SR
Alverno College	WI	16,930	LC
Arkansas State Univ	AR	7,480	C
Audrey Cohen College	NY	17,715	C
Baldwin-Wallace College	OH	22,010	VC+
Bemidji State Univ	MN	7,957	C
Bethel College	KS	17,355	C+
Emory & Henry College	VA	19,462	C
Humphreys College	CA	6,900	NC
Martin Univ	IN	8,370	SP
Midland Lutheran College	NE	18,600	C
NAES College	IL	5,140	SP
Northern Arizona Univ	AZ	7,398	C
Northern State Univ	SD	6,279	LC
Ohio Univ	OH	11,769	C
Portland State Univ	OR	11,220	C
Prescott College	AZ	13,430	C
Providence College	RI	27,620	HC
St. Martin's College	WA	20,566	C
St. Mary's College	MI	13,314	LC
Samford Univ	AL	16,340	VC
Southern Arkansas Univ	AR	5,740	LC
SUNY/College at Plattsburgh	NY	9,729	C
SUNY/Empire State College	NY	3,545	SP
Thomas Edison State College	NJ	2,750	SP
Univ of Calif at Riverside	CA	12,479	C
Univ of Calif at Santa Cruz	CA	13,655	VC
Univ of Delaware	DE	10,824	VC
Univ of Mass Boston	MA	4,227	C
Univ of Toledo	OH	11,206	NC
Winona State Univ	MN	8,570	C
Woodbury College	VT	12,060	LC

COMPARATIVE LITERATURE

School	ST	$IS	SR
Beloit College	WI	27,482	HC
Bennington College	VT	31,350	VC
Brandeis Univ	MA	34,481	MC
Brigham Young Univ	UT	7,840	HC
Brown Univ	RI	34,973	MC
Bryn Mawr College	PA	33,580	HC+
Cal State, Fullerton	CA	5,440	LC
Cal State, Long Beach	CA	7,400	LC
Case Western Reserve Univ	OH	27,418	C
Cedar Crest College	PA	25,145	C+
CUNY/Brooklyn College	NY	3,403	LC
CUNY/City College	NY	3,309	LC
CUNY/Herbert H. Lehman College	NY	3,320	LC
CUNY/Hunter College	NY	5,147	C+
CUNY/Queens College	NY	3,403	VC
Clark Univ	MA	29,170	HC
College of Wooster	OH	28,350	VC
Colo College	CO	31,525	HC+
Columbia Univ/Barnard College	NY	33,694	MC
Columbia Univ/Columbia College	NY	35,190	MC
Columbia Univ/School of General Studies	NY	35,000	C
Conn College	CT	33,585	MC
Cornell Univ	NY	34,614	MC
Dartmouth College	NH	34,458	MC
DePaul Univ	IL	23,590	VC
Eckerd College	FL	25,500	C+
Emory Univ	GA	33,792	MC
Fordham Univ	NY	30,710	VC
Georgetown Univ	DC	34,847	MC
Hamilton College	NY	34,150	HC
Hampshire College	MA	33,881	HC+
Haverford College	PA	34,300	MC
Hillsdale College	MI	20,586	VC+
Hobart and William Smith Colleges	NY	33,195	VC
Hofstra Univ	NY	23,252	C
Indiana Univ Bloomington	IN	10,712	C+
Mills College	CA	27,950	C
New England College	NH	20,706	LC
New York Univ	NY	35,200	MC
Northwestern Univ	IL	33,615	MC
Oberlin College	OH	33,140	HC+
Occidental College	CA	32,288	HC
Penn State Univ/Univ Park Campus	PA	11,126	VC
Princeton Univ	NJ	35,072	MC
Purdue Univ/West Lafayette	IN	10,284	VC
Rutgers, The State Univ of New Jersey New Brunswick Campus	NJ	12,709	C
San Diego State Univ	CA	9,716	C+
San Francisco State Univ	CA	7,139	LC
Smith College	MA	33,302	HC+
Stanford Univ	CA	34,222	MC
SUNY/College at Geneseo	NY	9,970	HC
SUNY/Univ at Binghamton	NY	10,653	HC
SUNY/Univ at Stony Brook	NY	10,998	VC
Swarthmore College	PA	34,538	MC
Syracuse Univ	NY	30,710	HC
Trinity College	CT	34,300	HC
Univ of Calif at Berkeley	CA	14,134	MC
Univ of Calif at Davis	CA	12,796	VC
Univ of Calif at Irvine	CA	11,756	C
Univ of Calif at Los Angeles	CA	13,227	MC
Univ of Calif at Riverside	CA	12,479	C
Univ of Calif at Santa Barbara	CA	11,732	VC
Univ of Chicago	IL	35,087	MC
Univ of Cincinnati	OH	12,491	LC
Univ of Delaware	DE	10,824	VC
Univ of Georgia	GA	8,656	VC
Univ of Illinois at Urbana-Champaign	IL	11,316	HC+
Univ of Iowa	IA	8,607	C+
Univ of La Verne	CA	24,280	C
Univ of Mass Amherst	MA	10,995	VC
Univ of Mich/Ann Arbor	MI	13,003	HC+
Univ of New Mexico	NM	8,026	C
Univ of N Car at Chapel Hill	NC	8,789	HC
Univ of Oregon	OR	9,969	C
Univ of Pennsylvania	PA	34,614	MC
Univ of PR/Rio Piedras	PR	5,510	
Univ of Rhode Island	RI	12,414	C
Univ of Rochester	NY	32,979	HC
Univ of Southern Calif	CA	33,647	MC
Univ of Tenn at Knoxville	TN	8,214	C
Univ of Virginia	VA	9,391	HC+
Univ of Washington	WA	10,361	VC
Univ of Wisc/Madison	WI	8,262	VC
Univ of Wisc/Milwaukee	WI	8,907	LC
Washington Univ in St. Louis	MO	34,593	MC
Wellesley College	MA	33,394	MC
West Chester Univ of Pennsylvania	PA	9,792	VC
Willamette Univ	OR	29,422	VC+
Yale Univ	CT	34,030	MC

COMPUTER EDUCATION

School	ST	$IS	SR
Baylor Univ	TX	18,298	VC+
College of St. Joseph	VT	17,400	NC
Concordia Univ, River Forest	IL	20,000	LC
East Texas Baptist Univ	TX	12,349	LC
Eastern Mich Univ	MI	9,855	C
Eastern Washington Univ	WA	7,972	LC
Illinois State Univ	IL	9,235	C
Northern Mich Univ	MI	9,693	C
St. Martin's College	WA	20,566	C
Stephen F. Austin State Univ	TX	6,905	C
Union College	NE	14,650	C
Univ of Illinois at Urbana-Champaign	IL	11,316	HC+
Viterbo Univ	WI	18,043	C
Youngstown State Univ	OH	9,318	NC

COMPUTER ENGINEERING

School	ST	$IS	SR
Arizona State Univ-Main	AZ	7,726	C
Auburn Univ	AL	5,510	C
Bellarmine Univ	KY	20,440	VC
Boston Univ	MA	34,358	MC
Bucknell Univ	PA	31,096	HC
Calif Polytechnic State Univ	CA	8,747	VC
Cal State, Chico	CA	8,598	LC
Cal State, Fresno	CA	7,762	C
Cal State, Long Beach	CA	7,400	LC
Cal State, Sacramento	CA	7,488	C
Capitol College	MD	18,462	LC
Carnegie Mellon Univ	PA	32,682	MC
Case Western Reserve Univ	OH	27,418	C
Christopher Newport Univ	VA	8,862	VC
Clarkson Univ	NY	29,884	VC
Clemson Univ	SC	7,600	C
Cogswell Polytechnical College	CA	14,400	LC
Colo Technical Univ	CO	9,425	LC
Columbia Univ/Fu Foundation School of Engineering and Applied Science	NY	35,190	MC
Cornell Univ	NY	34,614	MC
DeVry Univ/Addison (DuPage County)	IL	8,805	LC
DeVry Univ/Alpharetta	GA	8,805	LC
DeVry Univ/Chicago	IL	8,805	LC
DeVry Univ/Decatur	GA	8,805	LC
DeVry Univ/Fremont	CA	9,865	C
DeVry Univ/Kansas City	MO	8,805	LC
DeVry Univ/Long Beach	CA	9,140	LC
DeVry Univ/Pomona	CA	9,205	LC
DeVry Univ/Seattle	WA	10,065	LC
DeVry Univ/West Hills	CA	9,205	LC
Drexel Univ	PA	27,657	VC
Eastern Nazarene College	MA	19,433	LC
Elizabethtown College	PA	26,000	VC
Embry-Riddle Aeronautical Univ	FL	24,790	C
Florida Atlantic Univ	FL	8,832	C
Florida Inst of Technology	FL	25,250	VC
Florida International Univ	FL	9,486	VC
Florida State Univ	FL	7,835	HC
George Mason Univ	VA	9,192	C
George Washington Univ	DC	32,170	HC
Georgia Inst of Technology	GA	9,028	HC+
Gonzaga Univ	WA	24,276	HC+
Howard Univ	DC	15,522	LC
Illinois Inst of Technology	IL	25,182	HC+
Indiana Inst of Technology	IN	18,806	C
Indiana Univ-Purdue Univ Indianapolis	IN	9,473	C
Iowa State Univ	IA	8,108	VC
Johns Hopkins Univ	MD	35,226	MC
Johnson C. Smith Univ	NC	16,560	C+
Kansas State Univ	KS	6,995	C
Kettering Univ	MI	23,256	HC
Lehigh Univ	PA	32,290	MC
LeTourneau Univ	TX	19,020	VC
Louisiana State Univ and A&M College	LA	8,014	VC
Marquette Univ	WI	24,836	C+
Mass Inst of Technology	MA	35,228	MC
Mich State Univ	MI	10,386	VC
Mich Tech Univ	MI	11,088	VC
Milwaukee School of Engineering	WI	25,680	VC+
Miss State Univ	MS	7,853	C
Montana State Univ-Bozeman	MT	8,431	C

ST = STATE $IS = IN-STATE COSTS SR = SELECTOR RATING

School	ST	$IS	SR
Montana Tech of The Univ of Montana	MT	7,845	C
New Jersey Inst of Technology	NJ	14,690	VC
New York Inst of Technology	NY	21,756	C
New York Univ	NY	35,200	MC
N Car State Univ	NC	8,680	HC
N Dak State Univ	ND	7,004	VC
Northeastern Univ	MA	30,078	VC
Northern Arizona Univ	AZ	7,398	C
Northwestern Univ	IL	33,615	MC
Oakland Univ	MI	9,418	C
Ohio Northern Univ	OH	27,765	VC
Ohio Univ	OH	11,769	C
Okla Christian Univ	OK	16,500	VC
Old Dominion Univ	VA	9,386	C
Oral Roberts Univ	OK	18,490	C
Oregon State Univ	OR	9,612	VC
Pacific Lutheran Univ	WA	23,318	VC
Penn State Univ at Erie/Behrend College	PA	12,326	C
Penn State Univ/Univ Park Campus	PA	11,126	VC
Pennsylvania College of Technology	PA	12,860	NC
Polytechnic Univ/Brooklyn	NY	33,090	HC
Portland State Univ	OR	11,220	C
Prairie View A&M Univ	TX	3,172	LC
Purdue Univ/Calumet	IN	6,630	NC
Purdue Univ/West Lafayette	IN	10,284	VC
Rensselaer Polytechnic Inst	NY	33,863	HC+
Rochester Inst of Technology	NY	26,232	VC+
Roger Williams Univ	RI	29,010	C
Rose-Hulman Inst of Technology	IN	27,707	HC+
St. Mary's Univ of San Antonio	TX	19,735	C
San Diego State Univ	CA	9,716	C+
San Jose State Univ	CA	8,187	C
Santa Clara Univ	CA	28,371	VC+
S Dak School of Mines and Technology	SD	7,438	C+
Southern Illinois Univ at Carbondale	IL	8,621	C
Southern Illinois Univ Edwardsville	IL	7,869	LC
Southern Methodist Univ	TX	28,349	VC
Southwestern Okla State Univ	OK	4,801	C
SUNY/Univ at Binghamton	NY	10,653	HC
SUNY/Univ at Buffalo	NY	11,033	VC
SUNY/Univ at New Paltz	NY	9,685	VC
SUNY/Univ at Stony Brook	NY	10,998	VC
Stevens Inst of Technology	NJ	31,510	HC+
Stonehill College	MA	26,852	HC
Suffolk Univ	MA	26,516	C
Syracuse Univ	NY	30,710	HC
Taylor Univ	IN	21,562	VC+
Texas A&M Univ	TX	8,988	VC
Ohio State Univ	OH	10,819	VC
Tufts Univ	MA	34,874	MC
Tulane Univ	LA	34,013	HC+
Union College	NY	32,646	HC
United States Air Force Academy	CO		MC
Univ of Akron	OH	10,530	NC
Univ of Alabama at Huntsville	AL	7,916	VC
Univ of Arizona	AZ	8,614	C
Univ of Arkansas	AR	8,334	VC
Univ of Bridgeport	CT	23,020	C
Univ of Calif at Berkeley	CA	14,134	MC
Univ of Calif at Davis	CA	12,796	VC
Univ of Calif at Irvine	CA	11,756	C
Univ of Calif at Los Angeles	CA	13,227	MC
Univ of Calif at San Diego	CA	11,372	HC
Univ of Calif at Santa Cruz	CA	13,655	VC
Univ of Central Florida	FL	8,251	VC
Univ of Cincinnati	OH	12,491	LC
Univ of Colo at Boulder	CO	9,255	VC
Univ of Conn	CT	12,122	VC
Univ of Dayton	OH	20,400	VC
Univ of Delaware	DE	10,824	VC
Univ of Denver	CO	28,783	VC
Univ of Evansville	IN	22,865	VC+
Univ of Florida	FL	7,874	HC
Univ of Hartford	CT	28,884	C
Univ of Houston	TX	8,410	C
Univ of Idaho	ID	7,026	C
Univ of Illinois at Chicago	IL	10,702	VC
Univ of Illinois at Urbana-Champaign	IL	11,316	HC+
Univ of Iowa	IA	8,607	C+
Univ of Kansas	KS	7,232	VC
Univ of La Verne	CA	24,280	C
Univ of Louisiana at Lafayette	LA	5,200	C
Univ of Louisville	KY	7,402	LC
Univ of Maine	ME	10,798	C
Univ of Maryland/Baltimore County	MD	12,190	VC
Univ of Maryland/College Park	MD	11,959	C
Univ of Mass Amherst	MA	10,995	VC
Univ of Mass Dartmouth	MA	9,852	C
Univ of Memphis	TN	7,271	C
Univ of Miami	FL	31,130	HC
Univ of Mich/Ann Arbor	MI	13,003	HC+
Univ of Mich/Dearborn	MI	4,677	VC
Univ of Minn/Duluth	MN	10,436	C
Univ of Missouri/Columbia	MO	9,803	HC
Univ of Missouri/Rolla	MO	10,034	C
Univ of Nebr at Lincoln	NE	8,325	C+
Univ of Nevada/Las Vegas	NV	8,281	VC
Univ of New Hampshire	NH	13,207	C
Univ of New Haven	CT	23,860	LC
Univ of New Mexico	NM	8,026	C
Univ of N Car at Charlotte	NC	7,254	C
Univ of Notre Dame	IN	30,707	MC
Univ of Okla	OK	7,616	VC
Univ of Pennsylvania	PA	34,614	MC
Univ of Pittsburgh at Pittsburgh	PA	13,592	HC
Univ of PR/Mayaguez	PR	5,285	
Univ of Rhode Island	RI	12,414	C
Univ of South Alabama	AL	6,976	LC
Univ of S Car at Columbia	SC	8,748	VC
Univ of South Florida	FL	8,154	C
Univ of Southern Calif	CA	33,647	MC
Univ of Texas at Arlington	TX	7,192	LC
Univ of the Pacific	CA	28,255	VC
Univ of Toledo	OH	11,206	NC
Univ of Utah	UT	7,703	C
Univ of Vermont	VT	14,761	C+
Univ of Washington	WA	10,361	VC
Univ of West Florida	FL	7,518	C
Univ of Wyoming	WY	7,143	LC
Vanderbilt Univ	TN	34,482	MC
Vermont Technical College	VT	11,704	C
Villanova Univ	PA	31,997	HC
Virginia Polytechnic Inst and State Univ	VA	7,652	C
Washington State Univ	WA	9,388	C
Washington Univ in St. Louis	MO	34,593	MC
West Virginia Univ	WV	8,304	C
Western Mich Univ	MI	10,016	C
Wichita State Univ	KS	6,879	C
Wright State Univ	OH	9,141	LC

COMPUTER GRAPHICS

School	ST	$IS	SR
Allegheny College	PA	27,780	VC
American Univ	DC	31,544	VC+
Andrews Univ	MI	17,696	LC
Art Inst of Atlanta	GA	20,624	SP
Art Inst of Portland	OR	13,725	SP
Atlanta College of Art	GA	18,600	SP
Carlow College	PA	19,366	C
Champlain College	VT	19,680	C
Cogswell Polytechnical College	CA	14,400	LC
Columbia College Chicago	IL	22,063	LC
Dakota State Univ	SD	6,950	C
Dominican Univ	IL	20,800	C
Eastern Mich Univ	MI	9,855	C
Embry-Riddle Aeronautical Univ	FL	24,790	C
Escuela de Artes Plasticas de PR	PR	1,874	
Fashion Inst of Technology/SUNY	NY	9,504	C+
Henry Cogswell College	WA	13,080	SP
Huntingdon College	AL	18,400	VC
Jacksonville Univ	FL	21,110	LC
La Salle Univ	PA	27,890	C
Lewis Univ	IL	20,960	C
Loyola Marymount Univ	CA	28,754	HC
Monmouth Univ	NJ	24,042	C
New York Inst of Technology	NY	21,756	C
Pratt Inst	NY	27,550	SP
Purdue Univ/West Lafayette	IN	10,284	VC
Ringling School of Art and Design	FL	22,500	SP
Rochester Inst of Technology	NY	26,232	VC+
Savannah College of Art and Design	GA	25,075	SP
School of Visual Arts	NY	26,000	SP
Springfield College	MA	24,520	C
Syracuse Univ	NY	30,710	HC
Taylor Univ	IN	21,562	VC+
Univ of Dubuque	IA	19,990	C
Univ of Great Falls	MT	15,360	C
Univ of Mary Hardin-Baylor	TX	13,929	C
Univ of Tampa	FL	22,612	C
Univ of the Arts	PA	24,230	SP
Woodbury Univ	CA	25,344	LC

COMPUTER MANAGEMENT

School	ST	$IS	SR
Caldwell College	NJ	20,940	LC
Cal State, Stanislaus	CA	8,895	C
Champlain College	VT	19,680	C
Clarion Univ of Pennsylvania	PA	11,272	LC
College of St. Mary	NE	18,726	C
Colo Christian Univ	CO	17,714	C
Concordia Univ	MI	20,500	C
Eastern Mennonite Univ	VA	20,700	VC
Johnson and Wales Univ	RI	21,558	LC
Johnson State College	VT	10,776	C
Metropolitan State College of Denver	CO	2,338	LC
Mount Olive College	NC	14,410	LC
New Jersey Inst of Technology	NJ	14,690	VC
Northwest Missouri State Univ	MO	7,922	LC
Northwood Univ	MI	18,360	LC
Northwood Univ	TX	18,135	C
Okla City Univ	OK	15,810	C
Peru State College	NE	6,342	NC
Rochester College	MI	15,404	C+
Southern Adventist Univ	TN	15,600	C
Southwest Texas State Univ	TX	8,730	VC
Univ of Great Falls	MT	15,360	C
Univ of New Haven	CT	23,860	LC
Univ of Scranton	PA	27,964	C+
Univ of the Incarnate Word	TX	18,478	C

COMPUTER MATHEMATICS

School	ST	$IS	SR
Albertson College of Idaho	ID	23,900	VC
College of Mount St. Joseph	OH	20,290	C
Colo College	CO	31,525	HC+
Hollins Univ	VA	24,328	VC
Ithaca College	NY	28,719	HC
Keene State College	NH	11,280	C
LeTourneau Univ	TX	19,020	VC
Marist College	NY	24,756	VC
Mary Baldwin College	VA	23,440	C
Missouri Southern State College	MO	6,666	C
Oakwood College	AL	14,904	C
Rochester Inst of Technology	NY	26,232	VC+
Saginaw Valley State Univ	MI	9,465	C
Salem International Univ	WV	17,263	LC
Univ of Calif at Los Angeles	CA	13,227	MC
Univ of Maine at Farmington	ME	9,163	C
Univ of S Car at Aiken	SC	7,828	LC
Western Conn State Univ	CT	10,074	C
Wheaton College	MA	32,940	VC
Wingate Univ	NC	19,140	C

COMPUTER PROGRAMMING

School	ST	$IS	SR
Baker College of Flint	MI	7,720	NC
Calif Univ of Pennsylvania	PA	10,388	C
Caribbean Univ	PR	3,000	
Carnegie Mellon Univ	PA	32,682	MC
Central Washington Univ	WA	8,985	LC
Champlain College	VT	19,680	C
City Univ	WA	7,425	NC
Cogswell Polytechnical College	CA	14,400	LC
Concord College	WV	7,122	C+
Concordia Univ, River Forest	IL	20,000	LC
Dakota State Univ	SD	6,950	C
Davenport Univ	MI	10,057	NC
DeVry Univ/Colo Springs	CO	9,465	LC
DeVry Univ/Crystal City	VA	10,065	C
DeVry Univ/Denver	CO	9,465	LC
DeVry Univ/Fremont	CA	9,865	C
DeVry Univ/Long Beach	CA	9,140	LC
DeVry Univ/Orlando	FL	9,865	LC
DeVry Univ/Phoenix	AZ	8,805	LC
DeVry Univ/Pomona	CA	9,205	LC
DeVry Univ/Seattle	WA	10,065	LC
DeVry Univ/Tinley Park	IL	8,805	LC
DeVry Univ/West Hills	CA	9,205	LC
Dickinson State Univ	ND	5,495	NC
Dordt College	IA	18,100	C+
Dowling College	NY	20,281	LC
Eastern Kentucky Univ	KY	6,552	C
Eastern Mich Univ	MI	9,855	C
Ferris State Univ	MI	10,816	C
Freed-Hardeman Univ	TN	14,290	VC
Gannon Univ	PA	18,848	C
Georgia Southwestern State Univ	GA	6,013	C
Goldey-Beacom College	DE	11,440	C
Goshen College	IN	18,950	VC+
Hannibal-LaGrange College	MO	12,530	C
Hawaii Pacific Univ	HI	17,790	C
Howard Univ	DC	15,522	LC
Husson College	ME	15,360	LC
Indiana Inst of Technology	IN	18,806	C
Indiana Univ-Purdue Univ Fort Wayne	IN	3,166	LC
Lamar Univ	TX	6,816	LC
Lee Univ	TN	10,198	LC
Limestone College	SC	16,900	C
Mayville State Univ	ND	6,440	NC
Midland Lutheran College	NE	18,600	C
Missouri Western State College	MO	6,662	NC
Monmouth College	IL	21,550	C
Monmouth Univ	NJ	24,042	C
Montana Tech of The Univ of Montana	MT	7,845	C
Murray State Univ	KY	6,672	C
Newbury College	MA	21,490	C
Northeastern Univ	MA	30,078	VC
Northern Mich Univ	MI	9,693	C
Oakland City Univ	IN	11,286	LC
Pacific Lutheran Univ	WA	23,318	VC
Peru State College	NE	6,342	NC
Pontifical Catholic Univ of PR/Ponce	PR	7,076	
Purdue Univ/Calumet	IN	6,630	NC
Rhode Island College	RI	8,700	LC
St. Thomas Univ	FL	19,500	LC
Salem State College	MA	4,481	LC
Southwestern College	KS	17,656	C
Southwestern Okla State Univ	OK	4,801	C
Stephen F. Austin State Univ	TX	6,905	C
Suffolk Univ	MA	26,516	C
Tarleton State Univ	TX	7,160	C
Turabo Univ	PR	4,110	
Univ of Evansville	IN	22,865	VC+
Univ of Great Falls	MT	15,360	C
Univ of Nebr at Kearney	NE	7,048	NC
Univ of St. Francis	IL	19,650	C
Univ of Wisc/Eau Claire	WI	7,032	VC
Univ of Wisc/River Falls	WI	6,356	LC
Univ of Wisc/Whitewater	WI	6,937	C
Washburn Univ of Topeka	KS	6,766	NC
Washington Univ in St. Louis	MO	34,593	MC
Weber State Univ	UT	6,897	NC
West Virginia Univ Inst of Technology	WV	7,518	NC
York College of Pennsylvania	PA	12,550	VC
Youngstown State Univ	OH	9,318	NC

COMPUTER SCIENCE

School	ST	$IS	SR
Abilene Christian Univ	TX	16,300	VC
Adams State College	CO	7,468	C
Adelphi Univ	NY	23,320	VC
Alabama A&M Univ	AL	5,100	LC
Albany State Univ	GA	5,764	C+
Albion College	MI	25,224	VC
Albright College	PA	27,642	C
Alcorn State Univ	MS	5,594	LC
Alderson-Broaddus College	WV	19,640	C
Alfred Univ	NY	27,212	C+
Allegheny College	PA	27,780	VC
Alma College	MI	22,586	VC
Alverno College	WI	16,930	LC
American Univ	DC	31,544	VC+
Amherst College	MA	34,340	MC
Anderson Univ	IN	19,430	LC
Andrews Univ	MI	17,696	LC
Angelo State Univ	TX	7,028	C
Appalachian State Univ	NC	6,353	C
Arcadia Univ	PA	26,650	C
Arizona State Univ-Main	AZ	7,726	C
Arkansas Baptist College	AR	5,530	LC
Arkansas State Univ	AR	7,480	C
Arkansas Tech Univ	AR	6,256	C
Armstrong Atlantic State Univ	GA	7,084	C
Ashland Univ	OH	22,182	LC
Assumption College	MA	26,320	C
Atlantic Union College	MA	34,034	LC
Auburn Univ	AL	5,510	C
Augsburg College	MN	22,978	C
Augusta State Univ	GA	2,282	C
Augustana College	IL	24,117	VC+
Augustana College	SD	20,760	VC
Aurora Univ	IL	18,551	C
Austin College	TX	22,150	VC+
Austin Peay State Univ	TN	5,814	LC
Averett Univ	VA	17,980	LC
Avila College	MO	17,720	C
Azusa Pacific Univ	CA	22,422	VC
Baker Univ	KS	14,780	C+
Baldwin-Wallace College	OH	22,010	VC+
Ball State Univ	IN	8,660	C
Barry Univ	FL	24,100	LC
Bartlesville Wesleyan College	OK	14,100	LC
Baylor Univ	TX	18,298	VC+
Belhaven College	MS	16,040	C+
Bellarmine Univ	KY	20,440	VC
Belmont Univ	TN	19,066	VC
Beloit College	WI	27,482	HC
Bemidji State Univ	MN	7,957	C
Benedict College	SC	12,662	LC
Benedictine College	KS	18,485	LC
Benedictine Univ	IL	21,330	C
Bennett College	NC	11,200	C
Bennington College	VT	31,350	VC
Berry College	GA	18,850	C
Bethany College	WV	18,566	C
Bethel College	IN	17,650	LC
Bethel College	KS	17,355	C+
Bethel College	MN	22,740	VC
Bethune-Cookman College	FL	15,746	C
Biola Univ	CA	21,902	VC

School	ST	$IS	SR
Birmingham-Southern College	AL	22,960	C
Blackburn College	IL	13,690	C
Bloomsburg Univ of Pennsylvania	PA	9,434	C
Bluefield State College	WV	2,178	LC
Bluffton College	OH	20,644	C
Boston College	MA	33,330	MC
Boston Univ	MA	34,358	MC
Bowdoin College	ME	32,650	MC
Bowie State Univ	MD	9,300	C+
Bowling Green State Univ	OH	10,794	C
Bradley Univ	IL	20,970	VC
Brandeis Univ	MA	34,481	MC
Brescia Univ	KY	14,225	C
Briar Cliff Univ	IA	18,657	LC
Bridgewater College	VA	22,950	C
Bridgewater State College	MA	7,589	C+
Brigham Young Univ	UT	7,840	HC
Brigham Young Univ/Hawaii	HI	6,890	C
Brown Univ	RI	34,973	MC
Bryan College	TN	16,400	VC
Bucknell Univ	PA	31,096	HC
Buena Vista Univ	IA	22,828	C
Butler Univ	IN	25,580	VC+
Caldwell College	NJ	20,940	LC
Calif Lutheran Univ	CA	23,500	LC
Calif Polytechnic State Univ	CA	8,747	VC
Calif State Polytechnic Univ, Pomona	CA	8,615	C
Cal State, Bakersfield	CA	6,090	LC
Cal State, Chico	CA	8,598	LC
Cal State, Dominguez Hills	CA	5,840	LC
Cal State, Fresno	CA	7,762	C
Cal State, Fullerton	CA	5,440	LC
Cal State, Hayward	CA	7,400	LC
Cal State, Long Beach	CA	7,400	LC
Cal State, Los Angeles	CA	5,050	C
Cal State, Monterey Bay	CA	6,250	LC
Cal State, Northridge	CA	7,781	C
Cal State, Sacramento	CA	7,488	C
Cal State, San Bernardino	CA	6,516	C
Cal State, San Marcos	CA	1,736	LC
Cal State, Stanislaus	CA	8,895	C
Calif Univ of Pennsylvania	PA	10,388	C
Calvin College	MI	20,050	NC
Cameron Univ	OK	5,560	NC
Campbell Univ	NC	16,599	C
Canisius College	NY	24,696	C+
Capital Univ	OH	23,630	C
Cardinal Stritch Univ	WI	17,620	C
Caribbean Univ	PR	3,000	
Carleton College	MN	30,780	MC
Carlow College	PA	19,366	C
Carnegie Mellon Univ	PA	32,682	MC
Carroll College	MT	19,140	C
Carroll College	WI	21,170	C
Case Western Reserve Univ	OH	27,418	C
Castleton State College	VT	10,922	LC
Catawba College	NC	19,620	C
Catholic Univ of America	DC	29,332	VC
Cedar Crest College	PA	25,145	C+
Cedarville Univ	OH	17,553	VC
Central College	IA	21,206	C
Central Conn State Univ	CT	10,404	C
Central Methodist College	MO	10,400	C
Central Mich Univ	MI	8,355	C
Central Missouri State Univ	MO	7,920	C
Central State Univ	OH	8,922	C+
Central Univ of Bayamon	PR	3,335	
Central Washington Univ	WA	8,985	LC
Centre College	KY	24,000	HC
Chapman Univ	CA	30,218	VC
Charleston Southern Univ	SC	17,122	C
Chatham College	PA	25,454	C+
Chestnut Hill College	PA	24,790	LC
Cheyney Univ of Pennsylvania	PA	9,993	C
Chicago State Univ	IL	8,851	C+
Christian Brothers Univ	TN	19,820	VC
Christopher Newport Univ	VA	8,862	VC
Citadel, The	SC	9,126	C
CUNY/Brooklyn College	NY	3,403	LC
CUNY/City College	NY	3,309	LC
CUNY/College of Staten Island	NY	3,358	NC
CUNY/Herbert H. Lehman College	NY	3,320	LC
CUNY/Hunter College	NY	5,147	C+
CUNY/Queens College	NY	3,403	VC
Claflin Univ	SC	12,735	C+
Clarion Univ of Pennsylvania	PA	11,272	LC
Clark Atlanta Univ	GA	17,174	C
Clark Univ	MA	29,170	HC
Clarke College	IA	20,625	C+
Clarkson Univ	NY	29,884	VC
Clemson Univ	SC	7,600	C
Cleveland State Univ	OH	10,146	NC
Coastal Carolina Univ	SC	9,220	C
Coe College	IA	24,750	VC
Coker College	SC	20,120	C
Colby College	ME	34,290	MC
Colgate Univ	NY	33,480	MC
College Misericordia	PA	23,380	LC

School	ST	$IS	SR
College of Charleston	SC	8,350	HC
College of Mount St. Vincent	NY	24,230	C
College of Mount St. Joseph	OH	20,290	C
College of New Jersey	NJ	13,425	HC
College of Notre Dame of Maryland	MD	23,100	LC
College of Our Lady of the Elms	MA	20,644	C
College of St. Benedict	MN	23,921	VC
College of St. Elizabeth	NJ	22,510	C
College of St. Joseph	VT	17,400	NC
College of St. Scholastica	MN	22,378	C+
College of Santa Fe	NM	20,250	LC
College of the Ozarks	MO	2,650	C+
College of William and Mary	VA	10,002	MC
College of Wooster	OH	28,350	VC
Colo State Univ	CO	9,672	C
Colo Technical Univ	CO	9,425	LC
Columbia College	MO	15,082	C
Columbia Union College	MD	19,027	C+
Columbia Univ/Barnard College	NY	33,694	MC
Columbia Univ/Columbia College	NY	35,190	MC
Columbia Univ/Fu Foundation School of Engineering and Applied Science	NY	35,190	MC
Columbia Univ/School of General Studies	NY	35,000	C
Columbus State Univ	GA	7,228	LC
Concord College	WV	7,122	C+
Concordia College/Moorhead	MN	18,835	C
Concordia Univ at Austin	TX	16,740	LC
Concordia Univ Nebr	NE	17,770	C
Concordia Univ, River Forest	IL	20,000	LC
Converse College	SC	21,990	VC
Coppin State College	MD	9,133	LC
Cornell College	IA	24,980	VC
Cornell Univ	NY	34,614	MC
Creighton Univ	NE	23,476	VC
Dakota State Univ	SD	6,950	C
Dallas Baptist Univ	TX	13,682	LC
Dana College	NE	18,046	C
Daniel Webster College	NH	24,870	C
Dartmouth College	NH	34,458	MC
David Lipscomb Univ	TN	16,158	VC
Davis and Elkins College	WV	19,270	LC
De Sales Univ	PA	22,610	VC
Delaware State Univ	DE	8,104	LC
Delaware Valley College	PA	24,213	LC
Denison Univ	OH	29,640	HC
DePaul Univ	IL	23,590	VC
DePauw Univ	IN	28,000	HC
Dickinson College	PA	32,210	VC+
Dickinson State Univ	ND	5,495	NC
Dillard Univ	LA	16,046	VC
Doane College	NE	17,600	LC
Dominican Univ	IL	20,800	C
Dordt College	IA	18,100	C+
Dowling College	NY	20,281	LC
Drake Univ	IA	22,830	VC
Drew Univ/College of Liberal Arts	NJ	32,152	VC
Drexel Univ	PA	27,657	VC
Drury Univ	MO	15,250	VC
Duke Univ	NC	34,396	MC
Duquesne Univ	PA	24,242	C+
Earlham College	IN	27,446	VC+
East Carolina Univ	NC	7,766	C
East Central Univ	OK	4,578	C
East Stroudsburg Univ of Pennsylvania	PA	8,430	LC
East Tenn State Univ	TN	7,127	C
Eastern Conn State Univ	CT	10,362	C
Eastern Illinois Univ	IL	10,101	C
Eastern Kentucky Univ	KY	6,552	C
Eastern Mennonite Univ	VA	20,700	VC
Eastern Mich Univ	MI	9,855	C
Eastern Nazarene College	MA	19,433	LC
Eastern New Mexico Univ	NM	4,113	LC
Eastern Oregon Univ	OR	8,772	C
Eastern Washington Univ	WA	7,972	LC
East-West Univ	IL	9,140	LC
Eckerd College	FL	25,500	C+
Edinboro Univ of Pennsylvania	PA	9,328	LC
Edward Waters College	FL	13,124	LC
Elizabeth City State Univ	NC	5,550	LC
Elizabethtown College	PA	26,000	VC
Elmhurst College	IL	21,750	C
Elon Univ	NC	19,430	VC
Embry-Riddle Aeronautical Univ	AZ	23,470	C+
Embry-Riddle Aeronautical Univ	FL	24,790	C
Emory & Henry College	VA	19,462	C
Emory Univ	GA	33,792	MC
Emporia State Univ	KS	6,198	LC
Eureka College	IL	22,200	C
Evangel Univ	MO	14,050	C
Fairfield Univ	CT	30,885	HC

School	ST	$IS	SR
Fairleigh Dickinson Univ/Madison campus	NJ	25,500	C
Fairleigh Dickinson Univ/Teaneck Campus	NJ	24,646	C
Fairmont State College	WV	7,010	NC
Fayetteville State Univ	NC	5,590	LC
Felician College	NJ	20,050	C
Ferrum College	VA	15,990	LC
Fitchburg State College	MA	7,836	C
Florida A&M Univ	FL	6,948	C
Florida Atlantic Univ	FL	8,832	C
Florida Inst of Technology	FL	25,250	VC
Florida International Univ	FL	9,486	VC
Florida Memorial College	FL	6,000	LC
Florida State Univ	FL	7,835	HC
Fontbonne Univ	MO	18,046	C
Fordham Univ	NY	30,710	VC
Fort Hays State Univ	KS	6,294	LC
Fort Valley State Univ	GA	6,014	LC
Framingham State College	MA	7,259	C
Francis Marion Univ	SC	7,682	C
Franciscan Univ of Steubenville	OH	19,100	C+
Franklin College of Indiana	IN	19,905	C
Franklin Pierce College	NH	26,125	LC
Franklin Univ	OH	6,324	SP
Freed-Hardeman Univ	TN	14,290	VC
Friends Univ	KS	15,962	LC
Frostburg State Univ	MD	9,680	C
Furman Univ	SC	25,492	HC
Gallaudet Univ	DC	16,554	SP
Gannon Univ	PA	18,848	C
Gardner-Webb Univ	NC	17,400	C
Geneva College	PA	19,990	C+
George Fox Univ	OR	24,095	VC
George Mason Univ	VA	9,192	C
George Washington Univ	DC	32,170	HC
Georgetown College	KY	18,400	VC
Georgetown Univ	DC	34,847	MC
Georgia College and State Univ	GA	7,344	C
Georgia Inst of Technology	GA	9,028	HC+
Georgia Southern Univ	GA	6,958	C
Georgia Southwestern State Univ	GA	6,013	C
Georgia State Univ	GA	7,792	LC
Gettysburg College	PA	32,070	HC
Glenville State College	WV	6,588	NC
Gonzaga Univ	WA	24,276	HC+
Gordon College	MA	23,594	VC+
Goucher College	MD	30,650	VC+
Graceland Univ	IA	15,845	C
Grambling State Univ	LA	5,325	NC
Grand Canyon Univ	AZ	30,000	LC
Grand Valley State Univ	MI	10,040	C
Grand View College	IA	17,596	NC
Greenville College	IL	19,226	LC
Grinnell College	IA	28,300	HC+
Grove City College	PA	12,280	MC
Gustavus Adolphus College	MN	24,190	VC+
Gwynedd-Mercy College	PA	22,350	C
Hamilton College	NY	34,150	HC
Hampden-Sydney College	VA	24,871	C
Hampshire College	MA	33,881	HC+
Hampton Univ	VA	17,112	C+
Hanover College	IN	17,560	VC
Harding Univ	AR	13,528	VC
Hardin-Simmons Univ	TX	14,165	C
Hartwick College	NY	33,090	C+
Harvard Univ/Harvard College	MA	34,269	MC
Harvey Mudd College	CA	31,605	MC
Hastings College	NE	17,854	C+
Hawaii Pacific Univ	HI	17,790	C
Heidelberg College	OH	23,879	C
Henderson State Univ	AR	6,269	C
Hendrix College	AR	18,463	HC
Henry Cogswell College	WA	13,080	SP
Heritage College	WA	6,450	NC
High Point Univ	NC	20,220	LC
Hiram College	OH	27,034	VC
Hobart and William Smith Colleges	NY	33,195	VC
Hofstra Univ	NY	23,252	C
Hollins Univ	VA	24,328	VC
Holy Names College	CA	23,220	C
Hood College	MD	26,020	VC
Hope College	MI	22,922	C+
Houghton College	NY	21,810	VC+
Howard Payne Univ	TX	13,834	C+
Howard Univ	DC	15,522	LC
Huntingdon College	AL	18,400	VC
Huron Univ	SD	10,450	C
Huston-Tillotson College	TX	12,977	LC
Idaho State Univ	ID	7,030	C+
Illinois College	IL	16,234	C
Illinois Inst of Technology	IL	25,182	HC+
Illinois State Univ	IL	9,235	C
Illinois Wesleyan Univ	IL	26,970	HC
Indiana Inst of Technology	IN	18,806	C
Indiana State Univ	IN	8,461	LC
Indiana Univ Bloomington	IN	10,712	C+
Indiana Univ of Pennsylvania	PA	9,133	C
Indiana Univ South Bend	IN	3,515	C
Indiana Univ Southeast	IN	3,459	C

School	ST	$IS	SR
Indiana Univ-Purdue Univ Fort Wayne	IN	3,166	LC
Indiana Univ-Purdue Univ Indianapolis	IN	9,473	C
Inter-American Univ of PR/Aguadilla Campus	PR	3,278	
Inter-American Univ of PR/Arecibo Campus	PR	3,300	
Inter-American Univ of PR/Bayamon Univ College	PR	3,700	
Inter-American Univ of PR/Fajardo Campus	PR	4,000	
Inter-American Univ of PR/Metropolitan Campus	PR	4,166	
Inter-American Univ of PR/Ponce Regional College	PR	3,700	
Inter-American Univ of PR/San GermÈn	PR	6,390	
Iona College	NY	26,556	C
Iowa State Univ	IA	8,108	VC
Iowa Wesleyan College	IA	18,840	C
Ithaca College	NY	28,719	HC
Jackson State Univ	MS	6,776	LC
Jacksonville State Univ	AL	6,568	LC
James Madison Univ	VA	9,552	HC
Jamestown College	ND	11,310	NC
Jarvis Christian College	TX	9,035	NC
John Carroll Univ	OH	24,140	VC
Johns Hopkins Univ	MD	35,226	MC
Johnson and Wales Univ	RI	21,558	LC
Johnson C. Smith Univ	NC	16,560	C+
Judson College	IL	18,980	LC
Juniata College	PA	26,080	VC
Kalamazoo College	MI	26,955	HC+
Kansas State Univ	KS	6,995	C
Kansas Wesleyan Univ	KS	17,400	C+
Kean Univ	NJ	11,159	C
Keene State College	NH	11,280	C
Kennesaw State Univ	GA	2,306	LC
Kent State Univ	OH	11,104	C
Kentucky State Univ	KY	6,146	NC
Kentucky Wesleyan College	KY	15,800	C
Kettering Univ	MI	23,256	HC
King College	TN	17,800	VC
King's College	PA	24,680	C
Knox College	IL	28,230	HC
Kutztown Univ of Pennsylvania	PA	8,907	C
La Roche College	PA	18,854	LC
La Salle Univ	PA	27,890	C
La Sierra Univ	CA	19,260	LC
Lafayette College	PA	32,655	MC
LaGrange College	GA	17,496	C
Lake Forest College	IL	27,460	VC
Lake Superior State Univ	MI	9,034	LC
Lakeland College	WI	17,950	C
Lamar Univ	TX	6,816	LC
Lander Univ	SC	8,618	LC
Lane College	TN	10,400	C+
Langston Univ	OK	2,308	LC
Lawrence Tech Univ	MI	11,429	C
Lawrence Univ	WI	27,711	HC
Lebanon Valley College of Pennsylvania	PA	25,700	VC
Lehigh Univ	PA	32,290	MC
LeMoyne Owen College	TN	8,450	NC
Lenoir-Rhyne College	NC	19,186	C
LeTourneau Univ	TX	19,020	VC
Lewis and Clark College	OR	29,010	VC
Lewis Univ	IL	20,960	C
Liberty Univ	VA	14,500	C
Limestone College	SC	16,900	C
Lincoln Univ	PA	11,198	C+
Lindenwood Univ	MO	17,250	C
Linfield College	OR	25,840	VC
Livingstone College	NC	13,360	LC
Lock Haven Univ of Pennsylvania	PA	9,534	C
LIU/Brooklyn Campus	NY	22,290	C
LIU/C.W. Post Campus	NY	25,380	C
Longwood College	VA	8,950	C
Loras College	IA	22,994	C+
Louisiana State Univ and A&M College	LA	8,014	VC
Louisiana State Univ in Shreveport	LA	2,480	NC
Louisiana Tech Univ	LA	6,506	C
Loyola College in Maryland	MD	30,900	HC
Loyola Marymount Univ	CA	28,754	HC
Loyola Univ New Orleans	LA	23,506	VC+
Loyola Univ of Chicago	IL	25,992	VC
Luther College	IA	23,300	VC+
Lycoming College	PA	24,780	C
Lynchburg College	VA	23,405	C
Lyon College	AR	16,500	VC
Macalester College	MN	28,814	HC+
MacMurray College	IL	17,790	LC
Madonna Univ	MI	11,504	VC
Maharishi Univ of Management	IA	20,660	VC
Malone College	OH	19,190	C
Manchester College	IN	22,010	C
Manhattan College	NY	25,500	VC
Manhattanville College	NY	28,730	VC
Mansfield Univ	PA	9,648	C
Marietta College	OH	24,580	C

ST = STATE **$IS** = IN-STATE COSTS **SR** = SELECTOR RATING

School	ST	$IS	SR
Marist College	NY	24,756	VC
Marlboro College	VT	26,410	VC+
Marquette Univ	WI	24,836	C+
Mars Hill College	NC	18,600	LC
Mary Baldwin College	VA	23,440	C
Mary Washington College	VA	9,032	VC+
Marymount College/Tarrytown	NY	23,850	C
Marymount Univ	VA	21,560	LC
Maryville College	TN	23,210	VC
Maryville Univ of St. Louis	MO	18,680	C
Mass College of Liberal Arts	MA	8,717	LC
Mass Inst of Technology	MA	35,228	MC
McKendree College	IL	18,300	C+
McMurry Univ	TX	15,287	C
McNeese State Univ	LA	5,259	LC
McPherson College	KS	17,710	C
Mercer Univ	GA	24,130	VC
Mercy College	NY	15,875	LC
Meredith College	NC	17,500	C
Merrimack College	MA	25,725	VC
Mesa State College	CO	8,051	C
Messiah College	PA	23,180	VC
Methodist College	NC	19,526	C
Metropolitan State College of Denver	CO	2,338	LC
Metropolitan State Univ	MN	2,943	SP
Miami Univ	OH	12,885	VC+
Mich State Univ	MI	10,386	VC
Mich Tech Univ	MI	11,088	VC
MidAmerica Nazarene Univ	KS	16,960	C
Middle Tenn State Univ	TN	6,994	C
Middlebury College	VT	34,300	MC
Midland Lutheran College	NE	18,600	C
Midwestern State Univ	TX	6,704	NC
Miles College	AL	7,870	NC
Millersville Univ of Pennsylvania	PA	10,153	VC
Milligan College	TN	17,550	C
Millikin Univ	IL	24,415	C+
Mills College	CA	27,950	C
Millsaps College	MS	22,608	VC+
Minot State Univ	ND	5,466	LC
Miss College	MS	14,574	C
Miss State Univ	MS	7,853	C
Miss Valley State Univ	MS	6,345	C
Missouri Southern State College	MO	6,666	C
Missouri Western State College	MO	6,662	NC
Molloy College	NY	13,940	C
Monmouth College	IL	21,550	C
Monmouth Univ	NJ	24,042	C
Montana State Univ-Bozeman	MT	8,431	C
Montana Tech of The Univ of Montana	MT	7,845	C
Montclair State Univ	NJ	10,287	LC
Moorhead State Univ	MN	7,000	LC
Moravian College	PA	27,065	VC
Morehouse College	GA	19,814	C
Morgan State Univ	MD	10,078	LC
Morningside College	IA	19,124	C
Morris Brown College	GA	15,993	LC
Mount Holyoke College	MA	34,128	HC
Mount Marty College	SD	15,656	LC
Mount Mary College	WI	18,024	C
Mount Mercy College	IA	19,390	VC
Mount St. Mary College	NY	18,825	C
Mount St. Mary's College	MD	25,740	C
Mount Union College	OH	21,120	C
Mount Vernon Nazarene College	OH	17,027	C
Mountain State Univ	WV	8,180	NC
Muhlenberg College	PA	28,170	HC
Murray State Univ	KY	6,672	C
Muskingum College	OH	18,760	C
National Univ	CA	7,755	SP
Nebr Wesleyan Univ	NE	18,767	VC
Neumann College	PA	22,040	NC
New Jersey City Univ	NJ	9,100	LC
New Jersey Inst of Technology	NJ	14,690	VC
New Mexico Highlands Univ	NM	6,256	NC
New Mexico Inst of Mining and Technology	NM	7,152	VC+
New Mexico State Univ	NM	7,302	C
New York Inst of Technology	NY	21,756	C
New York Univ	NY	35,200	MC
Newberry College	SC	19,670	LC
Newbury College	MA	21,490	C
Niagara Univ	NY	22,250	C+
Nicholls State Univ	LA	5,290	NC
Norfolk State Univ	VA	8,382	LC
N Car Agricultural and Technical State Univ	NC	6,659	LC
N Car Central Univ	NC	6,418	LC
N Car State Univ	NC	8,680	HC
North Central College	IL	22,944	C+
N Dak State Univ	ND	7,004	VC
North Georgia College and State Univ	GA	6,322	C+
Northeastern Illinois Univ	IL	2,898	NC
Northeastern State Univ	OK	4,704	LC
Northeastern Univ	MA	30,078	VC
Northern Arizona Univ	AZ	7,398	C
Northern Illinois Univ	IL	9,545	C
Northern Kentucky Univ	KY	6,352	NC
Northern Mich Univ	MI	9,693	C
Northwest Missouri State Univ	MO	7,922	LC
Northwest Nazarene Univ	ID	18,380	C
Northwestern College of Iowa	IA	17,630	C+
Northwestern Okla State Univ	OK	4,542	NC
Northwestern Univ	IL	33,615	MC
Norwich Univ	VT	21,064	LC
Notre Dame de Namur Univ	CA	26,932	LC
Nova Southeastern Univ	FL	20,104	LC
Nyack College	NY	18,540	C
Oakland City Univ	IN	11,286	LC
Oakland Univ	MI	9,418	C
Oakwood College	AL	14,904	C
Oberlin College	OH	33,140	HC+
Oglethorpe Univ	GA	19,100	LC
Ohio Dominican College	OH	18,100	LC
Ohio Northern Univ	OH	27,765	VC
Ohio Univ	OH	11,769	C
Ohio Wesleyan Univ	OH	29,670	VC+
Okla Baptist Univ	OK	13,878	VC
Okla Christian Univ	OK	16,500	VC
Okla City Univ	OK	15,810	C
Okla State Univ	OK	7,650	VC
Old Dominion Univ	VA	9,386	C
Olivet College	MI	17,410	C
Olivet Nazarene Univ	IL	18,444	C
Oral Roberts Univ	OK	18,490	C
Oregon State Univ	OR	9,612	VC
Otterbein College	OH	23,439	C
Ouachita Baptist Univ	AR	16,460	VC
Pace Univ	NY	24,200	C
Pacific Lutheran Univ	WA	23,318	VC
Pacific Union College	CA	20,250	VC
Pacific Univ	OR	24,250	C
Palm Beach Atlantic College	FL	23,310	C
Park Univ	MO	9,816	C
Paul Quinn College	TX	8,150	LC
Penn State Univ at Erie/Behrend College	PA	12,326	C
Penn State Univ/Univ Park Campus	PA	11,126	VC
Pepperdine Univ	CA	32,830	VC
Peru State College	NE	6,342	NC
Philadelphia Univ	PA	24,722	C
Philander Smith College	AR	7,380	NC
Pikeville College	KY	12,000	NC
Pittsburg State Univ	KS	6,228	NC
Plymouth State College	NH	11,024	LC
Point Loma Nazarene Univ	CA	21,380	VC
Point Park College	PA	20,290	C
Polytechnic Univ/Brooklyn	NY	33,090	HC
Pomona College	CA	33,960	MC
Portland State Univ	OR	11,220	C
Prairie View A&M Univ	TX	3,172	LC
Princeton Univ	NJ	35,072	MC
Principia College	IL	23,865	C+
Providence College	RI	27,620	HC
Purdue Univ/Calumet	IN	6,630	NC
Purdue Univ/West Lafayette	IN	10,284	VC
Quincy Univ	IL	20,450	C
Quinnipiac Univ	CT	27,370	C
Radford Univ	VA	8,302	C
Ramapo College of New Jersey	NJ	13,550	VC
Randolph-Macon College	VA	24,395	C
Regis College	MA	26,750	C
Regis Univ	CO	25,740	C+
Rensselaer Polytechnic Inst	NY	33,863	HC+
Rhode Island College	RI	8,700	LC
Rhodes College	TN	26,466	HC+
Richard Stockton College of New Jersey	NJ	12,165	VC
Ripon College	WI	24,180	VC+
Rivier College	NH	24,215	C
Roanoke College	VA	24,689	VC
Roberts Wesleyan College	NY	20,160	C+
Rochester Inst of Technology	NY	26,232	VC+
Rockford College	IL	23,930	C
Rockhurst Univ	MO	20,090	C
Rocky Mountain College	MT	18,113	C
Roger Williams Univ	RI	29,010	C
Rollins College	FL	31,223	HC
Roosevelt Univ	IL	20,240	LC
Rose-Hulman Inst of Technology	IN	27,707	HC+
Russell Sage College	NY	23,674	C+
Rust College	MS	7,800	C+
Rutgers, The State Univ of New Jersey New Brunswick Campus	NJ	12,709	C
Rutgers, The State Univ of New Jersey/CamdenCampus	NJ	6,484	C
Rutgers, The State Univ of New Jersey/Newark Campus	NJ	6,394	C
Sacred Heart Univ	CT	26,588	VC
Saginaw Valley State Univ	MI	9,465	C
St. Ambrose Univ	IA	19,994	C
St. Anselm College	NH	27,405	C
St. Augustine's College	NC	12,990	C+
St. Bonaventure Univ	NY	21,956	C
St. Cloud State Univ	MN	7,180	C
St. Edward's Univ	TX	17,846	C
St. Francis Univ	PA	24,486	LC
St. John Fisher College	NY	21,800	C
St. John's Univ	MN	23,640	VC
St. John's Univ	NY	26,660	C
St. Joseph's College	IN	21,640	C
St. Joseph's Univ	PA	29,715	VC+
St. Lawrence Univ	NY	32,605	VC
St. Louis Univ	MO	26,590	VC+
St. Martin's College	WA	20,566	C
St. Mary-of-the-Woods College	IN	21,320	LC
St. Mary's College	MI	13,314	LC
St. Mary's College of Maryland	MD	14,104	HC
St. Mary's Univ of Minn	MN	19,975	C
St. Mary's Univ of San Antonio	TX	19,735	C
St. Michael's College	VT	26,935	VC
St. Norbert College	WI	23,169	VC
St. Peter's College	NJ	22,292	LC
St. Thomas Univ	FL	19,500	LC
St. Vincent College	PA	22,942	VC
St. Xavier Univ	IL	21,104	C
Salisbury Univ	MD	10,576	VC
Sam Houston State Univ	TX	6,076	LC
Samford Univ	AL	16,340	VC
San Diego State Univ	CA	9,716	C+
San Francisco State Univ	CA	7,139	LC
San Jose State Univ	CA	8,187	C
Santa Clara Univ	CA	28,371	VC+
Savannah State Univ	GA	2,550	LC
Seattle Pacific Univ	WA	22,674	C+
Seattle Univ	WA	24,183	VC
Seton Hall Univ	NJ	26,910	LC
Seton Hill College	PA	21,875	C
Shaw Univ	NC	12,810	C
Shepherd College	WV	7,062	LC
Shippensburg Univ of Pennsylvania	PA	9,652	C
Siena College	NY	22,685	VC
Silver Lake College of the Holy Family	WI	15,516	LC
Simmons College	MA	30,418	VC
Simpson College	IA	21,200	C+
Skidmore College	NY	34,201	VC+
Slippery Rock Univ	PA	9,152	LC
Smith College	MA	33,302	HC+
Sonoma State Univ	CA	8,953	C
S Car State Univ	SC	6,586	LC
S Dak School of Mines and Technology	SD	7,438	C+
S Dak State Univ	SD	6,848	C
Southeast Missouri State Univ	MO	8,367	C+
Southeastern Louisiana Univ	LA	6,047	LC
Southeastern Okla State Univ	OK	4,917	C
Southern Adventist Univ	TN	15,600	C
Southern Arkansas Univ	AR	5,740	LC
Southern Conn State Univ	CT	10,310	C
Southern Illinois Univ Edwardsville	IL	7,869	LC
Southern Methodist Univ	TX	28,349	VC
Southern Nazarene Univ	OK	14,634	NC
Southern Oregon Univ	OR	9,429	C
Southern Polytechnic State Univ	GA	6,662	C
Southern Univ and A&M College	LA	6,365	C+
Southern Univ at New Orleans	LA	995	NC
Southern Utah Univ	UT	7,254	C
Southwest Baptist Univ	MO	13,426	LC
Southwest Missouri State Univ	MO	7,600	LC
Southwest State Univ	MN	7,117	LC
Southwest Texas State Univ	TX	8,730	VC
Southwestern Adventist Univ	TX	14,798	C
Southwestern College	KS	17,656	C
Southwestern Okla State Univ	OK	4,801	C
Southwestern Univ	TX	22,550	HC
Spalding Univ	KY	15,196	C
Spelman College	GA	19,215	C+
Spring Arbor Univ	MI	17,976	C
Spring Hill College	AL	23,250	C
Stanford Univ	CA	34,222	MC
SUNY/College at Brockport	NY	10,267	C
SUNY/College at Fredonia	NY	10,125	C
SUNY/College at Geneseo	NY	9,970	HC
SUNY/College at Old Westbury	NY	9,818	LC
SUNY/College at Oneonta	NY	9,981	C
SUNY/College at Oswego	NY	10,856	C
SUNY/College at Plattsburgh	NY	9,729	C
SUNY/College at Potsdam	NY	10,519	C
SUNY/Univ at Albany	NY	10,997	VC
SUNY/Univ at Binghamton	NY	10,653	HC
SUNY/Univ at Buffalo	NY	11,033	VC
SUNY/Univ at New Paltz	NY	9,685	VC
SUNY/Univ at Stony Brook	NY	10,998	VC
State Univ of West Georgia	GA	7,101	C
Stephen F. Austin State Univ	TX	6,905	C
Sterling College	KS	16,370	VC
Stetson Univ	FL	25,640	VC
Stevens Inst of Technology	NJ	31,510	HC+
Stillman College	AL	11,370	LC
Stonehill College	MA	26,852	HC
Suffolk Univ	MA	26,516	C
Sul Ross State Univ	TX	6,582	LC
Susquehanna Univ	PA	27,270	VC
Swarthmore College	PA	34,538	MC
Sweet Briar College	VA	25,310	VC
Syracuse Univ	NY	30,710	HC
Tabor College	KS	17,600	LC
Talladega College	AL	10,110	LC
Taylor Univ	IN	21,562	VC+
Temple Univ	PA	14,124	C
Tenn State Univ	TN	7,058	VC
Tenn Tech Univ	TN	6,968	C
Texas A&M Univ	TX	8,988	VC
Texas A&M Univ at Commerce	TX	7,326	C
Texas A&M Univ at Kingsville	TX	6,446	LC
Texas Christian Univ	TX	19,910	C
Texas Lutheran Univ	TX	17,660	C
Texas Southern Univ	TX	6,576	NC
Texas Tech Univ	TX	8,825	C
Texas Wesleyan Univ	TX	14,710	C
Texas Woman's Univ	TX	5,855	LC
Ohio State Univ	OH	10,819	VC
Thiel College	PA	18,419	LC
Thomas Edison State College	NJ	2,750	SP
Thomas More College	KY	17,700	LC
Touro College	NY	14,950	VC
Towson Univ	MD	11,088	VC
Transylvania Univ	KY	21,780	VC+
Trinity Christian College	IL	19,415	C
Trinity College	CT	34,300	HC
Trinity International Univ	IL	20,640	C+
Trinity Univ	TX	21,444	HC
Tri-State Univ-Main Campus	IN	21,200	C
Troy State Univ	AL	7,696	C
Troy State Univ/Dothan	AL	3,296	C
Troy State Univ/Montgomery	AL	3,080	NC
Truman State Univ	MO	8,568	VC+
Tufts Univ	MA	34,874	MC
Tulane Univ	LA	34,013	HC+
Tusculum College	TN	17,900	LC
Tuskegee Univ	AL	14,600	LC
Union College	NE	14,650	C
Union College	NY	32,646	HC
Union Univ	TN	18,930	C+
United States Air Force Academy	CO		MC
United States Military Academy	NY		MC
United States Naval Academy	MD		MC
Universidad Adventista de las Antillas	PR	6,675	
Univ of Akron	OH	10,530	NC
Univ of Alabama	AL	7,402	C
Univ of Alabama at Birmingham	AL	10,110	C
Univ of Alabama at Huntsville	AL	7,916	VC
Univ of Alaska Anchorage	AK	9,100	NC
Univ of Alaska Fairbanks	AK	8,265	NC
Univ of Arizona	AZ	8,614	C
Univ of Arkansas	AR	8,334	VC
Univ of Arkansas at Little Rock	AR	5,637	NC
Univ of Arkansas at Pine Bluff	AR	7,925	C
Univ of Bridgeport	CT	23,020	C
Univ of Calif at Berkeley	CA	14,134	MC
Univ of Calif at Davis	CA	12,796	VC
Univ of Calif at Los Angeles	CA	13,227	MC
Univ of Calif at Riverside	CA	12,479	C
Univ of Calif at San Diego	CA	11,372	HC
Univ of Calif at Santa Barbara	CA	11,732	VC
Univ of Calif at Santa Cruz	CA	13,655	VC
Univ of Central Arkansas	AR	6,388	C
Univ of Central Florida	FL	8,251	VC
Univ of Central Okla	OK	5,205	C
Univ of Chicago	IL	35,087	MC
Univ of Cincinnati	OH	12,491	LC
Univ of Colo at Boulder	CO	9,255	VC
Univ of Colo at Colo Springs	CO	9,403	C
Univ of Colo at Denver	CO	3,673	C
Univ of Conn	CT	12,122	VC
Univ of Dallas	TX	22,128	VC+
Univ of Dayton	OH	20,400	VC

ST = STATE $IS = IN-STATE COSTS SR = SELECTOR RATING

School	ST	$IS	SR
Univ of Delaware	DE	10,824	VC
Univ of Denver	CO	28,783	VC
Univ of Detroit Mercy	MI	21,620	LC
Univ of Dubuque	IA	19,990	C
Univ of Evansville	IN	22,865	VC+
Univ of Findlay	OH	23,962	NC
Univ of Florida	FL	7,874	HC
Univ of Georgia	GA	8,656	VC
Univ of Great Falls	MT	15,360	C
Univ of Hartford	CT	28,884	C
Univ of Hawaii at Hilo	HI	6,497	C
Univ of Hawaii at Manoa	HI	7,862	VC
Univ of Houston	TX	8,410	C
Univ of Houston-Downtown	TX	2,006	NC
Univ of Idaho	ID	7,026	C
Univ of Illinois at Chicago	IL	10,702	VC
Univ of Illinois at Urbana-Champaign	IL	11,316	HC+
Univ of Indianapolis	IN	20,840	C
Univ of Iowa	IA	8,607	C+
Univ of Kansas	KS	7,232	VC
Univ of Kentucky	KY	7,765	C
Univ of La Verne	CA	24,280	C
Univ of Louisiana at Lafayette	LA	5,200	C
Univ of Louisiana at Monroe	LA	5,207	NC
Univ of Louisville	KY	7,402	LC
Univ of Maine	ME	10,798	C
Univ of Maine at Farmington	ME	9,163	C
Univ of Maine at Fort Kent	ME	7,450	LC
Univ of Mary Hardin-Baylor	TX	13,929	C
Univ of Maryland/Baltimore County	MD	12,190	VC
Univ of Maryland/College Park	MD	11,959	C
Univ of Maryland/Eastern Shore	MD	9,258	C
Univ of Maryland/Univ College	MD	5,910	SP
Univ of Mass Amherst	MA	10,095	VC
Univ of Mass Boston	MA	4,227	C
Univ of Mass Dartmouth	MA	9,852	C
Univ of Mass Lowell	MA	9,470	VC
Univ of Memphis	TN	7,271	C
Univ of Miami	FL	31,130	HC
Univ of Mich/Ann Arbor	MI	13,003	HC+
Univ of Mich/Dearborn	MI	4,677	VC
Univ of Mich/Flint	MI	4,323	C
Univ of Minn/Duluth	MN	10,436	C
Univ of Minn/Morris	MN	10,716	VC
Univ of Minn/Twin Cities	MN	11,123	VC
Univ of Miss	MS	7,666	C
Univ of Missouri/Columbia	MO	9,803	HC
Univ of Missouri/Kansas City	MO	9,685	VC
Univ of Missouri/Rolla	MO	10,034	C
Univ of Missouri/St. Louis	MO	9,966	C
Univ of Mobile	AL	13,620	LC
Univ of Montana	MT	8,038	C
Univ of Nebr at Kearney	NE	7,048	NC
Univ of Nebr at Lincoln	NE	8,325	C+
Univ of Nebr at Omaha	NE	6,867	C
Univ of Nevada/Las Vegas	NV	8,281	VC
Univ of Nevada/Reno	NV	8,737	C
Univ of New Hampshire	NH	13,207	C
Univ of New Haven	CT	23,860	LC
Univ of New Mexico	NM	8,026	C
Univ of New Orleans	LA	10,160	C
Univ of North Alabama	AL	7,016	NC
Univ of N Car at Asheville	NC	6,896	VC
Univ of N Car at Charlotte	NC	7,254	C
Univ of N Car at Pembroke	NC	5,914	LC
Univ of N Car at Wilmington	NC	7,769	C
Univ of N Dak	ND	7,067	VC
Univ of North Florida	FL	8,089	VC
Univ of North Texas	TX	7,629	C
Univ of Northern Colo	CO	8,082	C+
Univ of Northern Iowa	IA	7,850	C
Univ of Notre Dame	IN	30,707	MC
Univ of Okla	OK	7,616	VC
Univ of Oregon	OR	9,969	C
Univ of Pittsburgh at Bradford	PA	12,696	C
Univ of Pittsburgh at Johnstown	PA	13,044	LC
Univ of Pittsburgh at Pittsburgh	PA	13,592	HC
Univ of Portland	OR	24,950	VC
Univ of PR/Arecibo	PR	1,095	
Univ of PR/Bayamon Univ College Campus	PR	1,600	
Univ of PR/Mayaguez	PR	5,285	
Univ of PR/Rio Piedras	PR	5,510	
Univ of Puget Sound	WA	28,285	HC
Univ of Redlands	CA	29,246	VC
Univ of Rhode Island	RI	12,414	C
Univ of Richmond	VA	27,300	HC
Univ of Rio Grande	OH	8,728	NC
Univ of Rochester	NY	32,979	HC
Univ of St. Francis	IL	19,650	C
Univ of St. Thomas	MN	24,044	VC
Univ of San Diego	CA	29,198	HC
Univ of San Francisco	CA	27,302	VC
Univ of Science and Arts of Okla	OK	5,245	C
Univ of Scranton	PA	27,964	C+
Univ of Sioux Falls	SD	16,390	C
Univ of South Alabama	AL	6,976	LC
Univ of S Car at Columbia	SC	8,748	VC
Univ of S Car at Spartanburg	SC	7,318	C+
Univ of S Dak	SD	7,036	C
Univ of Southern Calif	CA	33,647	MC
Univ of Southern Maine	ME	10,569	C
Univ of Southern Miss	MS	6,155	LC
Univ of Tenn at Chattanooga	TN	7,783	C
Univ of Tenn at Knoxville	TN	8,214	C
Univ of Tenn at Martin	TN	8,268	C
Univ of Texas at Arlington	TX	7,192	LC
Univ of Texas at Austin	TX	9,437	HC
Univ of Texas at Dallas	TX	9,305	VC
Univ of Texas at El Paso	TX	5,076	LC
Univ of Texas at San Antonio	TX	9,088	NC
Univ of Texas-Pan American	TX	4,823	C
Univ of the District of Columbia	DC	2,844	NC
Univ of the Pacific	CA	28,255	VC
Univ of the Sacred Heart	PR	5,375	
Univ of the South	TN	27,290	HC
Univ of Toledo	OH	11,206	NC
Univ of Tulsa	OK	19,090	HC
Univ of Utah	UT	7,703	C
Univ of Vermont	VT	14,761	C+
Univ of Virginia	VA	9,391	HC+
Univ of Washington	WA	10,361	VC
Univ of West Alabama	AL	6,048	C
Univ of West Florida	FL	7,518	C
Univ of Wisc/Eau Claire	WI	7,032	VC
Univ of Wisc/Green Bay	WI	7,148	C
Univ of Wisc/La Crosse	WI	7,250	VC
Univ of Wisc/Madison	WI	8,262	VC
Univ of Wisc/Milwaukee	WI	8,907	LC
Univ of Wisc/Oshkosh	WI	6,130	LC
Univ of Wisc/Parkside	WI	6,160	LC
Univ of Wisc/Platteville	WI	7,282	C
Univ of Wisc/Superior	WI	7,051	C+
Univ of Wyoming	WY	7,143	LC
Ursinus College	PA	31,350	VC
Utah State Univ	UT	6,771	C
Utica College of Syracuse Univ	NY	24,400	LC
Valdosta State Univ	GA	6,988	C
Valparaiso Univ	IN	23,570	VC+
Vassar College	NY	33,450	MC
Villanova Univ	PA	31,997	HC
Virginia Commonwealth Univ	VA	9,030	C
Virginia Military Inst	VA	9,968	C+
Virginia Polytechnic Inst and State Univ	VA	7,652	C
Virginia Wesleyan College	VA	22,350	LC
Voorhees College	SC	9,976	C+
Wagner College	NY	27,000	C
Wake Forest Univ	NC	30,290	MC
Walla Walla College	WA	20,925	C
Walsh Univ	OH	16,880	C
Wartburg College	IA	21,165	VC
Washington and Lee Univ	VA	25,095	MC
Washington College	MD	20,040	VC
Washington State Univ	WA	9,388	C
Washington Univ in St. Louis	MO	34,593	MC
Wayne State College	NE	6,255	NC
Wayne State Univ	MI	6,720	C
Waynesburg College	PA	17,610	LC
Weber State Univ	UT	6,897	NC
Webster Univ	MO	19,804	VC
Wellesley College	MA	33,394	MC
Wells College	NY	19,350	VC
Wentworth Inst of Technology	MA	20,450	C
Wesleyan Univ	CT	3,405	MC
West Chester Univ of Pennsylvania	PA	9,792	VC
West Texas A&M Univ	TX	6,538	C
West Virginia Univ	WV	8,304	C
West Virginia Univ Inst of Technology	WV	7,518	NC
West Virginia Wesleyan College	WV	22,920	C
Western Baptist College	OR	19,700	C+
Western Carolina Univ	NC	5,667	C
Western Conn State Univ	CT	10,074	C
Western Illinois Univ	IL	9,571	C
Western Kentucky Univ	KY	6,834	C
Western Mich Univ	MI	10,016	C
Western New England College	MA	23,882	C
Western New Mexico Univ	NM	5,950	LC
Western Oregon Univ	OR	8,829	C
Western Washington Univ	WA	8,624	VC
Westfield State College	MA	8,394	C
Westminster College	MO	19,990	C+
Westminster College	PA	22,960	C
Westminster College	UT	17,226	C
Westmont College	CA	29,748	VC
Wheaton College	IL	21,934	HC
Wheaton College	MA	32,940	VC
Wheeling Jesuit Univ	WV	22,660	C
Whitworth College	WA	23,938	VC
Wichita State Univ	KS	6,879	C
Widener Univ	PA	26,920	C
Wilberforce Univ	OH	14,937	LC
Wiley College	TX	8,100	LC
Wilkes Univ	PA	25,800	C
Willamette Univ	OR	29,422	VC+
William Jewell College	MO	17,150	VC
William Paterson Univ of New Jersey	NJ	11,000	LC
William Penn Univ	IA	17,575	C
William Woods Univ	MO	19,390	LC
Williams Baptist College	AR	10,750	C
Williams College	MA	32,270	MC
Wilmington College	OH	21,826	C
Winona State Univ	MN	8,570	C
Winston-Salem State Univ	NC	5,927	LC
Winthrop Univ	SC	9,106	C
Wittenberg Univ	OH	28,766	VC
Wofford College	SC	23,995	VC
Worcester Polytechnic Inst	MA	34,480	HC+
Worcester State College	MA	7,901	LC
Wright State Univ	OH	9,141	LC
Xavier Univ	OH	23,880	C
Xavier Univ of Louisiana	LA	17,000	LC
Yale Univ	CT	34,030	MC
Yeshiva Univ	NY	21,400	C
Youngstown State Univ	OH	9,318	NC

COMPUTER TECHNOLOGY

School	ST	$IS	SR
Albertus Magnus College	CT	22,154	C
Andrews Univ	MI	17,696	LC
Bowie State Univ	MD	9,300	C+
Bowling Green State Univ	OH	10,794	C
Calif State Polytechnic Univ, Pomona	CA	8,615	C
Daniel Webster College	NH	24,870	C
DeVry/New York	NY	9,865	LC
DeVry Univ/Colo Springs	CO	9,465	LC
DeVry Univ/Columbus	OH	8,805	LC
DeVry Univ/Crystal City	VA	10,065	C
DeVry Univ/Dallas	TX	8,805	LC
DeVry Univ/Kansas City	MO	8,805	LC
DeVry Univ/Phoenix	AZ	8,805	LC
DeVry Univ/Tinley Park	IL	8,805	LC
Eastern Mich Univ	MI	9,855	C
Eastern Washington Univ	WA	7,972	LC
Endicott College	MA	23,704	C
Excelsior College	NY	915	SP
Georgia Southwestern State Univ	GA	6,013	C
Idaho State Univ	ID	7,030	C+
Indiana State Univ	IN	8,461	LC
Indiana Univ-Purdue Univ Indianapolis	IN	9,473	C
LeTourneau Univ	TX	19,020	VC
Martin Univ	IN	8,370	SP
Methodist College	NC	19,526	C
Missouri Southern State College	MO	6,666	C
Mountain State Univ	WV	8,180	NC
Murray State Univ	KY	6,672	C
Norfolk State Univ	VA	8,382	LC
Northeastern Univ	MA	30,078	VC
Oregon Inst of Technology	OR	8,718	C
Pennsylvania College of Technology	PA	12,860	NC
Purdue Univ/Calumet	IN	6,630	NC
Purdue Univ/West Lafayette	IN	10,284	VC
Rochester Inst of Technology	NY	26,232	VC+
Rockhurst Univ	MO	20,090	C
St. John's Univ	NY	26,660	C
St. Louis Univ	MO	26,590	VC+
Shawnee State Univ	OH	8,634	NC
Southern Polytechnic State Univ	GA	6,662	C
Southwestern College	KS	17,656	C
SUNY/College of Technology at Alfred	NY	9,188	C
SUNY/College of Technology at Farmingdale	NY	11,269	C
Thomas Edison State College	NJ	2,750	SP
Univ of Arkansas at Little Rock	AR	5,637	NC
Univ of Houston	TX	8,410	C
Univ of Maryland/Univ College	MD	5,910	SP
Univ of Memphis	TN	7,271	C
Univ of Miami	FL	31,130	HC
Univ of Phoenix	AZ	7,000	SP
Univ of Rio Grande	OH	8,728	NC
Univ of St. Francis	IL	19,650	C
Univ of Southern Miss	MS	6,155	LC
Wayne State Univ	MI	6,720	C
Wentworth Inst of Technology	MA	20,450	C
Youngstown State Univ	OH	9,318	NC

CONSERVATION AND REGULATION

School	ST	$IS	SR
Alaska Pacific Univ	AK	16,450	C
Alverno College	WI	16,930	LC
Austin Peay State Univ	TN	5,814	LC
Central Missouri State Univ	MO	7,920	C
Kent State Univ	OH	11,104	C
LIU/C.W. Post Campus	NY	25,380	C
Muskingum College	OH	18,760	C
N Car State Univ	NC	8,680	HC
Northwest Missouri State Univ	MO	7,922	LC
Northwestern Okla State Univ	OK	4,542	NC
Purdue Univ/West Lafayette	IN	10,284	VC
Southeastern Okla State Univ	OK	4,917	C
Southwest Missouri State Univ	MO	7,600	LC
Sterling College	VT	19,695	C
Unity College	ME	19,845	LC
Univ of Arkansas at Pine Bluff	AR	7,925	C
Univ of Maryland/College Park	MD	11,959	C
Univ of Tenn at Martin	TN	8,268	C
Univ of Wisc/Madison	WI	8,262	VC
Univ of Wisc/Milwaukee	WI	8,907	LC
Univ of Wisc/River Falls	WI	6,356	LC
Upper Iowa Univ	IA	17,438	C

CONSTRUCTION ENGINEERING

School	ST	$IS	SR
Arizona State Univ-Main	AZ	7,726	C
Bradley Univ	IL	20,970	VC
Fairleigh Dickinson Univ/Teaneck Campus	NJ	24,646	C
Iowa State Univ	IA	8,108	VC
Louisiana Tech Univ	LA	6,506	C
Montana State Univ-Bozeman	MT	8,431	C
Moorhead State Univ	MN	7,000	LC
N Dak State Univ	ND	7,004	VC
Purdue Univ/West Lafayette	IN	10,284	VC
Rensselaer Polytechnic Inst	NY	33,863	HC+
Southern Illinois Univ Edwardsville	IL	7,869	LC
Southern Polytechnic State Univ	GA	6,662	C
Texas A&M Univ	TX	8,988	VC
Thomas Edison State College	NJ	2,750	SP
Univ of Florida	FL	7,874	HC
Univ of Louisiana at Monroe	LA	5,207	NC
Univ of New Mexico	NM	8,026	C
Univ of the District of Columbia	DC	2,844	NC
Univ of Washington	WA	10,361	VC
Virginia Polytechnic Inst and State Univ	VA	7,652	C
Western Mich Univ	MI	10,016	C

CONSTRUCTION MANAGEMENT

School	ST	$IS	SR
Andrews Univ	MI	17,696	LC
Auburn Univ	AL	5,510	C
Boise State Univ	ID	6,531	LC
Brigham Young Univ	UT	7,840	HC
Calif Polytechnic State Univ	CA	8,747	VC
Cal State, Chico	CA	8,598	LC
Cal State, Fresno	CA	7,762	C
Central Missouri State Univ	MO	7,920	C
Clemson Univ	SC	7,600	C
Colo State Univ	CO	9,672	C
Drexel Univ	PA	27,657	VC
East Carolina Univ	NC	7,766	C
Eastern Mich Univ	MI	9,855	C
Ferris State Univ	MI	10,816	C
Florida International Univ	FL	9,486	VC
Georgia Inst of Technology	GA	9,028	HC+
Georgia Southern Univ	GA	6,958	C
John Brown Univ	AR	15,080	VC
Kansas State Univ	KS	6,995	C
Louisiana State Univ and A&M College	LA	8,014	VC
Mich State Univ	MI	10,386	VC
Milwaukee School of Engineering	WI	25,680	VC+
Minn State Univ, Mankato	MN	7,296	LC
N Car State Univ	NC	8,680	HC
N Dak State Univ	ND	7,004	VC
Northern Mich Univ	MI	9,693	C
Okla State Univ	OK	7,650	VC
Oregon State Univ	OR	9,612	VC
Pennsylvania College of Technology	PA	12,860	NC
Pratt Inst	NY	27,550	SP
Roger Williams Univ	RI	29,010	C
S Dak State Univ	SD	6,848	C
Southern Utah Univ	UT	7,254	C
Southwest Missouri State Univ	MO	7,600	LC

School	ST	$IS	SR
SUNY/College of Environmental Science and Forestry	NY	12,446	VC
SUNY/College of Technology at Alfred	NY	9,188	C
SUNY/College of Technology at Farmingdale	NY	11,269	C
Tuskegee Univ	AL	14,600	LC
Univ of Cincinnati	OH	12,491	LC
Univ of Denver	CO	28,783	VC
Univ of Houston	TX	8,410	C
Univ of Nebr at Lincoln	NE	8,325	C+
Univ of Nevada/Las Vegas	NV	8,281	VC
Univ of North Florida	FL	8,089	VC
Univ of Northern Iowa	IA	7,850	C
Univ of Okla	OK	7,616	VC
Univ of Texas at San Antonio	TX	9,088	NC
Utica College of Syracuse Univ	NY	24,400	LC
Virginia Polytechnic Inst and State Univ	VA	7,652	C
Washington State Univ	WA	9,388	C
Wentworth Inst of Technology	MA	20,450	C
Western Mich Univ	MI	10,016	C

CONSTRUCTION TECHNOLOGY

School	ST	$IS	SR
Appalachian State Univ	NC	6,353	C
Bowling Green State Univ	OH	10,794	C
Calif State Polytechnic Univ, Pomona	CA	8,615	C
Central Conn State Univ	CT	10,404	C
Eastern Kentucky Univ	KY	6,552	C
Indiana State Univ	IN	8,461	LC
Indiana Univ-Purdue Univ Indianapolis	IN	9,473	C
Montana State Univ-Northern	MT	8,600	NC
Murray State Univ	KY	6,672	C
Norfolk State Univ	VA	8,382	LC
Northern Kentucky Univ	KY	6,352	NC
Purdue Univ/Calumet	IN	6,630	NC
Purdue Univ/West Lafayette	IN	10,284	VC
Southwest Texas State Univ	TX	8,730	VC
Texas Southern Univ	TX	6,576	NC
Texas Tech Univ	TX	8,825	C
Univ of Akron	OH	10,530	NC
Univ of Arkansas at Little Rock	AR	5,637	NC
Univ of Houston	TX	8,410	C
Univ of Maine	ME	10,798	C
Univ of Maryland/Eastern Shore	MD	9,258	C
Univ of Mass Amherst	MA	10,995	VC
Univ of Nebr at Lincoln	NE	8,325	C+
Univ of Southern Miss	MS	6,155	LC
Univ of Wisc/Stout	WI	7,192	C
Wentworth Inst of Technology	MA	20,450	C

CONSUMER SERVICES

School	ST	$IS	SR
Indiana Univ of Pennsylvania	PA	9,133	C
Norfolk State Univ	VA	8,382	LC
Purdue Univ/West Lafayette	IN	10,284	VC
S Dak State Univ	SD	6,848	C
Syracuse Univ	NY	30,710	HC
Texas Woman's Univ	TX	5,855	LC
Univ of Delaware	DE	10,824	VC
Univ of Memphis	TN	7,271	C
Univ of Wisc/Madison	WI	8,262	VC

CORRECTIONS

School	ST	$IS	SR
CUNY/John Jay College of Criminal Justice	NY	3,251	C
College of the Ozarks	MO	2,650	C+
Eastern Kentucky Univ	KY	6,552	C
Jackson State Univ	MS	6,776	LC
Minn State Univ, Mankato	MN	7,296	LC
Northern Mich Univ	MI	9,693	C
Southeast Missouri State Univ	MO	8,367	C+
Southwest Texas State Univ	TX	8,730	VC
Stephen F. Austin State Univ	TX	6,905	C
Tiffin Univ	OH	17,250	C
Univ of Indianapolis	IN	20,840	C
Univ of New Haven	CT	23,860	LC
Univ of Texas-Pan American	TX	4,823	C
Washburn Univ of Topeka	KS	6,766	NC
Western Oregon Univ	OR	8,829	C
Youngstown State Univ	OH	9,318	NC

COUNSELING/PSYCHOLOGY

School	ST	$IS	SR
Dallas Baptist Univ	TX	13,682	LC
Eastern Mich Univ	MI	9,855	C
Geneva College	PA	19,990	C+
Goddard College	VT	21,056	C+
Grace College	IN	16,768	C
Kentucky Christian College	KY	13,472	C
Limestone College	SC	16,900	C
Martin Univ	IN	8,370	SP
Metropolitan State Univ	MN	2,943	SP
Moravian College	PA	27,065	VC
Newman Univ	KS	14,098	LC
Samford Univ	AL	16,340	VC
Toccoa Falls College	GA	14,220	C
Univ of Great Falls	MT	15,360	C
Univ of North Texas	TX	7,629	C
Wayne State College	NE	6,255	NC
Williams Baptist College	AR	10,750	C

COURT REPORTING

School	ST	$IS	SR
Central Mich Univ	MI	8,355	C
Humphreys College	CA	6,900	NC
Johnson and Wales Univ	RI	21,558	LC
Univ of Miss	MS	7,666	C

CRAFTS

School	ST	$IS	SR
Cal State, Fullerton	CA	5,440	LC
Kent State Univ	OH	11,104	C
Kutztown Univ of Pennsylvania	PA	8,907	C
Norfolk State Univ	VA	8,382	LC
Purdue Univ/West Lafayette	IN	10,284	VC
Rochester Inst of Technology	NY	26,232	VC+
Univ of Illinois at Urbana-Champaign	IL	11,316	HC+

CREATIVE WRITING

School	ST	$IS	SR
Agnes Scott College	GA	24,950	VC
Albertson College of Idaho	ID	23,900	VC
Alderson-Broaddus College	WV	19,640	C
Andrews Univ	MI	17,696	LC
Arkansas Tech Univ	AR	6,256	C
Ashland Univ	OH	22,182	LC
Bard College	NY	33,912	HC
Baylor Univ	TX	18,298	VC+
Beloit College	WI	27,482	HC
Bennington College	VT	31,350	VC
Bowling Green State Univ	OH	10,794	C
Cal State, San Marcos	CA	1,736	LC
Cardinal Stritch Univ	WI	17,620	C
Carlow College	PA	19,366	C
Carroll College	MT	19,140	C
Christopher Newport Univ	VA	8,862	VC
CUNY/Brooklyn College	NY	3,403	LC
CUNY/Hunter College	NY	5,147	C+
Colby College	ME	34,290	MC
College of Santa Fe	NM	20,250	LC
Colo College	CO	31,525	HC+
Columbia College Chicago	IL	22,063	LC
Concordia College/Moorhead	MN	18,835	C
Dartmouth College	NH	34,458	MC
Dominican Univ of Calif	CA	27,948	C
Drexel Univ	PA	27,657	VC
Eastern College	PA	19,641	LC
Eastern Washington Univ	WA	7,972	LC
Eckerd College	FL	25,500	C+
Edinboro Univ of Pennsylvania	PA	9,328	LC
Emerson College	MA	29,978	HC
Emory & Henry College	VA	19,462	C
Emory Univ	GA	33,792	MC
Eugene Lang College of New School Univ	NY	30,300	C
Florida State Univ	FL	7,835	HC
Fordham Univ	NY	30,710	VC
Geneva College	PA	19,990	C+
Goddard College	VT	21,056	C+
Green Mountain College	VT	24,130	C
Hamilton College	NY	34,150	HC
Hampshire College	MA	33,881	HC+
Harvard Univ/Harvard College	MA	34,269	MC
Hollins Univ	VA	24,328	VC
Houghton College	NY	21,810	VC+
Indiana Wesleyan Univ	IN	17,680	C
Ithaca College	NY	28,719	HC
Johnson State College	VT	10,776	C
Kansas City Art Inst	MO	25,880	SP
Knox College	IL	28,230	HC
La Roche College	PA	18,854	LC
Lakeland College	WI	17,950	C
Le Moyne College	NY	23,840	C
Lindenwood Univ	MO	17,250	C
Linfield College	OR	25,840	VC
Loras College	IA	22,994	C+
Loyola College in Maryland	MD	30,900	HC
Loyola Univ New Orleans	LA	23,506	VC+
Marlboro College	VT	26,410	VC+
Maryville College	TN	23,210	VC
Mass Inst of Technology	MA	35,228	MC
Methodist College	NC	19,526	C
Millikin Univ	IL	24,415	C+
Mills College	CA	27,950	C
Mount Union College	OH	21,120	C
Naropa Univ	CO	22,416	SP
New England College	NH	20,706	LC
Norfolk State Univ	VA	8,382	LC
Northland College	WI	21,435	C+
Oberlin College	OH	33,140	HC+
Ohio Northern Univ	OH	27,765	VC
Ohio Univ	OH	11,769	C
Okla Christian Univ	OK	16,500	VC
Pacific Univ	OR	24,250	C
Pratt Inst	NY	27,550	SP
Purdue Univ/West Lafayette	IN	10,284	VC
Roger Williams Univ	RI	29,010	C
St. Andrews Presbyterian College	NC	19,720	LC
St. Edward's Univ	TX	17,846	C
St. Joseph's College	IN	21,640	C
St. Mary's Univ of Minn	MN	19,975	C
Sarah Lawrence College	NY	37,516	HC
Seattle Univ	WA	24,183	VC
Simon's Rock College of Bard	MA	32,450	HC
Southern Methodist Univ	TX	28,349	VC
Southern Nazarene Univ	OK	14,634	NC
Southern Vermont College	VT	17,685	C
Southwest State Univ	MN	7,117	LC
SUNY/College at Purchase	NY	10,587	VC
Stephens College	MO	22,295	C
Sweet Briar College	VA	25,310	VC
Univ of Arizona	AZ	8,614	C
Univ of Calif at Riverside	CA	12,479	C
Univ of Central Okla	OK	5,205	C
Univ of Colo at Denver	CO	3,673	C
Univ of Evansville	IN	22,865	VC+
Univ of Houston	TX	8,410	C
Univ of Maine at Farmington	ME	9,163	C
Univ of Miami	FL	31,130	HC
Univ of Mich/Ann Arbor	MI	13,003	HC+
Univ of Montana--Western	MT	6,915	NC
Univ of New Haven	CT	23,860	LC
Univ of New Mexico	NM	8,026	C
Univ of N Car at Wilmington	NC	7,769	C
Univ of Pittsburgh at Greensburg	PA	12,842	C
Univ of Pittsburgh at Johnstown	PA	13,044	LC
Univ of Pittsburgh at Pittsburgh	PA	13,592	HC
Univ of Tampa	FL	22,612	C
Wartburg College	IA	21,165	VC
Washington Univ in St. Louis	MO	34,593	MC
Western Mich Univ	MI	10,016	C
Wheaton College	MA	32,940	VC

CRIMINAL JUSTICE

School	ST	$IS	SR
Abilene Christian Univ	TX	16,300	VC
Adrian College	MI	19,670	C
Alabama State Univ	AL	6,404	C
Albany State Univ	GA	5,764	C+
Albright College	PA	27,642	C
Alcorn State Univ	MS	5,594	LC
Alfred Univ	NY	27,212	C+
Alvernia College	PA	20,790	C
American International College	MA	22,268	LC
American Univ	DC	31,544	VC+
Anderson Univ	IN	19,430	LC
Angelo State Univ	TX	7,028	C
Anna Maria College	MA	22,800	LC
Appalachian State Univ	NC	6,353	C
Arizona State Univ-Main	AZ	7,726	C
Armstrong Atlantic State Univ	GA	7,084	C
Ashland Univ	OH	22,182	LC
Auburn Univ	AL	5,510	C
Auburn Univ Montgomery	AL	5,330	NC
Augusta State Univ	GA	2,282	C
Aurora Univ	IL	18,551	C
Averett Univ	VA	17,980	LC
Baldwin-Wallace College	OH	22,010	VC+
Ball State Univ	IN	8,660	C
Barton College	NC	16,834	LC
Bay Path College	MA	22,308	LC
Becker College	MA	21,230	LC
Bellevue Univ	NE	4,125	NC
Bemidji State Univ	MN	7,957	C
Benedict College	SC	12,662	LC
Bethel College	IN	17,650	LC
Bethune-Cookman College	FL	15,746	C
Bloomsburg Univ of Pennsylvania	PA	9,434	C
Bluefield College	VA	14,200	C
Bluefield State College	WV	2,178	LC
Bluffton College	OH	20,644	C
Boise State Univ	ID	6,531	LC
Bowie State Univ	MD	9,300	C+
Bowling Green State Univ	OH	10,794	C
Bradley Univ	IL	20,970	VC
Bridgewater State College	MA	7,589	C+
Buena Vista Univ	IA	22,828	C
Butler Univ	IN	25,580	VC+
Cabrini College	PA	25,950	LC
Caldwell College	NJ	20,940	LC
Calif Baptist Univ	CA	16,736	C
Calif Lutheran Univ	CA	23,500	LC
Cal State, Bakersfield	CA	6,090	LC
Cal State, Fullerton	CA	5,440	LC
Cal State, Hayward	CA	7,400	LC
Cal State, Los Angeles	CA	5,050	C
Cal State, Sacramento	CA	7,488	C
Cal State, San Bernardino	CA	6,516	C
Cal State, Stanislaus	CA	8,895	C
Calumet College of St. Joseph	IN	7,500	LC
Calvin College	MI	20,050	NC
Cameron Univ	OK	5,560	NC
Campbell Univ	NC	16,599	C
Canisius College	NY	24,696	C+
Capital Univ	OH	23,630	C
Caribbean Univ	PR	3,000	
Carlow College	PA	19,366	C
Carroll College	WI	21,170	C
Carthage College	WI	23,670	C
Castleton State College	VT	10,922	LC
Cedarville Univ	OH	17,553	VC
Centenary College	NJ	22,430	C
Central Methodist College	MO	16,460	C
Central Missouri State Univ	MO	7,920	C
Central Washington Univ	WA	8,985	LC
Chadron State College	NE	6,211	NC
Chaminade Univ of Honolulu	HI	17,370	C
Champlain College	VT	19,680	C
Charleston Southern Univ	SC	17,122	C
Chicago State Univ	IL	8,851	C+
Christopher Newport Univ	VA	8,862	VC
Citadel, The	SC	9,126	C
CUNY/John Jay College of Criminal Justice	NY	3,251	C
College of New Jersey	NJ	13,425	HC
College of the Ozarks	MO	2,650	C+
College of the Southwest	NM	8,456	NC
Columbia College	MO	15,082	C
Columbus State Univ	GA	7,228	LC
Concordia Univ	MI	20,500	C
Concordia Univ	MN	19,912	C
Concordia Univ Wisc	WI	16,600	LC
Coppin State College	MD	9,133	LC
Culver-Stockton College	MO	15,400	LC
Curry College	MA	26,025	LC
Dakota Wesleyan Univ	SD	15,512	C
Dallas Baptist Univ	TX	13,682	LC
De Sales Univ	PA	22,610	VC
Defiance College	OH	19,580	LC
Delaware Valley College	PA	24,213	LC
Delta State Univ	MS	5,416	C
Dillard Univ	LA	16,046	VC
East Carolina Univ	NC	7,766	C
East Central Univ	OK	4,578	C
East Tenn State Univ	TN	7,127	C
Eastern Mich Univ	MI	9,855	C
Eastern New Mexico Univ	NM	4,113	LC
Eastern Washington Univ	WA	7,972	LC
Edgewood College	WI	18,304	C
Edinboro Univ of Pennsylvania	PA	9,328	LC
Edward Waters College	FL	13,124	LC
Elizabeth City State Univ	NC	5,550	LC
Elmira College	NY	31,070	VC+
Endicott College	MA	23,704	C
Evangel Univ	MO	14,050	C
Fairleigh Dickinson Univ/Teaneck Campus	NJ	24,646	C
Fairmont State College	WV	7,010	NC
Fayetteville State Univ	NC	5,590	LC
Ferris State Univ	MI	10,816	C
Ferrum College	VA	15,990	LC
Fitchburg State College	MA	7,836	C
Florida A&M Univ	FL	6,948	C
Florida Atlantic Univ	FL	8,832	C
Florida Gulf Coast Univ	FL	9,201	C
Florida International Univ	FL	9,486	VC
Florida Memorial College	FL	6,000	LC
Florida Southern College	FL	19,430	C
Fordham Univ	NY	30,710	VC
Fort Hays State Univ	KS	6,294	LC
Fort Valley State Univ	GA	6,014	LC
Franklin Pierce College	NH	26,125	LC
Frostburg State Univ	MD	9,680	C
Gannon Univ	PA	18,848	C
George Mason Univ	VA	9,192	C
George Washington Univ	DC	32,170	HC
Georgia College and State Univ	GA	7,344	C
Georgia Southern Univ	GA	6,958	C
Georgia State Univ	GA	7,792	LC
Gonzaga Univ	WA	24,276	HC+
Grace College	IN	16,768	C
Graceland Univ	IA	15,845	C
Grambling State Univ	LA	5,325	NC
Grand Canyon Univ	AZ	30,000	LC
Grand Valley State Univ	MI	10,040	C
Grand View College	IA	17,596	NC
Guilford College	NC	23,255	C
Gustavus Adolphus College	MN	24,190	VC+
Gwynedd-Mercy College	PA	22,350	C
Hamline Univ	MN	23,339	C+
Hannibal-LaGrange College	MO	12,530	C

School	ST	$IS	SR
Hardin-Simmons Univ	TX	14,165	C
Hawaii Pacific Univ	HI	17,790	C
Hesser College	NH	16,210	LC
High Point Univ	NC	20,220	LC
Hilbert College	NY	16,830	LC
Holy Family College	PA	13,710	LC
Howard Univ	DC	15,522	LC
Huron Univ	SD	10,450	C
Husson College	ME	15,360	LC
Illinois State Univ	IL	9,235	C
Indiana Univ Bloomington	IN	10,712	C+
Indiana Univ Kokomo	IN	3,422	LC
Indiana Univ Northwest	IN	3,447	C
Indiana Univ South Bend	IN	3,515	C
Indiana Univ-Purdue Univ Fort Wayne	IN	3,166	LC
Indiana Univ-Purdue Univ Indianapolis	IN	9,473	C
Indiana Wesleyan Univ	IN	17,680	C
Inter-American Univ of PR/Aguadilla Campus	PR	3,278	
Inter-American Univ of PR/Arecibo Campus	PR	3,300	
Inter-American Univ of PR/Barranquitas Regional College	PR	3,300	LC
Inter-American Univ of PR/Bayamon Univ College	PR	3,700	
Inter-American Univ of PR/Fajardo Campus	PR	4,000	
Inter-American Univ of PR/Metropolitan Campus	PR	4,166	
Inter-American Univ of PR/Ponce Regional College	PR	3,700	
International College	FL	7,230	NC
Iona College	NY	26,556	C
Iowa Wesleyan College	IA	18,840	C
Jackson State Univ	MS	6,776	LC
Jacksonville State Univ	AL	6,568	LC
Jamestown College	ND	11,310	NC
Jarvis Christian College	TX	9,035	NC
Johnson and Wales Univ	RI	21,558	LC
Judson College	AL	13,790	C
Juniata College	PA	26,080	VC
Kansas Wesleyan Univ	KS	17,400	C+
Kean Univ	NJ	11,159	C
Kendall College	IL	19,119	LC
Kent State Univ	OH	11,104	C
Kentucky State Univ	KY	6,146	NC
Kentucky Wesleyan College	KY	15,800	C
Keuka College	NY	21,170	C
Keystone College	PA	19,066	LC
King's College	PA	24,680	C
Kutztown Univ of Pennsylvania	PA	8,907	C
La Roche College	PA	18,854	LC
La Salle Univ	PA	27,890	C
Lake Superior State Univ	MI	9,034	LC
Lakeland College	WI	17,950	C
Lamar Univ	TX	6,816	LC
Langston Univ	OK	2,308	LC
Lasell College	MA	24,100	C
Lees-McRae College	NC	17,106	LC
Lewis Univ	IL	20,960	C
Lewis-Clark State College	ID	6,496	C
Limestone College	SC	16,900	C
Lincoln Univ	MO	7,158	NC
Lincoln Univ	PA	11,198	C+
Lindenwood Univ	MO	17,250	C
Lindsey Wilson College	KY	16,392	LC
LIU/C.W. Post Campus	NY	25,380	C
Loras College	IA	22,994	C+
Louisiana College	LA	11,516	C
Lourdes College	OH	13,100	LC
Loyola Univ New Orleans	LA	23,506	VC+
Loyola Univ of Chicago	IL	25,992	VC
Lycoming College	PA	24,780	C
MacMurray College	IL	17,790	LC
Madonna Univ	MI	11,504	VC
Mansfield Univ	PA	9,648	C
Marian College of Fond du Lac	WI	17,935	LC
Marist College	NY	24,756	VC
Marshall Univ	WV	7,752	LC
Martin Univ	IN	8,370	SP
Marymount Univ	VA	21,560	LC
Marywood Univ	PA	24,639	C
McNeese State Univ	LA	5,259	LC
Medaille College	NY	18,320	C
Mercy College	NY	15,875	LC
Mercyhurst College	PA	20,694	C
Methodist College	NC	19,526	C
Metropolitan State College of Denver	CO	2,338	LC
Metropolitan State Univ	MN	2,943	SP
Mich State Univ	MI	10,386	VC
MidAmerica Nazarene Univ	KS	16,960	C
Middle Tenn State Univ	TN	6,994	C
Midwestern State Univ	TX	6,704	NC
Minot State Univ	ND	5,466	LC
Miss College	MS	14,574	C
Miss Valley State Univ	MS	6,345	C
Missouri Baptist College	MO	15,762	LC
Missouri Southern State College	MO	6,666	C
Missouri Valley College	MO	17,400	LC
Missouri Western State College	MO	6,662	NC
Mitchell College	CT	23,950	C
Molloy College	NY	13,940	C
Monmouth Univ	NJ	24,042	C
Moorhead State Univ	MN	7,000	LC
Moravian College	PA	27,065	VC
Morris Brown College	GA	15,993	LC
Morris College	SC	9,995	LC
Mount Ida College	MA	25,375	LC
Mount Marty College	SD	15,656	LC
Mount Mary College	WI	18,024	C
Mount Mercy College	IA	19,390	VC
Mount Olive College	NC	14,410	LC
Mount St. Clare College	IA	19,050	LC
Mount St. Mary College	NY	18,825	C
Mount Senario College	WI	17,750	C
Mountain State Univ	WV	8,180	NC
Murray State Univ	KY	6,672	C
National Univ	CA	7,755	SP
New England College	NH	20,706	LC
New Jersey City Univ	NJ	9,100	LC
New Mexico State Univ	NM	7,302	C
Newbury College	MA	21,490	C
Newman Univ	KS	14,098	LC
Niagara Univ	NY	22,250	C+
N Car Central Univ	NC	6,418	LC
N Car State Univ	NC	8,680	HC
N Car Wesleyan College	NC	15,650	LC
N Dak State Univ	ND	7,004	VC
North Georgia College and State Univ	GA	6,322	C+
Northeastern Illinois Univ	IL	2,898	NC
Northeastern State Univ	OK	4,704	LC
Northeastern Univ	MA	30,078	VC
Northern Arizona Univ	AZ	7,398	C
Northern Mich Univ	MI	9,693	C
Northern State Univ	SD	6,279	LC
Northwestern College	MN	19,816	C+
Northwestern College of Iowa	IA	17,630	C+
Northwestern Okla State Univ	OK	4,542	NC
Northwestern State Univ of Louisiana	LA	5,745	NC
Norwich Univ	VT	21,064	LC
Ohio Dominican College	OH	18,100	LC
Ohio Northern Univ	OH	27,765	VC
Ohio Univ	OH	11,769	C
Okla City Univ	OK	15,810	C
Old Dominion Univ	VA	9,386	C
Olivet College	MI	17,410	C
Pace Univ	NY	24,200	C
Park Univ	MO	9,816	C
Penn State Univ/Altoona	PA	12,578	C
Penn State Univ/Univ Park Campus	PA	11,126	VC
Pfeiffer Univ	NC	18,580	C
Pikeville College	KY	12,000	NC
Pittsburg State Univ	KS	6,228	NC
Point Park College	PA	20,290	C
Portland State Univ	OR	11,220	C
Prairie View A&M Univ	TX	3,172	LC
Prescott College	AZ	13,430	LC
Purdue Univ/Calumet	IN	6,630	NC
Quincy Univ	IL	20,450	C
Quinnipiac Univ	CT	27,070	C
Radford Univ	VA	8,302	C
Richard Stockton College of New Jersey	NJ	12,165	VC
Roanoke College	VA	24,689	VC
Roberts Wesleyan College	NY	20,160	C+
Rochester Inst of Technology	NY	26,232	VC+
Rockford College	IL	23,930	C
Roger Williams Univ	RI	29,010	C
Rowan Univ	NJ	12,365	VC
Russell Sage College	NY	23,674	C+
Rutgers, The State Univ of New Jersey/New Brunswick Campus	NJ	12,709	C
Rutgers, The State Univ of New Jersey/Newark Campus	NJ	6,394	C
Sacred Heart Univ	CT	26,588	VC
Saginaw Valley State Univ	MI	9,465	C
St. Ambrose Univ	IA	19,994	C
St. Anselm College	NH	27,405	C
St. Augustine's College	NC	12,990	C+
St. Cloud State Univ	MN	7,180	C
St. Edward's Univ	TX	17,846	C
St. Francis College	NY	9,610	C
St. Francis Univ	PA	24,486	LC
St. John's Univ	NY	26,660	C
St. Joseph's College	IN	21,640	C
St. Joseph's College of Maine	ME	22,500	LC
St. Joseph's Univ	PA	29,715	VC+
St. Louis Univ	MO	26,590	VC+
St. Martin's College	WA	20,566	C
St. Mary's Univ of Minn	MN	19,975	C
St. Mary's Univ of San Antonio	TX	19,735	C
St. Peter's College	NJ	22,292	LC
St. Thomas Aquinas College	NY	20,590	LC
St. Thomas Univ	FL	19,500	LC
St. Xavier Univ	IL	21,104	C
Salem International Univ	WV	17,263	LC
Salem State College	MA	4,481	LC
Salve Regina Univ	RI	26,460	C
Sam Houston State Univ	TX	6,076	LC
San Diego State Univ	CA	9,716	C+
San Jose State Univ	CA	8,187	C
Savannah State Univ	GA	2,550	LC
Seattle Univ	WA	24,183	VC
Seton Hall Univ	NJ	26,910	LC
Shaw Univ	NC	12,810	C
Shippensburg Univ of Pennsylvania	PA	9,652	C
Siena Heights Univ	MI	16,140	LC
Simpson College	IA	21,200	C+
Sojourner-Douglass College	MD	4,170	LC
Sonoma State Univ	CA	8,953	C
S Car State Univ	SC	6,586	LC
Southeast Missouri State Univ	MO	8,367	C+
Southeastern Louisiana Univ	LA	6,047	LC
Southeastern Okla State Univ	OK	4,917	C
Southern Illinois Univ at Carbondale	IL	8,621	C
Southern Illinois Univ Edwardsville	IL	7,869	LC
Southern Nazarene Univ	OK	14,634	NC
Southern Univ at New Orleans	LA	995	NC
Southern Utah Univ	UT	7,254	C
Southern Vermont College	VT	17,685	C
Southwest Baptist Univ	MO	13,426	LC
Southwest Texas State Univ	TX	8,730	VC
Southwestern Adventist Univ	TX	14,798	C
Southwestern College	KS	17,656	C
Southwestern Okla State Univ	OK	4,801	C
SUNY/College at Brockport	NY	10,267	C
SUNY/College at Buffalo	NY	8,025	C
SUNY/College at Oswego	NY	10,856	C
SUNY/College at Plattsburgh	NY	9,729	C
SUNY/College at Potsdam	NY	10,519	C
SUNY/Univ at Albany	NY	10,997	VC
Stephen F. Austin State Univ	TX	6,905	C
Stonehill College	MA	26,852	HC
Suffolk Univ	MA	26,516	C
Sul Ross State Univ	TX	6,582	LC
Tarleton State Univ	TX	7,160	C
Teikyo Post Univ	CT	21,800	C
Temple Univ	PA	14,124	C
Tenn State Univ	TN	7,058	VC
Texas A&M Univ at Commerce	TX	7,326	C
Texas Christian Univ	TX	19,910	C
Texas Southern Univ	TX	6,576	NC
Texas Wesleyan Univ	TX	14,710	C
Texas Woman's Univ	TX	5,855	LC
Thomas Edison State College	NJ	2,750	SP
Thomas More College	KY	17,700	LC
Thomas Univ	GA	8,770	NC
Tri-State Univ-Main Campus	IN	21,200	C
Troy State Univ	AL	7,696	C
Troy State Univ/Dothan	AL	3,296	C
Truman State Univ	MO	8,568	VC+
Union College	KY	15,920	C
Univ of Akron	OH	10,530	NC
Univ of Alabama	AL	7,402	C
Univ of Alabama at Birmingham	AL	10,110	C
Univ of Alaska Anchorage	AK	9,100	NC
Univ of Alaska Fairbanks	AK	8,265	NC
Univ of Arizona	AZ	8,614	C
Univ of Arkansas	AR	8,334	VC
Univ of Arkansas at Little Rock	AR	5,637	NC
Univ of Arkansas at Monticello	AR	5,940	NC
Univ of Arkansas at Pine Bluff	AR	7,925	C
Univ of Central Florida	FL	8,251	VC
Univ of Central Okla	OK	5,205	C
Univ of Cincinnati	OH	12,491	LC
Univ of Dayton	OH	20,400	VC
Univ of Delaware	DE	10,824	VC
Univ of Detroit Mercy	MI	21,620	LC
Univ of Evansville	IN	22,865	VC+
Univ of Findlay	OH	23,962	NC
Univ of Florida	FL	7,874	HC
Univ of Georgia	GA	8,656	VC
Univ of Great Falls	MT	15,360	C
Univ of Hartford	CT	28,884	C
Univ of Hawaii at Hilo	HI	6,497	C
Univ of Houston-Downtown	TX	2,006	NC
Univ of Idaho	ID	7,026	C
Univ of Illinois at Chicago	IL	10,702	VC
Univ of Louisiana at Lafayette	LA	5,200	C
Univ of Louisiana at Monroe	LA	5,207	NC
Univ of Louisville	KY	7,402	LC
Univ of Maine at Presque Isle	ME	7,964	LC
Univ of Mary Hardin-Baylor	TX	13,929	C
Univ of Maryland/College Park	MD	11,959	C
Univ of Maryland/Eastern Shore	MD	9,258	C
Univ of Maryland/Univ College	MD	5,910	SP
Univ of Mass Boston	MA	4,227	C
Univ of Mass Dartmouth	MA	9,852	C
Univ of Mass Lowell	MA	9,470	VC
Univ of Memphis	TN	7,271	C
Univ of Mich/Flint	MI	4,323	C
Univ of Missouri/Kansas City	MO	9,685	VC
Univ of Missouri/St. Louis	MO	9,966	C
Univ of Nebr at Kearney	NE	7,048	NC
Univ of Nebr at Omaha	NE	6,867	C
Univ of Nevada/Las Vegas	NV	8,281	VC
Univ of Nevada/Reno	NV	8,737	C
Univ of New Haven	CT	23,860	LC
Univ of New Mexico	NM	8,026	C
Univ of North Alabama	AL	7,016	NC
Univ of N Car at Charlotte	NC	7,254	C
Univ of N Car at Pembroke	NC	5,914	LC
Univ of N Car at Wilmington	NC	7,769	C
Univ of N Dak	ND	7,067	VC
Univ of North Florida	FL	8,089	VC
Univ of North Texas	TX	7,629	C
Univ of Northern Colo	CO	8,082	C+
Univ of Phoenix	AZ	7,000	SP
Univ of Pittsburgh at Bradford	PA	12,696	C
Univ of Portland	OR	24,950	VC
Univ of Richmond	VA	27,300	HC
Univ of St. Francis	IL	19,650	C
Univ of St. Thomas	MN	24,044	VC
Univ of Scranton	PA	27,964	C+
Univ of South Alabama	AL	6,976	LC
Univ of S Car at Columbia	SC	8,748	VC
Univ of S Car at Spartanburg	SC	7,318	C+
Univ of S Dak	SD	7,036	C
Univ of Southern Miss	MS	6,155	LC
Univ of Tenn at Chattanooga	TN	7,783	C
Univ of Tenn at Martin	TN	8,268	C
Univ of Texas at Arlington	TX	7,192	LC
Univ of Texas at El Paso	TX	5,076	LC
Univ of Texas at San Antonio	TX	9,088	NC
Univ of Texas-Pan American	TX	4,823	C
Univ of the District of Columbia	DC	2,844	NC
Univ of the Sacred Heart	PR	5,375	
Univ of Toledo	OH	11,206	NC
Univ of Virginia's College at Wise	VA	8,302	C
Univ of West Florida	FL	7,518	C
Univ of Wisc/Eau Claire	WI	7,032	VC
Univ of Wisc/Milwaukee	WI	8,907	LC
Univ of Wisc/Oshkosh	WI	6,130	LC
Univ of Wisc/Platteville	WI	7,282	C
Univ of Wisc/Superior	WI	7,051	C+
Univ of Wyoming	WY	7,143	LC
Urbana Univ	OH	17,004	C
Utica College of Syracuse Univ	NY	24,400	LC
Valdosta State Univ	GA	6,988	C
Villanova Univ	PA	31,997	HC
Virginia Commonwealth Univ	VA	9,030	C
Virginia Wesleyan College	VA	22,350	LC
Viterbo Univ	WI	18,043	C
Voorhees College	SC	9,976	C+
Washington State Univ	WA	9,388	C
Wayland Baptist Univ	TX	11,271	NC
Wayne State College	NE	6,255	NC
Wayne State Univ	MI	6,720	C
Waynesburg College	PA	17,610	LC
Weber State Univ	UT	6,897	NC
West Chester Univ of Pennsylvania	PA	9,792	VC
West Liberty State College	WV	6,056	LC
West Texas A&M Univ	TX	6,538	C
West Virginia State College	WV	6,264	NC
Western Carolina Univ	NC	5,667	C
Western Conn State Univ	CT	10,074	C
Western Illinois Univ	IL	9,571	C
Western International Univ	AZ	5,800	SP
Western Mich Univ	MI	10,016	C
Western New England College	MA	23,882	C
Westfield State College	MA	8,394	C
Westminster College	PA	22,960	C
Wheeling Jesuit Univ	WV	22,660	C
Wichita State Univ	KS	6,879	C
Widener Univ	PA	26,920	C
Wilmington College	DE	6,530	NC
Wilmington College	OH	21,826	C
Winona State Univ	MN	8,570	C
Worcester State College	MA	7,901	LC

School	ST	$IS	SR
Xavier Univ	OH	23,880	C
York College of Pennsylvania	PA	12,550	VC
Youngstown State Univ	OH	9,318	NC

CRIMINOLOGY

School	ST	$IS	SR
Adams State College	CO	7,468	C
Albertus Magnus College	CT	22,154	C
Arkansas State Univ	AR	7,480	C
Auburn Univ	AL	5,510	C
Barber-Scotia College	NC	13,100	C
Barry Univ	FL	24,100	LC
Cal State, Fresno	CA	7,762	C
Cal State, Northridge	CA	7,781	C
Central Conn State Univ	CT	10,404	C
Christopher Newport Univ	VA	8,862	VC
CUNY/John Jay College of Criminal Justice	NY	3,251	C
College of the Ozarks	MO	2,650	C+
Dominican Univ	IL	20,800	C
Drury Univ	MO	15,250	VC
Florida State Univ	FL	7,835	HC
Hilbert College	NY	16,830	LC
Indiana State Univ	IN	8,461	LC
Indiana Univ of Pennsylvania	PA	9,133	C
Le Moyne College	NY	23,840	C
Marquette Univ	WI	24,836	C+
Maryville Univ of St. Louis	MO	18,680	C
Mount Aloysius College	PA	18,186	LC
Pontifical Catholic Univ of PR/Ponce	PR	7,076	
St. Leo Univ	FL	19,250	LC
Southern Oregon Univ	OR	9,429	C
Southwest Texas State Univ	TX	8,730	VC
SUNY/College at Old Westbury	NY	9,818	LC
State Univ of West Georgia	GA	7,101	C
Ohio State Univ	OH	10,819	VC
Tiffin Univ	OH	17,250	C
Turabo Univ	PR	4,110	
Univ of Calif at Irvine	CA	11,756	C
Univ of La Verne	CA	24,280	C
Univ of Maryland/College Park	MD	11,959	C
Univ of Memphis	TN	7,271	C
Univ of Miami	FL	31,130	HC
Univ of Minn/Duluth	MN	10,436	C
Univ of Northern Iowa	IA	7,850	C
Univ of South Florida	FL	8,154	C
Univ of Southern Colo	CO	7,821	LC
Univ of Tampa	FL	22,612	C
Univ of Texas at Dallas	TX	9,305	VC
Upper Iowa Univ	IA	17,438	C
Valparaiso Univ	IN	23,570	VC+
Virginia Union Univ	VA	15,358	LC
Wilkes Univ	PA	25,800	C
William Penn Univ	IA	17,575	C

CROSSCULTURAL STUDIES

School	ST	$IS	SR
Alfred Univ	NY	27,212	C+
Andrews Univ	MI	17,696	LC
Antioch College	OH	25,072	LC
Azusa Pacific Univ	CA	22,422	VC
Biola Univ	CA	21,902	VC
Chatham College	PA	25,454	C+
Drake Univ	IA	22,830	VC
Eugene Lang College of New School Univ	NY	30,300	C
Goddard College	VT	21,056	C+
Hampshire College	MA	33,881	HC+
Hofstra Univ	NY	23,252	C
Hope International Univ	CA	16,940	NC
Houghton College	NY	21,810	VC+
John Brown Univ	AR	15,080	VC
Johns Hopkins Univ	MD	35,226	MC
Lee Univ	TN	10,198	LC
Montreat College	NC	17,164	C
Murray State Univ	KY	6,672	C
National-Louis Univ	IL	13,995	NC
Nyack College	NY	18,540	C
St. Olaf College	MN	25,880	HC
Simon's Rock College of Bard	MA	32,450	HC
Stanford Univ	CA	34,222	MC
Towson Univ	MD	11,088	VC
Univ of Calif at Irvine	CA	11,756	C
Univ of Calif at Los Angeles	CA	13,227	MC
Univ of Maryland/Baltimore County	MD	12,190	VC
Waynesburg College	PA	17,610	LC
Western Baptist College	OR	19,700	C+
Whitworth College	WA	23,938	VC
Wofford College	SC	23,995	VC

CYBERNETICS

School	ST	$IS	SR
Univ of Calif at Los Angeles	CA	13,227	MC

CYTOTECHNOLOGY

School	ST	$IS	SR
Alderson-Broaddus College	WV	19,640	C
Barry Univ	FL	24,100	LC
College of St. Elizabeth	NJ	22,510	C
College of St. Rose	NY	19,084	C
Edgewood College	WI	18,304	C
Indiana Univ-Purdue Univ Indianapolis	IN	9,473	C
Jewish Hospital College of Nursing and Allied Health	MO	11,200	SP
Kent State Univ	OH	11,104	C
Luther College	IA	23,300	VC+
Marian College of Fond du Lac	WI	17,935	LC
Mount St. Clare College	IA	19,050	LC
Northern Mich Univ	MI	9,693	C
St. John's Univ	NY	26,660	C
St. Mary's Univ of Minn	MN	19,975	C
Salve Regina Univ	RI	26,460	C
SUNY/Univ at Stony Brook	NY	10,998	VC
Suffolk Univ	MA	26,516	C
Thiel College	PA	18,419	LC
Thomas Edison State College	NJ	2,750	SP
Univ of Alabama at Birmingham	AL	10,110	C
Univ of Conn	CT	12,122	VC
Univ of Kansas	KS	7,232	VC
Univ of Miami	FL	31,130	HC
Univ of N Dak	ND	7,067	VC
Univ of North Texas	TX	7,629	C
Winona State Univ	MN	8,570	C

DAIRY SCIENCE

School	ST	$IS	SR
Calif Polytechnic State Univ	CA	8,747	VC
Delaware Valley College	PA	24,213	LC
Iowa State Univ	IA	8,108	VC
Penn State Univ/Univ Park Campus	PA	11,126	VC
S Dak State Univ	SD	6,848	C
Texas A&M Univ	TX	8,988	VC
Univ of Florida	FL	7,874	HC
Univ of Georgia	GA	8,656	VC
Univ of New Hampshire	NH	13,207	C
Univ of Wisc/Madison	WI	8,262	VC
Utah State Univ	UT	6,771	C
Virginia Polytechnic Inst and State Univ	VA	7,652	C

DANCE

School	ST	$IS	SR
Adelphi Univ	NY	23,320	VC
Amherst College	MA	34,340	MC
Arizona State Univ-Main	AZ	7,726	C
Baldwin-Wallace College	OH	22,010	VC+
Ball State Univ	IN	8,660	C
Bard College	NY	33,912	HC
Belhaven College	MS	16,040	C+
Bennington College	VT	31,350	VC
Birmingham-Southern College	AL	22,960	C
Boston Conservatory	MA	26,900	SP
Bowling Green State Univ	OH	10,794	C
Brenau Univ Women's College	GA	20,100	C
Brigham Young Univ	UT	7,840	HC
Butler Univ	IN	25,580	VC+
Calif Inst of the Arts	CA	27,275	SP
Cal State, Fullerton	CA	5,440	LC
Cal State, Long Beach	CA	7,400	LC
Cal State, Los Angeles	CA	5,050	C
Cal State, Northridge	CA	7,781	C
Cedar Crest College	PA	25,145	C+
Centenary College of Louisiana	LA	21,600	C+
CUNY/Brooklyn College	NY	3,403	LC
CUNY/Herbert H. Lehman College	NY	3,320	LC
CUNY/Hunter College	NY	5,147	C+
CUNY/Queens College	NY	3,403	VC
Coker College	SC	20,120	C
Colo College	CO	31,525	HC+
Columbia College	SC	19,050	LC
Columbia College Chicago	IL	22,063	LC
Columbia Univ/Barnard College	NY	33,694	MC
Columbia Univ/Columbia College	NY	35,190	MC
Columbia Univ/School of General Studies	NY	35,000	C
Conn College	CT	33,585	MC
Cornell Univ	NY	34,614	MC
Cornish College of the Arts	WA	16,200	SP
De Sales Univ	PA	22,610	VC
Denison Univ	OH	29,640	HC
Dickinson College	PA	32,210	VC+
East Carolina Univ	NC	7,766	C
Eastern Mich Univ	MI	9,855	C
Eastern Washington Univ	WA	7,972	LC
Emory Univ	GA	33,792	MC
Florida International Univ	FL	9,486	VC
Florida State Univ	FL	7,835	HC
Fordham Univ	NY	30,710	VC
Franklin Pierce College	NH	26,125	LC
George Mason Univ	VA	9,192	C
George Washington Univ	DC	32,170	HC
Georgia State Univ	GA	7,792	LC
Goucher College	MD	30,650	VC+
Gustavus Adolphus College	MN	24,190	VC+
Hamilton College	NY	34,150	HC
Hampshire College	MA	33,881	HC+
Hobart and William Smith Colleges	NY	33,195	VC
Hofstra Univ	NY	23,252	C
Hollins Univ	VA	24,328	VC
Hope College	MI	22,922	C+
Howard Univ	DC	15,522	LC
Huntingdon College	AL	18,400	VC
Illinois State Univ	IL	9,235	C
Indiana Univ Bloomington	IN	10,712	C+
Jacksonville Univ	FL	21,110	LC
James Madison Univ	VA	9,552	HC
Juilliard School	NY	28,200	SP
Kent State Univ	OH	11,104	C
Kenyon College	OH	32,130	HC+
La Roche College	PA	18,854	LC
Lake Erie College	OH	21,350	LC
Lindenwood Univ	MO	17,250	C
LIU/C.W. Post Campus	NY	25,380	C
Loyola Marymount Univ	CA	28,754	HC
Luther College	IA	23,300	VC+
Manhattanville College	NY	28,730	VC
Marlboro College	VT	26,410	VC+
Marygrove College	MI	16,075	C
Marymount Manhattan College	NY	23,195	VC
Mercyhurst College	PA	20,694	C
Meredith College	NC	17,500	C
Middlebury College	VT	34,300	MC
Mills College	CA	27,950	C
Minn State Univ, Mankato	MN	7,296	LC
Montclair State Univ	NJ	10,287	LC
Mount Holyoke College	MA	34,128	HC
Muhlenberg College	PA	28,170	HC
New Mexico State Univ	NM	7,302	C
New York Univ	NY	35,200	MC
N Car School of the Arts	NC	7,797	SP
Northwestern Univ	IL	33,615	MC
Oberlin College	OH	33,140	HC+
Ohio Univ	OH	11,769	C
Okla City Univ	OK	15,810	C
Old Dominion Univ	VA	9,386	C
Pitzer College	CA	33,930	HC
Point Park College	PA	20,290	C
Radford Univ	VA	8,302	C
Randolph-Macon Woman's College	VA	25,820	VC+
Richard Stockton College of New Jersey	NJ	12,165	VC
Roger Williams Univ	RI	29,010	C
Rutgers, The State Univ of New Jersey New Brunswick Campus	NJ	12,709	C
St. Olaf College	MN	25,880	HC
Sam Houston State Univ	TX	6,076	LC
San Diego State Univ	CA	9,716	C+
San Francisco State Univ	CA	7,139	LC
San Jose State Univ	CA	8,187	C
Sarah Lawrence College	NY	37,516	HC
Scripps College	CA	30,400	HC+
Shenandoah Univ	VA	22,550	NC
Simon's Rock College of Bard	MA	32,450	HC
Skidmore College	NY	34,201	VC+
Slippery Rock Univ	PA	9,152	LC
Smith College	MA	33,302	HC+
Southern Illinois Univ Edwardsville	IL	7,869	LC
Southern Methodist Univ	TX	28,349	VC
Southern Utah Univ	UT	7,254	C
Southwest Missouri State Univ	MO	7,600	LC
Southwest Texas State Univ	TX	8,730	VC
SUNY/College at Brockport	NY	10,267	C
SUNY/College at Potsdam	NY	10,519	C
SUNY/College at Purchase	NY	10,587	VC
SUNY/Univ at Buffalo	NY	11,033	VC
Stephen F. Austin State Univ	TX	6,905	C
Stephens College	MO	22,295	C
Swarthmore College	PA	34,538	MC
Sweet Briar College	VA	25,310	VC
Temple Univ	PA	14,124	C
Texas Christian Univ	TX	19,910	C
Texas Tech Univ	TX	8,825	C
Texas Woman's Univ	TX	5,855	LC
Ohio State Univ	OH	10,819	VC
Towson Univ	MD	11,088	VC
Trinity College	CT	34,300	HC
Tulane Univ	LA	34,013	HC+
Univ of Akron	OH	10,530	NC
Univ of Alabama	AL	7,402	C
Univ of Arizona	AZ	8,614	C
Univ of Calif at Irvine	CA	11,756	C
Univ of Calif at Riverside	CA	12,479	C
Univ of Calif at San Diego	CA	11,372	HC
Univ of Calif at Santa Barbara	CA	11,732	VC
Univ of Cincinnati	OH	12,491	LC
Univ of Colo at Boulder	CO	9,255	VC
Univ of Hartford	CT	28,884	C
Univ of Hawaii at Manoa	HI	7,862	VC
Univ of Idaho	ID	7,026	C
Univ of Illinois at Urbana-Champaign	IL	11,316	HC+
Univ of Iowa	IA	8,607	C+
Univ of Kansas	KS	7,232	VC
Univ of Louisiana at Lafayette	LA	5,200	C
Univ of Maryland/Baltimore County	MD	12,190	VC
Univ of Maryland/College Park	MD	11,959	C
Univ of Mass Amherst	MA	10,995	VC
Univ of Mich/Ann Arbor	MI	13,003	HC+
Univ of Minn/Twin Cities	MN	11,123	VC
Univ of Missouri/Kansas City	MO	9,685	VC
Univ of Nebr at Lincoln	NE	8,325	C+
Univ of Nevada/Las Vegas	NV	8,281	VC
Univ of New Mexico	NM	8,026	C
Univ of N Car at Charlotte	NC	7,254	C
Univ of N Car at Greensboro	NC	6,858	C
Univ of North Texas	TX	7,629	C
Univ of Northern Colo	CO	8,082	C+
Univ of Okla	OK	7,616	VC
Univ of Oregon	OR	9,969	C
Univ of South Florida	FL	8,154	C
Univ of Southern Miss	MS	6,155	LC
Univ of Texas at Austin	TX	9,437	HC
Univ of the Arts	PA	24,230	SP
Univ of Utah	UT	7,703	C
Univ of Washington	WA	10,361	VC
Univ of Wisc/Milwaukee	WI	8,907	LC
Univ of Wisc/Stevens Point	WI	7,116	C
Utah State Univ	UT	6,771	C
Virginia Commonwealth Univ	VA	9,030	C
Virginia Intermont College	VA	17,510	C
Washington Univ in St. Louis	MO	34,593	MC
Wayne State Univ	MI	6,720	C
Weber State Univ	UT	6,897	NC
Webster Univ	MO	19,804	VC
Wells College	NY	19,350	VC
Wesleyan Univ	CT	3,405	MC
West Texas A&M Univ	TX	6,538	C
Western Mich Univ	MI	10,016	C
Western Oregon Univ	OR	8,829	C
Winthrop Univ	SC	9,106	C
Wright State Univ	OH	9,141	LC

DANCE EDUCATION

School	ST	$IS	SR
Brenau Univ Women's College	GA	20,100	C
Columbia College	SC	19,050	LC
East Carolina Univ	NC	7,766	C
Huntingdon College	AL	18,400	VC
Jacksonville Univ	FL	21,110	LC
Point Park College	PA	20,290	C
Shenandoah Univ	VA	22,550	NC
Southern Utah Univ	UT	7,254	C
Towson Univ	MD	11,088	VC
Univ of Central Okla	OK	5,205	C
Univ of N Car at Charlotte	NC	7,254	C
Univ of the Arts	PA	24,230	SP

DATA PROCESSING

School	ST	$IS	SR
Chicago State Univ	IL	8,851	C+
East Carolina Univ	NC	7,766	C
St. John's Univ	NY	26,660	C
Youngstown State Univ	OH	9,318	NC

DENTAL HYGIENE

School	ST	$IS	SR
Armstrong Atlantic State Univ	GA	7,084	C
Clayton College and State Univ	GA	2,322	C+
East Tenn State Univ	TN	7,127	C
Eastern Washington Univ	WA	7,972	LC
Idaho State Univ	ID	7,030	C+
Indiana Univ-Purdue Univ Indianapolis	IN	9,473	C
Marquette Univ	WI	24,836	C+
Midwestern State Univ	TX	6,704	NC
Minn State Univ, Mankato	MN	7,296	LC
Northeastern Univ	MA	30,078	VC
Old Dominion Univ	VA	9,386	C
Oregon Inst of Technology	OR	8,718	C
Pennsylvania College of Technology	PA	12,860	NC
Southern Illinois Univ at Carbondale	IL	8,621	C
Tenn State Univ	TN	7,058	VC
Texas Woman's Univ	TX	5,855	LC
Ohio State Univ	OH	10,819	VC
Thomas Edison State College	NJ	2,750	SP
Univ of Bridgeport	CT	23,020	C
Univ of Detroit Mercy	MI	21,620	LC
Univ of Hawaii at Manoa	HI	7,862	VC
Univ of Louisiana at Monroe	LA	5,207	NC
Univ of Maine at Augusta	ME	3,928	C

School	ST	$IS	SR
Univ of Mich/Ann Arbor	MI	13,003	HC+
Univ of Minn/Twin Cities	MN	11,123	VC
Univ of Missouri/Kansas City	MO	9,685	VC
Univ of Nebr at Lincoln	NE	8,325	C+
Univ of New England	ME	24,110	LC
Univ of New Haven	CT	23,860	LC
Univ of New Mexico	NM	8,026	C
Univ of N Car at Chapel Hill	NC	8,789	HC
Univ of Rhode Island	RI	12,414	C
Univ of S Dak	SD	7,036	C
Univ of Washington	WA	10,361	VC
Univ of Wyoming	WY	7,143	LC
Weber State Univ	UT	6,897	NC
West Liberty State College	WV	6,056	LC
West Virginia Univ	WV	8,304	C
Western Kentucky Univ	KY	6,834	C
Youngstown State Univ	OH	9,318	NC

DENTAL LABORATORY TECHNOLOGY

School	ST	$IS	SR
Minot State Univ	ND	5,466	LC

DESIGN

School	ST	$IS	SR
Abilene Christian Univ	TX	16,300	VC
Adelphi Univ	NY	23,320	VC
Alma College	MI	22,586	VC
Andrews Univ	MI	17,696	LC
Art Center College of Design	CA	21,110	SP
Art Inst of Boston at Lesley Univ	MA	23,685	SP
Atlanta College of Art	GA	18,600	SP
Auburn Univ	AL	5,510	C
Becker College	MA	21,230	LC
Bowling Green State Univ	OH	10,794	C
Cal State, Long Beach	CA	7,400	LC
Carnegie Mellon Univ	PA	32,682	MC
Clemson Univ	SC	7,600	C
Cleveland Inst of Art	OH	22,680	SP
Colby-Sawyer College	NH	27,850	LC
College of Santa Fe	NM	20,250	LC
Cornell Univ	NY	34,614	MC
Cornish College of the Arts	WA	16,200	SP
Drexel Univ	PA	27,657	VC
East Carolina Univ	NC	7,766	C
Eastern Mich Univ	MI	9,855	C
Evangel Univ	MO	14,050	C
Fashion Inst of Technology/SUNY	NY	9,504	C+
Frostburg State Univ	MD	9,680	C
Grand Valley State Univ	MI	10,040	C
Harding Univ	AR	13,528	VC
Howard Univ	DC	15,522	LC
Iowa State Univ	IA	8,108	VC
John Brown Univ	AR	15,080	VC
Kansas City Art Inst	MO	25,880	SP
Kent State Univ	OH	11,104	C
Lamar Univ	TX	6,816	LC
Lynn Univ	FL	24,550	C
Marywood Univ	PA	24,639	C
Memphis College of Art	TN	19,460	SP
Minneapolis College of Art and Design	MN	23,560	SP
Nebr Wesleyan Univ	NE	[illegible]	VC
New Jersey City Univ	NJ	9,100	LC
N Car State Univ	NC	8,680	HC
Northern Arizona Univ	AZ	7,398	C
Northern Mich Univ	MI	9,693	C
Okla Christian Univ	OK	16,500	VC
Okla State Univ	OK	7,650	VC
Olivet College	MI	17,410	C
Otis College of Art and Design	CA	20,290	SP
Parsons School of Design	NY	32,242	SP
Purdue Univ/West Lafayette	IN	10,284	VC
Radford Univ	VA	8,302	C
Rhode Island School of Design	RI	30,227	SP
Rivier College	NH	24,215	C
Rochester Inst of Technology	NY	26,232	VC+
Saginaw Valley State Univ	MI	9,465	C
Salem State College	MA	4,481	LC
San Jose State Univ	CA	8,187	C
School of the Art Inst of Chicago	IL	27,800	SP
Seton Hill College	PA	21,875	C
Southern Illinois Univ at Carbondale	IL	8,621	C
Southern Illinois Univ Edwardsville	IL	7,869	LC
Southwest Missouri State Univ	MO	7,600	LC
SUNY/College at Buffalo	NY	8,025	C
SUNY/Univ at New Paltz	NY	9,685	VC
Syracuse Univ	NY	30,710	HC
Texas Southern Univ	TX	6,576	NC
Texas Tech Univ	TX	8,825	C
Texas Woman's Univ	TX	5,855	LC
Univ of Akron	OH	10,530	NC
Univ of Calif at Davis	CA	12,796	VC
Univ of Calif at Los Angeles	CA	13,227	MC
Univ of Cincinnati	OH	12,491	LC
Univ of Dayton	OH	20,400	VC
Univ of Georgia	GA	8,656	VC
Univ of Idaho	ID	7,026	C
Univ of Illinois at Chicago	IL	10,702	VC
Univ of Kansas	KS	7,232	VC
Univ of Mass Amherst	MA	10,995	VC
Univ of Mass Dartmouth	MA	9,852	C
Univ of Mich/Ann Arbor	MI	13,003	HC+
Univ of Miss	MS	7,666	C
Univ of Missouri/Columbia	MO	9,803	HC
Univ of Nebr at Lincoln	NE	8,325	C+
Univ of N Car at Greensboro	NC	6,858	C
Univ of Southern Miss	MS	6,155	LC
Univ of Texas at Austin	TX	9,437	HC
Villa Julie College	MD	16,026	C
Virginia Commonwealth Univ	VA	9,030	C
Washington Univ in St. Louis	MO	34,593	MC
Wayne State Univ	MI	6,720	C

DEVELOPMENTAL PSYCHOLOGY

School	ST	$IS	SR
Bard College	NY	33,912	HC
Bennington College	VT	31,350	VC
Moravian College	PA	27,065	VC
Univ of Kansas	KS	7,232	VC

DIETETICS

School	ST	$IS	SR
Abilene Christian Univ	TX	16,300	VC
Andrews Univ	MI	17,696	LC
Ball State Univ	IN	8,660	C
Baylor Univ	TX	18,298	VC+
Bennett College	NC	11,200	C
Berea College	KY	4,070	VC
Bluffton College	OH	20,644	C
Bowling Green State Univ	OH	10,794	C
Bradley Univ	IL	20,970	VC
Brigham Young Univ	UT	7,840	HC
Cal State, Los Angeles	CA	5,050	C
Central Missouri State Univ	MO	7,920	C
Chicago State Univ	IL	8,851	C+
CUNY/Herbert H. Lehman College	NY	3,320	LC
College of St. Benedict	MN	23,921	VC
College of St. Catherine	MN	22,324	VC
College of the Ozarks	MO	2,650	C+
Concordia College/Moorhead	MN	18,835	C
David Lipscomb Univ	TN	16,158	VC
Dominican Univ	IL	20,800	C
D'Youville College	NY	18,704	C
East Carolina Univ	NC	7,766	C
Eastern Kentucky Univ	KY	6,552	C
Eastern Mich Univ	MI	9,855	C
Florida International Univ	FL	9,486	VC
Florida State Univ	FL	7,835	HC
Fontbonne Univ	MO	18,046	C
Gannon Univ	PA	18,848	C
Harding Univ	AR	13,528	VC
Howard Univ	DC	15,522	LC
Idaho State Univ	ID	7,030	C+
Immaculata College	PA	22,400	LC
Indiana State Univ	IN	8,461	LC
Indiana Univ Bloomington	IN	10,712	C+
Indiana Univ of Pennsylvania	PA	9,133	C
Iowa State Univ	IA	8,108	VC
James Madison Univ	VA	9,552	HC
Kansas State Univ	KS	6,995	C
Keene State College	NH	11,280	C
Louisiana State Univ and A&M College	LA	8,014	VC
Louisiana Tech Univ	LA	6,506	C
Madonna Univ	MI	11,504	VC
Mansfield Univ	PA	9,648	C
Marshall Univ	WV	7,752	LC
Marywood Univ	PA	24,639	C
Mercyhurst College	PA	20,694	C
Messiah College	PA	23,180	VC
Miami Univ	OH	12,885	VC+
Mich State Univ	MI	10,386	VC
Minn State Univ, Mankato	MN	7,296	LC
Mount Mary College	WI	18,024	C
Murray State Univ	KY	6,672	C
Nicholls State Univ	LA	5,290	NC
Northern Arizona Univ	AZ	7,398	C
Northern Illinois Univ	IL	9,545	C
Northern Mich Univ	MI	9,693	C
Oakwood College	AL	14,904	C
Ohio Univ	OH	11,769	C
Olivet Nazarene Univ	IL	18,444	C
Ouachita Baptist Univ	AR	16,460	VC
Point Loma Nazarene Univ	CA	21,380	VC
Prairie View A&M Univ	TX	3,172	LC
Purdue Univ/West Lafayette	IN	10,284	VC
Rochester Inst of Technology	NY	26,232	VC+
St. John's Univ	MN	23,640	VC
St. Joseph College	CT	25,960	LC
San Francisco State Univ	CA	7,139	LC
Seton Hill College	PA	21,875	C
Simmons College	MA	30,418	VC
Southern Illinois Univ at Carbondale	IL	8,621	C
Southwest Missouri State Univ	MO	7,600	LC
SUNY/College at Buffalo	NY	8,025	C
SUNY/College at Oneonta	NY	9,981	C
SUNY/College at Plattsburgh	NY	9,729	C
Stephen F. Austin State Univ	TX	6,905	C
Syracuse Univ	NY	30,710	HC
Texas Christian Univ	TX	19,910	C
Texas Southern Univ	TX	6,576	NC
Texas Tech Univ	TX	8,825	C
Texas Woman's Univ	TX	5,855	LC
Tuskegee Univ	AL	14,600	LC
Univ of Akron	OH	10,530	NC
Univ of Calif at Davis	CA	12,796	VC
Univ of Central Arkansas	AR	6,388	C
Univ of Conn	CT	12,122	VC
Univ of Dayton	OH	20,400	VC
Univ of Delaware	DE	10,824	VC
Univ of Georgia	GA	8,656	VC
Univ of Idaho	ID	7,026	C
Univ of Louisiana at Lafayette	LA	5,200	C
Univ of Maryland/College Park	MD	11,959	C
Univ of Missouri/Columbia	MO	9,803	HC
Univ of Nebr at Kearney	NE	7,048	NC
Univ of Nebr at Lincoln	NE	8,325	C+
Univ of New Haven	CT	23,860	LC
Univ of New Mexico	NM	8,026	C
Univ of N Car at Greensboro	NC	6,858	C
Univ of N Dak	ND	7,067	VC
Univ of Northern Colo	CO	8,082	C+
Univ of Northern Iowa	IA	7,850	C
Univ of Rhode Island	RI	12,414	C
Univ of Tenn at Martin	TN	8,268	C
Univ of Texas at Austin	TX	9,437	HC
Univ of Texas-Pan American	TX	4,823	C
Univ of the Incarnate Word	TX	18,478	C
Univ of Vermont	VT	14,761	C+
Univ of Wisc/Madison	WI	8,262	VC
Univ of Wisc/Stevens Point	WI	7,116	C
Univ of Wisc/Stout	WI	7,744	C
Viterbo Univ	WI	18,043	C
Wayne State Univ	MI	6,720	C
Western Carolina Univ	NC	5,667	C
Western Kentucky Univ	KY	6,834	C
Western Mich Univ	MI	10,016	C
Youngstown State Univ	OH	9,318	NC

DIGITAL ARTS/TECHNOLOGY

School	ST	$IS	SR
Bethel College	IN	17,650	LC
Cal State, Dominguez Hills	CA	5,840	LC
Canisius College	NY	24,696	C+
Cogswell Polytechnical College	CA	14,400	LC
Dominican Univ of Calif	CA	27,948	C
Drexel Univ	PA	27,657	VC
Henry Cogswell College	WA	13,080	SP
Huntingdon College	AL	18,400	VC
Illinois State Univ	IL	9,235	C
Pacific Union College	CA	20,250	VC
Quinnipiac Univ	CT	27,370	C
School of the Art Inst of Chicago	IL	27,800	SP
Univ of Central Florida	FL	8,251	VC
Univ of Denver	CO	28,783	VC
Walla Walla College	WA	20,925	C

DRAFTING AND DESIGN

School	ST	$IS	SR
Appalachian State Univ	NC	6,353	C
Pennsylvania College of Technology	PA	12,860	NC
Southwest Missouri State Univ	MO	7,600	LC
Thomas Edison State College	NJ	2,750	SP
Youngstown State Univ	OH	9,318	NC

DRAFTING AND DESIGN TECHNOLOGY

School	ST	$IS	SR
Alabama A&M Univ	AL	5,100	LC
Baker College of Flint	MI	7,720	NC
Central Missouri State Univ	MO	7,920	C
Montana State Univ-Northern	MT	8,600	NC
Norfolk State Univ	VA	8,382	LC
School of the Art Inst of Chicago	IL	27,800	SP
Texas Southern Univ	TX	6,576	NC
Tri-State Univ-Main Campus	IN	21,200	C
Univ of Houston	TX	8,410	C
Univ of Nebr at Lincoln	NE	8,325	C+
Univ of Rio Grande	OH	8,728	NC
Youngstown State Univ	OH	9,318	NC

DRAMA EDUCATION

School	ST	$IS	SR
Appalachian State Univ	NC	6,353	C
Augustana College	SD	20,760	VC
Baylor Univ	TX	18,298	VC+
Boston Univ	MA	34,358	MC
Catholic Univ of America	DC	29,332	VC
Culver-Stockton College	MO	15,400	LC
Dana College	NE	18,046	C
East Carolina Univ	NC	7,766	C
East Central Univ	OK	4,578	C
East Texas Baptist Univ	TX	12,349	LC
Eastern Mich Univ	MI	9,855	C
Elmhurst College	IL	21,750	C
Grambling State Univ	LA	5,325	NC
Greensboro College	NC	19,080	LC
Greenville College	IL	19,226	LC
Kean Univ	NJ	11,159	C
Mars Hill College	NC	18,600	LC
Minot State Univ	ND	5,466	LC
Missouri Southern State College	MO	6,666	C
Oral Roberts Univ	OK	18,490	C
Palm Beach Atlantic College	FL	23,310	C
Piedmont College	GA	16,900	C
Point Park College	PA	20,290	C
Simpson College	IA	21,200	C+
Southern Utah Univ	UT	7,254	C
Southwestern College	KS	17,656	C
Stephen F. Austin State Univ	TX	6,905	C
Univ of Arizona	AZ	8,614	C
Univ of Maryland/College Park	MD	11,959	C
Univ of N Car at Charlotte	NC	7,254	C
Viterbo Univ	WI	18,043	C
West Texas A&M Univ	TX	6,538	C
Youngstown State Univ	OH	9,318	NC

DRAMATIC ARTS

School	ST	$IS	SR
Abilene Christian Univ	TX	16,300	VC
Adams State College	CO	7,468	C
Adelphi Univ	NY	23,320	VC
Adrian College	MI	19,670	C
Agnes Scott College	GA	24,950	VC
Albany State Univ	GA	5,764	C+
Albertson College of Idaho	ID	23,900	VC
Albertus Magnus College	CT	22,154	C
Albright College	PA	27,642	C
Alfred Univ	NY	27,212	C+
Allegheny College	PA	27,780	VC
Alma College	MI	22,586	VC
American Univ	DC	31,544	VC+
Amherst College	MA	34,340	MC
Anderson Univ	IN	19,430	LC
Angelo State Univ	TX	7,028	C
Appalachian State Univ	NC	6,353	C
Arcadia Univ	PA	26,650	C
Arizona State Univ-Main	AZ	7,726	C
Arkansas State Univ	AR	7,480	C
Armstrong Atlantic State Univ	GA	7,081	C
Ashland Univ	OH	22,182	LC
Auburn Univ	AL	5,510	C
Augsburg College	MN	22,978	C
Augustana College	IL	24,117	VC+
Augustana College	SD	20,760	VC
Averett Univ	VA	17,980	LC
Avila College	MO	17,720	C
Baker Univ	KS	14,780	C+
Baldwin-Wallace College	OH	22,010	VC+
Ball State Univ	IN	8,660	C
Bard College	NY	33,912	HC
Barry Univ	FL	24,100	LC
Barton College	NC	16,834	LC
Bates College	ME	34,100	MC
Baylor Univ	TX	18,298	VC+
Belhaven College	MS	16,040	C+
Beloit College	WI	27,482	HC
Benedictine College	KS	18,485	LC
Bennington College	VT	31,350	VC
Berea College	KY	4,070	VC
Berry College	GA	18,850	C
Bethany College	KS	16,602	C+
Bethel College	IN	17,650	LC
Bethel College	MN	22,740	VC
Birmingham-Southern College	AL	22,960	C
Bloomsburg Univ of Pennsylvania	PA	9,434	C
Blue Mountain College	MS	9,100	LC
Boise State Univ	ID	6,531	LC
Boston College	MA	33,330	MC
Boston Univ	MA	34,358	MC
Bowling Green State Univ	OH	10,794	C
Bradley Univ	IL	20,970	VC
Brandeis Univ	MA	34,481	MC
Brenau Univ Women's College	GA	20,100	C
Bucknell Univ	PA	31,096	HC
Butler Univ	IN	25,580	VC+
Calif Inst of the Arts	CA	27,275	SP

School	ST	$IS	SR
Calif Lutheran Univ	CA	23,500	LC
Calif State Polytechnic Univ, Pomona	CA	8,615	C
Cal State, Bakersfield	CA	6,090	LC
Cal State, Chico	CA	8,598	LC
Cal State, Dominguez Hills	CA	5,840	LC
Cal State, Fresno	CA	7,762	C
Cal State, Fullerton	CA	5,440	LC
Cal State, Hayward	CA	7,400	LC
Cal State, Long Beach	CA	7,400	LC
Cal State, Los Angeles	CA	5,050	C
Cal State, Northridge	CA	7,781	C
Cal State, Sacramento	CA	7,488	C
Cal State, San Bernardino	CA	6,516	C
Cal State, Stanislaus	CA	8,895	C
Calif Univ of Pennsylvania	PA	10,388	C
Cameron Univ	OK	5,560	NC
Campbell Univ	NC	16,599	C
Capital Univ	OH	23,630	C
Cardinal Stritch Univ	WI	17,620	C
Carnegie Mellon Univ	PA	32,682	MC
Carroll College	MT	19,140	C
Carroll College	WI	21,170	C
Case Western Reserve Univ	OH	27,418	C
Castleton State College	VT	10,922	LC
Catawba College	NC	19,620	C
Catholic Univ of America	DC	29,332	VC
Cedar Crest College	PA	25,145	C+
Cedarville Univ	OH	17,553	VC
Centenary College	NJ	22,430	C
Central College	IA	21,206	C
Central Conn State Univ	CT	10,404	C
Central Methodist College	MO	16,460	C
Central Mich Univ	MI	8,355	C
Central Washington Univ	WA	8,985	LC
Centre College	KY	24,000	HC
Chadron State College	NE	6,211	NC
Chapman Univ	CA	30,218	VC
Charleston Southern Univ	SC	17,122	C
Chatham College	PA	25,454	C+
Cheyney Univ of Pennsylvania	PA	9,993	C
Christopher Newport Univ	VA	8,862	VC
CUNY/Brooklyn College	NY	3,403	LC
CUNY/City College	NY	3,309	LC
CUNY/College of Staten Island	NY	3,358	NC
CUNY/Hunter College	NY	5,147	C+
CUNY/Queens College	NY	3,403	VC
CUNY/York College	NY	3,292	NC
Claremont McKenna College	CA	32,700	MC
Clarion Univ of Pennsylvania	PA	11,272	LC
Clark Univ	MA	29,170	HC
Clarke College	IA	20,625	C+
Cleveland State Univ	OH	10,146	NC
Coastal Carolina Univ	SC	9,220	C
Coe College	IA	24,750	VC
Coker College	SC	20,120	C
Colgate Univ	NY	33,480	MC
College of Charleston	SC	8,350	HC
College of St. Benedict	MN	23,921	VC
College of St. Catherine	MN	22,324	VC
College of Santa Fe	NM	20,250	LC
College of the Holy Cross	MA	32,780	MC
College of Wooster	OH	28,350	VC
Colo Christian Univ	CO	17,714	C
Colo College	CO	31,525	HC+
Columbia College Chicago	IL	22,063	LC
Columbia Univ/Barnard College	NY	33,694	MC
Columbia Univ/Columbia College	NY	35,190	MC
Columbia Univ/School of General Studies	NY	35,000	C
Columbus State Univ	GA	7,228	LC
Concordia College/Moorhead	MN	18,835	C
Concordia Univ	CA	22,290	C
Concordia Univ	MN	19,912	C
Concordia Univ	OR	20,500	LC
Concordia Univ Nebr	NE	17,770	C
Conn College	CT	33,585	MC
Cornell College	IA	24,980	VC
Cornell Univ	NY	34,614	MC
Cornish College of the Arts	WA	16,200	SP
Creighton Univ	NE	23,476	VC
Culver-Stockton College	MO	15,400	LC
Cumberland College	KY	14,864	C
Dakota Wesleyan Univ	SD	15,512	C
Dartmouth College	NH	34,458	MC
Davidson College	NC	30,823	MC
Davis and Elkins College	WV	19,270	LC
De Sales Univ	PA	22,610	VC
Denison Univ	OH	29,640	HC
DePaul Univ	IL	23,590	VC
Dickinson College	PA	32,210	VC+
Dillard Univ	LA	16,046	VC
Doane College	NE	17,600	LC
Dominican Univ	IL	20,800	C
Dordt College	IA	18,100	C+
Drake Univ	IA	22,830	VC
Drew Univ/College of Liberal Arts	NJ	32,152	VC
Drury Univ	MO	15,250	VC
Duke Univ	NC	34,396	MC
Duquesne Univ	PA	24,242	C+
Earlham College	IN	27,446	VC+
East Carolina Univ	NC	7,766	C
East Central Univ	OK	4,578	C
East Stroudsburg Univ of Pennsylvania	PA	8,430	LC
East Texas Baptist Univ	TX	12,349	LC
Eastern Illinois Univ	IL	10,101	C
Eastern Kentucky Univ	KY	6,552	C
Eastern Mennonite Univ	VA	20,700	VC
Eastern Mich Univ	MI	9,855	C
Eastern Nazarene College	MA	19,433	LC
Eastern New Mexico Univ	NM	4,113	LC
Eastern Oregon Univ	OR	8,772	C
Eastern Washington Univ	WA	7,972	LC
Eckerd College	FL	25,500	C+
Edinboro Univ of Pennsylvania	PA	9,328	LC
Elmhurst College	IL	21,750	C
Elmira College	NY	31,070	VC+
Elon Univ	NC	19,430	VC
Emerson College	MA	29,978	HC
Emory & Henry College	VA	19,462	C
Emory Univ	GA	33,792	MC
Emporia State Univ	KS	6,198	LC
Eugene Lang College of New School Univ	NY	30,300	C
Eureka College	IL	22,200	C
Evangel Univ	MO	14,050	C
Fairleigh Dickinson Univ/Madison campus	NJ	25,500	C
Fairleigh Dickinson Univ/Teaneck Campus	NJ	24,646	C
Fayetteville State Univ	NC	5,590	LC
Ferrum College	VA	15,990	LC
Fisk Univ	TN	13,700	LC
Five Towns College	NY	18,850	SP
Flagler College	FL	10,550	VC+
Florida A&M Univ	FL	6,948	C
Florida Atlantic Univ	FL	8,832	C
Florida International Univ	FL	9,486	VC
Florida Southern College	FL	19,430	C
Florida State Univ	FL	7,835	HC
Fordham Univ	NY	30,710	VC
Fort Lewis College	CO	7,659	LC
Francis Marion Univ	SC	7,682	C
Franklin and Marshall College	PA	32,410	HC
Franklin College of Indiana	IN	19,905	C
Franklin Pierce College	NH	26,125	LC
Freed-Hardeman Univ	TN	14,290	VC
Frostburg State Univ	MD	9,680	C
Furman Univ	SC	25,492	HC
Gallaudet Univ	DC	16,554	SP
Gannon Univ	PA	18,848	C
George Mason Univ	VA	9,192	C
George Washington Univ	DC	32,170	HC
Georgia College and State Univ	GA	7,344	C
Georgia Southern Univ	GA	6,958	C
Georgia State Univ	GA	7,792	LC
Gettysburg College	PA	32,070	HC
Gonzaga Univ	WA	24,276	HC+
Goshen College	IN	18,950	VC+
Goucher College	MD	30,650	VC+
Graceland Univ	IA	15,845	C
Grambling State Univ	LA	5,325	NC
Grand Canyon Univ	AZ	30,000	LC
Grand Valley State Univ	MI	10,040	C
Greensboro College	NC	19,080	LC
Greenville College	IL	19,226	LC
Grinnell College	IA	28,300	HC+
Guilford College	NC	23,255	C
Gustavus Adolphus College	MN	24,190	VC+
Hamilton College	NY	34,150	HC
Hamline Univ	MN	23,339	C+
Hampshire College	MA	33,881	HC+
Hampton Univ	VA	17,112	C+
Hannibal-LaGrange College	MO	12,530	C
Hanover College	IN	17,560	VC
Harding Univ	AR	13,528	VC
Hartwick College	NY	33,090	C+
Hastings College	NE	17,854	C+
Heidelberg College	OH	23,879	C
Henderson State Univ	AR	6,269	C
Hendrix College	AR	18,463	HC
High Point Univ	NC	20,220	LC
Hillsdale College	MI	20,586	VC+
Hiram College	OH	27,034	VC
Hofstra Univ	NY	23,252	C
Hollins Univ	VA	24,328	VC
Hope College	MI	22,922	C+
Howard Payne Univ	TX	13,834	C+
Howard Univ	DC	15,522	LC
Humboldt State Univ	CA	8,582	C
Huntingdon College	AL	18,400	VC
Idaho State Univ	ID	7,030	C+
Illinois College	IL	16,234	C
Illinois State Univ	IL	9,235	C
Illinois Wesleyan Univ	IL	26,970	HC
Indiana State Univ	IN	8,461	LC
Indiana Univ Bloomington	IN	10,712	C+
Indiana Univ Northwest	IN	3,447	C
Indiana Univ of Pennsylvania	PA	9,133	C
Indiana Univ South Bend	IN	3,515	C
Iona College	NY	26,556	C
Ithaca College	NY	28,719	HC
Jacksonville State Univ	AL	6,568	LC
Jacksonville Univ	FL	21,110	LC
James Madison Univ	VA	9,552	HC
Judson College	IL	18,980	LC
Juilliard School	NY	28,200	SP
Kalamazoo College	MI	26,955	HC+
Kansas State Univ	KS	6,995	C
Kansas Wesleyan Univ	KS	17,400	C+
Kean Univ	NJ	11,159	C
Keene State College	NH	11,280	C
Kennesaw State Univ	GA	2,306	LC
Kent State Univ	OH	11,104	C
Kentucky Wesleyan College	KY	15,800	C
Kenyon College	OH	32,130	HC+
King's College	PA	24,680	C
Knox College	IL	28,230	HC
Kutztown Univ of Pennsylvania	PA	8,907	C
LaGrange College	GA	17,496	C
Lakeland College	WI	17,950	C
Lamar Univ	TX	6,816	LC
Lambuth Univ	TN	14,254	C
Lander Univ	SC	8,618	LC
Langston Univ	OK	2,308	LC
Lawrence Univ	WI	27,711	HC
Le Moyne College	NY	23,840	C
Lees-McRae College	NC	17,106	LC
Lehigh Univ	PA	32,290	MC
Lenoir-Rhyne College	NC	19,186	C
Lewis and Clark College	OR	29,010	VC
Lewis Univ	IL	20,960	C
Lindenwood Univ	MO	17,250	C
Linfield College	OR	25,840	VC
LIU/C.W. Post Campus	NY	25,380	C
Louisiana College	LA	11,516	C
Louisiana State Univ and A&M College	LA	8,014	VC
Loyola Marymount Univ	CA	28,754	HC
Loyola Univ New Orleans	LA	23,506	VC+
Loyola Univ of Chicago	IL	25,992	VC
Luther College	IA	23,300	VC+
Lycoming College	PA	24,780	C
Lynchburg College	VA	23,405	C
Lyon College	AR	16,500	VC
Macalester College	MN	28,814	HC+
MacMurray College	IL	17,790	LC
Maharishi Univ of Management	IA	20,660	VC
Manhattanville College	NY	28,730	VC
Mansfield Univ	PA	9,648	C
Marian College	IN	21,020	C
Marietta College	OH	24,580	C
Marlboro College	VT	26,410	VC+
Marquette Univ	WI	24,836	C+
Mars Hill College	NC	18,600	LC
Mary Baldwin College	VA	23,440	C
Mary Washington College	VA	9,032	VC+
Marymount College/Tarrytown	NY	23,850	C
Marymount Manhattan College	NY	23,195	VC
Maryville College	TN	23,210	VC
Mass Inst of Technology	MA	35,228	MC
McMurry Univ	TX	15,287	C
McNeese State Univ	LA	5,259	LC
Meredith College	NC	17,500	C
Messiah College	PA	23,180	VC
Methodist College	NC	19,526	C
Metropolitan State Univ	MN	2,943	SP
Miami Univ	OH	12,885	VC+
Middle Tenn State Univ	TN	6,994	C
Middlebury College	VT	34,300	MC
Midwestern State Univ	TX	6,704	NC
Millikin Univ	IL	24,415	C+
Mills College	CA	27,950	C
Millsaps College	MS	22,608	VC+
Minn State Univ, Mankato	MN	7,296	LC
Missouri Southern State College	MO	6,666	C
Missouri Valley College	MO	17,400	LC
Monmouth College	IL	21,550	C
Montana State Univ-Billings	MT	7,653	NC
Montana State Univ-Bozeman	MT	8,431	C
Montana State Univ-Northern	MT	8,600	NC
Montclair State Univ	NJ	10,287	LC
Moorhead State Univ	MN	7,000	LC
Moravian College	PA	27,065	VC
Morehead State Univ	KY	6,510	C
Morgan State Univ	MD	10,078	LC
Morningside College	IA	19,124	C
Morris Brown College	GA	15,993	LC
Mount Holyoke College	MA	34,128	HC
Mount Mercy College	IA	19,390	VC
Mount Union College	OH	21,120	C
Muhlenberg College	PA	28,170	HC
Murray State Univ	KY	6,672	C
Muskingum College	OH	18,760	C
Nazareth College of Rochester	NY	22,036	VC
Nebr Wesleyan Univ	NE	18,767	VC
New College of Calif	CA	8,900	NC
New England College	NH	20,706	LC
New Mexico State Univ	NM	7,302	C
New York Univ	NY	35,200	MC
Newberry College	SC	19,670	LC
Niagara Univ	NY	22,250	C+
Norfolk State Univ	VA	8,382	LC
N Car Agricultural and Technical State Univ	NC	6,659	LC
N Car Central Univ	NC	6,418	LC
N Car School of the Arts	NC	7,797	SP
N Car Wesleyan College	NC	15,650	LC
N Dak State Univ	ND	7,004	VC
Northeastern Univ	MA	30,078	VC
Northern Arizona Univ	AZ	7,398	C
Northern Illinois Univ	IL	9,545	C
Northern Kentucky Univ	KY	6,352	NC
Northern Mich Univ	MI	9,693	C
Northwest Missouri State Univ	MO	7,922	LC
Northwestern College	MN	19,816	C+
Northwestern College of Iowa	IA	17,630	C+
Northwestern Okla State Univ	OK	4,542	NC
Northwestern State Univ of Louisiana	LA	5,745	NC
Northwestern Univ	IL	33,615	MC
Notre Dame de Namur Univ	CA	26,932	LC
Oberlin College	OH	33,140	HC+
Occidental College	CA	32,288	HC
Ohio Northern Univ	OH	27,765	VC
Ohio Univ	OH	11,769	C
Ohio Wesleyan Univ	OH	29,670	VC+
Okla Baptist Univ	OK	13,878	VC
Okla City Univ	OK	15,810	C
Okla State Univ	OK	7,650	VC
Old Dominion Univ	VA	9,386	C
Oral Roberts Univ	OK	18,490	C
Oregon State Univ	OR	9,612	VC
Ottawa Univ	KS	11,800	LC
Otterbein College	OH	23,439	C
Ouachita Baptist Univ	AR	16,460	VC
Our Lady of the Lake Univ of San Antonio	TX	17,336	C
Pace Univ	NY	24,200	C
Pacific Univ	OR	24,250	C
Palm Beach Atlantic College	FL	23,310	C
Penn State Univ/Univ Park Campus	PA	11,126	VC
Pepperdine Univ	CA	32,830	VC
Pfeiffer Univ	NC	18,580	C
Piedmont College	GA	16,900	C
Pitzer College	CA	33,930	HC
Point Loma Nazarene Univ	CA	21,380	VC
Point Park College	PA	20,290	C
Pomona College	CA	33,960	MC
Portland State Univ	OR	11,220	C
Prairie View A&M Univ	TX	3,172	LC
Principia College	IL	23,865	C+
Providence College	RI	27,620	HC
Purdue Univ/West Lafayette	IN	10,284	VC
Queens College	NC	17,250	C
Radford Univ	VA	8,302	C
Randolph-Macon Woman's College	VA	25,820	VC+
Regis College	MA	26,750	C
Rhode Island College	RI	8,700	LC
Rhodes College	TN	26,466	HC+
Richard Stockton College of New Jersey	NJ	12,165	VC
Ripon College	WI	24,180	VC+
Roanoke College	VA	24,689	VC
Rockford College	IL	23,930	C
Rockhurst Univ	MO	20,090	C
Rocky Mountain College	MT	18,113	C
Roger Williams Univ	RI	29,010	C
Rollins College	FL	31,223	HC
Roosevelt Univ	IL	20,240	LC
Rowan Univ	NJ	12,365	VC
Russell Sage College	NY	23,674	C+
Rutgers, The State Univ of New Jersey New Brunswick Campus	NJ	12,709	C
Rutgers, The State Univ of New Jersey/CamdenCampus	NJ	6,484	C
Saginaw Valley State Univ	MI	9,465	C
St. Cloud State Univ	MN	7,180	C
St. Edward's Univ	TX	17,846	C
St. John's Univ	MN	23,640	VC
St. Lawrence Univ	NY	32,605	VC
St. Louis Univ	MO	26,590	VC+
St. Mary College	KS	17,298	C
St. Mary's College	IN	24,474	VC
St. Mary's College of Maryland	MD	14,104	HC
St. Mary's Univ of Minn	MN	19,975	C
St. Michael's College	VT	26,935	VC
St. Olaf College	MN	25,880	HC
Salem State College	MA	4,481	LC
Salve Regina Univ	RI	26,460	C
Sam Houston State Univ	TX	6,076	LC
Samford Univ	AL	16,340	VC

ST = STATE $IS = IN-STATE COSTS SR = SELECTOR RATING

DRAWING

DUTCH

EARLY CHILDHOOD EDUCATION

INDEX OF COLLEGE MAJORS

School	ST	$IS	SR
CUNY/Queens College	NY	3,403	VC
Clarion Univ of Pennsylvania	PA	11,272	LC
Clarke College	IA	20,625	C+
Clemson Univ	SC	7,600	C
Cleveland State Univ	OH	10,146	NC
Coastal Carolina Univ	SC	9,220	C
Coker College	SC	20,120	C
Colby-Sawyer College	NH	27,850	LC
College Misericordia	PA	23,380	LC
College of Mount St. Joseph	OH	20,290	C
College of New Jersey	NJ	13,425	HC
College of New Rochelle	NY	20,000	C
College of Notre Dame of Maryland	MD	23,100	LC
College of Our Lady of the Elms	MA	20,644	C
College of St. Catherine	MN	22,324	VC
College of St. Elizabeth	NJ	22,510	C
College of St. Joseph	VT	17,400	NC
College of St. Mary	NE	18,726	C
Columbia College	SC	19,050	LC
Columbia College Chicago	IL	22,063	LC
Columbus State Univ	GA	7,228	LC
Concord College	WV	7,122	C+
Concordia College	AL	9,307	NC
Concordia College	NY	19,200	VC
Concordia Univ	CA	22,290	C
Concordia Univ	MN	19,912	C
Concordia Univ	OR	20,500	LC
Concordia Univ Nebr	NE	17,770	C
Concordia Univ Wisc	WI	16,600	LC
Concordia Univ, River Forest	IL	20,000	LC
Converse College	SC	21,990	VC
Curry College	MA	26,025	LC
Defiance College	OH	19,580	LC
Delaware State Univ	DE	8,104	LC
DePaul Univ	IL	23,590	VC
Dickinson State Univ	ND	5,495	NC
Duquesne Univ	PA	24,242	C+
East Carolina Univ	NC	7,766	C
East Central Univ	OK	4,578	C
East Stroudsburg Univ of Pennsylvania	PA	8,430	LC
Eastern Conn State Univ	CT	10,362	C
Eastern Illinois Univ	IL	10,101	C
Eastern Mennonite Univ	VA	20,700	VC
Eastern Mich Univ	MI	9,855	C
Edgewood College	WI	18,304	C
Edinboro Univ of Pennsylvania	PA	9,328	LC
Edward Waters College	FL	13,124	LC
Elizabethtown College	PA	26,000	VC
Elmhurst College	IL	21,750	C
Erskine College	SC	21,399	VC
Evangel Univ	MO	14,050	C
Fairmont State College	WV	7,010	NC
Fayetteville State Univ	NC	5,590	LC
Fitchburg State College	MA	7,836	C
Florida A&M Univ	FL	6,948	C
Florida Gulf Coast Univ	FL	9,201	C
Florida Southern College	FL	19,430	C
Florida State Univ	FL	7,835	HC
Fontbonne Univ	MO	18,046	C
Fort Valley State Univ	GA	6,014	LC
Framingham State College	MA	7,259	C
Francis Marion Univ	SC	7,682	C
Freed-Hardeman Univ	TN	14,290	VC
Frostburg State Univ	MD	9,680	C
Gallaudet Univ	DC	16,554	SP
Gannon Univ	PA	18,848	C
Georgia College and State Univ	GA	7,344	C
Georgia Southern Univ	GA	6,958	C
Georgia Southwestern State Univ	GA	6,013	C
Georgia State Univ	GA	7,792	LC
Glenville State College	WV	6,588	NC
Gordon College	MA	23,594	VC+
Goshen College	IN	18,950	VC+
Grambling State Univ	LA	5,325	NC
Greensboro College	NC	19,080	LC
Greenville College	IL	19,226	LC
Hannibal-LaGrange College	MO	12,530	C
Harding Univ	AR	13,528	VC
Hardin-Simmons Univ	TX	14,165	C
Harris-Stowe State College	MO	2,310	SP
Hillsdale College	MI	20,586	VC+
Hofstra Univ	NY	23,252	C
Holy Family College	PA	13,710	LC
Hood College	MD	26,020	VC
Houston Baptist Univ	TX	15,300	LC
Howard Univ	DC	15,522	LC
Humphreys College	CA	6,900	NC
Idaho State Univ	ID	7,030	C+
Illinois State Univ	IL	9,235	C
Immaculata College	PA	22,400	LC
Indiana State Univ	IN	8,461	LC
Indiana Univ Bloomington	IN	10,712	C+
Indiana Univ of Pennsylvania	PA	9,133	C
Inter-American Univ of PR/ Aguadilla Campus	PR	3,278	
Inter-American Univ of PR/ Barranquitas Regional College	PR	3,300	LC
Inter-American Univ of PR/ Bayamon Univ College	PR	3,700	
Inter-American Univ of PR/ Fajardo Campus	PR	4,000	
Inter-American Univ of PR/ Metropolitan Campus	PR	4,166	
Inter-American Univ of PR/ Ponce Regional College	PR	3,700	
Inter-American Univ of PR/ San GermÈn	PR	6,390	
Iowa State Univ	IA	8,108	VC
Iowa Wesleyan College	IA	18,840	C
Jacksonville State Univ	AL	6,568	LC
John Brown Univ	AR	15,080	VC
John Carroll Univ	OH	24,140	VC
Judson College	IL	18,980	LC
Juniata College	PA	26,080	VC
Kean Univ	NJ	11,159	C
Keene State College	NH	11,280	C
Kendall College	IL	19,119	LC
Kennesaw State Univ	GA	2,306	LC
Kent State Univ	OH	11,104	C
Kentucky State Univ	KY	6,146	NC
Keystone College	PA	19,066	LC
King's College	PA	24,680	C
Knoxville College	TN	6,200	LC
Kutztown Univ of Pennsylvania	PA	8,907	C
La Roche College	PA	18,854	LC
LaGrange College	GA	17,496	C
Lake Superior State Univ	MI	9,034	LC
Lakeland College	WI	17,950	C
Lamar Univ	TX	6,816	LC
Lander Univ	SC	8,618	LC
Lasell College	MA	24,100	C
Lenoir-Rhyne College	NC	19,186	C
Lesley College	MA	25,325	LC
Lincoln Memorial Univ	TN	12,620	LC
Lincoln Univ	PA	11,198	C+
Lindenwood Univ	MO	17,250	C
Livingstone College	NC	13,360	LC
Lock Haven Univ of Pennsylvania	PA	9,534	C
LIU/Brooklyn Campus	NY	22,290	C
LIU/C.W. Post Campus	NY	25,380	C
Loras College	IA	22,994	C+
Louisiana Tech Univ	LA	6,506	C
Luther College	IA	23,300	VC+
Lyndon State College	VT	11,313	LC
Lynn Univ	FL	24,550	C
Malone College	OH	19,190	C
Manhattan College	NY	25,500	VC
Mansfield Univ	PA	9,648	C
Marian College	IN	21,020	C
Marian College of Fond du Lac	WI	17,935	LC
Martin Univ	IN	8,370	SP
Mary Baldwin College	VA	23,440	C
Marygrove College	MI	16,075	C
Maryville Univ of St. Louis	MO	18,680	C
Marywood Univ	PA	24,639	C
McNeese State Univ	LA	5,259	LC
Mercer Univ	GA	24,130	VC
Mercyhurst College	PA	20,694	C
Messiah College	PA	23,180	VC
Miami Univ	OH	12,885	VC+
Mich State Univ	MI	10,386	VC
Middle Tenn State Univ	TN	6,994	C
Midland Lutheran College	NE	18,600	C
Miles College	AL	7,870	NC
Milligan College	TN	17,550	C
Mills College	CA	27,950	C
Miss Valley State Univ	MS	6,345	C
Missouri Baptist College	MO	15,762	LC
Missouri Southern State College	MO	6,666	C
Missouri Western State College	MO	6,662	NC
Mitchell College	CT	23,950	C
Montana State Univ-Billings	MT	7,653	NC
Moorhead State Univ	MN	7,000	LC
Morris Brown College	GA	15,993	LC
Morris College	SC	9,995	LC
Mount Holyoke College	MA	34,128	HC
Mount Ida College	MA	25,375	LC
Mount Mary College	WI	18,024	C
Mount Union College	OH	21,120	C
Mount Vernon Nazarene College	OH	17,027	C
Murray State Univ	KY	6,672	C
Muskingum College	OH	18,760	C
Naropa Univ	CO	22,416	SP
National-Louis Univ	IL	13,995	NC
Neumann College	PA	22,040	NC
New Jersey City Univ	NJ	9,100	LC
New Mexico Highlands Univ	NM	6,256	NC
New Mexico State Univ	NM	7,302	C
New York Univ	NY	35,200	MC
Newberry College	SC	19,670	LC
Norfolk State Univ	VA	8,382	LC
N Car Agricultural and Technical State Univ	NC	6,659	LC
North Georgia College and State Univ	GA	6,322	C+
North Park Univ	IL	24,030	C
Northeastern Illinois Univ	IL	2,898	NC
Northeastern State Univ	OK	4,704	LC
Northeastern Univ	MA	30,078	VC
Northern Arizona Univ	AZ	7,398	C
Northern Illinois Univ	IL	9,545	C
Northern Mich Univ	MI	9,693	C
Northern State Univ	SD	6,279	LC
Northwest Missouri State Univ	MO	7,922	LC
Northwestern College	MN	19,816	C+
Northwestern College of Iowa	IA	17,630	C+
Northwestern Okla State Univ	OK	4,542	NC
Northwestern State Univ of Louisiana	LA	5,745	NC
Notre Dame College	OH	20,425	C
Nova Southeastern Univ	FL	20,104	LC
Oglethorpe Univ	GA	19,100	LC
Ohio Dominican College	OH	18,100	LC
Ohio Northern Univ	OH	27,765	VC
Ohio Univ	OH	11,769	C
Ohio Wesleyan Univ	OH	29,670	VC+
Okla Baptist Univ	OK	13,878	VC
Okla Christian Univ	OK	16,500	VC
Okla City Univ	OK	15,810	C
Olivet Nazarene Univ	IL	18,444	C
Oral Roberts Univ	OK	18,490	C
Ouachita Baptist Univ	AR	16,460	VC
Our Lady of the Lake Univ of San Antonio	TX	17,336	C
Pace Univ	NY	24,200	C
Pacific Union College	CA	20,250	VC
Paine College	GA	11,896	LC
Palm Beach Atlantic College	FL	23,310	C
Park Univ	MO	9,816	C
Philander Smith College	AR	7,380	NC
Piedmont College	GA	16,900	C
Point Park College	PA	20,290	C
Prescott College	AZ	13,430	C
Purdue Univ/Calumet	IN	6,630	NC
Rhode Island College	RI	8,700	LC
Rider Univ	NJ	27,400	C
Ripon College	WI	24,180	VC+
Rivier College	NH	24,215	C
Rockford College	IL	23,930	C
Roosevelt Univ	IL	20,240	LC
Rowan Univ	NJ	12,365	VC
St. Cloud State Univ	MN	7,180	C
St. John Fisher College	NY	21,800	C
St. John's Univ	NY	26,660	C
St. Joseph's College, New York	NY	9,802	C
St. Mary-of-the-Woods College	IN	21,320	LC
St. Norbert College	WI	23,169	VC
St. Xavier Univ	IL	21,104	C
Salve Regina Univ	RI	26,460	C
Samford Univ	AL	16,340	VC
San Francisco State Univ	CA	7,139	LC
San Jose State Univ	CA	8,187	C
Seton Hill College	PA	21,875	C
Shorter College	GA	15,185	C
Silver Lake College of the Holy Family	WI	15,516	LC
Simmons College	MA	30,418	VC
Sinte Gleska Univ	SD	2,268	NC
Slippery Rock Univ	PA	9,152	LC
Smith College	MA	33,302	HC+
Sojourner-Douglass College	MD	4,170	LC
S Car State Univ	SC	6,586	LC
S Dak State Univ	SD	6,848	C
Southeast Missouri State Univ	MO	8,367	C+
Southeastern Okla State Univ	OK	4,917	C
Southern Conn State Univ	CT	10,310	C
Southern Illinois Univ at Carbondale	IL	8,621	C
Southern Illinois Univ Edwardsville	IL	7,869	LC
Southern Nazarene Univ	OK	14,634	NC
Southern Univ and A&M College	LA	6,365	C+
Southwest Baptist Univ	MO	13,426	LC
Southwest Missouri State Univ	MO	7,600	LC
Southwest State Univ	MN	7,117	LC
Southwest Texas State Univ	TX	8,730	VC
Southwestern College	KS	17,656	C
Spalding Univ	KY	15,196	C
Spring Hill College	AL	23,250	C
Springfield College	MA	24,520	C
SUNY/College at Fredonia	NY	10,125	C
SUNY/College at Potsdam	NY	10,519	C
SUNY/Univ at New Paltz	NY	9,685	VC
State Univ of West Georgia	GA	7,101	C
Stephen F. Austin State Univ	TX	6,905	C
Stephens College	MO	22,295	C
Susquehanna Univ	PA	27,270	VC
Syracuse Univ	NY	30,710	HC
Temple Univ	PA	14,124	C
Tenn State Univ	TN	7,058	VC
Texas A&M Univ at Commerce	TX	7,326	C
Texas Christian Univ	TX	19,910	C
Texas Southern Univ	TX	6,576	NC
Texas Tech Univ	TX	8,825	C
Texas Wesleyan Univ	TX	14,710	C
Thomas Univ	GA	8,770	NC
Toccoa Falls College	GA	14,220	C
Towson Univ	MD	11,088	VC
Trevecca Nazarene Univ	TN	15,752	C
Trinity College	DC	21,370	LC
Troy State Univ	AL	7,696	C
Troy State Univ/Dothan	AL	3,296	C
Tufts Univ	MA	34,874	MC
Tusculum College	TN	17,900	LC
Tuskegee Univ	AL	14,600	LC
Univ of Akron	OH	10,530	NC
Univ of Alabama	AL	7,402	C
Univ of Alabama at Birmingham	AL	10,110	C
Univ of Arizona	AZ	8,614	C
Univ of Arkansas	AR	8,334	VC
Univ of Arkansas at Little Rock	AR	5,637	NC
Univ of Arkansas at Pine Bluff	AR	7,925	C
Univ of Central Arkansas	AR	6,388	C
Univ of Central Florida	FL	8,251	VC
Univ of Central Okla	OK	5,205	C
Univ of Cincinnati	OH	12,491	LC
Univ of Dayton	OH	20,400	VC
Univ of Delaware	DE	10,824	VC
Univ of Detroit Mercy	MI	21,620	LC
Univ of Georgia	GA	8,656	VC
Univ of Hartford	CT	28,884	C
Univ of Idaho	ID	7,026	C
Univ of Illinois at Urbana-Champaign	IL	11,316	HC+
Univ of Kentucky	KY	7,765	C
Univ of Louisiana at Monroe	LA	5,207	NC
Univ of Louisville	KY	7,402	LC
Univ of Maine at Farmington	ME	9,163	C
Univ of Mary	ND	12,900	LC
Univ of Mary Hardin-Baylor	TX	13,929	C
Univ of Maryland/College Park	MD	11,959	C
Univ of Mass Amherst	MA	10,995	VC
Univ of Mich/Dearborn	MI	4,677	VC
Univ of Mich/Flint	MI	4,323	C
Univ of Minn/Twin Cities	MN	11,123	VC
Univ of Missouri/Columbia	MO	9,803	HC
Univ of Missouri/St. Louis	MO	9,966	C
Univ of Mobile	AL	13,620	LC
Univ of Montevallo	AL	7,266	C
Univ of Nebr at Kearney	NE	7,048	NC
Univ of Nebr at Lincoln	NE	8,325	C+
Univ of Nebr at Omaha	NE	6,867	C
Univ of New England	ME	24,110	LC
Univ of New Mexico	NM	8,026	C
Univ of North Alabama	AL	7,016	NC
Univ of N Car at Chapel Hill	NC	8,789	HC
Univ of N Car at Greensboro	NC	6,858	C
Univ of N Car at Wilmington	NC	7,769	C
Univ of N Dak	ND	7,067	VC
Univ of North Texas	TX	7,629	C
Univ of Northern Iowa	IA	7,850	C
Univ of Okla	OK	7,616	VC
Univ of PR/Bayamon Univ College Campus	PR	1,600	
Univ of Rio Grande	OH	8,728	NC
Univ of Science and Arts of Okla	OK	5,245	C
Univ of Scranton	PA	27,964	C+
Univ of Sioux Falls	SD	16,390	C
Univ of South Alabama	AL	6,976	LC
Univ of S Car at Aiken	SC	7,828	LC
Univ of S Car at Columbia	SC	8,748	VC
Univ of S Car at Spartanburg	SC	7,318	C+
Univ of Southern Miss	MS	6,155	LC
Univ of Tenn at Martin	TN	8,268	C
Univ of the District of Columbia	DC	2,844	NC
Univ of the Incarnate Word	TX	18,478	C
Univ of the Ozarks	AR	13,904	C
Univ of Toledo	OH	11,206	NC
Univ of Vermont	VT	14,761	C+
Univ of West Alabama	AL	6,048	C
Univ of West Florida	FL	7,518	C
Univ of Wisc/Stevens Point	WI	7,116	C
Univ of Wisc/Stout	WI	7,192	C
Univ of Wisc/Whitewater	WI	6,937	C
Ursuline College	OH	19,430	LC
Utah State Univ	UT	6,771	C
Valdosta State Univ	GA	6,988	C
Vanderbilt Univ	TN	34,482	MC
Virginia Polytechnic Inst and State Univ	VA	7,652	C
Virginia Union Univ	VA	15,358	LC
Viterbo Univ	WI	18,043	C
Walsh Univ	OH	16,880	C

School	ST	$IS	SR
Washburn Univ of Topeka	KS	6,766	NC
Weber State Univ	UT	6,897	NC
Wesleyan College	GA	17,050	VC
West Chester Univ of Pennsylvania	PA	9,792	VC
West Liberty State College	WV	6,056	LC
West Virginia State College	WV	6,264	NC
Western Carolina Univ	NC	5,667	C
Western Washington Univ	WA	8,624	VC
Westfield State College	MA	8,394	C
Westminster College	UT	17,226	C
Wheelock College	MA	25,520	C
Widener Univ	PA	26,920	C
William Woods Univ	MO	19,390	LC
Wilmington College	DE	6,530	NC
Wilmington College	OH	21,826	C
Winona State Univ	MN	8,570	C
Winthrop Univ	SC	9,106	C
Worcester State College	MA	7,901	LC
Xavier Univ	OH	23,880	C
Xavier Univ of Louisiana	LA	17,000	LC
Youngstown State Univ	OH	9,318	NC

EARLY CHILDHOOD STUDIES

School	ST	$IS	SR
Grace Bible College	MI	12,600	C
Kentucky Wesleyan College	KY	15,800	C
Langston Univ	OK	2,308	LC
Ohio Univ	OH	11,769	C
Plymouth State College	NH	11,024	LC
Southwestern Univ	TX	22,550	HC
Univ of Minn/Duluth	MN	10,436	C
Wayne State College	NE	6,255	NC
Weber State Univ	UT	6,897	NC
Youngstown State Univ	OH	9,318	NC

EARTH SCIENCE

School	ST	$IS	SR
Adams State College	CO	7,468	C
Adelphi Univ	NY	23,320	VC
Adrian College	MI	19,670	C
Albion College	MI	25,224	VC
Augustana College	IL	24,117	VC+
Baldwin-Wallace College	OH	22,010	VC+
Baylor Univ	TX	18,298	VC+
Bemidji State Univ	MN	7,957	C
Bloomsburg Univ of Pennsylvania	PA	9,434	C
Boston Univ	MA	34,358	MC
Bridgewater State College	MA	7,589	C+
Cal State, Long Beach	CA	7,400	LC
Cal State, Monterey Bay	CA	6,250	LC
Cal State, Northridge	CA	7,781	C
Cal State, Stanislaus	CA	8,895	C
Calif Univ of Pennsylvania	PA	10,388	C
Central Conn State Univ	CT	10,404	C
Central Mich Univ	MI	8,355	C
Central Missouri State Univ	MO	7,920	C
Central Washington Univ	WA	8,985	LC
CUNY/City College	NY	3,309	LC
Clarion Univ of Pennsylvania	PA	11,272	LC
Columbia Univ/Columbia College	NY	35,190	MC
Cornell Univ	NY	34,614	MC
Dartmouth College	NH	34,458	MC
DePauw Univ	IN	28,000	HC
Dickinson State Univ	ND	5,495	NC
East Stroudsburg Univ of Pennsylvania	PA	8,430	LC
Eastern Mich Univ	MI	9,855	C
Edinboro Univ of Pennsylvania	PA	9,328	LC
Emporia State Univ	KS	6,198	LC
Fitchburg State College	MA	7,836	C
George Mason Univ	VA	9,192	C
Georgia Inst of Technology	GA	9,028	HC+
Indiana Univ Bloomington	IN	10,712	C+
Indiana Univ-Purdue Univ Fort Wayne	IN	3,166	LC
Iowa State Univ	IA	8,108	VC
Johns Hopkins Univ	MD	35,226	MC
Kean Univ	NJ	11,159	C
Kent State Univ	OH	11,104	C
Lock Haven Univ of Pennsylvania	PA	9,534	C
Mass Inst of Technology	MA	35,228	MC
Mercyhurst College	PA	20,694	C
Mich State Univ	MI	10,386	VC
Millersville Univ of Pennsylvania	PA	10,153	VC
Minn State Univ, Mankato	MN	7,296	LC
Minot State Univ	ND	5,466	LC
Montana State Univ-Bozeman	MT	8,431	C
Morehead State Univ	KY	6,510	C
Murray State Univ	KY	6,672	C
Muskingum College	OH	18,760	C
National Univ	CA	7,755	SP
New Jersey City Univ	NJ	9,100	LC
N Car State Univ	NC	8,680	HC
N Dak State Univ	ND	7,004	VC
Northeastern Illinois Univ	IL	2,898	NC
Northern Mich Univ	MI	9,693	C
Northland College	WI	21,435	C+
Northwest Missouri State Univ	MO	7,922	LC
Ohio Univ	OH	11,769	C
Ohio Wesleyan Univ	OH	29,670	VC+
Penn State Univ/Univ Park Campus	PA	11,126	VC
Prescott College	AZ	13,430	C
Purdue Univ/West Lafayette	IN	10,284	VC
Rocky Mountain College	MT	18,113	C
St. Cloud State Univ	MN	7,180	C
St. Louis Univ	MO	26,590	VC+
St. Mary's Univ of San Antonio	TX	19,735	C
Salem State College	MA	4,481	LC
Shippensburg Univ of Pennsylvania	PA	9,652	C
Slippery Rock Univ	PA	9,152	LC
Southeast Missouri State Univ	MO	8,367	C+
Southern Conn State Univ	CT	10,310	C
Southwest Missouri State Univ	MO	7,600	LC
Stanford Univ	CA	34,222	MC
SUNY/College at Brockport	NY	10,267	C
SUNY/College at Buffalo	NY	8,025	C
SUNY/College at Fredonia	NY	10,125	C
SUNY/College at Oneonta	NY	9,981	C
SUNY/Univ at Albany	NY	10,997	VC
SUNY/Univ at Stony Brook	NY	10,998	VC
State Univ of West Georgia	GA	7,101	C
Stephen F. Austin State Univ	TX	6,905	C
Tarleton State Univ	TX	7,160	C
Temple Univ	PA	14,124	C
Texas A&M Univ at Commerce	TX	7,326	C
Texas Wesleyan Univ	TX	14,710	C
Towson Univ	MD	11,088	VC
Tulane Univ	LA	34,013	HC+
Univ of Akron	OH	10,530	NC
Univ of Alaska Fairbanks	AK	8,265	NC
Univ of Arizona	AZ	8,614	C
Univ of Arkansas	AR	8,334	VC
Univ of Calif at Berkeley	CA	14,134	MC
Univ of Calif at Los Angeles	CA	13,227	MC
Univ of Calif at San Diego	CA	11,372	HC
Univ of Calif at Santa Cruz	CA	13,655	VC
Univ of Houston	TX	8,410	C
Univ of Indianapolis	IN	20,840	C
Univ of Mass Amherst	MA	10,995	VC
Univ of Mich/Flint	MI	4,323	C
Univ of Minn/Duluth	MN	10,436	C
Univ of Missouri/Kansas City	MO	9,685	VC
Univ of Nevada/Las Vegas	NV	8,281	VC
Univ of New Hampshire	NH	13,207	C
Univ of New Mexico	NM	8,026	C
Univ of N Car at Charlotte	NC	7,254	C
Univ of N Car at Greensboro	NC	6,858	C
Univ of Northern Colo	CO	8,082	C+
Univ of Northern Iowa	IA	7,850	C
Univ of S Dak	SD	7,036	C
Univ of Texas at El Paso	TX	5,076	LC
Univ of Wisc/Green Bay	WI	7,148	C
Utah State Univ	UT	6,771	C
Virginia Wesleyan College	VA	22,350	LC
Washington Univ in St. Louis	MO	34,593	MC
Weber State Univ	UT	6,897	NC
Wesleyan Univ	CT	3,405	MC
West Chester Univ of Pennsylvania	PA	9,792	VC
Western Conn State Univ	CT	10,074	C
Western Mich Univ	MI	10,016	C
Western Oregon Univ	OR	8,829	C
Whittier College	CA	29,108	C
Wilkes Univ	PA	25,800	C
Winona State Univ	MN	8,570	C
Wittenberg Univ	OH	28,766	VC
Youngstown State Univ	OH	9,318	NC

EAST ASIAN LANGUAGES AND LITERATURE

School	ST	$IS	SR
Bates College	ME	34,100	MC
Beloit College	WI	27,482	HC
Indiana Univ Bloomington	IN	10,712	C+
Rutgers, The State Univ of New Jersey New Brunswick Campus	NJ	12,709	C
Smith College	MA	33,302	HC+
Univ of Kansas	KS	7,232	VC
Washington Univ in St. Louis	MO	34,593	MC

EAST ASIAN STUDIES

School	ST	$IS	SR
Augsburg College	MN	22,978	C
Boston Univ	MA	34,358	MC
Brown Univ	RI	34,973	MC
Bryn Mawr College	PA	33,580	HC+
Bucknell Univ	PA	31,096	HC
CUNY/Queens College	NY	3,403	VC
Colby College	ME	34,290	MC
Columbia Univ/Barnard College	NY	33,694	MC
Columbia Univ/Columbia College	NY	35,190	MC
Columbia Univ/School of General Studies	NY	35,000	C
Conn College	CT	33,585	MC
Denison Univ	OH	29,640	HC
DePauw Univ	IN	28,000	HC
Dickinson College	PA	32,210	VC+
Emory & Henry College	VA	19,462	C
George Washington Univ	DC	32,170	HC
Hamline Univ	MN	23,339	C+
Haverford College	PA	34,300	MC
Indiana Univ Bloomington	IN	10,712	C+
Johns Hopkins Univ	MD	35,226	MC
Lawrence Univ	WI	27,711	HC
Lewis and Clark College	OR	29,010	VC
Mass Inst of Technology	MA	35,228	MC
Middlebury College	VT	34,300	MC
Naropa Univ	CO	22,416	SP
New York Univ	NY	35,200	MC
Oakland Univ	MI	9,418	C
Oberlin College	OH	33,140	HC+
Penn State Univ/Univ Park Campus	PA	11,126	VC
Princeton Univ	NJ	35,072	MC
Simmons College	MA	30,418	VC
Simon's Rock College of Bard	MA	32,450	HC
Stanford Univ	CA	34,222	MC
Union College	NY	32,646	HC
Univ of Arizona	AZ	8,614	C
Univ of Calif at Davis	CA	12,796	VC
Univ of Calif at Irvine	CA	11,756	C
Univ of Calif at Los Angeles	CA	13,227	MC
Univ of Florida	FL	7,874	HC
Univ of Illinois at Urbana-Champaign	IL	11,316	HC+
Univ of Minn/Twin Cities	MN	11,123	VC
Univ of N Car at Chapel Hill	NC	8,789	HC
Univ of Pennsylvania	PA	34,614	MC
Univ of St. Thomas	MN	24,044	VC
Ursinus College	PA	31,350	VC
Vanderbilt Univ	TN	34,482	MC
Washington and Lee Univ	VA	25,095	MC
Washington Univ in St. Louis	MO	34,593	MC
Western Washington Univ	WA	8,624	VC
Wittenberg Univ	OH	28,766	VC
Yale Univ	CT	34,030	MC

EASTERN EUROPEAN STUDIES

School	ST	$IS	SR
Bard College	NY	33,912	HC
Florida State Univ	FL	7,835	HC
Kent State Univ	OH	11,104	C
Simon's Rock College of Bard	MA	32,450	HC
SUNY/Univ at Albany	NY	10,997	VC
Univ of Conn	CT	12,122	VC
Univ of Kansas	KS	7,232	VC
Univ of Texas at Austin	TX	9,437	HC
Washington Univ in St Louis	MO	34,593	MC
Yale Univ	CT	34,030	MC

ECOLOGY

School	ST	$IS	SR
Adams State College	CO	7,468	C
Appalachian State Univ	NC	6,353	C
Bard College	NY	33,912	HC
Beloit College	WI	27,482	HC
Bennington College	VT	31,350	VC
Boston Univ	MA	34,358	MC
Calif Polytechnic State Univ	CA	8,747	VC
Cal State, Long Beach	CA	7,400	LC
Defiance College	OH	19,580	LC
Florida State Univ	FL	7,835	HC
Hampshire College	MA	33,881	HC+
Idaho State Univ	ID	7,030	C+
Iona College	NY	26,556	C
Johns Hopkins Univ	MD	35,226	MC
Juniata College	PA	26,080	VC
Mich Tech Univ	MI	11,088	VC
Missouri Southern State College	MO	6,666	C
Montana State Univ-Northern	MT	8,600	NC
Morehead State Univ	KY	6,510	C
Northern Mich Univ	MI	9,693	C
Penn State Univ/Univ Park Campus	PA	11,126	VC
Purdue Univ/West Lafayette	IN	10,284	VC
Rutgers, The State Univ of New Jersey New Brunswick Campus	NJ	12,709	C
St. John's Univ	NY	26,660	C
San Francisco State Univ	CA	7,139	LC
Seattle Univ	WA	24,183	VC
Simon's Rock College of Bard	MA	32,450	HC
SUNY/College of Environmental Science and Forestry	NY	12,446	VC
Tulane Univ	LA	34,013	HC+
Unity College	ME	19,845	LC
Univ of Arizona	AZ	8,614	C
Univ of Calif at Davis	CA	12,796	VC
Univ of Calif at Irvine	CA	11,756	C
Univ of Calif at San Diego	CA	11,372	HC
Univ of Georgia	GA	8,656	VC
Univ of Mich/Ann Arbor	MI	13,003	HC+
Univ of Mich/Flint	MI	4,323	C
Univ of Minn/Twin Cities	MN	11,123	VC
Univ of New Hampshire	NH	13,207	C
Univ of Pittsburgh at Pittsburgh	PA	13,592	HC
Univ of Rochester	NY	32,979	HC
Univ of Vermont	VT	14,761	C+

ECONOMICS

School	ST	$IS	SR
Adelphi Univ	NY	23,320	VC
Adrian College	MI	19,670	C
Agnes Scott College	GA	24,950	VC
Alabama A&M Univ	AL	5,100	LC
Albertson College of Idaho	ID	23,900	VC
Albertus Magnus College	CT	22,154	C
Albion College	MI	25,224	VC
Albright College	PA	27,642	C
Alcorn State Univ	MS	5,594	LC
Alfred Univ	NY	27,212	C+
Allegheny College	PA	27,780	VC
Alma College	MI	22,586	VC
American International College	MA	22,268	LC
American Univ	DC	31,544	VC+
Amherst College	MA	34,340	MC
Anderson Univ	IN	19,430	LC
Andrews Univ	MI	17,696	LC
Appalachian State Univ	NC	6,353	C
Aquinas College	MI	20,052	C+
Arizona State Univ-Main	AZ	7,726	C
Arkansas State Univ	AR	7,480	C
Arkansas Tech Univ	AR	6,256	C
Armstrong Atlantic State Univ	GA	7,084	C
Ashland Univ	OH	22,182	LC
Assumption College	MA	26,320	C
Auburn Univ	AL	5,510	C
Augsburg College	MN	22,978	C
Augustana College	IL	24,117	VC+
Augustana College	SD	20,760	VC
Austin College	TX	22,150	VC+
Austin Peay State Univ	TN	5,814	LC
Baker Univ	KS	14,780	C+
Baldwin-Wallace College	OH	22,010	VC+
Ball State Univ	IN	8,660	C
Bard College	NY	33,912	HC
Barry Univ	FL	24,100	LC
Bates College	ME	34,100	MC
Baylor Univ	TX	18,298	VC+
Bellarmine Univ	KY	20,440	VC
Belmont Abbey College	NC	19,630	LC
Belmont Univ	TN	19,066	VC
Beloit College	WI	27,482	HC
Bemidji State Univ	MN	7,957	C
Benedictine College	KS	18,485	LC
Benedictine Univ	IL	21,330	C
Berea College	KY	4,070	VC
Berry College	GA	18,850	C
Bethany College	KS	16,602	C+
Bethany College	WV	18,566	C
Bethel College	MN	22,740	VC
Birmingham-Southern College	AL	22,960	C
Bloomsburg Univ of Pennsylvania	PA	9,434	C
Bluffton College	OH	20,644	C
Boise State Univ	ID	6,531	LC
Boston College	MA	33,330	MC
Boston Univ	MA	34,358	MC
Bowdoin College	ME	32,650	MC
Bowling Green State Univ	OH	10,794	C
Bradley Univ	IL	20,970	VC
Brandeis Univ	MA	34,481	MC
Bridgewater College	VA	22,950	C
Bridgewater State College	MA	7,589	C+
Brigham Young Univ	UT	7,840	HC
Brown Univ	RI	34,973	MC
Bryant College	RI	25,980	VC
Bryn Mawr College	PA	33,580	HC+
Bucknell Univ	PA	31,096	HC
Buena Vista Univ	IA	22,828	C
Butler Univ	IN	25,580	VC+
Calif Inst of Technology	CA	27,663	MC
Calif Lutheran Univ	CA	23,500	LC
Calif Polytechnic State Univ	CA	8,747	VC
Calif State Polytechnic Univ, Pomona	CA	8,615	C
Cal State, Bakersfield	CA	6,090	LC
Cal State, Chico	CA	8,598	LC
Cal State, Dominguez Hills	CA	5,840	LC
Cal State, Fresno	CA	7,762	C
Cal State, Fullerton	CA	5,440	LC
Cal State, Hayward	CA	7,400	LC
Cal State, Long Beach	CA	7,400	LC

School	ST	$IS	SR
Cal State, Los Angeles	CA	5,050	C
Cal State, Northridge	CA	7,781	C
Cal State, Sacramento	CA	7,488	C
Cal State, San Bernardino	CA	6,516	C
Cal State, San Marcos	CA	1,736	LC
Cal State, Stanislaus	CA	8,895	C
Calif Univ of Pennsylvania	PA	10,388	C
Calvin College	MI	20,050	NC
Campbell Univ	NC	16,599	C
Campbellsville Univ	KY	14,340	C
Canisius College	NY	24,696	C+
Capital Univ	OH	23,630	C
Carleton College	MN	30,780	MC
Carnegie Mellon Univ	PA	32,682	MC
Carson-Newman College	TN	16,490	C
Carthage College	WI	23,670	C
Case Western Reserve Univ	OH	27,418	C
Catholic Univ of America	DC	29,332	VC
Centenary College of Louisiana	LA	21,600	C+
Central College	IA	21,206	C
Central Conn State Univ	CT	10,404	C
Central Methodist College	MO	16,460	C
Central Mich Univ	MI	8,355	C
Central Missouri State Univ	MO	7,920	C
Central State Univ	OH	8,922	C+
Central Washington Univ	WA	8,985	LC
Centre College	KY	24,000	HC
Chapman Univ	CA	30,218	VC
Charleston Southern Univ	SC	17,122	C
Chatham College	PA	25,454	C+
Chestnut Hill College	PA	24,790	LC
Cheyney Univ of Pennsylvania	PA	9,993	C
Chicago State Univ	IL	8,851	C+
Christopher Newport Univ	VA	8,862	VC
CUNY/Baruch College	NY	3,275	VC+
CUNY/Brooklyn College	NY	3,403	LC
CUNY/City College	NY	3,309	LC
CUNY/College of Staten Island	NY	3,358	NC
CUNY/Herbert H. Lehman College	NY	3,320	LC
CUNY/Hunter College	NY	5,147	C+
CUNY/Queens College	NY	3,403	VC
CUNY/York College	NY	3,292	NC
Claremont McKenna College	CA	32,700	MC
Clarion Univ of Pennsylvania	PA	11,272	LC
Clark Atlanta Univ	GA	17,174	C
Clark Univ	MA	29,170	HC
Clarkson Univ	NY	29,884	VC
Clemson Univ	SC	7,600	C
Cleveland State Univ	OH	10,146	NC
Coe College	IA	24,750	VC
Colby College	ME	34,290	MC
Colgate Univ	NY	33,480	MC
College of Charleston	SC	8,350	HC
College of Mount St. Vincent	NY	24,230	C
College of New Jersey	NJ	13,425	HC
College of New Rochelle	NY	20,000	C
College of Notre Dame of Maryland	MD	23,100	LC
College of St. Benedict	MN	23,921	VC
College of St. Catherine	MN	22,324	VC
College of St. Elizabeth	NJ	22,510	C
College of St. Scholastica	MN	22,378	C+
College of the Holy Cross	MA	32,780	MC
College of William and Mary	VA	10,002	MC
College of Wooster	OH	28,350	VC
Colo College	CO	31,525	HC+
Colo School of Mines	CO	11,578	HC
Colo State Univ	CO	9,672	C
Columbia Univ/Barnard College	NY	33,694	MC
Columbia Univ/Columbia College	NY	35,190	MC
Columbia Univ/School of General Studies	NY	35,000	C
Concordia College/Moorhead	MN	18,835	C
Conn College	CT	33,585	MC
Converse College	SC	21,990	VC
Cornell College	IA	24,980	VC
Cornell Univ	NY	34,614	MC
Covenant College	GA	21,970	C+
Creighton Univ	NE	23,476	VC
Dartmouth College	NH	34,458	MC
David N. Myers College	OH	9,475	C
Davidson College	NC	30,823	MC
Davis and Elkins College	WV	19,270	LC
Delaware State Univ	DE	8,104	LC
Denison Univ	OH	29,640	HC
DePaul Univ	IL	23,590	VC
DePauw Univ	IN	28,000	HC
Dickinson College	PA	32,210	VC+
Dillard Univ	LA	16,046	VC
Doane College	NE	17,600	LC
Dowling College	NY	20,281	LC
Drake Univ	IA	22,830	VC
Drew Univ/College of Liberal Arts	NJ	32,152	VC
Drury Univ	MO	15,250	VC
Duke Univ	NC	34,396	MC
Earlham College	IN	27,446	VC+
East Carolina Univ	NC	7,766	C
East Stroudsburg Univ of Pennsylvania	PA	8,430	LC
East Tenn State Univ	TN	7,127	C
Eastern College	PA	19,641	LC
Eastern Conn State Univ	CT	10,362	C
Eastern Illinois Univ	IL	10,101	C
Eastern Kentucky Univ	KY	6,552	C
Eastern Mennonite Univ	VA	20,700	VC
Eastern Mich Univ	MI	9,855	C
Eastern New Mexico Univ	NM	4,113	LC
Eastern Washington Univ	WA	7,972	LC
Eckerd College	FL	25,500	C+
Edgewood College	WI	18,304	C
Edinboro Univ of Pennsylvania	PA	9,328	LC
Elizabethtown College	PA	26,000	VC
Elmhurst College	IL	21,750	C
Elon Univ	NC	19,430	VC
Emory & Henry College	VA	19,462	C
Emory Univ	GA	33,792	MC
Emporia State Univ	KS	6,198	LC
Eugene Lang College of New School Univ	NY	30,300	C
Fairfield Univ	CT	30,885	HC
Fairleigh Dickinson Univ/Madison campus	NJ	25,500	C
Fairleigh Dickinson Univ/Teaneck Campus	NJ	24,646	C
Fayetteville State Univ	NC	5,590	LC
Fisk Univ	TN	13,700	LC
Fitchburg State College	MA	7,836	C
Florida A&M Univ	FL	6,948	C
Florida Atlantic Univ	FL	8,832	C
Florida International Univ	FL	9,486	VC
Florida Southern College	FL	19,430	C
Florida State Univ	FL	7,835	HC
Fordham Univ	NY	30,710	VC
Fort Hays State Univ	KS	6,294	LC
Fort Lewis College	CO	7,659	LC
Fort Valley State Univ	GA	6,014	LC
Framingham State College	MA	7,259	C
Francis Marion Univ	SC	7,682	C
Franciscan Univ of Steubenville	OH	19,100	C+
Franklin and Marshall College	PA	32,410	HC
Franklin College of Indiana	IN	19,905	C
Frostburg State Univ	MD	9,680	C
Furman Univ	SC	25,492	HC
Gallaudet Univ	DC	16,554	SP
George Fox Univ	OR	24,095	VC
George Mason Univ	VA	9,192	C
George Washington Univ	DC	32,170	HC
Georgetown Univ	DC	34,847	MC
Georgia College and State Univ	GA	7,344	C
Georgia Inst of Technology	GA	9,028	HC+
Georgia Southern Univ	GA	6,958	C
Georgia State Univ	GA	7,792	LC
Gettysburg College	PA	32,070	HC
Gonzaga Univ	WA	24,276	HC+
Gordon College	MA	23,594	VC+
Goshen College	IN	18,950	VC+
Goucher College	MD	30,650	VC+
Graceland Univ	IA	15,845	C
Grand Canyon Univ	AZ	30,000	LC
Grand Valley State Univ	MI	10,040	C
Grinnell College	IA	28,300	HC+
Grove City College	PA	12,280	MC
Guilford College	NC	23,255	C
Gustavus Adolphus College	MN	24,190	VC+
Hamilton College	NY	34,150	HC
Hamline Univ	MN	23,339	C+
Hampden-Sydney College	VA	24,871	C
Hampshire College	MA	33,881	HC+
Hampton Univ	VA	17,112	C+
Hanover College	IN	17,560	VC
Harding Univ	AR	13,528	VC
Hartwick College	NY	33,090	C+
Harvard Univ/Harvard College	MA	34,269	MC
Hastings College	NE	17,854	C+
Haverford College	PA	34,300	MC
Hawaii Pacific Univ	HI	17,790	C
Heidelberg College	OH	23,879	C
Hillsdale College	MI	20,586	VC+
Hiram College	OH	27,034	VC
Hobart and William Smith Colleges	NY	33,195	VC
Hofstra Univ	NY	23,252	C
Hollins Univ	VA	24,328	VC
Holy Family College	PA	13,710	LC
Hood College	MD	26,020	VC
Hope College	MI	22,922	C+
Howard Univ	DC	15,522	LC
Idaho State Univ	ID	7,030	C+
Illinois College	IL	16,234	C
Illinois State Univ	IL	9,235	C
Illinois Wesleyan Univ	IL	26,970	HC
Immaculata College	PA	22,400	LC
Indiana State Univ	IN	8,461	LC
Indiana Univ Bloomington	IN	10,712	C+
Indiana Univ Northwest	IN	3,447	C
Indiana Univ of Pennsylvania	PA	9,133	C
Indiana Univ South Bend	IN	3,515	C
Indiana Univ Southeast	IN	3,459	C
Indiana Univ-Purdue Univ Fort Wayne	IN	3,166	LC
Indiana Univ-Purdue Univ Indianapolis	IN	9,473	C
Indiana Wesleyan Univ	IN	17,680	C
Inter-American Univ of PR/San GermÈn	PR	6,390	
Iona College	NY	26,556	C
Iowa State Univ	IA	8,108	VC
Ithaca College	NY	28,719	HC
Jackson State Univ	MS	6,776	LC
Jacksonville State Univ	AL	6,568	LC
Jacksonville Univ	FL	21,110	LC
James Madison Univ	VA	9,552	HC
John Carroll Univ	OH	24,140	VC
Johns Hopkins Univ	MD	35,226	MC
Johnson C. Smith Univ	NC	16,560	C+
Juniata College	PA	26,080	VC
Kansas State Univ	KS	6,995	C
Kean Univ	NJ	11,159	C
Kent State Univ	OH	11,104	C
Kentucky State Univ	KY	6,146	NC
Kenyon College	OH	32,130	HC+
King's College	PA	24,680	C
Knox College	IL	28,230	HC
La Salle Univ	PA	27,890	C
Lafayette College	PA	32,655	MC
Lake Forest College	IL	27,460	VC
Lake Superior State Univ	MI	9,034	LC
Lakeland College	WI	17,950	C
Lamar Univ	TX	6,816	LC
Langston Univ	OK	2,308	LC
Lawrence Univ	WI	27,711	HC
Le Moyne College	NY	23,840	C
Lebanon Valley College of Pennsylvania	PA	25,700	VC
Lehigh Univ	PA	32,290	MC
Lenoir-Rhyne College	NC	19,186	C
Lewis and Clark College	OR	29,010	VC
Lewis Univ	IL	20,960	C
Limestone College	SC	16,900	C
Lincoln Univ	MO	7,158	NC
Lincoln Univ	PA	11,198	C+
Linfield College	OR	25,840	VC
Lock Haven Univ of Pennsylvania	PA	9,534	C
LIU/Brooklyn Campus	NY	22,290	C
LIU/C.W. Post Campus	NY	25,380	C
Longwood College	VA	8,950	C
Loras College	IA	22,994	C+
Louisiana College	LA	11,516	C
Louisiana State Univ and A&M College	LA	8,014	VC
Louisiana State Univ in Shreveport	LA	2,480	NC
Loyola College in Maryland	MD	30,900	HC
Loyola Marymount Univ	CA	28,754	HC
Loyola Univ New Orleans	LA	23,506	VC+
Loyola Univ of Chicago	IL	25,992	VC
Luther College	IA	23,300	VC+
Lycoming College	PA	24,780	C
Lynchburg College	VA	23,405	C
Lyon College	AR	16,500	VC
Macalester College	MN	28,814	HC+
Manchester College	IN	22,010	C
Manhattan College	NY	25,500	VC
Manhattanville College	NY	28,730	VC
Mansfield Univ	PA	9,648	C
Marian College	IN	21,020	C
Marian College of Fond du Lac	WI	17,935	LC
Marietta College	OH	24,580	C
Marist College	NY	24,756	VC
Marlboro College	VT	26,410	VC+
Marquette Univ	WI	24,836	C+
Marshall Univ	WV	7,752	LC
Mary Baldwin College	VA	23,440	C
Mary Washington College	VA	9,032	VC+
Marymount College/Tarrytown	NY	23,850	C
Marymount Univ	VA	21,560	LC
Maryville College	TN	23,210	VC
Mass Inst of Technology	MA	35,228	MC
McKendree College	IL	18,300	C
McMurry Univ	TX	15,287	C
McNeese State Univ	LA	5,259	LC
Mercer Univ	GA	24,130	VC
Meredith College	NC	17,500	C
Merrimack College	MA	25,725	VC
Messiah College	PA	23,180	VC
Methodist College	NC	19,526	C
Metropolitan State College of Denver	CO	2,338	LC
Metropolitan State Univ	MN	2,943	SP
Miami Univ	OH	12,885	VC+
Mich State Univ	MI	10,386	VC
Middle Tenn State Univ	TN	6,994	C
Middlebury College	VT	34,300	MC
Midland Lutheran College	NE	18,600	C
Midwestern State Univ	TX	6,704	NC
Millersville Univ of Pennsylvania	PA	10,153	VC
Millikin Univ	IL	24,415	C+
Mills College	CA	27,950	C
Millsaps College	MS	22,608	VC+
Minn State Univ, Mankato	MN	7,296	LC
Minot State Univ	ND	5,466	LC
Miss State Univ	MS	7,853	C
Missouri Southern State College	MO	6,666	C
Missouri Valley College	MO	17,400	LC
Missouri Western State College	MO	6,662	NC
Montana State Univ-Bozeman	MT	8,431	C
Montclair State Univ	NJ	10,287	LC
Moorhead State Univ	MN	7,000	LC
Moravian College	PA	27,065	VC
Morehouse College	GA	19,814	C
Morgan State Univ	MD	10,078	LC
Morris Brown College	GA	15,993	LC
Mount Holyoke College	MA	34,128	HC
Mount St. Mary's College	MD	25,740	C
Mount Union College	OH	21,120	C
Muhlenberg College	PA	28,170	HC
Murray State Univ	KY	6,672	C
Muskingum College	OH	18,760	C
Nazareth College of Rochester	NY	22,036	VC
Nebr Wesleyan Univ	NE	18,767	VC
New College of Florida	FL	8,130	HC+
New Jersey City Univ	NJ	9,100	LC
New Mexico State Univ	NM	7,302	C
New York Univ	NY	35,200	MC
Newberry College	SC	19,670	LC
Nichols College	MA	24,610	LC
Norfolk State Univ	VA	8,382	LC
N Car Agricultural and Technical State Univ	NC	6,659	LC
N Car State Univ	NC	8,680	HC
North Central College	IL	22,944	C+
N Dak State Univ	ND	7,004	VC
North Park Univ	IL	24,030	C
Northeastern Illinois Univ	IL	2,898	NC
Northeastern Univ	MA	30,078	VC
Northern Arizona Univ	AZ	7,398	C
Northern Illinois Univ	IL	9,545	C
Northern Kentucky Univ	KY	6,352	NC
Northern Mich Univ	MI	9,693	C
Northern State Univ	SD	6,279	LC
Northwest Missouri State Univ	MO	7,922	LC
Northwest Nazarene Univ	ID	18,380	C
Northwestern College of Iowa	IA	17,630	C+
Northwestern Okla State Univ	OK	4,542	NC
Northwestern Univ	IL	33,615	MC
Notre Dame College	OH	20,425	C
Oakland Univ	MI	9,418	C
Oberlin College	OH	33,140	HC+
Occidental College	CA	32,288	HC
Oglethorpe Univ	GA	19,100	LC
Ohio Dominican College	OH	18,100	LC
Ohio Univ	OH	11,769	C
Ohio Wesleyan Univ	OH	29,670	VC+
Okla City Univ	OK	15,810	C
Okla State Univ	OK	7,650	VC
Old Dominion Univ	VA	9,386	C
Olivet College	MI	17,410	C
Olivet Nazarene Univ	IL	18,444	C
Oregon State Univ	OR	9,612	VC
Otterbein College	OH	23,439	C
Ouachita Baptist Univ	AR	16,460	VC
Pace Univ	NY	24,200	C
Pacific Lutheran Univ	WA	23,318	VC
Pacific Univ	OR	24,250	C
Park Univ	MO	9,816	C
Penn State Univ at Erie/Behrend College	PA	12,326	C
Penn State Univ/Univ Park Campus	PA	11,126	VC
Pepperdine Univ	CA	32,830	VC
Pfeiffer Univ	NC	18,580	C
Pittsburg State Univ	KS	6,228	NC
Pitzer College	CA	33,930	HC
Plymouth State College	NH	11,024	LC
Point Loma Nazarene Univ	CA	21,380	VC
Pomona College	CA	33,960	MC
Portland State Univ	OR	11,220	C
Presbyterian College	SC	23,356	VC
Prescott College	AZ	13,430	C
Princeton Univ	NJ	35,072	MC
Principia College	IL	23,865	C+
Providence College	RI	27,620	HC
Purdue Univ/West Lafayette	IN	10,284	VC
Quinnipiac Univ	CT	27,370	C
Radford Univ	VA	8,302	C
Ramapo College of New Jersey	NJ	13,550	VC
Randolph-Macon College	VA	24,395	C
Randolph-Macon Woman's College	VA	25,820	VC+
Reed College	OR	33,350	HC+
Regis College	MA	26,750	C
Regis Univ	CO	25,740	C+
Rensselaer Polytechnic Inst	NY	33,863	HC+
Rhode Island College	RI	8,700	LC

School	ST	$IS	SR
Rhodes College	TN	26,466	HC+
Richard Stockton College of New Jersey	NJ	12,165	VC
Rider Univ	NJ	27,400	C
Ripon College	WI	24,180	VC+
Roanoke College	VA	24,689	VC
Robert Morris Univ	PA	18,730	C
Rochester Inst of Technology	NY	26,232	VC+
Rockford College	IL	23,930	C
Rockhurst Univ	MO	20,090	C
Rocky Mountain College	MT	18,113	C
Rollins College	FL	31,223	HC
Roosevelt Univ	IL	20,240	LC
Rose-Hulman Inst of Technology	IN	27,707	HC+
Rosemont College	PA	24,060	C
Rowan Univ	NJ	12,365	VC
Rutgers, The State Univ of New Jersey New Brunswick Campus	NJ	12,709	C
Rutgers, The State Univ of New Jersey/ CamdenCampus	NJ	6,484	C
Rutgers, The State Univ of New Jersey/Newark Campus	NJ	6,394	C
Sacred Heart Univ	CT	26,588	VC
Saginaw Valley State Univ	MI	9,465	C
St. Ambrose Univ	IA	19,994	C
St. Anselm College	NH	27,405	C
St. Cloud State Univ	MN	7,180	C
St. Edward's Univ	TX	17,846	C
St. Francis College	NY	9,610	C
St. Francis Univ	PA	24,486	LC
St. John Fisher College	NY	21,800	C
St. John's Univ	MN	23,640	VC
St. John's Univ	NY	26,660	C
St. Joseph's College	IN	21,640	C
St. Joseph's Univ	PA	29,715	VC+
St. Lawrence Univ	NY	32,605	VC
St. Louis Univ	MO	26,590	VC+
St. Martin's College	WA	20,566	C
St. Mary's College	IN	24,474	VC
St. Mary's College of Calif	CA	27,575	C
St. Mary's College of Maryland	MD	14,104	HC
St. Mary's Univ of San Antonio	TX	19,735	C
St. Michael's College	VT	26,935	VC
St. Norbert College	WI	23,169	VC
St. Olaf College	MN	25,880	HC
St. Peter's College	NJ	22,292	LC
St. Thomas Univ	FL	19,500	LC
St. Vincent College	PA	22,942	VC
Salem College	NC	23,065	VC
Salem State College	MA	4,481	LC
Salisbury Univ	MD	10,576	VC
Salve Regina Univ	RI	26,460	C
Sam Houston State Univ	TX	6,076	LC
San Diego State Univ	CA	9,716	C+
San Francisco State Univ	CA	7,139	LC
San Jose State Univ	CA	8,187	C
Santa Clara Univ	CA	28,371	VC+
Sarah Lawrence College	NY	37,516	HC
Scripps College	CA	30,400	HC+
Seattle Pacific Univ	WA	22,671	C+
Seattle Univ	WA	24,183	VC
Seton Hall Univ	NJ	26,910	LC
Seton Hill College	PA	21,875	C
Shepherd College	WV	7,062	LC
Shippensburg Univ of Pennsylvania	PA	9,652	C
Shorter College	GA	15,185	C
Siena College	NY	22,685	VC
Simmons College	MA	30,418	VC
Simpson College	IA	21,200	C+
Skidmore College	NY	34,201	VC+
Slippery Rock Univ	PA	9,152	LC
Smith College	MA	33,302	HC+
Sonoma State Univ	CA	8,953	C
S Dak State Univ	SD	6,848	C
Southeast Missouri State Univ	MO	8,367	C+
Southeastern Okla State Univ	OK	4,917	C
Southern Conn State Univ	CT	10,310	C
Southern Illinois Univ at Carbondale	IL	8,621	C
Southern Illinois Univ Edwardsville	IL	7,869	LC
Southern Methodist Univ	TX	28,349	VC
Southern New Hampshire Univ	NH	23,852	C
Southern Oregon Univ	OR	9,429	C
Southern Univ at New Orleans	LA	995	NC
Southern Utah Univ	UT	7,254	C
Southwest Missouri State Univ	MO	7,600	LC
Southwest Texas State Univ	TX	8,730	VC
Southwestern Univ	TX	22,550	HC
Spelman College	GA	19,215	C+
Spring Hill College	AL	23,250	C
Stanford Univ	CA	34,222	MC

School	ST	$IS	SR
SUNY/College at Buffalo	NY	8,025	C
SUNY/College at Cortland	NY	10,564	C
SUNY/College at Geneseo	NY	9,970	HC
SUNY/College at Oneonta	NY	9,981	C
SUNY/College at Oswego	NY	10,856	C
SUNY/College at Plattsburgh	NY	9,729	C
SUNY/College at Potsdam	NY	10,519	C
SUNY/College at Purchase	NY	10,587	VC
SUNY/Empire State College	NY	3,545	SP
SUNY/Univ at Albany	NY	10,997	VC
SUNY/Univ at Binghamton	NY	10,653	HC
SUNY/Univ at Buffalo	NY	11,033	VC
SUNY/Univ at New Paltz	NY	9,685	VC
SUNY/Univ at Stony Brook	NY	10,998	VC
State Univ of West Georgia	GA	7,101	C
Stephen F. Austin State Univ	TX	6,905	C
Stetson Univ	FL	25,640	VC
Stonehill College	MA	26,852	HC
Strayer Univ	DC	8,789	SP
Suffolk Univ	MA	26,516	C
Susquehanna Univ	PA	27,270	VC
Swarthmore College	PA	34,538	MC
Sweet Briar College	VA	25,310	VC
Syracuse Univ	NY	30,710	HC
Talladega College	AL	10,110	LC
Tarleton State Univ	TX	7,160	C
Taylor Univ	IN	21,562	VC+
Temple Univ	PA	14,124	C
Tenn Tech Univ	TN	6,968	C
Texas A&M Univ	TX	8,988	VC
Texas A&M Univ at Commerce	TX	7,326	C
Texas Christian Univ	TX	19,910	C
Texas Lutheran Univ	TX	17,660	C
Texas Southern Univ	TX	6,576	NC
Texas Tech Univ	TX	8,825	C
Texas Wesleyan Univ	TX	14,710	C
Texas Woman's Univ	TX	5,855	LC
Ohio State Univ	OH	10,819	VC
Thomas Edison State College	NJ	2,750	SP
Thomas More College	KY	17,700	LC
Tougaloo College	MS	9,200	NC
Touro College	NY	14,950	VC
Towson Univ	MD	11,088	VC
Transylvania Univ	KY	21,780	VC+
Trinity College	CT	34,300	HC
Trinity College	DC	21,370	LC
Trinity Univ	TX	21,444	HC
Truman State Univ	MO	8,568	VC+
Tufts Univ	MA	34,874	MC
Tulane Univ	LA	34,013	HC+
Turabo Univ	PR	4,110	
Union College	NY	32,646	HC
Union Univ	TN	18,930	C+
United States Air Force Academy	CO		MC
United States Military Academy	NY		MC
United States Naval Academy	MD		MC
Univ of Akron	OH	10,530	NC
Univ of Alabama	AL	7,402	C
Univ of Alabama at Birmingham	AL	10,110	C
Univ of Alaska Anchorage	AK	9,100	NC
Univ of Arizona	AZ	8,614	C
Univ of Arkansas	AR	8,334	VC
Univ of Arkansas at Little Rock	AR	5,637	NC
Univ of Bridgeport	CT	23,020	C
Univ of Calif at Berkeley	CA	14,134	MC
Univ of Calif at Davis	CA	12,796	VC
Univ of Calif at Irvine	CA	11,756	C
Univ of Calif at Los Angeles	CA	13,227	MC
Univ of Calif at Riverside	CA	12,479	C
Univ of Calif at San Diego	CA	11,372	HC
Univ of Calif at Santa Barbara	CA	11,732	VC
Univ of Calif at Santa Cruz	CA	13,655	VC
Univ of Central Arkansas	AR	6,388	C
Univ of Central Florida	FL	8,251	VC
Univ of Central Okla	OK	5,205	C
Univ of Chicago	IL	35,087	MC
Univ of Cincinnati	OH	12,491	LC
Univ of Colo at Boulder	CO	9,255	VC
Univ of Colo at Colo Springs	CO	9,403	C
Univ of Colo at Denver	CO	3,673	C
Univ of Conn	CT	12,122	VC
Univ of Dallas	TX	22,128	VC+
Univ of Dayton	OH	20,400	VC
Univ of Delaware	DE	10,824	VC
Univ of Denver	CO	28,783	VC
Univ of Detroit Mercy	MI	21,620	LC
Univ of Evansville	IN	22,865	VC+
Univ of Findlay	OH	23,962	NC
Univ of Florida	FL	7,874	HC
Univ of Georgia	GA	8,656	VC
Univ of Hartford	CT	28,884	C
Univ of Hawaii at Hilo	HI	6,497	C
Univ of Hawaii at Manoa	HI	7,862	VC
Univ of Houston	TX	8,410	C
Univ of Idaho	ID	7,026	C

School	ST	$IS	SR
Univ of Illinois at Chicago	IL	10,702	VC
Univ of Illinois at Urbana-Champaign	IL	11,316	HC+
Univ of Indianapolis	IN	20,840	C
Univ of Iowa	IA	8,607	C+
Univ of Kansas	KS	7,232	VC
Univ of Kentucky	KY	7,765	C
Univ of Louisiana at Lafayette	LA	5,200	C
Univ of Louisiana at Monroe	LA	5,207	NC
Univ of Maine	ME	10,798	C
Univ of Mary Hardin-Baylor	TX	13,929	C
Univ of Maryland/Baltimore County	MD	12,190	VC
Univ of Maryland/College Park	MD	11,959	C
Univ of Mass Amherst	MA	10,995	VC
Univ of Mass Boston	MA	4,227	C
Univ of Mass Dartmouth	MA	9,852	C
Univ of Mass Lowell	MA	9,470	VC
Univ of Memphis	TN	7,271	C
Univ of Miami	FL	31,130	HC
Univ of Mich/Ann Arbor	MI	13,003	HC+
Univ of Mich/Dearborn	MI	4,677	VC
Univ of Mich/Flint	MI	4,323	C
Univ of Minn/Duluth	MN	10,436	C
Univ of Minn/Morris	MN	10,716	VC
Univ of Minn/Twin Cities	MN	11,123	VC
Univ of Miss	MS	7,666	C
Univ of Missouri/Columbia	MO	9,803	HC
Univ of Missouri/Kansas City	MO	9,685	VC
Univ of Missouri/Rolla	MO	10,034	C
Univ of Missouri/St. Louis	MO	9,966	C
Univ of Mobile	AL	13,620	LC
Univ of Montana	MT	8,038	C
Univ of Nebr at Kearney	NE	7,048	NC
Univ of Nebr at Lincoln	NE	8,325	C+
Univ of Nebr at Omaha	NE	6,867	C
Univ of Nevada/Las Vegas	NV	8,281	VC
Univ of New Hampshire	NH	13,207	C
Univ of New Mexico	NM	8,026	C
Univ of New Orleans	LA	10,160	C
Univ of N Car at Asheville	NC	6,896	VC
Univ of N Car at Chapel Hill	NC	8,789	HC
Univ of N Car at Charlotte	NC	7,254	C
Univ of N Car at Greensboro	NC	6,858	C
Univ of N Dak	ND	7,067	VC
Univ of North Florida	FL	8,089	VC
Univ of North Texas	TX	7,629	C
Univ of Northern Colo	CO	8,082	C+
Univ of Northern Iowa	IA	7,850	C
Univ of Notre Dame	IN	30,707	MC
Univ of Okla	OK	7,616	VC
Univ of Oregon	OR	9,969	C
Univ of Pennsylvania	PA	34,614	MC
Univ of Pittsburgh at Bradford	PA	12,696	C
Univ of Pittsburgh at Johnstown	PA	13,044	LC
Univ of Pittsburgh at Pittsburgh	PA	13,592	HC
Univ of PR/Cayey Univ College	PR	1,245	
Univ of PR/Mayaguez	PR	5,285	
Univ of PR/Rio Piedras	PR	5,510	
Univ of Puget Sound	WA	28,285	HC
Univ of Redlands	CA	29,246	VC
Univ of Rhode Island	RI	12,414	C
Univ of Richmond	VA	27,300	HC
Univ of Rio Grande	OH	8,728	NC
Univ of Rochester	NY	32,979	HC
Univ of St. Thomas	MN	24,044	VC
Univ of St. Thomas	TX	18,752	VC
Univ of San Diego	CA	29,198	HC
Univ of San Francisco	CA	27,302	VC
Univ of Science and Arts of Okla	OK	5,245	C
Univ of Scranton	PA	27,964	C+
Univ of S Car at Columbia	SC	8,748	VC
Univ of S Car at Spartanburg	SC	7,318	C+
Univ of S Dak	SD	7,036	C
Univ of South Florida	FL	8,154	C
Univ of Southern Calif	CA	33,647	MC
Univ of Southern Colo	CO	7,821	LC
Univ of Southern Indiana	IN	8,655	LC
Univ of Southern Maine	ME	10,569	C
Univ of Southern Miss	MS	6,155	LC
Univ of Tampa	FL	22,612	C
Univ of Tenn at Chattanooga	TN	7,783	C
Univ of Tenn at Knoxville	TN	8,214	C
Univ of Tenn at Martin	TN	8,268	C
Univ of Texas at Arlington	TX	7,192	LC
Univ of Texas at Austin	TX	9,437	HC
Univ of Texas at Dallas	TX	9,305	VC
Univ of Texas at El Paso	TX	5,076	LC
Univ of Texas at San Antonio	TX	9,088	NC
Univ of Texas-Pan American	TX	4,823	C
Univ of the District of Columbia	DC	2,844	NC
Univ of the Pacific	CA	28,255	VC

School	ST	$IS	SR
Univ of the South	TN	27,290	HC
Univ of Toledo	OH	11,206	NC
Univ of Tulsa	OK	19,090	HC
Univ of Utah	UT	7,703	C
Univ of Vermont	VT	14,761	C+
Univ of Virginia	VA	9,391	HC+
Univ of Virginia's College at Wise	VA	8,302	C
Univ of Washington	WA	10,361	VC
Univ of Wisc/Eau Claire	WI	7,032	VC
Univ of Wisc/Green Bay	WI	7,148	C
Univ of Wisc/La Crosse	WI	7,250	VC
Univ of Wisc/Madison	WI	8,262	VC
Univ of Wisc/Milwaukee	WI	8,907	LC
Univ of Wisc/Oshkosh	WI	6,130	LC
Univ of Wisc/Parkside	WI	6,160	LC
Univ of Wisc/Platteville	WI	7,282	C
Univ of Wisc/River Falls	WI	6,356	LC
Univ of Wisc/Stevens Point	WI	7,116	C
Univ of Wisc/Whitewater	WI	6,937	C
Univ of Wyoming	WY	7,143	LC
Ursinus College	PA	31,350	VC
Utah State Univ	UT	6,771	C
Utica College of Syracuse Univ	NY	24,400	LC
Valparaiso Univ	IN	23,570	VC+
Vanderbilt Univ	TN	34,482	MC
Vassar College	NY	33,450	MC
Villanova Univ	PA	31,997	HC
Virginia Commonwealth Univ	VA	9,030	C
Virginia Polytechnic Inst and State Univ	VA	7,652	C
Virginia State Univ	VA	8,182	LC
Wabash College	IN	25,335	HC
Wake Forest Univ	NC	30,290	MC
Wartburg College	IA	21,165	VC
Washburn Univ of Topeka	KS	6,766	NC
Washington and Jefferson College	PA	26,255	VC
Washington and Lee Univ	VA	25,095	MC
Washington College	MD	28,040	VC
Washington State Univ	WA	9,388	C
Washington Univ in St. Louis	MO	34,593	MC
Wayne State Univ	MI	6,720	C
Weber State Univ	UT	6,897	NC
Webster Univ	MO	19,804	VC
Wellesley College	MA	33,394	MC
Wells College	NY	19,350	VC
Wesleyan College	GA	17,050	VC
Wesleyan Univ	CT	3,405	MC
West Chester Univ of Pennsylvania	PA	9,792	VC
West Liberty State College	WV	6,056	LC
West Texas A&M Univ	TX	6,538	C
West Virginia State College	WV	6,264	NC
West Virginia Univ	WV	8,304	C
West Virginia Wesleyan College	WV	22,920	C
Western Carolina Univ	NC	5,667	C
Western Conn State Univ	CT	10,074	C
Western Illinois Univ	IL	9,571	C
Western Kentucky Univ	KY	6,834	C
Western Maryland College	MD	26,000	VC
Western Mich Univ	MI	10,016	C
Western New England College	MA	23,882	C
Western Oregon Univ	OR	8,829	C
Western State College of Colo	CO	7,585	LC
Western Washington Univ	WA	8,624	VC
Westfield State College	MA	8,394	C
Westminster College	MO	19,990	C+
Westminster College	PA	22,960	C
Westminster College	UT	17,226	C
Wheaton College	IL	21,934	HC
Wheaton College	MA	32,940	VC
Whitman College	WA	29,086	HC
Whittier College	CA	29,108	C
Whitworth College	WA	23,938	VC
Wichita State Univ	KS	6,879	C
Widener Univ	PA	26,920	C
Wilberforce Univ	OH	14,937	LC
Wilkes Univ	PA	25,800	C
Willamette Univ	OR	29,422	VC+
William Paterson Univ of New Jersey	NJ	11,000	LC
Williams College	MA	32,270	MC
Wingate Univ	NC	19,140	C
Winona State Univ	MN	8,570	C
Winston-Salem State Univ	NC	5,927	LC
Wittenberg Univ	OH	28,766	VC
Wofford College	SC	23,995	VC
Worcester Polytechnic Inst	MA	34,480	HC+
Worcester State College	MA	7,901	LC
Wright State Univ	OH	9,141	LC
Xavier Univ	OH	23,880	C
Yale Univ	CT	34,030	MC
Yeshiva Univ	NY	21,400	C
Youngstown State Univ	OH	9,318	NC

EDUCATION

School	ST	$IS	SR
Aquinas College	MI	20,052	C+
Belmont Abbey College	NC	19,630	LC

ST = STATE **$IS** = IN-STATE COSTS **SR** = SELECTOR RATING

School	ST	$IS	SR
Beloit College	WI	27,482	HC
Bennington College	VT	31,350	VC
Biola Univ	CA	21,902	VC
Boise State Univ	ID	6,531	LC
Brown Univ	RI	34,973	MC
Bryn Athyn College of the New Church	PA	10,590	NC
Bucknell Univ	PA	31,096	HC
Cabrini College	PA	25,950	LC
Calif Lutheran Univ	CA	23,500	LC
Cal State, Monterey Bay	CA	6,250	LC
Catawba College	NC	19,620	C
Catholic Univ of America	DC	29,332	VC
Central Mich Univ	MI	8,355	C
Christian Heritage College	CA	18,000	LC
CUNY/College of Staten Island	NY	3,358	NC
Claremont McKenna College	CA	32,700	MC
Coker College	SC	20,120	C
Colgate Univ	NY	33,480	MC
College of St. Mary	NE	18,726	C
College of St. Scholastica	MN	22,378	C+
College of Santa Fe	NM	20,250	LC
Columbia Univ/Columbia College	NY	35,190	MC
Concordia College	NY	19,200	VC
Cornell Univ	NY	34,614	MC
Culver-Stockton College	MO	15,400	LC
Denison Univ	OH	29,640	HC
Drexel Univ	PA	27,657	VC
Earlham College	IN	27,446	VC+
East Texas Baptist Univ	TX	12,349	LC
Eastern Mich Univ	MI	9,855	C
Eastern Nazarene College	MA	19,433	LC
Eastern Oregon Univ	OR	8,772	C
Eugene Lang College of New School Univ	NY	30,300	C
Eureka College	IL	22,200	C
Fordham Univ	NY	30,710	VC
Franklin Pierce College	NH	26,125	LC
Furman Univ	SC	25,492	HC
Goddard College	VT	21,056	C+
Hampshire College	MA	33,881	HC+
Hope International Univ	CA	16,940	NC
Huntington College	IN	15,480	LC
Huston-Tillotson College	TX	12,977	LC
Ithaca College	NY	28,719	HC
Johnson State College	VT	10,776	C
Kent State Univ	OH	11,104	C
Lake Forest College	IL	27,460	VC
LeMoyne-Owen College	TN	8,450	NC
Lourdes College	OH	13,100	LC
Lynchburg College	VA	23,405	C
Lynn Univ	FL	24,550	C
Maharishi Univ of Management	IA	20,660	VC
Martin Univ	IN	8,370	SP
Mary Baldwin College	VA	23,440	C
Mass College of Liberal Arts	MA	8,717	LC
Midway College	KY	15,815	C
Miss State Univ	MS	7,853	C
Montana State Univ-Billings	MT	7,653	NC
New York Inst of Technology	NY	21,756	C
N Car State Univ	NC	8,680	HC
Northwest College	WA	17,471	C
Northwestern Univ	IL	33,615	MC
Ohio State Univ at Lima	OH	3,603	NC
Pacific Lutheran Univ	WA	23,318	VC
Palm Beach Atlantic College	FL	23,310	C
Philadelphia Biblical Univ	PA	16,295	C+
Prescott College	AZ	13,430	C
Rice Univ	TX	24,325	MC
Rocky Mountain College	MT	18,113	C
St. Louis Univ	MO	26,590	VC+
St. Mary's College	MI	13,314	LC
Salem State College	MA	4,481	LC
Shawnee State Univ	OH	8,634	NC
Spalding Univ	KY	15,196	C
SUNY/Empire State College	NY	3,545	SP
Stephen F. Austin State Univ	TX	6,905	C
Stonehill College	MA	26,852	HC
Susquehanna Univ	PA	27,270	VC
Swarthmore College	PA	34,538	MC
Temple Univ	PA	14,124	C
Tenn Wesleyan College	TN	13,030	C
Texas Southern Univ	TX	6,576	NC
Texas Tech Univ	TX	8,825	C
Towson Univ	MD	11,088	VC
Trevecca Nazarene Univ	TN	15,752	C
Trinity Christian College	IL	19,415	C
Trinity College	CT	34,300	HC
Tusculum College	TN	17,900	LC
Union Univ	TN	18,930	C+
Univ of Alabama at Huntsville	AL	7,916	VC
Univ of Conn	CT	12,122	VC
Univ of Delaware	DE	10,824	VC
Univ of Dubuque	IA	19,990	C
Univ of Illinois at Chicago	IL	10,702	VC
Univ of Missouri/Columbia	MO	9,803	HC
Univ of Nebr at Lincoln	NE	8,325	C+
Univ of N Car at Chapel Hill	NC	8,789	HC
Univ of Oregon	OR	9,969	C
Univ of Pennsylvania	PA	34,614	MC
Univ of Puget Sound	WA	28,285	HC
Univ of St. Thomas	TX	18,752	VC
Univ of Science and Arts of Okla	OK	5,245	C
Univ of South Alabama	AL	6,976	LC
Univ of South Florida	FL	8,154	C
Univ of Tenn at Chattanooga	TN	7,783	C
Univ of Texas at Austin	TX	9,437	HC
Univ of the Pacific	CA	28,255	VC
Univ of Tulsa	OK	19,090	HC
Univ of Vermont	VT	14,761	C+
Univ of Wisc/Green Bay	WI	7,148	C
Univ of Wisc/Milwaukee	WI	8,907	LC
Univ of Wisc/Parkside	WI	6,160	LC
Vanderbilt Univ	TN	34,482	MC
Virginia Intermont College	VA	17,510	C
Wake Forest Univ	NC	30,290	MC
Washington State Univ	WA	9,388	C
Washington Univ in St. Louis	MO	34,593	MC
Webster Univ	MO	19,804	VC
Western Baptist College	OR	19,700	C+
Western Mich Univ	MI	10,016	C
Western Oregon Univ	OR	8,829	C
Xavier Univ	OH	23,880	C
York College	NE	13,500	C
Youngstown State Univ	OH	9,318	NC

EDUCATION ADMINISTRATION

School	ST	$IS	SR
Ashland Univ	OH	22,182	LC
Bay Path College	MA	22,308	C
Philander Smith College	AR	7,380	NC
Southwestern Okla State Univ	OK	4,801	C

EDUCATION OF THE DEAF AND HEARING IMPAIRED

School	ST	$IS	SR
Adelphi Univ	NY	23,320	VC
Augustana College	SD	20,760	VC
Ball State Univ	IN	8,660	C
Barton College	NC	16,834	LC
Boston Univ	MA	34,358	MC
Cal State, Northridge	CA	7,781	C
CUNY/Brooklyn College	NY	3,403	LC
College of New Jersey	NJ	13,425	HC
Eastern Kentucky Univ	KY	6,552	C
Eastern Mich Univ	MI	9,855	C
Flagler College	FL	10,550	VC+
Fontbonne Univ	MO	18,046	C
Indiana Univ of Pennsylvania	PA	9,133	C
Ithaca College	NY	28,719	HC
Lenoir-Rhyne College	NC	19,186	C
MacMurray College	IL	17,790	LC
Mercy College	NY	15,875	LC
Minot State Univ	ND	5,466	LC
Rochester Inst of Technology	NY	26,232	VC+
St. John's Univ	NY	26,660	C
Southern Univ at New Orleans	LA	995	NC
SUNY/College at Plattsburgh	NY	9,729	C
Stephen F. Austin State Univ	TX	6,905	C
Texas Christian Univ	TX	19,910	C
Towson Univ	MD	11,088	VC
Univ of Arkansas at Little Rock	AR	5,637	NC
Univ of Montevallo	AL	7,266	C
Univ of Science and Arts of Okla	OK	5,245	C
Univ of Tulsa	OK	19,090	HC

EDUCATION OF THE EMOTIONALLY HANDICAPPED

School	ST	$IS	SR
East Carolina Univ	NC	7,766	C
Eastern Mich Univ	MI	9,855	C
Florida International Univ	FL	9,486	VC
Florida State Univ	FL	7,835	HC
Stephen F. Austin State Univ	TX	6,905	C
Univ of Maine at Farmington	ME	9,163	C
Univ of South Florida	FL	8,154	C
Youngstown State Univ	OH	9,318	NC

EDUCATION OF THE EXCEPTIONAL CHILD

School	ST	$IS	SR
Ashland Univ	OH	22,182	LC
Bethel College	TN	12,980	C
Bethune-Cookman College	FL	15,746	C
Brewton-Parker College	GA	10,810	LC
Edgewood College	WI	18,304	C
Jacksonville Univ	FL	21,110	LC
Mansfield Univ	PA	9,648	C
Minot State Univ	ND	5,466	LC
Nova Southeastern Univ	FL	20,104	LC
St. Augustine's College	NC	12,990	C+
St. Leo Univ	FL	19,250	LC
Southeastern College	FL	11,648	LC
Stephen F. Austin State Univ	TX	6,905	C
Texas Christian Univ	TX	19,910	C
Univ of Central Arkansas	AR	6,388	C
Univ of Central Florida	FL	8,251	VC
Univ of Great Falls	MT	15,360	C
Univ of Maine at Farmington	ME	9,163	C
Univ of Wisc/Stevens Point	WI	7,116	C

EDUCATION OF THE MENTALLY HANDICAPPED

School	ST	$IS	SR
Augusta State Univ	GA	2,282	C
Calif Univ of Pennsylvania	PA	10,388	C
East Carolina Univ	NC	7,766	C
Eastern Mich Univ	MI	9,855	C
Florida International Univ	FL	9,486	VC
Florida State Univ	FL	7,835	HC
Indiana Univ of Pennsylvania	PA	9,133	C
Minot State Univ	ND	5,466	LC
Northern Mich Univ	MI	9,693	C
Northwest Missouri State Univ	MO	7,922	LC
Ohio Univ	OH	11,769	C
Stephen F. Austin State Univ	TX	6,905	C
Univ of Maine at Farmington	ME	9,163	C
Univ of Rio Grande	OH	8,728	NC
Univ of South Florida	FL	8,154	C
Youngstown State Univ	OH	9,318	NC

EDUCATION OF THE MULTIPLY HANDICAPPED

School	ST	$IS	SR
Eastern Mich Univ	MI	9,855	C
Ohio Univ	OH	11,769	C
Stephen F. Austin State Univ	TX	6,905	C
Univ of Alabama	AL	7,402	C
Youngstown State Univ	OH	9,318	NC

EDUCATION OF THE PHYSICALLY HANDICAPPED

School	ST	$IS	SR
Calif Univ of Pennsylvania	PA	10,388	C
Eastern Mich Univ	MI	9,855	C
Indiana Univ of Pennsylvania	PA	9,133	C
Ohio Univ	OH	11,769	C
Stephen F. Austin State Univ	TX	6,905	C

EDUCATION OF THE VISUALLY HANDICAPPED

School	ST	$IS	SR
Eastern Mich Univ	MI	9,855	C
Florida State Univ	FL	7,835	HC
Stephen F. Austin State Univ	TX	6,905	C

EDUCATIONAL MEDIA

School	ST	$IS	SR
Ball State Univ	IN	8,660	C
College of St. Scholastica	MN	22,378	C+
Duquesne Univ	PA	24,242	C+
Eastern Mich Univ	MI	9,855	C
Indiana State Univ	IN	8,461	LC
Indiana Univ Bloomington	IN	10,712	C+
Ithaca College	NY	28,719	HC
Purdue Univ/West Lafayette	IN	10,284	VC

EDUCATIONAL STATISTICS AND RESEARCH

School	ST	$IS	SR
Bucknell Univ	PA	31,096	HC
Emory Univ	GA	33,792	MC

ELECTRICAL/ELECTRONICS ENGINEERING

School	ST	$IS	SR
Alabama A&M Univ	AL	5,100	LC
Alfred Univ	NY	27,212	C+
Andrews Univ	MI	17,696	LC
Arizona State Univ-Main	AZ	7,726	C
Auburn Univ	AL	5,510	C
Bethel College	IN	17,650	LC
Bloomsburg Univ of Pennsylvania	PA	9,434	C
Boston Univ	MA	34,358	MC
Bradley Univ	IL	20,970	VC
Brigham Young Univ	UT	7,840	HC
Bucknell Univ	PA	31,096	HC
Calif Inst of Technology	CA	27,663	MC
Calif Polytechnic State Univ	CA	8,747	VC
Calif State Polytechnic Univ, Pomona	CA	8,615	C
Cal State, Chico	CA	8,598	LC
Cal State, Fresno	CA	7,762	C
Cal State, Fullerton	CA	5,440	LC
Cal State, Long Beach	CA	7,400	LC
Cal State, Los Angeles	CA	5,050	C
Cal State, Sacramento	CA	7,488	C
Calvin College	MI	20,050	NC
Capitol College	MD	18,462	LC
Carnegie Mellon Univ	PA	32,682	MC
Case Western Reserve Univ	OH	27,418	C
Catholic Univ of America	DC	29,332	VC
Cedarville Univ	OH	17,553	VC
Central Missouri State Univ	MO	7,920	C
Central Washington Univ	WA	8,985	LC
Christian Brothers Univ	TN	19,820	VC
Citadel, The	SC	9,126	C
CUNY/City College	NY	3,309	LC
Clarkson Univ	NY	29,884	VC
Clemson Univ	SC	7,600	C
Cleveland State Univ	OH	10,146	NC
Cogswell Polytechnical College	CA	14,400	LC
Colo State Univ	CO	9,672	C
Colo Technical Univ	CO	9,425	LC
Columbia Univ/Fu Foundation School of Engineering and Applied Science	NY	35,190	MC
Cooper Union for the Advancement of Science and Art	NY	6,500	MC
Cornell Univ	NY	34,614	MC
Delaware State Univ	DE	8,104	LC
Dordt College	IA	18,100	C+
Drexel Univ	PA	27,657	VC
Duke Univ	NC	34,396	MC
Embry-Riddle Aeronautical Univ	AZ	23,470	C+
Embry-Riddle Aeronautical Univ	FL	24,790	C
Fairleigh Dickinson Univ/Teaneck Campus	NJ	24,646	C
Florida A&M Univ	FL	6,948	C
Florida Atlantic Univ	FL	8,832	C
Florida Inst of Technology	FL	25,250	VC
Florida International Univ	FL	9,486	VC
Florida State Univ	FL	7,835	HC
Gannon Univ	PA	18,848	C
George Mason Univ	VA	9,192	C
George Washington Univ	DC	32,170	HC
Georgia Inst of Technology	GA	9,028	HC+
Gonzaga Univ	WA	24,276	HC+
Grove City College	PA	12,280	MC
Hampton Univ	VA	17,112	C+
Henry Cogswell College	WA	13,080	SP
Hofstra Univ	NY	23,252	C
Howard Univ	DC	15,522	LC
Illinois Inst of Technology	IL	25,182	HC+
Indiana Inst of Technology	IN	18,806	C
Indiana Univ-Purdue Univ Fort Wayne	IN	3,166	LC
Indiana Univ-Purdue Univ Indianapolis	IN	9,473	C
Iowa State Univ	IA	8,108	VC
Jacksonville Univ	FL	21,110	LC
John Brown Univ	AR	15,080	VC
Johns Hopkins Univ	MD	35,226	MC
Johnson and Wales Univ	RI	21,558	LC
Kansas State Univ	KS	6,995	C
Kettering Univ	MI	23,256	HC
Lafayette College	PA	32,655	MC
Lake Superior State Univ	MI	9,034	LC
Lamar Univ	TX	6,816	LC
Lawrence Tech Univ	MI	11,429	C
Lehigh Univ	PA	32,290	MC
LeTourneau Univ	TX	19,020	VC
Loras College	IA	22,994	C+
Louisiana State Univ and A&M College	LA	8,014	VC
Loyola College in Maryland	MD	30,900	HC
Loyola Marymount Univ	CA	28,754	HC
Maharishi Univ of Management	IA	20,660	VC
Manhattan College	NY	25,500	VC
Marquette Univ	WI	24,836	C+
Mass Inst of Technology	MA	35,228	MC
McNeese State Univ	LA	5,259	LC
Mercer Univ	GA	24,130	VC
Merrimack College	MA	25,725	VC
Mich State Univ	MI	10,386	VC
Mich Tech Univ	MI	11,088	VC
Milwaukee School of Engineering	WI	25,680	VC+
Minn State Univ, Mankato	MN	7,296	LC
Miss State Univ	MS	7,853	C
Montana State Univ-Bozeman	MT	8,431	C
Morgan State Univ	MD	10,078	LC
New Jersey Inst of Technology	NJ	14,690	VC
New Mexico Inst of Mining and Technology	NM	7,152	VC+
New Mexico State Univ	NM	7,302	C
New York Inst of Technology	NY	21,756	C

School	ST	$IS	SR
New York Univ	NY	35,200	MC
N Car Agricultural and Technical State Univ	NC	6,659	LC
N Car State Univ	NC	8,680	HC
N Dak State Univ	ND	7,004	VC
Northeastern Univ	MA	30,078	VC
Northern Arizona Univ	AZ	7,398	C
Northern Illinois Univ	IL	9,545	C
Northwestern Univ	IL	33,615	MC
Norwich Univ	VT	21,064	LC
Oakland Univ	MI	9,418	C
Occidental College	CA	32,288	HC
Ohio Northern Univ	OH	27,765	VC
Ohio Univ	OH	11,769	C
Okla Christian Univ	OK	16,500	VC
Okla State Univ	OK	7,650	VC
Old Dominion Univ	VA	9,386	C
Oral Roberts Univ	OK	18,490	C
Penn State Univ/Univ Park Campus	PA	11,126	VC
Polytechnic Univ/Brooklyn	NY	33,090	HC
Portland State Univ	OR	11,220	C
Prairie View A&M Univ	TX	3,172	LC
Princeton Univ	NJ	35,072	MC
Purdue Univ/Calumet	IN	6,630	NC
Purdue Univ/West Lafayette	IN	10,284	VC
Rensselaer Polytechnic Inst	NY	33,863	HC+
Rochester Inst of Technology	NY	26,232	VC+
Rose-Hulman Inst of Technology	IN	27,707	HC+
Rutgers, The State Univ of New Jersey New Brunswick Campus	NJ	12,709	C
Saginaw Valley State Univ	MI	9,465	C
St. Cloud State Univ	MN	7,180	C
St. Louis Univ	MO	26,590	VC+
St. Mary's Univ of San Antonio	TX	19,735	C
San Diego State Univ	CA	9,716	C+
San Francisco State Univ	CA	7,139	LC
San Jose State Univ	CA	8,187	C
Santa Clara Univ	CA	28,371	VC+
Seattle Pacific Univ	WA	22,674	C+
Seattle Univ	WA	24,183	VC
S Dak School of Mines and Technology	SD	7,438	C+
S Dak State Univ	SD	6,848	C
Southern Illinois Univ at Carbondale	IL	8,621	C
Southern Illinois Univ Edwardsville	IL	7,869	LC
Southern Methodist Univ	TX	28,349	VC
Southern Univ and A&M College	LA	6,365	C+
Stanford Univ	CA	34,222	MC
SUNY/Maritime College	NY	10,025	LC
SUNY/Univ at Binghamton	NY	10,653	HC
SUNY/Univ at Buffalo	NY	11,033	VC
SUNY/Univ at New Paltz	NY	9,685	VC
SUNY/Univ at Stony Brook	NY	10,998	VC
Stevens Inst of Technology	NJ	31,510	HC+
Suffolk Univ	MA	26,516	C
Syracuse Univ	NY	30,710	HC
Temple Univ	PA	14,124	C
Tenn State Univ	TN	7,058	VC
Tenn Tech Univ	TN	6,968	C
Texas A&M Univ	TX	8,988	VC
Texas A&M Univ at Kingsville	TX	6,446	LC
Texas Tech Univ	TX	8,825	C
Ohio State Univ	OH	10,819	VC
Tri-State Univ-Main Campus	IN	21,200	C
Tufts Univ	MA	34,874	MC
Tulane Univ	LA	34,013	HC+
Tuskegee Univ	AL	14,600	LC
Union College	NY	32,646	HC
United States Air Force Academy	CO		MC
United States Coast Guard Academy	CT		MC
United States Military Academy	NY		MC
United States Naval Academy	MD		MC
Universidad Politecnica de PR	PR	4,695	
Univ of Akron	OH	10,530	NC
Univ of Alabama	AL	7,402	C
Univ of Alabama at Birmingham	AL	10,110	C
Univ of Alabama at Huntsville	AL	7,916	VC
Univ of Alaska Fairbanks	AK	8,265	NC
Univ of Arizona	AZ	8,614	C
Univ of Arkansas	AR	8,334	VC
Univ of Calif at Berkeley	CA	14,134	MC
Univ of Calif at Davis	CA	12,796	VC
Univ of Calif at Irvine	CA	11,756	C
Univ of Calif at Los Angeles	CA	13,227	MC
Univ of Calif at Riverside	CA	12,479	C
Univ of Calif at San Diego	CA	11,372	HC
Univ of Calif at Santa Barbara	CA	11,732	VC
Univ of Central Florida	FL	8,251	VC
Univ of Cincinnati	OH	12,491	LC
Univ of Colo at Boulder	CO	9,255	VC
Univ of Colo at Colo Springs	CO	9,403	C
Univ of Colo at Denver	CO	3,673	C
Univ of Conn	CT	12,122	VC
Univ of Dayton	OH	20,400	VC
Univ of Delaware	DE	10,824	VC
Univ of Denver	CO	28,783	VC
Univ of Detroit Mercy	MI	21,620	LC
Univ of Evansville	IN	22,865	VC+
Univ of Florida	FL	7,874	HC
Univ of Hartford	CT	28,884	C
Univ of Hawaii at Manoa	HI	7,862	VC
Univ of Houston	TX	8,410	C
Univ of Houston-Downtown	TX	2,006	NC
Univ of Idaho	ID	7,026	C
Univ of Illinois at Chicago	IL	10,702	VC
Univ of Illinois at Urbana-Champaign	IL	11,316	HC+
Univ of Indianapolis	IN	20,840	C
Univ of Iowa	IA	8,607	C+
Univ of Kansas	KS	7,232	VC
Univ of Kentucky	KY	7,765	C
Univ of Louisiana at Lafayette	LA	5,200	C
Univ of Louisville	KY	7,402	LC
Univ of Maine	ME	10,798	C
Univ of Maryland/College Park	MD	11,959	C
Univ of Mass Amherst	MA	10,995	VC
Univ of Mass Dartmouth	MA	9,852	C
Univ of Mass Lowell	MA	9,470	VC
Univ of Memphis	TN	7,271	C
Univ of Miami	FL	31,130	HC
Univ of Mich/Ann Arbor	MI	13,003	HC+
Univ of Mich/Dearborn	MI	4,677	VC
Univ of Minn/Duluth	MN	10,436	C
Univ of Minn/Twin Cities	MN	11,123	VC
Univ of Miss	MS	7,666	C
Univ of Missouri/Columbia	MO	9,803	HC
Univ of Missouri/Kansas City	MO	9,685	VC
Univ of Missouri/Rolla	MO	10,034	C
Univ of Missouri/St. Louis	MO	9,966	C
Univ of Nebr at Lincoln	NE	8,325	C+
Univ of Nevada/Las Vegas	NV	8,281	VC
Univ of Nevada/Reno	NV	8,737	C
Univ of New Hampshire	NH	13,207	C
Univ of New Haven	CT	23,860	LC
Univ of New Mexico	NM	8,026	C
Univ of New Orleans	LA	10,160	C
Univ of N Car at Charlotte	NC	7,254	C
Univ of N Dak	ND	7,067	VC
Univ of North Florida	FL	8,089	VC
Univ of Notre Dame	IN	30,707	MC
Univ of Okla	OK	7,616	VC
Univ of Pennsylvania	PA	34,614	MC
Univ of Pittsburgh at Pittsburgh	PA	13,592	HC
Univ of Portland	OR	24,950	VC
Univ of PR/Mayaguez	PR	5,285	
Univ of Rhode Island	RI	12,414	C
Univ of Rochester	NY	32,979	HC
Univ of St. Thomas	MN	24,044	VC
Univ of San Diego	CA	29,198	HC
Univ of Scranton	PA	27,964	C+
Univ of South Alabama	AL	6,976	LC
Univ of S Car at Columbia	SC	8,748	VC
Univ of South Florida	FL	8,154	C
Univ of Southern Calif	CA	33,647	MC
Univ of Southern Maine	ME	10,569	C
Univ of Tenn at Knoxville	TN	8,214	C
Univ of Texas at Arlington	TX	7,192	LC
Univ of Texas at Austin	TX	9,437	HC
Univ of Texas at Dallas	TX	9,305	VC
Univ of Texas at El Paso	TX	5,076	LC
Univ of Texas at San Antonio	TX	9,088	NC
Univ of Texas-Pan American	TX	4,823	C
Univ of the District of Columbia	DC	2,844	NC
Univ of the Pacific	CA	28,255	VC
Univ of Toledo	OH	11,206	NC
Univ of Tulsa	OK	19,090	HC
Univ of Utah	UT	7,703	C
Univ of Vermont	VT	14,761	C+
Univ of Virginia	VA	9,391	HC+
Univ of Washington	WA	10,361	VC
Univ of West Florida	FL	7,518	C
Univ of Wisc/Madison	WI	8,262	VC
Univ of Wisc/Milwaukee	WI	8,907	LC
Univ of Wisc/Platteville	WI	7,282	C
Univ of Wyoming	WY	7,143	LC
Utah State Univ	UT	6,771	C
Valparaiso Univ	IN	23,570	VC+
Vanderbilt Univ	TN	34,482	MC
Villanova Univ	PA	31,997	HC
Virginia Commonwealth Univ	VA	9,030	C
Virginia Military Inst	VA	9,968	C+
Virginia Polytechnic Inst and State Univ	VA	7,652	C
Washington State Univ	WA	9,388	C
Washington Univ in St Louis	MO	34,593	MC
Wayne State Univ	MI	6,720	C
West Virginia Univ	WV	8,304	C
West Virginia Univ Inst of Technology	WV	7,518	NC
Western Kentucky Univ	KY	6,834	C
Western Mich Univ	MI	10,016	C
Western New England College	MA	23,882	C
Wichita State Univ	KS	6,879	C
Widener Univ	PA	26,920	C
Wilkes Univ	PA	25,800	C
Worcester Polytechnic Inst	MA	34,480	HC+
Wright State Univ	OH	9,141	LC
Yale Univ	CT	34,030	MC
Youngstown State Univ	OH	9,318	NC

ELECTRICAL/ELECTRONICS ENGINEERING TECHNOLOGY

School	ST	$IS	SR
Alabama A&M Univ	AL	5,100	LC
Andrews Univ	MI	17,696	LC
Appalachian State Univ	NC	6,353	C
Baker College of Flint	MI	7,720	NC
Brigham Young Univ	UT	7,840	HC
Calif Univ of Pennsylvania	PA	10,388	C
Central Conn State Univ	CT	10,404	C
Central Missouri State Univ	MO	7,920	C
Colo Technical Univ	CO	9,425	LC
DeVry College of Technology/North Brunswick	NJ	8,805	LC
DeVry/New York	NY	9,865	LC
DeVry Univ/Addison (DuPage County)	IL	8,805	LC
DeVry Univ/Alpharetta	GA	8,805	LC
DeVry Univ/Chicago	IL	8,805	LC
DeVry Univ/Colo Springs	CO	9,465	LC
DeVry Univ/Columbus	OH	8,805	LC
DeVry Univ/Crystal City	VA	10,065	C
DeVry Univ/Dallas	TX	8,805	LC
DeVry Univ/Decatur	GA	8,805	LC
DeVry Univ/Denver	CO	9,465	LC
DeVry Univ/Fremont	CA	9,865	C
DeVry Univ/Kansas City	MO	8,805	LC
DeVry Univ/Long Beach	CA	9,140	LC
DeVry Univ/Orlando	FL	9,865	LC
DeVry Univ/Phoenix	AZ	8,805	LC
DeVry Univ/Pomona	CA	9,205	LC
DeVry Univ/Seattle	WA	10,065	LC
DeVry Univ/Tinley Park	IL	8,805	LC
DeVry Univ/West Hills	CA	9,205	LC
East Carolina Univ	NC	7,766	C
Eastern New Mexico Univ	NM	4,113	LC
East-West Univ	IL	9,140	LC
Excelsior College	NY	915	SP
Fairleigh Dickinson Univ/Teaneck Campus	NJ	24,646	C
Fairmont State College	WV	7,010	NC
Fort Valley State Univ	GA	6,014	LC
Georgia Southern Univ	GA	6,958	C
Indiana State Univ	IN	8,461	LC
Indiana Univ-Purdue Univ Indianapolis	IN	9,473	C
Inter-American Univ of PR/Aguadilla Campus	PR	3,278	
Inter-American Univ of PR/Bayamon Univ College	PR	3,700	
Inter-American Univ of PR/Fajardo Campus	PR	4,000	
Inter-American Univ of PR/Ponce Regional College	PR	3,700	
Kansas State Univ	KS	6,995	C
Louisiana Tech Univ	LA	6,506	C
Maharishi Univ of Management	IA	20,660	VC
Metropolitan State College of Denver	CO	2,338	LC
Minn State Univ, Mankato	MN	7,296	LC
Montana State Univ-Northern	MT	8,600	NC
Murray State Univ	KY	6,672	C
New York Inst of Technology	NY	21,756	C
Norfolk State Univ	VA	8,382	LC
Northeastern Univ	MA	30,078	VC
Northern Mich Univ	MI	9,693	C
Northwestern State Univ of Louisiana	LA	5,745	NC
Okla State Univ	OK	7,650	VC
Old Dominion Univ	VA	9,386	C
Oregon Inst of Technology	OR	8,718	C
Pacific Union College	CA	20,250	VC
Pennsylvania College of Technology	PA	12,860	NC
Point Park College	PA	20,290	C
Purdue Univ/Calumet	IN	6,630	NC
Purdue Univ/West Lafayette	IN	10,284	VC
Rochester Inst of Technology	NY	26,232	VC+
Roosevelt Univ	IL	20,240	LC
Savannah State Univ	GA	2,550	LC
S Car State Univ	SC	6,586	LC
S Dak State Univ	SD	6,848	C
Southern Polytechnic State Univ	GA	6,662	C
Southwest Missouri State Univ	MO	7,600	LC
Southwestern Okla State Univ	OK	4,801	C
SUNY/College at Buffalo	NY	8,025	C
SUNY/College of Technology at Alfred	NY	9,188	C
SUNY/College of Technology at Farmingdale	NY	11,269	C
Temple Univ	PA	14,124	C
Texas Southern Univ	TX	6,576	NC
Texas Tech Univ	TX	8,825	C
Thomas Edison State College	NJ	2,750	SP
Univ of Arkansas at Little Rock	AR	5,637	NC
Univ of Central Florida	FL	8,251	VC
Univ of Cincinnati	OH	12,491	LC
Univ of Dayton	OH	20,400	VC
Univ of Hartford	CT	28,884	C
Univ of Houston	TX	8,410	C
Univ of Maine	ME	10,798	C
Univ of Memphis	TN	7,271	C
Univ of Nebr at Lincoln	NE	8,325	C+
Univ of N Car at Charlotte	NC	7,254	C
Univ of Pittsburgh at Johnstown	PA	13,044	LC
Univ of PR/Bayamon Univ College Campus	PR	1,600	
Univ of Rio Grande	OH	8,728	NC
Univ of Southern Colo	CO	7,821	LC
Univ of Southern Miss	MS	6,155	LC
Weber State Univ	UT	6,897	NC
Wentworth Inst of Technology	MA	20,450	C
West Virginia Univ Inst of Technology	WV	7,518	NC
Western Carolina Univ	NC	5,667	C
Western Kentucky Univ	KY	6,834	C
Western Washington Univ	WA	8,624	VC
Youngstown State Univ	OH	9,318	NC

ELECTROMECHANICAL TECHNOLOGY

School	ST	$IS	SR
CUNY/New York City Technical College	NY	3,319	NC
Cleveland State Univ	OH	10,146	NC
Penn State Univ/Altoona	PA	12,578	C
SUNY/College of Technology at Alfred	NY	9,188	C
Univ of Houston	TX	8,410	C
Univ of Northern Iowa	IA	7,850	C
Univ of the District of Columbia	DC	2,844	NC
Univ of Toledo	OH	11,206	NC
Vermont Technical College	VT	11,704	C
Wentworth Inst of Technology	MA	20,450	C
Western Kentucky Univ	KY	6,834	C

ELECTRONIC BUSINESS

School	ST	$IS	SR
Bay Path College	MA	22,308	C
Dakota State Univ	SD	6,950	C
De Sales Univ	PA	22,610	VC
Dominican Univ of Calif	CA	27,948	C
Ithaca College	NY	28,719	HC
King College	TN	17,800	VC
La Sierra Univ	CA	19,260	LC
Maryville Univ of St. Louis	MO	18,680	C
Mountain State Univ	WV	8,180	NC
Old Dominion Univ	VA	9,386	C
Temple Univ	PA	14,124	C
Texas Christian Univ	TX	19,910	C
Univ of La Verne	CA	24,280	C
Univ of Missouri/Rolla	MO	10,034	C
Univ of Scranton	PA	27,964	C+
Univ of South Alabama	AL	6,976	LC

ELEMENTARY EDUCATION

School	ST	$IS	SR
Abilene Christian Univ	TX	16,300	VC
Adams State College	CO	7,468	C
Adelphi Univ	NY	23,320	VC
Alabama A&M Univ	AL	5,100	LC
Alabama State Univ	AL	6,404	C
Alaska Pacific Univ	AK	16,450	C
Albright College	PA	27,642	C
Alcorn State Univ	MS	5,594	LC
Alderson-Broaddus College	WV	19,640	C
Alfred Univ	NY	27,212	C+
Alice Lloyd College	KY	1,785	VC
Alma College	MI	22,586	VC
Alvernia College	PA	20,790	C
Alverno College	WI	16,930	LC
American Indian College of the Assemblies of God	AZ	7,810	NC
American International College	MA	22,268	LC
American Univ	DC	31,544	VC+
Anderson Univ	IN	19,430	LC

School	ST	$IS	SR
Andrews Univ	MI	17,696	LC
Anna Maria College	MA	22,800	LC
Appalachian State Univ	NC	6,353	C
Aquinas College	TN	10,050	LC
Arcadia Univ	PA	26,650	C
Arizona State Univ-Main	AZ	7,726	C
Arkansas Baptist College	AR	5,530	LC
Arkansas State Univ	AR	7,480	C
Arkansas Tech Univ	AR	6,256	C
Armstrong Atlantic State Univ	GA	7,084	C
Asbury College	KY	18,540	VC
Ashland Univ	OH	22,182	LC
Atlantic Union College	MA	34,034	LC
Auburn Univ	AL	5,510	C
Auburn Univ Montgomery	AL	5,330	NC
Augsburg College	MN	22,978	C
Augusta State Univ	GA	2,282	C
Augustana College	IL	24,117	VC+
Augustana College	SD	20,760	VC
Aurora Univ	IL	18,551	C
Austin Peay State Univ	TN	5,814	LC
Avila College	MO	17,720	C
Baker Univ	KS	14,780	C+
Baldwin-Wallace College	OH	22,010	VC+
Ball State Univ	IN	8,660	C
Bartlesville Wesleyan College	OK	14,100	LC
Barton College	NC	16,834	LC
Bay Path College	MA	22,308	C
Baylor Univ	TX	18,298	VC+
Becker College	MA	21,230	LC
Belhaven College	MS	16,040	C+
Bellarmine Univ	KY	20,440	VC
Belmont Abbey College	NC	19,630	LC
Belmont Univ	TN	19,066	VC
Bemidji State Univ	MN	7,957	C
Benedict College	SC	12,662	LC
Benedictine College	KS	18,485	LC
Benedictine Univ	IL	21,330	C
Bennett College	NC	11,200	C
Berea College	KY	4,070	VC
Bethany College	KS	16,602	C+
Bethany College	WV	18,566	C
Bethel College	IN	17,650	LC
Bethel College	KS	17,355	C+
Bethel College	MN	22,740	VC
Bethune-Cookman College	FL	15,746	C
Birmingham-Southern College	AL	22,960	C
Black Hills State Univ	SD	6,652	LC
Blackburn College	IL	13,690	C
Bloomsburg Univ of Pennsylvania	PA	9,434	C
Blue Mountain College	MS	9,100	LC
Bluefield State College	WV	2,178	LC
Bluffton College	OH	20,644	C
Boise State Univ	ID	6,531	LC
Boricua College	NY	7,375	C
Boston College	MA	33,330	MC
Boston Univ	MA	34,358	MC
Bowie State Univ	MD	9,300	C+
Bowling Green State Univ	OH	10,794	C
Bradley Univ	IL	20,970	VC
Brescia Univ	KY	14,225	C
Briar Cliff Univ	IA	18,657	LC
Bridgewater State College	MA	7,589	C+
Brigham Young Univ	UT	7,840	HC
Brigham Young Univ/Hawaii	HI	6,890	C
Bryan College	TN	16,400	VC
Bucknell Univ	PA	31,096	HC
Buena Vista Univ	IA	22,828	C
Butler Univ	IN	25,580	VC+
Cabrini College	PA	25,950	LC
Caldwell College	NJ	20,940	LC
Cal State, Long Beach	CA	7,400	LC
Calif Univ of Pennsylvania	PA	10,388	C
Calumet College of St. Joseph	IN	7,500	LC
Calvin College	MI	20,050	NC
Cameron Univ	OK	5,560	NC
Campbell Univ	NC	16,599	C
Campbellsville Univ	KY	14,340	C
Canisius College	NY	24,696	C+
Capital Univ	OH	23,630	C
Cardinal Stritch Univ	WI	17,620	C
Caribbean Univ	PR	3,000	
Carlos Albizu Univ	FL	9,309	C
Carlow College	PA	19,366	C
Carroll College	MT	19,140	C
Carroll College	WI	21,170	C
Carson-Newman College	TN	16,490	C
Carthage College	WI	23,670	C
Catawba College	NC	19,620	C
Catholic Univ of America	DC	29,332	VC
Cazenovia College	NY	19,885	LC
Cedar Crest College	PA	25,145	C+
Cedarville Univ	OH	17,553	VC
Centenary College	NJ	22,430	C
Centenary College of Louisiana	LA	21,600	C+
Central College	IA	21,206	C
Central Conn State Univ	CT	10,404	C
Central Methodist College	MO	16,460	C
Central Mich Univ	MI	8,355	C
Central Missouri State Univ	MO	7,920	C

School	ST	$IS	SR
Central State Univ	OH	8,922	C+
Central Univ of Bayamon	PR	3,335	
Central Washington Univ	WA	8,985	LC
Centre College	KY	24,000	HC
Chadron State College	NE	6,211	NC
Chaminade Univ of Honolulu	HI	17,370	C
Champlain College	VT	19,680	C
Charleston Southern Univ	SC	17,122	C
Chestnut Hill College	PA	24,790	LC
Cheyney Univ of Pennsylvania	PA	9,993	C
Chicago State Univ	IL	8,851	C+
City Univ	WA	7,425	NC
CUNY/Brooklyn College	NY	3,403	LC
CUNY/City College	NY	3,309	LC
CUNY/Herbert H. Lehman College	NY	3,320	LC
CUNY/Hunter College	NY	5,147	C+
CUNY/Medgar Evers College	NY	3,282	NC
CUNY/Queens College	NY	3,403	VC
Claflin Univ	SC	12,735	C+
Clarion Univ of Pennsylvania	PA	11,272	LC
Clarke College	IA	20,625	C+
Clearwater Christian College	FL	13,160	LC
Clemson Univ	SC	7,600	C
Cleveland State Univ	OH	10,146	NC
Coastal Carolina Univ	SC	9,220	C
Coe College	IA	24,750	VC
Coker College	SC	20,120	C
College Misericordia	PA	23,380	LC
College of Charleston	SC	8,350	HC
College of Mount St. Joseph	OH	20,290	C
College of New Jersey	NJ	13,425	HC
College of New Rochelle	NY	20,000	C
College of Notre Dame of Maryland	MD	23,100	LC
College of Our Lady of the Elms	MA	20,644	C
College of St. Benedict	MN	23,921	VC
College of St. Catherine	MN	22,324	VC
College of St. Elizabeth	NJ	22,510	C
College of St. Joseph	VT	17,400	NC
College of St. Mary	NE	18,726	C
College of St. Rose	NY	19,084	C
College of St. Scholastica	MN	22,378	C+
College of the Ozarks	MO	2,650	C+
College of the Southwest	NM	8,456	NC
Columbia College	MO	15,082	C
Columbia College	SC	19,050	LC
Columbia Union College	MD	19,027	C+
Concord College	WV	7,122	C+
Concordia College	AL	9,307	NC
Concordia College	NY	19,200	VC
Concordia College/ Moorhead	MN	18,835	C
Concordia Univ	MI	20,500	C
Concordia Univ	MN	19,912	C
Concordia Univ	OR	20,500	LC
Concordia Univ at Austin	TX	16,740	LC
Concordia Univ Nebr	NE	17,770	C
Concordia Univ Wisc	WI	16,600	LC
Concordia Univ, River Forest	IL	20,000	LC
Converse College	SC	21,990	VC
Coppin State College	MD	9,133	LC
Cornell College	IA	24,980	VC
Cornerstone Univ and Grand Rapids Baptist Seminary	MI	18,092	C
Covenant College	GA	21,970	C+
Creighton Univ	NE	23,476	VC
Crichton College	TN	12,680	LC
Cumberland College	KY	14,864	C
Cumberland Univ	TN	11,970	LC
Curry College	MA	26,025	LC
Daemen College	NY	20,620	C
Dakota State Univ	SD	6,950	C
Dakota Wesleyan Univ	SD	15,512	C
Dallas Baptist Univ	TX	13,682	LC
Dana College	NE	18,046	C
David Lipscomb Univ	TN	16,158	VC
Davis and Elkins College	WV	19,270	LC
De Sales Univ	PA	22,610	VC
Defiance College	OH	19,580	LC
Delaware State Univ	DE	8,104	LC
Delta State Univ	MS	5,416	C
DePaul Univ	IL	23,590	VC
DePauw Univ	IN	28,000	HC
Dickinson State Univ	ND	5,495	NC
Dillard Univ	LA	16,046	VC
Doane College	NE	17,600	LC
Dominican College	NY	20,400	LC
Dordt College	IA	18,100	C+
Dowling College	NY	20,281	LC
Drake Univ	IA	22,830	VC
Drury Univ	MO	15,250	VC
Duquesne Univ	PA	24,242	C+
D'Youville College	NY	18,704	C
East Carolina Univ	NC	7,766	C
East Central Univ	OK	4,578	C

School	ST	$IS	SR
East Stroudsburg Univ of Pennsylvania	PA	8,430	LC
East Texas Baptist Univ	TX	12,349	LC
Eastern College	PA	19,641	LC
Eastern Illinois Univ	IL	10,101	C
Eastern Kentucky Univ	KY	6,552	C
Eastern Mennonite Univ	VA	20,700	VC
Eastern Mich Univ	MI	9,855	C
Eastern Nazarene College	MA	19,433	LC
Eastern New Mexico Univ	NM	4,113	LC
Eastern Washington Univ	WA	7,972	LC
Edgewood College	WI	18,304	C
Edinboro Univ of Pennsylvania	PA	9,328	LC
Edward Waters College	FL	13,124	LC
Elizabeth City State Univ	NC	5,550	LC
Elizabethtown College	PA	26,000	VC
Elmhurst College	IL	21,750	C
Elmira College	NY	31,070	VC+
Elon Univ	NC	19,430	VC
Emmanuel College	MA	23,802	C+
Emporia State Univ	KS	6,198	LC
Erskine College	SC	21,399	VC
Eureka College	IL	22,200	C
Evangel Univ	MO	14,050	C
Fairmont State College	WV	7,010	NC
Faulkner Univ	AL	13,000	C
Fayetteville State Univ	NC	5,590	LC
Felician College	NJ	20,050	C
Fitchburg State College	MA	7,836	C
Five Towns College	NY	18,850	SP
Flagler College	FL	10,550	VC+
Florida A&M Univ	FL	6,948	C
Florida Atlantic Univ	FL	8,832	C
Florida Gulf Coast Univ	FL	9,201	C
Florida International Univ	FL	9,486	VC
Florida Memorial College	FL	6,000	LC
Florida Southern College	FL	19,430	C
Florida State Univ	FL	7,835	HC
Fontbonne Univ	MO	18,046	C
Fort Hays State Univ	KS	6,294	LC
Framingham State College	MA	7,259	C
Francis Marion Univ	SC	7,682	C
Franciscan Univ of Steubenville	OH	19,100	C+
Franklin College of Indiana	IN	19,905	C
Franklin Pierce College	NH	26,125	LC
Freed-Hardeman Univ	TN	14,290	VC
Friends Univ	KS	15,962	LC
Frostburg State Univ	MD	9,680	C
Furman Univ	SC	25,492	HC
Gallaudet Univ	DC	16,554	SP
Gannon Univ	PA	18,848	C
Gardner-Webb Univ	NC	17,400	C
Geneva College	PA	19,990	C+
George Fox Univ	OR	24,095	VC
Georgetown College	KY	18,400	VC
Georgia Southwestern State Univ	GA	6,013	C
Georgian Court College	NJ	19,040	LC
Gettysburg College	PA	32,070	HC
Glenville State College	WV	6,588	NC
Gordon College	MA	23,594	VC+
Goshen College	IN	18,950	VC+
Goucher College	MD	30,650	VC+
Grace Bible College	MI	12,600	C
Grace College	IN	16,768	C
Graceland Univ	IA	15,845	C
Grambling State Univ	LA	5,325	NC
Grand Canyon Univ	AZ	30,000	LC
Grand Valley State Univ	MI	10,040	C
Grand View College	IA	17,596	NC
Green Mountain College	VT	24,130	C
Greensboro College	NC	19,080	LC
Greenville College	IL	19,226	LC
Grove City College	PA	12,280	MC
Guilford College	NC	23,255	C
Gustavus Adolphus College	MN	24,190	VC+
Gwynedd-Mercy College	PA	22,350	C
Hamline Univ	MN	23,339	C+
Hannibal-LaGrange College	MO	12,530	C
Hanover College	IN	17,560	VC
Harding Univ	AR	13,528	VC
Hardin-Simmons Univ	TX	14,165	C
Harris-Stowe State College	MO	2,310	SP
Hastings College	NE	17,854	C+
Heidelberg College	OH	23,879	C
Hellenic College/Holy Cross Greek Orthodox School of Theology	MA	17,215	C
Henderson State Univ	AR	6,269	C
Heritage College	WA	6,450	NC
High Point Univ	NC	20,220	LC
Hillsdale College	MI	20,586	VC+
Hiram College	OH	27,034	VC
Hofstra Univ	NY	23,252	C
Holy Family College	PA	13,710	LC
Hope College	MI	22,922	C+
Houghton College	NY	21,810	VC+
Houston Baptist Univ	TX	15,300	LC
Howard Payne Univ	TX	13,834	C+
Howard Univ	DC	15,522	LC
Humboldt State Univ	CA	8,582	C
Huntington College	IN	15,480	LC
Huron Univ	SD	10,450	C
Huston-Tillotson College	TX	12,977	LC

School	ST	$IS	SR
Idaho State Univ	ID	7,030	C+
Illinois College	IL	16,234	C
Illinois State Univ	IL	9,235	C
Illinois Wesleyan Univ	IL	26,970	HC
Immaculata College	PA	22,400	LC
Indiana State Univ	IN	8,461	LC
Indiana Univ Bloomington	IN	10,712	C+
Indiana Univ East	IN	3,415	C
Indiana Univ Kokomo	IN	3,422	LC
Indiana Univ Northwest	IN	3,447	C
Indiana Univ of Pennsylvania	PA	9,133	C
Indiana Univ South Bend	IN	3,515	C
Indiana Univ Southeast	IN	3,459	C
Indiana Univ-Purdue Univ Fort Wayne	IN	3,166	LC
Indiana Univ-Purdue Univ Indianapolis	IN	9,473	C
Indiana Wesleyan Univ	IN	17,680	C
Inter-American Univ of PR/ Aguadilla Campus	PR	3,278	
Inter-American Univ of PR/ Arecibo Campus	PR	3,300	
Inter-American Univ of PR/ Barranquitas Regional College	PR	3,300	LC
Inter-American Univ of PR/ Bayamon Univ College	PR	3,700	
Inter-American Univ of PR/ Fajardo Campus	PR	4,000	
Inter-American Univ of PR/ Metropolitan Campus	PR	4,166	
Inter-American Univ of PR/ Ponce Regional College	PR	3,700	
Inter-American Univ of PR/ San GermEn	PR	6,390	
Iona College	NY	26,556	C
Iowa State Univ	IA	8,108	VC
Iowa Wesleyan College	IA	18,840	C
Jackson State Univ	MS	6,776	LC
Jacksonville State Univ	AL	6,568	LC
Jacksonville Univ	FL	21,110	LC
Jamestown College	ND	11,310	NC
Jarvis Christian College	TX	9,035	NC
John Brown Univ	AR	15,080	VC
John Carroll Univ	OH	24,140	VC
Johnson C. Smith Univ	NC	16,560	C+
Johnson State College	VT	10,776	C
Judson College	AL	13,790	C
Judson College	IL	18,980	LC
Juniata College	PA	26,080	VC
Kansas State Univ	KS	6,995	C
Kean Univ	NJ	11,159	C
Keene State College	NH	11,280	C
Kennesaw State Univ	GA	2,306	LC
Kent State Univ	OH	11,104	C
Kentucky Christian College	KY	13,472	C
Kentucky State Univ	KY	6,146	NC
Kentucky Wesleyan College	KY	15,800	C
Keuka College	NY	21,170	C
Keystone College	PA	19,066	LC
King College	TN	17,800	VC
King's College	PA	24,680	C
Knox College	IL	28,230	HC
Knoxville College	TN	6,200	LC
Kutztown Univ of Pennsylvania	PA	8,907	C
La Roche College	PA	18,854	LC
La Salle Univ	PA	27,890	C
La Sierra Univ	CA	19,260	LC
Lake Erie College	OH	21,350	LC
Lake Superior State Univ	MI	9,034	LC
Lakeland College	WI	17,950	C
Lamar Univ	TX	6,816	LC
Lambuth Univ	TN	14,254	C
Lander Univ	SC	8,618	LC
Lane College	TN	10,400	C+
Langston Univ	OK	2,308	LC
Lasell College	MA	24,100	C
Le Moyne College	NY	23,840	C
Lebanon Valley College of Pennsylvania	PA	25,700	VC
Lee Univ	TN	10,198	LC
Lees-McRae College	NC	17,106	LC
Lenoir-Rhyne College	NC	19,186	C
Lesley College	MA	25,325	LC
LeTourneau Univ	TX	19,020	VC
Lewis Univ	IL	20,960	C
Lewis-Clark State College	ID	6,496	C
Liberty Univ	VA	14,500	C
Limestone College	SC	16,900	C
Lincoln Memorial Univ	TN	12,620	LC
Lincoln Univ	MO	7,158	NC
Lincoln Univ	PA	11,198	C+
Lindenwood Univ	MO	17,250	C
Lindsey Wilson College	KY	16,392	LC
Linfield College	OR	25,840	VC
Livingstone College	NC	13,360	LC
Lock Haven Univ of Pennsylvania	PA	9,534	C
LIU/Brooklyn Campus	NY	22,290	C
LIU/C.W. Post Campus	NY	25,380	C
LIU/Southampton College	NY	26,270	C
Longwood College	VA	8,950	C
Loras College	IA	22,994	C+
Louisiana College	LA	11,516	C

ST = STATE $IS = IN-STATE COSTS SR = SELECTOR RATING

School	ST	$IS	SR
Univ of Missouri/St. Louis	MO	9,966	C
Univ of Mobile	AL	13,620	LC
Univ of Montana	MT	8,038	C
Univ of Montana--Western	MT	6,915	NC
Univ of Montevallo	AL	7,266	C
Univ of Nebr at Kearney	NE	7,048	NC
Univ of Nebr at Lincoln	NE	8,325	C+
Univ of Nebr at Omaha	NE	6,867	C
Univ of Nevada/Las Vegas	NV	8,281	VC
Univ of Nevada/Reno	NV	8,737	C
Univ of New England	ME	24,110	LC
Univ of New Mexico	NM	8,026	C
Univ of New Orleans	LA	10,160	C
Univ of North Alabama	AL	7,016	NC
Univ of N Car at Chapel Hill	NC	8,789	HC
Univ of N Car at Charlotte	NC	7,254	C
Univ of N Car at Greensboro	NC	6,858	C
Univ of N Car at Pembroke	NC	5,914	LC
Univ of N Car at Wilmington	NC	7,769	C
Univ of N Dak	ND	7,067	VC
Univ of North Florida	FL	8,089	VC
Univ of North Texas	TX	7,629	C
Univ of Northern Iowa	IA	7,850	C
Univ of Okla	OK	7,616	VC
Univ of Pennsylvania	PA	34,614	MC
Univ of Pittsburgh at Johnstown	PA	13,044	LC
Univ of Portland	OR	24,950	VC
Univ of PR at Humacao	PR	1,245	
Univ of PR/Arecibo	PR	1,095	
Univ of PR/Bayamon Univ College Campus	PR	1,600	
Univ of PR/Cayey Univ College	PR	1,245	
Univ of PR/Rio Piedras	PR	5,510	
Univ of Rhode Island	RI	12,414	C
Univ of Rio Grande	OH	8,728	NC
Univ of St. Francis	IL	19,650	C
Univ of St. Francis	IN	17,790	LC
Univ of St. Thomas	MN	24,044	VC
Univ of San Diego	CA	29,198	HC
Univ of San Francisco	CA	27,302	VC
Univ of Science and Arts of Okla	OK	5,245	C
Univ of Scranton	PA	27,964	C+
Univ of Sioux Falls	SD	16,390	C
Univ of South Alabama	AL	6,976	LC
Univ of S Car at Aiken	SC	7,828	LC
Univ of S Car at Columbia	SC	8,748	VC
Univ of S Car at Spartanburg	SC	7,318	C+
Univ of S Dak	SD	7,036	C
Univ of South Florida	FL	8,154	C
Univ of Southern Indiana	IN	8,655	LC
Univ of Southern Miss	MS	6,155	LC
Univ of Tampa	FL	22,612	C
Univ of Tenn at Knoxville	TN	8,214	C
Univ of Tenn at Martin	TN	8,268	C
Univ of the District of Columbia	DC	2,844	NC
Univ of the Incarnate Word	TX	18,478	C
Univ of the Sacred Heart	PR	5,375	
Univ of Toledo	OH	11,206	NC
Univ of Tulsa	OK	19,090	HC
Univ of Utah	UT	7,703	C
Univ of Vermont	VT	14,761	C+
Univ of West Alabama	AL	6,048	C
Univ of West Florida	FL	7,518	C
Univ of Wisc/Eau Claire	WI	7,032	VC
Univ of Wisc/La Crosse	WI	7,250	VC
Univ of Wisc/Madison	WI	8,262	VC
Univ of Wisc/Oshkosh	WI	6,130	LC
Univ of Wisc/Platteville	WI	7,282	C
Univ of Wisc/River Falls	WI	6,356	LC
Univ of Wisc/Stevens Point	WI	7,116	C
Univ of Wisc/Superior	WI	7,051	C+
Univ of Wisc/Whitewater	WI	6,937	C
Univ of Wyoming	WY	7,143	LC
Upper Iowa Univ	IA	17,438	C
Urbana Univ	OH	17,004	C
Ursuline College	OH	19,430	LC
Utah State Univ	UT	6,771	C
Valley City State Univ	ND		LC
Valparaiso Univ	IN	23,570	VC+
Vanderbilt Univ	TN	34,482	MC
Vanguard Univ of Southern Calif	CA	20,212	C
Villanova Univ	PA	31,997	HC
Virginia Commonwealth Univ	VA	9,030	C
Virginia Union Univ	VA	15,358	LC
Viterbo Univ	WI	18,043	C
Wagner College	NY	27,000	C
Walla Walla College	WA	20,925	C
Walsh Univ	OH	16,880	C
Warren Wilson College	NC	19,968	C
Wartburg College	IA	21,165	VC
Washburn Univ of Topeka	KS	6,766	NC
Washington Univ in St. Louis	MO	34,593	MC
Wayne State College	NE	6,255	NC
Wayne State Univ	MI	6,720	C
Waynesburg College	PA	17,610	LC
Weber State Univ	UT	6,897	NC
Wellesley College	MA	33,394	MC
Wells College	NY	19,350	VC
Wesley College	DE	17,869	C
West Chester Univ of Pennsylvania	PA	9,792	VC
West Liberty State College	WV	6,056	LC
West Virginia State College	WV	6,264	NC
West Virginia Univ	WV	8,304	C
West Virginia Wesleyan College	WV	22,920	C
Western Carolina Univ	NC	5,667	C
Western Conn State Univ	CT	10,074	C
Western Illinois Univ	IL	9,571	C
Western Kentucky Univ	KY	6,834	C
Western Mich Univ	MI	10,016	C
Western New England College	MA	23,882	C
Western New Mexico Univ	NM	5,950	LC
Western State College of Colo	CO	7,585	LC
Western Washington Univ	WA	8,624	VC
Westfield State College	MA	8,394	C
Westminster College	MO	19,990	C+
Westminster College	PA	22,960	C
Westminster College	UT	17,226	C
Wheaton College	IL	21,934	HC
Wheelock College	MA	25,520	C
Whitworth College	WA	23,938	VC
Wichita State Univ	KS	6,879	C
Widener Univ	PA	26,920	C
Wiley College	TX	8,100	LC
Wilkes Univ	PA	25,800	C
William Carey College	MS	10,150	LC
William Jewell College	MO	17,150	VC
William Penn Univ	IA	17,575	C
William Woods Univ	MO	19,390	LC
Williams Baptist College	AR	10,750	C
Wilmington College	DE	6,530	NC
Wilmington College	OH	21,826	C
Wilson College	PA	21,337	LC
Wingate Univ	NC	19,140	C
Winona State Univ	MN	8,570	C
Winston-Salem State Univ	NC	5,927	LC
Winthrop Univ	SC	9,106	C
Wisc Lutheran College	WI	19,216	VC
Wittenberg Univ	OH	28,766	VC
Worcester State College	MA	7,901	LC
Wright State Univ	OH	9,141	LC
Xavier Univ of Louisiana	LA	17,000	LC
York College of Pennsylvania	PA	12,550	VC
Youngstown State Univ	OH	9,318	NC

ELEMENTARY PARTICLE PHYSICS

School	ST	$IS	SR
Catholic Univ of America	DC	29,332	VC

EMERGENCY MEDICAL TECHNOLOGIES

School	ST	$IS	SR
Creighton Univ	NE	23,476	VC
George Washington Univ	DC	32,170	HC
MCP Hahnemann Univ	PA	18,510	SP
Springfield College	MA	24,520	C
Univ of Akron	OH	10,530	NC
Univ of Maryland/Baltimore County	MD	12,190	VC
Univ of New Mexico	NM	8,026	C
Univ of Pittsburgh at Pittsburgh	PA	13,592	HC
Western Carolina Univ	NC	5,667	C

EMERGENCY/DISASTER SCIENCE

School	ST	$IS	SR
Arkansas Tech Univ	AR	6,256	C
Thomas Edison State College	NJ	2,750	SP
Univ of Akron	OH	10,530	NC
Univ of North Texas	TX	7,629	C
West Texas A&M Univ	TX	6,538	C

ENERGY MANAGEMENT TECHNOLOGY

School	ST	$IS	SR
CUNY/Hunter College	NY	5,147	C+
Penn State Univ/Univ Park Campus	PA	11,126	VC
Univ of New Hampshire	NH	13,207	C
Univ of Northern Iowa	IA	7,850	C

ENGINEERING

School	ST	$IS	SR
Alabama State Univ	AL	6,404	C
Andrews Univ	MI	17,696	LC
Arcadia Univ	PA	26,650	C
Arizona State Univ-Main	AZ	7,726	C
Arkansas State Univ	AR	7,480	C
Arkansas Tech Univ	AR	6,256	C
Baldwin-Wallace College	OH	22,010	VC+
Baylor Univ	TX	18,298	VC+
Biola Univ	CA	21,902	VC
Boston Univ	MA	34,358	MC
Brown Univ	RI	34,973	MC
Bucknell Univ	PA	31,096	HC
Calif Inst of Technology	CA	27,663	MC
Calif Polytechnic State Univ	CA	8,747	VC
Cal State, Hayward	CA	7,400	LC
Cal State, Los Angeles	CA	5,050	C
Cal State, Northridge	CA	7,781	C
Calvin College	MI	20,050	NC
Carnegie Mellon Univ	PA	32,682	MC
Case Western Reserve Univ	OH	27,418	C
Catholic Univ of America	DC	29,332	VC
Central Missouri State Univ	MO	7,920	C
Clark Atlanta Univ	GA	17,174	C
Colo School of Mines	CO	11,578	HC
Cooper Union for the Advancement of Science and Art	NY	6,500	MC
Dillard Univ	LA	16,046	VC
Dominican Univ	IL	20,800	C
Dordt College	IA	18,100	C+
Eastern Illinois Univ	IL	10,101	C
Elizabethtown College	PA	26,000	VC
Franciscan Univ of Steubenville	OH	19,100	C+
Geneva College	PA	19,990	C+
George Fox Univ	OR	24,095	VC
George Washington Univ	DC	32,170	HC
Grand Valley State Univ	MI	10,040	C
Harvard Univ/Harvard College	MA	34,269	MC
Harvey Mudd College	CA	31,605	MC
Hofstra Univ	NY	23,252	C
Hope College	MI	22,922	C+
Idaho State Univ	ID	7,030	C+
Indiana Univ-Purdue Univ Fort Wayne	IN	3,166	LC
Indiana Univ-Purdue Univ Indianapolis	IN	9,473	C
Iowa State Univ	IA	8,108	VC
John Brown Univ	AR	15,080	VC
Johns Hopkins Univ	MD	35,226	MC
Lafayette College	PA	32,655	MC
Lake Superior State Univ	MI	9,034	LC
Lebanon Valley College of Pennsylvania	PA	25,700	VC
LeTourneau Univ	TX	19,020	VC
Lincoln Univ	MO	7,158	NC
Lindenwood Univ	MO	17,250	C
Loyola College in Maryland	MD	30,900	HC
Lubbock Christian Univ	TX	14,226	LC
Lynchburg College	VA	23,405	C
Maine Maritime Academy	ME	10,911	C
Manchester College	IN	22,010	C
Marquette Univ	WI	24,836	C+
Maryville College	TN	23,210	VC
Messiah College	PA	23,180	VC
Miami Univ	OH	12,885	VC+
Mich State Univ	MI	10,386	VC
Mich Tech Univ	MI	11,088	VC
Montana Tech of The Univ of Montana	MT	7,845	C
Morningside College	IA	19,124	C
New Mexico Highlands Univ	NM	6,256	NC
New Mexico Inst of Mining and Technology	NM	7,152	VC+
Norfolk State Univ	VA	8,382	LC
N Car State Univ	NC	8,680	HC
Northeastern Univ	MA	30,078	VC
Northern Arizona Univ	AZ	7,398	C
Northwestern Univ	IL	33,615	MC
Okla State Univ	OK	7,650	VC
Olivet Nazarene Univ	IL	18,444	C
Oral Roberts Univ	OK	18,490	C
Penn State Univ at Erie/Behrend College	PA	12,326	C
Penn State Univ/Univ Park Campus	PA	11,126	VC
Pepperdine Univ	CA	32,830	VC
Principia College	IL	23,865	C+
Purdue Univ/Calumet	IN	6,630	NC
Purdue Univ/West Lafayette	IN	10,284	VC
Quincy Univ	IL	20,450	C
Regis Univ	CO	25,740	C+
Rensselaer Polytechnic Inst	NY	33,863	HC+
Rice Univ	TX	24,325	MC
Robert Morris Univ	PA	18,730	C
Rochester Inst of Technology	NY	26,232	VC+
Roger Williams Univ	RI	29,010	C
Rowan Univ	NJ	12,365	VC
St. Anselm College	NH	27,405	C
St. Mary's Univ of San Antonio	TX	19,735	C
San Francisco State Univ	CA	7,139	LC
San Jose State Univ	CA	8,187	C
Santa Clara Univ	CA	28,371	VC+
Scripps College	CA	30,400	HC+
Smith College	MA	33,302	HC+
Spelman College	GA	19,215	C+
Spring Hill College	AL	23,250	C
Stanford Univ	CA	34,222	MC
SUNY/Maritime College	NY	10,025	LC
Swarthmore College	PA	34,538	MC
Temple Univ	PA	14,124	C
Tenn Tech Univ	TN	6,968	C
Texas Christian Univ	TX	19,910	C
Texas Tech Univ	TX	8,825	C
Trinity College	CT	34,300	HC
Tufts Univ	MA	34,874	MC
Tulane Univ	LA	34,013	HC+
United States Air Force Academy	CO		MC
United States Merchant Marine Academy	NY		VC
United States Naval Academy	MD		MC
Univ of Arizona	AZ	8,614	C
Univ of Calif at Irvine	CA	11,756	C
Univ of Calif at San Diego	CA	11,372	HC
Univ of Cincinnati	OH	12,491	LC
Univ of Colo at Boulder	CO	9,255	VC
Univ of Dayton	OH	20,400	VC
Univ of Detroit Mercy	MI	21,620	LC
Univ of Hartford	CT	28,884	C
Univ of Illinois at Chicago	IL	10,702	VC
Univ of Illinois at Urbana-Champaign	IL	11,316	HC+
Univ of Iowa	IA	8,607	C+
Univ of Louisville	KY	7,402	LC
Univ of Maryland/College Park	MD	11,959	C
Univ of Miami	FL	31,130	HC
Univ of Mich/Ann Arbor	MI	13,003	HC+
Univ of Mich/Flint	MI	4,323	C
Univ of Miss	MS	7,666	C
Univ of Missouri/Rolla	MO	10,034	C
Univ of Missouri/St. Louis	MO	9,966	C
Univ of New Haven	CT	23,862	LC
Univ of Okla	OK	7,616	VC
Univ of Pennsylvania	PA	34,614	MC
Univ of Portland	OR	24,950	VC
Univ of PR/Mayaguez	PR	5,285	
Univ of South Florida	FL	8,154	C
Univ of Tenn at Chattanooga	TN	7,783	C
Univ of Tenn at Knoxville	TN	8,214	C
Univ of Tenn at Martin	TN	8,268	C
Univ of Toledo	OH	11,206	NC
Univ of Washington	WA	10,361	VC
Univ of Wisc/Milwaukee	WI	8,907	LC
Univ of Wisc/Platteville	WI	7,282	C
Utah State Univ	UT	6,771	C
Walla Walla College	WA	20,925	C
Washington Univ in St. Louis	MO	34,593	MC
Waynesburg College	PA	17,610	LC
West Virginia Univ	WV	8,304	C
Western Mich Univ	MI	10,016	C
Yale Univ	CT	34,030	MC
Youngstown State Univ	OH	9,318	NC

ENGINEERING AND APPLIED SCIENCE

School	ST	$IS	SR
Abilene Christian Univ	TX	16,300	VC
Benedictine Univ	IL	21,330	C
Bethel College	MN	22,740	VC
Calif Inst of Technology	CA	27,663	MC
Cal State, Fullerton	CA	5,440	LC
CUNY/College of Staten Island	NY	3,358	NC
College of New Jersey	NJ	13,425	HC
Colo State Univ	CO	9,672	C
Dartmouth College	NH	34,458	MC
Hofstra Univ	NY	23,252	C
New Jersey Inst of Technology	NJ	14,690	VC
Oakland Univ	MI	9,418	C
Pacific Lutheran Univ	WA	23,318	VC
Seattle Pacific Univ	WA	22,674	C+
Southern Polytechnic State Univ	GA	6,662	C
SUNY/Univ at Stony Brook	NY	10,998	VC
Trinity Univ	TX	21,444	HC
Tufts Univ	MA	34,874	MC
United States Air Force Academy	CO		MC
Univ of Calif at Berkeley	CA	14,134	MC
Univ of Florida	FL	7,874	HC
Univ of Mich/Ann Arbor	MI	13,003	HC+
Univ of Rochester	NY	32,979	HC
Univ of Southern Calif	CA	33,647	MC
Univ of Tenn at Knoxville	TN	8,214	C
Univ of Virginia	VA	9,391	HC+
Vanderbilt Univ	TN	34,482	MC
Wartburg College	IA	21,165	VC
Wilkes Univ	PA	25,800	C
Yale Univ	CT	34,030	MC

ENGINEERING MANAGEMENT

School	ST	$IS	SR
Clarkson Univ	NY	29,884	VC
Columbia Univ/Fu Foundation School of Engineering and Applied Science	NY	35,190	MC
Idaho State Univ	ID	7,030	C+
Lake Superior State Univ	MI	9,034	LC
Miami Univ	OH	12,885	VC+
Oral Roberts Univ	OK	18,490	C
Park Univ	MO	9,816	C
Point Park College	PA	20,290	C

School	ST	$IS	SR
St. Louis Univ	MO	26,590	VC+
Southern Illinois Univ at Carbondale	IL	8,621	C
Stevens Inst of Technology	NJ	31,510	HC+
Texas A&M Univ at Kingsville	TX	6,446	LC
Tri-State Univ-Main Campus	IN	21,200	C
United States Military Academy	NY		MC
Univ of Evansville	IN	22,865	VC+
Univ of Illinois at Chicago	IL	10,702	VC
Univ of Louisville	KY	7,402	LC
Univ of Missouri/Rolla	MO	10,034	C
Univ of Portland	OR	24,950	VC
Univ of Southern Calif	CA	33,647	MC
Univ of Tenn at Chattanooga	TN	7,783	C
Univ of the Pacific	CA	28,255	VC
Univ of Vermont	VT	14,761	C+
Western Mich Univ	MI	10,016	C
Wilkes Univ	PA	25,800	C
York College of Pennsylvania	PA	12,550	VC

ENGINEERING MECHANICS

School	ST	$IS	SR
Columbia Univ/Fu Foundation School of Engineering and Applied Science	NY	35,190	MC
Johns Hopkins Univ	MD	35,226	MC
Lehigh Univ	PA	32,290	MC
New Mexico Inst of Mining and Technology	NM	7,152	VC+
United States Air Force Academy	CO		MC
Univ of Cincinnati	OH	12,491	LC
Univ of Illinois at Urbana-Champaign	IL	11,316	HC+
Univ of Missouri/Rolla	MO	10,034	C
Univ of Wisc/Madison	WI	8,262	VC
Washington Univ in St. Louis	MO	34,593	MC

ENGINEERING PHYSICS

School	ST	$IS	SR
Abilene Christian Univ	TX	16,300	VC
Augustana College	IL	24,117	VC+
Augustana College	SD	20,760	VC
Bradley Univ	IL	20,970	VC
Case Western Reserve Univ	OH	27,418	C
Christian Brothers Univ	TN	19,820	VC
Conn College	CT	33,585	MC
Cornell Univ	NY	34,614	MC
Dartmouth College	NH	34,458	MC
Eastern Nazarene College	MA	19,433	LC
Edinboro Univ of Pennsylvania	PA	9,328	LC
Elizabethtown College	PA	26,000	VC
Embry-Riddle Aeronautical Univ	FL	24,790	C
Jacksonville Univ	FL	21,110	LC
John Carroll Univ	OH	24,140	VC
Lehigh Univ	PA	32,290	MC
Loyola Marymount Univ	CA	28,754	HC
Miami Univ	OH	12,885	VC+
Miss College	MS	14,574	C
Morgan State Univ	MD	10,078	LC
New York Univ	NY	35,200	MC
N Car Agricultural and Technical State Univ	NC	6,659	LC
Northwest Nazarene Univ	ID	18,380	C
Oakland Univ	MI	9,418	C
Okla Christian Univ	OK	16,500	VC
Point Loma Nazarene Univ	CA	21,380	VC
Rensselaer Polytechnic Inst	NY	33,863	HC+
St. Ambrose Univ	IA	19,994	C
St. Bonaventure Univ	NY	21,956	C
Samford Univ	AL	16,340	VC
Santa Clara Univ	CA	28,371	VC+
S Dak State Univ	SD	6,848	C
Southwest Missouri State Univ	MO	7,600	LC
Southwestern Okla State Univ	OK	4,801	C
SUNY/Univ at Buffalo	NY	11,033	VC
Stevens Inst of Technology	NJ	31,510	HC+
Syracuse Univ	NY	30,710	HC
Taylor Univ	IN	21,562	VC+
Texas Tech Univ	TX	8,825	C
Ohio State Univ	OH	10,819	VC
Tufts Univ	MA	34,874	MC
United States Military Academy	NY		MC
Univ of Arizona	AZ	8,614	C
Univ of Calif at Berkeley	CA	14,134	MC
Univ of Calif at San Diego	CA	11,372	HC
Univ of Central Okla	OK	5,205	C
Univ of Colo at Boulder	CO	9,255	VC
Univ of Illinois at Chicago	IL	10,702	VC
Univ of Illinois at Urbana-Champaign	IL	11,316	HC+
Univ of Kansas	KS	7,232	VC
Univ of Maine	ME	10,798	C
Univ of Mass Boston	MA	4,227	C
Univ of Mich/Ann Arbor	MI	13,003	HC+
Univ of Nebr at Omaha	NE	6,867	C
Univ of Nevada/Reno	NV	8,737	C
Univ of Okla	OK	7,616	VC
Univ of Pittsburgh at Pittsburgh	PA	13,592	HC
Univ of Tenn at Knoxville	TN	8,214	C
Univ of the Pacific	CA	28,255	VC
Univ of Tulsa	OK	19,090	HC
Univ of Wisc/Madison	WI	8,262	VC
Washington and Lee Univ	VA	25,095	MC
Washington Univ in St. Louis	MO	34,593	MC
West Virginia Wesleyan College	WV	22,920	C
Westmont College	CA	29,748	VC
Worcester Polytechnic Inst	MA	34,480	HC+
Wright State Univ	OH	9,141	LC

ENGINEERING TECHNOLOGY

School	ST	$IS	SR
Austin Peay State Univ	TN	5,814	LC
Bluefield State College	WV	2,178	LC
Calif Maritime Academy	CA	12,256	C
Calif State Polytechnic Univ, Pomona	CA	8,615	C
Cal State, Long Beach	CA	7,400	LC
Cal State, Sacramento	CA	7,488	C
Capitol College	MD	18,462	LC
Central Conn State Univ	CT	10,404	C
Central Mich Univ	MI	8,355	C
Central Missouri State Univ	MO	7,920	C
Central Washington Univ	WA	8,985	LC
East Tenn State Univ	TN	7,127	C
Embry-Riddle Aeronautical Univ	FL	24,790	C
Fairmont State College	WV	7,010	NC
Ferris State Univ	MI	10,816	C
Florida A&M Univ	FL	6,948	C
Francis Marion Univ	SC	7,682	C
Gallaudet Univ	DC	16,554	SP
Georgia Southern Univ	GA	6,958	C
Grambling State Univ	LA	5,325	NC
Indiana Univ-Purdue Univ Fort Wayne	IN	3,166	LC
Indiana Univ-Purdue Univ Indianapolis	IN	9,473	C
Iowa State Univ	IA	8,108	VC
Kent State Univ	OH	11,104	C
Lake Superior State Univ	MI	9,034	LC
Lawrence Tech Univ	MI	11,429	C
LeTourneau Univ	TX	19,020	VC
Maine Maritime Academy	ME	10,911	C
Miami Univ	OH	12,885	VC+
Mich Tech Univ	MI	11,088	VC
Middle Tenn State Univ	TN	6,994	C
Midwestern State Univ	TX	6,704	NC
Milwaukee School of Engineering	WI	25,680	VC+
Minn State Univ, Mankato	MN	7,296	LC
Missouri Western State College	MO	6,662	NC
Montana State Univ-Northern	MT	8,600	NC
Murray State Univ	KY	6,672	C
New Jersey Inst of Technology	NJ	14,690	VC
New Mexico State Univ	NM	7,302	C
New York Inst of Technology	NY	21,756	C
Northeastern Univ	MA	30,078	VC
Northern Illinois Univ	IL	9,545	C
Old Dominion Univ	VA	9,386	C
Oregon Inst of Technology	OR	8,718	C
Pacific Union College	CA	20,250	VC
Penn State Univ at Erie/Behrend College	PA	12,326	C
Pittsburg State Univ	KS	6,228	NC
Prairie View A&M Univ	TX	3,172	LC
Purdue Univ/Calumet	IN	6,630	NC
Rice Univ	TX	24,325	MC
Rochester Inst of Technology	NY	26,232	VC+
St. Cloud State Univ	MN	7,180	C
Savannah State Univ	GA	2,550	LC
Silver Lake College of the Holy Family	WI	15,516	LC
S Car State Univ	SC	6,586	LC
S Dak State Univ	SD	6,848	C
Southeast Missouri State Univ	MO	8,367	C+
Southern Illinois Univ at Carbondale	IL	8,621	C
Southern Univ and A&M College	LA	6,365	C+
Southern Utah Univ	UT	7,254	C
Southwest Texas State Univ	TX	8,730	VC
Southwestern Okla State Univ	OK	4,801	C
Temple Univ	PA	14,124	C
Texas A&M Univ	TX	8,988	VC
Texas A&M Univ at Commerce	TX	7,326	C
Texas Southern Univ	TX	6,576	NC
Univ of Central Florida	FL	8,251	VC
Univ of Cincinnati	OH	12,491	LC
Univ of Dayton	OH	20,400	VC
Univ of Delaware	DE	10,824	VC
Univ of Houston-Downtown	TX	2,006	NC
Univ of Maryland/Eastern Shore	MD	9,258	C
Univ of Mass Lowell	MA	9,470	VC
Univ of Miami	FL	31,130	HC
Univ of New Hampshire	NH	13,207	C
Univ of North Texas	TX	7,629	C
Univ of Southern Indiana	IN	8,655	LC
Univ of Southern Miss	MS	6,155	LC
Univ of Toledo	OH	11,206	NC
Virginia State Univ	VA	8,182	LC
West Texas A&M Univ	TX	6,538	C
West Virginia Univ Inst of Technology	WV	7,518	NC
Western Carolina Univ	NC	5,667	C
Western Washington Univ	WA	8,024	VC
Youngstown State Univ	OH	9,318	NC

ENGLISH

School	ST	$IS	SR
Abilene Christian Univ	TX	16,300	VC
Adams State College	CO	7,468	C
Adelphi Univ	NY	23,320	VC
Adrian College	MI	19,670	C
Agnes Scott College	GA	24,950	VC
Alabama A&M Univ	AL	5,100	LC
Alabama State Univ	AL	6,404	C
Albany State Univ	GA	5,764	C+
Albertson College of Idaho	ID	23,900	VC
Albertus Magnus College	CT	22,154	C
Albion College	MI	25,224	VC
Albright College	PA	27,642	C
Alcorn State Univ	MS	5,594	LC
Alfred Univ	NY	27,212	C+
Alice Lloyd College	KY	1,785	VC
Allegheny College	PA	27,780	VC
Allen Univ	SC	9,600	NC
Alma College	MI	22,586	VC
Alvernia College	PA	20,790	C
Alverno College	WI	16,930	LC
American International College	MA	22,268	LC
Amherst College	MA	34,340	MC
Anderson Univ	IN	19,430	LC
Andrews Univ	MI	17,696	LC
Angelo State Univ	TX	7,028	C
Anna Maria College	MA	22,800	LC
Appalachian State Univ	NC	6,353	C
Aquinas College	MI	20,052	C+
Arcadia Univ	PA	26,650	C
Arizona State Univ-Main	AZ	7,726	C
Arkansas State Univ	AR	7,480	C
Arkansas Tech Univ	AR	6,256	C
Armstrong Atlantic State Univ	GA	7,084	C
Asbury College	KY	18,540	VC
Ashland Univ	OH	22,182	LC
Assumption College	MA	26,320	C
Atlantic Union College	MA	34,034	LC
Auburn Univ	AL	5,510	C
Auburn Univ Montgomery	AL	5,330	NC
Augsburg College	MN	22,978	C
Augusta State Univ	GA	2,282	C
Augustana College	IL	24,117	VC+
Augustana College	SD	20,760	VC
Aurora Univ	IL	18,551	C
Austin College	TX	22,150	VC+
Austin Peay State Univ	TN	5,814	LC
Averett Univ	VA	17,980	LC
Avila College	MO	17,720	C
Azusa Pacific Univ	CA	22,422	VC
Baker Univ	KS	14,780	C+
Baldwin-Wallace College	OH	22,010	VC+
Ball State Univ	IN	8,660	C
Barber-Scotia College	NC	13,100	C
Bard College	NY	33,912	HC
Barry Univ	FL	24,100	LC
Bartlesville Wesleyan College	OK	14,100	LC
Barton College	NC	16,834	LC
Bates College	ME	34,100	MC
Baylor Univ	TX	18,298	VC+
Belhaven College	MS	16,040	C+
Bellarmine Univ	KY	20,440	VC
Bellevue Univ	NE	4,125	NC
Belmont Abbey College	NC	19,630	LC
Belmont Univ	TN	19,066	VC
Beloit College	WI	27,482	HC
Bemidji State Univ	MN	7,957	C
Benedict College	SC	12,662	LC
Benedictine College	KS	18,485	LC
Bennett College	NC	11,200	C
Bennington College	VT	31,350	VC
Bentley College	MA	31,060	HC
Berea College	KY	4,070	VC
Berry College	GA	18,850	C
Bethany College	KS	16,602	C+
Bethany College	WV	18,566	C
Bethel College	IN	17,650	LC
Bethel College	KS	17,355	C+
Bethel College	MN	22,740	VC
Bethel College	TN	12,980	C
Bethune-Cookman College	FL	15,716	C
Biola Univ	CA	21,902	VC
Birmingham-Southern College	AL	22,960	C
Black Hills State Univ	SD	6,652	LC
Bloomfield College	NJ	17,000	C
Bloomsburg Univ of Pennsylvania	PA	9,434	C
Blue Mountain College	MS	9,100	LC
Bluefield College	VA	14,200	C
Bluffton College	OH	20,644	C
Boise State Univ	ID	6,531	LC
Boston College	MA	33,330	MC
Boston Univ	MA	34,358	MC
Bowdoin College	ME	32,650	MC
Bowie State Univ	MD	9,300	C+
Bowling Green State Univ	OH	10,794	C
Bradley Univ	IL	20,970	VC
Brandeis Univ	MA	34,481	MC
Brenau Univ Women's College	GA	20,100	C
Brescia Univ	KY	14,225	C
Brewton-Parker College	GA	10,810	LC
Briar Cliff Univ	IA	18,657	LC
Bridgewater College	VA	22,950	C
Bridgewater State College	MA	7,589	C+
Brigham Young Univ	UT	7,840	HC
Brigham Young Univ/Hawaii	HI	6,890	C
Brown Univ	RI	34,973	MC
Bryan College	TN	16,400	VC
Bryant College	RI	25,980	VC
Bryn Athyn College of the New Church	PA	10,590	NC
Bryn Mawr College	PA	33,580	HC+
Bucknell Univ	PA	31,096	HC
Buena Vista Univ	IA	22,828	C
Butler Univ	IN	25,580	VC+
Cabrini College	PA	25,950	LC
Caldwell College	NJ	20,940	LC
Calif Baptist Univ	CA	16,736	C
Calif Lutheran Univ	CA	23,500	LC
Calif Polytechnic State Univ	CA	8,747	VC
Calif State Polytechnic Univ, Pomona	CA	8,615	C
Cal State, Bakersfield	CA	6,090	LC
Cal State, Chico	CA	8,598	LC
Cal State, Dominguez Hills	CA	5,840	LC
Cal State, Fresno	CA	7,762	C
Cal State, Fullerton	CA	5,440	LC
Cal State, Hayward	CA	7,400	LC
Cal State, Long Beach	CA	7,400	LC
Cal State, Los Angeles	CA	5,050	C
Cal State, Northridge	CA	7,781	C
Cal State, Sacramento	CA	7,488	C
Cal State, San Bernardino	CA	6,516	C
Cal State, Stanislaus	CA	8,895	C
Calif Univ of Pennsylvania	PA	10,388	C
Calumet College of St. Joseph	IN	7,500	LC
Calvin College	MI	20,050	NC
Cameron Univ	OK	5,560	NC
Campbell Univ	NC	16,599	C
Campbellsville Univ	KY	14,340	C
Canisius College	NY	24,696	C+
Capital Univ	OH	23,630	C
Cardinal Stritch Univ	WI	17,620	C
Carleton College	MN	30,780	MC
Carlow College	PA	19,366	C
Carnegie Mellon Univ	PA	32,682	MC
Carroll College	MT	19,140	C
Carroll College	WI	21,170	C
Carson-Newman College	TN	16,490	C
Carthage College	WI	23,670	C
Case Western Reserve Univ	OH	27,418	C
Catawba College	NC	19,620	C
Catholic Univ of America	DC	29,332	VC
Cazenovia College	NY	19,885	LC
Cedar Crest College	PA	25,145	C+
Cedarville Univ	OH	17,553	VC
Centenary College	NJ	22,430	C
Centenary College of Louisiana	LA	21,600	C+
Central College	IA	21,206	C
Central Conn State Univ	CT	10,404	C
Central Methodist College	MO	16,460	C
Central Mich Univ	MI	8,355	C
Central Missouri State Univ	MO	7,920	C
Central State Univ	OH	8,922	C+
Central Washington Univ	WA	8,985	LC
Centre College	KY	24,000	HC
Chadron State College	NE	6,211	NC
Chaminade Univ of Honolulu	HI	17,370	C
Chapman Univ	CA	30,218	VC
Charleston Southern Univ	SC	17,122	C
Chatham College	PA	25,454	C+
Chestnut Hill College	PA	24,790	LC
Cheyney Univ of Pennsylvania	PA	9,993	C
Chicago State Univ	IL	8,851	C+
Christendom College	VA	16,700	VC+
Christian Brothers Univ	TN	19,820	VC
Christian Heritage College	CA	18,000	LC
Christopher Newport Univ	VA	8,862	VC
Citadel, The	SC	9,126	C

School	ST	$IS	SR
CUNY/Baruch College	NY	3,275	VC+
CUNY/Brooklyn College	NY	3,403	LC
CUNY/City College	NY	3,309	LC
CUNY/College of Staten Island	NY	3,358	NC
CUNY/Herbert H. Lehman College	NY	3,320	LC
CUNY/Hunter College	NY	5,147	C+
CUNY/Queens College	NY	3,403	VC
CUNY/York College	NY	3,292	NC
Claflin Univ	SC	12,735	C+
Clarion Univ of Pennsylvania	PA	11,272	LC
Clark Atlanta Univ	GA	17,174	C
Clark Univ	MA	29,170	HC
Clarke College	IA	20,625	C+
Clearwater Christian College	FL	13,160	LC
Clemson Univ	SC	7,600	C
Cleveland State Univ	OH	10,146	NC
Coastal Carolina Univ	SC	9,220	C
Coe College	IA	24,750	VC
Coker College	SC	20,120	C
Colby College	ME	34,290	MC
Colby-Sawyer College	NH	27,850	LC
Colgate Univ	NY	33,480	MC
College Misericordia	PA	23,380	LC
College of Charleston	SC	8,350	HC
College of Mount St. Vincent	NY	24,230	C
College of Mount St. Joseph	OH	20,290	C
College of New Jersey	NJ	13,425	HC
College of New Rochelle	NY	20,000	C
College of Notre Dame of Maryland	MD	23,100	LC
College of Our Lady of the Elms	MA	20,644	C
College of St. Benedict	MN	23,921	VC
College of St. Catherine	MN	22,324	VC
College of St. Elizabeth	NJ	22,510	C
College of St. Joseph	VT	17,400	NC
College of St. Mary	NE	18,726	C
College of St. Rose	NY	19,084	C
College of St. Scholastica	MN	22,378	C+
College of Santa Fe	NM	20,250	LC
College of the Holy Cross	MA	32,780	MC
College of the Ozarks	MO	2,650	C+
College of the Southwest	NM	8,456	NC
College of William and Mary	VA	10,002	MC
College of Wooster	OH	28,350	VC
Colo Christian Univ	CO	17,714	C
Colo College	CO	31,525	HC+
Colo State Univ	CO	9,672	C
Columbia College	MO	15,082	C
Columbia College	SC	19,050	LC
Columbia Union College	MD	19,027	C+
Columbia Univ/Barnard College	NY	33,694	MC
Columbia Univ/Columbia College	NY	35,190	MC
Columbus State Univ	GA	7,228	LC
Concord College	WV	7,122	C+
Concordia College	NY	19,200	VC
Concordia College/Moorhead	MN	18,835	C
Concordia Univ	CA	22,290	C
Concordia Univ	MI	20,500	C
Concordia Univ	MN	19,912	C
Concordia Univ	OR	20,500	LC
Concordia Univ at Austin	TX	16,740	LC
Concordia Univ Nebr	NE	17,770	C
Concordia Univ Wisc	WI	16,600	LC
Concordia Univ, River Forest	IL	20,000	LC
Conn College	CT	33,585	MC
Converse College	SC	21,990	VC
Coppin State College	MD	9,133	LC
Cornell College	IA	24,980	VC
Cornell Univ	NY	34,614	MC
Cornerstone Univ and Grand Rapids Baptist Seminary	MI	18,092	C
Covenant College	GA	21,970	C+
Creighton Univ	NE	23,476	VC
Crichton College	TN	12,680	LC
Culver-Stockton College	MO	15,400	LC
Cumberland College	KY	14,864	C
Curry College	MA	26,025	LC
Daemen College	NY	20,620	C
Dakota State Univ	SD	6,950	C
Dakota Wesleyan Univ	SD	15,512	C
Dallas Baptist Univ	TX	13,682	LC
Dana College	NE	18,046	C
Dartmouth College	NH	34,458	MC
David Lipscomb Univ	TN	16,158	VC
Davidson College	NC	30,823	MC
Davis and Elkins College	WV	19,270	LC
De Sales Univ	PA	22,610	VC
Delaware State Univ	DE	8,104	LC
Delaware Valley College	PA	24,213	LC
Delta State Univ	MS	5,416	C
Denison Univ	OH	29,640	HC
DePaul Univ	IL	23,590	VC
DePauw Univ	IN	28,000	HC
Dickinson College	PA	32,210	VC+
Dickinson State Univ	ND	5,495	NC
Dillard Univ	LA	16,046	VC
Doane College	NE	17,600	LC
Dominican College	NY	20,400	LC
Dominican Univ	IL	20,800	C
Dordt College	IA	18,100	C+
Dowling College	NY	20,281	LC
Drake Univ	IA	22,830	VC
Drew Univ/College of Liberal Arts	NJ	32,152	VC
Drury Univ	MO	15,250	VC
Duke Univ	NC	34,396	MC
Duquesne Univ	PA	24,242	C+
D'Youville College	NY	18,704	C
Earlham College	IN	27,446	VC+
East Carolina Univ	NC	7,766	C
East Central Univ	OK	4,578	C
East Stroudsburg Univ of Pennsylvania	PA	8,430	LC
East Tenn State Univ	TN	7,127	C
East Texas Baptist Univ	TX	12,349	LC
Eastern Conn State Univ	CT	10,362	C
Eastern Illinois Univ	IL	10,101	C
Eastern Kentucky Univ	KY	6,552	C
Eastern Mennonite Univ	VA	20,700	VC
Eastern Mich Univ	MI	9,855	C
Eastern Nazarene College	MA	19,433	LC
Eastern New Mexico Univ	NM	4,113	LC
Eastern Oregon Univ	OR	8,772	C
Eastern Washington Univ	WA	7,972	LC
East-West Univ	IL	9,140	LC
Eckerd College	FL	25,500	C+
Edgewood College	WI	18,304	C
Edinboro Univ of Pennsylvania	PA	9,328	LC
Edward Waters College	FL	13,124	LC
Elizabeth City State Univ	NC	5,550	LC
Elizabethtown College	PA	26,000	VC
Elmhurst College	IL	21,750	C
Elon Univ	NC	19,430	VC
Emmanuel College	MA	23,802	C+
Emory Univ	GA	33,792	MC
Emporia State Univ	KS	6,198	C
Erskine College	SC	21,399	VC
Eugene Lang College of New School Univ	NY	30,300	C
Eureka College	IL	22,200	C
Evangel Univ	MO	14,050	C
Fairfield Univ	CT	30,885	HC
Fairleigh Dickinson Univ/Madison campus	NJ	25,500	C
Fairleigh Dickinson Univ/Teaneck Campus	NJ	24,646	C
Fairmont State College	WV	7,010	NC
Faulkner Univ	AL	13,000	C
Fayetteville State Univ	NC	5,590	LC
Felician College	NJ	20,050	C
Ferrum College	VA	15,990	LC
Fisk Univ	TN	13,700	LC
Fitchburg State College	MA	7,836	C
Flagler College	FL	10,550	VC+
Florida A&M Univ	FL	6,948	C
Florida Atlantic Univ	FL	8,832	C
Florida International Univ	FL	9,486	VC
Florida Memorial College	FL	6,000	LC
Florida Southern College	FL	19,430	C
Florida State Univ	FL	7,835	HC
Fontbonne Univ	MO	18,046	C
Fordham Univ	NY	30,710	VC
Fort Hays State Univ	KS	6,294	LC
Fort Lewis College	CO	7,659	LC
Fort Valley State Univ	GA	6,014	LC
Framingham State College	MA	7,259	C
Francis Marion Univ	SC	7,682	C
Franciscan Univ of Steubenville	OH	19,100	C+
Franklin and Marshall College	PA	32,410	HC
Franklin College of Indiana	IN	19,905	C
Franklin Pierce College	NH	26,125	LC
Freed-Hardeman Univ	TN	14,290	VC
Fresno Pacific Univ	CA	19,740	C
Friends Univ	KS	15,962	LC
Frostburg State Univ	MD	9,680	C
Furman Univ	SC	25,492	HC
Gallaudet Univ	DC	16,554	SP
Gannon Univ	PA	18,848	C
Gardner-Webb Univ	NC	17,400	C
Geneva College	PA	19,990	C+
George Mason Univ	VA	9,192	C
George Washington Univ	DC	32,170	HC
Georgetown College	KY	18,400	VC
Georgetown Univ	DC	34,847	MC
Georgia College and State Univ	GA	7,344	C
Georgia Southern Univ	GA	6,958	C
Georgia Southwestern State Univ	GA	6,013	C
Georgia State Univ	GA	7,792	LC
Georgian Court College	NJ	19,040	LC
Gettysburg College	PA	32,070	HC
Glenville State College	WV	6,588	NC
Gonzaga Univ	WA	24,276	HC+
Gordon College	MA	23,594	VC+
Goshen College	IN	18,950	VC+
Goucher College	MD	30,650	VC+
Grace College	IN	16,768	C
Graceland Univ	IA	15,845	C
Grambling State Univ	LA	5,325	NC
Grand Canyon Univ	AZ	30,000	LC
Grand Valley State Univ	MI	10,040	C
Grand View College	IA	17,596	NC
Green Mountain College	VT	24,130	C
Greensboro College	NC	19,080	LC
Greenville College	IL	19,226	LC
Grinnell College	IA	28,300	HC+
Grove City College	PA	12,280	MC
Guilford College	NC	23,255	C
Gustavus Adolphus College	MN	24,190	VC+
Gwynedd-Mercy College	PA	22,350	C
Hamilton College	NY	34,150	HC
Hamline Univ	MN	23,339	C+
Hampden-Sydney College	VA	24,871	C
Hampton Univ	VA	17,112	C+
Hannibal-LaGrange College	MO	12,530	C
Hanover College	IN	17,560	VC
Harding Univ	AR	13,528	VC
Hardin-Simmons Univ	TX	14,165	C
Hartwick College	NY	33,090	C+
Harvard Univ/Harvard College	MA	34,269	MC
Hastings College	NE	17,854	C+
Haverford College	PA	34,300	MC
Hawaii Pacific Univ	HI	17,790	C
Heidelberg College	OH	23,879	C
Henderson State Univ	AR	6,269	C
Hendrix College	AR	18,463	HC
Heritage College	WA	6,450	NC
High Point Univ	NC	20,220	LC
Hilbert College	NY	16,830	LC
Hillsdale College	MI	20,586	VC+
Hiram College	OH	27,034	VC
Hobart and William Smith Colleges	NY	33,195	VC
Hofstra Univ	NY	23,252	C
Hollins Univ	VA	24,328	VC
Holy Family College	PA	13,710	LC
Holy Names College	CA	23,220	C
Hood College	MD	26,020	VC
Hope College	MI	22,922	C+
Houghton College	NY	21,810	VC+
Houston Baptist Univ	TX	15,300	LC
Howard Payne Univ	TX	13,834	C+
Howard Univ	DC	15,522	LC
Humboldt State Univ	CA	8,582	C
Huntingdon College	AL	18,400	VC
Huntington College	IN	15,480	LC
Huston-Tillotson College	TX	12,977	LC
Idaho State Univ	ID	7,030	C+
Illinois College	IL	16,234	C
Illinois State Univ	IL	9,235	C
Illinois Wesleyan Univ	IL	26,970	HC
Immaculata College	PA	22,400	LC
Indiana State Univ	IN	8,461	LC
Indiana Univ Bloomington	IN	10,712	C+
Indiana Univ East	IN	3,415	C
Indiana Univ Kokomo	IN	3,422	LC
Indiana Univ Northwest	IN	3,447	C
Indiana Univ of Pennsylvania	PA	9,133	C
Indiana Univ South Bend	IN	3,515	C
Indiana Univ Southeast	IN	3,459	C
Indiana Univ-Purdue Univ Fort Wayne	IN	3,166	LC
Indiana Univ-Purdue Univ Indianapolis	IN	9,473	C
Indiana Wesleyan Univ	IN	17,680	C
Inter-American Univ of PR/San GermÈn	PR	6,390	
Iona College	NY	26,556	C
Iowa State Univ	IA	8,108	VC
Iowa Wesleyan College	IA	18,840	C
Ithaca College	NY	28,719	HC
Jackson State Univ	MS	6,776	LC
Jacksonville State Univ	AL	6,568	LC
Jacksonville Univ	FL	21,110	LC
James Madison Univ	VA	9,552	HC
Jamestown College	ND	11,310	NC
Jarvis Christian College	TX	9,035	NC
John Brown Univ	AR	15,080	VC
John Carroll Univ	OH	24,140	VC
Johns Hopkins Univ	MD	35,226	MC
Johnson C. Smith Univ	NC	16,560	C+
Johnson State College	VT	10,776	C
Judson College	AL	13,790	C
Judson College	IL	18,980	LC
Juniata College	PA	26,080	VC
Kalamazoo College	MI	26,955	HC+
Kansas State Univ	KS	6,995	C
Kansas Wesleyan Univ	KS	17,400	C+
Kean Univ	NJ	11,159	C
Keene State College	NH	11,280	C
Kennesaw State Univ	GA	2,306	LC
Kent State Univ	OH	11,104	C
Kentucky State Univ	KY	6,146	NC
Kentucky Wesleyan College	KY	15,800	C
Kenyon College	OH	32,130	HC+
Keuka College	NY	21,170	C
King College	TN	17,800	VC
King's College	PA	24,680	C
Knoxville College	TN	6,200	LC
Kutztown Univ of Pennsylvania	PA	8,907	C
La Roche College	PA	18,854	LC
La Salle Univ	PA	27,890	C
La Sierra Univ	CA	19,260	LC
Lafayette College	PA	32,655	MC
LaGrange College	GA	17,496	C
Lake Erie College	OH	21,350	LC
Lake Forest College	IL	27,460	VC
Lake Superior State Univ	MI	9,034	LC
Lakeland College	WI	17,950	C
Lamar Univ	TX	6,816	LC
Lambuth Univ	TN	14,254	C
Lander Univ	SC	8,618	LC
Lane College	TN	10,400	C+
Langston Univ	OK	2,308	LC
Lawrence Univ	WI	27,711	HC
Le Moyne College	NY	23,840	C
Lebanon Valley College of Pennsylvania	PA	25,700	VC
Lee Univ	TN	10,198	LC
Lees-McRae College	NC	17,106	LC
Lehigh Univ	PA	32,290	MC
LeMoyne-Owen College	TN	8,450	NC
Lenoir-Rhyne College	NC	19,186	C
LeTourneau Univ	TX	19,020	VC
Lewis and Clark College	OR	29,010	VC
Lewis Univ	IL	20,960	C
Lewis-Clark State College	ID	6,496	C
Liberty Univ	VA	14,500	C
Limestone College	SC	16,900	C
Lincoln Memorial Univ	TN	12,620	LC
Lincoln Univ	MO	7,158	NC
Lincoln Univ	PA	11,198	C+
Lindenwood Univ	MO	17,250	C
Lindsey Wilson College	KY	16,392	LC
Linfield College	OR	25,840	VC
Livingstone College	NC	13,360	LC
Lock Haven Univ of Pennsylvania	PA	9,534	C
LIU/Brooklyn Campus	NY	22,290	C
LIU/C.W. Post Campus	NY	25,380	C
LIU/Southampton College	NY	26,270	C
Longwood College	VA	8,950	C
Louisiana College	LA	11,516	C
Louisiana State Univ and A&M College	LA	8,014	VC
Louisiana State Univ in Shreveport	LA	2,480	NC
Louisiana Tech Univ	LA	6,506	C
Lourdes College	OH	13,100	LC
Loyola College in Maryland	MD	30,900	HC
Loyola Marymount Univ	CA	28,754	HC
Loyola Univ New Orleans	LA	23,506	VC+
Loyola Univ of Chicago	IL	25,992	VC
Luther College	IA	23,300	VC+
Lycoming College	PA	24,780	C
Lynchburg College	VA	23,405	C
Lyndon State College	VT	11,313	LC
Lyon College	AR	16,500	VC
Macalester College	MN	28,814	HC+
MacMurray College	IL	17,790	LC
Madonna Univ	MI	11,504	VC
Malone College	OH	19,190	C
Manchester College	IN	22,010	C
Manhattan College	NY	25,500	VC
Manhattanville College	NY	28,730	VC
Mansfield Univ	PA	9,648	C
Marian College	IN	21,020	C
Marian College of Fond du Lac	WI	17,935	LC
Marietta College	OH	24,580	C
Marist College	NY	24,756	VC
Marlboro College	VT	26,410	VC+
Marquette Univ	WI	24,836	C+
Mars Hill College	NC	18,600	LC
Marshall Univ	WV	7,752	LC
Martin Univ	IN	8,370	SP
Mary Baldwin College	VA	23,440	C
Mary Washington College	VA	9,032	VC+
Marygrove College	MI	16,075	C
Marymount College/Tarrytown	NY	23,850	C
Marymount Manhattan College	NY	23,195	VC
Marymount Univ	VA	21,560	LC
Maryville College	TN	23,210	VC
Maryville Univ of St. Louis	MO	18,680	C
Marywood Univ	PA	24,639	C
Mass College of Liberal Arts	MA	8,717	LC
Master's College	CA	21,500	C+
Mayville State Univ	ND	6,440	NC
McKendree College	IL	18,300	C+
McMurry Univ	TX	15,287	C
McNeese State Univ	LA	5,259	LC
McPherson College	KS	17,710	C
Mercer Univ	GA	24,130	VC
Mercy College	NY	15,875	LC
Mercyhurst College	PA	20,694	C
Meredith College	NC	17,500	C
Merrimack College	MA	25,725	VC
Mesa State College	CO	8,051	C
Messiah College	PA	23,180	VC
Methodist College	NC	19,526	C

ST = STATE **$IS** = IN-STATE COSTS **SR** = SELECTOR RATING

School	ST	$IS	SR
Metropolitan State College of Denver	CO	2,338	LC
Metropolitan State Univ	MN	2,943	SP
Miami Univ	OH	12,885	VC+
Mich State Univ	MI	10,386	VC
MidAmerica Nazarene Univ	KS	16,960	C
Middle Tenn State Univ	TN	6,994	C
Middlebury College	VT	34,300	MC
Midland Lutheran College	NE	18,600	C
Midway College	KY	15,815	C
Midwestern State Univ	TX	6,704	NC
Miles College	AL	7,870	NC
Millersville Univ of Pennsylvania	PA	10,153	VC
Milligan College	TN	17,550	C
Millikin Univ	IL	24,415	C+
Mills College	CA	27,950	C
Millsaps College	MS	22,608	VC+
Minn State Univ, Mankato	MN	7,296	LC
Minot State Univ	ND	5,466	LC
Miss College	MS	14,574	C
Miss State Univ	MS	7,853	C
Miss Univ for Women	MS	5,446	LC
Miss Valley State Univ	MS	6,345	C
Missouri Baptist College	MO	15,762	LC
Missouri Southern State College	MO	6,666	C
Missouri Valley College	MO	17,400	LC
Missouri Western State College	MO	6,662	NC
Molloy College	NY	13,940	C
Monmouth College	IL	21,550	C
Monmouth Univ	NJ	24,042	C
Montana State Univ-Billings	MT	7,653	NC
Montana State Univ-Bozeman	MT	8,431	C
Montana State Univ-Northern	MT	8,600	NC
Montclair State Univ	NJ	10,287	LC
Montreat College	NC	17,164	C
Moorhead State Univ	MN	7,000	LC
Moravian College	PA	27,065	VC
Morehead State Univ	KY	6,510	C
Morehouse College	GA	19,814	C
Morgan State Univ	MD	10,078	LC
Morningside College	IA	19,124	C
Morris Brown College	GA	15,993	LC
Morris College	SC	9,995	LC
Mount Aloysius College	PA	18,186	LC
Mount Holyoke College	MA	34,128	HC
Mount Marty College	SD	15,656	LC
Mount Mary College	WI	18,024	C
Mount Mercy College	IA	19,390	VC
Mount Olive College	NC	14,410	LC
Mount St. Clare College	IA	19,050	LC
Mount St. Mary College	NY	18,825	C
Mount St. Mary's College	CA	24,430	C
Mount St. Mary's College	MD	25,740	C
Mount Senario College	WI	17,750	C
Mount Union College	OH	21,120	C
Mount Vernon Nazarene College	OH	17,027	C
Muhlenberg College	PA	28,170	HC
Murray State Univ	KY	6,672	C
Muskingum College	OH	18,760	C
National Univ	CA	7,755	SP
National-Louis Univ	IL	13,995	NC
Nazareth College of Rochester	NY	22,036	VC
Nebr Wesleyan Univ	NE	18,767	VC
Neumann College	PA	22,040	NC
New College of Calif	CA	8,900	NC
New Jersey City Univ	NJ	9,100	LC
New Mexico Highlands Univ	NM	6,256	NC
New Mexico State Univ	NM	7,302	C
New York Inst of Technology	NY	21,756	C
New York Univ	NY	35,200	MC
Newberry College	SC	19,670	LC
Newman Univ	KS	14,098	LC
Niagara Univ	NY	22,250	C+
Nicholls State Univ	LA	5,290	NC
Nichols College	MA	24,610	LC
Norfolk State Univ	VA	8,382	LC
N Car Agricultural and Technical State Univ	NC	6,659	LC
N Car Central Univ	NC	6,418	LC
N Car State Univ	NC	8,680	HC
N Car Wesleyan College	NC	15,650	LC
North Central College	IL	22,944	C+
N Dak State Univ	ND	7,004	VC
North Georgia College and State Univ	GA	6,322	C+
North Park Univ	IL	24,030	C
Northeastern Illinois Univ	IL	2,898	NC
Northeastern State Univ	OK	4,704	LC
Northeastern Univ	MA	30,078	VC
Northern Arizona Univ	AZ	7,398	C
Northern Illinois Univ	IL	9,545	C
Northern Kentucky Univ	KY	6,352	NC
Northern Mich Univ	MI	9,693	C
Northern State Univ	SD	6,279	LC
Northland College	WI	21,435	C+
Northwest Missouri State Univ	MO	7,922	LC
Northwest Nazarene Univ	ID	18,380	C
Northwestern College	MN	19,816	C+
Northwestern College of Iowa	IA	17,630	C+
Northwestern Okla State Univ	OK	4,542	NC
Northwestern State Univ of Louisiana	LA	5,745	NC
Northwestern Univ	IL	33,615	MC
Norwich Univ	VT	21,064	LC
Notre Dame College	OH	20,425	C
Notre Dame de Namur Univ	CA	26,932	LC
Nyack College	NY	18,540	C
Oakland City Univ	IN	11,286	LC
Oakland Univ	MI	9,418	C
Oakwood College	AL	14,904	C
Oberlin College	OH	33,140	HC+
Oglethorpe Univ	GA	19,100	LC
Ohio Dominican College	OH	18,100	LC
Ohio Northern Univ	OH	27,765	VC
Ohio State Univ at Lima	OH	3,603	NC
Ohio State Univ at Marion	OH	3,606	NC
Ohio State Univ at Newark	OH	8,103	NC
Ohio Univ	OH	11,769	C
Ohio Wesleyan Univ	OH	29,670	VC+
Okla Baptist Univ	OK	13,878	VC
Okla Christian Univ	OK	16,500	VC
Okla City Univ	OK	15,810	C
Okla Panhandle State Univ	OK	3,812	NC
Okla State Univ	OK	7,650	VC
Old Dominion Univ	VA	9,386	C
Olivet College	MI	17,410	C
Olivet Nazarene Univ	IL	18,444	C
Oral Roberts Univ	OK	18,490	C
Oregon State Univ	OR	9,612	VC
Ottawa Univ	KS	11,800	LC
Otterbein College	OH	23,439	C
Ouachita Baptist Univ	AR	16,460	VC
Our Lady of Holy Cross College	LA	5,140	NC
Our Lady of the Lake Univ of San Antonio	TX	17,336	C
Pace Univ	NY	24,200	C
Pacific Lutheran Univ	WA	23,318	VC
Pacific Union College	CA	20,250	VC
Paine College	GA	11,896	LC
Palm Beach Atlantic College	FL	23,310	C
Park Univ	MO	9,816	C
Paul Quinn College	TX	8,150	LC
Penn State Univ at Erie/Behrend College	PA	12,326	C
Penn State Univ/Altoona	PA	12,578	C
Penn State Univ/Univ Park Campus	PA	11,126	VC
Pepperdine Univ	CA	32,830	VC
Peru State College	NE	6,342	NC
Piedmont College	GA	16,900	C
Pikeville College	KY	12,000	NC
Pine Manor College	MA	19,344	LC
Pittsburg State Univ	KS	6,228	NC
Pitzer College	CA	33,930	HC
Plymouth State College	NH	11,024	LC
Point Park College	PA	20,290	C
Pomona College	CA	33,960	MC
Pontifical Catholic Univ of PR/Ponce	PR	7,076	
Portland State Univ	OR	11,220	C
Prairie View A&M Univ	TX	3,172	LC
Presbyterian College	SC	23,356	VC
Prescott College	AZ	13,430	C
Princeton Univ	NJ	35,072	MC
Principia College	IL	23,865	C+
Providence College	RI	27,620	HC
Purdue Univ/Calumet	IN	6,630	NC
Purdue Univ/West Lafayette	IN	10,284	VC
Queens College	NC	17,250	C
Quincy Univ	IL	20,450	C
Quinnipiac Univ	CT	27,370	C
Radford Univ	VA	8,302	C
Randolph-Macon College	VA	24,395	C
Randolph-Macon Woman's College	VA	25,820	VC+
Regis College	MA	26,750	C
Regis Univ	CO	25,740	C+
Rhode Island College	RI	8,700	LC
Rhodes College	TN	26,466	HC+
Rice Univ	TX	24,325	MC
Rider Univ	NJ	27,400	C
Ripon College	WI	24,180	VC+
Rivier College	NH	24,215	C
Roanoke College	VA	24,689	VC
Robert Morris Univ	PA	18,730	C
Roberts Wesleyan College	NY	20,160	C+
Rochester College	MI	15,404	C+
Rockford College	IL	23,930	C
Rockhurst Univ	MO	20,090	C
Roger Williams Univ	RI	29,010	C
Rollins College	FL	31,223	HC
Roosevelt Univ	IL	20,240	LC
Rosemont College	PA	24,060	C
Rowan Univ	NJ	12,365	VC
Russell Sage College	NY	23,674	C+
Rust College	MS	7,800	C+
Rutgers, The State Univ of New Jersey New Brunswick Campus	NJ	12,709	C
Rutgers, The State Univ of New Jersey/ CamdenCampus	NJ	6,484	C
Rutgers, The State Univ of New Jersey/Newark Campus	NJ	6,394	C
Sacred Heart Univ	CT	26,588	VC
Saginaw Valley State Univ	MI	9,465	C
St. Ambrose Univ	IA	19,994	C
St. Andrews Presbyterian College	NC	19,720	LC
St. Anselm College	NH	27,405	C
St. Augustine's College	NC	12,990	C+
St. Bonaventure Univ	NY	21,956	C
St. Cloud State Univ	MN	7,180	C
St. Edward's Univ	TX	17,846	C
St. Francis College	NY	9,610	C
St. Francis Univ	PA	24,486	LC
St. John Fisher College	NY	21,800	C
St. John's Univ	MN	23,640	VC
St. John's Univ	NY	26,660	C
St. Joseph College	CT	25,960	LC
St. Joseph's College	IN	21,640	C
St. Joseph's College of Maine	ME	22,500	LC
St. Joseph's College, New York	NY	9,802	C
St. Joseph's Univ	PA	29,715	VC+
St. Lawrence Univ	NY	32,605	VC
St. Leo Univ	FL	19,250	LC
St. Louis Univ	MO	26,590	VC+
St. Martin's College	WA	20,566	C
St. Mary College	KS	17,298	C
St. Mary-of-the-Woods College	IN	21,320	LC
St. Mary's College	IN	24,474	VC
St. Mary's College	MI	13,314	LC
St. Mary's College of Calif	CA	27,575	C
St. Mary's College of Maryland	MD	14,104	HC
St. Mary's Univ of San Antonio	TX	19,735	C
St. Michael's College	VT	26,935	VC
St. Norbert College	WI	23,169	VC
St. Olaf College	MN	25,880	HC
St. Paul's College	VA	13,340	C
St. Peter's College	NJ	22,292	LC
St. Thomas Aquinas College	NY	20,590	LC
St. Thomas Univ	FL	19,500	LC
St. Vincent College	PA	22,942	VC
St. Xavier Univ	IL	21,104	C
Salem College	NC	23,065	VC
Salem State College	MA	4,481	LC
Salisbury Univ	MD	10,576	VC
Salve Regina Univ	RI	26,460	C
Sam Houston State Univ	TX	6,076	LC
Samford Univ	AL	16,340	VC
San Diego State Univ	CA	9,716	C+
San Francisco State Univ	CA	7,139	LC
San Jose State Univ	CA	8,187	C
Santa Clara Univ	CA	28,371	VC+
Sarah Lawrence College	NY	37,516	HC
Savannah State Univ	GA	2,550	LC
Schreiner Univ	TX	19,254	C
Scripps College	CA	30,400	HC+
Seattle Pacific Univ	WA	22,671	C+
Seattle Univ	WA	24,183	VC
Seton Hall Univ	NJ	26,910	LC
Seton Hill College	PA	21,875	C
Shaw Univ	NC	12,810	C
Shawnee State Univ	OH	8,634	NC
Shenandoah Univ	VA	22,550	NC
Shepherd College	WV	7,062	LC
Shippensburg Univ of Pennsylvania	PA	9,652	C
Shorter College	GA	15,185	C
Siena College	NY	22,685	VC
Siena Heights Univ	MI	16,140	LC
Silver Lake College of the Holy Family	WI	15,516	LC
Simmons College	MA	30,418	VC
Simpson College	CA	19,200	C
Simpson College	IA	21,200	C+
Skidmore College	NY	34,201	VC+
Slippery Rock Univ	PA	9,152	LC
Smith College	MA	33,302	HC+
Sonoma State Univ	CA	8,953	C
S Car State Univ	SC	6,586	LC
S Dak State Univ	SD	6,848	C
Southeast Missouri State Univ	MO	8,367	C+
Southeastern College	FL	11,648	LC
Southeastern Louisiana Univ	LA	6,047	LC
Southeastern Okla State Univ	OK	4,917	C
Southern Adventist Univ	TN	15,600	C
Southern Arkansas Univ	AR	5,740	LC
Southern Conn State Univ	CT	10,310	C
Southern Illinois Univ Edwardsville	IL	7,869	LC
Southern Methodist Univ	TX	28,349	VC
Southern Nazarene Univ	OK	14,634	NC
Southern New Hampshire Univ	NH	23,852	C
Southern Oregon Univ	OR	0,120	C
Southern Univ and A&M College	LA	6,365	C+
Southern Univ at New Orleans	LA	995	NC
Southern Utah Univ	UT	7,254	C
Southern Vermont College	VT	17,685	C
Southern Wesleyan Univ	SC	17,280	C
Southwest Baptist Univ	MO	13,426	LC
Southwest Missouri State Univ	MO	7,600	LC
Southwest Texas State Univ	TX	8,730	VC
Southwestern Adventist Univ	TX	14,798	C
Southwestern College	KS	17,650	C
Southwestern Okla State Univ	OK	4,801	C
Southwestern Univ	TX	22,550	HC
Spalding Univ	KY	15,196	C
Spelman College	GA	19,215	C+
Spring Arbor Univ	MI	17,976	C
Spring Hill College	AL	23,250	C
Springfield College	MA	24,520	C
Stanford Univ	CA	34,222	MC
SUNY/College at Brockport	NY	10,267	C
SUNY/College at Buffalo	NY	8,025	C
SUNY/College at Cortland	NY	10,564	C
SUNY/College at Fredonia	NY	10,125	C
SUNY/College at Geneseo	NY	9,970	HC
SUNY/College at Oneonta	NY	9,981	C
SUNY/College at Oswego	NY	10,856	C
SUNY/College at Plattsburgh	NY	9,729	C
SUNY/College at Potsdam	NY	10,519	C
SUNY/Univ at Albany	NY	10,997	VC
SUNY/Univ at Binghamton	NY	10,653	HC
SUNY/Univ at Buffalo	NY	11,033	VC
SUNY/Univ at New Paltz	NY	9,685	VC
SUNY/Univ at Stony Brook	NY	10,998	VC
State Univ of West Georgia	GA	7,101	C
Stephen F. Austin State Univ	TX	6,905	C
Stephens College	MO	22,295	C
Sterling College	KS	16,370	VC
Stetson Univ	FL	25,640	VC
Stillman College	AL	11,370	LC
Stonehill College	MA	26,852	HC
Suffolk Univ	MA	26,516	C
Sul Ross State Univ	TX	6,582	LC
Susquehanna Univ	PA	27,270	VC
Sweet Briar College	VA	25,310	VC
Syracuse Univ	NY	30,710	HC
Tabor College	KS	17,600	LC
Talladega College	AL	10,110	LC
Tarleton State Univ	TX	7,160	C
Taylor Univ	IN	21,562	VC+
Teikyo Post Univ	CT	21,800	C
Temple Univ	PA	14,124	C
Tenn State Univ	TN	7,058	VC
Tenn Tech Univ	TN	6,968	C
Tenn Wesleyan College	TN	13,030	C
Texas A&M Univ	TX	8,988	VC
Texas A&M Univ at Commerce	TX	7,326	C
Texas A&M Univ at Kingsville	TX	6,446	LC
Texas Christian Univ	TX	19,910	C
Texas Lutheran Univ	TX	17,660	C
Texas Southern Univ	TX	6,576	NC
Texas Tech Univ	TX	8,825	C
Texas Wesleyan Univ	TX	14,710	C
Texas Woman's Univ	TX	5,855	LC
Ohio State Univ	OH	10,819	VC
Thiel College	PA	18,419	LC
Thomas More College	KY	17,700	LC
Thomas Univ	GA	8,770	NC
Toccoa Falls College	GA	14,220	C
Tougaloo College	MS	9,200	NC
Touro College	NY	14,950	VC
Towson Univ	MD	11,088	VC
Transylvania Univ	KY	21,780	VC+
Trevecca Nazarene Univ	TN	15,752	C
Trinity Christian College	IL	19,415	C
Trinity College	CT	34,300	HC
Trinity College	DC	21,370	LC
Trinity International Univ	IL	20,640	C+
Trinity Univ	TX	21,444	HC
Troy State Univ	AL	7,696	C
Troy State Univ/Dothan	AL	3,296	C
Troy State Univ/ Montgomery	AL	3,080	NC
Truman State Univ	MO	8,568	VC+
Tufts Univ	MA	34,874	MC
Tulane Univ	LA	34,013	HC+
Turabo Univ	PR	4,110	
Tusculum College	TN	17,900	LC
Tuskegee Univ	AL	14,600	LC
Union College	KY	15,920	C
Union College	NE	14,650	C
Union College	NY	32,646	HC
Union Univ	TN	18,930	C+
United States Air Force Academy	CO		MC
United States Naval Academy	MD		MC

ST = STATE **$IS** = IN-STATE COSTS **SR** = SELECTOR RATING

School	ST	$IS	SR
Univ of Akron	OH	10,530	NC
Univ of Alabama	AL	7,402	C
Univ of Alabama at Birmingham	AL	10,110	C
Univ of Alabama at Huntsville	AL	7,916	VC
Univ of Alaska Anchorage	AK	9,100	NC
Univ of Alaska Fairbanks	AK	8,265	NC
Univ of Arizona	AZ	8,614	C
Univ of Arkansas	AR	8,334	VC
Univ of Arkansas at Little Rock	AR	5,637	NC
Univ of Arkansas at Monticello	AR	5,940	NC
Univ of Arkansas at Pine Bluff	AR	7,925	C
Univ of Bridgeport	CT	23,020	C
Univ of Calif at Berkeley	CA	14,134	MC
Univ of Calif at Davis	CA	12,796	VC
Univ of Calif at Irvine	CA	11,756	C
Univ of Calif at Los Angeles	CA	13,227	MC
Univ of Calif at Riverside	CA	12,479	C
Univ of Calif at Santa Barbara	CA	11,732	VC
Univ of Central Arkansas	AR	6,388	C
Univ of Central Florida	FL	8,251	VC
Univ of Central Okla	OK	5,205	C
Univ of Charleston	WV	20,640	C
Univ of Chicago	IL	35,087	MC
Univ of Cincinnati	OH	12,491	LC
Univ of Colo at Boulder	CO	9,255	VC
Univ of Colo at Colo Springs	CO	9,403	C
Univ of Colo at Denver	CO	3,673	C
Univ of Conn	CT	12,122	VC
Univ of Dallas	TX	22,128	VC+
Univ of Dayton	OH	20,400	VC
Univ of Delaware	DE	10,824	VC
Univ of Denver	CO	28,783	VC
Univ of Detroit Mercy	MI	21,620	LC
Univ of Dubuque	IA	19,990	C
Univ of Evansville	IN	22,865	VC+
Univ of Findlay	OH	23,962	NC
Univ of Florida	FL	7,874	HC
Univ of Georgia	GA	8,656	VC
Univ of Great Falls	MT	15,360	C
Univ of Hartford	CT	28,884	C
Univ of Hawaii at Hilo	HI	6,497	C
Univ of Hawaii at Manoa	HI	7,862	VC
Univ of Houston	TX	8,410	C
Univ of Houston-Downtown	TX	2,006	NC
Univ of Idaho	ID	7,026	C
Univ of Illinois at Urbana-Champaign	IL	11,316	HC+
Univ of Indianapolis	IN	20,840	C
Univ of Iowa	IA	8,607	C+
Univ of Kansas	KS	7,232	VC
Univ of Kentucky	KY	7,765	C
Univ of La Verne	CA	24,280	C
Univ of Louisiana at Lafayette	LA	5,200	C
Univ of Louisiana at Monroe	LA	5,207	NC
Univ of Louisville	KY	7,402	LC
Univ of Maine	ME	10,798	C
Univ of Maine at Augusta	ME	3,928	C
Univ of Maine at Farmington	ME	9,163	C
Univ of Maine at Fort Kent	ME	7,450	LC
Univ of Maine at Machias	ME	7,689	LC
Univ of Maine at Presque Isle	ME	7,964	LC
Univ of Mary	ND	12,900	LC
Univ of Mary Hardin-Baylor	TX	13,929	C
Univ of Maryland/Baltimore County	MD	12,190	VC
Univ of Maryland/College Park	MD	11,959	C
Univ of Maryland/Eastern Shore	MD	9,258	C
Univ of Maryland/Univ College	MD	5,910	SP
Univ of Mass Amherst	MA	10,995	VC
Univ of Mass Boston	MA	4,227	C
Univ of Mass Dartmouth	MA	9,852	C
Univ of Mass Lowell	MA	9,470	VC
Univ of Memphis	TN	7,271	C
Univ of Miami	FL	31,130	HC
Univ of Mich/Ann Arbor	MI	13,003	HC+
Univ of Mich/Dearborn	MI	4,677	VC
Univ of Mich/Flint	MI	4,323	C
Univ of Minn/Duluth	MN	10,436	C
Univ of Minn/Morris	MN	10,716	VC
Univ of Minn/Twin Cities	MN	11,123	VC
Univ of Miss	MS	7,666	C
Univ of Missouri/Columbia	MO	9,803	HC
Univ of Missouri/Kansas City	MO	9,685	VC
Univ of Missouri/Rolla	MO	10,034	C
Univ of Missouri/St. Louis	MO	9,966	C
Univ of Mobile	AL	13,620	LC
Univ of Montana	MT	8,038	C
Univ of Montevallo	AL	7,266	C
Univ of Nebr at Kearney	NE	7,048	NC
Univ of Nebr at Lincoln	NE	8,325	C+
Univ of Nebr at Omaha	NE	6,867	C
Univ of Nevada/Las Vegas	NV	8,281	VC
Univ of Nevada/Reno	NV	8,737	C
Univ of New England	ME	24,110	LC
Univ of New Hampshire	NH	13,207	C
Univ of New Haven	CT	23,860	LC
Univ of New Mexico	NM	8,026	C
Univ of New Orleans	LA	10,160	C
Univ of North Alabama	AL	7,016	NC
Univ of N Car at Chapel Hill	NC	8,789	HC
Univ of N Car at Charlotte	NC	7,254	C
Univ of N Car at Greensboro	NC	6,858	C
Univ of N Car at Pembroke	NC	5,914	LC
Univ of N Car at Wilmington	NC	7,769	C
Univ of N Dak	ND	7,067	VC
Univ of North Florida	FL	8,089	VC
Univ of North Texas	TX	7,629	C
Univ of Northern Colo	CO	8,082	C+
Univ of Northern Iowa	IA	7,850	C
Univ of Notre Dame	IN	30,707	MC
Univ of Okla	OK	7,616	VC
Univ of Oregon	OR	9,969	C
Univ of Pennsylvania	PA	34,614	MC
Univ of Pittsburgh at Bradford	PA	12,696	C
Univ of Pittsburgh at Johnstown	PA	13,044	LC
Univ of Portland	OR	24,950	VC
Univ of PR at Humacao	PR	1,245	
Univ of PR/Cayey Univ College	PR	1,245	
Univ of PR/Mayaguez	PR	5,285	
Univ of PR/Rio Piedras	PR	5,510	
Univ of Puget Sound	WA	28,285	HC
Univ of Redlands	CA	29,246	VC
Univ of Rhode Island	RI	12,414	C
Univ of Richmond	VA	27,300	HC
Univ of Rio Grande	OH	8,728	NC
Univ of Rochester	NY	32,979	HC
Univ of St. Francis	IL	19,650	C
Univ of St. Francis	IN	17,790	LC
Univ of St. Thomas	MN	24,044	VC
Univ of St. Thomas	TX	18,752	VC
Univ of San Diego	CA	29,198	HC
Univ of San Francisco	CA	27,302	VC
Univ of Science and Arts of Okla	OK	5,245	C
Univ of Scranton	PA	27,964	C+
Univ of Sioux Falls	SD	16,390	C
Univ of South Alabama	AL	6,976	LC
Univ of S Car at Aiken	SC	7,828	LC
Univ of S Car at Columbia	SC	8,748	VC
Univ of S Car at Spartanburg	SC	7,318	C+
Univ of S Dak	SD	7,036	C
Univ of Southern Calif	CA	33,647	MC
Univ of Southern Colo	CO	7,821	LC
Univ of Southern Indiana	IN	8,655	LC
Univ of Southern Maine	ME	10,569	C
Univ of Southern Miss	MS	6,155	LC
Univ of Tampa	FL	22,612	C
Univ of Tenn at Chattanooga	TN	7,783	C
Univ of Tenn at Knoxville	TN	8,214	C
Univ of Tenn at Martin	TN	8,268	C
Univ of Texas at Arlington	TX	7,192	LC
Univ of Texas at Austin	TX	9,437	HC
Univ of Texas at El Paso	TX	5,076	LC
Univ of Texas at San Antonio	TX	9,088	NC
Univ of Texas-Pan American	TX	4,823	C
Univ of the District of Columbia	DC	2,844	NC
Univ of the Incarnate Word	TX	18,478	C
Univ of the Ozarks	AR	13,904	C
Univ of the Pacific	CA	28,255	VC
Univ of the South	TN	27,290	HC
Univ of Toledo	OH	11,206	NC
Univ of Tulsa	OK	19,090	HC
Univ of Utah	UT	7,703	C
Univ of Vermont	VT	14,761	C+
Univ of Virginia	VA	9,391	HC+
Univ of Virginia's College at Wise	VA	8,302	C
Univ of Washington	WA	10,361	VC
Univ of West Alabama	AL	6,048	C
Univ of West Florida	FL	7,518	C
Univ of Wisc/Eau Claire	WI	7,032	VC
Univ of Wisc/Green Bay	WI	7,148	C
Univ of Wisc/La Crosse	WI	7,250	VC
Univ of Wisc/Madison	WI	8,262	VC
Univ of Wisc/Milwaukee	WI	8,907	LC
Univ of Wisc/Oshkosh	WI	6,130	LC
Univ of Wisc/Parkside	WI	6,160	LC
Univ of Wisc/Platteville	WI	7,282	C
Univ of Wisc/River Falls	WI	6,356	LC
Univ of Wisc/Stevens Point	WI	7,116	C
Univ of Wisc/Superior	WI	7,051	C+
Univ of Wisc/Whitewater	WI	6,937	C
Univ of Wyoming	WY	7,143	LC
Upper Iowa Univ	IA	17,438	C
Urbana Univ	OH	17,004	C
Ursinus College	PA	31,350	VC
Ursuline College	OH	19,430	LC
Utah State Univ	UT	6,771	C
Utica College of Syracuse Univ	NY	24,400	LC
Valdosta State Univ	GA	6,988	C
Valley City State Univ	ND		LC
Valparaiso Univ	IN	23,570	VC+
Vanderbilt Univ	TN	34,482	MC
Vanguard Univ of Southern Calif	CA	20,212	C
Vassar College	NY	33,450	MC
Villa Julie College	MD	16,026	C
Villanova Univ	PA	31,997	HC
Virginia Commonwealth Univ	VA	9,030	C
Virginia Intermont College	VA	17,510	C
Virginia Military Inst	VA	9,968	C+
Virginia Polytechnic Inst and State Univ	VA	7,652	C
Virginia Union Univ	VA	15,358	LC
Virginia Wesleyan College	VA	22,350	LC
Viterbo Univ	WI	18,043	C
Voorhees College	SC	9,976	C+
Wabash College	IN	25,335	HC
Wagner College	NY	27,000	C
Wake Forest Univ	NC	30,290	MC
Walla Walla College	WA	20,925	C
Walsh Univ	OH	16,880	C
Warner Pacific College	OR	20,370	LC
Warren Wilson College	NC	19,968	C
Wartburg College	IA	21,165	VC
Washburn Univ of Topeka	KS	6,766	NC
Washington and Jefferson College	PA	26,255	VC
Washington and Lee Univ	VA	25,095	MC
Washington College	MD	28,040	VC
Washington State Univ	WA	9,388	C
Washington Univ in St. Louis	MO	34,593	MC
Wayland Baptist Univ	TX	11,271	NC
Wayne State College	NE	6,255	NC
Wayne State Univ	MI	6,720	C
Waynesburg College	PA	17,610	LC
Weber State Univ	UT	6,897	NC
Webster Univ	MO	19,804	VC
Wellesley College	MA	33,394	MC
Wells College	NY	19,350	VC
Wesley College	DE	17,869	C
Wesleyan College	GA	17,050	VC
Wesleyan Univ	CT	3,405	MC
West Chester Univ of Pennsylvania	PA	9,792	VC
West Liberty State College	WV	6,056	LC
West Texas A&M Univ	TX	6,538	C
West Virginia State College	WV	6,264	NC
West Virginia Univ	WV	8,304	C
West Virginia Wesleyan College	WV	22,920	C
Western Baptist College	OR	19,700	C+
Western Carolina Univ	NC	5,667	C
Western Conn State Univ	CT	10,074	C
Western Illinois Univ	IL	9,571	C
Western Kentucky Univ	KY	6,834	C
Western Maryland College	MD	26,000	VC
Western Mich Univ	MI	10,016	C
Western New England College	MA	23,882	C
Western New Mexico Univ	NM	5,950	LC
Western Oregon Univ	OR	8,829	C
Western State College of Colo	CO	7,585	LC
Western Washington Univ	WA	8,624	VC
Westfield State College	MA	8,394	C
Westminster College	MO	19,990	C+
Westminster College	PA	22,960	C
Westminster College	UT	17,226	C
Westmont College	CA	29,748	VC
Wheaton College	IL	21,934	HC
Wheaton College	MA	32,940	VC
Wheeling Jesuit Univ	WV	22,660	C
Whitman College	WA	29,086	HC
Whittier College	CA	29,108	C
Whitworth College	WA	23,938	VC
Wichita State Univ	KS	6,879	C
Widener Univ	PA	26,920	C
Wiley College	TX	8,100	LC
Wilkes Univ	PA	25,800	C
Willamette Univ	OR	29,422	VC+
William Carey College	MS	10,150	LC
William Jewell College	MO	17,150	VC
William Paterson Univ of New Jersey	NJ	11,000	LC
William Penn Univ	IA	17,575	C
William Tyndale College	MI	11,150	C
William Woods Univ	MO	19,390	LC
Williams Baptist College	AR	10,750	C
Williams College	MA	32,270	MC
Wilmington College	OH	21,826	C
Wilson College	PA	21,337	LC
Wingate Univ	NC	19,140	C
Winona State Univ	MN	8,570	C
Winston-Salem State Univ	NC	5,927	LC
Winthrop Univ	SC	9,106	C
Wisc Lutheran College	WI	19,216	VC
Wittenberg Univ	OH	28,766	VC
Wofford College	SC	23,995	VC
Worcester State College	MA	7,901	LC
Wright State Univ	OH	9,141	LC
Xavier Univ	OH	23,880	C
Xavier Univ of Louisiana	LA	17,000	LC
Yale Univ	CT	34,030	MC
Yeshiva Univ	NY	21,400	C
York College	NE	13,500	C
York College of Pennsylvania	PA	12,550	VC
Youngstown State Univ	OH	9,318	NC

ENGLISH AS A SECOND/ FOREIGN LANGUAGE

School	ST	$IS	SR
Doane College	NE	17,600	LC
Eastern Mich Univ	MI	9,855	C
Holy Names College	CA	23,220	C
La Sierra Univ	CA	19,260	LC
Liberty Univ	VA	14,500	C
Maryville College	TN	23,210	VC
Salem International Univ	WV	17,263	LC
Simmons College	MA	30,418	VC
Union Univ	TN	18,930	C+
Univ of Findlay	OH	23,962	NC
Univ of Nebr at Lincoln	NE	8,325	C+
Univ of PR/Rio Piedras	PR	5,510	

ENGLISH EDUCATION

School	ST	$IS	SR
Adams State College	CO	7,468	C
Adelphi Univ	NY	23,320	VC
Alabama State Univ	AL	6,404	C
Alfred Univ	NY	27,212	C+
Andrews Univ	MI	17,696	LC
Arkansas State Univ	AR	7,480	C
Asbury College	KY	18,540	VC
Ashland Univ	OH	22,182	LC
Auburn Univ	AL	5,510	C
Bartlesville Wesleyan College	OK	14,100	LC
Baylor Univ	TX	18,298	VC+
Bennett College	NC	11,200	C
Bethany College	KS	16,602	C+
Bethany College	WV	18,566	C
Bethel College	IN	17,650	LC
Bethune-Cookman College	FL	15,746	C
Blackburn College	IL	13,690	C
Blue Mountain College	MS	9,100	LC
Boise State Univ	ID	6,531	LC
Boston Univ	MA	34,358	MC
Bowie State Univ	MD	9,300	C+
Brewton-Parker College	GA	10,810	LC
Brigham Young Univ/Hawaii	HI	6,890	C
Calif Univ of Pennsylvania	PA	10,388	C
Canisius College	NY	24,696	C+
Carthage College	WI	23,670	C
Catholic Univ of America	DC	29,332	VC
Central Missouri State Univ	MO	7,920	C
Central Univ of Bayamon	PR	3,335	
CUNY/Brooklyn College	NY	3,403	LC
Coastal Carolina Univ	SC	9,220	C
Coker College	SC	20,120	C
Colby-Sawyer College	NH	27,850	LC
College of New Jersey	NJ	13,425	HC
College of St. Rose	NY	19,084	C
College of Santa Fe	NM	20,250	LC
College of the Ozarks	MO	2,650	C+
Columbia Union College	MD	19,027	C+
Concordia Univ	MN	19,912	C
Cumberland College	KY	14,864	C
Daemen College	NY	20,620	C
Dakota State Univ	SD	6,950	C
Dana College	NE	18,046	C
Delta State Univ	MS	5,416	C
Duquesne Univ	PA	24,242	C+
East Carolina Univ	NC	7,766	C
East Central Univ	OK	4,578	C
East Texas Baptist Univ	TX	12,349	LC
Eastern College	PA	19,641	LC
Eastern Mich Univ	MI	9,855	C
Edinboro Univ of Pennsylvania	PA	9,328	LC
Florida Atlantic Univ	FL	8,832	C
Florida International Univ	FL	9,486	VC
Florida State Univ	FL	7,835	HC
Fresno Pacific Univ	CA	19,740	C
Friends Univ	KS	15,962	LC
Georgia Southwestern State Univ	GA	6,013	C
Grace College	IN	16,768	C
Grambling State Univ	LA	5,325	NC
Green Mountain College	VT	24,130	C
Greensboro College	NC	19,080	LC
Greenville College	IL	19,226	LC
Hood College	MD	26,020	VC
Humboldt State Univ	CA	8,582	C
Huntington College	IN	15,480	LC
Indiana Univ of Pennsylvania	PA	9,133	C
Indiana Wesleyan Univ	IN	17,680	C
Ithaca College	NY	28,719	HC
Johnson State College	VT	10,776	C
Judson College	AL	13,790	C
Judson College	IL	18,980	LC
Juniata College	PA	26,080	VC
Kennesaw State Univ	GA	2,306	LC
Kent State Univ	OH	11,104	C

School	ST	$IS	SR
La Roche College	PA	18,854	LC
Le Moyne College	NY	23,840	C
Limestone College	SC	16,900	C
LIU/C.W. Post Campus	NY	25,380	C
Louisiana College	LA	11,516	C
Lyndon State College	VT	11,313	LC
Mansfield Univ	PA	9,648	C
Mary Baldwin College	VA	23,440	C
MidAmerica Nazarene Univ	KS	16,960	C
Minot State Univ	ND	5,466	LC
Miss Valley State Univ	MS	6,345	C
Missouri Southern State College	MO	6,666	C
Monmouth Univ	NJ	24,042	C
Montreat College	NC	17,164	C
Morningside College	IA	19,124	C
Morris College	SC	9,995	LC
Mount Vernon Nazarene College	OH	17,027	C
Nazareth College of Rochester	NY	22,036	VC
New York Univ	NY	35,200	MC
Niagara Univ	NY	22,250	C+
N Car Agricultural and Technical State Univ	NC	6,659	LC
Northwest Nazarene Univ	ID	18,380	C
Northwestern College	MN	19,816	C+
Northwestern Okla State Univ	OK	4,542	NC
Oakwood College	AL	14,904	C
Okla Christian Univ	OK	16,500	VC
Okla Panhandle State Univ	OK	3,812	NC
Old Dominion Univ	VA	9,386	C
Oral Roberts Univ	OK	18,490	C
Palm Beach Atlantic College	FL	23,310	C
Philander Smith College	AR	7,380	NC
Providence College	RI	27,620	HC
Purdue Univ/West Lafayette	IN	10,284	VC
Rivier College	NH	24,215	C
Rocky Mountain College	MT	18,113	C
Saginaw Valley State Univ	MI	9,465	C
St. Augustine's College	NC	12,990	C+
St. John's Univ	NY	26,660	C
St. Mary's Univ of Minn	MN	19,975	C
St. Olaf College	MN	25,880	HC
Seattle Pacific Univ	WA	22,674	C+
Seton Hill College	PA	21,875	C
Shaw Univ	NC	12,810	C
Shepherd College	WV	7,062	LC
Southeast Missouri State Univ	MO	8,367	C+
Southeastern Louisiana Univ	LA	6,047	LC
Southern New Hampshire Univ	NH	23,852	C
Southern Univ at New Orleans	LA	995	NC
Southern Utah Univ	UT	7,254	C
Southwestern College	KS	17,656	C
Southwestern Okla State Univ	OK	4,801	C
SUNY/College at Oneonta	NY	9,981	C
SUNY/College at Plattsburgh	NY	9,729	C
SUNY/Univ at Albany	NY	10,997	VC
Stephen F. Austin State Univ	TX	6,905	C
Syracuse Univ	NY	30,710	HC
Taylor Univ	IN	21,562	VC+
Temple Univ	PA	14,124	C
Texas Christian Univ	TX	19,910	C
Texas Southern Univ	TX	6,576	NC
Trevecca Nazarene Univ	TN	15,752	C
Tri-State Univ-Main Campus	IN	21,200	C
Troy State Univ	AL	7,696	C
Troy State Univ/Dothan	AL	3,296	C
Turabo Univ	PR	4,110	
Union College	NE	14,650	C
Univ of Arkansas at Pine Bluff	AR	7,925	C
Univ of Central Florida	FL	8,251	VC
Univ of Central Okla	OK	5,205	C
Univ of Charleston	WV	20,640	C
Univ of Conn	CT	12,122	VC
Univ of Delaware	DE	10,824	VC
Univ of Evansville	IN	22,865	VC+
Univ of Georgia	GA	8,656	VC
Univ of Illinois at Chicago	IL	10,702	VC
Univ of Louisiana at Lafayette	LA	5,200	C
Univ of Louisiana at Monroe	LA	5,207	NC
Univ of Maine at Farmington	ME	9,163	C
Univ of Mary	ND	12,900	LC
Univ of Maryland/College Park	MD	11,959	C
Univ of Minn/Duluth	MN	10,436	C
Univ of Minn/Twin Cities	MN	11,123	VC
Univ of Miss	MS	7,666	C
Univ of New Hampshire	NH	13,207	C
Univ of New Orleans	LA	10,160	C
Univ of N Car at Charlotte	NC	7,254	C
Univ of N Car at Pembroke	NC	5,914	LC
Univ of Pittsburgh at Johnstown	PA	13,044	LC
Univ of Rio Grande	OH	8,728	NC
Univ of St. Francis	IN	17,790	LC
Univ of S Car at Spartanburg	SC	7,318	C+
Univ of South Florida	FL	8,154	C
Univ of Vermont	VT	14,761	C+
Valley City State Univ	ND		LC
Warren Wilson College	NC	19,968	C
Wartburg College	IA	21,165	VC
Wesley College	DE	17,869	C
West Texas A&M Univ	TX	6,538	C
West Virginia Univ	WV	8,304	C
Western Carolina Univ	NC	5,667	C
Westmont College	CA	29,748	VC
Whitworth College	WA	23,938	VC
Wiley College	TX	8,100	LC
Wingate Univ	NC	19,140	C
Xavier Univ of Louisiana	LA	17,000	LC
Youngstown State Univ	OH	9,318	NC

ENGLISH LITERATURE

School	ST	$IS	SR
Bard College	NY	33,912	HC
Blackburn College	IL	13,690	C
Brandeis Univ	MA	34,481	MC
Chatham College	PA	25,454	C+
Christopher Newport Univ	VA	8,862	VC
CUNY/Hunter College	NY	5,147	C+
Claremont McKenna College	CA	32,700	MC
Columbia Univ/School of General Studies	NY	35,000	C
Dartmouth College	NH	34,458	MC
DePauw Univ	IN	28,000	HC
Dominican Univ of Calif	CA	27,948	C
Eastern College	PA	19,641	LC
Eastern Mich Univ	MI	9,855	C
Edinboro Univ of Pennsylvania	PA	9,328	LC
Elmira College	NY	31,070	VC+
Knox College	IL	28,230	HC
Loras College	IA	22,994	C+
New England College	NH	20,706	LC
New York Univ	NY	35,200	MC
Oral Roberts Univ	OK	18,490	C
Pfeiffer Univ	NC	18,580	C
Reed College	OR	33,350	HC+
St. Edward's Univ	TX	17,846	C
Simon's Rock College of Bard	MA	32,450	HC
Southern Illinois Univ at Carbondale	IL	8,621	C
Southern New Hampshire Univ	NH	23,852	C
Swarthmore College	PA	34,538	MC
Syracuse Univ	NY	30,710	HC
Union Univ	TN	18,930	C+
Univ of Calif at San Diego	CA	11,372	HC
Univ of Montana--Western	MT	6,915	NC
Univ of Pittsburgh at Greensburg	PA	12,842	C
Univ of Pittsburgh at Pittsburgh	PA	13,592	HC
Univ of South Florida	FL	8,154	C
Virginia State Univ	VA	8,182	LC
Washington Univ in St. Louis	MO	34,593	MC
Western Mich Univ	MI	10,016	C

ENTOMOLOGY

School	ST	$IS	SR
Auburn Univ	AL	5,510	C
Cornell Univ	NY	34,614	MC
Iowa State Univ	IA	8,108	VC
Mich State Univ	MI	10,386	VC
Okla State Univ	OK	7,650	VC
Oregon State Univ	OR	9,612	VC
Purdue Univ/West Lafayette	IN	10,284	VC
SUNY/College of Environmental Science and Forestry	NY	12,446	VC
Texas A&M Univ	TX	8,988	VC
Ohio State Univ	OH	10,819	VC
Univ of Calif at Davis	CA	12,796	VC
Univ of Calif at Riverside	CA	12,479	C
Univ of Delaware	DE	10,824	VC
Univ of Florida	FL	7,874	HC
Univ of Georgia	GA	8,656	VC
Univ of Hawaii at Manoa	HI	7,862	VC
Univ of Idaho	ID	7,026	C
Univ of Wisc/Madison	WI	8,262	VC
Washington State Univ	WA	9,388	C

ENTREPRENEURIAL STUDIES

School	ST	$IS	SR
American International College	MA	22,268	LC
Antioch College	OH	25,072	LC
Baylor Univ	TX	18,298	VC+
Central Conn State Univ	CT	10,404	C
Chatham College	PA	25,454	C+
Fairleigh Dickinson Univ/Madison campus	NJ	25,500	C
Fairleigh Dickinson Univ/Teaneck Campus	NJ	24,646	C
Florida State Univ	FL	7,835	HC
Gallaudet Univ	DC	16,554	SP
Gannon Univ	PA	18,848	C
Indiana Univ Bloomington	IN	10,712	C+
Johnson and Wales Univ	RI	21,558	LC
Lourdes College	OH	13,100	LC
Middle Tenn State Univ	TN	6,994	C
Mountain State Univ	WV	8,180	NC
Norfolk State Univ	VA	8,382	LC
Northern Mich Univ	MI	9,693	C
Quinnipiac Univ	CT	27,370	C
Seton Hill College	PA	21,875	C
Southern Adventist Univ	TN	15,600	C
Suffolk Univ	MA	26,516	C
Syracuse Univ	NY	30,710	HC
Temple Univ	PA	14,124	C
Texas Christian Univ	TX	19,910	C
Univ of Arizona	AZ	8,614	C
Univ of Hartford	CT	28,884	C
Univ of Miami	FL	31,130	HC
Univ of New Mexico	NM	8,026	C
Univ of N Dak	ND	7,067	VC
Univ of North Texas	TX	7,629	C
Univ of Pennsylvania	PA	34,614	MC
Univ of St. Thomas	MN	24,044	VC
Univ of Texas at San Antonio	TX	9,088	NC
Univ of Vermont	VT	14,761	C+
Washington State Univ	WA	9,388	C
Wichita State Univ	KS	6,879	C
Xavier Univ	OH	23,880	C

ENVIRONMENTAL BIOLOGY

School	ST	$IS	SR
Arizona State Univ-Main	AZ	7,726	C
Beloit College	WI	27,482	HC
Bennington College	VT	31,350	VC
Bethel College	IN	17,650	LC
Cal State, Northridge	CA	7,781	C
Columbia Univ/Columbia College	NY	35,190	MC
East Texas Baptist Univ	TX	12,349	LC
Grand Canyon Univ	AZ	30,000	LC
Greenville College	IL	19,226	LC
Heidelberg College	OH	23,879	C
Lewis-Clark State College	ID	6,496	C
Lock Haven Univ of Pennsylvania	PA	9,534	C
Mount Union College	OH	21,120	C
Norfolk State Univ	VA	8,382	LC
Ohio Univ	OH	11,769	C
Plymouth State College	NH	11,024	LC
St. Mary's Univ of Minn	MN	19,975	C
SUNY/College of Environmental Science and Forestry	NY	12,446	VC
Taylor Univ	IN	21,562	VC+
Unity College	ME	19,845	LC
Univ of Calif at Davis	CA	12,796	VC
Univ of Colo at Boulder	CO	9,255	VC
Univ of Dayton	OH	20,400	VC
Univ of Missouri/Rolla	MO	10,034	C
Univ of New England	ME	24,110	LC
Univ of North Alabama	AL	7,016	NC
Western Carolina Univ	NC	5,667	C

ENVIRONMENTAL DESIGN

School	ST	$IS	SR
Art Center College of Design	CA	21,110	SP
Ball State Univ	IN	8,660	C
Bowling Green State Univ	OH	10,794	C
Hampshire College	MA	33,881	HC+
Harvard Univ/Harvard College	MA	34,269	MC
Miami Univ	OH	12,885	VC+
Montana State Univ-Bozeman	MT	8,431	C
New York Inst of Technology	NY	21,756	C
N Car State Univ	NC	8,680	HC
N Dak State Univ	ND	7,004	VC
Olivet Nazarene Univ	IL	18,444	C
Otis College of Art and Design	CA	20,290	SP
SUNY/College of Environmental Science and Forestry	NY	12,446	VC
SUNY/Univ at Buffalo	NY	11,033	VC
Syracuse Univ	NY	30,710	HC
Texas A&M Univ	TX	8,988	VC
Univ of Calif at Davis	CA	12,796	VC
Univ of Calif at Irvine	CA	11,756	C
Univ of Colo at Boulder	CO	9,255	VC
Univ of Houston	TX	8,410	C
Univ of Mass Amherst	MA	10,995	VC
Univ of Minn/Twin Cities	MN	11,123	VC
Univ of New Mexico	NM	8,026	C
Univ of Okla	OK	7,616	VC
Univ of Pennsylvania	PA	34,614	MC
Univ of PR/Rio Piedras	PR	5,510	

ENVIRONMENTAL EDUCATION

School	ST	$IS	SR
Johnson State College	VT	10,776	C
Montreat College	NC	17,164	C
Prescott College	AZ	13,430	C
SUNY/College of Environmental Science and Forestry	NY	12,446	VC
Ohio State Univ	OH	10,819	VC
Unity College	ME	19,845	LC
West Virginia Univ	WV	8,304	C

ENVIRONMENTAL ENGINEERING

School	ST	$IS	SR
Calif Polytechnic State Univ	CA	8,747	VC
Drexel Univ	PA	27,657	VC
Florida State Univ	FL	7,835	HC
Humboldt State Univ	CA	8,582	C
Johns Hopkins Univ	MD	35,226	MC
Louisiana State Univ and A&M College	LA	8,014	VC
Manhattan College	NY	25,500	VC
Marietta College	OH	24,580	C
Marquette Univ	WI	24,836	C+
Mass Inst of Technology	MA	35,228	MC
Mass Maritime Academy	MA	9,969	C
Mercer Univ	GA	24,130	VC
Mich Tech Univ	MI	11,088	VC
Montana Tech of The Univ of Montana	MT	7,845	C
New Mexico Inst of Mining and Technology	NM	7,152	VC+
New Mexico State Univ	NM	7,302	C
New York Univ	NY	35,200	MC
N Car State Univ	NC	8,680	HC
Northern Arizona Univ	AZ	7,398	C
Northwestern Univ	IL	33,615	MC
Old Dominion Univ	VA	9,386	C
Penn State Univ/Univ Park Campus	PA	11,126	VC
Rensselaer Polytechnic Inst	NY	33,863	HC+
Roger Williams Univ	RI	29,010	C
San Diego State Univ	CA	9,716	C+
Seattle Univ	WA	24,183	VC
S Dak State Univ	SD	6,848	C
Southern Methodist Univ	TX	28,349	VC
SUNY/College of Environmental Science and Forestry	NY	12,446	VC
SUNY/Univ at Buffalo	NY	11,033	VC
Stevens Inst of Technology	NJ	31,510	HC+
Suffolk Univ	MA	26,516	C
Syracuse Univ	NY	30,710	HC
Taylor Univ	IN	21,562	VC+
Tenn Tech Univ	TN	6,968	C
Texas Tech Univ	TX	8,825	C
Tulane Univ	LA	34,013	HC+
United States Air Force Academy	CO		MC
United States Military Academy	NY		MC
Universidad Politecnica de PR	PR	4,695	
Univ of Calif at Berkeley	CA	14,134	MC
Univ of Calif at Irvine	CA	11,756	C
Univ of Calif at Riverside	CA	12,479	C
Univ of Central Florida	FL	8,251	VC
Univ of Colo at Boulder	CO	9,255	VC
Univ of Conn	CT	12,122	VC
Univ of Delaware	DE	10,824	VC
Univ of Florida	FL	7,874	HC
Univ of Hartford	CT	28,884	C
Univ of Miami	FL	31,130	HC
Univ of Mich/Ann Arbor	MI	13,003	HC+
Univ of New Hampshire	NH	13,207	C
Univ of Notre Dame	IN	30,707	MC
Univ of Okla	OK	7,616	VC
Univ of Southern Calif	CA	33,647	MC
Univ of Utah	UT	7,703	C
Univ of Vermont	VT	14,761	C+
Wentworth Inst of Technology	MA	20,450	C
Wilkes Univ	PA	25,800	C

ENVIRONMENTAL ENGINEERING TECHNOLOGY

School	ST	$IS	SR
Azusa Pacific Univ	CA	22,422	VC
Cornell Univ	NY	34,614	MC
East Carolina Univ	NC	7,766	C
Lake Superior State Univ	MI	9,034	LC
Mesa State College	CO	8,051	C
New York Inst of Technology	NY	21,756	C
Rochester Inst of Technology	NY	26,232	VC+
Shawnee State Univ	OH	8,634	NC
Southwestern Okla State Univ	OK	4,801	C
Suffolk Univ	MA	26,516	C
Temple Univ	PA	14,124	C
Texas Southern Univ	TX	6,576	NC
Univ of Minn/Crookston	MN	9,626	NC

School	ST	$IS	SR
Univ of N Dak	ND	7,067	VC

ENVIRONMENTAL HEALTH SCIENCE

School	ST	$IS	SR
Benedict College	SC	12,662	LC
Boise State Univ	ID	6,531	LC
Bowling Green State Univ	OH	10,794	C
Cal State, Sacramento	CA	7,488	C
Cal State, San Bernardino	CA	6,516	C
CUNY/York College	NY	3,292	NC
Colo State Univ	CO	9,672	C
Delaware State Univ	DE	8,104	LC
Dickinson College	PA	32,210	VC+
East Carolina Univ	NC	7,766	C
East Central Univ	OK	4,578	C
East Tenn State Univ	TN	7,127	C
Eastern Kentucky Univ	KY	6,552	C
Illinois State Univ	IL	9,235	C
Indiana State Univ	IN	8,461	LC
Indiana Univ of Pennsylvania	PA	9,133	C
Indiana Univ-Purdue Univ Indianapolis	IN	9,473	C
Iowa Wesleyan College	IA	18,840	C
Miss Valley State Univ	MS	6,345	C
Missouri Southern State College	MO	6,666	C
Oakland Univ	MI	9,418	C
Old Dominion Univ	VA	9,386	C
Oregon State Univ	OR	9,612	VC
Purdue Univ/West Lafayette	IN	10,284	VC
Salisbury Univ	MD	10,576	VC
Springfield College	MA	24,520	C
Texas Southern Univ	TX	6,576	NC
Unity College	ME	19,845	LC
Univ of Arkansas at Little Rock	AR	5,637	NC
Univ of Calif at Davis	CA	12,796	VC
Univ of Georgia	GA	8,656	VC
Univ of Miami	FL	31,130	HC
Univ of Mich/Flint	MI	4,323	C
Univ of Missouri/Rolla	MO	10,034	C
Univ of Southern Colo	CO	7,821	LC
Univ of Southern Maine	ME	10,569	C
Univ of Washington	WA	10,361	VC
Western Carolina Univ	NC	5,667	C
Wright State Univ	OH	9,141	LC

ENVIRONMENTAL SCIENCE

School	ST	$IS	SR
Abilene Christian Univ	TX	16,300	VC
Adrian College	MI	19,670	C
Alabama A&M Univ	AL	5,100	LC
Alaska Pacific Univ	AK	16,450	C
Albright College	PA	27,642	C
Alfred Univ	NY	27,212	C+
Allegheny College	PA	27,780	VC
Alverno College	WI	16,930	LC
American Univ	DC	31,544	VC+
Andrews Univ	MI	17,696	LC
Antioch College	OH	25,072	LC
Appalachian State Univ	NC	6,353	C
Aquinas College	MI	20,052	C+
Arcadia Univ	PA	26,650	C
Ashland Univ	OH	22,182	LC
Assumption College	MA	26,320	C
Auburn Univ	AL	5,510	C
Augustana College	IL	24,117	VC+
Aurora Univ	IL	18,551	C
Austin Peay State Univ	TN	5,814	LC
Averett Univ	VA	17,980	LC
Baker Univ	KS	14,780	C+
Bard College	NY	33,912	HC
Barton College	NC	16,834	LC
Bates College	ME	34,100	MC
Baylor Univ	TX	18,298	VC+
Beloit College	WI	27,482	HC
Benedictine Univ	IL	21,330	C
Bennington College	VT	31,350	VC
Berry College	GA	18,850	C
Bethel College	MN	22,740	VC
Boston College	MA	33,330	MC
Boston Univ	MA	34,358	MC
Bowdoin College	ME	32,650	MC
Bowling Green State Univ	OH	10,794	C
Bradley Univ	IL	20,970	VC
Brenau Univ Women's College	GA	20,100	C
Brown Univ	RI	34,973	MC
Bucknell Univ	PA	31,096	HC
Cabrini College	PA	25,950	LC
Cal State, Chico	CA	8,598	LC
Cal State, Hayward	CA	7,400	LC
Calif Univ of Pennsylvania	PA	10,388	C
Calvin College	MI	20,050	NC
Canisius College	NY	24,696	C+
Capital Univ	OH	23,630	C
Carroll College	MT	19,140	C
Carroll College	WI	21,170	C
Case Western Reserve Univ	OH	27,418	C
Castleton State College	VT	10,922	LC
Catawba College	NC	19,620	C
Catholic Univ of America	DC	29,332	VC
Cedar Crest College	PA	25,145	C+
Centenary College of Louisiana	LA	21,600	C+
Central College	IA	21,206	C
Central Methodist College	MO	16,460	C
Chapman Univ	CA	30,218	VC
Charleston Southern Univ	SC	17,122	C
Chatham College	PA	25,454	C+
Chestnut Hill College	PA	24,790	LC
Christopher Newport Univ	VA	8,862	VC
CUNY/Hunter College	NY	5,147	C+
CUNY/Medgar Evers College	NY	3,282	NC
CUNY/Queens College	NY	3,403	VC
Claremont McKenna College	CA	32,700	MC
Clarion Univ of Pennsylvania	PA	11,272	LC
Clark Univ	MA	29,170	HC
Clarkson Univ	NY	29,884	VC
Cleveland State Univ	OH	10,146	NC
Coe College	IA	24,750	VC
Colby College	ME	34,290	MC
Colgate Univ	NY	33,480	MC
College of St. Rose	NY	19,084	C
College of Santa Fe	NM	20,250	LC
Colo College	CO	31,525	HC+
Columbia Univ/Barnard College	NY	33,694	MC
Columbia Univ/Columbia College	NY	35,190	MC
Columbia Univ/School of General Studies	NY	35,000	C
Concordia College	NY	19,200	VC
Concordia College/ Moorhead	MN	18,835	C
Concordia Univ	MN	19,912	C
Concordia Univ	OR	20,500	LC
Concordia Univ at Austin	TX	16,740	LC
Conn College	CT	33,585	MC
Cornell College	IA	24,980	VC
Creighton Univ	NE	23,476	VC
Curry College	MA	26,025	LC
Dana College	NE	18,046	C
Dartmouth College	NH	34,458	MC
Davis and Elkins College	WV	19,270	LC
De Sales Univ	PA	22,610	VC
Defiance College	OH	19,580	LC
Delta State Univ	MS	5,416	C
Denison Univ	OH	29,640	HC
DePaul Univ	IL	23,590	VC
Dickinson College	PA	32,210	VC+
Doane College	NE	17,600	LC
Dominican Univ	IL	20,800	C
Dordt College	IA	18,100	C+
Drake Univ	IA	22,830	VC
Drexel Univ	PA	27,657	VC
Drury Univ	MO	15,250	VC
Duke Univ	NC	34,396	MC
Duquesne Univ	PA	24,242	C+
Earlham College	IN	27,446	VC+
East Stroudsburg Univ of Pennsylvania	PA	8,430	LC
Eastern College	PA	19,641	LC
Eastern Conn State Univ	CT	10,362	C
Eastern Kentucky Univ	KY	6,552	C
Eastern Mennonite Univ	VA	20,700	VC
Eastern Nazarene College	MA	19,433	LC
Eckerd College	FL	25,500	C+
Edinboro Univ of Pennsylvania	PA	9,328	LC
Elizabethtown College	PA	26,000	VC
Elmhurst College	IL	21,750	C
Elmira College	NY	31,070	VC+
Elon Univ	NC	19,430	VC
Emory & Henry College	VA	19,462	C
Fairleigh Dickinson Univ/ Teaneck Campus	NJ	24,646	C
Ferrum College	VA	15,990	LC
Florida Inst of Technology	FL	25,250	VC
Florida International Univ	FL	9,486	VC
Florida Southern College	FL	19,430	C
Florida State Univ	FL	7,835	HC
Franklin Pierce College	NH	26,125	LC
Fresno Pacific Univ	CA	19,740	C
Friends Univ	KS	15,962	LC
Frostburg State Univ	MD	9,680	C
Furman Univ	SC	25,492	HC
Gannon Univ	PA	18,848	C
George Washington Univ	DC	32,170	HC
Georgetown College	KY	18,400	VC
Gettysburg College	PA	32,070	HC
Goddard College	VT	21,056	C+
Goshen College	IN	18,950	VC+
Guilford College	NC	23,255	C
Hamline Univ	MN	23,339	C+
Hampshire College	MA	33,881	HC+
Harvard Univ/Harvard College	MA	34,269	MC
Hawaii Pacific Univ	HI	17,790	C
Heritage College	WA	6,450	NC
Hiram College	OH	27,034	VC
Hobart and William Smith Colleges	NY	33,195	VC
Hood College	MD	26,020	VC
Houghton College	NY	21,810	VC+
Humboldt State Univ	CA	8,582	C
Illinois College	IL	16,234	C
Indiana Univ Bloomington	IN	10,712	C+
Indiana Univ-Purdue Univ Indianapolis	IN	9,473	C
Iowa State Univ	IA	8,108	VC
Ithaca College	NY	28,719	HC
Jacksonville Univ	FL	21,110	LC
Johns Hopkins Univ	MD	35,226	MC
Johnson State College	VT	10,776	C
Juniata College	PA	26,080	VC
Keene State College	NH	11,280	C
Kettering Univ	MI	23,256	HC
Keuka College	NY	21,170	C
Knox College	IL	28,230	HC
Kutztown Univ of Pennsylvania	PA	8,907	C
La Salle Univ	PA	27,890	C
Lake Erie College	OH	21,350	LC
Lake Forest College	IL	27,460	VC
Lake Superior State Univ	MI	9,034	LC
Lander Univ	SC	8,618	LC
Lawrence Univ	WI	27,711	HC
Lehigh Univ	PA	32,290	MC
Lewis Univ	IL	20,960	C
Lincoln Memorial Univ	TN	12,620	LC
Louisiana State Univ in Shreveport	LA	2,480	NC
Louisiana Tech Univ	LA	6,506	C
Lourdes College	OH	13,100	LC
Loyola Marymount Univ	CA	28,754	HC
Lubbock Christian Univ	TX	14,226	LC
Lynchburg College	VA	23,405	C
Macalester College	MN	28,814	HC+
Mansfield Univ	PA	9,648	C
Marian College	IN	21,020	C
Marietta College	OH	24,580	C
Marist College	NY	24,756	VC
Mary Washington College	VA	9,032	VC+
Marygrove College	MI	16,075	C
Marymount Univ	VA	21,560	LC
Maryville Univ of St. Louis	MO	18,680	C
Marywood Univ	PA	24,639	C
McMurry Univ	TX	15,287	C
McNeese State Univ	LA	5,259	LC
Mercyhurst College	PA	20,694	C
Merrimack College	MA	25,725	VC
Messiah College	PA	23,180	VC
Metropolitan State College of Denver	CO	2,338	LC
Miami Univ	OH	12,885	VC+
Middle Tenn State Univ	TN	6,994	C
Middlebury College	VT	34,300	MC
Midway College	KY	15,815	C
Midwestern State Univ	TX	6,704	NC
Miles College	AL	7,870	NC
Minn State Univ, Mankato	MN	7,296	LC
Molloy College	NY	13,940	C
Monmouth College	IL	21,550	C
Montana State Univ-Billings	MT	7,653	NC
Montana State Univ-Bozeman	MT	8,431	C
Montana State Univ-Northern	MT	8,600	NC
Montreat College	NC	17,164	C
Mount Marty College	SD	15,656	LC
Mount Olive College	NC	14,410	LC
Muhlenberg College	PA	28,170	HC
Muskingum College	OH	18,760	C
Naropa Univ	CO	22,416	SP
Nazareth College of Rochester	NY	22,036	VC
New College of Florida	FL	8,130	HC+
New England College	NH	20,706	LC
New Jersey Inst of Technology	NJ	14,690	VC
New Mexico Highlands Univ	NM	6,256	NC
New Mexico Inst of Mining and Technology	NM	7,152	VC+
New Mexico State Univ	NM	7,302	C
N Car Central Univ	NC	6,418	LC
N Car State Univ	NC	8,680	HC
N Car Wesleyan College	NC	15,650	LC
Northern State Univ	SD	6,279	LC
Northland College	WI	21,435	C+
Norwich Univ	VT	21,064	LC
Notre Dame College	OH	20,425	C
Nova Southeastern Univ	FL	20,104	LC
Oberlin College	OH	33,140	HC+
Occidental College	CA	32,288	HC
Ohio Univ	OH	11,769	C
Ohio Wesleyan Univ	OH	29,670	VC+
Okla State Univ	OK	7,650	VC
Olivet College	MI	17,410	C
Olivet Nazarene Univ	IL	18,444	C
Oregon Inst of Technology	OR	8,718	C
Oregon State Univ	OR	9,612	VC
Pacific Lutheran Univ	WA	23,318	VC
Pfeiffer Univ	NC	18,580	C
Philadelphia Univ	PA	24,722	C
Pitzer College	CA	33,930	HC
Point Park College	PA	20,290	C
Portland State Univ	OR	11,220	C
Prescott College	AZ	13,430	C
Principia College	IL	23,865	C+
Providence College	RI	27,620	HC
Quincy Univ	IL	20,450	C
Ramapo College of New Jersey	NJ	13,550	VC
Rice Univ	TX	24,325	MC
Richard Stockton College of New Jersey	NJ	12,165	VC
Rider Univ	NJ	27,400	C
Ripon College	WI	24,180	VC+
Roanoke College	VA	24,689	VC
Rochester Inst of Technology	NY	26,232	VC+
Roger Williams Univ	RI	29,010	C
Rollins College	FL	31,223	HC
Roosevelt Univ	IL	20,240	LC
Rosemont College	PA	24,060	C
Rutgers, The State Univ of New Jersey New Brunswick Campus	NJ	12,709	C
Sacred Heart Univ	CT	26,588	VC
Saginaw Valley State Univ	MI	9,465	C
St. Anselm College	NH	27,405	C
St. Bonaventure Univ	NY	21,956	C
St. John's Univ	NY	26,660	C
St. Joseph College	CT	25,960	LC
St. Joseph's College	IN	21,640	C
St. Joseph's College of Maine	ME	22,500	LC
St. Joseph's Univ	PA	29,715	VC+
St. Lawrence Univ	NY	32,605	VC
St. Leo Univ	FL	19,250	LC
St. Louis Univ	MO	26,590	VC+
St. Michael's College	VT	26,935	VC
St. Norbert College	WI	23,169	VC
St. Olaf College	MN	25,880	HC
St. Paul's College	VA	13,340	C
St. Vincent College	PA	22,942	VC
Salem International Univ	WV	17,263	LC
Sam Houston State Univ	TX	6,076	LC
Samford Univ	AL	16,340	VC
Savannah State Univ	GA	2,550	LC
Scripps College	CA	30,400	HC+
Shaw Univ	NC	12,810	C
Shenandoah Univ	VA	22,550	NC
Shepherd College	WV	7,062	LC
Shippensburg Univ of Pennsylvania	PA	9,652	C
Siena College	NY	22,685	VC
Sierra Nevada College-Lake Tahoe	NV	21,060	LC
Simmons College	MA	30,418	VC
Simpson College	IA	21,200	C+
Sonoma State Univ	CA	8,953	C
Southeast Missouri State Univ	MO	8,367	C+
Southern Vermont College	VT	17,685	C
Southwest Texas State Univ	TX	8,730	VC
Spring Hill College	AL	23,250	C
SUNY/College at Cortland	NY	10,564	C
SUNY/College at Oneonta	NY	9,981	C
SUNY/College at Plattsburgh	NY	9,729	C
SUNY/College at Purchase	NY	10,587	VC
SUNY/Maritime College	NY	10,025	LC
SUNY/Univ at Binghamton	NY	10,653	HC
State Univ of West Georgia	GA	7,101	C
Stephen F. Austin State Univ	TX	6,905	C
Stephens College	MO	22,295	C
Stetson Univ	FL	25,640	VC
Suffolk Univ	MA	26,516	C
Sul Ross State Univ	TX	6,582	LC
Susquehanna Univ	PA	27,270	VC
Sweet Briar College	VA	25,310	VC
Syracuse Univ	NY	30,710	HC
Taylor Univ	IN	21,562	VC+
Temple Univ	PA	14,124	C
Texas A&M Univ	TX	8,988	VC
Texas A&M Univ at Galveston	TX	7,269	C+
Texas Christian Univ	TX	19,910	C
Ohio State Univ	OH	10,819	VC
Thiel College	PA	18,419	LC
Thomas Edison State College	NJ	2,750	SP
Towson Univ	MD	11,088	VC
Trinity College	DC	21,370	LC
Tri-State Univ-Main Campus	IN	21,200	C
Tufts Univ	MA	34,874	MC
Tulane Univ	LA	34,013	HC+
Tusculum College	TN	17,900	LC
Union College	NY	32,646	HC
United States International Univ	CA	18,675	LC
Unity College	ME	19,845	LC
Univ of Alabama	AL	7,402	C
Univ of Alaska Fairbanks	AK	8,265	NC
Univ of Alaska Southeast	AK	7,900	LC
Univ of Arizona	AZ	8,614	C
Univ of Arkansas	AR	8,334	VC
Univ of Calif at Berkeley	CA	14,134	MC
Univ of Calif at Davis	CA	12,796	VC
Univ of Calif at Riverside	CA	12,479	C
Univ of Calif at San Diego	CA	11,372	HC

ST = STATE $IS = IN-STATE COSTS SR = SELECTOR RATING

School	ST	$IS	SR
Univ of Calif at Santa Barbara	CA	11,732	VC
Univ of Central Arkansas	AR	6,388	C
Univ of Charleston	WV	20,640	C
Univ of Chicago	IL	35,087	MC
Univ of Colo at Boulder	CO	9,255	VC
Univ of Conn	CT	12,122	VC
Univ of Delaware	DE	10,824	VC
Univ of Denver	CO	28,783	VC
Univ of Dubuque	IA	19,990	C
Univ of Evansville	IN	22,865	VC+
Univ of Findlay	OH	23,962	NC
Univ of Georgia	GA	8,656	VC
Univ of Hawaii at Manoa	HI	7,862	VC
Univ of Illinois at Urbana-Champaign	IL	11,316	HC+
Univ of Indianapolis	IN	20,840	C
Univ of Iowa	IA	8,607	C+
Univ of La Verne	CA	24,280	C
Univ of Maine	ME	10,798	C
Univ of Maine at Farmington	ME	9,163	C
Univ of Maine at Fort Kent	ME	7,450	LC
Univ of Maine at Machias	ME	7,689	LC
Univ of Maine at Presque Isle	ME	7,964	LC
Univ of Maryland/College Park	MD	11,959	C
Univ of Maryland/Eastern Shore	MD	9,258	C
Univ of Maryland/Univ College	MD	5,910	SP
Univ of Mass Amherst	MA	10,995	VC
Univ of Mass Lowell	MA	9,470	VC
Univ of Miami	FL	31,130	HC
Univ of Mich/Ann Arbor	MI	13,003	HC+
Univ of Mich/Dearborn	MI	4,677	VC
Univ of Minn/Duluth	MN	10,436	C
Univ of Missouri/Kansas City	MO	9,685	VC
Univ of Montana--Western	MT	6,915	NC
Univ of Nebr at Lincoln	NE	8,325	C+
Univ of Nevada/Las Vegas	NV	8,281	VC
Univ of Nevada/Reno	NV	8,737	C
Univ of New England	ME	24,110	LC
Univ of New Hampshire	NH	13,207	C
Univ of New Haven	CT	23,860	LC
Univ of N Car at Asheville	NC	6,896	VC
Univ of N Car at Wilmington	NC	7,769	C
Univ of Notre Dame	IN	30,707	MC
Univ of Okla	OK	7,616	VC
Univ of Oregon	OR	9,969	C
Univ of Pennsylvania	PA	34,614	MC
Univ of Pittsburgh at Bradford	PA	12,696	C
Univ of Pittsburgh at Pittsburgh	PA	13,592	HC
Univ of Portland	OR	24,950	VC
Univ of PR/Rio Piedras	PR	5,510	
Univ of Redlands	CA	29,246	VC
Univ of Rhode Island	RI	12,414	C
Univ of Rio Grande	OH	8,728	NC
Univ of Rochester	NY	32,979	HC
Univ of St. Francis	IL	19,650	C
Univ of St. Francis	IN	17,790	LC
Univ of St. Thomas	MN	24,044	VC
Univ of St. Thomas	TX	18,762	VC
Univ of San Francisco	CA	27,302	VC
Univ of Scranton	PA	27,964	C+
Univ of South Florida	FL	8,154	C
Univ of Southern Calif	CA	33,647	MC
Univ of Southern Maine	ME	10,569	C
Univ of Tampa	FL	22,612	C
Univ of Tenn at Chattanooga	TN	7,783	C
Univ of Tenn at Knoxville	TN	8,214	C
Univ of the District of Columbia	DC	2,844	NC
Univ of the Incarnate Word	TX	18,478	C
Univ of the Ozarks	AR	13,904	C
Univ of the Pacific	CA	28,255	VC
Univ of the Sciences in Philadelphia	PA	24,826	VC
Univ of Toledo	OH	11,206	NC
Univ of Tulsa	OK	19,090	HC
Univ of Vermont	VT	14,761	C+
Univ of Virginia	VA	9,391	HC+
Univ of Virginia's College at Wise	VA	8,302	C
Univ of West Alabama	AL	6,048	C
Univ of Wisc/Green Bay	WI	7,148	C
Univ of Wyoming	WY	7,143	LC
Ursinus College	PA	31,350	VC
Utah State Univ	UT	6,771	C
Valdosta State Univ	GA	6,988	C
Valparaiso Univ	IN	23,570	VC+
Vassar College	NY	33,450	MC
Virginia Polytechnic Inst and State Univ	VA	7,652	C
Walla Walla College	WA	20,925	C
Washington and Lee Univ	VA	25,095	MC
Washington College	MD	28,040	VC
Washington State Univ	WA	9,388	C
Washington Univ in St. Louis	MO	34,593	MC
Waynesburg College	PA	17,610	LC
Weber State Univ	UT	6,897	NC
Webster Univ	MO	19,804	VC
Wells College	NY	19,350	VC
Wesley College	DE	17,869	C
West Texas A&M Univ	TX	6,538	C
West Virginia Univ	WV	8,304	C
Western Conn State Univ	CT	10,074	C
Western Kentucky Univ	KY	6,834	C
Western Mich Univ	MI	10,016	C
Western New England College	MA	23,882	C
Western Washington Univ	WA	8,624	VC
Westfield State College	MA	8,394	C
Westminster College	MO	19,990	C+
Wheaton College	IL	21,934	HC
Wheaton College	MA	32,940	VC
Wheeling Jesuit Univ	WV	22,660	C
Whitman College	WA	29,086	HC
Whitworth College	WA	23,938	VC
Widener Univ	PA	26,920	C
Willamette Univ	OR	29,422	VC+
William Paterson Univ of New Jersey	NJ	11,000	LC
William Penn Univ	IA	17,575	C
Wilson College	PA	21,337	LC
Youngstown State Univ	OH	9,318	NC

ENVIRONMENTAL STUDIES

School	ST	$IS	SR
Adelphi Univ	NY	23,320	VC
Barton College	NC	16,834	LC
Cal State, Hayward	CA	7,400	LC
Catawba College	NC	19,620	C
CUNY/Queens College	NY	3,403	VC
Colby-Sawyer College	NH	27,850	LC
Dominican Univ of Calif	CA	27,948	C
Florida State Univ	FL	7,835	HC
Green Mountain College	VT	24,130	C
King's College	PA	24,680	C
Lewis and Clark College	OR	29,010	VC
Lyon College	AR	16,500	VC
Maharishi Univ of Management	IA	20,660	VC
Maryville College	TN	23,210	VC
Maryville Univ of St. Louis	MO	18,680	C
Mills College	CA	27,950	C
Northeastern Illinois Univ	IL	2,898	NC
Ohio Northern Univ	OH	27,765	VC
Penn State Univ/Altoona	PA	12,578	C
Prescott College	AZ	13,430	C
Randolph-Macon College	VA	24,395	C
Randolph-Macon Woman's College	VA	25,820	VC+
Roanoke College	VA	24,689	VC
Southwestern Univ	TX	22,550	HC
SUNY/College at Brockport	NY	10,267	C
SUNY/College of Environmental Science and Forestry	NY	12,446	VC
SUNY/Univ at Stony Brook	NY	10,998	VC
State Univ of West Georgia	GA	7,101	C
Sweet Briar College	VA	25,310	VC
Temple Univ	PA	14,124	C
Texas A&M Univ at Galveston	TX	7,269	C+
Thomas Edison State College	NJ	2,750	SP
Univ of Calif at Santa Cruz	CA	13,655	VC
Univ of Kansas	KS	7,232	VC
Univ of Montana	MT	8,038	C
Univ of Nebr at Lincoln	NE	8,325	C+
Univ of Pittsburgh at Johnstown	PA	13,044	LC
Univ of Puget Sound	WA	28,285	HC
Univ of Rochester	NY	32,979	HC
Univ of Vermont	VT	14,761	C+
Warren Wilson College	NC	19,968	C

EQUINE SCIENCE

School	ST	$IS	SR
Averett Univ	VA	17,980	LC
Centenary College	NJ	22,430	C
Colo State Univ	CO	9,672	C
Johnson and Wales Univ	RI	21,558	LC
Lake Erie College	OH	21,350	LC
Midway College	KY	15,815	C
Mount Ida College	MA	25,375	LC
N Dak State Univ	ND	7,004	VC
Otterbein College	OH	23,439	C
Rocky Mountain College	MT	18,113	C
St. Mary-of-the-Woods College	IN	21,320	LC
Salem International Univ	WV	17,263	LC
Stephens College	MO	22,295	C
Sul Ross State Univ	TX	6,582	LC
Truman State Univ	MO	8,568	VC+
Univ of Findlay	OH	23,962	NC
Univ of Louisville	KY	7,402	LC
Univ of New Hampshire	NH	13,207	C
Univ of Vermont	VT	14,761	C+
Virginia Intermont College	VA	17,510	C
William Woods Univ	MO	19,390	LC
Wilson College	PA	21,337	LC

ESKIMO

School	ST	$IS	SR
Univ of Alaska Fairbanks	AK	8,265	NC

ETHICS, POLITICS, AND SOCIAL POLICY

School	ST	$IS	SR
Bloomsburg Univ of Pennsylvania	PA	9,434	C
Drake Univ	IA	22,830	VC
Pine Manor College	MA	19,344	LC
Simon's Rock College of Bard	MA	32,450	HC
Syracuse Univ	NY	30,710	HC
Univ of Judaism College of A&S	CA	24,230	C
Univ of Mass Amherst	MA	10,995	VC
Univ of Mass Boston	MA	4,227	C
Wells College	NY	19,350	VC
Wheeling Jesuit Univ	WV	22,660	C
Yale Univ	CT	34,030	MC

ETHNIC STUDIES

School	ST	$IS	SR
Bethel College	MN	22,740	VC
Bowling Green State Univ	OH	10,794	C
Cal State, Chico	CA	8,598	LC
Cal State, Hayward	CA	7,400	LC
Chatham College	PA	25,454	C+
CUNY/City College	NY	3,309	LC
Drew Univ/College of Liberal Arts	NJ	32,152	VC
Kent State Univ	OH	11,104	C
Metropolitan State Univ	MN	2,943	SP
Mills College	CA	27,950	C
Minn State Univ, Mankato	MN	7,296	LC
SUNY/College at Purchase	NY	10,587	VC
SUNY/Univ at Stony Brook	NY	10,998	VC
Univ of Alaska Fairbanks	AK	8,265	NC
Univ of Arizona	AZ	8,614	C
Univ of Calif at Berkeley	CA	14,134	MC
Univ of Calif at Riverside	CA	12,479	C
Univ of Calif at San Diego	CA	11,372	HC
Univ of Colo at Boulder	CO	9,255	VC
Univ of Hawaii at Manoa	HI	7,862	VC
Univ of Oregon	OR	9,969	C
Univ of Texas at Austin	TX	9,437	HC
Univ of Washington	WA	10,361	VC
Washington Univ in St. Louis	MO	34,593	MC
Wichita State Univ	KS	6,879	C
Yale Univ	CT	34,030	MC

EUROPEAN STUDIES

School	ST	$IS	SR
Amherst College	MA	34,340	MC
Bard College	NY	33,912	HC
Bennington College	VT	31,350	VC
Brandeis Univ	MA	34,481	MC
Brigham Young Univ	UT	7,840	HC
Canisius College	NY	24,696	C+
Claremont McKenna College	CA	32,700	MC
Columbia Univ/Barnard College	NY	33,694	MC
Emory & Henry College	VA	19,462	C
Emory Univ	GA	33,792	MC
George Washington Univ	DC	32,170	HC
Georgetown College	KY	18,400	VC
Hamline Univ	MN	23,339	C+
Harvard Univ/Harvard College	MA	34,269	MC
Hillsdale College	MI	20,586	VC+
Huntingdon College	AL	18,400	VC
Loyola Marymount Univ	CA	28,754	HC
Millsaps College	MS	22,608	VC+
Mount Holyoke College	MA	34,128	HC
New York Univ	NY	35,200	MC
Ohio Univ	OH	11,769	C
Pitzer College	CA	33,930	HC
Rollins College	FL	31,223	HC
San Diego State Univ	CA	9,716	C+
Scripps College	CA	30,400	HC+
Seattle Pacific Univ	WA	22,674	C+
Simon's Rock College of Bard	MA	32,450	HC
Southwest Texas State Univ	TX	8,730	VC
Syracuse Univ	NY	30,710	HC
Univ of Calif at Los Angeles	CA	13,227	MC
Univ of Kansas	KS	7,232	VC
Univ of Minn/Morris	MN	10,716	VC
Univ of New Mexico	NM	8,026	C
Univ of Northern Iowa	IA	7,850	C
Univ of S Car at Columbia	SC	8,748	VC
Univ of Vermont	VT	14,761	C+
Valparaiso Univ	IN	23,570	VC+
Vanderbilt Univ	TN	34,482	MC
Washington Univ in St. Louis	MO	34,593	MC
Wellesley College	MA	33,394	MC
Western Mich Univ	MI	10,016	C
Westmont College	CA	29,748	VC

EVOLUTIONARY BIOLOGY

School	ST	$IS	SR
Case Western Reserve Univ	OH	27,418	C
Cornell Univ	NY	34,614	MC
Dartmouth College	NH	34,458	MC
Florida State Univ	FL	7,835	HC
Rutgers, The State Univ of New Jersey New Brunswick Campus	NJ	12,709	C
Tulane Univ	LA	34,013	HC+
Univ of Arizona	AZ	8,614	C
Univ of Calif at Santa Barbara	CA	11,732	VC
Univ of Conn	CT	12,122	VC
Univ of Minn/Twin Cities	MN	11,123	VC
Univ of Pittsburgh at Pittsburgh	PA	13,592	HC

EXERCISE SCIENCE

School	ST	$IS	SR
Albertson College of Idaho	ID	23,900	VC
Andrews Univ	MI	17,696	LC
Angelo State Univ	TX	7,028	C
Appalachian State Univ	NC	6,353	C
Arkansas State Univ	AR	7,480	C
Asbury College	KY	18,540	VC
Augustana College	SD	20,760	VC
Austin College	TX	22,150	VC+
Becker College	MA	21,230	LC
Belhaven College	MS	16,040	C+
Bluefield College	VA	14,200	C
Boston Univ	MA	34,358	MC
Bowling Green State Univ	OH	10,794	C
Bryan College	TN	16,400	VC
Calif Baptist Univ	CA	16,736	C
Cal State, Chico	CA	8,598	LC
Cal State, Northridge	CA	7,781	C
Carroll College	WI	21,170	C
Central College	IA	21,206	C
CUNY/York College	NY	3,292	NC
Colby-Sawyer College	NH	27,850	LC
College of St. Scholastica	MN	22,378	C+
Columbus State Univ	GA	7,228	LC
Concordia Univ	CA	22,290	C
Concordia Univ Nebr	NE	17,770	C
Drury Univ	MO	15,250	VC
East Carolina Univ	NC	7,766	C
East Central Univ	OK	4,578	C
Fort Lewis College	CO	7,659	LC
Georgia College and State Univ	GA	7,344	C
Georgia Southern Univ	GA	6,958	C
Gonzaga Univ	WA	24,276	HC+
Greensboro College	NC	19,080	LC
High Point Univ	NC	20,220	LC
Howard Payne Univ	TX	13,834	C+
Huntingdon College	AL	18,400	VC
Ithaca College	NY	28,719	HC
La Sierra Univ	CA	19,260	LC
Lake Superior State Univ	MI	9,034	LC
Lander Univ	SC	8,618	LC
Lasell College	MA	24,100	C
Liberty Univ	VA	14,500	C
Linfield College	OR	25,840	VC
Loras College	IA	22,994	C+
Louisiana College	LA	11,516	C
Lubbock Christian Univ	TX	14,226	LC
Lynchburg College	VA	23,405	C
Malone College	OH	19,190	C
Marquette Univ	WI	24,836	C+
Meredith College	NC	17,500	C
Messiah College	PA	23,180	VC
Miami Univ	OH	12,885	VC+
Milligan College	TN	17,550	C
Missouri Valley College	MO	17,400	LC
Mount Vernon Nazarene College	OH	17,027	C
Nebr Wesleyan Univ	NE	18,767	VC
Norfolk State Univ	VA	8,382	LC
N Car Wesleyan College	NC	15,650	LC
Purdue Univ/West Lafayette	IN	10,284	VC
Rutgers, The State Univ of New Jersey New Brunswick Campus	NJ	12,709	C
St. Louis Univ	MO	26,590	VC+
Samford Univ	AL	16,340	VC
San Diego State Univ	CA	9,716	C+
Seattle Pacific Univ	WA	22,674	C+
Skidmore College	NY	34,201	VC+
Southern Illinois Univ Edwardsville	IL	7,869	LC
Southern Nazarene Univ	OK	14,634	NC
Southwest Texas State Univ	TX	8,730	VC
Southwestern Adventist Univ	TX	14,798	C
Spring Arbor Univ	MI	17,976	C
SUNY/Univ at Buffalo	NY	11,033	VC
Stetson Univ	FL	25,640	VC
Syracuse Univ	NY	30,710	HC
Texas Tech Univ	TX	8,825	C
Towson Univ	MD	11,080	VC
Transylvania Univ	KY	21,780	VC+
Tulane Univ	LA	34,013	HC+

School	ST	$IS	SR
Univ of Arkansas	AR	8,334	VC
Univ of Central Arkansas	AR	6,388	C
Univ of Colo at Boulder	CO	9,255	VC
Univ of Conn	CT	12,122	VC
Univ of Mary Hardin-Baylor	TX	13,929	C
Univ of Mass Amherst	MA	10,995	VC
Univ of Mass Lowell	MA	9,470	VC
Univ of Memphis	TN	7,271	C
Univ of Miss	MS	7,666	C
Univ of Nebr at Lincoln	NE	8,325	C+
Univ of Nevada/Las Vegas	NV	8,281	VC
Univ of New Mexico	NM	8,026	C
Univ of Oregon	OR	9,969	C
Univ of Pittsburgh at Pittsburgh	PA	13,592	HC
Univ of Puget Sound	WA	28,285	HC
Univ of San Francisco	CA	27,302	VC
Univ of Scranton	PA	27,964	C+
Univ of S Car at Columbia	SC	8,748	VC
Univ of Southern Colo	CO	7,821	LC
Univ of Tampa	FL	22,612	C
Univ of Tulsa	OK	19,090	HC
Univ of Utah	UT	7,703	C
Univ of Wisc/La Crosse	WI	7,250	VC
Univ of Wyoming	WY	7,143	LC
Valdosta State Univ	GA	6,988	C
Valparaiso Univ	IN	23,570	VC+
Wake Forest Univ	NC	30,290	MC
Washington State Univ	WA	9,388	C
Waynesburg College	PA	17,610	LC
West Texas A&M Univ	TX	6,538	C
Western Mich Univ	MI	10,016	C
Westmont College	CA	29,748	VC
Willamette Univ	OR	29,422	VC+
Wilson College	PA	21,337	LC

EXPERIMENTAL PSYCHOLOGY

School	ST	$IS	SR
Drake Univ	IA	22,830	VC
Millikin Univ	IL	24,415	C+
Moravian College	PA	27,065	VC
Rochester Inst of Technology	NY	26,232	VC+
Tufts Univ	MA	34,874	MC

FAMILY AND COMMUNITY SERVICES

School	ST	$IS	SR
Bluffton College	OH	20,644	C
East Carolina Univ	NC	7,766	C
John Brown Univ	AR	15,080	VC
Kansas State Univ	KS	6,995	C
Ohio Univ	OH	11,769	C
Point Loma Nazarene Univ	CA	21,380	VC
Prairie View A&M Univ	TX	3,172	LC
Purdue Univ/West Lafayette	IN	10,284	VC
Union Univ	TN	18,930	C+
Univ of Delaware	DE	10,824	VC
Univ of Northern Iowa	IA	7,850	C
Univ of Oregon	OR	9,969	C
Youngstown State Univ	OH	9,318	NC

FAMILY/CONSUMER RESOURCE MANAGEMENT

School	ST	$IS	SR
Arizona State Univ-Main	AZ	7,726	C
Bowling Green State Univ	OH	10,794	C
East Central Univ	OK	4,578	C
Iowa State Univ	IA	8,108	VC
Mich State Univ	MI	10,386	VC
Northwest Missouri State Univ	MO	7,922	LC
Ohio State Univ at Lima	OH	3,603	NC
Ohio Univ	OH	11,769	C
St. Olaf College	MN	25,880	HC
Seton Hill College	PA	21,875	C
Southern Illinois Univ at Carbondale	IL	8,621	C
Texas Tech Univ	TX	8,825	C
Univ of Alabama	AL	7,402	C
Univ of Arizona	AZ	8,614	C
Univ of Hawaii at Manoa	HI	7,862	VC
West Virginia Univ	WV	8,304	C

FAMILY/CONSUMER STUDIES

School	ST	$IS	SR
Abilene Christian Univ	TX	16,300	VC
Alabama A&M Univ	AL	5,100	LC
Alcorn State Univ	MS	5,594	LC
Anderson Univ	IN	19,430	LC
Andrews Univ	MI	17,696	LC
Appalachian State Univ	NC	6,353	C
Baylor Univ	TX	18,298	VC+
Berry College	GA	18,850	C
Bradley Univ	IL	20,970	VC
Bridgewater College	VA	22,950	C
Brigham Young Univ	UT	7,840	HC
Cal State, Fresno	CA	7,762	C
Cal State, Los Angeles	CA	5,050	C
Cal State, Northridge	CA	7,781	C
Campbell Univ	NC	16,599	C
CUNY/Queens College	NY	3,403	VC
College of St. Catherine	MN	22,324	VC
College of the Ozarks	MO	2,650	C+
Concordia College/Moorhead	MN	18,835	C
Concordia Univ	MI	20,500	C
Cornell Univ	NY	34,614	MC
De Sales Univ	PA	22,610	VC
Delta State Univ	MS	5,416	C
Eastern Illinois Univ	IL	10,101	C
Eastern Mich Univ	MI	9,855	C
Fairmont State College	WV	7,010	NC
Florida State Univ	FL	7,835	HC
Fontbonne Univ	MO	18,046	C
Framingham State College	MA	7,259	C
Freed-Hardeman Univ	TN	14,290	VC
Gallaudet Univ	DC	16,554	SP
Georgia Southern Univ	GA	6,958	C
Hampshire College	MA	33,881	HC+
Henderson State Univ	AR	6,269	C
Indiana Univ Bloomington	IN	10,712	C+
Indiana Univ of Pennsylvania	PA	9,133	C
Iowa State Univ	IA	8,108	VC
Kansas State Univ	KS	6,995	C
Lamar Univ	TX	6,816	LC
Liberty Univ	VA	14,500	C
Louisiana State Univ and A&M College	LA	8,014	VC
Madonna Univ	MI	11,504	VC
Marygrove College	MI	16,075	C
McNeese State Univ	LA	5,259	LC
Mercyhurst College	PA	20,694	C
Meredith College	NC	17,500	C
Messiah College	PA	23,180	VC
Miami Univ	OH	12,885	VC+
Middle Tenn State Univ	TN	6,994	C
Minn State Univ, Mankato	MN	7,296	LC
Miss College	MS	14,574	C
Mitchell College	CT	23,950	C
Mount Vernon Nazarene College	OH	17,027	C
New Mexico State Univ	NM	7,302	C
Nicholls State Univ	LA	5,290	NC
Norfolk State Univ	VA	8,382	LC
Northwestern State Univ of Louisiana	LA	5,745	NC
Oakwood College	AL	14,904	C
Ohio Univ	OH	11,769	C
Olivet Nazarene Univ	IL	18,444	C
Oregon State Univ	OR	9,612	VC
Pittsburg State Univ	KS	6,228	NC
St. Joseph College	CT	25,960	LC
Seattle Pacific Univ	WA	22,674	C+
Seton Hill College	PA	21,875	C
Shepherd College	WV	7,062	LC
S Dak State Univ	SD	6,848	C
Southeast Missouri State Univ	MO	8,367	C+
Southeastern Louisiana Univ	LA	6,047	LC
Southern Univ and A&M College	LA	6,365	C+
Southern Utah Univ	UT	7,254	C
Southwest Texas State Univ	TX	8,730	VC
Syracuse Univ	NY	30,710	HC
Tenn State Univ	TN	7,058	VC
Texas Southern Univ	TX	6,576	NC
Texas Tech Univ	TX	8,825	C
Texas Woman's Univ	TX	5,855	LC
Towson Univ	MD	11,088	VC
Univ of Akron	OH	10,530	NC
Univ of Arizona	AZ	8,614	C
Univ of Arkansas at Pine Bluff	AR	7,925	C
Univ of Central Arkansas	AR	6,388	C
Univ of Central Okla	OK	5,205	C
Univ of Georgia	GA	8,656	VC
Univ of Houston	TX	8,410	C
Univ of Illinois at Urbana-Champaign	IL	11,316	HC+
Univ of Louisiana at Monroe	LA	5,207	NC
Univ of Maryland/College Park	MD	11,959	C
Univ of Miss	MS	7,666	C
Univ of Nebr at Kearney	NE	7,048	NC
Univ of Nebr at Lincoln	NE	8,325	C+
Univ of New Hampshire	NH	13,207	C
Univ of New Mexico	NM	8,026	C
Univ of PR/Rio Piedras	PR	5,510	
Univ of Rhode Island	RI	12,414	C
Univ of Utah	UT	7,703	C
Univ of Vermont	VT	14,761	C+
Univ of Wisc/Madison	WI	8,262	VC
Univ of Wisc/Stevens Point	WI	7,116	C
Univ of Wisc/Stout	WI	7,192	C
Univ of Wyoming	WY	7,143	LC
Villa Julie College	MD	16,026	C
Wayne State College	NE	6,255	NC
Weber State Univ	UT	6,897	NC
Western Illinois Univ	IL	9,571	C
Western Mich Univ	MI	10,016	C
Youngstown State Univ	OH	9,318	NC

FAMILY/JUVENILE JUSTICE

School	ST	$IS	SR
Thiel College	PA	18,419	LC
William Woods Univ	MO	19,390	LC

FASHION DESIGN AND TECHNOLOGY

School	ST	$IS	SR
American InterContinental Univ	GA	12,000	NC
Baylor Univ	TX	18,298	VC+
Calif College of Arts and Crafts	CA	27,366	SP
Centenary College	NJ	22,430	C
Columbus College of Art and Design	OH	22,210	SP
Dominican Univ	IL	20,800	C
Drexel Univ	PA	27,657	VC
Fashion Inst of Technology/SUNY	NY	9,504	C+
Florida State Univ	FL	7,835	HC
Georgia Southern Univ	GA	6,958	C
Illinois State Univ	IL	9,235	C
Iowa State Univ	IA	8,108	VC
Kent State Univ	OH	11,104	C
Lasell College	MA	24,100	C
Lindenwood Univ	MO	17,250	C
Marist College	NY	24,756	VC
Marymount College/Tarrytown	NY	23,850	C
Marymount Univ	VA	21,560	LC
Mass College of Art	MA	13,703	SP
Moore College of Art and Design	PA	23,125	SP
Mount Ida College	MA	25,375	LC
Mount Mary College	WI	18,024	C
Norfolk State Univ	VA	8,382	LC
Oregon State Univ	OR	9,612	VC
Otis College of Art and Design	CA	20,290	SP
Parsons School of Design	NY	32,242	SP
Philadelphia Univ	PA	24,722	C
Pratt Inst	NY	27,550	SP
Savannah College of Art and Design	GA	25,075	SP
School of the Art Inst of Chicago	IL	27,800	SP
Stephens College	MO	22,295	C
Syracuse Univ	NY	30,710	HC
Texas Tech Univ	TX	8,825	C
Texas Woman's Univ	TX	5,855	LC
Univ of Alabama	AL	7,402	C
Univ of Delaware	DE	10,824	VC
Univ of North Texas	TX	7,629	C
Univ of San Francisco	CA	27,302	VC
Univ of the Incarnate Word	TX	18,478	C
Ursuline College	OH	19,430	LC
Washington Univ in St. Louis	MO	34,593	MC
Western Mich Univ	MI	10,016	C
Woodbury Univ	CA	25,344	LC
Youngstown State Univ	OH	9,318	NC

FASHION MERCHANDISING

School	ST	$IS	SR
Adrian College	MI	19,670	C
Albright College	PA	27,642	C
American InterContinental Univ	GA	12,000	NC
Ashland Univ	OH	22,182	LC
Auburn Univ	AL	5,510	C
Baylor Univ	TX	18,298	VC+
Bennett College	NC	11,200	C
Bowling Green State Univ	OH	10,794	C
Brenau Univ Women's College	GA	20,100	C
Chicago State Univ	IL	8,851	C+
College of St. Catherine	MN	22,324	VC
David Lipscomb Univ	TN	16,158	VC
Delaware State Univ	DE	8,104	LC
Delta State Univ	MS	5,416	C
Dominican Univ	IL	20,800	C
Drexel Univ	PA	27,657	VC
East Central Univ	OK	4,578	C
Eastern Mich Univ	MI	9,855	C
Fashion Inst of Technology/SUNY	NY	9,504	C+
Florida State Univ	FL	7,835	HC
Fontbonne Univ	MO	18,046	C
Georgia Southern Univ	GA	6,958	C
Immaculata College	PA	22,400	LC
Indiana Univ of Pennsylvania	PA	9,133	C
Iowa State Univ	IA	8,108	VC
Johnson and Wales Univ	RI	21,558	LC
Judson College	AL	13,790	C
Kent State Univ	OH	11,104	C
Laboratory Inst of Merchandising	NY	13,550	SP
Lasell College	MA	24,100	C
Lynn Univ	FL	24,550	C
Marist College	NY	24,756	VC
Mars Hill College	NC	18,600	LC
Marymount College/Tarrytown	NY	23,850	C
Marymount Univ	VA	21,560	LC
Mercyhurst College	PA	20,694	C
Meredith College	NC	17,500	C
Miss Univ for Women	MS	5,446	LC
Mount Ida College	MA	25,375	LC
Mount Mary College	WI	18,024	C
New Mexico State Univ	NM	7,302	C
Norfolk State Univ	VA	8,382	LC
Northwood Univ	MI	18,360	LC
Ohio Univ	OH	11,769	C
Old Dominion Univ	VA	9,386	C
Olivet Nazarene Univ	IL	18,444	C
Philadelphia Univ	PA	24,722	C
Southeast Missouri State Univ	MO	8,367	C+
Southwest Texas State Univ	TX	8,730	VC
SUNY/College at Oneonta	NY	9,981	C
Stephen F. Austin State Univ	TX	6,905	C
Stephens College	MO	22,295	C
Tarleton State Univ	TX	7,160	C
Texas A&M Univ at Kingsville	TX	6,446	LC
Texas Christian Univ	TX	19,910	C
Texas Woman's Univ	TX	5,855	LC
Univ of Alabama	AL	7,402	C
Univ of Bridgeport	CT	23,020	C
Univ of Central Okla	OK	5,205	C
Univ of Georgia	GA	8,656	VC
Univ of Hawaii at Manoa	HI	7,862	VC
Univ of Louisiana at Lafayette	LA	5,200	C
Univ of Rhode Island	RI	12,414	C
Univ of the Incarnate Word	TX	18,478	C
Ursuline College	OH	19,430	LC
Utah State Univ	UT	6,771	C
West Virginia Univ	WV	8,304	C
Woodbury Univ	CA	25,344	LC
Youngstown State Univ	OH	9,318	NC

FIBER/TEXTILES/WEAVING

School	ST	$IS	SR
Edinboro Univ of Pennsylvania	PA	9,328	LC
Fashion Inst of Technology/SUNY	NY	9,504	C+
Florida State Univ	FL	7,835	HC
Kansas City Art Inst	MO	25,880	SP
Maryland Inst College of Art	MD	27,720	SP
Mass College of Art	MA	13,703	SP
Ohio Univ	OH	11,769	C
Savannah College of Art and Design	GA	25,075	SP
School of the Art Inst of Chicago	IL	27,800	SP
Syracuse Univ	NY	30,710	HC
Univ of Mass Dartmouth	MA	9,852	C
Univ of Mich/Ann Arbor	MI	13,003	HC+
Univ of North Texas	TX	7,629	C
Univ of Oregon	OR	9,969	C
Univ of the Arts	PA	24,230	SP
Univ of Washington	WA	10,361	VC

FILM ARTS

School	ST	$IS	SR
American Univ	DC	31,544	VC+
Art Center College of Design	CA	21,110	SP
Ball State Univ	IN	8,660	C
Bard College	NY	33,912	HC
Bennington College	VT	31,350	VC
Biola Univ	CA	21,902	VC
Boston College	MA	33,330	MC
Boston Univ	MA	34,358	MC
Bowling Green State Univ	OH	10,794	C
Burlington College	VT	10,640	SP
Calif College of Arts and Crafts	CA	27,366	SP
Calif Inst of the Arts	CA	27,275	SP
Cal State, Fullerton	CA	5,440	LC
Cal State, Long Beach	CA	7,400	LC
Cal State, Northridge	CA	7,781	C
Chapman Univ	CA	30,218	VC
CUNY/Brooklyn College	NY	3,403	LC
CUNY/City College	NY	3,309	LC
CUNY/College of Staten Island	NY	3,358	NC
CUNY/Hunter College	NY	5,147	C+
CUNY/Queens College	NY	3,403	VC
Claremont McKenna College	CA	32,700	MC
Clark Univ	MA	29,170	HC
College of Santa Fe	NM	20,250	LC
Colo College	CO	31,525	HC+
Columbia College Chicago	IL	22,063	LC
Columbia Univ/Columbia College	NY	35,190	MC
Columbia Univ/School of General Studies	NY	35,000	C
Cornell Univ	NY	34,614	MC
Dartmouth College	NH	34,458	MC
De Sales Univ	PA	22,610	VC
Denison Univ	OH	29,640	HC
Drexel Univ	PA	27,657	VC
Eastern Mich Univ	MI	9,855	C
Edinboro Univ of Pennsylvania	PA	9,328	LC
Elon Univ	NC	19,430	VC
Emerson College	MA	29,978	HC
Emory Univ	GA	33,792	MC

School	ST	$IS	SR
Florida State Univ	FL	7,835	HC
Fordham Univ	NY	00,710	VC
Georgia State Univ	GA	7,792	LC
Grand Valley State Univ	MI	10,040	C
Hampshire College	MA	33,881	HC+
Hofstra Univ	NY	23,252	C
Howard Univ	DC	15,522	LC
Indiana State Univ	IN	8,461	LC
Iona College	NY	26,556	C
Ithaca College	NY	28,719	HC
Kent State Univ	OH	11,104	C
LIU/C.W. Post Campus	NY	25,380	C
Mass College of Art	MA	13,703	SP
Middlebury College	VT	34,300	MC
Minneapolis College of Art and Design	MN	23,560	SP
New College of Calif	CA	8,900	NC
New York Univ	NY	35,200	MC
N Car School of the Arts	NC	7,797	SP
Northern Mich Univ	MI	9,693	C
Oral Roberts Univ	OK	18,490	C
Penn State Univ/Univ Park Campus	PA	11,126	VC
Pitzer College	CA	33,930	HC
Point Park College	PA	20,290	C
Pratt Inst	NY	27,550	SP
Purdue Univ/West Lafayette	IN	10,284	VC
Rhode Island College	RI	8,700	LC
Rhode Island School of Design	RI	30,227	SP
Rochester Inst of Technology	NY	26,232	VC+
St. John's Univ	NY	26,660	C
San Francisco Art Inst	CA	19,300	SP
San Francisco State Univ	CA	7,139	LC
San Jose State Univ	CA	8,187	C
Sarah Lawrence College	NY	37,516	HC
School of the Art Inst of Chicago	IL	27,800	SP
School of Visual Arts	NY	26,000	SP
Southern Adventist Univ	TN	15,600	C
Southern Illinois Univ at Carbondale	IL	8,621	C
Southern Methodist Univ	TX	28,349	VC
Southwest Missouri State Univ	MO	7,600	LC
SUNY/College at Cortland	NY	10,564	C
SUNY/College at Purchase	NY	10,587	VC
SUNY/Univ at Binghamton	NY	10,653	HC
SUNY/Univ at Stony Brook	NY	10,998	VC
Syracuse Univ	NY	30,710	HC
Temple Univ	PA	14,124	C
Texas Christian Univ	TX	19,910	C
Univ of Calif at Berkeley	CA	14,134	MC
Univ of Calif at Irvine	CA	11,756	C
Univ of Calif at Los Angeles	CA	13,227	MC
Univ of Calif at Santa Barbara	CA	11,732	VC
Univ of Calif at Santa Cruz	CA	13,655	VC
Univ of Central Florida	FL	8,251	VC
Univ of Chicago	IL	35,087	MC
Univ of Colo at Boulder	CO	9,255	VC
Univ of Hartford	CT	28,884	C
Univ of Iowa	IA	8,607	C+
Univ of Louisiana at Monroe	LA	5,207	NC
Univ of Miami	FL	31,130	HC
Univ of Mich/Ann Arbor	MI	13,003	HC+
Univ of Minn/Twin Cities	MN	11,123	VC
Univ of Nebr at Lincoln	NE	8,325	C+
Univ of Nevada/Las Vegas	NV	8,281	VC
Univ of N Car at Greensboro	NC	6,858	C
Univ of N Car at Wilmington	NC	7,769	C
Univ of North Texas	TX	7,629	C
Univ of Notre Dame	IN	30,707	MC
Univ of Okla	OK	7,616	VC
Univ of Pittsburgh at Pittsburgh	PA	13,592	HC
Univ of Rochester	NY	32,979	HC
Univ of Southern Calif	CA	33,647	MC
Univ of Tenn at Knoxville	TN	8,214	C
Univ of Texas at Austin	TX	9,437	HC
Univ of the Arts	PA	24,230	SP
Univ of Toledo	OH	11,206	NC
Univ of Tulsa	OK	19,090	HC
Univ of Utah	UT	7,703	C
Univ of Wisc/Milwaukee	WI	8,907	LC
Vassar College	NY	33,450	MC
Washington Univ in St. Louis	MO	34,593	MC
Wayne State Univ	MI	6,720	C
Webster Univ	MO	19,804	VC
Wesleyan Univ	CT	3,405	MC
Wright State Univ	OH	9,141	LC
Yale Univ	CT	34,030	MC

FINE ARTS

School	ST	$IS	SR
Abilene Christian Univ	TX	16,300	VC
Adelphi Univ	NY	23,320	VC
Agnes Scott College	GA	24,950	VC
Alabama State Univ	AL	6,404	C
Albany State Univ	GA	5,764	C+
Albertus Magnus College	CT	22,154	C
Alfred Univ	NY	27,212	C+
American Univ	DC	31,544	VC+
Amherst College	MA	34,340	MC
Anderson Univ	IN	19,430	LC
Aquinas College	MI	20,052	C+
Arcadia Univ	PA	26,650	C
Arkansas State Univ	AR	7,480	C
Art Academy of Cincinnati	OH	16,550	SP
Art Center College of Design	CA	21,110	SP
Art Inst of Boston at Lesley Univ	MA	23,685	SP
Ashland Univ	OH	22,182	LC
Atlanta College of Art	GA	18,600	SP
Auburn Univ Montgomery	AL	5,330	NC
Averett Univ	VA	17,980	LC
Baker Univ	KS	14,780	C+
Baldwin-Wallace College	OH	22,010	VC+
Ball State Univ	IN	8,660	C
Bay Path College	MA	22,308	C
Bellevue Univ	NE	4,125	NC
Bemidji State Univ	MN	7,957	C
Bennington College	VT	31,350	VC
Bethany College	KS	16,602	C+
Bethany College	WV	18,566	C
Bethel College	KS	17,355	C+
Bethel College	MN	22,740	VC
Birmingham-Southern College	AL	22,960	C
Black Hills State Univ	SD	6,652	LC
Bloomfield College	NJ	17,000	C
Bluefield College	VA	14,200	C
Boise State Univ	ID	6,531	LC
Bowie State Univ	MD	9,300	C+
Bowling Green State Univ	OH	10,794	C
Brandeis Univ	MA	34,481	MC
Brenau Univ Women's College	GA	20,100	C
Briar Cliff Univ	IA	18,657	LC
Brigham Young Univ/Hawaii	HI	6,890	C
Bryn Mawr College	PA	33,580	HC+
Bucknell Univ	PA	31,096	HC
Burlington College	VT	10,640	SP
Caldwell College	NJ	20,940	LC
Calif Baptist Univ	CA	16,736	C
Calif Inst of the Arts	CA	27,275	SP
Cal State, Chico	CA	8,598	LC
Cal State, Fullerton	CA	5,440	LC
Cal State, Stanislaus	CA	8,895	C
Calumet College of St. Joseph	IN	7,500	LC
Cameron Univ	OK	5,560	NC
Capital Univ	OH	23,630	C
Cardinal Stritch Univ	WI	17,620	C
Carnegie Mellon Univ	PA	32,682	MC
Carson-Newman College	TN	16,490	C
Carthage College	WI	23,670	C
Cedar Crest College	PA	25,145	C+
Central College	IA	21,206	C
Central Mich Univ	MI	8,355	C
Central Washington Univ	WA	8,985	LC
Centre College	KY	24,000	HC
Charleston Southern Univ	SC	17,122	C
Chestnut Hill College	PA	24,790	LC
Christopher Newport Univ	VA	8,862	VC
CUNY/City College	NY	3,309	LC
CUNY/Herbert H. Lehman College	NY	3,320	LC
CUNY/Hunter College	NY	5,147	C+
Claflin Univ	SC	12,735	C+
Claremont McKenna College	CA	32,700	MC
Clark Univ	MA	29,170	HC
Clarke College	IA	20,625	C+
Clemson Univ	SC	7,600	C
Coastal Carolina Univ	SC	9,220	C
College For Creative Studies	MI	20,938	SP
College of Mount St. Joseph	OH	20,290	C
College of New Jersey	NJ	13,425	HC
College of New Rochelle	NY	20,000	C
College of Our Lady of the Elms	MA	20,644	C
College of St. Benedict	MN	23,921	VC
College of St. Catherine	MN	22,324	VC
College of St. Elizabeth	NJ	22,510	C
College of Visual Arts	MN	12,185	SP
College of William and Mary	VA	10,002	MC
College of Wooster	OH	28,350	VC
Colo Christian Univ	CO	17,714	C
Columbia College	MO	15,082	C
Columbus College of Art and Design	OH	22,210	SP
Concordia Univ Nebr	NE	17,770	C
Converse College	SC	21,990	VC
Cooper Union for the Advancement of Science and Art	NY	6,500	MC
Corcoran School of Art and Design	DC	21,035	SP
Cornell College	IA	24,980	VC
Cornell Univ	NY	34,614	MC
Cornerstone Univ and Grand Rapids Baptist Seminary	MI	18,092	C
Cornish College of the Arts	WA	16,200	SP
Creighton Univ	NE	23,476	VC
Daemen College	NY	20,620	C
Dakota State Univ	SD	6,950	C
Dallas Baptist Univ	TX	13,682	LC
Denison Univ	OH	29,640	HC
DePaul Univ	IL	23,590	VC
Dickinson College	PA	32,210	VC+
Dickinson State Univ	ND	5,495	NC
Dominican Univ	IL	20,800	C
Dordt College	IA	18,100	C+
Dowling College	NY	20,281	LC
Drury Univ	MO	15,250	VC
East Stroudsburg Univ of Pennsylvania	PA	8,430	LC
East Tenn State Univ	TN	7,127	C
Eastern Conn State Univ	CT	10,362	C
Eastern Mich Univ	MI	9,855	C
Eastern New Mexico Univ	NM	4,113	LC
Edinboro Univ of Pennsylvania	PA	9,328	LC
Elmira College	NY	31,070	VC+
Emmanuel College	MA	23,802	C+
Endicott College	MA	23,704	C
Eureka College	IL	22,200	C
Fairfield Univ	CT	30,885	HC
Fairleigh Dickinson Univ/ Madison campus	NJ	25,500	C
Fairleigh Dickinson Univ/ Teaneck Campus	NJ	24,646	C
Ferrum College	VA	15,990	LC
Fisk Univ	TN	13,700	LC
Flagler College	FL	10,550	VC+
Florida A&M Univ	FL	6,948	C
Florida Atlantic Univ	FL	8,832	C
Florida Memorial College	FL	6,000	LC
Fontbonne Univ	MO	18,046	C
Fordham Univ	NY	30,710	VC
Fort Hays State Univ	KS	6,294	LC
Framingham State College	MA	7,259	C
Francis Marion Univ	SC	7,682	C
Franklin and Marshall College	PA	32,410	HC
Franklin Pierce College	NH	26,125	LC
Freed-Hardeman Univ	TN	14,290	VC
Friends Univ	KS	15,962	LC
George Washington Univ	DC	32,170	HC
Georgetown Univ	DC	34,847	MC
Georgia Southwestern State Univ	GA	6,013	C
Georgia State Univ	GA	7,792	LC
Grand Canyon Univ	AZ	30,000	LC
Grand Valley State Univ	MI	10,040	C
Green Mountain College	VT	24,130	C
Guilford College	NC	23,255	C
Gustavus Adolphus College	MN	24,190	VC+
Hamline Univ	MN	23,339	C+
Hampden-Sydney College	VA	24,871	C
Hampshire College	MA	33,881	HC+
Harding Univ	AR	13,528	VC
Harvard Univ/Harvard College	MA	34,269	MC
Hastings College	NE	17,854	C+
Haverford College	PA	34,300	MC
High Point Univ	NC	20,220	LC
Hillsdale College	MI	20,586	VC+
Hobart and William Smith Colleges	NY	33,195	VC
Hofstra Univ	NY	23,252	C
Hope College	MI	22,922	C+
Houston Baptist Univ	TX	15,300	LC
Howard Univ	DC	15,522	LC
Humboldt State Univ	CA	8,582	C
Idaho State Univ	ID	7,030	C+
Illinois College	IL	16,234	C
Illinois Wesleyan Univ	IL	26,970	HC
Indiana State Univ	IN	8,461	LC
Indiana Univ Bloomington	IN	10,712	C+
Indiana Univ Northwest	IN	3,447	C
Indiana Univ of Pennsylvania	PA	9,133	C
Indiana Univ South Bend	IN	3,515	C
Indiana Univ Southeast	IN	3,459	C
Indiana Univ-Purdue Univ Fort Wayne	IN	3,166	LC
Indiana Univ-Purdue Univ Indianapolis	IN	9,473	C
Inter-American Univ of PR/ San GermÈn	PR	6,390	
Iowa State Univ	IA	8,108	VC
Iowa Wesleyan College	IA	18,840	C
Ithaca College	NY	28,719	HC
James Madison Univ	VA	9,552	HC
Jamestown College	ND	11,310	NC
Johnson State College	VT	10,776	C
Judson College	IL	18,980	LC
Kean Univ	NJ	11,159	C
Keene State College	NH	11,280	C
Kendall College of Art and Design of Ferris State Univ	MI	8,820	SP
Kent State Univ	OH	11,104	C
Kentucky State Univ	KY	6,146	NC
Kutztown Univ of Pennsylvania	PA	8,907	C
La Salle Univ	PA	27,890	C
La Sierra Univ	CA	19,260	LC
LaGrange College	GA	17,496	C
Lake Erie College	OH	21,350	LC
Lake Superior State Univ	MI	9,034	LC
Lamar Univ	TX	6,816	LC
Lambuth Univ	TN	14,254	C
Lewis and Clark College	OR	29,010	VC
Lincoln Memorial Univ	TN	12,620	LC
Lock Haven Univ of Pennsylvania	PA	9,534	C
LIU/Brooklyn Campus	NY	22,290	C
LIU/C.W. Post Campus	NY	25,380	C
LIU/Southampton College	NY	26,270	C
Louisiana State Univ and A&M College	LA	8,014	VC
Louisiana State Univ in Shreveport	LA	2,480	NC
Louisiana Tech Univ	LA	6,506	C
Lourdes College	OH	13,100	LC
Loyola College in Maryland	MD	30,900	HC
Loyola Univ New Orleans	LA	23,506	VC+
Loyola Univ of Chicago	IL	25,992	VC
Lynn Univ	FL	24,550	C
Madonna Univ	MI	11,504	VC
Maharishi Univ of Management	IA	20,660	VC
Manhattanville College	NY	28,730	VC
Marietta College	OH	24,580	C
Marist College	NY	24,756	VC
Marlboro College	VT	26,410	VC+
Marshall Univ	WV	7,752	LC
Martin Univ	IN	8,370	SP
Mary Baldwin College	VA	23,440	C
Maryland Inst College of Art	MD	27,720	SP
Marylhurst Univ	OR	15,343	NC
Marymount College/ Tarrytown	NY	23,850	C
Marymount Manhattan College	NY	23,195	VC
Maryville College	TN	23,210	VC
Mass College of Art	MA	13,703	SP
Mass College of Liberal Arts	MA	8,717	LC
McNeese State Univ	LA	5,259	LC
Memphis College of Art	TN	19,460	SP
Meredith College	NC	17,500	C
Mesa State College	CO	8,051	C
Metropolitan State College of Denver	CO	2,338	LC
Miami Univ	OH	12,885	VC+
Midland Lutheran College	NE	18,600	C
Midwestern State Univ	TX	6,704	NC
Milligan College	TN	17,550	C
Milwaukee Inst of Art and Design	WI	24,388	SP
Minneapolis College of Art and Design	MN	23,560	SP
Miss Univ for Women	MS	5,446	LC
Miss Valley State Univ	MS	6,345	C
Missouri Southern State College	MO	6,666	C
Missouri Western State College	MO	6,662	NC
Montana State Univ-Billings	MT	7,653	NC
Montana State Univ- Bozeman	MT	8,431	C
Montana State Univ- Northern	MT	8,600	NC
Montclair State Univ	NJ	10,287	LC
Montserrat College of Art	MA	20,335	SP
Moore College of Art and Design	PA	23,125	SP
Moorhead State Univ	MN	7,000	LC
Morgan State Univ	MD	10,078	LC
Morris Brown College	GA	15,993	LC
Mount Mary College	WI	18,024	C
Mount Olive College	NC	14,410	LC
Mount St. Mary's College	MD	25,740	C
Muhlenberg College	PA	28,170	HC
Murray State Univ	KY	6,672	C
National-Louis Univ	IL	13,995	NC
Nazareth College of Rochester	NY	22,036	VC
New College of Calif	CA	8,900	NC
New College of Florida	FL	8,130	HC+
New England College	NH	20,706	LC
New Jersey City Univ	NJ	9,100	LC
New Mexico State Univ	NM	7,302	C
New York Inst of Technology	NY	21,756	C
New York Univ	NY	35,200	MC
Norfolk State Univ	VA	8,382	LC
North Central College	IL	22,944	C+
Northeastern Illinois Univ	IL	2,898	NC
Northeastern State Univ	OK	4,704	LC
Northern Arizona Univ	AZ	7,398	C
Northern Illinois Univ	IL	9,545	C
Northern Mich Univ	MI	9,693	C
Northern State Univ	SD	6,279	LC
Northland College	WI	21,435	C+
Northwest Missouri State Univ	MO	7,922	LC
Northwestern College of Iowa	IA	17,630	C+
Notre Dame de Namur Univ	CA	26,932	LC
Oakland City Univ	IN	11,286	LC
Oakland Univ	MI	9,418	C
Oberlin College	OH	33,140	HC+

ST = STATE $IS = IN-STATE COSTS SR = SELECTOR RATING

School	ST	$IS	SR
Ohio Northern Univ	OH	27,765	VC
Ohio Univ	OH	11,769	C
Ohio Wesleyan Univ	OH	29,670	VC+
Okla Baptist Univ	OK	13,878	VC
Old Dominion Univ	VA	9,386	C
Olivet College	MI	17,410	C
Otis College of Art and Design	CA	20,290	SP
Our Lady of the Lake Univ of San Antonio	TX	17,336	C
Pace Univ	NY	24,200	C
Pacific Lutheran Univ	WA	23,318	VC
Pacific Northwest College of Art	OR	16,507	SP
Pacific Union College	CA	20,250	VC
Park Univ	MO	9,816	C
Parsons School of Design	NY	32,242	SP
Penn State Univ/Univ Park Campus	PA	11,126	VC
Pomona College	CA	33,960	MC
Pontifical Catholic Univ of PR/Ponce	PR	7,076	
Portland State Univ	OR	11,220	C
Pratt Inst	NY	27,550	SP
Presbyterian College	SC	23,356	VC
Prescott College	AZ	13,430	C
Principia College	IL	23,865	C+
Purdue Univ/West Lafayette	IN	10,284	VC
Queens College	NC	17,250	C
Radford Univ	VA	8,302	C
Ramapo College of New Jersey	NJ	13,550	VC
Rhode Island College	RI	8,700	LC
Richard Stockton College of New Jersey	NJ	12,165	VC
Rider Univ	NJ	27,400	C
Ringling School of Art and Design	FL	22,500	SP
Roberts Wesleyan College	NY	20,160	C+
Rochester Inst of Technology	NY	26,232	VC+
Rockford College	IL	23,930	C
Rosemont College	PA	24,060	C
Rowan Univ	NJ	12,365	VC
Saginaw Valley State Univ	MI	9,465	C
St. Ambrose Univ	IA	19,994	C
St. Anselm College	NH	27,405	C
St. Augustine's College	NC	12,990	C+
St. Cloud State Univ	MN	7,180	C
St. Edward's Univ	TX	17,846	C
St. John's Univ	MN	23,640	VC
St. John's Univ	NY	26,660	C
St. Joseph's Univ	PA	29,715	VC+
St. Lawrence Univ	NY	32,605	VC
St. Mary-of-the-Woods College	IN	21,320	LC
St. Mary's College	IN	24,474	VC
St. Mary's College of Maryland	MD	14,104	HC
St. Michael's College	VT	26,935	VC
St. Norbert College	WI	23,169	VC
St. Olaf College	MN	25,880	HC
St. Peter's College	NJ	22,292	LC
St. Thomas Aquinas College	NY	20,590	LC
St. Vincent College	PA	22,942	VC
Salem State College	MA	4,481	LC
Salisbury Univ	MD	10,576	VC
San Diego State Univ	CA	9,716	C+
San Francisco Art Inst	CA	19,300	SP
San Francisco State Univ	CA	7,139	LC
San Jose State Univ	CA	8,187	C
Sarah Lawrence College	NY	37,516	HC
School of Visual Arts	NY	26,000	SP
Schreiner Univ	TX	19,254	C
Seattle Univ	WA	24,183	VC
Seton Hill College	PA	21,875	C
Shawnee State Univ	OH	8,634	NC
Siena Heights Univ	MI	16,140	LC
Sierra Nevada College-Lake Tahoe	NV	21,060	LC
Silver Lake College of the Holy Family	WI	15,516	LC
Simon's Rock College of Bard	MA	32,450	HC
Skidmore College	NY	34,201	VC+
Slippery Rock Univ	PA	9,152	LC
Sonoma State Univ	CA	8,953	C
S Car State Univ	SC	6,586	LC
Southeastern Okla State Univ	OK	4,917	C
Southern Adventist Univ	TN	15,600	C
Southern Conn State Univ	CT	10,310	C
Southern Illinois Univ at Carbondale	IL	8,621	C
Southern Nazarene Univ	OK	14,634	NC
Southern Univ and A&M College	LA	6,365	C+
Southern Univ at New Orleans	LA	995	NC
Southwest Texas State Univ	TX	8,730	VC
Spelman College	GA	19,215	C+
Springfield College	MA	24,520	C
Stanford Univ	CA	34,222	MC
SUNY/College at Buffalo	NY	8,025	C
SUNY/College at Fredonia	NY	10,125	C
SUNY/College at Oneonta	NY	9,981	C
SUNY/College at Potsdam	NY	10,519	C
SUNY/Univ at Albany	NY	10,997	VC
SUNY/Univ at Binghamton	NY	10,653	HC
SUNY/Univ at Buffalo	NY	11,033	VC
SUNY/Univ at New Paltz	NY	9,685	VC
State Univ of West Georgia	GA	7,101	C
Stephen F. Austin State Univ	TX	6,905	C
Sterling College	KS	16,370	VC
Stonehill College	MA	26,852	HC
Suffolk Univ	MA	26,516	C
Sul Ross State Univ	TX	6,582	LC
Syracuse Univ	NY	30,710	HC
Tarleton State Univ	TX	7,160	C
Temple Univ	PA	14,124	C
Tenn Tech Univ	TN	6,968	C
Texas A&M Univ at Commerce	TX	7,326	C
Texas A&M Univ at Kingsville	TX	6,446	LC
Texas Southern Univ	TX	6,576	NC
Texas Wesleyan Univ	TX	14,710	C
Texas Woman's Univ	TX	5,855	LC
Thomas More College	KY	17,700	LC
Trinity College	CT	34,300	HC
Truman State Univ	MO	8,568	VC+
Tusculum College	TN	17,900	LC
Union College	NY	32,646	HC
Univ of Akron	OH	10,530	NC
Univ of Alabama at Birmingham	AL	10,110	C
Univ of Alabama at Huntsville	AL	7,916	VC
Univ of Alaska Anchorage	AK	9,100	NC
Univ of Arizona	AZ	8,614	C
Univ of Bridgeport	CT	23,020	C
Univ of Calif at Davis	CA	12,796	VC
Univ of Calif at Irvine	CA	11,756	C
Univ of Central Florida	FL	8,251	VC
Univ of Central Okla	OK	5,205	C
Univ of Chicago	IL	35,087	MC
Univ of Cincinnati	OH	12,491	LC
Univ of Colo at Boulder	CO	9,255	VC
Univ of Colo at Colo Springs	CO	9,403	C
Univ of Colo at Denver	CO	3,673	C
Univ of Dayton	OH	20,400	VC
Univ of Delaware	DE	10,824	VC
Univ of Great Falls	MT	15,360	C
Univ of Hartford	CT	28,884	C
Univ of Hawaii at Manoa	HI	7,862	VC
Univ of Houston	TX	8,410	C
Univ of Idaho	ID	7,026	C
Univ of Iowa	IA	8,607	C+
Univ of Louisiana at Lafayette	LA	5,200	C
Univ of Maine at Machias	ME	7,689	LC
Univ of Mary Hardin-Baylor	TX	13,929	C
Univ of Maryland/Baltimore County	MD	12,190	VC
Univ of Mass Lowell	MA	9,470	VC
Univ of Miami	FL	31,130	HC
Univ of Missouri/Kansas City	MO	9,685	VC
Univ of Missouri/St. Louis	MO	9,966	C
Univ of Montana	MT	8,038	C
Univ of Nebr at Kearney	NE	7,048	NC
Univ of Nebr at Lincoln	NE	8,325	C+
Univ of Nebr at Omaha	NE	6,867	C
Univ of Nevada/Las Vegas	NV	8,281	VC
Univ of New Hampshire	NH	13,207	C
Univ of New Mexico	NM	8,026	C
Univ of New Orleans	LA	10,160	C
Univ of N Car at Charlotte	NC	7,254	C
Univ of N Car at Greensboro	NC	6,858	C
Univ of N Dak	ND	7,067	VC
Univ of North Florida	FL	8,089	VC
Univ of Northern Colo	CO	8,082	C+
Univ of Northern Iowa	IA	7,850	C
Univ of Okla	OK	7,616	VC
Univ of Oregon	OR	9,969	C
Univ of Pennsylvania	PA	34,614	MC
Univ of Pittsburgh at Pittsburgh	PA	13,592	HC
Univ of PR/Mayaguez	PR	5,285	
Univ of PR/Rio Piedras	PR	5,510	
Univ of Puget Sound	WA	28,285	HC
Univ of Rhode Island	RI	12,414	C
Univ of Rio Grande	OH	8,728	NC
Univ of Rochester	NY	32,979	HC
Univ of St. Francis	IL	19,650	C
Univ of St. Francis	IN	17,790	LC
Univ of St. Thomas	TX	18,752	VC
Univ of San Diego	CA	29,198	HC
Univ of San Francisco	CA	27,302	VC
Univ of South Alabama	AL	6,976	LC
Univ of S Car at Aiken	SC	7,828	LC
Univ of S Car at Columbia	SC	8,748	VC
Univ of Southern Calif	CA	33,647	MC
Univ of Southern Maine	ME	10,569	C
Univ of Southern Miss	MS	6,155	LC
Univ of Tampa	FL	22,612	C
Univ of Tenn at Chattanooga	TN	7,783	C
Univ of Tenn at Knoxville	TN	8,214	C
Univ of Tenn at Martin	TN	8,268	C
Univ of Texas at San Antonio	TX	9,088	NC
Univ of Texas-Pan American	TX	4,823	C
Univ of the District of Columbia	DC	2,844	NC
Univ of Toledo	OH	11,206	NC
Univ of Wisc/Eau Claire	WI	7,032	VC
Univ of Wisc/Green Bay	WI	7,148	C
Univ of Wisc/La Crosse	WI	7,250	VC
Univ of Wisc/Milwaukee	WI	8,907	LC
Univ of Wisc/Oshkosh	WI	6,130	LC
Univ of Wisc/Parkside	WI	6,160	LC
Univ of Wisc/Platteville	WI	7,282	C
Univ of Wisc/River Falls	WI	6,356	LC
Univ of Wisc/Stevens Point	WI	7,116	C
Univ of Wisc/Stout	WI	7,192	C
Univ of Wisc/Superior	WI	7,051	C+
Upper Iowa Univ	IA	17,438	C
Utah State Univ	UT	6,771	C
Utica College of Syracuse Univ	NY	24,400	LC
Vanderbilt Univ	TN	34,482	MC
Vassar College	NY	33,450	MC
Virginia Commonwealth Univ	VA	9,030	C
Virginia Intermont College	VA	17,510	C
Viterbo Univ	WI	18,043	C
Wagner College	NY	27,000	C
Washington College	MD	28,040	VC
Washington State Univ	WA	9,388	C
Washington Univ in St. Louis	MO	34,593	MC
Wayne State Univ	MI	6,720	C
Weber State Univ	UT	6,897	NC
Wellesley College	MA	33,394	MC
Wells College	NY	19,350	VC
West Liberty State College	WV	6,056	LC
West Virginia State College	WV	6,264	NC
Western Kentucky Univ	KY	6,834	C
Western Maryland College	MD	26,000	VC
Western New Mexico Univ	NM	5,950	LC
Western State College of Colo	CO	7,585	LC
Western Washington Univ	WA	8,624	VC
Westfield State College	MA	8,394	C
Westminster College	PA	22,960	C
Westminster College	UT	17,226	C
Wheaton College	MA	32,940	VC
Whitman College	WA	29,086	HC
Wilberforce Univ	OH	14,937	LC
William Paterson Univ of New Jersey	NJ	11,000	LC
William Penn Univ	IA	17,575	C
Williams College	MA	32,270	MC
Wilson College	PA	21,337	LC
Wingate Univ	NC	19,140	C
Winona State Univ	MN	8,570	C
Winthrop Univ	SC	9,106	C
Wittenberg Univ	OH	28,766	VC
Wright State Univ	OH	9,141	LC
Xavier Univ	OH	23,880	C
Xavier Univ of Louisiana	LA	17,000	LC
York College of Pennsylvania	PA	12,550	VC

FIRE CONTROL AND SAFETY TECHNOLOGY

School	ST	$IS	SR
Cogswell Polytechnical College	CA	14,400	LC
Okla State Univ	OK	7,650	VC
Univ of New Haven	CT	23,860	LC
Univ of N Car at Charlotte	NC	7,254	C

FIRE PROTECTION

School	ST	$IS	SR
Cal State, Los Angeles	CA	5,050	C
Cogswell Polytechnical College	CA	14,400	LC
Eastern Kentucky Univ	KY	6,552	C
Okla Panhandle State Univ	OK	3,812	NC
Park Univ	MO	9,816	C
Southern Illinois Univ at Carbondale	IL	8,621	C
Thomas Edison State College	NJ	2,750	SP
Western Oregon Univ	OR	8,829	C

FIRE PROTECTION ENGINEERING

School	ST	$IS	SR
Univ of Maryland/College Park	MD	11,959	C
Univ of Nebr at Lincoln	NE	8,325	C+
Univ of New Haven	CT	23,860	LC

FIRE SCIENCE

School	ST	$IS	SR
Anna Maria College	MA	22,800	LC
CUNY/John Jay College of Criminal Justice	NY	3,251	C
Lake Superior State Univ	MI	9,034	LC
Madonna Univ	MI	11,504	VC
Univ of Maryland/Univ College	MD	5,910	SP
Univ of New Haven	CT	23,860	LC
Univ of the District of Columbia	DC	2,844	NC

FISH AND GAME MANAGEMENT

School	ST	$IS	SR
Delaware State Univ	DE	8,104	LC
Frostburg State Univ	MD	9,680	C
Kansas State Univ	KS	6,995	C
Lake Superior State Univ	MI	9,034	LC
Okla State Univ	OK	7,650	VC
S Dak State Univ	SD	6,848	C
Stephen F. Austin State Univ	TX	6,905	C
Tenn Tech Univ	TN	6,968	C
Texas A&M Univ	TX	8,988	VC
Univ of Nebr at Lincoln	NE	8,325	C+
Univ of N Dak	ND	7,067	VC
West Virginia Univ	WV	8,304	C

FISHING AND FISHERIES

School	ST	$IS	SR
Auburn Univ	AL	5,510	C
Ball State Univ	IN	8,660	C
Colo State Univ	CO	9,672	C
Humboldt State Univ	CA	8,582	C
Mansfield Univ	PA	9,648	C
Miss State Univ	MS	7,853	C
Murray State Univ	KY	6,672	C
N Car State Univ	NC	8,680	HC
Oregon State Univ	OR	9,612	VC
Penn State Univ/Univ Park Campus	PA	11,126	VC
Texas A&M Univ	TX	8,988	VC
Texas A&M Univ at Galveston	TX	7,269	C+
Ohio State Univ	OH	10,819	VC
Unity College	ME	19,845	LC
Univ of Alaska Fairbanks	AK	8,265	NC
Univ of Arkansas at Pine Bluff	AR	7,925	C
Univ of Georgia	GA	8,656	VC
Univ of Idaho	ID	7,026	C
Univ of Maine	ME	10,798	C
Univ of Minn/Twin Cities	MN	11,123	VC
Univ of Rhode Island	RI	12,414	C
Univ of Tenn at Knoxville	TN	8,214	C
Univ of Vermont	VT	14,761	C+
Univ of Washington	WA	10,361	VC
West Virginia Univ	WV	8,304	C

FLUID AND THERMAL SCIENCE

School	ST	$IS	SR
Case Western Reserve Univ	OH	27,418	C

FOLKLORE AND MYTHOLOGY

School	ST	$IS	SR
Harvard Univ/Harvard College	MA	34,269	MC
Indiana Univ Bloomington	IN	10,712	C+
Univ of Pennsylvania	PA	34,614	MC

FOOD PRODUCTION/ MANAGEMENT/SERVICES

School	ST	$IS	SR
Ball State Univ	IN	8,660	C
Cornell Univ	NY	34,614	MC
David Lipscomb Univ	TN	16,158	VC
Delaware Valley College	PA	24,213	LC
Dominican Univ	IL	20,800	C
Drexel Univ	PA	27,657	VC
Georgia Southern Univ	GA	6,958	C
Grambling State Univ	LA	5,325	NC
Indiana Univ of Pennsylvania	PA	9,133	C
Johnson and Wales Univ	RI	21,558	LC
Kansas State Univ	KS	6,995	C
Kendall College	IL	19,119	LC
Marygrove College	MI	16,075	C
Mich State Univ	MI	10,386	VC
Miss Univ for Women	MS	5,446	LC
Mount Marty College	SD	15,656	LC
Newbury College	MA	21,490	C
Nicholls State Univ	LA	5,290	NC
Ohio Univ	OH	11,769	C
Rochester Inst of Technology	NY	26,232	VC+
St. Joseph's Univ	PA	29,715	VC+
Seton Hill College	PA	21,875	C
S Dak State Univ	SD	6,848	C
Stephen F. Austin State Univ	TX	6,905	C
Syracuse Univ	NY	30,710	HC
Texas A&M Univ at Kingsville	TX	6,446	LC
Texas Christian Univ	TX	19,910	C

School	ST	$IS	SR
Texas Tech Univ	TX	8,825	C
Univ of Alabama	AL	7,402	C
Univ of Minn/Crookston	MN	9,626	NC
Univ of Nevada/Las Vegas	NV	8,281	VC
Univ of Wisc/Stout	WI	7,192	C
Wayne State College	NE	6,255	NC
Western Mich Univ	MI	10,016	C

FOOD SCIENCE

School	ST	$IS	SR
Alabama A&M Univ	AL	5,100	LC
Ashland Univ	OH	22,182	LC
Auburn Univ	AL	5,510	C
Bluffton College	OH	20,644	C
Bowling Green State Univ	OH	10,794	C
Brigham Young Univ	UT	7,840	HC
Calif Polytechnic State Univ	CA	8,747	VC
Calif State Polytechnic Univ, Pomona	CA	8,615	C
Cal State, Fresno	CA	7,762	C
Cal State, San Bernardino	CA	6,516	C
Central Washington Univ	WA	8,985	LC
Chapman Univ	CA	30,218	VC
Clemson Univ	SC	7,600	C
College of the Ozarks	MO	2,650	C+
Cornell Univ	NY	34,614	MC
Delaware Valley College	PA	24,213	LC
Dominican Univ	IL	20,800	C
Florida State Univ	FL	7,835	HC
Framingham State College	MA	7,259	C
Georgia Southern Univ	GA	6,958	C
Immaculata College	PA	22,400	LC
Indiana State Univ	IN	8,461	LC
Indiana Univ of Pennsylvania	PA	9,133	C
Iowa State Univ	IA	8,108	VC
Kansas State Univ	KS	6,995	C
Louisiana State Univ and A&M College	LA	8,014	VC
Madonna Univ	MI	11,504	VC
Marygrove College	MI	16,075	C
Marymount College/ Tarrytown	NY	23,850	C
Meredith College	NC	17,500	C
Mich State Univ	MI	10,386	VC
Minn State Univ, Mankato	MN	7,296	LC
Miss State Univ	MS	7,853	C
Norfolk State Univ	VA	8,382	LC
N Car State Univ	NC	8,680	HC
N Dak State Univ	ND	7,004	VC
Northwest Missouri State Univ	MO	7,922	LC
Ohio Univ	OH	11,769	C
Oregon State Univ	OR	9,612	VC
Pacific Union College	CA	20,250	VC
Penn State Univ/Univ Park Campus	PA	11,126	VC
Purdue Univ/West Lafayette	IN	10,284	VC
Radford Univ	VA	8,302	C
Rutgers, The State Univ of New Jersey New Brunswick Campus	NJ	12,709	C
San Jose State Univ	CA	8,187	C
Seattle Pacific Univ	WA	22,674	C+
Simmons College	MA	30,418	VC
S Car State Univ	SC	6,586	LC
S Dak State Univ	SD	6,848	C
Southeast Missouri State Univ	MO	8,367	C+
Southern Illinois Univ at Carbondale	IL	8,621	C
Southwest Texas State Univ	TX	8,730	VC
Stephen F. Austin State Univ	TX	6,905	C
Texas A&M Univ at Kingsville	TX	6,446	LC
Texas Tech Univ	TX	8,825	C
Tuskegee Univ	AL	14,600	LC
Univ of Alabama	AL	7,402	C
Univ of Arkansas	AR	8,334	VC
Univ of Calif at Davis	CA	12,796	VC
Univ of Delaware	DE	10,824	VC
Univ of Florida	FL	7,874	HC
Univ of Georgia	GA	8,656	VC
Univ of Hawaii at Manoa	HI	7,862	VC
Univ of Idaho	ID	7,026	C
Univ of Illinois at Urbana-Champaign	IL	11,316	HC+
Univ of Kentucky	KY	7,765	C
Univ of Maine	ME	10,798	C
Univ of Maryland/College Park	MD	11,959	C
Univ of Mass Amherst	MA	10,995	VC
Univ of Minn/Twin Cities	MN	11,123	VC
Univ of Missouri/Columbia	MO	9,803	HC
Univ of Nebr at Lincoln	NE	8,325	C+
Univ of Rhode Island	RI	12,414	C
Univ of Tenn at Knoxville	TN	8,214	C
Univ of the District of Columbia	DC	2,844	NC
Univ of Vermont	VT	14,761	C+
Univ of Washington	WA	10,361	VC
Univ of Wisc/Madison	WI	8,262	VC
Univ of Wisc/River Falls	WI	6,356	LC
Utah State Univ	UT	6,771	C
Virginia Polytechnic Inst and State Univ	VA	7,652	C
Washington State Univ	WA	9,388	C
Wayne State Univ	MI	6,720	C
Winthrop Univ	SC	9,106	C

FOOD SERVICES TECHNOLOGY

School	ST	$IS	SR
Delaware Valley College	PA	24,213	LC
Johnson and Wales Univ	RI	21,558	LC
Kent State Univ	OH	11,104	C
Mount Mary College	WI	18,024	C
Pennsylvania College of Technology	PA	12,860	NC
Univ of Tenn at Knoxville	TN	8,214	C

FOREIGN LANGUAGES EDUCATION

School	ST	$IS	SR
Abilene Christian Univ	TX	16,300	VC
Adams State College	CO	7,468	C
Adelphi Univ	NY	23,320	VC
Alabama State Univ	AL	6,404	C
Alfred Univ	NY	27,212	C+
American International College	MA	22,268	LC
Anderson Univ	IN	19,430	LC
Appalachian State Univ	NC	6,353	C
Arkansas State Univ	AR	7,480	C
Asbury College	KY	18,540	VC
Ashland Univ	OH	22,182	LC
Auburn Univ	AL	5,510	C
Baldwin-Wallace College	OH	22,010	VC+
Ball State Univ	IN	8,660	C
Baylor Univ	TX	18,298	VC+
Bemidji State Univ	MN	7,957	C
Berea College	KY	4,070	VC
Bethany College	WV	18,566	C
Bethel College	MN	22,740	VC
Bethune-Cookman College	FL	15,746	C
Blue Mountain College	MS	9,100	LC
Boston Univ	MA	34,358	MC
Bowling Green State Univ	OH	10,794	C
Bradley Univ	IL	20,970	VC
Calif Univ of Pennsylvania	PA	10,388	C
Canisius College	NY	24,696	C+
Carroll College	MT	19,140	C
Carroll College	WI	21,170	C
Carson-Newman College	TN	16,490	C
Carthage College	WI	23,670	C
Cedarville Univ	OH	17,553	VC
Centenary College of Louisiana	LA	21,600	C+
Central Methodist College	MO	16,460	C
Central Mich Univ	MI	8,355	C
Central Missouri State Univ	MO	7,920	C
Central Washington Univ	WA	8,985	LC
Christopher Newport Univ	VA	8,862	VC
CUNY/Brooklyn College	NY	3,403	LC
CUNY/City College	NY	3,309	LC
CUNY/Herbert H. Lehman College	NY	3,320	LC
CUNY/Hunter College	NY	5,147	C+
Clarion Univ of Pennsylvania	PA	11,272	LC
College of New Rochelle	NY	20,000	C
College of Notre Dame of Maryland	MD	23,100	LC
College of Our Lady of the Elms	MA	20,644	C
College of St. Rose	NY	19,084	C
College of the Ozarks	MO	2,650	C+
Concordia College/ Moorhead	MN	18,835	C
Conn College	CT	33,585	MC
Converse College	SC	21,990	VC
Cornell College	IA	24,980	VC
Daemen College	NY	20,620	C
Dana College	NE	18,046	C
David Lipscomb Univ	TN	16,158	VC
Delta State Univ	MS	5,416	C
DePaul Univ	IL	23,590	VC
Dordt College	IA	18,100	C+
Duquesne Univ	PA	24,242	C+
East Carolina Univ	NC	7,766	C
East Stroudsburg Univ of Pennsylvania	PA	8,430	LC
East Tenn State Univ	TN	7,127	C
Eastern Kentucky Univ	KY	6,552	C
Eastern Mich Univ	MI	9,855	C
Eastern Washington Univ	WA	7,972	LC
Edinboro Univ of Pennsylvania	PA	9,328	LC
Elmira College	NY	31,070	VC+
Elon Univ	NC	19,430	VC
Emporia State Univ	KS	6,198	LC
Erskine College	SC	21,399	VC
Evangel Univ	MO	14,050	C
Fairmont State College	WV	7,010	NC
Florida Atlantic Univ	FL	8,832	C
Florida International Univ	FL	9,486	VC
Florida Southern College	FL	19,430	C
Florida State Univ	FL	7,835	HC
Friends Univ	KS	15,962	LC
Gannon Univ	PA	18,848	C
Gardner-Webb Univ	NC	17,400	C
George Mason Univ	VA	9,192	C
Georgetown College	KY	18,400	VC
Georgia Southwestern State Univ	GA	6,013	C
Gettysburg College	PA	32,070	HC
Goshen College	IN	18,950	VC+
Grace College	IN	16,768	C
Grambling State Univ	LA	5,325	NC
Grand Valley State Univ	MI	10,040	C
Greensboro College	NC	19,080	LC
Greenville College	IL	19,226	LC
Gustavus Adolphus College	MN	24,190	VC+
Hamline Univ	MN	23,339	C+
Harding Univ	AR	13,528	VC
Hardin-Simmons Univ	TX	14,165	C
Hastings College	NE	17,854	C+
Heidelberg College	OH	23,879	C
Hillsdale College	MI	20,586	VC+
Hofstra Univ	NY	23,252	C
Holy Family College	PA	13,710	LC
Hood College	MD	26,020	VC
Hope College	MI	22,922	C+
Houston Baptist Univ	TX	15,300	LC
Illinois College	IL	16,234	C
Immaculata College	PA	22,400	LC
Indiana State Univ	IN	8,461	LC
Indiana Univ of Pennsylvania	PA	9,133	C
Indiana Univ-Purdue Univ Fort Wayne	IN	3,166	LC
Iona College	NY	26,556	C
Ithaca College	NY	28,719	HC
Juniata College	PA	26,080	VC
Keene State College	NH	11,280	C
Kennesaw State Univ	GA	2,306	LC
Kent State Univ	OH	11,104	C
King's College	PA	24,680	C
La Roche College	PA	18,854	LC
La Salle Univ	PA	27,890	C
Lamar Univ	TX	6,816	LC
Le Moyne College	NY	23,840	C
Lenoir-Rhyne College	NC	19,186	C
Lock Haven Univ of Pennsylvania	PA	9,534	C
LIU/C.W. Post Campus	NY	25,380	C
Loras College	IA	22,994	C+
Louisiana Tech Univ	LA	6,506	C
Luther College	IA	23,300	VC+
Malone College	OH	19,190	C
Manhattan College	NY	25,500	VC
Mansfield Univ	PA	9,648	C
Mary Baldwin College	VA	23,440	C
Marymount College/ Tarrytown	NY	23,850	C
McNeese State Univ	LA	5,259	LC
Miami Univ	OH	12,885	VC+
Mich State Univ	MI	10,386	VC
Millikin Univ	IL	24,415	C+
Minn State Univ, Mankato	MN	7,296	LC
Minot State Univ	ND	5,466	LC
Missouri Southern State College	MO	6,666	C
Missouri Western State College	MO	6,662	NC
Monmouth Univ	NJ	24,042	C
Moorhead State Univ	MN	7,000	LC
Morris Brown College	GA	15,993	LC
Mount Mary College	WI	18,024	C
Mount Vernon Nazarene College	OH	17,027	C
Murray State Univ	KY	6,672	C
Muskingum College	OH	18,760	C
Nazareth College of Rochester	NY	22,036	VC
New York Univ	NY	35,200	MC
Niagara Univ	NY	22,250	C+
N Car State Univ	NC	8,680	HC
North Georgia College and State Univ	GA	6,322	C+
Northern Arizona Univ	AZ	7,398	C
Northern Mich Univ	MI	9,693	C
Northern State Univ	SD	6,279	LC
Northwest Nazarene Univ	ID	18,380	C
Northwestern College of Iowa	IA	17,630	C+
Ohio Wesleyan Univ	OH	29,670	VC+
Okla Baptist Univ	OK	13,878	VC
Okla City Univ	OK	15,810	C
Old Dominion Univ	VA	9,386	C
Oral Roberts Univ	OK	18,490	C
Ouachita Baptist Univ	AR	16,460	VC
Pittsburg State Univ	KS	6,228	NC
Prescott College	AZ	13,430	C
Providence College	RI	27,620	HC
Purdue Univ/Calumet	IN	6,630	NC
Purdue Univ/West Lafayette	IN	10,284	VC
Radford Univ	VA	8,302	C
Rhode Island College	RI	8,700	LC
Rice Univ	TX	24,325	MC
Rider Univ	NJ	27,400	C
Rivier College	NH	24,215	C
Rockhurst Univ	MO	20,090	C
Rosemont College	PA	24,060	C
Rowan Univ	NJ	12,365	VC
Saginaw Valley State Univ	MI	9,465	C
St. Cloud State Univ	MN	7,180	C
St. John's Univ	NY	26,660	C
St. Mary-of-the-Woods College	IN	21,320	LC
St. Mary's Univ of Minn	MN	19,975	C
St. Michael's College	VT	26,935	VC
St. Olaf College	MN	25,880	HC
St. Thomas Aquinas College	NY	20,590	LC
St. Xavier Univ	IL	21,104	C
Seton Hill College	PA	21,875	C
Slippery Rock Univ	PA	9,152	LC
Southeast Missouri State Univ	MO	8,367	C+
Southeastern Louisiana Univ	LA	6,047	LC
Southern Conn State Univ	CT	10,310	C
Southern Nazarene Univ	OK	14,634	NC
Southern Univ at New Orleans	LA	995	NC
Southern Utah Univ	UT	7,254	C
Southwest Missouri State Univ	MO	7,600	LC
Southwest Texas State Univ	TX	8,730	VC
Southwestern College	KS	17,656	C
SUNY/College at Buffalo	NY	8,025	C
SUNY/College at Cortland	NY	10,564	C
SUNY/College at Fredonia	NY	10,125	C
SUNY/College at Old Westbury	NY	9,818	LC
SUNY/College at Oneonta	NY	9,981	C
SUNY/College at Oswego	NY	10,856	C
SUNY/College at Potsdam	NY	10,519	C
SUNY/Univ at Albany	NY	10,997	VC
SUNY/Univ at New Paltz	NY	9,685	VC
Taylor Univ	IN	21,562	VC+
Temple Univ	PA	14,124	C
Texas Southern Univ	TX	6,576	NC
Thomas Edison State College	NJ	2,750	SP
Trinity Univ	TX	21,444	HC
Troy State Univ	AL	7,696	C
Turabo Univ	PR	4,110	
Univ of Akron	OH	10,530	NC
Univ of Central Arkansas	AR	6,388	C
Univ of Central Florida	FL	8,251	VC
Univ of Central Okla	OK	5,205	C
Univ of Cincinnati	OH	12,491	LC
Univ of Conn	CT	12,122	VC
Univ of Delaware	DE	10,824	VC
Univ of Findlay	OH	23,962	NC
Univ of Georgia	GA	8,656	VC
Univ of Idaho	ID	7,026	C
Univ of Illinois at Chicago	IL	10,702	VC
Univ of Illinois at Urbana-Champaign	IL	11,316	HC+
Univ of Indianapolis	IN	20,840	C
Univ of Iowa	IA	8,607	C+
Univ of Kentucky	KY	7,765	C
Univ of Louisiana at Lafayette	LA	5,200	C
Univ of Louisiana at Monroe	LA	5,207	NC
Univ of Louisville	KY	7,402	LC
Univ of Mary Hardin-Baylor	TX	13,929	C
Univ of Maryland/College Park	MD	11,959	C
Univ of Mich/Flint	MI	4,323	C
Univ of Minn/Duluth	MN	10,436	C
Univ of Miss	MS	7,666	C
Univ of Nebr at Kearney	NE	7,048	NC
Univ of Nebr at Lincoln	NE	8,325	C+
Univ of New Orleans	LA	10,160	C
Univ of North Alabama	AL	7,016	NC
Univ of N Car at Chapel Hill	NC	8,789	HC
Univ of N Car at Charlotte	NC	7,254	C
Univ of N Car at Greensboro	NC	6,858	C
Univ of Northern Iowa	IA	7,850	C
Univ of Okla	OK	7,616	VC
Univ of PR/Mayaguez	PR	5,285	
Univ of South Florida	FL	8,154	C
Univ of Southern Miss	MS	6,155	LC
Univ of Tenn at Martin	TN	8,268	C
Univ of Toledo	OH	11,206	NC
Univ of Vermont	VT	14,761	C+
Univ of Wisc/Eau Claire	WI	7,032	VC
Univ of Wisc/River Falls	WI	6,356	LC
Univ of Wisc/Whitewater	WI	6,937	C
Utah State Univ	UT	6,771	C
Vassar College	NY	33,450	MC
Wartburg College	IA	21,165	VC
Washington Univ in St. Louis	MO	34,593	MC
Wayne State College	NE	6,255	NC
Weber State Univ	UT	6,897	NC
West Chester Univ of Pennsylvania	PA	9,792	VC
West Texas A&M Univ	TX	6,538	C
West Virginia Univ	WV	8,304	C
Western Carolina Univ	NC	5,667	C
Western State College of Colo	CO	7,585	LC
Western Washington Univ	WA	8,624	VC
Whitworth College	WA	23,938	VC

ST = STATE $IS = IN-STATE COSTS SR = SELECTOR RATING

School	ST	$IS	SR
Widener Univ	PA	26,920	C
Winona State Univ	MN	8,570	C
Wittenberg Univ	OH	28,766	VC
Wright State Univ	OH	9,141	LC
Youngstown State Univ	OH	9,318	NC

FORENSIC STUDIES

School	ST	$IS	SR
Albany State Univ	GA	5,764	C+
Alvernia College	PA	20,790	C
Bay Path College	MA	22,308	C
Baylor Univ	TX	18,298	VC+
Chaminade Univ of Honolulu	HI	17,370	C
CUNY/John Jay College of Criminal Justice	NY	3,251	C
Columbia College	MO	15,082	C
Defiance College	OH	19,580	LC
Eastern Kentucky Univ	KY	6,552	C
Edinboro Univ of Pennsylvania	PA	9,328	LC
Mercyhurst College	PA	20,694	C
Mountain State Univ	WV	8,180	NC
Univ of Central Florida	FL	8,251	VC
Univ of Central Okla	OK	5,205	C
Univ of Miss	MS	7,666	C
Univ of New Haven	CT	23,860	LC
Univ of N Dak	ND	7,067	VC
Waynesburg College	PA	17,610	LC

FOREST ENGINEERING

School	ST	$IS	SR
Auburn Univ	AL	5,510	C
Oregon State Univ	OR	9,612	VC
SUNY/College of Environmental Science and Forestry	NY	12,446	VC
Univ of Maine	ME	10,798	C
Univ of Washington	WA	10,361	VC

FORESTRY AND RELATED SCIENCES

School	ST	$IS	SR
Alabama A&M Univ	AL	5,100	LC
Baylor Univ	TX	18,298	VC+
Catawba College	NC	19,620	C
Clemson Univ	SC	7,600	C
College of St. Benedict	MN	23,921	VC
Colo State Univ	CO	9,672	C
Eastern Mich Univ	MI	9,855	C
Eastern Oregon Univ	OR	8,772	C
Elizabethtown College	PA	26,000	VC
High Point Univ	NC	20,220	LC
Humboldt State Univ	CA	8,582	C
Iowa State Univ	IA	8,108	VC
Louisiana State Univ and A&M College	LA	8,014	VC
Louisiana Tech Univ	LA	6,506	C
Mich State Univ	MI	10,386	VC
Mich Tech Univ	MI	11,088	VC
N Car State Univ	NC	8,680	HC
Northern Arizona Univ	AZ	7,398	C
Northwest Missouri State Univ	MO	7,922	LC
Okla State Univ	OK	7,650	VC
Oregon State Univ	OR	9,612	VC
Penn State Univ/Univ Park Campus	PA	11,126	VC
Purdue Univ/West Lafayette	IN	10,284	VC
St. John's Univ	MN	23,640	VC
Southern Illinois Univ at Carbondale	IL	8,621	C
Southern Univ and A&M College	LA	6,365	C+
SUNY/College of Environmental Science and Forestry	NY	12,446	VC
Stephen F. Austin State Univ	TX	6,905	C
Texas A&M Univ	TX	8,988	VC
Ohio State Univ	OH	10,819	VC
Thomas Edison State College	NJ	2,750	SP
Univ of Arkansas at Monticello	AR	5,940	NC
Univ of Florida	FL	7,874	HC
Univ of Georgia	GA	8,656	VC
Univ of Illinois at Urbana-Champaign	IL	11,316	HC+
Univ of Kentucky	KY	7,765	C
Univ of Maine	ME	10,798	C
Univ of Mass Amherst	MA	10,995	VC
Univ of Minn/Twin Cities	MN	11,123	VC
Univ of Montana	MT	8,038	C
Univ of New Hampshire	NH	13,207	C
Univ of Tenn at Knoxville	TN	8,214	C
Univ of the South	TN	27,290	HC
Univ of Vermont	VT	14,761	C+
Univ of Wisc/Madison	WI	8,262	VC
Univ of Wisc/Stevens Point	WI	7,116	C
Utah State Univ	UT	6,771	C
Virginia Polytechnic Inst and State Univ	VA	7,652	C
Washington and Lee Univ	VA	25,095	MC
Washington State Univ	WA	9,388	C
West Virginia Univ	WV	8,304	C
Western New Mexico Univ	NM	5,950	LC

FORESTRY PRODUCTION AND PROCESSING

School	ST	$IS	SR
Auburn Univ	AL	5,510	C
Clemson Univ	SC	7,600	C
Miss State Univ	MS	7,853	C
Oregon State Univ	OR	9,612	VC
Penn State Univ/Univ Park Campus	PA	11,126	VC
Stephen F. Austin State Univ	TX	6,905	C
Univ of Idaho	ID	7,026	C
Univ of Minn/Twin Cities	MN	11,123	VC
Univ of Washington	WA	10,361	VC

FRENCH

School	ST	$IS	SR
Abilene Christian Univ	TX	16,300	VC
Adelphi Univ	NY	23,320	VC
Adrian College	MI	19,670	C
Agnes Scott College	GA	24,950	VC
Alabama A&M Univ	AL	5,100	LC
Alabama State Univ	AL	6,404	C
Albany State Univ	GA	5,764	C+
Albertus Magnus College	CT	22,154	C
Albion College	MI	25,224	VC
Albright College	PA	27,642	C
Alfred Univ	NY	27,212	C+
Allegheny College	PA	27,780	VC
Alma College	MI	22,586	VC
Amherst College	MA	34,340	MC
Anderson Univ	IN	19,430	LC
Andrews Univ	MI	17,696	LC
Angelo State Univ	TX	7,028	C
Appalachian State Univ	NC	6,353	C
Aquinas College	MI	20,052	C+
Arizona State Univ-Main	AZ	7,726	C
Arkansas State Univ	AR	7,480	C
Asbury College	KY	18,540	VC
Ashland Univ	OH	22,182	LC
Assumption College	MA	26,320	C
Atlantic Union College	MA	34,034	LC
Auburn Univ	AL	5,510	C
Augsburg College	MN	22,978	C
Augusta State Univ	GA	2,282	C
Augustana College	IL	24,117	VC+
Augustana College	SD	20,760	VC
Austin College	TX	22,150	VC+
Austin Peay State Univ	TN	5,814	LC
Baker Univ	KS	14,780	C+
Baldwin-Wallace College	OH	22,010	VC+
Ball State Univ	IN	8,660	C
Bard College	NY	33,912	HC
Barry Univ	FL	24,100	LC
Bates College	ME	34,100	MC
Baylor Univ	TX	18,298	VC+
Belmont Univ	TN	19,066	VC
Beloit College	WI	27,482	HC
Benedictine College	KS	18,485	LC
Bennington College	VT	31,350	VC
Berea College	KY	4,070	VC
Berry College	GA	18,850	C
Bethany College	WV	18,566	C
Birmingham-Southern College	AL	22,960	C
Bloomfield College	NJ	17,000	C
Bloomsburg Univ of Pennsylvania	PA	9,434	C
Boston College	MA	33,330	MC
Boston Univ	MA	34,358	MC
Bowdoin College	ME	32,650	MC
Bowling Green State Univ	OH	10,794	C
Bradley Univ	IL	20,970	VC
Brandeis Univ	MA	34,481	MC
Bridgewater College	VA	22,950	C
Brigham Young Univ	UT	7,840	HC
Brown Univ	RI	34,973	MC
Bryn Mawr College	PA	33,580	HC+
Bucknell Univ	PA	31,096	HC
Butler Univ	IN	25,580	VC+
Cabrini College	PA	25,950	LC
Caldwell College	NJ	20,940	LC
Calif Lutheran Univ	CA	23,500	LC
Cal State, Chico	CA	8,598	LC
Cal State, Fresno	CA	7,762	C
Cal State, Fullerton	CA	5,440	LC
Cal State, Hayward	CA	7,400	LC
Cal State, Long Beach	CA	7,400	LC
Cal State, Los Angeles	CA	5,050	C
Cal State, Northridge	CA	7,781	C
Cal State, Sacramento	CA	7,488	C
Cal State, San Bernardino	CA	6,516	C
Cal State, Stanislaus	CA	8,895	C
Calif Univ of Pennsylvania	PA	10,388	C
Calvin College	MI	20,050	NC
Campbell Univ	NC	16,599	C
Canisius College	NY	24,696	C+
Capital Univ	OH	23,630	C
Cardinal Stritch Univ	WI	17,620	C
Carleton College	MN	30,780	MC
Carnegie Mellon Univ	PA	32,682	MC
Carroll College	MT	19,140	C
Carson-Newman College	TN	16,490	C
Carthage College	WI	23,670	C
Case Western Reserve Univ	OH	27,418	C
Catawba College	NC	19,620	C
Catholic Univ of America	DC	29,332	VC
Cedar Crest College	PA	25,145	C+
Centenary College of Louisiana	LA	21,600	C+
Central College	IA	21,206	C
Central Conn State Univ	CT	10,404	C
Central Methodist College	MO	16,460	C
Central Mich Univ	MI	8,355	C
Central Missouri State Univ	MO	7,920	C
Central Washington Univ	WA	8,985	LC
Centre College	KY	24,000	HC
Chapman Univ	CA	30,218	VC
Chatham College	PA	25,454	C+
Chestnut Hill College	PA	24,790	LC
Christendom College	VA	16,700	VC+
Christopher Newport Univ	VA	8,862	VC
Citadel, The	SC	9,126	C
CUNY/Brooklyn College	NY	3,403	LC
CUNY/City College	NY	3,309	LC
CUNY/Herbert H. Lehman College	NY	3,320	LC
CUNY/Hunter College	NY	5,147	C+
CUNY/Queens College	NY	3,403	VC
CUNY/York College	NY	3,292	NC
Claremont McKenna College	CA	32,700	MC
Clarion Univ of Pennsylvania	PA	11,272	LC
Clark Univ	MA	29,170	HC
Clarke College	IA	20,625	C+
Clemson Univ	SC	7,600	C
Cleveland State Univ	OH	10,146	NC
Coe College	IA	24,750	VC
Coker College	SC	20,120	C
Colgate Univ	NY	33,480	MC
College of Charleston	SC	8,350	HC
College of Mount St. Vincent	NY	24,230	C
College of New Rochelle	NY	20,000	C
College of St. Benedict	MN	23,921	VC
College of St. Catherine	MN	22,324	VC
College of the Holy Cross	MA	32,780	MC
College of the Ozarks	MO	2,650	C+
College of William and Mary	VA	10,002	MC
College of Wooster	OH	28,350	VC
Colo College	CO	31,525	HC+
Colo State Univ	CO	9,672	C
Columbia College	SC	19,050	LC
Columbia Univ/Barnard College	NY	33,694	MC
Columbia Univ/Columbia College	NY	35,190	MC
Columbia Univ/School of General Studies	NY	35,000	C
Concordia College/ Moorhead	MN	18,835	C
Conn College	CT	33,585	MC
Converse College	SC	21,990	VC
Cornell College	IA	24,980	VC
Cornell Univ	NY	34,614	MC
Creighton Univ	NE	23,476	VC
Daemen College	NY	20,620	C
Dartmouth College	NH	34,458	MC
David Lipscomb Univ	TN	16,158	VC
Davidson College	NC	30,823	MC
Delaware State Univ	DE	8,104	LC
Denison Univ	OH	29,640	HC
DePaul Univ	IL	23,590	VC
DePauw Univ	IN	28,000	HC
Dickinson College	PA	32,210	VC+
Dillard Univ	LA	16,046	VC
Doane College	NE	17,600	LC
Dominican Univ	IL	20,800	C
Drew Univ/College of Liberal Arts	NJ	32,152	VC
Drury Univ	MO	15,250	VC
Earlham College	IN	27,446	VC+
East Carolina Univ	NC	7,766	C
East Stroudsburg Univ of Pennsylvania	PA	8,430	LC
Eastern College	PA	19,641	LC
Eastern Kentucky Univ	KY	6,552	C
Eastern Mennonite Univ	VA	20,700	VC
Eastern Mich Univ	MI	9,855	C
Eastern Nazarene College	MA	19,433	LC
Eastern Washington Univ	WA	7,972	LC
Eckerd College	FL	25,500	C+
Edgewood College	WI	18,304	C
Elizabethtown College	PA	26,000	VC
Elmhurst College	IL	21,750	C
Elmira College	NY	31,070	VC+
Elon Univ	NC	19,430	VC
Emory Univ	GA	33,792	MC
Fairfield Univ	CT	30,885	HC
Fairleigh Dickinson Univ/ Teaneck Campus	NJ	24,646	C
Fairmont State College	WV	7,010	NC
Ferrum College	VA	15,990	LC
Fisk Univ	TN	13,700	LC
Florida Atlantic Univ	FL	8,832	C
Florida International Univ	FL	9,486	VC
Florida State Univ	FL	7,835	HC
Fordham Univ	NY	30,710	VC
Fort Hays State Univ	KS	6,294	LC
Framingham State College	MA	7,259	C
Francis Marion Univ	SC	7,682	C
Franciscan Univ of Steubenville	OH	19,100	C+
Franklin and Marshall College	PA	32,410	HC
Franklin College of Indiana	IN	19,905	C
Furman Univ	SC	25,492	HC
Gallaudet Univ	DC	16,554	SP
Gardner-Webb Univ	NC	17,400	C
George Mason Univ	VA	9,192	C
George Washington Univ	DC	32,170	HC
Georgetown College	KY	18,400	VC
Georgetown Univ	DC	34,847	MC
Georgia College and State Univ	GA	7,344	C
Georgia Southern Univ	GA	6,958	C
Georgia State Univ	GA	7,792	LC
Georgian Court College	NJ	19,040	LC
Gettysburg College	PA	32,070	HC
Gonzaga Univ	WA	24,276	HC+
Gordon College	MA	23,594	VC+
Goshen College	IN	18,950	VC+
Goucher College	MD	30,650	VC+
Grace College	IN	16,768	C
Grambling State Univ	LA	5,325	NC
Greensboro College	NC	19,080	LC
Greenville College	IL	19,226	LC
Grinnell College	IA	28,300	HC+
Grove City College	PA	12,280	MC
Guilford College	NC	23,255	C
Gustavus Adolphus College	MN	24,190	VC+
Hamilton College	NY	34,150	HC
Hamline Univ	MN	23,339	C+
Hampden-Sydney College	VA	24,871	C
Hanover College	IN	17,560	VC
Harding Univ	AR	13,528	VC
Hardin-Simmons Univ	TX	14,165	C
Hartwick College	NY	33,090	C+
Harvard Univ/Harvard College	MA	34,269	MC
Haverford College	PA	34,300	MC
Hendrix College	AR	18,463	HC
High Point Univ	NC	20,220	LC
Hillsdale College	MI	20,586	VC+
Hiram College	OH	27,034	VC
Hobart and William Smith Colleges	NY	33,195	VC
Hofstra Univ	NY	23,252	C
Hollins Univ	VA	24,328	VC
Holy Family College	PA	13,710	LC
Hood College	MD	26,020	VC
Hope College	MI	22,922	C+
Houghton College	NY	21,810	VC+
Houston Baptist Univ	TX	15,300	LC
Howard Univ	DC	15,522	LC
Humboldt State Univ	CA	8,582	C
Idaho State Univ	ID	7,030	C+
Illinois College	IL	16,234	C
Illinois State Univ	IL	9,235	C
Illinois Wesleyan Univ	IL	26,970	HC
Immaculata College	PA	22,400	LC
Indiana State Univ	IN	8,461	LC
Indiana Univ Bloomington	IN	10,712	C+
Indiana Univ Northwest	IN	3,447	C
Indiana Univ of Pennsylvania	PA	9,133	C
Indiana Univ South Bend	IN	3,515	C
Indiana Univ Southeast	IN	3,459	C
Indiana Univ-Purdue Univ Fort Wayne	IN	3,166	LC
Indiana Univ-Purdue Univ Indianapolis	IN	9,473	C
Iona College	NY	26,556	C
Iowa State Univ	IA	8,108	VC
Ithaca College	NY	28,719	HC
Jacksonville Univ	FL	21,110	LC
John Carroll Univ	OH	24,140	VC
Johns Hopkins Univ	MD	35,226	MC
Juniata College	PA	26,080	VC
Kalamazoo College	MI	26,955	HC+
Keene State College	NH	11,280	C
Kennesaw State Univ	GA	2,306	LC
Kent State Univ	OH	11,104	C
Kenyon College	OH	32,130	HC+
King College	TN	17,800	VC
King's College	PA	24,680	C
Knox College	IL	28,230	HC
Kutztown Univ of Pennsylvania	PA	8,907	C
La Salle Univ	PA	27,890	C
Lafayette College	PA	32,655	MC
Lake Erie College	OH	21,350	LC
Lake Forest College	IL	27,460	VC
Lamar Univ	TX	6,816	LC
Lambuth Univ	TN	14,254	C
Lawrence Univ	WI	27,711	HC
Le Moyne College	NY	23,840	C
Lebanon Valley College of Pennsylvania	PA	25,700	VC
Lee Univ	TN	10,198	LC
Lehigh Univ	PA	32,290	MC
Lenoir-Rhyne College	NC	19,186	C

School	ST	$IS	SR
Lincoln Univ	MO	7,158	NC
Lincoln Univ	PA	11,198	C+
Lindenwood Univ	MO	17,250	C
Linfield College	OR	25,840	VC
Lock Haven Univ of Pennsylvania	PA	9,534	C
LIU/C.W. Post Campus	NY	25,380	C
Loras College	IA	22,994	C+
Louisiana College	LA	11,516	C
Louisiana State Univ and A&M College	LA	8,014	VC
Louisiana State Univ in Shreveport	LA	2,480	NC
Louisiana Tech Univ	LA	6,506	C
Loyola College in Maryland	MD	30,900	HC
Loyola Marymount Univ	CA	28,754	HC
Loyola Univ New Orleans	LA	23,506	VC+
Loyola Univ of Chicago	IL	25,992	VC
Luther College	IA	23,300	VC+
Lycoming College	PA	24,780	C
Lynchburg College	VA	23,405	C
Macalester College	MN	28,814	HC+
MacMurray College	IL	17,790	LC
Manchester College	IN	22,010	C
Manhattan College	NY	25,500	VC
Manhattanville College	NY	28,730	VC
Mansfield Univ	PA	9,648	C
Marian College	IN	21,020	C
Marietta College	OH	24,580	C
Marist College	NY	24,756	VC
Marlboro College	VT	26,410	VC+
Marquette Univ	WI	24,836	C+
Mary Baldwin College	VA	23,440	C
Mary Washington College	VA	9,032	VC+
Marymount College/Tarrytown	NY	23,850	C
Marywood Univ	PA	24,639	C
Mercer Univ	GA	24,130	VC
Meredith College	NC	17,500	C
Messiah College	PA	23,180	VC
Methodist College	NC	19,526	C
Miami Univ	OH	12,885	VC+
Mich State Univ	MI	10,386	VC
Middle Tenn State Univ	TN	6,994	C
Middlebury College	VT	34,300	MC
Millersville Univ of Pennsylvania	PA	10,153	VC
Millikin Univ	IL	24,415	C+
Mills College	CA	27,950	C
Millsaps College	MS	22,608	VC+
Minn State Univ, Mankato	MN	7,296	LC
Minot State Univ	ND	5,466	LC
Miss College	MS	14,574	C
Missouri Southern State College	MO	6,666	C
Missouri Western State College	MO	6,662	NC
Monmouth College	IL	21,550	C
Montana State Univ-Northern	MT	8,600	NC
Montclair State Univ	NJ	10,287	LC
Moorhead State Univ	MN	7,000	LC
Moravian College	PA	27,065	VC
Morehouse College	GA	19,814	C
Morris Brown College	GA	15,993	LC
Mount Holyoke College	MA	34,128	HC
Mount Mary College	WI	18,024	C
Mount St. Mary's College	CA	24,430	C
Mount St. Mary's College	MD	25,740	C
Mount Union College	OH	21,120	C
Muhlenberg College	PA	28,170	HC
Murray State Univ	KY	6,672	C
Muskingum College	OH	18,760	C
Nazareth College of Rochester	NY	22,036	VC
Nebr Wesleyan Univ	NE	18,767	VC
New York Univ	NY	35,200	MC
Newberry College	SC	19,670	LC
Niagara Univ	NY	22,250	C+
Nicholls State Univ	LA	5,290	NC
Norfolk State Univ	VA	8,382	LC
N Car Agricultural and Technical State Univ	NC	6,659	LC
N Car Central Univ	NC	6,418	LC
N Car State Univ	NC	8,680	HC
North Central College	IL	22,944	C+
N Dak State Univ	ND	7,004	VC
North Georgia College and State Univ	GA	6,322	C+
Northeastern Illinois Univ	IL	2,898	NC
Northeastern Univ	MA	30,078	VC
Northern Arizona Univ	AZ	7,398	C
Northern Illinois Univ	IL	9,545	C
Northern Kentucky Univ	KY	6,352	NC
Northern Mich Univ	MI	9,693	C
Northern State Univ	SD	6,279	LC
Northwest Missouri State Univ	MO	7,922	LC
Northwestern College of Iowa	IA	17,630	C+
Northwestern Univ	IL	33,615	MC
Notre Dame de Namur Univ	CA	26,932	LC
Oakland Univ	MI	9,418	C
Oakwood College	AL	14,904	C
Oberlin College	OH	33,140	HC+
Occidental College	CA	32,288	HC
Ohio Northern Univ	OH	27,765	VC
Ohio Univ	OH	11,769	C
Ohio Wesleyan Univ	OH	29,670	VC+
Okla Baptist Univ	OK	13,878	VC
Okla City Univ	OK	15,810	C
Okla State Univ	OK	7,650	VC
Old Dominion Univ	VA	9,386	C
Oral Roberts Univ	OK	18,490	C
Oregon State Univ	OR	9,612	VC
Otterbein College	OH	23,439	C
Ouachita Baptist Univ	AR	16,460	VC
Pace Univ	NY	24,200	C
Pacific Lutheran Univ	WA	23,318	VC
Pacific Union College	CA	20,250	VC
Penn State Univ/Univ Park Campus	PA	11,126	VC
Pepperdine Univ	CA	32,830	VC
Pittsburg State Univ	KS	6,228	NC
Pitzer College	CA	33,930	HC
Plymouth State College	NH	11,024	LC
Pomona College	CA	33,960	MC
Portland State Univ	OR	11,220	C
Presbyterian College	SC	23,356	VC
Principia College	IL	23,865	C+
Providence College	RI	27,620	HC
Purdue Univ/Calumet	IN	6,630	NC
Purdue Univ/West Lafayette	IN	10,284	VC
Queens College	NC	17,250	C
Randolph-Macon College	VA	24,395	C
Randolph-Macon Woman's College	VA	25,820	VC+
Regis College	MA	26,750	C
Regis Univ	CO	25,740	C+
Rhode Island College	RI	8,700	LC
Rhodes College	TN	26,466	HC+
Rider Univ	NJ	27,400	C
Ripon College	WI	24,180	VC+
Rivier College	NH	24,215	C
Roanoke College	VA	24,689	VC
Rockford College	IL	23,930	C
Rockhurst Univ	MO	20,090	C
Rollins College	FL	31,223	HC
Roosevelt Univ	IL	20,240	LC
Rosemont College	PA	24,060	C
Rutgers, The State Univ of New Jersey New Brunswick Campus	NJ	12,709	C
Rutgers, The State Univ of New Jersey/CamdenCampus	NJ	6,484	C
Saginaw Valley State Univ	MI	9,465	C
St. Ambrose Univ	IA	19,994	C
St. Anselm College	NH	27,405	C
St. Augustine's College	NC	12,990	C+
St. Bonaventure Univ	NY	21,956	C
St. Francis Univ	PA	24,486	LC
St. John Fisher College	NY	21,800	C
St. John's Univ	MN	23,640	VC
St. John's Univ	NY	26,660	C
St. Joseph's Univ	PA	29,715	VC+
St. Lawrence Univ	NY	32,605	VC
St. Louis Univ	MO	26,590	VC+
St. Mary's College	IN	24,474	VC
St. Mary's College of Calif	CA	27,575	C
St. Mary's Univ of Minn	MN	19,975	C
St. Mary's Univ of San Antonio	TX	19,735	C
St. Michael's College	VT	26,935	VC
St. Norbert College	WI	23,169	VC
St. Olaf College	MN	25,880	HC
St. Xavier Univ	IL	21,104	C
Salem College	NC	23,065	VC
Salisbury Univ	MD	10,576	VC
Salve Regina Univ	RI	26,460	C
Sam Houston State Univ	TX	6,076	LC
Samford Univ	AL	16,340	VC
San Diego State Univ	CA	9,716	C+
San Francisco State Univ	CA	7,139	LC
San Jose State Univ	CA	8,187	C
Santa Clara Univ	CA	28,371	VC+
Sarah Lawrence College	NY	37,516	HC
Seattle Pacific Univ	WA	22,674	C+
Seattle Univ	WA	24,183	VC
Seton Hall Univ	NJ	26,910	LC
Shippensburg Univ of Pennsylvania	PA	9,652	C
Shorter College	GA	15,185	C
Siena College	NY	22,685	VC
Simmons College	MA	30,418	VC
Simon's Rock College of Bard	MA	32,450	HC
Simpson College	IA	21,200	C+
Skidmore College	NY	34,201	VC+
Slippery Rock Univ	PA	9,152	LC
Smith College	MA	33,302	HC+
Sonoma State Univ	CA	8,953	C
S Car State Univ	SC	6,586	LC
Southeast Missouri State Univ	MO	8,367	C+
Southeastern Louisiana Univ	LA	6,047	LC
Southern Conn State Univ	CT	10,310	C
Southern Illinois Univ at Carbondale	IL	8,621	C
Southern Methodist Univ	TX	28,349	VC
Southern Univ and A&M College	LA	6,365	C+
Southern Utah Univ	UT	7,254	C
Southwest Missouri State Univ	MO	7,600	LC
Southwest Texas State Univ	TX	8,730	VC
Southwestern College	KS	17,656	C
Southwestern Univ	TX	22,550	HC
Spelman College	GA	19,215	C+
Stanford Univ	CA	34,222	MC
SUNY/College at Brockport	NY	10,267	C
SUNY/College at Buffalo	NY	8,025	C
SUNY/College at Fredonia	NY	10,125	C
SUNY/College at Geneseo	NY	9,970	HC
SUNY/College at Oneonta	NY	9,981	C
SUNY/College at Oswego	NY	10,856	C
SUNY/College at Plattsburgh	NY	9,729	C
SUNY/College at Potsdam	NY	10,519	C
SUNY/Univ at Albany	NY	10,997	VC
SUNY/Univ at Binghamton	NY	10,653	HC
SUNY/Univ at Buffalo	NY	11,033	VC
SUNY/Univ at New Paltz	NY	9,685	VC
SUNY/Univ at Stony Brook	NY	10,998	VC
State Univ of West Georgia	GA	7,101	C
Stephen F. Austin State Univ	TX	6,905	C
Stetson Univ	FL	25,640	VC
Suffolk Univ	MA	26,516	C
Susquehanna Univ	PA	27,270	VC
Swarthmore College	PA	34,538	MC
Sweet Briar College	VA	25,310	VC
Syracuse Univ	NY	30,710	HC
Taylor Univ	IN	21,562	VC+
Temple Univ	PA	14,124	C
Tenn Tech Univ	TN	6,968	C
Texas A&M Univ	TX	8,988	VC
Texas A&M Univ at Commerce	TX	7,326	C
Texas Christian Univ	TX	19,910	C
Texas Southern Univ	TX	6,576	NC
Texas Tech Univ	TX	8,825	C
Thiel College	PA	18,419	LC
Towson Univ	MD	11,088	VC
Transylvania Univ	KY	21,780	VC+
Trinity College	CT	34,300	HC
Trinity College	DC	21,370	LC
Trinity Univ	TX	21,444	HC
Truman State Univ	MO	8,568	VC+
Tufts Univ	MA	34,874	MC
Tulane Univ	LA	34,013	HC+
Union College	NY	32,646	HC
Union Univ	TN	18,930	C+
Univ of Akron	OH	10,530	NC
Univ of Alabama	AL	7,402	C
Univ of Alabama at Birmingham	AL	10,110	C
Univ of Alabama at Huntsville	AL	7,916	VC
Univ of Arizona	AZ	8,614	C
Univ of Arkansas	AR	8,334	VC
Univ of Arkansas at Little Rock	AR	5,637	NC
Univ of Calif at Berkeley	CA	14,134	MC
Univ of Calif at Davis	CA	12,796	VC
Univ of Calif at Irvine	CA	11,756	C
Univ of Calif at Los Angeles	CA	13,227	MC
Univ of Calif at Riverside	CA	12,479	C
Univ of Calif at Santa Barbara	CA	11,732	VC
Univ of Calif at Santa Cruz	CA	13,655	VC
Univ of Central Arkansas	AR	6,388	C
Univ of Central Florida	FL	8,251	VC
Univ of Central Okla	OK	5,205	C
Univ of Cincinnati	OH	12,491	LC
Univ of Colo at Boulder	CO	9,255	VC
Univ of Colo at Denver	CO	3,673	C
Univ of Conn	CT	12,122	VC
Univ of Dallas	TX	22,128	VC+
Univ of Dayton	OH	20,400	VC
Univ of Denver	CO	28,783	VC
Univ of Evansville	IN	22,865	VC+
Univ of Florida	FL	7,874	HC
Univ of Georgia	GA	8,656	VC
Univ of Hawaii at Manoa	HI	7,862	VC
Univ of Houston	TX	8,410	C
Univ of Idaho	ID	7,026	C
Univ of Illinois at Chicago	IL	10,702	VC
Univ of Illinois at Urbana-Champaign	IL	11,316	HC+
Univ of Indianapolis	IN	20,840	C
Univ of Iowa	IA	8,607	C+
Univ of Kansas	KS	7,232	VC
Univ of Kentucky	KY	7,765	C
Univ of La Verne	CA	24,280	C
Univ of Louisiana at Lafayette	LA	5,200	C
Univ of Louisiana at Monroe	LA	5,207	NC
Univ of Louisville	KY	7,402	LC
Univ of Maine	ME	10,798	C
Univ of Maine at Fort Kent	ME	7,450	LC
Univ of Maryland/Baltimore County	MD	12,190	VC
Univ of Maryland/College Park	MD	11,959	C
Univ of Mass Amherst	MA	10,995	VC
Univ of Mass Boston	MA	4,227	C
Univ of Mass Dartmouth	MA	9,852	C
Univ of Miami	FL	31,130	HC
Univ of Mich/Ann Arbor	MI	13,003	HC+
Univ of Mich/Flint	MI	4,323	C
Univ of Minn/Morris	MN	10,716	VC
Univ of Minn/Twin Cities	MN	11,123	VC
Univ of Miss	MS	7,666	C
Univ of Missouri/Columbia	MO	9,803	HC
Univ of Missouri/Kansas City	MO	9,685	VC
Univ of Missouri/St. Louis	MO	9,966	C
Univ of Montana	MT	8,038	C
Univ of Montevallo	AL	7,266	C
Univ of Nebr at Kearney	NE	7,048	NC
Univ of Nebr at Lincoln	NE	8,325	C+
Univ of Nebr at Omaha	NE	6,867	C
Univ of Nevada/Las Vegas	NV	8,281	VC
Univ of Nevada/Reno	NV	8,737	C
Univ of New Hampshire	NH	13,207	C
Univ of New Mexico	NM	8,026	C
Univ of New Orleans	LA	10,160	C
Univ of North Alabama	AL	7,016	NC
Univ of N Car at Asheville	NC	6,896	VC
Univ of N Car at Chapel Hill	NC	8,789	HC
Univ of N Car at Charlotte	NC	7,254	C
Univ of N Car at Greensboro	NC	6,858	C
Univ of N Car at Wilmington	NC	7,769	C
Univ of N Dak	ND	7,067	VC
Univ of North Texas	TX	7,629	C
Univ of Northern Colo	CO	8,082	C+
Univ of Northern Iowa	IA	7,850	C
Univ of Notre Dame	IN	30,707	MC
Univ of Okla	OK	7,616	VC
Univ of Oregon	OR	9,969	C
Univ of Pennsylvania	PA	34,614	MC
Univ of Pittsburgh at Pittsburgh	PA	13,592	HC
Univ of PR/Mayaguez	PR	5,285	
Univ of PR/Rio Piedras	PR	5,510	
Univ of Puget Sound	WA	28,285	HC
Univ of Redlands	CA	29,246	VC
Univ of Rhode Island	RI	12,414	C
Univ of Richmond	VA	27,300	HC
Univ of Rochester	NY	32,979	HC
Univ of St. Thomas	MN	24,044	VC
Univ of St. Thomas	TX	18,752	VC
Univ of San Diego	CA	29,198	HC
Univ of San Francisco	CA	27,302	VC
Univ of Scranton	PA	27,964	C+
Univ of South Alabama	AL	6,976	LC
Univ of S Car at Columbia	SC	8,748	VC
Univ of S Car at Spartanburg	SC	7,318	C+
Univ of South Florida	FL	8,154	C
Univ of Southern Calif	CA	33,647	MC
Univ of Southern Maine	ME	10,569	C
Univ of Tenn at Chattanooga	TN	7,783	C
Univ of Tenn at Knoxville	TN	8,214	C
Univ of Tenn at Martin	TN	8,268	C
Univ of Texas at Arlington	TX	7,192	LC
Univ of Texas at Austin	TX	9,437	HC
Univ of Texas at El Paso	TX	5,076	LC
Univ of Texas at San Antonio	TX	9,088	NC
Univ of the District of Columbia	DC	2,844	NC
Univ of the Pacific	CA	28,255	VC
Univ of the South	TN	27,290	HC
Univ of Toledo	OH	11,206	NC
Univ of Tulsa	OK	19,090	HC
Univ of Utah	UT	7,703	C
Univ of Vermont	VT	14,761	C+
Univ of Virginia	VA	9,391	HC+
Univ of Virginia's College at Wise	VA	8,302	C
Univ of Washington	WA	10,361	VC
Univ of Wisc/Eau Claire	WI	7,032	VC
Univ of Wisc/Green Bay	WI	7,148	C
Univ of Wisc/La Crosse	WI	7,250	VC
Univ of Wisc/Madison	WI	8,262	VC
Univ of Wisc/Milwaukee	WI	8,907	LC
Univ of Wisc/Oshkosh	WI	6,130	LC
Univ of Wisc/Parkside	WI	6,160	LC
Univ of Wisc/Platteville	WI	7,282	C
Univ of Wisc/Stevens Point	WI	7,116	C
Univ of Wisc/Whitewater	WI	6,937	C
Univ of Wyoming	WY	7,143	LC
Ursinus College	PA	31,350	VC
Utah State Univ	UT	6,771	C
Valdosta State Univ	GA	6,988	C
Valparaiso Univ	IN	23,570	VC+
Vanderbilt Univ	TN	34,482	MC
Villanova Univ	PA	31,997	HC
Virginia Polytechnic Inst and State Univ	VA	7,652	C
Virginia Wesleyan College	VA	22,350	LC
Wabash College	IN	25,335	HC
Wake Forest Univ	NC	30,290	MC
Walla Walla College	WA	20,925	C
Walsh Univ	OH	16,880	C
Wartburg College	IA	21,165	VC
Washburn Univ of Topeka	KS	6,766	NC

ST = STATE **$IS** = IN-STATE COSTS **SR** = SELECTOR RATING

School	ST	$IS	SR
Washington and Jefferson College	PA	26,255	VC
Washington and Lee Univ	VA	25,095	MC
Washington College	MD	28,040	VC
Washington State Univ	WA	9,388	C
Washington Univ in St. Louis	MO	34,593	MC
Weber State Univ	UT	6,897	NC
Webster Univ	MO	19,804	VC
Wellesley College	MA	33,394	MC
Wells College	NY	19,350	VC
Wesleyan College	GA	17,050	VC
Wesleyan Univ	CT	3,405	MC
West Chester Univ of Pennsylvania	PA	9,792	VC
Western Carolina Univ	NC	5,667	C
Western Illinois Univ	IL	9,571	C
Western Kentucky Univ	KY	6,834	C
Western Maryland College	MD	26,000	VC
Western Mich Univ	MI	10,016	C
Western Washington Univ	WA	8,624	VC
Westminster College	MO	19,990	C+
Westminster College	PA	22,960	C
Westmont College	CA	29,748	VC
Wheaton College	IL	21,934	HC
Wheaton College	MA	32,940	VC
Wheeling Jesuit Univ	WV	22,660	C
Whitman College	WA	29,086	HC
Whittier College	CA	29,108	C
Whitworth College	WA	23,938	VC
Wichita State Univ	KS	6,879	C
Wilkes Univ	PA	25,800	C
Willamette Univ	OR	29,422	VC+
William Jewell College	MO	17,150	VC
Williams College	MA	32,270	MC
Wilson College	PA	21,337	LC
Winona State Univ	MN	8,570	C
Winthrop Univ	SC	9,106	C
Wittenberg Univ	OH	28,766	VC
Wofford College	SC	23,995	VC
Wright State Univ	OH	9,141	LC
Xavier Univ	OH	23,880	C
Xavier Univ of Louisiana	LA	17,000	LC
Yale Univ	CT	34,030	MC
Yeshiva Univ	NY	21,400	C
Youngstown State Univ	OH	9,318	NC

FRENCH STUDIES

School	ST	$IS	SR
American Univ	DC	31,544	VC+
Assumption College	MA	26,320	C
Bard College	NY	33,912	HC
Case Western Reserve Univ	OH	27,418	C
Colby College	ME	34,290	MC
Columbia Univ/School of General Studies	NY	35,000	C
Duke Univ	NC	34,396	MC
Emory Univ	GA	33,792	MC
Fairleigh Dickinson Univ/ Madison campus	NJ	25,500	C
Fordham Univ	NY	30,710	VC
Lewis and Clark College	OR	29,010	VC
New College of Florida	FL	8,130	HC+
Reed College	OR	33,350	HC+
St. Joseph's Univ	PA	29,715	VC+
Scripps College	CA	30,400	HC+
Simon's Rock College of Bard	MA	32,450	HC
Skidmore College	NY	34,201	VC+
Smith College	MA	33,302	HC+
S Dak State Univ	SD	6,848	C
SUNY/Univ at Stony Brook	NY	10,998	VC
Univ of Calif at San Diego	CA	11,372	HC
Univ of New Hampshire	NH	13,207	C
Univ of S Dak	SD	7,036	C
Univ of the South	TN	27,290	HC
Wartburg College	IA	21,165	VC
Wesleyan Univ	CT	3,405	MC

FUNERAL HOME SERVICES

School	ST	$IS	SR
Cincinnati College of Mortuary Science	OH	10,850	SP
Mount Ida College	MA	25,375	LC
Point Park College	PA	20,290	C
St. John's Univ	NY	26,660	C
Southern Illinois Univ at Carbondale	IL	8,621	C
Univ of Central Okla	OK	5,205	C
Wayne State Univ	MI	6,720	C

FURNITURE DESIGN

School	ST	$IS	SR
Calif College of Arts and Crafts	CA	27,366	SP
Kendall College of Art and Design of Ferris State Univ	MI	8,820	SP
Minneapolis College of Art and Design	MN	23,560	SP
N Car State Univ	NC	8,680	HC
Northern Mich Univ	MI	9,693	C
Rhode Island School of Design	RI	30,227	SP
Rochester Inst of Technology	NY	26,232	VC+
Savannah College of Art and Design	GA	25,075	SP

GENDER STUDIES

School	ST	$IS	SR
Brown Univ	RI	34,973	MC
Conn College	CT	33,585	MC
Indiana Univ Bloomington	IN	10,712	C+
Lawrence Univ	WI	27,711	HC
Univ of Calif at San Diego	CA	11,372	HC
Univ of Chicago	IL	35,087	MC
Univ of Texas at Dallas	TX	9,305	VC

GENETICS

School	ST	$IS	SR
Ball State Univ	IN	8,660	C
Canisius College	NY	24,696	C+
Cedar Crest College	PA	25,145	C+
Cornell Univ	NY	34,614	MC
Dartmouth College	NH	34,458	MC
Florida State Univ	FL	7,835	HC
Iowa State Univ	IA	8,108	VC
Missouri Southern State College	MO	6,666	C
Ohio Wesleyan Univ	OH	29,670	VC+
Rutgers, The State Univ of New Jersey New Brunswick Campus	NJ	12,709	C
Texas A&M Univ	TX	8,988	VC
Univ of Calif at Davis	CA	12,796	VC
Univ of Conn	CT	12,122	VC
Univ of Georgia	GA	8,656	VC
Univ of Maryland/College Park	MD	11,959	C
Univ of Minn/Twin Cities	MN	11,123	VC
Univ of Rochester	NY	32,979	HC
Univ of Vermont	VT	14,761	C+
Univ of Wisc/Madison	WI	8,262	VC
Washington State Univ	WA	9,388	C
Western Kentucky Univ	KY	6,834	C

GEOCHEMISTRY

School	ST	$IS	SR
Calif Inst of Technology	CA	27,663	MC
Columbia Univ/Columbia College	NY	35,190	MC
Occidental College	CA	32,288	HC
SUNY/College at Cortland	NY	10,564	C
SUNY/College at Geneseo	NY	9,970	HC
SUNY/College at Oswego	NY	10,856	C
Univ of Maine at Farmington	ME	9,163	C

GEODETIC SCIENCE

School	ST	$IS	SR
Univ of Arkansas at Monticello	AR	5,940	NC

GEOGRAPHY

School	ST	$IS	SR
Appalachian State Univ	NC	6,353	C
Aquinas College	MI	20,052	C+
Arizona State Univ-Main	AZ	7,726	C
Arkansas State Univ	AR	7,480	C
Auburn Univ	AL	5,510	C
Augustana College	IL	24,117	VC+
Austin Peay State Univ	TN	5,814	LC
Ball State Univ	IN	8,660	C
Baylor Univ	TX	18,298	VC+
Bellevue Univ	NE	4,125	NC
Bemidji State Univ	MN	7,957	C
Bloomsburg Univ of Pennsylvania	PA	9,434	C
Boston Univ	MA	34,358	MC
Bowling Green State Univ	OH	10,794	C
Bridgewater State College	MA	7,589	C+
Brigham Young Univ	UT	7,840	HC
Bucknell Univ	PA	31,096	HC
Calif State Polytechnic Univ, Pomona	CA	8,615	C
Cal State, Chico	CA	8,598	LC
Cal State, Dominguez Hills	CA	5,840	LC
Cal State, Fresno	CA	7,762	C
Cal State, Fullerton	CA	5,440	LC
Cal State, Hayward	CA	7,400	LC
Cal State, Long Beach	CA	7,400	LC
Cal State, Los Angeles	CA	5,050	C
Cal State, Northridge	CA	7,781	C
Cal State, Sacramento	CA	7,488	C
Cal State, San Bernardino	CA	6,516	C
Cal State, Stanislaus	CA	8,895	C
Calif Univ of Pennsylvania	PA	10,388	C
Calvin College	MI	20,050	NC
Carroll College	WI	21,170	C
Carthage College	WI	23,670	C
Central Conn State Univ	CT	10,404	C
Central Mich Univ	MI	8,355	C
Central Missouri State Univ	MO	7,920	C
Central Washington Univ	WA	8,985	LC
Charleston Southern Univ	SC	17,122	C
Cheyney Univ of Pennsylvania	PA	9,993	C
Chicago State Univ	IL	8,851	C+
CUNY/Herbert H. Lehman College	NY	3,320	LC
CUNY/Hunter College	NY	5,147	C+
Clarion Univ of Pennsylvania	PA	11,272	LC
Clark Univ	MA	29,170	HC
Colgate Univ	NY	33,480	MC
Concord College	WV	7,122	C+
Concordia Univ Nebr	NE	17,770	C
Concordia Univ, River Forest	IL	20,000	LC
Dartmouth College	NH	34,458	MC
DePaul Univ	IL	23,590	VC
DePauw Univ	IN	28,000	HC
Dickinson State Univ	ND	5,495	NC
East Carolina Univ	NC	7,766	C
East Stroudsburg Univ of Pennsylvania	PA	8,430	LC
East Tenn State Univ	TN	7,127	C
Eastern Illinois Univ	IL	10,101	C
Eastern Kentucky Univ	KY	6,552	C
Eastern Mich Univ	MI	9,855	C
Eastern Washington Univ	WA	7,972	LC
Edinboro Univ of Pennsylvania	PA	9,328	LC
Elmhurst College	IL	21,750	C
Emory & Henry College	VA	19,462	C
Fayetteville State Univ	NC	5,590	LC
Fitchburg State College	MA	7,836	C
Florida Atlantic Univ	FL	8,832	C
Florida State Univ	FL	7,835	HC
Framingham State College	MA	7,259	C
Francis Marion Univ	SC	7,682	C
Frostburg State Univ	MD	9,680	C
George Mason Univ	VA	9,192	C
George Washington Univ	DC	32,170	HC
Georgia Southern Univ	GA	6,958	C
Georgia State Univ	GA	7,792	LC
Grand Valley State Univ	MI	10,040	C
Gustavus Adolphus College	MN	24,190	VC+
Hampshire College	MA	33,881	HC+
Hofstra Univ	NY	23,252	C
Humboldt State Univ	CA	8,582	C
Illinois State Univ	IL	9,235	C
Indiana State Univ	IN	8,461	LC
Indiana Univ Bloomington	IN	10,712	C+
Indiana Univ of Pennsylvania	PA	9,133	C
Indiana Univ Southeast	IN	3,459	C
Indiana Univ-Purdue Univ Indianapolis	IN	9,473	C
Jacksonville State Univ	AL	6,568	LC
Jacksonville Univ	FL	21,110	LC
James Madison Univ	VA	9,552	HC
Johns Hopkins Univ	MD	35,226	MC
Kansas State Univ	KS	6,995	C
Keene State College	NH	11,280	C
Kent State Univ	OH	11,104	C
Kutztown Univ of Pennsylvania	PA	8,907	C
Lock Haven Univ of Pennsylvania	PA	9,534	C
LIU/C.W. Post Campus	NY	25,380	C
Louisiana State Univ and A&M College	LA	8,014	VC
Louisiana State Univ in Shreveport	LA	2,480	NC
Louisiana Tech Univ	LA	6,506	C
Macalester College	MN	28,814	HC+
Mansfield Univ	PA	9,648	C
Marshall Univ	WV	7,752	LC
Mary Washington College	VA	9,032	VC+
Miami Univ	OH	12,885	VC+
Mich State Univ	MI	10,386	VC
Middle Tenn State Univ	TN	6,994	C
Middlebury College	VT	34,300	MC
Millersville Univ of Pennsylvania	PA	10,153	VC
Minn State Univ, Mankato	MN	7,296	LC
Montclair State Univ	NJ	10,287	LC
Morehead State Univ	KY	6,510	C
Mount Holyoke College	MA	34,128	HC
Murray State Univ	KY	6,672	C
New Jersey City Univ	NJ	9,100	LC
New Mexico State Univ	NM	7,302	C
N Car Central Univ	NC	6,418	LC
Northeastern Illinois Univ	IL	2,898	NC
Northeastern State Univ	OK	4,704	LC
Northern Arizona Univ	AZ	7,398	C
Northern Illinois Univ	IL	9,545	C
Northern Kentucky Univ	KY	6,352	NC
Northern Mich Univ	MI	9,693	C
Northwest Missouri State Univ	MO	7,922	LC
Ohio Univ	OH	11,769	C
Ohio Wesleyan Univ	OH	29,670	VC+
Okla State Univ	OK	7,650	VC
Old Dominion Univ	VA	9,386	C
Oregon State Univ	OR	9,612	VC
Penn State Univ/Univ Park Campus	PA	11,126	VC
Pittsburg State Univ	KS	6,228	NC
Plymouth State College	NH	11,024	LC
Portland State Univ	OR	11,220	C
Prairie View A&M Univ	TX	3,172	LC
Radford Univ	VA	8,302	C
Rhode Island College	RI	8,700	LC
Rutgers, The State Univ of New Jersey New Brunswick Campus	NJ	12,709	C
St. Cloud State Univ	MN	7,180	C
Salem State College	MA	4,481	LC
Salisbury Univ	MD	10,576	VC
Sam Houston State Univ	TX	6,076	LC
Samford Univ	AL	16,340	VC
San Diego State Univ	CA	9,716	C+
San Francisco State Univ	CA	7,139	LC
San Jose State Univ	CA	8,187	C
Shippensburg Univ of Pennsylvania	PA	9,652	C
Slippery Rock Univ	PA	9,152	LC
Sonoma State Univ	CA	8,953	C
S Dak State Univ	SD	6,848	C
Southeast Missouri State Univ	MO	8,367	C+
Southern Conn State Univ	CT	10,310	C
Southern Illinois Univ at Carbondale	IL	8,621	C
Southern Illinois Univ Edwardsville	IL	7,869	LC
Southern Oregon Univ	OR	9,429	C
Southwest Missouri State Univ	MO	7,600	LC
Southwest Texas State Univ	TX	8,730	VC
SUNY/College at Buffalo	NY	8,025	C
SUNY/College at Cortland	NY	10,564	C
SUNY/College at Geneseo	NY	9,970	HC
SUNY/College at Oneonta	NY	9,981	C
SUNY/College at Plattsburgh	NY	9,729	C
SUNY/Univ at Albany	NY	10,997	VC
SUNY/Univ at Binghamton	NY	10,653	HC
SUNY/Univ at Buffalo	NY	11,033	VC
SUNY/Univ at New Paltz	NY	9,685	VC
State Univ of West Georgia	GA	7,101	C
Stephen F. Austin State Univ	TX	6,905	C
Stetson Univ	FL	25,640	VC
Syracuse Univ	NY	30,710	HC
Taylor Univ	IN	21,562	VC+
Temple Univ	PA	14,124	C
Texas A&M Univ at Commerce	TX	7,326	C
Texas A&M Univ at Kingsville	TX	6,446	LC
Texas Southern Univ	TX	6,576	NC
Texas Tech Univ	TX	8,825	C
Ohio State Univ	OH	10,819	VC
Towson Univ	MD	11,088	VC
United States Air Force Academy	CO		MC
United States Military Academy	NY		MC
Univ of Akron	OH	10,530	NC
Univ of Alabama	AL	7,402	C
Univ of Alaska Fairbanks	AK	8,265	NC
Univ of Arizona	AZ	8,614	C
Univ of Arkansas	AR	8,334	VC
Univ of Calif at Berkeley	CA	14,134	MC
Univ of Calif at Davis	CA	12,796	VC
Univ of Calif at Irvine	CA	11,756	C
Univ of Calif at Los Angeles	CA	13,227	MC
Univ of Calif at Santa Barbara	CA	11,732	VC
Univ of Central Arkansas	AR	6,388	C
Univ of Central Okla	OK	5,205	C
Univ of Chicago	IL	35,087	MC
Univ of Cincinnati	OH	12,491	LC
Univ of Colo at Boulder	CO	9,255	VC
Univ of Colo at Colo Springs	CO	9,403	C
Univ of Colo at Denver	CO	3,673	C
Univ of Conn	CT	12,122	VC
Univ of Delaware	DE	10,824	VC
Univ of Denver	CO	28,783	VC
Univ of Florida	FL	7,874	HC
Univ of Georgia	GA	8,656	VC
Univ of Hawaii at Hilo	HI	6,497	C
Univ of Hawaii at Manoa	HI	7,862	VC
Univ of Idaho	ID	7,026	C
Univ of Illinois at Chicago	IL	10,702	VC
Univ of Illinois at Urbana-Champaign	IL	11,316	HC+
Univ of Iowa	IA	8,607	C+
Univ of Kansas	KS	7,232	VC
Univ of Kentucky	KY	7,765	C
Univ of Louisiana at Monroe	LA	5,207	NC
Univ of Louisville	KY	7,402	LC
Univ of Maine at Farmington	ME	9,163	C
Univ of Maryland/Baltimore County	MD	12,190	VC
Univ of Maryland/College Park	MD	11,959	C
Univ of Mass Amherst	MA	10,995	VC
Univ of Mass Boston	MA	4,227	C
Univ of Memphis	TN	7,271	C
Univ of Miami	FL	31,130	HC
Univ of Mich/Ann Arbor	MI	13,003	HC+
Univ of Mich/Flint	MI	4,323	C
Univ of Minn/Duluth	MN	10,436	C

School	ST	$IS	SR
Univ of Minn/Twin Cities	MN	11,123	VC
Univ of Missouri/Columbia	MO	9,803	HC
Univ of Missouri/Kansas City	MO	9,685	VC
Univ of Montana	MT	8,038	C
Univ of Nebr at Kearney	NE	7,048	NC
Univ of Nebr at Lincoln	NE	8,325	C+
Univ of Nebr at Omaha	NE	6,867	C
Univ of Nevada/Reno	NV	8,737	C
Univ of New Hampshire	NH	13,207	C
Univ of New Mexico	NM	8,026	C
Univ of New Orleans	LA	10,160	C
Univ of North Alabama	AL	7,016	NC
Univ of N Car at Chapel Hill	NC	8,789	HC
Univ of N Car at Charlotte	NC	7,254	C
Univ of N Car at Greensboro	NC	6,858	C
Univ of N Car at Wilmington	NC	7,769	C
Univ of N Dak	ND	7,067	VC
Univ of North Texas	TX	7,629	C
Univ of Northern Colo	CO	8,082	C+
Univ of Northern Iowa	IA	7,850	C
Univ of Okla	OK	7,616	VC
Univ of Oregon	OR	9,969	C
Univ of Pittsburgh at Johnstown	PA	13,044	LC
Univ of PR/Rio Piedras	PR	5,510	
Univ of Rhode Island	RI	12,414	C
Univ of St. Thomas	MN	24,044	VC
Univ of South Alabama	AL	6,976	LC
Univ of S Car at Columbia	SC	8,748	VC
Univ of South Florida	FL	8,154	C
Univ of Southern Calif	CA	33,647	MC
Univ of Southern Maine	ME	10,569	C
Univ of Southern Miss	MS	6,155	LC
Univ of Tenn at Knoxville	TN	8,214	C
Univ of Tenn at Martin	TN	8,268	C
Univ of Texas at Austin	TX	9,437	HC
Univ of Texas at Dallas	TX	9,305	VC
Univ of Texas at San Antonio	TX	9,088	NC
Univ of the District of Columbia	DC	2,844	NC
Univ of Toledo	OH	11,206	NC
Univ of Utah	UT	7,703	C
Univ of Vermont	VT	14,761	C+
Univ of Washington	WA	10,361	VC
Univ of Wisc/Eau Claire	WI	7,032	VC
Univ of Wisc/La Crosse	WI	7,250	VC
Univ of Wisc/Madison	WI	8,262	VC
Univ of Wisc/Milwaukee	WI	8,907	LC
Univ of Wisc/Oshkosh	WI	6,130	LC
Univ of Wisc/Parkside	WI	6,160	LC
Univ of Wisc/Platteville	WI	7,282	C
Univ of Wisc/River Falls	WI	6,356	LC
Univ of Wisc/Stevens Point	WI	7,116	C
Univ of Wisc/Whitewater	WI	6,937	C
Univ of Wyoming	WY	7,143	LC
Utah State Univ	UT	6,771	C
Valparaiso Univ	IN	23,570	VC+
Vassar College	NY	33,450	MC
Villanova Univ	PA	31,997	HC
Virginia Polytechnic Inst and State Univ	VA	7,652	C
Wayne State Univ	MI	6,720	C
Weber State Univ	UT	6,897	NC
West Chester Univ of Pennsylvania	PA	9,792	VC
West Texas A&M Univ	TX	6,538	C
West Virginia Univ	WV	8,304	C
Western Carolina Univ	NC	5,667	C
Western Illinois Univ	IL	9,571	C
Western Kentucky Univ	KY	6,834	C
Western Mich Univ	MI	10,016	C
Western Oregon Univ	OR	8,829	C
Western Washington Univ	WA	8,624	VC
William Paterson Univ of New Jersey	NJ	11,000	LC
Wittenberg Univ	OH	28,766	VC
Worcester State College	MA	7,901	LC
Wright State Univ	OH	9,141	LC
Youngstown State Univ	OH	9,318	NC

GEOLOGICAL ENGINEERING

School	ST	$IS	SR
Auburn Univ	AL	5,510	C
Brigham Young Univ	UT	7,840	HC
Colo School of Mines	CO	11,578	HC
Columbia Univ/Fu Foundation School of Engineering and Applied Science	NY	35,190	MC
Mich Tech Univ	MI	11,088	VC
Montana Tech of The Univ of Montana	MT	7,845	C
New Mexico State Univ	NM	7,302	C
Purdue Univ/West Lafayette	IN	10,284	VC
S Dak School of Mines and Technology	SD	7,438	C+
Univ of Alaska Fairbanks	AK	8,265	NC
Univ of Arizona	AZ	8,614	C
Univ of Calif at Los Angeles	CA	13,227	MC
Univ of Idaho	ID	7,026	C
Univ of Minn/Twin Cities	MN	11,123	VC
Univ of Miss	MS	7,666	C
Univ of Missouri/Rolla	MO	10,034	C
Univ of Nevada/Reno	NV	8,737	C
Univ of N Dak	ND	7,067	VC
Univ of Okla	OK	7,616	VC
Univ of Rochester	NY	32,979	HC
Univ of Utah	UT	7,703	C
Univ of Wisc/Madison	WI	8,262	VC
Washington Univ in St. Louis	MO	34,593	MC

GEOLOGY

School	ST	$IS	SR
Abilene Christian Univ	TX	16,300	VC
Adams State College	CO	7,468	C
Alfred Univ	NY	27,212	C+
Allegheny College	PA	27,780	VC
Amherst College	MA	34,340	MC
Appalachian State Univ	NC	6,353	C
Arizona State Univ-Main	AZ	7,726	C
Arkansas Tech Univ	AR	6,256	C
Ashland Univ	OH	22,182	LC
Auburn Univ	AL	5,510	C
Augustana College	IL	24,117	VC+
Austin Peay State Univ	TN	5,814	LC
Baldwin-Wallace College	OH	22,010	VC+
Ball State Univ	IN	8,660	C
Bates College	ME	34,100	MC
Baylor Univ	TX	18,298	VC+
Beloit College	WI	27,482	HC
Bemidji State Univ	MN	7,957	C
Bloomsburg Univ of Pennsylvania	PA	9,434	C
Boise State Univ	ID	6,531	LC
Boston College	MA	33,330	MC
Bowdoin College	ME	32,650	MC
Bowling Green State Univ	OH	10,794	C
Bridgewater State College	MA	7,589	C+
Brigham Young Univ	UT	7,840	HC
Brown Univ	RI	34,973	MC
Bryn Mawr College	PA	33,580	HC+
Bucknell Univ	PA	31,096	HC
Calif Inst of Technology	CA	27,663	MC
Calif Lutheran Univ	CA	23,500	LC
Calif State Polytechnic Univ, Pomona	CA	8,615	C
Cal State, Bakersfield	CA	6,090	LC
Cal State, Chico	CA	8,598	LC
Cal State, Dominguez Hills	CA	5,840	LC
Cal State, Fresno	CA	7,762	C
Cal State, Fullerton	CA	5,440	LC
Cal State, Hayward	CA	7,400	LC
Cal State, Long Beach	CA	7,400	LC
Cal State, Los Angeles	CA	5,050	C
Cal State, Northridge	CA	7,781	C
Cal State, Sacramento	CA	7,488	C
Cal State, San Bernardino	CA	6,516	C
Cal State, Stanislaus	CA	8,805	C
Calif Univ of Pennsylvania	PA	10,388	C
Calvin College	MI	20,050	NC
Carleton College	MN	30,780	MC
Case Western Reserve Univ	OH	27,418	C
Castleton State College	VT	10,922	LC
Centenary College of Louisiana	LA	21,600	C+
Central Mich Univ	MI	8,355	C
Central Missouri State Univ	MO	7,920	C
Central Washington Univ	WA	8,985	LC
Charleston Southern Univ	SC	17,122	C
CUNY/Brooklyn College	NY	3,403	LC
CUNY/City College	NY	3,309	LC
CUNY/Herbert H. Lehman College	NY	3,320	LC
CUNY/Queens College	NY	3,403	VC
CUNY/York College	NY	3,292	NC
Claremont McKenna College	CA	32,700	MC
Clarion Univ of Pennsylvania	PA	11,272	LC
Clemson Univ	SC	7,600	C
Cleveland State Univ	OH	10,146	NC
Colby College	ME	34,290	MC
Colgate Univ	NY	33,480	MC
College of Charleston	SC	8,350	HC
College of William and Mary	VA	10,002	MC
College of Wooster	OH	28,350	VC
Colo College	CO	31,525	HC+
Colo State Univ	CO	9,672	C
Columbia Univ/Columbia College	NY	35,190	MC
Columbus State Univ	GA	7,228	LC
Cornell College	IA	24,980	VC
Cornell Univ	NY	34,614	MC
Denison Univ	OH	29,640	HC
DePauw Univ	IN	28,000	HC
Dickinson College	PA	32,210	VC+
Duke Univ	NC	34,396	MC
Earlham College	IN	27,446	VC+
East Carolina Univ	NC	7,766	C
Eastern Illinois Univ	IL	10,101	C
Eastern Kentucky Univ	KY	6,552	C
Eastern Mich Univ	MI	9,855	C
Eastern New Mexico Univ	NM	4,113	LC
Eastern Washington Univ	WA	7,972	LC
Edinboro Univ of Pennsylvania	PA	9,328	LC
Elizabeth City State Univ	NC	5,550	LC
Florida Atlantic Univ	FL	8,832	C
Florida International Univ	FL	9,486	VC
Florida State Univ	FL	7,835	HC
Fort Hays State Univ	KS	6,294	LC
Fort Lewis College	CO	7,659	LC
Franklin and Marshall College	PA	32,410	HC
Furman Univ	SC	25,492	HC
George Mason Univ	VA	9,192	C
George Washington Univ	DC	32,170	HC
Georgia Southern Univ	GA	6,958	C
Georgia Southwestern State Univ	GA	6,013	C
Georgia State Univ	GA	7,792	LC
Grand Valley State Univ	MI	10,040	C
Guilford College	NC	23,255	C
Gustavus Adolphus College	MN	24,190	VC+
Hamilton College	NY	34,150	HC
Hampshire College	MA	33,881	HC+
Hanover College	IN	17,560	VC
Hardin-Simmons Univ	TX	14,165	C
Hartwick College	NY	33,090	C+
Harvard Univ/Harvard College	MA	34,269	MC
Haverford College	PA	34,300	MC
Hofstra Univ	NY	23,252	C
Hope College	MI	22,922	C+
Humboldt State Univ	CA	8,582	C
Idaho State Univ	ID	7,030	C+
Illinois State Univ	IL	9,235	C
Indiana State Univ	IN	8,461	LC
Indiana Univ Bloomington	IN	10,712	C+
Indiana Univ Northwest	IN	3,447	C
Indiana Univ of Pennsylvania	PA	9,133	C
Indiana Univ-Purdue Univ Fort Wayne	IN	3,166	LC
Indiana Univ-Purdue Univ Indianapolis	IN	9,473	C
Iowa State Univ	IA	8,108	VC
James Madison Univ	VA	9,552	HC
Johns Hopkins Univ	MD	35,226	MC
Juniata College	PA	26,080	VC
Kansas State Univ	KS	6,995	C
Keene State College	NH	11,280	C
Kent State Univ	OH	11,104	C
Kutztown Univ of Pennsylvania	PA	8,907	C
La Salle Univ	PA	27,890	C
Lafayette College	PA	32,655	MC
Lake Superior State Univ	MI	9,034	LC
Lamar Univ	TX	6,816	LC
Lawrence Univ	WI	27,711	HC
Lock Haven Univ of Pennsylvania	PA	9,534	C
LIU/C.W. Post Campus	NY	25,380	C
Louisiana State Univ and A&M College	LA	8,014	VC
Louisiana Tech Univ	LA	6,506	C
Macalester College	MN	28,814	HC+
Marietta College	OH	24,580	C
Marshall Univ	WV	7,752	LC
Mary Washington College	VA	9,032	VC+
McNeese State Univ	LA	5,259	LC
Mercyhurst College	PA	20,694	C
Miami Univ	OH	12,885	VC+
Mich State Univ	MI	10,386	VC
Mich Tech Univ	MI	11,088	VC
Middlebury College	VT	34,300	MC
Midwestern State Univ	TX	6,704	NC
Millersville Univ of Pennsylvania	PA	10,153	VC
Millsaps College	MS	22,608	VC+
Minot State Univ	ND	5,466	LC
Morehead State Univ	KY	6,510	C
Mount Holyoke College	MA	34,128	HC
Mount Union College	OH	21,120	C
Murray State Univ	KY	6,672	C
Muskingum College	OH	18,760	C
New Jersey City Univ	NJ	9,100	LC
New Mexico Inst of Mining and Technology	NM	7,152	VC+
New Mexico State Univ	NM	7,302	C
N Car State Univ	NC	8,680	HC
Northeastern Univ	MA	30,078	VC
Northern Arizona Univ	AZ	7,398	C
Northern Illinois Univ	IL	9,545	C
Northern Kentucky Univ	KY	6,352	NC
Northwest Missouri State Univ	MO	7,922	LC
Northwestern Univ	IL	33,615	MC
Norwich Univ	VT	21,064	LC
Oberlin College	OH	33,140	HC+
Occidental College	CA	32,288	HC
Ohio Univ	OH	11,769	C
Ohio Wesleyan Univ	OH	29,670	VC+
Okla State Univ	OK	7,650	VC
Old Dominion Univ	VA	9,386	C
Olivet Nazarene Univ	IL	18,444	C
Oregon State Univ	OR	9,612	VC
Pomona College	CA	33,960	MC
Portland State Univ	OR	11,220	C
Prescott College	AZ	13,430	C
Princeton Univ	NJ	35,072	MC
Purdue Univ/West Lafayette	IN	10,284	VC
Radford Univ	VA	8,302	C
Rensselaer Polytechnic Inst	NY	33,863	HC+
Rider Univ	NJ	27,400	C
Rutgers, The State Univ of New Jersey New Brunswick Campus	NJ	12,709	C
St. Cloud State Univ	MN	7,180	C
St. Lawrence Univ	NY	32,605	VC
St. Louis Univ	MO	26,590	VC+
St. Norbert College	WI	23,169	VC
Salem State College	MA	4,481	LC
Sam Houston State Univ	TX	6,076	LC
San Diego State Univ	CA	9,716	C+
San Francisco State Univ	CA	7,139	LC
San Jose State Univ	CA	8,187	C
Skidmore College	NY	34,201	VC+
Slippery Rock Univ	PA	9,152	LC
Smith College	MA	33,302	HC+
Sonoma State Univ	CA	8,953	C
S Dak School of Mines and Technology	SD	7,438	C+
Southern Illinois Univ at Carbondale	IL	8,621	C
Southern Methodist Univ	TX	28,349	VC
Southern Oregon Univ	OR	9,429	C
Southern Utah Univ	UT	7,254	C
Southwest Missouri State Univ	MO	7,600	LC
Stanford Univ	CA	34,222	MC
SUNY/College at Brockport	NY	10,267	C
SUNY/College at Buffalo	NY	8,025	C
SUNY/College at Cortland	NY	10,564	C
SUNY/College at Fredonia	NY	10,125	C
SUNY/College at Geneseo	NY	9,970	HC
SUNY/College at Oneonta	NY	9,981	C
SUNY/College at Oswego	NY	10,856	C
SUNY/College at Plattsburgh	NY	9,729	C
SUNY/College at Potsdam	NY	10,519	C
SUNY/Univ at Albany	NY	10,997	VC
SUNY/Univ at Binghamton	NY	10,653	HC
SUNY/Univ at Buffalo	NY	11,033	VC
SUNY/Univ at New Paltz	NY	9,685	VC
SUNY/Univ at Stony Brook	NY	10,998	VC
State Univ of West Georgia	GA	7,101	C
Stephen F. Austin State Univ	TX	6,905	C
Sul Ross State Univ	TX	6,582	LC
Syracuse Univ	NY	30,710	HC
Tarleton State Univ	TX	7,160	C
Temple Univ	PA	14,124	C
Tenn Tech Univ	TN	6,968	C
Texas A&M Univ	TX	8,988	VC
Texas A&M Univ at Commerce	TX	7,326	C
Texas A&M Univ at Kingsville	TX	6,446	LC
Texas Christian Univ	TX	19,910	C
Texas Southern Univ	TX	6,576	NC
Texas Tech Univ	TX	8,825	C
Ohio State Univ	OH	10,819	VC
Thiel College	PA	18,419	LC
Towson Univ	MD	11,088	VC
Tufts Univ	MA	34,874	MC
Tulane Univ	LA	34,013	HC+
Union College	NY	32,646	HC
Univ of Akron	OH	10,530	NC
Univ of Alabama	AL	7,402	C
Univ of Alaska Fairbanks	AK	8,265	NC
Univ of Arizona	AZ	8,614	C
Univ of Arkansas	AR	8,334	VC
Univ of Arkansas at Little Rock	AR	5,637	NC
Univ of Calif at Berkeley	CA	14,134	MC
Univ of Calif at Davis	CA	12,796	VC
Univ of Calif at Los Angeles	CA	13,227	MC
Univ of Calif at Riverside	CA	12,479	C
Univ of Calif at Santa Barbara	CA	11,732	VC
Univ of Calif at Santa Cruz	CA	13,655	VC
Univ of Cincinnati	OH	12,491	LC
Univ of Colo at Boulder	CO	9,255	VC
Univ of Colo at Denver	CO	3,673	C
Univ of Conn	CT	12,122	VC
Univ of Dayton	OH	20,400	VC
Univ of Delaware	DE	10,824	VC
Univ of Florida	FL	7,874	HC
Univ of Georgia	GA	8,656	VC
Univ of Hawaii at Hilo	HI	6,497	C
Univ of Hawaii at Manoa	HI	7,862	VC
Univ of Houston	TX	8,410	C
Univ of Idaho	ID	7,026	C
Univ of Illinois at Chicago	IL	10,702	VC
Univ of Illinois at Urbana-Champaign	IL	11,316	HC+
Univ of Iowa	IA	8,607	C+
Univ of Kansas	KS	7,232	VC
Univ of Kentucky	KY	7,765	C
Univ of Louisiana at Lafayette	LA	5,200	C
Univ of Louisiana at Monroe	LA	5,207	NC
Univ of Maine	ME	10,798	C
Univ of Maine at Farmington	ME	9,163	C
Univ of Maryland/College Park	MD	11,959	C
Univ of Mass Amherst	MA	10,995	VC

School	ST	$IS	SR
Univ of Memphis	TN	7,271	C
Univ of Miami	FL	31,130	HC
Univ of Minn/Duluth	MN	10,436	C
Univ of Minn/Morris	MN	10,716	VC
Univ of Minn/Twin Cities	MN	11,123	VC
Univ of Miss	MS	7,666	C
Univ of Missouri/Columbia	MO	9,803	HC
Univ of Missouri/Kansas City	MO	9,685	VC
Univ of Missouri/Rolla	MO	10,034	C
Univ of Montana	MT	8,038	C
Univ of Nebr at Lincoln	NE	8,325	C+
Univ of Nebr at Omaha	NE	6,867	C
Univ of Nevada/Las Vegas	NV	8,281	VC
Univ of Nevada/Reno	NV	8,737	C
Univ of New Hampshire	NH	13,207	C
Univ of New Orleans	LA	10,160	C
Univ of North Alabama	AL	7,016	NC
Univ of N Car at Chapel Hill	NC	8,789	HC
Univ of N Car at Charlotte	NC	7,254	C
Univ of N Car at Wilmington	NC	7,769	C
Univ of N Dak	ND	7,067	VC
Univ of Northern Colo	CO	8,082	C+
Univ of Northern Iowa	IA	7,850	C
Univ of Okla	OK	7,616	VC
Univ of Oregon	OR	9,969	C
Univ of Pennsylvania	PA	34,614	MC
Univ of Pittsburgh at Bradford	PA	12,696	C
Univ of Pittsburgh at Johnstown	PA	13,044	LC
Univ of Pittsburgh at Pittsburgh	PA	13,592	HC
Univ of PR/Mayaguez	PR	5,285	
Univ of Puget Sound	WA	28,285	HC
Univ of Rhode Island	RI	12,414	C
Univ of Rochester	NY	32,979	HC
Univ of St. Thomas	MN	24,044	VC
Univ of South Alabama	AL	6,976	LC
Univ of S Car at Columbia	SC	8,748	VC
Univ of South Florida	FL	8,154	C
Univ of Southern Calif	CA	33,647	MC
Univ of Southern Maine	ME	10,569	C
Univ of Southern Miss	MS	6,155	LC
Univ of Tenn at Chattanooga	TN	7,783	C
Univ of Tenn at Knoxville	TN	8,214	C
Univ of Tenn at Martin	TN	8,268	C
Univ of Texas at Arlington	TX	7,192	LC
Univ of Texas at Austin	TX	9,437	HC
Univ of Texas at El Paso	TX	5,076	LC
Univ of Texas at San Antonio	TX	9,088	NC
Univ of the Pacific	CA	28,255	VC
Univ of the South	TN	27,290	HC
Univ of Toledo	OH	11,206	NC
Univ of Tulsa	OK	19,090	HC
Univ of Utah	UT	7,703	C
Univ of Vermont	VT	14,761	C+
Univ of Washington	WA	10,361	VC
Univ of Wisc/Eau Claire	WI	7,032	VC
Univ of Wisc/Madison	WI	8,262	VC
Univ of Wisc/Milwaukee	WI	8,907	LC
Univ of Wisc/Oshkosh	WI	6,130	LC
Univ of Wisc/Parkside	WI	6,160	LC
Univ of Wisc/River Falls	WI	6,356	LC
Univ of Wyoming	WY	7,143	LC
Utah State Univ	UT	6,771	C
Valparaiso Univ	IN	23,570	VC+
Vanderbilt Univ	TN	34,482	MC
Vassar College	NY	33,450	MC
Virginia Polytechnic Inst and State Univ	VA	7,652	C
Washington and Lee Univ	VA	25,095	MC
Washington State Univ	WA	9,388	C
Wayne State Univ	MI	6,720	C
Weber State Univ	UT	6,897	NC
Wellesley College	MA	33,394	MC
West Texas A&M Univ	TX	6,538	C
West Virginia Univ	WV	8,304	C
Western Carolina Univ	NC	5,667	C
Western Illinois Univ	IL	9,571	C
Western Kentucky Univ	KY	6,834	C
Western Mich Univ	MI	10,016	C
Western State College of Colo	CO	7,585	LC
Western Washington Univ	WA	8,624	VC
Wheaton College	IL	21,934	HC
Whitman College	WA	29,086	HC
Wichita State Univ	KS	6,879	C
Williams College	MA	32,270	MC
Winona State Univ	MN	8,570	C
Wittenberg Univ	OH	28,766	VC
Wright State Univ	OH	9,141	LC
Yale Univ	CT	34,030	MC
Youngstown State Univ	OH	9,318	NC

GEOPHYSICAL ENGINEERING

School	ST	$IS	SR
Colo School of Mines	CO	11,578	HC
Montana Tech of The Univ of Montana	MT	7,845	C
New Jersey Inst of Technology	NJ	14,690	VC
Univ of Calif at Los Angeles	CA	13,227	MC
Univ of Texas at Austin	TX	9,437	HC

GEOPHYSICS AND SEISMOLOGY

School	ST	$IS	SR
Baylor Univ	TX	18,298	VC+
Boise State Univ	ID	6,531	LC
Boston College	MA	33,330	MC
Calif Inst of Technology	CA	27,663	MC
Colgate Univ	NY	33,480	MC
Columbia Univ/Columbia College	NY	35,190	MC
Harvard Univ/Harvard College	MA	34,269	MC
Johns Hopkins Univ	MD	35,226	MC
Kansas State Univ	KS	6,995	C
Mich Tech Univ	MI	11,088	VC
New Mexico Inst of Mining and Technology	NM	7,152	VC+
Occidental College	CA	32,288	HC
St. Louis Univ	MO	26,590	VC+
Southern Methodist Univ	TX	28,349	VC
SUNY/College at Cortland	NY	10,564	C
SUNY/College at Geneseo	NY	9,970	HC
Texas A&M Univ	TX	8,988	VC
Texas Tech Univ	TX	8,825	C
Univ of Calif at Los Angeles	CA	13,227	MC
Univ of Calif at Riverside	CA	12,479	C
Univ of Calif at Santa Barbara	CA	11,732	VC
Univ of Delaware	DE	10,824	VC
Univ of Hawaii at Manoa	HI	7,862	VC
Univ of Houston	TX	8,410	C
Univ of Minn/Twin Cities	MN	11,123	VC
Univ of Missouri/Rolla	MO	10,034	C
Univ of Nevada/Reno	NV	8,737	C
Univ of New Orleans	LA	10,160	C
Univ of Okla	OK	7,616	VC
Univ of S Car at Columbia	SC	8,748	VC
Univ of Texas at Austin	TX	9,437	HC
Univ of Texas at El Paso	TX	5,076	LC
Univ of the Pacific	CA	28,255	VC
Univ of Utah	UT	7,703	C
Western Mich Univ	MI	10,016	C
Wright State Univ	OH	9,141	LC

GEOSCIENCE

School	ST	$IS	SR
Albion College	MI	25,224	VC
Bradley Univ	IL	20,970	VC
Cal State, Chico	CA	8,598	LC
Columbia Univ/School of General Studies	NY	35,000	C
Earlham College	IN	27,446	VC+
Hobart and William Smith Colleges	NY	33,195	VC
Indiana Univ of Pennsylvania	PA	9,133	C
Lewis-Clark State College	ID	6,496	C
Miss State Univ	MS	7,853	C
Montclair State Univ	NJ	10,287	LC
Pacific Lutheran Univ	WA	23,318	VC
Penn State Univ/Univ Park Campus	PA	11,126	VC
Southeast Missouri State Univ	MO	8,367	C+
Stanford Univ	CA	34,222	MC
Texas Tech Univ	TX	8,825	C
Towson Univ	MD	11,088	VC
Trinity Univ	TX	21,444	HC
Univ of Arizona	AZ	8,614	C
Univ of Chicago	IL	35,087	MC
Univ of Mich/Ann Arbor	MI	13,003	HC+
Univ of Okla	OK	7,616	VC
Univ of Southern Maine	ME	10,569	C
Univ of Texas at Dallas	TX	9,305	VC
Univ of Tulsa	OK	19,090	HC
Univ of Wisc/Milwaukee	WI	8,907	LC
West Chester Univ of Pennsylvania	PA	9,792	VC
West Virginia Univ	WV	8,304	C

GERMAN

School	ST	$IS	SR
Adrian College	MI	19,670	C
Agnes Scott College	GA	24,950	VC
Albion College	MI	25,224	VC
Alfred Univ	NY	27,212	C+
Allegheny College	PA	27,780	VC
Alma College	MI	22,586	VC
Amherst College	MA	34,340	MC
Anderson Univ	IN	19,430	LC
Angelo State Univ	TX	7,028	C
Aquinas College	MI	20,052	C+
Arizona State Univ-Main	AZ	7,726	C
Auburn Univ	AL	5,510	C
Augsburg College	MN	22,978	C
Augustana College	IL	24,117	VC+
Augustana College	SD	20,760	VC
Austin College	TX	22,150	VC+
Austin Peay State Univ	TN	5,814	LC
Baker Univ	KS	14,780	C+
Baldwin-Wallace College	OH	22,010	VC+
Ball State Univ	IN	8,660	C
Bard College	NY	33,912	HC
Bates College	ME	34,100	MC
Baylor Univ	TX	18,298	VC+
Beloit College	WI	27,482	HC
Bemidji State Univ	MN	7,957	C
Bennington College	VT	31,350	VC
Berea College	KY	4,070	VC
Berry College	GA	18,850	C
Bethany College	WV	18,566	C
Bethel College	KS	17,355	C+
Birmingham-Southern College	AL	22,960	C
Bloomsburg Univ of Pennsylvania	PA	9,434	C
Boston Univ	MA	34,358	MC
Bowdoin College	ME	32,650	MC
Bowling Green State Univ	OH	10,794	C
Bradley Univ	IL	20,970	VC
Brandeis Univ	MA	34,481	MC
Brigham Young Univ	UT	7,840	HC
Brown Univ	RI	34,973	MC
Bryn Mawr College	PA	33,580	HC+
Bucknell Univ	PA	31,096	HC
Butler Univ	IN	25,580	VC+
Calif Lutheran Univ	CA	23,500	LC
Cal State, Chico	CA	8,598	LC
Cal State, Fullerton	CA	5,440	LC
Cal State, Long Beach	CA	7,400	LC
Cal State, Northridge	CA	7,781	C
Cal State, Sacramento	CA	7,488	C
Cal State, Stanislaus	CA	8,895	C
Calif Univ of Pennsylvania	PA	10,388	C
Calvin College	MI	20,050	NC
Canisius College	NY	24,696	C+
Carleton College	MN	30,780	MC
Carnegie Mellon Univ	PA	32,682	MC
Carthage College	WI	23,670	C
Case Western Reserve Univ	OH	27,418	C
Catholic Univ of America	DC	29,332	VC
Centenary College of Louisiana	LA	21,600	C+
Central College	IA	21,206	C
Central Conn State Univ	CT	10,404	C
Central Mich Univ	MI	8,355	C
Central Missouri State Univ	MO	7,920	C
Central Washington Univ	WA	8,985	LC
Centre College	KY	24,000	HC
Christopher Newport Univ	VA	8,862	VC
Citadel, The	SC	9,126	C
CUNY/Brooklyn College	NY	3,403	LC
CUNY/Herbert H. Lehman College	NY	3,320	LC
CUNY/Hunter College	NY	5,147	C+
CUNY/Queens College	NY	3,403	VC
Claremont McKenna College	CA	32,700	MC
Clemson Univ	SC	7,600	C
Cleveland State Univ	OH	10,146	NC
Coe College	IA	24,750	VC
Colby College	ME	34,290	MC
Colgate Univ	NY	33,480	MC
College of Charleston	SC	8,350	HC
College of St. Benedict	MN	23,921	VC
College of the Holy Cross	MA	32,780	MC
College of the Ozarks	MO	2,650	C+
College of William and Mary	VA	10,002	MC
College of Wooster	OH	28,350	VC
Colo College	CO	31,525	HC+
Colo State Univ	CO	9,672	C
Columbia Univ/Barnard College	NY	33,694	MC
Columbia Univ/Columbia College	NY	35,190	MC
Columbia Univ/School of General Studies	NY	35,000	C
Concordia College/Moorhead	MN	18,835	C
Conn College	CT	33,585	MC
Cornell College	IA	24,980	VC
Cornell Univ	NY	34,614	MC
Creighton Univ	NE	23,476	VC
Dana College	NE	18,046	C
Dartmouth College	NH	34,458	MC
David Lipscomb Univ	TN	16,158	VC
Davidson College	NC	30,823	MC
Denison Univ	OH	29,640	HC
DePaul Univ	IL	23,590	VC
DePauw Univ	IN	28,000	HC
Dickinson College	PA	32,210	VC+
Doane College	NE	17,600	LC
Dordt College	IA	18,100	C+
Drew Univ/College of Liberal Arts	NJ	32,152	VC
Drury Univ	MO	15,250	VC
Earlham College	IN	27,446	VC+
East Carolina Univ	NC	7,766	C
Eastern Mennonite Univ	VA	20,700	VC
Eastern Mich Univ	MI	9,855	C
Eastern Washington Univ	WA	7,972	LC
Eckerd College	FL	25,500	C+
Edinboro Univ of Pennsylvania	PA	9,328	LC
Elizabethtown College	PA	26,000	VC
Elmhurst College	IL	21,750	C
Fairfield Univ	CT	30,885	HC
Florida Atlantic Univ	FL	8,832	C
Florida International Univ	FL	9,486	VC
Florida State Univ	FL	7,835	HC
Fordham Univ	NY	30,710	VC
Fort Hays State Univ	KS	6,294	LC
Francis Marion Univ	SC	7,682	C
Franklin and Marshall College	PA	32,410	HC
Furman Univ	SC	25,492	HC
Gallaudet Univ	DC	16,554	SP
George Mason Univ	VA	9,192	C
George Washington Univ	DC	32,170	HC
Georgetown College	KY	18,400	VC
Georgetown Univ	DC	34,847	MC
Georgia Southern Univ	GA	6,958	C
Georgia State Univ	GA	7,792	LC
Gettysburg College	PA	32,070	HC
Gonzaga Univ	WA	24,276	HC+
Gordon College	MA	23,594	VC+
Goshen College	IN	18,950	VC+
Grace College	IN	16,768	C
Graceland Univ	IA	15,845	C
Grinnell College	IA	28,300	HC+
Guilford College	NC	23,255	C
Gustavus Adolphus College	MN	24,190	VC+
Hamilton College	NY	34,150	HC
Hamline Univ	MN	23,339	C+
Hampden-Sydney College	VA	24,871	C
Hanover College	IN	17,560	VC
Hardin-Simmons Univ	TX	14,165	C
Hartwick College	NY	33,090	C+
Harvard Univ/Harvard College	MA	34,269	MC
Hastings College	NE	17,854	C+
Haverford College	PA	34,300	MC
Heidelberg College	OH	23,879	C
Hendrix College	AR	18,463	HC
Hillsdale College	MI	20,586	VC+
Hiram College	OH	27,034	VC
Hofstra Univ	NY	23,252	C
Hollins Univ	VA	24,328	VC
Hood College	MD	26,020	VC
Hope College	MI	22,922	C+
Howard Univ	DC	15,522	LC
Humboldt State Univ	CA	8,582	C
Idaho State Univ	ID	7,030	C+
Illinois College	IL	16,234	C
Illinois State Univ	IL	9,235	C
Illinois Wesleyan Univ	IL	26,970	HC
Immaculata College	PA	22,400	LC
Indiana State Univ	IN	8,461	LC
Indiana Univ Bloomington	IN	10,712	C+
Indiana Univ of Pennsylvania	PA	9,133	C
Indiana Univ South Bend	IN	3,515	C
Indiana Univ-Purdue Univ Fort Wayne	IN	3,166	LC
Indiana Univ-Purdue Univ Indianapolis	IN	9,473	C
Iowa State Univ	IA	8,108	VC
Ithaca College	NY	28,719	HC
John Carroll Univ	OH	24,140	VC
Johns Hopkins Univ	MD	35,226	MC
Juniata College	PA	26,080	VC
Kalamazoo College	MI	26,955	HC+
Kent State Univ	OH	11,104	C
Kenyon College	OH	32,130	HC+
Knox College	IL	28,230	HC
La Salle Univ	PA	27,890	C
Lafayette College	PA	32,655	MC
Lake Erie College	OH	21,350	LC
Lake Forest College	IL	27,460	VC
Lakeland College	WI	17,950	C
Lawrence Univ	WI	27,711	HC
Lebanon Valley College of Pennsylvania	PA	25,700	VC
Lee Univ	TN	10,198	LC
Lehigh Univ	PA	32,290	MC
Lenoir-Rhyne College	NC	19,186	C
Lincoln Univ	PA	11,198	C+
Linfield College	OR	25,840	VC
Lock Haven Univ of Pennsylvania	PA	9,534	C
LIU/C.W. Post Campus	NY	25,380	C
Loras College	IA	22,994	C+
Louisiana State Univ and A&M College	LA	8,014	VC
Loyola College in Maryland	MD	30,900	HC
Loyola Univ New Orleans	LA	23,506	VC+
Loyola Univ of Chicago	IL	25,992	VC
Luther College	IA	23,300	VC+
Lycoming College	PA	24,780	C
Manchester College	IN	22,010	C
Manhattanville College	NY	28,730	VC
Mansfield Univ	PA	9,648	C
Marlboro College	VT	26,410	VC+
Marquette Univ	WI	24,836	C+
Mary Baldwin College	VA	23,440	C
Mary Washington College	VA	9,032	VC+
Mass Inst of Technology	MA	35,228	MC
Mercer Univ	GA	24,130	VC
Messiah College	PA	23,180	VC
Miami Univ	OH	12,885	VC+
Mich State Univ	MI	10,386	VC
Middle Tenn State Univ	TN	6,994	C
Middlebury College	VT	34,300	MC
Millersville Univ of Pennsylvania	PA	10,153	VC
Millikin Univ	IL	24,415	C+

School	ST	$IS	SR
Mills College	CA	27,950	C
Millsaps College	MS	22,608	VC+
Minn State Univ, Mankato	MN	7,296	LC
Minot State Univ	ND	5,466	LC
Missouri Southern State College	MO	6,666	C
Montclair State Univ	NJ	10,287	LC
Moorhead State Univ	MN	7,000	LC
Moravian College	PA	27,065	VC
Morehouse College	GA	19,814	C
Mount Holyoke College	MA	34,128	HC
Mount St. Mary's College	MD	25,740	C
Mount Union College	OH	21,120	C
Muhlenberg College	PA	28,170	HC
Murray State Univ	KY	6,672	C
Muskingum College	OH	18,760	C
Nazareth College of Rochester	NY	22,036	VC
Nebr Wesleyan Univ	NE	18,767	VC
New York Univ	NY	35,200	MC
Newberry College	SC	19,670	LC
North Central College	IL	22,944	C+
Northern Arizona Univ	AZ	7,398	C
Northern Illinois Univ	IL	9,545	C
Northern State Univ	SD	6,279	LC
Northwestern Univ	IL	33,615	MC
Oakland Univ	MI	9,418	C
Oberlin College	OH	33,140	HC+
Occidental College	CA	32,288	HC
Ohio Univ	OH	11,769	C
Ohio Wesleyan Univ	OH	29,670	VC+
Okla Baptist Univ	OK	13,878	VC
Okla City Univ	OK	15,810	C
Okla State Univ	OK	7,650	VC
Old Dominion Univ	VA	9,386	C
Oral Roberts Univ	OK	18,490	C
Oregon State Univ	OR	9,612	VC
Pacific Lutheran Univ	WA	23,318	VC
Penn State Univ/Univ Park Campus	PA	11,126	VC
Pepperdine Univ	CA	32,830	VC
Pomona College	CA	33,960	MC
Portland State Univ	OR	11,220	C
Presbyterian College	SC	23,356	VC
Purdue Univ/Calumet	IN	6,630	NC
Purdue Univ/West Lafayette	IN	10,284	VC
Randolph-Macon College	VA	24,395	C
Randolph-Macon Woman's College	VA	25,820	VC+
Rhodes College	TN	26,466	HC+
Rider Univ	NJ	27,400	C
Ripon College	WI	24,180	VC+
Rockford College	IL	23,930	C
Rosemont College	PA	24,060	C
Rutgers, The State Univ of New Jersey New Brunswick Campus	NJ	12,709	C
Rutgers, The State Univ of New Jersey/ CamdenCampus	NJ	6,484	C
St. Ambrose Univ	IA	19,994	C
St. John Fisher College	NY	21,800	C
St. John's Univ	MN	23,640	VC
St. John's Univ	NY	26,660	C
St. Joseph's Univ	PA	29,715	VC+
St. Lawrence Univ	NY	32,605	VC
St. Louis Univ	MO	26,590	VC+
St. Mary's Univ of San Antonio	TX	19,735	C
St. Norbert College	WI	23,169	VC
St. Olaf College	MN	25,880	HC
Salem College	NC	23,065	VC
Sam Houston State Univ	TX	6,076	LC
Samford Univ	AL	16,340	VC
San Diego State Univ	CA	9,716	C+
San Francisco State Univ	CA	7,139	LC
San Jose State Univ	CA	8,187	C
Santa Clara Univ	CA	28,371	VC+
Sarah Lawrence College	NY	37,516	HC
Seattle Pacific Univ	WA	22,674	C+
Seattle Univ	WA	24,183	VC
Simon's Rock College of Bard	MA	32,450	HC
Simpson College	IA	21,200	C+
Skidmore College	NY	34,201	VC+
Slippery Rock Univ	PA	9,152	LC
Sonoma State Univ	CA	8,953	C
S Dak State Univ	SD	6,848	C
Southeast Missouri State Univ	MO	8,367	C+
Southern Conn State Univ	CT	10,310	C
Southern Illinois Univ at Carbondale	IL	8,621	C
Southern Methodist Univ	TX	28,349	VC
Southern Utah Univ	UT	7,254	C
Southwest Missouri State Univ	MO	7,600	LC
Southwest Texas State Univ	TX	8,730	VC
Southwestern Univ	TX	22,550	HC
SUNY/College at Oswego	NY	10,856	C
SUNY/Univ at Binghamton	NY	10,653	HC
SUNY/Univ at Buffalo	NY	11,033	VC
SUNY/Univ at New Paltz	NY	9,685	VC
Stetson Univ	FL	25,640	VC
Susquehanna Univ	PA	27,270	VC
Swarthmore College	PA	34,538	MC
Sweet Briar College	VA	25,310	VC
Temple Univ	PA	14,124	C
Tenn Tech Univ	TN	6,968	C
Texas A&M Univ	TX	8,988	VC
Texas A&M Univ at Commerce	TX	7,326	C
Texas Lutheran Univ	TX	17,660	C
Texas Tech Univ	TX	8,825	C
Ohio State Univ	OH	10,819	VC
Towson Univ	MD	11,088	VC
Trinity College	CT	34,300	HC
Trinity Univ	TX	21,444	HC
Truman State Univ	MO	8,568	VC+
Tufts Univ	MA	34,874	MC
Tulane Univ	LA	34,013	HC+
Union College	NY	32,646	HC
Univ of Akron	OH	10,530	NC
Univ of Alabama	AL	7,402	C
Univ of Alabama at Huntsville	AL	7,916	VC
Univ of Arizona	AZ	8,614	C
Univ of Arkansas	AR	8,334	VC
Univ of Calif at Berkeley	CA	14,134	MC
Univ of Calif at Davis	CA	12,796	VC
Univ of Calif at Irvine	CA	11,756	C
Univ of Calif at Los Angeles	CA	13,227	MC
Univ of Calif at Riverside	CA	12,479	C
Univ of Calif at Santa Barbara	CA	11,732	VC
Univ of Central Okla	OK	5,205	C
Univ of Chicago	IL	35,087	MC
Univ of Cincinnati	OH	12,401	LC
Univ of Conn	CT	12,122	VC
Univ of Dallas	TX	22,128	VC+
Univ of Dayton	OH	20,400	VC
Univ of Denver	CO	28,783	VC
Univ of Evansville	IN	22,865	VC+
Univ of Florida	FL	7,874	HC
Univ of Georgia	GA	8,656	VC
Univ of Hawaii at Manoa	HI	7,862	VC
Univ of Houston	TX	8,410	C
Univ of Idaho	ID	7,026	C
Univ of Indianapolis	IN	20,840	C
Univ of Iowa	IA	8,607	C+
Univ of Kansas	KS	7,232	VC
Univ of Kentucky	KY	7,765	C
Univ of La Verne	CA	24,280	C
Univ of Maine	ME	10,798	C
Univ of Maryland/Baltimore County	MD	12,190	VC
Univ of Mass Amherst	MA	10,995	VC
Univ of Miami	FL	31,130	HC
Univ of Mich/Ann Arbor	MI	13,003	HC+
Univ of Mich/Flint	MI	4,323	C
Univ of Minn/Morris	MN	10,710	VC
Univ of Minn/Twin Cities	MN	11,123	VC
Univ of Miss	MS	7,666	C
Univ of Missouri/Columbia	MO	9,803	HC
Univ of Missouri/Kansas City	MO	9,685	VC
Univ of Missouri/St. Louis	MO	9,966	C
Univ of Montana	MT	8,038	C
Univ of Nebr at Kearney	NE	7,048	NC
Univ of Nebr at Lincoln	NE	8,325	C+
Univ of Nebr at Omaha	NE	6,867	C
Univ of Nevada/Las Vegas	NV	8,281	VC
Univ of Nevada/Reno	NV	8,737	C
Univ of New Hampshire	NH	13,207	C
Univ of New Mexico	NM	8,026	C
Univ of North Alabama	AL	7,016	NC
Univ of N Car at Asheville	NC	6,896	VC
Univ of N Car at Chapel Hill	NC	8,789	HC
Univ of N Car at Charlotte	NC	7,254	C
Univ of N Car at Greensboro	NC	6,858	C
Univ of N Dak	ND	7,067	VC
Univ of North Texas	TX	7,629	C
Univ of Northern Colo	CO	8,082	C+
Univ of Northern Iowa	IA	7,850	C
Univ of Notre Dame	IN	30,707	MC
Univ of Okla	OK	7,616	VC
Univ of Oregon	OR	9,969	C
Univ of Pennsylvania	PA	34,614	MC
Univ of Pittsburgh at Pittsburgh	PA	13,592	HC
Univ of Puget Sound	WA	28,285	HC
Univ of Redlands	CA	29,246	VC
Univ of Rhode Island	RI	12,414	C
Univ of Richmond	VA	27,300	HC
Univ of Rochester	NY	32,979	HC
Univ of St. Thomas	MN	24,044	VC
Univ of Scranton	PA	27,964	C+
Univ of South Alabama	AL	6,976	LC
Univ of S Car at Columbia	SC	8,748	VC
Univ of S Dak	SD	7,036	C
Univ of South Florida	FL	8,154	C
Univ of Southern Calif	CA	33,647	MC
Univ of Southern Indiana	IN	8,655	LC
Univ of Tenn at Knoxville	TN	8,214	C
Univ of Texas at Arlington	TX	7,192	LC
Univ of Texas at Austin	TX	9,437	HC
Univ of Texas at El Paso	TX	5,076	LC
Univ of Texas at San Antonio	TX	9,088	NC
Univ of the Pacific	CA	28,255	VC
Univ of the South	TN	27,290	HC
Univ of Toledo	OH	11,206	NC
Univ of Tulsa	OK	19,090	HC
Univ of Utah	UT	7,703	C
Univ of Vermont	VT	14,761	C+
Univ of Virginia	VA	9,391	HC+
Univ of Wisc/Eau Claire	WI	7,032	VC
Univ of Wisc/Green Bay	WI	7,148	C
Univ of Wisc/Madison	WI	8,262	VC
Univ of Wisc/Milwaukee	WI	8,907	LC
Univ of Wisc/Oshkosh	WI	6,130	LC
Univ of Wisc/Parkside	WI	6,160	LC
Univ of Wisc/Platteville	WI	7,282	C
Univ of Wisc/Stevens Point	WI	7,116	C
Univ of Wisc/Whitewater	WI	6,937	C
Univ of Wyoming	WY	7,143	LC
Ursinus College	PA	31,350	VC
Utah State Univ	UT	6,771	C
Valparaiso Univ	IN	23,570	VC+
Vanderbilt Univ	TN	34,482	MC
Villanova Univ	PA	31,997	HC
Virginia Polytechnic Inst and State Univ	VA	7,652	C
Virginia Wesleyan College	VA	22,350	LC
Wabash College	IN	25,335	HC
Wake Forest Univ	NC	30,290	MC
Walla Walla College	WA	20,925	C
Wartburg College	IA	21,165	VC
Washburn Univ of Topeka	KS	6,766	NC
Washington and Jefferson College	PA	26,255	VC
Washington and Lee Univ	VA	25,095	MC
Washington College	MD	28,040	VC
Washington State Univ	WA	9,388	C
Washington Univ in St. Louis	MO	34,593	MC
Wayne State Univ	MI	6,720	C
Weber State Univ	UT	6,897	NC
Webster Univ	MO	19,804	VC
Wellesley College	MA	33,394	MC
Wells College	NY	19,350	VC
Wesleyan Univ	CT	3,405	MC
West Chester Univ of Pennsylvania	PA	9,792	VC
Western Carolina Univ	NC	5,667	C
Western Kentucky Univ	KY	6,834	C
Western Maryland College	MD	26,000	VC
Western Mich Univ	MI	10,016	C
Western Washington Univ	WA	8,624	VC
Westminster College	PA	22,960	C
Wheaton College	IL	21,934	HC
Wheaton College	MA	32,940	VC
Whitman College	WA	29,086	HC
Willamette Univ	OR	29,422	VC+
Williams College	MA	32,270	MC
Winona State Univ	MN	8,570	C
Wittenberg Univ	OH	28,766	VC
Wofford College	SC	23,995	VC
Wright State Univ	OH	9,141	LC
Xavier Univ	OH	23,880	C
Yale Univ	CT	34,030	MC

GERMAN AREA STUDIES

School	ST	$IS	SR
American Univ	DC	31,544	VC+
Boston College	MA	00,000	MC
Case Western Reserve Univ	OH	27,418	C
Columbia Univ/School of General Studies	NY	35,000	C
Cornell Univ	NY	34,614	MC
Dartmouth College	NH	34,458	MC
Emory Univ	GA	33,792	MC
Fordham Univ	NY	30,710	VC
Indiana Univ Southeast	IN	3,459	C
Knox College	IL	28,230	HC
Lewis and Clark College	OR	29,010	VC
Macalester College	MN	28,814	HC+
Muhlenberg College	PA	28,170	HC
Pomona College	CA	33,960	MC
Principia College	IL	23,865	C+
Scripps College	CA	30,400	HC+
Simon's Rock College of Bard	MA	32,450	HC
Southern Methodist Univ	TX	28,349	VC
Stanford Univ	CA	34,222	MC
Swarthmore College	PA	34,538	MC
Sweet Briar College	VA	25,310	VC
Tufts Univ	MA	34,874	MC
Univ of Arizona	AZ	8,614	C
Univ of Calif at Santa Cruz	CA	13,655	VC
Univ of Colo at Boulder	CO	9,255	VC
Univ of Houston	TX	8,410	C
Univ of Illinois at Chicago	IL	10,702	VC
Univ of Mass Boston	MA	4,227	C
Univ of the South	TN	27,290	HC
Univ of Wisc/La Crosse	WI	7,250	VC
Wartburg College	IA	21,165	VC
Yale Univ	CT	34,030	MC

GERMANIC LANGUAGES AND LITERATURE

School	ST	$IS	SR
Bard College	NY	33,912	HC
Colby College	ME	34,290	MC
Columbia Univ/Columbia College	NY	35,190	MC
Duke Univ	NC	34,396	MC
New College of Florida	FL	8,130	HC+
New York Univ	NY	35,200	MC
Princeton Univ	NJ	35,072	MC
Reed College	OR	33,350	HC+
Scripps College	CA	30,400	HC+
Simon's Rock College of Bard	MA	32,450	HC
Smith College	MA	33,302	HC+
SUNY/Univ at Stony Brook	NY	10,998	VC
Syracuse Univ	NY	30,710	HC
Temple Univ	PA	14,124	C
Univ of Calif at San Diego	CA	11,372	HC
Univ of Calif at Santa Barbara	CA	11,732	VC
Univ of Colo at Boulder	CO	9,255	VC
Univ of Georgia	GA	8,656	VC
Univ of Illinois at Urbana-Champaign	IL	11,316	HC+
Univ of Kansas	KS	7,232	VC
Univ of Maryland/College Park	MD	11,959	C
Univ of Mich/Flint	MI	4,323	C
Univ of Washington	WA	10,361	VC
Washington and Lee Univ	VA	25,095	MC

GERONTOLOGY

School	ST	$IS	SR
Alfred Univ	NY	27,212	C+
Audrey Cohen College	NY	17,715	C
Bay Path College	MA	22,308	C
Bethune-Cookman College	FL	15,746	C
Bowling Green State Univ	OH	10,794	C
Cal State, Los Angeles	CA	5,050	C
Calif Univ of Pennsylvania	PA	10,388	C
Case Western Reserve Univ	OH	27,418	C
CUNY/York College	NY	3,292	NC
College of Mount St. Joseph	OH	20,290	C
College of the Holy Cross	MA	32,780	MC
College of the Ozarks	MO	2,650	C+
Drake Univ	IA	22,830	VC
East Central Univ	OK	4,578	C
Eastern Mich Univ	MI	9,855	C
Gwynedd-Mercy College	PA	22,350	C
Kent State Univ	OH	11,104	C
King's College	PA	24,680	C
Langston Univ	OK	2,308	LC
Lourdes College	OH	13,100	LC
Madonna Univ	MI	11,504	VC
Molloy College	NY	13,940	C
Mount St. Mary's College	CA	24,430	C
Pontifical Catholic Univ of PR/Ponce	PR	7,076	
Quinnipiac Univ	CT	27,370	C
St. Mary-of-the-Woods College	IN	21,320	LC
San Diego State Univ	CA	9,716	C+
Shaw Univ	NC	12,810	C
Sojourner-Douglass College	MD	4,170	LC
Southeastern Okla State Univ	OK	4,917	C
Southwest Missouri State Univ	MO	7,600	LC
Springfield College	MA	24,520	C
SUNY/College at Oneonta	NY	9,981	C
Stephen F. Austin State Univ	TX	6,905	C
Thomas Edison State College	NJ	2,750	SP
Towson Univ	MD	11,088	VC
Univ of Arkansas at Pine Bluff	AR	7,925	C
Univ of Central Arkansas	AR	6,388	C
Univ of Evansville	IN	22,865	VC+
Univ of Mass Boston	MA	4,227	C
Univ of Northern Colo	CO	8,082	C+
Univ of Scranton	PA	27,964	C+
Univ of South Florida	FL	8,154	C
Univ of Southern Calif	CA	33,647	MC
Wagner College	NY	27,000	C
Weber State Univ	UT	6,897	NC
Wichita State Univ	KS	6,879	C

GLASS

School	ST	$IS	SR
Alfred Univ	NY	27,212	C+
Calif College of Arts and Crafts	CA	27,366	SP
College For Creative Studies	MI	20,938	SP
Mass College of Art	MA	13,703	SP
Rhode Island School of Design	RI	30,227	SP
Rochester Inst of Technology	NY	26,232	VC+

GRAPHIC AND PRINTING PRODUCTION

School	ST	$IS	SR
CUNY/New York City Technical College	NY	3,319	NC

School	ST	$IS	SR
Rochester Inst of Technology	NY	26,232	VC+
Southwest Texas State Univ	TX	8,730	VC
Univ of Wisc/Stout	WI	7,192	C

GRAPHIC ARTS TECHNOLOGY

School	ST	$IS	SR
American Univ	DC	31,544	VC+
Andrews Univ	MI	17,696	LC
Appalachian State Univ	NC	6,353	C
Ball State Univ	IN	8,660	C
Bloomfield College	NJ	17,000	C
Calif Univ of Pennsylvania	PA	10,388	C
Carroll College	WI	21,170	C
Central Missouri State Univ	MO	7,920	C
Central State Univ	OH	8,922	C+
Clemson Univ	SC	7,600	C
College of the Ozarks	MO	2,650	C+
Florida State Univ	FL	7,835	HC
Kean Univ	NJ	11,159	C
New York Univ	NY	35,200	MC
Northwestern State Univ of Louisiana	LA	5,745	NC
Pacific Union College	CA	20,250	VC
Purdue Univ/West Lafayette	IN	10,284	VC
Rochester Inst of Technology	NY	26,232	VC+
SUNY/College of Technology at Farmingdale	NY	11,269	C
Stetson Univ	FL	25,640	VC
Texas Southern Univ	TX	6,576	NC
Univ of Houston	TX	8,410	C
Univ of Wisc/Stout	WI	7,192	C

GRAPHIC DESIGN

School	ST	$IS	SR
American Univ	DC	31,544	VC+
Anderson Univ	IN	19,430	LC
Andrews Univ	MI	17,696	LC
Appalachian State Univ	NC	6,353	C
Arcadia Univ	PA	26,650	C
Arizona State Univ-Main	AZ	7,726	C
Art Academy of Cincinnati	OH	16,550	SP
Art Center College of Design	CA	21,110	SP
Art Inst of Atlanta	GA	20,624	SP
Art Inst of Portland	OR	13,725	SP
Art Inst of Southern Calif	CA	14,500	SP
Atlanta College of Art	GA	18,600	SP
Ball State Univ	IN	8,660	C
Barton College	NC	16,834	LC
Bay Path College	MA	22,308	C
Becker College	MA	21,230	LC
Boston Univ	MA	34,358	MC
Bradley Univ	IL	20,970	VC
Brescia Univ	KY	14,225	C
Brigham Young Univ	UT	7,840	HC
Buena Vista Univ	IA	22,828	C
Cabrini College	PA	25,950	LC
Calif College of Arts and Crafts	CA	27,366	SP
Calif Polytechnic State Univ	CA	8,747	VC
Cal State, Fresno	CA	7,762	C
Cal State, Fullerton	CA	5,440	LC
Cal State, Los Angeles	CA	5,050	C
Carlow College	PA	19,366	C
Carthage College	WI	23,670	C
Central Conn State Univ	CT	10,404	C
Champlain College	VT	19,680	C
Cleveland Inst of Art	OH	22,680	SP
Coker College	SC	20,120	C
Colby-Sawyer College	NH	27,850	LC
College For Creative Studies	MI	20,938	SP
College of Mount St. Joseph	OH	20,290	C
College of New Jersey	NJ	13,425	HC
College of Notre Dame of Maryland	MD	23,100	LC
College of St. Rose	NY	19,084	C
College of Visual Arts	MN	12,185	SP
Columbus College of Art and Design	OH	22,210	SP
Concordia Univ Wisc	WI	16,600	LC
Cooper Union for the Advancement of Science and Art	NY	6,500	MC
Corcoran School of Art and Design	DC	21,035	SP
Daemen College	NY	20,620	C
Defiance College	OH	19,580	LC
Dominican Univ	IL	20,800	C
Dordt College	IA	18,100	C+
Drake Univ	IA	22,830	VC
Drexel Univ	PA	27,657	VC
Eastern Mich Univ	MI	9,855	C
Eastern Washington Univ	WA	7,972	LC
Edgewood College	WI	18,304	C
Edinboro Univ of Pennsylvania	PA	9,328	LC
Escuela de Artes Plasticas de PR	PR	1,874	
Fashion Inst of Technology/SUNY	NY	9,504	C+
Flagler College	FL	10,550	VC+
Florida Atlantic Univ	FL	8,832	C
Franklin Pierce College	NH	26,125	LC
Gallaudet Univ	DC	16,554	SP
Grace College	IN	16,768	C
Graceland Univ	IA	15,845	C
Grand Canyon Univ	AZ	30,000	LC
Grand View College	IA	17,596	NC
Harding Univ	AR	13,528	VC
Iowa State Univ	IA	8,108	VC
Kean Univ	NJ	11,159	C
Kent State Univ	OH	11,104	C
Kutztown Univ of Pennsylvania	PA	8,907	C
La Roche College	PA	18,854	LC
La Sierra Univ	CA	19,260	LC
Limestone College	SC	16,900	C
LIU/Southampton College	NY	26,270	C
Louisiana College	LA	11,516	C
Loyola Univ New Orleans	LA	23,506	VC+
Lyndon State College	VT	11,313	LC
Lynn Univ	FL	24,550	C
Madonna Univ	MI	11,504	VC
Maine College of Art	ME	26,367	SP
Marian College	IN	21,020	C
Marietta College	OH	24,580	C
Maryland Inst College of Art	MD	27,720	SP
Marymount Univ	VA	21,560	LC
Maryville Univ of St. Louis	MO	18,680	C
Mass College of Art	MA	13,703	SP
Mercyhurst College	PA	20,694	C
Middle Tenn State Univ	TN	6,994	C
Milwaukee Inst of Art and Design	WI	24,388	SP
Minneapolis College of Art and Design	MN	23,560	SP
Miss College	MS	14,574	C
Missouri Southern State College	MO	6,666	C
Montserrat College of Art	MA	20,335	SP
Moore College of Art and Design	PA	23,125	SP
Moravian College	PA	27,065	VC
Morningside College	IA	19,124	C
Mount Ida College	MA	25,375	LC
Mount Mary College	WI	18,024	C
New Mexico Highlands Univ	NM	6,256	NC
New York Inst of Technology	NY	21,756	C
Norfolk State Univ	VA	8,382	LC
N Car State Univ	NC	8,680	HC
Northern Kentucky Univ	KY	6,352	NC
Northern Mich Univ	MI	9,693	C
Northwest Nazarene Univ	ID	18,380	C
Northwestern College	MN	19,816	C+
Notre Dame College	OH	20,425	C
Notre Dame de Namur Univ	CA	26,932	LC
Ohio Dominican College	OH	18,100	LC
Ohio Northern Univ	OH	27,765	VC
Ohio Univ	OH	11,769	C
Okla City Univ	OK	15,810	C
Old Dominion Univ	VA	9,386	C
Otis College of Art and Design	CA	20,290	SP
Pacific Northwest College of Art	OR	16,507	SP
Pacific Union College	CA	20,250	VC
Park Univ	MO	9,816	C
Parsons School of Design	NY	32,242	SP
Pennsylvania College of Technology	PA	12,860	NC
Philadelphia Univ	PA	24,722	C
Plymouth State College	NH	11,024	LC
Rhode Island School of Design	RI	30,227	SP
Ringling School of Art and Design	FL	22,500	SP
Rivier College	NH	24,215	C
Rochester Inst of Technology	NY	26,232	VC+
St. John's Univ	NY	26,660	C
St. Mary's Univ of Minn	MN	19,975	C
St. Norbert College	WI	23,169	VC
Sam Houston State Univ	TX	6,076	LC
Samford Univ	AL	16,340	VC
Savannah College of Art and Design	GA	25,075	SP
School of Visual Arts	NY	26,000	SP
Shepherd College	WV	7,062	LC
Simmons College	MA	30,418	VC
S Dak State Univ	SD	6,848	C
Southern Adventist Univ	TN	15,600	C
Southwest Texas State Univ	TX	8,730	VC
Southwestern Okla State Univ	OK	4,801	C
Spring Hill College	AL	23,250	C
SUNY/College at Fredonia	NY	10,125	C
SUNY/College at Oswego	NY	10,856	C
Stephens College	MO	22,295	C
Suffolk Univ	MA	26,516	C
Syracuse Univ	NY	30,710	HC
Texas Christian Univ	TX	19,910	C
Union Univ	TN	18,930	C+
Univ of Bridgeport	CT	23,020	C
Univ of Central Okla	OK	5,205	C
Univ of Evansville	IN	22,865	VC+
Univ of Florida	FL	7,874	HC
Univ of Hartford	CT	28,884	C
Univ of Illinois at Chicago	IL	10,702	VC
Univ of Illinois at Urbana-Champaign	IL	11,316	HC+
Univ of Mass Dartmouth	MA	9,852	C
Univ of Miami	FL	31,130	HC
Univ of Mich/Ann Arbor	MI	13,003	HC+
Univ of Minn/Duluth	MN	10,436	C
Univ of New Haven	CT	23,860	LC
Univ of Northern Colo	CO	8,082	C+
Univ of Northern Iowa	IA	7,850	C
Univ of Oregon	OR	9,969	C
Univ of San Francisco	CA	27,302	VC
Univ of S Car at Spartanburg	SC	7,318	C+
Univ of Tampa	FL	22,612	C
Univ of Tenn at Knoxville	TN	8,214	C
Univ of the Arts	PA	24,230	SP
Univ of the Pacific	CA	28,255	VC
Univ of Washington	WA	10,361	VC
Upper Iowa Univ	IA	17,438	C
Ursuline College	OH	19,430	LC
Viterbo Univ	WI	18,043	C
Walla Walla College	WA	20,925	C
Wartburg College	IA	21,165	VC
Washington Univ in St. Louis	MO	34,593	MC
Wayne State College	NE	6,255	NC
Weber State Univ	UT	6,897	NC
West Liberty State College	WV	6,056	LC
West Texas A&M Univ	TX	6,538	C
Western Conn State Univ	CT	10,074	C
Western Mich Univ	MI	10,016	C
Wichita State Univ	KS	6,879	C
William Woods Univ	MO	19,390	LC
York College of Pennsylvania	PA	12,550	VC
Youngstown State Univ	OH	9,318	NC

GREEK

School	ST	$IS	SR
Amherst College	MA	34,340	MC
Asbury College	KY	18,540	VC
Brigham Young Univ	UT	7,840	HC
Bryn Mawr College	PA	33,580	HC+
Butler Univ	IN	25,580	VC+
Calvin College	MI	20,050	NC
Carleton College	MN	30,780	MC
CUNY/Brooklyn College	NY	3,403	LC
CUNY/Herbert H. Lehman College	NY	3,320	LC
CUNY/Hunter College	NY	5,147	C+
CUNY/Queens College	NY	3,403	VC
Colgate Univ	NY	33,480	MC
Columbia Univ/Barnard College	NY	33,694	MC
Columbia Univ/Columbia College	NY	35,190	MC
Cornell Univ	NY	34,614	MC
Creighton Univ	NE	23,476	VC
DePauw Univ	IN	28,000	HC
Dickinson College	PA	32,210	VC+
Duquesne Univ	PA	24,242	C+
Florida State Univ	FL	7,835	HC
Franklin and Marshall College	PA	32,410	HC
Furman Univ	SC	25,492	HC
Gettysburg College	PA	32,070	HC
Hampden-Sydney College	VA	24,871	C
Harvard Univ/Harvard College	MA	34,269	MC
Howard Univ	DC	15,522	LC
John Carroll Univ	OH	24,140	VC
Loyola Marymount Univ	CA	28,754	HC
Loyola Univ of Chicago	IL	25,992	VC
Luther College	IA	23,300	VC+
Marlboro College	VT	26,410	VC+
Mercer Univ	GA	24,130	VC
Miami Univ	OH	12,885	VC+
Monmouth College	IL	21,550	C
Moravian College	PA	27,065	VC
Mount Holyoke College	MA	34,128	HC
New York Univ	NY	35,200	MC
Randolph-Macon College	VA	24,395	C
St. Louis Univ	MO	26,590	VC+
St. Olaf College	MN	25,880	HC
Samford Univ	AL	16,340	VC
Santa Clara Univ	CA	28,371	VC+
Sarah Lawrence College	NY	37,516	HC
Smith College	MA	33,302	HC+
Swarthmore College	PA	34,538	MC
Sweet Briar College	VA	25,310	VC
Temple Univ	PA	14,124	C
Tufts Univ	MA	34,874	MC
Union Univ	TN	18,930	C+
Univ of Calif at Berkeley	CA	14,134	MC
Univ of Calif at Davis	CA	12,796	VC
Univ of Calif at Los Angeles	CA	13,227	MC
Univ of Georgia	GA	8,656	VC
Univ of Iowa	IA	8,607	C+
Univ of Mich/Ann Arbor	MI	13,003	HC+
Univ of Minn/Twin Cities	MN	11,123	VC
Univ of Nebr at Lincoln	NE	8,325	C+
Univ of New Hampshire	NH	13,207	C
Univ of N Car at Chapel Hill	NC	8,789	HC
Univ of N Car at Greensboro	NC	6,858	C
Univ of Notre Dame	IN	30,707	MC
Univ of Oregon	OR	9,969	C
Univ of Richmond	VA	27,300	HC
Univ of Scranton	PA	27,964	C+
Univ of S Car at Columbia	SC	8,748	VC
Univ of Tenn at Chattanooga	TN	7,783	C
Univ of Texas at Austin	TX	9,437	HC
Univ of the South	TN	27,290	HC
Univ of Vermont	VT	14,761	C+
Univ of Wisc/Madison	WI	8,262	VC
Wabash College	IN	25,335	HC
Wake Forest Univ	NC	30,290	MC
Wellesley College	MA	33,394	MC

GREEK (CLASSICAL)

School	ST	$IS	SR
Baylor Univ	TX	18,298	VC+
Boston Univ	MA	34,358	MC
College of Wooster	OH	28,350	VC
Kenyon College	OH	32,130	HC+
New York Univ	NY	35,200	MC
Ohio Univ	OH	11,769	C
Univ of Mass Boston	MA	4,227	C
Washington Univ in St. Louis	MO	34,593	MC

GREEK (MODERN)

School	ST	$IS	SR
Boston Univ	MA	34,358	MC

GUIDANCE EDUCATION

School	ST	$IS	SR
Central Mich Univ	MI	8,355	C
Eastern Washington Univ	WA	7,972	LC
McNeese State Univ	LA	5,259	LC
Prescott College	AZ	13,430	C
St. Cloud State Univ	MN	7,180	C
S Car State Univ	SC	6,586	LC
Texas A&M Univ at Commerce	TX	7,326	C
Univ of Akron	OH	10,530	NC
Univ of Central Arkansas	AR	6,388	C
Univ of Cincinnati	OH	12,491	LC
Univ of Nebr at Lincoln	NE	8,325	C+
Univ of Southern Miss	MS	6,155	LC
Westminster College	PA	22,960	C

GUITAR

School	ST	$IS	SR
Ball State Univ	IN	8,660	C
Boston Conservatory	MA	26,900	SP
Indiana Univ Bloomington	IN	10,712	C+
Roosevelt Univ	IL	20,240	LC
Stetson Univ	FL	25,640	VC
Temple Univ	PA	14,124	C
Univ of Miami	FL	31,130	HC

HAWAIIAN

School	ST	$IS	SR
Univ of Hawaii at Manoa	HI	7,862	VC

HAWAIIAN STUDIES

School	ST	$IS	SR
Brigham Young Univ/Hawaii	HI	6,890	C
Univ of Hawaii at Hilo	HI	6,497	C
Univ of Hawaii at Manoa	HI	7,862	VC

HEALTH

School	ST	$IS	SR
Aquinas College	MI	20,052	C+
Azusa Pacific Univ	CA	22,422	VC
Becker College	MA	21,230	LC
Bloomsburg Univ of Pennsylvania	PA	9,434	C
Brewton-Parker College	GA	10,810	LC
Cal State, Northridge	CA	7,781	C
Chicago State Univ	IL	8,851	C+
College of Mount St. Joseph	OH	20,290	C
Concordia College/Moorhead	MN	18,835	C
Concordia Univ Nebr	NE	17,770	C
Cumberland College	KY	14,864	C
Eastern Oregon Univ	OR	8,772	C
Georgetown Univ	DC	34,847	MC
Georgia Southern Univ	GA	6,958	C
Graceland Univ	IA	15,845	C
Ithaca College	NY	28,719	HC
LeTourneau Univ	TX	19,020	VC
Lourdes College	OH	13,100	LC
Luther College	IA	23,300	VC+
Mass College of Pharmacy and Health Sciences	MA	27,131	SP
Miami Univ	OH	12,885	VC+
Montana State Univ-Billings	MT	7,653	NC
Montana State Univ-Bozeman	MT	8,431	C
New Mexico Highlands Univ	NM	6,256	NC
Ohio Northern Univ	OH	27,765	VC
Olivet College	MI	17,410	C

School	ST	$IS	SR
Oregon State Univ	OR	9,612	VC
Prairie View A&M Univ	TX	3,172	LC
Rust College	MS	7,800	C+
Sam Houston State Univ	TX	6,076	LC
Samford Univ	AL	16,340	VC
Southern Oregon Univ	OR	9,429	C
Southwestern Adventist Univ	TX	14,798	C
SUNY/College at Buffalo	NY	8,025	C
Tenn Wesleyan College	TN	13,030	C
Texas Christian Univ	TX	19,910	C
Texas Southern Univ	TX	6,576	NC
Texas Tech Univ	TX	8,825	C
Thomas Edison State College	NJ	2,750	SP
Univ of Houston	TX	8,410	C
Univ of Louisiana at Monroe	LA	5,207	NC
Univ of Louisville	KY	7,402	LC
Univ of Rochester	NY	32,979	HC
Univ of St. Francis	IL	19,650	C
Univ of Texas at San Antonio	TX	9,088	NC
Univ of Texas-Pan American	TX	4,823	C
Upper Iowa Univ	IA	17,438	C
Voorhees College	SC	9,976	C+
Walla Walla College	WA	20,925	C
West Chester Univ of Pennsylvania	PA	9,792	VC
Worcester State College	MA	7,901	LC
Youngstown State Univ	OH	9,318	NC

HEALTH CARE ADMINISTRATION

School	ST	$IS	SR
Albertus Magnus College	CT	22,154	C
Alfred Univ	NY	27,212	C+
Alvernia College	PA	20,790	C
Appalachian State Univ	NC	6,353	C
Arcadia Univ	PA	26,650	C
Auburn Univ	AL	5,510	C
Austin Peay State Univ	TN	5,814	LC
Baker College of Flint	MI	7,720	NC
Benedictine Univ	IL	21,330	C
Black Hills State Univ	SD	6,652	LC
Bowling Green State Univ	OH	10,794	C
Cal State, Long Beach	CA	7,400	LC
Cal State, Northridge	CA	7,781	C
Cal State, San Bernardino	CA	6,516	C
Carroll College	MT	19,140	C
CUNY/Herbert H. Lehman College	NY	3,320	LC
Clayton College and State Univ	GA	2,322	C+
Cleary College	MI	10,350	LC
College of Mount St. Joseph	OH	20,290	C
College of St. Catherine	MN	22,324	VC
College of St. Scholastica	MN	22,378	C+
Columbia Union College	MD	19,027	C+
Concordia College/Moorhead	MN	18,835	C
Concordia Univ	MI	20,500	C
Concordia Univ	OR	20,500	LC
Daemen College	NY	20,620	C
David N. Myers College	OH	9,475	C
Duquesne Univ	PA	24,242	C+
Eastern College	PA	19,641	LC
Eastern Kentucky Univ	KY	6,552	C
Eastern Mich Univ	MI	9,855	C
Eastern Washington Univ	WA	7,972	LC
Emmanuel College	MA	23,802	C+
Ferris State Univ	MI	10,816	C
Florida Atlantic Univ	FL	8,832	C
Florida International Univ	FL	9,486	VC
Franklin Univ	OH	6,324	SP
Gwynedd-Mercy College	PA	22,350	C
Hastings College	NE	17,854	C+
Huron Univ	SD	10,450	C
Idaho State Univ	ID	7,030	C+
Illinois State Univ	IL	9,235	C
Indiana Univ Northwest	IN	3,447	C
Indiana Univ South Bend	IN	3,515	C
Indiana Univ-Purdue Univ Indianapolis	IN	9,473	C
Iona College	NY	26,556	C
Ithaca College	NY	28,719	HC
Johnson and Wales Univ	RI	21,558	LC
Kean Univ	NJ	11,159	C
King's College	PA	24,680	C
Knoxville College	TN	6,200	LC
Langston Univ	OK	2,308	LC
Lasell College	MA	24,100	C
Lewis Univ	IL	20,960	C
LIU/C.W. Post Campus	NY	25,380	C
Lynn Univ	FL	24,550	C
Mary Baldwin College	VA	23,440	C
Marymount Univ	VA	21,560	LC
Maryville Univ of St. Louis	MO	18,680	C
Marywood Univ	PA	24,639	C
Metropolitan State College of Denver	CO	2,338	LC
Midwestern State Univ	TX	6,704	NC
Milligan College	TN	17,550	C
Montana State Univ-Billings	MT	7,653	NC
Montana State Univ-Bozeman	MT	8,431	C
Mount Marty College	SD	15,656	LC
Mount Mercy College	IA	19,390	VC
Mountain State Univ	WV	8,180	NC
National-Louis Univ	IL	13,995	NC
Newbury College	MA	21,490	C
Norfolk State Univ	VA	8,382	LC
Ohio Univ	OH	11,769	C
Oregon State Univ	OR	9,612	VC
Pacific Union College	CA	20,250	VC
Park Univ	MO	9,816	C
Penn State Univ/Univ Park Campus	PA	11,126	VC
Point Park College	PA	20,290	C
Presentation College	SD	13,508	NC
Providence College	RI	27,620	HC
Quinnipiac Univ	CT	27,370	C
Robert Morris Univ	PA	18,730	C
St. Francis College	NY	9,610	C
St. John's Univ	NY	26,660	C
St. Joseph's College, New York	NY	9,802	C
St. Joseph's Univ	PA	29,715	VC+
St. Leo Univ	FL	19,250	LC
St. Louis Univ	MO	26,590	VC+
St. Peter's College	NJ	22,292	LC
Sojourner-Douglass College	MD	4,170	LC
Southern Adventist Univ	TN	15,600	C
Southern Illinois Univ at Carbondale	IL	8,621	C
Southern Univ at New Orleans	LA	995	NC
Southwest Texas State Univ	TX	8,730	VC
Southwestern Okla State Univ	OK	4,801	C
Springfield College	MA	24,520	C
SUNY/College at Fredonia	NY	10,125	C
Stonehill College	MA	26,852	HC
Tenn State Univ	TN	7,058	VC
Texas Southern Univ	TX	6,576	NC
Thomas Edison State College	NJ	2,750	SP
Towson Univ	MD	11,088	VC
Univ of Alabama	AL	7,402	C
Univ of Arizona	AZ	8,614	C
Univ of Central Arkansas	AR	6,388	C
Univ of Central Florida	FL	8,251	VC
Univ of Colo at Colo Springs	CO	9,403	C
Univ of Conn	CT	12,122	VC
Univ of Detroit Mercy	MI	21,620	LC
Univ of Great Falls	MT	15,360	C
Univ of La Verne	CA	24,280	C
Univ of Miami	FL	31,130	HC
Univ of Mich/Flint	MI	4,323	C
Univ of Minn/Crookston	MN	9,626	NC
Univ of Nevada/Las Vegas	NV	8,281	VC
Univ of New England	ME	24,110	LC
Univ of New Hampshire	NH	13,207	C
Univ of Pennsylvania	PA	34,614	MC
Univ of Phoenix	AZ	7,000	SP
Univ of Rhode Island	RI	12,414	C
Univ of Scranton	PA	27,964	C+
Univ of S Dak	SD	7,036	C
Univ of Washington	WA	10,361	VC
Univ of Wisc/Eau Claire	WI	7,032	VC
Univ of Wisc/Milwaukee	WI	8,907	LC
Upper Iowa Univ	IA	17,438	C
Ursuline College	OH	19,430	LC
Viterbo Univ	WI	18,043	C
Waynesburg College	PA	17,610	LC
Weber State Univ	UT	6,897	NC
West Virginia Univ Inst of Technology	WV	7,518	NC
Western Carolina Univ	NC	5,667	C
Western Kentucky Univ	KY	6,834	C
Wichita State Univ	KS	6,879	C
Wilberforce Univ	OH	14,937	LC

HEALTH EDUCATION

School	ST	$IS	SR
Albany State Univ	GA	5,764	C+
Anderson Univ	IN	19,430	LC
Appalachian State Univ	NC	6,353	C
Arkansas State Univ	AR	7,480	C
Arkansas Tech Univ	AR	6,256	C
Ashland Univ	OH	22,182	LC
Auburn Univ	AL	5,510	C
Augsburg College	MN	22,978	C
Augusta State Univ	GA	2,282	C
Austin Peay State Univ	TN	5,814	LC
Baldwin-Wallace College	OH	22,010	VC+
Ball State Univ	IN	8,660	C
Baylor Univ	TX	18,298	VC+
Bemidji State Univ	MN	7,957	C
Bethel College	MN	22,740	VC
Bethel College	TN	12,980	C
Black Hills State Univ	SD	6,652	LC
Bluffton College	OH	20,644	C
Bowling Green State Univ	OH	10,794	C
Briar Cliff Univ	IA	18,657	LC
Cal State, Sacramento	CA	7,488	C
Cal State, San Bernardino	CA	6,516	C
Cameron Univ	OK	5,560	NC
Carson-Newman College	TN	16,490	C
Central Mich Univ	MI	8,355	C
Central State Univ	OH	8,922	C+
Central Washington Univ	WA	8,985	LC
Chadron State College	NE	6,211	NC
Citadel, The	SC	9,126	C
CUNY/Brooklyn College	NY	3,403	LC
CUNY/Herbert H. Lehman College	NY	3,320	LC
CUNY/Hunter College	NY	5,147	C+
College of Mount St. Vincent	NY	24,230	C
College of New Jersey	NJ	13,425	HC
Concordia College/Moorhead	MN	18,835	C
Cumberland College	KY	14,864	C
Cumberland Univ	TN	11,970	LC
Curry College	MA	26,025	LC
Dakota State Univ	SD	6,950	C
Defiance College	OH	19,580	LC
Delaware State Univ	DE	8,104	LC
Delta State Univ	MS	5,416	C
East Carolina Univ	NC	7,766	C
East Central Univ	OK	4,578	C
East Stroudsburg Univ of Pennsylvania	PA	8,430	LC
Eastern Illinois Univ	IL	10,101	C
Eastern Kentucky Univ	KY	6,552	C
Eastern Mich Univ	MI	9,855	C
Eastern Washington Univ	WA	7,972	LC
Edinboro Univ of Pennsylvania	PA	9,328	LC
Elon Univ	NC	19,430	VC
Emporia State Univ	KS	6,198	LC
Fairmont State College	WV	7,010	NC
Fayetteville State Univ	NC	5,590	LC
Florida International Univ	FL	9,486	VC
Florida State Univ	FL	7,835	HC
Freed-Hardeman Univ	TN	14,290	VC
Friends Univ	KS	15,962	LC
Gardner-Webb Univ	NC	17,400	C
George Fox Univ	OR	24,095	VC
Georgia Southern Univ	GA	6,958	C
Georgia State Univ	GA	7,792	LC
Gustavus Adolphus College	MN	24,190	VC+
Hardin-Simmons Univ	TX	14,165	C
Hofstra Univ	NY	23,252	C
Howard Univ	DC	15,522	LC
Idaho State Univ	ID	7,030	C+
Illinois State Univ	IL	9,235	C
Indiana State Univ	IN	8,461	LC
Indiana Univ Bloomington	IN	10,712	C+
Indiana Univ-Purdue Univ Indianapolis	IN	9,473	C
Inter-American Univ of PR/San GermÈn	PR	6,390	
Iowa State Univ	IA	8,108	VC
Ithaca College	NY	28,719	HC
Jackson State Univ	MS	6,776	LC
Jacksonville State Univ	AL	6,568	LC
Johnson C. Smith Univ	NC	16,560	C+
Kennesaw State Univ	GA	2,306	LC
Kent State Univ	OH	11,104	C
Knoxville College	TN	6,200	LC
Lamar Univ	TX	6,816	LC
Lenoir Rhyne College	NC	19,186	C
Lincoln Memorial Univ	TN	12,620	LC
Linfield College	OR	25,840	VC
LIU/C.W. Post Campus	NY	25,380	C
Louisiana College	LA	11,516	C
Malone College	OH	19,190	C
Manchester College	IN	22,010	C
Manhattan College	NY	25,500	VC
Mayville State Univ	ND	6,440	NC
McNeese State Univ	LA	5,259	LC
Miami Univ	OH	12,885	VC+
MidAmerica Nazarene Univ	KS	16,960	C
Middle Tenn State Univ	TN	6,994	C
Minn State Univ, Mankato	MN	7,296	LC
Missouri Southern State College	MO	6,666	C
Montana State Univ-Billings	MT	7,653	NC
Montclair State Univ	NJ	10,287	LC
Moorhead State Univ	MN	7,000	LC
Morehead State Univ	KY	6,510	C
Morgan State Univ	MD	10,078	LC
Mountain State Univ	WV	8,180	NC
Murray State Univ	KY	6,672	C
New Jersey City Univ	NJ	9,100	LC
New York Inst of Technology	NY	21,756	C
Norfolk State Univ	VA	8,382	LC
N Car Central Univ	NC	6,418	LC
Northeastern State Univ	OK	4,704	LC
Northern Arizona Univ	AZ	7,398	C
Northern Mich Univ	MI	9,693	C
Northern State Univ	SD	6,279	LC
Ohio Northern Univ	OH	27,765	VC
Ohio Univ	OH	11,769	C
Okla Panhandle State Univ	OK	3,812	NC
Okla State Univ	OK	7,650	VC
Oral Roberts Univ	OK	18,490	C
Oregon State Univ	OR	9,612	VC
Otterbein College	OH	23,439	C
Ouachita Baptist Univ	AR	16,460	VC
Penn State Univ/Univ Park Campus	PA	11,126	VC
Plymouth State College	NH	11,024	LC
Portland State Univ	OR	11,220	C
Purdue Univ/West Lafayette	IN	10,284	VC
Rhode Island College	RI	8,700	LC
St. Cloud State Univ	MN	7,180	C
St. Mary's College of Calif	CA	27,575	C
Salisbury Univ	MD	10,576	VC
Shepherd College	WV	7,062	LC
Slippery Rock Univ	PA	9,152	LC
S Car State Univ	SC	6,586	LC
S Dak State Univ	SD	6,848	C
Southern Arkansas Univ	AR	5,740	LC
Southern Conn State Univ	CT	10,310	C
Southern Illinois Univ at Carbondale	IL	8,621	C
Southern Illinois Univ Edwardsville	IL	7,869	LC
Southwest Missouri State Univ	MO	7,600	LC
Southwest State Univ	MN	7,117	LC
Southwest Texas State Univ	TX	8,730	VC
Southwestern Okla State Univ	OK	4,801	C
Springfield College	MA	24,520	C
SUNY/College at Cortland	NY	10,564	C
Stephen F. Austin State Univ	TX	6,905	C
Tabor College	KS	17,600	LC
Tenn State Univ	TN	7,058	VC
Texas A&M Univ	TX	8,988	VC
Texas A&M Univ at Commerce	TX	7,326	C
Texas A&M Univ at Kingsville	TX	6,446	LC
Thomas Edison State College	NJ	2,750	SP
Tougaloo College	MS	9,200	NC
Troy State Univ	AL	7,696	C
Univ of Akron	OH	10,530	NC
Univ of Alabama	AL	7,402	C
Univ of Alabama at Birmingham	AL	10,110	C
Univ of Arizona	AZ	8,614	C
Univ of Arkansas at Little Rock	AR	5,637	NC
Univ of Arkansas at Monticello	AR	5,940	NC
Univ of Cincinnati	OH	12,491	LC
Univ of Dayton	OH	20,400	VC
Univ of Detroit Mercy	MI	21,620	LC
Univ of Florida	FL	7,874	HC
Univ of Georgia	GA	8,656	VC
Univ of Great Falls	MT	15,360	C
Univ of Iowa	IA	8,607	C+
Univ of Kansas	KS	7,232	VC
Univ of Kentucky	KY	7,765	C
Univ of Louisiana at Lafayette	LA	5,200	C
Univ of Maine	ME	10,798	C
Univ of Maine at Farmington	ME	9,163	C
Univ of Maine at Presque Isle	ME	7,964	LC
Univ of Mary Hardin-Baylor	TX	13,929	C
Univ of Maryland/College Park	MD	11,959	C
Univ of Maryland/Eastern Shore	MD	9,258	C
Univ of Minn/Duluth	MN	10,436	C
Univ of Missouri/Kansas City	MO	9,685	VC
Univ of Nebr at Kearney	NE	7,048	NC
Univ of Nebr at Lincoln	NE	8,325	C+
Univ of Nebr at Omaha	NE	6,867	C
Univ of Nevada/Las Vegas	NV	8,281	VC
Univ of New Mexico	NM	8,026	C
Univ of N Car at Greensboro	NC	6,858	C
Univ of North Texas	TX	7,629	C
Univ of Northern Iowa	IA	7,850	C
Univ of Rio Grande	OH	8,728	NC
Univ of St. Francis	IN	17,790	LC
Univ of St. Thomas	MN	24,044	VC
Univ of South Alabama	AL	6,976	LC
Univ of Southern Miss	MS	6,155	LC
Univ of Tenn at Knoxville	TN	8,214	C
Univ of Tenn at Martin	TN	8,268	C
Univ of the District of Columbia	DC	2,844	NC
Univ of Toledo	OH	11,206	NC
Univ of Utah	UT	7,703	C
Univ of Vermont	VT	14,761	C+
Univ of Virginia	VA	9,391	HC+
Univ of West Florida	FL	7,518	C
Univ of Wisc/La Crosse	WI	7,250	VC
Univ of Wisc/Stevens Point	WI	7,116	C
Univ of Wyoming	WY	7,143	C
Utah State Univ	UT	6,771	C
Valdosta State Univ	GA	6,988	C
Valley City State Univ	ND		LC
Virginia Commonwealth Univ	VA	9,030	C

School	ST	$IS	SR
Virginia Polytechnic Inst and State Univ	VA	7,652	C
Wayne State College	NE	6,255	NC
Weber State Univ	UT	6,897	NC
West Chester Univ of Pennsylvania	PA	9,792	VC
West Liberty State College	WV	6,056	LC
Western Conn State Univ	CT	10,074	C
Western Kentucky Univ	KY	6,834	C
Western Mich Univ	MI	10,016	C
Western Oregon Univ	OR	8,829	C
Western Washington Univ	WA	8,624	VC
William Paterson Univ of New Jersey	NJ	11,000	LC
William Penn Univ	IA	17,575	C
Winona State Univ	MN	8,570	C
Youngstown State Univ	OH	9,318	NC

HEALTH SCIENCE

School	ST	$IS	SR
Alcorn State Univ	MS	5,594	LC
Alma College	MI	22,586	VC
Alverno College	WI	16,930	LC
American Univ	DC	31,544	VC+
Appalachian State Univ	NC	6,353	C
Armstrong Atlantic State Univ	GA	7,084	C
Ball State Univ	IN	8,660	C
Baylor Univ	TX	18,298	VC+
Benedictine Univ	IL	21,330	C
Bethel College	KS	17,355	C+
Boise State Univ	ID	6,531	LC
Boston Univ	MA	34,358	MC
Bowling Green State Univ	OH	10,794	C
Bradley Univ	IL	20,970	VC
Bridgewater College	VA	22,950	C
Brigham Young Univ	UT	7,840	HC
Cal State, Chico	CA	8,598	LC
Cal State, Dominguez Hills	CA	5,840	LC
Cal State, Fresno	CA	7,762	C
Cal State, Fullerton	CA	5,440	LC
Cal State, Hayward	CA	7,400	LC
Cal State, Long Beach	CA	7,400	LC
Cal State, Los Angeles	CA	5,050	C
Carlow College	PA	19,366	C
Castleton State College	VT	10,922	LC
Centenary College of Louisiana	LA	21,600	C+
Chapman Univ	CA	30,218	VC
CUNY/Brooklyn College	NY	3,403	LC
CUNY/Queens College	NY	3,403	VC
College of Our Lady of the Elms	MA	20,644	C
College of St. Scholastica	MN	22,378	C+
Columbus State Univ	GA	7,228	LC
Dordt College	IA	18,100	C+
Duquesne Univ	PA	24,242	C+
East Tenn State Univ	TN	7,127	C
Erskine College	SC	21,399	VC
Florida Atlantic Univ	FL	8,832	C
Florida Gulf Coast Univ	FL	9,201	C
Furman Univ	SC	25,492	HC
George Mason Univ	VA	9,192	C
Gettysburg College	PA	32,070	HC
Grand Valley State Univ	MI	10,040	C
Guilford College	NC	23,255	C
Hampshire College	MA	33,881	HC+
Hope International Univ	CA	16,940	NC
Indiana Univ Bloomington	IN	10,712	C+
Ithaca College	NY	28,719	HC
James Madison Univ	VA	9,552	HC
Johnson State College	VT	10,776	C
Kalamazoo College	MI	26,955	HC+
Keene State College	NH	11,280	C
Kent State Univ	OH	11,104	C
La Sierra Univ	CA	19,260	LC
Lincoln Univ	PA	11,198	C+
Lock Haven Univ of Pennsylvania	PA	9,534	C
Marymount Univ	VA	21,560	LC
Maryville College	TN	23,210	VC
Maryville Univ of St. Louis	MO	18,680	C
MCP Hahnemann Univ	PA	18,510	SP
Middle Tenn State Univ	TN	6,994	C
Midwestern State Univ	TX	6,704	NC
Minn State Univ, Mankato	MN	7,296	LC
Missouri Baptist College	MO	15,762	LC
New England College	NH	20,706	LC
Nicholls State Univ	LA	5,290	NC
Norfolk State Univ	VA	8,382	LC
Northeastern Univ	MA	30,078	VC
Oakland Univ	MI	9,418	C
Old Dominion Univ	VA	9,386	C
Oral Roberts Univ	OK	18,490	C
Oregon Inst of Technology	OR	8,718	C
Our Lady of Holy Cross College	LA	5,140	NC
Pennsylvania College of Technology	PA	12,860	NC
Purdue Univ/West Lafayette	IN	10,284	VC
Quinnipiac Univ	CT	27,370	C
Randolph-Macon Woman's College	VA	25,820	VC+
Rice Univ	TX	24,325	MC
St. Ambrose Univ	IA	19,994	C
St. Francis College	NY	9,610	C
St. Mary's College	MI	13,314	LC
St. Mary's College of Calif	CA	27,575	C
San Diego State Univ	CA	9,716	C+
San Francisco State Univ	CA	7,139	LC
Southern Adventist Univ	TN	15,600	C
Southwestern Okla State Univ	OK	4,801	C
SUNY/College at Brockport	NY	10,267	C
SUNY/College at Cortland	NY	10,564	C
SUNY/Univ at Stony Brook	NY	10,998	VC
Stephen F. Austin State Univ	TX	6,905	C
Syracuse Univ	NY	30,710	HC
Taylor Univ	IN	21,562	VC+
Temple Univ	PA	14,124	C
Texas Southern Univ	TX	6,576	NC
Towson Univ	MD	11,088	VC
Truman State Univ	MO	8,568	VC+
Universidad Adventista de las Antillas	PR	6,675	
Univ of Arkansas	AR	8,334	VC
Univ of Arkansas at Little Rock	AR	5,637	NC
Univ of Central Arkansas	AR	6,388	C
Univ of Central Florida	FL	8,251	VC
Univ of Findlay	OH	23,962	NC
Univ of Hartford	CT	28,884	C
Univ of Hawaii at Manoa	HI	7,862	VC
Univ of Maryland/Baltimore County	MD	12,190	VC
Univ of Miami	FL	31,130	HC
Univ of Mich/Flint	MI	4,323	C
Univ of Missouri/St. Louis	MO	9,966	C
Univ of North Florida	FL	8,089	VC
Univ of Okla	OK	7,616	VC
Univ of South Alabama	AL	6,976	LC
Univ of Southern Maine	ME	10,569	C
Univ of Tenn at Knoxville	TN	8,214	C
Univ of Texas at El Paso	TX	5,076	LC
Univ of Wisc/Milwaukee	WI	8,907	LC
Univ of Wyoming	WY	7,143	LC
West Chester Univ of Pennsylvania	PA	9,792	VC
Western Baptist College	OR	19,700	C+
Western Illinois Univ	IL	9,571	C
William Paterson Univ of New Jersey	NJ	11,000	LC
Worcester State College	MA	7,901	LC
Yeshiva Univ	NY	21,400	C
Youngstown State Univ	OH	9,318	NC

HEBREW

School	ST	$IS	SR
CUNY/Brooklyn College	NY	3,403	LC
CUNY/Herbert H. Lehman College	NY	3,320	LC
CUNY/Hunter College	NY	5,147	C+
CUNY/Queens College	NY	3,403	VC
Harvard Univ/Harvard College	MA	34,269	MC
Hofstra Univ	NY	23,252	C
New York Univ	NY	35,200	MC
SUNY/Univ at Albany	NY	10,997	VC
SUNY/Univ at Binghamton	NY	10,653	HC
Temple Univ	PA	14,124	C
Ohio State Univ	OH	10,819	VC
Touro College	NY	14,950	VC
Univ of Calif at Los Angeles	CA	13,227	MC
Univ of Mich/Ann Arbor	MI	13,003	HC+
Univ of Minn/Twin Cities	MN	11,123	VC
Univ of Texas at Austin	TX	9,437	HC
Univ of Wisc/Madison	WI	8,262	VC
Univ of Wisc/Milwaukee	WI	8,907	LC
Washington Univ in St. Louis	MO	34,593	MC
Yeshiva Univ	NY	21,400	C

HISPANIC AMERICAN STUDIES

School	ST	$IS	SR
Arizona State Univ-Main	AZ	7,726	C
Boston College	MA	33,330	MC
Brown Univ	RI	34,973	MC
Cal State, Long Beach	CA	7,400	LC
CUNY/Brooklyn College	NY	3,403	LC
CUNY/Hunter College	NY	5,147	C+
Columbia Univ/Columbia College	NY	35,190	MC
Columbia Univ/School of General Studies	NY	35,000	C
Conn College	CT	33,585	MC
Dartmouth College	NH	34,458	MC
East Carolina Univ	NC	7,766	C
Lewis and Clark College	OR	29,010	VC
Mills College	CA	27,950	C
Mount St. Mary College	NY	18,825	C
Northwestern Univ	IL	33,615	MC
Rutgers, The State Univ of New Jersey New Brunswick Campus	NJ	12,709	C
St. Olaf College	MN	25,880	HC
Scripps College	CA	30,400	HC+
SUNY/College at Oneonta	NY	9,981	C
SUNY/Univ at Albany	NY	10,997	VC
Univ of Calif at Berkeley	CA	14,134	MC
Univ of Calif at Los Angeles	CA	13,227	MC
Univ of Mich/Ann Arbor	MI	13,003	HC+
Univ of PR/Cayey Univ College	PR	1,245	
Univ of PR/Rio Piedras	PR	5,510	
Western New Mexico Univ	NM	5,950	LC
Wheaton College	MA	32,940	VC

HISTORIC PRESERVATION

School	ST	$IS	SR
Eastern Mich Univ	MI	9,855	C
Goucher College	MD	30,650	VC+
Mary Washington College	VA	9,032	VC+
Roger Williams Univ	RI	29,010	C
Salve Regina Univ	RI	26,460	C
Savannah College of Art and Design	GA	25,075	SP
Univ of Delaware	DE	10,824	VC
Ursuline College	OH	19,430	LC

HISTORY

School	ST	$IS	SR
Abilene Christian Univ	TX	16,300	VC
Adams State College	CO	7,468	C
Adelphi Univ	NY	23,320	VC
Adrian College	MI	19,670	C
Agnes Scott College	GA	24,950	VC
Alabama A&M Univ	AL	5,100	LC
Alabama State Univ	AL	6,404	C
Albany State Univ	GA	5,764	C+
Albertson College of Idaho	ID	23,900	VC
Albertus Magnus College	CT	22,154	C
Albion College	MI	25,224	VC
Albright College	PA	27,642	C
Alcorn State Univ	MS	5,594	LC
Alderson-Broaddus College	WV	19,640	C
Alfred Univ	NY	27,212	C+
Alice Lloyd College	KY	1,785	VC
Allegheny College	PA	27,780	VC
Allen Univ	SC	9,600	NC
Alma College	MI	22,586	VC
Alvernia College	PA	20,790	C
Alverno College	WI	16,930	LC
American International College	MA	22,268	LC
American Univ	DC	31,544	VC+
Amherst College	MA	34,340	MC
Anderson Univ	IN	19,430	LC
Andrews Univ	MI	17,696	LC
Angelo State Univ	TX	7,028	C
Anna Maria College	MA	22,800	LC
Appalachian State Univ	NC	6,353	C
Aquinas College	MI	20,052	C+
Arcadia Univ	PA	26,650	C
Arizona State Univ-Main	AZ	7,726	C
Arkansas State Univ	AR	7,480	C
Arkansas Tech Univ	AR	6,256	C
Armstrong Atlantic State Univ	GA	7,084	C
Asbury College	KY	18,540	VC
Ashland Univ	OH	22,182	LC
Assumption College	MA	26,320	C
Atlantic Union College	MA	34,034	LC
Auburn Univ	AL	5,510	C
Auburn Univ Montgomery	AL	5,330	NC
Augsburg College	MN	22,978	C
Augusta State Univ	GA	2,282	C
Augustana College	IL	24,117	VC+
Augustana College	SD	20,760	VC
Aurora Univ	IL	18,551	C
Austin College	TX	22,150	VC+
Austin Peay State Univ	TN	5,814	LC
Averett Univ	VA	17,980	LC
Avila College	MO	17,720	C
Azusa Pacific Univ	CA	22,422	VC
Baker Univ	KS	14,780	C+
Baldwin-Wallace College	OH	22,010	VC+
Ball State Univ	IN	8,660	C
Bard College	NY	33,912	HC
Barry Univ	FL	24,100	LC
Bartlesville Wesleyan College	OK	14,100	LC
Barton College	NC	16,834	LC
Bates College	ME	34,100	MC
Baylor Univ	TX	18,298	VC+
Belhaven College	MS	16,040	C+
Bellarmine Univ	KY	20,440	VC
Bellevue Univ	NE	4,125	NC
Belmont Abbey College	NC	19,630	LC
Belmont Univ	TN	19,066	VC
Beloit College	WI	27,482	HC
Bemidji State Univ	MN	7,957	C
Benedictine College	KS	18,485	LC
Benedictine Univ	IL	21,330	C
Bennington College	VT	31,350	VC
Bentley College	MA	31,060	HC
Berea College	KY	4,070	VC
Berry College	GA	18,850	C
Bethany College	KS	16,602	C+
Bethany College	WV	18,566	C
Bethel College	IN	17,650	LC
Bethel College	KS	17,355	C+
Bethel College	MN	22,740	VC
Bethel College	TN	12,980	C
Bethune-Cookman College	FL	15,746	C
Biola Univ	CA	21,902	VC
Birmingham-Southern College	AL	22,960	C
Black Hills State Univ	SD	6,652	LC
Blackburn College	IL	13,690	C
Bloomfield College	NJ	17,000	C
Bloomsburg Univ of Pennsylvania	PA	9,434	C
Blue Mountain College	MS	9,100	LC
Bluefield College	VA	14,200	C
Bluffton College	OH	20,644	C
Boise State Univ	ID	6,531	LC
Boston College	MA	33,330	MC
Boston Univ	MA	34,358	MC
Bowdoin College	ME	32,650	MC
Bowie State Univ	MD	9,300	C+
Bowling Green State Univ	OH	10,794	C
Bradley Univ	IL	20,970	VC
Brandeis Univ	MA	34,481	MC
Brenau Univ Women's College	GA	20,100	C
Brescia Univ	KY	14,225	C
Brewton-Parker College	GA	10,810	LC
Briar Cliff Univ	IA	18,657	LC
Bridgewater College	VA	22,950	C
Bridgewater State College	MA	7,589	C+
Brigham Young Univ	UT	7,840	HC
Brigham Young Univ/Hawaii	HI	6,890	C
Brown Univ	RI	34,973	MC
Bryan College	TN	16,400	VC
Bryant College	RI	25,980	VC
Bryn Athyn College of the New Church	PA	10,590	NC
Bryn Mawr College	PA	33,580	HC+
Bucknell Univ	PA	31,096	HC
Buena Vista Univ	IA	22,828	C
Butler Univ	IN	25,580	VC+
Cabrini College	PA	25,950	LC
Caldwell College	NJ	20,940	LC
Calif Baptist Univ	CA	16,736	C
Calif Inst of Technology	CA	27,663	MC
Calif Lutheran Univ	CA	23,500	LC
Calif Polytechnic State Univ	CA	8,747	VC
Calif State Polytechnic Univ, Pomona	CA	8,615	C
Cal State, Bakersfield	CA	6,090	LC
Cal State, Chico	CA	8,598	LC
Cal State, Dominguez Hills	CA	5,840	LC
Cal State, Fresno	CA	7,762	C
Cal State, Fullerton	CA	5,440	LC
Cal State, Hayward	CA	7,400	LC
Cal State, Long Beach	CA	7,400	LC
Cal State, Los Angeles	CA	5,050	C
Cal State, Northridge	CA	7,781	C
Cal State, Sacramento	CA	7,488	C
Cal State, San Bernardino	CA	6,516	C
Cal State, San Marcos	CA	1,736	LC
Cal State, Stanislaus	CA	8,895	C
Calif Univ of Pennsylvania	PA	10,388	C
Calumet College of St. Joseph	IN	7,500	LC
Calvin College	MI	20,050	NC
Cameron Univ	OK	5,560	NC
Campbell Univ	NC	16,599	C
Campbellsville Univ	KY	14,340	C
Canisius College	NY	24,696	C+
Capital Univ	OH	23,630	C
Cardinal Stritch Univ	WI	17,620	C
Carleton College	MN	30,780	MC
Carlow College	PA	19,366	C
Carnegie Mellon Univ	PA	32,682	MC
Carroll College	MT	19,140	C
Carroll College	WI	21,170	C
Carson-Newman College	TN	16,490	C
Carthage College	WI	23,670	C
Case Western Reserve Univ	OH	27,418	C
Castleton State College	VT	10,922	LC
Catawba College	NC	19,620	C
Catholic Univ of America	DC	29,332	VC
Cedar Crest College	PA	25,145	C+
Cedarville Univ	OH	17,553	VC
Centenary College	NJ	22,430	C
Centenary College of Louisiana	LA	21,600	C+
Central College	IA	21,206	C
Central Conn State Univ	CT	10,404	C
Central Methodist College	MO	16,460	C
Central Mich Univ	MI	8,355	C
Central Missouri State Univ	MO	7,920	C
Central State Univ	OH	8,922	C+
Central Washington Univ	WA	8,985	LC
Centre College	KY	24,000	HC
Chadron State College	NE	6,211	NC
Chaminade Univ of Honolulu	HI	17,370	C
Chapman Univ	CA	30,218	VC
Charleston Southern Univ	SC	17,122	C
Chatham College	PA	25,454	C+
Chestnut Hill College	PA	24,790	LC
Chicago State Univ	IL	8,851	C+
Christendom College	VA	16,700	VC+
Christian Brothers Univ	TN	19,820	VC
Christian Heritage College	CA	18,000	LC
Christopher Newport Univ	VA	8,862	VC
Citadel, The	SC	9,126	C
CUNY/Baruch College	NY	3,275	VC+

School	ST	$IS	SR
CUNY/Brooklyn College	NY	3,403	LC
CUNY/City College	NY	3,309	LC
CUNY/College of Staten Island	NY	3,358	NC
CUNY/Herbert H. Lehman College	NY	3,320	LC
CUNY/Hunter College	NY	5,147	C+
CUNY/Queens College	NY	3,403	VC
CUNY/York College	NY	3,292	NC
Claflin Univ	SC	12,735	C+
Claremont McKenna College	CA	32,700	MC
Clarion Univ of Pennsylvania	PA	11,272	LC
Clark Atlanta Univ	GA	17,174	C
Clark Univ	MA	29,170	HC
Clarke College	IA	20,625	C+
Clarkson Univ	NY	29,884	VC
Clearwater Christian College	FL	13,160	LC
Clemson Univ	SC	7,600	C
Cleveland State Univ	OH	10,146	NC
Coastal Carolina Univ	SC	9,220	C
Coe College	IA	24,750	VC
Coker College	SC	20,120	C
Colby College	ME	34,290	MC
Colby-Sawyer College	NH	27,850	LC
Colgate Univ	NY	33,480	MC
College Misericordia	PA	23,380	LC
College of Charleston	SC	8,350	HC
College of Mount St. Vincent	NY	24,230	C
College of Mount St. Joseph	OH	20,290	C
College of New Jersey	NJ	13,425	HC
College of New Rochelle	NY	20,000	C
College of Notre Dame of Maryland	MD	23,100	LC
College of St. Benedict	MN	23,921	VC
College of St. Catherine	MN	22,324	VC
College of St. Elizabeth	NJ	22,510	C
College of St. Joseph	VT	17,400	NC
College of St. Rose	NY	19,084	C
College of St. Scholastica	MN	22,378	C+
College of the Holy Cross	MA	32,780	MC
College of the Ozarks	MO	2,650	C+
College of the Southwest	NM	8,456	NC
College of William and Mary	VA	10,002	MC
College of Wooster	OH	28,350	VC
Colo Christian Univ	CO	17,714	C
Colo College	CO	31,525	HC+
Colo State Univ	CO	9,672	C
Columbia College	MO	15,082	C
Columbia College	SC	19,050	LC
Columbia Union College	MD	19,027	C+
Columbia Univ/Barnard College	NY	33,694	MC
Columbia Univ/Columbia College	NY	35,190	MC
Columbia Univ/School of General Studies	NY	35,000	C
Columbus State Univ	GA	7,228	LC
Concord College	WV	7,122	C+
Concordia College	NY	19,200	VC
Concordia College/Moorhead	MN	18,835	C
Concordia Univ	CA	22,290	C
Concordia Univ	MI	20,500	C
Concordia Univ	MN	19,912	C
Concordia Univ at Austin	TX	16,740	LC
Concordia Univ Nebr	NE	17,770	C
Concordia Univ Wisc	WI	16,600	LC
Concordia Univ, River Forest	IL	20,000	LC
Conn College	CT	33,585	MC
Converse College	SC	21,990	VC
Coppin State College	MD	9,133	LC
Cornell College	IA	24,980	VC
Cornell Univ	NY	34,614	MC
Cornerstone Univ and Grand Rapids Baptist Seminary	MI	18,092	C
Covenant College	GA	21,970	C+
Creighton Univ	NE	23,476	VC
Crichton College	TN	12,680	LC
Culver-Stockton College	MO	15,400	LC
Cumberland College	KY	14,864	C
Curry College	MA	26,025	LC
Daemen College	NY	20,620	C
Dakota Wesleyan Univ	SD	15,512	C
Dallas Baptist Univ	TX	13,682	LC
Dana College	NE	18,046	C
Dartmouth College	NH	34,458	MC
David Lipscomb Univ	TN	16,158	VC
Davidson College	NC	30,823	MC
Davis and Elkins College	WV	19,270	LC
De Sales Univ	PA	22,610	VC
Defiance College	OH	19,580	LC
Delaware State Univ	DE	8,104	LC
Delta State Univ	MS	5,416	C
Denison Univ	OH	29,640	HC
DePaul Univ	IL	23,590	VC
DePauw Univ	IN	28,000	HC
Dickinson College	PA	32,210	VC+
Dickinson State Univ	ND	5,495	NC
Dillard Univ	LA	16,046	VC

School	ST	$IS	SR
Doane College	NE	17,600	LC
Dominican College	NY	20,400	LC
Dominican Univ	IL	20,800	C
Dominican Univ of Calif	CA	27,948	C
Dordt College	IA	18,100	C+
Dowling College	NY	20,281	LC
Drake Univ	IA	22,830	VC
Drew Univ/College of Liberal Arts	NJ	32,152	VC
Drexel Univ	PA	27,657	VC
Drury Univ	MO	15,250	VC
Duke Univ	NC	34,396	MC
Duquesne Univ	PA	24,242	C+
D'Youville College	NY	18,704	C
Earlham College	IN	27,446	VC+
East Carolina Univ	NC	7,766	C
East Central Univ	OK	4,578	C
East Stroudsburg Univ of Pennsylvania	PA	8,430	LC
East Tenn State Univ	TN	7,127	C
East Texas Baptist Univ	TX	12,349	LC
Eastern College	PA	19,641	LC
Eastern Conn State Univ	CT	10,362	C
Eastern Illinois Univ	IL	10,101	C
Eastern Kentucky Univ	KY	6,552	C
Eastern Mennonite Univ	VA	20,700	VC
Eastern Mich Univ	MI	9,855	C
Eastern Nazarene College	MA	19,433	LC
Eastern New Mexico Univ	NM	4,113	LC
Eastern Oregon Univ	OR	8,772	C
Eastern Washington Univ	WA	7,972	LC
Eckerd College	FL	25,500	C+
Edgewood College	WI	18,304	C
Edinboro Univ of Pennsylvania	PA	9,328	LC
Edward Waters College	FL	13,124	LC
Elizabeth City State Univ	NC	5,550	LC
Elizabethtown College	PA	26,000	VC
Elmhurst College	IL	21,750	C
Elmira College	NY	31,070	VC+
Elon Univ	NC	19,430	VC
Emory & Henry College	VA	19,462	C
Emory Univ	GA	33,792	MC
Emporia State Univ	KS	6,198	LC
Erskine College	SC	21,399	VC
Eugene Lang College of New School Univ	NY	30,300	C
Eureka College	IL	22,200	C
Evangel Univ	MO	14,050	C
Fairfield Univ	CT	30,885	HC
Fairleigh Dickinson Univ/Madison campus	NJ	25,500	C
Fairleigh Dickinson Univ/Teaneck Campus	NJ	24,646	C
Fairmont State College	WV	7,010	NC
Fayetteville State Univ	NC	5,590	LC
Felician College	NJ	20,050	C
Ferrum College	VA	15,990	LC
Fisk Univ	TN	13,700	LC
Fitchburg State College	MA	7,836	C
Flagler College	FL	10,550	VC+
Florida A&M Univ	FL	6,948	C
Florida Atlantic Univ	FL	8,832	C
Florida International Univ	FL	9,486	VC
Florida Southern College	FL	19,430	C
Florida State Univ	FL	7,835	HC
Fontbonne Univ	MO	18,046	C
Fordham Univ	NY	30,710	VC
Fort Hays State Univ	KS	6,294	LC
Fort Lewis College	CO	7,659	LC
Framingham State College	MA	7,259	C
Francis Marion Univ	SC	7,682	C
Franciscan Univ of Steubenville	OH	19,100	C+
Franklin and Marshall College	PA	32,410	HC
Franklin College of Indiana	IN	19,905	C
Franklin Pierce College	NH	26,125	LC
Freed-Hardeman Univ	TN	14,290	VC
Fresno Pacific Univ	CA	19,740	C
Friends Univ	KS	15,962	LC
Frostburg State Univ	MD	9,680	C
Furman Univ	SC	25,492	HC
Gallaudet Univ	DC	16,554	SP
Gannon Univ	PA	18,848	C
Gardner-Webb Univ	NC	17,400	C
Geneva College	PA	19,990	C+
George Fox Univ	OR	24,095	VC
George Mason Univ	VA	9,192	C
George Washington Univ	DC	32,170	HC
Georgetown College	KY	18,400	VC
Georgetown Univ	DC	34,847	MC
Georgia College and State Univ	GA	7,344	C
Georgia Inst of Technology	GA	9,028	HC+
Georgia Southern Univ	GA	6,958	C
Georgia Southwestern State Univ	GA	6,013	C
Georgia State Univ	GA	7,792	LC
Georgian Court College	NJ	19,040	LC
Gettysburg College	PA	32,070	HC
Glenville State College	WV	6,588	NC
Gonzaga Univ	WA	24,276	HC+
Gordon College	MA	23,594	VC+
Goshen College	IN	18,950	VC+
Goucher College	MD	30,650	VC+

School	ST	$IS	SR
Graceland Univ	IA	15,845	C
Grambling State Univ	LA	5,325	NC
Grand Canyon Univ	AZ	30,000	LC
Grand Valley State Univ	MI	10,040	C
Green Mountain College	VT	24,130	C
Greensboro College	NC	19,080	LC
Greenville College	IL	19,226	LC
Grinnell College	IA	28,300	HC+
Grove City College	PA	12,280	MC
Guilford College	NC	23,255	C
Gustavus Adolphus College	MN	24,190	VC+
Gwynedd-Mercy College	PA	22,350	C
Hamilton College	NY	34,150	HC
Hamline Univ	MN	23,339	C+
Hampden-Sydney College	VA	24,871	C
Hampshire College	MA	33,881	HC+
Hampton Univ	VA	17,112	C+
Hannibal-LaGrange College	MO	12,530	C
Hanover College	IN	17,560	VC
Harding Univ	AR	13,528	VC
Hardin-Simmons Univ	TX	14,165	C
Hartwick College	NY	33,090	C+
Harvard Univ/Harvard College	MA	34,269	MC
Hastings College	NE	17,854	C+
Haverford College	PA	34,300	MC
Hawaii Pacific Univ	HI	17,790	C
Heidelberg College	OH	23,879	C
Henderson State Univ	AR	6,269	C
Hendrix College	AR	18,463	HC
High Point Univ	NC	20,220	LC
Hillsdale College	MI	20,586	VC+
Hiram College	OH	27,034	VC
Hobart and William Smith Colleges	NY	33,195	VC
Hofstra Univ	NY	23,252	C
Hollins Univ	VA	24,328	VC
Holy Family College	PA	13,710	LC
Holy Names College	CA	23,220	C
Hood College	MD	26,020	VC
Hope College	MI	22,922	C+
Houghton College	NY	21,810	VC+
Houston Baptist Univ	TX	15,300	LC
Howard Payne Univ	TX	13,834	C+
Howard Univ	DC	15,522	LC
Humboldt State Univ	CA	8,582	C
Huntingdon College	AL	18,400	VC
Huntington College	IN	15,480	LC
Idaho State Univ	ID	7,030	C+
Illinois College	IL	16,234	C
Illinois State Univ	IL	9,235	C
Illinois Wesleyan Univ	IL	26,970	HC
Immaculata College	PA	22,400	LC
Indiana State Univ	IN	8,461	LC
Indiana Univ Bloomington	IN	10,712	C+
Indiana Univ Northwest	IN	3,447	C
Indiana Univ of Pennsylvania	PA	9,133	C
Indiana Univ South Bend	IN	3,515	C
Indiana Univ Southeast	IN	3,459	C
Indiana Univ-Purdue Univ Fort Wayne	IN	3,166	LC
Indiana Univ-Purdue Univ Indianapolis	IN	9,473	C
Indiana Wesleyan Univ	IN	17,680	C
Inter-American Univ of PR/Bayamon Univ College	PR	3,700	
Inter-American Univ of PR/Fajardo Campus	PR	4,000	
Inter-American Univ of PR/Metropolitan Campus	PR	4,166	
Inter-American Univ of PR/Ponce Regional College	PR	3,700	
Inter-American Univ of PR/San GermÈn	PR	6,390	
Iona College	NY	26,556	C
Iowa State Univ	IA	8,108	VC
Iowa Wesleyan College	IA	18,840	C
Ithaca College	NY	28,719	HC
Jackson State Univ	MS	6,776	LC
Jacksonville State Univ	AL	6,568	LC
Jacksonville Univ	FL	21,110	LC
James Madison Univ	VA	9,552	HC
Jamestown College	ND	11,310	NC
Jarvis Christian College	TX	9,035	NC
John Brown Univ	AR	15,080	VC
John Carroll Univ	OH	24,140	VC
Johns Hopkins Univ	MD	35,226	MC
Johnson C. Smith Univ	NC	16,560	C+
Johnson State College	VT	10,776	C
Judson College	AL	13,790	C
Judson College	IL	18,980	LC
Juniata College	PA	26,080	VC
Kalamazoo College	MI	26,955	HC+
Kansas State Univ	KS	6,995	C
Kansas Wesleyan Univ	KS	17,400	C+
Kean Univ	NJ	11,159	C
Keene State College	NH	11,280	C
Kennesaw State Univ	GA	2,306	LC
Kent State Univ	OH	11,104	C
Kentucky Christian College	KY	13,472	C
Kentucky State Univ	KY	6,146	NC
Kentucky Wesleyan College	KY	15,800	C
Kenyon College	OH	32,130	HC+
King College	TN	17,800	VC
King's College	PA	24,680	C

School	ST	$IS	SR
Knox College	IL	28,230	HC
Kutztown Univ of Pennsylvania	PA	8,907	C
La Roche College	PA	18,854	LC
La Salle Univ	PA	27,890	C
La Sierra Univ	CA	19,260	LC
Lafayette College	PA	32,655	MC
LaGrange College	GA	17,496	C
Lake Forest College	IL	27,460	VC
Lake Superior State Univ	MI	9,034	LC
Lakeland College	WI	17,950	C
Lamar Univ	TX	6,816	LC
Lambuth Univ	TN	14,254	C
Lander Univ	SC	8,618	LC
Lane College	TN	10,400	C+
Langston Univ	OK	2,308	LC
Lawrence Univ	WI	27,711	HC
Le Moyne College	NY	23,840	C
Lebanon Valley College of Pennsylvania	PA	25,700	VC
Lee Univ	TN	10,198	LC
Lees-McRae College	NC	17,106	LC
Lehigh Univ	PA	32,290	MC
LeMoyne-Owen College	TN	8,450	NC
Lenoir-Rhyne College	NC	19,186	C
LeTourneau Univ	TX	19,020	VC
Lewis and Clark College	OR	29,010	VC
Lewis Univ	IL	20,960	C
Lewis-Clark State College	ID	6,496	C
Liberty Univ	VA	14,500	C
Limestone College	SC	16,900	C
Lincoln Memorial Univ	TN	12,620	LC
Lincoln Univ	MO	7,158	NC
Lincoln Univ	PA	11,198	C+
Lindenwood Univ	MO	17,250	C
Lindsey Wilson College	KY	16,392	LC
Linfield College	OR	25,840	VC
Livingstone College	NC	13,360	LC
Lock Haven Univ of Pennsylvania	PA	9,534	C
LIU/Brooklyn Campus	NY	22,290	C
LIU/C.W. Post Campus	NY	25,380	C
LIU/Southampton College	NY	26,270	C
Longwood College	VA	8,950	C
Loras College	IA	22,994	C+
Louisiana College	LA	11,516	C
Louisiana State Univ and A&M College	LA	8,014	VC
Louisiana State Univ in Shreveport	LA	2,480	NC
Louisiana Tech Univ	LA	6,506	C
Lourdes College	OH	13,100	LC
Loyola College in Maryland	MD	30,900	HC
Loyola Marymount Univ	CA	28,754	HC
Loyola Univ New Orleans	LA	23,506	VC+
Loyola Univ of Chicago	IL	25,992	VC
Luther College	IA	23,300	VC+
Lycoming College	PA	24,780	C
Lynchburg College	VA	23,405	C
Lynn Univ	FL	24,550	C
Lyon College	AR	16,500	VC
Macalester College	MN	28,814	HC+
MacMurray College	IL	17,790	LC
Madonna Univ	MI	11,504	VC
Malone College	OH	19,190	C
Manchester College	IN	22,010	C
Manhattan College	NY	25,500	VC
Manhattanville College	NY	28,730	VC
Mansfield Univ	PA	9,648	C
Marian College	IN	21,020	C
Marian College of Fond du Lac	WI	17,935	LC
Marietta College	OH	24,580	C
Marist College	NY	24,756	VC
Marlboro College	VT	26,410	VC+
Marquette Univ	WI	24,836	C+
Mars Hill College	NC	18,600	LC
Marshall Univ	WV	7,752	LC
Martin Univ	IN	8,370	SP
Mary Baldwin College	VA	23,440	C
Mary Washington College	VA	9,032	VC+
Marygrove College	MI	16,075	C
Marymount College/Tarrytown	NY	23,850	C
Marymount Manhattan College	NY	23,195	VC
Marymount Univ	VA	21,560	LC
Maryville College	TN	23,210	VC
Maryville Univ of St. Louis	MO	18,680	C
Marywood Univ	PA	24,639	C
Mass College of Liberal Arts	MA	8,717	LC
Mass Inst of Technology	MA	35,228	MC
Master's College	CA	21,500	C+
McKendree College	IL	18,300	C+
McMurry Univ	TX	15,287	C
McNeese State Univ	LA	5,259	LC
McPherson College	KS	17,710	C
Mercer Univ	GA	24,130	VC
Mercy College	NY	15,875	LC
Mercyhurst College	PA	20,694	C
Meredith College	NC	17,500	C
Merrimack College	MA	25,725	VC
Mesa State College	CO	8,051	C
Messiah College	PA	23,180	VC
Methodist College	NC	19,526	C

ST = STATE $IS = IN-STATE COSTS SR = SELECTOR RATING

School	ST	$IS	SR
Metropolitan State College of Denver	CO	2,338	LC
Metropolitan State Univ	MN	2,943	SP
Miami Univ	OH	12,885	VC+
Mich State Univ	MI	10,386	VC
MidAmerica Nazarene Univ	KS	16,960	C
Middle Tenn State Univ	TN	6,994	C
Middlebury College	VT	34,300	MC
Midland Lutheran College	NE	18,600	C
Midwestern State Univ	TX	6,704	NC
Millersville Univ of Pennsylvania	PA	10,153	VC
Milligan College	TN	17,550	C
Millikin Univ	IL	24,415	C+
Mills College	CA	27,950	C
Millsaps College	MS	22,608	VC+
Minn State Univ, Mankato	MN	7,296	LC
Minot State Univ	ND	5,466	LC
Miss College	MS	14,574	C
Miss State Univ	MS	7,853	C
Miss Univ for Women	MS	5,446	LC
Miss Valley State Univ	MS	6,345	C
Missouri Baptist College	MO	15,762	LC
Missouri Southern State College	MO	6,666	C
Missouri Valley College	MO	17,400	LC
Missouri Western State College	MO	6,662	NC
Molloy College	NY	13,940	C
Monmouth College	IL	21,550	C
Monmouth Univ	NJ	24,042	C
Montana State Univ-Billings	MT	7,653	NC
Montana State Univ-Bozeman	MT	8,431	C
Montana State Univ-Northern	MT	8,600	NC
Montclair State Univ	NJ	10,287	LC
Montreat College	NC	17,164	C
Moorhead State Univ	MN	7,000	LC
Moravian College	PA	27,065	VC
Morehead State Univ	KY	6,510	C
Morehouse College	GA	19,814	C
Morgan State Univ	MD	10,078	LC
Morningside College	IA	19,124	C
Morris Brown College	GA	15,993	LC
Morris College	SC	9,995	LC
Mount Holyoke College	MA	34,128	HC
Mount Marty College	SD	15,656	LC
Mount Mary College	WI	18,024	C
Mount Mercy College	IA	19,390	VC
Mount Olive College	NC	14,410	LC
Mount St. Mary College	NY	18,825	C
Mount St. Mary's College	CA	24,430	C
Mount St. Mary's College	MD	25,740	C
Mount Senario College	WI	17,750	C
Mount Union College	OH	21,120	C
Mount Vernon Nazarene College	OH	17,027	C
Muhlenberg College	PA	28,170	HC
Murray State Univ	KY	6,672	C
Muskingum College	OH	18,760	C
Nazareth College of Rochester	NY	22,036	VC
Nebr Wesleyan Univ	NE	18,767	VC
New College of Florida	FL	8,130	HC+
New Jersey City Univ	NJ	9,100	LC
New Jersey Inst of Technology	NJ	14,690	VC
New Mexico Highlands Univ	NM	6,256	NC
New Mexico State Univ	NM	7,302	C
New York Univ	NY	35,200	MC
Newberry College	SC	19,670	LC
Newman Univ	KS	14,098	LC
Niagara Univ	NY	22,250	C+
Nicholls State Univ	LA	5,290	NC
Nichols College	MA	24,610	LC
Norfolk State Univ	VA	8,382	LC
N Car Agricultural and Technical State Univ	NC	6,659	LC
N Car Central Univ	NC	6,418	LC
N Car State Univ	NC	8,680	HC
N Car Wesleyan College	NC	15,650	LC
North Central College	IL	22,944	C+
N Dak State Univ	ND	7,004	VC
North Georgia College and State Univ	GA	6,322	C+
North Park Univ	IL	24,030	C
Northeastern Illinois Univ	IL	2,898	NC
Northeastern State Univ	OK	4,704	LC
Northeastern Univ	MA	30,078	VC
Northern Arizona Univ	AZ	7,398	C
Northern Illinois Univ	IL	9,545	C
Northern Kentucky Univ	KY	6,352	NC
Northern Mich Univ	MI	9,693	C
Northern State Univ	SD	6,279	LC
Northland College	WI	21,435	C+
Northwest Missouri State Univ	MO	7,922	LC
Northwest Nazarene Univ	ID	18,380	C
Northwestern College	MN	19,816	C+
Northwestern College of Iowa	IA	17,630	C+
Northwestern Okla State Univ	OK	4,542	NC
Northwestern State Univ of Louisiana	LA	5,745	NC
Northwestern Univ	IL	33,615	MC
Norwich Univ	VT	21,064	LC
Notre Dame College	OH	20,425	C
Notre Dame de Namur Univ	CA	26,932	LC
Nyack College	NY	18,540	C
Oakland Univ	MI	9,418	C
Oakwood College	AL	14,904	C
Oberlin College	OH	33,140	HC+
Occidental College	CA	32,288	HC
Oglala Lakota College	SD	1,950	NC
Oglethorpe Univ	GA	19,100	LC
Ohio Dominican College	OH	18,100	LC
Ohio Northern Univ	OH	27,765	VC
Ohio State Univ at Lima	OH	3,603	NC
Ohio State Univ at Newark	OH	8,103	NC
Ohio Univ	OH	11,769	C
Ohio Wesleyan Univ	OH	29,670	VC+
Okla Baptist Univ	OK	13,878	VC
Okla Christian Univ	OK	16,500	VC
Okla City Univ	OK	15,810	C
Okla Panhandle State Univ	OK	3,812	NC
Okla State Univ	OK	7,650	VC
Old Dominion Univ	VA	9,386	C
Olivet College	MI	17,410	C
Olivet Nazarene Univ	IL	18,444	C
Oral Roberts Univ	OK	18,490	C
Oregon State Univ	OR	9,612	VC
Ottawa Univ	KS	11,800	LC
Otterbein College	OH	23,439	C
Ouachita Baptist Univ	AR	16,460	VC
Our Lady of Holy Cross College	LA	5,140	NC
Our Lady of the Lake Univ of San Antonio	TX	17,336	C
Pace Univ	NY	24,200	C
Pacific Lutheran Univ	WA	23,318	VC
Pacific Union College	CA	20,250	VC
Pacific Univ	OR	24,250	C
Paine College	GA	11,896	LC
Palm Beach Atlantic College	FL	23,310	C
Park Univ	MO	9,816	C
Paul Quinn College	TX	8,150	LC
Penn State Univ at Erie/Behrend College	PA	12,326	C
Penn State Univ/Univ Park Campus	PA	11,126	VC
Pepperdine Univ	CA	32,830	VC
Peru State College	NE	6,342	NC
Pfeiffer Univ	NC	18,580	C
Piedmont College	GA	16,900	C
Pikeville College	KY	12,000	NC
Pine Manor College	MA	19,344	LC
Pittsburg State Univ	KS	6,228	NC
Pitzer College	CA	33,930	HC
Plymouth State College	NH	11,024	LC
Point Loma Nazarene Univ	CA	21,380	VC
Point Park College	PA	20,290	C
Pomona College	CA	33,960	MC
Pontifical Catholic Univ of PR/Ponce	PR	7,076	
Portland State Univ	OR	11,220	C
Prairie View A&M Univ	TX	3,172	LC
Presbyterian College	SC	23,356	VC
Princeton Univ	NJ	35,072	MC
Principia College	IL	23,865	C+
Providence College	RI	27,620	HC
Purdue Univ/Calumet	IN	6,630	NC
Purdue Univ/West Lafayette	IN	10,284	VC
Queens College	NC	17,250	C
Quincy Univ	IL	20,450	C
Quinnipiac Univ	CT	27,370	C
Radford Univ	VA	8,302	C
Ramapo College of New Jersey	NJ	13,550	VC
Randolph-Macon College	VA	24,395	C
Randolph-Macon Woman's College	VA	25,820	VC+
Reed College	OR	33,350	HC+
Regis College	MA	26,750	C
Regis Univ	CO	25,740	C+
Rhode Island College	RI	8,700	LC
Rhodes College	TN	26,466	HC+
Richard Stockton College of New Jersey	NJ	12,165	VC
Rider Univ	NJ	27,400	C
Ripon College	WI	24,180	VC+
Rivier College	NH	24,215	C
Roanoke College	VA	24,689	VC
Roberts Wesleyan College	NY	20,160	C+
Rochester College	MI	15,404	C+
Rockford College	IL	23,930	C
Rockhurst Univ	MO	20,090	C
Rocky Mountain College	MT	18,113	C
Roger Williams Univ	RI	29,010	C
Rollins College	FL	31,223	HC
Roosevelt Univ	IL	20,240	LC
Rosemont College	PA	24,060	C
Rowan Univ	NJ	12,365	VC
Russell Sage College	NY	23,674	C+
Rutgers, The State Univ of New Jersey New Brunswick Campus	NJ	12,709	C
Rutgers, The State Univ of New Jersey/CamdenCampus	NJ	6,484	C
Rutgers, The State Univ of New Jersey/Newark Campus	NJ	6,394	C
Sacred Heart Univ	CT	26,588	VC
Saginaw Valley State Univ	MI	9,465	C
St. Ambrose Univ	IA	19,994	C
St. Andrews Presbyterian College	NC	19,720	LC
St. Anselm College	NH	27,405	C
St. Augustine's College	NC	12,990	C+
St. Bonaventure Univ	NY	21,956	C
St. Cloud State Univ	MN	7,180	C
St. Edward's Univ	TX	17,846	C
St. Francis College	NY	9,610	C
St. Francis Univ	PA	24,486	LC
St. John Fisher College	NY	21,800	C
St. John's Univ	MN	23,640	VC
St. John's Univ	NY	26,660	C
St. Joseph College	CT	25,960	LC
St. Joseph's College	IN	21,640	C
St. Joseph's College of Maine	ME	22,500	LC
St. Joseph's College, New York	NY	9,802	C
St. Joseph's Univ	PA	29,715	VC+
St. Lawrence Univ	NY	32,605	VC
St. Leo Univ	FL	19,250	LC
St. Louis Univ	MO	26,590	VC+
St. Martin's College	WA	20,566	C
St. Mary College	KS	17,298	C
St. Mary's College	IN	24,474	VC
St. Mary's College of Calif	CA	27,575	C
St. Mary's College of Maryland	MD	14,104	HC
St. Mary's Univ of Minn	MN	19,975	C
St. Mary's Univ of San Antonio	TX	19,735	C
St. Michael's College	VT	26,935	VC
St. Norbert College	WI	23,169	VC
St. Olaf College	MN	25,880	HC
St. Peter's College	NJ	22,292	LC
St. Thomas Aquinas College	NY	20,590	LC
St. Thomas Univ	FL	19,500	LC
St. Vincent College	PA	22,942	VC
St. Xavier Univ	IL	21,104	C
Salem College	NC	23,065	VC
Salem State College	MA	4,481	LC
Salisbury Univ	MD	10,576	VC
Salve Regina Univ	RI	26,460	C
Sam Houston State Univ	TX	6,076	LC
Samford Univ	AL	16,340	VC
San Diego State Univ	CA	9,716	C+
San Francisco State Univ	CA	7,139	LC
San Jose State Univ	CA	8,187	C
Santa Clara Univ	CA	28,371	VC+
Sarah Lawrence College	NY	37,516	HC
Savannah State Univ	GA	2,550	LC
Schreiner Univ	TX	19,254	C
Scripps College	CA	30,400	HC+
Seattle Pacific Univ	WA	22,674	C+
Seattle Univ	WA	24,183	VC
Seton Hall Univ	NJ	26,910	LC
Seton Hill College	PA	21,875	C
Shawnee State Univ	OH	8,634	NC
Shenandoah Univ	VA	22,550	NC
Shepherd College	WV	7,062	LC
Shippensburg Univ of Pennsylvania	PA	9,652	C
Shorter College	GA	15,185	C
Siena College	NY	22,685	VC
Siena Heights Univ	MI	16,140	LC
Silver Lake College of the Holy Family	WI	15,516	LC
Simmons College	MA	30,418	VC
Simpson College	CA	19,200	C
Simpson College	IA	21,200	C+
Skidmore College	NY	34,201	VC+
Slippery Rock Univ	PA	9,152	LC
Smith College	MA	33,302	HC+
Sonoma State Univ	CA	8,953	C
S Car State Univ	SC	6,586	LC
S Dak State Univ	SD	6,848	C
Southeast Missouri State Univ	MO	8,367	C+
Southeastern Louisiana Univ	LA	6,047	LC
Southeastern Okla State Univ	OK	4,917	C
Southern Adventist Univ	TN	15,600	C
Southern Arkansas Univ	AR	5,740	LC
Southern Conn State Univ	CT	10,310	C
Southern Illinois Univ at Carbondale	IL	8,621	C
Southern Illinois Univ Edwardsville	IL	7,869	LC
Southern Methodist Univ	TX	28,349	VC
Southern Nazarene Univ	OK	14,634	NC
Southern Oregon Univ	OR	9,429	C
Southern Univ and A&M College	LA	6,365	C+
Southern Univ at New Orleans	LA	995	NC
Southern Utah Univ	UT	7,254	C
Southern Wesleyan Univ	SC	17,280	C
Southwest Baptist Univ	MO	13,426	LC
Southwest Missouri State Univ	MO	7,600	LC
Southwest State Univ	MN	7,117	LC
Southwest Texas State Univ	TX	8,730	VC
Southwestern Adventist Univ	TX	14,798	C
Southwestern College	KS	17,656	C
Southwestern Okla State Univ	OK	4,801	C
Southwestern Univ	TX	22,550	HC
Spalding Univ	KY	15,196	C
Spelman College	GA	19,215	C+
Spring Arbor Univ	MI	17,976	C
Spring Hill College	AL	23,250	C
Springfield College	MA	24,520	C
Stanford Univ	CA	34,222	MC
SUNY/College at Brockport	NY	10,267	C
SUNY/College at Buffalo	NY	8,025	C
SUNY/College at Cortland	NY	10,564	C
SUNY/College at Fredonia	NY	10,125	C
SUNY/College at Geneseo	NY	9,970	HC
SUNY/College at Oneonta	NY	9,981	C
SUNY/College at Oswego	NY	10,856	C
SUNY/College at Plattsburgh	NY	9,729	C
SUNY/College at Potsdam	NY	10,519	C
SUNY/College at Purchase	NY	10,587	VC
SUNY/Empire State College	NY	3,545	SP
SUNY/Univ at Albany	NY	10,997	VC
SUNY/Univ at Binghamton	NY	10,653	HC
SUNY/Univ at Buffalo	NY	11,033	VC
SUNY/Univ at New Paltz	NY	9,685	VC
SUNY/Univ at Stony Brook	NY	10,998	VC
State Univ of West Georgia	GA	7,101	C
Stephen F. Austin State Univ	TX	6,905	C
Sterling College	KS	16,370	VC
Stetson Univ	FL	25,640	VC
Stevens Inst of Technology	NJ	31,510	HC+
Stillman College	AL	11,370	LC
Stonehill College	MA	26,852	HC
Suffolk Univ	MA	26,516	C
Sul Ross State Univ	TX	6,582	LC
Susquehanna Univ	PA	27,270	VC
Swarthmore College	PA	34,538	MC
Sweet Briar College	VA	25,310	VC
Syracuse Univ	NY	30,710	HC
Tabor College	KS	17,600	LC
Talladega College	AL	10,110	LC
Tarleton State Univ	TX	7,160	C
Taylor Univ	IN	21,562	VC+
Teikyo Post Univ	CT	21,800	C
Temple Univ	PA	14,124	C
Tenn State Univ	TN	7,058	VC
Tenn Tech Univ	TN	6,968	C
Tenn Wesleyan College	TN	13,030	C
Texas A&M Univ	TX	8,988	VC
Texas A&M Univ at Commerce	TX	7,326	C
Texas A&M Univ at Kingsville	TX	6,446	LC
Texas Christian Univ	TX	19,910	C
Texas Lutheran Univ	TX	17,660	C
Texas Southern Univ	TX	6,576	NC
Texas Tech Univ	TX	8,825	C
Texas Wesleyan Univ	TX	14,710	C
Texas Woman's Univ	TX	5,855	LC
Ohio State Univ	OH	10,819	VC
Thiel College	PA	18,419	LC
Thomas Edison State College	NJ	2,750	SP
Thomas More College	KY	17,700	LC
Tougaloo College	MS	9,200	NC
Touro College	NY	14,950	VC
Towson Univ	MD	11,088	VC
Transylvania Univ	KY	21,780	VC+
Trevecca Nazarene Univ	TN	15,752	C
Trinity Christian College	IL	19,415	C
Trinity College	CT	34,300	HC
Trinity College	DC	21,370	LC
Trinity International Univ	IL	20,640	C+
Trinity Univ	TX	21,444	HC
Troy State Univ	AL	7,696	C
Troy State Univ/Montgomery	AL	3,080	NC
Truman State Univ	MO	8,568	VC+
Tufts Univ	MA	34,874	MC
Tulane Univ	LA	34,013	HC+
Turabo Univ	PR	4,110	
Tusculum College	TN	17,900	LC
Tuskegee Univ	AL	14,600	LC
Union College	KY	15,920	C
Union College	NE	14,650	C
Union College	NY	32,646	HC
Union Univ	TN	18,930	C+
United States Air Force Academy	CO		MC
United States Military Academy	NY		MC
United States Naval Academy	MD		MC
Universidad Adventista de las Antillas	PR	6,675	
Univ of Akron	OH	10,530	NC
Univ of Alabama	AL	7,402	C

School	ST	$IS	SR
Univ of Alabama at Birmingham	AL	10,110	C
Univ of Alabama at Huntsville	AL	7,916	VC
Univ of Alaska Anchorage	AK	9,100	NC
Univ of Alaska Fairbanks	AK	8,265	NC
Univ of Arizona	AZ	8,614	C
Univ of Arkansas	AR	8,334	VC
Univ of Arkansas at Little Rock	AR	5,637	NC
Univ of Arkansas at Monticello	AR	5,940	NC
Univ of Arkansas at Pine Bluff	AR	7,925	C
Univ of Calif at Berkeley	CA	14,134	MC
Univ of Calif at Davis	CA	12,796	VC
Univ of Calif at Irvine	CA	11,756	C
Univ of Calif at Los Angeles	CA	13,227	MC
Univ of Calif at Riverside	CA	12,479	C
Univ of Calif at San Diego	CA	11,372	HC
Univ of Calif at Santa Barbara	CA	11,732	VC
Univ of Calif at Santa Cruz	CA	13,655	VC
Univ of Central Arkansas	AR	6,388	C
Univ of Central Florida	FL	8,251	VC
Univ of Central Okla	OK	5,205	C
Univ of Charleston	WV	20,640	C
Univ of Chicago	IL	35,087	MC
Univ of Cincinnati	OH	12,491	LC
Univ of Colo at Boulder	CO	9,255	VC
Univ of Colo at Colo Springs	CO	9,403	C
Univ of Colo at Denver	CO	3,673	C
Univ of Conn	CT	12,122	VC
Univ of Dallas	TX	22,128	VC+
Univ of Dayton	OH	20,400	VC
Univ of Delaware	DE	10,824	VC
Univ of Denver	CO	28,783	VC
Univ of Detroit Mercy	MI	21,620	LC
Univ of Evansville	IN	22,865	VC+
Univ of Findlay	OH	23,962	NC
Univ of Florida	FL	7,874	HC
Univ of Georgia	GA	8,656	VC
Univ of Great Falls	MT	15,360	C
Univ of Hartford	CT	28,884	C
Univ of Hawaii at Hilo	HI	6,497	C
Univ of Hawaii at Manoa	HI	7,862	VC
Univ of Houston	TX	8,410	C
Univ of Idaho	ID	7,026	C
Univ of Illinois at Chicago	IL	10,702	VC
Univ of Illinois at Urbana-Champaign	IL	11,316	HC+
Univ of Indianapolis	IN	20,840	C
Univ of Iowa	IA	8,607	C+
Univ of Kansas	KS	7,232	VC
Univ of Kentucky	KY	7,765	C
Univ of La Verne	CA	24,280	C
Univ of Louisiana at Lafayette	LA	5,200	C
Univ of Louisiana at Monroe	LA	5,207	NC
Univ of Louisville	KY	7,402	LC
Univ of Maine	ME	10,798	C
Univ of Maine at Farmington	ME	9,163	C
Univ of Maine at Machias	ME	7,689	LC
Univ of Mary Hardin-Baylor	TX	13,929	C
Univ of Maryland/Baltimore County	MD	12,190	VC
Univ of Maryland/College Park	MD	11,959	C
Univ of Maryland/Eastern Shore	MD	9,258	C
Univ of Maryland/Univ College	MD	5,910	SP
Univ of Mass Amherst	MA	10,995	VC
Univ of Mass Boston	MA	4,227	C
Univ of Mass Dartmouth	MA	9,852	C
Univ of Mass Lowell	MA	9,470	VC
Univ of Memphis	TN	7,271	C
Univ of Miami	FL	31,130	HC
Univ of Mich/Ann Arbor	MI	13,003	HC+
Univ of Mich/Dearborn	MI	4,677	VC
Univ of Mich/Flint	MI	4,323	C
Univ of Minn/Duluth	MN	10,436	C
Univ of Minn/Morris	MN	10,716	VC
Univ of Minn/Twin Cities	MN	11,123	VC
Univ of Miss	MS	7,666	C
Univ of Missouri/Columbia	MO	9,803	HC
Univ of Missouri/Kansas City	MO	9,685	VC
Univ of Missouri/Rolla	MO	10,034	C
Univ of Missouri/St. Louis	MO	9,966	C
Univ of Mobile	AL	13,620	LC
Univ of Montana	MT	8,038	C
Univ of Montevallo	AL	7,266	C
Univ of Nebr at Kearney	NE	7,048	NC
Univ of Nebr at Lincoln	NE	8,325	C+
Univ of Nebr at Omaha	NE	6,867	C
Univ of Nevada/Las Vegas	NV	8,281	VC
Univ of Nevada/Reno	NV	8,737	C
Univ of New Hampshire	NH	13,207	C
Univ of New Haven	CT	23,860	LC
Univ of New Mexico	NM	8,026	C
Univ of New Orleans	LA	10,160	C
Univ of North Alabama	AL	7,016	NC
Univ of N Car at Asheville	NC	6,896	VC
Univ of N Car at Chapel Hill	NC	8,789	HC
Univ of N Car at Charlotte	NC	7,254	C
Univ of N Car at Greensboro	NC	6,858	C
Univ of N Car at Pembroke	NC	5,914	LC
Univ of N Car at Wilmington	NC	7,769	C
Univ of N Dak	ND	7,067	VC
Univ of North Florida	FL	8,089	VC
Univ of North Texas	TX	7,629	C
Univ of Northern Colo	CO	8,082	C+
Univ of Northern Iowa	IA	7,850	C
Univ of Notre Dame	IN	30,707	MC
Univ of Okla	OK	7,616	VC
Univ of Oregon	OR	9,969	C
Univ of Pennsylvania	PA	34,614	MC
Univ of Pittsburgh at Bradford	PA	12,696	C
Univ of Pittsburgh at Johnstown	PA	13,044	LC
Univ of Pittsburgh at Pittsburgh	PA	13,592	HC
Univ of Portland	OR	24,950	VC
Univ of PR/Cayey Univ College	PR	1,245	
Univ of PR/Mayaguez	PR	5,285	
Univ of PR/Rio Piedras	PR	5,510	
Univ of Puget Sound	WA	28,285	HC
Univ of Redlands	CA	29,246	VC
Univ of Rhode Island	RI	12,414	C
Univ of Richmond	VA	27,300	HC
Univ of Rio Grande	OH	8,728	NC
Univ of Rochester	NY	32,979	HC
Univ of St. Francis	IL	19,650	C
Univ of St. Francis	IN	17,790	LC
Univ of St. Thomas	MN	24,044	VC
Univ of St. Thomas	TX	18,752	VC
Univ of San Diego	CA	29,198	HC
Univ of San Francisco	CA	27,302	VC
Univ of Science and Arts of Okla	OK	5,245	C
Univ of Scranton	PA	27,964	C+
Univ of Sioux Falls	SD	16,390	C
Univ of South Alabama	AL	6,976	LC
Univ of S Car at Aiken	SC	7,828	LC
Univ of S Car at Columbia	SC	8,748	VC
Univ of S Car at Spartanburg	SC	7,318	C+
Univ of S Dak	SD	7,036	C
Univ of South Florida	FL	8,154	C
Univ of Southern Calif	CA	33,647	MC
Univ of Southern Colo	CO	7,821	LC
Univ of Southern Indiana	IN	8,655	LC
Univ of Southern Maine	ME	10,569	C
Univ of Southern Miss	MS	6,155	LC
Univ of Tampa	FL	22,612	C
Univ of Tenn at Chattanooga	TN	7,783	C
Univ of Tenn at Knoxville	TN	8,214	C
Univ of Tenn at Martin	TN	8,268	C
Univ of Texas at Arlington	TX	7,192	LC
Univ of Texas at Austin	TX	9,437	HC
Univ of Texas at Dallas	TX	9,305	VC
Univ of Texas at El Paso	TX	5,076	LC
Univ of Texas at San Antonio	TX	9,088	NC
Univ of Texas-Pan American	TX	4,823	C
Univ of the District of Columbia	DC	2,844	NC
Univ of the Incarnate Word	TX	18,478	C
Univ of the Ozarks	AR	13,904	C
Univ of the Pacific	CA	28,255	VC
Univ of the South	TN	27,290	HC
Univ of Toledo	OH	11,206	NC
Univ of Tulsa	OK	19,090	HC
Univ of Utah	UT	7,703	C
Univ of Vermont	VT	14,761	C+
Univ of Virginia	VA	9,391	HC+
Univ of Virginia's College at Wise	VA	8,302	C
Univ of Washington	WA	10,361	VC
Univ of West Alabama	AL	6,048	C
Univ of West Florida	FL	7,518	C
Univ of Wisc/Eau Claire	WI	7,032	VC
Univ of Wisc/Green Bay	WI	7,148	C
Univ of Wisc/La Crosse	WI	7,250	VC
Univ of Wisc/Madison	WI	8,262	VC
Univ of Wisc/Milwaukee	WI	8,907	LC
Univ of Wisc/Oshkosh	WI	6,130	LC
Univ of Wisc/Parkside	WI	6,160	LC
Univ of Wisc/Platteville	WI	7,282	C
Univ of Wisc/River Falls	WI	6,356	LC
Univ of Wisc/Stevens Point	WI	7,116	C
Univ of Wisc/Superior	WI	7,051	C+
Univ of Wisc/Whitewater	WI	6,937	C
Univ of Wyoming	WY	7,143	LC
Ursinus College	PA	31,350	VC
Ursuline College	OH	19,430	LC
Utah State Univ	UT	6,771	C
Utica College of Syracuse Univ	NY	24,400	LC
Valdosta State Univ	GA	6,988	C
Valley City State Univ	ND		LC
Valparaiso Univ	IN	23,570	VC+
Vanderbilt Univ	TN	34,482	MC
Vanguard Univ of Southern Calif	CA	20,212	C
Vassar College	NY	33,450	MC
Villanova Univ	PA	31,997	HC
Virginia Commonwealth Univ	VA	9,030	C
Virginia Intermont College	VA	17,510	C
Virginia Military Inst	VA	9,968	C+
Virginia Polytechnic Inst and State Univ	VA	7,652	C
Virginia State Univ	VA	8,182	LC
Virginia Union Univ	VA	15,358	LC
Virginia Wesleyan College	VA	22,350	LC
Wabash College	IN	25,335	HC
Wagner College	NY	27,000	C
Wake Forest Univ	NC	30,290	MC
Walla Walla College	WA	20,925	C
Walsh Univ	OH	16,880	C
Warner Pacific College	OR	20,370	LC
Warren Wilson College	NC	19,968	C
Wartburg College	IA	21,165	VC
Washburn Univ of Topeka	KS	6,766	NC
Washington and Jefferson College	PA	26,255	VC
Washington and Lee Univ	VA	25,095	MC
Washington College	MD	28,040	VC
Washington State Univ	WA	9,388	C
Washington Univ in St. Louis	MO	34,593	MC
Wayland Baptist Univ	TX	11,271	NC
Wayne State College	NE	6,255	NC
Wayne State Univ	MI	6,720	C
Waynesburg College	PA	17,610	LC
Weber State Univ	UT	6,897	NC
Webster Univ	MO	19,804	VC
Wellesley College	MA	33,394	MC
Wells College	NY	19,350	VC
Wesley College	DE	17,869	C
Wesleyan College	GA	17,050	VC
Wesleyan Univ	CT	3,405	MC
West Chester Univ of Pennsylvania	PA	9,792	VC
West Liberty State College	WV	6,056	LC
West Texas A&M Univ	TX	6,538	C
West Virginia State College	WV	6,264	NC
West Virginia Univ	WV	8,304	C
West Virginia Univ Inst of Technology	WV	7,518	NC
West Virginia Wesleyan College	WV	22,920	C
Western Baptist College	OR	19,700	C+
Western Carolina Univ	NC	5,667	C
Western Conn State Univ	CT	10,074	C
Western Illinois Univ	IL	9,571	C
Western Kentucky Univ	KY	6,834	C
Western Maryland College	MD	26,000	VC
Western Mich Univ	MI	10,016	C
Western New England College	MA	23,882	C
Western New Mexico Univ	NM	5,950	LC
Western Oregon Univ	OR	8,829	C
Western State College of Colo	CO	7,585	LC
Western Washington Univ	WA	8,624	VC
Westfield State College	MA	8,394	C
Westminster College	MO	19,990	C+
Westminster College	PA	22,960	C
Westminster College	UT	17,226	C
Westmont College	CA	29,748	VC
Wheaton College	IL	21,934	HC
Wheaton College	MA	32,940	VC
Wheeling Jesuit Univ	WV	22,660	C
Whitman College	WA	29,086	HC
Whittier College	CA	29,108	C
Whitworth College	WA	23,938	VC
Wichita State Univ	KS	6,879	C
Widener Univ	PA	26,920	C
Wiley College	TX	8,100	LC
Wilkes Univ	PA	25,800	C
Willamette Univ	OR	29,422	VC+
William Carey College	MS	10,150	LC
William Jewell College	MO	17,150	VC
William Paterson Univ of New Jersey	NJ	11,000	LC
William Penn Univ	IA	17,575	C
William Tyndale College	MI	11,150	C
William Woods Univ	MO	19,390	LC
Williams Baptist College	AR	10,750	C
Williams College	MA	32,270	MC
Wilmington College	OH	21,826	C
Wilson College	PA	21,337	LC
Wingate Univ	NC	19,140	C
Winona State Univ	MN	8,570	C
Winston-Salem State Univ	NC	5,927	LC
Winthrop Univ	SC	9,106	C
Wisc Lutheran College	WI	19,216	VC
Wittenberg Univ	OH	28,766	VC
Wofford College	SC	23,995	VC
Woodbury Univ	CA	25,344	LC
Worcester State College	MA	7,901	LC
Wright State Univ	OH	9,141	LC
Xavier Univ	OH	23,880	C
Xavier Univ of Louisiana	LA	17,000	LC
Yale Univ	CT	34,030	MC
Yeshiva Univ	NY	21,400	LC
York College	NE	13,500	C
York College of Pennsylvania	PA	12,550	VC
Youngstown State Univ	OH	9,318	NC

HISTORY OF PHILOSOPHY

School	ST	$IS	SR
Bard College	NY	33,912	HC
Bennington College	VT	31,350	VC
Colo College	CO	31,525	HC+

HISTORY OF SCIENCE

School	ST	$IS	SR
Bard College	NY	33,912	HC
Case Western Reserve Univ	OH	27,418	C
Johns Hopkins Univ	MD	35,226	MC
Univ of Wisc/Madison	WI	8,262	VC
Yale Univ	CT	34,030	MC

HOME ECONOMICS

School	ST	$IS	SR
Alverno College	WI	16,930	LC
Ball State Univ	IN	8,660	C
CUNY/Queens College	NY	3,403	VC
College of the Ozarks	MO	2,650	C+
Colo State Univ	CO	9,672	C
David Lipscomb Univ	TN	16,158	VC
Florida State Univ	FL	7,835	HC
George Fox Univ	OR	24,095	VC
Harding Univ	AR	13,528	VC
Idaho State Univ	ID	7,030	C+
Illinois State Univ	IL	9,235	C
Indiana State Univ	IN	8,461	LC
Langston Univ	OK	2,308	LC
Marygrove College	MI	16,075	C
Marymount College/Tarrytown	NY	23,850	C
Master's College	CA	21,500	C+
Montclair State Univ	NJ	10,287	LC
Morgan State Univ	MD	10,078	LC
Northwest Missouri State Univ	MO	7,922	LC
Oakwood College	AL	14,904	C
Oregon State Univ	OR	9,612	VC
Point Loma Nazarene Univ	CA	21,380	VC
Rice Univ	TX	24,325	MC
Sam Houston State Univ	TX	6,076	LC
Southwest Texas State Univ	TX	8,730	VC
SUNY/College at Oneonta	NY	9,981	C
SUNY/College at Plattsburgh	NY	9,729	C
Stephen F. Austin State Univ	TX	6,905	C
Tarleton State Univ	TX	7,160	C
Texas A&M Univ at Kingsville	TX	6,446	LC
Texas Tech Univ	TX	8,825	C
Texas Woman's Univ	TX	5,855	LC
Univ of Akron	OH	10,530	NC
Univ of Alabama	AL	7,402	C
Univ of Florida	FL	7,874	HC
Univ of Maryland/Eastern Shore	MD	9,258	C
Univ of Tenn at Chattanooga	TN	7,783	C
Utah State Univ	UT	6,771	C
Virginia State Univ	VA	8,182	LC
Washington State Univ	WA	9,388	C
Western Mich Univ	MI	10,016	C
Winthrop Univ	SC	9,106	C
Youngstown State Univ	OH	9,318	NC

HOME ECONOMICS EDUCATION

School	ST	$IS	SR
Abilene Christian Univ	TX	16,300	VC
Alabama A&M Univ	AL	5,100	LC
Ashland Univ	OH	22,182	LC
Auburn Univ	AL	5,510	C
Baldwin-Wallace College	OH	22,010	VC+
Ball State Univ	IN	8,660	C
Baylor Univ	TX	18,298	VC+
Berea College	KY	4,070	VC
Bluffton College	OH	20,644	C
Bowling Green State Univ	OH	10,794	C
Bradley Univ	IL	20,970	VC
Cal State, Northridge	CA	7,781	C
Carson-Newman College	TN	16,490	C
Central Mich Univ	MI	8,355	C
Central Missouri State Univ	MO	7,920	C
Central Washington Univ	WA	8,985	LC
Cheyney Univ of Pennsylvania	PA	9,993	C
CUNY/Queens College	NY	3,403	VC
College of St. Catherine	MN	22,324	VC
Colo State Univ	CO	9,672	C
Concordia College/Moorhead	MN	18,835	C
Concordia Univ Nebr	NE	17,770	C
Delaware State Univ	DE	8,104	LC
East Central Univ	OK	4,578	C
Eastern Kentucky Univ	KY	6,552	C
Eastern New Mexico Univ	NM	4,113	LC
Florida International Univ	FL	9,486	VC

School	ST	$IS	SR
Florida State Univ	FL	7,835	HC
Fort Valley State Univ	GA	6,014	LC
Gallaudet Univ	DC	16,554	SP
George Fox Univ	OR	24,095	VC
Grambling State Univ	LA	5,325	NC
Immaculata College	PA	22,400	LC
Indiana State Univ	IN	8,461	LC
Jacksonville State Univ	AL	6,568	LC
Keene State College	NH	11,280	C
Langston Univ	OK	2,308	LC
Lincoln Univ	MO	7,158	NC
Marshall Univ	WV	7,752	LC
Marymount College/ Tarrytown	NY	23,850	C
Marywood Univ	PA	24,639	C
McNeese State Univ	LA	5,259	LC
Mercyhurst College	PA	20,694	C
Mich State Univ	MI	10,386	VC
Morehead State Univ	KY	6,510	C
Mount Vernon Nazarene College	OH	17,027	C
Murray State Univ	KY	6,672	C
New Mexico State Univ	NM	7,302	C
N Car Agricultural and Technical State Univ	NC	6,659	LC
N Dak State Univ	ND	7,004	VC
Northeastern State Univ	OK	4,704	LC
Northern Illinois Univ	IL	9,545	C
Oakwood College	AL	14,904	C
Ohio Univ	OH	11,769	C
Ouachita Baptist Univ	AR	16,460	VC
Pontifical Catholic Univ of PR/Ponce	PR	7,076	
San Francisco State Univ	CA	7,139	LC
Seattle Pacific Univ	WA	22,674	C+
Seton Hill College	PA	21,875	C
Shepherd College	WV	7,062	LC
S Car State Univ	SC	6,586	LC
S Dak State Univ	SD	6,848	C
Southwest Missouri State Univ	MO	7,600	LC
Southwest Texas State Univ	TX	8,730	VC
SUNY/College at Oneonta	NY	9,981	C
Stephen F. Austin State Univ	TX	6,905	C
Tarleton State Univ	TX	7,160	C
Tenn Tech Univ	TN	6,968	C
Univ of Akron	OH	10,530	NC
Univ of Alabama	AL	7,402	C
Univ of Arizona	AZ	8,614	C
Univ of Arkansas at Pine Bluff	AR	7,925	C
Univ of Idaho	ID	7,026	C
Univ of Louisiana at Lafayette	LA	5,200	C
Univ of Maryland/Eastern Shore	MD	9,258	C
Univ of Minn/Twin Cities	MN	11,123	VC
Univ of Miss	MS	7,666	C
Univ of Montevallo	AL	7,266	C
Univ of Nebr at Kearney	NE	7,048	NC
Univ of Nebr at Lincoln	NE	8,325	C+
Univ of North Alabama	AL	7,016	NC
Univ of N Car at Greensboro	NC	6,858	C
Univ of Southern Miss	MS	6,155	LC
Univ of Tenn at Martin	TN	8,268	C
Univ of Wisc/Stevens Point	WI	7,116	C
Utah State Univ	UT	6,771	C
Virginia Polytechnic Inst and State Univ	VA	7,652	C
Wayne State College	NE	6,255	NC
Western Kentucky Univ	KY	6,834	C
Western Mich Univ	MI	10,016	C
Winthrop Univ	SC	9,106	C
Youngstown State Univ	OH	9,318	NC

HOME FURNISHINGS AND EQUIPMENT MANAGEMENT/ PRODUCTION/SERVICES

School	ST	$IS	SR
Auburn Univ	AL	5,510	C
Fashion Inst of Technology/ SUNY	NY	9,504	C+
High Point Univ	NC	20,220	LC
Univ of Georgia	GA	8,656	VC
Univ of North Texas	TX	7,629	C

HORTICULTURE

School	ST	$IS	SR
Alabama A&M Univ	AL	5,100	LC
Andrews Univ	MI	17,696	LC
Auburn Univ	AL	5,510	C
Berry College	GA	18,850	C
Brigham Young Univ	UT	7,840	HC
Calif Polytechnic State Univ	CA	8,747	VC
Calif State Polytechnic Univ, Pomona	CA	8,615	C
Christopher Newport Univ	VA	8,862	VC
Clemson Univ	SC	7,600	C
College of the Ozarks	MO	2,650	C+
Colo State Univ	CO	9,672	C
Cornell Univ	NY	34,614	MC
Delaware Valley College	PA	24,213	LC
Eastern Kentucky Univ	KY	6,552	C
Florida A&M Univ	FL	6,948	C
Florida Southern College	FL	19,430	C
Fort Valley State Univ	GA	6,014	LC
Iowa State Univ	IA	8,108	VC
Kansas State Univ	KS	6,995	C
Mich State Univ	MI	10,386	VC
Miss State Univ	MS	7,853	C
Montana State Univ-Bozeman	MT	8,431	C
Murray State Univ	KY	6,672	C
New Mexico State Univ	NM	7,302	C
N Car State Univ	NC	8,680	HC
N Dak State Univ	ND	7,004	VC
Northwest Missouri State Univ	MO	7,922	LC
Okla State Univ	OK	7,650	VC
Oregon State Univ	OR	9,612	VC
Penn State Univ/Univ Park Campus	PA	11,126	VC
Purdue Univ/West Lafayette	IN	10,284	VC
Sam Houston State Univ	TX	6,076	LC
S Dak State Univ	SD	6,848	C
Southeast Missouri State Univ	MO	8,367	C+
Southeastern Louisiana Univ	LA	6,047	LC
Southwest Missouri State Univ	MO	7,600	LC
Stephen F. Austin State Univ	TX	6,905	C
Tarleton State Univ	TX	7,160	C
Temple Univ	PA	14,124	C
Texas A&M Univ	TX	8,988	VC
Texas Tech Univ	TX	8,825	C
Thomas Edison State College	NJ	2,750	SP
Tuskegee Univ	AL	14,600	LC
Univ of Arkansas	AR	8,334	VC
Univ of Conn	CT	12,122	VC
Univ of Florida	FL	7,874	HC
Univ of Georgia	GA	8,656	VC
Univ of Hawaii at Manoa	HI	7,862	VC
Univ of Idaho	ID	7,026	C
Univ of Illinois at Urbana-Champaign	IL	11,316	HC+
Univ of Maine	ME	10,798	C
Univ of Maryland/College Park	MD	11,959	C
Univ of Nebr at Lincoln	NE	8,325	C+
Univ of New Hampshire	NH	13,207	C
Univ of PR/Mayaguez	PR	5,285	
Univ of Rhode Island	RI	12,414	C
Univ of Vermont	VT	14,761	C+
Univ of Wisc/Madison	WI	8,262	VC
Univ of Wisc/River Falls	WI	6,356	LC
Virginia Polytechnic Inst and State Univ	VA	7,652	C
Washington State Univ	WA	9,388	C
West Virginia Univ	WV	8,304	C

HOSPICE CARE

School	ST	$IS	SR
Madonna Univ	MI	11,504	VC

HOSPITAL ADMINISTRATION

School	ST	$IS	SR
Indiana Univ Northwest	IN	3,447	C
Ithaca College	NY	28,719	HC
Ohio Univ	OH	11,769	C
Southwest Texas State Univ	TX	8,730	VC
Thomas Edison State College	NJ	2,750	SP

HOSPITALITY MANAGEMENT SERVICES

School	ST	$IS	SR
Appalachian State Univ	NC	6,353	C
Bay Path College	MA	22,308	C
Becker College	MA	21,230	LC
Bowling Green State Univ	OH	10,794	C
Brigham Young Univ/Hawaii	HI	6,890	C
Central Conn State Univ	CT	10,404	C
Champlain College	VT	19,680	C
Chicago State Univ	IL	8,851	C+
Davis and Elkins College	WV	19,270	LC
Delta State Univ	MS	5,416	C
East Carolina Univ	NC	7,766	C
Eastern Mich Univ	MI	9,855	C
Ferris State Univ	MI	10,816	C
Florida International Univ	FL	9,486	VC
Georgia State Univ	GA	7,792	LC
Howard Univ	DC	15,522	LC
Husson College	ME	15,360	LC
James Madison Univ	VA	9,552	HC
Johnson and Wales Univ	RI	21,558	LC
Johnson State College	VT	10,776	C
Kendall College	IL	19,119	LC
Lakeland College	WI	17,950	C
Lasell College	MA	24,100	C
Madonna Univ	MI	11,504	VC
Marywood Univ	PA	24,639	C
Metropolitan State College of Denver	CO	2,338	LC
Metropolitan State Univ	MN	2,943	SP
Morgan State Univ	MD	10,078	LC
Mount Ida College	MA	25,375	LC
New York Inst of Technology	NY	21,756	C
Norfolk State Univ	VA	8,382	LC
Northwestern State Univ of Louisiana	LA	5,745	NC
Northwood Univ	FL	19,179	LC
Northwood Univ	MI	18,360	LC
Nova Southeastern Univ	FL	20,104	LC
Ohio State Univ at Lima	OH	3,603	NC
Philander Smith College	AR	7,380	NC
Robert Morris Univ	PA	18,730	C
St. John's Univ	NY	26,660	C
St. Thomas Univ	FL	19,500	LC
Shepherd College	WV	7,062	LC
Southern New Hampshire Univ	NH	23,852	C
SUNY/College at Buffalo	NY	8,025	C
Stephen F. Austin State Univ	TX	6,905	C
Ohio State Univ	OH	10,819	VC
Tuskegee Univ	AL	14,600	LC
Univ of Akron	OH	10,530	NC
Univ of Central Florida	FL	8,251	VC
Univ of Denver	CO	28,783	VC
Univ of Findlay	OH	23,962	NC
Univ of Memphis	TN	7,271	C
Univ of San Francisco	CA	27,302	VC
Univ of Wisc/Stout	WI	7,192	C
Western Carolina Univ	NC	5,667	C
Widener Univ	PA	26,920	C
Youngstown State Univ	OH	9,318	NC

HOTEL/MOTEL AND RESTAURANT MANAGEMENT

School	ST	$IS	SR
Arkansas Tech Univ	AR	6,256	C
Ashland Univ	OH	22,182	LC
Auburn Univ	AL	5,510	C
Belmont Univ	TN	19,066	VC
Bethune-Cookman College	FL	15,746	C
Black Hills State Univ	SD	6,652	LC
Boston Univ	MA	34,358	MC
Bowling Green State Univ	OH	10,794	C
Calif State Polytechnic Univ, Pomona	CA	8,615	C
Central Missouri State Univ	MO	7,920	C
Champlain College	VT	19,680	C
Cheyney Univ of Pennsylvania	PA	9,993	C
Chicago State Univ	IL	8,851	C+
CUNY/New York City Technical College	NY	3,319	NC
College of the Ozarks	MO	2,650	C+
Colo State Univ	CO	9,672	C
Concord College	WV	7,122	C+
Cornell Univ	NY	34,614	MC
Davenport Univ	MI	10,057	NC
Delaware State Univ	DE	8,104	LC
Drexel Univ	PA	27,657	VC
East Stroudsburg Univ of Pennsylvania	PA	8,430	LC
Endicott College	MA	23,704	C
Fairleigh Dickinson Univ/ Madison campus	NJ	25,500	C
Fairleigh Dickinson Univ/ Teaneck Campus	NJ	24,646	C
Florida Southern College	FL	19,430	C
Florida State Univ	FL	7,835	HC
Georgia Southern Univ	GA	6,958	C
Grambling State Univ	LA	5,325	NC
Grand Valley State Univ	MI	10,040	C
Howard Univ	DC	15,522	LC
Indiana State Univ	IN	8,461	LC
Indiana Univ of Pennsylvania	PA	9,133	C
Iowa State Univ	IA	8,108	VC
Johnson and Wales Univ	RI	21,558	LC
Kansas State Univ	KS	6,995	C
Kendall College	IL	19,119	LC
Keuka College	NY	21,170	C
Lasell College	MA	24,100	C
Lebanon Valley College of Pennsylvania	PA	25,700	VC
Lynn Univ	FL	24,550	C
Mercyhurst College	PA	20,694	C
Moorhead State Univ	MN	7,000	LC
Mountain State Univ	WV	8,180	NC
New Mexico State Univ	NM	7,302	C
New York Univ	NY	35,200	MC
Newbury College	MA	21,490	C
Niagara Univ	NY	22,250	C+
N Car Wesleyan College	NC	15,650	LC
N Dak State Univ	ND	7,004	VC
Northern Arizona Univ	AZ	7,398	C
Northwood Univ	MI	18,360	LC
Northwood Univ	TX	18,135	C
Okla State Univ	OK	7,650	VC
Oregon State Univ	OR	9,612	VC
Penn State Univ/Univ Park Campus	PA	11,126	VC
Purdue Univ/Calumet	IN	6,630	NC
Purdue Univ/West Lafayette	IN	10,284	VC
Rochester Inst of Technology	NY	26,232	VC+
Roosevelt Univ	IL	20,240	LC
St. Thomas Univ	FL	19,500	LC
Siena Heights Univ	MI	16,140	LC
S Dak State Univ	SD	6,848	C
Southern New Hampshire Univ	NH	23,852	C
Southern Vermont College	VT	17,685	C
Southwest Missouri State Univ	MO	7,600	LC
SUNY/College at Plattsburgh	NY	9,729	C
Tenn State Univ	TN	7,058	VC
Texas Tech Univ	TX	8,825	C
Thomas Edison State College	NJ	2,750	SP
Tiffin Univ	OH	17,250	C
United States International Univ	CA	18,675	LC
Univ of Alaska Anchorage	AK	9,100	NC
Univ of Central Okla	OK	5,205	C
Univ of Delaware	DE	10,824	VC
Univ of Houston	TX	8,410	C
Univ of Kentucky	KY	7,765	C
Univ of Louisiana at Lafayette	LA	5,200	C
Univ of Maryland/Eastern Shore	MD	9,258	C
Univ of Mass Amherst	MA	10,995	VC
Univ of Minn/Crookston	MN	9,626	NC
Univ of Missouri/Columbia	MO	9,803	HC
Univ of Nevada/Las Vegas	NV	8,281	VC
Univ of New Hampshire	NH	13,207	C
Univ of New Haven	CT	23,860	LC
Univ of New Orleans	LA	10,160	C
Univ of N Car at Greensboro	NC	6,858	C
Univ of North Texas	TX	7,629	C
Univ of S Car at Columbia	SC	8,748	VC
Univ of Southern Miss	MS	6,155	LC
Univ of Tenn at Knoxville	TN	8,214	C
Univ of the Incarnate Word	TX	18,478	C
Virginia Polytechnic Inst and State Univ	VA	7,652	C
Virginia State Univ	VA	8,182	LC
Washington State Univ	WA	9,388	C
Webber International Univ	FL	14,695	LC
Western Kentucky Univ	KY	6,834	C
Wiley College	TX	8,100	LC
Youngstown State Univ	OH	9,318	NC

HUMAN DEVELOPMENT

School	ST	$IS	SR
Alabama A&M Univ	AL	5,100	LC
Andrews Univ	MI	17,696	LC
Anna Maria College	MA	22,800	LC
Auburn Univ	AL	5,510	C
Bard College	NY	33,912	HC
Becker College	MA	21,230	LC
Boston College	MA	33,330	MC
Brescia Univ	KY	14,225	C
Calif Polytechnic State Univ	CA	8,747	VC
Cal State, Hayward	CA	7,400	LC
Cal State, Long Beach	CA	7,400	LC
Cal State, San Bernardino	CA	6,516	C
Cal State, San Marcos	CA	1,736	LC
Christian Brothers Univ	TN	19,820	VC
Christian Heritage College	CA	18,000	LC
Colo State Univ	CO	9,672	C
Conn College	CT	33,585	MC
Cornell Univ	NY	34,614	MC
East Tenn State Univ	TN	7,127	C
Eckerd College	FL	25,500	C+
Hellenic College/Holy Cross Greek Orthodox School of Theology	MA	17,215	C
Howard Univ	DC	15,522	LC
Indiana Univ Bloomington	IN	10,712	C+
Kalamazoo College	MI	26,955	HC+
Kent State Univ	OH	11,104	C
Lee Univ	TN	10,198	LC
Lynchburg College	VA	23,405	C
Marylhurst Univ	OR	15,343	NC
Miss Univ for Women	MS	5,446	LC
Mitchell College	CT	23,950	C
Montana State Univ-Bozeman	MT	8,431	C
National-Louis Univ	IL	13,995	NC
Northwestern Univ	IL	33,615	MC
Oakwood College	AL	14,904	C
Oregon State Univ	OR	9,612	VC
Penn State Univ/Altoona	PA	12,578	C
Penn State Univ/Univ Park Campus	PA	11,126	VC
Radford Univ	VA	8,302	C
Rivier College	NH	24,215	C
St. Mary's College of Maryland	MD	14,104	HC
Samford Univ	AL	16,340	VC
Sonoma State Univ	CA	8,953	C
S Dak State Univ	SD	6,848	C
Southern Christian Univ	AL	8,480	LC
SUNY/College at Oswego	NY	10,856	C
SUNY/Empire State College	NY	3,545	SP
SUNY/Univ at Binghamton	NY	10,653	HC

ST = STATE $IS = IN-STATE COSTS SR = SELECTOR RATING

School	ST	$IS	SR
Suffolk Univ	MA	26,516	C
Tenn Wesleyan College	TN	13,030	C
Texas Tech Univ	TX	8,825	C
Texas Wesleyan Univ	TX	14,710	C
Ohio State Univ	OH	10,819	VC
Univ of Alabama	AL	7,402	C
Univ of Arkansas	AR	8,334	VC
Univ of Calif at Davis	CA	12,796	VC
Univ of Calif at Riverside	CA	12,479	C
Univ of Calif at San Diego	CA	11,372	HC
Univ of Conn	CT	12,122	VC
Univ of Delaware	DE	10,824	VC
Univ of Houston	TX	8,410	C
Univ of Illinois at Urbana-Champaign	IL	11,316	HC+
Univ of Memphis	TN	7,271	C
Univ of Nebr at Kearney	NE	7,048	NC
Univ of Nebr at Lincoln	NE	8,325	C+
Univ of New England	ME	24,110	LC
Univ of Rhode Island	RI	12,414	C
Univ of Utah	UT	7,703	C
Univ of Vermont	VT	14,761	C+
Univ of Wisc/Green Bay	WI	7,148	C
Utah State Univ	UT	6,771	C
Vanderbilt Univ	TN	34,482	MC
Warner Pacific College	OR	20,370	LC
Washington State Univ	WA	9,388	C
Wayne State Univ	MI	6,720	C
Westminster College	UT	17,226	C
Wheelock College	MA	25,520	C

HUMAN ECOLOGY

School	ST	$IS	SR
Brenau Univ Women's College	GA	20,100	C
College of the Atlantic	ME	26,994	VC+
Ferrum College	VA	15,990	LC
Goddard College	VT	21,056	C+
Kansas State Univ	KS	6,995	C
Lambuth Univ	TN	14,254	C
Montclair State Univ	NJ	10,287	LC
Ramapo College of New Jersey	NJ	13,550	VC
Tenn Tech Univ	TN	6,968	C
Ohio State Univ	OH	10,819	VC
Unity College	ME	19,845	LC
Univ of Calif at Davis	CA	12,796	VC
Univ of Calif at Irvine	CA	11,756	C
Univ of Calif at Los Angeles	CA	13,227	MC
Univ of Nevada/Reno	NV	8,737	C
Univ of Texas at Austin	TX	9,437	HC
Virginia Wesleyan College	VA	22,350	LC
Youngstown State Univ	OH	9,318	NC

HUMAN RESOURCES

School	ST	$IS	SR
American International College	MA	22,268	LC
American Univ	DC	31,544	VC+
Bartlesville Wesleyan College	OK	14,100	LC
Barton College	NC	16,834	LC
Baylor Univ	TX	18,298	VC+
Becker College	MA	21,230	LC
Black Hills State Univ	SD	6,652	LC
Boston College	MA	33,330	MC
Brescia Univ	KY	14,225	C
Briar Cliff Univ	IA	18,657	LC
Cabrini College	PA	25,950	LC
Calif State Polytechnic Univ, Pomona	CA	8,615	C
Cal State, Los Angeles	CA	5,050	C
Carlow College	PA	19,366	C
Catholic Univ of America	DC	29,332	VC
Central Missouri State Univ	MO	7,920	C
Cleary College	MI	10,350	LC
Colo Christian Univ	CO	17,714	C
De Sales Univ	PA	22,610	VC
Defiance College	OH	19,580	LC
Excelsior College	NY	915	SP
Ferris State Univ	MI	10,816	C
Franklin Univ	OH	6,324	SP
George Fox Univ	OR	24,095	VC
George Washington Univ	DC	32,170	HC
Georgia State Univ	GA	7,792	LC
Golden Gate Univ	CA	8,592	NC
Grand Canyon Univ	AZ	30,000	LC
Gwynedd-Mercy College	PA	22,350	C
Harding Univ	AR	13,528	VC
Hawaii Pacific Univ	HI	17,790	C
Holy Names College	CA	23,220	C
Huron Univ	SD	10,450	C
Idaho State Univ	ID	7,030	C+
Indiana Univ of Pennsylvania	PA	9,133	C
Indiana Univ-Purdue Univ Indianapolis	IN	9,473	C
Ithaca College	NY	28,719	HC
Johns Hopkins Univ	MD	35,226	MC
Juniata College	PA	26,080	VC
Kentucky Wesleyan College	KY	15,800	C
Keystone College	PA	19,066	LC
Le Moyne College	NY	23,840	C
Lewis Univ	IL	20,960	C
Limestone College	SC	16,900	C
Lindenwood Univ	MO	17,250	C
Lourdes College	OH	13,100	LC
Marietta College	OH	24,580	C
Marquette Univ	WI	24,836	C+
Marymount Univ	VA	21,560	LC
Medaille College	NY	18,320	C
Metropolitan State Univ	MN	2,943	SP
Montana State Univ-Billings	MT	7,653	NC
Mount Olive College	NC	14,410	LC
Niagara Univ	NY	22,250	C+
Northeastern Univ	MA	30,078	VC
Notre Dame College	OH	20,425	C
Oakland Univ	MI	9,418	C
Ohio Univ	OH	11,769	C
Ohio Valley College	WV	13,650	C+
Our Lady of the Lake Univ of San Antonio	TX	17,336	C
Park Univ	MO	9,816	C
Point Park College	PA	20,290	C
Rider Univ	NJ	27,400	C
Robert Morris Univ	PA	18,730	C
Rockhurst Univ	MO	20,090	C
St. Leo Univ	FL	19,250	LC
St. Louis Univ	MO	26,590	VC+
St. Mary-of-the-Woods College	IN	21,320	LC
St. Mary's Univ of San Antonio	TX	19,735	C
St. Thomas Univ	FL	19,500	LC
Samford Univ	AL	16,340	VC
Silver Lake College of the Holy Family	WI	15,516	LC
Simpson College	CA	19,200	C
Southern Christian Univ	AL	8,480	LC
Southwestern College	KS	17,656	C
SUNY/College at Oswego	NY	10,856	C
SUNY/College at Potsdam	NY	10,519	C
Tarleton State Univ	TX	7,160	C
Temple Univ	PA	14,124	C
Ohio State Univ	OH	10,819	VC
Thomas Edison State College	NJ	2,750	SP
Univ of Arizona	AZ	8,614	C
Univ of Central Okla	OK	5,205	C
Univ of Colo at Boulder	CO	9,255	VC
Univ of Findlay	OH	23,962	NC
Univ of Hawaii at Manoa	HI	7,862	VC
Univ of Maryland/College Park	MD	11,959	C
Univ of Maryland/Univ College	MD	5,910	SP
Univ of Miami	FL	31,130	HC
Univ of Mich/Flint	MI	4,323	C
Univ of Nevada/Las Vegas	NV	8,281	VC
Univ of North Texas	TX	7,629	C
Univ of St. Francis	IN	17,790	LC
Univ of Scranton	PA	27,964	C+
Univ of Texas at San Antonio	TX	9,088	NC
Univ of Wisc/Oshkosh	WI	6,130	LC
Ursuline College	OH	19,430	LC
Valley City State Univ	ND		LC
Viterbo Univ	WI	18,043	C
Washington Univ in St. Louis	MO	34,593	MC
Wichita State Univ	KS	6,879	C
Xavier Univ	OH	23,880	C
York College	NE	13,500	C

HUMAN SERVICES

School	ST	$IS	SR
Adrian College	MI	19,670	C
Alaska Pacific Univ	AK	16,450	C
Albertus Magnus College	CT	22,154	C
Arkansas Baptist College	AR	5,530	LC
Audrey Cohen College	NY	17,715	C
Beacon College	FL	24,900	C
Bethel College	IN	17,650	LC
Bethel College	TN	12,980	C
Black Hills State Univ	SD	6,652	LC
Boricua College	NY	7,375	C
Burlington College	VT	10,640	SP
Cal State, Dominguez Hills	CA	5,840	LC
Cal State, Fullerton	CA	5,440	LC
Cal State, San Bernardino	CA	6,516	C
Cazenovia College	NY	19,885	LC
CUNY/New York City Technical College	NY	3,319	NC
Coe College	IA	24,750	VC
College of Mount St. Joseph	OH	20,290	C
College of St. Joseph	VT	17,400	NC
College of St. Mary	NE	18,726	C
College of Santa Fe	NM	20,250	LC
Dakota Wesleyan Univ	SD	15,512	C
East Central Univ	OK	4,578	C
Eastern New Mexico Univ	NM	4,113	LC
Elmira College	NY	31,070	VC+
Elon Univ	NC	19,430	VC
Fitchburg State College	MA	7,836	C
Florida Gulf Coast Univ	FL	9,201	C
Fontbonne Univ	MO	18,046	C
Friends Univ	KS	15,962	LC
Geneva College	PA	19,990	C+
George Washington Univ	DC	32,170	HC
Georgetown College	KY	18,400	VC
Georgia College and State Univ	GA	7,344	C
Grace Bible College	MI	12,600	C
Graceland Univ	IA	15,845	C
Grand View College	IA	17,596	NC
Hannibal-LaGrange College	MO	12,530	C
Hastings College	NE	17,854	C+
Hawaii Pacific Univ	HI	17,790	C
Henderson State Univ	AR	6,269	C
High Point Univ	NC	20,220	LC
Hilbert College	NY	16,830	LC
Holy Names College	CA	23,220	C
Hope International Univ	CA	16,940	NC
Indiana Inst of Technology	IN	18,806	C
Kendall College	IL	19,119	LC
La Roche College	PA	18,854	LC
LaGrange College	GA	17,496	C
Lake Superior State Univ	MI	9,034	LC
Lasell College	MA	24,100	C
Lenoir-Rhyne College	NC	19,186	C
Lesley College	MA	25,325	LC
Lincoln Univ	PA	11,198	C+
Lindenwood Univ	MO	17,250	C
Lindsey Wilson College	KY	16,392	LC
Lyndon State College	VT	11,313	LC
Lynn Univ	FL	24,550	C
Marian College of Fond du Lac	WI	17,935	LC
Marymount Univ	VA	21,560	LC
Maryville College	TN	23,210	VC
Medaille College	NY	18,320	C
Metropolitan State College of Denver	CO	2,338	LC
Metropolitan State Univ	MN	2,943	SP
Millikin Univ	IL	24,415	C+
Missouri Baptist College	MO	15,762	LC
Missouri Valley College	MO	17,400	LC
Montreat College	NC	17,164	C
Mount Olive College	NC	14,410	LC
Mount St. Mary College	NY	18,825	C
National-Louis Univ	IL	13,995	NC
N Car Central Univ	NC	6,418	LC
Northeastern Univ	MA	30,078	VC
Northern State Univ	SD	6,279	LC
Notre Dame de Namur Univ	CA	26,932	LC
Oglala Lakota College	SD	1,950	NC
Old Dominion Univ	VA	9,386	C
Ottawa Univ	KS	11,800	LC
Park Univ	MO	9,816	C
Pennsylvania College of Technology	PA	12,860	NC
Pfeiffer Univ	NC	18,580	C
Pikeville College	KY	12,000	NC
Quincy Univ	IL	20,450	C
Rockford College	IL	23,930	C
St. John's Univ	NY	26,660	C
St. Joseph's College	IN	21,640	C
St. Joseph's Univ	PA	29,715	VC+
St. Leo Univ	FL	19,250	LC
St. Mary-of-the-Woods College	IN	21,320	LC
St. Mary's College	MI	13,314	LC
St. Mary's Univ of Minn	MN	19,975	C
St. Thomas Univ	FL	19,500	LC
Salem International Univ	WV	17,263	LC
Seton Hill College	PA	21,875	C
Siena Heights Univ	MI	16,140	LC
Simmons College	MA	30,418	VC
Sinte Gleska Univ	SD	2,268	NC
S Car State Univ	SC	6,586	LC
Southern Vermont College	VT	17,685	C
Southwest Baptist Univ	MO	13,426	LC
Springfield College	MA	24,520	C
SUNY/College at Cortland	NY	10,564	C
Suffolk Univ	MA	26,516	C
Tenn Wesleyan College	TN	13,030	C
Texas Southern Univ	TX	6,576	NC
Thomas Edison State College	NJ	2,750	SP
Touro College	NY	14,950	VC
Troy State Univ	AL	7,696	C
Univ of Alaska Anchorage	AK	9,100	NC
Univ of Bridgeport	CT	23,020	C
Univ of Detroit Mercy	MI	21,620	LC
Univ of Great Falls	MT	15,360	C
Univ of Hartford	CT	28,884	C
Univ of Maine at Machias	ME	7,689	LC
Univ of Mass Boston	MA	4,227	C
Univ of Phoenix	AZ	7,000	SP
Univ of Rhode Island	RI	12,414	C
Univ of St. Francis	IN	17,790	LC
Univ of Scranton	PA	27,964	C+
Univ of Tenn at Chattanooga	TN	7,783	C
Univ of Tenn at Knoxville	TN	8,214	C
Univ of Wisc/Oshkosh	WI	6,130	LC
Upper Iowa Univ	IA	17,438	C
Villanova Univ	PA	31,997	HC
Viterbo Univ	WI	18,043	C
Washburn Univ of Topeka	KS	6,766	NC
Wayland Baptist Univ	TX	11,271	NC
Western New Mexico Univ	NM	5,950	LC
Western Washington Univ	WA	8,624	VC
William Penn Univ	IA	17,575	C
Wingate Univ	NC	19,140	C
Woodbury College	VT	12,060	LC
York College	NE	13,500	C

HUMANITIES

School	ST	$IS	SR
Albertus Magnus College	CT	22,154	C
Arizona State Univ-Main	AZ	7,726	C
Aurora Univ	IL	18,551	C
Belhaven College	MS	16,040	C+
Bennington College	VT	31,350	VC
Biola Univ	CA	21,902	VC
Bloomfield College	NJ	17,000	C
Bloomsburg Univ of Pennsylvania	PA	9,434	C
Bluefield State College	WV	2,178	LC
Brigham Young Univ	UT	7,840	HC
Bucknell Univ	PA	31,096	HC
Burlington College	VT	10,640	SP
Cal State, Chico	CA	8,598	LC
Cal State, Northridge	CA	7,781	C
Calif Univ of Pennsylvania	PA	10,388	C
Canisius College	NY	24,696	C+
Chaminade Univ of Honolulu	HI	17,370	C
Charleston Southern Univ	SC	17,122	C
Clarion Univ of Pennsylvania	PA	11,272	LC
Clarkson Univ	NY	29,884	VC
Clearwater Christian College	FL	13,160	LC
Colgate Univ	NY	33,480	MC
College of Mount St. Joseph	OH	20,290	C
College of St. Benedict	MN	23,921	VC
College of St. Mary	NE	18,726	C
College of St. Scholastica	MN	22,378	C+
College of Santa Fe	NM	20,250	LC
Concordia College/Moorhead	MN	18,835	C
Concordia Univ	CA	22,290	C
Concordia Univ	OR	20,500	LC
Concordia Univ Wisc	WI	16,600	LC
Daemen College	NY	20,620	C
Defiance College	OH	19,580	LC
Dominican College	NY	20,400	LC
Dominican Univ of Calif	CA	27,948	C
Dowling College	NY	20,281	LC
Eastern Washington Univ	WA	7,972	LC
Eckerd College	FL	25,500	C+
Edinboro Univ of Pennsylvania	PA	9,328	LC
Fairleigh Dickinson Univ/Madison campus	NJ	25,500	C
Fairleigh Dickinson Univ/Teaneck Campus	NJ	24,646	C
Felician College	NJ	20,050	C
Florida Inst of Technology	FL	25,250	VC
Florida International Univ	FL	9,486	VC
Florida Southern College	FL	19,430	C
Florida State Univ	FL	7,835	HC
Fort Lewis College	CO	7,659	LC
George Washington Univ	DC	32,170	HC
Georgian Court College	NJ	19,040	LC
Guilford College	NC	23,255	C
Hampden-Sydney College	VA	24,871	C
Hampshire College	MA	33,881	HC+
Harvard Univ/Harvard College	MA	34,269	MC
Hawaii Pacific Univ	HI	17,790	C
Hofstra Univ	NY	23,252	C
Holy Family College	PA	13,710	LC
Holy Names College	CA	23,220	C
Houghton College	NY	21,810	VC+
Indiana Univ Kokomo	IN	3,422	LC
Jacksonville Univ	FL	21,110	LC
John Carroll Univ	OH	24,140	VC
Johns Hopkins Univ	MD	35,226	MC
Johnson State College	VT	10,776	C
Juniata College	PA	26,080	VC
Kansas State Univ	KS	6,995	C
Lawrence Tech Univ	MI	11,429	C
Lees-McRae College	NC	17,106	LC
LeMoyne-Owen College	TN	8,450	NC
Lesley College	MA	25,325	LC
Loyola Marymount Univ	CA	28,754	HC
Lubbock Christian Univ	TX	14,226	LC
Lynn Univ	FL	24,550	C
Marshall Univ	WV	7,752	LC
Martin Univ	IN	8,370	SP
MCP Hahnemann Univ	PA	18,510	SP
Medaille College	NY	18,320	C
Messiah College	PA	23,180	VC
Mich State Univ	MI	10,386	VC
Midwestern State Univ	TX	6,704	NC
Milligan College	TN	17,550	C
Minn State Univ, Mankato	MN	7,296	LC
Montana State Univ-Northern	MT	8,600	NC
Montclair State Univ	NJ	10,287	LC
New College of Florida	FL	8,130	HC+
N Dak State Univ	ND	7,004	VC
Northwest Missouri State Univ	MO	7,922	LC
Notre Dame de Namur Univ	CA	26,932	LC
Nova Southeastern Univ	FL	20,104	LC
Oberlin College	OH	33,140	HC+
Okla City Univ	OK	15,810	C

School	ST	$IS	SR
Okla Panhandle State Univ	OK	3,812	NC
Pacific Univ	OR	24,250	C
Pepperdine Univ	CA	32,830	VC
Plymouth State College	NH	11,024	LC
Polytechnic Univ/Brooklyn	NY	33,090	HC
Providence College	RI	27,620	HC
Quincy Univ	IL	20,450	C
Rockford College	IL	23,930	C
Rosemont College	PA	24,060	C
Rutgers, The State Univ of New Jersey New Brunswick Campus	NJ	12,709	C
St. John's Univ	MN	23,640	VC
St. Joseph College	CT	25,960	LC
St. Joseph's Univ	PA	29,715	VC+
St. Louis Univ	MO	26,590	VC+
St. Martin's College	WA	20,566	C
St. Mary-of-the-Woods College	IN	21,320	LC
St. Mary's College	IN	24,474	VC
St. Norbert College	WI	23,169	VC
St. Peter's College	NJ	22,292	LC
Samford Univ	AL	16,340	VC
San Diego State Univ	CA	9,716	C+
San Francisco State Univ	CA	7,139	LC
Schreiner Univ	TX	19,254	C
Scripps College	CA	30,400	HC+
Seattle Univ	WA	24,183	VC
Shawnee State Univ	OH	8,634	NC
Shimer College	IL	17,560	LC
Siena Heights Univ	MI	16,140	LC
Sierra Nevada College-Lake Tahoe	NV	21,060	LC
Southern Methodist Univ	TX	28,349	VC
Southern New Hampshire Univ	NH	23,852	C
Spring Hill College	AL	23,250	C
SUNY/College at Buffalo	NY	8,025	C
SUNY/College at Old Westbury	NY	9,818	LC
SUNY/Maritime College	NY	10,025	LC
SUNY/Univ at Stony Brook	NY	10,998	VC
Stephen F. Austin State Univ	TX	6,905	C
Stetson Univ	FL	25,640	VC
Suffolk Univ	MA	26,516	C
Tabor College	KS	17,600	LC
Texas Wesleyan Univ	TX	14,710	C
Thomas Edison State College	NJ	2,750	SP
Thomas Univ	GA	8,770	NC
Trinity International Univ	IL	20,640	C+
Turabo Univ	PR	4,110	
Union College	NY	32,646	HC
United States Air Force Academy	CO		MC
Universidad Metropolitana	PR	3,324	
Univ of Akron	OH	10,530	NC
Univ of Arizona	AZ	8,614	C
Univ of Calif at Irvine	CA	11,756	C
Univ of Calif at Riverside	CA	12,479	C
Univ of Central Florida	FL	8,251	VC
Univ of Chicago	IL	35,087	MC
Univ of Colo at Boulder	CO	9,255	VC
Univ of Houston-Downtown	TX	2,006	NC
Univ of Illinois at Urbana-Champaign	IL	11,316	HC+
Univ of Kansas	KS	7,232	VC
Univ of Louisville	KY	7,402	LC
Univ of Maryland/Univ College	MD	5,910	SP
Univ of Mich/Ann Arbor	MI	13,003	HC+
Univ of Mich/Dearborn	MI	4,677	VC
Univ of Minn/Twin Cities	MN	11,123	VC
Univ of New Hampshire	NH	13,207	C
Univ of Northern Iowa	IA	7,850	C
Univ of Oregon	OR	9,969	C
Univ of Pennsylvania	PA	34,614	MC
Univ of Pittsburgh at Greensburg	PA	12,842	C
Univ of Pittsburgh at Johnstown	PA	13,044	LC
Univ of Pittsburgh at Pittsburgh	PA	13,592	HC
Univ of PR/Cayey Univ College	PR	1,245	
Univ of Rio Grande	OH	8,728	NC
Univ of San Diego	CA	29,198	HC
Univ of South Florida	FL	8,154	C
Univ of Tenn at Chattanooga	TN	7,783	C
Univ of Texas at Austin	TX	9,437	HC
Univ of Texas at Dallas	TX	9,305	VC
Univ of Texas at San Antonio	TX	9,088	NC
Univ of Toledo	OH	11,206	NC
Univ of Wisc/Green Bay	WI	7,148	C
Univ of Wisc/Madison	WI	8,262	VC
Univ of Wisc/Parkside	WI	6,160	LC
Univ of Wyoming	WY	7,143	LC
Ursuline College	OH	19,430	LC
Virginia Wesleyan College	VA	22,350	LC
Walla Walla College	WA	20,925	C
Warren Wilson College	NC	19,968	C
Washington College	MD	28,040	VC
Washington State Univ	WA	9,388	C
Washington Univ in St. Louis	MO	34,593	MC
Wesleyan College	GA	17,050	VC
Western Baptist College	OR	19,700	C+
Western New Mexico Univ	NM	5,950	LC
Western Oregon Univ	OR	8,829	C
Widener Univ	PA	26,920	C
Willamette Univ	OR	29,422	VC+
Wofford College	SC	23,995	VC
Woodbury Univ	CA	25,344	LC
Worcester Polytechnic Inst	MA	34,480	HC+
Wright State Univ	OH	9,141	LC
Xavier Univ	OH	23,880	C
Yale Univ	CT	34,030	MC
York College of Pennsylvania	PA	12,550	VC

HUMANITIES AND SOCIAL SCIENCE

School	ST	$IS	SR
Antioch College	OH	25,072	LC
Conn College	CT	33,585	MC
Franciscan Univ of Steubenville	OH	19,100	C+
Lock Haven Univ of Pennsylvania	PA	9,534	C
Montana Tech of The Univ of Montana	MT	7,845	C
SUNY/Empire State College	NY	3,545	SP
Univ of Mass Dartmouth	MA	9,852	C
Univ of N Dak	ND	7,067	VC

HYDROLOGY

School	ST	$IS	SR
Univ of Arizona	AZ	8,614	C
Univ of Calif at Davis	CA	12,796	VC
Univ of Calif at Santa Barbara	CA	11,732	VC
Univ of Nevada/Reno	NV	8,737	C
Univ of New Hampshire	NH	13,207	C
Western Mich Univ	MI	10,016	C

ILLUSTRATION

School	ST	$IS	SR
Arcadia Univ	PA	26,650	C
Art Academy of Cincinnati	OH	16,550	SP
Art Center College of Design	CA	21,110	SP
Art Inst of Boston at Lesley Univ	MA	23,685	SP
Art Inst of Southern Calif	CA	14,500	SP
Atlanta College of Art	GA	18,600	SP
Brigham Young Univ	UT	7,840	HC
Calif College of Arts and Crafts	CA	27,366	SP
Cal State, Fullerton	CA	5,440	LC
College For Creative Studies	MI	20,938	SP
College of Visual Arts	MN	12,185	SP
Columbus College of Art and Design	OH	22,210	SP
Fashion Inst of Technology/SUNY	NY	9,504	C+
Kansas City Art Inst	MO	25,880	SP
Kendall College of Art and Design of Ferris State Univ	MI	8,820	SP
Lewis Univ	IL	20,960	C
Maryland Inst College of Art	MD	27,720	SP
Mass College of Art	MA	13,703	SP
Milwaukee Inst of Art and Design	WI	24,388	SP
Minneapolis College of Art and Design	MN	23,560	SP
Montserrat College of Art	MA	20,335	SP
Moore College of Art and Design	PA	23,125	SP
Northern Mich Univ	MI	9,693	C
Olivet College	MI	17,410	C
Otis College of Art and Design	CA	20,290	SP
Pacific Northwest College of Art	OR	16,507	SP
Parsons School of Design	NY	32,242	SP
Rhode Island School of Design	RI	30,227	SP
Ringling School of Art and Design	FL	22,500	SP
Rivier College	NH	24,215	C
Rochester Inst of Technology	NY	26,232	VC+
St. John's Univ	NY	26,660	C
Savannah College of Art and Design	GA	25,075	SP
School of Visual Arts	NY	26,000	SP
Syracuse Univ	NY	30,710	HC
Univ of Bridgeport	CT	23,020	C
Univ of Findlay	OH	23,962	NC
Univ of Hartford	CT	28,884	C
Univ of Mass Dartmouth	MA	9,852	C
Univ of San Francisco	CA	27,302	VC
Univ of the Arts	PA	24,230	SP
Western Conn State Univ	CT	10,074	C

INDUSTRIAL ADMINISTRATION/ MANAGEMENT

School	ST	$IS	SR
Alcorn State Univ	MS	5,594	LC
Aurora Univ	IL	18,551	C
Cal State, Los Angeles	CA	5,050	C
Calif Univ of Pennsylvania	PA	10,388	C
Calumet College of St. Joseph	IN	7,500	LC
Central Mich Univ	MI	8,355	C
Clarion Univ of Pennsylvania	PA	11,272	LC
Clarkson Univ	NY	29,884	VC
Clemson Univ	SC	7,600	C
David N. Myers College	OH	9,475	C
Gardner-Webb Univ	NC	17,400	C
Georgia Southern Univ	GA	6,958	C
Grove City College	PA	12,280	MC
Indiana Univ South Bend	IN	3,515	C
Kent State Univ	OH	11,104	C
Lawrence Tech Univ	MI	11,429	C
LeTourneau Univ	TX	19,020	VC
Metropolitan State College of Denver	CO	2,338	LC
Millikin Univ	IL	24,415	C+
Norfolk State Univ	VA	8,382	LC
Northern State Univ	SD	6,279	LC
Oregon Inst of Technology	OR	8,718	C
Pace Univ	NY	24,200	C
Penn State Univ/Univ Park Campus	PA	11,126	VC
Purdue Univ/West Lafayette	IN	10,284	VC
Rockhurst Univ	MO	20,090	C
Saginaw Valley State Univ	MI	9,465	C
St. Augustine's College	NC	12,990	C+
San Francisco State Univ	CA	7,139	LC
Southwest Missouri State Univ	MO	7,600	LC
Southwestern Okla State Univ	OK	4,801	C
SUNY/College of Technology at Farmingdale	NY	11,269	C
Tri-State Univ-Main Campus	IN	21,200	C
Universidad Politecnica de PR	PR	4,695	
Univ of Alabama	AL	7,402	C
Univ of Alabama at Birmingham	AL	10,110	C
Univ of Arkansas at Little Rock	AR	5,637	NC
Univ of Cincinnati	OH	12,491	LC
Univ of Houston	TX	8,410	C
Univ of Iowa	IA	8,607	C+
Univ of Mass Lowell	MA	9,470	VC
Univ of N Car at Asheville	NC	6,896	VC
Univ of N Car at Chapel Hill	NC	8,789	HC
Univ of N Car at Charlotte	NC	7,254	C
Univ of North Texas	TX	7,629	C
Univ of Southern Colo	CO	7,821	LC
Univ of Wisc/Milwaukee	WI	8,907	LC
Univ of Wisc/Parkside	WI	6,160	LC
Univ of Wisc/Stout	WI	7,192	C
Wentworth Inst of Technology	MA	20,450	C
West Virginia Univ Inst of Technology	WV	7,518	NC
William Penn Univ	IA	17,575	C
Youngstown State Univ	OH	9,318	NC

INDUSTRIAL AND ORGANIZATIONAL PSYCHOLOGY

School	ST	$IS	SR
Albertus Magnus College	CT	22,154	C
Bay Path College	MA	22,308	C
Calif Univ of Pennsylvania	PA	10,388	C
CUNY/Baruch College	NY	3,275	VC+
High Point Univ	NC	20,220	LC
Ithaca College	NY	28,719	HC
Lincoln Univ	PA	11,198	C+
Moravian College	PA	27,065	VC
Nichols College	MA	24,610	LC
Northwest Missouri State Univ	MO	7,922	LC
Oregon Inst of Technology	OR	8,718	C
Point Loma Nazarene Univ	CA	21,380	VC
St. Joseph's Univ	PA	29,715	VC+
St. Mary College	KS	17,298	C
Suffolk Univ	MA	26,516	C
Ohio State Univ	OH	10,819	VC

INDUSTRIAL ARTS EDUCATION

School	ST	$IS	SR
Alabama A&M Univ	AL	5,100	LC
Alcorn State Univ	MS	5,594	LC
Appalachian State Univ	NC	6,353	C
Auburn Univ	AL	5,510	C
Ball State Univ	IN	8,660	C
Bemidji State Univ	MN	7,957	C
Calif Polytechnic State Univ	CA	8,747	VC
Cal State, Los Angeles	CA	5,050	C
Calif Univ of Pennsylvania	PA	10,388	C
Central Mich Univ	MI	8,355	C
Central Missouri State Univ	MO	7,920	C
Central Washington Univ	WA	8,985	LC
Chicago State Univ	IL	8,851	C+
Clemson Univ	SC	7,600	C
College of the Ozarks	MO	2,650	C+
Concordia Univ Nebr	NE	17,770	C
Eastern Kentucky Univ	KY	6,552	C
Eastern Mich Univ	MI	9,855	C
Elizabeth City State Univ	NC	5,550	LC
Fitchburg State College	MA	7,836	C
Florida A&M Univ	FL	6,948	C
Grambling State Univ	LA	5,325	NC
Humboldt State Univ	CA	8,582	C
Indiana State Univ	IN	8,461	LC
Iowa State Univ	IA	8,108	VC
Jackson State Univ	MS	6,776	LC
Kean Univ	NJ	11,159	C
Keene State College	NH	11,280	C
Langston Univ	OK	2,308	LC
Middle Tenn State Univ	TN	6,994	C
Minn State Univ, Mankato	MN	7,296	LC
Montana State Univ-Northern	MT	8,600	NC
Moorhead State Univ	MN	7,000	LC
Morehead State Univ	KY	6,510	C
Murray State Univ	KY	6,672	C
N Car Agricultural and Technical State Univ	NC	6,659	LC
N Car State Univ	NC	8,680	HC
Northeastern State Univ	OK	4,704	LC
Northern Arizona Univ	AZ	7,398	C
Northern Illinois Univ	IL	9,545	C
Northern Kentucky Univ	KY	6,352	NC
Northern Mich Univ	MI	9,693	C
Northern State Univ	SD	6,279	LC
Ohio Univ	OH	11,769	C
Penn State Univ/Univ Park Campus	PA	11,126	VC
Purdue Univ/West Lafayette	IN	10,284	VC
Rhode Island College	RI	8,700	LC
St. Cloud State Univ	MN	7,180	C
San Francisco State Univ	CA	7,139	LC
S Car State Univ	SC	6,586	LC
Southeast Missouri State Univ	MO	8,367	C+
Southwest Missouri State Univ	MO	7,600	LC
Southwestern Okla State Univ	OK	4,801	C
SUNY/College at Buffalo	NY	8,025	C
Tarleton State Univ	TX	7,160	C
Temple Univ	PA	14,124	C
Texas A&M Univ at Commerce	TX	7,326	C
Univ of Arkansas at Pine Bluff	AR	7,925	C
Univ of Central Okla	OK	5,205	C
Univ of Cincinnati	OH	12,491	LC
Univ of Idaho	ID	7,026	C
Univ of Louisiana at Lafayette	LA	5,200	C
Univ of Maryland/Eastern Shore	MD	9,258	C
Univ of Minn/Twin Cities	MN	11,123	VC
Univ of Montana--Western	MT	6,915	NC
Univ of Nebr at Lincoln	NE	8,325	C+
Univ of Southern Miss	MS	6,155	LC
Univ of Wyoming	WY	7,143	LC
Utah State Univ	UT	6,771	C
Wayne State College	NE	6,255	NC
Western Illinois Univ	IL	9,571	C

INDUSTRIAL DESIGN

School	ST	$IS	SR
Arizona State Univ-Main Campus	AZ	7,726	C
Art Center College of Design	CA	21,110	SP
Auburn Univ	AL	5,510	C
Berea College	KY	4,070	VC
Brigham Young Univ	UT	7,840	HC
Calif College of Arts and Crafts	CA	27,366	SP
Cleveland Inst of Art	OH	22,680	SP
College For Creative Studies	MI	20,938	SP
Columbus College of Art and Design	OH	22,210	SP
Georgia Inst of Technology	GA	9,028	HC+
Kean Univ	NJ	11,159	C
Kendall College of Art and Design of Ferris State Univ	MI	8,820	SP
Kent State Univ	OH	11,104	C
Mass College of Art	MA	13,703	SP
Metropolitan State College of Denver	CO	2,338	LC
Milwaukee Inst of Art and Design	WI	24,388	SP
N Car State Univ	NC	8,680	HC
Philadelphia Univ	PA	24,722	C
Pratt Inst	NY	27,550	SP
Purdue Univ/West Lafayette	IN	10,284	VC
Rhode Island School of Design	RI	30,227	SP

ST = STATE $IS = IN-STATE COSTS SR = SELECTOR RATING

School	ST	$IS	SR
Rochester Inst of Technology	NY	26,232	VC+
Savannah College of Art and Design	GA	25,075	SP
Syracuse Univ	NY	30,710	HC
Ohio State Univ	OH	10,819	VC
Univ of Bridgeport	CT	23,020	C
Univ of Illinois at Chicago	IL	10,702	VC
Univ of Illinois at Urbana-Champaign	IL	11,316	HC+
Univ of Mich/Ann Arbor	MI	13,003	HC+
Univ of the Arts	PA	24,230	SP
Wentworth Inst of Technology	MA	20,450	C
Western Mich Univ	MI	10,016	C

INDUSTRIAL ENGINEERING

School	ST	$IS	SR
Andrews Univ	MI	17,696	LC
Arizona State Univ-Main	AZ	7,726	C
Boston Univ	MA	34,358	MC
Bradley Univ	IL	20,970	VC
Calif Polytechnic State Univ	CA	8,747	VC
Calif State Polytechnic Univ, Pomona	CA	8,615	C
Cal State, Fresno	CA	7,762	C
Cal State, Hayward	CA	7,400	LC
Clemson Univ	SC	7,600	C
Cleveland State Univ	OH	10,146	NC
Elizabethtown College	PA	26,000	VC
Florida A&M Univ	FL	6,948	C
Florida International Univ	FL	9,486	VC
Florida State Univ	FL	7,835	HC
Georgia Inst of Technology	GA	9,028	HC+
Hofstra Univ	NY	23,252	C
Indiana Inst of Technology	IN	18,806	C
Johns Hopkins Univ	MD	35,226	MC
Kansas State Univ	KS	6,995	C
Kettering Univ	MI	23,256	HC
Lamar Univ	TX	6,816	LC
Lehigh Univ	PA	32,290	MC
Louisiana State Univ and A&M College	LA	8,014	VC
Louisiana Tech Univ	LA	6,506	C
Mass Maritime Academy	MA	9,969	C
Mercer Univ	GA	24,130	VC
Milwaukee School of Engineering	WI	25,680	VC+
Miss State Univ	MS	7,853	C
Montana State Univ-Bozeman	MT	8,431	C
New Jersey Inst of Technology	NJ	14,690	VC
New Mexico State Univ	NM	7,302	C
New York Inst of Technology	NY	21,756	C
N Car Agricultural and Technical State Univ	NC	6,659	LC
N Car State Univ	NC	8,680	HC
N Dak State Univ	ND	7,004	VC
Northeastern Univ	MA	30,078	VC
Northern Illinois Univ	IL	9,545	C
Northwestern Univ	IL	33,615	MC
Oakland Univ	MI	9,418	C
Ohio Univ	OH	11,769	C
Okla State Univ	OK	7,650	VC
Penn State Univ/Univ Park Campus	PA	11,126	VC
Purdue Univ/West Lafayette	IN	10,284	VC
Rensselaer Polytechnic Inst	NY	33,863	HC+
Rochester Inst of Technology	NY	26,232	VC+
Rutgers, The State Univ of New Jersey New Brunswick Campus	NJ	12,709	C
St. Ambrose Univ	IA	19,994	C
St. Augustine's College	NC	12,990	C+
St. Mary's Univ of San Antonio	TX	19,735	C
San Jose State Univ	CA	8,187	C
S Dak School of Mines and Technology	SD	7,438	C+
Southern Illinois Univ Edwardsville	IL	7,869	LC
Stanford Univ	CA	34,222	MC
SUNY/Univ at Binghamton	NY	10,653	HC
SUNY/Univ at Buffalo	NY	11,033	VC
Tenn Tech Univ	TN	6,968	C
Ohio State Univ	OH	10,819	VC
Universidad Politecnica de PR	PR	4,695	
Univ of Alabama	AL	7,402	C
Univ of Alabama at Huntsville	AL	7,916	VC
Univ of Arizona	AZ	8,614	C
Univ of Arkansas	AR	8,334	VC
Univ of Calif at Berkeley	CA	14,134	MC
Univ of Houston	TX	8,410	C
Univ of Illinois at Urbana-Champaign	IL	11,316	HC+
Univ of Iowa	IA	8,607	C+
Univ of Louisiana at Lafayette	LA	5,200	C
Univ of Louisville	KY	7,402	LC
Univ of Mass Amherst	MA	10,995	VC
Univ of Memphis	TN	7,271	C
Univ of Miami	FL	31,130	HC
Univ of Mich/Ann Arbor	MI	13,003	HC+
Univ of Mich/Dearborn	MI	4,677	VC
Univ of Minn/Duluth	MN	10,436	C
Univ of Minn/Twin Cities	MN	11,123	VC
Univ of Missouri/Columbia	MO	9,803	HC
Univ of Missouri/Rolla	MO	10,034	C
Univ of Missouri/St. Louis	MO	9,966	C
Univ of Nebr at Lincoln	NE	8,325	C+
Univ of New Haven	CT	23,860	LC
Univ of Okla	OK	7,616	VC
Univ of Pittsburgh at Pittsburgh	PA	13,592	HC
Univ of PR/Mayaguez	PR	5,285	
Univ of Rhode Island	RI	12,414	C
Univ of San Diego	CA	29,198	HC
Univ of South Florida	FL	8,154	C
Univ of Southern Colo	CO	7,821	LC
Univ of Tenn at Knoxville	TN	8,214	C
Univ of Toledo	OH	11,206	NC
Univ of Wisc/Madison	WI	8,262	VC
Univ of Wisc/Milwaukee	WI	8,907	LC
Univ of Wisc/Platteville	WI	7,282	C
Utah State Univ	UT	6,771	C
Western Mich Univ	MI	10,016	C
Western New England College	MA	23,882	C
Wichita State Univ	KS	6,879	C
Worcester Polytechnic Inst	MA	34,480	HC+
Youngstown State Univ	OH	9,318	NC

INDUSTRIAL ENGINEERING TECHNOLOGY

School	ST	$IS	SR
Alabama A&M Univ	AL	5,100	LC
Appalachian State Univ	NC	6,353	C
Bemidji State Univ	MN	7,957	C
Berea College	KY	4,070	VC
Bowling Green State Univ	OH	10,794	C
Cal State, Chico	CA	8,598	LC
Cal State, Fresno	CA	7,762	C
Cal State, Los Angeles	CA	5,050	C
Caribbean Univ	PR	3,000	
Central Conn State Univ	CT	10,404	C
Central Missouri State Univ	MO	7,920	C
Chadron State College	NE	6,211	NC
Chicago State Univ	IL	8,851	C+
College of the Ozarks	MO	2,650	C+
Colo State Univ	CO	9,672	C
Columbia Univ/Fu Foundation School of Engineering and Applied Science	NY	35,190	MC
East Carolina Univ	NC	7,766	C
Eastern Illinois Univ	IL	10,101	C
Elizabeth City State Univ	NC	5,550	LC
Fitchburg State College	MA	7,836	C
Georgia Southern Univ	GA	6,958	C
Grand Valley State Univ	MI	10,040	C
Humboldt State Univ	CA	8,582	C
Illinois State Univ	IL	9,235	C
Indiana State Univ	IN	8,461	LC
Indiana Univ-Purdue Univ Fort Wayne	IN	3,166	LC
Iowa State Univ	IA	8,108	VC
Kean Univ	NJ	11,159	C
Keene State College	NH	11,280	C
Kent State Univ	OH	11,104	C
Lamar Univ	TX	6,816	LC
Langston Univ	OK	2,308	LC
Marquette Univ	WI	24,836	C+
McPherson College	KS	17,710	C
Metropolitan State College of Denver	CO	2,338	LC
Middle Tenn State Univ	TN	6,994	C
Millersville Univ of Pennsylvania	PA	10,153	VC
Miss State Univ	MS	7,853	C
Miss Valley State Univ	MS	6,345	C
Morehead State Univ	KY	6,510	C
Morgan State Univ	MD	10,078	LC
Northern Kentucky Univ	KY	6,352	NC
Northern Mich Univ	MI	9,693	C
Northern State Univ	SD	6,279	LC
Northwestern State Univ of Louisiana	LA	5,745	NC
Okla Panhandle State Univ	OK	3,812	NC
Oregon State Univ	OR	9,612	VC
Prairie View A&M Univ	TX	3,172	LC
Purdue Univ/Calumet	IN	6,630	NC
Purdue Univ/West Lafayette	IN	10,284	VC
Rhode Island College	RI	8,700	LC
Southeast Missouri State Univ	MO	8,367	C+
Southeastern Louisiana Univ	LA	6,047	LC
Southern Illinois Univ at Carbondale	IL	8,621	C
Southern Polytechnic State Univ	GA	6,662	C
Southwest Texas State Univ	TX	8,730	VC
Southwestern Okla State Univ	OK	4,801	C
SUNY/College at Buffalo	NY	8,025	C
SUNY/College of Technology at Farmingdale	NY	11,269	C
Sul Ross State Univ	TX	6,582	LC
Tarleton State Univ	TX	7,160	C
Tenn Tech Univ	TN	6,968	C
Texas A&M Univ	TX	8,988	VC
Texas A&M Univ at Kingsville	TX	6,446	LC
Texas Southern Univ	TX	6,576	NC
Texas Tech Univ	TX	8,825	C
Univ of Arkansas at Pine Bluff	AR	7,925	C
Univ of Central Florida	FL	8,251	VC
Univ of Cincinnati	OH	12,491	LC
Univ of Dayton	OH	20,400	VC
Univ of Detroit Mercy	MI	21,620	LC
Univ of Florida	FL	7,874	HC
Univ of Houston	TX	8,410	C
Univ of Houston-Downtown	TX	2,006	NC
Univ of Illinois at Chicago	IL	10,702	VC
Univ of Mass Lowell	MA	9,470	VC
Univ of Nebr at Lincoln	NE	8,325	C+
Univ of New Haven	CT	23,860	LC
Univ of N Dak	ND	7,067	VC
Univ of Northern Iowa	IA	7,850	C
Univ of Rio Grande	OH	8,728	NC
Univ of Southern Maine	ME	10,569	C
Univ of Texas at Arlington	TX	7,192	LC
Univ of Texas at El Paso	TX	5,076	LC
Univ of West Alabama	AL	6,048	C
Univ of Wisc/Platteville	WI	7,282	C
Univ of Wisc/Stout	WI	7,192	C
Utah State Univ	UT	6,771	C
Wayne State Univ	MI	6,720	C
West Virginia Univ Inst of Technology	WV	7,518	NC
Western Carolina Univ	NC	5,667	C
Western Illinois Univ	IL	9,571	C
Western Kentucky Univ	KY	6,834	C
William Penn Univ	IA	17,575	C

INDUSTRIAL HYGIENE

School	ST	$IS	SR
Clarkson Univ	NY	29,884	VC
Doane College	NE	17,600	LC
Oakland Univ	MI	9,418	C
St. Augustine's College	NC	12,990	C+
Univ of Central Okla	OK	5,205	C
Univ of North Alabama	AL	7,016	NC

INFORMATION SCIENCES AND SYSTEMS

School	ST	$IS	SR
Abilene Christian Univ	TX	16,300	VC
Alabama State Univ	AL	6,404	C
Albany State Univ	GA	5,764	C+
Albright College	PA	27,642	C
Alvernia College	PA	20,790	C
Alverno College	WI	16,930	LC
American InterContinental Univ	GA	12,000	NC
American Univ	DC	31,544	VC+
Andrews Univ	MI	17,696	LC
Appalachian State Univ	NC	6,353	C
Aquinas College	MI	20,052	C+
Arizona State Univ-Main	AZ	7,726	C
Asbury College	KY	18,540	VC
Atlantic Union College	MA	34,034	LC
Auburn Univ Montgomery	AL	5,330	NC
Avila College	MO	17,720	C
Azusa Pacific Univ	CA	22,422	VC
Baker Univ	KS	14,780	C+
Bartlesville Wesleyan College	OK	14,100	LC
Barton College	NC	16,834	LC
Bay Path College	MA	22,308	C
Baylor Univ	TX	18,298	VC+
Belhaven College	MS	16,040	C+
Bellarmine Univ	KY	20,440	VC
Bellevue Univ	NE	4,125	NC
Belmont Abbey College	NC	19,630	LC
Bethel College	KS	17,355	C+
Bethune-Cookman College	FL	15,746	C
Bloomfield College	NJ	17,000	C
Boise State Univ	ID	6,531	LC
Boston College	MA	33,330	MC
Boston Univ	MA	34,358	MC
Bowling Green State Univ	OH	10,794	C
Bradley Univ	IL	20,970	VC
Bridgewater College	VA	22,950	C
Brigham Young Univ/Hawaii	HI	6,890	C
Bryant College	RI	25,980	VC
Cabrini College	PA	25,950	LC
Caldwell College	NJ	20,940	LC
Calif Baptist Univ	CA	16,736	C
Calif Lutheran Univ	CA	23,500	LC
Calif State Polytechnic Univ, Pomona	CA	8,615	C
Cal State, Chico	CA	8,598	LC
Cal State, Los Angeles	CA	5,050	C
Cal State, Stanislaus	CA	8,895	C
Calumet College of St. Joseph	IN	7,500	LC
Campbell Univ	NC	16,599	C
Campbellsville Univ	KY	14,340	C
Carlow College	PA	19,366	C
Carnegie Mellon Univ	PA	32,682	MC
Carroll College	WI	21,170	C
Catawba College	NC	19,620	C
Cedar Crest College	PA	25,145	C+
Cedarville Univ	OH	17,553	VC
Central Missouri State Univ	MO	7,920	C
Central Washington Univ	WA	8,985	LC
Champlain College	VT	19,680	C
Chapman Univ	CA	30,218	VC
Chicago State Univ	IL	8,851	C+
Christian Brothers Univ	TN	19,820	VC
Christopher Newport Univ	VA	8,862	VC
CUNY/Baruch College	NY	3,275	VC+
CUNY/Brooklyn College	NY	3,403	LC
CUNY/College of Staten Island	NY	3,358	NC
CUNY/John Jay College of Criminal Justice	NY	3,251	C
CUNY/York College	NY	3,292	NC
Claremont McKenna College	CA	32,700	MC
Clarion Univ of Pennsylvania	PA	11,272	LC
Clarke College	IA	20,625	C+
Clayton College and State Univ	GA	2,322	C+
Cleary College	MI	10,350	LC
Clemson Univ	SC	7,600	C
Cleveland State Univ	OH	10,146	NC
College Misericordia	PA	23,380	LC
College of Charleston	SC	8,350	HC
College of Notre Dame of Maryland	MD	23,100	LC
College of St. Catherine	MN	22,324	VC
College of St. Rose	NY	19,084	C
College of St. Scholastica	MN	22,378	C+
College of Santa Fe	NM	20,250	LC
College of the Ozarks	MO	2,650	C+
Colo State Univ	CO	9,672	C
Columbia College	MO	15,082	C
Columbia College	SC	19,050	LC
Columbia Union College	MD	19,027	C+
Concord College	WV	7,122	C+
Concordia Univ	MI	20,500	C
Covenant College	GA	21,970	C+
Culver-Stockton College	MO	15,400	LC
Cumberland College	KY	14,864	C
Dakota State Univ	SD	6,950	C
Daniel Webster College	NH	24,870	C
David N. Myers College	OH	9,475	C
Delta State Univ	MS	5,416	C
DePaul Univ	IL	23,590	VC
DeVry/New York	NY	0,865	LC
DeVry Univ/Addison (DuPage County)	IL	8,805	LC
DeVry Univ/Alpharetta	GA	8,805	LC
DeVry Univ/Chicago	IL	8,805	LC
DeVry Univ/Colo Springs	CO	9,465	LC
DeVry Univ/Columbus	OH	8,805	LC
DeVry Univ/Crystal City	VA	10,065	C
DeVry Univ/Dallas	TX	8,805	LC
DeVry Univ/Decatur	GA	8,805	LC
DeVry Univ/Denver	CO	9,465	LC
DeVry Univ/Fremont	CA	9,865	C
DeVry Univ/Kansas City	MO	8,805	LC
DeVry Univ/Long Beach	CA	9,140	LC
DeVry Univ/Orlando	FL	9,865	LC
DeVry Univ/Phoenix	AZ	8,805	LC
DeVry Univ/Pomona	CA	9,205	LC
DeVry Univ/Seattle	WA	10,065	LC
DeVry Univ/Tinley Park	IL	8,805	LC
DeVry Univ/West Hills	CA	9,205	LC
Dominican Univ	IL	20,800	C
Dordt College	IA	18,100	C+
Dowling College	NY	20,281	LC
Drake Univ	IA	22,830	VC
Drexel Univ	PA	27,657	VC
Drury Univ	MO	15,250	VC
Duquesne Univ	PA	24,242	C+
D'Youville College	NY	18,704	C
East Tenn State Univ	TN	7,127	C
East Texas Baptist Univ	TX	12,349	LC
Eastern Illinois Univ	IL	10,101	C
Eastern Mich Univ	MI	9,855	C
Eastern New Mexico Univ	NM	4,113	LC
Eastern Washington Univ	WA	7,972	LC
Edgewood College	WI	18,304	C
Elmhurst College	IL	21,750	C
Emporia State Univ	KS	6,198	LC
Excelsior College	NY	915	SP
Fairfield Univ	CT	30,885	HC
Florida Atlantic Univ	FL	8,832	C
Florida Gulf Coast Univ	FL	9,201	C
Florida Inst of Technology	FL	25,250	VC
Florida Southern College	FL	19,430	C
Florida State Univ	FL	7,835	HC
Fontbonne Univ	MO	18,046	C
Fordham Univ	NY	30,710	VC
Fort Hays State Univ	KS	6,294	LC
Fort Lewis College	CO	7,659	LC
Fort Valley State Univ	GA	6,014	LC
Francis Marion Univ	SC	7,682	C
Franklin College of Indiana	IN	19,905	C
Franklin Pierce College	NH	26,125	LC

School	ST	$IS	SR
Freed-Hardeman Univ	TN	14,290	VC
Friends Univ	KS	15,962	LC
Gardner-Webb Univ	NC	17,400	C
George Fox Univ	OR	24,095	VC
George Washington Univ	DC	32,170	HC
Georgia College and State Univ	GA	7,344	C
Georgia Southern Univ	GA	6,958	C
Graceland Univ	IA	15,845	C
Grambling State Univ	LA	5,325	NC
Grand View College	IA	17,596	NC
Gwynedd-Mercy College	PA	22,350	C
Hampton Univ	VA	17,112	C+
Hannibal-LaGrange College	MO	12,530	C
Hartwick College	NY	33,090	C+
Heidelberg College	OH	23,879	C
High Point Univ	NC	20,220	LC
Holy Family College	PA	13,710	LC
Hood College	MD	26,020	VC
Houston Baptist Univ	TX	15,300	LC
Howard Univ	DC	15,522	LC
Humboldt State Univ	CA	8,582	C
Huntington College	IN	15,480	LC
Idaho State Univ	ID	7,030	C+
Illinois College	IL	16,234	C
Illinois Inst of Technology	IL	25,182	HC+
Illinois State Univ	IL	9,235	C
Immaculata College	PA	22,400	LC
Indiana Inst of Technology	IN	18,806	C
Indiana Univ Bloomington	IN	10,712	C+
Indiana Univ East	IN	3,415	C
Indiana Univ Kokomo	IN	3,422	LC
Indiana Univ Northwest	IN	3,447	C
Indiana Univ-Purdue Univ Fort Wayne	IN	3,166	LC
Indiana Univ-Purdue Univ Indianapolis	IN	9,473	C
International College	FL	7,230	NC
Iona College	NY	26,556	C
Ithaca College	NY	28,719	HC
Jacksonville Univ	FL	21,110	LC
James Madison Univ	VA	9,552	HC
Jamestown College	ND	11,310	NC
Johns Hopkins Univ	MD	35,226	MC
Johnson and Wales Univ	RI	21,558	LC
Johnson State College	VT	10,776	C
Juniata College	PA	26,080	VC
Kansas State Univ	KS	6,995	C
Kennesaw State Univ	GA	2,306	LC
Kent State Univ	OH	11,104	C
Keystone College	PA	19,066	LC
King's College	PA	24,680	C
La Roche College	PA	18,854	LC
La Salle Univ	PA	27,890	C
La Sierra Univ	CA	19,260	LC
Lamar Univ	TX	6,816	LC
Le Moyne College	NY	23,840	C
Lehigh Univ	PA	32,290	MC
Limestone College	SC	16,900	C
Lincoln Memorial Univ	TN	12,620	LC
Lincoln Univ	MO	7,158	NC
Lock Haven Univ of Pennsylvania	PA	9,534	C
LIU/Brooklyn Campus	NY	22,290	C
LIU/C.W. Post Campus	NY	25,380	C
Loyola Univ New Orleans	LA	23,506	VC+
Lubbock Christian Univ	TX	14,226	LC
Madonna Univ	MI	11,504	VC
Manhattan College	NY	25,500	VC
Mansfield Univ	PA	9,648	C
Marian College of Fond du Lac	WI	17,935	LC
Marietta College	OH	24,580	C
Marist College	NY	24,756	VC
Marquette Univ	WI	24,836	C+
Marshall Univ	WV	7,752	LC
Marygrove College	MI	16,075	C
Marymount College/ Tarrytown	NY	23,850	C
Marymount Univ	VA	21,560	LC
Maryville Univ of St. Louis	MO	18,680	C
Marywood Univ	PA	24,639	C
Master's College	CA	21,500	C+
McKendree College	IL	18,300	C+
McNeese State Univ	LA	5,259	LC
Medaille College	NY	18,320	C
Mercy College	NY	15,875	LC
Meredith College	NC	17,500	C
Metropolitan State College of Denver	CO	2,338	LC
Metropolitan State Univ	MN	2,943	SP
Middle Tenn State Univ	TN	6,994	C
Midwestern State Univ	TX	6,704	NC
Milligan College	TN	17,550	C
Minn State Univ, Mankato	MN	7,296	LC
Miss State Univ	MS	7,853	C
Missouri Baptist College	MO	15,762	LC
Missouri Southern State College	MO	6,666	C
Missouri Valley College	MO	17,400	LC
Missouri Western State College	MO	6,662	NC
Molloy College	NY	13,940	C
Montana State Univ-Billings	MT	7,653	NC
Moravian College	PA	27,065	VC
Morgan State Univ	MD	10,078	LC

School	ST	$IS	SR
Mount Mercy College	IA	19,390	VC
Mount Olive College	NC	14,410	LC
Mount St. Clare College	IA	19,050	LC
Mount St. Mary College	NY	18,825	C
Mount Union College	OH	21,120	C
National American Univ	SD	13,680	NC
National Univ	CA	7,755	SP
National-Louis Univ	IL	13,995	NC
Nazareth College of Rochester	NY	22,036	VC
Nebr Wesleyan Univ	NE	18,767	VC
Neumann College	PA	22,040	NC
New Jersey Inst of Technology	NJ	14,690	VC
New York Univ	NY	35,200	MC
Newman Univ	KS	14,098	LC
Niagara Univ	NY	22,250	C+
Nicholls State Univ	LA	5,290	NC
N Car Wesleyan College	NC	15,650	LC
Northeastern State Univ	OK	4,704	LC
Northeastern Univ	MA	30,078	VC
Northern Arizona Univ	AZ	7,398	C
Northern Kentucky Univ	KY	6,352	NC
Northern Mich Univ	MI	9,693	C
Northland College	WI	21,435	C+
Northwest Missouri State Univ	MO	7,922	LC
Northwestern State Univ of Louisiana	LA	5,745	NC
Norwich Univ	VT	21,064	LC
Notre Dame College	OH	20,425	C
Notre Dame de Namur Univ	CA	26,932	LC
Nova Southeastern Univ	FL	20,104	LC
Oakland Univ	MI	9,418	C
Oakwood College	AL	14,904	C
Ohio Dominican College	OH	18,100	LC
Okla Baptist Univ	OK	13,878	VC
Okla Christian Univ	OK	16,500	VC
Okla Panhandle State Univ	OK	3,812	NC
Old Dominion Univ	VA	9,386	C
Ottawa Univ	KS	11,800	LC
Our Lady of the Lake Univ of San Antonio	TX	17,336	C
Pace Univ	NY	24,200	C
Park Univ	MO	9,816	C
Peirce College	PA	10,650	C
Pfeiffer Univ	NC	18,580	C
Pittsburg State Univ	KS	6,228	NC
Plymouth State College	NH	11,024	LC
Point Park College	PA	20,290	C
Polytechnic Univ/Brooklyn	NY	33,090	HC
Portland State Univ	OR	11,220	C
Purdue Univ/Calumet	IN	6,630	NC
Purdue Univ/West Lafayette	IN	10,284	VC
Quincy Univ	IL	20,450	C
Radford Univ	VA	8,302	C
Ramapo College of New Jersey	NJ	13,550	VC
Rhode Island College	RI	8,700	LC
Rice Univ	TX	24,325	MC
Richard Stockton College of New Jersey	NJ	12,165	VC
Rider Univ	NJ	27,400	C
Roanoke College	VA	24,689	VC
Robert Morris Univ	PA	18,730	C
Rochester Inst of Technology	NY	26,232	VC+
Rockhurst Univ	MO	20,090	C
Rocky Mountain College	MT	18,113	C
Roger Williams Univ	RI	29,010	C
Roosevelt Univ	IL	20,240	LC
Russell Sage College	NY	23,674	C+
Rutgers, The State Univ of New Jersey/Newark Campus	NJ	6,394	C
St. Augustine's College	NC	12,990	C+
St. Edward's Univ	TX	17,846	C
St. Joseph's Univ	PA	29,715	VC+
St. Leo Univ	FL	19,250	LC
St. Louis Univ	MO	26,590	VC+
St. Mary College	KS	17,298	C
St. Mary-of-the-Woods College	IN	21,320	LC
St. Norbert College	WI	23,169	VC
St. Vincent College	PA	22,942	VC
Salem International Univ	WV	17,263	LC
Salve Regina Univ	RI	26,460	C
San Diego State Univ	CA	9,716	C+
San Francisco State Univ	CA	7,139	LC
Santa Clara Univ	CA	28,371	VC+
Shepherd College	WV	7,062	LC
Shippensburg Univ of Pennsylvania	PA	9,652	C
Siena Heights Univ	MI	16,140	LC
Simpson College	IA	21,200	C+
Slippery Rock Univ	PA	9,152	LC
Southeastern Okla State Univ	OK	4,917	C
Southeastern Univ	DC	8,505	LC
Southern Adventist Univ	TN	15,600	C
Southern New Hampshire Univ	NH	23,852	C
Southern Utah Univ	UT	7,254	C
Southern Wesleyan Univ	SC	17,280	C
Southwest Baptist Univ	MO	13,426	LC

School	ST	$IS	SR
Southwest Missouri State Univ	MO	7,600	LC
Southwest Texas State Univ	TX	8,730	VC
Southwestern Adventist Univ	TX	14,798	C
Southwestern Okla State Univ	OK	4,801	C
Springfield College	MA	24,520	C
SUNY/College at Brockport	NY	10,267	C
SUNY/College at Buffalo	NY	8,025	C
SUNY/College at Oswego	NY	10,856	C
SUNY/College of Technology at Alfred	NY	9,188	C
SUNY/Univ at Albany	NY	10,997	VC
SUNY/Univ at Stony Brook	NY	10,998	VC
Stephen F. Austin State Univ	TX	6,905	C
Stetson Univ	FL	25,640	VC
Strayer Univ	DC	8,789	SP
Suffolk Univ	MA	26,516	C
Susquehanna Univ	PA	27,270	VC
Syracuse Univ	NY	30,710	HC
Tarleton State Univ	TX	7,160	C
Temple Univ	PA	14,124	C
Texas Christian Univ	TX	19,910	C
Texas Wesleyan Univ	TX	14,710	C
Ohio State Univ	OH	10,819	VC
Thomas College	ME	18,915	LC
Thomas Edison State College	NJ	2,750	SP
Tiffin Univ	OH	17,250	C
Towson Univ	MD	11,088	VC
Trevecca Nazarene Univ	TN	15,752	C
Trinity Christian College	IL	19,415	C
Tri-State Univ-Main Campus	IN	21,200	C
Tulane Univ	LA	34,013	HC+
Tusculum College	TN	17,900	LC
Union College	NY	32,646	HC
Univ of Arkansas at Little Rock	AR	5,637	NC
Univ of Calif at Irvine	CA	11,756	C
Univ of Calif at Riverside	CA	12,479	C
Univ of Calif at San Diego	CA	11,372	HC
Univ of Calif at Santa Cruz	CA	13,655	VC
Univ of Central Arkansas	AR	6,388	C
Univ of Charleston	WV	20,640	C
Univ of Cincinnati	OH	12,491	LC
Univ of Colo at Boulder	CO	9,255	VC
Univ of Dayton	OH	20,400	VC
Univ of Delaware	DE	10,824	VC
Univ of Detroit Mercy	MI	21,620	LC
Univ of Hawaii at Manoa	HI	7,862	VC
Univ of Houston	TX	8,410	C
Univ of Houston-Downtown	TX	2,006	NC
Univ of Idaho	ID	7,026	C
Univ of Illinois at Chicago	IL	10,702	VC
Univ of Iowa	IA	8,607	C+
Univ of Louisville	KY	7,402	LC
Univ of Maine at Augusta	ME	3,928	C
Univ of Mary Hardin-Baylor	TX	13,929	C
Univ of Maryland/Baltimore County	MD	12,190	VC
Univ of Maryland/College Park	MD	11,959	C
Univ of Maryland/Univ College	MD	5,910	SP
Univ of Mass Lowell	MA	9,470	VC
Univ of Minn/Crookston	MN	9,626	NC
Univ of Missouri/Kansas City	MO	9,685	VC
Univ of Missouri/Rolla	MO	10,034	C
Univ of Nebr at Kearney	NE	7,048	NC
Univ of Nevada/Reno	NV	8,737	C
Univ of North Alabama	AL	7,016	NC
Univ of N Car at Charlotte	NC	7,254	C
Univ of N Car at Greensboro	NC	6,858	C
Univ of North Florida	FL	8,089	VC
Univ of North Texas	TX	7,629	C
Univ of Northern Colo	CO	8,082	C+
Univ of Northern Iowa	IA	7,850	C
Univ of Okla	OK	7,616	VC
Univ of Phoenix	AZ	7,000	SP
Univ of Pittsburgh at Pittsburgh	PA	13,592	HC
Univ of PR/Bayamon Univ College Campus	PR	1,600	
Univ of PR/Mayaguez	PR	5,285	
Univ of St. Francis	IL	19,650	C
Univ of San Francisco	CA	27,302	VC
Univ of Scranton	PA	27,964	C+
Univ of S Car at Spartanburg	SC	7,318	C+
Univ of Southern Colo	CO	7,821	LC
Univ of Southern Miss	MS	6,155	LC
Univ of Tampa	FL	22,612	C
Univ of Texas at Arlington	TX	7,192	LC
Univ of Texas at San Antonio	TX	9,088	NC
Univ of Texas-Pan American	TX	4,823	C
Univ of the Incarnate Word	TX	18,478	C
Univ of the Pacific	CA	28,255	VC
Univ of Toledo	OH	11,206	NC

School	ST	$IS	SR
Univ of Tulsa	OK	19,090	HC
Univ of Vermont	VT	14,761	C+
Univ of Virginia's College at Wise	VA	8,302	C
Univ of Washington	WA	10,361	VC
Univ of Wisc/Eau Claire	WI	7,032	VC
Univ of Wisc/Green Bay	WI	7,148	C
Univ of Wisc/La Crosse	WI	7,250	VC
Univ of Wisc/Madison	WI	8,262	VC
Univ of Wisc/Stevens Point	WI	7,116	C
Univ of Wisc/Superior	WI	7,051	C+
Utah State Univ	UT	6,771	C
Valdosta State Univ	GA	6,988	C
Valparaiso Univ	IN	23,570	VC+
Villa Julie College	MD	16,026	C
Villanova Univ	PA	31,997	HC
Virginia Commonwealth Univ	VA	9,030	C
Virginia Intermont College	VA	17,510	C
Viterbo Univ	WI	18,043	C
Walla Walla College	WA	20,925	C
Wartburg College	IA	21,165	VC
Washburn Univ of Topeka	KS	6,766	NC
Washington Univ in St. Louis	MO	34,593	MC
Wayne State Univ	MI	6,720	C
Waynesburg College	PA	17,610	LC
Weber State Univ	UT	6,897	NC
Webster Univ	MO	19,804	VC
West Liberty State College	WV	6,056	LC
West Texas A&M Univ	TX	6,538	C
Western Carolina Univ	NC	5,667	C
Western International Univ	AZ	5,800	SP
Western Kentucky Univ	KY	6,834	C
Western Mich Univ	MI	10,016	C
Western New England College	MA	23,882	C
Western Oregon Univ	OR	8,829	C
Westfield State College	MA	8,394	C
Widener Univ	PA	26,920	C
Wilberforce Univ	OH	14,937	LC
Wilkes Univ	PA	25,800	C
William Jewell College	MO	17,150	VC
William Woods Univ	MO	19,390	LC
Woodbury Univ	CA	25,344	LC
Xavier Univ	OH	23,880	C
York College of Pennsylvania	PA	12,550	VC
Youngstown State Univ	OH	9,318	NC

INSTITUTIONAL MANAGEMENT

School	ST	$IS	SR
Bowling Green State Univ	OH	10,794	C
Crichton College	TN	12,680	LC
Felician College	NJ	20,050	C
Johnson and Wales Univ	RI	21,558	LC
N Dak State Univ	ND	7,004	VC
Rockhurst Univ	MO	20,090	C
Southwest Missouri State Univ	MO	7,600	LC

INSURANCE

School	ST	$IS	SR
Ball State Univ	IN	8,660	C
Baylor Univ	TX	18,298	VC+
Cal State, Sacramento	CA	7,488	C
Delta State Univ	MS	5,416	C
Ferris State Univ	MI	10,816	C
Howard Univ	DC	15,522	LC
Illinois State Univ	IL	9,235	C
Indiana State Univ	IN	8,461	LC
Indiana Univ Bloomington	IN	10,712	C+
Indiana Univ-Purdue Univ Indianapolis	IN	9,473	C
Inter-American Univ of PR/ Bayamon Univ College	PR	3,700	
Inter-American Univ of PR/ Fajardo Campus	PR	4,000	
Inter-American Univ of PR/ Ponce Regional College	PR	3,700	
Martin Univ	IN	8,370	SP
Miss State Univ	MS	7,853	C
Northeastern Univ	MA	30,078	VC
Olivet College	MI	17,410	C
Penn State Univ/Univ Park Campus	PA	11,126	VC
Roosevelt Univ	IL	20,240	LC
Southwest Missouri State Univ	MO	7,600	LC
Texas Southern Univ	TX	6,576	NC
Thomas Edison State College	NJ	2,750	SP
Univ of Central Okla	OK	5,205	C
Univ of Florida	FL	7,874	HC
Univ of Hartford	CT	28,884	C
Univ of Louisiana at Monroe	LA	5,207	NC
Univ of Miss	MS	7,666	C
Univ of North Texas	TX	7,629	C
Univ of S Car at Columbia	SC	8,748	VC
Western Mich Univ	MI	10,016	C

ST = STATE **$IS** = IN-STATE COSTS **SR** = SELECTOR RATING

INSURANCE AND RISK MANAGEMENT

School	ST	$IS	SR
Appalachian State Univ	NC	6,353	C
Bradley Univ	IL	20,970	VC
Drake Univ	IA	22,830	VC
Eastern Mich Univ	MI	9,855	C
Excelsior College	NY	915	SP
Florida State Univ	FL	7,835	HC
Georgia State Univ	GA	7,792	LC
Illinois Wesleyan Univ	IL	26,970	HC
Mercyhurst College	PA	20,694	C
Roosevelt Univ	IL	20,240	LC
St. John's Univ	NY	26,660	C
Southwestern Adventist Univ	TX	14,798	C
Univ of Central Arkansas	AR	6,388	C
Univ of Conn	CT	12,122	VC
Univ of Memphis	TN	7,271	C
Univ of Pennsylvania	PA	34,614	MC
Univ of Wisc/Madison	WI	8,262	VC
Washington State Univ	WA	9,388	C

INTERDISCIPLINARY STUDIES

School	ST	$IS	SR
Adams State College	CO	7,468	C
Alfred Univ	NY	27,212	C+
American Univ	DC	31,544	VC+
Amherst College	MA	34,340	MC
Andrews Univ	MI	17,696	LC
Angelo State Univ	TX	7,028	C
Antioch College	OH	25,072	LC
Appalachian State Univ	NC	6,353	C
Aquinas College	MI	20,052	C+
Arizona State Univ-Main	AZ	7,726	C
Austin College	TX	22,150	VC+
Austin Peay State Univ	TN	5,814	LC
Bard College	NY	33,912	HC
Baylor Univ	TX	18,298	VC+
Beloit College	WI	27,482	HC
Bennett College	NC	11,200	C
Bennington College	VT	31,350	VC
Bentley College	MA	31,060	HC
Berry College	GA	18,850	C
Bloomfield College	NJ	17,000	C
Bluefield College	VA	14,200	C
Boise State Univ	ID	6,531	LC
Boston Univ	MA	34,358	MC
Bowie State Univ	MD	9,300	C+
Brigham Young Univ/Hawaii	HI	6,890	C
Bryn Athyn College of the New Church	PA	10,590	NC
Bucknell Univ	PA	31,096	HC
Calif Lutheran Univ	CA	23,500	LC
Cal State, Dominguez Hills	CA	5,840	LC
Cal State, Long Beach	CA	7,400	LC
Cal State, Los Angeles	CA	5,050	C
Cascade College	OR	14,800	NC
Centenary College	NJ	22,430	C
Central Methodist College	MO	16,460	C
Chatham College	PA	25,454	C+
Christian Heritage College	CA	18,000	LC
Christopher Newport Univ	VA	8,862	VC
CUNY/Queens College	NY	3,403	VC
Clayton College and State Univ	GA	2,322	C+
Coastal Carolina Univ	SC	9,220	C
Coe College	IA	24,750	VC
College Misericordia	PA	23,380	LC
College of Notre Dame of Maryland	MD	23,100	LC
College of St. Rose	NY	19,084	C
College of the Ozarks	MO	2,650	C+
College of William and Mary	VA	10,002	MC
College of Wooster	OH	28,350	VC
Columbia College	MO	15,082	C
Concordia College	NY	19,200	VC
Cornerstone Univ and Grand Rapids Baptist Seminary	MI	18,092	C
Covenant College	GA	21,970	C+
Dallas Baptist Univ	TX	13,682	LC
Dana College	NE	18,046	C
Davidson College	NC	30,823	MC
DePauw Univ	IN	28,000	HC
East Tenn State Univ	TN	7,127	C
Eastern Mich Univ	MI	9,855	C
Emerson College	MA	29,978	HC
Emory & Henry College	VA	19,462	C
Ferrum College	VA	15,990	LC
Florida Atlantic Univ	FL	8,832	C
Florida Inst of Technology	FL	25,250	VC
Friends World Program	NY	26,240	C
Geneva College	PA	19,990	C+
George Mason Univ	VA	9,192	C
George Washington Univ	DC	32,170	HC
Georgetown Univ	DC	34,847	MC
Georgia State Univ	GA	7,792	LC
Goddard College	VT	21,056	C+
Gonzaga Univ	WA	24,276	HC+
Goucher College	MD	30,650	VC+
Grace Bible College	MI	12,600	C
Hendrix College	AR	18,463	HC
Heritage College	WA	6,450	NC
Hofstra Univ	NY	23,252	C
Hollins Univ	VA	24,328	VC
Hope International Univ	CA	16,940	NC
Indiana State Univ	IN	8,461	LC
International College	FL	7,230	NC
Ithaca College	NY	28,719	HC
John Brown Univ	AR	15,080	VC
Johns Hopkins Univ	MD	35,226	MC
Judson College	AL	13,790	C
Kalamazoo College	MI	26,955	HC+
Lafayette College	PA	32,655	MC
Lambuth Univ	TN	14,254	C
Lander Univ	SC	8,618	LC
Lees-McRae College	NC	17,106	LC
LeTourneau Univ	TX	19,020	VC
Lewis and Clark College	OR	29,010	VC
Liberty Univ	VA	14,500	C
Lyndon State College	VT	11,313	LC
Manchester College	IN	22,010	C
Marist College	NY	24,756	VC
Marlboro College	VT	26,410	VC+
Marquette Univ	WI	24,836	C+
Marylhurst Univ	OR	15,343	NC
Marymount College/Tarrytown	NY	23,850	C
Mass College of Liberal Arts	MA	8,717	LC
McMurry Univ	TX	15,287	C
Mercy College	NY	15,875	LC
Miami Univ	OH	12,885	VC+
Middle Tenn State Univ	TN	6,994	C
Midwestern State Univ	TX	6,704	NC
Miss State Univ	MS	7,853	C
Molloy College	NY	13,940	C
Monmouth Univ	NJ	24,042	C
Montana State Univ-Northern	MT	8,600	NC
Mount St. Clare College	IA	19,050	LC
Mount St. Mary College	NY	18,825	C
Mount St. Mary's College	MD	25,740	C
Mountain State Univ	WV	8,180	NC
Naropa Univ	CO	22,416	SP
National Univ	CA	7,755	SP
New York Inst of Technology	NY	21,756	C
Norfolk State Univ	VA	8,382	LC
N Car State Univ	NC	8,680	HC
Northeastern Univ	MA	30,078	VC
Northwest Christian College	OR	19,680	LC
Northwest College	WA	17,471	C
Nyack College	NY	18,540	C
Ohio Dominican College	OH	18,100	LC
Old Dominion Univ	VA	9,386	C
Palm Beach Atlantic College	FL	23,310	C
Plymouth State College	NH	11,024	LC
Prairie View A&M Univ	TX	3,172	LC
Radford Univ	VA	8,302	C
Rensselaer Polytechnic Inst	NY	33,863	HC+
Rhodes College	TN	26,466	HC+
Rice Univ	TX	24,325	MC
Rochester College	MI	15,404	C+
Russell Sage College	NY	23,674	C+
Saginaw Valley State Univ	MI	9,465	C
St. John Fisher College	NY	21,800	C
St. Lawrence Univ	NY	32,605	VC
St. Mary College	KS	17,298	C
Salisbury Univ	MD	10,570	VC
San Francisco State Univ	CA	7,139	LC
Santa Clara Univ	CA	28,371	VC+
Shawnee State Univ	OH	8,634	NC
Sheldon Jackson College	AK	14,940	LC
Shippensburg Univ of Pennsylvania	PA	9,652	C
Simon's Rock College of Bard	MA	32,450	HC
S Dak School of Mines and Technology	SD	7,438	C+
Southeastern College	FL	11,648	LC
Southern Utah Univ	UT	7,254	C
Southwest State Univ	MN	7,117	LC
Southwest Texas State Univ	TX	8,730	VC
SUNY/College at Brockport	NY	10,267	C
SUNY/College at Fredonia	NY	10,125	C
SUNY/College at Oneonta	NY	9,981	C
SUNY/College at Plattsburgh	NY	9,729	C
SUNY/College at Potsdam	NY	10,519	C
SUNY/Empire State College	NY	3,545	SP
SUNY/Univ at Binghamton	NY	10,653	HC
SUNY/Univ at Stony Brook	NY	10,998	VC
Stephen F. Austin State Univ	TX	6,905	C
Stonehill College	MA	26,852	HC
Tarleton State Univ	TX	7,160	C
Temple Univ	PA	14,124	C
Tenn Wesleyan College	TN	13,030	C
Texas Wesleyan Univ	TX	14,710	C
Texas Woman's Univ	TX	5,855	LC
Touro College	NY	14,950	VC
Towson Univ	MD	11,088	VC
Trinity College	CT	34,300	HC
Union College	NY	32,646	HC
Unity College	ME	19,845	LC
Univ of Alabama	AL	7,402	C
Univ of Alaska Anchorage	AK	9,100	NC
Univ of Alaska Fairbanks	AK	8,265	NC
Univ of Arizona	AZ	8,614	C
Univ of Bridgeport	CT	23,020	C
Univ of Calif at Los Angeles	CA	13,227	MC
Univ of Calif at Santa Barbara	CA	11,732	VC
Univ of Colo at Denver	CO	3,673	C
Univ of Delaware	DE	10,824	VC
Univ of Florida	FL	7,874	HC
Univ of Georgia	GA	8,656	VC
Univ of Hartford	CT	28,884	C
Univ of Houston	TX	8,410	C
Univ of Houston-Downtown	TX	2,006	NC
Univ of Idaho	ID	7,026	C
Univ of Maine at Augusta	ME	3,928	C
Univ of Maine at Farmington	ME	9,163	C
Univ of Maryland/Baltimore County	MD	12,190	VC
Univ of Mass Amherst	MA	10,995	VC
Univ of Mass Dartmouth	MA	9,852	C
Univ of Memphis	TN	7,271	C
Univ of Minn/Duluth	MN	10,436	C
Univ of Nebr at Omaha	NE	6,867	C
Univ of Nevada/Las Vegas	NV	8,281	VC
Univ of N Dak	ND	7,067	VC
Univ of North Texas	TX	7,629	C
Univ of Northern Colo	CO	8,082	C+
Univ of Portland	OR	24,950	VC
Univ of PR/Rio Piedras	PR	5,510	
Univ of Richmond	VA	27,300	HC
Univ of Science and Arts of Okla	OK	5,245	C
Univ of S Car at Aiken	SC	7,828	LC
Univ of S Car at Columbia	SC	8,748	VC
Univ of S Car at Spartanburg	SC	7,318	C+
Univ of Texas at Arlington	TX	7,192	LC
Univ of Texas at Dallas	TX	9,305	VC
Univ of Texas at San Antonio	TX	9,088	NC
Univ of Texas-Pan American	TX	4,823	C
Univ of Virginia	VA	9,391	HC+
Vanderbilt Univ	TN	34,482	MC
Villa Julie College	MD	16,026	C
Virginia Intermont College	VA	17,510	C
Virginia State Univ	VA	8,182	LC
Virginia Wesleyan College	VA	22,350	LC
Washington and Lee Univ	VA	25,095	MC
Wayland Baptist Univ	TX	11,271	NC
Wayne State College	NE	6,255	NC
Weber State Univ	UT	6,897	NC
Wesleyan College	GA	17,050	VC
West Liberty State College	WV	6,056	LC
West Texas A&M Univ	TX	6,538	C
West Virginia Univ	WV	8,304	C
Western Mich Univ	MI	10,016	C
Western Oregon Univ	OR	8,829	C
Westfield State College	MA	8,394	C
Wheaton College	IL	21,934	HC
William Woods Univ	MO	19,390	LC
Wisc Lutheran College	WI	19,216	VC
Woodbury College	VT	12,060	LC
Worcester Polytechnic Inst	MA	34,480	HC+

INTERIOR DESIGN

School	ST	$IS	SR
Adrian College	MI	19,670	C
American InterContinental Univ	GA	12,000	NC
Appalachian State Univ	NC	6,353	C
Arcadia Univ	PA	26,650	C
Arizona State Univ-Main	AZ	7,726	C
Art Inst of Atlanta	GA	20,624	SP
Art Inst of Portland	OR	13,725	SP
Atlanta College of Art	GA	18,600	SP
Auburn Univ	AL	5,510	C
Baker College of Flint	MI	7,720	NC
Bay Path College	MA	22,308	C
Baylor Univ	TX	18,298	VC+
Becker College	MA	21,230	LC
Bethel College	IN	17,650	LC
Boston Architectural Center	MA	6,405	SP
Bowling Green State Univ	OH	10,794	C
Brenau Univ Women's College	GA	20,100	C
Calif College of Arts and Crafts	CA	27,366	SP
Cal State, Fresno	CA	7,762	C
Cazenovia College	NY	19,885	LC
Central Missouri State Univ	MO	7,920	C
Chaminade Univ of Honolulu	HI	17,370	C
College For Creative Studies	MI	20,938	SP
College of Mount St. Joseph	OH	20,290	C
Colo State Univ	CO	9,672	C
Columbus College of Art and Design	OH	22,210	SP
Concordia Univ Wisc	WI	16,600	LC
Converse College	SC	21,990	VC
Drexel Univ	PA	27,657	VC
East Carolina Univ	NC	7,766	C
Eastern Kentucky Univ	KY	6,552	C
Eastern Mich Univ	MI	9,855	C
Endicott College	MA	23,704	C
Fashion Inst of Technology/SUNY	NY	9,504	C+
Florida International Univ	FL	9,486	VC
Florida State Univ	FL	7,835	HC
Georgia Southern Univ	GA	6,958	C
Harding Univ	AR	13,528	VC
High Point Univ	NC	20,220	LC
Indiana State Univ	IN	8,461	LC
Indiana Univ Bloomington	IN	10,712	C+
Indiana Univ of Pennsylvania	PA	9,133	C
Iowa State Univ	IA	8,108	VC
Kansas State Univ	KS	6,995	C
Kean Univ	NJ	11,159	C
Kendall College of Art and Design of Ferris State Univ	MI	8,820	SP
Kent State Univ	OH	11,104	C
La Roche College	PA	18,854	LC
Louisiana State Univ and A&M College	LA	8,014	VC
Maryland Inst College of Art	MD	27,720	SP
Marymount College/Tarrytown	NY	23,850	C
Marymount Univ	VA	21,560	LC
Maryville Univ of St. Louis	MO	18,680	C
Mercyhurst College	PA	20,694	C
Meredith College	NC	17,500	C
Miami Univ	OH	12,885	VC+
Mich State Univ	MI	10,386	VC
Middle Tenn State Univ	TN	6,994	C
Milwaukee Inst of Art and Design	WI	24,388	SP
Minn State Univ, Mankato	MN	7,296	LC
Miss College	MS	14,574	C
Moore College of Art and Design	PA	23,125	SP
Mount Ida College	MA	25,375	LC
Mount Mary College	WI	18,024	C
New York Inst of Technology	NY	21,756	C
Newbury College	MA	21,490	C
N Dak State Univ	ND	7,004	VC
Ohio Univ	OH	11,769	C
Okla Christian Univ	OK	16,500	VC
Park Univ	MO	9,816	C
Parsons School of Design	NY	32,242	SP
Philadelphia Univ	PA	24,722	C
Pratt Inst	NY	27,550	SP
Purdue Univ/West Lafayette	IN	10,284	VC
Rhode Island School of Design	RI	30,227	SP
Ringling School of Art and Design	FL	22,500	SP
Rochester Inst of Technology	NY	26,232	VC+
Salem College	NC	23,065	VC
Samford Univ	AL	16,340	VC
San Francisco State Univ	CA	7,139	LC
San Jose State Univ	CA	8,187	C
Savannah College of Art and Design	GA	25,075	SP
School of the Art Inst of Chicago	IL	27,000	SP
School of Visual Arts	NY	26,000	SP
S Dak State Univ	SD	6,848	C
Southeast Missouri State Univ	MO	8,367	C+
Southern Illinois Univ at Carbondale	IL	8,621	C
Southwest Missouri State Univ	MO	7,600	LC
Southwest Texas State Univ	TX	8,730	VC
Stephen F. Austin State Univ	TX	6,905	C
Suffolk Univ	MA	26,516	C
Syracuse Univ	NY	30,710	HC
Texas A&M Univ at Kingsville	TX	6,446	LC
Texas Christian Univ	TX	19,910	C
Texas Tech Univ	TX	8,825	C
Univ of Alabama	AL	7,402	C
Univ of Arkansas	AR	8,334	VC
Univ of Bridgeport	CT	23,020	C
Univ of Central Arkansas	AR	6,388	C
Univ of Central Okla	OK	5,205	C
Univ of Charleston	WV	20,640	C
Univ of Florida	FL	7,874	HC
Univ of Georgia	GA	8,656	VC
Univ of Houston	TX	8,410	C
Univ of Idaho	ID	7,026	C
Univ of Louisiana at Lafayette	LA	5,200	C
Univ of Mich/Ann Arbor	MI	13,003	HC+
Univ of Minn/Twin Cities	MN	11,123	VC
Univ of Nevada/Las Vegas	NV	8,281	VC
Univ of Nevada/Reno	NV	8,737	C
Univ of New Haven	CT	23,860	LC
Univ of North Alabama	AL	7,016	NC
Univ of North Texas	TX	7,629	C
Univ of Okla	OK	7,616	VC
Univ of Oregon	OR	9,969	C
Univ of Tenn at Knoxville	TN	8,214	C

ST = STATE $IS = IN-STATE COSTS   SR = SELECTOR RATING

School	ST	$IS	SR
Univ of Tenn at Martin	TN	8,268	C
Univ of Texas at Arlington	TX	7,192	LC
Univ of Texas at Austin	TX	9,437	HC
Univ of Texas at San Antonio	TX	9,088	NC
Univ of the Incarnate Word	TX	18,478	C
Univ of Wisc/Madison	WI	8,262	VC
Univ of Wisc/Stevens Point	WI	7,116	C
Ursuline College	OH	19,430	LC
Utah State Univ	UT	6,771	C
Valdosta State Univ	GA	6,988	C
Virginia Polytechnic Inst and State Univ	VA	7,652	C
Washington State Univ	WA	9,388	C
Wentworth Inst of Technology	MA	20,450	C
West Virginia Univ	WV	8,304	C
Western Carolina Univ	NC	5,667	C
Western Kentucky Univ	KY	6,834	C
Western Mich Univ	MI	10,016	C
Woodbury Univ	CA	25,344	LC

INTERNATIONAL AGRICULTURE

School	ST	$IS	SR
Cornell Univ	NY	34,614	MC
Eastern Mennonite Univ	VA	20,700	VC
Iowa State Univ	IA	8,108	VC
MidAmerica Nazarene Univ	KS	16,960	C
Univ of Calif at Davis	CA	12,796	VC
Utah State Univ	UT	6,771	C

INTERNATIONAL BUSINESS MANAGEMENT

School	ST	$IS	SR
Adams State College	CO	7,468	C
Adrian College	MI	19,670	C
Alaska Pacific Univ	AK	16,450	C
Albertson College of Idaho	ID	23,900	VC
Alma College	MI	22,586	VC
Alverno College	WI	16,930	LC
American International College	MA	22,268	LC
American Univ	DC	31,544	VC+
Aquinas College	MI	20,052	C+
Arkansas State Univ	AR	7,480	C
Assumption College	MA	26,320	C
Auburn Univ	AL	5,510	C
Augsburg College	MN	22,978	C
Avila College	MO	17,720	C
Baker Univ	KS	14,780	C+
Barry Univ	FL	24,100	LC
Bay Path College	MA	22,308	C
Baylor Univ	TX	18,298	VC+
Bellarmine Univ	KY	20,440	VC
Benedictine Univ	IL	21,330	C
Berkeley College	NY	21,545	LC
Berkeley College of New York City	NY	12,500	LC
Bethune-Cookman College	FL	15,746	C
Birmingham-Southern College	AL	22,960	C
Blackburn College	IL	13,690	C
Boston Univ	MA	34,358	MC
Bowling Green State Univ	OH	10,794	C
Bradley Univ	IL	20,970	VC
Brigham Young Univ/Hawaii	HI	6,890	C
Buena Vista Univ	IA	22,828	C
Butler Univ	IN	25,580	VC+
Caldwell College	NJ	20,940	LC
Calif State Polytechnic Univ, Pomona	CA	8,615	C
Cal State, Fullerton	CA	5,440	LC
Cal State, Long Beach	CA	7,400	LC
Cal State, Los Angeles	CA	5,050	C
Cal State, Sacramento	CA	7,488	C
Cal State, San Bernardino	CA	6,516	C
Campbell Univ	NC	16,599	C
Cardinal Stritch Univ	WI	17,620	C
Carlow College	PA	19,366	C
Catawba College	NC	19,620	C
Central College	IA	21,206	C
Central Conn State Univ	CT	10,404	C
Central Washington Univ	WA	8,985	LC
Champlain College	VT	19,680	C
Chatham College	PA	25,454	C+
Christopher Newport Univ	VA	8,862	VC
Clarion Univ of Pennsylvania	PA	11,272	LC
College of New Jersey	NJ	13,425	HC
College of Notre Dame of Maryland	MD	23,100	LC
College of Our Lady of the Elms	MA	20,644	C
College of St. Scholastica	MN	22,378	C+
College of the Ozarks	MO	2,650	C+
Concordia College/Moorhead	MN	18,835	C
Cornell College	IA	24,980	VC
Creighton Univ	NE	23,476	VC
Dickinson College	PA	32,210	VC+
Dominican College	NY	20,400	LC
Dominican Univ	IL	20,800	C
Dominican Univ of Calif	CA	27,948	C
Dowling College	NY	20,281	LC

School	ST	$IS	SR
Drake Univ	IA	22,830	VC
Drury Univ	MO	15,250	VC
Duquesne Univ	PA	24,242	C+
D'Youville College	NY	18,704	C
Eastern Mennonite Univ	VA	20,700	VC
Eastern Mich Univ	MI	9,855	C
Eckerd College	FL	25,500	C+
Elizabethtown College	PA	26,000	VC
Elmhurst College	IL	21,750	C
Elmira College	NY	31,070	VC+
Excelsior College	NY	915	SP
Fairfield Univ	CT	30,885	HC
Ferris State Univ	MI	10,816	C
Ferrum College	VA	15,990	LC
Florida Atlantic Univ	FL	8,832	C
Florida International Univ	FL	9,486	VC
Florida Southern College	FL	19,430	C
Florida State Univ	FL	7,835	HC
Fordham Univ	NY	30,710	VC
Friends Univ	KS	15,962	LC
Gannon Univ	PA	18,848	C
Gardner-Webb Univ	NC	17,400	C
George Washington Univ	DC	32,170	HC
Georgetown College	KY	18,400	VC
Georgetown Univ	DC	34,847	MC
Golden Gate Univ	CA	8,592	NC
Goldey-Beacom College	DE	11,440	C
Graceland Univ	IA	15,845	C
Grand Canyon Univ	AZ	30,000	LC
Grand Valley State Univ	MI	10,040	C
Grove City College	PA	12,280	MC
Gustavus Adolphus College	MN	24,190	VC+
Gwynedd-Mercy College	PA	22,350	C
Hamline Univ	MN	23,339	C+
Harding Univ	AR	13,528	VC
Hawaii Pacific Univ	HI	17,790	C
High Point Univ	NC	20,220	LC
Hillsdale College	MI	20,586	VC+
Hofstra Univ	NY	23,252	C
Howard Univ	DC	15,522	LC
Illinois State Univ	IL	9,235	C
Illinois Wesleyan Univ	IL	26,970	HC
Indiana Univ of Pennsylvania	PA	9,133	C
Iowa State Univ	IA	8,108	VC
Iowa Wesleyan College	IA	18,840	C
Ithaca College	NY	28,719	HC
Jacksonville Univ	FL	21,110	LC
James Madison Univ	VA	9,552	HC
Johnson and Wales Univ	RI	21,558	LC
Judson College	IL	18,980	LC
Juniata College	PA	26,080	VC
King's College	PA	24,680	C
Kutztown Univ of Pennsylvania	PA	8,907	C
La Roche College	PA	18,854	LC
La Sierra Univ	CA	19,260	LC
Lake Erie College	OH	21,350	LC
Lakeland College	WI	17,950	C
Lasell College	MA	24,100	C
Lebanon Valley College of Pennsylvania	PA	25,700	VC
Lenoir-Rhyne College	NC	19,186	C
Linfield College	OR	25,840	VC
Loras College	IA	22,994	C+
Lourdes College	OH	13,100	LC
Loyola Univ New Orleans	LA	23,506	VC+
Madonna Univ	MI	11,504	VC
Maine Maritime Academy	ME	10,911	C
Manchester College	IN	22,010	C
Manhattan College	NY	25,500	VC
Mansfield Univ	PA	9,648	C
Marietta College	OH	24,580	C
Marquette Univ	WI	24,836	C+
Marymount College/Tarrytown	NY	23,850	C
Marymount Univ	VA	21,560	LC
Marywood Univ	PA	24,639	C
Mass Maritime Academy	MA	9,969	C
Menlo College	CA	24,000	LC
Meredith College	NC	17,500	C
Merrimack College	MA	25,725	VC
Messiah College	PA	23,180	VC
Metropolitan State Univ	MN	2,943	SP
Millikin Univ	IL	24,415	C+
Milwaukee School of Engineering	WI	25,680	VC+
Minn State Univ, Mankato	MN	7,296	LC
Minot State Univ	ND	5,466	LC
Missouri Southern State College	MO	6,666	C
Moorhead State Univ	MN	7,000	LC
Moravian College	PA	27,065	VC
Mount Union College	OH	21,120	C
Muskingum College	OH	18,760	C
Nebr Wesleyan Univ	NE	18,767	VC
Neumann College	PA	22,040	NC
New Mexico State Univ	NM	7,302	C
New York Univ	NY	35,200	MC
Newbury College	MA	21,490	C
North Central College	IL	22,944	C+
North Park Univ	IL	24,030	C
Northeastern Univ	MA	30,078	VC
Northern State Univ	SD	6,279	LC
Northwest Missouri State Univ	MO	7,922	LC

School	ST	$IS	SR
Northwest Nazarene Univ	ID	18,380	C
Northwestern College	MN	19,816	C+
Northwood Univ	FL	19,179	LC
Northwood Univ	MI	18,360	LC
Northwood Univ	TX	18,135	C
Notre Dame de Namur Univ	CA	26,932	LC
Ohio Dominican College	OH	18,100	LC
Ohio Northern Univ	OH	27,765	VC
Ohio Univ	OH	11,769	C
Ohio Wesleyan Univ	OH	29,670	VC+
Okla State Univ	OK	7,650	VC
Old Dominion Univ	VA	9,386	C
Olivet College	MI	17,410	C
Oral Roberts Univ	OK	18,490	C
Pace Univ	NY	24,200	C
Palm Beach Atlantic College	FL	23,310	C
Penn State Univ/Univ Park Campus	PA	11,126	VC
Pepperdine Univ	CA	32,830	VC
Philadelphia Univ	PA	24,722	C
Quinnipiac Univ	CT	27,370	C
Ramapo College of New Jersey	NJ	13,550	VC
Regis Univ	CO	25,740	C+
Rider Univ	NJ	27,400	C
Rochester Inst of Technology	NY	26,232	VC+
Roger Williams Univ	RI	29,010	C
Rollins College	FL	31,223	HC
Sacred Heart Univ	CT	26,588	VC
St. Andrews Presbyterian College	NC	19,720	LC
St. Augustine's College	NC	12,990	C+
St. Cloud State Univ	MN	7,180	C
St. Edward's Univ	TX	17,846	C
St. Joseph's College	IN	21,640	C
St. Louis Univ	MO	26,590	VC+
St. Mary College	KS	17,298	C
St. Mary's Univ of Minn	MN	19,975	C
St. Mary's Univ of San Antonio	TX	19,735	C
St. Norbert College	WI	23,169	VC
St. Peter's College	NJ	22,292	LC
St. Thomas Univ	FL	19,500	LC
St. Xavier Univ	IL	21,104	C
Salem College	NC	23,065	VC
Samford Univ	AL	16,340	VC
San Diego State Univ	CA	9,716	C+
San Francisco State Univ	CA	7,139	LC
San Jose State Univ	CA	4,717	C
Seattle Univ	WA	24,183	VC
Seton Hill College	PA	21,875	C
Simpson College	IA	21,200	C+
Slippery Rock Univ	PA	9,152	LC
Southern Adventist Univ	TN	15,600	C
Southern New Hampshire Univ	NH	23,852	C
Southwest Texas State Univ	TX	8,730	VC
Spring Hill College	AL	23,250	C
SUNY/College at Brockport	NY	10,267	C
Stephen F. Austin State Univ	TX	6,905	C
Stetson Univ	FL	25,640	VC
Strayer Univ	DC	8,789	SP
Suffolk Univ	MA	26,516	C
Taylor Univ	IN	21,562	VC+
Temple Univ	PA	14,124	C
Texas A&M Univ at Galveston	TX	7,269	C+
Texas Christian Univ	TX	19,910	C
Texas Tech Univ	TX	8,825	C
Texas Wesleyan Univ	TX	14,710	C
Ohio State Univ	OH	10,819	VC
Thiel College	PA	18,419	LC
Thomas Edison State College	NJ	2,750	SP
United States International Univ	CA	18,675	LC
Univ of Akron	OH	10,530	NC
Univ of Arkansas	AR	8,334	VC
Univ of Bridgeport	CT	23,020	C
Univ of Colo at Boulder	CO	9,255	VC
Univ of Denver	CO	28,783	VC
Univ of Evansville	IN	22,865	VC+
Univ of Findlay	OH	23,962	NC
Univ of Georgia	GA	8,656	VC
Univ of Hawaii at Manoa	HI	7,862	VC
Univ of Indianapolis	IN	20,840	C
Univ of La Verne	CA	24,280	C
Univ of Maryland/College Park	MD	11,959	C
Univ of Memphis	TN	7,271	C
Univ of Miami	FL	31,130	HC
Univ of Miss	MS	7,666	C
Univ of Nebr at Lincoln	NE	8,325	C+
Univ of Nevada/Las Vegas	NV	8,281	VC
Univ of New Haven	CT	23,860	LC
Univ of New Mexico	NM	8,026	C
Univ of N Car at Charlotte	NC	7,254	C
Univ of Okla	OK	7,616	VC
Univ of Portland	OR	24,950	VC
Univ of Rio Grande	OH	8,728	NC
Univ of St. Thomas	MN	24,044	VC
Univ of San Francisco	CA	27,302	VC

School	ST	$IS	SR
Univ of Scranton	PA	27,964	C+
Univ of Southern Miss	MS	6,155	LC
Univ of Tampa	FL	22,612	C
Univ of Tenn at Martin	TN	8,268	C
Univ of Texas at San Antonio	TX	9,088	NC
Univ of Texas-Pan American	TX	4,823	C
Univ of the Incarnate Word	TX	18,478	C
Univ of Tulsa	OK	19,090	HC
Univ of Vermont	VT	14,761	C+
Univ of Washington	WA	10,361	VC
Univ of Wisc/La Crosse	WI	7,250	VC
Utah State Univ	UT	6,771	C
Valparaiso Univ	IN	23,570	VC+
Vanguard Univ of Southern Calif	CA	20,212	C
Wartburg College	IA	21,165	VC
Washington and Jefferson College	PA	26,255	VC
Washington State Univ	WA	9,388	C
Washington Univ in St. Louis	MO	34,593	MC
Waynesburg College	PA	17,610	LC
Webber International Univ	FL	14,695	LC
Wesleyan College	GA	17,050	VC
Western Carolina Univ	NC	5,667	C
Western International Univ	AZ	5,800	SP
Western New Mexico Univ	NM	5,950	LC
Western Washington Univ	WA	8,624	VC
Westminster College	MO	19,990	C+
Westminster College	PA	22,960	C
Wheeling Jesuit Univ	WV	22,660	C
Whitworth College	WA	23,938	VC
Wichita State Univ	KS	6,879	C
Widener Univ	PA	26,920	C
William Jewell College	MO	17,150	VC
Woodbury Univ	CA	25,344	LC
Xavier Univ	OH	23,880	C
York College of Pennsylvania	PA	12,550	VC

INTERNATIONAL ECONOMICS

School	ST	$IS	SR
Albertson College of Idaho	ID	23,900	VC
Assumption College	MA	26,320	C
Austin College	TX	22,150	VC+
Blackburn College	IL	13,690	C
Carthage College	WI	23,670	C
Catholic Univ of America	DC	29,332	VC
College of St. Catherine	MN	22,324	VC
Colo College	CO	31,525	HC+
Franklin Pierce College	NH	26,125	LC
Georgia Southern Univ	GA	6,958	C
Hiram College	OH	27,034	VC
Kent State Univ	OH	11,104	C
La Salle Univ	PA	27,890	C
Lafayette College	PA	32,655	MC
Louisiana State Univ and A&M College	LA	8,014	VC
Middlebury College	VT	34,300	MC
Midwestern State Univ	TX	6,704	NC
Pontifical Catholic Univ of PR/Ponce	PR	7,076	
St. Norbert College	WI	23,169	VC
Southwestern Adventist Univ	TX	14,798	C
SUNY/College at Oswego	NY	10,856	C
State Univ of West Georgia	GA	7,101	C
Suffolk Univ	MA	26,516	C
Texas Christian Univ	TX	19,910	C
Texas Tech Univ	TX	8,825	C
Univ of Calif at Los Angeles	CA	13,227	MC
Univ of Calif at Santa Cruz	CA	13,655	VC
Univ of Maryland/College Park	MD	11,959	C
Univ of Puget Sound	WA	28,285	HC
Valparaiso Univ	IN	23,570	VC+
Washington Univ in St. Louis	MO	34,593	MC
Youngstown State Univ	OH	9,318	NC

INTERNATIONAL PUBLIC SERVICE

School	ST	$IS	SR
Baylor Univ	TX	18,298	VC+
Christopher Newport Univ	VA	8,862	VC
Lehigh Univ	PA	32,290	MC
Valparaiso Univ	IN	23,570	VC+

INTERNATIONAL RELATIONS

School	ST	$IS	SR
Abilene Christian Univ	TX	16,300	VC
Agnes Scott College	GA	24,950	VC
Alverno College	WI	16,930	LC
American International College	MA	22,268	LC
Augsburg College	MN	22,978	C
Augustana College	SD	20,760	VC
Baldwin-Wallace College	OH	22,010	VC+
Beloit College	WI	27,482	HC
Bennington College	VT	31,350	VC
Bethel College	MN	22,740	VC
Birmingham-Southern College	AL	22,960	C

School	ST	$IS	SR
Boston Univ	MA	34,358	MC
Brown Univ	RI	34,973	MC
Bucknell Univ	PA	31,096	HC
Cal State, Chico	CA	8,598	LC
Cal State, Sacramento	CA	7,488	C
Canisius College	NY	24,696	C+
Capital Univ	OH	23,630	C
Carleton College	MN	30,780	MC
Carroll College	MT	19,140	C
Carroll College	WI	21,170	C
Centre College	KY	24,000	HC
Chaminade Univ of Honolulu	HI	17,370	C
Chatham College	PA	25,454	C+
Christopher Newport Univ	VA	8,862	VC
CUNY/Herbert H. Lehman College	NY	3,320	LC
CUNY/Hunter College	NY	5,147	C+
Claremont McKenna College	CA	32,700	MC
Clark Univ	MA	29,170	HC
Cleveland State Univ	OH	10,146	NC
Colgate Univ	NY	33,480	MC
College of Notre Dame of Maryland	MD	23,100	LC
College of St. Catherine	MN	22,324	VC
College of William and Mary	VA	10,002	MC
College of Wooster	OH	28,350	VC
Concordia College/Moorhead	MN	18,835	C
Conn College	CT	33,585	MC
Cornell College	IA	24,980	VC
Dana College	NE	18,046	C
Dominican Univ	IL	20,800	C
Drake Univ	IA	22,830	VC
Duquesne Univ	PA	24,242	C+
Eastern Mich Univ	MI	9,855	C
Eastern Washington Univ	WA	7,972	LC
Eckerd College	FL	25,500	C+
Edgewood College	WI	18,304	C
Florida International Univ	FL	9,486	VC
Florida State Univ	FL	7,835	HC
George Washington Univ	DC	32,170	HC
Georgetown Univ	DC	34,847	MC
Georgia Inst of Technology	GA	9,028	HC+
Gettysburg College	PA	32,070	HC
Goucher College	MD	30,650	VC+
Grand Valley State Univ	MI	10,040	C
Hamilton College	NY	34,150	HC
Hamline Univ	MN	23,339	C+
Hampshire College	MA	33,881	HC+
Hawaii Pacific Univ	HI	17,790	C
Hendrix College	AR	18,463	HC
Hobart and William Smith Colleges	NY	33,195	VC
Hope College	MI	22,922	C+
Houghton College	NY	21,810	VC+
Howard Univ	DC	15,522	LC
Illinois College	IL	16,234	C
Immaculata College	PA	22,400	LC
Iona College	NY	26,556	C
Iowa State Univ	IA	8,108	VC
Kalamazoo College	MI	26,955	HC+
Kent State Univ	OH	11,104	C
Knox College	IL	28,230	HC
Lafayette College	PA	32,655	MC
Lake Forest College	IL	27,400	VC
Lambuth Univ	TN	14,254	C
Lawrence Univ	WI	27,711	HC
Lehigh Univ	PA	32,290	MC
Lewis and Clark College	OR	29,010	VC
Lincoln Univ	PA	11,198	C+
Luther College	IA	23,300	VC+
Lynchburg College	VA	23,405	C
Macalester College	MN	28,814	HC+
Marquette Univ	WI	24,836	C+
Marshall Univ	WV	7,752	LC
Mary Baldwin College	VA	23,440	C
Mary Washington College	VA	9,032	VC+
Maryville College	TN	23,210	VC
McKendree College	IL	18,300	C+
Miami Univ	OH	12,885	VC+
Mich State Univ	MI	10,386	VC
Middle Tenn State Univ	TN	6,994	C
Middlebury College	VT	34,300	MC
Mills College	CA	27,950	C
Morehouse College	GA	19,814	C
Mount Holyoke College	MA	34,128	HC
Muskingum College	OH	18,760	C
North Park Univ	IL	24,030	C
Northeastern Univ	MA	30,078	VC
Northern Arizona Univ	AZ	7,398	C
Occidental College	CA	32,288	HC
Ohio Univ	OH	11,769	C
Ohio Wesleyan Univ	OH	29,670	VC+
Oral Roberts Univ	OK	18,490	C
Penn State Univ/Univ Park Campus	PA	11,126	VC
Pitzer College	CA	33,930	HC
Pomona College	CA	33,960	MC
Princeton Univ	NJ	35,072	MC
Principia College	IL	23,865	C+
Purdue Univ/Calumet	IN	6,630	NC
Randolph-Macon College	VA	24,395	C
Randolph-Macon Woman's College	VA	25,820	VC+
Roanoke College	VA	21,680	VC
Rockhurst Univ	MO	20,090	C
Rollins College	FL	31,223	HC
St. Cloud State Univ	MN	7,180	C
St. Joseph's Univ	PA	29,715	VC+
St. Mary's Univ of San Antonio	TX	19,735	C
St. Thomas Univ	FL	19,500	LC
Salem College	NC	23,065	VC
Samford Univ	AL	16,340	VC
San Francisco State Univ	CA	7,139	LC
Seton Hall Univ	NJ	26,910	LC
Shaw Univ	NC	12,810	C
Shawnee State Univ	OH	8,634	NC
Simmons College	MA	30,418	VC
Simpson College	IA	21,200	C+
Southern Illinois Univ at Carbondale	IL	8,621	C
Southwest Texas State Univ	TX	8,730	VC
Southwestern Adventist Univ	TX	14,798	C
Stanford Univ	CA	34,222	MC
SUNY/College at Geneseo	NY	9,970	HC
SUNY/Univ at New Paltz	NY	9,685	VC
Sweet Briar College	VA	25,310	VC
Syracuse Univ	NY	30,710	HC
Trinity Univ	TX	21,444	HC
Troy State Univ	AL	7,696	C
Tufts Univ	MA	34,874	MC
United States International Univ	CA	18,675	LC
Univ of Arkansas	AR	8,334	VC
Univ of Calif at Davis	CA	12,796	VC
Univ of Colo at Boulder	CO	9,255	VC
Univ of Delaware	DE	10,824	VC
Univ of Idaho	ID	7,026	C
Univ of Indianapolis	IN	20,840	C
Univ of Memphis	TN	7,271	C
Univ of Minn/Twin Cities	MN	11,123	VC
Univ of Nebr at Lincoln	NE	8,325	C+
Univ of Nevada/Reno	NV	8,737	C
Univ of Northern Colo	CO	8,082	C+
Univ of Pennsylvania	PA	34,614	MC
Univ of Redlands	CA	29,246	VC
Univ of San Diego	CA	29,198	HC
Univ of Scranton	PA	27,964	C+
Univ of S Car at Columbia	SC	8,748	VC
Univ of South Florida	FL	8,154	C
Univ of Southern Calif	CA	33,647	MC
Univ of the Pacific	CA	28,255	VC
Univ of Toledo	OH	11,206	NC
Univ of Virginia	VA	9,391	HC+
Univ of Washington	WA	10,361	VC
Univ of Wisc/Madison	WI	8,262	VC
Ursinus College	PA	31,350	VC
Utah State Univ	UT	6,771	C
Virginia Wesleyan College	VA	22,350	LC
Wartburg College	IA	21,165	VC
Washington Univ in St. Louis	MO	34,593	MC
Webster Univ	MO	19,804	VC
Wellesley College	MA	33,394	MC
Wesleyan College	GA	17,050	VC
Westminster College	PA	22,960	C
Wheaton College	MA	32,940	VC
Widener Univ	PA	26,020	C
William Jewell College	MO	17,150	VC
Winona State Univ	MN	8,570	C
Wittenberg Univ	OH	28,766	VC
Wright State Univ	OH	9,141	LC
Xavier Univ	OH	23,880	C

INTERNATIONAL STUDIES

School	ST	$IS	SR
Adrian College	MI	19,670	C
Albion College	MI	25,224	VC
Allegheny College	PA	27,780	VC
American Univ	DC	31,544	VC+
Aquinas College	MI	20,052	C+
Arkansas Tech Univ	AR	6,256	C
Ashland Univ	OH	22,182	LC
Assumption College	MA	26,320	C
Auburn Univ Montgomery	AL	5,330	NC
Augustana College	SD	20,760	VC
Austin College	TX	22,150	VC+
Azusa Pacific Univ	CA	22,422	VC
Barry Univ	FL	24,100	LC
Bay Path College	MA	22,308	C
Benedictine Univ	IL	21,330	C
Bentley College	MA	31,060	HC
Berry College	GA	18,850	C
Bethany College	WV	18,566	C
Bethel College	IN	17,650	LC
Bethune-Cookman College	FL	15,746	C
Bowling Green State Univ	OH	10,794	C
Bradley Univ	IL	20,970	VC
Brenau Univ Women's College	GA	20,100	C
Bridgewater College	VA	22,950	C
Brigham Young Univ/Hawaii	HI	6,890	C
Bryant College	RI	25,980	VC
Butler Univ	IN	25,580	VC+
Calif Lutheran Univ	CA	23,500	LC
Cal State, Hayward	CA	7,400	LC
Cal State, Long Beach	CA	7,400	LC
Cal State, Monterey Bay	CA	6,250	LC
Calif Univ of Pennsylvania	PA	10,388	C
Case Western Reserve Univ	OH	27,418	C
Cedarville Univ	OH	17,553	VC
Centenary College	NJ	22,430	C
Central College	IA	21,206	C
Central Conn State Univ	CT	10,404	C
CUNY/City College	NY	3,309	LC
CUNY/College of Staten Island	NY	3,358	NC
Clark Univ	MA	29,170	HC
Colby College	ME	34,290	MC
College of New Jersey	NJ	13,425	HC
College of New Rochelle	NY	20,000	C
College of Our Lady of the Elms	MA	20,644	C
College of St. Elizabeth	NJ	22,510	C
College of the Holy Cross	MA	32,780	MC
College of William and Mary	VA	10,002	MC
Columbia Univ/Barnard College	NY	33,694	MC
Concordia College	NY	19,200	VC
Denison Univ	OH	29,640	HC
DePaul Univ	IL	23,590	VC
Dickinson College	PA	32,210	VC+
Doane College	NE	17,600	LC
Dominican Univ of Calif	CA	27,948	C
Drexel Univ	PA	27,657	VC
Drury Univ	MO	15,250	VC
Eastern Illinois Univ	IL	10,101	C
Elmira College	NY	31,070	VC+
Elon Univ	NC	19,430	VC
Emory Univ	GA	33,792	MC
Evangel Univ	MO	14,050	C
Fairleigh Dickinson Univ/Teaneck Campus	NJ	24,646	C
Ferrum College	VA	15,990	LC
Fordham Univ	NY	30,710	VC
Francis Marion Univ	SC	7,682	C
Frostburg State Univ	MD	9,680	C
Gannon Univ	PA	18,848	C
George Fox Univ	OR	24,095	VC
Georgia Southern Univ	GA	6,958	C
Gonzaga Univ	WA	24,276	HC+
Gordon College	MA	23,594	VC+
Goucher College	MD	30,650	VC+
Graceland Univ	IA	15,845	C
Guilford College	NC	23,255	C
Hampshire College	MA	33,881	HC+
Hanover College	IN	17,560	VC
Harding Univ	AR	13,528	VC
Hawaii Pacific Univ	HI	17,790	C
Heidelberg College	OH	23,879	C
High Point Univ	NC	20,220	LC
Hollins Univ	VA	24,328	VC
Huntingdon College	AL	18,400	VC
Idaho State Univ	ID	7,030	C+
Illinois Wesleyan Univ	IL	26,970	HC
Indiana Univ Bloomington	IN	10,712	C+
Indiana Univ of Pennsylvania	PA	9,133	C
Jacksonville Univ	FL	21,110	LC
James Madison Univ	VA	9,552	HC
John Brown Univ	AR	15,080	VC
Johns Hopkins Univ	MD	35,226	MC
Juniata College	PA	26,080	VC
Kalamazoo College	MI	26,955	HC+
Kennesaw State Univ	GA	2,306	LC
Kenyon College	OH	32,130	HC+
La Roche College	PA	18,854	LC
Le Moyne College	NY	23,840	C
Lees-McRae College	NC	17,106	LC
Lindenwood Univ	MO	17,250	C
Lock Haven Univ of Pennsylvania	PA	9,534	C
LIU/C.W. Post Campus	NY	25,380	C
Loras College	IA	22,994	C+
Louisiana State Univ and A&M College	LA	8,014	VC
Lycoming College	PA	24,780	C
Manhattanville College	NY	28,730	VC
Mansfield Univ	PA	9,648	C
Marlboro College	VT	26,410	VC+
Mars Hill College	NC	18,600	LC
Marymount College/Tarrytown	NY	23,850	C
Marymount Manhattan College	NY	23,195	VC
Meredith College	NC	17,500	C
Methodist College	NC	19,526	C
Miami Univ	OH	12,885	VC+
Middlebury College	VT	34,300	MC
Millersville Univ of Pennsylvania	PA	10,153	VC
Millikin Univ	IL	24,415	C+
Missouri Southern State College	MO	6,666	C
Mount Mary College	WI	18,024	C
Mount Mercy College	IA	19,390	VC
Mount St. Mary College	NY	18,825	C
Mount St. Mary's College	MD	25,740	C
Mount Union College	OH	21,120	C
Muhlenberg College	PA	28,170	HC
National Univ	CA	7,755	SP
Nazareth College of Rochester	NY	22,036	VC
Nebr Wesleyan Univ	NE	18,767	VC
New College of Florida	FL	8,130	HC+
Niagara Univ	NY	22,250	C+
N Dak State Univ	ND	7,004	VC
Northern Kentucky Univ	KY	6,352	NC
Northern Mich Univ	MI	9,693	C
Northwest Christian College	OR	19,680	LC
Northwest Nazarene Univ	ID	18,380	C
Northwestern Univ	IL	33,615	MC
Norwich Univ	VT	21,064	LC
Oakwood College	AL	14,904	C
Oglethorpe Univ	GA	19,100	LC
Ohio Northern Univ	OH	27,765	VC
Ohio Univ	OH	11,769	C
Old Dominion Univ	VA	9,386	C
Oral Roberts Univ	OK	18,490	C
Otterbein College	OH	23,439	C
Pacific Lutheran Univ	WA	23,318	VC
Pepperdine Univ	CA	32,830	VC
Point Park College	PA	20,290	C
Portland State Univ	OR	11,220	C
Queens College	NC	17,250	C
Ramapo College of New Jersey	NJ	13,550	VC
Randolph-Macon College	VA	24,395	C
Rhodes College	TN	26,466	HC+
Ripon College	WI	24,180	VC+
Roosevelt Univ	IL	20,240	LC
Russell Sage College	NY	23,674	C+
Sacred Heart Univ	CT	26,588	VC
Saginaw Valley State Univ	MI	9,465	C
St. Edward's Univ	TX	17,846	C
St. Francis Univ	PA	24,486	LC
St. John Fisher College	NY	21,800	C
St. Joseph College	CT	25,960	LC
St. Joseph's College	IN	21,640	C
St. Lawrence Univ	NY	32,605	VC
St. Leo Univ	FL	19,250	LC
St. Louis Univ	MO	26,590	VC+
St. Mary-of-the-Woods College	IN	21,320	LC
St. Mary's Univ of San Antonio	TX	19,735	C
St. Norbert College	WI	23,169	VC
Samford Univ	AL	16,340	VC
Seattle Univ	WA	24,183	VC
Seton Hill College	PA	21,875	C
Shaw Univ	NC	12,810	C
Southern Adventist Univ	TN	15,600	C
Southern Methodist Univ	TX	28,349	VC
Southern Nazarene Univ	OK	14,634	NC
Southern Oregon Univ	OR	9,429	C
Southwest Texas State Univ	TX	8,730	VC
Southwestern Univ	TX	22,550	HC
Spring Hill College	AL	23,250	C
SUNY/College at Brockport	NY	10,267	C
SUNY/College at Cortland	NY	10,564	C
SUNY/College at Old Westbury	NY	9,818	LC
SUNY/College at Oneonta	NY	9,981	C
SUNY/College at Oswego	NY	10,856	C
State Univ of West Georgia	GA	7,101	C
Stephens College	MO	22,295	C
Stetson Univ	FL	25,640	VC
Stonehill College	MA	26,852	HC
Susquehanna Univ	PA	27,270	VC
Tabor College	KS	17,600	LC
Taylor Univ	IN	21,562	VC+
Texas A&M Univ	TX	8,988	VC
Texas Wesleyan Univ	TX	14,710	C
Ohio State Univ	OH	10,819	VC
Thomas College	ME	18,915	LC
Thomas More College	KY	17,700	LC
Tiffin Univ	OH	17,250	C
Towson Univ	MD	11,088	VC
Trinity College	CT	34,300	HC
Trinity College	DC	21,370	LC
Union College	NE	14,650	C
United States Air Force Academy	CO		MC
United States Military Academy	NY		MC
Univ of Alabama	AL	7,402	C
Univ of Alabama at Birmingham	AL	10,110	C
Univ of Arkansas at Little Rock	AR	5,637	NC
Univ of Bridgeport	CT	23,020	C
Univ of Calif at Irvine	CA	11,756	C
Univ of Calif at Los Angeles	CA	13,227	MC
Univ of Chicago	IL	35,087	MC
Univ of Cincinnati	OH	12,491	LC
Univ of Dayton	OH	20,400	VC
Univ of Denver	CO	28,783	VC
Univ of Evansville	IN	22,865	VC+
Univ of Findlay	OH	23,962	NC
Univ of Hartford	CT	28,884	C
Univ of Illinois at Urbana-Champaign	IL	11,316	HC+
Univ of Kansas	KS	7,232	VC
Univ of La Verne	CA	24,280	C
Univ of Maine	ME	10,798	C

School	ST	$IS	SR
Univ of Maine at Farmington	ME	9,163	C
Univ of Maine at Presque Isle	ME	7,964	LC
Univ of Memphis	TN	7,271	C
Univ of Miami	FL	31,130	HC
Univ of Mich/Dearborn	MI	4,677	VC
Univ of Mich/Flint	MI	4,323	C
Univ of Minn/Duluth	MN	10,436	C
Univ of Miss	MS	7,666	C
Univ of Missouri/Columbia	MO	9,803	HC
Univ of Nebr at Kearney	NE	7,048	NC
Univ of New Hampshire	NH	13,207	C
Univ of N Car at Chapel Hill	NC	8,789	HC
Univ of N Car at Charlotte	NC	7,254	C
Univ of N Dak	ND	7,067	VC
Univ of Okla	OK	7,616	VC
Univ of Oregon	OR	9,969	C
Univ of Richmond	VA	27,300	HC
Univ of St. Thomas	MN	24,044	VC
Univ of St. Thomas	TX	18,752	VC
Univ of South Alabama	AL	6,976	LC
Univ of S Dak	SD	7,036	C
Univ of Southern Miss	MS	6,155	LC
Univ of Tampa	FL	22,612	C
Univ of Tenn at Martin	TN	8,268	C
Univ of the Pacific	CA	28,255	VC
Univ of Virginia's College at Wise	VA	8,302	C
Univ of Wisc/Oshkosh	WI	6,130	LC
Univ of Wisc/Parkside	WI	6,160	LC
Univ of Wisc/Platteville	WI	7,282	C
Univ of Wisc/Stevens Point	WI	7,116	C
Univ of Wisc/Superior	WI	7,051	C+
Univ of Wisc/Whitewater	WI	6,937	C
Univ of Wyoming	WY	7,143	LC
Utica College of Syracuse Univ	NY	24,400	LC
Vassar College	NY	33,450	MC
Villanova Univ	PA	31,997	HC
Virginia Military Inst	VA	9,968	C+
Virginia Polytechnic Inst and State Univ	VA	7,652	C
Walsh Univ	OH	16,880	C
Washington College	MD	28,040	VC
Washington Univ in St. Louis	MO	34,593	MC
Wayne State Univ	MI	6,720	C
Wells College	NY	19,350	VC
West Virginia Univ	WV	8,304	C
West Virginia Wesleyan College	WV	22,920	C
Western New England College	MA	23,882	C
Western Oregon Univ	OR	8,829	C
Westminster College	MO	19,990	C+
Wheeling Jesuit Univ	WV	22,660	C
Whittier College	CA	29,108	C
Whitworth College	WA	23,938	VC
Wilkes Univ	PA	25,800	C
Willamette Univ	OR	29,422	VC+
William Woods Univ	MO	19,390	LC
Wilson College	PA	21,337	LC

INTERPRETER FOR THE DEAF

School	ST	$IS	SR
Bethel College	IN	17,650	LC
Bloomsburg Univ of Pennsylvania	PA	9,434	C
Columbia College Chicago	IL	22,063	LC
Gallaudet Univ	DC	16,554	SP
Gardner-Webb Univ	NC	17,400	C
MacMurray College	IL	17,790	LC
Madonna Univ	MI	11,504	VC
Maryville College	TN	23,210	VC
Mount Aloysius College	PA	18,186	LC
Northeastern Univ	MA	30,078	VC
Rochester Inst of Technology	NY	26,232	VC+
Univ of Arkansas at Little Rock	AR	5,637	NC
Univ of New Mexico	NM	8,026	C
Univ of Rochester	NY	32,979	HC
Western Oregon Univ	OR	8,829	C
William Woods Univ	MO	19,390	LC

INVESTMENTS AND SECURITIES

School	ST	$IS	SR
Campbell Univ	NC	16,599	C
CUNY/Baruch College	NY	3,275	VC+
Duquesne Univ	PA	24,242	C+
Johnson and Wales Univ	RI	21,558	LC
Univ of Miss	MS	7,666	C

ISLAMIC STUDIES

School	ST	$IS	SR
Brandeis Univ	MA	34,481	MC
Ohio State Univ	OH	10,819	VC
Univ of Calif at Santa Barbara	CA	11,732	VC
Univ of Mich/Ann Arbor	MI	13,003	HC+
Univ of Texas at Austin	TX	9,437	HC
Washington Univ in St. Louis	MO	34,593	MC

ITALIAN

School	ST	$IS	SR
Arizona State Univ-Main	AZ	7,726	C
Bard College	NY	33,912	HC
Bennington College	VT	31,350	VC
Boston College	MA	33,330	MC
Boston Univ	MA	34,358	MC
Brigham Young Univ	UT	7,840	HC
Brown Univ	RI	34,973	MC
Bryn Mawr College	PA	33,580	HC+
Central Conn State Univ	CT	10,404	C
CUNY/Brooklyn College	NY	3,403	LC
CUNY/Herbert H. Lehman College	NY	3,320	LC
CUNY/Hunter College	NY	5,147	C+
CUNY/Queens College	NY	3,403	VC
College of the Holy Cross	MA	32,780	MC
Columbia Univ/Barnard College	NY	33,694	MC
Columbia Univ/School of General Studies	NY	35,000	C
Conn College	CT	33,585	MC
Cornell Univ	NY	34,614	MC
Dartmouth College	NH	34,458	MC
DePaul Univ	IL	23,590	VC
Dominican Univ	IL	20,800	C
Fairfield Univ	CT	30,885	HC
Florida Atlantic Univ	FL	8,832	C
Florida State Univ	FL	7,835	HC
Fordham Univ	NY	30,710	VC
Georgetown Univ	DC	34,847	MC
Harvard Univ/Harvard College	MA	34,269	MC
Haverford College	PA	34,300	MC
Hofstra Univ	NY	23,252	C
Indiana Univ Bloomington	IN	10,712	C+
Iona College	NY	26,556	C
Johns Hopkins Univ	MD	35,226	MC
La Salle Univ	PA	27,890	C
Lake Erie College	OH	21,350	LC
LIU/C.W. Post Campus	NY	25,380	C
Loyola Univ of Chicago	IL	25,992	VC
Marlboro College	VT	26,410	VC+
Middlebury College	VT	34,300	MC
Montclair State Univ	NJ	10,287	LC
Mount Holyoke College	MA	34,128	HC
Nazareth College of Rochester	NY	22,036	VC
New York Univ	NY	35,200	MC
Northwestern Univ	IL	33,615	MC
Penn State Univ/Univ Park Campus	PA	11,126	VC
Providence College	RI	27,620	HC
Rutgers, The State Univ of New Jersey New Brunswick Campus	NJ	12,709	C
St. John Fisher College	NY	21,800	C
St. John's Univ	NY	26,660	C
San Francisco State Univ	CA	7,139	LC
Santa Clara Univ	CA	28,371	VC+
Sarah Lawrence College	NY	37,516	HC
Scripps College	CA	30,400	HC+
Seton Hall Univ	NJ	26,910	LC
Smith College	MA	33,302	HC+
Southern Conn State Univ	CT	10,310	C
Stanford Univ	CA	34,222	MC
SUNY/College at Buffalo	NY	8,025	C
SUNY/Univ at Albany	NY	10,997	VC
SUNY/Univ at Binghamton	NY	10,653	HC
SUNY/Univ at Buffalo	NY	11,033	VC
Temple Univ	PA	14,124	C
Ohio State Univ	OH	10,819	VC
Trinity College	CT	34,300	HC
Tulane Univ	LA	34,013	HC+
Univ of Arizona	AZ	8,614	C
Univ of Calif at Berkeley	CA	14,134	MC
Univ of Calif at Davis	CA	12,796	VC
Univ of Calif at Los Angeles	CA	13,227	MC
Univ of Colo at Boulder	CO	9,255	VC
Univ of Delaware	DE	10,824	VC
Univ of Denver	CO	28,783	VC
Univ of Georgia	GA	8,656	VC
Univ of Illinois at Chicago	IL	10,702	VC
Univ of Illinois at Urbana-Champaign	IL	11,316	HC+
Univ of Iowa	IA	8,607	C+
Univ of Kentucky	KY	7,765	C
Univ of Mass Boston	MA	4,227	C
Univ of Miami	FL	31,130	HC
Univ of Mich/Ann Arbor	MI	13,003	HC+
Univ of Minn/Twin Cities	MN	11,123	VC
Univ of N Car at Chapel Hill	NC	8,789	HC
Univ of Notre Dame	IN	30,707	MC
Univ of Oregon	OR	9,969	C
Univ of Pennsylvania	PA	34,614	MC
Univ of Pittsburgh at Pittsburgh	PA	13,592	HC
Univ of Rhode Island	RI	12,414	C
Univ of S Car at Columbia	SC	8,748	VC
Univ of South Florida	FL	8,154	C
Univ of Tenn at Knoxville	TN	8,214	C
Univ of Texas at Austin	TX	9,437	HC
Univ of Virginia	VA	9,391	HC+
Univ of Washington	WA	10,361	VC
Univ of Wisc/Madison	WI	8,262	VC
Univ of Wisc/Milwaukee	WI	8,907	LC
Washington Univ in St. Louis	MO	34,593	MC
Wayne State Univ	MI	6,720	C
Wellesley College	MA	33,394	MC
Wesleyan Univ	CT	3,405	MC
Yale Univ	CT	34,030	MC
Youngstown State Univ	OH	9,318	NC

ITALIAN STUDIES

School	ST	$IS	SR
Bard College	NY	33,912	HC
Columbia Univ/Columbia College	NY	35,190	MC
Columbia Univ/School of General Studies	NY	35,000	C
Conn College	CT	33,585	MC
Dickinson College	PA	32,210	VC+
Duke Univ	NC	34,396	MC
Florida International Univ	FL	9,486	VC
Fordham Univ	NY	30,710	VC
Gonzaga Univ	WA	24,276	HC+
Purdue Univ/West Lafayette	IN	10,284	VC
Rosemont College	PA	24,060	C
Scripps College	CA	30,400	HC+
Southern Methodist Univ	TX	28,349	VC
SUNY/Univ at Stony Brook	NY	10,998	VC
Sweet Briar College	VA	25,310	VC
Syracuse Univ	NY	30,710	HC
Univ of Calif at Los Angeles	CA	13,227	MC
Univ of Calif at San Diego	CA	11,372	HC
Univ of Calif at Santa Barbara	CA	11,732	VC
Univ of Calif at Santa Cruz	CA	13,655	VC
Univ of Conn	CT	12,122	VC
Univ of Houston	TX	8,410	C
Univ of Maryland/College Park	MD	11,959	C
Univ of Mass Amherst	MA	10,995	VC
Univ of Pennsylvania	PA	34,614	MC
Wheaton College	MA	32,940	VC

JAPANESE

School	ST	$IS	SR
Arizona State Univ-Main	AZ	7,726	C
Bates College	ME	34,100	MC
Brigham Young Univ	UT	7,840	HC
Cal State, Fullerton	CA	5,440	LC
Cal State, Long Beach	CA	7,400	LC
Cal State, Los Angeles	CA	5,050	C
Conn College	CT	33,585	MC
Eastern Mich Univ	MI	9,855	C
Florida Atlantic Univ	FL	8,832	C
George Washington Univ	DC	32,170	HC
Georgetown Univ	DC	34,847	MC
Harvard Univ/Harvard College	MA	34,269	MC
Hobart and William Smith Colleges	NY	33,195	VC
Lincoln Univ	PA	11,198	C+
Macalester College	MN	28,814	HC+
Middlebury College	VT	34,300	MC
Mount Union College	OH	21,120	C
North Central College	IL	22,944	C+
Oakland Univ	MI	9,418	C
Pacific Univ	OR	24,250	C
Pomona College	CA	33,960	MC
Portland State Univ	OR	11,220	C
Purdue Univ/West Lafayette	IN	10,284	VC
San Diego State Univ	CA	9,716	C+
San Francisco State Univ	CA	7,139	LC
Stanford Univ	CA	34,222	MC
Ohio State Univ	OH	10,819	VC
Tufts Univ	MA	34,874	MC
Univ of Calif at Berkeley	CA	14,134	MC
Univ of Calif at Davis	CA	12,796	VC
Univ of Calif at Irvine	CA	11,756	C
Univ of Calif at Los Angeles	CA	13,227	MC
Univ of Calif at Santa Barbara	CA	11,732	VC
Univ of Chicago	IL	35,087	MC
Univ of Colo at Boulder	CO	9,255	VC
Univ of Findlay	OH	23,962	NC
Univ of Hawaii at Manoa	HI	7,862	VC
Univ of Maryland/College Park	MD	11,959	C
Univ of Mass Amherst	MA	10,995	VC
Univ of Mich/Ann Arbor	MI	13,003	HC+
Univ of Minn/Twin Cities	MN	11,123	VC
Univ of Montana	MT	8,038	C
Univ of Notre Dame	IN	30,707	MC
Univ of Oregon	OR	9,969	C
Univ of Pittsburgh at Pittsburgh	PA	13,592	HC
Univ of Rochester	NY	32,979	HC
Univ of the Pacific	CA	28,255	VC
Univ of Utah	UT	7,703	C
Univ of Washington	WA	10,361	VC
Univ of Wisc/Madison	WI	8,262	VC
Washington Univ in St. Louis	MO	34,593	MC
Wellesley College	MA	33,394	MC
Yale Univ	CT	34,030	MC

JAPANESE STUDIES

School	ST	$IS	SR
Case Western Reserve Univ	OH	27,418	C
Dillard Univ	LA	16,046	VC
Earlham College	IN	27,446	VC+
Salem International Univ	WV	17,263	LC
Univ of Alaska Fairbanks	AK	8,265	NC
Univ of Calif at San Diego	CA	11,372	HC
Univ of Georgia	GA	8,656	VC
Univ of Hawaii at Hilo	HI	6,497	C
Willamette Univ	OR	29,422	VC+
William Jewell College	MO	17,150	VC

JAZZ

School	ST	$IS	SR
Berklee College of Music	MA	27,005	SP
Bowling Green State Univ	OH	10,794	C
DePaul Univ	IL	23,590	VC
Eastman School of Music	NY	30,684	SP
Five Towns College	NY	18,850	SP
Florida State Univ	FL	7,835	HC
Howard Univ	DC	15,522	LC
Indiana Univ Bloomington	IN	10,712	C+
Ithaca College	NY	28,719	HC
Johnson State College	VT	10,776	C
Loyola Univ New Orleans	LA	23,506	VC+
Manhattan School of Music	NY	31,500	SP
New England Conservatory of Music	MA	31,200	SP
N Car Central Univ	NC	6,418	LC
Roosevelt Univ	IL	20,240	LC
Shenandoah Univ	VA	22,550	NC
Temple Univ	PA	14,124	C
Ohio State Univ	OH	10,819	VC
Univ of Cincinnati	OH	12,491	LC
Univ of Denver	CO	28,783	VC
Univ of Hartford	CT	28,884	C
Univ of Maine at Augusta	ME	3,928	C
Univ of Miami	FL	31,130	HC
Univ of Mich/Ann Arbor	MI	13,003	HC+
Univ of Minn/Duluth	MN	10,436	C
Univ of North Florida	FL	8,089	VC
Univ of North Texas	TX	7,629	C
Univ of Oregon	OR	9,969	C
Univ of Rochester	NY	32,979	HC
Univ of Southern Calif	CA	33,647	MC
Univ of the Arts	PA	24,230	SP
Univ of Washington	WA	10,361	VC
Western Mich Univ	MI	10,016	C

JOURNALISM

School	ST	$IS	SR
Abilene Christian Univ	TX	16,300	VC
Adams State College	CO	7,468	C
American Univ	DC	31,544	VC+
Andrews Univ	MI	17,696	LC
Angelo State Univ	TX	7,028	C
Appalachian State Univ	NC	6,353	C
Arizona State Univ-Main	AZ	7,726	C
Arkansas State Univ	AR	7,480	C
Arkansas Tech Univ	AR	6,256	C
Asbury College	KY	18,540	VC
Ashland Univ	OH	22,182	LC
Auburn Univ	AL	5,510	C
Augustana College	SD	20,760	VC
Averett Univ	VA	17,980	LC
Ball State Univ	IN	8,660	C
Baylor Univ	TX	18,298	VC+
Bemidji State Univ	MN	7,957	C
Benedict College	SC	12,662	LC
Benedictine College	KS	18,485	LC
Bethany College	WV	18,566	C
Boston Univ	MA	34,358	MC
Bowling Green State Univ	OH	10,794	C
Butler Univ	IN	25,580	VC+
Calif Polytechnic State Univ	CA	8,747	VC
Cal State, Chico	CA	8,598	LC
Cal State, Fresno	CA	7,762	C
Cal State, Fullerton	CA	5,440	LC
Cal State, Hayward	CA	7,400	LC
Cal State, Long Beach	CA	7,400	LC
Cal State, Northridge	CA	7,781	C
Cal State, Sacramento	CA	7,488	C
Cameron Univ	OK	5,560	NC
Campbell Univ	NC	16,599	C
Carnegie Mellon Univ	PA	32,682	MC
Central Mich Univ	MI	8,355	C
Central Missouri State Univ	MO	7,920	C
Central State Univ	OH	8,922	C+
Central Univ of Bayamon	PR	3,335	
Central Washington Univ	WA	8,985	LC
Champlain College	VT	19,680	C
Christopher Newport Univ	VA	8,862	VC
CUNY/Baruch College	NY	3,275	VC+
CUNY/Brooklyn College	NY	3,403	LC
College of New Jersey	NJ	13,425	HC
College of St. Joseph	VT	17,400	NC
College of the Ozarks	MO	2,650	C+
Colo State Univ	CO	9,672	C
Columbia College Chicago	IL	22,063	LC
Columbia Union College	MD	19,027	C+
Concordia College/Moorhead	MN	18,835	C
Creighton Univ	NE	23,476	VC

School	ST	$IS	SR
Delaware State Univ	DE	8,104	LC
Delta State Univ	MS	5,416	C
Dickinson State Univ	ND	5,495	NC
Dominican Univ	IL	20,800	C
Dordt College	IA	18,100	C+
Drake Univ	IA	22,830	VC
Drury Univ	MO	15,250	VC
Duquesne Univ	PA	24,242	C+
East Central Univ	OK	4,578	C
Eastern Illinois Univ	IL	10,101	C
Eastern Kentucky Univ	KY	6,552	C
Eastern Mich Univ	MI	9,855	C
Eastern Nazarene College	MA	19,433	LC
Eastern New Mexico Univ	NM	4,113	LC
Eastern Washington Univ	WA	7,972	LC
Elon Univ	NC	19,430	VC
Emerson College	MA	20,978	HC
Emory & Henry College	VA	19,462	C
Evangel Univ	MO	14,050	C
Florida A&M Univ	FL	6,948	C
Florida Atlantic Univ	FL	8,832	C
Florida Southern College	FL	19,430	C
Fordham Univ	NY	30,710	VC
Franklin College of Indiana	IN	19,905	C
George Washington Univ	DC	32,170	HC
Georgia Southern Univ	GA	6,958	C
Georgia State Univ	GA	7,792	LC
Gonzaga Univ	WA	24,276	HC+
Grand Valley State Univ	MI	10,040	C
Grand View College	IA	17,596	NC
Hampshire College	MA	33,881	HC+
Hawaii Pacific Univ	HI	17,790	C
Hofstra Univ	NY	23,252	C
Howard Univ	DC	15,522	LC
Humboldt State Univ	CA	8,582	C
Indiana State Univ	IN	8,461	LC
Indiana Univ Bloomington	IN	10,712	C+
Indiana Univ of Pennsylvania	PA	9,133	C
Indiana Univ-Purdue Univ Indianapolis	IN	9,473	C
Iona College	NY	26,556	C
Iowa State Univ	IA	8,108	VC
Ithaca College	NY	28,719	HC
John Brown Univ	AR	15,080	VC
Johnson State College	VT	10,776	C
Kansas State Univ	KS	6,995	C
Keene State College	NH	11,280	C
Kent State Univ	OH	11,104	C
Lehigh Univ	PA	32,290	MC
Lewis Univ	IL	20,960	C
Lincoln Univ	MO	7,158	NC
Lincoln Univ	PA	11,198	C+
Lock Haven Univ of Pennsylvania	PA	9,534	C
LIU/Brooklyn Campus	NY	22,290	C
LIU/C.W. Post Campus	NY	25,300	C
Loras College	IA	22,994	C+
Louisiana College	LA	11,516	C
Louisiana State Univ in Shreveport	LA	2,480	NC
Louisiana Tech Univ	LA	6,506	C
Lyndon State College	VT	11,313	LC
MacMurray College	IL	17,790	LC
Madonna Univ	MI	11,504	VC
Mansfield Univ	PA	9,648	C
Marietta College	OH	24,580	C
Marquette Univ	WI	24,836	C+
Marshall Univ	WV	7,752	LC
Mercy College	NY	15,875	LC
Mercyhurst College	PA	20,694	C
Messiah College	PA	23,180	VC
Metropolitan State College of Denver	CO	2,338	LC
Mich State Univ	MI	10,386	VC
Midland Lutheran College	NE	18,600	C
Minn State Univ, Mankato	MN	7,296	LC
Moorhead State Univ	MN	7,000	LC
Morris College	SC	9,995	LC
Mount Ida College	MA	25,375	LC
Mount Marty College	SD	15,656	LC
Murray State Univ	KY	6,672	C
Muskingum College	OH	18,760	C
New Mexico State Univ	NM	7,302	C
New York Univ	NY	35,200	MC
Nicholls State Univ	LA	5,290	NC
Norfolk State Univ	VA	8,382	LC
Northeastern State Univ	OK	4,704	LC
Northeastern Univ	MA	30,078	VC
Northern Arizona Univ	AZ	7,398	C
Northern Illinois Univ	IL	9,545	C
Northern Kentucky Univ	KY	6,352	NC
Northwest Missouri State Univ	MO	7,922	LC
Northwestern College	MN	19,816	C+
Northwestern State Univ of Louisiana	LA	5,745	NC
Northwestern Univ	IL	33,615	MC
Oakland Univ	MI	9,418	C
Ohio Northern Univ	OH	27,765	VC
Ohio Univ	OH	11,769	C
Ohio Wesleyan Univ	OH	29,670	VC+
Okla Baptist Univ	OK	13,878	VC
Okla Christian Univ	OK	16,500	VC
Okla City Univ	OK	15,810	C
Okla State Univ	OK	7,650	VC
Old Dominion Univ	VA	9,386	C
Olivet College	MI	17,410	C
Otterbein College	OH	23,439	C
Pace Univ	NY	24,200	C
Pacific Union College	CA	20,250	VC
Penn State Univ/Univ Park Campus	PA	11,126	VC
Pepperdine Univ	CA	32,830	VC
Point Loma Nazarene Univ	CA	21,380	VC
Point Park College	PA	20,290	C
Prairie View A&M Univ	TX	3,172	LC
Prescott College	AZ	13,430	C
Purdue Univ/West Lafayette	IN	10,284	VC
Quinnipiac Univ	CT	27,370	C
Rider Univ	NJ	27,400	C
Roosevelt Univ	IL	20,240	LC
Rowan Univ	NJ	12,365	VC
Rust College	MS	7,800	C+
Rutgers, The State Univ of New Jersey New Brunswick Campus	NJ	12,709	C
St. Bonaventure Univ	NY	21,956	C
St. Cloud State Univ	MN	7,180	C
St. John's Univ	NY	26,660	C
St. Mary-of-the-Woods College	IN	21,320	LC
St. Michael's College	VT	26,935	VC
Sam Houston State Univ	TX	6,076	LC
Samford Univ	AL	16,340	VC
San Diego State Univ	CA	9,716	C+
San Francisco State Univ	CA	7,139	LC
San Jose State Univ	CA	8,187	C
Seattle Univ	WA	24,183	VC
Seton Hill College	PA	21,875	C
Simpson College	IA	21,200	C+
S Dak State Univ	SD	6,848	C
Southeast Missouri State Univ	MO	8,367	C+
Southern Adventist Univ	TN	15,600	C
Southern Arkansas Univ	AR	5,740	LC
Southern Conn State Univ	CT	10,310	C
Southern Illinois Univ at Carbondale	IL	8,621	C
Southern Methodist Univ	TX	28,349	VC
Southern Nazarene Univ	OK	14,634	NC
Southern Univ at New Orleans	LA	995	NC
Southwest Texas State Univ	TX	8,730	VC
Southwestern Adventist Univ	TX	14,798	C
Spring Hill College	AL	23,250	C
SUNY/College at Brockport	NY	10,267	C
SUNY/College at Buffalo	NY	8,025	C
SUNY/College at Oswego	NY	10,856	C
SUNY/College at Plattsburgh	NY	9,729	C
SUNY/College at Purchase	NY	10,587	VC
SUNY/Univ at New Paltz	NY	9,685	VC
Stephen F. Austin State Univ	TX	6,905	C
Suffolk Univ	MA	26,516	C
Syracuse Univ	NY	30,710	HC
Taylor Univ	IN	21,562	VC+
Temple Univ	PA	14,124	C
Tenn Tech Univ	TN	6,968	C
Texas A&M Univ	TX	8,088	VC
Texas A&M Univ at Commerce	TX	7,326	C
Texas Christian Univ	TX	19,910	C
Texas Southern Univ	TX	6,576	NC
Texas Tech Univ	TX	8,825	C
Ohio State Univ	OH	10,819	VC
Thomas Edison State College	NJ	2,750	SP
Toccoa Falls College	GA	14,220	C
Troy State Univ	AL	7,696	C
Truman State Univ	MO	8,568	VC+
Union College	NE	14,650	C
Union Univ	TN	18,930	C+
Univ of Alabama	AL	7,402	C
Univ of Alaska Anchorage	AK	9,100	NC
Univ of Alaska Fairbanks	AK	8,265	NC
Univ of Arizona	AZ	8,614	C
Univ of Arkansas	AR	8,334	VC
Univ of Arkansas at Little Rock	AR	5,637	NC
Univ of Arkansas at Pine Bluff	AR	7,925	C
Univ of Bridgeport	CT	23,020	C
Univ of Central Arkansas	AR	6,388	C
Univ of Central Florida	FL	8,251	VC
Univ of Central Okla	OK	5,205	C
Univ of Colo at Boulder	CO	9,255	VC
Univ of Conn	CT	12,122	VC
Univ of Dayton	OH	20,400	VC
Univ of Delaware	DE	10,824	VC
Univ of Denver	CO	28,783	VC
Univ of Florida	FL	7,874	HC
Univ of Georgia	GA	8,656	VC
Univ of Hawaii at Manoa	HI	7,862	VC
Univ of Houston	TX	8,410	C
Univ of Idaho	ID	7,026	C
Univ of Illinois at Urbana-Champaign	IL	11,316	HC+
Univ of Indianapolis	IN	20,840	C
Univ of Iowa	IA	8,607	C+
Univ of Judaism College of A&S	CA	24,230	C
Univ of Kansas	KS	7,232	VC
Univ of Kentucky	KY	7,765	C
Univ of La Verne	CA	24,280	C
Univ of Louisiana at Monroe	LA	5,207	NC
Univ of Maine	ME	10,798	C
Univ of Mary Hardin-Baylor	TX	13,929	C
Univ of Maryland/College Park	MD	11,959	C
Univ of Mass Amherst	MA	10,995	VC
Univ of Memphis	TN	7,271	C
Univ of Miami	FL	31,130	HC
Univ of Mich/Ann Arbor	MI	13,003	HC+
Univ of Miss	MS	7,666	C
Univ of Missouri/Columbia	MO	9,803	HC
Univ of Montana	MT	8,038	C
Univ of Montevallo	AL	7,266	C
Univ of Nebr at Kearney	NE	7,048	NC
Univ of Nebr at Lincoln	NE	8,325	C+
Univ of Nebr at Omaha	NE	6,867	C
Univ of Nevada/Reno	NV	8,737	C
Univ of New Hampshire	NH	13,207	C
Univ of New Mexico	NM	8,026	C
Univ of North Alabama	AL	7,016	NC
Univ of N Car at Chapel Hill	NC	8,789	HC
Univ of N Car at Pembroke	NC	5,914	LC
Univ of North Texas	TX	7,629	C
Univ of Northern Colo	CO	8,082	C+
Univ of Okla	OK	7,616	VC
Univ of Oregon	OR	9,969	C
Univ of Pittsburgh at Johnstown	PA	13,044	LC
Univ of Rhode Island	RI	12,414	C
Univ of Richmond	VA	27,300	HC
Univ of St. Francis	IL	19,650	C
Univ of St. Thomas	MN	24,044	VC
Univ of S Car at Columbia	SC	8,748	VC
Univ of S Dak	SD	7,036	C
Univ of Southern Calif	CA	33,647	MC
Univ of Southern Colo	CO	7,821	LC
Univ of Southern Indiana	IN	8,655	LC
Univ of Southern Miss	MS	6,155	LC
Univ of Tenn at Knoxville	TN	8,214	C
Univ of Texas at Arlington	TX	7,192	LC
Univ of Texas at Austin	TX	9,437	HC
Univ of Texas at El Paso	TX	5,076	LC
Univ of Texas-Pan American	TX	4,823	C
Univ of Wisc/Eau Claire	WI	7,032	VC
Univ of Wisc/Madison	WI	8,262	VC
Univ of Wisc/Oshkosh	WI	6,130	LC
Univ of Wisc/River Falls	WI	6,356	LC
Univ of Wisc/Whitewater	WI	6,937	C
Univ of Wyoming	WY	7,143	LC
Utah State Univ	UT	6,771	C
Utica College of Syracuse Univ	NY	24,400	LC
Valparaiso Univ	IN	23,570	VC+
Virginia Union Univ	VA	15,358	LC
Virginia Wesleyan College	VA	22,350	LC
Wartburg College	IA	21,165	VC
Washington and Lee Univ	VA	25,095	MC
Washington State Univ	WA	9,388	C
Wayne State Univ	MI	6,720	C
Weber State Univ	UT	6,007	NC
Webster Univ	MO	19,804	VC
West Virginia Univ	WV	8,304	C
Western Illinois Univ	IL	9,571	C
Western Kentucky Univ	KY	6,834	C
Western Mich Univ	MI	10,016	C
Western Washington Univ	WA	8,624	VC
Whitworth College	WA	23,938	VC
William Penn Univ	IA	17,575	C
William Woods Univ	MO	19,390	LC
Winona State Univ	MN	8,570	C
Youngstown State Univ	OH	9,318	NC

JOURNALISM EDUCATION

School	ST	$IS	SR
Ball State Univ	IN	8,660	C
Baylor Univ	TX	18,298	VC+
Stephen F. Austin State Univ	TX	6,905	C
Wartburg College	IA	21,165	VC

JUDAIC STUDIES

School	ST	$IS	SR
Albert A. List College of Jewish Studies	NY	18,500	HC+
American Univ	DC	31,544	VC+
Baltimore Hebrew Univ	MD	8,030	SP
Bard College	NY	33,912	HC
Brandeis Univ	MA	34,481	MC
Brown Univ	RI	34,973	MC
CUNY/Brooklyn College	NY	3,403	LC
CUNY/Hunter College	NY	5,147	C+
CUNY/Queens College	NY	3,403	VC
DePaul Univ	IL	23,590	VC
Dickinson College	PA	32,210	VC+
Emory Univ	GA	33,792	MC
Florida Atlantic Univ	FL	8,832	C
George Washington Univ	DC	32,170	HC
Hampshire College	MA	33,881	HC+
Hofstra Univ	NY	23,252	C
Indiana Univ Bloomington	IN	10,712	C+
Mount Holyoke College	MA	34,128	HC
New York Univ	NY	35,200	MC
Oberlin College	OH	33,140	HC+
Purdue Univ/West Lafayette	IN	10,284	VC
Rutgers, The State Univ of New Jersey New Brunswick Campus	NJ	12,709	C
Scripps College	CA	30,400	HC+
SUNY/Univ at Binghamton	NY	10,653	HC
Ohio State Univ	OH	10,819	VC
Touro College	NY	14,950	VC
Trinity College	CT	34,300	HC
Tufts Univ	MA	34,874	MC
Tulane Univ	LA	34,013	HC+
Univ of Arizona	AZ	8,614	C
Univ of Calif at Los Angeles	CA	13,227	MC
Univ of Calif at San Diego	CA	11,372	HC
Univ of Chicago	IL	35,087	MC
Univ of Cincinnati	OH	12,491	LC
Univ of Florida	FL	7,874	HC
Univ of Hartford	CT	28,884	C
Univ of Judaism College of A&S	CA	24,230	C
Univ of Maryland/College Park	MD	11,959	C
Univ of Mass Amherst	MA	10,995	VC
Univ of Miami	FL	31,130	HC
Univ of Mich/Ann Arbor	MI	13,003	HC+
Univ of Missouri/Kansas City	MO	9,685	VC
Univ of Oregon	OR	9,969	C
Univ of Pennsylvania	PA	34,614	MC
Univ of Washington	WA	10,361	VC
Univ of Wisc/Madison	WI	8,262	VC
Vassar College	NY	33,450	MC
Washington Univ in St. Louis	MO	34,593	MC
Wellesley College	MA	33,394	MC
Yale Univ	CT	34,030	MC

KOREAN

School	ST	$IS	SR
Brigham Young Univ	UT	7,840	HC
Univ of Calif at Los Angeles	CA	13,227	MC
Univ of Chicago	IL	35,087	MC
Univ of Hawaii at Manoa	HI	7,862	VC

LABOR STUDIES

School	ST	$IS	SR
Bowling Green State Univ	OH	10,794	C
Cal State, Dominguez Hills	CA	5,840	LC
CUNY/Queens College	NY	3,403	VC
Cleveland State Univ	OH	10,146	NC
Cornell Univ	NY	34,614	MC
Eastern Mich Univ	MI	9,855	C
Indiana Univ Bloomington	IN	10,712	C+
Indiana Univ Kokomo	IN	3,422	LC
Indiana Univ Northwest	IN	3,447	C
Indiana Univ South Bend	IN	3,515	C
Indiana Univ Southeast	IN	3,459	C
Indiana Univ-Purdue Univ Indianapolis	IN	9,473	C
Le Moyne College	NY	23,840	C
Middle Tenn State Univ	TN	6,994	C
Northern Kentucky Univ	KY	6,352	NC
Penn State Univ/Univ Park Campus	PA	11,126	VC
Rhode Island College	RI	8,700	LC
Rutgers, The State Univ of New Jersey New Brunswick Campus	NJ	12,709	C
St. Joseph's Univ	PA	29,715	VC+
San Francisco State Univ	CA	7,139	LC
SUNY/Empire State College	NY	3,545	SP
Thomas Edison State College	NJ	2,750	SP
Univ of PR/Rio Piedras	PR	5,510	
Wayne State Univ	MI	6,720	C
Youngstown State Univ	OH	9,318	NC

LAND USE MANAGEMENT AND RECLAMATION

School	ST	$IS	SR
Alverno College	WI	16,930	LC
Cal State, Bakersfield	CA	6,090	LC
Eastern Mich Univ	MI	9,855	C
Humboldt State Univ	CA	8,582	C
Metropolitan State College of Denver	CO	2,338	LC
Montana State Univ-Bozeman	MT	8,431	C
Northern Mich Univ	MI	9,693	C
Univ of Louisiana at Lafayette	LA	5,200	C
Univ of Okla	OK	7,616	VC
Univ of Wisc/Platteville	WI	7,282	C
Univ of Wisc/River Falls	WI	6,356	LC

LANDSCAPE ARCHITECTURE/DESIGN

School	ST	$IS	SR
Andrews Univ	MI	17,696	LC
Arizona State Univ-Main	AZ	7,726	C
Auburn Univ	AL	5,510	C

School	ST	$IS	SR
Augustana College	IL	24,117	VC+
Ball State Univ	IN	8,660	C
Calif Polytechnic State Univ	CA	8,747	VC
Calif State Polytechnic Univ, Pomona	CA	8,615	C
Clemson Univ	SC	7,600	C
Colo State Univ	CO	9,672	C
Cornell Univ	NY	34,614	MC
Iowa State Univ	IA	8,108	VC
Kansas State Univ	KS	6,995	C
Louisiana State Univ and A&M College	LA	8,014	VC
Mich State Univ	MI	10,386	VC
Miss State Univ	MS	7,853	C
N Car Agricultural and Technical State Univ	NC	6,659	LC
N Car State Univ	NC	8,680	HC
N Dak State Univ	ND	7,004	VC
Okla State Univ	OK	7,650	VC
Oregon State Univ	OR	9,612	VC
Penn State Univ/Univ Park Campus	PA	11,126	VC
Purdue Univ/West Lafayette	IN	10,284	VC
S Dak State Univ	SD	6,848	C
SUNY/College of Environmental Science and Forestry	NY	12,446	VC
Temple Univ	PA	14,124	C
Texas A&M Univ	TX	8,988	VC
Texas Tech Univ	TX	8,825	C
Ohio State Univ	OH	10,819	VC
Univ of Arizona	AZ	8,614	C
Univ of Arkansas	AR	8,334	VC
Univ of Calif at Berkeley	CA	14,134	MC
Univ of Calif at Davis	CA	12,796	VC
Univ of Conn	CT	12,122	VC
Univ of Delaware	DE	10,824	VC
Univ of Florida	FL	7,874	HC
Univ of Georgia	GA	8,656	VC
Univ of Idaho	ID	7,026	C
Univ of Illinois at Urbana-Champaign	IL	11,316	HC+
Univ of Kentucky	KY	7,765	C
Univ of Maryland/College Park	MD	11,959	C
Univ of Mass Amherst	MA	10,995	VC
Univ of Mich/Ann Arbor	MI	13,003	HC+
Univ of Minn/Twin Cities	MN	11,123	VC
Univ of Nevada/Las Vegas	NV	8,281	VC
Univ of Oregon	OR	9,969	C
Univ of Rhode Island	RI	12,414	C
Univ of Tenn at Knoxville	TN	8,214	C
Univ of Texas at Arlington	TX	7,192	LC
Univ of Vermont	VT	14,761	C+
Univ of Washington	WA	10,361	VC
Univ of Wisc/Madison	WI	8,262	VC
Utah State Univ	UT	6,771	C
Virginia Polytechnic Inst and State Univ	VA	7,652	C
Washington State Univ	WA	9,388	C
West Virginia Univ	WV	8,304	C

LANGUAGE ARTS

School	ST	$IS	SR
Christian Brothers Univ	TN	19,820	VC
Doane College	NE	17,600	LC
Hiram College	OH	27,034	VC
Malone College	OH	19,190	C
Marygrove College	MI	16,075	C
Miles College	AL	7,870	NC
Ohio Northern Univ	OH	27,765	VC
St. Edward's Univ	TX	17,846	C
Samford Univ	AL	16,340	VC
Spring Arbor Univ	MI	17,976	C
Univ of Arizona	AZ	8,614	C
Univ of Maine at Farmington	ME	9,163	C
Wells College	NY	19,350	VC

LANGUAGES

School	ST	$IS	SR
Adelphi Univ	NY	23,320	VC
Antioch College	OH	25,072	LC
Arkansas Tech Univ	AR	6,256	C
Assumption College	MA	26,320	C
Auburn Univ	AL	5,510	C
Austin Peay State Univ	TN	5,814	LC
Baylor Univ	TX	18,298	VC+
Bemidji State Univ	MN	7,957	C
Bennington College	VT	31,350	VC
Bethany College	WV	18,566	C
Canisius College	NY	24,696	C+
Carnegie Mellon Univ	PA	32,682	MC
Carson-Newman College	TN	16,490	C
Carthage College	WI	23,670	C
Central College	IA	21,206	C
Central Mich Univ	MI	8,355	C
CUNY/Brooklyn College	NY	3,403	LC
CUNY/Herbert H. Lehman College	NY	3,320	LC
CUNY/Hunter College	NY	5,147	C+
Clark Atlanta Univ	GA	17,174	C
Clark Univ	MA	29,170	HC
College of St. Scholastica	MN	22,378	C+
Columbia College	SC	19,050	LC
Converse College	SC	21,990	VC
Cornell College	IA	24,980	VC
Cornell Univ	NY	34,614	MC
David Lipscomb Univ	TN	16,158	VC
Davis and Elkins College	WV	19,270	LC
Denison Univ	OH	29,640	HC
Dillard Univ	LA	16,046	VC
Dominican College	NY	20,400	LC
Dordt College	IA	18,100	C+
Dowling College	NY	20,281	LC
Duquesne Univ	PA	24,242	C+
Eastern Illinois Univ	IL	10,101	C
Elmira College	NY	31,070	VC+
Frostburg State Univ	MD	9,680	C
Gannon Univ	PA	18,848	C
Gordon College	MA	23,594	VC+
Grand Valley State Univ	MI	10,040	C
Hamilton College	NY	34,150	HC
Hartwick College	NY	33,090	C+
Hofstra Univ	NY	23,252	C
Ithaca College	NY	28,719	HC
Jackson State Univ	MS	6,776	LC
Judson College	AL	13,790	C
King's College	PA	24,680	C
Lewis and Clark College	OR	29,010	VC
LIU/Brooklyn Campus	NY	22,290	C
Louisiana College	LA	11,516	C
Mary Washington College	VA	9,032	VC+
McNeese State Univ	LA	5,259	LC
Mercyhurst College	PA	20,694	C
Miss College	MS	14,574	C
Miss State Univ	MS	7,853	C
Murray State Univ	KY	6,672	C
New College of Florida	FL	8,130	HC+
New Mexico State Univ	NM	7,302	C
Newberry College	SC	19,670	LC
Northeastern Univ	MA	30,078	VC
Occidental College	CA	32,288	HC
Pomona College	CA	33,960	MC
Portland State Univ	OR	11,220	C
Principia College	IL	23,865	C+
Purdue Univ/West Lafayette	IN	10,284	VC
Roger Williams Univ	RI	29,010	C
Roosevelt Univ	IL	20,240	LC
St. Cloud State Univ	MN	7,180	C
St. John's Univ	NY	26,660	C
St. Mary-of-the-Woods College	IN	21,320	LC
St. Mary's College of Maryland	MD	14,104	HC
Salem College	NC	23,065	VC
Scripps College	CA	30,400	HC+
Southern Illinois Univ Edwardsville	IL	7,869	LC
Southern Methodist Univ	TX	28,349	VC
Southern Oregon Univ	OR	9,429	C
Stonehill College	MA	26,852	HC
Syracuse Univ	NY	30,710	HC
Tenn State Univ	TN	7,058	VC
Texas A&M Univ at Commerce	TX	7,326	C
United States Military Academy	NY		MC
Univ of Alabama at Huntsville	AL	7,916	VC
Univ of Alaska Anchorage	AK	9,100	NC
Univ of Calif at Riverside	CA	12,479	C
Univ of Central Florida	FL	8,251	VC
Univ of Delaware	DE	10,824	VC
Univ of Denver	CO	28,783	VC
Univ of Hartford	CT	28,884	C
Univ of Memphis	TN	7,271	C
Univ of Mich/Dearborn	MI	4,677	VC
Univ of Minn/Twin Cities	MN	11,123	VC
Univ of Nebr at Lincoln	NE	8,325	C+
Univ of New Mexico	NM	8,026	C
Univ of Okla	OK	7,616	VC
Univ of South Florida	FL	8,154	C
Univ of Southern Miss	MS	6,155	LC
Univ of Tenn at Knoxville	TN	8,214	C
Univ of Texas at El Paso	TX	5,076	LC
Vassar College	NY	33,450	MC
Virginia Commonwealth Univ	VA	9,030	C
Virginia Wesleyan College	VA	22,350	LC
Washington Univ in St. Louis	MO	34,593	MC
Wellesley College	MA	33,394	MC
Wilson College	PA	21,337	LC
Youngstown State Univ	OH	9,318	NC

LASER ELECTRO-OPTICS TECHNOLOGY

School	ST	$IS	SR
Oregon Inst of Technology	OR	8,718	C

LATIN

School	ST	$IS	SR
Amherst College	MA	34,340	MC
Asbury College	KY	18,540	VC
Austin College	TX	22,150	VC+
Baylor Univ	TX	18,298	VC+
Boston Univ	MA	34,358	MC
Bowling Green State Univ	OH	10,794	C
Bryn Mawr College	PA	33,580	HC+
Butler Univ	IN	25,580	VC+
Calvin College	MI	20,050	NC
Carleton College	MN	30,780	MC
Catholic Univ of America	DC	29,332	VC
CUNY/Brooklyn College	NY	3,403	LC
CUNY/Herbert H. Lehman College	NY	3,320	LC
CUNY/Hunter College	NY	5,147	C+
CUNY/Queens College	NY	3,403	VC
Colgate Univ	NY	33,480	MC
College of Wooster	OH	28,350	VC
Columbia Univ/Barnard College	NY	33,694	MC
Columbia Univ/Columbia College	NY	35,190	MC
Concordia College/Moorhead	MN	18,835	C
Cornell Univ	NY	34,614	MC
Creighton Univ	NE	23,476	VC
Denison Univ	OH	29,640	HC
DePauw Univ	IN	28,000	HC
Dickinson College	PA	32,210	VC+
Duquesne Univ	PA	24,242	C+
Emory Univ	GA	33,792	MC
Florida State Univ	FL	7,835	HC
Franklin and Marshall College	PA	32,410	HC
Furman Univ	SC	25,492	HC
Gettysburg College	PA	32,070	HC
Hampden-Sydney College	VA	24,871	C
Harvard Univ/Harvard College	MA	34,269	MC
Howard Univ	DC	15,522	LC
Indiana State Univ	IN	8,461	LC
Indiana Univ Bloomington	IN	10,712	C+
John Carroll Univ	OH	24,140	VC
Kent State Univ	OH	11,104	C
Kenyon College	OH	32,130	HC+
Louisiana State Univ and A&M College	LA	8,014	VC
Loyola College in Maryland	MD	30,900	HC
Loyola Marymount Univ	CA	28,754	HC
Loyola Univ of Chicago	IL	25,992	VC
Luther College	IA	23,300	VC+
Marlboro College	VT	26,410	VC+
Mary Washington College	VA	9,032	VC+
Mercer Univ	GA	24,130	VC
Miami Univ	OH	12,885	VC+
Mich State Univ	MI	10,386	VC
Monmouth College	IL	21,550	C
Montclair State Univ	NJ	10,287	LC
Mount Holyoke College	MA	34,128	HC
New York Univ	NY	35,200	MC
Ohio Univ	OH	11,769	C
Purdue Univ/West Lafayette	IN	10,284	VC
Randolph-Macon College	VA	24,395	C
Rutgers, The State Univ of New Jersey New Brunswick Campus	NJ	12,709	C
St. Louis Univ	MO	26,590	VC+
St. Olaf College	MN	25,880	HC
Samford Univ	AL	16,340	VC
Santa Clara Univ	CA	28,371	VC+
Sarah Lawrence College	NY	37,516	HC
Seattle Pacific Univ	WA	22,674	C+
Smith College	MA	33,302	HC+
Southwest Missouri State Univ	MO	7,600	LC
Southwestern Univ	TX	22,550	HC
SUNY/Univ at Albany	NY	10,997	VC
SUNY/Univ at Binghamton	NY	10,653	HC
Swarthmore College	PA	34,538	MC
Sweet Briar College	VA	25,310	VC
Texas Tech Univ	TX	8,825	C
Tufts Univ	MA	34,874	MC
Univ of Akron	OH	10,530	NC
Univ of Arizona	AZ	8,614	C
Univ of Calif at Berkeley	CA	14,134	MC
Univ of Calif at Davis	CA	12,796	VC
Univ of Calif at Los Angeles	CA	13,227	MC
Univ of Georgia	GA	8,656	VC
Univ of Idaho	ID	7,026	C
Univ of Iowa	IA	8,607	C+
Univ of Maine	ME	10,798	C
Univ of Mass Boston	MA	4,227	C
Univ of Mich/Ann Arbor	MI	13,003	HC+
Univ of Minn/Twin Cities	MN	11,123	VC
Univ of Nebr at Lincoln	NE	8,325	C+
Univ of New Hampshire	NH	13,207	C
Univ of N Car at Chapel Hill	NC	8,789	HC
Univ of N Car at Greensboro	NC	6,858	C
Univ of Notre Dame	IN	30,707	MC
Univ of Oregon	OR	9,969	C
Univ of Richmond	VA	27,300	HC
Univ of St. Thomas	MN	24,044	VC
Univ of Scranton	PA	27,964	C+
Univ of S Car at Columbia	SC	8,748	VC
Univ of Tenn at Chattanooga	TN	7,783	C
Univ of Texas at Austin	TX	9,437	HC
Univ of the South	TN	27,290	HC
Univ of Vermont	VT	14,761	C+
Univ of Wisc/Madison	WI	8,262	VC
Wabash College	IN	25,335	HC
Wake Forest Univ	NC	30,290	MC
Washington Univ in St. Louis	MO	34,593	MC
Wellesley College	MA	33,394	MC
West Chester Univ of Pennsylvania	PA	9,792	VC
Westminster College	PA	22,960	C
Wichita State Univ	KS	6,879	C

LATIN AMERICAN STUDIES

School	ST	$IS	SR
Adelphi Univ	NY	23,320	VC
Albright College	PA	27,642	C
American Univ	DC	31,544	VC+
Assumption College	MA	26,320	C
Austin College	TX	22,150	VC+
Ball State Univ	IN	8,660	C
Bard College	NY	33,912	HC
Baylor Univ	TX	18,298	VC+
Boston Univ	MA	34,358	MC
Bowdoin College	ME	32,650	MC
Brandeis Univ	MA	34,481	MC
Brigham Young Univ	UT	7,840	HC
Brown Univ	RI	34,973	MC
Bucknell Univ	PA	31,096	HC
Cal State, Chico	CA	8,598	LC
Cal State, Fullerton	CA	5,440	LC
Cal State, Hayward	CA	7,400	LC
Cal State, Los Angeles	CA	5,050	C
Carleton College	MN	30,780	MC
CUNY/Brooklyn College	NY	3,403	LC
CUNY/City College	NY	3,309	LC
CUNY/Hunter College	NY	5,147	C+
CUNY/Queens College	NY	3,403	VC
Colby College	ME	34,290	MC
Colgate Univ	NY	33,480	MC
College of the Holy Cross	MA	32,780	MC
Columbia Univ/Columbia College	NY	35,190	MC
Columbia Univ/School of General Studies	NY	35,000	C
Conn College	CT	33,585	MC
Cornell College	IA	24,980	VC
Dartmouth College	NH	34,458	MC
Denison Univ	OH	29,640	HC
DePaul Univ	IL	23,590	VC
Earlham College	IN	27,446	VC+
Emory Univ	GA	33,792	MC
Flagler College	FL	10,550	VC+
Florida Atlantic Univ	FL	8,832	C
Florida State Univ	FL	7,835	HC
Fordham Univ	NY	30,710	VC
George Washington Univ	DC	32,170	HC
Hamline Univ	MN	23,339	C+
Hampshire College	MA	33,881	HC+
Hanover College	IN	17,560	VC
Hood College	MD	26,020	VC
Johns Hopkins Univ	MD	35,226	MC
Kent State Univ	OH	11,104	C
Lake Forest College	IL	27,460	VC
Lock Haven Univ of Pennsylvania	PA	9,534	C
Macalester College	MN	28,814	HC+
Mass Inst of Technology	MA	35,228	MC
Mount Holyoke College	MA	34,128	HC
New York Univ	NY	35,200	MC
Notre Dame de Namur Univ	CA	26,932	LC
Oakland Univ	MI	9,418	C
Oberlin College	OH	33,140	HC+
Ohio Univ	OH	11,769	C
Penn State Univ/Univ Park Campus	PA	11,126	VC
Pitzer College	CA	33,930	HC
Pomona College	CA	33,960	MC
Rhode Island College	RI	8,700	LC
Rhodes College	TN	26,466	HC+
Ripon College	WI	24,180	VC+
Rollins College	FL	31,223	HC
Rutgers, The State Univ of New Jersey New Brunswick Campus	NJ	12,709	C
St. Mary's Univ of San Antonio	TX	19,735	C
Samford Univ	AL	16,340	VC
San Diego State Univ	CA	9,716	C+
Scripps College	CA	30,400	HC+
Seattle Pacific Univ	WA	22,674	C+
Simon's Rock College of Bard	MA	32,450	HC
Smith College	MA	33,302	HC+
Southern Methodist Univ	TX	28,349	VC
SUNY/College at Plattsburgh	NY	9,729	C
SUNY/Univ at Albany	NY	10,997	VC
SUNY/Univ at Binghamton	NY	10,653	HC
SUNY/Univ at New Paltz	NY	9,685	VC
Stetson Univ	FL	25,640	VC
Syracuse Univ	NY	30,710	HC
Temple Univ	PA	14,124	C
Texas Christian Univ	TX	19,910	C
Texas Tech Univ	TX	8,825	C
Tulane Univ	LA	34,013	HC+
Union College	NY	32,646	HC
Univ of Alabama	AL	7,402	C
Univ of Arizona	AZ	8,614	C
Univ of Calif at Berkeley	CA	14,134	MC
Univ of Calif at Los Angeles	CA	13,227	MC

School	ST	$IS	SR
Univ of Calif at Riverside	CA	12,479	C
Univ of Calif at San Diego	CA	11,372	HC
Univ of Calif at Santa Barbara	CA	11,732	VC
Univ of Calif at Santa Cruz	CA	13,655	VC
Univ of Chicago	IL	35,087	MC
Univ of Cincinnati	OH	12,491	LC
Univ of Conn	CT	12,122	VC
Univ of Delaware	DE	10,824	VC
Univ of Idaho	ID	7,026	C
Univ of Illinois at Chicago	IL	10,702	VC
Univ of Illinois at Urbana-Champaign	IL	11,316	HC+
Univ of Kansas	KS	7,232	VC
Univ of Kentucky	KY	7,765	C
Univ of Miami	FL	31,130	HC
Univ of Mich/Ann Arbor	MI	13,003	HC+
Univ of Minn/Morris	MN	10,716	VC
Univ of Nebr at Lincoln	NE	8,325	C+
Univ of New Mexico	NM	8,026	C
Univ of N Car at Chapel Hill	NC	8,789	HC
Univ of Northern Iowa	IA	7,850	C
Univ of Pennsylvania	PA	34,614	MC
Univ of Puget Sound	WA	28,285	HC
Univ of Rhode Island	RI	12,414	C
Univ of S Car at Columbia	SC	8,748	VC
Univ of Tenn at Knoxville	TN	8,214	C
Univ of Texas at Austin	TX	9,437	HC
Univ of Texas at El Paso	TX	5,076	LC
Univ of Texas-Pan American	TX	4,823	C
Univ of Vermont	VT	14,761	C+
Univ of Wisc/Eau Claire	WI	7,032	VC
Univ of Wisc/Madison	WI	8,262	VC
Vanderbilt Univ	TN	34,482	MC
Vassar College	NY	33,450	MC
Villanova Univ	PA	31,997	HC
Washington Univ in St. Louis	MO	34,593	MC
Wellesley College	MA	33,394	MC
Wesleyan Univ	CT	3,405	MC
Willamette Univ	OR	29,422	VC+
Yale Univ	CT	34,030	MC

LAW

School	ST	$IS	SR
American Univ	DC	31,544	VC+
Amherst College	MA	34,340	MC
Bay Path College	MA	22,308	C
Baylor Univ	TX	18,298	VC+
Becker College	MA	21,230	LC
Chapman Univ	CA	30,218	VC
Christopher Newport Univ	VA	8,862	VC
Drake Univ	IA	22,830	VC
Hampshire College	MA	33,881	HC+
Hood College	MD	26,020	VC
Lasell College	MA	24,100	C
Mount Ida College	MA	25,375	LC
Mountain State Univ	WV	8,180	NC
National Univ	CA	7,755	SP
Oberlin College	OH	33,140	HC+
Park Univ	MO	9,816	C
Purdue Univ/West Lafayette	IN	10,284	VC
Ramapo College of New Jersey	NJ	13,550	VC
Rice Univ	TX	24,325	MC
Rivier College	NH	24,215	C
Southeastern Univ	DC	8,505	LC
Texas Wesleyan Univ	TX	14,710	C
Towson Univ	MD	11,088	VC
Union College	NY	32,646	HC
United States Air Force Academy	CO		MC
United States Military Academy	NY		MC
Univ of Calif at Santa Barbara	CA	11,732	VC
Univ of Calif at Santa Cruz	CA	13,655	VC
Univ of Central Florida	FL	8,251	VC
Univ of Mass Amherst	MA	10,995	VC
Univ of Nebr at Lincoln	NE	8,325	C+
Univ of Pittsburgh at Pittsburgh	PA	13,592	HC
Univ of Wisc/Milwaukee	WI	8,907	LC
Univ of Wisc/Superior	WI	7,051	C+
Webster Univ	MO	19,804	VC
Wilson College	PA	21,337	LC
Wingate Univ	NC	19,140	C
Woodbury College	VT	12,060	LC

LAW ENFORCEMENT AND CORRECTIONS

School	ST	$IS	SR
CUNY/John Jay College of Criminal Justice	NY	3,251	C
College of the Ozarks	MO	2,650	C+
Frostburg State Univ	MD	9,680	C
Hardin-Simmons Univ	TX	14,165	C
Metropolitan State Univ	MN	2,943	SP
Minn State Univ, Mankato	MN	7,296	LC
St. Paul's College	VA	13,340	C
Sam Houston State Univ	TX	6,076	LC
Shenandoah Univ	VA	22,550	NC
Southeast Missouri State Univ	MO	8,367	C+
Southern Christian Univ	AL	8,480	LC
Southwest Texas State Univ	TX	8,730	VC
Stephen F. Austin State Univ	TX	6,905	C
Tarleton State Univ	TX	7,160	C
Tiffin Univ	OH	17,250	C
Univ of Great Falls	MT	15,360	C
Univ of Indianapolis	IN	20,840	C
Univ of New Haven	CT	23,860	LC
Univ of Pittsburgh at Pittsburgh	PA	13,592	HC
Univ of San Francisco	CA	27,302	VC
Univ of Virginia's College at Wise	VA	8,302	C
Washburn Univ of Topeka	KS	6,766	NC
Western Conn State Univ	CT	10,074	C
Western Illinois Univ	IL	9,571	C
Western New England College	MA	23,882	C
Western New Mexico Univ	NM	5,950	LC
Western Oregon Univ	OR	8,829	C
Youngstown State Univ	OH	9,318	NC

LIBERAL ARTS/GENERAL STUDIES

School	ST	$IS	SR
Adelphi Univ	NY	23,320	VC
Alaska Pacific Univ	AK	16,450	C
Albertus Magnus College	CT	22,154	C
Alcorn State Univ	MS	5,594	LC
Alderson-Broaddus College	WV	19,640	C
Alvernia College	PA	20,790	C
Alverno College	WI	16,930	LC
American International College	MA	22,268	LC
American Univ	DC	31,544	VC+
Angelo State Univ	TX	7,028	C
Anna Maria College	MA	22,800	LC
Aquinas College	TN	10,050	LC
Arcadia Univ	PA	26,650	C
Arkansas State Univ	AR	7,480	C
Armstrong Atlantic State Univ	GA	7,084	C
Atlantic Union College	MA	34,034	LC
Auburn Univ Montgomery	AL	5,330	NC
Averett Univ	VA	17,980	LC
Avila College	MO	17,720	C
Azusa Pacific Univ	CA	22,422	VC
Ball State Univ	IN	8,660	C
Barry Univ	FL	24,100	LC
Bartlesville Wesleyan College	OK	14,100	LC
Bay Path College	MA	22,308	C
Beacon College	FL	24,900	C
Bellarmine Univ	KY	20,440	VC
Belmont Abbey College	NC	19,630	LC
Belmont Univ	TN	19,066	VC
Benedictine College	KS	18,485	LC
Bennington College	VT	31,350	VC
Bentley College	MA	31,060	HC
Bethel College	IN	17,650	LC
Bethel College	TN	12,980	C
Bethune-Cookman College	FL	15,746	C
Boricua College	NY	7,375	C
Bowling Green State Univ	OH	10,794	C
Brenau Univ Women's College	GA	20,100	C
Brescia Univ	KY	14,225	C
Brewton-Parker College	GA	10,810	LC
Bridgewater College	VA	22,950	C
Bryan College	TN	16,400	VC
Cabrini College	PA	25,950	LC
Calif Baptist Univ	CA	16,736	C
Calif Lutheran Univ	CA	23,500	LC
Calif State Polytechnic Univ, Pomona	CA	8,615	C
Cal State, Bakersfield	CA	6,090	LC
Cal State, Chico	CA	8,598	LC
Cal State, Dominguez Hills	CA	5,840	LC
Cal State, Fresno	CA	7,762	C
Cal State, Fullerton	CA	5,140	LC
Cal State, Hayward	CA	7,400	LC
Cal State, Los Angeles	CA	5,050	C
Cal State, Monterey Bay	CA	6,250	LC
Cal State, Northridge	CA	7,781	C
Cal State, San Bernardino	CA	6,516	C
Cal State, San Marcos	CA	1,736	LC
Cal State, Stanislaus	CA	8,895	C
Calumet College of St. Joseph	IN	7,500	LC
Carlow College	PA	19,366	C
Cascade College	OR	14,800	NC
Catholic Univ of America	DC	29,332	VC
Cazenovia College	NY	19,885	LC
Cedar Crest College	PA	25,145	C+
Centenary College of Louisiana	LA	21,600	C+
Champlain College	VT	19,680	C
Chapman Univ	CA	30,218	VC
Charter Oak State College	CT		SP
Christian Brothers Univ	TN	19,820	VC
Christian Heritage College	CA	18,000	LC
City Univ	WA	7,425	NC
CUNY/College of Staten Island	NY	3,358	NC
CUNY/Medgar Evers College	NY	3,282	NC
CUNY/York College	NY	3,292	NC
Clarion Univ of Pennsylvania	PA	11,272	LC
Cleveland State Univ	OH	10,146	NC
College for Lifelong Learning	NH	4,100	SP
College Misericordia	PA	23,380	LC
College of Mount St. Vincent	NY	24,230	C
College of Mount St. Joseph	OH	20,290	C
College of New Rochelle - School of New Resources	NY	4,970	SP
College of Notre Dame of Maryland	MD	23,100	LC
College of St. Benedict	MN	23,921	VC
College of St. Joseph	VT	17,400	NC
College of St. Mary	NE	18,726	C
Colo Christian Univ	CO	17,714	C
Colo College	CO	31,525	HC+
Colo State Univ	CO	9,672	C
Columbia Union College	MD	19,027	C+
Columbus State Univ	GA	7,228	LC
Concordia Univ	CA	22,290	C
Concordia Univ at Austin	TX	16,740	LC
Crichton College	TN	12,680	LC
Dallas Baptist Univ	TX	13,682	LC
Dana College	NE	18,046	C
De Sales Univ	PA	22,610	VC
Dominican Univ of Calif	CA	27,948	C
Dowling College	NY	20,281	LC
Duquesne Univ	PA	24,242	C+
East Carolina Univ	NC	7,766	C
East Central Univ	OK	4,578	C
East Tenn State Univ	TN	7,127	C
Eastern Conn State Univ	CT	10,362	C
Eastern Mennonite Univ	VA	20,700	VC
Eastern Mich Univ	MI	9,855	C
Eastern Oregon Univ	OR	8,772	C
Edinboro Univ of Pennsylvania	PA	9,328	LC
Elmhurst College	IL	21,750	C
Emporia State Univ	KS	6,198	LC
Endicott College	MA	23,704	C
Eureka College	IL	22,200	C
Evergreen State College	WA	8,707	C
Excelsior College	NY	915	SP
Fairleigh Dickinson Univ/Teaneck Campus	NJ	24,646	C
Faulkner Univ	AL	13,000	C
Ferrum College	VA	15,990	LC
Fitchburg State College	MA	7,836	C
Florida Atlantic Univ	FL	8,832	C
Florida Gulf Coast Univ	FL	9,201	C
Florida International Univ	FL	9,486	VC
Fontbonne Univ	MO	18,046	C
Fort Hays State Univ	KS	6,294	LC
Francis Marion Univ	SC	7,682	C
Frostburg State Univ	MD	9,680	C
Gannon Univ	PA	18,848	C
George Washington Univ	DC	32,170	HC
Georgia College and State Univ	GA	7,344	C
Georgia Southern Univ	GA	6,958	C
Gonzaga Univ	WA	24,276	HC+
Graceland Univ	IA	15,845	C
Green Mountain College	VT	24,130	C
Greenville College	IL	19,226	LC
Hannibal-LaGrange College	MO	12,530	C
Harding Univ	AR	13,528	VC
Hilbert College	NY	16,830	LC
Hofstra Univ	NY	23,252	C
Holy Names College	CA	23,220	C
Hope International Univ	CA	16,940	NC
Howard Payne Univ	TX	13,834	C+
Humboldt State Univ	CA	8,582	C
Idaho State Univ	ID	7,030	C+
Indiana State Univ	IN	8,461	LC
Indiana Univ Bloomington	IN	10,712	C+
Indiana Univ East	IN	3,415	C
Indiana Univ Kokomo	IN	3,422	LC
Indiana Univ Northwest	IN	3,447	C
Indiana Univ South Bend	IN	3,515	C
Indiana Univ Southeast	IN	3,459	C
Indiana Univ-Purdue Univ Indianapolis	IN	9,473	C
Iowa State Univ	IA	8,108	VC
Ithaca College	NY	28,719	HC
James Madison Univ	VA	9,552	HC
Johnson C. Smith Univ	NC	16,560	C+
Johnson State College	VT	10,776	C
Kent State Univ	OH	11,104	C
Kentucky State Univ	KY	6,146	NC
Kutztown Univ of Pennsylvania	PA	8,907	C
La Roche College	PA	18,854	LC
La Sierra Univ	CA	19,260	LC
Lasell College	MA	24,100	C
Lewis Univ	IL	20,960	C
Lewis-Clark State College	ID	6,496	C
Liberty Univ	VA	14,500	C
Limestone College	SC	16,900	C
Lincoln Univ	MO	7,158	NC
Lindenwood Univ	MO	17,250	C
Lindsey Wilson College	KY	16,002	LC
Lock Haven Univ of Pennsylvania	PA	9,534	C
LIU/Southampton College	NY	26,270	C
Longwood College	VA	8,950	C
Loras College	IA	22,994	C+
Louisiana State Univ and A&M College	LA	8,014	VC
Louisiana State Univ in Shreveport	LA	2,480	NC
Louisiana Tech Univ	LA	6,506	C
Loyola Marymount Univ	CA	28,754	HC
MacMurray College	IL	17,790	LC
Madonna Univ	MI	11,504	VC
Malone College	OH	19,190	C
Manhattanville College	NY	28,730	VC
Mansfield Univ	PA	9,648	C
Marymount College/Tarrytown	NY	23,850	C
Marymount Manhattan College	NY	23,195	VC
Marymount Univ	VA	21,560	LC
Maryville Univ of St. Louis	MO	18,680	C
Master's College	CA	21,500	C+
Mayville State Univ	ND	6,440	NC
McNeese State Univ	LA	5,259	LC
Medaille College	NY	18,320	C
Menlo College	CA	24,000	LC
Mesa State College	CO	8,051	C
Metropolitan State Univ	MN	2,943	SP
Mich Tech Univ	MI	11,088	VC
Midway College	KY	15,815	C
Mills College	CA	27,950	C
Minot State Univ	ND	5,466	LC
Miss State Univ	MS	7,853	C
Missouri Southern State College	MO	6,666	C
Missouri Valley College	MO	17,400	LC
Mitchell College	CT	23,950	C
Montana State Univ-Billings	MT	7,653	NC
Montana Tech of The Univ of Montana	MT	7,845	C
Montreat College	NC	17,164	C
Morehead State Univ	KY	6,510	C
Morris College	SC	9,995	LC
Mount Ida College	MA	25,375	LC
Mount Olive College	NC	14,410	LC
Mount St. Clare College	IA	19,050	LC
Mount St. Mary's College	CA	24,430	C
Murray State Univ	KY	6,672	C
National Univ	CA	7,755	SP
Neumann College	PA	22,040	NC
New Mexico Inst of Mining and Technology	NM	7,152	VC+
Norfolk State Univ	VA	8,382	LC
Northern Illinois Univ	IL	9,545	C
Northwest Nazarene Univ	ID	18,380	C
Northwestern State Univ of Louisiana	LA	5,745	NC
Norwich Univ	VT	21,064	LC
Notre Dame de Namur Univ	CA	26,932	LC
Nova Southeastern Univ	FL	20,104	LC
Oakland Univ	MI	9,418	C
Ohio Univ	OH	11,769	C
Ohio Valley College	WV	13,650	C+
Okla Christian Univ	OK	16,500	VC
Okla State Univ	OK	7,650	VC
Olivet Nazarene Univ	IL	18,444	C
Oral Roberts Univ	OK	18,490	C
Oregon State Univ	OR	9,612	VC
Otterbein College	OH	23,439	C
Our Lady of Holy Cross College	LA	5,140	NC
Our Lady of the Lake Univ of San Antonio	TX	17,336	C
Park Univ	MO	9,816	C
Penn State Univ/Altoona	PA	12,578	C
Penn State Univ/Univ Park Campus	PA	11,126	VC
Pepperdine Univ	CA	32,830	VC
Point Loma Nazarene Univ	CA	21,380	VC
Point Park College	PA	20,290	C
Polytechnic Univ/Brooklyn	NY	33,090	HC
Pontifical Catholic Univ of PR/Ponce	PR	7,076	
Portland State Univ	OR	11,220	C
Purdue Univ/West Lafayette	IN	10,284	VC
Quinnipiac Univ	CT	27,370	C
Radford Univ	VA	8,302	C
Reinhardt College	GA	13,300	C
Rice Univ	TX	24,325	MC
Richard Stockton College of New Jersey	NJ	12,165	VC
Rider Univ	NJ	27,400	C
Rivier College	NH	24,215	C
Roosevelt Univ	IL	20,240	LC
Rosemont College	PA	24,060	C
Rowan Univ	NJ	12,365	VC
Rutgers, The State Univ of New Jersey/CamdenCampus	NJ	6,484	C
Sacred Heart Univ	CT	26,588	VC
St. Andrews Presbyterian College	NC	19,720	LC
St. Anselm College	NH	27,405	C
St. Edward's Univ	TX	17,846	C

School	ST	$IS	SR
St. John's College	MD	32,760	HC+
St. John's College	NM	32,835	VC+
St. John's Univ	NY	26,660	C
St. Mary College	KS	17,298	C
St. Mary's College of Calif	CA	27,575	C
St. Thomas Univ	FL	19,500	LC
St. Vincent College	PA	22,942	VC
Salem International Univ	WV	17,263	LC
Samford Univ	AL	16,340	VC
San Francisco State Univ	CA	7,139	LC
Santa Clara Univ	CA	28,371	VC+
Sarah Lawrence College	NY	37,516	HC
Seattle Pacific Univ	WA	22,674	C+
Seattle Univ	WA	24,183	VC
Seton Hall Univ	NJ	26,910	LC
Seton Hill College	PA	21,875	C
Shaw Univ	NC	12,810	C
Sheldon Jackson College	AK	14,940	LC
Shenandoah Univ	VA	22,550	NC
Siena Heights Univ	MI	16,140	LC
Simpson College	CA	19,200	C
Skidmore College	NY	34,201	VC+
Southeast Missouri State Univ	MO	8,367	C+
Southeastern Louisiana Univ	LA	6,047	LC
Southeastern Univ	DC	8,505	LC
Southern Christian Univ	AL	8,480	LC
Southern Illinois Univ at Carbondale	IL	8,621	C
Southern Illinois Univ Edwardsville	IL	7,869	LC
Southern Methodist Univ	TX	28,349	VC
Southern Oregon Univ	OR	9,429	C
Southern Vermont College	VT	17,685	C
Southwestern College	KS	17,656	C
Spalding Univ	KY	15,196	C
Spring Hill College	AL	23,250	C
SUNY/College at Purchase	NY	10,587	VC
SUNY/Empire State College	NY	3,545	SP
Stephens College	MO	22,295	C
Sweet Briar College	VA	25,310	VC
Teikyo Post Univ	CT	21,800	C
Texas Christian Univ	TX	19,910	C
Texas Tech Univ	TX	8,825	C
Thomas Aquinas College	CA	20,500	HC+
Thomas Edison State College	NJ	2,750	SP
Thomas More College	KY	17,700	LC
Thomas Univ	GA	8,770	NC
Tiffin Univ	OH	17,250	C
Touro College	NY	14,950	VC
Trinity International Univ	IL	20,640	C+
United States International Univ	CA	18,675	LC
Univ of Alaska Southeast	AK	7,900	LC
Univ of Arizona	AZ	8,614	C
Univ of Arkansas at Little Rock	AR	5,637	NC
Univ of Arkansas at Pine Bluff	AR	7,925	C
Univ of Calif at Riverside	CA	12,479	C
Univ of Central Florida	FL	8,251	VC
Univ of Central Okla	OK	5,205	C
Univ of Charleston	WV	20,640	C
Univ of Detroit Mercy	MI	21,620	LC
Univ of Evansville	IN	22,865	VC+
Univ of Hawaii at Hilo	HI	6,497	C
Univ of Hawaii at Manoa	HI	7,862	VC
Univ of Illinois at Urbana-Champaign	IL	11,316	HC+
Univ of Iowa	IA	8,607	C+
Univ of Judaism College of A&S	CA	24,230	C
Univ of La Verne	CA	24,280	C
Univ of Louisiana at Monroe	LA	5,207	NC
Univ of Louisville	KY	7,402	LC
Univ of Maine at Farmington	ME	9,163	C
Univ of Maine at Fort Kent	ME	7,450	LC
Univ of Maine at Machias	ME	7,689	LC
Univ of Maine at Presque Isle	ME	7,964	LC
Univ of Maryland/Eastern Shore	MD	9,258	C
Univ of Maryland/Univ College	MD	5,910	SP
Univ of Mass Amherst	MA	10,995	VC
Univ of Mass Lowell	MA	9,470	VC
Univ of Mich/Ann Arbor	MI	13,003	HC+
Univ of Mich/Dearborn	MI	4,677	VC
Univ of Minn/Morris	MN	10,716	VC
Univ of Miss	MS	7,666	C
Univ of Missouri/Kansas City	MO	9,685	VC
Univ of Mobile	AL	13,620	LC
Univ of Montana	MT	8,038	C
Univ of Montana--Western	MT	6,915	NC
Univ of Nevada/Reno	NV	8,737	C
Univ of New Haven	CT	23,860	LC
Univ of N Car at Chapel Hill	NC	8,789	HC
Univ of N Dak	ND	7,067	VC
Univ of North Texas	TX	7,629	C
Univ of Northern Iowa	IA	7,850	C
Univ of Notre Dame	IN	30,707	MC
Univ of Okla	OK	7,616	VC
Univ of Pittsburgh at Pittsburgh	PA	13,592	HC
Univ of PR/Rio Piedras	PR	5,510	
Univ of Redlands	CA	29,246	VC
Univ of St. Francis	IL	19,650	C
Univ of St. Francis	IN	17,790	LC
Univ of St. Thomas	TX	18,752	VC
Univ of San Diego	CA	29,198	HC
Univ of S Dak	SD	7,036	C
Univ of South Florida	FL	8,154	C
Univ of Tampa	FL	22,612	C
Univ of Texas at Austin	TX	9,437	HC
Univ of Texas-Pan American	TX	4,823	C
Univ of the Ozarks	AR	13,904	C
Univ of the Pacific	CA	28,255	VC
Univ of Virginia's College at Wise	VA	8,302	C
Univ of Washington	WA	10,361	VC
Univ of Wisc/Green Bay	WI	7,148	C
Univ of Wisc/Oshkosh	WI	6,130	LC
Univ of Wisc/Stevens Point	WI	7,116	C
Urbana Univ	OH	17,004	C
Utah State Univ	UT	6,771	C
Valdosta State Univ	GA	6,988	C
Valley City State Univ	ND		LC
Villa Julie College	MD	16,026	C
Villanova Univ	PA	31,997	HC
Virginia Intermont College	VA	17,510	C
Virginia Polytechnic Inst and State Univ	VA	7,652	C
Virginia Wesleyan College	VA	22,350	LC
Viterbo Univ	WI	18,043	C
Warner Pacific College	OR	20,370	LC
Washburn Univ of Topeka	KS	6,766	NC
Washington State Univ	WA	9,388	C
Wayne State Univ	MI	6,720	C
Wesley College	DE	17,869	C
West Chester Univ of Pennsylvania	PA	9,792	VC
West Texas A&M Univ	TX	6,538	C
West Virginia Univ	WV	8,304	C
Western Mich Univ	MI	10,016	C
Westmont College	CA	29,748	VC
Wichita State Univ	KS	6,879	C
Wilberforce Univ	OH	14,937	LC
Wiley College	TX	8,100	LC
Wilkes Univ	PA	25,800	C
William Carey College	MS	10,150	LC
Wilmington College	OH	21,826	C
Wingate Univ	NC	19,140	C
Xavier Univ	OH	23,880	C
York College	NE	13,500	C

LIBRARY SCIENCE

School	ST	$IS	SR
Clarion Univ of Pennsylvania	PA	11,272	LC
Eastern Conn State Univ	CT	10,362	C
Kutztown Univ of Pennsylvania	PA	8,907	C
Northwestern Okla State Univ	OK	4,542	NC
Rice Univ	TX	24,325	MC
Southern Conn State Univ	CT	10,310	C
Texas Woman's Univ	TX	5,855	LC
Univ of Central Arkansas	AR	6,388	C
Univ of Maine at Augusta	ME	3,928	C
Western Kentucky Univ	KY	6,834	C

LIFE SCIENCE

School	ST	$IS	SR
Atlantic Union College	MA	34,034	LC
Azusa Pacific Univ	CA	22,422	VC
Baylor Univ	TX	18,298	VC+
Bowling Green State Univ	OH	10,794	C
Husson College	ME	15,360	LC
Iowa Wesleyan College	IA	18,840	C
Johns Hopkins Univ	MD	35,226	MC
Kansas State Univ	KS	6,995	C
Kent State Univ	OH	11,104	C
Malone College	OH	19,190	C
Morehead State Univ	KY	6,510	C
National Univ	CA	7,755	SP
New York Inst of Technology	NY	21,756	C
Niagara Univ	NY	22,250	C+
Northwest College	WA	17,471	C
Nova Southeastern Univ	FL	20,104	LC
Otterbein College	OH	23,439	C
Stephen F. Austin State Univ	TX	6,905	C
United States Military Academy	NY		MC
Univ of Missouri/Rolla	MO	10,034	C
Univ of New Mexico	NM	8,026	C
Wayne State College	NE	6,255	NC

LINGUISTICS

School	ST	$IS	SR
Boston College	MA	33,330	MC
Boston Univ	MA	34,358	MC
Brandeis Univ	MA	34,481	MC
Brigham Young Univ	UT	7,840	HC
Brown Univ	RI	34,973	MC
Cal State, Fresno	CA	7,762	C
Cal State, Fullerton	CA	5,440	LC
Cal State, Northridge	CA	7,781	C
Central College	IA	21,206	C
CUNY/Brooklyn College	NY	3,403	LC
CUNY/Herbert H. Lehman College	NY	3,320	LC
CUNY/Queens College	NY	3,403	VC
Cleveland State Univ	OH	10,146	NC
Columbia Univ/Barnard College	NY	33,694	MC
Columbia Univ/Columbia College	NY	35,190	MC
Cornell Univ	NY	34,614	MC
Dartmouth College	NH	34,458	MC
Duke Univ	NC	34,396	MC
Eastern Mich Univ	MI	9,855	C
Florida Atlantic Univ	FL	8,832	C
Florida State Univ	FL	7,835	HC
Georgetown Univ	DC	34,847	MC
Hampshire College	MA	33,881	HC+
Harvard Univ/Harvard College	MA	34,269	MC
Indiana Univ Bloomington	IN	10,712	C+
Iowa State Univ	IA	8,108	VC
Lawrence Univ	WI	27,711	HC
Macalester College	MN	28,814	HC+
Marlboro College	VT	26,410	VC+
Miami Univ	OH	12,885	VC+
Mich State Univ	MI	10,386	VC
Montclair State Univ	NJ	10,287	LC
New York Univ	NY	35,200	MC
Northeastern Univ	MA	30,078	VC
Northwestern Univ	IL	33,615	MC
Oakland Univ	MI	9,418	C
Ohio Univ	OH	11,769	C
Pitzer College	CA	33,930	HC
Pomona College	CA	33,960	MC
Portland State Univ	OR	11,220	C
Purdue Univ/West Lafayette	IN	10,284	VC
Rutgers, The State Univ of New Jersey/New Brunswick Campus	NJ	12,709	C
San Diego State Univ	CA	9,716	C+
Southern Illinois Univ at Carbondale	IL	8,621	C
Stanford Univ	CA	34,222	MC
SUNY/College at Oswego	NY	10,856	C
SUNY/Univ at Albany	NY	10,997	VC
SUNY/Univ at Binghamton	NY	10,653	HC
SUNY/Univ at Buffalo	NY	11,033	VC
SUNY/Univ at Stony Brook	NY	10,998	VC
Swarthmore College	PA	34,538	MC
Syracuse Univ	NY	30,710	HC
Temple Univ	PA	14,124	C
Ohio State Univ	OH	10,819	VC
Tulane Univ	LA	34,013	HC+
Univ of Alabama at Birmingham	AL	10,110	C
Univ of Alaska Fairbanks	AK	8,265	NC
Univ of Arizona	AZ	8,614	C
Univ of Calif at Berkeley	CA	14,134	MC
Univ of Calif at Davis	CA	12,796	VC
Univ of Calif at Irvine	CA	11,756	C
Univ of Calif at Los Angeles	CA	13,227	MC
Univ of Calif at Riverside	CA	12,479	C
Univ of Calif at San Diego	CA	11,372	HC
Univ of Calif at Santa Barbara	CA	11,732	VC
Univ of Calif at Santa Cruz	CA	13,655	VC
Univ of Chicago	IL	35,087	MC
Univ of Cincinnati	OH	12,491	LC
Univ of Colo at Boulder	CO	9,255	VC
Univ of Conn	CT	12,122	VC
Univ of Florida	FL	7,874	HC
Univ of Georgia	GA	8,656	VC
Univ of Hawaii at Hilo	HI	6,497	C
Univ of Illinois at Urbana-Champaign	IL	11,316	HC+
Univ of Iowa	IA	8,607	C+
Univ of Kansas	KS	7,232	VC
Univ of Kentucky	KY	7,765	C
Univ of Louisville	KY	7,402	LC
Univ of Maryland/Baltimore County	MD	12,190	VC
Univ of Maryland/College Park	MD	11,959	C
Univ of Mass Amherst	MA	10,995	VC
Univ of Mich/Ann Arbor	MI	13,003	HC+
Univ of Minn/Twin Cities	MN	11,123	VC
Univ of Miss	MS	7,666	C
Univ of New Hampshire	NH	13,207	C
Univ of New Mexico	NM	8,026	C
Univ of N Car at Chapel Hill	NC	8,789	HC
Univ of Okla	OK	7,616	VC
Univ of Oregon	OR	9,969	C
Univ of Pennsylvania	PA	34,614	MC
Univ of Pittsburgh at Pittsburgh	PA	13,592	HC
Univ of Rochester	NY	32,979	HC
Univ of Southern Calif	CA	33,647	MC
Univ of Tenn at Knoxville	TN	8,214	C
Univ of Texas at Austin	TX	9,437	HC
Univ of Texas at El Paso	TX	5,076	LC
Univ of Toledo	OH	11,206	NC
Univ of Utah	UT	7,703	C
Univ of Wisc/Madison	WI	8,262	VC
Univ of Wisc/Milwaukee	WI	8,907	LC
Washington State Univ	WA	9,388	C
Wayne State Univ	MI	6,720	C
Western Washington Univ	WA	8,624	VC
Yale Univ	CT	34,030	MC

LITERATURE

School	ST	$IS	SR
Alderson-Broaddus College	WV	19,640	C
American Univ	DC	31,544	VC+
Andrews Univ	MI	17,696	LC
Aurora Univ	IL	18,551	C
Austin Peay State Univ	TN	5,814	LC
Beloit College	WI	27,482	HC
Benedictine Univ	IL	21,330	C
Bennington College	VT	31,350	VC
Burlington College	VT	10,640	SP
Calif Inst of Technology	CA	27,663	MC
Cal State, San Marcos	CA	1,736	LC
Castleton State College	VT	10,922	LC
Claremont McKenna College	CA	32,700	MC
Coe College	IA	24,750	VC
Columbia Univ/School of General Studies	NY	35,000	C
Concordia College/Moorhead	MN	18,835	C
Drake Univ	IA	22,830	VC
Drexel Univ	PA	27,657	VC
Duke Univ	NC	34,396	MC
Duquesne Univ	PA	24,242	C+
Eastern Mich Univ	MI	9,855	C
Eastern Nazarene College	MA	19,433	LC
Eastern Washington Univ	WA	7,972	LC
Emory & Henry College	VA	19,462	C
George Fox Univ	OR	24,095	VC
George Washington Univ	DC	32,170	HC
Gonzaga Univ	WA	24,276	HC+
Graceland Univ	IA	15,845	C
Hampshire College	MA	33,881	HC+
Harvard Univ/Harvard College	MA	34,269	MC
Hawaii Pacific Univ	HI	17,790	C
John Carroll Univ	OH	24,140	VC
Kentucky Christian College	KY	13,472	C
Maharishi Univ of Management	IA	20,660	VC
Mass Inst of Technology	MA	35,228	MC
Middlebury College	VT	34,300	MC
Naropa Univ	CO	22,416	SP
New College of Florida	FL	8,130	HC+
Norfolk State Univ	VA	8,382	LC
Ohio Northern Univ	OH	27,765	VC
Oral Roberts Univ	OK	18,490	C
Pacific Univ	OR	24,250	C
Point Loma Nazarene Univ	CA	21,380	VC
Pomona College	CA	33,960	MC
Ramapo College of New Jersey	NJ	13,550	VC
Rocky Mountain College	MT	18,113	C
Roosevelt Univ	IL	20,240	LC
St. John's Univ	NY	26,660	C
St. Mary's Univ of Minn	MN	19,975	C
Sarah Lawrence College	NY	37,516	HC
Simon's Rock College of Bard	MA	32,450	HC
Southern Vermont College	VT	17,685	C
Southwest State Univ	MN	7,117	LC
SUNY/College at Purchase	NY	10,587	VC
Stevens Inst of Technology	NJ	31,510	HC+
Swarthmore College	PA	34,538	MC
Sweet Briar College	VA	25,310	VC
Thomas Edison State College	NJ	2,750	SP
Thomas More College of Liberal Arts	NH	17,700	C
Touro College	NY	14,950	VC
Union College	NE	14,650	C
United States Military Academy	NY		MC
Univ of Alaska Southeast	AK	7,900	LC
Univ of Bridgeport	CT	23,020	LC
Univ of Calif at San Diego	CA	11,372	HC
Univ of Calif at Santa Barbara	CA	11,732	VC
Univ of Calif at Santa Cruz	CA	13,655	VC
Univ of Evansville	IN	22,865	VC+
Univ of Illinois at Chicago	IL	10,702	VC
Univ of Judaism College of A&S	CA	24,230	C
Univ of Mich/Ann Arbor	MI	13,003	HC+
Univ of New Haven	CT	23,860	LC
Univ of N Car at Asheville	NC	6,896	VC
Univ of Rhode Island	RI	12,414	C
Univ of St. Thomas	MN	24,044	VC
Univ of Texas at Dallas	TX	9,305	VC
Washington Univ in St. Louis	MO	34,593	MC
Waynesburg College	PA	17,610	LC
Webster Univ	MO	19,804	VC
West Chester Univ of Pennsylvania	PA	9,792	VC
Wheaton College	MA	32,940	VC
Wilberforce Univ	OH	14,937	LC
Williams College	MA	32,270	MC

School	ST	$IS	SR
Yale Univ	CT	34,030	MC

LUSO-BRAZILIAN STUDIES

School	ST	$IS	SR
New York Univ	NY	35,200	MC
Smith College	MA	33,302	HC+

MANAGEMENT ENGINEERING

School	ST	$IS	SR
Claremont McKenna College	CA	32,700	MC
Marywood Univ	PA	24,639	C
Pitzer College	CA	33,930	HC
Univ of Mich/Flint	MI	4,323	C
Univ of PR/Bayamon Univ College Campus	PR	1,600	
Worcester Polytechnic Inst	MA	34,480	HC+

MANAGEMENT INFORMATION SYSTEMS

School	ST	$IS	SR
Adams State College	CO	7,468	C
Adelphi Univ	NY	23,320	VC
Adrian College	MI	19,670	C
Albertus Magnus College	CT	22,154	C
Alderson-Broaddus College	WV	19,640	C
American Univ	DC	31,544	VC+
Andrews Univ	MI	17,696	LC
Arkansas State Univ	AR	7,480	C
Ashland Univ	OH	22,182	LC
Augsburg College	MN	22,978	C
Augustana College	SD	20,760	VC
Aurora Univ	IL	18,551	C
Barry Univ	FL	24,100	LC
Bay Path College	MA	22,308	C
Baylor Univ	TX	18,298	VC+
Benedictine Univ	IL	21,330	C
Bentley College	MA	31,060	HC
Boston Univ	MA	34,358	MC
Bowling Green State Univ	OH	10,794	C
Bradley Univ	IL	20,970	VC
Brigham Young Univ	UT	7,840	HC
Cal State, Fullerton	CA	5,440	LC
Cal State, Long Beach	CA	7,400	LC
Cal State, Northridge	CA	7,781	C
Cal State, Sacramento	CA	7,488	C
Cal State, San Bernardino	CA	6,516	C
Canisius College	NY	24,696	C+
Cedarville Univ	OH	17,553	VC
Central Conn State Univ	CT	10,404	C
Champlain College	VT	19,680	C
Chatham College	PA	25,454	C+
Clarkson Univ	NY	29,884	VC
Cleveland State Univ	OH	10,146	NC
Colo Christian Univ	CO	17,714	C
Colo Technical Univ	CO	9,425	LC
Columbus State Univ	GA	7,228	LC
Concordia Univ	MN	19,912	C
Creighton Univ	NE	23,476	VC
Dallas Baptist Univ	TX	13,682	LC
Daniel Webster College	NH	24,870	C
De Sales Univ	PA	22,610	VC
East Carolina Univ	NC	7,766	C
East Central Univ	OK	4,578	C
Eastern College	PA	19,641	LC
Eastern Mich Univ	MI	9,855	C
Emporia State Univ	KS	6,198	LC
Eureka College	IL	22,200	C
Excelsior College	NY	915	SP
Ferrum College	VA	15,990	LC
Florida International Univ	FL	9,486	VC
Florida State Univ	FL	7,835	HC
Fort Hays State Univ	KS	6,294	LC
Friends Univ	KS	15,962	LC
Gannon Univ	PA	18,848	C
George Mason Univ	VA	9,192	C
Georgetown College	KY	18,400	VC
Georgia State Univ	GA	7,792	LC
Grace College	IN	16,768	C
Greenville College	IL	19,226	LC
Grove City College	PA	12,280	MC
Hofstra Univ	NY	23,252	C
Humphreys College	CA	6,900	NC
Huron Univ	SD	10,450	C
Indiana State Univ	IN	8,461	LC
Indiana Univ Bloomington	IN	10,712	C+
Indiana Univ of Pennsylvania	PA	9,133	C
Inter-American Univ of PR/ Bayamon Univ College	PR	3,700	
Inter-American Univ of PR/ Fajardo Campus	PR	4,000	
Inter-American Univ of PR/ Metropolitan Campus	PR	4,166	
Inter-American Univ of PR/ Ponce Regional College	PR	3,700	
Iona College	NY	26,556	C
Johnson and Wales Univ	RI	21,558	LC
Johnson State College	VT	10,776	C
Juniata College	PA	26,080	VC
Kansas State Univ	KS	6,995	C
La Salle Univ	PA	27,890	C
Lasell College	MA	24,100	C
LeTourneau Univ	TX	19,020	VC
Lewis Univ	IL	20,960	C
Limestone College	SC	16,900	C
Lindenwood Univ	MO	17,250	C
Loras College	IA	22,994	C+
Louisiana State Univ and A&M College	LA	8,014	VC
Luther College	IA	23,300	VC+
MacMurray College	IL	17,790	LC
Marietta College	OH	24,580	C
Marquette Univ	WI	24,836	C+
McMurry Univ	TX	15,287	C
Menlo College	CA	24,000	LC
Mercyhurst College	PA	20,694	C
Metropolitan State Univ	MN	2,943	SP
Miami Univ	OH	12,885	VC+
Midland Lutheran College	NE	18,600	C
Millikin Univ	IL	24,415	C+
Milwaukee School of Engineering	WI	25,680	VC+
Minot State Univ	ND	5,466	LC
Missouri Southern State College	MO	6,666	C
National Univ	CA	7,755	SP
New Mexico Highlands Univ	NM	6,256	NC
New Mexico State Univ	NM	7,302	C
Nichols College	MA	24,610	LC
Norfolk State Univ	VA	8,382	LC
N Dak State Univ	ND	7,004	VC
Northeastern Univ	MA	30,078	VC
Northwestern College	MN	19,816	C+
Northwood Univ	FL	19,179	LC
Northwood Univ	TX	18,135	C
Oakland Univ	MI	9,418	C
Ohio Dominican College	OH	18,100	LC
Ohio Univ	OH	11,769	C
Okla State Univ	OK	7,650	VC
Old Dominion Univ	VA	9,386	C
Oral Roberts Univ	OK	18,490	C
Oregon Inst of Technology	OR	8,718	C
Ottawa Univ	KS	11,800	LC
Our Lady of the Lake Univ of San Antonio	TX	17,336	C
Palm Beach Atlantic College	FL	23,310	C
Park Univ	MO	9,816	C
Penn State Univ at Erie/ Behrend College	PA	12,326	C
Penn State Univ/Univ Park Campus	PA	11,126	VC
Philadelphia Univ	PA	24,722	C
Point Loma Nazarene Univ	CA	21,380	VC
Rensselaer Polytechnic Inst	NY	33,863	HC+
Rivier College	NH	24,215	C
Rochester Inst of Technology	NY	26,232	VC+
Rockhurst Univ	MO	20,090	C
Rutgers, The State Univ of New Jersey New Brunswick Campus	NJ	12,709	C
St. Edward's Univ	TX	17,846	C
St. Francis Univ	PA	24,486	LC
St. Joseph's College	IN	21,640	C
Salisbury Univ	MD	10,576	VC
Sam Houston State Univ	TX	6,076	LC
Savannah State Univ	GA	2,550	LC
Schreiner Univ	TX	19,254	C
Seton Hall Univ	NJ	26,910	LC
Shippensburg Univ of Pennsylvania	PA	9,652	C
Simmons College	MA	30,418	VC
Southern Christian Univ	AL	8,480	LC
Southern Illinois Univ Edwardsville	IL	7,869	LC
Southern Methodist Univ	TX	28,349	VC
Southern Nazarene Univ	OK	14,634	NC
Southwestern College	KS	17,656	C
Southwestern Okla State Univ	OK	4,801	C
Spring Arbor Univ	MI	17,976	C
SUNY/College at Old Westbury	NY	9,818	LC
State Univ of West Georgia	GA	7,101	C
Stephen F. Austin State Univ	TX	6,905	C
Syracuse Univ	NY	30,710	HC
Temple Univ	PA	14,124	C
Texas Lutheran Univ	TX	17,660	C
Texas Tech Univ	TX	8,825	C
Texas Wesleyan Univ	TX	14,710	C
Ohio State Univ	OH	10,819	VC
Thiel College	PA	18,419	LC
Thomas College	ME	18,915	LC
Thomas Edison State College	NJ	2,750	SP
Tusculum College	TN	17,900	LC
Univ of Alabama	AL	7,402	C
Univ of Alabama at Huntsville	AL	7,916	VC
Univ of Alaska Anchorage	AK	9,100	NC
Univ of Arizona	AZ	8,614	C
Univ of Arkansas at Monticello	AR	5,940	NC
Univ of Bridgeport	CT	23,020	C
Univ of Central Florida	FL	8,251	VC
Univ of Central Okla	OK	5,205	C
Univ of Conn	CT	12,122	VC
Univ of Dayton	OH	20,400	VC
Univ of Georgia	GA	8,050	VC
Univ of Hartford	CT	28,884	C
Univ of Hawaii at Manoa	HI	7,862	VC
Univ of Houston	TX	8,410	C
Univ of Idaho	ID	7,026	C
Univ of Indianapolis	IN	20,840	C
Univ of Louisiana at Monroe	LA	5,207	NC
Univ of Mary	ND	12,900	LC
Univ of Maryland/College Park	MD	11,959	C
Univ of Mass Dartmouth	MA	9,852	C
Univ of Memphis	TN	7,271	C
Univ of Miami	FL	31,130	HC
Univ of Miss	MS	7,666	C
Univ of Missouri/Rolla	MO	10,034	C
Univ of Missouri/St. Louis	MO	9,966	C
Univ of Nebr at Omaha	NE	6,867	C
Univ of Nevada/Las Vegas	NV	8,281	VC
Univ of N Car at Charlotte	NC	7,254	C
Univ of N Dak	ND	7,067	VC
Univ of North Texas	TX	7,629	C
Univ of Northern Iowa	IA	7,050	C
Univ of Notre Dame	IN	30,707	MC
Univ of Okla	OK	7,616	VC
Univ of Pennsylvania	PA	34,614	MC
Univ of PR/Rio Piedras	PR	5,510	
Univ of Rhode Island	RI	12,414	C
Univ of St. Thomas	TX	18,752	VC
Univ of San Francisco	CA	27,302	VC
Univ of South Florida	FL	8,154	C
Univ of Texas at Austin	TX	9,437	HC
Univ of Texas at El Paso	TX	5,076	LC
Univ of Texas at San Antonio	TX	9,088	NC
Univ of the Sacred Heart	PR	5,375	
Univ of Tulsa	OK	19,090	HC
Univ of Vermont	VT	14,761	C+
Univ of Wisc/Milwaukee	WI	8,907	LC
Univ of Wisc/Oshkosh	WI	6,130	LC
Univ of Wyoming	WY	7,143	LC
Upper Iowa Univ	IA	17,438	C
Utah State Univ	UT	6,771	C
Valley City State Univ	ND		LC
Villanova Univ	PA	31,997	HC
Virginia State Univ	VA	8,182	LC
Viterbo Univ	WI	18,043	C
Washington State Univ	WA	9,388	C
Wayne State Univ	MI	6,720	C
Weber State Univ	UT	6,897	NC
Western Conn State Univ	CT	10,074	C
Western Illinois Univ	IL	9,571	C
Western Mich Univ	MI	10,016	C
Western New Mexico Univ	NM	5,950	LC
Westminster College	MO	19,990	C+
William Jewell College	MO	17,150	VC
Wingate Univ	NC	19,140	C
Winona State Univ	MN	8,570	C
Winston-Salem State Univ	NC	5,927	LC
Worcester Polytechnic Inst	MA	34,480	HC+
Wright State Univ	OH	9,141	LC
Youngstown State Univ	OH	9,318	NC

MANAGEMENT SCIENCE

School	ST	$IS	SR
Abilene Christian Univ	TX	16,300	VC
Alfred Univ	NY	27,212	C+
Anderson Univ	IN	19,430	LC
Arizona State Univ-Main	AZ	7,726	C
Aurora Univ	IL	18,551	C
Austin Peay State Univ	TN	5,814	LC
Averett Univ	VA	17,980	LC
Avila College	MO	17,720	C
Ball State Univ	IN	8,660	C
Barry Univ	FL	24,100	LC
Belmont Univ	TN	19,066	VC
Bethel College	TN	12,980	C
Bluffton College	OH	20,644	C
Boston College	MA	33,330	MC
Bridgewater State College	MA	7,589	C+
Caldwell College	NJ	20,940	LC
Cal State, Fullerton	CA	5,440	LC
Cal State, Los Angeles	CA	5,050	C
Cal State, Monterey Bay	CA	6,250	LC
Cal State, San Bernardino	CA	6,516	C
Catholic Univ of America	DC	29,332	VC
Cazenovia College	NY	19,885	LC
Central Mich Univ	MI	8,355	C
Central Missouri State Univ	MO	7,920	C
Champlain College	VT	19,680	C
Chatham College	PA	25,454	C+
Chestnut Hill College	PA	24,790	LC
Chicago State Univ	IL	8,851	C+
Christian Brothers Univ	TN	19,820	VC
CUNY/Baruch College	NY	3,275	VC+
CUNY/Herbert H. Lehman College	NY	3,320	LC
Clemson Univ	SC	7,600	C
Cleveland State Univ	OH	10,146	NC
College for Lifelong Learning	NH	4,100	SP
College of New Jersey	NJ	13,425	HC
College of St. Benedict	MN	23,921	VC
Colo Christian Univ	CO	17,714	C
Colo Technical Univ	CO	9,425	LC
Columbia Union College	MD	19,027	C+
Concordia Univ Wisc	WI	16,600	LC
Covenant College	GA	21,970	C+
Culver-Stockton College	MO	15,400	LC
Davis and Elkins College	WV	19,270	LC
Defiance College	OH	19,580	LC
Delta State Univ	MS	5,416	C
Drake Univ	IA	22,830	VC
Earlham College	IN	27,446	VC+
East Central Univ	OK	4,578	C
East Tenn State Univ	TN	7,127	C
Eastern Mich Univ	MI	9,855	C
Eastern Washington Univ	WA	7,972	LC
Eckerd College	FL	25,500	C+
Emporia State Univ	KS	6,198	LC
Evangel Univ	MO	14,050	C
Florida Gulf Coast Univ	FL	9,201	C
Florida International Univ	FL	9,486	VC
Florida State Univ	FL	7,835	HC
Francis Marion Univ	SC	7,682	C
Franklin Pierce College	NH	26,125	LC
Franklin Univ	OH	6,324	SP
Gallaudet Univ	DC	16,554	SP
George Fox Univ	OR	24,095	VC
Georgetown College	KY	18,400	VC
Georgia College and State Univ	GA	7,344	C
Georgia Inst of Technology	GA	9,028	HC+
Goucher College	MD	30,650	VC+
Grand Valley State Univ	MI	10,040	C
Gwynedd-Mercy College	PA	22,350	C
Hawaii Pacific Univ	HI	17,790	C
Heidelberg College	OH	23,879	C
Henry Cogswell College	WA	13,080	SP
Hiram College	OH	27,034	VC
Hood College	MD	26,020	VC
Huron Univ	SD	10,450	C
Idaho State Univ	ID	7,030	C+
Illinois State Univ	IL	9,235	C
Iona College	NY	26,556	C
Iowa State Univ	IA	8,108	VC
Ithaca College	NY	28,719	HC
Johns Hopkins Univ	MD	35,226	MC
Johnson and Wales Univ	RI	21,558	LC
Keene State College	NH	11,280	C
Kennesaw State Univ	GA	2,306	LC
Kent State Univ	OH	11,104	C
Kentucky State Univ	KY	6,146	NC
Langston Univ	OK	2,308	LC
Lesley College	MA	25,325	LC
Louisiana State Univ and A&M College	LA	8,014	VC
Louisiana State Univ in Shreveport	LA	2,480	NC
Louisiana Tech Univ	LA	6,506	C
Loyola Univ New Orleans	LA	23,506	VC+
Lynchburg College	VA	23,405	C
Madonna Univ	MI	11,504	VC
Maharishi Univ of Management	IA	20,660	VC
Manhattanville College	NY	28,730	VC
Marian College of Fond du Lac	WI	17,935	LC
Marietta College	OH	24,580	C
Marylhurst Univ	OR	15,343	NC
Marymount Univ	VA	21,560	LC
Maryville Univ of St. Louis	MO	18,680	C
Mass Inst of Technology	MA	35,228	MC
McMurry Univ	TX	15,287	C
Metropolitan State College of Denver	CO	2,338	LC
Midwestern State Univ	TX	6,704	NC
Minn State Univ, Mankato	MN	7,296	LC
Minot State Univ	ND	5,466	LC
Missouri Baptist College	MO	15,762	LC
Missouri Southern State College	MO	6,666	C
Moravian College	PA	27,065	VC
Morehead State Univ	KY	6,510	C
National-Louis Univ	IL	13,995	NC
New Jersey Inst of Technology	NJ	14,690	VC
Northern Kentucky Univ	KY	6,352	NC
Notre Dame College	OH	20,425	C
Ohio Northern Univ	OH	27,765	VC
Ohio Univ	OH	11,769	C
Okla State Univ	OK	7,650	VC
Oral Roberts Univ	OK	18,490	C
Palm Beach Atlantic College	FL	23,310	C
Penn State Univ/Univ Park Campus	PA	11,126	VC
Philadelphia Univ	PA	24,722	C
Point Park College	PA	20,290	C
Portland State Univ	OR	11,220	C
Purdue Univ/West Lafayette	IN	10,284	VC
Quinnipiac Univ	CT	27,370	C
Regis College	MA	26,750	C
Rensselaer Polytechnic Inst	NY	33,863	HC+
Richard Stockton College of New Jersey	NJ	12,165	VC
Rivier College	NH	24,215	C
Robert Morris Univ	PA	18,730	C
Rochester Inst of Technology	NY	26,232	VC+
Rockhurst Univ	MO	20,090	C
Roosevelt Univ	IL	20,240	LC

School	ST	$IS	SR
Rutgers, The State Univ of New Jersey New Brunswick Campus	NJ	12,709	C
Rutgers, The State Univ of New Jersey/ CamdenCampus	NJ	6,484	C
Rutgers, The State Univ of New Jersey/Newark Campus	NJ	6,394	C
Sacred Heart Univ	CT	26,588	VC
St. Ambrose Univ	IA	19,994	C
St. Bonaventure Univ	NY	21,956	C
St. Francis Univ	PA	24,486	LC
St. John Fisher College	NY	21,800	C
St. John's Univ	MN	23,640	VC
St. John's Univ	NY	26,660	C
St. Joseph College	CT	25,960	LC
St. Joseph's Univ	PA	29,715	VC+
St. Louis Univ	MO	26,590	VC+
St. Martin's College	WA	20,566	C
Salve Regina Univ	RI	26,460	C
San Francisco State Univ	CA	7,139	LC
Shenandoah Univ	VA	22,550	NC
Southern Methodist Univ	TX	28,349	VC
Southern New Hampshire Univ	NH	23,852	C
Southwestern Adventist Univ	TX	14,798	C
Southwestern College	KS	17,656	C
Southwestern Okla State Univ	OK	4,801	C
SUNY/College at Cortland	NY	10,564	C
SUNY/College at Geneseo	NY	9,970	HC
SUNY/College at Oswego	NY	10,856	C
SUNY/Empire State College	NY	3,545	SP
State Univ of West Georgia	GA	7,101	C
Stephen F. Austin State Univ	TX	6,905	C
Stetson Univ	FL	25,640	VC
Suffolk Univ	MA	26,516	C
Tarleton State Univ	TX	7,160	C
Taylor Univ	IN	21,562	VC+
Teikyo Post Univ	CT	21,800	C
Tenn Tech Univ	TN	6,968	C
Texas A&M Univ	TX	8,988	VC
Texas A&M Univ at Kingsville	TX	6,446	LC
Texas Christian Univ	TX	19,910	C
Texas Southern Univ	TX	6,576	NC
Thomas College	ME	18,915	LC
Thomas Edison State College	NJ	2,750	SP
Touro College	NY	14,950	VC
Tri-State Univ-Main Campus	IN	21,200	C
Tulane Univ	LA	34,013	HC+
Turabo Univ	PR	4,110	
Tusculum College	TN	17,900	LC
Tuskegee Univ	AL	14,600	LC
Union College	NE	14,650	C
Union College	NY	32,646	HC
Union Univ	TN	18,930	C+
United States Air Force Academy	CO		MC
United States Coast Guard Academy	CT		MC
United States Military Academy	NY		MC
Universidad Metropolitana	PR	3,324	
Univ of Alabama	AL	7,402	C
Univ of Arizona	AZ	8,614	C
Univ of Arkansas at Little Rock	AR	5,637	NC
Univ of Bridgeport	CT	23,020	C
Univ of Calif at San Diego	CA	11,372	HC
Univ of Central Florida	FL	8,251	VC
Univ of Cincinnati	OH	12,491	LC
Univ of Colo at Boulder	CO	9,255	VC
Univ of Dayton	OH	20,400	VC
Univ of Delaware	DE	10,824	VC
Univ of Florida	FL	7,874	HC
Univ of Georgia	GA	8,656	VC
Univ of Great Falls	MT	15,360	C
Univ of Hartford	CT	28,884	C
Univ of Hawaii at Manoa	HI	7,862	VC
Univ of Illinois at Chicago	IL	10,702	VC
Univ of Iowa	IA	8,607	C+
Univ of La Verne	CA	24,280	C
Univ of Louisiana at Lafayette	LA	5,200	C
Univ of Louisiana at Monroe	LA	5,207	NC
Univ of Louisville	KY	7,402	LC
Univ of Maryland/Univ College	MD	5,910	SP
Univ of Mass Boston	MA	4,227	C
Univ of Memphis	TN	7,271	C
Univ of Minn/Crookston	MN	9,626	NC
Univ of Minn/Morris	MN	10,716	VC
Univ of Minn/Twin Cities	MN	11,123	VC
Univ of Miss	MS	7,666	C
Univ of Montevallo	AL	7,266	C
Univ of Nebr at Lincoln	NE	8,325	C+
Univ of Nebr at Omaha	NE	6,867	C
Univ of Nevada/Las Vegas	NV	8,281	VC
Univ of Nevada/Reno	NV	8,737	C
Univ of New Mexico	NM	8,026	C
Univ of N Dak	ND	7,067	VC
Univ of North Texas	TX	7,629	C
Univ of Northern Colo	CO	8,082	C+
Univ of Northern Iowa	IA	7,850	C
Univ of Notre Dame	IN	30,707	MC
Univ of Pennsylvania	PA	34,614	MC
Univ of Phoenix	AZ	7,000	SP
Univ of Pittsburgh at Greensburg	PA	12,842	C
Univ of Pittsburgh at Pittsburgh	PA	13,592	HC
Univ of PR at Humacao	PR	1,245	
Univ of PR/Cayey Univ College	PR	1,245	
Univ of Science and Arts of Okla	OK	5,245	C
Univ of S Car at Columbia	SC	8,748	VC
Univ of S Dak	SD	7,036	C
Univ of South Florida	FL	8,154	C
Univ of Tenn at Knoxville	TN	8,214	C
Univ of Texas at Arlington	TX	7,192	LC
Univ of Texas at Austin	TX	9,437	HC
Univ of Texas at El Paso	TX	5,076	LC
Univ of Texas at San Antonio	TX	9,088	NC
Univ of Texas-Pan American	TX	4,823	C
Univ of the Incarnate Word	TX	18,478	C
Univ of Tulsa	OK	19,090	HC
Univ of Utah	UT	7,703	C
Univ of Wisc/Platteville	WI	7,282	C
Univ of Wisc/Stevens Point	WI	7,116	C
Univ of Wisc/Stout	WI	7,192	C
Upper Iowa Univ	IA	17,438	C
Virginia Polytechnic Inst and State Univ	VA	7,652	C
Viterbo Univ	WI	18,043	C
Washington State Univ	WA	9,388	C
Wayne State Univ	MI	6,720	C
Waynesburg College	PA	17,610	LC
Webster Univ	MO	19,804	VC
Wesley College	DE	17,869	C
West Liberty State College	WV	6,056	LC
West Texas A&M Univ	TX	6,538	C
Western Carolina Univ	NC	5,667	C
Western International Univ	AZ	5,800	SP
Western Mich Univ	MI	10,016	C
Western New England College	MA	23,882	C
Western Washington Univ	WA	8,624	VC
Wheeling Jesuit Univ	WV	22,660	C
Wichita State Univ	KS	6,879	C
Wilberforce Univ	OH	14,937	LC
Woodbury Univ	CA	25,344	LC
Worcester Polytechnic Inst	MA	34,480	HC+
Wright State Univ	OH	9,141	LC
Xavier Univ	OH	23,880	C
York College of Pennsylvania	PA	12,550	VC

MANUFACTURING ENGINEERING

School	ST	$IS	SR
Boston Univ	MA	34,358	MC
Bradley Univ	IL	20,970	VC
Calif Polytechnic State Univ	CA	8,747	VC
Calif State Polytechnic Univ, Pomona	CA	8,615	C
Cal State, Los Angeles	CA	5,050	C
Central State Univ	OH	8,922	C+
Indiana Inst of Technology	IN	18,806	C
Kansas State Univ	KS	6,995	C
Kettering Univ	MI	23,256	HC
Miami Univ	OH	12,885	VC+
Midwestern State Univ	TX	6,704	NC
New Jersey Inst of Technology	NJ	14,690	VC
New York Inst of Technology	NY	21,756	C
N Dak State Univ	ND	7,004	VC
Northern Kentucky Univ	KY	6,352	NC
Pennsylvania College of Technology	PA	12,860	NC
Rochester Inst of Technology	NY	26,232	VC+
St. Cloud State Univ	MN	7,180	C
Seattle Univ	WA	24,183	VC
Silver Lake College of the Holy Family	WI	15,516	LC
Southern Illinois Univ Edwardsville	IL	7,869	LC
Southern Polytechnic State Univ	GA	6,662	C
Southwestern Okla State Univ	OK	4,801	C
Tenn Tech Univ	TN	6,968	C
Univ of Arkansas at Little Rock	AR	5,637	NC
Univ of Calif at Berkeley	CA	14,134	MC
Univ of Conn	CT	12,122	VC
Univ of Hartford	CT	28,884	C
Univ of Memphis	TN	7,271	C
Univ of Miami	FL	31,130	HC
Univ of Mich/Dearborn	MI	4,677	VC
Univ of Missouri/Rolla	MO	10,034	C
Univ of New Mexico	NM	8,026	C
Univ of N Car at Charlotte	NC	7,254	C
Univ of Texas-Pan American	TX	4,823	C
Univ of Wisc/Stout	WI	7,192	C
Washington State Univ	WA	9,388	C
Wichita State Univ	KS	6,879	C
Worcester Polytechnic Inst	MA	34,480	HC+

MANUFACTURING TECHNOLOGY

School	ST	$IS	SR
Arkansas State Univ	AR	7,480	C
Bowling Green State Univ	OH	10,794	C
Bradley Univ	IL	20,970	VC
Brigham Young Univ	UT	7,840	HC
Calif Univ of Pennsylvania	PA	10,388	C
Central Conn State Univ	CT	10,404	C
Central Missouri State Univ	MO	7,920	C
East Carolina Univ	NC	7,766	C
Eastern Kentucky Univ	KY	6,552	C
Eastern Mich Univ	MI	9,855	C
Fairmont State College	WV	7,010	NC
Illinois Inst of Technology	IL	25,182	HC+
Indiana State Univ	IN	8,461	LC
Indiana Univ-Purdue Univ Indianapolis	IN	9,473	C
Lake Superior State Univ	MI	9,034	LC
Minn State Univ, Mankato	MN	7,296	LC
Missouri Southern State College	MO	6,666	C
Montana State Univ-Northern	MT	8,600	NC
Northern Kentucky Univ	KY	6,352	NC
Northern Mich Univ	MI	9,693	C
Oregon Inst of Technology	OR	8,718	C
Rochester Inst of Technology	NY	26,232	VC+
Silver Lake College of the Holy Family	WI	15,516	LC
S Dak State Univ	SD	6,848	C
Southern Arkansas Univ	AR	5,740	LC
Southwest Missouri State Univ	MO	7,600	LC
Southwestern College	KS	17,656	C
Southwestern Okla State Univ	OK	4,801	C
SUNY/College of Technology at Farmingdale	NY	11,269	C
Texas Southern Univ	TX	6,576	NC
Thomas Edison State College	NJ	2,750	SP
Univ of Akron	OH	10,530	NC
Univ of Dayton	OH	20,400	VC
Univ of Houston	TX	8,410	C
Univ of Nebr at Lincoln	NE	8,325	C+
Univ of Northern Iowa	IA	7,850	C
Univ of Rio Grande	OH	8,728	NC
Wayne State Univ	MI	6,720	C
Weber State Univ	UT	6,897	NC
Western Carolina Univ	NC	5,667	C
Western Illinois Univ	IL	9,571	C
Western Mich Univ	MI	10,016	C
Western Washington Univ	WA	8,624	VC

MARINE BIOLOGY

School	ST	$IS	SR
Auburn Univ	AL	5,510	C
Barry Univ	FL	24,100	LC
Boston Univ	MA	34,358	MC
Carroll College	WI	21,170	C
College of Charleston	SC	8,350	HC
Dowling College	NY	20,281	LC
Eastern Nazarene College	MA	19,433	LC
Fairleigh Dickinson Univ/ Madison campus	NJ	25,500	C
Fairleigh Dickinson Univ/ Teaneck Campus	NJ	24,646	C
Florida Atlantic Univ	FL	8,832	C
Florida Inst of Technology	FL	25,250	VC
Florida State Univ	FL	7,835	HC
Hampshire College	MA	33,881	HC+
Hofstra Univ	NY	23,252	C
Missouri Southern State College	MO	6,666	C
Ohio Univ	OH	11,769	C
Palm Beach Atlantic College	FL	23,310	C
Roger Williams Univ	RI	29,010	C
St. Paul's College	VA	13,340	C
San Francisco State Univ	CA	7,139	LC
Savannah State Univ	GA	2,550	LC
Southwest Texas State Univ	TX	8,730	VC
Southwestern College	KS	17,656	C
Spring Hill College	AL	23,250	C
Stetson Univ	FL	25,640	VC
Texas A&M Univ at Galveston	TX	7,269	C+
Troy State Univ	AL	7,696	C
Univ of Alaska Southeast	AK	7,900	LC
Univ of Calif at Los Angeles	CA	13,227	MC
Univ of Calif at Santa Barbara	CA	11,732	VC
Univ of Calif at Santa Cruz	CA	13,655	VC
Univ of Maine at Machias	ME	7,689	LC
Univ of Maryland/College Park	MD	11,959	C
Univ of Mass Dartmouth	MA	9,852	C
Univ of New England	ME	24,110	LC
Univ of New Hampshire	NH	13,207	C
Univ of New Haven	CT	23,860	LC
Univ of N Car at Wilmington	NC	7,769	C
Univ of PR at Humacao	PR	1,245	
Univ of West Alabama	AL	6,048	C
Univ of West Florida	FL	7,518	C
Waynesburg College	PA	17,610	LC

MARINE ENGINEERING

School	ST	$IS	SR
Calif Maritime Academy	CA	12,256	C
Maine Maritime Academy	ME	10,911	C
Mass Maritime Academy	MA	9,969	C
SUNY/Maritime College	NY	10,025	LC
Texas A&M Univ at Galveston	TX	7,269	C+
Thomas Edison State College	NJ	2,750	SP
United States Merchant Marine Academy	NY		VC
United States Naval Academy	MD		MC
Univ of New Orleans	LA	10,160	C

MARINE SCIENCE

School	ST	$IS	SR
Cal State, Stanislaus	CA	8,895	C
Coastal Carolina Univ	SC	9,220	C
East Stroudsburg Univ of Pennsylvania	PA	8,430	LC
Eckerd College	FL	25,500	C+
Hawaii Pacific Univ	HI	17,790	C
Jacksonville Univ	FL	21,110	LC
Juniata College	PA	26,080	VC
Kutztown Univ of Pennsylvania	PA	8,907	C
LIU/Southampton College	NY	26,270	C
Richard Stockton College of New Jersey	NJ	12,165	VC
Rider Univ	NJ	27,400	C
Rutgers, The State Univ of New Jersey New Brunswick Campus	NJ	12,709	C
St. Paul's College	VA	13,340	C
Samford Univ	AL	16,340	VC
SUNY/Maritime College	NY	10,025	LC
Suffolk Univ	MA	26,516	C
Texas A&M Univ at Galveston	TX	7,269	C+
United States Coast Guard Academy	CT		MC
Univ of Alabama	AL	7,402	C
Univ of Conn	CT	12,122	VC
Univ of Hawaii at Hilo	HI	6,497	C
Univ of Maine	ME	10,798	C
Univ of Miami	FL	31,130	HC
Univ of N Car at Wilmington	NC	7,769	C
Univ of Rhode Island	RI	12,414	C
Univ of San Diego	CA	29,198	HC
Univ of S Car at Columbia	SC	8,748	VC
Univ of Tampa	FL	22,612	C

MARITIME SCIENCE

School	ST	$IS	SR
Maine Maritime Academy	ME	10,911	C
SUNY/Maritime College	NY	10,025	LC
Texas A&M Univ at Galveston	TX	7,269	C+
United States Merchant Marine Academy	NY		VC

MARKETING AND DISTRIBUTION

School	ST	$IS	SR
Alvernia College	PA	20,790	C
Becker College	MA	21,230	LC
Caldwell College	NJ	20,940	LC
Carlow College	PA	19,366	C
Clayton College and State Univ	GA	2,322	C+
Duquesne Univ	PA	24,242	C+
Florida Gulf Coast Univ	FL	9,201	C
Franklin Univ	OH	6,324	SP
Georgia College and State Univ	GA	7,344	C
Gwynedd-Mercy College	PA	22,350	C
Indiana State Univ	IN	8,461	LC
Inter-American Univ of PR/ Arecibo Campus	PR	3,300	
Johnson and Wales Univ	RI	21,558	LC
Mountain State Univ	WV	8,180	NC
Neumann College	PA	22,040	NC
New York Inst of Technology	NY	21,756	C
Northwest Nazarene Univ	ID	18,380	C
Our Lady of Holy Cross College	LA	5,140	NC
St. Edward's Univ	TX	17,846	C
St. John's Univ	NY	26,660	C

School	ST	$IS	SR
Southern Polytechnic State Univ	GA	6,662	C
Tarleton State Univ	TX	7,160	C
Taylor Univ	IN	21,562	VC+
Ohio State Univ	OH	10,819	VC
Thomas Edison State College	NJ	2,750	SP
Union College	NE	14,650	C
Univ of Houston	TX	8,410	C
Univ of La Verne	CA	24,280	C
Univ of Memphis	TN	7,271	C
Univ of Phoenix	AZ	7,000	SP
West Virginia Univ	WV	8,304	C
Western Carolina Univ	NC	5,667	C
Youngstown State Univ	OH	9,318	NC

MARKETING AND DISTRIBUTION EDUCATION

School	ST	$IS	SR
Bowling Green State Univ	OH	10,794	C
Dakota State Univ	SD	6,950	C
Eastern Washington Univ	WA	7,972	LC
Fayetteville State Univ	NC	5,590	LC
Johnson and Wales Univ	RI	21,558	LC
Middle Tenn State Univ	TN	6,994	C
N Car State Univ	NC	8,680	HC
Rider Univ	NJ	27,400	C
Southern New Hampshire Univ	NH	23,852	C
Temple Univ	PA	14,124	C
Univ of Central Okla	OK	5,205	C
Univ of Georgia	GA	8,656	VC
Univ of Idaho	ID	7,026	C
Univ of Tenn at Knoxville	TN	8,214	C
Univ of Wisc/Stout	WI	7,192	C
Virginia Polytechnic Inst and State Univ	VA	7,652	C
Western Mich Univ	MI	10,016	C

MARKETING MANAGEMENT

School	ST	$IS	SR
Alaska Pacific Univ	AK	16,450	C
American Univ	DC	31,544	VC+
Assumption College	MA	26,320	C
Baker College of Flint	MI	7,720	NC
Benedictine Univ	IL	21,330	C
Bentley College	MA	31,060	HC
Carthage College	WI	23,670	C
Champlain College	VT	19,680	C
Chatham College	PA	25,454	C+
Christopher Newport Univ	VA	8,862	VC
CUNY/Baruch College	NY	3,275	VC+
Clarke College	IA	20,625	C+
Cleary College	MI	10,350	LC
College of St. Elizabeth	NJ	22,510	C
College of the Ozarks	MO	2,650	C+
Colo Christian Univ	CO	17,714	C
Columbia College Chicago	IL	22,063	LC
Concordia Univ	MN	19,912	C
Coppin State College	MD	9,133	LC
Drake Univ	IA	22,830	VC
East Carolina Univ	NC	7,766	C
East Texas Baptist Univ	TX	12,349	LC
Edinboro Univ of Pennsylvania	PA	9,328	LC
Emerson College	MA	29,978	HC
Fordham Univ	NY	30,710	HC
George Washington Univ	DC	32,170	HC
Hawaii Pacific Univ	HI	17,790	C
Indiana Univ Kokomo	IN	3,422	LC
Ithaca College	NY	28,719	HC
Johns Hopkins Univ	MD	35,226	MC
Johnson and Wales Univ	RI	21,558	LC
La Sierra Univ	CA	19,260	LC
Lakeland College	WI	17,950	C
LeTourneau Univ	TX	19,020	VC
Limestone College	SC	16,900	C
Metropolitan State Univ	MN	2,943	SP
Mich State Univ	MI	10,386	VC
Montana State Univ-Billings	MT	7,653	NC
Morehead State Univ	KY	6,510	C
Northwestern College	MN	19,816	C+
Northwood Univ	FL	19,179	LC
Northwood Univ	TX	18,135	C
Ohio Univ	OH	11,769	C
Old Dominion Univ	VA	9,386	C
Olivet College	MI	17,410	C
Oregon State Univ	OR	9,612	VC
Our Lady of the Lake Univ of San Antonio	TX	17,336	C
Palm Beach Atlantic College	FL	23,310	C
Park Univ	MO	9,816	C
Penn State Univ at Erie/Behrend College	PA	12,326	C
Plymouth State College	NH	11,024	LC
Purdue Univ/West Lafayette	IN	10,284	VC
Rochester College	MI	15,404	C+
Rochester Inst of Technology	NY	26,232	VC+
Saginaw Valley State Univ	MI	9,465	C
Siena College	NY	22,685	VC
Southern Utah Univ	UT	7,254	C
Spring Hill College	AL	23,250	C
Stephen F. Austin State Univ	TX	6,905	C
Syracuse Univ	NY	30,710	HC
Thomas College	ME	18,915	LC
Troy State Univ/Dothan	AL	3,296	C
Troy State Univ/Montgomery	AL	3,080	NC
Tulane Univ	LA	34,013	HC+
Union Univ	TN	18,930	C+
Univ of Alabama	AL	7,402	C
Univ of Arkansas	AR	8,334	VC
Univ of Colo at Boulder	CO	9,255	VC
Univ of Maryland/College Park	MD	11,959	C
Univ of Maryland/Univ College	MD	5,910	SP
Univ of Mass Amherst	MA	10,995	VC
Univ of Memphis	TN	7,271	C
Univ of Miami	FL	31,130	HC
Univ of N Car at Charlotte	NC	7,254	C
Univ of North Florida	FL	8,089	VC
Univ of PR/Rio Piedras	PR	5,510	
Univ of Rio Grande	OH	8,728	NC
Univ of St. Thomas	MN	24,044	VC
Univ of S Car at Spartanburg	SC	7,318	C+
Univ of Texas at Austin	TX	9,437	HC
Univ of the Sciences in Philadelphia	PA	24,826	VC
Univ of Vermont	VT	14,761	C+
Ursuline College	OH	19,430	LC
Virginia State Univ	VA	8,182	LC
Washington State Univ	WA	9,388	C
Washington Univ in St. Louis	MO	34,593	MC
Weber State Univ	UT	6,897	NC
Western Carolina Univ	NC	5,667	C
Western Conn State Univ	CT	10,074	C
Western International Univ	AZ	5,800	SP
Youngstown State Univ	OH	9,318	NC

MARKETING/RETAILING/MERCHANDISING

School	ST	$IS	SR
Abilene Christian Univ	TX	16,300	VC
Adams State College	CO	7,468	C
Alabama A&M Univ	AL	5,100	LC
Alabama State Univ	AL	6,404	C
Albany State Univ	GA	5,764	C+
Alfred Univ	NY	27,212	C+
American International College	MA	22,268	LC
Anderson Univ	IN	19,430	LC
Andrews Univ	MI	17,696	LC
Angelo State Univ	TX	7,028	C
Appalachian State Univ	NC	6,353	C
Arcadia Univ	PA	26,650	C
Arizona State Univ-Main	AZ	7,726	C
Arkansas State Univ	AR	7,480	C
Ashland Univ	OH	22,182	LC
Assumption College	MA	26,320	C
Auburn Univ	AL	5,510	C
Auburn Univ Montgomery	AL	5,330	NC
Augsburg College	MN	22,978	C
Augusta State Univ	GA	2,282	C
Aurora Univ	IL	18,551	C
Austin Peay State Univ	TN	5,814	LC
Averett Univ	VA	17,980	LC
Avila College	MO	17,720	C
Azusa Pacific Univ	CA	22,422	VC
Baldwin-Wallace College	OH	22,010	VC+
Ball State Univ	IN	8,660	C
Barry Univ	FL	24,100	LC
Bay Path College	MA	22,308	C
Baylor Univ	TX	18,298	VC+
Belmont Univ	TN	19,066	VC
Benedictine Univ	IL	21,330	C
Berkeley College	NY	21,545	LC
Berkeley College of New York City	NY	12,500	LC
Bethel College	MN	22,740	VC
Birmingham-Southern College	AL	22,960	C
Black Hills State Univ	SD	6,652	LC
Bluffton College	OH	20,644	C
Boise State Univ	ID	6,531	LC
Boston College	MA	33,330	MC
Boston Univ	MA	34,358	MC
Bowling Green State Univ	OH	10,794	C
Bradley Univ	IL	20,970	VC
Brenau Univ Women's College	GA	20,100	C
Bryant College	RI	25,980	VC
Buena Vista Univ	IA	22,828	C
Butler Univ	IN	25,580	VC+
Cabrini College	PA	25,950	LC
Calif Lutheran Univ	CA	23,500	LC
Calif State Polytechnic Univ, Pomona	CA	8,615	C
Cal State, Fullerton	CA	5,440	LC
Cal State, Hayward	CA	7,400	LC
Cal State, Long Beach	CA	7,400	LC
Cal State, Los Angeles	CA	5,050	C
Cal State, Northridge	CA	7,781	C
Cal State, Sacramento	CA	7,488	C
Cal State, San Bernardino	CA	6,516	C
Cameron Univ	OK	5,560	NC
Canisius College	NY	24,696	C+
Caribbean Univ	PR	3,000	
Carnegie Mellon Univ	PA	32,682	MC
Cedarville Univ	OH	17,553	VC
Central Conn State Univ	CT	10,404	C
Central Mich Univ	MI	8,355	C
Central Missouri State Univ	MO	7,920	C
Central State Univ	OH	8,922	C+
Central Univ of Bayamon	PR	3,335	
Central Washington Univ	WA	8,985	LC
Chaminade Univ of Honolulu	HI	17,370	C
Chestnut Hill College	PA	24,790	LC
Chicago State Univ	IL	8,851	C+
Christian Brothers Univ	TN	19,820	VC
Christopher Newport Univ	VA	8,862	VC
City Univ	WA	7,425	NC
CUNY/Baruch College	NY	3,275	VC+
CUNY/York College	NY	3,292	NC
Clarion Univ of Pennsylvania	PA	11,272	LC
Clarkson Univ	NY	29,884	VC
Clemson Univ	SC	7,600	C
Cleveland State Univ	OH	10,146	NC
Coastal Carolina Univ	SC	9,220	C
College Misericordia	PA	23,380	LC
College of New Jersey	NJ	13,425	HC
College of Notre Dame of Maryland	MD	23,100	LC
College of Our Lady of the Elms	MA	20,644	C
College of the Southwest	NM	8,456	NC
Colo State Univ	CO	9,672	C
Columbus State Univ	GA	7,228	LC
Concord College	WV	7,122	C+
Concordia Univ Wisc	WI	16,600	LC
Cornerstone Univ and Grand Rapids Baptist Seminary	MI	18,092	C
Creighton Univ	NE	23,476	VC
Dallas Baptist Univ	TX	13,682	LC
Davenport Univ	MI	10,057	NC
David Lipscomb Univ	TN	16,158	VC
David N. Myers College	OH	9,475	C
Davis and Elkins College	WV	19,270	LC
De Sales Univ	PA	22,610	VC
Defiance College	OH	19,580	LC
Delaware State Univ	DE	8,104	LC
Delaware Valley College	PA	24,213	LC
Delta State Univ	MS	5,416	C
DePaul Univ	IL	23,590	VC
Dominican College	NY	20,400	LC
Dowling College	NY	20,281	LC
Drake Univ	IA	22,830	VC
Drexel Univ	PA	27,057	VC
Duquesne Univ	PA	24,242	C+
East Central Univ	OK	4,578	C
East Tenn State Univ	TN	7,127	C
Eastern College	PA	19,641	LC
Eastern Illinois Univ	IL	10,101	C
Eastern Kentucky Univ	KY	6,552	C
Eastern Mich Univ	MI	9,855	C
Eastern New Mexico Univ	NM	4,113	LC
Eastern Washington Univ	WA	7,972	LC
Elmhurst College	IL	21,750	C
Elmira College	NY	31,070	VC+
Emory Univ	GA	33,792	MC
Emporia State Univ	KS	6,198	LC
Evangel Univ	MO	14,050	C
Excelsior College	NY	915	SP
Fairfield Univ	CT	30,885	HC
Fairleigh Dickinson Univ/Madison campus	NJ	25,500	C
Fairleigh Dickinson Univ/Teaneck Campus	NJ	24,646	C
Fairmont State College	WV	7,010	NC
Fashion Inst of Technology/SUNY	NY	9,504	C+
Ferris State Univ	MI	10,816	C
Ferrum College	VA	15,990	LC
Florida Atlantic Univ	FL	8,832	C
Florida International Univ	FL	9,486	VC
Florida Southern College	FL	19,430	C
Florida State Univ	FL	7,835	HC
Fort Hays State Univ	KS	6,294	LC
Fort Valley State Univ	GA	6,014	LC
Francis Marion Univ	SC	7,682	C
Franklin Pierce College	NH	26,125	LC
Freed-Hardeman Univ	TN	14,290	VC
Gannon Univ	PA	18,848	C
George Mason Univ	VA	9,192	C
Georgetown College	KY	18,400	VC
Georgetown Univ	DC	34,847	MC
Georgia Southern Univ	GA	6,958	C
Georgia Southwestern State Univ	GA	6,013	C
Georgia State Univ	GA	7,792	LC
Glenville State College	WV	6,588	NC
Goldey-Beacom College	DE	11,440	C
Grambling State Univ	LA	5,325	NC
Grand Canyon Univ	AZ	30,000	LC
Grand Valley State Univ	MI	10,040	C
Greenville College	IL	19,226	LC
Grove City College	PA	12,280	MC
Hampton Univ	VA	17,112	C+
Harding Univ	AR	13,528	VC
Hardin-Simmons Univ	TX	14,165	C
Hesser College	NH	16,210	LC
High Point Univ	NC	20,220	LC
Hillsdale College	MI	20,586	VC+
Hofstra Univ	NY	23,252	C
Holy Family College	PA	13,710	LC
Houston Baptist Univ	TX	15,300	LC
Howard Univ	DC	15,522	LC
Huron Univ	SD	10,450	C
Husson College	ME	15,360	LC
Huston-Tillotson College	TX	12,977	LC
Idaho State Univ	ID	7,030	C+
Illinois State Univ	IL	9,235	C
Indiana State Univ	IN	8,461	LC
Indiana Univ Bloomington	IN	10,712	C+
Indiana Univ of Pennsylvania	PA	9,133	C
Indiana Univ South Bend	IN	3,515	C
Indiana Univ Southeast	IN	3,459	C
Indiana Univ-Purdue Univ Fort Wayne	IN	3,166	LC
Indiana Univ-Purdue Univ Indianapolis	IN	9,473	C
Indiana Wesleyan Univ	IN	17,680	C
Inter-American Univ of PR/Aguadilla Campus	PR	3,278	
Inter-American Univ of PR/Bayamon Univ College	PR	3,700	
Inter-American Univ of PR/Fajardo Campus	PR	4,000	
Inter-American Univ of PR/Metropolitan Campus	PR	4,166	
Inter-American Univ of PR/Ponce Regional College	PR	3,700	
Inter-American Univ of PR/San GermÈn	PR	6,390	
Iona College	NY	26,556	C
Iowa State Univ	IA	8,108	VC
Ithaca College	NY	28,719	HC
Jackson State Univ	MS	6,776	LC
Jacksonville State Univ	AL	6,568	LC
Jacksonville Univ	FL	21,110	LC
James Madison Univ	VA	9,552	HC
John Carroll Univ	OH	24,140	VC
Johnson and Wales Univ	RI	21,558	LC
Juniata College	PA	26,080	VC
Kansas State Univ	KS	6,995	C
Kean Univ	NJ	11,159	C
Kennesaw State Univ	GA	2,306	LC
Kent State Univ	OH	11,104	C
Kentucky State Univ	KY	6,146	NC
Keuka College	NY	21,170	C
King's College	PA	24,680	C
Kutztown Univ of Pennsylvania	PA	8,907	C
La Salle Univ	PA	27,890	C
Laboratory Inst of Merchandising	NY	13,550	SP
Lake Superior State Univ	MI	9,034	LC
Lamar Univ	TX	6,816	LC
Lasell College	MA	24,100	C
Lehigh Univ	PA	32,290	MC
LeTourneau Univ	TX	19,020	VC
Lewis Univ	IL	20,960	C
Lincoln Univ	MO	7,158	NC
Lindenwood Univ	MO	17,250	C
LIU/Brooklyn Campus	NY	22,290	C
LIU/C.W. Post Campus	NY	25,380	C
Loras College	IA	22,994	C+
Louisiana State Univ and A&M College	LA	8,014	VC
Louisiana State Univ in Shreveport	LA	2,480	NC
Louisiana Tech Univ	LA	6,506	C
Loyola Univ New Orleans	LA	23,506	VC+
Loyola Univ of Chicago	IL	25,992	VC
Lynchburg College	VA	23,405	C
Lynn Univ	FL	24,550	C
MacMurray College	IL	17,790	LC
Madonna Univ	MI	11,504	VC
Manhattan College	NY	25,500	VC
Mansfield Univ	PA	9,648	C
Marian College of Fond du Lac	WI	17,935	LC
Marietta College	OH	24,580	C
Marquette Univ	WI	24,836	C+
Marshall Univ	WV	7,752	LC
Martin Univ	IN	8,370	SP
Marymount Univ	VA	21,560	LC
Maryville Univ of St. Louis	MO	18,680	C
Marywood Univ	PA	24,639	C
McKendree College	IL	18,300	C+
McMurry Univ	TX	15,287	C
McNeese State Univ	LA	5,259	LC
Mercer Univ	GA	24,130	VC
Mercyhurst College	PA	20,694	C
Merrimack College	MA	25,725	VC
Messiah College	PA	23,180	VC
Methodist College	NC	19,526	C
Metropolitan State College of Denver	CO	2,338	LC
Miami Univ	OH	12,885	VC+
Mich State Univ	MI	10,386	VC
Middle Tenn State Univ	TN	6,994	C
Midland Lutheran College	NE	18,600	C

School	ST	$IS	SR
Midwestern State Univ	TX	6,704	NC
Millikin Univ	IL	24,415	C+
Minn State Univ, Mankato	MN	7,296	LC
Minot State Univ	ND	5,466	LC
Miss College	MS	14,574	C
Miss State Univ	MS	7,853	C
Missouri Southern State College	MO	6,666	C
Missouri Western State College	MO	6,662	NC
Monmouth Univ	NJ	24,042	C
Moorhead State Univ	MN	7,000	LC
Morehouse College	GA	19,814	C
Morgan State Univ	MD	10,078	LC
Mount Ida College	MA	25,375	LC
Mount Mercy College	IA	19,390	VC
Murray State Univ	KY	6,672	C
New Jersey City Univ	NJ	9,100	LC
New Mexico Highlands Univ	NM	6,256	NC
New Mexico State Univ	NM	7,302	C
New York Inst of Technology	NY	21,756	C
New York Univ	NY	35,200	MC
Newman Univ	KS	14,098	LC
Niagara Univ	NY	22,250	C+
Nicholls State Univ	LA	5,290	NC
Nichols College	MA	24,610	LC
North Central College	IL	22,944	C+
North Georgia College and State Univ	GA	6,322	C+
North Park Univ	IL	24,030	C
Northeastern Illinois Univ	IL	2,898	NC
Northeastern State Univ	OK	4,704	LC
Northeastern Univ	MA	30,078	VC
Northern Arizona Univ	AZ	7,398	C
Northern Illinois Univ	IL	9,545	C
Northern Kentucky Univ	KY	6,352	NC
Northern Mich Univ	MI	9,693	C
Northern State Univ	SD	6,279	LC
Northwest Missouri State Univ	MO	7,922	LC
Notre Dame College	OH	20,425	C
Notre Dame de Namur Univ	CA	26,932	LC
Oakland Univ	MI	9,418	C
Ohio Univ	OH	11,769	C
Okla Baptist Univ	OK	13,878	VC
Okla Christian Univ	OK	16,500	VC
Okla State Univ	OK	7,650	VC
Oral Roberts Univ	OK	18,490	C
Oregon State Univ	OR	9,612	VC
Pace Univ	NY	24,200	C
Parsons School of Design	NY	32,242	SP
Penn State Univ/Univ Park Campus	PA	11,126	VC
Peru State College	NE	6,342	NC
Philadelphia Univ	PA	24,722	C
Pittsburg State Univ	KS	6,228	NC
Pontifical Catholic Univ of PR/Ponce	PR	7,076	
Portland State Univ	OR	11,220	C
Prairie View A&M Univ	TX	3,172	LC
Providence College	RI	27,620	HC
Purdue Univ/Calumet	IN	6,630	NC
Quincy Univ	IL	20,450	C
Quinnipiac Univ	CT	27,370	C
Radford Univ	VA	8,302	C
Regis Univ	CO	25,740	C+
Rhode Island College	RI	8,700	LC
Rice Univ	TX	24,325	MC
Rider Univ	NJ	27,400	C
Robert Morris Univ	PA	18,730	C
Rockhurst Univ	MO	20,090	C
Roger Williams Univ	RI	29,010	C
Roosevelt Univ	IL	20,240	LC
Rowan Univ	NJ	12,365	VC
Rutgers, The State Univ of New Jersey New Brunswick Campus	NJ	12,709	C
Rutgers, The State Univ of New Jersey/ CamdenCampus	NJ	6,484	C
Rutgers, The State Univ of New Jersey/Newark Campus	NJ	6,394	C
St. Ambrose Univ	IA	19,994	C
St. Bonaventure Univ	NY	21,956	C
St. Cloud State Univ	MN	7,180	C
St. Joseph's College	IN	21,640	C
St. Joseph's Univ	PA	29,715	VC+
St. Louis Univ	MO	26,590	VC+
St. Martin's College	WA	20,566	C
St. Mary-of-the-Woods College	IN	21,320	LC
St. Mary's Univ of Minn	MN	19,975	C
St. Mary's Univ of San Antonio	TX	19,735	C
St. Peter's College	NJ	22,292	LC
St. Thomas Aquinas College	NY	20,590	LC
St. Thomas Univ	FL	19,500	LC
St. Xavier Univ	IL	21,104	C
Salem State College	MA	4,481	LC
Sam Houston State Univ	TX	6,076	LC
San Diego State Univ	CA	9,716	C+
San Francisco State Univ	CA	7,139	LC
San Jose State Univ	CA	8,187	C
Santa Clara Univ	CA	28,371	VC+
Savannah State Univ	GA	2,550	LC
Schreiner Univ	TX	19,254	C
Seattle Univ	WA	24,183	VC
Seton Hall Univ	NJ	26,910	LC
Seton Hill College	PA	21,875	C
Shippensburg Univ of Pennsylvania	PA	9,652	C
Simmons College	MA	30,418	VC
Simpson College	IA	21,200	C+
Slippery Rock Univ	PA	9,152	LC
S Car State Univ	SC	6,586	LC
Southeast Missouri State Univ	MO	8,367	C+
Southeastern College	FL	11,648	LC
Southeastern Louisiana Univ	LA	6,047	LC
Southeastern Univ	DC	8,505	LC
Southern Adventist Univ	TN	15,600	C
Southern Conn State Univ	CT	10,310	C
Southern Illinois Univ at Carbondale	IL	8,621	C
Southern Methodist Univ	TX	28,349	VC
Southern Nazarene Univ	OK	14,634	NC
Southern New Hampshire Univ	NH	23,852	C
Southern Oregon Univ	OR	9,429	C
Southern Univ and A&M College	LA	6,365	C+
Southern Utah Univ	UT	7,254	C
Southwest Missouri State Univ	MO	7,600	LC
Southwest State Univ	MN	7,117	LC
Southwest Texas State Univ	TX	8,730	VC
Southwestern Okla State Univ	OK	4,801	C
SUNY/College at Old Westbury	NY	9,818	LC
SUNY/College at Oswego	NY	10,856	C
SUNY/Univ at New Paltz	NY	9,685	VC
State Univ of West Georgia	GA	7,101	C
Stephen F. Austin State Univ	TX	6,905	C
Stetson Univ	FL	25,640	VC
Stonehill College	MA	26,852	HC
Suffolk Univ	MA	26,516	C
Syracuse Univ	NY	30,710	HC
Tabor College	KS	17,600	LC
Tarleton State Univ	TX	7,160	C
Teikyo Post Univ	CT	21,800	C
Temple Univ	PA	14,124	C
Tenn Tech Univ	TN	6,968	C
Texas A&M Univ	TX	8,988	VC
Texas A&M Univ at Commerce	TX	7,326	C
Texas A&M Univ at Kingsville	TX	6,446	LC
Texas Christian Univ	TX	19,910	C
Texas Southern Univ	TX	6,576	NC
Texas Tech Univ	TX	8,825	C
Texas Wesleyan Univ	TX	14,710	C
Texas Woman's Univ	TX	5,855	LC
Tiffin Univ	OH	17,250	C
Touro College	NY	14,950	VC
Trevecca Nazarene Univ	TN	15,752	C
Trinity International Univ	IL	20,640	C+
Tri-State Univ-Main Campus	IN	21,200	C
Troy State Univ	AL	7,696	C
Turabo Univ	PR	4,110	
Tuskegee Univ	AL	14,600	LC
Union Univ	TN	18,930	C+
Univ of Akron	OH	10,530	NC
Univ of Alabama at Birmingham	AL	10,110	C
Univ of Alabama at Huntsville	AL	7,916	VC
Univ of Alaska Anchorage	AK	9,100	NC
Univ of Arizona	AZ	8,614	C
Univ of Arkansas	AR	8,334	VC
Univ of Arkansas at Little Rock	AR	5,637	NC
Univ of Bridgeport	CT	23,020	C
Univ of Central Arkansas	AR	6,388	C
Univ of Central Florida	FL	8,251	VC
Univ of Central Okla	OK	5,205	C
Univ of Cincinnati	OH	12,491	LC
Univ of Conn	CT	12,122	VC
Univ of Dayton	OH	20,400	VC
Univ of Delaware	DE	10,824	VC
Univ of Denver	CO	28,783	VC
Univ of Evansville	IN	22,865	VC+
Univ of Findlay	OH	23,962	NC
Univ of Florida	FL	7,874	HC
Univ of Georgia	GA	8,656	VC
Univ of Great Falls	MT	15,360	C
Univ of Hartford	CT	28,884	C
Univ of Hawaii at Manoa	HI	7,862	VC
Univ of Houston	TX	8,410	C
Univ of Houston-Downtown	TX	2,006	NC
Univ of Idaho	ID	7,026	C
Univ of Illinois at Chicago	IL	10,702	VC
Univ of Illinois at Urbana-Champaign	IL	11,316	HC+
Univ of Indianapolis	IN	20,840	C
Univ of Iowa	IA	8,607	C+
Univ of Kentucky	KY	7,765	C
Univ of Louisiana at Lafayette	LA	5,200	C
Univ of Louisiana at Monroe	LA	5,207	NC
Univ of Louisville	KY	7,402	LC
Univ of Maine at Machias	ME	7,689	LC
Univ of Mary Hardin-Baylor	TX	13,929	C
Univ of Mass Dartmouth	MA	9,852	C
Univ of Mich/Flint	MI	4,323	C
Univ of Minn/Twin Cities	MN	11,123	VC
Univ of Miss	MS	7,666	C
Univ of Missouri/Columbia	MO	9,803	HC
Univ of Mobile	AL	13,620	LC
Univ of Montana	MT	8,038	C
Univ of Montevallo	AL	7,266	C
Univ of Nebr at Kearney	NE	7,048	NC
Univ of Nebr at Lincoln	NE	8,325	C+
Univ of Nebr at Omaha	NE	6,867	C
Univ of Nevada/Las Vegas	NV	8,281	VC
Univ of Nevada/Reno	NV	8,737	C
Univ of New Haven	CT	23,860	LC
Univ of New Mexico	NM	8,026	C
Univ of New Orleans	LA	10,160	C
Univ of North Alabama	AL	7,016	NC
Univ of N Car at Charlotte	NC	7,254	C
Univ of N Car at Greensboro	NC	6,858	C
Univ of N Car at Wilmington	NC	7,769	C
Univ of N Dak	ND	7,067	VC
Univ of North Texas	TX	7,629	C
Univ of Northern Colo	CO	8,082	C+
Univ of Northern Iowa	IA	7,850	C
Univ of Notre Dame	IN	30,707	MC
Univ of Okla	OK	7,616	VC
Univ of Pennsylvania	PA	34,614	MC
Univ of Pittsburgh at Pittsburgh	PA	13,592	HC
Univ of Portland	OR	24,950	VC
Univ of PR/Bayamon Univ College Campus	PR	1,600	
Univ of PR/Mayaguez	PR	5,285	
Univ of Rhode Island	RI	12,414	C
Univ of St. Francis	IL	19,650	C
Univ of St. Thomas	TX	18,752	VC
Univ of San Francisco	CA	27,302	VC
Univ of Scranton	PA	27,964	C+
Univ of Sioux Falls	SD	16,390	C
Univ of South Alabama	AL	6,976	LC
Univ of S Car at Columbia	SC	8,748	VC
Univ of South Florida	FL	8,154	C
Univ of Southern Indiana	IN	8,655	LC
Univ of Southern Miss	MS	6,155	LC
Univ of Tampa	FL	22,612	C
Univ of Tenn at Knoxville	TN	8,214	C
Univ of Tenn at Martin	TN	8,268	C
Univ of Texas at Arlington	TX	7,192	LC
Univ of Texas at El Paso	TX	5,076	LC
Univ of Texas at San Antonio	TX	9,088	NC
Univ of Texas-Pan American	TX	4,823	C
Univ of the District of Columbia	DC	2,844	NC
Univ of the Incarnate Word	TX	18,478	C
Univ of the Ozarks	AR	13,904	C
Univ of the Sacred Heart	PR	5,375	
Univ of Toledo	OH	11,206	NC
Univ of Tulsa	OK	19,090	HC
Univ of Utah	UT	7,703	C
Univ of Washington	WA	10,361	VC
Univ of West Florida	FL	7,518	C
Univ of Wisc/Eau Claire	WI	7,032	VC
Univ of Wisc/La Crosse	WI	7,250	VC
Univ of Wisc/Madison	WI	8,262	VC
Univ of Wisc/Milwaukee	WI	8,907	LC
Univ of Wisc/Oshkosh	WI	6,130	LC
Univ of Wisc/Whitewater	WI	6,937	C
Univ of Wyoming	WY	7,143	LC
Upper Iowa Univ	IA	17,438	C
Utah State Univ	UT	6,771	C
Valdosta State Univ	GA	6,988	C
Valparaiso Univ	IN	23,570	VC+
Vanguard Univ of Southern Calif	CA	20,212	C
Villanova Univ	PA	31,997	HC
Virginia Commonwealth Univ	VA	9,030	C
Virginia Polytechnic Inst and State Univ	VA	7,652	C
Viterbo Univ	WI	18,043	C
Walsh Univ	OH	16,880	C
Wartburg College	IA	21,165	VC
Washburn Univ of Topeka	KS	6,766	NC
Washington Univ in St. Louis	MO	34,593	MC
Wayne State Univ	MI	6,720	C
Waynesburg College	PA	17,610	LC
Webber International Univ	FL	14,695	LC
Wesley College	DE	17,869	C
West Chester Univ of Pennsylvania	PA	9,792	VC
West Liberty State College	WV	6,056	LC
West Texas A&M Univ	TX	6,538	C
West Virginia State College	WV	6,264	NC
West Virginia Wesleyan College	WV	22,920	C
Western Illinois Univ	IL	9,571	C
Western Kentucky Univ	KY	6,834	C
Western Mich Univ	MI	10,016	C
Western New England College	MA	23,882	C
Western New Mexico Univ	NM	5,950	LC
Western Washington Univ	WA	8,624	VC
Westminster College	PA	22,960	C
Westminster College	UT	17,226	C
Wheeling Jesuit Univ	WV	22,660	C
Wichita State Univ	KS	6,879	C
Wilberforce Univ	OH	14,937	LC
Wingate Univ	NC	19,140	C
Winona State Univ	MN	8,570	C
Woodbury Univ	CA	25,344	LC
Wright State Univ	OH	9,141	LC
Xavier Univ	OH	23,880	C
Xavier Univ of Louisiana	LA	17,000	LC
Yeshiva Univ	NY	21,400	C
York College of Pennsylvania	PA	12,550	VC
Youngstown State Univ	OH	9,318	NC

MATERIALS ENGINEERING

School	ST	$IS	SR
Alfred Univ	NY	27,212	C+
Calif Polytechnic State Univ	CA	8,747	VC
Calif State Polytechnic Univ, Pomona	CA	8,615	C
Drexel Univ	PA	27,657	VC
Florida State Univ	FL	7,835	HC
Georgia Inst of Technology	GA	9,028	HC+
Iowa State Univ	IA	8,108	VC
Johns Hopkins Univ	MD	35,226	MC
Lehigh Univ	PA	32,290	MC
Mass Inst of Technology	MA	35,228	MC
Mich State Univ	MI	10,386	VC
New Mexico Inst of Mining and Technology	NM	7,152	VC+
New York Univ	NY	35,200	MC
Purdue Univ/West Lafayette	IN	10,284	VC
Rensselaer Polytechnic Inst	NY	33,863	HC+
San Jose State Univ	CA	8,187	C
Stevens Inst of Technology	NJ	31,510	HC+
Ohio State Univ	OH	10,819	VC
Univ of Alabama at Birmingham	AL	10,110	C
Univ of Arizona	AZ	8,614	C
Univ of Calif at Berkeley	CA	14,134	MC
Univ of Calif at Davis	CA	12,796	VC
Univ of Calif at Los Angeles	CA	13,227	MC
Univ of Cincinnati	OH	12,491	LC
Univ of Conn	CT	12,122	VC
Univ of Florida	FL	7,874	HC
Univ of Kentucky	KY	7,765	C
Univ of Maryland/College Park	MD	11,959	C
Univ of Mich/Ann Arbor	MI	13,003	HC+
Univ of Minn/Twin Cities	MN	11,123	VC
Univ of Missouri/Rolla	MO	10,034	C
Univ of Pennsylvania	PA	34,614	MC
Univ of Pittsburgh at Pittsburgh	PA	13,592	HC
Univ of Tenn at Knoxville	TN	8,214	C
Univ of Utah	UT	7,703	C
Univ of Wisc/Milwaukee	WI	8,907	LC
Virginia Polytechnic Inst and State Univ	VA	7,652	C
Washington State Univ	WA	9,388	C
Western Mich Univ	MI	10,016	C
Wilkes Univ	PA	25,800	C
Winona State Univ	MN	8,570	C
Wright State Univ	OH	9,141	LC
Youngstown State Univ	OH	9,318	NC

MATERIALS SCIENCE

School	ST	$IS	SR
Arizona State Univ-Main	AZ	7,726	C
Case Western Reserve Univ	OH	27,418	C
Columbia Univ/Fu Foundation School of Engineering and Applied Science	NY	35,190	MC
Cornell Univ	NY	34,614	MC
Duke Univ	NC	34,396	MC
Georgia Inst of Technology	GA	9,028	HC+
Johns Hopkins Univ	MD	35,226	MC
Mass Inst of Technology	MA	35,228	MC
N Car State Univ	NC	8,680	HC
Northwestern Univ	IL	33,615	MC
Penn State Univ/Univ Park Campus	PA	11,126	VC
Rochester Inst of Technology	NY	26,232	VC+
Stanford Univ	CA	34,222	MC
Temple Univ	PA	14,124	C
Ohio State Univ	OH	10,819	VC
Thomas Edison State College	NJ	2,750	SP
Univ of Calif at Berkeley	CA	14,134	MC
Univ of Illinois at Urbana-Champaign	IL	11,316	HC+
Univ of Mass Dartmouth	MA	9,852	C

School	ST	$IS	SR
Univ of Mich/Ann Arbor	MI	13,003	HC+
Univ of Minn/Twin Cities	MN	11,123	VC
Univ of New Haven	CT	23,860	LC
Univ of Pittsburgh at Pittsburgh	PA	13,592	HC
Univ of Tenn at Knoxville	TN	8,214	C
Univ of Washington	WA	10,361	VC
Univ of Wisc/Madison	WI	8,262	VC

MATHEMATICS

School	ST	$IS	SR
Abilene Christian Univ	TX	16,300	VC
Adams State College	CO	7,468	C
Adelphi Univ	NY	23,320	VC
Adrian College	MI	19,670	C
Agnes Scott College	GA	24,950	VC
Alabama A&M Univ	AL	5,100	LC
Alabama State Univ	AL	6,404	C
Albany State Univ	GA	5,764	C+
Albertson College of Idaho	ID	23,900	VC
Albertus Magnus College	CT	22,154	C
Albion College	MI	25,224	VC
Albright College	PA	27,642	C
Alcorn State Univ	MS	5,594	LC
Alderson-Broaddus College	WV	19,640	C
Alfred Univ	NY	27,212	C+
Allegheny College	PA	27,780	VC
Allen Univ	SC	9,600	NC
Alma College	MI	22,586	VC
Alvernia College	PA	20,790	C
Alverno College	WI	16,930	LC
American International College	MA	22,268	LC
American Univ	DC	31,544	VC+
Amherst College	MA	34,340	MC
Anderson Univ	IN	19,430	LC
Andrews Univ	MI	17,696	LC
Angelo State Univ	TX	7,028	C
Appalachian State Univ	NC	6,353	C
Aquinas College	MI	20,052	C+
Arcadia Univ	PA	26,650	C
Arizona State Univ-Main	AZ	7,726	C
Arkansas State Univ	AR	7,480	C
Arkansas Tech Univ	AR	6,256	C
Armstrong Atlantic State Univ	GA	7,084	C
Asbury College	KY	18,540	VC
Ashland Univ	OH	22,182	LC
Assumption College	MA	26,320	C
Atlantic Union College	MA	34,034	LC
Auburn Univ	AL	5,510	C
Auburn Univ Montgomery	AL	5,330	NC
Augsburg College	MN	22,978	C
Augusta State Univ	GA	2,282	C
Augustana College	IL	24,117	VC+
Augustana College	SD	20,760	VC
Aurora Univ	IL	18,551	C
Austin College	TX	22,150	VC+
Austin Peay State Univ	TN	5,814	LC
Averett Univ	VA	17,980	LC
Avila College	MO	17,720	C
Azusa Pacific Univ	CA	22,422	VC
Baker Univ	KS	14,780	C+
Baldwin-Wallace College	OH	22,010	VC+
Ball State Univ	IN	8,660	C
Barber-Scotia College	NC	13,100	C
Bard College	NY	33,912	HC
Barry Univ	FL	24,100	LC
Bartlesville Wesleyan College	OK	14,100	LC
Barton College	NC	16,834	LC
Bates College	ME	34,100	MC
Baylor Univ	TX	18,298	VC+
Belhaven College	MS	16,040	C+
Bellarmine Univ	KY	20,440	VC
Belmont Univ	TN	19,066	VC
Beloit College	WI	27,482	HC
Bemidji State Univ	MN	7,957	C
Benedict College	SC	12,662	LC
Benedictine College	KS	18,485	LC
Benedictine Univ	IL	21,330	C
Bennett College	NC	11,200	C
Bennington College	VT	31,350	VC
Bentley College	MA	31,060	HC
Berea College	KY	4,070	VC
Berry College	GA	18,850	C
Bethany College	KS	16,602	C+
Bethany College	WV	18,566	C
Bethel College	IN	17,650	LC
Bethel College	KS	17,355	C+
Bethel College	MN	22,740	VC
Bethel College	TN	12,980	C
Bethune-Cookman College	FL	15,746	C
Biola Univ	CA	21,902	VC
Birmingham-Southern College	AL	22,960	C
Black Hills State Univ	SD	6,652	LC
Blackburn College	IL	13,690	C
Bloomsburg Univ of Pennsylvania	PA	9,434	C
Blue Mountain College	MS	9,100	LC
Bluefield College	VA	14,200	C
Bluffton College	OH	20,644	C
Boise State Univ	ID	6,531	LC
Boston College	MA	33,330	MC
Boston Univ	MA	34,358	MC
Bowdoin College	ME	32,650	MC
Bowie State Univ	MD	9,300	C+
Bowling Green State Univ	OH	10,794	C
Bradley Univ	IL	20,970	VC
Brandeis Univ	MA	34,481	MC
Brescia Univ	KY	14,225	C
Briar Cliff Univ	IA	18,657	LC
Bridgewater College	VA	22,950	C
Bridgewater State College	MA	7,589	C+
Brigham Young Univ	UT	7,840	HC
Brigham Young Univ/Hawaii	HI	6,890	C
Brown Univ	RI	34,973	MC
Bryan College	TN	16,400	VC
Bryn Mawr College	PA	33,580	HC+
Bucknell Univ	PA	31,096	HC
Buena Vista Univ	IA	22,828	C
Butler Univ	IN	25,580	VC+
Cabrini College	PA	25,950	LC
Caldwell College	NJ	20,940	LC
Calif Baptist Univ	CA	16,736	C
Calif Inst of Technology	CA	27,663	MC
Calif Lutheran Univ	CA	23,500	LC
Calif Polytechnic State Univ	CA	8,747	VC
Calif State Polytechnic Univ, Pomona	CA	8,615	C
Cal State, Bakersfield	CA	6,090	LC
Cal State, Chico	CA	8,598	LC
Cal State, Dominguez Hills	CA	5,840	LC
Cal State, Fresno	CA	7,762	C
Cal State, Fullerton	CA	5,440	LC
Cal State, Hayward	CA	7,400	LC
Cal State, Long Beach	CA	7,400	LC
Cal State, Los Angeles	CA	5,050	C
Cal State, Northridge	CA	7,781	C
Cal State, Sacramento	CA	7,488	C
Cal State, San Bernardino	CA	6,516	C
Cal State, San Marcos	CA	1,736	LC
Cal State, Stanislaus	CA	8,895	C
Calif Univ of Pennsylvania	PA	10,388	C
Calvin College	MI	20,050	NC
Cameron Univ	OK	5,560	NC
Campbell Univ	NC	16,599	C
Campbellsville Univ	KY	14,340	C
Canisius College	NY	24,696	C+
Capital Univ	OH	23,630	C
Cardinal Stritch Univ	WI	17,620	C
Caribbean Univ	PR	3,000	
Carleton College	MN	30,780	MC
Carlow College	PA	19,366	C
Carnegie Mellon Univ	PA	32,682	MC
Carroll College	MT	19,140	C
Carroll College	WI	21,170	C
Carthage College	WI	23,670	C
Case Western Reserve Univ	OH	27,418	C
Castleton State College	VT	10,922	LC
Catawba College	NC	19,620	C
Catholic Univ of America	DC	29,332	VC
Cedar Crest College	PA	25,145	C+
Cedarville Univ	OH	17,553	VC
Centenary College	NJ	22,430	C
Centenary College of Louisiana	LA	21,600	C+
Central College	IA	21,206	C
Central Conn State Univ	CT	10,404	C
Central Methodist College	MO	16,460	C
Central Mich Univ	MI	8,355	C
Central Missouri State Univ	MO	7,920	C
Central State Univ	OH	8,922	C+
Central Washington Univ	WA	8,985	LC
Centre College	KY	24,000	HC
Chadron State College	NE	6,211	NC
Chaminade Univ of Honolulu	HI	17,370	C
Chapman Univ	CA	30,218	VC
Charleston Southern Univ	SC	17,122	C
Chatham College	PA	25,454	C+
Chestnut Hill College	PA	24,790	LC
Cheyney Univ of Pennsylvania	PA	9,993	C
Chicago State Univ	IL	8,851	C+
Christian Brothers Univ	TN	19,820	VC
Christian Heritage College	CA	18,000	LC
Christopher Newport Univ	VA	8,862	VC
Citadel, The	SC	9,126	C
CUNY/Baruch College	NY	3,275	VC+
CUNY/Brooklyn College	NY	3,403	LC
CUNY/City College	NY	3,309	LC
CUNY/College of Staten Island	NY	3,358	NC
CUNY/Herbert H. Lehman College	NY	3,320	LC
CUNY/Hunter College	NY	5,147	C+
CUNY/Queens College	NY	3,403	VC
CUNY/York College	NY	3,292	NC
Claflin Univ	SC	12,735	C+
Claremont McKenna College	CA	32,700	MC
Clarion Univ of Pennsylvania	PA	11,272	LC
Clark Atlanta Univ	GA	17,174	C
Clark Univ	MA	29,170	HC
Clarke College	IA	20,625	C+
Clarkson Univ	NY	29,884	VC
Clearwater Christian College	FL	13,160	LC
Clemson Univ	SC	7,600	C
Cleveland State Univ	OH	10,146	NC
Coastal Carolina Univ	SC	9,220	C
Coe College	IA	24,750	VC
Coker College	SC	20,120	C
Colby College	ME	34,290	MC
Colgate Univ	NY	33,480	MC
College Misericordia	PA	23,380	LC
College of Charleston	SC	8,350	HC
College of Mount St. Vincent	NY	24,230	C
College of Mount St. Joseph	OH	20,290	C
College of New Jersey	NJ	13,425	HC
College of New Rochelle	NY	20,000	C
College of Notre Dame of Maryland	MD	23,100	LC
College of Our Lady of the Elms	MA	20,644	C
College of St. Benedict	MN	23,921	VC
College of St. Catherine	MN	22,324	VC
College of St. Elizabeth	NJ	22,510	C
College of St. Mary	NE	18,726	C
College of St. Rose	NY	19,084	C
College of St. Scholastica	MN	22,378	C+
College of Santa Fe	NM	20,250	LC
College of the Holy Cross	MA	32,780	MC
College of the Ozarks	MO	2,650	C+
College of the Southwest	NM	8,456	NC
College of William and Mary	VA	10,002	MC
College of Wooster	OH	28,350	VC
Colo Christian Univ	CO	17,714	C
Colo College	CO	31,525	HC+
Colo School of Mines	CO	11,178	HC
Colo State Univ	CO	9,672	C
Columbia College	SC	19,050	LC
Columbia Union College	MD	19,027	C+
Columbia Univ/Barnard College	NY	33,694	MC
Columbia Univ/Columbia College	NY	35,190	MC
Columbia Univ/School of General Studies	NY	35,000	C
Columbus State Univ	GA	7,228	LC
Concord College	WV	7,122	C+
Concordia College	NY	19,200	VC
Concordia College/Moorhead	MN	18,835	C
Concordia Univ	CA	22,290	C
Concordia Univ	MI	20,500	C
Concordia Univ Nebr	NE	17,770	C
Concordia Univ Wisc	WI	16,600	LC
Concordia Univ, River Forest	IL	20,000	LC
Conn College	CT	33,585	MC
Converse College	SC	21,990	VC
Coppin State College	MD	9,133	LC
Cornell College	IA	24,980	VC
Cornell Univ	NY	34,614	MC
Covenant College	GA	21,970	C+
Creighton Univ	NE	23,476	VC
Culver-Stockton College	MO	15,400	LC
Cumberland College	KY	14,864	C
Daemen College	NY	20,620	C
Dakota State Univ	SD	6,950	C
Dakota Wesleyan Univ	SD	15,512	C
Dallas Baptist Univ	TX	13,682	LC
Dana College	NE	18,046	C
Dartmouth College	NH	34,458	MC
David Lipscomb Univ	TN	16,158	VC
Davidson College	NC	30,823	MC
Davis and Elkins College	WV	19,270	LC
De Sales Univ	PA	22,610	VC
Defiance College	OH	19,580	LC
Delaware State Univ	DE	8,104	LC
Delaware Valley College	PA	24,213	LC
Delta State Univ	MS	5,416	C
Denison Univ	OH	29,640	HC
DePaul Univ	IL	23,590	VC
DePauw Univ	IN	28,000	HC
Dickinson College	PA	32,210	VC+
Dickinson State Univ	ND	5,495	NC
Dillard Univ	LA	16,046	VC
Doane College	NE	17,600	LC
Dominican College	NY	20,400	LC
Dominican Univ	IL	20,800	C
Dominican Univ of Calif	CA	27,948	C
Dordt College	IA	18,100	C+
Dowling College	NY	20,281	LC
Drake Univ	IA	22,830	VC
Drew Univ/College of Liberal Arts	NJ	32,152	VC
Drexel Univ	PA	27,657	VC
Drury Univ	MO	15,250	VC
Duke Univ	NC	34,396	MC
Duquesne Univ	PA	24,242	C+
Earlham College	IN	27,446	VC+
East Carolina Univ	NC	7,766	C
East Central Univ	OK	4,578	C
East Stroudsburg Univ of Pennsylvania	PA	8,430	LC
East Tenn State Univ	TN	7,127	C
East Texas Baptist Univ	TX	12,349	LC
Eastern College	PA	19,641	LC
Eastern Conn State Univ	CT	10,362	C
Eastern Illinois Univ	IL	10,101	C
Eastern Kentucky Univ	KY	6,552	C
Eastern Mennonite Univ	VA	20,700	VC
Eastern Mich Univ	MI	9,855	C
Eastern Nazarene College	MA	19,433	LC
Eastern New Mexico Univ	NM	4,113	LC
Eastern Oregon Univ	OR	8,772	C
Eastern Washington Univ	WA	7,972	LC
Eckerd College	FL	25,500	C+
Edgewood College	WI	18,304	C
Edinboro Univ of Pennsylvania	PA	9,328	LC
Edward Waters College	FL	13,124	LC
Elizabeth City State Univ	NC	5,550	LC
Elizabethtown College	PA	26,000	VC
Elmhurst College	IL	21,750	C
Elmira College	NY	31,070	VC+
Elon Univ	NC	19,430	VC
Emmanuel College	MA	23,802	C+
Emory & Henry College	VA	19,462	C
Emory Univ	GA	33,792	MC
Emporia State Univ	KS	6,198	LC
Erskine College	SC	21,399	VC
Eureka College	IL	22,200	C
Evangel Univ	MO	14,050	C
Fairfield Univ	CT	30,885	HC
Fairleigh Dickinson Univ/Madison campus	NJ	25,500	C
Fairleigh Dickinson Univ/Teaneck Campus	NJ	24,646	C
Fairmont State College	WV	7,010	NC
Fayetteville State Univ	NC	5,590	LC
Felician College	NJ	20,050	C
Ferrum College	VA	15,990	LC
Fisk Univ	TN	13,700	LC
Fitchburg State College	MA	7,836	C
Florida A&M Univ	FL	6,948	C
Florida Atlantic Univ	FL	8,832	C
Florida International Univ	FL	9,486	VC
Florida Memorial College	FL	6,000	LC
Florida Southern College	FL	19,430	C
Florida State Univ	FL	7,835	HC
Fontbonne Univ	MO	18,046	C
Fordham Univ	NY	30,710	VC
Fort Hays State Univ	KS	6,294	LC
Fort Lewis College	CO	7,659	LC
Fort Valley State Univ	GA	6,014	LC
Framingham State College	MA	7,259	C
Francis Marion Univ	SC	7,682	C
Franciscan Univ of Steubenville	OH	19,100	C+
Franklin and Marshall College	PA	32,410	HC
Franklin College of Indiana	IN	19,905	C
Franklin Pierce College	NH	26,125	LC
Freed-Hardeman Univ	TN	14,290	VC
Fresno Pacific Univ	CA	19,740	C
Friends Univ	KS	15,962	LC
Frostburg State Univ	MD	9,680	C
Furman Univ	SC	25,492	HC
Gallaudet Univ	DC	16,554	SP
Gannon Univ	PA	18,848	C
Gardner-Webb Univ	NC	17,400	C
George Fox Univ	OR	24,095	VC
George Mason Univ	VA	9,192	C
George Washington Univ	DC	32,170	HC
Georgetown College	KY	18,400	VC
Georgetown Univ	DC	34,847	MC
Georgia College and State Univ	GA	7,344	C
Georgia Inst of Technology	GA	9,028	HC+
Georgia Southern Univ	GA	6,958	C
Georgia Southwestern State Univ	GA	6,013	C
Georgia State Univ	GA	7,792	LC
Georgian Court College	NJ	19,040	LC
Gettysburg College	PA	32,070	HC
Gonzaga Univ	WA	24,276	HC+
Gordon College	MA	23,594	VC+
Goshen College	IN	18,950	VC+
Goucher College	MD	30,650	VC+
Grace College	IN	16,768	C
Graceland Univ	IA	15,845	C
Grambling State Univ	LA	5,325	NC
Grand Canyon Univ	AZ	30,000	LC
Grand Valley State Univ	MI	10,040	C
Greensboro College	NC	19,080	LC
Greenville College	IL	19,226	LC
Grinnell College	IA	28,300	HC+
Grove City College	PA	12,280	MC
Guilford College	NC	23,255	C
Gustavus Adolphus College	MN	24,190	VC+
Gwynedd-Mercy College	PA	22,350	C
Hamilton College	NY	34,150	HC
Hamline Univ	MN	23,339	C+
Hampden-Sydney College	VA	24,871	C
Hampshire College	MA	33,881	HC+
Hampton Univ	VA	17,112	C+
Hannibal-LaGrange College	MO	12,530	C
Hanover College	IN	17,560	VC
Harding Univ	AR	13,528	VC
Hardin-Simmons Univ	TX	14,165	C
Hartwick College	NY	33,090	C+
Harvard Univ/Harvard College	MA	34,269	MC
Harvey Mudd College	CA	31,605	MC
Hastings College	NE	17,854	C+

ST = STATE   **$IS** = IN-STATE COSTS   **SR** = SELECTOR RATING

INDEX OF COLLEGE MAJORS

School	ST	$IS	SR
Haverford College	PA	34,300	MC
Heidelberg College	OH	23,879	C
Henderson State Univ	AR	6,269	C
Hendrix College	AR	18,463	HC
Heritage College	WA	6,450	NC
High Point Univ	NC	20,220	LC
Hillsdale College	MI	20,586	VC+
Hiram College	OH	27,034	VC
Hobart and William Smith Colleges	NY	33,195	VC
Hofstra Univ	NY	23,252	C
Hollins Univ	VA	24,328	VC
Holy Family College	PA	13,710	LC
Hood College	MD	26,020	VC
Hope College	MI	22,922	C+
Houghton College	NY	21,810	VC+
Houston Baptist Univ	TX	15,300	LC
Howard Payne Univ	TX	13,834	C+
Howard Univ	DC	15,522	LC
Humboldt State Univ	CA	8,582	C
Huntingdon College	AL	18,400	VC
Huntington College	IN	15,480	LC
Huston-Tillotson College	TX	12,977	LC
Idaho State Univ	ID	7,030	C+
Illinois College	IL	16,234	C
Illinois State Univ	IL	9,235	C
Illinois Wesleyan Univ	IL	26,970	HC
Immaculata College	PA	22,400	LC
Indiana State Univ	IN	8,461	LC
Indiana Univ Bloomington	IN	10,712	C+
Indiana Univ Kokomo	IN	3,422	LC
Indiana Univ Northwest	IN	3,447	C
Indiana Univ of Pennsylvania	PA	9,133	C
Indiana Univ South Bend	IN	3,515	C
Indiana Univ Southeast	IN	3,459	C
Indiana Univ-Purdue Univ Fort Wayne	IN	3,166	LC
Indiana Univ-Purdue Univ Indianapolis	IN	9,473	C
Indiana Wesleyan Univ	IN	17,680	C
Inter-American Univ of PR/ Bayamon Univ College	PR	3,700	
Inter-American Univ of PR/ Fajardo Campus	PR	4,000	
Inter-American Univ of PR/ Metropolitan Campus	PR	4,166	
Inter-American Univ of PR/ Ponce Regional College	PR	3,700	
Inter-American Univ of PR/ San GermÈn	PR	6,390	
Iona College	NY	26,556	C
Iowa State Univ	IA	8,108	VC
Iowa Wesleyan College	IA	18,840	C
Ithaca College	NY	28,719	HC
Jackson State Univ	MS	6,776	LC
Jacksonville State Univ	AL	6,568	LC
Jacksonville Univ	FL	21,110	LC
James Madison Univ	VA	9,552	HC
Jamestown College	ND	11,310	NC
Jarvis Christian College	TX	9,035	NC
John Brown Univ	AR	15,080	VC
John Carroll Univ	OH	24,140	VC
Johns Hopkins Univ	MD	35,226	MC
Johnson C. Smith Univ	NC	16,560	C+
Johnson State College	VT	10,776	C
Judson College	AL	13,790	C
Judson College	IL	18,980	LC
Juniata College	PA	26,080	VC
Kalamazoo College	MI	26,955	HC+
Kansas State Univ	KS	6,995	C
Kansas Wesleyan Univ	KS	17,400	C+
Kean Univ	NJ	11,159	C
Keene State College	NH	11,280	C
Kennesaw State Univ	GA	2,306	LC
Kent State Univ	OH	11,104	C
Kentucky Christian College	KY	13,472	C
Kentucky State Univ	KY	6,146	NC
Kenyon College	OH	32,130	HC+
King College	TN	17,800	VC
King's College	PA	24,680	C
Knox College	IL	28,230	HC
Kutztown Univ of Pennsylvania	PA	8,907	C
La Salle Univ	PA	27,890	C
La Sierra Univ	CA	19,260	LC
Lafayette College	PA	32,655	MC
LaGrange College	GA	17,496	C
Lake Erie College	OH	21,350	LC
Lake Forest College	IL	27,460	VC
Lake Superior State Univ	MI	9,034	LC
Lakeland College	WI	17,950	C
Lamar Univ	TX	6,816	LC
Lambuth Univ	TN	14,254	C
Lander Univ	SC	8,618	LC
Lane College	TN	10,400	C+
Langston Univ	OK	2,308	LC
Lawrence Tech Univ	MI	11,429	C
Lawrence Univ	WI	27,711	HC
Le Moyne College	NY	23,840	C
Lebanon Valley College of Pennsylvania	PA	25,700	VC
Lee Univ	TN	10,198	LC
Lees-McRae College	NC	17,106	LC
Lehigh Univ	PA	32,290	MC
LeMoyne-Owen College	TN	8,450	NC
Lenoir-Rhyne College	NC	19,186	C
LeTourneau Univ	TX	19,020	VC
Lewis and Clark College	OR	29,010	VC
Lewis Univ	IL	20,960	C
Lewis-Clark State College	ID	6,496	C
Liberty Univ	VA	14,500	C
Lincoln Memorial Univ	TN	12,620	LC
Lincoln Univ	MO	7,158	NC
Lincoln Univ	PA	11,198	C+
Lindenwood Univ	MO	17,250	C
Linfield College	OR	25,840	VC
Livingstone College	NC	13,360	LC
Lock Haven Univ of Pennsylvania	PA	9,534	C
LIU/Brooklyn Campus	NY	22,290	C
LIU/C.W. Post Campus	NY	25,380	C
Longwood College	VA	8,950	C
Loras College	IA	22,994	C+
Louisiana College	LA	11,516	C
Louisiana State Univ and A&M College	LA	8,014	VC
Louisiana State Univ in Shreveport	LA	2,480	NC
Louisiana Tech Univ	LA	6,506	C
Loyola College in Maryland	MD	30,900	HC
Loyola Marymount Univ	CA	28,754	HC
Loyola Univ New Orleans	LA	23,506	VC+
Loyola Univ of Chicago	IL	25,992	VC
Lubbock Christian Univ	TX	14,226	LC
Luther College	IA	23,300	VC+
Lycoming College	PA	24,780	C
Lynchburg College	VA	23,405	C
Lyndon State College	VT	11,313	LC
Lyon College	AR	16,500	VC
Macalester College	MN	28,814	HC+
MacMurray College	IL	17,790	LC
Madonna Univ	MI	11,504	VC
Maharishi Univ of Management	IA	20,660	VC
Malone College	OH	19,190	C
Manchester College	IN	22,010	C
Manhattan College	NY	25,500	VC
Manhattanville College	NY	28,730	VC
Mansfield Univ	PA	9,648	C
Marian College	IN	21,020	C
Marian College of Fond du Lac	WI	17,935	LC
Marietta College	OH	24,580	C
Marist College	NY	24,756	VC
Marlboro College	VT	26,410	VC+
Marquette Univ	WI	24,836	C+
Mars Hill College	NC	18,600	LC
Marshall Univ	WV	7,752	LC
Martin Univ	IN	8,370	SP
Mary Baldwin College	VA	23,440	C
Mary Washington College	VA	9,032	VC+
Marygrove College	MI	16,075	C
Marymount College/ Tarrytown	NY	23,850	C
Marymount Univ	VA	21,560	LC
Maryville College	TN	23,210	VC
Maryville Univ of St. Louis	MO	18,680	C
Marywood Univ	PA	24,639	C
Mass College of Liberal Arts	MA	8,717	LC
Mass Inst of Technology	MA	35,228	MC
Master's College	CA	21,500	C+
Mayville State Univ	ND	6,440	NC
McKendree College	IL	18,300	C+
McMurry Univ	TX	15,287	C
McNeese State Univ	LA	5,259	LC
McPherson College	KS	17,710	C
Mercer Univ	GA	24,130	VC
Mercy College	NY	15,875	LC
Mercyhurst College	PA	20,694	C
Meredith College	NC	17,500	C
Merrimack College	MA	25,725	VC
Mesa State College	CO	8,051	C
Messiah College	PA	23,180	VC
Methodist College	NC	19,526	C
Metropolitan State College of Denver	CO	2,338	LC
Miami Univ	OH	12,885	VC+
Mich State Univ	MI	10,386	VC
Mich Tech Univ	MI	11,088	VC
MidAmerica Nazarene Univ	KS	16,960	C
Middle Tenn State Univ	TN	6,994	C
Middlebury College	VT	34,300	MC
Midland Lutheran College	NE	18,600	C
Midway College	KY	15,815	C
Midwestern State Univ	TX	6,704	NC
Miles College	AL	7,870	NC
Milligan College	TN	17,550	C
Millikin Univ	IL	24,415	C+
Mills College	CA	27,950	C
Millsaps College	MS	22,608	VC+
Minn State Univ, Mankato	MN	7,296	LC
Minot State Univ	ND	5,466	LC
Miss College	MS	14,574	C
Miss State Univ	MS	7,853	C
Miss Univ for Women	MS	5,446	LC
Miss Valley State Univ	MS	6,345	C
Missouri Baptist College	MO	15,762	LC
Missouri Southern State College	MO	6,666	C
Missouri Valley College	MO	17,400	LC
Missouri Western State College	MO	6,662	NC
Molloy College	NY	13,940	C
Monmouth College	IL	21,550	C
Monmouth Univ	NJ	24,042	C
Montana State Univ-Billings	MT	7,653	NC
Montana State Univ-Bozeman	MT	8,431	C
Montana Tech of The Univ of Montana	MT	7,845	C
Montclair State Univ	NJ	10,287	LC
Montreat College	NC	17,164	C
Moorhead State Univ	MN	7,000	LC
Moravian College	PA	27,065	VC
Morehead State Univ	KY	6,510	C
Morehouse College	GA	19,814	C
Morgan State Univ	MD	10,078	LC
Morningside College	IA	19,124	C
Morris Brown College	GA	15,993	LC
Morris College	SC	9,995	LC
Mount Holyoke College	MA	34,128	HC
Mount Marty College	SD	15,656	LC
Mount Mary College	WI	18,024	C
Mount Mercy College	IA	19,390	VC
Mount Olive College	NC	14,410	LC
Mount St. Mary College	NY	18,825	C
Mount St. Mary's College	CA	24,430	C
Mount St. Mary's College	MD	25,740	C
Mount Senario College	WI	17,750	C
Mount Union College	OH	21,120	C
Mount Vernon Nazarene College	OH	17,027	C
Muhlenberg College	PA	28,170	HC
Murray State Univ	KY	6,672	C
Muskingum College	OH	18,760	C
National Univ	CA	7,755	SP
National-Louis Univ	IL	13,995	NC
Nazareth College of Rochester	NY	22,036	VC
Nebr Wesleyan Univ	NE	18,767	VC
New College of Florida	FL	8,130	HC+
New England College	NH	20,706	LC
New Jersey City Univ	NJ	9,100	LC
New Mexico Highlands Univ	NM	6,256	NC
New Mexico Inst of Mining and Technology	NM	7,152	VC+
New Mexico State Univ	NM	7,302	C
New York Inst of Technology	NY	21,756	C
New York Univ	NY	35,200	MC
Newberry College	SC	19,670	LC
Newman Univ	KS	14,098	LC
Niagara Univ	NY	22,250	C+
Nicholls State Univ	LA	5,290	NC
Nichols College	MA	24,610	LC
Norfolk State Univ	VA	8,382	LC
N Car Agricultural and Technical State Univ	NC	6,659	LC
N Car Central Univ	NC	6,418	LC
N Car State Univ	NC	8,680	HC
N Car Wesleyan College	NC	15,650	LC
North Central College	IL	22,944	C+
N Dak State Univ	ND	7,004	VC
North Georgia College and State Univ	GA	6,322	C+
North Park Univ	IL	24,030	C
Northeastern Illinois Univ	IL	2,898	NC
Northeastern State Univ	OK	4,704	LC
Northeastern Univ	MA	30,078	VC
Northern Arizona Univ	AZ	7,398	C
Northern Illinois Univ	IL	9,545	C
Northern Kentucky Univ	KY	6,352	NC
Northern Mich Univ	MI	9,693	C
Northern State Univ	SD	6,279	LC
Northland College	WI	21,435	C+
Northwest Missouri State Univ	MO	7,922	LC
Northwest Nazarene Univ	ID	18,380	C
Northwestern College	MN	19,816	C+
Northwestern College of Iowa	IA	17,630	C+
Northwestern Okla State Univ	OK	4,542	NC
Northwestern State Univ of Louisiana	LA	5,745	NC
Northwestern Univ	IL	33,615	MC
Norwich Univ	VT	21,064	LC
Notre Dame College	OH	20,425	C
Notre Dame de Namur Univ	CA	26,932	LC
Nyack College	NY	18,540	C
Oakland City Univ	IN	11,286	LC
Oakland Univ	MI	9,418	C
Oakwood College	AL	14,904	C
Oberlin College	OH	33,140	HC+
Occidental College	CA	32,283	HC
Oglethorpe Univ	GA	19,100	LC
Ohio Dominican College	OH	18,100	LC
Ohio Northern Univ	OH	27,765	VC
Ohio Univ	OH	11,769	C
Ohio Wesleyan Univ	OH	29,670	VC+
Okla Baptist Univ	OK	13,878	VC
Okla Christian Univ	OK	16,500	VC
Okla City Univ	OK	15,810	C
Okla Panhandle State Univ	OK	3,812	NC
Okla State Univ	OK	7,650	VC
Old Dominion Univ	VA	9,386	C
Olivet College	MI	17,410	C
Olivet Nazarene Univ	IL	18,444	C
Oral Roberts Univ	OK	18,490	C
Oregon State Univ	OR	9,612	VC
Ottawa Univ	KS	11,800	LC
Otterbein College	OH	23,439	C
Ouachita Baptist Univ	AR	16,460	VC
Our Lady of the Lake Univ of San Antonio	TX	17,336	C
Pace Univ	NY	24,200	C
Pacific Lutheran Univ	WA	23,318	VC
Pacific Union College	CA	20,250	VC
Pacific Univ	OR	24,250	C
Paine College	GA	11,896	LC
Palm Beach Atlantic College	FL	23,310	C
Park Univ	MO	9,816	C
Paul Quinn College	TX	8,150	LC
Penn State Univ at Erie/ Behrend College	PA	12,326	C
Penn State Univ/Univ Park Campus	PA	11,126	VC
Pepperdine Univ	CA	32,830	VC
Peru State College	NE	6,342	NC
Pfeiffer Univ	NC	18,580	C
Piedmont College	GA	16,900	C
Pikeville College	KY	12,000	NC
Pittsburg State Univ	KS	6,228	NC
Pitzer College	CA	33,930	HC
Plymouth State College	NH	11,024	LC
Point Loma Nazarene Univ	CA	21,380	VC
Polytechnic Univ/Brooklyn	NY	33,090	HC
Pomona College	CA	33,960	MC
Pontifical Catholic Univ of PR/Ponce	PR	7,076	
Portland State Univ	OR	11,220	C
Prairie View A&M Univ	TX	3,172	LC
Presbyterian College	SC	23,356	VC
Princeton Univ	NJ	35,072	MC
Principia College	IL	23,865	C+
Providence College	RI	27,620	HC
Purdue Univ/Calumet	IN	6,630	NC
Purdue Univ/West Lafayette	IN	10,284	VC
Queens College	NC	17,250	C
Quincy Univ	IL	20,450	C
Quinnipiac Univ	CT	27,370	C
Radford Univ	VA	8,302	C
Ramapo College of New Jersey	NJ	13,550	VC
Randolph-Macon College	VA	24,395	C
Randolph-Macon Woman's College	VA	25,820	VC+
Reed College	OR	33,350	HC+
Regis College	MA	26,750	C
Regis Univ	CO	25,740	C+
Rensselaer Polytechnic Inst	NY	33,863	HC+
Rhode Island College	RI	8,700	LC
Rhodes College	TN	26,466	HC+
Richard Stockton College of New Jersey	NJ	12,165	VC
Rider Univ	NJ	27,400	C
Ripon College	WI	24,180	VC+
Rivier College	NH	24,215	C
Roanoke College	VA	24,689	VC
Robert Morris Univ	PA	18,730	C
Roberts Wesleyan College	NY	20,160	C+
Rochester Inst of Technology	NY	26,232	VC+
Rockford College	IL	23,930	C
Rockhurst Univ	MO	20,090	C
Rocky Mountain College	MT	18,113	C
Roger Williams Univ	RI	29,010	C
Rollins College	FL	31,223	HC
Roosevelt Univ	IL	20,240	LC
Rose-Hulman Inst of Technology	IN	27,707	HC+
Rosemont College	PA	24,060	C
Russell Sage College	NY	23,674	C+
Rust College	MS	7,800	C+
Rutgers, The State Univ of New Jersey New Brunswick Campus	NJ	12,709	C
Rutgers, The State Univ of New Jersey/ CamdenCampus	NJ	6,484	C
Sacred Heart Univ	CT	26,588	VC
Saginaw Valley State Univ	MI	9,465	C
St. Ambrose Univ	IA	19,994	C
St. Andrews Presbyterian College	NC	19,720	LC
St. Anselm College	NH	27,405	C
St. Augustine's College	NC	12,990	C+
St. Bonaventure Univ	NY	21,956	C
St. Cloud State Univ	MN	7,180	C
St. Edward's Univ	TX	17,846	C
St. Francis College	NY	9,610	C
St. Francis Univ	PA	24,486	LC
St. John Fisher College	NY	21,800	C
St. John's Univ	MN	23,640	VC
St. John's Univ	NY	26,660	C
St. Joseph College	CT	25,960	LC
St. Joseph's College	IN	21,640	C
St. Joseph's College of Maine	ME	22,500	LC
St. Joseph's College, New York	NY	9,802	C

School	ST	$IS	SR
St. Joseph's Univ	PA	29,715	VC+
St. Lawrence Univ	NY	32,605	VC
St. Louis Univ	MO	26,590	VC+
St. Martin's College	WA	20,566	C
St. Mary College	KS	17,298	C
St. Mary-of-the-Woods College	IN	21,320	LC
St. Mary's College	IN	24,474	VC
St. Mary's College of Calif	CA	27,575	C
St. Mary's College of Maryland	MD	14,104	HC
St. Mary's Univ of Minn	MN	19,975	C
St. Mary's Univ of San Antonio	TX	19,735	C
St. Michael's College	VT	26,935	VC
St. Norbert College	WI	23,169	VC
St. Olaf College	MN	25,880	HC
St. Paul's College	VA	13,340	C
St. Peter's College	NJ	22,292	LC
St. Vincent College	PA	22,942	VC
St. Xavier Univ	IL	21,104	C
Salem College	NC	23,065	VC
Salem State College	MA	4,481	LC
Salisbury Univ	MD	10,576	VC
Salve Regina Univ	RI	26,460	C
Sam Houston State Univ	TX	6,076	LC
Samford Univ	AL	16,340	VC
San Diego State Univ	CA	9,716	C+
San Francisco State Univ	CA	7,139	LC
San Jose State Univ	CA	8,187	C
Santa Clara Univ	CA	28,371	VC+
Sarah Lawrence College	NY	37,516	HC
Savannah State Univ	GA	2,550	LC
Schreiner Univ	TX	19,254	C
Scripps College	CA	30,400	HC+
Seattle Pacific Univ	WA	22,674	C+
Seattle Univ	WA	24,183	VC
Seton Hall Univ	NJ	26,910	LC
Seton Hill College	PA	21,875	C
Shaw Univ	NC	12,810	C
Shawnee State Univ	OH	8,634	NC
Shepherd College	WV	7,062	LC
Shippensburg Univ of Pennsylvania	PA	9,652	C
Shorter College	GA	15,185	C
Siena College	NY	22,685	VC
Siena Heights Univ	MI	16,140	LC
Silver Lake College of the Holy Family	WI	15,516	LC
Simmons College	MA	30,418	VC
Simon's Rock College of Bard	MA	32,450	HC
Simpson College	CA	19,200	C
Simpson College	IA	21,200	C+
Skidmore College	NY	34,201	VC+
Slippery Rock Univ	PA	9,152	LC
Smith College	MA	33,302	HC+
Sonoma State Univ	CA	8,953	C
S Car State Univ	SC	6,586	LC
S Dak School of Mines and Technology	SD	7,438	C+
S Dak State Univ	SD	6,848	C
Southeast Missouri State Univ	MO	8,367	C+
Southeastern Louisiana Univ	LA	6,047	LC
Southeastern Okla State Univ	OK	4,917	C
Southern Adventist Univ	TN	15,600	C
Southern Arkansas Univ	AR	5,740	LC
Southern Conn State Univ	CT	10,310	C
Southern Illinois Univ at Carbondale	IL	8,621	C
Southern Illinois Univ Edwardsville	IL	7,869	LC
Southern Methodist Univ	TX	28,349	VC
Southern Nazarene Univ	OK	14,634	NC
Southern Oregon Univ	OR	9,429	C
Southern Polytechnic State Univ	GA	6,662	C
Southern Univ and A&M College	LA	6,365	C+
Southern Univ at New Orleans	LA	995	NC
Southern Utah Univ	UT	7,254	C
Southern Wesleyan Univ	SC	17,280	C
Southwest Baptist Univ	MO	13,426	LC
Southwest Missouri State Univ	MO	7,600	LC
Southwest State Univ	MN	7,117	LC
Southwest Texas State Univ	TX	8,730	VC
Southwestern Adventist Univ	TX	14,798	C
Southwestern College	KS	17,656	C
Southwestern Okla State Univ	OK	4,801	C
Southwestern Univ	TX	22,550	HC
Spalding Univ	KY	15,196	C
Spelman College	GA	19,215	C+
Spring Arbor Univ	MI	17,976	C
Spring Hill College	AL	23,250	C
Springfield College	MA	24,520	C
Stanford Univ	CA	34,222	MC
SUNY/College at Brockport	NY	10,267	C
SUNY/College at Buffalo	NY	8,025	C

School	ST	$IS	SR
SUNY/College at Cortland	NY	10,661	C
SUNY/College at Fredonia	NY	10,125	C
SUNY/College at Geneseo	NY	9,970	HC
SUNY/College at Old Westbury	NY	9,818	LC
SUNY/College at Oneonta	NY	9,981	C
SUNY/College at Oswego	NY	10,856	C
SUNY/College at Plattsburgh	NY	9,729	C
SUNY/College at Potsdam	NY	10,519	C
SUNY/College at Purchase	NY	10,587	VC
SUNY/Empire State College	NY	3,545	SP
SUNY/Univ at Albany	NY	10,997	VC
SUNY/Univ at Binghamton	NY	10,653	HC
SUNY/Univ at Buffalo	NY	11,033	VC
SUNY/Univ at New Paltz	NY	9,685	VC
SUNY/Univ at Stony Brook	NY	10,998	VC
State Univ of West Georgia	GA	7,101	C
Stephen F. Austin State Univ	TX	6,905	C
Stephens College	MO	22,295	C
Sterling College	KS	16,370	VC
Stetson Univ	FL	25,640	VC
Stevens Inst of Technology	NJ	31,510	HC+
Stillman College	AL	11,370	LC
Stonehill College	MA	26,852	HC
Suffolk Univ	MA	26,516	C
Sul Ross State Univ	TX	6,582	LC
Susquehanna Univ	PA	27,270	VC
Swarthmore College	PA	34,538	MC
Sweet Briar College	VA	25,310	VC
Syracuse Univ	NY	30,710	HC
Tabor College	KS	17,600	LC
Talladega College	AL	10,110	LC
Tarleton State Univ	TX	7,160	C
Taylor Univ	IN	21,562	VC+
Temple Univ	PA	14,124	C
Tenn State Univ	TN	7,058	VC
Tenn Tech Univ	TN	6,968	C
Tenn Wesleyan College	TN	13,030	C
Texas A&M Univ	TX	8,988	VC
Texas A&M Univ at Commerce	TX	7,326	C
Texas A&M Univ at Kingsville	TX	6,446	LC
Texas Christian Univ	TX	19,910	C
Texas Lutheran Univ	TX	17,660	C
Texas Southern Univ	TX	6,576	NC
Texas Tech Univ	TX	8,825	C
Texas Wesleyan Univ	TX	14,710	C
Texas Woman's Univ	TX	5,855	LC
Ohio State Univ	OH	10,819	VC
Thiel College	PA	18,419	LC
Thomas Edison State College	NJ	2,750	SP
Thomas More College	KY	17,700	LC
Tougaloo College	MS	9,200	NC
Touro College	NY	14,950	VC
Towson Univ	MD	11,088	VC
Transylvania Univ	KY	21,780	VC+
Trevecca Nazarene Univ	TN	15,752	C
Trinity Christian College	IL	19,415	C
Trinity College	CT	34,300	HC
Trinity International Univ	IL	20,640	C+
Trinity Univ	TX	21,444	HC
Tri-State Univ-Main Campus	IN	21,200	C
Troy State Univ	AL	7,696	C
Troy State Univ/Dothan	AL	3,296	C
Troy State Univ/Montgomery	AL	3,080	NC
Truman State Univ	MO	8,568	VC+
Tufts Univ	MA	34,874	MC
Tulane Univ	LA	34,013	HC+
Turabo Univ	PR	4,110	
Tuskegee Univ	AL	14,600	LC
Union College	NE	14,650	C
Union College	NY	32,646	HC
Union Univ	TN	18,930	C+
United States Air Force Academy	CO		MC
United States Military Academy	NY		MC
United States Naval Academy	MD		MC
Univ of Akron	OH	10,530	NC
Univ of Alabama	AL	7,402	C
Univ of Alabama at Birmingham	AL	10,110	C
Univ of Alabama at Huntsville	AL	7,916	VC
Univ of Alaska Anchorage	AK	9,100	NC
Univ of Alaska Fairbanks	AK	8,265	NC
Univ of Alaska Southeast	AK	7,900	LC
Univ of Arizona	AZ	8,614	C
Univ of Arkansas	AR	8,334	VC
Univ of Arkansas at Little Rock	AR	5,637	NC
Univ of Arkansas at Monticello	AR	5,940	NC
Univ of Arkansas at Pine Bluff	AR	7,925	C
Univ of Bridgeport	CT	23,020	C
Univ of Calif at Berkeley	CA	14,134	MC
Univ of Calif at Davis	CA	12,796	VC
Univ of Calif at Irvine	CA	11,756	C

School	ST	$IS	SR
Univ of Calif at Los Angeles	CA	13,227	MC
Univ of Calif at Riverside	CA	12,479	C
Univ of Calif at San Diego	CA	11,372	HC
Univ of Calif at Santa Barbara	CA	11,732	VC
Univ of Calif at Santa Cruz	CA	13,655	VC
Univ of Central Arkansas	AR	6,388	C
Univ of Central Florida	FL	8,251	VC
Univ of Central Okla	OK	5,205	C
Univ of Chicago	IL	35,087	MC
Univ of Cincinnati	OH	12,491	LC
Univ of Colo at Boulder	CO	9,255	VC
Univ of Colo at Colo Springs	CO	9,403	C
Univ of Colo at Denver	CO	3,673	C
Univ of Conn	CT	12,122	VC
Univ of Dallas	TX	22,128	VC+
Univ of Dayton	OH	20,400	VC
Univ of Delaware	DE	10,824	VC
Univ of Denver	CO	28,783	VC
Univ of Detroit Mercy	MI	21,620	LC
Univ of Evansville	IN	22,865	VC+
Univ of Findlay	OH	23,962	NC
Univ of Florida	FL	7,874	HC
Univ of Georgia	GA	8,656	VC
Univ of Great Falls	MT	15,360	C
Univ of Hartford	CT	28,884	C
Univ of Hawaii at Hilo	HI	6,497	C
Univ of Hawaii at Manoa	HI	7,862	VC
Univ of Houston	TX	8,410	C
Univ of Idaho	ID	7,026	C
Univ of Illinois at Chicago	IL	10,702	VC
Univ of Illinois at Urbana-Champaign	IL	11,316	HC+
Univ of Indianapolis	IN	20,840	C
Univ of Iowa	IA	8,607	C+
Univ of Kansas	KS	7,232	VC
Univ of Kentucky	KY	7,765	C
Univ of La Verne	CA	24,280	C
Univ of Louisiana at Lafayette	LA	5,200	C
Univ of Louisiana at Monroe	LA	5,207	NC
Univ of Louisville	KY	7,402	LC
Univ of Maine	ME	10,798	C
Univ of Maine at Farmington	ME	9,163	C
Univ of Maine at Presque Isle	ME	7,964	LC
Univ of Mary	ND	12,900	LC
Univ of Mary Hardin-Baylor	TX	13,929	C
Univ of Maryland/Baltimore County	MD	12,190	VC
Univ of Maryland/College Park	MD	11,959	C
Univ of Maryland/Eastern Shore	MD	9,258	C
Univ of Mass Amherst	MA	10,995	VC
Univ of Mass Boston	MA	4,227	C
Univ of Mass Dartmouth	MA	9,852	C
Univ of Mass Lowell	MA	9,470	VC
Univ of Memphis	TN	7,271	C
Univ of Miami	FL	31,130	HC
Univ of Mich/Ann Arbor	MI	13,003	HC+
Univ of Mich/Dearborn	MI	4,677	VC
Univ of Mich/Flint	MI	4,323	C
Univ of Minn/Duluth	MN	10,436	C
Univ of Minn/Morris	MN	10,716	VC
Univ of Minn/Twin Cities	MN	11,123	VC
Univ of Missouri/Columbia	MO	9,803	HC
Univ of Missouri/Kansas City	MO	9,685	VC
Univ of Missouri/Rolla	MO	10,034	C
Univ of Missouri/St. Louis	MO	9,966	C
Univ of Mobile	AL	13,620	LC
Univ of Montana	MT	8,038	C
Univ of Montevallo	AL	7,266	C
Univ of Nebr at Kearney	NE	7,048	NC
Univ of Nebr at Lincoln	NE	8,325	C+
Univ of Nebr at Omaha	NE	6,867	C
Univ of Nevada/Las Vegas	NV	8,281	VC
Univ of Nevada/Reno	NV	8,737	C
Univ of New Hampshire	NH	13,207	C
Univ of New Haven	CT	23,860	LC
Univ of New Mexico	NM	8,026	C
Univ of New Orleans	LA	10,160	C
Univ of North Alabama	AL	7,016	NC
Univ of N Car at Asheville	NC	6,896	VC
Univ of N Car at Chapel Hill	NC	8,789	HC
Univ of N Car at Charlotte	NC	7,254	C
Univ of N Car at Greensboro	NC	6,858	C
Univ of N Car at Pembroke	NC	5,914	LC
Univ of N Car at Wilmington	NC	7,769	C
Univ of N Dak	ND	7,067	VC
Univ of North Florida	FL	8,089	VC
Univ of North Texas	TX	7,629	C
Univ of Northern Colo	CO	8,082	C+
Univ of Northern Iowa	IA	7,850	C
Univ of Notre Dame	IN	30,707	MC
Univ of Okla	OK	7,616	VC
Univ of Oregon	OR	9,969	C
Univ of Pennsylvania	PA	34,614	MC
Univ of Pittsburgh at Bradford	PA	12,696	C
Univ of Pittsburgh at Johnstown	PA	13,044	LC

School	ST	$IS	SR
Univ of Pittsburgh at Pittsburgh	PA	13,592	HC
Univ of Portland	OR	24,950	VC
Univ of PR at Humacao	PR	1,245	
Univ of PR/Cayey Univ College	PR	1,245	
Univ of PR/Mayaguez	PR	5,285	
Univ of PR/Rio Piedras	PR	5,510	
Univ of Puget Sound	WA	28,285	HC
Univ of Redlands	CA	29,246	VC
Univ of Rhode Island	RI	12,414	C
Univ of Richmond	VA	27,300	HC
Univ of Rio Grande	OH	8,728	NC
Univ of Rochester	NY	32,979	HC
Univ of St. Francis	IL	19,650	C
Univ of St. Thomas	MN	24,044	VC
Univ of St. Thomas	TX	18,752	VC
Univ of San Diego	CA	29,198	HC
Univ of San Francisco	CA	27,302	VC
Univ of Science and Arts of Okla	OK	5,245	C
Univ of Scranton	PA	27,964	C+
Univ of Sioux Falls	SD	16,390	C
Univ of South Alabama	AL	6,976	LC
Univ of S Car at Columbia	SC	8,748	VC
Univ of S Car at Spartanburg	SC	7,318	C+
Univ of S Dak	SD	7,036	C
Univ of South Florida	FL	8,154	C
Univ of Southern Calif	CA	33,647	MC
Univ of Southern Colo	CO	7,821	LC
Univ of Southern Indiana	IN	8,655	LC
Univ of Southern Maine	ME	10,569	C
Univ of Southern Miss	MS	6,155	LC
Univ of Tampa	FL	22,612	C
Univ of Tenn at Chattanooga	TN	7,783	C
Univ of Tenn at Knoxville	TN	8,214	C
Univ of Tenn at Martin	TN	8,268	C
Univ of Texas at Arlington	TX	7,192	LC
Univ of Texas at Austin	TX	9,437	HC
Univ of Texas at Dallas	TX	9,305	VC
Univ of Texas at El Paso	TX	5,076	LC
Univ of Texas at San Antonio	TX	9,088	NC
Univ of Texas-Pan American	TX	4,823	C
Univ of the District of Columbia	DC	2,844	NC
Univ of the Incarnate Word	TX	18,478	C
Univ of the Ozarks	AR	13,904	C
Univ of the Pacific	CA	28,255	VC
Univ of the Sacred Heart	PR	5,375	
Univ of the South	TN	27,290	HC
Univ of Toledo	OH	11,206	NC
Univ of Tulsa	OK	19,090	HC
Univ of Utah	UT	7,703	C
Univ of Vermont	VT	14,761	C+
Univ of Virginia	VA	9,391	HC+
Univ of Virginia's College at Wise	VA	8,302	C
Univ of Washington	WA	10,361	VC
Univ of West Alabama	AL	6,048	C
Univ of West Florida	FL	7,518	C
Univ of Wisc/Eau Claire	WI	7,032	VC
Univ of Wisc/Green Bay	WI	7,110	C
Univ of Wisc/La Crosse	WI	7,250	VC
Univ of Wisc/Madison	WI	8,262	VC
Univ of Wisc/Milwaukee	WI	8,907	LC
Univ of Wisc/Oshkosh	WI	6,130	LC
Univ of Wisc/Parkside	WI	6,160	LC
Univ of Wisc/Platteville	WI	7,282	C
Univ of Wisc/River Falls	WI	6,356	LC
Univ of Wisc/Stevens Point	WI	7,116	C
Univ of Wisc/Superior	WI	7,051	C+
Univ of Wisc/Whitewater	WI	6,937	C
Univ of Wyoming	WY	7,143	LC
Upper Iowa Univ	IA	17,438	C
Ursinus College	PA	31,350	VC
Ursuline College	OH	19,430	LC
Utah State Univ	UT	6,771	C
Utica College of Syracuse Univ	NY	24,400	LC
Valdosta State Univ	GA	6,988	C
Valley City State Univ	ND		LC
Valparaiso Univ	IN	23,570	VC+
Vanderbilt Univ	TN	34,482	MC
Vanguard Univ of Southern Calif	CA	20,212	C
Vassar College	NY	33,450	MC
Villanova Univ	PA	31,997	HC
Virginia Commonwealth Univ	VA	9,030	C
Virginia Military Inst	VA	9,968	C+
Virginia Polytechnic Inst and State Univ	VA	7,652	C
Virginia State Univ	VA	8,182	LC
Virginia Union Univ	VA	15,358	LC
Virginia Wesleyan College	VA	22,350	LC
Viterbo Univ	WI	18,043	C
Voorhees College	SC	9,976	C+
Wabash College	IN	25,335	HC
Wagner College	NY	27,000	C
Wake Forest Univ	NC	30,290	MC
Walla Walla College	WA	20,925	C
Walsh Univ	OH	16,880	C

School	ST	$IS	SR
Warren Wilson College	NC	19,968	C
Wartburg College	IA	21,165	VC
Washburn Univ of Topeka	KS	6,766	NC
Washington and Jefferson College	PA	26,255	VC
Washington and Lee Univ	VA	25,095	MC
Washington College	MD	28,040	VC
Washington State Univ	WA	9,388	C
Washington Univ in St. Louis	MO	34,593	MC
Wayland Baptist Univ	TX	11,271	NC
Wayne State College	NE	6,255	NC
Wayne State Univ	MI	6,720	C
Waynesburg College	PA	17,610	LC
Weber State Univ	UT	6,897	NC
Webster Univ	MO	19,804	VC
Wellesley College	MA	33,394	MC
Wells College	NY	19,350	VC
Wesleyan College	GA	17,050	VC
Wesleyan Univ	CT	3,405	MC
West Chester Univ of Pennsylvania	PA	9,792	VC
West Liberty State College	WV	6,056	LC
West Texas A&M Univ	TX	6,538	C
West Virginia State College	WV	6,264	NC
West Virginia Univ	WV	8,304	C
West Virginia Wesleyan College	WV	22,920	C
Western Baptist College	OR	19,700	C+
Western Carolina Univ	NC	5,667	C
Western Conn State Univ	CT	10,074	C
Western Illinois Univ	IL	9,571	C
Western Kentucky Univ	KY	6,834	C
Western Maryland College	MD	26,000	VC
Western Mich Univ	MI	10,016	C
Western New England College	MA	23,882	C
Western New Mexico Univ	NM	5,950	LC
Western Oregon Univ	OR	8,829	C
Western State College of Colo	CO	7,585	LC
Western Washington Univ	WA	8,624	VC
Westfield State College	MA	8,394	C
Westminster College	MO	19,990	C+
Westminster College	PA	22,960	C
Westminster College	UT	17,226	C
Westmont College	CA	29,748	VC
Wheaton College	IL	21,934	HC
Wheaton College	MA	32,940	VC
Wheeling Jesuit Univ	WV	22,660	C
Whitman College	WA	29,086	HC
Whittier College	CA	29,108	C
Whitworth College	WA	23,938	VC
Wichita State Univ	KS	6,879	C
Widener Univ	PA	26,920	C
Wilberforce Univ	OH	14,937	LC
Wiley College	TX	8,100	LC
Wilkes Univ	PA	25,800	C
Willamette Univ	OR	29,422	VC+
William Carey College	MS	10,150	LC
William Jewell College	MO	17,150	VC
William Paterson Univ of New Jersey	NJ	11,000	LC
William Tyndale College	MI	11,150	C
William Woods Univ	MO	19,390	LC
Williams College	MA	32,270	MC
Wilmington College	OH	21,826	C
Wilson College	PA	21,337	LC
Wingate Univ	NC	19,140	C
Winona State Univ	MN	8,570	C
Winston-Salem State Univ	NC	5,927	LC
Winthrop Univ	SC	9,106	C
Wisc Lutheran College	WI	19,216	VC
Wittenberg Univ	OH	28,766	VC
Wofford College	SC	23,995	VC
Worcester Polytechnic Inst	MA	34,480	HC+
Worcester State College	MA	7,901	LC
Wright State Univ	OH	9,141	LC
Xavier Univ	OH	23,880	C
Xavier Univ of Louisiana	LA	17,000	LC
Yale Univ	CT	34,030	MC
Yeshiva Univ	NY	21,400	C
York College of Pennsylvania	PA	12,550	VC
Youngstown State Univ	OH	9,318	NC

MATHEMATICS EDUCATION

School	ST	$IS	SR
Adams State College	CO	7,468	C
Adelphi Univ	NY	23,320	VC
Alfred Univ	NY	27,212	C+
Andrews Univ	MI	17,696	LC
Arkansas State Univ	AR	7,480	C
Asbury College	KY	18,540	VC
Auburn Univ	AL	5,510	C
Bartlesville Wesleyan College	OK	14,100	LC
Baylor Univ	TX	18,298	VC+
Bennett College	NC	11,200	C
Berry College	GA	18,850	C
Bethany College	KS	16,602	C+
Bethel College	IN	17,650	LC
Bethel College	MN	22,740	VC
Bethune-Cookman College	FL	15,746	C
Blue Mountain College	MS	9,100	LC
Boston Univ	MA	34,358	MC
Brewton-Parker College	GA	10,810	LC
Brigham Young Univ/Hawaii	HI	6,890	C
Cal State, Long Beach	CA	7,400	LC
Calif Univ of Pennsylvania	PA	10,388	C
Canisius College	NY	24,696	C+
Carthage College	WI	23,670	C
Catholic Univ of America	DC	29,332	VC
Cedarville Univ	OH	17,553	VC
Central Missouri State Univ	MO	7,920	C
CUNY/Brooklyn College	NY	3,403	LC
Coastal Carolina Univ	SC	9,220	C
Coker College	SC	20,120	C
College of St. Rose	NY	19,084	C
College of Santa Fe	NM	20,250	LC
College of the Ozarks	MO	2,650	C+
Columbia Union College	MD	19,027	C+
Concordia Univ	MN	19,912	C
Cumberland College	KY	14,864	C
Daemen College	NY	20,620	C
Dana College	NE	18,046	C
Defiance College	OH	19,580	LC
Delta State Univ	MS	5,416	C
Drake Univ	IA	22,830	VC
Duquesne Univ	PA	24,242	C+
East Carolina Univ	NC	7,766	C
East Central Univ	OK	4,578	C
East Texas Baptist Univ	TX	12,349	LC
Eastern Mich Univ	MI	9,855	C
Eastern Washington Univ	WA	7,972	LC
Edinboro Univ of Pennsylvania	PA	9,328	LC
Elmhurst College	IL	21,750	C
Elon Univ	NC	19,430	VC
Ferris State Univ	MI	10,816	C
Florida International Univ	FL	9,486	VC
Florida State Univ	FL	7,835	HC
Fordham Univ	NY	30,710	VC
Fort Valley State Univ	GA	6,014	LC
Fresno Pacific Univ	CA	19,740	C
Geneva College	PA	19,990	C+
George Fox Univ	OR	24,095	VC
Georgia Southern Univ	GA	6,958	C
Georgia Southwestern State Univ	GA	6,013	C
Grace College	IN	16,768	C
Grambling State Univ	LA	5,325	NC
Greensboro College	NC	19,080	LC
Greenville College	IL	19,226	LC
Gwynedd-Mercy College	PA	22,350	C
Hood College	MD	26,020	VC
Humboldt State Univ	CA	8,582	C
Huntington College	IN	15,480	LC
Indiana Univ of Pennsylvania	PA	9,133	C
Ithaca College	NY	28,719	HC
Jackson State Univ	MS	6,776	LC
John Carroll Univ	OH	24,140	VC
Johnson State College	VT	10,776	C
Judson College	AL	13,790	C
Judson College	IL	18,980	LC
Juniata College	PA	26,080	VC
Keene State College	NH	11,280	C
Kennesaw State Univ	GA	2,306	LC
Kent State Univ	OH	11,104	C
Kentucky State Univ	KY	6,146	NC
Knoxville College	TN	6,200	LC
Langston Univ	OK	2,308	LC
Le Moyne College	NY	23,840	C
Limestone College	SC	16,900	C
Lincoln Univ	PA	11,198	C+
Louisiana College	LA	11,516	C
Mansfield Univ	PA	9,648	C
Mars Hill College	NC	18,600	LC
Mary Baldwin College	VA	23,440	C
Marymount College/Tarrytown	NY	23,850	C
Mercyhurst College	PA	20,694	C
Messiah College	PA	23,180	VC
MidAmerica Nazarene Univ	KS	16,960	C
Minot State Univ	ND	5,466	LC
Miss Valley State Univ	MS	6,345	C
Missouri Southern State College	MO	6,666	C
Monmouth Univ	NJ	24,042	C
Montana State Univ-Billings	MT	7,653	NC
Montreat College	NC	17,164	C
Morningside College	IA	19,124	C
Morris College	SC	9,995	LC
Mount Holyoke College	MA	34,128	HC
Mount Vernon Nazarene College	OH	17,027	C
Nazareth College of Rochester	NY	22,036	VC
New York Univ	NY	35,200	MC
Niagara Univ	NY	22,250	C+
N Car Agricultural and Technical State Univ	NC	6,659	LC
N Car State Univ	NC	8,680	HC
North Georgia College and State Univ	GA	6,322	C+
Northwest Missouri State Univ	MO	7,922	LC
Northwest Nazarene Univ	ID	18,380	C
Northwestern College	MN	19,816	C+
Northwestern Okla State Univ	OK	4,542	NC
Oakwood College	AL	14,904	C
Okla Christian Univ	OK	16,500	VC
Okla Panhandle State Univ	OK	3,812	NC
Old Dominion Univ	VA	9,386	C
Oral Roberts Univ	OK	18,490	C
Palm Beach Atlantic College	FL	23,310	C
Philander Smith College	AR	7,380	NC
Plymouth State College	NH	11,024	LC
Pontifical Catholic Univ of PR/Ponce	PR	7,076	
Providence College	RI	27,620	HC
Purdue Univ/West Lafayette	IN	10,284	VC
Rice Univ	TX	24,325	MC
Rivier College	NH	24,215	C
Rocky Mountain College	MT	18,113	C
Saginaw Valley State Univ	MI	9,465	C
St. Augustine's College	NC	12,990	C+
St. John's Univ	NY	26,660	C
Seattle Pacific Univ	WA	22,674	C+
Seton Hill College	PA	21,875	C
Shaw Univ	NC	12,810	C
Sheldon Jackson College	AK	14,940	LC
Shepherd College	WV	7,062	LC
Shorter College	GA	15,185	C
Southeast Missouri State Univ	MO	8,367	C+
Southeastern Louisiana Univ	LA	6,047	LC
Southern Univ and A&M College	LA	6,365	C+
Southern Univ at New Orleans	LA	995	NC
Southern Utah Univ	UT	7,254	C
Southwest State Univ	MN	7,117	LC
Southwestern College	KS	17,656	C
Southwestern Okla State Univ	OK	4,801	C
SUNY/College at Old Westbury	NY	9,818	LC
SUNY/College at Oneonta	NY	9,981	C
SUNY/College at Plattsburgh	NY	9,729	C
SUNY/Univ at Albany	NY	10,997	VC
Stephen F. Austin State Univ	TX	6,905	C
Syracuse Univ	NY	30,710	HC
Taylor Univ	IN	21,562	VC+
Temple Univ	PA	14,124	C
Texas Southern Univ	TX	6,576	NC
Trevecca Nazarene Univ	TN	15,752	C
Tri-State Univ-Main Campus	IN	21,200	C
Troy State Univ	AL	7,696	C
Troy State Univ/Dothan	AL	3,296	C
Turabo Univ	PR	4,110	
Union College	NE	14,650	C
Univ of Arkansas at Pine Bluff	AR	7,925	C
Univ of Calif at San Diego	CA	11,372	HC
Univ of Central Florida	FL	8,251	VC
Univ of Central Okla	OK	5,205	C
Univ of Conn	CT	12,122	VC
Univ of Delaware	DE	10,824	VC
Univ of Evansville	IN	22,865	VC+
Univ of Georgia	GA	8,656	VC
Univ of Great Falls	MT	15,360	C
Univ of Illinois at Chicago	IL	10,702	VC
Univ of Indianapolis	IN	20,840	C
Univ of Kentucky	KY	7,765	C
Univ of Louisiana at Lafayette	LA	5,200	C
Univ of Louisiana at Monroe	LA	5,207	NC
Univ of Maine at Farmington	ME	9,163	C
Univ of Mary	ND	12,900	LC
Univ of Maryland/College Park	MD	11,959	C
Univ of Maryland/Eastern Shore	MD	9,258	C
Univ of Minn/Duluth	MN	10,436	C
Univ of Minn/Twin Cities	MN	11,123	VC
Univ of Miss	MS	7,666	C
Univ of New Hampshire	NH	13,207	C
Univ of New Orleans	LA	10,160	C
Univ of N Car at Charlotte	NC	7,254	C
Univ of N Car at Pembroke	NC	5,914	LC
Univ of North Florida	FL	8,089	VC
Univ of Okla	OK	7,616	VC
Univ of Pittsburgh at Johnstown	PA	13,044	LC
Univ of Rio Grande	OH	8,728	NC
Univ of S Car at Spartanburg	SC	7,318	C+
Univ of South Florida	FL	8,154	C
Univ of Vermont	VT	14,761	C+
Univ of Wisc/Superior	WI	7,051	C+
Utah State Univ	UT	6,771	C
Valley City State Univ	ND		LC
Wartburg College	IA	21,165	VC
Washington Univ in St. Louis	MO	34,593	MC
Wayne State Univ	MI	6,720	C
West Texas A&M Univ	TX	6,538	C
West Virginia Univ	WV	8,304	C
Western Carolina Univ	NC	5,667	C
Westmont College	CA	29,748	VC
Whitworth College	WA	23,938	VC
Wiley College	TX	8,100	LC
Wingate Univ	NC	19,140	C
Xavier Univ of Louisiana	LA	17,000	LC
Youngstown State Univ	OH	9,318	NC

MECHANICAL DESIGN TECHNOLOGY

School	ST	$IS	SR
Bowling Green State Univ	OH	10,794	C
Lincoln Univ	MO	7,158	NC
Pennsylvania College of Technology	PA	12,860	NC
Southwest Missouri State Univ	MO	7,600	LC

MECHANICAL ENGINEERING

School	ST	$IS	SR
Alabama A&M Univ	AL	5,100	LC
Alfred Univ	NY	27,212	C+
Arizona State Univ-Main	AZ	7,726	C
Auburn Univ	AL	5,510	C
Baylor Univ	TX	18,298	VC+
Bethel College	IN	17,650	LC
Boston Univ	MA	34,358	MC
Bradley Univ	IL	20,970	VC
Brigham Young Univ	UT	7,840	HC
Bucknell Univ	PA	31,096	HC
Calif Inst of Technology	CA	27,663	MC
Calif Maritime Academy	CA	12,256	C
Calif Polytechnic State Univ	CA	8,747	VC
Calif State Polytechnic Univ, Pomona	CA	8,615	C
Cal State, Chico	CA	8,598	LC
Cal State, Fresno	CA	7,762	C
Cal State, Fullerton	CA	5,440	LC
Cal State, Long Beach	CA	7,400	LC
Cal State, Los Angeles	CA	5,050	C
Cal State, Sacramento	CA	7,488	C
Calvin College	MI	20,050	NC
Carnegie Mellon Univ	PA	32,682	MC
Case Western Reserve Univ	OH	27,418	C
Catholic Univ of America	DC	29,332	VC
Cedarville Univ	OH	17,553	VC
Central Washington Univ	WA	8,985	LC
Christian Brothers Univ	TN	19,820	VC
CUNY/City College	NY	3,309	LC
Clarkson Univ	NY	29,884	VC
Clemson Univ	SC	7,600	C
Cleveland State Univ	OH	10,146	NC
Colo State Univ	CO	9,672	C
Columbia Univ/Fu Foundation School of Engineering and Applied Science	NY	35,190	MC
Cooper Union for the Advancement of Science and Art	NY	6,500	MC
Cornell Univ	NY	34,614	MC
Delaware State Univ	DE	8,104	LC
Dordt College	IA	18,100	C+
Drexel Univ	PA	27,657	VC
Duke Univ	NC	34,396	MC
Florida A&M Univ	FL	6,948	C
Florida Atlantic Univ	FL	8,832	C
Florida Inst of Technology	FL	25,250	VC
Florida International Univ	FL	9,486	VC
Florida State Univ	FL	7,835	HC
Gannon Univ	PA	18,848	C
George Washington Univ	DC	32,170	HC
Georgia Inst of Technology	GA	9,029	HC+
Gonzaga Univ	WA	24,276	HC+
Grove City College	PA	12,280	MC
Henry Cogswell College	WA	13,080	SP
Hofstra Univ	NY	23,252	C
Howard Univ	DC	15,522	LC
Illinois Inst of Technology	IL	25,182	HC+
Indiana Inst of Technology	IN	18,806	C
Indiana Univ-Purdue Univ Fort Wayne	IN	3,166	LC
Indiana Univ-Purdue Univ Indianapolis	IN	9,473	C
Iowa State Univ	IA	8,108	VC
Jacksonville Univ	FL	21,110	LC
Johns Hopkins Univ	MD	35,226	MC
Kansas State Univ	KS	6,995	C
Kettering Univ	MI	23,256	HC
Lafayette College	PA	32,655	MC
Lake Superior State Univ	MI	9,034	LC
Lamar Univ	TX	6,816	LC
Lawrence Tech Univ	MI	11,429	C
Lehigh Univ	PA	32,290	MC
LeTourneau Univ	TX	19,020	VC
Louisiana State Univ and A&M College	LA	8,014	VC
Louisiana Tech Univ	LA	6,506	C
Loyola Marymount Univ	CA	28,754	HC
Manhattan College	NY	25,500	VC
Marquette Univ	WI	24,836	C+
Mass Inst of Technology	MA	35,228	MC
McNeese State Univ	LA	5,259	LC
Mercer Univ	GA	24,130	VC
Mich State Univ	MI	10,386	VC

School	ST	$IS	SR
Mich Tech Univ	MI	11,088	VC
Milwaukee School of Engineering	WI	25,680	VC+
Minn State Univ, Mankato	MN	7,296	LC
Miss State Univ	MS	7,853	C
Montana State Univ-Bozeman	MT	8,431	C
New Jersey Inst of Technology	NJ	14,690	VC
New Mexico State Univ	NM	7,302	C
New York Inst of Technology	NY	21,756	C
New York Univ	NY	35,200	MC
N Car Agricultural and Technical State Univ	NC	6,659	LC
N Car State Univ	NC	8,680	HC
N Dak State Univ	ND	7,004	VC
Northeastern Univ	MA	30,078	VC
Northern Arizona Univ	AZ	7,398	C
Northern Illinois Univ	IL	9,545	C
Northwestern Univ	IL	33,615	MC
Norwich Univ	VT	21,064	LC
Oakland Univ	MI	9,418	C
Occidental College	CA	32,288	HC
Ohio Northern Univ	OH	27,765	VC
Ohio Univ	OH	11,769	C
Okla Christian Univ	OK	16,500	VC
Okla State Univ	OK	7,650	VC
Old Dominion Univ	VA	9,386	C
Oral Roberts Univ	OK	18,490	C
Oregon State Univ	OR	9,612	VC
Penn State Univ/Univ Park Campus	PA	11,126	VC
Polytechnic Univ/Brooklyn	NY	33,090	HC
Portland State Univ	OR	11,220	C
Prairie View A&M Univ	TX	3,172	LC
Princeton Univ	NJ	35,072	MC
Purdue Univ/Calumet	IN	6,630	NC
Purdue Univ/West Lafayette	IN	10,284	VC
Rensselaer Polytechnic Inst	NY	33,863	HC+
Rochester Inst of Technology	NY	26,232	VC+
Rose-Hulman Inst of Technology	IN	27,707	HC+
Rutgers, The State Univ of New Jersey New Brunswick Campus	NJ	12,709	C
Saginaw Valley State Univ	MI	9,465	C
St. Louis Univ	MO	26,590	VC+
St. Martin's College	WA	20,566	C
San Diego State Univ	CA	9,716	C+
San Francisco State Univ	CA	7,139	LC
San Jose State Univ	CA	8,187	C
Santa Clara Univ	CA	28,371	VC+
Savannah State Univ	GA	2,550	LC
Seattle Univ	WA	21,183	VC
S Dak School of Mines and Technology	SD	7,438	C+
S Dak State Univ	SD	6,848	C
Southern Illinois Univ at Carbondale	IL	8,621	C
Southern Illinois Univ Edwardsville	IL	7,869	LC
Southern Methodist Univ	TX	28,349	VC
Southern Univ and A&M College	LA	6,365	C+
Stanford Univ	CA	34,222	MC
SUNY/Univ at Binghamton	NY	10,653	HC
SUNY/Univ at Buffalo	NY	11,033	VC
SUNY/Univ at Stony Brook	NY	10,998	VC
Stevens Inst of Technology	NJ	31,510	HC+
Syracuse Univ	NY	30,710	HC
Temple Univ	PA	14,124	C
Tenn State Univ	TN	7,058	VC
Tenn Tech Univ	TN	6,968	C
Texas A&M Univ	TX	8,988	VC
Texas A&M Univ at Kingsville	TX	6,446	LC
Texas Tech Univ	TX	8,825	C
Ohio State Univ	OH	10,819	VC
Tri-State Univ-Main Campus	IN	21,200	C
Tufts Univ	MA	34,874	MC
Tulane Univ	LA	34,013	HC+
Tuskegee Univ	AL	14,600	LC
Union College	NY	32,646	HC
United States Air Force Academy	CO		MC
United States Coast Guard Academy	CT		MC
United States Military Academy	NY		MC
United States Naval Academy	MD		MC
Universidad Politecnica de PR	PR	4,695	
Univ of Akron	OH	10,530	NC
Univ of Alabama	AL	7,402	C
Univ of Alabama at Birmingham	AL	10,110	C
Univ of Alabama at Huntsville	AL	7,916	VC
Univ of Alaska Fairbanks	AK	8,265	NC
Univ of Arizona	AZ	8,614	C
Univ of Arkansas	AR	8,334	VC
Univ of Calif at Berkeley	CA	14,134	MC
Univ of Calif at Davis	CA	12,700	VC
Univ of Calif at Irvine	CA	11,756	C
Univ of Calif at Los Angeles	CA	13,227	MC
Univ of Calif at Riverside	CA	12,479	C
Univ of Calif at San Diego	CA	11,372	HC
Univ of Calif at Santa Barbara	CA	11,732	VC
Univ of Central Florida	FL	8,251	VC
Univ of Cincinnati	OH	12,491	LC
Univ of Colo at Boulder	CO	9,255	VC
Univ of Colo at Denver	CO	3,673	C
Univ of Conn	CT	12,122	VC
Univ of Dayton	OH	20,400	VC
Univ of Delaware	DE	10,824	VC
Univ of Denver	CO	28,783	VC
Univ of Detroit Mercy	MI	21,620	LC
Univ of Evansville	IN	22,865	VC+
Univ of Florida	FL	7,874	HC
Univ of Hartford	CT	28,884	C
Univ of Hawaii at Manoa	HI	7,862	VC
Univ of Houston	TX	8,410	C
Univ of Idaho	ID	7,026	C
Univ of Illinois at Chicago	IL	10,702	VC
Univ of Illinois at Urbana-Champaign	IL	11,316	HC+
Univ of Indianapolis	IN	20,840	C
Univ of Iowa	IA	8,607	C+
Univ of Kansas	KS	7,232	VC
Univ of Kentucky	KY	7,765	C
Univ of Louisiana at Lafayette	LA	5,200	C
Univ of Louisville	KY	7,402	LC
Univ of Maine	ME	10,798	C
Univ of Maryland/Baltimore County	MD	12,190	VC
Univ of Maryland/College Park	MD	11,959	C
Univ of Mass Amherst	MA	10,995	VC
Univ of Mass Dartmouth	MA	9,852	C
Univ of Mass Lowell	MA	9,470	VC
Univ of Memphis	TN	7,271	C
Univ of Miami	FL	31,130	HC
Univ of Mich/Ann Arbor	MI	13,003	HC+
Univ of Mich/Dearborn	MI	4,677	VC
Univ of Minn/Twin Cities	MN	11,123	VC
Univ of Miss	MS	7,666	C
Univ of Missouri/Columbia	MO	9,803	HC
Univ of Missouri/Kansas City	MO	9,685	VC
Univ of Missouri/Rolla	MO	10,034	C
Univ of Missouri/St. Louis	MO	9,966	C
Univ of Nebr at Lincoln	NE	8,325	C+
Univ of Nevada/Las Vegas	NV	8,281	VC
Univ of Nevada/Reno	NV	8,737	C
Univ of New Hampshire	NH	13,207	C
Univ of New Haven	CT	23,860	LC
Univ of New Mexico	NM	8,026	C
Univ of New Orleans	LA	10,160	C
Univ of N Car at Charlotte	NC	7,254	C
Univ of N Dak	ND	7,067	VC
Univ of North Florida	FL	8,089	VC
Univ of Notre Dame	IN	30,707	MC
Univ of Okla	OK	7,616	VC
Univ of Pennsylvania	PA	34,614	MC
Univ of Pittsburgh at Pittsburgh	PA	13,592	HC
Univ of Portland	OR	24,950	VC
Univ of PR/Mayaguez	PR	5,285	
Univ of Rhode Island	RI	12,414	C
Univ of Rochester	NY	32,979	HC
Univ of St. Thomas	MN	24,044	VC
Univ of South Alabama	AL	6,976	LC
Univ of S Car at Columbia	SC	8,748	VC
Univ of South Florida	FL	8,154	C
Univ of Southern Calif	CA	33,647	MC
Univ of Tenn at Knoxville	TN	8,214	C
Univ of Texas at Arlington	TX	7,192	LC
Univ of Texas at Austin	TX	9,437	HC
Univ of Texas at El Paso	TX	5,076	LC
Univ of Texas at San Antonio	TX	9,088	NC
Univ of Texas-Pan American	TX	4,823	C
Univ of the District of Columbia	DC	2,844	NC
Univ of the Pacific	CA	28,255	VC
Univ of Toledo	OH	11,206	NC
Univ of Tulsa	OK	19,090	HC
Univ of Utah	UT	7,703	C
Univ of Vermont	VT	14,761	C+
Univ of Virginia	VA	9,391	HC+
Univ of Wisc/Madison	WI	8,262	VC
Univ of Wisc/Milwaukee	WI	8,907	LC
Univ of Wisc/Platteville	WI	7,282	C
Univ of Wyoming	WY	7,143	LC
Utah State Univ	UT	6,771	C
Valparaiso Univ	IN	23,570	VC+
Vanderbilt Univ	TN	34,482	MC
Villanova Univ	PA	31,997	HC
Virginia Commonwealth Univ	VA	9,030	C
Virginia Military Inst	VA	9,968	C+
Virginia Polytechnic Inst and State Univ	VA	7,652	C
Washington Univ in St. Louis	MO	34,593	MC
Wayne State Univ	MI	6,720	C
West Virginia Univ	WV	8,304	C
West Virginia Univ Inst of Technology	WV	7,518	NC
Western Kentucky Univ	KY	6,834	C
Western Mich Univ	MI	10,016	C
Western New England College	MA	23,882	C
Wichita State Univ	KS	6,879	C
Widener Univ	PA	26,920	C
Wilkes Univ	PA	25,800	C
Worcester Polytechnic Inst	MA	34,480	HC+
Wright State Univ	OH	9,141	LC
Yale Univ	CT	34,030	MC
York College of Pennsylvania	PA	12,550	VC
Youngstown State Univ	OH	9,318	NC

MECHANICAL ENGINEERING TECHNOLOGY

School	ST	$IS	SR
Alabama A&M Univ	AL	5,100	LC
Andrews Univ	MI	17,696	LC
Central Conn State Univ	CT	10,404	C
Cleveland State Univ	OH	10,146	NC
Eastern Washington Univ	WA	7,972	LC
Fairleigh Dickinson Univ/Teaneck Campus	NJ	24,646	C
Fairmont State College	WV	7,010	NC
Georgia Southern Univ	GA	6,958	C
Henry Cogswell College	WA	13,080	SP
Indiana State Univ	IN	8,461	LC
Indiana Univ-Purdue Univ Indianapolis	IN	9,473	C
Kansas State Univ	KS	6,995	C
Metropolitan State College of Denver	CO	2,338	LC
Montana State Univ-Bozeman	MT	8,431	C
Northeastern Univ	MA	30,078	VC
Okla State Univ	OK	7,650	VC
Old Dominion Univ	VA	9,386	C
Oregon Inst of Technology	OR	8,718	C
Penn State Univ at Erie/Behrend College	PA	12,326	C
Pennsylvania College of Technology	PA	12,860	NC
Point Park College	PA	20,290	C
Purdue Univ/Calumet	IN	6,630	NC
Purdue Univ/West Lafayette	IN	10,284	VC
Rochester Inst of Technology	NY	26,232	VC+
S Car State Univ	SC	6,586	LC
Southern Polytechnic State Univ	GA	6,662	C
Southern Univ and A&M College	LA	6,365	C+
SUNY/College at Buffalo	NY	8,025	C
SUNY/College of Technology at Alfred	NY	9,188	C
Temple Univ	PA	14,124	C
Texas A&M Univ at Galveston	TX	7,269	C+
Texas Tech Univ	TX	8,825	C
Thomas Edison State College	NJ	2,750	SP
Univ of Akron	OH	10,530	NC
Univ of Arkansas at Little Rock	AR	5,637	NC
Univ of Cincinnati	OH	12,491	LC
Univ of Dayton	OH	20,400	VC
Univ of Hartford	CT	28,884	C
Univ of Houston	TX	8,410	C
Univ of Maine	ME	10,798	C
Univ of New Hampshire	NH	13,207	C
Univ of N Car at Charlotte	NC	7,254	C
Univ of Pittsburgh at Johnstown	PA	13,044	LC
Univ of Southern Colo	CO	7,821	LC
Univ of Southern Miss	MS	6,155	LC
Wayne State Univ	MI	6,720	C
Weber State Univ	UT	6,897	NC
Wentworth Inst of Technology	MA	20,450	C
Western Kentucky Univ	KY	6,834	C
Youngstown State Univ	OH	9,318	NC

MEDIA ARTS

School	ST	$IS	SR
Arizona State Univ-Main	AZ	7,726	C
Arkansas State Univ	AR	7,480	C
Ashland Univ	OH	22,182	LC
Champlain College	VT	19,680	C
Chatham College	PA	25,454	C+
CUNY/Hunter College	NY	5,147	C+
CUNY/Queens College	NY	3,403	VC
College of the Ozarks	MO	2,650	C+
Columbus College of Art and Design	OH	22,210	SP
Denison Univ	OH	29,640	HC
East Stroudsburg Univ of Pennsylvania	PA	8,430	LC
Edinboro Univ of Pennsylvania	PA	9,328	LC
Emerson College	MA	29,978	HC
Gallaudet Univ	DC	16,554	SP
Goddard College	VT	21,056	C+
Hampshire College	MA	33,881	HC+
Hofstra Univ	NY	23,252	C
Hollins Univ	VA	24,328	VC
Indiana Univ of Pennsylvania	PA	9,133	C
Indiana Univ-Purdue Univ Indianapolis	IN	9,473	C
Ithaca College	NY	28,719	HC
James Madison Univ	VA	9,552	HC
Johns Hopkins Univ	MD	35,226	MC
Judson College	IL	18,980	LC
Kendall College of Art and Design of Ferris State Univ	MI	8,820	SP
Loyola Marymount Univ	CA	28,754	HC
Mass College of Art	MA	13,703	SP
Mass Inst of Technology	MA	35,228	MC
Mills College	CA	27,950	C
Minneapolis College of Art and Design	MN	23,560	SP
Montana State Univ-Bozeman	MT	8,431	C
Mount Ida College	MA	25,375	LC
Mount St. Mary College	NY	18,825	C
Mount Union College	OH	21,120	C
National Univ	CA	7,755	SP
New Jersey City Univ	NJ	9,100	LC
Pitzer College	CA	33,930	HC
Point Park College	PA	20,290	C
Pomona College	CA	33,960	MC
Purdue Univ/West Lafayette	IN	10,284	VC
Rensselaer Polytechnic Inst	NY	33,863	HC+
Roosevelt Univ	IL	20,240	LC
Sacred Heart Univ	CT	26,588	VC
Salve Regina Univ	RI	26,460	C
Savannah College of Art and Design	GA	25,075	SP
Southern Methodist Univ	TX	28,349	VC
SUNY/College at Fredonia	NY	10,125	C
SUNY/College at Old Westbury	NY	9,818	LC
SUNY/Univ at Buffalo	NY	11,033	VC
Syracuse Univ	NY	30,710	HC
Towson Univ	MD	11,088	VC
Tulane Univ	LA	34,013	HC+
Univ of Arizona	AZ	8,614	C
Univ of Illinois at Urbana-Champaign	IL	11,316	HC+
Univ of Mich/Ann Arbor	MI	13,003	HC+
Univ of New Mexico	NM	8,026	C
Univ of San Francisco	CA	27,302	VC
Univ of S Car at Columbia	SC	8,748	VC
Univ of the Arts	PA	24,230	SP
Univ of the District of Columbia	DC	2,844	NC
Valdosta State Univ	GA	6,988	C
Washburn Univ of Topeka	KS	6,766	NC
Weber State Univ	UT	6,897	NC
Webster Univ	MO	19,804	VC
Western Illinois Univ	IL	9,571	C
Western Mich Univ	MI	10,016	C
Wilmington College	DE	6,530	NC
Wisc Lutheran College	WI	19,216	VC
Xavier Univ	OH	23,880	C

MEDICAL LABORATORY SCIENCE

School	ST	$IS	SR
Bethune-Cookman College	FL	15,746	C
Eastern Illinois Univ	IL	10,101	C
Northeastern Univ	MA	30,078	VC
Oakland Univ	MI	9,418	C
Shawnee State Univ	OH	8,634	NC
Univ of Illinois at Chicago	IL	10,702	VC
Univ of Mary	ND	12,900	LC
Univ of Mass Dartmouth	MA	9,852	C
Univ of New Hampshire	NH	13,207	C
Univ of Utah	UT	7,703	C
Univ of Vermont	VT	14,761	C+

MEDICAL LABORATORY TECHNOLOGY

School	ST	$IS	SR
Alabama A&M Univ	AL	5,100	LC
American International College	MA	22,268	LC
Anderson Univ	IN	19,430	LC
Andrews Univ	MI	17,696	LC
Angelo State Univ	TX	7,028	C
Arkansas State Univ	AR	7,480	C
Arkansas Tech Univ	AR	6,256	C
Armstrong Atlantic State Univ	GA	7,084	C
Asbury College	KY	18,540	VC
Auburn Univ	AL	5,510	C
Austin Peay State Univ	TN	5,814	LC
Averett Univ	VA	17,980	LC
Avila College	MO	17,720	C
Baldwin-Wallace College	OH	22,010	VC+
Ball State Univ	IN	8,660	C
Barton College	NC	16,834	LC
Baylor Univ	TX	18,298	VC+
Belmont Abbey College	NC	19,630	LC

School	ST	$IS	SR
Bemidji State Univ	MN	7,957	C
Bethany College	KS	16,602	C+
Blackburn College	IL	13,690	C
Bloomsburg Univ of Pennsylvania	PA	9,434	C
Boise State Univ	ID	6,531	LC
Bowling Green State Univ	OH	10,794	C
Briar Cliff Univ	IA	18,657	LC
Cabrini College	PA	25,950	LC
Caldwell College	NJ	20,940	LC
Cal State, Los Angeles	CA	5,050	C
Cal State, Northridge	CA	7,781	C
Cal State, Sacramento	CA	7,488	C
Calif Univ of Pennsylvania	PA	10,388	C
Calumet College of St. Joseph	IN	7,500	LC
Cameron Univ	OK	5,560	NC
Campbellsville Univ	KY	14,340	C
Canisius College	NY	24,696	C+
Catholic Univ of America	DC	29,332	VC
Cedar Crest College	PA	25,145	C+
Central Missouri State Univ	MO	7,920	C
Cheyney Univ of Pennsylvania	PA	9,993	C
CUNY/Hunter College	NY	5,147	C+
CUNY/York College	NY	3,292	NC
Clemson Univ	SC	7,600	C
Coe College	IA	24,750	VC
Coker College	SC	20,120	C
College Misericordia	PA	23,380	LC
College of Mount St. Joseph	OH	20,290	C
College of Our Lady of the Elms	MA	20,644	C
College of St. Benedict	MN	23,921	VC
College of St. Mary	NE	18,726	C
College of St. Rose	NY	19,084	C
Columbia College	SC	19,050	LC
Concord College	WV	7,122	C+
Concordia College/Moorhead	MN	18,835	C
Concordia Univ Nebr	NE	17,770	C
Cumberland College	KY	14,864	C
Dakota State Univ	SD	6,950	C
Defiance College	OH	19,580	LC
DePaul Univ	IL	23,590	VC
Dordt College	IA	18,100	C+
East Central Univ	OK	4,578	C
East Stroudsburg Univ of Pennsylvania	PA	8,430	LC
Eastern Mennonite Univ	VA	20,700	VC
Eastern Mich Univ	MI	9,855	C
Eastern New Mexico Univ	NM	4,113	LC
Eastern Washington Univ	WA	7,972	LC
Edinboro Univ of Pennsylvania	PA	9,328	LC
Elmira College	NY	31,070	VC+
Emmanuel College	MA	23,802	C+
Emory & Henry College	VA	19,462	C
Erskine College	SC	21,399	VC
Eureka College	IL	22,200	C
Evangel Univ	MO	14,050	C
Fairleigh Dickinson Univ/Madison campus	NJ	25,500	C
Fairleigh Dickinson Univ/Teaneck Campus	NJ	24,646	C
Fayetteville State Univ	NC	5,590	LC
Ferrum College	VA	15,990	LC
Fitchburg State College	MA	7,836	C
Florida Atlantic Univ	FL	8,832	C
Florida International Univ	FL	9,486	VC
Francis Marion Univ	SC	7,682	C
Gannon Univ	PA	18,848	C
George Washington Univ	DC	32,170	HC
Georgetown College	KY	18,400	VC
Graceland Univ	IA	15,845	C
Grand Valley State Univ	MI	10,040	C
Gwynedd-Mercy College	PA	22,350	C
High Point Univ	NC	20,220	LC
Holy Family College	PA	13,710	LC
Howard Univ	DC	15,522	LC
Huntington College	IN	15,480	LC
Idaho State Univ	ID	7,030	C+
Illinois College	IL	16,234	C
Illinois State Univ	IL	9,235	C
Indiana State Univ	IN	8,461	LC
Indiana Univ Kokomo	IN	3,422	LC
Indiana Univ-Purdue Univ Indianapolis	IN	9,473	C
Indiana Wesleyan Univ	IN	17,680	C
Inter-American Univ of PR/San GermÈn	PR	6,390	
Iona College	NY	26,556	C
John Brown Univ	AR	15,080	VC
Judson College	IL	18,980	LC
Kentucky State Univ	KY	6,146	NC
Keuka College	NY	21,170	C
King College	TN	17,800	VC
King's College	PA	24,680	C
Knoxville College	TN	6,200	LC
Kutztown Univ of Pennsylvania	PA	8,907	C
Lake Superior State Univ	MI	9,034	LC
Lamar Univ	TX	6,816	LC
Langston Univ	OK	2,308	LC

School	ST	$IS	SR
Lebanon Valley College of Pennsylvania	PA	25,700	VC
Lee Univ	TN	10,198	LC
Lenoir-Rhyne College	NC	19,186	C
Lincoln Memorial Univ	TN	12,620	LC
Lock Haven Univ of Pennsylvania	PA	9,534	C
LIU/C.W. Post Campus	NY	25,380	C
Louisiana College	LA	11,516	C
Louisiana Tech Univ	LA	6,506	C
Luther College	IA	23,300	VC+
Madonna Univ	MI	11,504	VC
Malone College	OH	19,190	C
Manchester College	IN	22,010	C
Marian College of Fond du Lac	WI	17,935	LC
Mary Baldwin College	VA	23,440	C
Marywood Univ	PA	24,639	C
McKendree College	IL	18,300	C+
McNeese State Univ	LA	5,259	LC
Mercy College	NY	15,875	LC
Mercyhurst College	PA	20,694	C
Mich State Univ	MI	10,386	VC
Mich Tech Univ	MI	11,088	VC
Midwestern State Univ	TX	6,704	NC
Minn State Univ, Mankato	MN	7,296	LC
Missouri Southern State College	MO	6,666	C
Missouri Western State College	MO	6,662	NC
Monmouth Univ	NJ	24,042	C
Moorhead State Univ	MN	7,000	LC
Morehead State Univ	KY	6,510	C
Morgan State Univ	MD	10,078	LC
Mount Mercy College	IA	19,390	VC
Mount St. Mary College	NY	18,825	C
National-Louis Univ	IL	13,995	NC
New Jersey City Univ	NJ	9,100	LC
N Car State Univ	NC	8,680	HC
North Park Univ	IL	24,030	C
Northeastern State Univ	OK	4,704	LC
Northern Mich Univ	MI	9,693	C
Northern State Univ	SD	6,279	LC
Northwestern College of Iowa	IA	17,630	C+
Northwestern Okla State Univ	OK	4,542	NC
Norwich Univ	VT	21,064	LC
Okla Christian Univ	OK	16,500	VC
Oral Roberts Univ	OK	18,490	C
Ouachita Baptist Univ	AR	16,460	VC
Pace Univ	NY	24,200	C
Pacific Union College	CA	20,250	VC
Pontifical Catholic Univ of PR/Ponce	PR	7,076	
Purdue Univ/Calumet	IN	6,630	NC
Quincy Univ	IL	20,450	C
Rhode Island College	RI	8,700	LC
Rochester Inst of Technology	NY	26,232	VC+
Rutgers, The State Univ of New Jersey/CamdenCampus	NJ	6,484	C
St. Augustine's College	NC	12,990	C+
St. Bonaventure Univ	NY	21,956	C
St. Francis College	NY	9,610	C
St. Francis Univ	PA	24,486	LC
St. John's Univ	MN	23,640	VC
St. Mary's Univ of Minn	MN	19,975	C
St. Norbert College	WI	23,169	VC
St. Peter's College	NJ	22,292	LC
St. Thomas Aquinas College	NY	20,590	LC
Salem College	NC	23,065	VC
Salem State College	MA	4,481	LC
Salve Regina Univ	RI	26,460	C
San Francisco State Univ	CA	7,139	LC
Seton Hill College	PA	21,875	C
Shorter College	GA	15,185	C
Slippery Rock Univ	PA	9,152	LC
Southeastern Okla State Univ	OK	4,917	C
Southern Arkansas Univ	AR	5,740	LC
Southern Wesleyan Univ	SC	17,280	C
Southwest Missouri State Univ	MO	7,600	LC
Southwest Texas State Univ	TX	8,730	VC
SUNY/College at Fredonia	NY	10,125	C
SUNY/College at Plattsburgh	NY	9,729	C
SUNY/Univ at Albany	NY	10,997	VC
SUNY/Univ at Buffalo	NY	11,033	VC
Suffolk Univ	MA	26,516	C
Tarleton State Univ	TX	7,160	C
Tenn State Univ	TN	7,058	VC
Texas A&M Univ at Kingsville	TX	6,446	LC
Thiel College	PA	18,419	LC
Thomas More College	KY	17,700	LC
Towson Univ	MD	11,088	VC
Trevecca Nazarene Univ	TN	15,752	C
Union College	NE	14,650	C
Union Univ	TN	18,930	C+
Univ of Akron	OH	10,530	NC
Univ of Bridgeport	CT	23,020	C

School	ST	$IS	SR
Univ of Central Florida	FL	8,251	VC
Univ of Central Okla	OK	5,205	C
Univ of Cincinnati	OH	12,491	LC
Univ of Conn	CT	12,122	VC
Univ of Delaware	DE	10,824	VC
Univ of Hartford	CT	28,884	C
Univ of Hawaii at Manoa	HI	7,862	VC
Univ of Idaho	ID	7,026	C
Univ of Indianapolis	IN	20,840	C
Univ of Iowa	IA	8,607	C+
Univ of Louisville	KY	7,402	LC
Univ of Maine	ME	10,798	C
Univ of Mass Amherst	MA	10,995	VC
Univ of Mich/Flint	MI	4,323	C
Univ of Minn/Twin Cities	MN	11,123	VC
Univ of Miss	MS	7,666	C
Univ of Nebr at Lincoln	NE	8,325	C+
Univ of New England	ME	24,110	LC
Univ of New Mexico	NM	8,026	C
Univ of N Car at Chapel Hill	NC	8,789	HC
Univ of N Car at Greensboro	NC	6,858	C
Univ of N Car at Wilmington	NC	7,769	C
Univ of North Texas	TX	7,629	C
Univ of Okla	OK	7,616	VC
Univ of Pittsburgh at Johnstown	PA	13,044	LC
Univ of Pittsburgh at Pittsburgh	PA	13,592	HC
Univ of Rhode Island	RI	12,414	C
Univ of St. Francis	IN	17,790	LC
Univ of Science and Arts of Okla	OK	5,245	C
Univ of Scranton	PA	27,964	C+
Univ of Sioux Falls	SD	16,390	C
Univ of S Car at Columbia	SC	8,748	VC
Univ of Southern Miss	MS	6,155	LC
Univ of Tenn at Chattanooga	TN	7,783	C
Univ of Texas at El Paso	TX	5,076	LC
Univ of the Incarnate Word	TX	18,478	C
Univ of Vermont	VT	14,761	C+
Univ of Virginia's College at Wise	VA	8,302	C
Univ of Washington	WA	10,361	VC
Univ of West Florida	FL	7,518	C
Univ of Wisc/La Crosse	WI	7,250	VC
Univ of Wisc/Madison	WI	8,262	VC
Univ of Wisc/Oshkosh	WI	6,130	LC
Utah State Univ	UT	6,771	C
Wagner College	NY	27,000	C
Wartburg College	IA	21,165	VC
Washburn Univ of Topeka	KS	6,766	NC
Waynesburg College	PA	17,610	LC
Wesley College	DE	17,869	C
Western Conn State Univ	CT	10,074	C
Western New Mexico Univ	NM	5,950	LC
Wichita State Univ	KS	6,879	C
William Carey College	MS	10,150	LC
William Jewell College	MO	17,150	VC
Winona State Univ	MN	8,570	C
Winthrop Univ	SC	9,106	C
Wright State Univ	OH	9,141	LC
Xavier Univ	OH	23,880	C
York College of Pennsylvania	PA	12,550	VC
Youngstown State Univ	OH	9,318	NC

MEDICAL RECORDS ADMINISTRATION/SERVICES

School	ST	$IS	SR
Chicago State Univ	IL	8,851	C+
Dakota State Univ	SD	6,950	C
East Carolina Univ	NC	7,766	C
East Central Univ	OK	4,578	C
LIU/C.W. Post Campus	NY	25,380	C
Louisiana Tech Univ	LA	6,506	C
Norfolk State Univ	VA	8,382	LC
Regis Univ	CO	25,740	C+
Southwest Texas State Univ	TX	8,730	VC
Southwestern Okla State Univ	OK	4,801	C
Tenn State Univ	TN	7,058	VC
Univ of Alabama at Birmingham	AL	10,110	C
Univ of Pittsburgh at Pittsburgh	PA	13,592	HC
Western Carolina Univ	NC	5,667	C

MEDICAL SCIENCE

School	ST	$IS	SR
Alderson-Broaddus College	WV	19,640	C
Oakland Univ	MI	9,418	C
Suffolk Univ	MA	26,516	C
Univ of Arkansas	AR	8,334	VC
Univ of Louisville	KY	7,402	LC
Univ of Wisc/Madison	WI	8,262	VC
Univ of Wisc/Milwaukee	WI	8,907	LC

MEDICAL TECHNOLOGY

School	ST	$IS	SR
Alderson-Broaddus College	WV	19,640	C
Aquinas College	MI	20,052	C+
Armstrong Atlantic State Univ	GA	7,084	C
Augustana College	SD	20,760	VC
Barry Univ	FL	24,100	LC
Blue Mountain College	MS	9,100	LC
Bradley Univ	IL	20,970	VC
Brescia Univ	KY	14,225	C
Bridgewater College	VA	22,950	C
Carroll College	WI	21,170	C
Catawba College	NC	19,620	C
Central Conn State Univ	CT	10,404	C
CUNY/College of Staten Island	NY	3,358	NC
Clarion Univ of Pennsylvania	PA	11,272	LC
Cleveland State Univ	OH	10,146	NC
College of St. Elizabeth	NJ	22,510	C
College of the Ozarks	MO	2,650	C+
Culver-Stockton College	MO	15,400	LC
DePauw Univ	IN	28,000	HC
Drake Univ	IA	22,830	VC
East Carolina Univ	NC	7,766	C
East Texas Baptist Univ	TX	12,349	LC
Edgewood College	WI	18,304	C
Elon Univ	NC	19,430	VC
Gardner-Webb Univ	NC	17,400	C
George Mason Univ	VA	9,192	C
Georgia Southern Univ	GA	6,958	C
Georgia State Univ	GA	7,792	LC
Harding Univ	AR	13,528	VC
Hartwick College	NY	33,090	C+
Houghton College	NY	21,810	VC+
Houston Baptist Univ	TX	15,300	LC
Indiana Univ of Pennsylvania	PA	9,133	C
Indiana Univ Southeast	IN	3,459	C
Indiana Univ-Purdue Univ Indianapolis	IN	9,473	C
Inter-American Univ of PR/Bayamon Univ College	PR	3,700	
Inter-American Univ of PR/Fajardo Campus	PR	4,000	
Inter-American Univ of PR/Metropolitan Campus	PR	4,166	
Inter-American Univ of PR/Ponce Regional College	PR	3,700	
Kansas State Univ	KS	6,995	C
Kean Univ	NJ	11,159	C
Kent State Univ	OH	11,104	C
King College	TN	17,800	VC
Lincoln Univ	MO	7,158	NC
Lindenwood Univ	MO	17,250	C
Loras College	IA	22,994	C+
Lubbock Christian Univ	TX	14,226	LC
Mansfield Univ	PA	9,648	C
Marist College	NY	24,756	VC
Miami Univ	OH	12,885	VC+
Miss State Univ	MS	7,853	C
Mount Marty College	SD	15,656	LC
Mount Vernon Nazarene College	OH	17,027	C
Norfolk State Univ	VA	8,382	LC
Northwestern State Univ of Louisiana	LA	5,745	NC
Oakwood College	AL	14,904	C
Ohio Northern Univ	OH	27,765	VC
Okla Panhandle State Univ	OK	3,812	NC
Okla State Univ	OK	7,650	VC
Old Dominion Univ	VA	9,386	C
Oregon State Univ	OR	9,612	VC
Pikeville College	KY	12,000	NC
Pittsburg State Univ	KS	6,228	NC
Prairie View A&M Univ	TX	3,172	LC
Purdue Univ/West Lafayette	IN	10,284	VC
Radford Univ	VA	8,302	C
Roanoke College	VA	24,689	VC
Rochester Inst of Technology	NY	26,232	VC+
Roosevelt Univ	IL	20,240	LC
Rutgers, The State Univ of New Jersey New Brunswick Campus	NJ	12,709	C
Sacred Heart Univ	CT	26,588	VC
St. John's Univ	NY	26,660	C
St. Joseph's College	IN	21,640	C
St. Leo Univ	FL	19,250	LC
St. Mary-of-the-Woods College	IN	21,320	LC
Sam Houston State Univ	TX	6,076	LC
Seattle Univ	WA	24,183	VC
Southern Adventist Univ	TN	15,600	C
Southwest Baptist Univ	MO	13,426	LC
Southwest State Univ	MN	7,117	LC
Southwestern Adventist Univ	TX	14,798	C
Southwestern Okla State Univ	OK	4,801	C
SUNY/College at Brockport	NY	10,267	C
Stetson Univ	FL	25,640	VC
Stonehill College	MA	26,852	HC
Texas Southern Univ	TX	6,576	NC
Ohio State Univ	OH	10,819	VC
Troy State Univ	AL	7,696	C
Truman State Univ	MO	8,568	VC+
Tusculum College	TN	17,900	LC

School	ST	$IS	SR
Univ of Alabama at Birmingham	AL	10,110	C
Univ of Arizona	AZ	8,614	C
Univ of Central Arkansas	AR	6,388	C
Univ of Mary Hardin-Baylor	TX	13,929	C
Univ of Mass Boston	MA	4,227	C
Univ of Miami	FL	31,130	HC
Univ of Mich/Ann Arbor	MI	13,003	HC+
Univ of Miss	MS	7,666	C
Univ of Missouri/Kansas City	MO	9,685	VC
Univ of Montana	MT	8,038	C
Univ of New Orleans	LA	10,160	C
Univ of N Car at Charlotte	NC	7,254	C
Univ of Rio Grande	OH	8,728	NC
Univ of St. Francis	IL	19,650	C
Univ of South Alabama	AL	6,976	LC
Univ of S Dak	SD	7,036	C
Univ of South Florida	FL	8,154	C
Univ of Southern Colo	CO	7,821	LC
Univ of Texas at Arlington	TX	7,192	LC
Univ of Texas at Austin	TX	9,437	HC
Univ of Texas-Pan American	TX	4,823	C
Univ of the Sacred Heart	PR	5,375	
Univ of the Sciences in Philadelphia	PA	24,826	VC
West Texas A&M Univ	TX	6,538	C
West Virginia Univ	WV	8,304	C
Western Illinois Univ	IL	9,571	C
Western Kentucky Univ	KY	6,834	C
Wilkes Univ	PA	25,800	C
William Jewell College	MO	17,150	VC
Winston-Salem State Univ	NC	5,927	LC
Youngstown State Univ	OH	9,318	NC

MEDIEVAL STUDIES

School	ST	$IS	SR
Bard College	NY	33,912	HC
Brown Univ	RI	34,973	MC
Catholic Univ of America	DC	29,332	VC
Columbia Univ/Barnard College	NY	33,694	MC
Columbia Univ/Columbia College	NY	35,190	MC
Conn College	CT	33,585	MC
Cornell College	IA	24,980	VC
Dickinson College	PA	32,210	VC+
Duke Univ	NC	34,396	MC
Emory Univ	GA	33,792	MC
Fordham Univ	NY	30,710	VC
Hanover College	IN	17,560	VC
Mass Inst of Technology	MA	35,228	MC
Mount Holyoke College	MA	34,128	HC
New College of Florida	FL	8,130	HC+
New York Univ	NY	35,200	MC
Penn State Univ/Univ Park Campus	PA	11,126	VC
Plymouth State College	NH	11,024	LC
Purdue Univ/West Lafayette	IN	10,284	VC
Rutgers, The State Univ of New Jersey New Brunswick Campus	NJ	12,709	C
St. Olaf College	MN	25,880	HC
Smith College	MA	33,002	HC+
Southern Methodist Univ	TX	28,349	VC
SUNY/Univ at Albany	NY	10,997	VC
SUNY/Univ at Binghamton	NY	10,653	HC
Swarthmore College	PA	34,538	MC
Syracuse Univ	NY	30,710	HC
Ohio State Univ	OH	10,819	VC
Tulane Univ	LA	34,013	HC+
Univ of Calif at Davis	CA	12,796	VC
Univ of Calif at Santa Barbara	CA	11,732	VC
Univ of Chicago	IL	35,087	MC
Univ of Mich/Ann Arbor	MI	13,003	HC+
Univ of Nebr at Lincoln	NE	8,325	C+
Univ of Notre Dame	IN	30,707	MC
Univ of Tenn at Knoxville	TN	8,214	C
Univ of the South	TN	27,290	HC
Vassar College	NY	33,450	MC
Washington and Lee Univ	VA	25,095	MC
Washington Univ in St. Louis	MO	34,593	MC
Wellesley College	MA	33,394	MC
Wesleyan Univ	CT	3,405	MC

MENTAL HEALTH/HUMAN SERVICES

School	ST	$IS	SR
Audrey Cohen College	NY	17,715	C
Franciscan Univ of Steubenville	OH	19,100	C+
MCP Hahnemann Univ	PA	18,510	SP
Morgan State Univ	MD	10,078	LC
Norfolk State Univ	VA	8,382	LC
Northern Kentucky Univ	KY	6,352	NC
Sinte Gleska Univ	SD	2,268	NC
Thomas Edison State College	NJ	2,750	SP
Univ of Maine at Augusta	ME	3,928	C

METAL/JEWELRY

School	ST	$IS	SR
Arizona State Univ-Main	AZ	7,726	C
Calif College of Arts and Crafts	CA	27,366	SP
College For Creative Studies	MI	20,938	SP
Edinboro Univ of Pennsylvania	PA	9,328	LC
Maine College of Art	ME	26,367	SP
Mass College of Art	MA	13,703	SP
Northern Mich Univ	MI	9,693	C
Rhode Island School of Design	RI	30,227	SP
Rochester Inst of Technology	NY	26,232	VC+
Savannah College of Art and Design	GA	25,075	SP
Syracuse Univ	NY	30,710	HC
Univ of Mass Dartmouth	MA	9,852	C
Univ of Mich/Ann Arbor	MI	13,003	HC+
Univ of North Texas	TX	7,629	C
Univ of Oregon	OR	9,969	C
Univ of the Arts	PA	24,230	SP
Univ of Washington	WA	10,361	VC

METALLURGICAL ENGINEERING

School	ST	$IS	SR
Calif Polytechnic State Univ	CA	8,747	VC
Colo School of Mines	CO	11,578	HC
Columbia Univ/Fu Foundation School of Engineering and Applied Science	NY	35,190	MC
Illinois Inst of Technology	IL	25,182	HC+
Montana Tech of The Univ of Montana	MT	7,845	C
New Mexico Inst of Mining and Technology	NM	7,152	VC+
S Dak School of Mines and Technology	SD	7,438	C+
Ohio State Univ	OH	10,819	VC
Univ of Alabama	AL	7,402	C
Univ of Cincinnati	OH	12,491	LC
Univ of Idaho	ID	7,026	C
Univ of Illinois at Urbana-Champaign	IL	11,316	HC+
Univ of Minn/Twin Cities	MN	11,123	VC
Univ of Missouri/Rolla	MO	10,034	C
Univ of Nevada/Reno	NV	8,737	C
Univ of Pittsburgh at Pittsburgh	PA	13,592	HC
Univ of Texas at El Paso	TX	5,076	LC
Univ of Utah	UT	7,703	C
Univ of Wisc/Madison	WI	8,262	VC

MEXICAN-AMERICAN/CHICANO STUDIES

School	ST	$IS	SR
Cal State, Dominguez Hills	CA	5,840	LC
Cal State, Fresno	CA	7,762	C
Cal State, Fullerton	CA	5,440	LC
Cal State, Los Angeles	CA	5,050	C
Cal State, Northridge	CA	7,781	C
Claremont McKenna College	CA	32,700	MC
Concordia Univ at Austin	TX	16,740	LC
Metropolitan State College of Denver	CO	2,338	LC
Pitzer College	CA	33,930	HC
San Diego State Univ	CA	9,716	C+
Scripps College	CA	30,400	HC+
Southern Methodist Univ	TX	28,349	VC
Sul Ross State Univ	TX	6,582	LC
Univ of Arizona	AZ	8,614	C
Univ of Calif at Davis	CA	12,796	VC
Univ of Calif at Riverside	CA	12,479	C
Univ of Calif at Santa Barbara	CA	11,732	VC
Univ of Minn/Twin Cities	MN	11,123	VC
Univ of Northern Colo	CO	8,082	C+
Univ of Texas at El Paso	TX	5,076	LC
Univ of Texas at San Antonio	TX	9,088	NC
Univ of Texas-Pan American	TX	4,823	C
Wayne State Univ	MI	6,720	C

MICROBIOLOGY

School	ST	$IS	SR
Arizona State Univ-Main	AZ	7,726	C
Auburn Univ	AL	5,510	C
Ball State Univ	IN	8,660	C
Bard College	NY	33,912	HC
Bowling Green State Univ	OH	10,794	C
Brigham Young Univ	UT	7,840	HC
Calif Polytechnic State Univ	CA	8,747	VC
Calif State Polytechnic Univ, Pomona	CA	8,615	C
Cal State, Chico	CA	8,598	LC
Cal State, Los Angeles	CA	5,050	C
Cal State, Northridge	CA	7,781	C
Cal State, Sacramento	CA	7,488	C
Clemson Univ	SC	7,600	C
Colo State Univ	CO	9,072	C
Duquesne Univ	PA	24,242	C+
Eastern Kentucky Univ	KY	6,552	C
Eastern Mich Univ	MI	9,855	C
Eastern Washington Univ	WA	7,972	LC
Howard Univ	DC	15,522	LC
Idaho State Univ	ID	7,030	C+
Indiana Univ Bloomington	IN	10,712	C+
Inter-American Univ of PR/Arecibo Campus	PR	3,300	
Iowa State Univ	IA	8,108	VC
Juniata College	PA	26,080	VC
Kansas State Univ	KS	6,995	C
Marlboro College	VT	26,410	VC+
Miami Univ	OH	12,885	VC+
Mich State Univ	MI	10,386	VC
Miss State Univ	MS	7,853	C
Miss Univ for Women	MS	5,446	LC
Missouri Southern State College	MO	6,666	C
Montana State Univ-Bozeman	MT	8,431	C
New Mexico State Univ	NM	7,302	C
N Car State Univ	NC	8,680	HC
N Dak State Univ	ND	7,004	VC
Northern Arizona Univ	AZ	7,398	C
Northern Mich Univ	MI	9,693	C
Ohio Univ	OH	11,769	C
Ohio Wesleyan Univ	OH	29,670	VC+
Okla State Univ	OK	7,650	VC
Oregon State Univ	OR	9,612	VC
Penn State Univ/Univ Park Campus	PA	11,126	VC
Purdue Univ/Calumet	IN	6,630	NC
Quinnipiac Univ	CT	27,370	C
Rutgers, The State Univ of New Jersey New Brunswick Campus	NJ	12,709	C
San Diego State Univ	CA	9,716	C+
San Francisco State Univ	CA	7,139	LC
San Jose State Univ	CA	8,187	C
S Dak State Univ	SD	6,848	C
Southern Illinois Univ at Carbondale	IL	8,621	C
Southwest Texas State Univ	TX	8,730	VC
SUNY/College of Environmental Science and Forestry	NY	12,446	VC
Texas A&M Univ	TX	8,988	VC
Texas Tech Univ	TX	8,825	C
Univ of Akron	OH	10,530	NC
Univ of Alabama	AL	7,402	C
Univ of Arizona	AZ	8,614	C
Univ of Arkansas	AR	8,334	VC
Univ of Calif at Davis	CA	12,796	VC
Univ of Calif at Los Angeles	CA	13,227	MC
Univ of Calif at San Diego	CA	11,372	HC
Univ of Calif at Santa Barbara	CA	11,732	VC
Univ of Central Florida	FL	8,251	VC
Univ of Florida	FL	7,874	HC
Univ of Georgia	GA	8,656	VC
Univ of Great Falls	MT	15,360	C
Univ of Hawaii at Manoa	HI	7,862	VC
Univ of Houston-Downtown	TX	2,006	NC
Univ of Idaho	ID	7,026	C
Univ of Illinois at Urbana-Champaign	IL	11,316	HC+
Univ of Iowa	IA	8,607	C+
Univ of Kansas	KS	7,232	VC
Univ of Maine	ME	10,798	C
Univ of Maryland/College Park	MD	11,959	C
Univ of Mass Amherst	MA	10,995	VC
Univ of Memphis	TN	7,271	C
Univ of Miami	FL	31,130	HC
Univ of Mich/Ann Arbor	MI	13,003	HC+
Univ of Mich/Dearborn	MI	4,677	VC
Univ of Minn/Twin Cities	MN	11,123	VC
Univ of Montana	MT	8,038	C
Univ of New Hampshire	NH	13,207	C
Univ of Northern Iowa	IA	7,850	C
Univ of Okla	OK	7,616	VC
Univ of Pittsburgh at Pittsburgh	PA	13,592	HC
Univ of PR at Humacao	PR	1,245	
Univ of PR/Arecibo	PR	1,095	
Univ of PR/Mayaguez	PR	5,285	
Univ of Rhode Island	RI	12,414	C
Univ of Rochester	NY	32,979	HC
Univ of South Florida	FL	8,154	C
Univ of Tenn at Knoxville	TN	8,214	C
Univ of Texas at Arlington	TX	7,192	LC
Univ of Texas at Austin	TX	9,437	HC
Univ of Texas at El Paso	TX	5,076	LC
Univ of the Sciences in Philadelphia	PA	24,826	VC
Univ of Vermont	VT	14,761	C+
Univ of Washington	WA	10,361	VC
Univ of Wisc/La Crosse	WI	7,250	VC
Univ of Wisc/Madison	WI	8,262	VC
Univ of Wisc/Milwaukee	WI	8,907	LC
Univ of Wisc/Oshkosh	WI	6,130	LC
Univ of Wyoming	WY	7,143	LC
Utah State Univ	UT	6,771	C
Wagner College	NY	27,000	C
Washington State Univ	WA	9,388	C
Weber State Univ	UT	6,897	NC
Xavier Univ of Louisiana	LA	17,000	LC

MIDDLE EASTERN STUDIES

School	ST	$IS	SR
Brandeis Univ	MA	34,481	MC
College of the Holy Cross	MA	32,780	MC
Columbia Univ/Barnard College	NY	33,694	MC
Columbia Univ/Columbia College	NY	35,190	MC
Columbia Univ/School of General Studies	NY	35,000	C
Dartmouth College	NH	34,458	MC
Emory & Henry College	VA	19,462	C
Emory Univ	GA	33,792	MC
Fordham Univ	NY	30,710	VC
George Washington Univ	DC	32,170	HC
Hampshire College	MA	33,881	HC+
Harvard Univ/Harvard College	MA	34,269	MC
New York Univ	NY	35,200	MC
Rutgers, The State Univ of New Jersey New Brunswick Campus	NJ	12,709	C
Tufts Univ	MA	34,874	MC
Univ of Arkansas	AR	8,334	VC
Univ of Calif at Berkeley	CA	14,134	MC
Univ of Conn	CT	12,122	VC
Univ of Mass Amherst	MA	10,995	VC
Univ of Mich/Ann Arbor	MI	13,003	HC+
Univ of Minn/Twin Cities	MN	11,123	VC
Univ of Texas at Austin	TX	9,437	HC
Univ of Utah	UT	7,703	C
Washington Univ in St. Louis	MO	34,593	MC

MIDDLE SCHOOL EDUCATION

School	ST	$IS	SR
Abilene Christian Univ	TX	16,300	VC
Alabama A&M Univ	AL	5,100	LC
Albany State Univ	GA	5,764	C+
Alice Lloyd College	KY	1,785	VC
Alverno College	WI	16,930	LC
American International College	MA	22,268	LC
Appalachian State Univ	NC	6,353	C
Arkansas State Univ	AR	7,480	C
Arkansas Tech Univ	AR	6,256	C
Armstrong Atlantic State Univ	GA	7,084	C
Asbury College	KY	18,540	VC
Auburn Univ	AL	5,510	C
Augusta State Univ	GA	2,282	C
Averett Univ	VA	17,980	LC
Avila College	MO	17,720	C
Ball State Univ	IN	8,660	C
Bartlesville Wesleyan College	OK	14,100	LC
Barton College	NC	16,834	LC
Bellarmine Univ	KY	20,440	VC
Bemidji State Univ	MN	7,957	C
Bennett College	NC	11,200	C
Berea College	KY	4,070	VC
Berry College	GA	18,850	C
Bethany College	KS	16,602	C+
Bluefield College	VA	14,200	C
Bluefield State College	WV	2,178	LC
Brenau Univ Women's College	GA	20,100	C
Brewton-Parker College	GA	10,810	LC
Buena Vista Univ	IA	22,828	C
Campbell Univ	NC	16,599	C
Campbellsville Univ	KY	14,340	C
Capital Univ	OH	23,630	C
Cardinal Stritch Univ	WI	17,620	C
Caribbean Univ	PR	3,000	
Carson-Newman College	TN	16,490	C
Carthage College	WI	23,670	C
Catawba College	NC	19,620	C
Cedarville Univ	OH	17,553	VC
Central Mich Univ	MI	8,355	C
Central Missouri State Univ	MO	7,920	C
Central Washington Univ	WA	8,985	LC
Christopher Newport Univ	VA	8,862	VC
City Univ	WA	7,425	NC
CUNY/Hunter College	NY	5,147	C+
Clayton College and State Univ	GA	2,322	C+
College of Mount St. Joseph	OH	20,290	C
College of New Rochelle	NY	20,000	C
College of Our Lady of the Elms	MA	20,644	C
College of the Ozarks	MO	2,650	C+
Columbus State Univ	GA	7,228	LC
Concord College	WV	7,122	C+
Concordia College/Moorhead	MN	18,835	C
Concordia Univ	MN	19,912	C
Concordia Univ Nebr	NE	17,770	C
Concordia Univ, River Forest	IL	20,000	LC

School	ST	$IS	SR
Cornerstone Univ and Grand Rapids Baptist Seminary	MI	18,092	C
Cumberland College	KY	14,864	C
Cumberland Univ	TN	11,970	LC
Dickinson State Univ	ND	5,495	NC
Drake Univ	IA	22,830	VC
East Carolina Univ	NC	7,766	C
Eastern Conn State Univ	CT	10,362	C
Eastern Illinois Univ	IL	10,101	C
Eastern Kentucky Univ	KY	6,552	C
Eastern Mich Univ	MI	9,855	C
Eastern Washington Univ	WA	7,972	LC
Elizabeth City State Univ	NC	5,550	LC
Elon Univ	NC	19,430	VC
Fairmont State College	WV	7,010	NC
Fayetteville State Univ	NC	5,590	LC
Fitchburg State College	MA	7,836	C
Florida Southern College	FL	19,430	C
Fontbonne Univ	MO	18,046	C
Fort Valley State Univ	GA	6,014	LC
Freed-Hardeman Univ	TN	14,290	VC
Frostburg State Univ	MD	9,680	C
Gardner-Webb Univ	NC	17,400	C
George Fox Univ	OR	24,095	VC
Georgia College and State Univ	GA	7,344	C
Georgia Southern Univ	GA	6,958	C
Georgia Southwestern State Univ	GA	6,013	C
Georgia State Univ	GA	7,792	LC
Glenville State College	WV	6,588	NC
Goshen College	IN	18,950	VC+
Grand Valley State Univ	MI	10,040	C
Greensboro College	NC	19,080	LC
Gustavus Adolphus College	MN	24,190	VC+
Harris-Stowe State College	MO	2,310	SP
Heidelberg College	OH	23,879	C
High Point Univ	NC	20,220	LC
Hillsdale College	MI	20,586	VC+
Humboldt State Univ	CA	8,582	C
Illinois State Univ	IL	9,235	C
Immaculata College	PA	22,400	LC
Indiana State Univ	IN	8,461	LC
Indiana Univ Bloomington	IN	10,712	C+
Iona College	NY	26,556	C
Ithaca College	NY	28,719	HC
Johnson C. Smith Univ	NC	16,560	C+
Johnson State College	VT	10,776	C
Judson College	AL	13,790	C
Kennesaw State Univ	GA	2,306	LC
Kent State Univ	OH	11,104	C
Kentucky Christian College	KY	13,472	C
Kentucky Wesleyan College	KY	15,800	C
King's College	PA	24,680	C
LaGrange College	GA	17,496	C
Lake Erie College	OH	21,350	LC
Lenoir-Rhyne College	NC	19,186	C
Lesley College	MA	25,325	LC
Lincoln Memorial Univ	TN	12,620	LC
Lubbock Christian Univ	TX	14,226	LC
Malone College	OH	19,190	C
Manchester College	IN	22,010	C
Manhattan College	NY	25,500	VC
Marian College of Fond du Lac	WI	17,935	LC
Mars Hill College	NC	18,600	LC
Marshall Univ	WV	7,752	LC
Mary Baldwin College	VA	23,440	C
Maryville Univ of St. Louis	MO	18,680	C
Methodist College	NC	19,526	C
Miami Univ	OH	12,885	VC+
Midland Lutheran College	NE	18,600	C
Millikin Univ	IL	24,415	C+
Missouri Baptist College	MO	15,762	LC
Missouri Southern State College	MO	6,666	C
Missouri Western State College	MO	6,662	NC
Montana State Univ-Billings	MT	7,653	NC
Morehead State Univ	KY	6,510	C
Mount Olive College	NC	14,410	LC
Mount Union College	OH	21,120	C
Mount Vernon Nazarene College	OH	17,027	C
Murray State Univ	KY	6,672	C
Nazareth College of Rochester	NY	22,036	VC
Nebr Wesleyan Univ	NE	18,767	VC
New York Inst of Technology	NY	21,756	C
Newman Univ	KS	14,098	LC
N Car Central Univ	NC	6,418	LC
N Car State Univ	NC	8,680	HC
N Car Wesleyan College	NC	15,650	LC
North Georgia College and State Univ	GA	6,322	C+
Northern Kentucky Univ	KY	6,352	NC
Northern State Univ	SD	6,279	LC
Northland College	WI	21,435	C+
Northwest Missouri State Univ	MO	7,922	LC
Northwestern College of Iowa	IA	17,630	C+
Notre Dame College	OH	20,425	C
Oakland City Univ	IN	11,286	LC
Oglethorpe Univ	GA	19,100	LC
Ohio Dominican College	OH	18,100	LC
Ohio Northern Univ	OH	27,765	VC
Ohio Univ	OH	11,769	C
Ohio Wesleyan Univ	OH	29,670	VC+
Okla Christian Univ	OK	16,500	VC
Ouachita Baptist Univ	AR	16,460	VC
Paine College	GA	11,896	LC
Palm Beach Atlantic College	FL	23,310	C
Piedmont College	GA	16,900	C
Pikeville College	KY	12,000	NC
Prescott College	AZ	13,430	C
Rhode Island College	RI	8,700	LC
Ripon College	WI	24,180	VC+
St. Francis College	NY	9,610	C
St. John's Univ	NY	26,660	C
St. Joseph's College	IN	21,640	C
St. Mary-of-the-Woods College	IN	21,320	LC
St. Mary's Univ of Minn	MN	19,975	C
St. Xavier Univ	IL	21,104	C
Shorter College	GA	15,185	C
Southeastern College	FL	11,648	LC
Southern Arkansas Univ	AR	5,740	LC
Southwest Baptist Univ	MO	13,426	LC
Southwest Missouri State Univ	MO	7,600	LC
Spalding Univ	KY	15,196	C
Springfield College	MA	24,520	C
SUNY/College at Cortland	NY	10,564	C
SUNY/College at Fredonia	NY	10,125	C
SUNY/College at Potsdam	NY	10,519	C
SUNY/Univ at New Paltz	NY	9,685	VC
State Univ of West Georgia	GA	7,101	C
Syracuse Univ	NY	30,710	HC
Tabor College	KS	17,600	LC
Temple Univ	PA	14,124	C
Texas Christian Univ	TX	19,910	C
Texas Wesleyan Univ	TX	14,710	C
Thomas More College	KY	17,700	LC
Thomas Univ	GA	8,770	NC
Toccoa Falls College	GA	14,220	C
Transylvania Univ	KY	21,780	VC+
Tusculum College	TN	17,900	LC
Union College	KY	15,920	C
Union Univ	TN	18,930	C+
Univ of Arkansas	AR	8,334	VC
Univ of Arkansas at Pine Bluff	AR	7,925	C
Univ of Central Arkansas	AR	6,388	C
Univ of Cincinnati	OH	12,491	LC
Univ of Detroit Mercy	MI	21,620	LC
Univ of Evansville	IN	22,865	VC+
Univ of Findlay	OH	23,962	NC
Univ of Georgia	GA	8,656	VC
Univ of Great Falls	MT	15,360	C
Univ of Indianapolis	IN	20,840	C
Univ of Iowa	IA	8,607	C+
Univ of Kansas	KS	7,232	VC
Univ of Kentucky	KY	7,765	C
Univ of Louisville	KY	7,402	LC
Univ of Maine at Machias	ME	7,689	LC
Univ of Mary Hardin-Baylor	TX	13,929	C
Univ of Missouri/Columbia	MO	9,803	HC
Univ of Montana--Western	MT	6,915	NC
Univ of Nebr at Kearney	NE	7,048	NC
Univ of Nebr at Lincoln	NE	8,325	C+
Univ of N Car at Chapel Hill	NC	8,789	HC
Univ of N Car at Charlotte	NC	7,254	C
Univ of N Car at Greensboro	NC	6,858	C
Univ of N Car at Pembroke	NC	5,914	LC
Univ of N Car at Wilmington	NC	7,769	C
Univ of N Dak	ND	7,067	VC
Univ of North Florida	FL	8,089	VC
Univ of Northern Iowa	IA	7,850	C
Univ of San Francisco	CA	27,302	VC
Univ of Sioux Falls	SD	16,390	C
Univ of South Alabama	AL	6,976	LC
Univ of Southern Indiana	IN	8,655	LC
Univ of Southern Miss	MS	6,155	LC
Univ of the Incarnate Word	TX	18,478	C
Univ of the Ozarks	AR	13,904	C
Univ of Vermont	VT	14,761	C+
Univ of West Alabama	AL	6,048	C
Univ of West Florida	FL	7,518	C
Univ of Wisc/Platteville	WI	7,282	C
Univ of Wisc/Whitewater	WI	6,937	C
Urbana Univ	OH	17,004	C
Valdosta State Univ	GA	6,988	C
Valparaiso Univ	IN	23,570	VC+
Wagner College	NY	27,000	C
Walsh Univ	OH	16,880	C
Warren Wilson College	NC	19,968	C
Washington Univ in St. Louis	MO	34,593	MC
Wesleyan College	GA	17,050	VC
West Liberty State College	WV	6,056	LC
Western Carolina Univ	NC	5,667	C
Western Kentucky Univ	KY	6,834	C
Westfield State College	MA	8,394	C
Westminster College	MO	19,990	C+
William Woods Univ	MO	19,390	LC
Wingate Univ	NC	19,140	C
Wittenberg Univ	OH	28,766	VC
Xavier Univ	OH	23,880	C
Youngstown State Univ	OH	9,318	NC

MILITARY SCIENCE

School	ST	$IS	SR
Austin Peay State Univ	TN	5,814	LC
Campbell Univ	NC	16,599	C
Drake Univ	IA	22,830	VC
Eastern Mich Univ	MI	9,855	C
Eastern Washington Univ	WA	7,972	LC
Elon Univ	NC	19,430	VC
Hawaii Pacific Univ	HI	17,790	C
Norfolk State Univ	VA	8,382	LC
Norwich Univ	VT	21,064	LC
Rice Univ	TX	24,325	MC
Rochester Inst of Technology	NY	26,232	VC+
Rockford College	IL	23,930	C
Texas Southern Univ	TX	6,576	NC
United States Air Force Academy	CO		MC
United States Military Academy	NY		MC

MINING AND MINERAL ENGINEERING

School	ST	$IS	SR
Colo School of Mines	CO	11,578	HC
Columbia Univ/Fu Foundation School of Engineering and Applied Science	NY	35,190	MC
Mich Tech Univ	MI	11,088	VC
Montana Tech of The Univ of Montana	MT	7,845	C
New Mexico Inst of Mining and Technology	NM	7,152	VC+
Penn State Univ/Univ Park Campus	PA	11,126	VC
S Dak School of Mines and Technology	SD	7,438	C+
Southern Illinois Univ at Carbondale	IL	8,621	C
Univ of Alaska Fairbanks	AK	8,265	NC
Univ of Arizona	AZ	8,614	C
Univ of Idaho	ID	7,026	C
Univ of Kentucky	KY	7,765	C
Univ of Missouri/Rolla	MO	10,034	C
Univ of Nevada/Reno	NV	8,737	C
Univ of Utah	UT	7,703	C
Virginia Polytechnic Inst and State Univ	VA	7,652	C
West Virginia Univ	WV	8,304	C

MINISTRIES

School	ST	$IS	SR
Abilene Christian Univ	TX	16,300	VC
American Indian College of the Assemblies of God	AZ	7,810	NC
Asbury College	KY	18,540	VC
Atlantic Union College	MA	34,034	LC
Averett Univ	VA	17,980	LC
Azusa Pacific Univ	CA	22,422	VC
Bethel College	IN	17,650	LC
Claflin Univ	SC	12,735	C+
Clearwater Christian College	FL	13,160	LC
College of St. Benedict	MN	23,921	VC
Concordia College	NY	19,200	VC
Concordia College/Moorhead	MN	18,835	C
Concordia Univ Wisc	WI	16,600	LC
Creighton Univ	NE	23,476	VC
Crichton College	TN	12,680	LC
Dakota Wesleyan Univ	SD	15,512	C
East Texas Baptist Univ	TX	12,349	LC
Eastern Mennonite Univ	VA	20,700	VC
Eastern Nazarene College	MA	19,433	LC
Freed-Hardeman Univ	TN	14,290	VC
Fresno Pacific Univ	CA	19,740	C
Geneva College	PA	19,990	C+
George Fox Univ	OR	24,095	VC
Greenville College	IL	19,226	LC
Harding Univ	AR	13,528	VC
Hardin-Simmons Univ	TX	14,165	C
Hope International Univ	CA	16,940	NC
Houghton College	NY	21,810	VC+
Huntington College	IN	15,480	LC
Indiana Wesleyan Univ	IN	17,680	C
John Brown Univ	AR	15,080	VC
Juniata College	PA	26,080	VC
Kentucky Christian College	KY	13,472	C
Loras College	IA	22,994	C+
Lubbock Christian Univ	TX	14,226	LC
Malone College	OH	19,190	C
Marylhurst Univ	OR	15,343	NC
Messiah College	PA	23,180	VC
Missouri Baptist College	MO	15,762	LC
Mount Ida College	MA	25,375	LC
Mount Olive College	NC	14,410	LC
North Central Univ	MN	12,744	LC
Northwest Christian College	OR	19,680	LC
Northwest College	WA	17,471	C
Northwest Nazarene Univ	ID	18,380	C
Northwestern College	MN	19,816	C+
Notre Dame College	OH	20,425	C
Oakwood College	AL	14,904	C
Okla Christian Univ	OK	16,500	VC
Oral Roberts Univ	OK	18,490	C
Ouachita Baptist Univ	AR	16,460	VC
Rochester College	MI	15,404	C+
Simpson College	CA	19,200	C
Southeastern College	FL	11,648	LC
Southern Christian Univ	AL	8,480	LC
Southwest Baptist Univ	MO	13,426	LC
Spalding Univ	KY	15,196	C
Spring Arbor Univ	MI	17,976	C
Tabor College	KS	17,600	LC
Tenn Wesleyan College	TN	13,030	C
Toccoa Falls College	GA	14,220	C
Trevecca Nazarene Univ	TN	15,752	C
Trinity Bible College	ND		
Union Univ	TN	18,930	C+
Univ of Mary	ND	12,900	LC
Univ of St. Francis	IN	17,790	LC
Valparaiso Univ	IN	23,570	VC+
Vanguard Univ of Southern Calif	CA	20,212	C
Viterbo Univ	WI	18,043	C
Warner Pacific College	OR	20,370	LC
Western Baptist College	OR	19,700	C+

MISSIONS

School	ST	$IS	SR
Abilene Christian Univ	TX	16,300	VC
Asbury College	KY	18,540	VC
Bethel College	IN	17,650	LC
Cascade College	OR	14,800	NC
Cedarville Univ	OH	17,553	VC
Covenant College	GA	21,970	C+
Eastern College	PA	19,641	LC
Evangel Univ	MO	14,050	C
Fresno Pacific Univ	CA	19,740	C
Grace Bible College	MI	12,600	C
King College	TN	17,800	VC
Milligan College	TN	17,550	C
Northwestern College	MN	19,816	C+
Nyack College	NY	18,540	C
Okla Christian Univ	OK	16,500	VC
Simpson College	CA	19,200	C
Southern Nazarene Univ	OK	14,634	NC
Toccoa Falls College	GA	14,220	C
Trinity Bible College	ND		
Union Univ	TN	18,930	C+

MODERN LANGUAGE

School	ST	$IS	SR
Augustana College	SD	20,760	VC
Beloit College	WI	27,482	HC
Bethune-Cookman College	FL	15,746	C
Clemson Univ	SC	7,600	C
College of Mount St. Vincent	NY	24,230	C
College of Notre Dame of Maryland	MD	23,100	LC
Converse College	SC	21,990	VC
Emory & Henry College	VA	19,462	C
Emory Univ	GA	33,792	MC
Fort Hays State Univ	KS	6,294	LC
Graceland Univ	IA	15,845	C
Greenville College	IL	19,226	LC
High Point Univ	NC	20,220	LC
Ithaca College	NY	28,719	HC
James Madison Univ	VA	9,552	HC
Kansas State Univ	KS	6,995	C
Kenyon College	OH	32,130	HC+
King College	TN	17,800	VC
Knox College	IL	28,230	HC
Longwood College	VA	8,950	C
Merrimack College	MA	25,725	VC
Metropolitan State College of Denver	CO	2,338	LC
MidAmerica Nazarene Univ	KS	16,960	C
Millikin Univ	IL	24,415	C+
Mills College	CA	27,950	C
Miss College	MS	14,574	C
Monmouth Univ	NJ	24,042	C
Montana State Univ-Bozeman	MT	8,431	C
St. Francis Univ	PA	24,486	LC
St. Mary's College	MI	13,314	LC
Seton Hall Univ	NJ	26,910	LC
Simon's Rock College of Bard	MA	32,450	HC
Sweet Briar College	VA	25,310	VC
Syracuse Univ	NY	30,710	HC
Trinity College	CT	34,300	HC
Union College	NE	14,650	C
Union College	NY	32,646	HC
Univ of Alaska Fairbanks	AK	8,265	NC
Univ of Maine	ME	10,798	C
Univ of Maryland/Baltimore County	MD	12,190	VC
Univ of Mass Lowell	MA	9,470	VC
Univ of PR/Rio Piedras	PR	5,510	
Univ of Wisc/River Falls	WI	6,356	LC
Wayne State College	NE	6,255	NC
Westmont College	CA	29,748	VC
Widener Univ	PA	26,920	C
Wright State Univ	OH	9,141	LC

MOLECULAR BIOLOGY

School	ST	$IS	SR
Alverno College	WI	16,930	LC
Andrews Univ	MI	17,696	LC
Arizona State Univ-Main	AZ	7,726	C
Auburn Univ	AL	5,510	C
Ball State Univ	IN	8,660	C
Bard College	NY	33,912	HC
Benedictine Univ	IL	21,330	C
Bradley Univ	IL	20,970	VC
Centre College	KY	24,000	HC
Chestnut Hill College	PA	24,790	LC
Clarion Univ of Pennsylvania	PA	11,272	LC
Clarkson Univ	NY	29,884	VC
Coe College	IA	24,750	VC
Colgate Univ	NY	33,480	MC
Florida State Univ	FL	7,835	HC
Goshen College	IN	18,950	VC+
Illinois Inst of Technology	IL	25,182	HC+
Johns Hopkins Univ	MD	35,226	MC
Juniata College	PA	26,080	VC
Kenyon College	OH	32,130	HC+
Lehigh Univ	PA	32,290	MC
LIU/C.W. Post Campus	NY	25,380	C
Mansfield Univ	PA	9,648	C
Marquette Univ	WI	24,836	C+
Marymount Univ	VA	21,560	LC
Middlebury College	VT	34,300	MC
Montclair State Univ	NJ	10,287	LC
Muskingum College	OH	18,760	C
Nebr Wesleyan Univ	NE	18,767	VC
Northwestern Univ	IL	33,615	MC
Ohio Northern Univ	OH	27,765	VC
Ohio Univ	OH	11,769	C
Okla State Univ	OK	7,650	VC
Otterbein College	OH	23,439	C
Penn State Univ/Univ Park Campus	PA	11,126	VC
Pomona College	CA	33,960	MC
Rutgers, The State Univ of New Jersey New Brunswick Campus	NJ	12,709	C
Salem International Univ	WV	17,263	LC
SUNY/College of Environmental Science and Forestry	NY	12,446	VC
SUNY/Univ at Albany	NY	10,997	VC
Stetson Univ	FL	25,640	VC
Sweet Briar College	VA	25,310	VC
Texas Tech Univ	TX	8,825	C
Towson Univ	MD	11,088	VC
Univ of Arizona	AZ	8,614	C
Univ of Calif at Berkeley	CA	14,134	MC
Univ of Calif at Los Angeles	CA	13,227	MC
Univ of Calif at San Diego	CA	11,372	HC
Univ of Colo at Boulder	CO	9,255	VC
Univ of Conn	CT	12,122	VC
Univ of Great Falls	MT	15,360	C
Univ of Idaho	ID	7,026	C
Univ of Illinois at Urbana-Champaign	IL	11,316	HC+
Univ of Maine	ME	10,798	C
Univ of Memphis	TN	7,271	C
Univ of New Hampshire	NH	13,207	C
Univ of Pittsburgh at Pittsburgh	PA	13,592	HC
Univ of Redlands	CA	29,246	VC
Univ of Richmond	VA	27,300	HC
Univ of Texas at Austin	TX	9,437	HC
Univ of Wisc/Madison	WI	8,262	VC
Univ of Wyoming	WY	7,143	LC
Vanderbilt Univ	TN	34,482	MC
Wells College	NY	19,350	VC
Wesleyan Univ	CT	3,405	MC
Westminster College	PA	22,960	C

MULTIMEDIA

School	ST	$IS	SR
Allegheny College	PA	27,780	VC
Appalachian State Univ	NC	6,353	C
Art Inst of Atlanta	GA	20,624	SP
Art Inst of Portland	OR	13,725	SP
Bethel College	MN	22,740	VC
Bradley Univ	IL	20,970	VC
Calif Lutheran Univ	CA	23,500	LC
Cedarville Univ	OH	17,553	VC
Champlain College	VT	19,680	C
Columbia College Chicago	IL	22,063	LC
Dakota Wesleyan Univ	SD	15,512	C
George Washington Univ	DC	32,170	HC
Howard Payne Univ	TX	13,834	C+
Kean Univ	NJ	11,159	C
Kendall College of Art and Design of Ferris State Univ	MI	8,820	SP
La Salle Univ	PA	27,890	C
Lewis Univ	IL	20,960	C
Louisiana College	LA	11,516	C
Lyndon State College	VT	11,313	LC
McMurry Univ	TX	15,287	C
Minot State Univ	ND	5,466	LC
St. John's Univ	NY	26,660	C
Univ of N Car at Asheville	NC	6,896	VC
Univ of the Arts	PA	24,230	SP
Waynesburg College	PA	17,610	LC
Wilmington College	DE	6,530	NC

MUSEUM STUDIES

School	ST	$IS	SR
Baylor Univ	TX	18,298	VC+
Juniata College	PA	26,080	VC
Regis College	MA	26,750	C
Tusculum College	TN	17,900	LC
Univ of Central Okla	OK	5,205	C

MUSIC

School	ST	$IS	SR
Abilene Christian Univ	TX	16,300	VC
Adams State College	CO	7,468	C
Adolphi Univ	NY	23,320	VC
Adrian College	MI	19,670	C
Agnes Scott College	GA	24,950	VC
Alabama State Univ	AL	6,404	C
Alaska Pacific Univ	AK	16,450	C
Albany State Univ	GA	5,764	C+
Albertson College of Idaho	ID	23,900	VC
Albion College	MI	25,224	VC
Alderson-Broaddus College	WV	19,640	C
Allegheny College	PA	27,780	VC
Allen Univ	SC	9,600	NC
Alma College	MI	22,586	VC
Alverno College	WI	16,930	LC
American Univ	DC	31,544	VC+
Amherst College	MA	34,340	MC
Andrews Univ	MI	17,696	LC
Angelo State Univ	TX	7,028	C
Anna Maria College	MA	22,800	LC
Aquinas College	MI	20,052	C+
Arizona State Univ-Main	AZ	7,726	C
Arkansas State Univ	AR	7,480	C
Arkansas Tech Univ	AR	6,256	C
Armstrong Atlantic State Univ	GA	7,084	C
Asbury College	KY	18,540	VC
Ashland Univ	OH	22,182	LC
Atlantic Union College	MA	34,034	LC
Augsburg College	MN	22,978	C
Augusta State Univ	GA	2,282	C
Augustana College	IL	24,117	VC+
Augustana College	SD	20,760	VC
Austin College	TX	22,150	VC+
Austin Peay State Univ	TN	5,814	LC
Averett Univ	VA	17,980	LC
Avila College	MO	17,720	C
Azusa Pacific Univ	CA	22,422	VC
Baker Univ	KS	14,780	C+
Ball State Univ	IN	8,660	C
Bartlesville Wesleyan College	OK	14,100	LC
Bates College	ME	34,100	MC
Baylor Univ	TX	18,298	VC+
Belhaven College	MS	16,040	C+
Bellarmine Univ	KY	20,440	VC
Belmont Univ	TN	19,066	VC
Beloit College	WI	27,482	HC
Bemidji State Univ	MN	7,957	C
Benedict College	SC	12,662	LC
Benedictine College	KS	18,485	LC
Benedictine Univ	IL	21,330	C
Bennett College	NC	11,200	C
Bennington College	VT	31,350	VC
Berea College	KY	4,070	VC
Berklee College of Music	MA	27,005	SP
Berry College	GA	18,850	C
Bethany College	KS	16,602	C+
Bethel College	IN	17,650	LC
Bethel College	KS	17,355	C+
Bethel College	MN	22,740	VC
Bethune-Cookman College	FL	15,746	C
Biola Univ	CA	21,902	VC
Birmingham-Southern College	AL	22,960	C
Black Hills State Univ	SD	6,652	LC
Bloomsburg Univ of Pennsylvania	PA	9,434	C
Blue Mountain College	MS	9,100	LC
Bluefield College	VA	14,200	C
Bluffton College	OH	20,644	C
Boise State Univ	ID	6,531	LC
Boston College	MA	33,330	MC
Boston Conservatory	MA	26,900	SP
Boston Univ	MA	34,358	MC
Bowdoin College	ME	32,650	MC
Bradley Univ	IL	20,970	VC
Brandeis Univ	MA	34,481	MC
Brewton-Parker College	GA	10,810	LC
Briar Cliff Univ	IA	18,657	LC
Bridgewater College	VA	22,950	C
Bridgewater State College	MA	7,589	C+
Brigham Young Univ	UT	7,840	HC
Brigham Young Univ/Hawaii	HI	6,890	C
Brown Univ	RI	34,973	MC
Bryan College	TN	16,400	VC
Bryn Mawr College	PA	33,580	HC+
Bucknell Univ	PA	31,096	HC
Buena Vista Univ	IA	22,828	C
Butler Univ	IN	25,580	VC+
Caldwell College	NJ	20,940	LC
Calif Baptist Univ	CA	16,736	C
Calif Inst of the Arts	CA	27,275	SP
Calif Lutheran Univ	CA	23,500	LC
Calif State Polytechnic Univ, Pomona	CA	8,615	C
Cal State, Bakersfield	CA	6,090	LC
Cal State, Chico	CA	8,598	LC
Cal State, Dominguez Hills	CA	5,840	LC
Cal State, Fresno	CA	7,762	C
Cal State, Fullerton	CA	5,440	LC
Cal State, Hayward	CA	7,400	LC
Cal State, Long Beach	CA	7,400	LC
Cal State, Los Angeles	CA	5,050	C
Cal State, Northridge	CA	7,781	C
Cal State, Sacramento	CA	7,488	C
Cal State, San Bernardino	CA	6,516	C
Cal State, Stanislaus	CA	8,895	C
Calvin College	MI	20,050	NC
Cameron Univ	OK	5,560	NC
Campbell Univ	NC	16,599	C
Campbellsville Univ	KY	14,340	C
Capital Univ	OH	23,630	C
Cardinal Stritch Univ	WI	17,620	C
Carleton College	MN	30,780	MC
Carnegie Mellon Univ	PA	32,682	MC
Carroll College	WI	21,170	C
Carson-Newman College	TN	16,490	C
Carthage College	WI	23,670	C
Case Western Reserve Univ	OH	27,418	C
Castleton State College	VT	10,922	LC
Catawba College	NC	19,620	C
Catholic Univ of America	DC	29,332	VC
Cedar Crest College	PA	25,145	C+
Cedarville Univ	OH	17,553	VC
Centenary College of Louisiana	LA	21,600	C+
Central College	IA	21,206	C
Central Conn State Univ	CT	10,404	C
Central Methodist College	MO	16,460	C
Central Mich Univ	MI	8,355	C
Central Missouri State Univ	MO	7,920	C
Central State Univ	OH	8,922	C+
Central Washington Univ	WA	8,985	LC
Centre College	KY	24,000	HC
Chadron State College	NE	6,211	NC
Chapman Univ	CA	30,218	VC
Charleston Southern Univ	SC	17,122	C
Chatham College	PA	25,454	C+
Chestnut Hill College	PA	24,790	LC
Cheyney Univ of Pennsylvania	PA	9,993	C
Chicago State Univ	IL	8,851	C+
Christian Heritage College	CA	18,000	LC
Christopher Newport Univ	VA	8,862	VC
CUNY/Baruch College	NY	3,275	VC+
CUNY/Brooklyn College	NY	3,403	LC
CUNY/City College	NY	3,309	LC
CUNY/College of Staten Island	NY	3,358	NC
CUNY/Herbert H. Lehman College	NY	3,320	LC
CUNY/Hunter College	NY	5,147	C+
CUNY/Queens College	NY	3,403	VC
CUNY/York College	NY	3,292	NC
Claflin Univ	SC	12,735	C+
Claremont McKenna College	CA	32,700	MC
Clarion Univ of Pennsylvania	PA	11,272	LC
Clark Atlanta Univ	GA	17,174	C
Clark Univ	MA	29,170	HC
Clarke College	IA	20,625	C+
Clayton College and State Univ	GA	2,322	C+
Clearwater Christian College	FL	13,160	LC
Cleveland Inst of Music	OH	25,880	SP
Cleveland State Univ	OH	10,146	NC
Coastal Carolina Univ	SC	9,220	C
Coe College	IA	24,750	VC
Coker College	SC	20,120	C
Colby College	ME	34,290	MC
Colgate Univ	NY	33,480	MC
College of Charleston	SC	8,350	HC
College of Mount St. Joseph	OH	20,290	C
College of New Jersey	NJ	13,425	HC
College of Notre Dame of Maryland	MD	23,100	LC
College of St. Benedict	MN	23,921	VC
College of St. Catherine	MN	22,324	VC
College of St. Elizabeth	NJ	22,510	C
College of St. Rose	NY	19,084	C
College of St. Scholastica	MN	22,378	C+
College of Santa Fe	NM	20,250	LC
College of the Holy Cross	MA	32,780	MC
College of the Ozarks	MO	2,650	C+
College of William and Mary	VA	10,002	MC
College of Wooster	OH	28,350	VC
Colo Christian Univ	CO	17,714	C
Colo College	CO	31,525	HC+
Colo State Univ	CO	9,672	C
Columbia College	SC	19,050	LC
Columbia College Chicago	IL	22,063	LC
Columbia Union College	MD	19,027	C+
Columbia Univ/Barnard College	NY	33,694	MC
Columbia Univ/Columbia College	NY	35,190	MC
Columbia Univ/School of General Studies	NY	35,000	C
Columbus State Univ	GA	7,228	LC
Concordia College	NY	19,200	VC
Concordia College/Moorhead	MN	18,835	C
Concordia Univ	CA	22,290	C
Concordia Univ	MI	20,500	C
Concordia Univ	MN	19,912	C
Concordia Univ at Austin	TX	16,740	LC
Concordia Univ Nebr	NE	17,770	C
Concordia Univ Wisc	WI	16,600	LC
Concordia Univ, River Forest	IL	20,000	LC
Conn College	CT	33,585	MC
Converse College	SC	21,990	VC
Cornell College	IA	24,980	VC
Cornell Univ	NY	34,614	MC
Cornerstone Univ and Grand Rapids Baptist Seminary	MI	18,092	C
Cornish College of the Arts	WA	16,200	SP
Covenant College	GA	21,970	C+
Creighton Univ	NE	23,476	VC
Culver-Stockton College	MO	15,400	LC
Cumberland College	KY	14,864	C
Curtis Inst of Music	PA		SP
Dakota State Univ	SD	6,950	C
Dallas Baptist Univ	TX	13,682	LC
Dana College	NE	18,046	C
Dartmouth College	NH	34,458	MC
David Lipscomb Univ	TN	16,158	VC
Davidson College	NC	30,823	MC
Davis and Elkins College	WV	19,270	LC
Delaware State Univ	DE	8,104	LC
Delta State Univ	MS	5,416	C
Denison Univ	OH	29,640	HC
DePaul Univ	IL	23,590	VC
DePauw Univ	IN	28,000	HC
Dickinson College	PA	32,210	VC+
Dickinson State Univ	ND	5,495	NC
Dillard Univ	LA	16,046	VC
Doane College	NE	17,600	LC
Dominican Univ	IL	20,800	C
Dominican Univ of Calif	CA	27,948	C
Dordt College	IA	18,100	C+
Dowling College	NY	20,281	LC
Drake Univ	IA	22,830	VC
Drew Univ/College of Liberal Arts	NJ	32,152	VC
Drexel Univ	PA	27,657	VC
Drury Univ	MO	15,250	VC
Duke Univ	NC	34,396	MC
Duquesne Univ	PA	24,242	C+
Earlham College	IN	27,446	VC+
East Central Univ	OK	4,578	C
East Stroudsburg Univ of Pennsylvania	PA	8,430	LC
East Tenn State Univ	TN	7,127	C
East Texas Baptist Univ	TX	12,349	LC
Eastern College	PA	19,641	LC
Eastern Illinois Univ	IL	10,101	C
Eastern Kentucky Univ	KY	6,552	C
Eastern Mennonite Univ	VA	20,700	VC
Eastern Mich Univ	MI	9,855	C
Eastern Nazarene College	MA	19,433	LC
Eastern New Mexico Univ	NM	4,113	LC
Eastern Oregon Univ	OR	8,772	C
Eastern Washington Univ	WA	7,972	LC
Eastman School of Music	NY	30,684	SP
Eckerd College	FL	25,500	C+
Edgewood College	WI	18,304	C
Edinboro Univ of Pennsylvania	PA	9,328	LC
Elizabeth City State Univ	NC	5,550	LC
Elizabethtown College	PA	26,000	VC
Elmhurst College	IL	21,750	C
Elmira College	NY	31,070	VC+
Elon Univ	NC	19,430	VC
Emory Univ	GA	33,792	MC
Emporia State Univ	KS	6,198	LC
Erskine College	SC	21,399	VC
Eureka College	IL	22,200	C
Evangel Univ	MO	14,050	C
Fisk Univ	TN	13,700	LC
Florida A&M Univ	FL	6,948	C
Florida Atlantic Univ	FL	8,832	C
Florida International Univ	FL	9,486	VC
Florida Memorial College	FL	6,000	LC
Florida Southern College	FL	19,430	C
Florida State Univ	FL	7,835	HC
Fordham Univ	NY	30,710	VC
Fort Hays State Univ	KS	6,294	LC
Fort Lewis College	CO	7,659	LC
Franklin and Marshall College	PA	32,410	HC
Franklin Pierce College	NH	26,125	LC
Fresno Pacific Univ	CA	19,740	C
Friends Univ	KS	15,962	LC
Frostburg State Univ	MD	9,680	C
Furman Univ	SC	25,492	HC
Gardner-Webb Univ	NC	17,400	C
Geneva College	PA	19,990	C+
George Fox Univ	OR	24,095	VC

School	ST	$IS	SR
George Mason Univ	VA	9,192	C
George Washington Univ	DC	32,170	HC
Georgetown College	KY	18,400	VC
Georgia College and State Univ	GA	7,344	C
Georgia Southern Univ	GA	6,958	C
Georgia Southwestern State Univ	GA	6,013	C
Georgia State Univ	GA	7,792	LC
Georgian Court College	NJ	19,040	LC
Gettysburg College	PA	32,070	HC
Gonzaga Univ	WA	24,276	HC+
Gordon College	MA	23,594	VC+
Goshen College	IN	18,950	VC+
Goucher College	MD	30,650	VC+
Grace College	IN	16,768	C
Graceland Univ	IA	15,845	C
Grambling State Univ	LA	5,325	NC
Grand Canyon Univ	AZ	30,000	LC
Grand Valley State Univ	MI	10,040	C
Greensboro College	NC	19,080	LC
Greenville College	IL	19,226	LC
Grinnell College	IA	28,300	HC+
Grove City College	PA	12,280	MC
Guilford College	NC	23,255	C
Gustavus Adolphus College	MN	24,190	VC+
Hamilton College	NY	34,150	HC
Hamline Univ	MN	23,339	C+
Hampshire College	MA	33,881	HC+
Hampton Univ	VA	17,112	C+
Hannibal-LaGrange College	MO	12,530	C
Hanover College	IN	17,560	VC
Harding Univ	AR	13,528	VC
Hardin-Simmons Univ	TX	14,165	C
Hartwick College	NY	33,090	C+
Harvard Univ/Harvard College	MA	34,269	MC
Hastings College	NE	17,854	C+
Haverford College	PA	34,300	MC
Heidelberg College	OH	23,879	C
Henderson State Univ	AR	6,269	C
Hendrix College	AR	18,463	HC
Hillsdale College	MI	20,586	VC+
Hiram College	OH	27,034	VC
Hobart and William Smith Colleges	NY	33,195	VC
Hofstra Univ	NY	23,252	C
Hollins Univ	VA	24,328	VC
Holy Names College	CA	23,220	C
Hood College	MD	26,020	VC
Hope College	MI	22,922	C+
Hope International Univ	CA	16,940	NC
Houston Baptist Univ	TX	15,300	LC
Howard Payne Univ	TX	13,834	C+
Howard Univ	DC	15,522	LC
Humboldt State Univ	CA	8,582	C
Huntingdon College	AL	18,400	VC
Huston-Tillotson College	TX	12,977	LC
Idaho State Univ	ID	7,030	C+
Illinois College	IL	16,234	C
Illinois State Univ	IL	9,235	C
Illinois Wesleyan Univ	IL	26,970	HC
Immaculata College	PA	22,400	LC
Indiana State Univ	IN	8,461	LC
Indiana Univ Bloomington	IN	10,712	C+
Indiana Univ of Pennsylvania	PA	9,133	C
Indiana Univ South Bend	IN	3,515	C
Indiana Univ Southeast	IN	3,459	C
Indiana Wesleyan Univ	IN	17,680	C
Inter-American Univ of PR/San GermÈn	PR	6,390	
Iowa State Univ	IA	8,108	VC
Iowa Wesleyan College	IA	18,840	C
Ithaca College	NY	28,719	HC
Jacksonville State Univ	AL	6,568	LC
Jacksonville Univ	FL	21,110	LC
James Madison Univ	VA	9,552	HC
Jamestown College	ND	11,310	NC
John Brown Univ	AR	15,080	VC
Johns Hopkins Univ	MD	35,226	MC
Johnson C. Smith Univ	NC	16,560	C+
Johnson State College	VT	10,776	C
Judson College	AL	13,790	C
Judson College	IL	18,980	LC
Kalamazoo College	MI	26,955	HC+
Kansas State Univ	KS	6,995	C
Kansas Wesleyan Univ	KS	17,400	C+
Kean Univ	NJ	11,159	C
Keene State College	NH	11,280	C
Kennesaw State Univ	GA	2,306	LC
Kent State Univ	OH	11,104	C
Kentucky Christian College	KY	13,472	C
Kentucky Wesleyan College	KY	15,800	C
Kenyon College	OH	32,130	HC+
Knox College	IL	28,230	HC
Knoxville College	TN	6,200	LC
Kutztown Univ of Pennsylvania	PA	8,907	C
La Salle Univ	PA	27,890	C
La Sierra Univ	CA	19,260	LC
Lafayette College	PA	32,655	MC
Lake Erie College	OH	21,350	LC
Lake Forest College	IL	27,460	VC
Lakeland College	WI	17,950	C
Lamar Univ	TX	6,816	LC
Lambuth Univ	TN	14,254	C
Lander Univ	SC	8,618	LC
Lane College	TN	10,400	C+
Langston Univ	OK	2,308	LC
Lebanon Valley College of Pennsylvania	PA	25,700	VC
Lee Univ	TN	10,198	LC
Lehigh Univ	PA	32,290	MC
Lenoir-Rhyne College	NC	19,186	C
Lewis and Clark College	OR	29,010	VC
Lewis Univ	IL	20,960	C
Liberty Univ	VA	14,500	C
Limestone College	SC	16,900	C
Lincoln Univ	PA	11,198	C+
Lindenwood Univ	MO	17,250	C
Linfield College	OR	25,840	VC
Livingstone College	NC	13,360	LC
Lock Haven Univ of Pennsylvania	PA	9,534	C
LIU/Brooklyn Campus	NY	22,290	C
LIU/C.W. Post Campus	NY	25,380	C
Longwood College	VA	8,950	C
Loras College	IA	22,994	C+
Louisiana College	LA	11,516	C
Louisiana State Univ and A&M College	LA	8,014	VC
Louisiana Tech Univ	LA	6,506	C
Loyola Marymount Univ	CA	28,754	HC
Lubbock Christian Univ	TX	14,226	LC
Luther College	IA	23,300	VC+
Lycoming College	PA	24,780	C
Lynchburg College	VA	23,405	C
Lyon College	AR	16,500	VC
Macalester College	MN	28,814	HC+
MacMurray College	IL	17,790	LC
Madonna Univ	MI	11,504	VC
Malone College	OH	19,190	C
Manchester College	IN	22,010	C
Manhattan School of Music	NY	31,500	SP
Manhattanville College	NY	28,730	VC
Mannes College of Music	NY	28,900	SP
Mansfield Univ	PA	9,648	C
Marian College	IN	21,020	C
Marian College of Fond du Lac	WI	17,935	LC
Marietta College	OH	24,580	C
Marlboro College	VT	26,410	VC+
Mars Hill College	NC	18,600	LC
Marshall Univ	WV	7,752	LC
Martin Univ	IN	8,370	SP
Mary Baldwin College	VA	23,440	C
Mary Washington College	VA	9,032	VC+
Marygrove College	MI	16,075	C
Marylhurst Univ	OR	15,343	NC
Maryville College	TN	23,210	VC
Maryville Univ of St. Louis	MO	18,680	C
Marywood Univ	PA	24,639	C
Mass Inst of Technology	MA	35,228	MC
McKendree College	IL	18,300	C+
McMurry Univ	TX	15,287	C
McNeese State Univ	LA	5,259	LC
McPherson College	KS	17,710	C
Mercer Univ	GA	24,130	VC
Mercy College	NY	15,875	LC
Mercyhurst College	PA	20,694	C
Meredith College	NC	17,500	C
Messiah College	PA	23,180	VC
Methodist College	NC	19,526	C
Miami Univ	OH	12,885	VC+
Mich State Univ	MI	10,386	VC
MidAmerica Nazarene Univ	KS	16,960	C
Middle Tenn State Univ	TN	6,994	C
Middlebury College	VT	34,300	MC
Midland Lutheran College	NE	18,600	C
Midwestern State Univ	TX	6,704	NC
Millersville Univ of Pennsylvania	PA	10,153	VC
Milligan College	TN	17,550	C
Millikin Univ	IL	24,415	C+
Mills College	CA	27,950	C
Millsaps College	MS	22,608	VC+
Minn State Univ, Mankato	MN	7,296	LC
Minot State Univ	ND	5,466	LC
Miss College	MS	14,574	C
Miss Univ for Women	MS	5,446	LC
Missouri Southern State College	MO	6,666	C
Missouri Western State College	MO	6,662	NC
Molloy College	NY	13,940	C
Monmouth College	IL	21,550	C
Monmouth Univ	NJ	24,042	C
Montana State Univ-Billings	MT	7,653	NC
Montana State Univ-Bozeman	MT	8,431	C
Montana State Univ-Northern	MT	8,600	NC
Montclair State Univ	NJ	10,287	LC
Moorhead State Univ	MN	7,000	LC
Moravian College	PA	27,065	VC
Morehead State Univ	KY	6,510	C
Morehouse College	GA	19,814	C
Morgan State Univ	MD	10,078	LC
Morningside College	IA	19,124	C
Morris Brown College	GA	15,993	LC
Mount Holyoke College	MA	34,128	HC
Mount Marty College	SD	15,656	LC
Mount Mary College	WI	18,024	C
Mount Mercy College	IA	19,390	VC
Mount Olive College	NC	14,410	LC
Mount St. Mary's College	CA	24,430	C
Mount Union College	OH	21,120	C
Mount Vernon Nazarene College	OH	17,027	C
Muhlenberg College	PA	28,170	HC
Murray State Univ	KY	6,672	C
Muskingum College	OH	18,760	C
Nazareth College of Rochester	NY	22,036	VC
Nebr Wesleyan Univ	NE	18,767	VC
New College of Calif	CA	8,900	NC
New College of Florida	FL	8,130	HC+
New England Conservatory of Music	MA	31,200	SP
New Jersey City Univ	NJ	9,100	LC
New Mexico Highlands Univ	NM	6,256	NC
New Mexico State Univ	NM	7,302	C
New York Univ	NY	35,200	MC
Newberry College	SC	19,670	LC
Nicholls State Univ	LA	5,290	NC
Norfolk State Univ	VA	8,382	LC
N Car Agricultural and Technical State Univ	NC	6,659	LC
N Car Central Univ	NC	6,418	LC
N Car School of the Arts	NC	7,797	SP
N Car Wesleyan College	NC	15,650	LC
North Central College	IL	22,944	C+
N Dak State Univ	ND	7,004	VC
North Georgia College and State Univ	GA	6,322	C+
North Park Univ	IL	24,030	C
Northeastern Illinois Univ	IL	2,898	NC
Northeastern State Univ	OK	4,704	LC
Northeastern Univ	MA	30,078	VC
Northern Arizona Univ	AZ	7,398	C
Northern Illinois Univ	IL	9,545	C
Northern Kentucky Univ	KY	6,352	NC
Northern Mich Univ	MI	9,693	C
Northern State Univ	SD	6,279	LC
Northwest Christian College	OR	19,680	LC
Northwest Missouri State Univ	MO	7,922	LC
Northwest Nazarene Univ	ID	18,380	C
Northwestern College	MN	19,816	C+
Northwestern College of Iowa	IA	17,630	C+
Northwestern Okla State Univ	OK	4,542	NC
Northwestern State Univ of Louisiana	LA	5,745	NC
Northwestern Univ	IL	33,615	MC
Notre Dame de Namur Univ	CA	26,932	LC
Nyack College	NY	18,540	C
Oakland City Univ	IN	11,286	LC
Oakland Univ	MI	9,418	C
Oakwood College	AL	14,904	C
Oberlin College	OH	33,140	HC+
Occidental College	CA	32,288	HC
Ohio Northern Univ	OH	27,765	VC
Ohio Univ	OH	11,769	C
Ohio Wesleyan Univ	OH	29,670	VC+
Okla Baptist Univ	OK	13,878	VC
Okla Christian Univ	OK	16,500	VC
Okla City Univ	OK	15,810	C
Okla Panhandle State Univ	OK	3,812	NC
Okla State Univ	OK	7,650	VC
Old Dominion Univ	VA	9,386	C
Olivet Nazarene Univ	IL	18,444	C
Oral Roberts Univ	OK	18,490	C
Oregon State Univ	OR	9,612	VC
Ottawa Univ	KS	11,800	LC
Otterbein College	OH	23,439	C
Ouachita Baptist Univ	AR	16,460	VC
Our Lady of the Lake Univ of San Antonio	TX	17,336	C
Pacific Lutheran Univ	WA	23,318	VC
Pacific Union College	CA	20,250	VC
Pacific Univ	OR	24,250	C
Palm Beach Atlantic College	FL	23,310	C
Paul Quinn College	TX	8,150	LC
Penn State Univ/Univ Park Campus	PA	11,126	VC
Pepperdine Univ	CA	32,830	VC
Peru State College	NE	6,342	NC
Pfeiffer Univ	NC	18,580	C
Philadelphia Biblical Univ	PA	16,295	C+
Philander Smith College	AR	7,380	NC
Piedmont College	GA	16,900	C
Pittsburg State Univ	KS	6,228	NC
Pitzer College	CA	33,930	HC
Plymouth State College	NH	11,024	LC
Point Loma Nazarene Univ	CA	21,380	VC
Pomona College	CA	33,960	MC
Portland State Univ	OR	11,220	C
Prairie View A&M Univ	TX	3,172	LC
Presbyterian College	SC	23,356	VC
Princeton Univ	NJ	35,072	MC
Principia College	IL	23,865	C+
Providence College	RI	27,620	HC
Queens College	NC	17,250	C
Quincy Univ	IL	20,450	C
Radford Univ	VA	8,302	C
Randolph-Macon Woman's College	VA	25,820	VC+
Reed College	OR	33,350	HC+
Rhode Island College	RI	8,700	LC
Rhodes College	TN	26,466	HC+
Richard Stockton College of New Jersey	NJ	12,165	VC
Ripon College	WI	24,180	VC+
Roanoke College	VA	24,689	VC
Roberts Wesleyan College	NY	20,160	C+
Rochester College	MI	15,404	C+
Rockford College	IL	23,930	C
Roosevelt Univ	IL	20,240	LC
Rowan Univ	NJ	12,365	VC
Rust College	MS	7,800	C+
Rutgers, The State Univ of New Jersey New Brunswick Campus	NJ	12,709	C
Rutgers, The State Univ of New Jersey/ CamdenCampus	NJ	6,484	C
Saginaw Valley State Univ	MI	9,465	C
St. Ambrose Univ	IA	19,994	C
St. Augustine's College	NC	12,990	C+
St. Cloud State Univ	MN	7,180	C
St. John's Univ	MN	23,640	VC
St. Joseph's College	IN	21,640	C
St. Lawrence Univ	NY	32,605	VC
St. Louis Univ	MO	26,590	VC+
St. Martin's College	WA	20,566	C
St. Mary-of-the-Woods College	IN	21,320	LC
St. Mary's College	IN	24,474	VC
St. Mary's College of Maryland	MD	14,104	HC
St. Mary's Univ of San Antonio	TX	19,735	C
St. Michael's College	VT	26,935	VC
St. Norbert College	WI	23,169	VC
St. Olaf College	MN	25,880	HC
St. Vincent College	PA	22,942	VC
St. Xavier Univ	IL	21,104	C
Salem College	NC	23,065	VC
Salisbury Univ	MD	10,576	VC
Salve Regina Univ	RI	26,460	C
Sam Houston State Univ	TX	6,076	LC
Samford Univ	AL	16,340	VC
San Diego State Univ	CA	9,716	C+
San Francisco Conservatory of Music	CA	20,780	SP
San Francisco State Univ	CA	7,139	LC
San Jose State Univ	CA	8,187	C
Santa Clara Univ	CA	28,371	VC+
Sarah Lawrence College	NY	37,516	HC
Savannah State Univ	GA	2,550	LC
Scripps College	CA	30,400	HC+
Seattle Pacific Univ	WA	22,674	C+
Seton Hall Univ	NJ	26,910	LC
Seton Hill College	PA	21,875	C
Shenandoah Univ	VA	22,550	NC
Shepherd College	WV	7,062	LC
Shorter College	GA	15,185	C
Siena Heights Univ	MI	16,140	LC
Sierra Nevada College-Lake Tahoe	NV	21,060	LC
Silver Lake College of the Holy Family	WI	15,516	LC
Simmons College	MA	30,418	VC
Simpson College	CA	19,200	C
Simpson College	IA	21,200	C+
Skidmore College	NY	34,201	VC+
Slippery Rock Univ	PA	9,152	LC
Smith College	MA	33,302	HC+
Sonoma State Univ	CA	8,953	C
S Dak State Univ	SD	6,848	C
Southeast Missouri State Univ	MO	8,367	C+
Southeastern College	FL	11,648	LC
Southeastern Louisiana Univ	LA	6,047	LC
Southeastern Okla State Univ	OK	4,917	C
Southern Adventist Univ	TN	15,600	C
Southern Illinois Univ at Carbondale	IL	8,621	C
Southern Illinois Univ Edwardsville	IL	7,869	LC
Southern Nazarene Univ	OK	14,634	NC
Southern Oregon Univ	OR	9,429	C
Southern Univ and A&M College	LA	6,365	C+
Southern Utah Univ	UT	7,254	C
Southern Wesleyan Univ	SC	17,280	C
Southwest Baptist Univ	MO	13,426	LC
Southwest Missouri State Univ	MO	7,600	LC
Southwest State Univ	MN	7,117	LC
Southwest Texas State Univ	TX	8,730	VC
Southwestern Adventist Univ	TX	14,798	C
Southwestern College	KS	17,656	C
Southwestern Univ	TX	22,550	HC
Spelman College	GA	19,215	C+
Spring Arbor Univ	MI	17,976	C

School	ST	$IS	SR
Stanford Univ	CA	34,222	MC
SUNY/College at Buffalo	NY	8,025	C
SUNY/College at Fredonia	NY	10,125	C
SUNY/College at Geneseo	NY	9,970	HC
SUNY/College at Oneonta	NY	9,981	C
SUNY/College at Oswego	NY	10,856	C
SUNY/College at Potsdam	NY	10,519	C
SUNY/College at Purchase	NY	10,587	VC
SUNY/Univ at Albany	NY	10,997	VC
SUNY/Univ at Binghamton	NY	10,653	HC
SUNY/Univ at Buffalo	NY	11,033	VC
SUNY/Univ at New Paltz	NY	9,685	VC
SUNY/Univ at Stony Brook	NY	10,998	VC
State Univ of West Georgia	GA	7,101	C
Stephen F. Austin State Univ	TX	6,905	C
Sterling College	KS	16,370	VC
Stetson Univ	FL	25,640	VC
Stillman College	AL	11,370	LC
Susquehanna Univ	PA	27,270	VC
Swarthmore College	PA	34,538	MC
Sweet Briar College	VA	25,310	VC
Syracuse Univ	NY	30,710	HC
Tabor College	KS	17,600	LC
Tarleton State Univ	TX	7,160	C
Taylor Univ	IN	21,562	VC+
Temple Univ	PA	14,124	C
Tenn State Univ	TN	7,058	VC
Tenn Wesleyan College	TN	13,030	C
Texas A&M Univ at Commerce	TX	7,326	C
Texas A&M Univ at Kingsville	TX	6,446	LC
Texas Christian Univ	TX	19,910	C
Texas Lutheran Univ	TX	17,660	C
Texas Southern Univ	TX	6,576	NC
Texas Tech Univ	TX	8,825	C
Texas Wesleyan Univ	TX	14,710	C
Texas Woman's Univ	TX	5,855	LC
Ohio State Univ	OH	10,819	VC
Thomas Edison State College	NJ	2,750	SP
Toccoa Falls College	GA	14,220	C
Tougaloo College	MS	9,200	NC
Towson Univ	MD	11,088	VC
Transylvania Univ	KY	21,780	VC+
Trevecca Nazarene Univ	TN	15,752	C
Trinity Christian College	IL	19,415	C
Trinity College	CT	34,300	HC
Trinity International Univ	IL	20,640	C+
Trinity Univ	TX	21,444	HC
Truman State Univ	MO	8,568	VC+
Tufts Univ	MA	34,874	MC
Tulane Univ	LA	34,013	HC+
Union College	KY	15,920	C
Union College	NE	14,650	C
Union College	NY	32,646	HC
Union Univ	TN	18,930	C+
Universidad Adventista de las Antillas	PR	6,675	
Univ of Akron	OH	10,530	NC
Univ of Alabama	AL	7,402	C
Univ of Alabama at Birmingham	AL	10,110	C
Univ of Alabama at Huntsville	AL	7,916	VC
Univ of Alaska Anchorage	AK	9,100	NC
Univ of Alaska Fairbanks	AK	8,265	NC
Univ of Arizona	AZ	8,614	C
Univ of Arkansas	AR	8,334	VC
Univ of Arkansas at Little Rock	AR	5,637	NC
Univ of Arkansas at Monticello	AR	5,940	NC
Univ of Arkansas at Pine Bluff	AR	7,925	C
Univ of Bridgeport	CT	23,020	C
Univ of Calif at Berkeley	CA	14,134	MC
Univ of Calif at Davis	CA	12,796	VC
Univ of Calif at Irvine	CA	11,756	C
Univ of Calif at Los Angeles	CA	13,227	MC
Univ of Calif at Riverside	CA	12,479	C
Univ of Calif at San Diego	CA	11,372	HC
Univ of Calif at Santa Barbara	CA	11,732	VC
Univ of Calif at Santa Cruz	CA	13,655	VC
Univ of Central Arkansas	AR	6,388	C
Univ of Central Florida	FL	8,251	VC
Univ of Central Okla	OK	5,205	C
Univ of Charleston	WV	20,640	C
Univ of Chicago	IL	35,087	MC
Univ of Cincinnati	OH	12,491	LC
Univ of Colo at Boulder	CO	9,255	VC
Univ of Colo at Denver	CO	3,673	C
Univ of Conn	CT	12,122	VC
Univ of Dayton	OH	20,400	VC
Univ of Delaware	DE	10,824	VC
Univ of Denver	CO	28,783	VC
Univ of Evansville	IN	22,865	VC+
Univ of Florida	FL	7,874	HC
Univ of Georgia	GA	8,656	VC
Univ of Hartford	CT	28,884	C
Univ of Hawaii at Hilo	HI	6,497	C
Univ of Hawaii at Manoa	HI	7,862	VC
Univ of Houston	TX	8,410	C
Univ of Idaho	ID	7,026	C
Univ of Illinois at Chicago	IL	10,702	VC
Univ of Illinois at Urbana-Champaign	IL	11,316	HC+
Univ of Indianapolis	IN	20,840	C
Univ of Iowa	IA	8,607	C+
Univ of Kentucky	KY	7,765	C
Univ of La Verne	CA	24,280	C
Univ of Louisiana at Lafayette	LA	5,200	C
Univ of Louisiana at Monroe	LA	5,207	NC
Univ of Louisville	KY	7,402	LC
Univ of Maine	ME	10,798	C
Univ of Maine at Farmington	ME	9,163	C
Univ of Mary	ND	12,900	LC
Univ of Mary Hardin-Baylor	TX	13,929	C
Univ of Maryland/Baltimore County	MD	12,190	VC
Univ of Maryland/College Park	MD	11,959	C
Univ of Mass Amherst	MA	10,995	VC
Univ of Mass Boston	MA	4,227	C
Univ of Mass Dartmouth	MA	9,852	C
Univ of Memphis	TN	7,271	C
Univ of Miami	FL	31,130	HC
Univ of Mich/Ann Arbor	MI	13,003	HC+
Univ of Mich/Flint	MI	4,323	C
Univ of Minn/Duluth	MN	10,436	C
Univ of Minn/Morris	MN	10,716	VC
Univ of Minn/Twin Cities	MN	11,123	VC
Univ of Miss	MS	7,666	C
Univ of Missouri/Columbia	MO	9,803	HC
Univ of Missouri/Kansas City	MO	9,685	VC
Univ of Missouri/St. Louis	MO	9,966	C
Univ of Mobile	AL	13,620	LC
Univ of Montana	MT	8,038	C
Univ of Montevallo	AL	7,266	C
Univ of Nebr at Kearney	NE	7,048	NC
Univ of Nebr at Lincoln	NE	8,325	C+
Univ of Nebr at Omaha	NE	6,867	C
Univ of Nevada/Las Vegas	NV	8,281	VC
Univ of Nevada/Reno	NV	8,737	C
Univ of New Hampshire	NH	13,207	C
Univ of New Haven	CT	23,860	LC
Univ of New Mexico	NM	8,026	C
Univ of New Orleans	LA	10,160	C
Univ of North Alabama	AL	7,016	NC
Univ of N Car at Asheville	NC	6,896	VC
Univ of N Car at Chapel Hill	NC	8,789	HC
Univ of N Car at Charlotte	NC	7,254	C
Univ of N Car at Greensboro	NC	6,858	C
Univ of N Car at Pembroke	NC	5,914	LC
Univ of N Car at Wilmington	NC	7,769	C
Univ of N Dak	ND	7,067	VC
Univ of North Florida	FL	8,089	VC
Univ of North Texas	TX	7,629	C
Univ of Northern Colo	CO	8,082	C+
Univ of Northern Iowa	IA	7,850	C
Univ of Notre Dame	IN	30,707	MC
Univ of Okla	OK	7,616	VC
Univ of Oregon	OR	9,969	C
Univ of Pennsylvania	PA	34,614	MC
Univ of Pittsburgh at Pittsburgh	PA	13,592	HC
Univ of Portland	OR	24,950	VC
Univ of PR/Rio Piedras	PR	5,510	
Univ of Puget Sound	WA	28,285	HC
Univ of Redlands	CA	29,246	VC
Univ of Rhode Island	RI	12,414	C
Univ of Richmond	VA	27,300	HC
Univ of Rio Grande	OH	8,728	NC
Univ of Rochester	NY	32,979	HC
Univ of St. Thomas	MN	24,044	VC
Univ of St. Thomas	TX	18,752	VC
Univ of San Diego	CA	29,198	HC
Univ of Science and Arts of Okla	OK	5,245	C
Univ of Sioux Falls	SD	16,390	C
Univ of South Alabama	AL	6,976	LC
Univ of S Car at Columbia	SC	8,748	VC
Univ of S Dak	SD	7,036	C
Univ of South Florida	FL	8,154	C
Univ of Southern Calif	CA	33,647	MC
Univ of Southern Maine	ME	10,569	C
Univ of Southern Miss	MS	6,155	LC
Univ of Tampa	FL	22,612	C
Univ of Tenn at Chattanooga	TN	7,783	C
Univ of Tenn at Knoxville	TN	8,214	C
Univ of Tenn at Martin	TN	8,268	C
Univ of Texas at Arlington	TX	7,192	LC
Univ of Texas at Austin	TX	9,437	HC
Univ of Texas at El Paso	TX	5,076	LC
Univ of Texas at San Antonio	TX	9,088	NC
Univ of Texas-Pan American	TX	4,823	C
Univ of the District of Columbia	DC	2,844	NC
Univ of the Incarnate Word	TX	18,478	C
Univ of the Ozarks	AR	13,904	C
Univ of the Pacific	CA	28,255	VC
Univ of the South	TN	27,290	HC
Univ of Toledo	OH	11,206	NC
Univ of Tulsa	OK	19,090	HC
Univ of Utah	UT	7,703	C
Univ of Vermont	VT	14,761	C+
Univ of Virginia	VA	9,391	HC+
Univ of West Florida	FL	7,518	C
Univ of Wisc/Eau Claire	WI	7,032	VC
Univ of Wisc/Green Bay	WI	7,148	C
Univ of Wisc/La Crosse	WI	7,250	VC
Univ of Wisc/Madison	WI	8,262	VC
Univ of Wisc/Milwaukee	WI	8,907	LC
Univ of Wisc/Oshkosh	WI	6,130	LC
Univ of Wisc/Parkside	WI	6,160	LC
Univ of Wisc/Platteville	WI	7,282	C
Univ of Wisc/River Falls	WI	6,356	LC
Univ of Wisc/Stevens Point	WI	7,116	C
Univ of Wisc/Superior	WI	7,051	C+
Univ of Wisc/Whitewater	WI	6,937	C
Univ of Wyoming	WY	7,143	LC
Upper Iowa Univ	IA	17,438	C
Ursinus College	PA	31,350	VC
Utah State Univ	UT	6,771	C
Valdosta State Univ	GA	6,988	C
Valley City State Univ	ND		LC
Valparaiso Univ	IN	23,570	VC+
Vanguard Univ of Southern Calif	CA	20,212	C
Vassar College	NY	33,450	MC
Virginia Commonwealth Univ	VA	9,030	C
Virginia Polytechnic Inst and State Univ	VA	7,652	C
Virginia Union Univ	VA	15,358	LC
Virginia Wesleyan College	VA	22,350	LC
Viterbo Univ	WI	18,043	C
Wabash College	IN	25,335	HC
Wagner College	NY	27,000	C
Wake Forest Univ	NC	30,290	MC
Walla Walla College	WA	20,925	C
Warner Pacific College	OR	20,370	LC
Wartburg College	IA	21,165	VC
Washburn Univ of Topeka	KS	6,766	NC
Washington and Jefferson College	PA	26,255	VC
Washington and Lee Univ	VA	25,095	MC
Washington College	MD	28,040	VC
Washington State Univ	WA	9,388	C
Washington Univ in St. Louis	MO	34,593	MC
Wayland Baptist Univ	TX	11,271	NC
Wayne State College	NE	6,255	NC
Wayne State Univ	MI	6,720	C
Weber State Univ	UT	6,897	NC
Webster Univ	MO	19,804	VC
Wellesley College	MA	33,394	MC
Wells College	NY	19,350	VC
Wesleyan College	GA	17,050	VC
Wesleyan Univ	CT	3,405	MC
West Chester Univ of Pennsylvania	PA	9,792	VC
West Liberty State College	WV	6,056	LC
West Texas A&M Univ	TX	6,538	C
West Virginia Univ	WV	8,304	C
West Virginia Wesleyan College	WV	22,920	C
Western Baptist College	OR	19,700	C+
Western Carolina Univ	NC	5,667	C
Western Conn State Univ	CT	10,074	C
Western Illinois Univ	IL	9,571	C
Western Kentucky Univ	KY	6,834	C
Western Maryland College	MD	26,000	VC
Western Mich Univ	MI	10,016	C
Western New Mexico Univ	NM	5,950	LC
Western Oregon Univ	OR	8,829	C
Western State College of Colo	CO	7,585	LC
Western Washington Univ	WA	8,624	VC
Westfield State College	MA	8,394	C
Westminster Choir College of Rider Univ	NJ	25,400	SP
Westminster College	PA	22,960	C
Westmont College	CA	29,748	VC
Wheaton College	IL	21,934	HC
Wheaton College	MA	32,940	VC
Whitman College	WA	29,086	HC
Whittier College	CA	29,108	C
Whitworth College	WA	23,938	VC
Wichita State Univ	KS	6,879	C
Wilberforce Univ	OH	14,937	LC
Wiley College	TX	8,100	LC
Wilkes Univ	PA	25,800	C
Willamette Univ	OR	29,422	VC+
William Carey College	MS	10,150	LC
William Jewell College	MO	17,150	VC
William Paterson Univ of New Jersey	NJ	11,000	LC
William Tyndale College	MI	11,150	C
Williams Baptist College	AR	10,750	C
Williams College	MA	32,270	MC
Wingate Univ	NC	19,140	C
Winona State Univ	MN	8,570	C
Winthrop Univ	SC	9,106	C
Wisc Lutheran College	WI	19,216	VC
Wittenberg Univ	OH	28,766	VC
Wright State Univ	OH	9,141	LC
Xavier Univ	OH	23,880	C
Xavier Univ of Louisiana	LA	17,000	LC
Yale Univ	CT	34,030	MC
Yeshiva Univ	NY	21,400	C
York College	NE	13,500	C
York College of Pennsylvania	PA	12,550	VC
Youngstown State Univ	OH	9,318	NC

MUSIC BUSINESS MANAGEMENT

School	ST	$IS	SR
Anderson Univ	IN	19,430	LC
Appalachian State Univ	NC	6,353	C
Baldwin-Wallace College	OH	22,010	VC+
Berklee College of Music	MA	27,005	SP
Blackburn College	IL	13,690	C
Butler Univ	IN	25,580	VC+
Columbia College Chicago	IL	22,063	LC
DePaul Univ	IL	23,590	VC
DePauw Univ	IN	28,000	HC
Dillard Univ	LA	16,046	VC
Drake Univ	IA	22,830	VC
Elmhurst College	IL	21,750	C
Five Towns College	NY	18,850	SP
Geneva College	PA	19,990	C+
Grove City College	PA	12,280	MC
Howard Univ	DC	15,522	LC
Jacksonville Univ	FL	21,110	LC
Johnson C. Smith Univ	NC	16,560	C+
Johnson State College	VT	10,776	C
Lewis Univ	IL	20,960	C
Loyola Univ New Orleans	LA	23,506	VC+
Mansfield Univ	PA	9,648	C
Marian College of Fond du Lac	WI	17,935	LC
Middle Tenn State Univ	TN	6,994	C
Minn State Univ, Mankato	MN	7,296	LC
Monmouth Univ	NJ	24,042	C
Montreat College	NC	17,164	C
New York Univ	NY	35,200	MC
Oakwood College	AL	14,904	C
Ohio Northern Univ	OH	27,765	VC
Peru State College	NE	6,342	NC
Point Loma Nazarene Univ	CA	21,380	VC
Quincy Univ	IL	20,450	C
St. Augustine's College	NC	12,990	C+
St. Mary's Univ of Minn	MN	19,975	C
S Car State Univ	SC	6,586	LC
S Dak State Univ	SD	6,848	C
Southern Nazarene Univ	OK	14,634	NC
Southern Oregon Univ	OR	9,429	C
SUNY/College at Oneonta	NY	9,981	C
SUNY/College at Potsdam	NY	10,519	C
Syracuse Univ	NY	30,710	HC
Trevecca Nazarene Univ	TN	15,752	C
Univ of Charleston	WV	20,640	C
Univ of Evansville	IN	22,865	VC+
Univ of Hartford	CT	28,884	C
Univ of Memphis	TN	7,271	C
Univ of Miami	FL	31,130	HC
Univ of New Haven	CT	23,860	LC
Univ of St. Thomas	MN	24,044	VC
Univ of Southern Calif	CA	33,647	MC
Univ of the Incarnate Word	TX	18,478	C
Univ of the Pacific	CA	28,255	VC
Wingate Univ	NC	19,140	C
Winston-Salem State Univ	NC	5,927	LC

MUSIC EDUCATION

School	ST	$IS	SR
Abilene Christian Univ	TX	16,300	VC
Adams State College	CO	7,468	C
Adelphi Univ	NY	23,320	VC
Adrian College	MI	19,670	C
Alabama A&M Univ	AL	5,100	LC
Alabama State Univ	AL	6,404	C
Albany State Univ	GA	5,764	C+
Alcorn State Univ	MS	5,594	LC
Alderson-Broaddus College	WV	19,640	C
Alverno College	WI	16,930	LC
Anderson Univ	IN	19,430	LC
Andrews Univ	MI	17,696	LC
Anna Maria College	MA	22,800	LC
Appalachian State Univ	NC	6,353	C
Arizona State Univ-Main	AZ	7,726	C
Arkansas State Univ	AR	7,480	C
Arkansas Tech Univ	AR	6,256	C
Armstrong Atlantic State Univ	GA	7,084	C
Asbury College	KY	18,540	VC
Ashland Univ	OH	22,182	LC
Atlantic Union College	MA	34,034	LC
Augsburg College	MN	22,978	C
Augusta State Univ	GA	2,282	C
Augustana College	IL	24,117	VC+
Augustana College	SD	20,760	VC
Azusa Pacific Univ	CA	22,422	VC
Baker Univ	KS	14,780	C+
Baldwin-Wallace College	OH	22,010	VC+
Ball State Univ	IN	8,660	C
Bartlesville Wesleyan College	OK	14,100	LC
Barton College	NC	16,834	LC
Baylor Univ	TX	18,298	VC+
Benedictine College	KS	18,485	LC
Bennett College	NC	11,200	C

School	ST	$IS	SR
Berea College	KY	4,070	VC
Berklee College of Music	MA	27,005	SP
Berry College	GA	18,850	C
Bethany College	KS	16,602	C+
Bethel College	IN	17,650	LC
Bethel College	MN	22,740	VC
Bethune-Cookman College	FL	15,746	C
Biola Univ	CA	21,902	VC
Birmingham-Southern College	AL	22,960	C
Black Hills State Univ	SD	6,652	LC
Blackburn College	IL	13,690	C
Blue Mountain College	MS	9,100	LC
Bluffton College	OH	20,644	C
Boise State Univ	ID	6,531	LC
Boston Conservatory	MA	26,900	SP
Boston Univ	MA	34,358	MC
Bowling Green State Univ	OH	10,794	C
Bradley Univ	IL	20,970	VC
Brenau Univ Women's College	GA	20,100	C
Bucknell Univ	PA	31,096	HC
Buena Vista Univ	IA	22,828	C
Butler Univ	IN	25,580	VC+
Cal State, Fullerton	CA	5,440	LC
Cal State, Los Angeles	CA	5,050	C
Cal State, San Bernardino	CA	6,516	C
Cameron Univ	OK	5,560	NC
Carnegie Mellon Univ	PA	32,682	MC
Carroll College	WI	21,170	C
Carson-Newman College	TN	16,490	C
Carthage College	WI	23,670	C
Case Western Reserve Univ	OH	27,418	C
Catawba College	NC	19,620	C
Catholic Univ of America	DC	29,332	VC
Cedarville Univ	OH	17,553	VC
Centenary College of Louisiana	LA	21,600	C+
Central College	IA	21,206	C
Central Conn State Univ	CT	10,404	C
Central Methodist College	MO	16,460	C
Central Mich Univ	MI	8,355	C
Central Missouri State Univ	MO	7,920	C
Central State Univ	OH	8,922	C+
Central Washington Univ	WA	8,985	LC
Charleston Southern Univ	SC	17,122	C
Chestnut Hill College	PA	24,790	LC
Chicago State Univ	IL	8,851	C+
Christopher Newport Univ	VA	8,862	VC
CUNY/Brooklyn College	NY	3,403	LC
CUNY/Hunter College	NY	5,147	C+
CUNY/Queens College	NY	3,403	VC
Claflin Univ	SC	12,735	C+
Clarion Univ of Pennsylvania	PA	11,272	LC
Clarke College	IA	20,625	C+
Clearwater Christian College	FL	13,160	LC
Cleveland Inst of Music	OH	25,880	SP
Coastal Carolina Univ	SC	9,220	C
Coe College	IA	24,750	VC
Coker College	SC	20,120	C
College of Mount St. Joseph	OH	20,290	C
College of New Jersey	NJ	13,425	HC
College of Notre Dame of Maryland	MD	23,100	LC
College of St. Catherine	MN	22,324	VC
College of St. Rose	NY	19,084	C
Colo Christian Univ	CO	17,714	C
Columbia College	SC	19,050	LC
Columbus State Univ	GA	7,228	LC
Concord College	WV	7,122	C+
Concordia College	NY	19,200	VC
Concordia College/ Moorhead	MN	18,835	C
Concordia Univ	MN	19,912	C
Concordia Univ Nebr	NE	17,770	C
Concordia Univ, River Forest	IL	20,000	LC
Conn College	CT	33,585	MC
Converse College	SC	21,990	VC
Cornell College	IA	24,980	VC
Cornerstone Univ and Grand Rapids Baptist Seminary	MI	18,092	C
Culver-Stockton College	MO	15,400	LC
Cumberland College	KY	14,864	C
Dakota State Univ	SD	6,950	C
Dana College	NE	18,046	C
David Lipscomb Univ	TN	16,158	VC
Delaware State Univ	DE	8,104	LC
Delta State Univ	MS	5,416	C
DePaul Univ	IL	23,590	VC
DePauw Univ	IN	28,000	HC
Dickinson State Univ	ND	5,495	NC
Dordt College	IA	18,100	C+
Dowling College	NY	20,281	LC
Drake Univ	IA	22,830	VC
Drury Univ	MO	15,250	VC
Duquesne Univ	PA	24,242	C+
East Carolina Univ	NC	7,766	C
East Central Univ	OK	4,578	C
East Texas Baptist Univ	TX	12,349	LC
Eastern Kentucky Univ	KY	6,552	C
Eastern Mich Univ	MI	9,855	C
Eastern Nazarene College	MA	19,433	LC
Eastern New Mexico Univ	NM	4,113	LC
Eastern Washington Univ	WA	7,972	LC
Eastman School of Music	NY	30,684	SP
Edinboro Univ of Pennsylvania	PA	9,328	LC
Elizabethtown College	PA	26,000	VC
Elmhurst College	IL	21,750	C
Elon Univ	NC	19,430	VC
Emporia State Univ	KS	6,198	LC
Erskine College	SC	21,399	VC
Eureka College	IL	22,200	C
Evangel Univ	MO	14,050	C
Fairmont State College	WV	7,010	NC
Fayetteville State Univ	NC	5,590	LC
Five Towns College	NY	18,850	SP
Florida A&M Univ	FL	6,948	C
Florida International Univ	FL	9,486	VC
Florida Southern College	FL	19,430	C
Florida State Univ	FL	7,835	HC
Fort Hays State Univ	KS	6,294	LC
Freed-Hardeman Univ	TN	14,290	VC
Fresno Pacific Univ	CA	19,740	C
Friends Univ	KS	15,962	LC
Furman Univ	SC	25,492	HC
Gardner-Webb Univ	NC	17,400	C
Geneva College	PA	19,990	C+
George Fox Univ	OR	24,095	VC
Georgetown College	KY	18,400	VC
Georgia College and State Univ	GA	7,344	C
Georgia Southern Univ	GA	6,958	C
Georgia Southwestern State Univ	GA	6,013	C
Gettysburg College	PA	32,070	HC
Glenville State College	WV	6,588	NC
Gonzaga Univ	WA	24,276	HC+
Gordon College	MA	23,594	VC+
Goshen College	IN	18,950	VC+
Grace College	IN	16,768	C
Graceland Univ	IA	15,845	C
Grambling State Univ	LA	5,325	NC
Grand Canyon Univ	AZ	30,000	LC
Grand Valley State Univ	MI	10,040	C
Greensboro College	NC	19,080	LC
Greenville College	IL	19,226	LC
Grove City College	PA	12,280	MC
Gustavus Adolphus College	MN	24,190	VC+
Hannibal-LaGrange College	MO	12,530	C
Harding Univ	AR	13,528	VC
Hardin-Simmons Univ	TX	14,165	C
Hartwick College	NY	33,090	C+
Hastings College	NE	17,854	C+
Heidelberg College	OH	23,879	C
Henderson State Univ	AR	6,269	C
Hillsdale College	MI	20,586	VC+
Hofstra Univ	NY	23,252	C
Hope College	MI	22,922	C+
Hope International Univ	CA	16,940	NC
Houghton College	NY	21,810	VC+
Houston Baptist Univ	TX	15,300	LC
Howard Univ	DC	15,522	LC
Humboldt State Univ	CA	8,582	C
Huntingdon College	AL	18,400	VC
Huntington College	IN	15,480	LC
Idaho State Univ	ID	7,030	C+
Illinois State Univ	IL	9,235	C
Immaculata College	PA	22,400	LC
Indiana State Univ	IN	8,461	LC
Indiana Univ Bloomington	IN	10,712	C+
Indiana Univ of Pennsylvania	PA	9,133	C
Indiana Univ South Bend	IN	3,515	C
Indiana Univ-Purdue Univ Fort Wayne	IN	3,166	LC
Indiana Wesleyan Univ	IN	17,680	C
Inter-American Univ of PR/ Bayamon Univ College	PR	3,700	
Inter-American Univ of PR/ Fajardo Campus	PR	4,000	
Inter-American Univ of PR/ Ponce Regional College	PR	3,700	
Inter-American Univ of PR/ San GermÈn	PR	6,390	
Iowa Wesleyan College	IA	18,840	C
Ithaca College	NY	28,719	HC
Jackson State Univ	MS	6,776	LC
Jacksonville State Univ	AL	6,568	LC
Jacksonville Univ	FL	21,110	LC
Jarvis Christian College	TX	9,035	NC
John Brown Univ	AR	15,080	VC
Johns Hopkins Univ	MD	35,226	MC
Johnson State College	VT	10,776	C
Judson College	AL	13,790	C
Judson College	IL	18,980	LC
Kansas State Univ	KS	6,995	C
Kansas Wesleyan Univ	KS	17,400	C+
Kean Univ	NJ	11,159	C
Keene State College	NH	11,280	C
Kennesaw State Univ	GA	2,306	LC
Kent State Univ	OH	11,104	C
Kentucky Christian College	KY	13,472	C
Kentucky State Univ	KY	6,146	NC
Kentucky Wesleyan College	KY	15,800	C
Knoxville College	TN	6,200	LC
La Sierra Univ	CA	19,260	LC
Lakeland College	WI	17,950	C
Lamar Univ	TX	6,816	LC
Lambuth Univ	TN	14,254	C
Lander Univ	SC	8,618	LC
Lawrence Univ	WI	27,711	HC
Lebanon Valley College of Pennsylvania	PA	25,700	VC
Lee Univ	TN	10,198	LC
Lenoir-Rhyne College	NC	19,186	C
Limestone College	SC	16,900	C
Lincoln Univ	MO	7,158	NC
Lincoln Univ	PA	11,198	C+
Lindenwood Univ	MO	17,250	C
Livingstone College	NC	13,360	LC
LIU/Brooklyn Campus	NY	22,290	C
LIU/C.W. Post Campus	NY	25,380	C
Longwood College	VA	8,950	C
Loras College	IA	22,994	C+
Louisiana College	LA	11,516	C
Louisiana State Univ and A&M College	LA	8,014	VC
Louisiana Tech Univ	LA	6,506	C
Loyola Univ New Orleans	LA	23,506	VC+
Lubbock Christian Univ	TX	14,226	LC
Luther College	IA	23,300	VC+
MacMurray College	IL	17,790	LC
Madonna Univ	MI	11,504	VC
Malone College	OH	19,190	C
Manhattanville College	NY	28,730	VC
Mansfield Univ	PA	9,648	C
Marian College of Fond du Lac	WI	17,935	LC
Marietta College	OH	24,580	C
Mars Hill College	NC	18,600	LC
Maryville College	TN	23,210	VC
Marywood Univ	PA	24,639	C
McMurry Univ	TX	15,287	C
Mercer Univ	GA	24,130	VC
Mercyhurst College	PA	20,694	C
Meredith College	NC	17,500	C
Messiah College	PA	23,180	VC
Methodist College	NC	19,526	C
Metropolitan State College of Denver	CO	2,338	LC
Miami Univ	OH	12,885	VC+
Mich State Univ	MI	10,386	VC
MidAmerica Nazarene Univ	KS	16,960	C
Midland Lutheran College	NE	18,600	C
Midwestern State Univ	TX	6,704	NC
Millersville Univ of Pennsylvania	PA	10,153	VC
Milligan College	TN	17,550	C
Millikin Univ	IL	24,415	C+
Minn State Univ, Mankato	MN	7,296	LC
Minot State Univ	ND	5,466	LC
Miss College	MS	14,574	C
Miss State Univ	MS	7,853	C
Miss Univ for Women	MS	5,446	LC
Miss Valley State Univ	MS	6,345	C
Missouri Baptist College	MO	15,762	LC
Missouri Southern State College	MO	6,666	C
Missouri Western State College	MO	6,662	NC
Monmouth Univ	NJ	24,042	C
Montana State Univ-Billings	MT	7,653	NC
Montana State Univ-Bozeman	MT	8,431	C
Montclair State Univ	NJ	10,287	LC
Moorhead State Univ	MN	7,000	LC
Moravian College	PA	27,065	VC
Morehead State Univ	KY	6,510	C
Morningside College	IA	19,124	C
Mount Mary College	WI	18,024	C
Mount Mercy College	IA	19,390	VC
Mount Senario College	WI	17,750	C
Mount Union College	OH	21,120	C
Mount Vernon Nazarene College	OH	17,027	C
Murray State Univ	KY	6,672	C
Muskingum College	OH	18,760	C
Nazareth College of Rochester	NY	22,036	VC
Nebr Wesleyan Univ	NE	18,767	VC
New England Conservatory of Music	MA	31,200	SP
New Jersey City Univ	NJ	9,100	LC
New Mexico State Univ	NM	7,302	C
New York Univ	NY	35,200	MC
Newberry College	SC	19,670	LC
Nicholls State Univ	LA	5,290	NC
Norfolk State Univ	VA	8,382	LC
N Car Agricultural and Technical State Univ	NC	6,659	LC
N Dak State Univ	ND	7,004	VC
North Georgia College and State Univ	GA	6,322	C+
Northeastern State Univ	OK	4,704	LC
Northern Arizona Univ	AZ	7,398	C
Northern Illinois Univ	IL	9,545	C
Northern Mich Univ	MI	9,693	C
Northern State Univ	SD	6,279	LC
Northland College	WI	21,435	C+
Northwest Missouri State Univ	MO	7,922	LC
Northwest Nazarene Univ	ID	18,380	C
Northwestern College	MN	19,816	C+
Northwestern College of Iowa	IA	17,630	C+
Northwestern Okla State Univ	OK	4,542	NC
Northwestern State Univ of Louisiana	LA	5,745	NC
Northwestern Univ	IL	33,615	MC
Nyack College	NY	18,540	C
Oakland City Univ	IN	11,286	LC
Oakland Univ	MI	9,418	C
Oakwood College	AL	14,904	C
Oberlin College	OH	33,140	HC+
Ohio Northern Univ	OH	27,765	VC
Ohio Univ	OH	11,769	C
Ohio Wesleyan Univ	OH	29,670	VC+
Okla Baptist Univ	OK	13,878	VC
Okla Christian Univ	OK	16,500	VC
Okla City Univ	OK	15,810	C
Okla Panhandle State Univ	OK	3,812	NC
Okla State Univ	OK	7,650	VC
Old Dominion Univ	VA	9,386	C
Oral Roberts Univ	OK	18,490	C
Otterbein College	OH	23,439	C
Ouachita Baptist Univ	AR	16,460	VC
Pacific Lutheran Univ	WA	23,318	VC
Paine College	GA	11,896	LC
Palm Beach Atlantic College	FL	23,310	C
Penn State Univ/Univ Park Campus	PA	11,126	VC
Peru State College	NE	6,342	NC
Pfeiffer Univ	NC	18,580	C
Piedmont College	GA	16,900	C
Pittsburg State Univ	KS	6,228	NC
Plymouth State College	NH	11,024	LC
Pontifical Catholic Univ of PR/Ponce	PR	7,076	
Presbyterian College	SC	23,356	VC
Providence College	RI	27,620	HC
Quincy Univ	IL	20,450	C
Rhode Island College	RI	8,700	LC
Roberts Wesleyan College	NY	20,160	C+
Rocky Mountain College	MT	18,113	C
Roosevelt Univ	IL	20,240	LC
Rowan Univ	NJ	12,365	VC
Saginaw Valley State Univ	MI	9,465	C
St. Ambrose Univ	IA	19,994	C
St. Augustine's College	NC	12,990	C+
St. Cloud State Univ	MN	7,180	C
St. Joseph's College	IN	21,640	C
St. Mary-of-the-Woods College	IN	21,320	LC
St. Mary's Univ of Minn	MN	19,975	C
St. Norbert College	WI	23,169	VC
St. Olaf College	MN	25,880	HC
St. Vincent College	PA	22,942	VC
St. Xavier Univ	IL	21,104	C
Samford Univ	AL	16,340	VC
Seattle Pacific Univ	WA	22,674	C+
Seton Hill College	PA	21,875	C
Shenandoah Univ	VA	22,550	NC
Shepherd College	WV	7,062	LC
Shorter College	GA	15,185	C
Siena Heights Univ	MI	16,140	LC
Silver Lake College of the Holy Family	WI	15,516	LC
Simpson College	IA	21,200	C+
Slippery Rock Univ	PA	9,152	LC
S Car State Univ	SC	6,586	LC
S Dak State Univ	SD	6,848	C
Southeast Missouri State Univ	MO	8,367	C+
Southeastern College	FL	11,648	LC
Southeastern Louisiana Univ	LA	6,047	LC
Southeastern Okla State Univ	OK	4,917	C
Southern Adventist Univ	TN	15,600	C
Southern Arkansas Univ	AR	5,740	LC
Southern Methodist Univ	TX	28,349	VC
Southern Nazarene Univ	OK	14,634	NC
Southern Univ and A&M College	LA	6,365	C+
Southern Univ at New Orleans	LA	995	NC
Southern Utah Univ	UT	7,254	C
Southern Wesleyan Univ	SC	17,280	C
Southwest Baptist Univ	MO	13,426	LC
Southwest Missouri State Univ	MO	7,600	LC
Southwest State Univ	MN	7,117	LC
Southwest Texas State Univ	TX	8,730	VC
Southwestern College	KS	17,656	C
Southwestern Okla State Univ	OK	4,801	C
SUNY/College at Fredonia	NY	10,125	C
SUNY/College at Potsdam	NY	10,519	C
State Univ of West Georgia	GA	7,101	C
Stephen F. Austin State Univ	TX	6,905	C
Sterling College	KS	16,370	VC
Stetson Univ	FL	25,640	VC
Susquehanna Univ	PA	27,270	VC

School	ST	$IS	SR
Syracuse Univ	NY	30,710	HC
Tabor College	KS	17,600	LC
Talladega College	AL	10,110	LC
Taylor Univ	IN	21,562	VC+
Temple Univ	PA	14,124	C
Tenn Tech Univ	TN	6,968	C
Tenn Wesleyan College	TN	13,030	C
Texas A&M Univ at Commerce	TX	7,326	C
Texas A&M Univ at Kingsville	TX	6,446	LC
Texas Christian Univ	TX	19,910	C
Texas Tech Univ	TX	8,825	C
Texas Wesleyan Univ	TX	14,710	C
Ohio State Univ	OH	10,819	VC
Toccoa Falls College	GA	14,220	C
Towson Univ	MD	11,088	VC
Trevecca Nazarene Univ	TN	15,752	C
Trinity Christian College	IL	19,415	C
Troy State Univ	AL	7,696	C
Union College	KY	15,920	C
Union College	NE	14,650	C
Union Univ	TN	18,930	C+
Universidad Adventista de las Antillas	PR	6,675	
Univ of Akron	OH	10,530	NC
Univ of Alabama	AL	7,402	C
Univ of Alaska Anchorage	AK	9,100	NC
Univ of Alaska Fairbanks	AK	8,265	NC
Univ of Arizona	AZ	8,614	C
Univ of Arkansas	AR	8,334	VC
Univ of Arkansas at Monticello	AR	5,940	NC
Univ of Arkansas at Pine Bluff	AR	7,925	C
Univ of Central Arkansas	AR	6,388	C
Univ of Central Florida	FL	8,251	VC
Univ of Central Okla	OK	5,205	C
Univ of Charleston	WV	20,640	C
Univ of Cincinnati	OH	12,491	LC
Univ of Colo at Boulder	CO	9,255	VC
Univ of Conn	CT	12,122	VC
Univ of Dayton	OH	20,400	VC
Univ of Delaware	DE	10,824	VC
Univ of Evansville	IN	22,865	VC+
Univ of Florida	FL	7,874	HC
Univ of Georgia	GA	8,656	VC
Univ of Hartford	CT	28,884	C
Univ of Idaho	ID	7,026	C
Univ of Illinois at Urbana-Champaign	IL	11,316	HC+
Univ of Iowa	IA	8,607	C+
Univ of Kansas	KS	7,232	VC
Univ of Kentucky	KY	7,765	C
Univ of La Verne	CA	24,280	C
Univ of Louisiana at Lafayette	LA	5,200	C
Univ of Louisiana at Monroe	LA	5,207	NC
Univ of Louisville	KY	7,402	LC
Univ of Maine	ME	10,798	C
Univ of Mary	ND	12,900	LC
Univ of Mary Hardin-Baylor	TX	13,929	C
Univ of Maryland/College Park	MD	11,959	C
Univ of Maryland/Eastern Shore	MD	9,258	C
Univ of Miami	FL	31,130	HC
Univ of Mich/Ann Arbor	MI	13,003	HC+
Univ of Mich/Flint	MI	4,323	C
Univ of Minn/Duluth	MN	10,436	C
Univ of Minn/Twin Cities	MN	11,123	VC
Univ of Missouri/Columbia	MO	9,803	HC
Univ of Missouri/Kansas City	MO	9,685	VC
Univ of Missouri/St. Louis	MO	9,966	C
Univ of Montana	MT	8,038	C
Univ of Montana--Western	MT	6,915	NC
Univ of Montevallo	AL	7,266	C
Univ of Nebr at Kearney	NE	7,048	NC
Univ of Nebr at Lincoln	NE	8,325	C+
Univ of Nevada/Reno	NV	8,737	C
Univ of New Hampshire	NH	13,207	C
Univ of New Mexico	NM	8,026	C
Univ of New Orleans	LA	10,160	C
Univ of North Alabama	AL	7,016	NC
Univ of N Car at Chapel Hill	NC	8,789	HC
Univ of N Car at Charlotte	NC	7,254	C
Univ of N Car at Greensboro	NC	6,858	C
Univ of N Car at Pembroke	NC	5,914	LC
Univ of N Car at Wilmington	NC	7,769	C
Univ of N Dak	ND	7,067	VC
Univ of North Florida	FL	8,089	VC
Univ of Northern Iowa	IA	7,850	C
Univ of Okla	OK	7,616	VC
Univ of Oregon	OR	9,969	C
Univ of Portland	OR	24,950	VC
Univ of Puget Sound	WA	28,285	HC
Univ of Rhode Island	RI	12,414	C
Univ of Rio Grande	OH	8,728	NC
Univ of Rochester	NY	32,979	HC
Univ of St. Thomas	MN	24,044	VC
Univ of St. Thomas	TX	18,752	VC
Univ of Sioux Falls	SD	16,390	C
Univ of South Alabama	AL	6,976	LC
Univ of S Car at Columbia	SC	8,748	VC
Univ of S Dak	SD	7,036	C
Univ of South Florida	FL	8,154	C
Univ of Southern Calif	CA	33,647	MC
Univ of Southern Colo	CO	7,821	LC
Univ of Southern Maine	ME	10,569	C
Univ of Southern Miss	MS	6,155	LC
Univ of Tenn at Chattanooga	TN	7,783	C
Univ of Tenn at Knoxville	TN	8,214	C
Univ of Tenn at Martin	TN	8,268	C
Univ of the Incarnate Word	TX	18,478	C
Univ of the Pacific	CA	28,255	VC
Univ of Toledo	OH	11,206	NC
Univ of Tulsa	OK	19,090	HC
Univ of Vermont	VT	14,761	C+
Univ of Washington	WA	10,361	VC
Univ of West Florida	FL	7,518	C
Univ of Wisc/Eau Claire	WI	7,032	VC
Univ of Wisc/Milwaukee	WI	8,907	LC
Univ of Wisc/Oshkosh	WI	6,130	LC
Univ of Wisc/Platteville	WI	7,282	C
Univ of Wisc/River Falls	WI	6,356	LC
Univ of Wisc/Stevens Point	WI	7,116	C
Univ of Wisc/Superior	WI	7,051	C+
Univ of Wisc/Whitewater	WI	6,937	C
Univ of Wyoming	WY	7,143	LC
Utah State Univ	UT	6,771	C
Valdosta State Univ	GA	6,988	C
Valley City State Univ	ND		LC
Valparaiso Univ	IN	23,570	VC+
VanderCook College of Music	IL	19,410	SP
Virginia Union Univ	VA	15,358	LC
Viterbo Univ	WI	18,043	C
Walla Walla College	WA	20,925	C
Warner Pacific College	OR	20,370	LC
Wartburg College	IA	21,165	VC
Washburn Univ of Topeka	KS	6,766	NC
Wayland Baptist Univ	TX	11,271	NC
Wayne State College	NE	6,255	NC
Weber State Univ	UT	6,897	NC
Webster Univ	MO	19,804	VC
West Chester Univ of Pennsylvania	PA	9,792	VC
West Liberty State College	WV	6,056	LC
West Texas A&M Univ	TX	6,538	C
West Virginia Wesleyan College	WV	22,920	C
Western Carolina Univ	NC	5,667	C
Western Conn State Univ	CT	10,074	C
Western Mich Univ	MI	10,016	C
Western State College of Colo	CO	7,585	LC
Western Washington Univ	WA	8,624	VC
Westfield State College	MA	8,394	C
Westminster Choir College of Rider Univ	NJ	25,400	SP
Westminster College	PA	22,960	C
Westmont College	CA	29,748	VC
Wheaton College	IL	21,934	HC
Whitworth College	WA	23,938	VC
Wichita State Univ	KS	6,879	C
Wiley College	TX	8,100	LC
Wilkes Univ	PA	25,800	C
Willamette Univ	OR	29,422	VC+
William Carey College	MS	10,150	LC
William Jewell College	MO	17,150	VC
William Paterson Univ of New Jersey	NJ	11,000	LC
Wingate Univ	NC	19,140	C
Winona State Univ	MN	8,570	C
Winston-Salem State Univ	NC	5,927	LC
Winthrop Univ	SC	9,106	C
Wittenberg Univ	OH	28,766	VC
Wright State Univ	OH	9,141	LC
Xavier Univ	OH	23,880	C
Xavier Univ of Louisiana	LA	17,000	LC
York College	NE	13,500	C
Youngstown State Univ	OH	9,318	NC

MUSIC HISTORY AND APPRECIATION

School	ST	$IS	SR
Bard College	NY	33,912	HC
Baylor Univ	TX	18,298	VC+
Boston Univ	MA	34,358	MC
Bucknell Univ	PA	31,096	HC
Catholic Univ of America	DC	29,332	VC
Florida State Univ	FL	7,835	HC
Howard Univ	DC	15,522	LC
Johnson State College	VT	10,776	C
Nazareth College of Rochester	NY	22,036	VC
New England Conservatory of Music	MA	31,200	SP
Oberlin College	OH	33,140	HC+
Ohio Univ	OH	11,769	C
Rollins College	FL	31,223	HC
Roosevelt Univ	IL	20,240	LC
Simmons College	MA	30,418	VC
Simon's Rock College of Bard	MA	32,450	HC
Temple Univ	PA	14,124	C
Texas Tech Univ	TX	8,825	C
Ohio State Univ	OH	10,819	VC
Univ of Calif at Los Angeles	CA	13,227	MC
Univ of Calif at San Diego	CA	11,372	HC
Univ of Cincinnati	OH	12,491	LC
Univ of Florida	FL	7,874	HC
Univ of Hartford	CT	28,884	C
Univ of Idaho	ID	7,026	C
Univ of Illinois at Urbana-Champaign	IL	11,316	HC+
Univ of Kansas	KS	7,232	VC
Univ of Mich/Ann Arbor	MI	13,003	HC+
Univ of Mich/Dearborn	MI	4,677	VC
Univ of New Hampshire	NH	13,207	C
Univ of North Texas	TX	7,629	C
Univ of the Pacific	CA	28,255	VC
Univ of Washington	WA	10,361	VC
Vanderbilt Univ	TN	34,482	MC
Western Mich Univ	MI	10,016	C
Wright State Univ	OH	9,141	LC
Youngstown State Univ	OH	9,318	NC

MUSIC PERFORMANCE

School	ST	$IS	SR
Adams State College	CO	7,468	C
Anderson Univ	IN	19,430	LC
Andrews Univ	MI	17,696	LC
Anna Maria College	MA	22,800	LC
Appalachian State Univ	NC	6,353	C
Arizona State Univ-Main	AZ	7,726	C
Arkansas State Univ	AR	7,480	C
Baldwin-Wallace College	OH	22,010	VC+
Ball State Univ	IN	8,660	C
Bard College	NY	33,912	HC
Barry Univ	FL	24,100	LC
Baylor Univ	TX	18,298	VC+
Belmont Univ	TN	19,066	VC
Berklee College of Music	MA	27,005	SP
Berry College	GA	18,850	C
Bethel College	IN	17,650	LC
Biola Univ	CA	21,902	VC
Blackburn College	IL	13,690	C
Boston Conservatory	MA	26,900	SP
Boston Univ	MA	34,358	MC
Bowling Green State Univ	OH	10,794	C
Bradley Univ	IL	20,970	VC
Brenau Univ Women's College	GA	20,100	C
Bucknell Univ	PA	31,096	HC
Butler Univ	IN	25,580	VC+
Cal State, Los Angeles	CA	5,050	C
Catholic Univ of America	DC	29,332	VC
Centenary College of Louisiana	LA	21,600	C+
Christopher Newport Univ	VA	8,862	VC
CUNY/Brooklyn College	NY	3,403	LC
Clayton College and State Univ	GA	2,322	C+
Colo Christian Univ	CO	17,714	C
Columbia College	SC	19,050	LC
Columbus State Univ	GA	7,228	LC
Concordia College/Moorhead	MN	18,835	C
Cornerstone Univ and Grand Rapids Baptist Seminary	MI	18,092	C
Dallas Baptist Univ	TX	13,682	LC
Delta State Univ	MS	5,416	C
DePauw Univ	IN	28,000	HC
Dillard Univ	LA	16,046	VC
Drake Univ	IA	22,830	VC
Duquesne Univ	PA	24,242	C+
East Carolina Univ	NC	7,766	C
East Texas Baptist Univ	TX	12,349	LC
Eastern Mich Univ	MI	9,855	C
Eastern Nazarene College	MA	19,433	LC
Eastern New Mexico Univ	NM	4,113	LC
Eastern Washington Univ	WA	7,972	LC
Eastman School of Music	NY	30,684	SP
Elon Univ	NC	19,430	VC
Emory & Henry College	VA	19,462	C
Evangel Univ	MO	14,050	C
Five Towns College	NY	18,850	SP
Florida State Univ	FL	7,835	HC
Fort Hays State Univ	KS	6,294	LC
Furman Univ	SC	25,492	HC
George Washington Univ	DC	32,170	HC
Georgia College and State Univ	GA	7,344	C
Georgia Southern Univ	GA	6,958	C
Gordon College	MA	23,594	VC+
Grove City College	PA	12,280	MC
Hannibal-LaGrange College	MO	12,530	C
Houghton College	NY	21,810	VC+
Houston Baptist Univ	TX	15,300	LC
Huntington College	IN	15,480	LC
Idaho State Univ	ID	7,030	C+
Illinois State Univ	IL	9,235	C
Indiana Univ Bloomington	IN	10,712	C+
Indiana Univ of Pennsylvania	PA	9,133	C
Ithaca College	NY	28,719	HC
Jacksonville Univ	FL	21,110	LC
Johns Hopkins Univ	MD	35,226	MC
Johnson State College	VT	10,776	C
Keene State College	NH	11,280	C
Kennesaw State Univ	GA	2,306	LC
Kentucky Christian College	KY	13,472	C
Kentucky State Univ	KY	6,146	NC
La Sierra Univ	CA	19,260	LC
LaGrange College	GA	17,496	C
Lawrence Univ	WI	27,711	HC
Lebanon Valley College of Pennsylvania	PA	25,700	VC
Louisiana Tech Univ	LA	6,506	C
Loyola Univ New Orleans	LA	23,506	VC+
Manhattan School of Music	NY	31,500	SP
Mannes College of Music	NY	28,900	SP
Mansfield Univ	PA	9,648	C
Mars Hill College	NC	18,600	LC
Maryville College	TN	23,210	VC
McMurry Univ	TX	15,287	C
Meredith College	NC	17,500	C
Methodist College	NC	19,526	C
Metropolitan State College of Denver	CO	2,338	LC
Miami Univ	OH	12,885	VC+
Millikin Univ	IL	24,415	C+
Missouri Baptist College	MO	15,762	LC
Montclair State Univ	NJ	10,287	LC
Montreat College	NC	17,164	C
Mount Union College	OH	21,120	C
Mount Vernon Nazarene College	OH	17,027	C
Nazareth College of Rochester	NY	22,036	VC
New England Conservatory of Music	MA	31,200	SP
New York Univ	NY	35,200	MC
Newberry College	SC	19,670	LC
Northwestern College	MN	19,816	C+
Nyack College	NY	18,540	C
Oakwood College	AL	14,904	C
Oberlin College	OH	33,140	HC+
Ohio Northern Univ	OH	27,765	VC
Ohio Univ	OH	11,769	C
Old Dominion Univ	VA	9,386	C
Oral Roberts Univ	OK	18,490	C
Pacific Lutheran Univ	WA	23,318	VC
Palm Beach Atlantic College	FL	23,310	C
Rocky Mountain College	MT	18,113	C
Rollins College	FL	31,223	HC
Roosevelt Univ	IL	20,240	LC
St. Mary's Univ of Minn	MN	19,975	C
St. Olaf College	MN	25,880	HC
St. Vincent College	PA	22,942	VC
Sam Houston State Univ	TX	6,076	LC
Samford Univ	AL	16,340	VC
Shenandoah Univ	VA	22,550	NC
Shepherd College	WV	7,062	LC
Simon's Rock College of Bard	MA	32,450	HC
Simpson College	IA	21,200	C+
Southeast Missouri State Univ	MO	8,367	C+
Southern Methodist Univ	TX	28,349	VC
Southern Nazarene Univ	OK	14,634	NC
Southwest Missouri State Univ	MO	7,600	LC
Southwest Texas State Univ	TX	8,730	VC
SUNY/College at Potsdam	NY	10,519	C
SUNY/Univ at Binghamton	NY	10,653	HC
SUNY/Univ at Buffalo	NY	11,033	VC
Stetson Univ	FL	25,640	VC
Susquehanna Univ	PA	27,270	VC
Syracuse Univ	NY	30,710	HC
Talladega College	AL	10,110	LC
Temple Univ	PA	14,124	C
Texas Christian Univ	TX	19,910	C
Texas Tech Univ	TX	8,825	C
Ohio State Univ	OH	10,819	VC
Toccoa Falls College	GA	14,220	C
Trinity Christian College	IL	19,415	C
Truman State Univ	MO	8,568	VC+
Union College	NE	14,650	C
Union Univ	TN	18,930	C+
Univ of Alabama	AL	7,402	C
Univ of Alaska Fairbanks	AK	8,265	NC
Univ of Arizona	AZ	8,614	C
Univ of Calif at Santa Barbara	CA	11,732	VC
Univ of Denver	CO	28,783	VC
Univ of Evansville	IN	22,865	VC+
Univ of Georgia	GA	8,656	VC
Univ of Hartford	CT	28,884	C
Univ of Idaho	ID	7,026	C
Univ of Indianapolis	IN	20,840	C
Univ of Kansas	KS	7,232	VC
Univ of Kentucky	KY	7,765	C
Univ of Maine	ME	10,798	C
Univ of Maryland/College Park	MD	11,959	C
Univ of Mass Lowell	MA	9,470	VC
Univ of Miami	FL	31,130	HC
Univ of Mich/Ann Arbor	MI	13,003	HC+
Univ of Minn/Duluth	MN	10,436	C
Univ of Missouri/Kansas City	MO	9,685	VC
Univ of Montana	MT	8,038	C
Univ of New Hampshire	NH	13,207	C
Univ of N Car at Wilmington	NC	7,769	C
Univ of N Dak	ND	7,067	VC
Univ of North Florida	FL	8,089	VC

School	ST	$IS	SR
Univ of North Texas	TX	7,629	C
Univ of Northern Iowa	IA	7,850	C
Univ of Oregon	OR	9,969	C
Univ of Puget Sound	WA	28,285	HC
Univ of South Alabama	AL	6,976	LC
Univ of S Car at Columbia	SC	8,748	VC
Univ of S Dak	SD	7,036	C
Univ of Southern Calif	CA	33,647	MC
Univ of Southern Colo	CO	7,821	LC
Univ of Southern Maine	ME	10,569	C
Univ of the Arts	PA	24,230	SP
Univ of the Pacific	CA	28,255	VC
Univ of Tulsa	OK	19,090	HC
Univ of Washington	WA	10,361	VC
Univ of Wisc/Superior	WI	7,051	C+
Univ of Wyoming	WY	7,143	LC
Valdosta State Univ	GA	6,988	C
Vanderbilt Univ	TN	34,482	MC
Virginia State Univ	VA	8,182	LC
Viterbo Univ	WI	18,043	C
Walla Walla College	WA	20,925	C
Wartburg College	IA	21,165	VC
Washburn Univ of Topeka	KS	6,766	NC
Washington State Univ	WA	9,388	C
Weber State Univ	UT	6,897	NC
West Chester Univ of Pennsylvania	PA	9,792	VC
Western Conn State Univ	CT	10,074	C
Western Kentucky Univ	KY	6,834	C
Westminster Choir College of Rider Univ	NJ	25,400	SP
Westminster College	PA	22,960	C
Wiley College	TX	8,100	LC
Willamette Univ	OR	29,422	VC+
William Carey College	MS	10,150	LC
William Tyndale College	MI	11,150	C
York College	NE	13,500	C
Youngstown State Univ	OH	9,318	NC

MUSIC TECHNOLOGY

School	ST	$IS	SR
Bloomfield College	NJ	17,000	C
Cogswell Polytechnical College	CA	14,400	LC
Conn College	CT	33,585	MC
LaGrange College	GA	17,496	C
Malone College	OH	19,190	C
Univ of Calif at San Diego	CA	11,372	HC
Univ of N Car at Asheville	NC	6,896	VC

MUSIC THEORY AND COMPOSITION

School	ST	$IS	SR
Arizona State Univ-Main	AZ	7,726	C
Bard College	NY	33,912	HC
Baylor Univ	TX	18,298	VC+
Berklee College of Music	MA	27,005	SP
Biola Univ	CA	21,902	VC
Boston Conservatory	MA	26,900	SP
Boston Univ	MA	34,358	MC
Bowling Green State Univ	OH	10,794	C
Bradley Univ	IL	20,970	VC
Bucknell Univ	PA	31,096	HC
Butler Univ	IN	25,580	VC+
Catholic Univ of America	DC	29,332	VC
Christopher Newport Univ	VA	8,862	VC
CUNY/Brooklyn College	NY	3,403	LC
Clayton College and State Univ	GA	2,322	C+
Cornerstone Univ and Grand Rapids Baptist Seminary	MI	18,092	C
DePauw Univ	IN	28,000	HC
East Carolina Univ	NC	7,766	C
Eastman School of Music	NY	30,684	SP
Emory & Henry College	VA	19,462	C
Five Towns College	NY	18,850	SP
Florida State Univ	FL	7,835	HC
Fort Hays State Univ	KS	6,294	LC
Furman Univ	SC	25,492	HC
Georgia Southern Univ	GA	6,958	C
Houghton College	NY	21,810	VC+
Houston Baptist Univ	TX	15,300	LC
Illinois Wesleyan Univ	IL	26,970	HC
Indiana Univ Bloomington	IN	10,712	C+
Ithaca College	NY	28,719	HC
Jacksonville Univ	FL	21,110	LC
Johns Hopkins Univ	MD	35,226	MC
Juilliard School	NY	28,200	SP
Lawrence Univ	WI	27,711	HC
Loyola Univ New Orleans	LA	23,506	VC+
Manhattan School of Music	NY	31,500	SP
Mannes College of Music	NY	28,900	SP
Mich State Univ	MI	10,386	VC
Miss College	MS	14,574	C
New England Conservatory of Music	MA	31,200	SP
New York Univ	NY	35,200	MC
Newberry College	SC	19,670	LC
Nyack College	NY	18,540	C
Oberlin College	OH	30,134	HC+
Ohio Northern Univ	OH	27,765	VC
Ohio Univ	OH	11,769	C
Old Dominion Univ	VA	9,386	C
Oral Roberts Univ	OK	18,490	C
Pacific Lutheran Univ	WA	23,318	VC
Palm Beach Atlantic College	FL	23,310	C
Roosevelt Univ	IL	20,240	LC
St. Olaf College	MN	25,880	HC
Sam Houston State Univ	TX	6,076	LC
Samford Univ	AL	16,340	VC
Shenandoah Univ	VA	22,550	NC
Shepherd College	WV	7,062	LC
Simon's Rock College of Bard	MA	32,450	HC
Southeast Missouri State Univ	MO	8,367	C+
Southern Methodist Univ	TX	28,349	VC
Southwest Texas State Univ	TX	8,730	VC
SUNY/College at Potsdam	NY	10,519	C
Stetson Univ	FL	25,640	VC
Syracuse Univ	NY	30,710	HC
Temple Univ	PA	14,124	C
Texas Christian Univ	TX	19,910	C
Texas Tech Univ	TX	8,825	C
Ohio State Univ	OH	10,819	VC
Toccoa Falls College	GA	14,220	C
Union Univ	TN	18,930	C+
Univ of Alabama	AL	7,402	C
Univ of Arizona	AZ	8,614	C
Univ of Calif at Santa Barbara	CA	11,732	VC
Univ of Cincinnati	OH	12,491	LC
Univ of Delaware	DE	10,824	VC
Univ of Georgia	GA	8,656	VC
Univ of Hartford	CT	28,884	C
Univ of Houston	TX	8,410	C
Univ of Idaho	ID	7,026	C
Univ of Illinois at Urbana-Champaign	IL	11,316	HC+
Univ of Kansas	KS	7,232	VC
Univ of Miami	FL	31,130	HC
Univ of Mich/Ann Arbor	MI	13,003	HC+
Univ of Missouri/Kansas City	MO	9,685	VC
Univ of New Hampshire	NH	13,207	C
Univ of North Texas	TX	7,629	C
Univ of Northern Iowa	IA	7,850	C
Univ of Oregon	OR	9,969	C
Univ of Rochester	NY	32,979	HC
Univ of Southern Calif	CA	33,647	MC
Univ of Southern Colo	CO	7,821	LC
Univ of Texas at Austin	TX	9,437	HC
Univ of the Arts	PA	24,230	SP
Univ of the Pacific	CA	28,255	VC
Univ of Wyoming	WY	7,143	LC
Vanderbilt Univ	TN	34,482	MC
Warner Pacific College	OR	20,370	LC
Wartburg College	IA	21,165	VC
Washington State Univ	WA	9,388	C
Washington Univ in St. Louis	MO	34,593	MC
West Chester Univ of Pennsylvania	PA	9,792	VC
West Texas A&M Univ	TX	6,538	C
Western Mich Univ	MI	10,016	C
Westminster Choir College of Rider Univ	NJ	25,400	SP
Westminster College	PA	22,960	C
Willamette Univ	OR	29,422	VC+
Wright State Univ	OH	9,141	LC
Youngstown State Univ	OH	9,318	NC

MUSIC THERAPY

School	ST	$IS	SR
Alverno College	WI	16,930	LC
Anna Maria College	MA	22,800	LC
Appalachian State Univ	NC	6,353	C
Arizona State Univ-Main	AZ	7,726	C
Augsburg College	MN	22,978	C
Baldwin-Wallace College	OH	22,010	VC+
Berklee College of Music	MA	27,005	SP
Chapman Univ	CA	30,218	VC
Charleston Southern Univ	SC	17,122	C
Duquesne Univ	PA	24,242	C+
East Carolina Univ	NC	7,766	C
Eastern Mich Univ	MI	9,855	C
Elizabethtown College	PA	26,000	VC
Florida State Univ	FL	7,835	HC
Georgia College and State Univ	GA	7,344	C
Howard Univ	DC	15,522	LC
Immaculata College	PA	22,400	LC
Louisiana College	LA	11,516	C
Loyola Univ New Orleans	LA	23,506	VC+
Mansfield Univ	PA	9,648	C
Maryville Univ of St. Louis	MO	18,680	C
Marywood Univ	PA	24,639	C
Mich State Univ	MI	10,386	VC
Molloy College	NY	13,940	C
Montclair State Univ	NJ	10,287	LC
Nazareth College of Rochester	NY	22,036	VC
Queens College	NC	17,250	C
St. Mary-of-the-Woods College	IN	21,320	LC
Sam Houston State Univ	TX	6,076	LC
Shenandoah Univ	VA	22,550	NC
Southern Methodist Univ	TX	28,349	VC
Southwestern Okla State Univ	OK	4,801	C
Temple Univ	PA	14,124	C
Tenn Tech Univ	TN	6,968	C
Texas Woman's Univ	TX	5,855	LC
Univ of Alabama	AL	7,402	C
Univ of Dayton	OH	20,400	VC
Univ of Evansville	IN	22,865	VC+
Univ of Georgia	GA	8,656	VC
Univ of Kansas	KS	7,232	VC
Univ of Miami	FL	31,130	HC
Univ of Minn/Twin Cities	MN	11,123	VC
Univ of Missouri/Kansas City	MO	9,685	VC
Univ of the Incarnate Word	TX	18,478	C
Univ of the Pacific	CA	28,255	VC
Univ of Wisc/Eau Claire	WI	7,032	VC
Univ of Wisc/Oshkosh	WI	6,130	LC
Utah State Univ	UT	6,771	C
Wartburg College	IA	21,165	VC
West Texas A&M Univ	TX	6,538	C
Western Mich Univ	MI	10,016	C
William Carey College	MS	10,150	LC

MUSICAL THEATER

School	ST	$IS	SR
Ashland Univ	OH	22,182	LC
Barton College	NC	16,834	LC
Boston Conservatory	MA	26,900	SP
Brenau Univ Women's College	GA	20,100	C
Cal State, Chico	CA	8,598	LC
Catawba College	NC	19,620	C
Catholic Univ of America	DC	29,332	VC
Coastal Carolina Univ	SC	9,220	C
Coker College	SC	20,120	C
College of the Ozarks	MO	2,650	C+
Elon Univ	NC	19,430	VC
Emerson College	MA	29,978	HC
Florida State Univ	FL	7,835	HC
Friends Univ	KS	15,962	LC
Howard Univ	DC	15,522	LC
Huntingdon College	AL	18,400	VC
Illinois Wesleyan Univ	IL	26,970	HC
Ithaca College	NY	28,719	HC
Jacksonville Univ	FL	21,110	LC
Lees-McRae College	NC	17,106	LC
Mars Hill College	NC	18,600	LC
Mercyhurst College	PA	20,694	C
Meredith College	NC	17,500	C
Millikin Univ	IL	24,415	C+
Otterbein College	OH	23,439	C
Ouachita Baptist Univ	AR	16,460	VC
Roosevelt Univ	IL	20,240	LC
Sam Houston State Univ	TX	6,076	LC
Samford Univ	AL	16,340	VC
Seton Hill College	PA	21,875	C
Shenandoah Univ	VA	22,550	NC
Shorter College	GA	15,185	C
SUNY/Univ at Buffalo	NY	11,033	VC
Syracuse Univ	NY	30,710	HC
Univ of Arizona	AZ	8,614	C
Univ of Hartford	CT	28,884	C
Univ of Indianapolis	IN	20,840	C
Univ of Miami	FL	31,130	HC
Univ of Mich/Ann Arbor	MI	13,003	HC+
Univ of the Arts	PA	24,230	SP
Univ of Tulsa	OK	19,090	HC
Viterbo Univ	WI	18,043	C
Weber State Univ	UT	6,897	NC
Webster Univ	MO	19,804	VC
West Texas A&M Univ	TX	6,538	C
Youngstown State Univ	OH	9,318	NC

NATIVE AMERICAN STUDIES

School	ST	$IS	SR
Colgate Univ	NY	33,480	MC
Dartmouth College	NH	34,458	MC
Humboldt State Univ	CA	8,582	C
Montana State Univ-Northern	MT	8,600	NC
Univ of Alaska Fairbanks	AK	8,265	NC
Univ of Calif at Berkeley	CA	14,134	MC
Univ of Calif at Davis	CA	12,796	VC
Univ of Calif at Riverside	CA	12,479	C
Univ of Minn/Duluth	MN	10,436	C
Univ of Montana	MT	8,038	C
Univ of N Dak	ND	7,067	VC
Univ of Okla	OK	7,616	VC
Univ of the Incarnate Word	TX	18,478	C

NATURAL RESOURCE MANAGEMENT

School	ST	$IS	SR
Alaska Pacific Univ	AK	16,450	C
Allegheny College	PA	27,780	VC
Ball State Univ	IN	8,660	C
Calif Polytechnic State Univ	CA	8,747	VC
Colo State Univ	CO	9,672	C
Cornell Univ	NY	34,614	MC
Delaware State Univ	DE	8,104	LC
Dominican Univ	IL	20,800	C
Hofstra Univ	NY	23,252	C
Humboldt State Univ	CA	8,582	C
Johnson State College	VT	10,776	C
Keystone College	PA	19,066	LC
Louisiana State Univ and A&M College	LA	8,014	VC
Montana State Univ-Bozeman	MT	8,431	C
New Mexico Highlands Univ	NM	6,256	NC
N Car State Univ	NC	8,680	HC
N Dak State Univ	ND	7,004	VC
Northland College	WI	21,435	C+
Penn State Univ/Univ Park Campus	PA	11,126	VC
Purdue Univ/West Lafayette	IN	10,284	VC
Rutgers, The State Univ of New Jersey New Brunswick Campus	NJ	12,709	C
SUNY/College of Environmental Science and Forestry	NY	12,446	VC
Sterling College	VT	19,695	C
Sul Ross State Univ	TX	6,582	LC
Texas A&M Univ at Galveston	TX	7,269	C+
Ohio State Univ	OH	10,819	VC
Univ of Alaska Fairbanks	AK	8,265	NC
Univ of Arizona	AZ	8,614	C
Univ of Conn	CT	12,122	VC
Univ of Delaware	DE	10,824	VC
Univ of Florida	FL	7,874	HC
Univ of Maine	ME	10,798	C
Univ of Maryland/College Park	MD	11,959	C
Univ of Mass Amherst	MA	10,995	VC
Univ of Mich/Ann Arbor	MI	13,003	HC+
Univ of Minn/Crookston	MN	9,626	NC
Univ of Minn/Twin Cities	MN	11,123	VC
Univ of Nebr at Lincoln	NE	8,325	C+
Univ of Nevada/Reno	NV	8,737	C
Univ of New Hampshire	NH	13,207	C
Univ of Northern Colo	CO	8,082	C+
Univ of Rhode Island	RI	12,414	C
Univ of Tenn at Martin	TN	8,268	C
Univ of the South	TN	27,290	HC
Univ of Vermont	VT	14,761	C+
Univ of Wisc/Stevens Point	WI	7,116	C
Utah State Univ	UT	6,771	C
Washington State Univ	WA	9,388	C
West Virginia Univ	WV	8,304	C
Western Carolina Univ	NC	5,667	C

NATURAL SCIENCES

School	ST	$IS	SR
Adelphi Univ	NY	23,320	VC
Arkansas Tech Univ	AR	6,256	C
Avila College	MO	17,720	C
Bard College	NY	33,912	HC
Benedictine College	KS	18,485	LC
Bennington College	VT	31,350	VC
Bethel College	KS	17,355	C+
Bloomsburg Univ of Pennsylvania	PA	9,434	C
Cal State, Fresno	CA	7,762	C
Cal State, Los Angeles	CA	5,050	C
Carthage College	WI	23,670	C
Case Western Reserve Univ	OH	27,418	C
Castleton State College	VT	10,922	LC
Charleston Southern Univ	SC	17,122	C
Christian Brothers Univ	TN	19,820	VC
Clarion Univ of Pennsylvania	PA	11,272	LC
Colgate Univ	NY	33,480	MC
College of Mount St. Joseph	OH	20,290	C
College of Our Lady of the Elms	MA	20,644	C
College of St. Benedict	MN	23,921	VC
College of St. Mary	NE	18,726	C
College of St. Scholastica	MN	22,378	C+
College of the Southwest	NM	8,456	NC
Columbia College	MO	15,082	C
Concordia Univ	MN	19,912	C
Concordia Univ Nebr	NE	17,770	C
Concordia Univ, River Forest	IL	20,000	LC
Covenant College	GA	21,970	C+
Daemen College	NY	20,620	C
Dowling College	NY	20,281	LC
Edgewood College	WI	18,304	C
Edinboro Univ of Pennsylvania	PA	9,328	LC
Erskine College	SC	21,399	VC
Fresno Pacific Univ	CA	19,740	C
Goshen College	IN	18,950	VC+
Gwynedd-Mercy College	PA	22,350	C
Hofstra Univ	NY	23,252	C
Illinois Wesleyan Univ	IL	26,970	HC
Indiana Univ of Pennsylvania	PA	9,133	C
Johns Hopkins Univ	MD	35,226	MC
Juniata College	PA	26,080	VC
Lehigh Univ	PA	32,290	MC
LeMoyne-Owen College	TN	8,450	NC
Lesley College	MA	25,325	LC
Lewis-Clark State College	ID	6,496	C
Loyola Marymount Univ	CA	28,754	HC
Lyndon State College	VT	11,313	LC

School	ST	$IS	SR
Madonna Univ	MI	11,504	VC
Master's College	CA	21,500	C+
McMurry Univ	TX	15,287	C
Mercer Univ	GA	24,130	VC
Missouri Western State College	MO	6,662	NC
Muhlenberg College	PA	28,170	HC
New College of Florida	FL	8,130	HC+
Norfolk State Univ	VA	8,382	LC
Northwest Nazarene Univ	ID	18,380	C
Oakwood College	AL	14,904	C
Our Lady of the Lake Univ of San Antonio	TX	17,336	C
Pacific Union College	CA	20,250	VC
Park Univ	MO	9,816	C
Pepperdine Univ	CA	32,830	VC
Rocky Mountain College	MT	18,113	C
St. Anselm College	NH	27,405	C
St. John's Univ	MN	23,640	VC
St. Joseph College	CT	25,960	LC
St. Mary's College of Maryland	MD	14,104	HC
St. Norbert College	WI	23,169	VC
St. Peter's College	NJ	22,292	LC
Shawnee State Univ	OH	8,634	NC
Shimer College	IL	17,560	LC
Shorter College	GA	15,185	C
Siena Heights Univ	MI	16,140	LC
Simon's Rock College of Bard	MA	32,450	HC
Southwestern Okla State Univ	OK	4,801	C
Spelman College	GA	19,215	C+
SUNY/College at Geneseo	NY	9,970	HC
Tabor College	KS	17,600	LC
Taylor Univ	IN	21,562	VC+
Texas A&M Univ at Galveston	TX	7,269	C+
Thomas Edison State College	NJ	2,750	SP
Turabo Univ	PR	4,110	
Universidad Metropolitana	PR	3,324	
Univ of Akron	OH	10,530	NC
Univ of Alabama at Birmingham	AL	10,110	C
Univ of Alaska Anchorage	AK	9,100	NC
Univ of Arizona	AZ	8,614	C
Univ of Hawaii at Hilo	HI	6,497	C
Univ of Houston-Downtown	TX	2,006	NC
Univ of La Verne	CA	24,280	C
Univ of New Haven	CT	23,860	LC
Univ of Pittsburgh at Greensburg	PA	12,842	C
Univ of Pittsburgh at Pittsburgh	PA	13,592	HC
Univ of PR/Cayey Univ College	PR	1,245	
Univ of Puget Sound	WA	28,285	HC
Univ of Science and Arts of Okla	OK	5,245	C
Univ of Wisc/Stevens Point	WI	7,116	C
Virginia Wesleyan College	VA	22,350	LC
Washington and Lee Univ	VA	25,095	MC
Western Oregon Univ	OR	8,829	C
Worcester State College	MA	7,901	LC
Xavier Univ	OH	23,880	C
York College	NE	13,500	C

NAVAL ARCHITECTURE AND MARINE ENGINEERING

School	ST	$IS	SR
Norfolk State Univ	VA	8,382	LC
SUNY/Maritime College	NY	10,025	LC
Texas A&M Univ at Galveston	TX	7,269	C+
United States Coast Guard Academy	CT		MC
United States Naval Academy	MD		MC
Univ of Mich/Ann Arbor	MI	13,003	HC+
Univ of New Orleans	LA	10,160	C
Webb Inst	NY	6,250	MC

NEAR EASTERN STUDIES

School	ST	$IS	SR
Brandeis Univ	MA	34,481	MC
Brigham Young Univ	UT	7,840	HC
Cornell Univ	NY	34,614	MC
Indiana Univ Bloomington	IN	10,712	C+
Johns Hopkins Univ	MD	35,226	MC
Mount Union College	OH	21,120	C
Oberlin College	OH	33,140	HC+
Princeton Univ	NJ	35,072	MC
Univ of Arizona	AZ	8,614	C
Univ of Calif at Los Angeles	CA	13,227	MC
Univ of Chicago	IL	35,087	MC
Univ of Mich/Ann Arbor	MI	13,003	HC+
Univ of Washington	WA	10,361	VC
Wayne State Univ	MI	6,720	C
William Tyndale College	MI	11,150	C
Yale Univ	CT	34,030	MC

NEUROSCIENCES

School	ST	$IS	SR
Allegheny College	PA	27,780	VC
Amherst College	MA	34,340	MC
Bates College	ME	34,100	MC
Baylor Univ	TX	18,298	VC+
Boston Univ	MA	34,358	MC
Bowdoin College	ME	32,650	MC
Bowling Green State Univ	OH	10,794	C
Brandeis Univ	MA	34,481	MC
Brown Univ	RI	34,973	MC
Cedar Crest College	PA	25,145	C+
Centenary College of Louisiana	LA	21,600	C+
Chatham College	PA	25,454	C+
Colgate Univ	NY	33,480	MC
Colo College	CO	31,525	HC+
Columbia Univ/Columbia College	NY	35,190	MC
Conn College	CT	33,585	MC
Drake Univ	IA	22,830	VC
Emory Univ	GA	33,792	MC
Fairfield Univ	CT	30,885	HC
Hamilton College	NY	34,150	HC
Johns Hopkins Univ	MD	35,226	MC
Kenyon College	OH	32,130	HC+
King's College	PA	24,680	C
Lafayette College	PA	32,655	MC
Lawrence Univ	WI	27,711	HC
Macalester College	MN	28,814	HC+
Muskingum College	OH	18,760	C
New York Univ	NY	35,200	MC
Northeastern Univ	MA	30,078	VC
Northwestern Univ	IL	33,615	MC
Oberlin College	OH	33,140	HC+
Pitzer College	CA	33,930	HC
Pomona College	CA	33,960	MC
Regis Univ	CO	25,740	C+
St. Lawrence Univ	NY	32,605	VC
Scripps College	CA	30,400	HC+
Smith College	MA	33,302	HC+
Texas Christian Univ	TX	19,910	C
Trinity College	CT	34,300	HC
Univ of Calif at Los Angeles	CA	13,227	MC
Univ of Calif at Riverside	CA	12,479	C
Univ of Pittsburgh at Pittsburgh	PA	13,592	HC
Univ of Rochester	NY	32,979	HC
Univ of St. Thomas	MN	24,044	VC
Univ of Scranton	PA	27,964	C+
Univ of Texas at Dallas	TX	9,305	VC
Univ of Washington	WA	10,361	VC
Washington and Lee Univ	VA	25,095	MC
Washington State Univ	WA	9,388	C
Washington Univ in St. Louis	MO	34,593	MC
Wellesley College	MA	33,394	MC
Wesleyan Univ	CT	3,405	MC
Westmont College	CA	29,748	VC

NUCLEAR ENGINEERING

School	ST	$IS	SR
Georgia Inst of Technology	GA	9,028	HC+
Kansas State Univ	KS	6,995	C
Mass Inst of Technology	MA	35,228	MC
N Car State Univ	NC	8,680	HC
Oregon State Univ	OR	9,612	VC
Penn State Univ/Univ Park Campus	PA	11,126	VC
Purdue Univ/West Lafayette	IN	10,284	VC
Rensselaer Polytechnic Inst	NY	33,863	HC+
Texas A&M Univ	TX	8,988	VC
United States Military Academy	NY		MC
Univ of Arizona	AZ	8,614	C
Univ of Calif at Berkeley	CA	14,134	MC
Univ of Cincinnati	OH	12,491	LC
Univ of Florida	FL	7,874	HC
Univ of Illinois at Urbana-Champaign	IL	11,316	HC+
Univ of Maryland/College Park	MD	11,959	C
Univ of Mich/Ann Arbor	MI	13,003	HC+
Univ of Missouri/Rolla	MO	10,034	C
Univ of New Mexico	NM	8,026	C
Univ of Tenn at Knoxville	TN	8,214	C
Univ of Wisc/Madison	WI	8,262	VC

NUCLEAR ENGINEERING TECHNOLOGY

School	ST	$IS	SR
Old Dominion Univ	VA	9,386	C
Thomas Edison State College	NJ	2,750	SP
Univ of Florida	FL	7,874	HC

NUCLEAR MEDICAL TECHNOLOGY

School	ST	$IS	SR
Alverno College	WI	16,930	LC
Aquinas College	MI	20,052	C+
Barry Univ	FL	24,100	LC
Benedictine Univ	IL	21,330	C
Cedar Crest College	PA	25,145	C+
Edinboro Univ of Pennsylvania	PA	9,328	LC
Ferris State Univ	MI	10,816	C
George Washington Univ	DC	32,170	HC
Indiana Univ of Pennsylvania	PA	9,133	C
Indiana Univ-Purdue Univ Indianapolis	IN	9,473	C
Loras College	IA	22,994	C+
Mass College of Pharmacy and Health Sciences	MA	27,131	SP
New Jersey City Univ	NJ	9,100	LC
Old Dominion Univ	VA	9,386	C
Rochester Inst of Technology	NY	26,232	VC+
Roosevelt Univ	IL	20,240	LC
St. Louis Univ	MO	26,590	VC+
St. Mary's Univ of Minn	MN	19,975	C
SUNY/Univ at Buffalo	NY	11,033	VC
Thomas Edison State College	NJ	2,750	SP
Univ of Alabama at Birmingham	AL	10,110	C
Univ of Central Arkansas	AR	6,388	C
Univ of Cincinnati	OH	12,491	LC
Univ of Detroit Mercy	MI	21,620	LC
Univ of Findlay	OH	23,962	NC
Univ of Iowa	IA	8,607	C+
Univ of Nevada/Las Vegas	NV	8,281	VC
Univ of St. Francis	IL	19,650	C
Univ of the Incarnate Word	TX	18,478	C
Univ of Vermont	VT	14,761	C+
Univ of Wisc/La Crosse	WI	7,250	VC
Wheeling Jesuit Univ	WV	22,660	C
York College of Pennsylvania	PA	12,550	VC

NUCLEAR TECHNOLOGY

School	ST	$IS	SR
Excelsior College	NY	915	SP
Peru State College	NE	6,342	NC
Thomas Edison State College	NJ	2,750	SP

NURSING

School	ST	$IS	SR
Abilene Christian Univ	TX	16,300	VC
Adelphi Univ	NY	23,320	VC
Albany State Univ	GA	5,764	C+
Alcorn State Univ	MS	5,594	LC
Alderson-Broaddus College	WV	19,640	C
Allen College	IA	17,088	SP
Alvernia College	PA	20,790	C
Alverno College	WI	16,930	LC
American International College	MA	22,268	LC
Anderson Univ	IN	19,430	LC
Andrews Univ	MI	17,696	LC
Angelo State Univ	TX	7,028	C
Anna Maria College	MA	22,800	LC
Aquinas College	TN	10,050	LC
Arizona State Univ-Main	AZ	7,726	C
Arkansas State Univ	AR	7,480	C
Arkansas Tech Univ	AR	6,256	C
Armstrong Atlantic State Univ	GA	7,084	C
Atlantic Union College	MA	34,034	LC
Auburn Univ	AL	5,510	C
Auburn Univ Montgomery	AL	5,330	NC
Augustana College	SD	20,760	VC
Aurora Univ	IL	18,551	C
Austin Peay State Univ	TN	5,814	LC
Avila College	MO	17,720	C
Azusa Pacific Univ	CA	22,422	VC
Baker Univ	KS	14,780	C+
Ball State Univ	IN	8,660	C
Barry Univ	FL	24,100	LC
Barton College	NC	16,834	LC
Baylor Univ	TX	18,298	VC+
Bellarmine Univ	KY	20,440	VC
Belmont Univ	TN	19,066	VC
Bemidji State Univ	MN	7,957	C
Benedictine Univ	IL	21,330	C
Berea College	KY	4,070	VC
Bethel College	IN	17,650	LC
Bethel College	KS	17,355	C+
Bethel College	MN	22,740	VC
Bethune-Cookman College	FL	15,746	C
Biola Univ	CA	21,902	VC
Bloomfield College	NJ	17,000	C
Bloomsburg Univ of Pennsylvania	PA	9,434	C
Blue Mountain College	MS	9,100	LC
Bluefield State College	WV	2,178	LC
Boise State Univ	ID	6,531	LC
Boston College	MA	33,330	MC
Bowie State Univ	MD	9,300	C+
Bowling Green State Univ	OH	10,794	C
Bradley Univ	IL	20,970	VC
Brenau Univ Women's College	GA	20,100	C
Briar Cliff Univ	IA	18,657	LC
Brigham Young Univ	UT	7,840	HC
Cal State, Bakersfield	CA	6,090	LC
Cal State, Chico	CA	8,598	LC
Cal State, Dominguez Hills	CA	5,840	LC
Cal State, Fresno	CA	7,762	C
Cal State, Fullerton	CA	5,440	LC
Cal State, Hayward	CA	7,400	LC
Cal State, Los Angeles	CA	5,050	C
Cal State, Northridge	CA	7,781	C
Cal State, Sacramento	CA	7,488	C
Cal State, San Bernardino	CA	6,516	C
Cal State, Stanislaus	CA	8,895	C
Calif Univ of Pennsylvania	PA	10,388	C
Calvin College	MI	20,050	NC
Capital Univ	OH	23,630	C
Cardinal Stritch Univ	WI	17,620	C
Caribbean Univ	PR	3,000	
Carlow College	PA	19,366	C
Carroll College	MT	19,140	C
Carroll College	WI	21,170	C
Carson-Newman College	TN	16,490	C
Case Western Reserve Univ	OH	27,418	C
Catholic Univ of America	DC	29,332	VC
Cedar Crest College	PA	25,145	C+
Cedarville Univ	OH	17,553	VC
Central Conn State Univ	CT	10,404	C
Central Methodist College	MO	16,460	C
Central Missouri State Univ	MO	7,920	C
Central Univ of Bayamon	PR	3,335	
Charleston Southern Univ	SC	17,122	C
Chicago State Univ	IL	8,851	C+
Christopher Newport Univ	VA	8,862	VC
CUNY/College of Staten Island	NY	3,358	NC
CUNY/Herbert H. Lehman College	NY	3,320	LC
CUNY/Hunter College	NY	5,147	C+
CUNY/Medgar Evers College	NY	3,282	NC
CUNY/York College	NY	3,292	NC
Clarion Univ of Pennsylvania	PA	11,272	LC
Clarke College	IA	20,625	C+
Clarkson College	NE	12,178	C
Clayton College and State Univ	GA	2,322	C+
Clemson Univ	SC	7,600	C
Cleveland State Univ	OH	10,146	NC
Coe College	IA	24,750	VC
Colby-Sawyer College	NH	27,850	LC
College Misericordia	PA	23,380	LC
College of Mount St. Vincent	NY	24,230	C
College of Mount St. Joseph	OH	20,290	C
College of New Jersey	NJ	13,425	HC
College of New Rochelle	NY	20,000	C
College of Notre Dame of Maryland	MD	23,100	LC
College of Our Lady of the Elms	MA	20,644	C
College of St. Benedict	MN	23,921	VC
College of St. Catherine	MN	22,324	VC
College of St. Elizabeth	NJ	22,510	C
College of St. Mary	NE	18,726	C
College of St. Scholastica	MN	22,378	C+
College of the Ozarks	MO	2,650	C+
Columbia Union College	MD	19,027	C+
Columbus State Univ	GA	7,228	LC
Concordia College/Moorhead	MN	18,835	C
Concordia Univ Wisc	WI	16,600	LC
Concordia Univ, River Forest	IL	20,000	LC
Coppin State College	MD	9,133	LC
Creighton Univ	NE	23,476	VC
Culver-Stockton College	MO	15,400	LC
Cumberland Univ	TN	11,970	LC
Curry College	MA	26,025	LC
Daemen College	NY	20,620	C
De Sales Univ	PA	22,610	VC
Deaconess College of Nursing	MO	12,700	SP
Delaware State Univ	DE	8,104	LC
Delta State Univ	MS	5,416	C
Dickinson State Univ	ND	5,495	NC
Dillard Univ	LA	16,046	VC
Dominican College	NY	20,400	LC
Dominican Univ of Calif	CA	27,948	C
Drury Univ	MO	15,250	VC
Duquesne Univ	PA	24,242	C+
D'Youville College	NY	18,704	C
East Carolina Univ	NC	7,766	C
East Central Univ	OK	4,578	C
East Stroudsburg Univ of Pennsylvania	PA	8,430	LC
East Tenn State Univ	TN	7,127	C
East Texas Baptist Univ	TX	12,349	LC
Eastern Kentucky Univ	KY	6,552	C
Eastern Mennonite Univ	VA	20,700	VC
Eastern Mich Univ	MI	9,855	C
Eastern New Mexico Univ	NM	4,113	LC
Eastern Oregon Univ	OR	8,772	C
Eastern Washington Univ	WA	7,972	LC
Edgewood College	WI	18,304	C
Edinboro Univ of Pennsylvania	PA	9,328	LC
Elmhurst College	IL	21,750	C
Elmira College	NY	31,070	VC+
Emmanuel College	MA	23,802	C+
Emory Univ	GA	33,792	MC
Emporia State Univ	KS	6,198	LC
Endicott College	MA	23,704	C

School	ST	$IS	SR
Excelsior College	NY	915	SP
Fairfield Univ	CT	30,885	HC
Fairleigh Dickinson Univ/ Teaneck Campus	NJ	24,646	C
Fayetteville State Univ	NC	5,590	LC
Felician College	NJ	20,050	C
Ferris State Univ	MI	10,816	C
Fitchburg State College	MA	7,836	C
Florida A&M Univ	FL	6,948	C
Florida Atlantic Univ	FL	8,832	C
Florida Gulf Coast Univ	FL	9,201	C
Florida Hospital College of Health Sciences	FL	5,790	C
Florida International Univ	FL	9,486	VC
Florida State Univ	FL	7,835	HC
Fort Hays State Univ	KS	6,294	LC
Franciscan Univ of Steubenville	OH	19,100	C+
Gannon Univ	PA	18,848	C
Gardner-Webb Univ	NC	17,400	C
George Mason Univ	VA	9,192	C
Georgetown College	KY	18,400	VC
Georgetown Univ	DC	34,847	MC
Georgia College and State Univ	GA	7,344	C
Georgia Southern Univ	GA	6,958	C
Georgia Southwestern State Univ	GA	6,013	C
Georgia State Univ	GA	7,792	LC
Glenville State College	WV	6,588	NC
Gonzaga Univ	WA	24,276	HC+
Goshen College	IN	18,950	VC+
Graceland Univ	IA	15,845	C
Grambling State Univ	LA	5,325	NC
Grand Canyon Univ	AZ	30,000	LC
Grand Valley State Univ	MI	10,040	C
Grand View College	IA	17,596	NC
Gustavus Adolphus College	MN	24,190	VC+
Gwynedd-Mercy College	PA	22,350	C
Hampton Univ	VA	17,112	C+
Hannibal-LaGrange College	MO	12,530	C
Harding Univ	AR	13,528	VC
Hardin-Simmons Univ	TX	14,165	C
Hartwick College	NY	33,090	C+
Hawaii Pacific Univ	HI	17,790	C
Henderson State Univ	AR	6,269	C
Holy Family College	PA	13,710	LC
Holy Names College	CA	23,220	C
Hope College	MI	22,922	C+
Houston Baptist Univ	TX	15,300	LC
Howard Univ	DC	15,522	LC
Humboldt State Univ	CA	8,582	C
Huron Univ	SD	10,450	C
Husson College	ME	15,360	LC
Idaho State Univ	ID	7,030	C+
Illinois State Univ	IL	9,235	C
Illinois Wesleyan Univ	IL	26,970	HC
Immaculata College	PA	22,400	LC
Indiana State Univ	IN	8,461	LC
Indiana Univ East	IN	3,415	C
Indiana Univ Kokomo	IN	3,422	LC
Indiana Univ Northwest	IN	3,447	C
Indiana Univ of Pennsylvania	PA	9,133	C
Indiana Univ South Bend	IN	3,515	C
Indiana Univ Southeast	IN	3,459	C
Indiana Univ-Purdue Univ Fort Wayne	IN	3,166	LC
Indiana Univ-Purdue Univ Indianapolis	IN	9,473	C
Inter-American Univ of PR/ Aguadilla Campus	PR	3,278	
Inter-American Univ of PR/ Arecibo Campus	PR	3,300	
Inter-American Univ of PR/ Bayamon Univ College	PR	3,700	
Inter-American Univ of PR/ Fajardo Campus	PR	4,000	
Inter-American Univ of PR/ Metropolitan Campus	PR	4,166	
Inter-American Univ of PR/ Ponce Regional College	PR	3,700	
Inter-American Univ of PR/ San GermÈn	PR	6,390	
Iowa Wesleyan College	IA	18,840	C
Jacksonville State Univ	AL	6,568	LC
Jacksonville Univ	FL	21,110	LC
James Madison Univ	VA	9,552	HC
Jamestown College	ND	11,310	NC
Jewish Hospital College of Nursing and Allied Health	MO	11,200	SP
Johns Hopkins Univ	MD	35,226	MC
Judson College	IL	18,980	LC
Kansas Wesleyan Univ	KS	17,400	C+
Kean Univ	NJ	11,159	C
Kennesaw State Univ	GA	2,306	LC
Kent State Univ	OH	11,104	C
Kentucky Wesleyan College	KY	15,800	C
Keuka College	NY	21,170	C
King College	TN	17,800	VC
Kutztown Univ of Pennsylvania	PA	8,907	C
La Roche College	PA	18,854	LC
La Salle Univ	PA	27,890	C
LaGrange College	GA	17,496	C
Lake Superior State Univ	MI	9,034	LC

School	ST	$IS	SR
Lamar Univ	TX	6,816	LC
Lander Univ	SC	8,618	LC
Langston Univ	OK	2,308	LC
Lenoir-Rhyne College	NC	19,186	C
Lester L. Cox College of Nursing and Health Sciences	MO	8,080	SP
Lewis Univ	IL	20,960	C
Lewis-Clark State College	ID	6,496	C
Liberty Univ	VA	14,500	C
Lincoln Memorial Univ	TN	12,620	LC
Lincoln Univ	MO	7,158	NC
LIU/Brooklyn Campus	NY	22,290	C
LIU/C.W. Post Campus	NY	25,380	C
Louisiana College	LA	11,516	C
Lourdes College	OH	13,100	LC
Loyola Univ New Orleans	LA	23,506	VC+
Loyola Univ of Chicago	IL	25,992	VC
Lubbock Christian Univ	TX	14,226	LC
Luther College	IA	23,300	VC+
Lynchburg College	VA	23,405	C
MacMurray College	IL	17,790	LC
Madonna Univ	MI	11,504	VC
Malone College	OH	19,190	C
Mansfield Univ	PA	9,648	C
Marian College	IN	21,020	C
Marian College of Fond du Lac	WI	17,935	LC
Marquette Univ	WI	24,836	C+
Marshall Univ	WV	7,752	LC
Martin Univ	IN	8,370	SP
Marymount Univ	VA	21,560	LC
Maryville College	TN	23,210	VC
Maryville Univ of St. Louis	MO	18,680	C
Marywood Univ	PA	24,639	C
McKendree College	IL	18,300	C+
McMurry Univ	TX	15,287	C
McNeese State Univ	LA	5,259	LC
MCP Hahnemann Univ	PA	18,510	SP
Mercy College	NY	15,875	LC
Mercy College of Health Sciences	IA	8,900	SP
Mesa State College	CO	8,051	C
Messiah College	PA	23,180	VC
Metropolitan State College of Denver	CO	2,338	LC
Metropolitan State Univ	MN	2,943	SP
Miami Univ	OH	12,885	VC+
Mich State Univ	MI	10,386	VC
MidAmerica Nazarene Univ	KS	16,960	C
Middle Tenn State Univ	TN	6,994	C
Midland Lutheran College	NE	18,600	C
Midway College	KY	15,815	C
Midwestern State Univ	TX	6,704	NC
Millersville Univ of Pennsylvania	PA	10,153	VC
Milligan College	TN	17,550	C
Millikin Univ	IL	24,415	C+
Milwaukee School of Engineering	WI	25,680	VC+
Minn State Univ, Mankato	MN	7,296	LC
Minot State Univ	ND	5,466	LC
Miss College	MS	14,574	C
Miss Univ for Women	MS	5,446	LC
Missouri Baptist College	MO	15,762	LC
Missouri Southern State College	MO	6,666	C
Missouri Western State College	MO	6,662	NC
Molloy College	NY	13,940	C
Monmouth Univ	NJ	24,042	C
Montana State Univ-Bozeman	MT	8,431	C
Montana State Univ-Northern	MT	8,600	NC
Moorhead State Univ	MN	7,000	LC
Moravian College	PA	27,065	VC
Morehead State Univ	KY	6,510	C
Morningside College	IA	19,124	C
Mount Aloysius College	PA	18,186	LC
Mount Marty College	SD	15,656	LC
Mount Mercy College	IA	19,390	VC
Mount St. Mary College	NY	18,825	C
Mount St. Mary's College	CA	24,430	C
Mountain State Univ	WV	8,180	NC
Murray State Univ	KY	6,672	C
National Univ	CA	7,755	SP
Nazareth College of Rochester	NY	22,036	VC
Nebr Methodist College of Nursing and Allied Health	NE	11,100	SP
Nebr Wesleyan Univ	NE	18,767	VC
Neumann College	PA	22,040	NC
New Jersey City Univ	NJ	9,100	LC
New Jersey Inst of Technology	NJ	14,690	VC
New Mexico State Univ	NM	7,302	C
New York Inst of Technology	NY	21,756	C
New York Univ	NY	35,200	MC
Newman Univ	KS	14,098	LC
Niagara Univ	NY	22,250	C+
Nicholls State Univ	LA	5,290	NC
Norfolk State Univ	VA	8,382	LC
N Car Agricultural and Technical State Univ	NC	6,659	LC

School	ST	$IS	SR
N Car Central Univ	NC	6,418	LC
North Central College	IL	22,944	C+
N Dak State Univ	ND	7,004	VC
North Georgia College and State Univ	GA	6,322	C+
North Park Univ	IL	24,030	C
Northeastern State Univ	OK	4,704	LC
Northeastern Univ	MA	30,078	VC
Northern Arizona Univ	AZ	7,398	C
Northern Illinois Univ	IL	9,545	C
Northern Kentucky Univ	KY	6,352	NC
Northern Mich Univ	MI	9,693	C
Northwest Nazarene Univ	ID	18,380	C
Northwestern Okla State Univ	OK	4,542	NC
Northwestern State Univ of Louisiana	LA	5,745	NC
Norwich Univ	VT	21,064	LC
Oakland Univ	MI	9,418	C
Oakwood College	AL	14,904	C
Ohio Univ	OH	11,769	C
Okla Baptist Univ	OK	13,878	VC
Okla City Univ	OK	15,810	C
Okla Panhandle State Univ	OK	3,812	NC
Old Dominion Univ	VA	9,386	C
Olivet Nazarene Univ	IL	18,444	C
Oral Roberts Univ	OK	18,490	C
Oregon State Univ	OR	9,612	VC
Otterbein College	OH	23,439	C
Our Lady of Holy Cross College	LA	5,140	NC
Pace Univ	NY	24,200	C
Pacific Lutheran Univ	WA	23,318	VC
Pacific Union College	CA	20,250	VC
Penn State Univ/Altoona	PA	12,578	C
Penn State Univ/Univ Park Campus	PA	11,126	VC
Pennsylvania College of Technology	PA	12,860	NC
Piedmont College	GA	16,900	C
Pittsburg State Univ	KS	6,228	NC
Point Loma Nazarene Univ	CA	21,380	VC
Pontifical Catholic Univ of PR/Ponce	PR	7,076	
Prairie View A&M Univ	TX	3,172	LC
Presentation College	SD	13,508	NC
Purdue Univ/Calumet	IN	6,630	NC
Purdue Univ/West Lafayette	IN	10,284	VC
Queens College	NC	17,250	C
Quincy Univ	IL	20,450	C
Quinnipiac Univ	CT	27,370	C
Radford Univ	VA	8,302	C
Ramapo College of New Jersey	NJ	13,550	VC
Regis College	MA	26,750	C
Regis Univ	CO	25,740	C+
Research College of Nursing	MO	20,310	SP
Rhode Island College	RI	8,700	LC
Richard Stockton College of New Jersey	NJ	12,165	VC
Rivier College	NH	24,215	C
Roberts Wesleyan College	NY	20,160	C+
Rockford College	IL	23,930	C
Rockhurst Univ	MO	20,090	C
Russell Sage College	NY	23,674	C+
Rutgers, The State Univ of New Jersey/ CamdenCampus	NJ	6,484	C
Sacred Heart Univ	CT	26,588	VC
Saginaw Valley State Univ	MI	9,465	C
St. Anselm College	NH	27,405	C
St. Francis Univ	PA	24,486	LC
St. John Fisher College	NY	21,800	C
St. John's Univ	MN	23,640	VC
St. John's Univ	NY	26,660	C
St. Joseph College	CT	25,960	LC
St. Joseph's College	IN	21,640	C
St. Joseph's College of Maine	ME	22,500	LC
St. Joseph's College, New York	NY	9,802	C
St. Louis Univ	MO	26,590	VC+
St. Mary's College	IN	24,474	VC
St. Mary's College of Calif	CA	27,575	C
St. Olaf College	MN	25,880	HC
St. Peter's College	NJ	22,292	LC
St. Xavier Univ	IL	21,104	C
Salem State College	MA	4,481	LC
Salisbury Univ	MD	10,576	VC
Salve Regina Univ	RI	26,460	C
Samford Univ	AL	16,340	VC
Samuel Merritt College	CA	22,073	SP
San Diego State Univ	CA	9,716	C+
San Francisco State Univ	CA	7,139	LC
San Jose State Univ	CA	8,187	C
Seattle Pacific Univ	WA	22,674	C+
Seattle Univ	WA	24,183	VC
Seton Hall Univ	NJ	26,910	LC
Seton Hill College	PA	21,875	C
Shawnee State Univ	OH	8,634	NC
Shenandoah Univ	VA	22,550	NC
Shepherd College	WV	7,062	LC
Simmons College	MA	30,418	VC
Slippery Rock Univ	PA	9,152	LC
Sonoma State Univ	CA	8,953	C

School	ST	$IS	SR
S Car State Univ	SC	6,586	LC
S Dak State Univ	SD	6,848	C
Southeast Missouri State Univ	MO	8,367	C+
Southeastern Louisiana Univ	LA	6,047	LC
Southern Adventist Univ	TN	15,600	C
Southern Conn State Univ	CT	10,310	C
Southern Illinois Univ Edwardsville	IL	7,869	LC
Southern Nazarene Univ	OK	14,634	NC
Southern Oregon Univ	OR	9,429	C
Southern Univ and A&M College	LA	6,365	C+
Southern Vermont College	VT	17,685	C
Southwest Baptist Univ	MO	13,426	LC
Southwest Missouri State Univ	MO	7,600	LC
Southwestern Adventist Univ	TX	14,798	C
Southwestern College	KS	17,656	C
Southwestern Okla State Univ	OK	4,801	C
Spalding Univ	KY	15,196	C
Spring Hill College	AL	23,250	C
SUNY/College at Brockport	NY	10,267	C
SUNY/College at Plattsburgh	NY	9,729	C
SUNY/Univ at Binghamton	NY	10,653	HC
SUNY/Univ at Buffalo	NY	11,033	VC
SUNY/Univ at Stony Brook	NY	10,998	VC
State Univ of West Georgia	GA	7,101	C
Stephen F. Austin State Univ	TX	6,905	C
Syracuse Univ	NY	30,710	HC
Tarleton State Univ	TX	7,160	C
Temple Univ	PA	14,124	C
Tenn State Univ	TN	7,058	VC
Tenn Tech Univ	TN	6,968	C
Tenn Wesleyan College	TN	13,030	C
Texas A&M Univ at Kingsville	TX	6,446	LC
Texas Christian Univ	TX	19,910	C
Texas Woman's Univ	TX	5,855	LC
Ohio State Univ	OH	10,819	VC
Thomas Edison State College	NJ	2,750	SP
Thomas More College	KY	17,700	LC
Thomas Univ	GA	8,770	NC
Towson Univ	MD	11,088	VC
Trinity Christian College	IL	19,415	C
Trinity College of Nursing	IL	4,300	SP
Troy State Univ	AL	7,696	C
Truman State Univ	MO	8,568	VC+
Tuskegee Univ	AL	14,600	LC
Union College	NE	14,650	C
Union Univ	TN	18,930	C+
Universidad Adventista de las Antillas	PR	6,675	
Universidad Metropolitana	PR	3,324	
Univ of Akron	OH	10,530	NC
Univ of Alabama	AL	7,402	C
Univ of Alabama at Birmingham	AL	10,110	C
Univ of Alabama at Huntsville	AL	7,916	VC
Univ of Alaska Anchorage	AK	9,100	NC
Univ of Arizona	AZ	8,614	C
Univ of Arkansas	AR	8,334	VC
Univ of Arkansas at Monticello	AR	5,940	NC
Univ of Arkansas at Pine Bluff	AR	7,925	C
Univ of Calif at Los Angeles	CA	13,227	MC
Univ of Central Arkansas	AR	6,388	C
Univ of Central Florida	FL	8,251	VC
Univ of Central Okla	OK	5,205	C
Univ of Charleston	WV	20,640	C
Univ of Cincinnati	OH	12,491	LC
Univ of Colo at Colo Springs	CO	9,403	C
Univ of Conn	CT	12,122	VC
Univ of Delaware	DE	10,824	VC
Univ of Detroit Mercy	MI	21,620	LC
Univ of Evansville	IN	22,865	VC+
Univ of Findlay	OH	23,962	NC
Univ of Florida	FL	7,874	HC
Univ of Hartford	CT	28,884	C
Univ of Hawaii at Hilo	HI	6,497	C
Univ of Hawaii at Manoa	HI	7,862	VC
Univ of Illinois at Chicago	IL	10,702	VC
Univ of Indianapolis	IN	20,840	C
Univ of Iowa	IA	8,607	C+
Univ of Kansas	KS	7,232	VC
Univ of Kentucky	KY	7,765	C
Univ of Louisiana at Lafayette	LA	5,200	C
Univ of Louisiana at Monroe	LA	5,207	NC
Univ of Louisville	KY	7,402	LC
Univ of Maine	ME	10,798	C
Univ of Maine at Fort Kent	ME	7,450	LC
Univ of Mary	ND	12,900	LC
Univ of Mary Hardin-Baylor	TX	13,929	C
Univ of Mass Amherst	MA	10,995	VC
Univ of Mass Boston	MA	4,227	C
Univ of Mass Dartmouth	MA	9,852	C

ST = STATE $IS = IN-STATE COSTS SR = SELECTOR RATING

School	ST	$IS	SR
Univ of Mass Lowell	MA	9,470	VC
Univ of Memphis	TN	7,271	C
Univ of Miami	FL	31,130	HC
Univ of Mich/Ann Arbor	MI	13,003	HC+
Univ of Mich/Flint	MI	4,323	C
Univ of Minn/Twin Cities	MN	11,123	VC
Univ of Missouri/Columbia	MO	9,803	HC
Univ of Missouri/Kansas City	MO	9,685	VC
Univ of Missouri/St. Louis	MO	9,966	C
Univ of Mobile	AL	13,620	LC
Univ of Nebr at Kearney	NE	7,048	NC
Univ of Nevada/Las Vegas	NV	8,281	VC
Univ of Nevada/Reno	NV	8,737	C
Univ of New England	ME	24,110	LC
Univ of New Hampshire	NH	13,207	C
Univ of New Mexico	NM	8,026	C
Univ of North Alabama	AL	7,016	NC
Univ of N Car at Chapel Hill	NC	8,789	HC
Univ of N Car at Charlotte	NC	7,254	C
Univ of N Car at Greensboro	NC	6,858	C
Univ of N Car at Wilmington	NC	7,769	C
Univ of N Dak	ND	7,067	VC
Univ of North Florida	FL	8,089	VC
Univ of Northern Colo	CO	8,082	C+
Univ of Pennsylvania	PA	34,614	MC
Univ of Phoenix	AZ	7,000	SP
Univ of Pittsburgh at Pittsburgh	PA	13,592	HC
Univ of Portland	OR	24,950	VC
Univ of PR at Humacao	PR	1,245	
Univ of PR/Arecibo	PR	1,095	
Univ of PR/Mayaguez	PR	5,285	
Univ of Rhode Island	RI	12,414	C
Univ of Rio Grande	OH	8,728	NC
Univ of Rochester	NY	32,979	HC
Univ of St. Francis	IL	19,650	C
Univ of St. Francis	IN	17,790	LC
Univ of San Diego	CA	29,198	HC
Univ of San Francisco	CA	27,302	VC
Univ of Scranton	PA	27,964	C+
Univ of South Alabama	AL	6,976	LC
Univ of S Car at Aiken	SC	7,828	LC
Univ of S Car at Columbia	SC	8,748	VC
Univ of S Car at Spartanburg	SC	7,318	C+
Univ of South Florida	FL	8,154	C
Univ of Southern Calif	CA	33,647	MC
Univ of Southern Colo	CO	7,821	LC
Univ of Southern Indiana	IN	8,655	LC
Univ of Southern Maine	ME	10,569	C
Univ of Southern Miss	MS	6,155	LC
Univ of Tampa	FL	22,612	C
Univ of Tenn at Chattanooga	TN	7,783	C
Univ of Tenn at Knoxville	TN	8,214	C
Univ of Tenn at Martin	TN	8,268	C
Univ of Texas at Arlington	TX	7,192	LC
Univ of Texas at Austin	TX	9,437	HC
Univ of Texas at El Paso	TX	5,076	LC
Univ of Texas-Pan American	TX	4,823	C
Univ of the District of Columbia	DC	2,844	NC
Univ of the Incarnate Word	TX	18,478	C
Univ of the Sacred Heart	PR	5,075	
Univ of Toledo	OH	11,206	NC
Univ of Tulsa	OK	19,090	HC
Univ of Utah	UT	7,703	C
Univ of Vermont	VT	14,761	C+
Univ of Virginia	VA	9,391	HC+
Univ of Virginia's College at Wise	VA	8,302	C
Univ of Washington	WA	10,361	VC
Univ of West Florida	FL	7,518	C
Univ of Wisc/Eau Claire	WI	7,032	VC
Univ of Wisc/Green Bay	WI	7,148	C
Univ of Wisc/Madison	WI	8,262	VC
Univ of Wisc/Milwaukee	WI	8,907	LC
Univ of Wisc/Oshkosh	WI	6,130	LC
Univ of Wisc/Stevens Point	WI	7,116	C
Univ of Wyoming	WY	7,143	LC
Ursuline College	OH	19,430	LC
Utica College of Syracuse Univ	NY	24,400	LC
Valdosta State Univ	GA	6,988	C
Valparaiso Univ	IN	23,570	VC+
Villa Julie College	MD	16,026	C
Villanova Univ	PA	31,997	HC
Virginia Commonwealth Univ	VA	9,030	C
Viterbo Univ	WI	18,043	C
Wagner College	NY	27,000	C
Walla Walla College	WA	20,925	C
Walsh Univ	OH	16,880	C
Washburn Univ of Topeka	KS	6,766	NC
Washington State Univ	WA	9,388	C
Wayne State Univ	MI	6,720	C
Waynesburg College	PA	17,610	LC
Weber State Univ	UT	6,897	NC
Webster Univ	MO	19,804	VC
West Chester Univ of Pennsylvania	PA	9,792	VC
West Liberty State College	WV	6,056	LC
West Suburban College of Nursing	IL	20,082	SP
West Texas A&M Univ	TX	6,538	C
West Virginia Univ	WV	8,304	C
West Virginia Univ Inst of Technology	WV	7,518	NC
West Virginia Wesleyan College	WV	22,920	C
Western Carolina Univ	NC	5,667	C
Western Conn State Univ	CT	10,074	C
Western Kentucky Univ	KY	6,834	C
Western Mich Univ	MI	10,016	C
Westminster College	UT	17,226	C
Wheeling Jesuit Univ	WV	22,660	C
Whitworth College	WA	23,938	VC
Wichita State Univ	KS	6,879	C
Widener Univ	PA	26,920	C
Wilkes Univ	PA	25,800	C
William Carey College	MS	10,150	LC
William Jewell College	MO	17,150	VC
William Paterson Univ of New Jersey	NJ	11,000	LC
Wilmington College	DE	6,530	NC
Winona State Univ	MN	8,570	C
Winston-Salem State Univ	NC	5,927	LC
Worcester State College	MA	7,901	LC
Wright State Univ	OH	9,141	LC
Xavier Univ	OH	23,880	C
York College of Pennsylvania	PA	12,550	VC
Youngstown State Univ	OH	9,318	NC

NURSING EDUCATION

School	ST	$IS	SR
Indiana Wesleyan Univ	IN	17,680	C

NUTRITION

School	ST	$IS	SR
Abilene Christian Univ	TX	16,300	VC
Alabama A&M Univ	AL	5,100	LC
Alcorn State Univ	MS	5,594	LC
Andrews Univ	MI	17,696	LC
Appalachian State Univ	NC	6,353	C
Auburn Univ	AL	5,510	C
Baylor Univ	TX	18,298	VC+
Benedictine Univ	IL	21,330	C
Bluffton College	OH	20,644	C
Boston Univ	MA	34,358	MC
Bowling Green State Univ	OH	10,794	C
Bridgewater College	VA	22,950	C
Brigham Young Univ	UT	7,840	HC
Cal State, Chico	CA	8,598	LC
Case Western Reserve Univ	OH	27,418	C
CUNY/Hunter College	NY	5,147	C+
College of St. Benedict	MN	23,921	VC
College of St. Catherine	MN	22,324	VC
College of St. Elizabeth	NJ	22,510	C
Colo State Univ	CO	9,672	C
Cornell Univ	NY	34,614	MC
Dominican Univ	IL	20,800	C
Drexel Univ	PA	27,657	VC
East Carolina Univ	NC	7,766	C
Edinboro Univ of Pennsylvania	PA	9,328	LC
Florida State Univ	FL	7,835	HC
Fort Valley State Univ	GA	6,011	LC
Framingham State College	MA	7,259	C
Georgia Southern Univ	GA	6,958	C
Georgia State Univ	GA	7,792	LC
Hampshire College	MA	33,881	HC+
Indiana Univ Bloomington	IN	10,712	C+
Iowa State Univ	IA	8,108	VC
Kansas State Univ	KS	6,995	C
Kent State Univ	OH	11,104	C
La Salle Univ	PA	27,890	C
Langston Univ	OK	2,308	LC
LIU/C.W. Post Campus	NY	25,380	C
Louisiana State Univ and A&M College	LA	8,014	VC
Madonna Univ	MI	11,504	VC
Marygrove College	MI	16,075	C
Meredith College	NC	17,500	C
Mich State Univ	MI	10,386	VC
Middle Tenn State Univ	TN	6,994	C
New Mexico State Univ	NM	7,302	C
New York Inst of Technology	NY	21,756	C
New York Univ	NY	35,200	MC
Norfolk State Univ	VA	8,382	LC
N Car Central Univ	NC	6,418	LC
N Dak State Univ	ND	7,004	VC
Ohio Univ	OH	11,769	C
Okla State Univ	OK	7,650	VC
Oregon State Univ	OR	9,612	VC
Penn State Univ/Univ Park Campus	PA	11,126	VC
Pepperdine Univ	CA	32,830	VC
Purdue Univ/West Lafayette	IN	10,284	VC
Radford Univ	VA	8,302	C
Rochester Inst of Technology	NY	26,232	VC+
Russell Sage College	NY	23,674	C+
Rutgers, The State Univ of New Jersey New Brunswick Campus	NJ	12,709	C
St. John's Univ	MN	23,640	VC
St. Louis Univ	MO	26,590	VC+
Samford Univ	AL	16,340	VC
San Diego State Univ	CA	9,716	C+
Simmons College	MA	30,418	VC
S Car State Univ	SC	6,586	LC
S Dak State Univ	SD	6,848	C
Southwest Missouri State Univ	MO	7,600	LC
Southwest Texas State Univ	TX	8,730	VC
Stephen F. Austin State Univ	TX	6,905	C
Syracuse Univ	NY	30,710	HC
Texas Christian Univ	TX	19,910	C
Texas Southern Univ	TX	6,576	NC
Univ of Arizona	AZ	8,614	C
Univ of Arkansas	AR	8,334	VC
Univ of Calif at Berkeley	CA	14,134	MC
Univ of Calif at Davis	CA	12,796	VC
Univ of Central Okla	OK	5,205	C
Univ of Conn	CT	12,122	VC
Univ of Dayton	OH	20,400	VC
Univ of Delaware	DE	10,824	VC
Univ of Georgia	GA	8,656	VC
Univ of Houston	TX	8,410	C
Univ of Illinois at Chicago	IL	10,702	VC
Univ of Maine	ME	10,798	C
Univ of Maryland/College Park	MD	11,959	C
Univ of Mass Amherst	MA	10,995	VC
Univ of Mich/Ann Arbor	MI	13,003	HC+
Univ of Minn/Twin Cities	MN	11,123	VC
Univ of Nevada/Reno	NV	8,737	C
Univ of New Hampshire	NH	13,207	C
Univ of New Mexico	NM	8,026	C
Univ of N Dak	ND	7,067	VC
Univ of Northern Iowa	IA	7,850	C
Univ of Pittsburgh at Pittsburgh	PA	13,592	HC
Univ of Rhode Island	RI	12,414	C
Univ of Tenn at Knoxville	TN	8,214	C
Univ of Texas at Austin	TX	9,437	HC
Univ of the Incarnate Word	TX	18,478	C
Univ of Vermont	VT	14,761	C+
Univ of Wisc/Green Bay	WI	7,148	C
Univ of Wisc/Madison	WI	8,262	VC
Viterbo Univ	WI	18,043	C
West Virginia Univ	WV	8,304	C
West Virginia Wesleyan College	WV	22,920	C
Western Carolina Univ	NC	5,667	C
Youngstown State Univ	OH	9,318	NC

NUTRITION EDUCATION

School	ST	$IS	SR
Indiana Univ of Pennsylvania	PA	9,133	C
Thomas Edison State College	NJ	2,750	SP
Univ of Cincinnati	OH	12,491	LC
Univ of Vermont	VT	14,761	C+

OCCUPATIONAL SAFETY AND HEALTH

School	ST	$IS	SR
Central Missouri State Univ	MO	7,920	C
Howard Payne Univ	TX	13,834	C+
Indiana Univ Bloomington	IN	10,712	C+
Keene State College	NH	11,280	C
Madonna Univ	MI	11,504	VC
Millersville Univ of Pennsylvania	PA	10,153	VC
Montana Tech of The Univ of Montana	MT	7,845	C
Murray State Univ	KY	6,672	C
N Car Agricultural and Technical State Univ	NC	6,659	LC
Southeastern Okla State Univ	OK	4,917	C
Southwest Baptist Univ	MO	13,426	LC
Univ of Findlay	OH	23,962	NC
Univ of New Haven	CT	23,860	LC
Univ of N Dak	ND	7,067	VC

OCCUPATIONAL THERAPY

School	ST	$IS	SR
Alvernia College	PA	20,790	C
American International College	MA	22,268	LC
Augustana College	IL	24,117	VC+
Baker College of Flint	MI	7,720	NC
Barry Univ	FL	24,100	LC
Bay Path College	MA	22,308	C
Boston Univ	MA	34,358	MC
Brenau Univ Women's College	GA	20,100	C
Cal State, Dominguez Hills	CA	5,840	LC
Chicago State Univ	IL	8,851	C+
CUNY/York College	NY	3,292	NC
Cleveland State Univ	OH	10,146	NC
College Misericordia	PA	23,380	LC
College of St. Benedict	MN	23,921	VC
College of St. Catherine	MN	22,324	VC
College of St. Mary	NE	18,726	C
Colo State Univ	CO	9,672	C
Concordia Univ Wisc	WI	16,600	LC
Dominican College	NY	20,400	LC
Dominican Univ of Calif	CA	27,948	C
Duquesne Univ	PA	24,242	C+
D'Youville College	NY	18,704	C
East Carolina Univ	NC	7,766	C
Eastern Kentucky Univ	KY	6,552	C
Eastern Mich Univ	MI	9,855	C
Elizabethtown College	PA	26,000	VC
Florida A&M Univ	FL	6,948	C
Florida International Univ	FL	9,486	VC
Howard Univ	DC	15,522	LC
Indiana Univ-Purdue Univ Indianapolis	IN	9,473	C
Ithaca College	NY	28,719	HC
Kean Univ	NJ	11,159	C
Keuka College	NY	21,170	C
Lamar Univ	TX	6,816	LC
Lebanon Valley College of Pennsylvania	PA	25,700	VC
Lenoir-Rhyne College	NC	19,186	C
LIU/Brooklyn Campus	NY	22,290	C
Mount Aloysius College	PA	18,186	LC
Mount Mary College	WI	18,024	C
New York Inst of Technology	NY	21,756	C
Newman Univ	KS	14,098	LC
North Park Univ	IL	24,030	C
Quinnipiac Univ	CT	27,370	C
Russell Sage College	NY	23,674	C+
Saginaw Valley State Univ	MI	9,465	C
St. Francis Univ	PA	24,486	LC
St. John's Univ	MN	23,640	VC
St. Louis Univ	MO	26,590	VC+
St. Vincent College	PA	22,942	VC
San Jose State Univ	CA	8,187	C
Shawnee State Univ	OH	8,634	NC
Spalding Univ	KY	15,196	C
SUNY/Univ at Buffalo	NY	11,033	VC
Temple Univ	PA	14,124	C
Tenn State Univ	TN	7,058	VC
Texas Woman's Univ	TX	5,855	LC
Ohio State Univ	OH	10,819	VC
Touro College	NY	14,950	VC
Towson Univ	MD	11,088	VC
Tuskegee Univ	AL	14,600	LC
Univ of Central Arkansas	AR	6,388	C
Univ of Findlay	OH	23,962	NC
Univ of Florida	FL	7,874	HC
Univ of Hartford	CT	28,884	C
Univ of Illinois at Chicago	IL	10,702	VC
Univ of Louisiana at Monroe	LA	5,207	NC
Univ of Mary	ND	12,900	LC
Univ of Minn/Twin Cities	MN	11,123	VC
Univ of Missouri/Columbia	MO	9,803	HC
Univ of New England	ME	24,110	LC
Univ of New Hampshire	NH	13,207	C
Univ of New Mexico	NM	8,026	C
Univ of N Dak	ND	7,067	VC
Univ of Pittsburgh at Pittsburgh	PA	13,592	HC
Univ of Puget Sound	WA	28,285	HC
Univ of Scranton	PA	27,964	C+
Univ of Southern Calif	CA	33,647	MC
Univ of Southern Colo	CO	7,821	LC
Univ of Southern Indiana	IN	8,655	LC
Univ of Tenn at Chattanooga	TN	7,783	C
Univ of Texas at San Antonio	TX	9,088	NC
Univ of Texas-Pan American	TX	4,823	C
Univ of the Sciences in Philadelphia	PA	24,826	VC
Univ of Utah	UT	7,703	C
Univ of Wisc/La Crosse	WI	7,250	VC
Univ of Wisc/Madison	WI	8,262	VC
Univ of Wisc/Milwaukee	WI	8,907	LC
Utica College of Syracuse Univ	NY	24,400	LC
Virginia Commonwealth Univ	VA	9,030	C
Wartburg College	IA	21,165	VC
Wayne State Univ	MI	6,720	C
West Virginia Univ	WV	8,304	C
Western Mich Univ	MI	10,016	C
Worcester State College	MA	7,901	LC
Xavier Univ	OH	23,880	C

OCEAN ENGINEERING

School	ST	$IS	SR
Florida Atlantic Univ	FL	8,832	C
Florida Inst of Technology	FL	25,250	VC
Mass Inst of Technology	MA	35,228	MC
Purdue Univ/West Lafayette	IN	10,284	VC
Texas A&M Univ at Galveston	TX	7,269	C+
United States Naval Academy	MD		MC
Univ of Rhode Island	RI	12,414	C
Univ of Washington	WA	10,361	VC
Virginia Polytechnic Inst and State Univ	VA	7,652	C

OCEANOGRAPHY

School	ST	$IS	SR
Florida Inst of Technology	FL	25,250	VC
Hawaii Pacific Univ	HI	17,790	C
Humboldt State Univ	CA	8,582	C
Johns Hopkins Univ	MD	35,226	MC
Maine Maritime Academy	ME	10,911	C
Millersville Univ of Pennsylvania	PA	10,153	VC
Nova Southeastern Univ	FL	20,104	LC
SUNY/Univ at Stony Brook	NY	10,998	VC
Texas A&M Univ at Galveston	TX	7,269	C+
United States Naval Academy	MD		MC
Univ of Mich/Ann Arbor	MI	13,003	HC+
Univ of San Diego	CA	29,198	HC
Univ of Washington	WA	10,361	VC

OFFICE SUPERVISION AND MANAGEMENT

School	ST	$IS	SR
Adams State College	CO	7,468	C
Alabama A&M Univ	AL	5,100	LC
Albany State Univ	GA	5,764	C+
Alcorn State Univ	MS	5,594	LC
Arkansas Tech Univ	AR	6,256	C
Baker College of Flint	MI	7,720	NC
Campbellsville Univ	KY	14,340	C
Central Conn State Univ	CT	10,404	C
College of St. Elizabeth	NJ	22,510	C
Concord College	WV	7,122	C+
Concordia College/Moorhead	MN	18,835	C
Cumberland College	KY	14,864	C
David N. Myers College	OH	9,475	C
East Central Univ	OK	4,578	C
Eastern Mich Univ	MI	9,855	C
Fayetteville State Univ	NC	5,590	LC
Fort Hays State Univ	KS	6,294	LC
Fort Valley State Univ	GA	6,014	LC
Georgia College and State Univ	GA	7,344	C
Gwynedd-Mercy College	PA	22,350	C
Indiana State Univ	IN	8,461	LC
Indiana Univ-Purdue Univ Indianapolis	IN	9,473	C
Jackson State Univ	MS	6,776	LC
John Brown Univ	AR	15,080	VC
Johnson and Wales Univ	RI	21,558	LC
Lincoln Univ	MO	7,158	NC
Mayville State Univ	ND	6,440	NC
Middle Tenn State Univ	TN	6,994	C
Miss Valley State Univ	MS	6,345	C
Mount Vernon Nazarene College	OH	17,027	C
Northwestern Okla State Univ	OK	4,542	NC
Philander Smith College	AR	7,380	NC
Purdue Univ/West Lafayette	IN	10,284	VC
St. John's Univ	NY	26,660	C
S Car State Univ	SC	6,586	LC
Southeast Missouri State Univ	MO	8,367	C+
Southern Nazarene Univ	OK	14,634	NC
Southwest State Univ	MN	7,117	LC
Southwestern Adventist Univ	TX	14,798	C
Stephen F. Austin State Univ	TX	6,905	C
Sul Ross State Univ	TX	6,582	LC
Tabor College	KS	17,600	LC
Tarleton State Univ	TX	7,160	C
Thomas Edison State College	NJ	2,750	SP
Universidad Adventista de las Antillas	PR	6,675	
Univ of Houston-Downtown	TX	2,006	NC
Univ of Idaho	ID	7,026	C
Univ of PR/Rio Piedras	PR	5,510	
Univ of S Car at Columbia	SC	8,748	VC
Univ of Tenn at Martin	TN	8,268	C
Univ of the District of Columbia	DC	2,844	NC
Univ of Wisc/Whitewater	WI	6,937	C
Valley City State Univ	ND		LC
Wiley College	TX	8,100	LC
Youngstown State Univ	OH	9,318	NC

OPERA

School	ST	$IS	SR
Boston Conservatory	MA	26,900	SP

OPERATIONS RESEARCH

School	ST	$IS	SR
Boston College	MA	33,330	MC
Boston Univ	MA	34,358	MC
Calif State Polytechnic Univ, Pomona	CA	8,615	C
CUNY/Baruch College	NY	3,275	VC+
Columbia Univ/Fu Foundation School of Engineering and Applied Science	NY	35,190	MC
Cornell Univ	NY	34,614	MC
Miami Univ	OH	12,885	VC+
New York Univ	NY	35,200	MC
Seattle Univ	WA	24,183	VC
United States Air Force Academy	CO		MC
United States Coast Guard Academy	CT		MC
United States Military Academy	NY		MC
Univ of Houston	TX	8,410	C
Univ of Maryland/College Park	MD	11,959	C
Univ of North Texas	TX	7,629	C
Univ of Scranton	PA	27,964	C+

OPHTHALMIC TECHNOLOGY

School	ST	$IS	SR
Alderson-Broaddus College	WV	19,640	C

OPTICAL ENGINEERING

School	ST	$IS	SR
Univ of Alabama at Huntsville	AL	7,916	VC
Univ of Arizona	AZ	8,614	C

OPTICS

School	ST	$IS	SR
Capitol College	MD	18,462	LC
Rose-Hulman Inst of Technology	IN	27,707	HC+
Saginaw Valley State Univ	MI	9,465	C
Univ of Rochester	NY	32,979	HC

OPTOMETRY

School	ST	$IS	SR
Baylor Univ	TX	18,298	VC+
Indiana Univ Bloomington	IN	10,712	C+
Oral Roberts Univ	OK	18,490	C
Purdue Univ/Calumet	IN	6,630	NC
Univ of Calif at Berkeley	CA	14,134	MC
Univ of Houston	TX	8,410	C

ORGANIZATIONAL BEHAVIOR

School	ST	$IS	SR
Benedictine Univ	IL	21,330	C
Boston Univ	MA	34,358	MC
Calif Baptist Univ	CA	16,736	C
Carroll College	WI	21,170	C
Central Missouri State Univ	MO	7,920	C
Chapman Univ	CA	30,218	VC
Concordia Univ	MN	19,912	C
Franklin Univ	OH	6,324	SP
Huntington College	IN	15,480	LC
Huron Univ	SD	10,450	C
Ithaca College	NY	28,719	HC
La Salle Univ	PA	27,890	C
Loyola Univ New Orleans	LA	23,506	VC+
Manhattanville College	NY	28,730	VC
Maryville Univ of St. Louis	MO	18,680	C
Methodist College	NC	19,526	C
Miami Univ	OH	12,885	VC+
Middle Tenn State Univ	TN	6,994	C
Mountain State Univ	WV	8,180	NC
National Univ	CA	7,755	SP
Northern Kentucky Univ	KY	6,352	NC
Oral Roberts Univ	OK	18,490	C
Pitzer College	CA	33,930	HC
Rider Univ	NJ	27,400	C
St. Louis Univ	MO	26,590	VC+
Santa Clara Univ	CA	28,371	VC+
Southern Methodist Univ	TX	28,349	VC
Univ of Calif at Davis	CA	12,796	VC
Univ of North Texas	TX	7,629	C
Univ of San Francisco	CA	27,302	VC
Wilmington College	OH	21,826	C
Xavier Univ	OH	23,880	C

PACIFIC AREA STUDIES

School	ST	$IS	SR
Brigham Young Univ/Hawaii	HI	6,890	C
Hawaii Pacific Univ	HI	17,790	C

PAINTING

School	ST	$IS	SR
Andrews Univ	MI	17,696	LC
Aquinas College	MI	20,052	C+
Arizona State Univ-Main	AZ	7,726	C
Art Inst of Southern Calif	CA	14,500	SP
Atlanta College of Art	GA	18,600	SP
Bard College	NY	33,912	HC
Barton College	NC	16,834	LC
Birmingham-Southern College	AL	22,960	C
Boston Univ	MA	34,358	MC
Calif College of Arts and Crafts	CA	27,366	SP
Catholic Univ of America	DC	29,332	VC
Cleveland Inst of Art	OH	22,680	SP
College For Creative Studies	MI	20,938	SP
College of Visual Arts	MN	12,185	SP
Edinboro Univ of Pennsylvania	PA	9,328	LC
Escuela de Artes Plasticas de PR	PR	1,874	
Harding Univ	AR	13,528	VC
Indiana Univ-Purdue Univ Indianapolis	IN	9,473	C
Kansas City Art Inst	MO	25,880	SP
Lewis Univ	IL	20,960	C
Maine College of Art	ME	26,367	SP
Maryland Inst College of Art	MD	27,720	SP
Mass College of Art	MA	13,703	SP
McMurry Univ	TX	15,287	C
Milwaukee Inst of Art and Design	WI	24,388	SP
Minneapolis College of Art and Design	MN	23,560	SP
Montserrat College of Art	MA	20,335	SP
Moore College of Art and Design	PA	23,125	SP
Northern Mich Univ	MI	9,693	C
Northwest Nazarene Univ	ID	18,380	C
Ohio Univ	OH	11,769	C
Pacific Northwest College of Art	OR	16,507	SP
Rhode Island School of Design	RI	30,227	SP
Rochester Inst of Technology	NY	26,232	VC+
San Francisco Art Inst	CA	19,300	SP
Savannah College of Art and Design	GA	25,075	SP
School of the Art Inst of Chicago	IL	27,800	SP
Shepherd College	WV	7,062	LC
Simon's Rock College of Bard	MA	32,450	HC
SUNY/College at Buffalo	NY	8,025	C
Syracuse Univ	NY	30,710	HC
Univ of Dallas	TX	22,128	VC+
Univ of Hartford	CT	28,884	C
Univ of Houston	TX	8,410	C
Univ of Illinois at Urbana-Champaign	IL	11,316	HC+
Univ of Kansas	KS	7,232	VC
Univ of Mass Dartmouth	MA	9,852	C
Univ of Miami	FL	31,130	HC
Univ of Mich/Ann Arbor	MI	13,003	HC+
Univ of North Texas	TX	7,629	C
Univ of Oregon	OR	9,969	C
Univ of PR/Rio Piedras	PR	5,510	
Univ of San Francisco	CA	27,302	VC
Univ of the Arts	PA	24,230	SP
Univ of Washington	WA	10,361	VC
Washington Univ in St. Louis	MO	34,593	MC
Western Mich Univ	MI	10,016	C
Youngstown State Univ	OH	9,318	NC

PALEONTOLOGY

School	ST	$IS	SR
Univ of Calif at Los Angeles	CA	13,227	MC

PAPER AND PULP SCIENCE

School	ST	$IS	SR
Miami Univ	OH	12,885	VC+
N Car State Univ	NC	8,680	HC
SUNY/College of Environmental Science and Forestry	NY	12,446	VC
Univ of Maine	ME	10,798	C
Univ of Washington	WA	10,361	VC
Univ of Wisc/Stevens Point	WI	7,116	C
Western Mich Univ	MI	10,016	C

PAPER ENGINEERING

School	ST	$IS	SR
SUNY/College of Environmental Science and Forestry	NY	12,446	VC
Western Mich Univ	MI	10,016	C

PARALEGAL STUDIES

School	ST	$IS	SR
Anna Maria College	MA	22,800	LC
Avila College	MO	17,720	C
Ball State Univ	IN	8,660	C
Bentley College	MA	31,060	HC
Brenau Univ Women's College	GA	20,100	C
Champlain College	VT	19,680	C
College of Mount St. Joseph	OH	20,290	C
College of Our Lady of the Elms	MA	20,644	C
College of St. Mary	NE	18,726	C
Concordia Univ Wisc	WI	16,600	LC
Davenport Univ	MI	10,057	NC
David N. Myers College	OH	9,475	C
East Central Univ	OK	4,578	C
Eastern Kentucky Univ	KY	6,552	C
Eastern Mich Univ	MI	9,855	C
Gannon Univ	PA	18,848	C
Hamline Univ	MN	23,339	C+
Hilbert College	NY	16,830	LC
Humphreys College	CA	6,900	NC
Husson College	ME	15,360	LC
International College	FL	7,230	NC
Johnson and Wales Univ	RI	21,558	LC
Lake Erie College	OH	21,350	LC
Lake Superior State Univ	MI	9,034	LC
Lasell College	MA	24,100	C
Marymount Univ	VA	21,560	LC
Maryville Univ of St. Louis	MO	18,680	C
Marywood Univ	PA	24,639	C
Mercy College	NY	15,875	LC
Miss College	MS	14,574	C
Miss Univ for Women	MS	5,446	LC
Moorhead State Univ	MN	7,000	LC
Morehead State Univ	KY	6,510	C
Morris Brown College	GA	15,993	LC
National American Univ	SD	13,680	NC
Nebr Wesleyan Univ	NE	18,767	VC
Newbury College	MA	21,490	C
Nova Southeastern Univ	FL	20,104	LC
Peirce College	PA	10,650	C
Pennsylvania College of Technology	PA	12,860	NC
Point Park College	PA	20,290	C
Quinnipiac Univ	CT	27,370	C
Rivier College	NH	24,215	C
Roger Williams Univ	RI	29,010	C
St. John's Univ	NY	26,660	C
Southern Illinois Univ at Carbondale	IL	8,621	C
Suffolk Univ	MA	26,516	C
Texas Wesleyan Univ	TX	14,710	C
Univ of Detroit Mercy	MI	21,620	LC
Univ of Evansville	IN	22,865	VC+
Univ of Great Falls	MT	15,360	C
Univ of La Verne	CA	24,280	C
Univ of Louisville	KY	7,402	LC
Univ of Maryland/Univ College	MD	5,910	SP
Univ of Pittsburgh at Pittsburgh	PA	13,592	HC
Univ of Tenn at Chattanooga	TN	7,783	C
Valdosta State Univ	GA	6,988	C
Villa Julie College	MD	16,026	C
Virginia Intermont College	VA	17,510	C
Wesley College	DE	17,869	C
Western Conn State Univ	CT	10,074	C
William Woods Univ	MO	19,390	LC
Winona State Univ	MN	8,570	C
Woodbury College	VT	12,060	LC

PARKS AND RECREATION MANAGEMENT

School	ST	$IS	SR
Arkansas Tech Univ	AR	6,256	C
Auburn Univ	AL	5,510	C
Aurora Univ	IL	18,551	C
Ball State Univ	IN	8,660	C
Bemidji State Univ	MN	7,957	C
Bethany College	KS	16,602	C+
Bowling Green State Univ	OH	10,794	C
Cal State, Chico	CA	8,598	LC
Cal State, Sacramento	CA	7,488	C
Calif Univ of Pennsylvania	PA	10,388	C
Central Mich Univ	MI	8,355	C
Central Washington Univ	WA	8,985	LC
Cheyney Univ of Pennsylvania	PA	9,993	C
Christopher Newport Univ	VA	8,862	VC
Clemson Univ	SC	7,600	C
Columbus State Univ	GA	7,228	LC
Concord College	WV	7,122	C+
Delaware State Univ	DE	8,104	LC
East Carolina Univ	NC	7,766	C
East Stroudsburg Univ of Pennsylvania	PA	8,430	LC
Eastern Mich Univ	MI	9,855	C
Eastern Washington Univ	WA	7,972	LC
Evangel Univ	MO	14,050	C
Florida International Univ	FL	9,486	VC
Gallaudet Univ	DC	16,554	SP
Guilford College	NC	23,255	C
Humboldt State Univ	CA	8,582	C
Huntington College	IN	15,480	LC
Illinois State Univ	IL	9,235	C
Indiana Inst of Technology	IN	18,806	C
Indiana State Univ	IN	8,461	LC
Indiana Univ Bloomington	IN	10,712	C+
Johnson and Wales Univ	RI	21,558	LC
Kansas State Univ	KS	6,995	C
Lake Superior State Univ	MI	9,034	LC
Marshall Univ	WV	7,752	LC
Midland Lutheran College	NE	18,600	C
Minn State Univ, Mankato	MN	7,296	LC
Missouri Western State College	MO	6,662	NC
Montclair State Univ	NJ	10,287	LC
Murray State Univ	KY	6,672	C
N Car State Univ	NC	8,680	HC
Northern Arizona Univ	AZ	7,398	C
Northern Mich Univ	MI	9,693	C
Northland College	WI	21,435	C+
Ohio Univ	OH	11,769	C
Penn State Univ/Univ Park Campus	PA	11,126	VC
Rice Univ	TX	24,325	MC
San Diego State Univ	CA	9,716	C+

School	ST	$IS	SR
Shorter College	GA	15,185	C
Slippery Rock Univ	PA	9,152	LC
S Dak State Univ	SD	6,848	C
Southeast Missouri State Univ	MO	8,367	C+
Southern Illinois Univ at Carbondale	IL	8,621	C
Southwest Missouri State Univ	MO	7,600	LC
Springfield College	MA	24,520	C
State Univ of West Georgia	GA	7,101	C
Stephen F. Austin State Univ	TX	6,905	C
Temple Univ	PA	14,124	C
Texas A&M Univ	TX	8,988	VC
Texas Tech Univ	TX	8,825	C
Unity College	ME	19,845	LC
Univ of Arkansas at Pine Bluff	AR	7,925	C
Univ of Delaware	DE	10,824	VC
Univ of Idaho	ID	7,026	C
Univ of Iowa	IA	8,607	C+
Univ of Maine	ME	10,798	C
Univ of Mary Hardin-Baylor	TX	13,929	C
Univ of Missouri/Columbia	MO	9,803	HC
Univ of Nebr at Lincoln	NE	8,325	C+
Univ of New Mexico	NM	8,026	C
Univ of N Car at Greensboro	NC	6,858	C
Univ of N Car at Pembroke	NC	5,914	LC
Univ of N Car at Wilmington	NC	7,769	C
Univ of Southern Miss	MS	6,155	LC
Univ of Tenn at Martin	TN	8,268	C
Univ of Utah	UT	7,703	C
Univ of Vermont	VT	14,761	C+
Univ of Wisc/La Crosse	WI	7,250	VC
Univ of Wyoming	WY	7,143	LC
Utah State Univ	UT	6,771	C
Virginia Wesleyan College	VA	22,350	LC
Wayne State College	NE	6,255	NC
Wayne State Univ	MI	6,720	C
West Virginia Univ	WV	8,304	C
Western Carolina Univ	NC	5,667	C
Western Illinois Univ	IL	9,571	C
Western Kentucky Univ	KY	6,834	C
Western Washington Univ	WA	8,624	VC
Wingate Univ	NC	19,140	C
Winona State Univ	MN	8,570	C
York College of Pennsylvania	PA	12,550	VC

PASTORAL STUDIES

School	ST	$IS	SR
Andrews Univ	MI	17,696	LC
Bartlesville Wesleyan College	OK	14,100	LC
Brescia Univ	KY	14,225	C
Cedarville Univ	OH	17,553	VC
Clearwater Christian College	FL	13,160	LC
College of Mount St. Joseph	OH	20,290	C
College of St. Benedict	MN	23,921	VC
Concordia Univ Wisc	WI	16,600	LC
Dallas Baptist Univ	TX	13,682	LC
Grace Bible College	MI	12,600	C
Greenville College	IL	19,226	LC
John Brown Univ	AR	15,080	VC
Madonna Univ	MI	11,504	VC
Marian College	IN	21,020	C
Morris College	SC	9,995	LC
Newman Univ	KS	14,098	LC
North Central Univ	MN	12,744	LC
Northwestern College	MN	19,816	C+
Nyack College	NY	18,540	C
St. John's Univ	MN	23,640	VC
St. Mary College	KS	17,298	C
Simpson College	CA	19,200	C
Southeastern College	FL	11,648	LC
Southwestern College	KS	17,656	C
Spalding Univ	KY	15,196	C
Tenn Wesleyan College	TN	13,030	C
Toccoa Falls College	GA	14,220	C
Union College	NE	14,650	C
Union Univ	TN	18,930	C+
Universidad Adventista de las Antillas	PR	6,675	
Univ of St. Thomas	TX	18,752	VC
Walsh Univ	OH	16,880	C
William Tyndale College	MI	11,150	C

PEACE STUDIES

School	ST	$IS	SR
Bethel College	KS	17,355	C+
Chapman Univ	CA	30,218	VC
Colgate Univ	NY	33,480	MC
College of St. Benedict	MN	23,921	VC
College of St. Elizabeth	NJ	22,510	C
College of the Holy Cross	MA	32,780	MC
DePauw Univ	IN	28,000	HC
Eastern Mennonite Univ	VA	20,700	VC
Fordham Univ	NY	30,710	VC
Goshen College	IN	18,950	VC+
Guilford College	NC	23,255	C
Hampshire College	MA	33,881	HC+
Juniata College	PA	26,080	VC
Kent State Univ	OH	11,104	C
Manchester College	IN	22,010	C
Manhattan College	NY	25,500	VC
Molloy College	NY	13,940	C
Northland College	WI	21,435	C+
Norwich Univ	VT	21,064	LC
Prescott College	AZ	13,430	C
Quincy Univ	IL	20,450	C
St. John's Univ	MN	23,640	VC
Salisbury Univ	MD	10,576	VC
San Diego State Univ	CA	9,716	C+
Syracuse Univ	NY	30,710	HC
Tufts Univ	MA	34,874	MC
Univ of Calif at Berkeley	CA	14,134	MC
Univ of N Car at Chapel Hill	NC	8,789	HC
Univ of St. Thomas	MN	24,044	VC
Univ of Washington	WA	10,361	VC
Villanova Univ	PA	31,997	HC
Wayne State Univ	MI	6,720	C
Wellesley College	MA	33,394	MC
Whitworth College	WA	23,938	VC

PERCUSSION

School	ST	$IS	SR
Drake Univ	IA	22,830	VC
Juilliard School	NY	28,200	SP
Northwestern Univ	IL	33,615	MC
Roosevelt Univ	IL	20,240	LC
Temple Univ	PA	14,124	C
Univ of Miami	FL	31,130	HC
Univ of Mich/Ann Arbor	MI	13,003	HC+
Youngstown State Univ	OH	9,318	NC

PERFORMING ARTS

School	ST	$IS	SR
Adelphi Univ	NY	23,320	VC
Alfred Univ	NY	27,212	C+
American Univ	DC	31,544	VC+
Bay Path College	MA	22,308	C
Baylor Univ	TX	18,298	VC+
Brandeis Univ	MA	34,481	MC
Brown Univ	RI	34,973	MC
Butler Univ	IN	25,580	VC+
Carroll College	MT	19,140	C
Carthage College	WI	23,670	C
Christopher Newport Univ	VA	8,862	VC
Colby College	ME	34,290	MC
College of the Ozarks	MO	2,650	C+
Colo State Univ	CO	9,672	C
Columbia College	SC	19,050	LC
De Sales Univ	PA	22,610	VC
Dominican Univ	IL	20,800	C
Drake Univ	IA	22,830	VC
Eastern Kentucky Univ	KY	6,552	C
Eastern Mich Univ	MI	9,855	C
Edgewood College	WI	18,304	C
Emerson College	MA	29,978	HC
Fontbonne Univ	MO	18,046	C
Fordham Univ	NY	30,710	VC
Franklin Pierce College	NH	26,125	LC
Hampshire College	MA	33,881	HC+
Ithaca College	NY	28,719	HC
Johns Hopkins Univ	MD	35,226	MC
Johnson State College	VT	10,776	C
Lindenwood Univ	MO	17,250	C
Mars Hill College	NC	18,600	LC
Marywood Univ	PA	24,039	C
Naropa Univ	CO	22,416	SP
N Car School of the Arts	NC	7,797	SP
Northeastern Univ	MA	30,078	VC
Northern Kentucky Univ	KY	6,352	NC
Northwestern Univ	IL	33,615	MC
Oakland Univ	MI	9,418	C
Plymouth State College	NH	11,024	LC
Roosevelt Univ	IL	20,240	LC
St. Mary's College of Calif	CA	27,575	C
Savannah College of Art and Design	GA	25,075	SP
Seton Hill College	PA	21,875	C
Shenandoah Univ	VA	22,550	NC
Simon's Rock College of Bard	MA	32,450	HC
Suffolk Univ	MA	26,516	C
Temple Univ	PA	14,124	C
Univ of Arizona	AZ	8,614	C
Univ of Florida	FL	7,874	HC
Univ of Hartford	CT	28,884	C
Univ of Mich/Ann Arbor	MI	13,003	HC+
Univ of Missouri/Kansas City	MO	9,685	VC
Univ of New Hampshire	NH	13,207	C
Univ of San Francisco	CA	27,302	VC
Univ of Tampa	FL	22,612	C
Univ of the Arts	PA	24,230	SP
Univ of Utah	UT	7,703	C
Virginia Intermont College	VA	17,510	C
Washington Univ in St. Louis	MO	34,593	MC
West Texas A&M Univ	TX	6,538	C
Western Kentucky Univ	KY	6,834	C
Youngstown State Univ	OH	9,318	NC

PERSONNEL MANAGEMENT

School	ST	$IS	SR
Arcadia Univ	PA	26,650	C
Auburn Univ	AL	5,510	C
Auburn Univ Montgomery	AL	5,330	NC
Baldwin-Wallace College	OH	22,010	VC+
Ball State Univ	IN	8,660	C
Baylor Univ	TX	18,298	VC+
Bellevue Univ	NE	4,125	NC
Bowling Green State Univ	OH	10,794	C
Cal State, Long Beach	CA	7,400	LC
Cal State, Los Angeles	CA	5,050	C
CUNY/Baruch College	NY	3,275	VC+
Columbia Union College	MD	19,027	C+
Dickinson State Univ	ND	5,495	NC
Eastern Mich Univ	MI	9,855	C
Eastern New Mexico Univ	NM	4,113	LC
Eastern Washington Univ	WA	7,972	LC
Faulkner Univ	AL	13,000	C
Florida International Univ	FL	9,486	VC
Florida Southern College	FL	19,430	C
Florida State Univ	FL	7,835	HC
Grand Canyon Univ	AZ	30,000	LC
Grand Valley State Univ	MI	10,040	C
Hannibal-LaGrange College	MO	12,530	C
Hawaii Pacific Univ	HI	17,790	C
Ithaca College	NY	28,719	HC
Kent State Univ	OH	11,104	C
King's College	PA	24,680	C
Lamar Univ	TX	6,816	LC
Loras College	IA	22,994	C+
Louisiana Tech Univ	LA	6,506	C
Loyola Univ of Chicago	IL	25,992	VC
Mansfield Univ	PA	9,648	C
Messiah College	PA	23,180	VC
Miami Univ	OH	12,885	VC+
Mich State Univ	MI	10,386	VC
Murray State Univ	KY	6,672	C
Nicholls State Univ	LA	5,290	NC
Nichols College	MA	24,610	LC
Northern Illinois Univ	IL	9,545	C
Northern State Univ	SD	6,279	LC
Northwest Missouri State Univ	MO	7,922	LC
Oakland Univ	MI	9,418	C
Ohio Univ	OH	11,769	C
Our Lady of the Lake Univ of San Antonio	TX	17,336	C
Portland State Univ	OR	11,220	C
Rhode Island College	RI	8,700	LC
Roberts Wesleyan College	NY	20,160	C+
Rockhurst Univ	MO	20,090	C
Roosevelt Univ	IL	20,240	LC
Rowan Univ	NJ	12,365	VC
St. Cloud State Univ	MN	7,180	C
St. Louis Univ	MO	26,590	VC+
San Francisco State Univ	CA	7,139	LC
Seton Hill College	PA	21,875	C
Silver Lake College of the Holy Family	WI	15,516	LC
Southern Nazarene Univ	OK	14,634	NC
Southern Wesleyan Univ	SC	17,280	C
Tarleton State Univ	TX	7,160	C
Temple Univ	PA	14,124	C
Texas A&M Univ	TX	8,988	VC
Tiffin Univ	OH	17,250	C
Troy State Univ/Dothan	AL	3,296	C
Univ of Akron	OH	10,530	NC
Univ of Houston	TX	8,410	C
Univ of Idaho	ID	7,026	C
Univ of Louisiana at Lafayette	LA	5,200	C
Univ of Mary Hardin-Baylor	TX	13,929	C
Univ of Montana	MT	8,038	C
Univ of Nebr at Kearney	NE	7,048	NC
Univ of New Mexico	NM	8,026	C
Univ of N Car at Greensboro	NC	6,858	C
Univ of North Texas	TX	7,629	C
Univ of PR at Humacao	PR	1,245	
Univ of PR/Rio Piedras	PR	5,510	
Univ of St. Thomas	MN	24,044	VC
Univ of Southern Miss	MS	6,155	LC
Univ of Texas at San Antonio	TX	9,088	NC
Univ of the Sacred Heart	PR	5,375	
Univ of Washington	WA	10,361	VC
Univ of Wisc/Whitewater	WI	6,937	C
Utah State Univ	UT	6,771	C
Vanguard Univ of Southern Calif	CA	20,212	C
Viterbo Univ	WI	18,043	C
Washington State Univ	WA	9,388	C
Weber State Univ	UT	6,897	NC
Western Illinois Univ	IL	9,571	C
Wilmington College	DE	6,530	NC
Winona State Univ	MN	8,570	C
Xavier Univ of Louisiana	LA	17,000	LC

PETROLEUM/NATURAL GAS ENGINEERING

School	ST	$IS	SR
Colo School of Mines	CO	11,578	HC
Louisiana State Univ and A&M College	LA	8,014	VC
Marietta College	OH	24,580	C
Montana Tech of The Univ of Montana	MT	7,845	C
New Mexico Inst of Mining and Technology	NM	7,152	VC+
Penn State Univ/Univ Park Campus	PA	11,126	VC
Savannah State Univ	GA	2,550	LC
Stanford Univ	CA	34,222	MC
Texas A&M Univ	TX	8,988	VC
Texas A&M Univ at Kingsville	TX	6,446	LC
Texas Tech Univ	TX	8,825	C
Univ of Alaska Fairbanks	AK	8,265	NC
Univ of Kansas	KS	7,232	VC
Univ of Louisiana at Lafayette	LA	5,200	C
Univ of Missouri/Rolla	MO	10,034	C
Univ of Okla	OK	7,616	VC
Univ of Texas at Austin	TX	9,437	HC
Univ of Tulsa	OK	19,090	HC
West Virginia Univ	WV	8,304	C

PHARMACOLOGY

School	ST	$IS	SR
SUNY/Univ at Stony Brook	NY	10,998	VC

PHARMACY

School	ST	$IS	SR
Albany College of Pharmacy	NY	19,470	SP
Auburn Univ	AL	5,510	C
Butler Univ	IN	25,580	VC+
Drake Univ	IA	22,830	VC
Duquesne Univ	PA	24,242	C+
Ferris State Univ	MI	10,816	C
Florida A&M Univ	FL	6,948	C
Howard Univ	DC	15,522	LC
Lamar Univ	TX	6,816	LC
LIU/Brooklyn Campus	NY	22,290	C
Mass College of Pharmacy and Health Sciences	MA	27,131	SP
N Dak State Univ	ND	7,004	VC
Northeastern Univ	MA	30,078	VC
Ohio Northern Univ	OH	27,765	VC
Purdue Univ/West Lafayette	IN	10,284	VC
Rutgers, The State Univ of New Jersey New Brunswick Campus	NJ	12,709	C
St. John's Univ	NY	26,660	C
S Dak State Univ	SD	6,848	C
SUNY/Univ at Buffalo	NY	11,033	VC
Temple Univ	PA	14,124	C
Texas Southern Univ	TX	6,576	NC
Univ of Arizona	AZ	8,614	C
Univ of Calif at Santa Barbara	CA	11,732	VC
Univ of Cincinnati	OH	12,491	LC
Univ of Conn	CT	12,122	VC
Univ of Florida	FL	7,874	HC
Univ of Georgia	GA	8,656	VC
Univ of Houston	TX	8,410	C
Univ of Illinois at Chicago	IL	10,702	VC
Univ of Iowa	IA	8,607	C+
Univ of Kansas	KS	7,232	VC
Univ of Louisiana at Monroe	LA	5,207	NC
Univ of Mich/Ann Arbor	MI	13,003	HC+
Univ of Minn/Twin Cities	MN	11,123	VC
Univ of Miss	MO	7,000	C
Univ of Montana	MT	8,038	C
Univ of New Mexico	NM	8,026	C
Univ of N Car at Chapel Hill	NC	8,789	HC
Univ of Rhode Island	RI	12,414	C
Univ of Texas at Austin	TX	9,437	HC
Univ of the Sciences in Philadelphia	PA	24,826	VC
Univ of Toledo	OH	11,206	NC
Univ of Utah	UT	7,703	C
Univ of Wisc/Madison	WI	8,262	VC
Washington Univ in St. Louis	MO	34,593	MC
Wayne State Univ	MI	6,720	C
West Virginia Univ	WV	8,304	C

PHILOSOPHY

School	ST	$IS	SR
Adelphi Univ	NY	23,320	VC
Agnes Scott College	GA	24,950	VC
Alaska Pacific Univ	AK	16,450	C
Albertson College of Idaho	ID	23,900	VC
Albertus Magnus College	CT	22,154	C
Albion College	MI	25,224	VC
Albright College	PA	27,642	C
Alfred Univ	NY	27,212	C+
Allegheny College	PA	27,780	VC
Alma College	MI	22,586	VC
Alvernia College	PA	20,790	C
Alverno College	WI	16,930	LC
American International College	MA	22,268	LC
American Univ	DC	31,544	VC+
Amherst College	MA	34,340	MC
Anderson Univ	IN	19,430	LC
Appalachian State Univ	NC	6,353	C
Aquinas College	MI	20,052	C+
Arcadia Univ	PA	26,650	C
Arizona State Univ-Main	AZ	7,726	C
Arkansas State Univ	AR	7,480	C

ST = STATE **$IS** = IN-STATE COSTS **SR** = SELECTOR RATING

INDEX OF COLLEGE MAJORS

School	ST	$IS	SR
Asbury College	KY	18,540	VC
Ashland Univ	OH	22,182	LC
Assumption College	MA	26,320	C
Auburn Univ	AL	5,510	C
Augsburg College	MN	22,978	C
Augustana College	IL	24,117	VC+
Augustana College	SD	20,760	VC
Aurora Univ	IL	18,551	C
Austin College	TX	22,150	VC+
Austin Peay State Univ	TN	5,814	LC
Azusa Pacific Univ	CA	22,422	VC
Baker Univ	KS	14,780	C+
Baldwin-Wallace College	OH	22,010	VC+
Ball State Univ	IN	8,660	C
Bard College	NY	33,912	HC
Barry Univ	FL	24,100	LC
Bates College	ME	34,100	MC
Baylor Univ	TX	18,298	VC+
Belhaven College	MS	16,040	C+
Bellarmine Univ	KY	20,440	VC
Bellevue Univ	NE	4,125	NC
Belmont Abbey College	NC	19,630	LC
Belmont Univ	TN	19,066	VC
Beloit College	WI	27,482	HC
Bemidji State Univ	MN	7,957	C
Benedict College	SC	12,662	LC
Benedictine College	KS	18,485	LC
Benedictine Univ	IL	21,330	C
Bennington College	VT	31,350	VC
Bentley College	MA	31,060	HC
Berea College	KY	4,070	VC
Berry College	GA	18,850	C
Bethany College	WV	18,566	C
Bethel College	IN	17,650	LC
Bethel College	MN	22,740	VC
Bethune-Cookman College	FL	15,746	C
Biola Univ	CA	21,902	VC
Birmingham-Southern College	AL	22,960	C
Bloomfield College	NJ	17,000	C
Bloomsburg Univ of Pennsylvania	PA	9,434	C
Boise State Univ	ID	6,531	LC
Boston College	MA	33,330	MC
Boston Univ	MA	34,358	MC
Bowdoin College	ME	32,650	MC
Bowling Green State Univ	OH	10,794	C
Bradley Univ	IL	20,970	VC
Brandeis Univ	MA	34,481	MC
Bridgewater College	VA	22,950	C
Bridgewater State College	MA	7,589	C+
Brigham Young Univ	UT	7,840	HC
Brown Univ	RI	34,973	MC
Bryn Mawr College	PA	33,580	HC+
Bucknell Univ	PA	31,096	HC
Buena Vista Univ	IA	22,828	C
Butler Univ	IN	25,580	VC+
Cabrini College	PA	25,950	LC
Calif Baptist Univ	CA	16,736	C
Calif Lutheran Univ	CA	23,500	LC
Calif Polytechnic State Univ	CA	8,747	VC
Calif State Polytechnic Univ, Pomona	CA	8,615	C
Cal State, Bakersfield	CA	6,090	LC
Cal State, Chico	CA	8,598	LC
Cal State, Dominguez Hills	CA	5,840	LC
Cal State, Fresno	CA	7,762	C
Cal State, Fullerton	CA	5,440	LC
Cal State, Hayward	CA	7,400	LC
Cal State, Long Beach	CA	7,400	LC
Cal State, Los Angeles	CA	5,050	C
Cal State, Northridge	CA	7,781	C
Cal State, Sacramento	CA	7,488	C
Cal State, San Bernardino	CA	6,516	C
Cal State, Stanislaus	CA	8,895	C
Calif Univ of Pennsylvania	PA	10,388	C
Calvin College	MI	20,050	NC
Canisius College	NY	24,696	C+
Capital Univ	OH	23,630	C
Carleton College	MN	30,780	MC
Carlow College	PA	19,366	C
Carnegie Mellon Univ	PA	32,682	MC
Carroll College	MT	19,140	C
Carson-Newman College	TN	16,490	C
Carthage College	WI	23,670	C
Case Western Reserve Univ	OH	27,418	C
Catawba College	NC	19,620	C
Catholic Univ of America	DC	29,332	VC
Cedar Crest College	PA	25,145	C+
Cedarville Univ	OH	17,553	VC
Centenary College of Louisiana	LA	21,600	C+
Central College	IA	21,206	C
Central Conn State Univ	CT	10,404	C
Central Methodist College	MO	16,460	C
Central Mich Univ	MI	8,355	C
Central Univ of Bayamon	PR	3,335	
Central Washington Univ	WA	8,985	LC
Centre College	KY	24,000	HC
Chaminade Univ of Honolulu	HI	17,370	C
Chapman Univ	CA	30,218	VC
Chatham College	PA	25,454	C+
Christendom College	VA	16,700	VC+
Christopher Newport Univ	VA	8,862	VC
CUNY/Baruch College	NY	3,275	VC+
CUNY/Brooklyn College	NY	3,403	LC
CUNY/City College	NY	3,309	LC
CUNY/College of Staten Island	NY	3,358	NC
CUNY/Herbert H. Lehman College	NY	3,320	LC
CUNY/Hunter College	NY	5,147	C+
CUNY/Queens College	NY	3,403	VC
CUNY/York College	NY	3,292	NC
Claremont McKenna College	CA	32,700	MC
Clarion Univ of Pennsylvania	PA	11,272	LC
Clark Atlanta Univ	GA	17,174	C
Clark Univ	MA	29,170	HC
Clarke College	IA	20,625	C+
Clemson Univ	SC	7,600	C
Cleveland State Univ	OH	10,146	NC
Coastal Carolina Univ	SC	9,220	C
Coe College	IA	24,750	VC
Colby College	ME	34,290	MC
Colgate Univ	NY	33,480	MC
College Misericordia	PA	23,380	LC
College of Charleston	SC	8,350	HC
College of Mount St. Vincent	NY	24,230	C
College of New Jersey	NJ	13,425	HC
College of New Rochelle	NY	20,000	C
College of St. Benedict	MN	23,921	VC
College of St. Catherine	MN	22,324	VC
College of St. Elizabeth	NJ	22,510	C
College of the Holy Cross	MA	32,780	MC
College of the Ozarks	MO	2,650	C+
College of William and Mary	VA	10,002	MC
College of Wooster	OH	28,350	VC
Colo College	CO	31,525	HC+
Colo State Univ	CO	9,672	C
Columbia Univ/Barnard College	NY	33,694	MC
Columbia Univ/Columbia College	NY	35,190	MC
Columbia Univ/School of General Studies	NY	35,000	C
Concordia College/Moorhead	MN	18,835	C
Concordia Univ, River Forest	IL	20,000	LC
Conn College	CT	33,585	MC
Cornell College	IA	24,980	VC
Cornell Univ	NY	34,614	MC
Covenant College	GA	21,970	C+
Creighton Univ	NE	23,476	VC
Curry College	MA	26,025	LC
Dakota Wesleyan Univ	SD	15,512	C
Dallas Baptist Univ	TX	13,682	LC
Dartmouth College	NH	34,458	MC
Davidson College	NC	30,823	MC
De Sales Univ	PA	22,610	VC
Denison Univ	OH	29,640	HC
DePaul Univ	IL	23,590	VC
DePauw Univ	IN	28,000	HC
Dickinson College	PA	32,210	VC+
Dillard Univ	LA	16,046	VC
Doane College	NE	17,600	LC
Dominican Univ	IL	20,800	C
Dordt College	IA	18,100	C+
Dowling College	NY	20,281	LC
Drake Univ	IA	22,830	VC
Drew Univ/College of Liberal Arts	NJ	32,152	VC
Drury Univ	MO	15,250	VC
Duke Univ	NC	34,396	MC
Duquesne Univ	PA	24,242	C+
D'Youville College	NY	18,704	C
Earlham College	IN	27,446	VC+
East Carolina Univ	NC	7,766	C
East Stroudsburg Univ of Pennsylvania	PA	8,430	LC
East Tenn State Univ	TN	7,127	C
Eastern College	PA	19,641	LC
Eastern Illinois Univ	IL	10,101	C
Eastern Kentucky Univ	KY	6,552	C
Eastern Mich Univ	MI	9,855	C
Eastern Washington Univ	WA	7,972	LC
Eckerd College	FL	25,500	C+
Edinboro Univ of Pennsylvania	PA	9,328	LC
Edward Waters College	FL	13,124	LC
Elizabethtown College	PA	26,000	VC
Elmhurst College	IL	21,750	C
Elmira College	NY	31,070	VC+
Elon Univ	NC	19,430	VC
Emory & Henry College	VA	19,462	C
Emory Univ	GA	33,792	MC
Erskine College	SC	21,399	VC
Eureka College	IL	22,200	C
Fairfield Univ	CT	30,885	HC
Fairleigh Dickinson Univ/Madison campus	NJ	25,500	C
Fairleigh Dickinson Univ/Teaneck Campus	NJ	24,646	C
Felician College	NJ	20,050	C
Ferrum College	VA	15,990	LC
Fisk Univ	TN	13,700	LC
Flagler College	FL	10,550	VC+
Florida Atlantic Univ	FL	8,832	C
Florida International Univ	FL	9,486	VC
Florida Memorial College	FL	6,000	LC
Florida State Univ	FL	7,835	HC
Fordham Univ	NY	30,710	VC
Fort Hays State Univ	KS	6,294	LC
Fort Lewis College	CO	7,659	LC
Franciscan Univ of Steubenville	OH	19,100	C+
Franklin and Marshall College	PA	32,410	HC
Franklin College of Indiana	IN	19,905	C
Fresno Pacific Univ	CA	19,740	C
Frostburg State Univ	MD	9,680	C
Furman Univ	SC	25,492	HC
Gallaudet Univ	DC	16,554	SP
Gannon Univ	PA	18,848	C
Geneva College	PA	19,990	C+
George Mason Univ	VA	9,192	C
George Washington Univ	DC	32,170	HC
Georgetown College	KY	18,400	VC
Georgetown Univ	DC	34,847	MC
Georgia Southern Univ	GA	6,958	C
Georgia State Univ	GA	7,792	LC
Gettysburg College	PA	32,070	HC
Gonzaga Univ	WA	24,276	HC+
Gordon College	MA	23,594	VC+
Goucher College	MD	30,650	VC+
Graceland Univ	IA	15,845	C
Grand Valley State Univ	MI	10,040	C
Green Mountain College	VT	24,130	C
Greenville College	IL	19,226	LC
Grinnell College	IA	28,300	HC+
Grove City College	PA	12,280	MC
Guilford College	NC	23,255	C
Gustavus Adolphus College	MN	24,190	VC+
Hamilton College	NY	34,150	HC
Hamline Univ	MN	23,339	C+
Hampden-Sydney College	VA	24,871	C
Hampshire College	MA	33,881	HC+
Hanover College	IN	17,560	VC
Hardin-Simmons Univ	TX	14,165	C
Hartwick College	NY	33,090	C+
Harvard Univ/Harvard College	MA	34,269	MC
Hastings College	NE	17,854	C+
Haverford College	PA	34,300	MC
Heidelberg College	OH	23,879	C
Hendrix College	AR	18,463	HC
High Point Univ	NC	20,220	LC
Hiram College	OH	27,034	VC
Hobart and William Smith Colleges	NY	33,195	VC
Hofstra Univ	NY	23,252	C
Hollins Univ	VA	24,328	VC
Holy Names College	CA	23,220	C
Hood College	MD	26,020	VC
Hope College	MI	22,922	C+
Houghton College	NY	21,810	VC+
Howard Univ	DC	15,522	LC
Humboldt State Univ	CA	8,582	C
Huntington College	IN	15,480	LC
Idaho State Univ	ID	7,030	C+
Illinois College	IL	16,234	C
Illinois State Univ	IL	9,235	C
Illinois Wesleyan Univ	IL	26,970	HC
Indiana State Univ	IN	8,461	LC
Indiana Univ Bloomington	IN	10,712	C+
Indiana Univ Northwest	IN	3,447	C
Indiana Univ of Pennsylvania	PA	9,133	C
Indiana Univ South Bend	IN	3,515	C
Indiana Univ Southeast	IN	3,459	C
Indiana Univ-Purdue Univ Fort Wayne	IN	3,166	LC
Indiana Univ-Purdue Univ Indianapolis	IN	9,473	C
Iona College	NY	26,556	C
Iowa State Univ	IA	8,108	VC
Ithaca College	NY	28,719	HC
Jacksonville Univ	FL	21,110	LC
James Madison Univ	VA	9,552	HC
Jamestown College	ND	11,310	NC
John Carroll Univ	OH	24,140	VC
Johns Hopkins Univ	MD	35,226	MC
Kalamazoo College	MI	26,955	HC+
Kansas State Univ	KS	6,995	C
Kean Univ	NJ	11,159	C
Kent State Univ	OH	11,104	C
Kentucky Christian College	KY	13,472	C
Kenyon College	OH	32,130	HC+
King's College	PA	24,680	C
Knox College	IL	28,230	HC
Kutztown Univ of Pennsylvania	PA	8,907	C
La Salle Univ	PA	27,890	C
Lafayette College	PA	32,655	MC
Lake Forest College	IL	27,460	VC
Lakeland College	WI	17,950	C
Lawrence Univ	WI	27,711	HC
Le Moyne College	NY	23,840	C
Lebanon Valley College of Pennsylvania	PA	25,700	VC
Lehigh Univ	PA	32,290	MC
Lenoir-Rhyne College	NC	19,186	C
Lewis and Clark College	OR	29,010	VC
Lewis Univ	IL	20,960	C
Lincoln Univ	MO	7,158	NC
Lincoln Univ	PA	11,198	C+
Linfield College	OR	25,840	VC
Lock Haven Univ of Pennsylvania	PA	9,534	C
LIU/Brooklyn Campus	NY	22,290	C
LIU/C.W. Post Campus	NY	25,380	C
Loras College	IA	22,994	C+
Louisiana College	LA	11,516	C
Louisiana State Univ and A&M College	LA	8,014	VC
Loyola College in Maryland	MD	30,900	HC
Loyola Marymount Univ	CA	28,754	HC
Loyola Univ New Orleans	LA	23,506	VC+
Loyola Univ of Chicago	IL	25,992	VC
Lycoming College	PA	24,780	C
Lynchburg College	VA	23,405	C
Macalester College	MN	28,814	HC+
MacMurray College	IL	17,790	LC
Manchester College	IN	22,010	C
Manhattan College	NY	25,500	VC
Manhattanville College	NY	28,730	VC
Mansfield Univ	PA	9,648	C
Marian College	IN	21,020	C
Marietta College	OH	24,580	C
Marlboro College	VT	26,410	VC+
Marquette Univ	WI	24,836	C+
Mary Baldwin College	VA	23,440	C
Mary Washington College	VA	9,032	VC+
Marymount Univ	VA	21,560	LC
Mass College of Liberal Arts	MA	8,717	LC
Mass Inst of Technology	MA	35,228	MC
McKendree College	IL	18,300	C+
McMurry Univ	TX	15,287	C
McPherson College	KS	17,710	C
Mercer Univ	GA	24,130	VC
Mercyhurst College	PA	20,694	C
Merrimack College	MA	25,725	VC
Messiah College	PA	23,180	VC
Metropolitan State College of Denver	CO	2,338	LC
Metropolitan State Univ	MN	2,943	SP
Miami Univ	OH	12,885	VC+
Mich State Univ	MI	10,386	VC
Middle Tenn State Univ	TN	6,994	C
Middlebury College	VT	34,300	MC
Millersville Univ of Pennsylvania	PA	10,153	VC
Millikin Univ	IL	24,415	C+
Mills College	CA	27,950	C
Millsaps College	MS	22,608	VC+
Minn State Univ, Mankato	MN	7,296	LC
Miss State Univ	MS	7,853	C
Missouri Valley College	MO	17,400	LC
Molloy College	NY	13,940	C
Monmouth College	IL	21,550	C
Montana State Univ-Bozeman	MT	8,431	C
Montclair State Univ	NJ	10,287	LC
Moorhead State Univ	MN	7,000	LC
Moravian College	PA	27,065	VC
Morehead State Univ	KY	6,510	C
Morehouse College	GA	19,814	C
Morgan State Univ	MD	10,078	LC
Morningside College	IA	19,124	C
Morris Brown College	GA	15,993	LC
Mount Holyoke College	MA	34,128	HC
Mount Mary College	WI	18,024	C
Mount St. Mary's College	CA	24,430	C
Mount St. Mary's College	MD	25,740	C
Mount Union College	OH	21,120	C
Mount Vernon Nazarene College	OH	17,027	C
Muhlenberg College	PA	28,170	HC
Murray State Univ	KY	6,672	C
Muskingum College	OH	18,760	C
Nazareth College of Rochester	NY	22,036	VC
Nebr Wesleyan Univ	NE	18,767	VC
New College of Florida	FL	8,130	HC+
New England College	NH	20,706	LC
New Jersey City Univ	NJ	9,100	LC
New Mexico State Univ	NM	7,302	C
New York Univ	NY	35,200	MC
Newberry College	SC	19,670	LC
Niagara Univ	NY	22,250	C+
N Car State Univ	NC	8,680	HC
North Central College	IL	22,944	C+
North Park Univ	IL	24,030	C
Northeastern Illinois Univ	IL	2,898	NC
Northeastern Univ	MA	30,078	VC
Northern Arizona Univ	AZ	7,398	C
Northern Illinois Univ	IL	9,545	C
Northern Kentucky Univ	KY	6,352	NC
Northern Mich Univ	MI	9,693	C
Northwest Missouri State Univ	MO	7,922	LC
Northwest Nazarene Univ	ID	18,380	C
Northwestern College of Iowa	IA	17,630	C+
Northwestern Univ	IL	33,615	MC
Notre Dame de Namur Univ	CA	26,932	LC
Nyack College	NY	18,540	C
Oakland Univ	MI	9,418	C

ST = STATE **$IS** = IN-STATE COSTS **SR** = SELECTOR RATING

School	ST	$IS	SR
Oberlin College	OH	33,140	HC+
Occidental College	CA	32,288	HC
Oglethorpe Univ	GA	19,100	LC
Ohio Dominican College	OH	18,100	LC
Ohio Northern Univ	OH	27,765	VC
Ohio Univ	OH	11,769	C
Ohio Wesleyan Univ	OH	29,670	VC+
Okla City Univ	OK	15,810	C
Okla State Univ	OK	7,650	VC
Old Dominion Univ	VA	9,386	C
Olivet Nazarene Univ	IL	18,444	C
Oral Roberts Univ	OK	18,490	C
Oregon State Univ	OR	9,612	VC
Otterbein College	OH	23,439	C
Ouachita Baptist Univ	AR	16,460	VC
Our Lady of the Lake Univ of San Antonio	TX	17,336	C
Pacific Lutheran Univ	WA	23,318	VC
Pacific Univ	OR	24,250	C
Paine College	GA	11,896	LC
Penn State Univ/Univ Park Campus	PA	11,126	VC
Pepperdine Univ	CA	32,830	VC
Piedmont College	GA	16,900	C
Pitzer College	CA	33,930	HC
Plymouth State College	NH	11,024	LC
Point Loma Nazarene Univ	CA	21,380	VC
Pomona College	CA	33,960	MC
Pontifical Catholic Univ of PR/Ponce	PR	7,076	
Portland State Univ	OR	11,220	C
Princeton Univ	NJ	35,072	MC
Principia College	IL	23,865	C+
Providence College	RI	27,620	HC
Purdue Univ/Calumet	IN	6,630	NC
Purdue Univ/West Lafayette	IN	10,284	VC
Queens College	NC	17,250	C
Quincy Univ	IL	20,450	C
Radford Univ	VA	8,302	C
Randolph-Macon College	VA	24,395	C
Randolph-Macon Woman's College	VA	25,820	VC+
Reed College	OR	33,350	HC+
Regis Univ	CO	25,740	C+
Rensselaer Polytechnic Inst	NY	33,863	HC+
Rhode Island College	RI	8,700	LC
Rhodes College	TN	26,466	HC+
Rice Univ	TX	24,325	MC
Richard Stockton College of New Jersey	NJ	12,165	VC
Rider Univ	NJ	27,400	C
Ripon College	WI	24,180	VC+
Roanoke College	VA	24,689	VC
Rockford College	IL	23,930	C
Rockhurst Univ	MO	20,090	C
Rocky Mountain College	MT	18,113	C
Roger Williams Univ	RI	29,010	C
Rollins College	FL	31,223	HC
Roosevelt Univ	IL	20,240	LC
Rosemont College	PA	24,060	C
Rutgers, The State Univ of New Jersey New Brunswick Campus	NJ	12,709	C
Rutgers, The State Univ of New Jersey/ CamdenCampus	NJ	6,484	C
Rutgers, The State Univ of New Jersey/Newark Campus	NJ	6,394	C
Sacred Heart Univ	CT	26,588	VC
St. Ambrose Univ	IA	19,994	C
St. Andrews Presbyterian College	NC	19,720	LC
St. Anselm College	NH	27,405	C
St. Bonaventure Univ	NY	21,956	C
St. Cloud State Univ	MN	7,180	C
St. Edward's Univ	TX	17,846	C
St. Francis College	NY	9,610	C
St. Francis Univ	PA	24,486	LC
St. John Fisher College	NY	21,800	C
St. John's Univ	MN	23,640	VC
St. John's Univ	NY	26,660	C
St. Joseph College	CT	25,960	LC
St. Joseph's College	IN	21,640	C
St. Joseph's College of Maine	ME	22,500	LC
St. Joseph's Univ	PA	29,715	VC+
St. Lawrence Univ	NY	32,605	VC
St. Louis Univ	MO	26,590	VC+
St. Mary's College	IN	24,474	VC
St. Mary's College	MI	13,314	LC
St. Mary's College of Calif	CA	27,575	C
St. Mary's College of Maryland	MD	14,104	HC
St. Mary's Univ of Minn	MN	19,975	C
St. Mary's Univ of San Antonio	TX	19,735	C
St. Michael's College	VT	26,935	VC
St. Norbert College	WI	23,169	VC
St. Olaf College	MN	25,880	HC
St. Peter's College	NJ	22,292	LC
St. Thomas Aquinas College	NY	20,590	LC
St. Vincent College	PA	22,942	VC
St. Xavier Univ	IL	21,104	C
Salem College	NC	23,065	VC
Salisbury Univ	MD	10,576	VC
Salve Regina Univ	RI	26,460	C
Sam Houston State Univ	TX	6,076	LC
Samford Univ	AL	16,340	VC
San Diego State Univ	CA	9,716	C+
San Francisco State Univ	CA	7,139	LC
San Jose State Univ	CA	8,187	C
Santa Clara Univ	CA	28,371	VC+
Sarah Lawrence College	NY	37,516	HC
Schreiner Univ	TX	19,254	C
Scripps College	CA	30,400	HC+
Seattle Pacific Univ	WA	22,674	C+
Seattle Univ	WA	24,183	VC
Seton Hall Univ	NJ	26,910	LC
Siena College	NY	22,685	VC
Siena Heights Univ	MI	16,140	LC
Simmons College	MA	30,418	VC
Simon's Rock College of Bard	MA	32,450	HC
Simpson College	IA	21,200	C+
Skidmore College	NY	34,201	VC+
Slippery Rock Univ	PA	9,152	LC
Smith College	MA	33,302	HC+
Sonoma State Univ	CA	8,953	C
Southeast Missouri State Univ	MO	8,367	C+
Southern Conn State Univ	CT	10,310	C
Southern Illinois Univ at Carbondale	IL	8,621	C
Southern Illinois Univ Edwardsville	IL	7,869	LC
Southern Methodist Univ	TX	28,349	VC
Southern Nazarene Univ	OK	14,634	NC
Southwest Missouri State Univ	MO	7,600	LC
Southwest Texas State Univ	TX	8,730	VC
Southwestern Univ	TX	22,550	HC
Spalding Univ	KY	15,196	C
Spelman College	GA	19,215	C+
Spring Arbor Univ	MI	17,976	C
Spring Hill College	AL	23,250	C
Stanford Univ	CA	34,222	MC
SUNY/College at Brockport	NY	10,267	C
SUNY/College at Buffalo	NY	8,025	C
SUNY/College at Cortland	NY	10,564	C
SUNY/College at Fredonia	NY	10,125	C
SUNY/College at Geneseo	NY	9,970	HC
SUNY/College at Old Westbury	NY	9,818	LC
SUNY/College at Oneonta	NY	9,981	C
SUNY/College at Oswego	NY	10,856	C
SUNY/College at Plattsburgh	NY	9,729	C
SUNY/College at Potsdam	NY	10,519	C
SUNY/College at Purchase	NY	10,587	VC
SUNY/Univ at Albany	NY	10,997	VC
SUNY/Univ at Binghamton	NY	10,653	HC
SUNY/Univ at Buffalo	NY	11,033	VC
SUNY/Univ at New Paltz	NY	9,685	VC
SUNY/Univ at Stony Brook	NY	10,998	VC
State Univ of West Georgia	GA	7,101	C
Stephens College	MO	22,295	C
Stetson Univ	FL	25,640	VC
Stevens Inst of Technology	NJ	31,510	HC+
Stonehill College	MA	26,852	HC
Suffolk Univ	MA	26,516	C
Susquehanna Univ	PA	27,270	VC
Swarthmore College	PA	34,538	MC
Sweet Briar College	VA	25,310	VC
Syracuse Univ	NY	30,710	HC
Tabor College	KS	17,600	LC
Taylor Univ	IN	21,562	VC+
Temple Univ	PA	14,124	C
Texas A&M Univ	TX	8,988	VC
Texas Christian Univ	TX	19,910	C
Texas Lutheran Univ	TX	17,660	C
Texas Southern Univ	TX	6,576	NC
Texas Tech Univ	TX	8,825	C
Ohio State Univ	OH	10,819	VC
Thiel College	PA	18,419	LC
Thomas Edison State College	NJ	2,750	SP
Thomas More College	KY	17,700	LC
Thomas More College of Liberal Arts	NH	17,700	C
Toccoa Falls College	GA	14,220	C
Touro College	NY	14,950	VC
Towson Univ	MD	11,088	VC
Transylvania Univ	KY	21,780	VC+
Trinity Christian College	IL	19,415	C
Trinity College	CT	34,300	HC
Trinity International Univ	IL	20,640	C+
Trinity Univ	TX	21,444	HC
Truman State Univ	MO	8,568	VC+
Tufts Univ	MA	34,874	MC
Tulane Univ	LA	34,013	HC+
Union College	NY	32,646	HC
Union Univ	TN	18,930	C+
United States Military Academy	NY		MC
Univ of Akron	OH	10,530	NC
Univ of Alabama	AL	7,402	C
Univ of Alabama at Birmingham	AL	10,110	C
Univ of Alabama at Huntsville	AL	7,916	VC
Univ of Alaska Fairbanks	AK	8,265	NC
Univ of Arizona	AZ	8,614	C
Univ of Arkansas	AR	8,334	VC
Univ of Arkansas at Little Rock	AR	5,637	NC
Univ of Calif at Berkeley	CA	14,134	MC
Univ of Calif at Davis	CA	12,796	VC
Univ of Calif at Irvine	CA	11,756	C
Univ of Calif at Los Angeles	CA	13,227	MC
Univ of Calif at Riverside	CA	12,479	C
Univ of Calif at San Diego	CA	11,372	HC
Univ of Calif at Santa Barbara	CA	11,732	VC
Univ of Calif at Santa Cruz	CA	13,055	VC
Univ of Central Arkansas	AR	6,388	C
Univ of Central Florida	FL	8,251	VC
Univ of Central Okla	OK	5,205	C
Univ of Charleston	WV	20,640	C
Univ of Chicago	IL	35,087	MC
Univ of Cincinnati	OH	12,491	LC
Univ of Colo at Boulder	CO	9,255	VC
Univ of Colo at Colo Springs	CO	9,403	C
Univ of Colo at Denver	CO	3,673	C
Univ of Conn	CT	12,122	VC
Univ of Dallas	TX	22,128	VC+
Univ of Dayton	OH	20,400	VC
Univ of Delaware	DE	10,824	VC
Univ of Denver	CO	28,783	VC
Univ of Detroit Mercy	MI	21,620	LC
Univ of Dubuque	IA	19,990	C
Univ of Evansville	IN	22,865	VC+
Univ of Findlay	OH	23,962	NC
Univ of Florida	FL	7,874	HC
Univ of Georgia	GA	8,656	VC
Univ of Hartford	CT	28,884	C
Univ of Hawaii at Hilo	HI	6,497	C
Univ of Hawaii at Manoa	HI	7,862	VC
Univ of Houston	TX	8,410	C
Univ of Idaho	ID	7,026	C
Univ of Illinois at Chicago	IL	10,702	VC
Univ of Illinois at Urbana-Champaign	IL	11,316	HC+
Univ of Indianapolis	IN	20,840	C
Univ of Iowa	IA	8,607	C+
Univ of Kansas	KS	7,232	VC
Univ of Kentucky	KY	7,765	C
Univ of La Verne	CA	24,280	C
Univ of Louisiana at Lafayette	LA	5,200	C
Univ of Louisville	KY	7,402	LC
Univ of Maine	ME	10,798	C
Univ of Maine at Farmington	ME	9,163	C
Univ of Maryland/Baltimore County	MD	12,190	VC
Univ of Maryland/College Park	MD	11,959	C
Univ of Mass Amherst	MA	10,995	VC
Univ of Mass Boston	MA	4,227	C
Univ of Mass Dartmouth	MA	9,852	C
Univ of Mass Lowell	MA	9,470	VC
Univ of Memphis	TN	7,271	C
Univ of Miami	FL	31,130	HC
Univ of Mich/Ann Arbor	MI	13,003	HC+
Univ of Mich/Dearborn	MI	4,677	VC
Univ of Mich/Flint	MI	4,323	C
Univ of Minn/Duluth	MN	10,436	C
Univ of Minn/Morris	MN	10,716	VC
Univ of Minn/Twin Cities	MN	11,123	VC
Univ of Miss	MS	7,666	C
Univ of Missouri/Columbia	MO	9,803	HC
Univ of Missouri/Kansas City	MO	9,685	VC
Univ of Missouri/Rolla	MO	10,034	C
Univ of Missouri/St. Louis	MO	9,966	C
Univ of Montana	MT	8,038	C
Univ of Nebr at Lincoln	NE	8,325	C+
Univ of Nebr at Omaha	NE	6,867	C
Univ of Nevada/Las Vegas	NV	8,281	VC
Univ of Nevada/Reno	NV	8,737	C
Univ of New Hampshire	NH	13,207	C
Univ of New Mexico	NM	8,026	C
Univ of New Orleans	LA	10,160	C
Univ of N Car at Asheville	NC	6,896	VC
Univ of N Car at Chapel Hill	NC	8,789	HC
Univ of N Car at Charlotte	NC	7,254	C
Univ of N Car at Greensboro	NC	6,858	C
Univ of N Car at Pembroke	NC	5,914	LC
Univ of N Car at Wilmington	NC	7,769	C
Univ of N Dak	ND	7,067	VC
Univ of North Florida	FL	8,089	VC
Univ of North Texas	TX	7,629	C
Univ of Northern Colo	CO	8,082	C+
Univ of Northern Iowa	IA	7,850	C
Univ of Notre Dame	IN	30,707	MC
Univ of Okla	OK	7,616	VC
Univ of Oregon	OR	9,969	C
Univ of Pennsylvania	PA	34,614	MC
Univ of Pittsburgh at Pittsburgh	PA	13,592	HC
Univ of Portland	OR	24,950	VC
Univ of PR/Mayaguez	PR	5,285	
Univ of PR/Rio Piedras	PR	5,510	
Univ of Puget Sound	WA	28,285	HC
Univ of Redlands	CA	29,246	VC
Univ of Rhode Island	RI	12,414	C
Univ of Richmond	VA	27,300	HC
Univ of Rochester	NY	32,979	HC
Univ of St. Thomas	MN	24,044	VC
Univ of St. Thomas	TX	18,752	VC
Univ of San Diego	CA	29,198	HC
Univ of San Francisco	CA	27,302	VC
Univ of Scranton	PA	27,964	C+
Univ of Sioux Falls	SD	16,390	C
Univ of South Alabama	AL	6,976	LC
Univ of S Car at Columbia	SC	8,748	VC
Univ of S Dak	SD	7,036	C
Univ of South Florida	FL	8,154	C
Univ of Southern Calif	CA	33,647	MC
Univ of Southern Indiana	IN	8,655	LC
Univ of Southern Maine	ME	10,569	C
Univ of Southern Miss	MS	6,155	LC
Univ of Tenn at Chattanooga	TN	7,783	C
Univ of Tenn at Knoxville	TN	8,214	C
Univ of Tenn at Martin	TN	8,268	C
Univ of Texas at Arlington	TX	7,192	LC
Univ of Texas at Austin	TX	9,437	HC
Univ of Texas at El Paso	TX	5,076	LC
Univ of Texas at San Antonio	TX	9,088	NC
Univ of Texas-Pan American	TX	4,823	C
Univ of the District of Columbia	DC	2,844	NC
Univ of the Incarnate Word	TX	18,478	C
Univ of the Pacific	CA	28,255	VC
Univ of the South	TN	27,290	HC
Univ of Toledo	OH	11,206	NC
Univ of Tulsa	OK	19,090	HC
Univ of Utah	UT	7,703	C
Univ of Vermont	VT	14,761	C+
Univ of Virginia	VA	9,391	HC+
Univ of Washington	WA	10,361	VC
Univ of West Florida	FL	7,518	C
Univ of Wisc/Eau Claire	WI	7,032	VC
Univ of Wisc/Green Bay	WI	7,148	C
Univ of Wisc/La Crosse	WI	7,250	VC
Univ of Wisc/Madison	WI	8,262	VC
Univ of Wisc/Milwaukee	WI	8,907	LC
Univ of Wisc/Oshkosh	WI	6,130	LC
Univ of Wisc/Parkside	WI	6,160	LC
Univ of Wisc/Platteville	WI	7,282	C
Univ of Wisc/Stevens Point	WI	7,116	C
Univ of Wyoming	WY	7,143	LC
Urbana Univ	OH	17,004	C
Ursuline College	OH	19,430	LC
Utah State Univ	UT	6,771	C
Utica College of Syracuse Univ	NY	24,400	LC
Valdosta State Univ	GA	6,988	C
Valparaiso Univ	IN	23,570	VC+
Vanderbilt Univ	TN	34,482	MC
Vassar College	NY	33,450	MC
Villanova Univ	PA	31,997	HC
Virginia Polytechnic Inst and State Univ	VA	7,652	C
Virginia Wesleyan College	VA	22,350	LC
Wabash College	IN	25,335	HC
Wake Forest Univ	NC	30,290	MC
Walsh Univ	OH	16,880	C
Wartburg College	IA	21,165	VC
Washburn Univ of Topeka	KS	6,766	NC
Washington and Jefferson College	PA	26,255	VC
Washington and Lee Univ	VA	25,095	MC
Washington College	MD	28,040	VC
Washington State Univ	WA	9,388	C
Washington Univ in St. Louis	MO	34,593	MC
Wayne State Univ	MI	6,720	C
Webster Univ	MO	19,804	VC
Wellesley College	MA	33,394	MC
Wells College	NY	19,350	VC
Wesleyan College	GA	17,050	VC
Wesleyan Univ	CT	3,405	MC
West Chester Univ of Pennsylvania	PA	9,792	VC
West Virginia Univ	WV	8,304	C
West Virginia Wesleyan College	WV	22,920	C
Western Carolina Univ	NC	5,667	C
Western Illinois Univ	IL	9,571	C
Western Kentucky Univ	KY	6,834	C
Western Maryland College	MD	26,000	VC
Western Mich Univ	MI	10,016	C
Western Oregon Univ	OR	8,829	C
Western Washington Univ	WA	8,624	VC
Westminster College	MO	19,990	C+
Westminster College	PA	22,960	C
Westminster College	UT	17,226	C
Westmont College	CA	29,748	VC
Wheaton College	IL	21,934	HC
Wheaton College	MA	32,940	VC
Wheeling Jesuit Univ	WV	22,660	C
Whitman College	WA	29,086	HC
Whittier College	CA	29,108	C
Whitworth College	WA	23,938	VC

School	ST	$IS	SR
Wichita State Univ	KS	6,879	C
Wiley College	TX	8,100	LC
Wilkes Univ	PA	25,800	C
Willamette Univ	OR	29,422	VC+
William Jewell College	MO	17,150	VC
William Paterson Univ of New Jersey	NJ	11,000	LC
Williams College	MA	32,270	MC
Wilson College	PA	21,337	LC
Wingate Univ	NC	19,140	C
Winthrop Univ	SC	9,106	C
Wittenberg Univ	OH	28,766	VC
Wofford College	SC	23,995	VC
Wright State Univ	OH	9,141	LC
Xavier Univ	OH	23,880	C
Xavier Univ of Louisiana	LA	17,000	LC
Yale Univ	CT	34,030	MC
Yeshiva Univ	NY	21,400	C
Youngstown State Univ	OH	9,318	NC

PHOTOGRAPHY

School	ST	$IS	SR
Andrews Univ	MI	17,696	LC
Aquinas College	MI	20,052	C+
Arcadia Univ	PA	26,650	C
Arizona State Univ-Main	AZ	7,726	C
Art Center College of Design	CA	21,110	SP
Art Inst of Atlanta	GA	20,624	SP
Art Inst of Boston at Lesley Univ	MA	23,685	SP
Atlanta College of Art	GA	18,600	SP
Ball State Univ	IN	8,660	C
Bard College	NY	33,912	HC
Barry Univ	FL	24,100	LC
Barton College	NC	16,834	LC
Bellevue Univ	NE	4,125	NC
Bennington College	VT	31,350	VC
Birmingham-Southern College	AL	22,960	C
Bradley Univ	IL	20,970	VC
Brigham Young Univ	UT	7,840	HC
Calif College of Arts and Crafts	CA	27,366	SP
Cal State, Fullerton	CA	5,440	LC
Central Missouri State Univ	MO	7,920	C
Cleveland Inst of Art	OH	22,680	SP
Coker College	SC	20,120	C
College For Creative Studies	MI	20,938	SP
College of Notre Dame of Maryland	MD	23,100	LC
College of Visual Arts	MN	12,185	SP
Columbia College Chicago	IL	22,063	LC
Corcoran School of Art and Design	DC	21,035	SP
Dominican Univ	IL	20,800	C
Drexel Univ	PA	27,657	VC
Edinboro Univ of Pennsylvania	PA	9,328	LC
Fordham Univ	NY	30,710	VC
Grand Valley State Univ	MI	10,040	C
Hampshire College	MA	33,881	HC+
Howard Univ	DC	15,522	LC
Indiana Univ-Purdue Univ Indianapolis	IN	9,473	C
Ithaca College	NY	28,719	HC
Kansas City Art Inst	MO	25,880	SP
Kent State Univ	OH	11,104	C
LIU/C.W. Post Campus	NY	25,380	C
Maine College of Art	ME	26,367	SP
Marlboro College	VT	26,410	VC+
Maryland Inst College of Art	MD	27,720	SP
Mass College of Art	MA	13,703	SP
Milwaukee Inst of Art and Design	WI	24,388	SP
Minneapolis College of Art and Design	MN	23,560	SP
Montserrat College of Art	MA	20,335	SP
Morningside College	IA	19,124	C
New Jersey City Univ	NJ	9,100	LC
New York Univ	NY	35,200	MC
Northern Mich Univ	MI	9,693	C
Ohio Univ	OH	11,769	C
Otis College of Art and Design	CA	20,290	SP
Pacific Northwest College of Art	OR	16,507	SP
Parsons School of Design	NY	32,242	SP
Point Park College	PA	20,290	C
Pratt Inst	NY	27,550	SP
Prescott College	AZ	13,430	C
Purdue Univ/West Lafayette	IN	10,284	VC
Rhode Island College	RI	8,700	LC
Rhode Island School of Design	RI	30,227	SP
Ringling School of Art and Design	FL	22,500	SP
Rivier College	NH	24,215	C
Rochester Inst of Technology	NY	26,232	VC+
St. Edward's Univ	TX	17,846	C
St. John's Univ	NY	26,660	C
Salem State College	MA	4,481	LC
Sam Houston State Univ	TX	6,076	LC
San Francisco Art Inst	CA	19,300	SP
Savannah College of Art and Design	GA	25,075	SP
School of the Art Inst of Chicago	IL	27,800	SP
School of Visual Arts	NY	26,000	SP
Shepherd College	WV	7,062	LC
Simon's Rock College of Bard	MA	32,450	HC
Southern Illinois Univ at Carbondale	IL	8,621	C
SUNY/College at Buffalo	NY	8,025	C
SUNY/Univ at New Paltz	NY	9,685	VC
Syracuse Univ	NY	30,710	HC
Temple Univ	PA	14,124	C
Texas A&M Univ at Commerce	TX	7,326	C
Texas Tech Univ	TX	8,825	C
Texas Woman's Univ	TX	5,855	LC
Thomas Edison State College	NJ	2,750	SP
Univ of Akron	OH	10,530	NC
Univ of Central Okla	OK	5,205	C
Univ of Dayton	OH	20,400	VC
Univ of Florida	FL	7,874	HC
Univ of Hartford	CT	28,884	C
Univ of Houston	TX	8,410	C
Univ of Idaho	ID	7,026	C
Univ of Illinois at Chicago	IL	10,702	VC
Univ of Illinois at Urbana-Champaign	IL	11,316	HC+
Univ of Louisiana at Monroe	LA	5,207	NC
Univ of Mass Dartmouth	MA	9,852	C
Univ of Miami	FL	31,130	HC
Univ of Mich/Ann Arbor	MI	13,003	HC+
Univ of North Texas	TX	7,629	C
Univ of Okla	OK	7,616	VC
Univ of Southern Calif	CA	33,647	MC
Univ of the Arts	PA	24,230	SP
Univ of Washington	WA	10,361	VC
Univ of Wisc/Eau Claire	WI	7,032	VC
Virginia Intermont College	VA	17,510	C
Washington Univ in St. Louis	MO	34,593	MC
Weber State Univ	UT	6,897	NC
Webster Univ	MO	19,804	VC
Western Conn State Univ	CT	10,074	C
Youngstown State Univ	OH	9,318	NC

PHYSICAL CHEMISTRY

School	ST	$IS	SR
Centre College	KY	24,000	HC
St. Mary's Univ of Minn	MN	19,975	C
Union Univ	TN	18,930	C+
Univ of Calif at San Diego	CA	11,372	HC
Washington and Jefferson College	PA	26,255	VC

PHYSICAL EDUCATION

School	ST	$IS	SR
Abilene Christian Univ	TX	16,300	VC
Adams State College	CO	7,468	C
Adelphi Univ	NY	23,320	VC
Adrian College	MI	19,670	C
Alabama A&M Univ	AL	5,100	LC
Albany State Univ	GA	5,764	C+
Albertson College of Idaho	ID	23,900	VC
Albion College	MI	25,224	VC
Alcorn State Univ	MS	5,594	LC
Alice Lloyd College	KY	1,785	VC
Anderson Univ	IN	19,430	LC
Andrews Univ	MI	17,696	LC
Appalachian State Univ	NC	6,353	C
Aquinas College	MI	20,052	C+
Arkansas State Univ	AR	7,480	C
Armstrong Atlantic State Univ	GA	7,084	C
Asbury College	KY	18,540	VC
Ashland Univ	OH	22,182	LC
Auburn Univ	AL	5,510	C
Augsburg College	MN	22,978	C
Augustana College	IL	24,117	VC+
Augustana College	SD	20,760	VC
Aurora Univ	IL	18,551	C
Averett Univ	VA	17,980	LC
Azusa Pacific Univ	CA	22,422	VC
Barry Univ	FL	24,100	LC
Bartlesville Wesleyan College	OK	14,100	LC
Barton College	NC	16,834	LC
Baylor Univ	TX	18,298	VC+
Bellevue Univ	NE	4,125	NC
Belmont Univ	TN	19,066	VC
Benedictine College	KS	18,485	LC
Berea College	KY	4,070	VC
Berry College	GA	18,850	C
Bethany College	KS	16,602	C+
Bethany College	WV	18,566	C
Bethel College	IN	17,650	LC
Bethel College	MN	22,740	VC
Bethel College	TN	12,980	C
Bethune-Cookman College	FL	15,746	C
Biola Univ	CA	21,902	VC
Black Hills State Univ	SD	6,652	LC
Blackburn College	IL	13,690	C
Blue Mountain College	MS	9,100	LC
Bluffton College	OH	20,644	C
Boise State Univ	ID	6,531	LC
Boston Univ	MA	34,358	MC
Bowling Green State Univ	OH	10,794	C
Bridgewater State College	MA	7,589	C+
Brigham Young Univ	UT	7,840	HC
Bryan College	TN	16,400	VC
Calif Baptist Univ	CA	16,736	C
Calif Lutheran Univ	CA	23,500	LC
Calif Polytechnic State Univ	CA	8,747	VC
Cal State, Chico	CA	8,598	LC
Cal State, Dominguez Hills	CA	5,840	LC
Cal State, Fullerton	CA	5,440	LC
Cal State, Los Angeles	CA	5,050	C
Cal State, Northridge	CA	7,781	C
Cal State, San Bernardino	CA	6,516	C
Cal State, Stanislaus	CA	8,895	C
Calvin College	MI	20,050	NC
Campbellsville Univ	KY	14,340	C
Canisius College	NY	24,696	C+
Capital Univ	OH	23,630	C
Carroll College	MT	19,140	C
Carroll College	WI	21,170	C
Carthage College	WI	23,670	C
Castleton State College	VT	10,922	LC
Catawba College	NC	19,620	C
Cedarville Univ	OH	17,553	VC
Central Conn State Univ	CT	10,404	C
Central Methodist College	MO	16,460	C
Central Missouri State Univ	MO	7,920	C
Central State Univ	OH	8,922	C+
Charleston Southern Univ	SC	17,122	C
Chicago State Univ	IL	8,851	C+
Citadel, The	SC	9,126	C
CUNY/Brooklyn College	NY	3,403	LC
CUNY/Queens College	NY	3,403	VC
CUNY/York College	NY	3,292	NC
Claflin Univ	SC	12,735	C+
Clearwater Christian College	FL	13,160	LC
Cleveland State Univ	OH	10,146	NC
Coastal Carolina Univ	SC	9,220	C
Coe College	IA	24,750	VC
Coker College	SC	20,120	C
College of Charleston	SC	8,350	HC
College of Mount St. Vincent	NY	24,230	C
College of Mount St. Joseph	OH	20,290	C
College of New Jersey	NJ	13,425	HC
College of St. Catherine	MN	22,324	VC
College of the Ozarks	MO	2,650	C+
College of the Southwest	NM	8,456	NC
Colo State Univ	CO	9,672	C
Concordia College/Moorhead	MN	18,835	C
Concordia Univ	CA	22,290	C
Concordia Univ	MI	20,500	C
Concordia Univ	MN	19,912	C
Concordia Univ Nebr	NE	17,770	C
Concordia Univ Wisc	WI	16,600	LC
Concordia Univ, River Forest	IL	20,000	LC
Cornerstone Univ and Grand Rapids Baptist Seminary	MI	18,092	C
Culver-Stockton College	MO	15,400	LC
Cumberland College	KY	14,864	C
Dakota Wesleyan Univ	SD	15,512	C
Dallas Baptist Univ	TX	13,682	LC
Dana College	NE	18,046	C
David Lipscomb Univ	TN	16,158	VC
Davis and Elkins College	WV	19,270	LC
Defiance College	OH	19,580	LC
Delaware State Univ	DE	8,104	LC
Denison Univ	OH	29,640	HC
DePaul Univ	IL	23,590	VC
Dillard Univ	LA	16,046	VC
Doane College	NE	17,600	LC
Drury Univ	MO	15,250	VC
East Carolina Univ	NC	7,766	C
East Central Univ	OK	4,578	C
East Tenn State Univ	TN	7,127	C
East Texas Baptist Univ	TX	12,349	LC
Eastern College	PA	19,641	LC
Eastern Conn State Univ	CT	10,362	C
Eastern Illinois Univ	IL	10,101	C
Eastern Kentucky Univ	KY	6,552	C
Eastern Mennonite Univ	VA	20,700	VC
Eastern Mich Univ	MI	9,855	C
Eastern New Mexico Univ	NM	4,113	LC
Eastern Oregon Univ	OR	8,772	C
Eastern Washington Univ	WA	7,972	LC
Edinboro Univ of Pennsylvania	PA	9,328	LC
Edward Waters College	FL	13,124	LC
Elizabeth City State Univ	NC	5,550	LC
Elmhurst College	IL	21,750	C
Elon Univ	NC	19,430	VC
Emory & Henry College	VA	19,462	C
Emporia State Univ	KS	6,198	LC
Endicott College	MA	23,704	C
Erskine College	SC	21,399	VC
Eureka College	IL	22,200	C
Evangel Univ	MO	14,050	C
Faulkner Univ	AL	13,000	C
Ferrum College	VA	15,990	LC
Florida Atlantic Univ	FL	8,832	C
Florida International Univ	FL	9,486	VC
Florida Memorial College	FL	6,000	LC
Florida State Univ	FL	7,835	HC
Fort Hays State Univ	KS	6,294	LC
Fort Valley State Univ	GA	6,014	LC
Franklin College of Indiana	IN	19,905	C
Freed-Hardeman Univ	TN	14,290	VC
Fresno Pacific Univ	CA	19,740	C
Frostburg State Univ	MD	9,680	C
Gallaudet Univ	DC	16,554	SP
Gardner-Webb Univ	NC	17,400	C
George Fox Univ	OR	24,095	VC
Georgetown College	KY	18,400	VC
Georgia College and State Univ	GA	7,344	C
Georgia Southern Univ	GA	6,958	C
Glenville State College	WV	6,588	NC
Gonzaga Univ	WA	24,276	HC+
Goshen College	IN	18,950	VC+
Grace College	IN	16,768	C
Graceland Univ	IA	15,845	C
Grambling State Univ	LA	5,325	NC
Grand Canyon Univ	AZ	30,000	LC
Greensboro College	NC	19,080	LC
Greenville College	IL	19,226	LC
Guilford College	NC	23,255	C
Hamline Univ	MN	23,339	C+
Hampton Univ	VA	17,112	C+
Hanover College	IN	17,560	VC
Hardin-Simmons Univ	TX	14,165	C
Heidelberg College	OH	23,879	C
Henderson State Univ	AR	6,269	C
Hendrix College	AR	18,463	HC
High Point Univ	NC	20,220	LC
Hillsdale College	MI	20,586	VC+
Hofstra Univ	NY	23,252	C
Houghton College	NY	21,810	VC+
Howard Univ	DC	15,522	LC
Humboldt State Univ	CA	8,582	C
Huntingdon College	AL	18,400	VC
Huntington College	IN	15,480	LC
Huron Univ	SD	10,450	C
Husson College	ME	15,360	LC
Huston-Tillotson College	TX	12,977	LC
Idaho State Univ	ID	7,030	C+
Illinois College	IL	16,234	C
Illinois State Univ	IL	9,235	C
Indiana State Univ	IN	8,461	LC
Indiana Univ Bloomington	IN	10,712	C+
Indiana Univ of Pennsylvania	PA	9,133	C
Indiana Univ-Purdue Univ Indianapolis	IN	9,473	C
Indiana Wesleyan Univ	IN	17,680	C
Iowa State Univ	IA	8,108	VC
Iowa Wesleyan College	IA	18,840	C
Ithaca College	NY	28,719	HC
Jacksonville Univ	FL	21,110	LC
Jamestown College	ND	11,310	NC
John Brown Univ	AR	15,080	VC
John Carroll Univ	OH	24,140	VC
Johnson C. Smith Univ	NC	16,560	C+
Johnson State College	VT	10,776	C
Judson College	IL	18,980	LC
Kansas Wesleyan Univ	KS	17,400	C+
Kean Univ	NJ	11,159	C
Keene State College	NH	11,280	C
Kennesaw State Univ	GA	2,306	LC
Kent State Univ	OH	11,104	C
Kentucky State Univ	KY	6,146	NC
Kentucky Wesleyan College	KY	15,800	C
Knoxville College	TN	6,200	LC
La Sierra Univ	CA	19,260	LC
Lambuth Univ	TN	14,254	C
Lander Univ	SC	8,618	LC
Lane College	TN	10,400	C+
Langston Univ	OK	2,308	LC
Lee Univ	TN	10,198	LC
Lees-McRae College	NC	17,106	LC
LeTourneau Univ	TX	19,020	VC
Liberty Univ	VA	14,500	C
Limestone College	SC	16,900	C
Lincoln Univ	MO	7,158	NC
Lincoln Univ	PA	11,198	C+
Lindenwood Univ	MO	17,250	C
Linfield College	OR	25,840	VC
Lock Haven Univ of Pennsylvania	PA	9,534	C
Longwood College	VA	8,950	C
Loras College	IA	22,994	C+
Louisiana Tech Univ	LA	6,506	C
Lubbock Christian Univ	TX	14,226	LC
Lyndon State College	VT	11,313	LC
MacMurray College	IL	17,790	LC
Malone College	OH	19,190	C
Manhattan College	NY	25,500	VC
Marian College	IN	21,020	C
Mars Hill College	NC	18,600	LC
Maryville College	TN	23,210	VC
Marywood Univ	PA	24,639	C
Master's College	CA	21,500	C+
Mayville State Univ	ND	6,440	NC
McKendree College	IL	18,300	C+
McMurry Univ	TX	15,287	C
McPherson College	KS	17,710	C

School	ST	$IS	SR
Messiah College	PA	23,180	VC
Methodist College	NC	19,526	C
Metropolitan State College of Denver	CO	2,338	LC
Miami Univ	OH	12,885	VC+
Mich State Univ	MI	10,386	VC
MidAmerica Nazarene Univ	KS	16,960	C
Middle Tenn State Univ	TN	6,994	C
Midwestern State Univ	TX	6,704	NC
Millikin Univ	IL	24,415	C+
Minn State Univ, Mankato	MN	7,296	LC
Minot State Univ	ND	5,466	LC
Miss State Univ	MS	7,853	C
Miss Valley State Univ	MS	6,345	C
Missouri Southern State College	MO	6,666	C
Missouri Valley College	MO	17,400	LC
Monmouth College	IL	21,550	C
Montana State Univ-Billings	MT	7,653	NC
Montana State Univ-Northern	MT	8,600	NC
Montclair State Univ	NJ	10,287	LC
Morehead State Univ	KY	6,510	C
Morehouse College	GA	19,814	C
Morgan State Univ	MD	10,078	LC
Mount Marty College	SD	15,656	LC
Mount Union College	OH	21,120	C
Mount Vernon Nazarene College	OH	17,027	C
Muskingum College	OH	18,760	C
Nebr Wesleyan Univ	NE	18,767	VC
New England College	NH	20,706	LC
New Mexico State Univ	NM	7,302	C
Newberry College	SC	19,670	LC
Norfolk State Univ	VA	8,382	LC
N Car Agricultural and Technical State Univ	NC	6,659	LC
N Car Central Univ	NC	6,418	LC
N Dak State Univ	ND	7,004	VC
North Georgia College and State Univ	GA	6,322	C+
Northeastern Illinois Univ	IL	2,898	NC
Northern Kentucky Univ	KY	6,352	NC
Northern Mich Univ	MI	9,693	C
Northern State Univ	SD	6,279	LC
Northwest Missouri State Univ	MO	7,922	LC
Northwest Nazarene Univ	ID	18,380	C
Northwestern College	MN	19,816	C+
Northwestern College of Iowa	IA	17,630	C+
Northwestern Okla State Univ	OK	4,542	NC
Northwestern State Univ of Louisiana	LA	5,745	NC
Norwich Univ	VT	21,064	LC
Oakwood College	AL	14,904	C
Ohio Northern Univ	OH	27,765	VC
Ohio Wesleyan Univ	OH	29,670	VC+
Okla Baptist Univ	OK	13,878	VC
Okla Christian Univ	OK	16,500	VC
Okla City Univ	OK	15,810	C
Okla Panhandle State Univ	OK	3,812	NC
Okla State Univ	OK	7,650	VC
Old Dominion Univ	VA	9,386	C
Olivet College	MI	17,410	C
Olivet Nazarene Univ	IL	18,444	C
Oral Roberts Univ	OK	18,490	C
Ottawa Univ	KS	11,800	LC
Otterbein College	OH	23,439	C
Pacific Lutheran Univ	WA	23,318	VC
Pacific Union College	CA	20,250	VC
Palm Beach Atlantic College	FL	23,310	C
Paul Quinn College	TX	8,150	LC
Pepperdine Univ	CA	32,830	VC
Peru State College	NE	6,342	NC
Pfeiffer Univ	NC	18,580	C
Philander Smith College	AR	7,380	NC
Plymouth State College	NH	11,024	LC
Point Loma Nazarene Univ	CA	21,380	VC
Pontifical Catholic Univ of PR/Ponce	PR	7,076	
Prairie View A&M Univ	TX	3,172	LC
Purdue Univ/West Lafayette	IN	10,284	VC
Quincy Univ	IL	20,450	C
Radford Univ	VA	8,302	C
Rhode Island College	RI	8,700	LC
Ripon College	WI	24,180	VC+
Roanoke College	VA	24,689	VC
Rockford College	IL	23,930	C
Rocky Mountain College	MT	18,113	C
Saginaw Valley State Univ	MI	9,465	C
St. Ambrose Univ	IA	19,994	C
St. Andrews Presbyterian College	NC	19,720	LC
St. Augustine's College	NC	12,990	C+
St. Bonaventure Univ	NY	21,956	C
St. Edward's Univ	TX	17,846	C
St. Francis College	NY	9,610	C
St. Joseph's College	IN	21,640	C
St. Joseph's College of Maine	ME	22,500	LC
St. Leo Univ	FL	19,250	LC
St. Mary's College of Calif	CA	27,575	C
St. Vincent College	PA	22,942	VC

School	ST	$IS	SR
Salisbury Univ	MD	10,576	VC
Sam Houston State Univ	TX	6,076	LC
Samford Univ	AL	16,340	VC
San Francisco State Univ	CA	7,139	LC
Shaw Univ	NC	12,810	C
Shepherd College	WV	7,062	LC
Simpson College	IA	21,200	C+
S Car State Univ	SC	6,586	LC
S Dak State Univ	SD	6,848	C
Southeast Missouri State Univ	MO	8,367	C+
Southeastern Okla State Univ	OK	4,917	C
Southern Adventist Univ	TN	15,600	C
Southern Conn State Univ	CT	10,310	C
Southern Illinois Univ at Carbondale	IL	8,621	C
Southern Nazarene Univ	OK	14,634	NC
Southern Oregon Univ	OR	9,429	C
Southern Univ at New Orleans	LA	995	NC
Southern Utah Univ	UT	7,254	C
Southern Wesleyan Univ	SC	17,280	C
Southwest Baptist Univ	MO	13,426	LC
Southwest Missouri State Univ	MO	7,600	LC
Southwest State Univ	MN	7,117	LC
Southwest Texas State Univ	TX	8,730	VC
Southwestern Adventist Univ	TX	14,798	C
Southwestern College	KS	17,656	C
Southwestern Okla State Univ	OK	4,801	C
Springfield College	MA	24,520	C
SUNY/College at Brockport	NY	10,267	C
SUNY/College at Cortland	NY	10,564	C
State Univ of West Georgia	GA	7,101	C
Stephen F. Austin State Univ	TX	6,905	C
Sterling College	KS	16,370	VC
Stillman College	AL	11,370	LC
Syracuse Univ	NY	30,710	HC
Tabor College	KS	17,600	LC
Tarleton State Univ	TX	7,160	C
Taylor Univ	IN	21,562	VC+
Temple Univ	PA	14,124	C
Tenn Tech Univ	TN	6,968	C
Tenn Wesleyan College	TN	13,030	C
Texas A&M Univ	TX	8,988	VC
Texas A&M Univ at Kingsville	TX	6,446	LC
Texas Christian Univ	TX	19,910	C
Texas Southern Univ	TX	6,576	NC
Texas Wesleyan Univ	TX	14,710	C
Tougaloo College	MS	9,200	NC
Towson Univ	MD	11,088	VC
Trevecca Nazarene Univ	TN	15,752	C
Tri-State Univ-Main Campus	IN	21,200	C
Troy State Univ	AL	7,696	C
Truman State Univ	MO	8,568	VC+
Turabo Univ	PR	4,110	
Tusculum College	TN	17,900	LC
Tuskegee Univ	AL	14,600	LC
Union College	NE	14,650	C
Union Univ	TN	18,930	C+
Univ of Akron	OH	10,530	NC
Univ of Alabama	AL	7,402	C
Univ of Alabama at Birmingham	AL	10,110	C
Univ of Alaska Anchorage	AK	9,100	NC
Univ of Arizona	AZ	8,614	C
Univ of Arkansas at Monticello	AR	5,940	NC
Univ of Arkansas at Pine Bluff	AR	7,925	C
Univ of Calif at Davis	CA	12,796	VC
Univ of Central Arkansas	AR	6,388	C
Univ of Central Florida	FL	8,251	VC
Univ of Central Okla	OK	5,205	C
Univ of Charleston	WV	20,640	C
Univ of Delaware	DE	10,824	VC
Univ of Dubuque	IA	19,990	C
Univ of Evansville	IN	22,865	VC+
Univ of Findlay	OH	23,962	NC
Univ of Great Falls	MT	15,360	C
Univ of Hawaii at Manoa	HI	7,862	VC
Univ of Idaho	ID	7,026	C
Univ of Illinois at Chicago	IL	10,702	VC
Univ of Illinois at Urbana-Champaign	IL	11,316	HC+
Univ of Indianapolis	IN	20,840	C
Univ of Kansas	KS	7,232	VC
Univ of Kentucky	KY	7,765	C
Univ of La Verne	CA	24,280	C
Univ of Louisiana at Monroe	LA	5,207	NC
Univ of Louisville	KY	7,402	LC
Univ of Maine	ME	10,798	C
Univ of Maine at Presque Isle	ME	7,964	LC
Univ of Mary	ND	12,900	LC
Univ of Maryland/College Park	MD	11,959	C
Univ of Maryland/Eastern Shore	MD	9,258	C

School	ST	$IS	SR
Univ of Mass Amherst	MA	10,995	VC
Univ of Mass Boston	MA	4,227	C
Univ of Mich/Ann Arbor	MI	13,003	HC+
Univ of Minn/Duluth	MN	10,436	C
Univ of Minn/Twin Cities	MN	11,123	VC
Univ of Missouri/Kansas City	MO	9,685	VC
Univ of Missouri/St. Louis	MO	9,966	C
Univ of Mobile	AL	13,620	LC
Univ of Montana	MT	8,038	C
Univ of Montevallo	AL	7,266	C
Univ of Nebr at Kearney	NE	7,048	NC
Univ of Nebr at Omaha	NE	6,867	C
Univ of Nevada/Las Vegas	NV	8,281	VC
Univ of New Hampshire	NH	13,207	C
Univ of New Mexico	NM	8,026	C
Univ of New Orleans	LA	10,160	C
Univ of North Alabama	AL	7,016	NC
Univ of N Car at Chapel Hill	NC	8,789	HC
Univ of N Car at Pembroke	NC	5,914	LC
Univ of N Car at Wilmington	NC	7,769	C
Univ of N Dak	ND	7,067	VC
Univ of North Florida	FL	8,089	VC
Univ of North Texas	TX	7,629	C
Univ of Northern Colo	CO	8,082	C+
Univ of Northern Iowa	IA	7,850	C
Univ of Rhode Island	RI	12,414	C
Univ of Rio Grande	OH	8,728	NC
Univ of St. Thomas	MN	24,044	VC
Univ of Science and Arts of Okla	OK	5,245	C
Univ of South Alabama	AL	6,976	LC
Univ of S Car at Columbia	SC	8,748	VC
Univ of S Car at Spartanburg	SC	7,318	C+
Univ of S Dak	SD	7,036	C
Univ of South Florida	FL	8,154	C
Univ of Southern Calif	CA	33,647	MC
Univ of Tenn at Knoxville	TN	8,214	C
Univ of Texas at Arlington	TX	7,192	LC
Univ of the District of Columbia	DC	2,844	NC
Univ of the Incarnate Word	TX	18,478	C
Univ of the Ozarks	AR	13,904	C
Univ of the Pacific	CA	28,255	VC
Univ of the Sacred Heart	PR	5,375	
Univ of Toledo	OH	11,206	NC
Univ of Vermont	VT	14,761	C+
Univ of Virginia	VA	9,391	HC+
Univ of West Alabama	AL	6,048	C
Univ of Wisc/Eau Claire	WI	7,032	VC
Univ of Wisc/La Crosse	WI	7,250	VC
Univ of Wisc/Madison	WI	8,262	VC
Univ of Wisc/Oshkosh	WI	6,130	LC
Univ of Wisc/Platteville	WI	7,282	C
Univ of Wisc/River Falls	WI	6,356	LC
Univ of Wisc/Stevens Point	WI	7,116	C
Univ of Wisc/Superior	WI	7,051	C+
Univ of Wisc/Whitewater	WI	6,937	C
Univ of Wyoming	WY	7,143	LC
Upper Iowa Univ	IA	17,438	C
Utah State Univ	UT	6,771	C
Valdosta State Univ	GA	6,988	C
Valley City State Univ	ND		LC
Valparaiso Univ	IN	23,570	VC+
Vanguard Univ of Southern Calif	CA	20,212	C
Virginia Polytechnic Inst and State Univ	VA	7,652	C
Virginia State Univ	VA	8,182	LC
Walla Walla College	WA	20,925	C
Walsh Univ	OH	16,880	C
Warner Pacific College	OR	20,370	LC
Wartburg College	IA	21,165	VC
Washburn Univ of Topeka	KS	6,766	NC
Washington State Univ	WA	9,388	C
Wayland Baptist Univ	TX	11,271	NC
Wayne State Univ	MI	6,720	C
Weber State Univ	UT	6,897	NC
Wesley College	DE	17,869	C
West Chester Univ of Pennsylvania	PA	9,792	VC
West Liberty State College	WV	6,056	LC
West Texas A&M Univ	TX	6,538	C
West Virginia Univ	WV	8,304	C
West Virginia Wesleyan College	WV	22,920	C
Western Baptist College	OR	19,700	C+
Western Carolina Univ	NC	5,667	C
Western Illinois Univ	IL	9,571	C
Western Kentucky Univ	KY	6,834	C
Western Maryland College	MD	26,000	VC
Western Mich Univ	MI	10,016	C
Western New Mexico Univ	NM	5,950	LC
Westminster College	MO	19,990	C+
Westmont College	CA	29,748	VC
Whittier College	CA	29,108	C
Wichita State Univ	KS	6,879	C
Wiley College	TX	8,100	LC
William Carey College	MS	10,150	LC
William Paterson Univ of New Jersey	NJ	11,000	LC
William Penn Univ	IA	17,575	C
William Woods Univ	MO	19,390	LC
Williams Baptist College	AR	10,750	C
Wilmington College	OH	21,826	C

School	ST	$IS	SR
Wingate Univ	NC	19,140	C
Winston-Salem State Univ	NC	5,927	LC
Winthrop Univ	SC	9,106	C
Wright State Univ	OH	9,141	LC
Xavier Univ of Louisiana	LA	17,000	LC
Youngstown State Univ	OH	9,318	NC

PHYSICAL FITNESS/ MOVEMENT

School	ST	$IS	SR
Adelphi Univ	NY	23,320	VC
Adrian College	MI	19,670	C
Arizona State Univ-Main	AZ	7,726	C
Ashland Univ	OH	22,182	LC
Auburn Univ	AL	5,510	C
Augustana College	SD	20,760	VC
Baldwin-Wallace College	OH	22,010	VC+
Ball State Univ	IN	8,660	C
Baylor Univ	TX	18,298	VC+
Berry College	GA	18,850	C
Bethel College	TN	12,980	C
Bloomsburg Univ of Pennsylvania	PA	9,434	C
Boston Univ	MA	34,358	MC
Bowling Green State Univ	OH	10,794	C
Brigham Young Univ/Hawaii	HI	6,890	C
Buena Vista Univ	IA	22,828	C
Calif State Polytechnic Univ, Pomona	CA	8,615	C
Cal State, Fresno	CA	7,762	C
Cal State, Hayward	CA	7,400	LC
Campbell Univ	NC	16,599	C
Capital Univ	OH	23,630	C
Chapman Univ	CA	30,218	VC
Christian Heritage College	CA	18,000	LC
Clarke College	IA	20,625	C+
College of St. Catherine	MN	22,324	VC
Concordia Univ Nebr	NE	17,770	C
Concordia Univ, River Forest	IL	20,000	LC
Dallas Baptist Univ	TX	13,682	LC
Defiance College	OH	19,580	LC
DePauw Univ	IN	28,000	HC
Drury Univ	MO	15,250	VC
East Carolina Univ	NC	7,766	C
East Stroudsburg Univ of Pennsylvania	PA	8,430	LC
East Texas Baptist Univ	TX	12,349	LC
Eastern Nazarene College	MA	19,433	LC
Eureka College	IL	22,200	C
George Washington Univ	DC	32,170	HC
Georgia Southern Univ	GA	6,958	C
Georgia State Univ	GA	7,792	LC
Gordon College	MA	23,594	VC+
Grand Canyon Univ	AZ	30,000	LC
Hardin-Simmons Univ	TX	14,165	C
High Point Univ	NC	20,220	LC
Hofstra Univ	NY	23,252	C
Hope College	MI	22,922	C+
Houston Baptist Univ	TX	15,300	LC
Humboldt State Univ	CA	8,582	C
Indiana Univ Bloomington	IN	10,712	C+
Ithaca College	NY	28,719	HC
James Madison Univ	VA	9,552	HC
Johnson State College	VT	10,776	C
Judson College	AL	13,790	C
Kansas State Univ	KS	6,995	C
Lakeland College	WI	17,950	C
Lasell College	MA	24,100	C
Lewis-Clark State College	ID	6,496	C
Limestone College	SC	16,900	C
Louisiana State Univ and A&M College	LA	8,014	VC
Lubbock Christian Univ	TX	14,226	LC
Lynchburg College	VA	23,405	C
Malone College	OH	19,190	C
Marshall Univ	WV	7,752	LC
Marymount Univ	VA	21,560	LC
Mesa State College	CO	8,051	C
Metropolitan State College of Denver	CO	2,338	LC
Miami Univ	OH	12,885	VC+
Minot State Univ	ND	5,466	LC
Miss Univ for Women	MS	5,446	LC
Missouri Baptist College	MO	15,762	LC
Mount Union College	OH	21,120	C
New England College	NH	20,706	LC
New Mexico Highlands Univ	NM	6,256	NC
N Dak State Univ	ND	7,004	VC
Northeastern Univ	MA	30,078	VC
Northern Kentucky Univ	KY	6,352	NC
Northern Mich Univ	MI	9,693	C
Northern State Univ	SD	6,279	LC
Northwestern College of Iowa	IA	17,630	C+
Oakwood College	AL	14,904	C
Occidental College	CA	32,288	HC
Penn State Univ/Univ Park Campus	PA	11,126	VC
Sacred Heart Univ	CT	26,588	VC
St. Augustine's College	NC	12,990	C+
St. Edward's Univ	TX	17,846	C
Sam Houston State Univ	TX	6,076	LC
Schreiner Univ	TX	19,254	C
Seattle Pacific Univ	WA	22,674	C+
Shenandoah Univ	VA	22,550	NC

School	ST	$IS	SR
Shepherd College	WV	7,062	LC
Southwestern Univ	TX	22,550	HC
Spring Arbor Univ	MI	17,976	C
Springfield College	MA	24,520	C
Stephen F. Austin State Univ	TX	6,905	C
Stetson Univ	FL	25,640	VC
Sul Ross State Univ	TX	6,582	LC
Tarleton State Univ	TX	7,160	C
Temple Univ	PA	14,124	C
Texas Christian Univ	TX	19,910	C
Texas Lutheran Univ	TX	17,660	C
Texas Woman's Univ	TX	5,855	LC
Truman State Univ	MO	8,568	VC+
Union College	NE	14,650	C
Univ of Alabama	AL	7,402	C
Univ of Central Okla	OK	5,205	C
Univ of Dayton	OH	20,400	VC
Univ of Delaware	DE	10,824	VC
Univ of Evansville	IN	22,865	VC+
Univ of Florida	FL	7,874	HC
Univ of Houston	TX	8,410	C
Univ of Maryland/College Park	MD	11,959	C
Univ of Mich/Ann Arbor	MI	13,003	HC+
Univ of Nevada/Las Vegas	NV	8,281	VC
Univ of New Hampshire	NH	13,207	C
Univ of New Mexico	NM	8,026	C
Univ of N Car at Charlotte	NC	7,254	C
Univ of North Texas	TX	7,629	C
Univ of Northern Colo	CO	8,082	C+
Univ of Pittsburgh at Pittsburgh	PA	13,592	HC
Univ of Puget Sound	WA	28,285	HC
Univ of Rio Grande	OH	8,728	NC
Univ of S Car at Aiken	SC	7,828	LC
Univ of Texas at Austin	TX	9,437	HC
Univ of Texas at El Paso	TX	5,076	LC
Univ of Texas at San Antonio	TX	9,088	NC
Univ of Texas-Pan American	TX	4,823	C
Univ of Toledo	OH	11,206	NC
Univ of Wisc/Stevens Point	WI	7,116	C
Upper Iowa Univ	IA	17,438	C
Urbana Univ	OH	17,004	C
West Liberty State College	WV	6,056	LC
Western State College of Colo	CO	7,585	LC
Westfield State College	MA	8,394	C
Wheaton College	IL	21,934	HC
Winona State Univ	MN	8,570	C
Youngstown State Univ	OH	9,318	NC

PHYSICAL SCIENCES

School	ST	$IS	SR
Alverno College	WI	16,930	LC
Antioch College	OH	25,072	LC
Arkansas Tech Univ	AR	6,256	C
Armstrong Atlantic State Univ	GA	7,084	C
Asbury College	KY	18,540	VC
Auburn Univ Montgomery	AL	5,330	NC
Augusta State Univ	GA	2,282	C
Biola Univ	CA	21,902	VC
Black Hills State Univ	SD	6,652	LC
Bowling Green State Univ	OH	10,794	C
Brescia Univ	KY	14,225	C
Bridgewater College	VA	22,950	C
Calif Polytechnic State Univ	CA	8,747	VC
Cal State, Chico	CA	8,598	LC
Cal State, Hayward	CA	7,400	LC
Cal State, Sacramento	CA	7,488	C
Cal State, Stanislaus	CA	8,895	C
Central Conn State Univ	CT	10,404	C
Central Mich Univ	MI	8,355	C
Colgate Univ	NY	33,480	MC
Colo State Univ	CO	9,672	C
Concordia Univ Nebr	NE	17,770	C
Concordia Univ, River Forest	IL	20,000	LC
Doane College	NE	17,600	LC
East Stroudsburg Univ of Pennsylvania	PA	8,430	LC
Emporia State Univ	KS	6,198	LC
Eureka College	IL	22,200	C
Fort Hays State Univ	KS	6,294	LC
Freed-Hardeman Univ	TN	14,290	VC
Harvard Univ/Harvard College	MA	34,269	MC
Kansas State Univ	KS	6,995	C
Kent State Univ	OH	11,104	C
Lynchburg College	VA	23,405	C
Malone College	OH	19,190	C
Mayville State Univ	ND	6,440	NC
Mesa State College	CO	8,051	C
Mich State Univ	MI	10,386	VC
Minot State Univ	ND	5,466	LC
Miss Univ for Women	MS	5,446	LC
Muhlenberg College	PA	28,170	HC
Okla Panhandle State Univ	OK	3,812	NC
Olivet Nazarene Univ	IL	18,444	C
Peru State College	NE	6,342	NC
Radford Univ	VA	8,302	C
Rice Univ	TX	24,325	MC
St. John's Univ	NY	26,660	C
St. Michael's College	VT	26,935	VC
San Diego State Univ	CA	9,716	C+
Shawnee State Univ	OH	8,634	NC
Stephen F. Austin State Univ	TX	6,905	C
Texas Wesleyan Univ	TX	14,710	C
Tri-State Univ-Main Campus	IN	21,200	C
Troy State Univ/Dothan	AL	3,296	C
Union Univ	TN	18,930	C+
Univ of Arkansas at Monticello	AR	5,940	NC
Univ of Calif at Berkeley	CA	14,134	MC
Univ of Calif at Riverside	CA	12,479	C
Univ of Dayton	OH	20,400	VC
Univ of Great Falls	MT	15,360	C
Univ of Maryland/College Park	MD	11,959	C
Univ of Mich/Flint	MI	4,323	C
Univ of Rio Grande	OH	8,728	NC
Univ of South Florida	FL	8,154	C
Univ of Southern Calif	CA	33,647	MC
Univ of Wisc/Eau Claire	WI	7,032	VC
Univ of Wisc/Platteville	WI	7,282	C
Warner Pacific College	OR	20,370	LC
Washington State Univ	WA	9,388	C
Washington Univ in St. Louis	MO	34,593	MC
Wayland Baptist Univ	TX	11,271	NC
Weber State Univ	UT	6,897	NC
Wesleyan College	GA	17,050	VC
Wheaton College	IL	21,934	HC
York College of Pennsylvania	PA	12,550	VC

PHYSICAL THERAPY

School	ST	$IS	SR
American International College	MA	22,268	LC
Arkansas State Univ	AR	7,480	C
Armstrong Atlantic State Univ	GA	7,084	C
Boston Univ	MA	34,358	MC
Bowling Green State Univ	OH	10,794	C
Bradley Univ	IL	20,970	VC
Cal State, Northridge	CA	7,781	C
Cal State, Sacramento	CA	7,488	C
Carson-Newman College	TN	16,490	C
CUNY/College of Staten Island	NY	3,358	NC
CUNY/Hunter College	NY	5,147	C+
Clarke College	IA	20,625	C+
Cleveland State Univ	OH	10,146	NC
Coe College	IA	24,750	VC
College Misericordia	PA	23,380	LC
College of St. Benedict	MN	23,921	VC
Concordia College	NY	19,200	VC
Daemen College	NY	20,620	C
Dominican College	NY	20,400	LC
Duquesne Univ	PA	24,242	C+
D'Youville College	NY	18,704	C
Florida A&M Univ	FL	6,948	C
Florida Gulf Coast Univ	FL	9,201	C
Georgia State Univ	GA	7,792	LC
Grand Valley State Univ	MI	10,040	C
Gustavus Adolphus College	MN	24,190	VC+
Howard Univ	DC	15,522	LC
Indiana Univ-Purdue Univ Indianapolis	IN	9,473	C
Ithaca College	NY	28,719	HC
Lamar Univ	TX	6,816	LC
Langston Univ	OK	2,308	LC
Lebanon Valley College of Pennsylvania	PA	25,700	VC
Lewis Univ	IL	20,960	C
LIU/Brooklyn Campus	NY	22,290	C
Loras College	IA	22,994	C+
Marquette Univ	WI	24,836	C+
Missouri Southern State College	MO	6,666	C
Nazareth College of Rochester	NY	22,036	VC
New York Inst of Technology	NY	21,756	C
North Park Univ	IL	24,030	C
Northeastern Univ	MA	30,078	VC
Northern Illinois Univ	IL	9,545	C
Oakland Univ	MI	9,418	C
Okla Baptist Univ	OK	13,878	VC
Purdue Univ/Calumet	IN	6,630	NC
Richard Stockton College of New Jersey	NJ	12,165	VC
Rivier College	NH	24,215	C
Russell Sage College	NY	23,674	C+
St. Edward's Univ	TX	17,846	C
St. Francis Univ	PA	24,486	LC
St. John's Univ	MN	23,640	VC
St. Mary's Univ of Minn	MN	19,975	C
St. Vincent College	PA	22,942	VC
San Francisco State Univ	CA	7,139	LC
Simmons College	MA	30,418	VC
Southern Nazarene Univ	OK	14,634	NC
Tarleton State Univ	TX	7,160	C
Tenn State Univ	TN	7,058	VC
Ohio State Univ	OH	10,819	VC
Thiel College	PA	18,419	LC
Touro College	NY	14,950	VC
Truman State Univ	MO	8,568	VC+
Univ of Central Arkansas	AR	6,388	C
Univ of Conn	CT	12,122	VC
Univ of Evansville	IN	22,865	VC+
Univ of Florida	FL	7,874	HC
Univ of Hartford	CT	28,884	C
Univ of Kentucky	KY	7,765	C
Univ of Mary	ND	12,900	LC
Univ of Maryland/Eastern Shore	MD	9,258	C
Univ of Miami	FL	31,130	HC
Univ of Mich/Flint	MI	4,323	C
Univ of Minn/Twin Cities	MN	11,123	VC
Univ of Missouri/Columbia	MO	9,803	HC
Univ of New England	ME	24,110	LC
Univ of New Mexico	NM	8,026	C
Univ of N Dak	ND	7,067	VC
Univ of Scranton	PA	27,964	C+
Univ of Southern Calif	CA	33,647	MC
Univ of the Sciences in Philadelphia	PA	24,826	VC
Univ of Toledo	OH	11,206	NC
Univ of Utah	UT	7,703	C
Utica College of Syracuse Univ	NY	24,400	LC
Virginia Commonwealth Univ	VA	9,030	C
Walsh Univ	OH	16,880	C
Waynesburg College	PA	17,610	LC
West Virginia Univ	WV	8,304	C
Western State College of Colo	CO	7,585	LC
Winona State Univ	MN	8,570	C
Winston-Salem State Univ	NC	5,927	LC
Youngstown State Univ	OH	9,318	NC

PHYSICIAN'S ASSISTANT

School	ST	$IS	SR
Butler Univ	IN	25,580	VC+
Catawba College	NC	19,620	C
CUNY/College of Staten Island	NY	3,358	NC
Daemen College	NY	20,620	C
De Sales Univ	PA	22,610	VC
Duquesne Univ	PA	24,242	C+
D'Youville College	NY	18,704	C
East Carolina Univ	NC	7,766	C
Gannon Univ	PA	18,848	C
Gardner-Webb Univ	NC	17,400	C
George Washington Univ	DC	32,170	HC
Grand Valley State Univ	MI	10,040	C
Howard Univ	DC	15,522	LC
Idaho State Univ	ID	7,030	C+
Le Moyne College	NY	23,840	C
Lenoir-Rhyne College	NC	19,186	C
LIU/Brooklyn Campus	NY	22,290	C
Marquette Univ	WI	24,836	C+
Mars Hill College	NC	18,600	LC
Marywood Univ	PA	24,639	C
MCP Hahnemann Univ	PA	18,510	SP
Methodist College	NC	19,526	C
Mountain State Univ	WV	8,180	NC
New York Inst of Technology	NY	21,756	C
Nova Southeastern Univ	FL	20,104	LC
Pace Univ	NY	24,200	C
Pennsylvania College of Technology	PA	12,860	NC
Philadelphia Univ	PA	24,722	C
Rochester Inst of Technology	NY	26,232	VC+
Rocky Mountain College	MT	18,113	C
St. Francis College	NY	9,610	C
St. Francis Univ	PA	24,486	LC
St. John's Univ	NY	26,660	C
St. Louis Univ	MO	26,590	VC+
St. Vincent College	PA	22,942	VC
Salem College	NC	23,065	VC
Seton Hill College	PA	21,875	C
South College	GA	8,720	LC
Southern Illinois Univ at Carbondale	IL	8,621	C
SUNY/Univ at Stony Brook	NY	10,998	VC
Union College	NE	14,650	C
Univ of Alabama at Birmingham	AL	10,110	C
Univ of Findlay	OH	23,962	NC
Univ of Florida	FL	7,874	HC
Univ of Kentucky	KY	7,765	C
Univ of New Mexico	NM	8,026	C
Univ of S Dak	SD	7,036	C
Univ of Southern Calif	CA	33,647	MC
Univ of Southern Colo	CO	7,821	LC
Univ of Texas-Pan American	TX	4,823	C
Univ of the Sciences in Philadelphia	PA	24,826	VC
Univ of Wisc/La Crosse	WI	7,250	VC
Univ of Wisc/Madison	WI	8,262	VC
Wagner College	NY	27,000	C
Wichita State Univ	KS	6,879	C

PHYSICS

School	ST	$IS	SR
Abilene Christian Univ	TX	16,300	VC
Adelphi Univ	NY	23,320	VC
Adrian College	MI	19,670	C
Agnes Scott College	GA	24,950	VC
Alabama A&M Univ	AL	5,100	LC
Alabama State Univ	AL	6,404	C
Albertson College of Idaho	ID	23,900	VC
Albion College	MI	25,224	VC
Albright College	PA	27,642	C
Alfred Univ	NY	27,212	C+
Allegheny College	PA	27,780	VC
Alma College	MI	22,586	VC
American Univ	DC	31,544	VC+
Amherst College	MA	34,340	MC
Anderson Univ	IN	19,430	LC
Andrews Univ	MI	17,696	LC
Angelo State Univ	TX	7,028	C
Appalachian State Univ	NC	6,353	C
Arizona State Univ-Main	AZ	7,726	C
Arkansas State Univ	AR	7,480	C
Ashland Univ	OH	22,182	LC
Auburn Univ	AL	5,510	C
Augsburg College	MN	22,978	C
Augusta State Univ	GA	2,282	C
Augustana College	IL	24,117	VC+
Augustana College	SD	20,760	VC
Austin College	TX	22,150	VC+
Austin Peay State Univ	TN	5,814	LC
Azusa Pacific Univ	CA	22,422	VC
Baker Univ	KS	14,780	C+
Baldwin-Wallace College	OH	22,010	VC+
Ball State Univ	IN	8,660	C
Bard College	NY	33,912	HC
Bates College	ME	34,100	MC
Baylor Univ	TX	18,298	VC+
Belmont Univ	TN	19,066	VC
Beloit College	WI	27,482	HC
Bemidji State Univ	MN	7,957	C
Benedict College	SC	12,662	LC
Benedictine College	KS	18,485	LC
Benedictine Univ	IL	21,330	C
Bennington College	VT	31,350	VC
Berea College	KY	4,070	VC
Berry College	GA	18,850	C
Bethany College	WV	18,566	C
Bethel College	IN	17,650	LC
Bethel College	KS	17,355	C+
Bethel College	MN	22,740	VC
Bethune-Cookman College	FL	15,746	C
Birmingham-Southern College	AL	22,960	C
Bloomsburg Univ of Pennsylvania	PA	9,434	C
Boise State Univ	ID	6,531	LC
Boston College	MA	33,330	MC
Boston Univ	MA	34,358	MC
Bowdoin College	ME	32,650	MC
Bowling Green State Univ	OH	10,794	C
Bradley Univ	IL	20,970	VC
Brandeis Univ	MA	34,481	MC
Bridgewater College	VA	22,950	C
Bridgewater State College	MA	7,589	C+
Brigham Young Univ	UT	7,840	HC
Brown Univ	RI	34,973	MC
Bryn Mawr College	PA	33,580	HC+
Bucknell Univ	PA	31,096	HC
Buena Vista Univ	IA	22,828	C
Butler Univ	IN	25,580	VC+
Calif Inst of Technology	CA	27,663	MC
Calif Lutheran Univ	CA	23,500	LC
Calif Polytechnic State Univ	CA	8,747	VC
Calif State Polytechnic Univ, Pomona	CA	8,615	C
Cal State, Bakersfield	CA	6,090	LC
Cal State, Chico	CA	8,598	LC
Cal State, Dominguez Hills	CA	5,840	LC
Cal State, Fresno	CA	7,762	C
Cal State, Fullerton	CA	5,440	LC
Cal State, Hayward	CA	7,400	LC
Cal State, Long Beach	CA	7,400	LC
Cal State, Los Angeles	CA	5,050	C
Cal State, Northridge	CA	7,781	C
Cal State, Sacramento	CA	7,488	C
Cal State, San Bernardino	CA	6,516	C
Cal State, Stanislaus	CA	8,895	C
Calif Univ of Pennsylvania	PA	10,388	C
Calvin College	MI	20,050	NC
Cameron Univ	OK	5,560	NC
Canisius College	NY	24,696	C+
Carleton College	MN	30,780	MC
Carnegie Mellon Univ	PA	32,682	MC
Carthage College	WI	23,670	C
Case Western Reserve Univ	OH	27,418	C
Catholic Univ of America	DC	29,332	VC
Cedarville Univ	OH	17,553	VC
Centenary College of Louisiana	LA	21,600	C+
Central College	IA	21,206	C
Central Conn State Univ	CT	10,404	C
Central Methodist College	MO	16,460	C
Central Mich Univ	MI	8,355	C
Central Missouri State Univ	MO	7,920	C
Central Washington Univ	WA	8,985	LC
Centre College	KY	24,000	HC
Chadron State College	NE	6,211	NC
Chatham College	PA	25,454	C+

School	ST	$IS	SR
Chicago State Univ	IL	8,851	C+
Christian Brothers Univ	TN	19,820	VC
Christopher Newport Univ	VA	8,862	VC
Citadel, The	SC	9,126	C
CUNY/Brooklyn College	NY	3,403	LC
CUNY/City College	NY	3,309	LC
CUNY/College of Staten Island	NY	3,358	NC
CUNY/Herbert H. Lehman College	NY	3,320	LC
CUNY/Hunter College	NY	5,147	C+
CUNY/Queens College	NY	3,403	VC
CUNY/York College	NY	3,292	NC
Claremont McKenna College	CA	32,700	MC
Clarion Univ of Pennsylvania	PA	11,272	LC
Clark Atlanta Univ	GA	17,174	C
Clark Univ	MA	29,170	HC
Clarkson Univ	NY	29,884	VC
Clemson Univ	SC	7,600	C
Cleveland State Univ	OH	10,146	NC
Coe College	IA	24,750	VC
Colby College	ME	34,290	MC
Colgate Univ	NY	33,480	MC
College of Charleston	SC	8,350	HC
College of Mount St. Vincent	NY	24,230	C
College of New Jersey	NJ	13,425	HC
College of New Rochelle	NY	20,000	C
College of Notre Dame of Maryland	MD	23,100	LC
College of St. Benedict	MN	23,921	VC
College of the Holy Cross	MA	32,780	MC
College of William and Mary	VA	10,002	MC
College of Wooster	OH	28,350	VC
Colo College	CO	31,525	HC+
Colo School of Mines	CO	11,578	HC
Colo State Univ	CO	9,672	C
Columbia Univ/Barnard College	NY	33,694	MC
Columbia Univ/Columbia College	NY	35,190	MC
Columbia Univ/School of General Studies	NY	35,000	C
Concordia College/Moorhead	MN	18,835	C
Conn College	CT	33,585	MC
Cornell College	IA	24,980	VC
Cornell Univ	NY	34,614	MC
Covenant College	GA	21,970	C+
Creighton Univ	NE	23,476	VC
Cumberland College	KY	14,864	C
Curry College	MA	26,025	LC
Dakota State Univ	SD	6,950	C
Dartmouth College	NH	34,458	MC
David Lipscomb Univ	TN	16,158	VC
Davidson College	NC	30,823	MC
Delaware State Univ	DE	8,104	LC
Denison Univ	OH	29,640	HC
DePaul Univ	IL	23,590	VC
DePauw Univ	IN	28,000	HC
Dickinson College	PA	32,210	VC+
Dillard Univ	LA	16,046	VC
Doane College	NE	17,600	LC
Dordt College	IA	18,100	C+
Drake Univ	IA	22,830	VC
Drew Univ/College of Liberal Arts	NJ	32,152	VC
Drexel Univ	PA	27,657	VC
Drury Univ	MO	15,250	VC
Duke Univ	NC	34,396	MC
Duquesne Univ	PA	24,242	C+
Earlham College	IN	27,446	VC+
East Carolina Univ	NC	7,766	C
East Central Univ	OK	4,578	C
East Tenn State Univ	TN	7,127	C
Eastern Illinois Univ	IL	10,101	C
Eastern Mich Univ	MI	9,855	C
Eastern Nazarene College	MA	19,433	LC
Eastern New Mexico Univ	NM	4,113	LC
Eastern Oregon Univ	OR	8,772	C
Eastern Washington Univ	WA	7,972	LC
Eckerd College	FL	25,500	C+
Edinboro Univ of Pennsylvania	PA	9,328	LC
Elizabeth City State Univ	NC	5,550	LC
Elizabethtown College	PA	26,000	VC
Elmhurst College	IL	21,750	C
Elon Univ	NC	19,430	VC
Emory & Henry College	VA	19,462	C
Emory Univ	GA	33,792	MC
Emporia State Univ	KS	6,198	LC
Erskine College	SC	21,399	VC
Fairfield Univ	CT	30,885	HC
Fisk Univ	TN	13,700	LC
Florida A&M Univ	FL	6,948	C
Florida Atlantic Univ	FL	8,832	C
Florida Inst of Technology	FL	25,250	VC
Florida International Univ	FL	9,486	VC
Florida Southern College	FL	19,430	C
Florida State Univ	FL	7,835	HC
Fordham Univ	NY	30,710	VC
Fort Hays State Univ	KS	6,294	LC
Fort Lewis College	CO	7,659	LC
Francis Marion Univ	SC	7,682	C
Franklin and Marshall College	PA	32,410	HC
Franklin College of Indiana	IN	19,905	C
Frostburg State Univ	MD	9,680	C
Furman Univ	SC	25,492	HC
Gallaudet Univ	DC	16,554	SP
Geneva College	PA	19,990	C+
George Mason Univ	VA	9,192	C
George Washington Univ	DC	32,170	HC
Georgetown College	KY	18,400	VC
Georgetown Univ	DC	34,847	MC
Georgia Inst of Technology	GA	9,028	HC+
Georgia Southern Univ	GA	6,958	C
Georgia State Univ	GA	7,792	LC
Georgian Court College	NJ	19,040	LC
Gettysburg College	PA	32,070	HC
Gonzaga Univ	WA	24,276	HC+
Gordon College	MA	23,594	VC+
Goshen College	IN	18,950	VC+
Goucher College	MD	30,650	VC+
Grambling State Univ	LA	5,325	NC
Grand Valley State Univ	MI	10,040	C
Greenville College	IL	19,226	LC
Grinnell College	IA	28,300	HC+
Grove City College	PA	12,280	MC
Guilford College	NC	23,255	C
Gustavus Adolphus College	MN	24,190	VC+
Hamilton College	NY	34,150	HC
Hamline Univ	MN	23,339	C+
Hampden-Sydney College	VA	24,871	C
Hampshire College	MA	33,881	HC+
Hampton Univ	VA	17,112	C+
Hanover College	IN	17,560	VC
Harding Univ	AR	13,528	VC
Hardin-Simmons Univ	TX	14,165	C
Hartwick College	NY	33,090	C+
Harvard Univ/Harvard College	MA	34,269	MC
Harvey Mudd College	CA	31,605	MC
Hastings College	NE	17,854	C+
Haverford College	PA	34,300	MC
Heidelberg College	OH	23,879	C
Henderson State Univ	AR	6,269	C
Hendrix College	AR	18,463	HC
Hillsdale College	MI	20,586	VC+
Hobart and William Smith Colleges	NY	33,195	VC
Hofstra Univ	NY	23,252	C
Hollins Univ	VA	24,328	VC
Hope College	MI	22,922	C+
Houghton College	NY	21,810	VC+
Houston Baptist Univ	TX	15,300	LC
Howard Univ	DC	15,522	LC
Humboldt State Univ	CA	8,582	C
Idaho State Univ	ID	7,030	C+
Illinois College	IL	16,234	C
Illinois Inst of Technology	IL	25,182	HC+
Illinois State Univ	IL	9,235	C
Illinois Wesleyan Univ	IL	26,970	HC
Indiana State Univ	IN	8,461	LC
Indiana Univ Bloomington	IN	10,712	C+
Indiana Univ of Pennsylvania	PA	9,133	C
Indiana Univ South Bend	IN	3,515	C
Indiana Univ-Purdue Univ Fort Wayne	IN	3,166	LC
Indiana Univ-Purdue Univ Indianapolis	IN	9,473	C
Iona College	NY	26,556	C
Iowa State Univ	IA	8,108	VC
Ithaca College	NY	28,719	HC
Jackson State Univ	MS	6,776	LC
Jacksonville State Univ	AL	6,568	LC
Jacksonville Univ	FL	21,110	LC
James Madison Univ	VA	9,552	HC
John Carroll Univ	OH	24,140	VC
Johns Hopkins Univ	MD	35,226	MC
Johnson C. Smith Univ	NC	16,560	C+
Juniata College	PA	26,080	VC
Kalamazoo College	MI	26,955	HC+
Kansas State Univ	KS	6,995	C
Kansas Wesleyan Univ	KS	17,400	C+
Kent State Univ	OH	11,104	C
Kentucky Wesleyan College	KY	15,800	C
Kenyon College	OH	32,130	HC+
King College	TN	17,800	VC
Knox College	IL	28,230	HC
Kutztown Univ of Pennsylvania	PA	8,907	C
La Sierra Univ	CA	19,260	LC
Lafayette College	PA	32,655	MC
Lake Forest College	IL	27,460	VC
Lamar Univ	TX	6,816	LC
Lane College	TN	10,400	C+
Lawrence Tech Univ	MI	11,429	C
Lawrence Univ	WI	27,711	HC
Le Moyne College	NY	23,840	C
Lebanon Valley College of Pennsylvania	PA	25,700	VC
Lehigh Univ	PA	32,290	MC
Lenoir-Rhyne College	NC	19,186	C
Lewis and Clark College	OR	29,010	VC
Lewis Univ	IL	20,960	C
Lincoln Univ	MO	7,158	NC
Lincoln Univ	PA	11,198	C+
Linfield College	OR	25,840	VC
Lock Haven Univ of Pennsylvania	PA	9,534	C
LIU/C.W. Post Campus	NY	25,380	C
Longwood College	VA	8,950	C
Loras College	IA	22,994	C+
Louisiana State Univ and A&M College	LA	8,014	VC
Louisiana State Univ in Shreveport	LA	2,480	NC
Louisiana Tech Univ	LA	6,506	C
Loyola College in Maryland	MD	30,900	HC
Loyola Marymount Univ	CA	28,754	HC
Loyola Univ New Orleans	LA	23,506	VC+
Loyola Univ of Chicago	IL	25,992	VC
Luther College	IA	23,300	VC+
Lycoming College	PA	24,780	C
Macalester College	MN	28,814	HC+
MacMurray College	IL	17,790	LC
Manchester College	IN	22,010	C
Manhattan College	NY	25,500	VC
Manhattanville College	NY	28,730	VC
Mansfield Univ	PA	9,648	C
Marietta College	OH	24,580	C
Marlboro College	VT	26,410	VC+
Marquette Univ	WI	24,836	C+
Marshall Univ	WV	7,752	LC
Mary Baldwin College	VA	23,440	C
Mary Washington College	VA	9,032	VC+
Maryville College	TN	23,210	VC
Mass College of Liberal Arts	MA	8,717	LC
Mass Inst of Technology	MA	35,228	MC
McMurry Univ	TX	15,287	C
McNeese State Univ	LA	5,259	LC
McPherson College	KS	17,710	C
Mercer Univ	GA	24,130	VC
Merrimack College	MA	25,725	VC
Messiah College	PA	23,180	VC
Metropolitan State College of Denver	CO	2,338	LC
Miami Univ	OH	12,885	VC+
Mich State Univ	MI	10,386	VC
Mich Tech Univ	MI	11,088	VC
MidAmerica Nazarene Univ	KS	16,960	C
Middle Tenn State Univ	TN	6,994	C
Middlebury College	VT	34,300	MC
Millersville Univ of Pennsylvania	PA	10,153	VC
Millikin Univ	IL	24,415	C+
Millsaps College	MS	22,608	VC+
Minn State Univ, Mankato	MN	7,296	LC
Minot State Univ	ND	5,466	LC
Miss College	MS	14,574	C
Miss State Univ	MS	7,853	C
Missouri Southern State College	MO	6,666	C
Monmouth College	IL	21,550	C
Montana State Univ-Bozeman	MT	8,431	C
Montclair State Univ	NJ	10,287	LC
Moorhead State Univ	MN	7,000	LC
Moravian College	PA	27,065	VC
Morehead State Univ	KY	6,510	C
Morehouse College	GA	19,814	C
Morgan State Univ	MD	10,078	LC
Morningside College	IA	19,124	C
Morris Brown College	GA	15,993	LC
Mount Holyoke College	MA	34,128	HC
Mount Union College	OH	21,120	C
Muhlenberg College	PA	28,170	HC
Murray State Univ	KY	6,672	C
Muskingum College	OH	18,760	C
Nebr Wesleyan Univ	NE	18,767	VC
New College of Florida	FL	8,130	HC+
New Jersey City Univ	NJ	9,100	LC
New Mexico Highlands Univ	NM	6,256	NC
New Mexico Inst of Mining and Technology	NM	7,152	VC+
New Mexico State Univ	NM	7,302	C
New York Inst of Technology	NY	21,756	C
New York Univ	NY	35,200	MC
Norfolk State Univ	VA	8,382	LC
N Car Agricultural and Technical State Univ	NC	6,659	LC
N Car Central Univ	NC	6,418	LC
N Car State Univ	NC	8,680	HC
North Central College	IL	22,944	C+
N Dak State Univ	ND	7,004	VC
North Georgia College and State Univ	GA	6,322	C+
North Park Univ	IL	24,030	C
Northeastern Illinois Univ	IL	2,898	NC
Northeastern State Univ	OK	4,704	LC
Northeastern Univ	MA	30,078	VC
Northern Arizona Univ	AZ	7,398	C
Northern Illinois Univ	IL	9,545	C
Northern Kentucky Univ	KY	6,352	NC
Northern Mich Univ	MI	9,693	C
Northwest Missouri State Univ	MO	7,922	LC
Northwest Nazarene Univ	ID	18,380	C
Northwestern Okla State Univ	OK	4,542	NC
Northwestern State Univ of Louisiana	LA	5,745	NC
Northwestern Univ	IL	33,615	MC
Norwich Univ	VT	21,064	LC
Oakland Univ	MI	9,418	C
Oberlin College	OH	33,140	HC+
Occidental College	CA	32,288	HC
Oglethorpe Univ	GA	19,100	LC
Ohio Northern Univ	OH	27,765	VC
Ohio Univ	OH	11,769	C
Ohio Wesleyan Univ	OH	29,670	VC+
Okla Baptist Univ	OK	13,878	VC
Okla City Univ	OK	15,810	C
Okla State Univ	OK	7,650	VC
Old Dominion Univ	VA	9,386	C
Oral Roberts Univ	OK	18,490	C
Oregon State Univ	OR	9,612	VC
Otterbein College	OH	23,439	C
Ouachita Baptist Univ	AR	16,460	VC
Pace Univ	NY	24,200	C
Pacific Lutheran Univ	WA	23,318	VC
Pacific Union College	CA	20,250	VC
Pacific Univ	OR	24,250	C
Penn State Univ at Erie/Behrend College	PA	12,326	C
Penn State Univ/Univ Park Campus	PA	11,126	VC
Pittsburg State Univ	KS	6,228	NC
Pitzer College	CA	33,930	HC
Point Loma Nazarene Univ	CA	21,380	VC
Polytechnic Univ/Brooklyn	NY	33,090	HC
Pomona College	CA	33,960	MC
Pontifical Catholic Univ of PR/Ponce	PR	7,076	
Portland State Univ	OR	11,220	C
Prairie View A&M Univ	TX	3,172	LC
Presbyterian College	SC	23,356	VC
Princeton Univ	NJ	35,072	MC
Principia College	IL	23,865	C+
Purdue Univ/Calumet	IN	6,630	NC
Purdue Univ/West Lafayette	IN	10,284	VC
Ramapo College of New Jersey	NJ	13,550	VC
Randolph-Macon College	VA	24,395	C
Randolph-Macon Woman's College	VA	25,820	VC+
Reed College	OR	33,350	HC+
Rensselaer Polytechnic Inst	NY	33,863	HC+
Rhode Island College	RI	8,700	LC
Rhodes College	TN	26,466	HC+
Richard Stockton College of New Jersey	NJ	12,165	VC
Rider Univ	NJ	27,400	C
Ripon College	WI	24,180	VC+
Roanoke College	VA	24,689	VC
Roberts Wesleyan College	NY	20,160	C+
Rochester Inst of Technology	NY	26,232	VC+
Rockhurst Univ	MO	20,090	C
Rollins College	FL	31,223	HC
Rose-Hulman Inst of Technology	IN	27,707	HC+
Rowan Univ	NJ	12,365	VC
Rutgers, The State Univ of New Jersey New Brunswick Campus	NJ	12,709	C
Rutgers, The State Univ of New Jersey/CamdenCampus	NJ	6,484	C
Saginaw Valley State Univ	MI	9,465	C
St. Ambrose Univ	IA	19,994	C
St. Bonaventure Univ	NY	21,956	C
St. Cloud State Univ	MN	7,180	C
St. John Fisher College	NY	21,800	C
St. John's Univ	MN	23,640	VC
St. John's Univ	NY	26,660	C
St. Joseph's Univ	PA	29,715	VC+
St. Lawrence Univ	NY	32,605	VC
St. Louis Univ	MO	26,590	VC+
St. Mary's College of Calif	CA	27,575	C
St. Mary's College of Maryland	MD	14,104	HC
St. Mary's Univ of Minn	MN	19,975	C
St. Mary's Univ of San Antonio	TX	19,735	C
St. Michael's College	VT	26,935	VC
St. Norbert College	WI	23,169	VC
St. Olaf College	MN	25,880	HC
St. Peter's College	NJ	22,292	LC
St. Vincent College	PA	22,942	VC
Salisbury Univ	MD	10,576	VC
Sam Houston State Univ	TX	6,076	LC
Samford Univ	AL	16,340	VC
San Diego State Univ	CA	9,716	C+
San Francisco State Univ	CA	7,139	LC
San Jose State Univ	CA	8,187	C
Santa Clara Univ	CA	28,371	VC+
Savannah State Univ	GA	2,550	LC
Scripps College	CA	30,400	HC+
Seattle Pacific Univ	WA	22,674	C+
Seattle Univ	WA	24,183	VC
Seton Hall Univ	NJ	26,910	LC
Seton Hill College	PA	21,875	C
Shaw Univ	NC	12,810	C
Shippensburg Univ of Pennsylvania	PA	9,652	C
Siena College	NY	22,685	VC

ST = STATE $IS = IN-STATE COSTS SR = SELECTOR RATING

School	ST	$IS	SR
Simon's Rock College of Bard	MA	32,450	HC
Skidmore College	NY	34,201	VC+
Slippery Rock Univ	PA	9,152	LC
Smith College	MA	33,302	HC+
Sonoma State Univ	CA	8,953	C
S Car State Univ	SC	6,586	LC
S Dak School of Mines and Technology	SD	7,438	C+
S Dak State Univ	SD	6,848	C
Southeast Missouri State Univ	MO	8,367	C+
Southeastern Louisiana Univ	LA	6,047	LC
Southeastern Okla State Univ	OK	4,917	C
Southern Adventist Univ	TN	15,600	C
Southern Conn State Univ	CT	10,310	C
Southern Illinois Univ at Carbondale	IL	8,621	C
Southern Illinois Univ Edwardsville	IL	7,869	LC
Southern Methodist Univ	TX	28,349	VC
Southern Nazarene Univ	OK	14,634	NC
Southern Oregon Univ	OR	9,429	C
Southern Polytechnic State Univ	GA	6,662	C
Southern Univ and A&M College	LA	6,365	C+
Southern Univ at New Orleans	LA	995	NC
Southwest Missouri State Univ	MO	7,600	LC
Southwest Texas State Univ	TX	8,730	VC
Southwestern Adventist Univ	TX	14,798	C
Southwestern College	KS	17,656	C
Southwestern Okla State Univ	OK	4,801	C
Southwestern Univ	TX	22,550	HC
Spelman College	GA	19,215	C+
Spring Arbor Univ	MI	17,976	C
Stanford Univ	CA	34,222	MC
SUNY/College at Brockport	NY	10,267	C
SUNY/College at Buffalo	NY	8,025	C
SUNY/College at Cortland	NY	10,564	C
SUNY/College at Fredonia	NY	10,125	C
SUNY/College at Geneseo	NY	9,970	HC
SUNY/College at Oneonta	NY	9,981	C
SUNY/College at Oswego	NY	10,856	C
SUNY/College at Plattsburgh	NY	9,729	C
SUNY/College at Potsdam	NY	10,519	C
SUNY/Univ at Albany	NY	10,997	VC
SUNY/Univ at Binghamton	NY	10,653	HC
SUNY/Univ at Buffalo	NY	11,033	VC
SUNY/Univ at New Paltz	NY	9,685	VC
SUNY/Univ at Stony Brook	NY	10,998	VC
State Univ of West Georgia	GA	7,101	C
Stephen F. Austin State Univ	TX	6,905	C
Stetson Univ	FL	25,640	VC
Stevens Inst of Technology	NJ	31,510	HC+
Suffolk Univ	MA	26,516	C
Susquehanna Univ	PA	27,270	VC
Swarthmore College	PA	34,538	MC
Sweet Briar College	VA	25,310	VC
Syracuse Univ	NY	30,710	HC
Talladega College	AL	10,110	LC
Tarleton State Univ	TX	7,160	C
Taylor Univ	IN	21,562	VC+
Temple Univ	PA	14,124	C
Tenn State Univ	TN	7,058	VC
Tenn Tech Univ	TN	6,968	C
Texas A&M Univ	TX	8,988	VC
Texas A&M Univ at Commerce	TX	7,326	C
Texas A&M Univ at Kingsville	TX	6,446	LC
Texas Christian Univ	TX	19,910	C
Texas Lutheran Univ	TX	17,660	C
Texas Southern Univ	TX	6,576	NC
Texas Tech Univ	TX	8,825	C
Ohio State Univ	OH	10,819	VC
Thiel College	PA	18,419	LC
Thomas Edison State College	NJ	2,750	SP
Thomas More College	KY	17,700	LC
Tougaloo College	MS	9,200	NC
Touro College	NY	14,950	VC
Towson Univ	MD	11,088	VC
Transylvania Univ	KY	21,780	VC+
Trevecca Nazarene Univ	TN	15,752	C
Trinity College	CT	34,300	HC
Trinity Univ	TX	21,444	HC
Truman State Univ	MO	8,568	VC+
Tufts Univ	MA	34,874	MC
Tulane Univ	LA	34,013	HC+
Tuskegee Univ	AL	14,600	LC
Union College	KY	15,920	C
Union College	NE	14,650	C
Union College	NY	32,646	HC
Union Univ	TN	18,930	C+
United States Air Force Academy	CO		MC
United States Military Academy	NY		MC
United States Naval Academy	MD		MC
Univ of Akron	OH	10,530	NC
Univ of Alabama	AL	7,402	C
Univ of Alabama at Birmingham	AL	10,110	C
Univ of Alabama at Huntsville	AL	7,916	VC
Univ of Alaska Fairbanks	AK	8,265	NC
Univ of Arizona	AZ	8,614	C
Univ of Arkansas	AR	8,334	VC
Univ of Arkansas at Little Rock	AR	5,637	NC
Univ of Arkansas at Pine Bluff	AR	7,925	C
Univ of Calif at Berkeley	CA	14,134	MC
Univ of Calif at Davis	CA	12,796	VC
Univ of Calif at Irvine	CA	11,756	C
Univ of Calif at Los Angeles	CA	13,227	MC
Univ of Calif at Riverside	CA	12,479	C
Univ of Calif at San Diego	CA	11,372	HC
Univ of Calif at Santa Barbara	CA	11,732	VC
Univ of Calif at Santa Cruz	CA	13,655	VC
Univ of Central Arkansas	AR	6,388	C
Univ of Central Florida	FL	8,251	VC
Univ of Chicago	IL	35,087	MC
Univ of Cincinnati	OH	12,491	LC
Univ of Colo at Boulder	CO	9,255	VC
Univ of Colo at Colo Springs	CO	9,403	C
Univ of Colo at Denver	CO	3,673	C
Univ of Conn	CT	12,122	VC
Univ of Dallas	TX	22,128	VC+
Univ of Dayton	OH	20,400	VC
Univ of Delaware	DE	10,824	VC
Univ of Denver	CO	28,783	VC
Univ of Evansville	IN	22,865	VC+
Univ of Florida	FL	7,874	HC
Univ of Georgia	GA	8,656	VC
Univ of Hartford	CT	28,884	C
Univ of Hawaii at Hilo	HI	6,497	C
Univ of Hawaii at Manoa	HI	7,862	VC
Univ of Houston	TX	8,410	C
Univ of Houston-Downtown	TX	2,006	NC
Univ of Idaho	ID	7,026	C
Univ of Illinois at Chicago	IL	10,702	VC
Univ of Illinois at Urbana-Champaign	IL	11,316	HC+
Univ of Indianapolis	IN	20,840	C
Univ of Iowa	IA	8,607	C+
Univ of Kansas	KS	7,232	VC
Univ of Kentucky	KY	7,765	C
Univ of La Verne	CA	24,280	C
Univ of Louisiana at Lafayette	LA	5,200	C
Univ of Louisiana at Monroe	LA	5,207	NC
Univ of Louisville	KY	7,402	LC
Univ of Maine	ME	10,798	C
Univ of Maryland/Baltimore County	MD	12,190	VC
Univ of Maryland/College Park	MD	11,959	C
Univ of Mass Amherst	MA	10,995	VC
Univ of Mass Boston	MA	4,227	C
Univ of Mass Dartmouth	MA	9,852	C
Univ of Mass Lowell	MA	9,470	VC
Univ of Memphis	TN	7,271	C
Univ of Miami	FL	31,130	HC
Univ of Mich/Ann Arbor	MI	13,003	HC+
Univ of Mich/Dearborn	MI	4,677	VC
Univ of Mich/Flint	MI	4,323	C
Univ of Minn/Duluth	MN	10,436	C
Univ of Minn/Morris	MN	10,716	VC
Univ of Minn/Twin Cities	MN	11,123	VC
Univ of Miss	MS	7,666	C
Univ of Missouri/Columbia	MO	9,803	HC
Univ of Missouri/Kansas City	MO	9,685	VC
Univ of Missouri/Rolla	MO	10,034	C
Univ of Missouri/St. Louis	MO	9,966	C
Univ of Montana	MT	8,038	C
Univ of Nebr at Kearney	NE	7,048	NC
Univ of Nebr at Lincoln	NE	8,325	C+
Univ of Nebr at Omaha	NE	6,867	C
Univ of Nevada/Las Vegas	NV	8,281	VC
Univ of Nevada/Reno	NV	8,737	C
Univ of New Hampshire	NH	13,207	C
Univ of New Mexico	NM	8,026	C
Univ of New Orleans	LA	10,160	C
Univ of North Alabama	AL	7,016	NC
Univ of N Car at Asheville	NC	6,896	VC
Univ of N Car at Chapel Hill	NC	8,789	HC
Univ of N Car at Charlotte	NC	7,254	C
Univ of N Car at Greensboro	NC	6,858	C
Univ of N Car at Wilmington	NC	7,769	C
Univ of N Dak	ND	7,067	VC
Univ of North Florida	FL	8,089	VC
Univ of North Texas	TX	7,629	C
Univ of Northern Colo	CO	8,082	C+
Univ of Northern Iowa	IA	7,850	C
Univ of Notre Dame	IN	30,707	MC
Univ of Okla	OK	7,616	VC
Univ of Oregon	OR	9,969	C
Univ of Pennsylvania	PA	34,614	MC
Univ of Pittsburgh at Pittsburgh	PA	13,592	HC
Univ of Portland	OR	24,950	VC
Univ of PR at Humacao	PR	1,245	
Univ of PR/Mayaguez	PR	5,285	
Univ of PR/Rio Piedras	PR	5,510	
Univ of Puget Sound	WA	28,285	HC
Univ of Redlands	CA	29,246	VC
Univ of Rhode Island	RI	12,414	C
Univ of Richmond	VA	27,300	HC
Univ of Rochester	NY	32,979	HC
Univ of St. Thomas	MN	24,044	VC
Univ of San Diego	CA	29,198	HC
Univ of San Francisco	CA	27,302	VC
Univ of Science and Arts of Okla	OK	5,245	C
Univ of Scranton	PA	27,964	C+
Univ of South Alabama	AL	6,976	LC
Univ of S Car at Columbia	SC	8,748	VC
Univ of S Dak	SD	7,036	C
Univ of South Florida	FL	8,154	C
Univ of Southern Calif	CA	33,647	MC
Univ of Southern Colo	CO	7,821	LC
Univ of Southern Maine	ME	10,569	C
Univ of Southern Miss	MS	6,155	LC
Univ of Tenn at Chattanooga	TN	7,783	C
Univ of Tenn at Knoxville	TN	8,214	C
Univ of Texas at Arlington	TX	7,192	LC
Univ of Texas at Austin	TX	9,437	HC
Univ of Texas at Dallas	TX	9,305	VC
Univ of Texas at El Paso	TX	5,076	LC
Univ of Texas at San Antonio	TX	9,088	NC
Univ of Texas-Pan American	TX	4,823	C
Univ of the District of Columbia	DC	2,844	NC
Univ of the Ozarks	AR	13,904	C
Univ of the Pacific	CA	28,255	VC
Univ of the South	TN	27,290	HC
Univ of Toledo	OH	11,206	NC
Univ of Tulsa	OK	19,090	HC
Univ of Utah	UT	7,703	C
Univ of Vermont	VT	14,761	C+
Univ of Virginia	VA	9,391	HC+
Univ of Washington	WA	10,361	VC
Univ of West Alabama	AL	6,048	C
Univ of West Florida	FL	7,518	C
Univ of Wisc/Eau Claire	WI	7,032	VC
Univ of Wisc/La Crosse	WI	7,250	VC
Univ of Wisc/Madison	WI	8,262	VC
Univ of Wisc/Milwaukee	WI	8,907	LC
Univ of Wisc/Oshkosh	WI	6,130	LC
Univ of Wisc/Parkside	WI	6,160	LC
Univ of Wisc/Platteville	WI	7,282	C
Univ of Wisc/River Falls	WI	6,356	LC
Univ of Wisc/Stevens Point	WI	7,116	C
Univ of Wisc/Whitewater	WI	6,937	C
Univ of Wyoming	WY	7,143	LC
Ursinus College	PA	31,350	VC
Utah State Univ	UT	6,771	C
Utica College of Syracuse Univ	NY	24,400	LC
Valdosta State Univ	GA	6,988	C
Valparaiso Univ	IN	23,570	VC+
Vanderbilt Univ	TN	34,482	MC
Vassar College	NY	33,450	MC
Villanova Univ	PA	31,997	HC
Virginia Commonwealth Univ	VA	9,030	C
Virginia Military Inst	VA	9,968	C+
Virginia Polytechnic Inst and State Univ	VA	7,652	C
Virginia State Univ	VA	8,182	LC
Wabash College	IN	25,335	HC
Wagner College	NY	27,000	C
Wake Forest Univ	NC	30,290	MC
Walla Walla College	WA	20,925	C
Wartburg College	IA	21,165	VC
Washburn Univ of Topeka	KS	6,766	NC
Washington and Jefferson College	PA	26,255	VC
Washington and Lee Univ	VA	25,095	MC
Washington College	MD	28,040	VC
Washington State Univ	WA	9,388	C
Washington Univ in St. Louis	MO	34,593	MC
Wayne State Univ	MI	6,720	C
Weber State Univ	UT	6,897	NC
Wellesley College	MA	33,394	MC
Wells College	NY	19,350	VC
Wesleyan College	GA	17,050	VC
Wesleyan Univ	CT	3,405	MC
West Chester Univ of Pennsylvania	PA	9,792	VC
West Texas A&M Univ	TX	6,538	C
West Virginia Univ	WV	8,304	C
West Virginia Univ Inst of Technology	WV	7,518	NC
West Virginia Wesleyan College	WV	22,920	C
Western Carolina Univ	NC	5,667	C
Western Illinois Univ	IL	9,571	C
Western Kentucky Univ	KY	6,834	C
Western Maryland College	MD	26,000	VC
Western Mich Univ	MI	10,016	C
Western State College of Colo	CO	7,585	LC
Western Washington Univ	WA	8,624	VC
Westminster College	MO	19,990	C+
Westminster College	PA	22,960	C
Westminster College	UT	17,226	C
Westmont College	CA	29,748	VC
Wheaton College	IL	21,934	HC
Wheaton College	MA	32,940	VC
Wheeling Jesuit Univ	WV	22,660	C
Whitman College	WA	29,086	HC
Whittier College	CA	29,108	C
Whitworth College	WA	23,938	VC
Wichita State Univ	KS	6,879	C
Widener Univ	PA	26,920	C
Wiley College	TX	8,100	LC
Willamette Univ	OR	29,422	VC+
William Jewell College	MO	17,150	VC
Williams College	MA	32,270	MC
Winona State Univ	MN	8,570	C
Wittenberg Univ	OH	28,766	VC
Wofford College	SC	23,995	VC
Worcester Polytechnic Inst	MA	34,480	HC+
Wright State Univ	OH	9,141	LC
Xavier Univ	OH	23,880	C
Xavier Univ of Louisiana	LA	17,000	LC
Yale Univ	CT	34,030	MC
Youngstown State Univ	OH	9,318	NC

PHYSIOLOGY

School	ST	$IS	SR
Andrews Univ	MI	17,696	LC
Boston Univ	MA	34,358	MC
Cal State, Long Beach	CA	7,400	LC
Florida State Univ	FL	7,835	HC
Hampshire College	MA	33,881	HC+
Iowa Wesleyan College	IA	18,840	C
Marquette Univ	WI	24,836	C+
Northern Mich Univ	MI	9,693	C
Okla State Univ	OK	7,650	VC
Rutgers, The State Univ of New Jersey New Brunswick Campus	NJ	12,709	C
San Francisco State Univ	CA	7,139	LC
Southern Illinois Univ at Carbondale	IL	8,621	C
Southwest Texas State Univ	TX	8,730	VC
Univ of Arizona	AZ	8,614	C
Univ of Calif at Davis	CA	12,796	VC
Univ of Calif at Los Angeles	CA	13,227	MC
Univ of Calif at San Diego	CA	11,372	HC
Univ of Calif at Santa Barbara	CA	11,732	VC
Univ of Conn	CT	12,122	VC
Univ of Great Falls	MT	15,360	C
Univ of Illinois at Urbana-Champaign	IL	11,316	HC+
Univ of Minn/Twin Cities	MN	11,123	VC

PIANO/ORGAN

School	ST	$IS	SR
Ball State Univ	IN	8,660	C
Blue Mountain College	MS	9,100	LC
Boston Conservatory	MA	26,900	SP
Catholic Univ of America	DC	29,332	VC
Columbia College	SC	19,050	LC
East Central Univ	OK	4,578	C
East Texas Baptist Univ	TX	12,349	LC
Eastern Mich Univ	MI	9,855	C
Florida State Univ	FL	7,835	HC
Furman Univ	SC	25,492	HC
Grand Canyon Univ	AZ	30,000	LC
Hannibal-LaGrange College	MO	12,530	C
Illinois Wesleyan Univ	IL	26,970	HC
Indiana Univ Bloomington	IN	10,712	C+
Indiana Univ South Bend	IN	3,515	C
Jackson State Univ	MS	6,776	LC
Juilliard School	NY	28,200	SP
Loyola Univ New Orleans	LA	23,506	VC+
Manhattan School of Music	NY	31,500	SP
Martin Univ	IN	8,370	SP
McMurry Univ	TX	15,287	C
Miss College	MS	14,574	C
Northwestern Univ	IL	33,615	MC
Nyack College	NY	18,540	C
Ohio Univ	OH	11,769	C
Okla City Univ	OK	15,810	C
Pacific Lutheran Univ	WA	23,318	VC
Roosevelt Univ	IL	20,240	LC
Samford Univ	AL	16,340	VC
Shenandoah Univ	VA	22,550	NC
Shorter College	GA	15,185	C
Southern Methodist Univ	TX	28,349	VC
Southern Nazarene Univ	OK	14,634	NC
Stetson Univ	FL	25,640	VC
Temple Univ	PA	14,124	C
Texas Christian Univ	TX	19,910	C
Union Univ	TN	18,930	C+
Univ of Cincinnati	OH	12,491	LC
Univ of Miami	FL	31,130	HC
Univ of Mich/Ann Arbor	MI	13,003	HC+
Univ of Tulsa	OK	19,090	HC

School	ST	$IS	SR
Weber State Univ	UT	6,897	NC
Westminster Choir College of Rider Univ	NJ	25,400	SP
Youngstown State Univ	OH	9,318	NC

PLANETARY AND SPACE SCIENCE

School	ST	$IS	SR
Boston Univ	MA	34,358	MC
Calif Inst of Technology	CA	27,663	MC
Florida Inst of Technology	FL	25,250	VC
SUNY/Univ at Stony Brook	NY	10,998	VC
Univ of New Mexico	NM	8,026	C

PLANT GENETICS

School	ST	$IS	SR
SUNY/College of Environmental Science and Forestry	NY	12,446	VC
Washington State Univ	WA	9,388	C

PLANT PATHOLOGY

School	ST	$IS	SR
Iowa State Univ	IA	8,108	VC
Oregon State Univ	OR	9,612	VC
Univ of Delaware	DE	10,824	VC
Univ of Florida	FL	7,874	HC
Univ of Wisc/Madison	WI	8,262	VC
Washington State Univ	WA	9,388	C

PLANT PHYSIOLOGY

School	ST	$IS	SR
Calif State Polytechnic Univ, Pomona	CA	8,615	C
SUNY/College of Environmental Science and Forestry	NY	12,446	VC
Ohio State Univ	OH	10,819	VC

PLANT PROTECTION (PEST MANAGEMENT)

School	ST	$IS	SR
Auburn Univ	AL	5,510	C
Iowa State Univ	IA	8,108	VC
Miss State Univ	MS	7,853	C
N Dak State Univ	ND	7,004	VC
Purdue Univ/West Lafayette	IN	10,284	VC
Univ of Arkansas	AR	8,334	VC
Univ of Georgia	GA	8,656	VC
Univ of Nebr at Lincoln	NE	8,325	C+
Washington State Univ	WA	9,388	C
West Texas A&M Univ	TX	6,538	C

PLANT SCIENCE

School	ST	$IS	SR
Arizona State Univ-Main	AZ	7,726	C
Arkansas State Univ	AR	7,480	C
Cal State, Fresno	CA	7,762	C
Cornell Univ	NY	34,614	MC
Florida State Univ	FL	7,835	HC
Fort Valley State Univ	GA	6,014	LC
Iowa State Univ	IA	8,108	VC
Louisiana State Univ and A&M College	LA	8,014	VC
Middle Tenn State Univ	TN	6,994	C
Montana State Univ-Bozeman	MT	8,431	C
N Dak State Univ	ND	7,004	VC
Ohio Univ	OH	11,769	C
Okla State Univ	OK	7,650	VC
Penn State Univ/Univ Park Campus	PA	11,126	VC
Rutgers, The State Univ of New Jersey New Brunswick Campus	NJ	12,709	C
Southern Illinois Univ at Carbondale	IL	8,621	C
SUNY/College of Agriculture and Technology at Cobleskill	NY	11,200	C+
SUNY/College of Environmental Science and Forestry	NY	12,446	VC
Tarleton State Univ	TX	7,160	C
Tenn Tech Univ	TN	6,968	C
Texas A&M Univ at Kingsville	TX	6,446	LC
Ohio State Univ	OH	10,819	VC
Univ of Arizona	AZ	8,614	C
Univ of Calif at Davis	CA	12,796	VC
Univ of Delaware	DE	10,824	VC
Univ of Florida	FL	7,874	HC
Univ of Maryland/College Park	MD	11,959	C
Univ of Mass Amherst	MA	10,995	VC
Univ of New Hampshire	NH	13,207	C
Univ of Tenn at Knoxville	TN	8,214	C
Univ of Tenn at Martin	TN	8,268	C
Univ of Vermont	VT	14,761	C+
Utah State Univ	UT	6,771	C
Washington Univ in St. Louis	MO	34,593	MC
West Texas A&M Univ	TX	6,538	C
West Virginia Univ	WV	8,304	C

PLASTICS ENGINEERING

School	ST	$IS	SR
Ferris State Univ	MI	10,816	C
Pennsylvania College of Technology	PA	12,860	NC
Univ of Mass Lowell	MA	9,470	VC
Univ of Missouri/Rolla	MO	10,034	C

PLASTICS TECHNOLOGY

School	ST	$IS	SR
Eastern Mich Univ	MI	9,855	C
Penn State Univ at Erie/Behrend College	PA	12,326	C
Shawnee State Univ	OH	8,634	NC

POLISH

School	ST	$IS	SR
Univ of Illinois at Chicago	IL	10,702	VC
Univ of Pittsburgh at Pittsburgh	PA	13,592	HC
Univ of Wisc/Madison	WI	8,262	VC

POLITICAL SCIENCE/GOVERNMENT

School	ST	$IS	SR
Abilene Christian Univ	TX	16,300	VC
Adams State College	CO	7,468	C
Adelphi Univ	NY	23,320	VC
Adrian College	MI	19,670	C
Agnes Scott College	GA	24,950	VC
Alabama A&M Univ	AL	5,100	LC
Alabama State Univ	AL	6,404	C
Albany State Univ	GA	5,764	C+
Albertson College of Idaho	ID	23,900	VC
Albertus Magnus College	CT	22,154	C
Albion College	MI	25,224	VC
Albright College	PA	27,642	C
Alcorn State Univ	MS	5,594	LC
Alderson-Broaddus College	WV	19,640	C
Alfred Univ	NY	27,212	C+
Allegheny College	PA	27,780	VC
Allen Univ	SC	9,600	NC
Alma College	MI	22,586	VC
Alvernia College	PA	20,790	C
American International College	MA	22,268	LC
American Univ	DC	31,544	VC+
Amherst College	MA	34,340	MC
Anderson Univ	IN	19,430	LC
Andrews Univ	MI	17,696	LC
Angelo State Univ	TX	7,028	C
Anna Maria College	MA	22,800	LC
Appalachian State Univ	NC	6,353	C
Aquinas College	MI	20,052	C+
Arcadia Univ	PA	26,650	C
Arizona State Univ-Main	AZ	7,726	C
Arkansas State Univ	AR	7,480	C
Armstrong Atlantic State Univ	GA	7,084	C
Ashland Univ	OH	22,182	LC
Assumption College	MA	26,320	C
Auburn Univ	AL	5,510	C
Auburn Univ Montgomery	AL	5,330	NC
Augsburg College	MN	22,978	C
Augusta State Univ	GA	2,282	C
Augustana College	IL	24,117	VC+
Augustana College	SD	20,760	VC
Aurora Univ	IL	18,551	C
Austin College	TX	22,150	VC+
Austin Peay State Univ	TN	5,814	LC
Averett Univ	VA	17,980	LC
Avila College	MO	17,720	C
Azusa Pacific Univ	CA	22,422	VC
Baker Univ	KS	14,780	C+
Baldwin-Wallace College	OH	22,010	VC+
Ball State Univ	IN	8,660	C
Barber-Scotia College	NC	13,100	C
Bard College	NY	33,912	HC
Barry Univ	FL	24,100	LC
Bartlesville Wesleyan College	OK	14,100	LC
Barton College	NC	16,834	LC
Bates College	ME	34,100	MC
Baylor Univ	TX	18,298	VC+
Belhaven College	MS	16,040	C+
Bellarmine Univ	KY	20,440	VC
Bellevue Univ	NE	4,125	NC
Belmont Abbey College	NC	19,630	LC
Belmont Univ	TN	19,066	VC
Beloit College	WI	27,482	HC
Bemidji State Univ	MN	7,957	C
Benedictine College	KS	18,485	LC
Benedictine Univ	IL	21,330	C
Bennett College	NC	11,200	C
Berea College	KY	4,070	VC
Berry College	GA	18,850	C
Bethany College	WV	18,566	C
Bethel College	MN	22,740	VC
Bethune-Cookman College	FL	15,746	C
Birmingham-Southern College	AL	22,960	C
Black Hills State Univ	SD	6,652	LC
Blackburn College	IL	13,690	C
Bloomfield College	NJ	17,000	C
Bloomsburg Univ of Pennsylvania	PA	9,434	C
Boise State Univ	ID	6,531	LC
Boston College	MA	33,330	MC
Boston Univ	MA	34,358	MC
Bowdoin College	ME	32,650	MC
Bowie State Univ	MD	9,300	C+
Bowling Green State Univ	OH	10,794	C
Bradley Univ	IL	20,970	VC
Brandeis Univ	MA	34,481	MC
Brenau Univ Women's College	GA	20,100	C
Bridgewater College	VA	22,950	C
Bridgewater State College	MA	7,589	C+
Brigham Young Univ	UT	7,840	HC
Brigham Young Univ/Hawaii	HI	6,890	C
Brown Univ	RI	34,973	MC
Bryn Mawr College	PA	33,580	HC+
Bucknell Univ	PA	31,096	HC
Buena Vista Univ	IA	22,828	C
Butler Univ	IN	25,580	VC+
Cabrini College	PA	25,950	LC
Caldwell College	NJ	20,940	LC
Calif Baptist Univ	CA	16,736	C
Calif Inst of Technology	CA	27,663	MC
Calif Lutheran Univ	CA	23,500	LC
Calif Polytechnic State Univ	CA	8,747	VC
Calif State Polytechnic Univ, Pomona	CA	8,615	C
Cal State, Bakersfield	CA	6,090	LC
Cal State, Chico	CA	8,598	LC
Cal State, Dominguez Hills	CA	5,840	LC
Cal State, Fresno	CA	7,762	C
Cal State, Fullerton	CA	5,440	LC
Cal State, Hayward	CA	7,400	LC
Cal State, Long Beach	CA	7,400	LC
Cal State, Los Angeles	CA	5,050	C
Cal State, Northridge	CA	7,781	C
Cal State, San Bernardino	CA	6,516	C
Cal State, San Marcos	CA	1,736	LC
Calif Univ of Pennsylvania	PA	10,388	C
Calvin College	MI	20,050	NC
Cameron Univ	OK	5,560	NC
Campbell Univ	NC	16,599	C
Campbellsville Univ	KY	14,340	C
Canisius College	NY	24,696	C+
Capital Univ	OH	23,630	C
Carleton College	MN	30,780	MC
Carnegie Mellon Univ	PA	32,682	MC
Carroll College	MT	19,140	C
Carroll College	WI	21,170	C
Carthage College	WI	23,670	C
Case Western Reserve Univ	OH	27,418	C
Catawba College	NC	19,620	C
Catholic Univ of America	DC	29,332	VC
Cedar Crest College	PA	25,145	C+
Cedarville Univ	OH	17,553	VC
Centenary College	NJ	22,430	C
Centenary College of Louisiana	LA	21,600	C+
Central College	IA	21,206	C
Central Conn State Univ	CT	10,404	C
Central Methodist College	MO	16,460	C
Central Mich Univ	MI	8,355	C
Central Missouri State Univ	MO	7,920	C
Central State Univ	OH	8,922	C+
Central Washington Univ	WA	8,985	LC
Centre College	KY	24,000	HC
Chadron State College	NE	6,211	NC
Chaminade Univ of Honolulu	HI	17,370	C
Chapman Univ	CA	30,218	VC
Charleston Southern Univ	SC	17,122	C
Chatham College	PA	25,454	C+
Chestnut Hill College	PA	24,790	LC
Cheyney Univ of Pennsylvania	PA	9,993	C
Chicago State Univ	IL	8,851	C+
Christendom College	VA	16,700	VC+
Christopher Newport Univ	VA	8,862	VC
Citadel, The	SC	9,126	C
CUNY/Baruch College	NY	3,275	VC+
CUNY/Brooklyn College	NY	3,403	LC
CUNY/City College	NY	3,309	LC
CUNY/College of Staten Island	NY	3,358	NC
CUNY/Herbert H. Lehman College	NY	3,320	LC
CUNY/Hunter College	NY	5,147	C+
CUNY/John Jay College of Criminal Justice	NY	3,251	C
CUNY/Queens College	NY	3,403	VC
CUNY/York College	NY	3,292	NC
Claflin Univ	SC	12,735	C+
Claremont McKenna College	CA	32,700	MC
Clarion Univ of Pennsylvania	PA	11,272	LC
Clark Atlanta Univ	GA	17,174	C
Clark Univ	MA	29,170	HC
Clarke College	IA	20,625	C+
Clarkson Univ	NY	29,884	VC
Clemson Univ	SC	7,600	C
Cleveland State Univ	OH	10,146	NC
Coastal Carolina Univ	SC	9,220	C
Coe College	IA	24,750	VC
Coker College	SC	20,120	C
Colby College	ME	34,290	MC
Colgate Univ	NY	33,480	MC
College of Charleston	SC	8,350	HC
College of New Jersey	NJ	13,425	HC
College of New Rochelle	NY	20,000	C
College of Notre Dame of Maryland	MD	23,100	LC
College of St. Benedict	MN	23,921	VC
College of St. Catherine	MN	22,324	VC
College of St. Joseph	VT	17,400	NC
College of the Holy Cross	MA	32,780	MC
College of the Ozarks	MO	2,650	C+
College of William and Mary	VA	10,002	MC
College of Wooster	OH	28,350	VC
Colo Christian Univ	CO	17,714	C
Colo College	CO	31,525	HC+
Colo State Univ	CO	9,672	C
Columbia College	MO	15,082	C
Columbia College	SC	19,050	LC
Columbia Univ/Barnard College	NY	33,694	MC
Columbia Univ/Columbia College	NY	35,190	MC
Columbia Univ/School of General Studies	NY	35,000	C
Columbus State Univ	GA	7,228	LC
Concord College	WV	7,122	C+
Concordia College/Moorhead	MN	18,835	C
Concordia Univ, River Forest	IL	20,000	LC
Conn College	CT	33,585	MC
Converse College	SC	21,990	VC
Cornell College	IA	24,980	VC
Cornell Univ	NY	34,614	MC
Creighton Univ	NE	23,476	VC
Cumberland College	KY	14,864	C
Daemen College	NY	20,620	C
Dartmouth College	NH	34,458	MC
David Lipscomb Univ	TN	16,158	VC
Davidson College	NC	30,823	MC
Davis and Elkins College	WV	19,270	LC
De Sales Univ	PA	22,610	VC
Delaware State Univ	DE	8,104	LC
Delta State Univ	MS	5,416	C
Denison Univ	OH	29,640	HC
DePaul Univ	IL	23,590	VC
DePauw Univ	IN	28,000	HC
Dickinson College	PA	32,210	VC+
Dickinson State Univ	ND	5,495	NC
Dillard Univ	LA	16,046	VC
Doane College	NE	17,600	LC
Dominican Univ	IL	20,800	C
Dominican Univ of Calif	CA	27,948	C
Dordt College	IA	18,100	C+
Dowling College	NY	20,281	LC
Drake Univ	IA	22,830	VC
Drew Univ/College of Liberal Arts	NJ	32,152	VC
Drexel Univ	PA	27,657	VC
Drury Univ	MO	15,250	VC
Duke Univ	NC	34,396	MC
Duquesne Univ	PA	24,242	C+
Earlham College	IN	27,446	VC+
East Carolina Univ	NC	7,766	C
East Central Univ	OK	4,578	C
East Stroudsburg Univ of Pennsylvania	PA	8,430	LC
East Tenn State Univ	TN	7,127	C
Eastern College	PA	19,641	LC
Eastern Conn State Univ	CT	10,362	C
Eastern Illinois Univ	IL	10,101	C
Eastern Kentucky Univ	KY	6,552	C
Eastern Mich Univ	MI	9,855	C
Eastern New Mexico Univ	NM	4,113	LC
Eastern Washington Univ	WA	7,972	LC
Eckerd College	FL	25,500	C+
Edgewood College	WI	18,304	C
Edinboro Univ of Pennsylvania	PA	9,328	LC
Edward Waters College	FL	13,124	LC
Elizabeth City State Univ	NC	5,550	LC
Elizabethtown College	PA	26,000	VC
Elmhurst College	IL	21,750	C
Elmira College	NY	31,070	VC+
Elon Univ	NC	19,430	VC
Emmanuel College	MA	23,802	C+
Emory & Henry College	VA	19,462	C
Emory Univ	GA	33,792	MC
Emporia State Univ	KS	6,198	LC
Eugene Lang College of New School Univ	NY	30,300	C
Eureka College	IL	22,200	C
Evangel Univ	MO	14,050	C
Fairfield Univ	CT	30,885	HC
Fairleigh Dickinson Univ/Madison campus	NJ	25,500	C
Fairleigh Dickinson Univ/Teaneck Campus	NJ	24,646	C
Fairmont State College	WV	7,010	NC
Fayetteville State Univ	NC	5,590	LC
Ferrum College	VA	15,990	LC
Fisk Univ	TN	13,700	LC
Fitchburg State College	MA	7,836	C

School	ST	$IS	SR
Flagler College	FL	10,550	VC+
Florida A&M Univ	FL	6,948	C
Florida Atlantic Univ	FL	8,832	C
Florida International Univ	FL	9,486	VC
Florida Memorial College	FL	6,000	LC
Florida Southern College	FL	19,430	C
Florida State Univ	FL	7,835	HC
Fordham Univ	NY	30,710	VC
Fort Hays State Univ	KS	6,294	LC
Fort Lewis College	CO	7,659	LC
Fort Valley State Univ	GA	6,014	LC
Framingham State College	MA	7,259	C
Francis Marion Univ	SC	7,682	C
Franciscan Univ of Steubenville	OH	19,100	C+
Franklin and Marshall College	PA	32,410	HC
Franklin College of Indiana	IN	19,905	C
Franklin Pierce College	NH	26,125	LC
Friends Univ	KS	15,962	LC
Frostburg State Univ	MD	9,680	C
Furman Univ	SC	25,492	HC
Gallaudet Univ	DC	16,554	SP
Gannon Univ	PA	18,848	C
Geneva College	PA	19,990	C+
George Fox Univ	OR	24,095	VC
George Mason Univ	VA	9,192	C
George Washington Univ	DC	32,170	HC
Georgetown College	KY	18,400	VC
Georgetown Univ	DC	34,847	MC
Georgia College and State Univ	GA	7,344	C
Georgia Southern Univ	GA	6,958	C
Georgia Southwestern State Univ	GA	6,013	C
Georgia State Univ	GA	7,792	LC
Gettysburg College	PA	32,070	HC
Gonzaga Univ	WA	24,276	HC+
Gordon College	MA	23,594	VC+
Goucher College	MD	30,650	VC+
Grambling State Univ	LA	5,325	NC
Grand Valley State Univ	MI	10,040	C
Grand View College	IA	17,596	NC
Greensboro College	NC	19,080	LC
Greenville College	IL	19,226	LC
Grinnell College	IA	28,300	HC+
Grove City College	PA	12,280	MC
Guilford College	NC	23,255	C
Gustavus Adolphus College	MN	24,190	VC+
Hamilton College	NY	34,150	HC
Hamline Univ	MN	23,339	C+
Hampden-Sydney College	VA	24,871	C
Hampshire College	MA	33,881	HC+
Hampton Univ	VA	17,112	C+
Hanover College	IN	17,560	VC
Harding Univ	AR	13,528	VC
Hardin-Simmons Univ	TX	14,165	C
Hartwick College	NY	33,090	C+
Harvard Univ/Harvard College	MA	34,269	MC
Hastings College	NE	17,854	C+
Haverford College	PA	34,300	MC
Hawaii Pacific Univ	HI	17,790	C
Heidelberg College	OH	23,879	C
Henderson State Univ	AR	6,269	C
Hendrix College	AR	18,463	HC
High Point Univ	NC	20,220	LC
Hillsdale College	MI	20,586	VC+
Hiram College	OH	27,034	VC
Hobart and William Smith Colleges	NY	33,195	VC
Hofstra Univ	NY	23,252	C
Hollins Univ	VA	24,328	VC
Hood College	MD	26,020	VC
Hope College	MI	22,922	C+
Houghton College	NY	21,810	VC+
Houston Baptist Univ	TX	15,300	LC
Howard Payne Univ	TX	13,834	C+
Howard Univ	DC	15,522	LC
Humboldt State Univ	CA	8,582	C
Huntingdon College	AL	18,400	VC
Huston-Tillotson College	TX	12,977	LC
Idaho State Univ	ID	7,030	C+
Illinois College	IL	16,234	C
Illinois Inst of Technology	IL	25,182	HC+
Illinois State Univ	IL	9,235	C
Illinois Wesleyan Univ	IL	26,970	HC
Indiana State Univ	IN	8,461	LC
Indiana Univ Bloomington	IN	10,712	C+
Indiana Univ Northwest	IN	3,447	C
Indiana Univ of Pennsylvania	PA	9,133	C
Indiana Univ South Bend	IN	3,515	C
Indiana Univ Southeast	IN	3,459	C
Indiana Univ-Purdue Univ Fort Wayne	IN	3,166	LC
Indiana Univ-Purdue Univ Indianapolis	IN	9,473	C
Indiana Wesleyan Univ	IN	17,680	C
Inter-American Univ of PR/ Bayamon Univ College	PR	3,700	
Inter-American Univ of PR/ Fajardo Campus	PR	4,000	
Inter-American Univ of PR/ Metropolitan Campus	PR	4,166	
Inter-American Univ of PR/ Ponce Regional College	PR	3,700	
Inter-American Univ of PR/ San GermÈn	PR	6,390	
Iona College	NY	26,556	C
Iowa State Univ	IA	8,108	VC
Ithaca College	NY	28,719	HC
Jackson State Univ	MS	6,776	LC
Jacksonville State Univ	AL	6,568	LC
Jacksonville Univ	FL	21,110	LC
James Madison Univ	VA	9,552	HC
Jamestown College	ND	11,310	NC
John Carroll Univ	OH	24,140	VC
Johns Hopkins Univ	MD	35,226	MC
Johnson C. Smith Univ	NC	16,560	C+
Johnson State College	VT	10,776	C
Judson College	IL	18,980	LC
Juniata College	PA	26,080	VC
Kalamazoo College	MI	26,955	HC+
Kansas State Univ	KS	6,995	C
Kean Univ	NJ	11,159	C
Keene State College	NH	11,280	C
Kennesaw State Univ	GA	2,306	LC
Kent State Univ	OH	11,104	C
Kentucky State Univ	KY	6,146	NC
Kentucky Wesleyan College	KY	15,800	C
Kenyon College	OH	32,130	HC+
Keuka College	NY	21,170	C
King College	TN	17,800	VC
King's College	PA	24,680	C
Knox College	IL	28,230	HC
Knoxville College	TN	6,200	LC
Kutztown Univ of Pennsylvania	PA	8,907	C
La Salle Univ	PA	27,890	C
La Sierra Univ	CA	19,260	LC
Lafayette College	PA	32,655	MC
LaGrange College	GA	17,496	C
Lake Forest College	IL	27,460	VC
Lake Superior State Univ	MI	9,034	LC
Lamar Univ	TX	6,816	LC
Lambuth Univ	TN	14,254	C
Lander Univ	SC	8,618	LC
Lawrence Univ	WI	27,711	HC
Le Moyne College	NY	23,840	C
Lebanon Valley College of Pennsylvania	PA	25,700	VC
Lehigh Univ	PA	32,290	MC
LeMoyne-Owen College	TN	8,450	NC
Lenoir-Rhyne College	NC	19,186	C
Lewis and Clark College	OR	29,010	VC
Lewis Univ	IL	20,960	C
Liberty Univ	VA	14,500	C
Lincoln Univ	MO	7,158	NC
Lindenwood Univ	MO	17,250	C
Linfield College	OR	25,840	VC
Livingstone College	NC	13,360	LC
Lock Haven Univ of Pennsylvania	PA	9,534	C
LIU/Brooklyn Campus	NY	22,290	C
LIU/C.W. Post Campus	NY	25,380	C
LIU/Southampton College	NY	26,270	C
Longwood College	VA	8,950	C
Loras College	IA	22,994	C+
Louisiana State Univ and A&M College	LA	8,014	VC
Louisiana State Univ in Shreveport	LA	2,480	NC
Louisiana Tech Univ	LA	6,506	C
Loyola College in Maryland	MD	30,900	HC
Loyola Marymount Univ	CA	28,754	HC
Loyola Univ New Orleans	LA	23,506	VC+
Loyola Univ of Chicago	IL	25,992	VC
Luther College	IA	23,300	VC+
Lycoming College	PA	24,780	C
Lynchburg College	VA	23,405	C
Lynn Univ	FL	24,550	C
Lyon College	AR	16,500	VC
Macalester College	MN	28,814	HC+
MacMurray College	IL	17,790	LC
Malone College	OH	19,190	C
Manchester College	IN	22,010	C
Manhattan College	NY	25,500	VC
Manhattanville College	NY	28,730	VC
Mansfield Univ	PA	9,648	C
Marian College	IN	21,020	C
Marist College	NY	24,756	VC
Marlboro College	VT	26,410	VC+
Marquette Univ	WI	24,836	C+
Mars Hill College	NC	18,600	LC
Marshall Univ	WV	7,752	LC
Martin Univ	IN	8,370	SP
Mary Baldwin College	VA	23,440	C
Mary Washington College	VA	9,032	VC+
Marygrove College	MI	16,075	C
Marymount College/ Tarrytown	NY	23,850	C
Marymount Manhattan College	NY	23,195	VC
Marymount Univ	VA	21,560	LC
Maryville College	TN	23,210	VC
Mass Inst of Technology	MA	35,228	MC
Master's College	CA	21,500	C+
McKendree College	IL	18,300	C+
McMurry Univ	TX	15,287	C
Medaille College	NY	18,320	C
Mercer Univ	GA	24,130	VC
Mercy College	NY	15,875	LC
Mercyhurst College	PA	20,694	C
Meredith College	NC	17,500	C
Merrimack College	MA	25,725	VC
Mesa State College	CO	8,051	C
Messiah College	PA	23,180	VC
Methodist College	NC	19,526	C
Metropolitan State College of Denver	CO	2,338	LC
Miami Univ	OH	12,885	VC+
Mich State Univ	MI	10,386	VC
Middle Tenn State Univ	TN	6,994	C
Middlebury College	VT	34,300	MC
Midwestern State Univ	TX	6,704	NC
Miles College	AL	7,870	NC
Millersville Univ of Pennsylvania	PA	10,153	VC
Millikin Univ	IL	24,415	C+
Mills College	CA	27,950	C
Millsaps College	MS	22,608	VC+
Minn State Univ, Mankato	MN	7,296	LC
Miss College	MS	14,574	C
Miss State Univ	MS	7,853	C
Miss Univ for Women	MS	5,446	LC
Miss Valley State Univ	MS	6,345	C
Missouri Southern State College	MO	6,666	C
Missouri Valley College	MO	17,400	LC
Missouri Western State College	MO	6,662	NC
Molloy College	NY	13,940	C
Monmouth College	IL	21,550	C
Monmouth Univ	NJ	24,042	C
Montana State Univ-Bozeman	MT	8,431	C
Montclair State Univ	NJ	10,287	LC
Moorhead State Univ	MN	7,000	LC
Moravian College	PA	27,065	VC
Morehead State Univ	KY	6,510	C
Morehouse College	GA	19,814	C
Morgan State Univ	MD	10,078	LC
Morningside College	IA	19,124	C
Morris Brown College	GA	15,993	LC
Morris College	SC	9,995	LC
Mount Holyoke College	MA	34,128	HC
Mount Mercy College	IA	19,390	VC
Mount St. Mary College	NY	18,825	C
Mount St. Mary's College	CA	24,430	C
Mount St. Mary's College	MD	25,740	C
Mount Union College	OH	21,120	C
Muhlenberg College	PA	28,170	HC
Murray State Univ	KY	6,672	C
Muskingum College	OH	18,760	C
Nazareth College of Rochester	NY	22,036	VC
Nebr Wesleyan Univ	NE	18,767	VC
Neumann College	PA	22,040	NC
New College of Calif	CA	8,900	NC
New College of Florida	FL	8,130	HC+
New England College	NH	20,706	LC
New Jersey City Univ	NJ	9,100	LC
New Mexico Highlands Univ	NM	6,256	NC
New Mexico State Univ	NM	7,302	C
New York Inst of Technology	NY	21,756	C
New York Univ	NY	35,200	MC
Newberry College	SC	19,670	LC
Niagara Univ	NY	22,250	C+
Nicholls State Univ	LA	5,290	NC
Norfolk State Univ	VA	8,382	LC
N Car Agricultural and Technical State Univ	NC	6,659	LC
N Car Central Univ	NC	6,418	LC
N Car State Univ	NC	8,680	HC
N Car Wesleyan College	NC	15,650	LC
North Central College	IL	22,944	C+
N Dak State Univ	ND	7,004	VC
North Georgia College and State Univ	GA	6,322	C+
North Park Univ	IL	24,030	C
Northeastern Illinois Univ	IL	2,898	NC
Northeastern State Univ	OK	4,704	LC
Northeastern Univ	MA	30,078	VC
Northern Arizona Univ	AZ	7,398	C
Northern Illinois Univ	IL	9,545	C
Northern Kentucky Univ	KY	6,352	NC
Northern Mich Univ	MI	9,693	C
Northern State Univ	SD	6,279	LC
Northwest Missouri State Univ	MO	7,922	LC
Northwest Nazarene Univ	ID	18,380	C
Northwestern College of Iowa	IA	17,630	C+
Northwestern Okla State Univ	OK	4,542	NC
Northwestern State Univ of Louisiana	LA	5,745	NC
Northwestern Univ	IL	33,615	MC
Norwich Univ	VT	21,064	LC
Notre Dame College	OH	20,425	C
Notre Dame de Namur Univ	CA	26,932	LC
Oakland Univ	MI	9,418	C
Oberlin College	OH	33,140	HC+
Occidental College	CA	32,288	HC
Oglethorpe Univ	GA	19,100	LC
Ohio Dominican College	OH	18,100	LC
Ohio Northern Univ	OH	27,765	VC
Ohio Univ	OH	11,769	C
Ohio Wesleyan Univ	OH	29,670	VC+
Okla Baptist Univ	OK	13,878	VC
Okla City Univ	OK	15,810	C
Okla State Univ	OK	7,650	VC
Old Dominion Univ	VA	9,386	C
Olivet Nazarene Univ	IL	18,444	C
Oral Roberts Univ	OK	18,490	C
Oregon State Univ	OR	9,612	VC
Ottawa Univ	KS	11,800	LC
Otterbein College	OH	23,439	C
Ouachita Baptist Univ	AR	16,460	VC
Our Lady of the Lake Univ of San Antonio	TX	17,336	C
Pace Univ	NY	24,200	C
Pacific Lutheran Univ	WA	23,318	VC
Pacific Univ	OR	24,250	C
Palm Beach Atlantic College	FL	23,310	C
Park Univ	MO	9,816	C
Penn State Univ at Erie/ Behrend College	PA	12,326	C
Penn State Univ/Univ Park Campus	PA	11,126	VC
Pepperdine Univ	CA	32,830	VC
Pfeiffer Univ	NC	18,580	C
Philander Smith College	AR	7,380	NC
Pittsburg State Univ	KS	6,228	NC
Pitzer College	CA	33,930	HC
Plymouth State College	NH	11,024	LC
Point Loma Nazarene Univ	CA	21,380	VC
Point Park College	PA	20,290	C
Pomona College	CA	33,960	MC
Pontifical Catholic Univ of PR/Ponce	PR	7,076	
Portland State Univ	OR	11,220	C
Prairie View A&M Univ	TX	3,172	LC
Presbyterian College	SC	23,356	VC
Princeton Univ	NJ	35,072	MC
Principia College	IL	23,865	C+
Providence College	RI	27,620	HC
Purdue Univ/Calumet	IN	6,630	NC
Purdue Univ/West Lafayette	IN	10,284	VC
Queens College	NC	17,250	C
Quincy Univ	IL	20,450	C
Quinnipiac Univ	CT	27,370	C
Radford Univ	VA	8,302	C
Ramapo College of New Jersey	NJ	13,550	VC
Randolph-Macon College	VA	24,395	C
Randolph-Macon Woman's College	VA	25,820	VC+
Reed College	OR	33,350	HC+
Regis College	MA	26,750	C
Regis Univ	CO	25,740	C+
Rhode Island College	RI	8,700	LC
Rhodes College	TN	26,466	HC+
Richard Stockton College of New Jersey	NJ	12,165	VC
Rider Univ	NJ	27,400	C
Ripon College	WI	24,180	VC+
Rivier College	NH	24,215	C
Roanoke College	VA	24,689	VC
Rockford College	IL	23,930	C
Rockhurst Univ	MO	20,090	C
Rocky Mountain College	MT	18,113	C
Roger Williams Univ	RI	29,010	C
Rollins College	FL	31,223	HC
Roosevelt Univ	IL	20,240	LC
Rosemont College	PA	24,060	C
Rowan Univ	NJ	12,365	VC
Russell Sage College	NY	23,674	C+
Rust College	MS	7,800	C+
Rutgers, The State Univ of New Jersey New Brunswick Campus	NJ	12,709	C
Rutgers, The State Univ of New Jersey/ CamdenCampus	NJ	6,484	C
Rutgers, The State Univ of New Jersey/Newark Campus	NJ	6,394	C
Sacred Heart Univ	CT	26,588	VC
Saginaw Valley State Univ	MI	9,465	C
St. Ambrose Univ	IA	19,994	C
St. Andrews Presbyterian College	NC	19,720	LC
St. Anselm College	NH	27,405	C
St. Augustine's College	NC	12,990	C+
St. Bonaventure Univ	NY	21,956	C
St. Cloud State Univ	MN	7,180	C
St. Edward's Univ	TX	17,846	C
St. Francis College	NY	9,610	C
St. Francis Univ	PA	24,486	LC
St. John Fisher College	NY	21,800	C
St. John's Univ	MN	23,640	VC
St. John's Univ	NY	26,660	C
St. Joseph College	CT	25,960	LC
St. Joseph's College	IN	21,640	C
St. Joseph's Univ	PA	29,715	VC+
St. Lawrence Univ	NY	32,605	VC
St. Leo Univ	FL	19,250	LC
St. Louis Univ	MO	26,590	VC+
St. Martin's College	WA	20,566	C

ST = STATE $IS = IN-STATE COSTS SR = SELECTOR RATING

School	ST	$IS	SR
St. Mary College	KS	17,298	C
St. Mary's College	IN	24,474	VC
St. Mary's College of Calif	CA	27,575	C
St. Mary's College of Maryland	MD	14,104	HC
St. Mary's Univ of Minn	MN	19,975	C
St. Mary's Univ of San Antonio	TX	19,735	C
St. Michael's College	VT	26,935	VC
St. Norbert College	WI	23,169	VC
St. Olaf College	MN	25,880	HC
St. Paul's College	VA	13,340	C
St. Peter's College	NJ	22,292	LC
St. Thomas Univ	FL	19,500	LC
St. Vincent College	PA	22,942	VC
St. Xavier Univ	IL	21,104	C
Salisbury Univ	MD	10,576	VC
Salve Regina Univ	RI	26,460	C
Sam Houston State Univ	TX	6,076	LC
Samford Univ	AL	16,340	VC
San Diego State Univ	CA	9,716	C+
San Francisco State Univ	CA	7,139	LC
San Jose State Univ	CA	8,187	C
Santa Clara Univ	CA	28,371	VC+
Sarah Lawrence College	NY	37,516	HC
Savannah State Univ	GA	2,550	LC
Scripps College	CA	30,400	HC+
Seattle Pacific Univ	WA	22,674	C+
Seattle Univ	WA	24,183	VC
Seton Hall Univ	NJ	26,910	LC
Seton Hill College	PA	21,875	C
Shaw Univ	NC	12,810	C
Shepherd College	WV	7,062	LC
Shippensburg Univ of Pennsylvania	PA	9,652	C
Siena College	NY	22,685	VC
Simmons College	MA	30,418	VC
Simon's Rock College of Bard	MA	32,450	HC
Simpson College	IA	21,200	C+
Skidmore College	NY	34,201	VC+
Slippery Rock Univ	PA	9,152	LC
Smith College	MA	33,302	HC+
Sonoma State Univ	CA	8,953	C
S Car State Univ	SC	6,586	LC
S Dak State Univ	SD	6,848	C
Southeast Missouri State Univ	MO	8,367	C+
Southeastern Louisiana Univ	LA	6,047	LC
Southeastern Okla State Univ	OK	4,917	C
Southern Arkansas Univ	AR	5,740	LC
Southern Conn State Univ	CT	10,310	C
Southern Illinois Univ at Carbondale	IL	8,621	C
Southern Illinois Univ Edwardsville	IL	7,869	LC
Southern Methodist Univ	TX	28,349	VC
Southern Nazarene Univ	OK	14,634	NC
Southern Oregon Univ	OR	9,429	C
Southern Univ and A&M College	LA	6,365	C+
Southern Univ at New Orleans	LA	995	NC
Southern Utah Univ	UT	7,254	C
Southwest Baptist Univ	MO	13,426	LC
Southwest Missouri State Univ	MO	7,600	LC
Southwest State Univ	MN	7,117	LC
Southwest Texas State Univ	TX	8,730	VC
Southwestern Okla State Univ	OK	4,801	C
Southwestern Univ	TX	22,550	HC
Spelman College	GA	19,215	C+
Spring Hill College	AL	23,250	C
Springfield College	MA	24,520	C
Stanford Univ	CA	34,222	MC
SUNY/College at Brockport	NY	10,267	C
SUNY/College at Buffalo	NY	8,025	C
SUNY/College at Cortland	NY	10,564	C
SUNY/College at Fredonia	NY	10,125	C
SUNY/College at Geneseo	NY	9,970	HC
SUNY/College at Old Westbury	NY	9,818	LC
SUNY/College at Oneonta	NY	9,981	C
SUNY/College at Oswego	NY	10,856	C
SUNY/College at Plattsburgh	NY	9,729	C
SUNY/College at Potsdam	NY	10,519	C
SUNY/College at Purchase	NY	10,587	VC
SUNY/Univ at Albany	NY	10,997	VC
SUNY/Univ at Binghamton	NY	10,653	HC
SUNY/Univ at Buffalo	NY	11,033	VC
SUNY/Univ at New Paltz	NY	9,685	VC
SUNY/Univ at Stony Brook	NY	10,998	VC
State Univ of West Georgia	GA	7,101	C
Stephen F. Austin State Univ	TX	6,905	C
Stephens College	MO	22,295	C
Stetson Univ	FL	25,640	VC
Stonehill College	MA	26,852	HC
Suffolk Univ	MA	26,516	C
Sul Ross State Univ	TX	6,582	LC
Susquehanna Univ	PA	27,270	VC
Swarthmore College	PA	34,538	MC
Sweet Briar College	VA	25,310	VC
Syracuse Univ	NY	30,710	HC
Tarleton State Univ	TX	7,160	C
Taylor Univ	IN	21,562	VC+
Temple Univ	PA	14,124	C
Tenn State Univ	TN	7,058	VC
Tenn Tech Univ	TN	6,968	C
Texas A&M Univ	TX	8,988	VC
Texas A&M Univ at Commerce	TX	7,326	C
Texas A&M Univ at Kingsville	TX	6,446	LC
Texas Christian Univ	TX	19,910	C
Texas Lutheran Univ	TX	17,660	C
Texas Southern Univ	TX	6,576	NC
Texas Tech Univ	TX	8,825	C
Texas Wesleyan Univ	TX	14,710	C
Texas Woman's Univ	TX	5,855	LC
Ohio State Univ	OH	10,819	VC
Thiel College	PA	18,419	LC
Thomas Edison State College	NJ	2,750	SP
Thomas More College of Liberal Arts	NH	17,700	C
Tougaloo College	MS	9,200	NC
Touro College	NY	14,950	VC
Towson Univ	MD	11,088	VC
Transylvania Univ	KY	21,780	VC+
Trevecca Nazarene Univ	TN	15,752	C
Trinity College	CT	34,300	HC
Trinity College	DC	21,370	LC
Trinity Univ	TX	21,444	HC
Troy State Univ	AL	7,696	C
Troy State Univ/ Montgomery	AL	3,080	NC
Truman State Univ	MO	8,568	VC+
Tufts Univ	MA	34,874	MC
Tulane Univ	LA	34,013	HC+
Tuskegee Univ	AL	14,600	LC
Union College	NY	32,646	HC
Union Univ	TN	18,930	C+
United States Air Force Academy	CO		MC
United States Coast Guard Academy	CT		MC
United States Military Academy	NY		MC
United States Naval Academy	MD		MC
Univ of Akron	OH	10,530	NC
Univ of Alabama	AL	7,402	C
Univ of Alabama at Birmingham	AL	10,110	C
Univ of Alabama at Huntsville	AL	7,916	VC
Univ of Alaska Anchorage	AK	9,100	NC
Univ of Alaska Fairbanks	AK	8,265	NC
Univ of Alaska Southeast	AK	7,900	LC
Univ of Arizona	AZ	8,614	C
Univ of Arkansas	AR	8,334	VC
Univ of Arkansas at Little Rock	AR	5,637	NC
Univ of Arkansas at Monticello	AR	5,940	NC
Univ of Arkansas at Pine Bluff	AR	7,026	C
Univ of Calif at Berkeley	CA	14,134	MC
Univ of Calif at Davis	CA	12,796	VC
Univ of Calif at Irvine	CA	11,756	C
Univ of Calif at Los Angeles	CA	13,227	MC
Univ of Calif at Riverside	CA	12,479	C
Univ of Calif at San Diego	CA	11,372	HC
Univ of Calif at Santa Barbara	CA	11,732	VC
Univ of Calif at Santa Cruz	CA	13,655	VC
Univ of Central Arkansas	AR	6,388	C
Univ of Central Florida	FL	8,251	VC
Univ of Central Okla	OK	5,205	C
Univ of Charleston	WV	20,640	C
Univ of Chicago	IL	35,087	MC
Univ of Cincinnati	OH	12,491	LC
Univ of Colo at Boulder	CO	9,255	VC
Univ of Colo at Colo Springs	CO	9,403	C
Univ of Colo at Denver	CO	3,673	C
Univ of Conn	CT	12,122	VC
Univ of Dallas	TX	22,128	VC+
Univ of Dayton	OH	20,400	VC
Univ of Delaware	DE	10,824	VC
Univ of Denver	CO	28,783	VC
Univ of Detroit Mercy	MI	21,620	LC
Univ of Evansville	IN	22,865	VC+
Univ of Findlay	OH	23,962	NC
Univ of Florida	FL	7,874	HC
Univ of Georgia	GA	8,656	VC
Univ of Great Falls	MT	15,360	C
Univ of Hartford	CT	28,884	C
Univ of Hawaii at Hilo	HI	6,497	C
Univ of Hawaii at Manoa	HI	7,862	VC
Univ of Houston	TX	8,410	C
Univ of Idaho	ID	7,026	C
Univ of Illinois at Chicago	IL	10,702	VC
Univ of Illinois at Urbana-Champaign	IL	11,316	HC+
Univ of Indianapolis	IN	20,840	C
Univ of Iowa	IA	8,607	C+
Univ of Judaism College of A&S	CA	24,230	C
Univ of Kansas	KS	7,232	VC
Univ of Kentucky	KY	7,765	C
Univ of La Verne	CA	24,280	C
Univ of Louisiana at Lafayette	LA	5,200	C
Univ of Louisiana at Monroe	LA	5,207	NC
Univ of Louisville	KY	7,402	LC
Univ of Maine	ME	10,798	C
Univ of Maine at Farmington	ME	9,163	C
Univ of Mary Hardin-Baylor	TX	13,929	C
Univ of Maryland/Baltimore County	MD	12,190	VC
Univ of Maryland/College Park	MD	11,959	C
Univ of Mass Amherst	MA	10,995	VC
Univ of Mass Boston	MA	4,227	C
Univ of Mass Dartmouth	MA	9,852	C
Univ of Mass Lowell	MA	9,470	VC
Univ of Memphis	TN	7,271	C
Univ of Miami	FL	31,130	HC
Univ of Mich/Ann Arbor	MI	13,003	HC+
Univ of Mich/Dearborn	MI	4,677	VC
Univ of Mich/Flint	MI	4,323	C
Univ of Minn/Duluth	MN	10,436	C
Univ of Minn/Morris	MN	10,716	VC
Univ of Minn/Twin Cities	MN	11,123	VC
Univ of Miss	MS	7,666	C
Univ of Missouri/Columbia	MO	9,803	HC
Univ of Missouri/Kansas City	MO	9,685	VC
Univ of Missouri/St. Louis	MO	9,966	C
Univ of Montana	MT	8,038	C
Univ of Montevallo	AL	7,266	C
Univ of Nebr at Kearney	NE	7,048	NC
Univ of Nebr at Lincoln	NE	8,325	C+
Univ of Nebr at Omaha	NE	6,867	C
Univ of Nevada/Las Vegas	NV	8,281	VC
Univ of Nevada/Reno	NV	8,737	C
Univ of New Hampshire	NH	13,207	C
Univ of New Haven	CT	23,860	LC
Univ of New Mexico	NM	8,026	C
Univ of New Orleans	LA	10,160	C
Univ of North Alabama	AL	7,016	NC
Univ of N Car at Asheville	NC	6,896	VC
Univ of N Car at Chapel Hill	NC	8,789	HC
Univ of N Car at Charlotte	NC	7,254	C
Univ of N Car at Greensboro	NC	6,858	C
Univ of N Car at Pembroke	NC	5,914	LC
Univ of N Car at Wilmington	NC	7,769	C
Univ of N Dak	ND	7,067	VC
Univ of North Florida	FL	8,089	VC
Univ of North Texas	TX	7,629	C
Univ of Northern Colo	CO	8,082	C+
Univ of Northern Iowa	IA	7,850	C
Univ of Notre Dame	IN	30,707	MC
Univ of Okla	OK	7,616	VC
Univ of Oregon	OR	9,969	C
Univ of Pennsylvania	PA	34,614	MC
Univ of Pittsburgh at Bradford	PA	12,696	C
Univ of Pittsburgh at Greensburg	PA	12,042	C
Univ of Pittsburgh at Johnstown	PA	13,044	LC
Univ of Pittsburgh at Pittsburgh	PA	13,592	HC
Univ of Portland	OR	24,950	VC
Univ of PR/Mayaguez	PR	5,285	
Univ of PR/Rio Piedras	PR	5,510	
Univ of Puget Sound	WA	28,285	HC
Univ of Redlands	CA	29,246	VC
Univ of Rhode Island	RI	12,414	C
Univ of Richmond	VA	27,300	HC
Univ of Rio Grande	OH	8,728	NC
Univ of Rochester	NY	32,979	HC
Univ of St. Francis	IL	19,650	C
Univ of St. Thomas	MN	24,044	VC
Univ of St. Thomas	TX	18,752	VC
Univ of San Diego	CA	29,198	HC
Univ of San Francisco	CA	27,302	VC
Univ of Science and Arts of Okla	OK	5,245	C
Univ of Scranton	PA	27,964	C+
Univ of Sioux Falls	SD	16,390	C
Univ of South Alabama	AL	6,976	LC
Univ of S Car at Aiken	SC	7,828	LC
Univ of S Car at Columbia	SC	8,748	VC
Univ of S Car at Spartanburg	SC	7,318	C+
Univ of S Dak	SD	7,036	C
Univ of South Florida	FL	8,154	C
Univ of Southern Calif	CA	33,647	MC
Univ of Southern Colo	CO	7,821	LC
Univ of Southern Indiana	IN	8,655	LC
Univ of Southern Maine	ME	10,569	C
Univ of Southern Miss	MS	6,155	LC
Univ of Tampa	FL	22,612	C
Univ of Tenn at Chattanooga	TN	7,783	C
Univ of Tenn at Knoxville	TN	8,214	C
Univ of Tenn at Martin	TN	8,268	C
Univ of Texas at Arlington	TX	7,192	LC
Univ of Texas at Austin	TX	9,437	HC
Univ of Texas at Dallas	TX	9,305	VC
Univ of Texas at El Paso	TX	5,076	LC
Univ of Texas at San Antonio	TX	9,088	NC
Univ of Texas-Pan American	TX	4,823	C
Univ of the District of Columbia	DC	2,844	NC
Univ of the Incarnate Word	TX	18,478	C
Univ of the Ozarks	AR	13,904	C
Univ of the Pacific	CA	28,255	VC
Univ of the South	TN	27,290	HC
Univ of Toledo	OH	11,206	NC
Univ of Tulsa	OK	19,090	HC
Univ of Utah	UT	7,703	C
Univ of Vermont	VT	14,761	C+
Univ of Virginia	VA	9,391	HC+
Univ of Virginia's College at Wise	VA	8,302	C
Univ of Washington	WA	10,361	VC
Univ of West Florida	FL	7,518	C
Univ of Wisc/Eau Claire	WI	7,032	VC
Univ of Wisc/Green Bay	WI	7,148	C
Univ of Wisc/La Crosse	WI	7,250	VC
Univ of Wisc/Madison	WI	8,262	VC
Univ of Wisc/Milwaukee	WI	8,907	LC
Univ of Wisc/Oshkosh	WI	6,130	LC
Univ of Wisc/Parkside	WI	6,160	LC
Univ of Wisc/Platteville	WI	7,282	C
Univ of Wisc/River Falls	WI	6,356	LC
Univ of Wisc/Stevens Point	WI	7,116	C
Univ of Wisc/Superior	WI	7,051	C+
Univ of Wisc/Whitewater	WI	6,937	C
Univ of Wyoming	WY	7,143	LC
Ursinus College	PA	31,350	VC
Utah State Univ	UT	6,771	C
Utica College of Syracuse Univ	NY	24,400	LC
Valdosta State Univ	GA	6,988	C
Valparaiso Univ	IN	23,570	VC+
Vanderbilt Univ	TN	34,482	MC
Vanguard Univ of Southern Calif	CA	20,212	C
Vassar College	NY	33,450	MC
Villanova Univ	PA	31,997	HC
Virginia Commonwealth Univ	VA	9,030	C
Virginia Polytechnic Inst and State Univ	VA	7,652	C
Virginia State Univ	VA	8,182	LC
Virginia Union Univ	VA	15,358	LC
Virginia Wesleyan College	VA	22,350	LC
Wabash College	IN	25,335	HC
Wagner College	NY	27,000	C
Wake Forest Univ	NC	30,290	MC
Walsh Univ	OH	16,880	C
Wartburg College	IA	21,165	VC
Washburn Univ of Topeka	KS	6,766	NC
Washington and Jefferson College	PA	26,255	VC
Washington and Lee Univ	VA	25,095	MC
Washington College	MD	28,040	VC
Washington State Univ	WA	9,388	C
Washington Univ in St. Louis	MO	34,593	MC
Wayland Baptist Univ	TX	11,271	NC
Wayne State College	NE	6,255	NC
Wayne State Univ	MI	6,720	C
Waynesburg College	PA	17,610	LC
Weber State Univ	UT	6,897	NC
Webster Univ	MO	19,804	VC
Wellesley College	MA	33,394	MC
Wells College	NY	19,350	VC
Wesley College	DE	17,869	C
Wesleyan College	GA	17,050	VC
Wesleyan Univ	CT	3,405	MC
West Chester Univ of Pennsylvania	PA	9,792	VC
West Liberty State College	WV	6,056	LC
West Texas A&M Univ	TX	6,538	C
West Virginia State College	WV	6,264	NC
West Virginia Univ	WV	8,304	C
West Virginia Wesleyan College	WV	22,920	C
Western Carolina Univ	NC	5,667	C
Western Conn State Univ	CT	10,074	C
Western Illinois Univ	IL	9,571	C
Western Kentucky Univ	KY	6,834	C
Western Maryland College	MD	26,000	VC
Western Mich Univ	MI	10,016	C
Western New England College	MA	23,882	C
Western Oregon Univ	OR	8,829	C
Western State College of Colo	CO	7,585	LC
Western Washington Univ	WA	8,624	VC
Westfield State College	MA	8,394	C
Westminster College	MO	19,990	C+
Westminster College	PA	22,960	C
Westmont College	CA	29,748	VC
Wheaton College	IL	21,934	HC
Wheaton College	MA	32,940	VC
Wheeling Jesuit Univ	WV	22,660	C
Whitman College	WA	29,086	HC

ST = STATE **$IS** = IN-STATE COSTS **SR** = SELECTOR RATING

School	ST	$IS	SR
Whittier College	CA	29,108	C
Whitworth College	WA	23,938	VC
Wichita State Univ	KS	6,879	C
Widener Univ	PA	26,920	C
Wilberforce Univ	OH	14,937	LC
Wilkes Univ	PA	25,800	C
Willamette Univ	OR	29,422	VC+
William Jewell College	MO	17,150	VC
William Paterson Univ of New Jersey	NJ	11,000	LC
William Penn Univ	IA	17,575	C
William Woods Univ	MO	19,390	LC
Williams College	MA	32,270	MC
Wilson College	PA	21,337	LC
Winona State Univ	MN	8,570	C
Winston-Salem State Univ	NC	5,927	LC
Winthrop Univ	SC	9,106	C
Wisc Lutheran College	WI	19,216	VC
Wittenberg Univ	OH	28,766	VC
Wofford College	SC	23,995	VC
Woodbury Univ	CA	25,344	LC
Wright State Univ	OH	9,141	LC
Xavier Univ	OH	23,880	C
Xavier Univ of Louisiana	LA	17,000	LC
Yale Univ	CT	34,030	MC
Yeshiva Univ	NY	21,400	C
York College of Pennsylvania	PA	12,550	VC
Youngstown State Univ	OH	9,318	NC

POLYMER SCIENCE

School	ST	$IS	SR
Case Western Reserve Univ	OH	27,418	C
Central Conn State Univ	CT	10,404	C
Eastern Mich Univ	MI	9,855	C
Georgia Inst of Technology	GA	9,028	HC+
Pennsylvania College of Technology	PA	12,860	NC
Rochester Inst of Technology	NY	26,232	VC+
SUNY/College of Environmental Science and Forestry	NY	12,446	VC
Stevens Inst of Technology	NJ	31,510	HC+
Univ of Calif at Davis	CA	12,796	VC
Univ of Missouri/Rolla	MO	10,034	C
Univ of Southern Calif	CA	33,647	MC
Univ of Southern Miss	MS	6,155	LC

PORTUGUESE

School	ST	$IS	SR
Brigham Young Univ	UT	7,840	HC
Florida International Univ	FL	9,486	VC
Georgetown Univ	DC	34,847	MC
Harvard Univ/Harvard College	MA	34,269	MC
Indiana Univ Bloomington	IN	10,712	C+
New York Univ	NY	35,200	MC
Ohio State Univ	OH	10,819	VC
Tulane Univ	LA	34,013	HC+
Univ of Arizona	AZ	8,614	C
Univ of Calif at Los Angeles	CA	13,227	MC
Univ of Calif at Santa Barbara	CA	11,732	VC
Univ of Conn	CT	12,122	VC
Univ of Florida	FL	7,874	HC
Univ of Illinois at Urbana-Champaign	IL	11,316	HC+
Univ of Iowa	IA	8,607	C+
Univ of Mass Amherst	MA	10,995	VC
Univ of Mass Dartmouth	MA	9,852	C
Univ of New Mexico	NM	8,026	C
Univ of N Car at Chapel Hill	NC	8,789	HC
Univ of Texas at Austin	TX	9,437	HC
Univ of Wisc/Madison	WI	8,262	VC
Yale Univ	CT	34,030	MC

POULTRY SCIENCE

School	ST	$IS	SR
Auburn Univ	AL	5,510	C
College of the Ozarks	MO	2,650	C+
Miss State Univ	MS	7,853	C
N Car State Univ	NC	8,680	HC
Oregon State Univ	OR	9,612	VC
Penn State Univ/Univ Park Campus	PA	11,126	VC
Texas A&M Univ	TX	8,988	VC
Univ of Arkansas	AR	8,334	VC
Univ of Florida	FL	7,874	HC
Univ of Georgia	GA	8,656	VC
Univ of Maryland/Eastern Shore	MD	9,258	C
Univ of Wisc/Madison	WI	8,262	VC
Virginia Polytechnic Inst and State Univ	VA	7,652	C

PREALLIED HEALTH

School	ST	$IS	SR
Juniata College	PA	26,080	VC
La Salle Univ	PA	27,890	C

PREDENTISTRY

School	ST	$IS	SR
Abilene Christian Univ	TX	16,300	VC
Adams State College	CO	7,468	C
Albertus Magnus College	CT	22,154	C
Albion College	MI	25,224	VC
American International College	MA	22,268	LC
Arcadia Univ	PA	26,650	C
Ashland Univ	OH	22,182	LC
Auburn Univ	AL	5,510	C
Austin Peay State Univ	TN	5,814	LC
Azusa Pacific Univ	CA	22,422	VC
Baker Univ	KS	14,780	C+
Baldwin-Wallace College	OH	22,010	VC+
Ball State Univ	IN	8,660	C
Bard College	NY	33,912	HC
Barry Univ	FL	24,100	LC
Bartlesville Wesleyan College	OK	14,100	LC
Baylor Univ	TX	18,298	VC+
Bellarmine Univ	KY	20,440	VC
Belmont Abbey College	NC	19,630	LC
Beloit College	WI	27,482	HC
Bemidji State Univ	MN	7,957	C
Berry College	GA	18,850	LC
Bethany College	KS	16,602	C+
Bethany College	WV	18,566	C
Bethel College	IN	17,650	LC
Boise State Univ	ID	6,531	LC
Boston Univ	MA	34,358	MC
Briar Cliff Univ	IA	18,657	LC
Brigham Young Univ/Hawaii	HI	6,890	C
Calif Lutheran Univ	CA	23,500	LC
Calif Univ of Pennsylvania	PA	10,388	C
Calvin College	MI	20,050	NC
Capital Univ	OH	23,630	C
Cardinal Stritch Univ	WI	17,620	C
Carroll College	MT	19,140	C
Catawba College	NC	19,620	C
Central Missouri State Univ	MO	7,920	C
Chadron State College	NE	6,211	NC
Chicago State Univ	IL	8,851	C+
Christopher Newport Univ	VA	8,862	VC
Citadel, The	SC	9,126	C
CUNY/Brooklyn College	NY	3,403	LC
CUNY/City College	NY	3,309	LC
CUNY/Herbert H. Lehman College	NY	3,320	LC
CUNY/Hunter College	NY	5,147	C+
CUNY/Queens College	NY	3,403	VC
Claflin Univ	SC	12,735	C+
Clark Univ	MA	29,170	HC
Clemson Univ	SC	7,600	C
Coastal Carolina Univ	SC	9,220	C
Coe College	IA	24,750	VC
College Misericordia	PA	23,380	LC
College of Charleston	SC	8,350	HC
College of New Rochelle	NY	20,000	C
College of Notre Dame of Maryland	MD	23,100	LC
College of Our Lady of the Elms	MA	20,644	C
College of St. Benedict	MN	23,921	VC
College of St. Elizabeth	NJ	22,510	C
Columbia Union College	MD	19,027	C+
Concord College	WV	7,122	C+
Concordia College/Moorhead	MN	18,835	C
Concordia Univ Nebr	NE	17,770	C
Converse College	SC	21,990	VC
Coppin State College	MD	9,133	LC
Cornerstone Univ and Grand Rapids Baptist Seminary	MI	18,092	C
Dakota Wesleyan Univ	SD	15,512	C
David Lipscomb Univ	TN	16,158	VC
Davis and Elkins College	WV	19,270	LC
Delta State Univ	MS	5,416	C
Dordt College	IA	18,100	C+
Drake Univ	IA	22,830	VC
Drexel Univ	PA	27,657	VC
Drury Univ	MO	15,250	VC
Eastern Mich Univ	MI	9,855	C
Eastern Washington Univ	WA	7,972	LC
Eckerd College	FL	25,500	C+
Edinboro Univ of Pennsylvania	PA	9,328	LC
Elmira College	NY	31,070	VC+
Emmanuel College	MA	23,802	C+
Fairleigh Dickinson Univ/Teaneck Campus	NJ	24,646	C
Florida A&M Univ	FL	6,948	C
Florida State Univ	FL	7,835	HC
Fordham Univ	NY	30,710	VC
Freed-Hardeman Univ	TN	14,290	VC
Gannon Univ	PA	18,848	C
George Fox Univ	OR	24,095	VC
Gettysburg College	PA	32,070	HC
Goshen College	IN	18,950	VC+
Grace College	IN	16,768	C
Graceland Univ	IA	15,845	C
Grand Valley State Univ	MI	10,040	C
Grove City College	PA	12,280	MC
Gustavus Adolphus College	MN	24,190	VC+
Hamline Univ	MN	23,339	C+
Harding Univ	AR	13,528	VC
Heidelberg College	OH	23,879	C
Hillsdale College	MI	20,586	VC+
Hope College	MI	22,922	C+
Houston Baptist Univ	TX	15,300	LC
Howard Univ	DC	15,522	LC
Humboldt State Univ	CA	8,582	C
Indiana State Univ	IN	8,461	LC
Indiana Univ-Purdue Univ Fort Wayne	IN	3,166	LC
Indiana Wesleyan Univ	IN	17,680	C
Iona College	NY	26,556	C
Iowa Wesleyan College	IA	18,840	C
Ithaca College	NY	28,719	HC
Johnson C. Smith Univ	NC	16,560	C+
Judson College	IL	18,980	LC
Juniata College	PA	26,080	VC
Kansas State Univ	KS	6,995	C
Kennesaw State Univ	GA	2,306	LC
Kent State Univ	OH	11,104	C
Kentucky Wesleyan College	KY	15,800	C
Keuka College	NY	21,170	C
King's College	PA	24,680	C
La Salle Univ	PA	27,890	C
LaGrange College	GA	17,496	C
Lake Superior State Univ	MI	9,034	LC
Lamar Univ	TX	6,816	LC
Le Moyne College	NY	23,840	C
Lebanon Valley College of Pennsylvania	PA	25,700	VC
Lehigh Univ	PA	32,290	MC
Lewis Univ	IL	20,960	C
Lincoln Memorial Univ	TN	12,620	LC
Livingstone College	NC	13,360	LC
LIU/Brooklyn Campus	NY	22,290	C
LIU/C.W. Post Campus	NY	25,380	C
Louisiana College	LA	11,516	C
Loyola Univ of Chicago	IL	25,992	VC
Luther College	IA	23,300	VC+
MacMurray College	IL	17,790	LC
Manhattan College	NY	25,500	VC
Mars Hill College	NC	18,600	LC
Mary Washington College	VA	9,032	VC+
Maryville College	TN	23,210	VC
Mercer Univ	GA	24,130	VC
Mercyhurst College	PA	20,694	C
Merrimack College	MA	25,725	VC
Methodist College	NC	19,526	C
Mich State Univ	MI	10,386	VC
Midland Lutheran College	NE	18,600	C
Midwestern State Univ	TX	6,704	NC
Miles College	AL	7,870	NC
Minn State Univ, Mankato	MN	7,296	LC
Missouri Southern State College	MO	6,666	C
Moorhead State Univ	MN	7,000	LC
Mount Mary College	WI	18,024	C
Murray State Univ	KY	6,672	C
New Jersey City Univ	NJ	9,100	LC
New Mexico Highlands Univ	NM	6,256	NC
New York Univ	NY	35,200	MC
Niagara Univ	NY	22,250	C+
N Car State Univ	NC	8,680	HC
North Central College	IL	22,944	C+
North Georgia College and State Univ	GA	6,322	C+
North Park Univ	IL	24,030	C
Northeastern State Univ	OK	4,704	LC
Northern Arizona Univ	AZ	7,398	C
Northern Kentucky Univ	KY	6,352	NC
Northern Mich Univ	MI	9,693	C
Northern State Univ	SD	6,279	LC
Northwest Missouri State Univ	MO	7,922	LC
Northwestern College of Iowa	IA	17,630	C+
Notre Dame de Namur Univ	CA	26,932	LC
Occidental College	CA	32,288	HC
Ohio Univ	OH	11,769	C
Ohio Wesleyan Univ	OH	29,670	VC+
Okla Baptist Univ	OK	13,878	VC
Olivet College	MI	17,410	C
Oral Roberts Univ	OK	18,490	C
Ouachita Baptist Univ	AR	16,460	VC
Pace Univ	NY	24,200	C
Palm Beach Atlantic College	FL	23,310	C
Purdue Univ/Calumet	IN	6,630	NC
Purdue Univ/West Lafayette	IN	10,284	VC
Quinnipiac Univ	CT	27,370	C
Rensselaer Polytechnic Inst	NY	33,863	HC+
Rider Univ	NJ	27,400	C
Rivier College	NH	24,215	C
Rochester Inst of Technology	NY	26,232	VC+
Rockford College	IL	23,930	C
Roosevelt Univ	IL	20,240	LC
Rosemont College	PA	24,060	C
Rutgers, The State Univ of New Jersey/CamdenCampus	NJ	6,484	C
Rutgers, The State Univ of New Jersey/Newark Campus	NJ	6,394	C
St. Anselm College	NH	27,405	C
St. Cloud State Univ	MN	7,180	C
St. Edward's Univ	TX	17,846	C
St. John's Univ	MN	23,640	VC
St. John's Univ	NY	26,660	C
St. Joseph's College	IN	21,640	C
St. Martin's College	WA	20,566	C
St. Mary-of-the-Woods College	IN	21,320	LC
St. Mary's Univ of Minn	MN	19,975	C
St. Mary's Univ of San Antonio	TX	19,735	C
St. Michael's College	VT	26,935	VC
St. Peter's College	NJ	22,292	LC
St. Thomas Univ	FL	19,500	LC
St. Vincent College	PA	22,942	VC
St. Xavier Univ	IL	21,104	C
Savannah State Univ	GA	2,550	LC
Schreiner Univ	TX	19,254	C
Seton Hill College	PA	21,875	C
Southern Arkansas Univ	AR	5,740	LC
Southern Nazarene Univ	OK	14,634	NC
Southwest Missouri State Univ	MO	7,600	LC
Spring Hill College	AL	23,250	C
Springfield College	MA	24,520	C
SUNY/College at Fredonia	NY	10,125	C
SUNY/College at Oneonta	NY	9,981	C
SUNY/College of Environmental Science and Forestry	NY	12,446	VC
SUNY/Univ at Albany	NY	10,997	VC
Stevens Inst of Technology	NJ	31,510	HC+
Syracuse Univ	NY	30,710	HC
Tarleton State Univ	TX	7,160	C
Temple Univ	PA	14,124	C
Texas A&M Univ at Commerce	TX	7,326	C
Texas A&M Univ at Kingsville	TX	6,446	LC
Texas Tech Univ	TX	8,825	C
Thiel College	PA	18,419	LC
Touro College	NY	14,950	VC
Trinity Christian College	IL	19,415	C
Truman State Univ	MO	8,568	VC+
Union Univ	TN	18,930	C+
Univ of Akron	OH	10,530	NC
Univ of Arkansas	AR	8,334	VC
Univ of Arkansas at Pine Bluff	AR	7,925	C
Univ of Bridgeport	CT	23,020	C
Univ of Central Arkansas	AR	6,388	C
Univ of Cincinnati	OH	12,491	LC
Univ of Dayton	OH	20,400	VC
Univ of Detroit Mercy	MI	21,620	LC
Univ of Georgia	GA	8,656	VC
Univ of Great Falls	MT	15,360	C
Univ of Hartford	CT	28,884	C
Univ of Iowa	IA	8,607	C+
Univ of Mass Amherst	MA	10,995	VC
Univ of Miami	FL	31,130	HC
Univ of Mich/Flint	MI	4,323	C
Univ of Minn/Twin Cities	MN	11,123	VC
Univ of Missouri/Rolla	MO	10,034	C
Univ of Nebr at Kearney	NE	7,048	NC
Univ of Nebr at Lincoln	NE	8,325	C+
Univ of New England	ME	24,110	LC
Univ of New Haven	CT	23,860	LC
Univ of New Mexico	NM	8,026	C
Univ of N Car at Greensboro	NC	6,858	C
Univ of North Florida	FL	8,089	VC
Univ of Notre Dame	IN	30,707	MC
Univ of Rio Grande	OH	8,728	NC
Univ of St. Francis	IL	19,650	C
Univ of St. Francis	IN	17,790	LC
Univ of Scranton	PA	27,964	C+
Univ of Southern Calif	CA	33,647	MC
Univ of Southern Colo	CO	7,821	LC
Univ of Southern Indiana	IN	8,655	LC
Univ of Southern Miss	MS	6,155	LC
Univ of Tenn at Knoxville	TN	8,214	C
Univ of Tenn at Martin	TN	8,268	C
Univ of the Incarnate Word	TX	18,478	C
Univ of West Alabama	AL	6,048	C
Univ of West Florida	FL	7,518	C
Univ of Wisc/Milwaukee	WI	8,907	LC
Utah State Univ	UT	6,771	C
Walsh Univ	OH	16,880	C
Washington State Univ	WA	9,388	C
Washington Univ in St. Louis	MO	34,593	MC
Waynesburg College	PA	17,610	LC
Weber State Univ	UT	6,897	NC
West Chester Univ of Pennsylvania	PA	9,792	VC
West Liberty State College	WV	6,056	LC
West Texas A&M Univ	TX	6,538	C
Western Carolina Univ	NC	5,667	C
Western Mich Univ	MI	10,016	C
Western New Mexico Univ	NM	5,950	LC
Western State College of Colo	CO	7,585	LC
Westminster College	PA	22,960	C
Whitworth College	WA	23,938	VC
Widener Univ	PA	26,920	C
Wilkes Univ	PA	25,800	C
Wilmington College	OH	21,826	C
Wingate Univ	NC	19,140	C
Winona State Univ	MN	8,570	C
Wittenberg Univ	OH	28,766	VC

School	ST	$IS	SR
Wright State Univ	OH	9,141	LC
Xavier Univ	OH	23,880	C
Xavier Univ of Louisiana	LA	17,000	LC
Youngstown State Univ	OH	9,318	NC

PREENGINEERING

School	ST	$IS	SR
Adams State College	CO	7,468	C
Alice Lloyd College	KY	1,785	VC
Augustana College	IL	24,117	VC+
Barry Univ	FL	24,100	LC
Bellarmine Univ	KY	20,440	VC
Belmont Abbey College	NC	19,630	LC
Berry College	GA	18,850	C
Bethel College	TN	12,980	C
Briar Cliff Univ	IA	18,657	LC
Campbell Univ	NC	16,599	C
CUNY/Brooklyn College	NY	3,403	LC
CUNY/Hunter College	NY	5,147	C+
Coe College	IA	24,750	VC
College of Notre Dame of Maryland	MD	23,100	LC
College of St. Benedict	MN	23,921	VC
College of the Ozarks	MO	2,650	C+
Concordia College/Moorhead	MN	18,835	C
Coppin State College	MD	9,133	LC
David Lipscomb Univ	TN	16,158	VC
DePauw Univ	IN	28,000	HC
Dominican College	NY	20,400	LC
Eastern Mich Univ	MI	9,855	C
Edgewood College	WI	18,304	C
Elon Univ	NC	19,430	VC
Emmanuel College	MA	23,802	C+
Fordham Univ	NY	30,710	VC
Framingham State College	MA	7,259	C
Freed-Hardeman Univ	TN	14,290	VC
Furman Univ	SC	25,492	HC
Goshen College	IN	18,950	VC+
Harvard Univ/Harvard College	MA	34,269	MC
Heidelberg College	OH	23,879	C
Indiana State Univ	IN	8,461	LC
Iowa Wesleyan College	IA	18,840	C
Johnson C. Smith Univ	NC	16,560	C+
Judson College	IL	18,980	LC
Juniata College	PA	26,080	VC
Kennesaw State Univ	GA	2,306	LC
Kentucky Wesleyan College	KY	15,800	C
Lewis Univ	IL	20,960	C
Lincoln Univ	PA	11,198	C+
LIU/C.W. Post Campus	NY	25,380	C
Luther College	IA	23,300	VC+
MacMurray College	IL	17,790	LC
Mansfield Univ	PA	9,648	C
Maryville College	TN	23,210	VC
Midwestern State Univ	TX	6,704	NC
Miles College	AL	7,870	NC
Minn State Univ, Mankato	MN	7,296	LC
Niagara Univ	NY	22,250	C+
North Central College	IL	22,944	C+
North Georgia College and State Univ	GA	6,322	C+
Northern Kentucky Univ	KY	6,352	NC
Northwest Missouri State Univ	MO	7,922	LC
Oral Roberts Univ	OK	18,490	C
Peru State College	NE	6,342	NC
Pfeiffer Univ	NC	18,580	C
Providence College	RI	27,620	HC
Purdue Univ/West Lafayette	IN	10,284	VC
Richard Stockton College of New Jersey	NJ	12,165	VC
Rockford College	IL	23,930	C
St. Edward's Univ	TX	17,846	C
St. John's Univ	MN	23,640	VC
St. John's Univ	NY	26,660	C
St. Mary's College of Calif	CA	27,575	C
St. Mary's Univ of Minn	MN	19,975	C
St. Michael's College	VT	26,935	VC
St. Norbert College	WI	23,169	VC
Scripps College	CA	30,400	HC+
Shaw Univ	NC	12,810	C
Southern Nazarene Univ	OK	14,634	NC
Stephen F. Austin State Univ	TX	6,905	C
Texas A&M Univ at Commerce	TX	7,326	C
Thiel College	PA	18,419	LC
Truman State Univ	MO	8,568	VC+
Union Univ	TN	18,930	C+
Univ of Arkansas at Pine Bluff	AR	7,925	C
Univ of Central Arkansas	AR	6,388	C
Univ of Findlay	OH	23,962	NC
Univ of Georgia	GA	8,656	VC
Univ of Rio Grande	OH	8,728	NC
Univ of Scranton	PA	27,964	C+
Univ of Southern Colo	CO	7,821	LC
Valley City State Univ	ND		LC
Weber State Univ	UT	6,897	NC
West Liberty State College	WV	6,056	LC
West Texas A&M Univ	TX	6,538	C
Western Carolina Univ	NC	5,667	C
Western State College of Colo	CO	7,585	LC

School	ST	$IS	SR
Wilberforce Univ	OH	14,937	LC
Wingate Univ	NC	19,140	C
Yeshiva Univ	NY	21,400	C
Youngstown State Univ	OH	9,318	NC

PRELAW

School	ST	$IS	SR
Abilene Christian Univ	TX	16,300	VC
Adams State College	CO	7,468	C
Albertus Magnus College	CT	22,154	C
American International College	MA	22,268	LC
Arcadia Univ	PA	26,650	C
Ashland Univ	OH	22,182	LC
Audrey Cohen College	NY	17,715	C
Austin Peay State Univ	TN	5,814	LC
Averett Univ	VA	17,980	LC
Baker Univ	KS	14,780	C+
Baldwin-Wallace College	OH	22,010	VC+
Ball State Univ	IN	8,660	C
Bard College	NY	33,912	HC
Barry Univ	FL	24,100	LC
Bartlesville Wesleyan College	OK	14,100	LC
Baylor Univ	TX	18,298	VC+
Bellarmine Univ	KY	20,440	VC
Belmont Abbey College	NC	19,630	LC
Beloit College	WI	27,482	HC
Bemidji State Univ	MN	7,957	C
Berry College	GA	18,850	C
Bethany College	KS	16,602	C+
Bethany College	WV	18,566	C
Bethel College	IN	17,650	LC
Black Hills State Univ	SD	6,652	LC
Blue Mountain College	MS	9,100	LC
Calif Lutheran Univ	CA	23,500	LC
Calvin College	MI	20,050	NC
Campbell Univ	NC	16,599	C
Capital Univ	OH	23,630	C
Cardinal Stritch Univ	WI	17,620	C
Carroll College	MT	19,140	C
Catawba College	NC	19,620	C
Cedar Crest College	PA	25,145	C+
Cedarville Univ	OH	17,553	VC
Centenary College of Louisiana	LA	21,600	C+
Central Missouri State Univ	MO	7,920	C
Chadron State College	NE	6,211	NC
Champlain College	VT	19,680	C
Chicago State Univ	IL	8,851	C+
Christopher Newport Univ	VA	8,862	VC
CUNY/Brooklyn College	NY	3,403	LC
CUNY/City College	NY	3,309	LC
CUNY/Herbert H. Lehman College	NY	3,320	LC
CUNY/Hunter College	NY	5,147	C+
Claflin Univ	SC	12,735	C+
Claremont McKenna College	CA	32,700	MC
Clark Univ	MA	29,170	HC
Clearwater Christian College	FL	13,160	LC
Clemson Univ	SC	7,600	C
Coastal Carolina Univ	SC	9,220	C
Coe College	IA	24,750	VC
College Misericordia	PA	23,380	LC
College of New Rochelle	NY	20,000	C
College of Notre Dame of Maryland	MD	23,100	LC
College of Our Lady of the Elms	MA	20,644	C
College of St. Benedict	MN	23,921	VC
College of St. Elizabeth	NJ	22,510	C
College of St. Joseph	VT	17,400	NC
College of the Southwest	NM	8,456	NC
Columbia Union College	MD	19,027	C+
Concord College	WV	7,122	C+
Concordia College/Moorhead	MN	18,835	C
Concordia Univ Nebr	NE	17,770	C
Concordia Univ, River Forest	IL	20,000	LC
Converse College	SC	21,990	VC
Cornerstone Univ and Grand Rapids Baptist Seminary	MI	18,092	C
Creighton Univ	NE	23,476	VC
Crichton College	TN	12,680	LC
Cumberland Univ	TN	11,970	LC
David Lipscomb Univ	TN	16,158	VC
Davis and Elkins College	WV	19,270	LC
Dominican College	NY	20,400	LC
Dordt College	IA	18,100	C+
Drake Univ	IA	22,830	VC
Drexel Univ	PA	27,657	VC
Drury Univ	MO	15,250	VC
East Central Univ	OK	4,578	C
Eastern Mich Univ	MI	9,855	C
Eastern Washington Univ	WA	7,972	LC
Eckerd College	FL	25,500	C+
Edgewood College	WI	18,304	C
Edinboro Univ of Pennsylvania	PA	9,328	LC
Elmira College	NY	31,070	VC+
Emmanuel College	MA	23,802	C+
Emory & Henry College	VA	19,462	C
Eugene Lang College of New School Univ	NY	30,300	C
Faulkner Univ	AL	13,000	C
Florida State Univ	FL	7,835	HC
Fontbonne Univ	MO	18,046	C
Fordham Univ	NY	30,710	VC
Fresno Pacific Univ	CA	19,740	C
Gannon Univ	PA	18,848	C
George Fox Univ	OR	24,095	VC
Gettysburg College	PA	32,070	HC
Grace College	IN	16,768	C
Grambling State Univ	LA	5,325	NC
Grand Valley State Univ	MI	10,040	C
Grove City College	PA	12,280	MC
Gustavus Adolphus College	MN	24,190	VC+
Hamline Univ	MN	23,339	C+
Heidelberg College	OH	23,879	C
Hillsdale College	MI	20,586	VC+
Holy Family College	PA	13,710	LC
Hope College	MI	22,922	C+
Humboldt State Univ	CA	8,582	C
Huntington College	IN	15,480	LC
Illinois College	IL	16,234	C
Immaculata College	PA	22,400	LC
Indiana State Univ	IN	8,461	LC
Indiana Univ of Pennsylvania	PA	9,133	C
Indiana Univ-Purdue Univ Fort Wayne	IN	3,166	LC
Iona College	NY	26,556	C
Iowa Wesleyan College	IA	18,840	C
Ithaca College	NY	28,719	HC
John Brown Univ	AR	15,080	VC
Johns Hopkins Univ	MD	35,226	MC
Johnson C. Smith Univ	NC	16,560	C+
Johnson State College	VT	10,776	C
Judson College	IL	18,980	LC
Juniata College	PA	26,080	VC
Kansas Wesleyan Univ	KS	17,400	C+
Kennesaw State Univ	GA	2,306	LC
Kentucky Wesleyan College	KY	15,800	C
Keuka College	NY	21,170	C
King's College	PA	24,680	C
La Salle Univ	PA	27,890	C
Lafayette College	PA	32,655	MC
LaGrange College	GA	17,496	C
Lake Superior State Univ	MI	9,034	LC
Lamar Univ	TX	6,816	LC
Le Moyne College	NY	23,840	C
Lebanon Valley College of Pennsylvania	PA	25,700	VC
Lenoir-Rhyne College	NC	19,186	C
LeTourneau Univ	TX	19,020	VC
Lewis Univ	IL	20,960	C
Limestone College	SC	16,900	C
Lincoln Memorial Univ	TN	12,620	LC
Lindenwood Univ	MO	17,250	C
Livingstone College	NC	13,360	LC
LIU/Brooklyn Campus	NY	22,290	C
LIU/C.W. Post Campus	NY	25,380	C
LIU/Southampton College	NY	26,270	C
Louisiana College	LA	11,516	C
Luther College	IA	23,300	VC+
Lynn Univ	FL	24,550	C
MacMurray College	IL	17,790	LC
Manchester College	IN	22,010	C
Manhattan College	NY	25,500	VC
Mansfield Univ	PA	9,648	C
Marlboro College	VT	26,470	VC+
Mars Hill College	NC	18,600	LC
Mary Washington College	VA	9,032	VC+
Maryville College	TN	23,210	VC
Mercer Univ	GA	24,130	VC
Mercyhurst College	PA	20,694	C
Merrimack College	MA	25,725	VC
Methodist College	NC	19,526	C
Miami Univ	OH	12,885	VC+
Mich State Univ	MI	10,386	VC
Middle Tenn State Univ	TN	6,994	C
Midland Lutheran College	NE	18,600	C
Midwestern State Univ	TX	6,704	NC
Minn State Univ, Mankato	MN	7,296	LC
Monmouth Univ	NJ	24,042	C
Moorhead State Univ	MN	7,000	LC
Moravian College	PA	27,065	VC
Mount Aloysius College	PA	18,186	LC
Mount Mary College	WI	18,024	C
Mount St. Mary College	NY	18,825	C
Murray State Univ	KY	6,672	C
New Jersey City Univ	NJ	9,100	LC
New Mexico Highlands Univ	NM	6,256	NC
New York Inst of Technology	NY	21,756	C
New York Univ	NY	35,200	MC
Newbury College	MA	21,490	C
Niagara Univ	NY	22,250	C+
Norfolk State Univ	VA	8,382	LC
N Car State Univ	NC	8,680	HC
North Central College	IL	22,944	C+
North Georgia College and State Univ	GA	6,322	C+
North Park Univ	IL	24,030	C
Northeastern State Univ	OK	4,704	LC
Northern Arizona Univ	AZ	7,398	C
Northern Kentucky Univ	KY	6,352	NC
Northern Mich Univ	MI	9,693	C
Northern State Univ	SD	6,279	LC
Northwest Missouri State Univ	MO	7,922	LC
Northwestern College of Iowa	IA	17,630	C+
Notre Dame de Namur Univ	CA	26,932	LC
Nova Southeastern Univ	FL	20,104	LC
Oakland City Univ	IN	11,286	LC
Ohio Univ	OH	11,769	C
Ohio Wesleyan Univ	OH	29,670	VC+
Okla Baptist Univ	OK	13,878	VC
Okla Christian Univ	OK	16,500	VC
Okla City Univ	OK	15,810	C
Okla State Univ	OK	7,650	VC
Olivet College	MI	17,410	C
Oral Roberts Univ	OK	18,490	C
Ouachita Baptist Univ	AR	16,460	VC
Penn State Univ/Univ Park Campus	PA	11,126	VC
Peru State College	NE	6,342	NC
Pfeiffer Univ	NC	18,580	C
Purdue Univ/Calumet	IN	6,630	NC
Purdue Univ/West Lafayette	IN	10,284	VC
Quinnipiac Univ	CT	27,370	C
Regis Univ	CO	25,740	C+
Rensselaer Polytechnic Inst	NY	33,863	HC+
Rhode Island College	RI	8,700	LC
Rider Univ	NJ	27,400	C
Rivier College	NH	24,215	C
Roberts Wesleyan College	NY	20,160	C+
Rochester Inst of Technology	NY	26,232	VC+
Rockford College	IL	23,930	C
Roger Williams Univ	RI	29,010	C
Roosevelt Univ	IL	20,240	LC
Rosemont College	PA	24,060	C
Rutgers, The State Univ of New Jersey/CamdenCampus	NJ	6,484	C
Rutgers, The State Univ of New Jersey/Newark Campus	NJ	6,394	C
St. Anselm College	NH	27,405	C
St. Augustine's College	NC	12,990	C+
St. Bonaventure Univ	NY	21,956	C
St. Cloud State Univ	MN	7,180	C
St. Edward's Univ	TX	17,846	C
St. John's Univ	MN	23,640	VC
St. John's Univ	NY	26,660	C
St. Joseph's College	IN	21,640	C
St. Martin's College	WA	20,566	C
St. Mary-of-the-Woods College	IN	21,320	LC
St. Mary's College	MI	13,314	LC
St. Mary's Univ of Minn	MN	19,975	C
St. Mary's Univ of San Antonio	TX	19,735	C
St. Michael's College	VT	26,935	VC
St. Peter's College	NJ	22,292	LC
St. Thomas Aquinas College	NY	20,590	LC
St. Thomas Univ	FL	19,500	LC
St. Vincent College	PA	22,942	VC
St. Xavier Univ	IL	21,104	C
Schreiner Univ	TX	19,254	C
Scripps College	CA	30,400	HC+
Seton Hill College	PA	21,075	C
Shawnee State Univ	OH	8,634	NC
Simmons College	MA	30,418	VC
Southern Nazarene Univ	OK	14,634	NC
Southern Oregon Univ	OR	9,429	C
Springfield College	MA	24,520	C
SUNY/College at Oneonta	NY	9,981	C
SUNY/College of Environmental Science and Forestry	NY	12,446	VC
SUNY/Univ at Albany	NY	10,997	VC
Stephen F. Austin State Univ	TX	6,905	C
Stephens College	MO	22,295	C
Stetson Univ	FL	25,640	VC
Stevens Inst of Technology	NJ	31,510	HC+
Stillman College	AL	11,370	LC
Syracuse Univ	NY	30,710	HC
Tarleton State Univ	TX	7,160	C
Temple Univ	PA	14,124	C
Texas A&M Univ at Commerce	TX	7,326	C
Texas A&M Univ at Kingsville	TX	6,446	LC
Texas Tech Univ	TX	8,825	C
Thiel College	PA	18,419	LC
Touro College	NY	14,950	VC
Trinity Christian College	IL	19,415	C
Trinity College	DC	21,370	LC
Truman State Univ	MO	8,568	VC+
Union Univ	TN	18,930	C+
Univ of Akron	OH	10,530	NC
Univ of Alabama	AL	7,402	C
Univ of Arkansas	AR	8,334	VC
Univ of Bridgeport	CT	23,020	C
Univ of Cincinnati	OH	12,491	LC
Univ of Detroit Mercy	MI	21,620	LC
Univ of Evansville	IN	22,865	VC+
Univ of Findlay	OH	23,962	NC
Univ of Great Falls	MT	15,360	C

School	ST	$IS	SR
Univ of Iowa	IA	8,607	C+
Univ of Louisiana at Monroe	LA	5,207	NC
Univ of Mary	ND	12,900	LC
Univ of Mary Hardin-Baylor	TX	13,929	C
Univ of Mass Amherst	MA	10,995	VC
Univ of Miami	FL	31,130	HC
Univ of Mich/Flint	MI	4,323	C
Univ of Minn/Morris	MN	10,716	VC
Univ of Minn/Twin Cities	MN	11,123	VC
Univ of Missouri/Rolla	MO	10,034	C
Univ of Nebr at Kearney	NE	7,048	NC
Univ of Nebr at Omaha	NE	6,867	C
Univ of New England	ME	24,110	LC
Univ of New Mexico	NM	8,026	C
Univ of N Car at Greensboro	NC	6,858	C
Univ of N Car at Pembroke	NC	5,914	LC
Univ of North Florida	FL	8,089	VC
Univ of Rio Grande	OH	8,728	NC
Univ of St. Francis	IL	19,650	C
Univ of Scranton	PA	27,964	C+
Univ of Sioux Falls	SD	16,390	C
Univ of Southern Calif	CA	33,647	MC
Univ of Southern Colo	CO	7,821	LC
Univ of Southern Indiana	IN	8,655	LC
Univ of Southern Miss	MS	6,155	LC
Univ of Tenn at Martin	TN	8,268	C
Univ of the Incarnate Word	TX	18,478	C
Univ of the Pacific	CA	28,255	VC
Univ of Tulsa	OK	19,090	HC
Univ of West Alabama	AL	6,048	C
Univ of West Florida	FL	7,518	C
Univ of Wisc/Milwaukee	WI	8,907	LC
Univ of Wisc/River Falls	WI	6,356	LC
Univ of Wisc/Whitewater	WI	6,937	C
Urbana Univ	OH	17,004	C
Ursinus College	PA	31,350	VC
Ursuline College	OH	19,430	LC
Utah State Univ	UT	6,771	C
Vanguard Univ of Southern Calif	CA	20,212	C
Vassar College	NY	33,450	MC
Walsh Univ	OH	16,880	C
Waynesburg College	PA	17,610	LC
Webber International Univ	FL	14,695	LC
West Chester Univ of Pennsylvania	PA	9,792	VC
West Liberty State College	WV	6,056	LC
West Texas A&M Univ	TX	6,538	C
Western Carolina Univ	NC	5,667	C
Western Mich Univ	MI	10,016	C
Western State College of Colo	CO	7,585	LC
Westminster College	PA	22,960	C
Whitworth College	WA	23,938	VC
Widener Univ	PA	26,920	C
Wilberforce Univ	OH	14,937	LC
Wilkes Univ	PA	25,800	C
William Tyndale College	MI	11,150	C
Wilmington College	OH	21,826	C
Wingate Univ	NC	19,140	C
Winona State Univ	MN	8,570	C
Wittenberg Univ	OH	28,766	VC
Wright State Univ	OH	9,141	LC
Xavier Univ	OH	23,880	C
Xavier Univ of Louisiana	LA	17,000	LC
York College of Pennsylvania	PA	12,550	VC
Youngstown State Univ	OH	9,318	NC

PREMEDICINE

School	ST	$IS	SR
Abilene Christian Univ	TX	16,300	VC
Adams State College	CO	7,468	C
Albertus Magnus College	CT	22,154	C
Albion College	MI	25,224	VC
American International College	MA	22,268	LC
Arcadia Univ	PA	26,650	C
Ashland Univ	OH	22,182	LC
Auburn Univ	AL	5,510	C
Augustana College	IL	24,117	VC+
Austin Peay State Univ	TN	5,814	LC
Averett Univ	VA	17,980	LC
Avila College	MO	17,720	C
Azusa Pacific Univ	CA	22,422	VC
Baker Univ	KS	14,780	C+
Baldwin-Wallace College	OH	22,010	VC+
Ball State Univ	IN	8,660	C
Bard College	NY	33,912	HC
Barry Univ	FL	24,100	LC
Bartlesville Wesleyan College	OK	14,100	LC
Baylor Univ	TX	18,298	VC+
Bellarmine Univ	KY	20,440	VC
Belmont Abbey College	NC	19,630	LC
Beloit College	WI	27,482	HC
Bemidji State Univ	MN	7,957	C
Bennington College	VT	31,350	VC
Berry College	GA	18,850	C
Bethany College	KS	16,602	C+
Bethany College	WV	18,566	C
Bethel College	IN	17,650	LC
Blue Mountain College	MS	9,100	LC
Boise State Univ	ID	6,531	LC
Boston Univ	MA	34,358	MC
Bowling Green State Univ	OH	10,794	C
Briar Cliff Univ	IA	18,657	LC
Brigham Young Univ/Hawaii	HI	6,890	C
Calif Lutheran Univ	CA	23,500	LC
Calif Univ of Pennsylvania	PA	10,388	C
Capital Univ	OH	23,630	C
Cardinal Stritch Univ	WI	17,620	C
Carroll College	MT	19,140	C
Catawba College	NC	19,620	C
Centenary College of Louisiana	LA	21,600	C+
Central Missouri State Univ	MO	7,920	C
Central Univ of Bayamon	PR	3,335	
Chadron State College	NE	6,211	NC
Chicago State Univ	IL	8,851	C+
Christopher Newport Univ	VA	8,862	VC
Citadel, The	SC	9,126	C
CUNY/Brooklyn College	NY	3,403	LC
CUNY/City College	NY	3,309	LC
CUNY/Herbert H. Lehman College	NY	3,320	LC
CUNY/Hunter College	NY	5,147	C+
CUNY/Queens College	NY	3,403	VC
Claremont McKenna College	CA	32,700	MC
Clark Univ	MA	29,170	HC
Clearwater Christian College	FL	13,160	LC
Clemson Univ	SC	7,600	C
Cleveland State Univ	OH	10,146	NC
Coastal Carolina Univ	SC	9,220	C
Coe College	IA	24,750	VC
College Misericordia	PA	23,380	LC
College of Charleston	SC	8,350	HC
College of Mount St. Joseph	OH	20,290	C
College of New Rochelle	NY	20,000	C
College of Notre Dame of Maryland	MD	23,100	LC
College of Our Lady of the Elms	MA	20,644	C
College of St. Benedict	MN	23,921	VC
College of St. Elizabeth	NJ	22,510	C
College of the Ozarks	MO	2,650	C+
Columbia Union College	MD	19,027	C+
Concord College	WV	7,122	C+
Concordia College/Moorhead	MN	18,835	C
Concordia Univ	OR	20,500	LC
Concordia Univ Nebr	NE	17,770	C
Concordia Univ, River Forest	IL	20,000	LC
Converse College	SC	21,990	VC
Cornerstone Univ and Grand Rapids Baptist Seminary	MI	18,092	C
Cumberland Univ	TN	11,970	LC
Dakota State Univ	SD	6,950	C
Dakota Wesleyan Univ	SD	15,512	C
David Lipscomb Univ	TN	16,158	VC
Davis and Elkins College	WV	19,270	LC
Delta State Univ	MS	5,416	C
Dillard Univ	LA	16,046	VC
Dominican College	NY	20,400	LC
Dominican Univ of Calif	CA	27,948	C
Dordt College	IA	18,100	C+
Drake Univ	IA	22,830	VC
Drexel Univ	PA	27,657	VC
Drury Univ	MO	15,250	VC
East Stroudsburg Univ of Pennsylvania	PA	8,430	LC
Eastern Mich Univ	MI	9,855	C
Eastern Washington Univ	WA	7,972	LC
Eckerd College	FL	25,500	C+
Edgewood College	WI	18,304	C
Edinboro Univ of Pennsylvania	PA	9,328	LC
Elmira College	NY	31,070	VC+
Emmanuel College	MA	23,802	C+
Emory & Henry College	VA	19,462	C
Fairleigh Dickinson Univ/Teaneck Campus	NJ	24,646	C
Florida A&M Univ	FL	6,948	C
Florida Inst of Technology	FL	25,250	VC
Florida State Univ	FL	7,835	HC
Fordham Univ	NY	30,710	VC
Freed-Hardeman Univ	TN	14,290	VC
Fresno Pacific Univ	CA	19,740	C
Friends Univ	KS	15,962	LC
Gannon Univ	PA	18,848	C
George Fox Univ	OR	24,095	VC
George Washington Univ	DC	32,170	HC
Gettysburg College	PA	32,070	HC
Goshen College	IN	18,950	VC+
Grace College	IN	16,768	C
Graceland Univ	IA	15,845	C
Grambling State Univ	LA	5,325	NC
Grand Valley State Univ	MI	10,040	C
Grove City College	PA	12,280	MC
Gustavus Adolphus College	MN	24,190	VC+
Hamline Univ	MN	23,339	C+
Hampshire College	MA	33,881	HC+
Harding Univ	AR	13,528	VC
Hawaii Pacific Univ	HI	17,790	C
Heidelberg College	OH	23,879	C
Hillsdale College	MI	20,586	VC+
Holy Family College	PA	13,710	LC
Hope College	MI	22,922	C+
Houston Baptist Univ	TX	15,300	LC
Howard Univ	DC	15,522	LC
Humboldt State Univ	CA	8,582	C
Huntington College	IN	15,480	LC
Immaculata College	PA	22,400	LC
Indiana State Univ	IN	8,461	LC
Indiana Univ of Pennsylvania	PA	9,133	C
Indiana Univ-Purdue Univ Fort Wayne	IN	3,166	LC
Indiana Wesleyan Univ	IN	17,680	C
Inter-American Univ of PR/San GermÈn	PR	6,390	
Iona College	NY	26,556	C
Iowa Wesleyan College	IA	18,840	C
Ithaca College	NY	28,719	HC
Jackson State Univ	MS	6,776	LC
Jarvis Christian College	TX	9,035	NC
Johns Hopkins Univ	MD	35,226	MC
Johnson C. Smith Univ	NC	16,560	C+
Johnson State College	VT	10,776	C
Judson College	IL	18,980	LC
Juniata College	PA	26,080	VC
Kansas State Univ	KS	6,995	C
Kennesaw State Univ	GA	2,306	LC
Kent State Univ	OH	11,104	C
Kentucky Wesleyan College	KY	15,800	C
Keuka College	NY	21,170	C
King's College	PA	24,680	C
La Salle Univ	PA	27,890	C
LaGrange College	GA	17,496	C
Lake Superior State Univ	MI	9,034	LC
Lamar Univ	TX	6,816	LC
Le Moyne College	NY	23,840	C
Lebanon Valley College of Pennsylvania	PA	25,700	VC
Lehigh Univ	PA	32,290	MC
Lenoir-Rhyne College	NC	19,186	C
LeTourneau Univ	TX	19,020	VC
Lewis Univ	IL	20,960	C
Lincoln Memorial Univ	TN	12,620	LC
Livingstone College	NC	13,360	LC
LIU/Brooklyn Campus	NY	22,290	C
LIU/C.W. Post Campus	NY	25,380	C
Louisiana College	LA	11,516	C
Loyola Univ of Chicago	IL	25,992	VC
Luther College	IA	23,300	VC+
MacMurray College	IL	17,790	LC
Manhattan College	NY	25,500	VC
Mansfield Univ	PA	9,648	C
Marlboro College	VT	26,410	VC+
Mars Hill College	NC	18,600	LC
Mary Washington College	VA	9,032	VC+
Marymount Manhattan College	NY	23,195	VC
Maryville College	TN	23,210	VC
Mass College of Pharmacy and Health Sciences	MA	27,131	SP
Mercer Univ	GA	24,130	VC
Mercyhurst College	PA	20,694	C
Merrimack College	MA	25,725	VC
Miami Univ	OH	12,885	VC+
Mich State Univ	MI	10,386	VC
Midland Lutheran College	NE	18,600	C
Midwestern State Univ	TX	6,704	NC
Miles College	AL	7,870	NC
Milligan College	TN	17,550	C
Minn State Univ, Mankato	MN	7,296	LC
Missouri Southern State College	MO	6,666	C
Monmouth Univ	NJ	24,042	C
Moorhead State Univ	MN	7,000	LC
Morris Brown College	GA	15,993	LC
Mount Mary College	WI	18,024	C
Mount St. Mary College	NY	18,825	C
Murray State Univ	KY	6,672	C
New Jersey City Univ	NJ	9,100	LC
New Mexico Highlands Univ	NM	6,256	NC
New York Univ	NY	35,200	MC
Niagara Univ	NY	22,250	C+
Norfolk State Univ	VA	8,382	LC
N Car State Univ	NC	8,680	HC
N Car Wesleyan College	NC	15,650	LC
North Central College	IL	22,944	C+
North Georgia College and State Univ	GA	6,322	C+
North Park Univ	IL	24,030	C
Northeastern State Univ	OK	4,704	LC
Northern Arizona Univ	AZ	7,398	C
Northern Kentucky Univ	KY	6,352	NC
Northern Mich Univ	MI	9,693	C
Northern State Univ	SD	6,279	LC
Northwest Missouri State Univ	MO	7,922	LC
Northwest Nazarene Univ	ID	18,380	C
Northwestern College of Iowa	IA	17,630	C+
Notre Dame de Namur Univ	CA	26,932	LC
Nova Southeastern Univ	FL	20,104	LC
Oakland City Univ	IN	11,286	LC
Occidental College	CA	32,288	HC
Ohio Univ	OH	11,769	C
Ohio Wesleyan Univ	OH	29,670	VC+
Okla Baptist Univ	OK	13,878	VC
Okla Christian Univ	OK	16,500	VC
Okla City Univ	OK	15,810	C
Okla State Univ	OK	7,650	VC
Olivet College	MI	17,410	C
Oral Roberts Univ	OK	18,490	C
Ouachita Baptist Univ	AR	16,460	VC
Pace Univ	NY	24,200	C
Palm Beach Atlantic College	FL	23,310	C
Penn State Univ/Univ Park Campus	PA	11,126	VC
Peru State College	NE	6,342	NC
Pfeiffer Univ	NC	18,580	C
Philadelphia Univ	PA	24,722	C
Purdue Univ/Calumet	IN	6,630	NC
Purdue Univ/West Lafayette	IN	10,284	VC
Quinnipiac Univ	CT	27,370	C
Rensselaer Polytechnic Inst	NY	33,863	HC+
Rider Univ	NJ	27,400	C
Rivier College	NH	24,215	C
Roberts Wesleyan College	NY	20,160	C+
Rochester Inst of Technology	NY	26,232	VC+
Rockford College	IL	23,930	C
Roger Williams Univ	RI	29,010	C
Roosevelt Univ	IL	20,240	LC
Rosemont College	PA	24,060	C
Rutgers, The State Univ of New Jersey/CamdenCampus	NJ	6,484	C
Rutgers, The State Univ of New Jersey/Newark Campus	NJ	6,394	C
St. Anselm College	NH	27,405	C
St. Augustine's College	NC	12,990	C+
St. Bonaventure Univ	NY	21,956	C
St. Cloud State Univ	MN	7,180	C
St. Edward's Univ	TX	17,846	C
St. Francis College	NY	9,610	C
St. John's Univ	MN	23,640	VC
St. John's Univ	NY	26,660	C
St. Joseph's College	IN	21,640	C
St. Martin's College	WA	20,566	C
St. Mary-of-the-Woods College	IN	21,320	LC
St. Mary's College	MI	13,314	LC
St. Mary's Univ of Minn	MN	19,975	C
St. Mary's Univ of San Antonio	TX	19,735	C
St. Peter's College	NJ	22,292	LC
St. Thomas Aquinas College	NY	20,590	LC
St. Thomas Univ	FL	19,500	LC
St. Vincent College	PA	22,942	VC
St. Xavier Univ	IL	21,104	C
Sarah Lawrence College	NY	37,516	HC
Schreiner Univ	TX	19,254	C
Seton Hill College	PA	21,875	C
Shawnee State Univ	OH	8,634	NC
Siena Heights Univ	MI	16,140	LC
Simmons College	MA	30,418	VC
Simon's Rock College of Bard	MA	32,450	HC
Southern Arkansas Univ	AR	5,740	LC
Southern Nazarene Univ	OK	14,634	NC
Southern Oregon Univ	OR	9,429	C
Spring Hill College	AL	23,250	C
Springfield College	MA	24,520	C
SUNY/College at Fredonia	NY	10,125	C
SUNY/College at Oneonta	NY	9,981	C
SUNY/College of Environmental Science and Forestry	NY	12,446	VC
SUNY/Univ at Albany	NY	10,997	VC
SUNY/Univ at New Paltz	NY	9,685	VC
Stephen F. Austin State Univ	TX	6,905	C
Stevens Inst of Technology	NJ	31,510	HC+
Stillman College	AL	11,370	LC
Syracuse Univ	NY	30,710	HC
Tarleton State Univ	TX	7,160	C
Temple Univ	PA	14,124	C
Texas A&M Univ at Commerce	TX	7,326	C
Texas A&M Univ at Kingsville	TX	6,446	LC
Texas Tech Univ	TX	8,825	C
Thiel College	PA	18,419	LC
Touro College	NY	14,950	VC
Trinity Christian College	IL	19,415	C
Trinity College	DC	21,370	LC
Trinity International Univ	IL	20,640	C+
Tri-State Univ-Main Campus	IN	21,200	C
Truman State Univ	MO	8,568	VC+
Tusculum College	TN	17,900	LC
Union Univ	TN	18,930	C+
Univ of Akron	OH	10,530	NC
Univ of Arkansas	AR	8,334	VC
Univ of Arkansas at Pine Bluff	AR	7,925	C
Univ of Bridgeport	CT	23,020	C
Univ of Calif at Riverside	CA	12,479	C
Univ of Central Arkansas	AR	6,388	C
Univ of Cincinnati	OH	12,491	LC
Univ of Dayton	OH	20,400	VC

ST = STATE **$IS** = IN-STATE COSTS **SR** = SELECTOR RATING

School	ST	$IS	SR
Univ of Detroit Mercy	MI	21,620	LC
Univ of Evansville	IN	22,865	VC+
Univ of Findlay	OH	23,962	NC
Univ of Georgia	GA	8,656	VC
Univ of Great Falls	MT	15,360	C
Univ of Hartford	CT	28,884	C
Univ of Iowa	IA	8,607	C+
Univ of Judaism College of A&S	CA	24,230	C
Univ of Louisiana at Monroe	LA	5,207	NC
Univ of Mary	ND	12,900	LC
Univ of Mary Hardin-Baylor	TX	13,929	C
Univ of Mass Amherst	MA	10,995	VC
Univ of Miami	FL	31,130	HC
Univ of Mich/Flint	MI	4,323	C
Univ of Minn/Morris	MN	10,716	VC
Univ of Minn/Twin Cities	MN	11,123	VC
Univ of Missouri/Rolla	MO	10,034	C
Univ of Nebr at Kearney	NE	7,048	NC
Univ of Nebr at Lincoln	NE	8,325	C+
Univ of Nebr at Omaha	NE	6,867	C
Univ of New England	ME	24,110	LC
Univ of New Haven	CT	23,860	LC
Univ of New Mexico	NM	8,026	C
Univ of New Orleans	LA	10,160	C
Univ of N Car at Greensboro	NC	6,858	C
Univ of N Car at Pembroke	NC	5,914	LC
Univ of Notre Dame	IN	30,707	MC
Univ of PR/Mayaguez	PR	5,285	
Univ of Rio Grande	OH	8,728	NC
Univ of St. Francis	IL	19,650	C
Univ of St. Francis	IN	17,790	LC
Univ of Scranton	PA	27,964	C+
Univ of Sioux Falls	SD	16,390	C
Univ of Southern Calif	CA	33,647	MC
Univ of Southern Colo	CO	7,821	LC
Univ of Southern Indiana	IN	8,655	LC
Univ of Southern Miss	MS	6,155	LC
Univ of Tenn at Knoxville	TN	8,214	C
Univ of Tenn at Martin	TN	8,268	C
Univ of the Incarnate Word	TX	18,478	C
Univ of the Sciences in Philadelphia	PA	24,826	VC
Univ of Tulsa	OK	19,090	HC
Univ of West Alabama	AL	6,048	C
Univ of West Florida	FL	7,518	C
Univ of Wisc/Milwaukee	WI	8,907	LC
Univ of Wisc/River Falls	WI	6,356	LC
Urbana Univ	OH	17,004	C
Ursinus College	PA	31,350	VC
Ursuline College	OH	19,430	LC
Utah State Univ	UT	6,771	C
Valley City State Univ	ND		LC
Vanguard Univ of Southern Calif	CA	20,212	C
Vassar College	NY	33,450	MC
Virginia Intermont College	VA	17,510	C
Walsh Univ	OH	16,880	C
Washington State Univ	WA	9,388	C
Washington Univ in St. Louis	MO	34,593	MC
Waynesburg College	PA	17,610	LC
Weber State Univ	UT	6,897	NC
West Chester Univ of Pennsylvania	PA	9,792	VC
West Liberty State College	WV	6,056	LC
West Texas A&M Univ	TX	6,538	C
Western Carolina Univ	NC	5,667	C
Western Mich Univ	MI	10,016	C
Western New Mexico Univ	NM	5,950	LC
Westminster College	PA	22,960	C
Whitworth College	WA	23,938	VC
Widener Univ	PA	26,920	C
Wilkes Univ	PA	25,800	C
Wilmington College	OH	21,826	C
Wingate Univ	NC	19,140	C
Winona State Univ	MN	8,570	C
Wittenberg Univ	OH	28,766	VC
Wright State Univ	OH	9,141	LC
Xavier Univ	OH	23,880	C
Xavier Univ of Louisiana	LA	17,000	LC
York College of Pennsylvania	PA	12,550	VC
Youngstown State Univ	OH	9,318	NC

PREOPTOMETRY

School	ST	$IS	SR
Adams State College	CO	7,468	C
Arcadia Univ	PA	26,650	C
Ashland Univ	OH	22,182	LC
Auburn Univ	AL	5,510	C
Berry College	GA	18,850	C
Cardinal Stritch Univ	WI	17,620	C
Carroll College	MT	19,140	C
Eastern Mich Univ	MI	9,855	C
Florida State Univ	FL	7,835	HC
Freed-Hardeman Univ	TN	14,290	VC
Gannon Univ	PA	18,848	C
Iowa Wesleyan College	IA	18,840	C
Juniata College	PA	26,080	VC
Le Moyne College	NY	23,840	C
Lehigh Univ	PA	32,290	MC
Lewis Univ	IL	20,960	C
Louisiana College	LA	11,516	C
Missouri Southern State College	MO	6,666	C
New York Univ	NY	35,200	MC
Ohio Univ	OH	11,769	C
Stephen F. Austin State Univ	TX	6,905	C
Trinity Christian College	IL	19,415	C
Truman State Univ	MO	8,568	VC+
Univ of Arkansas	AR	8,334	VC
Univ of Central Arkansas	AR	6,388	C
Univ of Hartford	CT	28,884	C
Univ of Southern Colo	CO	7,821	LC
Univ of Tenn at Martin	TN	8,268	C
Valley City State Univ	ND		LC
Western Carolina Univ	NC	5,667	C
Youngstown State Univ	OH	9,318	NC

PREOSTEOPATHY

School	ST	$IS	SR
Gannon Univ	PA	18,848	C
Mercyhurst College	PA	20,694	C
Minn State Univ, Mankato	MN	7,296	LC
New York Inst of Technology	NY	21,756	C
Univ of Southern Colo	CO	7,821	LC
Youngstown State Univ	OH	9,318	NC

PREPHARMACY

School	ST	$IS	SR
Adams State College	CO	7,468	C
Alice Lloyd College	KY	1,785	VC
Austin Peay State Univ	TN	5,814	LC
Ball State Univ	IN	8,660	C
Barry Univ	FL	24,100	LC
Bellarmine Univ	KY	20,440	VC
Belmont Abbey College	NC	19,630	LC
Berry College	GA	18,850	C
Briar Cliff Univ	IA	18,657	LC
Campbell Univ	NC	16,599	C
Carroll College	MT	19,140	C
Clemson Univ	SC	7,600	C
College of Notre Dame of Maryland	MD	23,100	LC
College of St. Benedict	MN	23,921	VC
College of the Ozarks	MO	2,650	C+
Concord College	WV	7,122	C+
Coppin State College	MD	9,133	LC
David Lipscomb Univ	TN	16,158	VC
Eastern Mich Univ	MI	9,855	C
Edgewood College	WI	18,304	C
Edinboro Univ of Pennsylvania	PA	9,328	LC
Florida State Univ	FL	7,835	HC
Freed-Hardeman Univ	TN	14,290	VC
Gannon Univ	PA	18,848	C
Goshen College	IN	18,950	VC+
Huntingdon College	AL	18,400	VC
Indiana State Univ	IN	8,461	LC
Iona College	NY	26,556	C
Juniata College	PA	26,080	VC
Kennesaw State Univ	GA	2,306	LC
Le Moyne College	NY	23,840	C
Lebanon Valley College of Pennsylvania	PA	25,700	VC
Lewis Univ	IL	20,960	C
LIU/C.W. Post Campus	NY	25,380	C
Mars Hill College	NC	18,600	LC
Mercer Univ	GA	24,130	VC
Mercyhurst College	PA	20,694	C
Midwestern State Univ	TX	6,704	NC
Minn State Univ, Mankato	MN	7,296	LC
Missouri Southern State College	MO	6,666	C
Moorhead State Univ	MN	7,000	LC
North Georgia College and State Univ	GA	6,322	C+
Northern Kentucky Univ	KY	6,352	NC
Northwest Missouri State Univ	MO	7,922	LC
Notre Dame de Namur Univ	CA	26,932	LC
Ohio Univ	OH	11,769	C
Peru State College	NE	6,342	NC
Purdue Univ/Calumet	IN	6,630	NC
Purdue Univ/West Lafayette	IN	10,284	VC
Roberts Wesleyan College	NY	20,160	C+
Rockford College	IL	23,930	C
Roosevelt Univ	IL	20,240	LC
St. John's Univ	MN	23,640	VC
St. Joseph's College of Maine	ME	22,500	LC
St. Martin's College	WA	20,566	C
St. Vincent College	PA	22,942	VC
St. Xavier Univ	IL	21,104	C
Southern Nazarene Univ	OK	14,634	NC
SUNY/College of Environmental Science and Forestry	NY	12,446	VC
Stephen F. Austin State Univ	TX	6,905	C
Tarleton State Univ	TX	7,160	C
Texas A&M Univ at Commerce	TX	7,326	C
Texas A&M Univ at Kingsville	TX	6,446	LC
Texas Tech Univ	TX	8,825	C
Thiel College	PA	18,419	LC
Truman State Univ	MO	8,568	VC+
Union Univ	TN	18,930	C+
Univ of Akron	OH	10,530	NC
Univ of Arkansas	AR	8,334	VC
Univ of Arkansas at Pine Bluff	AR	7,925	C
Univ of Central Arkansas	AR	6,388	C
Univ of Houston	TX	8,410	C
Univ of Miami	FL	31,130	HC
Univ of Mich/Flint	MI	4,323	C
Univ of Minn/Twin Cities	MN	11,123	VC
Univ of Nebr at Lincoln	NE	8,325	C+
Univ of New England	ME	24,110	LC
Univ of Southern Calif	CA	33,647	MC
Univ of Southern Colo	CO	7,821	LC
Univ of Tenn at Martin	TN	8,268	C
Univ of the Pacific	CA	28,255	VC
Univ of Wisc/River Falls	WI	6,356	LC
Valley City State Univ	ND		LC
Washington Univ in St. Louis	MO	34,593	MC
West Liberty State College	WV	6,056	LC
West Texas A&M Univ	TX	6,538	C
Western Carolina Univ	NC	5,667	C
Western New Mexico Univ	NM	5,950	LC
Wilkes Univ	PA	25,800	C
Wingate Univ	NC	19,140	C
Xavier Univ	OH	23,880	C
Youngstown State Univ	OH	9,318	NC

PREPODIATRY

School	ST	$IS	SR
Gannon Univ	PA	18,848	C
Juniata College	PA	26,080	VC
Le Moyne College	NY	23,840	C
Minn State Univ, Mankato	MN	7,296	LC
New York Univ	NY	35,200	MC
Univ of Arkansas	AR	8,334	VC
Univ of Southern Colo	CO	7,821	LC
Wilkes Univ	PA	25,800	C

PREVETERINARY SCIENCE

School	ST	$IS	SR
Adams State College	CO	7,468	C
Alabama A&M Univ	AL	5,100	LC
Albertus Magnus College	CT	22,154	C
Andrews Univ	MI	17,696	LC
Arcadia Univ	PA	26,650	C
Ashland Univ	OH	22,182	LC
Auburn Univ	AL	5,510	C
Bellarmine Univ	KY	20,440	VC
Beloit College	WI	27,482	HC
Bennington College	VT	31,350	VC
Berry College	GA	18,850	C
Cardinal Stritch Univ	WI	17,620	C
Carroll College	MT	19,140	C
Clemson Univ	SC	7,600	C
College of St. Benedict	MN	23,921	VC
College of the Ozarks	MO	2,650	C+
Concordia College/Moorhead	MN	18,835	C
Cornerstone Univ and Grand Rapids Baptist Seminary	MI	18,092	C
Drake Univ	IA	22,830	VC
Drury Univ	MO	15,250	VC
Eastern Washington Univ	WA	7,972	LC
Edgewood College	WI	18,304	C
Edinboro Univ of Pennsylvania	PA	9,328	LC
Emmanuel College	MA	23,802	C+
Fairleigh Dickinson Univ/Teaneck Campus	NJ	24,646	C
Florida State Univ	FL	7,835	HC
Fordham Univ	NY	30,710	VC
Freed-Hardeman Univ	TN	14,290	VC
Gannon Univ	PA	18,848	C
George Fox Univ	OR	24,095	VC
Goshen College	IN	18,950	VC+
Graceland Univ	IA	15,845	C
Hillsdale College	MI	20,586	VC+
Indiana State Univ	IN	8,461	LC
Indiana Wesleyan Univ	IN	17,680	C
Iona College	NY	26,556	C
Iowa Wesleyan College	IA	18,840	C
Juniata College	PA	26,080	VC
Kennesaw State Univ	GA	2,306	LC
Kent State Univ	OH	11,104	C
Keuka College	NY	21,170	C
Le Moyne College	NY	23,840	C
Lebanon Valley College of Pennsylvania	PA	25,700	VC
LeTourneau Univ	TX	19,020	VC
Lewis Univ	IL	20,960	C
Louisiana College	LA	11,516	C
Loyola Univ of Chicago	IL	25,992	VC
MacMurray College	IL	17,790	LC
Mars Hill College	NC	18,600	LC
Mary Washington College	VA	9,032	VC+
Mercyhurst College	PA	20,694	C
Midwestern State Univ	TX	6,704	NC
Miles College	AL	7,870	NC
Minn State Univ, Mankato	MN	7,296	LC
Missouri Southern State College	MO	6,666	C
Moorhead State Univ	MN	7,000	LC
Mount St. Mary College	NY	10,025	C
New Mexico Highlands Univ	NM	6,256	NC
Norfolk State Univ	VA	8,382	LC
N Car State Univ	NC	8,680	HC
North Central College	IL	22,944	C+
N Dak State Univ	ND	7,004	VC
North Georgia College and State Univ	GA	6,322	C+
Northern Kentucky Univ	KY	6,352	NC
Northern Mich Univ	MI	9,693	C
Northwest Missouri State Univ	MO	7,922	LC
Notre Dame de Namur Univ	CA	26,932	LC
Ohio Wesleyan Univ	OH	29,670	VC+
Okla State Univ	OK	7,650	VC
Olivet College	MI	17,410	C
Palm Beach Atlantic College	FL	23,310	C
Peru State College	NE	6,342	NC
Purdue Univ/Calumet	IN	6,630	NC
Rivier College	NH	24,215	C
Roberts Wesleyan College	NY	20,160	C+
Rochester Inst of Technology	NY	26,232	VC+
Rockford College	IL	23,930	C
Roger Williams Univ	RI	29,010	C
Roosevelt Univ	IL	20,240	LC
St. John's Univ	MN	23,640	VC
St. Martin's College	WA	20,566	C
St. Mary's Univ of Minn	MN	19,975	C
St. Vincent College	PA	22,942	VC
Seton Hill College	PA	21,875	C
Spring Hill College	AL	23,250	C
Stephen F. Austin State Univ	TX	6,905	C
Syracuse Univ	NY	30,710	HC
Tarleton State Univ	TX	7,160	C
Texas A&M Univ at Kingsville	TX	6,446	LC
Thiel College	PA	18,419	LC
Truman State Univ	MO	8,568	VC+
Univ of Akron	OH	10,530	NC
Univ of Central Arkansas	AR	6,388	C
Univ of Findlay	OH	23,962	NC
Univ of Georgia	GA	8,656	VC
Univ of Maryland/College Park	MD	11,959	C
Univ of Mass Amherst	MA	10,995	VC
Univ of Miami	FL	31,130	HC
Univ of Mich/Flint	MI	4,323	C
Univ of Minn/Twin Cities	MN	11,123	VC
Univ of New Hampshire	NH	13,207	C
Univ of New Haven	CT	23,860	LC
Univ of New Orleans	LA	10,160	C
Univ of Rio Grande	OH	8,728	NC
Univ of St. Francis	IL	19,650	C
Univ of Southern Colo	CO	7,821	LC
Univ of Tenn at Knoxville	TN	8,214	C
Univ of Vermont	VT	14,761	C+
Valley City State Univ	ND		LC
Virginia Intermont College	VA	17,510	C
Walsh Univ	OH	16,880	C
Washington Univ in St. Louis	MO	34,593	MC
Waynesburg College	PA	17,610	LC
West Texas A&M Univ	TX	6,538	C
Western Carolina Univ	NC	5,667	C
Wilkes Univ	PA	25,800	C
Wilmington College	OH	21,826	C
Wingate Univ	NC	19,140	C
Winona State Univ	MN	8,570	C
Youngstown State Univ	OH	9,318	NC

PRINTING TECHNOLOGY

School	ST	$IS	SR
Arkansas State Univ	AR	7,480	C
Georgia Southern Univ	GA	6,958	C
Pennsylvania College of Technology	PA	12,860	NC
Pittsburg State Univ	KS	6,228	NC
Rochester Inst of Technology	NY	26,232	VC+
Southwest Missouri State Univ	MO	7,600	LC
Western Mich Univ	MI	10,016	C

PRINTMAKING

School	ST	$IS	SR
Aquinas College	MI	20,052	C+
Arizona State Univ-Main	AZ	7,726	C
Atlanta College of Art	GA	18,600	SP
Birmingham-Southern College	AL	22,960	C
Bradley Univ	IL	20,970	VC
Calif College of Arts and Crafts	CA	27,366	SP
Cal State, Fullerton	CA	5,440	LC
College For Creative Studies	MI	20,938	SP
College of Visual Arts	MN	12,185	SP
Drake Univ	IA	22,830	VC
Edinboro Univ of Pennsylvania	PA	9,328	LC
Howard Univ	DC	15,522	LC
Indiana Univ-Purdue Univ Indianapolis	IN	9,473	C

School	ST	$IS	SR
Kansas City Art Inst	MO	25,880	SP
Maine College of Art	ME	26,367	SP
Maryland Inst College of Art	MD	27,720	SP
Mass College of Art	MA	13,703	SP
Milwaukee Inst of Art and Design	WI	24,388	SP
Minneapolis College of Art and Design	MN	23,560	SP
Montserrat College of Art	MA	20,335	SP
Moore College of Art and Design	PA	23,125	SP
Northern Mich Univ	MI	9,693	C
Ohio Univ	OH	11,769	C
Pacific Northwest College of Art	OR	16,507	SP
Rhode Island School of Design	RI	30,227	SP
San Francisco Art Inst	CA	19,300	SP
School of the Art Inst of Chicago	IL	27,800	SP
Shepherd College	WV	7,062	LC
SUNY/College at Buffalo	NY	8,025	C
Syracuse Univ	NY	30,710	HC
Texas A&M Univ at Commerce	TX	7,326	C
Univ of Dallas	TX	22,128	VC+
Univ of Hartford	CT	28,884	C
Univ of Houston	TX	8,410	C
Univ of Kansas	KS	7,232	VC
Univ of Miami	FL	31,130	HC
Univ of Mich/Ann Arbor	MI	13,003	HC+
Univ of North Texas	TX	7,629	C
Univ of Oregon	OR	9,969	C
Univ of the Arts	PA	24,230	SP
Univ of Washington	WA	10,361	VC
Washington Univ in St. Louis	MO	34,593	MC
Youngstown State Univ	OH	9,318	NC

PSYCHOBIOLOGY

School	ST	$IS	SR
Albright College	PA	27,642	C
Arcadia Univ	PA	26,650	C
Centre College	KY	24,000	HC
Chatham College	PA	25,454	C+
Claremont McKenna College	CA	32,700	MC
Drew Univ/College of Liberal Arts	NJ	32,152	VC
Florida Atlantic Univ	FL	8,832	C
Hamilton College	NY	34,150	HC
Hiram College	OH	27,034	VC
La Sierra Univ	CA	19,260	LC
Lebanon Valley College of Pennsylvania	PA	25,700	VC
Lincoln Univ	PA	11,198	C+
Mount Holyoke College	MA	34,128	HC
Occidental College	CA	32,288	HC
Quinnipiac Univ	CT	27,370	C
Ripon College	WI	24,180	VC+
Simmons College	MA	30,418	VC
SUNY/Univ at Binghamton	NY	10,653	HC
Swarthmore College	PA	34,538	MC
Univ of Calif at Los Angeles	CA	13,227	MC
Univ of Calif at Riverside	CA	12,479	C
Univ of Calif at Santa Cruz	CA	13,655	VC
Univ of Evansville	IN	22,865	VC+
Univ of Miami	FL	31,130	HC
Wellesley College	MA	33,394	MC
Wilson College	PA	21,337	LC

PSYCHOLOGY

School	ST	$IS	SR
Abilene Christian Univ	TX	16,300	VC
Adams State College	CO	7,468	C
Adelphi Univ	NY	23,320	VC
Adrian College	MI	19,670	C
Agnes Scott College	GA	24,950	VC
Alabama A&M Univ	AL	5,100	LC
Alabama State Univ	AL	6,404	C
Alaska Pacific Univ	AK	16,450	C
Albany State Univ	GA	5,764	C+
Albertson College of Idaho	ID	23,900	VC
Albertus Magnus College	CT	22,154	C
Albion College	MI	25,224	VC
Albright College	PA	27,642	C
Alcorn State Univ	MS	5,594	LC
Alderson-Broaddus College	WV	19,640	C
Alfred Univ	NY	27,212	C+
Allegheny College	PA	27,780	VC
Alma College	MI	22,586	VC
Alvernia College	PA	20,790	C
Alverno College	WI	16,930	LC
American International College	MA	22,268	LC
American Univ	DC	31,544	VC+
Amherst College	MA	34,340	MC
Anderson Univ	IN	19,430	LC
Andrews Univ	MI	17,696	LC
Angelo State Univ	TX	7,028	C
Anna Maria College	MA	22,800	LC
Appalachian State Univ	NC	6,353	C
Aquinas College	MI	20,052	C+
Arcadia Univ	PA	26,650	C
Arizona State Univ-Main	AZ	7,726	C
Arkansas State Univ	AR	7,480	C
Arkansas Tech Univ	AR	6,256	C
Armstrong Atlantic State Univ	GA	7,084	C
Asbury College	KY	18,540	VC
Ashland Univ	OH	22,182	LC
Assumption College	MA	26,320	C
Atlantic Union College	MA	34,034	LC
Auburn Univ	AL	5,510	C
Auburn Univ Montgomery	AL	5,330	NC
Audrey Cohen College	NY	17,715	C
Augsburg College	MN	22,978	C
Augusta State Univ	GA	2,282	C
Augustana College	IL	24,117	VC+
Augustana College	SD	20,760	VC
Aurora Univ	IL	18,551	C
Austin College	TX	22,150	VC+
Austin Peay State Univ	TN	5,814	LC
Averett Univ	VA	17,980	LC
Avila College	MO	17,720	C
Azusa Pacific Univ	CA	22,422	VC
Baker Univ	KS	14,780	C+
Baldwin-Wallace College	OH	22,010	VC+
Ball State Univ	IN	8,660	C
Barry Univ	FL	24,100	LC
Barton College	NC	16,834	LC
Bates College	ME	34,100	MC
Bay Path College	MA	22,308	C
Baylor Univ	TX	18,298	VC+
Becker College	MA	21,230	LC
Belhaven College	MS	16,040	C+
Bellarmine Univ	KY	20,440	VC
Bellevue Univ	NE	4,125	NC
Belmont Abbey College	NC	19,630	LC
Belmont Univ	TN	19,066	VC
Beloit College	WI	27,482	HC
Bemidji State Univ	MN	7,957	C
Benedictine College	KS	18,485	LC
Benedictine Univ	IL	21,330	C
Bennett College	NC	11,200	C
Bennington College	VT	31,350	VC
Berea College	KY	4,070	VC
Berry College	GA	18,850	C
Bethany College	KS	16,602	C+
Bethany College	WV	18,566	C
Bethel College	IN	17,650	LC
Bethel College	KS	17,355	C+
Bethel College	MN	22,740	VC
Bethel College	TN	12,980	C
Bethune-Cookman College	FL	15,746	C
Biola Univ	CA	21,902	VC
Birmingham-Southern College	AL	22,960	C
Black Hills State Univ	SD	6,652	LC
Blackburn College	IL	13,690	C
Bloomfield College	NJ	17,000	C
Bloomsburg Univ of Pennsylvania	PA	9,434	C
Blue Mountain College	MS	9,100	LC
Bluefield College	VA	14,200	C
Bluffton College	OH	20,644	C
Boise State Univ	ID	6,531	LC
Boston College	MA	33,330	MC
Boston Univ	MA	34,358	MC
Bowdoin College	ME	32,650	MC
Bowie State Univ	MD	9,300	C+
Bowling Green State Univ	OH	10,794	C
Bradley Univ	IL	20,970	VC
Brandeis Univ	MA	34,481	MC
Brenau Univ Women's College	GA	20,100	C
Brescia Univ	KY	14,225	C
Brewton-Parker College	GA	10,810	LC
Briar Cliff Univ	IA	18,657	LC
Bridgewater College	VA	22,950	C
Bridgewater State College	MA	7,589	C+
Brigham Young Univ	UT	7,840	HC
Brigham Young Univ/Hawaii	HI	6,890	C
Brown Univ	RI	34,973	MC
Bryan College	TN	16,400	VC
Bryant College	RI	25,980	VC
Bryn Mawr College	PA	33,580	HC+
Bucknell Univ	PA	31,096	HC
Buena Vista Univ	IA	22,828	C
Burlington College	VT	10,640	SP
Butler Univ	IN	25,580	VC+
Cabrini College	PA	25,950	LC
Caldwell College	NJ	20,940	LC
Calif Baptist Univ	CA	16,736	C
Calif Lutheran Univ	CA	23,500	LC
Calif Polytechnic State Univ	CA	8,747	VC
Calif State Polytechnic Univ, Pomona	CA	8,615	C
Cal State, Bakersfield	CA	6,090	LC
Cal State, Chico	CA	8,598	LC
Cal State, Dominguez Hills	CA	5,840	LC
Cal State, Fresno	CA	7,762	C
Cal State, Fullerton	CA	5,440	LC
Cal State, Hayward	CA	7,400	LC
Cal State, Long Beach	CA	7,400	LC
Cal State, Los Angeles	CA	5,050	C
Cal State, Northridge	CA	7,781	C
Cal State, Sacramento	CA	7,488	C
Cal State, San Bernardino	CA	6,516	C
Cal State, San Marcos	CA	1,736	LC
Cal State, Stanislaus	CA	8,895	C
Calif Univ of Pennsylvania	PA	10,388	C
Calvin College	MI	20,050	NC
Cameron Univ	OK	5,560	NC
Campbell Univ	NC	16,599	C
Campbellsville Univ	KY	14,340	C
Canisius College	NY	24,696	C+
Capital Univ	OH	23,630	C
Cardinal Stritch Univ	WI	17,620	C
Carleton College	MN	30,780	MC
Carlos Albizu Univ	FL	9,309	C
Carlow College	PA	19,366	C
Carnegie Mellon Univ	PA	32,682	MC
Carroll College	MT	19,140	C
Carroll College	WI	21,170	C
Carson-Newman College	TN	16,490	C
Carthage College	WI	23,670	C
Cascade College	OR	14,800	NC
Case Western Reserve Univ	OH	27,418	C
Castleton State College	VT	10,922	LC
Catawba College	NC	19,620	C
Catholic Univ of America	DC	29,332	VC
Cazenovia College	NY	19,885	LC
Cedar Crest College	PA	25,145	C+
Cedarville Univ	OH	17,553	VC
Centenary College	NJ	22,430	C
Centenary College of Louisiana	LA	21,600	C+
Central College	IA	21,206	C
Central Conn State Univ	CT	10,404	C
Central Methodist College	MO	16,460	C
Central Mich Univ	MI	8,355	C
Central Missouri State Univ	MO	7,920	C
Central State Univ	OH	8,922	C+
Central Univ of Bayamon	PR	3,335	
Central Washington Univ	WA	8,985	LC
Centre College	KY	24,000	HC
Chadron State College	NE	6,211	NC
Chaminade Univ of Honolulu	HI	17,370	C
Champlain College	VT	19,680	C
Chapman Univ	CA	30,218	VC
Charleston Southern Univ	SC	17,122	C
Chatham College	PA	25,454	C+
Chestnut Hill College	PA	24,790	LC
Cheyney Univ of Pennsylvania	PA	9,993	C
Chicago State Univ	IL	8,851	C+
Christian Brothers Univ	TN	19,820	VC
Christian Heritage College	CA	18,000	LC
Christopher Newport Univ	VA	8,862	VC
Citadel, The	SC	9,126	C
CUNY/Baruch College	NY	3,275	VC+
CUNY/Brooklyn College	NY	3,403	LC
CUNY/City College	NY	3,309	LC
CUNY/College of Staten Island	NY	3,358	NC
CUNY/Herbert H. Lehman College	NY	3,320	LC
CUNY/Hunter College	NY	5,147	C+
CUNY/Medgar Evers College	NY	3,282	NC
CUNY/Queens College	NY	3,403	VC
CUNY/York College	NY	3,292	NC
Claremont McKenna College	CA	32,700	MC
Clarion Univ of Pennsylvania	PA	11,272	LC
Clark Atlanta Univ	GA	17,174	C
Clark Univ	MA	29,170	HC
Clarke College	IA	20,625	C+
Clarkson Univ	NY	29,884	VC
Clearwater Christian College	FL	13,160	LC
Clemson Univ	SC	7,600	C
Cleveland State Univ	OH	10,146	NC
Coastal Carolina Univ	SC	9,220	C
Coe College	IA	24,750	VC
Coker College	SC	20,120	C
Colby College	ME	34,290	MC
Colby-Sawyer College	NH	27,850	LC
Colgate Univ	NY	33,480	MC
College Misericordia	PA	23,380	LC
College of Charleston	SC	8,350	HC
College of Mount St. Vincent	NY	24,230	C
College of Mount St. Joseph	OH	20,290	C
College of New Jersey	NJ	13,425	HC
College of New Rochelle	NY	20,000	C
College of Notre Dame of Maryland	MD	23,100	LC
College of Our Lady of the Elms	MA	20,644	C
College of St. Benedict	MN	23,921	VC
College of St. Catherine	MN	22,324	VC
College of St. Elizabeth	NJ	22,510	C
College of St. Joseph	VT	17,400	NC
College of St. Mary	NE	18,726	C
College of St. Rose	NY	19,084	C
College of St. Scholastica	MN	22,378	C+
College of Santa Fe	NM	20,250	LC
College of the Holy Cross	MA	32,780	MC
College of the Ozarks	MO	2,650	C+
College of the Southwest	NM	8,456	NC
College of William and Mary	VA	10,002	MC
College of Wooster	OH	28,350	VC
Colo Christian Univ	CO	17,714	C
Colo College	CO	31,525	HC+
Colo State Univ	CO	9,672	C
Columbia College	MO	15,082	C
Columbia College	SC	19,050	LC
Columbia Union College	MD	19,027	C+
Columbia Univ/Barnard College	NY	33,694	MC
Columbia Univ/Columbia College	NY	35,190	MC
Columbia Univ/School of General Studies	NY	35,000	C
Columbus State Univ	GA	7,228	LC
Concord College	WV	7,122	C+
Concordia College/Moorhead	MN	18,835	C
Concordia Univ	CA	22,290	C
Concordia Univ	MI	20,500	C
Concordia Univ	MN	19,912	C
Concordia Univ	OR	20,500	LC
Concordia Univ Nebr	NE	17,770	C
Concordia Univ Wisc	WI	16,600	LC
Concordia Univ, River Forest	IL	20,000	LC
Conn College	CT	33,585	MC
Converse College	SC	21,990	VC
Coppin State College	MD	9,133	LC
Cornell College	IA	24,980	VC
Cornell Univ	NY	34,614	MC
Cornerstone Univ and Grand Rapids Baptist Seminary	MI	18,092	C
Covenant College	GA	21,970	C+
Creighton Univ	NE	23,476	VC
Crichton College	TN	12,680	LC
Culver-Stockton College	MO	15,400	LC
Cumberland College	KY	14,864	C
Curry College	MA	26,025	LC
Daemen College	NY	20,620	C
Dakota Wesleyan Univ	SD	15,512	C
Dallas Baptist Univ	TX	13,682	LC
Dana College	NE	18,046	C
Dartmouth College	NH	34,458	MC
David Lipscomb Univ	TN	16,158	VC
Davidson College	NC	30,823	MC
Davis and Elkins College	WV	19,270	LC
De Sales Univ	PA	22,610	VC
Defiance College	OH	19,580	LC
Delaware State Univ	DE	8,104	LC
Delta State Univ	MS	5,416	C
Denison Univ	OH	29,640	HC
DePaul Univ	IL	23,590	VC
DePauw Univ	IN	28,000	HC
Dickinson College	PA	32,210	VC+
Dillard Univ	LA	16,046	VC
Doane College	NE	17,600	LC
Dominican College	NY	20,400	LC
Dominican Univ	IL	20,800	C
Dominican Univ of Calif	CA	27,948	C
Dordt College	IA	18,100	C+
Dowling College	NY	20,281	LC
Drake Univ	IA	22,830	VC
Drew Univ/College of Liberal Arts	NJ	32,152	VC
Drexel Univ	PA	27,657	VC
Drury Univ	MO	15,250	VC
Duke Univ	NC	34,396	MC
Duquesne Univ	PA	24,242	C+
D'Youville College	NY	18,704	C
Earlham College	IN	27,446	VC+
East Carolina Univ	NC	7,766	C
East Central Univ	OK	4,578	C
East Stroudsburg Univ of Pennsylvania	PA	8,430	LC
East Tenn State Univ	TN	7,127	C
East Texas Baptist Univ	TX	12,349	LC
Eastern College	PA	19,641	LC
Eastern Conn State Univ	CT	10,362	C
Eastern Illinois Univ	IL	10,101	C
Eastern Kentucky Univ	KY	6,552	C
Eastern Mennonite Univ	VA	20,700	VC
Eastern Mich Univ	MI	9,855	C
Eastern Nazarene College	MA	19,433	LC
Eastern New Mexico Univ	NM	4,113	LC
Eastern Oregon Univ	OR	8,772	C
Eastern Washington Univ	WA	7,972	LC
Eckerd College	FL	25,500	C+
Edgewood College	WI	18,304	C
Edinboro Univ of Pennsylvania	PA	9,328	LC
Edward Waters College	FL	13,124	LC
Elizabeth City State Univ	NC	5,550	LC
Elizabethtown College	PA	26,000	VC
Elmhurst College	IL	21,750	C
Elmira College	NY	31,070	VC+
Elon Univ	NC	19,430	VC
Emmanuel College	MA	23,802	C+
Emory & Henry College	VA	19,462	C
Emory Univ	GA	33,792	MC
Emporia State Univ	KS	6,198	LC
Endicott College	MA	23,704	C
Erskine College	SC	21,399	VC
Eugene Lang College of New School Univ	NY	30,300	C
Eureka College	IL	22,200	C
Evangel Univ	MO	14,050	C

School	ST	$IS	SR
Fairfield Univ	CT	30,885	HC
Fairleigh Dickinson Univ/ Madison campus	NJ	25,500	C
Fairleigh Dickinson Univ/ Teaneck Campus	NJ	24,646	C
Fairmont State College	WV	7,010	NC
Fayetteville State Univ	NC	5,590	LC
Felician College	NJ	20,050	C
Ferrum College	VA	15,990	LC
Fisk Univ	TN	13,700	LC
Fitchburg State College	MA	7,836	C
Flagler College	FL	10,550	VC+
Florida A&M Univ	FL	6,948	C
Florida Atlantic Univ	FL	8,832	C
Florida Inst of Technology	FL	25,250	VC
Florida International Univ	FL	9,486	VC
Florida Memorial College	FL	6,000	LC
Florida Southern College	FL	19,430	C
Florida State Univ	FL	7,835	HC
Fordham Univ	NY	30,710	VC
Fort Hays State Univ	KS	6,294	LC
Fort Lewis College	CO	7,659	LC
Fort Valley State Univ	GA	6,014	LC
Framingham State College	MA	7,259	C
Francis Marion Univ	SC	7,682	C
Franciscan Univ of Steubenville	OH	19,100	C+
Franklin and Marshall College	PA	32,410	HC
Franklin College of Indiana	IN	19,905	C
Franklin Pierce College	NH	26,125	LC
Freed-Hardeman Univ	TN	14,290	VC
Fresno Pacific Univ	CA	19,740	C
Friends Univ	KS	15,962	LC
Frostburg State Univ	MD	9,680	C
Furman Univ	SC	25,492	HC
Gallaudet Univ	DC	16,554	SP
Gannon Univ	PA	18,848	C
Gardner-Webb Univ	NC	17,400	C
Geneva College	PA	19,990	C+
George Fox Univ	OR	24,095	VC
George Mason Univ	VA	9,192	C
George Washington Univ	DC	32,170	HC
Georgetown College	KY	18,400	VC
Georgetown Univ	DC	34,847	MC
Georgia College and State Univ	GA	7,344	C
Georgia Inst of Technology	GA	9,028	HC+
Georgia Southern Univ	GA	6,958	C
Georgia Southwestern State Univ	GA	6,013	C
Georgia State Univ	GA	7,792	LC
Georgian Court College	NJ	19,040	LC
Gettysburg College	PA	32,070	HC
Gonzaga Univ	WA	24,276	HC+
Gordon College	MA	23,594	VC+
Goshen College	IN	18,950	VC+
Goucher College	MD	30,650	VC+
Grace College	IN	16,768	C
Graceland Univ	IA	15,845	C
Grambling State Univ	LA	5,325	NC
Grand Canyon Univ	AZ	30,000	LC
Grand Valley State Univ	MI	10,040	C
Grand View College	IA	17,556	NC
Green Mountain College	VT	24,130	C
Greensboro College	NC	19,080	LC
Greenville College	IL	19,220	LC
Grinnell College	IA	28,300	HC+
Grove City College	PA	12,280	MC
Guilford College	NC	23,255	C
Gustavus Adolphus College	MN	24,190	VC+
Gwynedd-Mercy College	PA	22,350	C
Hamilton College	NY	34,150	HC
Hamline Univ	MN	23,339	C+
Hampden-Sydney College	VA	24,871	C
Hampshire College	MA	33,881	HC+
Hampton Univ	VA	17,112	C+
Hannibal-LaGrange College	MO	12,530	C
Hanover College	IN	17,560	VC
Harding Univ	AR	13,528	VC
Hardin-Simmons Univ	TX	14,165	C
Hartwick College	NY	33,090	C+
Harvard Univ/Harvard College	MA	34,269	MC
Hastings College	NE	17,854	C+
Haverford College	PA	34,300	MC
Hawaii Pacific Univ	HI	17,790	C
Heidelberg College	OH	23,879	C
Henderson State Univ	AR	6,269	C
Hendrix College	AR	18,463	HC
Heritage College	WA	6,450	NC
High Point Univ	NC	20,220	LC
Hilbert College	NY	16,830	LC
Hillsdale College	MI	20,586	VC+
Hiram College	OH	27,034	VC
Hobart and William Smith Colleges	NY	33,195	VC
Hofstra Univ	NY	23,252	C
Hollins Univ	VA	24,328	VC
Holy Family College	PA	13,710	LC
Holy Names College	CA	23,220	C
Hood College	MD	26,020	VC
Hope College	MI	22,922	C+
Hope International Univ	CA	16,940	NC
Houghton College	NY	21,810	VC+
Houston Baptist Univ	TX	15,300	LC

School	ST	$IS	SR
Howard Payne Univ	TX	13,834	C+
Howard Univ	DC	15,522	LC
Humboldt State Univ	CA	8,582	C
Huntingdon College	AL	18,400	VC
Huntington College	IN	15,480	LC
Husson College	ME	15,360	LC
Idaho State Univ	ID	7,030	C+
Illinois College	IL	16,234	C
Illinois Inst of Technology	IL	25,182	HC+
Illinois State Univ	IL	9,235	C
Illinois Wesleyan Univ	IL	26,970	HC
Immaculata College	PA	22,400	LC
Indiana State Univ	IN	8,461	LC
Indiana Univ Bloomington	IN	10,712	C+
Indiana Univ Kokomo	IN	3,422	LC
Indiana Univ Northwest	IN	3,447	C
Indiana Univ of Pennsylvania	PA	9,133	C
Indiana Univ South Bend	IN	3,515	C
Indiana Univ Southeast	IN	3,459	C
Indiana Univ-Purdue Univ Fort Wayne	IN	3,166	LC
Indiana Univ-Purdue Univ Indianapolis	IN	9,473	C
Indiana Wesleyan Univ	IN	17,680	C
Inter-American Univ of PR/ Bayamon Univ College	PR	3,700	
Inter-American Univ of PR/ Fajardo Campus	PR	4,000	
Inter-American Univ of PR/ Metropolitan Campus	PR	4,166	
Inter-American Univ of PR/ Ponce Regional College	PR	3,700	
Inter-American Univ of PR/ San GermÈn	PR	6,390	
Iona College	NY	26,556	C
Iowa State Univ	IA	8,108	VC
Iowa Wesleyan College	IA	18,840	C
Ithaca College	NY	28,719	HC
Jackson State Univ	MS	6,776	LC
Jacksonville State Univ	AL	6,568	LC
Jacksonville Univ	FL	21,110	LC
James Madison Univ	VA	9,552	HC
Jamestown College	ND	11,310	NC
John Brown Univ	AR	15,080	VC
John Carroll Univ	OH	24,140	VC
Johns Hopkins Univ	MD	35,226	MC
Johnson C. Smith Univ	NC	16,560	C+
Johnson State College	VT	10,776	C
Judson College	AL	13,790	C
Judson College	IL	18,980	LC
Juniata College	PA	26,080	VC
Kalamazoo College	MI	26,955	HC+
Kansas State Univ	KS	6,995	C
Kansas Wesleyan Univ	KS	17,400	C+
Kean Univ	NJ	11,159	C
Keene State College	NH	11,280	C
Kennesaw State Univ	GA	2,306	LC
Kent State Univ	OH	11,104	C
Kentucky Christian College	KY	13,472	C
Kentucky State Univ	KY	6,146	NC
Kentucky Wesleyan College	KY	15,800	C
Kenyon College	OH	32,130	HC+
Keuka College	NY	21,170	C
King College	TN	17,800	VC
King's College	PA	24,680	C
Knox College	IL	28,230	HC
Knoxville College	TN	6,200	LC
Kutztown Univ of Pennsylvania	PA	8,907	C
La Roche College	PA	18,854	LC
La Salle Univ	PA	27,890	C
La Sierra Univ	CA	19,260	LC
Lafayette College	PA	32,655	MC
LaGrange College	GA	17,496	C
Lake Erie College	OH	21,350	LC
Lake Forest College	IL	27,460	VC
Lake Superior State Univ	MI	9,034	LC
Lakeland College	WI	17,950	C
Lamar Univ	TX	6,816	LC
Lambuth Univ	TN	14,254	C
Lander Univ	SC	8,618	LC
Langston Univ	OK	2,308	LC
Lasell College	MA	24,100	C
Lawrence Univ	WI	27,711	HC
Le Moyne College	NY	23,840	C
Lebanon Valley College of Pennsylvania	PA	25,700	VC
Lee Univ	TN	10,198	LC
Lees-McRae College	NC	17,106	LC
Lehigh Univ	PA	32,290	MC
Lenoir-Rhyne College	NC	19,186	C
LeTourneau Univ	TX	19,020	VC
Lewis and Clark College	OR	29,010	VC
Lewis Univ	IL	20,960	C
Lewis-Clark State College	ID	6,496	C
Liberty Univ	VA	14,500	C
Limestone College	SC	16,900	C
Lincoln Memorial Univ	TN	12,620	LC
Lincoln Univ	MO	7,158	NC
Lincoln Univ	PA	11,198	C+
Lindenwood Univ	MO	17,250	C
Linfield College	OR	25,840	VC
Livingstone College	NC	13,360	LC
Lock Haven Univ of Pennsylvania	PA	9,534	C

School	ST	$IS	SR
LIU/Brooklyn Campus	NY	22,290	C
LIU/C.W. Post Campus	NY	25,380	C
LIU/Southampton College	NY	26,270	C
Longwood College	VA	8,950	C
Loras College	IA	22,994	C+
Louisiana College	LA	11,516	C
Louisiana State Univ and A&M College	LA	8,014	VC
Louisiana State Univ in Shreveport	LA	2,480	NC
Louisiana Tech Univ	LA	6,506	C
Lourdes College	OH	13,100	LC
Loyola College in Maryland	MD	30,900	HC
Loyola Marymount Univ	CA	28,754	HC
Loyola Univ New Orleans	LA	23,506	VC+
Loyola Univ of Chicago	IL	25,992	VC
Lubbock Christian Univ	TX	14,226	LC
Luther College	IA	23,300	VC+
Lycoming College	PA	24,780	C
Lynchburg College	VA	23,405	C
Lyndon State College	VT	11,313	LC
Lynn Univ	FL	24,550	C
Lyon College	AR	16,500	VC
Macalester College	MN	28,814	HC+
MacMurray College	IL	17,790	LC
Madonna Univ	MI	11,504	VC
Maharishi Univ of Management	IA	20,660	VC
Malone College	OH	19,190	C
Manchester College	IN	22,010	C
Manhattan College	NY	25,500	VC
Manhattanville College	NY	28,730	VC
Mansfield Univ	PA	9,648	C
Marian College	IN	21,020	C
Marian College of Fond du Lac	WI	17,935	LC
Marietta College	OH	24,580	C
Marist College	NY	24,756	VC
Marlboro College	VT	26,410	VC+
Marquette Univ	WI	24,836	C+
Mars Hill College	NC	18,600	LC
Marshall Univ	WV	7,752	LC
Martin Univ	IN	8,370	SP
Mary Baldwin College	VA	23,440	C
Mary Washington College	VA	9,032	VC+
Marygrove College	MI	16,075	C
Marymount College/ Tarrytown	NY	23,850	C
Marymount Manhattan College	NY	23,195	VC
Marymount Univ	VA	21,560	LC
Maryville College	TN	23,210	VC
Maryville Univ of St. Louis	MO	18,680	C
Marywood Univ	PA	24,639	C
Mass College of Liberal Arts	MA	8,717	LC
Mass College of Pharmacy and Health Sciences	MA	27,131	SP
Mass Inst of Technology	MA	35,228	MC
McKendree College	IL	18,300	C+
McMurry Univ	TX	15,287	C
McNeese State Univ	LA	5,259	LC
McPherson College	KS	17,710	C
Medaille College	NY	18,320	C
Menlo College	CA	24,000	LC
Mercer Univ	GA	24,130	VC
Mercy College	NY	15,875	LC
Mercyhurst College	PA	20,694	C
Meredith College	NC	17,500	C
Merrimack College	MA	25,725	VC
Mesa State College	CO	8,051	C
Messiah College	PA	23,180	VC
Methodist College	NC	19,526	C
Metropolitan State College of Denver	CO	2,338	LC
Metropolitan State Univ	MN	2,943	SP
Miami Univ	OH	12,885	VC+
Mich State Univ	MI	10,386	VC
MidAmerica Nazarene Univ	KS	16,960	C
Middle Tenn State Univ	TN	6,994	C
Middlebury College	VT	34,300	MC
Midland Lutheran College	NE	18,600	C
Midway College	KY	15,815	C
Midwestern State Univ	TX	6,704	NC
Millersville Univ of Pennsylvania	PA	10,153	VC
Milligan College	TN	17,550	C
Millikin Univ	IL	24,415	C+
Mills College	CA	27,950	C
Millsaps College	MS	22,608	VC+
Minn State Univ, Mankato	MN	7,296	LC
Minot State Univ	ND	5,466	LC
Miss College	MS	14,574	C
Miss State Univ	MS	7,853	C
Miss Univ for Women	MS	5,446	LC
Missouri Baptist College	MO	15,762	LC
Missouri Southern State College	MO	6,666	C
Missouri Valley College	MO	17,400	LC
Missouri Western State College	MO	6,662	NC
Molloy College	NY	13,940	C
Monmouth College	IL	21,550	C
Monmouth Univ	NJ	24,042	C
Montana State Univ-Billings	MT	7,653	NC

School	ST	$IS	SR
Montana State Univ-Bozeman	MT	8,431	C
Montclair State Univ	NJ	10,287	LC
Moorhead State Univ	MN	7,000	LC
Moravian College	PA	27,065	VC
Morehead State Univ	KY	6,510	C
Morehouse College	GA	19,814	C
Morgan State Univ	MD	10,078	LC
Morningside College	IA	19,124	C
Morris Brown College	GA	15,993	LC
Mount Aloysius College	PA	18,186	LC
Mount Holyoke College	MA	34,128	HC
Mount Mary College	WI	18,024	C
Mount Mercy College	IA	19,390	VC
Mount Olive College	NC	14,410	LC
Mount St. Mary College	NY	18,825	C
Mount St. Mary's College	CA	24,430	C
Mount St. Mary's College	MD	25,740	C
Mount Senario College	WI	17,750	C
Mount Union College	OH	21,120	C
Mount Vernon Nazarene College	OH	17,027	C
Muhlenberg College	PA	28,170	HC
Murray State Univ	KY	6,672	C
Muskingum College	OH	18,760	C
Naropa Univ	CO	22,416	SP
National Univ	CA	7,755	SP
National-Louis Univ	IL	13,995	NC
Nazareth College of Rochester	NY	22,036	VC
Nebr Wesleyan Univ	NE	18,767	VC
Neumann College	PA	22,040	NC
New College of Calif	CA	8,900	NC
New College of Florida	FL	8,130	HC+
New England College	NH	20,706	LC
New Jersey City Univ	NJ	9,100	LC
New Mexico Highlands Univ	NM	6,256	NC
New Mexico Inst of Mining and Technology	NM	7,152	VC+
New Mexico State Univ	NM	7,302	C
New York Univ	NY	35,200	MC
Newberry College	SC	19,670	LC
Newbury College	MA	21,490	C
Newman Univ	KS	14,098	LC
Niagara Univ	NY	22,250	C+
Nicholls State Univ	LA	5,290	NC
Nichols College	MA	24,610	LC
Norfolk State Univ	VA	8,382	LC
N Car Agricultural and Technical State Univ	NC	6,659	LC
N Car Central Univ	NC	6,418	LC
N Car State Univ	NC	8,680	HC
N Car Wesleyan College	NC	15,650	LC
North Central College	IL	22,944	C+
N Dak State Univ	ND	7,004	VC
North Georgia College and State Univ	GA	6,322	C+
North Park Univ	IL	24,030	C
Northeastern Illinois Univ	IL	2,898	NC
Northeastern State Univ	OK	4,704	LC
Northeastern Univ	MA	30,078	VC
Northern Arizona Univ	AZ	7,398	C
Northern Illinois Univ	IL	9,545	C
Northern Kentucky Univ	KY	6,352	NC
Northern Mich Univ	MI	9,693	C
Northern State Univ	SD	6,070	LC
Northland College	WI	21,435	C+
Northwest Christian College	OR	19,680	LC
Northwest Missouri State Univ	MO	7,922	LC
Northwest Nazarene Univ	ID	18,380	C
Northwestern College	MN	19,816	C+
Northwestern College of Iowa	IA	17,630	C+
Northwestern Okla State Univ	OK	4,542	NC
Northwestern State Univ of Louisiana	LA	5,745	NC
Northwestern Univ	IL	33,615	MC
Norwich Univ	VT	21,064	LC
Notre Dame College	OH	20,425	C
Notre Dame de Namur Univ	CA	26,932	LC
Nova Southeastern Univ	FL	20,104	LC
Nyack College	NY	18,540	C
Oakland Univ	MI	9,418	C
Oakwood College	AL	14,904	C
Oberlin College	OH	33,140	HC+
Occidental College	CA	32,288	HC
Oglethorpe Univ	GA	19,100	LC
Ohio Dominican College	OH	18,100	LC
Ohio Northern Univ	OH	27,765	VC
Ohio State Univ at Lima	OH	3,603	NC
Ohio State Univ at Marion	OH	3,606	NC
Ohio State Univ at Newark	OH	8,103	NC
Ohio Univ	OH	11,769	C
Ohio Valley College	WV	13,650	C+
Ohio Wesleyan Univ	OH	29,670	VC+
Okla Baptist Univ	OK	13,878	VC
Okla Christian Univ	OK	16,500	VC
Okla City Univ	OK	15,810	C
Okla Panhandle State Univ	OK	3,812	NC
Okla State Univ	OK	7,650	VC
Old Dominion Univ	VA	9,386	C
Olivet College	MI	17,410	C
Olivet Nazarene Univ	IL	18,444	C
Oral Roberts Univ	OK	18,490	C

School	ST	$IS	SR
Oregon State Univ	OR	9,612	VC
Ottawa Univ	KS	11,800	LC
Otterbein College	OH	23,439	C
Ouachita Baptist Univ	AR	16,460	VC
Our Lady of the Lake Univ of San Antonio	TX	17,336	C
Pace Univ	NY	24,200	C
Pacific Lutheran Univ	WA	23,318	VC
Pacific Union College	CA	20,250	VC
Pacific Univ	OR	24,250	C
Paine College	GA	11,896	LC
Palm Beach Atlantic College	FL	23,310	C
Park Univ	MO	9,816	C
Penn State Univ at Erie/Behrend College	PA	12,326	C
Penn State Univ/Univ Park Campus	PA	11,126	VC
Pepperdine Univ	CA	32,830	VC
Peru State College	NE	6,342	NC
Pfeiffer Univ	NC	18,580	C
Philadelphia Univ	PA	24,722	C
Philander Smith College	AR	7,380	NC
Piedmont College	GA	16,900	C
Pikeville College	KY	12,000	NC
Pine Manor College	MA	19,344	LC
Pittsburg State Univ	KS	6,228	NC
Pitzer College	CA	33,930	HC
Plymouth State College	NH	11,024	LC
Point Loma Nazarene Univ	CA	21,380	VC
Point Park College	PA	20,290	C
Pomona College	CA	33,960	MC
Pontifical Catholic Univ of PR/Ponce	PR	7,076	
Portland State Univ	OR	11,220	C
Prairie View A&M Univ	TX	3,172	LC
Presbyterian College	SC	23,356	VC
Prescott College	AZ	13,430	C
Princeton Univ	NJ	35,072	MC
Providence College	RI	27,620	HC
Purdue Univ/Calumet	IN	6,630	NC
Purdue Univ/West Lafayette	IN	10,284	VC
Queens College	NC	17,250	C
Quincy Univ	IL	20,450	C
Quinnipiac Univ	CT	27,370	C
Radford Univ	VA	8,302	C
Ramapo College of New Jersey	NJ	13,550	VC
Randolph-Macon College	VA	24,395	C
Randolph-Macon Woman's College	VA	25,820	VC+
Reed College	OR	33,350	HC+
Regis College	MA	26,750	C
Regis Univ	CO	25,740	C+
Rensselaer Polytechnic Inst	NY	33,863	HC+
Rhode Island College	RI	8,700	LC
Rhodes College	TN	26,466	HC+
Rice Univ	TX	24,325	MC
Richard Stockton College of New Jersey	NJ	12,165	VC
Rider Univ	NJ	27,400	C
Ripon College	WI	24,180	VC+
Rivier College	NH	24,215	C
Roanoke College	VA	24,689	VC
Roberts Wesleyan College	NY	20,160	C+
Rochester College	MI	15,404	C+
Rochester Inst of Technology	NY	26,232	VC+
Rockford College	IL	23,930	C
Rockhurst Univ	MO	20,090	C
Rocky Mountain College	MT	18,113	C
Roger Williams Univ	RI	29,010	C
Rollins College	FL	31,223	HC
Roosevelt Univ	IL	20,240	LC
Rosemont College	PA	24,060	C
Rowan Univ	NJ	12,365	VC
Russell Sage College	NY	23,674	C+
Rutgers, The State Univ of New Jersey New Brunswick Campus	NJ	12,709	C
Rutgers, The State Univ of New Jersey/CamdenCampus	NJ	6,484	C
Rutgers, The State Univ of New Jersey/Newark Campus	NJ	6,394	C
Sacred Heart Univ	CT	26,588	VC
Saginaw Valley State Univ	MI	9,465	C
St. Ambrose Univ	IA	19,994	C
St. Andrews Presbyterian College	NC	19,720	LC
St. Anselm College	NH	27,405	C
St. Augustine's College	NC	12,990	C+
St. Bonaventure Univ	NY	21,956	C
St. Cloud State Univ	MN	7,180	C
St. Edward's Univ	TX	17,846	C
St. Francis College	NY	9,610	C
St. Francis Univ	PA	24,486	LC
St. John Fisher College	NY	21,800	C
St. John's Univ	MN	23,640	VC
St. John's Univ	NY	26,660	C
St. Joseph College	CT	25,960	LC
St. Joseph's College	IN	21,640	C
St. Joseph's College of Maine	ME	22,500	LC

School	ST	$IS	SR
St. Joseph's College, New York	NY	9,802	C
St. Joseph's Univ	PA	29,715	VC+
St. Lawrence Univ	NY	32,605	VC
St. Leo Univ	FL	19,250	LC
St. Louis Univ	MO	26,590	VC+
St. Martin's College	WA	20,566	C
St. Mary College	KS	17,298	C
St. Mary-of-the-Woods College	IN	21,320	LC
St. Mary's College	IN	24,474	VC
St. Mary's College	MI	13,314	LC
St. Mary's College of Calif	CA	27,575	C
St. Mary's College of Maryland	MD	14,104	HC
St. Mary's Univ of Minn	MN	19,975	C
St. Mary's Univ of San Antonio	TX	19,735	C
St. Michael's College	VT	26,935	VC
St. Norbert College	WI	23,169	VC
St. Olaf College	MN	25,880	HC
St. Peter's College	NJ	22,292	LC
St. Thomas Aquinas College	NY	20,590	LC
St. Thomas Univ	FL	19,500	LC
St. Vincent College	PA	22,942	VC
St. Xavier Univ	IL	21,104	C
Salem College	NC	23,065	VC
Salem State College	MA	4,481	LC
Salisbury Univ	MD	10,576	VC
Salve Regina Univ	RI	26,460	C
Sam Houston State Univ	TX	6,076	LC
Samford Univ	AL	16,340	VC
San Diego State Univ	CA	9,716	C+
San Francisco State Univ	CA	7,139	LC
San Jose State Univ	CA	8,187	C
Santa Clara Univ	CA	28,371	VC+
Sarah Lawrence College	NY	37,516	HC
Schreiner Univ	TX	19,254	C
Scripps College	CA	30,400	HC+
Seattle Pacific Univ	WA	22,674	C+
Seattle Univ	WA	24,183	VC
Seton Hall Univ	NJ	26,910	LC
Seton Hill College	PA	21,875	C
Shaw Univ	NC	12,810	C
Shawnee State Univ	OH	8,634	NC
Shenandoah Univ	VA	22,550	NC
Shepherd College	WV	7,062	LC
Shippensburg Univ of Pennsylvania	PA	9,652	C
Shorter College	GA	15,185	C
Siena College	NY	22,685	VC
Siena Heights Univ	MI	16,140	LC
Silver Lake College of the Holy Family	WI	15,516	LC
Simmons College	MA	30,418	VC
Simon's Rock College of Bard	MA	32,450	HC
Simpson College	CA	19,200	C
Simpson College	IA	21,200	C+
Skidmore College	NY	34,201	VC+
Slippery Rock Univ	PA	9,152	LC
Smith College	MA	33,302	HC+
Sojourner-Douglass College	MD	4,170	LC
Sonoma State Univ	CA	8,953	C
S Car State Univ	SC	6,586	LC
S Dak State Univ	SD	6,848	C
Southeast Missouri State Univ	MO	8,367	C+
Southeastern College	FL	11,648	LC
Southeastern Louisiana Univ	LA	6,047	LC
Southeastern Okla State Univ	OK	4,917	C
Southern Adventist Univ	TN	15,600	C
Southern Arkansas Univ	AR	5,740	LC
Southern Conn State Univ	CT	10,310	C
Southern Illinois Univ at Carbondale	IL	8,621	C
Southern Illinois Univ Edwardsville	IL	7,869	LC
Southern Methodist Univ	TX	28,349	VC
Southern Nazarene Univ	OK	14,634	NC
Southern New Hampshire Univ	NH	23,852	C
Southern Oregon Univ	OR	9,429	C
Southern Univ and A&M College	LA	6,365	C+
Southern Univ at New Orleans	LA	995	NC
Southern Utah Univ	UT	7,254	C
Southern Vermont College	VT	17,685	C
Southern Wesleyan Univ	SC	17,280	C
Southwest Baptist Univ	MO	13,426	LC
Southwest Missouri State Univ	MO	7,600	LC
Southwest State Univ	MN	7,117	LC
Southwest Texas State Univ	TX	8,730	VC
Southwestern Adventist Univ	TX	14,798	C
Southwestern College	KS	17,656	C
Southwestern Okla State Univ	OK	4,801	C
Southwestern Univ	TX	22,550	HC
Spalding Univ	KY	15,196	C

School	ST	$IS	SR
Spelman College	GA	19,215	C+
Spring Arbor Univ	MI	17,976	C
Spring Hill College	AL	23,250	C
Springfield College	MA	24,520	C
Stanford Univ	CA	34,222	MC
SUNY/College at Brockport	NY	10,267	C
SUNY/College at Buffalo	NY	8,025	C
SUNY/College at Cortland	NY	10,564	C
SUNY/College at Fredonia	NY	10,125	C
SUNY/College at Geneseo	NY	9,970	HC
SUNY/College at Old Westbury	NY	9,818	LC
SUNY/College at Oneonta	NY	9,981	C
SUNY/College at Oswego	NY	10,856	C
SUNY/College at Potsdam	NY	10,519	C
SUNY/College at Purchase	NY	10,587	VC
SUNY/Univ at Albany	NY	10,997	VC
SUNY/Univ at Binghamton	NY	10,653	HC
SUNY/Univ at Buffalo	NY	11,033	VC
SUNY/Univ at New Paltz	NY	9,685	VC
SUNY/Univ at Stony Brook	NY	10,998	VC
State Univ of West Georgia	GA	7,101	C
Stephen F. Austin State Univ	TX	6,905	C
Stetson Univ	FL	25,640	VC
Stonehill College	MA	26,852	HC
Suffolk Univ	MA	26,516	C
Sul Ross State Univ	TX	6,582	LC
Susquehanna Univ	PA	27,270	VC
Swarthmore College	PA	34,538	MC
Sweet Briar College	VA	25,310	VC
Syracuse Univ	NY	30,710	HC
Tabor College	KS	17,600	LC
Talladega College	AL	10,110	LC
Taylor Univ	IN	21,562	VC+
Teikyo Post Univ	CT	21,800	C
Temple Univ	PA	14,124	C
Tenn State Univ	TN	7,058	VC
Tenn Tech Univ	TN	6,968	C
Tenn Wesleyan College	TN	13,030	C
Texas A&M Univ	TX	8,988	VC
Texas A&M Univ at Commerce	TX	7,326	C
Texas A&M Univ at Kingsville	TX	6,446	LC
Texas Christian Univ	TX	19,910	C
Texas Lutheran Univ	TX	17,660	C
Texas Southern Univ	TX	6,576	NC
Texas Tech Univ	TX	8,825	C
Texas Wesleyan Univ	TX	14,710	C
Texas Woman's Univ	TX	5,855	LC
Ohio State Univ	OH	10,819	VC
Thiel College	PA	18,419	LC
Thomas Edison State College	NJ	2,750	SP
Thomas More College	KY	17,700	LC
Thomas Univ	GA	8,770	NC
Tougaloo College	MS	9,200	NC
Touro College	NY	14,950	VC
Towson Univ	MD	11,088	VC
Transylvania Univ	KY	21,780	VC+
Trevecca Nazarene Univ	TN	15,752	C
Trinity Christian College	IL	19,415	C
Trinity College	CT	34,300	HC
Trinity College	DC	21,370	LC
Trinity International Univ	IL	20,640	C+
Trinity Univ	TX	21,444	HC
Tri-State Univ-Main Campus	IN	21,200	C
Troy State Univ	AL	7,696	C
Troy State Univ/Dothan	AL	3,296	C
Troy State Univ/Montgomery	AL	3,080	NC
Truman State Univ	MO	8,568	VC+
Tufts Univ	MA	34,874	MC
Tulane Univ	LA	34,013	HC+
Turabo Univ	PR	4,110	
Tusculum College	TN	17,900	LC
Tuskegee Univ	AL	14,600	LC
Union College	KY	15,920	C
Union College	NE	14,650	C
Union College	NY	32,646	HC
Union Univ	TN	18,930	C+
United States Air Force Academy	CO		MC
United States International Univ	CA	18,675	LC
Universidad Metropolitana	PR	3,324	
Univ of Akron	OH	10,530	NC
Univ of Alabama	AL	7,402	C
Univ of Alabama at Birmingham	AL	10,110	C
Univ of Alabama at Huntsville	AL	7,916	VC
Univ of Alaska Anchorage	AK	9,100	NC
Univ of Alaska Fairbanks	AK	8,265	NC
Univ of Arizona	AZ	8,614	C
Univ of Arkansas	AR	8,334	VC
Univ of Arkansas at Little Rock	AR	5,637	NC
Univ of Arkansas at Monticello	AR	5,940	NC
Univ of Arkansas at Pine Bluff	AR	7,925	C
Univ of Calif at Berkeley	CA	14,134	MC
Univ of Calif at Davis	CA	12,796	VC

School	ST	$IS	SR
Univ of Calif at Irvine	CA	11,756	C
Univ of Calif at Los Angeles	CA	13,227	MC
Univ of Calif at Riverside	CA	12,479	C
Univ of Calif at San Diego	CA	11,372	HC
Univ of Calif at Santa Barbara	CA	11,732	VC
Univ of Calif at Santa Cruz	CA	13,655	VC
Univ of Central Arkansas	AR	6,388	C
Univ of Central Florida	FL	8,251	VC
Univ of Central Okla	OK	5,205	C
Univ of Charleston	WV	20,640	C
Univ of Chicago	IL	35,087	MC
Univ of Cincinnati	OH	12,491	LC
Univ of Colo at Boulder	CO	9,255	VC
Univ of Colo at Colo Springs	CO	9,403	C
Univ of Colo at Denver	CO	3,673	C
Univ of Conn	CT	12,122	VC
Univ of Dallas	TX	22,128	VC+
Univ of Dayton	OH	20,400	VC
Univ of Delaware	DE	10,824	VC
Univ of Denver	CO	28,783	VC
Univ of Detroit Mercy	MI	21,620	LC
Univ of Dubuque	IA	19,990	C
Univ of Evansville	IN	22,865	VC+
Univ of Findlay	OH	23,962	NC
Univ of Florida	FL	7,874	HC
Univ of Georgia	GA	8,656	VC
Univ of Great Falls	MT	15,360	C
Univ of Hartford	CT	28,884	C
Univ of Hawaii at Hilo	HI	6,497	C
Univ of Hawaii at Manoa	HI	7,862	VC
Univ of Houston	TX	8,410	C
Univ of Idaho	ID	7,026	C
Univ of Illinois at Chicago	IL	10,702	VC
Univ of Illinois at Urbana-Champaign	IL	11,316	HC+
Univ of Indianapolis	IN	20,840	C
Univ of Iowa	IA	8,607	C+
Univ of Judaism College of A&S	CA	24,230	C
Univ of Kansas	KS	7,232	VC
Univ of Kentucky	KY	7,765	C
Univ of La Verne	CA	24,280	C
Univ of Louisiana at Lafayette	LA	5,200	C
Univ of Louisiana at Monroe	LA	5,207	NC
Univ of Louisville	KY	7,402	LC
Univ of Maine	ME	10,798	C
Univ of Maine at Farmington	ME	9,163	C
Univ of Mary	ND	12,900	LC
Univ of Mary Hardin-Baylor	TX	13,929	C
Univ of Maryland/Baltimore County	MD	12,190	VC
Univ of Maryland/College Park	MD	11,959	C
Univ of Maryland/Univ College	MD	5,910	SP
Univ of Mass Amherst	MA	10,995	VC
Univ of Mass Boston	MA	4,227	C
Univ of Mass Dartmouth	MA	9,852	C
Univ of Mass Lowell	MA	9,470	VC
Univ of Memphis	TN	7,271	C
Univ of Miami	FL	31,130	HC
Univ of Mich/Ann Arbor	MI	13,003	HC+
Univ of Mich/Dearborn	MI	4,677	VC
Univ of Mich/Flint	MI	4,323	C
Univ of Minn/Duluth	MN	10,436	C
Univ of Minn/Morris	MN	10,716	VC
Univ of Minn/Twin Cities	MN	11,123	VC
Univ of Miss	MS	7,666	C
Univ of Missouri/Columbia	MO	9,803	HC
Univ of Missouri/Kansas City	MO	9,685	VC
Univ of Missouri/Rolla	MO	10,034	C
Univ of Missouri/St. Louis	MO	9,966	C
Univ of Mobile	AL	13,620	LC
Univ of Montana	MT	8,038	C
Univ of Montevallo	AL	7,266	C
Univ of Nebr at Kearney	NE	7,048	NC
Univ of Nebr at Lincoln	NE	8,325	C+
Univ of Nebr at Omaha	NE	6,867	C
Univ of Nevada/Las Vegas	NV	8,281	VC
Univ of Nevada/Reno	NV	8,737	C
Univ of New England	ME	24,110	LC
Univ of New Hampshire	NH	13,207	C
Univ of New Haven	CT	23,860	LC
Univ of New Mexico	NM	8,026	C
Univ of New Orleans	LA	10,160	C
Univ of North Alabama	AL	7,016	NC
Univ of N Car at Asheville	NC	6,896	VC
Univ of N Car at Chapel Hill	NC	8,789	HC
Univ of N Car at Charlotte	NC	7,254	C
Univ of N Car at Greensboro	NC	6,858	C
Univ of N Car at Pembroke	NC	5,914	LC
Univ of N Car at Wilmington	NC	7,769	C
Univ of N Dak	ND	7,067	VC
Univ of North Florida	FL	8,089	VC
Univ of North Texas	TX	7,629	C
Univ of Northern Colo	CO	8,082	C+
Univ of Northern Iowa	IA	7,850	C
Univ of Notre Dame	IN	30,707	MC
Univ of Okla	OK	7,616	VC
Univ of Oregon	OR	9,969	C

ST = STATE $IS = IN-STATE COSTS SR = SELECTOR RATING

School	ST	$IS	SR
Univ of Pennsylvania	PA	34,614	MC
Univ of Pittsburgh at Bradford	PA	12,696	C
Univ of Pittsburgh at Greensburg	PA	12,842	C
Univ of Pittsburgh at Johnstown	PA	13,044	LC
Univ of Pittsburgh at Pittsburgh	PA	13,592	HC
Univ of Portland	OR	24,950	VC
Univ of PR/Cayey Univ College	PR	1,245	
Univ of PR/Mayaguez	PR	5,285	
Univ of PR/Rio Piedras	PR	5,510	
Univ of Puget Sound	WA	28,285	HC
Univ of Redlands	CA	29,246	VC
Univ of Rhode Island	RI	12,414	C
Univ of Richmond	VA	27,300	HC
Univ of Rio Grande	OH	8,728	NC
Univ of Rochester	NY	32,979	HC
Univ of St. Francis	IL	19,650	C
Univ of St. Francis	IN	17,790	LC
Univ of St. Thomas	MN	24,044	VC
Univ of St. Thomas	TX	18,752	VC
Univ of San Diego	CA	29,198	HC
Univ of San Francisco	CA	27,302	VC
Univ of Science and Arts of Okla	OK	5,245	C
Univ of Scranton	PA	27,964	C+
Univ of Sioux Falls	SD	16,390	C
Univ of South Alabama	AL	6,976	LC
Univ of S Car at Aiken	SC	7,828	LC
Univ of S Car at Columbia	SC	8,748	VC
Univ of S Car at Spartanburg	SC	7,318	C+
Univ of S Dak	SD	7,036	C
Univ of South Florida	FL	8,154	C
Univ of Southern Calif	CA	33,647	MC
Univ of Southern Colo	CO	7,821	LC
Univ of Southern Indiana	IN	8,655	LC
Univ of Southern Maine	ME	10,569	C
Univ of Southern Miss	MS	6,155	LC
Univ of Tampa	FL	22,612	C
Univ of Tenn at Chattanooga	TN	7,783	C
Univ of Tenn at Knoxville	TN	8,214	C
Univ of Tenn at Martin	TN	8,268	C
Univ of Texas at Arlington	TX	7,192	LC
Univ of Texas at Austin	TX	9,437	HC
Univ of Texas at Dallas	TX	9,305	VC
Univ of Texas at El Paso	TX	5,076	LC
Univ of Texas at San Antonio	TX	9,088	NC
Univ of Texas-Pan American	TX	4,823	C
Univ of the District of Columbia	DC	2,844	NC
Univ of the Incarnate Word	TX	18,478	C
Univ of the Ozarks	AR	13,904	C
Univ of the Pacific	CA	28,255	VC
Univ of the Sacred Heart	PR	5,375	
Univ of the Sciences in Philadelphia	PA	24,826	VC
Univ of the South	TN	27,290	HC
Univ of Toledo	OH	11,206	NC
Univ of Tulsa	OK	19,090	HC
Univ of Utah	UT	7,703	C
Univ of Vermont	VT	14,761	C+
Univ of Virginia	VA	9,391	HC+
Univ of Virginia's College at Wise	VA	8,302	C
Univ of Washington	WA	10,361	VC
Univ of West Alabama	AL	6,048	C
Univ of West Florida	FL	7,518	C
Univ of Wisc/Eau Claire	WI	7,032	VC
Univ of Wisc/Green Bay	WI	7,148	C
Univ of Wisc/La Crosse	WI	7,250	VC
Univ of Wisc/Madison	WI	8,262	VC
Univ of Wisc/Milwaukee	WI	8,907	LC
Univ of Wisc/Oshkosh	WI	6,130	LC
Univ of Wisc/Parkside	WI	6,160	LC
Univ of Wisc/Platteville	WI	7,282	C
Univ of Wisc/River Falls	WI	6,356	LC
Univ of Wisc/Stevens Point	WI	7,116	C
Univ of Wisc/Stout	WI	7,192	C
Univ of Wisc/Superior	WI	7,051	C+
Univ of Wisc/Whitewater	WI	6,937	C
Univ of Wyoming	WY	7,143	LC
Upper Iowa Univ	IA	17,438	C
Urbana Univ	OH	17,004	C
Ursinus College	PA	31,350	VC
Ursuline College	OH	19,430	LC
Utah State Univ	UT	6,771	C
Utica College of Syracuse Univ	NY	24,400	LC
Valdosta State Univ	GA	6,988	C
Valparaiso Univ	IN	23,570	VC+
Vanderbilt Univ	TN	34,482	MC
Vanguard Univ of Southern Calif	CA	20,212	C
Vassar College	NY	33,450	MC
Villa Julie College	MD	16,026	C
Villanova Univ	PA	31,997	HC
Virginia Commonwealth Univ	VA	9,030	C
Virginia Intermont College	VA	17,510	C
Virginia Military Inst	VA	9,968	C+
Virginia Polytechnic Inst and State Univ	VA	7,652	C
Virginia State Univ	VA	8,182	LC
Virginia Union Univ	VA	15,358	LC
Virginia Wesleyan College	VA	22,350	LC
Viterbo Univ	WI	18,043	C
Wabash College	IN	25,335	HC
Wagner College	NY	27,000	C
Wake Forest Univ	NC	30,290	MC
Walla Walla College	WA	20,925	C
Walsh Univ	OH	16,880	C
Warren Wilson College	NC	19,968	C
Wartburg College	IA	21,165	VC
Washburn Univ of Topeka	KS	6,766	NC
Washington and Jefferson College	PA	26,255	VC
Washington and Lee Univ	VA	25,095	MC
Washington College	MD	28,040	VC
Washington State Univ	WA	9,388	C
Washington Univ in St. Louis	MO	34,593	MC
Wayland Baptist Univ	TX	11,271	NC
Wayne State College	NE	6,255	NC
Wayne State Univ	MI	6,720	C
Waynesburg College	PA	17,610	LC
Weber State Univ	UT	6,897	NC
Webster Univ	MO	19,804	VC
Wellesley College	MA	33,394	MC
Wells College	NY	19,350	VC
Wesley College	DE	17,869	C
Wesleyan College	GA	17,050	VC
Wesleyan Univ	CT	3,405	MC
West Chester Univ of Pennsylvania	PA	9,792	VC
West Liberty State College	WV	6,056	LC
West Texas A&M Univ	TX	6,538	C
West Virginia State College	WV	6,264	NC
West Virginia Univ	WV	8,304	C
West Virginia Wesleyan College	WV	22,920	C
Western Baptist College	OR	19,700	C+
Western Carolina Univ	NC	5,667	C
Western Conn State Univ	CT	10,074	C
Western Illinois Univ	IL	9,571	C
Western Kentucky Univ	KY	6,834	C
Western Maryland College	MD	26,000	VC
Western Mich Univ	MI	10,016	C
Western New England College	MA	23,882	C
Western New Mexico Univ	NM	5,950	LC
Western Oregon Univ	OR	8,829	C
Western State College of Colo	CO	7,585	LC
Western Washington Univ	WA	8,624	VC
Westfield State College	MA	8,394	C
Westminster College	MO	19,990	C+
Westminster College	PA	22,960	C
Westminster College	UT	17,226	C
Westmont College	CA	29,748	VC
Wheaton College	IL	21,934	HC
Wheaton College	MA	32,940	VC
Wheeling Jesuit Univ	WV	22,660	C
Whitman College	WA	29,086	HC
Whittier College	CA	29,108	C
Whitworth College	WA	23,938	VC
Wichita State Univ	KS	6,879	C
Widener Univ	PA	26,920	C
Wilberforce Univ	OH	14,937	LC
Wilkes Univ	PA	25,800	C
Willamette Univ	OR	29,422	VC+
William Carey College	MS	10,150	LC
William Jewell College	MO	17,150	VC
William Paterson Univ of New Jersey	NJ	11,000	LC
William Penn Univ	IA	17,575	C
William Tyndale College	MI	11,150	C
William Woods Univ	MO	19,390	LC
Williams Baptist College	AR	10,750	C
Williams College	MA	32,270	MC
Wilmington College	OH	21,826	C
Wingate Univ	NC	19,140	C
Winona State Univ	MN	8,570	C
Winston-Salem State Univ	NC	5,927	LC
Winthrop Univ	SC	9,106	C
Wisc Lutheran College	WI	19,216	VC
Wittenberg Univ	OH	28,766	VC
Wofford College	SC	23,995	VC
Woodbury Univ	CA	25,344	LC
Worcester State College	MA	7,901	LC
Wright State Univ	OH	9,141	LC
Xavier Univ	OH	23,880	C
Xavier Univ of Louisiana	LA	17,000	LC
Yale Univ	CT	34,030	MC
Yeshiva Univ	NY	21,400	C
York College	NE	13,500	C
York College of Pennsylvania	PA	12,550	VC
Youngstown State Univ	OH	9,318	NC

PSYCHOLOGY EDUCATION

School	ST	$IS	SR
Eastern Mich Univ	MI	9,855	C
Rocky Mountain College	MT	18,113	C
St. Vincent College	PA	22,942	VC
Shenandoah Univ	VA	22,550	NC
Univ of Delaware	DE	10,824	VC
Univ of Rio Grande	OH	8,728	NC

PUBLIC ADMINISTRATION

School	ST	$IS	SR
Abilene Christian Univ	TX	16,300	VC
Alfred Univ	NY	27,212	C+
American International College	MA	22,268	LC
Auburn Univ	AL	5,510	C
Augustana College	IL	24,117	VC+
Austin Peay State Univ	TN	5,814	LC
Baylor Univ	TX	18,298	VC+
Blackburn College	IL	13,690	C
Bowling Green State Univ	OH	10,794	C
Brown Univ	RI	34,973	MC
Buena Vista Univ	IA	22,828	C
Cal State, Bakersfield	CA	6,090	LC
Cal State, Chico	CA	8,598	LC
Cal State, Dominguez Hills	CA	5,840	LC
Cal State, Fresno	CA	7,762	C
Cal State, Fullerton	CA	5,440	LC
Cal State, Sacramento	CA	7,488	C
Cal State, San Bernardino	CA	6,516	C
Cal State, Stanislaus	CA	8,895	C
Carnegie Mellon Univ	PA	32,682	MC
Carroll College	MT	19,140	C
Catawba College	NC	19,620	C
Cedarville Univ	OH	17,553	VC
Central Methodist College	MO	16,460	C
Central State Univ	OH	8,922	C+
Central Washington Univ	WA	8,985	LC
Christopher Newport Univ	VA	8,862	VC
CUNY/John Jay College of Criminal Justice	NY	3,251	C
CUNY/Medgar Evers College	NY	3,282	NC
College of Santa Fe	NM	20,250	LC
David N. Myers College	OH	9,475	C
Doane College	NE	17,600	LC
Dominican College	NY	20,400	LC
Eastern Mich Univ	MI	9,855	C
Edgewood College	WI	18,304	C
Elon Univ	NC	19,430	VC
Evangel Univ	MO	14,050	C
Fayetteville State Univ	NC	5,590	LC
Florida A&M Univ	FL	6,948	C
Florida Atlantic Univ	FL	8,832	C
Florida International Univ	FL	9,486	VC
Florida Memorial College	FL	6,000	LC
George Mason Univ	VA	9,192	C
Grambling State Univ	LA	5,325	NC
Grand Valley State Univ	MI	10,040	C
Harding Univ	AR	13,528	VC
Hawaii Pacific Univ	HI	17,790	C
Heidelberg College	OH	23,879	C
Henderson State Univ	AR	6,269	C
Heritage College	WA	6,450	NC
Huntingdon College	AL	18,400	VC
Indiana Univ Bloomington	IN	10,712	C+
Indiana Univ Northwest	IN	3,447	C
Indiana Univ-Purdue Univ Fort Wayne	IN	3,166	LC
Inter-American Univ of PR/ Bayamon Univ College	PR	3,700	
Inter-American Univ of PR/ Fajardo Campus	PR	4,000	
Inter-American Univ of PR/ Ponce Regional College	PR	3,700	
Inter-American Univ of PR/ San GermÈn	PR	6,390	
James Madison Univ	VA	9,552	HC
John Carroll Univ	OH	24,140	VC
Juniata College	PA	26,080	VC
Kean Univ	NJ	11,159	C
Kentucky State Univ	KY	6,146	NC
Kutztown Univ of Pennsylvania	PA	8,907	C
La Salle Univ	PA	27,890	C
Lakeland College	WI	17,950	C
Lamar Univ	TX	6,816	LC
LeTourneau Univ	TX	19,020	VC
Lewis Univ	IL	20,960	C
Lincoln Univ	MO	7,158	NC
Lindenwood Univ	MO	17,250	C
LIU/C.W. Post Campus	NY	25,380	C
Louisiana College	LA	11,516	C
Metropolitan State Univ	MN	2,943	SP
Miami Univ	OH	12,885	VC+
Mich State Univ	MI	10,386	VC
Middle Tenn State Univ	TN	6,994	C
Mills College	CA	27,950	C
Miss Valley State Univ	MS	6,345	C
Missouri Valley College	MO	17,400	LC
Mount Ida College	MA	25,375	LC
Mountain State Univ	WV	8,180	NC
New College of Florida	FL	8,130	HC+
Norfolk State Univ	VA	8,382	LC
Northern Arizona Univ	AZ	7,398	C
Northern Kentucky Univ	KY	6,352	NC
Northern Mich Univ	MI	9,693	C
Northland College	WI	21,435	C+
Northwest Missouri State Univ	MO	7,922	LC
Oakland Univ	MI	9,418	C
Occidental College	CA	32,288	HC
Ohio Univ	OH	11,769	C
Park Univ	MO	9,816	C
Penn State Univ/Univ Park Campus	PA	11,126	VC
Plymouth State College	NH	11,024	LC
Point Park College	PA	20,290	C
Pontifical Catholic Univ of PR/Ponce	PR	7,076	
Rhode Island College	RI	8,700	LC
Rice Univ	TX	24,325	MC
Roosevelt Univ	IL	20,240	LC
Saginaw Valley State Univ	MI	9,465	C
St. Ambrose Univ	IA	19,994	C
St. Cloud State Univ	MN	7,180	C
St. Francis Univ	PA	24,486	LC
St. John's Univ	NY	26,660	C
St. Joseph's Univ	PA	29,715	VC+
St. Leo Univ	FL	19,250	LC
St. Mary's Univ of Minn	MN	19,975	C
St. Thomas Univ	FL	19,500	LC
Samford Univ	AL	16,340	VC
San Diego State Univ	CA	9,716	C+
Seattle Univ	WA	24,183	VC
Shaw Univ	NC	12,810	C
Shenandoah Univ	VA	22,550	NC
Shippensburg Univ of Pennsylvania	PA	9,652	C
Siena Heights Univ	MI	16,140	LC
Silver Lake College of the Holy Family	WI	15,516	LC
Slippery Rock Univ	PA	9,152	LC
Sojourner-Douglass College	MD	4,170	LC
Southeastern Univ	DC	8,505	LC
Southern Adventist Univ	TN	15,600	C
Southwest Missouri State Univ	MO	7,600	LC
Southwest Texas State Univ	TX	8,730	VC
Stephen F. Austin State Univ	TX	6,905	C
Stonehill College	MA	26,852	HC
Suffolk Univ	MA	26,516	C
Talladega College	AL	10,110	LC
Texas A&M Univ at Kingsville	TX	6,446	LC
Thomas Edison State College	NJ	2,750	SP
Turabo Univ	PR	4,110	
Univ of Akron	OH	10,530	NC
Univ of Alaska Southeast	AK	7,900	LC
Univ of Arizona	AZ	8,614	C
Univ of Arkansas	AR	8,334	VC
Univ of Central Arkansas	AR	6,388	C
Univ of Central Florida	FL	8,251	VC
Univ of Central Okla	OK	5,205	C
Univ of La Verne	CA	24,280	C
Univ of Maine	ME	10,798	C
Univ of Maine at Augusta	ME	3,928	C
Univ of Mich/Flint	MI	4,323	C
Univ of Miss	MS	7,666	C
Univ of Missouri/St. Louis	MO	9,966	C
Univ of Nebr at Omaha	NE	6,867	C
Univ of Nevada/Las Vegas	NV	8,281	VC
Univ of N Car at Greensboro	NC	6,858	C
Univ of N Car at Pembroke	NC	5,914	LC
Univ of N Dak	ND	7,067	VC
Univ of Northern Iowa	IA	7,850	C
Univ of Oregon	OR	9,969	C
Univ of Pittsburgh at Pittsburgh	PA	13,592	HC
Univ of Puget Sound	WA	28,285	HC
Univ of San Francisco	CA	27,302	VC
Univ of Southern Calif	CA	33,647	MC
Univ of Tenn at Knoxville	TN	8,214	C
Univ of Tenn at Martin	TN	8,268	C
Univ of Texas at Dallas	TX	9,305	VC
Univ of the District of Columbia	DC	2,844	NC
Univ of Wisc/Green Bay	WI	7,148	C
Univ of Wisc/La Crosse	WI	7,250	VC
Univ of Wisc/Stevens Point	WI	7,116	C
Univ of Wisc/Superior	WI	7,051	C+
Univ of Wisc/Whitewater	WI	6,937	C
Virginia Polytechnic Inst and State Univ	VA	7,652	C
Virginia State Univ	VA	8,182	LC
Wagner College	NY	27,000	C
Washburn Univ of Topeka	KS	6,766	NC
West Chester Univ of Pennsylvania	PA	9,792	VC
West Texas A&M Univ	TX	6,538	C
West Virginia Univ Inst of Technology	WV	7,518	NC
Western Mich Univ	MI	10,016	C
Western New Mexico Univ	NM	5,950	LC
Western Oregon Univ	OR	8,829	C
Winona State Univ	MN	8,570	C
Winston-Salem State Univ	NC	5,927	LC
Youngstown State Univ	OH	9,318	NC

PUBLIC AFFAIRS

School	ST	$IS	SR
Albion College	MI	25,224	VC
Bentley College	MA	31,060	HC
Chatham College	PA	25,454	C+

School	ST	$IS	SR
CUNY/Baruch College	NY	3,275	VC+
Columbia College	SC	19,050	LC
Cornell Univ	NY	34,614	MC
Dickinson College	PA	32,210	VC+
Duke Univ	NC	34,396	MC
Emory & Henry College	VA	19,462	C
Georgia Inst of Technology	GA	9,028	HC+
Hamilton College	NY	34,150	HC
Huntingdon College	AL	18,400	VC
Indiana Univ Bloomington	IN	10,712	C+
Indiana Univ South Bend	IN	3,515	C
Indiana Univ-Purdue Univ Indianapolis	IN	9,473	C
Johns Hopkins Univ	MD	35,226	MC
Lincoln Univ	PA	11,198	C+
Marymount College/ Tarrytown	NY	23,850	C
Meredith College	NC	17,500	C
Mills College	CA	27,950	C
Muskingum College	OH	18,760	C
Olivet Nazarene Univ	IL	18,444	C
Pomona College	CA	33,960	MC
Rochester Inst of Technology	NY	26,232	VC+
St. Mary's College of Maryland	MD	14,104	HC
St. Vincent College	PA	22,942	VC
Simmons College	MA	30,418	VC
Southern Methodist Univ	TX	28,349	VC
Stanford Univ	CA	34,222	MC
Syracuse Univ	NY	30,710	HC
Texas Lutheran Univ	TX	17,660	C
Texas Southern Univ	TX	6,576	NC
Trinity College	CT	34,300	HC
Univ of Calif at Santa Barbara	CA	11,732	VC
Univ of Chicago	IL	35,087	MC
Univ of Denver	CO	28,783	VC
Univ of N Car at Chapel Hill	NC	8,789	HC
Univ of Okla	OK	7,616	VC
Univ of Pennsylvania	PA	34,614	MC
Vanderbilt Univ	TN	34,482	MC
Washington State Univ	WA	9,388	C
Wayne State Univ	MI	6,720	C
Wells College	NY	19,350	VC

PUBLIC HEALTH

School	ST	$IS	SR
Andrews Univ	MI	17,696	LC
Arkansas State Univ	AR	7,480	C
Central Washington Univ	WA	8,985	LC
CUNY/Hunter College	NY	5,147	C+
Cumberland College	KY	14,864	C
Dillard Univ	LA	16,046	VC
East Tenn State Univ	TN	7,127	C
Edinboro Univ of Pennsylvania	PA	9,328	LC
Indiana Univ Bloomington	IN	10,712	C+
Indiana Univ-Purdue Univ Indianapolis	IN	9,473	C
Ithaca College	NY	28,719	HC
Johns Hopkins Univ	MD	35,226	MC
Minn State Univ, Mankato	MN	7,296	LC
New Jersey City Univ	NJ	9,100	LC
Penn State Univ/Univ Park Campus	PA	11,126	VC
Richard Stockton College of New Jersey	NJ	12,165	VC
Rutgers, The State Univ of New Jersey New Brunswick Campus	NJ	12,709	C
St. Cloud State Univ	MN	7,180	C
San Francisco State Univ	CA	7,139	LC
Simmons College	MA	30,418	VC
Southern Conn State Univ	CT	10,310	C
Univ of Illinois at Urbana-Champaign	IL	11,316	HC+
Univ of Nebr at Lincoln	NE	8,325	C+
Univ of N Car at Chapel Hill	NC	8,789	HC
Univ of N Car at Greensboro	NC	6,858	C
Univ of Rochester	NY	32,979	HC
Univ of Wisc/Eau Claire	WI	7,032	VC
Utah State Univ	UT	6,771	C
West Chester Univ of Pennsylvania	PA	9,792	VC
Western Kentucky Univ	KY	6,834	C
Western New Mexico Univ	NM	5,950	LC
Winona State Univ	MN	8,570	C

PUBLIC RELATIONS

School	ST	$IS	SR
American Univ	DC	31,544	VC+
Andrews Univ	MI	17,696	LC
Appalachian State Univ	NC	6,353	C
Auburn Univ	AL	5,510	C
Barry Univ	FL	24,100	LC
Boston Univ	MA	34,358	MC
Brigham Young Univ	UT	7,840	HC
Cal State, Fullerton	CA	5,440	LC
Cal State, Los Angeles	CA	5,050	C
Capital Univ	OH	23,630	C
Cardinal Stritch Univ	WI	17,620	C
Carroll College	MT	19,140	C
Central Missouri State Univ	MO	7,920	C
Champlain College	VT	19,680	C
Coe College	IA	24,750	VC
College of St. Rose	NY	19,084	C
Concordia College/ Moorhead	MN	18,835	C
David Lipscomb Univ	TN	16,158	VC
Drake Univ	IA	22,830	VC
Drury Univ	MO	15,250	VC
East Central Univ	OK	4,578	C
Eastern Kentucky Univ	KY	6,552	C
Emerson College	MA	29,978	HC
Ferris State Univ	MI	10,816	C
Florida Southern College	FL	19,430	C
Florida State Univ	FL	7,835	HC
Freed-Hardeman Univ	TN	14,290	VC
George Washington Univ	DC	32,170	HC
Georgia Southern Univ	GA	6,958	C
Gonzaga Univ	WA	24,276	HC+
Greenville College	IL	19,226	LC
Gwynedd-Mercy College	PA	22,350	C
Heidelberg College	OH	23,879	C
Hofstra Univ	NY	23,252	C
Illinois State Univ	IL	9,235	C
Indiana Univ Northwest	IN	3,447	C
Ithaca College	NY	28,719	HC
John Brown Univ	AR	15,080	VC
Kent State Univ	OH	11,104	C
Lewis Univ	IL	20,960	C
LIU/C.W. Post Campus	NY	25,380	C
Loras College	IA	22,994	C+
Mansfield Univ	PA	9,648	C
Marietta College	OH	24,580	C
Marquette Univ	WI	24,836	C+
Mary Baldwin College	VA	23,440	C
Mercyhurst College	PA	20,694	C
Metropolitan State Univ	MN	2,943	SP
Middle Tenn State Univ	TN	6,994	C
Montana State Univ-Billings	MT	7,653	NC
Moorhead State Univ	MN	7,000	LC
Mount Mary College	WI	18,024	C
Mount Mercy College	IA	19,390	VC
Mount St. Mary College	NY	18,825	C
Northeastern Univ	MA	30,078	VC
Northern Mich Univ	MI	9,693	C
Northwest Missouri State Univ	MO	7,922	LC
Northwestern Okla State Univ	OK	4,542	NC
Ohio Dominican College	OH	18,100	LC
Ohio Northern Univ	OH	27,765	VC
Ohio Univ	OH	11,769	C
Otterbein College	OH	23,439	C
Pacific Union College	CA	20,250	VC
Park Univ	MO	9,816	C
Pepperdine Univ	CA	32,830	VC
Pontifical Catholic Univ of PR/Ponce	PR	7,076	
Purdue Univ/West Lafayette	IN	10,284	VC
Quinnipiac Univ	CT	27,370	C
Roosevelt Univ	IL	20,240	LC
St. Mary's Univ of Minn	MN	19,975	C
Shorter College	GA	15,185	C
Simmons College	MA	30,418	VC
Southeast Missouri State Univ	MO	8,367	C+
Southern Adventist Univ	TN	15,600	C
Southern Methodist Univ	TX	28,349	VC
Southwest Texas State Univ	TX	8,730	VC
Spring Hill College	AL	23,250	C
SUNY/College at Oswego	NY	10,856	C
Stephens College	MO	22,295	C
Suffolk Univ	MA	26,516	C
Syracuse Univ	NY	30,710	HC
Texas Tech Univ	TX	8,825	C
Toccoa Falls College	GA	14,220	C
Trevecca Nazarene Univ	TN	15,752	C
Union College	NE	14,650	C
Union Univ	TN	18,930	C+
Univ of Alabama	AL	7,402	C
Univ of Central Florida	FL	8,251	VC
Univ of Central Okla	OK	5,205	C
Univ of Dayton	OH	20,400	VC
Univ of Florida	FL	7,874	HC
Univ of Georgia	GA	8,656	VC
Univ of Indianapolis	IN	20,840	C
Univ of Louisiana at Lafayette	LA	5,200	C
Univ of Miami	FL	31,130	HC
Univ of North Alabama	AL	7,016	NC
Univ of Northern Colo	CO	8,082	C+
Univ of Northern Iowa	IA	7,850	C
Univ of Okla	OK	7,616	VC
Univ of Pittsburgh at Bradford	PA	12,696	C
Univ of Rio Grande	OH	8,728	NC
Univ of S Car at Columbia	SC	8,748	VC
Univ of Southern Calif	CA	33,647	MC
Univ of Texas at Austin	TX	9,437	HC
Univ of Wisc/Whitewater	WI	6,937	C
Ursuline College	OH	19,430	LC
Utica College of Syracuse Univ	NY	24,400	LC
Wartburg College	IA	21,165	VC
Washington State Univ	WA	9,388	C
Wayne State Univ	MI	6,720	C
Weber State Univ	UT	6,897	NC
Webster Univ	MO	19,804	VC
West Texas A&M Univ	TX	6,538	C
West Virginia Univ	WV	8,304	C
West Virginia Wesleyan College	WV	22,920	C
Western Kentucky Univ	KY	6,834	C
Western Mich Univ	MI	10,016	C
Westminster College	PA	22,960	C
William Penn Univ	IA	17,575	C
Winthrop Univ	SC	9,106	C
Xavier Univ	OH	23,880	C
Youngstown State Univ	OH	9,318	NC

PUBLISHING

School	ST	$IS	SR
Benedictine Univ	IL	21,330	C
Emerson College	MA	29,978	HC
Rochester Inst of Technology	NY	26,232	VC+
St. Mary's Univ of Minn	MN	19,975	C
Syracuse Univ	NY	30,710	HC
West Texas A&M Univ	TX	6,538	C

PURCHASING/INVENTORY MANAGEMENT

School	ST	$IS	SR
Arizona State Univ-Main	AZ	7,726	C
Bowling Green State Univ	OH	10,794	C
College of Mount St. Joseph	OH	20,290	C
Duquesne Univ	PA	24,242	C+
Miami Univ	OH	12,885	VC+
Southwestern College	KS	17,656	C
Thomas Edison State College	NJ	2,750	SP
Univ of Houston-Downtown	TX	2,006	NC
Weber State Univ	UT	6,897	NC

QUANTITATIVE METHODS

School	ST	$IS	SR
Johns Hopkins Univ	MD	35,226	MC
Ohio Univ	OH	11,769	C
Simon's Rock College of Bard	MA	32,450	HC
Univ of Cincinnati	OH	12,491	LC
Univ of Houston	TX	8,410	C
Univ of Houston-Downtown	TX	2,006	NC
Univ of Washington	WA	10,361	VC
Univ of Wisc/Madison	WI	8,262	VC
Whitworth College	WA	23,938	VC

RADIATION THERAPY

School	ST	$IS	SR
Gwynedd-Mercy College	PA	22,350	C
Indiana Univ-Purdue Univ Indianapolis	IN	9,473	C
National-Louis Univ	IL	13,995	NC
Southwest Texas State Univ	TX	8,730	VC
Thomas Edison State College	NJ	2,750	SP
Univ of Mich/Flint	MI	4,323	C
Univ of St. Francis	IL	19,650	C
Univ of Vermont	VT	14,761	C+
Univ of Wisc/La Crosse	WI	7,250	VC
Wayne State Univ	MI	6,720	C

RADIO/TELEVISION TECHNOLOGY

School	ST	$IS	SR
Arkansas State Univ	AR	7,480	C
Biola Univ	CA	21,902	VC
CUNY/Brooklyn College	NY	3,403	LC
Columbia College Chicago	IL	22,063	LC
Emerson College	MA	29,978	HC
Kent State Univ	OH	11,104	C
Lewis Univ	IL	20,960	C
Lyndon State College	VT	11,313	LC
Mount Ida College	MA	25,375	LC
New York Univ	NY	35,200	MC
Northern Kentucky Univ	KY	6,352	NC
Northwestern Univ	IL	33,615	MC
Southeast Missouri State Univ	MO	8,367	C+
Texas Christian Univ	TX	19,910	C
Univ of Arkansas at Little Rock	AR	5,637	NC
Univ of Houston	TX	8,410	C
Univ of Louisiana at Monroe	LA	5,207	NC
Univ of Miss	MS	7,666	C
Univ of Montana	MT	8,038	C
Univ of North Texas	TX	7,629	C
Univ of Southern Miss	MS	6,155	LC
Univ of the Arts	PA	24,230	SP

RADIOGRAPH MEDICAL TECHNOLOGY

School	ST	$IS	SR
Alderson-Broaddus College	WV	19,640	C
Champlain College	VT	19,680	C
Clarkson College	NE	12,178	C
College Misericordia	PA	23,380	LC
Florida Hospital College of Health Sciences	FL	5,790	C
Howard Univ	DC	15,522	LC
La Roche College	PA	18,854	LC
Oregon Inst of Technology	OR	8,718	C
Southwest Missouri State Univ	MO	7,600	LC
Ohio State Univ	OH	10,819	VC
Univ of St. Francis	IL	19,650	C
Univ of St. Francis	IN	17,790	LC
Weber State Univ	UT	6,897	NC

RADIOLOGICAL SCIENCE

School	ST	$IS	SR
Arkansas State Univ	AR	7,480	C
Armstrong Atlantic State Univ	GA	7,084	C
Gannon Univ	PA	18,848	C
George Washington Univ	DC	32,170	HC
Idaho State Univ	ID	7,030	C+
Jewish Hospital College of Nursing and Allied Health	MO	11,200	SP
Manhattan College	NY	25,500	VC
Midwestern State Univ	TX	6,704	NC
Quinnipiac Univ	CT	27,370	C
St. Francis College	NY	9,610	C
Suffolk Univ	MA	26,516	C
Univ of Alabama at Birmingham	AL	10,110	C
Univ of Central Arkansas	AR	6,388	C
Univ of Central Florida	FL	8,251	VC
Univ of Charleston	WV	20,640	C
Univ of Missouri/Columbia	MO	9,803	HC
Univ of New Mexico	NM	8,026	C
Univ of N Car at Chapel Hill	NC	8,789	HC
Univ of South Alabama	AL	6,976	LC

RADIOLOGICAL TECHNOLOGY

School	ST	$IS	SR
Austin Peay State Univ	TN	5,814	LC
Avila College	MO	17,720	C
Bloomsburg Univ of Pennsylvania	PA	9,434	C
Boise State Univ	ID	6,531	LC
Cal State, Northridge	CA	7,781	C
Clarion Univ of Pennsylvania	PA	11,272	LC
Clarkson College	NE	12,178	C
Concordia Univ Wisc	WI	16,600	LC
Fairleigh Dickinson Univ/ Madison campus	NJ	25,500	C
Fairleigh Dickinson Univ/ Teaneck Campus	NJ	24,646	C
Fort Hays State Univ	KS	6,294	LC
Friends Univ	KS	15,962	LC
Jamestown College	ND	11,310	NC
LIU/C.W. Post Campus	NY	25,380	C
Marian College of Fond du Lac	WI	17,935	LC
Marygrove College	MI	16,075	C
Mass College of Pharmacy and Health Sciences	MA	27,131	SP
McNeese State Univ	LA	5,259	LC
Minot State Univ	ND	5,466	LC
Mount Marty College	SD	15,656	LC
N Dak State Univ	ND	7,004	VC
Northwestern State Univ of Louisiana	LA	5,745	NC
Presentation College	SD	13,508	NC
Rhode Island College	RI	8,700	LC
St. Mary's College	MI	13,314	LC
Southern Illinois Univ at Carbondale	IL	8,621	C
Univ of Hartford	CT	28,884	C
Univ of Louisiana at Monroe	LA	5,207	NC
Univ of Mary	ND	12,900	LC
Univ of Nevada/Las Vegas	NV	8,281	VC
William Carey College	MS	10,150	LC

RANGE/FARM MANAGEMENT

School	ST	$IS	SR
Colo State Univ	CO	9,672	C
Eastern Oregon Univ	OR	8,772	C
Montana State Univ-Bozeman	MT	8,431	C
New Mexico State Univ	NM	7,302	C
N Dak State Univ	ND	7,004	VC
Oregon State Univ	OR	9,612	VC
S Dak State Univ	SD	6,848	C
Stephen F. Austin State Univ	TX	6,905	C
Tarleton State Univ	TX	7,160	C
Texas A&M Univ	TX	8,988	VC
Texas A&M Univ at Kingsville	TX	6,446	LC
Texas Tech Univ	TX	8,825	C
Univ of Arizona	AZ	8,614	C
Univ of Calif at Davis	CA	12,796	VC
Univ of Idaho	ID	7,026	C
Univ of Nebr at Lincoln	NE	8,325	C+
Univ of Wyoming	WY	7,143	LC
Utah State Univ	UT	6,771	C
Washington State Univ	WA	9,388	C

READING EDUCATION

School	ST	$IS	SR
Baylor Univ	TX	18,298	VC+

School	ST	$IS	SR
Defiance College	OH	19,580	LC
Eastern Mich Univ	MI	9,855	C
Florida State Univ	FL	7,835	HC
Hardin-Simmons Univ	TX	14,165	C
Houston Baptist Univ	TX	15,300	LC
Jarvis Christian College	TX	9,035	NC
Missouri Southern State College	MO	6,666	C
Muskingum College	OH	18,760	C
S Car State Univ	SC	6,586	LC
Southwest Texas State Univ	TX	8,730	VC
Stephen F. Austin State Univ	TX	6,905	C
Texas Southern Univ	TX	6,576	NC
Texas Wesleyan Univ	TX	14,710	C
Univ of Great Falls	MT	15,360	C
Univ of North Texas	TX	7,629	C
Univ of Rio Grande	OH	8,728	NC
West Texas A&M Univ	TX	6,538	C
Wingate Univ	NC	19,140	C

REAL ESTATE

School	ST	$IS	SR
Arizona State Univ-Main	AZ	7,726	C
Ball State Univ	IN	8,660	C
Baylor Univ	TX	18,298	VC+
Calif State Polytechnic Univ, Pomona	CA	8,615	C
Cal State, Los Angeles	CA	5,050	C
Cal State, Sacramento	CA	7,488	C
Christopher Newport Univ	VA	8,862	VC
CUNY/Baruch College	NY	3,275	VC+
Clarion Univ of Pennsylvania	PA	11,272	LC
David N. Myers College	OH	9,475	C
Eastern Mich Univ	MI	9,855	C
Florida Atlantic Univ	FL	8,832	C
Florida International Univ	FL	9,486	VC
Georgia State Univ	GA	7,792	LC
Indiana Univ Bloomington	IN	10,712	C+
Indiana Univ-Purdue Univ Indianapolis	IN	9,473	C
Kent State Univ	OH	11,104	C
Miss State Univ	MS	7,853	C
Morehead State Univ	KY	6,510	C
Penn State Univ/Univ Park Campus	PA	11,126	VC
St. John's Univ	NY	26,660	C
San Diego State Univ	CA	9,716	C+
San Francisco State Univ	CA	7,139	LC
Schreiner Univ	TX	19,254	C
Southern Methodist Univ	TX	28,349	VC
State Univ of West Georgia	GA	7,101	C
Temple Univ	PA	14,124	C
Texas A&M Univ at Kingsville	TX	6,446	LC
Ohio State Univ	OH	10,819	VC
Thomas Edison State College	NJ	2,750	SP
Univ of Cincinnati	OH	12,491	LC
Univ of Conn	CT	12,122	VC
Univ of Denver	CO	28,783	VC
Univ of Florida	FL	7,874	HC
Univ of Georgia	GA	8,656	VC
Univ of Hawaii at Manoa	HI	7,862	VC
Univ of Memphis	TN	7,271	C
Univ of Miami	FL	31,130	HC
Univ of Miss	MS	7,666	C
Univ of Missouri/Columbia	MO	9,803	HC
Univ of Nevada/Las Vegas	NV	8,281	VC
Univ of North Texas	TX	7,629	C
Univ of Okla	OK	7,616	VC
Univ of Pennsylvania	PA	34,614	MC
Univ of St. Thomas	MN	24,044	VC
Univ of S Car at Columbia	SC	8,748	VC
Univ of Texas at Arlington	TX	7,192	LC
Univ of Wisc/Madison	WI	8,262	VC
Univ of Wisc/Milwaukee	WI	8,907	LC
Washington State Univ	WA	9,388	C

RECREATION AND LEISURE SERVICES

School	ST	$IS	SR
Arizona State Univ-Main	AZ	7,726	C
Arkansas Tech Univ	AR	6,256	C
Asbury College	KY	18,540	VC
Austin Peay State Univ	TN	5,814	LC
Belmont Abbey College	NC	19,630	LC
Bethune-Cookman College	FL	15,746	C
Bowling Green State Univ	OH	10,794	C
Calif Polytechnic State Univ	CA	8,747	VC
Cal State, Dominguez Hills	CA	5,840	LC
Cal State, Hayward	CA	7,400	LC
Cal State, Northridge	CA	7,781	C
Calvin College	MI	20,050	NC
Catawba College	NC	19,620	C
Central Missouri State Univ	MO	7,920	C
Central Washington Univ	WA	8,985	LC
Chicago State Univ	IL	8,851	C+
Christopher Newport Univ	VA	8,862	VC
East Central Univ	OK	4,578	C
Eastern Conn State Univ	CT	10,362	C
Eastern Mich Univ	MI	9,855	C
Eastern Washington Univ	WA	7,972	LC
Emory & Henry College	VA	19,462	C
Emporia State Univ	KS	6,198	LC
Ferrum College	VA	15,990	LC
Florida State Univ	FL	7,835	HC
Franklin College of Indiana	IN	19,905	C
Frostburg State Univ	MD	9,680	C
Gallaudet Univ	DC	16,554	SP
Georgetown College	KY	18,400	VC
Georgia Southern Univ	GA	6,958	C
Georgia State Univ	GA	7,792	LC
Gordon College	MA	23,594	VC+
Graceland Univ	IA	15,845	C
Grambling State Univ	LA	5,325	NC
Green Mountain College	VT	24,130	C
Greenville College	IL	19,226	LC
Henderson State Univ	AR	6,260	C
High Point Univ	NC	20,220	LC
Houghton College	NY	21,810	VC+
Indiana State Univ	IN	8,461	LC
Indiana Univ Bloomington	IN	10,712	C+
Ithaca College	NY	28,719	HC
James Madison Univ	VA	9,552	HC
Johnson and Wales Univ	RI	21,558	LC
Kean Univ	NJ	11,159	C
Kent State Univ	OH	11,104	C
Lyndon State College	VT	11,313	LC
Mars Hill College	NC	18,600	LC
Maryville College	TN	23,210	VC
Metropolitan State College of Denver	CO	2,338	LC
Middle Tenn State Univ	TN	6,994	C
Montclair State Univ	NJ	10,287	LC
Morris College	SC	9,005	LC
Mount Olive College	NC	14,410	LC
Mountain State Univ	WV	8,180	NC
New Mexico Highlands Univ	NM	6,256	NC
New York Univ	NY	35,200	MC
N Car State Univ	NC	8,680	HC
N Dak State Univ	ND	7,004	VC
North Georgia College and State Univ	GA	6,322	C+
Northwest Missouri State Univ	MO	7,922	LC
Northwest Nazarene Univ	ID	18,380	C
Ohio Univ	OH	11,769	C
Okla State Univ	OK	7,650	VC
Old Dominion Univ	VA	9,386	C
Oral Roberts Univ	OK	18,490	C
Pacific Lutheran Univ	WA	23,318	VC
Pacific Union College	CA	20,250	VC
Plymouth State College	NH	11,024	LC
Purdue Univ/West Lafayette	IN	10,284	VC
Radford Univ	VA	8,302	C
St. Thomas Aquinas College	NY	20,590	LC
Shaw Univ	NC	12,810	C
Shepherd College	WV	7,062	LC
Southeastern Okla State Univ	OK	4,917	C
Southern Conn State Univ	CT	10,310	C
Southern Wesleyan Univ	SC	17,280	C
Southwest Baptist Univ	MO	13,426	LC
Southwest Missouri State Univ	MO	7,600	LC
SUNY/College at Brockport	NY	10,267	C
Taylor Univ	IN	21,562	VC+
Tenn Wesleyan College	TN	13,030	C
Texas Tech Univ	TX	8,825	C
Thomas Edison State College	NJ	2,750	SP
Tougaloo College	MS	9,200	NC
Tri-State Univ-Main Campus	IN	21,200	C
Univ of Delaware	DE	10,824	VC
Univ of Florida	FL	7,874	HC
Univ of Georgia	GA	8,656	VC
Univ of Hawaii at Manoa	HI	7,862	VC
Univ of Illinois at Urbana-Champaign	IL	11,316	HC+
Univ of Iowa	IA	8,607	C+
Univ of Maine at Machias	ME	7,689	LC
Univ of Maine at Presque Isle	ME	7,964	LC
Univ of Memphis	TN	7,271	C
Univ of Mich/Ann Arbor	MI	13,003	HC+
Univ of Minn/Twin Cities	MN	11,123	VC
Univ of Miss	MS	7,666	C
Univ of New Hampshire	NH	13,207	C
Univ of N Car at Chapel Hill	NC	8,789	HC
Univ of N Dak	ND	7,067	VC
Univ of North Texas	TX	7,629	C
Univ of Northern Iowa	IA	7,850	C
Univ of South Alabama	AL	6,976	LC
Univ of S Dak	SD	7,036	C
Univ of Southern Colo	CO	7,821	LC
Univ of Tenn at Chattanooga	TN	7,783	C
Univ of Toledo	OH	11,206	NC
Univ of Utah	UT	7,703	C
Univ of Wisc/Madison	WI	8,262	VC
Univ of Wisc/Milwaukee	WI	8,907	LC
Upper Iowa Univ	IA	17,438	C
Voorhees College	SC	9,976	C+
Wartburg College	IA	21,165	VC
Weber State Univ	UT	6,897	NC
West Texas A&M Univ	TX	6,538	C
West Virginia Univ	WV	8,304	C
Western Kentucky Univ	KY	6,834	C
Western Mich Univ	MI	10,016	C
Western State College of Colo	CO	7,585	LC
William Penn Univ	IA	17,575	C

RECREATION EDUCATION

School	ST	$IS	SR
Alcorn State Univ	MS	5,594	LC
Alderson-Broaddus College	WV	19,640	C
Baylor Univ	TX	18,298	VC+
Campbellsville Univ	KY	14,340	C
Eastern Washington Univ	WA	7,972	LC
Georgia College and State Univ	GA	7,344	C
Georgia Southwestern State Univ	GA	6,013	C
Howard Univ	DC	15,522	LC
Johnson State College	VT	10,776	C
Knoxville College	TN	6,200	LC
Lyndon State College	VT	11,313	LC
Northwest Missouri State Univ	MO	7,922	LC
Oral Roberts Univ	OK	18,490	C
Prescott College	AZ	13,430	C
St. Mary's College of Calif	CA	27,575	C
San Francisco State Univ	CA	7,139	LC
Southern Univ at New Orleans	LA	995	NC
SUNY/College at Cortland	NY	10,564	C
Sterling College	VT	19,695	C
Univ of Arkansas	AR	8,334	VC
Univ of Conn	CT	12,122	VC
Univ of Hawaii at Manoa	HI	7,862	VC
Univ of Idaho	ID	7,026	C
Univ of Maine	ME	10,798	C
Univ of Minn/Duluth	MN	10,436	C
Univ of Nevada/Las Vegas	NV	8,281	VC
Univ of New Hampshire	NH	13,207	C
Univ of Tenn at Knoxville	TN	8,214	C
Warren Wilson College	NC	19,968	C
Washington State Univ	WA	9,388	C
West Texas A&M Univ	TX	6,538	C

RECREATION THERAPY

School	ST	$IS	SR
Ashland Univ	OH	22,182	LC
Cal State, Northridge	CA	7,781	C
Catawba College	NC	19,620	C
College of Mount St. Joseph	OH	20,290	C
East Carolina Univ	NC	7,766	C
Eastern Mich Univ	MI	9,855	C
Eastern Washington Univ	WA	7,972	LC
Gallaudet Univ	DC	16,554	SP
Green Mountain College	VT	24,130	C
Hampton Univ	VA	17,112	C+
Indiana Inst of Technology	IN	18,806	C
Ithaca College	NY	28,719	HC
Lake Superior State Univ	MI	9,034	LC
Lincoln Univ	PA	11,198	C+
Longwood College	VA	8,950	C
Mercy College	NY	15,875	LC
Messiah College	PA	23,180	VC
Morris Brown College	GA	15,993	LC
Ohio Univ	OH	11,769	C
Shaw Univ	NC	12,810	C
Shepherd College	WV	7,062	LC
Springfield College	MA	24,520	C
Univ of N Car at Wilmington	NC	7,769	C
Univ of Southern Maine	ME	10,569	C
Univ of Wisc/La Crosse	WI	7,250	VC
Utica College of Syracuse Univ	NY	24,400	LC
West Virginia State College	WV	6,264	NC
Western Carolina Univ	NC	5,667	C
Winston-Salem State Univ	NC	5,927	LC

RECREATIONAL FACILITIES MANAGEMENT

School	ST	$IS	SR
Appalachian State Univ	NC	6,353	C
Ashland Univ	OH	22,182	LC
Barber-Scotia College	NC	13,100	C
Bluffton College	OH	20,644	C
Cal State, Fresno	CA	7,762	C
Central Methodist College	MO	16,460	C
College of St. Joseph	VT	17,400	NC
Colo State Univ	CO	9,672	C
Culver-Stockton College	MO	15,400	LC
East Carolina Univ	NC	7,766	C
East Texas Baptist Univ	TX	12,349	LC
Eastern Illinois Univ	IL	10,101	C
Eastern Mennonite Univ	VA	20,700	VC
Elmhurst College	IL	21,750	C
Graceland Univ	IA	15,845	C
Green Mountain College	VT	24,130	C
Hannibal-LaGrange College	MO	12,530	C
Indiana Wesleyan Univ	IN	17,680	C
Johnson and Wales Univ	RI	21,558	LC
Johnson State College	VT	10,776	C
Keystone College	PA	19,066	LC
Lynn Univ	FL	24,550	C
Malone College	OH	19,190	C
Missouri Valley College	MO	17,400	LC
New Mexico State Univ	NM	7,302	C
Savannah State Univ	GA	2,550	LC
Shorter College	GA	15,185	C
Sierra Nevada College-Lake Tahoe	NV	21,060	LC
Southwest Texas State Univ	TX	8,730	VC
Southwestern Okla State Univ	OK	4,801	C
Thomas Univ	GA	8,770	NC
Univ of Central Okla	OK	5,205	C
Univ of Minn/Twin Cities	MN	11,123	VC
Univ of Miss	MS	7,666	C
Univ of Nevada/Las Vegas	NV	8,281	VC
Univ of St. Francis	IL	19,650	C
Webber International Univ	FL	14,695	LC

REHABILITATION THERAPY

School	ST	$IS	SR
Arkansas Tech Univ	AR	6,256	C
Assumption College	MA	26,320	C
Boston Univ	MA	34,358	MC
Cal State, Los Angeles	CA	5,050	C
Clarion Univ of Pennsylvania	PA	11,272	LC
East Carolina Univ	NC	7,766	C
East Central Univ	OK	4,578	C
Emporia State Univ	KS	6,198	LC
Florida International Univ	FL	9,486	VC
Florida State Univ	FL	7,835	HC
Indiana Univ of Pennsylvania	PA	9,133	C
Ithaca College	NY	28,719	HC
Kean Univ	NJ	11,159	C
Montana State Univ-Billings	MT	7,653	NC
Northeastern Univ	MA	30,078	VC
Penn State Univ/Univ Park Campus	PA	11,126	VC
Shaw Univ	NC	12,810	C
Southern Illinois Univ at Carbondale	IL	8,621	C
Southern Univ and A&M College	LA	6,365	C+
Springfield College	MA	24,520	C
Stephen F. Austin State Univ	TX	6,905	C
Thomas Univ	GA	8,770	NC
Univ of Arkansas at Pine Bluff	AR	7,925	C
Univ of Maine at Farmington	ME	9,163	C
Univ of Maryland/Eastern Shore	MD	9,258	C
Univ of N Dak	ND	7,067	VC
Univ of North Texas	TX	7,629	C
Univ of Northern Colo	CO	8,082	C+
Univ of Tenn at Chattanooga	TN	7,783	C
Univ of Texas-Pan American	TX	4,823	C
Univ of Wisc/Stout	WI	7,192	C
Wilberforce Univ	OH	14,937	LC
Wright State Univ	OH	9,141	LC

RELIGION

School	ST	$IS	SR
Abilene Christian Univ	TX	16,300	VC
Adrian College	MI	19,670	C
Agnes Scott College	GA	24,950	VC
Albertson College of Idaho	ID	23,900	VC
Albertus Magnus College	CT	22,154	C
Albion College	MI	25,224	VC
Albright College	PA	27,642	C
Allegheny College	PA	27,780	VC
Alma College	MI	22,586	VC
Alverno College	WI	16,930	LC
American Univ	DC	31,544	VC+
Amherst College	MA	34,340	MC
Anderson Univ	IN	19,430	LC
Andrews Univ	MI	17,696	LC
Appalachian State Univ	NC	6,353	C
Arizona State Univ-Main	AZ	7,726	C
Arkansas Baptist College	AR	5,530	LC
Ashland Univ	OH	22,182	LC
Atlantic Union College	MA	34,034	LC
Auburn Univ	AL	5,510	C
Augsburg College	MN	22,978	C
Augustana College	IL	24,117	VC+
Augustana College	SD	20,760	VC
Aurora Univ	IL	18,551	C
Austin College	TX	22,150	VC+
Averett Univ	VA	17,980	LC
Azusa Pacific Univ	CA	22,422	VC
Baker Univ	KS	14,780	C+
Baldwin-Wallace College	OH	22,010	VC+
Ball State Univ	IN	8,660	C
Bard College	NY	33,912	HC
Bartlesville Wesleyan College	OK	14,100	LC
Barton College	NC	16,834	LC
Bates College	ME	34,100	MC
Baylor Univ	TX	18,298	VC+
Belmont Univ	TN	19,066	VC
Beloit College	WI	27,482	HC
Benedict College	SC	12,662	LC

School	ST	$IS	SR
Benedictine College	KS	18,485	LC
Berea College	KY	4,070	VC
Berry College	GA	18,850	C
Bethany College	WV	18,566	C
Bethel College	IN	17,650	LC
Bethel College	KS	17,355	C+
Bethel College	MN	22,740	VC
Bethune-Cookman College	FL	15,746	C
Bloomfield College	NJ	17,000	C
Bluefield College	VA	14,200	C
Bluffton College	OH	20,644	C
Boston Univ	MA	34,358	MC
Bowdoin College	ME	32,650	MC
Bradley Univ	IL	20,970	VC
Brescia Univ	KY	14,225	C
Bridgewater College	VA	22,950	C
Bryan College	TN	16,400	VC
Bryn Athyn College of the New Church	PA	10,590	NC
Bryn Mawr College	PA	33,580	HC+
Bucknell Univ	PA	31,096	HC
Buena Vista Univ	IA	22,828	C
Butler Univ	IN	25,580	VC+
Cabrini College	PA	25,950	LC
Caldwell College	NJ	20,940	LC
Calif Lutheran Univ	CA	23,500	LC
Cal State, Bakersfield	CA	6,090	LC
Cal State, Chico	CA	8,598	LC
Cal State, Fullerton	CA	5,440	LC
Cal State, Long Beach	CA	7,400	LC
Calvin College	MI	20,050	NC
Campbell Univ	NC	16,599	C
Canisius College	NY	24,696	C+
Capital Univ	OH	23,630	C
Cardinal Stritch Univ	WI	17,620	LC
Carleton College	MN	30,780	MC
Carroll College	MT	19,140	C
Carroll College	WI	21,170	C
Carson-Newman College	TN	16,490	C
Carthage College	WI	23,670	C
Case Western Reserve Univ	OH	27,418	C
Catawba College	NC	19,620	C
Catholic Univ of America	DC	29,332	VC
Centenary College of Louisiana	LA	21,600	C+
Central College	IA	21,206	C
Central Methodist College	MO	16,460	C
Central Mich Univ	MI	8,355	C
Central Univ of Bayamon	PR	3,335	
Centre College	KY	24,000	HC
Chaminade Univ of Honolulu	HI	17,370	C
Chapman Univ	CA	30,218	VC
Charleston Southern Univ	SC	17,122	C
Christian Brothers Univ	TN	19,820	VC
Christopher Newport Univ	VA	8,862	VC
CUNY/Brooklyn College	NY	3,403	LC
CUNY/Hunter College	NY	5,147	C+
CUNY/Queens College	NY	3,403	VC
Claflin Univ	SC	12,735	C+
Claremont McKenna College	CA	32,700	MC
Clark Atlanta Univ	GA	17,174	C
Clarke College	IA	20,625	C+
Cleveland State Univ	OH	10,146	NC
Coe College	IA	24,750	VC
Coker College	SC	20,120	C
Colby College	ME	34,290	MC
Colgate Univ	NY	33,480	MC
College of Charleston	SC	8,350	HC
College of Mount St. Vincent	NY	24,230	C
College of Mount St. Joseph	OH	20,290	C
College of New Rochelle	NY	20,000	C
College of Notre Dame of Maryland	MD	23,100	LC
College of Our Lady of the Elms	MA	20,644	C
College of St. Rose	NY	19,084	C
College of St. Scholastica	MN	22,378	C+
College of Santa Fe	NM	20,250	LC
College of the Holy Cross	MA	32,780	MC
College of the Ozarks	MO	2,650	C+
College of William and Mary	VA	10,002	MC
College of Wooster	OH	28,350	VC
Colo Christian Univ	CO	17,714	C
Colo College	CO	31,525	HC+
Columbia College	SC	19,050	LC
Columbia Union College	MD	19,027	C+
Columbia Univ/Barnard College	NY	33,694	MC
Columbia Univ/Columbia College	NY	35,190	MC
Columbia Univ/School of General Studies	NY	35,000	C
Concordia College	NY	19,200	VC
Concordia College/Moorhead	MN	18,835	C
Concordia Univ	CA	22,290	C
Concordia Univ	MI	20,500	C
Concordia Univ	MN	19,912	C
Concordia Univ Wisc	WI	16,600	LC
Concordia Univ, River Forest	IL	20,000	LC
Conn College	CT	33,585	MC
Converse College	SC	21,990	VC
Cornell College	IA	24,980	VC
Cornell Univ	NY	34,614	MC
Cornerstone Univ and Grand Rapids Baptist Seminary	MI	18,092	C
Covenant College	GA	21,970	C+
Culver-Stockton College	MO	15,400	LC
Cumberland College	KY	14,864	C
Daemen College	NY	20,620	C
Dakota Wesleyan Univ	SD	15,512	C
Dana College	NE	18,046	C
Dartmouth College	NH	34,458	MC
David Lipscomb Univ	TN	16,158	VC
Davidson College	NC	30,823	MC
Davis and Elkins College	WV	19,270	LC
Defiance College	OH	19,580	LC
Denison Univ	OH	29,640	HC
DePaul Univ	IL	23,590	VC
DePauw Univ	IN	28,000	HC
Dickinson College	PA	32,210	VC+
Dillard Univ	LA	16,046	VC
Doane College	NE	17,600	LC
Dominican Univ	IL	20,800	C
Dominican Univ of Calif	CA	27,948	C
Dordt College	IA	18,100	C+
Drake Univ	IA	22,830	VC
Drew Univ/College of Liberal Arts	NJ	32,152	VC
Duke Univ	NC	34,396	MC
Earlham College	IN	27,446	VC+
East Texas Baptist Univ	TX	12,349	LC
Eastern Mennonite Univ	VA	20,700	VC
Eastern Nazarene College	MA	19,433	LC
Eastern New Mexico Univ	NM	4,113	LC
Eckerd College	FL	25,500	C+
Edgewood College	WI	18,304	C
Edward Waters College	FL	13,124	LC
Elizabethtown College	PA	26,000	VC
Elmhurst College	IL	21,750	C
Elon Univ	NC	19,430	VC
Emory & Henry College	VA	19,462	C
Emory Univ	GA	33,792	MC
Erskine College	SC	21,399	VC
Eureka College	IL	22,200	C
Evangel Univ	MO	14,050	C
Fairfield Univ	CT	30,885	HC
Felician College	NJ	20,050	C
Ferrum College	VA	15,990	LC
Fisk Univ	TN	13,700	LC
Flagler College	FL	10,550	VC+
Florida International Univ	FL	9,486	VC
Florida Memorial College	FL	6,000	LC
Florida Southern College	FL	19,430	C
Florida State Univ	FL	7,835	HC
Fordham Univ	NY	30,710	VC
Franciscan Univ of Steubenville	OH	19,100	C+
Franklin and Marshall College	PA	32,410	HC
Franklin College of Indiana	IN	19,905	C
Fresno Pacific Univ	CA	19,740	C
Friends Univ	KS	15,962	LC
Furman Univ	SC	25,492	HC
Gallaudet Univ	DC	16,554	SP
Gardner-Webb Univ	NC	17,400	C
George Fox Univ	OR	24,095	VC
George Mason Univ	VA	9,192	C
George Washington Univ	DC	32,170	HC
Georgetown College	KY	18,400	VC
Georgetown Univ	DC	34,847	MC
Georgia State Univ	GA	7,792	LC
Georgian Court College	NJ	19,040	LC
Gettysburg College	PA	32,070	HC
Gonzaga Univ	WA	24,276	HC+
Goshen College	IN	18,950	VC+
Grace Bible College	MI	12,600	C
Grace College	IN	16,768	C
Graceland Univ	IA	15,845	C
Greensboro College	NC	19,080	LC
Greenville College	IL	19,226	LC
Grinnell College	IA	28,300	HC+
Grove City College	PA	12,280	MC
Guilford College	NC	23,255	C
Gustavus Adolphus College	MN	24,190	VC+
Hamilton College	NY	34,150	HC
Hamline Univ	MN	23,339	C+
Hampden-Sydney College	VA	24,871	C
Hampshire College	MA	33,881	HC+
Harding Univ	AR	13,528	VC
Hardin-Simmons Univ	TX	14,165	C
Hartwick College	NY	33,090	C+
Harvard Univ/Harvard College	MA	34,269	MC
Hastings College	NE	17,854	C+
Haverford College	PA	34,300	MC
Heidelberg College	OH	23,879	C
Hellenic College/Holy Cross Greek Orthodox School of Theology	MA	17,215	C
Hendrix College	AR	18,463	HC
High Point Univ	NC	20,220	LC
Hillsdale College	MI	20,586	VC+
Hiram College	OH	27,034	VC
Hobart and William Smith Colleges	NY	33,195	VC
Hollins Univ	VA	24,328	VC
Holy Family College	PA	13,710	LC
Holy Names College	CA	23,220	C
Hood College	MD	26,020	VC
Hope College	MI	22,922	C+
Houghton College	NY	21,810	VC+
Humboldt State Univ	CA	8,582	C
Huntingdon College	AL	18,400	VC
Illinois College	IL	16,234	C
Illinois Wesleyan Univ	IL	26,970	HC
Indiana State Univ	IN	8,461	LC
Indiana Univ Bloomington	IN	10,712	C+
Indiana Univ of Pennsylvania	PA	9,133	C
Indiana Univ-Purdue Univ Indianapolis	IN	9,473	C
Indiana Wesleyan Univ	IN	17,680	C
Iona College	NY	26,556	C
Iowa State Univ	IA	8,108	VC
James Madison Univ	VA	9,552	HC
Jamestown College	ND	11,310	NC
Jarvis Christian College	TX	9,035	NC
John Carroll Univ	OH	24,140	VC
Judson College	AL	13,790	C
Kalamazoo College	MI	26,955	HC+
Kansas Wesleyan Univ	KS	17,400	C+
Kenyon College	OH	32,130	HC+
La Roche College	PA	18,854	LC
La Salle Univ	PA	27,890	C
La Sierra Univ	CA	19,260	LC
Lafayette College	PA	32,655	MC
LaGrange College	GA	17,496	C
Lakeland College	WI	17,950	C
Lambuth Univ	TN	14,254	C
Lane College	TN	10,400	C+
Lawrence Univ	WI	27,711	HC
Le Moyne College	NY	23,840	C
Lebanon Valley College of Pennsylvania	PA	25,700	VC
Lees-McRae College	NC	17,106	LC
Lehigh Univ	PA	32,290	MC
Lewis and Clark College	OR	29,010	VC
Lewis Univ	IL	20,960	C
Liberty Univ	VA	14,500	C
Lincoln Univ	PA	11,198	C+
Lindenwood Univ	MO	17,250	C
Linfield College	OR	25,840	VC
Loras College	IA	22,994	C+
Louisiana College	LA	11,516	C
Lourdes College	OH	13,100	LC
Loyola Univ New Orleans	LA	23,506	VC+
Loyola Univ of Chicago	IL	25,992	VC
Lycoming College	PA	24,780	C
Lynchburg College	VA	23,405	C
Lyon College	AR	16,500	VC
Macalester College	MN	28,814	HC+
MacMurray College	IL	17,790	LC
Madonna Univ	MI	11,504	VC
Manchester College	IN	22,010	C
Manhattan College	NY	25,500	VC
Manhattanville College	NY	28,730	VC
Mars Hill College	NC	18,600	LC
Martin Univ	IN	8,370	SP
Mary Washington College	VA	9,032	VC+
Marygrove College	MI	16,075	C
Maryville College	TN	23,210	VC
Marywood Univ	PA	24,639	C
McKendree College	IL	18,300	C+
McMurry Univ	TX	15,287	C
McPherson College	KS	17,710	C
Mercer Univ	GA	24,130	VC
Mercyhurst College	PA	20,694	C
Meredith College	NC	17,500	C
Merrimack College	MA	25,725	VC
Messiah College	PA	23,180	VC
Methodist College	NC	19,526	C
Miami Univ	OH	12,885	VC+
Mich State Univ	MI	10,386	VC
MidAmerica Nazarene Univ	KS	16,960	C
Middlebury College	VT	34,300	MC
Midland Lutheran College	NE	18,600	C
Millikin Univ	IL	24,415	C+
Millsaps College	MS	22,608	VC+
Missouri Baptist College	MO	15,762	LC
Missouri Valley College	MO	17,400	LC
Monmouth College	IL	21,550	C
Montclair State Univ	NJ	10,287	LC
Montreat College	NC	17,164	C
Moravian College	PA	27,065	VC
Morehouse College	GA	19,814	C
Morgan State Univ	MD	10,078	LC
Morningside College	IA	19,124	C
Morris Brown College	GA	15,993	LC
Mount Holyoke College	MA	34,128	HC
Mount Marty College	SD	15,656	LC
Mount Mercy College	IA	19,390	VC
Mount Olive College	NC	14,410	LC
Mount St. Clare College	IA	19,050	LC
Mount St. Mary's College	CA	24,430	C
Mount Union College	OH	21,120	C
Mount Vernon Nazarene College	OH	17,027	C
Muhlenberg College	PA	28,170	HC
Muskingum College	OH	18,760	C
Naropa Univ	CO	22,416	SP
Nazareth College of Rochester	NY	22,036	VC
Nebr Wesleyan Univ	NE	18,767	VC
New College of Florida	FL	8,130	HC+
New York Univ	NY	35,200	MC
Newberry College	SC	19,670	LC
Newman Univ	KS	14,098	LC
Niagara Univ	NY	22,250	C+
N Car State Univ	NC	8,680	HC
N Car Wesleyan College	NC	15,650	LC
North Central College	IL	22,944	C+
North Central Univ	MN	12,744	LC
North Park Univ	IL	24,030	C
Northern Arizona Univ	AZ	7,398	C
Northland College	WI	21,435	C+
Northwest College	WA	17,471	C
Northwest Nazarene Univ	ID	18,380	C
Northwestern College of Iowa	IA	17,630	C+
Northwestern Univ	IL	33,615	MC
Notre Dame de Namur Univ	CA	26,932	LC
Nyack College	NY	18,540	C
Oakland City Univ	IN	11,286	LC
Oakwood College	AL	14,904	C
Oberlin College	OH	33,140	HC+
Occidental College	CA	32,288	HC
Ohio Northern Univ	OH	27,765	VC
Ohio Valley College	WV	13,650	C+
Ohio Wesleyan Univ	OH	29,670	VC+
Okla Baptist Univ	OK	13,878	VC
Okla City Univ	OK	15,810	C
Olivet Nazarene Univ	IL	18,444	C
Oral Roberts Univ	OK	18,490	C
Ottawa Univ	KS	11,800	LC
Otterbein College	OH	23,439	C
Ouachita Baptist Univ	AR	16,460	VC
Our Lady of the Lake Univ of San Antonio	TX	17,336	C
Pacific Lutheran Univ	WA	23,318	VC
Pacific Union College	CA	20,250	VC
Palm Beach Atlantic College	FL	23,310	C
Paul Quinn College	TX	8,150	LC
Penn State Univ/Univ Park Campus	PA	11,126	VC
Pepperdine Univ	CA	32,830	VC
Pfeiffer Univ	NC	18,580	C
Piedmont College	GA	16,900	C
Pikeville College	KY	12,000	NC
Point Loma Nazarene Univ	CA	21,380	VC
Pomona College	CA	33,960	MC
Pontifical Catholic Univ of PR/Ponce	PR	7,076	
Presbyterian College	SC	23,356	VC
Princeton Univ	NJ	35,072	MC
Principia College	IL	23,865	C+
Purdue Univ/West Lafayette	IN	10,284	VC
Queens College	NC	17,250	C
Radford Univ	VA	8,302	C
Randolph-Macon College	VA	24,395	C
Randolph-Macon Woman's College	VA	25,820	VC+
Reed College	OR	33,350	HC+
Regis Univ	CO	25,740	C+
Rhodes College	TN	26,466	HC+
Rice Univ	TX	24,325	MC
Richard Stockton College of New Jersey	NJ	12,165	VC
Ripon College	WI	24,180	VC+
Roanoke College	VA	24,689	VC
Rockford College	IL	23,930	C
Rocky Mountain College	MT	18,113	C
Rollins College	FL	31,223	HC
Rosemont College	PA	24,060	C
Rutgers, The State Univ of New Jersey New Brunswick Campus	NJ	12,709	C
Sacred Heart Univ	CT	26,588	VC
St. Andrews Presbyterian College	NC	19,720	LC
St. Edward's Univ	TX	17,846	C
St. Francis Univ	PA	24,486	LC
St. John Fisher College	NY	21,800	C
St. Joseph College	CT	25,960	LC
St. Joseph's College	IN	21,640	C
St. Joseph's Univ	PA	29,715	VC+
St. Lawrence Univ	NY	32,605	VC
St. Leo Univ	FL	19,250	LC
St. Martin's College	WA	20,566	C
St. Mary's College	IN	24,474	VC
St. Mary's College of Calif	CA	27,575	C
St. Mary's College of Maryland	MD	14,104	HC
St. Michael's College	VT	26,935	VC
St. Norbert College	WI	23,169	VC
St. Olaf College	MN	25,880	HC
St. Thomas Aquinas College	NY	20,590	LC
St. Thomas Univ	FL	19,500	LC
St. Xavier Univ	IL	21,104	C
Salem College	NC	23,065	VC
Salve Regina Univ	RI	26,460	C
Samford Univ	AL	16,340	VC
San Diego State Univ	CA	9,716	C+
San Jose State Univ	CA	8,187	C

ST = STATE **$IS** = IN-STATE COSTS **SR** = SELECTOR RATING

School	ST	$IS	SR
Santa Clara Univ	CA	28,371	VC+
Sarah Lawrence College	NY	37,516	HC
Schreiner Univ	TX	19,254	C
Scripps College	CA	30,400	HC+
Seattle Pacific Univ	WA	22,674	C+
Seattle Univ	WA	24,183	VC
Seton Hall Univ	NJ	26,910	LC
Seton Hill College	PA	21,875	C
Shaw Univ	NC	12,810	C
Shenandoah Univ	VA	22,550	NC
Shorter College	GA	15,185	C
Siena College	NY	22,685	VC
Siena Heights Univ	MI	16,140	LC
Silver Lake College of the Holy Family	WI	15,516	LC
Simpson College	CA	19,200	C
Simpson College	IA	21,200	C+
Skidmore College	NY	34,201	VC+
Smith College	MA	33,302	HC+
Southeastern College	FL	11,648	LC
Southern Methodist Univ	TX	28,349	VC
Southern Nazarene Univ	OK	14,634	NC
Southern Wesleyan Univ	SC	17,280	C
Southwest Baptist Univ	MO	13,426	LC
Southwest Missouri State Univ	MO	7,600	LC
Southwestern Adventist Univ	TX	14,798	C
Southwestern Univ	TX	22,550	HC
Spalding Univ	KY	15,196	C
Spelman College	GA	19,215	C+
Spring Arbor Univ	MI	17,976	C
Stanford Univ	CA	34,222	MC
SUNY/Univ at Albany	NY	10,007	VC
SUNY/Univ at Stony Brook	NY	10,998	VC
Stetson Univ	FL	25,640	VC
Stillman College	AL	11,370	LC
Stonehill College	MA	26,852	HC
Susquehanna Univ	PA	27,270	VC
Swarthmore College	PA	34,538	MC
Sweet Briar College	VA	25,310	VC
Syracuse Univ	NY	30,710	HC
Tabor College	KS	17,600	LC
Temple Univ	PA	14,124	C
Texas A&M Univ at Commerce	TX	7,326	C
Texas Christian Univ	TX	19,910	C
Texas Wesleyan Univ	TX	14,710	C
Thiel College	PA	18,419	LC
Thomas Edison State College	NJ	2,750	SP
Toccoa Falls College	GA	14,220	C
Towson Univ	MD	11,088	VC
Transylvania Univ	KY	21,780	VC+
Trevecca Nazarene Univ	TN	15,752	C
Trinity College	CT	34,300	HC
Trinity International Univ	IL	20,040	C+
Trinity Univ	TX	21,444	HC
Truman State Univ	MO	8,568	VC+
Tufts Univ	MA	34,874	MC
Tulane Univ	LA	34,013	HC+
Union College	NE	14,650	C
Union Univ	TN	18,930	C+
Universidad Adventista de las Antillas	PR	6,675	
Univ of Alabama	AL	7,402	C
Univ of Arizona	AZ	8,614	C
Univ of Bridgeport	CT	23,020	C
Univ of Calif at Berkeley	CA	14,134	MC
Univ of Calif at Davis	CA	12,796	VC
Univ of Calif at Los Angeles	CA	13,227	MC
Univ of Calif at Riverside	CA	12,479	C
Univ of Calif at San Diego	CA	11,372	HC
Univ of Calif at Santa Barbara	CA	11,732	VC
Univ of Calif at Santa Cruz	CA	13,655	VC
Univ of Central Arkansas	AR	6,388	C
Univ of Charleston	WV	20,640	C
Univ of Chicago	IL	35,087	MC
Univ of Colo at Boulder	CO	9,255	VC
Univ of Dayton	OH	20,400	VC
Univ of Denver	CO	28,783	VC
Univ of Detroit Mercy	MI	21,620	LC
Univ of Dubuque	IA	19,990	C
Univ of Evansville	IN	22,865	VC+
Univ of Findlay	OH	23,962	NC
Univ of Florida	FL	7,874	HC
Univ of Georgia	GA	8,656	VC
Univ of Great Falls	MT	15,360	C
Univ of Hawaii at Manoa	HI	7,862	VC
Univ of Illinois at Urbana-Champaign	IL	11,316	HC+
Univ of Indianapolis	IN	20,840	C
Univ of Iowa	IA	8,607	C+
Univ of La Verne	CA	24,280	C
Univ of Mary Hardin-Baylor	TX	13,929	C
Univ of Miami	FL	31,130	HC
Univ of Mich/Ann Arbor	MI	13,003	HC+
Univ of Missouri/Columbia	MO	9,803	HC
Univ of Mobile	AL	13,620	LC
Univ of N Car at Chapel Hill	NC	8,789	HC
Univ of N Car at Charlotte	NC	7,254	C
Univ of N Car at Greensboro	NC	6,858	C
Univ of N Car at Pembroke	NC	5,914	LC
Univ of N Car at Wilmington	NC	7,769	C
Univ of N Dak	ND	7,067	VC
Univ of Northern Iowa	IA	7,850	C
Univ of Okla	OK	7,616	VC
Univ of Oregon	OR	9,969	C
Univ of Pennsylvania	PA	34,614	MC
Univ of Pittsburgh at Pittsburgh	PA	13,592	HC
Univ of Puget Sound	WA	28,285	HC
Univ of Redlands	CA	29,246	VC
Univ of Richmond	VA	27,300	HC
Univ of Rochester	NY	32,979	HC
Univ of St. Francis	IN	17,790	LC
Univ of San Diego	CA	29,198	HC
Univ of San Francisco	CA	27,302	VC
Univ of Sioux Falls	SD	16,390	C
Univ of S Car at Columbia	SC	8,748	VC
Univ of South Florida	FL	8,154	C
Univ of Southern Calif	CA	33,647	MC
Univ of Tenn at Knoxville	TN	8,214	C
Univ of Texas at Austin	TX	9,437	HC
Univ of the Incarnate Word	TX	18,478	C
Univ of the Ozarks	AR	13,904	C
Univ of the Pacific	CA	28,255	VC
Univ of the South	TN	27,290	HC
Univ of Tulsa	OK	19,090	HC
Univ of Vermont	VT	14,761	C+
Univ of Virginia	VA	9,391	HC+
Univ of Washington	WA	10,361	VC
Univ of West Florida	FL	7,518	C
Univ of Wisc/Eau Claire	WI	7,032	VC
Univ of Wisc/Milwaukee	WI	8,907	LC
Univ of Wisc/Oshkosh	WI	6,130	LC
Ursinus College	PA	31,350	VC
Ursuline College	OH	19,130	LC
Valparaiso Univ	IN	23,570	VC+
Vanderbilt Univ	TN	34,482	MC
Vassar College	NY	33,450	MC
Villanova Univ	PA	31,997	HC
Virginia Commonwealth Univ	VA	9,030	C
Virginia Intermont College	VA	17,510	C
Virginia Union Univ	VA	15,358	LC
Virginia Wesleyan College	VA	22,350	LC
Viterbo Univ	WI	18,043	C
Wabash College	IN	25,335	HC
Wake Forest Univ	NC	30,290	MC
Walla Walla College	WA	20,925	C
Walsh Univ	OH	16,880	C
Wartburg College	IA	21,165	VC
Washburn Univ of Topeka	KS	6,766	NC
Washington and Lee Univ	VA	25,095	MC
Washington State Univ	WA	9,388	C
Washington Univ in St. Louis	MO	34,593	MC
Wayland Baptist Univ	TX	11,271	NC
Webster Univ	MO	19,804	VC
Wellesley College	MA	33,394	MC
Wells College	NY	19,350	VC
Wesleyan College	GA	17,050	VC
Wesleyan Univ	CT	3,405	MC
West Chester Univ of Pennsylvania	PA	9,792	VC
West Virginia Wesleyan College	WV	22,920	C
Western Kentucky Univ	KY	6,834	C
Western Maryland College	MD	26,000	VC
Western Mich Univ	MI	10,016	C
Westminster College	MO	19,990	C+
Westminster College	PA	22,960	C
Westmont College	CA	29,748	VC
Wheaton College	IL	21,934	HC
Wheaton College	MA	32,940	VC
Wheeling Jesuit Univ	WV	22,660	C
Whittier College	CA	29,108	C
Whitworth College	WA	23,938	VC
Wiley College	TX	8,100	LC
Willamette Univ	OR	29,422	VC+
William Carey College	MS	10,150	LC
William Jewell College	MO	17,150	VC
Williams Baptist College	AR	10,750	C
Williams College	MA	32,270	MC
Wilmington College	OH	21,826	C
Wilson College	PA	21,337	LC
Wingate Univ	NC	19,140	C
Winthrop Univ	SC	9,106	C
Wittenberg Univ	OH	28,766	VC
Wofford College	SC	23,995	VC
Wright State Univ	OH	9,141	LC
Yale Univ	CT	34,030	MC
Yeshiva Univ	NY	21,400	C
Youngstown State Univ	OH	9,318	NC

RELIGIOUS EDUCATION

School	ST	$IS	SR
Andrews Univ	MI	17,696	LC
Baylor Univ	TX	18,298	VC+
Campbellsville Univ	KY	14,340	C
Clearwater Christian College	FL	13,160	LC
College of Mount St. Joseph	OH	20,290	C
Concordia Univ	MN	19,912	C
Cornerstone Univ and Grand Rapids Baptist Seminary	MI	18,092	C
Dallas Baptist Univ	TX	13,682	LC
Grace Bible College	MI	12,600	C
Huntingdon College	AL	18,400	VC
Kansas Wesleyan Univ	KS	17,400	C+
La Roche College	PA	18,854	LC
Lee Univ	TN	10,198	LC
Lenoir-Rhyne College	NC	19,186	C
Louisiana College	LA	11,516	C
Loyola Univ New Orleans	LA	23,506	VC+
Marian College	IN	21,020	C
Mercyhurst College	PA	20,694	C
Missouri Baptist College	MO	15,762	LC
Morris College	SC	9,995	LC
Mount Vernon Nazarene College	OH	17,027	C
Muskingum College	OH	18,760	C
North Central Univ	MN	12,744	LC
Nyack College	NY	18,540	C
Oakwood College	AL	14,904	C
Okla Christian Univ	OK	16,500	VC
Oral Roberts Univ	OK	18,490	C
Pfeiffer Univ	NC	18,580	C
Point Loma Nazarene Univ	CA	21,380	VC
Quincy Univ	IL	20,450	C
St. Mary's College	MI	13,314	LC
St. Vincent College	PA	22,942	VC
Seattle Pacific Univ	WA	22,674	C+
Simpson College	CA	19,200	C
Southern Adventist Univ	TN	15,600	C
Southern Nazarene Univ	OK	14,634	NC
Southwest Baptist Univ	MO	13,426	LC
Southwestern Christian College	TX	7,500	NC
Sterling College	KS	16,370	VC
Tenn Wesleyan College	TN	13,030	C
Thiel College	PA	18,419	LC
Toccoa Falls College	GA	14,220	C
Trinity Bible College	ND		
Union College	NE	14,650	C
Vanguard Univ of Southern Calif	CA	20,212	C
Wayland Baptist Univ	TX	11,271	NC
West Virginia Wesleyan College	WV	22,920	C
Williams Baptist College	AR	10,750	C

RELIGIOUS MUSIC

School	ST	$IS	SR
Alderson-Broaddus College	WV	19,640	C
Bartlesville Wesleyan College	OK	14,100	LC
Baylor Univ	TX	18,298	VC+
Belhaven College	MS	16,040	C+
Bethel College	IN	17,650	LC
Campbellsville Univ	KY	14,340	C
Cedarville Univ	OH	17,553	VC
Centenary College of Louisiana	LA	21,600	C+
Charleston Southern Univ	SC	17,122	C
Clearwater Christian College	FL	13,160	LC
College of the Ozarks	MO	2,650	C+
Columbia College	SC	19,050	LC
Concordia College	NY	19,200	VC
Concordia Univ	MN	19,912	C
Concordia Univ at Austin	TX	16,740	LC
Concordia Univ Wisc	WI	16,600	LC
Cumberland College	KY	14,004	C
Drake Univ	IA	22,830	VC
East Texas Baptist Univ	TX	12,349	LC
Eastern Nazarene College	MA	19,433	LC
Evangel Univ	MO	14,050	C
Furman Univ	SC	25,492	HC
Gardner-Webb Univ	NC	17,400	C
Georgetown College	KY	18,400	VC
Georgia College and State Univ	GA	7,344	C
Grace Bible College	MI	12,600	C
Grand Canyon Univ	AZ	30,000	LC
Greenville College	IL	19,226	LC
Grove City College	PA	12,280	MC
Hannibal-LaGrange College	MO	12,530	C
Houston Baptist Univ	TX	15,300	LC
Indiana Wesleyan Univ	IN	17,680	C
Kentucky Christian College	KY	13,472	C
LaGrange College	GA	17,496	C
Lenoir-Rhyne College	NC	19,186	C
Louisiana College	LA	11,516	C
Madonna Univ	MI	11,504	VC
Malone College	OH	19,190	C
Marywood Univ	PA	24,639	C
Milligan College	TN	17,550	C
Miss College	MS	14,574	C
Missouri Baptist College	MO	15,762	LC
North Central Univ	MN	12,744	LC
Northwest College	WA	17,471	C
Northwestern College of Iowa	IA	17,630	C+
Nyack College	NY	18,540	C
Oral Roberts Univ	OK	18,490	C
Palm Beach Atlantic College	FL	23,310	C
Pfeiffer Univ	NC	18,580	C
St. Olaf College	MN	25,880	HC
Samford Univ	AL	16,340	VC
Seton Hill College	PA	21,875	C
Shenandoah Univ	VA	22,550	NC
Shorter College	GA	15,185	C
Southeastern College	FL	11,648	LC
Southwest Baptist Univ	MO	13,426	LC
Susquehanna Univ	PA	27,270	VC
Tenn Wesleyan College	TN	13,030	C
Texas Christian Univ	TX	19,910	C
Toccoa Falls College	GA	14,220	C
Trevecca Nazarene Univ	TN	15,752	C
Union Univ	TN	18,930	C+
Warner Pacific College	OR	20,370	LC
Wartburg College	IA	21,165	VC
Wayland Baptist Univ	TX	11,271	NC
Westminster Choir College of Rider Univ	NJ	25,400	SP
Westminster College	PA	22,960	C
William Carey College	MS	10,150	LC
William Tyndale College	MI	11,150	C
Williams Baptist College	AR	10,750	C

RESPIRATORY THERAPY

School	ST	$IS	SR
Armstrong Atlantic State Univ	GA	7,084	C
Boise State Univ	ID	6,531	LC
Columbia Union College	MD	19,027	C+
Columbus State Univ	GA	7,228	LC
Dakota State Univ	SD	6,950	C
Gannon Univ	PA	18,848	C
Georgia State Univ	GA	7,792	LC
Gwynedd-Mercy College	PA	22,350	C
Indiana Univ of Pennsylvania	PA	9,133	C
Indiana Univ-Purdue Univ Indianapolis	IN	9,473	C
La Roche College	PA	18,854	LC
Midwestern State Univ	TX	6,704	NC
Mountain State Univ	WV	8,180	NC
National-Louis Univ	IL	13,995	NC
Nebr Methodist College of Nursing and Allied Health	NE	11,100	SP
N Dak State Univ	ND	7,004	VC
Point Park College	PA	20,290	C
Quinnipiac Univ	CT	27,370	C
Salisbury Univ	MD	10,576	VC
Shenandoah Univ	VA	22,550	NC
Southwest Missouri State Univ	MO	7,600	LC
Southwest Texas State Univ	TX	8,730	VC
SUNY/Univ at Stony Brook	NY	10,998	VC
Tenn State Univ	TN	7,058	VC
Texas Southern Univ	TX	6,576	NC
Ohio State Univ	OH	10,819	VC
Thiel College	PA	18,419	LC
Thomas Edison State College	NJ	2,750	SP
Univ of Alabama at Birmingham	AL	10,110	C
Univ of Bridgeport	CT	23,020	C
Univ of Central Florida	FL	8,251	VC
Univ of Charleston	WV	20,640	C
Univ of Hartford	CT	28,884	C
Univ of Kansas	KS	7,232	VC
Univ of Mary	ND	12,900	LC
Univ of Missouri/Columbia	MO	9,803	HC
Univ of South Alabama	AL	6,976	LC
Weber State Univ	UT	6,897	NC
Wheeling Jesuit Univ	WV	22,660	C
York College of Pennsylvania	PA	12,550	VC
Youngstown State Univ	OH	9,318	NC

RETAILING

School	ST	$IS	SR
Cal State, Los Angeles	CA	5,050	C
Central Mich Univ	MI	8,355	C
David N. Myers College	OH	9,475	C
Johnson and Wales Univ	RI	21,558	LC
Marymount Univ	VA	21,560	LC
Mount Ida College	MA	25,375	LC
New Jersey City Univ	NJ	9,100	LC
Philadelphia Univ	PA	24,722	C
Purdue Univ/West Lafayette	IN	10,284	VC
Siena Heights Univ	MI	16,140	LC
Southern New Hampshire Univ	NH	23,852	C
Syracuse Univ	NY	30,710	HC
Thomas Edison State College	NJ	2,750	SP
Univ of Arizona	AZ	8,614	C
Univ of Memphis	TN	7,271	C
Univ of Minn/Twin Cities	MN	11,123	VC
Univ of S Car at Columbia	SC	8,748	VC
Univ of Tenn at Knoxville	TN	8,214	C
Univ of Wisc/Madison	WI	8,262	VC
Univ of Wisc/Stout	WI	7,192	C
Youngstown State Univ	OH	9,318	NC

ROMANCE LANGUAGES AND LITERATURE

School	ST	$IS	SR
Albertus Magnus College	CT	22,154	C
Boston College	MA	33,330	MC
Bowdoin College	ME	32,650	MC
Bryn Mawr College	PA	33,580	HC+

School	ST	$IS	SR
Cameron Univ	OK	5,560	NC
Carleton College	MN	30,780	MC
Clark Univ	MA	29,170	HC
Colo College	CO	31,525	HC+
Dartmouth College	NH	34,458	MC
DePauw Univ	IN	28,000	HC
Dowling College	NY	20,281	LC
Haverford College	PA	34,300	MC
Johns Hopkins Univ	MD	35,226	MC
Manhattanville College	NY	28,730	VC
Mount Holyoke College	MA	34,128	HC
New York Univ	NY	35,200	MC
Oberlin College	OH	33,140	HC+
Ohio Univ	OH	11,769	C
Olivet Nazarene Univ	IL	18,444	C
Point Loma Nazarene Univ	CA	21,380	VC
Princeton Univ	NJ	35,072	MC
St. Thomas Aquinas College	NY	20,590	LC
Univ of Chicago	IL	35,087	MC
Univ of Georgia	GA	8,656	VC
Univ of Maine	ME	10,798	C
Univ of Maryland/College Park	MD	11,959	C
Univ of Mich/Ann Arbor	MI	13,003	HC+
Univ of Nevada/Las Vegas	NV	8,281	VC
Univ of Oregon	OR	9,969	C
Univ of Pennsylvania	PA	34,614	MC
Washington and Lee Univ	VA	25,095	MC
Washington Univ in St. Louis	MO	34,593	MC
Wesleyan Univ	CT	3,405	MC
Wheeling Jesuit Univ	WV	22,660	C

RURAL ECONOMICS

School	ST	$IS	SR
Univ of Alaska Fairbanks	AK	8,265	NC
Univ of Idaho	ID	7,026	C

RURAL SOCIOLOGY

School	ST	$IS	SR
Auburn Univ	AL	5,510	C
Cornell Univ	NY	34,614	MC
S Dak State Univ	SD	6,848	C
Univ of Wisc/Madison	WI	8,262	VC

RUSSIAN

School	ST	$IS	SR
Amherst College	MA	34,340	MC
Arizona State Univ-Main	AZ	7,726	C
Bard College	NY	33,912	HC
Bates College	ME	34,100	MC
Baylor Univ	TX	18,298	VC+
Beloit College	WI	27,482	HC
Boston Univ	MA	34,358	MC
Bowdoin College	ME	32,650	MC
Bowling Green State Univ	OH	10,794	C
Brandeis Univ	MA	34,481	MC
Brigham Young Univ	UT	7,840	HC
Bryn Mawr College	PA	33,580	HC+
Bucknell Univ	PA	31,096	HC
Carleton College	MN	30,780	MC
CUNY/Brooklyn College	NY	3,403	LC
CUNY/Herbert H. Lehman College	NY	3,320	LC
CUNY/Hunter College	NY	5,147	C+
CUNY/Queens College	NY	3,403	VC
Claremont McKenna College	CA	32,700	MC
Colgate Univ	NY	33,480	MC
College of the Holy Cross	MA	32,780	MC
Colo College	CO	31,525	HC+
Columbia Univ/Barnard College	NY	33,694	MC
Columbia Univ/Columbia College	NY	35,190	MC
Cornell College	IA	24,980	VC
Cornell Univ	NY	34,614	MC
Dartmouth College	NH	34,458	MC
Dickinson College	PA	32,210	VC+
Drew Univ/College of Liberal Arts	NJ	32,152	VC
Eckerd College	FL	25,500	C+
Ferrum College	VA	15,990	LC
Florida State Univ	FL	7,835	HC
Fordham Univ	NY	30,710	VC
Gallaudet Univ	DC	16,554	SP
George Washington Univ	DC	32,170	HC
Georgetown Univ	DC	34,847	MC
Goucher College	MD	30,650	VC+
Grace College	IN	16,768	C
Grinnell College	IA	28,300	HC+
Gustavus Adolphus College	MN	24,190	VC+
Harvard Univ/Harvard College	MA	34,269	MC
Haverford College	PA	34,300	MC
Hofstra Univ	NY	23,252	C
Howard Univ	DC	15,522	LC
Illinois Wesleyan Univ	IL	26,970	HC
Indiana State Univ	IN	8,461	LC
Indiana Univ Bloomington	IN	10,712	C+
Indiana Univ of Pennsylvania	PA	9,133	C
Iowa State Univ	IA	8,108	VC
Juniata College	PA	26,080	VC
Kent State Univ	OH	11,104	C
Knox College	IL	28,230	HC
La Salle Univ	PA	27,890	C
Lawrence Univ	WI	27,711	HC
Lincoln Univ	PA	11,198	C+
Loyola Univ New Orleans	LA	23,506	VC+
Macalester College	MN	28,814	HC+
Marlboro College	VT	26,410	VC+
Miami Univ	OH	12,885	VC+
Mich State Univ	MI	10,386	VC
Middlebury College	VT	34,300	MC
Mount Holyoke College	MA	34,128	HC
New York Univ	NY	35,200	MC
Northern Illinois Univ	IL	9,545	C
Oakland Univ	MI	9,418	C
Oberlin College	OH	33,140	HC+
Ohio Univ	OH	11,769	C
Okla State Univ	OK	7,650	VC
Penn State Univ/Univ Park Campus	PA	11,126	VC
Pomona College	CA	33,960	MC
Portland State Univ	OR	11,220	C
Purdue Univ/West Lafayette	IN	10,284	VC
Rider Univ	NJ	27,400	C
Rutgers, The State Univ of New Jersey New Brunswick Campus	NJ	12,709	C
St. Louis Univ	MO	26,590	VC+
St. Olaf College	MN	25,880	HC
San Diego State Univ	CA	9,716	C+
San Francisco State Univ	CA	7,139	LC
Sarah Lawrence College	NY	37,516	HC
Seattle Pacific Univ	WA	22,674	C+
Smith College	MA	33,302	HC+
Southern Illinois Univ at Carbondale	IL	8,621	C
Southern Methodist Univ	TX	28,349	VC
SUNY/Univ at Albany	NY	10,997	VC
Swarthmore College	PA	34,538	MC
Syracuse Univ	NY	30,710	HC
Temple Univ	PA	14,124	C
Texas A&M Univ	TX	8,988	VC
Ohio State Univ	OH	10,819	VC
Trinity College	CT	34,300	HC
Trinity Univ	TX	21,444	HC
Truman State Univ	MO	8,568	VC+
Tufts Univ	MA	34,874	MC
Tulane Univ	LA	34,013	HC+
Univ of Akron	OH	10,530	NC
Univ of Alabama	AL	7,402	C
Univ of Arizona	AZ	8,614	C
Univ of Calif at Davis	CA	12,796	VC
Univ of Calif at Irvine	CA	11,756	C
Univ of Calif at Riverside	CA	12,479	C
Univ of Chicago	IL	35,087	MC
Univ of Florida	FL	7,874	HC
Univ of Hawaii at Manoa	HI	7,862	VC
Univ of Illinois at Chicago	IL	10,702	VC
Univ of Iowa	IA	8,607	C+
Univ of Kentucky	KY	7,765	C
Univ of Maryland/Baltimore County	MD	12,190	VC
Univ of Maryland/College Park	MD	11,959	C
Univ of Mass Boston	MA	4,227	C
Univ of Mich/Ann Arbor	MI	13,003	HC+
Univ of Minn/Twin Cities	MN	11,123	VC
Univ of Missouri/Columbia	MO	9,803	HC
Univ of Montana	MT	8,038	C
Univ of Nebr at Lincoln	NE	8,325	C+
Univ of New Hampshire	NH	13,207	C
Univ of N Car at Chapel Hill	NC	8,789	HC
Univ of Notre Dame	IN	30,707	MC
Univ of Okla	OK	7,616	VC
Univ of Oregon	OR	9,969	C
Univ of Pennsylvania	PA	34,614	MC
Univ of Pittsburgh at Pittsburgh	PA	13,592	HC
Univ of Rochester	NY	32,979	HC
Univ of St. Thomas	MN	24,044	VC
Univ of South Alabama	AL	6,976	LC
Univ of South Florida	FL	8,154	C
Univ of Southern Calif	CA	33,647	MC
Univ of Tenn at Knoxville	TN	8,214	C
Univ of Texas at Arlington	TX	7,192	LC
Univ of Texas at Austin	TX	9,437	HC
Univ of the South	TN	27,290	HC
Univ of Utah	UT	7,703	C
Univ of Vermont	VT	14,761	C+
Univ of Wisc/Madison	WI	8,262	VC
Univ of Wisc/Milwaukee	WI	8,907	LC
Univ of Wyoming	WY	7,143	LC
Vanderbilt Univ	TN	34,482	MC
Washington State Univ	WA	9,388	C
Washington Univ in St. Louis	MO	34,593	MC
Wayne State Univ	MI	6,720	C
Wellesley College	MA	33,394	MC
Wesleyan Univ	CT	3,405	MC
West Chester Univ of Pennsylvania	PA	9,792	VC
Wheaton College	MA	32,940	VC
Williams College	MA	32,270	MC
Wittenberg Univ	OH	28,766	VC
Yale Univ	CT	34,030	MC

RUSSIAN AND SLAVIC STUDIES

School	ST	$IS	SR
American Univ	DC	31,544	VC+
Augsburg College	MN	22,978	C
Bard College	NY	33,912	HC
Baylor Univ	TX	18,298	VC+
Boston College	MA	33,330	MC
Boston Univ	MA	34,358	MC
Brown Univ	RI	34,973	MC
Cal State, Fullerton	CA	5,440	LC
Colgate Univ	NY	33,480	MC
College of Wooster	OH	28,350	VC
Columbia Univ/Columbia College	NY	35,190	MC
Concordia College/Moorhead	MN	18,835	C
Conn College	CT	33,585	MC
Cornell Univ	NY	34,614	MC
Dartmouth College	NH	34,458	MC
DePauw Univ	IN	28,000	HC
Dickinson College	PA	32,210	VC+
Emory Univ	GA	33,792	MC
Florida State Univ	FL	7,835	HC
Fordham Univ	NY	30,710	VC
George Mason Univ	VA	9,192	C
Hamilton College	NY	34,150	HC
Harvard Univ/Harvard College	MA	34,269	MC
Hobart and William Smith Colleges	NY	33,195	VC
Indiana Univ Bloomington	IN	10,712	C+
Kent State Univ	OH	11,104	C
Knox College	IL	28,230	HC
Lafayette College	PA	32,655	MC
Lehigh Univ	PA	32,290	MC
Louisiana State Univ and A&M College	LA	8,014	VC
Macalester College	MN	28,814	HC+
Mass Inst of Technology	MA	35,228	MC
Middlebury College	VT	34,300	MC
Muhlenberg College	PA	28,170	HC
Oakland Univ	MI	9,418	C
Principia College	IL	23,865	C+
Randolph-Macon Woman's College	VA	25,820	VC+
Rhodes College	TN	26,466	HC+
Rutgers, The State Univ of New Jersey New Brunswick Campus	NJ	12,709	C
St. Olaf College	MN	25,880	HC
San Diego State Univ	CA	9,716	C+
Sarah Lawrence College	NY	37,516	HC
Simon's Rock College of Bard	MA	32,450	HC
Smith College	MA	33,302	HC+
Southern Methodist Univ	TX	28,349	VC
Southwest Texas State Univ	TX	8,730	VC
SUNY/Univ at Albany	NY	10,997	VC
Stetson Univ	FL	25,640	VC
Syracuse Univ	NY	30,710	HC
Texas Tech Univ	TX	8,825	C
Tufts Univ	MA	34,874	MC
Tulane Univ	LA	34,013	HC+
Union College	NY	32,646	HC
Univ of Alabama at Huntsville	AL	7,916	VC
Univ of Alaska Fairbanks	AK	8,265	NC
Univ of Calif at Los Angeles	CA	13,227	MC
Univ of Calif at San Diego	CA	11,372	HC
Univ of Calif at Santa Cruz	CA	13,655	VC
Univ of Colo at Boulder	CO	9,255	VC
Univ of Denver	CO	28,783	VC
Univ of Houston	TX	8,410	C
Univ of Illinois at Urbana-Champaign	IL	11,316	HC+
Univ of Iowa	IA	8,607	C+
Univ of Maryland/College Park	MD	11,959	C
Univ of Mass Amherst	MA	10,995	VC
Univ of Mich/Ann Arbor	MI	13,003	HC+
Univ of Minn/Twin Cities	MN	11,123	VC
Univ of N Car at Chapel Hill	NC	8,789	HC
Univ of Northern Iowa	IA	7,850	C
Univ of St. Thomas	MN	24,044	VC
Univ of Tenn at Knoxville	TN	8,214	C
Univ of Texas at Austin	TX	9,437	HC
Univ of the South	TN	27,290	HC
Univ of Tulsa	OK	19,090	HC
Univ of Vermont	VT	14,761	C+
Univ of Washington	WA	10,361	VC
Villanova Univ	PA	31,997	HC
Washington and Lee Univ	VA	25,095	MC
Washington Univ in St. Louis	MO	34,593	MC
Wesleyan Univ	CT	3,405	MC
Wheaton College	MA	32,940	VC

RUSSIAN LANGUAGES AND LITERATURE

School	ST	$IS	SR
New College of Florida	FL	8,130	HC+
Ouachita Baptist Univ	AR	16,460	VC
Reed College	OR	33,350	HC+
SUNY/Univ at Stony Brook	NY	10,998	VC
Univ of Calif at Los Angeles	CA	13,227	MC
Univ of Illinois at Urbana-Champaign	IL	11,316	HC+

SAFETY AND SECURITY TECHNOLOGY

School	ST	$IS	SR
Indiana Univ of Pennsylvania	PA	9,133	C
Lewis Univ	IL	20,960	C
Madonna Univ	MI	11,504	VC
Marshall Univ	WV	7,752	LC
St. John's Univ	NY	26,660	C
SUNY/College of Technology at Farmingdale	NY	11,269	C
Univ of Wisc/Whitewater	WI	6,937	C
Youngstown State Univ	OH	9,318	NC

SAFETY MANAGEMENT

School	ST	$IS	SR
Central Missouri State Univ	MO	7,920	C
CUNY/John Jay College of Criminal Justice	NY	3,251	C
College of the Ozarks	MO	2,650	C+
Franklin Univ	OH	6,324	SP
Illinois State Univ	IL	9,235	C
Indiana State Univ	IN	8,461	LC
Keene State College	NH	11,280	C
Rivier College	NH	24,215	C
Southern Christian Univ	AL	8,480	LC

SANSKRIT AND INDIAN STUDIES

School	ST	$IS	SR
Harvard Univ/Harvard College	MA	34,269	MC

SCANDINAVIAN LANGUAGES

School	ST	$IS	SR
Augsburg College	MN	22,978	C
Augustana College	IL	24,117	VC+
Gustavus Adolphus College	MN	24,190	VC+
Pacific Lutheran Univ	WA	23,318	VC
St. Olaf College	MN	25,880	HC
Univ of Calif at Berkeley	CA	14,134	MC
Univ of Calif at Los Angeles	CA	13,227	MC
Univ of Minn/Twin Cities	MN	11,123	VC
Univ of N Dak	ND	7,067	VC
Univ of Texas at Austin	TX	9,437	HC
Univ of Washington	WA	10,361	VC

SCANDINAVIAN STUDIES

School	ST	$IS	SR
Augsburg College	MN	22,978	C
Concordia College/Moorhead	MN	18,835	C
Luther College	IA	23,300	VC+
Pacific Lutheran Univ	WA	23,318	VC
Univ of Mich/Ann Arbor	MI	13,003	HC+
Univ of Wisc/Madison	WI	8,262	VC

SCHOOL PSYCHOLOGY

School	ST	$IS	SR
Eastern Mich Univ	MI	9,855	C
Indiana Univ Bloomington	IN	10,712	C+
Southwestern Okla State Univ	OK	4,801	C

SCIENCE

School	ST	$IS	SR
Alfred Univ	NY	27,212	C+
Alvernia College	PA	20,790	C
Alverno College	WI	16,930	LC
American International College	MA	22,268	LC
Arcadia Univ	PA	26,650	C
Bartlesville Wesleyan College	OK	14,100	LC
Brandeis Univ	MA	34,481	MC
Buena Vista Univ	IA	22,828	C
Caribbean Univ	PR	3,000	
Cheyney Univ of Pennsylvania	PA	9,993	C
Claremont McKenna College	CA	32,700	MC
Clarkson Univ	NY	29,884	VC
Coe College	IA	24,750	VC
Colo Christian Univ	CO	17,714	C
Concordia Univ	MI	20,500	C
Drexel Univ	PA	27,657	VC
East Stroudsburg Univ of Pennsylvania	PA	8,430	LC
Eastern Nazarene College	MA	19,433	LC
Elizabethtown College	PA	26,000	VC
Fairleigh Dickinson Univ/Teaneck Campus	NJ	24,646	C
Ferrum College	VA	15,990	LC
Fordham Univ	NY	30,710	VC
Fort Hays State Univ	KS	6,294	LC
Frostburg State Univ	MD	9,680	C
Gannon Univ	PA	18,848	C
Grace College	IN	16,768	C

School	ST	$IS	SR
Graceland Univ	IA	15,845	C
Grinnell College	IA	20,000	HC+
Hampshire College	MA	33,881	HC+
Hawaii Pacific Univ	HI	17,790	C
Heritage College	WA	6,450	NC
Houghton College	NY	21,810	VC+
Indiana Univ Bloomington	IN	10,712	C+
Indiana Wesleyan Univ	IN	17,680	C
John Brown Univ	AR	15,080	VC
Kentucky Christian College	KY	13,472	C
King's College	PA	24,680	C
Le Moyne College	NY	23,840	C
Lee Univ	TN	10,198	LC
Linfield College	OR	25,840	VC
Loras College	IA	22,994	C+
Lyndon State College	VT	11,313	LC
Madonna Univ	MI	11,504	VC
Malone College	OH	19,190	C
Marygrove College	MI	16,075	C
Marylhurst Univ	OR	15,343	NC
Maryville Univ of St. Louis	MO	18,680	C
Mayville State Univ	ND	6,440	NC
Mich State Univ	MI	10,386	VC
Middle Tenn State Univ	TN	6,994	C
Miss State Univ	MS	7,853	C
Missouri Baptist College	MO	15,762	LC
Montana Tech of The Univ of Montana	MT	7,845	C
National-Louis Univ	IL	13,995	NC
Northwest Missouri State Univ	MO	7,922	LC
Okla City Univ	OK	15,810	C
Oregon State Univ	OR	9,612	VC
Penn State Univ at Erie/ Behrend College	PA	12,326	C
Penn State Univ/Altoona	PA	12,578	C
Penn State Univ/Univ Park Campus	PA	11,126	VC
Philander Smith College	AR	7,380	NC
Pitzer College	CA	33,930	HC
Pomona College	CA	33,960	MC
Portland State Univ	OR	11,220	C
Purdue Univ/West Lafayette	IN	10,284	VC
Rochester College	MI	15,404	C+
Rockford College	IL	23,930	C
Rutgers, The State Univ of New Jersey/ CamdenCampus	NJ	6,484	C
San Francisco State Univ	CA	7,139	LC
Santa Clara Univ	CA	28,371	VC+
Seattle Univ	WA	24,183	VC
Sierra Nevada College-Lake Tahoe	NV	21,060	LC
Simon's Rock College of Bard	MA	32,450	HC
Southern Oregon Univ	OR	9,429	C
SUNY/Empire State College	NY	3,545	SP
Trevecca Nazarene Univ	TN	15,752	C
Troy State Univ/Dothan	AL	3,296	C
Union College	NE	14,650	C
United States Air Force Academy	CO		MC
United States Naval Academy	MD		MC
Univ of Alaska Fairbanks	AK	8,265	NC
Univ of Denver	CO	28,783	VC
Univ of Findlay	OH	23,962	NC
Univ of Great Falls	MT	15,000	C
Univ of Mass Amherst	MA	10,995	VC
Univ of Mich/Dearborn	MI	4,677	VC
Univ of Northern Iowa	IA	7,850	C
Univ of Oregon	OR	9,969	C
Univ of PR/Rio Piedras	PR	5,510	
Univ of St. Francis	IN	17,790	LC
Univ of Texas at El Paso	TX	5,076	LC
Univ of Wisc/Parkside	WI	6,160	LC
Univ of Wisc/Platteville	WI	7,282	C
Univ of Wisc/River Falls	WI	6,356	LC
Univ of Wisc/Stout	WI	7,192	C
Upper Iowa Univ	IA	17,438	C
Urbana Univ	OH	17,004	C
Villanova Univ	PA	31,997	HC
Walsh Univ	OH	16,880	C
Warner Pacific College	OR	20,370	LC
Washburn Univ of Topeka	KS	6,766	NC
Washington State Univ	WA	9,388	C
Wayland Baptist Univ	TX	11,271	NC
West Virginia Univ	WV	8,304	C
Western New Mexico Univ	NM	5,950	LC
Wheeling Jesuit Univ	WV	22,660	C
Wilberforce Univ	OH	14,937	LC
William Woods Univ	MO	19,390	LC
Youngstown State Univ	OH	9,318	NC

SCIENCE AND MANAGEMENT

School	ST	$IS	SR
Claremont McKenna College	CA	32,700	MC
Nova Southeastern Univ	FL	20,104	LC
Pitzer College	CA	33,930	HC
Scripps College	CA	30,400	HC+

SCIENCE EDUCATION

School	ST	$IS	SR
Abilene Christian Univ	TX	16,300	VC
Adams State College	CO	7,468	C
Adelphi Univ	NY	23,320	VC
Alabama A&M Univ	AL	5,100	LC
Albany State Univ	GA	5,764	C+
Alfred Univ	NY	27,212	C+
Alverno College	WI	16,930	LC
American International College	MA	22,268	LC
Anderson Univ	IN	19,430	LC
Andrews Univ	MI	17,696	LC
Appalachian State Univ	NC	6,353	C
Arkansas State Univ	AR	7,480	C
Asbury College	KY	18,540	VC
Ashland Univ	OH	22,182	LC
Auburn Univ	AL	5,510	C
Baldwin-Wallace College	OH	22,010	VC+
Ball State Univ	IN	8,660	C
Bartlesville Wesleyan College	OK	14,100	LC
Barton College	NC	16,834	LC
Baylor Univ	TX	18,298	VC+
Belmont Univ	TN	19,066	VC
Bemidji State Univ	MN	7,957	C
Bennett College	NC	11,200	C
Bethany College	KS	16,602	C+
Bethany College	WV	18,566	C
Bethel College	IN	17,650	LC
Bethel College	MN	22,740	VC
Bethune-Cookman College	FL	15,746	C
Black Hills State Univ	SD	6,652	LC
Bloomsburg Univ of Pennsylvania	PA	9,434	C
Blue Mountain College	MS	9,100	LC
Boston Univ	MA	34,358	MC
Bowie State Univ	MD	9,300	C+
Brewton-Parker College	GA	10,810	LC
Brigham Young Univ/Hawaii	HI	6,890	C
Bryan College	TN	16,400	VC
Buena Vista Univ	IA	22,828	C
Cal State, Long Beach	CA	7,400	LC
Calif Univ of Pennsylvania	PA	10,388	C
Calumet College of St. Joseph	IN	7,500	LC
Canisius College	NY	24,696	C+
Caribbean Univ	PR	3,000	
Carroll College	WI	21,170	C
Carson-Newman College	TN	16,490	C
Catawba College	NC	19,620	C
Cedar Crest College	PA	25,145	C+
Cedarville Univ	OH	17,553	VC
Centenary College of Louisiana	LA	21,600	C+
Central Methodist College	MO	16,460	C
Central Mich Univ	MI	8,355	C
Central Missouri State Univ	MO	7,920	C
Central Univ of Bayamon	PR	3,335	
Central Washington Univ	WA	8,985	LC
Chadron State College	NE	6,211	NC
Charleston Southern Univ	SC	17,122	C
Christopher Newport Univ	VA	8,862	VC
CUNY/Brooklyn College	NY	3,403	LC
CUNY/Herbert H. Lehman College	NY	3,320	LC
CUNY/Hunter College	NY	5,147	C+
Colby-Sawyer College	NH	27,850	LC
College of Mount St. Joseph	OH	20,290	C
College of Notre Dame of Maryland	MD	23,100	LC
College of Our Lady of the Elms	MA	20,644	C
College of St. Rose	NY	19,084	C
Concord College	WV	7,122	C+
Concordia College/ Moorhead	MN	18,835	C
Concordia Univ	MN	19,912	C
Concordia Univ Nebr	NE	17,770	C
Concordia Univ, River Forest	IL	20,000	LC
Conn College	CT	33,585	MC
Converse College	SC	21,990	VC
Cornell College	IA	24,980	VC
Cornerstone Univ and Grand Rapids Baptist Seminary	MI	18,092	C
Cumberland College	KY	14,864	C
Daemen College	NY	20,620	C
Dana College	NE	18,046	C
David Lipscomb Univ	TN	16,158	VC
Defiance College	OH	19,580	LC
Delaware State Univ	DE	8,104	LC
Delta State Univ	MS	5,416	C
Dickinson State Univ	ND	5,495	NC
Doane College	NE	17,600	LC
Dominican College	NY	20,400	LC
Drake Univ	IA	22,830	VC
Duquesne Univ	PA	24,242	C+
East Carolina Univ	NC	7,766	C
East Central Univ	OK	4,578	C
East Texas Baptist Univ	TX	12,349	LC
Eastern Mich Univ	MI	9,855	C
Eastern Nazarene College	MA	19,433	LC
Eastern Washington Univ	WA	7,972	LC
Edgewood College	WI	18,304	C
Edinboro Univ of Pennsylvania	PA	9,328	LC
Elmira College	NY	31,070	VC+

School	ST	$IS	SR
Elon Univ	NC	19,430	VC
Eureka College	IL	22,200	C
Evangel Univ	MO	14,050	C
Fairmont State College	WV	7,010	NC
Florida A&M Univ	FL	6,948	C
Florida Inst of Technology	FL	25,250	VC
Florida International Univ	FL	9,486	VC
Florida Southern College	FL	19,430	C
Florida State Univ	FL	7,835	HC
Freed-Hardeman Univ	TN	14,290	VC
Fresno Pacific Univ	CA	19,740	C
Friends Univ	KS	15,962	LC
George Fox Univ	OR	24,095	VC
Georgia Southwestern State Univ	GA	6,013	C
Gettysburg College	PA	32,070	HC
Glenville State College	WV	6,588	NC
Goshen College	IN	18,950	VC+
Grace College	IN	16,768	C
Grambling State Univ	LA	5,325	NC
Grand Canyon Univ	AZ	30,000	LC
Grand Valley State Univ	MI	10,040	C
Greensboro College	NC	19,080	LC
Greenville College	IL	19,226	LC
Grove City College	PA	12,280	MC
Gustavus Adolphus College	MN	24,190	VC+
Gwynedd-Mercy College	PA	22,350	C
Hamline Univ	MN	23,339	C+
Hardin-Simmons Univ	TX	14,165	C
Hastings College	NE	17,854	C+
Heidelberg College	OH	23,879	C
Heritage College	WA	6,450	NC
Hillsdale College	MI	20,586	VC+
Hofstra Univ	NY	23,252	C
Holy Family College	PA	13,710	LC
Hood College	MD	26,020	VC
Hope College	MI	22,922	C+
Houghton College	NY	21,810	VC+
Houston Baptist Univ	TX	15,300	LC
Humboldt State Univ	CA	8,582	C
Huntington College	IN	15,480	LC
Huron Univ	SD	10,450	C
Illinois College	IL	16,234	C
Immaculata College	PA	22,400	LC
Indiana State Univ	IN	8,461	LC
Indiana Univ of Pennsylvania	PA	9,133	C
Indiana Univ South Bend	IN	3,515	C
Indiana Univ Southeast	IN	3,459	C
Indiana Univ-Purdue Univ Fort Wayne	IN	3,166	LC
Indiana Wesleyan Univ	IN	17,680	C
Inter-American Univ of PR/ San GermEn	PR	6,390	
Iona College	NY	26,556	C
Iowa Wesleyan College	IA	18,840	C
John Brown Univ	AR	15,080	VC
Johnson State College	VT	10,776	C
Judson College	AL	13,790	C
Judson College	IL	18,980	LC
Juniata College	PA	26,080	VC
Keene State College	NH	11,280	C
Kennesaw State Univ	GA	2,306	LC
Kent State Univ	OH	11,104	C
King's College	PA	24,680	C
Knoxville College	TN	6,200	LC
La Roche College	PA	18,854	LC
La Salle Univ	PA	27,890	C
Lamar Univ	TX	6,816	LC
Lander Univ	SC	8,618	LC
Langston Univ	OK	2,308	LC
Le Moyne College	NY	23,840	C
Lenoir-Rhyne College	NC	19,186	C
LeTourneau Univ	TX	19,020	VC
Limestone College	SC	16,900	C
Lincoln Memorial Univ	TN	12,620	LC
Lindenwood Univ	MO	17,250	C
Livingstone College	NC	13,360	LC
Lock Haven Univ of Pennsylvania	PA	9,534	C
LIU/Brooklyn Campus	NY	22,290	C
LIU/C.W. Post Campus	NY	25,380	C
Loras College	IA	22,994	C+
Louisiana College	LA	11,516	C
Lubbock Christian Univ	TX	14,226	LC
Luther College	IA	23,300	VC+
Lyndon State College	VT	11,313	LC
MacMurray College	IL	17,790	LC
Malone College	OH	19,190	C
Manhattan College	NY	25,500	VC
Mansfield Univ	PA	9,648	C
Mars Hill College	NC	18,600	LC
Mary Baldwin College	VA	23,440	C
Marymount College/ Tarrytown	NY	23,850	C
Maryville College	TN	23,210	VC
Marywood Univ	PA	24,639	C
Mayville State Univ	ND	6,440	NC
McNeese State Univ	LA	5,259	LC
Mercyhurst College	PA	20,694	C
Messiah College	PA	23,180	VC
Miami Univ	OH	12,885	VC+
Mich State Univ	MI	10,386	VC
MidAmerica Nazarene Univ	KS	16,960	C
Midland Lutheran College	NE	18,600	C
Miles College	AL	7,870	NC

School	ST	$IS	SR
Millikin Univ	IL	24,415	C+
Minn State Univ, Mankato	MN	7,296	LC
Minot State Univ	ND	5,466	LC
Miss Valley State Univ	MS	6,345	C
Missouri Southern State College	MO	6,666	C
Monmouth Univ	NJ	24,042	C
Montana State Univ-Billings	MT	7,653	NC
Montana State Univ-Northern	MT	8,600	NC
Moorhead State Univ	MN	7,000	LC
Morningside College	IA	19,124	C
Morris College	SC	9,995	LC
Mount Holyoke College	MA	34,128	HC
Mount Mary College	WI	18,024	C
Mount St. Clare College	IA	19,050	LC
Mount Senario College	WI	17,750	C
Mount Vernon Nazarene College	OH	17,027	C
Muskingum College	OH	18,760	C
Nazareth College of Rochester	NY	22,036	VC
New Mexico Highlands Univ	NM	6,256	NC
New York Inst of Technology	NY	21,756	C
New York Univ	NY	35,200	MC
Niagara Univ	NY	22,250	C+
N Car State Univ	NC	8,680	HC
North Georgia College and State Univ	GA	6,322	C+
Northeastern State Univ	OK	4,704	LC
Northern Arizona Univ	AZ	7,398	C
Northern Kentucky Univ	KY	6,052	NC
Northern Mich Univ	MI	9,693	C
Northern State Univ	SD	6,279	LC
Northwest Missouri State Univ	MO	7,922	LC
Northwest Nazarene Univ	ID	18,380	C
Northwestern College of Iowa	IA	17,630	C+
Northwestern Okla State Univ	OK	4,542	NC
Nova Southeastern Univ	FL	20,104	LC
Oakland City Univ	IN	11,286	LC
Oakwood College	AL	14,904	C
Ohio Univ	OH	11,769	C
Ohio Wesleyan Univ	OH	29,670	VC+
Okla Baptist Univ	OK	13,878	VC
Okla Christian Univ	OK	16,500	VC
Okla City Univ	OK	15,810	C
Okla Panhandle State Univ	OK	3,812	NC
Old Dominion Univ	VA	9,386	C
Oral Roberts Univ	OK	18,490	C
Ouachita Baptist Univ	AR	16,460	VC
Palm Beach Atlantic College	FL	23,310	C
Peru State College	NE	6,342	NC
Pfeiffer Univ	NC	18,580	C
Philander Smith College	AR	7,380	NC
Plymouth State College	NH	11,024	LC
Pontifical Catholic Univ of PR/Ponce	PR	7,076	
Providence College	RI	27,620	HC
Purdue Univ/Calumet	IN	6,630	NC
Purdue Univ/West Lafayette	IN	10,284	VC
Quincy Univ	IL	20,450	C
Rhode Island College	RI	8,700	LC
Rider Univ	NJ	27,400	C
Rivier College	NH	24,215	C
Rocky Mountain College	MT	18,113	C
Rowan Univ	NJ	12,365	VC
St. Augustine's College	NC	12,990	C+
St. Cloud State Univ	MN	7,180	C
St. John's Univ	NY	26,660	C
St. Joseph's College	IN	21,640	C
St. Mary-of-the-Woods College	IN	21,320	LC
St. Mary's Univ of Minn	MN	19,975	C
St. Mary's Univ of San Antonio	TX	19,735	C
St. Michael's College	VT	26,935	VC
St. Thomas Aquinas College	NY	20,590	LC
St. Vincent College	PA	22,942	VC
St. Xavier Univ	IL	21,104	C
Salem State College	MA	4,481	LC
Samford Univ	AL	16,340	VC
Seattle Pacific Univ	WA	22,674	C+
Seton Hill College	PA	21,875	C
Shaw Univ	NC	12,810	C
Sheldon Jackson College	AK	14,940	LC
Shepherd College	WV	7,062	LC
Slippery Rock Univ	PA	9,152	LC
Southeast Missouri State Univ	MO	8,367	C+
Southeastern Louisiana Univ	LA	6,047	LC
Southeastern Okla State Univ	OK	4,917	C
Southern Arkansas Univ	AR	5,740	LC
Southern Conn State Univ	CT	10,310	C
Southern Illinois Univ Edwardsville	IL	7,869	LC
Southern Univ at New Orleans	LA	995	NC
Southern Utah Univ	UT	7,254	C

School	ST	$IS	SR
Southwest Missouri State Univ	MO	7,600	LC
Southwest Texas State Univ	TX	8,730	VC
Southwestern College	KS	17,656	C
Southwestern Okla State Univ	OK	4,801	C
Springfield College	MA	24,520	C
SUNY/College at Buffalo	NY	8,025	C
SUNY/College at Fredonia	NY	10,125	C
SUNY/College at Old Westbury	NY	9,818	LC
SUNY/College at Oneonta	NY	9,981	C
SUNY/College at Plattsburgh	NY	9,729	C
SUNY/College at Potsdam	NY	10,519	C
SUNY/College of Environmental Science and Forestry	NY	12,446	VC
SUNY/Univ at Albany	NY	10,997	VC
SUNY/Univ at New Paltz	NY	9,685	VC
Stephen F. Austin State Univ	TX	6,905	C
Syracuse Univ	NY	30,710	HC
Tabor College	KS	17,600	LC
Taylor Univ	IN	21,562	VC+
Temple Univ	PA	14,124	C
Texas A&M Univ at Commerce	TX	7,326	C
Texas Christian Univ	TX	19,910	C
Trevecca Nazarene Univ	TN	15,752	C
Tri-State Univ-Main Campus	IN	21,200	C
Troy State Univ	AL	7,696	C
Troy State Univ/Dothan	AL	3,296	C
Turabo Univ	PR	4,110	
Univ of Akron	OH	10,530	NC
Univ of Arizona	AZ	8,614	C
Univ of Arkansas at Pine Bluff	AR	7,925	C
Univ of Calif at San Diego	CA	11,372	HC
Univ of Central Arkansas	AR	6,388	C
Univ of Central Florida	FL	8,251	VC
Univ of Central Okla	OK	5,205	C
Univ of Charleston	WV	20,640	C
Univ of Cincinnati	OH	12,491	LC
Univ of Conn	CT	12,122	VC
Univ of Delaware	DE	10,824	VC
Univ of Evansville	IN	22,865	VC+
Univ of Georgia	GA	8,656	VC
Univ of Great Falls	MT	15,360	C
Univ of Idaho	ID	7,026	C
Univ of Illinois at Chicago	IL	10,702	VC
Univ of Indianapolis	IN	20,840	C
Univ of Iowa	IA	8,607	C+
Univ of Kentucky	KY	7,765	C
Univ of Louisiana at Lafayette	LA	5,200	C
Univ of Louisiana at Monroe	LA	5,207	NC
Univ of Louisville	KY	7,402	LC
Univ of Maine at Farmington	ME	9,163	C
Univ of Mary	ND	12,900	LC
Univ of Mary Hardin-Baylor	TX	13,929	C
Univ of Maryland/College Park	MD	11,959	C
Univ of Maryland/Eastern Shore	MD	9,258	C
Univ of Mich/Dearborn	MI	4,677	VC
Univ of Mich/Flint	MI	4,323	C
Univ of Minn/Duluth	MN	10,436	C
Univ of Minn/Twin Cities	MN	11,123	VC
Univ of Miss	MS	7,666	C
Univ of Montana	MT	8,038	C
Univ of Montana--Western	MT	6,915	NC
Univ of Nebr at Kearney	NE	7,048	NC
Univ of Nebr at Lincoln	NE	8,325	C+
Univ of New England	ME	24,110	LC
Univ of New Mexico	NM	8,026	C
Univ of New Orleans	LA	10,160	C
Univ of North Alabama	AL	7,016	NC
Univ of N Car at Chapel Hill	NC	8,789	HC
Univ of N Car at Charlotte	NC	7,254	C
Univ of N Car at Greensboro	NC	6,858	C
Univ of N Car at Pembroke	NC	5,914	LC
Univ of N Dak	ND	7,067	VC
Univ of North Florida	FL	8,089	VC
Univ of Northern Colo	CO	8,082	C+
Univ of Northern Iowa	IA	7,850	C
Univ of Notre Dame	IN	30,707	MC
Univ of Okla	OK	7,616	VC
Univ of Pittsburgh at Johnstown	PA	13,044	LC
Univ of Rio Grande	OH	8,728	NC
Univ of St. Francis	IN	17,790	LC
Univ of St. Thomas	MN	24,044	VC
Univ of Scranton	PA	27,964	C+
Univ of Sioux Falls	SD	16,390	C
Univ of South Florida	FL	8,154	C
Univ of Southern Indiana	IN	8,655	LC
Univ of Southern Miss	MS	6,155	LC
Univ of Tenn at Martin	TN	8,268	C
Univ of the Incarnate Word	TX	18,478	C
Univ of Toledo	OH	11,206	NC
Univ of Vermont	VT	14,761	C+
Univ of West Alabama	AL	6,048	C
Univ of Wisc/Eau Claire	WI	7,032	VC
Univ of Wisc/La Crosse	WI	7,250	VC
Univ of Wisc/Oshkosh	WI	6,130	LC
Univ of Wisc/Platteville	WI	7,282	C
Univ of Wisc/Superior	WI	7,051	C+
Univ of Wisc/Whitewater	WI	6,937	C
Utah State Univ	UT	6,771	C
Valley City State Univ	ND		LC
Vanguard Univ of Southern Calif	CA	20,212	C
Wartburg College	IA	21,165	VC
Washington Univ in St. Louis	MO	34,593	MC
Wayne State College	NE	6,255	NC
Wayne State Univ	MI	6,720	C
Weber State Univ	UT	6,897	NC
West Liberty State College	WV	6,056	LC
West Texas A&M Univ	TX	6,538	C
Western Carolina Univ	NC	5,667	C
Western Kentucky Univ	KY	6,834	C
Western Mich Univ	MI	10,016	C
Western New Mexico Univ	NM	5,950	LC
Western State College of Colo	CO	7,585	LC
Western Washington Univ	WA	8,624	VC
Westfield State College	MA	8,394	C
Wheaton College	IL	21,934	HC
Whitworth College	WA	23,938	VC
Widener Univ	PA	26,920	C
William Penn Univ	IA	17,575	C
Wingate Univ	NC	19,140	C
Winona State Univ	MN	8,570	C
Wittenberg Univ	OH	28,766	VC
Wright State Univ	OH	9,141	LC
Xavier Univ	OH	23,880	C
Xavier Univ of Louisiana	LA	17,000	LC
York College of Pennsylvania	PA	12,550	VC
Youngstown State Univ	OH	9,318	NC

SCIENCE TECHNOLOGY

School	ST	$IS	SR
Colby College	ME	34,290	MC
Cornell Univ	NY	34,614	MC
James Madison Univ	VA	9,552	HC
Lehigh Univ	PA	32,290	MC
New Jersey Inst of Technology	NJ	14,690	VC
Olivet Nazarene Univ	IL	18,444	C
Rensselaer Polytechnic Inst	NY	33,863	HC+
St. John Fisher College	NY	21,800	C
Scripps College	CA	30,400	HC+
Wesleyan Univ	CT	3,405	MC

SCULPTURE

School	ST	$IS	SR
Aquinas College	MI	20,052	C+
Arizona State Univ-Main	AZ	7,726	C
Atlanta College of Art	GA	18,600	SP
Bard College	NY	33,912	HC
Birmingham-Southern College	AL	22,960	C
Boston Univ	MA	34,358	MC
Bradley Univ	IL	20,970	VC
Calif College of Arts and Crafts	CA	27,366	SP
Cal State, Fullerton	CA	5,440	LC
Catholic Univ of America	DC	29,332	VC
College For Creative Studies	MI	20,938	SP
College of Visual Arts	MN	12,185	SP
Edinboro Univ of Pennsylvania	PA	9,328	LC
Escuela de Artes Plasticas de PR	PR	1,874	
Indiana Univ-Purdue Univ Indianapolis	IN	9,473	C
Kansas City Art Inst	MO	25,880	SP
Maine College of Art	ME	26,367	SP
Maryland Inst College of Art	MD	27,720	SP
Mass College of Art	MA	13,703	SP
Milwaukee Inst of Art and Design	WI	24,388	SP
Minneapolis College of Art and Design	MN	23,560	SP
Montserrat College of Art	MA	20,335	SP
Moore College of Art and Design	PA	23,125	SP
Northern Mich Univ	MI	9,693	C
Northwest Nazarene Univ	ID	18,380	C
Pacific Northwest College of Art	OR	16,507	SP
Rhode Island School of Design	RI	30,227	SP
Rochester Inst of Technology	NY	26,232	VC+
San Francisco Art Inst	CA	19,300	SP
School of the Art Inst of Chicago	IL	27,800	SP
Shepherd College	WV	7,062	LC
SUNY/College at Buffalo	NY	8,025	C
Syracuse Univ	NY	30,710	HC
Univ of Dallas	TX	22,128	VC+
Univ of Hartford	CT	28,884	C
Univ of Houston	TX	8,410	C
Univ of Illinois at Urbana-Champaign	IL	11,316	HC+
Univ of Kansas	KS	7,232	VC
Univ of Mass Dartmouth	MA	9,852	C
Univ of Miami	FL	31,130	HC
Univ of Mich/Ann Arbor	MI	13,003	HC+
Univ of North Texas	TX	7,629	C
Univ of Oregon	OR	9,969	C
Univ of the Arts	PA	24,230	SP
Univ of Washington	WA	10,361	VC
Washington Univ in St. Louis	MO	34,593	MC

SECONDARY EDUCATION

School	ST	$IS	SR
Abilene Christian Univ	TX	16,300	VC
Adams State College	CO	7,468	C
Adelphi Univ	NY	23,320	VC
Adrian College	MI	19,670	C
Alabama A&M Univ	AL	5,100	LC
Alabama State Univ	AL	6,404	C
Albright College	PA	27,642	C
Alderson-Broaddus College	WV	19,640	C
Alfred Univ	NY	27,212	C+
Alice Lloyd College	KY	1,785	VC
Alma College	MI	22,586	VC
Alvernia College	PA	20,790	C
Alverno College	WI	16,930	LC
American International College	MA	22,268	LC
American Univ	DC	31,544	VC+
Andrews Univ	MI	17,696	LC
Appalachian State Univ	NC	6,353	C
Arcadia Univ	PA	26,650	C
Arizona State Univ-Main	AZ	7,726	C
Arkansas Tech Univ	AR	6,256	C
Armstrong Atlantic State Univ	GA	7,084	C
Asbury College	KY	18,540	VC
Ashland Univ	OH	22,182	LC
Auburn Univ	AL	5,510	C
Auburn Univ Montgomery	AL	5,330	NC
Augsburg College	MN	22,978	C
Augustana College	IL	24,117	VC+
Augustana College	SD	20,760	VC
Averett Univ	VA	17,980	LC
Baker Univ	KS	14,780	C+
Baldwin-Wallace College	OH	22,010	VC+
Ball State Univ	IN	8,660	C
Bartlesville Wesleyan College	OK	14,100	LC
Baylor Univ	TX	18,298	VC+
Bellarmine Univ	KY	20,440	VC
Belmont Abbey College	NC	19,630	LC
Bemidji State Univ	MN	7,957	C
Benedictine College	KS	18,485	LC
Bennett College	NC	11,200	C
Berea College	KY	4,070	VC
Bethany College	KS	16,602	C+
Bethany College	WV	18,566	C
Bethel College	IN	17,650	LC
Bethel College	MN	22,740	VC
Black Hills State Univ	SD	6,652	LC
Blackburn College	IL	13,690	C
Bloomsburg Univ of Pennsylvania	PA	9,434	C
Blue Mountain College	MS	9,100	LC
Bluefield College	VA	14,200	C
Bluffton College	OH	20,644	C
Boise State Univ	ID	6,531	LC
Boston College	MA	33,330	MC
Bowling Green State Univ	OH	10,794	C
Bradley Univ	IL	20,970	VC
Briar Cliff Univ	IA	18,657	LC
Brigham Young Univ	UT	7,840	HC
Bucknell Univ	PA	31,096	HC
Buena Vista Univ	IA	22,828	C
Butler Univ	IN	25,580	VC+
Cal State, Stanislaus	CA	8,895	C
Calif Univ of Pennsylvania	PA	10,388	C
Calumet College of St. Joseph	IN	7,500	LC
Calvin College	MI	20,050	NC
Canisius College	NY	24,696	C+
Capital Univ	OH	23,630	C
Cardinal Stritch Univ	WI	17,620	C
Caribbean Univ	PR	3,000	
Carlow College	PA	19,366	C
Carroll College	MT	19,140	C
Carson-Newman College	TN	16,490	C
Carthage College	WI	23,670	C
Catholic Univ of America	DC	29,332	VC
Cedar Crest College	PA	25,145	C+
Centenary College	NJ	22,430	C
Central College	IA	21,206	C
Central Mich Univ	MI	8,355	C
Central Missouri State Univ	MO	7,920	C
Central State Univ	OH	8,922	C+
Central Univ of Bayamon	PR	3,335	
Central Washington Univ	WA	8,985	LC
Chadron State College	NE	6,211	NC
Chaminade Univ of Honolulu	HI	17,370	C
Cheyney Univ of Pennsylvania	PA	9,993	C
Chicago State Univ	IL	8,851	C+
Christopher Newport Univ	VA	8,862	VC
Citadel, The	SC	9,126	C
CUNY/Brooklyn College	NY	3,403	LC
CUNY/City College	NY	3,309	LC
CUNY/Herbert H. Lehman College	NY	3,320	LC
CUNY/Hunter College	NY	5,147	C+
CUNY/Queens College	NY	3,403	VC
Claflin Univ	SC	12,735	C+
Clarion Univ of Pennsylvania	PA	11,272	LC
Clarke College	IA	20,625	C+
Clearwater Christian College	FL	13,160	LC
Clemson Univ	SC	7,600	C
Cleveland State Univ	OH	10,146	NC
Coastal Carolina Univ	SC	9,220	C
Coe College	IA	24,750	VC
Coker College	SC	20,120	C
College Misericordia	PA	23,380	LC
College of New Rochelle	NY	20,000	C
College of Notre Dame of Maryland	MD	23,100	LC
College of Our Lady of the Elms	MA	20,644	C
College of St. Joseph	VT	17,400	NC
College of the Ozarks	MO	2,650	C+
College of the Southwest	NM	8,456	NC
Columbia College	MO	15,082	C
Columbus State Univ	GA	7,228	LC
Concord College	WV	7,122	C+
Concordia College	NY	19,200	VC
Concordia College/Moorhead	MN	18,835	C
Concordia Univ	MI	20,500	C
Concordia Univ	MN	19,912	C
Concordia Univ	OR	20,500	LC
Concordia Univ at Austin	TX	16,740	LC
Concordia Univ Nebr	NE	17,770	C
Concordia Univ Wisc	WI	16,600	LC
Concordia Univ, River Forest	IL	20,000	LC
Converse College	SC	21,990	VC
Cornell College	IA	24,980	VC
Cornerstone Univ and Grand Rapids Baptist Seminary	MI	18,092	C
Creighton Univ	NE	23,476	VC
Crichton College	TN	12,680	LC
Cumberland Univ	TN	11,970	LC
Dakota State Univ	SD	6,950	C
Dakota Wesleyan Univ	SD	15,512	C
Dana College	NE	18,046	C
Davis and Elkins College	WV	19,270	LC
Defiance College	OH	19,580	LC
Delaware Valley College	PA	24,213	LC
Delta State Univ	MS	5,416	C
DePaul Univ	IL	23,590	VC
Dickinson State Univ	ND	5,495	NC
Dillard Univ	LA	16,046	VC
Dominican College	NY	20,400	LC
Dordt College	IA	18,100	C+
Dowling College	NY	20,281	LC
Drake Univ	IA	22,830	VC
Drury Univ	MO	15,250	VC
Duquesne Univ	PA	24,242	C+
East Central Univ	OK	4,578	C
East Stroudsburg Univ of Pennsylvania	PA	8,430	LC
East Texas Baptist Univ	TX	12,349	LC
Eastern College	PA	19,641	LC
Eastern Illinois Univ	IL	10,101	C
Eastern Kentucky Univ	KY	6,552	C
Eastern Mennonite Univ	VA	20,700	VC
Eastern Mich Univ	MI	9,855	C
Eastern Washington Univ	WA	7,972	LC
Edinboro Univ of Pennsylvania	PA	9,328	LC
Elizabethtown College	PA	26,000	VC
Elmhurst College	IL	21,750	C
Elmira College	NY	31,070	VC+
Elon Univ	NC	19,430	VC
Emmanuel College	MA	23,802	C+
Emporia State Univ	KS	6,198	LC
Eureka College	IL	22,200	C
Evangel Univ	MO	14,050	C
Fairmont State College	WV	7,010	NC
Faulkner Univ	AL	13,000	C
Fayetteville State Univ	NC	5,590	LC
Fitchburg State College	MA	7,836	C
Flagler College	FL	10,550	VC+
Florida Memorial College	FL	6,000	LC
Florida Southern College	FL	19,430	C
Fort Valley State Univ	GA	6,014	LC
Franklin Pierce College	NH	26,125	LC
Freed-Hardeman Univ	TN	14,290	VC
Friends Univ	KS	15,962	LC
Gallaudet Univ	DC	16,554	SP
Gannon Univ	PA	18,848	C
Gardner-Webb Univ	NC	17,400	C
George Fox Univ	OR	24,095	VC
Georgia Southern Univ	GA	6,958	C
Georgia Southwestern State Univ	GA	6,013	C
Gettysburg College	PA	32,070	HC
Glenville State College	WV	6,588	NC

School	ST	$IS	SR
Goshen College	IN	18,950	VC+
Grace Bible College	MI	12,600	C
Grand Canyon Univ	AZ	30,000	LC
Grand Valley State Univ	MI	10,040	C
Grand View College	IA	17,596	NC
Green Mountain College	VT	24,130	C
Greensboro College	NC	19,080	LC
Greenville College	IL	19,226	LC
Grove City College	PA	12,280	MC
Guilford College	NC	23,255	C
Gustavus Adolphus College	MN	24,190	VC+
Gwynedd-Mercy College	PA	22,350	C
Hamline Univ	MN	23,339	C+
Hannibal-LaGrange College	MO	12,530	C
Harding Univ	AR	13,528	VC
Hardin-Simmons Univ	TX	14,165	C
Hastings College	NE	17,854	C+
Heidelberg College	OH	23,879	C
Heritage College	WA	6,450	NC
High Point Univ	NC	20,220	LC
Hillsdale College	MI	20,586	VC+
Hofstra Univ	NY	23,252	C
Holy Family College	PA	13,710	LC
Hood College	MD	26,020	VC
Hope College	MI	22,922	C+
Hope International Univ	CA	16,940	NC
Houghton College	NY	21,810	VC+
Houston Baptist Univ	TX	15,300	LC
Howard Payne Univ	TX	13,834	C+
Howard Univ	DC	15,522	LC
Humboldt State Univ	CA	8,582	C
Huron Univ	SD	10,450	C
Idaho State Univ	ID	7,030	C+
Illinois College	IL	16,234	C
Immaculata College	PA	22,400	LC
Indiana State Univ	IN	8,461	LC
Indiana Univ Bloomington	IN	10,712	C+
Indiana Univ East	IN	3,415	C
Indiana Univ Northwest	IN	3,447	C
Indiana Univ South Bend	IN	3,515	C
Indiana Univ Southeast	IN	3,459	C
Indiana Univ-Purdue Univ Fort Wayne	IN	3,166	LC
Indiana Univ-Purdue Univ Indianapolis	IN	9,473	C
Inter-American Univ of PR/ Aguadilla Campus	PR	3,278	
Inter-American Univ of PR/ Arecibo Campus	PR	3,300	
Inter-American Univ of PR/ Barranquitas Regional College	PR	3,300	LC
Inter-American Univ of PR/ Bayamon Univ College	PR	3,700	
Inter-American Univ of PR/ Fajardo Campus	PR	4,000	
Inter-American Univ of PR/ Metropolitan Campus	PR	4,166	
Inter-American Univ of PR/ Ponce Regional College	PR	3,700	
Inter-American Univ of PR/ San GermÈn	PR	6,390	
Iona College	NY	26,556	C
Iowa State Univ	IA	8,108	VC
Iowa Wesleyan College	IA	18,840	C
Ithaca College	NY	28,719	HC
Jacksonville State Univ	AL	6,568	LC
Jacksonville Univ	FL	21,110	LC
Jarvis Christian College	TX	9,035	NC
John Brown Univ	AR	15,080	VC
John Carroll Univ	OH	24,140	VC
Johnson C. Smith Univ	NC	16,560	C+
Johnson State College	VT	10,776	C
Judson College	AL	13,790	C
Judson College	IL	18,980	LC
Juniata College	PA	26,080	VC
Kansas State Univ	KS	6,995	C
Kansas Wesleyan Univ	KS	17,400	C+
Keene State College	NH	11,280	C
Kent State Univ	OH	11,104	C
Kentucky State Univ	KY	6,146	NC
Kentucky Wesleyan College	KY	15,800	C
Keuka College	NY	21,170	C
King College	TN	17,800	VC
King's College	PA	24,680	C
Knox College	IL	28,230	HC
Kutztown Univ of Pennsylvania	PA	8,907	C
La Salle Univ	PA	27,890	C
La Sierra Univ	CA	19,260	LC
LaGrange College	GA	17,496	C
Lake Superior State Univ	MI	9,034	LC
Lakeland College	WI	17,950	C
Lamar Univ	TX	6,816	LC
Lambuth Univ	TN	14,254	C
Lasell College	MA	24,100	C
Lawrence Univ	WI	27,711	HC
Le Moyne College	NY	23,840	C
Lebanon Valley College of Pennsylvania	PA	25,700	VC
Lenoir-Rhyne College	NC	19,186	C
LeTourneau Univ	TX	19,020	VC
Lewis Univ	IL	20,960	C
Lewis-Clark State College	ID	6,496	C
Lincoln Memorial Univ	TN	12,620	LC
Lincoln Univ	PA	11,198	C+
Lindenwood Univ	MO	17,250	C
Lindsey Wilson College	KY	16,392	LC
Livingstone College	NC	13,360	LC
Lock Haven Univ of Pennsylvania	PA	9,534	C
LIU/Brooklyn Campus	NY	22,290	C
LIU/C.W. Post Campus	NY	25,380	C
Loras College	IA	22,994	C+
Louisiana College	LA	11,516	C
Louisiana State Univ and A&M College	LA	8,014	VC
Louisiana State Univ in Shreveport	LA	2,480	NC
Louisiana Tech Univ	LA	6,506	C
Lubbock Christian Univ	TX	14,226	LC
Luther College	IA	23,300	VC+
Lynn Univ	FL	24,550	C
MacMurray College	IL	17,790	LC
Madonna Univ	MI	11,504	VC
Malone College	OH	19,190	C
Manchester College	IN	22,010	C
Manhattan College	NY	25,500	VC
Mansfield Univ	PA	9,648	C
Marian College of Fond du Lac	WI	17,935	LC
Marquette Univ	WI	24,836	C+
Marymount College/ Tarrytown	NY	23,850	C
Marymount Manhattan College	NY	23,195	VC
Maryville College	TN	23,210	VC
Maryville Univ of St. Louis	MO	18,680	C
Marywood Univ	PA	24,639	C
Master's College	CA	21,500	C+
Mayville State Univ	ND	6,440	NC
McPherson College	KS	17,710	C
Mercer Univ	GA	24,130	VC
Mercyhurst College	PA	20,694	C
Merrimack College	MA	25,725	VC
Methodist College	NC	19,526	C
Miami Univ	OH	12,885	VC+
Mich State Univ	MI	10,386	VC
Midland Lutheran College	NE	18,600	C
Miles College	AL	7,870	NC
Millikin Univ	IL	24,415	C+
Minn State Univ, Mankato	MN	7,296	LC
Miss State Univ	MS	7,853	C
Missouri Southern State College	MO	6,666	C
Missouri Western State College	MO	6,662	NC
Molloy College	NY	13,940	C
Monmouth College	IL	21,550	C
Monmouth Univ	NJ	24,042	C
Montana State Univ-Billings	MT	7,653	NC
Montana State Univ-Bozeman	MT	8,431	C
Montana State Univ-Northern	MT	8,600	NC
Montreat College	NC	17,164	C
Moorhead State Univ	MN	7,000	LC
Moravian College	PA	27,065	VC
Mount Marty College	SD	15,656	LC
Mount Mary College	WI	18,024	C
Mount Olive College	NC	14,410	LC
Mount St. Mary College	NY	18,825	C
Mount St. Mary's College	CA	24,430	C
Mount St. Mary's College	MD	25,740	C
Mount Senario College	WI	17,750	C
Mount Vernon Nazarene College	OH	17,027	C
Murray State Univ	KY	6,672	C
Muskingum College	OH	18,760	C
New England College	NH	20,706	LC
New Jersey City Univ	NJ	9,100	LC
New Mexico State Univ	NM	7,302	C
New York Inst of Technology	NY	21,756	C
New York Univ	NY	35,200	MC
Newman Univ	KS	14,098	LC
Niagara Univ	NY	22,250	C+
Nicholls State Univ	LA	5,290	NC
Norfolk State Univ	VA	8,382	LC
N Car State Univ	NC	8,680	HC
North Central College	IL	22,944	C+
N Dak State Univ	ND	7,004	VC
North Georgia College and State Univ	GA	6,322	C+
North Park Univ	IL	24,030	C
Northeastern Illinois Univ	IL	2,898	NC
Northeastern State Univ	OK	4,704	LC
Northern Arizona Univ	AZ	7,398	C
Northern Kentucky Univ	KY	6,352	NC
Northern Mich Univ	MI	9,693	C
Northern State Univ	SD	6,279	LC
Northland College	WI	21,435	C+
Northwest Missouri State Univ	MO	7,922	LC
Northwestern College of Iowa	IA	17,630	C+
Northwestern Okla State Univ	OK	4,542	NC
Northwestern State Univ of Louisiana	LA	5,745	NC
Northwestern Univ	IL	33,615	MC
Notre Dame College	OH	20,425	C
Nova Southeastern Univ	FL	20,104	LC
Nyack College	NY	18,540	C
Oakland City Univ	IN	11,286	LC
Oglethorpe Univ	GA	19,100	LC
Ohio Univ	OH	11,769	C
Ohio Valley College	WV	13,650	C+
Ohio Wesleyan Univ	OH	29,670	VC+
Okla Baptist Univ	OK	13,878	VC
Okla State Univ	OK	7,650	VC
Old Dominion Univ	VA	9,386	C
Olivet College	MI	17,410	C
Ouachita Baptist Univ	AR	16,460	VC
Our Lady of Holy Cross College	LA	5,140	NC
Pace Univ	NY	24,200	C
Paine College	GA	11,896	LC
Palm Beach Atlantic College	FL	23,310	C
Paul Quinn College	TX	8,150	LC
Penn State Univ/Univ Park Campus	PA	11,126	VC
Pepperdine Univ	CA	32,830	VC
Peru State College	NE	6,342	NC
Pfeiffer Univ	NC	18,580	C
Philander Smith College	AR	7,380	NC
Pikeville College	KY	12,000	NC
Point Park College	PA	20,290	C
Pontifical Catholic Univ of PR/Ponce	PR	7,076	
Presbyterian College	SC	23,356	VC
Prescott College	AZ	13,430	C
Principia College	IL	23,865	C+
Providence College	RI	27,620	HC
Purdue Univ/Calumet	IN	6,630	NC
Purdue Univ/West Lafayette	IN	10,284	VC
Quincy Univ	IL	20,450	C
Rhode Island College	RI	8,700	LC
Rider Univ	NJ	27,400	C
Ripon College	WI	24,180	VC+
Rivier College	NH	24,215	C
Rockhurst Univ	MO	20,090	C
Roger Williams Univ	RI	29,010	C
Roosevelt Univ	IL	20,240	LC
Rosemont College	PA	24,060	C
Rutgers, The State Univ of New Jersey/ CamdenCampus	NJ	6,484	C
St. Ambrose Univ	IA	19,994	C
St. Anselm College	NH	27,405	C
St. Cloud State Univ	MN	7,180	C
St. Edward's Univ	TX	17,846	C
St. Francis College	NY	9,610	C
St. Francis Univ	PA	24,486	LC
St. John's Univ	NY	26,660	C
St. Joseph's College	IN	21,640	C
St. Joseph's College, New York	NY	9,802	C
St. Joseph's Univ	PA	29,715	VC+
St. Leo Univ	FL	19,250	LC
St. Mary-of-the-Woods College	IN	21,320	LC
St. Mary's Univ of San Antonio	TX	19,735	C
St. Michael's College	VT	26,395	VC
St. Paul's College	VA	13,340	C
St. Peter's College	NJ	22,292	LC
St. Thomas Aquinas College	NY	20,590	LC
St. Thomas Univ	FL	19,500	LC
St. Xavier Univ	IL	21,104	C
Salem International Univ	WV	17,263	LC
Salem State College	MA	4,481	LC
Salve Regina Univ	RI	26,460	C
San Francisco State Univ	CA	7,139	LC
Schreiner Univ	TX	19,254	C
Seton Hall Univ	NJ	26,910	LC
Seton Hill College	PA	21,875	C
Shaw Univ	NC	12,810	C
Sheldon Jackson College	AK	14,940	LC
Shepherd College	WV	7,062	LC
Silver Lake College of the Holy Family	WI	15,516	LC
Simmons College	MA	30,418	VC
Simpson College	CA	19,200	C
Slippery Rock Univ	PA	9,152	LC
S Dak State Univ	SD	6,848	C
Southeast Missouri State Univ	MO	8,367	C+
Southeastern College	FL	11,648	LC
Southeastern Okla State Univ	OK	4,917	C
Southern Arkansas Univ	AR	5,740	LC
Southern Conn State Univ	CT	10,310	C
Southern Nazarene Univ	OK	14,634	NC
Southern Univ and A&M College	LA	6,365	C+
Southern Univ at New Orleans	LA	995	NC
Southwest Missouri State Univ	MO	7,600	LC
Southwest Texas State Univ	TX	8,730	VC
Southwestern Adventist Univ	TX	14,798	C
Southwestern Okla State Univ	OK	4,801	C
Spalding Univ	KY	15,196	C
Spring Hill College	AL	23,250	C
Springfield College	MA	24,520	C
SUNY/College at Buffalo	NY	8,025	C
SUNY/College at Cortland	NY	10,564	C
SUNY/College at Fredonia	NY	10,125	C
SUNY/College at Old Westbury	NY	9,818	LC
SUNY/College at Oneonta	NY	9,981	C
SUNY/College at Oswego	NY	10,856	C
SUNY/College at Plattsburgh	NY	9,729	C
SUNY/College at Potsdam	NY	10,519	C
SUNY/Univ at Albany	NY	10,997	VC
SUNY/Univ at New Paltz	NY	9,685	VC
Stephen F. Austin State Univ	TX	6,905	C
Stetson Univ	FL	25,640	VC
Syracuse Univ	NY	30,710	HC
Tabor College	KS	17,600	LC
Temple Univ	PA	14,124	C
Tenn Tech Univ	TN	6,968	C
Texas A&M Univ	TX	8,988	VC
Texas A&M Univ at Commerce	TX	7,326	C
Texas A&M Univ at Kingsville	TX	6,446	LC
Texas Wesleyan Univ	TX	14,710	C
Thiel College	PA	18,419	LC
Thomas More College	KY	17,700	LC
Toccoa Falls College	GA	14,220	C
Trinity International Univ	IL	20,640	C+
Tri-State Univ-Main Campus	IN	21,200	C
Troy State Univ	AL	7,696	C
Troy State Univ/Dothan	AL	3,296	C
Turabo Univ	PR	4,110	
Tuskegee Univ	AL	14,600	LC
Union College	KY	15,920	C
Union College	NE	14,650	C
Union Univ	TN	18,930	C+
Universidad Adventista de las Antillas	PR	6,675	
Universidad Metropolitana	PR	3,324	
Univ of Akron	OH	10,530	NC
Univ of Alabama	AL	7,402	C
Univ of Alabama at Birmingham	AL	10,110	C
Univ of Alaska Anchorage	AK	9,100	NC
Univ of Arizona	AZ	8,614	C
Univ of Central Arkansas	AR	6,388	C
Univ of Cincinnati	OH	12,491	LC
Univ of Dayton	OH	20,400	VC
Univ of Delaware	DE	10,824	VC
Univ of Detroit Mercy	MI	21,620	LC
Univ of Evansville	IN	22,865	VC+
Univ of Findlay	OH	23,962	NC
Univ of Great Falls	MT	15,360	C
Univ of Hartford	CT	28,884	C
Univ of Hawaii at Manoa	HI	7,862	VC
Univ of Houston-Downtown	TX	2,006	NC
Univ of Idaho	ID	7,026	C
Univ of Illinois at Chicago	IL	10,702	VC
Univ of Illinois at Urbana-Champaign	IL	11,316	HC+
Univ of Indianapolis	IN	20,040	C
Univ of Iowa	IA	8,607	C+
Univ of Kansas	KS	7,232	VC
Univ of Kentucky	KY	7,765	C
Univ of Louisiana at Lafayette	LA	5,200	C
Univ of Louisville	KY	7,402	LC
Univ of Maine	ME	10,798	C
Univ of Maine at Farmington	ME	9,163	C
Univ of Maine at Presque Isle	ME	7,964	LC
Univ of Mary Hardin-Baylor	TX	13,929	C
Univ of Maryland/College Park	MD	11,959	C
Univ of Maryland/Eastern Shore	MD	9,258	C
Univ of Mass Amherst	MA	10,995	VC
Univ of Miami	FL	31,130	HC
Univ of Mich/Ann Arbor	MI	13,003	HC+
Univ of Mich/Dearborn	MI	4,677	VC
Univ of Mich/Flint	MI	4,323	C
Univ of Minn/Morris	MN	10,716	VC
Univ of Missouri/Columbia	MO	9,803	HC
Univ of Missouri/Kansas City	MO	9,685	VC
Univ of Missouri/Rolla	MO	10,034	C
Univ of Missouri/St. Louis	MO	9,966	C
Univ of Mobile	AL	13,620	LC
Univ of Montana	MT	8,038	C
Univ of Montana--Western	MT	6,915	NC
Univ of Nebr at Kearney	NE	7,048	NC
Univ of Nebr at Lincoln	NE	8,325	C+
Univ of Nebr at Omaha	NE	6,867	C
Univ of Nevada/Las Vegas	NV	8,281	VC
Univ of Nevada/Reno	NV	8,737	C
Univ of New England	ME	24,110	LC
Univ of New Orleans	LA	10,160	C
Univ of North Alabama	AL	7,016	NC
Univ of N Car at Chapel Hill	NC	8,789	HC
Univ of N Car at Pembroke	NC	5,914	LC

ST = STATE $IS = IN-STATE COSTS SR = SELECTOR RATING

School	ST	$IS	SR
Univ of N Car at Wilmington	NC	7,769	C
Univ of North Florida	FL	8,089	VC
Univ of Pittsburgh at Johnstown	PA	13,044	LC
Univ of Portland	OR	24,950	VC
Univ of PR/Cayey Univ College	PR	1,245	
Univ of PR/Rio Piedras	PR	5,510	
Univ of Rhode Island	RI	12,414	C
Univ of Rio Grande	OH	8,728	NC
Univ of St. Francis	IN	17,790	LC
Univ of St. Thomas	MN	24,044	VC
Univ of San Diego	CA	29,198	HC
Univ of San Francisco	CA	27,302	VC
Univ of Scranton	PA	27,964	C+
Univ of Sioux Falls	SD	16,390	C
Univ of South Alabama	AL	6,976	LC
Univ of S Car at Aiken	SC	7,828	LC
Univ of S Car at Columbia	SC	8,748	VC
Univ of S Car at Spartanburg	SC	7,318	C+
Univ of S Dak	SD	7,036	C
Univ of Southern Indiana	IN	8,655	LC
Univ of Southern Miss	MS	6,155	LC
Univ of Tampa	FL	22,612	C
Univ of Tenn at Chattanooga	TN	7,783	C
Univ of Tenn at Martin	TN	8,268	C
Univ of Texas-Pan American	TX	4,823	C
Univ of the Incarnate Word	TX	18,478	C
Univ of Toledo	OH	11,206	NC
Univ of Vermont	VT	14,761	C+
Univ of West Alabama	AL	6,048	C
Univ of West Florida	FL	7,518	C
Univ of Wisc/Eau Claire	WI	7,032	VC
Univ of Wisc/La Crosse	WI	7,250	VC
Univ of Wisc/Madison	WI	8,262	VC
Univ of Wisc/Oshkosh	WI	6,130	LC
Univ of Wisc/Platteville	WI	7,282	C
Univ of Wisc/River Falls	WI	6,356	LC
Univ of Wisc/Superior	WI	7,051	C+
Univ of Wisc/Whitewater	WI	6,937	C
Univ of Wyoming	WY	7,143	LC
Urbana Univ	OH	17,004	C
Ursinus College	PA	31,350	VC
Ursuline College	OH	19,430	LC
Utah State Univ	UT	6,771	C
Valdosta State Univ	GA	6,988	C
Valley City State Univ	ND		LC
Valparaiso Univ	IN	23,570	VC+
Vanderbilt Univ	TN	34,482	MC
Vanguard Univ of Southern Calif	CA	20,212	C
Villanova Univ	PA	31,997	HC
Virginia Intermont College	VA	17,510	C
Virginia Union Univ	VA	15,358	LC
Wagner College	NY	27,000	C
Walsh Univ	OH	16,880	C
Wartburg College	IA	21,165	VC
Washburn Univ of Topeka	KS	6,766	NC
Washington State Univ	WA	9,388	C
Washington Univ in St. Louis	MO	34,593	MC
Weber State Univ	UT	6,897	NC
Wellesley College	MA	33,394	MC
Wesley College	DE	17,869	C
Wesleyan College	GA	17,050	VC
West Chester Univ of Pennsylvania	PA	9,792	VC
West Liberty State College	WV	6,056	LC
West Virginia State College	WV	6,264	NC
West Virginia Univ	WV	8,304	C
West Virginia Wesleyan College	WV	22,920	C
Western Carolina Univ	NC	5,667	C
Western Conn State Univ	CT	10,074	C
Western Mich Univ	MI	10,016	C
Western New England College	MA	23,882	C
Western New Mexico Univ	NM	5,950	LC
Western State College of Colo	CO	7,585	LC
Western Washington Univ	WA	8,624	VC
Westfield State College	MA	8,394	C
Westminster College	MO	19,990	C+
Westminster College	PA	22,960	C
Westminster College	UT	17,226	C
Wheaton College	IL	21,934	HC
Whitworth College	WA	23,938	VC
Wichita State Univ	KS	6,879	C
Widener Univ	PA	26,920	C
Wiley College	TX	8,100	LC
William Jewell College	MO	17,150	VC
William Penn Univ	IA	17,575	C
Williams Baptist College	AR	10,750	C
Wilmington College	OH	21,826	C
Winona State Univ	MN	8,570	C
Winthrop Univ	SC	9,106	C
Wittenberg Univ	OH	28,766	VC
Wright State Univ	OH	9,141	LC
Xavier Univ of Louisiana	LA	17,000	LC
York College of Pennsylvania	PA	12,550	VC
Youngstown State Univ	OH	9,318	NC

SECRETARIAL STUDIES/ OFFICE MANAGEMENT

School	ST	$IS	SR
Bennett College	NC	11,200	C
Caribbean Univ	PR	3,000	
David N. Myers College	OH	9,475	C
Delta State Univ	MS	5,416	C
Eastern Mich Univ	MI	9,855	C
Inter-American Univ of PR/ Aguadilla Campus	PR	3,278	
Inter-American Univ of PR/ Barranquitas Regional College	PR	3,300	LC
Inter-American Univ of PR/ Bayamon Univ College	PR	3,700	
Inter-American Univ of PR/ Fajardo Campus	PR	4,000	
Inter-American Univ of PR/ Metropolitan Campus	PR	4,166	
Inter-American Univ of PR/ Ponce Regional College	PR	3,700	
Inter-American Univ of PR/ San GermÈn	PR	6,390	
Johnson and Wales Univ	RI	21,558	LC
Southeastern Okla State Univ	OK	4,917	C
Southern Univ at New Orleans	LA	995	NC
Turabo Univ	PR	4,110	
Univ of PR at Humacao	PR	1,245	
Univ of PR/Arecibo	PR	1,095	
Univ of PR/Cayey Univ College	PR	1,245	
Univ of the Sacred Heart	PR	5,375	
Youngstown State Univ	OH	9,318	NC

SLAVIC LANGUAGES

School	ST	$IS	SR
Brown Univ	RI	34,973	MC
Columbia Univ/School of General Studies	NY	35,000	C
Duke Univ	NC	34,396	MC
Northwestern Univ	IL	33,615	MC
Princeton Univ	NJ	35,072	MC
Stanford Univ	CA	34,222	MC
Univ of Calif at Berkeley	CA	14,134	MC
Univ of Calif at Los Angeles	CA	13,227	MC
Univ of Calif at Santa Barbara	CA	11,732	VC
Univ of Kansas	KS	7,232	VC
Univ of N Car at Chapel Hill	NC	8,789	HC
Univ of Texas at Austin	TX	9,437	HC
Univ of Virginia	VA	9,391	HC+
Univ of Washington	WA	10,361	VC
Wayne State Univ	MI	6,720	C

SMALL BUSINESS MANAGEMENT

School	ST	$IS	SR
Adams State College	CO	7,468	C
Cal State, Los Angeles	CA	5,050	C
Cal State, San Bernardino	CA	6,516	C
Concord College	WV	7,122	C+
Ferris State Univ	MI	10,816	C
Florida Atlantic Univ	FL	8,832	C
Florida State Univ	FL	7,835	HC
Hawaii Pacific Univ	HI	17,790	C
Johnson and Wales Univ	RI	21,558	LC
Johnson State College	VT	10,776	C
Lawrence Tech Univ	MI	11,429	C
Mount Ida College	MA	25,375	LC
Northeastern Univ	MA	30,078	VC
Rowan Univ	NJ	12,365	VC
Thomas Edison State College	NJ	2,750	SP
Tusculum College	TN	17,900	LC
Union College	NE	14,650	C
Univ of Colo at Boulder	CO	9,255	VC
Univ of Montana	MT	8,038	C
Univ of North Texas	TX	7,629	C
Univ of Wyoming	WY	7,143	LC
Waynesburg College	PA	17,610	C

SOCIAL FOUNDATIONS

School	ST	$IS	SR
Eastern Mich Univ	MI	9,855	C
Lehigh Univ	PA	32,290	MC
Southern Christian Univ	AL	8,480	LC
Univ of Wisc/Green Bay	WI	7,148	C

SOCIAL PSYCHOLOGY

School	ST	$IS	SR
Bard College	NY	33,912	HC
Florida Atlantic Univ	FL	8,832	C
Our Lady of Holy Cross College	LA	5,140	NC
Park Univ	MO	9,816	C
Wheaton College	MA	32,940	VC

SOCIAL SCIENCE

School	ST	$IS	SR
Abilene Christian Univ	TX	16,300	VC
Adelphi Univ	NY	23,320	VC
Alvernia College	PA	20,790	C
Alverno College	WI	16,930	LC
Anna Maria College	MA	22,800	LC
Arkansas State Univ	AR	7,480	C
Ashland Univ	OH	22,182	LC
Averett Univ	VA	17,980	LC
Azusa Pacific Univ	CA	22,422	VC
Bard College	NY	33,912	HC
Bellevue Univ	NE	4,125	NC
Bemidji State Univ	MN	7,957	C
Benedict College	SC	12,662	LC
Benedictine College	KS	18,485	LC
Benedictine Univ	IL	21,330	C
Bennington College	VT	31,350	VC
Berry College	GA	18,850	C
Bethany College	KS	16,602	C+
Bethel College	IN	17,650	LC
Bethel College	KS	17,355	C+
Biola Univ	CA	21,902	VC
Black Hills State Univ	SD	6,652	LC
Bloomsburg Univ of Pennsylvania	PA	9,434	C
Blue Mountain College	MS	9,100	LC
Bluefield State College	WV	2,178	LC
Boise State Univ	ID	6,531	LC
Bowling Green State Univ	OH	10,794	C
Buena Vista Univ	IA	22,828	C
Calif Baptist Univ	CA	16,736	C
Calif Inst of Technology	CA	27,663	MC
Calif Lutheran Univ	CA	23,500	LC
Calif Polytechnic State Univ	CA	8,747	VC
Calif State Polytechnic Univ, Pomona	CA	8,615	C
Cal State, Chico	CA	8,598	LC
Cal State, Los Angeles	CA	5,050	C
Cal State, Monterey Bay	CA	6,250	LC
Cal State, Sacramento	CA	7,488	C
Cal State, San Bernardino	CA	6,516	C
Cal State, San Marcos	CA	1,736	LC
Cal State, Stanislaus	CA	8,895	C
Calif Univ of Pennsylvania	PA	10,388	C
Calumet College of St. Joseph	IN	7,500	LC
Canisius College	NY	24,696	C+
Cardinal Stritch Univ	WI	17,620	C
Caribbean Univ	PR	3,000	
Carnegie Mellon Univ	PA	32,682	MC
Carroll College	MT	19,140	C
Carson-Newman College	TN	16,490	C
Carthage College	WI	23,670	C
Castleton State College	VT	10,922	LC
Cazenovia College	NY	19,885	LC
Cedarville Univ	OH	17,553	VC
Central Washington Univ	WA	8,985	LC
Chadron State College	NE	6,211	NC
Chaminade Univ of Honolulu	HI	17,370	C
Chapman Univ	CA	30,218	VC
Charleston Southern Univ	SC	17,122	C
Cheyney Univ of Pennsylvania	PA	9,993	C
CUNY/Hunter College	NY	5,147	C+
Claflin Univ	SC	12,735	C+
Clarion Univ of Pennsylvania	PA	11,272	LC
Clarkson Univ	NY	29,884	VC
Cleveland State Univ	OH	10,146	NC
Coker College	SC	20,120	C
Colgate Univ	NY	33,480	MC
College of St. Benedict	MN	23,921	VC
Colo Christian Univ	CO	17,714	C
Concord College	WV	7,122	C+
Concordia Univ Wisc	WI	16,600	LC
Concordia Univ, River Forest	IL	20,000	LC
Coppin State College	MD	9,133	LC
Cumberland Univ	TN	11,970	LC
Dana College	NE	18,046	C
Daniel Webster College	NH	24,870	C
Dartmouth College	NH	34,458	MC
David N. Myers College	OH	9,475	C
Delta State Univ	MS	5,416	C
DePaul Univ	IL	23,590	VC
Dominican College	NY	20,400	LC
Dominican Univ	IL	20,800	C
Dordt College	IA	18,100	C+
Dowling College	NY	20,281	LC
Duquesne Univ	PA	24,242	C+
Eastern Conn State Univ	CT	10,362	C
Eastern Mennonite Univ	VA	20,700	VC
Eastern Mich Univ	MI	9,855	C
Eastern Washington Univ	WA	7,972	LC
Edinboro Univ of Pennsylvania	PA	9,328	LC
Elizabeth City State Univ	NC	5,550	LC
Emory & Henry College	VA	19,462	C
Emporia State Univ	KS	6,198	LC
Eugene Lang College of New School Univ	NY	30,300	C
Eureka College	IL	22,200	C
Evangel Univ	MO	14,050	C
Fayetteville State Univ	NC	5,590	LC
Flagler College	FL	10,550	VC+
Florida A&M Univ	FL	6,948	C
Florida Atlantic Univ	FL	8,832	C
Florida Southern College	FL	19,430	C
Florida State Univ	FL	7,835	HC
Fordham Univ	NY	30,710	VC
Fresno Pacific Univ	CA	19,740	C
Frostburg State Univ	MD	9,680	C
Gannon Univ	PA	18,848	C
Gardner-Webb Univ	NC	17,400	C
Goddard College	VT	21,056	C+
Goucher College	MD	30,650	VC+
Graceland Univ	IA	15,845	C
Grand Canyon Univ	AZ	30,000	LC
Grand Valley State Univ	MI	10,040	C
Gustavus Adolphus College	MN	24,190	VC+
Hamline Univ	MN	23,339	C+
Harding Univ	AR	13,528	VC
Hardin-Simmons Univ	TX	14,165	C
Harvard Univ/Harvard College	MA	34,269	MC
Hastings College	NE	17,854	C+
Hawaii Pacific Univ	HI	17,790	C
Heidelberg College	OH	23,879	C
Hillsdale College	MI	20,586	VC+
Hofstra Univ	NY	23,252	C
Hope International Univ	CA	16,940	NC
Humboldt State Univ	CA	8,582	C
Illinois State Univ	IL	9,235	C
Immaculata College	PA	22,400	LC
Indiana Univ Kokomo	IN	3,422	LC
Indiana Univ of Pennsylvania	PA	9,133	C
Indiana Univ-Purdue Univ Fort Wayne	IN	3,166	LC
Iona College	NY	26,556	C
James Madison Univ	VA	9,552	HC
Johns Hopkins Univ	MD	35,226	MC
Johnson C. Smith Univ	NC	16,560	C+
Juniata College	PA	26,080	VC
Kansas State Univ	KS	6,995	C
Keene State College	NH	11,280	C
Kendall College	IL	19,119	LC
Lake Erie College	OH	21,350	LC
Lake Superior State Univ	MI	9,034	LC
Lamar Univ	TX	6,816	LC
Langston Univ	OK	2,308	LC
Lee Univ	TN	10,198	LC
LeMoyne-Owen College	TN	8,450	NC
Lesley College	MA	25,325	LC
Lewis-Clark State College	ID	6,496	C
Liberty Univ	VA	14,500	C
Lincoln Memorial Univ	TN	12,620	LC
Lindsey Wilson College	KY	16,392	LC
Lock Haven Univ of Pennsylvania	PA	9,534	C
LIU/Brooklyn Campus	NY	22,290	C
LIU/Southampton College	NY	26,270	C
Loyola Univ New Orleans	LA	23,506	VC+
Lyndon State College	VT	11,313	LC
Madonna Univ	MI	11,504	VC
Mansfield Univ	PA	9,648	C
Marlboro College	VT	26,410	VC+
Marygrove College	MI	16,075	C
Marylhurst Univ	OR	15,343	NC
Maryville College	TN	23,210	VC
Marywood Univ	PA	24,639	C
Mayville State Univ	ND	6,440	NC
McKendree College	IL	18,300	C+
MCP Hahnemann Univ	PA	18,510	SP
Medaille College	NY	18,320	C
Mercer Univ	GA	24,130	VC
Mesa State College	CO	8,051	C
Metropolitan State Univ	MN	2,943	SP
Miami Univ	OH	12,885	VC+
Mich State Univ	MI	10,386	VC
Mich Tech Univ	MI	11,088	VC
Midland Lutheran College	NE	18,600	C
Millikin Univ	IL	24,415	C+
Minot State Univ	ND	5,466	LC
Miss Univ for Women	MS	5,446	LC
Missouri Baptist College	MO	15,762	LC
Missouri Southern State College	MO	6,666	C
Montana State Univ-Northern	MT	8,600	NC
Moorhead State Univ	MN	7,000	LC
Moravian College	PA	27,065	VC
Morehead State Univ	KY	6,510	C
Morris Brown College	GA	15,993	LC
Mount Marty College	SD	15,656	LC
Mount St. Clare College	IA	19,050	LC
Mount St. Mary College	NY	18,825	C
Mount St. Mary's College	CA	24,430	C
Mount Senario College	WI	17,750	C
Mount Union College	OH	21,120	C
Muhlenberg College	PA	28,170	HC
Muskingum College	OH	18,760	C
National-Louis Univ	IL	13,995	NC
Nazareth College of Rochester	NY	22,036	VC
New College of Calif	CA	8,900	NC
New College of Florida	FL	8,130	HC+
Niagara Univ	NY	22,250	C+
N Car State Univ	NC	8,680	HC
North Central College	IL	22,944	C+
N Dak State Univ	ND	7,004	VC
North Georgia College and State Univ	GA	6,322	C+
Northeastern State Univ	OK	4,704	LC
Northern Kentucky Univ	KY	6,352	NC

School	ST	$IS	SR
Northern State Univ	SD	6,279	LC
Northwest Missouri State Univ	MO	7,922	LC
Northwestern College	MN	19,816	C+
Northwestern Okla State Univ	OK	4,542	NC
Northwestern State Univ of Louisiana	LA	5,745	NC
Notre Dame de Namur Univ	CA	26,932	LC
Nyack College	NY	18,540	C
Ohio Wesleyan Univ	OH	29,670	VC+
Okla Baptist Univ	OK	13,878	VC
Olivet Nazarene Univ	IL	18,444	C
Our Lady of Holy Cross College	LA	5,140	NC
Pace Univ	NY	24,200	C
Palm Beach Atlantic College	FL	23,310	C
Pepperdine Univ	CA	32,830	VC
Peru State College	NE	6,342	NC
Pikeville College	KY	12,000	NC
Pittsburg State Univ	KS	6,228	NC
Point Loma Nazarene Univ	CA	21,380	VC
Polytechnic Univ/Brooklyn	NY	33,090	HC
Pontifical Catholic Univ of PR/Ponce	PR	7,076	
Providence College	RI	27,620	HC
Quinnipiac Univ	CT	27,370	C
Radford Univ	VA	8,302	C
Ramapo College of New Jersey	NJ	13,550	VC
Rhode Island College	RI	8,700	LC
Rice Univ	TX	24,325	MC
Robert Morris Univ	PA	18,730	C
Rockford College	IL	23,930	C
Roger Williams Univ	RI	29,010	C
Roosevelt Univ	IL	20,240	LC
Rosemont College	PA	24,060	C
St. Bonaventure Univ	NY	21,956	C
St. Cloud State Univ	MN	7,180	C
St. John's Univ	MN	23,640	VC
St. John's Univ	NY	26,660	C
St. Joseph College	CT	25,960	LC
St. Joseph's College, New York	NY	9,802	C
St. Louis Univ	MO	26,590	VC+
St. Mary-of-the-Woods College	IN	21,320	LC
St. Mary's College	MI	13,314	LC
St. Mary's Univ of Minn	MN	19,975	C
St. Paul's College	VA	13,340	C
St. Peter's College	NJ	22,292	LC
St. Thomas Aquinas College	NY	20,590	LC
St. Xavier Univ	IL	21,104	C
Samford Univ	AL	16,340	VC
San Diego State Univ	CA	9,716	C+
San Jose State Univ	CA	8,187	C
Seton Hall Univ	NJ	26,910	LC
Shawnee State Univ	OH	8,634	NC
Shimer College	IL	17,560	LC
Shorter College	GA	15,185	C
Siena Heights Univ	MI	16,140	LC
Silver Lake College of the Holy Family	WI	15,516	LC
Simpson College	CA	19,200	C
Skidmore College	NY	34,201	VC+
Slippery Rock Univ	PA	9,152	LC
Southeastern Okla State Univ	OK	4,917	C
Southern Illinois Univ at Carbondale	IL	8,621	C
Southern Methodist Univ	TX	28,349	VC
Southern Nazarene Univ	OK	14,634	NC
Southern New Hampshire Univ	NH	23,852	C
Southern Oregon Univ	OR	9,429	C
Southern Wesleyan Univ	SC	17,280	C
Southwest Missouri State Univ	MO	7,600	LC
Southwest Texas State Univ	TX	8,730	VC
Southwestern Adventist Univ	TX	14,798	C
Spring Arbor Univ	MI	17,976	C
SUNY/Univ at Buffalo	NY	11,033	VC
SUNY/Univ at New Paltz	NY	9,685	VC
SUNY/Univ at Stony Brook	NY	10,998	VC
Stephens College	MO	22,295	C
Stetson Univ	FL	25,640	VC
Suffolk Univ	MA	26,516	C
Sul Ross State Univ	TX	6,582	LC
Syracuse Univ	NY	30,710	HC
Tabor College	KS	17,600	LC
Temple Univ	PA	14,124	C
Texas Wesleyan Univ	TX	14,710	C
Thomas Edison State College	NJ	2,750	SP
Thomas Univ	GA	8,770	NC
Touro College	NY	14,950	VC
Towson Univ	MD	11,088	VC
Trevecca Nazarene Univ	TN	15,752	C
Trinity International Univ	IL	20,640	C+
Tri-State Univ-Main Campus	IN	21,200	C
Troy State Univ	AL	7,696	C
Troy State Univ/Dothan	AL	3,296	C
Troy State Univ/Montgomery	AL	3,080	NC
Turabo Univ	PR	4,110	
Union College	NE	14,650	C
United States Air Force Academy	CO		MC
Universidad Metropolitana	PR	3,324	
Univ of Akron	OH	10,530	NC
Univ of Alaska Southeast	AK	7,900	LC
Univ of Arizona	AZ	8,614	C
Univ of Bridgeport	CT	23,020	C
Univ of Calif at Berkeley	CA	14,134	MC
Univ of Calif at Davis	CA	12,796	VC
Univ of Calif at Irvine	CA	11,756	C
Univ of Calif at Riverside	CA	12,479	C
Univ of Central Florida	FL	8,251	VC
Univ of Chicago	IL	35,087	MC
Univ of Cincinnati	OH	12,491	LC
Univ of Denver	CO	28,783	VC
Univ of Georgia	GA	8,656	VC
Univ of Great Falls	MT	15,360	C
Univ of Houston	TX	8,410	C
Univ of Houston-Downtown	TX	2,006	NC
Univ of Indianapolis	IN	20,840	C
Univ of Iowa	IA	8,607	C+
Univ of La Verne	CA	24,280	C
Univ of Maine at Augusta	ME	3,928	C
Univ of Maine at Fort Kent	ME	7,450	LC
Univ of Mary	ND	12,900	LC
Univ of Mary Hardin-Baylor	TX	13,929	C
Univ of Maryland/Univ College	MD	5,910	SP
Univ of Miami	FL	31,130	HC
Univ of Mich/Ann Arbor	MI	13,003	HC+
Univ of Mich/Dearborn	MI	4,677	VC
Univ of Mich/Flint	MI	4,323	C
Univ of Minn/Morris	MN	10,716	VC
Univ of Missouri/Columbia	MO	9,803	HC
Univ of Montana--Western	MT	6,915	NC
Univ of Montevallo	AL	7,266	C
Univ of Nebr at Kearney	NE	7,048	NC
Univ of Nevada/Las Vegas	NV	8,281	VC
Univ of N Car at Greensboro	NC	6,858	C
Univ of N Dak	ND	7,067	VC
Univ of North Texas	TX	7,629	C
Univ of Northern Colo	CO	8,082	C+
Univ of Northern Iowa	IA	7,850	C
Univ of Pittsburgh at Bradford	PA	12,696	C
Univ of Pittsburgh at Greensburg	PA	12,842	C
Univ of Pittsburgh at Johnstown	PA	13,044	LC
Univ of Pittsburgh at Pittsburgh	PA	13,592	HC
Univ of PR/Mayaguez	PR	5,285	
Univ of PR/Rio Piedras	PR	5,510	
Univ of St. Thomas	MN	24,044	VC
Univ of South Florida	FL	8,154	C
Univ of Southern Calif	CA	33,647	MC
Univ of Southern Colo	CO	7,821	LC
Univ of Southern Miss	MS	6,155	LC
Univ of Tampa	FL	22,612	C
Univ of the Ozarks	AR	13,904	C
Univ of the Pacific	CA	20,255	VC
Univ of the South	TN	27,290	HC
Univ of Utah	UT	7,703	C
Univ of Virginia's College at Wise	VA	8,302	C
Univ of West Alabama	AL	6,048	C
Univ of West Florida	FL	7,518	C
Univ of Wisc/Eau Claire	WI	7,032	VC
Univ of Wisc/Platteville	WI	7,282	C
Univ of Wisc/Stevens Point	WI	7,116	C
Univ of Wyoming	WY	7,143	LC
Upper Iowa Univ	IA	17,438	C
Valley City State Univ	ND		LC
Virginia Wesleyan College	VA	22,350	LC
Warner Pacific College	OR	20,370	LC
Washington State Univ	WA	9,388	C
Washington Univ in St. Louis	MO	34,593	MC
Wayland Baptist Univ	TX	11,271	NC
Wayne State College	NE	6,255	NC
Waynesburg College	PA	17,610	LC
Webster Univ	MO	19,804	VC
Wesleyan College	GA	17,050	VC
West Liberty State College	WV	6,056	LC
West Texas A&M Univ	TX	6,538	C
West Virginia Wesleyan College	WV	22,920	C
Western Baptist College	OR	19,700	C+
Western Carolina Univ	NC	5,667	C
Western Conn State Univ	CT	10,074	C
Western Mich Univ	MI	10,016	C
Western New Mexico Univ	NM	5,950	LC
Western Oregon Univ	OR	8,829	C
Westminster College	PA	22,960	C
Westminster College	UT	17,226	C
Westmont College	CA	29,748	VC
Wheaton College	IL	21,934	HC
Widener Univ	PA	26,920	C
Wilberforce Univ	OH	14,937	LC
Wiley College	TX	8,100	LC
William Carey College	MS	10,150	LC
William Tyndale College	MI	11,150	C
Wilmington College	OH	21,826	C
Winona State Univ	MN	8,570	C
Wisc Lutheran College	WI	19,216	VC
Worcester Polytechnic Inst	MA	34,480	HC+
Youngstown State Univ	OH	9,318	NC

SOCIAL SCIENCE EDUCATION

School	ST	$IS	SR
Appalachian State Univ	NC	6,353	C
Armstrong Atlantic State Univ	GA	7,084	C
Auburn Univ	AL	5,510	C
Baylor Univ	TX	18,298	VC+
Bethune-Cookman College	FL	15,746	C
Blackburn College	IL	13,690	C
Blue Mountain College	MS	9,100	LC
Brigham Young Univ/Hawaii	HI	6,890	C
Calumet College of St. Joseph	IN	7,500	LC
Central Methodist College	MO	16,460	C
College of St. Scholastica	MN	22,378	C+
Dana College	NE	18,046	C
Delta State Univ	MS	5,416	C
Doane College	NE	17,600	LC
Eastern Illinois Univ	IL	10,101	C
Eastern Mich Univ	MI	9,855	C
Eastern Nazarene College	MA	19,433	LC
Eastern Washington Univ	WA	7,972	LC
Elon Univ	NC	19,430	VC
Fayetteville State Univ	NC	5,590	LC
Florida State Univ	FL	7,835	HC
Fresno Pacific Univ	CA	19,740	C
Friends Univ	KS	15,962	LC
Georgia Southwestern State Univ	GA	6,013	C
Hope International Univ	CA	16,940	NC
Humboldt State Univ	CA	8,582	C
Indiana Univ of Pennsylvania	PA	9,133	C
Jackson State Univ	MS	6,776	LC
Lincoln Univ	MO	7,158	NC
Mercyhurst College	PA	20,694	C
Miles College	AL	7,870	NC
Miss Valley State Univ	MS	6,345	C
Missouri Southern State College	MO	6,666	C
Montana State Univ-Billings	MT	7,653	NC
Montana State Univ-Northern	MT	8,600	NC
Mount Holyoke College	MA	34,128	HC
N Car Agricultural and Technical State Univ	NC	6,659	LC
North Georgia College and State Univ	GA	6,322	C+
Northwest Nazarene Univ	ID	18,380	C
Oakwood College	AL	14,904	C
Palm Beach Atlantic College	FL	23,310	C
Plymouth State College	NH	11,024	LC
Rocky Mountain College	MT	18,113	C
St. John's Univ	NY	26,660	C
St. Mary's Univ of Minn	MN	19,975	C
Seattle Pacific Univ	WA	22,674	C+
Seton Hill College	PA	21,875	C
Sheldon Jackson College	AK	14,940	LC
Southern Utah Univ	UT	7,254	C
Southwest Baptist Univ	MO	13,426	LC
Southwestern Okla State Univ	OK	4,801	C
SUNY/College at Oneonta	NY	9,981	C
Stetson Univ	FL	25,640	VC
Tri-State Univ-Main Campus	IN	21,200	C
Troy State Univ	AL	7,696	C
Troy State Univ/Dothan	AL	3,296	C
Turabo Univ	PR	4,110	
Union College	NE	14,650	C
Univ of Arkansas at Pine Bluff	AR	7,925	C
Univ of Central Florida	FL	8,251	VC
Univ of Georgia	GA	8,656	VC
Univ of Maine at Farmington	ME	9,163	C
Univ of Mary	ND	12,900	LC
Univ of Maryland/Eastern Shore	MD	9,258	C
Univ of Miss	MS	7,666	C
Univ of North Alabama	AL	7,016	NC
Univ of Pittsburgh at Johnstown	PA	13,044	LC
Univ of Rio Grande	OH	8,728	NC
Univ of Southern Calif	CA	33,647	MC
Univ of Utah	UT	7,703	C
Univ of Wisc/Milwaukee	WI	8,907	LC
Univ of Wisc/Oshkosh	WI	6,130	LC
Valley City State Univ	ND		LC
Washington Univ in St. Louis	MO	34,593	MC
Weber State Univ	UT	6,897	NC
Western Carolina Univ	NC	5,667	C
Westmont College	CA	29,748	VC
Wiley College	TX	8,100	LC
Youngstown State Univ	OH	9,318	NC

SOCIAL STUDIES

School	ST	$IS	SR
Alverno College	WI	16,930	LC
Andrews Univ	MI	17,696	LC
Bartlesville Wesleyan College	OK	14,100	LC
Barton College	NC	16,834	LC
Bluefield College	VA	14,200	C
Brescia Univ	KY	14,225	C
Caldwell College	NJ	20,940	LC
Carlow College	PA	19,366	C
Christian Brothers Univ	TN	19,820	VC
Cleveland State Univ	OH	10,146	NC
College of St. Catherine	MN	22,324	VC
Concordia Univ	MI	20,500	C
DePaul Univ	IL	23,590	VC
East Stroudsburg Univ of Pennsylvania	PA	8,430	LC
Eastern Nazarene College	MA	19,433	LC
Eastern New Mexico Univ	NM	4,113	LC
Elizabethtown College	PA	26,000	VC
Erskine College	SC	21,399	VC
Ferrum College	VA	15,990	LC
Grand Canyon Univ	AZ	30,000	LC
Harvard Univ/Harvard College	MA	34,269	MC
Hiram College	OH	27,034	VC
Indiana Univ Bloomington	IN	10,712	C+
Indiana Wesleyan Univ	IN	17,680	C
Ithaca College	NY	28,719	HC
John Brown Univ	AR	15,080	VC
Methodist College	NC	19,526	C
Minn State Univ, Mankato	MN	7,296	LC
Miss College	MS	14,574	C
Missouri Southern State College	MO	6,666	C
Mount St. Mary's College	MD	25,740	C
New York Inst of Technology	NY	21,756	C
Northern Mich Univ	MI	9,693	C
Ohio Northern Univ	OH	27,765	VC
Ohio Univ	OH	11,769	C
Okla Panhandle State Univ	OK	3,812	NC
Olivet College	MI	17,410	C
Our Lady of the Lake Univ of San Antonio	TX	17,336	C
Pacific Union College	CA	20,250	VC
Pfeiffer Univ	NC	18,580	C
St. Francis College	NY	9,610	C
St. Joseph's Univ	PA	29,715	VC+
Shippensburg Univ of Pennsylvania	PA	9,652	C
S Car State Univ	SC	6,586	LC
Southwestern Adventist Univ	TX	14,798	C
Spalding Univ	KY	15,196	C
Univ of Arizona	AZ	8,614	C
Univ of St. Thomas	MN	24,044	VC
Univ of Wisc/River Falls	WI	6,356	LC
Univ of Wisc/Superior	WI	7,051	C+
Utica College of Syracuse Univ	NY	24,400	LC
Vassar College	NY	33,450	MC
Virginia Wesleyan College	VA	22,350	LC
Viterbo Univ	WI	18,043	C
Washington State Univ	WA	0,000	O
Wayland Baptist Univ	TX	11,271	NC
Western Kentucky Univ	KY	6,834	C
Wisc Lutheran College	WI	19,216	VC
Youngstown State Univ	OH	9,318	NC

SOCIAL STUDIES EDUCATION

School	ST	$IS	SR
Adams State College	CO	7,468	C
Adelphi Univ	NY	23,320	VC
Alabama State Univ	AL	6,404	C
Alfred Univ	NY	27,212	C+
Alice Lloyd College	KY	1,785	VC
Anderson Univ	IN	19,430	LC
Andrews Univ	MI	17,696	LC
Asbury College	KY	18,540	VC
Augustana College	SD	20,760	VC
Baldwin-Wallace College	OH	22,010	VC+
Ball State Univ	IN	8,660	C
Bartlesville Wesleyan College	OK	14,100	LC
Baylor Univ	TX	18,298	VC+
Bethel College	IN	17,650	LC
Bloomsburg Univ of Pennsylvania	PA	9,434	C
Boston Univ	MA	34,358	MC
Calif Univ of Pennsylvania	PA	10,388	C
Canisius College	NY	24,696	C+
Cedarville Univ	OH	17,553	VC
Centenary College of Louisiana	LA	21,600	C+
Central Missouri State Univ	MO	7,920	C
CUNY/Brooklyn College	NY	3,403	LC
Clearwater Christian College	FL	13,160	LC
Coastal Carolina Univ	SC	9,220	C
Colby-Sawyer College	NH	27,850	LC
College of St. Rose	NY	19,084	C
College of the Ozarks	MO	2,650	C+

ST = STATE $IS = IN-STATE COSTS SR = SELECTOR RATING

School	ST	$IS	SR
Concordia College/Moorhead	MN	18,835	C
Concordia Univ	MN	19,912	C
Cumberland College	KY	14,864	C
Daemen College	NY	20,620	C
Dana College	NE	18,046	C
Defiance College	OH	19,580	LC
Delta State Univ	MS	5,416	C
Drake Univ	IA	22,830	VC
Duquesne Univ	PA	24,242	C+
East Texas Baptist Univ	TX	12,349	LC
Edgewood College	WI	18,304	C
Edinboro Univ of Pennsylvania	PA	9,328	LC
Florida International Univ	FL	9,486	VC
George Fox Univ	OR	24,095	VC
Green Mountain College	VT	24,130	C
Greensboro College	NC	19,080	LC
Greenville College	IL	19,226	LC
Gwynedd-Mercy College	PA	22,350	C
Heritage College	WA	6,450	NC
Huntington College	IN	15,480	LC
Indiana State Univ	IN	8,461	LC
Indiana Univ South Bend	IN	3,515	C
Indiana Univ Southeast	IN	3,459	C
Indiana Univ-Purdue Univ Indianapolis	IN	9,473	C
Indiana Wesleyan Univ	IN	17,680	C
Ithaca College	NY	28,719	HC
Johnson C. Smith Univ	NC	16,560	C+
Judson College	AL	13,790	C
Juniata College	PA	26,080	VC
Kennesaw State Univ	GA	2,306	LC
Kent State Univ	OH	11,104	C
Kentucky State Univ	KY	6,146	NC
La Salle Univ	PA	27,890	C
Le Moyne College	NY	23,840	C
Limestone College	SC	16,900	C
Louisiana College	LA	11,516	C
Malone College	OH	19,190	C
Mansfield Univ	PA	9,648	C
Mars Hill College	NC	18,600	LC
Mary Baldwin College	VA	23,440	C
Marygrove College	MI	16,075	C
Messiah College	PA	23,180	VC
MidAmerica Nazarene Univ	KS	16,960	C
Millersville Univ of Pennsylvania	PA	10,153	VC
Missouri Southern State College	MO	6,666	C
Missouri Valley College	MO	17,400	LC
Montana State Univ-Billings	MT	7,653	NC
Montreat College	NC	17,164	C
Moorhead State Univ	MN	7,000	LC
Morningside College	IA	19,124	C
Morris College	SC	9,995	LC
Mount Vernon Nazarene College	OH	17,027	C
Nazareth College of Rochester	NY	22,036	VC
New York Univ	NY	35,200	MC
Niagara Univ	NY	22,250	C+
N Car State Univ	NC	8,680	HC
Northwestern College	MN	19,816	C+
Notre Dame de Namur Univ	CA	26,932	LC
Okla Christian Univ	OK	16,500	VC
Okla Panhandle State Univ	OK	3,812	NC
Old Dominion Univ	VA	9,386	C
Oral Roberts Univ	OK	18,490	C
Pontifical Catholic Univ of PR/Ponce	PR	7,076	
Providence College	RI	27,620	HC
Purdue Univ/West Lafayette	IN	10,284	VC
Rider Univ	NJ	27,400	C
Rivier College	NH	24,215	C
Rocky Mountain College	MT	18,113	C
St. Augustine's College	NC	12,990	C+
St. Edward's Univ	TX	17,846	C
St. John's Univ	NY	26,660	C
St. Martin's College	WA	20,566	C
St. Olaf College	MN	25,880	HC
St. Thomas Univ	FL	19,500	LC
Shaw Univ	NC	12,810	C
Shepherd College	WV	7,062	LC
Simmons College	MA	30,418	VC
Southeast Missouri State Univ	MO	8,367	C+
Southeastern Louisiana Univ	LA	6,047	LC
Southern Univ at New Orleans	LA	995	NC
Southern Utah Univ	UT	7,254	C
SUNY/College at Plattsburgh	NY	9,729	C
SUNY/Univ at Albany	NY	10,997	VC
Syracuse Univ	NY	30,710	HC
Taylor Univ	IN	21,562	VC+
Temple Univ	PA	14,124	C
Texas Christian Univ	TX	19,910	C
Univ of Central Okla	OK	5,205	C
Univ of Charleston	WV	20,640	C
Univ of Conn	CT	12,122	VC
Univ of Evansville	IN	22,865	VC+
Univ of Great Falls	MT	15,360	C
Univ of Indianapolis	IN	20,840	C
Univ of Kentucky	KY	7,765	C
Univ of Louisiana at Lafayette	LA	5,200	C
Univ of Louisiana at Monroe	LA	5,207	NC
Univ of Mich/Dearborn	MI	4,677	VC
Univ of Minn/Duluth	MN	10,436	C
Univ of Minn/Twin Cities	MN	11,123	VC
Univ of N Car at Charlotte	NC	7,254	C
Univ of N Car at Pembroke	NC	5,914	LC
Univ of N Dak	ND	7,067	VC
Univ of Okla	OK	7,616	VC
Univ of Rio Grande	OH	8,728	NC
Univ of St. Francis	IN	17,790	LC
Univ of S Car at Spartanburg	SC	7,318	C+
Univ of South Florida	FL	8,154	C
Univ of Vermont	VT	14,761	C+
Univ of Wisc/La Crosse	WI	7,250	VC
Univ of Wisc/Whitewater	WI	6,937	C
Wartburg College	IA	21,165	VC
Washington Univ in St. Louis	MO	34,593	MC
Wesley College	DE	17,869	C
West Chester Univ of Pennsylvania	PA	9,792	VC
West Texas A&M Univ	TX	6,538	C
Whitworth College	WA	23,938	VC
Xavier Univ of Louisiana	LA	17,000	LC
Youngstown State Univ	OH	9,318	NC

SOCIAL WORK

School	ST	$IS	SR
Abilene Christian Univ	TX	16,300	VC
Adams State College	CO	7,468	C
Adelphi Univ	NY	23,320	VC
Alabama A&M Univ	AL	5,100	LC
Alabama State Univ	AL	6,404	C
Albany State Univ	GA	5,764	C+
Alvernia College	PA	20,790	C
Anderson Univ	IN	19,430	LC
Andrews Univ	MI	17,696	LC
Anna Maria College	MA	22,800	LC
Appalachian State Univ	NC	6,353	C
Arizona State Univ-Main	AZ	7,726	C
Arkansas State Univ	AR	7,480	C
Asbury College	KY	18,540	VC
Ashland Univ	OH	22,182	LC
Atlantic Union College	MA	34,034	LC
Auburn Univ	AL	5,510	C
Audrey Cohen College	NY	17,715	C
Augsburg College	MN	22,978	C
Augustana College	SD	20,760	VC
Aurora Univ	IL	18,551	C
Austin Peay State Univ	TN	5,814	LC
Avila College	MO	17,720	C
Azusa Pacific Univ	CA	22,422	VC
Ball State Univ	IN	8,660	C
Barton College	NC	16,834	LC
Baylor Univ	TX	18,298	VC+
Belhaven College	MS	16,040	C+
Belmont Univ	TN	19,066	VC
Bemidji State Univ	MN	7,957	C
Benedict College	SC	12,662	LC
Bennett College	NC	11,200	C
Bethany College	KS	16,602	C+
Bethany College	WV	18,566	C
Bethel College	KS	17,355	C+
Bethel College	MN	22,740	VC
Bloomsburg Univ of Pennsylvania	PA	9,434	C
Bluffton College	OH	20,644	C
Boise State Univ	ID	6,531	LC
Bowie State Univ	MD	9,300	C+
Bowling Green State Univ	OH	10,794	C
Bradley Univ	IL	20,970	VC
Brescia Univ	KY	14,225	C
Briar Cliff Univ	IA	18,657	LC
Bridgewater State College	MA	7,589	C+
Brigham Young Univ	UT	7,840	HC
Brigham Young Univ/Hawaii	HI	6,890	C
Buena Vista Univ	IA	22,828	C
Cabrini College	PA	25,950	LC
Cal State, Chico	CA	8,598	LC
Cal State, Fresno	CA	7,762	C
Cal State, Los Angeles	CA	5,050	C
Cal State, Sacramento	CA	7,488	C
Calif Univ of Pennsylvania	PA	10,388	C
Calumet College of St. Joseph	IN	7,500	LC
Calvin College	MI	20,050	NC
Campbell Univ	NC	16,599	C
Campbellsville Univ	KY	14,340	C
Capital Univ	OH	23,630	C
Caribbean Univ	PR	3,000	
Carlow College	PA	19,366	C
Carroll College	MT	19,140	C
Carroll College	WI	21,170	C
Carthage College	WI	23,670	C
Castleton State College	VT	10,922	LC
Catholic Univ of America	DC	29,332	VC
Cedar Crest College	PA	25,145	C+
Cedarville Univ	OH	17,553	VC
Central Conn State Univ	CT	10,404	C
Central Missouri State Univ	MO	7,920	C
Central State Univ	OH	8,922	C+
Central Univ of Bayamon	PR	3,335	
Central Washington Univ	WA	8,985	LC
Chadron State College	NE	6,211	NC
Champlain College	VT	19,680	C
Chatham College	PA	25,454	C+
Christopher Newport Univ	VA	8,862	VC
CUNY/College of Staten Island	NY	3,358	NC
CUNY/Herbert H. Lehman College	NY	3,320	LC
CUNY/Queens College	NY	3,403	VC
CUNY/York College	NY	3,292	NC
Clark Atlanta Univ	GA	17,174	C
Clarke College	IA	20,625	C+
Cleveland State Univ	OH	10,146	NC
College Misericordia	PA	23,380	LC
College of Mount St. Joseph	OH	20,290	C
College of New Rochelle	NY	20,000	C
College of Our Lady of the Elms	MA	20,644	C
College of St. Benedict	MN	23,921	VC
College of St. Catherine	MN	22,324	VC
College of St. Rose	NY	19,084	C
College of St. Scholastica	MN	22,378	C+
College of the Ozarks	MO	2,650	C+
Colo State Univ	CO	9,672	C
Columbia College	MO	15,082	C
Columbia College	SC	19,050	LC
Concord College	WV	7,122	C+
Concordia College	NY	19,200	VC
Concordia College/Moorhead	MN	18,835	C
Concordia Univ	OR	20,500	LC
Concordia Univ Wisc	WI	16,600	LC
Concordia Univ, River Forest	IL	20,000	LC
Coppin State College	MD	9,133	LC
Cornerstone Univ and Grand Rapids Baptist Seminary	MI	18,092	C
Creighton Univ	NE	23,476	VC
Cumberland College	KY	14,864	C
Daemen College	NY	20,620	C
Dana College	NE	18,046	C
David Lipscomb Univ	TN	16,158	VC
De Sales Univ	PA	22,610	VC
Defiance College	OH	19,580	LC
Delaware State Univ	DE	8,104	LC
Delta State Univ	MS	5,416	C
Dickinson State Univ	ND	5,495	NC
Dillard Univ	LA	16,046	VC
Dominican College	NY	20,400	LC
Dordt College	IA	18,100	C+
East Carolina Univ	NC	7,766	C
East Central Univ	OK	4,578	C
East Tenn State Univ	TN	7,127	C
Eastern College	PA	19,641	LC
Eastern Conn State Univ	CT	10,362	C
Eastern Kentucky Univ	KY	6,552	C
Eastern Mennonite Univ	VA	20,700	VC
Eastern Mich Univ	MI	9,855	C
Eastern Nazarene College	MA	19,433	LC
Eastern Washington Univ	WA	7,972	LC
Edinboro Univ of Pennsylvania	PA	9,328	LC
Elizabeth City State Univ	NC	5,550	LC
Elizabethtown College	PA	26,000	VC
Evangel Univ	MO	14,050	C
Ferris State Univ	MI	10,816	C
Ferrum College	VA	15,990	LC
Florida A&M Univ	FL	6,948	C
Florida Atlantic Univ	FL	8,832	C
Florida International Univ	FL	9,486	VC
Florida State Univ	FL	7,835	HC
Fordham Univ	NY	30,710	VC
Fort Hays State Univ	KS	6,294	LC
Fort Valley State Univ	GA	6,014	LC
Franklin Pierce College	NH	26,125	LC
Freed-Hardeman Univ	TN	14,290	VC
Fresno Pacific Univ	CA	19,740	C
Frostburg State Univ	MD	9,680	C
Gallaudet Univ	DC	16,554	SP
Gannon Univ	PA	18,848	C
George Fox Univ	OR	24,095	VC
George Mason Univ	VA	9,192	C
Georgia State Univ	GA	7,792	LC
Georgian Court College	NJ	19,040	LC
Gordon College	MA	23,594	VC+
Goshen College	IN	18,950	VC+
Grace College	IN	16,768	C
Grambling State Univ	LA	5,325	NC
Grand Valley State Univ	MI	10,040	C
Greenville College	IL	19,226	LC
Gwynedd-Mercy College	PA	22,350	C
Harding Univ	AR	13,528	VC
Hardin-Simmons Univ	TX	14,165	C
Hawaii Pacific Univ	HI	17,790	C
Heritage College	WA	6,450	NC
Holy Family College	PA	13,710	LC
Hood College	MD	26,020	VC
Hope College	MI	22,922	C+
Howard Payne Univ	TX	13,834	C+
Humboldt State Univ	CA	8,582	C
Idaho State Univ	ID	7,030	C+
Illinois College	IL	16,234	C
Illinois State Univ	IL	9,235	C
Indiana State Univ	IN	8,461	LC
Indiana Univ East	IN	3,415	C
Indiana Univ-Purdue Univ Indianapolis	IN	9,473	C
Indiana Wesleyan Univ	IN	17,680	C
Inter-American Univ of PR/Arecibo Campus	PR	3,300	
Inter-American Univ of PR/Bayamon Univ College	PR	3,700	
Inter-American Univ of PR/Fajardo Campus	PR	4,000	
Inter-American Univ of PR/Metropolitan Campus	PR	4,166	
Inter-American Univ of PR/Ponce Regional College	PR	3,700	
Iona College	NY	26,556	C
Jackson State Univ	MS	6,776	LC
Jacksonville State Univ	AL	6,568	LC
James Madison Univ	VA	9,552	HC
Johnson C. Smith Univ	NC	16,560	C+
Juniata College	PA	26,080	VC
Kansas State Univ	KS	6,995	C
Kean Univ	NJ	11,159	C
Kentucky Christian College	KY	13,472	C
Kentucky State Univ	KY	6,146	NC
Keuka College	NY	21,170	C
Kutztown Univ of Pennsylvania	PA	8,907	C
La Salle Univ	PA	27,890	C
La Sierra Univ	CA	19,260	LC
LaGrange College	GA	17,496	C
Lamar Univ	TX	6,816	LC
LeMoyne-Owen College	TN	8,450	NC
Lewis Univ	IL	20,960	C
Lewis-Clark State College	ID	6,496	C
Limestone College	SC	16,900	C
Lincoln Memorial Univ	TN	12,620	LC
Lindenwood Univ	MO	17,250	C
Livingstone College	NC	13,360	LC
Lock Haven Univ of Pennsylvania	PA	9,534	C
LIU/Brooklyn Campus	NY	22,290	C
LIU/C.W. Post Campus	NY	25,380	C
Longwood College	VA	8,950	C
Loras College	IA	22,994	C+
Louisiana College	LA	11,516	C
Lourdes College	OH	13,100	LC
Loyola Univ of Chicago	IL	25,992	VC
Lubbock Christian Univ	TX	14,226	LC
Luther College	IA	23,300	VC+
MacMurray College	IL	17,790	LC
Madonna Univ	MI	11,504	VC
Malone College	OH	19,190	C
Manchester College	IN	22,010	C
Mansfield Univ	PA	9,648	C
Marian College of Fond du Lac	WI	17,935	LC
Marist College	NY	24,756	VC
Mars Hill College	NC	18,600	LC
Marshall Univ	WV	7,752	LC
Mary Baldwin College	VA	23,440	C
Marygrove College	MI	16,075	C
Marymount College/Tarrytown	NY	23,850	C
Marywood Univ	PA	24,639	C
Mercy College	NY	15,875	LC
Mercyhurst College	PA	20,694	C
Meredith College	NC	17,500	C
Messiah College	PA	23,180	VC
Methodist College	NC	19,526	C
Metropolitan State College of Denver	CO	2,338	LC
Metropolitan State Univ	MN	2,943	SP
Miami Univ	OH	12,885	VC+
Mich State Univ	MI	10,386	VC
Middle Tenn State Univ	TN	6,994	C
Midwestern State Univ	TX	6,704	NC
Miles College	AL	7,870	NC
Millersville Univ of Pennsylvania	PA	10,153	VC
Minn State Univ, Mankato	MN	7,296	LC
Minot State Univ	ND	5,466	LC
Miss College	MS	14,574	C
Miss State Univ	MS	7,853	C
Miss Valley State Univ	MS	6,345	C
Missouri Western State College	MO	6,662	NC
Molloy College	NY	13,940	C
Monmouth Univ	NJ	24,042	C
Moorhead State Univ	MN	7,000	LC
Morehead State Univ	KY	6,510	C
Morgan State Univ	MD	10,078	LC
Mount Mary College	WI	18,024	C
Mount Mercy College	IA	19,390	VC
Mount Senario College	WI	17,750	C
Mount Vernon Nazarene College	OH	17,027	C
Mountain State Univ	WV	8,180	NC
Murray State Univ	KY	6,672	C
Nazareth College of Rochester	NY	22,036	VC
Nebr Wesleyan Univ	NE	18,767	VC
New Mexico Highlands Univ	NM	6,256	NC
New Mexico State Univ	NM	7,302	C
New York Univ	NY	35,200	MC
Niagara Univ	NY	22,250	C+
Norfolk State Univ	VA	8,382	LC

ST = STATE **$IS** = IN-STATE COSTS **SR** = SELECTOR RATING

School	ST	$IS	SR
N Car Agricultural and Technical State Univ	NC	6,659	LC
N Car Central Univ	NC	6,418	LC
N Car State Univ	NC	8,680	HC
Northeastern Illinois Univ	IL	2,898	NC
Northeastern State Univ	OK	4,704	LC
Northern Arizona Univ	AZ	7,398	C
Northern Kentucky Univ	KY	6,352	NC
Northern Mich Univ	MI	9,693	C
Northwest Nazarene Univ	ID	18,380	C
Northwestern College of Iowa	IA	17,630	C+
Northwestern Okla State Univ	OK	4,542	NC
Northwestern State Univ of Louisiana	LA	5,745	NC
Nyack College	NY	18,540	C
Oakwood College	AL	14,904	C
Oglethorpe Univ	GA	19,100	LC
Ohio Dominican College	OH	18,100	LC
Ohio Univ	OH	11,769	C
Okla Baptist Univ	OK	13,878	VC
Olivet Nazarene Univ	IL	18,444	C
Oral Roberts Univ	OK	18,490	C
Our Lady of the Lake Univ of San Antonio	TX	17,336	C
Pacific Lutheran Univ	WA	23,318	VC
Pacific Union College	CA	20,250	VC
Pacific Univ	OR	24,250	C
Philadelphia Biblical Univ	PA	16,295	C+
Philander Smith College	AR	7,380	NC
Pittsburg State Univ	KS	6,228	NC
Plymouth State College	NH	11,024	LC
Point Loma Nazarene Univ	CA	21,380	VC
Pontifical Catholic Univ of PR/Ponce	PR	7,076	
Prairie View A&M Univ	TX	3,172	LC
Prescott College	AZ	13,430	C
Presentation College	SD	13,508	NC
Providence College	RI	27,620	HC
Purdue Univ/Calumet	IN	6,630	NC
Quincy Univ	IL	20,450	C
Radford Univ	VA	8,302	C
Ramapo College of New Jersey	NJ	13,550	VC
Regis College	MA	26,750	C
Rhode Island College	RI	8,700	LC
Richard Stockton College of New Jersey	NJ	12,165	VC
Roberts Wesleyan College	NY	20,160	C+
Rochester Inst of Technology	NY	26,232	VC+
Rockford College	IL	23,930	C
Rust College	MS	7,800	C+
Rutgers, The State Univ of New Jersey New Brunswick Campus	NJ	12,709	C
Rutgers, The State Univ of New Jersey/ CamdenCampus	NJ	6,484	C
Rutgers, The State Univ of New Jersey/Newark Campus	NJ	6,394	C
Sacred Heart Univ	CT	26,588	VC
Saginaw Valley State Univ	MI	9,465	C
St. Cloud State Univ	MN	7,180	C
St. Edward's Univ	TX	17,846	C
St. Francis Univ	PA	24,486	LC
St. John's Univ	MN	23,640	VC
St. Joseph College	CT	25,960	LC
St. Joseph's College	IN	21,640	C
St. Leo Univ	FL	19,250	LC
St. Louis Univ	MO	26,590	VC+
St. Mary-of-the-Woods College	IN	21,320	LC
St. Mary's College	IN	24,474	VC
St. Olaf College	MN	25,880	HC
Salem State College	MA	4,481	LC
Salisbury Univ	MD	10,576	VC
Salve Regina Univ	RI	26,460	C
San Diego State Univ	CA	9,716	C+
San Francisco State Univ	CA	7,139	LC
San Jose State Univ	CA	8,187	C
Savannah State Univ	GA	2,550	LC
Seattle Univ	WA	24,183	VC
Seton Hall Univ	NJ	26,910	LC
Seton Hill College	PA	21,875	C
Shaw Univ	NC	12,810	C
Shepherd College	WV	7,062	LC
Shippensburg Univ of Pennsylvania	PA	9,652	C
Siena College	NY	22,685	VC
Siena Heights Univ	MI	16,140	LC
Skidmore College	NY	34,201	VC+
Slippery Rock Univ	PA	9,152	LC
Sojourner-Douglass College	MD	4,170	LC
S Car State Univ	SC	6,586	LC
Southeast Missouri State Univ	MO	8,367	C+
Southeastern College	FL	11,648	LC
Southeastern Louisiana Univ	LA	6,047	LC
Southern Adventist Univ	TN	15,600	C
Southern Conn State Univ	CT	10,310	C
Southern Illinois Univ at Carbondale	IL	8,621	C
Southern Illinois Univ Edwardsville	IL	7,869	LC
Southern Univ and A&M College	LA	6,365	C+
Southern Univ at New Orleans	LA	995	NC
Southern Vermont College	VT	17,685	C
Southwest Missouri State Univ	MO	7,600	LC
Southwest State Univ	MN	7,117	LC
Southwest Texas State Univ	TX	8,730	VC
Southwestern Adventist Univ	TX	14,798	C
Southwestern Okla State Univ	OK	4,801	C
Spalding Univ	KY	15,196	C
Spring Arbor Univ	MI	17,976	C
SUNY/College at Brockport	NY	10,267	C
SUNY/College at Buffalo	NY	8,025	C
SUNY/College at Fredonia	NY	10,125	C
SUNY/College at Plattsburgh	NY	9,729	C
SUNY/Univ at Albany	NY	10,997	VC
SUNY/Univ at Stony Brook	NY	10,998	VC
Stephen F. Austin State Univ	TX	6,905	C
Syracuse Univ	NY	30,710	HC
Talladega College	AL	10,110	LC
Tarleton State Univ	TX	7,160	C
Taylor Univ	IN	21,562	VC+
Temple Univ	PA	14,124	C
Tenn State Univ	TN	7,058	VC
Texas A&M Univ at Commerce	TX	7,326	C
Texas Christian Univ	TX	19,910	C
Texas Lutheran Univ	TX	17,660	C
Texas Southern Univ	TX	6,576	NC
Texas Tech Univ	TX	8,825	C
Texas Woman's Univ	TX	5,855	LC
Ohio State Univ	OH	10,819	VC
Thomas Univ	GA	8,770	NC
Trevecca Nazarene Univ	TN	15,752	C
Trinity Christian College	IL	19,415	C
Troy State Univ	AL	7,696	C
Tuskegee Univ	AL	14,600	LC
Union College	NE	14,650	C
Union Univ	TN	18,930	C+
Univ of Akron	OH	10,530	NC
Univ of Alabama	AL	7,402	C
Univ of Alabama at Birmingham	AL	10,110	C
Univ of Alaska Anchorage	AK	9,100	NC
Univ of Alaska Fairbanks	AK	8,265	NC
Univ of Arkansas	AR	8,334	VC
Univ of Arkansas at Monticello	AR	5,940	NC
Univ of Arkansas at Pine Bluff	AR	7,925	C
Univ of Calif at Berkeley	CA	14,134	MC
Univ of Central Florida	FL	8,251	VC
Univ of Cincinnati	OH	12,491	LC
Univ of Detroit Mercy	MI	21,620	LC
Univ of Findlay	OH	23,962	NC
Univ of Georgia	GA	8,656	VC
Univ of Hawaii at Manoa	HI	7,862	VC
Univ of Illinois at Chicago	IL	10,702	VC
Univ of Indianapolis	IN	20,840	C
Univ of Iowa	IA	8,607	C+
Univ of Kansas	KS	7,232	VC
Univ of Kentucky	KY	7,765	C
Univ of Louisiana at Monroe	LA	5,207	NC
Univ of Maine	ME	10,798	C
Univ of Maine at Presque Isle	ME	7,964	LC
Univ of Mary	ND	12,900	LC
Univ of Mary Hardin-Baylor	TX	13,929	C
Univ of Maryland/Baltimore County	MD	12,190	VC
Univ of Memphis	TN	7,271	C
Univ of Mich/Flint	MI	4,323	C
Univ of Miss	MS	7,666	C
Univ of Missouri/Columbia	MO	9,803	HC
Univ of Missouri/St. Louis	MO	9,966	C
Univ of Montana	MT	8,038	C
Univ of Montevallo	AL	7,266	C
Univ of Nebr at Kearney	NE	7,048	NC
Univ of Nebr at Omaha	NE	6,867	C
Univ of Nevada/Las Vegas	NV	8,281	VC
Univ of Nevada/Reno	NV	8,737	C
Univ of New Hampshire	NH	13,207	C
Univ of North Alabama	AL	7,016	NC
Univ of N Car at Charlotte	NC	7,254	C
Univ of N Car at Greensboro	NC	6,858	C
Univ of N Car at Pembroke	NC	5,914	LC
Univ of N Car at Wilmington	NC	7,769	C
Univ of N Dak	ND	7,067	VC
Univ of North Texas	TX	7,629	C
Univ of Northern Iowa	IA	7,850	C
Univ of Okla	OK	7,616	VC
Univ of Pittsburgh at Pittsburgh	PA	13,592	HC
Univ of Portland	OR	24,950	VC
Univ of PR at Humacao	PR	1,245	
Univ of PR/Rio Piedras	PR	5,510	
Univ of Rio Grande	OH	8,728	NC
Univ of St. Francis	IL	19,650	C
Univ of St. Francis	IN	17,790	LC
Univ of St. Thomas	MN	24,044	VC
Univ of Sioux Falls	SD	16,390	C
Univ of S Dak	SD	7,036	C
Univ of South Florida	FL	8,154	C
Univ of Southern Colo	CO	7,821	LC
Univ of Southern Indiana	IN	8,655	LC
Univ of Southern Maine	ME	10,569	C
Univ of Southern Miss	MS	6,155	LC
Univ of Tenn at Chattanooga	TN	7,783	C
Univ of Tenn at Knoxville	TN	8,214	C
Univ of Tenn at Martin	TN	8,268	C
Univ of Texas at Arlington	TX	7,192	LC
Univ of Texas at Austin	TX	9,437	HC
Univ of Texas at El Paso	TX	5,076	LC
Univ of Texas-Pan American	TX	4,823	C
Univ of the District of Columbia	DC	2,844	NC
Univ of the Sacred Heart	PR	5,375	
Univ of Toledo	OH	11,206	NC
Univ of Vermont	VT	14,761	C+
Univ of Washington	WA	10,361	VC
Univ of West Florida	FL	7,518	C
Univ of Wisc/Eau Claire	WI	7,032	VC
Univ of Wisc/Green Bay	WI	7,148	C
Univ of Wisc/Madison	WI	8,262	VC
Univ of Wisc/Milwaukee	WI	8,907	LC
Univ of Wisc/Oshkosh	WI	6,130	LC
Univ of Wisc/River Falls	WI	6,356	LC
Univ of Wisc/Superior	WI	7,051	C+
Univ of Wisc/Whitewater	WI	6,937	C
Univ of Wyoming	WY	7,143	LC
Ursuline College	OH	19,430	LC
Utah State Univ	UT	6,771	C
Valparaiso Univ	IN	23,570	VC+
Virginia Commonwealth Univ	VA	9,030	C
Virginia Intermont College	VA	17,510	C
Virginia State Univ	VA	8,182	LC
Virginia Union Univ	VA	15,358	LC
Virginia Wesleyan College	VA	22,350	LC
Viterbo Univ	WI	18,043	C
Wagner College	NY	27,000	C
Walla Walla College	WA	20,925	C
Warner Pacific College	OR	20,370	LC
Warren Wilson College	NC	19,968	C
Wartburg College	IA	21,165	VC
Washburn Univ of Topeka	KS	6,766	NC
Washington State Univ	WA	9,388	C
Wayne State Univ	MI	6,720	C
Weber State Univ	UT	6,897	NC
West Chester Univ of Pennsylvania	PA	9,792	VC
West Texas A&M Univ	TX	6,538	C
West Virginia State College	WV	6,264	NC
West Virginia Univ	WV	8,304	C
Western Carolina Univ	NC	5,667	C
Western Conn State Univ	CT	10,074	C
Western Illinois Univ	IL	9,571	C
Western Kentucky Univ	KY	6,834	C
Western Maryland College	MD	26,000	VC
Western Mich Univ	MI	10,016	C
Western New England College	MA	23,882	C
Western New Mexico Univ	NM	5,950	LC
Westfield State College	MA	8,394	C
Wheelock College	MA	25,520	C
Whittier College	CA	29,108	C
Wichita State Univ	KS	6,879	C
Widener Univ	PA	26,920	C
Wilberforce Univ	OH	14,937	LC
William Woods Univ	MO	19,390	LC
Wilmington College	OH	21,826	C
Winona State Univ	MN	8,570	C
Winthrop Univ	SC	9,106	C
Wright State Univ	OH	9,141	LC
Xavier Univ	OH	23,880	C
Youngstown State Univ	OH	9,318	NC

SOCIOLOGY

School	ST	$IS	SR
Abilene Christian Univ	TX	16,300	VC
Adams State College	CO	7,468	C
Adelphi Univ	NY	23,320	VC
Adrian College	MI	19,670	C
Agnes Scott College	GA	24,950	VC
Alabama A&M Univ	AL	5,100	LC
Alabama State Univ	AL	6,404	C
Albany State Univ	GA	5,764	C+
Albertus Magnus College	CT	22,154	C
Albion College	MI	25,224	VC
Alcorn State Univ	MS	5,594	LC
Alfred Univ	NY	27,212	C+
Allen Univ	SC	9,600	NC
Alma College	MI	22,586	VC
American International College	MA	22,268	LC
American Univ	DC	31,544	VC+
Amherst College	MA	34,340	MC
Anderson Univ	IN	19,430	LC
Andrews Univ	MI	17,696	LC
Angelo State Univ	TX	7,028	C
Appalachian State Univ	NC	0,353	C
Aquinas College	MI	20,052	C+
Arcadia Univ	PA	26,650	C
Arizona State Univ-Main	AZ	7,726	C
Arkansas State Univ	AR	7,480	C
Arkansas Tech Univ	AR	6,256	C
Asbury College	KY	18,540	VC
Ashland Univ	OH	22,182	LC
Assumption College	MA	26,320	C
Auburn Univ	AL	5,510	C
Auburn Univ Montgomery	AL	5,330	NC
Augsburg College	MN	22,978	C
Augusta State Univ	GA	2,282	C
Augustana College	IL	24,117	VC+
Augustana College	SD	20,760	VC
Aurora Univ	IL	18,551	C
Austin College	TX	22,150	VC+
Austin Peay State Univ	TN	5,814	LC
Averett Univ	VA	17,980	LC
Avila College	MO	17,720	C
Azusa Pacific Univ	CA	22,422	VC
Baker Univ	KS	14,780	C+
Baldwin-Wallace College	OH	22,010	VC+
Ball State Univ	IN	8,660	C
Barber-Scotia College	NC	13,100	C
Bard College	NY	33,912	HC
Barry Univ	FL	24,100	LC
Bartlesville Wesleyan College	OK	14,100	LC
Bates College	ME	34,100	MC
Baylor Univ	TX	18,298	VC+
Bellarmine Univ	KY	20,440	VC
Bellevue Univ	NE	4,125	NC
Belmont Abbey College	NC	19,630	LC
Beloit College	WI	27,482	HC
Bemidji State Univ	MN	7,957	C
Benedictine College	KS	18,485	LC
Benedictine Univ	IL	21,330	C
Bennett College	NC	11,200	C
Bennington College	VT	31,350	VC
Berea College	KY	4,070	VC
Berry College	GA	18,850	C
Bethany College	KS	16,602	C+
Bethel College	IN	17,650	LC
Bethel College	TN	12,980	C
Bethune-Cookman College	FL	15,746	C
Biola Univ	CA	21,902	VC
Birmingham-Southern College	AL	22,960	C
Black Hills State Univ	SD	6,652	LC
Bloomfield College	NJ	17,000	C
Bloomsburg Univ of Pennsylvania	PA	9,434	C
Bluffton College	OH	20,644	C
Boise State Univ	ID	6,531	LC
Boston College	MA	33,330	MC
Boston Univ	MA	34,358	MC
Bowdoin College	ME	32,650	MC
Bowie State Univ	MD	9,300	C+
Bowling Green State Univ	OH	10,794	C
Bradley Univ	IL	20,970	VC
Brandeis Univ	MA	34,481	MC
Brewton-Parker College	GA	10,810	LC
Briar Cliff Univ	IA	18,657	LC
Bridgewater College	VA	22,950	C
Bridgewater State College	MA	7,589	C+
Brigham Young Univ	UT	7,840	HC
Brown Univ	RI	34,973	MC
Bryn Mawr College	PA	33,580	HC+
Bucknell Univ	PA	31,096	HC
Butler Univ	IN	25,580	VC+
Cabrini College	PA	25,950	LC
Caldwell College	NJ	20,940	LC
Calif Lutheran Univ	CA	23,500	LC
Calif State Polytechnic Univ, Pomona	CA	8,615	C
Cal State, Bakersfield	CA	6,090	LC
Cal State, Chico	CA	8,598	LC
Cal State, Dominguez Hills	CA	5,840	LC
Cal State, Fresno	CA	7,762	C
Cal State, Fullerton	CA	5,440	LC
Cal State, Hayward	CA	7,400	LC
Cal State, Long Beach	CA	7,400	LC
Cal State, Los Angeles	CA	5,050	C
Cal State, Northridge	CA	7,781	C
Cal State, Sacramento	CA	7,488	C
Cal State, San Bernardino	CA	6,516	C
Cal State, San Marcos	CA	1,736	LC
Cal State, Stanislaus	CA	8,895	C
Calif Univ of Pennsylvania	PA	10,388	C
Calumet College of St. Joseph	IN	7,500	LC
Calvin College	MI	20,050	NC
Cameron Univ	OK	5,560	NC
Campbellsville Univ	KY	14,340	C
Canisius College	NY	24,696	C+
Capital Univ	OH	23,630	C
Cardinal Stritch Univ	WI	17,620	C
Carleton College	MN	30,780	MC
Carlow College	PA	19,366	C
Carroll College	MT	19,140	C
Carroll College	WI	21,170	C
Carson-Newman College	TN	16,490	C
Carthage College	WI	23,670	C
Case Western Reserve Univ	OH	27,418	C

ST = STATE $IS = IN-STATE COSTS SR = SELECTOR RATING

INDEX OF COLLEGE MAJORS

School	ST	$IS	SR
Castleton State College	VT	10,922	LC
Catawba College	NC	19,620	C
Catholic Univ of America	DC	29,332	VC
Cedar Crest College	PA	25,145	C+
Cedarville Univ	OH	17,553	VC
Centenary College	NJ	22,430	C
Centenary College of Louisiana	LA	21,600	C+
Central College	IA	21,206	C
Central Conn State Univ	CT	10,404	C
Central Methodist College	MO	16,460	C
Central Mich Univ	MI	8,355	C
Central Missouri State Univ	MO	7,920	C
Central State Univ	OH	8,922	C+
Central Univ of Bayamon	PR	3,335	
Central Washington Univ	WA	8,985	LC
Centre College	KY	24,000	HC
Chadron State College	NE	6,211	NC
Chapman Univ	CA	30,218	VC
Charleston Southern Univ	SC	17,122	C
Chestnut Hill College	PA	24,790	LC
Chicago State Univ	IL	8,851	C+
Christopher Newport Univ	VA	8,862	VC
CUNY/Baruch College	NY	3,275	VC+
CUNY/Brooklyn College	NY	3,403	LC
CUNY/City College	NY	3,309	LC
CUNY/College of Staten Island	NY	3,358	NC
CUNY/Herbert H. Lehman College	NY	3,320	LC
CUNY/Hunter College	NY	5,147	C+
CUNY/Queens College	NY	3,403	VC
CUNY/York College	NY	3,292	NC
Claflin Univ	SC	12,735	C+
Claremont McKenna College	CA	32,700	MC
Clarion Univ of Pennsylvania	PA	11,272	LC
Clark Atlanta Univ	GA	17,174	C
Clark Univ	MA	29,170	HC
Clarke College	IA	20,625	C+
Clarkson Univ	NY	29,884	VC
Clemson Univ	SC	7,600	C
Cleveland State Univ	OH	10,146	NC
Coastal Carolina Univ	SC	9,220	C
Coe College	IA	24,750	VC
Coker College	SC	20,120	C
Colby College	ME	34,290	MC
Colgate Univ	NY	33,480	MC
College of Charleston	SC	8,350	HC
College of Mount St. Vincent	NY	24,230	C
College of Mount St. Joseph	OH	20,290	C
College of New Jersey	NJ	13,425	HC
College of New Rochelle	NY	20,000	C
College of Our Lady of the Elms	MA	20,644	C
College of St. Benedict	MN	23,921	VC
College of St. Catherine	MN	22,324	VC
College of St. Elizabeth	NJ	22,510	C
College of St. Rose	NY	19,084	C
College of the Holy Cross	MA	32,780	MC
College of the Ozarks	MO	2,650	C
College of the Southwest	NM	8,456	NC
College of William and Mary	VA	10,002	MC
College of Wooster	OH	28,350	VC
Colo College	CO	31,525	HC+
Colo State Univ	CO	9,672	C
Columbia College	MO	15,082	C
Columbia College	SC	19,050	LC
Columbia Univ/Barnard College	NY	33,694	MC
Columbia Univ/Columbia College	NY	35,190	MC
Columbia Univ/School of General Studies	NY	35,000	C
Columbus State Univ	GA	7,228	LC
Concord College	WV	7,122	C+
Concordia College/Moorhead	MN	18,835	C
Concordia Univ	MI	20,500	C
Concordia Univ	MN	19,912	C
Concordia Univ, River Forest	IL	20,000	LC
Conn College	CT	33,585	MC
Converse College	SC	21,990	VC
Cornell College	IA	24,980	VC
Cornell Univ	NY	34,614	MC
Cornerstone Univ and Grand Rapids Baptist Seminary	MI	18,092	C
Covenant College	GA	21,970	C+
Creighton Univ	NE	23,476	VC
Culver-Stockton College	MO	15,400	LC
Curry College	MA	26,025	LC
Dakota Wesleyan Univ	SD	15,512	C
Dallas Baptist Univ	TX	13,682	LC
Dana College	NE	18,046	C
Dartmouth College	NH	34,458	MC
Davidson College	NC	30,823	MC
Davis and Elkins College	WV	19,270	LC
Delaware State Univ	DE	8,104	LC
Delta State Univ	MS	5,416	C
DePaul Univ	IL	23,590	VC
DePauw Univ	IN	28,000	HC
Dickinson College	PA	32,210	VC+
Dickinson State Univ	ND	5,495	NC
Dillard Univ	LA	16,046	VC
Doane College	NE	17,600	LC
Dominican Univ	IL	20,800	C
Dordt College	IA	18,100	C+
Dowling College	NY	20,281	LC
Drake Univ	IA	22,830	VC
Drew Univ/College of Liberal Arts	NJ	32,152	VC
Drexel Univ	PA	27,657	VC
Drury Univ	MO	15,250	VC
Duke Univ	NC	34,396	MC
Duquesne Univ	PA	24,242	C+
D'Youville College	NY	18,704	C
Earlham College	IN	27,446	VC+
East Carolina Univ	NC	7,766	C
East Central Univ	OK	4,578	C
East Stroudsburg Univ of Pennsylvania	PA	8,430	LC
East Tenn State Univ	TN	7,127	C
East Texas Baptist Univ	TX	12,349	LC
Eastern College	PA	19,641	LC
Eastern Conn State Univ	CT	10,362	C
Eastern Illinois Univ	IL	10,101	C
Eastern Kentucky Univ	KY	6,552	C
Eastern Mennonite Univ	VA	20,700	VC
Eastern Mich Univ	MI	9,855	C
Eastern Nazarene College	MA	19,433	LC
Eastern New Mexico Univ	NM	4,113	LC
Eastern Oregon Univ	OR	8,772	C
Eastern Washington Univ	WA	7,972	LC
Eckerd College	FL	25,500	C+
Edgewood College	WI	18,304	C
Edinboro Univ of Pennsylvania	PA	9,328	LC
Edward Waters College	FL	13,124	LC
Elizabeth City State Univ	NC	5,550	LC
Elizabethtown College	PA	26,000	VC
Elmhurst College	IL	21,750	C
Elmira College	NY	31,070	VC+
Elon Univ	NC	19,430	VC
Emmanuel College	MA	23,802	C+
Emory & Henry College	VA	19,462	C
Emory Univ	GA	33,792	MC
Emporia State Univ	KS	6,198	LC
Eugene Lang College of New School Univ	NY	30,300	C
Eureka College	IL	22,200	C
Evangel Univ	MO	14,050	C
Fairfield Univ	CT	30,885	HC
Fairleigh Dickinson Univ/Madison campus	NJ	25,500	C
Fairleigh Dickinson Univ/Teaneck Campus	NJ	24,646	C
Fairmont State College	WV	7,010	NC
Fayetteville State Univ	NC	5,590	LC
Fisk Univ	TN	13,700	LC
Fitchburg State College	MA	7,836	C
Florida A&M Univ	FL	6,948	C
Florida Atlantic Univ	FL	8,832	C
Florida International Univ	FL	9,486	VC
Florida Memorial College	FL	6,000	LC
Florida Southern College	FL	19,430	C
Florida State Univ	FL	7,835	HC
Fordham Univ	NY	30,710	VC
Fort Hays State Univ	KS	6,294	LC
Fort Lewis College	CO	7,659	LC
Fort Valley State Univ	GA	6,014	LC
Framingham State College	MA	7,259	C
Francis Marion Univ	SC	7,682	C
Franciscan Univ of Steubenville	OH	19,100	C+
Franklin and Marshall College	PA	32,410	HC
Franklin College of Indiana	IN	19,905	C
Franklin Pierce College	NH	26,125	LC
Frostburg State Univ	MD	9,680	C
Furman Univ	SC	25,492	HC
Gardner-Webb Univ	NC	17,400	C
Geneva College	PA	19,990	C+
George Fox Univ	OR	24,095	VC
George Mason Univ	VA	9,192	C
George Washington Univ	DC	32,170	HC
Georgetown College	KY	18,400	VC
Georgetown Univ	DC	34,847	MC
Georgia College and State Univ	GA	7,344	C
Georgia Southern Univ	GA	6,958	C
Georgia Southwestern State Univ	GA	6,013	C
Georgia State Univ	GA	7,792	LC
Georgian Court College	NJ	19,040	LC
Gettysburg College	PA	32,070	HC
Gonzaga Univ	WA	24,276	HC+
Gordon College	MA	23,594	VC+
Goshen College	IN	18,950	VC+
Goucher College	MD	30,650	VC+
Grace College	IN	16,768	C
Graceland Univ	IA	15,845	C
Grambling State Univ	LA	5,325	NC
Grand Canyon Univ	AZ	30,000	LC
Grand Valley State Univ	MI	10,040	C
Greensboro College	NC	19,080	LC
Greenville College	IL	19,226	LC
Grinnell College	IA	28,300	HC+
Guilford College	NC	23,255	C
Gustavus Adolphus College	MN	24,190	VC+
Gwynedd-Mercy College	PA	22,350	C
Hamilton College	NY	34,150	HC
Hamline Univ	MN	23,339	C+
Hampshire College	MA	33,881	HC+
Hampton Univ	VA	17,112	C+
Hanover College	IN	17,560	VC
Harding Univ	AR	13,528	VC
Hardin-Simmons Univ	TX	14,165	C
Hartwick College	NY	33,090	C+
Harvard Univ/Harvard College	MA	34,269	MC
Hastings College	NE	17,854	C+
Haverford College	PA	34,300	MC
Hawaii Pacific Univ	HI	17,790	C
Henderson State Univ	AR	6,269	C
Hendrix College	AR	18,463	HC
Heritage College	WA	6,450	NC
High Point Univ	NC	20,220	LC
Hillsdale College	MI	20,586	VC+
Hiram College	OH	27,034	VC
Hobart and William Smith Colleges	NY	33,195	VC
Hofstra Univ	NY	23,252	C
Hollins Univ	VA	24,328	VC
Holy Family College	PA	13,710	LC
Holy Names College	CA	23,220	C
Hood College	MD	26,020	VC
Hope College	MI	22,922	C+
Houghton College	NY	21,810	VC+
Houston Baptist Univ	TX	15,300	LC
Howard Payne Univ	TX	13,834	C+
Howard Univ	DC	15,522	LC
Humboldt State Univ	CA	8,582	C
Huntington College	IN	15,480	LC
Huston-Tillotson College	TX	12,977	LC
Idaho State Univ	ID	7,030	C+
Illinois College	IL	16,234	C
Illinois State Univ	IL	9,235	C
Illinois Wesleyan Univ	IL	26,970	HC
Immaculata College	PA	22,400	LC
Indiana State Univ	IN	8,461	LC
Indiana Univ Bloomington	IN	10,712	C+
Indiana Univ Kokomo	IN	3,422	LC
Indiana Univ Northwest	IN	3,447	C
Indiana Univ of Pennsylvania	PA	9,133	C
Indiana Univ South Bend	IN	3,515	C
Indiana Univ Southeast	IN	3,459	C
Indiana Univ-Purdue Univ Fort Wayne	IN	3,166	LC
Indiana Univ-Purdue Univ Indianapolis	IN	9,473	C
Indiana Wesleyan Univ	IN	17,680	C
Inter-American Univ of PR/Bayamon Univ College	PR	3,700	
Inter-American Univ of PR/Fajardo Campus	PR	4,000	
Inter-American Univ of PR/Metropolitan Campus	PR	4,166	
Inter-American Univ of PR/Ponce Regional College	PR	3,700	
Inter-American Univ of PR/San GermÈn	PR	6,390	
Iona College	NY	26,556	C
Iowa State Univ	IA	8,108	VC
Iowa Wesleyan College	IA	18,840	C
Ithaca College	NY	28,719	HC
Jackson State Univ	MS	6,776	LC
Jacksonville State Univ	AL	6,568	LC
Jacksonville Univ	FL	21,110	LC
James Madison Univ	VA	9,552	HC
Jarvis Christian College	TX	9,035	NC
John Carroll Univ	OH	24,140	VC
Johns Hopkins Univ	MD	35,226	MC
Johnson C. Smith Univ	NC	16,560	C+
Johnson State College	VT	10,776	C
Judson College	IL	18,980	LC
Juniata College	PA	26,080	VC
Kalamazoo College	MI	26,955	HC+
Kansas State Univ	KS	6,995	C
Kansas Wesleyan Univ	KS	17,400	C+
Kean Univ	NJ	11,159	C
Keene State College	NH	11,280	C
Kent State Univ	OH	11,104	C
Kentucky State Univ	KY	6,146	NC
Kentucky Wesleyan College	KY	15,800	C
Kenyon College	OH	32,130	HC+
Keuka College	NY	21,170	C
King's College	PA	24,680	C
Knox College	IL	28,230	HC
Knoxville College	TN	6,200	LC
Kutztown Univ of Pennsylvania	PA	8,907	C
La Roche College	PA	18,854	LC
La Salle Univ	PA	27,890	C
La Sierra Univ	CA	19,260	LC
Lafayette College	PA	32,655	MC
Lake Forest College	IL	27,460	VC
Lake Superior State Univ	MI	9,034	LC
Lakeland College	WI	17,950	C
Lamar Univ	TX	6,816	LC
Lambuth Univ	TN	14,254	C
Lander Univ	SC	8,618	LC
Lane College	TN	10,400	C+
Langston Univ	OK	2,308	LC
Lasell College	MA	24,100	C
Le Moyne College	NY	23,840	C
Lebanon Valley College of Pennsylvania	PA	25,700	VC
Lee Univ	TN	10,198	LC
Lees-McRae College	NC	17,106	LC
Lehigh Univ	PA	32,290	MC
LeMoyne-Owen College	TN	8,450	NC
Lenoir-Rhyne College	NC	19,186	C
Lewis and Clark College	OR	29,010	VC
Lewis Univ	IL	20,960	C
Lincoln Univ	MO	7,158	NC
Lincoln Univ	PA	11,198	C+
Lindenwood Univ	MO	17,250	C
Linfield College	OR	25,840	VC
Livingstone College	NC	13,360	LC
Lock Haven Univ of Pennsylvania	PA	9,534	C
LIU/Brooklyn Campus	NY	22,290	C
LIU/Southampton College	NY	26,270	C
Longwood College	VA	8,950	C
Loras College	IA	22,994	C+
Louisiana College	LA	11,516	C
Louisiana State Univ and A&M College	LA	8,014	VC
Louisiana State Univ in Shreveport	LA	2,480	NC
Louisiana Tech Univ	LA	6,506	C
Lourdes College	OH	13,100	LC
Loyola College in Maryland	MD	30,900	HC
Loyola Marymount Univ	CA	28,754	HC
Loyola Univ New Orleans	LA	23,506	VC+
Loyola Univ of Chicago	IL	25,992	VC
Luther College	IA	23,300	VC+
Lycoming College	PA	24,780	C
Lynchburg College	VA	23,405	C
Lynn Univ	FL	24,550	C
Macalester College	MN	28,814	HC+
Madonna Univ	MI	11,504	VC
Manchester College	IN	22,010	C
Manhattan College	NY	25,500	VC
Manhattanville College	NY	28,730	VC
Mansfield Univ	PA	9,648	C
Marian College	IN	21,020	C
Marlboro College	VT	26,410	VC+
Marquette Univ	WI	24,836	C+
Mars Hill College	NC	18,600	LC
Marshall Univ	WV	7,752	LC
Martin Univ	IN	8,370	SP
Mary Baldwin College	VA	23,440	C
Mary Washington College	VA	9,032	VC+
Marymount College/Tarrytown	NY	23,850	C
Marymount Manhattan College	NY	23,195	VC
Marymount Univ	VA	21,560	LC
Maryville College	TN	23,210	VC
Maryville Univ of St. Louis	MO	18,680	C
Marywood Univ	PA	24,639	C
Mass College of Liberal Arts	MA	8,717	LC
McKendree College	IL	18,300	C+
McMurry Univ	TX	15,287	C
McNeese State Univ	LA	5,259	LC
McPherson College	KS	17,710	C
Mercer Univ	GA	24,130	VC
Mercy College	NY	15,875	LC
Mercyhurst College	PA	20,694	C
Meredith College	NC	17,500	C
Merrimack College	MA	25,725	VC
Mesa State College	CO	8,051	C
Messiah College	PA	23,180	VC
Methodist College	NC	19,526	C
Metropolitan State College of Denver	CO	2,338	LC
Miami Univ	OH	12,885	VC+
Mich State Univ	MI	10,386	VC
MidAmerica Nazarene Univ	KS	16,960	C
Middle Tenn State Univ	TN	6,994	C
Middlebury College	VT	34,300	MC
Midland Lutheran College	NE	18,600	C
Midwestern State Univ	TX	6,704	NC
Millersville Univ of Pennsylvania	PA	10,153	VC
Milligan College	TN	17,550	C
Millikin Univ	IL	24,415	C+
Mills College	CA	27,950	C
Millsaps College	MS	22,608	VC+
Minn State Univ, Mankato	MN	7,296	LC
Minot State Univ	ND	5,466	LC
Miss College	MS	14,574	C
Miss State Univ	MS	7,853	C
Miss Valley State Univ	MS	6,345	C
Missouri Southern State College	MO	6,666	C
Missouri Valley College	MO	17,400	LC
Molloy College	NY	13,940	C
Monmouth College	IL	21,550	C
Montana State Univ-Billings	MT	7,653	NC
Montana State Univ-Bozeman	MT	8,431	C
Montclair State Univ	NJ	10,287	LC
Moorhead State Univ	MN	7,000	LC
Moravian College	PA	27,065	VC
Morehead State Univ	KY	6,510	C

ST = STATE **$IS** = IN-STATE COSTS **SR** = SELECTOR RATING

School	ST	$IS	SR
Morehouse College	GA	19,814	C
Morgan State Univ	MD	10,078	LC
Morris Brown College	GA	15,993	LC
Morris College	SC	9,995	LC
Mount Holyoke College	MA	34,128	HC
Mount Mercy College	IA	19,390	VC
Mount St. Mary College	NY	18,825	C
Mount St. Mary's College	CA	24,430	C
Mount St. Mary's College	MD	25,740	C
Mount Union College	OH	21,120	C
Mount Vernon Nazarene College	OH	17,027	C
Muhlenberg College	PA	28,170	HC
Murray State Univ	KY	6,672	C
Muskingum College	OH	18,760	C
Nazareth College of Rochester	NY	22,036	VC
Nebr Wesleyan Univ	NE	18,767	VC
New College of Florida	FL	8,130	HC+
New England College	NH	20,706	LC
New Jersey City Univ	NJ	9,100	LC
New Mexico Highlands Univ	NM	6,256	NC
New Mexico State Univ	NM	7,302	C
New York Inst of Technology	NY	21,756	C
New York Univ	NY	35,200	MC
Newberry College	SC	19,670	LC
Newman Univ	KS	14,098	LC
Niagara Univ	NY	22,250	C+
Nicholls State Univ	LA	5,290	NC
Norfolk State Univ	VA	8,382	LC
N Car Agricultural and Technical State Univ	NC	6,659	LC
N Car Central Univ	NC	6,418	LC
N Car State Univ	NC	8,680	HC
N Car Wesleyan College	NC	15,650	LC
North Central College	IL	22,944	C+
N Dak State Univ	ND	7,004	VC
North Georgia College and State Univ	GA	6,322	C+
North Park Univ	IL	24,030	C
Northeastern Illinois Univ	IL	2,898	NC
Northeastern State Univ	OK	4,704	LC
Northeastern Univ	MA	30,078	VC
Northern Arizona Univ	AZ	7,398	C
Northern Illinois Univ	IL	9,545	C
Northern Kentucky Univ	KY	6,352	NC
Northern Mich Univ	MI	9,693	C
Northern State Univ	SD	6,279	LC
Northland College	WI	21,435	C+
Northwest Missouri State Univ	MO	7,922	LC
Northwestern College of Iowa	IA	17,630	C+
Northwestern Okla State Univ	OK	4,542	NC
Northwestern State Univ of Louisiana	LA	5,745	NC
Northwestern Univ	IL	33,615	MC
Notre Dame de Namur Univ	CA	26,932	LC
Oakland Univ	MI	9,418	C
Oberlin College	OH	33,140	HC+
Occidental College	CA	32,288	HC
Oglala Lakota College	SD	1,950	NC
Oglethorpe Univ	GA	19,100	LC
Ohio Dominican College	OH	18,100	LC
Ohio Northern Univ	OH	27,765	VC
Ohio Univ	OH	11,769	C
Ohio Wesleyan Univ	OH	29,670	VC+
Okla Baptist Univ	OK	13,878	VC
Okla City Univ	OK	15,810	C
Okla State Univ	OK	7,650	VC
Old Dominion Univ	VA	9,386	C
Olivet College	MI	17,410	C
Olivet Nazarene Univ	IL	18,444	C
Oregon State Univ	OR	9,612	VC
Ottawa Univ	KS	11,800	LC
Otterbein College	OH	23,439	C
Ouachita Baptist Univ	AR	16,460	VC
Our Lady of the Lake Univ of San Antonio	TX	17,336	C
Pace Univ	NY	24,200	C
Pacific Lutheran Univ	WA	23,318	VC
Pacific Union College	CA	20,250	VC
Pacific Univ	OR	24,250	C
Paine College	GA	11,896	LC
Park Univ	MO	9,816	C
Paul Quinn College	TX	8,150	LC
Penn State Univ/Univ Park Campus	PA	11,126	VC
Pepperdine Univ	CA	32,830	VC
Peru State College	NE	6,342	NC
Pfeiffer Univ	NC	18,580	C
Philander Smith College	AR	7,380	NC
Piedmont College	GA	16,900	C
Pikeville College	KY	12,000	NC
Pittsburg State Univ	KS	6,228	NC
Pitzer College	CA	33,930	HC
Point Loma Nazarene Univ	CA	21,380	VC
Pomona College	CA	33,960	MC
Pontifical Catholic Univ of PR/Ponce	PR	7,076	
Portland State Univ	OR	11,220	C
Prairie View A&M Univ	TX	3,172	LC
Presbyterian College	SC	23,356	VC
Prescott College	AZ	13,430	C
Princeton Univ	NJ	35,072	MC
Principia College	IL	23,865	C+
Providence College	RI	27,620	HC
Purdue Univ/Calumet	IN	6,630	NC
Purdue Univ/West Lafayette	IN	10,284	VC
Quincy Univ	IL	20,450	C
Quinnipiac Univ	CT	27,370	C
Radford Univ	VA	8,302	C
Ramapo College of New Jersey	NJ	13,550	VC
Randolph-Macon College	VA	24,395	C
Randolph-Macon Woman's College	VA	25,820	VC+
Reed College	OR	33,350	HC+
Regis College	MA	26,750	C
Regis Univ	CO	25,740	C+
Rhode Island College	RI	8,700	LC
Rhodes College	TN	26,466	HC+
Rider Univ	NJ	27,400	C
Ripon College	WI	24,180	VC+
Rivier College	NH	24,215	C
Roanoke College	VA	24,689	VC
Roberts Wesleyan College	NY	20,160	C+
Rockford College	IL	23,930	C
Rockhurst Univ	MO	20,090	C
Rocky Mountain College	MT	18,113	C
Rollins College	FL	31,223	HC
Roosevelt Univ	IL	20,240	LC
Rosemont College	PA	24,060	C
Rowan Univ	NJ	12,365	VC
Russell Sage College	NY	23,674	C+
Rust College	MS	7,800	C+
Rutgers, The State Univ of New Jersey New Brunswick Campus	NJ	12,709	C
Rutgers, The State Univ of New Jersey/ CamdenCampus	NJ	6,484	C
Rutgers, The State Univ of New Jersey/Newark Campus	NJ	6,394	C
Sacred Heart Univ	CT	26,588	VC
Saginaw Valley State Univ	MI	9,465	C
St. Ambrose Univ	IA	19,994	C
St. Anselm College	NH	27,405	C
St. Augustine's College	NC	12,990	C+
St. Bonaventure Univ	NY	21,956	C
St. Cloud State Univ	MN	7,180	C
St. Edward's Univ	TX	17,846	C
St. Francis College	NY	9,610	C
St. Francis Univ	PA	24,486	LC
St. John Fisher College	NY	21,800	C
St. John's Univ	MN	23,640	VC
St. John's Univ	NY	26,660	C
St. Joseph College	CT	25,960	LC
St. Joseph's College	IN	21,640	C
St. Joseph's College of Maine	ME	22,500	LC
St. Joseph's Univ	PA	29,715	VC+
St. Lawrence Univ	NY	32,605	VC
St. Leo Univ	FL	19,250	LC
St. Louis Univ	MO	26,590	VC+
St. Mary College	KS	17,298	C
St. Mary's College	IN	24,474	VC
St. Mary's College	MI	13,314	LC
St. Mary's College of Maryland	MD	14,104	HC
St. Mary's Univ of Minn	MN	19,975	C
St. Mary's Univ of San Antonio	TX	19,735	C
St. Michael's College	VT	26,935	VC
St. Norbert College	WI	23,169	VC
St. Olaf College	MN	25,880	HC
St. Paul's College	VA	13,340	C
St. Peter's College	NJ	22,292	LC
St. Thomas Univ	FL	19,500	LC
St. Vincent College	PA	22,942	VC
St. Xavier Univ	IL	21,104	C
Salem College	NC	23,065	VC
Salem State College	MA	4,481	LC
Salisbury Univ	MD	10,576	VC
Salve Regina Univ	RI	26,460	C
Sam Houston State Univ	TX	6,076	LC
Samford Univ	AL	16,340	VC
San Diego State Univ	CA	9,716	C+
San Francisco State Univ	CA	7,139	LC
San Jose State Univ	CA	8,187	C
Santa Clara Univ	CA	28,371	VC+
Sarah Lawrence College	NY	37,516	HC
Savannah State Univ	GA	2,550	LC
Seattle Pacific Univ	WA	22,674	C+
Seattle Univ	WA	24,183	VC
Seton Hall Univ	NJ	26,910	LC
Seton Hill College	PA	21,875	C
Shaw Univ	NC	12,810	C
Shawnee State Univ	OH	8,634	NC
Shenandoah Univ	VA	22,550	NC
Shepherd College	WV	7,062	LC
Shippensburg Univ of Pennsylvania	PA	9,652	C
Shorter College	GA	15,185	C
Siena College	NY	22,685	VC
Simmons College	MA	30,418	VC
Simpson College	IA	21,200	C+
Skidmore College	NY	34,201	VC+
Slippery Rock Univ	PA	9,152	LC
Smith College	MA	33,302	HC+
Sonoma State Univ	CA	8,953	C
S Car State Univ	SC	6,586	LC
S Dak State Univ	SD	6,848	C
Southeast Missouri State Univ	MO	8,367	C+
Southeastern Louisiana Univ	LA	6,047	LC
Southeastern Okla State Univ	OK	4,917	C
Southern Arkansas Univ	AR	5,740	LC
Southern Conn State Univ	CT	10,310	C
Southern Illinois Univ at Carbondale	IL	8,621	C
Southern Illinois Univ Edwardsville	IL	7,869	LC
Southern Methodist Univ	TX	28,349	VC
Southern Nazarene Univ	OK	14,634	NC
Southern Oregon Univ	OR	9,429	C
Southern Univ and A&M College	LA	6,365	C+
Southern Univ at New Orleans	LA	995	NC
Southern Utah Univ	UT	7,254	C
Southwest Baptist Univ	MO	13,426	LC
Southwest Missouri State Univ	MO	7,600	LC
Southwest State Univ	MN	7,117	LC
Southwest Texas State Univ	TX	8,730	VC
Southwestern Univ	TX	22,550	HC
Spalding Univ	KY	15,196	C
Spelman College	GA	19,215	C+
Spring Arbor Univ	MI	17,976	C
Springfield College	MA	24,520	C
Stanford Univ	CA	34,222	MC
SUNY/College at Brockport	NY	10,267	C
SUNY/College at Buffalo	NY	8,025	C
SUNY/College at Cortland	NY	10,564	C
SUNY/College at Fredonia	NY	10,125	C
SUNY/College at Geneseo	NY	9,970	HC
SUNY/College at Old Westbury	NY	9,818	LC
SUNY/College at Oneonta	NY	9,981	C
SUNY/College at Oswego	NY	10,856	C
SUNY/College at Plattsburgh	NY	9,729	C
SUNY/College at Potsdam	NY	10,519	C
SUNY/College at Purchase	NY	10,587	VC
SUNY/Empire State College	NY	3,545	SP
SUNY/Univ at Albany	NY	10,997	VC
SUNY/Univ at Binghamton	NY	10,653	HC
SUNY/Univ at Buffalo	NY	11,033	VC
SUNY/Univ at New Paltz	NY	9,685	VC
SUNY/Univ at Stony Brook	NY	10,998	VC
State Univ of West Georgia	GA	7,101	C
Stephen F. Austin State Univ	TX	6,905	C
Stetson Univ	FL	25,640	VC
Stonehill College	MA	26,852	HC
Suffolk Univ	MA	26,516	C
Susquehanna Univ	PA	27,270	VC
Swarthmore College	PA	34,538	MC
Sweet Briar College	VA	25,310	VC
Syracuse Univ	NY	30,710	HC
Tabor College	KS	17,600	LC
Talladega College	AL	10,110	LC
Tarleton State Univ	TX	7,160	C
Taylor Univ	IN	21,562	VC+
Teikyo Post Univ	CT	21,800	C
Temple Univ	PA	14,124	C
Tenn State Univ	TN	7,058	VC
Tenn Tech Univ	TN	6,968	C
Texas A&M Univ	TX	8,988	VC
Texas A&M Univ at Commerce	TX	7,326	C
Texas A&M Univ at Kingsville	TX	6,446	LC
Texas Christian Univ	TX	19,910	C
Texas Lutheran Univ	TX	17,660	C
Texas Southern Univ	TX	6,576	NC
Texas Tech Univ	TX	8,825	C
Texas Woman's Univ	TX	5,855	LC
Ohio State Univ	OH	10,819	VC
Thiel College	PA	18,419	LC
Thomas Edison State College	NJ	2,750	SP
Thomas More College	KY	17,700	LC
Tougaloo College	MS	9,200	NC
Touro College	NY	14,950	VC
Towson Univ	MD	11,088	VC
Transylvania Univ	KY	21,780	VC+
Trinity Christian College	IL	19,415	C
Trinity College	CT	34,300	HC
Trinity Univ	TX	21,444	HC
Troy State Univ/Dothan	AL	3,296	C
Truman State Univ	MO	8,568	VC+
Tufts Univ	MA	34,874	MC
Tulane Univ	LA	34,013	HC+
Turabo Univ	PR	4,110	
Tuskegee Univ	AL	14,600	LC
Union College	NY	32,646	HC
Union Univ	TN	18,930	C+
Universidad Metropolitana	PR	3,324	
Univ of Akron	OH	10,530	NC
Univ of Alabama at Birmingham	AL	10,110	C
Univ of Alabama at Huntsville	AL	7,916	VC
Univ of Alaska Anchorage	AK	9,100	NC
Univ of Alaska Fairbanks	AK	8,265	NC
Univ of Arizona	AZ	8,614	C
Univ of Arkansas	AR	8,334	VC
Univ of Arkansas at Little Rock	AR	5,637	NC
Univ of Arkansas at Pine Bluff	AR	7,925	C
Univ of Calif at Berkeley	CA	14,134	MC
Univ of Calif at Davis	CA	12,796	VC
Univ of Calif at Irvine	CA	11,756	C
Univ of Calif at Los Angeles	CA	13,227	MC
Univ of Calif at Riverside	CA	12,479	C
Univ of Calif at San Diego	CA	11,372	HC
Univ of Calif at Santa Barbara	CA	11,732	VC
Univ of Calif at Santa Cruz	CA	13,655	VC
Univ of Central Arkansas	AR	6,388	C
Univ of Central Florida	FL	8,251	VC
Univ of Central Okla	OK	5,205	C
Univ of Chicago	IL	35,087	MC
Univ of Cincinnati	OH	12,491	LC
Univ of Colo at Boulder	CO	9,255	VC
Univ of Colo at Colo Springs	CO	9,403	C
Univ of Colo at Denver	CO	3,673	C
Univ of Conn	CT	12,122	VC
Univ of Dayton	OH	20,400	VC
Univ of Delaware	DE	10,824	VC
Univ of Denver	CO	28,783	VC
Univ of Detroit Mercy	MI	21,620	LC
Univ of Dubuque	IA	19,990	C
Univ of Evansville	IN	22,865	VC+
Univ of Findlay	OH	23,962	NC
Univ of Florida	FL	7,874	HC
Univ of Georgia	GA	8,656	VC
Univ of Great Falls	MT	15,360	C
Univ of Hartford	CT	28,884	C
Univ of Hawaii at Hilo	HI	6,497	C
Univ of Hawaii at Manoa	HI	7,862	VC
Univ of Houston	TX	8,410	C
Univ of Idaho	ID	7,026	C
Univ of Illinois at Chicago	IL	10,702	VC
Univ of Illinois at Urbana-Champaign	IL	11,316	HC+
Univ of Indianapolis	IN	20,840	C
Univ of Iowa	IA	8,607	C+
Univ of Kansas	KS	7,232	VC
Univ of Kentucky	KY	7,765	C
Univ of La Verne	CA	24,280	C
Univ of Louisiana at Lafayette	LA	5,200	C
Univ of Louisiana at Monroe	LA	5,207	NC
Univ of Louisville	KY	7,402	LC
Univ of Maine	ME	10,798	C
Univ of Maine at Farmington	ME	9,163	C
Univ of Mary Hardin-Baylor	TX	13,929	C
Univ of Maryland/Baltimore County	MD	12,190	VC
Univ of Maryland/College Park	MD	11,959	C
Univ of Maryland/Eastern Shore	MD	9,258	C
Univ of Mass Amherst	MA	10,995	VC
Univ of Mass Boston	MA	4,227	C
Univ of Mass Dartmouth	MA	9,852	C
Univ of Mass Lowell	MA	9,470	VC
Univ of Memphis	TN	7,271	C
Univ of Miami	FL	31,130	HC
Univ of Mich/Ann Arbor	MI	13,003	HC+
Univ of Mich/Dearborn	MI	4,677	VC
Univ of Mich/Flint	MI	4,323	C
Univ of Minn/Duluth	MN	10,436	C
Univ of Minn/Morris	MN	10,716	VC
Univ of Minn/Twin Cities	MN	11,123	VC
Univ of Miss	MS	7,666	C
Univ of Missouri/Columbia	MO	9,803	HC
Univ of Missouri/Kansas City	MO	9,685	VC
Univ of Missouri/St. Louis	MO	9,966	C
Univ of Mobile	AL	13,620	LC
Univ of Montana	MT	8,038	C
Univ of Montevallo	AL	7,266	C
Univ of Nebr at Kearney	NE	7,048	NC
Univ of Nebr at Lincoln	NE	8,325	C+
Univ of Nebr at Omaha	NE	6,867	C
Univ of Nevada/Las Vegas	NV	8,281	VC
Univ of Nevada/Reno	NV	8,737	C
Univ of New Hampshire	NH	13,207	C
Univ of New Mexico	NM	8,026	C
Univ of New Orleans	LA	10,160	C
Univ of North Alabama	AL	7,016	NC
Univ of N Car at Asheville	NC	6,896	VC
Univ of N Car at Chapel Hill	NC	8,789	HC
Univ of N Car at Charlotte	NC	7,254	C
Univ of N Car at Greensboro	NC	6,858	C
Univ of N Car at Pembroke	NC	5,914	LC
Univ of N Car at Wilmington	NC	7,769	C
Univ of N Dak	ND	7,067	VC
Univ of North Florida	FL	8,089	VC

School	ST	$IS	SR
Univ of North Texas	TX	7,629	C
Univ of Northern Colo	CO	8,082	C+
Univ of Northern Iowa	IA	7,850	C
Univ of Notre Dame	IN	30,707	MC
Univ of Okla	OK	7,616	VC
Univ of Oregon	OR	9,969	C
Univ of Pennsylvania	PA	34,614	MC
Univ of Pittsburgh at Bradford	PA	12,696	C
Univ of Pittsburgh at Johnstown	PA	13,044	LC
Univ of Pittsburgh at Pittsburgh	PA	13,592	HC
Univ of Portland	OR	24,950	VC
Univ of PR/Mayaguez	PR	5,285	
Univ of PR/Rio Piedras	PR	5,510	
Univ of Puget Sound	WA	28,285	HC
Univ of Redlands	CA	29,246	VC
Univ of Rhode Island	RI	12,414	C
Univ of Richmond	VA	27,300	HC
Univ of Rio Grande	OH	8,728	NC
Univ of St. Thomas	MN	24,044	VC
Univ of San Diego	CA	29,198	HC
Univ of San Francisco	CA	27,302	VC
Univ of Science and Arts of Okla	OK	5,245	C
Univ of Scranton	PA	27,964	C+
Univ of Sioux Falls	SD	16,390	C
Univ of South Alabama	AL	6,976	LC
Univ of S Car at Aiken	SC	7,828	LC
Univ of S Car at Columbia	SC	8,748	VC
Univ of S Car at Spartanburg	SC	7,318	C+
Univ of S Dak	SD	7,036	C
Univ of South Florida	FL	8,154	C
Univ of Southern Calif	CA	33,647	MC
Univ of Southern Colo	CO	7,821	LC
Univ of Southern Indiana	IN	8,655	LC
Univ of Southern Maine	ME	10,569	C
Univ of Southern Miss	MS	6,155	LC
Univ of Tampa	FL	22,612	C
Univ of Tenn at Chattanooga	TN	7,783	C
Univ of Tenn at Knoxville	TN	8,214	C
Univ of Tenn at Martin	TN	8,268	C
Univ of Texas at Arlington	TX	7,192	LC
Univ of Texas at Austin	TX	9,437	HC
Univ of Texas at Dallas	TX	9,305	VC
Univ of Texas at El Paso	TX	5,076	LC
Univ of Texas at San Antonio	TX	9,088	NC
Univ of Texas-Pan American	TX	4,823	C
Univ of the District of Columbia	DC	2,844	NC
Univ of the Incarnate Word	TX	18,478	C
Univ of the Ozarks	AR	13,904	C
Univ of the Pacific	CA	28,255	VC
Univ of Toledo	OH	11,206	NC
Univ of Tulsa	OK	19,090	HC
Univ of Utah	UT	7,703	C
Univ of Vermont	VT	14,761	C+
Univ of Virginia	VA	9,391	HC+
Univ of Washington	WA	10,361	VC
Univ of West Alabama	AL	6,048	C
Univ of West Florida	FL	7,518	C
Univ of Wisc/Eau Claire	WI	7,032	VC
Univ of Wisc/La Crosse	WI	7,250	VC
Univ of Wisc/Madison	WI	8,262	VC
Univ of Wisc/Milwaukee	WI	8,907	LC
Univ of Wisc/Oshkosh	WI	6,130	LC
Univ of Wisc/Parkside	WI	6,160	LC
Univ of Wisc/River Falls	WI	6,356	LC
Univ of Wisc/Stevens Point	WI	7,116	C
Univ of Wisc/Superior	WI	7,051	C+
Univ of Wisc/Whitewater	WI	6,937	C
Univ of Wyoming	WY	7,143	LC
Upper Iowa Univ	IA	17,438	C
Urbana Univ	OH	17,004	C
Ursinus College	PA	31,350	VC
Ursuline College	OH	19,430	LC
Utah State Univ	UT	6,771	C
Utica College of Syracuse Univ	NY	24,400	LC
Valdosta State Univ	GA	6,988	C
Valparaiso Univ	IN	23,570	VC+
Vanderbilt Univ	TN	34,482	MC
Vanguard Univ of Southern Calif	CA	20,212	C
Vassar College	NY	33,450	MC
Villanova Univ	PA	31,997	HC
Virginia Commonwealth Univ	VA	9,030	C
Virginia Polytechnic Inst and State Univ	VA	7,652	C
Virginia State Univ	VA	8,182	LC
Virginia Union Univ	VA	15,358	LC
Virginia Wesleyan College	VA	22,350	LC
Viterbo Univ	WI	18,043	C
Voorhees College	SC	9,976	C+
Wagner College	NY	27,000	C
Wake Forest Univ	NC	30,290	MC
Walla Walla College	WA	20,925	C
Walsh Univ	OH	16,880	C
Warner Pacific College	OR	20,370	LC
Wartburg College	IA	21,165	VC
Washburn Univ of Topeka	KS	6,766	NC
Washington and Jefferson College	PA	26,255	VC
Washington and Lee Univ	VA	25,095	MC
Washington College	MD	28,040	VC
Washington State Univ	WA	9,388	C
Wayne State College	NE	6,255	NC
Wayne State Univ	MI	6,720	C
Waynesburg College	PA	17,610	LC
Weber State Univ	UT	6,897	NC
Webster Univ	MO	19,804	VC
Wellesley College	MA	33,394	MC
Wells College	NY	19,350	VC
Wesleyan College	GA	17,050	VC
Wesleyan Univ	CT	3,405	MC
West Chester Univ of Pennsylvania	PA	9,792	VC
West Liberty State College	WV	6,056	LC
West Texas A&M Univ	TX	6,538	C
West Virginia State College	WV	6,264	NC
West Virginia Univ	WV	8,304	C
West Virginia Wesleyan College	WV	22,920	C
Western Carolina Univ	NC	5,667	C
Western Conn State Univ	CT	10,074	C
Western Illinois Univ	IL	9,571	C
Western Kentucky Univ	KY	6,834	C
Western Maryland College	MD	26,000	VC
Western Mich Univ	MI	10,016	C
Western New England College	MA	23,882	C
Western New Mexico Univ	NM	5,950	LC
Western Oregon Univ	OR	8,829	C
Western State College of Colo	CO	7,585	LC
Western Washington Univ	WA	8,624	VC
Westfield State College	MA	8,394	C
Westminster College	MO	19,990	C+
Westminster College	PA	22,960	C
Westminster College	UT	17,226	C
Westmont College	CA	29,748	VC
Wheaton College	IL	21,934	HC
Wheaton College	MA	32,940	VC
Whitman College	WA	29,086	HC
Whittier College	CA	29,108	C
Whitworth College	WA	23,938	VC
Wichita State Univ	KS	6,879	C
Widener Univ	PA	26,920	C
Wilberforce Univ	OH	14,937	LC
Wiley College	TX	8,100	LC
Wilkes Univ	PA	25,800	C
Willamette Univ	OR	29,422	VC+
William Paterson Univ of New Jersey	NJ	11,000	LC
William Penn Univ	IA	17,575	C
Williams College	MA	32,270	MC
Wilmington College	OH	21,826	C
Wingate Univ	NC	19,140	C
Winona State Univ	MN	8,570	C
Winston-Salem State Univ	NC	5,927	LC
Winthrop Univ	SC	9,106	C
Wittenberg Univ	OH	28,766	VC
Wofford College	SC	23,995	VC
Worcester State College	MA	7,901	LC
Wright State Univ	OH	9,141	LC
Xavier Univ	OH	23,880	C
Xavier Univ of Louisiana	LA	17,000	LC
Yale Univ	CT	34,030	MC
Yeshiva Univ	NY	21,400	C
York College of Pennsylvania	PA	12,550	VC
Youngstown State Univ	OH	9,318	NC

SOIL SCIENCE

School	ST	$IS	SR
Alabama A&M Univ	AL	5,100	LC
Auburn Univ	AL	5,510	C
Baylor Univ	TX	18,298	VC+
Calif Polytechnic State Univ	CA	8,747	VC
Clemson Univ	SC	7,600	C
Cornell Univ	NY	34,614	MC
Eastern Oregon Univ	OR	8,772	C
Huntingdon College	AL	18,400	VC
Mich State Univ	MI	10,386	VC
Montana State Univ-Bozeman	MT	8,431	C
New Mexico State Univ	NM	7,302	C
N Car State Univ	NC	8,680	HC
N Dak State Univ	ND	7,004	VC
Oregon State Univ	OR	9,612	VC
Penn State Univ/Univ Park Campus	PA	11,126	VC
SUNY/College of Environmental Science and Forestry	NY	12,446	VC
Tenn Tech Univ	TN	6,968	C
Texas A&M Univ at Kingsville	TX	6,446	LC
Univ of Arizona	AZ	8,614	C
Univ of Calif at Davis	CA	12,796	VC
Univ of Delaware	DE	10,824	VC
Univ of Florida	FL	7,874	HC
Univ of Idaho	ID	7,026	C
Univ of Mass Amherst	MA	10,995	VC
Univ of Missouri/Columbia	MO	9,803	HC
Univ of Nebr at Lincoln	NE	8,325	C+
Univ of New Hampshire	NH	13,207	C
Univ of Tenn at Knoxville	TN	8,214	C
Univ of Wisc/Madison	WI	8,262	VC
Univ of Wisc/Platteville	WI	7,282	C
Univ of Wisc/River Falls	WI	6,356	LC
Univ of Wisc/Stevens Point	WI	7,116	C
Utah State Univ	UT	6,771	C
Virginia Polytechnic Inst and State Univ	VA	7,652	C
Washington State Univ	WA	9,388	C
West Texas A&M Univ	TX	6,538	C

SOUTH ASIAN STUDIES

School	ST	$IS	SR
Brown Univ	RI	34,973	MC
Oakland Univ	MI	9,418	C
Univ of Calif at Santa Cruz	CA	13,655	VC
Univ of Minn/Twin Cities	MN	11,123	VC
Univ of Pennsylvania	PA	34,614	MC
Univ of Washington	WA	10,361	VC
Univ of Wisc/Madison	WI	8,262	VC
Washington Univ in St. Louis	MO	34,593	MC

SOUTHWEST AMERICAN STUDIES

School	ST	$IS	SR
College of Santa Fe	NM	20,250	LC
Colo College	CO	31,525	HC+
Fort Lewis College	CO	7,659	LC
Southern Methodist Univ	TX	28,349	VC

SPANISH

School	ST	$IS	SR
Abilene Christian Univ	TX	16,300	VC
Adams State College	CO	7,468	C
Adelphi Univ	NY	23,320	VC
Adrian College	MI	19,670	C
Agnes Scott College	GA	24,950	VC
Alabama State Univ	AL	6,404	C
Albany State Univ	GA	5,764	C+
Albertson College of Idaho	ID	23,900	VC
Albertus Magnus College	CT	22,154	C
Albion College	MI	25,224	VC
Albright College	PA	27,642	C
Alfred Univ	NY	27,212	C+
Allegheny College	PA	27,780	VC
Alma College	MI	22,586	VC
American International College	MA	22,268	LC
Amherst College	MA	34,340	MC
Anderson Univ	IN	19,430	LC
Andrews Univ	MI	17,696	LC
Angelo State Univ	TX	7,028	C
Appalachian State Univ	NC	6,353	C
Aquinas College	MI	20,052	C+
Arizona State Univ-Main	AZ	7,726	C
Arkansas State Univ	AR	7,480	C
Armstrong Atlantic State Univ	GA	7,084	C
Asbury College	KY	18,540	VC
Ashland Univ	OH	22,182	LC
Assumption College	MA	26,320	C
Atlantic Union College	MA	34,034	LC
Auburn Univ	AL	5,510	C
Augsburg College	MN	22,978	C
Augusta State Univ	GA	2,282	C
Augustana College	IL	24,117	VC+
Augustana College	SD	20,760	VC
Austin College	TX	22,150	VC+
Austin Peay State Univ	TN	5,814	LC
Azusa Pacific Univ	CA	22,422	VC
Baker Univ	KS	14,780	C+
Baldwin-Wallace College	OH	22,010	VC+
Ball State Univ	IN	8,660	C
Bard College	NY	33,912	HC
Barry Univ	FL	24,100	LC
Bates College	ME	34,100	MC
Baylor Univ	TX	18,298	VC+
Beloit College	WI	27,482	HC
Bemidji State Univ	MN	7,957	C
Benedictine College	KS	18,485	LC
Benedictine Univ	IL	21,330	C
Bennington College	VT	31,350	VC
Berea College	KY	4,070	VC
Berry College	GA	18,850	C
Bethany College	WV	18,566	C
Bethel College	KS	17,355	C+
Bethel College	MN	22,740	VC
Biola Univ	CA	21,902	VC
Birmingham-Southern College	AL	22,960	C
Black Hills State Univ	SD	6,652	LC
Blackburn College	IL	13,690	C
Bloomfield College	NJ	17,000	C
Bloomsburg Univ of Pennsylvania	PA	9,434	C
Bluffton College	OH	20,644	C
Boston Univ	MA	34,358	MC
Bowdoin College	ME	32,650	MC
Bowling Green State Univ	OH	10,794	C
Bradley Univ	IL	20,970	VC
Brandeis Univ	MA	34,481	MC
Briar Cliff Univ	IA	18,657	LC
Bridgewater College	VA	22,950	C
Bridgewater State College	MA	7,589	C+
Brigham Young Univ	UT	7,840	HC
Bryan College	TN	16,400	VC
Bryn Mawr College	PA	33,580	HC+
Bucknell Univ	PA	31,096	HC
Buena Vista Univ	IA	22,828	C
Butler Univ	IN	25,580	VC+
Cabrini College	PA	25,950	LC
Caldwell College	NJ	20,940	LC
Calif Lutheran Univ	CA	23,500	LC
Calif State Polytechnic Univ, Pomona	CA	8,615	C
Cal State, Bakersfield	CA	6,090	LC
Cal State, Chico	CA	8,598	LC
Cal State, Dominguez Hills	CA	5,840	LC
Cal State, Fresno	CA	7,762	C
Cal State, Fullerton	CA	5,440	LC
Cal State, Hayward	CA	7,400	LC
Cal State, Long Beach	CA	7,400	LC
Cal State, Los Angeles	CA	5,050	C
Cal State, Northridge	CA	7,781	C
Cal State, Sacramento	CA	7,488	C
Cal State, San Bernardino	CA	6,516	C
Cal State, San Marcos	CA	1,736	LC
Cal State, Stanislaus	CA	8,895	C
Calif Univ of Pennsylvania	PA	10,388	C
Calvin College	MI	20,050	NC
Campbell Univ	NC	16,599	C
Canisius College	NY	24,696	C+
Capital Univ	OH	23,630	C
Cardinal Stritch Univ	WI	17,620	C
Carleton College	MN	30,780	MC
Carlow College	PA	19,366	C
Carnegie Mellon Univ	PA	32,682	MC
Carroll College	MT	19,140	C
Carroll College	WI	21,170	C
Carson-Newman College	TN	16,490	C
Carthage College	WI	23,670	C
Case Western Reserve Univ	OH	27,418	C
Castleton State College	VT	10,922	LC
Catawba College	NC	19,620	C
Catholic Univ of America	DC	29,332	VC
Cedar Crest College	PA	25,145	C+
Cedarville Univ	OH	17,553	VC
Centenary College of Louisiana	LA	21,600	C+
Central College	IA	21,206	C
Central Conn State Univ	CT	10,404	C
Central Methodist College	MO	16,460	C
Central Mich Univ	MI	8,355	C
Central Missouri State Univ	MO	7,920	C
Central Univ of Bayamon	PR	3,335	
Central Washington Univ	WA	8,985	LC
Centre College	KY	24,000	HC
Chapman Univ	CA	30,218	VC
Charleston Southern Univ	SC	17,122	C
Chatham College	PA	25,454	C+
Chestnut Hill College	PA	24,790	LC
Chicago State Univ	IL	8,851	C+
Christopher Newport Univ	VA	8,862	VC
Citadel, The	SC	9,126	C
CUNY/Baruch College	NY	3,275	VC+
CUNY/Brooklyn College	NY	3,403	LC
CUNY/City College	NY	3,309	LC
CUNY/College of Staten Island	NY	3,358	NC
CUNY/Herbert H. Lehman College	NY	3,320	LC
CUNY/Hunter College	NY	5,147	C+
CUNY/Queens College	NY	3,403	VC
CUNY/York College	NY	3,292	NC
Claremont McKenna College	CA	32,700	MC
Clarion Univ of Pennsylvania	PA	11,272	LC
Clark Univ	MA	29,170	HC
Clarke College	IA	20,625	C+
Clemson Univ	SC	7,600	C
Cleveland State Univ	OH	10,146	NC
Coastal Carolina Univ	SC	9,220	C
Coe College	IA	24,750	VC
Coker College	SC	20,120	C
Colby College	ME	34,290	MC
Colgate Univ	NY	33,480	MC
College of Charleston	SC	8,350	HC
College of Mount St. Vincent	NY	24,230	C
College of New Jersey	NJ	13,425	HC
College of New Rochelle	NY	20,000	C
College of Our Lady of the Elms	MA	20,644	C
College of St. Benedict	MN	23,921	VC
College of St. Catherine	MN	22,324	VC
College of St. Elizabeth	NJ	22,510	C
College of St. Rose	NY	19,084	C
College of the Holy Cross	MA	32,780	MC
College of the Ozarks	MO	2,650	C+
College of William and Mary	VA	10,002	MC
College of Wooster	OH	28,350	VC
Colo College	CO	31,525	HC+
Colo State Univ	CO	9,672	C
Columbia College	SC	19,050	LC
Columbia Univ/Barnard College	NY	33,694	MC

School	ST	$IS	SR
Columbia Univ/Columbia College	NY	35,190	MC
Columbia Univ/School of General Studies	NY	35,000	C
Concordia College/Moorhead	MN	18,835	C
Concordia Univ at Austin	TX	16,740	LC
Concordia Univ Wisc	WI	16,600	LC
Converse College	SC	21,990	VC
Cornell College	IA	24,980	VC
Cornell Univ	NY	34,614	MC
Creighton Univ	NE	23,476	VC
Daemen College	NY	20,620	C
Dana College	NE	18,046	C
Dartmouth College	NH	34,458	MC
David Lipscomb Univ	TN	16,158	VC
Davidson College	NC	30,823	MC
De Sales Univ	PA	22,610	VC
Delaware State Univ	DE	8,104	LC
Denison Univ	OH	29,640	HC
DePaul Univ	IL	23,590	VC
DePauw Univ	IN	28,000	HC
Dickinson College	PA	32,210	VC+
Dickinson State Univ	ND	5,495	NC
Dillard Univ	LA	16,046	VC
Doane College	NE	17,600	LC
Dominican College	NY	20,400	LC
Dominican Univ	IL	20,800	C
Dordt College	IA	18,100	C+
Drew Univ/College of Liberal Arts	NJ	32,152	VC
Drury Univ	MO	15,250	VC
Duke Univ	NC	34,396	MC
Duquesne Univ	PA	24,242	C+
Earlham College	IN	27,446	VC+
East Stroudsburg Univ of Pennsylvania	PA	8,430	LC
East Texas Baptist Univ	TX	12,349	LC
Eastern College	PA	19,641	LC
Eastern Conn State Univ	CT	10,362	C
Eastern Kentucky Univ	KY	6,552	C
Eastern Mennonite Univ	VA	20,700	VC
Eastern Mich Univ	MI	9,855	C
Eastern Nazarene College	MA	19,433	LC
Eastern New Mexico Univ	NM	4,113	LC
Eastern Washington Univ	WA	7,972	LC
Eckerd College	FL	25,500	C+
Edgewood College	WI	18,304	C
Edinboro Univ of Pennsylvania	PA	9,328	LC
Elizabethtown College	PA	26,000	VC
Elmhurst College	IL	21,750	C
Elmira College	NY	31,070	VC+
Elon Univ	NC	19,430	VC
Emmanuel College	MA	23,802	C+
Emory Univ	GA	33,792	MC
Evangel Univ	MO	14,050	C
Fairfield Univ	CT	30,885	HC
Fairleigh Dickinson Univ/Teaneck Campus	NJ	24,646	C
Fayetteville State Univ	NC	5,590	LC
Ferrum College	VA	15,990	LC
Fisk Univ	TN	13,700	LC
Flagler College	FL	10,550	VC+
Florida Atlantic Univ	FL	8,832	C
Florida International Univ	FL	9,486	VC
Florida Southern College	FL	19,430	C
Florida State Univ	FL	7,835	HC
Fordham Univ	NY	30,710	VC
Fort Hays State Univ	KS	6,294	LC
Fort Lewis College	CO	7,659	LC
Framingham State College	MA	7,259	C
Francis Marion Univ	SC	7,682	C
Franciscan Univ of Steubenville	OH	19,100	C+
Franklin and Marshall College	PA	32,410	HC
Franklin College of Indiana	IN	19,905	C
Fresno Pacific Univ	CA	19,740	C
Friends Univ	KS	15,962	LC
Furman Univ	SC	25,492	HC
Gallaudet Univ	DC	16,554	SP
Gardner-Webb Univ	NC	17,400	C
Geneva College	PA	19,990	C+
George Fox Univ	OR	24,095	VC
George Mason Univ	VA	9,192	C
George Washington Univ	DC	32,170	HC
Georgetown College	KY	18,400	VC
Georgetown Univ	DC	34,847	MC
Georgia College and State Univ	GA	7,344	C
Georgia Southern Univ	GA	6,958	C
Georgia State Univ	GA	7,792	LC
Georgian Court College	NJ	19,040	LC
Gettysburg College	PA	32,070	HC
Gonzaga Univ	WA	24,276	HC+
Gordon College	MA	23,594	VC+
Goshen College	IN	18,950	VC+
Goucher College	MD	30,650	VC+
Grace College	IN	16,768	C
Graceland Univ	IA	15,845	C
Grambling State Univ	LA	5,325	NC
Grand Canyon Univ	AZ	30,000	LC
Greensboro College	NC	19,080	LC
Greenville College	IL	19,226	LC
Grinnell College	IA	28,300	HC+
Grove City College	PA	12,280	MC
Guilford College	NC	23,255	C
Gustavus Adolphus College	MN	24,190	VC+
Hamilton College	NY	34,150	HC
Hamline Univ	MN	23,339	C+
Hampden-Sydney College	VA	24,871	C
Hanover College	IN	17,560	VC
Harding Univ	AR	13,528	VC
Hardin-Simmons Univ	TX	14,165	C
Hartwick College	NY	33,090	C+
Harvard Univ/Harvard College	MA	34,269	MC
Hastings College	NE	17,854	C+
Haverford College	PA	34,300	MC
Heidelberg College	OH	23,879	C
Henderson State Univ	AR	6,269	C
Hendrix College	AR	18,463	HC
Heritage College	WA	6,450	NC
High Point Univ	NC	20,220	LC
Hillsdale College	MI	20,586	VC+
Hiram College	OH	27,034	VC
Hobart and William Smith Colleges	NY	33,195	VC
Hofstra Univ	NY	23,252	C
Hollins Univ	VA	24,328	VC
Holy Family College	PA	13,710	LC
Hood College	MD	26,020	VC
Hope College	MI	22,922	C+
Hope International Univ	CA	16,940	NC
Houghton College	NY	21,810	VC+
Houston Baptist Univ	TX	15,300	LC
Howard Payne Univ	TX	13,834	C+
Howard Univ	DC	15,622	LC
Humboldt State Univ	CA	8,582	C
Idaho State Univ	ID	7,030	C+
Illinois College	IL	16,234	C
Illinois State Univ	IL	9,235	C
Illinois Wesleyan Univ	IL	26,970	HC
Immaculata College	PA	22,400	LC
Indiana State Univ	IN	8,461	LC
Indiana Univ Bloomington	IN	10,712	C+
Indiana Univ Northwest	IN	3,447	C
Indiana Univ of Pennsylvania	PA	9,133	C
Indiana Univ South Bend	IN	3,515	C
Indiana Univ Southeast	IN	3,459	C
Indiana Univ-Purdue Univ Fort Wayne	IN	3,166	LC
Indiana Univ-Purdue Univ Indianapolis	IN	9,473	C
Indiana Wesleyan Univ	IN	17,680	C
Inter-American Univ of PR/Bayamon Univ College	PR	3,700	
Inter-American Univ of PR/Fajardo Campus	PR	4,000	
Inter-American Univ of PR/Metropolitan Campus	PR	4,166	
Inter-American Univ of PR/Ponce Regional College	PR	3,700	
Inter-American Univ of PR/San GermÈn	PR	6,390	
Iona College	NY	26,556	C
Iowa State Univ	IA	8,108	VC
Ithaca College	NY	28,719	HC
Jacksonville Univ	FL	21,110	LC
John Carroll Univ	OH	24,140	VC
Johns Hopkins Univ	MD	35,226	MC
Juniata College	PA	26,080	VC
Kalamazoo College	MI	26,955	HC+
Kansas Wesleyan Univ	KS	17,400	C+
Kean Univ	NJ	11,159	C
Keene State College	NH	11,280	C
Kennesaw State Univ	GA	2,306	LC
Kent State Univ	OH	11,104	C
Kenyon College	OH	32,130	HC+
King College	TN	17,800	VC
King's College	PA	24,680	C
Knox College	IL	28,230	HC
Kutztown Univ of Pennsylvania	PA	8,907	C
La Salle Univ	PA	27,890	C
La Sierra Univ	CA	19,260	LC
Lafayette College	PA	32,655	MC
LaGrange College	GA	17,496	C
Lake Erie College	OH	21,350	LC
Lake Forest College	IL	27,460	VC
Lakeland College	WI	17,950	C
Lamar Univ	TX	6,816	LC
Lambuth Univ	TN	14,254	C
Lander Univ	SC	8,618	LC
Lawrence Univ	WI	27,711	HC
Le Moyne College	NY	23,840	C
Lebanon Valley College of Pennsylvania	PA	25,700	VC
Lee Univ	TN	10,198	LC
Lehigh Univ	PA	32,290	MC
Lenoir-Rhyne College	NC	19,186	C
Liberty Univ	VA	14,500	C
Lincoln Univ	MO	7,158	NC
Lincoln Univ	PA	11,198	C+
Lindenwood Univ	MO	17,250	C
Linfield College	OR	25,840	VC
Lock Haven Univ of Pennsylvania	PA	9,534	C
LIU/C.W. Post Campus	NY	25,380	C
Loras College	IA	22,994	C+
Louisiana State Univ and A&M College	LA	8,014	VC
Louisiana State Univ in Shreveport	LA	2,480	NC
Louisiana Tech Univ	LA	6,506	C
Loyola College in Maryland	MD	30,900	HC
Loyola Marymount Univ	CA	28,754	HC
Loyola Univ New Orleans	LA	23,506	VC+
Loyola Univ of Chicago	IL	25,992	VC
Lycoming College	PA	24,780	C
Lynchburg College	VA	23,405	C
Lyon College	AR	16,500	VC
Macalester College	MN	28,814	HC+
MacMurray College	IL	17,790	LC
Madonna Univ	MI	11,504	VC
Malone College	OH	19,190	C
Manchester College	IN	22,010	C
Manhattan College	NY	25,500	VC
Manhattanville College	NY	28,730	VC
Mansfield Univ	PA	9,648	C
Marian College	IN	21,020	C
Marian College of Fond du Lac	WI	17,935	LC
Marietta College	OH	24,580	C
Marist College	NY	24,756	VC
Marlboro College	VT	26,410	VC+
Marquette Univ	WI	24,836	C+
Mars Hill College	NC	18,600	LC
Mary Baldwin College	VA	23,440	C
Mary Washington College	VA	9,032	VC+
Marymount College/Tarrytown	NY	23,850	C
Maryville College	TN	23,210	VC
Marywood Univ	PA	24,639	C
McMurry Univ	TX	15,287	C
McPherson College	KS	17,710	C
Mercer Univ	GA	24,130	VC
Meredith College	NC	17,500	C
Messiah College	PA	23,180	VC
Methodist College	NC	19,526	C
Metropolitan State College of Denver	CO	2,338	LC
Miami Univ	OH	12,885	VC+
Mich State Univ	MI	10,386	VC
MidAmerica Nazarene Univ	KS	16,960	C
Middle Tenn State Univ	TN	6,994	C
Middlebury College	VT	34,300	MC
Midwestern State Univ	TX	6,704	NC
Millersville Univ of Pennsylvania	PA	10,153	VC
Millikin Univ	IL	24,415	C+
Millsaps College	MS	22,608	VC+
Minn State Univ, Mankato	MN	7,296	LC
Minot State Univ	ND	5,466	LC
Miss College	MS	14,574	C
Miss Univ for Women	MS	5,446	LC
Missouri Southern State College	MO	6,666	C
Missouri Western State College	MO	6,662	NC
Molloy College	NY	13,940	C
Monmouth College	IL	21,550	C
Montclair State Univ	NJ	10,287	LC
Moorhead State Univ	MN	7,000	LC
Moravian College	PA	27,065	VC
Morehouse College	GA	19,814	C
Morningside College	IA	19,124	C
Morris Brown College	GA	15,993	LC
Mount Holyoke College	MA	34,128	HC
Mount Mary College	WI	18,024	C
Mount St. Mary's College	CA	24,430	C
Mount St. Mary's College	MD	25,740	C
Mount Union College	OH	21,120	C
Mount Vernon Nazarene College	OH	17,027	C
Muhlenberg College	PA	28,170	HC
Murray State Univ	KY	6,672	C
Muskingum College	OH	18,760	C
Nazareth College of Rochester	NY	22,036	VC
Nebr Wesleyan Univ	NE	18,767	VC
New College of Calif	CA	8,900	NC
New Jersey City Univ	NJ	9,100	LC
New Mexico Highlands Univ	NM	6,256	NC
New York Univ	NY	35,200	MC
Newberry College	SC	19,670	LC
Niagara Univ	NY	22,250	C+
Norfolk State Univ	VA	8,382	LC
N Car Central Univ	NC	6,418	LC
N Car State Univ	NC	8,680	HC
North Central College	IL	22,944	C+
N Dak State Univ	ND	7,004	VC
North Georgia College and State Univ	GA	6,322	C+
North Park Univ	IL	24,030	C
Northeastern Illinois Univ	IL	2,898	NC
Northeastern State Univ	OK	4,704	LC
Northeastern Univ	MA	30,078	VC
Northern Arizona Univ	AZ	7,398	C
Northern Illinois Univ	IL	9,545	C
Northern Kentucky Univ	KY	6,352	NC
Northern Mich Univ	MI	9,693	C
Northern State Univ	SD	6,279	LC
Northwest Missouri State Univ	MO	7,922	LC
Northwest Nazarene Univ	ID	18,380	C
Northwestern College	MN	19,810	C+
Northwestern College of Iowa	IA	17,630	C+
Northwestern Univ	IL	33,615	MC
Oakland Univ	MI	9,418	C
Oakwood College	AL	14,904	C
Oberlin College	OH	33,140	HC+
Occidental College	CA	32,288	HC
Ohio Northern Univ	OH	27,765	VC
Ohio Univ	OH	11,769	C
Ohio Wesleyan Univ	OH	29,670	VC+
Okla Baptist Univ	OK	13,878	VC
Okla Christian Univ	OK	16,500	VC
Okla City Univ	OK	15,810	C
Okla State Univ	OK	7,650	VC
Old Dominion Univ	VA	9,386	C
Oral Roberts Univ	OK	18,490	C
Oregon State Univ	OR	9,612	VC
Otterbein College	OH	23,439	C
Ouachita Baptist Univ	AR	16,460	VC
Our Lady of the Lake Univ of San Antonio	TX	17,336	C
Pace Univ	NY	24,200	C
Pacific Lutheran Univ	WA	23,318	VC
Pacific Union College	CA	20,250	VC
Pacific Univ	OR	24,250	C
Park Univ	MO	9,816	C
Penn State Univ/Univ Park Campus	PA	11,126	VC
Pepperdine Univ	CA	32,830	VC
Piedmont College	GA	16,900	C
Pittsburg State Univ	KS	6,228	NC
Pitzer College	CA	33,930	HC
Plymouth State College	NH	11,024	LC
Point Loma Nazarene Univ	CA	21,380	VC
Pomona College	CA	33,960	MC
Pontifical Catholic Univ of PR/Ponce	PR	7,076	
Portland State Univ	OR	11,220	C
Prairie View A&M Univ	TX	3,172	LC
Presbyterian College	SC	23,356	VC
Prescott College	AZ	13,430	C
Principia College	IL	23,865	C+
Providence College	RI	27,620	HC
Purdue Univ/Calumet	IN	6,630	NC
Purdue Univ/West Lafayette	IN	10,284	VC
Queens College	NC	17,250	C
Quinnipiac Univ	CT	27,370	C
Randolph-Macon College	VA	24,395	C
Randolph-Macon Woman's College	VA	25,820	VC+
Regis College	MA	26,750	C
Regis Univ	CO	25,740	C+
Rhode Island College	RI	8,700	LC
Rhodes College	TN	26,466	HC+
Rider Univ	NJ	27,400	C
Ripon College	WI	24,180	VC+
Rivier College	NH	24,215	C
Roanoke College	VA	24,689	VC
Rockford College	IL	23,930	C
Rockhurst Univ	MO	20,090	C
Rollins College	FL	31,223	HC
Roosevelt Univ	IL	20,240	LC
Rosemont College	PA	24,060	C
Rowan Univ	NJ	12,365	VC
Russell Sage College	NY	23,674	C+
Rutgers, The State Univ of New Jersey New Brunswick Campus	NJ	12,709	C
Rutgers, The State Univ of New Jersey/CamdenCampus	NJ	6,484	C
Sacred Heart Univ	CT	26,588	VC
Saginaw Valley State Univ	MI	9,465	C
St. Ambrose Univ	IA	19,994	C
St. Anselm College	NH	27,405	C
St. Augustine's College	NC	12,990	C+
St. Bonaventure Univ	NY	21,956	C
St. Edward's Univ	TX	17,846	C
St. Francis Univ	PA	24,486	LC
St. John Fisher College	NY	21,800	C
St. John's Univ	MN	23,640	VC
St. John's Univ	NY	26,660	C
St. Joseph College	CT	25,960	LC
St. Joseph's College, New York	NY	9,802	C
St. Joseph's Univ	PA	29,715	VC+
St. Lawrence Univ	NY	32,605	VC
St. Louis Univ	MO	26,590	VC+
St. Mary's College	IN	24,474	VC
St. Mary's College of Calif	CA	27,575	C
St. Mary's Univ of Minn	MN	19,975	C
St. Mary's Univ of San Antonio	TX	19,735	C
St. Michael's College	VT	26,935	VC
St. Norbert College	WI	23,169	VC
St. Olaf College	MN	25,880	HC
St. Peter's College	NJ	22,292	LC
St. Thomas Aquinas College	NY	20,590	LC
St. Thomas Univ	FL	19,500	LC
St. Vincent College	PA	22,942	VC
St. Xavier Univ	IL	21,104	C
Salem College	NC	23,065	VC
Salisbury Univ	MD	10,576	VC
Salve Regina Univ	RI	26,460	C

School	ST	$IS	SR
Sam Houston State Univ	TX	6,076	LC
Samford Univ	AL	16,340	VC
San Diego State Univ	CA	9,716	C+
San Jose State Univ	CA	8,187	C
Santa Clara Univ	CA	28,371	VC+
Sarah Lawrence College	NY	37,516	HC
Seattle Pacific Univ	WA	22,674	C+
Seattle Univ	WA	24,183	VC
Seton Hall Univ	NJ	26,910	LC
Seton Hill College	PA	21,875	C
Shippensburg Univ of Pennsylvania	PA	9,652	C
Shorter College	GA	15,185	C
Siena College	NY	22,685	VC
Siena Heights Univ	MI	16,140	LC
Simmons College	MA	30,418	VC
Simon's Rock College of Bard	MA	32,450	HC
Simpson College	IA	21,200	C+
Skidmore College	NY	34,201	VC+
Slippery Rock Univ	PA	9,152	LC
Smith College	MA	33,302	HC+
Sonoma State Univ	CA	8,953	C
S Car State Univ	SC	6,586	LC
S Dak State Univ	SD	6,848	C
Southeast Missouri State Univ	MO	8,367	C+
Southeastern Louisiana Univ	LA	6,047	LC
Southern Arkansas Univ	AR	5,740	LC
Southern Conn State Univ	CT	10,310	C
Southern Illinois Univ at Carbondale	IL	8,621	C
Southern Methodist Univ	TX	28,349	VC
Southern Nazarene Univ	OK	14,634	NC
Southern Oregon Univ	OR	9,429	C
Southern Univ and A&M College	LA	6,365	C+
Southern Univ at New Orleans	LA	995	NC
Southern Utah Univ	UT	7,254	C
Southwest Baptist Univ	MO	13,426	LC
Southwest Missouri State Univ	MO	7,600	LC
Southwest State Univ	MN	7,117	LC
Southwest Texas State Univ	TX	8,730	VC
Southwestern College	KS	17,656	C
Southwestern Univ	TX	22,550	HC
Spelman College	GA	19,215	C+
Spring Arbor Univ	MI	17,976	C
Spring Hill College	AL	23,250	C
Stanford Univ	CA	34,222	MC
SUNY/College at Brockport	NY	10,267	C
SUNY/College at Buffalo	NY	8,025	C
SUNY/College at Fredonia	NY	10,125	C
SUNY/College at Geneseo	NY	9,970	HC
SUNY/College at Old Westbury	NY	9,818	LC
SUNY/College at Oneonta	NY	9,981	C
SUNY/College at Oswego	NY	10,856	C
SUNY/College at Plattsburgh	NY	9,729	C
SUNY/College at Potsdam	NY	10,519	C
SUNY/Univ at Albany	NY	10,997	VC
SUNY/Univ at Binghamton	NY	10,653	HC
SUNY/Univ at Buffalo	NY	11,033	VC
SUNY/Univ at New Paltz	NY	9,685	VC
State Univ of West Georgia	GA	7,101	C
Stephen F. Austin State Univ	TX	6,905	C
Stephens College	MO	22,295	C
Stetson Univ	FL	25,640	VC
Suffolk Univ	MA	26,516	C
Sul Ross State Univ	TX	6,582	LC
Susquehanna Univ	PA	27,270	VC
Swarthmore College	PA	34,538	MC
Sweet Briar College	VA	25,310	VC
Syracuse Univ	NY	30,710	HC
Tarleton State Univ	TX	7,160	C
Taylor Univ	IN	21,562	VC+
Temple Univ	PA	14,124	C
Tenn Tech Univ	TN	6,968	C
Texas A&M Univ	TX	8,988	VC
Texas A&M Univ at Commerce	TX	7,326	C
Texas A&M Univ at Kingsville	TX	6,446	LC
Texas Christian Univ	TX	19,910	C
Texas Lutheran Univ	TX	17,660	C
Texas Southern Univ	TX	6,576	NC
Texas Tech Univ	TX	8,825	C
Texas Wesleyan Univ	TX	14,710	C
Texas Woman's Univ	TX	5,855	LC
Ohio State Univ	OH	10,819	VC
Thiel College	PA	18,419	LC
Towson Univ	MD	11,088	VC
Transylvania Univ	KY	21,780	VC+
Trinity Christian College	IL	19,415	C
Trinity College	CT	34,300	HC
Trinity College	DC	21,370	LC
Trinity Univ	TX	21,444	HC
Truman State Univ	MO	8,568	VC+
Tufts Univ	MA	34,874	MC
Tulane Univ	LA	34,013	HC+
Turabo Univ	PR	4,110	
Union College	NY	32,646	HC
Union Univ	TN	18,930	C+
Universidad Adventista de las Antillas	PR	6,675	
Univ of Akron	OH	10,530	NC
Univ of Alabama	AL	7,402	C
Univ of Alabama at Birmingham	AL	10,110	C
Univ of Alabama at Huntsville	AL	7,916	VC
Univ of Arizona	AZ	8,614	C
Univ of Arkansas	AR	8,334	VC
Univ of Arkansas at Little Rock	AR	5,637	NC
Univ of Calif at Berkeley	CA	14,134	MC
Univ of Calif at Davis	CA	12,796	VC
Univ of Calif at Irvine	CA	11,756	C
Univ of Calif at Los Angeles	CA	13,227	MC
Univ of Calif at Riverside	CA	12,479	C
Univ of Calif at Santa Barbara	CA	11,732	VC
Univ of Central Arkansas	AR	6,388	C
Univ of Central Florida	FL	8,251	VC
Univ of Central Okla	OK	5,205	C
Univ of Cincinnati	OH	12,491	LC
Univ of Colo at Boulder	CO	9,255	VC
Univ of Colo at Colo Springs	CO	9,403	C
Univ of Colo at Denver	CO	3,673	C
Univ of Conn	CT	12,122	VC
Univ of Dallas	TX	22,128	VC+
Univ of Dayton	OH	20,400	VC
Univ of Denver	CO	28,783	VC
Univ of Evansville	IN	22,865	VC+
Univ of Findlay	OH	23,962	NC
Univ of Florida	FL	7,874	HC
Univ of Georgia	GA	8,656	VC
Univ of Hawaii at Manoa	HI	7,862	VC
Univ of Houston	TX	8,410	C
Univ of Idaho	ID	7,026	C
Univ of Illinois at Chicago	IL	10,702	VC
Univ of Illinois at Urbana-Champaign	IL	11,316	HC+
Univ of Indianapolis	IN	20,840	C
Univ of Iowa	IA	8,607	C+
Univ of Kansas	KS	7,232	VC
Univ of Kentucky	KY	7,765	C
Univ of La Verne	CA	24,280	C
Univ of Louisiana at Lafayette	LA	5,200	C
Univ of Louisiana at Monroe	LA	5,207	NC
Univ of Louisville	KY	7,402	LC
Univ of Maine	ME	10,798	C
Univ of Mary Hardin-Baylor	TX	13,929	C
Univ of Maryland/Baltimore County	MD	12,190	VC
Univ of Maryland/College Park	MD	11,959	C
Univ of Mass Amherst	MA	10,995	VC
Univ of Mass Boston	MA	4,227	C
Univ of Mass Dartmouth	MA	9,852	C
Univ of Miami	FL	31,130	HC
Univ of Mich/Ann Arbor	MI	13,003	HC+
Univ of Mich/Flint	MI	4,323	C
Univ of Minn/Duluth	MN	10,436	C
Univ of Minn/Morris	MN	10,716	VC
Univ of Minn/Twin Cities	MN	11,123	VC
Univ of Miss	MS	7,666	C
Univ of Missouri/Columbia	MO	9,803	HC
Univ of Missouri/Kansas City	MO	9,685	VC
Univ of Missouri/St. Louis	MO	9,966	C
Univ of Montana	MT	8,038	C
Univ of Montevallo	AL	7,266	C
Univ of Nebr at Kearney	NE	7,048	NC
Univ of Nebr at Lincoln	NE	8,325	C+
Univ of Nebr at Omaha	NE	6,867	C
Univ of Nevada/Las Vegas	NV	8,281	VC
Univ of Nevada/Reno	NV	8,737	C
Univ of New Hampshire	NH	13,207	C
Univ of New Mexico	NM	8,026	C
Univ of New Orleans	LA	10,160	C
Univ of North Alabama	AL	7,016	NC
Univ of N Car at Asheville	NC	6,896	VC
Univ of N Car at Chapel Hill	NC	8,789	HC
Univ of N Car at Charlotte	NC	7,254	C
Univ of N Car at Greensboro	NC	6,858	C
Univ of N Car at Wilmington	NC	7,769	C
Univ of N Dak	ND	7,067	VC
Univ of North Florida	FL	8,089	VC
Univ of North Texas	TX	7,629	C
Univ of Northern Colo	CO	8,082	C+
Univ of Northern Iowa	IA	7,850	C
Univ of Notre Dame	IN	30,707	MC
Univ of Okla	OK	7,616	VC
Univ of Oregon	OR	9,969	C
Univ of Pennsylvania	PA	34,614	MC
Univ of Pittsburgh at Pittsburgh	PA	13,592	HC
Univ of Portland	OR	24,950	VC
Univ of Puget Sound	WA	28,285	HC
Univ of Redlands	CA	29,246	VC
Univ of Rhode Island	RI	12,414	C
Univ of Richmond	VA	27,300	HC
Univ of Rochester	NY	32,979	HC
Univ of St. Thomas	MN	24,044	VC
Univ of St. Thomas	TX	18,752	VC
Univ of San Diego	CA	29,198	HC
Univ of San Francisco	CA	27,302	VC
Univ of Scranton	PA	27,964	C+
Univ of South Alabama	AL	6,976	LC
Univ of S Car at Columbia	SC	8,748	VC
Univ of S Car at Spartanburg	SC	7,318	C+
Univ of S Dak	SD	7,036	C
Univ of South Florida	FL	8,154	C
Univ of Southern Calif	CA	33,647	MC
Univ of Southern Colo	CO	7,821	LC
Univ of Southern Indiana	IN	8,655	LC
Univ of Tampa	FL	22,612	C
Univ of Tenn at Chattanooga	TN	7,783	C
Univ of Tenn at Knoxville	TN	8,214	C
Univ of Tenn at Martin	TN	8,268	C
Univ of Texas at Arlington	TX	7,192	LC
Univ of Texas at Austin	TX	9,437	HC
Univ of Texas at El Paso	TX	5,076	LC
Univ of Texas at San Antonio	TX	9,088	NC
Univ of Texas-Pan American	TX	4,823	C
Univ of the District of Columbia	DC	2,844	NC
Univ of the Incarnate Word	TX	18,478	C
Univ of the Pacific	CA	28,255	VC
Univ of the South	TN	27,290	HC
Univ of Toledo	OH	11,206	NC
Univ of Tulsa	OK	19,090	HC
Univ of Utah	UT	7,703	C
Univ of Vermont	VT	14,761	C+
Univ of Virginia	VA	9,391	HC+
Univ of Virginia's College at Wise	VA	8,302	C
Univ of Washington	WA	10,361	VC
Univ of Wisc/Eau Claire	WI	7,032	VC
Univ of Wisc/Green Bay	WI	7,148	C
Univ of Wisc/La Crosse	WI	7,250	VC
Univ of Wisc/Madison	WI	8,262	VC
Univ of Wisc/Milwaukee	WI	8,907	LC
Univ of Wisc/Oshkosh	WI	6,130	LC
Univ of Wisc/Parkside	WI	6,160	LC
Univ of Wisc/Platteville	WI	7,282	C
Univ of Wisc/Stevens Point	WI	7,116	C
Univ of Wisc/Whitewater	WI	6,937	C
Univ of Wyoming	WY	7,143	LC
Ursinus College	PA	31,350	VC
Utah State Univ	UT	6,771	C
Valdosta State Univ	GA	6,988	C
Valley City State Univ	ND		LC
Valparaiso Univ	IN	23,570	VC+
Vanderbilt Univ	TN	34,482	MC
Vanguard Univ of Southern Calif	CA	20,212	C
Villanova Univ	PA	31,997	HC
Virginia Polytechnic Inst and State Univ	VA	7,652	C
Virginia Wesleyan College	VA	22,350	LC
Viterbo Univ	WI	18,043	C
Wabash College	IN	25,335	HC
Wake Forest Univ	NC	30,290	MC
Walla Walla College	WA	20,925	C
Walsh Univ	OH	16,880	C
Wartburg College	IA	21,165	VC
Washburn Univ of Topeka	KS	6,766	NC
Washington and Jefferson College	PA	26,255	VC
Washington and Lee Univ	VA	25,095	MC
Washington College	MD	28,040	VC
Washington State Univ	WA	9,388	C
Washington Univ in St. Louis	MO	34,593	MC
Wayland Baptist Univ	TX	11,271	NC
Wayne State College	NE	6,255	NC
Wayne State Univ	MI	6,720	C
Weber State Univ	UT	6,897	NC
Webster Univ	MO	19,804	VC
Wellesley College	MA	33,394	MC
Wells College	NY	19,350	VC
Wesleyan College	GA	17,050	VC
Wesleyan Univ	CT	3,405	MC
West Chester Univ of Pennsylvania	PA	9,792	VC
West Texas A&M Univ	TX	6,538	C
Western Carolina Univ	NC	5,667	C
Western Conn State Univ	CT	10,074	C
Western Illinois Univ	IL	9,571	C
Western Kentucky Univ	KY	6,834	C
Western Maryland College	MD	26,000	VC
Western Mich Univ	MI	10,016	C
Western New Mexico Univ	NM	5,950	LC
Western Oregon Univ	OR	8,829	C
Western State College of Colo	CO	7,585	LC
Western Washington Univ	WA	8,624	VC
Westminster College	MO	19,990	C+
Westminster College	PA	22,960	C
Westmont College	CA	29,748	VC
Wheaton College	IL	21,934	HC
Wheeling Jesuit Univ	WV	22,660	C
Whitman College	WA	29,086	HC
Whittier College	CA	29,108	C
Whitworth College	WA	23,938	VC
Wichita State Univ	KS	6,879	C
Wilkes Univ	PA	25,800	C
Willamette Univ	OR	29,422	VC+
William Carey College	MS	10,150	LC
William Jewell College	MO	17,150	VC
William Paterson Univ of New Jersey	NJ	11,000	LC
Williams College	MA	32,270	MC
Wilmington College	OH	21,826	C
Wilson College	PA	21,337	LC
Wingate Univ	NC	19,140	C
Winona State Univ	MN	8,570	C
Winston-Salem State Univ	NC	5,927	LC
Winthrop Univ	SC	9,106	C
Wisc Lutheran College	WI	19,216	VC
Wittenberg Univ	OH	28,766	VC
Wofford College	SC	23,995	VC
Worcester State College	MA	7,901	LC
Wright State Univ	OH	9,141	LC
Xavier Univ	OH	23,880	C
Xavier Univ of Louisiana	LA	17,000	LC
Yale Univ	CT	34,030	MC
York College of Pennsylvania	PA	12,550	VC
Youngstown State Univ	OH	9,318	NC

SPANISH STUDIES

School	ST	$IS	SR
American Univ	DC	31,544	VC+
Assumption College	MA	26,320	C
Bard College	NY	33,912	HC
Barton College	NC	16,834	LC
Dartmouth College	NH	34,458	MC
Fairleigh Dickinson Univ/ Madison campus	NJ	25,500	C
Fordham Univ	NY	30,710	VC
Holy Names College	CA	23,220	C
Montana State Univ-Billings	MT	7,653	NC
New College of Florida	FL	8,130	HC+
Reed College	OR	33,350	HC+
SUNY/Univ at Stony Brook	NY	10,998	VC
Sweet Briar College	VA	25,310	VC
Univ of Calif at San Diego	CA	11,372	HC
Vassar College	NY	33,450	MC

SPECIAL EDUCATION

School	ST	$IS	SR
Alabama A&M Univ	AL	5,100	LC
Alabama State Univ	AL	6,404	C
Albany State Univ	GA	5,764	C+
Albright College	PA	27,642	C
Alcorn State Univ	MS	5,594	LC
American International College	MA	22,268	LC
Appalachian State Univ	NC	6,353	C
Arcadia Univ	PA	26,650	C
Arizona State Univ-Main	AZ	7,726	C
Arkansas State Univ	AR	7,480	C
Auburn Univ	AL	5,510	C
Augusta State Univ	GA	2,282	C
Augustana College	SD	20,760	VC
Austin Peay State Univ	TN	5,814	LC
Avila College	MO	17,720	C
Baldwin-Wallace College	OH	22,010	VC+
Ball State Univ	IN	8,660	C
Baylor Univ	TX	18,298	VC+
Bellarmine Univ	KY	20,440	VC
Benedictine College	KS	18,485	LC
Benedictine Univ	IL	21,330	C
Bennett College	NC	11,200	C
Bethany College	WV	18,566	C
Black Hills State Univ	SD	6,652	LC
Bloomsburg Univ of Pennsylvania	PA	9,434	C
Boston College	MA	33,330	MC
Boston Univ	MA	34,358	MC
Bowling Green State Univ	OH	10,794	C
Bradley Univ	IL	20,970	VC
Brenau Univ Women's College	GA	20,100	C
Brescia Univ	KY	14,225	C
Bridgewater State College	MA	7,589	C+
Brigham Young Univ	UT	7,840	HC
Brigham Young Univ/Hawaii	HI	6,890	C
Buena Vista Univ	IA	22,828	C
Cabrini College	PA	25,950	LC
Cal State, Long Beach	CA	7,400	LC
Calif Univ of Pennsylvania	PA	10,388	C
Calvin College	MI	20,050	NC
Canisius College	NY	24,696	C+
Cardinal Stritch Univ	WI	17,620	C
Caribbean Univ	PR	3,000	
Carlow College	PA	19,366	C
Catawba College	NC	19,620	C
Cedarville Univ	OH	17,553	VC
Central Conn State Univ	CT	10,404	C
Central Mich Univ	MI	8,355	C
Central Missouri State Univ	MO	7,920	C
Central State Univ	OH	8,922	C+
Central Washington Univ	WA	8,985	LC
Cheyney Univ of Pennsylvania	PA	9,993	C
Chicago State Univ	IL	8,851	C+
CUNY/Brooklyn College	NY	3,403	LC
CUNY/City College	NY	3,309	LC

School	ST	$IS	SR
CUNY/Medgar Evers College	NY	3,282	NC
Clarion Univ of Pennsylvania	PA	11,272	LC
Clarke College	IA	20,625	C+
Clearwater Christian College	FL	13,160	LC
Clemson Univ	SC	7,600	C
Cleveland State Univ	OH	10,146	NC
Coastal Carolina Univ	SC	9,220	C
College Misericordia	PA	23,380	LC
College of Charleston	SC	8,350	HC
College of Mount St. Vincent	NY	24,230	C
College of Mount St. Joseph	OH	20,290	C
College of New Jersey	NJ	13,425	HC
College of Notre Dame of Maryland	MD	23,100	LC
College of Our Lady of the Elms	MA	20,644	C
College of St. Elizabeth	NJ	22,510	C
College of St. Joseph	VT	17,400	NC
College of St. Mary	NE	18,726	C
College of St. Rose	NY	19,084	C
College of the Southwest	NM	8,456	NC
Columbia College	SC	19,050	LC
Columbus State Univ	GA	7,228	LC
Concord College	WV	7,122	C+
Concordia Univ Nebr	NE	17,770	C
Coppin State College	MD	9,133	LC
Creighton Univ	NE	23,476	VC
Cumberland College	KY	14,864	C
Curry College	MA	26,025	LC
Daemen College	NY	20,620	LC
Dana College	NE	18,046	C
Delaware State Univ	DE	8,104	LC
Delta State Univ	MS	5,416	C
Dillard Univ	LA	16,046	VC
Doane College	NE	17,600	LC
Dominican College	NY	20,400	LC
Dowling College	NY	20,281	LC
Drury Univ	MO	15,250	VC
D'Youville College	NY	18,704	C
East Carolina Univ	NC	7,766	C
East Central Univ	OK	4,578	C
East Stroudsburg Univ of Pennsylvania	PA	8,430	LC
East Tenn State Univ	TN	7,127	C
Eastern Illinois Univ	IL	10,101	C
Eastern Kentucky Univ	KY	6,552	C
Eastern Mennonite Univ	VA	20,700	VC
Eastern Mich Univ	MI	9,855	C
Eastern New Mexico Univ	NM	4,113	LC
Edinboro Univ of Pennsylvania	PA	9,328	LC
Elizabeth City State Univ	NC	5,550	LC
Elmhurst College	IL	21,750	C
Elon Univ	NC	19,430	VC
Erskine College	SC	21,399	VC
Evangel Univ	MO	14,050	C
Felician College	NJ	20,050	C
Fitchburg State College	MA	7,836	C
Florida Atlantic Univ	FL	8,832	C
Florida Gulf Coast Univ	FL	9,201	C
Florida International Univ	FL	9,486	VC
Florida Southern College	FL	19,430	C
Fontbonne Univ	MO	18,046	C
Freed-Hardeman Univ	TN	14,290	VC
Gannon Univ	PA	18,848	C
Georgia College and State Univ	GA	7,344	C
Georgia Southern Univ	GA	6,958	C
Georgia Southwestern State Univ	GA	6,013	C
Georgian Court College	NJ	19,040	LC
Glenville State College	WV	6,588	NC
Gonzaga Univ	WA	24,276	HC+
Gordon College	MA	23,594	VC+
Goucher College	MD	30,650	VC+
Grambling State Univ	LA	5,325	NC
Grand Canyon Univ	AZ	30,000	LC
Green Mountain College	VT	24,130	C
Greensboro College	NC	19,080	LC
Greenville College	IL	19,226	LC
Gwynedd-Mercy College	PA	22,350	C
Hastings College	NE	17,854	C+
High Point Univ	NC	20,220	LC
Holy Family College	PA	13,710	LC
Hood College	MD	26,020	VC
Hope College	MI	22,922	C+
Houston Baptist Univ	TX	15,300	LC
Idaho State Univ	ID	7,030	C+
Illinois State Univ	IL	9,235	C
Indiana State Univ	IN	8,461	LC
Indiana Univ Bloomington	IN	10,712	C+
Indiana Univ of Pennsylvania	PA	9,133	C
Indiana Univ South Bend	IN	3,515	C
Indiana Univ Southeast	IN	3,459	C
Inter-American Univ of PR/Arecibo Campus	PR	3,300	
Inter-American Univ of PR/Bayamon Univ College	PR	3,700	
Inter-American Univ of PR/Fajardo Campus	PR	4,000	
Inter-American Univ of PR/Metropolitan Campus	PR	4,166	
Inter-American Univ of PR/Ponce Regional College	PR	3,700	
Inter-American Univ of PR/San GermÈn	PR	6,390	
Jackson State Univ	MS	6,776	LC
Jacksonville State Univ	AL	6,568	LC
Jarvis Christian College	TX	9,035	NC
Juniata College	PA	26,080	VC
Kansas Wesleyan Univ	KS	17,400	C+
Kean Univ	NJ	11,159	C
Keene State College	NH	11,280	C
Kent State Univ	OH	11,104	C
Kutztown Univ of Pennsylvania	PA	8,907	C
La Salle Univ	PA	27,890	C
Lamar Univ	TX	6,816	LC
Lambuth Univ	TN	14,254	C
Lander Univ	SC	8,618	LC
Lasell College	MA	24,100	C
Lesley College	MA	25,325	LC
Lewis Univ	IL	20,960	C
Lincoln Univ	MO	7,158	NC
Lock Haven Univ of Pennsylvania	PA	9,534	C
LIU/Brooklyn Campus	NY	22,290	C
Longwood College	VA	8,950	C
Loras College	IA	22,994	C+
Louisiana College	LA	11,516	C
Louisiana Tech Univ	LA	6,506	C
Loyola Univ of Chicago	IL	25,992	VC
Luther College	IA	23,300	VC+
MacMurray College	IL	17,790	LC
Malone College	OH	19,190	C
Manhattan College	NY	25,500	VC
Mansfield Univ	PA	9,648	C
Marian College	IN	21,020	C
Marist College	NY	24,756	VC
Marygrove College	MI	16,075	C
Marymount College/Tarrytown	NY	23,850	C
Marymount Manhattan College	NY	23,195	VC
Marywood Univ	PA	24,639	C
McNeese State Univ	LA	5,259	LC
McPherson College	KS	17,710	C
Mercer Univ	GA	24,130	VC
Mercy College	NY	15,875	LC
Mercyhurst College	PA	20,694	C
Methodist College	NC	19,526	C
Miami Univ	OH	12,885	VC+
Mich State Univ	MI	10,386	VC
Middle Tenn State Univ	TN	6,994	C
Millersville Univ of Pennsylvania	PA	10,153	VC
Miss College	MS	14,574	C
Miss State Univ	MS	7,853	C
Missouri Southern State College	MO	6,666	C
Molloy College	NY	13,940	C
Monmouth Univ	NJ	24,042	C
Montana State Univ-Billings	MT	7,653	NC
Moorhead State Univ	MN	7,000	LC
Morehead State Univ	KY	6,510	C
Morningside College	IA	19,124	C
Mount Marty College	SD	15,656	LC
Mount St. Mary College	NY	18,825	C
Mount Vernon Nazarene College	OH	17,027	C
Muskingum College	OH	18,760	C
Nazareth College of Rochester	NY	22,036	VC
Nebr Wesleyan Univ	NE	18,767	VC
New England College	NH	20,706	LC
New Jersey City Univ	NJ	9,100	LC
New Mexico Highlands Univ	NM	6,256	NC
New Mexico State Univ	NM	7,302	C
New York Univ	NY	35,200	MC
Newberry College	SC	19,670	LC
Nicholls State Univ	LA	5,290	NC
Norfolk State Univ	VA	8,382	LC
N Car Agricultural and Technical State Univ	NC	6,659	LC
North Georgia College and State Univ	GA	6,322	C+
Northeastern Illinois Univ	IL	2,898	NC
Northeastern State Univ	OK	4,704	LC
Northern Arizona Univ	AZ	7,398	C
Northern State Univ	SD	6,279	LC
Northwest Missouri State Univ	MO	7,922	LC
Northwestern College of Iowa	IA	17,630	C+
Northwestern Okla State Univ	OK	4,542	NC
Northwestern State Univ of Louisiana	LA	5,745	NC
Ohio Dominican College	OH	18,100	LC
Okla Christian Univ	OK	16,500	VC
Oral Roberts Univ	OK	18,490	C
Our Lady of the Lake Univ of San Antonio	TX	17,336	C
Palm Beach Atlantic College	FL	23,310	C
Penn State Univ/Univ Park Campus	PA	11,126	VC
Peru State College	NE	6,342	NC
Pfeiffer Univ	NC	18,580	C
Philander Smith College	AR	7,380	NC
Piedmont College	GA	16,900	C
Pontifical Catholic Univ of PR/Ponce	PR	7,076	
Presbyterian College	SC	23,356	VC
Prescott College	AZ	13,430	C
Providence College	RI	27,620	HC
Purdue Univ/West Lafayette	IN	10,284	VC
Quincy Univ	IL	20,450	C
Rhode Island College	RI	8,700	LC
Rivier College	NH	24,215	C
Saginaw Valley State Univ	MI	9,465	C
St. John Fisher College	NY	21,800	C
St. John's Univ	NY	26,660	C
St. Joseph College	CT	25,960	LC
St. Joseph's College, New York	NY	9,802	C
St. Martin's College	WA	20,566	C
St. Mary-of-the-Woods College	IN	21,320	LC
St. Thomas Aquinas College	NY	20,590	LC
Salve Regina Univ	RI	26,460	C
Samford Univ	AL	16,340	VC
San Francisco State Univ	CA	7,139	LC
Seattle Pacific Univ	WA	22,674	C+
Seton Hall Univ	NJ	26,910	LC
Seton Hill College	PA	21,875	C
Shaw Univ	NC	12,810	C
Silver Lake College of the Holy Family	WI	15,516	LC
Simmons College	MA	30,418	VC
Slippery Rock Univ	PA	9,152	LC
S Car State Univ	SC	6,586	LC
Southeast Missouri State Univ	MO	8,367	C+
Southeastern Louisiana Univ	LA	6,047	LC
Southern Conn State Univ	CT	10,310	C
Southern Illinois Univ at Carbondale	IL	8,621	C
Southern Illinois Univ Edwardsville	IL	7,869	LC
Southern Univ and A&M College	LA	6,365	C+
Southern Utah Univ	UT	7,254	C
Southern Wesleyan Univ	SC	17,280	C
Southwest Missouri State Univ	MO	7,600	LC
Southwest Texas State Univ	TX	8,730	VC
Southwestern Okla State Univ	OK	4,801	C
SUNY/College at Buffalo	NY	8,025	C
SUNY/College at Geneseo	NY	9,970	HC
SUNY/College at Old Westbury	NY	9,818	LC
SUNY/College at Plattsburgh	NY	9,729	C
State Univ of West Georgia	GA	7,101	C
Stephen F. Austin State Univ	TX	6,905	C
Syracuse Univ	NY	30,710	HC
Tabor College	KS	17,600	LC
Tenn State Univ	TN	7,058	VC
Tenn Tech Univ	TN	6,968	C
Texas Southern Univ	TX	6,576	NC
Touro College	NY	14,950	VC
Towson Univ	MD	11,088	VC
Trinity Christian College	IL	19,415	C
Troy State Univ	AL	7,696	C
Troy State Univ/Dothan	AL	3,296	C
Turabo Univ	PR	4,110	
Tusculum College	TN	17,900	LC
Tuskegee Univ	AL	14,600	LC
Union College	KY	15,920	C
Union Univ	TN	18,930	C+
Univ of Akron	OH	10,530	NC
Univ of Alabama	AL	7,402	C
Univ of Alabama at Birmingham	AL	10,110	C
Univ of Arizona	AZ	8,614	C
Univ of Arkansas	AR	8,334	VC
Univ of Arkansas at Monticello	AR	5,940	NC
Univ of Arkansas at Pine Bluff	AR	7,925	C
Univ of Central Arkansas	AR	6,388	C
Univ of Central Florida	FL	8,251	VC
Univ of Central Okla	OK	5,205	C
Univ of Cincinnati	OH	12,491	LC
Univ of Conn	CT	12,122	VC
Univ of Dayton	OH	20,400	VC
Univ of Delaware	DE	10,824	VC
Univ of Detroit Mercy	MI	21,620	LC
Univ of Evansville	IN	22,865	VC+
Univ of Florida	FL	7,874	HC
Univ of Georgia	GA	8,656	VC
Univ of Great Falls	MT	15,360	C
Univ of Hartford	CT	28,884	C
Univ of Hawaii at Manoa	HI	7,862	VC
Univ of Idaho	ID	7,026	C
Univ of Illinois at Urbana-Champaign	IL	11,316	HC+
Univ of Kentucky	KY	7,765	C
Univ of Louisiana at Lafayette	LA	5,200	C
Univ of Louisiana at Monroe	LA	5,207	NC
Univ of Maine at Farmington	ME	9,163	C
Univ of Mary	ND	12,900	LC
Univ of Mary Hardin-Baylor	TX	13,929	C
Univ of Maryland/College Park	MD	11,959	C
Univ of Memphis	TN	7,271	C
Univ of Miami	FL	31,130	HC
Univ of Miss	MS	7,666	C
Univ of Missouri/St. Louis	MO	9,966	C
Univ of Nebr at Kearney	NE	7,048	NC
Univ of Nebr at Lincoln	NE	8,325	C+
Univ of Nebr at Omaha	NE	6,867	C
Univ of Nevada/Las Vegas	NV	8,281	VC
Univ of Nevada/Reno	NV	8,737	C
Univ of New Mexico	NM	8,026	C
Univ of N Car at Pembroke	NC	5,914	LC
Univ of N Car at Wilmington	NC	7,769	C
Univ of North Florida	FL	8,089	VC
Univ of Northern Iowa	IA	7,850	C
Univ of Okla	OK	7,616	VC
Univ of PR/Cayey Univ College	PR	1,245	
Univ of St. Francis	IN	17,790	LC
Univ of Scranton	PA	27,964	C+
Univ of South Alabama	AL	6,976	LC
Univ of S Car at Spartanburg	SC	7,318	C+
Univ of S Dak	SD	7,036	C
Univ of South Florida	FL	8,154	C
Univ of Tenn at Chattanooga	TN	7,783	C
Univ of Tenn at Knoxville	TN	8,214	C
Univ of the Incarnate Word	TX	18,478	C
Univ of Toledo	OH	11,206	NC
Univ of West Alabama	AL	6,048	C
Univ of Wisc/Eau Claire	WI	7,032	VC
Univ of Wisc/Oshkosh	WI	6,130	LC
Univ of Wisc/Whitewater	WI	6,937	C
Univ of Wyoming	WY	7,143	LC
Utah State Univ	UT	6,771	C
Valdosta State Univ	GA	6,988	C
Vanderbilt Univ	TN	34,482	MC
Virginia Union Univ	VA	15,358	LC
Walla Walla College	WA	20,925	C
Walsh Univ	OH	16,880	C
Wayne State College	NE	6,255	NC
Wayne State Univ	MI	6,720	C
Waynesburg College	PA	17,610	LC
West Chester Univ of Pennsylvania	PA	9,792	VC
West Liberty State College	WV	6,056	LC
West Texas A&M Univ	TX	6,538	C
Western Carolina Univ	NC	5,667	C
Western Illinois Univ	IL	9,571	C
Western Kentucky Univ	KY	6,834	C
Western New Mexico Univ	NM	5,950	LC
Westfield State College	MA	8,394	C
Wheelock College	MA	25,520	C
Wichita State Univ	KS	6,879	C
Wiley College	TX	8,100	LC
William Paterson Univ of New Jersey	NJ	11,000	LC
William Penn Univ	IA	17,575	C
William Woods Univ	MO	19,390	LC
Winona State Univ	MN	8,570	C
Winston-Salem State Univ	NC	5,927	LC
Winthrop Univ	SC	9,106	C
Wittenberg Univ	OH	28,766	VC
Wright State Univ	OH	9,141	LC
Xavier Univ	OH	23,880	C
York College of Pennsylvania	PA	12,550	VC
Youngstown State Univ	OH	9,318	NC

SPECIFIC LEARNING DISABILITIES

School	ST	$IS	SR
Barton College	NC	16,834	LC
Florida International Univ	FL	9,486	VC
Florida State Univ	FL	7,835	HC
Northwest Missouri State Univ	MO	7,922	LC
Palm Beach Atlantic College	FL	23,310	C
Univ of South Florida	FL	8,154	C
Youngstown State Univ	OH	9,318	NC

SPEECH CORRECTION

School	ST	$IS	SR
Columbia College	SC	19,050	LC
Ithaca College	NY	28,719	HC
Lewis Univ	IL	20,960	C
Longwood College	VA	8,950	C
Southeast Missouri State Univ	MO	8,367	C+
Western Carolina Univ	NC	5,667	C

SPEECH PATHOLOGY/ AUDIOLOGY

School	ST	$IS	SR
Abilene Christian Univ	TX	16,300	VC
Adelphi Univ	NY	23,320	VC
Alabama A&M Univ	AL	5,100	LC
Andrews Univ	MI	17,696	LC
Arizona State Univ-Main	AZ	7,726	C
Arkansas State Univ	AR	7,480	C
Armstrong Atlantic State Univ	GA	7,084	C
Auburn Univ	AL	5,510	C
Augustana College	IL	24,117	VC+
Augustana College	SD	20,760	VC
Baldwin-Wallace College	OH	22,010	VC+
Ball State Univ	IN	8,660	C
Baylor Univ	TX	18,298	VC+
Biola Univ	CA	21,902	VC
Bloomsburg Univ of Pennsylvania	PA	9,434	C
Boston Univ	MA	34,358	MC
Bowling Green State Univ	OH	10,794	C
Brescia Univ	KY	14,225	C
Brigham Young Univ	UT	7,840	HC
Butler Univ	IN	25,580	VC+
Cal State, Chico	CA	8,598	LC
Cal State, Fresno	CA	7,762	C
Cal State, Fullerton	CA	5,440	LC
Cal State, Hayward	CA	7,400	LC
Cal State, Los Angeles	CA	5,050	C
Cal State, Northridge	CA	7,781	C
Cal State, Sacramento	CA	7,488	C
Calif Univ of Pennsylvania	PA	10,388	C
Central Mich Univ	MI	8,355	C
Central Missouri State Univ	MO	7,920	C
CUNY/Brooklyn College	NY	3,403	LC
CUNY/Herbert H. Lehman College	NY	3,320	LC
Clarion Univ of Pennsylvania	PA	11,272	LC
Clemson Univ	SC	7,600	C
College of Our Lady of the Elms	MA	20,644	C
College of St. Rose	NY	19,084	C
College of the Ozarks	MO	2,650	C+
Delta State Univ	MS	5,416	C
Duquesne Univ	PA	24,242	C+
East Carolina Univ	NC	7,766	C
East Stroudsburg Univ of Pennsylvania	PA	8,430	LC
Eastern Illinois Univ	IL	10,101	C
Eastern Mich Univ	MI	9,855	C
Eastern New Mexico Univ	NM	4,113	LC
Eastern Washington Univ	WA	7,972	LC
Edinboro Univ of Pennsylvania	PA	9,328	LC
Elmhurst College	IL	21,750	C
Elmira College	NY	31,070	VC+
Emerson College	MA	29,978	HC
Florida State Univ	FL	7,835	HC
Fontbonne Univ	MO	18,046	C
Fort Hays State Univ	KS	6,294	LC
Geneva College	PA	19,990	C+
George Washington Univ	DC	32,170	HC
Grambling State Univ	LA	5,325	NC
Hampton Univ	VA	17,112	C+
Harding Univ	AR	13,528	VC
Hardin-Simmons Univ	TX	14,165	C
Hofstra Univ	NY	23,252	C
Howard Univ	DC	15,522	LC
Idaho State Univ	ID	7,030	C+
Illinois State Univ	IL	9,235	C
Indiana State Univ	IN	8,461	LC
Indiana Univ Bloomington	IN	10,712	C+
Indiana Univ of Pennsylvania	PA	9,133	C
Indiana Univ-Purdue Univ Fort Wayne	IN	3,166	LC
Iona College	NY	26,556	C
Ithaca College	NY	28,719	HC
James Madison Univ	VA	9,552	HC
Kansas State Univ	KS	6,995	C
Kean Univ	NJ	11,159	C
Kent State Univ	OH	11,104	C
Kutztown Univ of Pennsylvania	PA	8,907	C
La Salle Univ	PA	27,890	C
Lamar Univ	TX	6,816	LC
Lambuth Univ	TN	14,254	C
LIU/C.W. Post Campus	NY	25,380	C
Louisiana College	LA	11,516	C
Louisiana State Univ and A&M College	LA	8,014	VC
Louisiana Tech Univ	LA	6,506	C
Loyola College in Maryland	MD	30,900	HC
Marquette Univ	WI	24,836	C+
Marymount Manhattan College	NY	23,195	VC
Marywood Univ	PA	24,639	C
Miami Univ	OH	12,885	VC+
Mich State Univ	MI	10,386	VC
Minn State Univ, Mankato	MN	7,296	LC
Minot State Univ	ND	5,466	LC
Miss Univ for Women	MS	5,446	LC
Molloy College	NY	13,940	C
Moorhead State Univ	MN	7,000	LC
Murray State Univ	KY	6,672	C
Nazareth College of Rochester	NY	22,036	VC
New Mexico State Univ	NM	7,302	C
New York Univ	NY	35,200	MC
Nicholls State Univ	LA	5,290	NC
Norfolk State Univ	VA	8,382	LC
N Car State Univ	NC	8,680	HC
Northeastern Univ	MA	30,078	VC
Northern Arizona Univ	AZ	7,398	C
Northern Illinois Univ	IL	9,545	C
Northern Mich Univ	MI	9,693	C
Northern State Univ	SD	6,279	LC
Northwestern Univ	IL	33,615	MC
Ohio Univ	OH	11,769	C
Okla State Univ	OK	7,650	VC
Old Dominion Univ	VA	9,386	C
Ouachita Baptist Univ	AR	16,460	VC
Our Lady of the Lake Univ of San Antonio	TX	17,336	C
Pace Univ	NY	24,200	C
Penn State Univ/Univ Park Campus	PA	11,126	VC
Purdue Univ/West Lafayette	IN	10,284	VC
Radford Univ	VA	8,302	C
Richard Stockton College of New Jersey	NJ	12,165	VC
Rockhurst Univ	MO	20,090	C
St. Cloud State Univ	MN	7,180	C
St. John's Univ	NY	26,660	C
St. Louis Univ	MO	26,590	VC+
St. Xavier Univ	IL	21,104	C
San Diego State Univ	CA	9,716	C+
San Francisco State Univ	CA	7,139	LC
San Jose State Univ	CA	8,187	C
Shaw Univ	NC	12,810	C
S Car State Univ	SC	6,586	LC
Southeast Missouri State Univ	MO	8,367	C+
Southeastern Louisiana Univ	LA	6,047	LC
Southern Illinois Univ at Carbondale	IL	8,621	C
Southern Illinois Univ Edwardsville	IL	7,869	LC
Southern Univ and A&M College	LA	6,365	C+
Southwest Missouri State Univ	MO	7,600	LC
Southwest Texas State Univ	TX	8,730	VC
SUNY/College at Buffalo	NY	8,025	C
SUNY/College at Cortland	NY	10,564	C
SUNY/College at Fredonia	NY	10,125	C
SUNY/College at Geneseo	NY	9,970	HC
SUNY/Univ at Buffalo	NY	11,033	VC
SUNY/Univ at New Paltz	NY	9,685	VC
State Univ of West Georgia	GA	7,101	C
Syracuse Univ	NY	30,710	HC
Tenn State Univ	TN	7,058	VC
Texas A&M Univ at Kingsville	TX	6,446	LC
Texas Christian Univ	TX	19,910	C
Texas Southern Univ	TX	6,576	NC
Thiel College	PA	18,419	LC
Towson Univ	MD	11,088	VC
Truman State Univ	MO	8,568	VC+
Univ of Akron	OH	10,530	NC
Univ of Alabama	AL	7,402	C
Univ of Arizona	AZ	8,614	C
Univ of Arkansas	AR	8,334	VC
Univ of Arkansas at Little Rock	AR	5,637	NC
Univ of Central Arkansas	AR	6,388	C
Univ of Central Florida	FL	8,251	VC
Univ of Central Okla	OK	5,205	C
Univ of Cincinnati	OH	12,491	LC
Univ of Colo at Boulder	CO	9,255	VC
Univ of Florida	FL	7,874	HC
Univ of Georgia	GA	8,656	VC
Univ of Hawaii at Manoa	HI	7,862	VC
Univ of Illinois at Urbana-Champaign	IL	11,316	HC+
Univ of Iowa	IA	8,607	C+
Univ of Kansas	KS	7,232	VC
Univ of Louisiana at Lafayette	LA	5,200	C
Univ of Louisiana at Monroe	LA	5,207	NC
Univ of Maine	ME	10,798	C
Univ of Mass Amherst	MA	10,995	VC
Univ of Minn/Duluth	MN	10,436	C
Univ of Minn/Twin Cities	MN	11,123	VC
Univ of Miss	MS	7,666	C
Univ of Montevallo	AL	7,266	C
Univ of Nebr at Lincoln	NE	8,325	C+
Univ of Nevada/Reno	NV	8,737	C
Univ of New Hampshire	NH	13,207	C
Univ of New Mexico	NM	8,026	C
Univ of N Car at Greensboro	NC	6,858	C
Univ of N Dak	ND	7,067	VC
Univ of North Texas	TX	7,629	C
Univ of Northern Colo	CO	8,082	C+
Univ of Northern Iowa	IA	7,850	C
Univ of Oregon	OR	9,969	C
Univ of Rhode Island	RI	12,414	C
Univ of Science and Arts of Okla	OK	5,245	C
Univ of South Alabama	AL	6,976	LC
Univ of S Dak	SD	7,036	C
Univ of Southern Colo	CO	7,821	LC
Univ of Southern Miss	MS	6,155	LC
Univ of Tenn at Knoxville	TN	8,214	C
Univ of Texas at Austin	TX	9,437	HC
Univ of Texas at Dallas	TX	9,305	VC
Univ of Texas-Pan American	TX	4,823	C
Univ of the District of Columbia	DC	2,844	NC
Univ of the Pacific	CA	28,255	VC
Univ of Toledo	OH	11,206	NC
Univ of Tulsa	OK	19,090	HC
Univ of Utah	UT	7,703	C
Univ of Vermont	VT	14,761	C+
Univ of Virginia	VA	9,391	HC+
Univ of Washington	WA	10,361	VC
Univ of Wisc/Eau Claire	WI	7,032	VC
Univ of Wisc/Madison	WI	8,262	VC
Univ of Wisc/Milwaukee	WI	8,907	LC
Univ of Wisc/Oshkosh	WI	6,130	LC
Univ of Wisc/River Falls	WI	6,356	LC
Univ of Wisc/Stevens Point	WI	7,116	C
Univ of Wyoming	WY	7,143	LC
Utah State Univ	UT	6,771	C
Valdosta State Univ	GA	6,988	C
Washington State Univ	WA	9,388	C
Wayne State Univ	MI	6,720	C
West Chester Univ of Pennsylvania	PA	9,792	VC
West Liberty State College	WV	6,056	LC
West Texas A&M Univ	TX	6,538	C
West Virginia Univ	WV	8,304	C
Western Illinois Univ	IL	9,571	C
Western Kentucky Univ	KY	6,834	C
Western Mich Univ	MI	10,016	C
Western Washington Univ	WA	8,624	VC
Wichita State Univ	KS	6,879	C
Winthrop Univ	SC	9,106	C
Worcester State College	MA	7,901	LC
Xavier Univ of Louisiana	LA	17,000	LC

SPEECH THERAPY

School	ST	$IS	SR
Baylor Univ	TX	18,298	VC+
Cal State, Fresno	CA	7,762	C
Cleveland State Univ	OH	10,146	NC
College Misericordia	PA	23,380	LC
Ithaca College	NY	28,719	HC
Stephen F. Austin State Univ	TX	6,905	C
Univ of Miss	MS	7,666	C

SPEECH/DEBATE/RHETORIC

School	ST	$IS	SR
Abilene Christian Univ	TX	16,300	VC
Adams State College	CO	7,468	C
Albany State Univ	GA	5,764	C+
Albion College	MI	25,224	VC
Arkansas State Univ	AR	7,480	C
Arkansas Tech Univ	AR	6,256	C
Ashland Univ	OH	22,182	LC
Auburn Univ	AL	5,510	C
Augsburg College	MN	22,978	C
Augustana College	IL	24,117	VC+
Austin Peay State Univ	TN	5,814	LC
Baldwin-Wallace College	OH	22,010	VC+
Ball State Univ	IN	8,660	C
Bates College	ME	34,100	MC
Baylor Univ	TX	18,298	VC+
Beloit College	WI	27,482	HC
Bethel College	MN	22,740	VC
Black Hills State Univ	SD	6,652	LC
Bloomsburg Univ of Pennsylvania	PA	9,434	C
Buena Vista Univ	IA	22,828	C
Butler Univ	IN	25,580	VC+
Cal State, Fresno	CA	7,762	C
Cal State, Fullerton	CA	5,440	LC
Cal State, Hayward	CA	7,400	LC
Cal State, Los Angeles	CA	5,050	C
Cal State, Northridge	CA	7,781	C
Cal State, Stanislaus	CA	8,895	C
Cameron Univ	OK	5,560	NC
Capital Univ	OH	23,630	C
Catawba College	NC	19,620	C
Centenary College of Louisiana	LA	21,600	C+
Central Missouri State Univ	MO	7,920	C
Central Washington Univ	WA	8,985	LC
Chadron State College	NE	6,211	NC
Charleston Southern Univ	SC	17,122	C
Chicago State Univ	IL	8,851	C+
CUNY/Brooklyn College	NY	3,403	LC
CUNY/Herbert H. Lehman College	NY	3,320	LC
CUNY/York College	NY	3,292	NC
Clarion Univ of Pennsylvania	PA	11,272	LC
Clark Atlanta Univ	GA	17,174	C
College of St. Catherine	MN	22,324	VC
College of William and Mary	VA	10,002	MC
Colo State Univ	CO	9,672	C
Concordia College/Moorhead	MN	18,835	C
Concordia Univ Nebr	NE	17,770	C
Concordia Univ Wisc	WI	16,600	LC
Cornerstone Univ and Grand Rapids Baptist Seminary	MI	18,092	C
Creighton Univ	NE	23,476	VC
Denison Univ	OH	29,640	HC
Dickinson State Univ	ND	5,495	NC
Dillard Univ	LA	16,046	VC
Doane College	NE	17,600	LC
Dordt College	IA	18,100	C+
Dowling College	NY	20,281	LC
Drake Univ	IA	22,830	VC
Drury Univ	MO	15,250	VC
East Central Univ	OK	4,578	C
East Tenn State Univ	TN	7,127	C
East Texas Baptist Univ	TX	12,349	LC
Eastern Kentucky Univ	KY	6,552	C
Eastern Mich Univ	MI	9,855	C
Eastern Nazarene College	MA	19,433	LC
Eastern New Mexico Univ	NM	4,113	LC
Eastern Washington Univ	WA	7,972	LC
Edinboro Univ of Pennsylvania	PA	9,328	LC
Emerson College	MA	29,978	HC
Evangel Univ	MO	14,050	C
Fairmont State College	WV	7,010	NC
Fayetteville State Univ	NC	5,590	LC
Fisk Univ	TN	13,700	LC
Florida State Univ	FL	7,835	HC
Freed-Hardeman Univ	TN	14,290	VC
Frostburg State Univ	MD	9,680	C
Geneva College	PA	19,990	C+
Georgia State Univ	GA	7,792	LC
Gonzaga Univ	WA	24,276	HC+
Graceland Univ	IA	15,845	C
Grand Canyon Univ	AZ	30,000	LC
Greenville College	IL	19,226	LC
Gustavus Adolphus College	MN	24,190	VC+
Hannibal-LaGrange College	MO	12,530	C
Hastings College	NE	17,854	C+
Henderson State Univ	AR	6,269	C
Hillsdale College	MI	20,586	VC+
Hofstra Univ	NY	23,252	C
Houston Baptist Univ	TX	15,300	LC
Humboldt State Univ	CA	8,582	C
Huntingdon College	AL	18,400	VC
Idaho State Univ	ID	7,030	C+
Illinois College	IL	16,234	C
Illinois State Univ	IL	9,235	C
Indiana Univ Bloomington	IN	10,712	C+
Indiana Univ South Bend	IN	3,515	C
Indiana Univ-Purdue Univ Fort Wayne	IN	3,166	LC
Indiana Univ-Purdue Univ Indianapolis	IN	9,473	C
Iowa State Univ	IA	8,108	VC
Ithaca College	NY	28,719	HC
Jackson State Univ	MS	6,776	LC
Jacksonville Univ	FL	21,110	LC
James Madison Univ	VA	9,552	HC
Kansas State Univ	KS	6,995	C
Kansas Wesleyan Univ	KS	17,400	C+
Kent State Univ	OH	11,104	C
Kutztown Univ of Pennsylvania	PA	8,907	C
Lamar Univ	TX	6,816	LC
Lander Univ	SC	8,618	LC
Langston Univ	OK	2,308	LC
Lock Haven Univ of Pennsylvania	PA	9,534	C
LIU/Brooklyn Campus	NY	22,290	C
Loras College	IA	22,994	C+
Louisiana College	LA	11,516	C
Louisiana State Univ and A&M College	LA	8,014	VC
Louisiana State Univ in Shreveport	LA	2,480	NC
Louisiana Tech Univ	LA	6,506	C
Luther College	IA	23,300	VC+
Mansfield Univ	PA	9,648	C
Marietta College	OH	24,580	C
McKendree College	IL	18,300	C+
McNeese State Univ	LA	5,259	LC
McPherson College	KS	17,710	C
Mercy College	NY	15,875	LC
Meredith College	NC	17,500	C
Metropolitan State College of Denver	CO	2,338	LC
Miami Univ	OH	12,885	VC+
Middle Tenn State Univ	TN	6,994	C
Minn State Univ, Mankato	MN	7,296	LC
Miss Valley State Univ	MS	6,345	C
Missouri Southern State College	MO	6,666	C
Missouri Valley College	MO	17,400	LC
Missouri Western State College	MO	6,662	NC
Montclair State Univ	NJ	10,287	LC
Moorhead State Univ	MN	7,000	LC
Morehead State Univ	KY	6,510	C
Morgan State Univ	MD	10,078	LC
Morris Brown College	GA	15,993	LC

ST = STATE $IS = IN-STATE COSTS SR = SELECTOR RATING

School	ST	$IS	SR
Mount Mercy College	IA	19,390	VC
Murray State Univ	KY	6,672	C
Muskingum College	OH	18,760	C
New York Univ	NY	35,200	MC
Norfolk State Univ	VA	8,382	LC
N Car Agricultural and Technical State Univ	NC	6,659	LC
North Central College	IL	22,944	C+
Northeastern Illinois Univ	IL	2,898	NC
Northeastern State Univ	OK	4,704	LC
Northern Arizona Univ	AZ	7,398	C
Northern Kentucky Univ	KY	6,352	NC
Northern Mich Univ	MI	9,693	C
Northwest Missouri State Univ	MO	7,922	LC
Northwestern Okla State Univ	OK	4,542	NC
Ohio Univ	OH	11,769	C
Okla Baptist Univ	OK	13,878	VC
Okla City Univ	OK	15,810	C
Olivet Nazarene Univ	IL	18,444	C
Oral Roberts Univ	OK	18,490	C
Oregon State Univ	OR	9,612	VC
Otterbein College	OH	23,439	C
Ouachita Baptist Univ	AR	16,460	VC
Palm Beach Atlantic College	FL	23,310	C
Penn State Univ/Univ Park Campus	PA	11,126	VC
Pepperdine Univ	CA	32,830	VC
Point Loma Nazarene Univ	CA	21,380	VC
Portland State Univ	OR	11,220	C
Prairie View A&M Univ	TX	3,172	LC
Radford Univ	VA	8,302	C
Rider Univ	NJ	27,400	C
Ripon College	WI	24,180	VC+
Rowan Univ	NJ	12,365	VC
St. Ambrose Univ	IA	19,994	C
St. Cloud State Univ	MN	7,180	C
St. John's Univ	NY	26,660	C
St. Joseph's College, New York	NY	9,802	C
St. Mary's Univ of San Antonio	TX	19,735	C
Sam Houston State Univ	TX	6,076	LC
Samford Univ	AL	16,340	VC
San Francisco State Univ	CA	7,139	LC
San Jose State Univ	CA	8,187	C
Shippensburg Univ of Pennsylvania	PA	9,652	C
Simpson College	IA	21,200	C+
Southeastern Okla State Univ	OK	4,917	C
Southern Illinois Univ at Carbondale	IL	8,621	C
Southern Illinois Univ Edwardsville	IL	7,869	LC
Southern Nazarene Univ	OK	14,634	NC
Southern Univ at New Orleans	LA	995	NC
Southwest Missouri State Univ	MO	7,600	LC
Southwest Texas State Univ	TX	8,730	VC
Southwestern Adventist Univ	TX	14,798	C
SUNY/College at Oneonta	NY	9,981	C
SUNY/College at Potsdam	NY	10,519	C
SUNY/Univ at Binghamton	NY	10,653	HC
SUNY/Univ at New Paltz	NY	9,685	VC
State Univ of West Georgia	GA	7,101	C
Stephen F. Austin State Univ	TX	6,905	C
Sterling College	KS	16,370	VC
Suffolk Univ	MA	26,516	C
Syracuse Univ	NY	30,710	HC
Tarleton State Univ	TX	7,160	C
Temple Univ	PA	14,124	C
Tenn State Univ	TN	7,058	VC
Texas A&M Univ	TX	8,988	VC
Texas Christian Univ	TX	19,910	C
Texas Southern Univ	TX	6,576	NC
Thomas More College	KY	17,700	LC
Touro College	NY	14,950	VC
Trevecca Nazarene Univ	TN	15,752	C
Trinity Univ	TX	21,444	HC
Troy State Univ	AL	7,696	C
Truman State Univ	MO	8,568	VC+
Univ of Akron	OH	10,530	NC
Univ of Alabama	AL	7,402	C
Univ of Alaska Southeast	AK	7,900	LC
Univ of Arkansas at Monticello	AR	5,940	NC
Univ of Arkansas at Pine Bluff	AR	7,925	C
Univ of Calif at Berkeley	CA	14,134	MC
Univ of Calif at Davis	CA	12,796	VC
Univ of Central Arkansas	AR	6,388	C
Univ of Central Okla	OK	5,205	C
Univ of Dubuque	IA	19,990	C
Univ of Florida	FL	7,874	HC
Univ of Georgia	GA	8,656	VC
Univ of Hawaii at Manoa	HI	7,862	VC
Univ of Houston	TX	8,410	C
Univ of Illinois at Chicago	IL	10,702	VC
Univ of Illinois at Urbana-Champaign	IL	11,316	HC+
Univ of Indianapolis	IN	20,840	C
Univ of Iowa	IA	8,607	C+
Univ of Kansas	KS	7,232	VC
Univ of Louisiana at Monroe	LA	5,207	NC
Univ of Maine	ME	10,798	C
Univ of Mary Hardin-Baylor	TX	13,929	C
Univ of Miami	FL	31,130	HC
Univ of Mich/Ann Arbor	MI	13,003	HC+
Univ of Mich/Flint	MI	4,323	C
Univ of Minn/Morris	MN	10,716	VC
Univ of Minn/Twin Cities	MN	11,123	VC
Univ of Missouri/Kansas City	MO	9,685	VC
Univ of Nebr at Kearney	NE	7,048	NC
Univ of Nebr at Lincoln	NE	8,325	C+
Univ of Nebr at Omaha	NE	6,867	C
Univ of Nevada/Reno	NV	8,737	C
Univ of N Car at Chapel Hill	NC	8,789	HC
Univ of N Car at Greensboro	NC	6,858	C
Univ of N Car at Wilmington	NC	7,769	C
Univ of Northern Iowa	IA	7,850	C
Univ of Pittsburgh at Pittsburgh	PA	13,592	HC
Univ of Rhode Island	RI	12,414	C
Univ of Richmond	VA	27,300	HC
Univ of Sioux Falls	SD	16,390	C
Univ of S Car at Columbia	SC	8,748	VC
Univ of South Florida	FL	8,154	C
Univ of Southern Indiana	IN	8,655	LC
Univ of Southern Miss	MS	6,155	LC
Univ of Tenn at Knoxville	TN	8,214	C
Univ of Texas at Arlington	TX	7,192	LC
Univ of Texas at Austin	TX	9,437	HC
Univ of Texas at El Paso	TX	5,076	LC
Univ of Utah	UT	7,703	C
Univ of Washington	WA	10,361	VC
Univ of Wisc/La Crosse	WI	7,250	VC
Univ of Wisc/Oshkosh	WI	6,130	LC
Univ of Wisc/Platteville	WI	7,282	C
Univ of Wisc/River Falls	WI	6,356	LC
Univ of Wisc/Superior	WI	7,051	C+
Univ of Wisc/Whitewater	WI	6,937	C
Valdosta State Univ	GA	6,988	C
Wabash College	IN	25,335	HC
Walla Walla College	WA	20,925	C
Washburn Univ of Topeka	KS	6,766	NC
Wayne State College	NE	6,255	NC
Weber State Univ	UT	6,897	NC
West Chester Univ of Pennsylvania	PA	9,792	VC
West Texas A&M Univ	TX	6,538	C
West Virginia Univ	WV	8,304	C
West Virginia Wesleyan College	WV	22,920	C
Western Carolina Univ	NC	5,667	C
Western Kentucky Univ	KY	6,834	C
Western Oregon Univ	OR	8,829	C
Whitworth College	WA	23,938	VC
Winona State Univ	MN	8,570	C
Winthrop Univ	SC	9,106	C
Yeshiva Univ	NY	21,400	C
York College of Pennsylvania	PA	12,550	VC
Youngstown State Univ	OH	0,318	NC

SPORTS MANAGEMENT

School	ST	$IS	SR
Adams State College	CO	7,468	C
Alaska Pacific Univ	AK	16,450	C
Albertson College of Idaho	ID	23,900	VC
Alvernia College	PA	20,790	C
Anderson Univ	IN	19,430	LC
Averett Univ	VA	17,980	LC
Baldwin-Wallace College	OH	22,010	VC+
Ball State Univ	IN	8,660	C
Barry Univ	FL	24,100	LC
Barton College	NC	16,834	LC
Becker College	MA	21,230	LC
Berry College	GA	18,850	C
Bethel College	IN	17,650	LC
Bluffton College	OH	20,644	C
Bowling Green State Univ	OH	10,794	C
Buena Vista Univ	IA	22,828	C
Campbell Univ	NC	16,599	C
Champlain College	VT	19,680	C
Colby-Sawyer College	NH	27,850	LC
College Misericordia	PA	23,380	LC
Concordia Univ	MI	20,500	C
Concordia Univ Nebr	NE	17,770	C
Dakota Wesleyan Univ	SD	15,512	C
Daniel Webster College	NH	24,870	C
De Sales Univ	PA	22,610	VC
Defiance College	OH	19,580	LC
Drury Univ	MO	15,250	VC
Edinboro Univ of Pennsylvania	PA	9,328	LC
Elon Univ	NC	19,430	VC
Erskine College	SC	21,399	VC
Faulkner Univ	AL	13,000	C
Flagler College	FL	10,550	VC+
Florida State Univ	FL	7,835	HC
Franklin Pierce College	NH	26,125	LC
Fresno Pacific Univ	CA	19,740	C
Gardner Webb Univ	NC	17,400	C
Georgia Southern Univ	GA	6,958	C
Guilford College	NC	23,255	C
Gwynedd-Mercy College	PA	22,350	C
Hampton Univ	VA	17,112	C+
Harding Univ	AR	13,528	VC
High Point Univ	NC	20,220	LC
Huron Univ	SD	10,450	C
Husson College	ME	15,360	LC
Indiana State Univ	IN	8,461	LC
Indiana Univ Bloomington	IN	10,712	C+
Iowa Wesleyan College	IA	18,840	C
Ithaca College	NY	28,719	HC
Johnson and Wales Univ	RI	21,558	LC
Judson College	IL	18,980	LC
Lewis Univ	IL	20,960	C
Liberty Univ	VA	14,500	C
Limestone College	SC	16,900	C
Lindenwood Univ	MO	17,250	C
Loras College	IA	22,994	C+
Lubbock Christian Univ	TX	14,226	LC
Lynchburg College	VA	23,405	C
Lyndon State College	VT	11,313	LC
Lynn Univ	FL	24,550	C
MacMurray College	IL	17,790	LC
Malone College	OH	19,190	C
Marian College	IN	21,020	C
Marian College of Fond du Lac	WI	17,935	LC
Marymount Univ	VA	21,560	LC
Medaille College	NY	18,320	C
Menlo College	CA	24,000	LC
Methodist College	NC	19,526	C
Miami Univ	OH	12,885	VC+
Miss Univ for Women	MS	5,446	LC
Missouri Baptist College	MO	15,762	LC
Mount Union College	OH	21,120	C
Mount Vernon Nazarene College	OH	17,027	C
Mountain State Univ	WV	8,180	NC
Nebr Wesleyan Univ	NE	18,767	VC
Neumann College	PA	22,040	NC
New England College	NH	20,706	LC
New York Univ	NY	35,200	MC
Nichols College	MA	24,610	LC
Northwestern College	MN	19,816	C+
Ohio Northern Univ	OH	27,765	VC
Ohio Univ	OH	11,769	C
Old Dominion Univ	VA	9,386	C
Peru State College	NE	6,342	NC
Pfeiffer Univ	NC	18,580	C
Principia College	IL	23,865	C+
Quincy Univ	IL	20,450	C
Robert Morris Univ	PA	18,730	C
St. John Fisher College	NY	21,800	C
St. John's Univ	NY	26,660	C
St. Leo Univ	FL	19,250	LC
St. Thomas Univ	FL	19,500	LC
Salem International Univ	WV	17,263	LC
Seton Hall Univ	NJ	26,910	LC
Shepherd College	WV	7,062	LC
Simpson College	IA	21,200	C+
Southern Nazarene Univ	OK	14,634	NC
Southern New Hampshire Univ	NH	23,852	C
Southwest Baptist Univ	MO	13,426	LC
Southwestern College	KS	17,656	C
Springfield College	MA	24,520	C
Taylor Univ	IN	21,562	VC+
Temple Univ	PA	14,124	C
Tenn Wesleyan College	TN	13,030	C
Thomas College	ME	18,915	LC
Towson Univ	MD	11,088	VC
Trinity International Univ	IL	20,640	C+
Tusculum College	TN	17,900	LC
Union College	KY	15,920	C
Union Univ	TN	18,930	C+
Univ of Charleston	WV	20,640	C
Univ of Dayton	OH	20,400	VC
Univ of Houston	TX	8,410	C
Univ of Idaho	ID	7,026	C
Univ of Indianapolis	IN	20,840	C
Univ of Louisville	KY	7,402	LC
Univ of Mass Amherst	MA	10,995	VC
Univ of Miami	FL	31,130	HC
Univ of Mich/Ann Arbor	MI	13,003	HC+
Univ of Minn/Crookston	MN	9,626	NC
Univ of New England	ME	24,110	LC
Univ of New Haven	CT	23,860	LC
Univ of Pittsburgh at Bradford	PA	12,696	C
Univ of S Car at Columbia	SC	8,748	VC
Univ of Tenn at Knoxville	TN	8,214	C
Univ of the Incarnate Word	TX	18,478	C
Univ of the Pacific	CA	28,255	VC
Univ of Tulsa	OK	19,090	HC
Urbana Univ	OH	17,004	C
Valparaiso Univ	IN	23,570	VC+
Virginia Intermont College	VA	17,510	C
Washington State Univ	WA	9,388	C
Wayne State College	NE	6,255	NC
West Virginia Univ	WV	8,304	C
Western Carolina Univ	NC	5,667	C
Western New England College	MA	23,882	C
Wheeling Jesuit Univ	WV	22,660	C
Wichita State Univ	KS	6,879	C
William Penn Univ	IA	17,575	C
Wilmington College	DE	6,530	NC
Wilmington College	OH	21,826	C
Wingate Univ	NC	19,140	C
Winston-Salem State Univ	NC	5,927	LC
Winthrop Univ	SC	9,106	C
Xavier Univ	OH	23,880	C
York College of Pennsylvania	PA	12,550	VC

SPORTS MEDICINE

School	ST	$IS	SR
Averett Univ	VA	17,980	LC
Avila College	MO	17,720	C
Baldwin-Wallace College	OH	22,010	VC+
Barton College	NC	16,834	LC
Cabrini College	PA	25,950	LC
Calif Lutheran Univ	CA	23,500	LC
Campbellsville Univ	KY	14,340	C
Capital Univ	OH	23,630	C
Castleton State College	VT	10,922	LC
Catawba College	NC	19,620	C
Central Mich Univ	MI	8,355	C
Concordia Univ Wisc	WI	16,600	LC
Eastern Mich Univ	MI	9,855	C
Eastern Nazarene College	MA	19,433	LC
Elon Univ	NC	19,430	VC
Georgia Southern Univ	GA	6,958	C
Guilford College	NC	23,255	C
Heidelberg College	OH	23,879	C
High Point Univ	NC	20,220	LC
Hope International Univ	CA	16,940	NC
Ithaca College	NY	28,719	HC
John Brown Univ	AR	15,080	VC
Johnson State College	VT	10,776	C
King's College	PA	24,680	C
Lander Univ	SC	8,618	LC
Lees-McRae College	NC	17,106	LC
Lynchburg College	VA	23,405	C
Lyndon State College	VT	11,313	LC
Marietta College	OH	24,580	C
Mercyhurst College	PA	20,694	C
Merrimack College	MA	25,725	VC
Missouri Baptist College	MO	15,762	LC
Northwestern College	MN	19,816	C+
Norwich Univ	VT	21,064	LC
Ohio Univ	OH	11,769	C
Old Dominion Univ	VA	9,386	C
Pepperdine Univ	CA	32,830	VC
Pfeiffer Univ	NC	18,580	C
Rivier College	NH	24,215	C
Samford Univ	AL	16,340	VC
Shawnee State Univ	OH	8,634	NC
Southeast Missouri State Univ	MO	8,367	C+
Stetson Univ	FL	25,640	VC
Towson Univ	MD	11,088	VC
Trinity International Univ	IL	20,640	C+
Tusculum College	TN	17,900	LC
Union Univ	TN	18,930	C+
Univ of Charleston	WV	20,640	C
Univ of Detroit Mercy	MI	21,620	LC
Univ of Evansville	IN	22,865	VC+
Univ of Nevada/Las Vegas	NV	8,281	VC
Univ of Southern Maine	ME	10,569	C
Univ of the Pacific	CA	28,255	VC
Urbana Univ	OH	17,004	C
Valdosta State Univ	GA	6,988	C
Wingate Univ	NC	19,140	C

STATISTICS

School	ST	$IS	SR
American Univ	DC	31,544	VC+
Appalachian State Univ	NC	6,353	C
Bowling Green State Univ	OH	10,794	C
Brigham Young Univ	UT	7,840	HC
Calif Polytechnic State Univ	CA	8,747	VC
Cal State, Hayward	CA	7,400	LC
Cal State, Long Beach	CA	7,400	LC
Carnegie Mellon Univ	PA	32,682	MC
Case Western Reserve Univ	OH	27,418	C
Central Mich Univ	MI	8,355	C
CUNY/Baruch College	NY	3,275	VC+
CUNY/Hunter College	NY	5,147	C+
College of New Jersey	NJ	13,425	HC
Colo State Univ	CO	9,672	C
Columbia Univ/Barnard College	NY	33,694	MC
Columbia Univ/Columbia College	NY	35,190	MC
Columbia Univ/School of General Studies	NY	35,000	C
Cornell Univ	NY	34,614	MC
Eastern Kentucky Univ	KY	6,552	C
Eastern Mich Univ	MI	9,855	C
Eastern New Mexico Univ	NM	4,113	LC
Florida International Univ	FL	9,486	VC
Florida State Univ	FL	7,835	HC
George Washington Univ	DC	32,170	HC
Harvard Univ/Harvard College	MA	34,269	MC
Iowa State Univ	IA	8,108	VC
James Madison Univ	VA	9,552	HC
Kansas State Univ	KS	6,995	C

School	ST	$IS	SR
Lehigh Univ	PA	32,290	MC
Marquette Univ	WI	24,836	C+
Miami Univ	OH	12,885	VC+
Mich State Univ	MI	10,386	VC
Mount Holyoke College	MA	34,128	HC
New Jersey Inst of Technology	NJ	14,690	VC
New York Univ	NY	35,200	MC
N Car State Univ	NC	8,680	HC
N Dak State Univ	ND	7,004	VC
Northwest Missouri State Univ	MO	7,922	LC
Northwestern Univ	IL	33,615	MC
Oakland Univ	MI	9,418	C
Ohio Northern Univ	OH	27,765	VC
Okla State Univ	OK	7,650	VC
Penn State Univ/Univ Park Campus	PA	11,126	VC
Purdue Univ/West Lafayette	IN	10,284	VC
Rochester Inst of Technology	NY	26,232	VC+
Roosevelt Univ	IL	20,240	LC
Rutgers, The State Univ of New Jersey New Brunswick Campus	NJ	12,709	C
St. Cloud State Univ	MN	7,180	C
San Diego State Univ	CA	9,716	C+
San Francisco State Univ	CA	7,139	LC
San Jose State Univ	CA	8,187	C
Southern Methodist Univ	TX	28,349	VC
SUNY/College at Oneonta	NY	9,981	C
SUNY/Univ at Stony Brook	NY	10,998	VC
Syracuse Univ	NY	30,710	HC
Temple Univ	PA	14,124	C
Univ of Akron	OH	10,530	NC
Univ of Alaska Fairbanks	AK	8,265	NC
Univ of Calif at Berkeley	CA	14,134	MC
Univ of Calif at Davis	CA	12,796	VC
Univ of Calif at Riverside	CA	12,479	C
Univ of Calif at Santa Barbara	CA	11,732	VC
Univ of Central Florida	FL	8,251	VC
Univ of Chicago	IL	35,087	MC
Univ of Conn	CT	12,122	VC
Univ of Denver	CO	28,783	VC
Univ of Florida	FL	7,874	HC
Univ of Georgia	GA	8,656	VC
Univ of Houston	TX	8,410	C
Univ of Illinois at Chicago	IL	10,702	VC
Univ of Illinois at Urbana-Champaign	IL	11,316	HC+
Univ of Iowa	IA	8,607	C+
Univ of Louisiana at Lafayette	LA	5,200	C
Univ of Mich/Ann Arbor	MI	13,003	HC+
Univ of Minn/Twin Cities	MN	11,123	VC
Univ of Missouri/Columbia	MO	9,803	HC
Univ of Missouri/Rolla	MO	10,034	C
Univ of Nebr at Kearney	NE	7,048	NC
Univ of N Car at Chapel Hill	NC	8,789	HC
Univ of N Car at Greensboro	NC	6,858	C
Univ of North Florida	FL	8,089	VC
Univ of Northern Colo	CO	8,082	C+
Univ of Pennsylvania	PA	34,614	MC
Univ of Pittsburgh at Pittsburgh	PA	13,592	HC
Univ of Rhode Island	RI	12,414	C
Univ of Rochester	NY	32,979	HC
Univ of South Alabama	AL	6,976	LC
Univ of S Car at Columbia	SC	8,748	VC
Univ of Southern Miss	MS	6,155	LC
Univ of Tenn at Knoxville	TN	8,214	C
Univ of Texas at Dallas	TX	9,305	VC
Univ of Texas at El Paso	TX	5,076	LC
Univ of Vermont	VT	14,761	C+
Univ of Washington	WA	10,361	VC
Univ of West Florida	FL	7,518	C
Univ of Wisc/Eau Claire	WI	7,032	VC
Univ of Wisc/Madison	WI	8,262	VC
Univ of Wyoming	WY	7,143	LC
Utah State Univ	UT	6,771	C
Virginia Polytechnic Inst and State Univ	VA	7,652	C
Washington Univ in St. Louis	MO	34,593	MC
West Virginia Univ	WV	8,304	C
Western Mich Univ	MI	10,016	C
Winona State Univ	MN	8,570	C
Xavier Univ of Louisiana	LA	17,000	LC

STRINGS

School	ST	$IS	SR
Drake Univ	IA	22,830	VC
Florida State Univ	FL	7,835	HC
Juilliard School	NY	28,200	SP
Manhattan School of Music	NY	31,500	SP
Roosevelt Univ	IL	20,240	LC
Temple Univ	PA	14,124	C
Univ of Mich/Ann Arbor	MI	13,003	HC+

STUDIO ART

School	ST	$IS	SR
Allegheny College	PA	27,780	VC
American Univ	DC	31,544	VC+
Anna Maria College	MA	22,800	LC
Appalachian State Univ	NC	6,353	C
Augsburg College	MN	22,978	C
Augusta State Univ	GA	2,282	C
Augustana College	IL	24,117	VC+
Baker Univ	KS	14,780	C+
Barton College	NC	16,834	LC
Baylor Univ	TX	18,298	VC+
Beloit College	WI	27,482	HC
Benedictine Univ	IL	21,330	C
Berry College	GA	18,850	C
Bloomsburg Univ of Pennsylvania	PA	9,434	C
Boston College	MA	33,330	MC
Bowdoin College	ME	32,650	MC
Bradley Univ	IL	20,970	VC
Brenau Univ Women's College	GA	20,100	C
Caldwell College	NJ	20,940	LC
Cal State, Fullerton	CA	5,440	LC
Cal State, Stanislaus	CA	8,895	C
Carleton College	MN	30,780	MC
Carthage College	WI	23,670	C
Cazenovia College	NY	19,885	LC
Central Missouri State Univ	MO	7,920	C
Chestnut Hill College	PA	24,790	LC
CUNY/Queens College	NY	3,403	VC
CUNY/York College	NY	3,292	NC
Clark Univ	MA	29,170	HC
Clarke College	IA	20,625	C+
Cleveland Inst of Art	OH	22,680	SP
Coastal Carolina Univ	SC	9,220	C
Colgate Univ	NY	33,480	MC
College of Charleston	SC	8,350	HC
College of Notre Dame of Maryland	MD	23,100	LC
College of St. Rose	NY	19,084	C
College of the Holy Cross	MA	32,780	MC
College of the Ozarks	MO	2,650	C+
Colo College	CO	31,525	HC+
Columbia College	SC	19,050	LC
Concordia College/Moorhead	MN	18,835	C
Concordia Univ	MN	19,912	C
Concordia Univ Nebr	NE	17,770	C
Dartmouth College	NH	34,458	MC
Denison Univ	OH	29,640	HC
DePauw Univ	IN	28,000	HC
Drake Univ	IA	22,830	VC
Duquesne Univ	PA	24,242	C+
East Carolina Univ	NC	7,766	C
Eastern College	PA	19,641	LC
Eastern Washington Univ	WA	7,972	LC
Emmanuel College	MA	23,802	C+
Florida State Univ	FL	7,835	HC
Franklin and Marshall College	PA	32,410	HC
Gallaudet Univ	DC	16,554	SP
George Mason Univ	VA	9,192	C
Georgia State Univ	GA	7,792	LC
Gettysburg College	PA	32,070	HC
Goucher College	MD	30,650	VC+
Graceland Univ	IA	15,845	C
Grand Canyon Univ	AZ	30,000	LC
Hamilton College	NY	34,150	HC
Henderson State Univ	AR	6,269	C
Hollins Univ	VA	24,328	VC
Indiana State Univ	IN	8,461	LC
Indiana Univ Bloomington	IN	10,712	C+
Indiana Univ of Pennsylvania	PA	9,133	C
Indiana Wesleyan Univ	IN	17,680	C
Ithaca College	NY	28,719	HC
Jacksonville Univ	FL	21,110	LC
Johnson State College	VT	10,776	C
Juniata College	PA	26,080	VC
Kansas Wesleyan Univ	KS	17,400	C+
Kean Univ	NJ	11,159	C
Kentucky State Univ	KY	6,146	NC
Kenyon College	OH	32,130	HC+
Knox College	IL	28,230	HC
Lawrence Univ	WI	27,711	HC
Lewis and Clark College	OR	29,010	VC
Lewis Univ	IL	20,960	C
Limestone College	SC	16,900	C
Lindenwood Univ	MO	17,250	C
Loras College	IA	22,994	C+
Louisiana College	LA	11,516	C
Loyola Marymount Univ	CA	28,754	HC
Loyola Univ New Orleans	LA	23,506	VC+
Lycoming College	PA	24,780	C
Mansfield Univ	PA	9,648	C
Marian College	IN	21,020	C
Marietta College	OH	24,580	C
Mary Washington College	VA	9,032	VC+
Maryville Univ of St. Louis	MO	18,680	C
Marywood Univ	PA	24,639	C
Mass College of Art	MA	13,703	SP
Mercyhurst College	PA	20,694	C
Messiah College	PA	23,180	VC
Mich State Univ	MI	10,386	VC
Middle Tenn State Univ	TN	6,994	C
Middlebury College	VT	34,300	MC
Mills College	CA	27,950	C
Minneapolis College of Art and Design	MN	23,560	SP
Moravian College	PA	27,065	VC
Mount Holyoke College	MA	34,128	HC
New York Univ	NY	35,200	MC
Northwestern College	MN	19,816	C+
Notre Dame College	OH	20,425	C
Old Dominion Univ	VA	9,386	C
Oral Roberts Univ	OK	18,490	C
Parsons School of Design	NY	32,242	SP
Pomona College	CA	33,960	MC
Principia College	IL	23,865	C+
Providence College	RI	27,620	HC
Randolph-Macon College	VA	24,395	C
Rivier College	NH	24,215	C
Rochester Inst of Technology	NY	26,232	VC+
Rollins College	FL	31,223	HC
St. Louis Univ	MO	26,590	VC+
St. Mary's Univ of Minn	MN	19,975	C
St. Olaf College	MN	25,880	HC
St. Vincent College	PA	22,942	VC
Salem College	NC	23,065	VC
Salve Regina Univ	RI	26,460	C
Santa Clara Univ	CA	28,371	VC+
Scripps College	CA	30,400	HC+
Seton Hill College	PA	21,875	C
Silver Lake College of the Holy Family	WI	15,516	LC
Simon's Rock College of Bard	MA	32,450	HC
Smith College	MA	33,302	HC+
Southern Conn State Univ	CT	10,310	C
Southern Methodist Univ	TX	28,349	VC
Southwest Texas State Univ	TX	8,730	VC
Spring Hill College	AL	23,250	C
SUNY/College at Brockport	NY	10,267	C
SUNY/College at Geneseo	NY	9,970	HC
SUNY/College at Potsdam	NY	10,519	C
SUNY/Univ at Binghamton	NY	10,653	HC
SUNY/Univ at Buffalo	NY	11,033	VC
SUNY/Univ at Stony Brook	NY	10,998	VC
Sweet Briar College	VA	25,310	VC
Texas Christian Univ	TX	19,910	C
Texas Tech Univ	TX	8,825	C
Transylvania Univ	KY	21,780	VC+
Trinity Christian College	IL	19,415	C
Trinity College	CT	34,300	HC
Tulane Univ	LA	34,013	HC+
Union College	NE	14,650	C
Union College	NY	32,646	HC
Univ of Alabama at Birmingham	AL	10,110	C
Univ of Arizona	AZ	8,614	C
Univ of Calif at Davis	CA	12,796	VC
Univ of Calif at Irvine	CA	11,756	C
Univ of Calif at San Diego	CA	11,372	HC
Univ of Evansville	IN	22,865	VC+
Univ of Findlay	OH	23,962	NC
Univ of Georgia	GA	8,656	VC
Univ of Houston	TX	8,410	C
Univ of Idaho	ID	7,026	C
Univ of Illinois at Chicago	IL	10,702	VC
Univ of Indianapolis	IN	20,840	C
Univ of Maryland/College Park	MD	11,959	C
Univ of Mass Amherst	MA	10,995	VC
Univ of Miami	FL	31,130	HC
Univ of Minn/Morris	MN	10,716	VC
Univ of Minn/Twin Cities	MN	11,123	VC
Univ of Missouri/Kansas City	MO	9,685	VC
Univ of Montevallo	AL	7,266	C
Univ of New Hampshire	NH	13,207	C
Univ of New Mexico	NM	8,026	C
Univ of N Car at Chapel Hill	NC	8,789	HC
Univ of N Car at Wilmington	NC	7,769	C
Univ of Northern Iowa	IA	7,850	C
Univ of Notre Dame	IN	30,707	MC
Univ of Pittsburgh at Pittsburgh	PA	13,592	HC
Univ of Richmond	VA	27,300	HC
Univ of Rochester	NY	32,979	HC
Univ of St. Thomas	TX	18,752	VC
Univ of South Alabama	AL	6,976	LC
Univ of S Car at Columbia	SC	8,748	VC
Univ of Southern Calif	CA	33,647	MC
Univ of Tenn at Knoxville	TN	8,214	C
Univ of Texas at Arlington	TX	7,192	LC
Univ of Texas at Austin	TX	9,437	HC
Univ of the Pacific	CA	28,255	VC
Univ of Washington	WA	10,361	VC
Univ of West Florida	FL	7,518	C
Univ of Wisc/Superior	WI	7,051	C+
Viterbo Univ	WI	18,043	C
Washington and Lee Univ	VA	25,095	MC
Washington Univ in St. Louis	MO	34,593	MC
Wellesley College	MA	33,394	MC
Wesleyan College	GA	17,050	VC
Wesleyan Univ	CT	3,405	MC
West Chester Univ of Pennsylvania	PA	9,792	VC
West Texas A&M Univ	TX	6,538	C
Western Carolina Univ	NC	5,667	C
Western Conn State Univ	CT	10,074	C
Western Kentucky Univ	KY	6,834	C
Whitman College	WA	29,086	HC
Wichita State Univ	KS	6,879	C
Willamette Univ	OR	29,422	VC+
William Paterson Univ of New Jersey	NJ	11,000	LC
William Woods Univ	MO	19,390	LC
Youngstown State Univ	OH	9,318	NC

SURVEY AND MAPPING TECHNOLOGY

School	ST	$IS	SR
East Tenn State Univ	TN	7,127	C
Metropolitan State College of Denver	CO	2,338	LC
Southern Polytechnic State Univ	GA	6,662	C
SUNY/College of Environmental Science and Forestry	NY	12,446	VC
SUNY/College of Technology at Alfred	NY	9,188	C
Thomas Edison State College	NJ	2,750	SP
Univ of Akron	OH	10,530	NC
Univ of Alaska Anchorage	AK	9,100	NC

SURVEYING ENGINEERING

School	ST	$IS	SR
Cal State, Fresno	CA	7,762	C
Ferris State Univ	MI	10,816	C
Metropolitan State College of Denver	CO	2,338	LC
Mich Tech Univ	MI	11,088	VC
New Mexico State Univ	NM	7,302	C
Oregon Inst of Technology	OR	8,718	C
Purdue Univ/West Lafayette	IN	10,284	VC
Universidad Metropolitana	PR	3,324	
Universidad Politecnica de PR	PR	4,695	
Univ of Arkansas at Little Rock	AR	5,637	NC
Univ of Florida	FL	7,874	HC
Univ of Maine	ME	10,798	C
Univ of PR/Mayaguez	PR	5,285	

SYSTEMS ANALYSIS

School	ST	$IS	SR
George Washington Univ	DC	32,170	HC
Johnson and Wales Univ	RI	21,558	LC
Rochester Inst of Technology	NY	26,232	VC+
Univ of Miami	FL	31,130	HC

SYSTEMS ENGINEERING

School	ST	$IS	SR
Case Western Reserve Univ	OH	27,418	C
George Mason Univ	VA	9,192	C
Huron Univ	SD	10,450	C
Milwaukee School of Engineering	WI	25,680	VC+
Northwood Univ	TX	18,135	C
Oakland Univ	MI	9,418	C
Point Park College	PA	20,290	C
Purdue Univ/West Lafayette	IN	10,284	VC
Texas A&M Univ at Galveston	TX	7,269	C+
United States Military Academy	NY		MC
United States Naval Academy	MD		MC
Univ of Arizona	AZ	8,614	C
Univ of Memphis	TN	7,271	C
Univ of Missouri/Rolla	MO	10,034	C
Univ of Pennsylvania	PA	34,614	MC
Univ of Virginia	VA	9,391	HC+
Washington Univ in St. Louis	MO	34,593	MC
West Virginia Univ	WV	8,304	C
Wright State Univ	OH	9,141	LC
Youngstown State Univ	OH	9,318	NC

SYSTEMS SCIENCE

School	ST	$IS	SR
Johnson and Wales Univ	RI	21,558	LC
Park Univ	MO	9,816	C
Stanford Univ	CA	34,222	MC
State Univ of West Georgia	GA	7,101	C
Washington Univ in St. Louis	MO	34,593	MC

TEACHING ENGLISH AS A SECOND/FOREIGN LANGUAGE (TESOL/TEFOL)

School	ST	$IS	SR
Abilene Christian Univ	TX	16,300	VC
Andrews Univ	MI	17,696	LC
Brigham Young Univ	UT	7,840	HC
Brigham Young Univ/Hawaii	HI	6,890	C
Caribbean Univ	PR	3,000	
Carroll College	MT	19,140	C
College of Our Lady of the Elms	MA	20,644	C
Eastern Mich Univ	MI	9,855	C
Goshen College	IN	18,950	VC+

School	ST	$IS	SR
Hawaii Pacific Univ	HI	17,790	C
Houston Baptist Univ	TX	15,300	LC
Howard Payne Univ	TX	13,834	C+
Inter-American Univ of PR/ Arecibo Campus	PR	3,300	
Inter-American Univ of PR/ San GermÈn	PR	6,390	
LIU/Brooklyn Campus	NY	22,290	C
Mercy College	NY	15,875	LC
Northern Arizona Univ	AZ	7,398	C
Northwestern College	MN	19,816	C+
Nyack College	NY	18,540	C
Ohio Dominican College	OH	18,100	LC
Okla Christian Univ	OK	16,500	VC
Pontifical Catholic Univ of PR/Ponce	PR	7,076	
Rider Univ	NJ	27,400	C
San Jose State Univ	CA	8,187	C
Temple Univ	PA	14,124	C
Texas Wesleyan Univ	TX	14,710	C
Toccoa Falls College	GA	14,220	C
Union Univ	TN	18,930	C+
United States International Univ	CA	18,675	LC
Univ of Louisville	KY	7,402	LC
Univ of Minn/Twin Cities	MN	11,123	VC
Univ of Nebr at Kearney	NE	7,048	NC
Univ of New Mexico	NM	8,026	C
Univ of Northern Iowa	IA	7,850	C
Univ of PR/Mayaguez	PR	5,285	
Univ of the Pacific	CA	28,255	VC

TECHNICAL AND BUSINESS WRITING

School	ST	$IS	SR
Bowling Green State Univ	OH	10,794	C
Carlow College	PA	19,366	C
Cedarville Univ	OH	17,553	VC
Christian Brothers Univ	TN	19,820	VC
Clarkson Univ	NY	29,884	VC
Colo State Univ	CO	9,672	C
Doane College	NE	17,600	LC
Dominican Univ	IL	20,800	C
Illinois Inst of Technology	IL	25,182	HC+
Lindenwood Univ	MO	17,250	C
Madonna Univ	MI	11,504	VC
Marylhurst Univ	OR	15,343	NC
Metropolitan State Univ	MN	2,943	SP
Mich Tech Univ	MI	11,088	VC
Milwaukee School of Engineering	WI	25,680	VC+
Mount Mary College	WI	18,024	C
New Jersey Inst of Technology	NJ	14,690	VC
New Mexico Inst of Mining and Technology	NM	7,152	VC+
New York Inst of Technology	NY	21,756	C
Ohio Dominican College	OH	18,100	LC
Pennsylvania College of Technology	PA	12,860	NC
Polytechnic Univ/Brooklyn	NY	33,090	HC
Southern Polytechnic State Univ	GA	6,662	C
Southwest Missouri State Univ	MO	7,600	LC
Tenn Tech Univ	TN	6,968	C
Thiel College	PA	18,419	LC
Univ of Arkansas at Little Rock	AR	5,637	NC
Univ of Findlay	OH	23,962	NC
Univ of Hartford	CT	28,884	C
Univ of Houston-Downtown	TX	2,006	NC
Univ of Mass Dartmouth	MA	9,852	C
Univ of Missouri/Rolla	MO	10,034	C
Univ of Montana--Western	MT	6,915	NC
Univ of New Mexico	NM	8,026	C
Univ of the Sciences in Philadelphia	PA	24,826	VC
Univ of Washington	WA	10,361	VC
Waynesburg College	PA	17,610	LC
Weber State Univ	UT	6,897	NC
Wheeling Jesuit Univ	WV	22,660	C
Youngstown State Univ	OH	9,318	NC

TECHNICAL EDUCATION

School	ST	$IS	SR
Andrews Univ	MI	17,696	LC
Ball State Univ	IN	8,660	C
Bowling Green State Univ	OH	10,794	C
Central Conn State Univ	CT	10,404	C
CUNY/New York City Technical College	NY	3,319	NC
College of New Jersey	NJ	13,425	HC
College of the Ozarks	MO	2,650	C+
Eastern Kentucky Univ	KY	6,552	C
Elizabeth City State Univ	NC	5,550	LC
Ferris State Univ	MI	10,816	C
Fort Hays State Univ	KS	6,294	LC
Georgia Southern Univ	GA	6,958	C
Kean Univ	NJ	11,159	C
Kent State Univ	OH	11,104	C
Millersville Univ of Pennsylvania	PA	10,153	VC
Miss State Univ	MS	7,853	C
Montana State Univ-Bozeman	MT	8,431	C
Montclair State Univ	NJ	10,287	LC
New Mexico Highlands Univ	NM	6,256	NC
New York Inst of Technology	NY	21,756	C
Norfolk State Univ	VA	8,382	LC
N Car State Univ	NC	8,680	HC
Okla State Univ	OK	7,650	VC
Southwestern Okla State Univ	OK	4,801	C
Tuskegee Univ	AL	14,600	LC
Univ of Akron	OH	10,530	NC
Univ of Northern Iowa	IA	7,850	C
Univ of Southern Maine	ME	10,569	C
Univ of Wisc/Platteville	WI	7,282	C
Univ of Wisc/Stout	WI	7,192	C
Valley City State Univ	ND		LC
Virginia Polytechnic Inst and State Univ	VA	7,652	C
Wayne State Univ	MI	6,720	C
Western Illinois Univ	IL	9,571	C

TECHNOLOGICAL MANAGEMENT

School	ST	$IS	SR
Arkansas State Univ	AR	7,480	C
Champlain College	VT	19,680	C
Clayton College and State Univ	GA	2,322	C+
DeVry Univ/Addison (DuPage County)	IL	8,805	LC
DeVry Univ/Alpharetta	GA	8,805	LC
DeVry Univ/Chicago	IL	8,805	LC
DeVry Univ/Colo Springs	CO	9,465	LC
DeVry Univ/Columbus	OH	8,805	LC
DeVry Univ/Crystal City	VA	10,065	C
DeVry Univ/Dallas	TX	8,805	LC
DeVry Univ/Decatur	GA	8,805	LC
DeVry Univ/Fremont	CA	9,865	C
DeVry Univ/Kansas City	MO	8,805	LC
DeVry Univ/Long Beach	CA	9,140	LC
DeVry Univ/Orlando	FL	9,865	LC
DeVry Univ/Phoenix	AZ	8,805	LC
DeVry Univ/Pomona	CA	9,205	LC
DeVry Univ/Tinley Park	IL	8,805	LC
DeVry Univ/West Hills	CA	9,205	LC
Excelsior College	NY	915	SP
Franklin Univ	OH	6,324	SP
Georgia Southern Univ	GA	6,958	C
Golden Gate Univ	CA	8,592	NC
Johnson and Wales Univ	RI	21,558	LC
Murray State Univ	KY	6,672	C
New York Inst of Technology	NY	21,756	C
Ohio Northern Univ	OH	27,765	VC
Pennsylvania College of Technology	PA	12,860	NC
Southern Illinois Univ at Carbondale	IL	8,621	C
Southern New Hampshire Univ	NH	23,852	C
Southern Univ at New Orleans	LA	995	NC
SUNY/College at Oswego	NY	10,856	C
State Univ of West Georgia	GA	7,101	C
Univ of Alaska Anchorage	AK	9,100	NC
Univ of Alaska Fairbanks	AK	8,265	NC
Univ of Findlay	OH	23,962	NC
Univ of Minn/Crookston	MN	9,626	NC
Washburn Univ of Topeka	KS	6,766	NC
Wayne State College	NE	6,255	NC
Wentworth Inst of Technology	MA	20,450	C

TECHNOLOGY AND PUBLIC AFFAIRS

School	ST	$IS	SR
Georgia Inst of Technology	GA	9,028	HC+
Pomona College	CA	33,960	MC
Univ of Georgia	GA	8,656	VC
Vassar College	NY	33,450	MC
Washington Univ in St. Louis	MO	34,593	MC
Wheeling Jesuit Univ	WV	22,660	C

TELECOMMUNICATIONS

School	ST	$IS	SR
Alabama A&M Univ	AL	5,100	LC
Ball State Univ	IN	8,660	C
Baylor Univ	TX	18,298	VC+
Bowling Green State Univ	OH	10,794	C
Butler Univ	IN	25,580	VC+
Cal State, Monterey Bay	CA	6,250	LC
Capitol College	MD	18,462	LC
Champlain College	VT	19,680	C
CUNY/New York City Technical College	NY	3,319	NC
Colo Technical Univ	CO	9,425	LC
Concordia Univ Wisc	WI	16,600	LC
DeVry College of Technology/North Brunswick	NJ	8,805	LC
DeVry Univ/New York	NY	9,865	LC
DeVry Univ/Addison (DuPage County)	IL	8,805	LC
DeVry Univ/Alpharetta	GA	8,805	LC
DeVry Univ/Chicago	IL	8,805	LC
DeVry Univ/Colo Springs	CO	9,465	LC
DeVry Univ/Crystal City	VA	10,065	C
DeVry Univ/Dallas	TX	8,805	LC
DeVry Univ/Decatur	GA	8,805	LC
DeVry Univ/Fremont	CA	9,865	C
DeVry Univ/Kansas City	MO	8,805	LC
DeVry Univ/Long Beach	CA	9,140	LC
DeVry Univ/Orlando	FL	9,865	LC
DeVry Univ/Phoenix	AZ	8,805	LC
DeVry Univ/Pomona	CA	9,205	LC
DeVry Univ/Seattle	WA	10,065	LC
DeVry Univ/Tinley Park	IL	8,805	LC
DeVry Univ/West Hills	CA	9,205	LC
Eastern Mich Univ	MI	9,855	C
Fort Hays State Univ	KS	6,294	LC
George Fox Univ	OR	24,095	VC
Illinois State Univ	IL	9,235	C
Indiana Univ Bloomington	IN	10,712	C+
Indiana Univ-Purdue Univ Fort Wayne	IN	3,166	LC
Ithaca College	NY	28,719	HC
Kean Univ	NJ	11,159	C
Kent State Univ	OH	11,104	C
Kutztown Univ of Pennsylvania	PA	8,907	C
Marywood Univ	PA	24,639	C
Miami Univ	OH	12,885	VC+
Mich State Univ	MI	10,386	VC
Morgan State Univ	MD	10,078	LC
Murray State Univ	KY	6,672	C
New York Inst of Technology	NY	21,756	C
Northern Arizona Univ	AZ	7,398	C
Ohio Univ	OH	11,769	C
Okla Baptist Univ	OK	13,878	VC
Pepperdine Univ	CA	32,830	VC
Purdue Univ/West Lafayette	IN	10,284	VC
Rochester Inst of Technology	NY	26,232	VC+
Roosevelt Univ	IL	20,240	LC
Syracuse Univ	NY	30,710	HC
Temple Univ	PA	14,124	C
Texas Southern Univ	TX	6,576	NC
Texas Tech Univ	TX	8,825	C
United States International Univ	CA	18,675	LC
Univ of Alabama	AL	7,402	C
Univ of Colo at Boulder	CO	9,255	VC
Univ of Florida	FL	7,874	HC
Univ of Georgia	GA	8,656	VC
Univ of Idaho	ID	7,026	C
Univ of Kentucky	KY	7,765	C
Univ of Louisiana at Lafayette	LA	5,200	C
Univ of Miami	FL	31,130	HC
Univ of Nebr at Kearney	NE	7,048	NC
Univ of Northern Colo	CO	8,082	C+
Univ of PR/Arecibo	PR	1,095	
Univ of Texas at Dallas	TX	9,305	VC
Univ of the Sacred Heart	PR	5,375	
Univ of Wisc/Stout	WI	7,192	C
Valdosta State Univ	GA	6,988	C
Weber State Univ	UT	6,897	NC
Western Mich Univ	MI	10,016	C
Youngstown State Univ	OH	9,318	NC

TEXTILE ENGINEERING

School	ST	$IS	SR
Auburn Univ	AL	5,510	C
Georgia Inst of Technology	GA	9,028	HC+
N Car State Univ	NC	8,680	HC
Philadelphia Univ	PA	24,722	C
Southern Polytechnic State Univ	GA	6,662	C
Texas Tech Univ	TX	8,825	C

TEXTILE TECHNOLOGY

School	ST	$IS	SR
Auburn Univ	AL	5,510	C
Clemson Univ	SC	7,600	C
Fashion Inst of Technology/ SUNY	NY	9,504	C+
Philadelphia Univ	PA	24,722	C
Southern Polytechnic State Univ	GA	6,662	C
Univ of Mass Dartmouth	MA	9,852	C
Univ of Wisc/Madison	WI	8,262	VC

TEXTILES AND CLOTHING

School	ST	$IS	SR
Albright College	PA	27,642	C
Auburn Univ	AL	5,510	C
Calif College of Arts and Crafts	CA	27,366	SP
Central Missouri State Univ	MO	7,920	C
College For Creative Studies	MI	20,938	SP
Cornell Univ	NY	34,614	MC
Fashion Inst of Technology/ SUNY	NY	9,504	C+
Framingham State College	MA	7,259	C
Georgia Inst of Technology	GA	9,028	HC+
Indiana State Univ	IN	8,461	LC
Iowa State Univ	IA	8,108	VC
Kansas State Univ	KS	6,995	C
Kentucky State Univ	KY	6,146	NC
Louisiana State Univ and A&M College	LA	8,014	VC
Middle Tenn State Univ	TN	6,994	C
Moore College of Art and Design	PA	23,125	SP
N Car State Univ	NC	8,680	HC
N Dak State Univ	ND	7,004	VC
Northwest Missouri State Univ	MO	7,922	LC
Oregon State Univ	OR	9,612	VC
Rhode Island School of Design	RI	30,227	SP
Syracuse Univ	NY	30,710	HC
Texas Woman's Univ	TX	5,855	LC
Univ of Calif at Davis	CA	12,796	VC
Univ of Delaware	DE	10,824	VC
Univ of Idaho	ID	7,026	C
Univ of Kentucky	KY	7,765	C
Univ of Minn/Twin Cities	MN	11,123	VC
Univ of Nebr at Lincoln	NE	8,325	C+
Univ of Rhode Island	RI	12,414	C
Univ of Tenn at Knoxville	TN	8,214	C
Univ of Texas at Austin	TX	9,437	HC
Univ of Wisc/Madison	WI	8,262	VC
Virginia Polytechnic Inst and State Univ	VA	7,652	C
Western Kentucky Univ	KY	6,834	C
Western Mich Univ	MI	10,016	C

THEATER DESIGN

School	ST	$IS	SR
Adelphi Univ	NY	23,320	VC
Arcadia Univ	PA	26,650	C
Baylor Univ	TX	18,298	VC+
Boston Univ	MA	34,358	MC
Central Missouri State Univ	MO	7,920	C
College of the Ozarks	MO	2,650	C+
Cornish College of the Arts	WA	16,200	SP
DePaul Univ	IL	23,590	VC
Dickinson College	PA	32,210	VC+
Emerson College	MA	29,978	HC
Florida State Univ	FL	7,835	HC
Franklin Pierce College	NH	26,125	LC
Ithaca College	NY	28,719	HC
Johnson State College	VT	10,776	C
N Car School of the Arts	NC	7,797	SP
Pace Univ	NY	24,200	C
Purdue Univ/West Lafayette	IN	10,284	VC
Roosevelt Univ	IL	20,240	LC
Seton Hill College	PA	21,875	C
Shenandoah Univ	VA	22,550	NC
SUNY/College at Purchase	NY	10,587	VC
Syracuse Univ	NY	30,710	HC
Texas Tech Univ	TX	8,825	C
Towson Univ	MD	11,088	VC
Univ of Arizona	AZ	8,614	C
Univ of Cincinnati	OH	12,491	LC
Univ of Conn	CT	12,122	VC
Univ of Evansville	IN	22,865	VC+
Univ of Florida	FL	7,874	HC
Univ of Kansas	KS	7,232	VC
Univ of Maryland/Baltimore County	MD	12,190	VC
Univ of Miami	FL	31,130	HC
Univ of Northern Iowa	IA	7,850	C
Univ of Southern Calif	CA	33,647	MC
Vanderbilt Univ	TN	34,482	MC
Washburn Univ of Topeka	KS	6,766	NC
Webster Univ	MO	19,804	VC
Western Mich Univ	MI	10,016	C
Wright State Univ	OH	9,141	LC

THEATER MANAGEMENT

School	ST	$IS	SR
Barry Univ	FL	24,100	LC
Barton College	NC	16,834	LC
Benedictine College	KS	18,485	LC
Boston Univ	MA	34,358	MC
Catawba College	NC	19,620	C
CUNY/Brooklyn College	NY	3,403	LC
Emerson College	MA	29,978	HC
Hardin-Simmons Univ	TX	14,165	C
Ithaca College	NY	28,719	HC
Johnson State College	VT	10,776	C
Luther College	IA	23,300	VC+
Marywood Univ	PA	24,639	C
Roosevelt Univ	IL	20,240	LC
Salisbury Univ	MD	10,576	VC
Seton Hill College	PA	21,875	C
Shenandoah Univ	VA	22,550	NC
Syracuse Univ	NY	30,710	HC
Texas Tech Univ	TX	8,825	C
Trinity College	CT	34,300	HC
Univ of Delaware	DE	10,824	VC
Univ of Evansville	IN	22,865	VC+
Univ of Hartford	CT	28,884	C
Univ of Miami	FL	31,130	HC
Univ of Portland	OR	24,950	VC
Univ of Southern Calif	CA	33,647	MC
Univ of Texas at El Paso	TX	5,076	LC
Yale Univ	CT	34,030	MC

THEOLOGICAL STUDIES

School	ST	$IS	SR
Alvernia College	PA	20,790	C
Andrews Univ	MI	17,696	LC
Aquinas College	MI	20,052	C+
Assumption College	MA	26,320	C
Atlantic Union College	MA	34,034	LC
Avila College	MO	17,720	C
Barry Univ	FL	24,100	LC
Bellarmine Univ	KY	20,440	VC
Belmont Abbey College	NC	19,630	LC
Berry College	GA	18,850	C
Boston College	MA	33,330	MC
Briar Cliff Univ	IA	18,657	LC
Calumet College of St. Joseph	IN	7,500	LC
Carlow College	PA	19,366	C
Christendom College	VA	16,700	VC+
College of Mount St. Joseph	OH	20,290	C
College of St. Benedict	MN	23,921	VC
College of St. Catherine	MN	22,324	VC
College of St. Elizabeth	NJ	22,510	C
Concordia Univ	MN	19,912	C
Concordia Univ	OR	20,500	LC
Concordia Univ Nebr	NE	17,770	C
Concordia Univ Wisc	WI	16,600	LC
Concordia Univ, River Forest	IL	20,000	LC
Creighton Univ	NE	23,476	VC
De Sales Univ	PA	22,610	VC
Duquesne Univ	PA	24,242	C+
Eastern College	PA	19,641	LC
Fordham Univ	NY	30,710	VC
Franciscan Univ of Steubenville	OH	19,100	C+
Gannon Univ	PA	18,848	C
Hanover College	IN	17,560	VC
Hardin-Simmons Univ	TX	14,165	C
Immaculata College	PA	22,400	LC
John Brown Univ	AR	15,080	VC
King's College	PA	24,680	C
Lenoir-Rhyne College	NC	19,186	C
Loyola College in Maryland	MD	30,900	HC
Loyola Marymount Univ	CA	28,754	HC
Loyola Univ of Chicago	IL	25,992	VC
Malone College	OH	19,190	C
Marian College	IN	21,020	C
Marquette Univ	WI	24,836	C+
Marymount Univ	VA	21,560	LC
Molloy College	NY	13,940	C
Mount Mary College	WI	18,024	C
Mount St. Mary's College	MD	25,740	C
Notre Dame College	OH	20,425	C
Ouachita Baptist Univ	AR	16,460	VC
Pacific Union College	CA	20,250	VC
Palm Beach Atlantic College	FL	23,310	C
Pontifical Catholic Univ of PR/Ponce	PR	7,076	
Providence College	RI	27,620	HC
Quincy Univ	IL	20,450	C
Rice Univ	TX	24,325	MC
Roanoke College	VA	24,689	VC
Rockhurst Univ	MO	20,090	C
St. Anselm College	NH	27,405	C
St. John's Univ	MN	23,640	VC
St. John's Univ	NY	26,660	C
St. Joseph's College of Maine	ME	22,500	LC
St. Louis Univ	MO	26,590	VC+
St. Mary College	KS	17,298	C
St. Mary-of-the-Woods College	IN	21,320	LC
St. Mary's College	MI	13,314	LC
St. Mary's Univ of Minn	MN	19,975	C
St. Mary's Univ of San Antonio	TX	19,735	C
St. Peter's College	NJ	22,292	LC
St. Vincent College	PA	22,942	VC
Seattle Pacific Univ	WA	22,674	C+
Southern Adventist Univ	TN	15,600	C
Southwestern Adventist Univ	TX	14,798	C
Spring Hill College	AL	23,250	C
Sterling College	KS	16,370	VC
Texas Lutheran Univ	TX	17,660	C
Thomas More College	KY	17,700	LC
Toccoa Falls College	GA	14,220	C
Trinity Christian College	IL	19,415	C
Union College	NE	14,650	C
Universidad Adventista de las Antillas	PR	6,675	
Univ of Arizona	AZ	8,614	C
Univ of Dallas	TX	22,128	VC+
Univ of Evansville	IN	22,865	VC+
Univ of Great Falls	MT	15,360	C
Univ of Kansas	KS	7,232	VC
Univ of Notre Dame	IN	30,707	MC
Univ of Portland	OR	24,950	VC
Univ of St. Francis	IL	19,650	C
Univ of St. Thomas	MN	24,044	VC
Univ of St. Thomas	TX	18,752	VC
Univ of San Francisco	CA	27,302	VC
Univ of Scranton	PA	27,964	C+
Valparaiso Univ	IN	23,570	VC+
Villanova Univ	PA	31,997	HC
Walla Walla College	WA	20,925	C
Walsh Univ	OH	16,880	C
Waynesburg College	PA	17,610	LC
William Tyndale College	MI	11,150	C
Wisc Lutheran College	WI	19,216	VC
Xavier Univ	OH	23,880	C
Xavier Univ of Louisiana	LA	17,000	LC

THIRD WORLD STUDIES

School	ST	$IS	SR
Pitzer College	CA	33,930	HC
Univ of Calif at San Diego	CA	11,372	HC
Univ of the South	TN	27,290	HC

TOTAL QUALITY MANAGEMENT (TQM)

School	ST	$IS	SR
Norfolk State Univ	VA	8,382	LC

TOURISM

School	ST	$IS	SR
Bowling Green State Univ	OH	10,794	C
Brigham Young Univ	UT	7,840	HC
Brigham Young Univ/Hawaii	HI	6,890	C
Cal State, Dominguez Hills	CA	5,840	LC
Cal State, Fullerton	CA	5,440	LC
Central Missouri State Univ	MO	7,920	C
Champlain College	VT	19,680	C
Dowling College	NY	20,281	LC
Eastern Mich Univ	MI	9,855	C
George Washington Univ	DC	32,170	HC
Hawaii Pacific Univ	HI	17,790	C
Indiana Univ Bloomington	IN	10,712	C+
Indiana Univ-Purdue Univ Indianapolis	IN	9,473	C
James Madison Univ	VA	9,552	HC
Johnson and Wales Univ	RI	21,558	LC
Johnson State College	VT	10,776	C
Lasell College	MA	24,100	C
Lynn Univ	FL	24,550	C
Mansfield Univ	PA	9,648	C
National American Univ	SD	13,680	NC
New Mexico State Univ	NM	7,302	C
Niagara Univ	NY	22,250	C+
Rochester Inst of Technology	NY	26,232	VC+
St. Thomas Univ	FL	19,500	LC
Sojourner-Douglass College	MD	4,170	LC
Southern New Hampshire Univ	NH	23,852	C
Southwest Texas State Univ	TX	8,730	VC
Temple Univ	PA	14,124	C
United States International Univ	CA	18,675	LC
Univ of Colo at Boulder	CO	9,255	VC
Univ of Hawaii at Manoa	HI	7,862	VC
Univ of Missouri/Columbia	MO	9,803	HC
Univ of Nebr at Kearney	NE	7,048	NC
Univ of New Hampshire	NH	13,207	C
Univ of New Haven	CT	23,860	LC
Univ of New Mexico	NM	8,026	C
Univ of New Orleans	LA	10,160	C
Univ of Tenn at Knoxville	TN	8,214	C
Univ of Texas at San Antonio	TX	9,088	NC
Univ of the Sacred Heart	PR	5,375	
Univ of Utah	UT	7,703	C
Webber International Univ	FL	14,695	LC
West Liberty State College	WV	6,056	LC
West Virginia Univ	WV	8,304	C
Western Mich Univ	MI	10,016	C

TOXICOLOGY

School	ST	$IS	SR
Ashland Univ	OH	22,182	LC
CUNY/John Jay College of Criminal Justice	NY	3,251	C
College of St. Elizabeth	NJ	22,510	C
Northeastern Univ	MA	30,078	VC
St. John's Univ	NY	26,660	C
Univ of Calif at Davis	CA	12,796	VC
Univ of Louisiana at Monroe	LA	5,207	NC
Univ of Miami	FL	31,130	HC
Univ of the Sciences in Philadelphia	PA	24,826	VC
Univ of Wisc/Madison	WI	8,262	VC
Xavier Univ of Louisiana	LA	17,000	LC

TOY DESIGN

School	ST	$IS	SR
Fashion Inst of Technology/SUNY	NY	9,504	C+

TRADE AND INDUSTRIAL EDUCATION

School	ST	$IS	SR
Alabama A&M Univ	AL	5,100	LC
Kent State Univ	OH	11,104	C
New York Inst of Technology	NY	21,756	C
Univ of Georgia	GA	8,656	VC
Univ of Houston	TX	8,410	C
Univ of Nevada/Las Vegas	NV	8,281	VC
Univ of Wyoming	WY	7,143	LC
Valdosta State Univ	GA	6,988	C
Virginia State Univ	VA	8,182	LC
Western Kentucky Univ	KY	6,834	C

TRADE AND INDUSTRIAL SUPERVISION AND MANAGEMENT

School	ST	$IS	SR
Alaska Pacific Univ	AK	16,450	C
Cal State, Los Angeles	CA	5,050	C
College of St. Joseph	VT	17,400	NC
Eastern College	PA	19,641	LC
Miss State Univ	MS	7,853	C
Moorhead State Univ	MN	7,000	LC
Rice Univ	TX	24,325	MC
Washington Univ in St. Louis	MO	34,593	MC

TRANSPORTATION AND TRAVEL MARKETING

School	ST	$IS	SR
Johnson and Wales Univ	RI	21,558	LC
Northwood Univ	FL	19,179	LC
Northwood Univ	MI	18,360	LC
Northwood Univ	TX	18,135	C
Ursuline College	OH	19,430	LC

TRANSPORTATION ENGINEERING

School	ST	$IS	SR
Purdue Univ/West Lafayette	IN	10,284	VC

TRANSPORTATION MANAGEMENT

School	ST	$IS	SR
Arkansas State Univ	AR	7,480	C
Auburn Univ	AL	5,510	C
Calif Maritime Academy	CA	12,256	C
Cal State, Los Angeles	CA	5,050	C
Dowling College	NY	20,281	LC
Elmhurst College	IL	21,750	C
Embry-Riddle Aeronautical Univ	FL	24,790	C
Florida International Univ	FL	9,486	VC
Florida Memorial College	FL	6,000	LC
Georgia Southern Univ	GA	6,958	C
Iowa State Univ	IA	8,108	VC
Mass Maritime Academy	MA	9,969	C
Niagara Univ	NY	22,250	C+
Northeastern Univ	MA	30,078	VC
Penn State Univ/Univ Park Campus	PA	11,126	VC
Robert Morris Univ	PA	18,730	C
St. John's Univ	NY	26,660	C
San Francisco State Univ	CA	7,139	LC
Southern Univ at New Orleans	LA	995	NC
SUNY/Maritime College	NY	10,025	LC
Texas A&M Univ at Galveston	TX	7,269	C+
Ohio State Univ	OH	10,819	VC
Thomas Edison State College	NJ	2,750	SP
United States Merchant Marine Academy	NY		VC
Univ of Alaska Anchorage	AK	9,100	NC
Univ of Arkansas	AR	8,334	VC
Univ of N Dak	ND	7,067	VC
Univ of North Florida	FL	8,089	VC
Univ of Tenn at Knoxville	TN	8,214	C

TRANSPORTATION TECHNOLOGY

School	ST	$IS	SR
Maine Maritime Academy	ME	10,911	C

ULTRASOUND TECHNOLOGY

School	ST	$IS	SR
Barry Univ	FL	24,100	LC
Champlain College	VT	19,680	C
Mountain State Univ	WV	8,180	NC
Nebr Methodist College of Nursing and Allied Health	NE	11,100	SP
Newman Univ	KS	14,098	LC
Oregon Inst of Technology	OR	8,718	C
Rochester Inst of Technology	NY	26,232	VC+
Seattle Univ	WA	24,183	VC

URBAN DESIGN

School	ST	$IS	SR
Arizona State Univ-Main	AZ	7,726	C
New York Univ	NY	35,200	MC
Oregon State Univ	OR	9,612	VC
SUNY/Univ at Albany	NY	10,997	VC

URBAN PLANNING TECHNOLOGY

School	ST	$IS	SR
Arizona State Univ-Main	AZ	7,726	C
Ball State Univ	IN	8,660	C
Eastern Mich Univ	MI	9,855	C
Florida Atlantic Univ	FL	8,832	C
Mass Inst of Technology	MA	35,228	MC
Southwest Missouri State Univ	MO	7,600	LC
Univ of Alabama	AL	7,402	C
Univ of Nevada/Las Vegas	NV	8,281	VC
Univ of Southern Calif	CA	33,647	MC
Univ of Utah	UT	7,703	C

URBAN STUDIES

School	ST	$IS	SR
Adams State College	CO	7,468	C
Albertus Magnus College	CT	22,154	C
Augsburg College	MN	22,978	C
Baylor Univ	TX	18,298	VC+
Bellevue Univ	NE	4,125	NC
Boston Univ	MA	34,358	MC
Brown Univ	RI	34,973	MC
Bryn Mawr College	PA	33,580	HC+
Calif State Polytechnic Univ, Pomona	CA	8,615	C
Cal State, Northridge	CA	7,781	C
Canisius College	NY	24,696	C+
Carnegie Mellon Univ	PA	32,682	MC
Central Washington Univ	WA	8,985	LC
CUNY/Brooklyn College	NY	3,403	LC
CUNY/Hunter College	NY	5,147	C+
CUNY/Queens College	NY	3,403	VC
Cleveland State Univ	OH	10,146	NC
College of Charleston	SC	8,350	HC
College of Mount St. Vincent	NY	24,230	C
College of Wooster	OH	28,350	VC
Columbia Univ/Barnard College	NY	33,694	MC
Columbia Univ/Columbia College	NY	35,190	MC
Columbia Univ/School of General Studies	NY	35,000	C
Conn College	CT	33,585	MC
Cornell Univ	NY	34,614	MC
David Lipscomb Univ	TN	16,158	VC
DePaul Univ	IL	23,590	VC
Dillard Univ	LA	16,046	VC
Eastern College	PA	19,641	LC
Eastern Washington Univ	WA	7,972	LC
Elmhurst College	IL	21,750	C
Eugene Lang College of New School Univ	NY	30,300	C
Florida International Univ	FL	9,486	VC
Fordham Univ	NY	30,710	VC
Furman Univ	SC	25,492	HC
Georgia State Univ	GA	7,792	LC
Hamline Univ	MN	23,339	C+
Hampshire College	MA	33,881	HC+
Haverford College	PA	34,300	MC
Hobart and William Smith Colleges	NY	33,195	VC
Indiana State Univ	IN	8,461	LC
Iona College	NY	26,556	C
Jackson State Univ	MS	6,776	LC
Johns Hopkins Univ	MD	35,226	MC
Langston Univ	OK	2,308	LC
Lehigh Univ	PA	32,290	MC
Loyola Marymount Univ	CA	28,754	HC
Macalester College	MN	28,814	HC+
Manhattan College	NY	25,500	VC
Metropolitan State College of Denver	CO	2,338	LC
Miami Univ	OH	12,885	VC+
Minn State Univ, Mankato	MN	7,296	LC
Morehouse College	GA	19,814	C
Mount Mercy College	IA	19,390	VC
New College of Florida	FL	8,130	HC+
New York Univ	NY	35,200	MC
Northwestern Univ	IL	33,615	MC
Occidental College	CA	32,288	HC
Ohio Univ	OH	11,769	C
Purdue Univ/West Lafayette	IN	10,284	VC
Rhode Island College	RI	8,700	LC
Rhodes College	TN	26,466	HC+
Rockford College	IL	23,930	C
Roosevelt Univ	IL	20,240	LC
Rutgers, The State Univ of New Jersey New Brunswick Campus	NJ	12,709	C
Rutgers, The State Univ of New Jersey/ CamdenCampus	NJ	6,484	C
St. Augustine's College	NC	12,990	C+
St. Cloud State Univ	MN	7,180	C
St. Louis Univ	MO	26,590	VC+
St. Peter's College	NJ	22,292	LC
San Diego State Univ	CA	9,716	C+
San Francisco State Univ	CA	7,139	LC
Stanford Univ	CA	34,222	MC
SUNY/College at Buffalo	NY	8,025	C
Temple Univ	PA	14,124	C
Trinity Univ	TX	21,444	HC
Univ of Calif at San Diego	CA	11,372	HC
Univ of Cincinnati	OH	12,491	LC
Univ of Conn	CT	12,122	VC
Univ of Mich/Flint	MI	4,323	C
Univ of Minn/Duluth	MN	10,436	C
Univ of Minn/Twin Cities	MN	11,123	VC

School	ST	$IS	SR
Univ of Missouri/Kansas City	MO	9,685	VC
Univ of Nebr at Omaha	NE	6,867	C
Univ of New Orleans	LA	10,160	C
Univ of Pennsylvania	PA	34,614	MC
Univ of Pittsburgh at Pittsburgh	PA	13,592	HC
Univ of Richmond	VA	27,300	HC
Univ of San Diego	CA	29,198	HC
Univ of Tampa	FL	22,612	C
Univ of Tenn at Knoxville	TN	8,214	C
Univ of the District of Columbia	DC	2,844	NC
Univ of the Sacred Heart	PR	5,375	
Univ of Wisc/Green Bay	WI	7,148	C
Univ of Wisc/Oshkosh	WI	6,130	LC
Vanderbilt Univ	TN	34,482	MC
Vassar College	NY	33,450	MC
Virginia Commonwealth Univ	VA	9,030	C
Virginia Polytechnic Inst and State Univ	VA	7,652	C
Washington Univ in St. Louis	MO	34,593	MC
Wayne State Univ	MI	6,720	C
Westfield State College	MA	8,394	C
Worcester State College	MA	7,901	LC
Wright State Univ	OH	9,141	LC

VETERINARY SCIENCE

School	ST	$IS	SR
Becker College	MA	21,230	LC
Fort Valley State Univ	GA	6,014	LC
Lincoln Memorial Univ	TN	12,620	LC
Mercy College	NY	15,875	LC
Mount Ida College	MA	25,375	LC
Murray State Univ	KY	6,672	C
National American Univ	SD	13,680	NC
Newberry College	SC	19,670	LC
N Dak State Univ	ND	7,004	VC
Purdue Univ/West Lafayette	IN	10,284	VC
Quinnipiac Univ	CT	27,370	C
Tuskegee Univ	AL	14,600	LC
Univ of Arizona	AZ	8,614	C
Univ of Idaho	ID	7,026	C
Univ of Illinois at Urbana-Champaign	IL	11,316	HC+
Univ of Nebr at Lincoln	NE	8,325	C+
Utah State Univ	UT	6,771	C
Washington State Univ	WA	9,388	C
West Virginia Univ	WV	8,304	C
Wilson College	PA	21,337	LC

VIDEO

School	ST	$IS	SR
American InterContinental Univ	GA	12,000	NC
Atlanta College of Art	GA	18,600	SP
Bloomfield College	NJ	17,000	C
Drexel Univ	PA	27,657	VC
Fairleigh Dickinson Univ/Madison campus	NJ	25,500	C
Five Towns College	NY	18,850	SP
Hampshire College	MA	33,881	HC+
Ithaca College	NY	28,719	HC
Kansas City Art Inst	MO	25,880	SP
Madonna Univ	MI	11,504	VC
Minneapolis College of Art and Design	MN	23,560	SP
Ohio Univ	OH	11,769	C
Point Park College	PA	20,290	C
Rochester Inst of Technology	NY	26,232	VC+
San Francisco Art Inst	CA	19,300	SP
Savannah College of Art and Design	GA	25,075	SP
School of the Art Inst of Chicago	IL	27,800	SP
School of Visual Arts	NY	26,000	SP
Syracuse Univ	NY	30,710	HC
Univ of Hartford	CT	28,884	C
Univ of Miami	FL	31,130	HC
Univ of Okla	OK	7,616	VC
Webster Univ	MO	19,804	VC
Wilmington College	DE	6,530	NC

VISUAL AND PERFORMING ARTS

School	ST	$IS	SR
Adelphi Univ	NY	23,320	VC
Albion College	MI	25,224	VC
Alverno College	WI	16,930	LC
Andrews Univ	MI	17,696	LC
Antioch College	OH	25,072	LC
Assumption College	MA	26,320	C
Bennett College	NC	11,200	C
Bennington College	VT	31,350	VC
Bowdoin College	ME	32,650	MC
Cabrini College	PA	25,950	LC
Cal State, Monterey Bay	CA	6,250	LC
Cal State, San Marcos	CA	1,736	LC
Chatham College	PA	25,454	C+
CUNY/Brooklyn College	NY	3,403	LC
Clark Univ	MA	29,170	HC
College of Santa Fe	NM	20,250	LC
Columbia Univ/Columbia College	NY	35,190	MC
Columbia Univ/School of General Studies	NY	35,000	C
Curry College	MA	26,025	LC
Dowling College	NY	20,281	LC
Duke Univ	NC	34,396	MC
Eckerd College	FL	25,500	C+
Fayetteville State Univ	NC	5,590	LC
Fordham Univ	NY	30,710	VC
Goddard College	VT	21,056	C+
Grand View College	IA	17,596	NC
Green Mountain College	VT	24,130	C
Indiana Univ Bloomington	IN	10,712	C+
Inter-American Univ of PR/Bayamon Univ College	PR	3,700	
Inter-American Univ of PR/Fajardo Campus	PR	4,000	
Inter-American Univ of PR/Ponce Regional College	PR	3,700	
Ithaca College	NY	28,719	HC
Johnson State College	VT	10,776	C
Kent State Univ	OH	11,104	C
King College	TN	17,800	VC
Kutztown Univ of Pennsylvania	PA	8,907	C
Lander Univ	SC	8,618	LC
Longwood College	VA	8,950	C
Loyola Univ New Orleans	LA	23,506	VC+
McNeese State Univ	LA	5,259	LC
Mount Mercy College	IA	19,390	VC
Mount St. Clare College	IA	19,050	LC
Naropa Univ	CO	22,416	SP
New England Conservatory of Music	MA	31,200	SP
Notre Dame College	OH	20,425	C
Ohio Univ	OH	11,769	C
Oregon State Univ	OR	9,612	VC
Otterbein College	OH	23,439	C
Presbyterian College	SC	23,356	VC
Rice Univ	TX	24,325	MC
Roger Williams Univ	RI	29,010	C
Rutgers, The State Univ of New Jersey New Brunswick Campus	NJ	12,709	C
St. Andrews Presbyterian College	NC	19,720	LC
St. Augustine's College	NC	12,990	C+
St. Bonaventure Univ	NY	21,956	C
St. Vincent College	PA	22,942	VC
Sarah Lawrence College	NY	37,516	HC
School of the Art Inst of Chicago	IL	27,800	SP
Seattle Pacific Univ	WA	22,674	C+
Shaw Univ	NC	12,810	C
Simon's Rock College of Bard	MA	32,450	HC
Sonoma State Univ	CA	8,953	C
Southern Oregon Univ	OR	9,429	C
SUNY/College at Old Westbury	NY	9,818	LC
SUNY/College at Purchase	NY	10,587	VC
Texas Tech Univ	TX	8,825	C
Univ of Alabama	AL	7,402	C
Univ of Arkansas at Little Rock	AR	5,637	NC
Univ of Calif at San Diego	CA	11,372	HC
Univ of Conn	CT	12,122	VC
Univ of Maine at Farmington	ME	9,163	C
Univ of Maryland/Baltimore County	MD	12,190	VC
Univ of N Dak	ND	7,067	VC
Univ of North Texas	TX	7,629	C
Univ of San Francisco	CA	27,302	VC
Univ of Texas at Austin	TX	9,437	HC
Univ of Texas at Dallas	TX	9,305	VC
Univ of the Sacred Heart	PR	5,375	
Virginia State Univ	VA	8,182	LC
Washington State Univ	WA	9,388	C
Washington Univ in St. Louis	MO	34,593	MC
Wells College	NY	19,350	VC
West Virginia Univ	WV	8,304	C
Wichita State Univ	KS	6,879	C

VOCATIONAL EDUCATION

School	ST	$IS	SR
Auburn Univ	AL	5,510	C
Cal State, Los Angeles	CA	5,050	C
Cal State, San Bernardino	CA	6,516	C
Cal State, Stanislaus	CA	8,895	C
Central Conn State Univ	CT	10,404	C
Chicago State Univ	IL	8,851	C+
CUNY/New York City Technical College	NY	3,319	NC
College of the Ozarks	MO	2,650	C+
Florida International Univ	FL	9,486	VC
Idaho State Univ	ID	7,030	C+
Indiana Univ of Pennsylvania	PA	9,133	C
Keene State College	NH	11,280	C
Kent State Univ	OH	11,104	C
Louisiana State Univ and A&M College	LA	8,014	VC
Martin Univ	IN	8,370	SP
N Car State Univ	NC	8,680	HC
Pittsburg State Univ	KS	6,228	NC
Rutgers, The State Univ of New Jersey New Brunswick Campus	NJ	12,709	C
San Diego State Univ	CA	9,716	C+
San Francisco State Univ	CA	7,139	LC
S Dak State Univ	SD	6,848	C
Southern Illinois Univ at Carbondale	IL	8,621	C
SUNY/College at Oswego	NY	10,856	C
Univ of Arkansas	AR	8,334	VC
Univ of Central Florida	FL	8,251	VC
Univ of Idaho	ID	7,026	C
Univ of N Dak	ND	7,067	VC
Univ of North Texas	TX	7,629	C
Univ of South Florida	FL	8,154	C
Univ of Toledo	OH	11,206	NC
Univ of Wisc/Stout	WI	7,192	C
Virginia Polytechnic Inst and State Univ	VA	7,652	C
Wayland Baptist Univ	TX	11,271	NC
Western New Mexico Univ	NM	5,950	LC
Youngstown State Univ	OH	9,318	NC

VOICE

School	ST	$IS	SR
Ball State Univ	IN	8,660	C
Catholic Univ of America	DC	29,332	VC
Drake Univ	IA	22,830	VC
East Central Univ	OK	4,578	C
East Texas Baptist Univ	TX	12,349	LC
Florida State Univ	FL	7,835	HC
Georgia College and State Univ	GA	7,344	C
Grand Canyon Univ	AZ	30,000	LC
Illinois Wesleyan Univ	IL	26,970	HC
Indiana Univ Bloomington	IN	10,712	C+
Juilliard School	NY	28,200	SP
Manhattan School of Music	NY	31,500	SP
Mannes College of Music	NY	28,900	SP
McMurry Univ	TX	15,287	C
Miss College	MS	14,574	C
New York Univ	NY	35,200	MC
Northwestern Univ	IL	33,615	MC
Nyack College	NY	18,540	C
Ohio Univ	OH	11,769	C
Pacific Lutheran Univ	WA	23,318	VC
Palm Beach Atlantic College	FL	23,310	C
Rollins College	FL	31,223	HC
Roosevelt Univ	IL	20,240	LC
Samford Univ	AL	16,340	VC
Shorter College	GA	15,185	C
Southern Nazarene Univ	OK	14,634	NC
Stetson Univ	FL	25,640	VC
Temple Univ	PA	14,124	C
Union Univ	TN	18,930	C+
Univ of Cincinnati	OH	12,491	LC
Univ of Illinois at Urbana-Champaign	IL	11,316	HC+
Univ of Kansas	KS	7,232	VC
Univ of Miami	FL	31,130	HC
Univ of Mich/Ann Arbor	MI	13,003	HC+
Univ of New Hampshire	NH	13,207	C
Univ of Tulsa	OK	19,090	HC
Weber State Univ	UT	6,897	NC
Westminster Choir College of Rider Univ	NJ	25,400	SP
Youngstown State Univ	OH	9,318	NC

WATER AND WASTEWATER TECHNOLOGY

School	ST	$IS	SR
Wright State Univ	OH	9,141	LC

WATER RESOURCES

School	ST	$IS	SR
Central State Univ	OH	8,922	C+
Colo State Univ	CO	9,672	C
Heidelberg College	OH	23,879	C
Northern Mich Univ	MI	9,693	C
Ohio Univ	OH	11,769	C
SUNY/College at Brockport	NY	10,267	C
SUNY/College at Oneonta	NY	9,981	C
Tarleton State Univ	TX	7,160	C
Univ of Arizona	AZ	8,614	C
Univ of Nebr at Lincoln	NE	8,325	C+
Univ of New Hampshire	NH	13,207	C
Univ of Rhode Island	RI	12,414	C
Univ of Wisc/Stevens Point	WI	7,116	C

WEB SERVICES

School	ST	$IS	SR
Champlain College	VT	19,680	C
Johnson and Wales Univ	RI	21,558	LC
Maharishi Univ of Management	IA	20,660	VC
Mercyhurst College	PA	20,694	C
Southern Adventist Univ	TN	15,600	C
Southern Wesleyan Univ	SC	17,280	C
SUNY/College of Technology at Alfred	NY	9,188	C

WEB TECHNOLOGY

School	ST	$IS	SR
Cabrini College	PA	25,950	LC
Cogswell Polytechnical College	CA	14,400	LC
Illinois Inst of Technology	IL	25,182	HC+
Mercyhurst College	PA	20,694	C
Strayer Univ	DC	8,789	SP

WELDING ENGINEERING

School	ST	$IS	SR
LeTourneau Univ	TX	19,020	VC
Pennsylvania College of Technology	PA	12,860	NC

WESTERN CIVILIZATION/CULTURE

School	ST	$IS	SR
St. John's College	MD	32,760	HC+
Univ of Kansas	KS	7,232	VC

WESTERN EUROPEAN STUDIES

School	ST	$IS	SR
New York Univ	NY	35,200	MC
St. John's College	MD	32,760	HC+
Univ of Mich/Ann Arbor	MI	13,003	HC+
Univ of Nebr at Lincoln	NE	8,325	C+
Washington Univ in St. Louis	MO	34,593	MC

WILDLIFE BIOLOGY

School	ST	$IS	SR
Auburn Univ	AL	5,510	C
Baker Univ	KS	14,780	C+
Ball State Univ	IN	8,660	C
Colo State Univ	CO	9,672	C
Humboldt State Univ	CA	8,582	C
Louisiana State Univ and A&M College	LA	8,014	VC
Murray State Univ	KY	6,672	C
New Mexico State Univ	NM	7,302	C
Northern Mich Univ	MI	9,693	C
Ohio Univ	OH	11,769	C
Oregon State Univ	OR	9,612	VC
Penn State Univ/Univ Park Campus	PA	11,126	VC
Southwest Texas State Univ	TX	8,730	VC
Unity College	ME	19,845	LC
Univ of Alaska Fairbanks	AK	8,265	NC
Univ of Arizona	AZ	8,614	C
Univ of Calif at Davis	CA	12,796	VC
Univ of Florida	FL	7,874	HC
Univ of Mich/Ann Arbor	MI	13,003	HC+
Univ of Minn/Twin Cities	MN	11,123	VC
Univ of Montana	MT	8,038	C
Univ of Tenn at Martin	TN	8,268	C
Univ of Vermont	VT	14,761	C+
Univ of Wisc/Madison	WI	8,262	VC
Univ of Wisc/Stevens Point	WI	7,116	C
Washington State Univ	WA	9,388	C
West Texas A&M Univ	TX	6,538	C

WILDLIFE MANAGEMENT

School	ST	$IS	SR
Arkansas State Univ	AR	7,480	C
Brigham Young Univ	UT	7,840	HC
Eastern Kentucky Univ	KY	6,552	C
Eastern New Mexico Univ	NM	4,113	LC
Frostburg State Univ	MD	9,680	C
Lake Superior State Univ	MI	9,034	LC
Lincoln Memorial Univ	TN	12,620	LC
Louisiana Tech Univ	LA	6,506	C
McNeese State Univ	LA	5,259	LC
Miss State Univ	MS	7,853	C
Northwest Missouri State Univ	MO	7,922	LC
Peru State College	NE	6,342	NC
Purdue Univ/West Lafayette	IN	10,284	VC
Southwest Missouri State Univ	MO	7,600	LC
Sterling College	VT	19,695	C
Sul Ross State Univ	TX	6,582	LC
Tenn Tech Univ	TN	6,968	C
Texas A&M Univ at Commerce	TX	7,326	C
Texas Tech Univ	TX	8,825	C
Univ of Alaska Fairbanks	AK	8,265	NC
Univ of Arkansas at Monticello	AR	5,940	NC
Univ of Georgia	GA	8,656	VC
Univ of Idaho	ID	7,026	C
Univ of Maine	ME	10,798	C
Univ of Mass Amherst	MA	10,995	VC
Univ of Miami	FL	31,130	HC
Univ of New Hampshire	NH	13,207	C
Univ of Rhode Island	RI	12,414	C
Univ of Wyoming	WY	7,143	LC
Utah State Univ	UT	6,771	C
Washington State Univ	WA	9,388	C

WINDS

School	ST	$IS	SR
Florida State Univ	FL	7,835	HC
Juilliard School	NY	28,200	SP
Miss College	MS	14,574	C
Northwestern Univ	IL	33,615	MC
Roosevelt Univ	IL	20,240	LC
Temple Univ	PA	14,124	C
Univ of Mich/Ann Arbor	MI	13,003	HC+
Youngstown State Univ	OH	9,318	NC

WOMEN'S STUDIES

School	ST	$IS	SR
Agnes Scott College	GA	24,950	VC
Allegheny College	PA	27,780	VC
American Univ	DC	31,544	VC+
Amherst College	MA	34,340	MC
Arizona State Univ-Main	AZ	7,726	C
Augsburg College	MN	22,978	C
Bates College	ME	34,100	MC
Beloit College	WI	27,482	HC
Berea College	KY	4,070	VC
Bowdoin College	ME	32,650	MC
Bowling Green State Univ	OH	10,794	C
Bucknell Univ	PA	31,096	HC
Cal State, Fresno	CA	7,762	C
Cal State, Fullerton	CA	5,440	LC
Cal State, Long Beach	CA	7,400	LC
Cal State, Northridge	CA	7,781	C
Cal State, San Marcos	CA	1,736	LC
Carleton College	MN	30,780	MC
Case Western Reserve Univ	OH	27,418	C
Chatham College	PA	25,454	C+
CUNY/Brooklyn College	NY	3,403	LC
CUNY/College of Staten Island	NY	3,358	NC
CUNY/Hunter College	NY	5,147	C+
CUNY/Queens College	NY	3,403	VC
Claremont McKenna College	CA	32,700	MC
Coe College	IA	24,750	VC
Colby College	ME	34,290	MC
Colgate Univ	NY	33,480	MC
College of Mount St. Joseph	OH	20,290	C
College of New Jersey	NJ	13,425	HC
College of Wooster	OH	28,350	VC
Colo College	CO	31,525	HC+
Columbia Univ/Barnard College	NY	33,694	MC
Columbia Univ/Columbia College	NY	35,190	MC
Columbia Univ/School of General Studies	NY	35,000	C
Cornell College	IA	24,980	VC
Cornell Univ	NY	34,614	MC
Dartmouth College	NH	34,458	MC
Denison Univ	OH	29,640	HC
DePaul Univ	IL	23,590	VC
DePauw Univ	IN	28,000	HC
Drake Univ	IA	22,830	VC
Drew Univ/College of Liberal Arts	NJ	32,152	VC
Duke Univ	NC	34,396	MC
East Carolina Univ	NC	7,766	C
Eastern Mich Univ	MI	9,855	C
Eckerd College	FL	25,500	C+
Emory Univ	GA	33,792	MC
Eugene Lang College of New School Univ	NY	30,300	C
Florida International Univ	FL	9,486	VC
Florida State Univ	FL	7,835	HC
Fordham Univ	NY	30,710	VC
Gettysburg College	PA	32,070	HC
Goddard College	VT	21,056	C+
Goucher College	MD	30,650	VC+
Guilford College	NC	23,255	C
Hamilton College	NY	34,150	HC
Hamline Univ	MN	23,339	C+
Hampshire College	MA	33,881	HC+
Harvard Univ/Harvard College	MA	34,269	MC
Hobart and William Smith Colleges	NY	33,195	VC
Hollins Univ	VA	24,328	VC
Indiana Univ Bloomington	IN	10,712	C+
Indiana Univ South Bend	IN	3,515	C
Knox College	IL	28,230	HC
Macalester College	MN	28,814	HC+
Mass Inst of Technology	MA	35,228	MC
Metropolitan State Univ	MN	2,943	SP
Middlebury College	VT	34,300	MC
Mills College	CA	27,950	C
Minn State Univ, Mankato	MN	7,296	LC
Mount Holyoke College	MA	34,128	HC
Nebr Wesleyan Univ	NE	18,767	VC
New College of Florida	FL	8,130	HC+
New England College	NH	20,706	LC
New York Univ	NY	35,200	MC
Oakland Univ	MI	9,418	C
Oberlin College	OH	33,140	HC+
Occidental College	CA	32,288	HC
Ohio Wesleyan Univ	OH	29,670	VC+
Old Dominion Univ	VA	9,386	C
Pacific Lutheran Univ	WA	23,318	VC
Penn State Univ/Univ Park Campus	PA	11,126	VC
Pitzer College	CA	33,930	HC
Pomona College	CA	33,960	MC
Portland State Univ	OR	11,220	C
Randolph-Macon College	VA	24,395	C
Rhode Island College	RI	8,700	LC
Roosevelt Univ	IL	20,240	LC
Rosemont College	PA	24,060	C
Rutgers, The State Univ of New Jersey New Brunswick Campus	NJ	12,709	C
St. Olaf College	MN	25,880	HC
San Diego State Univ	CA	9,716	C+
San Francisco State Univ	CA	7,139	LC
Sarah Lawrence College	NY	37,516	HC
Scripps College	CA	30,400	HC+
Simmons College	MA	30,418	VC
Skidmore College	NY	34,201	VC+
Smith College	MA	33,302	HC+
Southwestern Univ	TX	22,550	HC
Spelman College	GA	19,215	C+
Stanford Univ	CA	34,222	MC
SUNY/College at Oswego	NY	10,856	C
SUNY/College at Purchase	NY	10,587	VC
SUNY/Univ at Albany	NY	10,997	VC
SUNY/Univ at Buffalo	NY	11,033	VC
SUNY/Univ at Stony Brook	NY	10,998	VC
Syracuse Univ	NY	30,710	HC
Temple Univ	PA	14,124	C
Ohio State Univ	OH	10,819	VC
Towson Univ	MD	11,088	VC
Trinity College	CT	34,300	HC
Tufts Univ	MA	34,874	MC
Tulane Univ	LA	34,013	HC+
Union College	NY	32,646	HC
Univ of Arizona	AZ	8,614	C
Univ of Calif at Berkeley	CA	14,134	MC
Univ of Calif at Davis	CA	12,796	VC
Univ of Calif at Irvine	CA	11,756	C
Univ of Calif at Los Angeles	CA	13,227	MC
Univ of Calif at Riverside	CA	12,479	C
Univ of Calif at Santa Barbara	CA	11,732	VC
Univ of Calif at Santa Cruz	CA	13,655	VC
Univ of Colo at Boulder	CO	9,255	VC
Univ of Conn	CT	12,122	VC
Univ of Delaware	DE	10,824	VC
Univ of Denver	CO	28,783	VC
Univ of Hartford	CT	28,884	C
Univ of Hawaii at Manoa	HI	7,862	VC
Univ of Kansas	KS	7,232	VC
Univ of Louisville	KY	7,402	LC
Univ of Maine	ME	10,798	C
Univ of Maine at Farmington	ME	9,163	C
Univ of Maryland/College Park	MD	11,959	C
Univ of Mass Amherst	MA	10,995	VC
Univ of Mass Boston	MA	4,227	C
Univ of Miami	FL	31,130	HC
Univ of Mich/Ann Arbor	MI	13,003	HC+
Univ of Minn/Duluth	MN	10,436	C
Univ of Minn/Morris	MN	10,716	VC
Univ of Minn/Twin Cities	MN	11,123	VC
Univ of Montana	MT	8,038	C
Univ of Nebr at Lincoln	NE	8,325	C+
Univ of Nevada/Las Vegas	NV	8,281	VC
Univ of New Hampshire	NH	13,207	C
Univ of N Car at Chapel Hill	NC	8,789	HC
Univ of Okla	OK	7,616	VC
Univ of Oregon	OR	9,969	C
Univ of Pennsylvania	PA	34,614	MC
Univ of Puget Sound	WA	28,285	HC
Univ of Rhode Island	RI	12,414	C
Univ of Richmond	VA	27,300	HC
Univ of Rochester	NY	32,979	HC
Univ of St. Thomas	MN	24,044	VC
Univ of S Car at Columbia	SC	8,748	VC
Univ of South Florida	FL	8,154	C
Univ of Southern Calif	CA	33,647	MC
Univ of Southern Maine	ME	10,569	C
Univ of Tenn at Chattanooga	TN	7,783	C
Univ of Tenn at Knoxville	TN	8,214	C
Univ of Toledo	OH	11,206	NC
Univ of Utah	UT	7,703	C
Univ of Vermont	VT	14,761	C+
Univ of Washington	WA	10,361	VC
Univ of Wisc/Madison	WI	8,262	VC
Univ of Wisc/Whitewater	WI	6,937	C
Univ of Wyoming	WY	7,143	LC
Vassar College	NY	33,450	MC
Villanova Univ	PA	31,997	HC
Washington State Univ	WA	9,388	C
Washington Univ in St. Louis	MO	34,593	MC
Wayne State Univ	MI	6,720	C
Wellesley College	MA	33,394	MC
Wells College	NY	19,350	VC
Wesleyan Univ	CT	3,405	MC
West Chester Univ of Pennsylvania	PA	9,792	VC
Western Mich Univ	MI	10,016	C
Wheaton College	MA	32,940	VC
Whitworth College	WA	23,938	VC
Wichita State Univ	KS	6,879	C
Yale Univ	CT	34,030	MC

WOOD SCIENCE

School	ST	$IS	SR
N Car State Univ	NC	8,680	HC
SUNY/College of Environmental Science and Forestry	NY	12,446	VC
Univ of Maine	ME	10,798	C
Univ of Washington	WA	10,361	VC

WOODWORKING

School	ST	$IS	SR
Edinboro Univ of Pennsylvania	PA	9,328	LC
Indiana Univ-Purdue Univ Indianapolis	IN	9,473	C
Rochester Inst of Technology	NY	26,232	VC+
Univ of Rio Grande	OH	8,728	NC

YOUTH MINISTRY

School	ST	$IS	SR
Andrews Univ	MI	17,696	LC
Bartlesville Wesleyan College	OK	14,100	LC
Benedictine College	KS	18,485	LC
Bethel College	IN	17,650	LC
Bethel College	MN	22,740	VC
Calif Baptist Univ	CA	16,736	C
Cascade College	OR	14,800	NC
Charleston Southern Univ	SC	17,122	C
Colo Christian Univ	CO	17,714	C
Concordia Univ	OR	20,500	LC
Dakota Wesleyan Univ	SD	15,512	C
Dordt College	IA	18,100	C+
Eastern College	PA	19,641	LC
Eastern Mennonite Univ	VA	20,700	VC
Georgetown College	KY	18,400	VC
Gordon College	MA	23,594	VC+
Grace Bible College	MI	12,600	C
Grace College	IN	16,768	C
Greenville College	IL	19,226	LC
Hope International Univ	CA	16,940	NC
Huntington College	IN	15,480	LC
John Brown Univ	AR	15,080	VC
Judson College	IL	18,980	LC
Kentucky Christian College	KY	13,472	C
King College	TN	17,800	VC
MacMurray College	IL	17,790	LC
Malone College	OH	19,190	C
Milligan College	TN	17,550	C
Mount Vernon Nazarene College	OH	17,027	C
Northwestern College	MN	19,816	C+
Nyack College	NY	18,540	C
Ohio Northern Univ	OH	27,765	VC
Okla Christian Univ	OK	16,500	VC
St. Mary's Univ of Minn	MN	19,975	C
Simpson College	CA	19,200	C
Southeastern College	FL	11,648	LC
Toccoa Falls College	GA	14,220	C
Trinity International Univ	IL	20,640	C+
Union Univ	TN	18,930	C+
Washington State Univ	WA	9,388	C

ZOOLOGY

School	ST	$IS	SR
Alabama A&M Univ	AL	5,100	LC
Andrews Univ	MI	17,696	LC
Auburn Univ	AL	5,510	C
Ball State Univ	IN	8,660	C
Bethel College	TN	12,980	C
Brigham Young Univ	UT	7,840	HC
Calif State Polytechnic Univ, Pomona	CA	8,615	C
Cal State, Long Beach	CA	7,400	LC
Central Washington Univ	WA	8,985	LC
Colo State Univ	CO	9,672	C
Conn College	CT	33,585	MC
Eastern Mich Univ	MI	9,855	C
Eastern Washington Univ	WA	7,972	LC
Florida State Univ	FL	7,835	HC
Fort Valley State Univ	GA	6,014	LC
Friends Univ	KS	15,962	LC
Howard Univ	DC	15,522	LC
Humboldt State Univ	CA	8,582	C
Idaho State Univ	ID	7,030	C+
Iowa State Univ	IA	8,108	VC
Juniata College	PA	26,080	VC
Kent State Univ	OH	11,104	C
Mars Hill College	NC	18,600	LC
Miami Univ	OH	12,885	VC+
Mich State Univ	MI	10,386	VC
N Car State Univ	NC	8,680	HC
North Central College	IL	22,944	C+
N Dak State Univ	ND	7,004	VC
Northeastern State Univ	OK	4,704	LC
Northern Arizona Univ	AZ	7,398	C
Northern Mich Univ	MI	9,693	C
Northwest Missouri State Univ	MO	7,922	LC
Ohio Wesleyan Univ	OH	29,670	VC+
Okla State Univ	OK	7,650	VC
Olivet Nazarene Univ	IL	18,444	C
Oregon State Univ	OR	9,612	VC
Purdue Univ/Calumet	IN	6,630	NC
San Francisco State Univ	CA	7,139	LC
San Jose State Univ	CA	8,187	C
Southern Illinois Univ at Carbondale	IL	8,621	C
Southwest Texas State Univ	TX	8,730	VC
SUNY/College at Oswego	NY	10,856	C
Texas A&M Univ	TX	8,988	VC
Texas Tech Univ	TX	8,825	C
Ohio State Univ	OH	10,819	VC
Univ of Akron	OH	10,530	NC
Univ of Arkansas	AR	8,334	VC
Univ of Calif at Davis	CA	12,796	VC
Univ of Calif at Santa Barbara	CA	11,732	VC
Univ of Florida	FL	7,874	HC
Univ of Georgia	GA	8,656	VC
Univ of Hawaii at Manoa	HI	7,862	VC
Univ of Idaho	ID	7,026	C
Univ of Kentucky	KY	7,765	C
Univ of Maine	ME	10,798	C
Univ of Maryland/College Park	MD	11,959	C
Univ of Mich/Ann Arbor	MI	13,003	HC+
Univ of Montana	MT	8,038	C
Univ of New Hampshire	NH	13,207	C
Univ of N Car at Chapel Hill	NC	8,789	HC
Univ of Okla	OK	7,616	VC
Univ of Rhode Island	RI	12,414	C
Univ of Texas at Austin	TX	9,437	HC
Univ of Vermont	VT	14,761	C+
Univ of Washington	WA	10,361	VC
Univ of Wisc/Madison	WI	8,262	VC
Univ of Wisc/Milwaukee	WI	8,907	LC
Univ of Wyoming	WY	7,143	LC
Washington State Univ	WA	9,388	C
Weber State Univ	UT	6,897	NC
Western New Mexico Univ	NM	5,950	LC

ST = STATE **$IS** = IN-STATE COSTS **SR** = SELECTOR RATING

PART IV

A CLOSE LOOK AT THE COLLEGES

This section will help you understand the college Profiles that are at the heart of this directory, so you can get the most out of them.

The College Admissions Selector explains Barron's unique system of comparing every school's degree of admissions competitiveness. Colleges are rated from Most Competitive to Less Competitive, and more.

Explanations of the ratings are followed by an in-depth look at the college capsule and essay.

Next comes the Profiles—some 1600 four-year accredited colleges and universities in the United States—followed by encapsulated descriptions of about fifty religious schools. Universities outside the boundaries of this country are profiled here, too, including Canadian, European, and more.

COLLEGE ADMISSIONS SELECTOR

This index groups all the colleges listed in this book according to degree of admissions competitiveness. The *Selector* is not a rating of colleges by academic standards or quality of education; it is rather an attempt to describe, in general terms, the situation a prospective student will meet when applying for admission.

THE CRITERIA USED

The factors used in determining the category for each college were: median entrance examination scores for the 2001-2002 freshman class (the SAT I score used was derived by averaging the median verbal reasoning and the median mathematics reasoning scores; the ACT score used was the median composite score); percentages of 2001-2002 freshmen scoring 500 and above and 600 and above on both the verbal reasoning and mathematics reasoning sections of the SAT I; percentages of 2001-2002 freshmen scoring 21 and above and 27 and above on the ACT; percentage of 2001-2002 freshmen who ranked in the upper fifth and the upper two-fifths of their high school graduating classes; minimum class rank and grade point average required for admission (if any); and percentage of applicants to the 2001-2002 freshman class who were accepted. The *Selector* cannot and does not take into account all the other factors that each college considers when making admissions decisions. Colleges place varying degrees of emphasis on the factors that comprise each of these categories.

USING THE SELECTOR

To use the *Selector* effectively, the prospective student's records should be compared realistically with the freshmen enrolled by the colleges in each category, as shown by the SAT I or ACT scores, the quality of high school record emphasized by the colleges in each category, and the kinds of risks that the applicant wishes to take.

The student should also be aware of what importance a particular school places on various nonacademic factors; when available, this information is presented in the profile of the school. If a student has unusual qualifications that may compensate for exam scores or high school record, the student should examine admissions policies of the colleges in the next higher category than the one that encompasses his or her score and consider those colleges that give major consideration to factors other than exam scores and high school grades. The "safety" college should usually be chosen from the next lower category, where the student can be reasonably sure that his or her scores and high school record will fall above the median scores and records of the freshmen enrolled in the college.

The listing within each category is alphabetical and not in any qualitative order. State-supported institutions have been classified according to the requirements for state residents, but standards for admission of out-of-state students are usually higher. Colleges that are experimenting with the admission of students of higher potential but lower achievement may appear in a less competitive category because of this fact.

A WORD OF CAUTION

The *Selector* is intended primarily for preliminary screening, to eliminate the majority of colleges that are not suitable for a particular student. Be sure to examine the admissions policies spelled out in the *Admissions* section of each profile. And remember that many colleges have to reject *qualified* students; the *Selector* will tell you what your chances are, not which college will accept you.

MOST COMPETITIVE

Even superior students will encounter a great deal of competition for admission to the colleges in this category. In general, these colleges require high school rank in the top 10% to 20% and grade averages of A to B+. Median freshman test scores at these colleges are generally between 655 and 800 on the SAT I and 29 and above on the ACT. In addition, many of these colleges admit only a small percentage of those who apply—usually fewer than one third.

Amherst College, MA
Bates College, ME
Boston College, MA
Boston University, MA
Bowdoin College, ME
Brandeis University, MA
Brown University, RI
California Institute of Technology, CA
Carleton College, MN
Carnegie Mellon University, PA
Case Western Reserve University
Claremont McKenna College, CA
Colby College, ME
Colgate University, NY
College of the Holy Cross, MA
College of William and Mary, VA
Columbia University/Barnard College, NY
Columbia University/Columbia College, NY
Columbia University/Fu Foundation School of Engineering, NY
Connecticut College, CT
Cooper Union for the Advancement of Science and Art, NY
Cornell University, NY
Dartmouth College, NH
Davidson College, NC
Duke University, NC
Emory University, GA
Georgetown University, DC
Grove City College, PA
Harvard University/Harvard College, MA
Harvey Mudd College, CA
Haverford College, PA
Johns Hopkins University, MD
Lafayette College, PA
Lehigh University, PA
Massachusetts Institute of Technology, MA
Middlebury College, VT
New York University, NY
Northwestern University, IL
Pomona College, CA
Princeton University, NJ
Rice University, TX
Stanford University, CA
Swarthmore College, PA
Tufts University, MA
United States Air Force Academy, CO
United States Coast Guard Academy, CT
United States Military Academy, NY
United States Naval Academy, MD
University of California at Berkeley, CA
University of California at Los Angeles, CA
University of Chicago, IL
University of Notre Dame, IN
University of Pennsylvania, PA
University of Southern California, CA
Vanderbilt University, TN
Vassar College, NY
Wake Forest University, NC
Washington and Lee University, VA
Washington University in St. Louis, MO
Webb Institute, NY
Wellesley College, MA
Wesleyan University, CT
Williams College, MA
Yale University, CT

HIGHLY COMPETITIVE

Colleges in this group look for students with grade averages of B+ to B and accept most of their students from the top 20% to 35% of the high school class. Median freshman test scores at these colleges range from 620 to 654 on the SAT I and 27 or 28 on the ACT. These schools generally accept between one third and one half of their applicants.

To provide for finer distinctions within this admissions category, a plus (+) symbol has been placed before some entries. These are colleges with median freshman scores of 645 or more on the SAT I or 28 or more on the ACT (depending on which test the college prefers), and colleges that accept fewer than one quarter of their applicants.

+Albert A. List College of Jewish Studies, NY
Babson College, MA
Bard College, NY
Beloit College, WI
Bentley College, MA
Brigham Young University, UT
+Bryn Mawr College, PA
Bucknell University, PA
Centre College, KY
Clark University, MA
College of Charleston, SC
College of New Jersey, The, NJ
+Colorado College, CO
Colorado School of Mines, CO
Denison University, OH
DePauw University, IN
Emerson College, MA
Fairfield University, CT
Florida State University, FL
Franklin and Marshall College, PA
Furman University, SC
George Washington University, DC
+Georgia Institute of Technology, GA
Gettysburg College, PA
+Gonzaga University, WA
+Grinnell College, IA
Hamilton College, NY
+Hampshire College, MA
Hendrix College, AR
+Illinois Institute of Technology, IL
Illinois Wesleyan University, IL
Ithaca College, NY
James Madison University, VA
+Kalamazoo College, MI
+Kenyon College, OH
Kettering University, MI
Knox College, IL
Lawrence University, WI
Loyola College in Maryland, MD
Loyola Marymount University, CA
+Macalester College, MN
Mount Holyoke College, MA
Muhlenberg College, PA
+New College of Florida, FL
North Carolina State University, NC
+Oberlin College, OH
Occidental College, CA
Pitzer College, CA
Polytechnic University/Brooklyn, NY
Providence College, RI
+Reed College, OR
+Rensselaer Polytechnic Institute, NY
+Rhodes College, TN
Rollins College, FL
+Rose-Hulman Institute of Technology, IN
+Saint John's College, MD
Saint Mary's College of Maryland, MD
Saint Olaf College, MN
Sarah Lawrence College, NY
+Scripps College, CA
Simon's Rock College of Bard, MA
+Smith College, MA
Southwestern University, TX
State University of New York/College at Geneseo, NY
State University of New York/University at Binghamton, NY
+Stevens Institute of Technology, NJ
Stonehill College, MA
Syracuse University, NY
+Thomas Aquinas College, CA
Trinity College, CT
Trinity University, TX
+Tulane University, LA
Union College, NY
University of California at San Diego, CA
University of Florida, FL
+University of Illinois at Urbana-Champaign, IL
University of Miami, FL
+University of Michigan/Ann Arbor, MI
University of Missouri/Columbia, MO
University of North Carolina at Chapel Hill, NC
University of Pittsburgh at Pittsburgh, PA
University of Puget Sound, WA
University of Richmond, VA
University of Rochester, NY
University of San Diego, CA
University of Texas at Austin, TX
University of the South, TN
University of Tulsa, OK
+University of Virginia, VA
Villanova University, PA
Wabash College, IN
Wheaton College, IL
Whitman College, WA
+Worcester Polytechnic Institute, MA

VERY COMPETITIVE

The colleges in this category admit students whose averages are no less than B- and who rank in the top 35% to 50% of their graduating class. They report median freshman test scores in the 573 to 619 range on the SAT I and from 24 to 26 on the ACT. These schools generally accept between one half and three quarters of their applicants.

The plus (+) has been placed before colleges with median freshman scores of 610 or above on the SAT I or 26 or better on the ACT (depending on which test the college prefers), and colleges that accept fewer than one third of their applicants.

Abilene Christian University, TX
Adelphi University, NY
Agnes Scott College, GA
Albertson College of Idaho, ID
Albion College, MI
Alice Lloyd College, KY
Allegheny College, PA
Alma College, MI
+American University, DC
Asbury College, KY
+Augustana College, IL
Augustana College, SD
+Austin College, TX
Azusa Pacific University, CA
+Baldwin-Wallace College, OH
+Baylor University, TX
Bellarmine University, KY
Belmont University, TN
Bennington College, VT
Berea College, KY
Bethel College, MN
Biola University, CA
Bradley University, IL
Bryan College, TN
Bryant College, RI
+Butler University, IN
California Polytechnic State University, CA
Catholic University of America, DC
Cedarville University, OH
Chapman University, CA
+Christendom College, VA
Christian Brothers University, TN
Christopher Newport University, VA
+City University of New York/Baruch College, NY
City University of New York/Queens College, NY
Clarkson University, NY
Coe College, IA
College of Saint Benedict, MN
College of Saint Catherine, MN
+College of the Atlantic, ME
College of Wooster, OH
Concordia College, NY
Converse College, SC
Cornell College, IA
Creighton University, NE
David Lipscomb University, TN
DePaul University, IL
DeSales University, PA
+Dickinson College, PA
Dillard University, LA
Drake University, IA
Drew University/College of Liberal Arts, NJ
Drexel University, PA
Drury University, MO
+Earlham College, IN
Eastern Mennonite University, VA
Elizabethtown College, PA
+Elmira College, NY
Elon University, NC
Erskine College, SC
+Flagler College, FL
Florida Institute of Technology, FL
Florida International University, FL
Fordham University, NY
Freed-Hardeman University, TN
George Fox University, OR
Georgetown College, KY
+Gordon College, MA
+Goshen College, IN
+Goucher College, MD
+Gustavus Adolphus College, MN
Hanover College, IN
Harding University, AR
+Hillsdale College, MI
Hiram College, OH
Hobart and William Smith Colleges, NY
Hollins University, VA
Hood College, MD
+Houghton College, NY
Huntingdon College, AL
Iowa State University, IA
John Brown University, AR
John Carroll University, OH
Juniata College, PA
King College, TN
Lake Forest College, IL
Lebanon Valley College of Pennsylvania, PA
LeTourneau University, TX
Lewis and Clark College, OR
Linfield College, OR
Louisiana State University and Agricultural and Mechanical College, LA
+Loyola University New Orleans, LA
Loyola University of Chicago, IL
+Luther College, IA
Lyon College, AR
Madonna University, MI
Maharishi University of Management, IA
Manhattan College, NY
Manhattanville College, NY
Marist College, NY
+Marlboro College, VT
+Mary Washington College, VA
Marymount Manhattan College, NY
Maryville College, TN
Mercer University, GA
Merrimack College, MA
Messiah College, PA
+Miami University, OH
Michigan State University, MI
Michigan Technological University, MI
Millersville University of Pennsylvania, PA
+Millsaps College, MS
+Milwaukee School of Engineering, WI
Moravian College, PA
Mount Mercy College, IA
Nazareth College of Rochester, NY
Nebraska Wesleyan University, NE
New Jersey Institute of Technology, NJ
+New Mexico Institute of Mining and Technology, NM
North Dakota State University, ND
Northeastern University, MA
Ohio Northern University, OH
The Ohio State University, OH
+Ohio Wesleyan University, OH
Oklahoma Baptist University, OK
Oklahoma Christian University, OK
Oklahoma State University, OK
Oregon State University, OR
Ouachita Baptist University, AR
Pacific Lutheran University, WA
Pacific Union College, CA
Penn State University/University Park Campus, PA
Pepperdine University, CA

Point Loma Nazarene University, CA
Presbyterian College, SC
Purdue University/West Lafayette, IN
Ramapo College of New Jersey, NJ
+Randolph-Macon Woman's College, VA
Richard Stockton College of New Jersey, NJ
+Ripon College, WI
Roanoke College, VA
+Rochester Institute of Technology, NY
Rowan University, NJ
Sacred Heart University, CT
+Saint John's College, NM
Saint John's University, MN
+Saint Joseph's University, PA
Saint Lawrence University, NY
+Saint Louis University, MO
Saint Mary's College, IN
Saint Michael's College, VT
Saint Norbert College, WI
Saint Vincent College, PA
Salem College, NC
Salisbury University, MD
Samford University, AL
+Santa Clara University, CA
Seattle University, WA
Siena College, NY
Simmons College, MA
+Skidmore College, NY
Southern Methodist University, TX
Southwest Texas State University, TX
State University of New York/College at Purchase, NY
State University of New York/College of Environmental Science and Forestry, NY
State University of New York/University at Albany, NY
State University of New York/University at Buffalo, NY
State University of New York/University at New Paltz, NY
State University of New York/University at Stony Brook, NY
Sterling College, KS
Stetson University, FL
Susquehanna University, PA
Sweet Briar College, VA
+Taylor University, IN
Tennessee State University, TN
Texas A&M University, TX
Touro College, NY
Towson University, MD
+Transylvania University, KY
+Truman State University, MO
United States Merchant Marine Academy, NY
University of Alabama at Huntsville, AL
University of Arkansas, AR
University of California at Davis, CA
University of California at Santa Barbara, CA
University of California at Santa Cruz, CA
University of Central Florida, FL
University of Colorado at Boulder, CO
University of Connecticut, CT
+University of Dallas, TX
University of Dayton, OH
University of Delaware, DE
University of Denver, CO
+University of Evansville, IN
University of Georgia, GA
University of Hawaii at Manoa, HI
University of Illinois at Chicago, IL
University of Kansas, KS
University of Maryland/Baltimore County, MD
University of Massachusetts Amherst, MA
University of Massachusetts Lowell, MA
University of Michigan/Dearborn, MI
University of Minnesota/Morris, MN
University of Minnesota/Twin Cities, MN
University of Missouri/Kansas City, MO
University of Nevada/Las Vegas, NV
University of North Carolina at Asheville, NC
University of North Dakota, ND
University of North Florida, FL
University of Oklahoma, OK
University of Portland, OR
University of Redlands, CA
University of Saint Thomas, MN
University of Saint Thomas, TX
University of San Francisco, CA
University of South Carolina at Columbia, SC
University of Texas at Dallas, TX
University of the Pacific, CA
University of the Sciences in Philadelphia, PA
University of Washington, WA
University of Wisconsin/Eau Claire, WI
University of Wisconsin/La Crosse, WI
University of Wisconsin/Madison, WI
Ursinus College, PA
+Valparaiso University, IN
Wartburg College, IA
Washington and Jefferson College, PA
Washington College, MD
Webster University, MO
Wells College, NY
Wesleyan College, GA
West Chester University of Pennsylvania, PA
Western Maryland College, MD
Western Washington University, WA
Westmont College, CA
Wheaton College, MA
Whitworth College, WA
+Willamette University, OR
William Jewell College, MO
Wisconsin Lutheran College, WI
Wittenberg University, OH
Wofford College, SC
York College of Pennsylvania, PA

COMPETITIVE

This category is a very broad one, covering colleges that generally have median freshman test scores between 500 and 572 on the SAT I and between 21 and 23 on the ACT. Some of these colleges require that students have high school averages of B- or better, although others state a minimum of C+ or C. Generally, these colleges prefer students in the top 50% to 65% of the graduating class and accept between 75% and 85% of their applicants.

Colleges with a plus (+) are those with median freshman SAT I scores of 563 or more or median freshman ACT scores of 24 or more (depending on which test the colleges prefers), and those that admit fewer than half of their applicants.

Adams State College, CO
Adrian College, MI
Alabama State University, AL
Alaska Pacific University, AK
+Albany State University, GA
Albertus Magnus College, CT
Albright College, PA
Alderson-Broaddus College, WV
+Alfred University, NY
Alvernia College, PA
Angelo State University, TX
Appalachian State University, NC
+Aquinas College, MI
Arcadia University, PA
Arizona State University-Main, AZ
Arkansas State University, AR
Arkansas Tech University, AR
Armstrong Atlantic State University, GA
Assumption College, MA
Auburn University, AL
Audrey Cohen College, NY
Augsburg College, MN
Augusta State University, GA
Aurora University, IL
Avila College, MO
+Baker University, KS
Ball State University, IN
Barber-Scotia College, NC
Bay Path College, MA
Beacon College, FL
+Belhaven College, MS
Bemidji State University, MN
Benedictine University, IL
Bennett College, NC
Berry College, GA
+Bethany College, KS
Bethany College, WV
+Bethel College, KS
Bethel College, TN
Bethune-Cookman College, FL
Birmingham-Southern College, AL
Blackburn College, IL
Bloomfield College, NJ
Bloomsburg University of Pennsylvania, PA
Bluefield College, VA
Bluffton College, OH
Boricua College, NY
+Bowie State University, MD
Bowling Green State University, OH
Brenau University Women's College, GA
Brescia University, KY
Bridgewater College, VA
+Bridgewater State College, MA
Brigham Young University/Hawaii, HI
Buena Vista University, IA
Cabarrus College of Health Sciences, NC
California Baptist University, CA
California Maritime Academy, CA
California State Polytechnic University, Pomona, CA
California State University, Fresno, CA
California State University, Los Angeles, CA
California State University, Northridge, CA
California State University, Sacramento, CA
California State University, San Bernardino, CA
California State University, Stanislaus, CA
California University of Pennsylvania, PA
Campbell University, NC
Campbellsville University, KY
+Canisius College, NY
Capital University, OH
Cardinal Stritch University, WI
Carlos Albizu University, FL
Carlow College, PA
Carroll College, MT
Carroll College, WI
Carson-Newman College, TN
Carthage College, WI
Case Western Reserve University, OH
Catawba College, NC
+Cedar Crest College, PA
Centenary College, NJ
+Centenary College of Louisiana, LA
Central College, IA
Central Connecticut State University, CT
Central Methodist College, MO
Central Michigan University, MI
Central Missouri State University, MO
+Central State University, OH
Chaminade University of Honolulu, HI
Champlain College, VT
Charleston Southern University, SC
+Chatham College, PA
Cheyney University of Pennsylvania, PA
+Chicago State University, IL
Citadel, The, SC
+City University of New York/Hunter College, NY
City University of New York/John Jay College of Criminal Justice, NY
+Claflin University, SC
Clark Atlanta University, GA
+Clarke College, IA
Clarkson College, NE
+Clayton College and State University, GA
Clemson University, SC
Coastal Carolina University, SC
Coker College, SC
College of Mount Saint Vincent, NY
College of Mount St. Joseph, OH
College of New Rochelle, NY
College of Our Lady of the Elms, MA
College of Saint Elizabeth, NJ
College of Saint Mary, NE
College of Saint Rose, NY
+College of Saint Scholastica, MN
+College of the Ozarks, MO
Colorado Christian University, CO
Colorado State University, CO
Columbia College, MO
+Columbia Union College, MD
Columbia University/School of General Studies, NY
+Concord College, WV
Concordia College/Moorhead, MN
Concordia University, CA
Concordia University, MI
Concordia University, MN
Concordia University Nebraska, NE
Cornerstone University and Grand Rapids Baptist Seminary, MI
+Covenant College, GA
Cumberland College, KY
Daemen College, NY
Dakota State University, SD
Dakota Wesleyan University, SD
Dana College, NE
Daniel Webster College, NH

David N. Myers College, OH
Delta State University, MS
DeVry University/Crystal City, VA
DeVry University/Fremont, CA
Dominican University, IL
Dominican University of California, CA
+Dordt College, IA
+Duquesne University, PA
D'Youville College, NY
East Carolina University, NC
East Central University, OK
East Tennessee State University, TN
Eastern Connecticut State University, CT
Eastern Illinois University, IL
Eastern Kentucky University, KY
Eastern Michigan University, MI
Eastern Oregon University, OR
+Eckerd College, FL
Edgewood College, WI
Elmhurst College, IL
+Embry-Riddle Aeronautical University, AZ
Embry-Riddle Aeronautical University, FL
+Emmanuel College, MA
Emory & Henry College, VA
Endicott College, MA
Eugene Lang College of New School University, NY
Eureka College, IL
Evangel University, MO
Evergreen State College, WA
Fairleigh Dickinson University/Madison campus, NJ
Fairleigh Dickinson University/Teaneck Campus, NJ
+Fashion Institute of Technology/State University of New York, NY
Faulkner University, AL
Felician College, NJ
Ferris State University, MI
Fisher College, MA
Fitchburg State College, MA
Florida Agricultural and Mechanical University, FL
Florida Atlantic University, FL
Florida Gulf Coast University, FL
Florida Hospital College of Health Sciences, FL
Florida Southern College, FL
Fontbonne University, MO
Framingham State College, MA
Francis Marion University, SC
+Franciscan University of Steubenville, OH
Franklin College of Indiana, IN
Fresno Pacific University, CA
Friends World Program, NY
Frostburg State University, MD
Gannon University, PA
Gardner-Webb University, NC
+Geneva College, PA
George Mason University, VA
Georgia College and State University, GA
Georgia Southern University, GA
Georgia Southwestern State University, GA
+Goddard College, VT
Goldey-Beacom College, DE
Grace Bible College, MI
Grace College, IN
Graceland University, IA
Grand Valley State University, MI
Green Mountain College, VT
Guilford College, NC
Gwynedd-Mercy College, PA
+Hamline University, MN
Hampden-Sydney College, VA
+Hampton University, VA
Hannibal-LaGrange College, MO
Hardin-Simmons University, TX
+Hartwick College, NY
+Hastings College, NE
Hawaii Pacific University, HI
Heidelberg College, OH
Hellenic College/Holy Cross Greek Orthodox School of Theology, MA
Henderson State University, AR
Hofstra University, NY
Holy Names College, CA
+Hope College, MI
+Howard Payne University, TX
Humboldt State University, CA
Huron University, SD
+Idaho State University, ID
Illinois College, IL
Illinois State University, IL
Indiana Institute of Technology, IN
+Indiana University Bloomington, IN
Indiana University East, IN
Indiana University Northwest, IN
Indiana University of Pennsylvania, PA
Indiana University South Bend, IN
Indiana University Southeast, IN
Indiana University-Purdue University Indianapolis, IN
Indiana Wesleyan University, IN
Iona College, NY
Iowa Wesleyan College, IA
+Johnson C. Smith University, NC
Johnson State College, VT
Judson College, AL
Kansas State University, KS
+Kansas Wesleyan University, KS
Kean University, NJ
Keene State College, NH
Kent State University, OH
Kentucky Christian College, KY
Kentucky Wesleyan College, KY
Keuka College, NY
King's College, PA
Kutztown University of Pennsylvania, PA
La Salle University, PA
LaGrange College, GA
Lakeland College, WI
Lambuth University, TN
+Lane College, TN
Lasell College, MA
Lawrence Technological University, MI
Le Moyne College, NY
Lenoir-Rhyne College, NC
Lewis University, IL
Lewis-Clark State College, ID
Liberty University, VA
Limestone College, SC
+Lincoln University, PA
Lindenwood University, MO
Lock Haven University of Pennsylvania, PA
Long Island University/Brooklyn Campus, NY
Long Island University/C.W. Post Campus, NY
Long Island University/Southampton College, NY
Longwood College, VA
+Loras College, IA
Louisiana College, LA
Louisiana Tech University, LA
Lycoming College, PA
Lynchburg College, VA
Lynn University, FL
Maine Maritime Academy, ME
Malone College, OH
Manchester College, IN
Mansfield University, PA
Marian College, IN
Marietta College, OH
+Marquette University, WI
Mary Baldwin College, VA
Marygrove College, MI
Marymount College/Tarrytown, NY
Maryville University of Saint Louis, MO
Marywood University, PA
Massachusetts Maritime Academy, MA
+Master's College, CA
+McKendree College, IL
McMurry University, TX
McPherson College, KS
Medaille College, NY
Mercyhurst College, PA
Meredith College, NC
Mesa State College, CO
Methodist College, NC
MidAmerica Nazarene University, KS
Middle Tennessee State University, TN
Midland Lutheran College, NE
Midway College, KY

Milligan College, TN
Millikin University, IL
Mills College, CA
Mississippi College, MS
Mississippi State University, MS
Mississippi Valley State University, MS
Missouri Southern State College, MO
Mitchell College, CT
Molloy College, NY
Monmouth College, IL
Monmouth University, NJ
Montana State University-Bozeman, MT
Montana Tech of The University of Montana, MT
Montreat College, NC
Morehead State University, KY
Morehouse College, GA
Morningside College, IA
Mount Mary College, WI
Mount Saint Mary College, NY
Mount Saint Mary's College, CA
Mount Saint Mary's College, MD
Mount Senario College, WI
Mount Union College, OH
Mount Vernon Nazarene College, OH
Murray State University, KY
Muskingum College, OH
New Mexico State University, NM
New York Institute of Technology, NY
Newbury College, MA
+Niagara University, NY
+North Central College, IL
+North Georgia College and State University, GA
North Park University, IL
Northern Arizona University, AZ
Northern Illinois University, IL
Northern Michigan University, MI
+Northland College, WI
Northwest College, WA
Northwest Nazarene University, ID
+Northwestern College, MN
+Northwestern College of Iowa, IA
Northwood University, TX
Notre Dame College, OH
Nyack College, NY
Oakland University, MI
Oakwood College, AL
Ohio University, OH
+Ohio Valley College, WV
Oklahoma City University, OK
Old Dominion University, VA
Olivet College, MI
Olivet Nazarene University, IL
Oral Roberts University, OK
Oregon Institute of Technology, OR
Otterbein College, OH
Our Lady of the Lake University of San Antonio, TX
Pace University, NY
Pacific University, OR
Palm Beach Atlantic College, FL
Park University, MO
Peirce College, PA
Penn State University at Erie/Behrend College, PA
Penn State University/Altoona, PA
Pfeiffer University, NC
+Philadelphia Biblical University, PA
Philadelphia University, PA
Piedmont College, GA
Point Park College, PA
Portland State University, OR
Prescott College, AZ
+Principia College, IL
Queens College, NC
Quincy University, IL
Quinnipiac University, CT
Radford University, VA
Randolph-Macon College, VA
Regis College, MA
+Regis University, CO
Reinhardt College, GA
Rider University, NJ
Rivier College, NH
Robert Morris University, PA
+Roberts Wesleyan College, NY
Rochester College, MI
Rockford College, IL
Rockhurst University, MO
Rocky Mountain College, MT
Roger Williams University, RI
Rosemont College, PA
+Russell Sage College, NY
+Rust College, MS
Rutgers, The State University of New Jersey/CamdenCampus, NJ
Rutgers, The State University of New Jersey/New Brunswick Campus, NJ
Rutgers, The State University of New Jersey/Newark Campus, NJ
Saginaw Valley State University, MI
Saint Ambrose University, IA
Saint Anselm College, NH
+Saint Augustine's College, NC
Saint Bonaventure University, NY
Saint Cloud State University, MN
Saint Edward's University, TX
Saint Francis College, NY
Saint John Fisher College, NY
Saint John's University, NY
Saint Joseph's College, IN
Saint Joseph's College, New York, NY
Saint Martin's College, WA
Saint Mary College, KS
Saint Mary's College of California, CA
Saint Mary's University of Minnesota, MN
Saint Mary's University of San Antonio, TX
Saint Paul's College, VA
Saint Xavier University, IL
Salve Regina University, RI
+San Diego State University, CA
San Jose State University, CA
Schreiner University, TX
+Seattle Pacific University, WA
Seton Hill College, PA
Shaw University, NC
Shippensburg University of Pennsylvania, PA
Shorter College, GA
Simpson College, CA
+Simpson College, IA
Sonoma State University, CA
+South Dakota School of Mines and Technology, SD
South Dakota State University, SD
+Southeast Missouri State University, MO
Southeastern Oklahoma State University, OK
Southern Adventist University, TN
Southern Connecticut State University, CT
Southern Illinois University at Carbondale, IL
Southern New Hampshire University, NH
Southern Oregon University, OR
Southern Polytechnic State University, GA
+Southern University and A&M College, LA
Southern Utah University, UT
Southern Vermont College, VT
Southern Wesleyan University, SC
Southwestern Adventist University, TX
Southwestern College, KS
Southwestern Oklahoma State University, OK
Spalding University, KY
+Spelman College, GA
Spring Arbor University, MI
Spring Hill College, AL
Springfield College, MA
State University of New York/College at Brockport, NY
State University of New York/College at Buffalo, NY
State University of New York/College at Cortland, NY
State University of New York/College at Fredonia, NY
State University of New York/College at Oneonta, NY
State University of New York/College at Oswego, NY
State University of New York/College at Plattsburgh, NY
State University of New York/College at Potsdam, NY
+State University of New York/College of Agriculture and Technology at Cobleskill, NY
State University of New York/College of Technology at Alfred, NY
State University of New York/College of Technology at Farmingdale, NY
State University of West Georgia, GA
Stephen F. Austin State University, TX

Stephens College, MO
Sterling College, VT
Suffolk University, MA
Tarleton State University, TX
Teikyo Post University, CT
Temple University, PA
Tennessee Technological University, TN
Tennessee Wesleyan College, TN
Texas A&M University at Commerce, TX
+Texas A&M University at Galveston, TX
Texas Christian University, TX
Texas Lutheran University, TX
Texas Tech University, TX
Texas Wesleyan University, TX
Thomas More College of Liberal Arts, NH
Tiffin University, OH
Toccoa Falls College, GA
Trevecca Nazarene University, TN
Trinity Christian College, IL
+Trinity International University, IL
Tri-State University-Main Campus, IN
Troy State University, AL
Troy State University Dothan, AL
Union College, KY
Union College, NE
+Union University, TN
University of Alabama, AL
University of Alabama at Birmingham, AL
University of Arizona, AZ
University of Arkansas at Pine Bluff, AR
University of Bridgeport, CT
University of California at Irvine, CA
University of California at Riverside, CA
University of Central Arkansas, AR
University of Central Oklahoma, OK
University of Charleston, WV
University of Colorado at Colorado Springs, CO
University of Colorado at Denver, CO
University of Dubuque, IA
University of Great Falls, MT
University of Hartford, CT
University of Hawaii at Hilo, HI
University of Houston, TX
University of Idaho, ID
University of Indianapolis, IN
+University of Iowa, IA
University of Judaism College of Arts and Sciences, CA
University of Kentucky, KY
University of La Verne, CA
University of Louisiana at Lafayette, LA
University of Maine, ME
University of Maine at Augusta, ME
University of Maine at Farmington, ME
University of Mary Hardin-Baylor, TX
University of Maryland/College Park, MD
University of Maryland/Eastern Shore, MD
University of Massachusetts Boston, MA
University of Massachusetts Dartmouth, MA
University of Memphis, TN
University of Michigan/Flint, MI
University of Minnesota/Duluth, MN
University of Mississippi, MS
University of Missouri/Rolla, MO
University of Missouri/St. Louis, MO
University of Montana, MT
University of Montevallo, AL
+University of Nebraska at Lincoln, NE
University of Nebraska at Omaha, NE
University of Nevada/Reno, NV
University of New Hampshire, NH
University of New Mexico, NM
University of New Orleans, LA
University of North Carolina at Charlotte, NC
University of North Carolina at Greensboro, NC
University of North Carolina at Wilmington, NC
University of North Texas, TX
+University of Northern Colorado, CO
University of Northern Iowa, IA
University of Oregon, OR
University of Pittsburgh at Bradford, PA
University of Pittsburgh at Greensburg, PA
University of Rhode Island, RI
University of Saint Francis, IL
University of Science and Arts of Oklahoma, OK
+University of Scranton, PA
University of Sioux Falls, SD
+University of South Carolina at Spartanburg, SC
University of South Dakota, SD
University of South Florida, FL
University of Southern Maine, ME
University of Tampa, FL
University of Tennessee at Chattanooga, TN
University of Tennessee at Knoxville, TN
University of Tennessee at Martin, TN
University of Texas-Pan American, TX
University of the Incarnate Word, TX
University of the Ozarks, AR
University of Utah, UT
+University of Vermont, VT
University of Virginia's College at Wise, VA
University of West Alabama, AL
University of West Florida, FL
University of Wisconsin/Green Bay, WI
University of Wisconsin/Platteville, WI
University of Wisconsin/Stevens Point, WI
University of Wisconsin/Stout, WI
+University of Wisconsin/Superior, WI
University of Wisconsin/Whitewater, WI
Upper Iowa University, IA
Urbana University, OH
Utah State University, UT
Valdosta State University, GA
Vanguard University of Southern California, CA
Vermont Technical College, VT
Villa Julie College, MD
Virginia Commonwealth University, VA
Virginia Intermont College, VA
+Virginia Military Institute, VA
Virginia Polytechnic Institute and State University, VA
Viterbo University, WI
+Voorhees College, SC
Wagner College, NY
Walla Walla College, WA
Walsh University, OH
Warren Wilson College, NC
Washington State University, WA
Wayne State University, MI
Wentworth Institute of Technology, MA
Wesley College, DE
West Texas A&M University, TX
West Virginia University, WV
West Virginia Wesleyan College, WV
+Western Baptist College, OR
Western Carolina University, NC
Western Connecticut State University, CT
Western Illinois University, IL
Western Kentucky University, KY
Western Michigan University, MI
Western New England College, MA
Western Oregon University, OR
Westfield State College, MA
+Westminster College, MO
Westminster College, PA
Westminster College, UT
Wheeling Jesuit University, WV
Wheelock College, MA
Whittier College, CA
Wichita State University, KS
Widener University, PA
Wilkes University, PA
William Penn University, IA
William Tyndale College, MI
Williams Baptist College, AR
Wilmington College, OH
Wingate University, NC
Winona State University, MN
Winthrop University, SC
Xavier University, OH
Yeshiva University, NY
York College, NE

LESS COMPETITIVE

Included in this category are colleges with median freshman test scores below 500 on the SAT I and below 21 on the ACT; some colleges that require entrance examinations but do not report median scores; and colleges that admit students with averages below C who rank in the top 65% of the graduating class. These colleges usually admit 85% or more of their applicants.

Alabama Agricultural and Mechanical University, AL
Alcorn State University, MS
Alverno College, WI
American International College, MA
Anderson University, IN
Andrews University, MI
Anna Maria College, MA
Antioch College, OH
Aquinas College, TN
Arkansas Baptist College, AR
Ashland University, OH
Atlantic Union College, MA
Austin Peay State University, TN
Averett University, VA
Barry University, FL
Bartlesville Wesleyan College, OK
Barton College, NC
Becker College, MA
Belmont Abbey College, NC
Benedict College, SC
Benedictine College, KS
Berkeley College, NY
Berkeley College of New York City, NY
Bethel College, IN
Black Hills State University, SD
Blue Mountain College, MS
Bluefield State College, WV
Boise State University, ID
Brewton-Parker College, GA
Briar Cliff University, IA
Cabrini College, PA
Caldwell College, NJ
California Lutheran University, CA
California State University, Bakersfield, CA
California State University, Chico, CA
California State University, Dominguez Hills, CA
California State University, Fullerton, CA
California State University, Hayward, CA
California State University, Long Beach, CA
California State University, Monterey Bay, CA
California State University, San Marcos, CA
Calumet College of St. Joseph, IN
Capitol College, MD
Castleton State College, VT
Cazenovia College, NY
Central Washington University, WA
Chestnut Hill College, PA
Christian Heritage College, CA
City University of New York/Brooklyn College, NY
City University of New York/City College, NY
City University of New York/Herbert H. Lehman College, NY
Clarion University of Pennsylvania, PA
Clearwater Christian College, FL
Cleary College, MI
Cogswell Polytechnical College, CA
Colby-Sawyer College, NH
College Misericordia, PA
College of Notre Dame of Maryland, MD
College of Santa Fe, NM
Colorado Technical University, CO
Columbia College, SC
Columbia College Chicago, IL
Columbus State University, GA
Concordia University, OR
Concordia University at Austin, TX
Concordia University Wisconsin, WI
Concordia University, River Forest, IL
Coppin State College, MD
Crichton College, TN
Culver-Stockton College, MO
Cumberland University, TN
Curry College, MA
Dallas Baptist University, TX
Davis and Elkins College, WV
Defiance College, OH
Delaware State University, DE
Delaware Valley College, PA
DeVry College of Technology/North Brunswick, NJ
DeVry Institute of Technology/New York, NY
DeVry University/Addison (DuPage County), IL
DeVry University/Alpharetta, GA
DeVry University/Chicago, IL
DeVry University/Colorado Springs, CO
DeVry University/Columbus, OH
DeVry University/Dallas, TX
DeVry University/Decatur, GA
DeVry University/Denver, CO
DeVry University/Kansas City, MO
DeVry University/Long Beach, CA
DeVry University/Orlando, FL
DeVry University/Phoenix, AZ
DeVry University/Pomona, CA
DeVry University/Seattle, WA
DeVry University/Tinley Park, IL
DeVry University/West Hills, CA
Doane College, NE
Dominican College, NY
Dowling College, NY
East Stroudsburg University of Pennsylvania, PA
East Texas Baptist University, TX
Eastern College, PA
Eastern Nazarene College, MA
Eastern New Mexico University, NM
Eastern Washington University, WA
East-West University, IL
Edinboro University of Pennsylvania, PA
Edward Waters College, FL
Elizabeth City State University, NC
Emporia State University, KS
Fayetteville State University, NC
Ferrum College, VA
Fisk University, TN
Florida Memorial College, FL
Fort Hays State University, KS
Fort Lewis College, CO
Fort Valley State University, GA
Franklin Pierce College, NH
Friends University, KS
Georgia State University, GA
Georgian Court College, NJ
Grand Canyon University, AZ
Greensboro College, NC
Greenville College, IL
Hesser College, NH
High Point University, NC
Hilbert College, NY
Holy Family College, PA
Houston Baptist University, TX
Howard University, DC
Huntington College, IN
Husson College, ME
Huston-Tillotson College, TX
Immaculata College, PA
Indiana State University, IN
Indiana University Kokomo, IN
Indiana University-Purdue University Fort Wayne, IN
Jackson State University, MS
Jacksonville State University, AL
Jacksonville University, FL
Johnson and Wales University, RI
Judson College, IL
Kendall College, IL

Kennesaw State University, GA
Keystone College, PA
Knoxville College, TN
La Roche College, PA
La Sierra University, CA
Lake Erie College, OH
Lake Superior State University, MI
Lamar University, TX
Lander University, SC
Langston University, OK
Lee University, TN
Lees-McRae College, NC
Lesley College, MA
Lincoln Memorial University, TN
Lindsey Wilson College, KY
Livingstone College, NC
Lourdes College, OH
Lubbock Christian University, TX
Lyndon State College, VT
MacMurray College, IL
Marian College of Fond du Lac, WI
Mars Hill College, NC
Marshall University, WV
Marymount University, VA
Massachusetts College of Liberal Arts, MA
McNeese State University, LA
Menlo College, CA
Mercy College, NY
Metropolitan State College of Denver, CO
Minnesota State University, Mankato, MN
Minot State University, ND
Mississippi University for Women, MS
Missouri Baptist College, MO
Missouri Valley College, MO
Monroe College, NY
Montclair State University, NJ
Moorhead State University, MN
Morgan State University, MD
Morris Brown College, GA
Morris College, SC
Mount Aloysius College, PA
Mount Ida College, MA
Mount Marty College, SD
Mount Olive College, NC
Mount Saint Clare College, IA
New England College, NH
New Jersey City University, NJ
Newberry College, SC
Newman University, KS
Nichols College, MA
Norfolk State University, VA
North Carolina Agricultural and Technical State University, NC
North Carolina Central University, NC
North Carolina Wesleyan College, NC
North Central University, MN
Northeastern State University, OK
Northern State University, SD
Northwest Christian College, OR
Northwest Missouri State University, MO
Northwood University, FL
Northwood University, MI
Norwich University, VT
Notre Dame de Namur University, CA
Nova Southeastern University, FL
Oakland City University, IN
Oglethorpe University, GA
Ohio Dominican College, OH
Ottawa University, KS
Paine College, GA
Paul Quinn College, TX
Pine Manor College, MA
Plymouth State College, NH
Prairie View A&M University, TX
Rhode Island College, RI
Roosevelt University, IL
Saint Andrews Presbyterian College, NC
Saint Francis University, PA
Saint Joseph College, CT
Saint Joseph's College of Maine, ME
Saint Leo University, FL
Saint Mary-of-the-Woods College, IN
Saint Mary's College, MI
Saint Peter's College, NJ
Saint Thomas Aquinas College, NY
Saint Thomas University, FL
Salem International University, WV
Salem State College, MA
Sam Houston State University, TX
San Francisco State University, CA
Savannah State University, GA
Seton Hall University, NJ
Sheldon Jackson College, AK
Shepherd College, WV
Shimer College, IL
Siena Heights University, MI
Sierra Nevada College-Lake Tahoe, NV
Silver Lake College of the Holy Family, WI
Slippery Rock University, PA
Sojourner-Douglass College, MD
South Carolina State University, SC
South College, GA
Southeastern College, FL
Southeastern Louisiana University, LA
Southeastern University, DC
Southern Arkansas University, AR
Southern Christian University, AL
Southern Illinois University Edwardsville, IL
Southwest Baptist University, MO
Southwest Missouri State University, MO
Southwest State University, MN
State University of New York/College at Old Westbury, NY
State University of New York/Maritime College, NY
Stillman College, AL
Sul Ross State University, TX
Tabor College, KS
Talladega College, AL
Texas A&M University at Kingsville, TX
Texas Woman's University, TX
Thiel College, PA
Thomas College, ME
Thomas More College, KY
Trinity College, DC
Tusculum College, TN
Tuskegee University, AL
United States International University, CA
Unity College, ME
University of Alaska Southeast, AK
University of Cincinnati, OH
University of Detroit Mercy, MI
University of Louisville, KY
University of Maine at Fort Kent, ME
University of Maine at Machias, ME
University of Maine at Presque Isle, ME
University of Mary, ND
University of Mobile, AL
University of New England, ME
University of New Haven, CT
University of North Carolina at Pembroke, NC
University of Pittsburgh at Johnstown, PA
University of Saint Francis, IN
University of South Alabama, AL
University of South Carolina at Aiken, SC
University of Southern Colorado, CO
University of Southern Indiana, IN
University of Southern Mississippi, MS
University of Texas at Arlington, TX
University of Texas at El Paso, TX
University of Wisconsin/Milwaukee, WI
University of Wisconsin/Oshkosh, WI
University of Wisconsin/Parkside, WI
University of Wisconsin/River Falls, WI
University of Wyoming, WY
Ursuline College, OH
Utica College of Syracuse University, NY
Valley City State University, ND
Virginia State University, VA
Virginia Union University, VA
Virginia Wesleyan College, VA
Warner Pacific College, OR
Waynesburg College, PA
Webber International University, FL
West Liberty State College, WV
Western New Mexico University, NM
Western State College of Colorado, CO

Wilberforce University, OH
Wiley College, TX
William Carey College, MS
William Paterson University of New Jersey, NJ
William Woods University, MO
Wilson College, PA
Winston-Salem State University, NC
Woodbury College, VT
Woodbury University, CA
Worcester State College, MA
Wright State University, OH
Xavier University of Louisiana, LA

NONCOMPETITIVE

The colleges in this category generally only require evidence of graduation from an accredited high school (although they may also require completion of a certain number of high school units). Some require that entrance examinations be taken for placement purposes only, or only by graduates of unaccredited high schools or only by out-of-state students. In some cases, insufficient capacity may compel a college in this category to limit the number of students that are accepted; generally, however, if a college accepts 98% or more of its applicants, it automatically falls in this category. Colleges are also rated Noncompetitive if they admit all state residents, but have some requirements for nonresidents.

Allen University, SC
American Indian College of the Assemblies of God, AZ
American InterContinental University, GA
Auburn University Montgomery, AL
Baker College of Flint, MI
Bellevue University, NE
Bryn Athyn College of the New Church, PA
Calvin College, MI
Cameron University, OK
Cascade College, OR
Chadron State College, NE
City University, WA
City University of New York/College of Staten Island, NY
City University of New York/Medgar Evers College, NY
City University of New York/New York City Technical College, NY
City University of New York/York College, NY
Cleveland State University, OH
College of Saint Joseph, VT
College of the Southwest, NM
Concordia College, AL
Davenport University, MI
Dickinson State University, ND
Fairmont State College, WV
Glenville State College, WV
Golden Gate University, CA
Grambling State University, LA
Grand View College, IA
Heritage College, WA
Hope International University, CA
Humphreys College, CA
International College, FL
Jamestown College, ND
Jarvis Christian College, TX
Kentucky State University, KY
LeMoyne-Owen College, TN
Lincoln University, MO
Louisiana State University in Shreveport, LA
Marylhurst University, OR
Mayville State University, ND
Midwestern State University, TX
Miles College, AL
Missouri Western State College, MO
Montana State University-Billings, MT
Montana State University-Northern, MT
Mountain State University, WV
National American University, SD
National-Louis University, IL
Neumann College, PA
New College of California, CA
New Mexico Highlands University, NM
Nicholls State University, LA
Northeastern Illinois University, IL
Northern Kentucky University, KY
Northwestern Oklahoma State University, OK
Northwestern State University of Louisiana, LA
Oglala Lakota College, SD
Ohio State University at Lima, OH
Ohio State University at Mansfield, OH
Ohio State University at Marion, OH
Ohio State University at Newark, OH
Oklahoma Panhandle State University, OK
Our Lady of Holy Cross College, LA
Pennsylvania College of Technology, PA
Peru State College, NE
Philander Smith College, AR
Pikeville College, KY
Pittsburg State University, KS
Presentation College, SD
Purdue University/Calumet, IN
Saint Gregory's University, OK
Shawnee State University, OH
Shenandoah University, VA
Sinte Gleska University, SD
Southern Nazarene University, OK
Southern University at New Orleans, LA
Southwestern Christian College, TX
Texas Southern University, TX
Thomas University, GA
Tougaloo College, MS
Troy State University/Montgomery, AL
University of Akron, OH
University of Alaska Anchorage, AK
University of Alaska Fairbanks, AK
University of Arkansas at Little Rock, AR
University of Arkansas at Monticello, AR
University of Findlay, OH
University of Houston-Downtown, TX
University of Louisiana at Monroe, LA
University of Minnesota/Crookston, MN
University of Montana—Western, MT
University of Nebraska at Kearney, NE
University of North Alabama, AL
University of Rio Grande, OH
University of Texas at San Antonio, TX
University of the District of Columbia, DC
University of Toledo, OH
Washburn University of Topeka, KS
Wayland Baptist University, TX
Wayne State College, NE
Weber State University, UT
West Virginia State College, WV
West Virginia University Institute of Technology, WV
Wilmington College, DE
Youngstown State University, OH

SPECIAL

Listed here are colleges whose programs of study are specialized; professional schools of art, music, nursing, and other disciplines. In general, the admissions requirements are not based primarily on academic criteria, but on evidence of talent or special interest in the field. Many other colleges and universities offer special-interest programs *in addition* to regular academic curricula, but such institutions have been given a regular competitive rating based on academic criteria. Schools oriented toward working adults have also been assigned this rating.

Albany College of Pharmacy, NY
Allen College, IA
Art Academy of Cincinnati, OH
Art Center College of Design, CA
Art Institute of Atlanta, GA
Art Institute of Boston at Lesley University, MA
Art Institute of Portland, OR
Art Institute of Southern California, CA
Atlanta College of Art, GA
Baltimore Hebrew University, MD
Benjamin Franklin Institute of Technology, MA
Berklee College of Music, MA
Boston Architectural Center, MA
Boston Conservatory, MA
Burlington College, VT
California College of Arts and Crafts, CA
California Institute of the Arts, CA
Cambridge College, MA
Charter Oak State College, CT
Cincinnati College of Mortuary Science, OH
Cleveland Institute of Art, OH
Cleveland Institute of Music, OH
College For Creative Studies, MI
College for Lifelong Learning, NH
College of Aeronautics, NY
College of New Rochelle - School of New Resources, NY
College of Visual Arts, MN
Columbus College of Art and Design, OH
Corcoran School of Art and Design, DC
Cornish College of the Arts, WA
Curtis Institute of Music, PA
Deaconess College of Nursing, MO
Eastman School of Music, NY
Excelsior College, NY
Five Towns College, NY
Franklin University, OH
Gallaudet University, DC
Harris-Stowe State College, MO
Henry Cogswell College, WA
Jewish Hospital College of Nursing and Allied Health, MO
Juilliard School, NY
Kansas City Art Institute, MO
Kendall College of Art and Design of Ferris State University, MI
Laboratory Institute of Merchandising, NY
Lester L. Cox College of Nursing and Health Sciences, MO
Maine College of Art, ME
Manhattan School of Music, NY
Mannes College of Music, NY
Martin University, IN
Maryland Institute College of Art, MD
Massachusetts College of Art, MA
Massachusetts College of Pharmacy and Health Sciences, MA
MCP Hahnemann University, PA
Memphis College of Art, TN
Mercy College of Health Sciences, IA
Metropolitan State University, MN
Milwaukee Institute of Art and Design, WI
Minneapolis College of Art and Design, MN
Montserrat College of Art, MA
Moore College of Art and Design, PA
NAES College, IL
Naropa University, CO
National University, CA
Nebraska Methodist College of Nursing and Allied Health, NE
New England Conservatory of Music, MA
North Carolina School of the Arts, NC
Otis College of Art and Design, CA
Pacific Northwest College of Art, OR
Parsons School of Design, NY
Pratt Institute, NY
Research College of Nursing, MO
Rhode Island School of Design, RI
Ringling School of Art and Design, FL
Samuel Merritt College, CA
San Francisco Art Institute, CA
San Francisco Conservatory of Music, CA
Savannah College of Art and Design, GA
School of the Art Institute of Chicago, IL
School of Visual Arts, NY
Southern California Institute of Architecture, CA
State University of New York/Empire State College, NY
Strayer University, DC
Thomas Edison State College, NJ
Trinity College of Nursing, IL
Union Institute and University, OH
University of Maryland/University College, MD
University of Phoenix, AZ
University of the Arts, PA
VanderCook College of Music, IL
West Suburban College of Nursing, IL
Western International University, AZ
Westminster Choir College of Rider University, NJ

AN EXPLANATION OF THE COLLEGE ENTRIES

THE BASICS

Some 1700 U.S. colleges and universities, public and private college systems, and Canadian and other foreign universities are described in detail in the Profiles that follow.

The Choice of Schools

Colleges and universities in this country may achieve recognition from a number of professional organizations, but we have based our choice of U.S. colleges on accreditation from two of the six U.S. regional accrediting associations.

Accreditation amounts to a stamp of approval given to a college. The accreditation process evaluates institutions and programs to determine whether they meet established standards of educational quality. The regional associations listed below supervise an aspect of the accrediting procedure—the study of a detailed report submitted by the institution applying for accreditation, and then an inspection visit by members of the accrediting agency. The six agencies are associated with the Commission on Recognition of Postsecondary Accreditation (CORPA). They include:

Middle States Association of Colleges and Schools
New England Association of Schools and Colleges
North Central Association of Colleges and Schools
Northwest Association of Schools and Colleges
Southern Association of Colleges and Schools
Western Association of Schools and Colleges

Getting accreditation for the first time can take a school several years. To acknowledge that schools have begun this process, the agencies accord them candidate status. Most candidates eventually are awarded full accreditation.

The U.S. schools included in this book are fully accredited or are candidates for that status. If the latter is the case, it is indicated below the address of the school. Because the U.S. regional accrediting bodies do not officially accredit Canadian colleges and universities, and because there is no equivalent accrediting system in Canada, we have chosen to include only the larger, English-language Canadian schools—those with total full-time undergraduate enrollment of more than 10,000. It should be understood that size in no way relates to quality; there are many excellent Canadian colleges and universities with fewer than 10,000 students.

Four-Year Colleges Only

This book presents Profiles for all accredited four-year colleges that grant bachelor's degrees and admit freshmen with no previous college experience. Most of these colleges also accept transfer students. Profiles of upper-division schools, which offer only the junior or senior year of undergraduate study, are not included, nor are junior or community colleges.

Consistent Entries

Each Profile of a U.S. college is organized in the same way; the only Profiles that vary are those of Canada, schools abroad, and religious schools. The following discussion applies to the U.S. college Profiles, but refers to the other Profiles as well.

Every Profile begins with a capsule and is followed by separate sections covering the campus environment, student life, programs of study, admissions, financial aid, information for international students, computers, graduates, and the admissions contact. These categories are always introduced in the same sequence, so you can find data and compare specific points easily. The following commentary will help you evaluate and interpret the information given for each college.

Data Collection

Barron's *Profiles of American Colleges* was first published in 1964. Since then, it has been revised almost every year; comprehensive revisions are undertaken every two years. Such frequent updating is necessary because so much information about colleges—particularly enrollment figures, costs, programs of study, and admissions standards—changes rapidly.

The facts in the capsule portion of each Profile in this edition were gathered in the fall of 2001 and apply to the 2001–2002 academic year. Figures on tuition and room-and-board costs generally change soon after the book is published. For the most up-to-date information on such items, you should always check with the colleges. Other information—such as the basic nature of the school, its campus, and the educational goals of its students—changes less rapidly. A few new programs of study might be added or new services made available, but the basic educational offerings generally will remain constant.

THE CAPSULE

The capsule of each Profile provides basic information about the college at a glance. An explanation of the standard capsule is shown in the accompanying box.

All toll-free phone numbers are presumed to be out-of-state or both in-state and out-of-state, unless noted.

A former name is given if the name has been changed recently. To use the map code to the right of the college name, turn to the appropriate college-locator map at the beginning of each chapter. Wherever "n/av" is used in the capsule, it means the information was not available. The abbreviation "n/app" means not applicable.

Full-time, Part-time, Graduate

Enrollment figures are the clearest indication of the size of a college, and show whether or not it is coeducational and what the

COMPLETE NAME OF SCHOOL
(Former Name, if any)
City, State, Zip Code
(Accreditation Status, if a candidate)

MAP CODE

Fax and Phone Numbers

Full-time: Full-time undergraduate enrollment
Part-time: Part-time undergraduate enrollment
Graduate: Graduate enrollment
Year: Semesters, quarters, summer sessions
Application Deadline: Fall admission deadline

Faculty: Number of full-time faculty; AAUP category of school, salary-level symbol
Ph.D.s: Percentage of faculty holding Ph.D.
Student/Faculty: Full-time student/full-time faculty ratio
Tuition: Yearly tuition and fees (out-of-state if different)
Room & Board: Yearly room-and-board costs

Freshman Class: Number of students who applied, number accepted, number enrolled
SAT I: Median Verbal, Median Math

ACT: Median composite ACT

ADMISSIONS SELECTOR RATING

male-female ratio is. Graduate enrollment is presented to give a better idea of the size of the entire student body; some schools have far more graduate students enrolled than undergraduates.

Year

Some of the more innovative college calendars include the 4-1-4, 3-2-3, 3-3-1, and 1-3-1-4-3 terms. College administrators sometimes utilize various intersessions or interims—special short terms—for projects, independent study, short courses, or travel programs. The early semester calendar, which allows students to finish spring semesters earlier than those of the traditional semester calendar, gives students a head start on finding summer jobs. A modified semester (4-1-4) system provides a January or winter term, approximately four weeks long, for special projects that usually earn the same credit as one semester-long course. The trimester calendar divides the year into three equal parts; students may attend college during all three but generally take a vacation during any one. The quarter calendar divides the year into four equal parts; students usually attend for three quarters each year. The term calendar is essentially the same as the quarter calendar without the summer quarter; it has three sessions between September and June. The capsule also indicates schools that offer a summer session.

Application Deadline

Indicated here is the deadline for applications for admission to the fall semester. If there are no specific deadlines, it will say "open." Application deadlines for admission to other semesters are, where available, given in the admissions section of the profile.

Faculty

The first number given refers to the number of full-time faculty members at the college or university.

The Roman numeral and symbol that follow represent the salary level of faculty at the school as compared with faculty salaries nationally. This information is based on the salary report* published by the American Association of University Professors (AAUP). The Roman numeral refers to the AAUP category to which the particular college or university is assigned. (This allows for comparison of faculty salaries at the same types of schools.) Category I includes "institutions that offer the doctorate degree, and that conferred in the most recent three years an annual average of fifteen or more earned doctorates covering a minimum of three nonrelated disciplines." Category IIA includes "institutions awarding degrees above the baccalaureate, but not included in Category I." Category IIB includes "institutions awarding only the baccalaureate or equivalent degree." Category III includes "institutions with academic ranks, mostly two-year institutions." Category IV includes "institutions without academic ranks." (With the exception of a few liberal arts colleges, this category includes mostly two-year institutions.)

The symbol that follows the Roman numeral indicates into which percentile range the average salary of professors, associate professors, assistant professors, and instructors at the school falls, as compared with other schools in the same AAUP category. The symbols used in this book represent the following:

++$	95th percentile
+$	80th percentile
av$	60th percentile
–$	40th percentile
––$	20th percentile and below

If the school is not a member of AAUP, nothing will appear.

Ph.D.s

The figure here indicates the percentage of full-time faculty who have Ph.D.s or the highest terminal degree.

*Source: Annual Report on the Economic Status of the Profession published in the March-April 2001 issue of *Academe:* Bulletin of the AAUP, 1012 Fourteenth St. N.W., Suite 500, Washington, D.C. 20005.

Student/Faculty

Student/faculty ratios may be deceptive because the faculties of many large universities include scholars and scientists who do little or no teaching. Nearly every college has some large lecture classes, usually in required or popular subjects, and many small classes in advanced or specialized fields. Here, the ratio reflects full-time students and full-time faculty, and some colleges utilize the services of a large part-time faculty. Additionally, some institutions factor in an FTE component in determining this ratio. We do not, and thus the Student/Faculty ratio that we report may differ somewhat from what the college reports. In general, a student/faculty ratio of 10 to 1 is very good.

If the faculty and student body are both mostly part-time, the entry will say "n/app."

Tuition

It is important to remember that tuition costs change continually and that in many cases, these changes are substantial. Particularly heavy increases have occurred recently and will continue to occur. On the other hand, some smaller colleges are being encouraged to lower tuitions, in order to make higher education more affordable. Students are therefore urged to contact individual colleges for the most current tuition figures.

The figure given here includes tuition and student fees for the school's standard academic year. If costs differ for state residents and out-of-state residents, the figure for nonresidents is given in parentheses. Where tuition costs are listed per credit hour (p/c), per course (p/course), or per unit (p/unit), student fees are not included. In some university systems, tuition is the same for all schools. However, student fees, and therefore the total tuition figure, may vary from school to school.

Room and Board

It is suggested that students check with individual schools for the most current room-and-board figures because, like tuition figures, they increase continually. The room-and-board figures given here represent the annual cost of a double room and all meals. The word "none" indicates that the college does not charge for room and board; "n/app" indicates that room and board are not provided.

Freshman Class

The numbers apply to the number of students who applied, were accepted, and enrolled in the 2001–2002 freshman class or in a recent class.

SAT I, ACT

Whenever available, the median SAT I scores—both Verbal and Mathematics—and the median ACT composite score for the 2001–2002 freshman class are given. If the school has not reported median SAT I or ACT scores, the capsule indicates whether the SAT I or ACT is required. Note: Test scores are reported for mainstream students.

Admissions Selector Rating

The College Admissions Selector Rating indicates the degree of competitiveness of admission to the college.

THE GENERAL DESCRIPTION

The Introductory Paragraph

This paragraph indicates, in general, what types of programs the college offers, when it was founded, whether it is public or private, and its religious affiliation. Baccalaureate program accreditation and information on the size of the school's library collection are also provided.

In evaluating the size of the collection, keep in mind the difference between college and university libraries: A university's graduate and professional schools require many specialized books that would be of no value to an undergraduate. For a university, a ratio of one undergraduate to 500 books generally means an outstanding library, one to 200 an adequate library, one to 100 an inferior library. For a college, a ratio of one to 400 is outstanding, one to 300 superior, one to 200 adequate, one to 50 inferior.

These figures are somewhat arbitrary, because a large university with many professional schools or campuses requires more books than a smaller university. Furthermore, a recently founded college would be expected to have fewer books than an older school, since it has not inherited from the past what might be a great quantity of outdated and useless books. Most libraries can make up for deficiencies through interlibrary loans.

The ratio of students to the number of subscriptions to periodicals is less meaningful, and again, a university requires more periodicals than a college. But for a university, subscription to more than 1500 periodicals is outstanding, and 6000 is generally more than adequate. For a college, 15,000 subscriptions are exceptional, 700 very good, and 400 adequate. Subscription to fewer than 200 periodicals generally implies an inferior library with a very tight budget. Microform items are assuming greater importance within a library's holdings, and this information is included when available. Services of a Learning Resource Center and special facilities, such as a museum, and radio or TV station are also described in this paragraph.

This paragraph also provides information on the campus: its size, the type of area in which it is located, and its proximity to a large city.

At most institutions, the existence of classrooms, administrative offices, and dining facilities may be taken for granted, and they generally are not mentioned in the entries unless they have been recently constructed or are considered exceptional.

Student Life

This section, with subdivisions that detail housing, campus activities, sports, facilities for disabled students, services offered to students, and campus safety concentrates on the everyday life of students.

The introductory paragraph, which includes various characteristics of the student body, gives an idea of the mix of attitudes and backgrounds. It includes, where available, percentages of students from out-of-state and from private or public high schools. It also indicates what percentage of the students belong to minority groups and what percentages are Protestant, Catholic, and Jewish. Finally, it tells the average age of all enrolled freshmen and of all undergraduates, and gives data on the freshman dropout rate and the percentage of freshmen who remain to graduate.

Housing. Availability of on-campus housing is described here. If you plan to live on campus, note the type, quantity, and capacity of the dormitory accommodations. Some colleges provide dormitory rooms for freshmen, but require upperclass students to make their own arrangements to live in fraternity or sorority houses, off-campus apartments, or rented rooms in private houses. Some small colleges require all students who do not live with parents or other relatives to live on campus. And some colleges have no residence halls.

This paragraph tells whether special housing is available and whether campus housing is single-sex or coed. It gives the percentage of those who live on campus and those who remain on campus on weekends. Finally, it states if alcohol is not permitted on campus and whether students may keep cars on campus.

Activities. Campus organizations play a vital part in students' social lives. This subsection lists types of activities, including student government, special interest or academic clubs, fraternities and sororities, and cultural and popular campus events sponsored at the college.

Sports. Sports are important on campus, so we indicate the extent of the athletic program by giving the number of intercollegiate and intramural sports offered for men and for women. We have also included the athletic and recreation facilities and campus stadium seating capacity.

Disabled Students. The colleges' own estimates of how accessible their campuses are to the physically disabled are provided. This information should be considered along with the specific kinds of special facilities available. If a Profile does not include a subsection on the disabled, the college did not provide the information.

Services. Services that may be available to students—free or for a fee—include health care, birth control information, day-care services, psychological, vocational, personal, and military students counseling, tutoring, remedial instruction, and reader service for the blind.

Safety. This section lists the safety and security measures that are in place on the campus. These vary among schools, but may include 24-hour foot and vehicle patrol, self-defense education, escort services, shuttle buses, informal discussions, pamphlets/posters/films, emergency telephones, and lighted pathways/sidewalks.

Programs of Study

Listed here are the bachelor's degrees granted, strongest and most popular majors, and whether associate, master's, and doctoral degrees are awarded. Major areas of study have been included under broader general areas (shown in capital letters in the profiles) for quicker reference; however, the general areas do not necessarily correspond to the academic divisions of the college or university but are more career-oriented.

Required. Wherever possible, information on specific required courses and distribution requirements is supplied, in addition to the number of credits or hours required for graduation. If the college requires students to maintain a certain grade point average (GPA) or pass comprehensive exams to graduate, that also is given.

Special. Special programs are described here. Students at almost every college now have the opportunity to study abroad, either through their college or through other institutions. Internships with businesses, schools, hospitals, and public agencies permit students to gain work experience as they learn. The pass/fail grading option, now quite prevalent, allows students to take courses in unfamiliar areas without threatening their academic average. Many schools offer students the opportunity to earn a combined B.A.-B.S. degree, pursue a general studies (no major) degree, or design their own major. Frequently students may take advantage of a cooperative program offered by two or more universities. Such a program might be referred to, for instance, as a 3-2 engineering program; a student in this program would spend three years at one institution and two at another. The number of national honor societies represented on campus is included. Schools also may conduct honors programs for qualified students, either university-wide or in specific major fields, and these also are listed.

Faculty/Classroom. The percentage of male and female faculty are mentioned here if provided by the college, along with the percentage of introductory courses taught by graduate students (if any). The average class size in an introductory lecture, laboratory, and regular class offering may also be indicated.

Admissions

The admissions section gives detailed information on standards so you can evaluate your chances for acceptance. Where the SAT I or ACT scores of the 2001–2002 freshman class are broken down, you may compare your own scores. Because the role of standardized tests in the admissions process has been subject to criticism, more colleges are considering other factors such as recommendations from high school officials, leadership record, special talents, extracurricular activities, and advanced placement or honors courses completed. A few schools may consider education of parents, ability to pay for college, and relationship to alumni. Some give preference to state residents; others seek a geographically diverse student body.

If a college indicates that it follows an open admissions policy, it is noncompetitive and generally accepts all applicants who meet certain basic requirements, such as graduation from an accredited high school. If a college has rolling admissions, it decides on each application as soon as possible if the applicant's file is complete and does not specify a notification deadline. As a general rule, it is best to submit applications as early as possible.

Some colleges offer special admissions programs for nontraditional applicants. Early admissions programs allow students to begin college either during the summer before their freshman year or during what would have been their last year of high school; in the latter case, a high school diploma is not required. These programs are designed for students who are emotionally and educationally prepared for college at an earlier age than usual.

Deferred admissions plans permit students to spend a year at another activity, such as working or traveling, before beginning college. Students who take advantage of this option can relax during the year off, because they already have been accepted at a college and have a space reserved. During the year off from study, many students become clearer about their educational goals, and they perform better when they do begin study.

Early decision plans allow students to be notified by their first-choice school during the first term of the senior year. This plan may eliminate the anxiety of deciding whether or not to send a deposit to a second-choice college that offers admission before the first-choice college responds.

The Ivy League institutions, along with the Massachusetts Institute of Technology, have adopted an early evaluation procedure under which applicants receive, between November 1 and February 15, an evaluation of their chances for admission. They are told that acceptance is likely, possible, or unlikely, or that the colleges have received insufficient evidence for evaluation. This information helps applicants decide whether to concentrate on another school. Final notification is made on a common date in April.

Requirements. This subsection specifies the minimum high school class rank and GPA, if any, required by the college for freshman applicants. It indicates what standardized tests (if any) are required, specifically the SAT I or ACT, or for Puerto Rican schools, the CEEB (the Spanish-language version of the SAT I). Additional requirements are given such as whether an essay, interview, or audition is necessary, and if AP*/CLEP credit is given. If a college accepts applications on computer disk or on-line, those facts are so noted and described. Other factors used by the school in the admissions decision are also listed.

Procedure. This subsection indicates when you should take entrance exams, the application deadlines for various sessions, the application fee, and when students are notified of the admissions decision. Some schools note that their application deadlines are open; this can mean either that they will consider applications until a class is filled, or that applications are considered right up until registration for the term in which the student wishes to enroll. If a waiting list is an active part of the admissions procedure, the college may indicate what percentage of applicants are placed on that list and the number of wait-listed applicants accepted.

Transfer. Nearly every college admits some transfer students. These students may have earned associate degrees at two-year colleges and want to continue their education at a four-year college or wish to attend a different school. One important thing to consider when transferring is how many credits earned at one school will be accepted at another, so entire semesters won't be spent making up lost work. Because most schools require students to spend a specified number of hours in residence to earn a degree, it is best not to wait too long to transfer if you decide to do so.

Visiting. Some colleges hold special orientation programs for prospective students to give them a better idea of what the school is like. Many also will provide guides for informal visits, often allowing students to spend a night in the residence halls. You should make arrangements with the college before visiting.

Financial Aid

This paragraph in each Profile describes the availability of financial aid. It includes the percentage of freshmen and continuing students who receive aid, the average scholarship, loan, and work contract aid to freshmen, the average amount of need-based scholarships from all sources and the types and sources of aid available, such as scholarships, grants, loans, and work-study. It indicates if there is a formal appeal process for obtaining more money for the second semester. Aid application deadlines and required forms are also indicated.

International Students

This section begins by telling how many of the school's students come from outside the United States. It tells which English proficiency exam, if any, applicants must take and the minimum score required, if there is one. Any necessary college entrance exams, including SAT II: Subject tests, are listed, as are any minimum scores required on those exams.

Computers

This section details the make and model of the mainframe and the scope of computerized facilities that are available for academic use. Limitations (if any) on student use of computer facilities are outlined. It also gives information on the required or recommended ownership of a personal computer.

Graduates

This section gives the number of graduates in the 2001 class, the most popular majors and percentage of graduates earning degrees in those fields, and the percentages of men and women in the 2000 class who enrolled in graduate school or found employment within 6 months of graduation.

Admissions Contact

This is the name or title of the person to whom all correspondence regarding your application should be sent. Internet and World Wide Web addresses are included here, along with the availability of a video of the campus.

* Advanced Placement and AP are registered trademarks owned by the College Entrance Examination Board. No endorsement of this product is implied or given.

PROFILES OF AMERICAN COLLEGES

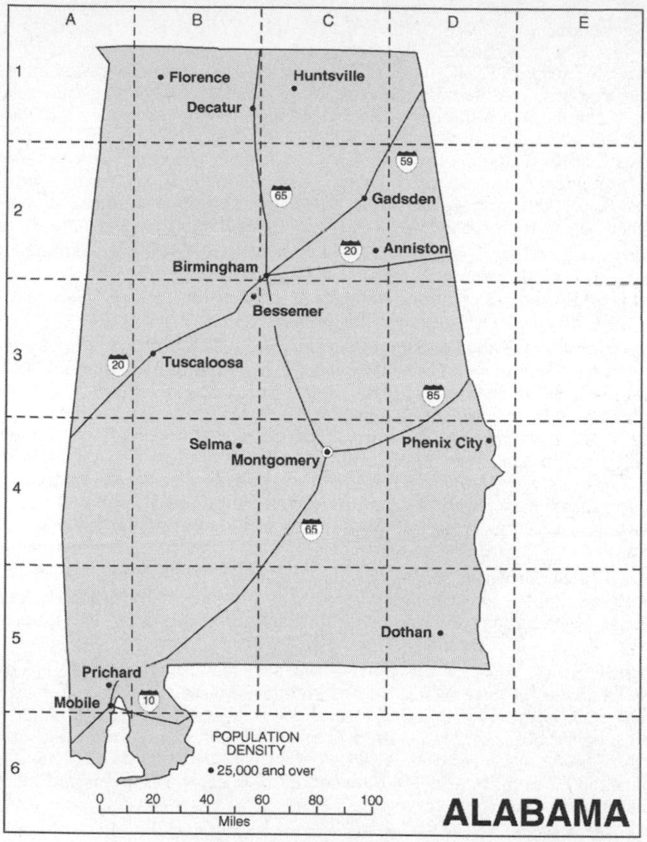

ALABAMA AGRICULTURAL AND MECHANICAL UNIVERSITY C-1

Normal, AL 35762 (256) 851-5245

(800) 553-0816; (256) 785-7456

Full-time: 1950 men, 2020 women
Part-time: 160 men, 190 women
Graduate: 360 men, 800 women
Year: semesters, summer session
Application Deadline: July 15
Freshman Class: n/av
SAT I: n/av

Faculty: 150; IIA, --$
Ph.D.s: 70%
Student/Faculty: 27 to 1
Tuition: $2400 ($4300)
Room & Board: $2700

ACT: required

LESS COMPETITIVE

Alabama Agricultural and Mechanical University, founded in 1875, is a public land-grant institution offering undergraduate and graduate studies in agriculture, home economics, arts and sciences, business, education, engineering, and technology. Figures in above capsule are approximate. There are 5 undergraduate schools and 1 graduate school. In addition to regional accreditation, A&M has baccalaureate program accreditation with ABET, ADA, AHEA, CSWE, FIDER, and NCATE. The library contains 253,620 volumes, 48,300 microform items, and 3010 audiovisual forms/CDs, and subscribes to 2070 periodicals. Computerized library services include the card catalog, interlibrary loans, and database searching. Special learning facilities include a learning resource center, art gallery, radio station, TV station, and State Black Archives. The 2001-acre campus is in a suburban area 90 miles north of Birmingham and 95 miles south of Nashville. Including residence halls, there are 55 buildings.

Student Life: 70% of undergraduates are from Alabama. Others are from 42 states, 29 foreign countries, and Canada. 90% are from public schools. 90% are African American. Most are Protestant. The average age of freshmen is 18; all undergraduates, 20. 30% do not continue beyond their first year; 60% remain to graduate.

Housing: 3100 students can be accommodated in college housing, which includes single-sex dormitories. On-campus housing is guaranteed for all 4 years. 60% of students live on campus; of those, 60% remain on campus on weekends. Alcohol is not permitted. All students may keep cars.

Activities: 7% of men belong to 4 national fraternities; 9% of women belong to 4 national sororities. There are 109 groups on campus, including band, cheerleading, choir, chorus, computers, dance, debate, drama, drill team, ethnic, forensics, honors, international, jazz band, marching band, newspaper, orchestra, pep band, political, professional, radio and TV, religious, social, student government, symphony, and yearbook. Popular campus events include Magic City Classic, Women's Week, and Men's Week.

Sports: There are 7 intercollegiate sports for men and 7 for women, and 7 intramural sports for men and 7 for women. Facilities include a 7000-seat gym, an Olympic-size pool, track and playing fields, and a 21,000-seat stadium/health education complex.

Disabled Students: 95% of the campus is accessible. Wheelchair ramps, elevators, special parking, specially equipped rest rooms, and lowered drinking fountains are available.

Services: Counseling and information services are available, as is tutoring in most subjects. There is a reader service for the blind.

Campus Safety and Security: Measures include 24-hour foot and vehicle patrol, self-defense education, escort service, and informal discussions. There are pamphlets/posters/films and lighted pathways/sidewalks.

Programs of Study: A&M confers B.A., B.S., B.S.C.E., B.S.E.E., B.S.E.T., B.S.M.E., and B.S.W. degrees. Associate, master's, and doctoral degrees are also awarded. Bachelor's degrees are awarded in AG RICULTURE (agricultural business management, agricultural economics, agronomy, animal science, forestry and related sciences, horticulture, and soil science), BIOLOGICAL SCIENCE (biology/biological science, nutrition, and zoology), BUSINESS (accounting, banking and finance, business administration and management, marketing/retailing/merchandising, and office supervision and management), COMMUNICATIONS AND THE ARTS (English, French, and telecommunications), COMPUTER AND PHYSICAL SCIENCE (chemistry, computer science, mathematics, and physics), EDUCATION (agricultural, art, early childhood, elementary, home economics, industrial arts, middle school, music, physical, science, secondary, special, and trade and industrial), ENGINEERING AND ENVIRONMENTAL DESIGN (city/community/regional planning, civil engineering, civil engineering technology, drafting and design technology, electrical/electronics engineering, electrical/electronics engineering technology, environmental science, industrial engineering technology, mechanical engineering, and mechanical engineering technology), HEALTH PROFESSIONS (medical laboratory technology, preveterinary science, and speech pathology/audiology), SOCIAL SCIENCE (economics, family/consumer studies, food science, history, human development, political science/government, psychology, social work, and sociology). Physics, food science, and teacher education are the strongest academically. Business administration, education, and computer science are the largest.

Required: All students are required to take at least 52 hours of general studies, including phys ed, music, and art, and to maintain a minimum GPA of 2.0. Students must complete a total of 120 to 126 credit hours, with 30 to 36 in the major. A comprehensive exam is required for some majors.

Special: Co-op programs with Georgia Institute of Technology and Tuskegee University, cross-registration with the University of Alabama in Huntsville, Oakwood College, Calhoun Community College, and Athens State College, internships with various government agencies, dual majors, and work-study programs are available. There is a 3-2 engineering degree program with Georgia Institute of Technology. There are 5 national honor societies, a freshman honors program, and 5 departmental honors programs.

Faculty/Classroom: 70% of faculty are male; 30%, female. 50% teach undergraduates, 30% do research, and 30% do both. No introductory courses are taught by graduate students. The average class size in an introductory lecture is 90; in a laboratory, 20; and in a regular course, 30.

Admissions: There were 16 National Merit finalists in a recent year.

Requirements: The ACT is required. In addition, the SAT I or ACT is required, with a minimum score of 18 on the ACT. Applicants must have 4 years each of English, math, science, social studies, and history. An interview is recommended. The GED is accepted. A GPA of 2.0 is required. AP and CLEP credits are accepted. Important factors in the admissions decision are advanced placement or honor courses, leadership record, and recommendations by school officials. Applications are accepted on-line at the school's web site.

Procedure: Freshmen are admitted to all sessions. There are early decision, early admissions, and deferred admissions plans. Applications should be filed by July 15 for fall entry, December 1 for spring entry, and May 15 for summer entry. Notification is sent on a rolling basis. The fall 2001 application fee was $10.

Transfer: 318 transfer students enrolled in a recent year. Transfer students must have a minimum GPA of 2.0 and have earned at least 12 semester credit hours. 30 to 36 credits of 120 to 126 must be completed at A&M.

Visiting: There are regularly scheduled orientations for prospective students, consisting of sessions in June, July, and November. There are guides for informal visits and visitors may stay overnight. To schedule a visit, contact Antonio Boyle, Director of Admissions at (256) 851-5248.

Financial Aid: In a recent year, 72% of all freshmen and 68% of continuing students received some form of financial aid. 75% of freshmen and 61% of continuing students received need-based aid. The average freshman award was $4150. Of that total, scholarships or need-based grants averaged $830 ($1868 maximum); loans averaged $1660 ($4150 maximum); and work contracts averaged $1660 ($2075 maximum). 50% of undergraduates work part time. Average annual earnings from campus work are $3600. The average financial indebtedness of a recent graduate was $25,000. The CSS/Profile, FAFSA, FFS or SFS, or the college's own financial statement are required. Check with the school for current deadlines.

International Students: There were 185 international students enrolled in a recent year. The school actively recruits these students. They must score 500 on the written TOEFL.

Computers: The mainframe is an IBM. In addition to the Mac/IBM computer center, there are IBM PCs located in the library, computer labs, and language and writing centers. All students may access the system. There are no time limits. The fee is $50. It is strongly recommended that all students have a personal computer.

Graduates: In an average class, 54% graduate in 6 years.

Admissions Contact: Antonio Boyle, Director of Admissions. A video is available. E-mail: *aboyle@asnaam.aamu.edu* Web: *www.aamu.edu*

ALABAMA STATE UNIVERSITY — C-4

Montgomery, AL 36101-0271 — (334) 229-4291
(800) 410-3522; Fax: (334) 229-4984

Full-time: 1756 men, 2379 women	**Faculty:** 223
Part-time: 211 men, 365 women	**Ph.D.s:** 57%
Graduate: 213 men, 666 women	**Student/Faculty:** 18 to 1
Year: semesters, summer session	**Tuition:** $2904 ($5808)
Application Deadline: July 30	**Room & Board:** $3500
Freshman Class: 6798 applied, 4322 accepted, 1645 enrolled	
SAT I Verbal/Math: 414/410	**ACT:** 17 **COMPETITIVE**

Alabama State University, founded in 1867, is a state-assisted institution offering undergraduate programs in liberal arts and sciences, business administration, education, music, social work, aerospace studies, and health science. There are 6 undergraduate schools and 1 graduate school. In addition to regional accreditation, ASU has baccalaureate program accreditation with ACBSP, ACOTE, CSWE, NASDTEC, NASM, and NCATE. The library contains 396,871 volumes, 2,559,000 microform items, and 42,319 audiovisual forms/CDs, and subscribes to 1307 periodicals. Computerized library services include the card catalog, interlibrary loans, and database searching. Special learning facilities include a learning resource center, art gallery, and radio station. The 168-acre campus is in an urban area 91 miles south of Birmingham. Including residence halls, there are 64 buildings.

Student Life: 70% of undergraduates are from Alabama. Others are from 39 states, 16 foreign countries, and Canada. 90% are African American. The average age of freshmen is 19; all undergraduates, 23. 36% do not continue beyond their first year; 21% remain to graduate.

Housing: 2330 students can be accommodated in college housing, which includes single-sex dormitories and on-campus apartments. In addition, there are honors houses. On-campus housing is available on a first-come, first-served basis. 62% of students commute. Alcohol is not permitted. All students may keep cars.

Activities: 8% of men belong to 4 national fraternities; 6% of women belong to 4 national sororities. There are 50 groups on campus, including art, band, cheerleading, choir, chorus, dance, debate, drama, drum and bugle corps, honors, international, jazz band, marching band, musical theater, newspaper, orchestra, pep band, political, professional, radio and TV, social service, student government, symphony, and yearbook. Popular campus events include Founders Day, Fall Convocation, and Honors Day Program.

Sports: There are 8 intercollegiate sports for men and 9 for women, and 6 intramural sports for men and 5 for women. Facilities include an 8000-seat acadome, a stadium, a gym, 12 tennis courts, a swimming pool, an 8-lane indoor track, and 2 weight rooms.

Disabled Students: 80% of the campus is accessible. Wheelchair ramps, elevators, special parking, specially equipped rest rooms, special class scheduling, lowered drinking fountains, lowered telephones, and semiautomatic doors are available.

Services: Counseling and information services are available, as is tutoring in some subjects, including math and English. There is remedial math, reading, and writing.

Campus Safety and Security: Measures include 24-hour foot and vehicle patrol, self-defense education, escort service, and informal discussions. There are pamphlets/posters/films, emergency telephones, lighted pathways/sidewalks, and a campus police department with 24 officers.

Programs of Study: ASU confers B.A., B.S., B.M.E., B.S.Ed., and B.S.W. degrees. Master's degrees are also awarded. Bachelor's degrees are awarded in BIOLOGICAL SCIENCE (biology/biological science), BUSINESS (accounting, banking and finance, business administration and management, business economics, and marketing/retailing/merchandising), COMMUNICATIONS AND THE ARTS (broadcasting, communications, English, fine arts, French, music, and Spanish), COMPUTER AND PHYSICAL SCIENCE (chemistry, information sciences and systems, mathematics, and physics), EDUCATION (art, business, early childhood, elementary, English, foreign languages, music, secondary, social studies, and special), ENGINEERING AND ENVIRONMENTAL DESIGN (engineering), SOCIAL SCIENCE (criminal justice, history, political science/government, psychology, social work, and sociology). Business and education are the strongest academically. Computer information systems and elementary education are the largest.

Required: All students must complete a 42-hour core curriculum and pass an English proficiency exam and a senior comprehensive exam. A total of 120 semester hours, with at least 27 in the major, and a minimum GPA of 2.0 are required for graduation.

Special: Cooperative programs are offered in all majors, including engineering and math with Auburn University and marine biology with Dauphin Island Sea Laboratory. The Division of Aerospace Studies, in conjunction with the AFROTC curriculum, offers programs leading to a commission in the U.S. Air Force. There is a 3-2 engineering program with Auburn University, and cross enrollment is possible. Internships, dual majors, a general studies degree, work study, nondegree study, and credit for military experience are available. There are 16 national honor societies, a freshman honors program, and 9 departmental honors program.

Faculty/Classroom: 49% of faculty are male; 51%, female. All teach undergraduates. No introductory courses are taught by graduate students. The average class size in an introductory lecture is 40; in a laboratory, 40; and in a regular course, 40.

Admissions: 64% of the 2001-2002 applicants were accepted. The SAT I scores for the 2001-2002 freshman class were: Verbal--87% below 500, 10% between 500 and 599, and 3% between 600 and 700; Math--86% below 500, 12% between 500 and 599, and 2% between 600 and 700. The ACT scores were 88% below 21, 9% between 21 and 23, 2% between 24 and 26, and 1% between 27 and 28. 4 freshmen graduated first in their class.

Requirements: The SAT I or ACT is recommended. In addition, applicants should be high school graduates with at least 3 units of English and 8 units combined in math, natural sciences, social sciences, and foreign languages. An interview is recommended. Applications may be submitted on-line. A GPA of 2.0 is required. AP and CLEP credits are accepted.

Procedure: Freshmen are admitted fall, spring, and summer. Entrance exams should be taken in the fall of the senior year. There are early decision, early admissions, and deferred admissions plans. Applications should be filed by July 30 for fall entry, December 1 for spring entry, and May 30 for summer entry. Notification is sent on a rolling basis.

Transfer: 171 transfer students enrolled in 2001-2002. A minimum college GPA of 2.0 is required. An interview is recommended. No more than 64 semester hours are accepted for credit from 2-year colleges. 30 credits of 120 must be completed at ASU.

Visiting: There are regularly scheduled orientations for prospective students, including visits for spring, January 5 to 7, and fall, July 6 to 11, and August 17 to 22. There are guides for informal visits. To schedule a visit, contact the Office of Admissions and Recruitment.

Financial Aid: In 2001-2002, 93% of all freshmen and 98% of continuing students received some form of financial aid. 94% of freshmen and 75% of continuing students received need-based aid. The average freshman award was $9660. Of that total, scholarships or need-based grants averaged $200 ($11,008 maximum); loans averaged $2625 ($4625 maximum); and work contracts averaged $1984 ($2976 maximum). Average annual earnings from campus work are $1984. The average financial indebtedness of the 2001 graduate was $25,000. ASU is a member of CSS. The FAFSA and Alabama Student Data Form are required. The fall application deadline is May 1.

International Students: There are 11 international students enrolled. They must score 500 on the written TOEFL and also take or complete ESL Level 109. and also take the SAT I or the ACT.

Computers: The mainframe is a multiprise 2003-225. About 350 PCs and Macs are available in student labs. All students may access the system 24 hours a day.

Graduates: In 2001, 437 bachelor's degrees were awarded. The most popular majors were computer information systems (12%), criminal justice (10%), and elementary education (6%). 278 companies recruited on campus in 2000-2001. Of the 2000 graduating class, 21% were enrolled in graduate school within 6 months of graduation.

Admissions Contact: Danielle Kennedy-Lamar, Director of Admissions. A video is available. E-mail: *dlamar@asunet.alasu.edu*
Web: *www.alasu.edu*

AUBURN UNIVERSITY SYSTEM

Auburn University, established in 1856, is a public system in Alabama. It is governed by a board of trustees whose chief administrator is the president. The primary goal of the system is service through its instruction, research, and extension divisions. The main priorities are to provide outstanding, economical instruction to its undergraduate, graduate, and professional students, to expand and diversify overall research effort, and to disseminate and apply knowledge through extension and public service programs. Total enrollment of both campuses is about 28,000; there are 1500 faculty members. Altogether there are approximately 160 baccalaureate, 74 master's, 10 educational specialist, and 40 doctoral programs offered in Auburn University. There are 4-year campuses located in Auburn and Montgomery. Profiles of the 4-year campuses are in this section.

AUBURN UNIVERSITY

Auburn University, AL 36849-5145 D-3
(334) 844-6428
(800) 392-8051

Full-time: 8752 men, 8344 women	**Faculty:** I, --$
Part-time: 1051 men, 651 women	**Ph.D.s:** 93%
Graduate: 1558 men, 1261 women	**Student/Faculty:** 15 to 1
Year: semesters, summer session	**Tuition:** $3380 ($9900)
Application Deadline: August 1	**Room & Board:** $2130
Freshman Class: 13,645 applied, 10,362 accepted, 3755 enrolled	
SAT I Verbal/Math: 540/560	**ACT:** 23 **COMPETITIVE**

Auburn University, founded in 1856, is a state-supported institution offering undergraduate and graduate degrees in agriculture, business, education, engineering, liberal arts, sciences and math, veterinary medicine, architecture/design and construction, forestry, human sciences, nursing, and pharmacy. There are 12 undergraduate schools and 1 graduate school. In addition to regional accreditation, Auburn has baccalaureate program accreditation with AACSB, ABET, ACEJMC, ACPE, ADA, AHEA, ASLA, CSWE, FIDER, NAAB, NASAD, NASM, NCATE, NLN, and SAF. The 3 libraries contain 2,591,255 volumes, 2,511,632 microform items, and 219,454 audiovisual forms/CDs, and subscribe to 23,121 periodicals. Computerized library services include the card catalog, interlibrary loans, and database searching. Special learning facilities include a learning resource center, art gallery, radio station, TV station, and a nuclear science center, an arboretum, and electron microscopy labs. The 1871-acre campus is in a small town 110 miles southwest of Atlanta, Georgia. Including residence halls, there are 144 buildings.

Student Life: 64% of undergraduates are from Alabama. Others are from 49 states, 95 foreign countries, and Canada. 78% are from public schools. 89% are white. The average age of freshmen is 18; all undergraduates, 21. 19% do not continue beyond their first year; 66% remain to graduate.

Housing: Housing includes single-sex and coed dormitories, on-campus apartments, married-student housing, and fraternity houses. In addition, there are honors houses and special housing for disabled students. On-campus housing is available on a first-come, first-served basis. 83% of students commute. Alcohol is not permitted. All students may keep cars.

Activities: 21% of men and about 1% of women belong to 27 national fraternities; 35% of women belong to 18 national sororities. There are 300 groups on campus, including art, band, cheerleading, chess, choir, chorale, chorus, computers, dance, debate, drama, drill team, ethnic, film, gay, honors, international, jazz band, literary magazine, marching band, musical theater, newspaper, opera, orchestra, pep band, photography, political, professional, radio and TV, religious, social, social service, student government, symphony, and yearbook. Popular campus events include Hey Day, ODK Cake Race, and pep rallies.

Sports: There are 7 intercollegiate sports for men and 9 for women, and 15 intramural sports for men and 15 for women. Facilities include a stadium, a coliseum, an athletic complex, a sports arena, a track, a park, a student activities center, intramural field houses, racquetball courts, tennis courts, and a swim center.

Disabled Students: 80% of the campus is accessible. Wheelchair ramps, elevators, special parking, specially equipped rest rooms, special class scheduling, lowered drinking fountains, braille elevators, and wheelchair lifts are available.

Services: Counseling and information services are available, as is tutoring in most subjects. There is a reader service for the blind.

Campus Safety and Security: Measures include 24-hour foot and vehicle patrol, self-defense education, escort service, and shuttle buses. There are informal discussions, pamphlets/posters/films, emergency telephones, and lighted pathways/sidewalks.

Programs of Study: Auburn confers B.A., B.S., B.Arch., B.En., B.F.A., B.Int. Arch., B.Int.Design, and B.Mus.Ed. degrees. Master's and doctoral degrees are also awarded. Bachelor's degrees are awarded in AGRICULTURE (agricultural business management, agriculture, animal science, fishing and fisheries, forest engineering, forestry production and processing, horticulture, plant protection (pest management), poultry science, and soil science), BIOLOGICAL SCIENCE (biochemistry, biology/biological science, botany, entomology, marine biology, microbiology, molecular biology, nutrition, wildlife biology, and zoology), BUSINESS (accounting, banking and finance, business administration and management, business economics, fashion merchandising, hotel/motel and restaurant management, international business management, marketing/retailing/merchandising, personnel management, and transportation management), COMMUNICATIONS AND THE ARTS (communications, design, dramatic arts, English, French, German, industrial design, journalism, languages, public relations, Spanish, and speech/debate/rhetoric), COMPUTER AND PHYSICAL SCIENCE (applied mathematics, chemistry, computer science, geology, mathematics, and physics), EDUCATION (business, early childhood, elementary, English, foreign languages, health, home economics, industrial arts, mathematics, middle school, physical, science, secondary, social science, special, and vocational), ENGINEERING AND ENVIRONMENTAL DESIGN (aeronautical engineering, agricultural engineering, architecture, aviation administration/management, chemical engineering, civil engineering, computer engineering, construction management, electrical/electronics engineering, environmental science, geological engineering, interior design, landscape architecture/design, mechanical engineering, textile engineering, and textile technology), HEALTH PROFESSIONS (health care administration, medical laboratory technology, nursing, pharmacy, predentistry, premedicine, preoptometry, preveterinary science, and speech pathology/audiology), SOCIAL SCIENCE (anthropology, criminal justice, criminology, economics, food science, geography, history, home furnishings and equipment management/production/services, human development, parks and recreation management, philosophy, physical fitness/movement, political science/government, psychology, public administration, religion, rural sociology, social work, sociology, and textiles and clothing). Engineering, architecture, and psychology are the strongest academically. Liberal arts, engineering, and business are the largest.

Required: All students must complete a core curriculum of 6 semester hours and 3 each in English composition, history, literature, and social science, 8 in science, 2 each in math, philosophy, and fine arts. A total of 120 to 130 semester hours, with a minimum overall GPA of 2.0, is required in order to graduate. Two upper-level writing reinforcement courses are required within various fields of study that include extensive writing assignments and are evaluated for both content and writing mechanics.

Special: Opportunities are available for co-op programs in most majors, and there are internships, work-study programs, and dual majors. A 3-2 engineering degree with several area institutions, credit by examination, nondegree study, pass/fail options, credit for life experience, and study abroad in more than 25 countries are also available. There is a chapter of Phi Beta Kappa, a freshman honors program, and campus-wide departmental honors programs.

Faculty/Classroom: 73% of faculty are male; 27%, female.

Admissions: 76% of the 2001-2002 applicants were accepted. The SAT I scores for the 2001-2002 freshman class were: Verbal--26% below 500, 49% between 500 and 599, 22% between 600 and 700, and 3% above 700; Math--19% below 500, 48% between 500 and 599, 28% between 600 and 700, and 4% above 700. The ACT scores were 23% below 21, 30% between 21 and 23, 26% between 24 and 26, 11% between 27 and 28, and 10% above 28. 41% of the current freshmen were in the top fifth of their class; 69% were in the top two fifths. There were 30 National Merit finalists.

Requirements: The SAT I or ACT is required. In addition, graduation from an accredited secondary school is required; a GED will be accepted. Applicants must have completed 4 years of high school English, 3 each of math and social studies, and 2 of science. It is recommended that students also complete 2 years each of a foreign language, an additional science course, and an additional social science. Admission is equally based on test scores and the GPA in completed core requirements. AP and CLEP credits are accepted. Important factors in the admissions decision are advanced placement or honor courses, evidence of special talent, and parents or siblings attending the school. Applications are accepted on-line.

Procedure: Freshmen are admitted to all sessions. Entrance exams should be taken in the spring of the junior year. There are early decision, early admissions, and deferred admissions plans. Early decision applications should be filed by November 1; regular applications, by August 1 for fall entry, December 10 for spring entry, and May 1 for summer entry, along with a $25 fee. Notification is sent on a rolling basis. A waiting list is an active part of the admissions procedure.

Transfer: 1332 transfer students enrolled in 2001-2002. Students who have attempted 48 quarter hours or 32 semester hours must have earned a cumulative 2.5 GPA in at least 30 quarter hours or 20 semester hours of standard academic courses as required in the core curriculum. These hours must include at least one course in each of the following areas: English (college-level composition or literature), history, math (college-level algebra or higher), and natural science with a lab. 25% of required credits of 120 must be completed at Auburn.

Visiting: There are regularly scheduled orientations for prospective students, including 3 War Eagle Days held on Saturdays, minority recruitment weekends, and informal visits. Agendas vary, but normally include campus tours, meetings with admissions counselors, tours of housing, and meetings with faculty in various academic areas as desired. There are guides for informal visits and visitors may sit in on classes and stay overnight. To schedule a visit, contact Admissions Office at (334) 844-4080.

Financial Aid: In 2001-2002, 49% of all freshmen received some form of financial aid. The average freshman award was $5171. Of that total, scholarships or need-based grants averaged $2506; and loans averaged $2843. The average financial indebtedness of the 2001 graduate was $17,236. The FAFSA and the college's own financial statement are required. The fall application deadline is March 1.

International Students: There are 150 international students enrolled. The school actively recruits these students. They must score 550 on the written TOEFL and take the SAT I.

Computers: The mainframe is an IBM 9672/EO3. More than 700 networked PCs and terminals are available in various academic buildings and the library. Student computer labs include spreadsheet, word processing, statistical, and other software programs. Students may also access the university's mainframe computers, the Internet, and the Alabama Supercomputer. All students may access the system 24 hours a day. There are no time limits. The fee varies.

Graduates: In 2001, 3885 bachelor's degrees were awarded. The most popular majors were business (26%), engineering (15%), and education (9%). In an average class, 29% graduate in 4 years, 61% in 5 years, and 65% in 6 years.

Admissions Contact: Dr. John Fletcher, Enrollment Management. A video is available. E-mail: *admissions@auburn.edu*
Web: *www.auburn.edu*

AUBURN UNIVERSITY MONTGOMERY C-4
Montgomery, AL 36124-4023 (334) 244-3611
(800) 227-2649; Fax: (334) 244-3795

Full-time: 869 men, 1671 women	**Faculty:** 182; IIA, -$
Part-time: 616 men, 1009 women	**Ph.D.s:** n/av
Graduate: 272 men, 545 women	**Student/Faculty:** 14 to 1
Year: semesters, summer session	**Tuition:** $3440 ($9860)
Application Deadline: open	**Room & Board:** $1890
Freshman Class: 613 enrolled	
SAT I or ACT: required	**NONCOMPETITIVE**

Auburn University Montgomery, founded in 1967, is a public institution. There are 5 undergraduate and 4 graduate schools. In addition to regional accreditation, AUM has baccalaureate program accreditation with AACSB and NCATE. The library contains 306,271 volumes, 2,376,000 microform items, and 24,864 audiovisual forms/CDs, and subscribes to 1443 periodicals. Computerized library services include the card catalog, interlibrary loans, and database searching. Special learning facilities include a learning resource center, an art gallery, a graphic arts center, and a mass communication lab. The 500-acre campus is in an urban area 7 miles east of downtown Montgomery. Including residence halls, there are 49 buildings.

Student Life: 95% of undergraduates are from Alabama. Others are from 34 states, 21 foreign countries, and Canada. 62% are white; 34% African American. The average age of freshmen is 20; all undergraduates, 25.

Housing: 576 students can be accommodated in college housing, which includes single-sex and coed on-campus apartments and married-student housing. On-campus housing is available on a first-come, first-served basis. 90% of students commute. Alcohol is not permitted. All students may keep cars.

Activities: 5% of men belong to 5 national fraternities; 4% of women belong to 6 national sororities. There are 40 groups on campus, including campus activities board, cheerleading, choir, chorus, computers, drama, ethnic, honors, international, literary magazine, newspaper, professional, religious, social, social service, and student government. Popular campus events include AUM Fest and Mardi Gras Parade.

Sports: There are 4 intercollegiate sports for men and 3 for women, and 9 intramural sports for men and 7 for women. Facilities include a multipurpose gym-auditorium, an indoor track, baseball and soccer fields, and tennis courts.

Disabled Students: 95% of the campus is accessible. Wheelchair ramps, elevators, special parking, specially equipped rest rooms, special class scheduling, lowered drinking fountains, lowered telephones, and specially equipped rooms in university housing are available.

Services: Counseling and information services are available, as is tutoring in every subject. There is a reader service for the blind, remedial math, reading, and writing, and help with study skills.

Campus Safety and Security: Measures include 24-hour foot and vehicle patrol, escort service, informal discussions, and pamphlets/posters/films. There are emergency telephones and lighted pathways/sidewalks.

Programs of Study: AUM confers B.A., B.S., B.L.A., B.S.B.A., and B.S.N. degrees. Master's and doctoral degrees are also awarded. Bachelor's degrees are awarded in BIOLOGICAL SCIENCE (biology/biological science), BUSINESS (accounting, banking and finance, business administration and management, business economics, marketing/retailing/merchandising, and personnel management), COMMUNICATIONS AND THE ARTS (communications, English, and fine arts), COMPUTER AND PHYSICAL SCIENCE (information sciences and systems, mathematics, and physical sciences), EDUCATION (elementary and secondary), HEALTH PROFESSIONS (nursing), SOCIAL SCIENCE (criminal justice, history, international studies, liberal arts/general studies, political science/government, psychology, and sociology). Education and liberal arts are the strongest academically. Elementary education, general business, and general studies are the largest.

Required: To graduate, students must complete a minimum of 120 credit hours with a minimum GPA of 2.0 in the major and overall. All students must fulfill English composition requirements and liberal education program requirements.

Special: AUM offers co-op programs in all majors, cross-registration with Alabama State University, Huntingdon College, and Faulkner University, and study abroad in England and other countries. There are 13 national honor societies, a freshman honors program, and 9 departmental honors programs.

Faculty/Classroom: 53% of faculty are male; 48%, female. The average class size in a laboratory is 22 and in a regular course, 20.

Admissions: The ACT scores for a recent freshman class were: 63% below 21, 21% between 21 and 23, 13% between 24 and 26, 3% between 27 and 28. In 2001-2002, 21 freshman graduated first in their class.The ACT or SAT is required. High school preparation should include English, math,social studies, science, and foreign language. The GED may be used for admission. Applications are accepted accepted on-line at the schools web site. A GPA of 2.3 is required. AP and CLEP credits are accepted.

Requirements: The ACT or SAT I is required. High school preparation should include English, math, social studies, science, and foreign language. The GED may be used for admission. A GPA of 2.3 is required. AP and CLEP credits are accepted. Applications are accepted on-line at the school's web site.

Procedure: Freshmen are admitted to all sessions. Entrance exams should be taken in the junior year. There are early admissions and deferred admissions plans. Application deadlines are open. The application fee is $25. Notification is sent on a rolling basis.

Transfer: Applicants for transfer must have a C average and be in good standing at their last school. 67 credits of 120 must be completed at AUM.

Visiting: There are regularly scheduled orientations for prospective students, which include meetings with faculty, staff, and advising and registration. There are guides for informal visits and visitors may sit in on classes. To schedule a visit, contact the Office of Enrollment Services at (334) 244-3668 or: *vsamuel@mickey.aum.edu.*

Financial Aid: The FAFSA and the college's own financial statement are required. The fall application deadline is March 15.

International Students: There were 85 international students enrolled in a recent year. The school actively recruits these students. They must score 500 on the written TOEFL or 173 on the electronic version, and must also take the ACT or SAT I, scoring 17 on the ACT or 820 on the SAT I.

Computers: The mainframe is an NCR 4300 with a Gateway server. There are 200 PCs available to students throughout the campus, with network access via Ethernet, TCP, or IP. All students may access the system from 7 A.M. to 1 A.M. There are no time limits and no fees. It is strongly recommended that all students have a personal computer.

Graduates: In 2001, 1004 bachelor's degrees were awarded. The most popular majors were business marketing (33%), education (25%), and professional services/public administration (10%). 260 companies recruited on campus in 2000-2001.

Admissions Contact: George Hill, Associate Director of Admissions and Records. A video is available. E-mail: *auminfo@mickey.aum.edu*
Web: *http://www.aum.edu*

BIRMINGHAM-SOUTHERN COLLEGE C-2
Birmingham, AL 35254 (205) 226-4698
(800) 523-5793; Fax: (205) 226-3074

Full-time: 528 men, 751 women	**Faculty:** 98; IIB, +$
Part-time: 13 men, 55 women	**Ph.D.s:** 92%
Graduate: 41 men, 36 women	**Student/Faculty:** 13 to 1
Year: 4-1-4, summer session	**Tuition:** $17,180
Application Deadline: January 15	**Room & Board:** $5780
Freshman Class: 1047 applied, 961 accepted, 388 enrolled	
SAT I or ACT: required	**COMPETITIVE**

Birmingham-Southern College, founded in 1856, is a private liberal arts college affiliated with the United Methodist Church. In addition to regional accreditation, BSC has baccalaureate program accreditation with AACSB, NASM, and NCATE. The library contains 231,815 volumes, 175,038 microform items, and 26,914 audiovisual forms/CDs, and subscribes to 955 periodicals. Computerized library services include the card catalog, interlibrary loans, and database searching. Special learning facilities include a learning resource center, art gallery, planetarium, environmental center, and outdoor educational center. The 198-acre campus is in an urban area 3 miles west of downtown Birmingham. Including residence halls, there are 28 buildings.

Student Life: 77% of undergraduates are from Alabama. Others are from 28 states, 18 foreign countries, and Canada. 89% are white. The average age of freshmen is 18; all undergraduates, 24.

Housing: 1220 students can be accommodated in college housing, which includes single-sex dormitories, on-campus apartments, married-student housing, fraternity houses, and sorority houses. In addition, there are honors houses. On-campus housing is guaranteed for all 4 years. 85% of students live on campus; of those, 70% remain on campus on weekends. All students may keep cars.

Activities: 54% of men belong to 6 national fraternities; 60% of women belong to 7 national sororities. There are more than 70 groups on campus, including art, band, cheerleading, choir, chorale, chorus, computers, dance, drama, drill team, ethnic, gay, honors, international, jazz band, literary magazine, musical theater, newspaper, opera, orchestra, pep band, political, professional, religious, social, social service, student government, and yearbook. Popular campus events include Southern Comfort, Honors Day, and Community Day.

Sports: There are 6 intercollegiate sports for men and 8 for women, and 17 intramural sports for men and 17 for women. Facilities include a coliseum, a baseball field, racquetball and tennis courts, 2 soccer fields, a weight room, an intramural athletic field, an indoor pool, a game room, an indoor jogging track, 3 gyms, and an aerobics studio.

Disabled Students: 80% of the campus is accessible. Wheelchair ramps, elevators, special parking, specially equipped rest rooms, special class scheduling, lowered drinking fountains, and lowered telephones are available.

Services: Counseling and information services are available, as is tutoring in some subjects, including math, English, computer science, and other subjects as requested. Tutoring is arranged on an individual basis; assistance in finding teachers is provided upon request.

Campus Safety and Security: Measures include 24-hour foot and vehicle patrol, self-defense education, escort service, and shuttle buses. There are informal discussions, pamphlets/posters/films, emergency telephones, and lighted pathways/sidewalks.

Programs of Study: BSC confers B.A., B.S., B.F.A., B.Mus., and B.Mus.Ed. degrees. Master's degrees are also awarded. Bachelor's degrees are awarded in BIOLOGICAL SCIENCE (biology/biological science), BUSINESS (accounting, business administration and management, international business management, and marketing/retailing/merchandising), COMMUNICATIONS AND THE ARTS (art history and appreciation, dance, dramatic arts, English, fine arts, French, German, music, painting, photography, printmaking, sculpture, and Spanish), COMPUTER AND PHYSICAL SCIENCE (chemistry, computer science, mathematics, and physics), EDUCATION (art, early childhood, elementary, and music), SOCIAL SCIENCE (economics, history, international relations, philosophy, political science/government, psychology, and sociology). Biology, English, and psychology are the strongest academically. Business administration is the largest.

Required: All students must complete 32 regular units with courses in English composition and literature, lab sciences, math, fine arts, foreign language, social sciences, history, philosophy, and religion as well as 4 interim (January) experiences. A total of 128 credits with a GPA of at least 2.0 is required to graduate.

Special: There is cross-registration with the University of Alabama at Birmingham, Miles College, University of Montevallo, and Samford University. Student-designed majors, dual majors, an interdisciplinary computer science/math major, a Washington semester, internships, work-study programs, and study abroad are offered. There is a 3-2 nursing program with Vanderbilt University and a 3-2 environmental studies program wih Duke University. A 3-2 engineering degree is offered with the University of Alabama at Birmingham, Auburn University, Columbia University, and Washington University at St. Louis. Limited pass/fail options are available. There are 22 national honor societies, including Phi Beta Kappa, a freshman honors program, and 1 departmental honors program.

Faculty/Classroom: 64% of faculty are male; 36%, female. All teach undergraduates and 80% both teach and do research.

Admissions: 92% of the 2001-2002 applicants were accepted. The SAT I scores for the 2001-2002 freshman class were: Verbal--7% below 500, 40% between 500 and 599, 41% between 600 and 700, and 12% above 700; Math--13% below 500, 43% between 500 and 599, 38% between 600 and 700, and 6% above 700. The ACT scores were 19% below 23, 60% between 24 and 29, and 21% above 30. 78% of the current freshmen were in the top fourth of their class; 90% were in the top half. 28 freshmen graduated first in their class.

Requirements: The SAT I or ACT is required. The minimum SAT I score should be 970 combined, and the minimum ACT score, 21. Applicants should have graduated from an accredited secondary school with 4 courses in English, 4 each in math, science, and social studies, and a recommended 2 in foreign language. The GED is also accepted. An essay is required and an interview is recommended. Fine arts majors are advised to submit a portfolio or arrange an audition. BSC requires applicants to be in the upper 50% of their class. A GPA of 2.0 is required. AP and CLEP credits are accepted. Important factors in the admissions decision are advanced placement or honor courses, leadership record, and recommendations by school officials. Applications are accepted on-line via Common App.

Procedure: Freshmen are admitted fall, spring, and summer. Entrance exams should be taken in the spring of the junior year. There are early admissions and deferred admissions plans. Applications should be filed by January 15 for fall entry, December 15 for winter entry, January 15 for spring entry, and May 1 for summer entry, along with a $25 fee. Notification is sent on a rolling basis.

Transfer: 38 transfer students enrolled in 2001-2002. Transfer applicants must have a minimum GPA of 2.0 and leave their former school in good standing. An essay and a school recommendation are required. An interview is recommended. 64 credits of 128 must be completed at BSC.

Visiting: There are regularly scheduled orientations for prospective students, including Preview Days, Scholarship Days, and individual visits. There are guides for informal visits and visitors may sit in on classes and stay overnight. To schedule a visit, contact the Office of Admission at (205) 226-4698.

Financial Aid: In 2001-2002, 90% of all students received some form of financial aid. 42% of freshmen and 39% of continuing students received need-based aid. The average freshman award was $13,422. Of that total, scholarships or need-based grants averaged $11,092; and loans averaged $2878. The average financial indebtedness of the 2001 graduate was $13,000. The CSS/Profile, FAFSA, FFS or SFS, and the college's own financial statement are required. The fall application deadline is March 31.

International Students: The school actively recruits international students. They must score 500 on the written TOEFL. The SAT I or ACT is required instead of the TOEFL for students whose primary language is English. The minimum score required on the ACT is 21.

Computers: The mainframe is an HP 9000/Series 835. There are 520 PCs in the computer center and other buildings on campus. All residence halls are wired to accept 2 PCs per room. All residence halls have computer labs. All students may access the system 24 hours a day. There are no time limits. The fee is $100. It is strongly recommended that all students have a personal computer.

Graduates: In 2001, 339 bachelor's degrees were awarded. The most popular majors were business administration (26%), education (9%), and English (8%). In an average class, 68% graduate in 4 years, 77% in 5 years, and 79% in 6 years.

Admissions Contact: DeeDee Barnes Bruns, VP for Admission and Financial Aid. A video is available. E-mail: *dbruns@bsc.edu*
Web: *www.bsc.edu*

CONCORDIA COLLEGE

Selma, AL 36701 — R-4
(334) 874-5700; Fax: (334) 874-5755

Full-time: 173 men, 457 women	**Faculty:** 17
Part-time: 17 men, 111 women	**Ph.D.s:** 53%
Graduate: none	**Student/Faculty:** 37 to 1
Year: semesters	**Tuition:** $5707
Application Deadline: August 8	**Room & Board:** $3600
Freshman Class: 366 enrolled	
SAT I: n/av	**ACT:** required

NONCOMPETITIVE

Concordia College, founded in 1922, is a historically black institution, where the christian faith as taught from the Holy Scriptures and subscribed to by the Lutheran Church-Missouri Synod is the foundation and guide for all programs, activities, and relationships. The library contains 58,814 volumes, 4405 microform items, and 1831 audiovisual forms/CDs, and subscribes to 168 periodicals. Computerized library services include the card catalog, interlibrary loans, and database searching. Special learning facilities include a learning resource center. The 22-acre campus is in a small town 50 miles west of Montgomery. Including residence halls, there are 13 buildings.

Student Life: 89% of undergraduates are from Alabama. Others are from 16 states and 6 foreign countries. 93% are African American. 56% are Baptist; 17% claim no religious affiliation.

Housing: 350 students can be accommodated in college housing, which includes single-sex dormitories. On-campus housing is guaranteed for all 4 years. 69% of students commute. Alcohol is not permitted. All students may keep cars.

Activities: There are no fraternities or sororities. There are 11 groups on campus, including cheerleading, choir, drama, international, religious, and student government. Popular campus events include Spiritual Enrichment Week.

Sports: There are 3 intercollegiate sports for men and 2 for women, and 3 intramural sports for men and 2 for women. Facilities include a gym, a swimming pool, a health and fitness center, and a game room.
Disabled Students: 80% of the campus is accessible. Wheelchair ramps, elevators, special parking, specially equipped rest rooms, lowered drinking fountains, and lowered telephones are available.
Services: Counseling and information services are available, as is tutoring in most subjects. There is remedial math, reading, and writing.
Campus Safety and Security: Measures include informal discussions, lighted pathways/sidewalks, and security guards and security gates.
Programs of Study: CC confers the B.A. degree. Associate degrees are also awarded. Bachelor's degrees are awarded in BUSINESS (business administration and management), EDUCATION (early childhood and elementary). Education is the strongest academically and has the largest enrollment.
Required: To graduate, students must complete 126 to 137 credit hours, depending on the major, with a minium 2.0 GPA and pass a comprehensive exam. General education requirements include 18 hours of humanities, 12 of social sciences, 9 of math, 6 of religion, 3 each of computer science and health/phys ed, and 1 of orientation to college.
Special: CC offers internships, a Lutheran teacher diploma program, and cross-registration with other schools in the Concordia University system. There is 1 national honor society and a freshman honors program.
Faculty/Classroom: 59% of faculty are male; 41%, female. All teach undergraduates. The average class size in an introductory lecture is 25; in a laboratory, 15; and in a regular course, 30.
Admissions: 4 freshmen graduated first in their class.
Requirements: The ACT is required. A GPA of 2.0 is required. AP and CLEP credits are accepted. Important factors in the admissions decision are advanced placement or honor courses, evidence of special talent, and leadership record.
Procedure: Freshmen are admitted fall and spring. There is a deferred admissions plan. Applications should be filed by August 8 for fall entry and January 15 for spring entry. The college accepts all applicants. Notification is sent August. The fall 2001 application fee was $10.
Transfer: 122 transfer students enrolled in 2001-2002. Courses completed with a passing grade of C or better at an accredited postsecondary institution will be accepted for transfer, but only work at Concordia is included in the cumultive GPA. 36 credits of the last 40 must be completed at CC. 126 to 137 credits are required for the bachelor's degree.
Visiting: There are regularly scheduled orientations for prospective students. There are guides for informal visits and visitors may sit in on classes and stay overnight. To schedule a visit, contact Evelyn Pickens, Director of Enrollment Management at E-Mail:
epickens@concordiaselma.edu.
Financial Aid: In 2001-2002, all students received some form of financial aid. Including need-based aid. The average freshman award was $4410. 15% of undergraduates work part time. Average annual earnings from campus work are $700. The FAFSA is required. The fall application deadline is April 15.
International Students: There are 33 international students enrolled. They must take the college's own test.
Computers: Students may access the network in the computer labs, in the library, or on their own computers. Approximately 100 terminals are available for student use. All students may access the system. There are no time limits. The fee is $10.
Graduates: In 2001, 11 bachelor's degrees were awarded.
Admissions Contact: Gwendolyn Moore, Acting Director of Admissions. A video is available. E-mail: *gmoore@concordiaselma.edu*
Web: *www.concordiaselma.edu*

FAULKNER UNIVERSITY C-4
Montgomery, AL 36109-3398 (334) 386-7200
(800) 879-9816; Fax: (334) 386-7137

Full-time: 678 men, 815 women	**Faculty:** 46
Part-time: 231 men, 574 women	**Ph.D.s:** 62%
Graduate: 155 men, 146 women	**Student/Faculty:** 26 to 1
Year: semesters, summer session	**Tuition:** $8700
Application Deadline: open	**Room & Board:** $4300
Freshman Class: 540 applied, 490 accepted, 281 enrolled	
ACT: 20	**COMPETITIVE**

Faulkner University, founded in 1942, is a private, multicampus university affiliated with the Church of Christ, offering undergraduate programs in Bible studies, business, education, and liberal arts and sciences. There are 4 undergraduate and 2 graduate schools. The 2 libraries contain 90,358 volumes, 4060 microform items, and 436 audiovisual forms/CDs, and subscribe to 550 periodicals. Computerized library services include the card catalog, interlibrary loans, and database searching. Special learning facilities include a learning resource center and a stellar observatory. The 92-acre campus is in an urban area. Including residence halls, there are 18 buildings.
Student Life: 89% of undergraduates are from Alabama. Others are from 19 states, 3 foreign countries, and Canada. 92% are from public schools. 61% are white; 38%, African American. Most are Protestant. The average age of freshmen is 19; all undergraduates, 28. 50% do not continue beyond their first year.
Housing: 403 students can be accommodated in college housing, which includes single-sex dormitories and on-campus apartments. On-campus housing is available on a first-come, first-served basis. Priority is given to out-of-town students. Alcohol is not permitted. All students may keep cars.
Activities: There are 4 local fraternities and 4 local sororities. There are 11 groups on campus, including cheerleading, chorus, drama, literary magazine, musical theater, newspaper, religious, social, social service, student government, and yearbook. Popular campus events include the Annual Bible Lectureship, Jamboree, and Fall Visitation Weekend.
Sports: There are 3 intercollegiate sports for men and 3 for women, and 6 intramural sports for men and 6 for women. Facilities include a gym, a weight room, baseball and softball fields, and lighted tennis courts.
Disabled Students: All of the campus is accessible. Wheelchair ramps, elevators, special parking, and specially equipped rest rooms are available. Special needs are met.
Services: Counseling and information services are available, as is tutoring in some subjects, including basic math, English, and reading comprehension. There is remedial math, reading, and writing.
Campus Safety and Security: Measures include 24-hour foot and vehicle patrol, informal discussions, pamphlets/posters/films, and lighted pathways/sidewalks.
Programs of Study: Faulkner confers B.A. and B.S. degrees. Associate, master's, and doctoral degrees are also awarded. Bachelor's degrees are awarded in BIOLOGICAL SCIENCE (biology/biological science), BUSINESS (business administration and management, business data processing, personnel management, and sports management), COMMUNICATIONS AND THE ARTS (English), EDUCATION (elementary, physical, and secondary), SOCIAL SCIENCE (biblical studies, liberal arts/general studies, and prelaw).
Required: Students must complete a 52-semester-hour core curriculum, including courses in Bible, history, social science, English composition, literature, art/music appreciation, speech communication, physical and natural science, math, computer literacy, and phys ed. B.A. students must take 2 semesters of foreign language. At least 120 semester hours with a minimum GPA of 2.0 are required to graduate.
Special: A second bachelor's degree in a separate major may be completed with a minimum of 24 semester hours earned beyond the first degree. Cross-registration with Auburn University at Montgomery and Huntingdon College, dual majors, credit for life/military/work experience, and nondegree study are offered. Internships in education, psychology, criminal justice, Bible, and sports management are available, as are accelerated degree programs in some majors. There are 4 national honor societies, a freshman honors program, and all departments have honors programs.
Faculty/Classroom: 61% of faculty are male; 39%, female. All teach undergraduates. No introductory courses are taught by graduate students. The average class size in an introductory lecture is 27; in a laboratory, 15; and in a regular course, 20.
Admissions: 91% of the 2001-2002 applicants were accepted.
Requirements: The ACT is required and the SAT I is recommended, with minimum composite scores of 735 on the SAT I or 17 on the ACT. Candidates must be graduates of an accredited secondary school, or have the GED equivalent, with a minimum of 15 academic units, including 3 in English. A GPA of 2.0 is required. AP and CLEP credits are accepted. Applications are accepted on computer disk and on-line at *www.faulkner.edu.*
Procedure: Freshmen are admitted to all sessions. Application deadlines are open. The application fee is $10.
Transfer: 68 transfer students enrolled in 2001-2002. Applicants must be in good academic standing from another accredited college. 30 credits of 120 must be completed at Faulkner.
Visiting: There are regularly scheduled orientations for prospective students. There are guides for informal visits and visitors may sit in on classes and stay overnight. To schedule a visit, contact the Admissions Office at *admissions@faulkner.ed.*
Financial Aid: 59% of undergraduates work part time. Average annual earnings from campus work are $1200. The FAFSA or FFS and the college's own financial statement are required. The fall application deadline is May 1.
International Students: They must score 450 on the written TOEFL.
Computers: PCs and Macs are available in the computer lab. All students may access the system. There are no time limits and no fees. It is strongly recommended that all students have a personal computer.
Graduates: In 2001, 236 bachelor's degrees were awarded. The most popular majors were business administration (41%), management of human resources (34%), and education (3%).
Admissions Contact: Keith Mock, Director of Admissions.
E-mail: *kmock@faulkner.edu*

HUNTINGDON COLLEGE C-4

Montgomery, AL 36106-2148 (334) 833-4497
(800) 763-0313; Fax: (334) 833-4347

Full-time: 205 men, 372 women	**Faculty:** 46; IIB, --$
Part-time: 13 men, 25 women	**Ph.D.s:** 80%
Graduate: none	**Student/Faculty:** 13 to 1
Year: 4-1-4, summer session	**Tuition:** $12,650
Application Deadline: open	**Room & Board:** $5750
Freshman Class: 579 applied, 473 accepted, 152 enrolled	
SAT I Verbal/Math: 590/580	**ACT:** 24 **VERY COMPETITIVE**

Huntingdon College, founded in 1854, is a private liberal arts institution related to the United Methodist Church. In addition to regional accreditation, Huntingdon has baccalaureate program accreditation with NASM. The library contains 102,074 volumes, 47,443 microform items, and 1517 audiovisual forms/CDs, and subscribes to 391 periodicals. Computerized library services include interlibrary loans and database searching. Special learning facilities include a learning resource center, art gallery, and recital hall and theater. The 58-acre campus is in a suburban area 90 miles south of Birmingham. Including residence halls, there are 18 buildings.

Student Life: 66% of undergraduates are from Alabama. Others are from 24 states, 12 foreign countries, and Canada. 75% are from public schools. 86% are white. 78% are Protestant; 12% claim no religious affiliation; 10% Catholic. The average age of freshmen is 18; all undergraduates, 20. 27% do not continue beyond their first year; 48% remain to graduate.

Housing: 656 students can be accommodated in college housing, which includes coed dormitories. On-campus housing is guaranteed for all 4 years. 72% of students live on campus; of those, 80% remain on campus on weekends. Alcohol is not permitted. All students may keep cars.

Activities: 29% of men belong to 2 national fraternities; 32% of women belong to 3 national sororities. There are 50 groups on campus, including art, cheerleading, choir, chorale, chorus, computers, dance, drama, ethnic, forensics, gay, honors, international, jazz band, literary magazine, musical theater, newspaper, opera, photography, political, professional, religious, social, social service, student government, and yearbook. Popular campus events include Stallworth Lecture Series, Performing Arts Series, and Madrigal Dinner.

Sports: There are 6 intercollegiate sports for men and 6 for women, and 16 intramural sports for men and 16 for women. Facilities include a student center with a 1500-seat gym for volleyball, basketball, and badminton, a swimming pool, weight and training rooms, Ping-Pong tables, pool tables, video games, 2 dance studios, and sports medicine facilities. There are also outdoor tennis courts, softball, baseball, and soccer fields, and an outdoor volleyball court.

Disabled Students: 80% of the campus is accessible. Wheelchair ramps, elevators, special parking, specially equipped rest rooms, special class scheduling, lowered drinking fountains, and lowered telephones are available.

Services: Counseling and information services are available, as is tutoring in most subjects. There is also a reading and writing lab.

Campus Safety and Security: Measures include 24-hour foot and vehicle patrol, self-defense education, escort service, and informal discussions. There are pamphlets/posters/films, emergency telephones, lighted pathways/sidewalks, controlled access to residence halls, and weather alert broadcasts.

Programs of Study: Huntingdon confers the B.A. degree. Associate degrees are also awarded. Bachelor's degrees are awarded in AGRICULTURE (soil science), BIOLOGICAL SCIENCE (biology/biological science), BUSINESS (accounting, and business administration and management), COMMUNICATIONS AND THE ARTS (art, arts administration/management, communications, dance, dramatic arts, English, music, musical theater, and speech/debate/rhetoric), COMPUTER AND PHYSICAL SCIENCE (chemistry, computer science, digital arts/technology, and mathematics), EDUCATION (art, athletic training, dance, music, and physical), ENGINEERING AND ENVIRONMENTAL DESIGN (computer graphics), HEALTH PROFESSIONS (exercise science, and prepharmacy), SOCIAL SCIENCE (American studies, European studies, history, international studies, political science/government, psychology, public administration, public affairs, religion, and religious education). Biology, chemistry, and psychology are the strongest academically. Biology, business, and education are the largest.

Required: Huntindon's core curriculum includes a 12 hour liberal arts symposium, up to 9 hours of foreign languages, a 3-hour rhetoric seminar, and a 3-hour senior captone course. Additionally, students take 12 hours of social and self-awareness, and 9 hours each of aesthetic expression and science and technology. Students must maintain a minimum GAP of 2.0 over 124 credits for the B.A. Major requirements range from 30 to 42 hours.

Special: The Huntingdon plan includes an opportunity for travel/study experiences offered as part of regular educational costs, hands-on learning experiences in every program of study, dual majors, internships, and co-op programs in business and computer science. The public affairs trisubject major combines politics with 2 other areas, including history, philosophy, psychology, and communications. Cross-registration is available with Auburn University Montgomery, Faulkner University, and the Marine Environmental Sciences Consortium in Dauphin Island. There are 14 national honor societies and 13 departmental honors programs.

Faculty/Classroom: 67% of faculty are male; 33%, female. The average class size in an introductory lecture is 16; in a laboratory, 13; and in a regular course, 13.

Admissions: 82% of the 2001-2002 applicants were accepted. The SAT I scores for the 2001-2002 freshman class were: Verbal--7% below 500, 46% between 500 and 599, 39% between 600 and 700, and 8% above 700; Math--30% below 500, 31% between 500 and 599, and 39% between 600 and 700. The ACT scores were 17% below 21, 25% between 21 and 23, 24% between 24 and 26, 19% between 27 and 28, and 15% above 28. 73% of the current freshmen were in the top fifth of their class; 93% were in the top two fifths. 12 freshmen graduated first in their class in a recent year.

Requirements: The SAT I or ACT is required. In addition, applicants should have completed 4 years of high school English, 3 credits each in math and history, and 2 credits each of science, foreign language, and humanities. An interview is recommended. A portfolio or audition may be required. A GPA of 2.25 is required. AP and CLEP credits are accepted. Important factors in the admissions decision are evidence of special talent, leadership record, and advanced placement or honor courses. Students can apply on-line via CollegeView and by using the Apply CD-ROM.

Procedure: Freshmen are admitted fall and spring. Entrance exams should be taken in the spring of the junior year. There is an early admissions plan. Application deadlines are open. The application fee is $25.

Transfer: 38 transfer students enrolled in a recent year. High school and college transcripts are required. An interview is recommended. 31 credits of 124 must be completed at Huntingdon.

Visiting: There are regularly scheduled orientations for prospective students, consisting of class visitation, a campus tour, a meeting with an admissions counselor, and student panel, financial aid, and faculty presentations. There are guides for informal visits and visitors may sit in on classes and stay overnight. To schedule a visit, contact the Office of Admission.

Financial Aid: In a recent year, 98% of all freshmen and 93% of continuing students received some form of financial aid. 61% of all students received need-based aid. The average freshman award was $9911. Of that total, scholarships or need-based grants averaged $6606 ($10,500 maximum); loans averaged $2348 ($6625 maximum); work contracts averaged $412 ($1236 maximum); and Alabama Student Grant averaged $545 ($768 maximum). 79% of undergraduates work part time. Average annual earnings from campus work are $850. The average financial indebtedness of the 2001 graduate was $15,262. The FAFSA and the college's own financial statement are required. The fall application deadline is April 15.

International Students: There were 28 international students enrolled in a recent year. The school actively recruits these students. They must score 500 on the written TOEFL. The SAT I or ACT is required only for students whose first language is English. A score of 930 is required on the SAT I.

Computers: The mainframe is a network of powerful PCs. All freshmen are provided a Gateway 2000 computer, which they may keep upon graduation. The computers include Windows 98, Netscape Communicator, Corel Word Perfect Suite 8.0, Oxford Biblical Library, and other required software. All residence hall rooms, classrooms, and faculty and administrative offices have direct access to the Internet. All students may access the system 24 hours a day, 7 days a week. There are no time limits and no fees.

Graduates: In a recent year, 122 bachelor's degrees were awarded. The most popular majors were business administration (13%), English (10%), and human performance and kinesiolo (8%). In an average class, 1% graduate in 3 years, 45% in 4 years, 66% in 5 years, and 70% in 6 years. 30 companies recruited on campus in 2000-2001. Of the 2000 graduating class, 45% were enrolled in graduate school within 6 months of graduation and 55% were employed.

Admissions Contact: Laura Duncan, Director of Admission.
E-mail: *admiss@huntingdon.edu* Web: *www.huntingdon.edu*

JACKSONVILLE STATE UNIVERSITY
D-2

Jacksonville, AL 36265

(256) 782-5400
(800) 231-5291; Fax: (256) 782-5121

Full-time: 2319 men, 3142 women
Part-time: 637 men, 911 women
Graduate: 438 men, 1031 women
Year: semesters, summer session
Application Deadline: open
Freshman Class: 2300 applied, 2009 accepted, 1077 enrolled
ACT: 17
Faculty: 268; IIA, --$
Ph.D.s: 70%
Student/Faculty: 20 to 1
Tuition: $2950 ($5890)
Room & Board: $3618
LESS COMPETITIVE

Jacksonville State University, founded in 1883, is a public institution offering programs in business, arts and sciences, criminal justice, education, and nursing. There are 4 undergraduate schools and 1 graduate school. In addition to regional accreditation, JSU has baccalaureate program accreditation with AACSB, CSWE, NASAD, NASM, NCATE, and NLN. The library contains 645,311 volumes, 1,273,105 microform items, and 32,875 audiovisual forms/CDs, and subscribes to 1695 periodicals. Computerized library services include the card catalog, interlibrary loans, and database searching. Special learning facilities include a learning resource center, a radio station, and a stellar observatory. The 318-acre campus is in a small town 75 miles east of Birmingham. Including residence halls, there are 58 buildings.

Student Life: 85% of undergraduates are from Alabama. Others are from 45 states, 72 foreign countries, and Canada. 85% are from public schools. 74% are white; 22%, African American. The average age of freshmen is 20; all undergraduates, 23. 34% do not continue beyond their first year; 66% remain to graduate.

Housing: 1245 students can be accommodated in college housing, which includes single-sex and coed dormitories, on-campus apartments, off-campus apartments, married-student housing, fraternity houses, and sorority houses. On-campus housing is guaranteed for all 4 years. 67% of students commute. Alcohol is not permitted. All students may keep cars.

Activities: 10% of men belong to 10 national fraternities; 10% of women belong to 9 national sororities. There are 100 groups on campus, including art, band, cheerleading, choir, chorus, computers, dance, drama, drill team, ethnic, honors, international, jazz band, marching band, musical theater, newspaper, pep band, political, professional, radio and TV, religious, social, social service, student government, symphony, and yearbook. Popular campus events include Visitation Day and Parents Day.

Sports: There are 7 intercollegiate sports for men and 7 for women, and 15 intramural sports for men and 15 for women. Facilities include a 15,000-seat football stadium, indoor and outdoor courts, athletic fields, a 5,000-seat indoor gym, an indoor pool, a weight room, and a fitness center.

Disabled Students: 85% of the campus is accessible. Wheelchair ramps, elevators, special parking, specially equipped rest rooms, lowered drinking fountains, and lowered telephones are available.

Services: Counseling and information services are available, as is tutoring in most subjects. There is remedial math, reading, and writing.

Campus Safety and Security: Measures include 24-hour foot and vehicle patrol, escort service, informal discussions, and pamphlets/posters/films. There are lighted pathways/sidewalks.

Programs of Study: JSU confers B.A., B.S., B.F.A., B.S.Ed., and B.S.W. degrees. Master's and doctoral degrees are also awarded. Bachelor's degrees are awarded in BIOLOGICAL SCIENCE (biology/biological science), BUSINESS (accounting, banking and finance, and marketing/retailing/merchandising), COMMUNICATIONS AND THE ARTS (communications, dramatic arts, English, and music), COMPUTER AND PHYSICAL SCIENCE (chemistry, computer science, mathematics, and physics), EDUCATION (early childhood, elementary, health, home economics, music, secondary, and special), HEALTH PROFESSIONS (nursing), SOCIAL SCIENCE (criminal justice, economics, geography, history, political science/government, psychology, social work, and sociology). Education is the strongest academically and is the largest.

Required: All students are required to complete a core curriculum of 46 semester hours, including 15 hours in fine arts and humanities, 8 each in communications and natural sciences, 6 each in analysis and social sciences, and 3 in wellness. English competency and courses in computer literacy are required. A total of 128 semester hours, with a minimum GPA of 2.2, is required in order to graduate.

Special: Co-op programs with major area employees are available. JSU has cross-registration with the Marine Environmental Sciences Consortium and internships in education, political science, communication, journalism, and criminal justice. Work-study programs, dual majors in most programs, and credit for military experience are offered. There are 8 national honor societies.

Faculty/Classroom: 56% of faculty are male; 44%, female. 99% teach undergraduates, 1% do research, and 70% do both. No introductory courses are taught by graduate students. The average class size in an introductory lecture is 50; in a laboratory, 25; and in a regular course, 25.

Admissions: 87% of the 2001-2002 applicants were accepted. The ACT scores for the 2001-2002 freshman class were: 71% below 21, and 29% between 21 and 23.

Requirements: The SAT I or ACT is required. Applicants should be graduates of an accredited high school; the GED is also accepted. 19 on the ACT or 900 on the SAT I is required for unconditional admission; 16 to 18 on the ACT or 750 to 890 on the SAT I is required for conditional admission. AP and CLEP credits are accepted. Students may apply on-line on the JSU home page.

Procedure: Freshmen are admitted to all sessions. Application deadlines are open. The application fee is $20. Notification is sent on a rolling basis.

Transfer: 764 transfer students enrolled in 2001-2002. Transfer applicants must be eligible to return to the last institution attended. 32 credits of 128 must be completed at JSU.

Visiting: There are regularly scheduled orientations for prospective students, consisting of 2-day orientations scheduled during the summer. There are guides for informal visits. To schedule a visit, contact Carra McWhorter, Senior Admissions Counselor, Information Center.

Financial Aid: In 2001-2002, 80% of all freshmen and 78% of continuing students received some form of financial aid. 66% of freshmen and 68% of continuing students received need-based aid. The average freshman award was $3500. Of that total, scholarships or need-based grants averaged $2517 ($3440 maximum); loans averaged $2000 ($2625 maximum); and work contracts averaged $1500 ($2500 maximum). 55% of undergraduates work part time. Average annual earnings from campus work are $2500. The average financial indebtedness of the 2001 graduate was $17,125. The FAFSA is required. The fall application deadline is March 15.

International Students: There are 194 international students enrolled. They must score 500 on the written TOEFL. The SAT I or ACT may be substituted.

Computers: The mainframe is an IBM 2003 Model 207. The mainframe is accessed via computer labs at various locations on campus. All students may access the system during specific lab hours. There are no time limits and no fees.

Graduates: In 2001, 1069 bachelor's degrees were awarded. The most popular majors were elementary education (10%), nursing (9%), and criminal justice (9%). 150 companies recruited on campus in 2000-2001.

Admissions Contact: Martha Mitchell and Kathy Cambron, Dean of Admissions and Records. E-mail: *info@jsucc.jsu.edu*
Web: *www.jsu.edu*

JUDSON COLLEGE
B-3

Marion, AL 36756

(334) 683-5110
(800) 447-9472; Fax: (334) 683-5158

Full-time: 6 men, 283 women
Part-time: 13 men, 43 women
Graduate: none
Year: semesters, summer session
Application Deadline: open
Freshman Class: 335 applied, 271 accepted, 102 enrolled
ACT: 23
Faculty: 31
Ph.D.s: 68%
Student/Faculty: 9 to 1
Tuition: $8490
Room & Board: $5300
COMPETITIVE

Judson College, founded in 1838, is a private women's liberal arts college affiliated with the Alabama Baptist Convention. In addition to regional accreditation, Judson has baccalaureate program accreditation with NASM. The library contains 55,000 volumes, 1943 microform items, and 5380 audiovisual forms/CDs, and subscribes to 223 periodicals. Computerized library services include the card catalog, interlibrary loans, and database searching. Special learning facilities include a learning resource center and the Alabama Women's Hall of Fame. The 80-acre campus is in a small town 27 miles west of Selma. Including residence halls, there are 18 buildings.

Student Life: 83% of undergraduates are from Alabama. Others are from 21 states and 2 foreign countries. 84% are from public schools. 86% are white; 11% African American. Most are Protestant. The average age of freshmen is 18; all undergraduates, 24. 40% do not continue beyond their first year.

Housing: 266 students can be accommodated in college housing, which includes dormitories. On-campus housing is guaranteed for all 4 years. 63% of students live on campus; of those, 33% remain on campus on weekends. Alcohol is not permitted. All students may keep cars.

Activities: There are no sororities. There are 25 groups on campus, including band, cheerleading, choir, chorale, chorus, computers, dance, drama, environmental, honors, literary magazine, marching band, musical theater, newspaper, orchestra, photography, political, professional, religious, social, social service, student government, woodwind ensemble, and yearbook. Popular campus events include Winter Ball, Junior-Sophomore Dance, and Hockey Day.

Sports: Facilities include an indoor swimming pool, riding stables and a riding arena, tennis courts, a wellness center, a gym, an aerobics room, a weight training facility, a hockey field, and a game room.

Disabled Students: 50% of the campus is accessible. Elevators, special parking, specially equipped rest rooms, lowered drinking fountains, and lowered telephones are available.

Services: Counseling and information services are available, as is tutoring in most subjects. There is remedial writing.

Campus Safety and Security: Measures include 24-hour foot and vehicle patrol, self-defense education, informal discussions, and pamphlets/posters/films. There are emergency telephones and lighted pathways/sidewalks.

Programs of Study: Judson confers B.A. and B.S. degrees. Bachelor's degrees are awarded in BIOLOGICAL SCIENCE (biology/biological science), BUSINESS (business administration and management and fashion merchandising), COMMUNICATIONS AND THE ARTS (applied music, art, English, languages, and music), COMPUTER AND PHYSICAL SCIENCE (chemistry and mathematics), EDUCATION (elementary, English, mathematics, middle school, music, science, secondary, and social studies), SOCIAL SCIENCE (criminal justice, history, interdisciplinary studies, physical fitness/movement, psychology, and religion). Biology, education, and psychology are the strongest academically. Biology, elementary education, and English are the largest.

Required: All students are required to complete courses in women's studies, multicultural studies, speech, religion, social science, math, humanities, computer literacy, and health/phys ed. A total of 128 credit hours, including at least 30 in the major, and a minimum GPA of 2.0 (2.5 for education majors) are required to graduate. B.A. students must also complete at least 6 hours of foreign languages at the 200 level or above; B.S. students must complete at least 12 hours of math or science electives in addition to the core competency.

Special: Cross-registration with the Marion Military Institute is available for ROTC students. B.A.-B.S. degrees are offered in criminal justice, fashion merchandising, math, business, biology, business and management information systems, psychology, and chemistry. Study abroad in 3 countries, dual majors, an interdisciplinary major, a 3-2 engineering degree with the University of Alabama, work-study programs, and internships are offered. There are preprofessional programs in health, engineering, and law. The Adult Studies Program offers credit for prior learning experience and provides individually paced instruction leading to a baccalaureate degree. There are 7 national honor societies and 15 departmental honors programs.

Faculty/Classroom: 56% of faculty are male; 44%, female. All teach undergraduates. The average class size in an introductory lecture is 20; in a laboratory, 10; and in a regular course, 7.

Admissions: 81% of the 2001-2002 applicants were accepted. The SAT I scores for the 2001-2002 freshman class were: Verbal--25% below 500, 50% between 500 and 599, and 25% between 600 and 700; Math -75% below 500, and 25% between 500 and 599. The ACT scores were 33% below 21, 29% between 21 and 23, 22% between 24 and 26, 4% between 27 and 28, and 12% above 28. 39% of the current freshmen were in the top fifth of their class; 73% were in the top two fifths. 3 freshmen graduated first in their class.

Requirements: The SAT I or ACT is required, with a minimum composite score of 18 on the ACT. Applicants should have completed 17 high school credits, including 4 in English, with at least a 2.0 GPA. Non-high school graduates must provide the GED equivalent. An interview is required. AP and CLEP credits are accepted. Important factors in the admissions decision are advanced placement or honor courses, evidence of special talent, and leadership record. Applications are accepted on-line.

Procedure: Freshmen are admitted fall and winter. Entrance exams should be taken in the spring of the junior year. There is an early admissions plan. Application deadlines are open. The fall 2001 application fee was $25. Notification is sent on a rolling basis.

Transfer: 30 transfer students enrolled in 2001-2002. Transfer students must have a minimum GPA of 2.0 and be eligible to return to the school from which they transfer. 32 credits of 128 must be completed at Judson.

Visiting: There are regularly scheduled orientations for prospective students, consisting of 2 college Preview Days, 1 in June and 1 in August. There are guides for informal visits and visitors may sit in on classes and stay overnight. To schedule a visit, contact Admissions.

Financial Aid: In 2001-2002, all students received some form of financial aid. 80% of freshmen and 72% of continuing students received need-based aid. The average freshman award was $9666. Of that total, scholarships or need-based grants averaged $6424 ($8150 maximum); loans averaged $1192 ($2625 maximum); work contracts averaged $1500 ($1700 maximum); and Parent Plus averaged $5547 ($10,000 maximum). 55% of undergraduates work part time. Average annual earnings from campus work are $1000. The average financial indebtedness of the 2001 graduate was $11,398. The FAFSA, the college's own financial statement, and the state aid form are required. The fall application deadline is March 1.

International Students: There are 2 international students enrolled. They must score 500 on the written TOEFL or 173 on the electronic version.

Computers: There is 1 general computer center with 24 PCs available for student use. Access is provided to the campus network and the Internet. The library has 5 PCs for general use. Additionally, specialized computer centers for music and technical writing students bring the total to 41 PCs. All students may access the system 8 A.M. to 1 A.M. 7 days a week. There are no time limits and no fees.

Graduates: In 2001, 50 bachelor's degrees were awarded. The most popular majors were business (18%), psychology (18%), and biology (16%). In an average class, 20% graduate in 3 years, 90% in 4 years, 99% in 5 years, and 100% in 6 years. Of the 2000 graduating class, 22% were enrolled in graduate school within 6 months of graduation and 73% were employed.

Admissions Contact: Charlotte Clements, Director of Admissions.
E-mail: *admissions@future.judson.edu* Web: *home.judson.edu*

MILES COLLEGE C-2
Birmingham, AL 35208 (205) 929-1656
(800) 445-0708; (205) 929-1668

Full-time: 1400 men and women	**Faculty:** 46
Part-time: none	**Ph.D.s:** 50%
Graduate: none	**Student/Faculty:** 30 to 1
Year: semesters, summer session	**Tuition:** $4770
Application Deadline: open	**Room & Board:** $3100
Freshman Class: n/av	
SAT I or ACT: required	**NONCOMPETITIVE**

Miles College, founded in 1908, is a private institution affiliated with and controlled by the Christian Methodist Episcopal Church. The college offers undergraduate programs in the liberal arts and sciences, business, and education. Figures given in above capsule are approximate. There are 5 undergraduate schools. The library contains 180,000 volumes and 850 microform items, and subscribes to 250 periodicals. Special learning facilities include a learning resource center and an Afro-American materials center, and a media center. The 35-acre campus is in an urban area 7 miles from downtown Birmingham. Including residence halls, there are 17 buildings.

Student Life: 98% are African American. The average age of freshmen is 18; all undergraduates, 22. 15% do not continue beyond their first year.

Housing: 490 students can be accommodated in college housing, which includes single-sex dormitories. On-campus housing is available on a first-come, first-served basis. Priority is given to out-of-town students. Alcohol is not permitted. All students may keep cars.

Activities: 15% of men belong to 4 local and 4 national fraternities; 15% of women belong to 4 local and 4 national sororities. There are 12 groups on campus, including choir, drama, ethnic, honors, international, literary magazine, newspaper, professional, radio and TV, religious, student government, and yearbook. Popular campus events include Senior Class Day, Spring Festival, and Honors Day.

Sports: There are 6 intercollegiate sports for men and 4 for women, and 5 intramural sports for men and 5 for women. Facilities include a 2000-seat football field, a 1500-seat gym, a weight room, and a baseball field.

Services: Counseling and information services are available, as is tutoring in every subject. There is remedial math, reading, and writing. Miles offers a Student Support Services Program for students with an academically challenged developmental background.

Programs of Study: Miles confers B.A., B.S., and B.S.W. degrees. Associate degrees are also awarded. Bachelor's degrees are awarded in BIOLOGICAL SCIENCE (biology/biological science), BUSINESS (accounting and business administration and management), COMMUNICATIONS AND THE ARTS (communications, English, and language arts), COMPUTER AND PHYSICAL SCIENCE (chemistry, computer science, and mathematics), EDUCATION (early childhood, elementary, science, secondary, and social science), ENGINEERING AND ENVIRONMENTAL DESIGN (environmental science and preengineering), HEALTH PROFESSIONS (predentistry, premedicine, and preveterinary science), SOCIAL SCIENCE (political science/government and social work). Business is the strongest academically. Early childhood and elementary education are the largest.

Required: To graduate, all students must complete a minimum of 51 hours of general education requirements, including the 33-hour freshman studies program. A minimum of 124 credit hours is required for a bachelor's degree, with a minimum GPA of 2.0 in the major. All students must pass English proficiency and exit exams.

Special: Miles offers co-op programs in all majors, internships, federal work-study, and cross-registration with the University of Alabama at Birmingham and other area colleges and universities. There are cooperative programs in allied health sciences with the University of Alabama at Birmingham, and in engineering, physics, veterinary medicine, and Asian studies. There is 1 national honor society, and a freshman honors program.

Faculty/Classroom: All teach undergraduates.

Requirements: The SAT I or ACT is required. In addition, students should be graduates of an accredited high school or hold a GED. A personal interview is recommended. A GPA of 2.0 is required.

Procedure: Freshmen are admitted to all sessions. Application deadlines are open. The fall 2001 application fee was $25.

Transfer: 32 credits of 124 must be completed at Miles.

Visiting: There are guides for informal visits and visitors may sit in on classes. To schedule a visit, contact Admissions.

Financial Aid: Miles is a member of CSS. The FAFSA is required. The fall priority application deadline is April 15.

International Students: They must score 450 on the written TOEFL or take the MELAB and also take the SAT I or the ACT.

Computers: All students may access the system. There are no time limits.

Admissions Contact: Admissions Director. A video is available.
Web: *www.miles.edu*

OAKWOOD COLLEGE C-1
Huntsville, AL 35896 (256) 726-7000
(800) 824-5312; Fax: (256) 726-7154

Full-time: 683 men, 899 women	**Faculty:** 96; IIB, --$
Part-time: 90 men, 106 women	**Ph.D.s:** 54%
Graduate: none	**Student/Faculty:** 16 to 1
Year: semesters, summer session	**Tuition:** $9420
Application Deadline: open	**Room & Board:** $5484
Freshman Class: 847 applied, 464 accepted, 399 enrolled	
SAT I Verbal/Math: 484/454	**ACT:** 18 **COMPETITIVE**

Oakwood College, founded in 1896, is a private, historically black, Seventh-day Adventist institution offering undergraduate programs in business and education, humanities, natural sciences and math, religion and theology, and social sciences. In addition to regional accreditation, Oakwood has baccalaureate program accreditation with ACBSP, ADA, CSWE, and NCATE. The library contains 125,373 volumes, 2140 microform items, and 4816 audiovisual forms/CDs, and subscribes to 630 periodicals. Computerized library services include the card catalog and database searching. Special learning facilities include a learning resource center, radio station, and a black history museum. The 105-acre campus is in a suburban area 5 miles northwest of Huntsville. Including residence halls, there are 30 buildings.

Student Life: 79% of undergraduates are from out of state, mostly the South. Others are from 39 states, 22 foreign countries, and Canada. 52% are from public schools. 79% are African American; 12% foreign nationals. The average age of freshmen is 19; all undergraduates, 23. 27% do not continue beyond their first year.

Housing: 1173 students can be accommodated in college housing, which includes single-sex dormitories and married-student housing. On-campus housing is available on a first-come, first-served basis. Priority is given to out-of-town students. 71% of students live on campus; of those, 98% remain on campus on weekends. Alcohol is not permitted. Upperclassmen may keep cars.

Activities: There are no fraternities or sororities. There are 20 groups on campus, including band, choir, chorale, drama, honors, international, newspaper, professional, radio and TV, religious, student government, and yearbook. Popular campus events include convocations, the arts and lecture series, and Centennial.

Sports: There are 4 intramural sports for men and 3 for women. Facilities include a gym, a skating rink, an Olympic-size pool, tennis courts, playing fields, racquetball courts, and a weight room.

Disabled Students: 80% of the campus is accessible. Wheelchair ramps, elevators, special parking, and specially equipped rest rooms are available.

Services: Counseling and information services are available, as is tutoring in most subjects. There is remedial math, reading, and writing. Testing, counseling, and developmental guidance services are available through the counseling center.

Campus Safety and Security: Measures include 24-hour foot and vehicle patrol, escort service, informal discussions, and pamphlets/posters/films. There are lighted pathways/sidewalks.

Programs of Study: Oakwood confers B.A., B.S., B.B.A., B.M., and B.S.W. degrees. Associate degrees are also awarded. Bachelor's degrees are awarded in BIOLOGICAL SCIENCE (biochemistry and biology/biological science), BUSINESS (accounting and business administration and management), COMMUNICATIONS AND THE ARTS (communications, English, French, music, music business management, music performance, and Spanish), COMPUTER AND PHYSICAL SCIENCE (chemistry, computer mathematics, computer science, information sciences and systems, mathematics, and natural sciences), EDUCATION (business, elementary, English, home economics, mathematics, music, physical, science, and social science), HEALTH PROFESSIONS (medical technology and nursing), SOCIAL SCIENCE (dietetics, family/consumer studies, history, home economics, human development, international studies, ministries, physical fitness/movement, psychology, religion, religious education, and social work). Biochemistry, chemistry, and nursing are the strongest academically. Business and biology are the largest.

Required: To graduate, students must complete 128 semester hours, including 30 in the major and 40 in upper-division courses, with a GPA of 2.0. Regular chapel attendance is required. All students must complete a liberal arts core and must meet English oral and written proficiency requirements.

Special: Students may cross-register with Alabama A&M, Athens State, or the University of Alabama at Huntsville. The college offers a student missionary abroad program as well as a study abroad program through the Adventist College Consortium. Internships, work-study, dual majors, independent study, life experience credit, and pass/fail options are also available. A second bachelor's degree is offered to students completing at least 160 semester credits. There is 1 national honor society and 2 departmental honors programs.

Faculty/Classroom: 51% of faculty are male; 49%, female. All teach undergraduates. The average class size in an introductory lecture is 30; in a laboratory, 30; and in a regular course, 40.

Admissions: 55% of the 2001-2002 applicants were accepted. The SAT I scores for the 2001-2002 freshman class were: Verbal--57% below 500, 31% between 500 and 599, 11% between 600 and 700, and 1% above 700; Math--64% below 500, 29% between 500 and 599, 6% between 600 and 700, and 1% above 700. The ACT scores were 68% below 21, 19% between 21 and 23, 10% between 24 and 26, 2% between 27 and 28, and 1% above 28. 38% of the current freshmen were in the top fifth of their class; 58% were in the top two fifths. 1 freshman graduated first in the class.

Requirements: The SAT I or ACT is recommended. In addition, applicants should be high school graduates with a minimum GPA of 2.0 and at least 11 academic units, distributed as follows: 4 in English, 2 each in math, science, and social studies, and 1 in typing. The GED is accepted. 2 character references are required. Students with GPAs between 1.7 and 2.0 may be admitted on probation. Applicants admitted without test scores must take the ACT during freshman orientation. A GPA of 2.0 is required. AP and CLEP credits are accepted. Important factors in the admissions decision are recommendations by school officials, ability to finance college education, and leadership record.

Procedure: Freshmen are admitted to all sessions. Entrance exams should be taken before high school graduation. There is an early decision plan. Application deadlines are open. The application fee is $20.

Transfer: 79 transfer students enrolled in a recent year. Applicants must submit a college transcript and a statement of honorable dismissal. Grades of C minus or better transfer for credit. 32 credits of 128 must be completed at Oakwood.

Visiting: There are guides for informal visits and visitors may sit in on classes and stay overnight. To schedule a visit, contact Fred Pullins, Enrollment Management at (256) 726-7030.

Financial Aid: Oakwood is a member of CSS. The FAFSA, the college's own financial statement, and student and parent federal income tax returns are required.

International Students: There were 217 international students enrolled in a recent year. They must score 500 on the written TOEFL and also take the college's own test and the SAT I or ACT. Students may take the ACT on campus prior to registration.

Computers: PCs are available in various departmental computer labs. A public computer lab is available in the library. There are no time limits. The fees vary.

Graduates: In a recent year, 225 bachelor's degrees were awarded. The most popular majors were biology (13%), social work (9%), and psychology (8%). 120 companies recruited on campus in a recent year.

Admissions Contact: Fred Pullins, Enrollment Management Director.
E-mail: *admission@oakwood.edu* Web: *www.oakwood.edu*

SAMFORD UNIVERSITY C-2
Birmingham, AL 35229 (205) 726-2871
(800) 888-7218; Fax: (205) 726-2171

Full-time: 988 men, 1691 women	**Faculty:** 166; IIA, av$
Part-time: 73 men, 138 women	**Ph.D.s:** 81%
Graduate: 708 men, 779 women	**Student/Faculty:** 11 to 1
Year: 4-1-4, summer session	**Tuition:** $11,490
Application Deadline: August 1	**Room & Board:** $4850
Freshman Class: 1903 applied, 1675 accepted, 663 enrolled	
SAT I Verbal/Math: 580/550	**ACT:** 25 **VERY COMPETITIVE**

Samford University, founded in 1841, is a private, liberal arts school and maintains a close relationship with the Alabama Baptist Convention. There are 5 undergraduate and 7 graduate schools. In addition to regional accreditation, Samford has baccalaureate program accreditation with AACSB, ACPE, FIDER, NASM, NCATE, and NLN. The 6 libraries contain 437,876 volumes, 905,508 microform items, and 13,574 audiovisual forms/CDs, and subscribe to 3789 periodicals. Computerized library services include the card catalog, interlibrary loans, and database searching. Special learning facilities include a learning resource center, art gallery, planetarium, radio station, TV station, and a global center, and a drug information center. The 180-acre campus is in a suburban area 4 miles south of Birmingham. Including residence halls, there are 62 buildings.

Student Life: 53% of undergraduates are from out of state, mostly the South. Others are from 41 states, 21 foreign countries, and Canada. 62% are from public schools. 90% are white. Most are Protestant. The average age of freshmen is 18; all undergraduates, 21. 16% do not continue beyond their first year.

Housing: 1894 students can be accommodated in college housing, which includes single-sex dormitories, fraternity houses, and sorority houses. On-campus housing is available on a first-come, first-served basis. 65% of students live on campus. Alcohol is not permitted. All students may keep cars.

Activities: 37% of men belong to 7 national fraternities; 44% of women belong to 8 national sororities. There are 133 groups on campus, including band, cheerleading, choir, chorale, chorus, computers, dance, debate, drama, drill team, ethnic, honors, international, jazz band, literary magazine, marching band, musical theater, newspaper, opera, orchestra, pep band, political, professional, radio and TV, religious, social, social service, student government, symphony, and yearbook. Popular campus events include Step Sing and Spring Fling.

Sports: There are 7 intercollegiate sports for men and 8 for women, and 10 intramural sports for men and 10 for women. 59% of men and women participate. Facilities include a 6700-seat stadium, a 4000-seat gym, intramural fields, tennis and racquetball courts, practice fields, baseball/soccer/softball fields, and a swimming pool.

Disabled Students: Most of the campus is accessible to the physically disabled. Wheelchair ramps, elevators, special parking, specially equipped rest rooms, special class scheduling, lowered drinking fountains, lowered telephones, and dormitory rooms with wheelchair access are available.

Services: Counseling and information services are available, as is tutoring in most subjects. There is a reader service for the blind.

Campus Safety and Security: Measures include 24-hour foot and vehicle patrol, self-defense education, escort service, and informal discussions. There are pamphlets/posters/films, emergency telephones, and lighted pathways/sidewalks.

Programs of Study: Samford confers B.A., B.S., B.G.S., B.Mus., B.S.B.A., B.S.Ed., and B.S.N. degrees. Associate, master's, and doctoral degrees are also awarded. Bachelor's degrees are awarded in BIOLOGICAL SCIENCE (biochemistry, biology/biological science, marine science, and nutrition), BUSINESS (accounting, business administration and management, human resources, and international business management), COMMUNICATIONS AND THE ARTS (art, classics, dramatic arts, English, French, German, graphic design, Greek, journalism, language arts, Latin, music, music performance, music theory and composition, musical theater, piano/organ, Spanish, speech/debate/rhetoric, and voice), COMPUTER AND PHYSICAL SCIENCE (chemistry, computer science, mathematics, and physics), EDUCATION (athletic training, early childhood, elementary, music, physical, science, and special), ENGINEERING AND ENVIRONMENTAL DESIGN (engineering physics, environmental science, and interior design), HEALTH PROFESSIONS (exercise science, health, nursing, and sports medicine), SOCIAL SCIENCE (Asian/Oriental studies, biblical studies, community services, counseling/psychology, geography, history, human development, humanities, international relations, international studies, Latin American studies, liberal arts/general studies, philosophy, political science/government, psychology, public administration, religion, religious music, social science, and sociology). Teacher education, business, and music are the strongest academically. Business management, early childhood education, and nursing are the largest.

Required: All students must receive an overall GPA of at least 2.0 and take at least 128 credits, including 30 semester hours in their major. Distribution requirements include 8 semester hours in cultural perspectives, 8 semester hours in communication arts, 4 hours in Biblical Perspectives, and 2 hours in phys ed. Students also must demonstrate writing proficiency.

Special: A 3-2 engineering degree is available with Auburn, Washington (St. Louis), and Mercer Universities and the University of Alabama. The School of Arts and Sciences offers an interdisciplinary core curriculum with team teaching. Cross-registration with Birmingham-Southern College, the University of Alabama at Birmingham, The University of Montevallo, and Miles College, study abroad in England and 15 other countries, additional major options, internships, credit for life experience, and pass/fail options are also offered. Accelerated degree programs are possible in some majors. There are 17 national honor societies, a freshman honors program, and 16 departmental honors program.

Faculty/Classroom: 55% of faculty are male; 45%, female. 70% teach undergraduates. No introductory courses are taught by graduate students. The average class size in an introductory lecture is 22; in a laboratory, 20; and in a regular course, 19.

Admissions: 88% of the 2001-2002 applicants were accepted. The SAT I scores for the 2001-2002 freshman class were: Verbal--19% below 500, 42% between 500 and 599, 28% between 600 and 700, and 11% above 700; Math--21% below 500, 45% between 500 and 599, 27% between 600 and 700, and 7% above 700. The ACT scores were 13% below 21, 29% between 21 and 23, 24% between 24 and 26, 16% between 27 and 28, and 18% above 28. 56% of the current freshmen were in the top fifth of their class; 82% were in the top two fifths. There were 9 National Merit finalists and 1 semifinalist. 29 freshmen graduated first in their class.

Requirements: The SAT I or ACT is required. In addition, applicants need 18 academic credits and 16 Carnegie units, including 4 in English. The university also recommends that students have 3 units in math and science, 2 units each in foreign language and social studies, and 3 units in math and science. An essay is required and an interview suggested. The GED is accepted. AP and CLEP credits are accepted. Important factors in the admissions decision are advanced placement or honor courses, leadership record, and recommendations by school officials.

Procedure: Freshmen are admitted fall, spring, and summer. Entrance exams should be taken in the junior year. Applications should be filed by August 1 for fall entry. The fee was $25 in 2001. Notification is sent on a rolling basis.

Transfer: 168 transfer students enrolled in 2001-2002. Transfer applicants may transfer a maximum of 96 credits from a 4-year institution and 64 units from a 2-year institution. 25 credits of 128 must be completed at Samford.

Visiting: There are regularly scheduled orientations for prospective students consisting of a 2-day program during which students stay on campus, take placement tests, meet advisors, and register for classes. There are guides for informal visits and visitors may sit in on classes and stay overnight. To schedule a visit, contact the Admissions Office at (205) 726-3673 or *admiss@samford.edu*.

Financial Aid: The FAFSA and a state aid form are required. The fall application deadline is March 1.

International Students: There are 24 international students enrolled. The school actively recruits these students. They must score 550 on the written TOEFL or 213 on the electronic version and also take the SAT I or the ACT.

Computers: The mainframe is an IBM RISC/6000 7026 H70. There are 6 computer labs available for general academic and student use. Near semester's end, hours of operation may be extended. PCs include Dell and Power Mac. There is a voice/data connection for every resident student. All students may access the system. There are no time limits and no fees.

Graduates: In 2001, 672 bachelor's degrees were awarded. The most popular majors were business (17%), education (13%), and nursing (8%). In an average class, 1% graduate in 3 years, 55% in 4 years, 64% in 5 years, and 68% in 6 years. 109 companies recruited on campus in 2000-2001.

Admissions Contact: Phil Kimrey, Dean Admission and Financial Aid.
E-mail: *admiss@samford.edu*
Web: *www.samford.edu/groups/admiss/index.html*

SOUTHERN CHRISTIAN UNIVERSITY C-4

Montgomery, AL 36117-3553 **(334) 387-3877, ext. 213**
(800) 351-4040; Fax: (334) 387-3878

Full-time: 132 men, 61 women	**Faculty:** 40
Part-time: 1 man, 1 woman	**Ph.D.s:** 63%
Graduate: 139 men, 85 women	**Student/Faculty:** 5 to 1
Year: semesters, summer session	**Tuition:** $8480
Application Deadline: open	**Room & Board:** n/app
Freshman Class: n/av	
SAT I or ACT: n/av	**LESS COMPETITIVE**

Southern Christian University, founded in 1967, merges traditional and on-line education; 90% of its students access SCU programs via Distance Learning. There are 2 undergraduate and 2 graduate schools. The library contains 73,000 volumes, 500 microform items, and 800 audiovisual forms/CDs, and subscribes to 1200 periodicals. Computerized library services include the card catalog, interlibrary loans, and database searching. Special learning facilities include a learning resource center. The 9-acre campus is in an urban area in Montgomery. There is one building.

Student Life: 65% of undergraduates are from out of state. Others are from 47 states and 3 foreign countries. 68% are white; 26% African American. Most are Protestant. The average age of freshmen is 28; all undergraduates, 35.

Housing: There are no residence halls. Alcohol is not permitted. All students may keep cars.

Activities: There are some groups and organizations on campus, including student government.

Disabled Students: Wheelchair ramps and special parking are available. All classrooms and the learning resource center are accessible.

Programs of Study: SCU confers B.A. and B.S. degrees. Master's and doctoral degrees are also awarded. Bachelor's degrees are awarded in BUSINESS (human resources and management information systems),

EDUCATION (social foundations), SOCIAL SCIENCE (biblical studies, human development, law enforcement and corrections, liberal arts/general studies, ministries, and safety management). Human and social development, management, communications, and ministry/Bible are the largest.

Required: Students must complete at least 128 credit hours, with 36 in the major and a minimum GPA of 2.0.

Faculty/Classroom: 77% of faculty are male; 23%, female. No introductory courses are taught by graduate students.

Requirements: CLEP credit is accepted. Applications are available on-line at *www.southernchristian.edu*.

Procedure: Freshmen are admitted to all sessions. Application deadlines are open. The application fee is $50.

Transfer: Unconditional admission requires a 2.0 GPA on prior course work; below 2.0, students are admitted on a conditional basis. 32 credits of 128 must be completed at SCU.

Financial Aid: In 2001-2002, 90% of all students received some form of financial aid, including need-based aid. The average freshman award was $9725. Of that total, scholarships or need-based grants averaged $7000 (maximum); and loans averaged $2725 (maximum). Undergraduate students enrolling full-time receive a 50% tuition scholarship. The average financial indebtedness of the 2001 graduate was $30,000. The FAFSA and the college's own financial statement are required.

International Students: There are 4 international students enrolled. They must score 440 on the written TOEFL and also take the SAT I or the ACT.

Computers: On-campus students may use PCs in the library. All students may access the system. All students are required to have personal computers. The school recommends a 200-MHz Intel Pentium processor running Windows, or Mac OS 8.1 or better.

Graduates: In 2001, 36 bachelor's degrees were awarded. The most popular majors were ministry (50%), Bible (25%), and liberal studies (14%). Of the 2000 graduating class, 50% were enrolled in graduate school within 6 months of graduation and 90% were employed.

Admissions Contact: Rick Johnson, Director of Enrollment Management. E-mail: *rickkjohnson@southernchristian.edu*
Web: *www.southernchristian.edu*

SPRING HILL COLLEGE
Mobile, AL 36608 — **A-5**
(251) 380-3030
(800) SHC-6704; Fax: (251) 460-2186

Full-time: 417 men, 605 women	**Faculty:** 69; IIB, --$
Part-time: 59 men, 163 women	**Ph.D.s:** 87%
Graduate: 71 men, 168 women	**Student/Faculty:** 15 to 1
Year: semesters, summer session	**Tuition:** $17,230
Application Deadline: July 1	**Room & Board:** $6020
Freshman Class: 1000 applied, 774 accepted, 251 enrolled	
SAT I Verbal/Math: 530/520	**ACT:** 23 **COMPETITIVE**

Spring Hill College, founded in 1830, is a private Catholic liberal arts and sciences college. In addition to regional accreditation, Spring Hill has baccalaureate program accreditation with ACBSP and CCNE. The 2 libraries contain 162,113 volumes and 282,213 microform items, and subscribe to 538 periodicals. Computerized library services include the card catalog, interlibrary loans, and database searching. Special learning facilities include a theater. The 400-acre campus is in a suburban area in Mobile. Including residence halls, there are 32 buildings.

Student Life: 51% of undergraduates are from Alabama. Others are from 33 states, 9 foreign countries, and Canada. 76% are white; 14%, African American. 58% are Catholic; 26%, Protestant. The average age of freshmen is 18; all undergraduates, 23. 18% do not continue beyond their first year.

Housing: 768 students can be accommodated in college housing, which includes single-sex and coed dormitories and on-campus apartments. On-campus housing is guaranteed for all 4 years. 58% of students live on campus; of those, 90% remain on campus on weekends. All students may keep cars.

Activities: 27% of men belong to 3 local and 2 national fraternities; 30% of women belong to 4 national sororities. There are 35 groups on campus, including art, cheerleading, chorale, computers, dance, drama, ethnic, honors, international, literary magazine, musical theater, newspaper, photography, political, professional, religious, social, social service, student government, and yearbook. Popular campus events include Mardi Gras, Oktoberfest, and Christmas on the Hill.

Sports: There are 7 intercollegiate sports for men and 8 for women, and 8 intramural sports for men and 8 for women. Facilities include an 18-hole golf course; tennis and basketball courts; an outdoor sand volleyball area; and baseball, softball, football, rugby, and soccer fields. A recreation center houses the intercollegiate basketball arena, 2 basketball courts, 2 racquetball courts, a cardiovascular exercise room, an indoor pool, and a running track.

Disabled Students: 80% of the campus is accessible. Wheelchair ramps, elevators, special parking, specially equipped rest rooms, special class scheduling, lowered drinking fountains, and lowered telephones are available.

Services: Counseling and information services are available, as is tutoring in some subjects, including English, theology, math, languages, philosophy, economics, biology, accounting, psychology, computer science, and political science. There is remedial math, reading, and writing.

Campus Safety and Security: Measures include 24-hour foot and vehicle patrol, self-defense education, escort service, and informal discussions. There are pamphlets/posters/films, emergency telephones, and lighted pathways/sidewalks.

Programs of Study: Spring Hill confers B.A., B.S., and B.S.N. degrees. Associate and master's degrees are also awarded. Bachelor's degrees are awarded in BIOLOGICAL SCIENCE (biochemistry, biology/biological science, and marine biology), BUSINESS (accounting, banking and finance, business administration and management, international business management, and marketing management), COMMUNICATIONS AND THE ARTS (advertising, arts administration/management, broadcasting, dramatic arts, English, graphic design, journalism, public relations, Spanish, and studio art), COMPUTER AND PHYSICAL SCIENCE (chemistry, computer science, and mathematics), EDUCATION (early childhood, elementary, and secondary), ENGINEERING AND ENVIRONMENTAL DESIGN (engineering and environmental science), HEALTH PROFESSIONS (art therapy, nursing, predentistry, premedicine, and preveterinary science), SOCIAL SCIENCE (economics, history, humanities, international studies, liberal arts/general studies, philosophy, political science/government, psychology, and theological studies). Theology, English, and business are the strongest academically. Business and management, biology, and communication arts are the largest.

Required: All students must take core curriculum courses in English composition and literature, history, philosophy, theology, math, science, social science, fine art, and foreign language. Graduation requirements include completion of a minimum of 128 semester hours with a minimum GPA of 2.0 and 30 to 36 upper-division semester hours in the major with a minimum grade of 2.0.

Special: SHC offers 3-2 engineering programs with the University of Alabama-Birmingham, Auburn University, the University of Florida, and Marquette University. It also offers 3-3 occupational therapy and physical therapy programs with Rockhurst University. The college is a member of the Marine Environmental Sciences Consortium and offers marine biology courses at the Dauphin Island Sea Lab. Several study-abroad options are available. Internships are also available in many majors. An accelerated degree program is offered in organizational management and communication, and most majors may be completed in 3 years by taking summer courses. Also available are dual majors, student-designed majors, a Washington semester, and pass/fail options. There are 8 national honor societies, a freshman honors program, and 5 departmental honors programs.

Faculty/Classroom: 61% of faculty are male; 39%, female. All teach undergraduates. No introductory courses are taught by graduate students. The average class size in an introductory lecture is 23; in a laboratory, 17; and in a regular course, 17.

Admissions: 77% of the 2001-2002 applicants were accepted. The SAT I scores for the 2001-2002 freshman class were: Verbal--36% below 500, 36% between 500 and 599, 22% between 600 and 700, and 6% above 700; Math--42% below 500, 35% between 500 and 599, 19% between 600 and 700, and 4% above 700. The ACT scores were 24% below 21, 27% between 21 and 23, 24% between 24 and 26, 13% between 27 and 28, and 12% above 28. 44% of the current freshmen were in the top fifth of their class; 70% were in the top two fifths. 6 freshmen graduated first in their class.

Requirements: The SAT I or ACT is required. The ACT is preferred. Applicants should have completed at least 16 high school units, including 4 in English, 2 each in math, science, and social studies, and 2 in other academic areas. The GED equivalent is accepted. An essay is required and an interview is recommended. Spring Hill requires applicants to be in the upper 50% of their class. A GPA of 2.5 is required. AP and CLEP credits are accepted. Important factors in the admissions decision are advanced placement or honor courses, recommendations by school officials, and leadership record. Applications are accepted on-line at the college's web site.

Procedure: Freshmen are admitted fall, spring, and summer. Entrance exams should be taken in spring of the junior year or fall of the senior year. Applications should be filed by July 1 for fall entry and December 15 for spring entry, along with a $25 fee. Notification is sent on a rolling basis.

Transfer: 44 transfer students enrolled in 2001-2002. Transfer applicants must have at least 20 semester hours of college credit, a minimum cumulative GPA of 2.5, good academic standing at the last college or university attended, and a satisfactory recommendation. 32 credits of 128 must be completed at Spring Hill.

Visiting: There are regularly scheduled orientations for prospective students, consisting of a campus tour, faculty appointments, attending a class, lunch with a student, and an interview with an admissions counselor. There are guides for informal visits and visitors may sit in on classes and stay overnight. To schedule a visit, contact the Office of Admissions.

Financial Aid: In 2001-2002, 95% of all freshmen and 93% of continuing students received some form of financial aid. 65% of freshmen and 66% of continuing students received need-based aid. The average freshman award was $15,655. Of that total, scholarships or need-based grants averaged $11,671 ($21,620 maximum); loans averaged $3093 ($4875 maximum); and work contracts averaged $891 ($2320 maximum). 27% of undergraduates work part time. Average annual earnings from campus work are $878. The average financial indebtedness of the 2001 graduate was $17,050. Spring Hill is a member of CSS. The FAFSA, the college's own financial statement, and, for Alabama residents, a state aid form are required.

International Students: There are 19 international students enrolled. The school actively recruits these students. They must score 550 on the written TOEFL or 213 on the electronic version, or take the MELAB. The SAT I or ACT is required of students with English as their first language.

Computers: The mainframe consists of 2 DEC VAX 3100 computers. The mainframe supports interactive users and functions as a server for the academic network of PCs and Macs. The academic network is connected to the Internet. Approximately 141 PCs and 14 Macs are available for general student use; these include machines in instructional labs that support teaching needs. All students may access the system Monday to Thursday, 8 A.M. to midnight; Friday, 8 A.M. to 7 P.M.; Saturday, noon to 5 P.M.; Sunday, 3 P.M. to midnight; and 24 hours per day via modem. There are no time limits and no fees.

Graduates: In 2001, 211 bachelor's degrees were awarded. The most popular majors were communication arts (19%), business and management (17%), and biology (11%). In an average class, 2% graduate in 3 years, 49% in 4 years, 59% in 5 years, and 60% in 6 years. 9 companies recruited on campus in 2000-2001. Of the 2000 graduating class, 28% were enrolled in graduate school within 6 months of graduation and 71% were employed.

Admissions Contact: Florence Hines, Dean of Enrollment Management. E-mail: *admit@shc.edu* Web: *http://www.shc.edu*

STILLMAN COLLEGE
Tuscaloosa, AL 35403-9990 — B-3

(205) 366-8817
(800) 841-5722; (205) 366-8996

Full-time: 640 men, 780 women	**Faculty:** 52
Part-time: 20 men, 20 women	**Ph.D.s:** 70%
Graduate: none	**Student/Faculty:** 27 to 1
Year: semesters, summer session	**Tuition:** $7370
Application Deadline: see profile	**Room & Board:** $4000
Freshman Class: n/av	
SAT I or ACT: required	**LESS COMPETITIVE**

Stillman College, founded in 1876, is a small, private liberal arts institution affiliated with the Presbyterian Church (U.S.A.). Figures in the above capsule are approximate. The library contains 113,120 volumes, 7240 microform items, and 3550 audiovisual forms/CDs, and subscribes to 360 periodicals. Computerized library services include the card catalog, interlibrary loans, and database searching. Special learning facilities include a learning resource center, art gallery, and radio station. The 100-acre campus is in a small town 60 miles from Birmingham and 105 miles from Montgomery. Including residence halls, there are 26 buildings.

Student Life: 70% of undergraduates are from Alabama. Others are from 27 states and 8 foreign countries. 95% are from public schools. 98% are African American. Most are Protestant. The average age of freshmen is 19.

Housing: 750 students can be accommodated in college housing, which includes single-sex dormitories and off-campus apartments. On-campus housing is available on a first-come, first-served basis. 50% of students live on campus. Alcohol is not permitted. All students may keep cars.

Activities: 10% of men belong to 4 national fraternities; 20% of women belong to 4 national sororities. There are 19 groups on campus, including art, band, cheerleading, choir, chorus, dance, debate, drama, honors, international, jazz band, marching band, newspaper, pep band, radio and TV, religious, social, social service, student government, and yearbook. Popular campus events include "S" Day, Founder's Day, and Coffee House.

Sports: There are 6 intercollegiate sports for men and 6 for women. Facilities include a college center, tennis courts, a stress center, bowling lanes, billiards, a swimming pool, a gym, a football field, and a weight room.

Disabled Students: Wheelchair ramps, elevators, special parking, and specially equipped rest rooms are available.

Services: Counseling and information services are available, as is tutoring in some subjects, including reading, writing, math, physics, and chemistry. There is remedial math, reading, and writing.

Campus Safety and Security: Measures include 24-hour foot and vehicle patrol, self-defense education, escort service, and informal discussions. There are pamphlets/posters/films and lighted pathways/sidewalks.

Programs of Study: Stillman confers B.A. and B.S. degrees. Bachelor's degrees are awarded in BIOLOGICAL SCIENCE (biology/biological science), BUSINESS (business administration and management), COMMUNICATIONS AND THE ARTS (art, English, and music), COMPUTER AND PHYSICAL SCIENCE (computer science and mathematics), EDUCATION (elementary and physical), HEALTH PROFESSIONS (premedicine), SOCIAL SCIENCE (history, prelaw, and religion).

Required: To graduate, students must complete a minimum of 124 credit hours, with at least 30 in the major, and maintain a minimum GPA of 2.0 overall and in the major. The 53-credit-hour general education core includes courses in religion, logic, English composition, public speaking, African heritage, African American experience, history, social science, physical and life sciences, math, computer literacy, health, and phys ed. All students must submit a senior thesis and take a senior departmental exam.

Special: Stillman offers local, national, and international opportunites for cooperative education and internships. Cross-registration is possible with the University of Alabama at Birmingham, with which there also are cooperative degree programs in nursing and allied health. Federal work-study is available on and off campus, and students may earn credit for prior learning experiences. There are 3 national honor societies.

Faculty/Classroom: 40% of faculty are male; 60%, female. All teach undergraduates. The average class size in an introductory lecture is 40; in a laboratory, 40; and in a regular course, 35.

Requirements: The SAT I or ACT is required. In addition, applicants should be high school graduates or have earned the GED. Secondary preparation should include 4 units of English and 1 unit each of math, science, and history. All applicants must have an interview. Music majors must audition. A GPA of 2.0 is required. AP and CLEP credits are accepted.

Procedure: Freshmen are admitted to all sessions. Notification is sent on a rolling basis. Check with the school for current application deadlines and fee.

Transfer: 70 transfer students enrolled in a recent year. Transfer applicants should present at least a C average in previous college work and must plan to spend at least a year in residence. 64 credits of 124 must be completed at Stillman.

Visiting: There are regularly scheduled orientations for prospective students. To schedule a visit, contact the director of recruitment.

Financial Aid: In a recent year, 90% of all freshmen received some form of financial aid. 50% of freshmen received need-based aid. The average freshman award was $6000. The CSS/Profile, FAFSA, FFS or SFS and the college's own financial statement are required.

International Students: There were 12 international students enrolled in a recent year. The school actively recruits these students. They must take the SAT I or the ACT.

Computers: The mainframe is a DEC ALPHA server. Terminals and PCs are available in computer labs and residence halls. Student accounts and e-mail addresses are issued. All students may access the system 8 A.M. to 9 P.M. Monday through Saturday. Students may access the system 69 hours per week. There are no fees.

Graduates: In a recent year, 165 bachelor's degrees were awarded. The most popular majors were business (27%), education (13%), and biology (9%). 15 companies recruited on campus in a recent year.

Admissions Contact: Mason Bonner, Director of Admissions. E-mail: *mbonner@www.stillman.edu* Web: *www.stillman.edu*

TALLADEGA COLLEGE
Talladega, AL 35160 — C-2

(256) 761-6416
(800) 633-2440; n/av

Full-time: 230 men, 400 women	**Faculty:** 40
Part-time: 10 men, 20 women	**Ph.D.s:** 60%
Graduate: none	**Student/Faculty:** 16 to 1
Year: semesters	**Tuition:** $6810
Application Deadline: open	**Room & Board:** $3300
Freshman Class: n/av	
SAT I or ACT: required	**LESS COMPETITIVE**

Talladega College, founded in 1867, is a private liberal arts institution offering emphases on business, sciences, and social work. Figures given in above capsule are approximate. In addition to regional accreditation, Dega has baccalaureate program accreditation with CSWE. The library contains 87,960 volumes and 350 audiovisual forms/CDs, and subscribes to 330 periodicals. Computerized library services include the card catalog and interlibrary loans. Special learning facilities include a learning resource center, art gallery, and science drop-in center, curriculum and writing labs, and financial computer lab. The 130-acre campus is in a small town 55 miles east of Birmingham and 115 miles west of Atlanta. Including residence halls, there are 42 buildings.

Student Life: 60% of undergraduates are from Alabama. Others are from 29 states and 2 foreign countries. 99% are African American. Most are Protestant. The average age of freshmen is 18; all undergraduates, 20. 22% do not continue beyond their first year; 45% remain to graduate.

Housing: 580 students can be accommodated in college housing, which includes single-sex dormitories and on-campus apartments. In addition, there are honors houses. On-campus housing is guaranteed for all 4 years. 70% of students live on campus; of those, 90% remain on campus on weekends. Alcohol is not permitted. All students may keep cars.

Activities: 14% of men belong to 4 national fraternities; 40% of women belong to 4 national sororities. There are 23 groups on campus, including art, cheerleading, choir, chorus, computers, dance, drama, honors, jazz band, newspaper, professional, social, student government, and yearbook. Popular campus events include Spring Concert, Carnival, and Coronation.

Sports: There are 4 intercollegiate sports for men and 4 for women, and 8 intramural sports for men and 3 for women. Facilities include a swimming pool, a 150-seat gym, lounges, game rooms, tennis courts, and a baseball field.

Disabled Students: 50% of the campus is accessible. Wheelchair ramps, elevators, special parking, and specially equipped rest rooms are available.

Services: Counseling and information services are available, as is tutoring in every subject. There is remedial math, reading, and writing.

Campus Safety and Security: Measures include 24-hour foot and vehicle patrol, escort service, informal discussions, and pamphlets/posters/films. There are lighted pathways/sidewalks.

Programs of Study: Dega confers the B.A. degree. Bachelor's degrees are awarded in BIOLOGICAL SCIENCE (biology/biological science), BUSINESS (accounting, banking and finance, and business administration and management), COMMUNICATIONS AND THE ARTS (English and music performance), COMPUTER AND PHYSICAL SCIENCE (chemistry, computer science, mathematics, and physics), EDUCATION (music), SOCIAL SCIENCE (economics, history, psychology, public administration, social work, and sociology). Business, biology, and chemistry are the strongest academically. Biology is the largest.

Required: To graduate, students must maintain a minimum GPA of 2.5 while taking 124 to 127 total semester hours, including 60 in the major and completion of a core curriculum. Distribution requirements at the freshman level include 8 semester hours in natural sciences, 6 each in communications, social sciences, and humanities, 2 in phys ed, and 1 in freshman orientation; additional hours in these subjects vary by major at the sophomore level.

Special: Talladega offers co-op programs with other schools through individual departments, a 3-2 engineering degree with Auburn University, internships involving historic preservation work, work-study plans with Adopt-a-Family and Adult Literacy, and B.A.-B.S. degrees in biology, business administration, chemistry, and computer science. There are dual majors available in law, nursing, engineering, and allied health. There are 4 national honor societies.

Faculty/Classroom: 60% of faculty are male; 40%, female. All teach undergraduates and 25% both teach and do research. The average class size in an introductory lecture is 30; in a laboratory, 20; and in a regular course, 18.

Requirements: The SAT I or ACT is required. In addition, applicants must be graduates of an accredited secondary school with 22 academic units, including 4 in English, 3 in social studies, and 2 each in math, science, health/phys ed, and electives. The GED is considered. An essay and interview are recommended. An audition is required for music majors. A GPA of 2.5 is required. CLEP credit is accepted. Important factors in the admissions decision are advanced placement or honor courses, recommendations by school officials, and recommendations by alumni. Applications are accepted at the school's web site.

Procedure: Freshmen are admitted fall and spring. Entrance exams should be taken in the junior year. There is a deferred admissions plan. Application deadlines are open. The fall 2001 application fee was $10.

Transfer: Applicants must have a cumulative GPA of 2.0 in college work. The SAT I or ACT is recommended. 60 credits of 124 to 127 must be completed at Dega.

Visiting: There are guides for informal visits and visitors may sit in on classes and stay overnight. To schedule a visit, contact the Admissions Office.

Financial Aid: The CSS/Profile, FAFSA, FFS or SFS and the college's own financial statement are required. Check with the school for current deadlines.

International Students: The school actively recruits these students. They must take the TOEFL or the college's own test, the SAT I or the ACT.

Computers: The mainframes are a DEC VAX 750 and an HP 835/41. Student computer labs in the library and in a classroom building provide 30 PCs and 3 mainframe terminals. All students may access the system from 8 A.M. to 4:30 P.M. and 7 P.M. to 10 P.M. daily. There are no time limits and no fees.

Admissions Contact: Admissions Office.
E-mail: *admissions@talladega.edu* Web: *www.talladega.edu*

TROY STATE UNIVERSITY SYSTEM

The Troy State University System, established in 1887, is a private system in Alabama. It is governed by a board of trustees whose chief administrator is the chancellor. The primary goal of the system is to provide an academic, cultural, and social environment conducive to the development of students as well as productive, individual members of society. The main priorities are the preprofessional and professional preparation of students in the arts and sciences, fine arts, business, education, communication, applied science, nursing, and allied health sciences. The total enrollment of the main campus is nearly 7000; there are more than 650 faculty members at the 12-campus system. Altogether there are 38 baccalaureate and 14 master's programs offered in the system. 4-year campuses are located in Troy, Phoenix City, Montgomery, and Dothan/Fort Rucker. Profiles of those campuses are included in this section.

TROY STATE UNIVERSITY

Troy, AL 36082 C-4

(334) 670-3179
(800) 551-9716; Fax: (334) 670-3733

Full-time: 1510 men, 2070 women	**Faculty:** 209; IIA, --$
Part-time: 347 men, 680 women	**Ph.D.s:** 53%
Graduate: 847 men, 1323 women	**Student/Faculty:** 17 to 1
Year: semesters, summer session	**Tuition:** $3296 ($6316)
Application Deadline: open	**Room & Board:** $4400

Freshman Class: 2428 applied, 1766 accepted, 857 enrolled
ACT: 21 **COMPETITIVE**

Troy State University, founded in 1887, is a liberal arts institution that is part of the public Troy State University system. There are 5 undergraduate and 3 graduate schools. In addition to regional accreditation, TSU has baccalaureate program accreditation with AACSB, ACBSP, CSWE, NASM, NCATE, and NLN. The library contains 389,524 volumes, 1,362,063 microform items, and 10,065 audiovisual forms/CDs, and subscribes to 4190 periodicals. Computerized library services include the card catalog, interlibrary loans, and database searching. Special learning facilities include a learning resource center, art gallery, TV station, and arboretum. The 577-acre campus is in a small town 50 miles south of Montgomery. Including residence halls, there are 73 buildings.

Student Life: 83% of undergraduates are from Alabama. Others are from 49 states, 55 foreign countries, and Canada. 62% are white; 25% African American.

Housing: 1527 students can be accommodated in college housing, which includes single-sex and coed dormitories, on-campus apartments, off-campus apartments, married-student housing, fraternity houses, and sorority houses. In addition, there are honors houses, special-interest houses, an international house, and substance free housing. On-campus housing is guaranteed for all 4 years. 72% of students commute. Alcohol is not permitted. All students may keep cars.

Activities: 18% of men belong to 11 national fraternities; 19% of women belong to 8 national sororities. There are 110 groups on campus, including art, band, cheerleading, choir, chorale, chorus, computers, dance, drama, drill team, ethnic, film, honors, international, jazz band, literary magazine, marching band, musical theater, newspaper, opera, orchestra, pep band, photography, political, professional, radio and TV, religious, social, social service, student government, symphony, and yearbook. Popular campus events include Greek Week, winter formals, and spring break weekends.

Sports: There are 7 intercollegiate sports for men and 9 for women, and 11 intramural sports for men and 11 for women. Facilities include a 17,500-seat football stadium, a 4000-seat gym, a natatorium, a baseball field, a golf course, and tennis courts.

Disabled Students: 95% of the campus is accessible. Wheelchair ramps, elevators, special parking, specially equipped rest rooms, special class scheduling, lowered drinking fountains, lowered telephones, and graded inclines, and specially equipped apartments are available.

Services: Counseling and information services are available, as is tutoring in most subjects. There is a reader service for the blind, and remedial math, reading, and writing.

Campus Safety and Security: Measures include 24-hour foot and vehicle patrol, self-defense education, escort service, and pamphlets/posters/films. There are lighted pathways/sidewalks.

Programs of Study: TSU confers B.A., B.S., B.A.Ed., B.Applied Sc., B.S.Ed., and B.S.N. degrees. Associate and master's degrees are also awarded. Bachelor's degrees are awarded in BIOLOGICAL SCIENCE (biology/biological science and marine biology), BUSINESS (accounting, banking and finance, business administration and management, and marketing/retailing/merchandising), COMMUNICATIONS AND THE ARTS (art history and appreciation, broadcasting, communications, dramatic arts, English, journalism, and speech/debate/rhetoric), COMPUTER AND PHYSICAL SCIENCE (chemistry, computer science, and mathematics), EDUCATION (art, early childhood, elementary, English, foreign languages, health, mathematics, music, physical, science, secondary, social science, and special), HEALTH PROFESSIONS (medical technology and nursing), SOCIAL SCIENCE (criminal justice, history, human services, international relations, political science/government, psychology, social science, and social work). Business and education are the strongest academically. Business is the largest.

Required: All students must maintain a minimum GPA of 2.0 while taking 120 to 140 semester credit hours, 54 of which must be in their major field. Distribution requirements include 48 hours of general studies, covering such subjects as English, math, history, science, and fine arts.

Special: Cross-registration with the Marine Biological Consortium, internships in education, journalism, and nursing, study abroad in 2 countries, work-study programs at the university, and student-designed majors in public relations, advertising, and other fields are offered. Credit for life experience and nondegree study are also offered. There are 21 national honor societies, including Phi Beta Kappa, a freshman honors program, and 8 departmental honors programs.

Faculty/Classroom: 52% of faculty are male; 48%, female. All teach undergraduates.

Admissions: 73% of the 2001-2002 applicants were accepted. The ACT scores for the 2001-2002 freshman class were: 51% below 21, 21% between 21 and 23, 13% between 24 and 26, 9% between 27 and 28, and 6% above 28.

Requirements: The SAT I or ACT is required, with recommended composite scores of 870 or 18, respectively. Applicants must have earned at least 15 Carnegie units, with 11 in academic courses and 3 to 4 in English. An interview is recommended, along with a portfolio or audition for some programs. The GED is accepted. Applications are accepted on-line. A GPA of 2.0 is required. AP and CLEP credits are accepted. Important factors in the admissions decision are ability to finance college education, evidence of special talent, and extracurricular activities record.

Procedure: Freshmen are admitted to all sessions. Entrance exams should be taken in the fall of the senior year. Application deadlines are open.

Transfer: 372 transfer students enrolled in 2001-2002. Transfer applicants need 20 semester hours attempted at their previous institution, with a GPA of at least 2.0.

Visiting: There are regularly scheduled orientations for prospective students, including a campus tour, classroom visitation, academic consultation, and interviews. There are guides for informal visits and visitors may sit in on classes. To schedule a visit, contact the Office of Enrollment Services.

Financial Aid: TSU is a member of CSS. The CSS/Profile, FAFSA, FFS or SFS and the college's own financial statement are required. The fall application deadline is May 1.

International Students: There are 224 international students enrolled. The school actively recruits these students. They must score 500 on the written TOEFL or 175 on the electronic version and also take the SAT I or the ACT, scoring 870 or 18, respectively.

Computers: The mainframes are an IBM ES 9000 and an IBM 9375. All students may access the system 7 days a week. There are no time limits and no fees.

Graduates: In 2001, 827 bachelor's degrees were awarded. The most popular majors were business (26%), education (24%), and nursing (7%). In an average class, 40% graduate in 4 years, and 52% in 5 years.

Admissions Contact: Buddy Starling, Dean of Enrollment Services. A video is available. E-mail: *bstar@trojan.troyst.edu*
Web: *www.troyst.edu*

TROY STATE UNIVERSITY DOTHAN D-5
Dothan, AL 36304 **(334) 983-6556; Fax: (334) 983-6322**

Full-time: 226 men, 442 women	**Faculty:** 52
Part-time: 310 men, 521 women	**Ph.D.s:** 41%
Graduate: 98 men, 258 women	**Student/Faculty:** 13 to 1
Year: semesters, summer session	**Tuition:** $3296 ($6316)
Application Deadline: open	**Room & Board:** n/app
Freshman Class: 106 applied, 62 accepted, 45 enrolled	
ACT: 22	**COMPETITIVE**

Troy State University Dothan, founded in 1965, is a public liberal arts school. As part of the Troy State University System, it established a permanent campus in Dothan in 1977 to serve the tri-state region. It continues to offer degree completion studies for the military at Fort Rucker. There are 3 undergraduate and 3 graduate schools. In addition to regional accreditation, TSUD has baccalaureate program accreditation with ACBSP and NCATE. The library contains 100,193 volumes, 278,829 microform items, and 7900 audiovisual forms/CDs, and subscribes to 564 periodicals. Computerized library services include the card catalog, interlibrary loans, and database searching. Special learning facilities include a learning resource center. The 250-acre campus is in an urban area 90 miles southeast of Montgomery. There are 3 buildings.

Student Life: 93% of undergraduates are from Alabama. Others are from 8 states and 1 foreign country. 74% are white; 19% African American. The average age of freshmen is 24; all undergraduates, 30. 54% do not continue beyond their first year.

Housing: There are no residence halls. All students commute. Alcohol is not permitted.

Activities: There are no fraternities or sororities. There are 10 groups on campus, including band, chess, computers, ethnic, honors, literary magazine, newspaper, professional, social, and student government.

Sports: There is no sports program at TSUD.

Disabled Students: All of the campus is accessible. Wheelchair ramps, elevators, special parking, specially equipped rest rooms, lowered drinking fountains, and lowered telephones are available.

Services: Counseling and information services are available, as is tutoring in most subjects. There is remedial math and writing.

Campus Safety and Security: Measures include 24-hour foot and vehicle patrol, pamphlets/posters/films, and lighted pathways/sidewalks.

Programs of Study: TSUD confers B.S., B.A.E., and B.Applied Sc. degrees. Associate and master's degrees are also awarded. Bachelor's degrees are awarded in BIOLOGICAL SCIENCE (biology/biological science), BUSINESS (accounting, banking and finance, business administration and management, business economics, marketing management, and personnel management), COMMUNICATIONS AND THE ARTS (English), COMPUTER AND PHYSICAL SCIENCE (computer science, mathematics, physical sciences, and science), EDUCATION (early childhood, elementary, English, mathematics, science, secondary, social science, and special), SOCIAL SCIENCE (criminal justice, psychology, social science, and sociology). Education is the strongest academically. Business and education are the largest.

Required: All students must take a minimum of 120 semester hours, including 30 in their major, and must maintain an overall GPA of at least 2.0. Distribution requirements include English composition I and II, 6 hours each of literature, history, and social science, 3 hours each of music and art, microcomputing and speech, math, biology, philosophy, and science.

Special: Internships in the accounting and education programs, nondegree study, and pass/fail options are available. There are 4 national honor societies.

Faculty/Classroom: 65% of faculty are male; 35%, female. All teach undergraduates. No introductory courses are taught by graduate students. The average class size in a regular course is 23.

Admissions: 58% of the 2001-2002 applicants were accepted. The ACT scores for the 2001-2002 freshman class were: 44% below 21, 38% between 21 and 23, 6% between 24 and 26, 6% between 27 and 28, and 6% above 28.

Requirements: A GPA of 2.0 is required. In addition, applicants must be graduates of an accredited high school. Beginning freshmen under age 21 must have a minimum ACT score of 19. The GED is accepted. AP and CLEP credits are accepted. Applications are accepted on-line.

Procedure: Freshmen are admitted fall, spring, and summer. Entrance exams should be taken during the junior year of high school. There is an early admissions plan. Application deadlines are open. The application fee is $20.

Transfer: 265 transfer students enrolled in 2001-2002. Transfer applicants receive unconditional acceptance if their GPA is 2.0 or above. 30 credits of 120 must be completed at TSUD.

Visiting: There are regularly scheduled orientations for prospective students, including review of program and services, introduction of department deans, and meetings with advisers. There are guides for informal visits and visitors may sit in on classes. To schedule a visit, contact Taylor Barbaree at (334) 983-6556, ext. 207 or *tbarbaree@tsud.edu*

Financial Aid: In a recent year, 53% of all freshmen and 64% of continuing students received some form of financial aid. 1% of undergraduates work part time. The FAFSA is required. The fall application deadline is July 1.

International Students: There is 1 international student enrolled. They must score 550 on the written TOEFL or 213 on the electronic version.

Computers: The mainframe is an IBM 4331. There are 90 PCs in 3 labs. All students may access the system between 9 A.M. and 10 P.M., Monday through Thursday and on weekends. There are no time limits and no fees.

Graduates: In 2001, 309 bachelor's degrees were awarded. The most popular majors were general business (32%), elementary education (14%), and computer and information science (13%). 56 companies recruited on campus in 2000-2001.

Admissions Contact: Bob Willis, Enrollment Services.
E-mail: *bwillis@tsud.edu* Web: *www.tsud.edu*

TROY STATE UNIVERSITY/MONTGOMERY C-4

Montgomery, AL 36103-4419 (334) 241-9506
(800) 355-TSUM; Fax: (334) 241-9714

Full-time: 264 men, 597 women
Part-time: 680 men, 1164 women
Graduate: 154 men, 274 women
Year: semesters, summer session
Application Deadline: open
Freshman Class: n/av
SAT I or ACT: not required
Faculty: 36; IIA, --$
Ph.D.s: 57%
Student/Faculty: 24 to 1
Tuition: $3080 ($6100)
Room & Board: n/app
NONCOMPETITIVE

Troy State University/Montgomery, founded in 1965 as a branch of the Troy State University System, is a public evening commuter institution offering undergraduate and graduate degrees in arts and sciences, education, and business. There are 3 undergraduate schools and 1 graduate school. In addition to regional accreditation, TSUM has baccalaureate program accreditation with ACBSP. The library contains 36,504 volumes, 78,323 microform items, and 9166 audiovisual forms/CDs, and subscribes to 484 periodicals. Computerized library services include the card catalog, interlibrary loans, and database searching. Special learning facilities include a learning resource center, planetarium, radio station, and TV station. The 6-acre campus is in an urban area in downtown Montgomery. There are 7 buildings.

Student Life: 99% of undergraduates are from Alabama. 51% are white; 43% African American. The average age of freshmen is 27; all undergraduates, 27.

Housing: There are no residence halls. All students commute. Alcohol is not permitted.

Activities: There are no fraternities or sororities. There are 7 groups on campus, including honors, professional, social service, and student government. Popular campus events include Golf Classic.

Sports: There is no sports program at TSUM.

Disabled Students: 95% of the campus is accessible. Wheelchair ramps, elevators, special parking, specially equipped rest rooms, lowered drinking fountains, and lowered telephones are available.

Services: Counseling and information services are available, as is tutoring in some subjects. There is a reader service for the blind, and remedial math, reading, and writing. Tutors may be provided for students upon request.

Campus Safety and Security: Measures include escort service, informal discussions, pamphlets/posters/films, and lighted pathways/sidewalks. In addition, there are foot and vehicle patrols during class hours.

Programs of Study: TSUM confers B.A. and B.S. degrees. Associate and master's degrees are also awarded. Bachelor's degrees are awarded in BUSINESS (accounting, banking and finance, business administration and management, and marketing management), COMMUNICATIONS AND THE ARTS (English), COMPUTER AND PHYSICAL SCIENCE (computer science and mathematics), SOCIAL SCIENCE (history, political science/government, psychology, and social science). Computer and information science are the strongest academically. Business administration and management are the largest.

Required: Students must complete a minimum of 120 semester hours, with 36 hours within the TSU system in the major area, and maintain a minimum GPA of 2.0. At least half of the required total hours must be composed of traditional credits, excluding credit by correspondence or by exam.

Special: TSUM offers an external degree program in professional studies for those unable to attend regularly scheduled classes because of handicap, work, or family restrictions. Credit may be granted for military service and experiential learning. Guided independent study/research, nondegree study, and pass/fail options are possible. Flexible schedules and televised courses are available to meet the needs of adult students. Cross-registration with Alabama State University is offered. There are 2 national honor societies.

Faculty/Classroom: 56% of faculty are male; 44%, female. 95% teach undergraduates. No introductory courses are taught by graduate students. The average class size in a regular course is 18.

Requirements: A GPA of 2.0 is required. In addition, graduates from accredited secondary schools should have 15 Carnegie units, with 3 or more in English and 11 others in academic courses. Graduates from nonaccredited secondary schools may be admitted if they meet the same requirements and are deemed capable of performing satisfactorily. The GED is accepted. Other applicants may be admitted as unclassified, nondegree-seeking students. For students under 21, the high school GPA and SAT I or ACT scores are used in a formula to determine admissions eligibility; those applicants not having a test score may be admitted with conditional status. For students over 21, requirements include a minimum high school GPA of 2.0. Applicants with a lower GPA may be admitted conditionally. Important factors in the admissions decision are ability to finance college education, recommendations by alumni, and geographic diversity.

Procedure: Freshmen are admitted to all sessions. Entrance exams should be taken by the fall of the senior year. There is an early admissions plan. Application deadlines are open. The application fee is $20.

Transfer: Transfer students must submit college transcripts from each college attended. Those with fewer than 15 quarter hours (or 9 semester hours) of credit are required to submit a high school transcript as well. Applicants should have a college GPA of at least 2.0 and be in good standing; others may be admitted conditionally. 120 credits are required for a bachelor's degree.

Visiting: There are guides for informal visits and visitors may sit in on classes.

Computers: The mainframes are a DEC ALPHA server 2000, a DEC ALPHA server 1000, and 4 Gateway ALR 7200 Series. Students may access compilers and other utilities via DEC terminals and PCs in several locations as well as through dial-up capability. Approximately 300 PCs have access to the Internet and the web. Students taking computer and information science courses may access the system 7 days a week. There are no time limits and no fees.

Graduates: In 2001, 272 bachelor's degrees were awarded. The most popular majors were human resources management (33%), psychology (14%), and business (11%). In an average class, 9% graduate in 6 years.

Admissions Contact: Frank Hrabe, Director of Enrollment Management. E-mail: *fhrabe@tsum.edu or admit@tsum.edu*
Web: *www.tsu.edu*

TUSKEGEE UNIVERSITY D-4

Tuskegee, AL 36088 (334) 727-8500
(800) 622-6531; Fax: (334) 724-4402

Full-time: 1000 men, 1500 women
Part-time: 60 men, 50 women
Graduate: 170 men, 230 women
Year: semesters, summer session
Application Deadline: see profile
Freshman Class: n/av
SAT I or ACT: required
Faculty: 231
Ph.D.s: 70%
Student/Faculty: 11 to 1
Tuition: $9500
Room & Board: $5100
LESS COMPETITIVE

Tuskegee University, founded in 1881 by Booker T. Washington, is an independent professional and technical institution offering degree programs in liberal arts and sciences, agriculture, architecture, business, education, engineering, and health professions. Figures in above capsule are approximate. There are 7 undergraduate and 5 graduate schools. In addition to regional accreditation, Tuskegee has baccalaureate program accreditation with ABET, CSWE, NAAB, NCATE, and NLN. The 3 libraries contain 293,660 volumes and 300 microform items, and subscribe to 1150 periodicals. Computerized library services include the card catalog, interlibrary loans, and database searching. Special learning facilities include a learning resource center, the Carver Museum, a child development center, and special engineering labs. The 5200-acre campus is in a rural area 40 miles east of Montgomery. Including residence halls, there are 150 buildings.

Student Life: 70% of undergraduates are from out of state, mostly the South. Others are from 41 states, 31 foreign countries, and Canada. 90% are from public schools. 90% are African American. The average age of freshmen is 18; all undergraduates, 22. 35% do not continue beyond their first year; 45% remain to graduate.

Housing: 2000 students can be accommodated in college housing, which includes single-sex dormitories, on-campus apartments, and married-student housing. In addition, there are honors houses. On-campus housing is guaranteed for the freshman year only. 60% of students live on campus. Alcohol is not permitted. All students may keep cars.

Activities: 4% of men belong to 6 local and 4 national fraternities; 4% of women belong to 5 local and 4 national sororities. There are 60 groups on campus, including band, cheerleading, choir, chorus, drama, honors, international, jazz band, marching band, newspaper, orchestra, religious, social service, and student government. Popular campus events include Spring Pageant, Campus All-Star Challenge, and Student Leadership Retreat.

Sports: There are 5 intercollegiate sports for men and 5 for women, and 7 intramural sports for men and 6 for women. Facilities include a 10000-seat stadium, a 5000-seat arena, a student center, tennis courts, a rifle range, playing fields, and an Olympic-size natatorium.

Disabled Students: Wheelchair ramps, elevators, special parking, specially equipped rest rooms, special class scheduling, lowered drinking fountains, and lowered telephones are available.

Services: Counseling and information services are available, as is tutoring in some subjects. There is a reader service for the blind.

Campus Safety and Security: Measures include 24-hour foot and vehicle patrol, escort service, informal discussions, and lighted pathways/sidewalks.

Programs of Study: Tuskegee confers B.A., B.S., and B.S.N. degrees. Master's and doctoral degrees are also awarded. Bachelor's degrees are awarded in AGRICULTURE (animal science and horticulture), BIOLOGICAL SCIENCE (biology/biological science), BUSINESS (accounting, banking and finance, business administration and management, business economics, hospitality management services, management science, and marketing/retailing/merchandising), COMMUNICATIONS AND THE ARTS (English), COMPUTER AND PHYSICAL SCIENCE (chemistry, computer science, mathematics, and physics), EDUCATION (early childhood, elementary, physical, secondary, special, and technical), ENGINEERING AND ENVIRONMENTAL DESIGN (chemical engineering, construction management, electrical/electronics engineering, and mechanical engineering), HEALTH PROFESSIONS (nursing, occupational therapy, and veterinary science), SOCIAL SCIENCE (dietetics, food science, history, political science/government, psychology, social work, and sociology). Engineering, biology, and veterinary science are the largest.

Required: All students must complete a general education curriculum, including courses in history, sociology, philosophy, art, English, humanities, political science, math, natural sciences, and phys ed. A minimum of 124 semester credits with a GPA of 2.0 is required for graduation.

Special: Cooperative programs, internships, work-study programs, dual majors, nondegree study, and a B.A.-B.S. degree are offered. There are 17 national honor societies, a freshman honors program, and 9 departmental honors programs.

Faculty/Classroom: 70% of faculty are male; 30%, female. No introductory courses are taught by graduate students.

Requirements: The SAT I or ACT is required, with the SAT I preferred. The recommended minimum composite score is 900 on the SAT I or 18 on the ACT. A GPA of 2.5 is recommended. Applicants should be graduates of an accredited secondary school or hold the GED. They should have completed 4 units of English, 3 each of social science and math, and 1 each of physical science and biological science. SAT II: Subject tests in mathematics (level I or II) and 1 other subject are recommended. An essay is required. A GPA of 2.0 is required. AP and CLEP credits are accepted.

Procedure: Freshmen are admitted to all sessions. There is an early admissions plan. Applications should be filed at least 4 weeks prior to registration. Notification is sent on a rolling basis. The fall 2001 application fee was $25.

Transfer: 56 transfer students enrolled in a recent year. Applicants must be in good standing at all previously attended institutions and have completed 12 or more semester hours with a GPA of 2.0. 44 credits of 124 must be completed at Tuskegee.

Visiting: Visitors may sit in on classes and stay overnight. To schedule a visit, contact the Office of Admissions.

Financial Aid: In a recent year, 91% of all freshmen and 92% of continuing students received some form of financial aid. Tuskegee is a member of CSS. The CSS/Profile and federal tax returns are required. Check with the school for current deadlines.

International Students: They must take the TOEFL and also take the SAT I or the ACT.

Computers: The mainframe is a DEC VAX 6420. There are more than 150 PCs and terminals in various campus departments. All students may access the system. There are no time limits and no fees.

Graduates: Of the 2000 graduating class, 22% were enrolled in graduate school within 6 months of graduation and 80% were employed.

Admissions Contact: Iolantha Spencer, Dean, Admissions and Records. E-mail: *admi@acd.tusk.edu* Web: *www.tusk.edu*

UNIVERSITY OF ALABAMA SYSTEM

The University of Alabama System, established in 1969, is a public system comprised of three research universities located in Tuscaloosa, Birmingham, and Huntsville. It is governed by a board of trustees whose chief administrator is the chancellor. The primary goal of the system is to serve all the people of the state through teaching, research, and public service. The main priorities are to promote the economic, cultural, and social welfare of Alabama through higher education; to educate and train the leaders and citizens of tomorrow; and to conduct research in all fields that address the critical needs of mankind. The total enrollment of all 3 campuses usually exceeds 40,000, with about 3000 faculty members. There are approximately 175 baccalaureate, 150 master's, and 90 doctoral programs offered through the University of Alabama System. Profiles of the 4-year campuses are included in this section.

UNIVERSITY OF ALABAMA

Tuscaloosa, AL 35487 — B-3

(205) 348-5666
(800) 933-BAMA; Fax: (205) 348-9046

Full-time: 6317 men, 7198 women	**Faculty:** 651; I, --$
Part-time: 853 men, 833 women	**Ph.D.s:** 97%
Graduate: 1441 men, 1899 women	**Student/Faculty:** 21 to 1
Year: semesters, summer session	**Tuition:** $3292 ($8912)
Application Deadline: June 1	**Room & Board:** $4110
Freshman Class: 7864 applied, 6250 accepted, 2435 enrolled	
SAT I Verbal/Math: 550/550	**ACT:** 23 **COMPETITIVE**

The University of Alabama, founded in 1831, is a public comprehensive research institution and part of the University of Alabama system. There are 8 undergraduate and 10 graduate schools. In addition to regional accreditation, UA has baccalaureate program accreditation with AACSB, AAFCS, ABET, ACEJMC, ADA, AHEA, CCNE, CSAB, CSWE, FIDER, NASAD, NASM, NCATE, and NLN. The 8 libraries contain 2,229,330 volumes, 3,628,724 microform items, and 480,498 audiovisual forms/CDs, and subscribe to 17,788 periodicals. Computerized library services include the card catalog, interlibrary loans, and database searching. Special learning facilities include a learning resource center, art gallery, natural history museum, radio station, TV station, special collections department, map library, observatory, specialized computer labs, and archeological site. The 1000-acre campus is in a suburban area 50 miles southwest of Birmingham. Including residence halls, there are 253 buildings.

Student Life: 75% of undergraduates are from Alabama. Others are from 50 states, 70 foreign countries, and Canada. 89% are from public schools. 79% are white; 14%, African American. The average age of freshmen is 18; all undergraduates, 21. 19% do not continue beyond their first year; 57% remain to graduate.

Housing: 5000 students can be accommodated in college housing, which includes single-sex and coed dormitories, on-campus apartments, married-student housing, fraternity houses, and sorority houses. In addition, there are honors houses, language houses, and special interest houses. On-campus housing is available on a first-come, first-served basis. 75% of students commute. All students may keep cars.

Activities: 15% of men belong to 1 local and 26 national fraternities; 25% of women belong to 19 national sororities. There are 272 groups on campus, including art, band, cheerleading, chess, choir, chorale, chorus, computers, dance, debate, drama, drill team, ethnic, film, forensics, gay, honors, international, jazz band, literary magazine, marching band, musical theater, newspaper, opera, orchestra, pep band, photography, political, professional, radio and TV, religious, social, social service, student government, symphony, and yearbook. Popular campus events include Honors Week and Get on Board Day.

Sports: There are 8 intercollegiate sports for men and 11 for women, and 17 intramural sports for men and 16 for women. Facilities include an 83,000-seat football stadium, a 15,000-seat basketball arena, a track and field facility, a 6,100-seat baseball stadium, a 1,600-foot softball stadium, an indoor football practice facility, lighted varsity and public tennis courts, an aquatic complex with Olympic-size and standard pools and a weight-lifing facility, a soccer field, racquetball, basketball, and volleyball courts, weight and exercise rooms, an indoor/outdoor pool, an 18-hole golf course with clubhouse and driving range, an outdoor Olympic-size pool, and fitness centers in the residence halls.

Disabled Students: 90% of the campus is accessible. Wheelchair ramps, elevators, special parking, specially equipped rest rooms, special class scheduling, lowered drinking fountains, lowered telephones, automatic doors, TDD, and adaptive technology are available.

Services: Counseling and information services are available, as is tutoring in some subjects, including math, chemistry, physics, computer science, accounting, finance, economics, and foreign languages. There is a reader service for the blind, remedial math, reading, and writing, a center for teaching and learning, a writing lab, a career center, and computer-based self-tutoring

Campus Safety and Security: Measures include 24-hour foot and vehicle patrol, self-defense education, escort service, and informal discussions. There are pamphlets/posters/films, emergency telephones, lighted pathways/sidewalks, community-oriented police service (COPS), a UA Police bike patrol, Project Hope, educational awareness for personal safety, and alcohol and domestic violence awareness programs.

Programs of Study: UA confers B.A., B.S., B.A.Com., B.F.A., B.M., B.S.A.E., B.S.C.B.A., B.S.C.E., B.S.Ch.E., B.S.Chem., B.S.C.S., B.S.Ed., B.S.E.E., B.S.Geo., B.S.H.E.S., B.S.I.E., B.S.M.E., B.S.Met., B.S.N., and B.S.W. degrees. Master's and doctoral degrees are also awarded. Bachelor's degrees are awarded in BIOLOGICAL SCIENCE (biology/biological science, marine science, and microbiology), BUSINESS (accounting, banking and finance, fashion merchandising, management information systems, management science, and marketing management), COMMUNICATIONS AND THE ARTS (advertising, art history and appreciation, classics, dance, English, French, German, journalism, music, music performance, music theory and composition, public relations, Russian, Spanish, speech/debate/rhetoric, telecommunications, and visual and performing arts), COMPUTER AND PHYSICAL SCIENCE (chemistry, computer science, geology, mathematics, and physics), EDUCATION (athletic training, early childhood, education of the multiply handicapped, elementary, health, home economics, music, physical, secondary, and special), ENGINEERING AND ENVIRONMENTAL DESIGN (aerospace studies, chemical engineering, civil engineering, electrical/electronics engineering, environmental science, industrial administration/management, industrial engineering, interior design, mechanical engineering, metallurgical engineering, and urban planning technology), HEALTH PROFESSIONS (health care administration, music therapy, nursing, and speech pathology/audiology), SOCIAL SCIENCE (American studies, anthropology, Asian/Oriental studies, clothing and textiles management/production/services, criminal justice, economics, family/consumer resource management, fashion design and technology, food production/management/services, food science, geography, history, home economics, human development, interdisciplinary studies, international studies, Latin American studies, philosophy, physical fitness/movement, political science/government, prelaw, psychology, religion, and social work). Advertising, accounting, and engineering are the strongest academically. Public relations, finance, and marketing are the largest.

Required: To graduate, all students must complete a minimum of 120 semester hours, including at least 27 in the major, with a minimum GPA of 2.0. Core curriculum requirements include 12 hours each of humanities/fine arts and history/social science, 11 of natural science/math, 6 of computer studies or a foreign language, 6 of English composition, and 6 of upper-level courses with a writing component.

Special: UA offers cross-registration with Stillman College and Shelton State Community College, internships, international study programs, a Washington semester, a 3-week May-June interim term, exchange study within the United States, work-study, co-op programs, accelerated programs in business, B.A.-B.S. degrees, dual majors, student-designed majors, interdisciplinary majors in the New College arts and sciences program, credit for life experiences, nondegree study, and pass/fail options. There are 3-2 engineering degree programs with the University of Montevallo, as well as cross-registration within the Engineering Foundation Coalition. There are 50 national honor societies, including Phi Beta Kappa, a freshman honors program, and 5 departmental honors programs.

Faculty/Classroom: 66% of faculty are male; 34%, female. 75% teach undergraduates, 4% do research, and 3% do both. Graduate students teach 36% of introductory courses. The average class size in an introductory lecture is 59; in a laboratory, 17; and in a regular course, 25.

Admissions: 79% of the 2001-2002 applicants were accepted. The SAT I scores for the 2001-2002 freshman class were: Verbal--27% below 500, 45% between 500 and 599, 23% between 600 and 700, and 5% above 700; Math--28% below 500, 42% between 500 and 599, 23% between 600 and 700, and 6% above 700. The ACT scores were 27% below 21, 30% between 21 and 23, 23% between 24 and 26, 12% between 27 and 28, and 13% above 28. 46% of the current freshmen were in the top fifth of their class; 74% were in the top two fifths. There were 33 National Merit finalists.

Requirements: The SAT I or ACT is required. Admission is based on a sliding scale of test scores and high school GPA: students with a 2.5 academic GPA and a 20 ACT composite or 970 SAT I combined score will generally be admitted. A minimum GPA of 2.0 is required. The GED is accepted. High school preparation should include 4 units each of English and social studies, 3 each of math and science, 1 of foreign language, and 5 of academic electives. AP and CLEP credits are accepted. Important factors in the admissions decision are advanced placement or honor courses, evidence of special tallent, and leadership record. Applications are accepted on-line at *admissions@ua.edu*

Procedure: Freshmen are admitted to all sessions. Entrance exams should be taken in the spring of the junior year. There is an early admissions plan. Applications should be filed by June 1 for fall entry and May 1 for summer entry, along with a $25 fee. Notification is sent on a rolling basis.

Transfer: 1146 transfer students enrolled in 2001-2002. Applicants need an overall minimum GPA of 2.0 with at least 24 semester hours earned. Those with fewer than 24 hours must meet freshman standards. 32 credits of 120 must be completed at UA.

Visiting: There are regularly scheduled orientations for prospective students, consisting of a campus tour followed by meetings with admissions counselors and faculty and staff. Customized visits to suit student and parent needs are possible. University Day each November offers tours and information sessions. There are guides for informal visits and visitors may sit in on classes and stay overnight. To schedule a visit, contact the Office of Undergraduate Admissions.

Financial Aid: In a recent year, 55% of all freshmen and 60% of continuing students received some form of financial aid. 35% of freshmen and 38% of continuing students received need-based aid. The average freshman award was $6562. Of that total, scholarships or need-based grants averaged $2579 ($15,000 maximum); loans averaged $5025 ($9625 maximum); work contracts averaged $1084 ($1880 maximum); and third-party billings, faculty/staff tuition grants, and institutional and department grants averaged $599 ($2470 maximum). 16% of undergraduates work part time. Average annual earnings from campus work are $1952. The average financial indebtedness of the 2001 graduate was $19,386. The FAFSA is required. The fall application deadline is March 1.

International Students: There are 479 international students enrolled. The school actively recruits these students. They must score 500 on the written TOEFL or 173 on the electronic version, or earn a proficiency certificate from the university's English Language Institute. The SAT I or ACT is required for scholarship consideration.

Computers: The mainframes are an R26 and a Sun E600. More than 60 computer labs with more than 1450 PCs are located on campus to provide network access. All students may access the system 24 hours a day. There are no time limits and no fees.

Graduates: In 2001, 2577 bachelor's degrees were awarded. The most popular majors were marketing (8%), finance (7%), and management (7%). In an average class, 1% graduate in 3 years, 27% in 4 years, 55% in 5 years, and 59% in 6 years. 596 companies recruited on campus in 2000-2001.

Admissions Contact: Lisa B. Harris, Assistant Vice President of Admissions and Financial Aid. A video is available.
E-mail: *admissions@ua.edu* Web: *http://www.ua.edu*

UNIVERSITY OF ALABAMA AT BIRMINGHAM C-2

Birmingham, AL 35294 (205) 934-8221
(800) 421-8743; Fax: (205) 975-7114

Full-time: 2722 men, 4056 women	**Faculty:** 728; I, --$
Part-time: 1385 men, 1791 women	**Ph.D.s:** 91%
Graduate: 1488 men, 2278 women	**Student/Faculty:** 9 to 1
Year: semesters, summer session	**Tuition:** $3640 ($6610)
Application Deadline: August 1	**Room & Board:** $6471

Freshman Class: 3172 applied, 2886 accepted, 1301 enrolled
ACT: 21 **COMPETITIVE**

The University of Alabama at Birmingham, founded in 1969, is a public institution offering degrees in the arts and humanities, business, education, engineering, natural sciences and math, health-related professions, and social and behavorial sciences. There are 8 undergraduate and 13 graduate schools. In addition to regional accreditation, UAB has baccalaureate program accreditation with AACSB, ABET, CAHEA, CSWE, NASAD, NASM, NCATE, and NLN. The 2 libraries contain 760,757 volumes, 1,271,750 microform items, and 78,017 audiovisual forms/CDs, and subscribe to 4090 periodicals. Computerized library services include the card catalog, interlibrary loans, and database searching. Special learning facilities include an art gallery, radio station, Reynolds Historical Library, and Alabama Museum of the Health Sciences. The 180-acre campus is in an urban area in Birmingham. Including residence halls, there are 110 buildings.

Student Life: 92% of undergraduates are from Alabama. Others are from 40 states, 77 foreign countries, and Canada. 92% are from public schools. 59% are white; 30% African American. The average age of freshmen is 19; all undergraduates, 24. 26% do not continue beyond their first year.

Housing: 1911 students can be accommodated in college housing, which includes single-sex and coed dormitories, on-campus apartments, and married-student housing. On-campus housing is available on a first-come, first-served basis. 89% of students commute. Alcohol is not permitted. All students may keep cars.

Activities: 6% of men belong to 9 national fraternities; 6% of women belong to 8 national sororities. There are 150 groups on campus, including band, cheerleading, chess, choir, dance, drama, ethnic, honors, international, jazz band, literary magazine, marching band, musical theater, pep band, political, professional, radio and TV, religious, social, social service, student government, and yearbook. Popular campus events include Springfest and Madrigal Feaste.

Sports: There are 7 intercollegiate sports for men and 9 for women, and 11 intramural sports for men and 11 for women. Facilities include 11 tennis courts; 3 enclosed, lighted fields; a quarter-mile running track; and the Wallace Physical Education Complex, which includes 2 gyms, 3 basketball courts, 4 volleyball courts, 6 racquetball/handball courts, 2 wallyball courts, a squash court, fitness weight areas, 2 cardio-fitness rooms with equipment, an indoor track, an indoor heated swimming pool, and equipment.

Disabled Students: 80% of the campus is accessible. Wheelchair ramps, elevators, special parking, specially equipped rest rooms, lowered drinking fountains, and lowered telephones are available.

Services: Counseling and information services are available, as is tutoring in most subjects. There is a reader service for the blind, and remedial math, reading, and writing.

Campus Safety and Security: Measures include 24-hour foot and vehicle patrol, self-defense education, escort service, and shuttle buses. There are informal discussions, pamphlets/posters/films, emergency telephones, lighted pathways/sidewalks, a bike and mounted patrol, and a campus watch program.

Programs of Study: UAB confers B.A., B.S., B.F.A., B.S.B.M.E., B.S.C.E., B.S.E.E., B.S.M.E., B.S.Mt.E., B.S.N., and B.S.S.W. degrees. Master's and doctoral degrees are also awarded. Bachelor's degrees are awarded in BIOLOGICAL SCIENCE (biology/biological science), BUSINESS (accounting, banking and finance, business economics, and marketing/retailing/merchandising), COMMUNICATIONS AND THE ARTS (communications, dramatic arts, English, fine arts, French, linguistics, music, Spanish, and studio art), COMPUTER AND PHYSICAL SCIENCE (chemistry, computer science, mathematics, natural sciences, and physics), EDUCATION (early childhood, elementary, health, physical, secondary, and special), ENGINEERING AND ENVIRONMENTAL DESIGN (biomedical engineering, civil engineering, electrical/electronics engineering, industrial administration/management, materials engineering, and mechanical engineering), HEALTH PROFESSIONS (allied health, cytotechnology, medical records administration/services, medical technology, nuclear medical technology, nursing, physician's assistant, radiological science, and respiratory therapy), SOCIAL SCIENCE (anthropology, criminal justice, economics, history, international studies, philosophy, political science/government, psychology, social work, and sociology). Biology, psychology, and criminal justice are the largest.

Required: All students must complete a core curriculum that includes courses in math, computers, English, history, science, social sciences, philosophy, fine arts, foreign language or culture, and literature. To receive a bachelor's degree, students must complete 128 semester hours for most programs, with a GPA of at least 2.0.

Special: UAB offers student-designed majors, cross-registration with the Birmingham Area Consortium for Higher Education, internships, study abroad in 12 countries, work-study programs, nondegree study, pass/fail options, and credit by exam and for life experience. Cooperative education programs in the student's area of interest provide full-time or part-time work. There are 28 national honor societies, and a freshman honors program.

Faculty/Classroom: 64% of faculty are male; 36%, female.

Admissions: 91% of the 2001-2002 applicants were accepted. The ACT scores for the 2001-2002 freshman class were: 44% below 21, 26% between 21 and 23, 15% between 24 and 26, 7% between 27 and 28, and 8% above 28. 5% of the current freshmen were in the top fifth of their class; 19% were in the top two fifths. There were 10 National Merit finalists.

Requirements: The SAT I or ACT is required. In addition, applicants should have completed 12 Carnegie units, including 4 in English and 2 each in math, science, and social studies. The GED is accepted if the student's score on the test is at least 52. A GPA of 2.0 is required. AP and CLEP credits are accepted.

Procedure: Freshmen are admitted to all sessions. Entrance exams should be taken by the beginning of the senior year. There is a deferred admissions plan. Applications should be filed by August 1 for fall entry, December 1 for spring entry, and May 10 for summer entry. The fall 2001 application fee was $25. Notification is sent on a rolling basis.

Transfer: 845 transfer students enrolled in 2001-2002. Applicants should have earned at least 24 semester hours at an accredited institution with a minimum GPA of 2.0. College transcripts and statements of good standing from prior colleges are required of all transfer students. 32 credits of 128 must be completed at UAB.

Visiting: There are regularly scheduled orientations for prospective students, including a question-and-answer session, academic advising, sessions for parents, and presentations on student life, financial aid, housing, and student development. There are guides for informal visits and visitors may sit in on classes. To schedule a visit, contact Yolanda Tait at (205) 934-8142.

Financial Aid: In 2001-2002, 46% of all freshmen and 50% of continuing students received some form of financial aid. The average freshman award was $8018. The average financial indebtedness of the 2001 graduate was $17,485. UAB is a member of CSS. The FAFSA and the college's own financial statement are required. The fall application deadline is May 1.

International Students: There were 306 international students enrolled in a recent year. They must score 500 on the written TOEFL.

Computers: The mainframe is comprised of a Hitachi DataSystems operating in IBM System/ESA/370 mode. An IBM 4381 is used as a server for Internet and Suranet, with access to the Alabama Supercomputer Cray X-MP24. PCs are available in various schools and labs for student use. All students may access the system. There are no time limits and no fees.

Graduates: In 2001, 1646 bachelor's degrees were awarded. The most popular majors were psychology (9%), management (7%), and nursing (7%). In an average class, 6% graduate in 4 years, 21% in 5 years, and 30% in 6 years. 60 companies recruited on campus in 2000-2001.

Admissions Contact: Office of Undergraduate Admissions.
E-mail: *undergradadmit@uab.edu* Web: *www.uab.edu/enrollment/*

UNIVERSITY OF ALABAMA AT HUNTSVILLE C-1

Huntsville, AL 35899 **(256) 890-6070**
(800) UAH-CALL; Fax: (256) 824-6841

Full-time: 1633 men, 1764 women	**Faculty:** 281; I, --$
Part-time: 1082 men, 987 women	**Ph.D.s:** 91%
Graduate: 764 men, 524 women	**Student/Faculty:** 12 to 1
Year: semesters, summer session	**Tuition:** $3536 ($7430)
Application Deadline: August 15	**Room & Board:** $4380
Freshman Class: 1198 applied, 1004 accepted, 592 enrolled	
SAT I Verbal/Math: 550/570	**ACT:** 24 **VERY COMPETITIVE**

The University of Alabama in Huntsville, founded in 1950 and part of the University of Alabama system, is a public institution offering programs in liberal arts and sciences, business, nursing, and engineering. There are 5 undergraduate schools and 1 graduate school. In addition to regional accreditation, UAH has baccalaureate program accreditation with AACSB, ABET, CCNE, CSAB, NASM, and NLN. The library contains 274,946 volumes, 763,978 microform items, and 2677 audiovisual forms/CDs, and subscribes to 1336 periodicals. Computerized library services include the card catalog, interlibrary loans, and database searching. Special learning facilities include an art gallery and radio station. The 376-acre campus is in a suburban area 100 miles north of Birmingham and 90 miles south of Nashville. Including residence halls, there are 34 buildings.

Student Life: 89% of undergraduates are from Alabama. Others are from 44 states, 80 foreign countries, and Canada. 91% are from public schools. 73% are white; 14% African American. 79% are Protestant; 11% Catholic. The average age of freshmen is 19; all undergraduates, 25. 29% do not continue beyond their first year; 35% remain to graduate.

Housing: 748 students can be accommodated in college housing, which includes coed dormitories, on-campus apartments, and married-student housing. On-campus housing is available on a first-come, first-served basis. 88% of students commute. Alcohol is not permitted. All students may keep cars.

Activities: 5% of men belong to 6 national fraternities; 6% of women belong to 5 national sororities. There are 110 groups on campus, including art, cheerleading, chess, choir, chorale, chorus, computers, dance, drama, ethnic, film, gay, honors, international, jazz band, literary magazine, newspaper, pep band, photography, political, professional, radio and TV, religious, social, social service, student government, and symphony. Popular campus events include FallFest, SpringFest, and Black History Month.

Sports: There are 5 intercollegiate sports for men and 6 for women, and 13 intramural sports for men and 13 for women. Facilities include a 2800-seat gym, a swimming pool, racquetball and tennis courts, soccer fields, softball diamonds, and a recreational facility.

Disabled Students: 80% of the campus is accessible. Wheelchair ramps, elevators, special parking, specially equipped rest rooms, special class scheduling, lowered drinking fountains, and a swimming pool lift are available.

Services: Counseling and information services are available, as is tutoring in most subjects. There is a reader service for the blind, remedial math, reading, and writing, and study skills classes.

Campus Safety and Security: Measures include 24-hour foot and vehicle patrol, escort service, informal discussions, and pamphlets/posters/films. There are lighted pathways/sidewalks.

Programs of Study: UAH confers B.A., B.S., B.S.B.A., B.S.E., and B.S.N. degrees. Master's and doctoral degrees are also awarded. Bachelor's degrees are awarded in BIOLOGICAL SCIENCE (biology/biological science), BUSINESS (accounting, banking and finance, business administration and management, management information systems, and marketing/retailing/merchandising), COMMUNICATIONS AND THE ARTS (communications, English, fine arts, French, German, languages, music, and Spanish), COMPUTER AND PHYSICAL SCIENCE (chemistry, computer science, mathematics, and physics), EDUCATION (education), ENGINEERING AND ENVIRONMENTAL DESIGN (chemical engineering, civil engineering, computer engineering, electrical/electronics engineering, industrial engineering, mechanical engineering, and optical engineering), HEALTH PROFESSIONS (nursing), SOCIAL SCIENCE (history, philosophy, political science/government, psychology, Russian and Slavic studies, and sociology). Engineering, nursuing, and management information systems are the largest.

Required: All students must earn a minimum GPA of 2.0 over 128 to 134 credit hours, including 21 to 36 in their major. The core curriculum includes courses in English composition, literature, world history, foreign language and communications, fine arts, math, science, and social sciences.

Special: UAH offers co-op programs in all majors, cross-registration with Alabama Agricultural and Mechanical University and Athens State and Calhoun Community Colleges, and internships in administrative science, communications, education, and political science. A 3-2 engineering degree is available with Oakwood College, Fisk University, Atlanta University Center, and the American University of Paris. Dual majors, B.A.-B.S. degrees in math and biology, nondegree study, and a pass/fail option are also offered. There are 22 national honor societies and a freshman honors program.

Faculty/Classroom: 65% of faculty are male; 35%, female. All both teach and do research. Graduate students teach 7% of introductory courses. The average class size in an introductory lecture is 28; in a laboratory, 16; and in a regular course, 19.

Admissions: 84% of the 2001-2002 applicants were accepted. The SAT I scores for the 2001-2002 freshman class were: Verbal--26% below 500, 42% between 500 and 599, 24% between 600 and 700, and 8% above 700; Math--25% below 500, 36% between 500 and 599, 30% between 600 and 700, and 9% above 700. The ACT scores were 18% below 21, 25% between 21 and 23, 30% between 24 and 26, 14% between 27 and 28, and 13% above 28. 47% of the current freshmen were in the top fifth of their class; 77% were in the top two fifths. There were 3 National Merit finalists. 1 freshman graduated first in the class.

Requirements: The SAT I or ACT is required. In addition, a sliding scale with the GPA determines the minimum test score needed. The

GED is accepted. Students should present a minimum of 20 Carnegie units, including 4 years of English, 3 each of math and social studies, and 2 of science. AP and CLEP credits are accepted. Applications are accepted on-line via CollegeNET.

Procedure: Freshmen are admitted to all sessions. Entrance exams should be taken during the junior year. There are early admissions and deferred admissions plans. Applications should be filed by August 15 for fall entry, January 15 for spring entry, and May 15 for summer entry. Notification is sent on a rolling basis. The fall 2001 application fee was $20.

Transfer: 614 transfer students enrolled in 2001-2002. Applicants need a minimum GPA of 2.0. 32 credits of 128 must be completed at UAH.

Visiting: There are regularly scheduled orientations for prospective students, including new student orientation, held prior to the beginning of each semester or during the first week of classes. There are guides for informal visits and visitors may sit in on classes and stay overnight. To schedule a visit, contact James Thomas in Admissions at (256) 824-7142 or *thomasj@email.uah.edu*.

Financial Aid: In 2001-2002, 85% of all freshmen and 49% of continuing students received some form of financial aid. 38% of freshmen and 34% of continuing students received need-based aid. The average freshman award was $3542. Of that total, scholarships or need-based grants averaged $2712 ($13,344 maximum); loans averaged $3605 ($12,625 maximum); and work contracts averaged $3590. 85% of undergraduates work part time. Average annual earnings from campus work are $2100. The average financial indebtedness of the 2001 graduate was $16,882. The FAFSA is required. The fall application deadline is July 1.

International Students: There are 151 international students enrolled. The school actively recruits these students. They must score 500 on the written TOEFL, take the college's own test, and also take the SAT I or the ACT.

Computers: The mainframe is a DEC 7000/610. Terminals are located in 8 buildings across campus. The campus is served by Ethernet and provides access to the Alabama Supercomputer. All students may access the system 24 hours a day. There are no time limits and no fees.

Graduates: In 2001, 646 bachelor's degrees were awarded. The most popular majors were nursing (20%), management information systems (10%), and electrical engineering (8%). In an average class, 10% graduate in 4 years, 29% in 5 years, and 39% in 6 years. 399 companies recruited on campus in 2000-2001. Of the 2000 graduating class, 15% were enrolled in graduate school within 6 months of graduation.

Admissions Contact: Scott Verzyl, Associate Vice President for Enrollment Services, Registrar, and Director of Admissions.
E-mail: *admitme@email.uah.edu* Web: *www.uah.edu*

UNIVERSITY OF MOBILE
Mobile, AL 36663-0220 — **A-5**
(251) 675-5990
(800) 946-7267; Fax: (251) 675-6329

Full-time: 495 men, 885 women	**Faculty:** 86
Part-time: 80 men, 343 women	**Ph.D.s:** 72%
Graduate: 51 men, 133 women	**Student/Faculty:** 16 to 1
Year: semesters, summer session	**Tuition:** $8770
Application Deadline: September 10	**Room & Board:** $4850
Freshman Class: 450 applied, 440 accepted, 220 enrolled	
ACT: required	**LESS COMPETITIVE**

The University of Mobile, founded in 1961, is a private liberal arts institution affiliated with the Southern Baptists. There are 6 undergraduate and 4 graduate schools. In addition to regional accreditation, Mobile has baccalaureate program accreditation with ACBSP, NASM, and NLN. The library contains 64,504 volumes, 253 microform items, and 959 audiovisual forms/CDs, and subscribes to 950 periodicals. Computerized library services include the card catalog, interlibrary loans, and database searching. Special learning facilities include a learning resource center, an art gallery and a forest learning center. The 830-acre campus is in a suburban area 10 miles northwest of Mobile. Including residence halls, there are 52 buildings.

Student Life: 83% of undergraduates are from Alabama. Others are from 23 states, 14 foreign countries, and Canada. 86% are from public schools. 73% are white; 19%, African American. Most are Protestant. The average age of freshmen is 18; all undergraduates, 26. 45% do not continue beyond their first year; 33% remain to graduate.

Housing: 372 students can be accommodated in college housing, which includes single-sex dormitories. On-campus housing is guaranteed for the freshman year only and is available on a first-come, first-served basis. 80% of students commute. Alcohol is not permitted. All students may keep cars.

Activities: There are no fraternities or sororities. There are 52 groups on campus, including art, band, cheerleading, choir, chorale, chorus, computers, dance, drama, ethnic, honors, international, musical theater, newspaper, orchestra, pep band, political, professional, religious, social, social service, student government, and symphony. Popular campus events include Boar's Head Festival, College Preview Day, and Upper Room Dinner Theater.

Sports: There are 6 intercollegiate sports for men and 7 for women, and 7 intramural sports for men and 6 for women. Facilities include an 800-seat gym, a tennis complex with 10 courts, a swimming pool, a track, baseball, softball, and soccer fields, and a golf driving range with 2 putting greens.

Disabled Students: 95% of the campus is accessible. Wheelchair ramps, elevators, special parking, specially equipped rest rooms, special class scheduling, and lowered drinking fountains are available.

Services: Counseling and information services are available, as is tutoring in some subjects, including writing, English, and math. There is remedial math, reading, and writing.

Campus Safety and Security: Measures include 24-hour foot and vehicle patrol, self-defense education, informal discussions, and pamphlets/posters/films. There are emergency telephones, lighted pathways/sidewalks, and a professional campus security service available 24 hours per day.

Programs of Study: Mobile confers B.A., B.S., and B.S.N. degrees. Associate and master's degrees are also awarded. Bachelor's degrees are awarded in BIOLOGICAL SCIENCE (biology/biological science), BUSINESS (accounting, business administration and management, and marketing/retailing/merchandising), COMMUNICATIONS AND THE ARTS (communications, English, and music), COMPUTER AND PHYSICAL SCIENCE (chemistry, computer science, and mathematics), EDUCATION (early childhood, elementary, physical, and secondary), HEALTH PROFESSIONS (nursing), SOCIAL SCIENCE (economics, history, liberal arts/general studies, psychology, religion, and sociology). Education and nursing are the strongest academically. Business administration, elementary education, and nursing are the largest.

Required: All students are required to complete 128 credit hours, with at least 30 in their major field, and earn a minimum GPA of 2.0. Distribution requirements include 12 hours in English, 8 hours in lab science, 6 hours each in religion and history, 6 hours from business, computer science, economics, political science, psychology, and sociology, 4 hours in health/phys ed and recreation, 3 hours each in speech and math, and 3 hours in art, music, or philosophy. Computer literacy must be demonstrated. Chapel attendance is also required.

Special: A variety of internships and work-study programs, B.A.-B.S. degrees, an accelerated degree program, and dual majors are available, as is a 3-2 engineering degree with Auburn University and the University of South Alabama. There are 10 national honor societies, a freshman honors program, and 7 departmental honors program.

Faculty/Classroom: 47% of faculty are male; 53%, female. All teach undergraduates. No introductory courses are taught by graduate students. The average class size in an introductory lecture is 25; in a laboratory, 16; and in a regular course, 20.

Admissions: 98% of the 2001-2002 applicants were accepted. The ACT scores for the 2001-2002 freshman class were: 50% below 21, 21% between 21 and 23, 15% between 24 and 26, 7% between 27 and 28, and 8% above 28. 2 freshmen graduated first in their class.

Requirements: The ACT is required with a minimum composite score of 19. In addition, applicants must have 22 Carnegie units. An essay, portfolio, and interview are recommended. The GED is accepted. The ACT is not required of applicants over age 30. A GPA of 2.0 is required. AP and CLEP credits are accepted. Important factors in the admissions decision are advanced placement or honor courses, ability to finance college education, and leadership record. Applications are accepted on-line at the university's web site.

Procedure: Freshmen are admitted fall, spring, and summer. Entrance exams should be taken in August before the junior year. There are early decision and deferred admissions plans. Early decision applications should be filed by October 31; regular applications, by September 10 for fall entry, January 24 for spring entry, and May 1 for summer entry, along with a $30 fee. Notification of early decision is sent November 1; regular decision, on a rolling basis.

Transfer: 239 transfer students enrolled in 2001-2002. Transfer students need to have earned a minimum GPA of 2.0 for previous college work. If fewer than 30 semester hours are accepted, a minimum score of 19 on the ACT and a high school transcript, or GED, are required. 32 credits of 128 must be completed at Mobile.

Visiting: There are regularly scheduled orientations for prospective students, including financial aid seminars, academic seminars, faculty advising, campus tours, and admissions counseling. There are guides for informal visits and visitors may sit in on classes and stay overnight. To schedule a visit, contact Brian Boyle, Director of Admissions at (251) 442-2287.

Financial Aid: In 2001-2002, 98% of all freshmen and 97% of continuing students received some form of financial aid. 36% of freshmen and 32% of continuing students received need-based aid. The average freshman award was $3525. Of that total, scholarships or need-based grants averaged $3130 ($6150 maximum); loans averaged $2625 (maximum); and work contracts averaged $1545. 15% of undergraduates work part time. Average annual earnings from campus work are $1545. The average financial indebtedness of the 2001 graduate was $8240. The FAFSA and the college's own financial statement are required. The fall application deadline is March 31.

International Students: There are 28 international students enrolled. The school actively recruits these students. They must score 500 on the written TOEFL and also take the college's own test and the ACT, scoring 19.

Computers: The mainframe is a DEC VAX 11/750. Students use the terminals located in 5 computer labs. All students may access the system 8 A.M. to 9 P.M. Monday through Friday and a half day Saturday. There are no time limits. The fee is $35 per semester. It is strongly recommended that all students have a personal computer.

Graduates: In 2001, 300 bachelor's degrees were awarded. The most popular majors were business administration (20%), education (20%), and nursing (15%). 50 companies recruited on campus in 2000-2001.

Admissions Contact: Brian Boyle, Director of Admissions.
E-mail: *brianb@mail.umobile.edu* Web: *www.umobile.edu*

UNIVERSITY OF MONTEVALLO

Montevallo, AL 35115-6030 C-3
(205) 665-6030
(800) 292-4349; Fax: (205) 665-6032

Full-time: 745 men, 1551 women	**Faculty:** 131; IIA, --$
Part-time: 79 men, 184 women	**Ph.D.s:** 84%
Graduate: 76 men, 300 women	**Student/Faculty:** 18 to 1
Year: semesters, summer session	**Tuition:** $3690 ($7100)
Application Deadline: August 1	**Room & Board:** $3576
Freshman Class: 1342 applied, 973 accepted, 533 enrolled	
ACT: 22	**COMPETITIVE**

The University of Montevallo, founded in 1896, is a public liberal arts institution offering courses in business, fine arts, music, preprofessional training, and teacher preparation. There are 4 undergraduate schools and 1 graduate school. In addition to regional accreditation, UM has baccalaureate program accreditation with AACSB, ADA, AHEA, CSWE, NASAD, NASM, and NCATE. The library contains 252,120 volumes, 768,856 microform items, and 2767 audiovisual forms/CDs, and subscribes to 738 periodicals. Computerized library services include the card catalog, interlibrary loans, and database searching. Special learning facilities include a learning resource center, art gallery, TV station, and a university theater. The 160-acre campus is in a small town 35 miles south of Birmingham. Including residence halls, there are 37 buildings.

Student Life: 98% of undergraduates are from Alabama. Others are from 18 states, 24 foreign countries, and Canada. 94% are from public schools. 80% are white; 14% African American. Most are Protestant. The average age of freshmen is 18; all undergraduates, 21. 28% do not continue beyond their first year.

Housing: 1276 students can be accommodated in college housing, which includes single-sex and coed dormitories and on-campus apartments. On-campus housing is available on a first-come, first-served basis. 63% of students commute. All students may keep cars.

Activities: 21% of men belong to 7 national fraternities; 16% of women belong to 7 national sororities. There are 74 groups on campus, including art, cheerleading, choir, chorus, dance, debate, drama, ethnic, forensics, gay, honors, international, jazz band, literary magazine, musical theater, newspaper, pep band, photography, political, professional, radio and TV, religious, social, social service, student government, and yearbook. Popular campus events include College Night, Springfest, and Honors Day.

Sports: There are 4 intercollegiate sports for men and 5 for women, and 7 intramural sports for men and 4 for women. Facilities include a 2200-seat gym, an indoor swimming pool, bowling lanes, soccer and other playing fields, a golf course, a walking track, and tennis courts.

Disabled Students: 90% of the campus is accessible. Wheelchair ramps, elevators, special parking, specially equipped rest rooms, special class scheduling, lowered drinking fountains, and lowered telephones are available.

Services: Counseling and information services are available, as is tutoring in some subjects, including study skills. There is a reader service for the blind, and remedial math, reading, and writing, and a speech and hearing center.

Campus Safety and Security: Measures include 24-hour foot and vehicle patrol, escort service, informal discussions, and pamphlets/posters/films. There are lighted pathways/sidewalks and campus lighting, and electronic access into residence halls.

Programs of Study: UM confers B.A., B.S., B.B.A., B.F.A., B.M., and B.M.E. degrees. Master's degrees are also awarded. Bachelor's degrees are awarded in BIOLOGICAL SCIENCE (biology/biological science), BUSINESS (accounting, banking and finance, business administration and management, management science, and marketing/retailing/merchandising), COMMUNICATIONS AND THE ARTS (art, communications, dramatic arts, English, French, journalism, music, Spanish, and studio art), COMPUTER AND PHYSICAL SCIENCE (chemistry and mathematics), EDUCATION (art, early childhood, education of the deaf and hearing impaired, elementary, home economics, music, and physical), HEALTH PROFESSIONS (speech pathology/audiology), SOCIAL SCIENCE (history, political science/government, psychology, social science, social work, and sociology). Elementary/early childhood education, speech pathology, and English are the largest.

Required: To graduate, students must complete a minimum of 130 semester hours with an overall 2.0 GPA while meeting core, major, and minor requirements. Core requirements include 12 hours of writing reinforcement courses (usually met with literature and major/minor courses), 7 hours of sciences (two branches), 6 hours each of foundations in writing, world literature, world civilizations, and institutions and issues courses, 4 hours of health/phys ed, and 3 hours each of oral communications, math, computer science, fine arts, and human behavior and inquiry courses.

Special: A 3-2 engineering degree is offered with Auburn University and the University of Alabama at Birmingham. Internships, study abroad, work-study, an accelerated degree plan, B.A.-B.S. degrees, dual degrees, and pass/fail options are available. There are 22 national honor societies and a freshman honors program.

Faculty/Classroom: 55% of faculty are male; 45%, female. 99% teach undergraduates. No introductory courses are taught by graduate students. The average class size in an introductory lecture is 27; in a laboratory, 24; and in a regular course, 24.

Admissions: 73% of the 2001-2002 applicants were accepted. The ACT scores for the 2001-2002 freshman class were: 39% below 21, 28% between 21 and 23, 9% between 24 and 26, 9% between 27 and 28, and 5% above 28. 25% of the current freshmen were in the top fifth of their class; 58% were in the top 50%. There were 2 National Merit finalists and 6 semifinalists.

Requirements: The ACT is required. In addition, applicants must be high school graduates with a minimum of 16 academic credits, including 4 units each of English, social studies, and academic electives, and 2 each of math and science. One year each of algebra and plane geometry is recommended. The GED is accepted with a minimum standard score average of 50. A GPA of 2.0 is required. AP and CLEP credits are accepted. Important factors in the admissions decision are advanced placement or honor courses, evidence of special talent, and geographic diversity.

Procedure: Freshmen are admitted to all sessions. Entrance exams should be taken in April or June of the junior year, or October of the senior year. There are early admissions and deferred admissions plans. Applications should be filed by August 1 for fall entry, December 1 for spring entry, and May 1 for summer entry. Notification is sent on a rolling basis. The fall 2001 application fee was $25.

Transfer: 263 transfer students enrolled in 2001-2002. Applicants need a minimum GPA of 2.0 on previous college study attempted. 30 credits of 130 must be completed at UM.

Visiting: There are regularly scheduled orientations for prospective students, consisting of 1 day of preregistration in July and 2 days of orientation in August, including on-site visits, mentor groups, play activities, and career and learning style assessments. There are guides for informal visits and visitors may sit in on classes and stay overnight. To schedule a visit, contact the Office of Admissions.

Financial Aid: In a recent year, 68% of all freshmen and 65% of continuing students received some form of financial aid. The average freshman award was $3288. Of that total, scholarships or need-based grants averaged $1673 ($7074 maximum); loans averaged $2384 ($9253 maximum); work contracts averaged $1274 ($1600 maximum); and (PAC-PrePaid Affordable College Tuition) $2834. 32% of undergraduates work part time. Average annual earnings from campus work are $1188. The average financial indebtedness of the 2001 graduate was $9749. The FAFSA is required. The fall application deadline is August 1.

International Students: There are 47 international students enrolled. They must score 525 on the written TOEFL.

Computers: The mainframe is a Compaq Alpha DS20E. About 170 Pentium class machines and 130 Power Macs are available in 9 computer labs. All students may access the system 7 A.M. to 11 P.M. Monday through Friday; hours vary on weekends. There are no time limits and no fees.

Graduates: In 2001, 491 bachelor's degrees were awarded. The most popular majors were elementary/early childhood education (12%), speech-language pathology (6%), and family and consumer science (6%). In an average class, 22% graduate in 4 years, 39% in 5 years, and 42% in 6 years. 80 companies recruited on campus in 2000-2001.

Admissions Contact: William J. Cannon, Jr., Director of Admissions.
E-mail: *admissions@um.montevallo.edu* Web: *www.montevallo.edu*

UNIVERSITY OF NORTH ALABAMA B-1
Florence, AL 35632-0001 (256) 765-4608
(800) TALKUNA; Fax: (256) 765-4960

Full-time: 1688 men, 2392 women	**Faculty:** 188; IIA, --$
Part-time: 323 men, 449 women	**Ph.D.s:** 72%
Graduate: 232 men, 438 women	**Student/Faculty:** 22 to 1
Year: semesters, summer session	**Tuition:** $2982 ($5646)
Application Deadline: July 1	**Room & Board:** $4034

Freshman Class: 1374 applied, 1374 accepted, 789 enrolled
ACT: 21 **NONCOMPETITIVE**

The University of North Alabama, founded in 1872, is a public institution offering degree programs in arts and sciences, business, education, and nursing. There are 4 undergraduate and 2 graduate schools. In addition to regional accreditation, UNA has baccalaureate program accreditation with ACBSP, CSWE, NASAD, NASM, NCATE, and NLN. The library contains 343,486 volumes, 968,776 microform items, and 8945 audiovisual forms/CDs, and subscribes to 1792 periodicals. Computerized library services include the card catalog, interlibrary loans, and database searching. Special learning facilities include a learning resource center, art gallery, planetarium, and radio station. The 125-acre campus is in an urban area 116 miles north of Birmingham. Including residence halls, there are 50 buildings.

Student Life: 82% of undergraduates are from Alabama. Others are from 30 states, 31 foreign countries, and Canada. 89% are from public schools. 80% are white; 10%, African American. The average age of freshmen is 19; all undergraduates, 23. 45% do not continue beyond their first year; 35% remain to graduate.

Housing: 1010 students can be accommodated in college housing, which includes single-sex and coed dormitories, on-campus apartments, and married-student housing. On-campus housing is available on a first-come, first-served basis. 81% of students commute. Alcohol is not permitted. All students may keep cars.

Activities: 5% of men belong to 6 national fraternities; 6% of women belong to 6 national sororities. There are 91 groups on campus, including band, cheerleading, choir, chorus, computers, drama, drill team, ethnic, film, honors, international, jazz band, literary magazine, marching band, musical theater, newspaper, opera, pep band, political, radio and TV, religious, social, social service, student government, and yearbook. Popular campus events include Spring Fling and George Lindsey Film Festival.

Sports: There are 6 intercollegiate sports for men and 6 for women, and 19 intramural sports for men and 19 for women. Facilities include a 13,500-seat football stadium, a 4000-seat gym, a baseball field, an outdoor track, an indoor swimming pool, and tennis courts.

Disabled Students: 96% of the campus is accessible. Wheelchair ramps, elevators, special parking, specially equipped rest rooms, special class scheduling, lowered drinking fountains, and lowered telephones are available.

Services: Counseling and information services are available, as is tutoring in some subjects, including math, English, history, biology, chemistry, accounting, finance, and economics. There is a reader service for the blind, remedial math and writing, and an academic resource center that features computer-assisted tutoring and faculty mentoring.

Campus Safety and Security: Measures include 24-hour foot and vehicle patrol, informal discussions, pamphlets/posters/films, and emergency telephones. There are lighted pathways/sidewalks.

Programs of Study: UNA confers B.A., B.S., B.A.M., B.B.A., B.F.A., B.G.S., B.M.M.Ed., B.S.Ed.,B.S.M., B.S.N., and B.S.W. degrees. Master's degrees are also awarded. Bachelor's degrees are awarded in BIOLOGICAL SCIENCE (biology/biological science and environmental biology), BUSINESS (accounting, banking and finance, business economics, and marketing/retailing/merchandising), COMMUNICATIONS AND THE ARTS (art, communications, dramatic arts, English, French, German, journalism, music, public relations, and Spanish), COMPUTER AND PHYSICAL SCIENCE (chemistry, computer science, geology, information sciences and systems, mathematics, and physics), EDUCATION (art, business, early childhood, elementary, foreign languages, home economics, music, physical, science, secondary, and social science), ENGINEERING AND ENVIRONMENTAL DESIGN (interior design), HEALTH PROFESSIONS (industrial hygiene and nursing), SOCIAL SCIENCE (criminal justice, geography, history, political science/government, psychology, social work, and sociology). Physical sciences, biological sciences, and math are the strongest academically. Management, accounting, and marketing are the largest.

Required: Students must complete a core curriculum, which includes 12 semester hours in history, social and behavioral sciences, humanities, and fine arts, 11 in natural sciences and math, and 6 in language composition. Passing grades in 1 writing emphasis and 1 computer course also are needed. A minimum of 128 semester hours and a minimum GPA of 2.0 are required in order to graduate.

Special: UNA offers cooperative programs in all majors, work-study programs, various B.A.-B.S. degrees, dual majors, and a general studies degree. Nondegree study is possible. There are 13 national honor societies, including Phi Beta Kappa, and 2 departmental honors program.

Faculty/Classroom: 62% of faculty are male; 38%, female. All teach undergraduates. No introductory courses are taught by graduate students.

Admissions: All of the 2001-2002 applicants were accepted. The ACT scores for the 2001-2002 freshman class were: 48% below 21, 24% between 21 and 23, 19% between 24 and 26, 5% between 27 and 28, and 4% above 28. 37% of the current freshmen were in the top fifth of their class; 72% were in the top two fifths.

Requirements: The SAT I or ACT is required. In addition, applicants should be graduates of an accredited high school or have earned a GED. A GPA of 2.0 is required. AP and CLEP credits are accepted. Applications are accepted on-line.

Procedure: Freshmen are admitted to all sessions. Entrance exams should be taken in the senior year. There is a deferred admissions plan. Applications should be filed by July 1 for fall entry, December 1 for spring entry, and May 25 for summer entry along with a $25 fee. Notification is sent on a rolling basis.

Transfer: 573 transfer students enrolled in a recent year. Applicants should be eligible to return to the school last attended. 30 credits of 128 must be completed at UNA.

Visiting: There are regularly scheduled orientations for prospective students, consisting of orientation programs conducted each summer prior to the fall semester. There are guides for informal visits. To schedule a visit, contact Kim Mauldin, Director of Admissions.

Financial Aid: In 2001-2002, 63% of all freshmen and 57% of continuing students received some form of financial aid. 53% of freshmen and 49% of continuing students received need-based aid. The average freshman award was $2144. Of that total, scholarships or need-based grants averaged $1602 ($3125 maximum); loans averaged $2945 ($4625 maximum); and work contracts averaged $1648 ($2000 maximum). 13% of undergraduates work part time. Average annual earnings from campus work are $2250. The average financial indebtedness of the 2001 graduate was $16,529. The FAFSA is required. The fall application deadline is April 1.

International Students: There are 159 international students enrolled. The school actively recruits these students. They must score 500 on the written TOEFL or 173 on the electronic version.

Computers: The mainframe is an IBM 4300 series. Terminals are located in the Computer Center and in computer labs in the Colleges of Business and Education. Macs and PCs are available in the Academic Resource Center, with additional units available in faculty and departmental offices. Computer labs are also available in each dormitory. All students may access the system. There are no time limits and no fees. It is strongly recommended that all students have a personal computer.

Graduates: In 2001, 808 bachelor's degrees were awarded. The most popular majors were business (27%), education (18%), and social sciences (10%). In an average class, 11% graduate in 4 years, 29% in 5 years, and 36% in 6 years. 100 companies recruited on campus in 2000-2001.

Admissions Contact: Kim Mauldin, Director of Admissions. A video is available. E-mail: *admis1@unanov.una.edu*
Web: *http://www.una.edu*

UNIVERSITY OF SOUTH ALABAMA A-5
Mobile, AL 36688 (334) 460-6141
(800) 872-5247; Fax: (334) 460-7023

Full-time: 2407 men, 3572 women	**Faculty:** 688; IIA, av$
Part-time: 1611 men, 1982 women	**Ph.D.s:** 81%
Graduate: 717 men, 1582 women	**Student/Faculty:** 9 to 1
Year: semesters, summer session	**Tuition:** $3230 ($6140)
Application Deadline: August 10	**Room & Board:** $3746

Freshman Class: 2444 applied, 2282 accepted, 1176 enrolled
ACT: 23 **LESS COMPETITIVE**

The University of South Alabama, a state-supported institution established in 1963, offers undergraduate and graduate degrees in the allied health professions, arts and sciences, business and management studies, education, engineering, nursing, computer and information sciences, and medicine. There are 8 undergraduate and 8 graduate schools. In addition to regional accreditation, USA has baccalaureate program accreditation with AACSB, ABET, ACOTE, AHEA, APTA, CAAHEP, CAHEA, CCNE, CSAB, LCME, NAACLS, NASAD, NASM, NCATE, and NLN. The 2 libraries contain 494,046 volumes and 1,424,457 microform items, and subscribe to 3145 periodicals. Computerized library services include the card catalog, interlibrary loans, and database searching. Special learning facilities include a learning resource center, art gallery, radio station, and TV station. The 1667-acre campus is in a suburban area 150 miles east of New Orleans. Including residence halls, there are 286 buildings.

Student Life: 78% of undergraduates are from Alabama. Others are from 40 states, 100 foreign countries, and Canada. 73% are white; 16%,

African American. The average age of all undergraduates is 24. 29% do not continue beyond their first year.

Housing: 1966 students can be accommodated in college housing, which includes coed dormitories, on-campus apartments, married-student housing, fraternity houses, and sorority houses. On-campus housing is available on a first-come, first-served basis. 81% of students commute. Alcohol is not permitted. All students may keep cars.

Activities: 10% of men belong to 12 national fraternities; 7% of women belong to 8 national sororities. There are 130 groups on campus, including band, cheerleading, chess, choir, chorale, chorus, dance, drama, ethnic, film, gay, honors, international, jazz band, literary magazine, musical theater, newspaper, opera, orchestra, pep band, political, professional, radio and TV, religious, social, social service, student government, and symphony. Popular campus events include Club South, Greek Week, and Chi Omega Songfest.

Sports: There are 7 intercollegiate sports for men and 8 for women, and 13 intramural sports for men and 12 for women. Facilities include a 10,000-seat arena and a 49,000-square-foot student recreation center, including 6 handball courts, fitness rooms, 2 basketball/volleyball courts, and an indoor track.

Disabled Students: 90% of the campus is accessible. Wheelchair ramps, elevators, special parking, specially equipped rest rooms, lowered drinking fountains, and lowered telephones are available.

Services: Counseling and information services are available, as is tutoring in some subjects. There is a reader service for the blind, and remedial math, reading, and writing.

Campus Safety and Security: Measures include 24-hour foot and vehicle patrol, escort service, informal discussions, and pamphlets/posters/films. There are emergency telephones and lighted pathways/sidewalks.

Programs of Study: USA confers B.A., B.S., B.F.A., B.Mus., B.S.C.E., B.S.Cardioresp.Care, B.S.Ch.E., B.S.C.L.S., B.S.Comp.Eng., B.S.H.S., B.S.O.T., B.S.R.S., and B.S.Sp. degrees. Master's and doctoral degrees are also awarded. Bachelor's degrees are awarded in BIOLOGICAL SCIENCE (biology/biological science), BUSINESS (banking and finance, business administration and management, business economics, electronic business, marketing/retailing/merchandising, and recreation and leisure services), COMMUNICATIONS AND THE ARTS (art, art history and appreciation, communications, dramatic arts, English, fine arts, French, German, music, music performance, Russian, Spanish, and studio art), COMPUTER AND PHYSICAL SCIENCE (atmospheric sciences and meteorology, chemistry, computer science, geology, mathematics, physics, and statistics), EDUCATION (early childhood, education, elementary, health, middle school, music, physical, secondary, and special), ENGINEERING AND ENVIRONMENTAL DESIGN (chemical engineering, civil engineering, computer engineering, electrical/electronics engineering, and mechanical engineering), HEALTH PROFESSIONS (biomedical science, clinical science, health science, medical technology, nursing, radiological science, respiratory therapy, and speech pathology/audiology), SOCIAL SCIENCE (anthropology, criminal justice, geography, history, international studies, philosophy, political science/government, psychology, and sociology). Business administration, nursing, and computer and information sciences are the largest.

Required: General education requirements consist of 12 hours in written composition, 12 hours in humanities and fine arts, 11 hours in natural science and math, and at least 12 hours in history and the social and behavioral sciences. A minimum of 128 semester hours, with a minimum GPA of 2.0, are required for graduation.

Special: A cooperative doctoral program in education is offered in conjunction with Auburn University. Also available are work-study programs, internships, study abroad in 4 countries, dual majors, an adult degree program, and a personalized studies program. There are 43 national honor societies and a freshman honors program.

Faculty/Classroom: 67% of faculty are male; 33%, female. No introductory courses are taught by graduate students. The average class size in an introductory lecture is 72; in a laboratory, 26; and in a regular course, 29.

Admissions: 93% of the 2001-2002 applicants were accepted. The ACT scores for the 2000-2001 freshman class were 25% below 20, 40% between 20 and 23, 24% between 24 and 27, 9% between 38 and 32, and 1% between 33 and 36. 46% of the current freshman were in the top quarter of their class; 84% were in the top half.

Requirements: The ACT is required. In addition, applicants should be high school graduates or have a GED certificate. A minimum ACT score of 19 is required for regular admission. AP and CLEP credits are accepted.

Procedure: Freshmen are admitted to all sessions. Entrance exams should be taken during the junior year or early in the senior year. There is an early admissions plan. Applications should be filed by August 10 for fall entry, December 15 for spring entry, and May 20 for summer entry, along with a $25 fee. Notification is sent on a rolling basis.

Transfer: 985 transfer students enrolled in 2001-2002. Transfer applicants must have at least a 2.0 GPA all college work attempted for regular admission. 32 credits of 128 must be completed at USA.

Visiting: There are regularly scheduled orientations for prospective students, including 3 Saturday visiting days in November, February, and April. There are guides for informal visits and visitors may sit in on classes. To schedule a visit, contact Melissa Jones, Director of Admissions at E-Mail: *admiss@usouthal.edu*.

Financial Aid: In 2001-2002, 57% of all students received some form of financial aid. 38% of all students received need-based aid. The average freshman award was $5900. Of that total, loans averaged $4400. The average financial indebtedness of the 2001 graduate was $9000. The FAFSA and the college's own financial statement are required.

International Students: There are 1020 international students enrolled. The school actively recruits these students. They must score 500 on the written TOEFL.

Computers: The mainframe is a Sun SPARCserver 10 Model 512. Students may access the academic host Sun SPARCserver through terminals in the terminal lab or through modem connections. Access to the Internet is provided through PCs on campus or via modem for computers off campus. All students may access the system at various times. The fee varies. All students are required to have access to personal computers. Students enrolled in the entry-level programming sequence are required to have laptops.

Graduates: In 2001, 1285 bachelor's degrees were awarded. The most popular majors were elementary education (10%), nursing (8%), and marketing (5%). In an average class, 11% graduate in 4 years, 22% in 5 years, and 30% in 6 years. 239 companies recruited on campus in 2000-2001. Of the 2000 graduating class, 93% were employed within 6 months of graduation.

Admissions Contact: Melissa Jones, Director of Admissions.
E-mail: *admiss@.usouthal.edu* Web: *www.southalabama.edu*

UNIVERSITY OF WEST ALABAMA

Livingston, AL 35470 — A-3
(205) 652-3578
(888) 636-8800; Fax: (205) 652-3522

Full-time: 660 men, 790 women	**Faculty:** 87; IIA, --$
Part-time: 54 men, 91 women	**Ph.D.s:** 65%
Graduate: 71 men, 258 women	**Student/Faculty:** 17 to 1
Year: semesters, summer session	**Tuition:** $3174 ($5958)
Application Deadline: open	**Room & Board:** $2874
Freshman Class: 844 applied, 582 accepted, 360 enrolled	
SAT I or ACT: required	**COMPETITIVE**

University of West Alabama, founded in 1835, is a state-controlled institution offering programs in liberal arts and sciences, business and commerce, general studies, and education. There are 5 undergraduate schools and 1 graduate school. In addition to regional accreditation, UWA has baccalaureate program accreditation with NCATE and NLN. The 2 libraries contain 135,000 volumes, 500,000 microform items, and 7500 audiovisual forms/CDs, and subscribe to 700 periodicals. Computerized library services include interlibrary loans and database searching. Special learning facilities include a learning resource center, art gallery, and TV station. The 600-acre campus is in a small town 35 miles east of Meridian, Mississippi. Including residence halls, there are 36 buildings.

Student Life: 80% of undergraduates are from Alabama. Others are from 21 states, 9 foreign countries, and Canada. 88% are from public schools. 61% are white; 37% African American. The average age of freshmen is 18; all undergraduates, 22. 39% do not continue beyond their first year.

Housing: 903 students can be accommodated in college housing, which includes single-sex dormitories, on-campus apartments, and married-student housing. In addition, there are honors houses. On-campus housing is guaranteed for all 4 years. Alcohol is not permitted. All students may keep cars.

Activities: 10% of men belong to 6 national fraternities; 6% of women belong to 4 national sororities. There are 30 groups on campus, including band, cheerleading, choir, chorus, drama, drill team, ethnic, honors, international, jazz band, marching band, newspaper, pep band, photography, political, professional, radio and TV, religious, social, student government, symphony, and yearbook. Popular campus events include Springfest and Club Luie.

Sports: There are 5 intercollegiate sports for men and 5 for women, and 8 intramural sports for men and 8 for women. Facilities include an 800-seat gym, a 7500-seat football stadium, a baseball field, tennis and racquetball courts, a pool, weight rooms, a lake, and hiking trails.

Disabled Students: 95% of the campus is accessible. Wheelchair ramps, elevators, special parking, specially equipped rest rooms, special class scheduling, and lowered drinking fountains are available.

Services: Counseling and information services are available, as is tutoring in most subjects. There is remedial math, reading, and writing.

Campus Safety and Security: Measures include 24-hour foot and vehicle patrol, informal discussions, pamphlets/posters/films, and lighted pathways/sidewalks.

Programs of Study: UWA confers B.A., B.S., B.B.A., and B.T. degrees. Associate and master's degrees are also awarded. Bachelor's degrees are awarded in BIOLOGICAL SCIENCE (biology/biological science and marine biology), BUSINESS (accounting and business administration and management), COMMUNICATIONS AND THE

ARTS (English), COMPUTER AND PHYSICAL SCIENCE (chemistry, computer science, mathematics, and physics), EDUCATION (athletic training, early childhood, elementary, middle school, physical, science, secondary, and special), ENGINEERING AND ENVIRONMENTAL DESIGN (environmental science and industrial engineering technology), HEALTH PROFESSIONS (predentistry and premedicine), SOCIAL SCIENCE (history, prelaw, psychology, social science, and sociology). English, business, and sciences are the strongest academically. Education and business are the largest.

Required: To graduate, all students must complete at least 120 semester hours with a minimum GPA of 2.0.

Special: There is a 3-2 engineering program with Auburn University and the University of Alabama at Birmingham. The 2-year technical division offers programs leading to a possible B.T. degree. B.A.-B.S. degrees, a co-op program in environmental science, and an accelerated degree are available. Nondegree study is possible. There are 5 national honor societies, a freshman honors program, and 4 departmental honors programs.

Faculty/Classroom: 60% of faculty are male; 40%, female. 90% teach undergraduates. Graduate students teach 4% of introductory courses. The average class size in an introductory lecture is 30; in a laboratory, 18; and in a regular course, 15.

Admissions: 69% of the 2001-2002 applicants were accepted.

Requirements: The SAT I or ACT is required with a minimum composite score of 18 on the ACT for unconditional admission. In addition, applicants should have completed 15 high school credits or the GED equivalent. Applications are accepted on-line via the UWA web page. AP and CLEP credits are accepted.

Procedure: Freshmen are admitted to all sessions. Entrance exams should be taken during the junior or senior year. There are early admissions and deferred admissions plans. Application deadlines are open.

Transfer: 179 transfer students enrolled in a recent year. Transfer applicants must have maintained a minimum GPA of 2.0 in all previous college courses. 30 credits of 120 must be completed at UWA.

Visiting: There are regularly scheduled orientations for prospective students. There are guides for informal visits and visitors may sit in on classes and stay overnight. To schedule a visit, contact the Admissions Office.

Financial Aid: The CSS/Profile, FAFSA, FFS or SFS is required. The fall application deadline is May 1.

International Students: There were 14 international students enrolled in a recent year. They must score 500 on the written TOEFL and also take the SAT I or the ACT, scoring 18 on the ACT.

Computers: The mainframe is an IBM 9375. All students may access the system. There are no time limits. The fee $20. It is strongly recommended that all students have a personal computer.

Graduates: In a recent year, 217 bachelor's degrees were awarded. The most popular majors were elementary education (14%), physical education (9%), and history (8%). In an average class, 17% graduate in 3 years, 28% in 4 years, 33% in 5 years, and 37% in 6 years. 25 companies recruited on campus in a recent year. Of a recent year's graduating class, 10% were enrolled in graduate school within 6 months of graduation and 90% were employed.

Admissions Contact: Richard Hester, Director of Admissions. A video is available. E-mail: *rhester@uwa.edu* Web: *www.uwa.edu*

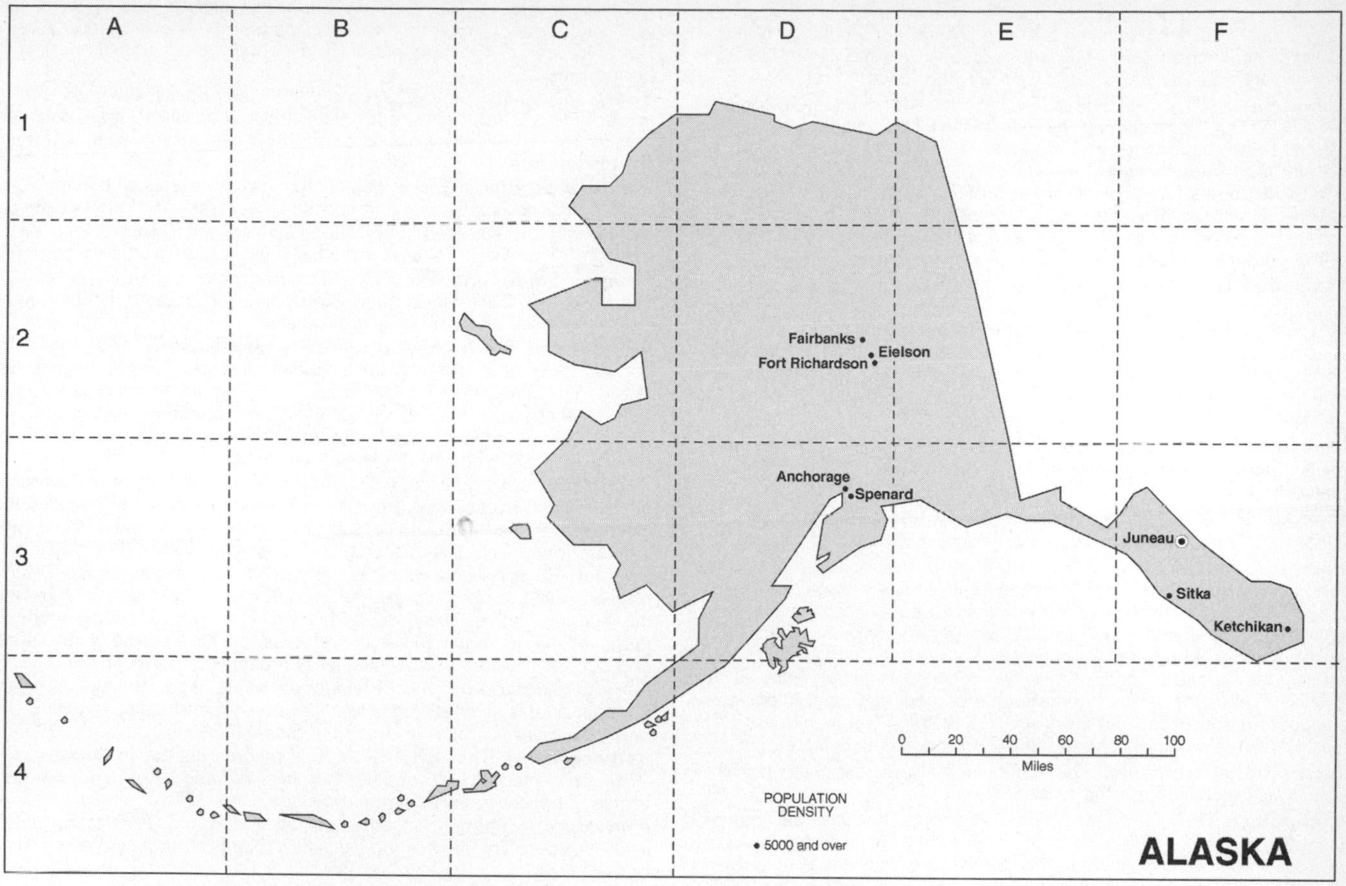

ALASKA PACIFIC UNIVERSITY

Anchorage, AK 99508-4672 D-3

(907) 564-8248

(800) 252-7528; Fax: (907) 564-8317

Full-time: 100 men, 154 women	**Faculty:** 30
Part-time: 52 men, 79 women	**Ph.D.s:** 77%
Graduate: 60 men, 111 women	**Student/Faculty:** 8 to 1
Year: 4-1-4, summer session	**Tuition:** $10,068 ($11,952)
Application Deadline: February 1	**Room & Board:** $5090
Freshman Class: 89 applied, 35 accepted, 33 enrolled	
SAT I Verbal/Math: 530/510	**ACT:** 20 **COMPETITIVE**

Alaska Pacific University, founded in 1957, is an independent institution offering undergraduate programs in business administration, elementary education, environmental science and outdoor studies, liberal studies, and psychology and human services. There are 5 graduate schools. The library contains 384,698 volumes, 37,619 microform items, and 7080 audiovisual forms/CDs, and subscribes to 3479 periodicals. Computerized library services include the card catalog and interlibrary loans. Special learning facilities include a learning resource center, radio station, and TV station. The 270-acre campus is in a suburban area in midtown Anchorage. Including residence halls, there are 7 buildings.

Student Life: Others are from 9 foreign countries and Canada. 68% are white; 12% Native American/Alaskan Native. The average age of freshmen is 20; all undergraduates, 26. 30% do not continue beyond their first year; 30% remain to graduate.

Housing: 125 students can be accommodated in college housing, which includes coed dormitories, on-campus apartments, off-campus apartments, and married-student housing. In addition, there are special-interest houses. On-campus housing is guaranteed for the freshman year only, is available on a first-come, first-served basis, and is available on a lottery system for upperclassmen. 74% of students commute. Alcohol is not permitted. All students may keep cars.

Activities: There are no fraternities or sororities. There are 15 groups on campus, including chorus, drama, ethnic, gay, international, literary magazine, newspaper, religious, student government, and yearbook. Popular campus events include the Outdoor Program.

Sports: There are 1 intercollegiate sports for men and 1 for women, and 5 intramural sports for men and 5 for women. Facilities include a 300-seat sports center, an indoor swimming pool, cross-country skiing and running trails, a climbing wall, a soccer field, a lake for boating, and a weight/exercise room.

Disabled Students: 75% of the campus is accessible. Wheelchair ramps, elevators, special parking, specially equipped rest rooms, lowered drinking fountains, and lowered telephones are available.

Services: Counseling and information services are available, as is tutoring in most subjects, including math, writing, and other subjects as needed. There is remedial math and writing.

Campus Safety and Security: Measures include 24-hour foot and vehicle patrol, informal discussions, pamphlets/posters/films, and emergency telephones. There are lighted pathways/sidewalks.

Programs of Study: APU confers the B.A. degree. Associate and master's degrees are also awarded. Bachelor's degrees are awarded in AGRICULTURE (conservation and regulation, and natural resource management), BUSINESS (accounting, business administration and management, hospitality management services, hotel/motel and restaurant management, international business management, marketing management, sports management, and trade and industrial supervision and management), COMMUNICATIONS AND THE ARTS (art, comparative literature, and music), COMPUTER AND PHYSICAL SCIENCE (information sciences and systems), EDUCATION (elementary), ENGINEERING AND ENVIRONMENTAL DESIGN (environmental science), SOCIAL SCIENCE (history, human services, liberal arts/general studies, philosophy, and psychology). All is the strongest academically. Environmental Science/Outdoor Studies and Liberal Studies are the largest.

Required: All students must complete 4 semester hours each in an orientation to active, learning class, a lab science, a course in social/behavioral science,and a course in ethics or religion; two courses in humanities; a sophomore seminar in the major; and a foreign language or American Sign Language course. Courses to meet writing, speech, and quantitative skills competencies are also required.

Special: The internship program is very strong. The Degree Completion Program for working adults leads to a B.A. in organizational management, accounting, or human services. There are 2 national honor societies, and 2 departmental honors program.

Faculty/Classroom: 56% of faculty are male; 44%, female. 90% teach undergraduates. No introductory courses are taught by graduate stu-

dents. The average class size in an introductory lecture is 11; in a laboratory, 14; and in a regular course, 8.

Admissions: 39% of the 2001-2002 applicants were accepted. The SAT I scores for the 2001-2002 freshman class were: Verbal--33% below 500, 38% between 500 and 599, and 29% between 600 and 700; Math--43% below 500, 48% between 500 and 599, and 9% between 600 and 700. The ACT scores were 64% below 21, 9% between 21 and 23, 18% between 24 and 26, and 9% between 27 and 28.

Requirements: The SAT I or ACT is required with a minimum composite score of 920 normally required on the SAT I or 19 on the ACT. Two teacher recommendations and an essay are required. A GED is acceptable in lieu of a high school transcript. . A GPA of 2.5 is required. AP and CLEP credits are accepted. Important factors in the admissions decision are advanced placement or honor courses, leadership record, and recommendations by school officials. Applications are accepted on-line at the school's web site.

Procedure: Freshmen are admitted to all sessions. Entrance exams should be taken before January of the senior year. There are early decision and early admissions plans. Early decision applications should be filed by December 1; regular applications, by February 1 for fall entry, application deadlines for spring or summer entry are open. Notification of early decision is sent December 15; regular decision, on a rolling basis. The fall 2001 application fee was $25.

Transfer: 39 transfer students enrolled in 2001-2002. Transfer applicants must have a 2.0 cumulative GPA. 32 credits of 128 must be completed at APU.

Visiting: There are guides for informal visits and visitors may sit in on classes and stay overnight. To schedule a visit, contact Admissions.

Financial Aid: In a recent year, 80% of all freshmen received some form of financial aid. 32% of freshmen received need-based aid. The average freshman award was $11,534. Of that total, scholarships or need-based grants averaged $6427 ($9900 maximum); loans averaged $4888 ($15,578 maximum); work contracts averaged $1242 ($1500 maximum); and Bureau of Indian Affairs scholarship grant is available. $2517 ($5950 maximum). 17% of undergraduates work part time. Average annual earnings from campus work are $1242. APU is a member of CSS. The FAFSA is required. The fall application deadline is March 15.

International Students: The school actively recruits these students. They must score 500 on the written TOEFL.

Computers: The mainframe is a Sun Solaris. The Academic Support Center provides 26 PCs for student and faculty use. Internet and Web access is provided free of charge to enrolled students and is available in faculty and administrative offices. All students may access the system. There are no time limits and no fees.

Graduates: In 2001, 39 bachelor's degrees were awarded. The most popular majors were business administration (21%), elementary education (18%), and outdoor studies (18%). In an average class, 30% graduate in 4 years.

Admissions Contact: Director of Admissions.
E-mail: *admissions@alaskapacific.edu*
Web: *http://www.alaskapacific.edu*

SHELDON JACKSON COLLEGE
Sitka, AK 99835 — F-3
(907) 747-5221
(800) 478-4556; Fax: (907) 747-6366

Full-time: 165 men and women	**Faculty:** 17
Part-time: 75 men and women	**Ph.D.s:** 71%
Graduate: none	**Student/Faculty:** 10 to 1
Year: semesters	**Tuition:** $8020
Application Deadline: open	**Room & Board:** $6920
Freshman Class: 45 applied	
SAT I or ACT: recommended	**LESS COMPETITIVE**

Sheldon Jackson College, founded in 1878, is a private liberal arts college offering emphases in natural and aquatic resources, outdoor recreation, fisheries, marine biology, business, elementary and secondary education, and interdisciplinary studies. In addition to regional accreditation, Sheldon Jackson College has baccalaureate program accreditation with NASDTEC. The library contains 80,000 volumes and subscribes to 500 periodicals. Computerized library services include the card catalog, interlibrary loans, and database searching. Special learning facilities include a learning resource center, a natural history museum, and a salmon hatchery. The 345-acre campus is in a small town in southeast Alaska. Including residence halls, there are 23 buildings.

Student Life: 70% of undergraduates are from out of state, mostly the Northwest. Others are from 35 states and 4 foreign countries. 99% are from public schools. 70% are white; 26%, Native American/Eskimo. The average age of freshmen is 20; all undergraduates, 24. 18% do not continue beyond their first year; 21% remain to graduate.

Housing: 240 students can be accommodated in college housing, which includes single-sex dormitories, on-campus apartments, and married-student housing. On-campus housing is guaranteed for the freshman year only and is available on a first-come, first-served basis. 75% of students live on campus; of those, all remain on campus on weekends. Alcohol is not permitted. All students may keep cars.

Activities: There are no fraternities or sororities. There are 14 groups on campus, including art, choir, chorus, computers, drama, ethnic, musical theater, outdoor, photography, political, religious, social, social service, and student government. Popular campus events include Alaska Day, Gathering of the People (Alaska native dances and dinner), and Spring Expo.

Sports: There are 5 intramural sports for men and 5 for women. Facilities include a 2-court gym, a 25-meter pool, a weight room, 2 racquetball courts, a wilderness center, a student center, sea kayaks, and a climbing wall.

Disabled Students: Wheelchair ramps, elevators, special parking, specially equipped rest rooms, and special class scheduling are available.

Services: Counseling and information services are available, as is tutoring in most subjects. There is remedial math, reading, and writing.

Campus Safety and Security: Measures include self-defense education, informal discussions, pamphlets/posters/films, and lighted pathways/sidewalks. There is a security officer.

Programs of Study: Sheldon Jackson College confers B.A. and B.S. degrees. Associate degrees are also awarded. Bachelor's degrees are awarded in EDUCATION (elementary, mathematics, science, secondary, and social science), SOCIAL SCIENCE (interdisciplinary studies and liberal arts/general studies). Environmental science/education is the strongest academically and has the largest enrollment.

Required: All students must complete a core curriculum in writing, math, speech, science, fine arts, computer competence, and multicultural awareness. A minimum GPA of 2.0 and a major of more than 30 credits out of a total of at least 120 credits are required for graduation.

Special: Business and education internships are required. Work-study programs with the U.S. Forest and Park Services, child care centers, and the Alaska Native Museum, combined B.A.-B.S. degrees, student-designed majors, a general studies degree, and a dual major in natural and aquatic resources are available. Nondegree study is possible.

Faculty/Classroom: 59% of faculty are male; 41%, female. All teach undergraduates. The average class size in an introductory lecture is 32; in a laboratory, 11; and in a regular course, 13.

Requirements: The SAT I or ACT is recommended. In addition, the GED is accepted. A GPA of 2.0 is required. AP and CLEP credits are accepted. Applications are accepted on-line.

Procedure: Freshmen are admitted fall and spring. Application deadlines are open. The application fee is $25. Notification is sent on a rolling basis.

Transfer: 24 transfer students enrolled in a recent year. The college follows a nonselective admissions policy for transfer applicants with a 2.0 GPA. 30 credits of 120 must be completed at Sheldon Jackson College.

Visiting: There are regularly scheduled orientations for prospective students, including campus tours, visits to classrooms, and meetings with financial aid counselors. There are guides for informal visits and visitors may sit in on classes and stay overnight. To schedule a visit, contact the Admissions Office.

Financial Aid: In a recent year, 95% of all freshmen and 98% of continuing students received some form of financial aid. 75% of freshmen and 90% of continuing students received need-based aid. The average freshman award was $8000. Of that total, scholarships or need-based grants averaged $3000; loans averaged $3000; and work contracts averaged $2000. 90% of undergraduates work part time. Average annual earnings from campus work are $1500. The average financial indebtedness of a recent graduate was $15,000. The FAFSA is required. The fall application deadline is July 15.

International Students: They must score 550 on the written TOEFL or 250 on the electronic version.

Computers: The mainframe is a Dell. A 20-unit center housing PCs and Macs is open from 8 A.M. to 10 P.M. weekdays, and part of the weekend. Hookups are available in every dorm room. All students may access the system. There are no time limits. The fee is $370 per year. It is strongly recommended that all students have a personal computer.

Graduates: In 2001, 20 bachelor's degrees were awarded. The most popular majors were aquatic resources (60%), elementary education (30%), and natural resource management (10%). In an average class, 40% graduate in 4 years, 50% in 5 years, and 60% in 6 years. Of the 2000 graduating class, 10% were enrolled in graduate school within 6 months of graduation and 80% were employed.

Admissions Contact: Elizabeth Lower, Director of Admissions.
E-mail: *elower@sj-alaska.edu* Web: *http://www.sj-alaska.edu*

UNIVERSITY OF ALASKA SYSTEM

The University of Alaska is the only public institution of higher learning in the state of Alaska. It is a statewide system consisting of three multimission main campuses located in Anchorage, Fairbanks, and Juneau, with extended satellite colleges and sites throughout Alaska. The university was established at Fairbanks in 1915 as the Alaska Agricultural College and School of Mines; in 1935 it was renamed the University of Alaska. The university now includes full-service universities in Fairbanks, Anchorage, and Juneau; lower division college centers in Bethel, Dillington, Ketchikan, Kodiak, Kotzebue, Nome, Palmer, Sitka, and Soldotna; a community college at Valdez; and vocational, rural education, and extension sites through the state. The university is governed by an eleven-member Board of Regents. The board is an autonomous organization and the highest authority in the administration of the university, governed by the Alaska Statutes, which provides for the appointment of the regents by the governor for overlapping terms of eight years. Since 1975, students have been represented on the board; they are appointed for two-year terms.

UNIVERSITY OF ALASKA ANCHORAGE — D-3

Anchorage, AK 99508 — (907) 786-1480; Fax: (907) 786-4888

Full-time: 2100 men, 2900 women	**Faculty:** 331; IIA, -$
Part-time: 2800 men, 4800 women	**Ph.D.s:** 80%
Graduate: 200 men, 400 women	**Student/Faculty:** 16 to 1
Year: semesters, summer session	**Tuition:** $2500 ($6800)
Application Deadline: see profile	**Room & Board:** $6600
Freshman Class: n/av	
SAT I or ACT: recommended	**NONCOMPETITIVE**

The University of Alaska Anchorage, founded in 1954, is a public institution and a major unit of the University of Alaska statewide system. Its baccalaureate programs are administered through the Colleges of Arts and Sciences, Business and Public Policy, Health, Education, and Social Welfare, and the School of Engineering, and the Community and Technical College. Tuition is based on the level of course work and number of credits taken; fees also vary by credits. Figures given in the above capsule are approximate. There are 5 undergraduate and 5 graduate schools. In addition to regional accreditation, UAA has baccalaureate program accreditation with AACSB, ABET, ACEJMC, ADA, CAHEA, CSWE, NASAD, NASDTEC, and NLN. The library contains 676,750 volumes, 574,010 microform items, and 7080 audiovisual forms/CDs, and subscribes to 3480 periodicals. Computerized library services include interlibrary loans and database searching. Special learning facilities include a learning resource center, art gallery, radio station, TV station, and a dental clinic, a welding lab, an auto-diesel garage, a theater, photography labs, and a student art museum show case. The 428-acre campus is in an urban area. Including residence halls, there are 27 buildings.

Student Life: 90% of undergraduates are from Alaska. Others are from 49 states, 41 foreign countries, and Canada. 80% are white. The average age of all undergraduates is 29. 37% do not continue beyond their first year.

Housing: 388 students can be accommodated in college housing, which includes single-sex and coed on-campus apartments. In addition, there is a house for Alaska Natives or American Indians who are engineering majors. On-campus housing is available on a first-come, first-served basis. Priority is given to out-of-town students. 97% of students commute. Alcohol is not permitted. All students may keep cars.

Activities: There are no fraternities or sororities. There are 75 groups on campus, including art, band, cheerleading, chess, choir, chorus, computers, dance, debate, drama, ethnic, film, gay, honors, international, jazz band, literary magazine, newspaper, orchestra, photography, political, professional, radio and TV, religious, social, social service, student government, and yearbook. Popular campus events include Great Alaska Shoot-Out, Northern Lights Invitational, and Student Showcase.

Sports: There are 6 intercollegiate sports for men and 4 for women, and 10 intramural sports for men and 10 for women. Facilities include an ice rink, an indoor jogging track, a gym, a swimming/diving pool, a weight room, and racquetball/squash courts.

Disabled Students: All of the campus is accessible. Wheelchair ramps, elevators, special parking, specially equipped rest rooms, lowered drinking fountains, and lowered telephones are available.

Services: Counseling and information services are available, as is tutoring in most subjects. There is a reader service for the blind, and remedial math, reading, and writing. Sign language, interpreters, and note takers are available.

Campus Safety and Security: Measures include 24-hour foot and vehicle patrol, self-defense education, escort service, and informal discussions. There are pamphlets/posters/films, emergency telephones, and lighted pathways/sidewalks.

Programs of Study: UAA confers B.A., B.S., B.B.A., B.Ed., B.F.A., B.Mus., and B.S.W. degrees. Associate and master's degrees are also awarded. Bachelor's degrees are awarded in BIOLOGICAL SCIENCE (biology/biological science), BUSINESS (accounting, banking and finance, business administration and management, hotel/motel and restaurant management, management information systems, marketing/retailing/merchandising, and transportation management), COMMUNICATIONS AND THE ARTS (art, communications, dramatic arts, English, fine arts, journalism, languages, and music), COMPUTER AND PHYSICAL SCIENCE (chemistry, computer science, mathematics, and natural sciences), EDUCATION (elementary, music, physical, and secondary), ENGINEERING AND ENVIRONMENTAL DESIGN (aeronautical technology, civil engineering, survey and mapping technology, and technological management), HEALTH PROFESSIONS (nursing), SOCIAL SCIENCE (anthropology, criminal justice, economics, history, human services, interdisciplinary studies, political science/government, psychology, social work, and sociology). Education, nursing, and social sciences are the strongest academically. Elementary education, accounting, and nursing are the largest.

Required: General education requirements include 7 credits in natural science, 6 each in written communications, humanities, and social sciences, and 3 each in oral communication, quantitative skills, and fine arts. A total of 120 to 132 credits, with 48 upper-division courses, and a minimum GPA of 2.0 are required to graduate.

Special: UAA participates in the National Student Exchange Program and offers study abroad. UAA also offers B.A.-B.S. degrees, student-designed and dual majors, internships, pass/fail options, a 3-2 electrical engineering degree, a general studies degree, nondegree study, and credit for life experience. The Community and Technical College provides educational and vocational courses for career development. There are 2 national honor societies, and 3 departmental honors programs.

Faculty/Classroom: 60% of faculty are male; 40%, female. The average class size in an introductory lecture is 50; in a laboratory, 20; and in a regular course, 35.

Requirements: The SAT I or ACT is recommended. In addition, applicants should be graduates of an accredited secondary school or have a high school or GED certificate. A GPA of 2.5 is required. AP and CLEP credits are accepted. Applications are accepted on-line at the school's web site.

Procedure: Freshmen are admitted to all sessions. Entrance exams should be taken by May of the senior year. There are early admissions and deferred admissions plans. The college accepts all applicants. Notification is sent on a rolling basis. Check with the school for current application deadlines. The fall 2001 application fee was $35.

Transfer: Applicants must meet admission requirements and must have a minimum GPA of 2.0 and at least 30 credit hours earned at an accredited postsecondary institution. 30 credits of 120 to 132 must be completed at UAA.

Visiting: There are regularly scheduled orientations for prospective students, consisting of registration orientation, application process, campus tours, student appointments, and classes. There are guides for informal visits and visitors may sit in on classes. To schedule a visit, contact the Office of Admissions.

Financial Aid: UAA is a member of CSS. The FAFSA and the college's own financial statement are required. Check with the school for current deadlines.

International Students: They must score 450 on the written TOEFL and also take the SAT I or the ACT.

Computers: The mainframe is a DEC AXP 2100 ALPHA open VMS system. There are also 120 Mac and IBM PCs available in various academic departments, the Learning Resource Center, the Reading and Writing Center, and the Campus Center. All students may access the system. There are no time limits and no fees.

Graduates: In an average class, 5% graduate in 4 years, 14% in 5 years, and 20% in 6 years.

Admissions Contact: Enrollment Services. A video is available.
Web: *www.uaa.alaska.edu*

UNIVERSITY OF ALASKA FAIRBANKS — D-2

Fairbanks, AK 99775-7480 — (907) 474-7500
(800) 478-1823; Fax: (907) 474-5379

Full-time: 1556 men, 1648 women	**Faculty:** 507; I, --$
Part-time: 1056 men, 2050 women	**Ph.D.s:** n/av
Graduate: 389 men, 443 women	**Student/Faculty:** 6 to 1
Year: semesters, summer session	**Tuition:** $3495 ($8565)
Application Deadline: August 1	**Room & Board:** $4770
Freshman Class: 1626 applied, 1343 accepted, 886 enrolled	
SAT I Verbal/Math: 510/510	**ACT:** 21 **NONCOMPETITIVE**

The University of Alaska Fairbanks, founded in 1917 and the nation's northernmost Land, Sea, and Space Grant university and international research center, advances and disseminates knowledge through creative teaching, research, and public service with an emphasis on Alaska, the North, and their diverse peoples. There are 9 undergraduate and 8 graduate schools. In addition to regional accreditation, UAF has baccalaureate program accreditation with AACSB, ABET, ACEJMC, CSWE, and NASM. The 3 libraries contain 608,575 volumes, 1,131,516 microform items, and 664,448 audiovisual forms/CDs, and subscribe to 2754 periodicals. Computerized library services include the card catalog, interlibrary loans, and database searching. Special learning facilities include a learning resource center, art gallery, natural history museum, radio station, and TV station. Several research institutes and labs for study in the physical and natural sciences are associated with the university. The 2250-acre campus is in a small town 4 miles northwest of Fairbanks. Including residence halls, there are 175 buildings.

Student Life: 86% of undergraduates are from Alaska. Others are from 49 states, 2 foreign countries, and Canada. 65% are white; 16%, Native American/Eskimo. The average age of freshmen is 33; all undergraduates, 42. 32% do not continue beyond their first year.

Housing: 1554 students can be accommodated in college housing, which includes coed dormitories, on-campus apartments, and married-student housing. On-campus housing is available on a first-come, first-served basis. 69% of students commute. All students may keep cars.

Activities: There is 1 national fraternitiy and 1 national sorority. There are 113 groups on campus, including art, band, cheerleading, chess, choir, chorus, computers, dance, drama, ethnic, film, gay, honors, international, jazz band, literary magazine, musical theater, newspaper, opera, orchestra, political, professional, radio and TV, religious, social, student government, and symphony. Popular campus events include All-Campus Day, Alcohol Awareness Week, and Meltdown (spring event).

Sports: There are 4 intercollegiate sports for men and 4 for women, and 21 intramural sports for men and 21 for women. Facilities include a 2500-seat arena, a 2000-seat gym, a 1500-seat skating rink, 2 racquetball courts, 2 weight rooms, 4 basketball courts, an Olympic-size swimming pool, a small-bore rifle range, and a lighted 30-mile ski trail.

Disabled Students: 90% of the campus is accessible. Wheelchair ramps, elevators, special parking, specially equipped rest rooms, special class scheduling, lowered drinking fountains, lowered telephones, a shuttle bus, and a swimming pool equipped with hydraulic lifts are available. Special residence hall accommodations are coordinated by the Disabled Student Service Office.

Services: Counseling and information services are available, as is tutoring in some subjects, including chemistry, calculus, languages, and biology. There is a reader service for the blind, and remedial math, reading, and writing.

Campus Safety and Security: Measures include self-defense education, escort service, shuttle buses, and informal discussions. There are pamphlets/posters/films, emergency telephones, lighted pathways/sidewalks, a 24-hour dormitory lockup, a 24-hour crisis line, evening patrols inside dormitories, and residence hall check-in.

Programs of Study: UAF confers B.A., B.S., B.B.A., B.Ed., B.F.A., B.M., and B.T. degrees. Associate, master's, and doctoral degrees are also awarded. Bachelor's degrees are awarded in AGRICULTURE (fishing and fisheries, natural resource management, and wildlife management), BIOLOGICAL SCIENCE (biology/biological science and wildlife biology), BUSINESS (accounting, business administration and management, and business economics), COMMUNICATIONS AND THE ARTS (art, communications, dramatic arts, English, Eskimo, journalism, linguistics, modern language, music, and music performance), COMPUTER AND PHYSICAL SCIENCE (applied physics, chemistry, computer science, earth science, geology, mathematics, physics, science, and statistics), EDUCATION (elementary and music), ENGINEERING AND ENVIRONMENTAL DESIGN (civil engineering, electrical/electronics engineering, environmental science, geological engineering, mechanical engineering, mining and mineral engineering, petroleum/natural gas engineering, and technological management), SOCIAL SCIENCE (anthropology, area studies, criminal justice, ethnic studies, geography, history, interdisciplinary studies, Japanese studies, Native American studies, philosophy, political science/government, psychology, rural economics, Russian and Slavic studies, social work, and sociology). Engineering, fisheries, and wildlife management are the strongest academically. Biological sciences, business administration, and computer science are the largest.

Required: All students must complete core courses in English and oral communication, library skills, humanities, social science, natural science, and math. A minimum of 120 credit hours, with 27 to 30 in the major, and a 2.0 GPA are required for graduation.

Special: The university's College of Rural Alaska offers satellite education programs to Alaska residents to reach students at remote sites. Study abroad is offered in 8 countries, and B.A.-B.S. degrees are available in 8 majors. Internships are offered through the Rural Alaska Honors Institute. Student-designed majors, credit/no credit options, nondegree study, and credit for life, military, and work experience are also available. There are 10 national honor societies and a freshman honors program.

Faculty/Classroom: 61% of faculty are male; 39%, female.

Admissions: 83% of the 2001-2002 applicants were accepted. The SAT I scores for the 2001-2002 freshman class were: Verbal--40% below 500, 37% between 500 and 599, 20% between 600 and 700, and 3% above 700; Math--46% below 500, 36% between 500 and 599, 17% between 600 and 700, and 2% above 700. The ACT scores were 48% below 21, 22% between 21 and 23, 17% between 24 and 26, 5% between 27 and 28, and 8% above 28. 26% of the current freshmen were in the top fifth of their class; 50% were in the top two fifths.

Requirements: The SAT I or ACT is required. In addition, applicants should be graduates of an accredited secondary school with 16 academic credits, including 4 in English and 3 each in math, natural or physical sciences, and social sciences, with a minimum GPA of 2.5 in these courses and 2.0 overall. The GED or its equivalent is accepted. AP and CLEP credits are accepted. Applications are accepted on-line.

Procedure: Freshmen are admitted to all sessions. Applications should be filed by August 1 for fall entry and December 1 for spring entry, along with a $35 fee. The college accepts all applicants. Notification is sent September 1.

Transfer: 537 transfer students enrolled in 2001-2002. A GPA of 2.0 in all previous college work and an honorable dismissal from all schools attended are required. Applicants with fewer than 30 semester hours of transferable credit also must have a high school GPA of 2.0 and ACT or SAT I scores. 30 credits of 120 must be completed at UAF.

Visiting: There are regularly scheduled orientations for prospective students. There are guides for informal visits and visitors may sit in on classes and stay overnight. To schedule a visit, contact the Admissions Counseling Office at *fngrs@uaf.edu*.

Financial Aid: The FAFSA is required. The fall application deadline is May 15.

International Students: There are 153 international students enrolled. They must score 550 on the written TOEFL and also take the SAT I or the ACT.

Computers: The mainframe is a DEC ALPHA 7000-640. PCs and Macs are available for student use in the library, the Bunnell Building, and various academic departments. All students may access the system 24 hours per day. There are no time limits and no fees.

Graduates: In 2001, 448 bachelor's degrees were awarded. The most popular majors were biological sciences (9%), business administration (8%), and education (8%).

Admissions Contact: Nancy Dix, Director of Admissions. A video is available. E-mail: *fyapply@uaf.edu* Web: *www.uaf.edu*

UNIVERSITY OF ALASKA SOUTHEAST — F-3

Juneau, AK 99801 (907) 465-6457

(877) 465-4827; Fax: (907) 465-6365

Full-time: 250 men, 310 women	**Faculty:** 60; IIA, --$
Part-time: 580 men, 850 women	**Ph.D.s:** 52%
Graduate: 40 men, 50 women	**Student/Faculty:** 50 to 1
Year: semesters, summer session	**Tuition:** $2500 ($7000)
Application Deadline: open	**Room & Board:** $5400
Freshman Class: n/av	
SAT I or ACT: recommended	**LESS COMPETITIVE**

The University of Alaska Southeast, a multicampus institution founded in 1972, is part of the University of Alaska statewide system, with baccalaureate programs offered in business and public administration, education, and liberal arts and science. Figures in the above capsule are approximate. There are 3 undergraduate and 2 graduate schools. The library contains 250,000 volumes, 250,000 microform items, and 1850 audiovisual forms/CDs, and subscribes to 1500 periodicals. Computerized library services include the card catalog, interlibrary loans, and database searching. Special learning facilities include a learning resource center and media and educational technology classrooms. The 198-acre campus is in a suburban area 10 miles north of Juneau. Including residence halls, there are 18 buildings.

Student Life: 75% of undergraduates are from Alaska. Others are from 37 states, 12 foreign countries, and Canada. 95% are from public schools. 70% are white; 17% Native American/Eskimo. The average age of freshmen is 18; all undergraduates, 24.

Housing: 250 students can be accommodated in college housing, which includes single-sex dormitories, on-campus apartments, and married-student housing. On-campus housing is available on a first-come, first-served basis. Priority is given to out-of-town students. 90% of students commute. All students may keep cars.

Activities: There are no fraternities or sororities. There are 16 groups on campus, including choir, ethnic, gay, honors, literary magazine, newspaper, political, professional, religious, and student government. Popular campus events include Ski Day, whale-watching, and Eagle Preserve field trips.

Sports: There are 3 intramural sports for men and 3 for women. Facilities include a community gym and pool, an activity center, and access to health club facilities.

Disabled Students: 95% of the campus is accessible. Wheelchair ramps, elevators, special parking, specially equipped rest rooms, lowered drinking fountains, and lowered telephones are available.

Services: Counseling and information services are available, as is tutoring in most subjects. There is a reader service for the blind, and remedial math, reading, and writing.

Campus Safety and Security: Measures include shuttle buses, informal discussions, pamphlets/posters/films, and emergency telephones. There are lighted pathways/sidewalks and late-night security at student housing.

Programs of Study: UAS confers B.A., B.S., B.B.A., B.Ed., and B.L.A. degrees. Associate and master's degrees are also awarded. Bachelor's degrees are awarded in BIOLOGICAL SCIENCE (biology/biological science and marine biology), BUSINESS (accounting, and business administration and management), COMMUNICATIONS AND THE ARTS (art, communications, literature, and speech/debate/rhetoric), COMPUTER AND PHYSICAL SCIENCE (mathematics), EDUCATION (elementary), ENGINEERING AND ENVIRONMENTAL DESIGN (environmental science), SOCIAL SCIENCE (liberal arts/general studies, political science/government, public administration, and social science). Accounting, marine biology, and environmental science are the strongest academically. Liberal arts is the largest.

Required: All students are required to complete general education courses, including 15 credits in humanities and social science, 10 in math and natural sciences, 6 in written communication skills, and 3 in speech. A total of 120 semester credits, with at least 36 in the major, and a minimum GPA of 2.0 are required in order to graduate. In the liberal arts program, a portfolio is required.

Special: UAS offers cross-registration through the National Student Exchange, and internships with federal and state agencies. Study abroad, work-study, dual and student-designed majors, credit/no credit options, and credit for military experience are also available. The School of Career and Continuing Education offers courses and certificate programs in technological skills.

Faculty/Classroom: 98% teach undergraduates. No introductory courses are taught by graduate students. The average class size in an introductory lecture is 20 and in a laboratory, 12.

Requirements: The SAT I or ACT is recommended. In addition, applicants should be graduates of an accredited secondary school or have the GED. A GPA of 2.0 is required. AP and CLEP credits are accepted.

Procedure: Freshmen are admitted fall and spring. There are early admissions and deferred admissions plans. Application deadlines are open. The fall 2001application fee was $35.

Transfer: A minimum GPA of 2.0 from an accredited institution is required. 30 credits of 120 must be completed at UAS.

Visiting: There are regularly scheduled orientations for prospective students. There are guides for informal visits and visitors may sit in on classes. To schedule a visit, contact Greg Wagner.

Financial Aid: UAS is a member of CSS. The FAFSA and the college's own financial statement are required. Check with the school for current application deadlines and fee.

International Students: They must score 550 on the written TOEFL and also take the SAT I or the ACT.

Computers: The mainframe is a DEC VAX 8600. There are 2 computer labs with 15 terminals each. There are also 68 IBM PCs and Macs. All students may access the system. There are no time limits and no fees.

Admissions Contact: Greg Wagner, Director of Admissions.
E-mail: *jyuas@alaska.edu* Web: *www.jun.alaska.edu*

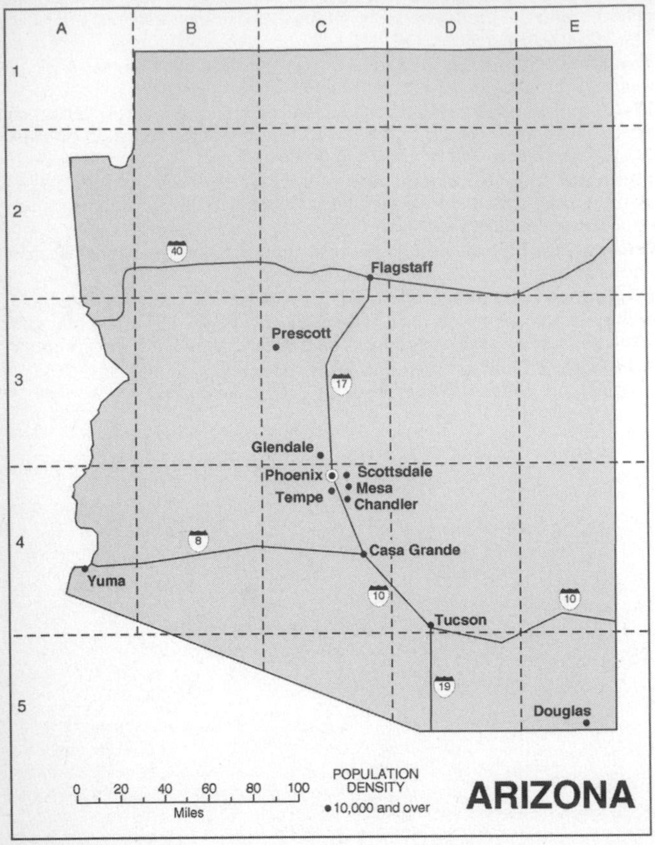

AMERICAN INDIAN COLLEGE OF THE ASSEMBLIES OF GOD C-4

Phoenix, AZ 85021 **(602) 944-3335, ext. 227**
(800) 933-3828; Fax: (602) 943-8299

Full-time: 26 men, 36 women	**Faculty:** 4
Part-time: 4 men, 5 women	**Ph.D.s:** n/av
Graduate: none	**Student/Faculty:** 16 to 1
Year: semesters	**Tuition:** $4330
Application Deadline: open	**Room & Board:** $3480
Freshman Class: 10 applied, 10 accepted, 10 enrolled	
SAT I Verbal/Math: 375/325	**ACT:** 13 **NONCOMPETITIVE**

American Indian College of the Assemblies of God, founded in 1957, is a Christian college with a specific mission of preparing American Indians for leadership in churches, education, and the community. The library contains 20,000 volumes and 7000 microform items, and subscribes to 102 periodicals. Computerized library services include the card catalog. Special learning facilities include a learning resource center and a student-led chapel. The 10-acre campus is in an urban area in north Phoenix, just east of I17 and the Metrocenter area. Including residence halls, there are 9 buildings.

Student Life: 60% of undergraduates are from Arizona. Others are from 12 states. 75% are Native American/Eskimo; 14%, white. Most are Protestant. The average age of freshmen is 23; all undergraduates, 26.

Housing: College-sponsered living facilities include single-sex dormitories and off-campus apartments. 66% of students live on campus. Alcohol is not permitted. All students may keep cars.

Activities: There are no fraternities or sororities. There are several groups and organizations on campus, including band, cheerleading, drama, ethnic, religious, student government, and yearbook. Popular campus events include missions conventions and College Days.

Sports: There is 1 intercollegiate sport for men and 1 for women, and 2 intramural sports for men and 2 for women. Facilities include a full-size gym with a locker room and a weight room.

Disabled Students: All of the campus is accessible. Wheelchair ramps, special parking, specially equipped rest rooms, and lowered drinking fountains are available.

Services: Counseling and information services are available, as is tutoring in most subjects. There is remedial math, reading, and writing.

Campus Safety and Security: Measures include informal discussions, pamphlets/posters/films, lighted pathways/sidewalks, and night security.

Programs of Study: AIC confers the B.A. degree. Associate degrees are also awarded. Bachelor's degrees are awarded in EDUCATION (elementary), and SOCIAL SCIENCE (ministries).

Required: To graduate, students must complete 128 credits. Students in the Christian ministry program are required to have 40 credits in general education, 24 in Bible, 9 in theology, 3 in Christian education, 3 in missions, and 13 in pastoral ministries. Students enrolled in the elementary education program must complete 56 credits in general education, 21 in Bible/theology, 45 in professional courses, and 6 in general electives.

Special: Internships and dual majors are available.

Faculty/Classroom: 51% of faculty are male; 39%, female. All teach undergraduates. The average class size in an introductory lecture is 7; in a laboratory, 9; and in a regular course, 7.

Admissions: All of the 2001-2002 applicants were accepted. The SAT I scores for the 2001-2002 freshman class were: Verbal--100% below 500; Math--100% below 500. The ACT scores were 75% below 21 and 25% between 21 and 23.

Requirements: The SAT I or ACT is required. In addition, transcripts from high school and any other secondary schools attended are required along with a pastor's reference form. Applicants are required to take placement tests with satisfactory results. A 2.0 GPA is required and the GED is accepted. AP and CLEP credits are accepted. Important factors in the admissions decision are advanced placement or honor courses, evidence of special talent, and extracurricular activities record.

Procedure: Freshmen are admitted to all sessions. Entrance exams should be taken prior to acceptance. There are early decision, early admissions, and deferred admissions plans. Application deadlines are open.

Transfer: Official transcripts from high school and each college attended, plus a pastor's reference form is required. Students must demonstrate proficiency in English, writing, math, and reading. 30 credits of 128 must be completed at AIC.

Visiting: There are regularly scheduled orientations for prospective students, There are College Days in the fall and spring semesters that include class visits, overnight stays in dorms, and meals in the cafeteria for 2 days. There are guides for informal visits and visitors may sit in on classes and stay overnight. To schedule a visit, contact Admissions at *sticeahkie@aicag.edu*.

Financial Aid: In 2001-2002, 89% of all freshmen and 91% of continuing students received some form of financial aid. 89% of freshmen and 84% of continuing students received need-based aid. The average freshman award was $5139. Of that total, scholarships or need-based grants averaged $3304 ($12,680 maximum). 38% of undergraduates work part time. Average annual earnings from campus work are $1772. The FAFSA is required. The fall application deadline is August.

International Students: They must take the TOEFL and the SAT I or the ACT.

Computers: A computer lab with 10 computers is open every day. Students sign in on the network with passwords. All computers have access to the Internet and the web. All students may access the system. There are no time limits and no fees. It is strongly recommended that all students have a personal computer.

Graduates: In 2001, 11 bachelor's degrees were awarded. The most popular majors were elementary education (57%) and Christian ministry (43%). In an average class, 35% graduate in 6 years.

Admissions Contact: Sandy Ticeahkie, Admissions Coordinator.
E-mail: *aicadm@juno.com* Web: *www.aicag.edu*

ARIZONA BOARD OF REGENTS

The Arizona Board of Regents governs Arizona's public university system, including Arizona State University, Northern Arizona University, and the University of Arizona. The universities enroll nearly 104,000 students at the three main campuses in Tempe, Flagstaff, and Tucson, at branch campuses in Glendale and Sierra Vista, and at more than 220 centers and sites throughout the state. The system consists of more than 1700 buildings. Recent initiatives of the Board include a review of the economics and demographics of higher education, and solicitation of recommendations from the business community to increase the effective use of university capital assets and increase the opportunities for privatization of Arizona's campuses. Partnerships between NAU and Arizona Western Community College, and between UA South and Cochise Community College have allowed students to attend community colleges for lower division courses and university courses for bachelor's degrees. The Board of Regents continues to improve teacher education programs, plan for enrollment growth, develop learner-centered approaches to teaching, and assure adequate resources to maintain the quality of education at Arizona's universities.

ARIZONA STATE UNIVERSITY-MAIN C-4
Tempe, AZ 85287-0112 (480) 965-7788

Full-time: 13,383 men, 14,584 women	**Faculty:** 1709; I, -$
Part-time: 3596 men, 3628 women	**Ph.D.s:** 85%
Graduate: 5127 men, 5375 women	**Student/Faculty:** 16 to 1
Year: semesters, summer session	**Tuition:** $2486 ($10,352)
Application Deadline: open	**Room & Board:** $5240
Freshman Class: 18,129 applied, 15,702 accepted, 6203 enrolled	
SAT I Verbal/Math: 542/555	**ACT:** 23 **COMPETITIVE**

Arizona State University-Main founded in 1885, is a publicly funded institution offering undergraduate programs in the arts and sciences, business, education, engineering, nursing, public programs, architecture and environmental design, social work, and fine arts. There are 9 undergraduate and 10 graduate schools. In addition to regional accreditation, ASU-Main has baccalaureate program accreditation with AACSB, ABET, ACCE, ACEJMC, ADA, CSAB, CSWE, FIDER, NAAB, NASM, NCATE, NLN, and NRPA. The 5 libraries contain 3,190,820 volumes, 5,733,474 microform items, and 1,315,373 audiovisual forms/CDs, and subscribe to 28,159 periodicals. Computerized library services include the card catalog, interlibrary loans, and database searching. Special learning facilities include an art gallery, planetarium, radio station, and TV station. The 716-acre campus is in an urban area 10 miles east of Phoenix.

Student Life: 73% of undergraduates are from Arizona. Others are from 50 states, 104 foreign countries, and Canada. 71% are white; 11%, Hispanic. The average age of freshmen is 18; all undergraduates, 22. 25% do not continue beyond their first year.

Housing: 5500 students can be accommodated in college housing, which includes coed dormitories, on-campus apartments, and fraternity houses. In addition, there are honors houses and special-interest houses. On-campus housing is available on a first-come, first-served basis. 82% of students commute. All students may keep cars.

Activities: 9% of men belong to 25 national fraternities; 7% of women belong to 19 national sororities. There are 453 groups on campus, including art, band, cheerleading, chess, choir, chorus, computers, dance, drama, ethnic, film, gay, honors, international, jazz band, literary magazine, marching band, musical theater, newspaper, opera, orchestra, photography, political, professional, radio and TV, religious, social, social service, student government, and symphony. Popular campus events include World Fest international food and cultural festival and Fiesta Bowl.

Sports: There are 10 intercollegiate sports for men and 11 for women, and 35 intramural sports for men and 35 for women. Facilities include 4 stadiums (including football and baseball), a tennis center, an aquatic complex, a golf course, 2 activity centers, a student recreation complex, and a track.

Disabled Students: 98% of the campus is accessible. Wheelchair ramps, elevators, special parking, specially equipped rest rooms, special class scheduling, lowered drinking fountains, lowered telephones, flashing alarms for the deaf, braille maps, modified residence hall rooms, and an adaptive exercise program and facility are available.

Services: Counseling and information services are available, as is tutoring in most subjects, including 125 different courses. There is a reader service for the blind, and remedial math, reading, and writing. There is also on-line tutoring and graduate test preparation.

Campus Safety and Security: Measures include 24-hour foot and vehicle patrol, self-defense education, escort service, and shuttle buses. There are informal discussions, pamphlets/posters/films, emergency telephones, and lighted pathways/sidewalks.

Programs of Study: ASU-Main confers B.A., B.S., B.A.E., B.F.A., B.I.S., B.Mus., B.S.D., B.S.E., B.S.L.A., B.S.N., B.S.P., and B.S.W. degrees. Master's and doctoral degrees are also awarded. Bachelor's degrees are awarded in AGRICULTURE (plant science), BIOLOGICAL SCIENCE (biochemistry, biology/biological science, environmental biology, microbiology, and molecular biology), BUSINESS (accounting, banking and finance, management science, marketing/retailing/merchandising, purchasing/inventory management, real estate, and recreation and leisure services), COMMUNICATIONS AND THE ARTS (art, art history and appreciation, broadcasting, ceramic art and design, Chinese, communications, dance, dramatic arts, drawing, English, French, German, graphic design, industrial design, Italian, Japanese, journalism, media arts, metal/jewelry, music, music performance, music theory and composition, painting, photography, printmaking, Russian, sculpture, and Spanish), COMPUTER AND PHYSICAL SCIENCE (chemistry, computer science, geology, information sciences and systems, mathematics, and physics), EDUCATION (early childhood, elementary, music, secondary, and special), ENGINEERING AND ENVIRONMENTAL DESIGN (aeronautical engineering, architecture, bioengineering, chemical engineering, civil engineering, computer engineering, construction engineering, electrical/electronics engineering, engineering, industrial engineering, interior design, landscape architecture/design, materials science, mechanical engineering, urban design, and urban planning technology), HEALTH PROFESSIONS (clinical science, music therapy, nursing, and speech pathology/audiology), SOCIAL SCIENCE (African American studies, American Indian studies, anthropology, criminal justice, economics, family/consumer resource management, geography, Hispanic American studies, history, humanities, interdisciplinary studies, philosophy, physical fitness/movement, political science/government, psychology, religion, social work, sociology, and women's studies). Engineering, architecture, and computer science are the strongest academically. Business, psychology, and communication are the largest.

Required: To graduate, students must have a minimum GPA of 2.0 and a total of at least 120 credit hours, including 50 hours of upper-level work. The number of hours in the major varies by degree program. All students must take English composition and fulfill the general studies requirement of 35 hours in the areas of numeracy, literacy and critical inquiry, humanities and fine arts, social and behavioral sciences, natural sciences, global awareness, and historical awareness.

Special: ASU offers internships in many disciplines, study abroad in 10 countries, and a variety of interdisciplinary undergraduate programs. Students may participate in educational programs supported by several institutes and centers, such as the National Center for Electron Microscopy, the American Indian Institute, and the Center for Medieval and Renaissance Studies. Also available are continuing education programs and a summer math and science program for high school students. There are 20 national honor societies, including Phi Beta Kappa, and a freshman honors program.

Faculty/Classroom: 63% of faculty are male; 37%, female. 75% teach undergraduates. The average class size in an introductory lecture is 40 and in a laboratory, 22.

Admissions: 87% of the 2001-2002 applicants were accepted. The SAT I scores for the 2001-2002 freshman class were: Verbal--30% below 500, 45% between 500 and 599, 20% between 600 and 700, and 5% above 700; Math--24% below 500, 44% between 500 and 599, 27% between 600 and 700, and 6% above 700. The ACT scores were 26% below 21, 28% between 21 and 23, 25% between 24 and 26, 11% between 27 and 28, and 11% above 28. 43% of the current freshmen were in the top fifth of their class; 72% were in the top two fifths. There were 112 National Merit finalists.

Requirements: The SAT I or ACT is required. The minimum composite score on the ACT is 22 for in-state students, 24 for out-of-state students; on the SAT I, 1040 for in-state students, 1110 for out-of-state students. Graduation from an accredited secondary school must include 4 years each of English and math, 3 years of lab science, 2 years each of social science (including American history) and the same foreign language, and 1 year of fine arts. The GED, minimum score 50, is also accepted. ASU-Main requires applicants to be in the upper 25% of their class. A GPA of 3.0 is required. AP and CLEP credits are accepted. Applications are accepted on-line.

Procedure: Freshmen are admitted to all sessions. Entrance exams should be taken late in the junior year. There is an early admissions plan. Application deadlines are open. The fee is $40 for nonresidents. Notification is sent on a rolling basis.

Transfer: 3622 transfer students enrolled in 2001-2002. Applicants with fewer than 36 transferable hours must meet the requirements for freshman admission. A minimum GPA of 2.0 is required for in-state applicants; 2.5 for out-of-state applicants. 30 credits of 120 must be completed at ASU-Main.

Visiting: There are regularly scheduled orientations for prospective students. There are guides for informal visits and visitors may sit in on classes. To schedule a visit, contact Undergraduate Admissions at (480) 727-7013 or *asuvisit@asu.edu*.

Financial Aid: in 2000-2001, 34% of all freshmen received some form of financial aid. 29% of freshmen received need-based aid. The average freshman award was $6183. The average financial indebtedness of the 2001 graduate was $17,662. ASU-Main is a member of CSS. The CSS/Profile, FAFSA, FFS, or SFS are required. The fall application deadline is March 1.

International Students: There are 1087 international students enrolled. They must score 500 on the written TOEFL or 173 on the electronic version.

Computers: There are IBM RS/6000/390s and 590s and an SGI Power Challenge as computer servers, HP 9000/735s as statistical servers, an IBM RS/6000 and an HP 9000/735 as file servers, Sun SPARC 20s, Sun SPARC 10s, HP 9000/712s, and IBM RS/6000/250s as translators, an HP T500 and an HP K200 for development as transaction servers, and Sun SPAR C 20s and Sun SPARC 10s as miscellaneous servers. Also available are 770 Rycom, MAG, HAL, Zenith, and Mac PCs in 7 areas on campus. All students may access the system; 1 site is open 24 hours per day. There are no time limits and no fees.

Graduates: In 2001, 6285 bachelor's degrees were awarded. The most popular majors were interdisciplinary studies (8%), communication (6%), and psychology (5%). In an average class, 1% graduate in 3 years, 22% in 4 years, 43% in 5 years, and 49% in 6 years.

Admissions Contact: Tim Desch, Director Undergraduate Admissions. E-mail: *ugradinq@asu.edu* Web: *www.asu.edu*

DEVRY UNIVERSITY/PHOENIX C-4

Phoenix, AZ 85021-2995 **(602) 870-9201**
(800) 528-0250; Fax: (602) 331-1494

Full-time: 1808 men, 539 women	**Faculty:** 37
Part-time: 520 men, 183 women	**Ph.D.s:** n/av
Graduate: none	**Student/Faculty:** 63 to 1
Year: semesters, summer session	**Tuition:** $8805
Application Deadline: open	**Room & Board:** n/app
Freshman Class: 1196 applied, 1078 accepted, 551 enrolled	
SAT I or ACT: recommended	**LESS COMPETITIVE**

The DeVry University/Phoenix, formerly Devry Institute of Technology, is a private institution opened in 1967; there are 22 other DeVry schools in the United States and Canada owned by DeVry University Inc. The school offers a hands-on technology-based curriculum in business administration, computer information systems, electronics, technical management, information technology, computer engineering technology, and telecommunications. In addition to regional accreditation, DeVry has baccalaureate program accreditation with ABET. The library contains 20,283 volumes, 125,000 microform items, and 1563 audiovisual forms/CDs, and subscribes to 125 periodicals. Computerized library services include database searching. Special learning facilities include a learning resource center and electronics and other labs. The 18-acre campus is in a suburban area of Phoenix. There is 1 building.

Student Life: 68% of undergraduates are from Arizona. Others are from 38 states and 4 foreign countries. 68% are white; 15% Hispanic. The average age of all undergraduates is 26. 59% do not continue beyond their first year; 36% remain to graduate.

Housing: There are no residence halls. All students commute. Alcohol is not permitted. All students may keep cars.

Activities: There are no fraternities or sororities. There are 13 groups on campus, including ethnic, honors, professional, radio and TV, religious, social, and yearbook. Popular campus events include Thanksgiving Dinner, Ethnic Day, and Cino de Mayo.

Sports: There is 1 intramural sport for men and 1 for women. Facilities include a game room. Students can obtain free passes for a fitness center.

Disabled Students: All of the campus is accessible. Wheelchair ramps, elevators, special parking, specially equipped rest rooms, special class scheduling, lowered drinking fountains, and lowered telephones are available.

Services: Counseling and information services are available, as is tutoring in every subject.

Campus Safety and Security: Measures include escort services, informal discussions, pamphlets/posters/films, and emergency telephones. There are lighted pathways/sidewalks and a security guard service Monday through Friday 8 A.M. to 11 P.M. and from 12 noon to 6 P.M. on Sunday. The building is guarded during hours of closure by a motion-detector system.

Programs of Study: DeVry confers the B.S. degree. Associate degrees are also awarded. Bachelor's degrees are awarded in BUSINESS (business administration and management), COMMUNICATIONS AND THE ARTS (telecommunications), COMPUTER AND PHYSICAL SCIENCE (computer programming and information sciences and systems), ENGINEERING AND ENVIRONMENTAL DESIGN (computer technology, electrical/electronics engineering technology, and technological management). Computer information systems and electronics engineering technology are the largest.

Required: To graduate, students must achieve a GPA of at least 2.0 and satisfactorily complete all curriculum requirements. Course requirements vary according to program. All first-semester students take courses in business organization, computer applications, algebra, psychology, and student success strategies.

Special: Accelerated degrees, co-op programs, nondegree study, and evening and weekend classes are possible. There is 1 national honor society.

Faculty/Classroom: All teach undergraduates. The average class size in an introductory lecture is 30; in a laboratory, 30; and in a regular course, 30.

Admissions: 90% of the 2001-2002 applicants were accepted.

Requirements: The SAT I or ACT is recommended. In addition, admissions requirements include graduation from a secondary school; the GED is also accepted. Applicants from accredited postsecondary schools must pass the DeVry entrance exam or present satisfactory ACT or SAT I scores. An interview is required. CLEP credit is accepted. Applications are accepted on-line at Embark.com.

Procedure: Freshmen are admitted fall, spring, and summer. There is a deferred admissions plan. Application deadlines are open. The application fee is $50.

Transfer: 256 transfer students enrolled in 2001-2002. Applicants must present passing grades in all completed college course work, demonstrate language skills proficiency with at least 24 completed semester hours, and evidence math proficiency by appropriate college-level credits. 35% of 48 to 154 credits must be completed at DeVry.

Visiting: There are regularly scheduled orientations for prospective students. There are guides for informal visits and visitors may sit in on classes. To schedule a visit, contact Raymond Toledo, Director of Admissions at (602) 870-9222.

Financial Aid: In a recent year, 32% of all freshmen and 85% of continuing students received some form of financial aid. 14% of freshmen and 42% of continuing students received need-based aid. 27% of undergraduates work part time. Average annual earnings from campus work are $6960. The average financial indebtedness of the 2001 graduate was $13,146. The FAFSA is required.

International Students: There are 26 international students enrolled. They must score 550 on the written TOEFL or 173 on the electronic version and also take DeVry's computerized placement test, achieving a minimum score that varies by program.

Computers: The mainframe is an IBM 3081K. Lab facilities include PCs in stand-alone and network configurations with access to the mainframe. LANs provide access to a wide range of applications software. Hard copy from the mainframe is provided through a local minicomputer and medium- and high-speed printers. Students in the computer information systems program may access the system during published lab hours. There are no time limits and no fees. It is recommended that students in the information technology program have DeVry-issued laptop computers. There is a $55 per hour technology fee.

Graduates: In 2001, 902 bachelor's degrees were awarded. The most popular majors were computer information (49%), business (28%), and electronics engineering technology (23%). 210 companies recruited on campus in 2000-2001.

Admissions Contact: Ray Toledo, Director of Admissions.
Web: *www.devry-phx.edu*

EMBRY-RIDDLE AERONAUTICAL UNIVERSITY C-3

Prescott, AZ 86301-3720 **(928) 777-6692**
(800) 442-ERAU; Fax: 9928) 777-6606

Full-time: 1322 men, 246 women	**Faculty:** 76
Part-time: 124 men, 32 women	**Ph.D.s:** 55%
Graduate: 10 men, 6 women	**Student/Faculty:** 21 to 1
Year: semesters, summer session	**Tuition:** $18,430
Application Deadline: open	**Room & Board:** $5040
Freshman Class: 1330 applied, 1045 accepted, 375 enrolled	
SAT I Verbal/Math: 540/560	**ACT:** 24 **COMPETITIVE+**

Embry-Riddle Aeronautical University, founded in 1926, is a private institution offering undergraduate programs in aviation, engineering, business, and professional training on 2 campuses: the Prescott campus, founded in 1978, and the Daytona Beach, Florida, campus. Graduate programs are also offered at both campuses. There are 3 undergraduate schools and 1 graduate school. In addition to regional accreditation, ERAU has baccalaureate program accreditation with ABET. The library contains 28,682 volumes, 186,626 microform items, and 2301 audiovisual forms/CDs, and subscribes to 628 periodicals. Computerized library services include the card catalog, interlibrary loans, and database searching. Special learning facilities include a learning resource center, 4 wind tunnels, an aviation safety center, and an aircraft structures lab. The Flight Training Center at Ernest A. Love Field offers a simulator lab and flight operations center. The 547-acre campus is in a rural area 100 miles north of Phoenix. Including residence halls, there are 57 buildings.

Student Life: 78% of undergraduates are from out of state, mostly the Southwest. Others are from 48 states, 33 foreign countries, and Canada. 76% are white. The average age of freshmen is 18; all undergraduates, 21. 23% do not continue beyond their first year.

Housing: 849 students can be accommodated in college housing, which includes coed dormitories and on-campus apartments. On-campus housing is guaranteed for the freshman year only and is available on a first-come, first-served basis. 51% of students commute. Alcohol is not permitted. All students may keep cars.

Activities: 11% of men belong to 3 national fraternities; 18% of women belong to 2 national sororities. There are 68 groups on campus, including ethnic, gay, honors, international, jazz band, literary magazine, newspaper, political, professional, radio and TV, religious, social, social service, and student government. Popular campus events include Octoberwest, Spring Fling, and Hawaii Luau Club.

Sports: There is 1 intercollegiate sport for men and 1 for women, and 19 intramural sports for men and 19 for women. Facilities include an activity center with 3 basketball courts and 3 volleyball courts, a gym/weight room, a multipurpose athletic playing field, a game room, a swimming pool complex, and a fitness facility.

Disabled Students: 20% of the campus is accessible. Wheelchair ramps, special parking, specially equipped rest rooms, special class scheduling, lowered drinking fountains, lowered telephones, specially equipped dorm rooms, and pneumatic doors are available.

Services: Counseling and information services are available, as is tutoring in most subjects. There is remedial math, reading, and writing.

Campus Safety and Security: Measures include 24-hour foot and vehicle patrol, self-defense education, escort service, and shuttle buses.

There are informal discussions, pamphlets/posters/films, emergency telephones, and lighted pathways/sidewalks.

Programs of Study: ERAU confers the B.S. degree. Associate and master's degrees are also awarded. Bachelor's degrees are awarded in COMPUTER AND PHYSICAL SCIENCE (computer science), ENGINEERING AND ENVIRONMENTAL DESIGN (aeronautical engineering, aeronautical science, aerospace studies, aviation administration/management, and electrical/electronics engineering). Engineering is the strongest academically. Aeronautical science is the largest.

Required: All students must complete 36 credits of general education requirements, including courses in communication skills, technical report writing, humanities/social sciences, math, physical science, economics, and computer science. A total of 120 to 135 credit hours with a minimum GPA of 2.0 is required to graduate.

Special: Cooperative work-study programs, internships in all majors, and study abroad in 19 countries are offered. Flight training may be taken in conjunction with aeronautical science and other degree programs. Credit is given for life and military experience. There are 2 national honor societies.

Faculty/Classroom: 74% of faculty are male; 26%, female. All teach undergraduates. The average class size in an introductory lecture is 24; in a laboratory, 13; and in a regular course, 23.

Admissions: 79% of the 2001-2002 applicants were accepted. The SAT I scores for the 2001-2002 freshman class were: Verbal--26% below 500, 49% between 500 and 599, 23% between 600 and 700, and 2% above 700; Math--19% below 500, 46% between 500 and 599, 30% between 600 and 700, and 5% above 700. The ACT scores were 21% below 21, 23% between 21 and 23, 27% between 24 and 26, 17% between 27 and 28, and 10% above 28. 38% of the current freshmen were in the top fifth of their class; 68% were in the top two fifths.

Requirements: The SAT I or ACT is required. In addition, applicants must be graduates of an accredited secondary school or have a GED equivalent. All admissions items are processed at Daytona Beach headquarters. Applications are available on the ERAU web site. AP and CLEP credits are accepted. Important factors in the admissions decision are advanced placement or honor courses, recommendations by school officials, and evidence of special talent.

Procedure: Freshman are admitted to all sessions. Entrance exams should be taken during the fall of the senior year. There are early decision and deferred admissions plans. Early decision applications should be filed by December 1; for regular applications, the deadlines are open. The fee is $30. Notification of early decision is sent December 31; regular decision, on a rolling basis. 44 early decision candidates were accepted for the 2001-2002 class.

Transfer: 101 transfer students enrolled in 2001-2002. Applicants must have a minimum GPA of 2.0 in at least 12 credit hours earned. 30 credits of 120 must be completed at ERAU.

Visiting: There are regularly scheduled orientations for prospective students. There are guides for informal visits. To schedule a visit, contact Bill Thompson at *thompsb@pr.erau.edu.*

Financial Aid: In 2001-2002, 80% of all freshmen and 87% of continuing students received some form of financial aid. 79% of freshmen and 76% of continuing students received need-based aid. The average freshman award was $15,784. Of that total, scholarships or need-based grants averaged $3671 ($7500 maximum); and loans averaged $2816 ($6500 maximum). 24% of undergraduates work part time. Average annual earnings from campus work are $2173. The average financial indebtedness of the 2001 graduate was $21,421. ERAU is a member of CSS. The FAFSA is required. The fall application deadline is April 15.

International Students: There are 56 international students enrolled. The school actively recruits these students. They must score 500 on the written TOEFL and also take the SAT I or the ACT.

Computers: The mainframe is a Sun SPARC Server 1000 with SPARC Storage Array. Some 200 UNIX, IBM, and Mac computers are available in student labs. All students may access the system. There are no time limits and no fees.

Graduates: In 2001, 306 bachelor's degrees were awarded. The most popular majors were aeronautical science (44%), aerospace engineering (18%), and electrical engineering (1%). In an average class, 31% graduate in 4 years, 51% in 5 years, and 53% in 6 years. 21 companies recruited on campus in 2000-2001. Of the 2000 graduating class, 5% were enrolled in graduate school within 6 months of graduation and 98% were employed.

Admissions Contact: Bill Thompson, Director of Admissions.
E-mail: *admit@pr.erau.edu* Web: *www.embryriddle.edu*

GRAND CANYON UNIVERSITY — C-4

Phoenix, AZ 85061-1097 — (602) 589-2855
(800) 800-9776, ext. 2855; Fax: (602) 589-2580

Full-time: 448 men, 879 women	**Faculty:** 96; IIB, --$
Part-time: 127 men, 155 women	**Ph.D.s:** 80%
Graduate: 569 men, 1935 women	**Student/Faculty:** 14 to 1
Year: semesters, summer session	**Tuition:** $21,000
Application Deadline: open	**Room & Board:** $9000
Freshman Class: 563 applied, 508 accepted, 305 enrolled	
SAT I or ACT: required	**LESS COMPETITIVE**

Grand Canyon University, founded in 1949, is a small, private, nonsectarian liberal arts institution. There are 5 undergraduate and 2 graduate schools. In addition to regional accreditation, Canyon has baccalaureate program accreditation with NLN. The library contains 166,000 volumes, 97,324 microform items, and 4100 audiovisual forms/CDs, and subscribes to 700 periodicals. Computerized library services include the card catalog, interlibrary loans, and database searching. Special learning facilities include an art gallery. The 90-acre campus is in a suburban area in Phoenix. Including residence halls, there are 32 buildings.

Student Life: 81% of undergraduates are from Arizona. Others are from 43 states, 6 foreign countries, and Canada. 77% are white; 10%, Hispanic. Most are Protestant. The average age of freshmen is 19; all undergraduates, 25.

Housing: 600 students can be accommodated in college housing, which includes single-sex dormitories and on-campus apartments. On-campus housing is available on a first-come, first-served basis. 52% of students live on campus. Alcohol is not permitted. All students may keep cars.

Activities: There are no fraternities or sororities. There are many groups and organizations on campus, including art, band, cheerleading, choir, chorale, chorus, computers, drama, ethnic, honors, international, jazz band, literary magazine, musical theater, newspaper, opera, orchestra, pep band, photography, political, professional, religious, social service, student government, and yearbook. Popular campus events include Spiritual Emphasis Week, Harvest Festival, and Spring Formal.

Sports: There are 5 intercollegiate sports for men and 4 for women. Facilities include a baseball field, a 500-seat gym, a 1750-seat gym, a 3000-seat stadium, 6 tennis courts, a weight room, and a swimming pool.

Disabled Students: All of the campus is accessible. Wheelchair ramps, elevators, special parking, and specially equipped rest rooms are available.

Services: Counseling and information services are available, as is tutoring in most subjects. There is a reader service for the blind and remedial reading and writing. Tutors are also trained in test-taking techniques, study skills, and time management.

Campus Safety and Security: Measures include 24-hour foot and vehicle patrol, self-defense education, escort service, and informal discussions. There are emergency telephones, lighted pathways/sidewalks, and a university safety committee that provides controlled after-hours access to residence halls.

Programs of Study: Canyon confers B.A., B.S., B.B.A., B.L.S., B.M., and B.S.N. degrees. Master's degrees are also awarded. Bachelor's degrees are awarded in BIOLOGICAL SCIENCE (biology/biological science and environmental biology), BUSINESS (accounting, banking and finance, business administration and management, human resources, international business management, marketing/retailing/merchandising, and personnel management), COMMUNICATIONS AND THE ARTS (applied music, communications, dramatic arts, English, fine arts, graphic design, music, piano/organ, Spanish, speech/debate/rhetoric, studio art, and voice), COMPUTER AND PHYSICAL SCIENCE (chemistry, computer science, and mathematics), EDUCATION (art, business, elementary, music, physical, science, secondary, and special), HEALTH PROFESSIONS (nursing), SOCIAL SCIENCE (Christian studies, criminal justice, economics, history, physical fitness/movement, psychology, religious music, social science, social studies, and sociology). Natural sciences, elementary education, and nursing are the strongest academically and have the largest enrollments.

Required: All students are required to complete 39 hours of general studies, including 3 hours each in Old Testament history and New Testament history, 6 each in English and humanities, 9 in social studies, 10 in science, and 2 in phys ed. Chapel attendance is required. A writing proficiency exam along with a total of 128 semester hours, with a minimum GPA of 2.0, are required to graduate.

Special: Co-op programs with several schools in the Christian College Coalition are available. Internships are offered for most majors through organizations, corporations, and agencies in the Phoenix area. Dual majors, study abroad in 5 countries, and a Washington semester are possible. A 3-2 engineering degree with Arizona State University is available. There is 1 national honor society, Phi Beta Kappa, a freshman honors program, and 1 departmental honors program.

Faculty/Classroom: 50% of faculty are male; 50%, female. All teach undergraduates. The average class size in an introductory lecture is 25; in a laboratory, 10; and in a regular course, 25.

Admissions: 90% of the 2001-2002 applicants were accepted.

Requirements: The SAT I or ACT is required. In addition, applicants should be graduates of an accredited high school or have a GED. Canyon requires applicants to be in the upper 50% of their class. A GPA of 2.14 is required. AP and CLEP credits are accepted. Important factors in the admissions decision are evidence of special talent, extracurricular activities record, and leadership record.

Procedure: Freshmen are admitted to all sessions. Entrance exams should be taken during the junior or senior year of high school. Application deadlines are open.The application fee is $50. Notification is sent on a rolling basis.

Transfer: 305 transfer students enrolled in 2001-2002. Transfer applicants must have a minimum GPA of 2.0 and a minimum of 24 transferable hours. 30 credits of 128 must be completed at Canyon.

Visiting: There are regularly scheduled orientations for prospective students, including High School Preview Days in February and Transfer Preview Days in March. There are guides for informal visits and visitors may sit in on classes and stay overnight. To schedule a visit, contact the Admission Office.

Financial Aid: In 2001-2002, 60% of all freshmen and 66% of continuing students received some form of financial aid. The average freshman award was $8405. The FAFSA is recommended.

International Students: There were 68 international students enrolled in a recent year. The school actively recruits these students. They must score 500 on the written TOEFL. The SAT I or ACT is required of students with English as their first language, with a 50 national percentile score or higher required.

Computers: The mainframe is a DEC ALPHA 4100 server. The computer lab facilities also include a large network of Macs and PCs, and a Motorola 6000 system. All students may access the system usually from morning until midnight. There are no time limits. The fee is $85 per semester.

Graduates: In 2001, 340 bachelor's degrees were awarded. The most popular majors were business (25%), health professions (18%), and education (12%). In an average class, 27% graduate in 4 years, 40% in 5 years, and 47% in 6 years.

Admissions Contact: April Chapman, Director of Admissions. A video is available. E-mail: *admiss@grand-canyon.edu*
Web: *www.grand-canyon.edu*

NORTHERN ARIZONA UNIVERSITY C-2

Flagstaff, AZ 86011 **(928) 523-5511**
(888) MORE-NAU; Fax: (928) 523-6023

Full-time: 4744 men, 6758 women	**Faculty:** 708; I, --$
Part-time: 817 men, 1421 women	**Ph.D.s:** 84%
Graduate: 1767 men, 4221 women	**Student/Faculty:** 16 to 1
Year: semesters, summer session	**Tuition:** $2488 ($10,354)
Application Deadline: March 1	**Room & Board:** $4910
Freshman Class: 10,952 applied, 8807 accepted, 2431 enrolled	
SAT I or ACT: required	**COMPETITIVE**

Northern Arizona University, founded in 1899, is a public institution offering undergraduate and graduate degrees in a full range of disciplines from liberal arts and sciences to professional and career-related fields. There are 11 undergraduate and 7 graduate schools. In addition to regional accreditation, NAU has baccalaureate program accreditation with AACSB, ABET, ADA, AHEA, APTA,CAPTE, NASM, NCATE, NLN, NRPA, and SAF. The library contains 1,462,816 volumes, 376,030 microform items, and 30,199 audiovisual forms/CDs, and subscribes to 6816 periodicals. Computerized library services include the card catalog, interlibrary loans, and database searching. Special learning facilities include a learning resource center, art gallery, radio station, TV station, observatory, research centers, and the Institute for Human Development. The 730-acre campus is in a small town 140 miles north of Phoenix. Including residence halls, there are 79 buildings.

Student Life: 83% of undergraduates are from Arizona. Others are from 50 states, 69 foreign countries, and Canada. 77% are white; 11% Hispanic. The average age of freshmen is 18; all undergraduates, 24. 36% do not continue beyond their first year.

Housing: 6106 students can be accommodated in college housing, which includes single-sex and coed dormitories, on-campus apartments, married-student housing, fraternity houses, and sorority houses. In addition, there are honors houses. On-campus housing is available on a first-come, first-served basis. Alcohol is not permitted. All students may keep cars.

Activities: 4% of men belong to 10 national fraternities; 3% of women belong to 7 national sororities. There are 133 groups on campus, including art, band, cheerleading, chess, choir, chorale, chorus, computers, dance, debate, drama, drill team, ethnic, film, forensics, gay, honors, international, jazz band, marching band, musical theater, newspaper, opera, orchestra, pep band, photography, political, professional, radio and TV, religious, social, social service, student government, and symphony. Popular campus events include Martin Luther King Jr. Day, Luminario Lighting, and Parents Weekend.

Sports: There are 5 intercollegiate sports for men and 8 for women, and 32 intramural sports for men and 32 for women. Facilities include the Skydome for football, basketball, and indoor track and field, 3 recreation centers with basketball and racquetball courts and weight rooms, a 50-meter indoor swimming pool with diving facilities, and numerous outdoor grass fields for soccer, rugby and lacrosse.

Disabled Students: 90% of the campus is accessible. Wheelchair ramps, elevators, special parking, specially equipped rest rooms, special class scheduling, lowered drinking fountains, and lowered telephones are available.

Services: Counseling and information services are available, as is tutoring in most subjects. There is a reader service for the blind, and remedial math, reading, and writing. Most counseling and tutoring is done by volunteers and student interns.

Campus Safety and Security: Measures include 24-hour foot and vehicle patrol, self-defense education, escort service, and shuttle buses. There are informal discussions, pamphlets/posters/films, emergency telephones, and lighted pathways/sidewalks.

Programs of Study: NAU confers B.A., B.S., B.F.A., B.Mus., B.Mus.Ed., B.S.B.A., B.S.C.S.E., B.S.D.H., B.S.E., B.S.Ed., B.S.F., B.S.J., B.S.N., and B.S.W. degrees. Master's and doctoral degrees are also awarded. Bachelor's degrees are awarded in AGRICULTURE (forestry and related sciences), BIOLOGICAL SCIENCE (biology/biological science, botany, microbiology, and zoology), BUSINESS (accounting, banking and finance, business administration and management, business economics, hotel/motel and restaurant management, and marketing/retailing/merchandising), COMMUNICATIONS AND THE ARTS (advertising, art history and appreciation, arts administration/management, broadcasting, communications, design, dramatic arts, English, fine arts, French, German, journalism, music, Spanish, speech/debate/rhetoric, and telecommunications), COMPUTER AND PHYSICAL SCIENCE (chemistry, computer science, geology, information sciences and systems, mathematics, and physics), EDUCATION (art, business, early childhood, elementary, foreign languages, health, industrial arts, music, science, secondary, special, and teaching English as a second/foreign language (TESOL/TEFOL)), ENGINEERING AND ENVIRONMENTAL DESIGN (civil engineering, computer engineering, electrical/electronics engineering, engineering, environmental engineering, and mechanical engineering), HEALTH PROFESSIONS (nursing, predentistry, premedicine, and speech pathology/audiology), SOCIAL SCIENCE (anthropology, community services, criminal justice, dietetics, economics, geography, history, international relations, parks and recreation management, philosophy, political science/government, prelaw, psychology, public administration, religion, social work, and sociology). Health professions, engineering, and business are the strongest academically. Education, hotel/restaurant management, and psychology are the largest.

Required: To graduate, students must have at least 120 credit hours, including 45 to 60 in the major, with a minimum GPA of 2.0; some majors require a higher GPA. Students must complete a 44-hour liberal studies curriculum, consisting of foundation courses (6 hours of English and 3 hours of college algebra) and discipline courses (9 hours each of creative arts, letters, and behavioral science and 8 each of natural science and math).

Special: NAU offers co-op programs in business, cross-registration with many universities through the National Student Exchange, and internships in most majors. Legislative internships are offered through the Arizona State Senate and House of Representatives. Students may study abroad in 15 countries. Work-study programs are available in engineering, business, park services, and arts management. Accelerated degrees, a general studies degree, dual majors, nondegree study, and pass/fail options are possible. There are 6 national honor societies, and a freshman honors program.

Faculty/Classroom: 53% of faculty are male; 47%, female. All both teach and do research.

Admissions: 80% of the 2001-2002 applicants were accepted. The SAT I scores for the 2001-2002 freshman class were: Verbal--33% below 500, 45% between 500 and 599, 19% between 600 and 700, and 3% above 700; Math--33% below 500, 43% between 500 and 599, 21% between 600 and 700, and 3% above 700. 41 freshmen graduated first in their class.

Requirements: The SAT I or ACT is required. In addition, students must have a minimum GPA of 2.5 or rank in the top 50% of their class or have minimum composite SAT I scores of 1040 for in-state and 1110 for out-of-state applicants, or minimum ACT scores of 22 for in-state and 24 for out-of-state applicants. Students should be graduates of an accredited secondary school or hold the GED. Requirements include 16 academic credits, with a grade of C or better in each class of 4 years of English, 3 of algebra, 3 of lab science, 2 of foreign language, and 1 each of geometry, social studies, fine art, and American history. AP and CLEP credits are accepted.

Procedure: Freshmen are admitted to all sessions. Entrance exams should be taken before the last semester of the senior year. Applications should be filed by March 1 for fall entry, December 1 for spring entry, and May 15 for summer entry. There is a $40 application fee (fall 2001) for nonresidents. Notification is sent on a rolling basis.

Transfer: 1610 transfer students enrolled in 2001-2002. Transfer students must be eligible to reenter the institution last attended. Requirements vary with the number of college credits being transferred. Generally, in-state applicants must have a minimum GPA of 2.0 and submit high school and/or college transcripts. Nonresident transfer students with a GPA below 2.5 are admitted on a space-available basis. 30 credits of 120 must be completed at NAU.

Visiting: There are regularly scheduled orientations for prospective students, including eight 2-day orientation/registration sessions for new students held mid-June through mid-July, and a 4-day program held the week before the fall and spring semesters. There are guides for informal visits and visitors may sit in on classes and stay overnight. To schedule a visit, contact the Office of Undergraduate Admissions at (928) 523-2491.

Financial Aid: In 2001-2002, 69% of all freshmen and 70% of continuing students received some form of financial aid. 57% of freshmen and 50% of continuing students received need-based aid. The average freshman award was $5877. Of that total, scholarships or need-based grants averaged $2572 ($20,500 maximum); loans averaged $4376 ($19,200 maximum); and work contracts averaged $2536 ($6382 maximum). 65% of undergraduates work part time. Average annual earnings from campus work are $1447. The average financial indebtedness of the 2001 graduate was $16,202. The FAFSA is required. The priority application deadline is April 15.

International Students: There are 282 international students enrolled. They must score 500 on the written TOEFL or 173 on the electronic version or take the MELAB.

Computers: The mainframes are a DEC VAX and an IBM 3083 and 9375-60. PCs are available to students at various campus locations. Mainframes are sponsored by the faculty. All students may access the system. There are no time limits and no fees.

Graduates: In 2001, 2912 bachelor's degrees were awarded. The most popular majors were elementary education (22%), business administration (17%), and liberal arts (10%). In an average class, 1% graduate in 3 years, 4% in 4 years, 30% in 5 years, and 41% in 6 years.

Admissions Contact: Molly S. Munger, Director of Admissions. A video is available. E-mail: *undergraduate.admissions@nau.edu*
Web: *www.nau.edu*

PRESCOTT COLLEGE

Prescott, AZ 86301 — **C-3**

(928) 778-2090, ext. 2101
(800) 628-6364; Fax: (928) 776-5137

Full-time: 303 men, 433 women	**Faculty:** 49
Part-time: 40 men, 51 women	**Ph.D.s:** 43%
Graduate: 61 men, 117 women	**Student/Faculty:** 15 to 1
Year: trimesters, summer session	**Tuition:** $13,430
Application Deadline: open	**Room & Board:** n/app
Freshman Class: 254 applied, 213 accepted, 85 enrolled	
SAT I or ACT: not required	**COMPETITIVE**

Prescott College, founded in 1966, is a private commuter institution offering a nontraditional undergraduate program in the liberal arts. The curriculum is organized into multidisciplinary courses that allow students to pursue individual areas of competency. Evaluations of a student's work are conducted through a portfolio/contract system and an ongoing series of student self-evaluations. There are 3 undergraduate schools and 1 graduate school. The library contains 22,417 volumes, 125 microform items, and 1304 audiovisual forms/CDs, and subscribes to 270 periodicals. Computerized library services include the card catalog, interlibrary loans, and database searching. Special learning facilities include a learning resource center, art gallery, a greenhouse, a weather station, and a recycling center. The 4-acre campus is in a small town 100 miles north of Phoenix. There are 16 buildings.

Student Life: 89% of undergraduates are from out of state, mostly the Northeast. Others are from 43 states, 5 foreign countries, and Canada. 96% are white. The average age of freshmen is 20; all undergraduates, 28. 5% do not continue beyond their first year; 78% remain to graduate.

Housing: There are no residence halls. All of students commute. Alcohol is not permitted. All students may keep cars.

Activities: There are no fraternities or sororities. There are 10 groups on campus, including agriculture, art, dance, drama, garden, gay, indigenous rights, literary magazine, martial arts, newspaper, photography, political, social, social service, and student government. Popular campus events include Earth Day, Southwest Writers Series, and Student-Directed Days.

Sports: There is no sports program at Prescott. There are no sports facilities on campus, but students have access to the local community pool, weight room, gym, and city league sports.

Disabled Students: 60% of the campus is accessible. Wheelchair ramps, special parking, and specially equipped rest rooms are available.

Services: There is remedial math and writing. There is a learning specialist on staff and untimed tests are available.

Campus Safety and Security: Measures include self-defense education, informal discussions, pamphlets/posters/films, and emergency telephones.

Programs of Study: Prescott confers the B.A. degree. Master's degrees are also awarded. Bachelor's degrees are awarded in AGRICULTURE (environmental studies), BIOLOGICAL SCIENCE (biology/biological science), COMMUNICATIONS AND THE ARTS (communications, English, fine arts, journalism, photography, and Spanish), COMPUTER AND PHYSICAL SCIENCE (earth science, and geology), EDUCATION (art, early childhood, education, elementary, environmental, foreign languages, guidance, middle school, recreation, secondary, and special), ENGINEERING AND ENVIRONMENTAL DESIGN (environmental science), SOCIAL SCIENCE (anthropology, community services, criminal justice, economics, peace studies, psychology, social work, and sociology). Environmental studies is the strongest academically. Education is the largest.

Required: Prescott does not specify any formal graduation requirements. Students may design an individual program of studies within 4 multidisciplinary areas: environmental studies, adventure education, arts and letters, and integrative studies. Each student is required to submit a graduation proposal at the end of the junior year to the Graduation Review Committee.

Special: Student-coordinated internships, study abroad in almost any country, dual majors, a general studies degree, pass/fail options, and credit for life experience are offered. All majors are student-designed.

Faculty/Classroom: 55% of faculty are male; 45%, female. All teach undergraduates. The average class size in an introductory lecture is 12; in a laboratory, 12; and in a regular course, 12.

Admissions: 84% of the 2001-2002 applicants were accepted. The SAT I scores for the 2001-2002 freshman class were: Verbal--30% below 500, 49% between 500 and 599, and 21% between 600 and 700; Math--14% below 500, 49% between 500 and 599, 33% between 600 and 700, and 4% above 700. The ACT scores were 71% below 17, 24% between 18 and 23, and 5% between 24 and 28.

Requirements: The GED is accepted. The school requires essays, transcripts, and letters of recommendation. Students may also submit portfolios and writing samples. Important factors in the admissions decision are extracurricular activities record, personality/intangible qualities, and leadership record.

Procedure: Freshmen are admitted fall and spring. Application deadlines are open.

Transfer: 170 transfer students enrolled in 2001-2002. Transfer applicants must meet the same requirements as entering freshmen and must also submit official college transcripts. Students who successfully completed 2 years of college work (60 semester hours or 90 quarter credits) need not submit high school transcripts. There is a 2-year residency requirement. 90 credits of 186 must be completed at Prescott.

Visiting: There are regularly scheduled orientations for prospective students, including a college video, a campus tour, and an interview with an admissions counselor. There are guides for informal visits and visitors may sit in on classes. To schedule a visit, contact the RDP Admissions Office.

Financial Aid: In 2001-2002, 33% of all freshmen and 73% of continuing students received some form of financial aid, including need-based aid. The average freshman award was $3264. Of that total, scholarships or need-based grants averaged $2884 ($11,286 maximum); loans averaged $2933 ($20,000 maximum); and work contracts averaged $796 ($1500 maximum). 17% of undergraduates work part time. Average annual earnings from campus work are $1780. The average financial indebtedness of the 2001 graduate was $15,891. The FAFSA is required.

International Students: There are 8 international students enrolled. They must score 500 on the written TOEFL.

Computers: The Learning Center has 20 PCs for student use. All students may access the system 100 hours per week. There are no time limits and no fees.

Graduates: In 2001, 264 bachelor's degrees were awarded. The most popular majors were environmental studies (40%), integrative studies (30%), and arts and letters (23%). In an average class, 25% graduate in 3 years, 45% in 4 years, and 52% in 5 years.

Admissions Contact: Shari Sterling, Director of Admissions.
E-mail: *rdpadmissions@prescott.edu* Web: *www.prescott.edu*

UNIVERSITY OF ARIZONA

D-4

Tucson, AZ 85721 (520) 621-3237; Fax: (520) 621-9799

Full-time: 11,028 men, 12,155 women	**Faculty:** 1495; I, av$
Part-time: 1729 men, 1966 women	**Ph.D.s:** 94%
Graduate: 3044 men, 3030 women	**Student/Faculty:** 16 to 1
Year: semesters, summer session	**Tuition:** $2490 ($10,356)
Application Deadline: April 1	**Room & Board:** $6124
Freshman Class: 19,719 applied, 16,613 accepted, 5949 enrolled	
SAT I or ACT: required	**COMPETITIVE**

The University of Arizona, founded in 1885, is a public land-grant institution controlled by the state of Arizona. Undergraduate programs are offered in agriculture, architecture, arts and sciences, business and public administration, education, engineering and mines, and nursing, pharmacy, and other health-related professions. There are 13 undergraduate and 5 graduate schools. In addition to regional accreditation, UA has baccalaureate program accreditation with AACSB, ABET, ACPE, ADA, ASLA, NAAB, NASAD, NASM, NCATE, and NLN. The 7 libraries contain 4,266,503 volumes, 5,196,499 microform items, and 49,171 audiovisual forms/CDs, and subscribe to 23,678 periodicals. Computerized library services include the card catalog, interlibrary loans, and database searching. Special learning facilities include a learning resource center, art gallery, natural history museum, planetarium, radio station, TV station, and the Ansel Adams Center for creative photography. The 353-acre campus is in an urban area in Tucson. Including residence halls, there are 172 buildings.

Student Life: 70% of undergraduates are from Arizona. Others are from 49 states, 131 foreign countries, and Canada. 90% are from public schools. 68% are white; 13% Hispanic. The average age of freshmen is 18; all undergraduates, 23. 23% do not continue beyond their first year.

Housing: 4600 students can be accommodated in college housing, which includes single-sex and coed dormitories, on-campus apartments, off-campus apartments, married-student housing, fraternity houses, and sorority houses. In addition, there are honors houses and special-interest houses. On-campus housing is available on a first-come, first-served basis. 80% of students commute. Alcohol is not permitted. All students may keep cars.

Activities: 15% of men belong to 3 local and 23 national fraternities; 15% of women belong to 3 local and 14 national sororities. There are 375 groups on campus, including art, band, cheerleading, chess, choir, chorale, chorus, computers, dance, drama, drill team, ethnic, film, gay, honors, international, jazz band, literary magazine, marching band, musical theater, newspaper, orchestra, pep band, photography, political, professional, radio and TV, religious, social, social service, student government, and yearbook. Popular campus events include the Spring Fling carnival and cultural programs.

Sports: There are 8 intercollegiate sports for men and 10 for women, and 27 intramural sports for men and 26 for women. Facilities include an athletic center, a 53,000-seat stadium, a 13,500-seat arena, and a student recreation facility with a weight room, a waveless swimming pool, two gyms, aerobics facilities, treadmills, stairclimbers, stationary bicycles, and racquetball, squash, and handball courts. Hiking, backpacking, and skiing trails as well as facilities for kayaking, caving, and scuba diving are available.

Disabled Students: 95% of the campus is accessible. Wheelchair ramps, elevators, special parking, specially equipped rest rooms, lowered drinking fountains, lowered telephones, and physical therapy, counseling, interpreters, note taking, equipment maintenance, and an adaptive athletics program are available.

Services: Counseling and information services are available, as is tutoring in most subjects. There is a reader service for the blind and remedial writing.

Campus Safety and Security: Measures include 24-hour foot and vehicle patrol, self-defense education, escort service, and shuttle buses. There are emergency telephones and lighted pathways/sidewalks.

Programs of Study: UA confers B.A., B.S., B.Arch., B.F.A., B.L.A., B.M., B.S.B.A., B.S.H.S., B.S.N., and B.S.P.A. degrees. Master's and doctoral degrees are also awarded. Bachelor's degrees are awarded in AGRICULTURE (agricultural economics, animal science, natural resource management, plant science, range/farm management, and soil science), BIOLOGICAL SCIENCE (biochemistry, biology/biological science, ecology, evolutionary biology, microbiology, molecular biology, nutrition, physiology, and wildlife biology), BUSINESS (accounting, banking and finance, business administration and management, business economics, entrepreneurial studies, human resources, management information systems, management science, marketing/retailing/merchandising, and retailing), COMMUNICATIONS AND THE ARTS (art history and appreciation, classics, communications, creative writing, dance, dramatic arts, English, fine arts, French, German, Italian, journalism, language arts, Latin, linguistics, media arts, music, music performance, music theory and composition, musical theater, performing arts, Portuguese, Russian, Spanish, studio art, and theater design), COMPUTER AND PHYSICAL SCIENCE (astronomy, atmospheric sciences and meteorology, chemistry, computer science, earth science, geology, geoscience, hydrology, mathematics, natural sciences, and physics), EDUCATION (agricultural, art, drama, early childhood, elementary, health, home economics, music, physical, science, secondary, and special), ENGINEERING AND ENVIRONMENTAL DESIGN (aeronautical engineering, aerospace studies, agricultural engineering, agricultural engineering technology, architecture, chemical engineering, city/community/regional planning, civil engineering, computer engineering, electrical/electronics engineering, engineering, engineering physics, environmental science, geological engineering, industrial engineering, landscape architecture/design, materials engineering, mechanical engineering, mining and mineral engineering, nuclear engineering, optical engineering, and systems engineering), HEALTH PROFESSIONS (health care administration, medical technology, nursing, pharmacy, speech pathology/audiology, and veterinary science), SOCIAL SCIENCE (anthropology, child care/child and family studies, criminal justice, East Asian studies, economics, ethnic studies, family/consumer resource management, family/consumer studies, geography, German area studies, history, humanities, interdisciplinary studies, Judaic studies, Latin American studies, liberal arts/general studies, Mexican-American/Chicano studies, Near Eastern studies, philosophy, political science/government, psychology, public administration, religion, social science, social studies, sociology, theological studies, water resources, and women's studies). Sciences, social sciences, and management information systems are the strongest academically. Social sciences and business are the largest.

Required: All students must complete a core curriculum of courses in natural sciences, traditions and cultures, individuals and societies, math, English, art, and a foreign language. A total of 125 credits, with a minimum GPA of 2.0, is required to graduate.

Special: Co-op programs are available in almost all majors. B.A.-B.S. degrees, dual majors, interdisciplinary degrees such as engineering-math and theater arts-education, a 3-2 arts and sciences-business degree, and student-designed majors are offered. Internships in almost all disciplines, a Washington semester, study abroad in numerous countries, work-study programs on campus, a general studies degree, and pass/fail options are offered. Nondegree study is possible. There are 19 national honor societies, including Phi Beta Kappa, and a freshman honors program. Most departments have honors programs.

Faculty/Classroom: 67% of faculty are male; 33%, female. 62% teach undergraduates and 94% do research. Graduate students teach 42% of introductory courses. The average class size in an introductory lecture is 47; in a laboratory, 19; and in a regular course, 29.

Admissions: 84% of the 2001-2002 applicants were accepted. There were 54 National Merit finalists and 105 freshmen graduated first in their class in a recent year.

Requirements: The SAT I or ACT is required. In addition, applicants should have completed 4 years each in high school English and math, 3 in science, 2 of a foreign language, and 1 each in history, fine arts, and social studies. A GED may be considered in place of a high school diploma. Some fine arts programs require auditions prior to admission. Applications are accepted on-line at the school's website. UA requires applicants to be in the upper 25% of their class. A GPA of 3.0 is required. AP and CLEP credits are accepted. Important factors in the admissions decision are advanced placement or honor courses, leadership record, and extracurricular activities record.

Procedure: Freshmen are admitted to all sessions. Entrance exams should be taken from March of the junior year through December of the senior year. Applications should be filed by April 1 for fall entry, October 1 for spring entry, and May 1 for summer entry, along with a $50 application fee for out-of-state only. Notification is sent on a rolling basis.

Transfer: 2086 transfer students enrolled in 2001-2002. Resident transfer applicants must have a minimum GPA of 2.0; nonresidents, 2.5. Some university divisions have higher requirements. Admission is competitive for out-of-state students. 30 credits of 125 must be completed at UA.

Visiting: There are regularly scheduled orientations for prospective students, consisting of an admissions presentation and tour. There are guides for informal visits and visitors may sit in on classes. To schedule a visit, contact the Tour Desk at (520) 621-3641 or E-Mail: *visitua@arizona.edu*.

Financial Aid: In a recent year, 85% of all students received some form of financial aid. 52% of all students received need-based aid. The average freshman award was $5635. Of that total, scholarships or need-based grants averaged $2426 ($4710 maximum); loans averaged $5499 ($10,500 maximum); and work contracts averaged $1292 ($3500 maximum). 31% of undergraduates work part time. Average annual earnings from campus work are $2200. The average financial indebtedness of a recent year's graduate was $17,772. UA is a member of CSS. The FAFSA is required. The fall application deadline is March 1.

International Students: There were 2434 international students enrolled in a recent year. The school actively recruits these students. They must score 500 on the written TOEFL or 173 on the electronic version or take the Comprehensive English Language Test. The SAT I, with a score of 1110 or the ACT is required only if the applicant is a graduate of a U.S. high school.

Computers: The mainframes are an IBM 9672 and UNIX systems using IBM and HP. There are 1913 terminals, all with Internet web access. All students may access the system 18 hours a day. Students may access the system depending on course work. There are no fees. It is recommended that students in architecture have personal computers.

Graduates: In 2001, 4922 bachelor's degrees were awarded. The most popular majors were business/marketing (19%), social sciences and history (10%), and communications/communication technology (9%). In an average class, 1% graduate in 3 years, 21% in 4 years, 46% in 5 years, and 53% in 6 years. 250 companies recruited on campus in a recent year.

Admissions Contact: Lori Goldman, Director of Admissions. A video is available. E-mail: *appinfo@arizona.edu*
Web: *admissions.arizona.edu*

UNIVERSITY OF PHOENIX C-4

Phoenix, AZ 85040 (408) 966-9577; (800) 228-7240

Full-time and Part-time: 65,000 men and women	**Faculty:** 250
	Ph.D.s: n/av
Graduate: 5000 men and women	**Student/Faculty:** n/av
Year: 5-week blocks	**Tuition:** $7000
Application Deadline: open	**Room & Board:** n/app
Freshman Class: n/av	
SAT I or ACT: not required	**SPECIAL**

The University of Phoenix, founded in 1976, is a private multicampus institution offering undergraduate and graduate programs in business to working adults. Figures given in the above capsule are approximate. There are 6 undergraduate schools. Computerized library services include database searching. Special learning facilities include a learning resource center. The campus is in an urban area in Phoenix, with additional campuses in 22 other states.

Student Life: The average age of freshmen is 34.

Housing: There are no residence halls. All students commute. Alcohol is not permitted. All students may keep cars.

Activities: There are no fraternities or sororities.

Sports: There is no sports program at UOP.

Disabled Students: Wheelchair ramps, elevators, special parking, and specially equipped rest rooms are available.

Services: Counseling and information services are available, as is tutoring in some subjects, including math and English. There is remedial math and writing.

Campus Safety and Security: Measures include escort service, emergency telephones, and lighted pathways/sidewalks.

Programs of Study: UOP confers the B.S. degree. Associate and master's degrees are also awarded. Bachelor's degrees are awarded in BUSINESS (accounting, business administration and management, management science, and marketing and distribution), COMPUTER AND PHYSICAL SCIENCE (information sciences and systems), ENGINEERING AND ENVIRONMENTAL DESIGN (computer technology), HEALTH PROFESSIONS (health care administration and nursing), SOCIAL SCIENCE (criminal justice and human services). Business is the strongest academically.

Required: To graduate, students must complete 120 credit hours, with 51 to 66 in the major.

Special: Accelerated degree programs are offered in all majors.

Faculty/Classroom: 60% of faculty are male; 40%, female. All teach undergraduates and 40% do research. The average class size in an introductory lecture is 17 and in a regular course, 13.

Requirements: In addition, applicants must be at least 23 years of age. Applications are accepted on-line. A GPA of 2.0 is required. CLEP credit is accepted. Ability to finance college education is an important factor in the admission decision.

Procedure: Freshmen are admitted to all sessions. Application deadlines are open. Check with the school for current application deadlines and fee.

Transfer: 30 credits of 120 must be completed at UOP.

Visiting: There are regularly scheduled orientations for prospective students, including annual information meetings and class auditing. There are guides for informal visits and visitors may sit in on classes. To schedule a visit, contact enrollment counselors.

Financial Aid: UOP is a member of CSS. The FAFSA is required. Check with the school for current deadlines.

International Students: They must score 580 on the written TOEFL and also take the Comprehensive English Language Test and also take the college's own entrance exam.

Computers: All students may access the system from 10 A.M. to 10 P.M. Monday through Friday and from 9 A.M. to 1 P.M. Saturday. It is strongly recommended that all students have a personal computer.

Admissions Contact: Office of Enrollment. Web: *www.phoenix.edu*

WESTERN INTERNATIONAL UNIVERSITY C-4

Phoenix, AZ 85021 (602) 943-2311; Fax: (602) 371-8637

Full-time: 500 men, 380 women	**Faculty:** n/av
Part-time: none	**Ph.D.s:** 30%
Graduate: 190 men, 150 women	**Student/Faculty:** n/av
Year: 2-month terms, summer session	**Tuition:** $5800
Application Deadline: open	**Room & Board:** n/app
Freshman Class: n/av	
SAT I or ACT: not required	**SPECIAL**

Western International University, founded in 1978, is a private arts and sciences institution designed to serve adult students and professionals. WIU offers 2-month semesters and evening and weekend courses. Figures given in the above capsule are approximate. There are 2 undergraduate and 3 graduate schools. In addition to regional accreditation, WIU has baccalaureate program accreditation with AACSB. The library contains 6000 volumes, 200 microform items, and 63 audiovisual forms/CDs, and subscribes to 150 periodicals. Computerized library services include database searching. Special learning facilities include a learning resource center. The 4-acre campus is in an urban area in Phoenix. There is one building.

Student Life: 90% of undergraduates are from Arizona. Others are from 52 foreign countries and Canada. 60% are white; 25% foreign nationals. The average age of all undergraduates is 33.

Housing: There are no residence halls. All students commute. Alcohol is not permitted. All students may keep cars.

Activities: There are no fraternities or sororities. There are 3 groups on campus, including ethnic, honors, and international. Popular campus events include International Day and cultural activities off and on campus.

Sports: There is no sports program at WIU.

Disabled Students: 95% of the campus is accessible. Wheelchair ramps, elevators, special parking, specially equipped rest rooms, and lowered telephones are available.

Services: There is remedial writing through the Learning Resource Center.

Campus Safety and Security: Measures include escort service and lighted pathways/sidewalks.

Programs of Study: WIU confers B.A. and B.S. degrees. Associate and master's degrees are also awarded. Bachelor's degrees are awarded in BUSINESS (accounting, banking and finance, business administration and management, international business management, management science, and marketing management), COMPUTER AND PHYSICAL SCIENCE (information sciences and systems), SOCIAL SCIENCE (behavioral science and criminal justice). Management is the strongest academically and is the largest are the strongest academically.

Required: All students must demonstrate competence or satisfactorily complete courses in a 32-hour major concentration, a 42-hour core, and a 60-hour general education curriculum, which includes courses in language and culture, humanities, social and behavioral sciences, math, and natural sceince. A 2.0 GPA and 126 credit hours are required to graduate.

Special: An accelerated degree program, independent study, credit by exam, credit for life and work experience, and nondegree study are possible. Course offerings are also available at Fort Huachuca and 9 corporate teaching sites. There is 1 national honor society.

Faculty/Classroom: 70% of faculty are male; 30%, female. No introductory courses are taught by graduate students. The average class size in an introductory lecture is 15 and in a regular course, 15.

Requirements: In addition, high school graduates from an accredited secondary school must meet one of the following requirements: a 2.5 cummulative GPA, a rank in the upper half of the class, a composite score of 22 on the ACT, or a combined score of 950 on the SAT I. The GED is accepted with a minimun average score of 50 and minimum standard scores of 35 in each section. A GPA of 2.5 is required. AP and CLEP credits are accepted. Important factors in the admissions decision are advanced placement or honor courses, leadership record, and personality/intangible qualities. Applications are accepted on-line.

Procedure: Freshmen are admitted to all sessions. There is a deferred admissions plan. Application deadlines are open. The fall 2001 application fee was $85.

Transfer: Applicants must have a cumulative college GPA of at least 2.0. Those with fewer than 12 transferable semester credits must also meet requirements for new freshmen. 36 credits of 126 must be completed at WIU.

Visiting: There are regularly scheduled orientations for prospective students. There are guides for informal visits and visitors may sit in on classes. To schedule a visit, contact the Enrollment Department.

Financial Aid: 1% of undergraduates work part time. The CSS/Profile, FAFSA, FFS or SFS, the college's own financial statement and the USAF Single File are required. Check with the school for current deadlines.

International Students: The school actively recruits these students. They must score 500 on the written TOEFL or 173 on the electronic version and also take the college's own test. Students may either participate in an intensive English program or submit minimum scores of 500 on the TOEFL or 75 on the Michigan English Test or successfully complete WIU's ESL program.

Computers: The mainframe is a Sequent. The computer facility includes 14 Compaq Pentium systems. HP Laserjet printers, word processing, MS Office, Lotus, and Harvard Graphics are available. The library system is connected to the Internet 24 hours a day by 7 terminals. All students may access the system. There are no time limits and no fees. It is strongly recommended that all students have a personal computer.

Graduates: In a recent year, 461 bachelor's degrees were awarded.

Admissions Contact: Enrollment Adviser. Web: *www.wintu.edu*

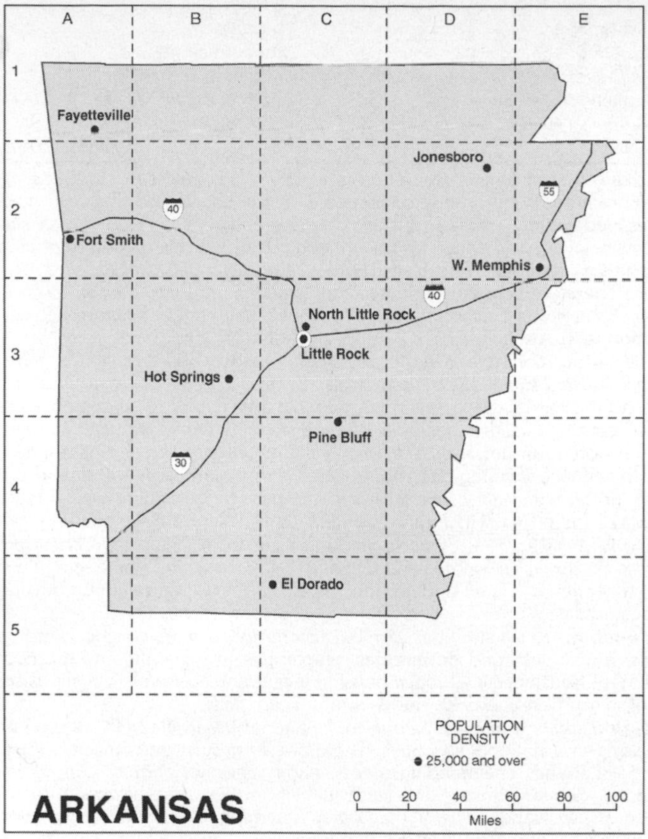

ARKANSAS BAPTIST COLLEGE C-3
Little Rock, AR 72202-6099 **(501) 374-7856, ext. 19**
Fax: (501) 375-9257

Full-time: 200 men and women
Part-time: none
Graduate: none
Year: semesters, summer session
Application Deadline: see profile
Freshman Class: n/av
SAT I or ACT: n/av
Faculty: n/av
Ph.D.s: n/av
Student/Faculty: n/av
Tuition: $2530
Room & Board: $3000
LESS COMPETITIVE

Arkansas Baptist College, founded in 1884, is a private liberal arts institution affiliated with American Baptist Churches, U.S.A. Figures given in the above capsule are approximate. The library contains 23,000 volumes, and subscribes to 6 periodicals. The campus is in an urban area in downtown Little Rock.

Housing: On-campus housing includes single-sex dormitories.

Programs of Study: The college confers B.A. and B.S. degrees. Associate degrees are also awarded. Bachelor's degrees are awarded in BUSINESS (accounting and business administration and management), COMPUTER AND PHYSICAL SCIENCE (computer science), EDUCATION (elementary), SOCIAL SCIENCE (human services and religion).

Required: Students must complete a minimim of 124 credit hours, with 45 in upper-division courses, and must maintain a minimum GPA of 2.0 overall and in the major. Required courses include the Old Testament, theology, humanities, liberal arts, and art or music appreciation.

Special: The college offers a co-op program with Ouachita Baptist University, work-study programs, combined B.A.-B.S. degrees, dual majors, and 1 general studies degree.

Requirements: In addition, for unconditional admission, applicants must be graduates of an accredited high school or have a GED. Others may be admitted conditionally.

Procedure: Freshmen are admitted fall, spring, and summer. Check with the school for current application deadlines. The fall 2001 application fee was $10.

Transfer: For unconditional admission, transfer applicants must have a cumulative GPA of 2.0 and not have been suspended from the previously attended institution. Others may be admitted conditionally.

Financial Aid: Check with the school for current deadlines.

International Students: They must score 500 on the written TOEFL.

Computers: There are no time limits and no fees.

Admissions Contact: Annie A. Hightower, Registrar.

Web: *www.arbaptcol.edu*

ARKANSAS STATE UNIVERSITY D-2
State University, AR 72467 **(870) 972-3024**
(800) 382-3030; Fax: (870) 910-8094

Full-time: 3125 men, 4388 women
Part-time: 835 men, 1078 women
Graduate: 398 men, 744 women
Year: semesters, summer session
Application Deadline: day before first class
Faculty: 394; IIA, --$
Ph.D.s: 87%
Student/Faculty: 19 to 1
Tuition: $4270 ($9490)
Room & Board: $3210
Freshman Class: 2757 applied, 2255 accepted, 1704 enrolled
ACT: 22 **COMPETITIVE**

Arkansas State University, founded in 1909 and part of the Arkansas State University System, is a state-supported institution offering undergraduate and graduate degrees in agriculture, arts and sciences, business, communications, education, engineering, fine arts, nursing, and health professions. There are 9 undergraduate schools and 1 graduate school. In addition to regional accreditation, ASU has baccalaureate program accreditation with AACSB, ABET, ACEJMC, ASLA, CAPTE, CSAB, CSWE, NAACLS, NASAD, NASM, NASPAA, NCATE, and NLN. The library contains 562,067 volumes, 624,520 microform items, and 10,689 audiovisual forms/CDs, and subscribes to 1739 periodicals. Computerized library services include the card catalog, interlibrary loans, and database searching. Special learning facilities include a learning resource center, art gallery, natural history museum, radio station, TV station, facilities for agriculture and environmental ecotoxicology research, a geographic information system facility, an electron microscope lab, and the Delta Studies Center. The 941-acre campus is in a small town 70 miles west of Memphis, Tennessee. Including residence halls, there are 80 buildings.

Student Life: 89% of undergraduates are from Arkansas. Others are from 42 states, 50 foreign countries, and Canada. 93% are from public schools. 84% are white; 12% African American. The average age of freshmen is 21; all undergraduates, 23. 33% do not continue beyond their first year; 32% remain to graduate.

Housing: 2410 students can be accommodated in college housing, which includes single-sex dormitories, on-campus apartments, married-student housing, and fraternity houses. On-campus housing is available on a first-come, first-served basis. 78% of students commute. Alcohol is not permitted. All students may keep cars.

Activities: 15% of men belong to 11 national fraternities; 11% of women belong to 9 national sororities. There are 203 groups on campus, including academic, art, cheerleading, choir, computers, dance, debate, drama, drill team, ethnic, forensics, gay, honors, international, jazz band, marching band, musical theater, newspaper, pep band, photography, political, professional, radio and TV, religious, social service, student government, symphony, and yearbook. Popular campus events include Springfest, Convocation of Scholars Week, and International Night.

Sports: There are 7 intercollegiate sports for men and 8 for women, and 27 intramural sports for men and 27 for women. Facilities include A 10,563-seat convocation center, a 33,410-seat football stadium, a 1,200-seat baseball complex, a 1,200-seat track facility, and a soccer field.

Disabled Students: 99% of the campus is accessible. Wheelchair ramps, elevators, special parking, specially equipped rest rooms, special class scheduling, lowered drinking fountains, lowered telephones, and automatic doors are available.

Services: Counseling and information services are available, as is tutoring in some subjects. There is a reader service for the blind, and remedial math, reading, and writing. Tutoring is available in basic courses.

Campus Safety and Security: Measures include 24-hour foot and vehicle patrol, pamphlets/posters/films, emergency telephones, and lighted pathways/sidewalks.

Programs of Study: ASU confers B.A., B.S., B.F.A., B.G.S., B.Mus., B.Mus.Ed., B.S.Ag., B.S.Ed., B.S. in Eng., B.S.N., and B.S.R.S. degrees. Associate, master's, and doctoral degrees are also awarded. Bachelor's degrees are awarded in AGRICULTURE (agricultural business management, agriculture, animal science, plant science, and wildlife management), BIOLOGICAL SCIENCE (biology/biological science), BUSINESS (accounting, banking and finance, business administration and management, business economics, business systems analysis, international business management, management information systems, marketing/retailing/merchandising, and transportation management), COMMUNICATIONS AND THE ARTS (dramatic arts, English, fine arts, French, journalism, media arts, music, music performance, radio/television technology, Spanish, and speech/debate/rhetoric), COMPUTER AND PHYS-

ICAL SCIENCE (chemistry, computer science, mathematics, and physics), EDUCATION (agricultural, art, business, early childhood, elementary, English, foreign languages, health, mathematics, middle school, music, physical, science, and special), ENGINEERING AND ENVIRONMENTAL DESIGN (engineering, manufacturing technology, printing technology, and technological management), HEALTH PROFESSIONS (exercise science, medical laboratory technology, nursing, physical therapy, public health, radiological science, and speech pathology/audiology), SOCIAL SCIENCE (community services, criminology, economics, geography, history, liberal arts/general studies, philosophy, political science/government, psychology, social science, social work, and sociology). Elementary education, business administration, and accounting are the strongest academically. Early childhood elementary education, business administration, and biology are the largest.

Required: All students must complete a 44-credit distribution of general education courses. A total of at least 124 credits, with a minimum GPA of 2.0, is required to graduate. All students must take a state-administered comprehensive exam.

Special: A general studies degree, co-op programs, study abroad in 17 countries, and work-study programs are offered. Dual majors and internships are available in many areas. Nondegree study is possible. There are 42 national honor societies, a freshman honors program, and 1 departmental honors program.

Faculty/Classroom: 55% of faculty are male; 45%, female. 90% teach undergraduates, 10% do research, and 8% do both. Graduate students teach 4% of introductory courses. The average class size in an introductory lecture is 24; in a laboratory, 26; and in a regular course, 23.

Admissions: 82% of the 2001-2002 applicants were accepted. The ACT scores for the 2001-2002 freshman class were: 41% below 21, 22% between 21 and 23, 24% between 24 and 26, 8% between 27 and 28, and 5% above 28.

Requirements: Applicants should have completed 18 high school units, including 4 in English, 3 in social studies, 3 each in math and science, and 2 in 1 foreign language. The university places those applicants scoring below 19 on the ACT in developmental or remedial courses. ACT, SAT, or ASSET scores are required, with ACT scores recommended. A high school transcript is also required. A GPA of 2.0 is required. AP and CLEP credits are accepted. Applications are available on the university's web site.

Procedure: Freshmen are admitted to all sessions. Entrance exams should be taken before April 1 of high school senior year. There are early admissions and deferred admissions plans. Notification is sent on a rolling basis. In fall 2001, the application fee was $15.

Transfer: 881 transfer students enrolled in 2001-2002. Transfer applicants should have a minimum GPA of 2.0. Those having completed 12 or fewer credit hours will be admitted on the same basis as freshmen. Official transcripts from every institution attended are required. 32 credits of 124 must be completed at ASU.

Visiting: There are regularly scheduled orientations for prospective students, consisting of sessions in February, September, and November. There are guides for informal visits and visitors may sit in on classes and stay overnight. To schedule a visit, contact the Office of Admissions.

Financial Aid: In 2001-2002, 81% of all freshmen and 44% of continuing students received some form of financial aid. 78% of freshmen and 62% of continuing students received need-based aid. The average freshman award was $2600. Of that total, scholarships or need-based grants averaged $2000 ($3000 maximum); loans averaged $1200 ($3000 maximum); and work contracts averaged $1000 ($2000 maximum) for the year. 15% of undergraduates work part time. Average annual earnings from campus work are $3000. The average financial indebtedness of the 2001 graduate was $13,800. The FAFSA and the university's own financial statement are required. The fall application deadline is July 1.

International Students: There are 104 international students enrolled. The school actively recruits these students. They must score 500 on the written TOEFL or 173 on the electronic version and also take the SAT I or the ACT, scoring 19 on the ACT.

Computers: The mainframe is an IBM 9121-260. 30 labs with 551 computers are located on campus. Some are restricted to certain majors and some are open to everyone. All students may access the system during the day and evening on weekdays and weekends. A schedule is posted. There are no time limits and no fees.

Graduates: In 2001, 1439 bachelor's degrees were awarded. The most popular majors were elementary education (8%), business administration (7%), and accounting (6%). In an average class, 2% graduate in 3 years, 14% in 4 years, 27% in 5 years, and 33% in 6 years. 184 companies recruited on campus in 2000-2001.

Admissions Contact: Paula James Lynn, Director of Admissions. A video is available. E-mail: *admissions@astate.edu*
Web: *www.astate.edu/admissions.htm*

ARKANSAS TECH UNIVERSITY — B-2

Russellville, AR 72801-2222 — (501) 968-0343
(800) 582-6953; Fax: (501) 964-0522

Full-time: 2161 men, 2217 women — **Faculty:** 196; IIB, --$
Part-time: 348 men, 479 women — **Ph.D.s:** 66%
Graduate: 145 men, 226 women — **Student/Faculty:** 22 to 1
Year: semesters, summer session — **Tuition:** $2976 ($6132)
Application Deadline: open — **Room & Board:** $3280
Freshman Class: 2597 applied, 1351 accepted, 1256 enrolled
ACT: 21 — **COMPETITIVE**

Arkansas Tech University, founded in 1909, is a state-supported institution offering undergraduate instruction in the liberal and fine arts, business, education, physical and life sciences, information technology, systems science, and other technical fields. Graduate instruction is offered in education, liberal arts, instructional technology, and fisheries and wildlife. There are 6 undergraduate schools and 1 graduate school. In addition to regional accreditation, Tech has baccalaureate program accreditation with AACSB, ABET, CAHEA, NASM, NCATE, NLN, and NRPA. The library contains 234,397 volumes and 809,384 microform items, and subscribes to 1225 periodicals. Computerized library services include the card catalog, interlibrary loans, and database searching. Special learning facilities include a learning resource center, art gallery, natural history museum, radio station, TV station,energy center, and a library with distance learning classrooms, satellite downlink, and 400 data drops for laptop computers. The 517-acre campus is in a small town 75 miles east of Little Rock. Including residence halls, there are 41 buildings.

Student Life: 94% of undergraduates are from Arkansas. Others are from 35 foreign countries and Canada. 89% are white. The average age of freshmen is 21; all undergraduates, 23. 36% do not continue beyond their first year.

Housing: 1319 students can be accommodated in college housing, which includes coed dormitories, on-campus apartments, and married-student housing. On-campus housing is guaranteed for all 4 years. Alcohol is not permitted. All students may keep cars.

Activities: 5% of men belong to 4 national fraternities; 3% of women belong to 2 national sororities. There are 90 groups on campus, including art, band, cheerleading, chess, choir, chorale, chorus, computers, dance, debate, drama, drill team, film, forensics, gay, honors, international, jazz band, literary magazine, marching band, musical theater, newspaper, orchestra, pep band, photography, political, professional, radio and TV, religious, social, social service, student government, and yearbook. Popular campus events include Greek Week, Family Day, and Spring Fling and Fall Fest.

Sports: There are 4 intercollegiate sports for men and 5 for women, and 28 intramural sports for men and 28 for women. Facilities include a coliseum, fields, an Olympic-size indoor pool, racquetball courts, and a 10,000-seat stadium. The Student Activities Building is the hub of indoor recreational activities.

Disabled Students: All of the campus is accessible. Wheelchair ramps, elevators, special parking, specially equipped rest rooms, lowered drinking fountains, and lowered telephones are available.

Services: Counseling and information services are available, as is tutoring in most subjects. There is a reader service for the blind, and remedial math, reading, and writing.

Campus Safety and Security: Measures include 24-hour foot and vehicle patrol, self-defense education, escort service, and informal discussions. There are lighted pathways/sidewalks.

Programs of Study: Tech confers B.A., B.S., and B.F.A. degrees. Associate and master's degrees are also awarded. Bachelor's degrees are awarded in AGRICULTURE (agricultural business management), BIOLOGICAL SCIENCE (biology/biological science), BUSINESS (accounting, business administration and management, hotel/motel and restaurant management, office supervision and management, and recreation and leisure services), COMMUNICATIONS AND THE ARTS (art, creative writing, English, journalism, languages, music, and speech/debate/rhetoric), COMPUTER AND PHYSICAL SCIENCE (chemistry, computer science, geology, mathematics, natural sciences, and physical sciences), EDUCATION (art, business, elementary, health, middle school, music, and secondary), ENGINEERING AND ENVIRONMENTAL DESIGN (emergency/disaster science, and engineering), HEALTH PROFESSIONS (medical laboratory technology, nursing, and rehabilitation therapy), SOCIAL SCIENCE (economics, history, international studies, parks and recreation management, psychology, and sociology). Elementary education and management marketing are the strongest academically. Computer science is the largest.

Required: Students must complete at least 124 semester hours, including 40 hours of upper-level courses to fulfill a major, and maintain a minimum GPA of 2.0. General education requirements include 12 hours of social studies, 8 to 12 of science, 6 of communications, 3 each of math, fine arts, and the humanities, and 2 of phys ed or military science. Activity credits are limited to 4 semester hours.

Special: Special academic features include internships and work-study programs. Independent study is available to seniors. Off-campus courses and on-line telecourses are also offered. There are 4 national honor societies, and there is a campus-wide honors program.

Faculty/Classroom: 61% of faculty are male; 39%, female. All both teach and do research. No introductory courses are taught by graduate students. The average class size in an introductory lecture is 48; in a laboratory, 23; and in a regular course, 40.

Admissions: 52% of the 2001-2002 applicants were accepted. The ACT scores for the 2001-2002 freshman class were: 45% below 21, 21% between 21 and 23, 22% between 24 and 26, 7% between 27 and 28, and 5% above 28. There were 4 National Merit semifinalists. 48 freshmen graduated first in their class.

Requirements: The ACT is required and the SAT I is recommended. In addition, applicants must be graduates of a secondary school on the Arkansas preparatory track. In addition, academic ability must be demonstrated by one of the following: a high school GPA of at least 2.0 on a 4.0 scale; a minimum ACT score of 15; attainment of Freshman Placement test score standards; or completion of 6 semester hours with a cumulative average of C or better in summer sessions or as a part-time student in regular sessions, with at least 3 of the hours being in English, math, social studies, or science. AP and CLEP credits are accepted. Applications are available on-line at *http://admissions.atu.edu/online.htm*.

Procedure: Freshmen are admitted to all sessions. Entrance exams should be taken no later than the second semester of the senior year. Application deadlines are open.

Transfer: 262 transfer students enrolled in a recent year. Transfers are accepted for second-semester freshman, sophomore, and junior classes. A C average is required; no D grades are accepted. 30 credits of 124 must be completed at Tech.

Visiting: There are regularly scheduled orientations for prospective students, including the opportunity to visit with or attend presentations by faculty in each academic discipline. There are guides for informal visits and visitors may sit in on classes. To schedule a visit, contact the Admissions Office at *tech.enroll@mail.atu.edu*

Financial Aid: In 2001-2002, 55% of all freshmen and 53% of continuing students received some form of financial aid. 50% of freshmen and 44% of continuing students received need-based aid. The average freshman award was $3585. Of that total, scholarships or need-based grants averaged $3200 and loans averaged $385. 11% of undergraduates work part time. Average annual earnings from campus work are $1258. The average financial indebtedness of the 2001 graduate was $14,762. The FAFSA,the university's own financial statement, and the federal application are required. The fall application deadline is May 1.

International Students: There are 171 international students enrolled. The school actively recruits these students. They must score 500 on the written TOEFL and also take the SAT I or the ACT.

Computers: The mainframe is an IBM 4381, which can be accessed by 120 terminals campuswide. All students may access the system. There are no time limits and no fees.

Graduates: In 2001, 427 bachelor's degrees were awarded. The most popular majors were elementary education (18%) and management marketing (6%). In an average class, 8% graduate in 3 years, 18% in 4 years, 32% in 5 years, and 36% in 6 years. 104 companies recruited on campus in 2000-2001.

Admissions Contact: Shauna Donnell, Director of Enrollment Management. A video is available. E-mail: *tech.enroll@mail.atu.edu*
Web: *www.atu.edu*

HARDING UNIVERSITY — C-2
Searcy, AR 72149-0001 — (501) 279-4407
(800) 477-4407; Fax: (501) 279-4076

Full-time: 1757 men, 2061 women	**Faculty:** 186
Part-time: 103 men, 157 women	**Ph.D.s:** 65%
Graduate: 194 men, 405 women	**Student/Faculty:** 21 to 1
Year: semesters, summer session	**Tuition:** $9030
Application Deadline: June 1	**Room & Board:** $4498
Freshman Class: 1967 applied, 1384 accepted, 1038 enrolled	
SAT I Verbal/Math: 550/540	**ACT:** 24 **VERY COMPETITIVE**

Harding University, founded in 1924, is a private Christian institution comprised of the Colleges of Arts and Sciences and Bible and Religion and the Schools of Business, Education, and Nursing. There are 7 undergraduate and 5 graduate schools. In addition to regional accreditation, Harding has baccalaureate program accreditation with ACBSP, CSWE, NASM, NCATE, and NLN. The library contains 459,351 volumes, 153,000 microform items, and 6750 audiovisual forms/CDs, and subscribes to 1442 periodicals. Computerized library services include the card catalog, interlibrary loans, and database searching. Special learning facilities include a learning resource center, art gallery, natural history museum, radio station, and TV station. The 200-acre campus is in a small town 50 miles northeast of Little Rock. Including residence halls, there are 50 buildings.

Student Life: 69% of undergraduates are from out of state, mostly the Southwest. Others are from 50 states, 48 foreign countries, and Canada. 73% are from public schools. 87% are white. Most are Protestant. The average age of freshmen is 18; all undergraduates, 21. 22% do not continue beyond their first year; 60% remain to graduate.

Housing: 2400 students can be accommodated in college housing, which includes single-sex dormitories, on-campus apartments, off-campus apartments, and married-student housing. On-campus housing is guaranteed for all 4 years. 71% of students live on campus; of those, 80% remain on campus on weekends. Alcohol is not permitted. All students may keep cars.

Activities: 50% of men belong to 14 local fraternities; 39% of women belong to 14 local sororities. There are 40 groups on campus, including art, band, cheerleading, choir, chorale, chorus, computers, debate, drama, drill team, ethnic, film, forensics, honors, international, jazz band, literary magazine, marching band, musical theater, newspaper, orchestra, pep band, photography, political, professional, radio and TV, religious, social, social service, student government, symphony, and yearbook. Popular campus events include Spring Sing, Parents Weekend, and Youth Forum.

Sports: There are 7 intercollegiate sports for men and 5 for women, and 10 intramural sports for men and 10 for women. Facilities include baseball and softball fields, racquetball, handball, and tennis courts, a football stadium, an indoor and outdoor track, a golf practice range, a gymnastics room, 2 weight rooms, 2 Olympic-size swimming pools, and 2 gyms. Harding owns a 2000-acre camp in the Ozark Mountains with horses, 25 rustic cabins, streams, and hiking trails.

Disabled Students: 95% of the campus is accessible. Wheelchair ramps, elevators, special parking, specially equipped rest rooms, special class scheduling, lowered drinking fountains, and lowered telephones are available.

Services: Counseling and information services are available, as is tutoring in every subject. There is a reader service for the blind, and remedial math, reading, and writing.

Campus Safety and Security: Measures include 24-hour foot and vehicle patrol, self-defense education, escort service, and informal discussions. There are pamphlets/posters/films, emergency telephones, and lighted pathways/sidewalks.

Programs of Study: Harding confers B.A., B.S., B.B.A., B.F.A, B.M.E., B.Mus., B.S.M.T., B.S.N., and B.S.W. degrees. Master's degrees are also awarded. Bachelor's degrees are awarded in BIOLOGICAL SCIENCE (biochemistry, and biology/biological science), BUSINESS (accounting, business administration and management, business economics, human resources, international business management, marketing/retailing/merchandising, and sports management), COMMUNICATIONS AND THE ARTS (advertising, art, broadcasting, communications, design, dramatic arts, English, fine arts, French, graphic design, music, painting, and Spanish), COMPUTER AND PHYSICAL SCIENCE (chemistry, computer science, mathematics, and physics), EDUCATION (early childhood, elementary, foreign languages, music, and secondary), ENGINEERING AND ENVIRONMENTAL DESIGN (interior design), HEALTH PROFESSIONS (medical technology, nursing, predentistry, premedicine, and speech pathology/audiology), SOCIAL SCIENCE (American studies, dietetics, economics, history, home economics, international studies, liberal arts/general studies, ministries, political science/government, psychology, public administration, religion, social science, social work, and sociology). Business, premedicine, and sciences are the strongest academically. Business and education are the largest.

Required: All students must complete 54 hours of general education courses, including religion, English composition, history, speech communications, social sciences, biology, physical science, math, Western literature, music and art appreciation, and phys ed. A total of 128 semester hours, with a minimum GPA of 2.0, is required to graduate.

Special: The Harding campus in Florence, Italy, and programs in Greece, England, and Australia offer international studies. Internships are given in in social work, teaching, nursing, and international missions. Co-op programs in all majors, work-study programs, dual majors, a general studies degree, nondegree study, and pass/fail options are available. A 3-2 engineering degree is offered with the University of Missouri, Georgia Institute of Technology, and the University of Southern California. There are 3 national honor societies, a freshman honors program, and 13 departmental honors program.

Faculty/Classroom: 64% of faculty are male; 36%, female. All teach undergraduates and 20% do research. No introductory courses are taught by graduate students. The average class size in an introductory lecture is 39; in a laboratory, 15; and in a regular course, 24.

Admissions: 70% of the 2001-2002 applicants were accepted. The SAT I scores for the 2001-2002 freshman class were: Verbal--15% below 500, 43% between 500 and 599, 36% between 600 and 700, and 6% above 700; Math--22% below 500, 40% between 500 and 599, 30% between 600 and 700, and 6% above 700. The ACT scores were 27% below 21, 23% between 21 and 23, 21% between 24 and 26, 12% between 27 and 28, and 17% above 28. There were 24 National Merit finalists and 20 semifinalists. 41 freshmen graduated first in their class.

Requirements: The SAT I or ACT is required. AP and CLEP credits are accepted. Applicants should be graduates of an accredited secondary school and have completed 19 high school hours, including 4 each in

English and math, 3 each in science and social studies, 3 in art, history, or music, and 2 in a foreign language. An interview is highly recommended. Harding requires applicants to be in the upper 50% of their class. A GPA of 3.0 is required. A lower GPA can be offset by higher test scores. AP and CLEP credits are accepted. Important factors in the admissions decision are leadership record, recommendations by school officials, and advanced placement or honor courses.

Procedure: Freshmen are admitted to all sessions. Entrance exams should be taken in the junior year or early in the senior year. There are early admissions and deferred admissions plans. Applications should be filed by June 1 for fall entry and November 1 for spring entry. Notification is sent on a rolling basis. 20% of all applicants are on a waiting list. In fall 2001, the application fee was $35.

Transfer: 249 transfer students enrolled in 2001-2002. Applicants with a minimum GPA of 2.0 and at least 14 semester hours earned are considered for admission. An interview is highly recommended. 32 credits of 128 must be completed at Harding.

Visiting: There are regularly scheduled orientations for prospective students. There are guides for informal visits and visitors may sit in on classes and stay overnight. To schedule a visit, contact the Admissions Office or e-mail: *mwilliams@harding.edu*

Financial Aid: In 2001-2002, 93% of all freshmen and 91% of continuing students received some form of financial aid. 52% of freshmen and 57% of continuing students received need-based aid. The average freshman award was $9173. Of that total, scholarships or need-based grants averaged $4046 ($12,305 maximum); loans averaged $6540 ($14,900 maximum); and work contracts averaged $1295 ($2884 maximum). 58% of undergraduates work part time. Average annual earnings from campus work are $866. The average financial indebtedness of the 2001 graduate was $19,711. Harding is a member of CSS. The CSS/Profile or FFS is required. The fall application deadline is May 1.

International Students: There are 228 international students enrolled. The school actively recruits these students. They must score 500 on the written TOEFL. For English-speaking foreign students, the SAT I or ACT is recommended.

Computers: The mainframe is a DEC VAX 3600. There are numerous terminals for accessing the mainframe and 200 PCs available for student use. Many students have their own computers. All students may access the system. The fee is $100. It is strongly recommended that all students have a personal computer.

Graduates: In 2001, 629 bachelor's degrees were awarded. The most popular majors were elementary education (10%), nursing (6%), and accounting (6%). In an average class, 10% graduate in 3 years, 39% in 4 years, 48% in 5 years, and 56% in 6 years. 330 companies recruited on campus in 2000-2001. Of the 2000 graduating class, 10% were enrolled in graduate school within 6 months of graduation and 98% were employed.

Admissions Contact: Mike Williams, Assistant Vice President of Admissions Services. A video is available.
E-mail: *mwilliams@harding.edu* Web: *www.harding.edu*

HENDERSON STATE UNIVERSITY

Arkadelphia, AR 71999-0001

	B-4
	(870) 230-5028
	Fax: (870) 230-5066
Full-time: 1210 men, 1569 women	**Faculty:** 167; IIB, -$
Part-time: 114 men, 157 women	**Ph.D.s:** 71%
Graduate: 110 men, 203 women	**Student/Faculty:** 17 to 1
Year: semesters, summer session	**Tuition:** $3021 ($5757)
Application Deadline: open	**Room & Board:** $3248
Freshman Class: 1697 applied, 1169 accepted, 658 enrolled	
SAT I Verbal/Math: 500/550 **ACT:** 22	**COMPETITIVE**

Henderson State University began in 1890 as Arkadelphia Methodist College, an affiliate of the Methodist Church. In 1929 it became a state institution offering liberal arts courses. There are 3 undergraduate schools and 1 graduate school. In addition to regional accreditation, HSU has baccalaureate program accreditation with AACSB, NASM, NCATE, and NLN. The library contains 255,567 volumes, 210,060 microform items, and 18,254 audiovisual forms/CDs, and subscribes to 1516 periodicals. Computerized library services include the card catalog, interlibrary loans, and database searching. Special learning facilities include an art gallery, planetarium, radio station, and TV station. The 148-acre campus is in a small town 60 miles southwest of Little Rock. Including residence halls, there are 46 buildings.

Student Life: 89% of undergraduates are from Arkansas. Others are from 24 states, 28 foreign countries, and Canada. 80% are white; 14% African American. The average age of freshmen is 18; all undergraduates, 22. 35% do not continue beyond their first year; 30% remain to graduate.

Housing: 878 students can be accommodated in college housing, which includes single-sex and coed dormitories and off-campus apartments. In addition, there are honors houses. On-campus housing is available on a first-come, first-served basis. 67% of students commute. Alcohol is not permitted. All students may keep cars.

Activities: There are 8 national fraternities and 8 national sororities. There are 85 groups on campus, including art, band, cheerleading, choir, chorale, chorus, dance, drama, ethnic, gay, honors, international, jazz band, marching band, musical theater, newspaper, pep band, political, professional, radio and TV, religious, social, social service, student government, and yearbook. Popular campus events include Spring Fling and orientation.

Sports: There are 6 intercollegiate sports for men and 6 for women, and 5 intramural sports for men and 5 for women. Facilities include a 9600-seat football stadium, a gym, an auxiliary gym, a weight room, an intramural practice field for football, a swimming pool, 6 tennis courts, baseball and softball fields, and a track.

Disabled Students: 67% of the campus is accessible. Wheelchair ramps, elevators, special parking, specially equipped rest rooms, special class scheduling, lowered drinking fountains, and lowered telephones are available.

Services: Counseling and information services are available, as is tutoring in most subjects. There is a reader service for the blind and remedial math and reading.

Campus Safety and Security: Measures include 24-hour foot and vehicle patrol, informal discussions, and lighted pathways/sidewalks.

Programs of Study: HSU confers B.A., B.S., B.B.A., B.F.A., B.M., B.S.E., and B.S.N. degrees. Associate and master's degrees are also awarded. Bachelor's degrees are awarded in BIOLOGICAL SCIENCE (biology/biological science), BUSINESS (accounting, business administration and management, and recreation and leisure services), COMMUNICATIONS AND THE ARTS (communications, dramatic arts, English, music, Spanish, speech/debate/rhetoric, and studio art), COMPUTER AND PHYSICAL SCIENCE (chemistry, computer science, mathematics, and physics), EDUCATION (athletic training, business, elementary, music, and physical), ENGINEERING AND ENVIRONMENTAL DESIGN (aviation administration/management), HEALTH PROFESSIONS (nursing), SOCIAL SCIENCE (family/consumer studies, history, human services, political science/government, psychology, public administration, and sociology). Elementary education, biology, and business administration are the largest.

Required: All students must complete a total of 124 credit hours, including 30 in the major, with a minimum GPA of 2.0. Core requirements include 12 semester hours in social science, 11 in natural science, 9 in English, 6 in humanities, 3 each in non-Western culture, math, and oral communication, and 2 in phys ed or military science. Students must take the comprehensive Rising Junior Examination.

Special: HSU offers co-op programs and cross-registration with Ouachita Baptist University, internships in business, psychology, political science, recreation, and education, work-study programs, credit for military experience, nondegree study, and pass/fail options. There are 10 national honor societies and a freshman honors program.

Faculty/Classroom: 56% of faculty are male; 44%, female. 97% teach undergraduates and 50% both teach and do research. Graduate students teach 1% of introductory courses. The average class size in an introductory lecture is 50; in a laboratory, 20; and in a regular course, 30.

Admissions: 69% of the 2001-2002 applicants were accepted. The SAT I scores for the 2001-2002 freshman class were: Verbal--44% below 500, 37% between 500 and 599, 15% between 600 and 700, and 4% above 700; Math--33% below 500, 33% between 500 and 599, 30% between 600 and 700, and 4% above 700. The ACT scores were 40% below 21, 25% between 21 and 23, 23% between 24 and 26, 8% between 27 and 28, and 4% above 28. 38% of the current freshmen were in the top fifth of their class; 69% were in the top two fifths.

Requirements: The ACT is required. In addition, applicants need at least 15 academic credits or 15 Carnegie units. Students with a predicted GPA of 1.5 or below will be admitted conditionally. 4 units of English, 3 of history, civics, or American government, 2 each of natural science, math, and foreign language, and a half unit of computer science are recommended. Applications are accepted on-line at *www.hsu.edu/dept/ura/application.html*. HSU requires applicants to be in the upper 50% of their class. A GPA of 2.5 is required. AP and CLEP credits are accepted.

Procedure: Freshmen are admitted fall, spring, and summer. Entrance exams should be taken during the senior year. Application deadlines are open.

Transfer: 294 transfer students enrolled in 2001-2002. Applicants with a cumulative GPA below 2.0 will be admitted conditionally. The entire academic record is considered. 30 credits of 124 must be completed at HSU.

Visiting: There are regularly scheduled orientations for prospective students. There are guides for informal visits and visitors may stay overnight. To schedule a visit, contact Vikita Hardwrick.

Financial Aid: In 2001-2002, 80% of all freshmen and 61% of continuing students received some form of financial aid. 52% of freshmen and 56% of continuing students received need-based aid. The average freshman award was $3725. 10% of undergraduates work part time. The FFS is required. The fall application deadline is March 1.

International Students: There are 76 international students enrolled. The school actively recruits these students. They must score 500 on the

written TOEFL or 173 on the electronic version or take the MELAB. They must also take the SAT I or ACT.

Computers: The mainframe is a Compaq DS2. The campus is networked for student access to the mainframe and LAN. Students have full access to the Internet, telnet access to computer services mainframe, and network access to file servers from all dorms to 10 labs. About 175 lab computers are available, not including computers in dorms. All students may access the system. There are no time limits and no fees.

Graduates: In 2001, 426 bachelor's degrees were awarded. The most popular majors were education (27%), business administration (17%), and social sciences (8%). In an average class, 9% graduate in 3 years, 25% in 4 years, 31% in 5 years, and 35% in 6 years. 125 companies recruited on campus in a recent year.

Admissions Contact: Vikita Hardwrick, Director of University Relations/Admissions. E-mail: *hardwrv@hsu.edu*
Web: *www.hsu.edu/dept/ura/index.html*

HENDRIX COLLEGE — C-3
Conway, AR 72032 — (501) 450-1362
(800) 277-9017; Fax: (501) 450-3843

Full-time: 495 men, 572 women	**Faculty:** 79; IIB, av$
Part-time: 5 men, 7 women	**Ph.D.s:** 95%
Graduate: 2 men, 4 women	**Student/Faculty:** 14 to 1
Year: semesters	**Tuition:** $13,711
Application Deadline: open	**Room & Board:** $4752–6075
Freshman Class: 1056 applied, 871 accepted, 279 enrolled	
SAT I Verbal/Math: 628/604	**ACT:** 27 **HIGHLY COMPETITIVE**

Hendrix College, founded in 1876, is a private liberal arts college affiliated with the United Methodist Church. In addition to regional accreditation, Hendrix has baccalaureate program accreditation with NASM and NCATE. The library contains 208,259 volumes, 176,029 microform items, and 3719 audiovisual forms/CDs, and subscribes to 747 periodicals. Computerized library services include the card catalog, interlibrary loans, and database searching. Special learning facilities include an art gallery, radio station, and a writing lab. The 65-acre campus is in a suburban area 25 miles northwest of Little Rock. Including residence halls, there are 37 buildings.

Student Life: 69% of undergraduates are from Arkansas. Others are from 39 states and 13 foreign countries. 75% are white. 56% are Protestant; 30% claim no religious affiliation; 11% Catholic. The average age of freshmen is 18; all undergraduates, 20. 16% do not continue beyond their first year.

Housing: 875 students can be accommodated in college housing, which includes single-sex and coed dormitories, on-campus apartments, and off-campus apartments. In addition, there are language houses. On-campus housing is guaranteed for the freshman year only, is available on a first-come, first-served basis, and is available on a lottery system for upperclassmen. 80% of students live on campus; of those, 80% remain on campus on weekends. All students may keep cars.

Activities: There are no fraternities or sororities. There are 56 groups on campus, including art, band, cheerleading, choir, chorale, chorus, dance, drama, ethnic, gay, honors, international, jazz band, literary magazine, musical theater, newspaper, opera, orchestra, pep band, photography, political, professional, radio and TV, religious, social, social service, student government, and yearbook. Popular campus events include Candlelight Carol Service, Basketball Homecoming, and Kampus Kitty Week.

Sports: There are 8 intercollegiate sports for men and 9 for women, and 14 intramural sports for men and 14 for women. Facilities include a 1600-seat gym, an indoor activity center with tennis and racquetball courts, intramural football and softball fields, a nature fitness trail, and NCAA regulation baseball and soccer fields.

Disabled Students: 95% of the campus is accessible. Wheelchair ramps, elevators, special parking, specially equipped rest rooms, and push-button door openers are available.

Services: Counseling and information services are available, as is tutoring in some subjects, including math, biology, and writing.

Campus Safety and Security: Measures include 24-hour foot and vehicle patrol, self-defense education, escort service, and informal discussions. There are pamphlets/posters/films, emergency telephones, and lighted pathways/sidewalks.

Programs of Study: Hendrix confers the B.A. degree. Master's degrees are also awarded. Bachelor's degrees are awarded in BIOLOGICAL SCIENCE (biology/biological science), BUSINESS (business economics), COMMUNICATIONS AND THE ARTS (art, dramatic arts, English, French, German, music, and Spanish), COMPUTER AND PHYSICAL SCIENCE (chemistry, computer science, mathematics, and physics), EDUCATION (physical), SOCIAL SCIENCE (anthropology, history, interdisciplinary studies, international relations, philosophy, political science/government, psychology, religion, and sociology). Chemistry, economics, and religion are the strongest academically. Biology, psychology, economics and business, and history are the largest.

Required: To graduate, students must complete a total of 32 courses with a 2.0 GPA. General education requirements consist of 3 components. (1) Collegiate Center, (2) Learning Domains, and (3) Capacities. The Collegiate Center includes Journeys (fresher common course) and 1 course from Challenges of the Contemporary World. Students must also take 7 courses across 6 distinct Learning Domains and must meet basic skill standards in four Capacities sections (writing skills, foreign language, quantitative skills, and physical activity).

Special: Internships and work-study may be arranged in all fields. The college offers 3-2 engineering programs with Columbia, Vanderbilt, and Washington Universities. Also available are a Washington semester, study abroad, dual majors, and student-designed interdisciplinary studies. Students can pursue minors in all academic departments, as well as gender studies and cultural anthropology. There are 5 national honor societies, including Phi Beta Kappa.

Faculty/Classroom: 63% of faculty are male; 37%, female. All teach undergraduates and 78% both teach and do research. No introductory courses are taught by graduate students. The average class size in an introductory lecture is 21; in a laboratory, 25; and in a regular course, 17.

Admissions: 82% of the 2001-2002 applicants were accepted. The SAT I scores for the 2001-2002 freshman class were: Verbal--5% below 500, 28% between 500 and 599, 47% between 600 and 700, and 20% above 700; Math--10% below 500, 34% between 500 and 599, 46% between 600 and 700, and 10% above 700. The ACT scores were 4% below 21, 9% between 21 and 23, 27% between 24 and 26, 19% between 27 and 28, and 41% above 28. 70% of the current freshmen were in the top fifth of their class; 91% were in the top two fifths. There were 6 National Merit finalists and 17 semifinalists. 16 freshmen graduated first in their class.

Requirements: The SAT I or ACT is required. In addition, Hendrix recommends that applicants have completed 4 high school units in English, 3 to 4 each in math and social studies, 2 to 3 in science, and 2 in a foreign language. The GED is accepted. AP and CLEP credits are accepted. Important factors in the admissions decision are leadership record, advanced placement or honor courses, and extracurricular activities record. Applications are accepted on-line.

Procedure: Freshmen are admitted fall, winter, and spring. Entrance exams should be taken during the junior and senior years. There is a deferred admissions plan. Application deadlines are open. The application fee is $40. 1% of all applicants are on a waiting list.

Transfer: 34 transfer students enrolled in 2001-2002. Official transcripts from all colleges previously attended must be submitted. An interview is recommended. 16 courses of 32 must be completed at Hendrix.

Visiting: There are regularly scheduled orientations for prospective students, including attendance at a class, visits with students and faculty, a campus tour, and a luncheon with speakers. Students may also stay overnight in a residence hall. There are guides for informal visits and visitors may sit in on classes and stay overnight. To schedule a visit, contact the Office of Admission.

Financial Aid: In 2001-2002, 94% of all freshmen and 95% of continuing students received some form of financial aid. 59% of freshmen and 44% of continuing students received need-based aid. The average freshman award was $12,417. Of that total, scholarships or need-based grants averaged $8676 ($21,178 maximum); loans averaged $1595 ($20,000 maximum); work contracts averaged $1440 ($1500 maximum); and veterans benefits, faculty/staff-related grants, and ministerial-related grants averaged $1268 ($11,440 maximum). 40% of undergraduates work part time. Average annual earnings from campus work are $1446. The average financial indebtedness of the 2001 graduate was $9048. Hendrix is a member of CSS. The FAFSA and the college's own financial statement are required. The fall application deadline is February 15.

International Students: There are 14 international students enrolled. The school actively recruits these students. They must score 550 on the written TOEFL or 223 on the electronic version and also take the SAT I or the ACT.

Computers: The mainframe is a DEC ALPHA Server 1000 time-sharing system. There are computer labs utilizing 44 Macs and 31 PCs. In addition, all dorm rooms are wired for computer hookup. All students may access the system 24 hours a day, 7 days a week. There are no time limits. The fee is $30.

Graduates: In 2001, 240 bachelor's degrees were awarded. The most popular majors were biology (15%), psychology (14%), and economics and business w(8%). In an average class, 1% graduate in 3 years, 53% in 4 years, 61% in 5 years, and 62% in 6 years. 88 companies recruited on campus in 2000-2001. Of the 2000 graduating class, 40% were enrolled in graduate school within 6 months of graduation and 38% were employed.

Admissions Contact: Art Weeden, Vice President for Enrollment.
E-mail: *adm@hendrix.edu* Web: *www.hendrix.edu*

JOHN BROWN UNIVERSITY

A-1

Siloam Springs, AR 72761

(479) 524-7190
(877) JBU-INFO; Fax: (479) 524-4196

Full-time: 652 men, 793 women	**Faculty:** 60; IIB, --$
Part-time: 54 men, 46 women	**Ph.D.s:** 73%
Graduate: 60 men, 79 women	**Student/Faculty:** 24 to 1
Year: semesters	**Tuition:** $12,374
Application Deadline: May 1	**Room & Board:** $4658
Freshman Class: 677 applied, 571 accepted, 278 enrolled	
SAT I Verbal/Math: 575/555	**ACT:** 25 **VERY COMPETITIVE**

John Brown University, founded in 1919, is a private, nondenominational Christian institution offering undergraduate programs in the arts and sciences, Bible studies, business, engineering and technology, health promotion and human performance, and teacher education. Some information in this profile is approximate. In addition to regional accreditation, JBU has baccalaureate program accreditation with NCATE. The library contains 95,000 volumes, 30,000 microform items, and 3000 audiovisual forms/CDs, and subscribes to 450 periodicals. Computerized library services include interlibrary loans and database searching. Special learning facilities include a learning resource center, radio station, TV station, and a wellness assessment laboratory. The 200-acre campus is in a small town 80 miles east of Tulsa. Including residence halls, there are 15 buildings.

Student Life: 58% of undergraduates are from out of state, mostly the Southwest. Students are from 44 states, 35 foreign countries, and Canada. 88% are white; 10%, foreign nationals. Most are Protestant. The average age of freshmen is 19; all undergraduates, 21. 24% do not continue beyond their first year; 45% remain to graduate.

Housing: 750 students can be accommodated in college housing, which includes single-sex dormitories, on-campus apartments, off-campus apartments, and married-student housing. On-campus housing is guaranteed for the freshman year only. 75% of students live on campus; of those, 80% remain on campus on weekends. Alcohol is not permitted. All students may keep cars.

Activities: There are no fraternities or sororities. There are many groups and organizations on campus, including band, cheerleading, choir, chorale, chorus, drama, ethnic, honors, newspaper, pep band, photography, radio and TV, religious, student government, and yearbook. Popular campus events include Christmas Candlelight Service, Spiritual Emphasis Week, and Welcome banquet.

Sports: There are 4 intercollegiate sports for men and 4 for women, and 8 intramural sports for men. Facilities include a 1500-seat gym, soccer and softball fields, a baseball diamond, a training room, and a swimming pool. The Lifetime Health Complex includes an indoor track, 4 racquetball courts, a Nautilus fitness center, an aerobics room, and a 3-court recreation center.

Disabled Students: 70% of the campus is accessible. Wheelchair ramps, elevators, special parking, specially equipped rest rooms, special class scheduling, lowered drinking fountains, and lowered telephones are available.

Services: Counseling and information services are available, as is tutoring in most subjects. There is remedial math, reading, and writing.

Campus Safety and Security: Measures include escort service, informal discussions, and lighted pathways/sidewalks.

Programs of Study: JBU confers B.A., B.S., B.E., B.Mus.Ed., and B.S.E. degrees. Associate degrees are also awarded. Bachelor's degrees are awarded in BIOLOGICAL SCIENCE (biochemistry and biology/biological science), BUSINESS (accounting, business administration and management, and office supervision and management), COMMUNICATIONS AND THE ARTS (art, broadcasting, design, English, journalism, music, and public relations), COMPUTER AND PHYSICAL SCIENCE (chemistry, mathematics, and science), EDUCATION (business, early childhood, elementary, music, physical, science, and secondary), ENGINEERING AND ENVIRONMENTAL DESIGN (construction management, electrical/electronics engineering, and engineering), HEALTH PROFESSIONS (community health work, medical laboratory technology, and sports medicine), SOCIAL SCIENCE (biblical studies, crosscultural studies, family and community services, history, interdisciplinary studies, international studies, ministries, pastoral studies, prelaw, psychology, social studies, theological studies, and youth ministry). Engineering and teacher education are the strongest academically. Business, broadcasting, and psychology are the largest.

Required: All students must complete 12 hours in Bible studies, 9 in general education, 6 each in English and science, and 3 each in American history and humanities, as well as competencies in communication and quantitative skills, physical fitness concepts, and health and hygiene. A total of 124 semester hours, with a minimum GPA of 2.0 (2.25 in teacher education and engineering), is required in order to graduate.

Special: Internships or field experiences are available in most majors. Study abroad in 3 countries, a Washington semester, and pass/fail options are offered. There is 1 national honor society and a freshman honors program.

Faculty/Classroom: 70% of faculty are male; 30%, female. 94% teach undergraduates. The average class size in an introductory lecture is 40; in a laboratory, 25; and in a regular course, 30.

Admissions: 84% of the 2001-2002 applicants were accepted. The SAT I scores for the 2001-2002 freshman class were: Verbal--18% below 500, 47% between 500 and 599, 24% between 600 and 700, and 11% above 700; Math--17% below 500, 51% between 500 and 599, 26% between 600 and 700, and 6% above 700. The ACT scores were 20% below 21, 22% between 21 and 23, 28% between 24 and 26, 12% between 27 and 28, and 18% above 28. 61% of the current freshmen were in the top fifth of their class; 85% were in the top two fifths.

Requirements: The SAT I or ACT is recommended. In addition, applicants should have completed 14 high school units, including 4 in English, 3 in math, 2 each in science, history, and foreign language, and 1 in social studies. Two references are required: one from a high school counselor or teacher, the other from a pastor or church leader. An essay and an interview are recommended. Applicants 21 years of age or older may be admitted without ACT or SAT scores. JBU requires applicants to be in the upper 50% of their class. A GPA of 2.5 is required. AP and CLEP credits are accepted. Important factors in the admissions decision are advanced placement or honor courses, leadership record, and evidence of special talent.

Procedure: Freshmen are admitted fall and spring. Entrance exams should be taken during the spring of the junior year or the fall of the senior year. There is an early admissions plan. Applications should be filed by May 1 for fall entry. The fall 2001 application fee was $25. Notification is sent on a rolling basis. A waiting list is an active part of the admissions procedure.

Transfer: Applicants must have completed at least 12 units of college work, with at least 9 transferable, and a minimum 2.0 GPA. 36 credits of 124 must be completed at JBU.

Visiting: There are regularly scheduled orientations for prospective students, including campus tours, consultations with faculty and coaches, and examination of financial aid opportunities. There are guides for informal visits and visitors may sit in on classes and stay overnight. To schedule a visit, contact the Admissions Office.

Financial Aid: In 2001-2002, 72% of all freshmen and 81% of continuing students received some form of financial aid. In a recent yar, 47% of freshmen and 44% of continuing students received need-based aid. The average freshman award was $10,060. The average financial indebtedness of a recent graduate was $12,260. JBU is a member of CSS. The FAFSA is required. Check with the school for current deadlines.

International Students: These students must score 550 on the written TOEFL.

Computers: There are 80 PCs and 20 Macs in 4 computer rooms, and local area networks are available. All students may access the system. There are no time limits. In a recent year, the fee was $15 per semester.

Admissions Contact: Nate Mouttet, Director of Admissions. A video is available. E-mail: *jbuinfo@jbu.edu* Web: *www.jbu.edu*

LYON COLLEGE

C-2

Batesville, AR 72503-2317

(870) 698-4250
(800) 423-2542; Fax: (870) 793-1791

Full-time: 214 men, 272 women	**Faculty:** 41; IIB, --$
Part-time: 13 men, 27 women	**Ph.D.s:** 85%
Graduate: none	**Student/Faculty:** 12 to 1
Year: semesters, summer session	**Tuition:** $11,375
Application Deadline: open	**Room & Board:** $5125
Freshman Class: 439 applied, 344 accepted, 127 enrolled	
SAT I Verbal/Math: 540/560	**ACT:** 25 **VERY COMPETITIVE**

Lyon College, founded in 1872, is a selective, independent, residential, liberal arts college affiliated with the Presbyterian Church (U.S.A.). In addition to regional accreditation, Lyon has baccalaureate program accreditation with NCATE. The library contains 158,392 volumes, 2921 microform items, and 5587 audiovisual forms/CDs, and subscribes to 1324 periodicals. Computerized library services include the card catalog, interlibrary loans, and database searching. Special learning facilities include a learning resource center, and a language lab, and a computer lab. The 136-acre campus is in a small town 90 miles north of Little Rock. Including residence halls, there are 28 buildings.

Student Life: 83% of undergraduates are from Arkansas. Others are from 21 states, 15 foreign countries, and Canada. 88% are white. 61% are Protestant; 25% claim no religious affiliation. The average age of freshmen is 18; all undergraduates, 21. 19% do not continue beyond their first year.

Housing: 409 students can be accommodated in college housing, which includes single-sex dormitories. On-campus housing is guaranteed for all 4 years. 76% of students live on campus; of those, 75% remain on campus on weekends. All students may keep cars.

Activities: 21% of men belong to 3 national fraternities; 31% of women belong to 1 local sorority and 2 national sororities. There are 36 groups on campus, including art, bagpipe band, band, cheerleading, choir, drama, ethnic, honors, international, literary magazine, newspaper, pep band, political, professional, religious, social, social service, student government, and yearbook. Popular campus events include LyonFest, Arkansas Scottish Festival, and Service Day.

Sports: There are 5 intercollegiate sports for men and 5 for women, and 25 intramural sports for men and 25 for women. Facilities include an 1,100-seat gym, softball, baseball, and soccer fields, a cross-country trail, a swimming pool, 6 tennis courts, and a weight room.

Disabled Students: 80% of the campus is accessible. Wheelchair ramps, elevators, special parking, specially equipped rest rooms, and lowered drinking fountains are available.

Services: Counseling and information services are available, as is tutoring in some subjects, including foreign language. There is remedial math and writing. Writing and math labs are available.

Campus Safety and Security: Measures include escort service, informal discussions, pamphlets/posters/films, and lighted pathways/sidewalks.

Programs of Study: Lyon confers B.A. and B.S. degrees. Bachelor's degrees are awarded in AGRICULTURE (environmental studies), BIOLOGICAL SCIENCE (biology/biological science), BUSINESS (accounting, and business administration and management), COMMUNICATIONS AND THE ARTS (art, dramatic arts, English, music, and Spanish), COMPUTER AND PHYSICAL SCIENCE (chemistry, computer science, and mathematics), SOCIAL SCIENCE (economics, history, political science/government, psychology, and religion). Biology, psychology, and business administration are the largest.

Required: All students are required to demonstrate proficiency in English composition, math, and foreign language; meet distribution requirements in social sciences, arts and literature, natural science and math, and religion and philosophy; take the 2-semester Western Tradition course sequence; complete the freshman orientation program; and take 1 semester of phys ed in each of the 4 years. A total of 120 credits, with a minimum GPA of 2.0, are required to graduate.

Special: Internships are offered and cross-registration (for certain courses) with the University of Arkansas Community College at Batesville and Ozarka College. A 2-2 engineering program is offered with the University of Missouri in Rolla, and a 3-2 program is offered with the University of Arkansas at Fayetteville. Work-study courses, study abroad in 4 countries, dual majors, student-designed majors, pass/fail options, and credit for military experience are available. There are 9 national honor societies.

Faculty/Classroom: 57% of faculty are male; 43%, female. All both teach and do research. The average class size in an introductory lecture is 18; in a laboratory, 17; and in a regular course, 15.

Admissions: 78% of the 2001-2002 applicants were accepted. The SAT I scores for the 2001-2002 freshman class were: Verbal--26% below 500, 45% between 500 and 599, and 29% between 600 and 700; Math--26% below 500, 41% between 500 and 599, 29% between 600 and 700, and 4% above 700. The ACT scores were 7% below 21, 27% between 21 and 23, 28% between 24 and 26, 24% between 27 and 28, and 14% above 28. 69% of the current freshmen were in the top fifth of their class; 92% were in the top two fifths. 18 freshmen graduated first in their class.

Requirements: The SAT I or ACT is required. In addition, applicants should have completed a minimum of 16 high school units, including 4 in English, 3 each in science and math, 3 in social sciences, and 2 in a foreign language. A letter of recommendation and an admission interview are recommended. Applications are available on the college's web site. AP credits are accepted.

Procedure: Freshmen are admitted fall and spring. Entrance exams should be taken in the spring of junior year and the fall of senior year. There is a deferred admissions plan. Application deadlines are open. In fall 2001, the application fee was $25.

Transfer: 32 transfer students enrolled in 2001-2002. Transfer applicants with 24 or more semester hours must submit a transcript and statement of good standing from each institution attended. Students with fewer than 24 semester hours must submit their final high school transcript and ACT or SAT I scores. 24 credits of 120 must be completed at Lyon.

Visiting: There are regularly scheduled orientations for prospective students, consisting of a campus tour, admission and financial aid orientation, and information sessions with faculty and students. There are guides for informal visits and visitors may sit in on classes and stay overnight. To schedule a visit, contact the Admission Office.

Financial Aid: In 2001-2002, 99% of all freshmen and 93% of continuing students received some form of financial aid. 60% of freshmen and 56% of continuing students received need-based aid. The average freshman award was $12,981. Of that total, scholarships or need-based grants averaged $7807 ($16,500 maximum); loans averaged $2543 ($4000 maximum); and work contracts averaged $608 ($1545 maximum). 40% of undergraduates work part time. The average financial indebtedness of the 2001 graduate was $13,104. The FAFSA is required. The fall application deadline is April 1.

International Students: There are 27 international students enrolled. They must score 550 on the written TOEFL or 213 on the electronic version and also take the SAT I or the ACT.

Computers: The mainframes include an IBM RISC 6000, 1 DEC ALPHA, and several Intel-based NT servers. Students have access to campus information resources from 84 computers in classrooms, residence hall lounges, the Union, and the library. Students may also access these resources in residence hall rooms using their own PCs. Access to the Internet is available from any network access point with a user ID and password. All students may access the system. There are no time limits. The fee is $200.

Graduates: In 2001, 82 bachelor's degrees were awarded. The most popular majors were psychology (17%), biology (12%), and English (12%). In an average class, 47% graduate in 4 years, 49% in 5 years, and 49% in 6 years. 5 companies recruited on campus in 2000-2001. Of the 2000 graduating class, 35% were enrolled in graduate school within 6 months of graduation and 60% were employed.

Admissions Contact: David Wilkey, Vice President for Enrollment Services. A video is available. E-mail: *admissions@lyon.edu*
Web: *www.lyon.edu*

OUACHITA BAPTIST UNIVERSITY — B-4

Arkadelphia, AR 71998-0001 — (870) 245-5110
(800) 342-5628; Fax: (870) 245-5500

Full-time: 730 men, 853 women	**Faculty:** 111; IIB, -$
Part-time: 49 men, 25 women	**Ph.D.s:** 76%
Graduate: none	**Student/Faculty:** 14 to 1
Year: semesters, summer session	**Tuition:** $12,010
Application Deadline: open	**Room & Board:** $4450
Freshman Class: 863 applied, 724 accepted, 427 enrolled	
SAT I Verbal/Math: 550/550	**ACT:** 24 **VERY COMPETITIVE**

Ouachita Baptist University, founded in 1886, is a private liberal arts institution affiliated with the Arkansas Baptist State Convention. There are 7 undergraduate schools. In addition to regional accreditation, Ouachita has baccalaureate program accreditation with NASM and NCATE. The 2 libraries contain 117,517 volumes, 205,614 microform items, and 3159 audiovisual forms/CDs, and subscribe to 1067 periodicals. Computerized library services include the card catalog, interlibrary loans, and database searching. Special learning facilities include a learning resource center, art gallery, and planetarium. The 60-acre campus is in a small town 65 miles southwest of Little Rock. Including residence halls, there are 33 buildings.

Student Life: 53% of undergraduates are from Arkansas. Others are from 32 states and 62 foreign countries. 95% are from public schools. 90% are white. Most are Protestant. The average age of freshmen is 18; all undergraduates, 21. 25% do not continue beyond their first year.

Housing: 1352 students can be accommodated in college housing, which includes single-sex dormitories, on-campus apartments, off-campus apartments, and married-student housing. On-campus housing is guaranteed for the freshman year only and is available on a first-come, first-served basis. 90% of students live on campus; of those, 60% remain on campus on weekends. Alcohol is not permitted. All students may keep cars.

Activities: 30% of men belong to 5 local fraternities; 30% of women belong to 5 local sororities. There are 30 groups on campus, including band, cheerleading, choir, chorale, chorus, computers, debate, drama, drill team, ethnic, film, honors, international, jazz band, marching band, musical theater, newspaper, opera, orchestra, pep band, photography, political, professional, religious, social, social service, student government, and yearbook. Popular campus events include International Student Fair, Tiger Tunes, and Tiger Traks.

Sports: There are 9 intercollegiate sports for men and 5 for women, and 4 intramural sports for men and 3 for women. Facilities include a 6000-seat football stadium, and an athletic complex featuring a 2500-seat basketball arena, a swimming pool, a weight room, and tennis, racquetball, and volleyball courts.

Disabled Students: 95% of the campus is accessible. Wheelchair ramps, elevators, special parking, specially equipped rest rooms, and special class scheduling are available.

Services: Counseling and information services are available, as is tutoring in most subjects. There is a reader service for the blind, and remedial math, reading, and writing.

Campus Safety and Security: Measures include 24-hour foot and vehicle patrol, informal discussions, pamphlets/posters/films, and emergency telephones. There are lighted pathways/sidewalks.

Programs of Study: Ouachita confers B.A., B.S., B.M., B.M.E., and B.S.E. degrees. Associate degrees are also awarded. Bachelor's degrees are awarded in BIOLOGICAL SCIENCE (biology/biological science), BUSINESS (accounting, business administration and management, and business economics), COMMUNICATIONS AND THE ARTS (communications, dramatic arts, English, French, music, musical theater, Russian languages and literature, Spanish, and speech/debate/rhetoric), COMPUTER AND PHYSICAL SCIENCE (chemistry, computer science, mathematics, and physics), EDUCATION (art, business, early childhood, elementary, foreign languages, health, home economics, middle school, music, science, and secondary), HEALTH PROFESSIONS (medical laboratory technology, predentistry, premedicine, and speech pathology/audiology), SOCIAL SCIENCE (biblical studies, dietetics, economics, history, ministries, philosophy, political science/government, prelaw, psychology, religion, sociology, and theological studies). Education, business, and religion are the largest.

Required: All students must fulfill 44 semester hours of general education courses, including 2 semesters of 1 foreign language, 7 chapel credits, and 2 semester hours of phys ed. A total of 128 semester hours, with a minimum GPA of 2.0, is required for graduation.

Special: Ouachita offers cross-registration with Henderson State University, a Washington semester for political science majors, internships and co-op programs for business majors, B.A.-B.S. degrees, dual majors, pass/fail options, and nondegree study. Study-abroad opportunities are available in Germany, England, France, Italy, Russia, Japan, China, Hong Kong, Kazakhstan, Austria, Israel, Belize, and Morocco. There is a freshman honors program.

Faculty/Classroom: 73% of faculty are male; 27%, female. All teach undergraduates. The average class size in an introductory lecture is 30; in a laboratory, 11; and in a regular course, 13.

Admissions: 84% of the 2001-2002 applicants were accepted. The SAT I scores for the 2001-2002 freshman class were: Verbal--27% below 500, 40% between 500 and 599, 29% between 600 and 700, and 7% above 700; Math--30% below 500, 39% between 500 and 599, 27% between 600 and 700, and 4% above 700. The ACT scores were 23% below 21, 27% between 21 and 23, 25% between 24 and 26, 10% between 27 and 28, and 15% above 28. 57% of the current freshmen were in the top fifth of their class; 76% were in the top two fifths. There were 6 National Merit finalists. 25 freshmen graduated first in their class.

Requirements: The SAT I or ACT is required. In addition, applicants should have completed 19 high school units, including 4 in English, 3 in social science, and 2 each in natural science and math; 2 in a foreign language and 1/2 in computer science are also recommended. Ouachita requires applicants to be in the upper 50% of their class. A GPA of 2.5 is required. AP and CLEP credits are accepted.

Procedure: Freshmen are admitted to all sessions. Entrance exams should be taken in the junior year. There are early decision, early admissions, and deferred admissions plans. Application deadlines are open. The application fee is $25. 10 early decision candidates were accepted for the 2001-2002 class.

Transfer: 53 transfer students enrolled in 2001-2002. Applicants must be eligible to return to their previous school. 60 credits of 128 must be completed at Ouachita.

Visiting: There are regularly scheduled orientations for prospective students, including a campus tour, a question-and-answer session, and meetings with professors and students. There are guides for informal visits and visitors may sit in on classes and stay overnight. To schedule a visit, contact the Admissions Counseling Office at *jonesr@obu.edu*

Financial Aid: In 2001-2002, 95% of all freshmen and 92% of continuing students received some form of financial aid. 50% of freshmen and 48% of continuing students received need-based aid. The average freshman award was $10,152. Of that total, scholarships or need-based grants averaged $8873 ($16,860 maximum); loans averaged $3928 ($16,810 maximum); and work contracts averaged $1488 ($1500 maximum). 52% of undergraduates work part time. Average annual earnings from campus work are $1500. The average financial indebtedness of the 2001 graduate was $6130. The FAFSA and the university's own financial statement are required. The fall application deadline is February 15.

International Students: There are 78 international students enrolled. The school actively recruits these students. They must score 550 on the written TOEFL and also take the SAT I or the ACT, scoring 20 on the ACT.

Computers: The mainframe is an AS/400. There are 5 computer labs available to students. All academic departments have PCs. All students may access the system. There are no time limits and no fees.

Graduates: In 2001, 312 bachelor's degrees were awarded. The most popular majors were education (20%), religion (14%), and business related (14%). In an average class, 30% graduate in 4 years, 45% in 5 years, and 50% in 6 years. 17 companies recruited on campus in 2000-2001. Of the 2000 graduating class, 10% were enrolled in graduate school within 6 months of graduation and 90% were employed.

Admissions Contact: Rebecca Jones, Director of Admissions Counseling. E-mail: *admissions@alpha.obu.edu* Web: *www.obu.edu*

PHILANDER SMITH COLLEGE — C-3
Little Rock, AR 72202 (501) 370-5221
(800) 446-6772; Fax: (501) 370-5225

Full-time: 800 men and women	**Faculty:** 32
Part-time: 200 men and women	**Ph.D.s:** 20%
Graduate: none	**Student/Faculty:** 24 to 1
Year: semesters, summer session	**Tuition:** $4330
Application Deadline: see profile	**Room & Board:** $3050
Freshman Class: 137 applied, 111 accepted, 75 enrolled	
ACT: 14	**NONCOMPETITIVE**

Philander Smith College, founded in 1877, is affiliated with the United Methodist Church. The college offers undergraduate degrees in education, humanities, natural and physical sciences, business, and social science. Figures given in the above capsule are approximate. The library contains 83,000 volumes, 170 microform items, and 60 audiovisual forms/CDs, and subscribes to 370 periodicals. Computerized library services include interlibrary loans. The 25-acre campus is in an urban area in Little Rock. There are 14 buildings.

Programs of Study: PSC confers B.A., B.S., and B.A.M. degrees. Bachelor's degrees are awarded in BIOLOGICAL SCIENCE (biology/biological science), BUSINESS (accounting, business administration and management, hospitality management services, and office supervision and management), COMMUNICATIONS AND THE ARTS (music), COMPUTER AND PHYSICAL SCIENCE (chemistry, computer science, and science), EDUCATION (business, early childhood, education administration, English, mathematics, physical, science, secondary, and special), SOCIAL SCIENCE (political science/government, psychology, social work, and sociology).

Required: To graduate, all students must complete at least 124 credit hours with a minimum 2.0 GPA and satisfy general education requirements, which include courses in speech, English composition, literature, philosophy and religion, physical and life science, math, computing, psychology, political science or sociology, economics, U.S. history, phys ed, and health.

Special: There are 2 national honor societies.

Admissions: 81% of the 2001-2002 applicants were accepted.

Requirements: The ACT is required, the SAT I is accepted. Applicants must be graduates of an accredited secondary school or have a GED certificate. A GPA of 2.0 is required for unconditional admission. Students should have completed 16 academic credits, including 4 units of English, 2 of math, and 2 of the following: foreign language, science, or social studies. AP and CLEP credits are accepted.

Procedure: There is an early admissions plan. Check with the school for current application deadlines. The fall 2001 application fee was $10.

Transfer: 22 credits of the last 32 must be completed at PSC.

Visiting: To schedule a visit, contact the Admissions Office.

Financial Aid: In 2001-2002, 90% of all freshmen and 80% of continuing students received some form of financial aid. PSC is a member of CSS. The FFS is required. Check with the school for current deadlines.

International Students: They must score 500 on the written TOEFL or 213 on the electronic version and also take or IELP, or present an ESL certificate and also take the ACT.

Computers: There are no time limits and no fees.

Admissions Contact: Office of Admissions.
Web: *www.philander.edu*

SOUTHERN ARKANSAS UNIVERSITY — B-5
Magnolia, AR 71754 (870) 235-4040
(800) 332-SAUM; Fax: (870) 235-4931

Full-time: 1134 men, 1339 women	**Faculty:** 137; IIB, --$
Part-time: 113 men, 277 women	**Ph.D.s:** 53%
Graduate: 52 men, 212 women	**Student/Faculty:** 18 to 1
Year: semesters, summer session	**Tuition:** $2670 ($3726)
Application Deadline: open	**Room & Board:** $3070
Freshman Class: 1142 applied, 938 accepted, 581 enrolled	
ACT: required	**LESS COMPETITIVE**

Southern Arkansas University, founded in 1909, is a state-supported liberal arts institution offering degrees in business administration, education, liberal and performing arts, and science and technology. There are 4 undergraduate schools and 1 graduate school. In addition to regional accreditation, SAU has baccalaureate program accreditation with NASAD, NASM, NCATE, and NLN. The library contains 148,462 volumes, 636,089 microform items, and 11,123 audiovisual forms/CDs, and subscribes to 910 periodicals. Computerized library services include the card catalog, interlibrary loans, and database searching. Special learning facilities include a learning resource center, art gallery, radio station, biological field station, and university farm. The 781-acre campus is in a small town. Including residence halls, there are 27 buildings.

Student Life: 64% of undergraduates are from Arkansas. Others are from 24 states, 33 foreign countries, and Canada. 99% are from public schools. 71% are white; 23% African American. The average age of freshmen is 19; all undergraduates, 27. 32% do not continue beyond their first year.

Housing: 1043 students can be accommodated in college housing, which includes single-sex and coed dormitories. In addition, there are honors houses. On-campus housing is guaranteed for all 4 years. 68% of students commute. Alcohol is not permitted. All students may keep cars.

Activities: 10% of men belong to 8 national fraternities; 10% of women belong to 7 national sororities. There are 80 groups on campus, including art, band, cheerleading, choir, chorale, computers, drama, drill team, ethnic, honors, international, jazz band, literary magazine, marching band, musical theater, newspaper, pep band, photography, political, professional, radio and TV, religious, social, student government, and yearbook. Popular campus events include Spring Fling and Celebration of Lights (Christmas).

Sports: There are 7 intercollegiate sports for men and 6 for women, and 15 intramural sports for men and 15 for women. Facilities include a 6500-seat stadium, a 2500-seat gym, 10 lighted tennis courts, a baseball field, an indoor pool, a dance studio, a multipurpose building with basketball and volleyball courts, and a wellness center.

Disabled Students: 95% of the campus is accessible. Wheelchair ramps, elevators, special parking, specially equipped rest rooms, special class scheduling, lowered drinking fountains, lowered telephones, and automatic doors are available.

Services: Counseling and information services are available, as is tutoring in most subjects. There is remedial math, reading, and writing, and supplemental instruction in courses with high drop/failure rates.

Campus Safety and Security: Measures include 24-hour foot and vehicle patrol, escort service, informal discussions, and pamphlets/posters/films. There are emergency telephones and lighted pathways/sidewalks.

Programs of Study: SAU confers B.A., B.S., B.A.S., B.B.A., B.M.E., B.S.E., and B.S.W. degrees. Associate and master's degrees are also awarded. Bachelor's degrees are awarded in AGRICULTURE (agricultural business management, and agriculture), BIOLOGICAL SCIENCE (biology/biological science), BUSINESS (accounting, and business administration and management), COMMUNICATIONS AND THE ARTS (art, broadcasting, communications, English, journalism, and Spanish), COMPUTER AND PHYSICAL SCIENCE (chemistry, computer science, and mathematics), EDUCATION (agricultural, art, business, elementary, health, middle school, music, science, and secondary), ENGINEERING AND ENVIRONMENTAL DESIGN (manufacturing technology), HEALTH PROFESSIONS (medical laboratory technology, predentistry, and premedicine), SOCIAL SCIENCE (community services, history, political science/government, psychology, and sociology). Accounting and physical science are the strongest academically. Business administration and health education/kinesiology are the largest.

Required: All students must complete 43 semester hours of general education courses, including 18 in humanities, 12 in social sciences, 4 each in biological and physical science, 3 in math, and 2 to 3 in physical and health education. A minimum of 124 total semester hours, with a minimum GPA of 2.0, is required to graduate.

Special: Work-study programs at SAU, business and Spanish internships, study abroad in Russia, and a general studies degree are offered. There is 1 national honor society, a freshman honors program, and 6 departmental honors program.

Faculty/Classroom: 54% of faculty are male; 46%, female. 95% teach undergraduates, 10% do research, and 10% do both. No introductory courses are taught by graduate students. The average class size in an introductory lecture is 35; in a laboratory, 25; and in a regular course, 20.

Admissions: 82% of the 2001-2002 applicants were accepted. The ACT scores for the 2001-2002 freshman class were: 53% below 21, 24% between 21 and 23, 17% between 24 and 26, 4% between 27 and 28, and 2% above 28.

Requirements: The ACT is required, with a minimum composite of 19. Applicants should have completed 4 high school units in English, 3 each in math and social studies, and 2 each in natural science and a foreign language. The GED is accepted. AP and CLEP credits are accepted. Important factors in the admissions decision are leadership record, recommendations by school officials, and evidence of special talent.

Procedure: Freshmen are admitted to all sessions. Entrance exams should be taken in the fall prior to enrollment. There is a deferred admissions plan. Application deadlines are open. Notification is sent on a rolling basis.

Transfer: 207 transfer students enrolled in 2001-2002. Applicants must be eligible to return to their previous school. Those with fewer than 24 credit hours must submit ACT or SAT I scores and a high school transcript or GED. 30 credits of 124 must be completed at SAU.

Visiting: There are regularly scheduled orientations for prospective students. There are guides for informal visits and visitors may sit in on classes. To schedule a visit, contact the Admissions Office.

Financial Aid: In 2001-2002, 92% of all freshmen and 75% of continuing students received some form of financial aid. 85% of freshmen and 70% of continuing students received need-based aid. The average freshman award was $5654. Of that total, scholarships or need-based grants averaged $3928 ($9346 maximum); loans averaged $2772 ($6625 maximum); and work contracts averaged $2503 ($2700 maximum). 35% of undergraduates work part time. Average annual earnings from campus work are $1077. The average financial indebtedness of the 2001 graduate was $15,075. The FAFSA is required. The fall application deadline is August 1.

International Students: There are 117 international students enrolled. The school actively recruits these students. They must score 500 on the written TOEFL or 173 on the electronic version and also take the SAT I or the ACT.

Computers: The school's 3 networked minicomputers include a DEC VAX 4000/600, a DEC ALPHA 2100 4/275, and a DEC ALPHA 3000/600. Computer resources are located in the library, 3 computer labs, and 3 computer classrooms. All students may access the system from 8 A.M. to 10 P.M. There are no time limits and no fees.

Graduates: In 2001, 313 bachelor's degrees were awarded. The most popular majors were business administration (26%), elementary teacher education (11%), and agricultural business management (10%). In an average class, 4% graduate in 3 years, 13% in 4 years, 26% in 5 years, and 33% in 6 years. More than 60 companies recruited on campus in 2000-2001.

Admissions Contact: Sarah Jennings, Dean of Enrollment Services. E-mail: *sejennings@saumag.edu* Web: *www.saumag.edu*

UNIVERSITY OF ARKANSAS SYSTEM

The University of Arkansas System, established in 1871, is governed by a board of trustees whose chief administrator is the president. The primary goals of the system are teaching, research, and public service. The total enrollment of all 5 campuses usually exceeds 32,000, with more than 2300 faculty members. Altogether there are 236 baccalaureate, 112 master's, and 30 doctoral programs offered in the system. Profiles of the 4-year campuses, located in Fayetteville, Little Rock, Pine Bluff, and Monticello, are included in this section.

UNIVERSITY OF ARKANSAS — A-1

Fayetteville, AR 72701 — (501) 575-5346

(800) 377-8632; Fax: (501) 575-7515

Full-time: 5533 men, 5292 women	**Faculty:** 663; I, --$
Part-time: 1076 men, 917 women	**Ph.D.s:** 92%
Graduate: 1527 men, 1407 women	**Student/Faculty:** 16 to 1
Year: semesters, summer session	**Tuition:** $3880 ($9438)
Application Deadline: August 15	**Room & Board:** $4454
Freshman Class: 4164 applied, 3994 accepted, 2332 enrolled	
SAT I Verbal/Math: 560/580	**ACT:** 24 **VERY COMPETITIVE**

The University of Arkansas, founded in 1871, is a land-grant institution offering undergraduate and graduate programs in liberal arts and sciences, agricultural, food, social and natural sciences, life sciences, business administration, engineering, architecture, education, law, and human environmental sciences. There are 8 undergraduate and 2 graduate schools. In addition to regional accreditation, U of A has baccalaureate program accreditation with AACSB, ABET, ACEJMC, ADA, ASLA, CSWE, FIDER, NAAB, NASM, NCATE, and NLN. The 6 libraries contain 1,696,015 volumes, 3,245,404 microform items, and 23,133 audiovisual forms/CDs, and subscribe to 14,990 periodicals. Computerized library services include the card catalog, interlibrary loans, and database searching. Special learning facilities include a learning resource center, art gallery, natural history museum, planetarium, radio station, TV station, and numerous research centers. The 357-acre campus is in an urban area 190 miles northwest of Little Rock. Including residence halls, there are 130 buildings.

Student Life: 90% of undergraduates are from Arkansas. Others are from 49 states, 109 foreign countries, and Canada. 95% are from public schools. 81% are white. The average age of freshmen is 18; all undergraduates, 22. 19% do not continue beyond their first year.

Housing: 3223 students can be accommodated in college housing, which includes single-sex and coed dormitories, on-campus apartments, and married-student housing. On-campus housing is guaranteed for the freshman year only and is available on a first-come, first-served basis. 60% of students commute. All students may keep cars.

Activities: 17% of men belong to 11 national fraternities; 19% of women belong to 11 national sororities. There are 263 groups on campus, including art, band, cheerleading, chess, choir, chorale, chorus, computers, dance, debate, drama, drill team, ethnic, film, gay, honors, international, jazz band, literary magazine, marching band, musical theater, newspaper, opera, orchestra, pep band, photography, political, professional, radio and TV, religious, social, social service, student government, symphony, and yearbook. Popular campus events include Academic Festival, Native American Pow Wow, and Martin Luther King Jr. Event.

Sports: There are 8 intercollegiate sports for men and 11 for women, and 43 intramural sports for men and 43 for women. Facilities include

a 72,000-seat stadium, a 20,000-seat basketball arena, a 3300-seat baseball stadium, a 9000-seat volleyball arena, a 1500-seat soccer stadium, 4 gyms, indoor and outdoor jogging tracks, 2 dance studios, 10 racquetball courts, a fitness and weight training center, a swimming pool, an outdoor recreation center, 20 outdoor and 4 indoor tennis courts, 10 multipurpose playing fields, an indoor practice football field, a 3000-seat indoor running track, and a 1500-seat softball stadium.

Disabled Students: All of the campus is accessible. Wheelchair ramps, elevators, special parking, specially equipped rest rooms, special class scheduling, lowered drinking fountains, lowered telephones, and automatic doors on entrances to buildings are available.

Services: Counseling and information services are available, as is tutoring in some subjects. There is a reader service for the blind, remedial math, reading, and writing, a math resource center, and a writing center, Student Support Services and individual colleges have labs and other facilities.

Campus Safety and Security: Measures include 24-hour foot and vehicle patrol, self-defense education, escort service, and shuttle buses. There are informal discussions, pamphlets/posters/films, emergency telephones, lighted pathways/sidewalks, crime prevention lectures, rape defense program, property engraving, bicycle patrol, and electronic card access in residence halls.

Programs of Study: U of A confers B.A., B.S., B.Arch., B.I.D., B.L.A., B.M., B.S.A., B.S.B.A., B.S.B.A.E., B.S.C.E., B.S.Ch.E., B.S.C.S.E, B.S.E., B.S.E.E., B.S.E.M., B.S.H.E.S., B.S.I.B., B.S.I.E., B.S.I.M., B.S.M.E., B.S.N., and B.S.P.A. degrees. Master's and doctoral degrees are also awarded. Bachelor's degrees are awarded in AGRICULTURE (agricultural business management, agricultural economics, animal science, horticulture, plant protection (pest management), and poultry science), BIOLOGICAL SCIENCE (biology/biological science, botany, microbiology, nutrition, and zoology), BUSINESS (accounting, apparel and accessories marketing, banking and finance, business administration and management, business economics, international business management, marketing management, marketing/retailing/merchandising, and transportation management), COMMUNICATIONS AND THE ARTS (art, classics, communications, dramatic arts, English, French, German, journalism, music, and Spanish), COMPUTER AND PHYSICAL SCIENCE (chemistry, computer science, earth science, geology, mathematics, and physics), EDUCATION (agricultural, early childhood, elementary, middle school, music, recreation, special, and vocational), ENGINEERING AND ENVIRONMENTAL DESIGN (agricultural engineering, architecture, bioengineering, chemical engineering, civil engineering, computer engineering, electrical/electronics engineering, environmental science, industrial engineering, interior design, landscape architecture/design, and mechanical engineering), HEALTH PROFESSIONS (exercise science, health science, medical science, nursing, predentistry, premedicine, preoptometry, prepharmacy, prepodiatry, and speech pathology/audiology), SOCIAL SCIENCE (American studies, anthropology, criminal justice, economics, food science, geography, history, human development, international relations, Middle Eastern studies, philosophy, political science/government, prelaw, psychology, public administration, social work, and sociology). Business, chemical and electrical engineering, and computer science are the strongest academically. Childhood education, accounting, and kinesiology are the largest.

Required: To graduate, all students must complete 35 hours of general education courses, including 9 in social studies, 8 in science, 6 in English, and 3 each in fine arts, math, humanities, and history/government. No more than 25% of the minimum total of 124 hours may be D or below.

Special: Co-op programs and internships are available, as well as dual majors, B.A.-B.S. degrees in many majors, and study abroad in 16 countries. There are 3-2 engineering degrees with several universities, a combined medical/dental degree, and a 6-year B.S./J.D. degree for highly qualified students. Non-degree study is possible. There are 60 national honor societies, including Phi Beta Kappa, a freshman honors program, and 30 departmental honors program.

Faculty/Classroom: 69% of faculty are male; 31%, female. 83% teach undergraduates. The average class size in an introductory lecture is 32; in a laboratory, 19; and in a regular course, 29.

Admissions: 96% of the 2001-2002 applicants were accepted. The SAT I scores for the 2001-2002 freshman class were: Math--19% below 500, 39% between 500 and 599, 35% between 600 and 700, and 7% above 700. The ACT scores for the 2001-2002 freshman class were: 16% below 21, 26% between 21 and 23, 25% between 24 and 26, 13% between 27 and 28, and 20% above 28. 54% of the current freshmen were in the top fifth of their class; 81% were in the top two fifths. There were 29 National Merit finalists and 23 semifinalists. 177 freshmen graduated first in their class.

Requirements: The SAT I or ACT is required. In addition, U of A recommends 4 years of English and math and 3 years each of social science and natural science. AP and honors level courses will enhance the applicant's opportunity for admission. A GPA of 3.0 is required. AP and CLEP credits are accepted. Important factors in the admissions decision are advanced placement or honor courses, leadership record, and evidence of special talent. Applications are accepted on computer disk and on-line.

Procedure: Freshmen are admitted fall, spring, and summer. Entrance exams should be taken in the junior year or in October or December of the senior year. There are early admissions and deferred admissions plans. Early decision application should be filed by February 15; regular applications, by August 15 for fall entry and January 1 for spring entry. Notification is sent on a rolling basis. The Fall 2001 application fee was $30.

Transfer: 1230 transfer students enrolled in 2001-2002. Applicants must present a GPA of 2.0 on all college course work attempted and be in good standing at the last institution attended. Those with fewer than 24 transferable semester credits must meet the requirements of entering freshmen. 30 credits of 124 must be completed at U of A.

Visiting: There are regularly scheduled orientations for prospective students, consisting of individual or group campus tours, meetings with an academic adviser, residence hall tours, and a meeting with an admissions counselor. Appointments are recommended, but not required. There are guides for informal visits and visitors may sit in on classes. To schedule a visit, contact the Admissions Office at: *seiwert@uark.edu*

Financial Aid: In 2001-2002, 74% of all freshmen and 70% of continuing students received some form of financial aid. 35% of freshmen and 50% of continuing students received need-based aid. The average freshman award was $7092. Of that total, scholarships or need-based grants averaged $1652 ($12,000 maximum); loans averaged $5298 ($6625 maximum); and work contracts averaged $142 ($3000 maximum). 4% of undergraduates work part time. Average annual earnings from campus work are $1887. The average financial indebtedness of the 2001 graduate was $10,271. U of A is a member of CSS. The FAFSA is required. The fall application deadline is March 1.

International Students: There are 396 international students enrolled. The school actively recruits these students. They must score 550 on the written TOEFL or 213 on the electronic version. Electrical engineering and computer systems engineering require a composite score of 1000 on the SAT I or 25 on the ACT, and a score of 5 on the TSE.

Computers: The mainframe is an IBM 9672 with a Sun Enterprise 5000. More than 600 Macs and PCs are available for academic use in student labs and in the computer center. E-mail and access to the Internet is available to all students. Networked servers provide access to word processing, spreadsheet, database, graphics, and statistical package applications. Dial-up password resets are available through a web interface. All students may access the system 24 hours daily. There are no time limits and no fees. It is recommended that students in architecture have personal computers.

Graduates: In 2001, 1935 bachelor's degrees were awarded. The most popular majors were marketing and transportation (8%), finance (5%), and information systems (4%). In an average class, 20% graduate in 4 years, 40% in 5 years, and 45% in 6 years. 200 companies recruited on campus in 2000-2001.

Admissions Contact: Maxine Jones, Interim Director. A video is available. E-mail: *uafadmis@uark.edu* Web: *http://www.uark.edu*

UNIVERSITY OF ARKANSAS AT LITTLE ROCK — C-3

Little Rock, AR 72204-1099 — **(501) 569-3492**
(800) 482-8892; Fax: (501) 569-8956

Full-time: 2139 men, 3308 women	**Faculty:** n/av
Part-time: 1347 men, 2390 women	**Ph.D.s:** 45%
Graduate: 503 men, 1255 women	**Student/Faculty:** n/av
Year: semesters, summer session	**Tuition:** $3037 ($6887)
Application Deadline: open	**Room & Board:** $2600
Freshman Class: 960 applied, 933 accepted, 803 enrolled	
ACT: 19	**NONCOMPETITIVE**

The University of Arkansas at Little Rock, which began in 1927 as Little Rock Junior College, and joined the University of Arkansas system in 1969, is a liberal arts institution. Some information in this profile is approximate. There are 5 undergraduate and 2 graduate schools. In addition to regional accreditation, UALR has baccalaureate program accreditation with AACSB, ABET, ACEJMC, ASLA, CSWE, NASAD, NASM, NCATE, and NLN. The library contains 394,780 volumes, 691,612 microform items, and 8300 audiovisual forms/CDs, and subscribes to 2626 periodicals. Computerized library services include the card catalog, interlibrary loans, and database searching. Special learning facilities include a learning resource center, art gallery, planetarium, radio station, TV station, and speech and hearing clinic. The 150-acre campus is in an urban area in Little Rock. Including residence halls, there are 38 buildings.

Student Life: 93% of undergraduates are from Arkansas. Others are from 44 states, 62 foreign countries, and Canada. 70% are white; 24%, African American. The average age of freshmen is 19; all undergraduates, 26. 41% do not continue beyond their first year.

Housing: 306 students can be accommodated in college housing, which includes coed dormitories and on-campus apartments. In addition, there are university-owned rental house. On-campus housing is available on a first-come, first-served basis. 97% of students commute. Alcohol is not permitted. All students may keep cars.

Activities: 5% of men belong to 6 national fraternities; 3% of women belong to 6 national sororities. There are 75 groups on campus, including cheerleading, chess, chorale, dance, drama, honors, jazz band, literary magazine, musical theater, newspaper, opera, pep band, political, professional, radio and TV, religious, social service, and student government. Popular campus events include International Week, Sunshine Days, and Art Spree.

Sports: There are 6 intercollegiate sports for men and 7 for women, and 18 intramural sports for men and 18 for women. Facilities include a 2000-seat gym, a swimming pool, tennis courts, baseball and intramural fields, a horseshoe pit, a bowling alley, a fitness and weight room, an indoor jogging track, a steam room, a sauna, and basketball, volleyball, and racquetball courts.

Disabled Students: 85% of the campus is accessible. Wheelchair ramps, elevators, special parking, specially equipped rest rooms, special class scheduling, lowered drinking fountains, and study rooms are available.

Services: Counseling and information services are available, as is tutoring in every subject. There is a reader service for the blind, and remedial math, reading, and writing. Also available are interpreters and a braille dictionary, typewriter, and reading machine.

Campus Safety and Security: Measures include 24-hour foot and vehicle patrol, self-defense education, escort service, and informal discussions. There are emergency telephones, lighted pathways/sidewalks, emergency phones, and a student patrol crime prevention unit.

Programs of Study: UALR confers B.A., B.S., B.B.A., and B.S.W. degrees. Associate, master's, and doctoral degrees are also awarded. Bachelor's degrees are awarded in BIOLOGICAL SCIENCE (biology/biological science), BUSINESS (accounting, banking and finance, business administration and management, management science, and marketing/retailing/merchandising), COMMUNICATIONS AND THE ARTS (advertising, art, art history and appreciation, dramatic arts, English, French, journalism, music, radio/television technology, Spanish, technical and business writing, and visual and performing arts), COMPUTER AND PHYSICAL SCIENCE (chemistry, computer science, geology, information sciences and systems, mathematics, and physics), EDUCATION (early childhood, education of the deaf and hearing impaired, elementary, and health), ENGINEERING AND ENVIRONMENTAL DESIGN (computer technology, construction technology, electrical/electronics engineering technology, industrial administration/management, manufacturing engineering, mechanical engineering technology, and surveying engineering), HEALTH PROFESSIONS (environmental health science, health science, and speech pathology/audiology), SOCIAL SCIENCE (criminal justice, economics, history, international studies, interpreter for the deaf, liberal arts/general studies, philosophy, political science/government, psychology, and sociology). Psychology, biology, and liberal arts are the largest.

Required: To graduate, all students must complete a minimum of 124 credit hours, including 45 at the upper level, while maintaining a GPA of 2.0. A minimum 44-hour core curriculum must be completed, and distribution requirements include freshman composition, speech and history, 3 hours of math, and 2 hours of leisure science. Each student must complete a major and a minor or a double major. There also is an exam in written English. Language proficiency is required for the B.A. degree.

Special: Study abroad in Mexico, France, Spain, and Austria is available; UALR has exchange relationships with more than 30 countries. In addition, internships, work-study programs with the university, cross-registration with the University of Arkansas Medical School, B.A.-B.S. degrees, a general studies degree, student-designed majors, nondegree study, and pass/fail options are offered. There are 3 national honor societies, including Phi Beta Kappa, a freshman honors program, and 5 departmental honors programs.

Faculty/Classroom: 53% of faculty are male; 47%, female.

Admissions: 97% of the 2001-2002 applicants were accepted. The ACT scores for the 2001-2002 freshman class were: 64% below 21, 18% between 21 and 23, 12% between 24 and 26, 3% between 27 and 28, and 3% above 28.

Requirements: The SAT I or ACT is required. In addition, 2 or more of the following criteria must be met: a high school GPA of at least 2.5 or a passing GED test score; an ACT composite score of at least 21 or a combined verbal/math SAT I score of 990 taken within the past 5 years; completion of a college-preparatory core in high school that includes 4 units of English, 3 each of math and social studies, and 2 each of natural science and a single foreign language. Students with test subscores below the state minimum requirement will be placed in the appropriate development courses. AP and CLEP credits are accepted.

Procedure: Freshmen are admitted to all sessions. Entrance exams should be taken during the fall of the senior year. There are early admissions and deferred admissions plans. Application deadlines are open. Notification is sent on a rolling basis.

Transfer: Applicants must have a minimum college GPA of 2.0. They must submit official transcripts from each college previously attended. Students who have 12 or fewer acceptable transfer credits must meet all the admission requirements for entering freshmen. 30 credits of 124 must be completed at UALR.

Visiting: There are regularly scheduled orientations for prospective students, which take place before each semester and at which attendance is required. There are guides for informal visits and visitors may sit in on classes. To schedule a visit, contact the Admissions Office.

Financial Aid: In 2001-2002, 65% of all freshmen received some form of financial aid. 4% of undergraduates work part time. Average annual earnings from campus work are $1400. The FAFSA is required. Check with the school for current deadlines.

International Students: These students must score 525 on the written TOEFL and at least 4 points on the Test of Written English (TWE), or take the ACT or the school's own test.

Computers: The mainframe is a DEC VAX 11/780. About 750 PCs and computer terminals are available for student use and are located throughout the campus. Students have access to e-mail, FTP, Telnet, Gopher, and the World Wide Web. All students may access the system 24 hours a day. There are no time limits and no fees.

Admissions Contact: John Noah, Director.
Web: *http://www.ualr.edu/~adminfo/*

UNIVERSITY OF ARKANSAS AT MONTICELLO C-4

Monticello, AR 71656-3596 (870) 460-1026
(800) 844-1826; Fax: (870) 460-1933

Full-time: 840 men, 1000 women	**Faculty:** 116
Part-time: 100 men, 190 women	**Ph.D.s:** 60%
Graduate: 50 men, 90 women	**Student/Faculty:** 16 to 1
Year: semesters, summer session	**Tuition:** $2950 ($6040)
Application Deadline: open	**Room & Board:** $2990
Freshman Class: n/av	
SAT I or ACT: required	**NONCOMPETITIVE**

The University of Arkansas at Monticello was established in 1909 as the Fourth District Agricultural School. Made part of the public University of Arkansas System in 1971, UAM offers liberal arts undergraduate courses and graduate programs. Figures in the above capsule are approximate. There are 6 undergraduate and 2 graduate schools. In addition to regional accreditation, UAM has baccalaureate program accreditation with NASM, NCATE, NLN, and SAF. The library contains 146,000 volumes, 221,000 microform items, and 640 audiovisual forms/CDs, and subscribes to 1140 periodicals. Computerized library services include the card catalog, interlibrary loans, and database searching. Special learning facilities include a learning resource center, natural history museum, planetarium, a university forest, and a university farm. The 1556-acre campus is in a small town 90 miles south of Little Rock. Including residence halls, there are 37 buildings.

Student Life: 90% of undergraduates are from Arkansas. Others are from 20 states and 3 foreign countries. 99% are from public schools. 75% are white; 20% African American. The average age of freshmen is 19; all undergraduates, 23. 44% do not continue beyond their first year; 26% remain to graduate.

Housing: 600 students can be accommodated in college housing, which includes single-sex dormitories, on-campus apartments, and married-student housing. On-campus housing is guaranteed for all 4 years. 75% of students commute. Alcohol is not permitted. All students may keep cars.

Activities: 10% of men belong to 6 national fraternities; 9% of women belong to 5 national sororities. There are 56 groups on campus, including art, band, cheerleading, chess, choir, chorus, debate, ethnic, honors, jazz band, literary magazine, marching band, musical theater, newspaper, pep band, political, professional, religious, social, social service, and student government. Popular campus events include Forestry Festival, Special Olympics, and All-Campus Talent Show.

Sports: There are 5 intercollegiate sports for men and 5 for women, and 6 intramural sports for men and 6 for women. Facilities include a 4000-seat stadium, a 2500-seat gym, a swimming pool, tennis and racquetball courts, and facilities for numerous intramural sports.

Disabled Students: All of the campus is accessible. Wheelchair ramps, elevators, special parking, specially equipped rest rooms, special class scheduling, lowered drinking fountains, lowered telephones, and extended test times, books on tape, note takers, quiet test facilites, and word processing assistance are available.

Services: Counseling and information services are available, as is tutoring in some subjects, including general education. There is a reader service for the blind, and remedial math, reading, and writing.

Campus Safety and Security: Measures include 24-hour foot and vehicle patrol, informal discussions, pamphlets/posters/films, and emergency telephones. There are lighted pathways/sidewalks.

Programs of Study: UAM confers B.A., B.S., B.B.A., B.M.Ed., and B.S.N. degrees. Associate and master's degrees are also awarded. Bachelor's degrees are awarded in AGRICULTURE (agriculture, forestry and related sciences, and wildlife management), BIOLOGICAL SCIENCE (biology/biological science), BUSINESS (accounting, business administration and management, and management information systems), COMMUNICATIONS AND THE ARTS (art, English, music, and speech/debate/rhetoric), COMPUTER AND PHYSICAL SCIENCE (chemistry, geodetic science, mathematics, and physical sciences), EDUCATION (business, elementary, health, music, physical, and special), HEALTH PROFESSIONS (nursing), SOCIAL SCIENCE (criminal justice, history, political science/government, psychology, and social work). Forestry and sciences are the strongest academically. Business administration, elementary education, and computer information systems are the largest.

Required: All students are required to complete 124 total semester hours, approximately 30 within their major, and maintain a minimum GPA of 2.0 (2.75 in education). Distribution requirements include 11 hours in basic sciences, 6 hours each in composition and humanities, and 3 hours each in fine arts, speech, U.S. history or government, psychology or sociology, social science, and math.

Special: A work-study program in forestry, a general studies degree, cross-registration within the University of Arkansas system, credit for military experience, dual majors, and nondegree study are available. There is 1 national honor society, a freshman honors program.

Faculty/Classroom: 65% of faculty are male; 35%, female. All teach undergraduates and 11% do research. No introductory courses are taught by graduate students. The average class size in an introductory lecture is 27; in a laboratory, 15; and in a regular course, 20.

Requirements: The SAT I or ACT is required. In addition, a high school diploma or GED is required. The Arkansas high school core curriculum is recommended. State law requires proof of immunization. AP and CLEP credits are accepted. Applications are accepted on-line at the school's web site.

Procedure: Freshmen are admitted to all sessions. Entrance exams should be taken by December of the senior year. Application deadlines are open. Check with the school for current fee.

Transfer: 176 transfer students enrolled in a recent year. Transfer students must be in good academic standing at the previous college. ACT or SAT I test scores are required only if the student has not successfully completed Freshman Composition I and College Algebra. 30 credits of 124 must be completed at UAM.

Visiting: There are regularly scheduled orientations for prospective students, including a review of admission requirements and financial aid opportunities and a visit to academic departments and faculty in the field of interest. There are guides for informal visits and visitors may sit in on classes and stay overnight. To schedule a visit, contact the Office of Admissions.

Financial Aid: In a recent year, 90% of all freshmen and 75% of continuing students received some form of financial aid. 66% of freshmen and 74% of continuing students received need-based aid. The average freshman award was $5047. Of that total, scholarships or need-based grants averaged $3914; loans averaged $2529 ($4125 maximum); work contracts averaged $2908 ($3400 maximum); and rehabilitation, veterans, and law enforcement officer dependent grants averaged $2237. 18% of undergraduates work part time. Average annual earnings from campus work are $1175. UAM is a member of CSS. The FAFSA is required. Check with the school for current deadlines.

International Students: There were 5 international students enrolled in a recent year. They must score 500 on the written TOEFL or 173 on the electronic version and also take the SAT I or the ACT.

Computers: The mainframe is a DEC ALPHA DS20. There are approximately 275 PCs in public computer labs for students use. Residence halls are wired for network access. All campus computers have access to the campus network and the Internet. All students are eligible for e-mail accounts and have web access to their grades, financial aid, and demographic information. All students may access the system. There are no time limits and no fees. It is strongly recommended that all students have a personal computer.

Graduates: In a recent year, 266 bachelor's degrees were awarded. The most popular majors were business administration (19%), elementary education (12%), and agriculture (10%). In an average class, 9% graduate in 4 years, 21% in 5 years, and 26% in 6 years.

Admissions Contact: Mary Whiting, Director of Admissions. A video is available. E-mail: *whitingm@uamont.edu* Web: *www.uamont.edu*

UNIVERSITY OF ARKANSAS AT PINE BLUFF — C-4

Pine Bluff, AR 71601-2799 (870) 575-8492

(800) 264-6585; Fax: (870) 543-8014

Full-time: 1234 men, 1495 women	**Faculty:** 171; IIB, --$
Part-time: 124 men, 199 women	**Ph.D.s:** 57%
Graduate: 23 men, 69 women	**Student/Faculty:** 16 to 1
Year: semesters, summer session	**Tuition:** $3209 ($6509)
Application Deadline: see profile	**Room & Board:** $4716

Freshman Class: 1632 applied, 1173 accepted, 715 enrolled

SAT I or ACT: required — **COMPETITIVE**

The University of Arkansas at Pine Bluff, established in 1873, is a historically black land-grant institution providing a liberal arts education as part of the public University of Arkansas system. There are 5 undergraduate schools and 1 graduate school. In addition to regional accreditation, UAPB has baccalaureate program accreditation with AHEA, CSWE, NASM, NCATE, and NLN. The library contains 271,547 volumes, 119,205 microform items, and 4299 audiovisual forms/CDs, and subscribes to 1050 periodicals. Computerized library services include the card catalog, interlibrary loans, and database searching. Special learning facilities include a learning resource center, art gallery, radio station, and TV station. The 318-acre campus is in a small town 40 miles southeast of Little Rock and approximately 142 miles southwest of Memphis. Including residence halls, there are 49 buildings.

Student Life: 80% of undergraduates are from Arkansas. Others are from 28 states, 17 foreign countries, and Canada. 94% are African American. The average age of freshmen is 18; all undergraduates, 22. 61% do not continue beyond their first year.

Housing: 1099 students can be accommodated in college housing, which includes single-sex dormitories. In addition, there are honors clusters in the dorms. On-campus housing is guaranteed for all 4 years. 65% of students commute. Alcohol is not permitted. All students may keep cars.

Activities: There are 4 local and 4 national fraternities and 4 local and 4 national sororities. There are 65 groups on campus, including art, band, cheerleading, choir, computers, drama, drill team, honors, jazz band, marching band, newspaper, orchestra, photography, political, professional, radio and TV, religious, social, social service, student government, and yearbook. Popular campus events include Founders Day, Spring Emphasis, and Unity Fest.

Sports: There are 7 intercollegiate sports for men and 8 for women, and 20 intramural sports for men and 19 for women. Facilities include a phys ed complex that provides activities such as flag football, basketball, volleyball, softball, tennis, handball, racquetball, track and field, and badminton. There is also a swimming pool and a 6,000-seat football stadium.

Disabled Students: 98% of the campus is accessible. Wheelchair ramps, elevators, special parking, specially equipped rest rooms, special class scheduling, lowered drinking fountains, and lowered telephones are available.

Services: Counseling and information services are available, as is tutoring in most subjects. There is a reader service for the blind, and remedial math, reading, and writing.

Campus Safety and Security: Measures include 24-hour foot and vehicle patrol, self-defense education, escort service, and informal discussions. There are pamphlets/posters/films, emergency telephones, lighted pathways/sidewalks. There is a department of public safety and security on campus.

Programs of Study: UAPB confers B.A. and B.S. degrees. Associate and master's degrees are also awarded. Bachelor's degrees are awarded in AGRICULTURE (agriculture, conservation and regulation, and fishing and fisheries), BIOLOGICAL SCIENCE (biology/biological science), BUSINESS (accounting and business administration and management), COMMUNICATIONS AND THE ARTS (art, English, journalism, music, and speech/debate/rhetoric), COMPUTER AND PHYSICAL SCIENCE (applied mathematics, chemistry, computer science, mathematics, and physics), EDUCATION (agricultural, art, business, early childhood, English, home economics, industrial arts, mathematics, middle school, music, physical, science, social science, and special), ENGINEERING AND ENVIRONMENTAL DESIGN (industrial engineering technology and preengineering), HEALTH PROFESSIONS (nursing, predentistry, premedicine, prepharmacy, and rehabilitation therapy), SOCIAL SCIENCE (criminal justice, family/consumer studies, gerontology, history, liberal arts/general studies, parks and recreation management, political science/government, psychology, social work, and sociology). Business administration, biology and computer science are the strongest academically and are the largest.

Required: All students must complete at least 124 hours of credit, including 30 hours in their major, while earning an overall 2.0 GPA (2.5 for teacher education majors) and a C or better in all major courses. Distribution requirements include English, math, social and natural science, and phys ed courses. Students must pass a comprehensive exam in their major.

Special: The university offers formal co-op education and work-study programs, concurrent registration with members of the University of Arkansas system, internships, B.A.-B.S. degrees, and dual and student-designed majors. Also offered are credit for military experience, nondegree study, individualized programs of study for honors college students, and study abroad. There are 4 national honor societies, a freshman honors program, and 6 departmental honors programs.

Faculty/Classroom: 54% of faculty are male; 46%, female. The average class size in a laboratory is 20 and in a regular course, 21.

Admissions: 72% of the 2001-2002 applicants were accepted.

Requirements: The SAT I or ACT is required. The ACT, with a minimum composite score of 19, is preferred. Applicants must have earned 15 credits, including 4 units of English and 3 each in social studies, math, and science. The GED is accepted. Students not meeting these requirements may apply for conditional admission. A GPA of 2.0 is required. AP and CLEP credits are accepted.

Procedure: Freshmen are admitted fall, spring, and summer. Entrance exams should be taken during the junior or senior year. There are early admissions and deferred admissions plans. Notification is sent on a rolling basis. Check with the school for current application deadlines and fees.

Transfer: 210 transfer students enrolled in 2001-2002. Transfer students must have a minimum GPA of 2.0. Applicants with fewer than 60 semester hours of college credit must submit an application, ACT or SAT I scores, and all college transcripts. 30 credits of 124 must be completed at UAPB.

Visiting: There are regularly scheduled orientations for prospective students. There are guides for informal visits and visitors may sit in on classes and stay overnight. To schedule a visit, contact the Director of Recruitment at (501) 575-8961 or (800) 525-5272.

Financial Aid: 70% of undergraduates work part time. Average annual earnings from campus work are $800. UAPB is a member of CSS. The FAFSA is required. Check with the school for current deadlines.

International Students: There are 44 international students enrolled. They must score 550 on the written TOEFL and also take the SAT I or ACT. The ACT, with a minimum score of 19, is preferred. SAT I scores may be used.

Computers: The mainframe is a Dec VAX 4500. The academic computer center is networked to the mainframe with a capacity for 60 PCs. All students may access the system 7 A.M. to 11 P.M. Monday through Friday, and during special weekend hours. There are no time limits. The fee a $15 lab fee.

Graduates: In 2001, 332 bachelor's degrees were awarded. The most popular majors were general studies (13%), business administration (13%), and criminal justice (9%). In an average class, 1% graduate in 3 years, 9% in 4 years, 20% in 5 years, and 26% in 6 years. 21 companies recruited on campus in 2000-2001. Of the 2000 graduating class, 10% were enrolled in graduate school within 6 months of graduation and 42% were employed.

Admissions Contact: Erica Fulton, Director of Admissions and Academic Records. E-mail: *fulton_e@4500.uabb.edu* Web: *www.uapb.edu*

UNIVERSITY OF CENTRAL ARKANSAS — C-3

Conway, AR 72035-0001 — **(501) 450-3128; (800) 243-8245**

Full-time: 2670 men, 4190 women	**Faculty:** IIA, --$
Part-time: 340 men, 450 women	**Ph.D.s:** 68%
Graduate: 270 men, 770 women	**Student/Faculty:** n/av
Year: semesters, summer session	**Tuition:** $3238 ($5902)
Application Deadline: August 1	**Room & Board:** $3150
Freshman Class: n/av	
SAT I or ACT: required	**COMPETITIVE**

The University of Central Arkansas, established in 1907, is a comprehensive public institution offering undergraduate and graduate degrees in liberal arts, business, health-related sciences, and education. Figures in the above capsule are approximate. There are 7 undergraduate schools and 1 graduate school. In addition to regional accreditation, UCA has baccalaureate program accreditation with AACSB, ADA, APTA, CAHEA, NASAD, NASM, NCATE, and NLN. The library contains 405,200 volumes, 866,600 microform items, and 6200 audiovisual forms/CDs, and subscribes to 2000 periodicals. Computerized library services include the card catalog, interlibrary loans, and database searching. Special learning facilities include a learning resource center, art gallery, planetarium, radio station, and TV station. The 262-acre campus is in a small town 29 miles north of Little Rock. Including residence halls, there are 52 buildings.

Student Life: 90% of undergraduates are from Arkansas. Others are from 35 states, 52 foreign countries, and Canada. 96% are from public schools. 90% are white; 10% African American. The average age of freshmen is 19; all undergraduates, 22. 38% do not continue beyond their first year; 30% remain to graduate.

Housing: 2120 students can be accommodated in college housing, which includes single-sex and coed dormitories. In addition, there are honors houses and an international students' residence hall. On-campus housing is available on a first-come, first-served basis. 75% of students commute. Alcohol is not permitted. All students may keep cars.

Activities: 10% of men belong to 9 national fraternities; 10% of women belong to 9 national sororities. There are 95 groups on campus, including art, band, cheerleading, choir, chorale, chorus, dance, drama, ethnic, gay, honors, international, jazz band, literary magazine, marching band, musical theater, newspaper, orchestra, pep band, photography, political, professional, radio and TV, religious, social, social service, student government, symphony, and yearbook. Popular campus events include Bear Facts Day.

Sports: There are 4 intercollegiate sports for men and 6 for women, and 18 intramural sports for men and 18 for women. Facilities include a gym, a swimming pool, a fitness center, racquetball and tennis courts, a track, soccer fields, and softball fields.

Disabled Students: 98% of the campus is accessible. Wheelchair ramps, elevators, special parking, specially equipped rest rooms, special class scheduling, lowered drinking fountains, lowered telephones, and special dorm rooms are available.

Services: Counseling and information services are available, as is tutoring in some subjects. There is a reader service for the blind, and remedial math, reading, and writing.

Campus Safety and Security: Measures include 24-hour foot and vehicle patrol, escort service, informal discussions, and pamphlets/posters/films. There are emergency telephones, lighted pathways/sidewalks, and security checkpoints.

Programs of Study: UCA confers B.A., B.S., B.B.A., B.M., B.M.E., and B.S.E. degrees. Associate, master's, and doctoral degrees are also awarded. Bachelor's degrees are awarded in BIOLOGICAL SCIENCE (biology/biological science), BUSINESS (accounting, banking and finance, business administration and management, business economics, insurance and risk management, and marketing/retailing/merchandising), COMMUNICATIONS AND THE ARTS (communications, English, French, journalism, music, Spanish, and speech/debate/rhetoric), COMPUTER AND PHYSICAL SCIENCE (chemistry, computer science, information sciences and systems, mathematics, and physics), EDUCATION (art, athletic training, early childhood, education of the exceptional child, elementary, foreign languages, guidance, library science, middle school, music, physical, science, secondary, and special), ENGINEERING AND ENVIRONMENTAL DESIGN (environmental science, interior design, and preengineering), HEALTH PROFESSIONS (exercise science, health care administration, health science, medical technology, nuclear medical technology, nursing, occupational therapy, physical therapy, predentistry, premedicine, preoptometry, prepharmacy, preveterinary science, radiological science, and speech pathology/audiology), SOCIAL SCIENCE (dietetics, economics, family/consumer studies, geography, gerontology, history, philosophy, political science/government, psychology, public administration, religion, and sociology). Business, health-related sciences, and education are the strongest academically. Business and health-related sciences are the largest.

Required: All students must earn a minimum of 124 semester hours, including 40 in upper-division courses. Distribution requirements include 7 hours in science, and 6 hours each in the humanities and social sciences. A minimum GPA of 2.25 is needed for the B.B.A., 2.5 for most education programs. Minimum requirements also include 2 semester hours in phys ed.

Special: Study abroad, work-study programs, a B.S.-B.A. degree, a 3-2 engineering degree with Arkansas State University, dual majors, nondegree study, and pass/fail options are available. Co-op programs in business, computer science, and health sciences, and internships in education are also possible. There are 18 national honor societies, a freshman honors program, and 25 departmental honors programs.

Faculty/Classroom: 60% of faculty are male; 40%, female. No introductory courses are taught by graduate students. The average class size in a laboratory is 20 and in a regular course, 34.

Requirements: The SAT I or ACT is required, with a minimum ACT score of 19. The GED is accepted. UCA requires applicants to be in the upper 33% of their class. A GPA of 3.0 is required. AP and CLEP credits are accepted. Important factors in the admissions decision are advanced placement or honor courses, evidence of special talent, and recommendations by school officials.

Procedure: Freshmen are admitted to all sessions. Applications should be filed by August 1 for fall entry and December 15 for spring entry. Notification is sent on a rolling basis. Check with the school for current fee.

Transfer: Applicants need, on UCA's scale, a minimum cumulative GPA of 2.0. 24 credits of 124 must be completed at UCA.

Visiting: There are regularly scheduled orientations for prospective students, including tours at 11 A.M. and 2 P.M.; departments and dormitories may be visited. There are also special visitation days that include a campus tour, departmental session, lunch, parents' session, optional residence hall tour, and classroom visit or planetarium show. Visitors may sit in on classes. To schedule a visit, contact the Admissions Office.

Financial Aid: 10% of undergraduates work part time. The FAFSA is required. The priority fall application deadline is April 15.

International Students: The school actively recruits these students. They must score 500 on the written TOEFL or 173 on the electronic version.

Computers: The mainframes are an IBM 5390, Multipurpose 2000. There are also 110 PCs and Macs available in academic buildings, the library, and dorms. All students may access the system. It is strongly recommended that all students have a personal computer.

Graduates: In a recent year, 1097 bachelor's degrees were awarded. The most popular majors were health sciences (30%), education (22%), and business (17%). In an average class, 20% graduate in 4 years, 25% in 5 years, and 30% in 6 years. 210 companies recruited on campus in a recent year.

Admissions Contact: Director of Admissions.
E-mail: *admissions@ecom.uca.edu* Web: *www.uca.edu*

UNIVERSITY OF THE OZARKS
B-2

Clarksville, AR 72830
(501) 979-1421
(800) 264-8636; Fax: (501) 979-1355

Full-time: 286 men, 338 women
Faculty: 41; IIB, --$
Part-time: 9 men, 21 women
Ph.D.s: 73%
Graduate: none
Student/Faculty: 15 to 1
Year: semesters, summer session
Tuition: $9624
Application Deadline: July 1
Room & Board: $4280
Freshman Class: 385 applied, 367 accepted, 194 enrolled
SAT I Verbal/Math: 506/425
ACT: 23
COMPETITIVE

The University of the Ozarks, founded in 1834, is a private liberal arts institution affiliated with the Presbyterian Church (U.S.A.). There are 4 undergraduate schools. In addition to regional accreditation, Ozarks has baccalaureate program accreditation with NCATE. The library contains 69,960 volumes, 6927 microform items, and 2955 audiovisual forms/CDs, and subscribes to 611 periodicals. Computerized library services include the card catalog, interlibrary loans, and database searching. Special learning facilities include a learning resource center, art gallery, TV station, and the Jones Learning Center for students with diagnosed learning disabilities. The 35-acre campus is in a small town 100 miles northwest of Little Rock. Including residence halls, there are 16 buildings.

Student Life: 58% of undergraduates are from Arkansas. Others are from 21 states and 13 foreign countries. 92% are from public schools. 77% are white; 10% foreign nationals. 59% are Protestant; 25% claim no religious affiliation; 15% Catholic. The average age of freshmen is 18; all undergraduates, 20. 34% do not continue beyond their first year.

Housing: 400 students can be accommodated in college housing, which includes single-sex and coed dormitories. On-campus housing is guaranteed for the freshman year only and is available on a first-come, first-served basis. Priority is given to out-of-town students. 67% of students live on campus; of those, 51% remain on campus on weekends. Alcohol is not permitted. All students may keep cars.

Activities: There are no fraternities or sororities. There are 30 groups on campus, including art, cheerleading, choir, chorale, dance, debate, drama, film, forensics, honors, international, literary magazine, newspaper, political, professional, religious, social, social service, student government, TV, and yearbook. Popular campus events include International Fair and Banquet, Family Weekend, and Freshman Matriculation Ceremony.

Sports: There are 6 intercollegiate sports for men and 5 for women, and 6 intramural sports for men and 5 for women. Facilities include a sports complex housing racquetball courts, a pool, and a 2200-seat basketball arena. In addition, there are softball, soccer, and baseball fields, a quarter-mile track, tennis courts, and a 700-seat stadium.

Disabled Students: 75% of the campus is accessible. Elevators, special parking, specially equipped rest rooms, special class scheduling, and lowered drinking fountains are available.

Services: Counseling and information services are available, as is tutoring in every subject. There is remedial math, reading, and writing.

Campus Safety and Security: Measures include 24-hour foot and vehicle patrol, informal discussions, emergency telephones, and lighted pathways/sidewalks.

Programs of Study: Ozarks confers B.A., B.S., and B.G.S. degrees. Bachelor's degrees are awarded in BIOLOGICAL SCIENCE (biology/biological science), BUSINESS (accounting, business administration and management, and marketing/retailing/merchandising), COMMUNICATIONS AND THE ARTS (art, communications, dramatic arts, English, and music), COMPUTER AND PHYSICAL SCIENCE (chemistry, mathematics, and physics), EDUCATION (business, early childhood, middle school, and physical), ENGINEERING AND ENVIRONMENTAL DESIGN (environmental science), SOCIAL SCIENCE (history, liberal arts/general studies, political science/government, psychology, religion, social science, and sociology). Chemistry and English are the strongest academically. Business is the largest.

Required: Students are required to earn 124 hours, with 30 to 42 in the major, and maintain a minimum GPA of 2.0. Distribution requirements include 7 hours in math and science and 6 hours each in the humanities and fine arts, and social science or business. Students must also take 4 hours in phys ed, 3 hours of composition, and a computer literacy exam. In addition, 6 hours of foreign language are required for the B.A.

Special: Internships, study abroad in 8 countries, including Japan, numerous work-study programs, dual majors, a general studies degree, and a 3-2 engineering degree with the University of Arkansas are available. There is 1 national honor society.

Faculty/Classroom: 73% of faculty are male; 27%, female. All teach undergraduates. The average class size in an introductory lecture is 16; in a laboratory, 20; and in a regular course, 16.

Admissions: 95% of the 2001-2002 applicants were accepted. The SAT I scores for the 2001-2002 freshman class were: Verbal--50% below 500, 26% between 500 and 599, and 24% between 600 and 700; Math--62% below 500, 29% between 500 and 599, and 9% between 600 and 700. The ACT scores were 20% below 21, 43% between 21 and 23, 20% between 24 and 26, 10% between 27 and 28, and 7% above 28. 41% of the current freshmen were in the top fifth of their class; 72% were in the top two fifths. There was 1 National Merit finalist and 5 semifinalists. 12 freshmen graduated first in their class.

Requirements: The SAT I or ACT is required, with a minimum composite score of 800 on the SAT I or 18 on the ACT. An interview is recommended. The GED is accepted. Ozarks requires applicants to be in the upper 50% of their class. A GPA of 2.0 is required. AP and CLEP credits are accepted. Important factors in the admissions decision are personality/intangible qualities, advanced placement or honor courses, and evidence of special talent. Applications are available on-line at the school's web site.

Procedure: Freshmen are admitted to all sessions. Entrance exams should be taken as early as possible. There is a deferred admissions plan. Applications should be filed by July 1 for fall entry and December 1 for spring entry. Notification is sent on a rolling basis. In fall 2001, the application fee was $10.

Transfer: 37 transfer students enrolled in 2001-2002. A GPA of 2.0 and college transcripts are required. Applicants with a GPA of less than 2.0 or fewer than 30 hours of college work must furnish high school transcripts. 30 credits of 124 must be completed at Ozarks.

Visiting: There are regularly scheduled orientations for prospective students, including a campus tour, meetings with faculty and students, admissions, and financial aid. In most cases, prospective students may meet with the President and coaches as requested, and may sit in on classes. There are guides for informal visits and visitors may sit in on classes and stay overnight. To schedule a visit, contact the Admissions Office.

Financial Aid: In 2001-2002, 82% of all freshmen and 92% of continuing students received some form of financial aid. 57% of freshmen and 43% of continuing students received need-based aid. The average freshman award was $11,000. Of that total, scholarships or need-based grants averaged $5820 ($9300 maximum); loans averaged $2400 ($2600 maximum); and work contracts averaged $1500. 50% of undergraduates work part time. Average annual earnings from campus work are $1100. The average financial indebtedness of the 2001 graduate was $13,200. The FAFSA is required. The fall application deadline is February 15.

International Students: There are 103 international students enrolled. The school actively recruits these students. They must score 500 on the written TOEFL.

Computers: The university provides 100 networked PCs with Internet access in computer labs. Each residence hall room has 2 Internet ports. All students may access the system. There are no time limits. The fee is $100. It is strongly recommended that all students have a personal computer.

Graduates: In 2001, 82 bachelor's degrees were awarded. The most popular majors were marketing (21%), management (17%), and business administration (14%). In an average class, 21% graduate in 4 years, 37% in 5 years, and 39% in 6 years. 50 companies recruited on campus in 2000-2001. Of the 2000 graduating class, 11% were enrolled in graduate school within 6 months of graduation and 68% were employed.

Admissions Contact: Jim Decker, Director of Admissions.
E-mail: *jdecker@ozarks.edu* Web: *www.ozarks.edu*

WILLIAMS BAPTIST COLLEGE
D-1

Walnut Ridge, AR 72476
(870) 759-4121
(800) 722-4434; Fax: (870) 886-3924

Full-time: 218 men, 287 women
Faculty: 28; IIB, --$
Part-time: 67 men, 116 women
Ph.D.s: 60%
Graduate: none
Student/Faculty: 18 to 1
Year: semesters, summer session
Tuition: $7250
Application Deadline: open
Room & Board: $3500
Freshman Class: 445 applied, 329 accepted, 149 enrolled
ACT: 21
COMPETITIVE

Williams Baptist College, founded in 1941, is a liberal arts institution providing undergraduate education in business, education, humanities, natural sciences, religion, and social sciences. WBC is affiliated with the Southern Baptist Church and is sponsored by the Arkansas Baptist Convention. In addition to regional accreditation, WBC has baccalaureate program accreditation with NCATE. The library contains 67,262 volumes and 18,626 microform items, and subscribes to 198 periodicals. Computerized library services include the card catalog, interlibrary loans, and database searching. Special learning facilities include a learning resource center, art gallery, and an education curriculum lab. The 180-acre campus is in a rural area 100 miles northwest of Memphis, Tennessee, and 125 miles north of Little Rock. Including residence halls, there are 40 buildings.

Student Life: 80% of undergraduates are from Arkansas. Others are from 14 states and 8 foreign countries. 94% are from public schools. 93% are white. Most are Protestant. The average age of freshmen is 18;

all undergraduates, 24. 49% do not continue beyond their first year; 20% remain to graduate.

Housing: 391 students can be accommodated in college housing, which includes single-sex dormitories, on-campus apartments, and married-student housing. On-campus housing is guaranteed for all 4 years. 68% of students live on campus; of those, 35% remain on campus on weekends. Alcohol is not permitted. All students may keep cars.

Activities: There are no fraternities or sororities. There are 32 groups on campus, including art, cheerleading, chess, choir, chorale, chorus, drama, honors, international, literary magazine, pep band, professional, religious, social, social service, student government, symphony, and yearbook. Popular campus events include Firstweek, October Days, and WOW! Wednesday.

Sports: There are 5 intercollegiate sports for men and 4 for women, and 4 intramural sports for men and 4 for women. Facilities include a gym, a weight room, racquetball and tennis courts, a jogging track, and a student center.

Disabled Students: 90% of the campus is accessible. Wheelchair ramps, special parking, specially equipped rest rooms, special class scheduling, and lowered drinking fountains are available.

Services: Counseling and information services are available, as is tutoring in some subjects, including English, math, and science. There is a reader service for the blind, and remedial math, reading, and writing.

Campus Safety and Security: Measures include lighted pathways/sidewalks and and vehicle and foot patrol.

Programs of Study: WBC confers B.A., B.S., B.F.A., B.S.B.A., and B.S.Ed. degrees. Associate degrees are also awarded. Bachelor's degrees are awarded in BIOLOGICAL SCIENCE (biology/biological science), BUSINESS (business administration and management), COMMUNICATIONS AND THE ARTS (art, English, and music), COMPUTER AND PHYSICAL SCIENCE (computer science), EDUCATION (elementary, physical, and secondary), SOCIAL SCIENCE (counseling/psychology, history, psychology, religion, religious education, and religious music). Education, psychology, and religion are the strongest academically. Education, religion, and phys ed are the largest.

Required: To graduate, all students must follow a core curriculum including humanities, social science/religion, natural science/math, and physical activity. Chapel attendance is mandatory. A total of 128 credits, with 36 to 64 hours in the major, and a minimum GPA of 2.0 are required to graduate.

Special: WBC offers study abroad in England, Latin America, the Middle East, and Russia, a Washington semester through the American Studies Program, and a general studies major. There are 4 national honor societies, and 3 departmental honors program.

Faculty/Classroom: 44% of faculty are male; 56%, female. All both teach and do research. The average class size in an introductory lecture is 21; in a laboratory, 23; and in a regular course, 9.

Admissions: 74% of the 2001-2002 applicants were accepted. The ACT scores for the 2001-2002 freshman class were: 55% below 21, 17% between 21 and 23, 19% between 24 and 26, 6% between 27 and 28, and 3% above 28. 33% of the current freshmen were in the top fifth of their class; 62% were in the top two fifths. 4 freshmen graduated first in their class.

Requirements: The ACT is required. In addition, applicants must be graduates of an accredited secondary school. A minimum of 16 academic credits is required and should include at least 12 in the areas of English, math, social science, and natural science. A GPA of 2.5 is required. AP and CLEP credits are accepted. Applications are accepted on-line at the college's web site.

Procedure: Freshmen are admitted to all sessions. Application deadlines are open. The application fee is $20.

Transfer: 63 transfer students enrolled in 2001-2002. Transfer students must have a GPA of 2.0 for unconditional admission. 32 credits of 128 must be completed at WBC.

Visiting: There are regularly scheduled orientations for prospective students, including visits with faculty in fields of interest, mock classes, financial aid sessions, campus tours, and a student panel discussion. There are guides for informal visits and visitors may sit in on classes and stay overnight. To schedule a visit, contact the Director of Admissions at *admissions@wbcoll.edu*

Financial Aid: In 2001-2002, 97% of all freshmen and 98% of continuing students received some form of financial aid. 74% of freshmen and 70% of continuing students received need-based aid. The average freshman award was $8305. Of that total, scholarships or need-based grants averaged $5797 ($11,875 maximum); loans averaged $2307 ($2645 maximum); and work contracts averaged $1296 ($2637 maximum). 44% of undergraduates work part time. Average annual earnings from campus work are $1385. The average financial indebtedness of the 2001 graduate was $15,818. The FAFSA is required. The fall application deadline is May 1.

International Students: There are 10 international students enrolled. The school actively recruits these students. They must score 500 on the written TOEFL and also take the SAT I or ACT, and the college's own interest inventory test, scoring 19 on the ACT.

Computers: WBC uses PCs for all computing, and a computer lab is available to students. All students may access the system. There are no time limits. The fee is $10.

Graduates: In 2001, 90 bachelor's degrees were awarded. The most popular majors were elementary education (26%), psychology (16%), and business administration (13%). In an average class, 14% graduate in 4 years, 23% in 5 years, and 25% in 6 years.

Admissions Contact: Angela Flippo, Director of Admissions. A video is available. E-mail: *admissions@wbclab.edu* Web: *wbc2.wbcoll.edu*

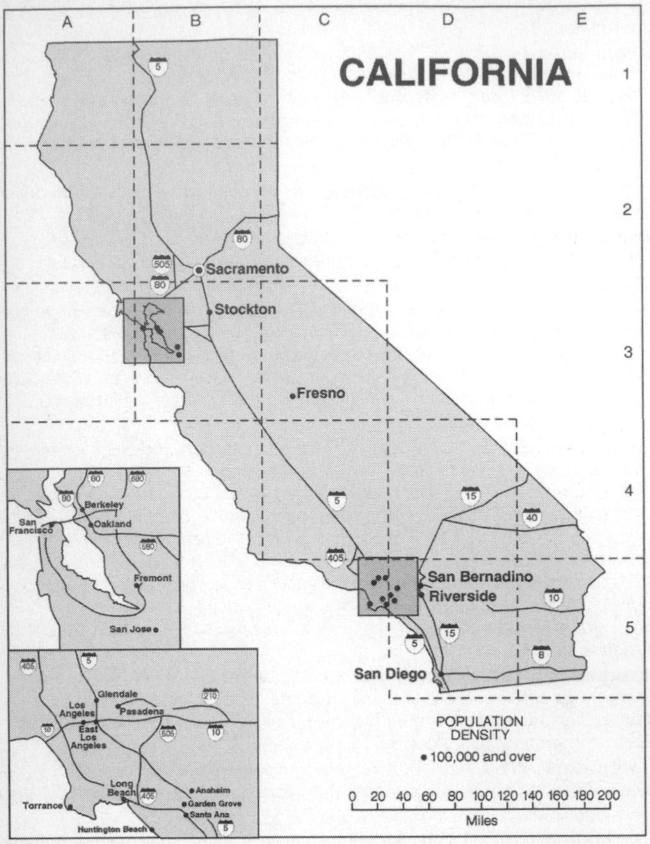

ART CENTER COLLEGE OF DESIGN — C-5

Pasadena, CA 91103 — (626) 396-2373; Fax: (626) 795-0578

Full-time: 831 men, 546 women
Part-time: none
Graduate: 49 men, 39 women
Year: trimesters, summer session
Application Deadline: open
Freshman Class: 1129 applied, 730 accepted, 544 enrolled
SAT I or ACT: required
Faculty: 66
Ph.D.s: 10%
Student/Faculty: 21 to 1
Tuition: $21,110
Room & Board: n/app
SPECIAL

Art Center College of Design, founded in 1930, is a private, nonprofit institution offering programs in fine arts and design. There is 1 graduate school. In addition to regional accreditation, Art Center has baccalaureate program accreditation with NASAD. The library contains 64,000 volumes, 60,000 microform items, and 4000 audiovisual forms/CDs, and subscribes to 400 periodicals. Computerized library services include the card catalog and database searching. Special learning facilities include an art gallery. The 175-acre campus is in a suburban area 10 miles northwest of Los Angeles. There is one building.

Student Life: 56% of undergraduates are from California. Others are from 43 states, 37 foreign countries, and Canada. 39% are white; 32% Asian American; 17% foreign nationals; 10% Hispanic. The average age of freshmen is 23; all undergraduates, 24. 5% do not continue beyond their first year; 60% remain to graduate.

Housing: There are no residence halls. All students commute. Alcohol is not permitted. All students may keep cars.

Activities: There are no fraternities or sororities. There are 12 groups on campus, including ethnic, gay, international, religious, social, and student government.

Sports: There is no sports program at Art Center. Students have access to athletic facilities at Occidental College and California Institute of Technology.

Disabled Students: All of the campus is accessible. Wheelchair ramps, elevators, special parking, specially equipped rest rooms, lowered drinking fountains, and lowered telephones are available.

Services: Counseling and information services are available, as is tutoring in some subjects, including some art classes.

Campus Safety and Security: Measures include 24-hour foot and vehicle patrol, emergency telephones, and lighted pathways/sidewalks.

Programs of Study: Art Center confers B.S. and B.F.A. degrees. Master's degrees are also awarded. Bachelor's degrees are awarded in COMMUNICATIONS AND THE ARTS (advertising, design, film arts, fine arts, graphic design, illustration, industrial design, and photography), ENGINEERING AND ENVIRONMENTAL DESIGN (environmental design). Illustration, graphic design, and industrial design are the largest.

Required: To graduate, students must complete a total of 135 credit hours, with 90 in the major, and 45 units of liberal arts and sciences. Course requirements vary by the program. A minimum GPA of 2.5 and a core curriculum of English Composition and Introduction to Modernism are also required.

Special: The college offers cross-registration with Occidental College and the California Institute of Technology, internships, and nondegree study.

Faculty/Classroom: 72% of faculty are male; 28%, female. 99% teach undergraduates. No introductory courses are taught by graduate students. The average class size in an introductory lecture is 22 and in a regular course, 30.

Admissions: 65% of the 2001-2002 applicants were accepted.

Requirements: The SAT I or ACT is required. In addition, applicants must be graduates of an accredited secondary school or have a GED. Official transcripts and a portfolio must be submitted. An interview is recommended. No applications are accepted on computer disk or on-line. A GPA of 2.5 is required. AP credits are accepted. Important factors in the admissions decision are evidence of special talent, advanced placement or honor courses, and extracurricular activities record.

Procedure: Freshmen are admitted to all sessions. Entrance exams should be taken in the senior year. Application deadlines are open.

Transfer: 466 transfer students enrolled in 2001-2002. Transfer applicants must have a minimum 2.5 GPA and provide official transcripts from all colleges attended. Up to 60 units of liberal arts and studio credits may be transferred. Portfolios are required, and interviews are recommended. Up to 32 of the 45 liberal arts and science units required for graduation may be transferred. There is a 4-semester residency requirement.

Visiting: There are regularly scheduled orientations for prospective students. There are guides for informal visits. To schedule a visit, contact Admissions.

Financial Aid: In 2001-2002, 70% of all freshmen received some form of financial aid. 69% of freshmen and 61% of continuing students received need-based aid. The average freshman award was $9258. 20% of undergraduates work part time. Average annual earnings from campus work are $1767. The average financial indebtedness of the 2001 graduate was $55,810. Art Center is a member of CSS. The FAFSA is required. The fall application deadline is March 1.

International Students: There are 249 international students enrolled. The school actively recruits these students. They must score 550 on the written TOEFL or 213 on the electronic version and also take the college's own test.

Computers: Many personal and graphics computers are available. . There are no time limits and no fees. It is strongly recommended that all students have a personal computer.

Graduates: In 2001, 354 bachelor's degrees were awarded. The most popular majors were illustration (20%), graphic design (19%), and product design (16%). In an average class, 70% graduate in 4 years, and 77% in 5 years. 200 companies recruited on campus in 2000-2001. Of the 2000 graduating class, 94% were employed within 6 months of graduation.

Admissions Contact: Kit Baron, Vice President of Student Services. A video is available. E-mail: *admissions@artcenter.edu*
Web: *www/artcenter.edu*

ART INSTITUTE OF SOUTHERN CALIFORNIA — D-5

Laguna Beach, CA 92651 — (949) 376-6000
(800) 255-0762; Fax: (949) 376-6009

Full-time: 100 men, 60 women
Part-time: 20 men, 30 women
Graduate: none
Year: semesters, summer session
Application Deadline: see profile
Freshman Class: n/av
SAT I or ACT: required
Faculty: 8
Ph.D.s: 85%
Student/Faculty: 20 to 1
Tuition: $14,500
Room & Board: n/app
SPECIAL

The Art Institute of Southern California, founded in 1961, is a nonprofit, independent, institution offering full- and part-time undergraduate art programs leading to the Bachelor of Fine Arts. In addition to regional accreditation, AISC has baccalaureate program accreditation with NASAD. The library contains 15,000 volumes and 300 audiovisual forms/CDs, and subscribes to 90 periodicals. Computerized library services include the card catalog and interlibrary loans. Special learning facilities include a learning resource center and art gallery. The 9-acre campus is in a small town 47 miles southeast of Los Angeles. There are 11 buildings.

Student Life: 60% of undergraduates are from California. Others are from 33 states, 13 foreign countries, and Canada. 85% are from public schools. 66% are white; 13% foreign nationals; 11% Asian American. The average age of freshmen is 19; all undergraduates, 23. 15% do not continue beyond their first year; 60% remain to graduate.

Housing: There are no residence halls. The Institute will assist in the location of off-campus housing. All students commute. Alcohol is not permitted. All students may keep cars.

Activities: There are no fraternities or sororities. There are 2 groups on campus, including art and student government.

Sports: There is no sports program at AISC.

Disabled Students: 90% of the campus is accessible. Special parking, specially equipped rest rooms, special class scheduling, and lowered drinking fountains are available.

Services: There is remedial reading and writing.

Campus Safety and Security: Measures include escort service and night security.

Programs of Study: AISC confers the B.F.A. degree. Bachelor's degrees are awarded in COMMUNICATIONS AND THE ARTS (animation, drawing, graphic design, illustration, and painting).

Required: All students must complete 122 credit hours, with approximately 55 in the major, including studio electives. General education requirements include 30 hours in liberal arts and 15 in art history. 22 hours of studio foundation courses are required, in which students explore all artistic mediums.

Special: Internships are possible, and work-study is available on campus. Students may petition the registrar if they wish to attempt more than 15 semester units.

Faculty/Classroom: 65% of faculty are male; 35%, female. All teach undergraduates. The average class size in an introductory lecture is 15 and in a regular course, 12.

Requirements: The SAT I or ACT is required for applicants currently in high school. Students must be high school graduates or hold an equivalent GED. A personal essay and letter of recommendation are required, as is a personal or telephone interview, and a 10-piece portfolio. A GPA of 2.5 is required. AP and CLEP credits are accepted. Important factors in the admissions decision are evidence of special talent, recommendations by school officials, and ability to finance college education. Applications are accepted on-line at the institute's web site.

Procedure: Freshmen are admitted fall and spring. There is a deferred admissions plan. Early decision applications should be filed by March 2; regular applications, by December 15 for spring entry. Notification is sent on a rolling basis. The fall 2001 application fee was $35.

Transfer: In addition to freshman requirements, transfer students must submit all prior college transcripts. 45 credits of 122 must be completed at AISC.

Visiting: There are regularly scheduled orientations for prospective students, consisting of national portfolio days and open house. There are guides for informal visits and visitors may sit in on classes. To schedule a visit, contact the Admissions Office.

Financial Aid: In a recent year, 92% of all freshmen and 88% of continuing students received some form of financial aid. 43% of freshmen and 48% of continuing students received need-based aid. The average freshman award was $4000. Of that total, scholarships or need-based grants averaged $1000 ($2000 maximum); loans averaged $2400 ($4000 maximum); work contracts averaged $1000 ($1500 maximum); and Cal grants averaged $5400 ($7200 maximum). 50% of undergraduates work part time. AISC is a member of CSS. The CSS/Profile, FAFSA, or FFS and SAAC for California grants are required. Check with the school for current deadlines.

International Students: The school actively recruits these students. They must score 550 on the written TOEFL or 213 on the electronic version and also take the college's own test.

Computers: There are 30 Macs available in a network for student use, with all necessary software for multimedia and full color computer animation. All students may access the system. There are no time limits and no fees. It is strongly recommended that all students have a personal computer.

Admissions Contact: Anthony Padilla, Dean of Admissions. A video is available. E-mail: *admissions@aisc.edu* Web: *www.aisc.edu*

AZUSA PACIFIC UNIVERSITY

Azusa, CA 91702-7000 **D-5**

(626) 812-3016
(800) TALK-APU; (626) 812-3096

Full-time: 1283 men, 2286 women	**Faculty:** 218; IIA, --$
Part-time: 43 men, 42 women	**Ph.D.s:** 73%
Graduate: 1649 men, 1532 women	**Student/Faculty:** 16 to 1
Year: semesters, summer session	**Tuition:** $16,192
Application Deadline: open	**Room & Board:** $6230
Freshman Class: 2257 applied, 1581 accepted, 763 enrolled	
SAT I or ACT: required	**VERY COMPETITIVE**

Azusa Pacific University, founded in 1899, is a private, interdenominational Christian institution offering undergraduate and graduate programs in the liberal arts and emphasizing spiritual growth. There are 6 undergraduate and 6 graduate schools. In addition to regional accreditation, APU has baccalaureate program accreditation with CSWE and NLN. The 2 libraries contain 181,666 volumes, 612,579 microform items, and 14,829 audiovisual forms/CDs, and subscribe to 1417 periodicals. Computerized library services include the card catalog, interlibrary loans, and database searching. Special learning facilities include a learning resource center, art gallery, radio station, and TV station. The 60-acre campus is in a small town 26 miles east of Los Angeles. Including residence halls, there are 67 buildings.

Student Life: 87% of undergraduates are from California. Others are from 32 states, 52 foreign countries, and Canada. 73% are white; 12% Hispanic. The average age of freshmen is 18; all undergraduates, 20. 21% do not continue beyond their first year.

Housing: 1960 students can be accommodated in college housing, which includes single-sex and coed dormitories, on-campus apartments, off-campus apartments, and married-student housing. On-campus housing is available on a first-come, first-served basis and is available on a lottery system for upperclassmen. 60% of students live on campus; of those, 50% remain on campus on weekends. Alcohol is not permitted. All students may keep cars.

Activities: There are no fraternities or sororities. There are 100 groups on campus, including art, band, cheerleading, choir, chorale, chorus, computers, drama, ethnic, honors, international, jazz band, newspaper, orchestra, pep band, photography, political, religious, social, student government, and yearbook. Popular campus events include Missions Week, International Week, and Black Culture Week.

Sports: There are 7 intercollegiate sports for men and 7 for women, and 6 intramural sports for men and 4 for women. Facilities include an all-weather track, a 3000-seat football stadium, a baseball field, a 1200-seat gym, a residence hall lounge, and a recreation room.

Disabled Students: All of the campus is accessible. Wheelchair ramps, elevators, special parking, specially equipped rest rooms, lowered drinking fountains, and lowered telephones are available.

Services: Counseling and information services are available, as is tutoring in most subjects. There is remedial math, reading, and writing.

Campus Safety and Security: Measures include 24-hour foot and vehicle patrol, escort service, shuttle buses, and informal discussions. There are pamphlets/posters/films and lighted pathways/sidewalks.

Programs of Study: APU confers B.A. and B.S. degrees. Master's and doctoral degrees are also awarded. Bachelor's degrees are awarded in BIOLOGICAL SCIENCE (biochemistry, biology/biological science, and life science), BUSINESS (accounting, business administration and management, and marketing/retailing/merchandising), COMMUNICATIONS AND THE ARTS (communications, English, music, and Spanish), COMPUTER AND PHYSICAL SCIENCE (chemistry, computer science, information sciences and systems, mathematics, and physics), EDUCATION (art, music, and physical), ENGINEERING AND ENVIRONMENTAL DESIGN (environmental engineering technology), HEALTH PROFESSIONS (health, nursing, predentistry, and premedicine), SOCIAL SCIENCE (biblical studies, crosscultural studies, history, international studies, liberal arts/general studies, ministries, philosophy, political science/government, psychology, religion, social science, social work, and sociology). Nursing, education, and religion are the strongest academically. Business administration is the largest.

Required: All students must take 126 semester units and earn a minimum GPA of 2.0. 15 units of Bible study, 120 hours of community ministry, and 2 units of health are required. General education requirements include courses in public speaking, fine arts, religion and philosophy, English, algebra, foreign language, and phys ed. Heritage and Institutions, Identity and Relationships, and Nature are also required courses.

Special: Internships in ministerial and American studies, study abroad in Japan, Latin America, Taiwan, and England, and a Washington semester are available. In addition, work-study with the university, a B.A.-B.S. degree, dual majors in all programs, and a 3-2 engineering degree are offered. APU awards credit for life experience and allows nondegree study. There are 2 national honor societies, and a freshman honors program.

Faculty/Classroom: 54% of faculty are male; 46%, female. The average class size in an introductory lecture is 40 and in a regular course, 35.

Admissions: 70% of the 2001-2002 applicants were accepted. The SAT I scores for the 2001-2002 freshman class were: Verbal--24% below 500, 25% between 500 and 599, 45% between 600 and 700, and 7% above 700; Math--24% below 500, 47% between 500 and 599, 25% between 600 and 700, and 4% above 700. The ACT scores were 56% below 23, 38% between 24 and 29, and 7% above 29. 59% of the current freshmen were in the top quarter of their class; 89% were in the top half.
Requirements: The SAT I or ACT is required, but no minimum score is necessary. An essay is required. A portfolio and an interview are recommended for certain programs. The GED is accepted. A GPA of 2.5 is required. AP and CLEP credits are accepted. Important factors in the admissions decision are personality/intangible qualities, evidence of special talent, and advanced placement or honor courses. Applications are accepted on-line at the school's web site.
Procedure: Freshmen are admitted to all sessions. Entrance exams should be taken prior to enrollment. There are early admissions and deferred admissions plans. Application deadlines are open. Application fee is $45. Notifcation is sent on a rolling basis. A waiting list is an active part of the admissions procedure.
Transfer: 398 transfer students enrolled in 2001-2002. Applicants must have a minimum GPA of 2.0 on previous college work. The SAT I or ACT is not required if 30 or more semester units have been completed. An associate degree and an interview are recommended. 30 credits of 126 must be completed at APU.
Visiting: There are regularly scheduled orientations for prospective students, including Seniors Only Day in November and a brother/sister weekend in February that is open to both juniors and seniors. There are guides for informal visits and visitors may sit in on classes and stay overnight. To schedule a visit, contact the Admissions Office.
Financial Aid: In 2001-2002, 60% of all freshmen and 55% of continuing students received some form of financial aid. 60% of freshmen received need-based aid. The average freshman award was $9121. The average financial indebtedness of the 2001 graduate was $18,440. The FAFSA and the college's own financial statement are required. The fall application deadline is July 1.
International Students: The school actively recruits these students. They must score 500 on the written TOEFL.
Computers: 268 computer workstations are available on campus. All students may access the system Monday through Friday 8 A.M. to 11 P.M., Saturday 8:30 A.M. to 8 P.M., and Sunday 1 P.M. to 6 P.M. There are no time limits and no fees. It is recommended that students in Human Development (degree completion program) have personal computers.
Graduates: In 2001, 766 bachelor's degrees were awarded. The most popular major was business administration (32%).
Admissions Contact: Deana Porterfield, Dean of Admissions. A video is available. E-mail: *admissions@apu.edu* Web: *http://www.apu.edu*

BIOLA UNIVERSITY

La Mirada, CA 90639-0001 — **D-5**
(562) 903-4752
(800) OK-BIOLA; Fax: (562) 903-4709

Full-time: 1020 men, 1656 women	**Faculty:** 124; IIA, --$
Part-time: 132 men, 142 women	**Ph.D.s:** n/av
Graduate: 849 men, 523 women	**Student/Faculty:** 22 to 1
Year: 4-1-4, summer session	**Tuition:** $16,630
Application Deadline: June 1	**Room & Board:** $5272
Freshman Class: 2351 applied, 1304 accepted, 640 enrolled	
SAT I Verbal/Math: 600/610	**ACT:** 24 **VERY COMPETITIVE**

Biola University, founded in 1908, is a private, interdenominational Christian institution offering undergraduate and graduate degrees in arts and sciences, psychology, theology, intercultural studies, and business. There are 6 undergraduate and 6 graduate schools. In addition to regional accreditation, Biola has baccalaureate program accreditation with ACBSP, APA, ATS, NASAD, NASM, and NLN. The library contains 273,364 volumes, 525,279 microform items, and 9900 audiovisual forms/CDs, and subscribes to 1123 periodicals. Computerized library services include the card catalog, interlibrary loans, and database searching. Special learning facilities include a learning resource center, art gallery, radio station, TV station, film studio and 3-D art facility, MIDI lab for music composition majors, electronic piano lab, listening lab with music archives, physical science labs, and scanning electron microscope. The 95-acre campus is in a suburban area 22 miles southeast of Los Angeles. Including residence halls, there are 39 buildings.
Student Life: 68% are white; 13% Asian American. Most are Protestant. The average age of freshmen is 18; all undergraduates, 20. 17% do not continue beyond their first year; 60% remain to graduate.
Housing: 1900 students can be accommodated in college housing, which includes single-sex and coed dormitories, on-campus apartments, and off-campus apartments. On-campus housing is available on a first-come, first-served basis. 69% of students live on campus. Alcohol is not permitted. All students may keep cars.
Activities: There are no fraternities or sororities. There are more than 52 groups on campus, including band, cheerleading, chess, chorale, dance, debate, drama, ethnic, film, forensics, gospel choir, honors, international, jazz band, ministries, missionary, musical theater, newspaper, orchestra, political, professional, radio and TV, religious, social, social service, student government, symphony, and yearbook. Popular campus events include Multicultural Week, Christmas Celebration, and Harvest Festival.
Sports: There are 7 intercollegiate sports for men and 8 for women, and 5 intramural sports for men and 5 for women. Facilities include a gym-swimming complex, a 450-seat auditorium, athletic fields, including one for soccer, a quarter-mile track, a baseball diamond, tennis, sand volleyball and basketball courts, and a fitness center.
Disabled Students: Wheelchair ramps, elevators, special parking, specially equipped rest rooms, special class scheduling, lowered drinking fountains, and lowered telephones are available.
Services: Counseling and information services are available, as is tutoring in most subjects. There is a reader service for the blind and a writing center.
Campus Safety and Security: Measures include 24-hour foot and vehicle patrol, self-defense education, escort service, and informal discussions. There are pamphlets/posters/films, emergency telephones, lighted pathways/sidewalks, and a bike patrol.
Programs of Study: Biola confers B.A., B.S., and B.M. degrees. Master's and doctoral degrees are also awarded. Bachelor's degrees are awarded in BIOLOGICAL SCIENCE (biochemistry, and biology/biological science), BUSINESS (business administration and management), COMMUNICATIONS AND THE ARTS (art, communications, English, film arts, music, music performance, music theory and composition, radio/television technology, and Spanish), COMPUTER AND PHYSICAL SCIENCE (computer science, mathematics, and physical sciences), EDUCATION (Christian, education, music, and physical), ENGINEERING AND ENVIRONMENTAL DESIGN (engineering), HEALTH PROFESSIONS (nursing, and speech pathology/audiology), SOCIAL SCIENCE (anthropology, biblical studies, crosscultural studies, history, humanities, philosophy, psychology, social science, and sociology). Business administration, biological science, and chemistry are the strongest academically. Business, organizational leadership, and liberal studies are the largest.
Required: To graduate, students must pass a writing competency exam, complete 30 units of biblical studies and theology, and fulfill the general education and phys ed requirements. At least 130 semester hours must be completed, with 30 hours in the major and 24 of these in upper-division work. Other requirements vary by major. A minimum 2.0 GPA is required.
Special: Cross-registration with the Au Sable Institute of Environmental Studies is possible. Biola offers internships, summer travel tours, study abroad, and an American studies program in Washington D.C., sponsored by the Christian College Coalition. Special programs include L.A. Film Studies, a semester in Hollywood working in the film industry; Biola Baja, a 3-week program at Vermillion Sea Field, Baja; a family studies course at Focus on the Family Institute in Colorado Springs; a China studies program at Fudan University in Shanghai, China; and a development theory studies program in Honduras. Also available are on- and off-campus work-study programs, a B.A.- B.S. degree, a 3-2 engineering degree with the University of Southern California, dual majors, and non-degree study. There are several preprofessional programs available, including prelaw, prephysical therapy, and prechiropractic. A 3-1 program with Los Angeles College of Chiropractic is offered. There are 2 national honor societies, a freshman honors program, and 7 departmental honors programs.
Faculty/Classroom: 75% of faculty are male; 25%, female. 76% teach undergraduates. No introductory courses are taught by graduate students. The average class size in an introductory lecture is 35 and in a laboratory, 15.
Admissions: 55% of the 2001-2002 applicants were accepted. The SAT I scores for the 2001-2002 freshman class were: Verbal--23% below 500, 39% between 500 and 599, 32% between 600 and 700, and 7% above 700; Math--23% below 500, 41% between 500 and 599, 32% between 600 and 700, and 4% above 700. The ACT scores were 23% below 21, 20% between 21 and 23, 23% between 24 and 26, 16% between 27 and 28, and 16% above 28. 68% of the current freshmen were in the top fifth of their class; 89% were in the top two fifths. 39 freshmen graduated first in their class.
Requirements: The SAT I or ACT is required. Applicants need not be graduates of an accredited secondary school. The GED is accepted. Students should have completed 15 academic credits, including 4 years of English and foreign language, 3 years of math, and 2 each of social studies and science. All students must be evangelical Christians who can demonstrate Christian character, leadership ability, and the aptitude for possible success in college. Applicants must submit 2 personal references: 1 from their pastor or someone on the pastoral staff, and 1 from the school last attended, or from an employer if they have been out of school for a year and have been working. An essay and an interview are required. Applications are accepted on-line. A GPA of 3.0 is required. AP and CLEP credits are accepted. Important factors in the admissions decision are personality/intangible qualities, recommendations by school officials, and leadership record.

Procedure: Freshmen are admitted to all sessions. There is a deferred admissions plan. Applications should be filed by June 1 for fall entry and January 1 for spring entry, along with a $45 fee. Notification is sent on a rolling basis.
Transfer: 238 transfer students enrolled in 2001-2002. Applicants with fewer than 27 credit hours must submit both college transcripts and SAT I scores. All students must provide high school transcripts. A minimum 2.0 GPA and an interview are required. 30 credits of 130 must be completed at Biola.
Visiting: There are regularly scheduled orientations for prospective students, including class visits; orientation with the departments of admissions, financial aid, and student affairs; chapel; a sporting event; and a Disneyland or Knott's Berry Farm visit. There are guides for informal visits and visitors may sit in on classes and stay overnight. To schedule a visit, contact the Admissions Office.
Financial Aid: In 2001-2002, 80% of all freshmen and 77% of continuing students received some form of financial aid. 63% of freshmen and 65% of continuing students received need-based aid. The average freshman award was $12,900. Of that total, scholarships or need-based grants averaged $6574; loans averaged $4750; and work contracts averaged $2864 ($3000 maximum). Average annual earnings from campus work are $3318. The FAFSA and the university's own financial statement are required. California residents should submit the Cal Grant GPA verification form. The fall application deadline is March 2.
International Students: There are 120 international students enrolled. The school actively recruits these students. They must score 600 on the written TOEFL or 250 on the electronic version and also take SAT I or the ACT, scoring 920 on the SAT I or 19 on the ACT.
Computers: The mainframes are an HP 9000/Series 300, a DEC VAX 3100, and a DEC VAX 2100. There is 1 main computer center for the HP and VAX terminals. In addition, Mac and IBM PC labs are located throughout the campus. All residence hall rooms have Internet access. All students may access the system every day. There are no time limits and no fees.
Graduates: In 2001, 562 bachelor's degrees were awarded. The most popular majors were organizational leadership (26%), communications (9%), and liberal studies (8%). In an average class, 2% graduate in 3 years, 40% in 4 years, 46% in 5 years, and 53% in 6 years. More than 90 companies recruited on campus in 2000-2001. Of the 2000 graduating class, 45% were employed within 6 months of graduation.
Admissions Contact: Gregory G. Vaughan, Director of Enrollment Management. E-mail: *admissions@biola.edu* Web: *www.biola.edu*

CALIFORNIA BAPTIST UNIVERSITY
Riverside, CA 92504-3297 — D-5
(909) 343-4212
(877)-228-8866; Fax: (909) 343-4525

Full-time: 437 men, 827 women	**Faculty:** 76
Part-time: 113 men, 203 women	**Ph.D.s:** 57%
Graduate: 134 men, 376 women	**Student/Faculty:** 17 to 1
Year: semesters, summer session	**Tuition:** $11,690
Application Deadline: open	**Room & Board:** $5046
Freshman Class: 793 applied, 625 accepted, 216 enrolled	
SAT I Verbal/Math: 504/490	**ACT:** 20 **COMPETITIVE**

California Baptist University, founded in 1950, is a private institution supported by the California Southern Baptist Convention and offering degree programs in the arts and sciences, business, and religious studies. There are 5 undergraduate and 3 graduate schools. In addition to regional accreditation, Cal Baptist has baccalaureate program accreditation with ACBSP and NASM. The library contains 90,953 volumes, 47,106 microform items, and 4367 audiovisual forms/CDs, and subscribes to 336 periodicals. Computerized library services include the card catalog, interlibrary loans, and database searching. Special learning facilities include a learning resource center and art gallery. The 60-acre campus is in a suburban area 60 miles east of Los Angeles. Including residence halls, there are 12 buildings.
Student Life: 95% of undergraduates are from California. Others are from 19 states, 15 foreign countries, and Canada. 56% are white; 12% Hispanic. 70% are Protestant; 22% claim no religious affiliation. The average age of freshmen is 19; all undergraduates, 28. 19% do not continue beyond their first year.
Housing: 808 students can be accommodated in college housing, which includes single-sex dormitories, on-campus apartments, off-campus apartments, and married-student housing. On-campus housing is guaranteed for all 4 years. 53% of students commute. Alcohol is not permitted. All students may keep cars.
Activities: There are no fraternities or sororities. There are 14 groups on campus, including art, choir, chorale, chorus, computers, debate, drama, ethnic, forensics, honors, international, musical theater, newspaper, pep band, political, professional, religious, social service, student government, and yearbook. Popular campus events include Campus Day, Twirp Week, and Christmas Yule.
Sports: There are 8 intercollegiate sports for men and 8 for women, and 8 intramural sports for men and 8 for women. Facilities include a 950-seat gym, baseball, soccer, and softball fields, tennis and sand volleyball courts, an Olympic swimming facility, and a fitness center.
Disabled Students: 95% of the campus is accessible. Wheelchair ramps, elevators, special parking, and specially equipped rest rooms are available.
Services: Counseling and information services are available, as is tutoring in most subjects. There is remedial math, reading, and writing.
Campus Safety and Security: Measures include 24-hour foot and vehicle patrol, self-defense education, escort service, and informal discussions. There are pamphlets/posters/films, emergency telephones, and lighted pathways/sidewalks.
Programs of Study: Cal Baptist confers B.A., B.S., and B.B.A. degrees. Master's degrees are also awarded. Bachelor's degrees are awarded in BIOLOGICAL SCIENCE (biology/biological science), BUSINESS (business administration and management, and organizational behavior), COMMUNICATIONS AND THE ARTS (art, communications, English, fine arts, and music), COMPUTER AND PHYSICAL SCIENCE (information sciences and systems and mathematics), EDUCATION (physical), HEALTH PROFESSIONS (exercise science), SOCIAL SCIENCE (behavioral science, Christian studies, criminal justice, history, liberal arts/general studies, philosophy, political science/government, psychology, social science, and youth ministry). Education, behavioral science, and English are the strongest academically. Behavioral sciences and education are the largest.
Required: All students must complete courses in fine arts, humanities, natural sciences, religion, social sciences, and phys ed. A total of 124 units, with a minimum GPA of 2.0, is required to graduate.
Special: Cal Baptist offers an accelerated program in several disciplines. Study abroad, in at least 6 countries, internships, work-study programs, a Washington semester, B.A.-B.S. degrees, and credit for military/work experience are available. There are 2 national honor societies.
Faculty/Classroom: 62% of faculty are male; 38%, female. 95% teach undergraduates. No introductory courses are taught by graduate students. The average class size in an introductory lecture is 30; in a laboratory, 10; and in a regular course, 19.
Admissions: 79% of the 2001-2002 applicants were accepted. The SAT I scores for the 2001-2002 freshman class were: Verbal--47% below 500, 37% between 500 and 599, 15% between 600 and 700, and 1% above 700; Math--52% below 500, 38% between 500 and 599, 8% between 600 and 700, and 2% above 700. The ACT scores were 53% below 21, 24% between 21 and 23, 11% between 24 and 26, 8% between 27 and 28, and 4% above 28.
Requirements: The SAT I or ACT is required. In addition, applicants should be graduates of an accredited high school or have a GED. An essay and interview are recommended, and 2 references, preferably from a church leader and an official of an academic institution, are required. A GPA of 2.5 is required. AP and CLEP credits are accepted. Important factors in the admissions decision are recommendations by school officials, leadership record, and advanced placement or honor courses. Applications are accepted on-line at *www.calbaptist.edu*
Procedure: Freshmen are admitted fall and spring. Entrance exams should be taken during the junior year. There is a deferred admissions plan. Application deadlines are open. The application fee is $45. Notification is sent on a rolling basis.
Transfer: 100 transfer students enrolled in 2001-2002. Applicants must have a minimum GPA of 2.0, if they are transferring in at least 30 transferable semester units. Only courses with a grade C- or better may transfer. If less than 30 units, their high school GPA must be at least 2.5 and they must submit SAT I or ACT scores. Only courses with a grade C -or better may transfer. 36 credits of 124 must be completed at Cal Baptist.
Visiting: There are regularly scheduled orientations for prospective students, consisting of a welcome, orientation, academic fair, and tours. There are guides for informal visits and visitors may sit in on classes and stay overnight. To schedule a visit, contact the Admissions Office.
Financial Aid: In 2001-2002, 89% of all freshmen and 95% of continuing students received some form of financial aid. 65% of freshmen and 79% of continuing students received need-based aid. The average freshman award was $8400. Of that total, scholarships or need-based grants averaged $4300; loans averaged $2500; and work contracts averaged $1100. 18% of undergraduates work part time. Average annual earnings from campus work are $1000. The average financial indebtedness of the 2001 graduate was $18,300. The FAFSA is required.
International Students: The school actively recruits these students. They must score 520 on the written TOEFL and also take an English proficiency exam. The college requires a minimum score of 19 on the ACT, 920 on the SAT I.
Computers: The mainframe is an HP 9000/Series 836. Academic computer labs house 63 computers available for student use. All students may access the system during open lab and library hours. There are no time limits and no fees.
Graduates: In 2001, 487 bachelor's degrees were awarded. The most popular majors were liberal studies (education) (47%), psychology/behavioral science (12%), and business (12%). In an average class, 3% graduate in 3 years, 34% in 4 years, 52% in 5 years, and 53% in 6 years. 9 companies recruited on campus in 2000-2001.

Admissions Contact: Allen Johnson, Director, Undergraduate Admissions. E-mail: *admissions@calbaptist.edu* Web: *www.calbaptist.edu*

CALIFORNIA COLLEGE OF ARTS AND CRAFTS B-3

San Francisco, CA 94107 (415) 703-9535
(800) 447-1ART; Fax: (415) 703-9539

Full-time: 406 men, 614 women	**Faculty:** 35
Part-time: 60 men, 84 women	**Ph.D.s:** 60%
Graduate: 41 men, 86 women	**Student/Faculty:** 29 to 1
Year: semesters, summer session	**Tuition:** $20,690
Application Deadline: February 15	**Room & Board:** $6676
Freshman Class: 451 applied, 321 accepted, 123 enrolled	
SAT I Verbal/Math: 547/507	**ACT:** 22 **SPECIAL**

California College of Arts and Crafts, established in 1907, is a private professional arts institution offering programs in fine arts, design, and architecture studies. There are 4 graduate schools. In addition to regional accreditation, CCAC has baccalaureate program accreditation with FIDER, NAAB, and NASAD. The 2 libraries contain 39,000 volumes, 50 microform items, and 520 audiovisual forms/CDs, and subscribe to 340 periodicals. Computerized library services include the card catalog, interlibrary loans, and database searching. Special learning facilities include a learning resource center and art gallery. The 4-acre campus is in an urban area. Including residence halls, there are 15 buildings.

Student Life: 70% of undergraduates are from California. Others are from 37 states, 25 foreign countries, and Canada. 82% are from public schools. 56% are white; 11% Asian American. The average age of freshmen is 18; all undergraduates, 24. 20% do not continue beyond their first year.

Housing: 275 students can be accommodated in college housing, which includes coed dormitories and on-campus apartments. On-campus housing is guaranteed for the freshman year only, is available on a first-come, first-served basis, and on a lottery system for upperclassmen. Priority is given to out-of-town students. 88% of students commute. Alcohol is not permitted. No one may keep cars.

Activities: There are no fraternities or sororities. There are 11 groups on campus, including art, ethnic, gay, honors, international, newspaper, professional, and student government. Popular campus events include All-College Honors, Holiday and Spring Fair, and Student Gala.

Sports: There is no sports program at CCAC.

Disabled Students: 80% of the campus is accessible. Wheelchair ramps, elevators, special parking, specially equipped rest rooms, special class scheduling, lowered drinking fountains, and lowered telephones are available.

Services: Counseling and information services are available, as is tutoring in some subjects, including humanities and sciences.

Campus Safety and Security: Measures include self-defense education, escort service, shuttle buses, and informal discussions. There are pamphlets/posters/films, emergency telephones, and lighted pathways/sidewalks.

Programs of Study: CCAC confers B.Arch. and B.F.A. degrees. Master's degrees are also awarded. Bachelor's degrees are awarded in COMMUNICATIONS AND THE ARTS (ceramic art and design, film arts, glass, graphic design, illustration, industrial design, metal/jewelry, painting, photography, printmaking, and sculpture), ENGINEERING AND ENVIRONMENTAL DESIGN (architecture, furniture design, and interior design), SOCIAL SCIENCE (fashion design and technology, and textiles and clothing). Design, painting/drawing, and illustration are the largest.

Required: Students must successfully complete 126 credits for the B.F.A., with 57 in the major, and 162 for the B.Arch., with 96 in the major. Distribution requirements are 51 credits in humanities and science plus 75 in studio work for fine arts majors and 111 in studio work for architecture majors. All students must complete the core curriculum and maintain a minimum GPA of 2.0.

Special: Co-op programs in design are available. Cross-registration is permitted with Mills and Holy Names colleges in Oakland and with the University of San Francisco in San Francisco. Opportunities are provided for internships, study abroad in 11 countries, student-designed majors, and nondegree study. The Association of Independent Colleges of Art and Design Mobility Program is also possible.

Faculty/Classroom: 55% of faculty are male; 45%, female. 98% teach undergraduates. No introductory courses are taught by graduate students. The average class size in an introductory lecture is 22 and in a regular course, 17.

Admissions: 71% of the 2001-2002 applicants were accepted. The SAT I scores for the 2001-2002 freshman class were: Verbal--26% below 500, 50% between 500 and 599, 19% between 600 and 700, and 5% above 700; Math--45% below 500, 37% between 500 and 599, and 18% between 600 and 700. The ACT scores were 14% below 21, 50% between 21 and 23, 27% between 24 and 26, and 9% between 27 and 28.

Requirements: The SAT I or ACT is recommended. In addition, graduation from an accredited secondary school is required; a GED will be accepted. An essay, portfolio, and letters of recommendation are required. An interview is strongly recommended. A GPA of 2.0 is required. AP credits are accepted. Important factors in the admissions decision are evidence of special talent, recommendations by school officials, and extracurricular activities record.

Procedure: Freshmen are admitted fall and spring. Applications should be filed by February 15 for fall entry and October 1 for spring entry, along with a $40 fee. Notification is sent on a rolling basis.

Transfer: 185 transfer students enrolled in 2001-2002. Applicants must submit a portfolio. 30 credits of 126 must be completed at CCAC.

Visiting: There are regularly scheduled orientations for prospective students, including fall and spring open houses and orientation for admitted students a week prior to the start of the semester. There are guides for informal visits and visitors may sit in on classes. To schedule a visit, contact the Office of Enrollment Services, at (800) 447-1ART or (415) 703-9523.

Financial Aid: In 2001-2002, 57% of all freshmen and 65% of continuing students received some form of financial aid. 53% of freshmen and 63% of continuing students received need-based aid. The average freshman award was $17,645. Of that total, scholarships or need-based grants averaged $9069 ($17,420 maximum); loans averaged $2655 ($5000 maximum); and work contracts averaged $2000 ($2500 maximum). All undergraduates work part time. Average annual earnings from campus work are $1500. The average financial indebtedness of the 2001 graduate was $25,361. The FAFSA and the college's own financial statement are required. The fall application deadline is March 1.

International Students: There are 84 international students enrolled. They must score 550 on the written TOEFL or 213 on the electronic version.

Computers: The mainframe is an HP 3000. Mulitmedia computer labs on both campuses house Mac Power PCs and Quadras, scanners, printers, removable media drives, CD recorders, and Quick Cam cameras. Various software is available. The labs are networked to the Internet. All students may access the system. There are no time limits and no fees.

Graduates: In 2001, 100 bachelor's degrees were awarded. The most popular majors were graphic design (30%), painting/drawing (14%), and individualized major (9%). In an average class, 57% graduate in 6 years.

Admissions Contact: Sheri Sivin McKenzie, Vice President for Enrollment Management. E-mail: *smckenzie@ccac-art.edu*
Web: *www.ccac-art.edu*

CALIFORNIA INSTITUTE OF TECHNOLOGY C-5

Pasadena, CA 91125 (626) 395-6341
(800) 568-8324; Fax: (626) 683-3026

Full-time: 633 men, 309 women	**Faculty:** 294; I, ++$
Part-time: none	**Ph.D.s:** 100%
Graduate: 836 men, 280 women	**Student/Faculty:** 3 to 1
Year: quarters	**Tuition:** $21,120
Application Deadline: January 1	**Room & Board:** $6543
Freshman Class: 3365 applied, 515 accepted, 214 enrolled	
SAT I Verbal/Math: 740/790	**MOST COMPETITIVE**

California Institute of Technology, founded in 1891, is a private institution offering programs in engineering, science, and math. In addition to regional accreditation, Caltech has baccalaureate program accreditation with ABET. The 16 libraries contain 3,165,000 volumes, 821 microform items, and 824 audiovisual forms/CDs, and subscribe to 4500 periodicals. Computerized library services include the card catalog, interlibrary loans, and database searching. Special learning facilities include a learning resource center. The 124-acre campus is in a suburban area 12 miles northeast of Los Angeles. Including residence halls, there are 103 buildings.

Student Life: 58% of undergraduates are from out of state, mostly the West. Others are from 47 states, 33 foreign countries, and Canada. 85% are from public schools. 56% are white; 25% Asian American; 10% foreign nationals. The average age of freshmen is 18; all undergraduates, 20. 2% do not continue beyond their first year.

Housing: 820 students can be accommodated in college housing, which includes coed dormitories, off-campus apartments, and married-student housing. On-campus housing is guaranteed for all 4 years. 87% of students live on campus. Alcohol is not permitted. All students may keep cars.

Activities: There are no fraternities or sororities. There are 85 groups on campus, including art, band, cheerleading, chess, choir, chorale, chorus, computers, dance, drama, ethnic, film, gay, honors, international, jazz band, literary magazine, musical theater, newspaper, orchestra, pep band, photography, political, professional, religious, social, social service, student government, symphony, and yearbook. Popular campus events include Ditch Day, International Day, and Pre-Frosh Weekend.

Sports: There are 10 intercollegiate sports for men and 8 for women, and 16 intramural sports for men and 13 for women. Facilities include 2 Olympic-size swimming pools, a 300-seat gym, a 440-meter track, a football field, 4 baseball fields, and 8 tennis courts. Another athletic facility includes a gym, a 4000-square foot exercise room with equipment, and racquetball courts.

Disabled Students: 98% of the campus is accessible. Wheelchair ramps, elevators, special parking, specially equipped rest rooms, and lowered telephones are available.
Services: Counseling and information services are available, as is tutoring in every subject. There is a reader service for the blind.
Campus Safety and Security: Measures include 24-hour foot and vehicle patrol, self-defense education, escort service, and informal discussions. There are pamphlets/posters/films, emergency telephones, and lighted pathways/sidewalks.
Programs of Study: Caltech confers the B.S. degree. Master's and doctoral degrees are also awarded. Bachelor's degrees are awarded in BIOLOGICAL SCIENCE (biology/biological science), COMMUNICATIONS AND THE ARTS (literature), COMPUTER AND PHYSICAL SCIENCE (astronomy, chemistry, geochemistry, geology, geophysics and seismology, mathematics, physics, and planetary and space science), ENGINEERING AND ENVIRONMENTAL DESIGN (aeronautical engineering, chemical engineering, civil engineering, electrical/electronics engineering, engineering, engineering and applied science, and mechanical engineering), SOCIAL SCIENCE (economics, history, political science/government, and social science). Engineering, applied science, and electrical engineering are the largest.
Required: All students must complete 108 units in humanities and social science, 90 each in math and physics, 21 in chemistry, 9 in biology, 6 in lab, and 9 in additional science courses, and 3 terms of phys ed. A total of 780 quarter units, including 516 in the major, and a minimum GPA of 1.9 are required to graduate.
Special: Caltech offers cross-registration with Scripps College, Occidental College, and Art Center College of Design, various work-study programs, including those with NASA's Jet Propulsion Laboratory, dual majors in any major, and independent studies degrees with faculty-approved student-designed majors. A 3-2 engineering degree is possible with several institutions. Pass/fail options are available for freshmen. A summer undergraduate research fellowship program is offered. Study abroad at Cambridge University in England is possible.
Faculty/Classroom: 85% of faculty are male; 15%, female. All both teach and do research. No introductory courses are taught by graduate students. The average class size in an introductory lecture is 150 and in a regular course, 12.
Admissions: 15% of the 2001-2002 applicants were accepted. The SAT I scores for the 2001-2002 freshman class were: Verbal--1% below 500, 1% between 500 and 599, 19% between 600 and 700, and 80% above 700; Math--2% between 600 and 700, and 98% above 700. All of the current freshmen were in the top fifth of their class. There were 53 National Merit finalists. 85 freshmen graduated first in their class.
Requirements: The SAT I is required. In addition, SAT II: Subject tests in writing, math level II, and one in physics, biology, or chemistry are also required. Applicants should have completed 4 years of high school math, 3 of English, 1 each of chemistry and history, and 5 units from other concentrations. Important factors in the admissions decision are advanced placement or honor courses, recommendations by school officials, and evidence of special talent.
Procedure: Freshmen are admitted in the fall. Entrance exams should be taken through December of the senior year. There are early action, early admissions, and deferred admissions plans. Early action applications should be filed by November 1; regular applications, by January 1 for fall entry, along with a $50 fee. Applications are accepted on-line at *embark.com*. Notification of early action is sent December 31; regular decision, April 1. 151 early action candidates were accepted for the 2001-2002 class. 2% of all applicants are on a waiting list.
Transfer: 18 transfer students enrolled in 2001-2002. Transfers, admitted only into sophomore and junior classes, need a minimum GPA of 3.0. Applicants must have completed 1 year (2 years for juniors) of calculus and calculus-based physics, and must take Caltech's entrance exams in math and physics. Chemistry or chemical engineering majors also should have completed 1 year of chemistry and must take an additional entrance exam. 216 credits of 780 must be completed at Caltech.
Visiting: There are regularly scheduled orientations for prospective students, including a campus tour leaving every day at 1:45 P.M. from Public Relations, followed by an Admissions Office information session. There are guides for informal visits and visitors may sit in on classes. To schedule a visit, contact the Admissions Office/Visitor's Center.
Financial Aid: In 2001-2002, 61% of all freshmen and 58% of continuing students received some form of financial aid. 53% of freshmen and 51% of continuing students received need-based aid. The average freshman award was $21,416. The average financial indebtedness of the 2001 graduate was $12,621. Caltech is a member of CSS. The CSS/Profile or FAFSA is required. The fall application deadline is January 15.
International Students: There are 92 international students enrolled. Students must take the SAT I and SAT II: Subject tests in Math level IIC, writing, and chemistry, physics, or biology.
Computers: The mainframe is a SUN/UNIX cluster. Terminals are located in all buildings, including student housing. The mainframe computer can also be accessed from student-owned PCs. All students may access the system anytime. There are no time limits and no fees. It is strongly recommended that all students have a personal computer.
Graduates: In 2001, 204 bachelor's degrees were awarded. The most popular majors were engineering and applied science (50%), physical sciences (33%), and biology (9%). In an average class, 81% graduate in 6 years. 130 companies recruited on campus in 2000-2001. Of the 2000 graduating class, 500% were enrolled in graduate school within 6 months of graduation and 50% were employed.
Admissions Contact: Charlene Liebau, Director of Admissions.
E-mail: *ugadmissions@caltech.edu* Web: *www.admissions.caltech.edu*

CALIFORNIA INSTITUTE OF THE ARTS
Valencia, CA 91355 — C-5
(661) 255-1050
(800) 545-ARTS; Fax: (805) 254-8352

Full-time: 467 men, 349 women	**Faculty:** n/av
Part-time: 6 men, 1 woman	**Ph.D.s:** n/av
Graduate: 205 men, 217 women	**Student/Faculty:** 7 to 1
Year: semesters	**Tuition:** $21,275
Application Deadline: January 11	**Room & Board:** $6000
Freshman Class: 1271 applied, 467 accepted, 135 enrolled	
SAT I or ACT: not required	**SPECIAL**

California Institute of the Arts, founded in 1961, is a private, nonprofit institution offering undergraduate and graduate programs in art, dance, film and video, music, and theater, and graduate majors in directing, integrated media, and writing. There are 6 undergraduate and 6 graduate schools. In addition to regional accreditation, Cal Arts has baccalaureate program accreditation with NASAD, NASD, NASM, and NAST. The library contains 96,306 volumes, 5320 microform items, and 17,718 audiovisual forms/CDs, and subscribes to 382 periodicals. Computerized library services include the card catalog, interlibrary loans, and database searching. Special learning facilities include an art gallery, radio station, TV station, movie theater, sound stages, scenery construction shops, and slide and film libraries. The 60-acre campus is in a suburban area 30 miles north of Los Angeles. Including residence halls, there are 3 buildings.
Student Life: 57% of undergraduates are from out of state, mostly the Midwest. Others are from 48 states, 39 foreign countries, and Canada. 70% are white; 14% foreign nationals; 11% Asian American; 10% Hispanic. The average age of freshmen is 19; all undergraduates, 22. 13% do not continue beyond their first year.
Housing: 450 students can be accommodated in college housing, which includes coed dormitories and on-campus apartments. On-campus housing is available on a first-come, first-served basis and is available on a lottery system for upperclassmen. Priority is given to out-of-town students. 53% of students live on campus. All students may keep cars.
Activities: There are no fraternities or sororities. There are 17 groups on campus, including art, choir, chorale, chorus, dance, drama, ethnic, film, gay, international, jazz band, literary magazine, newspaper, opera, orchestra, photography, radio and TV, religious, student government, and symphony. Popular campus events include music festivals, theater productions, and poetry readings.
Sports: There is no sports program at Cal Arts. Facilities include tennis courts, sand volleyball courts and a swimming pool.
Disabled Students: 95% of the campus is accessible. Wheelchair ramps, elevators, special parking, specially equipped rest rooms, special class scheduling, lowered drinking fountains, and lowered telephones are available.
Services: Counseling and information services are available, as is tutoring in some subjects, as well as all-computerized media systems used in the 6 major departments, and other subjects, which vary each year. There is a reader service for the blind.
Campus Safety and Security: Measures include 24-hour foot and vehicle patrol, escort service, informal discussions, and pamphlets/posters/films. There are lighted pathways/sidewalks.
Programs of Study: Cal Arts confers the B.F.A. degree. Master's degrees are also awarded. Bachelor's degrees are awarded in COMMUNICATIONS AND THE ARTS (dance, dramatic arts, film arts, fine arts, and music). Art and music are the strongest academically. Film and video and art are the largest.
Required: To graduate, all students must complete a total of 120 credit hours, with 48 in critical studies and 72 in the major, and must satisfy all curriculum and degree requirements of the particular school.
Special: Cal Arts offers internships with local and national companies, student-designed majors, interdisciplinary studies, study abroad in 6 countries, and a cooperative education program.
Faculty/Classroom: 60% of faculty are male; 40%, female. No introductory courses are taught by graduate students. The average class size in an introductory lecture is 15 and in a regular course, 8.
Admissions: 37% of the 2001-2002 applicants were accepted. There was 1 National Merit semifinalist.
Requirements: Applicants must be graduates of an accredited secondary school or have a GED certificate. They must submit an official transcript and an essay. Portfolios and auditions are required and an interview is recommended. AP credits are accepted. Important factors in the

admissions decision are evidence of special talent and advanced placement or honor courses.

Procedure: Freshmen are admitted fall and spring. There is a deferred admissions plan. Applications should be filed by January 11 for fall entry and November 15 for spring entry. Notification is sent on a rolling basis. 1% of all applicants are on a waiting list. The fall 2001 application fee was $60.

Transfer: 147 transfer students enrolled in 2001-2002. Applicants must submit official college and high school transcripts. An audition or a portfolio is required. Depending on the program, at least 1 or 2 years, including the final semester, must be completed in residence.

Visiting: There are regularly scheduled orientations for prospective students, including tours held Monday through Friday at 12 P.M. throughout the academic year. Visitors may sit in on classes. To schedule a visit, contact the Office of Admissions.

Financial Aid: In 2001-2002, 72% of all freshmen and 79% of continuing students received some form of financial aid. 62% of freshmen and 68% of continuing students received need-based aid. The average freshman award was $18,688. Of that total, scholarships or need-based grants averaged $7880 ($22,792 maximum); loans averaged $12,924 ($32,073 maximum); work contracts averaged $2361 ($2400 maximum); and tutiton remission averaged $20,930 (maximum). 23% of undergraduates work part time. Average annual earnings from campus work are $1536. The average financial indebtedness of the 2001 graduate was $25,069. Cal Arts is a member of CSS. The FAFSA is required. The fall application deadline is March 2.

International Students: There are 176 international students enrolled. They must score 550 on the written TOEFL.

Computers: In addition to the library's computer center, the graphic design school has a Mac computer-imaging, text, and visual motion lab. The film and video school offers computer animation labs and editing equipment. The theater and dance schools feature computerized lighting facilities, and the music school has computerized composition and digital synthesis systems. All students may access the system. There are no time limits and no fees.

Graduates: In 2001, 151 bachelor's degrees were awarded. The most popular majors were animation (20%), art/photography (20%), and music performance (20%). In an average class, 52% graduate in 4 years. 25 companies recruited on campus in a recent year.

Admissions Contact: Carol Kim, Director of Enrollment Services. E-mail: *admiss@calarts.edu* Web: *www.calarts.edu*

CALIFORNIA LUTHERAN UNIVERSITY C-5
Thousand Oaks, CA 91360-2700 (805) 493-3135
(877) 258-3678; Fax: (805) 493-3114

Full-time: 1570 men and women	**Faculty:** 90; IIA, --$
Part-time: 260 men and women	**Ph.D.s:** 85%
Graduate: 940 men and women	**Student/Faculty:** 18 to 1
Year: semesters, summer session	**Tuition:** $17,000
Application Deadline: March 1	**Room & Board:** $6500
Freshman Class: n/av	
SAT I or ACT: required	**LESS COMPETITIVE**

California Lutheran University, founded in 1959, is a private, nonprofit liberal arts institution affiliated with the Evangelical Lutheran Church of America. The comprehensive university offers undergraduate programs in arts and sciences and education. Figures in the above capsule are approximate. There are 3 undergraduate and 4 graduate schools. The library contains 114,280 volumes, 18,080 microform items, and 1140 audiovisual forms/CDs, and subscribes to 610 periodicals. Computerized library services include the card catalog, interlibrary loans, and database searching. Special learning facilities include a learning resource center, radio station, TV station, and a state-of-the-art science center. The 290-acre campus is in an urban area 45 miles north of Los Angeles in Ventura County, midway between Santa Barbara and L.A. Including residence halls, there are 40 buildings.

Student Life: 80% of undergraduates are from California. Others are from 28 states, 40 foreign countries, and Canada. 85% are from public schools. 80% are white; 10% Hispanic. 55% are Protestant; 30% claim no religious affiliation; 20% Catholic. The average age of freshmen is 18; all undergraduates, 20. 30% do not continue beyond their first year; 50% remain to graduate.

Housing: 860 students can be accommodated in college housing, which includes coed dormitories, a quiet hall, and graduate housing; there are senior singles. On-campus housing is guaranteed for all 4 years. 60% of students live on campus; of those, 75% remain on campus on weekends. Alcohol is not permitted. All students may keep cars.

Activities: There are no fraternities or sororities. There are 35 groups on campus, including art, band, cheerleading, choir, chorale, chorus, computers, dance, debate, drama, drum and bugle corps, environmental, ethnic, honors, international, jazz band, literary magazine, marching band, musical theater, newspaper, orchestra, pep band, photography, political, professional, radio and TV, religious, social, social service, student alumni, student government, symphony, and yearbook. Popular campus events include Santa Lucia, Scandinavian Day, and the Pulitzer Prize Symposium.

Sports: There are 8 intercollegiate sports for men and 7 for women, and 5 intramural sports for men and 5 for women. Facilities include a 400-seat gym, 2 fields, a swimming pool, tennis courts, and a 2000-seat stadium.

Disabled Students: 60% of the campus is accessible. Wheelchair ramps, elevators, special parking, specially equipped rest rooms, lowered drinking fountains, and lowered telephones are available.

Services: Counseling and information services are available, as is tutoring in every subject. The learning resources and writing centers offer help with study and writing skills. There is remedial math, reading, and writing. A student support services program helps low-income first-generation students adapt to the academic and social life of the campus.

Campus Safety and Security: Measures include 24-hour foot and vehicle patrol, escort service, informal discussions, and pamphlets/posters/films. There are emergency telephones and lighted pathways/sidewalks. All residence halls are equipped with security systems.

Programs of Study: CLU confers B.A. and B.S. degrees. Master's degrees are also awarded. Bachelor's degrees are awarded in BIOLOGICAL SCIENCE (biochemistry and biology/biological science), BUSINESS (accounting, business administration and management, and marketing/retailing/merchandising), COMMUNICATIONS AND THE ARTS (art, communications, dramatic arts, English, French, German, multimedia, music, and Spanish), COMPUTER AND PHYSICAL SCIENCE (chemistry, computer science, geology, information sciences and systems, mathematics, and physics), EDUCATION (education and physical), HEALTH PROFESSIONS (predentistry, premedicine, and sports medicine), SOCIAL SCIENCE (criminal justice, economics, history, interdisciplinary studies, international studies, liberal arts/general studies, philosophy, political science/government, prelaw, psychology, religion, social science, and sociology). Biology, accounting, and humanities are the strongest academically. Business, psychology, and communication arts are the largest.

Required: To graduate, all students must complete a core curriculum including 16 to 20 units in social science, 8 each in religion, foreign language, and science, 7 in English, 4 to 6 in creative arts, 4 in math, and 3 in phys ed. Students must also fulfill content requirements of a freshman cluster and take 2 writing-intensive courses, global studies, gender and ethnic studies, and a senior-level capstone course. Also needed are a total of 124 units, 36 of which must be upper division with 32 hours in the major for a B.A. and a minimum of 36 hours for a B.S. The final 30 credits before graduation must be completed at CLU. Students must have a minimum 2.0 GPA, with 2.25 in the major.

Special: CLU offers co-op programs, cross-registration with Wagner College, internships, and study abroad in 20 countries. Also available are work-study, accelerated degrees in business, computer science, and accounting, a general studies degree, and dual and student-designed interdisciplinary degree majors. A 3-2 engineering degree with Washington University of St. Louis, credit for experiential learning, special student status for nondegree study, pass/fail options, continuing education, English as a second language, and an adult degree evening program are also offered. There are 4 national honor societies, and a freshman honors program.

Faculty/Classroom: 65% of faculty are male; 35%, female. 94% teach undergraduates. No introductory courses are taught by graduate students. The average class size in an introductory lecture is 35; in a laboratory, 17; and in a regular course, 22.

Requirements: The SAT I or ACT is required. Minimum composite scores are 800 for the SAT I (400 verbal) and 19 for the ACT. Applicants must be graduates of an accredited secondary school and have completed a minimum of 4 years of English, 2 years each of math, foreign language, and social studies, and 1 of lab science. The GED is accepted. An essay is required and an interview is recommended. A GPA of 2.75 is required. AP and CLEP credits are accepted. Important factors in the admissions decision are advanced placement or honor courses, recommendations by school officials, and evidence of special talent. Applications are accepted on computer disk.

Procedure: Freshmen are admitted fall and spring. Entrance exams should be taken in the fall. There are early decision and deferred admissions plans. Applications should be filed by March 1 for fall entry and October 1 for spring entry. Notification is sent on a rolling basis. The fall 2001 application fee was $45.

Transfer: Transfers must have a minimum 2.25 GPA and at least 24 credit hours earned. An application is required. An interview is recommended. Applicants must be in good standing at the previous college and may submit a recommendation from a college professor in lieu of a high school recommendation. 30 credits of 124 must be completed at CLU.

Visiting: There are regularly scheduled orientations for prospective students, including an admission and financial aid interview, a tour, visits with faculty or coaches, and lunch. There are guides for informal visits and visitors may sit in on classes and stay overnight. To schedule a visit, contact the Admission Office.

Financial Aid: In a recent year, 90% of all freshmen and 80% of continuing students received some form of financial aid. 45% of undergraduates work part time. Average annual earnings from campus work are $1000. The FAFSA is required. The priority application deadline for financiad aid is March 1.
International Students: The school actively recruits these students. They must score 530 on the written TOEFL and also take the college's own test.
Computers: The mainframes are an HP 9000-825, and a DEC VAX 11/750. Students may access the network through 72 terminals in the library and labs. Mac and IBM labs are in the computer science building. The Ahmanson Science Center has a hypermedia lab with 14 Macs. 6 halls contain 3 Macs with printers. All students may access the system any time. There are no time limits and no fees.
Admissions Contact: Marc D. Meredith, Director of Admission. E-mail: *meredith@clunet.edu* Web: *www.clunet.edu*

CALIFORNIA MARITIME ACADEMY B-3
Vallejo, CA 94590-0644 (707) 654-1330
(800) 561-1945; Fax: (707) 654-1336

Full-time: 459 men, 115 women	**Faculty:** 49; IIA, av$
Part-time: 15 men, 64 women	**Ph.D.s:** 31%
Graduate: none	**Student/Faculty:** 12 to 1
Year: semesters, summer session	**Tuition:** $6356 ($12,308)
Application Deadline: see profile	**Room & Board:** $5900
Freshman Class: 352 applied, 204 accepted, 150 enrolled	
SAT I Verbal/Math: 512/532	**ACT:** 21 **COMPETITIVE**

California Maritime Academy, founded in 1929, is a public college that awards undergraduate degrees in marine transportation, business, engineering, and technology. In addition to regional accreditation, Cal Maritime has baccalaureate program accreditation with ABET. The library contains 25,000 volumes and 15,000 microform items, and subscribes to 225 periodicals. Computerized library services include the card catalog, interlibrary loans, and database searching. Special learning facilities include a learning resource center and a training ship, navigation, steam plant, and diesel engine simulators, and a fluid dynamics lab with wind tunnels and a miniature jet turbine engine. The 67-acre campus is in a suburban area 30 miles northeast of San Francisco. Including residence halls, there are 26 buildings.
Student Life: 82% of undergraduates are from California. Others are from 19 states and 14 foreign countries. 80% are from public schools. 55% are white; 13% Asian American. The average age of freshmen is 21; all undergraduates, 22. 7% do not continue beyond their first year.
Housing: 457 students can be accommodated in college housing, which includes single-sex and coed dormitories. There are also 24-hour quiet residences. On-campus housing is guaranteed for all 4 years. 65% of students live on campus; of those, 30% remain on campus on weekends. Alcohol is not permitted. All students may keep cars.
Activities: There are no fraternities or sororities. There are 16 groups on campus, including auto shop, drill team, engineering, ethnic, international, photography, professional, religious, social, social service, student government, surf club, and yearbook. Popular campus events include movie nights, cave exploring, and cafe night.
Sports: There are 7 intercollegiate sports for men and 5 for women, and 10 intramural sports for men and 8 for women. Facilities include a gym, a weight room, physical therapy and exercise rooms, a 25-meter pool, tennis and racquetball courts, and a sports field.
Disabled Students: 70% of the campus is accessible. Wheelchair ramps, special parking, specially equipped rest rooms, lowered drinking fountains, and lowered telephones are available.
Services: Counseling and information services are available, as is tutoring in some subjects, including math, English, engineering, and science. There is remedial math, reading, and writing.
Campus Safety and Security: Measures include 24-hour foot and vehicle patrol, self-defense education, escort service, and informal discussions. There are pamphlets/posters/films, lighted pathways/sidewalks, and surveilance cameras.
Programs of Study: Cal Maritime confers the B.S degree. Bachelor's degrees are awarded in BUSINESS (business administration and management and transportation management), ENGINEERING AND ENVIRONMENTAL DESIGN (engineering technology, marine engineering, and mechanical engineering). Mechanical engineering is the strongest academically. Marine transportation is the largest.
Required: Graduation requirements for all students include a minimum 2.0 GPA and completion of English composition, American government, U.S. history, algebra and trigonometry, computer science, and survival swimming courses. All students must participate in at least one 2-month training cruise. A total of 129 to 187 credits is required for graduation.
Special: The academy has simulator training and requires a 2-month session aboard the academy's ship. Lab time is a major part of each program. Industry internships are available during the summer. Dual majors and co-op programs are available, as is cross-registration with other Cal State institutions. There are B.A.- B.S. degrees in mechanical engineering, business, marine transportation, facilities engineering, and marine engineering.
Faculty/Classroom: 85% of faculty are male; 15%, female. All teach undergraduates. The average class size in an introductory lecture is 20; in a laboratory, 9; and in a regular course, 20.
Admissions: 58% of the 2001-2002 applicants were accepted.
Requirements: The SAT I or ACT is required. In addition, secondary school courses must include 4 years of English, 3 of math, 3 of electives, 2 of language, and 1 each of lab science, history, and a visual or performing art. A GPA of 2.0 is required. AP and CLEP credits are accepted. Important factors in the admissions decision are leadership record, advanced placement or honor courses, and evidence of special talent. Applications are accepted on-line at *www.csumentor.edu*
Procedure: Freshmen are admitted in the fall. Entrance exams should be taken by December of the senior year. Students should apply for fall admission during the CSU "priority" month of November. Cal Maritime will accept applications on a rolling basis up to May 1 (or earlier if the campus becomes oversubscribed). The fall 2001 application fee was $55. Notification is sent on a rolling basis beginning in January.
Transfer: 50 transfer students enrolled in 2001-2002. Applicants must have a 2.0 GPA, provide SAT I or ACT scores, and be in good standing at the last institution attended.
Visiting: There are regularly scheduled orientations for prospective students. There are guides for informal visits and visitors may sit in on classes and stay overnight. To schedule a visit, contact the Admissions Office.
Financial Aid: In 2001-2002, 59% of all freshmen and 69% of continuing students received some form of financial aid. 59% of freshmen and 60% of continuing students received need-based aid. The average freshman award was $8042. Of that total, scholarships or need-based grants averaged $2130 ($4920 maximum); loans averaged $8201 ($10,234 maximum); work contracts averaged $213 ($1500 maximum); and California Veteran Dependent Fee Waiver averaged $107 ($2084 maximum). 80% of undergraduates work part time. Average annual earnings from campus work are $700. The average financial indebtedness of the 2001 graduate was $5147. The FAFSA is required.
International Students: There are 39 international students enrolled. They must score 550 on the written TOEFL or 213 on the electronic version and also take the SAT I or the ACT.
Computers: There are 22 self-contained PCs in the computer center and 4 PCs in the library. There are also 5 Macs in the residence halls. All students may access the system. There are no time limits and no fees.
Graduates: In 2001, 64 bachelor's degrees were awarded. The most popular majors were marine transportation (31%), business administration (28%), and mechanical engineering (23%). In an average class, 49% graduate in 4 years, 8% in 5 years, and 3% in 6 years. 30 companies recruited on campus in 2000-2001. Of the 2000 graduating class, 1% were enrolled in graduate school within 6 months of graduation and all were employed.
Admissions Contact: Chris Krzak, Director of Admissions and Outreach. E-mail: *admission@csum.edu* Web: *www.csum.edu*

CALIFORNIA POLYTECHNIC STATE UNIVERSITY B-4
San Luis Obispo, CA 93407 (805) 756-2311
Fax: (805) 756-5400

Full-time: 8882 men, 7213 women	**Faculty:** 654; IIA, ++$
Part-time: 564 men, 407 women	**Ph.D.s:** 73%
Graduate: 447 men, 566 women	**Student/Faculty:** 20 to 1
Year: quarters, summer session	**Tuition:** $2153 ($9533)
Application Deadline: November 30	**Room & Board:** $6594
Freshman Class: 18,755 applied, 8760 accepted, 3003 enrolled	
SAT I or ACT: required	**VERY COMPETITIVE**

California Polytechnic State University, founded in 1901, is a public institution that is part of the California State University system. It offers programs in agriculture, architecture and environmental design, business, education, engineering, liberal arts, sciences and math, and preprofessional studies. There are 6 undergraduate and 19 graduate schools. In addition to regional accreditation, Cal Poly has baccalaureate program accreditation with AACSB, ABET, ACCE, ADA, AHEA, ASLA, CSAB, NAAB, NRPA, and SAF. The library contains 1,206,340 volumes, 2,055,543 microform items, and 37,256 audiovisual forms/CDs, and subscribes to 3198 periodicals. Computerized library services include the card catalog, interlibrary loans, and database searching. Special learning facilities include a learning resource center, art gallery, radio station, and TV station. The 6000-acre campus is in a suburban area 200 miles from both San Francisco and Los Angeles. Including residence halls, there are 130 buildings.
Student Life: 96% of undergraduates are from California. Others are from 48 states, 41 foreign countries, and Canada. 61% are white; 11% Asian American; 10% Hispanic. The average age of freshmen is 19; all undergraduates, 22. 11% do not continue beyond their first year.
Housing: 2783 students can be accommodated in college housing, which includes single-sex and coed dormitories. In addition, there are special-interest houses and living/learning centers with an academic

theme. On-campus housing is available on a first-come, first-served basis. 83% of students commute. Alcohol is not permitted. All students may keep cars.

Activities: 8% of men belong to 1 local fraternity and 26 national fraternities; 9% of women belong to 8 national sororities. There are 400 groups on campus, including art, band, cheerleading, chess, choir, chorale, chorus, computers, dance, drama, ethnic, film, gay, honors, international, jazz band, literary magazine, marching band, musical theater, newspaper, orchestra, pep band, photography, political, professional, radio and TV, religious, social, social service, student government, and symphony. Popular campus events include Rose Float, Week of Welcome (WOW), and Civil Rights Awareness Week.

Sports: There are 9 intercollegiate sports for men and 8 for women, and 19 intramural sports for men and 19 for women. Facilities include an indoor/outdoor swimming pool, volleyball, tennis, basketball, and racquetball courts, weight rooms, playing fields, and a track.

Disabled Students: 95% of the campus is accessible. Wheelchair ramps, elevators, special parking, specially equipped rest rooms, and lowered telephones are available.

Services: Counseling and information services are available, as is tutoring in most subjects. There is a reader service for the blind, a writing skills lab, and a test office. Psychological and career services are available.

Campus Safety and Security: Measures include 24-hour foot and vehicle patrol, escort service, pamphlets/posters/films, and emergency telephones. There are lighted pathways/sidewalks.

Programs of Study: Cal Poly confers B.A., B.S., and B.Arch. degrees. Master's degrees are also awarded. Bachelor's degrees are awarded in AGRICULTURE (agricultural business management, agriculture, dairy science, horticulture, natural resource management, and soil science), BIOLOGICAL SCIENCE (biochemistry, biology/biological science, ecology, and microbiology), BUSINESS (business administration and management and recreation and leisure services), COMMUNICATIONS AND THE ARTS (English, graphic design, and journalism), COMPUTER AND PHYSICAL SCIENCE (chemistry, computer science, mathematics, physical sciences, physics, and statistics), EDUCATION (industrial arts and physical), ENGINEERING AND ENVIRONMENTAL DESIGN (aeronautical engineering, agricultural engineering, architectural engineering, architecture, city/community/regional planning, civil engineering, computer engineering, construction management, electrical/electronics engineering, engineering, environmental engineering, industrial engineering, landscape architecture/design, manufacturing engineering, materials engineering, mechanical engineering, and metallurgical engineering), SOCIAL SCIENCE (economics, food science, history, human development, philosophy, political science/government, psychology, and social science). Agricultural management, architecture, and business administration are the largest.

Required: Students must have a minimum 2.0 GPA and complete general education and breadth requirements, including the following: 18 units each of physical and life sciences, social sciences, and literature and the arts; 14 units of English; and 5 units of psychology and health. Math and computer literacy courses and a senior project are required. 186 to 263 quarter units are needed to graduate.

Special: Cal Poly offers work-study programs, co-op programs in numerous majors, study abroad in 11 countries, dual majors, and internships in many majors. Credit for military experience and pass/fail options are available.

Faculty/Classroom: 69% of faculty are male; 31%, female.

Admissions: 47% of the 2001-2002 applicants were accepted. The SAT I scores for the 2001-2002 freshman class were: Verbal--19% below 500, 48% between 500 and 599, 30% between 600 and 700, and 4% above 700; Math--9% below 500, 34% between 500 and 599, 45% between 600 and 700, and 11% above 700. The ACT scores were 38% below 23, 55% between 24 and 29, and 8% above 29. 67% of the current freshmen were in the top quarter of their class; 93% were in the top half.

Requirements: The SAT I or ACT is required. In addition, applicants must be graduates of an accredited high school or have a GED. 15 academic credits are required, including 4 years of English, 3 each of math and science, 2 of a foreign language, and 1 each of history and visual or performing arts. A GPA of 2.0 is required. AP and CLEP credits are accepted. An on-line application is Cal Poly's preferred method of application.

Procedure: Freshmen are admitted fall and summer. Entrance exams should be taken January 15. There are early decision and early admissions plans. Early decision applications should be filed by October 31; regular applications, by November 30 for fall entry and February 28 for summer entry, along with a $55 fee. Notification of early decision is sent December 15; regular decision, on a rolling basis beginning March 1.

Transfer: 1030 transfer students enrolled in 2001-2002. Applicants must have completed 56 semester or 84 quarter units with a minimum GPA of 2.0. 50 quarter credits of 186 must be completed at Cal Poly.

Visiting: There are regularly scheduled orientations for prospective students, held on Mondays and Wednesdays at 10 A.M. and 2 P.M. There are guides for informal visits and visitors may stay overnight. To schedule a visit, contact the Admissions Office at (805) 756-2792.

Financial Aid: In 2001-2002, 29% of all freshmen and 34% of continuing students received some form of financial aid. The average freshman award was $6299. Of that total, scholarships or need-based grants averaged $3141; and loans averaged $2252. The average financial indebtedness of the 2001 graduate was $12,908. The FAFSA and the college's own financial statement are required. The fall application deadline is March 2.

International Students: There are 79 international students enrolled. The school actively recruits these students. They must score 550 on the written TOEFL.

Computers: The mainframe is an IBM ES/9000 Model 732. There are also more than 1000 Macs and PCs available throughout campus. All students may access the system. There are no time limits and no fees. It is strongly recommended that all students have a personal computer.

Graduates: In 2001, 2838 bachelor's degrees were awarded. The most popular majors were engineering (22%), business (18%), and agriculture (15%). In an average class, 64% graduate in 6 years.

Admissions Contact: James L. Maraviglia, Director of Admissions.
E-mail: *admprosp@calpoly.edu* Web: *www.calpoly.edu*

CALIFORNIA STATE POLYTECHNIC UNIVERSITY, POMONA — D-5

Pomona, CA 91768-4019 — **(909) 869-2392; Fax: (909) 869-4529**

Full-time: 7797 men, 5976 women	**Faculty:** 663; IIA, ++$
Part-time: 1830 men, 1402 women	**Ph.D.s:** 46%
Graduate: 840 men, 1196 women	**Student/Faculty:** 21 to 1
Year: quarters, summer session	**Tuition:** $1772 ($9152)
Application Deadline: November 1	**Room & Board:** $6843
Freshman Class: 11,003 applied, 7389 accepted, 2544 enrolled	
SAT I Verbal/Math: 481/530	**ACT:** 20 **COMPETITIVE**

California State Polytechnic University, Pomona, an occupationally oriented institution founded in 1938, is part of the state-supported university system. It offers undergraduate and graduate programs in agriculture, liberal arts and sciences, business, engineering, and technical and professional training. There are 8 undergraduate and 7 graduate schools. In addition to regional accreditation, Cal Poly Pomona has baccalaureate program accreditation with AACSB, ABET, ADA, ASLA, CSAB, and NAAB. The library contains 443,973 volumes, 2,453,273 microform items, and 12,066 audiovisual forms/CDs, and subscribes to 5919 periodicals. Computerized library services include the card catalog, interlibrary loans, and database searching. Special learning facilities include a learning resource center, art gallery, TV station, and an interactive TV studio. The 1438-acre campus is in a suburban area 30 miles east of Los Angeles. Including residence halls, there are 80 buildings.

Student Life: 96% of undergraduates are from California. Others are from 50 states, 54 foreign countries, and Canada. 87% are from public schools. 38% are Asian American; 30% white; 27% Hispanic. The average age of freshmen is 18; all undergraduates, 22. 22% do not continue beyond their first year; 42% remain to graduate.

Housing: 2025 students can be accommodated in college housing, which includes coed dormitories and on-campus apartments. In addition, there are special interest houses. On-campus housing is available on a first-come, first-served basis. 92% of students commute. All students may keep cars.

Activities: 1% of men belong to 6 local and 11 national fraternities; 1% of women belong to 3 local and 4 national sororities. There are 220 groups on campus, including art, band, cheerleading, choir, chorale, chorus, computers, ethnic, film, gay, honors, international, literary magazine, musical theater, newspaper, pep band, photography, political, professional, religious, social, social service, student government, and yearbook. Popular campus events include Rose Float and Back-to-School parties.

Sports: There are 6 intercollegiate sports for men and 6 for women. Facilities include a 5000-seat stadium, tennis and racquetball courts, basketball and volleyball courts, soccer, baseball, and softball fields, a track, a swimming pool, gymnastics and weight rooms, a horse arena, and dance studios.

Disabled Students: 96% of the campus is accessible. Wheelchair ramps, elevators, special parking, specially equipped rest rooms, special class scheduling, lowered drinking fountains, lowered telephones, and specialized tram, van, and shuttle transportation are available.

Services: Counseling and information services are available, as is tutoring in most subjects. There is a reader service for the blind and remedial math and writing.

Campus Safety and Security: Measures include 24-hour foot and vehicle patrol, self-defense education, escort service, and shuttle buses. There are informal discussions, pamphlets/posters/films, emergency telephones, lighted pathways/sidewalks, vehicle assists, and crime prevention programs.

Programs of Study: Cal Poly Pomona confers B.A. and B.S. degrees. Master's degrees are also awarded. Bachelor's degrees are awarded in

AGRICULTURE (agricultural business management, agriculture, agronomy, animal science, and horticulture), BIOLOGICAL SCIENCE (biology/biological science, biotechnology, botany, microbiology, plant physiology, and zoology), BUSINESS (accounting, apparel and accessories marketing, banking and finance, business administration and management, hotel/motel and restaurant management, human resources, international business management, marketing/retailing/merchandising, operations research, and real estate), COMMUNICATIONS AND THE ARTS (art, communications, dramatic arts, English, music, and Spanish), COMPUTER AND PHYSICAL SCIENCE (chemistry, computer science, geology, information sciences and systems, mathematics, and physics), ENGINEERING AND ENVIRONMENTAL DESIGN (aeronautical engineering, architecture, chemical engineering, civil engineering, computer technology, construction technology, electrical/electronics engineering, engineering technology, industrial engineering, landscape architecture/design, manufacturing engineering, materials engineering, and mechanical engineering), SOCIAL SCIENCE (anthropology, behavioral science, economics, food science, geography, history, liberal arts/general studies, philosophy, physical fitness/movement, political science/government, psychology, social science, sociology, and urban studies). Engineering, architecture, and business are the strongest academically. Computer information systems and electrical engineering are the largest.
Required: All students must complete general education requirements, including courses in written and oral communications, critical thinking, math, humanities, natural sciences, and social sciences, and must pass a graduation writing test. A total of 186 (B.A.) to 198 (B.S.) quarter units with a minimum GPA of 2.0 is required to graduate.
Special: Cross-registration is possible with any California State University school. Internships and co-op programs are available in agriculture, business, environmental design, engineering, science, political science, behavioral science, and phys ed. An international study program in 17 countries, work-study programs, B.A.-B.S. degrees, a liberal studies degree, credit for military experience, an external degree program, and credit/no credit options are offered. Nondegree study is possible. There are 30 national honor societies.
Faculty/Classroom: 64% of faculty are male; 36%, female. The average class size in an introductory lecture is 40; in a laboratory, 24; and in a regular course, 27.
Admissions: 67% of the 2001-2002 applicants were accepted. The SAT I scores for the 2001-2002 freshman class were: Verbal--58% below 500, 33% between 500 and 599, 8% between 600 and 700, and 1% above 700; Math--35% below 500, 40% between 500 and 599, 21% between 600 and 700, and 3% above 700. The ACT scores were 56% below 21, 26% between 21 and 23, 12% between 24 and 26, 4% between 27 and 28, and 2% above 28.
Requirements: The SAT I or ACT is recommended. In addition, applicants must be graduates of an accredited secondary school or have a GED equivalent. Secondary school courses must include 4 years of high school English, 3 each of math and electives, 2 of foreign language, and 1 each of science, history, and art. A GPA of 2.0 is required. AP and CLEP credits are accepted. Applications are accepted on computer disk and on-line via XAPplication and at *www.csumentor.edu*.
Procedure: Freshmen are admitted to all sessions. Entrance exams should be taken during the fall of the senior year. There is a deferred admissions plan. Applications should be filed by November 1 for fall entry, June 1 for winter entry, August 1 for spring entry, and February 1 for summer entry. The fall 2001 application fee was $55. Notification is sent on a rolling basis.
Transfer: 1367 transfer students enrolled in 2001-2002. Applicants must have completed 56 semester or 84 quarter units including college preparatory subjects. A 2.0 GPA (2.4 for nonresidents) is required. 50 credits of 186 must be completed at Cal Poly Pomona.
Visiting: There are regularly scheduled orientations for prospective students, consisting of tours of the campus led by current undergraduate students and a 90 minute walking tour. There are guides for informal visits and visitors may sit in on classes and stay overnight. To schedule a visit, contact Visitor Services at (909) 869-3529.
Financial Aid: In 2001-2002, 41% of all freshmen and 54% of continuing students received some form of financial aid. 38% of freshmen and 48% of continuing students received need-based aid. The average freshman award was $6545. Average annual earnings from campus work are $1560. The average financial indebtedness of the 2001 graduate was $10,165. The FAFSA is required. The fall application deadline is March 2.
International Students: There are 802 international students enrolled. They must score 525 on the written TOEFL and also take the SAT I or the ACT.
Computers: The mainframe is a DEC ALPHA 7000-620. PC clusters are available in labs on campus. All students may access the system 24 hours per day. There are no time limits and no fees. It is recommended that students in environmental design have personal computers.
Graduates: In 2001, 2763 bachelor's degrees were awarded. The most popular majors were computer information (10%), liberal studies (8%), and marketing (7%). In an average class, 8% graduate in 4 years, 28% in 5 years, and 43% in 6 years.
Admissions Contact: George A. Gaines, Associate Director of Admissions. A video is available. E-mail: *ggaines@csupomona.edu*
Web: *www.csupomona.edu*

CALIFORNIA STATE UNIVERSITY SYSTEM

The California State University System, established in 1961, is California's comprehensive public university system offering bachelor's, master's, and joint doctoral degrees. It is governed by a 24-member board of trustees and its chief administrator is the chancellor. CSU's main priorities are to emphasize quality in instruction; to provide an environment in which scholarship, research, creative, artistic, and professional activity are valued and supported; and to stress the importance of the liberal arts and sciences. Total enrollment of all 22 campuses is usually around 350,000, with some 19,500 faculty members. The California State University System offers more than 900 baccalaureate, 600 master's, and 14 joint doctoral programs. CSU campuses are located in Bakersfield, Chico, Dominguez Hills (in Carson), Fresno, Fullerton, Hayward, Humboldt (in Arcata), Long Beach, Los Angeles, Maritime Academy (in Vallejo), Monterey Bay)in Seaside), Northridge, Pomona, Sacramento, San Bernardino, San Diego, San Francisco, San Jose, San Luis Obispo, San Marcos, Sonoma (in Rohnert Park), and Stanislaus (in Turlock). Profiles of the 14 4-year campuses are included in this section.

CALIFORNIA STATE UNIVERSITY, BAKERSFIELD C-4

Bakersfield, CA 93311-1099 (661) 664-2160
(800) 788-2782; Fax: (661) 664-3389

Full-time: 1436 men, 2699 women	**Faculty:** 234; IIA, +$
Part-time: 392 men, 701 women	**Ph.D.s:** 50%
Graduate: 566 men, 1256 women	**Student/Faculty:** 18 to 1
Year: quarters, summer session	**Tuition:** $1960 ($9340)
Application Deadline: open	**Room & Board:** $4130
Freshman Class: n/av	
SAT I Verbal/Math: 450/470	**LESS COMPETITIVE**

California State University/Bakersfield, founded in 1965, is part of the California State University System and offers undergraduate and graduate programs in liberal arts and sciences, business, public administration, education, health fields, preengineering, and preprofessional training. Some information in this profile is approximate. There are 3 undergraduate and 10 graduate schools. In addition to regional accreditation, Cal State Bakersfield has baccalaureate program accreditation with AACSB, NCATE, and NLN. The library contains 339,900 volumes, 603,300 microform items, and 5180 audiovisual forms/CDs, and subscribes to 2700 periodicals. Computerized library services include the card catalog, interlibrary loans, and database searching. Special learning facilities include a learning resource center, art gallery, natural history museum, geological data sample repository, archeological information center, instructional television network, applied research center, and animal care and treatment facility. The 375-acre campus is in an urban area in southwest Bakersfield. Including residence halls, there are 30 buildings.
Student Life: 98% of undergraduates are from California. Others are from 25 states, 50 foreign countries, and Canada. 98% are from public schools. 51% are white; 25%, Hispanic. The average age of freshmen is 19; all undergraduates, 25. 15% do not continue beyond their first year.
Housing: 330 students can be accommodated in college housing, which includes single-sex and coed dormitories. On-campus housing is guaranteed for all 4 years. 98% of students commute. Alcohol is not permitted. All students may keep cars.
Activities: 2% of men belong to 3 national fraternities; 2% of women belong to 4 national sororities. There are 74 groups on campus, including art, band, cheerleading, chess, choir, chorale, computers, dance, drama, ethnic, film, gay, honors, international, jazz band, literary magazine, musical theater, newspaper, opera, orchestra, pep band, photography, political, professional, radio and TV, religious, social, social service, student government, and symphony. Popular campus events include Cinco de Mayo, Open Campus, and Jazz Festival.
Sports: There are 7 intercollegiate sports for men and 6 for women, and 12 intramural sports for men and 12 for women. Facilities include a 4000-seat gym, a wrestling sport center, an aquatic center, tennis and racquetball courts, and softball and soccer fields.
Disabled Students: Wheelchair ramps, elevators, special parking, specially equipped rest rooms, special class scheduling, lowered drinking fountains, and lowered telephones are available.
Services: Counseling and information services are available, as is tutoring in most subjects, as well as in study skills. There is a reader service for the blind, and remedial math, reading, and writing.
Campus Safety and Security: Measures include 24-hour foot and vehicle patrol, self-defense education, escort service, and informal discussions. There are pamphlets/posters/films, emergency telephones, and lighted pathways/sidewalks.
Programs of Study: Cal State Bakersfield confers B.A. and B.S. degrees. Master's degrees are also awarded. Bachelor's degrees are award-

ed in BIOLOGICAL SCIENCE (biology/biological science), BUSINESS (business administration and management), COMMUNICATIONS AND THE ARTS (art, communications, dramatic arts, English, music, and Spanish), COMPUTER AND PHYSICAL SCIENCE (chemistry, computer science, geology, mathematics, and physics), ENGINEERING AND ENVIRONMENTAL DESIGN (land use management and reclamation), HEALTH PROFESSIONS (clinical science, and nursing), SOCIAL SCIENCE (anthropology, child psychology/development, criminal justice, economics, history, liberal arts/general studies, philosophy, political science/government, psychology, public administration, religion, and sociology). Business, education, and public administration are the strongest academically. Business is the largest.

Required: All students must complete 72 quarter units of general education requirements in basic skills, Western civilization, non-Western culture, philosophy, fine arts, literature, technology, and physical, social, and life sciences. They must also take a comprehensive writing exam or complete an upper-division writing course with a grade of C or better, demonstrate understanding of American history and government institutions, and complete a senior seminar. A total of 186 quarter units with a minimum GPA of 2.0 is required to graduate.

Special: Cal State Bakersfield offers co-op programs in education and business administration, cross-registration through the National Student Exchange Program, study abroad at 36 universities in 16 countries, a 3-2 engineering degree with California Polytechnic State University/San Luis Obispo, and student-designed majors. Credit for life experience, pass/fail options, and nondegree study are available. Students may also earn credits as interns and participate in work-study programs on and off campus. There is a freshman honors program.

Faculty/Classroom: 62% of faculty are male; 38%, female. All both teach and do research. No introductory courses are taught by graduate students. The average class size in an introductory lecture is 40; in a laboratory, 24; and in a regular course, 30.

Admissions: The SAT I scores for the 2001-2002 freshman class were: Verbal--70% below 500, 24% between 500 and 599, and 5% between 600 and 700; Math--60% below 500, 33% between 500 and 599, 7% between 600 and 700, and 1% above 700.

Requirements: The SAT I or ACT is required if the GPA is below 3.0 (3.6 for nonresidents). A minimum GPA of 2.0 is required. Admission is based on an eligibility index that weights the GPA and standardized test scores. In addition, applicants must be graduates of an accredited secondary school or GED equivalent, and have a total of 15 academic units, including 4 years of English, 3 of math, 2 of foreign language, 1 each of lab science, U.S. history/government, and visual and performing arts, and 3 of electives. Cal State Bakersfield requires applicants to be in the upper 33% of their class. AP and CLEP credits are accepted.

Procedure: Freshmen are admitted fall, winter, and spring. Entrance exams should be taken by December of the senior year. There are early decision, early admissions, and deferred admissions plans. Check with the school for current application deadline. The application fee is $55. Notification is sent on a rolling basis.

Transfer: A 2.0 GPA (2.4 for nonresidents) is required in a minimum of 56 semester or 84 quarter units earned, including English and math. 45 quarter credits of 186 must be completed at Cal State Bakersfield.

Visiting: There are regularly scheduled orientations for prospective students, consisting of a day-long orientation that includes meetings with faculty advisers and school deans. There are guides for informal visits and visitors may sit in on classes. To schedule a visit, contact the Office of Outreach Services at (661) 664-3138.

Financial Aid: In 2001-2002, 50% of all freshmen received some form of financial aid. 9% of undergraduates work part time. Cal State Bakersfield is a member of CSS. The FAFSA is required. Check with the school for current deadlines.

International Students: The school actively recruits these students. They must score 500 on the written TOEFL or 173 on the electronic version. The SAT I or ACT is required if the GPA is below 3.0.

Computers: The mainframes are a CDC CYBER 830 and a DEC VAX 8350. There are about 300 PCs available in student labs located throughout the campus. All students may access the system. There are no time limits and no fees.

Graduates: In an average class, 28% graduate in 5 years.

Admissions Contact: Dr. Homer Montalvo, Dean of Admissions.
E-mail: *hmontalvo@csubak.edu* Web: *http://www.csub.edu*

CALIFORNIA STATE UNIVERSITY, CHICO — B-2

Chico, CA 95929-0722 — (530) 898-4428
(800) 542-4426; Fax: (530) 898-6456

Full-time: 6179 men, 6995 women	**Faculty:** 615; IIA, +$
Part-time: 681 men, 779 women	**Ph.D.s:** 62%
Graduate: 821 men, 1249 women	**Student/Faculty:** 21 to 1
Year: semesters, summer session	**Tuition:** $2070 ($9450)
Application Deadline: November 30	**Room & Board:** $6528
Freshman Class: 7899 applied, 7139 accepted, 2128 enrolled	
SAT I Verbal/Math: 500/510	**ACT:** 21 **LESS COMPETITIVE**

California State University/Chico, founded in 1887, is a public institution offering undergraduate programs in behavioral and social sciences, business, communication and education, engineering, computer science and technology, humanities and fine arts, natural sciences, agriculture, and nursing. The university offers web-based classes. There are 7 undergraduate schools and 1 graduate school. In addition to regional accreditation, CSU, Chico has baccalaureate program accreditation with AACSB, ABET, ACCE, ADA, CSAB, CSWE, NASAD, NASM, NLN, and NRPA. The library contains 948,564 volumes, 1,140,465 microform items, and 22,968 audiovisual forms/CDs, and subscribes to 20,404 periodicals. Computerized library services include the card catalog, interlibrary loans, and database searching. Special learning facilities include a learning resource center, art gallery, planetarium, radio station, an instructional media center, university farm, biological field station, anthropology museum, media preparation lab, computer graphics lab, and recording arts studio. The 130-acre campus is in a small town 100 miles north of Sacramento. Including residence halls, there are 72 buildings.

Student Life: 99% of undergraduates are from California. Others are from 44 states, 48 foreign countries, and Canada. 94% are from public schools. 67% are white; 10% Hispanic. The average age of freshmen is 18; all undergraduates, 22. 21% do not continue beyond their first year; 64% remain to graduate.

Housing: 1700 students can be accommodated in college housing, which includes coed dormitories, on-campus apartments, and off-campus apartments. In addition, there are honors houses, language houses, and special- interest houses. On-campus housing is available on a first-come, first-served basis. 90% of students commute. Alcohol is not permitted. All students may keep cars.

Activities: 8% of men belong to 4 local and 14 national fraternities; 8% of women belong to 8 local and 10 national sororities. There are more than 200 groups on campus, including art, band, cheerleading, chess, choir, chorale, chorus, computers, dance, debate, departmental, drama, drill team, ethnic, film, forensics, gay, honors, international, intramural and club sports, jazz band, literary magazine, musical theater, newspaper, opera, orchestra, pep band, political, professional, radio and TV, reentry, religious, social, social service, student government, symphony, and yearbook. Popular campus events include International Festival, Greek Week, and Fun Without Alcohol Fair.

Sports: There are 6 intercollegiate sports for men and 7 for women, and 17 intramural sports for men and 16 for women. Facilities include 2 gyms, athletic training rooms, a dance studio, swimming and diving pools, a par course, putting greens and sand trap, handball/racquetball courts, baseball/softball fields, an all-weather track, a soccer stadium, a 7500-seat football stadium, and a residence hall sports center.

Disabled Students: 95% of the campus is accessible. Wheelchair ramps, elevators, special parking, specially equipped rest rooms, special class scheduling, lowered drinking fountains, lowered telephones, sign language interpreters, on-campus transportation, Braille signage, books on tape, adaptive computer lab, and disability support services are available.

Services: Counseling and information services are available, as is tutoring in every subject. There is a reader service for the blind, and remedial math, reading, and writing. A student learning center offers a tutorial program, study skills development, and learning assistance workshops.

Campus Safety and Security: Measures include 24-hour foot and vehicle patrol, self-defense education, escort service, and shuttle buses. There are informal discussions, pamphlets/posters/films, emergency telephones, lighted pathways/sidewalks, a victim awareness program, and crime prevention workshops.

Programs of Study: CSU, Chico confers B.A., B.S., and B.F.A. degrees. Master's degrees are also awarded. Bachelor's degrees are awarded in AGRICULTURE (agricultural business management and agriculture), BIOLOGICAL SCIENCE (biology/biological science, microbiology, and nutrition), BUSINESS (business administration and management), COMMUNICATIONS AND THE ARTS (art, communications, dramatic arts, English, fine arts, French, German, journalism, music, musical theater, and Spanish), COMPUTER AND PHYSICAL SCIENCE (chemistry, computer science, geology, geoscience, information sciences and systems, mathematics, physical sciences, and physics), EDUCATION (physical), ENGINEERING AND ENVIRONMENTAL DESIGN (civil engineering, computer engineering, construction management, electrical/electronics engineering, environmental science, industrial engineering technology, and mechanical engineering), HEALTH PROFESSIONS (exercise science, health science, nursing, and speech pathology/audiology), SOCIAL SCIENCE (American studies, anthropology, Asian/Oriental studies, child psychology/development, economics, ethnic studies, geography, history, humanities, international relations, Latin American studies, liberal arts/general studies, parks and recreation management, philosophy, political science/government, psychology, public administration, religion, social science, social work, and sociology). Nursing, accounting, and biology are the strongest academically. Business administration, liberal studies, and communications are the largest.

Required: Graduation requirements for all students include the completion of math, writing proficiency, ethnic studies, non-Western studies, U.S. history, U.S. Constitution, and U.S./California government courses. Also required are a 48-unit general education program, a 2.0 minimum GPA, 124 to 132 total credit hours, and 24 to 115 hours in the major.

Special: The university offers co-op programs and cross-registration as part of the National Student Exchange. Internships, distance learning, teacher certification, study abroad in 16 countries, work-study, student-designed majors, independent study, credit for experience, nondegree study, and pass/fail options are available. There are 4 national honor societies, a freshman honors program, and 28 departmental honors programs.

Faculty/Classroom: 59% of faculty are male; 41%, female. All teach undergraduates. Graduate students teach 2% of introductory courses. The average class size in an introductory lecture is 25; in a laboratory, 21; and in a regular course, 22.

Admissions: 90% of the 2001-2002 applicants were accepted.

Requirements: The SAT I or ACT is required. An index combining GPA and SAT I and ACT scores is used to determine eligibility for admission. Applicants must be graduates of secondary school or have a GED and have completed 4 years of English, 3 years each of math and college preparatory electives, 2 years of a foreign language, and 1 year each of history, science, art and/or music. Applicants are accepted on-line at *www.csumentor.edu* AP and CLEP credits are accepted.

Procedure: Freshmen are admitted fall and spring. Entrance exams should be taken in fall of the senior year. There is a deferred admissions plan. Applications should be filed by November 30 for fall entry, along with a $55 fee. Notification is sent on a rolling basis.

Transfer: 1660 transfer students enrolled in 2001-2002. Transfer students who are California residents must have a minimum 2.0 GPA, and nonresidents need 2.4. A minimum of 56 transferable credit hours are needed, and students must have made up any missing college preparatory subjects and provide a statement of good standing from prior institutions. 30 credits of 124 must be completed at CSU, Chico.

Visiting: There are guides for informal visits and visitors may sit in on classes. To schedule a visit, contact University Outreach.

Financial Aid: The FAFSA is required. The fall application deadline is March 2.

International Students: There are 282 international students enrolled. The school actively recruits these students. They must score 500 on the written TOEFL or 173 on the electronic version.

Computers: The mainframes are an IBM 4381, an IBM 3090, and a DEC VAX 6310. There are 1000 PCs available, with about 200 networked. There are also over 50 terminals. In addition, there are large department based central computers. All students may access the system. There are no time limits and no fees. It is strongly recommended that all students have a personal computer.

Graduates: In 2001, 2696 bachelor's degrees were awarded. The most popular majors were business administration (16%), liberal studies (13%), and psychology (5%). In an average class, 10% graduate in 4 years, 38% in 5 years, and 49% in 6 years. 282 companies recruited on campus in 2000-2001.

Admissions Contact: John Swiney, Director of Admissions.
E-mail: *info@csuchico.edu* Web: *http://www.csuchico.edu*

CALIFORNIA STATE UNIVERSITY, DOMINGUEZ HILLS C-5

Carson, CA 90747-0005 **(310) 243-3696**

Full-time: 1470 men, 3140 women	**Faculty:** 290; IIA, +$
Part-time: 790 men, 2280 women	**Ph.D.s:** 80%
Graduate: 1480 men, 3360 women	**Student/Faculty:** 16 to 1
Year: semesters, summer session	**Tuition:** $1740 ($9140)
Application Deadline: see profile	**Room & Board:** $4100
Freshman Class: n/av	
SAT I or ACT: required	**LESS COMPETITIVE**

California State University Dominguez Hills, founded in 1960 as part of the state-supported university system, offers graduate and undergraduate programs in liberal arts and sciences, business, fine arts, health sciences, and technology to a primarily commuter student body. Figures in above capsule are approximate. There are 4 undergraduate and 4 graduate schools. In addition to regional accreditation, CSU Dominguez Hills has baccalaureate program accreditation with CAHEA, NASAD, NASM, NCATE, and NLN. The library contains 396,520 volumes, 569,630 microform items, and 17,130 audiovisual forms/CDs, and subscribes to 4740 periodicals. Computerized library services include the card catalog and database searching. Special learning facilities include a learning resource center, art gallery, planetarium, and TV station. The 350-acre campus is in an urban area 10 miles south of Los Angeles. There are 40 buildings.

Student Life: Most undergraduates are from California. Others are from 29 states, 79 foreign countries, and Canada. 98% are from public schools. 30% are African American; 30% Hispanic; 20% white; 10% Asian American. The average age of freshmen is 19; all undergraduates, 29. 30% do not continue beyond their first year; 30% remain to graduate.

Housing: There are no residence halls. 710 students can be accommodated in college housing, which includes single-sex and coed on-campus apartments. On-campus housing is guaranteed for all 4 years. Most students commute. All students may keep cars.

Activities: There are 4 national fraternities and 1 local and 2 national sororities. There are 69 groups on campus, including art, band, cheerleading, choir, chorale, computers, dance, drama, drill team, ethnic, gay, honors, international, jazz band, literary magazine, musical theater, newspaper, orchestra, photography, political, professional, radio and TV, religious, social, social service, student government, symphony, and yearbook.

Sports: There are 4 intercollegiate sports for men and 4 for women. Facilities include the Olympic Velodrome (bicycle racing stadium), a gym, tennis courts, a baseball field, a track, a weight room, a swimming pool, and a soccer field.

Disabled Students: Wheelchair ramps, elevators, special parking, specially equipped rest rooms, lowered drinking fountains, and lowered telephones are available.

Services: Counseling and information services are available, as is tutoring in most subjects. There is a reader service for the blind, and remedial math, reading, and writing.

Campus Safety and Security: Measures include 24-hour foot and vehicle patrol, escort service, informal discussions, and pamphlets/posters/films. There are emergency telephones and lighted pathways/sidewalks.

Programs of Study: CSU Dominguez Hills confers B.A. and B.S. degrees. Master's degrees are also awarded. Bachelor's degrees are awarded in BIOLOGICAL SCIENCE (biology/biological science), BUSINESS (business administration and management, labor studies, recreation and leisure services, and tourism), COMMUNICATIONS AND THE ARTS (art, communications, dramatic arts, English, music, and Spanish), COMPUTER AND PHYSICAL SCIENCE (chemistry, computer science, digital arts/technology, geology, mathematics, and physics), EDUCATION (physical), HEALTH PROFESSIONS (clinical science, health science, nursing, and occupational therapy), SOCIAL SCIENCE (African studies, anthropology, behavioral science, economics, geography, history, human services, interdisciplinary studies, liberal arts/general studies, Mexican-American/Chicano studies, philosophy, political science/government, psychology, public administration, and sociology). Liberal studies is the strongest academically. Business administration is the largest.

Required: To graduate, students must complete 120 to 132 semester units, including 54 to 60 units in general education, 40 units in upper-division courses, and specific courses or proficiency tests in U.S. history and politics, math, and writing. A minimum GPA of 2.0 must be maintained.

Special: Cross-registration is offered with 7 other California State University schools. Study abroad in 15 countries, co-op programs in all majors, on-campus work-study, internships, B.A.-B.S. degrees, dual and student-designed majors, credit for life experience, and pass/fail options are available. A B.A. in interdisciplinary studies, in which an accelerated degree is possible, and in liberal studies is offered. Many majors have evening programs. There are 2 national honor societies, a freshman honors program, and 13 departmental honors programs.

Faculty/Classroom: 50% of faculty are male; 50%, female. 95% teach undergraduates. The average class size in an introductory lecture is 45; in a laboratory, 19; and in a regular course, 32.

Requirements: The SAT I or ACT is required, except of those with a GPA of at least 3.0 (3.6 for nonresidents). Students must be high school graduates with a GPA of at least 2.0 and 15 academic units, including 4 in English, 3 in math, 2 in foreign language, and 1 each in U.S. history, lab science, and visual and performing arts. The GED is accepted. CSU Dominguez Hills requires applicants to be in the upper 33% of their class. AP and CLEP credits are accepted.

Procedure: Freshmen are admitted fall and spring. Entrance exams should be taken prior to submitting an application. There are early decision and early admissions plans. Notification is sent on a rolling basis. Check with the school for current deadlines. The fall 2001 application fee was $55.

Transfer: 1239 transfer students enrolled in a recent year. Applicants should have a college GPA of at least 2.0 (2.4 for nonresidents) and submit SAT I or ACT scores if transferring fewer than 56 semester or 84 quarter units. 30 credits of 120 to 132 must be completed at CSU Dominguez Hills.

Visiting: There are regularly scheduled orientations for prospective students. There are guides for informal visits and visitors may sit in on classes. To schedule a visit, contact the Outreach Office for group visits at (310) 516-3699 or the Information at Center for individual visits at (310) 516-3696.

Financial Aid: The FAFSA is required. The fall application deadline is March 2.

International Students: The school actively recruits these students. They must score 550 on the written TOEFL and also take the SAT I or the ACT.

Computers: The mainframes are a CDC CYBER 960 and a DEC VAX 6500. About 450 Mac and IBM PCs are available in the library, student labs, and individual departments. All students may access the system. There are no time limits and no fees. It is strongly recommended that all students have a personal computer.

Graduates: In a recent year, 1806 bachelor's degrees were awarded. The most popular majors were nursing (20%), business administration (16%), and liberal studies (16%). In an average class, 4% graduate in 4 years, 13% in 5 years, and 30% in 6 years. 180 companies recruited on campus in a recent year.

Admissions Contact: Information and Services Center.
Web: *www.csudh.edu*

CALIFORNIA STATE UNIVERSITY, FRESNO C-3

Fresno, CA 93740-8027 (559) 278-2261; Fax: (559) 278-4812

Full-time: 5313 men, 7484 women	**Faculty:** 662; IIA, +$
Part-time: 1435 men, 1856 women	**Ph.D.s:** n/av
Graduate: 1401 men, 2524 women	**Student/Faculty:** 19 to 1
Year: semesters, summer session	**Tuition:** $1762 ($7666)
Application Deadline: May 15	**Room & Board:** $6000
Freshman Class: 8015 applied, 5906 accepted, 4465 enrolled	
SAT I Verbal/Math: 460/470	**ACT:** 18 **COMPETITIVE**

California State University, Fresno, founded in 1911, is part of the state-supported university system. The school offers undergraduate and graduate programs in agriculture and technology, liberal arts and sciences, business administration, education, engineering, health fields, and pre-professional training. There are 8 undergraduate and 8 graduate schools. In addition to regional accreditation, Fresno State has baccalaureate program accreditation with AACSB, ABET, ACCE, ACEJMC, ADA, AHEA, APTA, ASLA, CSWE, FIDER, NASM, NCATE, NLN, and NRPA. The library contains 976,196 volumes, 1,469,875 microform items, and 73,369 audiovisual forms/CDs, and subscribes to 2450 periodicals. Computerized library services include the card catalog, interlibrary loans, and database searching. Special learning facilities include a learning resource center, art gallery, planetarium, radio station, and and various farm lab units. The 327-acre campus is in a suburban area 300 miles southeast of San Francisco. Including residence halls, there are 47 buildings.

Student Life: 97% of undergraduates are from California. Others are from 42 states, 66 foreign countries, and Canada. 99% are from public schools. 40% are white; 27% Hispanic; 14% Asian American. The average age of freshmen is 18; all undergraduates, 23. 20% do not continue beyond their first year; 55% remain to graduate.

Housing: 1036 students can be accommodated in college housing, which includes single-sex and coed dormitories. In addition, there are special-interest houses. On-campus housing is available on a first-come, first-served basis. 94% of students commute. Alcohol is not permitted. All students may keep cars.

Activities: 3% of men belong to 4 local and 15 national fraternities; 3% of women belong to 4 local and 9 national sororities. There are 270 groups on campus, including art, band, cheerleading, chess, choir, chorale, chorus, computers, dance, drama, drill team, ethnic, film, gay, honors, international, jazz band, marching band, musical theater, newspaper, orchestra, pep band, photography, political, professional, radio and TV, religious, social, social service, and student government. Popular campus events include Vintage Days, International Week, and Black History Month.

Sports: There are 10 intercollegiate sports for men and 12 for women, and 4 intramural sports for men and 4 for women. Facilities include 2 gyms, an indoor/outdoor swimming pool, 12 tennis courts, 6 indoor handball/racquetball courts, and 2 putting greens and driving areas. There are sports clubs in cycling, fencing, judo, karate, rodeo, and rugby. The campus stadium seats 41,031, the baseball stadium seats 6575, and the softball stadium seats 5467. There is also a 10,800-square-foot strength and conditioning center.

Disabled Students: All of the campus is accessible. Wheelchair ramps, elevators, special parking, specially equipped rest rooms, special class scheduling, lowered drinking fountains, and lowered telephones are available.

Services: Counseling and information services are available, as is tutoring in most subjects. There is a reader service for the blind, and remedial math, reading, and writing.

Campus Safety and Security: Measures include 24-hour foot and vehicle patrol, self-defense education, escort service, and informal discussions. There are pamphlets/posters/films, emergency telephones, lighted pathways/sidewalks, closed circuit television cameras, and bicycle safety patrols.

Programs of Study: Fresno State confers B.A. and B.S. degrees. Master's and doctoral degrees are also awarded. Bachelor's degrees are awarded in AGRICULTURE (agricultural business management, animal science, and plant science), BIOLOGICAL SCIENCE (biology/biological science), BUSINESS (business administration and management, and recreational facilities management), COMMUNICATIONS AND THE ARTS (art, communications, dramatic arts, English, French, graphic design, journalism, linguistics, music, Spanish, and speech/debate/rhetoric), COMPUTER AND PHYSICAL SCIENCE (chemistry, computer science, geology, mathematics, natural sciences, and physics), EDUCATION (agricultural), ENGINEERING AND ENVIRONMENTAL DESIGN (civil engineering, computer engineering, construction management, electrical/electronics engineering, industrial engineering, industrial engineering technology, interior design, mechanical engineering, and surveying engineering), HEALTH PROFESSIONS (health science, nursing, speech pathology/audiology, and speech therapy), SOCIAL SCIENCE (African American studies, anthropology, child psychology/development, criminology, economics, family/consumer studies, food science, geography, history, liberal arts/general studies, Mexican-American/Chicano studies, philosophy, physical fitness/movement, political science/government, psychology, public administration, social work, sociology, and women's studies). Business and liberal arts are the largest.

Required: All students must complete general education requirements. A minimum of 124 to 137 semester units, with a GPA of 2.0, is required to graduate.

Special: Study abroad in London, China, and the South Pacific, co-op programs, internships, work-study programs, B.A.-B.S. degrees, dual majors, and student-designed majors are offered. A liberal studies major, credit for military experience, pass/fail options, and nondegree study are available. There are 21 national honor societies, a freshman honors program, and 2 departmental honors programs.

Faculty/Classroom: 60% of faculty are male; 40%, female. All both teach undergraduates and do research. The average class size in an introductory lecture is 28; in a laboratory, 20; and in a regular course, 26.

Admissions: 74% of the 2001-2002 applicants were accepted. The SAT I scores for the 2001-2002 freshman class were: Verbal--65% below 500, 27% between 500 and 599, 7% between 600 and 700, and 1% above 700; Math--59% below 500, 30% between 500 and 599, 10% between 600 and 700, and 1% above 700. The ACT scores were 68% below 21, 17% between 21 and 23, 10% between 24 and 26, 3% between 27 and 28, and 2% above 28.

Requirements: The SAT I or ACT is required. Only students with a GPA below 3.0 are required to submit the SAT I or ACT scores. Applicants must be graduates of an accredited secondary school or have a GED. Secondary school courses must include 15 academic credits: 4 years of high school English, 3 each of math and electives, 2 of a foreign language, and 1 each of science, history/government, and visual/performing arts. A GPA of 2.0 is required. Applications are accepted on-line at the school's web site via CSU Mentor. AP and CLEP credits are accepted.

Procedure: Freshmen are admitted fall and spring. Entrance exams should be taken as early as possible, by the first semester of the senior year. Applications should be filed by May 15 for fall entry and October 15 for spring entry. The fall 2001 application fee was $55. Notification is sent on a rolling basis.

Transfer: 1993 transfer students enrolled in 2001-2002. Transfer applicants must have a minimum GPA of 2.0 and 56 transferable semester units earned, including English and math. 30 credits of 124 must be completed at Fresno State.

Visiting: There are regularly scheduled orientations for prospective students, including 1- and 2-day overnight programs for entering students. There are guides for informal visits and visitors may stay overnight. To schedule a visit, contact Orientation and Transition Services or University Outreach Services at (559) 278-7533 or (559) 278-2048.

Financial Aid: In 2001-2002, 61% of all freshmen and 78% of continuing students received some form of financial aid. 23% of freshmen and 50% of continuing students received need-based aid. The average freshman award was $5312. Of that total, scholarships or need-based grants averaged $4209 ($10,000 maximum); loans averaged $2342 ($2625 maximum); and work contracts averaged $2818 ($4000 maximum). 3% of undergraduates work part time. Average annual earnings from campus work are $3000. The average financial indebtedness of the 2001 graduate was $14,458. Fresno State is a member of CSS. The FAFSA is required. The fall application deadline is March 2.

International Students: There are 392 international students enrolled. The school actively recruits these students. They must score 500 on the written TOEFL and also take the SAT I or the ACT.

Computers: The mainframe is an IBM 3090. There are 1500 PCs and Macs available for student use. All students may access the system anytime. There are no time limits and no fees. All students are required to have personal computers.

Graduates: In 2001, 2859 bachelor's degrees were awarded. The most popular majors were liberal studies (25%), business administration

(16%), and criminology (5%). In an average class, 11% graduate in 4 years, 31% in 5 years, and 40% in 6 years. 259 companies recruited on campus in 2000-2001.

Admissions Contact: Vivian Franco, Director of Admissions. E-mail: *vivian-franco@csufresno.edu* Web: *www.csufresno.edu*

CALIFORNIA STATE UNIVERSITY, FULLERTON D-5
Fullerton, CA 92834 (714) 278-2370; (714) 278-2356

Full-time: 6450 men, 9360 women	**Faculty:** 630; IIA, +$
Part-time: 2960 men, 3680 women	**Ph.D.s:** 90%
Graduate: 1680 men, 3040 women	**Student/Faculty:** 25 to 1
Year: semesters, summer session	**Tuition:** $1740 ($9140)
Application Deadline: open	**Room & Board:** $3700
Freshman Class: n/av	
SAT I or ACT: required	**LESS COMPETITIVE**

California State University, Fullerton, founded in 1957, is part of the California State University system. The school offers programs in the arts, business and economics, communications, engineering and computer science, human development and community services, humanities and social science, and natural science and math. Figures in above capsule are approximate. There are 7 undergraduate and 7 graduate schools. In addition to regional accreditation, Cal State Fullerton has baccalaureate program accreditation with AACSB, ABET, ACEJMC, NASAD, NASM, NCATE, and NLN. The library contains 654,790 volumes, 964,340 microform items, and 15,790 audiovisual forms/CDs, and subscribes to 2500 periodicals. Computerized library services include the card catalog, interlibrary loans, and database searching. Special learning facilities include a learning resource center, art gallery, and an arboretum, an herbarium, a center for economic education, a developmental research center, a foreign language lab, an institute for economic and environmental studies, an institute for molecular biology and nutrition, a phonetic research lab, a social science research center, and a sport and movement institute. The 225-acre campus is in a suburban area 30 miles east of Los Angeles. Including residence halls, there are 22 buildings.

Student Life: Most undergraduates are from California. Others are from 40 states, 105 foreign countries, and Canada. 40% are white; 20% Asian American; 20% Hispanic. The average age of freshmen is 18; all undergraduates, 23. 20% do not continue beyond their first year; 60% remain to graduate.

Housing: 400 students can be accommodated in college housing, which includes coed on-campus apartments, fraternity houses, and sorority houses. On-campus housing is available on a first-come, first-served basis. Most students commute. All students may keep cars.

Activities: There are 5 local and 13 national fraternities and 1 local and 8 national sororities. There are 200 groups on campus, including art, band, cheerleading, choir, chorus, computers, dance, drama, ethnic, gay, honors, international, jazz band, literary magazine, musical theater, newspaper, orchestra, pep band, photography, political, professional, religious, social, social service, student government, and yearbook.

Sports: There are 7 intercollegiate sports for men and 9 for women, and 7 intramural sports for men and 9 for women. Facilities include a gym, a swimming pool, tennis and racquetball courts, baseball/softball, track, and soccer fields, a bowling alley, and a stadium.

Disabled Students: All of the campus is accessible. Wheelchair ramps, elevators, special parking, specially equipped rest rooms, lowered drinking fountains, lowered telephones, and automatic doors are available.

Services: Counseling and information services are available, as is tutoring in some subjects, including English and math. There is a reader service for the blind, and remedial math, reading, and writing.

Campus Safety and Security: Measures include 24-hour foot and vehicle patrol, self-defense education, escort service, and shuttle buses. There are pamphlets/posters/films, emergency telephones, and lighted pathways/sidewalks.

Programs of Study: Cal State Fullerton confers B.A., B.S., B.F.A., and B.M. degrees. Master's degrees are also awarded. Bachelor's degrees are awarded in BIOLOGICAL SCIENCE (biochemistry and biology/biological science), BUSINESS (accounting, banking and finance, business administration and management, business economics, international business management, management information systems, management science, marketing/retailing/merchandising, and tourism), COMMUNICATIONS AND THE ARTS (advertising, animation, art history and appreciation, broadcasting, ceramic art and design, communications, comparative literature, crafts, dance, dramatic arts, drawing, English, film arts, fine arts, French, German, graphic design, illustration, Japanese, journalism, linguistics, music, photography, printmaking, public relations, sculpture, Spanish, speech/debate/rhetoric, and studio art), COMPUTER AND PHYSICAL SCIENCE (chemistry, computer science, geology, mathematics, and physics), EDUCATION (art, music, and physical), ENGINEERING AND ENVIRONMENTAL DESIGN (civil engineering, electrical/electronics engineering, engineering and applied science, and mechanical engineering), HEALTH PROFESSIONS (health science, nursing, and speech pathology/audiology), SOCIAL SCIENCE (African American studies, American studies, anthropology, Asian/American studies, child psychology/development, criminal justice, economics, geography, history, human services, Latin American studies, liberal arts/general studies, Mexican-American/Chicano studies, philosophy, political science/government, psychology, public administration, religion, Russian and Slavic studies, sociology, and women's studies). Business administration, communications, and psychology are the largest.

Required: Graduation requirements for all students include the completion of a minimum of 51 units of general education courses, a 2.0 GPA, and an upper-division writing course designated by the major department. 120 to 135 credit hours must be completed for graduation, and students must pass a writing proficiency exam.

Special: The university offers cross-registration with other schools in the California State University system, the University of California, and California Community colleges, internships and co-op programs in 45 academic areas, study abroad in 18 countries, and work-study programs both on and off campus. A B.A.-B.S. degree in chemistry, dual and student-designed majors, and pass/fail options are also available. There are 16 national honor societies, a freshman honors program, and 13 departmental honors programs.

Faculty/Classroom: 70% of faculty are male; 30%, female. No introductory courses are taught by graduate students. The average class size in an introductory lecture is 50; in a laboratory, 24; and in a regular course, 25.

Requirements: The SAT I or ACT is required. In addition, applicants must be graduates of an accredited secondary school or have a GED certificate. Secondary school courses must include 4 years of English, 3 years of math, 2 years each of a foreign language, science, and history, and 1 year of visual or performing arts. Admission is based on the Qualifiable Eligibility Index, a combination of the high school GPA and either the SAT I or ACT score. Auditions are required for music majors. Applications are accepted on-line. A GPA of 2.0 is required. AP and CLEP credits are accepted.

Procedure: Freshmen are admitted fall and spring. Entrance exams should be taken during the senior year of high school. There is an early admissions plan. Application deadlines are open. The fall 2001 application fee was $55.

Transfer: Applicants must have a minimum 2.0 GPA. The SAT I or ACT is required for students with fewer than 56 transferable units earned. Students with 56 transferable units or more must have 30 units of general education completed with a C or better, including English composition, math, speech, and critical thinking. 30 credits of 120 to 135 must be completed at Cal State Fullerton.

Visiting: There are regularly scheduled orientations for prospective students. There are guides for informal visits. To schedule a visit, contact New Student Orientation at (714) 278-3120.

Financial Aid: Cal State Fullerton is a member of CSS. The FAFSA is required. The fall application deadline is March 2.

International Students: They must score 500 on the written TOEFL or 173 on the electronic version.

Computers: The mainframes are a DEC VAX 8550 and an IBM 3090/150E. Students may access the mainframe via school-based and computer center labs. All students may access the system 24 hours a day. There are no time limits and no fees.

Graduates: In an average class, 8% graduate in 4 years, and 23% in 5 years.

Admissions Contact: Nancy Dority, Associate Director, Admissions and Records. Web: *www.fullerton.edu*

CALIFORNIA STATE UNIVERSITY, HAYWARD B-3
Hayward, CA 94542-3095 (510) 885-2784; (510) 885-4059

Full-time: 2700 men, 5000 women	**Faculty:** 370; IIA, +$
Part-time: 1200 men, 1900 women	**Ph.D.s:** 90%
Graduate: 700 men, 1300 women	**Student/Faculty:** 21 to 1
Year: quarters, summer session	**Tuition:** $1200 ($6200)
Application Deadline: July 12	**Room & Board:** $6200
Freshman Class: n/av	
SAT I or ACT: required	**LESS COMPETITIVE**

California State University, Hayward, founded in 1957, is part of the California State University system. The institution offers degree programs in the arts, sciences, business and economics, and education to a primarily commuter student body. Figures given in the above capsule are approximate. There are 4 undergraduate and 4 graduate schools. In addition to regional accreditation, CSUH has baccalaureate program accreditation with AACSB, NASAD, NASM, NCATE, and NLN. The library contains 850,000 volumes, 700,000 microform items, and 26,000 audiovisual forms/CDs, and subscribes to 2000 periodicals. Computerized library services include the card catalog, interlibrary loans, and database searching. Special learning facilities include a learning resource center, art gallery, natural history museum, radio station, TV station, a marine biology lab, and a geology summer field camp. The 342-acre campus is in a suburban area 20 miles southeast of San Francisco in the Hayward Hills. Including residence halls, there are 17 buildings.

Student Life: 90% of undergraduates are from California. 85% are from public schools. 50% are white; 25% Asian American; 10% African American; 10% Hispanic. The average age of freshmen is 20; all undergraduates, 25. 15% do not continue beyond their first year; 60% remain to graduate.

Housing: 400 students can be accommodated in college housing, which includes coed on-campus apartments. On-campus housing is guaranteed for the freshman year only and is available on a first-come, first-served basis. Most students commute. All students may keep cars.

Activities: 1% of men belong to 4 national fraternities; 1% of women belong to 3 national sororities. There are 90 groups on campus, including art, cheerleading, chorale, chorus, computers, dance, drama, ethnic, film, gay, honors, international, jazz band, literary magazine, musical theater, newspaper, opera, orchestra, pep band, photography, political, professional, radio and TV, religious, social, social service, student government, symphony, and yearbook. Popular campus events include Science Fair and several leadership conferences.

Sports: There are 4 intercollegiate sports for men and 7 for women. Facilities include tennis and racquetball courts, 2 swimming pools, a track, a football field, a martial arts facility, a gymnastics center, a dance studio, baseball and softball diamonds, a 9000-seat stadium, a 5000-seat gym, and a 500-seat theater.

Disabled Students: 90% of the campus is accessible. Wheelchair ramps, elevators, special parking, specially equipped rest rooms, lowered drinking fountains, and lowered telephones are available. The Disabled Student Services Center provides tutorial, scribe, interpretive, and translation services are available.

Services: Counseling and information services are available, as is tutoring in most subjects. There is a reader service for the blind, and remedial math, reading, and writing.

Campus Safety and Security: Measures include 24-hour foot and vehicle patrol, self-defense education, escort service, and shuttle buses. There are informal discussions, pamphlets/posters/films, emergency telephones, and lighted pathways/sidewalks.

Programs of Study: CSUH confers B.A. and B.S. degrees. Master's degrees are also awarded. Bachelor's degrees are awarded in AGRICULTURE (environmental studies), BIOLOGICAL SCIENCE (biochemistry and biology/biological science), BUSINESS (accounting, business administration and management, marketing/retailing/merchandising, and recreation and leisure services), COMMUNICATIONS AND THE ARTS (advertising, art, arts administration/management, broadcasting, communications, dramatic arts, English, French, journalism, music, Spanish, and speech/debate/rhetoric), COMPUTER AND PHYSICAL SCIENCE (chemistry, computer science, geology, mathematics, physical sciences, physics, and statistics), ENGINEERING AND ENVIRONMENTAL DESIGN (engineering, environmental science, and industrial engineering), HEALTH PROFESSIONS (health science, nursing, and speech pathology/audiology), SOCIAL SCIENCE (anthropology, criminal justice, economics, ethnic studies, geography, history, human development, international studies, Latin American studies, liberal arts/general studies, philosophy, physical fitness/movement, political science/government, psychology, and sociology). Business administration, liberal studies, and computer science are the strongest academically. Business administration and liberal studies are the largest.

Required: In order to graduate, students must fulfill the university writing skills requirement, have a 2.0 minimum GPA, and complete 186 quarter units, including 72 in distribution requirements. The number of hours in the major varies by program from 56 to 153 quarter units.

Special: CSUH offers cross-registration with local community colleges, other CSU campuses, and the University of California/Berkeley. Internships, study abroad in 15 countries, work-study programs, and student-designed majors are also available. The PACE program provides degree opportunities in liberal studies and in human development to working adults. There is 1 national honor society, a freshman honors program, and 1 departmental honors program.

Requirements: The SAT I or ACT is required. All students must meet the eligibility index, a combination of the high school GPA and SAT I or ACT scores. Applicants must be graduates of an accredited secondary school or have a GED certificate. Secondary school courses must include 4 years of English, 3 each of math and electives, 2 of foreign language, and 1 each of history, science, and art, dance, drama/theater, or music. A GPA of 2.0 is required. AP and CLEP credits are accepted. Important factors in the admissions decision are advanced placement or honor courses, leadership record, and evidence of special talent.

Procedure: Freshmen are admitted to all sessions. There are early decision, early admissions, and deferred admissions plans. Applications should be filed by July 12 for fall entry, November 2 for winter entry, January 14 for spring entry, and April 19 for summer entry. Notification is sent on a rolling basis.

Transfer: 2215 transfer students enrolled in a recent year. Applicants must have a minimum 2.0 GPA (2.45 for nonresidents), be in good standing at the last college attended, and either meet freshman admission requirements or have completed at least 56 transferable semester (84 quarter) units. 45 quarter credits of 186 must be completed at CSUH.

Visiting: There are regularly scheduled orientations for prospective students. There are guides for informal visits. To schedule a visit, contact Enrollment Services at (510) 885-2556.

Financial Aid: All undergraduates work part time. CSUH is a member of CSS. The FAFSA is required. The priority deadline date for financial application is March 2.

International Students: They must score 525 on the written TOEFL or 197 on the electronic version. Graduates of a U.S. high school must also take the SAT I or ACT.

Computers: The mainframes are an E/XSI and an IBM 9370. There are 300 IBM, AT&T, and Mac PCs available throughout campus. All students may access the system on a 24-hour basis from home and 16 hours per day on campus. There are no time limits and no fees.

Admissions Contact: Admissions. E-mail: *adminfo@csuhayward.edu* Web: *www.csuhayward.edu*

CALIFORNIA STATE UNIVERSITY, LONG BEACH — D-5

Long Beach, CA 90840-0106 — **(562) 985-4141; Fax: 985-4973**

Full-time: 7450 men, 10,910 women	**Faculty:** 900; IIA, +$
Part-time: 2660 men, 3090 women	**Ph.D.s:** 85%
Graduate: 2250 men, 3660 women	**Student/Faculty:** 20 to 1
Year: semesters, summer session	**Tuition:** $1800 ($8100)
Application Deadline: November 30	**Room & Board:** $5600
Freshman Class: n/av	
SAT I or ACT: required	**LESS COMPETITIVE**

California State University, Long Beach, founded in 1949, is a nonprofit institution that is part of the California State University system. The commuter university offers undergraduate programs through the Colleges of Health and Human Services, Liberal Arts, Natural Sciences and Math, Business Administration, Engineering, the Arts, and Education. Figures given in the above capsule are approximate. There are 7 undergraduate and 7 graduate schools. In addition to regional accreditation, CSULB has baccalaureate program accreditation with AACSB, ABET, ACEJMC, AHEA, APTA, CSWE, FIDER, NASAD, NASM, NLN, and NRPA. The 2 libraries contain 1,100,000 volumes, 1,600,000 microform items, and 38,000 audiovisual forms/CDs, and subscribe to 3600 periodicals. Computerized library services include the card catalog and database searching. Special learning facilities include a learning resource center, art gallery, radio station, and TV station. The 322-acre campus is in a suburban area 25 miles southeast of Los Angeles. Including residence halls, there are 84 buildings.

Student Life: 90% of undergraduates are from California. Others are from 47 states, 105 foreign countries, and Canada. 90% are from public schools. 40% are white; 30% Asian American; 25% Hispanic; 10% African American. The average age of freshmen is 18; all undergraduates, 22. 20% do not continue beyond their first year; 50% remain to graduate.

Housing: 1830 students can be accommodated in college housing, which includes single-sex and coed dormitories. The international house has 44 foreign students, each of whom is paired with a resident student. On-campus housing is available on a first-come, first-served basis. 90% of students commute. All students may keep cars.

Activities: 6% of men belong to 15 national fraternities; 5% of women belong to 11 national sororities. There are 150 groups on campus, including art, band, cheerleading, choir, chorale, chorus, computers, dance, drama, drill team, ethnic, film, gay, honors, international, jazz band, literary magazine, musical theater, newspaper, opera, orchestra, pep band, photography, political, professional, radio and TV, religious, social, social service, student government, symphony, and yearbook. Popular campus events include the Kaleidoscope Spring Festival and Engineering Day, Blues Festival, and Odyssey Theme Year.

Sports: There are 10 intercollegiate sports for men and 9 for women, and 14 intramural sports for men and 12 for women. Facilities include the Long Beach Arena (seats 11,500 for basketball), a baseball field (seats 1500), the Pyramid Sports Arena (seats 5000) and an indoor gym (seats 2000).

Disabled Students: 98% of the campus is accessible. Wheelchair ramps, elevators, special parking, specially equipped rest rooms, special class scheduling, lowered drinking fountains, and lowered telephones are available. The university also offers registration and mobility assistance, adaptive equipment, counseling, community referrals, and services to the learning-disabled are available.

Services: Counseling and information services are available, as is tutoring in most subjects. There is a reader service for the blind, and remedial math, reading, and writing.

Campus Safety and Security: Measures include 24-hour foot and vehicle patrol, escort service, shuttle buses, and informal discussions. There are pamphlets/posters/films, emergency telephones, and lighted pathways/sidewalks.

Programs of Study: CSULB confers B.A., B.S., B.F.A., B.M., and B.Voc.Ed. degrees. Master's degrees are also awarded. Bachelor's degrees are awarded in BIOLOGICAL SCIENCE (biochemistry, biology/biological science, botany, cell biology, ecology, physiology, and zoology), BUSINESS (accounting, banking and finance, business administration and management, international business management, management information systems, marketing/retailing/merchandising, and personnel management), COMMUNICATIONS AND THE ARTS (art, communications, comparative literature, dance, design, dramatic arts, English, film arts, French, German, Japanese, journalism, music, and Spanish), COMPUTER AND PHYSICAL SCIENCE (applied mathematics, chemistry, computer science, earth science, geology, mathematics, physics, and statistics), EDUCATION (elementary, mathematics, science, and special), ENGINEERING AND ENVIRONMENTAL DESIGN (aerospace studies, chemical engineering, civil engineering, computer engineering, electrical/electronics engineering, engineering technology, and mechanical engineering), HEALTH PROFESSIONS (health care administration, and health science), SOCIAL SCIENCE (African American studies, anthropology, Asian/Oriental studies, economics, geography, Hispanic American studies, history, human development, interdisciplinary studies, international studies, philosophy, political science/government, psychology, religion, sociology, and women's studies). Art, biological sciences, and music are the strongest academically. Business administration, psychology, and liberal studies are the largest.

Required: Graduation requirements for all students include the completion of 51 units in general education (45 for engineering majors), 40 units of upper-division coursework, and 30 units in residence at the university. Students must have a minimum 2.0 GPA and a total of 124 to 140 credit hours, depending on the major. Required courses include University 100: "The University in Your Future.[3]

Special: The university offers cross-registration with California State University, Dominguez Hills for courses not offered at CSULB. Internships, study abroad in 22 countries, dual majors in engineering, a 3-2 engineering degree, student-designed majors, and pass/fail options are also available. There are 23 national honor societies, including Phi Beta Kappa, and a freshman honors program.

Faculty/Classroom: 65% of faculty are male; 35%, female. All teach undergraduates, 60% do research, and 60% do both. Graduate students teach 3% of introductory courses. The average class size in an introductory lecture is 68; in a laboratory, 24; and in a regular course, 26.

Admissions: There were 13 National Merit finalists and 2 semifinalists in a recent year. 53 freshmen graduated first in their class.

Requirements: The SAT I or ACT is required. In addition, applicants must be graduates of an accredited secondary school and have completed 4 years of English, 3 years each of math and electives, 2 years of foreign language, and 1 year each of lab science, U.S. history or U.S. history and government, and 1 visual and performing arts. Students are admitted on the basis of the eligibility index, which is computed from the secondary school GPA and the SAT I or ACT scores. California residents with a minimum 3.0 GPA are automatically admissible. A portfolio is required for art and design students. An audition is required for dance, music, and theater students. CSULB requires applicants to be in the upper 33% of their class. A GPA of 2.0 is required. AP and CLEP credits are accepted. The university accepts applications on computer disk and on-line.

Procedure: Freshmen are admitted fall and spring. Entrance exams should be taken during the fall semester of the senior year. Applications should be filed by November 30 for fall entry and August 31 for spring entry. Notification is sent on a rolling basis.

Transfer: 3120 transfer students enrolled in a recent year. Upper-division students must have completed a minimum of 60 semester units, and have a minimum 2.0 GPA, lower-division students must meet the same requirements as entering freshmen. 30 credits of 124 must be completed at CSULB.

Visiting: There are regularly scheduled orientations for prospective students, consisting of Student Orientation, Advising, and Registration (SOAR) sessions. Students may participate in SOAR I, which consists of advising and registration, or SOAR II, which involves a campus tour and an orientation to activities. There are guides for informal visits. To schedule a visit, contact the Office of School Relations at (562) 985-5358.

Financial Aid: In a recent year, 48% of all freshmen and 40% of continuing students received some form of financial aid. 42% of freshmen and 36% of continuing students received need-based aid. The average freshman award was $5461. Of that total, scholarships or need-based grants averaged $3417 ($6000 maximum); loans averaged $2000 ($4125 maximum); and work contracts averaged $1125 ($2000 maximum). 75% of undergraduates work part time. Average annual earnings from campus work are $1900. The average financial indebtedness of a recent year's graduate was $6400. CSULB is a member of CSS. The FAFSA is required. The fall application deadline is March 2.

International Students: There were 1138 international students enrolled in a recent year. The school actively recruits these students. They must score 500 on the written TOEFL and also take the SAT I or the ACT.

Computers: Four main labs with a total of approximately 550 PC-based or Mac-based systems, plus 54 college-based labs with a total of between 550 and 1100 PC or Mac-based systems, are open for student use 5 or more days a week. Internet and web access are automatically available on most of the available systems. All students may access the system during open lab hours, which vary across campus. There are no time limits and no fees.

Graduates: In a recent year, 4078 bachelor's degrees were awarded. The most popular majors were psychology (7%), liberal studies (6%), and criminal justice (5%). In an average class, 1% graduate in 3 years, 7% in 4 years, 24% in 5 years, and 37% in 6 years. 400 companies recruited on campus in a recent year.

Admissions Contact: Thomas Enders, Assistant Vice President, Enrollment Services. Web: *www.csulb.edu*

CALIFORNIA STATE UNIVERSITY, LOS ANGELES C-5

Los Angeles, CA 90032 **(323) 343-3901; Fax: (323) 343-3888**

Full-time: 3821 men, 6175 women	**Faculty:** 458; IIA, +$
Part-time: 1624 men, 2278 women	**Ph.D.s:** n/av
Graduate: 2378 men, 4399 women	**Student/Faculty:** 22 to 1
Year: quarters, summer session	**Tuition:** $1782 ($9162)
Application Deadline: June 15	**Room & Board:** $3268

Freshman Class: 9207 applied, 4856 accepted, 1280 enrolled

SAT I or ACT: required **COMPETITIVE**

California State University, Los Angeles, founded in 1947 as part of the state system, offers undergraduate and graduate programs in liberal arts and sciences, business education, engineering, health science, and professional training. There are 6 undergraduate schools. In addition to regional accreditation, Cal State, LA has baccalaureate program accreditation with AACSB, ABET, ADA, AHEA, CSWE, NASAD, NASM, NCATE, and NLN. The library contains 1,702,916 volumes, 1,040,737 microform items, and 4764 audiovisual forms/CDs, and subscribes to 2639 periodicals. Computerized library services include the card catalog, interlibrary loans, and database searching. Special learning facilities include a learning resource center, art gallery, and TV station. The 173-acre campus is in an urban area 5 miles east of downtown Los Angeles. Including residence halls, there are 22 buildings.

Student Life: 95% of undergraduates are from California. Others are from Canada. 53% are Hispanic; 22% Asian American; 16% white. The average age of freshmen is 18; all undergraduates, 25.

Housing: 1006 students can be accommodated in college housing, which includes single-sex and coed on-campus apartments. In addition, there are special-interest houses. On-campus housing is available on a first-come, first-served basis. 97% of students commute. All students may keep cars.

Activities: There are 4 national fraternities and 2 local and 3 national sororities. There are 115 groups on campus, including band, choir, chorale, chorus, computers, dance, drama, ethnic, gay, honors, international, jazz band, literary magazine, musical theater, newspaper, opera, orchestra, political, professional, radio and TV, religious, social, social service, student government, symphony, and yearbook. Popular campus events include Christmas Toy and Food Drive, Earth Week, and Career Day.

Sports: There are 6 intercollegiate sports for men and 6 for women, and 9 intramural sports for men and 7 for women. Facilities include a 4800-seat stadium, a 5500-seat gym, a swimming pool, tennis and racquetball courts, a track, and athletic fields.

Disabled Students: 95% of the campus is accessible. Wheelchair ramps, elevators, special parking, specially equipped rest rooms, and lowered telephones are available.

Services: Counseling and information services are available, as is tutoring in most subjects. There is a reader service for the blind, and remedial math, reading, and writing.

Campus Safety and Security: Measures include escort service, shuttle buses, emergency telephones, and lighted pathways/sidewalks.

Programs of Study: Cal State, LA confers B.A., B.S., B.M., and B.Voc.Ed. degrees. Master's and doctoral degrees are also awarded. Bachelor's degrees are awarded in BIOLOGICAL SCIENCE (biochemistry, biology/biological science, and microbiology), BUSINESS (accounting, banking and finance, business administration and management, business economics, business statistics, human resources, international business management, management science, marketing/retailing/merchandising, personnel management, real estate, retailing, small business management, trade and industrial supervision and management, and transportation management), COMMUNICATIONS AND THE ARTS (art history and appreciation, dance, dramatic arts, English, French, graphic design, Japanese, music, music performance, public relations, Spanish, and speech/debate/rhetoric), COMPUTER AND PHYSICAL SCIENCE (applied mathematics, chemistry, computer science, geology, information sciences and systems, mathematics, natural sciences, and physics), EDUCATION (industrial arts, music, physical, and vocational), ENGINEERING AND ENVIRONMENTAL DESIGN (automotive technology, aviation administration/management, civil engineering, electrical/electronics engineering, engineering, industrial administration/management, industrial engineering technology, manufacturing engineering, and mechanical engineering), HEALTH PROFESSIONS (community health work, health science, medical laboratory technology, nursing, rehabilitation therapy, and speech pathology/audiology), SO-

CIAL SCIENCE (African American studies, anthropology, child psychology/development, criminal justice, dietetics, economics, family/consumer studies, fire protection, geography, gerontology, history, interdisciplinary studies, Latin American studies, liberal arts/general studies, Mexican-American/Chicano studies, philosophy, political science/government, psychology, social science, social work, and sociology). Child development, computer information systems, and criminal justice are the largest.

Required: To graduate, students must complete 186 to 203 quarter units, with a minimum 2.0 GPA, and must demonstrate skills in math and oral and written communications. General education requirements include 72 quarter units in the social sciences, natural sciences, and humanities.

Special: Cross-registration is offered with other California State University schools. The school, as part of the state university system, is part of the California Desert Studies Consortium, which provides a field facility in the Mojave Desert to develop desert studies educational programs. It is also part of the Ocean Studies Institute, which facilitates marine educational and research activities. Students may design their own majors. Internships, study-abroad in 17 countries, work-study programs, B.A.-B.S. degrees, dual majors, pass/fail options, and credit for life experience are available. An accelerated degree program in nursing is offered. There are 21 national honor societies, including Phi Beta Kappa, a freshman honors program, and 5 departmental honors programs.

Faculty/Classroom: 55% of faculty are male; 45%, female. All teach undergraduates. No introductory courses are taught by graduate students. The average class size in an introductory lecture is 40; in a laboratory, 8; and in a regular course, 40.

Admissions: 53% of the 2001-2002 applicants were accepted.

Requirements: The SAT I or ACT is required. In addition, applicants should be graduates of accredited secondary schools or have a GED equivalent. 15 academic credits are required, including 4 years of English, 3 each of math and electives, 2 of a foreign language, and 1 each of science, history, and the visual and performing arts. Cal State, LA requires applicants to be in the upper 33% of their class. AP and CLEP credits are accepted. Applications are accepted on-line at CSUMentor

Procedure: Freshmen are admitted to all sessions. Entrance exams should be taken during the senior year. Applications should be filed by June 15 for fall entry, November 1 for winter entry, February 1 for spring entry, and April 1 for summer entry. The fall 2001 application fee was $55. Notification is sent on a rolling basis.

Transfer: 1546 transfer students enrolled in 2001-2002. Applicants must have 56 semester units (84 quarter units) and a 2.0 GPA (2.4 GPA for nonresidents) or meet freshman admission requirements. 45 credits of 186 must be completed at Cal State, LA.

Visiting: There are guides for informal visits.

Financial Aid: In 2001-2002, 87% of all freshmen received some form of financial aid. Scholarships or need-based grants averaged $5203; and loans averaged $2135. The CSS/Profile, FAFSA, and the SAAC (in-state) are required. The fall application deadline is March 1.

International Students: They must score 550 on the written TOEFL or 213 on the electronic version and also take the SAT I or the ACT.

Computers: The mainframe is a 35-server network of Sun servers. Students use the network system through both general access computing labs and electronic classrooms, and remote access via modems. Currently, there are 1500 workstations available to students, including PCs, Sun UNIX workstations, and MACs. All students may access the system 24 hours a day. There is a 2-hour limit in the open access labs during peak demand periods. There are no fees.

Graduates: In 2001, 2490 bachelor's degrees were awarded.

Admissions Contact: Vince Lopez, Director of Outreach and Recruitment.

CALIFORNIA STATE UNIVERSITY, MONTEREY BAY B-3

Seaside, CA 93955 **(831) 582-3518; Fax: (831) 582-3783**

Recognized candidate for accreditation

Full-time: 595 men, 1196 women	**Faculty:** 102; IIA, av$
Part-time: 100 men, 100 women	**Ph.D.s:** n/av
Graduate: 95 men, 175 women	**Student/Faculty:** 18 to 1
Year: semesters, summer session	**Tuition:** $1815 ($9195)
Application Deadline: open	**Room & Board:** $4900
Freshman Class: n/av	
SAT I or ACT: required	**LESS COMPETITIVE**

California State University, Monterey Bay, founded in 1994, is a public institution with 12 undergraduate divisions, including arts and sciences, communications, education and professional training, and science and technology. Figures in the above capsule are approximate. There are 12 undergraduate and 2 graduate schools. The library contains 40,000 volumes and 500 audiovisual forms/CDs, and subscribes to 445 periodicals. Computerized library services include interlibrary loans and database searching. Special learning facilities include a learning resource center. The 1300-acre campus is in a suburban area 80 miles south of San Francisco. Including residence halls, there are 51 buildings.

Student Life: 99% of undergraduates are from California. Others are from 25 states, 11 foreign countries, and Canada. 46% are white; 21% Hispanic; 10% Asian American.

Housing: 2100 students can be accommodated in college housing, which includes single-sex and coed dormitories, on-campus apartments, and married-student housing. On-campus housing is available on a first-come, first-served basis. 62% of students live on campus. Alcohol is not permitted. All students may keep cars.

Activities: There are no fraternities or sororities. There are 39 groups on campus, including choir, chorus, computers, dance, disabilities, drama, ethnic, gay, multicultural, musical theater, newspaper, photography, religious, sports, social service, and student government.

Sports: There are 5 intercollegiate sports for men and 4 for women, and 5 intramural sports for men and 5 for women. Facilities include 3 racquetball courts, a 2500-square-foot fitness room, saunas, and a 10,000-square-foot gym with facilities for basketball, volleyball, badminton, indoor soccer, aerobics, and dance.

Disabled Students: Wheelchair ramps, elevators, special parking, specially equipped rest rooms, and special class scheduling are available.

Services: Counseling and information services are available, as is tutoring in some subjects, including computer skills and others by demand. There is a reader service for the blind, and remedial math, reading, and writing.

Campus Safety and Security: Measures include self-defense education, escort service, shuttle buses, and informal discussions. There are pamphlets/posters/films, emergency telephones, and lighted pathways/sidewalks.

Programs of Study: CSUMB confers B.A. and B.S. degrees. Master's degrees are also awarded. Bachelor's degrees are awarded in BUSINESS (management science), COMMUNICATIONS AND THE ARTS (communications technology, telecommunications, and visual and performing arts), COMPUTER AND PHYSICAL SCIENCE (computer science and earth science), EDUCATION (education), SOCIAL SCIENCE (behavioral science, international studies, liberal arts/general studies, and social science). Computer science and technology, and liberal studies are the strongest academically.

Required: To graduate, students must complete 124 credit hours, including general education requirements and at least 24 hours in the major.

Special: Study abroad in 16 countries and an integrated studies major are available.

Faculty/Classroom: 55% of faculty are male; 45%, female. All teach undergraduates. The average class size in an introductory lecture is 23; in a laboratory, 17; and in a regular course, 22.

Requirements: The SAT I or ACT is required. Applications are accepted on-line. A GPA of 2.0 is required. AP and CLEP credits are accepted.

Procedure: Freshmen are admitted to all sessions. Application deadlines are open. The application fee is $55. Notification is sent on a rolling basis.

Transfer: 464 transfer students enrolled in 2001-2002. Applicants must have a college GPA of 2.0 and 56 transferable semester units, including 30 units of general education courses.

Visiting: There are regularly scheduled orientations for prospective students, onsite advising and registration, campus tours, and faculty one-on-one sessions. There are guides for informal visits and visitors may sit in on classes and stay overnight. To schedule a visit, contact Valarie E. Brown at *valarie_brown@csumb.edu*.

Financial Aid: In 2001-2002, 69% of all freshmen and 64% of continuing students received some form of financial aid. 54% of freshmen and 55% of continuing students received need-based aid. The average freshman award was $6179. Of that total, scholarships or need-based grants averaged $4873 ($10,676 maximum); loans averaged $3546 ($10,828 maximum); and work contracts averaged $3780 ($4000 maximum). The average financial indebtedness of the 2001 graduate was $8604. The FAFSA is required. The fall application deadline is March 2.

International Students: There were 6 international students enrolled in a recent year. They must score 525 on the written TOEFL and also take the SAT I or the ACT.

Computers: The mainframe is an IBM. All students have their own web page, e-mail account, and space on the campuswide server. All students may access the system. There are no time limits and no fees. It is strongly recommended that all students have a personal computer.

Graduates: In a recent year, 200 bachelor's degrees were awarded. The most popular major was liberal studies (33%). In an average class, 15% graduate in 4 years, 36% in 5 years, and 43% in 6 years.

Admissions Contact: Student Information Center. A video is available. E-mail: *student-infor-center@monterey.edu*
Web: *www.monterey.edu*

CALIFORNIA STATE UNIVERSITY, NORTHRIDGE C-5

Northridge, CA 91328 (818) 677-3700; Fax: (818) 677-3766

Full-time: 7484 men, 10,841 women	**Faculty:** 841; IIA, +$
Part-time: 2578 men, 3560 women	**Ph.D.s:** 84%
Graduate: 2108 men, 4877 women	**Student/Faculty:** 22 to 1
Year: semesters, summer session	**Tuition:** $1916 ($9790)
Application Deadline: November 30	**Room & Board:** $5865
Freshman Class: 10,600 applied, 8788 accepted, 3299 enrolled	
SAT I Verbal/Math: 466/448	**COMPETITIVE**

California State University, Northridge, founded in 1958, is part of the state-supported university system offering degree programs in the liberal arts and sciences, business administration, education, engineering, music, health fields, and fine arts. There are 8 undergraduate schools and 1 graduate school. In addition to regional accreditation, CSUN has baccalaureate program accreditation with AACSB, ABET, ACEJMC, AHEA, APTA, CAHEA, CSAB, NASAD, NASM, NCATE, and NRPA. The 3 libraries contain 2.13 million volumes, 3.1 million microform items, and 37,000 audiovisual forms/CDs, and subscribe to 4300 periodicals. Computerized library services include the card catalog, interlibrary loans, and database searching. Special learning facilities include a learning resource center, art gallery, planetarium, radio station, TV station, observatory, anthropological museum, botanical gardens, urban archives center, Natural Center on Deafness, and Center for the Study of Cancer and Development Biology. The 353-acre campus is in a suburban area 25 miles north of Los Angeles. Including residence halls, there are 47 buildings.

Student Life: 93% of undergraduates are from California. Others are from 46 states and Canada. 93% are from public schools. 35% are white; 24% Hispanic, 12% Asian American. The average age of freshmen is 18; all undergraduates, 24.

Housing: 2400 students can be accommodated in college housing, which includes coed on-campus apartments. In addition, there is an international house. On-campus housing is guaranteed for all 4 years and is available on a first-come, first-served basis. All students may keep cars.

Activities: There are 5 local and 13 national fraternities and 6 local and 8 national sororities. There are 181 groups on campus, including art, band, cheerleading, choir, chorale, chorus, computers, dance, drama, ethnic, film, gay, honors, international, jazz band, literary magazine, marching band, musical theater, newspaper, opera, orchestra, photography, political, professional, radio and TV, religious, social, social service, student government, symphony, and yearbook. Popular campus events include International Student Days, Campus Community Day, and Welcome Week.

Sports: There are 10 intercollegiate sports for men and 12 for women, and 9 intramural sports for men and 9 for women. Facilities include 2 gyms, 2 swimming pools, softball and soccer fields, handball, racquetball, and tennis courts, a baseball field, and a track.

Disabled Students: 98% of the campus is accessible. Wheelchair ramps, elevators, special parking, specially equipped rest rooms, special class scheduling, lowered drinking fountains, lowered telephones, and electric doors are available.

Services: Counseling and information services are available, as is tutoring in some subjects, including English and math. There is a reader service for the blind, and remedial math, reading, and writing. Student tutors are available for other selected subjects as well.

Campus Safety and Security: Measures include 24-hour foot and vehicle patrol, escort service, shuttle buses, and informal discussions. There are pamphlets/posters/films, emergency telephones, and lighted pathways/sidewalks.

Programs of Study: CSUN confers B.A., B.S., and B.M. degrees. Master's degrees are also awarded. Bachelor's degrees are awarded in BIOLOGICAL SCIENCE (biochemistry, biology/biological science, environmental biology, and microbiology), BUSINESS (accounting, banking and finance, business administration and management, management information systems, marketing/retailing/merchandising, and recreation and leisure services), COMMUNICATIONS AND THE ARTS (art, dance, dramatic arts, English, film arts, French, German, journalism, linguistics, music, Spanish, and speech/debate/rhetoric), COMPUTER AND PHYSICAL SCIENCE (astrophysics, chemistry, computer science, earth science, geology, mathematics, physics, and radiological technology), EDUCATION (business, education of the deaf and hearing impaired, home economics, and physical), ENGINEERING AND ENVIRONMENTAL DESIGN (engineering), HEALTH PROFESSIONS (biomedical science, exercise science, health, health care administration, medical laboratory technology, nursing, physical therapy, recreation therapy, and speech pathology/audiology), SOCIAL SCIENCE (African American studies, anthropology, Asian/American studies, child psychology/development, criminology, economics, family/consumer studies, geography, history, humanities, liberal arts/general studies, Mexican-American/Chicano studies, philosophy, political science/government, psychology, sociology, urban studies, and women's studies). Liberal studies is the strongest academically. Business administration and economics, psychology, and liberal studies are the largest.

Required: All students must complete 52 units of general education requirements in 6 areas, including courses in American history, U.S. Constitution, state and local government, English, math, logic, and oral and written communication. A total of 124 semester units for the B.A., 128 to 132 for the B.S., and 132 for the B.M., with a minimum GPA of 2.0, is required to graduate. At least 30 semester units must be completed in residence.

Special: Cross-registration is offered through the Intra System Visitor Program. Study abroad in 16 countries, internships, university work-study programs, dual majors, student-designed majors, credit for military experience, and pass/fail options for elective courses are offered. There are 4 national honor societies, a freshman honors program, and 8 departmental honors programs.

Faculty/Classroom: 61% of faculty are male; 39%, female. All teach undergraduates. Graduate students teach 12% of introductory courses. The average class size in an introductory lecture is 33 and in a laboratory, 20.

Admissions: 83% of the 2001-2002 applicants were accepted. The SAT I scores for the 2001-2002 freshman class were: Verbal--68% below 500, 25% between 500 and 599, and 7% between 600 and 700; Math--60% below 500, 31% between 500 and 599, 8% between 600 and 700, and 1% above 700.

Requirements: The SAT I or ACT is required for students with a GPA below 3.0 (3.6 for nonresidents). Applicants should have completed 4 years of high school English, 3 each of math and academic electives, 2 of foreign language, and 1 each of lab science, U.S. history/government, and visual/performing arts. CSUN requires applicants to be in the upper 33% of their class. A GPA of 2.0 is required. AP and CLEP credits are accepted. Important factors in the admissions decision are recommendations by school officials, evidence of special talent, and leadership record. Applications are accepted on-line through CSU-Mentor.

Procedure: Freshmen are admitted fall and spring. Entrance exams should be taken by December of the senior year. There is an early decision plan. Applications should be filed by November 30 for fall entry and August 31 for spring entry. The fall 2001 application fee was $55. Notification is sent on a rolling basis.

Transfer: 2902 transfer students enrolled in a recent year. A GPA of 2.0 (2.4 for nonresidents) is required in a minimum of 56 transferable semester units. Basic courses in writing, math, speech, and logic must be completed with a grade of C or better. 30 credits of 124 must be completed at CSUN.

Visiting: There are regularly scheduled orientations for prospective students, held in June and July for fall entrance and in November for spring entrance. There are guides for informal visits and visitors may sit in on classes and stay overnight. To schedule a visit, contact Student Outreach and Recruitment at (818) 677-2879 or *jason.roberts@csun.edu*

Financial Aid: Scholarships or need-based grants averaged $1435; loans averaged $3873; and work contracts averaged $1403 in a recent year. The average financial indebtedness of a recent year graduate was $12,000. CSUN is a member of CSS. The SAAC financial statement is required. The fall application deadline is March 2.

International Students: There are 1126 international students enrolled. They must score 500 on the written TOEFL.

Computers: The mainframe is an IBM 4381. There are 1700 PCs on campus; 300 are networked by DOS and UNIX. The computers are located in some labs and classrooms, libraries, and student housing. All students may access the system 24 hours a day, 7 days a week. There are no time limits and no fees.

Graduates: In 2001, 4387 bachelor's degrees were awarded. The most popular majors were business administration (18%), liberal studies (9%), and psychology (8%). In an average class, 3% graduate in 4 years, 15% in 5 years, and 25% in 6 years. 400 companies recruited on campus in 2000-2001.

Admissions Contact: Eric Forbes, Registrar and Director of Operations, Admissions, and Records. Web: *http://www.csun.edu/index.html*

CALIFORNIA STATE UNIVERSITY, SACRAMENTO B-3

Sacramento, CA 95819-6048 (916) 278-3901
(800) 722-4748; Fax: (916) 278-5603

Full-time: 6876 men, 9174 women	**Faculty:** 784; IIA, ++$	
Part-time: 2430 men, 3023 women	**Ph.D.s:** 79%	
Graduate: 1787 men, 3633 women	**Student/Faculty:** 20 to 1	
Year: semesters, summer session	**Tuition:** $1887 ($9267)	
Application Deadline: open	**Room & Board:** $5601	
Freshman Class: 9713 applied, 4973 accepted, 2420 enrolled		
SAT I Verbal/Math: 475/470	**ACT:** 20	**COMPETITIVE**

California State University/Sacramento, founded in 1947, is part of the state-supported university system. The school offers graduate and undergraduate programs in the liberal arts and sciences, business administration, education, engineering, music, and health and human service fields. There are 8 undergraduate schools. In addition to regional accreditation, Sac State has baccalaureate program accreditation with AACSB, ABET, AHEA, CSWE, NASAD, NASM, NLN, and NRPA. The library contains 770,779 volumes, 2,269,028 microform items, and 152,128 audiovisual forms/CDs, and subscribes to 4040 periodicals. Computerized library services include the card catalog, interlibrary loans, and database searching. Special learning facilities include a learning resource center, art gallery, planetarium, radio station, TV station, an aquatic center, and an anthropology museum. The 282-acre campus is in an urban area 90 miles northeast of San Francisco. Including residence halls, there are 51 buildings.

Student Life: 98% of undergraduates are from California. Others are from 45 states, 82 foreign countries, and Canada. 94% are from public schools. 47% are white; 17% Asian American; 10% Hispanic. The average age of freshmen is 18; all undergraduates, 24. 19% do not continue beyond their first year; 52% remain to graduate.

Housing: 1299 students can be accommodated in college housing, which includes coed dormitories. On-campus housing is available on a first-come, first-served basis. 96% of students commute. All students may keep cars.

Activities: 8% of men belong to 1 local and 18 national fraternities; 4% of women belong to 2 local and 8 national sororities. There are 250 groups on campus, including art, band, cheerleading, chess, choir, chorale, chorus, computers, dance, drama, ethnic, film, gay, honors, international, jazz band, marching band, musical theater, newspaper, opera, orchestra, pep band, photography, political, professional, radio and TV, religious, social, social service, student government, and symphony. Popular campus events include Greek Week, Festival of New American Music, and River City Days.

Sports: There are 8 intercollegiate sports for men and 8 for women, and 13 intramural sports for men and 13 for women. Facilities include a 15,000-seat stadium, 2 gyms, 2 swimming pools, an all-weather outdoor track, baseball, softball, and soccer fields, and an aquatic center, with sailing, wind-surfing, rowing, and canoeing.

Disabled Students: 90% of the campus is accessible. Wheelchair ramps, elevators, special parking, specially equipped rest rooms, special class scheduling, lowered drinking fountains, and lowered telephones are available.

Services: Counseling and information services are available, as is tutoring in most subjects. There is a reader service for the blind, and remedial math, reading, and writing.

Campus Safety and Security: Measures include 24-hour foot and vehicle patrol, self-defense education, escort service, and shuttle buses. There are informal discussions, pamphlets/posters/films, emergency telephones, and lighted pathways/sidewalks.

Programs of Study: Sac State confers B.A., B.S., and B.M. degrees. Master's degrees are also awarded. Bachelor's degrees are awarded in BIOLOGICAL SCIENCE (biology/biological science and microbiology), BUSINESS (accounting, banking and finance, business administration and management, insurance, international business management, management information systems, marketing/retailing/merchandising, and real estate), COMMUNICATIONS AND THE ARTS (communications, dramatic arts, English, French, German, journalism, music, and Spanish), COMPUTER AND PHYSICAL SCIENCE (chemistry, computer science, geology, mathematics, physical sciences, and physics), EDUCATION (business, early childhood, and health), ENGINEERING AND ENVIRONMENTAL DESIGN (civil engineering, computer engineering, electrical/electronics engineering, engineering technology, and mechanical engineering), HEALTH PROFESSIONS (environmental health science, medical laboratory technology, nursing, physical therapy, and speech pathology/audiology), SOCIAL SCIENCE (anthropology, criminal justice, economics, geography, history, international relations, parks and recreation management, philosophy, psychology, public administration, social science, social work, and sociology). Nursing, criminal justice, and business administration are the strongest academically. Business administration, communications, and criminal justice are the largest.

Required: In order to graduate, students must complete a minimum of 124 semester hours, including 30 to 86 hours in the major, with a minimum 2.0 GPA. Students must complete 51 units in general education requirements and take proficiency exams in writing and a foreign language. A course in race and ethnicity in American society is required.

Special: The university offers cross-registration with other California State University schools, co-op programs in many academic programs, internships, a Washington semester, study abroad in 12 countries, and dual and student-designed majors. There are 12 national honor societies, including Phi Beta Kappa.

Faculty/Classroom: 55% of faculty are male; 45%, female. All both teach and do research. The average class size in an introductory lecture is 40; in a laboratory, 20; and in a regular course, 40.

Admissions: 51% of the 2001-2002 applicants were accepted. The SAT I scores for the 2001-2002 freshman class were: Verbal--58% below 500, 33% between 500 and 599, 8% between 600 and 700, and 1% above 700; Math--50% below 500, 36% between 500 and 599, 13% between 600 and 700, and 1% above 700. The ACT scores were 59% below 21, 23% between 21 and 23, 13% between 24 and 26, 3% between 27 and 28, and 2% above 28.

Requirements: The SAT I or ACT is required as is a GPA of 2.0. The SAT I or ACT is required of applicants with a high school GPA below 3.0. Applicants should have completed 4 years of high school English, 3 years of math, 2 years of a foreign language, 1 year each of lab science, history, and visual/performing arts and 3 years of college preparatory electives. AP and CLEP credits are accepted. Applications are accepted on computer disk and on line at *http://www.csumentor.edu/admissionapp*

Procedure: Freshmen are admitted fall and spring. Entrance exams should be taken before December of the senior year. There is an early admissions plan. The fall 2001 application fee was $55. Application deadlines are open.

Transfer: Applicants must have a 2.0 GPA and 56 transferable semester units, including 30 units of specific general education courses to include oral and written communication, critical thinking, and math. 30 credits of 124 must be completed at Sac State.

Visiting: There are regularly scheduled orientations for prospective students. There are guides for informal visits and visitors may sit in on classes. To schedule a visit, contact the University Outreach Services Office at (916) 278-7362 or *outreach@csus.edu*

Financial Aid: 75% of undergraduates work part time. Sac State is a member of CSS. The FAFSA and SAAC are required. The fall application deadline is March 2.

International Students: There were 607 international students enrolled in a recent year. They must score 510 on the written TOEFL or 180 on the electronic version and also take the SAT I or the ACT.

Computers: The mainframes are an IBM 4381, an IBM 3090/150E, and a DEC VAX 880. There are 400 terminals or PC workstations located in 10 computer labs. All students may obtain accounts to access e-mail and Internet services and all campus computers. All students may access the system. There are no fees. It is strongly recommended that all students have a personal computer.

Graduates: In 2001, 4087 bachelor's degrees were awarded. The most popular majors were liberal studies (6%), communication studies (6%), and criminal justice (6%). In an average class, 15% graduate in 4 years, 40% in 5 years, and 3% in 6 years. Of the 2000 graduating class, 20% were enrolled in graduate school within 6 months of graduation.

Admissions Contact: Larry D. Glasmire, Assistant to Vice President for Student Affairs. E-mail: *admissions@csus.edu*
Web: *http://www.csus.edu/admr/*

CALIFORNIA STATE UNIVERSITY, SAN BERNARDINO D-5
San Bernardino, CA 92407-2397 **(909) 880-5188**
Fax: (909) 880-7034

Full-time: 3356 men, 5707 women	**Faculty:** IIA, +$
Part-time: 770 men, 1187 women	**Ph.D.s:** 92%
Graduate: 1721 men, 3244 women	**Student/Faculty:** 19 to 1
Year: quarters, summer session	**Tuition:** $1733 ($9244)
Application Deadline: November 1	**Room & Board:** $4783
Freshman Class: 4114 applied, 2813 accepted, 1195 enrolled	
SAT I Verbal/Math: 440/450	**ACT:** 18 **COMPETITIVE**

California State University, San Bernardino, founded in 1965, is a public, comprehensive regional university offering programs in business and public administration, natural sciences, education, arts and letters, and social and behavioral sciences. There are 5 undergraduate and 19 graduate schools. In addition to regional accreditation, CSUSB has baccalaureate program accreditation with AACSB, ADA, CSAB, CSWE, NASAD, and NLN. The library contains 731,259 volumes, 643,292 microform items, and 15,252 audiovisual forms/CDs, and subscribes to 2028 periodicals. Computerized library services include the card catalog, interlibrary loans, and database searching. Special learning facilities include a learning resource center, art gallery, and radio station. The 430-acre campus is in a suburban area 60 miles east of Los Angeles. Including residence halls, there are 45 buildings.

Student Life: 96% of undergraduates are from California. Others are from 29 states, 49 foreign countries, and Canada. 83% are from public schools. 40% are white; 27% Hispanic; 10% African American. The average age of freshmen is 19; all undergraduates, 22. 23% do not continue beyond their first year.

Housing: 747 students can be accommodated in college housing, which includes single-sex and coed dormitories. On-campus housing is available on a first-come, first-served basis. 96% of students commute. All students may keep cars.

Activities: 5% of men belong to 1 local and 8 national fraternities; 3% of women belong to 6 national sororities. There are 80 groups on campus, including art, band, cheerleading, choir, chorale, chorus, computers, dance, drama, ethnic, film, gay, honors, international, jazz band, literary magazine, musical theater, newspaper, opera, orchestra, pep band, political, professional, radio and TV, religious, social, social service, and student government. Popular campus events include Dia de los Muertos, California Indian Cultural Awareness Conference, and Around the World.

Sports: There are 4 intercollegiate sports for men and 7 for women. Facilities include an arena for basketball and volleyball, baseball, softball,

and soccer fields, tennis courts, swimming pools for water polo and recreational swimming, and a gym for recreational workouts.
Disabled Students: 98% of the campus is accessible. Wheelchair ramps, elevators, special parking, specially equipped rest rooms, lowered drinking fountains, lowered telephones, student assistants, cart service, and special equipment such as TSS, phonic ear, and VisualTek are available.
Services: Counseling and information services are available, as is tutoring in most subjects. There is a reader service for the blind and remedial math and writing.
Campus Safety and Security: Measures include 24-hour foot and vehicle patrol, self-defense education, escort service, and emergency telephones. There are lighted pathways/sidewalks and e-mail and web site alerts.
Programs of Study: CSUSB confers B.A., B.S., and B.V.E. degrees. Master's degrees are also awarded. Bachelor's degrees are awarded in BIOLOGICAL SCIENCE (biochemistry and biology/biological science), BUSINESS (accounting, banking and finance, business administration and management, business economics, international business management, management information systems, management science, marketing/retailing/merchandising, and small business management), COMMUNICATIONS AND THE ARTS (art, communications, dramatic arts, English, French, music, and Spanish), COMPUTER AND PHYSICAL SCIENCE (chemistry, computer science, geology, mathematics, and physics), EDUCATION (bilingual/bicultural, health, music, physical, and vocational), HEALTH PROFESSIONS (environmental health science, health care administration, and nursing), SOCIAL SCIENCE (American studies, anthropology, criminal justice, economics, food science, geography, history, human development, human services, liberal arts/general studies, philosophy, political science/government, psychology, public administration, social science, and sociology). Liberal arts and business administration are the largest.
Required: To graduate, students must complete 180 to 198 quarter hours, including 60 in upper-division courses and requirements for the major, with a minimum GPA of 2.0. The 82-credit general education program includes courses in basic skills, natural sciences, humanities, social and behavioral sciences, lifelong understanding, upper-division writing, multicultural/gender studies, and electives. Students must also demonstrate an understanding of the U.S. Constitution, American history, and California government.
Special: The university offers cross-registration with other CSU campuses and with Loma Linda University, and study abroad through the National Student Exchange Program and CSU International Programs. Also available are internships, campus and community work-study programs, B.A.-B.S. degrees, dual and student-designed majors, credit for vocational education and military experience, and nondegree study. There is 1 national honor society, a chapter of Phi Beta Kappa, and a freshman honors program.
Faculty/Classroom: 60% of faculty are male; 40%, female. The average class size in an introductory lecture is 40; in a laboratory, 18; and in a regular course, 24.
Admissions: 68% of the 2001-2002 applicants were accepted. The SAT I scores for the 2001-2002 freshman class were: Verbal--75% below 500, 21% between 500 and 599, and 4% between 600 and 700; Math--71% below 500, 24% between 500 and 599, and 5% between 600 and 700. The ACT scores were 78% below 21, 15% between 21 and 23, and 6% between 24 and 26.
Requirements: The SAT I or ACT is required. In addition, applicants must be graduates of an accredited secondary school. Preparatory work should include 4 years of English, 3 of math, 2 of foreign language, 1 each of U.S. history/government, lab science, and visual and performing arts, and 3 of electives. Admission is based on an eligibility index that weighs the high school GPA and the SAT I or ACT score. Students with GPAs of 3.0 or better (3.6 for nonresidents) are exempt from test score requirements. A GPA of 2.0 is required. AP and CLEP credits are accepted. Important factors in the admissions decision are advanced placement or honor courses, recommendations by school officials, and leadership record. Applications are accepted on-line via *www.csumentor.edu*
Procedure: Freshmen are admitted to all sessions. Entrance exams should be taken prior to applying. Applications should be filed by November 1 for fall entry, June 1 for winter entry, August 1 for spring entry, and February 1 for summer entry. The fall 2001 application fee was $55. Notification is sent on a rolling basis.
Transfer: 6187 transfer students enrolled in 2001-2002. Applicants must have a minimum college GPA of 2.0 (2.4 for nonresidents) and be in good standing at the previously attended institution. Those with fewer than 56 transferable semester units must meet freshman entrance requirements. 45 credits of 180 to 198 must be completed at CSUSB.
Visiting: There are regularly scheduled orientations for prospective students, including sessions on admissions requirements, financial aid information, and campus (student) life information. There are guides for informal visits and visitors may sit in on classes and stay overnight. To schedule a visit, contact the Outreach Services Office.
Financial Aid: The FAFSA is required. The fall application deadline is March 2.
International Students: There are 626 international students enrolled. The school actively recruits these students. They must score 500 on the written TOEFL or 173 on the electronic version.
Computers: The mainframes are an IBM 4381 and a DEC VAX 3500. Macs and PCs are available in various buildings. All students may access the system. There are no time limits and no fees.
Graduates: In 2001, 2097 bachelor's degrees were awarded. The most popular majors were business administration (23%), liberal studies (15%), and education (8%). In an average class, 38% graduate in 6 years. Of the 2000 graduating class, 17% were enrolled in graduate school within 6 months of graduation.
Admissions Contact: Enrollment Services. A video is available.
E-mail: *www.moreinfo@mail.csusb,edu*
Web: *http://enrollment.csusb.edu*

CALIFORNIA STATE UNIVERSITY, SAN MARCOS D-5

San Marcos, CA 92096-0001 **(760) 750-4848**
Fax: (760) 750-3248

Full-time: 5757 men and women	**Faculty:** 170; IIA, av$
Part-time: none	**Ph.D.s:** 92%
Graduate: 746 men and women	**Student/Faculty:** n/av
Year: semesters, summer session	**Tuition:** $1736 ($10,000)
Application Deadline: November 30	**Room & Board:** n/app
Freshman Class: n/av	
SAT I or ACT: recommended	**LESS COMPETITIVE**

California State University, San Marcos, founded in 1989, is a public commuter institution that is part of the California State University system. There are 2 undergraduate and 3 graduate schools. In addition to regional accreditation, Cal State San Marcos has baccalaureate program accreditation with NCATE. The library contains 148,114 volumes, 755,260 microform items, and 5668 audiovisual forms/CDs, and subscribes to 1871 periodicals. Computerized library services include the card catalog, interlibrary loans, and database searching. Special learning facilities include a learning resource center. The 304-acre campus is in a suburban area 32 miles northeast of San Diego. There are 8 buildings.
Student Life: 98% of undergraduates are from California. Others are from Canada. 55% are white; 18% Hispanic. The average age of freshmen is 19; all undergraduates, 25.
Housing: There are no residence halls. All students commute. Alcohol is not permitted.
Activities: 3% of men belong to 2 national fraternities; 2% of women belong to 2 national sororities. There are 35 groups on campus, including computers, ethnic, gay, honors, international, political, professional, religious, social, student government, and yearbook. Popular campus events include Admissions Day, San Marcos Grand Festival, and Preview Day.
Sports: There are 3 intercollegiate sports for men and 3 for women, and 5 intramural sports for men and 5 for women. Facilities include an Olympic-quality track.
Disabled Students: All of the campus is accessible. Wheelchair ramps, elevators, special parking, specially equipped rest rooms, special class scheduling, lowered drinking fountains, and lowered telephones are available.
Services: There is a reader service for the blind, and remedial math, reading, and writing, a writing center, and math, accounting, and computer labs.
Campus Safety and Security: Measures include 24-hour foot and vehicle patrol, escort service, informal discussions, and pamphlets/posters/films. There are emergency telephones and lighted pathways/sidewalks.
Programs of Study: Cal State San Marcos confers B.A. and B.S. degrees. Master's degrees are also awarded. Bachelor's degrees are awarded in BIOLOGICAL SCIENCE (biology/biological science), BUSINESS (business administration and management), COMMUNICATIONS AND THE ARTS (communications, creative writing, literature, Spanish, and visual and performing arts), COMPUTER AND PHYSICAL SCIENCE (chemistry, computer science, and mathematics), SOCIAL SCIENCE (economics, history, human development, liberal arts/general studies, political science/government, psychology, social science, sociology, and women's studies). Business administration, psychology, and liberal studies are the largest.
Required: To graduate, students must attain foreign language proficiency at the intermediate level, demonstrate computer competency, fulfill a writing requirement, and maintain a GPA of 2.0. The number of credits required for graduation varies from 124 to 132 depending on the major.
Special: There is cross-registration with other CSU campuses. Internships, study abroad in 16 countries, and work-study programs are available.
Faculty/Classroom: 53% of faculty are male; 47%, female. Graduate students teach 5% of introductory courses. The average class size in an introductory lecture is 25; in a laboratory, 25; and in a regular course, 25.

Requirements: The SAT I or ACT is recommended. Applications are accepted on-line at *www.csumentor.edu*. A GPA of 2.0 is required. AP and CLEP credits are accepted.

Procedure: Freshmen are admitted fall and spring. Applications should be filed by November 30 for fall entry and August 31 for spring entry, along with a $55 fee.

Transfer: 1086 transfer students enrolled in 2001-2002. Requirements include 56 units completed and a 2.0 GPA for California residents, 2.4 for nonresidents. 30 credits of 124 to 132 must be completed at Cal State San Marcos.

Visiting: There are regularly scheduled orientations for prospective students, including workshops and a campus tour. There are guides for informal visits and visitors may sit in on classes. To schedule a visit, contact the Office of Admissions.

Financial Aid: In 2001-2002, 39% of all freshmen and 50% of continuing students received some form of financial aid. 32% of freshmen and 36% of continuing students received need-based aid. The average freshman award was $5046. Of that total, scholarships or need-based grants averaged $1726 ($10,000 maximum); loans averaged $5582 ($18,500 maximum); and work contracts averaged $1596 ($3600 maximum). The average financial indebtedness of the 2001 graduate was $15,027. Cal State San Marcos is a member of CSS. The FAFSA is required. The fall application deadline is March 2.

International Students: There were 82 international students enrolled in a recent year. The school actively recruits these students. They must score 550 on the written TOEFL.

Computers: All students may access the system. There are no time limits and no fees. It is strongly recommended that all students have a personal computer.

Graduates: In 2001, 1100 bachelor's degrees were awarded. Of the 2000 graduating class, 33% were enrolled in graduate school within 6 months of graduation and 79% were employed.

Admissions Contact: Cherine Heckman, Director of Admissions. A video is available. E-mail: *apply@csusm.edu* Web: *www.csusm.edu*

CALIFORNIA STATE UNIVERSITY, STANISLAUS B-3

Turlock, CA 95382 (209) 667-3070
(800) 828-7733; Fax: (209) 667-3788

Full-time: 1310 men, 2537 women	**Faculty:** 262; IIA, +$
Part-time: 554 men, 1223 women	**Ph.D.s:** 56%
Graduate: 538 men, 1372 women	**Student/Faculty:** 15 to 1
Year: 4-1-4, summer session	**Tuition:** $1875 ($9255)
Application Deadline: open	**Room & Board:** $7020
Freshman Class: 1875 applied, 1281 accepted, 562 enrolled	
SAT I Verbal/Math: 480/480	**ACT:** 20 **COMPETITIVE**

California State University, Stanislaus, founded in 1957, is a state-supported institution offering undergraduate and graduate programs in liberal and fine arts, business, health science, and teacher preparation. There are 3 undergraduate schools and 1 graduate school. In addition to regional accreditation, CSU/Stanislaus has baccalaureate program accreditation with AACSB, ACS, CCTC, CSWE, NASAD, NASM, NCATE, and NLN. The library contains 347,651 volumes, 1,315,053 microform items, and 4302 audiovisual forms/CDs, and subscribes to 1974 periodicals. Computerized library services include the card catalog, interlibrary loans, and database searching. Special learning facilities include a learning resource center, art gallery, radio station, theater and laser lab, marine sciences station, greenhouse, art gallery, mainstage theater, recital hall, observatory, art complex, and distance learning studios. The 220-acre campus is in a rural area in the San Joaquin Valley, about 100 miles from San Francisco. Including residence halls, there are 20 buildings.

Student Life: 99% of undergraduates are from California. Others are from 22 states, 20 foreign countries, and Canada. 96% are from public schools. 50% are white; 23% Hispanic, 10% foreign nationals. The average age of freshmen is 18; all undergraduates, 25. 60% of freshmen remain to graduate.

Housing: 350 students can be accommodated in college housing, which includes coed dormitories and on-campus apartments. On-campus housing is available on a first-come, first-served basis. 95% of students commute. All students may keep cars.

Activities: 2% of men belong to 5 national fraternities; 3% of women belong to 9 national sororities. There are 79 groups on campus, including art, band, cheerleading, choir, chorale, chorus, computers, dance, drama, ethnic, gay, honors, international, jazz band, marching band, newspaper, opera, orchestra, pep band, photography, political, professional, radio, religious, social, student government, and symphony. Popular campus events include College Day, Warrior Day, and Wellness Day.

Sports: There are 7 intercollegiate sports for men and 7 for women, and 9 intramural sports for men and 9 for women. Facilities include a field house, a 2300-seat gym, softball and baseball diamonds, a soccer field, tennis courts, an all-weather track, a swimming pool, and a weight room.

Disabled Students: 99% of the campus is accessible. Wheelchair ramps, elevators, special parking, specially equipped rest rooms, lowered drinking fountains, lowered telephones, tutors, and note taking are available.

Services: Counseling and information services are available, as is tutoring in most subjects. There is a reader service for the blind, and remedial math, reading, and writing.

Campus Safety and Security: Measures include 24-hour foot and vehicle patrol, self-defense education, escort service, and shuttle buses. There are informal discussions, pamphlets/posters/films, emergency telephones, and lighted pathways/sidewalks. There are also 24-hour security officers, safety awareness programs, motorist assistance, and CPR and first-aid training.

Programs of Study: CSU/Stanislaus confers B.A., B.S., B.F.A., B.M., and B.V.E. degrees. Master's degrees are also awarded. Bachelor's degrees are awarded in BIOLOGICAL SCIENCE (biology/biological science and marine science), BUSINESS (business administration and management), COMMUNICATIONS AND THE ARTS (communications, dramatic arts, English, fine arts, French, German, music, Spanish, speech/debate/rhetoric, and studio art), COMPUTER AND PHYSICAL SCIENCE (chemistry, computer management, computer science, earth science, geology, information sciences and systems, mathematics, physical sciences, and physics), EDUCATION (physical, secondary, and vocational), HEALTH PROFESSIONS (nursing), SOCIAL SCIENCE (anthropology, child psychology/development, cognitive science, criminal justice, economics, geography, history, liberal arts/general studies, philosophy, psychology, public administration, social science, and sociology). Liberal studies, business and psychology are the strongest academically. Liberal studies is the largest.

Required: To graduate, students must complete at least 120 semester units, including 51 in the general education program and 40 in upper-division courses, with a minimum GPA of 2.0. Distribution requirements consist of 12 units of social science, 9 each of communication skills, natural science and math, and humanities, and 3 of computer study or health.

Special: Numerous co-op programs and internships are offered. Cross-registration with the Higher Education Consortium of Central California, study abroad in 16 countries, work-study programs, nondegree study, a Washington semester, an accelerated degree program, B.A.-B.S. degrees, dual majors, student-designed majors, and pass/fail options are also available. There is a freshman honors program.

Faculty/Classroom: 53% of faculty are male; 47%, female. All teach undergraduates and 80% both teach and do research. Graduate students teach 1% of introductory courses. The average class size in an introductory lecture is 50; in a laboratory, 25; and in a regular course, 30.

Admissions: 68% of the 2001-2002 applicants were accepted. The SAT I scores for the 2001-2002 freshman class were: Verbal--43% below 500, 48% between 500 and 599, 8% between 600 and 700, and 1% above 700; Math--43% below 500, 48% between 500 and 599, 8% between 600 and 700, and 1% above 700. The ACT scores were 62% below 21, 18% between 21 and 23, 14% between 24 and 26, 3% between 27 and 28, and 3% above 28.

Requirements: The SAT I or ACT is recommended. Admission is based on an eligibility index that weights GPA and the SAT I or ACT scores. Applicants with a GPA of 3.0 (3.4 for nonresidents) are exempt from test score requirements. Applicants should be graduates of an accredited secondary school. Preparatory course work should include 4 years of English, 3 of math, 2 of foreign language, and 1 each of history, lab science, and visual and performing arts. A GPA of 3.0 is required. AP and CLEP credits are accepted. Important factors in the admissions decision are advanced placement or honor courses, evidence of special talent, and geographic diversity. Applications are accepted on-line.

Procedure: Freshmen are admitted to all sessions. Entrance exams should be taken in the spring. There are early decision, early admissions, and deferred admissions plans. Application deadlines are open. The fall 2001 application fee was $55. Notification is sent on a rolling basis.

Transfer: Applicants must have a college GPA of 2.0 (2.4 for nonresidents) and have completed their lower-division general education English and math courses. Those with fewer than 56 transferable semester credits must meet freshman entrance requirements. 30 credits of 120 must be completed at CSU/Stanislaus.

Visiting: There are regularly scheduled orientations for prospective students. There are guides for informal visits and visitors may sit in on classes. To schedule a visit, contact University Outreach Services at *outreach_help_desk@stan.csustan.edu*

Financial Aid: In 2001-2002, 63% of all freshmen and 49% of continuing students received some form of financial aid. 66% of freshmen and 44% of continuing students received need-based aid. The average freshman award was $943. Of that total, scholarships or need-based grants averaged $752 ($1181 maximum); loans averaged $1185 ($1333 maximum); and work contracts averaged $596 ($1357 maximum). Grants, loans, and work-study programs are available. 15% of undergraduates work part time. Average annual earnings from campus work are $1554. The average financial indebtedness of the 2001 graduate was $13,000.

CSU/Stanislaus is a member of CSS. The FAFSA and the SAAC for California residents are required. The fall application deadline is March 2.
International Students: They must score 500 on the written TOEFL or 173 on the electronic version and also take the SAT I or the ACT.
Computers: The mainframe is an IBM. Terminals are located for student access and may be used for class assignments and personal business. All students may access the system. There are no time limits and no fees.
Graduates: In 2001, 1267 bachelor's degrees were awarded. The most popular majors were liberal studies (25%), business (15%), and psychology (6%). In an average class, 21% graduate in 4 years, 40% in 5 years, and 48% in 6 years.
Admissions Contact: Ardean Teo Campbell, Admissions and Records Counselor. A video is available. E-mail: *outreach@toto.csuston.edu*
Web: *http://www.csustan.edu*

CHAPMAN UNIVERSITY

Orange, CA 92866 D-5
(714) 997-6711
(888) CUAPPLY; Fax: (714) 997-6713

Full-time: 1264 men, 1617 women	**Faculty:** 181; IIA, +$
Part-time: 121 men, 125 women	**Ph.D.s:** 85%
Graduate: 387 men, 678 women	**Student/Faculty:** 16 to 1
Year: 4-1-4, summer session	**Tuition:** $22,256
Application Deadline: January 31	**Room & Board:** $7962
Freshman Class: 2423 applied, 1691 accepted, 730 enrolled	
SAT I Verbal/Math: 583/590	**ACT:** 24 VERY COMPETITIVE

Chapman University, founded in 1861, is an independent institution affiliated with the Disciples of Christ Christian Church, offering degree programs in liberal and fine arts, business, education, and the health sciences. There are 7 undergraduate and 8 graduate schools. In addition to regional accreditation, Chapman has baccalaureate program accreditation with AACSB, APTA, and NASM. The library contains 203,915 volumes, 11,375 microform items, and 3350 audiovisual forms/CDs, and subscribes to 2121 periodicals. Computerized library services include the card catalog, interlibrary loans, and database searching. Special learning facilities include a learning resource center, art gallery, radio station, TV station, and a food science sensory lab. The 60-acre campus is in a suburban area 35 miles southeast of Los Angeles. Including residence halls, there are 25 buildings.
Student Life: 74% of undergraduates are from California. Others are from 40 states, 40 foreign countries, and Canada. 65% are from public schools. 65% are white. 35% are Protestant; 24% Catholic. The average age of freshmen is 19; all undergraduates, 22. 13% do not continue beyond their first year.
Housing: 1200 students can be accommodated in college housing, which includes coed dormitories and on-campus apartments. In addition, there are special interest houses. On-campus housing is guaranteed for the freshman year only, is available on a first-come, first-served basis, and is available on a lottery system for upperclassmen. Priority is given to out-of-town students. 57% of students commute. All students may keep cars.
Activities: 10% of men belong to 6 national fraternities; 11% of women belong to 5 national sororities. There are 59 groups on campus, including art, cheerleading, choir, chorale, chorus, community service, dance, debate, drama, ethnic, film, gay, honors, international, jazz band, literary magazine, newspaper, opera, orchestra, pep band, photography, political, professional, radio and TV, religious, social, social service, student government, symphony, and yearbook. Popular campus events include lunchtime concerts, Spring Sizzle, and All University Formal.
Sports: There are 9 intercollegiate sports for men and 9 for women, and 10 intramural sports for men and 10 for women. Facilities include a gym, a weight room, 3 practice fields, and 4 tennis courts. Baseball and softball fields, a track, and a pool are available for student use nearby in the city of Orange.
Disabled Students: 75% of the campus is accessible. Wheelchair ramps, elevators, special parking, specially equipped rest rooms, special class scheduling, lowered drinking fountains, lowered telephones, and designated rooms in the residence halls are available.
Services: Counseling and information services are available, as is tutoring in most subjects, including math, sciences, business, and English. There is a reader service for the blind, and remedial math, reading, and writing. In addition, there are note takers, readers, and tapes for deaf, blind, and international students; special study skills workshops; and help for the learning disabled.
Campus Safety and Security: Measures include 24-hour foot and vehicle patrol, self-defense education, escort service, and informal discussions. There are pamphlets/posters/films, emergency telephones, lighted pathways/sidewalks, and rape awareness and victim assistance programs.
Programs of Study: Chapman confers B.A., B.S., B.F.A., B.M., and B.S.B.A. degrees. Master's and doctoral degrees are also awarded. Bachelor's degrees are awarded in BIOLOGICAL SCIENCE (biology/biological science), BUSINESS (accounting, business administration and management, and organizational behavior), COMMUNICATIONS AND THE ARTS (art, communications, dramatic arts, English, film arts, French, music, and Spanish), COMPUTER AND PHYSICAL SCIENCE (chemistry, computer science, information sciences and systems, and mathematics), ENGINEERING AND ENVIRONMENTAL DESIGN (environmental science), HEALTH PROFESSIONS (health science and music therapy), SOCIAL SCIENCE (economics, food science, history, law, liberal arts/general studies, peace studies, philosophy, physical fitness/movement, political science/government, psychology, religion, social science, and sociology). Business is the strongest academically. Business, communications, and film and television are the largest.
Required: Students in the B.A., B.F.A., B.S., and B.S.B.A. programs must complete a total of 124 credits with at least a 2.0 GPA. In addition, students must meet requirements in basic subjects such as writing, oral communication, freshman seminar, math, and phys ed through course work, advanced credit, or exam. General education requirements include 10 credits in natural sciences and 9 each in humanities and social sciences. Also required are 6 credits each of cultural heritage/human diversity and foreign language, and a junior writing proficiency exam.
Special: Cooperative and internship programs are available. Students may study abroad for a semester or spend a semester in Washington, D.C. Dual and student-designed majors are possible. A general studies degree, B.A.-B.S. degrees, nondegree study options, and pass/fail options are also permitted. A 3-2 engineering degree with the University of California, Irvine, is possible. There is 1 national honor society and a freshman honors program.
Faculty/Classroom: 61% of faculty are male; 39%, female. 94% teach undergraduates. No introductory courses are taught by graduate students. The average class size in an introductory lecture is 21; in a laboratory, 17; and in a regular course, 19.
Admissions: 70% of the 2001-2002 applicants were accepted. The SAT I scores for the 2001-2002 freshman class were: Verbal--12% below 500, 50% between 500 and 599, 33% between 600 and 700, and 6% above 700; Math--9% below 500, 48% between 500 and 599, 39% between 600 and 700, and 5% above 700. The ACT scores were 3% below 21, 47% between 21 and 23, 22% between 24 and 26, 23% between 27 and 28, and 5% above 28. 41% of the current freshmen were in the top fifth of their class; 81% were in the top two fifths. 9 freshmen graduated first in their class.
Requirements: The SAT I or ACT is required. In addition, applicants should be graduates of accredited high schools or have earned the GED. Secondary preparation should include 3 years of social science or electives, 2 each of composition and/or literature, science, a foreign language, and math, including algebra II. Prospective art or music majors should show some preparation in those fields. A personal essay is required. An on-campus interview is recommended. A GPA of 2.75 is required. AP and CLEP credits are accepted. Important factors in the admissions decision are advanced placement or honor courses, evidence of special talent, and leadership record. Applications are accepted on-line, and may be submitted at the university's web site *www.chapman.edu*
Procedure: Freshmen are admitted fall and spring. Entrance exams should be taken by fall of the senior year. There is an early admissions plan. Applications should be filed by January 31 for fall entry, November 15 for spring entry, and June 1 for summer entry, along with a $40 fee. Notification is sent on February 28. 4% of all applicants are on a waiting list.
Transfer: 297 transfer students enrolled in 2001-2002. Transfer applicants should have completed at least 12 credits of transferable college work with a 2.25 minimum GPA. High school records and SAT I or ACT scores should be submitted if fewer than 30 transferable credits have been completed. 24 credits of 124 must be completed at Chapman.
Visiting: There are regularly scheduled orientations for prospective students, consisting of fall and spring campus exploration day events. Weekday appointments and campus tours are also available. There are guides for informal visits and visitors may sit in on classes. To schedule a visit, contact the Office of Admissions.
Financial Aid: In 2001-2002, 88% of all freshmen and 80% of continuing students received some form of financial aid. 56% of freshmen and 60% of continuing students received need-based aid. The average freshman award was $18,034. Of that total, scholarships or need-based grants averaged $14,180; loans averaged $3719; and work contracts averaged $1900. All undergraduates work part time. Average annual earnings from campus work are $2200. The average financial indebtedness of the 2001 graduate was $17,700. The FAFSA is required. The fall application deadline is March 2.
International Students: There are 130 international students enrolled. The school actively recruits these students. They must score 500 on the written TOEFL or 213 on the electronic version and also take the SAT I or the ACT.
Computers: The mainframe is an HP 3000/957. There are 46 Mac II SIs and SEs, 50 PCs, 3 DEC MicroVAX II UNIX-based minicomputers, 2 DEC workstations that are networked and have access to the Internet, 25 Power Mac 6100/60s, 1 DEC ALPHA, and 1 SGT. All students may access the system 8 A.M. to 11 P.M. There are no time limits and no fees.

Graduates: In 2001, 472 bachelor's degrees were awarded. In an average class, 63% graduate in 6 years. 80 companies recruited on campus in 2000-2001. Of the 2000 graduating class, 40% were enrolled in graduate school within 6 months of graduation and 93% were employed.

Admissions Contact: Mike Drummy, Associate Dean of Enrollment/Chief Admission Officer. E-mail: *admit@chapman.edu*
Web: *www.chapman.edu*

CHRISTIAN HERITAGE COLLEGE D-5
El Cajon, CA 92019-1157 (619) 588-7747
(800) 676-2242; (619) 440-0209

Full-time: 500 men and women	**Faculty:** 30
Part-time: 100 men and women	**Ph.D.s:** 50%
Graduate: none	**Student/Faculty:** 18 to 1
Year: semesters, summer session	**Tuition:** $12,600
Application Deadline: see profile	**Room & Board:** $5400
Freshman Class: n/av	
SAT I or ACT: required	**LESS COMPETITIVE**

Christian Heritage College is a small, private institution founded in 1970 by the Scott Memorial Baptist Church of San Diego, with which it is still affiliated. It offers programs in the liberal arts, business, and education. Figures given in the above capsule are approximate. The library contains 70,000 volumes, 80 microform items, and 3820 audiovisual forms/CDs, and subscribes to 250 periodicals. Computerized library services include database searching. Special learning facilities include the nearby Institute for Creation Research. The 32-acre campus is in a suburban area 15 miles east of San Diego. Including residence halls, there are 14 buildings.

Student Life: 80% of undergraduates are from California. 75% are from public schools. 70% are white; 10% African American; 10% Hispanic. All are Protestant. The average age of freshmen is 18; all undergraduates, 21. 40% do not continue beyond their first year; 30% remain to graduate.

Housing: 200 students can be accommodated in college housing, which includes single-sex dormitories and off-campus apartments. On-campus housing is guaranteed for all 4 years. 50% of students live on campus; of those, 30% remain on campus on weekends. Alcohol is not permitted. All students may keep cars.

Activities: There are no fraternities or sororities. There are 14 groups on campus, including art, choir, chorale, chorus, computers, honors, international, newspaper, pep band, political, religious, social, student government, and yearbook. Popular campus events include spring, winter, and Valentine's Day banquets, and the Missions Conference.

Sports: There are 2 intercollegiate sports for men and 2 for women, and 5 intramural sports for men and 4 for women. Facilities include a swimming pool, a gym, outdoor courts for tennis, volleyball, and basketball, and soccer and softball fields.

Disabled Students: 90% of the campus is accessible. Wheelchair ramps, elevators, and special parking are available.

Services: Counseling and information services are available, as is tutoring in some subjects.

Campus Safety and Security: Measures include 24-hour foot and vehicle patrol, lighted pathways/sidewalks, and a fenced campus.

Programs of Study: CHC confers B.A. and B.S. degrees. Associate degrees are also awarded. Bachelor's degrees are awarded in BIOLOGICAL SCIENCE (biology/biological science), BUSINESS (business administration and management), COMMUNICATIONS AND THE ARTS (communications, English, and music), COMPUTER AND PHYSICAL SCIENCE (mathematics), EDUCATION (education), ENGINEERING AND ENVIRONMENTAL DESIGN (aviation administration/management), SOCIAL SCIENCE (biblical studies, history, human development, interdisciplinary studies, liberal arts/general studies, physical fitness/movement, and psychology). Counseling psychology, education, and business are the strongest academically. Business, education, and human development are the largest.

Required: The required credits for graduation vary by degree program and major. All students must take 46 to 52 credits in sciences and math, social science, and humanities; 20 credits in personal Christian development and biblical studies; and the balance in major field requirements and electives. A 2.0 GPA is required for graduation.

Special: Students attend chapel 3 times each week, participate in an annual Bible conference, and complete a student ministry assignment each semester. Independent study for 1 to 3 credits can be arranged. There are internships in psychology, pastoral studies, and education.

Faculty/Classroom: 60% of faculty are male; 40%, female. All teach undergraduates. The average class size in an introductory lecture is 40; in a laboratory, 15; and in a regular course, 16.

Requirements: The SAT I or ACT is required; the ACT is preferred. Applicants must have a high school diploma or the GED, or have successfully completed the California State High School Proficiency Exam. Secondary preparation should include 4 units of English, 3 each of math, natural science, and social studies, and 2 of a single foreign language. A personal essay is also required. In addition, applicants must meet certain spiritual requirements. CHC requires applicants to be in the upper 50% of their class. A GPA of 2.25 is required. AP and CLEP credits are accepted. Important factors in the admissions decision are recommendations by school officials, leadership record, and extracurricular activities record.

Procedure: Freshmen are admitted fall and spring. Entrance exams should be taken during the junior year. Notification is sent on a rolling basis. Check with the school for current application deadlines. The fall 2001 application fee was $25.

Transfer: 30 credits of 124 must be completed at CHC.

Visiting: There are regularly scheduled orientations for prospective students, including a campus tour, cafeteria meal, and class and chapel attendance. There are guides for informal visits and visitors may sit in on classes and stay overnight. To schedule a visit, contact the Admissions Office.

Financial Aid: 70% of undergraduates work part time. CHC is a member of CSS. The FAFSA and the college's own financial statement are required. The fall application deadline is March 2.

International Students: There were 15 international students enrolled in a recent year. The school actively recruits these students. They must score 500 on the written TOEFL or take the college's own test.

Computers: There are 32 networked PCs at 3 campus locations, all with e-mail, Internet, and World Wide Web access. All students may access the system. There are no time limits and no fees. It is strongly recommended that all students have a personal computer.

Graduates: In an average class, 1% graduate in 3 years, 78% in 4 years, 97% in 5 years, and 99% in 6 years.

Admissions Contact: Jennifer Wiersma, Director of Admissions.
E-mail: *chcadm@adm.christianheritage.edu*
Web: *www.christianheritage.edu*

CLAREMONT COLLEGES, THE

Established in 1925, this prestigious group of seven private colleges is a consortium of higher education institutions. It is comprised of five undergraduate liberal arts colleges: Claremont McKenna, Harvey Mudd, Pitzer, Pomona, and Scripps; and two graduate institutions: Claremont Graduate University and the recently established (1997) Leck Graduate Institute of Applied Life Sciences. Together, the institutions serve nearly 6,000 students from 50 states and more than 80 foreign countries. 2,500 courses are taught each year by 600 professors, often with class sizes under 20. Six continguous campuses with 175 buildings are spread over 350 acres of land with the seventh campus located nearby. Each institution is independent, with its own faculty, student body, administration, curricular emphasis, and distinctive style. However, each is enriched by the presence of the others. The consortium offers students a variety of intellectual, cultural, and social activities in facilities and shared academic resources. Claremont University Consortium (CUC) is the central coordinating and support organization for The Claremont Colleges. Some of the 23 services include campus safety, libraries, health and counseling services, ethnic student centers, an interfaith office of chaplains, a centralized bookstore, food services, information technology, human resources, real estate, risk management, and employee benefits. In the words of the founding father, Dr. Robert J. Bernard, "This pioneering enterprise has given national leadership in demonstrating how the advantages of small colleges and the advantages of a university can be combined to build a notable center of learning."

CLAREMONT MCKENNA COLLEGE D-5
Claremont, CA 91711-6425 (909) 621-8088; Fax: (909) 621-8516

Full-time: 558 men, 483 women	**Faculty:** 139; IIB, ++$
Part-time: 3 women	**Ph.D.s:** 100%
Graduate: none	**Student/Faculty:** 7 to 1
Year: semesters	**Tuition:** $24,540
Application Deadline: January 1	**Room & Board:** $8160
Freshman Class: 2898 applied, 831 accepted, 262 enrolled	
SAT I Verbal/Math: 690/700	**ACT:** 30 **MOST COMPETITIVE**

Claremont McKenna College, founded in 1946, is a highly selective liberal arts college with a curricular emphasis on economics, government, international relations, and public affairs. In addition to regional accreditation, CMC has baccalaureate program accreditation with WASC. The 5 libraries contain 2,008,476 volumes, 1,448,021 microform items, and 15,400 audiovisual forms/CDs, and subscribe to 5592 periodicals. Computerized library services include the card catalog, interlibrary loans, and database searching. Special learning facilities include a learning resource center, art gallery, radio station, and 9 research institutes. The 50-acre campus is in a small town 35 miles east of downtown Los Angeles. Including residence halls, there are 29 buildings.

Student Life: 51% of undergraduates are from California. Others are from 48 states, 26 foreign countries, and Canada. 76% are from public schools. 65% are white; 15% Asian American. 40% are Protestant; 30% claim no religious affiliation; 19% Catholic. The average age of freshmen is 18; all undergraduates, 20. 6% do not continue beyond their first year; 86% remain to graduate.

Housing: 946 students can be accommodated in college housing, which includes coed dormitories, on-campus apartments, and substance-free housing. On-campus housing is guaranteed for all 4 years. 96% of students live on campus; of those, 80% remain on campus on weekends. All students may keep cars.

Activities: There are no fraternities or sororities. There are 185 groups on campus, including art, band, cheerleading, choir, chorus, computers, dance, debate, drama, ethnic, film, forensics, gay, honors, international, jazz band, literary magazine, newspaper, orchestra, photography, political, professional, radio and TV, religious, social, social service, student government, and yearbook. Popular campus events include International Festival, Madrigal Dinners, and Monte Carlo Night.

Sports: There are 10 intercollegiate sports for men and 10 for women, and 6 intramural sports for men and 6 for women. Facilities include gym facilities, a weight room, a swimming pool, courts for squash, tennis, and volleyball, and various playing fields.

Disabled Students: 90% of the campus is accessible. Wheelchair ramps, elevators, special parking, specially equipped rest rooms, special class scheduling, and lowered drinking fountains are available.

Services: Counseling and information services are available, as is tutoring in most subjects. There is remedial writing. The Writing Center offers writing help and specialized workshops.

Campus Safety and Security: Measures include 24-hour foot and vehicle patrol, self-defense education, escort service, and informal discussions. There are pamphlets/posters/films, emergency telephones, and lighted pathways/sidewalks.

Programs of Study: CMC confers the B.A. degree. Bachelor's degrees are awarded in BIOLOGICAL SCIENCE (biochemistry and biology/biological science), BUSINESS (accounting, business economics, and management engineering), COMMUNICATIONS AND THE ARTS (Chinese, classics, dramatic arts, English literature, film arts, fine arts, French, German, literature, music, Russian, and Spanish), COMPUTER AND PHYSICAL SCIENCE (chemistry, geology, information sciences and systems, mathematics, physics, science, and science and management), EDUCATION (education), ENGINEERING AND ENVIRONMENTAL DESIGN (environmental science), HEALTH PROFESSIONS (premedicine), SOCIAL SCIENCE (African American studies, American studies, anthropology, Asian/Oriental studies, economics, European studies, history, international relations, Mexican-American/Chicano studies, philosophy, political science/government, prelaw, psychobiology, psychology, religion, sociology, and women's studies). Economics, government, and international relations are the strongest academically and the largest.

Required: All students must complete 32 courses (128 semester hours) with a C average. Required courses include a minimum of 3 semesters each of social science and phys ed; 2 each of sciences and humanities; 1 each of English, calculus, and civilization; and foreign language proficiency equal to 3 college semesters. A thesis is required of all students. At least 16 courses must be taken in residence.

Special: CMC students may cross-register at any of the Claremont Colleges and may participate in exchange programs with Haverford, Spelman, or Colby Colleges. Students may study abroad in 32 countries or spend a semester in Washington, D.C. Part-time and full-time internships and dual and student designed majors are available. There are 3-2 programs in management-engineering with Stanford University, Harvey Mudd College, and others, and a 3-3 program with Columbia Law School. A multidisciplinary program in leadership studies and an interdisciplinary program in legal studies are offered. There are limited pass/fail options. There are 5 national honor societies, including Phi Beta Kappa, and all departments have honors programs.

Faculty/Classroom: 66% of faculty are male; 34%, female. All both teach and do research. The average class size in an introductory lecture is 19 and in a regular course, 19.

Admissions: 29% of the 2001-2002 applicants were accepted. 97% of the current freshmen were in the top fifth of their class; All were in the top two fifths. There were 17 National Merit finalists. 32 freshmen graduated first in their class.

Requirements: The SAT I is required. In addition, applicants must be graduates of an accredited high school or have earned the GED. Secondary preparation must include 4 years of English, 3 years (preferably 4) of math, at least 2 years of a foreign language and science, and 1 year of history. A personal essay is required, and an interview is recommended. AP credits are accepted. Important factors in the admissions decision are advanced placement or honor courses, leadership record, and extracurricular activities record. The application is available on computer disk. Applications are accepted on-line.

Procedure: Freshmen are admitted fall and spring. Entrance exams should be taken during the junior year or between October and January of the senior year. There is an early decision plan. Early decision application should be filed by November 15; regular applications, by January 1 for fall entry and November 1 for spring entry. The fall 2001 application fee was $50. Notification of early decision is sent December 15; regular decision, April 1. 48 early decision candidates were accepted for the 2001-2002 class. 1% of all applicants are on a waiting list; 17 were accepted in 2001.

Transfer: 70 transfer students enrolled in 2001-2002. Applicants must submit the SAT I or ACT scores, high school and college transcripts, essays, a college report form, midsemester grades, and recommendations from a college professor or counselor. 64 credits of 128 must be completed at CMC.

Visiting: There are regularly scheduled orientations for prospective students, including a campus tour, faculty presentations, student discussions, and admissions and financial aid workshops. There are guides for informal visits and visitors may sit in on classes and stay overnight. To schedule a visit, contact the Admissions Office.

Financial Aid: In 2001-2002, 52% of all freshmen and 58% of continuing students received some form of financial aid, including need-based aid. The average freshman award was $22,275. Of that total, scholarships or need-based grants averaged $18,250; loans averaged $2750; and work contracts averaged $1275. 65% of undergraduates work part time. Average annual earnings from campus work are $1550. The average financial indebtedness of the 2001 graduate was $12,000. CMC is a member of CSS. The CSS/Profile or FAFSA is required. The fall application deadline is February 1.

International Students: There are 32 international students enrolled. The school actively recruits these students. They must score 550 on the written TOEFL and also take the SAT I or the ACT.

Computers: The mainframes are 2 DEC VAXs. Students have access to the VAXs through lab terminals. In addition, Macs, PCs, and an extensive software library are available. All students may access the system. There are no time limits and no fees.

Graduates: In 2001, 253 bachelor's degrees were awarded. The most popular majors were government (28%), economics (23%), and accounting (10%). In an average class, 84% graduate in 4 years, 86% in 5 years, and 87% in 6 years. 87 companies recruited on campus in 2000-2001.

Admissions Contact: Richard C. Vos, VP, Dean of Admission and Financial Aid. E-mail: *admission@claremontmckenna.edu*
Web: *www.mckennna.edu*

COGSWELL POLYTECHNICAL COLLEGE — B-3

Sunnyvale, CA 94089 — **(408) 541-0100, ext. 131**
(800)-264-7955 (COGSWLL); Fax: (408) 747-0764

Full-time: 200 men and women	**Faculty:** 10
Part-time: 300 men and women	**Ph.D.s:** 35%
Graduate: none	**Student/Faculty:** 20 to 1
Year: trimesters, summer session	**Tuition:** $14,400
Application Deadline: see profile	**Room & Board:** n/app
Freshman Class: n/av	
SAT I or ACT: not required	**LESS COMPETITIVE**

Cogswell Polytechnical College, founded in 1887, is a small, independent engineering and arts college. Figures in the above capsule are approximate. The library contains 13,000 volumes, 250 microform items, and 200 audiovisual forms/CDs, and subscribes to 125 periodicals. Computerized library services include the card catalog and database searching. Special learning facilities include an art gallery and a commercial studio, and a video postproduction company. The 4-acre campus is in a suburban area 40 miles south of San Francisco in California's Silicon Valley. There is one building.

Student Life: 70% of undergraduates are from California. 65% are from public schools. The average age of freshmen is 19; all undergraduates, 28. 10% do not continue beyond their first year; 70% remain to graduate.

Housing: There are no residence halls. Arrangements can be made to accommodate students in private houses or at nearby corporate apartments. Alcohol is not permitted. All students may keep cars.

Activities: There are no fraternities or sororities. There are 7 groups on campus, including art, computers, honors, international, jazz band, professional, and student government. Popular campus events include Founders Day, club competitions, and ski trips.

Sports: There is no sports program at Cogswell College. Facilities include a game room, a student lounge, and access to community athletic facilities.

Disabled Students: Wheelchair ramps, special parking, specially equipped rest rooms, special class scheduling, lowered drinking fountains, and lowered telephones are available.

Services: Counseling and information services are available, as is tutoring in every subject. There is remedial writing.

Campus Safety and Security: Measures include pamphlets/posters/films, lighted pathways/sidewalks, an emergency evacuation plan, and maps in the classrooms.

Programs of Study: Cogswell College confers B.A.C.V.I. (Computer and Video Imaging), B.S.E.E., B.S.F.S. (Fire Science), and B.S.S.W.E. (Software Engineering) degrees. Bachelor's degrees are awarded in COMMUNICATIONS AND THE ARTS (animation, audio technology, and music technology), COMPUTER AND PHYSICAL SCIENCE (computer programming, digital arts/technology, and web technology), ENGINEERING AND ENVIRONMENTAL DESIGN (computer engineering, computer graphics, and electrical/electronics engineering), SOCIAL SCIENCE (fire control and safety technology, and fire protection). Engineering and animation are the strongest academically. Computer video imaging is the largest.

Required: To graduate, students must complete a total of 120 to 128 credits with 18 to 27 in the major and have a 2.0 GPA. 45 to 56 credits in general education core courses are required, depending on the major, and include courses in English, math, natural sciences, social sciences, and humanities.

Special: Cogswell offers various internships and work-study programs. The college administers the Open Learning for the Fire Service (OLFS) program for Arizona, California, and Nevada, through which nonresident students can earn a B.S. in fire science. Nondegree study and pass/fail options are possible. There is a freshman honors program.

Faculty/Classroom: 65% of faculty are male; 35%, female. The average class size in an introductory lecture is 15; in a laboratory, 8; and in a regular course, 25.

Requirements: Applicants must be high school graduates or have the GED. Secondary preparation must include 3 years of English, 2 to 3 of math, including algebra, geometry, and trigonometry, and 1 year of science. Cogswell requires a personal essay and recommends a personal interview. A portfolio is required for computer and video imaging programs. A GPA of 2.7 is required. AP and CLEP credits are accepted. Important factors in the admissions decision are advanced placement or honor courses, recommendations by school officials, and ability to finance college education.

Procedure: Freshmen are admitted to all sessions. There are early decision and early admissions plans. Notification is sent on a rolling basis. Check with the school for current application deadlines. The fall 2001 application fee was $50.

Transfer: Applicants must have completed at least 12 college credits with a 2.2 GPA. An interview is recommended. 27 credits of 120 must be completed at Cogswell College.

Visiting: Visitors may sit in on classes. To schedule a visit, contact the dean of marketing and recruiting.

Financial Aid: 2% of undergraduates work part time. Cogswell College is a member of CSS. The FAFSA and the college's own financial statement are required. The fall application deadline is March 2 for a Cal Grant but othervise open.

International Students: The school actively recruits these students. They must score 550 on the written TOEFL.

Computers: The mainframe is a DEC VAX 11/780. There are also 35 IBM PC-PS2 PCs available in computer labs and the library. The Internet is accessible in computer labs. All students may access the system during school hours. There are no time limits and no fees. It is strongly recommended that all students have a personal computer.

Graduates: In a recent year, 100 bachelor's degrees were awarded. The most popular majors were computer and video imaging (78%), electrical engineering (12%), and software engineering (10%). In an average class, 50% graduate in 6 years. 5 companies recruited on campus in a recent year. Of a recent graduating class, 95% were employed within 6 months of graduation.

Admissions Contact: David Pullman, Registrar/Director of Admissions. E-mail: *admin@cogswell.edu* Web: *www.cogswell.edu*

COLLEGE OF NOTRE DAME
(See Notre Dame de Namur University)

(See Notre Dame de Namur University)

CONCORDIA UNIVERSITY
Irvine, CA 92612-3299 — D-5

(949) 854-8002 ext. 1170
(800) 229-1200; Fax: (949) 854-6894

Full-time: 332 men, 677 women	**Faculty:** 52; IIB, --$
Part-time: 33 men, 70 women	**Ph.D.s:** 62%
Graduate: 76 men, 126 women	**Student/Faculty:** 19 to 1
Year: semesters, summer session	**Tuition:** $16,480
Application Deadline: May 1	**Room & Board:** $5810
Freshman Class: 978 applied, 646 accepted, 266 enrolled	
SAT I Verbal/Math: 500/510	**ACT:** 22 **COMPETITIVE**

Concordia University, founded in 1972, is a private liberal arts institution affiliated with the Lutheran Church-Missouri Synod. There are 4 undergraduate and 3 graduate schools. The library contains 99,500 volumes, 56,000 microform items, and 5230 audiovisual forms/CDs, and subscribes to 750 periodicals. Computerized library services include the card catalog, interlibrary loans, and database searching. Special learning facilities include a learning resource center, art gallery, and radio station. The 70-acre campus is in a suburban area 40 miles south of Los Angeles. Including residence halls, there are 18 buildings.

Student Life: 80% of undergraduates are from California. Others are from 21 states, 12 foreign countries, and Canada. 76% are white. The average age of freshmen is 18; all undergraduates, 21. 23% do not continue beyond their first year.

Housing: 874 students can be accommodated in college housing, which includes coed dormitories, on-campus apartments, and off-campus apartments. On-campus housing is guaranteed for all 4 years. 68% of students live on campus. All students may keep cars.

Activities: There are no fraternities or sororities. There are 18 groups on campus, including art, choir, chorale, chorus, dance, drama, ethnic, international, newspaper, pep band, professional, radio and TV, religious, social, social service, student government, and yearbook. Popular campus events include Closing Banquet, Christmas Dance, and Octoberfest.

Sports: There are 5 intercollegiate sports for men and 6 for women, and 7 intramural sports for men and 7 for women. Facilities include a 1500-seat gym, a soccer field, a baseball/softball diamond, volleyball, tennis, and racquetball courts, a track field, a weight room, a dance room, team rooms, and locker rooms.

Disabled Students: 90% of the campus is accessible. Wheelchair ramps, special parking, specially equipped rest rooms, and lowered drinking fountains are available.

Services: Counseling and information services are available, as is tutoring in some subjects, including math, chemistry, critical thinking, Spanish, biology, and calculus.

Campus Safety and Security: Measures include 24-hour foot and vehicle patrol, escort service, informal discussions, and pamphlets/posters/films. There are lighted pathways/sidewalks.

Programs of Study: Concordia Irvine confers the B.A. degree. Associate and master's degrees are also awarded. Bachelor's degrees are awarded in BIOLOGICAL SCIENCE (biology/biological science), BUSINESS (business administration and management), COMMUNICATIONS AND THE ARTS (art, communications, dramatic arts, English, and music), COMPUTER AND PHYSICAL SCIENCE (mathematics), EDUCATION (Christian, early childhood, and physical), HEALTH PROFESSIONS (exercise science), SOCIAL SCIENCE (behavioral science, history, humanities, liberal arts/general studies, psychology, and religion). Education, social science, and business administration are the strongest academically and have the largest enrollments.

Required: All students must complete 49 semester hours of general education requirements, including courses in humanities and fine arts, math and science, social science, religion, and exercise and sport science. A total of 128 credits, including 36 to 45 in the major, is required to graduate. A GPA of 2.0 in major and program course work must be maintained.

Special: Cross-registration is possible with 9 Concordia Universities/Colleges nationwide. Internships, an accelerated degree program in the liberal arts major with an emphasis on business and teacher education, and dual and student-designed majors are available. There is a freshman honors program.

Faculty/Classroom: 54% of faculty are male; 46%, female. 97% teach undergraduates and 2% do research. No introductory courses are taught by graduate students. The average class size in a laboratory is 24 and in a regular course, 26.

Admissions: 66% of the 2001-2002 applicants were accepted. The SAT I scores for the 2001-2002 freshman class were: Verbal--45% below 500, 41% between 500 and 599, 12% between 600 and 700, and 1% above 700; Math--44% below 500, 41% between 500 and 599, 13% between 600 and 700, and 1% above 700. The ACT scores were 36% below 21, 39% between 21 and 23, 13% between 24 and 26, 5% between 27 and 28, and 7% above 28. 40% of the current freshmen were in the top fifth of their class; 75% were in the top two fifths. There were 3 National Merit finalists. 3 freshmen graduated first in their class.

Requirements: The SAT I or ACT is required. In addition, applicants should be high school graduates with 4 years of English, 3 each of math and science, and 2 each of social studies and a foreign language. The GED is accepted. A school reference is also required. Concordia Irvine requires applicants to be in the upper 50% of their class. A GPA of 2.8 is required. AP and CLEP credits are accepted. Important factors in the admissions decision are leadership record, extracurricular activities record, and recommendations by school officials. Applications are accepted on computer disk or on-line via XAPplication.

Procedure: Freshmen are admitted fall and spring. Entrance exams should be taken by the fall of the senior year. There is a deferred admissions plan. Applications should be filed by May 1 for fall entry and December 1 for spring entry, along with a $40 fee. Notification is sent on a rolling basis.

Transfer: 103 transfer students enrolled in 2001-2002. A GPA of 2.3 is required in a minimum of 24 semester or 36 quarter units completed. An academic reference is required, as are official high school transcripts. 32 credits of 128 must be completed at Concordia Irvine.

Visiting: There are regularly scheduled orientations for prospective students. There are guides for informal visits and visitors may sit in on classes and stay overnight. To schedule a visit, contact the Admission Office at (949) 854-8002 ext. 1106 or *admission@cui.edu*.

Financial Aid: In 2001-2002, 95% of all freshmen and 90% of continuing students received some form of financial aid. 59% of freshmen and 61% of continuing students received need-based aid. The average freshman award was $10,700. Of that total, scholarships or need-based grants averaged $8000 ($24,590 maximum); loans averaged $2300

($2625 maximum); and work contracts averaged $1800 ($2000 maximum). 39% of undergraduates work part time. Average annual earnings from campus work are $2000. The average financial indebtedness of the 2001 graduate was $17,000. The FAFSA and the college's own financial statement are required. The fall application priority deadline is March 2.

International Students: There are 87 international students enrolled. The school actively recruits these students. They must score 525 on the written TOEFL or 195 on the electronic version and also take the SAT I or the ACT.

Computers: The mainframe is a VAX. Students have access to a computer center, e-mail to on-campus addresses, the Internet and World Wide Web, and a campuswide network. All students may access the system. There are no fees.

Graduates: In 2001, 163 bachelor's degrees were awarded. The most popular majors were business management (21%), philosophy and religion (18%), and education (16%). In an average class, 44% graduate in 4 years, 47% in 5 years, and 54% in 6 years. 50 companies recruited on campus in 2000-2001.

Admissions Contact: Lori McDonald, Director of Enrollment Services. E-mail: *lori.mcdonald@cui.edu* Web: *www.cui.edu*

DEVRY UNIVERSITY/FREMONT B-3

Fremont, CA 94555 (510) 574-1100
(888) 393-3879; Fax: (510) 742-0868

Full-time: 1467 men, 406 women	**Faculty:** 54
Part-time: 307 men, 98 women	**Ph.D.s:** n/av
Graduate: none	**Student/Faculty:** 35 to 1
Year: semesters, summer session	**Tuition:** $9865
Application Deadline: open	**Room & Board:** n/app
Freshman Class: 810 applied, 680 accepted, 389 enrolled	
SAT I or ACT: recommended	**COMPETITIVE**

DeVry University/Fremont, formerly DeVry Institute of Technology, founded in 1998, is a private institution offering hands-on programs in electronics, business administration, computer information systems, telecommunications management, computer engineering technology, and technical management. The school is 1 of 23 DeVry schools throughout the United States and Canada. In addition to regional accreditation, DeVry has baccalaureate program accreditation with ABET. The library contains 13,000 volumes and 206 audiovisual forms/CDs, and subscribes to 50 periodicals. Computerized library services include the card catalog, interlibrary loans, and database searching. Special learning facilities include a learning resource center and electronic labs. The 17-acre campus is in a suburban area. There is 1 building.

Student Life: 97% of undergraduates are from California. Others are from 22 states and 15 foreign countries. 40% are Asian American; 28% white, 17% Hispanic. The average age of all undergraduates is 24. 40% do not continue beyond their first year.

Housing: There are no residence halls. Housing referrals can be obtained through the Student Housing Office. All students commute. Alcohol is not permitted. All students may keep cars.

Activities: There are no fraternities or sororities. There are 6 groups on campus, including chess, ethnic, professional, and religious. Popular campus events include Thanksgiving Dinner, Summer BBQ, and Book Fair.

Sports: There is no sports program at DeVry.

Disabled Students: 90% of the campus is accessible. Wheelchair ramps, elevators, special parking, specially equipped rest rooms, and lowered drinking fountains are available.

Services: Counseling and information services are available, as is tutoring in every subject.

Campus Safety and Security: Measures include 24-hour foot and vehicle patrol, self-defense education, escort service, and informal discussions. There are pamphlets/posters/films, emergency telephones, and lighted pathways/sidewalks.

Programs of Study: DeVry confers the B.S. degree. Associate degrees are also awarded. Bachelor's degrees are awarded in BUSINESS (business administration and management), COMMUNICATIONS AND THE ARTS (telecommunications), COMPUTER AND PHYSICAL SCIENCE (computer programming and information sciences and systems), ENGINEERING AND ENVIRONMENTAL DESIGN (computer engineering, electrical/electronics engineering technology, and technological management). Electronics, telecommunications, and computer information systems are the largest.

Required: To graduate, students must achieve a cumulative GPA of at least 2.0 and satisfactorily complete all curriculum requirements. Course requirements vary according to program. All first-semester students take courses in business organization, computer applications, algebra, psychology, and student success strategies.

Special: Accelerated degrees, co-op programs, nondegree study, and evening and weekend classes are possible.

Faculty/Classroom: All teach undergraduates. The average class size in an introductory lecture is 30; in a laboratory, 30; and in a regular course, 30.

Admissions: 84% of the 2001-2002 applicants were accepted.

Requirements: The SAT I or ACT is recommended. Admissions requirements include graduation from a secondary school; the GED is also accepted. Applicants must pass the DeVry entrance exam or present satisfactory ACT or SAT I scores. An interview is required. CLEP credit is accepted. Applications are accepted on-line at Embark.com

Procedure: Freshmen are admitted fall, spring, and summer. There is a deferred admissions plan. Application deadlines are open. The application fee is $50. Notification is sent on a rolling basis.

Transfer: 28 transfer students enrolled in 2001-2002. Applicants must present passing grades in all completed college course work, demonstrate language skills proficiency in at least 24 completed semester hours, and present evidence of math proficiency by appropriate college-level credits. 35% of 48 to 154 credits must be completed at DeVry.

Visiting: There are regularly scheduled orientations for prospective students. There are guides for informal visits and visitors may sit in on classes. To schedule a visit, contact Bruce Williams, New Student Coordinator.

Financial Aid: In a recent year, 20% of all freshmen and 74% of continuing students received some form of financial aid. 10% of freshmen and 45% of continuing students received need-based aid. 4% of undergraduates work part time. Average annual earnings from campus work are $8000. The average financial indebtedness of a recent graduate was $10,344. The FAFSA is required.

International Students: There are 55 international students enrolled. They must score 500 on the written TOEFL or 173 on the electronic version and also take the college's own entrance exam.

Computers: Lab facilities include PCs in stand-alone and network configurations with access to the mainframe. LANs provide access to a wide range of applications software. Hard copy from the mainframe is provided through a local minicomputer and medium- and high-speed printers. All students may access the system during lab hours. There are no fees. It is strongly recommended that all students have personal computers. It is recommended that students in the Information Technology program have DeVry-issued laptop computers.

Graduates: In 2001, 135 bachelor's degrees were awarded. The most popular majors were business (71%), electronics engineering technology (15%), and computer information systems (14%). 40 companies recruited on campus in 2000-2001.

Admissions Contact: Jade Muranka, Director of Admissions. Web: *www.fre.devry.edu*

DEVRY UNIVERSITY/LONG BEACH C-5

Long Beach, CA 90806 (562) 427-0861
(800) 597-0444; Fax: (562) 427-4162

Full-time: 1479 men, 542 women	**Faculty:** 41
Part-time: 584 men, 248 women	**Ph.D.s:** n/av
Graduate: none	**Student/Faculty:** 49 to 1
Year: semesters, summer session	**Tuition:** $9205
Application Deadline: open	**Room & Board:** n/app
Freshman Class: 829 applied, 675 accepted, 491 enrolled	
SAT I or ACT: recommended	**LESS COMPETITIVE**

DeVry University/Long Beach, formerly DeVry Institute of Technology, is 1 of 23 DeVry schools in the United States and Canada. The school offers programs in business administration, computer information systems, electronics, telecommunications management, technical management, information technology, and computer engineering technology. In addition to regional accreditation, DeVry has baccalaureate program accreditation with ABET. The library contains 9276 volumes, 315 microform items, and 741 audiovisual forms/CDs, and subscribes to 80 periodicals. Computerized library services include the card catalog, interlibrary loans, and database searching. Special learning facilities include a learning resource center and electronics and other labs. The 11-acre campus is in an urban area midway between Los Angeles and Orange County. There is 1 building.

Student Life: 97% of undergraduates are from California. Others are from 23 states and 13 foreign countries. 32% are Asian American; 26% Hispanic, 20% white, 13% African American. The average age of all undergraduates is 26. 55% do not continue beyond their first year.

Housing: There are no residence halls. Housing referrals may be obtained through the Student Housing Office. All students commute. Alcohol is not permitted. All students may keep cars.

Activities: There are no fraternities or sororities. There are 13 groups on campus, including ethnic and professional. Popular campus events include Welcome BBQ, Cleo's Cafe, and Winter Formal.

Sports: There is 1 intramural sport for men and 1 for women.

Disabled Students: 90% of the campus is accessible. Wheelchair ramps, elevators, special parking, specially equipped rest rooms, lowered drinking fountains, and lowered telephones are available.

Services: Counseling and information services are available, as is tutoring in every subject.

Campus Safety and Security: Measures include escort service, informal discussions, pamphlets/posters/films, and emergency telephones.

There are lighted pathways/sidewalks. A DeVry employee patrols the building from 4 P.M. to midnight, and a guard service patrols the lot from 6:30 A.M. to midnight.

Programs of Study: DeVry confers the B.S. degree. Associate degrees are also awarded. Bachelor's degrees are awarded in BUSINESS (business administration and management), COMMUNICATIONS AND THE ARTS (telecommunications), COMPUTER AND PHYSICAL SCIENCE (computer programming and information sciences and systems), ENGINEERING AND ENVIRONMENTAL DESIGN (computer engineering, electrical/electronics engineering technology, and technological management). Computer information systems, telecommunications, and business are the largest.

Required: In order to graduate, students must achieve a cumulative GPA of at least 2.0 and satisfactorily complete all curriculum requirements. Course requirements vary according to program. All first-semester students take courses in business organization, computer applications, algebra, psychology, and student success strategies.

Special: Evening and weekend classes, co-op programs, and nondegree study are possible. There is 1 national honor society.

Faculty/Classroom: All teach undergraduates. The average class size in an introductory lecture is 30; in a laboratory, 30; and in a regular course, 30.

Admissions: 81% of the 2001-2002 applicants were accepted.

Requirements: The SAT I or ACT is recommended. Admissions requirements include graduation from a secondary school; the GED is also accepted. Applicants from accredited postsecondary institutions must pass the DeVry entrance exam, or present satisfactory ACT or SAT I scores. An interview is required. CLEP credit is accepted. Applications are accepted on-line at *Embark.com*

Procedure: Freshmen are admitted fall, spring, and summer. There is a deferred admissions plan. Application deadlines are open. The application fee is $50. Notification is sent on a rolling basis.

Transfer: 1 transfer student enrolled in 2001-2002. Applicants must present passing grades in all completed college course work, demonstrate language skills proficiency with at least 24 completed semester hours, and evidence math proficiency by appropriate college-level credits. 35% of 48 to 154 credits must be completed at DeVry.

Visiting: There are regularly scheduled orientations for prospective students. There are guides for informal visits and visitors may sit in on classes. To schedule a visit, contact Lisa Flores, New Student Coordinator.

Financial Aid: In a recent year, 83% of all students received some form of financial aid. 51% of freshmen and 47% of continuing students received need-based aid. 75% of undergraduates work part time. Average annual earnings from campus work are $7500. The average financial indebtedness of the 2001 graduate was $15,493. DeVry is a member of CSS. The FAFSA is required.

International Students: There are 51 international students enrolled. They must score 500 on the written TOEFL or 173 on the electronic version and also take the college's own entrance exam and the DeVry computerized placement test.

Computers: The mainframe is an IBM. Lab facilities include PCs in stand-alone and network configurations, with access to the mainframe. LANs provide access to a wide range of applications software. Hard copy from the mainframe is provided through a local minicomputer and medium- and high-speed printers. Computer information systems students may access the system during published lab hours. There are no fees.

Graduates: In 2001, 462 bachelor's degrees were awarded. The most popular majors were business (51%), computer information systems (35%), and electronics engineering technology (14%). 86 companies recruited on campus in 2000-2001.

Admissions Contact: Elaine Francisco, Director of Admissions.
Web: *www.lb.devry.edu*

DEVRY UNIVERSITY/POMONA D-5
Pomona, CA 91768-2642 (909) 622-8866
(800) 882-7536; Fax: (909) 623-3338

Full-time: 1945 men, 638 women	**Faculty:** 47
Part-time: 784 men, 302 women	**Ph.D.s:** n/av
Graduate: none	**Student/Faculty:** 55 to 1
Year: semesters, summer session	**Tuition:** $9205
Application Deadline: open	**Room & Board:** n/app
Freshman Class: 1178 applied, 1003 accepted, 740 enrolled	
SAT I or ACT: recommended	**LESS COMPETITIVE**

DeVry University/Pomona, formerly DeVry Institute of Technology, is 1 of 23 DeVry schools in the United States and Canada. The school offers programs in business administration, computer information systems, electronics, telecommunications management, technical management, information technology, and computer engineering technology. In addition to regional accreditation, DeVry has baccalaureate program accreditation with ABET. The library contains 9149 volumes and 875 audiovisual forms/CDs, and subscribes to 79 periodicals. Computerized library services include the card catalog, interlibrary loans, and database searching. Special learning facilities include a learning resource center and electronics and other labs. The 11-acre campus is in an urban area 30 miles east of Los Angeles. There is 1 building.

Student Life: 98% of undergraduates are from California. Others are from 21 states and 24 foreign countries. 34% are Asian American; 31% Hispanic, 22% white. The average age of all undergraduates is 26. 51% do not continue beyond their first year; 40% remain to graduate.

Housing: There are no residence halls. Housing referrals may be obtained through the Student Housing Office. All students commute. Alcohol is not permitted. All students may keep cars.

Activities: There are no fraternities or sororities. There are 14 groups on campus, including computers, ethnic, honors, professional, and social. Popular campus events include Welcome Barbecue, Winter Formal, and Part-time Jobs Fair.

Sports: There is 1 intramural sport for men and 1 for women.

Disabled Students: 90% of the campus is accessible. Wheelchair ramps, elevators, special parking, specially equipped rest rooms, lowered drinking fountains, and lowered telephones are available.

Services: Counseling and information services are available, as is tutoring in every subject.

Campus Safety and Security: Measures include escort service, informal discussions, pamphlets/posters/films, and emergency telephones. There are lighted pathways/sidewalks. A DeVry employee patrols the building from 4 P.M. to midnight, and a guard service patrols the lot from 6:30 A.M. to midnight.

Programs of Study: DeVry confers the B.S. degree. Associate degrees are also awarded. Bachelor's degrees are awarded in BUSINESS (business administration and management), COMMUNICATIONS AND THE ARTS (telecommunications), COMPUTER AND PHYSICAL SCIENCE (computer programming and information sciences and systems), ENGINEERING AND ENVIRONMENTAL DESIGN (computer engineering, electrical/electronics engineering technology, and technological management). Computer information systems and telecommunications are the largest.

Required: To graduate, students must achieve a cumulative GPA of at least 2.0 and satisfactorily complete all curriculum requirements. Course requirements vary according to program. All first-semester students take courses in business organization, computer applications, algebra, psychology, and student success strategies.

Special: Evening and weekend classes, nondegree study, and co-op programs in all majors are possible. There are 5 national honor societies.

Faculty/Classroom: All teach undergraduates. The average class size in an introductory lecture is 30; in a laboratory, 30; and in a regular course, 30.

Admissions: 85% of the 2001-2002 applicants were accepted.

Requirements: The SAT I or ACT is recommended. Admissions requirements include graduation from a secondary school; the GED is also accepted. Applicants from accredited postsecondary institutions must pass the DeVry entrance exam, or present satisfactory ACT or SAT I scores. An interview is required. CLEP credit is accepted. Applications are accepted on-line at *Embark.com*

Procedure: Freshmen are admitted fall, spring, and summer. There is a deferred admissions plan. Application deadlines are open. The Application fee is $50. Notification is sent on a rolling basis.

Transfer: 1 transfer student enrolled in 2001-2002. Applicants must present passing grades in all completed college course work, demonstrate language skills proficiency with at least 24 completed semester hours, and evidence math proficiency by appropriate college-level credits. 35% of 48 to 154 credits must be completed at DeVry.

Visiting: There are regularly scheduled orientations for prospective students. There are guides for informal visits and visitors may sit in on classes. To schedule a visit, contact Melanie Guerra, New Student Coordinator.

Financial Aid: In a recent year, 84% of all freshmen and 85% of continuing students received some form of financial aid. 52% of freshmen and 51% of continuing students received need-based aid. Scholarships or need-based grants averaged $2090 and loans averaged $6582. 10% of undergraduates work part time. Average annual earnings from campus work are $7500. DeVry is a member of CSS. The FAFSA is required.

International Students: There are 89 international students enrolled. They must score 500 on the written TOEFL or 173 on the electronic version and also take the college's own entrance exam and DeVry's computerized placement test, achieving a minimum score that varies by program.

Computers: The mainframe is an IBM. Lab facilities include PCs in stand-alone and network configurations, with access to the mainframe. LANs provide access to a wide range of applications software. Hard copy from the mainframe is provided through a local minicomputer and medium- and high-speed printers. Computer information systems students may access the system during published lab hours. There are no time limits and no fees.

Graduates: In 2001, 574 bachelor's degrees were awarded. The most popular majors were business (53%), computer information (31%), and

electronics engineering (16%). 16 companies recruited on campus in 2000-2001.
Admissions Contact: Byron Chung, Director of Admissions.
Web: *www.pom.devry.edu*

DEVRY UNIVERSITY/WEST HILLS C-5
West Hills, CA 91304 (818) 932-3001
(888) 393-3879; Fax: (818) 713-8118

Full-time: 657 men, 197 women	**Faculty:** 19
Part-time: 367 men, 130 women	**Ph.D.s:** n/av
Graduate: none	**Student/Faculty:** 45 to 1
Year: semesters, summer session	**Tuition:** $9205
Application Deadline: open	**Room & Board:** n/app
Freshman Class: 612 applied, 477 accepted, 348 enrolled	
SAT I or ACT: recommended	**LESS COMPETITIVE**

DeVry University/West Hills, formerly DeVry Institute of Technology, founded in 1999, is a private institution offering hands-on programs in electronics, business administration, computer information systems, telecommunications management, information technology, computer engineering technology, and technical management. The school is 1 of 23 DeVry schools throughout the United States and Canada. The library contains 4731 volumes and 91 audiovisual forms/CDs, and subscribes to 75 periodicals. Computerized library services include the card catalog, interlibrary loans, and database searching. Special learning facilities include a learning resource center and electronics and other labs. The 15-acre campus is in a suburban area in the San Fernando Valley. There is 1 building.
Student Life: 99% of undergraduates are from California. Others are from 9 states and 7 foreign countries. 34% are white; 31% Asian American, 26% Hispanic. The average age of all undergraduates is 26. 44% do not continue beyond their first year.
Housing: All of students commute.Housing referrals can be obtained through the Student Housing Office. Alcohol is not permitted. All students may keep cars.
Activities: There are no fraternities or sororities. There are 10 groups on campus, including computers, ethnic, international, professional, religious, and social. Popular campus events include Welcome BBQ, Cosmic Bowling, and Winter Formal.
Sports: There are 3 intramural sports for men and 3 for women.
Disabled Students: All of the campus is accessible. Wheelchair ramps, elevators, special parking, specially equipped rest rooms, lowered drinking fountains, and lowered telephones are available.
Services: Counseling and information services are available, as is tutoring in every subject.
Campus Safety and Security: Measures include emergency telephones and lighted pathways/sidewalks.
Programs of Study: DeVry confers the B.S. degree. Associate degrees are also awarded. Bachelor's degrees are awarded in BUSINESS (business administration and management), COMMUNICATIONS AND THE ARTS (telecommunications), COMPUTER AND PHYSICAL SCIENCE (computer programming and information sciences and systems), ENGINEERING AND ENVIRONMENTAL DESIGN (computer engineering, electrical/electronics engineering technology, and technological management). Computer information systems and business are the largest.
Required: To graduate, students must achieve a cumulative GPA of at least 2.0 and satisfactorily complete all curriculum requirements. Course requirements vary according to program. All first-semester students take courses in business organization, computer applications, algebra, psychology, and student success strategies.
Special: Co-op programs, nondegree study, and evening and weekend classes are possible.
Faculty/Classroom: All teach undergraduates. The average class size in an introductory lecture is 30; in a laboratory, 30; and in a regular course, 30.
Admissions: 78% of the 2001-2002 applicants were accepted.
Requirements: The SAT I or ACT is recommended. Admissions requirements include graduation from a secondary school; the GED is also accepted. Applicants must pass the DeVry entrance exam or present satisfactory ACT or SAT I scores. An interview is required. CLEP credit is accepted. Applications are accepted on-line at *Embark.com*
Procedure: Freshmen are admitted fall, spring, and summer. There is a deferred admissions plan. Application deadlines are open. The application fee is $50. Notification is sent on a rolling basis.
Transfer: 1 transfer student enrolled in 2001-2002. Applicants must present passing grades in all completed college course work, demonstrate language skills proficiency in at least 24 completed semester hours, and present evidence of math proficiency by appropriate college-level credits. 35% of 48 to 154 credits must be completed at DeVry.
Visiting: There are regularly scheduled orientations for prospective students. There are guides for informal visits and visitors may sit in on classes. To schedule a visit, contact the New Student Coordinator.
Financial Aid: In 2001-2002, 31% of all freshmen received some form of financial aid. 21% of freshmen received need-based aid. 5% of undergraduates work part time. Average annual earnings from campus work are $3120. The FAFSA is required.
International Students: There are 10 international students enrolled. They must score 500 on the written TOEFL or 173 on the electronic version and also take the college's own entrance exam.
Computers: Lab facilities include PCs in stand-alone and network configurations, with access to the mainframe. LANs provide access to a wide range of applications software. Hard copy from the mainframe is provided through a local microcomputer and medium- and high-speed printers. Computer information students may access the system during published lab hours. Students may access the system. There are no fees.
Graduates: In 2001, 2 bachelor's degrees were awarded. The most popular major was business (100%). 7 companies recruited on campus in 2000-2001.
Admissions Contact: Denise Barba, Acting Director of Admissions.
Web: *www.wh.devry.edu*

DOMINICAN UNIVERSITY OF CALIFORNIA B-3
San Rafael, CA 94901-2298 (415) 485-3204
(888) 323-6763; Fax: (415) 485-3214

Full-time: 164 men, 508 women	**Faculty:** 40; IIA, av$
Part-time: 49 men, 225 women	**Ph.D.s:** 69%
Graduate: 130 men, 360 women	**Student/Faculty:** 12 to 1
Year: semesters, summer session	**Tuition:** $18,998
Application Deadline: March 2	**Room & Board:** $8950
Freshman Class: 489 accepted, 128 enrolled	
SAT I Verbal/Math: 508/480	**COMPETITIVE**

Dominican University of California, formerly Dominican College of San Rafael, founded in 1890, is a Catholic, international university. There are 5 undergraduate and 4 graduate schools. In addition to regional accreditation, Dominican has baccalaureate program accreditation with NLN. The library contains 102,813 volumes, 2821 microform items, and 1107 audiovisual forms/CDs, and subscribes to 389 periodicals. Computerized library services include the card catalog, interlibrary loans, and database searching. Special learning facilities include a learning resource center, art gallery, natural history museum, radio station, music library, and art history slide and print collection. The 80-acre campus is in a suburban area 11 miles north of San Francisco. Including residence halls, there are 21 buildings.
Student Life: 91% of undergraduates are from California. Others are from 17 states, 18 foreign countries, and Canada. 69% are from public schools. 66% are white; 12% Asian American; 10% Hispanic. 32% are Catholic; 16% Protestant. The average age of freshmen is 18; all undergraduates, 28. 22% do not continue beyond their first year.
Housing: 240 students can be accommodated in college housing, which includes coed dormitories. On-campus housing is guaranteed for the freshman year only, is available on a first-come, first-served basis, and is available on a lottery system for upperclassmen. 77% of students commute. All students may keep cars.
Activities: There are no fraternities or sororities. There are 16 groups on campus, including art, cheerleading, chorus, computers, drama, ethnic, honors, international, literary magazine, newspaper, orchestra, radio and TV, religious, social service, student government, and yearbook. Popular campus events include an ecumenical Thanksgiving dinner, boat dance, and Shield Day (welcoming the freshman class).
Sports: There are 3 intercollegiate sports for men and 5 for women. Facilities include a gym, a fitness center, a swimming pool, tennis courts, a soccer field and a sand volleyball court.
Disabled Students: 50% of the campus is accessible. Wheelchair ramps, elevators, special parking, specially equipped rest rooms, special class scheduling, and lowered drinking fountains are available.
Services: Counseling and information services are available, as is tutoring in some subjects, including writing, math, chemistry, economics, time management, and study skills. There is remedial math and writing.
Campus Safety and Security: Measures include 24-hour foot and vehicle patrol, escort service, informal discussions, and lighted pathways/sidewalks.
Programs of Study: Dominican confers B.A., B.S., B.F.A., and B.S.N. degrees. Master's degrees are also awarded. Bachelor's degrees are awarded in AGRICULTURE (environmental studies), BIOLOGICAL SCIENCE (biology/biological science), BUSINESS (electronic business and international business management), COMMUNICATIONS AND THE ARTS (art, art history and appreciation, communications, creative writing, English literature, and music), COMPUTER AND PHYSICAL SCIENCE (digital arts/technology and mathematics), HEALTH PROFESSIONS (nursing, occupational therapy, and premedicine), SOCIAL SCIENCE (history, humanities, international studies, liberal arts/general studies, political science/government, psychology, and religion). Biology, psychology, and English literature are the strongest academically. Nursing, psychology, and humanities are the largest.
Required: All students must complete 124 credit hours including at least 24 in upper-division work, with a minimum 2.0 GPA. Core requirements include a cultural heritage colloquium of 12 units, 6 units in religious her-

itage, 3 to 4 units in the natural world, and 3 units each in human nature, verbal expression, quantitative reasoning, cultural perspectives, human relationships, and creativity in the arts. A senior thesis, project, recital, or comprehensive exam is required.

Special: Students may cross-register with the University of California at Berkeley. There is a semester interchange program with colleges in Michigan, Florida, or New York. Dominican also offers study abroad, dual majors, student-designed majors, internships, pass/fail options outside of the major and general education courses, and an evening/weekend bachelor's degree program. There is a freshman honors program.

Faculty/Classroom: 39% of faculty are male; 61%, female. 73% teach undergraduates. No introductory courses are taught by graduate students. The average class size in an introductory lecture is 25; in a laboratory, 20; and in a regular course, 17.

Admissions: The SAT I scores for the 2001-2002 freshman class were: Verbal--42% below 500, 35% between 500 and 599, 20% between 600 and 700, and 2% above 700; Math--45% below 500, 41% between 500 and 599, and 13% between 600 and 700. The ACT scores were 31% below 21, 38% between 21 and 23, 22% between 24 and 26, 6% between 27 and 28, and 3% above 28.

Requirements: The SAT I is required. In addition, applicants must be graduates of an accredited high school or have earned the GED. Secondary preparation must include 4 years of English, 2 each of math and a foreign language, and 1 each of lab science and history. An essay and a recommendation are required. An interview and a visit to the campus are highly recommended. Prospective music majors are encouraged to schedule an audition. A GPA of 2.5 is required. AP and CLEP credits are accepted. Important factors in the admissions decision are recommendations by school officials, extracurricular activities record, and evidence of special talent. Applications are accepted on-line at the school's web site.

Procedure: Freshmen are admitted to all sessions. Entrance exams should be taken in the late fall or early spring of the senior year. There is a deferred admissions plan. Applications should be filed by March 2 for fall entry, December 15 for spring entry, and May 1 for summer entry, along with a $40 fee. Notification is sent on a rolling basis.

Transfer: 98 transfer students enrolled in 2001-2002. Applicants must have a 2.0 GPA at an accredited college. They must also submit official high school and college transcripts and a letter of recommendation from a professor, academic dean, or counselor. 30 credits of 124 must be completed at Dominican.

Visiting: There are regularly scheduled orientations for prospective students, including financial aid conferences, math and writing placement testing, and a meeting with the prospective academic adviser. There are guides for informal visits and visitors may sit in on classes and stay overnight. To schedule a visit, contact the Admissions Office.

Financial Aid: In 2001-2002, 99% of all freshmen and 85% of continuing students received some form of financial aid. 70% of freshmen and 66% of continuing students received need-based aid. The average freshman award was $21,187. Of that total, scholarships or need-based grants averaged $8490 ($15,500 maximum); loans averaged $2888 ($4625 maximum); work contracts averaged $2505 ($2750 maximum); and athletic awards averaged $5756 ($13,620 maximum). 3% of undergraduates work part time. Average annual earnings from campus work are $2524. The FAFSA and the college's own financial statement are required. The fall application deadline is March 2.

International Students: There are 37 international students enrolled. The school actively recruits these students. They must score 550 on the written TOEFL and also take the SAT I or the ACT.

Computers: The mainframe is an IBM RF/6000 Model 530H. Students have access to 20 PCs, 6 PowerMacs, 3 graphics workstations, laser printers, an optical scanner, Ethernet and TCP/IP running on a Novell network, and numerous software programs. They also have access to e-mail, the Internet, and the Web. All students may access the system Monday through Thursday, 8 A.M. to 11 P.M.; Friday, 8 A.M. to 6 P.M.; Saturday, 10 A.M. to 6 P.M., and Sunday, noon to 11 P.M. There is a 2-hour time limit only when other students are waiting. There are no fees.

Graduates: In 2001, 235 bachelor's degrees were awarded. The most popular majors were nursing (18%), business (17%), and psychology (16%). In an average class, 35% graduate in 4 years, 40% in 5 years, and 51% in 6 years. Of the 2000 graduating class, 20% were enrolled in graduate school within 6 months of graduation and 70% were employed.

Admissions Contact: Art Cross, Director of Admissions (Day Program). E-mail: *enroll@dominican.edu* Web: *www.dominican.edu*

FRESNO PACIFIC UNIVERSITY — C-3

Fresno, CA 93702 — (559) 453-2039
(800) 660-6089; Fax: (559) 453-2007

Full-time: 297 men, 645 women	**Faculty:** 49
Part-time: 40 men, 74 women	**Ph.D.s:** 53%
Graduate: 270 men, 655 women	**Student/Faculty:** 19 to 1
Year: semesters, summer session	**Tuition:** $15,310
Application Deadline: July 31	**Room & Board:** $4430
Freshman Class: n/av	
SAT I Verbal/Math: 512/517	**ACT:** 22 **COMPETITIVE**

Fresno Pacific University, founded in 1944, is a private Christian liberal arts college affiliated with the Mennonite Brethren. The library contains 158,000 volumes, 300,000 microform items, and 10,000 audiovisual forms/CDs, and subscribes to 2583 periodicals. Computerized library services include the card catalog, interlibrary loans, and database searching. Special learning facilities include a learning resource center and the Center for Mennonite Brethren Studies, the Center for Conflict Studies and Peacemaking, and the Center for Degree Completion. The 42-acre campus is in a suburban area 150 miles southeast of San Francisco. Including residence halls, there are 18 buildings.

Student Life: 97% of undergraduates are from California. Others are from 14 states, 12 foreign countries, and Canada. 86% are from public schools. 65% are white; 19% Hispanic. Most are Protestant. The average age of freshmen is 20; all undergraduates, 22. 18% do not continue beyond their first year; 54% remain to graduate.

Housing: 510 students can be accommodated in college housing, which includes single-sex dormitories, on-campus apartments, and married-student housing. On-campus housing is available on a first-come, first-served basis and on a lottery system for upperclassmen. Priority is given to out-of-town students. 52% of students live on campus; of those, 40% remain on campus on weekends. Alcohol is not permitted. All students may keep cars.

Activities: There are no fraternities or sororities. There are 17 groups on campus, including art, choir, chorale, chorus, drama, ethnic, honors, international, jazz band, newspaper, pep band, professional, religious, social, social service, student government, and yearbook. Popular campus events include Carol Sing, Winter Ball, and Junior/Senior Banquet.

Sports: There are 4 intercollegiate sports for men and 5 for women, and 6 intramural sports for men and 6 for women. Facilities include a gym, 2 soccer fields, a swimming pool, and a track and field facility.

Disabled Students: All of the campus is accessible. Wheelchair ramps, elevators, special parking, specially equipped rest rooms, lowered drinking fountains, and lowered telephones are available.

Services: Counseling and information services are available, as is tutoring in every subject. There is a reader service for the blind, and remedial math, reading, and writing.

Campus Safety and Security: Measures include 24-hour foot and vehicle patrol, self-defense education, escort service, and informal discussions. There are pamphlets/posters/films, emergency telephones, and lighted pathways/sidewalks.

Programs of Study: FPU confers the B.A. degree. Associate and master's degrees are also awarded. Bachelor's degrees are awarded in BIOLOGICAL SCIENCE (biology/biological science), BUSINESS (accounting, business administration and management, and sports management), COMMUNICATIONS AND THE ARTS (English, music, and Spanish), COMPUTER AND PHYSICAL SCIENCE (chemistry, mathematics, and natural sciences), EDUCATION (English, mathematics, music, physical, science, and social science), ENGINEERING AND ENVIRONMENTAL DESIGN (environmental science), HEALTH PROFESSIONS (premedicine), SOCIAL SCIENCE (history, ministries, missions, philosophy, prelaw, psychology, religion, social science, and social work). Business, education, and religion are the strongest academically. Business, education, and psychology are the largest.

Required: Students must complete 124 semester units, 40 of which are in upper division courses, with at least a 2.0 GPA. General education requirements include a biblical studies/world civilization series, and 2 courses each in humanities, natural sciences, social sciences, phys ed, and math. Students are required to attend College Hour, a twice-weekly program of lectures, films, and concerts. Students are encouraged to volunteer 2 hours of community service per week. Several majors require internships.

Special: Internships are available, as is a one-semester cooperative program with the University of California, Davis. Cross-registration is possible with San Joaquin College of Law and California State University, Fresno. A B.A. in management and organizational development is offered to working adults. Other off-campus learning opportunities include programs in American studies in Washington, D.C., urban studies in Chicago, and study abroad in Israel, Japan, Costa Rica, and Brethren Colleges in England, Spain, France, Germany, or China. A summer semester in Mexico is offered. There is 1 national honor society and a freshman honors program.

Faculty/Classroom: 67% of faculty are male; 33%, female. 64% teach undergraduates. No introductory courses are taught by graduate students. The average class size in a regular course is 25.
Admissions: The SAT I scores for the 2001-2002 freshman class were: Verbal--49% below 500, 35% between 500 and 599, 15% between 600 and 700, and 1% above 700; Math--49% below 500, 36% between 500 and 599, and 15% between 600 and 700. The ACT scores were 40% below 21, 25% between 21 and 23, 15% between 24 and 26, 15% between 27 and 28, and 5% above 28.
Requirements: The SAT I or ACT is required. In addition, applicants should be graduates of an accredited high school or have the GED. Required secondary preparation includes 4 years of college prep English, 2 years of social studies, algebra 1 and 2, geometry, and at least 1 year of a lab science. The university recommends that applicants also take courses in art, music, and 2 years of the same foreign language, all with a grade of C or better. An essay is required, and an audition is recommended for prospective music majors. A GPA of 3.1 is required. AP and CLEP credits are accepted. Important factors in the admissions decision are recommendations by school officials, advanced placement or honor courses, and extracurricular activities record.
Procedure: Freshmen are admitted fall and spring. Entrance exams should be taken during the fall of the senior year. Early decision applications should be filed by January 31; regular applications, by July 31 for fall entry and December 5 for spring entry. The fall 2001application fee was $30. Notification is sent on a rolling basis.
Transfer: 143 transfer students enrolled in 2001-2002. Applicants should have completed at least 24 transferable units of college work with a 2.4 GPA. Those with fewer credits may apply any time but must meet freshman admission requirements. The SAT I or ACT scores are recommended. 30 credits of 124 must be completed at FPU.
Visiting: There are regularly scheduled orientations for prospective students. There are guides for informal visits and visitors may sit in on classes and stay overnight. To schedule a visit, contact Jon Endicott, Director of Admissions at *ugadmis@fresno.edu*
Financial Aid: In a recent year, 99% of all freshmen and 93% of continuing students received some form of financial aid. 85% of freshmen and 79% of continuing students received need-based aid. The average freshman award was $14,068. Of that total, scholarships or need-based grants averaged $10,956 ($18,384 maximum); loans averaged $3782 ($6625 maximum); and work contracts averaged $1718 ($2000 maximum). The average financial indebtedness of a recent graduate was $13,573. The FAFSA and the college's own financial statement are required. The fall application deadline is May 1.
International Students: There were 34 international students enrolled in a recent year. The school actively recruits these students. They must score 500 on the written TOEFL.
Computers: The mainframe is an HP 9000G. The university provides 12 PCs for academic use in the library. There are also Mac and PC labs with 20 computers in each. Students may access university systems through dial up procedures. All students may access the system 8 A.M. to 12 P.M. weekdays, 1 P.M. to 4 P.M. weekends. There are no time limits and no fees. It is strongly recommended that all students have personal computers.
Graduates: In 2001, 251 bachelor's degrees were awarded. The most popular majors were business (44%), liberal studies (20%), and biblical studies (8%). In an average class, 48% graduate in 4 years, 63% in 5 years, and 64% in 6 years. 45 companies recruited on campus in 2000-2001. Of the 2000 graduating class, 41% were enrolled in graduate school within 6 months of graduation.
Admissions Contact: Jon Endicott, Director of Admissions. A video is available. E-mail: *jendicot@fresno.edu* Web: *www.fresno.edu*

GOLDEN GATE UNIVERSITY

San Francisco, CA 94105-2968 — B-3 — (415) 442-7800
(800) 448-4968; Fax: (415) 442-7807

Full-time: 150 men, 190 women	**Faculty:** 35
Part-time: 390 men, 575 women	**Ph.D.s:** 98%
Graduate: 2060 men, 2050 women	**Student/Faculty:** 9 to 1
Year: trimesters, summer session	**Tuition:** $8600
Application Deadline: June 1	**Room & Board:** n/app
Freshman Class: 50 applied, 50 accepted, 50 enrolled	
SAT I or ACT: not required	**NONCOMPETITIVE**

Golden Gate University, founded in 1901, is a private, nonprofit, independent, commuter institution offering undergraduate and graduate degrees in business administration, accounting, human and social sciences, and special programs. There are 3 undergraduate and 4 graduate schools. Figures in the above capsule are approximate. The 2 libraries contain 300,000 volumes, and subscribe to 2500 periodicals. Computerized library services include interlibrary loans and database searching. Special learning facilities include a learning resource center and an English as a second language center. The 1-acre campus is in an urban area in San Francisco. There are 2 buildings.
Student Life: Others are from Canada. 51% are white; 19% Asian American; 18% foreign nationals; 10% African American; 10% Hispanic. The average age of freshmen is 21; all undergraduates, 37. 12% do not continue beyond their first year.

Housing: There are no residence halls. All students commute. Alcohol is not permitted.

Activities: There are no fraternities or sororities. There are 5 groups on campus, including ethnic, international, newspaper, professional, and social. Popular campus events include Commencement Ball and other social functions.

Sports: There is no sports program at Golden Gate.

Disabled Students: All of the campus is accessible. Wheelchair ramps, elevators, special parking, and specially equipped rest rooms are available.

Services: Counseling and information services are available, as is tutoring in some subjects. There is remedial math, reading, and writing.

Campus Safety and Security: Measures include escort service, informal discussions, and pamphlets/posters/films.

Programs of Study: Golden Gate confers B.S. and B.B.A. degrees. Master's and doctoral degrees are also awarded. Bachelor's degrees are awarded in BUSINESS (accounting, international business management, management science, and marketing), COMMUNICATIONS AND THE ARTS (telecommunications), COMPUTER AND PHYSICAL SCIENCE (information sciences and systems), SOCIAL SCIENCE (human services). Accounting, finance, and information systems are the strongest academically. Finance, accounting, and management are the largest.

Required: A total of 123 trimester hours, with 21 to 33 in the major, are required to graduate. A minimum GPA of 2.0 is also required.

Special: The university offers cooperative programs, cross-registration with the San Francisco Consortium, internships, an accelerated degree program, dual majors, credit for military experience, nondegree study, and credit/no credit options. Also available are weekend classes and 10-week terms.

Faculty/Classroom: 66% of faculty are male; 34%, female. All teach undergraduates. No introductory courses are taught by graduate students. The average class size in an introductory lecture is 25; in a laboratory, 15; and in a regular course, 20.

Admissions: All of the 2001-2002 applicants were accepted.

Requirements: Applicants must be graduates of an accredited secondary school or have a GED. Applications are accepted on-line via the school's web site and CollegeNet.com. A GPA of 2.5 is required. AP and CLEP credits are accepted.

Procedure: Freshmen are admitted in fall, spring, and summer. There is a deferred admissions and deferred admissions plan. Applications for fall entry should be filed by June 1 along with a $55 fee ($90 international). Notification is sent on a rolling basis.

Transfer: 50 transfer students enrolled in 2001-2002. At least 24 transferable units and a 2.0 overall GPA are required. A minimum of 30 units out of 123, including 21 in the major, must be completed at GGU. 30 credits of 123 must be completed at Golden Gate.

Visiting: Visitors may sit in on classes. To schedule a visit, contact Admissions Office.

Financial Aid: In a recent year, 25% of all freshmen and 22% of continuing students received some form of financial aid. 10% of freshmen and 17% of continuing students received need-based aid. The average freshman award was $18,483. Of that total, scholarships or need-based grants averaged $2415 ($5926 maximum); loans averaged $5086 ($6540 maximum); and work contracts averaged $111 ($3000 maximum). 96% of undergraduates work part time. The FAFSA is required. The fall application deadline is open.

International Students: There are 226 international students enrolled. The school actively recruits these students. They must score 525 on the written TOEFL or 197 on the electronic version. Check with the web site for further information.

Computers: The mainframe is an HP 3000/Series 64. PCs are available in the computer center. All students may access the system at designated hours.

Graduates: In 2001, 201 bachelor's degrees were awarded. The most popular majors were management (25%), accounting (15%), and human relations (8%). 74 companies recruited on campus in 2000-2001. Of the 2000 graduating class, 9% were enrolled in graduate school within 6 months of graduation and 64% were employed.

Admissions Contact: Office of Enrollment Services.
E-mail: *info@ggu.edu* Web: *www.ggu.edu*

HARVEY MUDD COLLEGE D-5

Claremont, CA 91711 **(909) 621-8011; Fax: (909) 607-7046**

Full-time: 480 men, 223 women **Faculty:** 82; IIB, +$
Part-time: 3 men **Ph.D.s:** 100%
Graduate: 1 man **Student/Faculty:** 9 to 1
Year: semesters **Tuition:** $23,187
Application Deadline: January 15 **Room & Board:** $8418
Freshman Class: 1421 applied, 516 accepted, 174 enrolled
SAT I Verbal/Math: 710/750 **MOST COMPETITIVE**

Harvey Mudd College, founded in 1955, is one of the Claremont Colleges. It is an independent college specializing in engineering and physical science education within a liberal arts tradition. In addition to regional accreditation, Harvey Mudd has baccalaureate program accreditation with ABET and ACS. The library contains 1.9 million volumes and subscribes to 6800 periodicals. Computerized library services include the card catalog, interlibrary loans, and database searching. Special learning facilities include an art gallery, planetarium, and radio station. The 30-acre campus is in a suburban area 35 miles east of Los Angeles. Including residence halls, there are 18 buildings.

Student Life: 57% of undergraduates are from out of state, mostly the Northwest. Students are from 45 states, 12 foreign countries, and Canada. 80% are from public schools. 65% are white; 22% Asian American. The average age of freshmen is 18; all undergraduates, 20. 3% do not continue beyond their first year.

Housing: 632 students can be accommodated in college housing, which includes single-sex and coed dormitories and on-campus apartments. On-campus housing is guaranteed for the freshman year only, is available on a first-come, first-served basis, and is available on a lottery system for upperclassmen. 97% of students live on campus; of those, 94% remain on campus on weekends. All students may keep cars.

Activities: There are no fraternities or sororities. There are 74 groups on campus, including art, band, chess, choir, chorale, chorus, computers, dance, drama, ethnic, gay, international, jazz band, literary magazine, musical theater, newspaper, orchestra, pep band, photography, political, professional, radio and TV, religious, social, social service, student government, symphony, and yearbook. Popular campus events include 5-class competition relay races, Wednesday night lecture/dinner series, and film nights.

Sports: There are 10 intercollegiate sports for men and 10 for women, and 6 intramural sports for men and 6 for women. Facilities include an athletic facility housing 2 gym floors, a weight room, a 400-meter track, a swimming pool, 9 tennis courts, and sports fields. The campus recreation facility houses a full-size gym floor, an aerobic/dance room, and a fitness room with treadmills, steppers, exercycles, and weight equipment.

Disabled Students: 99% of the campus is accessible. Wheelchair ramps, elevators, special parking, specially equipped rest rooms, special class scheduling, and lowered drinking fountains are available.

Services: Counseling and information services are available, as is tutoring in most subjects. Support is offered on a case-by-case basis.

Campus Safety and Security: Measures include 24-hour foot and vehicle patrol, self-defense education, escort service, and informal discussions. There are pamphlets/posters/films, emergency telephones, lighted pathways/sidewalks, and a biweekly, electronic newsletter on campus security issues.

Programs of Study: Harvey Mudd confers the B.S. degree. Bachelor's degrees are awarded in BIOLOGICAL SCIENCE (biology/biological science), COMPUTER AND PHYSICAL SCIENCE (chemistry, computer science, mathematics, and physics), ENGINEERING AND ENVIRONMENTAL DESIGN (engineering). Physics and chemistry are the strongest academically. Engineering and computer engineering are the largest.

Required: To graduate, all students must have a 2.0 GPA and complete a total of 128 hours, including 45 hours in a common core. This consists of 4 semesters of math, 3 semesters of physics, 2 semesters of chemistry, and courses in biology, programming, and system engineering, plus 2 electives chosen from core offerings. Another 37 hours are required in humanities and social sciences, including literature, psychology, philosophy, history, and institutions, and 46 in the major and electives. All students take 3 semesters of noncredit phys ed courses. A senior research or corporate clinic project is required.

Special: Students may cross-register at any of the other Claremont Colleges. Internships are available for engineering and math majors. Study abroad, a Washington semester, work-study, joint computer science/math and math/biology majors, and student-designed majors are available. A 3-2 engineering degree with Claremont McKenna College is possible, as is a 4-1 B.S./M.B.A. with Claremont Graduate University. Some courses may be audited. The first semester for freshmen is taken on a pass/fail basis; thereafter, only 1 noncore and nonmajor course per semester may be taken on that basis. There is 1 national honor society and 7 departmental honors programs.

Faculty/Classroom: 71% of faculty are male; 29%, female. All both teach and do research. Graduate students teach 1% of introductory courses. The average class size in an introductory lecture is 80; in a laboratory, 10; and in a regular course, 15.

Admissions: 36% of the 2001-2002 applicants were accepted. The SAT I scores for the 2001-2002 freshman class were: Verbal--4% between 500 and 599, 45% between 600 and 700, and 51% above 700; Math--17% between 600 and 700, and 83% above 700. 94% of the current freshmen were in the top fifth of their class; All were in the top two fifths. There were 37 National Merit finalists and 51 semifinalists. 36 freshmen graduated first in their class.

Requirements: The SAT I is required. In addition, applicants must be graduates of an accredited secondary school and have completed 4 years each of English and math (including algebra, demonstrative and analytic geometry, trigonometry, and calculus) and 1 year each of physics and chemistry. The college strongly recommends that applicants take 2 years of a foreign language and 1 year each of history and biology. SAT II: Subject tests in math II, writing, and 1 other subject are required. Applicants must submit 2 personal essays and are encouraged to seek an interview. AP credits are accepted. Important factors in the admissions decision are leadership record, recommendations by school officials, and advanced placement or honor courses. Applications are accepted on-line via CollegeLink, Common App, Harvey Mudd's on-line application, Next Stop College, Embark, and Apply.

Procedure: Freshmen are admitted in the fall. Entrance exams should be taken by January of the senior year. There are early decision and deferred admissions plans. Early decision applications should be filed by November 15; regular applications, by January 15 for fall entry, along with a $50 fee. Notification of early decision is sent December 15; regular decision, April 1. 53 early decision candidates were accepted for the 2001-2002 class. 19% of all applicants are on a waiting list; 39 were accepted in 2001.

Transfer: 5 transfer students enrolled in 2001-2002. Applicants must submit SAT II: Subject test scores, transcripts, course descriptions, and references from a college math, science, or engineering teacher and from a counselor. An interview is recommended. Students must have completed courses in calculus, physics, chemistry, and English composition. 80 credits of 128 must be completed at Harvey Mudd.

Visiting: There are regularly scheduled orientations for prospective students, including tours and interviews conducted Monday through Friday and Saturday mornings in the fall. There are guides for informal visits and visitors may sit in on classes and stay overnight. To schedule a visit, contact the Admission Office.

Financial Aid: In 2001-2002, 85% of all freshmen and 81% of continuing students received some form of financial aid. 62% of freshmen and 55% of continuing students received need-based aid. The average freshman award was $15,335. Of that total, scholarships or need-based grants averaged $11,750 ($30,135 maximum); loans averaged $3027 ($4000 maximum); and work contracts averaged $575 ($1875 maximum). 27% of undergraduates work part time. Average annual earnings from campus work are $782. The average financial indebtedness of the 2001 graduate was $17,968. Harvey Mudd is a member of CSS. The CSS/Profile or FAFSA is required. The fall application deadline is February 1.

International Students: There are 18 international students enrolled. They must score 600 on the written TOEFL and also take the SAT I. Students must take SAT II: Subject tests in math, writing, and 1 other subject.

Computers: The mainframes are a Sun Ultra Enterprise 2 and others. Students may access systems from dorm rooms, academic labs, and classrooms. 90% of students own PCs that are attached to the campus network via Ethernet. More than 150 systems ranging from Mac and Windows PCs to SGI, Sun, and HP UNIX workstations are available on the network for student use. All students may access the system 24 hours a day. There are no time limits and no fees. It is strongly recommended that all students have a personal computer.

Graduates: In 2001, 147 bachelor's degrees were awarded. The most popular majors were engineering (52%), computer science (28%), and physics (25%). In an average class, 74% graduate in 4 years, 79% in 5 years, and 79% in 6 years. 50 companies recruited on campus in 2000-2001. Of the 2000 graduating class, 36% were enrolled in graduate school within 6 months of graduation and 95% were employed.

Admissions Contact: Deren Finks, Vice President, Dean of Admissions and Financial Aid. E-mail: *admission@hmc.edu*
Web: *www.hmc.edu*

HOLY NAMES COLLEGE
Oakland, CA 94619 B-3

(510) 436-1321
(800) 430-1321; Fax: (510) 436-1325

Full-time: 91 men, 209 women	**Faculty:** 30
Part-time: 19 men, 187 women	**Ph.D.s:** 87%
Graduate: 58 men, 268 women	**Student/Faculty:** 10 to 1
Year: semesters, summer session	**Tuition:** $16,620
Application Deadline: August 1	**Room & Board:** $6600

Freshman Class: 167 applied, 119 accepted, 46 enrolled
SAT I Verbal/Math: 440/460 **COMPETITIVE**

Holy Names College, founded in 1868, is an independent college affiliated with the Roman Catholic Church. It offers education in the liberal arts and preparation for some professions. In addition to regional accreditation, Holy Names has baccalaureate program accreditation with NASM and NLN. The library contains 111,174 volumes, 50,931 microform items, and 4298 audiovisual forms/CDs, and subscribes to 198 periodicals. Computerized library services include database searching. Special learning facilities include a learning resource center, art gallery, a performing arts center, a 400-seat theater, and a black box theater. The 60-acre campus is in an urban area 20 miles east of San Francisco. Including residence halls, there are 15 buildings.

Student Life: 97% of undergraduates are from California. Others are from 10 states, 12 foreign countries, and Canada. 65% are from public schools. 34% are African American; 24% white; 15% Hispanic. 19% do not continue beyond their first year; 46% remain to graduate.

Housing: 351 students can be accommodated in college housing, which includes coed dormitories. On-campus housing is guaranteed for all 4 years. 55% of students commute. Alcohol is not permitted. All students may keep cars.

Activities: There are no fraternities or sororities. There are 19 groups on campus, including cheerleading, choir, chorale, computers, drama, ethnic, honors, international, orchestra, religious, social service, and student government. Popular campus events include Humanistic Studies Days and Founders Day.

Sports: There are 4 intercollegiate sports for men and 4 for women, and 8 intramural sports for men and 8 for women. Facilities include a gym, a pool, a fitness center, locker rooms and training rooms, and an outdoor fitness course.

Disabled Students: 85% of the campus is accessible. Elevators, special parking, specially equipped rest rooms, lowered drinking fountains, lowered telephones, a learning disability program, and special accommodations based on student need and eligibility are available.

Services: Counseling and information services are available, as is tutoring in most subjects. There is remedial math and writing. Note takers and extended time for tests may be arranged.

Campus Safety and Security: Measures include self-defense education, escort service, informal discussions, and lighted pathways/sidewalks. There is a 24-hour manned entrance gate and nighttime foot patrol.

Programs of Study: Holy Names confers B.A., B.S., B.Mus., and B.S.N. degrees. Master's degrees are also awarded. Bachelor's degrees are awarded in BIOLOGICAL SCIENCE (biology/biological science), BUSINESS (business administration and management and human resources), COMMUNICATIONS AND THE ARTS (communications, English, English as a second/foreign language, and music), COMPUTER AND PHYSICAL SCIENCE (computer science), HEALTH PROFESSIONS (nursing), SOCIAL SCIENCE (history, human services, humanities, liberal arts/general studies, philosophy, psychology, religion, sociology, and Spanish studies). Business administration, nursing, and psychology are the largest.

Required: Students must have a 2.0 GPA and complete at least 120 hours with 24 to 36 in the major and 20 upper-division hours taken outside the major field. Students must complete a core curriculum, including foundation courses in critical thinking and communication, and courses in disciplinary studies, integrative studies across cultures, and writing across the curriculum. In some cases these requirements may be satisfied by secondary record, advanced placement, or challenge test. All students must take multidisciplinary courses in humanistic studies, a senior colloquium, and health or phys ed.

Special: Students may cross-register for 1 course per semester at any of 9 members of the Regional Association of East Bay Colleges and Universities. Internships, study abroad, and cooperative exchange programs with Central College in Iowa, Anna Maria College in Massachusetts, the Center for Bilingual Multicultural Studies in Mexico, and Kansai University of Foreign Studies in Japan are available. Dual and student-designed majors and interdisciplinary majors, including business administration and communication and business administration and philosophy are offered. Accelerated degrees are available in all B.A. programs. A weekend college for adults, limited nondegree study, and pass/fail options are available. There are 10 national honor societies and 1 departmental honors program.

Faculty/Classroom: 40% of faculty are male; 60%, female. No introductory courses are taught by graduate students. The average class size in an introductory lecture is 13; in a laboratory, 7; and in a regular course, 15.

Admissions: 71% of the 2001-2002 applicants were accepted. The SAT I scores for the 2001-2002 freshman class were: Verbal--68% below 500, 21% between 500 and 599, and 6% between 600 and 700; Math--73% below 500, 19% between 500 and 599, and 8% between 600 and 700. 37% of the current freshmen were in the top fifth of their class; 71% were in the top two fifths.

Requirements: The SAT I or ACT is required. In addition, applicants must be graduates of an accredited secondary school or have earned the GED. Secondary preparation should include at least 4 years of English, 3 years of math, 2 years of a single foreign language, 1 year each of lab science and U.S. history, 1 additional year of advanced courses in math, lab science, or foreign language, and 3 other 1-year college preparatory electives. In addition, the college requires a personal essay. Music auditions are required for scholarship applicants and recommended for others. AP and CLEP credits are accepted. Important factors in the admissions decision are advanced placement or honor courses, leadership record, and recommendations by school officials.

Procedure: Freshmen are admitted fall and spring. Entrance exams should be taken during the fall of the senior year. There is a deferred admissions plan. Applications should be filed by August 1 for fall entry and December 1 for spring entry, along with a $35 fee. Notification is sent on a rolling basis.

Transfer: 47 transfer students enrolled in 2001-2002. Applicants must have at least a 2.2 GPA in college work or a minimum of 30 transferable units. They must submit college records, a letter of recommendation from a college teacher or counselor, and a personal statement of their educational goals. 24 credits of 120 must be completed at Holy Names.

Visiting: There are guides for informal visits and visitors may sit in on classes and stay overnight. To schedule a visit, contact the Admissions Office at (510) 436-1351.

Financial Aid: In 2001-2002, 80% of all freshmen and 87% of continuing students received some form of financial aid. 78% of freshmen and 82% of continuing students received need-based aid. The average freshman award was $21,225. Of that total, scholarships or need-based grants averaged $10,500 ($16,500 maximum); loans averaged $2625 ($10,500 maximum); and work contracts averaged $2000. 25% of undergraduates work part time. Average annual earnings from campus work are $2000. The average financial indebtedness of the 2001 graduate was $17,000. The FAFSA is required. The fall application deadline is March 2.

International Students: There are 28 international students enrolled. The school actively recruits these students. They must score 490 on the written TOEFL or 163 on the electronic version or take the MELAB.

Computers: The mainframe is A DEC ALPHA 4000. 24 IBM PCs and 12 Macs are available in 2 large computer labs open to all students. Additional computers are located in the music resource lab, the nursing department, and the library. There are 16 PCs in a lab in the residence hall. Microsoft Office and Internet access is available. The entire campus has fiber optic cable connection. All students may access the system 8 A.M. to 10 P.M. daily in the labs. Network access is available 24 hours a day. There are no time limits and no fees.

Graduates: In 2001, 94 bachelor's degrees were awarded. The most popular majors were business and marketing (27%), nursing (23%), and liberal studies (11%). In an average class, 15% graduate in 4 years, 26% in 5 years, and 28% in 6 years. 12 companies recruited on campus in a recent year.

Admissions Contact: Jeffrey Miller, Vice President for Enrollment Management. E-mail: *admissions@hnc.edu* Web: *www.hnc.edu*

HOPE INTERNATIONAL UNIVERSITY
Fullerton, CA 92831 D-5

(714) 879-3901, ext. 2215
(800) 762-1294; Fax: (714) 524-0231

Full-time: 300 men, 400 women	**Faculty:** 29
Part-time: 40 men, 100 women	**Ph.D.s:** 48%
Graduate: 80 men, 80 women	**Student/Faculty:** 24 to 1
Year: 4-1-4, summer session	**Tuition:** $12,500
Application Deadline: May 1	**Room & Board:** $4440

Freshman Class: n/av
SAT I or ACT: required **NONCOMPETITIVE**

Hope International University, founded in 1928, is a small, private liberal arts institution affiliated with the Independent Christian Church/Churches of Christ. Figures given in the above capsule are approximate. There are 2 undergraduate schools and 1 graduate school. The library contains 65,000 volumes, 100 microform items, and 3300 audiovisual forms/CDs, and subscribes to 300 periodicals. Computerized library services include the card catalog and database searching. Special learning facilities include a learning resource center and a 1000-seat theater. The 15-acre campus is in an urban area 45 miles southeast of Los Angeles. Including residence halls, there are 9 buildings.

Student Life: 53% of undergraduates are from California. Others are from 25 states, 27 foreign countries, and Canada. 88% are from public schools. 61% are white; 20% foreign nationals. Most are Protestant. The average age of freshmen is 18; all undergraduates, 21. 19% do not continue beyond their first year; 48% remain to graduate.

Housing: 450 students can be accommodated in college housing, which includes single-sex dormitories. On-campus housing is guaranteed for all 4 years. 52% of students live on campus; of those, 75% remain on campus on weekends. Alcohol is not permitted. All students may keep cars.

Activities: There are no fraternities or sororities. There are 17 groups on campus, including band, cheerleading, choir, chorale, chorus, drama, international, literary magazine, newspaper, orchestra, religious, social service, student government, and yearbook. Popular campus events include Sadie Hawkins, Spring Formal, and Service on Saturday (community outreach).

Sports: There are 4 intercollegiate sports for men and 5 for women, and 10 intramural sports for men and 8 for women. Facilities include a swimming pool and game rooms.

Disabled Students: 95% of the campus is accessible. Elevators, special parking, and specially equipped rest rooms are available. Priority is given to disabled students for first-floor housing.

Services: Counseling and information services are available, as is tutoring in most subjects. There is a reader service for the blind, and remedial math, reading, and writing.

Campus Safety and Security: Measures include 24-hour foot and vehicle patrol, escort service, and lighted pathways/sidewalks.

Programs of Study: Hope confers B.A., B.S., B.M., and B.M.E. degrees. Associate and master's degrees are also awarded. Bachelor's degrees are awarded in BUSINESS (business administration and management), COMMUNICATIONS AND THE ARTS (music and Spanish), EDUCATION (education, music, secondary, and social science), HEALTH PROFESSIONS (health science and sports medicine), SOCIAL SCIENCE (biblical studies, child psychology/development, crosscultural studies, human services, interdisciplinary studies, liberal arts/general studies, ministries, psychology, social science, and youth ministry). Education, business, and church ministry are the largest.

Required: Regular attendance at convocation and Christian service is required. To graduate, students must complete at least 124 credit units with 36 to 51 in the major, and demonstrate 80% or better competency on the university placement test. A minimum GPA of 2.0 must be maintained. Distribution requirements include 18 credits in biblical studies and 55 in general education courses.

Special: Hope International offers co-op programs and cross-registration with California State University, Fullerton. Internships, study abroad in 3 countries, work-study programs, dual and student-designed majors, nondegree study, pass/fail options, and credit for life, military, and work experience are also offered. There is a freshman honors program.

Faculty/Classroom: 69% of faculty are male; 31%, female. 83% teach undergraduates. No introductory courses are taught by graduate students. The average class size in an introductory lecture is 33; in a laboratory, 20; and in a regular course, 30.

Admissions: 45% of the current freshmen were in the top fifth of their class; 77% were in the top two fifths.

Requirements: The SAT I or ACT is required. In addition, applicants must be high school graduates with a GPA of 2.5. The GED is accepted. A personal essay and references from a church leader and an academic counselor are required. AP and CLEP credits are accepted.

Procedure: Freshmen are admitted fall and spring. Entrance exams should be taken before enrolling. There are early admissions and deferred admissions plans. Applications should be filed by May 1 for fall entry and December 1 for spring entry. The college accepts all applicants. Notification is sent on a rolling basis. The fall 2001 application fee was $30.

Transfer: 51 transfer students were enrolled in a recent year. Transfer students must submit copies of college transcripts and SAT I scores if fewer than 30 college units have been completed. A minimum GPA of 2.0 is required. 30 credits of 124 must be completed at Hope.

Visiting: There are regularly scheduled orientations for prospective students. There are guides for informal visits and visitors may sit in on classes and stay overnight. To schedule a visit, contact the Admissions Office.

Financial Aid: 80% of undergraduates work part time. The FAFSA and the college's own financial statement are required. The priority deadline date for financial application is March 2.

International Students: There were 67 international students enrolled in a recent year. The school actively recruits these students. They must score 500 on the written TOEFL and also take the college's own entrance exam.

Computers: PC facilities are available for student use at the campus learning center. All students may access the system at any time. There are no time limits and no fees. It is strongly recommended that all students have a personal computer.

Graduates: In an average class, 42% graduate in 4 years, 54% in 5 years, and 56% in 6 years. 16 companies recruited on campus in a recent year.

Admissions Contact: Kaylene Carr, Director of Admissions. A video is available. E-mail: *twinston@hiu.edu* Web: *www.hiu.ed*

HUMBOLDT STATE UNIVERSITY — A-1

Arcata, CA 95521-8299 — **(707) 826-4402; Fax: (707) 826-6194**

Full-time: 2888 men, 3530 women	**Faculty:** 308; IIA, +$
Part-time: 343 men, 353 women	**Ph.D.s:** 99%
Graduate: 399 men, 565 women	**Student/Faculty:** 21 to 1
Year: semesters, summer session	**Tuition:** $1892 ($7796)
Application Deadline: open	**Room & Board:** $6690
Freshman Class: 3833 applied, 2829 accepted, 732 enrolled	
SAT I Verbal/Math: 530/520	**ACT:** 22 **COMPETITIVE**

Humboldt State University, founded in 1913, is a liberal arts institution and the northernmost campus of the California State University system. There are 3 undergraduate schools and 1 graduate school. In addition to regional accreditation, Humboldt has baccalaureate program accreditation with ABET, ACEJMC, CSWE, NASAD, NASM, NLN, and SAF. The library contains 570,552 volumes, 600,254 microform items, and 18,562 audiovisual forms/CDs, and subscribes to 2782 periodicals. Computerized library services include the card catalog, interlibrary loans, and database searching. Special learning facilities include an art gallery, natural history museum, radio station, observatory, greenhouse, solar hydrogen project, wildlife sanctuaries, the Center for Appropriate Technology, child development lab, and ceramics lab. The 161-acre campus is in a small town 275 miles north of San Francisco. Including residence halls, there are 77 buildings.

Student Life: 91% of undergraduates are from California. Others are from 48 states, 16 foreign countries, and Canada. 79% are from public schools. 65% are white. The average age of freshmen is 18; all undergraduates, 24. 24% do not continue beyond their first year.

Housing: 1356 students can be accommodated in college housing, which includes single-sex and coed dormitories and on-campus apartments. In addition, there are special-interest houses, and living learning houses. On-campus housing is available on a first-come, first-served basis. 82% of students commute. Alcohol is not permitted. All students may keep cars.

Activities: There are 2 national fraternities and 4 local sororities. There are 124 groups on campus, including art, band, cheerleading, chorale, chorus, computers, dance, drama, environmental, ethnic, film, gay, honors, international, jazz band, literary magazine, musical theater, newspaper, opera, orchestra, pep band, photography, political, professional, radio and TV, religious, social, social service, student government, and symphony. Popular campus events include Lumberjack Days, Native American Motivation Day, and Cinco de Mayo.

Sports: There are 5 intercollegiate sports for men and 7 for women, and 5 intramural sports for men and 5 for women. Facilities include a 7000-seat stadium, an all-weather track, a swimming pool, a field house, tennis and racquetball courts, playing fields, 2 gyms, a weight room, and a rock-climbing wall.

Disabled Students: 60% of the campus is accessible. Wheelchair ramps, elevators, special parking, specially equipped rest rooms, special class scheduling, lowered drinking fountains, lowered telephones, and wheelchair-accessible transportation, and a study center are available.

Services: Counseling and information services are available, as is tutoring in every subject. There is a reader service for the blind, and remedial math, reading, and writing.

Campus Safety and Security: Measures include 24-hour foot and vehicle patrol, escort service, informal discussions, and pamphlets/posters/films. There are emergency telephones, lighted pathways/sidewalks, and escort and emergency transportation services.

Programs of Study: Humboldt confers B.A. and B.S. degrees. Master's degrees are also awarded. Bachelor's degrees are awarded in AGRICULTURE (fishing and fisheries, forestry and related sciences, and natural resource management), BIOLOGICAL SCIENCE (biology/biological science, botany, wildlife biology, and zoology), BUSINESS (business administration and management and business economics), COMMUNICATIONS AND THE ARTS (art, communications, dramatic arts, English, fine arts, French, German, journalism, music, Spanish, and speech/debate/rhetoric), COMPUTER AND PHYSICAL SCIENCE (chemistry, geology, information sciences and systems, mathematics, oceanography, and physics), EDUCATION (business, elementary, English, industrial arts, mathematics, middle school, music, physical, science, secondary, and social science), ENGINEERING AND ENVIRONMENTAL DESIGN (environmental engineering, environmental science, industrial engineering technology, and land use management and reclamation), HEALTH PROFESSIONS (nursing, predentistry, and premedicine), SOCIAL SCIENCE (anthropology, child psychology/development, geography, history, liberal arts/general studies, Native American studies, parks and recreation management, philosophy, physical fitness/movement, political science/government, prelaw, psychology, religion, social science, social work, and sociology). Environmental resources engineering, natural resources, and performing arts are the strongest academically. Biological sciences is the largest.

Required: To graduate, students must complete 124 to 132 semester credits, including 48 in general education courses and at least 24 to 36 in the major, with a minimum overall GPA of 2.0. Requirements in freshman reading and composition, American institutions, U.S. history and the Constitution, and California government may be met through course work or exams.

Special: HSU offers campus work-study programs, co-op programs with a variety of public and private agencies, internships, and study abroad in 16 countries, with semesters in London, China, and Greece. Dual majors, student-designed majors, credit for life and military experience, and credit/no credit grading options are also offered. There are 5 national honor societies, and 6 departmental honors programs.

Faculty/Classroom: 68% of faculty are male; 32%, female. No introductory courses are taught by graduate students. The average class size in an introductory lecture is 32; in a laboratory, 19; and in a regular course, 25.

Admissions: 74% of the 2001-2002 applicants were accepted. The SAT I scores for the 2001-2002 freshman class were: Verbal--37% below 500, 41% between 500 and 599, 20% between 600 and 700, and 2% above 700; Math--41% below 500, 41% between 500 and 599, 18% between 600 and 700, and 1% above 700. The ACT scores were 38% below 21, 27% between 21 and 23, 23% between 24 and 26, 7% between 27 and 28, and 5% above 28.

Requirements: The SAT I or ACT is recommended. In addition, applicants must be high school graduates with a minimium GPA of 2.0 and 15 academic credits, to include 4 years in English, 3 years in college prep math, 2 years in foreign language, and 1 year each of U.S. history/government, science with lab, and visual and performing arts. The GED is accepted. HSU uses an eligibility index that combines GPA and ACT or SAT I scores for admission. Requirements are higher for out-of-state applicants. For an applicaton diskette, write to the Office of Admissions and School Relations, or download it from Humboldt's web site. A GPA of 2.0 is required. AP and CLEP credits are accepted.

Procedure: Freshmen are admitted fall and spring. Entrance exams should be taken prior to admission. There are early decision and early admissions plans. Application deadlines are open. Notification is sent in November and December. The fall 2001 application fee was $55.

Transfer: Applicants must have a minimum college GPA of 2.0 (2.4 for nonresidents). To enter, students need 30 general education units with a grade of C or better, including courses in written and speech communication, critical thinking, and math. Students with fewer than 56 transferable semester units must meet freshman requirements. 30 credits of 124 to 132 must be completed at Humboldt.

Visiting: There are regularly scheduled orientations for prospective students, including Preview Day in the spring and mandatory summer orientation for new students, which provides peer and academic counseling, registration, and a variety of social activities. There are guides for informal visits and visitors may sit in on classes and stay overnight. To schedule a visit, contact the Office of Admissions and School Relations.

Financial Aid: In 2001-2002, 49% of all freshmen and 54% of continuing students received some form of financial aid. 45% of freshmen and 47% of continuing students received need-based aid. The average freshman award was $5044. Of that total, scholarships or need-based grants averaged $4100; and loans averaged $3106. Humboldt is a member of CSS. The FAFSA is required. The fall application deadline is March 2.

International Students: They must score 550 on the written TOEFL.

Computers: The mainframe is a DEC ALPHA. More than 200 Mac and IBM PCs are available in numerous locations. Students also have access to Internet, academic specialty centers, and specialized software programs. All students may access the system 24 hours a day. There are no time limits and no fees. It is strongly recommended that all students have a personal computer.

Graduates: In 2001, 1391 bachelor's degrees were awarded. The most popular majors were liberal studies (11%), art (7%), and biology (7%). In an average class, 8% graduate in 4 years, 27% in 5 years, and 38% in 6 years.

Admissions Contact: Dr. Ronald P. Maggiore, Dean, Enrollment Management. E-mail: *hsuinfo@humboldt.edu*
Web: *www.humboldt.edu*

HUMPHREYS COLLEGE

Stockton, CA 95207 — B-3

(209) 478-0800; Fax: (209) 478-8721

Full-time: 260 men, 400 women	**Faculty:** 22
Part-time: 30 men, 70 women	**Ph.D.s:** 46%
Graduate: 40 men, 20 women	**Student/Faculty:** 30 to 1
Year: quarters, summer session	**Tuition:** $6900
Application Deadline: open	**Room & Board:** n/av
Freshman Class: n/av	
SAT I or ACT: not required	**NONCOMPETITIVE**

Humphreys College, founded in 1896, is an independent institution offering undergraduate degrees in business management, accounting, paralegal studies, computer management, and liberal arts to a primarily commuter student body. Figures given in the above capsule are approximate. The library contains 21,000 volumes and 1000 audiovisual forms/CDs, and subscribes to 110 periodicals. Computerized library services include the card catalog and database searching. The 10-acre campus is in a suburban area 40 miles south of Sacramento. Including residence halls, there are 9 buildings.

Student Life: 97% of undergraduates are from California. Others are from 4 states and 5 foreign countries. 97% are from public schools. 70% are white; 17% Hispanic. The average age of freshmen is 23; all undergraduates, 25. 20% do not continue beyond their first year; 50% remain to graduate.

Housing: 64 students can be accommodated in college housing, which includes single-sex on-campus apartments and married-student housing. On-campus housing is available on a first-come, first-served basis. Priority is given to out-of-town students. 90% of students commute. Alcohol is not permitted. All students may keep cars.

Activities: There are no fraternities or sororities. There are 4 groups on campus, including professional and student government. Popular campus events include a Halloween party, a Christmas dinner, and a quarterly Hot Dog Day barbecue.

Sports: There is no sports program at Humphreys. Facilities include a swimming pool, a basketball court, a tennis court, and sports fields.

Disabled Students: All of the campus is accessible. Wheelchair ramps, special parking, specially equipped rest rooms, special class scheduling, lowered drinking fountains, and lowered telephones are available.

Services: Counseling and information services are available, as is tutoring in some subjects, including accounting. There is remedial math and writing.

Campus Safety and Security: Measures include 24-hour foot and vehicle patrol, escort service, and lighted pathways/sidewalks.

Programs of Study: Humphreys confers the B.S. degree. Associate and doctoral degrees are also awarded. Bachelor's degrees are awarded in BUSINESS (accounting, business administration and management, court reporting, and management information systems), EDUCATION (early childhood), SOCIAL SCIENCE (community services, and paralegal studies). Paralegal studies is the largest.

Required: To graduate, students must complete a total of 180 quarter units, including 56 in the major and 72 in general education courses, with a minimum GPA of 2.0.

Special: Local internship positions are available for students of paralegal studies and business administration. Dual majors in business studies are possible.

Faculty/Classroom: 51% of faculty are male; 49%, female. All teach undergraduates. No introductory courses are taught by graduate students. The average class size in an introductory lecture is 17.

Requirements: Applicants must be graduates of an accredited secondary school or have earned a GED. AP and CLEP credits are accepted.

Procedure: Freshmen are admitted to all sessions. Entrance exams should be taken at any time. There are early admissions and deferred admissions plans. Application deadlines are open. Check with the school for current application fee.

Transfer: Applicants must submit official transcripts and have a GPA of at least 2.0. 36 quarter credits of 180 must be completed at Humphreys.

Visiting: There are regularly scheduled orientations for prospective students, including a campus tour, classroom visits, and meetings with admissions, financial aid, and academic advisers. There are guides for informal visits and visitors may sit in on classes. To schedule a visit, contact Santa Lopez in Admissions.

Financial Aid: In a recent year, 95% of all freshmen and 93% of continuing students received some form of financial aid. 94% of freshmen and 93% of continuing students received need-based aid. The average freshman award was $7900. Of that total, scholarships or need-based grants averaged $3500 ($6533 maximum); and loans averaged $2625 ($4000 maximum). 64% of undergraduates work part time. Average annual earnings from campus work are $1200. The average financial indebtedness of a recent graduate was $24,000. Humphreys is a member of CSS. The FAFSA is required. Check with the school for current deadines.

International Students: They must score 450 on the written TOEFL or take the MELAB.

Computers: The mainframe is an IBM AS/400. There are 30 PCs available in 2 campus labs. All students may access the system when a lab aide or instructor is present or with an instructor's permission. There are no time limits and no fees.

Admissions Contact: Director of Admissions.
Web: *www.humphreys.edu*

LA SIERRA UNIVERSITY D-5
Riverside, CA 92515-8247 (909) 785-2176
(800) 874-5587; Fax: (909) 785-2447

Full-time: 440 men, 490 women	**Faculty:** 98; IIA, --$
Part-time: 50 men, 70 women	**Ph.D.s:** 76%
Graduate: 70 men, 80 women	**Student/Faculty:** 10 to 1
Year: quarters, summer session	**Tuition:** $15,060
Application Deadline: August 15	**Room & Board:** $4200
Freshman Class: n/av	
SAT I or ACT: required	**LESS COMPETITIVE**

La Sierra University, founded originally as La Sierra Academy in 1922, is a Seventh-day Adventist, private university, offering undergraduate and graduate programs in applied and liberal arts and sciences, business and management, religion, and education. Figures in the above capsule are approximate. There are 5 undergraduate and 4 graduate schools. In addition to regional accreditation, La Sierra has baccalaureate program accreditation with ABET. The library contains 230,000 volumes and 285,000 microform items, and subscribes to 1500 periodicals. Computerized library services include the card catalog, interlibrary loans, and database searching. Special learning facilities include a learning resource center, art gallery, natural history museum, radio station, and an observatory, a missionary museum, and an arboretum. The 300-acre campus is in a suburban area 40 miles east of Los Angeles. Including residence halls, there are 48 buildings.

Student Life: 71% of undergraduates are from California. Others are from 34 states, 58 foreign countries, and Canada. 39% are from public schools. 35% are white; 31% Asian American; 19% Hispanic. 90% are Protestant; 12% claim no religious affiliation. The average age of freshmen is 19; all undergraduates, 22.

Housing: 650 students can be accommodated in college housing, which includes single-sex dormitories, on-campus apartments, off-campus apartments, and married-student housing. In addition, there are honors houses. On-campus housing is available on a first-come, first-served basis. 56% of students commute. Alcohol is not permitted. All students may keep cars.

Activities: There are no fraternities or sororities. There are 30 groups on campus, including band, choir, chorus, computers, drama, ethnic, international, literary magazine, newspaper, orchestra, professional, religious, social service, student government, and yearbook. Popular campus events include University Experience, Academic Expo, and Community Service Day.

Sports: There are 3 intercollegiate sports for men and 2 for women, and 9 intramural sports for men and 9 for women. Facilities include a gym, soccer and flag football fields, a running track, a swimming pool, and a fitness center.

Disabled Students: 99% of the campus is accessible. Wheelchair ramps, elevators, special parking, specially equipped rest rooms, and special class scheduling are available.

Services: Counseling and information services are available, as is tutoring in most subjects. There is a reader service for the blind, and remedial math, reading, and writing. and a learning support center.

Campus Safety and Security: Measures include 24-hour foot and vehicle patrol, escort service, informal discussions, and lighted pathways/sidewalks.

Programs of Study: La Sierra confers B.A., B.S., B.B.A., B.F.A., B.Mus., and B.S.W. degrees. Associate, master's, and doctoral degrees are also awarded. Bachelor's degrees are awarded in BIOLOGICAL SCIENCE (biochemistry, biology/biological science, biometrics and biostatistics, and biophysics), BUSINESS (accounting, banking and finance, business administration and management, electronic business, international business management, and marketing management), COMMUNICATIONS AND THE ARTS (art, communications, English, English as a second/foreign language, fine arts, graphic design, music, music performance, and Spanish), COMPUTER AND PHYSICAL SCIENCE (chemistry, computer science, information sciences and systems, mathematics, and physics), EDUCATION (elementary, music, physical, and secondary), HEALTH PROFESSIONS (exercise science, and health science), SOCIAL SCIENCE (history, liberal arts/general studies, political science/government, psychobiology, psychology, religion, social work, and sociology). English and history are the strongest academically. Biology, psychology, and business are the largest.

Required: To graduate, students must complete 190 units, at least 60 of which must be upper division, with a GPA of 2.0. All students must complete a University Studies curriculum consisting of a 29-unit core curriculum and the distribution requirements, and 15 clock hours of community service per year.

Special: Cross-registration with Walla Walla College is necessary for engineering students. Study abroad is available in 3 countries through the Adventist Colleges Abroad Consortium. Liberal studies students work with an adviser to design their own major. There is a freshman honors program.

Faculty/Classroom: 71% of faculty are male; 29%, female. All teach undergraduates, 70% do research, and 70% do both. Graduate students teach 1% of introductory courses. The average class size in an introductory lecture is 30; in a laboratory, 21; and in a regular course, 20.

Requirements: The SAT I or ACT is required. In addition, prospective students should have a high school diploma or equivalent. Test scores above the 50th percentile and a personal interview are recommended. Provisional acceptance may be considered with lesser credentials, following a more exhaustive examination. A GPA of 2.5 is required. AP and CLEP credits are accepted. Important factors in the admissions decision are recommendations by school officials, leadership record, and evidence of special talent.

Procedure: Freshmen are admitted to all sessions. Entrance exams should be taken during the senior year. Applications should be filed by August 15 for fall entry, December 1 for winter entry, March 1 for spring entry, and May 1 for summer entry. Notification is sent on a rolling basis. The fall 2001 application fee was $30.

Transfer: Transcripts from all previous colleges are required. 36 credits of 190 must be completed at La Sierra.

Visiting: There are regularly scheduled orientations for prospective students, including a tour and meetings with faculty and administrators. There are guides for informal visits and visitors may sit in on classes and stay overnight. To schedule a visit, contact Recruitment/Admissions.

Financial Aid: In a recent year, 93% of all freshmen and 85% of continuing students received some form of financial aid. 80% of freshmen and 75% of continuing students received need-based aid. The average freshman award was $11,325. Of that total, scholarships or need-based grants averaged $6200 ($9600 maximum); loans averaged $3925 ($4425 maximum); and work contracts averaged $1200 ($2500 maximum). 45% of undergraduates work part time. Average annual earnings from campus work are $1800. The average financial indebtedness of a recent graduate was $23,000. La Sierra is a member of CSS. The FAFSA is required. The piority deadline date for financial application is March 2.

International Students: The school actively recruits these students. They must score 550 on the written TOEFL and also take the MELAB and also take the SAT I or the ACT.

Computers: The mainframe is a Sun SPARC 1000. Terminals accessing the mainframe are available in every building on campus, and Mac, AT&T, and IBM PCs are available in the PC lab. All systems are connected to an Ethernet network and a Micom Dataswitch. All students may access the system 24 hours a day. There are no time limits and no fees.

Admissions Contact: C. Tom Smith, Associate Vice Preseident, Enrollment Services. E-mail: *admissions@lasierra.edu*
Web: *www.lasierra.edu*

LOYOLA MARYMOUNT UNIVERSITY C-5
Los Angeles, CA 90045 (310) 338-2750
(800) LMU-INFO; Fax: (310) 338-2797

Full-time: 1983 men, 2765 women	**Faculty:** 375; IIA, +$
Part-time: 101 men, 110 women	**Ph.D.s:** 87%
Graduate: 606 men, 789 women	**Student/Faculty:** 13 to 1
Year: semesters, summer session	**Tuition:** $20,954
Application Deadline: February 1	**Room & Board:** $7800
Freshman Class: 7468 applied, 4446 accepted, 1258 enrolled	
SAT I Verbal/Math: 369/581 (mean)	**HIGHLY COMPETITIVE**

Loyola Marymount University, a private institution founded in 1911 and affiliated with the Roman Catholic Church, offers programs in liberal arts, business administration, fine arts, science, and engineering. There are 4 undergraduate schools and 1 graduate school. In addition to regional accreditation, LMU has baccalaureate program accreditation with AACSB, ABET, and NCATE. The 2 libraries contain 899,186 volumes, 1,538,857 microform items, and 20,638 audiovisual forms/CDs. Computerized library services include the card catalog, interlibrary loans, and database searching. Special learning facilities include a learning resource center, art gallery, radio station, the Burns Fine Arts Center, and the Little Theatre. The 128-acre campus is in a suburban area 15 miles southwest of downtown Los Angeles on a mesa overlooking Marina del Rey. Including residence halls, there are 36 buildings.

Student Life: 77% of undergraduates are from California. Others are from 47 states, 76 foreign countries, and Canada. 45% are from public schools. 51% are white; 19% Hispanic; 11% Asian American. 58% are Catholic; 25% Christian, Buddhist, other; 15% claim no religious affiliation. The average age of freshmen is 18; all undergraduates, 20. 13% do not continue beyond their first year.

Housing: 2773 students can be accommodated in college housing, which includes single-sex and coed dormitories and on-campus apartments. In addition, there are honors houses and special-interest houses. On-campus housing is available on a lottery system for upperclassmen. 57% of students live on campus. All students may keep cars.

Activities: 6% of men belong to 4 national fraternities; 6% of women belong to 3 national sororities. There are 120 groups on campus, including art, cheerleading, chess, choir, chorale, chorus, computers, dance, drama, ethnic, film, gay, honors, international, literary magazine, newspaper, orchestra, pep band, political, professional, radio and TV, religious, social, social service, student government, and yearbook. Popular campus events include Cinco de Mayo, Special Games (disabled children), and the ASLMU Formal Dance.

Sports: There are 8 intercollegiate sports for men and 9 for women, and 6 intramural sports for men and 6 for women. Facilities include an athletic pavilion, a 4166-seat gym, a swimming pool, tennis, handball, and racquetball courts, a baseball stadium, a floating crew shell house, soccer, rugby, and football fields, and a recreation center.

Disabled Students: 95% of the campus is accessible. Wheelchair ramps, elevators, special parking, specially equipped rest rooms, special class scheduling, lowered drinking fountains, and lowered telephones are available. Special arrangements are possible for placement tests and registration. Hearing aid equipment is provided for disabled students in the library.

Services: Counseling and information services are available, as is tutoring in most subjects. There is a reader service for the blind, and remedial math, reading, and writing. There is an extensive learning resource center with full-time specialists in reading, writing, and study skills as well as a peer tutoring staff and computer-aided instruction. Note takers and special equipment and materials are available.

Campus Safety and Security: Measures include 24-hour foot and vehicle patrol, escort service, informal discussions, and emergency telephones. There are lighted pathways/sidewalks.

Programs of Study: LMU confers B.A., B.S., B.B.A., B.S.A., and B.S.E. degrees. Master's degrees are also awarded. Bachelor's degrees are awarded in BIOLOGICAL SCIENCE (biochemistry and biology/biological science), BUSINESS (accounting and business administration and management), COMMUNICATIONS AND THE ARTS (art history and appreciation, classics, communications, dance, dramatic arts, English, French, Greek, Latin, media arts, music, Spanish, and studio art), COMPUTER AND PHYSICAL SCIENCE (chemistry, computer science, mathematics, natural sciences, and physics), ENGINEERING AND ENVIRONMENTAL DESIGN (civil engineering, computer graphics, electrical/electronics engineering, engineering physics, environmental science, and mechanical engineering), SOCIAL SCIENCE (African American studies, Asian/Oriental studies, classical/ancient civilization, economics, European studies, history, humanities, liberal arts/general studies, philosophy, political science/government, psychology, sociology, theological studies, and urban studies). Communication arts, political science, and engineering are the strongest academically. Psychology, communication studies, and business administration are the largest.

Required: The core curriculum required for all students in the liberal arts college includes 6 hours each of communication skills, history, science/technology, philosophy, and theology and 3 hours of fine arts, literature/psychology, and social studies. A minimum 2.0 GPA is required, as are at least 120 semester credits, with at least 40 hours in the major. The last 30 semester hours of academic work and at least 12 hours of the major must be completed at LMU.

Special: LMU offers internships and volunteer work experience with local firms, study abroad in Europe, Mexico, Japan, and China, a Washington semester, dual majors, work-study, student-designed and individualized studies majors, accelerated degree programs in all majors, a general studies degree, nondegree study, and pass/fail options for electives. There are 2 national honor societies, and a freshman honors program.

Faculty/Classroom: 61% of faculty are male; 39%, female. No introductory courses are taught by graduate students. The average class size in an introductory lecture is 17; in a laboratory, 16; and in a regular course, 17.

Admissions: 60% of the 2001-2002 applicants were accepted. The SAT I scores for the 2001-2002 freshman class were: Verbal--14% below 500, 51% between 500 and 599, 31% between 600 and 700, and 4% above 700; Math--12% below 500, 47% between 500 and 599, 36% between 600 and 700, and 5% above 700. 95% of the current freshmen were in the top fifth of their class; 99% were in the top two fifths.

Requirements: The SAT I or ACT is required. In addition, prospective students must be graduates of an accredited secondary school and have completed 4 years of English, 3 each of a foreign language, math, and social studies, 2 of science, and 1 of an academic elective. A recommendation from an official of a previous school and essays are required. An interview is recommended. A GPA of 2.9 is required. AP credits are accepted. Important factors in the admissions decision are advanced placement or honor courses, recommendations by school officials, and evidence of special talent. Applications are accepted on computer disk (disks are available from LMU) and on-line at the school's web site.

Procedure: Freshmen are admitted fall and spring. Entrance exams should be taken during the spring of the junior year or fall of the senior year. There is a deferred admissions plan. Applications should be filed by February 1 for fall entry and December 1 for spring entry. The fall 2001 application fee was $45. Notification is sent on a rolling basis. A waiting list is an active part of the admissions procedure.

Transfer: 188 transfer students enrolled in 2001-2002. Applicants must have a minimum 2.75 GPA and at least 30 credit hours earned. No minimum credit hours are necessary for students who meet freshman requirements. The SAT I and an interview are recommended. 30 credits of 120 must be completed at LMU.

Visiting: There are regularly scheduled orientations for prospective students, consisting of an open house in the fall. There are guides for informal visits and visitors may sit in on classes. To schedule a visit, contact the Admissions Office.

Financial Aid: In 2001-2002, 52% of all freshmen and 64% of continuing students received some form of financial aid. 41% of freshmen and 63% of continuing students received need-based aid. The average freshman award was $16,180. Of that total, scholarships or need-based grants averaged $4830; loans averaged $3536; and work contracts averaged $2533. 32% of undergraduates work part time. Average annual earnings from campus work are $3000. The average financial indebtedness of the 2001 graduate was $20,893. The CSS/Profile or FAFSA is required. The fall application deadline is February 15.

International Students: There are 142 international students enrolled. They must score 550 on the written TOEFL.

Computers: The mainframe is an IBM 4381. There are 40 PCs in a student lab networked with Internet access. The library houses 30 PCs with Internet access. Residence halls are wired for access to a campuswide network through students' personal computers. The system may be accessed through a 24-hour dial-in service. All students may access the system. Lab hours are Monday to Thursday 8 A.M. to 2 A.M., Friday 8 A.M. to 10 P.M., Saturday 9 A.M. to 6 P.M., and Sunday noon to 2 A.M. Students may access the system 2 hours for remote access. There are no fees. It is strongly recommended that all students have a personal computer.

Graduates: In 2001, 1084 bachelor's degrees were awarded. The most popular majors were business administration (31%), psychology (9%), and communication studies (6%). In an average class, 1% graduate in 3 years, 57% in 4 years, 69% in 5 years, and 73% in 6 years. 112 companies recruited on campus in 2000-2001. Of the 2000 graduating class, 11% were enrolled in graduate school within 6 months of graduation and 75% were employed.

Admissions Contact: Matthew Fissinger, Director of Undergraduate Admissions. A video is available. E-mail: *admissions@lmu.edu*
Web: *www.lmu.edu*

MASTER'S COLLEGE C-5
Santa Clarita, CA 91321-1200 **(661) 259-3540, ext. 3365**
(800) 568-6248; Fax: (661) 288-1037

Full-time: 527 men, 579 women	**Faculty:** 48
Part-time: 46 men, 22 women	**Ph.D.s:** 66%
Graduate: 299 men, 49 women	**Student/Faculty:** 23 to 1
Year: semesters, summer session	**Tuition:** $15,720
Application Deadline: March 2	**Room & Board:** $5780
Freshman Class: 597 applied, 492 accepted, 242 enrolled	
SAT I Verbal/Math: 575/557	**ACT:** 24 **COMPETITIVE+**

The Master's College, founded in 1927, is a private, nondenominational Christian liberal arts institution. The library contains 143,567 volumes, 2090 microform items, and 2791 audiovisual forms/CDs, and subscribes to 547 periodicals. Computerized library services include the card catalog, interlibrary loans, and database searching. Special learning facilities include a learning resource center. The 110-acre campus is in a rural area 35 miles north of Los Angeles. Including residence halls, there are 27 buildings.

Student Life: 65% of undergraduates are from California. Others are from 43 states, 29 foreign countries, and Canada. 69% are from public schools. 86% are white. All are Protestant. The average age of freshmen is 18; all undergraduates, 20. 20% do not continue beyond their first year.

Housing: 600 students can be accommodated in college housing, which includes single-sex dormitories and off-campus apartments. In addition, there are special-interest houses. On-campus housing is guaranteed for the freshman year only and is available on a first-come, first-served basis. 85% of students live on campus; of those, 95% remain on campus on weekends. Alcohol is not permitted. All students may keep cars.

Activities: There are no fraternities or sororities. There are 14 groups on campus, including band, choir, chorale, drama, film, jazz band, musical theater, opera, orchestra, pep band, radio and TV, religious, social service, and student government. Popular campus events include College View Weekend, Community Day, and Mission Conference.

Sports: There are 4 intercollegiate sports for men and 4 for women, and 4 intramural sports for men and 3 for women. Facilities include a gym, a sports field, tennis and volleyball courts, an intramural field, a swimming pool, and a fitness center.

Disabled Students: All of the campus is accessible. Wheelchair ramps, special parking, specially equipped rest rooms, lowered drinking fountains, and lowered telephones are available.

Services: Counseling and information services are available, as is tutoring in most subjects. There is remedial math.

Campus Safety and Security: Measures include 24-hour foot and vehicle patrol, shuttle buses, and lighted pathways/sidewalks.

Programs of Study: TMC confers B.A., B.S., and B.Th. degrees. Master's degrees are also awarded. Bachelor's degrees are awarded in BIOLOGICAL SCIENCE (biology/biological science), BUSINESS (business administration and management), COMMUNICATIONS AND THE ARTS (communications and English), COMPUTER AND PHYSICAL SCIENCE (information sciences and systems, mathematics, and natural sciences), EDUCATION (elementary, physical, and secondary), SOCIAL SCIENCE (biblical studies, history, home economics, liberal arts/general studies, and political science/government). Biological sciences, biblical studies, and business administration are the strongest academically. Biblical studies, education, and business administration are the largest.

Required: Students must complete at least 122 semester hours, including 78 distributed as follows: 24 hours in Bible studies, 18 in social sciences, 9 in English, 7 in natural science, 6 in cross-cultural studies, 3 each in communication, business, logical reasoning, and fine arts, and 2 in phys ed. Students must complete at least 40 semester hours in upper-division courses and at least 40 in the major and must maintain a minimum GPA of 2.0.

Special: Students may cross-register with the Coalition of Christian Colleges and Universities and may participate in a co-op program with the College of the Canyon. Internships are offered with local churches, radio stations, and newspapers. A Washington semester, study abroad, dual majors in music plus a second discipline, and a general studies degree are available. The Master's Institute, a 1-year certificate Bible program, is also offered.

Faculty/Classroom: 80% of faculty are male; 20%, female. All teach undergraduates. No introductory courses are taught by graduate students. The average class size in an introductory lecture is 39; in a laboratory, 14; and in a regular course, 20.

Admissions: 82% of the 2001-2002 applicants were accepted. The SAT I scores for the 2001-2002 freshman class were: Verbal--18% below 500, 38% between 500 and 599, 35% between 600 and 700, and 9% above 700; Math--25% below 500, 40% between 500 and 599, 30% between 600 and 700, and 5% above 700. The ACT scores were 18% below 21, 29% between 21 and 23, 30% between 24 and 26, 11% between 27 and 28, and 11% above 28. 32% of the current freshmen were in the top fifth of their class; 49% were in the top two fifths. There was 1 National Merit finalist. 9 freshmen graduated first in their class.

Requirements: The SAT I or ACT is required. In addition, applicants must have completed 4 years of English, 3 each of math and science, 2 of history, and 8 units of electives. A GPA of 2.5 is required. AP and CLEP credits are accepted. Important factors in the admissions decision are personality/intangible qualities, recommendations by school officials, and leadership record. Applications are accepted on-line.

Procedure: Freshmen are admitted fall and spring. Entrance exams should be taken in the fall. There is a deferred admissions plan. Applications should be filed by March 2 for fall entry and November 15 for spring entry, along with a $35 fee. Notification is sent March 20.

Transfer: 127 transfer students enrolled in 2001-2002. Applicants must meet freshman requirements. A maximum of 70 units can be transferred. 24 credits of 122 must be completed at TMC.

Visiting: There are regularly scheduled orientations for prospective students, including class visitation, meetings with faculty, interviews, athletic events, an overnight stay, and college activities. There are guides for informal visits and visitors may sit in on classes and stay overnight. To schedule a visit, contact the Admissions Office at (800) 568-6428, ext. 3371 *hkeller@masters.edu*

Financial Aid: In 2001-2002, 65% of all freshmen and 80% of continuing students received some form of financial aid. 58% of freshmen and 66% of continuing students received need-based aid. The average freshman award was $13,251. Of that total, scholarships or need-based grants averaged $8325 ($24,220 maximum); loans averaged $4313 ($23,624 maximum); and work contracts averaged $613 ($3500 maximum). 19% of undergraduates work part time. Average annual earnings from campus work are $1612. The average financial indebtedness of the 2001 graduate was $13,000. TMC is a member of CSS. The FAFSA and the college's own financial statement are required.

International Students: They must score 525 on the written TOEFL.

Computers: The mainframe is a DEC ALPHA 1000 4/233 server. Computer access is available in the library, business center, math lab, and computer center. All students may access the system during specified times. There are no time limits and no fees. It is strongly recommended that all students have personal computers.

Graduates: In 2001, 203 bachelor's degrees were awarded. The most popular majors were biblical studies (31%), business (15%), and education (9%). In an average class, 4% graduate in 3 years, 44% in 4 years, 49% in 5 years, and 51% in 6 years. 20 companies recruited on campus in 2000-2001.

Admissions Contact: Yaphet N. Peterson, Director of Enrollment Management. A video is available. E-mail: *enrollment@masters.edu* Web: *http://www.masters.edu*

MENLO COLLEGE — B-3
Atherton, CA 94027 — (650) 688-3762
(800) 55-MENLO; (650) 617-2395

Full-time: 290 men, 200 women	**Faculty:** 21; IIB, +$
Part-time: 60 men, 80 women	**Ph.D.s:** 80%
Graduate: none	**Student/Faculty:** 23 to 1
Year: semesters, summer session	**Tuition:** $17,000
Application Deadline: open	**Room & Board:** $7000
Freshman Class: n/av	
SAT I or ACT: required	**LESS COMPETITIVE**

Menlo College, founded in 1927, is a private college offering preprofessional programs in the liberal arts and management. Figures in the above capsule are approximate. The library contains 61,000 volumes, 670 microform items, and 330 audiovisual forms/CDs, and subscribes to 740 periodicals. Computerized library services include the card catalog, interlibrary loans, and database searching. Special learning facilities include a learning resource center, radio station, TV station, and a photo lab, a newspaper production facility, and an observation room for the psychology program. The 62-acre campus is in a suburban area 30 miles south of San Francisco. Including residence halls, there are 16 buildings.

Student Life: 75% of undergraduates are from California. Others are from 18 states and 17 foreign countries. 60% are from public schools. 54% are white; 13% Asian American; 12% foreign nationals. The average age of freshmen is 18; all undergraduates, 23. 51% do not continue beyond their first year; 33% remain to graduate.

Housing: 400 students can be accommodated in college housing, which includes single-sex and coed dormitories and on-campus apartments. In addition, there are special-interest houses. On-campus housing is guaranteed for all 4 years. 62% of students live on campus; of those, 55% remain on campus on weekends. All students may keep cars.

Activities: There are no fraternities or sororities. There are 14 groups on campus, including cheerleading, chess, computers, debate, drama, ethnic, honors, international, newspaper, professional, radio and TV, social, social service, and student government. Popular campus events include Spring Fest, SBA Day, and Communication Career Day.

Sports: There are 8 intercollegiate sports for men and 6 for women, and 4 intramural sports for men and 4 for women. Facilities include 2 swimming pools, a soccer field, tennis courts, a track, and a 600-seat gym. The campus stadium seats 1000, the largest auditorium/arena, 220.

Disabled Students: 95% of the campus is accessible. Wheelchair ramps, elevators, special parking, specially equipped rest rooms, lowered drinking fountains, and lowered telephones are available.

Services: Counseling and information services are available, as is tutoring in every subject. There is a reader service for the blind.

Campus Safety and Security: Measures include 24-hour foot and vehicle patrol, informal discussions, pamphlets/posters/films, and lighted pathways/sidewalks.

Programs of Study: Menlo confers B.A. and B.S. degrees. Bachelor's degrees are awarded in BUSINESS (business administration and management, international business management, management information systems, and sports management), COMMUNICATIONS AND THE ARTS (communications), SOCIAL SCIENCE (liberal arts/general studies and psychology). Management and mass communications are the strongest academically and the largest.

Required: All students must complete 59 units in the general education curriculum, including 9 units each of English, math, management, and economics, 7 of science, 6 of diversity, 4 of quantitative skills, and 3 each of American institutions and computer competency. A total of 124 units, including 21 to 30 in the major and 18 in a concentration, and a minimum 2.0 GPA, are required to graduate.

Special: Students may earn up to 12 credits through internships. Menlo also offers study abroad in England, China, and Chile, dual and student-designed majors, B.A.-B.S. degrees, and an accelerated degree program in management. There are 2 national honor societies, and 1 departmental honors program.

Faculty/Classroom: 59% of faculty are male; 41%, female. All teach undergraduates. The average class size in an introductory lecture is 23; in a laboratory, 20; and in a regular course, 16.

Requirements: The SAT I or ACT is required. In addition, a personal essay and letter of recommendation should be submitted. The GED is accepted. A GPA of 2.5 is required. AP and CLEP credits are accepted. Important factors in the admissions decision are advanced placement or honor courses, evidence of special talent, and leadership record. Applications are available on-line.

Procedure: Freshmen are admitted fall and spring. Entrance exams should be taken during the junior or senior year. There are early decision, early admissions, and deferred admissions plans. Application deadlines are open, with a priority date of February 1. 35 early decision candidates were accepted for the 2001-2002 class. Check with the school for current application deadlines and fee.

Transfer: Transfer applicants must show potential for success indicated by a 2.5 GPA at the college level. Those with fewer than 24 credits must meet freshman requirements. 30 credits of 124 must be completed at Menlo.

Visiting: There are regularly scheduled orientations for prospective students, including a fall preview with an introduction to college life and college decision making. The spring visit for accepted students provides an in-depth view of Menlo. There are guides for informal visits and visitors may sit in on classes and stay overnight. To schedule a visit, contact the Office of Admissions at (650) 688-3753 or (800) 55-Menlo.

Financial Aid: 40% of undergraduates work part time. Average annual earnings from campus work are $2000. Menlo is a member of CSS. The CSS/Profile or FAFSA is required. The priority fall application deadline is March 2.

International Students: The school actively recruits these students. They must score 500 on the written TOEFL and also take or take the SAT I or ACT if English is their first language.

Computers: The mainframes are an HP 3000/Series 44 and an HP 9000/Series 300. There are 56 HP PCs and 10 Macs located in academic buildings. All students may access the system 8 A.M. to 11 P.M. daily. There are no time limits and no fees.

Graduates: In a recent year, 45 bachelor's degrees were awarded.

Admissions Contact: Sara Sargent, Director of Admissions Outreach Programs. E-mail: *ssargent@menlo.edu* Web: *www.menlo.edu*

MILLS COLLEGE

Oakland, CA 94613 — B-3

(510) 430-2135
(800) 87-MILLS; 430-3314

Full-time: 690 women	**Faculty:** 81
Part-time: 40 women	**Ph.D.s:** 95%
Graduate: 80 men, 320 women	**Student/Faculty:** 9 to 1
Year: semesters	**Tuition:** $20,650
Application Deadline: February 1	**Room & Board:** $7300
Freshman Class: n/av	
SAT I or ACT: required	**COMPETITIVE**

Mills College, founded in 1852, is a private women's college offering instruction in liberal and fine arts, sciences, and teacher preparation. Graduate programs are coeducational. Figures in the above capsule are approximate. The library contains 206,600 volumes, 7700 microform items, and 5000 audiovisual forms/CDs, and subscribes to 700 periodicals. Computerized library services include the card catalog, interlibrary loans, and database searching. Special learning facilities include an art gallery and a children's school, a small book press, an electronic/computer music studio, a botanical garden, and a computer learning studio. The 135-acre campus is in an urban area 12 miles east of San Francisco. Including residence halls, there are 84 buildings.

Student Life: 79% of undergraduates are from California. Others are from 39 states and 10 foreign countries. 80% are from public schools. 58% are white. The average age of freshmen is 19; all undergraduates, 22. 20% do not continue beyond their first year; 60% remain to graduate.

Housing: 780 students can be accommodated in college housing, which includes dormitories, on-campus apartments, and married-student housing. In addition, there are language houses and speial interest houses. Married-student housing is offered on an equal basis to domestic partners of lesbian and gay students, and a student co-op house is available for juniors and seniors. On-campus housing is guaranteed for all 4 years. 58% of students live on campus; of those, 75% remain on campus on weekends. All students may keep cars.

Activities: There are no fraternities. There are 30 groups on campus, including art, band, choir, chorale, chorus, dance, drama, ethnic, gay, honors, international, literary magazine, newspaper, political, professional, religious, social, social service, student government, and yearbook. Popular campus events include Boat Dance, Black and White Ball, and Fine Arts Festival.

Sports: Facilities include an 872-seat gym, a weight room/fitness center, athletic fields, a pool, and 6 tennis courts.

Disabled Students: 90% of the campus is accessible. Wheelchair ramps, elevators, special parking, specially equipped rest rooms, special class scheduling, lowered telephones, and dorm housing are available.

Services: Counseling and information services are available, as is tutoring in every subject. There is a reader service for the blind.

Campus Safety and Security: Measures include 24-hour foot and vehicle patrol, self-defense education, escort service, and shuttle buses. There are informal discussions, pamphlets/posters/films, emergency telephones, and lighted pathways/sidewalks.

Programs of Study: Mills confers the B.A. degree. Master's degrees are also awarded. Bachelor's degrees are awarded in AGRICULTURE (environmental studies), BIOLOGICAL SCIENCE (biochemistry and biology/biological science), BUSINESS (business economics), COMMUNICATIONS AND THE ARTS (art history and appreciation, comparative literature, creative writing, dance, dramatic arts, English, French, German, media arts, modern language, music, and studio art), COMPUTER AND PHYSICAL SCIENCE (chemistry, computer science, and mathematics), EDUCATION (early childhood), SOCIAL SCIENCE (American studies, anthropology, child psychology/development, economics, ethnic studies, Hispanic American studies, history, international relations, liberal arts/general studies, philosophy, political science/government, psychology, public administration, public affairs, sociology, and women's studies). Art, biology, and computer science are the strongest academically. Communications, English, and psychology are the largest.

Required: All students must fulfill an English writing requirement and a core curriculum of a first-year seminar, a 2-semester sophomore course, and a cross-cultural course. Distribution requirements include 2 courses in each of 4 curricular areas. A total of 34 semester course credits is required, with 10 to 17 of them in the major. The minimum GPA is 2.0.

Special: There is cross-registration with the University of California/Berkeley and California State University, among others. Mills offers co-op programs, internships, study abroad, a Washington semester, work-study programs, dual, student-designed and interdisciplinary majors, including political, legal, and economic analysis, an accelerated degree program, a general studies degree, a 3-2 engineering program, credit by examination, and pass/fail options. There is 1 national honor society, Phi Beta Kappa.

Faculty/Classroom: 46% of faculty are male; 54%, female. All both teach and do research. No introductory courses are taught by graduate students. The average class size in a regular course is 14.

Admissions: 2 freshmen graduated first in their class in a recent year.

Requirements: The SAT I or ACT is required. In addition, SAT II: Subject tests are recommended. Applicants should graduate from an accredited secondary school or have a GED. An essay is required; an interview, recommended. Mills requires applicants to be in the upper 50% of their class. A GPA of 3.0 is required. AP credits are accepted. Important factors in the admissions decision are advanced placement or honor courses, personality/intangible qualities, and recommendations by school officials. The Common App is accepted on-line.

Procedure: Freshmen are admitted fall and spring. Entrance exams should be taken no later than 1 month prior to application. There are early action, early admissions, and deferred admissions plans. Early action applications should be filed by November 15; regular applications, by February 1 for fall entry and November 1 for spring entry. Notification of early action is sent December 20; regular decision, March 30. The fall 2001 application fee was $40.

Transfer: 93 transfer students enrolled in a recent year. Transfer applicants with fewer than 12 credits should take the SAT I or ACT. 12 credits of 34 must be completed at Mills.

Visiting: There are regularly scheduled orientations for prospective students, consisting of class visits, campus tours, lunch with faculty, financial aid workshops, an admissions interview, and an overnight stay. There are guides for informal visits and visitors may sit in on classes and stay overnight. To schedule a visit, contact the Admission Office.

Financial Aid: In a recent year, 86% of all freshmen received some form of financial aid. Mills is a member of CSS. The FAFSA and the college's own financial statement are required. Check with the school for current deadlines.

International Students: There were 16 international students enrolled in a recent year. The school actively recruits these students. They must score 550 on the written TOEFL and also take the SAT I.

Computers: The mainframe is a Sun SPARC 10. Students can access any 1 of 3 central systems servers from many locations on campus. The 3 systems provide e-mail services, file storage and sharing, and student financial and academic records. A mix of 132 Macs and PCs in residence halls, computing labs, academic departmental labs, the library, and student lounges give students access to the Internet and Web. All students may access the system 24 hours a day, year round. There are no time limits. It is recommended that students in computer science and book arts have personal computers. Mac is recommended.

Graduates: 25 companies recruited on campus in a recent year.

Admissions Contact: Avis E. Hinkson, Dean of Admission. A video is available. E-mail: *admission@mills.edu* Web: *www.mills.edu*

MOUNT SAINT MARY'S COLLEGE

Los Angeles, CA 90049 — C-5

(310) 954-4250
(800) 999-9893; (310) 954-4259

Full-time: 20 men, 870 women	**Faculty:** 91; IIB, +$
Part-time: 30 women	**Ph.D.s:** 43%
Graduate: 80 men, 230 women	**Student/Faculty:** 10 to 1
Year: semesters	**Tuition:** $17,630
Application Deadline: February 15	**Room & Board:** $6800
Freshman Class: n/av	
SAT I or ACT: required	**COMPETITIVE**

Mount Saint Mary's College, founded in 1925 and affiliated with the Catholic Church, is a private, primarily women's institution that offers programs in the liberal arts and sciences. Figures in the above capsule are approximate. In addition to regional accreditation, The Mount has baccalaureate program accreditation with NASM and NLN. The library contains 132,000 volumes, 320 microform items, and 2520 audiovisual forms/CDs, and subscribes to 690 periodicals. Computerized library services include the card catalog, interlibrary loans, and database searching. Special learning facilities include a learning resource center and art gallery. The 72-acre campus is in an urban area 10 miles west of Los Angeles. Including residence halls, there are 26 buildings.

Student Life: 94% of undergraduates are from California. Others are from 18 states, 4 foreign countries, and Canada. 77% are from public schools. 39% are Hispanic; 23% Asian American; 21% white. Most are Catholic. The average age of freshmen is 18; all undergraduates, 23. 25% do not continue beyond their first year; 68% remain to graduate.

Housing: 433 students can be accommodated in college housing, which includes single-sex dormitories. On-campus housing is guaranteed for all 4 years. 53% of students commute. All students may keep cars.

Activities: 66% of women belong to 2 local and 1 national sororities. There are no fraternities. There are 29 groups on campus, including art, choir, chorale, chorus, computers, dance, departmental, drama, ethnic, honors, musical theater, newspaper, political, professional, religious, social, social service, student government, and yearbook. Popular campus events include Mary's Day (honors and awards), Horizon's Day, and Spring Sing.

Sports: There are 4 intramural sports for women. Facilities include a pool, tennis courts, exercise and weight rooms, and cardiovascular equipment.

Disabled Students: Wheelchair ramps, elevators, and special parking are available.

Services: Counseling and information services are available, as is tutoring in most subjects. A peer tutoring program is available.

Campus Safety and Security: Measures include 24-hour foot and vehicle patrol, self-defense education, shuttle buses, and informal discussions. There are pamphlets/posters/films and lighted pathways/sidewalks.

Programs of Study: The Mount confers B.A., B.S., and B.A.M. degrees. Associate and master's degrees are also awarded. Bachelor's degrees are awarded in BIOLOGICAL SCIENCE (biochemistry and biology/biological science), BUSINESS (business administration and management), COMMUNICATIONS AND THE ARTS (art, English, French, music, and Spanish), COMPUTER AND PHYSICAL SCIENCE (chemistry and mathematics), EDUCATION (elementary and secondary), HEALTH PROFESSIONS (nursing), SOCIAL SCIENCE (American studies, child psychology/development, gerontology, history, liberal arts/general studies, philosophy, political science/government, psychology, religion, social science, and sociology). Premedicine is the strongest academically. Nursing and biological science are the largest.

Required: Requirements for graduation include completion of 59 units of distribution requirements and 124 total credit hours, with the number of hours in the major varying by department. English courses and a minimum 2.0 GPA are required.

Special: The Mount offers cross-registration with UCLA, internships within the Business Department, study abroad in Spain, England, and France, a Washington semester through American University, the B.A.-B.S. degree in business, dual and student-designed majors, credit for prior experiences, and pass/fail options. There are 11 national honor societies, a freshman honors program, and 9 departmental honors programs.

Faculty/Classroom: 25% of faculty are male; 75%, female. No introductory courses are taught by graduate students. The average class size in an introductory lecture is 20; in a laboratory, 20; and in a regular course, 19.

Requirements: The SAT I or ACT is required. In addition, applicants must be graduates of an accredited secondary school or have earned the GED, with 16 academic credits and 16 Carnegie units, including 4 years of English literature and composition, 2 or 3 years each of math, science, and social studies, and 1 or 2 years of history. An essay is required, and an interview is recommended. A GPA of 3.25 is required. AP and CLEP credits are accepted. Important factors in the admissions decision are recommendations by school officials, recommendations by alumni, and advanced placement or honor courses. Applications are accepted on computer disk.

Procedure: Freshmen are admitted in the fall. Entrance exams should be taken at the end of the junior year or the beginning of the senior year. Applications should be filed by February 15 for priority consideration for fall entry and November 1 for spring entry. Notification is sent on a rolling basis. The fall 2001 application fee was $40.

Transfer: 125 transfer students enrolled in a recent year. Transfer students must have a minimum 2.25 GPA with at least 24 completed credit hours. 30 credits of 124 must be completed at The Mount.

Visiting: There are regularly scheduled orientations for prospective students, including workshops, student panels, tours, class visits, and faculty presentations. There are guides for informal visits and visitors may sit in on classes. To schedule a visit, contact the Admissions Office.

Financial Aid: In a recent year, 86% of all freshmen and 82% of continuing students received some form of financial aid. 66% of freshmen and 60% of continuing students received need-based aid. The average freshman award was $13,500. Of that total, scholarships or need-based grants averaged $8375 ($14,716 maximum); loans averaged $2625 ($6625 maximum); and work contracts averaged $2500 ($3000 maximum). 45% of undergraduates work part time. Average annual earnings from campus work are $1800. The average financial indebtedness of a recent graduate was $15,000. The Mount is a member of CSS. The FAFSA is required. Check with the school for current deadlines.

International Students: There are 3 international students enrolled. They must score 550 on the written TOEFL.

Computers: The mainframe is a Sequent S27. There are 40 PCs available in a lab for word processing, database use, computer programming, and Internet access. All students may access the system during regular working hours, 4 nights per week, and from 3 P.M. to 11 P.M. on Sunday. There are no time limits and no fees.

Graduates: In a recent year, 274 bachelor's degrees were awarded. The most popular majors were nursing (25%), liberal studies (11%), and business (10%). In an average class, 66% graduate in 5 years.

Admissions Contact: Katy Murphy, Executive Director of Enrollment. E-mail: *admissions@msmc.la.edu* Web: *www.msmc.la.edu*

NATIONAL UNIVERSITY — D-5

La Jolla, CA 92037 — (858) 541-7701
(800) NAT-UNIV; Fax: (858) 541-7792

Full-time: 1138 men, 1599 women	**Faculty:** 103; IIA, --$
Part-time: 1173 men, 1450 women	**Ph.D.s:** 90%
Graduate: 4979 men, 7928 women	**Student/Faculty:** 27 to 1
Year: quarters, summer session	**Tuition:** $7755
Application Deadline: open	**Room & Board:** n/app
Freshman Class: 168 applied, 168 accepted, 63 enrolled	
SAT I or ACT: not required	**SPECIAL**

National University, founded in 1971, is a private, nonprofit institution offering lifelong learning opportunities to adult learners in 11 major metropolitan areas. Disciplines include business, technology, criminal justice, computers, education, human services, nursing, counseling, arts and sciences, and math. There are 3 undergraduate and 3 graduate schools. In addition to regional accreditation, National has baccalaureate program accreditation with CCNEand IACBE. The library contains 162,413 volumes, 1,266,660 microform items, and 100 audiovisual forms/CDs, and subscribes to 5825 periodicals. Computerized library services include the card catalog, interlibrary loans, and database searching. Special learning facilities include a learning resource center. The 15-acre campus is in an urban area 3 miles northeast of downtown San Diego. There are 8 buildings.

Student Life: All students are from California. 58% are white; 16% Hispanic; 10% African American. The average age of freshmen is 29; all undergraduates, 32. 32% do not continue beyond their first year.

Housing: There are no residence halls. All students commute. Alcohol is not permitted. All students may keep cars.

Activities: There are no fraternities or sororities. There is 1 honors organization on campus.

Sports: There is no sports program at National.

Disabled Students: All of the campus is accessible. Wheelchair ramps, elevators, special parking, specially equipped rest rooms, special class scheduling, lowered drinking fountains, and lowered telephones are available.

Services: Counseling and information services are available. Instruction is offered in math and English through the writing center. There is remedial math, reading, and writing.

Campus Safety and Security: Measures include 24-hour foot and vehicle patrol and lighted pathways/sidewalks.

Programs of Study: National confers B.A., B.S., B.B.A., and B.S.N. degrees. Associate and master's degrees are also awarded. Bachelor's degrees are awarded in BIOLOGICAL SCIENCE (life science), BUSINESS (accounting, banking and finance, business administration and management, management information systems, and organizational behavior), COMMUNICATIONS AND THE ARTS (communications, English, and media arts), COMPUTER AND PHYSICAL SCIENCE (computer science, earth science, information sciences and systems, and mathematics), HEALTH PROFESSIONS (nursing), SOCIAL SCIENCE (behavioral science, criminal justice, interdisciplinary studies, international studies, law, liberal arts/general studies, and psychology). Computer science, accounting, and psychology are the strongest academically. Business and computer science are the largest.

Required: To graduate, students must complete a total of 180 quarter hours, including 36 upper-division quarter units with a minimum GPA of 2.0. A minimum of 45 hours in the major and 67 quarter units in general education is required.

Special: There are 3 national honor societies and 2 departmental honors programs.

Faculty/Classroom: 67% of faculty are male; 33%, female. All both teach undergraduates and do research. No introductory courses are taught by graduate students. The average class size in an introductory lecture is 18 and in a regular course, 18.

Admissions: All of the 2001-2002 applicants were accepted.

Requirements: Graduation from an accredited secondary school or satisfactory scores on the GED are required for admission. Applicants

are generally expected to have 5 or more years of successful work experience. National requires an interview. AP and CLEP credits are accepted. Important factors in the admissions decision are leadership record, evidence of special talent, and advanced placement or honor courses. Applications are accepted on-line at *www.nu.edu/getmoreinfo.html*
Procedure: Freshmen are admitted to all sessions. There is a deferred admissions plan. Application deadlines are open. The fall 2001 application fee was $60.
Transfer: 5297 transfer students enrolled in 2001-2002. Transfer applicants must have a minimum GPA of 2.0. Transcripts from all previous institutions attended must be submitted. 45 quarter hours of 180 must be completed at National.
Visiting: There are guides for informal visits and visitors may sit in on classes. To schedule a visit, contact the Associate Regional Dean.
Financial Aid: In 2001-2002, about 70% of all students received some form of financial aid, including need-based aid. National is a member of CSS. The CSS/Profile, FAFSA, and the college's own financial statement are required. Applications deadlines are open.
International Students: There are 222 international students enrolled. The school actively recruits these students. They must score 525 on the written TOEFL or take the MELAB.
Computers: The mainframe is an IBM 3081-GX. Students have access to National's PC labs. All students may access the system Monday through Friday, 8 A.M. to 9 P.M., and Saturday, 8 A.M. to 2 P.M. There are no time limits and no fees.
Graduates: In 2001, 1370 bachelor's degrees were awarded. The most popular majors were interdisciplinary studies (13%), behavioral sciences (10%), and computer science/information technology (9%).
Admissions Contact: Nancy Rohland, Associate Regional Dean.
E-mail: *admissions@nu.edu* Web: *www.nu.edu*

NEW COLLEGE OF CALIFORNIA — B-3
San Francisco, CA 94110 (415) 437-3460
(888) 437-3460; (415) 437-3417

Full-time: 60 men, 80 women	**Faculty:** 16
Part-time: 10 women	**Ph.D.s:** 20%
Graduate: 10 men, 10 women	**Student/Faculty:** 11 to 1
Year: semesters, summer session	**Tuition:** $8900
Application Deadline: see profile	**Room & Board:** n/app
Freshman Class: n/av	
SAT I or ACT: not required	**NONCOMPETITIVE**

New College of California, founded in 1971, is a private college offering a liberal arts program. Figures in the above capsule are approximate. The library contains 30,000 volumes. Computerized library services include the card catalog, interlibrary loans, and database searching. Special learning facilities include a learning resource center and a video-editing lab, and a theater. The 2-acre campus is in an urban area in the mission district of San Francisco. There are 3 buildings.
Student Life: 70% of undergraduates are from California. Others are from 10 states, 5 foreign countries, and Canada. 80% are from public schools. 61% are white; 16% African American; 10% Hispanic. The average age of freshmen is 25; all undergraduates, 28. 30% do not continue beyond their first year; 70% remain to graduate.
Housing: There are no residence halls. All students commute. Alcohol is not permitted.
Activities: There are no fraternities or sororities. There are 10 groups on campus, including band, drama, ethnic, film, gay, literary magazine, newspaper, political, professional, social, social service, and student government. Popular campus events include an arts and social change showcase, movie nights, and acoustic band nights.
Sports: There is 1 intercollegiate sports for men.
Disabled Students: 60% of the campus is accessible. Wheelchair ramps, specially equipped rest rooms, and special class scheduling are available.
Services: There is remedial math, reading, and writing.
Campus Safety and Security: Measures include front-desk security in all buildings.
Programs of Study: New College confers the B.A. degree. Master's degrees are also awarded. Bachelor's degrees are awarded in COMMUNICATIONS AND THE ARTS (dramatic arts, English, film arts, fine arts, music, and Spanish), SOCIAL SCIENCE (anthropology, political science/government, psychology, and social science). Humanities is the strongest academically and the largest.
Required: To graduate, students must complete at least 120 credit hours, including 30 in the major. Requirements include 6 units of core humanities and 3 units each of arts, literature or writing, social sciences, scientific reasoning, quantitative reasoning, research methods, a practicum, and a senior project. A minimum GPA of 2.0 is required.
Special: Internships include a required 3-unit practicum on or off campus. New College offers work-study programs, independent study, study abroad in Mexico and Nepal, an accelerated degree program, student-designed majors, and pass/fail options. Students can earn up to 30 units of credit for prior life, military, and work experience.
Faculty/Classroom: 60% of faculty are male; 40%, female. 80% teach undergraduates. The average class size in an introductory lecture is 12; in a laboratory, 10; and in a regular course, 12.
Requirements: In addition, new College requires graduation from an accredited secondary school; the GED is also accepted. An essay is required. AP and CLEP credits are accepted.
Procedure: Freshmen are admitted fall and spring. There is a deferred admissions plan. The college accepts all applicants. Notification is sent on a rolling basis. Check with the school for current application deadlines and fee.
Transfer: 30 credits of 120 must be completed at New College.
Visiting: There are regularly scheduled orientations for prospective students, consisting of monthly open houses. There are guides for informal visits and visitors may sit in on classes. To schedule a visit, contact the Admissions Coordinator.
Financial Aid: 85% of undergraduates work part time. Average annual earnings from campus work are $3500. New College is a member of CSS. The FAFSA, the college's own financial statement and the are required. The fall application deadline is March 2.
International Students: They must score 500 on the written TOEFL.
Computers: The mainframe is a Prime unit. Terminals are located in the library. IBMs and Macs are available for word processing and layout and design. All students may access the system. There are no time limits and no fees.
Graduates: In an average class, 50% graduate in 4 years, 80% in 5 years, and 100% in 6 years. Of a recent graduating class, 30% were enrolled in graduate school within 6 months of graduation and 75% were employed.
Admissions Contact: Admissions Coordinator.
E-mail: *admissions@newcollege.edu* Web: *www.newcollege.edu*

NOTRE DAME DE NAMUR UNIVERSITY — B-3
Belmont, CA 94002 (650) 508-3607
(800) 263-0545; Fax: (650) 508-3426

Full-time: 172 men, 420 women	**Faculty:** 44; IIA, av$
Part-time: 103 men, 272 women	**Ph.D.s:** 75%
Graduate: 158 men, 444 women	**Student/Faculty:** 13 to 1
Year: semesters, summer session	**Tuition:** $18,456
Application Deadline: see profile	**Room & Board:** $8476
Freshman Class: n/av	
SAT I Verbal/Math: 460/460	**ACT:** 19 **LESS COMPETITIVE**

Notre Dame de Namur University, founded in 1851, is an independent liberal arts institution affiliated with the Roman Catholic Church. Some information in this profile is approximate. There is 1 graduate school. In addition to regional accreditation, NDNU has baccalaureate program accreditation with NASM and NCATE. The library contains 100,000 volumes, 68,975 microform items, and 7960 audiovisual forms/CDs, and subscribes to 750 periodicals. Computerized library services include the card catalog, interlibrary loans, and database searching. Special learning facilities include an art gallery and and the Archives of Modern Christian Art. The 80-acre campus is in a suburban area 25 miles south of San Francisco. Including residence halls, there are 23 buildings.
Student Life: 80% of undergraduates are from California. Others are from 23 states, 18 foreign countries, and Canada. 70% are from public schools. 38% are white; 25%, Asian American; 17%, foreign nationals; 13%, Hispanic. 55% are Catholic; 30% claim no religious affiliation. The average age of freshmen is 18; all undergraduates, 24. 19% do not continue beyond their first year; 60% remain to graduate.
Housing: 300 students can be accommodated in college housing, which includes coed dormitories and on-campus apartments. On-campus housing is guaranteed for all 4 years. 63% of students commute. All students may keep cars.
Activities: There are no fraternities or sororities. There are 27 groups on campus, including art, band, cheerleading, choir, chorale, chorus, computers, dance, drama, ethnic, gay, honors, international, jazz band, literary magazine, musical theater, newspaper, orchestra, photography, political, professional, religious, social, social service, student government, symphony, and yearbook. Popular campus events include Honors Day, Ralston Concert Series, and Fiesta Latina.
Sports: There are 5 intercollegiate sports for men and 6 for women, and 2 intramural sports for men and 2 for women. Facilities include a gym, a recreation center, tennis courts, a soccer field, a weight room, a swimming pool, a par course, an arcade, and pool and Ping-Pong tables.
Disabled Students: 90% of the campus is accessible. Wheelchair ramps, special parking, specially equipped rest rooms, and special class scheduling are available.
Services: Counseling and information services are available, as is tutoring in every subject. There is remedial math, reading, and writing.
Campus Safety and Security: Measures include 24-hour foot and vehicle patrol, escort service, informal discussions, and pamphlets/posters/films. There are lighted pathways/sidewalks.
Programs of Study: NDNU confers B.A., B.S., B.F.A., and B.Mus. degrees. Associate and master's degrees are also awarded. Bachelor's de-

grees are awarded in BIOLOGICAL SCIENCE (biochemistry and biology/biological science), BUSINESS (accounting, banking and finance, business administration and management, business economics, international business management, and marketing/retailing/merchandising), COMMUNICATIONS AND THE ARTS (art, communications, dramatic arts, English, fine arts, French, graphic design, and music), COMPUTER AND PHYSICAL SCIENCE (computer science, information sciences and systems, and mathematics), EDUCATION (social studies), HEALTH PROFESSIONS (predentistry, premedicine, prepharmacy, and preveterinary science), SOCIAL SCIENCE (history, human services, humanities, Latin American studies, liberal arts/general studies, philosophy, political science/government, prelaw, psychology, religion, social science, and sociology). Biology, premedicine, and English are the strongest academically. Business administration, liberal studies, and psychology are the largest.

Required: All students must complete general education requirements, 3 units of career development, and a writing proficiency exam. American history is required for those students who have not completed this course in an American high school. A total of 124 semester units with an overall GPA of 2.0 is required in order to graduate.

Special: The university offers a Washington semester through Trinity College, an exchange program with Emmanuel College in Boston, and study abroad in 7 countries. Internships, accelerated degree programs in business administration and human service, B.A.-B.S. degrees in biology and biochemistry, a 3-2 engineering degree with Boston University, dual and student-designed majors, a general studies degree, credit for military experience, and pass/fail options are offered. Nondegree study is possible. There are 3 national honor societies and a freshman honors program.

Faculty/Classroom: 46% of faculty are male; 54%, female. 71% teach undergraduates. No introductory courses are taught by graduate students. The average class size in an introductory lecture is 25; in a laboratory, 10; and in a regular course, 15.

Admissions: 84% of the 2001-2002 applicants were accepted.The SAT I scores for the 2001-2002 freshman class were: Verbal--69% below 500, 22% between 500 and 599, and 9% between 600 and 700; Math--64% below 500, 27% between 500 and 599, 8% between 600 and 700, and 1% above 700. The ACT scores were 66% below 21, 20% between 21 and 23, and 14% between 24 and 26. 29% of the current freshmen were in the top fifth of their class; 57% were in the top two fifths.

Requirements: The SAT I or ACT is required. In addition, applicants should have completed 13 Carnegie units, including 4 years of high school English, 2 each of math, history/social studies, foreign language, and 1 of lab science, along with 1 year in 3 of these areas beyond the basic requirements. An essay is required. An audition is required for music majors. A GPA of 2.0 is required; the average GPA is a 3.2. AP and CLEP credits are accepted. Important factors in the admissions decision are advanced placement or honor courses, evidence of special talent, and leadership record.

Procedure: Freshmen are admitted to all sessions. Entrance exams should be taken by the December test date of the senior year. There is a deferred admissions plan. Check with the school for current application deadlines. The application fee is $40. Notification is sent on a rolling basis.

Transfer: Applicants must have a 2.0 GPA to be considered for admission. 24 credits of 124 must be completed at NDNU.

Visiting: There are regularly scheduled orientations for prospective students, consisting of tours and information on student life, financial aid, and academics. There are guides for informal visits and visitors may sit in on classes and stay overnight. To schedule a visit, contact the Admission Office.

Financial Aid: In 2001-2002, the average freshman award was $19,753. Of that total, scholarships or need-based grants averaged $11,904 ($28,000 maximum); loans averaged $7122 ($28,000 maximum); and work contracts averaged $727 ($2000 maximum). 25% of undergraduates work part time. Average annual earnings from campus work are $1168. NDNU is a member of CSS. The FAFSA and the college's own financial statement are required. Check with the school for current deadlines.

International Students: The school actively recruits these students. They must score 500 on the written TOEFL or 173 on the electronic version.

Computers: The mainframe is an IBM AS/400. 3 computer labs are available offering Mac and DOS workstations. All students may access the system 7 days a week. There are no time limits and no fees.

Graduates: In an average class, 56% graduate in 4 years.

Admissions Contact: Katy Murphy, Dean of Enrollment.
E-mail: *admiss@ndnu.edu* Web: *www.ndnu.edu*

OCCIDENTAL COLLEGE C-5
Los Angeles, CA 90041 **(323) 259-2700**
800-825-5262; Fax: (323) 259-2958

Full-time: 1730 men and women **Faculty:** 138; IIB, +$
Part-time: 40 men and women **Ph.D.s:** 93%
Graduate: 26 men and women **Student/Faculty:** 13 to 1
Year: semesters, summer session **Tuition:** $25,195
Application Deadline: January 15 **Room & Board:** $7093
Freshman Class: 3636 applied, 1745 accepted, 458 enrolled
SAT I Verbal/Math: 610/610 **HIGHLY COMPETITIVE**

Occidental College, founded in 1887, is a nonsectarian school of liberal arts and sciences. Some information in this profile is approximate. The library contains 500,000 volumes, 390,000 microform items, and 12,000 audiovisual forms/CDs, and subscribes to 1450 periodicals. Computerized library services include the card catalog, interlibrary loans, and database searching. Special learning facilities include a learning resource center, art gallery, radio station, ocean-going research vessel, and small nuclear reactor. The 120-acre campus is in an urban area in Los Angeles. Including residence halls, there are 44 buildings.

Student Life: 60% of undergraduates are from California. Others are from 47 states, 45 foreign countries, and Canada. 57% are from public schools. 55% are white; 20%, Asian American; 14%, Hispanic. 55% are Protestant; 20%, Catholic; 10%, Jewish; 10% claim no religious affiliation. The average age of freshmen is 18; all undergraduates, 19. 10% do not continue beyond their first year; 78% remain to graduate.

Housing: 1250 students can be accommodated in college housing, which includes single-sex and coed dormitories, fraternity houses, and sorority houses. In addition, there are special-interest houses and language floors. On-campus housing is guaranteed for all 4 years. 79% of students live on campus; of those, 85% remain on campus on weekends. All students may keep cars.

Activities: 16% of men belong to 2 national fraternities; 13% of women belong to 3 local sororities. There are 90 groups on campus, including art, cheerleading, chess, choir, chorale, dance, debate, drama, drum and bugle corps, ethnic, film, gay, honors, international, jazz band, literary magazine, musical theater, newspaper, orchestra, pep band, photography, political, professional, radio and TV, religious, social, social service, student government, symphony, and yearbook. Popular campus events include Da Getaway, Oxy-Gras, and Asian Pacific Heritage Week.

Sports: There are 10 intercollegiate sports for men and 10 for women. Facilities include playing fields, an all-weather track, tennis courts, an outdoor pool, a dance studio, a sports medicine center, gyms, and a weight room.

Disabled Students: 80% of the campus is accessible. Wheelchair ramps, elevators, special parking, specially equipped rest rooms, lowered drinking fountains, and lowered telephones are available.

Services: Counseling and information services are available, as is tutoring in most subjects. There is a reader service for the blind and remedial math and writing.

Campus Safety and Security: Measures include 24-hour foot and vehicle patrol, self-defense education, escort service, and shuttle buses. There are informal discussions, pamphlets/posters/films, emergency telephones, and lighted pathways/sidewalks.

Programs of Study: Oxy confers the A.B. degree. Master's degrees are also awarded. Bachelor's degrees are awarded in BIOLOGICAL SCIENCE (biochemistry and biology/biological science), COMMUNICATIONS AND THE ARTS (art history and appreciation, comparative literature, dramatic arts, French, German, languages, music, and Spanish), COMPUTER AND PHYSICAL SCIENCE (chemistry, geochemistry, geology, geophysics and seismology, mathematics, and physics), ENGINEERING AND ENVIRONMENTAL DESIGN (electrical/electronics engineering, environmental science, and mechanical engineering), HEALTH PROFESSIONS (predentistry and premedicine), SOCIAL SCIENCE (American studies, anthropology, Asian/Oriental studies, cognitive science, economics, history, international relations, philosophy, physical fitness/movement, political science/government, psychobiology, psychology, public administration, religion, sociology, urban studies, and women's studies). Social sciences, biology, and chemistry are the strongest academically. Social sciences, biology, and diplomacy and world affairs are the largest.

Required: To graduate, students must complete 32 courses of 4 semester hours or 6 quarter units each, and must maintain a minimum GPA of 2.0. In addition, all students must fulfill core course requirements in science, math, fine arts, language proficiency, and American, European, and world cultures. Proficiency in English can be demonstrated by course work or testing.

Special: Cross-registration is permitted with the California Institute of Technology and the Art Center College of Design. Cooperative programs are available with Columbia University. Students may study abroad in 18 countries in Europe, Asia, and Latin America. Opportunities are provided for internships, a Washington semester, a U.N. semester in New York City, work-study programs, B.A.-B.S. degrees, dual and student-designed majors, a 3-2 engineering degree with the California

Institute of Technology, credit by exam, nondegree study, and pass/fail options. There are 9 national honor societies, including Phi Beta Kappa.
Faculty/Classroom: 55% of faculty are male; 45%, female. All teach undergraduates. No introductory courses are taught by graduate students. The average class size in an introductory lecture is 40; in a laboratory, 15; and in a regular course, 23.
Admissions: 48% of the 2001-2002 applicants were accepted. 81% of the current freshmen were in the top fifth of their class; 97% were in the top two fifths. In a recent year, 20 freshmen graduated first in their class.
Requirements: The SAT I or ACT is required. In addition, applicants should be high school graduates of high academic standing with 4 years of English, 3 to 4 of math, 3 each of foreign language and social studies, and 1 each of biological and physical science. The GED is accepted. An essay is required, and an interview is recommended. AP credits are accepted. Important factors in the admissions decision are extracurricular activities record, advanced placement or honor courses, and recommendations by school officials. Applications are accepted on disk via Common App or on-line at the school's web site.
Procedure: Freshmen are admitted in the fall. Entrance exams should be taken no later than January of the senior year. There are early decision and deferred admissions plans. Early decision applications should be filed by November 15; regular applications, by January 15 for fall entry, along with a $50 fee. Notification of early decision is sent December 15; regular decision, April 1. 29 early decision candidates were accepted in a recent year. 14% of all applicants are on a waiting list; 101 were accepted in a recent year.
Transfer: 66 transfer students enrolled in a recent year. Students must have at least a 3.0 GPA in all courses submitted for transfer credit. The SAT I or ACT is required. 64 credits of 128 must be completed at Oxy.
Visiting: There are regularly scheduled orientations for prospective students, including campus tours followed by information sessions with an admission officer. There are guides for informal visits and visitors may sit in on classes and stay overnight. To schedule a visit, contact the Office of Admission.
Financial Aid: In 2001-2002, 70% of continuing students received some form of financial aid. In a recent year, 48% of freshmen and 50% of continuing students received need-based aid. The average freshman award was $23,507. Oxy is a member of CSS. The CSS/Profile or FAFSA and the SAAC for California residents are required. Check with the school for current deadlines.
International Students: In a recent year, there were 50 international students enrolled. The school actively recruits these students. They must score 600 on the written TOEFL and also take the SAT I or the ACT.
Computers: The mainframe is a Sun SPARC Station 10 Model 512. Macs and PCs are available in the library's computer center. All students may access the system at any time. There are no time limits and no fees.
Admissions Contact: Vince Cuseo, Director of Admission.
E-mail: *admission@oxy.edu* Web: *www.oxy.edu*

OTIS COLLEGE OF ART AND DESIGN — C-2
Los Angeles, CA 90045 — (310) 665-6820
(800) 527-6847; Fax: (310) 665-6821

Full-time: 331 men, 577 women	**Faculty:** 28
Part-time: 10 men, 9 women	**Ph.D.s:** 94%
Graduate: 18 men, 20 women	**Student/Faculty:** 32 to 1
Year: semesters, summer session	**Tuition:** $20,290
Application Deadline: February 15	**Room & Board:** n/app
Freshman Class: 563 applied, 361 accepted, 151 enrolled	
SAT I Verbal/Math: 474/521	**ACT:** 22 — **SPECIAL**

Otis College of Art and Design, founded in 1918, is a private, not-for-profit college offering undergraduate programs in fine arts, ceramics, graphic design and illustration, environmental design, fashion design, toy design, and digital media design and graduate programs in fine arts and writing. As part of their instruction, students work directly with professional artists, designers, critics, and writers. There are 3 undergraduate schools and 1 graduate school. In addition to regional accreditation, Otis has baccalaureate program accreditation with NASAD. The library contains 39,000 volumes and 2000 audiovisual forms/CDs, and subscribes to 125 periodicals. Computerized library services include the card catalog and database searching. Special learning facilities include an art gallery, a photographic darkroom, printmaking studios, a fine books press room, a woodworking studio, a digital imaging room, a metalworking shop, and multiuse studios. The 5-acre campus is in an urban area on the west side of Los Angeles. There are 3 buildings.
Student Life: 61% of undergraduates are from California. Others are from 50 states, 32 foreign countries, and Canada. 75% are from public schools. 38% are white; 28% Asian American, 11% foreign nationals, 11% Hispanic. The average age of freshmen is 20; all undergraduates, 22. 12% do not continue beyond their first year; 80% remain to graduate.
Housing: There are no residence halls. 60 students can be accommodated in college-sponsored housing, which includes single-sex and coed off-campus apartments. Housing is guaranteed for the freshman year only and is available on a first-come, first-served basis. Priority is given to out-of-town students. 94% of students commute. Alcohol is not permitted. All students may keep cars.
Activities: There are no fraternities or sororities. There are 8 groups and organizations on campus, including art, computers, film, gay, literary magazine, photography, social, and student government. Popular campus events include gallery openings, a yearly fashion design show, and a student leadership retreat.
Sports: There is no sports program at Otis.
Disabled Students: All of the campus is accessible. Wheelchair ramps, elevators, special parking, specially equipped rest rooms, lowered drinking fountains, and lowered telephones are available.
Services: Counseling and information services are available, as is tutoring in most subjects, including drawing. There is remedial math, reading, and writing.
Campus Safety and Security: Measures include 24-hour foot and vehicle patrol, self-defense education, escort service, and informal discussions. There are pamphlets/posters/films, emergency telephones, and lighted pathways/sidewalks.
Programs of Study: Otis confers the B.F.A. degree. Master's degrees are also awarded. Bachelor's degrees are awarded in COMMUNICATIONS AND THE ARTS (design, fine arts, graphic design, illustration, and photography), ENGINEERING AND ENVIRONMENTAL DESIGN (environmental design), SOCIAL SCIENCE (fashion design and technology). Graphic design and digital media are the strongest academically. Digital media design, communication arts (graphic design and illustration), and fashion design are the largest.
Required: Requirements for graduation include courses in liberal arts and sciences, art history, and studio arts. A senior thesis and a minimum of 134 total credit hours with a 2.0 minimum GPA are also required.
Special: Study abroad is available in London, Paris, and Stockholm. Internships are also available. There is a freshman honors program.
Faculty/Classroom: 52% of faculty are male; 48%, female. All teach undergraduates. The average class size in an introductory lecture is 25; in a laboratory, 10; and in a regular course, 18.
Admissions: 64% of the 2001-2002 applicants were accepted. The SAT I scores for the 2001-2002 freshman class were: Verbal--57% below 500, 30% between 500 and 599, 13% between 600 and 700, and 1% above 700; Math--41% below 500, 39% between 500 and 599, 18% between 600 and 700, and 2% above 700. The ACT scores were 42% below 21, 21% between 21 and 23, 21% between 24 and 26, 11% between 27 and 28, and 5% above 28.
Requirements: The SAT I or ACT is required. In addition, applicants must be graduates of an accredited secondary school or have a GED certificate, and submit a portfolio. Interviews are recommended, and essays are required. A GPA of 2.5 is required. AP credits are accepted. Important factors in the admissions decision are evidence of special talent, advanced placement or honor courses, and recommendations by school officials. Applications are accepted on-line at the school's web site.
Procedure: Freshmen are admitted fall and spring. Entrance exams should be taken in the fall. There is a deferred admissions plan. Applications should be filed by February 15 for fall entry and December 1 for spring entry, along with a $50 fee. Notification is sent on a rolling basis. 2% of all applicants are on a waiting list; 24 were accepted in 2001.
Transfer: 154 transfer students enrolled in 2001-2002. Transfer students must have a minimum 2.5 GPA and at least 18 studio art credit hours earned. An interview is recommended. 63 credits of 134 must be completed at Otis.
Visiting: There are regularly scheduled orientations for prospective students, including a campus tour and departmental, portfolio, and financial aid presentations. There are guides for informal visits and visitors may sit in on classes. To schedule a visit, contact the Admissions Office.
Financial Aid: In 2001-2002, 63% of all freshmen and 66% of continuing students received some form of financial aid. 62% of freshmen and 65% of continuing students received need-based aid. The average freshman award was $12,800. Of that total, scholarships or need-based grants averaged $6000 ($8500 maximum); loans averaged $6625 (maximum); and work contracts averaged $1000 ($3000 maximum). 18% of undergraduates work part time. Average annual earnings from campus work are $1200. The average financial indebtedness of the 2001 graduate was $23,000. The FAFSA and the college's own financial statement are required.
International Students: There are 106 international students enrolled. The school actively recruits these students. They must score 550 on the written TOEFL or 213 on the electronic version and also take the SAT I or the ACT.
Computers: The mainframe is an Apple 8150 server. There are 27 Power Mac 7100s and 15 Mac IICIs. There is also an Internet access station. All students may access the system. There are no time limits and no fees. It is strongly recommended that all students have personal computers.
Graduates: In 2001, 137 bachelor's degrees were awarded. The most popular majors were digital media (23%), communication arts (23%), and fine arts (20%). In an average class, 32% graduate in 6 years.

Admissions Contact: Marc D. Meredith, Dean of Admissions. E-mail: *otisart@otisart.edu* Web: *http://www.otisart.edu*

PACIFIC UNION COLLEGE
Angwin, CA 94508-9707 B-2
(707) 965-6336
(800) 862-7080; Fax: (707) 965-6432

Full-time: 625 men, 866 women	**Faculty:** 100; IIB, --$
Part-time: 38 men, 70 women	**Ph.D.s:** 56%
Graduate: 2 men, 2 women	**Student/Faculty:** 15 to 1
Year: quarters, summer session	**Tuition:** $15,585
Application Deadline: open	**Room & Board:** $4665
Freshman Class: 1128 applied, 689 accepted, 481 enrolled	
ACT: recommended	**VERY COMPETITIVE**

Pacific Union College, founded in 1888, is a private college affiliated with the Seventh-day Adventist Church, offering programs in liberal arts, religion, business, health science, and teacher preparation, among others. In addition to regional accreditation, PUC has baccalaureate program accreditation with ADA, CAADE, CCTC, CSWE, NASM,and NLN. The library contains 132,573 volumes, 116,673 microform items, and 54,549 audiovisual forms/CDs, and subscribes to 879 periodicals. Computerized library services include the card catalog and interlibrary loans. Special learning facilities include a learning resource center, art gallery, natural history museum, radio station, video production studio, and an observatory. The 2000-acre campus is in a small town 70 miles north of San Francisco. Including residence halls, there are 60 buildings.

Student Life: 72% of undergraduates are from California. Others are from 34 states, 37 foreign countries, and Canada. 47% are white; 19% Asian American; 10% foreign nationals; 10% Hispanic.

Housing: 1344 students can be accommodated in college housing, which includes single-sex dormitories and married-student housing. On-campus housing is guaranteed for all 4 years. 80% of students live on campus. Alcohol is not permitted. All students may keep cars.

Activities: There are no fraternities or sororities. There are 50 groups on campus, including academic, art, band, campus ministry, chess, choir, chorale, computers, drama, ethnic, film, honors, literary magazine, musical theater, newspaper, orchestra, photography, political, radio and TV, religious, social, student government, symphony, and yearbook. Popular campus events include picnic and ski days and All-College Get-Acquainted Party.

Sports: There are 3 intercollegiate sports for men and 3 for women, and 4 intramural sports for men and 4 for women. Facilities include a gym, a pool, a stadium, lighted tennis courts, and 3 athletic fields for softball, soccer, volleyball, flagball, and track and field.

Disabled Students: 95% of the campus is accessible. Wheelchair ramps, elevators, and special parking are available.

Services: Counseling and information services are available, as is tutoring in most subjects. There is a reader service for the blind, and remedial math, reading, and writing.

Campus Safety and Security: Measures include 24-hour foot and vehicle patrol, self-defense education, escort service, and informal discussions. There are pamphlets/posters/films, emergency telephones, lighted pathways/sidewalks, and a safety committee.

Programs of Study: PUC confers B.A., B.S., B.B.A., B.Mus., B.S.Med.Tech., and B.S.W. degrees. Associate and master's degrees are also awarded. Bachelor's degrees are awarded in BIOLOGICAL SCIENCE (biology/biological science and biophysics), BUSINESS (business administration and management, and recreation and leisure services), COMMUNICATIONS AND THE ARTS (communications, English, fine arts, French, graphic design, journalism, music, public relations, and Spanish), COMPUTER AND PHYSICAL SCIENCE (applied mathematics, chemistry, computer science, digital arts/technology, mathematics, natural sciences, and physics), EDUCATION (business, early childhood, and physical), ENGINEERING AND ENVIRONMENTAL DESIGN (airline piloting and navigation, electrical/electronics engineering technology, engineering technology, and graphic arts technology), HEALTH PROFESSIONS (health care administration, medical laboratory technology, and nursing), SOCIAL SCIENCE (behavioral science, food science, history, psychology, religion, social studies, social work, sociology, and theological studies). Sciences and behavioral science are the strongest academically. Nursing and business administration are the largest.

Required: To graduate, a student must complete a minimum of 192 quarter hours, including 60 in upper-level courses. The student must maintain a minimum GPA of 2.0 overall and 2.25 in the major. The required total hours in the major and the general education requirements vary according to the major. A religion course is required.

Special: Students may study abroad in Austria, Spain, France, Argentina, and Italy, earn B.A.-B.S. degrees, take dual majors, and pursue a major in interdisciplinary studies. Internships and accelerated degree programs are also offered. The college offers nondegree study and credit for life, military, and work experience. There are 8 national honor societies and a freshman honors program.

Faculty/Classroom: 61% of faculty are male; 39%, female. 99% teach undergraduates. The average class size in an introductory lecture is 19; in a laboratory, 18; and in a regular course, 17.

Admissions: 61% of the 2001-2002 applicants were accepted.

Requirements: The ACT is recommended. Scores are used only for advising purposes. Candidates for admission should have completed 4 years of English, 2 of math, and 1 each of science and history. A GPA of 2.3 is required. AP and CLEP credits are accepted. Important factors in the admissions decision are recommendations by school officials, leadership record, and advanced placement or honor courses. Applications are accepted on-line at the school's web site.

Procedure: Freshmen are admitted to all sessions. Entrance exams should be taken in the junior or senior year. Application deadlines are open. The application fee is $30.

Transfer: 183 transfer students enrolled in 2001-2002. Admission requirements are the same as for nontransfer students. 36 credits of 192 must be completed at PUC.

Visiting: There are regularly scheduled orientations for prospective students. There are guides for informal visits and visitors may sit in on classes and stay overnight. To schedule a visit, contact the Admissions Office at (707) 965-6425.

Financial Aid: In 2001-2002, 99% of all students received some form of financial aid. 96% of freshmen and 95% of continuing students received need-based aid. The average freshman award was $13,136. Of that total, scholarships or need-based grants averaged $9011 ($15,014 maximum); and loans averaged $4125 (maximum). 80% of undergraduates work part time. Average annual earnings from campus work are $1500. The average financial indebtedness of the 2001 graduate was $12,000. The FAFSA and the college's own financial statement are required. The fall application deadline is March 2.

International Students: There are 216 international students enrolled. They must score 450 to 525 on the written TOEFL or 133 to 197 on the electronic version and also take the SAT I or the ACT.

Computers: All students may access the system at any time. There are no time limits and no fees. It is strongly recommended that all students have personal computers.

Graduates: In 2001, 282 bachelor's degrees were awarded. The most popular majors were business (19%) and nursing (13%).

Admissions Contact: Sean Kootsey, Director of Enrollment Services. A video is available. E-mail: *enroll@puc.edu* Web: *www.puc.edu*

PEPPERDINE UNIVERSITY
Malibu, CA 90263-4392 C-5
(310) 506-4392; Fax: (310) 506-4861

Full-time: 1050 men, 1610 women	**Faculty:** 167; IIA, ++$
Part-time: 50 men, 80 women	**Ph.D.s:** 100%
Graduate: 2270 men, 2380 women	**Student/Faculty:** 16 to 1
Year: semesters, summer session	**Tuition:** $25,250
Application Deadline: January 15	**Room & Board:** $7580
Freshman Class: n/av	
SAT I or ACT: required	**VERY COMPETITIVE**

Pepperdine University, founded in 1937, is a private liberal arts university affiliated with the Church of Christ. Figures in above capsule are approximate. The library contains 470,236 volumes, 455,162 microform items, and 5817 audiovisual forms/CDs, and subscribes to 3134 periodicals. Computerized library services include the card catalog, interlibrary loans, and database searching. Special learning facilities include an art gallery, radio station, TV station, writing center, and Japanese tea ceremony room. The 830-acre campus is in a suburban area 35 miles northwest of Los Angeles, overlooking the Pacific Ocean. Including residence halls, there are 76 buildings.

Student Life: 51% of undergraduates are from California. Others are from 49 states, 53 foreign countries, and Canada. 65% are from public schools. 60% are white. 65% are Protestant; 17% Catholic; 12% undeclared, 6% other, 1% Islamic, 1% Jewish, 1% Buddist. The average age of freshmen is 18; all undergraduates, 20. 15% do not continue beyond their first year; 70% remain to graduate.

Housing: 1863 students can be accommodated in college housing, which includes single-sex dormitories, on-campus apartments, and married-student housing. On-campus housing is guaranteed for all 4 years. 65% of students live on campus; of those, 55% remain on campus on weekends. Alcohol is not permitted. All students may keep cars.

Activities: 25% of men belong to 6 national fraternities; 25% of women belong to 8 national sororities. There are 50 groups on campus, including art, band, cheerleading, chess, choir, chorale, chorus, computers, cycling, dance, debate, drama, equestrian, ethnic, honors, international, jazz band, literary magazine, musical theater, newspaper, opera, orchestra, pep band, photography, political, professional, radio and TV, religious, social, social service, student government, symphony, and yearbook. Popular campus events include Midnight Madness, Songfest, and Parents Weekend.

Sports: There are 7 intercollegiate sports for men and 7 for women, and 11 intramural sports for men and 11 for women. Facilities include a field house, a pool, a weight room, basketball, racquetball, and tennis courts, playing fields, an all-weather track, an aerobics room, and a whirlpool/hot tub.

Disabled Students: Wheelchair ramps, elevators, special parking, specially equipped rest rooms, special class scheduling, lowered drinking fountains, and lowered telephones are available.

Services: Counseling and information services are available, as is tutoring in most subjects.

Campus Safety and Security: Measures include 24-hour foot and vehicle patrol, self-defense education, escort service, and shuttle buses. There are informal discussions, pamphlets/posters/films, emergency telephones, lighted pathways/sidewalks, guarded entrances to campus, security cameras, late-night escort service, and a campus crimewatch program.

Programs of Study: Pepperdine confers B.A., B.S., and B.S.M. degrees. Master's and doctoral degrees are also awarded. Bachelor's degrees are awarded in BIOLOGICAL SCIENCE (biology/biological science and nutrition), BUSINESS (accounting, business administration and management, and international business management), COMMUNICATIONS AND THE ARTS (advertising, art, communications, dramatic arts, English, French, German, journalism, music, public relations, Spanish, speech/debate/rhetoric, and telecommunications), COMPUTER AND PHYSICAL SCIENCE (chemistry, computer science, mathematics, and natural sciences), EDUCATION (elementary, physical, and secondary), ENGINEERING AND ENVIRONMENTAL DESIGN (engineering), HEALTH PROFESSIONS (sports medicine), SOCIAL SCIENCE (economics, history, humanities, international studies, liberal arts/general studies, philosophy, political science/government, psychology, religion, social science, and sociology). Natural sciences (premedical), sports medicine, and political science are the strongest academically. Communication and business are the largest.

Required: To graduate, students must complete 128 units, including 64 units of general education requirements. 2 years of a broad liberal arts core curriculum are needed. Courses are required in English, religion, Western heritage, non-Western heritage, American heritage, behavioral science, foreign language, lab science, math, speech and rhetoric, freshman seminar, and phys ed. Students must take at least 40 upper-division units and complete a 28-unit residency requirement. Pepperdine requires a minimum GPA of 2.0 for graduation.

Special: Students may earn 1 to 4 units for an internship, available in most majors, participate in a Washington or a Sacramento semester, and study abroad in 8 countries. The school offers a 3-2 engineering degree with Washington University in St. Louis, the University of Southern California, and Boston University. There are dual majors in any discipline, student-designed contract majors, federal work-study programs, nondegree study, and pass/fail options. There are 12 national honor societies, a freshman honors program, and 3 departmental honors programs.

Faculty/Classroom: All teach undergraduates. No introductory courses are taught by graduate students. The average class size in an introductory lecture is 18; in a laboratory, 15; and in a regular course, 17.

Requirements: The SAT I or ACT is required. In addition, it is strongly recommended that candidates for admission present a college preparatory program that includes 4 years of English, 3 of math, 2 each of foreign language and science, and courses in speech communication, humanities, and social science. Applications are available on-line at *www.wavelink.edu*. AP and CLEP credits are accepted. Important factors in the admissions decision are advanced placement or honor courses, recommendations by school officials, and evidence of special talent.

Procedure: Freshmen are admitted fall and spring. Entrance exams should be taken in the fall. There are early action and deferred admissions plans. Early action applications should be filed by November 15; regular applications, by January 15 for fall entry, and October 15 for spring entry, along with a $55 fee. Notification of early action is sent December 15; regular decision, April 1. A waiting list is an active part of the admissions procedure.

Transfer: 85 transfer students enrolled in a recent year. Transfer applicants should have a minimum GPA of 2.7 from an accredited college. SAT I or ACT scores are required for applicants who have completed fewer than 30 transferable semester hours at an accredited college. 28 credits of 128 must be completed at Pepperdine.

Visiting: There are regularly scheduled orientations for prospective students, including tours of the campus, meetings with faculty and current students, and sessions on admission and financial aid; interviews may be arranged on the hour with admission counselors. There are guides for informal visits and visitors may sit in on classes and stay overnight. To schedule a visit, contact the Admissions Office.

Financial Aid: In a recent year, 79% of all freshmen and 70% of continuing students received some form of financial aid. 55% of students received need-based aid. The average freshman award was $23,364. Of that total, scholarships or need-based grants averaged $11,277; loans averaged $4744; and work contracts averaged $1914. 97% of undergraduates work part time. Average annual earnings from campus work are $1500. Pepperdine is a member of CSS. The FAFSA, the college's own financial statement and the federal income tax form, state scholarship/grant form (California residents), and W-2 wage statement are required. Check with the school for current deadlines.

International Students: There were 226 international students enrolled in a recent year. The school actively recruits these students. They must score 550 on the written TOEFL and also take the college's own test and also take the SAT I or the ACT.

Computers: The mainframe is an IBM ES/9000 Model 210. 292 PCs are available to students in residence halls, computer labs, electronic classrooms, the library, and the student center. Access to the minicomputer and mainframe, the library system, and the Internet is available. Students may access the system with permission from the faculty. They may access the system any time. Word-processing labs are open to all students. There are no time limits and no fees.

Graduates: In a recent year, 568 bachelor's degrees were awarded. The most popular majors were business administration (14%), psychology (8%), and telecommunications (6%). In an average class, 4% graduate in 3 years, 67% in 4 years, 65% in 5 years, and 75% in 6 years. 73 companies recruited on campus in a recent year.

Admissions Contact: Paul A. Long, Dean of Admission and Enrollment Management. A video is available.
E-mail: *admission-seaver@pepperdine.edu* Web: *www.pepperdine.edu*

PITZER COLLEGE — D-5
Claremont, CA 91711-6101 — (909) 621-8129
(800) PITZER-1; Fax: (909) 621-8770

Full-time: 331 men, 538 women	**Faculty:** 56; IIB, +$
Part-time: 15 men, 37 women	**Ph.D.s:** 99%
Graduate: none	**Student/Faculty:** 16 to 1
Year: semesters	**Tuition:** $27,030
Application Deadline: January 15	**Room & Board:** $6900
Freshman Class: 2282 applied, 1228 accepted, 224 enrolled	
SAT I Verbal/Math: 620/610	**ACT:** 25 **HIGHLY COMPETITIVE**

Pitzer College, founded in 1963, is a private liberal arts college emphasizing the social and behavioral sciences. It is one of the Claremont Colleges. There are 5 undergraduate and 2 graduate schools. The library contains 2 million volumes and 1,338,751 microform items, and subscribes to 6000 periodicals. Computerized library services include the card catalog, interlibrary loans, and database searching. Special learning facilities include an art gallery, radio station, TV station, a social science lab, and an arboretum. The 30-acre campus is in a suburban area 35 miles east of Los Angeles. Including residence halls, there are 13 buildings.

Student Life: 54% of undergraduates are from California. Others are from 44 states, 14 foreign countries, and Canada. 51% are white; 13% Asian American; 13% Hispanic. The average age of freshmen is 18. 18% do not continue beyond their first year.

Housing: 601 students can be accommodated in college housing, which includes single-sex and coed dormitories. On-campus housing is guaranteed for all 4 years. 92% of students live on campus. All students may keep cars.

Activities: There are no fraternities or sororities. There are 200 groups on campus, including art, choir, chorus, computers, dance, debate, drama, ethnic, film, gay, honors, international, literary magazine, musical theater, newspaper, photography, political, professional, radio and TV, religious, social, social service, student government, symphony, and yearbook. Popular campus events include the Kohoutek Festival, Atherton dinners, and Marquis Library Firesides.

Sports: There are 10 intercollegiate sports for men and 9 for women. Facilities include some of those shared by all the Claremont Colleges, including 3 gyms, 5 swimming pools, 20 tennis courts, numerous playing fields, and lighted volleyball courts. The campus stadium seats 1200. There are also shared intercollegiate sports with Pomona College, at the Gold Student Center.

Disabled Students: 95% of the campus is accessible. Wheelchair ramps, elevators, special parking, specially equipped rest rooms, lowered drinking fountains, and lowered telephones are available.

Services: Counseling and information services are available, as is tutoring in every subject, and tutoring software and programs for the learning disabled. There is a reader service for the blind and remedial writing.

Campus Safety and Security: Measures include 24-hour foot and vehicle patrol, self-defense education, escort service, and informal discussions. There are pamphlets/posters/films, emergency telephones, and lighted pathways/sidewalks.

Programs of Study: Pitzer confers the B.A. degree. Bachelor's degrees are awarded in BIOLOGICAL SCIENCE (biochemistry, biology/biological science, and neurosciences), BUSINESS (management engineering, and organizational behavior), COMMUNICATIONS AND THE ARTS (art, classics, dance, dramatic arts, English, film arts, French, linguistics, media arts, music, and Spanish), COMPUTER AND PHYSICAL SCIENCE (chemistry, mathematics, physics, science, and science and management), ENGINEERING AND ENVIRONMENTAL DESIGN (environmental science), SOCIAL SCIENCE (African American studies, American studies, anthropology, Asian/American studies, Asian/Oriental studies, Caribbean studies, economics, European studies, history, international relations, Latin American studies, Mexican-American/Chicano studies, philosophy, political science/government, psychology, sociology, Third World studies, and women's studies). Social and behavioral sciences are the strongest academically and the largest.

Required: Students must complete a total of 32 courses with a 2.0 GPA. Although requirements vary according to major, most students take introductory or preparatory courses in their first 2 years and courses in or related to their major in the last 2 years. All students must fufill educational objectives in the following areas: interdisciplinary and intercultural exploration; social responsibility and the ethical implications of knowledge and action; breadth of knowledge; and written expression.

Special: Students may cross-register at any of the other Claremont Colleges, or study abroad in Africa, Asia, Europe, Latin America, North America, or Oceania. There are co-op programs, internships, dual majors, student-designed majors, an extensive freshman seminar program, and interdisciplinary study offered in science and technology, and international or intercultural studies. Joint advanced degrees are offered in math, business administration, and public policy. There are independent study and limited pass/fail options.

Faculty/Classroom: 58% of faculty are male; 42%, female. All both teach and do research. The average class size in an introductory lecture is 35; in a laboratory, 50; and in a regular course, 17.

Admissions: 54% of the 2001-2002 applicants were accepted. The SAT I scores for the 2001-2002 freshman class were: Verbal--5% below 500, 32% between 500 and 599, 48% between 600 and 700, and 15% above 700; Math--9% below 500, 38% between 500 and 599, 48% between 600 and 700, and 5% above 700. The ACT scores were 7% below 21, 10% between 21 and 23, 47% between 24 and 26, 12% between 27 and 28, and 23% above 28. 55% of the current freshmen were in the top fifth of their class; 84% were in the top two fifths.

Requirements: The SAT I or ACT is required. In addition, applicants must be graduates of an accredited secondary school or have earned the GED. Secondary school courses must include 4 years of English courses requiring extensive writing, and 3 years each of social and behavioral sciences including history, lab science, foreign language, and math. A personal essay is required and a personal interview is recommended. AP credits are accepted. Important factors in the admissions decision are advanced placement or honor courses, leadership record, and evidence of special talent. Applications are accepted on-line via Apply Yourself, Common App, or Next Stop College.

Procedure: Freshmen are admitted fall and spring. Entrance exam scores must be submitted by January 15. There are early admissions and deferred admissions plans. Early decision application should be filed by December 1; regular applications, by January 15 for fall entry and October 15 for spring entry. The fall 2001 application fee was $40. Notification of early decision is sent January 1; regular decision, April 1. A waiting list is an active part of the admissions procedure.

Transfer: 22 transfer students enrolled in 2001-2002. No more than 2 years of previous credits may be transferred. 16 courses of 32 must be completed at Pitzer.

Visiting: There are regularly scheduled orientations for prospective students. There are guides for informal visits and visitors may sit in on classes and stay overnight. To schedule a visit, contact the Office of Admissions at *campus_visit@pitzer.edu*

Financial Aid: In 2001-2002, 53% of all freshmen and 55% of continuing students received some form of financial aid. 39% of freshmen and 52% of continuing students received need-based aid. The average freshman award was $24,686. Of that total, scholarships or need-based grants averaged $20,177 ($30,320 maximum); loans averaged $3463 ($3700 maximum); and work contracts averaged $2454 ($2460 maximum). 60% of undergraduates work part time. Average annual earnings from campus work are $2300. The average financial indebtedness of the 2001 graduate was $20,900. Pitzer is a member of CSS. The CSS/Profile or FAFSA is required. The fall application deadline is February 1.

International Students: There are 36 international students enrolled. The school actively recruits these students. They must score 587 on the written TOEFL or 240 on the electronic version and also take the SAT I or the ACT.

Computers: The mainframes are a VAX 4000/200, VAXstation 3100, and 16 NeXT workstations. Macs and PCs are available in labs. All students may access the system. There are no time limits and no fees.

Graduates: In 2001, 217 bachelor's degrees were awarded. The most popular majors were psychology (18%), English and world literature (10%), and political studies (9%). In an average class, 1% graduate in 3 years, 64% in 4 years, and 9% in 5 years. 25 companies recruited on campus in 2000-2001.

Admissions Contact: Arnaldo Rodriguez, Vice President, Admission and Financial Aid. E-mail: *admission@pitzer.edu* Web: *www.pitzer.edu*

POINT LOMA NAZARENE UNIVERSITY — D-5

San Diego, CA 92106-2899 — (619) 849-2565
(800) 733-7770; Fax: (619) 849-2601

Full-time: 919 men, 1362 women — **Faculty:** 115; IIB, av$
Part-time: 33 men, 39 women — **Ph.D.s:** 61%
Graduate: 192 men, 336 women — **Student/Faculty:** 20 to 1
Year: semesters, summer session — **Tuition:** $15,300
Application Deadline: March 1 — **Room & Board:** $6080
Freshman Class: 1365 applied, 1038 accepted, 546 enrolled
SAT I Verbal/Math: 553/553 — **ACT:** 23 — **VERY COMPETITIVE**

Point Loma Nazarene University, founded in 1902, is a private liberal arts university affiliated with the Church of the Nazarene. In addition to regional accreditation, PLNU has baccalaureate program accreditation with ACBSP and NLN. The library contains 143,577 volumes, 35,037 microform items, and 10,700 audiovisual forms/CDs, and subscribes to 613 periodicals. Computerized library services include the card catalog, interlibrary loans, and database searching. Special learning facilities include a learning resource center, radio station, and a laboratory preschool. The 90-acre campus is in a suburban area 5 miles southwest of San Diego. Including residence halls, there are 42 buildings.

Student Life: 77% of undergraduates are from California. Others are from 36 states, 14 foreign countries, and Canada. 82% are from public schools. 84% are white. Most are Protestant. The average age of freshmen is 18; all undergraduates, 20. 21% do not continue beyond their first year; 89% remain to graduate.

Housing: 1460 students can be accommodated in college housing, which includes single-sex dormitories, on-campus apartments, off-campus apartments, and married-student housing. On-campus housing is available on a first-come, first-served basis and on a lottery system for upperclassmen. 67% of students live on campus. Alcohol is not permitted. Upperclassmen may keep cars.

Activities: There are 3 local fraternities and 1 national and 2 local sororities. There are 41 groups on campus, including art, band, cheerleading, choir, chorale, computers, debate, drama, ethnic, forensics, honors, international, jazz band, literary magazine, newspaper, opera, orchestra, pep band, political, professional, radio and TV, religious, social, social service, student government, and yearbook. Popular campus events include Spiritual Emphasis Week and Christmas Messiah Concert.

Sports: There are 7 intercollegiate sports for men and 5 for women, and 18 intramural sports for men and 17 for women. Facilities include a gym, baseball and soccer fields, a track, tennis courts, dormitory lounges, and table tennis and pool tables.

Disabled Students: 75% of the campus is accessible. Wheelchair ramps, elevators, special parking, specially equipped rest rooms, special class scheduling, lowered drinking fountains, and lowered telephones are available.

Services: Counseling and information services are available, as is tutoring in most subjects. There is a reader service for the blind, and remedial math, reading, and writing.

Campus Safety and Security: Measures include 24-hour foot and vehicle patrol, self-defense education, escort service, and shuttle buses. There are informal discussions, pamphlets/posters/films, emergency telephones, and lighted pathways/sidewalks.

Programs of Study: PLNU confers B.A., B.S., and B.S.N. degrees. Master's degrees are also awarded. Bachelor's degrees are awarded in BIOLOGICAL SCIENCE (biology/biological science), BUSINESS (accounting, business administration and management, and management information systems), COMMUNICATIONS AND THE ARTS (art, communications, dramatic arts, journalism, literature, music, music business management, romance languages and literature, Spanish, and speech/debate/rhetoric), COMPUTER AND PHYSICAL SCIENCE (chemistry, computer science, mathematics, and physics), EDUCATION (physical), ENGINEERING AND ENVIRONMENTAL DESIGN (engineering physics), HEALTH PROFESSIONS (nursing), SOCIAL SCIENCE (child psychology/development, dietetics, economics, family and community services, history, home economics, industrial and organizational psychology, liberal arts/general studies, philosophy, political science/government, psychology, religion, religious education, social science, social work, and sociology). Biology, chemistry, and art are the strongest academically. Liberal studies and business are the largest.

Required: To graduate, students must complete a minimum of 128 semester units. At least 24 upper-division semester units are needed for the major. A minimum GPA of 2.0 is required. Students must complete the general education requirements, though B.S.N. candidates need not take a foreign language. General education requirements include 9 courses in cultural studies, 5 in the sciences, 4 in cognitive studies, and 3 in religious studies. Students must demonstrate proficiency in writing and math.

Special: PLNU offers internships in the church, in state and national governments, in journalism, in small business, and in the film industry. Students may study abroad in several world capitals and in Russia, the Middle East, and Costa Rica. There are Washington and United Nations semester programs. Various dual or interdepartmental majors are offered, including biology-chemistry, graphic communications, human environmental science-business, and church music-youth ministries. There are preprofessional programs in medicine/dentistry, law, and engineering. A general studies degree in liberal studies is available, as is credit for life, military, and work experience for nursing students. PLNU also offers nondegree study and credit/no credit options. There is 1 national honor society, a freshman honors program, and 1 departmental honors program.

Faculty/Classroom: 55% of faculty are male; 45%, female. 95% teach undergraduates and 10% both teach and do research. No introductory courses are taught by graduate students. The average class size in an introductory lecture is 75; in a laboratory, 18; and in a regular course, 25.

Admissions: 76% of the 2001-2002 applicants were accepted. The SAT I scores for the 2001-2002 freshman class were: Verbal--25% below 500, 47% between 500 and 599, 24% between 600 and 700, and 4% above 700; Math--23% below 500, 46% between 500 and 599, 28% between 600 and 700, and 3% above 700. The ACT scores were 19% below 21, 37% between 21 and 23, 24% between 24 and 26, 10% between 27 and 28, and 11% above 28. 53% of the current freshmen were in the top fifth of their class; 81% were in the top two fifths. 18 freshmen graduated first in their class.

Requirements: The SAT I or ACT is required. In addition, candidates for admission should have completed 4 years of English, 2 years each of foreign language and math, and 1 year each of history and science. A GPA of 2.8 is required. AP and CLEP credits are accepted. Important factors in the admissions decision are personality/intangible qualities, leadership record, and advanced placement or honor courses.

Procedure: Freshmen are admitted to all sessions. Entrance exams should be taken in the junior year or early in the senior year. There are early admissions and deferred admissions plans. Applications should be filed by March 1 for fall entry. The fall 2001 application fee was $45. Notification is sent on a rolling basis.

Transfer: 165 transfer students enrolled in 2001-2002. Transfer students must have a C average in all college work and present transcripts, including certificates of honorable dismissal. Credits submitted from nonaccredited schools will be evaluated individually. Advanced standing is provisional for at least one term, in which the student must maintain at least a C average. 24 credits of 128 must be completed at PLNU.

Visiting: There are regularly scheduled orientations for prospective students, including campus tours and appointments with major advisers. There are guides for informal visits and visitors may sit in on classes and stay overnight. To schedule a visit, contact the Admissions Office at (619) 221-2273.

Financial Aid: In 2001-2002, 85% of all students received some form of financial aid. 28% of undergraduates work part time. PLNU is a member of CSS. The CSS/Profile or FAFSA and the college's own financial statement are required. The fall application deadline is April 10.

International Students: There are 19 international students enrolled. They must score 550 on the written TOEFL or 216 on the electronic version and also take the SAT I.

Computers: The mainframes are a Data General MV/10,000. Terminals are located in the computer center and the business and science areas. There are 125 PCs and 20 Apple IIes in computer labs available for classes and for general use. All students may access the system when computer labs are open. There are no time limits and no fees. It is recommended that students in business administration have personal computers.

Graduates: In 2001, 447 bachelor's degrees were awarded. The most popular majors were business (21%), liberal studies (17%), and nursing (13%). In an average class, 31% graduate in 4 years, 46% in 5 years, and 52% in 6 years. 140 companies recruited on campus in 2000-2001.

Admissions Contact: Scott Shoemaker, Director, Admissions. A video is available. E-mail: *admissions@ptloma.edu*
Web: *www.ptloma.edu/admissions*

POMONA COLLEGE

Claremont, CA 91711 — D-5
(909) 621-8134; Fax: (909) 621-8952

Full-time: 783 men, 754 women	**Faculty:** 155; IIB, ++$
Part-time: 18 men, 15 women	**Ph.D.s:** 100%
Graduate: none	**Student/Faculty:** 10 to 1
Year: semesters	**Tuition:** $25,010
Application Deadline: January 2	**Room & Board:** $8950
Freshman Class: 3712 applied, 1079 accepted, 394 enrolled	
SAT I Verbal/Math: 720/720	**ACT:** 31 **MOST COMPETITIVE**

Pomona College, the oldest and largest of the Claremont Colleges (a consortium of colleges), is an independent, national liberal arts and sciences institution founded in 1887. Some information in this profile is approximate. There are 5 undergraduate and 2 graduate schools. The 3 libraries contain 2,022,481 volumes, 1,382,687 microform items, and 777 audiovisual forms/CDs, and subscribe to 6624 periodicals. Computerized library services include the card catalog, interlibrary loans, and database searching. Special learning facilities include an art gallery, radio station, observatory, and modern languages and international relations center. The 140-acre campus is in a suburban area 35 miles east of Los Angeles. Including residence halls, there are 47 buildings.

Student Life: 61% of undergraduates are from out of state, mostly the Northwest. Students are from 49 states, 31 foreign countries, and Canada. 69% are from public schools. 51% are white; 21%, Asian American; 10%, Hispanic. The average age of freshmen is 18; all undergraduates, 20. 1% do not continue beyond their first year; 94% remain to graduate.

Housing: 1335 students can be accommodated in college housing, which includes coed dormitories and on-campus apartments. In addition, there are language houses. On-campus housing is guaranteed for all 4 years. 97% of students live on campus; of those, 95% remain on campus on weekends. All students may keep cars.

Activities: 6% of men and about 4% of women belong to 6 local fraternities. There are no sororities. There are 280 groups on campus, including art, band, chess, choir, chorus, dance, debate, drama, ethnic, film, gay, honors, international, jazz band, literary magazine, musical theater, newspaper, orchestra, pep band, photography, political, professional, radio and TV, religious, social, social service, student government, symphony, and yearbook.

Sports: There are 10 intercollegiate sports for men and 10 for women, and 13 intramural sports for men and 13 for women. Facilities include an all-weather track, 2 swimming pools, a weight room, a fitness center, a dance studio, various playing fields, and courts for tennis, squash, racquetball, basketball, volleyball, and badminton.

Disabled Students: 80% of the campus is accessible. Wheelchair ramps, elevators, special parking, specially equipped rest rooms, special class scheduling, lowered drinking fountains, and lowered telephones are available.

Services: Counseling and information services are available, as is tutoring in most subjects. There is a reader service for the blind.

Campus Safety and Security: Measures include 24-hour foot and vehicle patrol, self-defense education, escort service, and informal discussions. There are pamphlets/posters/films, emergency telephones, and lighted pathways/sidewalks.

Programs of Study: Pomona confers the B.A. degree. Bachelor's degrees are awarded in BIOLOGICAL SCIENCE (biology/biological science, molecular biology, and neurosciences), COMMUNICATIONS AND THE ARTS (art history and appreciation, Chinese, classics, dramatic arts, English, fine arts, French, German, Japanese, languages, linguistics, literature, media arts, music, Russian, Spanish, and studio art), COMPUTER AND PHYSICAL SCIENCE (chemistry, computer science, geology, mathematics, physics, and science), ENGINEERING AND ENVIRONMENTAL DESIGN (technology and public affairs), SOCIAL SCIENCE (African American studies, American studies, anthropology, Asian/Oriental studies, economics, German area studies, history, international relations, Latin American studies, philosophy, political science/government, psychology, public affairs, religion, sociology, and women's studies). Social sciences and sciences are the largest.

Required: Students must pass 1 course in each of the following categories: read literature critically, use and understand scientific method, use and understand formal reasoning, understand and analyze data, analyze creative art critically, perform or produce creative art, explore and understand human behavior, explore and understand historical culture, compare and contrast contemporary culture, and think critically about values and rationality. To graduate, students must complete 32 semester courses with a 6.0 GPA on a 12.0 scale.

Special: Students may cross-register at any of the Claremont Colleges, study abroad in 22 countries, and spend a semester in Washington, D.C. Dual and student-designed majors, internships, and independent study are possible. A 3-2 engineering program is offered with California Institute of Technology or Washington University in St. Louis. Students may study for 1 semester at Colby, Smith, Spelman, or Swarthmore Colleges. There are pass/fail options. There are 9 national honor societies, including Phi Beta Kappa.

Faculty/Classroom: 58% of faculty are male; 42%, female. All both teach and do research. The average class size in an introductory lecture is 30; in a laboratory, 14; and in a regular course, 14.

Admissions: 29% of the 2001-2002 applicants were accepted. The SAT I scores for the 2001-2002 freshman class were: Verbal--4% between 500 and 599, 30% between 600 and 700, and 66% above 700; Math--5% between 500 and 599, 30% between 600 and 700, and 66% above 700. The ACT scores were 1% between 21 and 23, 6% between 24 and 26, 23% between 27 and 28, and 70% above 28. 97% of the current freshmen were in the top fifth of their class; all were in the top two fifths. In a recent year, there were 41 National Merit finalists. 32 freshmen graduated first in their class.

Requirements: The SAT I or ACT is required. Although applicants need not be graduates of accredited high schools (some may be admitted after the junior year), most are, or have earned the GED. Secondary preparation must include 4 years of English, 3 each of math and foreign languages, and 2 each of lab and social sciences. An essay is required and an interview is strongly recommended. AP credits are accepted. Important factors in the admissions decision are recommendations by school officials, leadership record, and recommendations by alumni. Applications are accepted on-line at CollegeLink, Embark, Apply, Common App, and the College Board's "Next Stop College."

Procedure: Freshmen are admitted in the fall. Entrance exams should be taken before December of the senior year. There are early decision, early admissions, and deferred admissions plans. Early decision applications should be filed by November 15 (round I) or December 28 (round II); regular applications, by January 2 for fall entry. The fall 2001 application fee was $55. Notification of early decision is sent December 15; regular decision, April 10. 82 early decision candidates were accepted for a recent class. A waiting list is an active part of the admissions procedure.

Transfer: 16 transfer students enrolled in 2001-2002. Applicants must have completed at least 1 year (24 semester hours) of college-level courses at the time of enrollment. 16 credits of 32 must be completed at Pomona.

Visiting: There are regularly scheduled orientations for prospective students, including interviews, information sessions, and tours. There are guides for informal visits and visitors may sit in on classes and stay overnight. To schedule a visit, contact the Admissions Office.

Financial Aid: In 2001-2002, 53% of all freshmen and 52% of continuing students received some form of financial aid. In a recent year, 49% of freshmen and 52% of continuing students received need-based aid. The average freshman award was $21,310. Of that total, scholarships or need-based grants averaged $16,500; loans averaged $3500; and work contracts averaged $2110. 65% of undergraduates work part time. Average annual earnings from campus work are $2000. The average financial indebtedness of a recent graduate was $15,800. Pomona is a member of CSS. The CSS/Profile or FAFSA and tax returns are required. Check with the school for current deadlines.

International Students: The school actively recruits these students. They must score 600 on the written TOEFL or 250 on the electronic version and also take the SAT I or the ACT.

Computers: The mainframe is a DEC ALPHA. Students may access the mainframe computer at several public facilities and from dormitory rooms. Macs and PCs are available in public work areas. All students may access the system. There are no time limits and no fees.

Graduates: In a recent class, 366 bachelor's degrees were awarded. The most popular majors were social sciences (28%), biology (13%), and psychology (9%). In an average class, 94% graduate in 4 years and 96% in 5 years. 165 companies recruited on campus in a recent year. Of a recent graduating class, 35% were enrolled in graduate school within 6 months of graduation and 60% were employed.

Admissions Contact: Bruce J. Poch, Vice President and Dean of Admissions. E-mail: *admissions@pomona.edu* Web: *www.pomona.edu*

SAINT MARY'S COLLEGE OF CALIFORNIA B-3

Moraga, CA 94575-4800 **(925) 631-4224**

(800) 800-4SMC; Fax: (925) 376-7193

Full-time: 975 men, 1493 women	**Faculty:** 150; IIA, +$
Part-time: 8 men, 11 women	**Ph.D.s:** 92%
Graduate: 505 men, 1135 women	**Student/Faculty:** 16 to 1
Year: 4-1-4	**Tuition:** $19,525
Application Deadline: February 1	**Room & Board:** $8050
Freshman Class: 3146 applied, 2496 accepted, 580 enrolled	
SAT I Verbal/Math: 540/550	**ACT:** 22 **COMPETITIVE**

Saint Mary's College of California, founded in 1863, is a private, independent, liberal arts college affiliated with the Roman Catholic Church. The school offers undergraduate and graduate programs in liberal arts, nursing, economics and business administration, education, and preprofessional studies. There are 5 undergraduate and 5 graduate schools. In addition to regional accreditation, Saint Mary's has baccalaureate program accreditation with NLN. The library contains 203,007 volumes, 462,907 microform items, and 7000 audiovisual forms/CDs, and subscribes to 2600 periodicals. Computerized library services include the card catalog, interlibrary loans, and database searching. Special learning facilities include an art gallery, radio station, and TV station. The 420-acre campus is in a suburban area 20 miles east of San Francisco. Including residence halls, there are 58 buildings.

Student Life: 89% of undergraduates are from California. Others are from 29 states, 14 foreign countries, and Canada. 58% are from public schools. 65% are white; 16% Hispanic. 55% are Catholic; 38% Protestant. The average age of freshmen is 18; all undergraduates, 20. 15% do not continue beyond their first year; 67% remain to graduate.

Housing: 1550 students can be accommodated in college housing, which includes single-sex and coed dormitories and on-campus apartments. On-campus housing is guaranteed for the freshman year only and is available on a lottery system for upperclassmen. 62% of students live on campus; of those, 68% remain on campus on weekends. All students may keep cars.

Activities: There are no fraternities or sororities. There are 42 groups on campus, including art, cheerleading, choir, chorus, dance, drama, ethnic, gay, honors, international, jazz band, literary magazine, musical theater, newspaper, pep band, political, professional, radio and TV, religious, social, social service, student government, and yearbook. Popular campus events include Welcome Back Dance, OASIS, and St. Mary's Day Off.

Sports: There are 7 intercollegiate sports for men and 8 for women, and 9 intramural sports for men and 9 for women. Facilities include a gym, football and baseball fields, a swimming pool, lighted tennis courts, a soccer field and rugby pitch, a weight room, and a workout facility.

Disabled Students: 90% of the campus is accessible. Wheelchair ramps, elevators, special parking, specially equipped rest rooms, special class scheduling, lowered drinking fountains, and lowered telephones are available.

Services: Counseling and information services are available, as is tutoring in most subjects in 1-on-1 sessions or group workshops. Readers, note takers, and other services are provided to learning or physically disabled students.

Campus Safety and Security: Measures include 24-hour foot and vehicle patrol, escort service, informal discussions, and pamphlets/posters/films. There are emergency telephones and lighted pathways/sidewalks.

Programs of Study: Saint Mary's confers B.A., B.S., and B.S.N. degrees. Master's and doctoral degrees are also awarded. Bachelor's degrees are awarded in BIOLOGICAL SCIENCE (biology/biological science), BUSINESS (accounting and business administration and management), COMMUNICATIONS AND THE ARTS (art, classical languages, communications, English, French, performing arts, and Spanish), COMPUTER AND PHYSICAL SCIENCE (chemistry, mathematics, and physics), EDUCATION (health, physical, and recreation), ENGINEERING AND ENVIRONMENTAL DESIGN (preengineering), HEALTH PROFESSIONS (health science and nursing), SOCIAL SCIENCE (anthropology, economics, history, liberal arts/general studies, philosophy, political science/government, psychology, and religion). Business administration, communications, and psychology are the largest.

Required: To graduate, students must complete 36 course credits, including 17 at the upper-division level, with a GPA of 2.0 overall and in the major. Specific requirements include the freshman seminar and 2 courses each in religious studies, humanities, math/science, and social sciences. All students must demonstrate competence in written English.

Special: Saint Mary's College and Samuel Merritt College confer the B.S.N. degree to students completing the Intercollegiate Nursing Program. The college offers seminars in all fields, dual and student-designed majors, study abroad in 10 countries, a Washington semester, cross-registration with the Regional Association of East Bay Colleges and Universities, and an integral liberal arts degree. There are 3-2 engineering programs with Washington University, the University of Southern California, and Boston University.

Faculty/Classroom: 53% of faculty are male; 47%, female. All both teach and do research. No introductory courses are taught by graduate students. The average class size in an introductory lecture is 25; in a laboratory, 16; and in a regular course, 20.

Admissions: 79% of the 2001-2002 applicants were accepted. The SAT I scores for the 2001-2002 freshman class were: Verbal--26% below 500, 50% between 500 and 599, 22% between 600 and 700, and 2% above 700; Math--23% below 500, 53% between 500 and 599, 21% between 600 and 700, and 3% above 700. The ACT scores were 33% below 21, 30% between 21 and 23, 22% between 24 and 26, 6% between 27 and 28, and 10% above 28.

Requirements: The SAT I or ACT is required. In addition, candidates should be graduates of an accredited secondary school, with 16 academic units, including 4 in English and 1 each in algebra, advanced algebra, geometry, and U.S. history. It is recommended that the remaining units be made up of foreign language, lab science, and additional academic electives in the student's areas of strength. The GED is accepted. An essay is required. AP and CLEP credits are accepted. Important factors in the admissions decision are recommendations by school officials, advanced placement or honor courses, and parents or siblings attending the school. Applications on disk are available through the Admissions Office. The application is available on the Apply Technologies CD-ROM, Apply web site, and on the college's web site.

Procedure: Freshmen are admitted to all sessions. Entrance exams should be taken by December of the senior year. There is a deferred admissions plan. Applications should be filed by February 1 for fall entry and January 1 for spring entry. The fall 2001 application fee was $45. Notification of early decision is sent January 1; regular decision, April 1. There is a waiting list; 248 wait-listed applicants were accepted in 2001.

Transfer: 162 transfer students enrolled in 2001-2002. Applicants must have a GPA of 2.3 and a minimum of 23 transferable academic semester units. 9 credits of 36 must be completed at Saint Mary's.

Visiting: There are regularly scheduled orientations for prospective students. There are guides for informal visits and visitors may sit in on classes and stay overnight. To schedule a visit, contact the Admissions Office at (925) 631-4106.

Financial Aid: In 2001-2002, 74% of all freshmen and 69% of continuing students received some form of financial aid. 60% of freshmen and 57% of continuing students received need-based aid. The average fresh-

man award was $15,349. Of that total, scholarships or need-based grants averaged $15,147 ($19,390 maximum); loans averaged $2430 ($7625 maximum); and work contracts averaged $1406 ($1500 maximum). 25% of undergraduates work part time. Average annual earnings from campus work are $1570. The average financial indebtedness of the 2001 graduate was $16,890. Saint Mary's is a member of CSS. The FAFSA and California GPA verification form for residents only are required. The fall application deadline is March 2.

International Students: There were 67 international students enrolled in a recent year. The school actively recruits these students. They must score 525 on the written TOEFL or 197 on the electronic version. Nonnative English speakers who submit a score of 525 or higher on the TOEFL may be admitted as full-time undergraduates. Others may be accepted conditionally and enrolled in the college's Intensive English Program.

Computers: There are 197 college-owned workstations available for general student use in the library and computer center. All students may access the system. There are no time limits and no fees.

Graduates: In 2001, 534 bachelor's degrees were awarded. The most popular majors were business administration (25%), psychology (13%), and communications (11%). In an average class, 64% graduate in 4 years, 66% in 5 years, and 67% in 6 years. 70 companies recruited on campus in 2000-2001.

Admissions Contact: Dorothy Benjamin, Dean of Admissions. A video is available. E-mail: *smcadmit@stmarys-ca.edu*
Web: *http://www.stmarys-ca.edu*

SAMUEL MERRITT COLLEGE — B-3
Oakland, CA 94609-9954 — (510) 869-6576
(800) 607-6377; Fax: (510) 869-6525

Full-time: 20 men, 225 women	**Faculty:** 27
Part-time: 10 men, 45 women	**Ph.D.s:** 59%
Graduate: 95 men, 365 women	**Student/Faculty:** 9 to 1
Year: 4-1-4	**Tuition:** $18,563
Application Deadline: see profile	**Room & Board:** $3510
Freshman Class: n/av	
SAT I: required	**SPECIAL**

Samuel Merritt College, founded in 1909, is a private, independent college offering a nursing program in cooperation with St. Mary's College of California. Graduate degrees are offered in nursing, physical therapy, and occupational therapy. Figures in above capsule are approximate. There are 3 graduate schools. In addition to regional accreditation, Samuel Merritt College has baccalaureate program accreditation with APTA and NLN. The library contains 12,500 volumes and 900 audiovisual forms/CDs, and subscribes to 550 periodicals. Computerized library services include the card catalog, interlibrary loans, and database searching. Special learning facilities include a health education center, television studio, and nursing resource, physical therapy, and occupational therapy labs. The 1-acre campus is in an urban area in Oakland, 10 miles east of San Francisco. Including residence halls, there are 3 buildings.

Student Life: 99% of undergraduates are from California. Others are from 4 states and 2 foreign countries. 84% are from public schools. 68% are white; 18% Asian American. 43% are Catholic; 27% Protestant; 18% claim no religious affiliation; 11% Muslim (4%), not specified (7%). The average age of freshmen is 19; all undergraduates, 28. 33% do not continue beyond their first year; 83% remain to graduate.

Housing: 93 students can be accommodated in college housing, which includes coed dormitories. On-campus housing is available on a first-come, first-served basis. 83% of students commute. Alcohol is not permitted. All students may keep cars.

Activities: There are no fraternities or sororities. There are 16 groups on campus, including ethnic, gay, honors, professional, religious, social, social service, student government, and yearbook. Popular campus events include Career Fair, Beginning and End of Year Bar-B-Ques, and Multicultural Spring Fair.

Sports: There is no sports program at Samuel Merritt College. Facilities include a swimming pool and an exercise room.

Disabled Students: All of the campus is accessible. Wheelchair ramps, elevators, special parking, specially equipped rest rooms, and lowered drinking fountains are available.

Services: Counseling and information services are available, as is tutoring in every subject. There is remedial math, reading, and writing.

Campus Safety and Security: Measures include 24-hour foot and vehicle patrol, self-defense education, escort service, and shuttle buses. There are informal discussions, pamphlets/posters/films, emergency telephones, and lighted pathways/sidewalks.

Programs of Study: Samuel Merritt College confers the B.S.N. degree. Master's degrees are also awarded. Bachelor's degrees are awarded in HEALTH PROFESSIONS (nursing).

Required: Students must take a basic core curriculum with a minimum of 129 total credit hours, including 69 lower-division and 60 upper-division courses. Students must take at least 60 hours in the major. A minimum GPA of 2.0 overall and in the nursing major is necessary.

Special: There is 1 national honor society, and 1 departmental honors program.

Faculty/Classroom: 19% of faculty are male; 81%, female. 48% teach undergraduates, 50% do research, and 50% do both. No introductory courses are taught by graduate students. The average class size in a laboratory is 8 and in a regular course, 27.

Requirements: The SAT I is required. In addition, students must be high school graduates or hold a GED. Candidates for admission should have completed 3 years of English and 2 years each of math, science, and social studies. A GPA of 2.5 is required. AP and CLEP credits are accepted. Important factors in the admissions decision are advanced placement or honor courses, leadership record, and extracurricular activities record.

Procedure: Freshmen are admitted fall and spring. Entrance exams should be taken within 3 to 4 months of admission. Notification is sent on a rolling basis. A waiting list is an active part of the admissions procedure. Check with the school for current deadlines. The fall 2001 application fee was $35.

Transfer: 102 transfer students enrolled in a recent year. A minimum college GPA of 2.5 is required for students with more than 30 prior credits, as well as completion of specified prerequisite courses. 18 credits of 129 must be completed at Samuel Merritt College.

Visiting: There are regularly scheduled orientations for prospective students, including a campus tour and meetings with students and faculty. There are guides for informal visits. To schedule a visit, contact the Office of Admission.

Financial Aid: In a recent year, 80% of all freshmen and 62% of continuing students received some form of financial aid. 50% of freshmen and 73% of continuing students received need-based aid. The average freshman award was $6486. Of that total, scholarships or need-based grants averaged $3000 ($9500 maximum); loans averaged $2625 ($6625 maximum); and work contracts averaged $300. All of undergraduates work part time. Samuel Merritt College is a member of CSS. The FAFSA is required. Check with the school for current deadlines.

International Students: There were 2 international students enrolled in a recent year. They must score 550 on the written TOEFL and also take the SAT I or the ACT.

Computers: The mainframe is an IBM RS/6000 Model 970. The academic computer lab at St. Mary's College is available to Samuel Merritt students. All students may access the system. There are no time limits and no fees.

Graduates: In an average class, 70% graduate in 4 years, 74% in 5 years, and 75% in 6 years.

Admissions Contact: Admission Office.
E-mail: *admissions@samuelmerritt.edu* Web: *samuelmerritt.edu*

SAN DIEGO STATE UNIVERSITY — D-5
San Diego, CA 92182 — (619) 594-7800; Fax: (619) 594-4902

Full-time: 9232 men, 12,288 women	**Faculty:** 1166; IIA, +$
Part-time: 2635 men, 3716 women	**Ph.D.s:** 78%
Graduate: 2375 men, 3925 women	**Student/Faculty:** 18 to 1
Year: semesters, summer session	**Tuition:** $1776 ($9156)
Application Deadline: November 30	**Room & Board:** $7940
Freshman Class: 23,932 applied, 15,946 accepted, 4255 enrolled	
SAT I Verbal/Math: 500/530	**ACT:** 21 **COMPETITIVE+**

San Diego State University, founded in 1897, is a public liberal arts university that is part of the California State University system. There are 8 undergraduate schools. In addition to regional accreditation, SDSU has baccalaureate program accreditation with ACEJMC, ADA, ASLA, CSWE, FIDER, NASAD, NASM, NCATE, NLN, and NRPA. The library contains 1,300,460 volumes, 4,153,642 microform items, and 11,955 audiovisual forms/CDs, and subscribes to 4851 periodicals. Computerized library services include the card catalog, interlibrary loans, and database searching. Special learning facilities include a learning resource center, art gallery, planetarium, radio station, TV station, theater, and recital hall. The 282-acre campus is in an urban area 8 miles east of downtown San Diego. Including residence halls, there are 56 buildings.

Student Life: 96% of undergraduates are from California. Others are from 50 states, 82 foreign countries, and Canada. 45% are white; 20% Hispanic; 14% Asian American. The average age of freshmen is 18.5; all undergraduates, 23. 25% do not continue beyond their first year; 35% remain to graduate.

Housing: 3087 students can be accommodated in college housing, which includes coed dormitories, on-campus apartments, fraternity houses, and sorority houses. In addition, there are honors houses and special-interest houses. On-campus housing is available on a first-come, first-served basis. 89% of students commute. All students may keep cars.

Activities: There are 15 national fraternities; 2% of women belong to 9 national sororities. There are 300 groups on campus, including art, band, cheerleading, choir, chorale, chorus, dance, drama, drill team, ethnic, film, gay, honors, international, jazz band, marching band, musical theater, newspaper, opera, orchestra, pep band, political, professional, radio and TV, religious, social, social service, student government, and symphony. Popular campus events include Ethnic Pride and Pow-Wow.

Sports: There are 6 intercollegiate sports for men and 11 for women, and 7 intramural sports for men and 7 for women. Facilities include a gym, basketball, racquetball, tennis, and volleyball courts, a swimming pool, a track, soccer, softball, baseball, and football fields, an aquatic center, a weight room, bowling and gymnastic equipment, a cardio room, and a 30-foot climbing wall.

Disabled Students: 95% of the campus is accessible. Wheelchair ramps, elevators, special parking, specially equipped rest rooms, special class scheduling, lowered drinking fountains, lowered telephones, orientation, counseling, transportation, books on tape, sign language interpreters, testing assistance, support equipment for loan, special computers, and note-taking services are available.

Services: Counseling and information services are available, as is tutoring in most subjects. There is a reader service for the blind, and remedial math, reading, and writing.

Campus Safety and Security: Measures include 24-hour foot and vehicle patrol, self-defense education, escort service, and informal discussions. There are pamphlets/posters/films, emergency telephones, and lighted pathways/sidewalks.

Programs of Study: SDSU confers B.A., B.S., and B.M. degrees. Master's and doctoral degrees are also awarded. Bachelor's degrees are awarded in BIOLOGICAL SCIENCE (biology/biological science, microbiology, and nutrition), BUSINESS (accounting, banking and finance, business administration and management, international business management, marketing/retailing/merchandising, and real estate), COMMUNICATIONS AND THE ARTS (broadcasting, classics, communications, comparative literature, dance, dramatic arts, English, fine arts, French, German, Japanese, journalism, linguistics, music, Russian, and Spanish), COMPUTER AND PHYSICAL SCIENCE (astronomy, chemistry, computer science, geology, information sciences and systems, mathematics, physical sciences, physics, and statistics), EDUCATION (vocational), ENGINEERING AND ENVIRONMENTAL DESIGN (aeronautical engineering, civil engineering, computer engineering, electrical/electronics engineering, environmental engineering, and mechanical engineering), HEALTH PROFESSIONS (exercise science, health science, nursing, and speech pathology/audiology), SOCIAL SCIENCE (African studies, American studies, anthropology, Asian/Oriental studies, child psychology/development, criminal justice, economics, European studies, geography, gerontology, history, humanities, Latin American studies, Mexican-American/Chicano studies, parks and recreation management, peace studies, philosophy, political science/government, psychology, public administration, religion, Russian and Slavic studies, social science, social work, sociology, urban studies, and women's studies). Business administration is the strongest academically and the largest.

Required: To graduate, students must complete 124 to 133 credit hours, including 49 general education units. The number of hours in the major varies by program. A 2.0 or higher GPA must be maintained, depending on the major. Students must demonstrate math and writing competency and fulfill requirements in upper-division writing and in American Institutions. History majors must complete a senior thesis.

Special: Students may study abroad in London and Paris and receive credit for life, military, and work experience. Cross-registration with the University of California, community colleges, and California State University, internships, dual majors, an interdisciplinary major, a political science internship in Sacramento or Washington, D.C., an off-campus public administration program, and a prelaw program in cooperation with California Western School of Law are available. There are 30 national honor societies, including Phi Beta Kappa, a freshman honors program, and 24 departmental honors programs.

Faculty/Classroom: 61% of faculty are male; 39%, female. Graduate students teach 13% of introductory courses. The average class size in an introductory lecture is 32 and in a regular course, 29.

Admissions: 67% of the 2001-2002 applicants were accepted. The SAT I scores for the 2001-2002 freshman class were: Verbal--45% below 500, 42% between 500 and 599, 11% between 600 and 700, and 1% above 700; Math--35% below 500, 46% between 500 and 599, 18% between 600 and 700, and 1% above 700. The ACT scores were 46% below 21, 29% between 21 and 23, 18% between 24 and 26, 6% between 27 and 28, and 1% above 28.

Requirements: The SAT I or ACT is required. In addition, applicants must have a qualifying CSU eligibility index, based on a combination of GPA and standardized test scores. Candidates for admission should have completed 4 years of English, 3 of math, 2 of a foreign language, 1 each of science with lab, U.S. history, and visual and performing arts, and 3 of electives. A GPA of 2.0 is required. Applications are accepted on-line via the admissions web site.

Procedure: Freshmen are admitted fall and spring. Entrance exams should be taken by October of the senior year. Applications should be filed by November 30 for fall entry and August 31 for spring entry. The fall 2001 application fee was $55. Notification is sent on a rolling basis, beginning in early March.

Transfer: 2838 transfer students enrolled in 2001-2002. A minimum 2.0 GPA is required. Students with fewer than 56 transferable semester units must complete the regular admission procedure. Any number of units are accepted from a 4-year institution, but a maximum of 70 units may transfer from a 2-year institution.

Visiting: There are regularly scheduled orientations for prospective students, including tours that can be scheduled with SDSU ambassadors. Visitors may stay overnight. To schedule a visit, contact Housing and Residential Life at (619) 594-6868.

Financial Aid: In 2001-2002, 62% of all freshmen and 53% of continuing students received some form of financial aid. 40% of all students received need-based aid. The average freshman award was $6500. The average financial indebtedness of the 2001 graduate was $13,500. SDSU is a member of CSS. The CSS/Profile or FAFSA and SAAC are required. The preferred fall application deadline is March 2.

International Students: There are 859 international students enrolled. They must score 550 on the written TOEFL and also take the college's own test.

Computers: The mainframes are an IBM-390 MVS System, a VAX Sun SPARC-1000E, and a SPARC-20. Student accounts are available by application; there is both on-campus and off-campus access. Various labs on campus with approximately 2000 computers are available. All students may access the system. There are no time limits and no fees.

Graduates: In 2001, 5083 bachelor's degrees were awarded. The most popular majors were liberal studies (9%), psychology (8%), and criminal justice administration (5%). In an average class, 4% graduate in 4 years, 23% in 5 years, and 33% in 6 years.

Admissions Contact: Kathleen Deaver, Director of Admissions.
E-mail: *arweb.sdsu.edu/es/admissions* Web: *www.csumentor.edu*

SAN FRANCISCO ART INSTITUTE — B-3

San Francisco, CA 94133 — (415) 749-4500
(800) 345-SFAI; Fax: (415) 749-4592

Full-time: 225 men, 200 women	**Faculty:** 35
Part-time: 40 men, 40 women	**Ph.D.s:** 99%
Graduate: 50 men, 80 women	**Student/Faculty:** 12 to 1
Year: semesters, summer session	**Tuition:** $19,400
Application Deadline: see profile	**Room & Board:** n/app
Freshman Class: n/av	
SAT I or ACT: required	**SPECIAL**

San Francisco Art Institute, founded in 1871, is a private, commuter college devoted solely to the fine arts. In addition to regional accreditation, SFAI has baccalaureate program accreditation with NASAD. Information in the above capsule, and in this profile, is approximate. The library contains 22,000 volumes and 1500 audiovisual forms/CDs, and subscribes to 210 periodicals. Special learning facilities include a learning resource center and art gallery. The 3-acre campus is in an urban area. There is one building.

Student Life: Others are from Canada. 66% are white; 11% foreign nationals. The average age of freshmen is 26; all undergraduates, 26. 12% do not continue beyond their first year; 15% remain to graduate.

Housing: There are no residence halls. All students commute. Alcohol is not permitted.

Activities: There are no fraternities or sororities. There are 7 groups on campus, including art, ethnic, gay, international, newspaper, and student government. Popular campus events include visiting artist lectures, symposia, and graduate open studios.

Sports: There is no sports program at SFAI.

Disabled Students: 70% of the campus is accessible. Wheelchair ramps, elevators, special parking, specially equipped rest rooms, and special class scheduling are available.

Services: Counseling and information services are available, as is tutoring in most subjects. There is remedial math, reading, and writing.

Campus Safety and Security: Measures include 24-hour foot and vehicle patrol, emergency telephones, and video security cameras.

Programs of Study: SFAI confers the B.F.A. degree. Master's degrees are also awarded. Bachelor's degrees are awarded in COMMUNICATIONS AND THE ARTS (film arts, fine arts, painting, photography, printmaking, sculpture, and video). Painting and photography are the largest.

Required: Students are required to complete at least 120 credit hours, 36 of which must be in the major. 6 liberal arts units, 24 studio units, and 15 art history units must be completed, as well as 33 units in the Letters and Science Program. SFAI requires a minimum GPA of 2.0.

Special: Students may participate in off-campus internships for credit. There are study-abroad opportunities in 9 countries. There is an interdisciplinary program in which studio curricula are chosen that best support specific artistic direction. The institute offers dual majors in all subjects, nondegree study, work-study with SFAI, and pass/fail options in the senior year.

Faculty/Classroom: 52% of faculty are male; 48%, female. 96% teach undergraduates. No introductory courses are taught by graduate students. The average class size in an introductory lecture is 100; in a laboratory, 17; and in a regular course, 17.

Admissions: 69% of the 2001-2002 applicants were accepted.

Requirements: The SAT I or ACT is required, with a minimum required score of 20 on the ACT or 420 on the SAT I verbal. A GPA of 2.5 is required. AP and CLEP credits are accepted. Important factors in the admissions decision are evidence of special talent, recommendations by school officials, and recommendations by alumni.
Procedure: Freshmen are admitted to all sessions. There is a deferred admissions plan. Check with the school for current application deadlines and fee. Notification is sent on a rolling basis.
Transfer: 136 transfer students enrolled in a recent year. Transfer students must have satisfactory prior college performance and a portfolio appropriate to their level of experience. College transcripts and an essay are required. 30 credits of 120 must be completed at SFAI.
Visiting: There are guides for informal visits and visitors may sit in on classes. To schedule a visit, contact the Office of Admissions.
Financial Aid: The FAFSA is required. Check with the school for current deadlines.
International Students: There were 48 international students enrolled in a recent year. The school actively recruits these students. They must score 500 on the written TOEFL.
Computers: The mainframe is an HP. Students have access to 3 computer labs. 6 Macs are for students in the tutoring center, and 6 Amigas can be used for video processing. 24 Macs are available in the Center for Digital Media. All students may access the system. Students registered in CDM classes may access the system from 9 A.M. to 10 P.M. There are no time limits.
Graduates: In a recent year, 149 bachelor's degrees were awarded. The most popular majors were multidisciplinary studies (38%), painting (32%), and photography (18%). In an average class, 33% graduate in 5 years.
Admissions Contact: Mark Takiguchi, Director of Admissions.
E-mail: *admissions@sfai.edu* Web: *www.sfai.edu*

SAN FRANCISCO CONSERVATORY OF MUSIC — B-3

San Francisco, CA 94122 (415) 759-3431; Fax: (415) 759-3499

Full-time: 60 men, 75 women	**Faculty:** 24
Part-time: 3 men, 3 women	**Ph.D.s:** 21%
Graduate: 45 men, 84 women	**Student/Faculty:** 6 to 1
Year: semesters	**Tuition:** $20,780
Application Deadline: February 1	**Room & Board:** n/app
Freshman Class: 116 applied, 73 accepted, 21 enrolled	
SAT I Verbal/Math: 580/550	**SPECIAL**

San Francisco Conservatory of Music, founded in 1917, is a private institution offering undergraduate, graduate, and nondegree programs in music. There is 1 graduate school. In addition to regional accreditation, SFCM has baccalaureate program accreditation with NASM. The library contains 44,782 volumes and 15,538 audiovisual forms/CDs, and subscribes to 72 periodicals. Computerized library services include the card catalog, interlibrary loans, and database searching. The 5-acre campus is in an urban area in a residential neighborhood of San Francisco. There are 3 buildings.
Student Life: 57% are white, 16% foreign nationals; 14% Asian Americans. The average age of freshmen is 18.5; all undergraduates, 21.
Housing: There are no residence halls. All students commute. All students may keep cars.
Activities: There are no fraternities or sororities. There are 5 groups on campus, including chorale, musical theater, opera, orchestra, student government, and symphony. Popular campus events include the nearly 300 recitals and concerts scheduled each year.
Sports: There is no sports program at SFCM.
Disabled Students: 90% of the campus is accessible. Wheelchair ramps, elevators, special parking, and specially equipped rest rooms are available.
Campus Safety and Security: Measures include self-defense education, informal discussions, pamphlets/posters/films, and emergency telephones. There are lighted pathways/sidewalks.
Programs of Study: SFCM confers the B.Mus. degree. Master's degrees are also awarded. Bachelor's degrees are awarded in COMMUNICATIONS AND THE ARTS (music). Voice, piano, and violin are the largest.
Required: Students must complete 130 credit hours, 100 of which must be music related, and the remainder in general education courses, including courses in fine arts, English, history, and humanities. Specific required courses and total number of hours in the major vary by instrument. Students must also pass the senior recital and maintain a minimum GPA of 2.0.
Special: Work-study programs and accelerated degree programs are available.
Faculty/Classroom: 67% of faculty are male; 33%, female. All teach undergraduates. No introductory courses are taught by graduate students. The average class size in an introductory lecture is 15 and in a regular course, 7.
Admissions: 63% of the 2001-2002 applicants were accepted. The SAT I scores for the 2001-2002 freshman class were: Verbal--27% below 500, 27% between 500 and 599, 37% between 600 and 700, and 9% above 700; Math--20% below 500, 53% between 500 and 599, 20% between 600 and 700, and 7% above 700. 36% of the current freshmen were in the top fifth of their class; 57% were in the top two fifths.
Requirements: The SAT I or ACT is required. In addition, all applicants must have reached a high level of musical proficiency. An audition is required. A GPA of 2.5 is required. AP and CLEP credits are accepted. Important factors in the admissions decision are evidence of special talent, personality/intangible qualities, and extracurricular activities record.
Procedure: Freshmen are admitted fall and spring. Entrance exams should be taken by the late fall or early spring. There is an early admissions plan. Applications should be filed by February 1 for fall entry and November 1 for spring entry. Notification is sent April 1. 12% of all applicants are on a waiting list; 12 were accepted in 2001. The fall 2001 application fee was $70.
Transfer: 19 transfer students enrolled in 2001-2002. Transfer students must demonstrate a high level of musical proficiency, submit 2 letters of recommendation, and have a good academic record. An audition is required. 30 credits of 130 must be completed at SFCM.
Visiting: There are guides for informal visits and visitors may sit in on classes. To schedule a visit, contact Alex Brose in the Admissions Office.
Financial Aid: In 2001-2002, 71% of all freshmen and 75% of continuing students received some form of financial aid. 71% of freshmen and 72% of continuing students received need-based aid. The average freshman award was $11,960. Of that total, scholarships or need-based grants averaged $10,320; and loans averaged $2330. 85% of undergraduates work part time. Average annual earnings from campus work are $1700. The average financial indebtedness of the 2001 graduate was $17,650. The FAFSA and the college's own financial statement are required. The fall application deadline is March 1.
International Students: There are 29 international students enrolled. They must score 500 on the written TOEFL or 173 on the electronic version and also take the SAT I or the ACT.
Computers: Students have access to a computer lab equipped with Mac PCs, electronic keyboards, and a laser printer. Software includes class tutorials and a variety of commercially available music programs. All students may access the system when the building is open. There are no time limits and no fees.
Graduates: In 2001, 24 bachelor's degrees were awarded. The most popular majors were piano (21%), voice (21%), and cello (12%). In an average class, 61% graduate in 4 years, 64% in 5 years, and 64% in 6 years. Of the 2000 graduating class, 44% were enrolled in graduate school within 6 months of graduation and 52% were employed.
Admissions Contact: Alex Brose, Admissions Office.
E-mail: *admit@sfcm.edu* Web: *www.sfcm.edu*

SAN FRANCISCO STATE UNIVERSITY — B-3

San Francisco, CA 94132 (415) 338-2355; Fax: (415) 338-0903

Full-time: 14,640 men and women	**Faculty:** 977; IIA, ++$
Part-time: 6090 men and women	**Ph.D.s:** n/av
Graduate: 6260 men and women	**Student/Faculty:** 15 to 1
Year: semesters, summer session	**Tuition:** $1826 ($9206)
Application Deadline: see profile	**Room & Board:** $5313
Freshman Class: n/av	
SAT I or ACT: required	**LESS COMPETITIVE**

San Francisco State University, founded in 1899, is a public liberal arts institution offering graduate and undergraduate programs as part of the California State University system. Figures given in above capsule are approximate. There are 8 undergraduate and 8 graduate schools. In addition to regional accreditation, San Francisco State has baccalaureate program accreditation with AACSB, ACEJMC, ADA, AHEA, NASM, and NLN. The library contains 636,000 volumes and 970,000 microform items, and subscribes to 560,000 periodicals. Computerized library services include the card catalog. Special learning facilities include a learning resource center, art gallery, natural history museum, planetarium, radio station, TV station, a field campus, the Labor Archives and Research Center, a Media Access Center, and an anthropology museum. The 130-acre campus is in an urban area. Including residence halls, there are 23 buildings.
Student Life: 78% of undergraduates are from California. Others are from 17 states, 12 foreign countries, and Canada. 48% are white; 28% Asian American; 10% Hispanic. The average age of all undergraduates is 24. 17% do not continue beyond their first year; 62% remain to graduate.
Housing: Housing includes coed dormitories. On-campus housing is available on a first-come, first-served basis. 95% of students commute. Alcohol is not permitted. All students may keep cars.
Activities: There are 12 national fraternities and 4 local and 8 national sororities. There are 200 groups on campus, including art, band, cheerleading, chorale, dance, drama, ethnic, film, gay, honors, jazz band, literary magazine, musical theater, newspaper, opera, orchestra, pep band, political, radio and TV, social service, student government, symphony, and yearbook. Popular campus events include Activities Fair and Crafts

Festival, Morrison Artists' Series Chamber Music Program, and the Alexander String Quartet.
Sports: There are 8 intercollegiate sports for men and 7 for women, and 10 intramural sports for men and 10 for women. Facilities include a 6500-seat stadium, 2 gyms, an indoor pool, a weight room, a training room, wrestling and gymnastics areas, an all-weather track, 14 tennis courts, softball and baseball fields, and auxiliary practice fields.
Disabled Students: Wheelchair ramps, elevators, special parking, specially equipped rest rooms, lowered drinking fountains, lowered telephones, and readers, interpreters, an equipment loan, on-campus transportation, and priority registration are available.
Services: Counseling and information services are available, as is tutoring in every subject.
Campus Safety and Security: Measures include escort service, shuttle buses, emergency telephones, and lighted pathways/sidewalks.
Programs of Study: San Francisco State confers B.A., B.S., B.M., and B.Voc.Ed. degrees. Associate, master's, and doctoral degrees are also awarded. Bachelor's degrees are awarded in BIOLOGICAL SCIENCE (biochemistry, biology/biological science, botany, cell biology, ecology, marine biology, microbiology, physiology, and zoology), BUSINESS (accounting, banking and finance, business administration and management, international business management, labor studies, management science, marketing/retailing/merchandising, personnel management, real estate, and transportation management), COMMUNICATIONS AND THE ARTS (broadcasting, Chinese, classics, comparative literature, dance, dramatic arts, English, film arts, fine arts, French, German, Italian, Japanese, journalism, music, Russian, and speech/debate/rhetoric), COMPUTER AND PHYSICAL SCIENCE (applied mathematics, chemistry, computer science, geology, information sciences and systems, mathematics, physics, science, and statistics), EDUCATION (early childhood, elementary, home economics, industrial arts, physical, recreation, secondary, special, and vocational), ENGINEERING AND ENVIRONMENTAL DESIGN (civil engineering, electrical/electronics engineering, engineering, industrial administration/management, interior design, and mechanical engineering), HEALTH PROFESSIONS (allied health, clinical science, health science, medical laboratory technology, nursing, physical therapy, public health, and speech pathology/audiology), SOCIAL SCIENCE (African American studies, American studies, anthropology, clothing and textiles management/production/services, dietetics, economics, geography, history, humanities, interdisciplinary studies, international relations, liberal arts/general studies, philosophy, political science/government, psychology, social work, sociology, urban studies, and women's studies).
Required: To graduate, students must complete 124 to 132 credits with a minimum GPA of 2.0. The required general education core includes 27 credits in arts and sciences, 12 in basic skills subjects, and 9 in upper-division courses. English composition and U.S. history and government competency requirements may be fulfilled by either exam or course work.
Special: Students may cross-register with the California College of Podiatric Medicine, the City College of San Francisco, Cogswell College of Engineering, and several other area universities. Study abroad in numerous countries, a Washington semester, campus work-study, a general studies degree, dual and student-designed majors, credit for life experience, nondegree study, and pass/fail options are also offered. There is a chapter of Phi Beta Kappa.
Faculty/Classroom: 61% of faculty are male; 39%, female. No introductory courses are taught by graduate students.
Requirements: The SAT I or ACT is required. In addition, applicants should be graduates of an accredited secondary school with a minimum GPA of 2.0. The GED is accepted. High school courses should include 4 years of English, 3 of math, 2 of foreign language, and 1 each of U.S. history or government, lab science, and visual and performing arts. A GPA of 2.0 is required. AP and CLEP credits are accepted.
Procedure: Freshmen are admitted fall and spring. Notification is sent on a rolling basis. The fall 2001 application fee was $55. Check with the school for current deadlines.
Transfer: Applicants must have a college GPA of 2.0 (2.4 for nonresidents). Those with fewer than 56 tranferable semester credits must meet freshman entrance requirements. 30 credits of 124 must be completed at San Francisco State.
Visiting: There are regularly scheduled orientations for prospective students. Visitors may sit in on classes. To schedule a visit, contact Student Outreach Services.
Financial Aid: San Francisco State is a member of CSS. The CSS/Profile or FFS is required. Check with the school for current application deadlines.
International Students: They must score 500 on the written TOEFL.
Computers: The mainframes are a DEC VAX 6420 and an IBM 4381/R22. There are 46 dial-in modems, 50 CD-ROM and on-line databases, more than 100 networked terminals, and more than 1000 IBM, Mac, and other PCs available for student use. All students may access the system 24 hours daily. There are no time limits and no fees.
Admissions Contact: Student Outreach Services.
E-mail: *outreach@sfsu.edu* Web: *www.sfsu.edu*

SAN JOSE STATE UNIVERSITY — B-3

San Jose, CA 95192 — (408) 924-2000; Fax: (408) 924-2050

Full-time: 6980 men, 7620 women — **Faculty:** 868
Part-time: 3440 men, 3400 women — **Ph.D.s:** 84%
Graduate: 1980 men, 3550 women — **Student/Faculty:** 17 to 1
Year: semesters, summer session — **Tuition:** $2000 ($7900)
Application Deadline: open — **Room & Board:** $6300
Freshman Class: 2406 enrolled
SAT I Verbal/Math: required — **COMPETITIVE**

San Jose State University, founded in 1857 and part of the California State University system, is a public institution offering undergraduate and graduate programs in applied arts and science, social science, and social work to a primarily commuter student body. There are 8 undergraduate and 8 graduate schools. Figures in the above capsule, and in this profile, are approximate. In addition to regional accreditation, SJSU has baccalaureate program accreditation with AACSB, ABET, ACEJMC, ADA, ASLA, NASAD, NASM, NCATE, and NLN. The 2 libraries contain 1,101,995 volumes, 1,621,426 microform items, and 37,146 audiovisual forms/CDs, and subscribe to 2504 periodicals. Computerized library services include the card catalog, interlibrary loans, and database searching. Special learning facilities include a learning resource center, art gallery, radio station, and TV station. The 104-acre campus is in an urban area in the center of San Jose. Including residence halls, there are 55 buildings.
Student Life: Others are from 40 states, 114 foreign countries, and Canada. 89% are from public schools. 36% are Asian American; 30% white; 14% Hispanic. The average age of freshmen is 20; all undergraduates, 25.
Housing: 2014 students can be accommodated in college housing, which includes coed dormitories, on-campus apartments, fraternity houses, and sorority houses. In addition, there are special-interest houses. On-campus housing is available on a first-come, first-served basis. Alcohol is not permitted. All students may keep cars.
Activities: 8% of men belong to 6 local and 15 national fraternities; 4% of women belong to 3 local and 9 national sororities. There are 175 groups on campus, including art, band, cheerleading, choir, chorale, chorus, dance, drama, ethnic, film, gay, international, literary magazine, marching band, musical theater, newspaper, photography, political, radio and TV, social, student government, and symphony. Popular campus events include International Food Bazaar, Welcome Day, and National Collegiate Alcohol Awareness Week.
Sports: There are 6 intercollegiate sports for men and 10 for women, and 17 intramural sports for men and 13 for women. Facilities include a gym, a pool, a track, a football field, and a recreation center with racquetball courts and a bowling alley.
Disabled Students: 95% of the campus is accessible. Wheelchair ramps, elevators, special parking, specially equipped rest rooms, special class scheduling, lowered drinking fountains, lowered telephones, and preadmission assistance are available.
Services: Counseling and information services are available, as is tutoring in most subjects. There is a reader service for the blind. There are also test accommodations, sign-language interpreters, liaisons to faculty, and note takers.
Campus Safety and Security: Measures include 24-hour foot and vehicle patrol, self-defense education, escort service, and shuttle buses. There are informal discussions, pamphlets/posters/films, emergency telephones, lighted pathways/sidewalks, and and a canine patrol.
Programs of Study: SJSU confers B.A., B.S., B.F.A., and B.Mus. degrees. Master's degrees are also awarded. Bachelor's degrees are awarded in BIOLOGICAL SCIENCE (biochemistry, biology/biological science, botany, microbiology, and zoology), BUSINESS (accounting, banking and finance, business administration and management, international business management, and marketing/retailing/merchandising), COMMUNICATIONS AND THE ARTS (advertising, broadcasting, dance, design, dramatic arts, English, film arts, fine arts, French, German, journalism, music, Spanish, and speech/debate/rhetoric), COMPUTER AND PHYSICAL SCIENCE (chemistry, computer science, geology, mathematics, physics, and statistics), EDUCATION (early childhood and teaching English as a second/foreign language (TESOL/TEFOL)), ENGINEERING AND ENVIRONMENTAL DESIGN (aeronautical engineering, chemical engineering, civil engineering, computer engineering, electrical/electronics engineering, engineering, industrial engineering, interior design, materials engineering, and mechanical engineering), HEALTH PROFESSIONS (nursing, occupational therapy, and speech pathology/audiology), SOCIAL SCIENCE (anthropology, criminal justice, economics, food science, geography, history, philosophy, political science/government, psychology, religion, social science, social work, and sociology). Accounting is the strongest academically. Accounting, electrical engineering, and management are the largest.
Required: Students must complete 39 units of core general education, including 12 units of upper-division courses in residence and 6 units of American history and institutions. A minimum of 124 credits, with at least 24 in the major, a minimum GPA of 2.0, and the successful com-

pletion of writing, English, and entry-level math tests are required to graduate.

Special: SJSU has opportunities for cooperative programs in business, science, engineering, arts, and the humanities, work-study with many employers, internships (some required, some optional), study abroad in 16 countries, field experiences, and student teaching. An accelerated program is offered in nursing, and the B.A.-B.S. degree and dual majors are available in various areas of study. A general studies degree, student-designed majors, nondegree study, and credit/no-credit options are possible. There are 3 national honor societies and 18 departmental honors programs.

Faculty/Classroom: 66% of faculty are male; 34%, female. The average class size in an introductory lecture is 30; in a laboratory, 20; and in a regular course, 25.

Requirements: The SAT I or ACT is required. In addition, scores are used to calculate an eligibility index rating, which determines qualification for admission. Graduation from an accredited secondary school is required; the GED is accepted. Applicants must have completed 4 years of English, 3 each of math and electives, 2 of a foreign language, and 1 each of history, science, and art. A GPA of 2.1 is required. AP and CLEP credits are accepted. Important factors in the admissions decision are personality/intangible qualities, recommendations by alumni, and recommendations by school officials. Applications are accepted on-line.

Procedure: Freshmen are admitted fall and spring. Entrance exams should be taken prior to the fall semester. There are early admissions and deferred admissions plans. Application deadlines are open. Check with the school for current fee.

Transfer: 2779 transfer students enrolled in a recent year. Applicants must have a minimum GPA of 2.0. The student's rating in the eligibility index is also considered in determining qualification for transfer. 30 credits of 124 must be completed at SJSU.

Visiting: There are regularly scheduled orientations for prospective students. There are guides for informal visits and visitors may sit in on classes. To schedule a visit, contact the Office of Relations with Schools at (408) 924-2564.

Financial Aid: SJSU is a member of CSS. The FAFSA is required. Check with the school for current deadlines.

International Students: There are 498 international students enrolled. The school actively recruits these students. They must score 500 on the written TOEFL and also take the SAT I or the ACT.

Computers: The mainframe is an IBM 3090. About 50% of students use the 1597 PCs available, about 300 of which are networked. All students may access the system 9 A.M. to 8 P.M. Monday through Friday and 9 A.M. to 5 P.M. Saturday.

Graduates: In a recent year, 4099 bachelor's degrees were awarded. The most popular majors were information resource management (7%), accounting (5%), and psychology (5%). In an average class, 9% graduate in 4 years, 39% in 5 years, and 70% in 6 years. 949 companies recruited on campus in a recent year.

Admissions Contact: John Bradbury, Director of Admissions.
E-mail: *contact@anrnet.sjsu.edu*

SANTA CLARA UNIVERSITY D-3

Santa Clara, CA 95053 **(408) 554-4700; Fax: (408) 554-5255**

Full-time: 1923 men, 2228 women	**Faculty:** 360; IIA, ++$
Part-time: 58 men, 70 women	**Ph.D.s:** 91%
Graduate: 1684 men, 1405 women	**Student/Faculty:** 12 to 1
Year: quarters, summer session	**Tuition:** $20,337
Application Deadline: January 15	**Room & Board:** $8034
Freshman Class: 6049 applied, 3823 accepted, 1018 enrolled	
SAT I Verbal/Math: 608/631	**ACT:** 27 **VERY COMPETITIVE+**

Santa Clara University, founded in 1851 by Jesuit priests, is a private institution offering undergraduate and graduate degrees in arts and sciences, engineering, business law, education, and counseling. There are 3 undergraduate and 5 graduate schools. In addition to regional accreditation, Santa Clara University has baccalaureate program accreditation with AACSB, ABET, and NASM. The 2 libraries contain 529,398 volumes, 764,430 microform items, and 8536 audiovisual forms/CDs, and subscribe to 5201 periodicals. Computerized library services include the card catalog, interlibrary loans, and database searching. Special learning facilities include a learning resource center, art gallery, planetarium, radio station, TV station, and California Mission (archeology lab). The 104-acre campus is in a suburban area 46 miles south of San Francisco. Including residence halls, there are 51 buildings.

Student Life: 69% of undergraduates are from California. Others are from 32 states, 10 foreign countries, and Canada. 52% are from public schools. 55% are white; 19% Asian American, 14% Hispanic. 51% are Catholic; 18% Protestant; 17% claim no religious affiliation. The average age of freshmen is 19; all undergraduates, 21. 8% do not continue beyond their first year; 80% remain to graduate.

Housing: 1803 students can be accommodated in college housing, which includes coed dormitories, on-campus apartments, and off-campus apartments. All freshman students select one of 9 residential learning communities (RLCs). Approximately 75% of sophomores participate in RLCs. Juniors and seniors can apply for the Sobrato apartment-style learning community. On-campus housing is guaranteed for the freshman year only, is available on a first-come, first-served basis, and on a lottery system for upperclassmen. Priority is given to out-of-town students. 51% of students commute. All students may keep cars.

Activities: There are no fraternities or sororities. There are 55 groups on campus, including art, cheerleading, choir, chorale, chorus, computers, dance, debate, drama, ethnic, film, forensics, gay, gospel choir, honors, international, jazz band, literary magazine, major-specific, musical theater, newspaper, opera, orchestra, pep band, photography, political, professional, radio and TV, religious, social, social service, student government, symphony, and yearbook. Popular campus events include Bronco Bust (Spirit Week), Special Olympics, and Cinco de Mayo.

Sports: There are 8 intercollegiate sports for men and 9 for women, and 6 intramural sports for men and 11 for women. Facilities include an activities center with a basketball pavilion, volleyball courts, a swimming pool, a weight-training section, and a sauna. There also is a 6,800-seat stadium with practice fields nearby, and several fields for general recreation and intramurals.

Disabled Students: All of the campus is accessible. Wheelchair ramps, elevators, special parking, specially equipped rest rooms, special class scheduling, lowered drinking fountains, lowered telephones, and TTY (hard-of-hearing phone system) are available. Residence halls have been restructured to allow disabled students to open all doors with a remote control. Scribes and notetakers are also provided.

Services: Counseling and information services are available, as is tutoring in most subjects. Text books on tape, reader service as needed, and print enlargement for students with poor vision is provided.

Campus Safety and Security: Measures include 24-hour foot and vehicle patrol, escort service, informal discussions, and pamphlets/posters/films. There are emergency telephones, lighted pathways/sidewalks, and self-help information, including meetings with local police on crime prevention and behavior ground rules.

Programs of Study: Santa Clara University confers B.A., B.S., B.S.C., and B.S.Ch. degrees. Master's and doctoral degrees are also awarded. Bachelor's degrees are awarded in BIOLOGICAL SCIENCE (biology/biological science), BUSINESS (accounting, banking and finance, business economics, marketing/retailing/merchandising, and organizational behavior), COMMUNICATIONS AND THE ARTS (art, art history and appreciation, classics, communications, dramatic arts, English, French, German, Greek, Italian, Latin, music, Spanish, and studio art), COMPUTER AND PHYSICAL SCIENCE (chemistry, computer science, information sciences and systems, mathematics, physics, and science), ENGINEERING AND ENVIRONMENTAL DESIGN (civil engineering, computer engineering, electrical/electronics engineering, engineering, engineering physics, and mechanical engineering), SOCIAL SCIENCE (anthropology, economics, history, interdisciplinary studies, liberal arts/general studies, philosophy, political science/government, psychology, religion, and sociology). Social sciences and engineering are the strongest academically. Social sciences and business are the largest.

Required: All students are required to maintain a GPA of at least 2.0 in both major and minor subjects. Students must take 175 quarter units for most bachelor's degrees. Core requirements include composition and literature, Western culture, foreign language, social sciences, math and natural sciences, technology, ethics, religious studies, United States, and World Cultures/Societies.

Special: Study abroad in 26 countries at 75 sites is offered, as are international internship and volunteer opportunities. A co-op program in engineering, dual majors, internships in business, government, and non-profit agencies, a general studies degree, student-designed majors, work-study, a Washington semester, and pass/fail options also are available. There are 21 national honor societies, including Phi Beta Kappa, a freshman honors program, and 4 departmental honors programs.

Faculty/Classroom: 63% of faculty are male; 37%, female. All both teach and do research. No introductory courses are taught by graduate students. The average class size in an introductory lecture is 29; in a laboratory, 13; and in a regular course, 22.

Admissions: 63% of the 2001-2002 applicants were accepted. The SAT I scores for the 2001-2002 freshman class were: Verbal--11% below 500, 42% between 500 and 599, 42% between 600 and 700, and 5% above 700; Math--5% below 500, 33% between 500 and 599, 52% between 600 and 700, and 10% above 700. 65% of the current freshmen were in the top fifth of their class; 92% were in the top two fifths. There were 54 National Merit finalists. 42 freshmen graduated first in their class.

Requirements: The SAT I is required. In addition, applicants should have 16 academic units, including 4 years of English, 3 each in math, foreign language, and science, 1 or 2 of which are a lab, 1 in history, and 2 1/2 to 4 in electives. An essay is required. An audition is recommended for theater arts majors.The GED is not accepted. AP credits are accepted. Important factors in the admissions decision are extracurricular activities record, advanced placement or honor courses, and recommendations by school officials. Applications are accepted on-line via Apply Yourself.

Procedure: Freshmen are admitted fall, winter, and spring. Entrance exams should be taken by February 1. There is an early admissions plan. Applications should be filed by January 15 for fall entry, along with a $55 fee. Notification is sent on a rolling basis. 8% of all applicants are on a waiting list.

Transfer: 193 transfer students enrolled in 2001-2002. Transfer students need a minimum GPA of 3.0. 87 quarter units of 175 must be completed at Santa Clara University.

Visiting: There are regularly scheduled orientations for prospective students, including an open house in October, with overviews of academic programs and student activities, and preview weekend in April for accepted students. There are guides for informal visits and accepted students may sit in on classes and stay overnight during the spring quarter. To schedule a visit, contact the Undergraduate Admissions Office.

Financial Aid: In 2001-2002, 64% of all freshmen and 61% of continuing students received some form of financial aid. 42% of freshmen and 45% of continuing students received need-based aid. The average freshman award was $16,987. Of that total, scholarships or need-based grants averaged $13,982 ($22,572 maximum); loans averaged $5910 ($6625 maximum); work contracts averaged $1970 ($2500 maximum); and athletic aid averaged $16,414 ($31,008 maximum). 57% of undergraduates work part time. Average annual earnings from campus work are $1324. The average financial indebtedness of the 2001 graduate was $24,810. Santa Clara University is a member of CSS. The CSS/Profile or FAFSA is required. The fall application deadline is February 1.

International Students: There are 120 international students enrolled. They must score 550 on the written TOEFL or 213 on the electronic version and also take the SAT I or the ACT.

Computers: The mainframes are an IBM 4381, a DEC VAX 8650, and a 750 DEC VAX. There are also PCs available in computer labs. All students may access the system. There are no time limits and no fees.

Graduates: In a recent year, 1073 bachelor's degrees were awarded. The most popular majors were finance (10%), marketing (8%), and psychology (8%). In an average class, 75% graduate in 4 years, 81% in 5 years, and 82% in 6 years. 230 companies recruited on campus in 2000-2001. Of the 2000 graduating class, 18% were enrolled in graduate school within 6 months of graduation.

Admissions Contact: Sandra Hayes, Dean of Admissions. A video is available. E-mail: *ugadmissions@scu.edu* Web: *www.scu.edu*

SCRIPPS COLLEGE

Claremont, CA 91711-3948 — D-5

(909) 621-8149
(800) 770-1333; Fax: (909) 607-7508

Full-time: 782 women	**Faculty:** 56; IIB, ++$
Part-time: 4 women	**Ph.D.s:** 97%
Graduate: none	**Student/Faculty:** 14 to 1
Year: semesters	**Tuition:** $22,600
Application Deadline: February 1	**Room & Board:** $7800
Freshman Class: 1200 applied, 771 accepted, 201 enrolled	
SAT I Verbal/Math: 650/620	**ACT:** 30

HIGHLY COMPETITIVE+

Scripps College, founded in 1926, is a private liberal arts institution for women. A member of the Claremont Colleges, Scripps emphasizes a challenging core curriculum based on interdisciplinary humanistic studies. The 4 libraries contain 2,088,476 volumes, 1,444,465 microform items, and 4361 audiovisual forms/CDs, and subscribe to 5733 periodicals. Computerized library services include the card catalog, interlibrary loans, and database searching. Special learning facilities include an art gallery, radio station, TV station, humanities museum, and biological field station. The 30-acre campus is in a suburban area 35 miles east of Los Angeles. Including residence halls, there are 20 buildings.

Student Life: 55% of undergraduates are from out of state, mostly the Northwest. Others are from 41 states and 15 foreign countries. 64% are from public schools. 58% are white; 16% Asian American. The average age of freshmen is 18; all undergraduates, 20. 12% do not continue beyond their first year; 76% remain to graduate.

Housing: 679 students can be accommodated in college housing, which includes dormitories and on-campus apartments. On-campus housing is guaranteed for all 4 years. 92% of students live on campus; of those, 80% remain on campus on weekends. All students may keep cars.

Activities: There are no fraternities. There are 200 groups on campus, including art, band, chess, choir, chorale, chorus, computers, dance, debate, drama, ethnic, film, gay, honors, international, jazz band, literary magazine, musical theater, newspaper, opera, orchestra, photography, political, professional, radio and TV, religious, social, social service, student government, symphony, and yearbook. Popular campus events include Break Away Series, Scripps Outdoor Adventure Program, and Freshman Mugging.

Sports: Facilities include 2 gyms, tennis and squash courts, 4 swimming pools, a climbing wall, a workout room, 2 outdoor tracks, and fields for baseball, softball, and soccer.

Disabled Students: 70% of the campus is accessible. Wheelchair ramps, elevators, special parking, specially equipped rest rooms, special class scheduling, lowered drinking fountains, and specialized dormitory space are available.

Services: Counseling and information services are available, as is tutoring in every subject. There is a reader service for the blind.

Campus Safety and Security: Measures include 24-hour foot and vehicle patrol, self-defense education, escort service, and informal discussions. There are pamphlets/posters/films, emergency telephones, and lighted pathways/sidewalks.

Programs of Study: Scripps confers the B.A. degree. Bachelor's degrees are awarded in BIOLOGICAL SCIENCE (biology/biological science and neurosciences), COMMUNICATIONS AND THE ARTS (art history and appreciation, classical languages, dance, dramatic arts, English, Germanic languages and literature, Italian, languages, music, and studio art), COMPUTER AND PHYSICAL SCIENCE (chemistry, mathematics, physics, science and management, and science technology), ENGINEERING AND ENVIRONMENTAL DESIGN (engineering, environmental science, and preengineering), SOCIAL SCIENCE (African American studies, American studies, anthropology, Asian/American studies, Asian/Oriental studies, classical/ancient civilization, economics, European studies, French studies, German area studies, Hispanic American studies, history, humanities, Italian studies, Judaic studies, Latin American studies, Mexican-American/Chicano studies, philosophy, political science/government, prelaw, psychology, religion, and women's studies). Premedicine, art, and English are the strongest academically. Social science is the largest.

Required: To graduate, students must complete a total of 128 credits, or 32 courses with a minimum C average. Core requirements include the 3-semester humanities core, 2 additional courses in humanities, and 1 course each in fine arts, letters, natural sciences, social sciences, and math. All students must also fulfill language and thesis requirements.

Special: Students may cross-register with any of the other Claremont Colleges. Scripps also offers internships, work-study programs, study abroad in 35 countries, a Washington semester, and student-designed, dual, and interdisciplinary majors, including organizational studies and science, technology, and society. Many courses are offered as seminars. There are 3-2 accelerated degree programs in the arts and business administration. A 3-2 engineering program (B.A.-B.S.) is offered with Harvey Mudd College, Washington University in St. Louis, USC, UC Berkeley, and Columbia, Stanford, and Boston Universities. There are 3 national honor societies, including Phi Beta Kappa.

Faculty/Classroom: 43% of faculty are male; 57%, female. All both teach and do research. The average class size in an introductory lecture is 30; in a laboratory, 20; and in a regular course, 17.

Admissions: 64% of the 2001-2002 applicants were accepted. The SAT I scores for the 2001-2002 freshman class were: Verbal--2% below 500, 18% between 500 and 599, 53% between 600 and 700, and 27% above 700; Math--4% below 500, 32% between 500 and 599, 50% between 600 and 700, and 14% above 700. The ACT scores were 15% between 27 and 28, and 84% above 28. 73% of the current freshmen were in the top fifth of their class; 95% were in the top two fifths. There were 15 National Merit finalists and 1 semifinalist. 5 freshmen graduated first in their class.

Requirements: The SAT I or ACT is required. In addition, applicants must have completed 4 units each of high school English and math, 3 each of lab science and social studies, and either 3 of a single foreign language or 2 each of 2 languages. SAT II: Subject tests and an interview are recommended. An essay and a graded writing assignment from the junior or senior year are required. Scripps requires applicants to be in the upper 50% of their class. A GPA of 3.0 is required. AP and CLEP credits are accepted. Important factors in the admissions decision are advanced placement or honor courses, evidence of special talent, and leadership record. Applications are accepted on computer disk and on-line.

Procedure: Freshmen are admitted fall and spring. Entrance exams should be taken by December of the senior year. There are early decision, early admissions, and deferred admissions plans. Early decision application should be filed by November 1 (fall) and January 1 (winter); regular applications, by February 1 for fall entry and November 15 for spring entry. The fall 2001 application fee was $50. Notification of early decision is sent December 15 (fall) and February 1 (winter); regular decision, April 1. 46 early decision candidates were accepted for the 2001-2002 class. 17% of all applicants are on a waiting list.

Transfer: 19 transfer students enrolled in 2001-2002. A cumulative college GPA of 3.0 is required. 64 credits of 128 must be completed at Scripps.

Visiting: There are guides for informal visits and visitors may sit in on classes and stay overnight. To schedule a visit, contact the Admission Office.

Financial Aid: In 2001-2002, 63% of all freshmen and 62% of continuing students received some form of financial aid. 51% of all students received need-based aid. The average freshman award was $21,430. Of that total, scholarships or need-based grants averaged $18,685 ($26,237 maximum); loans averaged $1786 ($3625 maximum); and work con-

tracts averaged $1704 ($1800 maximum). Average annual earnings from campus work are $1024. The average financial indebtedness of the 2001 graduate was $13,394. Scripps is a member of CSS. The CSS/Profile or FAFSA is required. The fall application deadline is February 1.
International Students: There were 19 international students enrolled in a recent year. The school actively recruits these students. They must score 600 on the written TOEFL and also take the SAT I or the ACT.
Computers: The mainframe is a DEC VAX. Macs and PCs are available in computer labs and dormitories. Students are served by the Novell Network, with access to the Internet, including direct access from their rooms. All students may access the system. There are no time limits and no fees.
Graduates: In 2001, 166 bachelor's degrees were awarded. The most popular majors were psychology (12%), biology (10%), and English (9%). In an average class, 1% graduate in 3 years, 69% in 4 years, 74% in 5 years, and 77% in 6 years. 180 companies recruited on campus in 2000-2001. Of the 2000 graduating class, 27% were enrolled in graduate school within 6 months of graduation and 69% were employed.
Admissions Contact: Patricia F. Goldsmith, Vice President and Dean of Admission, Financial Aid. E-mail: *admofc@ad.scrippscol.edu*
Web: *www.scrippscol.edu*

SIMPSON COLLEGE
Redding, CA 96003 B-3
(530) 226-4606
(800) 598-2493; Fax: (530) 226-4861

Full-time: 331 men, 633 women	**Faculty:** 36
Part-time: 7 men, 15 women	**Ph.D.s:** 64%
Graduate: 71 men, 104 women	**Student/Faculty:** 27 to 1
Year: semesters, summer session	**Tuition:** $13,680
Application Deadline: open	**Room & Board:** $5520
Freshman Class: 683 applied, 419 accepted, 146 enrolled	
SAT I Verbal/Math: 530/510	**ACT:** 21 **COMPETITIVE**

Simpson College, founded in 1921, is a private Christian liberal arts institution affiliated with the Christian and Missionary Alliance. Some information in this profile is approximate. There is 1 graduate school. The library contains 69,000 volumes, 178,355 microform items, and 1475 audiovisual forms/CDs, and subscribes to 419 periodicals. Computerized library services include the card catalog, interlibrary loans, and database searching. The 60-acre campus is in a suburban area 3 miles northeast of Redding. Including residence halls, there are 11 buildings.
Student Life: 75% of undergraduates are from California. Others are from 28 states, 8 foreign countries, and Canada. 60% are from public schools. 87% are white. Most are Protestant. The average age of freshmen is 18; all undergraduates, 25. 65% do not continue beyond their first year.
Housing: 536 students can be accommodated in college housing, which includes single-sex dormitories and off-campus apartments. On-campus housing is guaranteed for all 4 years. 71% of students live on campus; of those, 90% remain on campus on weekends. Alcohol is not permitted. All students may keep cars.
Activities: There are no fraternities or sororities. There are 14 groups on campus, including choir, chorale, drama, literary magazine, newspaper, pep band, photography, professional, religious, social, social service, student government, and yearbook. Popular campus events include Spring and Winter Banquet, Missions Emphasis Week, and Multicultural Appreciation Day.
Sports: There are 4 intercollegiate sports for men and 4 for women, and 5 intramural sports for men and 5 for women. Facilities include a soccer field, 1450-seat gym, weight and training rooms, softball field, and outdoor volleyball and basketball courts. Students have access to nearby facilities for swimming, boating, mountain climbing, and skiing.
Disabled Students: 95% of the campus is accessible. Wheelchair ramps, elevators, special parking, specially equipped rest rooms, lowered drinking fountains, lowered telephones, and specially equipped dormitory rooms are available.
Services: Counseling and information services are available, as is tutoring in some subjects, depending on student requests. There is remedial math, reading, and writing, and instruction in English as a second language.
Campus Safety and Security: Measures include 24-hour foot and vehicle patrol, shuttle buses, informal discussions, and lighted pathways/sidewalks. There is an emergency whistle program and local police patrols.
Programs of Study: Simpson confers the B.A. degree. Associate and master's degrees are also awarded. Bachelor's degrees are awarded in BUSINESS (accounting, business administration and management, and human resources), COMMUNICATIONS AND THE ARTS (communications, English, and music), COMPUTER AND PHYSICAL SCIENCE (mathematics), EDUCATION (elementary and secondary), SOCIAL SCIENCE (biblical studies, history, liberal arts/general studies, ministries, missions, pastoral studies, psychology, religion, religious education, social science, and youth ministry). Psychology, education, and business are the largest.
Required: To graduate, students must complete at least 124 credits, including a minimum of 36 upper-division credits and 30 in the major, with a minimum GPA of 2.0. General education requirements include 24 credits in humanities, 12 each in natural sciences and math, English and communication, and social sciences and history, and 2 in phys ed. All students also must complete a biblical studies requirement of 24 credits.
Special: Students may take internships in Christian education, pastoral studies, and youth ministries or study abroad in Central America or the Middle East. Simpson also offers work-study programs in elementary education with the federal government, programs for American studies (Washington, D.C.) and film studies (Los Angeles), and a variety of options for dual majors and student-designed majors. There is a 1-year, nondegree Bible certificate program. An accelerated degree program in business and human resources management, psychology, or liberal arts is possible for students with 60 college credits and 5 years of full-time work experience. There is 1 national honor society.
Faculty/Classroom: 76% of faculty are male; 24%, female. No introductory courses are taught by graduate students. The average class size in an introductory lecture is 45; in a laboratory, 20; and in a regular course, 30.
Admissions: 61% of the 2001-2002 applicants were accepted. The SAT I scores for the 2001-2002 freshman class were: Verbal--44% below 500, 40% between 500 and 599, 15% between 600 and 700, and 1% above 700; Math--55% below 500, 30% between 500 and 599, 13% between 600 and 700, and 1% above 700. The ACT scores were 50% below 21, 22% between 21 and 23, 18% between 24 and 26, 8% between 27 and 28, and 3% above 28. 38% of the current freshmen were in the top fifth of their class; 66% were in the top two fifths.
Requirements: The SAT I or ACT is required. In addition, applicants must be graduates of an accredited high school or have a GED. It is recommended that applicants have completed 4 years of high school English, 3 each of math, science, and social studies/history, and 2 of a foreign language. A GPA of 2.0 is required. AP and CLEP credits are accepted. Important factors in the admissions decision are leadership record, personality/intangible qualities, and recommendations by school officials. Applications are accepted on-line at Simpson's web site.
Procedure: Freshmen are admitted to all sessions. There is a deferred admissions plan. Application deadlines are open. The application fee is $20. Notification is sent on a rolling basis.
Transfer: 88 transfer students enrolled in a recent year. Applicants with at least 30 semester college credits need not submit SAT I or ACT scores. 30 credits of 124 must be completed at Simpson.
Visiting: There are regularly scheduled orientations for prospective students, consisting of College Days weekend, offered each spring. There are guides for informal visits and visitors may sit in on classes and stay overnight. To schedule a visit, contact Matt Bridgen, Telecounseling Coordinator.
Financial Aid: In 2001-2002, 81% of all freshmen and 93% of continuing students received some form of financial aid. In a recent year, 65% of freshmen and 76% of continuing students received need-based aid. The average freshman award was $11,837. Of that total, scholarships or need-based grants averaged $4360; loans averaged $6227; work contracts averaged $750; and outside scholarships averaged $500. 21% of undergraduates work part time. Average annual earnings from campus work are $769. The average financial indebtedness of a recent graduate was $17,600. Simpson is a member of CSS. The FAFSA and the college's own financial statement are required. Check with the school for current deadlines.
International Students: These students must score 500 on the written TOEFL.
Computers: The mainframe is an IBM AS/400 B-70. The college provides PCs for academic use. There are 16 Power Macs with DOS capability available in the computer lab and 6 terminals to access library software. All students may access the system. There are no fees.
Graduates: In an average class, 4% graduate in 3 years, 85% in 4 years, 9% in 5 years, and 87% in 6 years.
Admissions Contact: Matt Bridgen, Telecounseling Coordinator.
E-mail: *admissions@simpsonca.edu* Web: *www.simpsonca.edu*

SONOMA STATE UNIVERSITY
Rohnert Park, CA 94928 B-3
(707) 664-2778; Fax: (707) 664-2060

Full-time: 1903 men, 3438 women	**Faculty:** 250; IIA, +$
Part-time: 376 men, 561 women	**Ph.D.s:** 89%
Graduate: 354 men, 958 women	**Student/Faculty:** 21 to 1
Year: semesters, summer session	**Tuition:** $2032 ($9382)
Application Deadline: November	**Room & Board:** $6921
Freshman Class: 5029 applied, 4638 accepted, 1058 enrolled	
SAT I Verbal/Math: 514/507	**COMPETITIVE**

Sonoma State University, founded in 1960 and part of the California State University system, offers undergraduate programs in business and economics, natural sciences, social sciences, and arts and humanities, and graduate programs in education, counseling, business, and other fields. There are 4 undergraduate schools and 1 graduate school. In addition to regional accreditation, Sonoma State has baccalaureate program accreditation with ACS, NASAD, NASM, and NLN. The library contains 666,393 volumes, 1,655,701 microform items, and 25,805 audiovisual forms/CDs, and subscribes to 1071 periodicals. Computerized library services include the card catalog, interlibrary loans, and database searching. Special learning facilities include a learning resource center, art gallery, radio station, and an observatory. The 253-acre campus is in a suburban area 45 miles north of San Francisco. Including residence halls, there are 62 buildings.

Student Life: 96% of undergraduates are from California. Others are from 39 states, 40 foreign countries, and Canada. 87% are from public schools. 64% are white; 10% Hispanic. The average age of freshmen is 18; all undergraduates, 23. 20% do not continue beyond their first year; 50% remain to graduate.

Housing: 1900 students can be accommodated in college housing, which includes single-sex and coed dormitories and on-campus apartments. In addition, there are special-interest houses. On-campus housing is guaranteed for the freshman year only and is available on a first-come, first-served basis. 71% of students commute. All students may keep cars.

Activities: 6% of men belong to 5 national fraternities; 5% of women belong to 4 national sororities. There are 100 groups on campus, including art, cheerleading, chess, choir, chorale, chorus, computers, dance, drama, ethnic, gay, honors, international, jazz band, literary magazine, musical theater, newspaper, orchestra, pep band, political, professional, radio and TV, religious, social, social service, and student government. Popular campus events include Science Night, Parents Day, and Unity Through Diversity Week.

Sports: There are 4 intercollegiate sports for men and 7 for women, and 5 intramural sports for men and 5 for women. Facilities include a 5000-seat stadium, a 3000-seat gym, a field house, tennis courts, a pool, a 500-seat auditorium, and various playing fields.

Disabled Students: All of the campus is accessible. Wheelchair ramps, elevators, special parking, specially equipped rest rooms, special class scheduling, lowered drinking fountains, lowered telephones, a reading machine, phonic listening devices, PC and mainframe access, and interpreters are also available.

Services: Counseling and information services are available, as is tutoring in most subjects. There is a reader service for the blind, remedial math, reading, and writing, and learning disability assessment.

Campus Safety and Security: Measures include 24-hour foot and vehicle patrol, self-defense education, escort service, and pamphlets/posters/films. There are emergency telephones and lighted pathways/sidewalks.

Programs of Study: Sonoma State confers B.A., B.S., and B.F.A. degrees. Master's degrees are also awarded. Bachelor's degrees are awarded in BIOLOGICAL SCIENCE (biology/biological science), BUSINESS (business administration and management), COMMUNICATIONS AND THE ARTS (art, communications, English, fine arts, French, German, music, Spanish, and visual and performing arts), COMPUTER AND PHYSICAL SCIENCE (chemistry, computer science, geology, mathematics, and physics), ENGINEERING AND ENVIRONMENTAL DESIGN (environmental science), HEALTH PROFESSIONS (nursing), SOCIAL SCIENCE (anthropology, criminal justice, economics, geography, history, human development, philosophy, political science/government, psychology, and sociology). Liberal arts, physics, and math are the strongest academically. Business, psychology, and liberal studies are the largest.

Required: Undergraduate students must complete 120 to 132 units, depending on the degree program, consisting of 48 to 51 units of general education, a concentration of study in a specific major, and electives. General education programs require experience in oral and written communications, critical thinking, natural science and math, arts and humanities, social sciences, and personal integration. All students must take an ethnic studies course and the equivalent of courses in U.S. government, U.S. history, and California government.

Special: Students may cross-register at Mills College, Oakland, and University of California, Berkeley. Study-abroad programs are available in 17 countries. Community service internships, work-study, nondegree study through Open University, and pass/fail grading options are available. B.A. and B.S. options in biology, chemistry, environmental studies, geology, interdisciplinary studies, math, and physics are offered. The Hutchins School B.A. in liberal studies offers small seminar classes and an interdisciplinary curriculum. Distance learning programs in nursing are available at 3 off-site centers. There are 6 national honor societies and 5 departmental honors programs.

Faculty/Classroom: 62% of faculty are male; 38%, female. 99% teach undergraduates. Graduate students teach 1% of introductory courses. The average class size in an introductory lecture is 40; in a laboratory, 8; and in a regular course, 24.

Admissions: 92% of the 2001-2002 applicants were accepted. 27% of the current freshmen were in the top fifth of their class; 61% were in the top two fifths.

Requirements: The SAT I or ACT is required, unless the applicant has a 3.0 GPA. Applicants should be graduates of accredited high schools or have earned the GED. Secondary school preparation should include 4 years each of arts and humanities, 3 each of English, math, social science, and academic electives, and 1 each of music, history, and a lab science. A GPA of 2.0 is required. AP and CLEP credits are accepted.

Procedure: Freshmen are admitted fall and spring. Applications should be filed by November for fall entry and August for spring entry. The fall 2001 application fee was $55. Notification is sent on a rolling basis.

Transfer: 863 transfer students enrolled in 2001-2002. Applicants must have a minimum 2.0 GPA. The maximum number of transferable credits is 70. 30 credits of 120 to 132 must be completed at Sonoma State.

Visiting: There are regularly scheduled orientations for prospective students, consisting of programs in the spring and summer. There are guides for informal visits and visitors may sit in on classes. To schedule a visit, contact the Admissions Development Office at (707) 664-3032.

Financial Aid: In 2001-2002, 34% of all freshmen received some form of financial aid. 27% of freshmen received need-based aid. The average freshman award was $5382. Of that total, scholarships or need-based grants averaged $4487 ($8000 maximum); loans averaged $5000 ($17,500 maximum); and work contracts averaged $2300. 5% of undergraduates work part time. Average annual earnings from campus work are $2300. The average financial indebtedness of the 2001 graduate was $15,000. The FAFSA is required.

International Students: There are 97 international students enrolled. The school actively recruits these students. They must score 500 on the written TOEFL or 173 on the electronic version.

Computers: The mainframes are a DEC VAX 6360, a MicroVAX 2000, and a MicroVAX II. Sonoma State provides more than 850 PCs, most of which are networked with Internet, CSUNSET, NeXT, or LAN systems, in labs, the library, and the computer center. All students may access the system. There are no time limits and no fees. It is strongly recommended that all students have personal computers.

Graduates: In 2001, 1445 bachelor's degrees were awarded. The most popular majors were business administration (16%), psychology (11%), and liberal studies (11%). In an average class, 2% graduate in 3 years, 15% in 4 years, 37% in 5 years, and 44% in 6 years. 300 companies recruited on campus in 2000-2001. Of the 2000 graduating class, 15% were enrolled in graduate school within 6 months of graduation and 88% were employed.

Admissions Contact: Gustavo Flores, Admissions Office. A video is available. E-mail: *gustavo.flores@sonoma.edu* Web: *www.sonoma.edu*

SOUTHERN CALIFORNIA INSTITUTE OF ARCHITECTURE — C-5

Los Angeles, CA 90013-1829 — (213) 613-2200
(800) 774-7242; Fax: (310) 574-3801

Full-time: 160 men, 50 women	**Faculty:** 36
Part-time: none	**Ph.D.s:** n/av
Graduate: 140 men, 80 women	**Student/Faculty:** 6 to 1
Year: semesters, summer session	**Tuition:** $16,740
Application Deadline: see profile	**Room & Board:** n/app
Freshman Class: n/av	
SAT I or ACT: required	**SPECIAL**

Southern California Institute of Architecture, founded in 1972, is a private, independent school offering a 5-year professional degree program. Figures given in the above capsule are approximate. There is 1 graduate school. In addition to regional accreditation, Sci-Arc has baccalaureate program accreditation with NAAB. The library contains 10,000 volumes and 700 audiovisual forms/CDs, and subscribes to 70 periodicals. Special learning facilities include an art gallery and a media center, a dark room, and a woodshop. The 2-acre campus is in an urban area. There is one building.

Student Life: Students are from 35 states, 17 foreign countries, and Canada. 53% are white; 34% Asian American; 25% foreign nationals; 10% Hispanic. The average age of freshmen is 22. 40% do not continue beyond their first year.

Housing: There are no residence halls. Housing includes off-campus apartments. Alcohol is not permitted.

Activities: There are no fraternities or sororities. There are some groups and organizations on campus, including literary magazine, photography, and student government.

Sports: There is no sports program at Sci-Arc.

Campus Safety and Security: Measures include private service and 24-hour service.

Programs of Study: Sci-Arc confers the B.Arch. degree. Master's degrees are also awarded. Bachelor's degrees are awarded in ENGINEERING AND ENVIRONMENTAL DESIGN (architecture).

Required: To graduate, students must complete 33 units in general studies, 150 units in the major, and a thesis.

Special: Exchange programs in Switzerland, Japan, Germany, England, Australia, and Mexico are offered.

Requirements: The SAT I or ACT is required. In addition, official transcripts, 3 letters of recommendation, a portfolio and an interview, and a statement of purpose are required. A GPA of 2.0 is required. AP and CLEP credits are accepted. Evidence of special talent is an important factor in the admission decision.

Procedure: Freshmen are admitted fall, spring, and summer. There is a deferred admissions plan. Notification is sent on a rolling basis. Check with the school for current deadlines and fees.

Transfer: Sci-Arc will accept courses with a grade of C- or better for credit. 60 credits of 150 must be completed at Sci-Arc.

Visiting: There are guides for informal visits and visitors may sit in on classes. To schedule a visit, contact the Admissions Office at (310) 574-3625.

Financial Aid: Sci-Arc is a member of CSS. The CSS/Profile or FAFSA and the college's own financial statement are required.

International Students: The school actively recruits these students. They must score 550 on the written TOEFL and also take the SAT I or the ACT.

Computers: A computer lab for design and a library for word processing are available to students. All students may access the system. There are no time limits and no fees.

Admissions Contact: Debra Abel, Admissions Director.
E-mail: *admissions@sciarc.edu*

STANFORD UNIVERSITY — B-3

Stanford, CA 94305-3005 — **(650) 725-2839; Fax: (650) 725-2846**

Full-time: 3329 men, 3114 women — **Faculty:** I, ++$
Part-time: none — **Ph.D.s:** 98%
Graduate: 6976 men, 4336 women — **Student/Faculty:** 7 to 1
Year: quarters, summer session — **Tuition:** $25,917
Application Deadline: December 15 — **Room & Board:** $8305
Freshman Class: 19,052 applied, 2406 accepted, 1618 enrolled
SAT I or ACT: required — **MOST COMPETITIVE**

Stanford University, founded in 1885, is a private research-intensive university offering a broad curriculum in undergraduate liberal arts, graduate education, and professional training. There are 3 undergraduate and 7 graduate schools. In addition to regional accreditation, Stanford has baccalaureate program accreditation with AACSB and ABET. The 18 libraries contain 8 million volumes and 4.9 million microform items. Computerized library services include interlibrary loans and database searching. Special learning facilities include a learning resource center, art gallery, radio station, TV station, art museum, biological preserve, and linear accelerator. The 8180-acre campus is in a suburban area 30 miles south of San Francisco. Including residence halls, there are 678 buildings.

Student Life: 51% of undergraduates are from out of state, mostly the Middle Atlantic. Others are from 49 states, 58 foreign countries, and Canada. 70% are from public schools. 49% are white; 24% Asian American; 11% Hispanic. 40% are Protestant; 30% Catholic; 10% claim no religious affiliation; 10% Jewish. The average age of freshmen is 18; all undergraduates, 20. 2% do not continue beyond their first year; 90% remain to graduate.

Housing: 9500 students can be accommodated in college housing, which includes single-sex and coed dormitories, on-campus apartments, off-campus apartments, married-student housing, fraternity houses, and sorority houses. In addition, there are language houses, special-interest houses, and ethnic theme houses. On-campus housing is guaranteed for all 4 years. 94% of students live on campus; of those, 95% remain on campus on weekends. Upperclassmen may keep cars.

Activities: 17% of men belong to 15 national fraternities; 12% of women belong to 8 national sororities. There are 500 groups on campus, including art, band, cheerleading, chess, choir, chorale, computers, dance, debate, drama, ethnic, film, gay, honors, international, jazz band, literary magazine, marching band, musical theater, newspaper, orchestra, pep band, photography, political, professional, radio and TV, religious, social, social service, student government, symphony, and yearbook. Popular campus events include the Big Game, Full Moon on the Quad, and Pow Wow.

Sports: There are 15 intercollegiate sports for men and 17 for women, and 37 intramural sports for men and 37 for women. Facilities include athletic fields, gyms, swimming pools, volleyball courts, lighted tennis courts, dance studios, an 18-hole golf course, a sailing center, a rowing facility, handball, racquetball, and squash courts, a baseball diamond, and a football stadium.

Disabled Students: 90% of the campus is accessible. Wheelchair ramps, elevators, special parking, specially equipped rest rooms, special class scheduling, lowered drinking fountains, and lowered telephones are available. Stanford has a Diversity and Access Office to provide help.

Services: Counseling and information services are available, as is tutoring in most subjects. There is a reader service for the blind. The Disability Resource Center provides many services to learning disabled students.

Campus Safety and Security: Measures include 24-hour foot and vehicle patrol, self-defense education, escort service, and shuttle buses. There are informal discussions, pamphlets/posters/films, emergency telephones, and lighted pathways/sidewalks.

Programs of Study: Stanford confers A.B., B.S., and B.A.S. degrees. Master's and doctoral degrees are also awarded. Bachelor's degrees are awarded in BIOLOGICAL SCIENCE (biology/biological science), COMMUNICATIONS AND THE ARTS (art, Chinese, classics, communications, comparative literature, dramatic arts, English, fine arts, French, Italian, Japanese, linguistics, music, Slavic languages, and Spanish), COMPUTER AND PHYSICAL SCIENCE (chemistry, computer science, earth science, geology, geoscience, mathematics, and physics), ENGINEERING AND ENVIRONMENTAL DESIGN (aeronautical science, chemical engineering, civil engineering, electrical/electronics engineering, engineering, industrial engineering, materials science, mechanical engineering, and petroleum/natural gas engineering), SOCIAL SCIENCE (African American studies, American studies, anthropology, archeology, crosscultural studies, East Asian studies, economics, German area studies, history, international relations, philosophy, political science/government, psychology, public affairs, religion, sociology, systems science, urban studies, and women's studies). Biology, economics, and computer science are the largest.

Required: To graduate, students must complete 180 units, including requirements for the major, a writing requirement, 1 year of a foreign language, 1 year of Introduction to the Humanities, 3 courses in natural sciences, applied science and technology, and math, 3 courses in humanities and social sciences, and 2 courses in world cultures, American cultures, and Gender Studies.

Special: Internships, study abroad, a Washington semester, student-designed majors, dual majors, a B.A.-B.S. degree, a 3-2 engineering degree, pass/no credit options, and numerous research opportunities are offered. There is a chapter of Phi Beta Kappa. Most departments have honors programs.

Faculty/Classroom: 78% of faculty are male; 22%, female. All both teach and do research. Graduate students teach 4% of undergraduate courses.

Admissions: 13% of the 2001-2002 applicants were accepted. 96% of the current freshmen were in the top fifth of their class; 99% were in the top two fifths. 265 freshmen received national Merit Scholarships.

Requirements: The SAT I or ACT is required. The SAT I is preferred. The university recommends that applicants have strong preparation in high school English, math, a foreign language, science, and social studies. SAT II: Subject tests are strongly recommended. Applications are accepted on-line. AP credits are accepted. Important factors in the admissions decision are advanced placement or honor courses, personality/intangible qualities, and recommendations by school officials.

Procedure: Freshmen are admitted in the fall. Entrance exams should be taken before December of the application year. There are early decision and deferred admissions plans. Early decision application should be filed by November 1; regular applications, by December 15 for fall entry. Notification of early decision is sent mid-December; regular decision, early April. 517 early decision candidates were accepted for the 2001-2002 class. 5% of all applicants are on a waiting list; 15 were accepted in 2001.

Transfer: 98 transfer students enrolled in 2001-2002. Transfer students must complete one full year of academic work prior to enrollment. There is only fall quarter enrollment for transfer students. The application deadline is March 15. 90 credits of 180 must be completed at Stanford.

Visiting: There are regularly scheduled orientations for prospective students, including group information sessions and campus tours. There are guides for informal visits and visitors may sit in on classes. To schedule a visit, contact the Undergraduate Admissions Office at (650) 723-2091 or *undergrad.admissions@forsythe.stanford.edu*.

Financial Aid: In 2001-2002, 79% of all freshmen and 62% of continuing students received some form of financial aid. 46% of freshmen received need-based aid. The average freshman need-based award was $27,474. Of that total, scholarships or need-based grants averaged $16,790 ($35,978 maximum); loans averaged $1846 ($23,769 maximum); and work contracts averaged $193 ($2500 maximum). The average financial indebtedness of the 2001 graduate was $17,185. Stanford is a member of CSS. The CSS/Profile or FAFSA is required. The fall application deadline is February 1.

International Students: There are 332 international students enrolled. The school actively recruits these students. They must take the TOEFL. A minimum score of 620 on the written version or 260 on the electronic version is recommended. The SAT I or ACT is required. SAT II: Subject tests are strongly recommended.

Computers: PCs are available in residences, libraries, and other campus clusters. All students may access the system. There are no time limits and no fees.

Graduates: In 2001, 1676 bachelor's degrees were awarded. The most popular majors were biology/human biology (20%), economics (12%), and computer science (8%). In an average class, 93% graduate in 6 years. 500 companies recruited on campus in 2000-2001.

Admissions Contact: Robin Mamlet, Director of Admission.
Web: *www.stanford.edu*

THOMAS AQUINAS COLLEGE — C-5
Santa Paula, CA 93060 (805) 525-4417, ext. 361
(800) 634-9797; Fax: (805) 525-0620

Full-time: 150 men, 151 women
Part-time: none
Graduate: none
Year: semesters
Application Deadline: open
Freshman Class: 178 applied, 131 accepted, 85 enrolled
SAT I Verbal/Math: 650/610
Faculty: 27
Ph.D.s: 79%
Student/Faculty: 11 to 1
Tuition: $15,900
Room & Board: $4600
ACT: 28
HIGHLY COMPETITIVE+

Thomas Aquinas College, founded in 1969 and affiliated with the Roman Catholic Church, is a small, private, liberal arts college offering an integrated studies curriculum based on the Great Books. All classes are conducted as conversations directed by teachers using the Socratic method. In addition to regional accreditation, TAC has baccalaureate program accreditation with AALE. The library contains 48,000 volumes and 7000 audiovisual forms/CDs, and subscribes to 48 periodicals. Computerized library services include the card catalog, interlibrary loans, and database searching. Special learning facilities include a learning resource center. The 170-acre campus is in a rural area 60 miles northwest of Los Angeles. Including residence halls, there are 22 buildings.

Student Life: 60% of undergraduates are from out of state, mostly the Midwest. Others are from 36 states, 3 foreign countries, and Canada. 24% are from public schools. 80% are white; 10% foreign nationals. Most are Catholic. The average age of freshmen is 18; all undergraduates, 20. 12% do not continue beyond their first year.

Housing: 382 students can be accommodated in college housing, which includes single-sex dormitories. On-campus housing is guaranteed for all 4 years. All students live on campus; of those, all remain on campus on weekends. Alcohol is not permitted. All students may keep cars.

Activities: There are no fraternities or sororities. There are some groups and organizations on campus, including choir, drama, literary magazine, and religious. Popular campus events include St. Thomas Aquinas Day, President's Day, and Alumni Day.

Sports: There are 4 intramural sports for men and 2 for women. Facilities include tennis, basketball, and volleyball courts, a soccer field, a swimming area, a weight-lifting room, and a softball field.

Disabled Students: All of the campus is accessible. Wheelchair ramps, elevators, special parking, specially equipped rest rooms, and lowered drinking fountains are available.

Services: All students may be tutored by the full-time teaching faculty.

Campus Safety and Security: Measures include lighted pathways/sidewalks.

Programs of Study: TAC confers the B.A. degree. Bachelor's degrees are awarded in SOCIAL SCIENCE (liberal arts/general studies).

Required: The entire curriculum is required of all students: 4 years of seminars in literature, history, and social sciences, 4 years each of philosophy, theology, math, and lab science, 2 years of language, and 1 year of music. A total of 146 semester hours, with a minimum GPA of 2.0, is required to graduate. A senior thesis is also required.

Special: There are no electives, majors, or minors. Students read original writings of Western civilization and discuss them in small seminar-style groups. Many exams are oral.

Faculty/Classroom: 90% of faculty are male; 10%, female. All teach undergraduates. The average class size in an introductory lecture is 17; in a laboratory, 16; and in a regular course, 17.

Admissions: 74% of the 2001-2002 applicants were accepted. The SAT I scores for the 2001-2002 freshman class were: Verbal--21% between 500 and 599, 58% between 600 and 700, and 21% above 700; Math--3% below 500, 42% between 500 and 599, 51% between 600 and 700, and 5% above 700. The ACT scores were 9% between 21 and 23, 26% between 24 and 26, 30% between 27 and 28, and 35% above 28. In a recent year, 2 freshmen graduated first in their class.

Requirements: The SAT I or ACT is required. In addition, candidates for admission should have completed 4 years of English, 3 years of math, and 2 years each of a foreign language, history, and science. Important factors in the admissions decision are personality/intangible qualities, advanced placement or honor courses, and recommendations by school officials.

Procedure: Freshmen are admitted in the fall. Entrance exams should be taken by March. There is a deferred admissions plan. Application deadlines are open.

Transfer: Transfers are not accepted.

Visiting: There are regularly scheduled orientations for prospective students, including hosting of prospective students by current students. Visits are for up to 5 days and consist of observing classes and attending lectures, concerts, and meals. There are guides for informal visits and visitors may sit in on classes and stay overnight. To schedule a visit, contact the Admissions Office at (800) 634-9797, ext. 360 or *admissions@thomasaquinas.edu*

Financial Aid: In 2001-2002, 79% of all students received some form of financial aid. 69% of freshmen and 75% of continuing students received need-based aid. The average freshman award was $12,167. Of that total, scholarships or need-based grants averaged $8178 ($16,500 maximum); loans averaged $2670 ($3300 maximum); and work contracts averaged $2938 ($3050 maximum). 67% of undergraduates work part time. Average annual earnings from campus work are $3050. The average financial indebtedness of the 2001 graduate was $13,250. TAC is a member of CSS. The FAFSA and the college's own financial statement are required. The fall application deadline is July 1.

International Students: There are 28 international students enrolled. They must score 570 on the written TOEFL or 230 on the electronic version and also take the SAT I.

Computers: 1 PC is available to students in each of the 7 dormitory buildings; there are 7 student computers in the library for e-mail, word processing, and limited access to the web. All students may access the system whenever available, or during library hours. There are no time limits and no fees.

Graduates: In 2001, 48 bachelor's degrees were awarded. In an average class, 62% graduate in 4 years, 65% in 5 years, and 71% in 6 years. 2 companies recruited on campus in 2000-2001. Of the 2000 graduating class, 9% were enrolled in graduate school within 6 months of graduation and 65% were employed.

Admissions Contact: Thomas J. Susanka, Director, Admissions. A video is available. E-mail: *admissions@thomasaquinas.edu*
Web: *thomasaquinas.edu*

UNITED STATES INTERNATIONAL UNIVERSITY — D-5
San Diego, CA 92131-1799 (858) 635-4772; Fax: (858) 635-4739

Full-time: 200 men, 270 women
Part-time: 20 men, 20 women
Graduate: 370 men, 490 women
Year: quarters, summer session
Application Deadline: open
Freshman Class: n/av
SAT I or ACT: required
Faculty: 34
Ph.D.s: 94%
Student/Faculty: 13 to 1
Tuition: $13,275
Room & Board: $5400
LESS COMPETITIVE

United States International University, established in 1952, is a private institution offering undergraduate and graduate programs in education, business, psychology, and international studies. The university also has campuses in Nairobi and Mexico City and a graduate center in Orange County. Figures in above capsule are approximate. There are 2 undergraduate and 2 graduate schools. The library contains 159,000 volumes and 291,461 microform items, and subscribes to 860 periodicals. Computerized library services include the card catalog, interlibrary loans, and database searching. Special learning facilities include a curriculum lab for education. The 160-acre campus is in a suburban area 15 miles north of downtown San Diego. Including residence halls, there are 68 buildings.

Student Life: 40% of undergraduates are from California. Others are from 47 states, 69 foreign countries, and Canada. 65% are from public schools. 51% are white; 26% foreign nationals. The average age of freshmen is 18; all undergraduates, 21.

Housing: 600 students can be accommodated in college housing, which includes single-sex dormitories. On-campus housing is guaranteed for all 4 years. 70% of students commute. All students may keep cars.

Activities: There are no fraternities or sororities. There are 35 groups on campus, including ethnic, gay, honors, international, literary magazine, newspaper, professional, social, social service, student government, and yearbook. Popular campus events include dances, harbor cruises, beach parties, and the International Friendship Festival.

Sports: There are 3 intercollegiate sports for men and 3 for women, and 7 intramural sports for men and 7 for women. Facilities include weight and exercise rooms, tennis courts, softball, baseball, and soccer fields, 4 swimming pools, an all-purpose playing field, and a basketball/volleyball indoor recreational facility.

Disabled Students: 80% of the campus is accessible. Wheelchair ramps, elevators, special parking, and specially equipped rest rooms are available.

Services: Counseling and information services are available, as is tutoring in most subjects. There is a reader service for the blind, and remedial math, reading, and writing.

Campus Safety and Security: Measures include 24-hour foot and vehicle patrol, pamphlets/posters/films, and lighted pathways/sidewalks.

Programs of Study: USIU confers B.A. and B.S. degrees. Associate, master's, and doctoral degrees are also awarded. Bachelor's degrees are awarded in BUSINESS (business administration and management, hotel/motel and restaurant management, international business management, and tourism), COMMUNICATIONS AND THE ARTS (telecommunications), EDUCATION (teaching English as a second/foreign language (TESOL/TEFOL)), ENGINEERING AND ENVIRONMENTAL DESIGN (environmental science), SOCIAL SCIENCE (international relations, liberal arts/general studies, and psychology). International relations and international business are the strongest academically. Business is the largest.

Required: To graduate, students must complete 186 quarter hours, including 96 in the major, with a minimum GPA of 2.0. Required courses

include English, math, science, international studies, Freshman Experience, and Senior Experience.
Special: USIU offers internships, study abroad at the university's international campuses, an accelerated degree program, a general studies degree, B.A.-B.S. degrees, nondegree study, and pass/fail options. There is 1 national honor society, a freshman honors program, and 1 departmental honors program.
Faculty/Classroom: 67% of faculty are male; 33%, female. The average class size in an introductory lecture is 25 and in a regular course, 18.
Requirements: The SAT I or ACT is required. In addition, applicants should be graduates of a regionally accredited secondary school with a GPA of 2.5. High school preparation should include 4 years each of English, history, and math, 3 of social studies, and 2 of science. An essay is required, along with a recommendation. A GPA of 2.0 is required. AP and CLEP credits are accepted. Important factors in the admissions decision are advanced placement or honor courses, leadership record, and evidence of special talent.
Procedure: Freshmen are admitted to all sessions. Entrance exams should be taken by the end of the senior year. There are early decision and deferred admissions plans. Application deadlines are open. The fall 2001 application fee was $40.
Transfer: A college GPA of 2.5 is recommended. All applicants must submit high school as well as college transcripts. Applicants with more than 1 full semester of college credit need not submit SAT I/ACT scores. 48 credits of 186 must be completed at USIU.
Visiting: There are regularly scheduled orientations for prospective students, including admissions and financial aid counseling, meeting with a student panel, an information fair, a campus tour, and dinner. There are guides for informal visits and visitors may sit in on classes and stay overnight. To schedule a visit, contact the Admissions Office.
Financial Aid: In a recent year, 60% of all freshmen and 57% of continuing students received some form of financial aid. 56% of freshmen and 52% of continuing students received need-based aid. The average freshman award was $12,482. Of that total, scholarships or need-based grants averaged $3000 ($9900 maximum); loans averaged $1400 ($2625 maximum); and work contracts averaged $2000 ($4200 maximum). 50% of undergraduates work part time. Average annual earnings from campus work are $3850. The average financial indebtedness of a recent year's graduate was $16,210. USIU is a member of CSS. The FAFSA and the college's own financial statement are required. Check with the school for current deadlines.
International Students: The school actively recruits these students. They must score 550 on the written TOEFL and also take the college's own test.
Computers: The mainframe is an HP 9000. The computer lab has about 57 IBM PCs and Macs, linked through a network, in 3 classroom areas. They are available to all students during off-peak hours and on a first-come, first-served basis when computer classes are in session. The lab is open daily from 9 A.M. to 10 P.M. All students may access the system. There are no time limits and no fees. It is strongly recommended that all students have a personal computer.
Admissions Contact: Susan Topham, Director of Admissions.
E-mail: *admissions@usiu.edu* Web: *www.usiu.edu*

UNIVERSITY OF CALIFORNIA SYSTEM

The University of California System, established in 1868, is a public system. It is governed by a board of regents whose chief administrator is the president. The primary goals of the system are teaching, research, and public service. The total enrollment of all 9 campuses is approximately 163,000, with more than 7000 faculty members. Altogether there are 565 baccalaureate, 250 master's, and 200 doctoral programs offered through the University of California. 4-year campuses are located in Berkeley, Davis, Irvine, Los Angeles, Riverside, San Diego, Santa Barbara, and Santa Cruz. Profiles of those campuses are included in this section.

UNIVERSITY OF CALIFORNIA AT BERKELEY — B-3

Berkeley, CA 94720-5800 — **(510) 642-3175; Fax: (510) 642-7333**

Full-time: 9958 men, 11,088 women	**Faculty:** 1444; I, ++$
Part-time: 870 men, 761 women	**Ph.D.s:** 98%
Graduate: 4615 men, 3984 women	**Student/Faculty:** 15 to 1
Year: semesters, summer session	**Tuition:** $4088 ($15,162)
Application Deadline: November 30	**Room & Board:** $10,046

Freshman Class: 32,963 applied, 8715 accepted, 3703 enrolled
SAT I Verbal/Math: 635/674 — **MOST COMPETITIVE**

The University of California at Berkeley, founded in 1868, is a public institution offering a wide variety of programs in the social and physical sciences, liberal arts, and professional fields. It is the oldest campus of the University of California system. There are 7 undergraduate and 14 graduate schools. In addition to regional accreditation, Cal has baccalaureate program accreditation with AACSB, ABET, ADA, ASLA, CSWE, NAAB, and SAF. The 30 libraries contain 9,107,757 volumes, 6,260,903 microform items, and 94,299 audiovisual forms/CDs, and subscribe to 78,891 periodicals. Computerized library services include the card catalog, interlibrary loans, and database searching. Special learning facilities include a learning resource center, art gallery, natural history museum, radio station, TV station, a botanical garden, an anthropology museum, a hall of science, the University Art Museum and Pacific Film Archive, a seismographic station, an herberia, the Hall for the Performing Arts, an observatory, and many off-campus facilities. The 1232-acre campus is in an urban area 10 miles east of San Francisco. Including residence halls, there are 100 buildings.
Student Life: 86% of undergraduates are from California. Others are from 50 states, 130 foreign countries, and Canada. 85% are from public schools. 40% are Asian American; 30%, white; 10%, Hispanic. The average age of freshmen is 19; all undergraduates, 21. 5% do not continue beyond their first year; 5% remain to graduate.
Housing: 9875 students can be accommodated in college housing, which includes single-sex and coed dormitories, off-campus apartments, married-student housing, fraternity houses, and sorority houses. In addition, there are honors houses, language houses, and special-interest houses. On-campus housing is guaranteed for the freshman year only and is available on a lottery system for upperclassmen. All students may keep cars.
Activities: 11% of men belong to 14 local and 38 national fraternities; 10% of women belong to 7 local and 13 national sororities. There are 400 groups on campus, including art, band, cheerleading, chess, choir, chorale, chorus, computers, dance, debate, drama, ethnic, film, forensics, gay, honors, international, jazz band, literary magazine, marching band, musical theater, newspaper, orchestra, pep band, photography, political, professional, radio and TV, religious, social, social service, student government, symphony, and yearbook. Popular campus events include The Big Game, Cal Performances, E-Week.
Sports: There are 13 intercollegiate sports for men and 13 for women, and 14 intramural sports for men and 14 for women. Facilities include a football stadium, a track stadium, a basketball pavilion, 4 gyms, a martial arts room, 7 swimming pools, 3 weight rooms, squash, racquetball, handball, volleyball, and tennis courts, and baseball and softball fields.
Disabled Students: 95% of the campus is accessible. Wheelchair ramps, elevators, special parking, specially equipped rest rooms, special class scheduling, lowered drinking fountains, lowered telephones, and disabled students program are available.
Services: Counseling and information services are available, as is tutoring in most subjects. There is a reader service for the blind, a workshop in study strategy and note taking, counseling, and an athletic study center.
Campus Safety and Security: Measures include 24-hour foot and vehicle patrol, self-defense education, escort service, and shuttle buses. There are informal discussions, pamphlets/posters/films, emergency telephones, lighted pathways/sidewalks, a rape prevention peer education program, and an earthquake emergency preparedness program.
Programs of Study: Cal confers B.A. AND B.S. degrees. Master's and doctoral degrees are also awarded. Bachelor's degrees are awarded in BIOLOGICAL SCIENCE (biology/biological science, molecular biology, and nutrition), BUSINESS (business administration and management), COMMUNICATIONS AND THE ARTS (Chinese, classical languages, communications, comparative literature, dramatic arts, Dutch, English, film arts, French, German, Greek, Italian, Japanese, Latin, linguistics, music, Scandinavian languages, Slavic languages, Spanish, and speech/debate/rhetoric), COMPUTER AND PHYSICAL SCIENCE (applied mathematics, astrophysics, chemistry, computer science, earth science, geology, mathematics, physical sciences, physics, and statistics), ENGINEERING AND ENVIRONMENTAL DESIGN (architecture, bioengineering, chemical engineering, civil engineering, computer engineering, electrical/electronics engineering, engineering and applied science, engineering physics, environmental engineering, environmental science, industrial engineering, landscape architecture/design, manufacturing engineering, materials engineering, materials science, mechanical engineering, and nuclear engineering), HEALTH PROFESSIONS (optometry), SOCIAL SCIENCE (African American studies, American studies, anthropology, archeology, Asian/American studies, Asian/Oriental studies, Celtic studies, classical/ancient civilization, cognitive science, economics, ethnic studies, geography, Hispanic American studies, history, Latin American studies, Middle Eastern studies, Native American studies, peace studies, philosophy, political science/government, psychology, religion, social science, social work, sociology, and women's studies). Electrical engineering and computer science, molecular and cell biology, and English are the largest.
Required: All undergraduate students are required to satisfy the general university requirements of English and writing proficiency, and integrative and comparative courses in American history, institutions, and cultures. Students must complete 120 units with a minimum GPA of 2.0.
Special: Co-op programs, cross-registration with many area schools, internships, work-study programs, and study abroad in 33 countries are available. Interdisciplinary majors are also available. Students may dou-

ble-major, earn dual degrees, design their own majors, study independently, and choose pass/fail options. Students have opportunities for independent or team research. There are 6 national honor societies, including Phi Beta Kappa. Most departments have honors programs.

Faculty/Classroom: 70% of faculty are male; 30%, female. All teach undergraduates, 80% do research, and 80% do both. The average class size in a regular course is 40.

Admissions: 26% of the 2001-2002 applicants were accepted. The SAT I scores for the 2001-2002 freshman class were: Verbal--8% below 500, 23% between 500 and 599, 39% between 600 and 700, and 30% above 700; Math--5% below 500, 14% between 500 and 599, 35% between 600 and 700, and 46% above 700. 95% of the current freshmen were in the top fifth of their class; 100% were in the top two fifths. There were 245 National Merit finalists.

Requirements: The SAT I or ACT is required and 3 SAT II: Subject tests. Also required are 4 years of English, 3 of math (4 recommended), 2 each of history/social sciences, lab science (3 recommended), foreign language (3 recommended), and college preparatory electives. A GPA of 2.8 is required. AP credits are accepted. Important factors in the admissions decision are advanced placement or honor courses, evidence of special talent, and leadership record. Applications are accepted on-line at *http://www.ucop.edu/pathways.*

Procedure: Freshmen are admitted in the fall. Entrance exams should be taken no later than December test dates in the senior year. There is a deferred admissions plan. Applications should be filed by November 30 for fall entry. Notification is sent March 30. The fall 2001application fee was $40.

Transfer: 1520 transfer students enrolled in 2001-2002. A minimum GPA of 2.4 generally is required for in-state students and 2.8 for out-of-state students. Admission is competitive so meeting the minimum does not guarantee admission. Students must have completed at least 60 transferable semester units and no more than 80 to 90 semester units (depending upon specific college). They must complete all lower-division courses for intended major prior to admission. 24 credits of 120 must be completed at Cal.

Visiting: There are regularly scheduled orientations for prospective students, including student-led tours by the visitor information center and group advising from the Office of Undergraduate Admission and Relations with Schools. There are guides for informal visits and visitors may sit in on classes. To schedule a visit, contact the Visitor Information Center at (510) 642-5215.

Financial Aid: In 2000-2001, 53% of all freshmen and 46% of continuing students received some form of financial aid. 49% of freshmen and 38% of continuing students received need-based aid. The average freshman award was $10,554. Of that total, scholarships or need-based grants averaged $7363; loans averaged $4252; and work contracts averaged $5343. 26% of undergraduates work part time. Average annual earnings from campus work are $2044. The average financial indebtedness of the 2001 graduate was $13,052. The FAFSA is required. The fall application deadline is March 2.

International Students: There are 794 international students enrolled. They must score 550 on the written TOEFL. Students must take SAT II: Subject tests in writing, math level I or IC, or IIC and 1 test in one of the following areas: English literature, foreign languages, science, or social studies.

Computers: The mainframes are an IBM 3090 and a DEC UNIX. There are 12 general-access computer facilities on campus, with about 600 computers, including Macs, PCs, and UNIX workstations. Additional computer labs are located in residence halls, libraries, and academic departments. Internet access and e-mail accounts are available. Home computers can be linked to the campus data network. All students may access the system. There are no time limits and no fees.

Graduates: In 2000-2001, 6169 bachelor's degrees were awarded. The most popular majors were molecular and cell biology (8%), English (7%), and electrical engineering and computer science (6%). In an average class, 48% graduate in 4 years, 78% in 5 years, and 83% in 6 years. 630 companies recruited on campus in 2000-2001.

Admissions Contact: Pamela Burnett, Director, Undergraduate Admission. E-mail: *ouars@uclink.berkeley.edu*
Web: *http://www.berkeley.edu*

UNIVERSITY OF CALIFORNIA AT DAVIS B-2

Davis, CA 95616-8507 **(530) 752-2971; Fax: (530) 752-1280**

Full-time: 8076 men, 10,616 women	**Faculty:** 1620; I, +$
Part-time: 1182 men, 1419 women	**Ph.D.s:** 98%
Graduate: 2618 men, 2601 women	**Student/Faculty:** 12 to 1
Year: quarters, summer session	**Tuition:** $4594 ($10,704)
Application Deadline: see profile	**Room & Board:** $8202
Freshman Class: 27,954 applied, 17,581 accepted, 4412 enrolled	
SAT I or ACT: required	**VERY COMPETITIVE**

University of California at Davis, founded in 1905, is a public, comprehensive institution offering programs in arts and science, agricultural and environmental sciences, and engineering. There are 3 undergraduate and 5 graduate schools. In addition to regional accreditation, UCD has baccalaureate program accreditation with ABET, ADA, and ASLA. The 5 libraries contain 3,180,865 volumes, 3,948,731 microform items, and 14,047 audiovisual forms/CDs, and subscribe to 44,232 periodicals. Computerized library services include the card catalog and database searching. Special learning facilities include a learning resource center, art gallery, radio station, experimental farms, a 150-acre arboretum, a raptor center, an equestrian center, a primate research center, and the Crocker Nuclear Laboratory. The 5980-acre campus is in a suburban area 15 miles west of Sacramento and 72 miles northeast of San Francisco. Including residence halls, there are 1083 buildings.

Student Life: 96% of undergraduates are from California. Others are from 47 states, 113 foreign countries, and Canada. 90% are from public schools. 43% are white; 32%, Asian American; 10%, Hispanic. The average age of freshmen is 18; all undergraduates, 21. 1% do not continue beyond their first year; 76% remain to graduate.

Housing: 5290 students can be accommodated in college housing, which includes single-sex and coed dormitories, on-campus apartments, off-campus apartments, and married-student housing. In addition, there are honors houses, language houses, and special-interest houses. On-campus housing is guaranteed for the freshman year only. 81% of students commute. Alcohol is not permitted. All students may keep cars.

Activities: 9% of men belong to 28 national fraternities; 9% of women belong to 20 national sororities. There are 320 groups on campus, including art, band, cheerleading, chess, choir, chorus, computers, dance, drama, ethnic, film, gay, honors, international, jazz band, literary magazine, marching band, musical theater, newspaper, orchestra, pep band, photography, political, professional, radio and TV, religious, social, social service, student government, symphony, and yearbook. Popular campus events include Picnic Day, Whole Earth Festival, and Asian Pacific Cultural Week.

Sports: There are 11 intercollegiate sports for men and 9 for women, and 18 intramural sports for men and 18 for women. Facilities include a football stadium, tennis and basketball courts, equestrian trails, a track field, baseball, soccer, and softball fields, a recreation hall, 2 gyms, 2 swimming pools, bowling alleys, weight-training facilities, and an outdoor roller hockey rink.

Disabled Students: 99% of the campus is accessible. Wheelchair ramps, elevators, special parking, specially equipped rest rooms, special class scheduling, lowered drinking fountains, lowered telephones, and lowered automatic teller machines are available.

Services: Counseling and information services are available, as is tutoring in most subjects. There is a reader service for the blind and remedial math and writing.

Campus Safety and Security: Measures include 24-hour foot and vehicle patrol, self-defense education, escort service, and shuttle buses. There are informal discussions, pamphlets/posters/films, emergency telephones, and lighted pathways/sidewalks. There is also a rape prevention program, a crime prevention unit, a bike patrol unit, and a K-9 program.

Programs of Study: UCD confers A.B., B.S., and B.A.S. degrees. Master's and doctoral degrees are also awarded. Bachelor's degrees are awarded in AGRICULTURE (agricultural business management, agricultural economics, animal science, international agriculture, plant science, range/farm management, and soil science), BIOLOGICAL SCIENCE (avian sciences, bacteriology, biochemistry, biology/biological science, botany, ecology, entomology, environmental biology, genetics, microbiology, nutrition, physiology, toxicology, wildlife biology, and zoology), BUSINESS (organizational behavior), COMMUNICATIONS AND THE ARTS (art history and appreciation, Chinese, communications, comparative literature, design, dramatic arts, English, fine arts, French, German, Greek, Italian, Japanese, Latin, linguistics, music, Russian, Spanish, speech/debate/rhetoric, and studio art), COMPUTER AND PHYSICAL SCIENCE (atmospheric sciences and meteorology, chemistry, computer science, geology, hydrology, mathematics, physics, polymer science, and statistics), EDUCATION (physical), ENGINEERING AND ENVIRONMENTAL DESIGN (aeronautical engineering, agricultural engineering, bioengineering, chemical engineering, civil engineering, computer engineering, electrical/electronics engineering, environmental design, environmental science, landscape architecture/design, materials engineering, and mechanical engineering), HEALTH PROFESSIONS (community health work, and environmental health science), SOCIAL SCIENCE (African studies, American studies, anthropology, behavioral science, classical/ancient civilization, dietetics, East Asian studies, economics, food science, geography, history, human development, human ecology, international relations, medieval studies, Mexican-American/Chicano studies, Native American studies, philosophy, political science/government, psychology, religion, social science, sociology, textiles and clothing, and women's studies). Agricultural, biological, and biotechnical sciences are the strongest academically. Biological science, biochemistry, and psychology are the largest.

Required: General education requirements vary by college but are based on 3 components: topical breadth, social-cultural diversity, and writing experience. A minimum of 180 quarter units with a minimum GPA of 2.0 are required for graduation, as is proficiency in English composition and an American History and Institutions requirement.

Special: There are credit and noncredit internship programs. Study abroad in more than 32 countries and a Washington semester are offered. Students may participate in college work-study, federal work-study, and California work-study programs. Several A.B.-B.S. degrees are offered. Students may design their own majors, take dual majors, and elect pass/fail options. Interdisciplinary majors are offered in African American and African studies, American Studies, Chicana/Chicano (Mexican American) studies, comparative literature, East Asian studies, exercise science, international relations, linguistics, medieval studies, Native American studies, religious studies, and women's studies. There are 24 national honor societies, including Phi Beta Kappa, a freshman honors program, and 3 departmental honors program.

Faculty/Classroom: 69% of faculty are male; 31%, female. No introductory courses are taught by graduate students. The average class size in a laboratory is 21 and in a regular course, 56.

Admissions: 63% of the 2001-2002 applicants were accepted. The SAT I scores for the 2001-2002 freshman class were: Math--8% below 500, 34% between 500 and 599, 45% between 600 and 700, and 13% above 700. The ACT scores for the 2001-2002 freshman class were: 21% below 21, 22% between 21 and 23, 29% between 24 and 26, 15% between 27 and 28, and 13% above 28. There were 92 National Merit finalists.

Requirements: The SAT I or ACT is required. In addition, candidates for admission should have completed 4 units of English, 3 of math, and 2 each of foreign language, history/social science, lab science, and college preparatory electives, for a total of 15 units. SAT II: Subject tests are required in writing, math, and 1 other subject chosen from English literature, foreign language, science, or social studies. A GPA of 3.3 is required. AP credits are accepted. Important factors in the admissions decision are advanced placement or honor courses, evidence of special talent, and leadership record. Applications are accepted on-line.

Procedure: Freshmen are admitted fall, winter, and spring. Entrance exams should be taken no later than December of the senior year. There is a deferred admissions plan. Check with the school for current application deadlines. In Fall 2001, the application fee was $40.

Transfer: 1903 transfer students enrolled in 2001-2002. Junior-level transfers have priority. Requirements vary by college, discipline, and major.

Visiting: There are regularly scheduled orientations for prospective students, including weekend tours of the campus, weekday tours by appointment, and drop-in counseling with staff and faculty. The campus also offers a 1-day preview for prospective students and their families. There are guides for informal visits and visitors may sit in on classes and stay overnight. To schedule a visit, contact Lanette Rodriguez, Information Services Office.

Financial Aid: 44% of undergraduates work part time. The average financial indebtedness of a recent graduate was $8300. UCD is a member of CSS. The CSS/Profile or FFS is required. Check with the school for current financial aid deadlines.

International Students: There are 302 international students enrolled. They must score 500 on the written TOEFL. Students must take SAT II: Subject tests in writing, math, and 1 other subject.

Computers: There are hundreds of PCs and terminals located in numerous computer labs and classrooms throughout the campus. In addition, many PCs are provided for student use in the residence halls. All students may access the system. There are no time limits and no fees.

Graduates: In 2001, 4955 bachelor's degrees were awarded. The most popular majors were social sciences (23%), human health & development (17%), and biological sciences (16%). In an average class, 1% graduate in 3 years, 28% in 4 years, 65% in 5 years, and 75% in 6 years. Of the 2000 graduating class, 38% were enrolled in graduate school within 6 months of graduation and 79% were employed.

Admissions Contact: Dr. Gary Tudor, Director of Undergraduate Admissions. E-mail: *thinkucd@ucdavis.edu*
Web: *http://www.ucdavis.edu/admissions@html*

UNIVERSITY OF CALIFORNIA AT IRVINE D-5

Irvine, CA 92697-1075 (949) 824-6701; Fax: (949) 824-2711

Full-time: 7260 men, 8130 women	**Faculty:** 1207; I, +$
Part-time: none	**Ph.D.s:** 99%
Graduate: 1700 men, 980 women	**Student/Faculty:** 13 to 1
Year: quarters, summer session	**Tuition:** $4556 ($15,260)
Application Deadline: November 30	**Room & Board:** $7200
Freshman Class: n/av	
SAT I or ACT: required	**COMPETITIVE**

The University of California, Irvine, founded in 1965, is a public research university and part of the University of California System. Figures in above capsule are approximate. There are 8 undergraduate and 3 graduate schools. In addition to regional accreditation, UCI has baccalaureate program accreditation with AACSB and ABET. The 3 libraries contain 2.3 million volumes, 2,284,641 microform items, and 87,375 audiovisual forms/CDs, and subscribe to 18,187 periodicals. Computerized library services include the card catalog, interlibrary loans, and database searching. Special learning facilities include a learning resource center, art gallery, planetarium, radio station, freshwater marsh reserve, arboretum, laser institute, and numerous research centers. The 1489-acre campus is in a suburban area 40 miles south of Los Angeles. Including residence halls, there are 418 buildings.

Student Life: 99% of undergraduates are from California. Others are from 49 states, 59 foreign countries, and Canada. 88% are from public schools. 55% are Asian American; 21% white; 11% Hispanic. The average age of freshmen is 18; all undergraduates, 21. 7% do not continue beyond their first year; 74% remain to graduate.

Housing: 4645 students can be accommodated in college housing, which includes single-sex and coed dormitories, on-campus apartments, and married-student housing. In addition, there are honors houses, language houses, special-interest houses, academic theme houses, an 80-space RV park (vehicles not included), and houses to lease for fraternities and sororities. On-campus housing is guaranteed for the freshman year only, is available on a first-come, first-served basis, and is available on a lottery system for upperclassmen. 68% of students commute. Alcohol is not permitted. All students may keep cars.

Activities: 7% of men belong to 12 national fraternities; 7% of women belong to 9 national sororities. There are 275 groups on campus, including art, band, cheerleading, choir, chorale, chorus, computers, dance, drama, ethnic, film, gay, honors, international, jazz band, literary magazine, musical theater, newspaper, opera, orchestra, pep band, political, professional, radio and TV, religious, social, social service, student government, symphony, and yearbook. Popular campus events include Celebrate UCI, Rainbow Festival, and Engineering Week.

Sports: There are 11 intercollegiate sports for men and 9 for women, and 23 intramural sports for men and 20 for women. Facilities include a 2500-seat track stadium, a 5000-seat events center, a 1000-seat soccer field, a 500-seat tennis stadium, baseball and other fields, a swimming pool, 6 indoor handball/racquetball/squash courts, and an activities hall with areas for badminton, basketball, volleyball, combatives, fencing, and weight training. A sailing and crew base is located in nearby Newport Beach.

Disabled Students: 99% of the campus is accessible. Wheelchair ramps, elevators, special parking, specially equipped rest rooms, special class scheduling, lowered drinking fountains, lowered telephones, and automatic doors, and transportation on and off campus are available.

Services: Counseling and information services are available, as is tutoring in most subjects. There is a reader service for the blind, and remedial math, reading, and writing.

Campus Safety and Security: Measures include 24-hour foot and vehicle patrol, self-defense education, escort service, and shuttle buses. There are informal discussions, pamphlets/posters/films, emergency telephones, and lighted pathways/sidewalks.

Programs of Study: UCI confers B.A., B.S., B.F.A., and B.Mus. degrees. Master's and doctoral degrees are also awarded. Bachelor's degrees are awarded in BIOLOGICAL SCIENCE (biology/biological science and ecology), COMMUNICATIONS AND THE ARTS (art history and appreciation, Chinese, classics, comparative literature, dance, dramatic arts, English, film arts, fine arts, French, German, Japanese, linguistics, music, Russian, Spanish, and studio art), COMPUTER AND PHYSICAL SCIENCE (chemistry, information sciences and systems, mathematics, and physics), ENGINEERING AND ENVIRONMENTAL DESIGN (aeronautical engineering, chemical engineering, civil engineering, computer engineering, electrical/electronics engineering, engineering, environmental design, environmental engineering, and mechanical engineering), SOCIAL SCIENCE (anthropology, classical/ancient civilization, criminology, crosscultural studies, East Asian studies, economics, geography, history, human ecology, humanities, international studies, philosophy, political science/government, psychology, social science, sociology, and women's studies). Biological sciences, political science, and economics are the strongest academically. Biological sciences, social ecology, and economics are the largest.

Required: To graduate, students must maintain a GPA of at least 2.0, earn 180 quarter units, and fulfill requirements in English composition and in American history and institutions. Under distribution requirements, 3 courses each must be completed in writing beyond the introductory level, natural sciences, social and behavioral sciences, humanistic inquiry, and math and symbolic systems, and 1 course each in multicultural studies and global issues.

Special: Students may study abroad in Spain, England, India, Kenya, Sweden, and Egypt. UCI also offers internships, a Washington semester, work-study programs with the university, B.A.-B.S. degrees, dual majors, and pass/fail options. There are 3 national honor societies, including Phi Beta Kappa, a freshman honors program, and 14 departmental honors programs.

Faculty/Classroom: 81% of faculty are male; 19%, female. All both teach and do research. The average class size in an introductory lecture is 250; in a laboratory, 24; and in a regular course, 37.

Admissions: There were 9 National Merit finalists in a recent.

Requirements: The SAT I or ACT is required, minimum scores are determined by an eligibility index. In addition, SAT II: Subject tests in writing, math, and a third chosen from science, social science, foreign language, or English literature are required. Applicants need 15 academic credits, including 4 years of English, 3 in math, and 2 each in foreign language, history/social science, lab science, and electives. An additional year each in foreign language, math, and science is recommended. An essay also is needed. The GED is accepted. Applications are accepted on-line at *www.ucop.edu/pathways/*. A GPA of 2.85 is required. AP credits are accepted.

Procedure: Freshmen are admitted in the fall. Entrance exams should be taken no later than December of the senior year. Applications should be filed by November 30 for fall entry, July 31 for winter entry, and October 31 for spring entry. Notification is sent March 1. Check with the school for current deadlines. The fall 2001 application fee was $40.

Transfer: 922 transfer students enrolled in a recent year. Applicants must have completed 60 transferable units, including 2 semesters of English composition and 1 semester of math. Some majors require completion of prerequisites. California Community College transfers receive preference. 36 credits of 180 must be completed at UCI.

Visiting: There are regularly scheduled orientations for prospective students. There are guides for informal visits and visitors may sit in on classes and stay overnight. To schedule a visit, contact the Office of Admissions and Relations with Schools and Colleges.

Financial Aid: In a recent year, 75% of all freshmen and 62% of continuing students received some form of financial aid. 50% of freshmen and 52% of continuing students received need-based aid. The average freshman award was $11,254. Of that total, scholarships or need-based grants averaged $5820; loans averaged $6450; and work contracts averaged $1640. Average annual earnings from campus work are $1640. The average financial indebtedness of a recent graduate was $9680. UCI is a member of CSS. The FAFSA is required. Check with the school for current deadlines.

International Students: They must score 550 on the written TOEFL and also take the SAT I or the ACT. Students must take SAT II: Subject tests in writing and math, and a third in area of the student's choice.

Computers: There are approximately 500 computer terminals/PCs located in the computer center, the student center, the library, and departmental computer labs. All students may access the system 24 hours a day. Students may access the system for 2-hour sessions. There are no fees.

Graduates: In a recent year, 3167 bachelor's degrees were awarded. The most popular majors were biological sciences (19%), social sciences (8%), and economics (7%). In an average class, 35% graduate in 4 years, 70% in 5 years, and 74% in 6 years.

Admissions Contact: Susan Wilbur, Ph.D., Director, Admissions.
Web: *www.reg.uci.edu/uci/admissions*

UNIVERSITY OF CALIFORNIA AT LOS ANGELES C-5

Los Angeles, CA 90095 **(213) 825-3101; Fax: (310) 206-1206**

Full-time: 11,381 men, 13,947 women	**Faculty:** 1806; I, +$
Part-time: none	**Ph.D.s:** 100%
Graduate: 6399 men, 5767 women	**Student/Faculty:** 17 to 1
Year: quarters, summer session	**Tuition:** $4236 ($15,309)
Application Deadline: November 30	**Room & Board:** $8991
Freshman Class: 40,739 applied, 10,953 accepted, 4247 enrolled	
SAT I Verbal/Math: 620/670	**ACT:** 27 **MOST COMPETITIVE**

University of California at Los Angeles (UCLA), founded in 1919, is a public institution offering undergraduate and graduate degrees in arts and sciences, engineering, applied science, nursing, and theater, film, and television. There are 5 undergraduate and 12 graduate schools. In addition to regional accreditation, UCLA has baccalaureate program accreditation with AACSB, ABET, ADA, CSWE, NAAB, and NLN. The 13 libraries contain 7,616,016 volumes, 6,027,333 microform items, and 250,358 audiovisual forms/CDs, and subscribe to 94,801 periodicals. Computerized library services include the card catalog and database searching. Special learning facilities include a learning resource center, art gallery, natural history museum, and radio station. The 419-acre campus is in an urban area. Including residence halls, there are 272 buildings.

Student Life: 94% of undergraduates are from California. Others are from 50 states, 100 foreign countries, and Canada. 81% are from public schools. 39% are white, 35% Asian American, 13% Hispanic. The average age of freshmen is 18; all undergraduates, 21. 4% do not continue beyond their first year; 72% remain to graduate.

Housing: 6915 students can be accommodated in college housing, which includes coed dormitories, off-campus apartments, married-student housing, fraternity houses, and sorority houses. On-campus housing is guaranteed for the freshman year only and is available on a lottery system for upperclassmen. 73% of students commute. Alcohol is not permitted.

Activities: 11% of men belong to 5 local and 23 national fraternities; 10% of women belong to 3 local and 17 national sororities. There are 700 groups on campus, including band, cheerleading, choir, chorale, chorus, computers, dance, drama, ethnic, film, gay, honors, international, literary magazine, marching band, newspaper, photography, political, professional, radio and TV, religious, social, social service, student government, and yearbook.

Sports: There are 10 intercollegiate sports for men and 11 for women, and 21 intramural sports for men and 17 for women. Facilities include a pavilion, a stadium, a tennis center, and a recreation and sports center.

Disabled Students: All of the campus is accessible. Wheelchair ramps, elevators, special parking, specially equipped rest rooms, special class scheduling, lowered drinking fountains, and lowered telephones are available.

Services: Counseling and information services are available, as is tutoring in most subjects. There is a reader service for the blind, and remedial math, reading, and writing.

Campus Safety and Security: Measures include 24-hour foot and vehicle patrol, self-defense education, escort service, and shuttle buses. There are informal discussions, pamphlets/posters/films, and lighted pathways/sidewalks.

Programs of Study: UCLA confers B.A. and B.S. degrees. Master's and doctoral degrees are also awarded. Bachelor's degrees are awarded in BIOLOGICAL SCIENCE (biochemistry, biology/biological science, botany, marine biology, microbiology, molecular biology, neurosciences, and physiology), BUSINESS (business economics and international economics), COMMUNICATIONS AND THE ARTS (African languages, Arabic, art, art history and appreciation, Chinese, communications, comparative literature, design, dramatic arts, English, film arts, French, German, Greek, Hebrew, Italian, Japanese, Korean, Latin, linguistics, music, music history and appreciation, Portuguese, Russian languages and literature, Scandinavian languages, Slavic languages, and Spanish), COMPUTER AND PHYSICAL SCIENCE (applied mathematics, applied physics, astrophysics, atmospheric sciences and meteorology, chemistry, computer mathematics, computer science, cybernetics, earth science, geology, geophysics and seismology, mathematics, paleontology, and physics), ENGINEERING AND ENVIRONMENTAL DESIGN (aeronautical engineering, chemical engineering, civil engineering, computer engineering, electrical/electronics engineering, geological engineering, geophysical engineering, materials engineering, and mechanical engineering), HEALTH PROFESSIONS (nursing), SOCIAL SCIENCE (African American studies, American studies, anthropology, Asian/American studies, classical/ancient civilization, cognitive science, crosscultural studies, East Asian studies, economics, European studies, geography, Hispanic American studies, history, human ecology, interdisciplinary studies, international studies, Italian studies, Judaic studies, Latin American studies, Near Eastern studies, philosophy, political science/government, psychobiology, psychology, religion, Russian and Slavic studies, sociology, and women's studies). Biology, psychology, and economics are the largest.

Required: Students must complete a minimum of 180 quarter units and maintain a minimum GPA of 2.0 in all courses. All students must demonstrate a proficiency in English composition, or take specific courses to achieve this proficiency, and must also meet course requirements in American history and institutions. Other requirements vary by major and college or school.

Special: Opportunities are provided for internships, work-study programs, study abroad in 33 countries, B.A.-B.S. degrees, student-designed majors, dual majors, and interdisciplinary majors, including chemistry and materials science, Chicana and Chicano studies, and math and engineering. There is a Washington, D.C., program for 20 to 30 students selected each fall and spring. There are 4 national honor societies, including Phi Beta Kappa, a freshman honors program, and 7 departmental honors programs.

Faculty/Classroom: 77% of faculty are male; 23%, female.

Admissions: 27% of the 2001-2002 applicants were accepted. The SAT I scores for the 2001-2002 freshman class were: Verbal--9% below 500, 28% between 500 and 599, 43% between 600 and 700, and 19% above 700; Math--4% below 500, 19% between 500 and 599, 41% between 600 and 700, and 36% above 700. The ACT scores were 2% below 17, 26% between 18 and 23, 48% between 24 and 29, and 24% between 30 and 36.

Requirements: The SAT I or ACT is required. Graduation from an accredited secondary school is required. Applicants must submit a challenging academic program, including honors and AP-level courses in English, math, a language other than English, science, and history and social science; most students complete at least 42 semester courses in these areas. SAT II: Subject tests in writing, math, and 1 subject of the student's choice are required. An essay is required, and a portfolio and audition are required for all art, theater, and film and television majors. UCLA requires applicants to be in the upper 13% of their class. A GPA of 3.3 is required. AP credits are accepted. Important factors in the admissions decision are advanced placement or honor courses, evidence of special talent, and leadership record. Applications may be submitted on-line at *www.ucop.edu/pathways* or via UC Application.

Procedure: Freshmen are admitted in the fall. Entrance exams should be taken preferably in the junior year, but no later than December of the senior year. Applications should be filed by November 30 for fall entry. The Fall 2001 application fee was $40. Notification is sent March 31.

Transfer: 2427 transfer students enrolled in 2001-2002. For minimum requirements, transfer students must have earned 90 quarter units at the previous college and have completed preparatory courses for the selected major. Most students selected present a GPA of 3.0 or better. 68 quarter credits of 180 must be completed at UCLA.
Visiting: There are regularly scheduled orientations for prospective students, including campus tours by current UCLA students, offered weekdays at 10:15 and 2:15. Reservations are required. Visitors may sit in on classes. To schedule a visit, contact Tours in Undergraduate Admissions at (310) 825-8764.
Financial Aid: In 2001-2002, 59% of all freshmen and 61% of continuing students received some form of financial aid. 45% of freshmen and 60% of continuing students received need-based aid. The average freshman award was $9800. Of that total, scholarships or need-based grants averaged $6900 ($9000 maximum); loans averaged $5600 ($6500 maximum); and work contracts averaged $1600 ($5000 maximum). 41% of undergraduates work part time. Average annual earnings from campus work are $3436. The average financial indebtedness of the 2001 graduate was $16,825. The FAFSA and the college's own financial statement are required. The fall application deadline is March 2.
International Students: There are 726 international students enrolled. They must score 550 on the written TOEFL and also take the SAT I or the ACT. Students must take SAT II: Subject tests in writing, math, and a choice of literature, foreign language, science, or social science.
Computers: The mainframe is an IBM 3090 Model 600S. There are also IBM, HP, Zenith, and DEC VAX PCs available throughout the campus. All students may access the system 24 hours a day, 7 days a week. Time limits vary by individual department. There are no fees.
Graduates: In 2001, 6309 bachelor's degrees were awarded. The most popular majors were psychology (13%), economics (13%), and political science (8%). In an average class, 75% graduate in 5 years and 80% in 6 years. 396 companies recruited on campus in a recent year.
Admissions Contact: Director of Undergraduate Admissions and Relations with Schools. E-mail: *ugadm@saonet.ucla.edu*
Web: *http://www.ucla.edu*

UNIVERSITY OF CALIFORNIA AT RIVERSIDE D-5

Riverside, CA 92521 **(909) 787-3411; Fax: (909) 787-6344**

Full-time: 5660 men, 6588 women	**Faculty:** 663; I, av$
Part-time: 239 men, 227 women	**Ph.D.s:** 98%
Graduate: 875 men, 840 women	**Student/Faculty:** 18 to 1
Year: quarters, summer session	**Tuition:** $4379 ($15,449)
Application Deadline: November 30	**Room & Board:** $8100
Freshman Class: 20,980 applied, 17,909 accepted, 3272 enrolled	
SAT I Verbal/Math: 500/560	**ACT:** 21 **COMPETITIVE**

University of California at Riverside, founded in 1954, is a public liberal arts institution with undergraduate programs in engineering, humanities, arts, social sciences, and natural and agricultural sciences. There are 3 undergraduate and 5 graduate schools. In addition to regional accreditation, UCR has baccalaureate program accreditation with ABET. The 6 libraries contain 1,896,960 volumes, 1,603,000 microform items, and 21,331 audiovisual forms/CDs, and subscribe to 13,316 periodicals. Computerized library services include the card catalog, interlibrary loans, and database searching. Special learning facilities include a learning resource center, art gallery, radio station, a museum of photography, botanical gardens, and various research centers. The 1200-acre campus is in an urban area 50 miles east of Los Angeles. Including residence halls, there are 476 buildings.
Student Life: 99% of undergraduates are from California. Others are from 35 states, 22 foreign countries, and Canada. 87% are from public schools. 42% are Asian American; 24%, white; 22%, Hispanic. The average age of freshmen is 18; all undergraduates, 21. 16% do not continue beyond their first year.
Housing: 2254 students can be accommodated in college housing, which includes coed dormitories, on-campus apartments, off-campus apartments, married-student housing, and fraternity houses. In addition, there are honors houses, special-interest houses, and an international village. On-campus housing is guaranteed for the freshman year only and is available on a first-come, first-served basis. 70% of students commute. All students may keep cars.
Activities: 3% of men belong to 5 local and 11 national fraternities; 3% of women belong to 5 local and 9 national sororities. There are 200 groups on campus, including art, bagpipe band, band, cheerleading, chess, choir, chorale, chorus, computers, dance, drama, ethnic, gay, honors, international, jazz band, literary magazine, marching band, musical theater, newspaper, orchestra, pep band, photography, political, professional, radio and TV, religious, social, social service, student government, and yearbook. Popular campus events include Highlander Days, Oktoberfest, and Winter Arts Festival.
Sports: There are 8 intercollegiate sports for men and 9 for women, and 10 intramural sports for men and 10 for women. Facilities include a heated Olympic-size pool, weight rooms, a track, a vita course, racquetball and tennis courts, basketball and volleyball courts, a gym, an aerobics room, a roller hockey rink, and a student recreation center.
Disabled Students: 90% of the campus is accessible. Wheelchair ramps, elevators, special parking, specially equipped rest rooms, special class scheduling, lowered drinking fountains, lowered telephones, and automatic doors are available.
Services: Counseling and information services are available, as is tutoring in every subject, including individual and group tutoring. There is a reader service for the blind, and remedial math, reading, and writing. There are also study skills classes, preparation sessions for graduate entrance exams, study groups, individual counseling and lab work, speed-reading classes, and English as a Second Language classes.
Campus Safety and Security: Measures include 24-hour foot and vehicle patrol, self-defense education, escort service, and shuttle buses. There are informal discussions, pamphlets/posters/films, emergency telephones, lighted pathways/sidewalks, and a ride-along program.
Programs of Study: UCR confers B.A. and B.S. degrees. Master's and doctoral degrees are also awarded. Bachelor's degrees are awarded in BIOLOGICAL SCIENCE (biochemistry, biology/biological science, botany, entomology, and neurosciences), BUSINESS (business administration and management and business economics), COMMUNICATIONS AND THE ARTS (art, art history and appreciation, Chinese, classics, comparative literature, creative writing, dance, dramatic arts, English, French, German, languages, linguistics, music, Russian, and Spanish), COMPUTER AND PHYSICAL SCIENCE (chemistry, computer science, geology, geophysics and seismology, information sciences and systems, mathematics, physical sciences, physics, and statistics), ENGINEERING AND ENVIRONMENTAL DESIGN (chemical engineering, electrical/electronics engineering, environmental engineering, environmental science, and mechanical engineering), HEALTH PROFESSIONS (premedicine), SOCIAL SCIENCE (African American studies, anthropology, Asian/Oriental studies, classical/ancient civilization, community services, economics, ethnic studies, history, human development, humanities, Latin American studies, liberal arts/general studies, Mexican-American/Chicano studies, Native American studies, philosophy, political science/government, psychobiology, psychology, religion, social science, sociology, and women's studies). Biomedical sciences is the strongest academically. Business administration, biology, and psychology are the largest.
Required: Students must demonstrate proficiency in English and a knowledge of American history and institutions and complete a maximum of 6 phys ed units. A total of 180 quarter credit hours with a minimum GPA of 2.0 is required in order to graduate. The number of hours in the major varies. All students must complete a 1-year sequence in English composition, in computers, math, or statistics, and in concepts/issues of ethnicity. There are breadth requirements in humanities, social sciences, and natural sciences/math for all students; the number of units/courses in each group depends on the student's college and major. A thesis is required for honors program students.
Special: Internships, work-study programs with various agencies and employers on and off campus, study abroad in 35 countries, and a semester in Washington in conjunction with the College of William and Mary are available. An accelerated degree in biomedical science is offered in conjunction with UCLA. Student-designed majors, dual majors, opportunities for undergraduate research, and pass/fail options in elective subjects are possible. Grants are available for research, fieldwork, or other creative activity. Academic internships and co-op programs are offered in all majors. There are 8 national honor societies, including Phi Beta Kappa, a freshman honors program, and 13 departmental honors program.
Faculty/Classroom: 69% of faculty are male; 31%, female. 93% teach undergraduates, 68% do research, and 68% do both. No introductory courses are taught by graduate students. The average class size in an introductory lecture is 25; in a laboratory, 20; and in a regular course, 22.
Admissions: 85% of the 2001-2002 applicants were accepted. The SAT I scores for the 2001-2002 freshman class were: Verbal--47% below 500, 36% between 500 and 599, 15% between 600 and 700, and 2% above 700; Math--26% below 500, 39% between 500 and 599, 28% between 600 and 700, and 7% above 700. The ACT scores were 47% below 21, 26% between 21 and 23, 16% between 24 and 26, 6% between 27 and 28, and 5% above 28.
Requirements: The SAT I or ACT is required. The minimum GPA varies from 2.8 to 3.3, depending on SAT I or ACT scores. Candidates for admission should have completed 4 years of English, 3 of math, and 2 of foreign language, history, science, and electives. SAT II: Subject tests are required in writing, mathematics, and 1 subject of the student's choice. A GPA of 2.8 is required. AP credits are accepted. Important factors in the admissions decision are advanced placement or honor courses, evidence of special talent, and extracurricular activities record. Applications are accepted on-line at *www.ucop.edu/pathways*.
Procedure: Freshmen are admitted fall, winter, and spring. Entrance exams should be taken by October or November of the senior year. There is an early admissions plan. Applications should be filed by November 30 for fall entry, July 31 for winter entry, and October 31 for spring entry, along with a $40 fee. Notification is sent March 31.
Transfer: 773 transfer students enrolled in 2001-2002. Applicants need a minimum college GPA of 2.4 (2.8 for nonresidents). 35 credits of 180 must be completed at UCR.

Visiting: There are regularly scheduled orientations for prospective students, Through the Host program, prospective students may attend classes and stay overnight in a residence hall. Along with University Preview Day in October and Open House in April, tours are available throughout the year. There are guides for informal visits and visitors may sit in on classes and stay overnight. To schedule a visit, contact the Office of Undergraduate Admissions at (909) 787-4531.

Financial Aid: In 2001-2002, 75% of all freshmen and 55% of continuing students received some form of financial aid. 60% of freshmen and 50% of continuing students received need-based aid. The average freshman award was $11,412. Of that total, scholarships or need-based grants averaged $6754; loans averaged $3621; and work contracts averaged $1037. 20% of undergraduates work part time. The average financial indebtedness of the 2001 graduate was $11,283. UCR is a member of CSS. The FAFSA is required. The fall application deadline is March 2.

International Students: There are 211 international students enrolled. They must score 550 on the written TOEFL.

Computers: The mainframe is a DEC 2100 ALPHA Server cluster (VMSAXP) with an IBM ES/9000-311 (MVS/ESA). There are more than 600 terminals and PCs, including NeXT, Power Mac, and high-end DOS/Windows PCs, plus more than 150 printers. They are located in dorms, the student center, and various campus buildings. All terminals have Internet access, including on-line access to the UC Library System, computer classes, and e-mail accounts. All students may access the system. There are no time limits and no fees.

Graduates: In 2001, 1966 bachelor's degrees were awarded. The most popular majors were business administration (25%), biology (8%), and psychology (8%). In an average class, 37% graduate in 4 years, 61% in 5 years, and 64% in 6 years. 280 companies recruited on campus in 2000-2001. Of the 2000 graduating class, 37% were enrolled in graduate school within 6 months of graduation and 60% were employed.

Admissions Contact: Laurie Nelson, Director of Undergraduate Admissions. E-mail: *discover@pop.ucr.edu* Web: *http://www.ucr.edu*

UNIVERSITY OF CALIFORNIA AT SAN DIEGO D-5
La Jolla, CA 92093 (858) 534-4831

Full-time: 7891 men, 8605 women	**Faculty:** I, +$
Part-time: none	**Ph.D.s:** 95%
Graduate: 3716 men and women	**Student/Faculty:** n/av
Year: quarters, summer session	**Tuition:** $3862 ($14,566)
Application Deadline: November 30	**Room & Board:** $7510
Freshman Class: 35,691 applied, 13,718 accepted, 3122 enrolled	
SAT I or ACT: required	**HIGHLY COMPETITIVE**

University of California at San Diego, founded in 1960, is a public liberal arts institution. There are 6 undergraduate and 5 graduate schools. In addition to regional accreditation, UCSD has baccalaureate program accreditation with ABET. The 8 libraries contain 2,616,776 volumes, 2,880,645 microform items, and 87,625 audiovisual forms/CDs, and subscribe to 24,986 periodicals. Computerized library services include the card catalog, interlibrary loans, and database searching. Special learning facilities include an art gallery, radio station, TV station, and aquarium-museum. The 1976-acre campus is in a suburban area 12 miles north of downtown San Diego. Including residence halls, there are 501 buildings.

Student Life: 98% of undergraduates are from California. Others are from 70 foreign countries and Canada. 90% are from public schools. 39% are white; 35%, Asian American; 10%, Hispanic. The average age of freshmen is 18; all undergraduates, 21. 7% do not continue beyond their first year.

Housing: 5108 students can be accommodated in college housing, which includes coed dormitories, on-campus apartments, off-campus apartments, and married-student housing. In addition, there are language houses and special-interest houses. On-campus housing is guaranteed for the freshman year only and is available on a lottery system for upperclassmen. 64% of students commute. All students may keep cars.

Activities: 10% of men belong to 14 national fraternities; 10% of women belong to 19 national sororities. There are 350 groups on campus, including art, band, cheerleading, chess, choir, chorale, chorus, computers, dance, debate, drama, ethnic, film, gay, honors, international, jazz band, literary magazine, musical theater, newspaper, opera, orchestra, pep band, photography, political, professional, radio and TV, religious, social, social service, student government, symphony, and yearbook. Popular campus events include Fall Festival on the Green, Spring Sun God Festival, and Asian Pacific Awareness Week.

Sports: There are 12 intercollegiate sports for men and 12 for women, and 27 intramural sports for men and 23 for women. Facilities include a 9-lane, all-weather track, soccer and softball fields, an athletic training facility, 2 pools, a spa, a weight room, tennis courts, playing fields, and a golf driving range. An 188,000-square-foot recreation complex features a 5000-seat arena, 8 handball/racquetball courts, 2 squash courts, a 12,000-square-foot weight-training facility, and basketball, volleyball, and badminton courts.

Disabled Students: 95% of the campus is accessible. Wheelchair ramps, elevators, special parking, specially equipped rest rooms, special class scheduling, lowered drinking fountains, lowered telephones, special accommodations, and administrative support services are available.

Services: Counseling and information services are available, as is tutoring in most subjects. There is a reader service for the blind.

Campus Safety and Security: Measures include 24-hour foot and vehicle patrol, self-defense education, escort service, and shuttle buses. There are informal discussions, pamphlets/posters/films, emergency telephones, lighted pathways/sidewalks, and , a student safety awareness program, peer educators, and an on-campus police department.

Programs of Study: UCSD confers B.A. and B.S. degrees. Master's and doctoral degrees are also awarded. Bachelor's degrees are awarded in AGRICULTURE (animal science), BIOLOGICAL SCIENCE (biochemistry, biology/biological science, biophysics, ecology, microbiology, molecular biology, and physiology), BUSINESS (management science), COMMUNICATIONS AND THE ARTS (art history and appreciation, Chinese, classics, communications, dance, dramatic arts, English literature, Germanic languages and literature, linguistics, literature, music, music history and appreciation, music technology, studio art, and visual and performing arts), COMPUTER AND PHYSICAL SCIENCE (applied mathematics, applied physics, chemistry, computer science, earth science, information sciences and systems, mathematics, physical chemistry, and physics), EDUCATION (mathematics and science), ENGINEERING AND ENVIRONMENTAL DESIGN (aerospace studies, bioengineering, chemical engineering, computer engineering, electrical/electronics engineering, engineering, engineering physics, environmental science, and mechanical engineering), SOCIAL SCIENCE (anthropology, cognitive science, economics, ethnic studies, French studies, gender studies, history, human development, Italian studies, Japanese studies, Judaic studies, Latin American studies, philosophy, political science/government, psychology, religion, Russian and Slavic studies, sociology, Spanish studies, Third World studies, and urban studies). Sciences, the arts, and social sciences are the strongest academically. Biology, psychology, and applied mechanics and engineering are the largest.

Required: Graduation requirements vary by college but students must complete 180 to 184 total quarter units or 45 to 46 courses, with a minimum of 60 credit hours or 12 to 22 courses in the major. Students must maintain a minimum GPA of 2.0.

Special: Internships in many fields, work-study, study abroad in more than 30 countries, and a Washington semester are offered. B.A.-B.S. degrees, an accelerated degree, dual majors, student-designed majors, and exchange programs with Dartmouth College, Spelman College, and Morehouse College are available. Nondegree study, credit for military experience, and pass/fail options are possible. There are 2 national honor societies, including Phi Beta Kappa, a freshman honors program, and 14 departmental honors program.

Faculty/Classroom: 76% of faculty are male; 24%, female. All both teach and do research. The average class size in an introductory lecture is 300; in a laboratory, 40; and in a regular course, 100.

Admissions: 38% of the 2001-2002 applicants were accepted. 100% of the current freshmen were in the top fifth of their class.

Requirements: The SAT I or ACT is required. In addition, 3 SAT II: Subject tests, including writing, math I or II, and a choice of English literature, foreign language, science, or social studies, are required. Candidates for admission should have completed 4 years of English, 3 of math, and 2 each of a foreign language, lab science, history, and college preparatory electives. A GPA of 2.8 is required for California residents. AP credits are accepted. Important factors in the admissions decision are advanced placement or honor courses, evidence of special talent, and extracurricular activities record. Applications are accepted on-line.

Procedure: Freshmen are admitted in the fall. Entrance exams should be taken by December of the senior year. Applications should be filed by November 30 for fall entry. Notification is sent March 30. The fall 2001 application fee was $40.

Transfer: 1250 transfer students enrolled in 2001-2002. California residents should have a competitive GPA; average 2001 GPA was 3.35. Transfers should have completed 90 quarter units. Preference is given to applicants from state community colleges. 36 credits of 180 must be completed at UCSD.

Visiting: There are regularly scheduled orientations for prospective students. There are guides for informal visits and visitors may sit in on classes. To schedule a visit, contact Campus Tours at (858) 534-1935 or *campustours@ucsd.edu*.

Financial Aid: In a recent year, 51% of all freshmen received some form of financial aid. Scholarships or need-based grants averaged $5504; and loans averaged $3733. 75% of undergraduates work part time. Average annual earnings from campus work are $1325. UCSD is a member of CSS. The FAFSA is required. The fall application deadline is May 1.

International Students: There are 206 international students enrolled. They must score 550 on the written TOEFL and also take the SAT I or the ACT. Students must take SAT II: Subject tests in writing, math I or II, and either English literature, foreign language, science, or social studies.

Computers: There are 1020 computer terminals available for student use in computer labs, libraries, the student center, and each undergraduate college. Students have access to e-mail, the Internet, and the World Wide Web. There is a campuswide network. All students may access the system 24 hours every day. There are no fees. It is strongly recommended that all students have a personal computer.

Graduates: In a recent year, 3574 bachelor's degrees were awarded. The most popular majors were social sciences (42%), science/math (32%), and engineering (13%). In an average class, 1% graduate in 3 years, 30% in 4 years, 66% in 5 years, and 74% in 6 years. 600 companies recruited on campus in 2000-2001.

Admissions Contact: Mae Brown, Dir, Office of Adms and Relations. E-mail: *admissionsinfo@ucsd.edu* Web: *http://admissions.ucsd.edu/*

UNIVERSITY OF CALIFORNIA AT SANTA BARBARA C-5

Santa Barbara, CA 93106 **(805) 893-2881; Fax: (805) 893-2676**

Full-time: 7782 men, 9208 women	**Faculty:** 792; I, +$
Part-time: 390 men, 344 women	**Ph.D.s:** 100%
Graduate: 1459 men, 1190 women	**Student/Faculty:** 21 to 1
Year: quarters, summer session	**Tuition:** $3841 ($14,915)
Application Deadline: November 30	**Room & Board:** $7891
Freshman Class: 34,022 applied, 17,018 accepted, 3649 enrolled	
SAT I Verbal/Math: 580/620	**ACT:** 25 **VERY COMPETITIVE**

The University of California at Santa Barbara, founded in 1909, is a public liberal arts institution offering programs in creative studies, engineering, and letters and science. There are 3 undergraduate schools and 1 graduate school. In addition to regional accreditation, UCSB has baccalaureate program accreditation with ABET and CSAB. The library contains 2,674,331 volumes, 3,669,358 microform items, and 103,495 audiovisual forms/CDs, and subscribes to 18,898 periodicals. Computerized library services include the card catalog, interlibrary loans, and database searching. Special learning facilities include a learning resource center, art gallery, radio station, language and learning lab, and numerous national and multicampus research institutes. The 813-acre campus is in a suburban area 10 miles west of Santa Barbara. Including residence halls, there are 300 buildings.

Student Life: 94% of undergraduates are from California. Others are from 48 states, 45 foreign countries, and Canada. 86% are from public schools. 56% are white; 15% Hispanic; 14% Asian American. The average age of freshmen is 18; all undergraduates, 21. 12% do not continue beyond their first year; 67% remain to graduate.

Housing: 4069 students can be accommodated in college housing, which includes coed dormitories, on-campus apartments, off-campus apartments, and married student housing. In addition, there are special-interest floors. On-campus housing is available on a first-come, first-served basis. 79% of students commute. All students may keep cars.

Activities: 15% of men belong to 2 local and 20 national fraternities; 16% of women belong to 4 local and 14 national sororities. There are 300 groups on campus, including band, cheerleading, chess, choir, chorale, chorus, computers, dance, drama, ethnic, film, gay, honors, international, jazz band, literary magazine, newspaper, pep band, photography, political, professional, radio and TV, religious, social, social service, student government, and yearbook. Popular campus events include Club Day, Activities Fair, and UCEN Cultural Festival.

Sports: There are 11 intercollegiate sports for men and 10 for women, and 18 intramural sports for men and 18 for women. Facilities include a football stadium, a track, 24 tennis courts, an aquatics complex plus a campus swimming pool, 2 gyms, a gymnastics area, a weight room, a Nautilus facility, a wellness institute, an aerobics studio, outdoor basketball courts, softball and baseball fields, a ropes course and climbing wall, and a sailing center.

Disabled Students: 98% of the campus is accessible. Wheelchair ramps, elevators, special parking, specially equipped rest rooms, special class scheduling, lowered drinking fountains, and lowered telephones are available.

Services: Counseling and information services are available, as is tutoring in most subjects. There is a reader service for the blind and remedial reading and writing.

Campus Safety and Security: Measures include 24-hour foot and vehicle patrol, self-defense education, escort service, and emergency telephones. There are lighted pathways/sidewalks.

Programs of Study: UCSB confers B.A., B.S., B.F.A., and B.M. degrees. Master's and doctoral degrees are also awarded. Bachelor's degrees are awarded in BIOLOGICAL SCIENCE (biochemistry, biology/biological science, cell biology, evolutionary biology, marine biology, microbiology, physiology, and zoology), BUSINESS (business economics), COMMUNICATIONS AND THE ARTS (art, art history and appreciation, Chinese, classics, communications, comparative literature, dance, dramatic arts, English, film arts, French, German, Germanic languages and literature, Japanese, linguistics, literature, music, music performance, music theory and composition, Portuguese, Slavic languages, and Spanish), COMPUTER AND PHYSICAL SCIENCE (chemistry, computer science, geology, geophysics and seismology, hydrology, mathematics, physics, and statistics), ENGINEERING AND ENVIRONMENTAL DESIGN (chemical engineering, electrical/electronics engineering, environmental science, and mechanical engineering), HEALTH PROFESSIONS (pharmacy), SOCIAL SCIENCE (African American studies, anthropology, Asian/American studies, Asian/Oriental studies, biopsychology, economics, geography, history, interdisciplinary studies, Islamic studies, Italian studies, Latin American studies, law, medieval studies, Mexican-American/Chicano studies, philosophy, political science/government, psychology, public affairs, religion, sociology, and women's studies). Business economics, political science, and biological science are the largest.

Required: Graduation requirements vary by college. Generally, students will take one third of their distribution in the major subject, one third in general education courses, and one third in elective courses. General subject requirements include courses in English, foreign language, science/math/technology, social sciences, civilization and thought, literature, and the arts; specific subject requirements include 6 writing-intensive courses and 1 course each in non-Western culture, quantitative relationships, and ethnic studies. To graduate, students must earn at least 180 quarter units, with a minimum GPA of 2.0, and have completed the American History and Institutions requirement.

Special: A Washington semester, internships, study abroad in 32 countries, work-study programs, student-designed majors, the B.A.-B.S. degree, and an accelerated degree program in electrical engineering are offered. There are 6 national honor societies, including Phi Beta Kappa, and a freshman honors program.

Faculty/Classroom: 69% of faculty are male; 31%, female. All both teach and do research. The average class size in an introductory lecture is 60; in a laboratory, 24; and in a regular course, 30.

Admissions: 50% of the 2001-2002 applicants were accepted. The SAT I scores for the 2001-2002 freshman class were: Verbal--15% below 500, 40% between 500 and 599, 37% between 600 and 700, and 8% above 700; Math--8% below 500, 31% between 500 and 599, 45% between 600 and 700, and 15% above 700.

Requirements: The SAT I or ACT is required, as well as SAT II: Subject tests in writing, math, and 1 other choice. Candidates for admission must have completed 4 years of English, 3 of math, and 2 each of foreign language, lab science, history/social science, and college-preparatory electives. An additional year each in foreign language, math, and science is recommended. AP and CLEP credits are accepted. Applications are accepted on line

Procedure: Freshmen are admitted in the fall. Entrance exams should be taken by November of the senior year. Applications should be filed by November 30 for fall entry. The fall application fee was $40. Notification is sent March 1.

Transfer: 1291 transfer students enrolled in 2001-2002. California residents should have a minimum 2.0 GPA in transferable course work; nonresidents, a 2.8 GPA. Students with fewer than 12 quarter or semester units of transferable course work must provide standardized test scores. 35 quarter credits of 180 must be completed at UCSB.

Visiting: There are regularly scheduled orientations for prospective students, consisting of a campus film, an information session, and a walking tour of the campus led by a student guide. There are guides for informal visits and visitors may sit in on classes and stay overnight. To schedule a visit, contact the Office of Relations with Schools at (805) 893-2485.

Financial Aid: In 2001-2002, 45% of all freshmen and 42% of continuing students received some form of financial aid. 36% of freshmen and 33% of continuing students received need-based aid. The average freshman award was $9446. The average financial indebtedness of the 2001 graduate was $16,426. UCSB is a member of CSS. The FAFSA is required. The fall application deadline is March 2.

International Students: They must score 500 on the written TOEFL and also take the SAT I or the ACT. Students must take SAT II: Subject tests in in writing, math, and 1 other choice.

Computers: They are accessed via numerous systems and networks on campus. There are more than 1800 terminals available in PC and departmental labs. All students may access the system at any time, if students have their own computer and modem. There are no time limits and no fees.

Graduates: The most popular majors among 2001 graduates were social sciences/history (24%), business/marketing (12%), and visual and performing arts (8%).

Admissions Contact: Undergraduate Admissions Office.
E-mail: *appinfo@sa.ucsb.edu* Web: *www.ucsb.edu*

UNIVERSITY OF CALIFORNIA AT SANTA CRUZ B-3

Santa Cruz, CA 95064 (831) 459-4008; Fax: (831) 459-4452

Full-time: 4914 men, 6468 women	**Faculty:** 485; I, av$
Part-time: 311 men, 341 women	**Ph.D.s:** 100%
Graduate: 541 men, 595 women	**Student/Faculty:** 23 to 1
Year: quarters, summer session	**Tuition:** $4300 ($15,004)
Application Deadline: November 30	**Room & Board:** $9355
Freshman Class: 19,578 applied, 15,833 accepted, 3020 enrolled	
SAT I Verbal/Math: 572/577	**ACT:** 23 **VERY COMPETITIVE**

The University of California, at Santa Cruz, opened in 1965, is a public institution in a small-college setting with the academic resources of a major university, offering programs in the arts, engineering, humanities, natural sciences, and social sciences. There are 10 undergraduate schools and 1 graduate school. In addition to regional accreditation, UCSC has baccalaureate program accreditation with ABET. The 10 libraries contain 1,302,295 volumes, 831,193 microform items, and 41,187 audiovisual forms/CDs, and subscribe to 9023 periodicals. Computerized library services include the card catalog, interlibrary loans, and database searching. Special learning facilities include a learning resource center, art gallery, radio station, agroecology program farm, arboretum, Long Marine Lab, and Lick Observatory on Mt. Hamilton. The 2000-acre campus is in a small town 40 miles north of Monterey and 75 miles south of San Francisco. Including residence halls, there are 467 buildings.

Student Life: 94% of undergraduates are from California. Others are from 49 states, 22 foreign countries, and Canada. 80% are from public schools. 61% are white; 18% Asian American; 15% Hispanic. The average age of freshmen is 18; all undergraduates, 21. 13% do not continue beyond their first year.

Housing: 4050 students can be accommodated in college housing, which includes single-sex and coed dormitories, on-campus apartments, off-campus apartments, and married-student housing. In addition, there are language houses, special-interest houses, and multicultural residence halls. On-campus housing is guaranteed for the freshman year only and is available on a lottery system for upperclassmen. 56% of students commute. Alcohol is not permitted. Upperclassmen may keep cars.

Activities: 1% of men belong to 4 national fraternities; 1% of women belong to 3 local and 3 national sororities. There are 100 groups on campus, including art, chess, choir, chorale, chorus, computers, dance, debate, drama, ethnic, film, gay, honors, international, jazz band, literary magazine, musical theater, orchestra, photography, political, professional, radio and TV, religious, social, social service, student government, symphony, and yearbook. Popular campus events include Multicultural Festival, Martin Luther King Jr. Convocation, and Preview Day.

Sports: There are 15 intercollegiate sports for men and 15 for women, and 5 intramural sports for men and 5 for women. Facilities include a 50-meter pool, 2 playing fields, a weight room, an all-weather jogging track, fully equipped gyms, a fitness course, racquetball, tennis, and basketball courts, and a 12,000-square-foot fitness center.

Disabled Students: 90% of the campus is accessible. Wheelchair ramps, elevators, special parking, specially equipped rest rooms, special class scheduling, lowered drinking fountains, lowered telephones, and wheelchair lift-equipped transportation are available.

Services: Counseling and information services are available, as is tutoring in some subjects, including writing. There is a reader service for the blind. A learning center helps SAA/EOP students with math and writing skills.

Campus Safety and Security: Measures include 24-hour foot and vehicle patrol, self-defense education, escort service, and shuttle buses. There are informal discussions, pamphlets/posters/films, emergency telephones, lighted pathways/sidewalks, a rape prevention program, seminars for residential staff, and guards at each entrance from 8 P.M. until dawn.

Programs of Study: UCSC confers B.A., B.S., and B.M. degrees. Master's and doctoral degrees are also awarded. Bachelor's degrees are awarded in AGRICULTURE (environmental studies), BIOLOGICAL SCIENCE (biochemistry, biology/biological science, and marine biology), BUSINESS (business economics and international economics), COMMUNICATIONS AND THE ARTS (art, art history and appreciation, classical languages, dramatic arts, film arts, French, linguistics, literature, and music), COMPUTER AND PHYSICAL SCIENCE (chemistry, computer science, earth science, geology, information sciences and systems, mathematics, and physics), ENGINEERING AND ENVIRONMENTAL DESIGN (computer engineering), SOCIAL SCIENCE (American studies, anthropology, community services, economics, German area studies, history, Italian studies, Latin American studies, law, philosophy, political science/government, psychobiology, psychology, religion, Russian and Slavic studies, sociology, South Asian studies, and women's studies). Psychology, biology, and literature are the largest.

Required: To graduate, all students must complete 36 full-credit courses (180 quarter units) with a minimum GPA of 2.0. They must satisfy university requirements in American history and institutions and in English composition, the senior residence, the core course, and a comprehensive exam or senior thesis. Particular college requirements and those of approved majors vary.

Special: Cross-registration is possible with other University of California campuses, Hampshire College, the University of New Hampshire, and the University of New Mexico. UCSC also offers work-study, internships in many arenas, study abroad in 34 countries, student-designed majors, dual majors, a 3-2 engineering degree with the University of California at Berkeley, and a B.A.-B.S. degree in earth sciences, chemistry and biochemistry, and computer science. There is a chapter of Phi Beta Kappa, a freshman honors program, and 1 departmental honors program.

Faculty/Classroom: 60% of faculty are male; 40%, female. All both teach and do research. Graduate students teach 1% of introductory courses. The average class size in an introductory lecture is 100.

Admissions: 81% of the 2001-2002 applicants were accepted. 96% of the current freshmen were in the top fifth of their class.

Requirements: The SAT I or ACT is required, as are SAT II: Subject tests in writing, math, and a choice of English literature, social science, foreign language, or science. Applicants must be graduates of an accredited secondary school or have a GED certificate. They should have completed 15 academic credits, including 4 years of English, 3 of math, and 2 each of foreign language, history, lab science, and college preparatory electives. Auditions are required for music majors, and portfolios are recommended for art majors. All students must submit a personal statement. Nonresidents must meet additional requirements. A GPA of 2.8 is required for in-stste students, 3.4 for out of state students. AP credits are accepted. Important factors in the admissions decision are advanced placement or honor courses, evidence of special talent, and extracurricular activities record. Applications are accepted on-line at *http://www.ucop.edu/pathways*.

Procedure: Freshmen are admitted in the fall. Entrance exams should be taken by December of the senior year. Applications should be filed by November 30 for fall entry and July 31 for winter entry. The fall 2001 application fee was $40. Notification is sent March 1.

Transfer: 963 transfer students enrolled in 2001-2002. Applicants should have completed 84 quarter credits, with a GPA of 2.4 required for California residents and 2.8 for nonresidents, and all subject areas must be completed. No senior transfers are accepted. 35 quarter credits of 180 must be completed at UCSC.

Visiting: There are guides for informal visits and visitors may sit in on classes and stay overnight. To schedule a visit, contact the Office of Admissions.

Financial Aid: The FAFSA is required. The fall application deadline is March 2.

International Students: There are 134 international students enrolled. They must score 550 on the written TOEFL or 220 on the electronic version and also take the SAT I or the ACT. Students must take SAT II: Subject tests in writing, math, and 1 other (not math).

Computers: The mainframe is a Sun SPARC Station 10. There are Macs and IBM PCs available in 13 open-access computer labs and in classrooms throughout the campus, providing e-mail and Internet access. ResNet provides Internet access to all students in university-sponsored housing. All students may sign up for e-mail addresses. All students may access the system. There are no time limits and no fees. It is strongly recommended that all students have a personal computer.

Graduates: In 2001, 2503 bachelor's degrees were awarded. In an average class, 1% graduate in 3 years, 41% in 4 years, 59% in 5 years, and 64% in 6 years.

Admissions Contact: Kevin Browne, Executive Director of Admissions and University Registrar. A video is available.
E-mail: *admissions@cats.ucsc.edu* Web: *http://admissions.ucsc.edu*

UNIVERSITY OF JUDAISM COLLEGE OF ARTS AND SCIENCES C-5

Bel Air, CA 90077 (310) 476-9777, ext. 261
(888) UJ FOR ME; Fax: (310) 471-3657

Full-time: 42 men, 56 women	**Faculty:** 10
Part-time: 4 men, 4 women	**Ph.D.s:** 100%
Graduate: 56 men, 67 women	**Student/Faculty:** 10 to 1
Year: semesters	**Tuition:** $15,550
Application Deadline: January 31	**Room & Board:** $8680
Freshman Class: 81 applied, 72 accepted, 26 enrolled	
SAT I or ACT: required	**COMPETITIVE**

The College of Arts and Sciences at the University of Judaism is distinguished by its core curriculum integrating the study of Western and Jewish civilizations. It prepares students for careers and graduate studies in law, business, psychology, education, and other fields. There are 3 graduate schools. The library contains 105,000 volumes, and subscribes to 400 periodicals. Computerized library services include the card catalog and interlibrary loans. Special learning facilities include a learning resource center, art gallery, and radio station. The 28-acre campus is in a suburban area. Including residence halls, there are 9 buildings.

Student Life: 71% of undergraduates are from California. Others are from 22 states and 2 foreign countries. 80% are from public schools.

81% are white; 10%, Hispanic. Most are Jewish. The average age of freshmen is 18; all undergraduates, 23. 5% do not continue beyond their first year; 90% remain to graduate.

Housing: 192 students can be accommodated in college housing, which includes coed dormitories, on-campus apartments, and married-student housing. On-campus housing is guaranteed for all 4 years. 85% of students live on campus; of those, 80% remain on campus on weekends. All students may keep cars.

Activities: There are no fraternities or sororities. There are many groups and organizations on campus, including art, chorus, dance, drama, literary magazine, newspaper, political, radio and TV, religious, social, social service, student government, and yearbook.

Sports: Facilities include a weight room, basketball and volleyball courts, and a soccer field.

Disabled Students: All of the campus is accessible. Elevators, special parking, specially equipped rest rooms, lowered drinking fountains, lowered telephones, and specially equipped dormitory rooms are available.

Services: Counseling and information services are available, as is tutoring in most subjects. There is remedial math and writing.

Campus Safety and Security: Measures include 24-hour foot and vehicle patrol, self-defense education, informal discussions, and pamphlets/posters/films. There are lighted pathways/sidewalks.

Programs of Study: UJ confers the B.A. degree. Master's degrees are also awarded. Bachelor's degrees are awarded in BUSINESS (business administration and management), COMMUNICATIONS AND THE ARTS (journalism and literature), HEALTH PROFESSIONS (premedicine), SOCIAL SCIENCE (ethics, politics, and social policy, Judaic studies, liberal arts/general studies, political science/government, and psychology).

Required: All students must complete a core curriculum combining the study of Jewish and Western civilizations, as well as courses in communications and foreign language, and 1 in computer science. There are distribution requirements in math, natural and behavioral sciences, and fine arts. Other requirements vary according to the major, with at least 32 to 36 upper-division credits needed. A total of 127 semester units, with a minimum GPA of 2.0, is required to graduate.

Special: There is a 5-year joint business management program with University of Judaism's Lieber School of Graduate Studies. Student-designed and dual majors are available. Internships in all available majors, study abroad, work-study programs, accelerated degree programs, and pass/fail options are offered. Students may apply for independent study projects.

Faculty/Classroom: 75% of faculty are male; 25%, female. All teach undergraduates and all both teach and do research. No introductory courses are taught by graduate students. The average class size in an introductory lecture is 13; in a laboratory, 6; and in a regular course, 9.

Admissions: 89% of the 2001-2002 applicants were accepted.

Requirements: The SAT I or ACT is required with scores of at least 1100 on the SAT I or 23 on the ACT preferred. Applicants must be graduates of an accredited secondary school or have the GED. A visit and an interview are recommended for all students. Two recommendations from teachers, an autobiographical essay, and a secondary school report/recommendation from an academic counselor also are required. Students scoring below 500 verbal on the SAT I or earning below a 3.2 GPA are occasionally admitted if their essay, recommendations, and grades in English and other humanities courses are exceptionally strong. AP credits are accepted.

Procedure: Freshmen are admitted fall and spring. Entrance exams should be taken no later than November of the year prior to enrollment. There are early decision and deferred admissions plans. Early decision application should be filed by November 15; regular applications, by January 31 for fall entry and November 1 for spring entry. Notification of early decision is sent December 15; regular decision, on a rolling basis. The fall 2001 application fee was $35.

Transfer: 19 transfer students enrolled in 2001-2002. Previous college work should be at the B level to transfer. Students with fewer than 60 college credits should also have a minimum 3.0 high school GPA, at least 1100 on the SAT I or 23 on the ACT, 2 recommendations, and an autobiographical essay. The SAT I or ACT requirement is waived if the applicant has 60 or more transferable credits. A visit and an interview are recommended. 34 credits of 127 must be completed at UJ.

Visiting: There are regularly scheduled orientations for prospective students, including meetings with admissions representatives and campus tours. There are guides for informal visits and visitors may sit in on classes and stay overnight. To schedule a visit, contact Amnon Finkelstein, Dean of Admissions at (310) 476-9777, ext. 252 or *finaid@uj.edu*

Financial Aid: In 2001-2002, 74% of all freshmen and 78% of continuing students received some form of financial aid. 68% of freshmen and 75% of continuing students received need-based aid. Scholarships or need-based grants averaged $7950 ($14,850 maximum); loans averaged $3839 ($10,500 maximum); and work contracts averaged $2000 ($3000 maximum). 78% of undergraduates work part time. Average annual earnings from campus work are $1694. The average financial indebtedness of the 2001 graduate was $8932. UJ is a member of CSS. The FAFSA, the college's own financial statement, and tax returns and W2s are required. The fall application deadline is March 2.

International Students: There are 2 international students enrolled. They must score 550 on the written TOEFL or 213 on the electronic version and also take the SAT I scoring 1100, or the ACT.

Computers: In total, there are 4 computer rooms housing 30 IBMs and Macs, and several printers. All students may access the system. There are no time limits and no fees.

Graduates: In 2001, 22 bachelor's degrees were awarded. The most popular majors were psychology (46%), literature (23%), and Judaic studies (15%). In an average class, 75% graduate in 4 years, and 25% in 5 years. Of the 2000 graduating class, 65% were enrolled in graduate school within 6 months of graduation.

Admissions Contact: Dr. Amnon Finkelstein, Dean of Admissions. E-mail: *afinkelstein@uj.edu* Web: *www.uj.edu*

UNIVERSITY OF LA VERNE — D-5
La Verne, CA 91750-4443 — 392-2800
(800) 876-4858; Fax: (909) 392-2714

Full-time: 538 men, 805 women	**Faculty:** 97; IIA, av$
Part-time: 33 men, 46 women	**Ph.D.s:** 84%
Graduate: 671 men, 1265 women	**Student/Faculty:** 14 to 1
Year: 4-1-4, summer session	**Tuition:** $18,000
Application Deadline: February 1	**Room & Board:** $6280
Freshman Class: 1164 applied, 838 accepted, 309 enrolled	
SAT I Verbal/Math: 490/500	**ACT:** 22 **COMPETITIVE**

The University of La Verne, founded in 1891, is an independent, liberal arts and graduate studies university. There are 4 undergraduate and 5 graduate schools. The library contains 215,000 volumes, and subscribes to 4500 periodicals. Computerized library services include the card catalog, interlibrary loans, and database searching. Special learning facilities include a learning resource center, art gallery, natural history museum, radio station, TV station, a theater, and an archaeology lab. The 26-acre campus is in a suburban area 35 miles east of Los Angeles. Including residence halls, there are 16 buildings.

Student Life: 95% of undergraduates are from California. Others are from 21 states. 38% are white; 36%, Hispanic. 34% are Catholic; 32%, Protestant; 30% claim no religious affiliation. The average age of freshmen is 18; all undergraduates, 20. 18% do not continue beyond their first year.

Housing: 500 students can be accommodated in college housing, which includes single-sex and coed dormitories. In addition, there are special-interest houses. On-campus housing is available on a first-come, first-served basis and is available on a lottery system for upperclassmen. Priority is given to out-of-town students. 65% of students commute. Alcohol is not permitted. All students may keep cars.

Activities: 7% of men belong to 3 national fraternities; 10% of women belong to 1 local sorority and 2 national sororities. There are 40 groups on campus, including art, cheerleading, choir, chorale, chorus, computers, dance, debate, drama, ethnic, forensics, gay, honors, international, jazz band, literary magazine, newspaper, photography, political, professional, radio and TV, religious, social, social service, student government, and yearbook. Popular campus events include Cinco de Mayo, International Week, and Kwanzaa.

Sports: There are 11 intercollegiate sports for men and 9 for women, and 6 intramural sports for men and 6 for women. Facilities include a football stadium, 2 gyms, a pool, a weight and fitness center, tennis courts, an outdoor track, and soccer and other playing fields.

Disabled Students: 95% of the campus is accessible. Wheelchair ramps, elevators, special parking, specially equipped rest rooms, and lowered telephones are available.

Services: Counseling and information services are available, as is tutoring in most subjects. There is a reader service for the blind, and remedial math, reading, and writing. Students may use the computerized Learning Enhancement Center or schedule tutoring free of charge.

Campus Safety and Security: Measures include 24-hour foot and vehicle patrol, escort service, informal discussions, and pamphlets/posters/films. There are emergency telephones and lighted pathways/sidewalks.

Programs of Study: ULV confers B.A. and B.S. degrees. Associate, master's, and doctoral degrees are also awarded. Bachelor's degrees are awarded in BIOLOGICAL SCIENCE (biology/biological science), BUSINESS (accounting, business administration and management, business economics, electronic business, international business management, management science, and marketing and distribution), COMMUNICATIONS AND THE ARTS (art, broadcasting, communications, comparative literature, dramatic arts, English, French, German, journalism, music, and Spanish), COMPUTER AND PHYSICAL SCIENCE (chemistry, computer science, mathematics, natural sciences, and physics), EDUCATION (elementary, music, and physical), ENGINEERING AND ENVIRONMENTAL DESIGN (computer engineering and environmental science), HEALTH PROFESSIONS (health care administration), SOCIAL SCIENCE (anthropology, behavioral science, criminology, history, international studies, liberal arts/general studies, paralegal studies, philosophy, political science/government, psychology, public administration, religion, social science, and sociology). Natural science, education, and psychology are the strongest academically. Business, liberal studies, and psychology are the largest.

Required: To graduate, students must complete a minimum of 128 credit hours, with a minimum GPA of 2.0. 24 to 48 hours in the major are required, and 6 in general education. Required core courses include Values and Critical Thinking, Service Learning, International/Intercultural Experience, The Human Condition, and Toward a Sustainable Planet.

Special: Internships, study abroad in 10 countries, work-study programs, B.A.-B.S. degrees, dual majors, and nondegree study are available. Pass/fail options are also available. There are programs for adult students and locations on military bases in California and Alaska. There are 2 national honor societies, a freshman honors program, and 6 departmental honors program.

Faculty/Classroom: 63% of faculty are male; 37%, female. 72% teach undergraduates. No introductory courses are taught by graduate students. The average class size in an introductory lecture is 15; in a laboratory, 15; and in a regular course, 15.

Admissions: 72% of the 2001-2002 applicants were accepted. The SAT I scores for the 2001-2002 freshman class were: Verbal--50% below 500, 40% between 500 and 599, 8% between 600 and 700, and 2% above 700; Math--49% below 500, 39% between 500 and 599, 11% between 600 and 700, and 1% above 700. The ACT scores were 48% below 21, 29% between 21 and 23, 12% between 24 and 26, 7% between 27 and 28, and 4% above 28. 55% of the current freshmen were in the top fifth of their class; 83% were in the top two fifths.

Requirements: The SAT I or ACT is required. In addition, applicants must be graduates of an accredited secondary school. The GED is not accepted for traditional age students. An essay is required, and an interview is recommended. AP and CLEP credits are accepted. Important factors in the admissions decision are advanced placement or honor courses, recommendations by school officials, and extracurricular activities record. Applications may be submitted on-line via Embark at *www.ulv.edu/admissions/app-opt*.

Procedure: Freshmen are admitted fall and spring. Entrance exams should be taken in the junior or senior year. There is a deferred admissions plan. Applications should be filed by February 1 for fall entry and December 1 for spring entry, along with a $50 fee. Notification is sent on a rolling basis.

Transfer: 122 transfer students enrolled in 2001-2002. Applicants must demonstrate academic ability at all previous colleges attended. Students with fewer than 32 transferable semester credits must submit SAT I or ACT scores and a high school transcript. 32 credits of 128 must be completed at ULV.

Visiting: There are regularly scheduled orientations for prospective students, consisting of a spotlight weekend in April and a Campus Preview Day in October. There are guides for informal visits and visitors may sit in on classes and stay overnight. To schedule a visit, contact the Admissions Office at *admissions@ulv.edu*

Financial Aid: In 2001-2002, 80% of all students received some form of financial aid. 79% of freshmen and 78% of continuing students received need-based aid. The average freshman award was $19,486. Of that total, scholarships or need-based grants averaged $14,082 ($26,400 maximum); loans averaged $5908 ($20,625 maximum); work contracts averaged $1771 ($1800 maximum); and annual endowed, restricted, and ICSC scholarship funds $1429 ($5000 maximum). 55% of undergraduates work part time. Average annual earnings from campus work are $1748. The FAFSA and Cal Grant Application are required. The fall application deadline is March 2.

International Students: There are 30 international students enrolled. The school actively recruits these students. International applicants must demonstrate English proficiency by presenting either a TOEFL score of 500, an SAT I verbal score of 480, a grade of 3.0 on ULV's own test, or 30 transferable college credits, including the equivalent of English 110.

Computers: The mainframe is a DEC VAX 1200. 5 PC labs and a campuswide network offer a variety of hardware, software, and operating environments. All students may access the system 24 hours, 7 days a week. There are no time limits and no fees.

Graduates: In 2001, 194 bachelor's degrees were awarded. The most popular majors were business administration (24%), liberal studies (14%), and psychology (10%). In an average class, 35% graduate in 4 years, 42% in 5 years, and 46% in 6 years. 85 companies recruited on campus in 2000-2001.

Admissions Contact: Lisa Meyer, Dean of Admissions.
E-mail: *admissions@ulv.edu* Web: *www.ulv.edu*

UNIVERSITY OF REDLANDS

D-5

Redlands, CA 92373-0999

(909) 335-4074
(800) 455-5064; Fax: (909) 335-4089

Full-time: 797 men, 1108 women	**Faculty:** 132; IIA, av$
Part-time: 19 men, 22 women	**Ph.D.s:** 86%
Graduate: 16 men, 55 women	**Student/Faculty:** 14 to 1
Year: 4-1-4	**Tuition:** $21,406
Application Deadline: February 1	**Room & Board:** $7840
Freshman Class: 2478 applied, 1909 accepted, 614 enrolled	
SAT I Verbal/Math: 560/560	**ACT:** 23 **VERY COMPETITIVE**

University of Redlands, founded in 1907, is an independent institution that offers programs in liberal and fine arts, business, and teacher preparation. There are 2 undergraduate and 4 graduate schools. In addition to regional accreditation, Redlands has baccalaureate program accreditation with WASC. The library contains 419,209 volumes, 168,228 microform items, and 9855 audiovisual forms/CDs, and subscribes to 1876 periodicals. Computerized library services include the card catalog, interlibrary loans, and database searching. Special learning facilities include an art gallery, language lab, computer center, and geographic information systems lab. The 130-acre campus is in a small town 60 miles east of Los Angeles. Including residence halls, there are 40 buildings.

Student Life: 72% of undergraduates are from California. Others are from 42 states and 13 foreign countries. 62% are white; 11%, Hispanic. The average age of freshmen is 18; all undergraduates, 20. 15% do not continue beyond their first year.

Housing: 1497 students can be accommodated in college housing, which includes single-sex and coed dormitories, on-campus apartments, off-campus apartments, married-student housing, fraternity houses, and sorority houses. In addition, there are honors houses and special-interest houses. On-campus housing is guaranteed for all 4 years. 77% of students live on campus. All students may keep cars.

Activities: 24% of men belong to 7 local fraternities; 27% of women belong to 5 local sororities. There are 95 groups on campus, including art, band, cheerleading, chess, choir, chorale, chorus, dance, debate, drama, drill team, ethnic, film, gay, honors, international, jazz band, literary magazine, musical theater, newspaper, opera, orchestra, pep band, photography, political, professional, radio and TV, religious, social, social service, student government, symphony, and yearbook. Popular campus events include Mayfest, Multicultural Festival, and Feast of Lights.

Sports: There are 11 intercollegiate sports for men and 11 for women, and 11 intramural sports for men and 11 for women. Facilities include a fitness center, an aquatic center a football stadium, tennis courts, and baseball, softball, soccer, and lacrosse fields.

Disabled Students: 25% of the campus is accessible. Wheelchair ramps, elevators, special parking, specially equipped rest rooms, special class scheduling, lowered drinking fountains, and lowered telephones are available.

Services: Counseling and information services are available, as is tutoring in every subject. There is a reader service for the blind.

Campus Safety and Security: Measures include 24-hour foot and vehicle patrol, self-defense education, escort service, and shuttle buses. There are informal discussions, pamphlets/posters/films, emergency telephones, lighted pathways/sidewalks, and safety whistles.

Programs of Study: Redlands confers B.A., B.S., and B.Mus. degrees. Master's degrees are also awarded. Bachelor's degrees are awarded in BIOLOGICAL SCIENCE (biochemistry, biology/biological science, and molecular biology), BUSINESS (accounting and business administration and management), COMMUNICATIONS AND THE ARTS (art, English, French, German, music, and Spanish), COMPUTER AND PHYSICAL SCIENCE (chemistry, computer science, mathematics, and physics), ENGINEERING AND ENVIRONMENTAL DESIGN (environmental science), SOCIAL SCIENCE (anthropology, Asian/Oriental studies, economics, history, international relations, liberal arts/general studies, philosophy, political science/government, psychology, religion, and sociology). Liberal arts is the strongest academically. Business is the largest.

Required: Requirements for graduation vary according to the degree and major. Students must complete at least 132 units with a minimum of 44 in the major, and maintain a minimum GPA of 2.0. Students pursuing a B.S. degree must fulfill an additional field requirement. A capstone in the major is required.

Special: Cross-registration with sister colleges, various internships, and study abroad in 50 countries are offered. A Washington semester, a Sacramento program, various work-study programs, B.A.-B.S. degrees, a liberal studies degree, dual majors, and accelerated degree programs are available. Students may pursue nondegree study, take advantage of pass/fail options, and receive credit for life or work experience. At the Johnston Center for Integrative Studies, students design their own majors and courses of study. There are 7 national honor societies, including Phi Beta Kappa, a freshman honors program, and 24 departmental honors program.

Faculty/Classroom: 55% of faculty are male; 45%, female. All teach undergraduates. No introductory courses are taught by graduate stu-

dents. The average class size in an introductory lecture is 20; in a laboratory, 10; and in a regular course, 12.

Admissions: 77% of the 2001-2002 applicants were accepted. The SAT I scores for the 2001-2002 freshman class were: Verbal--17% below 500, 52% between 500 and 599, 26% between 600 and 700, and 5% above 700; Math--18% below 500, 51% between 500 and 599, 29% between 600 and 700, and 3% above 700. The ACT scores were 26% below 21, 30% between 21 and 23, 24% between 24 and 26, 12% between 27 and 28, and 8% above 28. There were 5 National Merit finalists.

Requirements: The SAT I or ACT is required. In addition, Redlands recommends that applicants have completed a minimum of 16 units in solid academic areas. The student should have completed at least 4 years of high school English, 2 to 3 years each of math, lab sciences, and social science, and 2 years of a foreign language. AP and CLEP credits are accepted. Important factors in the admissions decision are advanced placement or honor courses, leadership record, and personality/intangible qualities. Applications are available and can be completed at the school's web site. The Common Application is accepted.

Procedure: Freshmen are admitted to all sessions. Entrance exams should be taken prior to application. There is a deferred admissions plan. Early decision application should be filed by December 15; regular applications, by February 1 for fall entry and January 1 for spring entry. Notification is sent on a rolling basis. The fall 2001 application fee was $40.

Transfer: 80 transfer students enrolled in 2001-2002. The SAT I or the ACT may be required of transfer applicants, depending on how many units are accepted. 30 credits of 132 must be completed at Redlands.

Visiting: There are regularly scheduled orientations for prospective students, including campus tours at 10 A.M., 1 P.M., and 4 P.M., on weekdays and 11 A.M. on Saturdays during the school year. There are guides for informal visits and visitors may sit in on classes and stay overnight. To schedule a visit, contact the Visit Coordinator at (909) 793-2121, ext. 4573 or *Tamie_Fawcett@redlands.edu*

Financial Aid: In 2001-2002, 90% of all students received some form of financial aid. 89% of freshmen and 85% of continuing students received need-based aid. The average freshman award was $21,348. Of that total, scholarships or need-based grants averaged $11,347 ($21,180 maximum); loans averaged $2315 ($4000 maximum); work contracts averaged $1987 ($2000 maximum); and outside grant aid, state grant, and federal grant averaged $8851 ($24,596 maximum). 51% of undergraduates work part time. Average annual earnings from campus work are $2063. The FAFSA, the college's own financial statement, and the GPA verification Form for California residents are required.

International Students: There are 14 international students enrolled. The school actively recruits these students. They must score 550 on the written TOEFL or 213 on the electronic version.

Computers: The academic computing center provides 150 networked Mac and Windows computers connecting to Mac, NT, and UNIX servers and the Internet. These include specialized graphics/desktop publishing and geographic information systems (GIS) labs as well as general-purpose teaching and drop-in labs. All students may access the system. There are no time limits. The fee is $300.

Graduates: In 2001, 315 bachelor's degrees were awarded. The most popular majors were liberal studies (21%), social sciences/history (20%), and business (14%). In an average class, 62% graduate in 4 years, 63% in 5 years, and 64% in 6 years.

Admissions Contact: Paul M. Driscoll, Dean of Admissions.
E-mail: *admissions@uor.edu* Web: *www.redlands.edu*

UNIVERSITY OF SAN DIEGO
San Diego, CA 92110 — D-5
(619) 260-4506
(800) 248-4873; Fax: (619) 260-6836

Full-time: 1865 men, 2774 women	**Faculty:** 315
Part-time: 79 men, 91 women	**Ph.D.s:** 98%
Graduate: 1049 men, 1202 women	**Student/Faculty:** 15 to 1
Year: 4-1-4, summer session	**Tuition:** $20,458
Application Deadline: January 5	**Room & Board:** $8740
Freshman Class: 6702 applied, 3378 accepted, 1004 enrolled	
SAT I Verbal/Math: 575/590	**ACT:** 26 **HIGHLY COMPETITIVE**

The University of San Diego, founded in 1949, is an independent, Catholic liberal arts university. There are 4 undergraduate and 5 graduate schools. In addition to regional accreditation, USD has baccalaureate program accreditation with AACSB, ABET, and NLN. The 2 libraries contain 475,000 volumes and 130,000 microform items, and subscribe to 2000 periodicals. Computerized library services include the card catalog, interlibrary loans, and database searching. Special learning facilities include a learning resource center, art gallery, a media center, and a child development center. The 180-acre campus is in an urban area 10 miles north of downtown San Diego. Including residence halls, there are 24 buildings.

Student Life: 63% of undergraduates are from California. Others are from 49 states, 62 foreign countries, and Canada. 66% are from public schools. 69% are white; 12% Hispanic; 10% Asian American. 57% are Catholic; 27% Protestant. The average age of freshmen is 18; all undergraduates, 20. 8% do not continue beyond their first year; 69% remain to graduate.

Housing: 1900 students can be accommodated in college housing, which includes single-sex and coed dormitories and on-campus apartments. In addition, there are honors houses and special-interest houses. On-campus housing is guaranteed for all 4 years. 55% of students live on campus; of those, 70% remain on campus on weekends. All students may keep cars.

Activities: 20% of men belong to 4 national fraternities; 20% of women belong to 4 national sororities. There are 68 groups on campus, including art, cheerleading, choir, chorus, dance, drama, ethnic, gay, honors, international, jazz band, newspaper, opera, orchestra, political, professional, religious, social, social service, student government, and yearbook. Popular campus events include the Annual Bike Race and Hunger Awareness Week.

Sports: There are 8 intercollegiate sports for men and 8 for women, and 15 intramural sports for men and 15 for women. Facilities include a sports center, a stadium, tennis courts, a golf course, a swimming pool, soccer, baseball, and softball fields, and the Mission Bay Aquatic Center.

Disabled Students: 80% of the campus is accessible. Wheelchair ramps, elevators, special parking, specially equipped rest rooms, and lowered drinking fountains are available. Individual needs can be accommodated.

Services: Counseling and information services are available, as is tutoring in every subject.

Campus Safety and Security: Measures include 24-hour foot and vehicle patrol, self-defense education, escort service, and shuttle buses. There are informal discussions, pamphlets/posters/films, emergency telephones, and lighted pathways/sidewalks.

Programs of Study: USD confers B.A., B.A./B.S., B.Acc., B.B.A., and B.S.N. degrees. Master's and doctoral degrees are also awarded. Bachelor's degrees are awarded in BIOLOGICAL SCIENCE (biology/biological science and marine science), BUSINESS (accounting, business administration and management, and business economics), COMMUNICATIONS AND THE ARTS (communications, English, fine arts, French, music, and Spanish), COMPUTER AND PHYSICAL SCIENCE (chemistry, computer science, mathematics, oceanography, and physics), EDUCATION (elementary and secondary), ENGINEERING AND ENVIRONMENTAL DESIGN (electrical/electronics engineering and industrial engineering), HEALTH PROFESSIONS (nursing), SOCIAL SCIENCE (anthropology, economics, history, humanities, international relations, liberal arts/general studies, philosophy, political science/government, psychology, religion, sociology, and urban studies). Business administration and communications are the largest.

Required: All students must take 124 credit hours, including 36 to 72 in their major, while maintaining a minimum GPA of 2.0. Distribution requirements include 9 units each of religious studies and humanities and fine arts, 6 each of philosophy, natural sciences, and social sciences, 3 or 4 of math, 3 of composition and literature, as well as 3 semesters of foreign language.

Special: A co-op program and a B.A.-B.S. degree are offered in electrical engineering. Internships in all disciplines, study abroad in 7 countries, work-study programs on campus, dual majors in marine science and ocean studies, nondegree study through the lawyer assistance program, and pass/fail options are available. There are 15 national honor societies and a freshman honors program.

Faculty/Classroom: 55% of faculty are male; 45%, female. 90% teach undergraduates; 50% do research. No introductory courses are taught by graduate students. The average class size in an introductory lecture is 30; in a laboratory, 15; and in a regular course, 22.

Admissions: 50% of the 2001-2002 applicants were accepted. The SAT I scores for the 2001-2002 freshman class were: Verbal--13% below 500, 47% between 500 and 599, 35% between 600 and 700, and 5% above 700; Math--10% below 500, 41% between 500 and 599, 43% between 600 and 700, and 5% above 700. The ACT scores were 33% between 21 and 23, 56% between 24 and 26, 16% between 27 and 28, and 8% above 28. 80% of the current freshmen were in the top fifth of their class; 97% were in the top two fifths. 53 freshmen graduated first in their class.

Requirements: The SAT I is required with a recommended score of 500 verbal and 500 math. In addition, the university recommends that applicants have 4 units each of high school English and math, 3 or 4 in foreign language, 2 or 3 in science, and 2 each in history and social studies. An essay also is necessary. The GED is accepted. AP and CLEP credits are accepted. Important factors in the admissions decision are advanced placement or honor courses, extracurricular activities record, and recommendations by school officials. Applications are accepted on-line via CollegeView, College Net, Apply, and XAPlication.

Procedure: Freshmen are admitted fall, spring, and summer. Entrance exams should be taken before December 30. There is an early admissions plan. Applications should be filed by January 5 for fall entry and November 1 for spring entry, along with a $55 fee. Notification is sent April 15. 8% of all applicants are on a waiting list; 26 were accepted in 2001.

Transfer: 323 transfer students enrolled in 2001-2002. Transfer students must have a minimum GPA of 3.0 and have earned 24 credit hours. 30 credits of 124 must be completed at USD.

Visiting: There are regularly scheduled orientations for prospective students, including tours and information sessions run by the Admissions Office, Monday through Friday at 10 A.M. and 2 P.M., and Saturday, from November through April at 10 A.M. and noon. There are guides for informal visits and visitors may sit in on classes. To schedule a visit, contact the Admissions Office at (800) 248-4873 or (619) 260-4506.

Financial Aid: In 2001-2002, 69% of all freshmen and 61% of continuing students received some form of financial aid. 50% of freshmen and 46% of continuing students received need-based aid. The average freshman award was $17,869. Of that total, scholarships or need-based grants averaged $8046; loans averaged $5000; work contracts averaged $2250; and athletic awards averaged $11,532. 21% of undergraduates work part time. Average annual earnings from campus work are $18,000. The average financial indebtedness of the 2001 graduate was $23,800. The FAFSA and the college's own financial statement are required. The fall application deadline is February 20.

International Students: There are 139 international students enrolled. The school actively recruits these students. They must score 550 on the written TOEFL or 213 on the electronic version, and also take the SAT I or the ACT. Students must also take the SAT II: Subject tests in writing.

Computers: The mainframes are a DEC VAX 6300 and a 6330. There are 300 Macs and PCs located in buildings across campus. All students may access the system. There are no time limits and no fees.

Graduates: In 2001, 1056 bachelor's degrees were awarded. The most popular majors were business administration (26%), communication (10%), and psychology (7%). In an average class, 62% graduate in 4 years, 68% in 5 years, and 67% in 6 years. 110 companies recruited on campus in 2000-2001. Of the 2000 graduating class, 36% were enrolled in graduate school within 6 months of graduation and 96% were employed.

Admissions Contact: Stephen Pultz, Director of Undergraduate Admissions. E-mail: *admissions@sandiego.edu* Web: *www.sandiego.edu*

UNIVERSITY OF SAN FRANCISCO B-3

San Francisco, CA 94117-1080 (415) 422-6563
(800) CALLUSF; Fax: (415) 422-2217

Full-time: 1556 men, 2649 women	**Faculty:** 250
Part-time: 120 men, 120 women	**Ph.D.s:** 92%
Graduate: 1237 men, 1918 women	**Student/Faculty:** 17 to 1
Year: 4-1-4, summer session	**Tuition:** $19,060
Application Deadline: February 15	**Room & Board:** $8242
Freshman Class: 3838 applied, 3038 accepted, 845 enrolled	
SAT I Verbal/Math: 550/550	**ACT:** 23 **VERY COMPETITIVE**

The University of San Francisco, founded in 1855, is a private Roman Catholic institution run by the Jesuit Fathers and offering degree programs in the arts and sciences, business, education, nursing, and law. There are 5 undergraduate and 6 graduate schools. In addition to regional accreditation, USF has baccalaureate program accreditation with AACSB, ACS, APA, CSAB, and NLN. The 2 libraries contain 877,303 volumes, 852,413 microform items, and 5420 audiovisual forms/CDs, and subscribe to 5000 periodicals. Computerized library services include the card catalog, interlibrary loans, and database searching. Special learning facilities include a learning resource center, art gallery, radio station, rare book room, the Institute for Chinese-Western Cultural History, and the Center for Pacific Rim Studies. The 55-acre campus is in an urban area in the heart of the city. Including residence halls, there are 17 buildings.

Student Life: 69% of undergraduates are from California. Others are from 50 states, 53 foreign countries, and Canada. 44% are from public schools. 39% are white; 27%, Asian American; 12%, Hispanic. 48% are Catholic; 33%, Buddhist, Hindu, or Muslim. The average age of freshmen is 18; all undergraduates, 21. 18% do not continue beyond their first year; 65% remain to graduate.

Housing: 1900 students can be accommodated in college housing, which includes single-sex and coed dormitories and off-campus apartments. In addition, there are special-interest houses. Alcohol is not permitted. All students may keep cars.

Activities: 1% of men belong to 2 local fraternities and 1 national fraternity; 2% of women belong to 4 local and 2 national sororities. There are 75 groups on campus, including cheerleading, choir, chorus, computers, drama, ethnic, honors, international, literary magazine, musical theater, newspaper, pep band, political, professional, radio and TV, religious, social, social service, and student government. Popular campus events include Founders Day and International Week.

Sports: There are 7 intercollegiate sports for men and 7 for women, and 8 intramural sports for men and 8 for women. Facilities include a 600-seat soccer stadium, a recreation center with a 50-meter swimming pool, a multipurpose gym, a weight room, a dance and aerobics room, a martial arts room, and 5 racquetball/handball courts.

Disabled Students: 95% of the campus is accessible. Wheelchair ramps, elevators, special parking, specially equipped rest rooms, lowered drinking fountains, and exam accommodations are available.

Services: Counseling and information services are available, as is tutoring in every subject. There is a reader service for the blind. There is a full-time counselor for learning-disabled students, as well as a learning and writing center for students in need of academic assistance.

Campus Safety and Security: Measures include 24-hour foot and vehicle patrol, self-defense education, escort service, and shuttle buses. There are informal discussions, pamphlets/posters/films, emergency telephones, and lighted pathways/sidewalks.

Programs of Study: USF confers B.A., B.S., B.Arch., B.F.A., B.P.A., B.S.B.A., and B.S.N. degrees. Master's and doctoral degrees are also awarded. Bachelor's degrees are awarded in BIOLOGICAL SCIENCE (biology/biological science), BUSINESS (accounting, banking and finance, business administration and management, hospitality management services, international business management, management information systems, marketing/retailing/merchandising, and organizational behavior), COMMUNICATIONS AND THE ARTS (communications, drawing, English, fine arts, French, graphic design, illustration, media arts, painting, performing arts, Spanish, and visual and performing arts), COMPUTER AND PHYSICAL SCIENCE (chemistry, computer science, information sciences and systems, mathematics, and physics), EDUCATION (athletic training, elementary, middle school, and secondary), ENGINEERING AND ENVIRONMENTAL DESIGN (architecture and environmental science), HEALTH PROFESSIONS (exercise science and nursing), SOCIAL SCIENCE (economics, fashion design and technology, history, law enforcement and corrections, philosophy, political science/government, psychology, public administration, religion, sociology, and theological studies). Sciences and business are the strongest academically. Communications, nursing, and psychology are the largest.

Required: All students must maintain a GPA of at least 2.0 and take 128 credit hours, including 58 in upper-division courses. The current general education requirements include 9 units each of basic skills and history/social science, 6 each of philosophy, religious studies, cultural perspectives, natural science, and literature and fine arts, and 3 of ethics.

Special: USF offers a Bachelor of Architecture with California College of Arts and Crafts, cross-registration with the San Francisco Consortium, and internships with local business, social services, and research opportunities. Study abroad in Europe and Japan, work-study programs both on and off campus, a B.A.-B.S. degree in exercise and sports medicine, dual majors in liberal arts and education, 3-2 engineering degrees with the University of Southern California, student-designed majors, nondegree study, and limited pass/fail options are also available. The College of Professional Studies is a degree completion program for working adults. There are 5 national honor societies, a freshman honors program, and 1 departmental honors program.

Faculty/Classroom: 59% of faculty are male; 41%, female. 90% teach undergraduates, 75% do research, and 90% do both. No introductory courses are taught by graduate students. The average class size in an introductory lecture is 31; in a laboratory, 14; and in a regular course, 19.

Admissions: 79% of the 2001-2002 applicants were accepted. The SAT I scores for the 2001-2002 freshman class were: Verbal--21% below 500, 47% between 500 and 599, 28% between 600 and 700, and 3% above 700; Math--17% below 500, 55% between 500 and 599, 25% between 600 and 700, and 3% above 700. The ACT scores were 24% below 21, 33% between 21 and 23, 21% between 24 and 26, 10% between 27 and 28, and 12% above 28. 51% of the current freshmen were in the top fifth of their class; 83% were in the top two fifths. 6 freshmen graduated first in their class.

Requirements: The SAT I or ACT is required. In addition, applicants are required to have 20 academic units, based on 6 years of academic electives, 4 of English, 3 each of math and social studies, and 2 each of foreign language and lab science. An essay is required. The GED is accepted. A GPA of 2.8 is required. AP and CLEP credits are accepted. Important factors in the admissions decision are extracurricular activities record, evidence of special talent, and leadership record. Upon request, the Office of Admissions will send for completion a prepared IBM or Mac disk to those students who wish to apply by computer, or students may apply on-line via the school's web site using Apply Web.

Procedure: Freshmen are admitted fall and spring. Entrance exams should be taken during the first half of the senior year. There are early admissions and deferred admissions plans. Early action application should be filed by November 15; regular applications, by February 15 for fall entry and December 15 for spring entry, along with a $45 fee. Notification of early action is sent January 1; regular decision, on a rolling basis.

Transfer: 354 transfer students enrolled in 2001-2002. Applicants need a minimum GPA of 2.0, or 2.8 if they have earned fewer than 24 semester units. 45 credits of 128 must be completed at USF.

Visiting: There are regularly scheduled orientations for prospective students, including a tour of campus, academic buildings, library, residence halls, and recreation centers, and a group information session hosted by an admissions staff member. There are guides for informal visits and visitors may sit in on classes and stay overnight. To schedule a visit, contact the Office of Admissions.

Financial Aid: In 2001-2002, 69% of all freshmen and 65% of continuing students received some form of financial aid. 56% of freshmen and 53% of continuing students received need-based aid. The average freshman award was $19,976. Of that total, scholarships or need-based grants averaged $16,184 ($33,626 maximum); loans averaged $5355 ($33,125 maximum); and work contracts averaged $2315 ($3800 maximum). 29% of undergraduates work part time. Average annual earnings from campus work are $2810. The average financial indebtedness of the 2001 graduate was $19,958. The FAFSA is required. The fall application deadline is February 15. The priority date for merit-based aid is December 1.

International Students: There are 347 international students enrolled. The school actively recruits these students. They must score 550 on the written TOEFL or 213 on the electronic version.

Computers: The mainframe is a DEC ALPHA/VMS administrative computer. There are 250 PCs available in 10 locations and operating on a LAN system. Each residence room is linked to the network, allowing e-mail and other applications. All students may access the system. There are no time limits and no fees.

Graduates: In 2001, 1081 bachelor's degrees were awarded. The most popular majors were communication (10%), business administration (9%), and psychology (8%). In an average class, 2% graduate in 3 years, 41% in 4 years, 62% in 5 years, and 64% in 6 years. 120 companies recruited on campus in 2000-2001. Of the 2000 graduating class, 15% were enrolled in graduate school within 6 months of graduation and 70% were employed.

Admissions Contact: William A. Henley, Director of Admissions.
E-mail: *admissions@usfca.edu* Web: *http://www.usfca.edu/*

UNIVERSITY OF SOUTHERN CALIFORNIA C-5

Los Angeles, CA 90089 **(213) 740-1111; Fax: (213) 740-6364**

Full-time: 7689 men, 7716 women	**Faculty:** 1304; I, +$
Part-time: 360 men, 255 women	**Ph.D.s:** 87%
Graduate: 7546 men, 6247 women	**Student/Faculty:** 12 to 1
Year: semesters, summer session	**Tuition:** $25,533
Application Deadline: January 10	**Room & Board:** $8114

Freshman Class: 26,294 applied, 8435 accepted, 2780 enrolled
SAT I Verbal/Math: 650/670 **ACT:** 29 **MOST COMPETITIVE**

University of Southern California, founded in 1880, is a private institution offering undergraduate and graduate programs in liberal arts, fine arts, education, business, law, dentistry, engineering, communications, health professions, and more. There are 14 undergraduate and 18 graduate schools. In addition to regional accreditation, USC has baccalaureate program accreditation with AACSB, ABET, ACEJMC, ACPE, ACS, ADA, ALA, AOTA, APTA, CAHEA, CSAB, CSWE, NAAB, NASM, NASPAA, NLN. The 25 libraries contain 3,654,985 volumes, 5,795,818 microform items, and 3,231,602 audiovisual forms/CDs, and subscribe to 28,561 periodicals. Computerized library services include the card catalog, interlibrary loans, and database searching. Special learning facilities include a learning resource center, art gallery, natural history museum, radio station, TV station, labs, state-of-the-art cinema/film-making facilities, wind tunnel, and marine science center. The 155-acre campus is in an urban area 3 miles south of the Los Angeles Civic Center. Including residence halls, there are 166 buildings.

Student Life: 69% of undergraduates are from California. Others are from 50 states, 108 foreign countries, and Canada. 60% are from public schools. 47% are white; 22%, Asian American; 14%, Hispanic. The average age of freshmen is 18; all undergraduates, 20. 6% do not continue beyond their first year; 73% remain to graduate.

Housing: 6400 students can be accommodated in college housing, which includes coed dormitories, on-campus apartments, off-campus apartments, married-student housing, fraternity houses, and sorority houses. In addition, there are special-interest houses, a Greek honors house, Latino, African American, multicultural, environmental, and cinema floors, and an international residence hall. On-campus housing is guaranteed for the freshman year only, is available on a first-come, first-served basis, and on a lottery system for upperclassmen. 65% of students commute. All students may keep cars.

Activities: 17% of men belong to 4 local and 21 national fraternities; 18% of women belong to 8 local and 10 national sororities. There are 303 groups on campus, including art, band, cheerleading, chess, choir, chorale, chorus, computers, dance, debate, drama, drill team, ethnic, film, gay, honors, international, jazz band, literary magazine, marching band, musical theater, newspaper, opera, orchestra, photography, political, professional, radio and TV, religious, service, social, social service, student government, symphony, volunteer, and yearbook. Popular campus events include Springfest, International Food and Cultural Fair, and Spectrum Concert Series.

Sports: There are 10 intercollegiate sports for men and 10 for women, and 24 intramural sports for men and 20 for women. Facilities include a student athletic center, a track, a gym, 2 Olympic pools, and tennis, swimming, and baseball stadiums.

Disabled Students: 95% of the campus is accessible. Wheelchair ramps, elevators, special parking, specially equipped rest rooms, special class scheduling, lowered drinking fountains, and lowered telephones are available.

Services: Counseling and information services are available, as is tutoring in every subject. There is a reader service for the blind. Accommodations are made for students with disabilities.

Campus Safety and Security: Measures include 24-hour foot and vehicle patrol, self-defense education, escort service, and shuttle buses. There are informal discussions, pamphlets/posters/films, emergency telephones, and lighted pathways/sidewalks. The safety department patrols an area 5 times the area of the campus.

Programs of Study: USC confers B.A., B.S., B.Arch., B.F.A., B. Land. Arch., and B.M. degrees. Master's and doctoral degrees are also awarded. Bachelor's degrees are awarded in BIOLOGICAL SCIENCE (biology/biological science and biophysics), BUSINESS (accounting and business administration and management), COMMUNICATIONS AND THE ARTS (art history and appreciation, broadcasting, classics, communications, comparative literature, dramatic arts, English, film arts, fine arts, French, German, jazz, journalism, linguistics, music, music business management, music performance, music theory and composition, photography, public relations, Russian, Spanish, studio art, theater design, and theater management), COMPUTER AND PHYSICAL SCIENCE (astronomy, chemistry, computer science, geology, mathematics, physical sciences, physics, and polymer science), EDUCATION (music, physical, and social science), ENGINEERING AND ENVIRONMENTAL DESIGN (aeronautical engineering, architecture, biomedical engineering, chemical engineering, civil engineering, computer engineering, electrical/electronics engineering, engineering and applied science, engineering management, environmental engineering, environmental science, mechanical engineering, and urban planning technology), HEALTH PROFESSIONS (nursing, occupational therapy, physical therapy, physician's assistant, predentistry, premedicine, and prepharmacy), SOCIAL SCIENCE (African American studies, American studies, anthropology, Asian/American studies, economics, geography, gerontology, history, international relations, philosophy, political science/government, prelaw, psychology, public administration, religion, social science, sociology, and women's studies). Business, engineering, and arts and sciences are the largest.

Required: All students must satisfy requirements in foreign language, freshman writing, and general education and take 1 multicultural course. Graduation requirements include a minimum of 128 credit hours and a minimum GPA of 2.0.

Special: Cross-registration is permitted with Hebrew Union College and Howard University. Internships in various majors, a Washington semester, study abroad in 28 countries, dual majors, a general studies degree, student-designed majors, a 3-2 engineering degree, and pass/fail options are available. Students are encouraged to pursue interdisciplinary study linking core art and science disciplines to professional programs. There are 41 national honor societies, including Phi Beta Kappa, and a freshman honors program.

Faculty/Classroom: 69% of faculty are male; 31%, female. All do research. No introductory courses are taught by graduate students. The average class size in an introductory lecture is 33; in a laboratory, 24; and in a regular course, 28.

Admissions: 32% of the 2001-2002 applicants were accepted. The SAT I scores for the 2001-2002 freshman class were: Verbal--1% below 500, 22% between 500 and 599, 52% between 600 and 700, and 25% above 700; Math--1% below 500, 13% between 500 and 599, 51% between 600 and 700, and 36% above 700. The ACT scores were 2% between 21 and 23, 10% between 24 and 26, 27% between 27 and 28, and 61% above 28. 85% of the current freshmen were in the top fifth of their class; 95% were in the top two fifths. There were 153 National Merit finalists.

Requirements: The SAT I or ACT is required. In addition, graduation from an accredited secondary school is required. Applicants must have completed 16 high school courses, including 4 years of English, 3 of math, 2 each of a foreign language, science, and social studies, plus 3 academic electives. An essay is required, and an interview is recommended. AP credits are accepted. Important factors in the admissions decision are advanced placement or honor courses, recommendations by school officials, and evidence of special talent. Applications are available on-line at USC's web site.

Procedure: Freshmen are admitted fall and spring. Entrance exams should be taken by November of the senior year for scholarship applicants; by December for all others. Applications should be filed by January 10 for fall entry, along with a $65 fee. Notification is sent April 1.

Transfer: 1244 transfer students enrolled in 2001-2002. Transfer applicants must submit 30 units of transferable work. Admissions is highly competitive and the average GPA for entering transfer students is 3.5. 48 credits of 128 must be completed at USC.

Visiting: There are regularly scheduled orientations for prospective students. There are guides for informal visits and visitors may sit in on classes and stay overnight. To schedule a visit, contact the Admission Office at (213) 740-6616.

Financial Aid: In 2001-2002, 74% of all freshmen and 72% of continuing students received some form of financial aid. 61% of freshmen and 59% of continuing students received need-based aid. The average freshman award was $19,952. Of that total, scholarships or need-based grants averaged $16,362 ($36,640 maximum); loans averaged $2650 ($36,640 maximum); and work contracts averaged $940 ($2500 maximum). The average financial indebtedness of the 2001 graduate was $20,619. USC is a member of CSS. The CSS/Profile or FAFSA and tax forms are required. The fall application deadline is January 22.

International Students: There are 1183 international students enrolled. The school actively recruits these students. They must take the college's own test.

Computers: There are approximately 2500 PCs available for student use on campus. These are linked via USCnet to the Internet. They are located in labs, residence halls, and libraries. All student rooms in university housing are wired for direct connection to the Internet. All students may access the system. There are no time limits and no fees.

Graduates: In 2001, 3746 bachelor's degrees were awarded. The most popular majors were business (26%), social sciences (13%), and visual and performing arts (13%). In an average class, 53% graduate in 4 years, 69% in 5 years, and 73% in 6 years. 664 companies recruited on campus in 2000-2001.

Admissions Contact: Laurel Tew, Director of Admissions. A video is available. Web: *www.usc.edu*

UNIVERSITY OF THE PACIFIC — B-3

Stockton, CA 95211-0197 — (209) 946-2211
(800) 959-2867; Fax: (209) 946-2413

Full-time: 1288 men, 1808 women	**Faculty:** 229; IIA, +$
Part-time: 50 men, 39 women	**Ph.D.s:** 90%
Graduate: 1128 men, 1384 women	**Student/Faculty:** 14 to 1
Year: semesters, summer session	**Tuition:** $21,525
Application Deadline: February 15	**Room & Board:** $6730
Freshman Class: 3162 applied, 2475 accepted, 732 enrolled	
SAT I Verbal/Math: 570/550	**ACT:** 23 **VERY COMPETITIVE**

The University of the Pacific, founded in 1851, is a private institution. It offers undergraduate and graduate programs in arts and sciences, and professional programs in pharmacy, law, and dentistry. There are 8 undergraduate schools and 1 graduate school. In addition to regional accreditation, UOP or Pacific has baccalaureate program accreditation with AACSB, ABET, ACPE, NASAD, NASM, and NCATE. The 2 libraries contain 276,882 volumes, 644,250 microform items, and 8594 audiovisual forms/CDs, and subscribe to 3909 periodicals. Computerized library services include the card catalog, interlibrary loans, and database searching. Special learning facilities include a learning resource center, art gallery, and radio station. The 175-acre campus is in a suburban area 80 miles east of San Francisco and 40 miles south of Sacramento. Including residence halls, there are 98 buildings.

Student Life: 80% of undergraduates are from California. Others are from Canada. 51% are white; 26%, Asian American; 10%, Hispanic. The average age of freshmen is 18; all undergraduates, 21. 14% do not continue beyond their first year.

Housing: 1987 students can be accommodated in college housing, which includes coed dormitories, on-campus apartments, married-student housing, fraternity houses, and sorority houses. In addition, there are honors houses and special-interest houses. On-campus housing is guaranteed for the freshman year only, is available on a first-come, first-served basis, and is available on a lottery system for upperclassmen. Priority is given to out-of-town students. 55% of students live on campus. Alcohol is not permitted. All students may keep cars.

Activities: 20% of men belong to 1 local fraternity and 5 national fraternities; 20% of women belong to 4 national sororities. There are 80 groups on campus, including art, band, cheerleading, choir, chorale, chorus, computers, dance, debate, drama, ethnic, forensics, gay, honors, international, jazz band, literary magazine, musical theater, newspaper, opera, orchestra, pep band, photography, political, professional, radio and TV, religious, social, social service, student government, and symphony. Popular campus events include men's basketball games, Pacific Boardwalk Carnival, and Cultural Diversity Week.

Sports: There are 7 intercollegiate sports for men and 9 for women, and 20 intramural sports for men and 20 for women. Facilities include a 6000-seat sports arena, an Olympic-size pool, tennis courts, a softball field, and a fitness center.

Disabled Students: 90% of the campus is accessible. Wheelchair ramps, elevators, special parking, specially equipped rest rooms, special class scheduling, lowered drinking fountains, and lowered telephones are available.

Services: Counseling and information services are available, as is tutoring in every subject. There is a reader service for the blind, and remedial math, reading, and writing.

Campus Safety and Security: Measures include 24-hour foot and vehicle patrol, escort service, informal discussions, and pamphlets/posters/films. There are emergency telephones and lighted pathways/sidewalks.

Programs of Study: UOP or Pacific confers B.A., B.S., B.F.A., B.M., and B.S. in Eng. degrees. Master's and doctoral degrees are also awarded. Bachelor's degrees are awarded in BIOLOGICAL SCIENCE (biochemistry and biology/biological science), BUSINESS (business administration and management and sports management), COMMUNICATIONS AND THE ARTS (art, art history and appreciation, arts administration/management, classics, communications, dramatic arts, English, French, German, graphic design, Japanese, music, music business management, music history and appreciation, music performance, music theory and composition, Spanish, and studio art), COMPUTER AND PHYSICAL SCIENCE (chemistry, computer science, geology, geophysics and seismology, information sciences and systems, mathematics, and physics), EDUCATION (art, athletic training, education, music, physical, and teaching English as a second/foreign language (TESOL/TEFOL)), ENGINEERING AND ENVIRONMENTAL DESIGN (civil engineering, computer engineering, electrical/electronics engineering, engineering management, engineering physics, environmental science, and mechanical engineering), HEALTH PROFESSIONS (music therapy, prepharmacy, speech pathology/audiology, and sports medicine), SOCIAL SCIENCE (economics, history, international relations, international studies, liberal arts/general studies, philosophy, political science/government, prelaw, psychology, religion, social science, and sociology). Natural sciences and the professions are the strongest academically. Arts and sciences, pharmacy, and business are the largest.

Required: Students must complete at least 124 credit hours to graduate. The required general education program consists of 3 "mentors seminars" and 6 to 9 other courses chosen from categories such as the Individual and Society, the Human Heritage, and the Natural World and Formal Systems of Thought.

Special: The engineering school requires and guarantees a co-op program for specialized training in the field. Internships for credit or pay in all majors, more than 230 study-abroad programs in more than 70 countries, a Washington semester, and more than 20 work-study programs also are available. Student-designed majors, dual majors in most disciplines, and pass/fail options are possible. There are 16 national honor societies and a freshman honors program. Almost all departments have honors programs.

Faculty/Classroom: 65% of faculty are male; 35%, female. No introductory courses are taught by graduate students. The average class size in an introductory lecture is 26; in a laboratory, 20; and in a regular course, 21.

Admissions: 78% of the 2001-2002 applicants were accepted. The SAT I scores for the 2001-2002 freshman class were: Verbal--25% below 500, 48% between 500 and 599, 24% between 600 and 700, and 4% above 700; Math--17% below 500, 42% between 500 and 599, 33% between 600 and 700, and 8% above 700. The ACT scores were 20% below 21, 30% between 21 and 23, 29% between 24 and 26, 12% between 27 and 28, and 8% above 28. 55% of the current freshmen were in the top fifth of their class; 85% were in the top two fifths.

Requirements: The SAT I or ACT is required. In addition, applicants must have 16 academic credits, including a recommended 4 years of high school English, 3 of math, 2 in the same foreign language, 2 of lab science, 1 of U.S. history or government, 1 of fine or performing arts, and 4 additional academic courses. An essay is required; an interview is recommended. An audition is necessary for music students. The GED is accepted. A GPA of 2.0 is required. AP and CLEP credits are accepted. Applications are accepted on computer disk and on-line via XAPplication and the school's web site.

Procedure: Freshmen are admitted fall and spring. Entrance exams should be taken in the spring of the junior year or fall of the senior year. There are early action and deferred admissions plans. Early action applications should be filed by December 15; regular applications, by February 15 for fall entry and December 15 for spring entry. Notification of early action is sent January 15; regular decision, on a rolling basis. 322 early action candidates were accepted for the 2001-2002 class. The fall 2001 application fee was $50.

Transfer: 230 transfer students enrolled in 2001-2002. Applicants should have a minimum GPA of 2.5 and at least 16 credit hours. The SAT I or ACT and high school transcripts are required if fewer than 30 units of college work have been completed. 32 credits of 124 must be completed at UOP.

Visiting: There are regularly scheduled orientations for prospective students. Individually scheduled visits may include a tour, appointments with faculty, admissions, financial aid personnel, and class visits. There are guides for informal visits and visitors may sit in on classes and stay overnight. To schedule a visit, contact Admissions.

Financial Aid: In 2001-2002, 82% of all freshmen and 88% of continuing students received some form of financial aid. 81% of freshmen and 67% of continuing students received need-based aid. The average freshman award was $9887. Of that total, loans averaged $2453. 36% of undergraduates work part time. Average annual earnings from campus work are $1300. UOP is a member of CSS. The FAFSA is required. The fall application deadline is February 15.

International Students: There are 111 international students enrolled. The school actively recruits these students. They must score 475 on the

written TOEFL or 150 on the electronic version and also take the SAT I or ACT is required if the student has attended a U.S.-style high school.

Computers: The mainframe is a SUN Enterprise 450. 185 PCs, primarily IBMs and Macs, are available for student use in residence halls and computer labs. All students may access the system any time. There are no time limits and no fees. It is recommended that students in pharmacy have personal computers.

Graduates: In 2001, 581 bachelor's degrees were awarded. The most popular majors were arts/sciences (61%), business (17%), and engineering (9%). In an average class, 1% graduate in 3 years, 48% in 4 years, 62% in 5 years, and 66% in 6 years. 125 companies recruited on campus in a recent year. Of a recent graduating class, 20% were enrolled in graduate school within 6 months of graduation and 75% were employed.

Admissions Contact: Marc McGee, Director of Admissions. E-mail: *admissions@uop.edu* Web: *www.uop.edu*

VANGUARD UNIVERSITY OF SOUTHERN CALIFORNIA D-5

Costa Mesa, CA 92626 (714) 556-3610
(800) 722-6279; Fax: (714) 966-5471

Full-time: 462 men, 734 women	**Faculty:** 43; IIB, av$
Part-time: 176 men, 206 women	**Ph.D.s:** 74%
Graduate: 102 men, 147 women	**Student/Faculty:** 28 to 1
Year: semesters, summer session	**Tuition:** $14,944
Application Deadline: open	**Room & Board:** $5268
Freshman Class: 667 applied, 583 accepted, 328 enrolled	
SAT I Verbal/Math: 501/491	**ACT:** 22 **COMPETITIVE**

Vanguard University, founded in 1920, is a Christian comprehensive university affiliated with the Assemblies of God, offering 27 majors and concentrations. The library contains 121,219 volumes, 14,217 microform items, and 2241 audiovisual forms/CDs, and subscribes to 1066 periodicals. Computerized library services include the card catalog, interlibrary loans, and database searching. Special learning facilities include a learning resource center. The 38-acre campus is in a suburban area 40 miles southeast of Los Angeles and 5 miles north of Newport Beach. Including residence halls, there are 20 buildings.

Student Life: 79% of undergraduates are from California. Others are from 42 states, 18 foreign countries, and Canada. 75% are from public schools. 75% are white; 11%, Hispanic. Most are Protestant. The average age of freshmen is 18; all undergraduates, 20. 29% do not continue beyond their first year; 71% remain to graduate.

Housing: 941 students can be accommodated in college housing, which includes single-sex dormitories, on-campus apartments, off-campus apartments, and married-student housing. On-campus housing is guaranteed for all 4 years. 58% of students live on campus. Alcohol is not permitted. All students may keep cars.

Activities: There are no fraternities or sororities. There are 50 groups on campus, including art, band, choir, chorale, chorus, debate, drama, ethnic, forensics, international, jazz band, musical theater, newspaper, orchestra, pep band, political, religious, student government, student ministries, and yearbook.

Sports: There are 6 intercollegiate sports for men and 7 for women, and 15 intramural sports for men and 15 for women. Facilities include a gym, and baseball, softball, and soccer fields.

Disabled Students: All of the campus is accessible. Wheelchair ramps, elevators, special parking, and specially equipped rest rooms are available.

Services: Counseling and information services are available, as is tutoring in every subject.

Campus Safety and Security: Measures include 24-hour foot and vehicle patrol, self-defense education, escort service, and informal discussions. There are lighted pathways/sidewalks.

Programs of Study: VU confers B.A. and B.S. degrees. Master's degrees are also awarded. Bachelor's degrees are awarded in BIOLOGICAL SCIENCE (biology/biological science), BUSINESS (accounting, banking and finance, business administration and management, international business management, marketing/retailing/merchandising, and personnel management), COMMUNICATIONS AND THE ARTS (communications, dramatic arts, English, music, and Spanish), COMPUTER AND PHYSICAL SCIENCE (chemistry and mathematics), EDUCATION (elementary, physical, science, and secondary), HEALTH PROFESSIONS (premedicine), SOCIAL SCIENCE (anthropology, biblical studies, history, ministries, political science/government, prelaw, psychology, religious education, and sociology). Religion, history/political science, and business are the strongest academically. Business, liberal studies, and religion are the largest.

Required: Students must complete a minimum of 124 credits, with 40 to 70 in the major. General education requirements include 16 credits in religion, 15 in humanities and fine arts, 12 in social science, 10 in natural sciences and math, and 2 in phys ed. VU requires a minimum GPA of 2.0 and a writing competency exam.

Special: Study abroad in Costa Rica and Russia, internships, a Washington semester, a general studies degree, work-study, and pass/fail options are available. 3 summer sessions are offered. There are 4 national honor societies and 4 departmental honors program.

Faculty/Classroom: 70% of faculty are male; 30%, female. 90% teach undergraduates. No introductory courses are taught by graduate students. The average class size in an introductory lecture is 30; in a laboratory, 12; and in a regular course, 16.

Admissions: 87% of the 2001-2002 applicants were accepted. The SAT I scores for the 2001-2002 freshman class were: Verbal--45% below 500, 43% between 500 and 599, 11% between 600 and 700, and 1% above 700; Math--54% below 500, 35% between 500 and 599, 10% between 600 and 700, and 1% above 700. 50% of the current freshmen were in the top fifth of their class; 78% were in the top two fifths. 1 freshman graduated first in the class.

Requirements: The SAT I or ACT is required. In addition, high school courses should include 4 years of English, 3 of social studies, and 2 of math and science. Applicants are required to write an application essay and submit references from a pastor/minister. A GPA of 2.5 is required. AP and CLEP credits are accepted. Important factors in the admissions decision are leadership record, advanced placement or honor courses, and evidence of special talent. Applications are accepted on-line at the school's web site.

Procedure: Freshmen are admitted fall and spring. Entrance exams should be taken in the junior year. Application deadlines are open. The application fee is $30.

Transfer: 245 transfer students enrolled in 2001-2002. Transfer applicants must submit college transcripts and have a minimum college GPA of 2.0. 24 credits of 124 must be completed at VU.

Visiting: There are regularly scheduled orientations for prospective students, consisting of University Preview on Veterans Day each year. There are guides for informal visits and visitors may sit in on classes and stay overnight. To schedule a visit, contact Undergraduate Admissions.

Financial Aid: The FAFSA, the university's own financial statement, and the state (or province) scholarship/grant forms are required. The fall application deadline is March 2.

International Students: There are 11 international students enrolled. They must score 550 on the written TOEFL or 213 on the electronic version.

Computers: There are 75 academic PCs in 4 locations on campus. All network computers have access to the Internet. All students may access the system. There are no time limits. The fee is $25 per semester. It is recommended that students in communications have personal computers.

Graduates: In 2001, 307 bachelor's degrees were awarded. The most popular majors were business (34%), psychology (15%), and religion (12%). In an average class, 31% graduate in 4 years, 36% in 5 years, and 39% in 6 years. 30 companies recruited on campus in 2000-2001.

Admissions Contact: Jessica Mireles, Director of Admissions. A video is available. E-mail: *admissions@vanguard.edu*
Web: *www.vanguard.edu*

WESTMONT COLLEGE C-5

Santa Barbara, CA 93108 (805) 565-6005
(800) 777-9011; Fax: (805) 565-6234

Full-time: 512 men, 853 women	**Faculty:** 85; IIB, av$
Part-time: 4 men, 12 women	**Ph.D.s:** 92%
Graduate: none	**Student/Faculty:** 16 to 1
Year: semesters, summer session	**Tuition:** $22,256
Application Deadline: February 15	**Room & Board:** $7092
Freshman Class: 1336 applied, 1001 accepted, 371 enrolled	
SAT I Verbal/Math: 610/600	**ACT:** 26 **VERY COMPETITIVE**

Westmont College, founded in 1937, is a selective, nondenominational Christian college devoted to the intellectual and spiritual development of students through a rigorous liberal arts curriculum. The library contains 162,274 volumes, 20,687 microform items, and 7926 audiovisual forms/CDs, and subscribes to 3211 periodicals. Computerized library services include the card catalog, interlibrary loans, and database searching. Special learning facilities include a learning resource center, art gallery, radio station, and observatory; science center with a premedical center; physiology lab; and a fitness center. The 133-acre campus is in a suburban area 90 miles north of Los Angeles. Including residence halls, there are 30 buildings.

Student Life: 65% of undergraduates are from California. Others are from 41 states, 8 foreign countries, and Canada. 71% are from public schools. 87% are white. Most are Protestant. The average age of freshmen is 18; all undergraduates, 20. 15% do not continue beyond their first year.

Housing: 1148 students can be accommodated in college housing, which includes single-sex and coed dormitories, off-campus apartments, and married-student housing. On-campus housing is guaranteed for all 4 years. 83% of students live on campus; of those, 65% remain on campus on weekends. Alcohol is not permitted. Upperclassmen may keep cars.

Activities: There are no fraternities or sororities. There are 50 groups on campus, including art, band, cheerleading, chess, choir, chorale, chorus, computers, dance, debate, drama, ethnic, film, honors, international, jazz band, leadership, literary magazine, musical theater, newspaper, orchestra, pep band, photography, political, professional, radio and TV, religious, social, social service, student government, symphony, and yearbook. Popular campus events include Community Service Day, Multicultural Fellowship Week, and theatrical and musical productions.

Sports: There are 6 intercollegiate sports for men and 6 for women, and 11 intramural sports for men and 11 for women. Facilities include a 2133-seat gym, a soccer/baseball field, a swimming pool, a fitness room, a dance studio, a track, and volleyball, tennis, basketball, and racquetball courts.

Disabled Students: 60% of the campus is accessible. Wheelchair ramps, elevators, special parking, specially equipped rest rooms, special class scheduling, lowered drinking fountains, lowered telephones, and ADA-compliant dormitory rooms for physically challenged students are available.

Services: Counseling and information services are available, as is tutoring in every subject. There is a reader service for the blind and remedial math. A writers' corner supervised by tutors is available.

Campus Safety and Security: Measures include 24-hour foot and vehicle patrol, self-defense education, escort service, and shuttle buses. There are informal discussions, pamphlets/posters/films, emergency telephones, and lighted pathways/sidewalks.

Programs of Study: Westmont confers B.A. and B.S. degrees. Bachelor's degrees are awarded in BIOLOGICAL SCIENCE (biology/biological science and neurosciences), BUSINESS (business economics), COMMUNICATIONS AND THE ARTS (art, communications, dramatic arts, English, French, modern language, music, and Spanish), COMPUTER AND PHYSICAL SCIENCE (chemistry, computer science, mathematics, and physics), EDUCATION (art, English, mathematics, music, physical, and social science), ENGINEERING AND ENVIRONMENTAL DESIGN (engineering physics), HEALTH PROFESSIONS (exercise science), SOCIAL SCIENCE (European studies, history, liberal arts/general studies, philosophy, political science/government, psychology, religion, social science, and sociology). Biology, communication studies, and economics/business are the largest.

Required: All students must earn a minimum GPA of 2.0 while taking at least 124 credit hours, including 36 to 66 in the major. A total of 60 units in general education courses is required, with 16 units in religious studies and 4 units in phys ed. Also required are courses in the history of Western civilization, English composition, and math.

Special: Westmont offers cross-registration with 12 Christian colleges, internships in local businesses and social agencies, study abroad in 11 countries, and semesters in Washington, D.C., San Francisco, and Los Angeles. B.A.-B.S. degrees, student-designed majors, work-study programs, a 3-2 engineering program with several California universities, University of Washington, and Boston University, and pass/fail options also are available. There are also preprofessional programs in dentistry, law, medicine, ministry/missions, optometry, pharmacology, physical therapy, and veterinary medicine. There are 7 national honor societies, a freshman honors program, and 9 departmental honors programs.

Faculty/Classroom: 71% of faculty are male; 29%, female. All both teach and do research. The average class size in an introductory lecture is 30; in a laboratory, 15; and in a regular course, 20.

Admissions: 75% of the 2001-2002 applicants were accepted. The SAT I scores for the 2001-2002 freshman class were: Verbal--4% below 500, 43% between 500 and 599, 40% between 600 and 700, and 13% above 700; Math--5% below 500, 39% between 500 and 599, 48% between 600 and 700, and 8% above 700. The ACT scores were 2% below 21, 21% between 21 and 23, 30% between 24 and 26, 24% between 27 and 28, and 23% above 28. 65% of the current freshmen were in the top fifth of their class; 92% were in the top two fifths. There were 12 National Merit finalists. 39 freshmen graduated first in their class.

Requirements: The SAT I or ACT is required. SAT I scores of 500 verbal and 500 math or an ACT composite score of 25 is recommended. Applicants need 16 academic credits, including 4 years of high school English, 3 of math, 2 each of a foreign language, social science, and physical science, and 1 each of history and biological science. Interviews are recommended. Essays are required. The GED is accepted. A GPA of 3.0 is required. AP and CLEP credits are accepted. Important factors in the admissions decision are advanced placement or honor courses, leadership record, and extracurricular activities record. Applications are accepted on computer disk, and on-line via CollegeLink, XAP, Princeton Review, and Westmont's web site.

Procedure: Freshmen are admitted fall and spring. Entrance exams should be taken during the spring of the junior year or the beginning of the senior year. Early decision application should be filed by December 1; regular applications, by February 15 for fall entry and November 1 for spring entry. Notification of early decision is sent January 15; regular decision, April 1. The fall 2001 application fee was $40 (on-line), $50 (paper).

Transfer: 54 transfer students enrolled in 2001-2002. Transfer students from 2-year colleges must have a minimum GPA of 2.8, and those students from 4-year colleges or universities, a 2.5. The college will not accept more than 64 transferable units from a community college; there is no maximum number of transferable units from a 4-year college. High school transcripts and test scores are required if the student has fewer than 24 transferable units. 32 credits of 124 must be completed at Westmont.

Visiting: There are regularly scheduled orientations for prospective students, consisting of meeting faculty and administrators and attending classes, academic seminars, student/parent panels, academic open houses, admission and financial aid sessions, student led small groups, campus tours, and various cultural events. There are guides for informal visits and visitors may sit in on classes and stay overnight. To schedule a visit, contact Admissions/Campus Visit Coordinator at (805) 565-6200.

Financial Aid: In 2001-2002, 76% of all freshmen and 83% of continuing students received some form of financial aid. 75% of freshmen and 82% of continuing students received need-based aid. The average freshman award was $15,623. Of that total, scholarships or need-based grants averaged $11,816; loans averaged $3848; and work contracts averaged $919. 54% of undergraduates work part time. Average annual earnings from campus work are $872. The average financial indebtedness of the 2001 graduate was $17,557. The FAFSA is required. The fall application deadline is March 2.

International Students: There are 6 international students enrolled. They must score 560 on the written TOEFL or 260 on the electronic version and also take the SAT I or the ACT.

Computers: The mainframes are 3 IBM RS/6000s. There are 11 PCs and 47 Macs available in the library. There are Ethernet connections in every office, every dorm room, and many classrooms. The complete network has access to the Internet. All students may access the system. There are no time limits and no fees. It is strongly recommended that all students have a personal computer.

Graduates: In 2001, 278 bachelor's degrees were awarded. The most popular majors were economics and business (16%), communication studies (14%), and biology (13%). In an average class, 3% graduate in 3 years, 61% in 4 years, 66% in 5 years, and 68% in 6 years. 52 companies recruited on campus in 2000-2001. Of the 2000 graduating class, 48% were enrolled in graduate school within 6 months of graduation and 85% were employed.

Admissions Contact: Joyce M. Luy, Director of Admissions. A video is available. E-mail: *admissions@westmont.edu*
Web: *http://www.westmont.edu*

WHITTIER COLLEGE

Whittier, CA 90608 — D-5 — **(562) 907-4238; Fax: (562) 907-4870**

Full-time: 533 men, 697 women	**Faculty:** 96; IIB, +$
Part-time: 27 men, 13 women	**Ph.D.s:** 88%
Graduate: 335 men, 493 women	**Student/Faculty:** 13 to 1
Year: 4-1-4, summer session	**Tuition:** $22,066
Application Deadline: February 1	**Room & Board:** $7042
Freshman Class: 1321 applied, 1209 accepted, 345 enrolled	
SAT I Verbal/Math: 539/541	**ACT:** 23 **COMPETITIVE**

Whittier College, founded in 1887 by the Society of Friends, is an independent liberal arts institution with no religious affiliation. Some information in this profile is approximate. There are 2 graduate schools. In addition to regional accreditation, Whittier has baccalaureate program accreditation with CSWE. The 2 libraries contain 225,337 volumes, 33,729 microform items, and 4650 audiovisual forms/CDs, and subscribe to 700 periodicals. Computerized library services include the card catalog, interlibrary loans, and database searching. Special learning facilities include a learning resource center, art gallery, radio station, the Fairchild Aerial Photography Collection, and performing arts, and writing centers. The 95-acre campus is in a suburban area 18 miles southeast of Los Angeles, in the foothills of the San Gabriel Mountains. Including residence halls, there are 50 buildings.

Student Life: 73% of undergraduates are from California. Others are from 27 states, 20 foreign countries, and Canada. 69% are from public schools. 50% are white; 30%, Hispanic; 10%, Asian American. The average age of freshmen is 18; all undergraduates, 21. 26% do not continue beyond their first year; 54% remain to graduate.

Housing: 813 students can be accommodated in college housing, which includes coed dormitories. In addition, there are special-interest houses, a multicultural community residence hall, and a substance-free residence hall. On-campus housing is guaranteed for all 4 years. 60% of students live on campus; of those, 75% remain on campus on weekends. All students may keep cars.

Activities: 15% of men belong to 4 local fraternities; 15% of women belong to 5 local sororities. There are 54 groups on campus, including art, band, cheerleading, choir, chorale, chorus, computers, dance, drama, ethnic, film, gay, honors, international, jazz band, literary magazine, musical theater, newspaper, photography, political, professional, radio and TV, religious, social, social service, student government, and yearbook. Popular campus events include the Spring Sing (annual talent show), Hawaiian Islander Club Luau, and Asian Night.

Sports: There are 11 intercollegiate sports for men and 10 for women, and 10 intramural sports for men and 10 for women. Facilities include a 7000-seat stadium, a 2000-seat gym, 3 playing fields, an athletics center, an aquatics center, a fitness center, and tennis courts.

Disabled Students: 75% of the campus is accessible. Wheelchair ramps, elevators, special parking, specially equipped rest rooms, special class scheduling, lowered drinking fountains, and lowered telephones are available.

Services: Counseling and information services are available, as is tutoring in every subject.

Campus Safety and Security: Measures include 24-hour foot and vehicle patrol, self-defense education, escort service, and informal discussions. There are pamphlets/posters/films, emergency telephones, and lighted pathways/sidewalks.

Programs of Study: Whittier confers the B.A. degree. Master's and doctoral degrees are also awarded. Bachelor's degrees are awarded in BIOLOGICAL SCIENCE (biochemistry and biology/biological science), BUSINESS (business administration and management), COMMUNICATIONS AND THE ARTS (art, dramatic arts, English, French, music, and Spanish), COMPUTER AND PHYSICAL SCIENCE (chemistry, earth science, mathematics, and physics), EDUCATION (physical), SOCIAL SCIENCE (child psychology/development, economics, history, international studies, philosophy, political science/government, psychology, religion, social work, and sociology). Business administration, political science, and English are the largest.

Required: To graduate, all students must complete a total of 120 credits, including at least 30 in the major field, with a minimum GPA of 2.0. Distribution requirements include 8 credits in natural sciences, 6 in paired courses from European and North American civilizations, Asian, African, and Latin American civilizations, or contemporary society and the individual, and 3 each in college writing, humanities, math, and fine arts.

Special: Internships are possible in business, counseling, teaching, and other areas. Study abroad is offered in 5 countries, with additional opportunities with 36 universities overseas through the University of Miami consortium. A Washington semester in January is optional. The Whittier Scholars Program offers self-designed interdisciplinary curricula. Nondegree study and pass/fail options are available. Whittier offers a 3-2 engineering program with the University of Southern California, Dartmouth College, and Columbia, Washington, Case Western Reserve, and Colorado State Universities. There are 10 national honor societies.

Faculty/Classroom: 60% of faculty are male; 40%, female. All teach undergraduates. No introductory courses are taught by graduate students. The average class size in an introductory lecture is 20; in a laboratory, 24; and in a regular course, 22.

Admissions: 92% of the 2001-2002 applicants were accepted. The SAT I scores for the 2001-2002 freshman class were: Verbal--34% below 500, 42% between 500 and 599, 21% between 600 and 700, and 3% above 700; Math--34% below 500, 40% between 500 and 599, 20% between 600 and 700, and 6% above 700. The ACT scores were 47% below 21, 21% between 21 and 23, 17% between 24 and 26, 7% between 27 and 28, and 8% above 28. 50% of the current freshmen were in the top fifth of their class; 80% were in the top two fifths.

Requirements: The SAT I or ACT is required; the SAT I is preferred. The college recommends that applicants have 4 years of high school English, 3 each of history, math, science, and 2 of a foreign language. An essay is required and an interview is recommended. A GPA of 2.0 is required. AP credits are accepted. Important factors in the admissions decision are advanced placement or honor courses, recommendations by school officials, and leadership record. Whittier provides DOS or Mac versions to any student wishing to apply via computer disk. On-line applications may be accessed via the school's web site.

Procedure: Freshmen are admitted in the fall. Entrance exams should be taken during the junior year or the fall of the senior year. There are early decision and deferred admissions plans. Early decision applications should be filed by December 1; regular applications, by February 1 for fall entry and December 1 for spring entry, along with a $35 fee. Notification of early decision is sent December 29; regular decision, on a rolling basis.

Transfer: Applicants are considered on a case-by-case basis, but a minimum GPA of 2.5 is recommended in academic course work. The SAT I or the ACT is required for students with fewer than 30 academic units. The GED is accepted for applicants with at least 30 academic units. 30 credits of 120 must be completed at Whittier.

Visiting: There are regularly scheduled orientations for prospective students, consisting of an interview with an admissions officer and a campus tour. Customized visits can be arranged to include meetings with faculty and coaches, extracurricular activities, class visits, and residence hall tours. There are guides for informal visits and visitors may sit in on classes and stay overnight. To schedule a visit, contact the Office of Admissions.

Financial Aid: In 2001-2002, 83% of all freshmen and 75% of continuing students received some form of financial aid. Whittier is a member of CSS. The CSS/Profile or FAFSA is required. Check with the school for current deadlines.

International Students: The school actively recruits these students. They must score 550 on the written TOEFL or 217 on the electronic version and also take the SAT I or the ACT.

Computers: The mainframe is a DEC ALPHA server. Computers are accessible in several labs around campus, in the library, and in many residence halls. Through the college network, students have access to the library OPAC, e-mail, other on-line resources, and the Internet. All students may access the system 24 hours a day. There are no time limits and no fees.

Graduates: In an average class, 51% graduate in 4 years, 57% in 5 years, and 58% in 6 years.

Admissions Contact: Urmi Kar, Dean of Enrollment.
E-mail: *admission@whittier.edu* Web: *www.whittier.edu*

WOODBURY UNIVERSITY C-5
Burbank, CA 91510-7846
(818) 767-0888
(800) 784-9663; Fax: (818) 767-7520

Full-time: 790 men and women	**Faculty:** 24; IIA, av$
Part-time: 230 men and women	**Ph.D.s:** 88%
Graduate: 150 men and women	**Student/Faculty:** 26 to 1
Year: semesters, summer session	**Tuition:** $18,344
Application Deadline: open	**Room & Board:** $7000
Freshman Class: n/av	
SAT I: required	**LESS COMPETITIVE**

Woodbury University, founded in 1884, is a private institution that emphasizes business and professional design education. Figures in above capsule are approximate. There are 3 undergraduate schools and 1 graduate school. In addition to regional accreditation, Woodbury has baccalaureate program accreditation with FIDER and NAAB. The library contains 70,699 volumes, 89,785 microform items, and 1341 audiovisual forms/CDs, and subscribes to 1500 periodicals. Computerized library services include the card catalog, interlibrary loans, and database searching. Special learning facilities include a learning resource center, art gallery, and architecture gallery. The 23-acre campus is in a suburban area 17 miles north of Los Angeles. Including residence halls, there are 15 buildings.

Student Life: Students are from 32 foreign countries. 33% are white; 24% Hispanic; 19% Asian American; 15% foreign nationals. The average age of freshmen is 18; all undergraduates, 21.

Housing: 198 students can be accommodated in college housing, which includes single-sex and coed dormitories and nonsmoking suites. On-campus housing is guaranteed for all 4 years. 80% of students commute. All students may keep cars.

Activities: 5% of men belong to 1 local and 1 national fraternity; 5% of women belong to 2 local sororities and 1 national sorority. There are 36 groups on campus, including computers, drama, ethnic, fashion, gay, international, newspaper, political, professional, religious, social, social service, and student government. Popular campus events include Chinese New Year, Black History Dinner, and Winter Formal.

Sports: There are 4 intramural sports for men and 4 for women. Facilities include a gym, basketball and volleyball courts, weight training and aerobics rooms, an outdoor swimming pool, a quarter-mile track, and a field for soccer and other sports.

Disabled Students: 90% of the campus is accessible. Wheelchair ramps, elevators, special parking, specially equipped rest rooms, and special class scheduling are available.

Services: Counseling and information services are available, as is tutoring in some subjects, including accounting, physics, architectural structures. There is remedial math and writing. Books on tape are available for the blind.

Campus Safety and Security: Measures include 24-hour foot and vehicle patrol, self-defense education, escort service, and informal discussions. There are pamphlets/posters/films, emergency telephones, and lighted pathways/sidewalks.

Programs of Study: Woodbury confers B.S. and B.Arch. degrees. Master's degrees are also awarded. Bachelor's degrees are awarded in BUSINESS (accounting, banking and finance, business administration and management, fashion merchandising, international business management, management science, and marketing/retailing/merchandising), COMPUTER AND PHYSICAL SCIENCE (information sciences and systems), ENGINEERING AND ENVIRONMENTAL DESIGN (architecture, computer graphics, and interior design), SOCIAL SCIENCE (fashion design and technology, history, humanities, political science/government, and psychology). Business and architecture are the strongest academically and have the largest enrollments.

Required: To graduate with a B.S., students must complete 126 semester units, including 44 to 66 in the major; with a B.Arch., 160 semester units, including 98 in the major. All students must maintain a minimum GPA of 2.0 and take freshman composition, comparative literature, computer literacy, and public speaking courses. Course work in behavioral sciences, economics, fine arts, history, natural science, math, and philosophy is also part of the curriculum.

Special: Internships are required for architecture, interior design, arts and sciences, fashion design, and fashion marketing majors and encouraged for all others. Current registration with area institutions, work-study programs, study abroad in France, dual majors, and pass/fail options also are offered. There are interdisciplinary majors in humanities and management and psychology and management.

Faculty/Classroom: 66% of faculty are male; 34%, female. 89% teach undergraduates, 3% do research, and 3% do both. No introductory courses are taught by graduate students. The average class size in an introductory lecture is 17; in a laboratory, 15; and in a regular course, 14.

Requirements: The SAT I or ACT is required. In addition, application form, essay, 2 academic references, official high school transcripts, and official SAT I or ACT scores are required for all applicants. Students applying to the animation arts major are also required to submit a portfolio. A GPA of 2.0 is required. AP and CLEP credits are accepted. Important factors in the admissions decision are advanced placement or honor courses, evidence of special talent, and recommendations by school officials.

Procedure: Freshmen are admitted fall, spring, and summer. Entrance exams should be taken prior to application. There is a deferred admissions plan. The application fee is $35. Check with the school for current deadlines.

Transfer: Applicants are required to have maintained a minimum GPA of 2.0 and to take the SAT I or ACT if they have completed fewer than 30 semester units. The priority application deadline for fall entry is April 15. 45 credits must be completed at Woodbury.

Visiting: There are regularly scheduled orientations for prospective students, consisting of meeting with admissions counselors, the president, faculty members, students, financial aid counselors, and student services staff. There are guides for informal visits and visitors may sit in on classes and stay overnight. To schedule a visit, contact the Admissions Office.

Financial Aid: In a recent year, 85% of all freshmen and 70% of continuing students received some form of financial aid. 80% of freshmen and 60% of continuing students received need-based aid. The average freshman award was $17,000. Of that total, scholarships or need-based grants averaged $10,155 ($20,005 maximum); loans averaged $6121 ($23,635 maximum); and work contracts averaged $1500. 15% of undergraduates work part time. Average annual earnings from campus work are $1173. Woodbury is a member of CSS. The FAFSA and the college's own financial statement are required. Check with the school for current deadlines.

International Students: The school actively recruits these students. They must score 550 on the written TOEFL.

Computers: The mainframe is a 2 DEC VAX 4200s. All full-time freshman are required to have and are provided with a multimedia notebook computer that allows access to the Internet and Web. Many PCs are available throughout campus. Because students have their own computers, there is 24-hour access. There are no time limits. The fee is $850.

Admissions Contact: Kyle Lynn Matthews.
E-mail: *admit@vaxb.woodbury.edu* Web: *www.woodbury.edu*

COLORADO

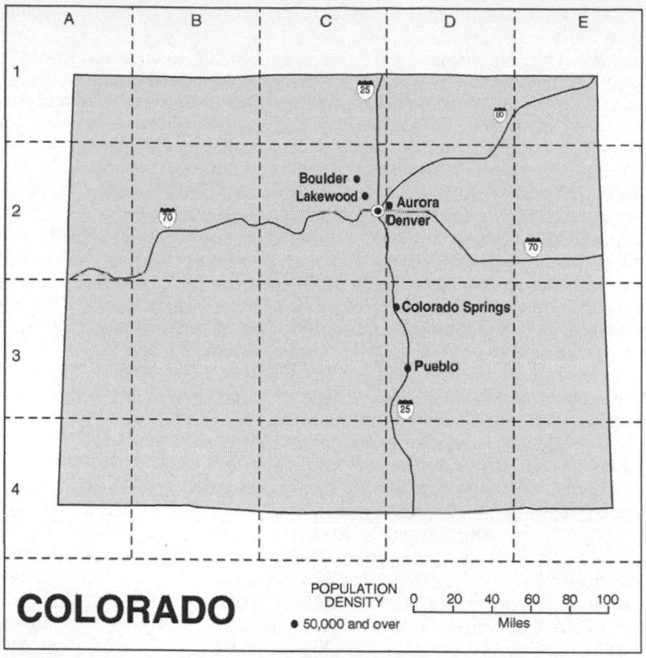

ADAMS STATE COLLEGE

Alamosa, CO 81102 — C-4

(719) 587-7712
(800) 824-6494; Fax: (719) 587-7522

Full-time: 852 men, 898 women	**Faculty:** 103; IIB, --$
Part-time: 83 men, 215 women	**Ph.D.s:** 91%
Graduate: 114 men, 278 women	**Student/Faculty:** 17 to 1
Year: semesters, summer session	**Tuition:** $2278 ($6910)
Application Deadline: August 1	**Room & Board:** $5190

Freshman Class: 1984 applied, 1865 accepted, 732 enrolled

ACT: 22 — **COMPETITIVE**

Adams State College, founded in 1921, is a public liberal arts college awarding undergraduate and graduate degrees. There are 4 undergraduate schools and 1 graduate school. In addition to regional accreditation, Adams State has baccalaureate program accreditation with NASM and NCATE. The library contains 154,603 volumes, 703,115 microform items, and 2090 audiovisual forms/CDs, and subscribes to 1086 periodicals. Computerized library services include the card catalog, interlibrary loans, and database searching. Special learning facilities include a learning resource center, art gallery, planetarium, and radio station. The 90-acre campus is in a small town 220 miles south of Denver and 200 miles north of Albuquerque, New Mexico. Including residence halls, there are 52 buildings.

Student Life: 85% of undergraduates are from Colorado. Others are from 38 states, 6 foreign countries, and Canada. 95% are from public schools. 67% are white; 27%, Hispanic. The average age of freshmen is 19; all undergraduates, 23. 42% do not continue beyond their first year; 33% remain to graduate.

Housing: 1052 students can be accommodated in college housing, which includes single-sex and coed dormitories, on-campus apartments, married-student housing, and freshman interest-group housing. On-campus housing is guaranteed for the freshman year only, is available on a first-come, first-served basis, and is available on a lottery system for upperclassmen. 50% of students commute. Alcohol is not permitted. All students may keep cars.

Activities: There are no fraternities or sororities. There are 40 groups on campus, including band, cheerleading, chess, choir, chorale, computers, drama, ethnic, gay, honors, international, jazz band, literary magazine, marching band, musical theater, pep band, photography, political, radio and TV, religious, social service, student government, and yearbook. Popular campus events include Student Appreciation Breakfast, Spud Bowl, and Snow Daze.

Sports: There are 6 intercollegiate sports for men and 5 for women, and 5 intramural sports for men and 5 for women. Facilities include a swimming pool, handball, racquetball, and tennis courts, horseshoe pits, indoor and outdoor tracks, a weight room, free weights and weight machines, an 1800-square-foot climbing wall, an aerobics studio, a cardiovascular area, and game facilities.

Disabled Students: 95% of the campus is accessible. Wheelchair ramps, elevators, special parking, specially equipped rest rooms, special class scheduling, lowered drinking fountains, and lowered telephones are available.

Services: Counseling and information services are available, as is tutoring in every subject. There is remedial math, reading, and writing.

Campus Safety and Security: Measures include 24-hour foot and vehicle patrol, escort service, informal discussions, and pamphlets/posters/films. There are emergency telephones, lighted pathways/sidewalks, and formal safety seminars.

Programs of Study: Adams State confers B.A. and B.S. degrees. Associate and master's degrees are also awarded. Bachelor's degrees are awarded in BIOLOGICAL SCIENCE (biology/biological science and ecology), BUSINESS (accounting, banking and finance, business administration and management, business economics, international business management, management information systems, marketing/retailing/merchandising, office supervision and management, small business management, and sports management), COMMUNICATIONS AND THE ARTS (advertising, art, dramatic arts, English, journalism, music, music performance, Spanish, and speech/debate/rhetoric), COMPUTER AND PHYSICAL SCIENCE (chemistry, computer science, earth science, geology, and mathematics), EDUCATION (art, athletic training, business, elementary, English, foreign languages, mathematics, music, physical, science, secondary, and social studies), ENGINEERING AND ENVIRONMENTAL DESIGN (preengineering), HEALTH PROFESSIONS (allied health, predentistry, premedicine, preoptometry, prepharmacy, and preveterinary science), SOCIAL SCIENCE (criminology, history, interdisciplinary studies, political science/government, prelaw, psychology, social work, sociology, and urban studies). Biology and allied health sciences are the strongest academically. Business and education are the largest.

Required: All students must maintain a GPA of at least 2.0 and complete 120 credit hours, including 24 in the major. General education requirements total 40 semester hours, with 6 each in communication arts, human behavior and institutions, history and culture, and arts and literature, 3 in quantitative thinking, and 2 in health and fitness. Students are also required to take 3 seminars in science foundations/issues and pass a technology proficiency exam.

Special: Cross-registration through the State Colleges of Colorado consortium is available. Work-study programs with the college, dual majors, a general studies degree, and student-designed majors are possible. Nondegree study is offered.

Faculty/Classroom: 63% of faculty are male; 37%, female. All teach undergraduates. No introductory courses are taught by graduate students. The average class size in an introductory lecture is 24; in a laboratory, 14; and in a regular course, 25.

Admissions: 94% of the 2001-2002 applicants were accepted. The ACT scores for the 2001-2002 freshman class were: 55% below 21, 28% between 21 and 23, 11% between 24 and 26, 4% between 27 and 28, and 2% above 28. 30% of recent freshmen were in the top fifth of their class; 67% were in the top two fifths.

Requirements: The SAT I or ACT is recommended. In addition, applicants are required to have at least 15 academic credits with 4 in English, 3 in social science, 2 each in math, lab science, and foreign language, and 1/2 in computer applications recommended. The GED is accepted. Adams State requires applicants to be in the upper 67% of their class. A GPA of 2.5 is required. AP and CLEP credits are accepted. Important factors in the admissions decision are advanced placement or honor courses, leadership record, and recommendations by school officials. Applications are accepted on-line via Colorado Mentor or the college's web site.

Procedure: Freshmen are admitted to all sessions. Entrance exams should be taken during the junior year. There is a deferred admissions plan. Applications should be filed by August 1 for fall entry and December 1 for spring entry, along with a $25 fee. Notification is sent on a rolling basis.

Transfer: 157 transfer students enrolled in 2001-2002. Applicants must have a minimum GPA of 2.0. If they have fewer than 12 credits, the SAT I or ACT test scores and official high school transcripts are also required. 30 credits of 120 must be completed at Adams State.

Visiting: There are regularly scheduled orientations for prospective students, including a meeting with academic faculty, a campus tour, information on financial aid and housing, and a free ticket to an athletic event (when applicable). There are guides for informal visits and visitors may sit in on classes and stay overnight. To schedule a visit, contact the Admissions Office.

Financial Aid: In 2001-2002, 91% of all students received some form of financial aid. 80% of all students received need-based aid. In a recent year, the average freshman award was $6392. Of that total, scholarships or need-based grants averaged $2531 ($4000 maximum); loans averaged $2625 ($4625 maximum); and work contracts averaged $1236

($3090 maximum). 65% of undergraduates work part time. Average annual earnings from campus work are $1719. The average financial indebtedness of a recent graduate was $13,644. The FAFSA is required. The fall application deadline is April 15.

International Students: There are 11 international students enrolled. The school actively recruits these students. They must score 550 on the written TOEFL or 213 on the electronic version and also take the SAT I or the ACT.

Computers: The mainframes are a network of 13 Dell and Compaq Servers. There are 30 stand-alone Pentium PCs and 75 networked Pentium clients located in 7 labs throughout the campus and supported by 13 file servers. All students may access the system.

Graduates: In 2001, 299 bachelor's degrees were awarded. The most popular majors were business (29%), education (14%), and psychology (9%). In an average class, 2% graduate in 3 years, 12% in 4 years, 40% in 5 years, and 50% in 6 years. 78 companies recruited on campus in 2000-2001. Of the 2000 graduating class, 93% were employed within 6 months of graduation.

Admissions Contact: Lori Lee Laske, Assistant Director of Admissions. A video is available. E-mail: *ascadmit@adams.edu*
Web: *www.adams.edu*

COLORADO CHRISTIAN UNIVERSITY C-2
Lakewood, CO 80226-7499 (303) 963-3200
(800) 44 FAITH; Fax: (303) 963-3201

Full-time: 523 men, 755 women	**Faculty:** 49
Part-time: 272 men, 213 women	**Ph.D.s:** 63%
Graduate: 31 men, 55 women	**Student/Faculty:** 26 to 1
Year: semesters, summer session	**Tuition:** $12,244
Application Deadline: August 1	**Room & Board:** $5470
Freshman Class: 906 applied, 675 accepted, 270 enrolled	
SAT I Verbal/Math: 540/530	**ACT:** 23 **COMPETITIVE**

Colorado Christian University, founded in 1914, is a private, Christian interdenominational institution offering undergraduate and graduate programs in the arts and sciences, biblical studies, music, and education. There are 6 undergraduate and 2 graduate schools. The library contains 53,532 volumes, 281,234 microform items, and 3917 audiovisual forms/CDs, and subscribes to 415 periodicals. Computerized library services include the card catalog, interlibrary loans, and database searching. Special learning facilities include an art gallery and radio station. The 29-acre campus is in a suburban area 10 miles west of Denver. Including residence halls, there are 13 buildings.

Student Life: 68% of undergraduates are from Colorado. Others are from 44 states, 16 foreign countries, and Canada. 81% are white. Most are Protestant. The average age of freshmen is 19; all undergraduates, 27. 33% do not continue beyond their first year.

Housing: 732 students can be accommodated in college housing, which includes single-sex on-campus apartments. On-campus housing is guaranteed for the freshman year only, is available on a first-come, first-served basis, and is available on a lottery system for upperclassmen. Priority is given to out-of-town students. 62% of students commute. Alcohol is not permitted. All students may keep cars.

Activities: There are no fraternities or sororities. There are 21 groups on campus, including band, cheerleading, choir, chorus, computers, drama, honors, international, jazz band, literary magazine, musical theater, orchestra, photography, professional, radio and TV, religious, social, social service, student government, symphony, and yearbook. Popular campus events include Preview Days, Spring Retreat, and New Student Retreat.

Sports: There are 5 intercollegiate sports for men and 5 for women, and 6 intramural sports for men and 6 for women. Facilities include a gym and soccer and practice fields.

Disabled Students: 85% of the campus is accessible. Wheelchair ramps, special parking, specially equipped rest rooms, special class scheduling, and lowered drinking fountains are available.

Services: Counseling and information services are available, as is tutoring in every subject. There is remedial math, reading, and writing.

Campus Safety and Security: Measures include 24-hour foot and vehicle patrol, emergency telephones, and lighted pathways/sidewalks.

Programs of Study: CCU confers B.A., B.S., B.F.A., B.M., B.M.M., and B.M.E. degrees. Associate and master's degrees are also awarded. Bachelor's degrees are awarded in BIOLOGICAL SCIENCE (biology/biological science), BUSINESS (accounting, business administration and management, human resources, management information systems, management science, and marketing management), COMMUNICATIONS AND THE ARTS (art, communications, dramatic arts, English, fine arts, music, and music performance), COMPUTER AND PHYSICAL SCIENCE (computer management, mathematics, and science), EDUCATION (music), SOCIAL SCIENCE (biblical studies, history, liberal arts/general studies, political science/government, psychology, religion, social science, and youth ministry). Human resources management, computer/information technology, and liberal arts are the largest.

Required: To graduate, students must complete at least 128 semester hours, including the 48-hour general education requirement and courses specified for the major, with a minimum cumulative GPA of 2.0; 2.5 in the major. The university requires 4 semesters of Christian service and regular chapel attendance. All students must complete 12 credits in biblical studies.

Special: The school offers co-op programs with Colorado Art Institute, Metro State College, and CU Boulder, internships, mission work abroad, and a Washington semester. Accelerated degree programs, dual and student-designed majors, nondegree study, pass/fail options, and credit for life, military, and work experience are also available. There are 2 national honor societies, and a freshman honors program.

Faculty/Classroom: 61% of faculty are male; 39%, female. No introductory courses are taught by graduate students.

Admissions: 75% of the 2001-2002 applicants were accepted. The SAT I scores for the 2001-2002 freshman class were: Verbal--34% below 500, 37% between 500 and 599, 27% between 600 and 700, and 2% above 700; Math--35% below 500, 41% between 500 and 599, 22% between 600 and 700, and 2% above 700. The ACT scores were 28% below 21, 26% between 21 and 23, 28% between 24 and 26, 10% between 27 and 28, and 8% above 28. There was 1 National Merit finalist.

Requirements: The SAT I or ACT is required. In addition, applicants must be graduates of an accredited secondary school. The GED is accepted. An essay is required. A campus visit is recommended. AP and CLEP credits are accepted. Applications are accepted on-line at *www.applyweb.com/apply/ccu/newmainmenu.html*.

Procedure: Freshmen are admitted to all sessions. There is a deferred admissions plan. Applications should be filed by August 1 for fall entry and December 15 for spring entry, along with a $40 fee. Notification is sent on a rolling basis.

Transfer: Applicants for transfer should have completed 12 college credits with a minimum GPA of 2.0. 30 credits of 128 must be completed at CCU.

Visiting: There are regularly scheduled orientations for prospective students. There are guides for informal visits and visitors may sit in on classes and stay overnight. To schedule a visit, contact the Office of Admissions at *admission@ccu.edu*

Financial Aid: In 2001-2002, 51% of all freshmen and 68% of continuing students received some form of financial aid. 45% of freshmen and 54% of continuing students received need-based aid. The average freshman award was $8149. 5% of undergraduates work part time. Average annual earnings from campus work are $1720. The FAFSA is required. The fall application deadline is March 15.

International Students: There are 13 international students enrolled. The school actively recruits these students. They must score 500 on the written TOEFL and also take the college's own test and the SAT I or the ACT.

Computers: The mainframe is a VAX cluster. PCs are available in the computer lab and in the library. Dorm apartments are wired for the Internet. All students may access the system. There are no time limits.

Graduates: In 2001, 478 bachelor's degrees were awarded. The most popular majors were human resources management (35%), computer information (30%), and liberal arts (11%). In an average class, 27% graduate in 4 years, 38% in 5 years, and 41% in 6 years.

Admissions Contact: Kim Myrick, Director of Admission. A video is available. E-mail: *kmyrick@ccu.edu* Web: *www.ccu.edu*

COLORADO COLLEGE D-3
Colorado Springs, CO 80903 (719) 389-6344
(800) 542-7214; Fax: (719) 389-6816

Full-time: 873 men, 1048 women	**Faculty:** 168; IIB, +$
Part-time: 6 men, 7 women	**Ph.D.s:** 96%
Graduate: 4 men, 14 women	**Student/Faculty:** 11 to 1
Year: see profile	**Tuition:** $24,893
Application Deadline: January 15	**Room & Board:** $6632
Freshman Class: 3402 applied, 2337 accepted, 551 enrolled	
SAT I Verbal/Math: 640/640	**ACT:** 28 **HIGHLY COMPETITIVE+**

Colorado College, founded in 1874, is an independent liberal arts and sciences institution. The academic year is based on the Block Plan, under which students take only 1 course during each of the eight 3-1/2-week-long blocks of study; there is also a 9-week 3-block summer session. Computerized library services include the card catalog, interlibrary loans, and database searching. Special learning facilities include a learning resource center, art gallery, radio station, electronic music studio, telescope dome, multimedia computer laboratory, the Colorado College Press, herbarium, Fourier transform nuclear magnetic resonance spectrometer, scanning electronic microscope and transmission electronic microscope, and environmental service van equipped for field research. The 90-acre campus is in a suburban area 70 miles south of Denver. Including residence halls, there are 52 buildings.

Student Life: 69% of undergraduates are from out of state, mostly the West. Students are from 49 states, 25 foreign countries, and Canada.

70% are from public schools. 78% are white. The average age of freshmen is 19; all undergraduates, 20. 6% do not continue beyond their first year; 82% remain to graduate.
Housing: 1476 students can be accommodated in college housing, which includes single-sex and coed dormitories and on-campus apartments. In addition, there are language, special-interest, substance-free, smoke-free, diversity, community arts, arts and crafts, and sustainable living houses. On-campus housing is guaranteed for all 4 years. 74% of students live on campus. Upperclassmen may keep cars.
Activities: 16% of men belong to 3 national fraternities; 18% of women belong to 3 national sororities. There are 80 groups on campus, including art, band, chess, choir, chorale, chorus, computers, dance, drama, ethnic, film, forensics, gay, honors, international, jazz band, literary magazine, musical theater, newspaper, orchestra, photography, political, professional, radio and TV, religious, social, social service, student government, symphony, and yearbook. Popular campus events include an afternoon and evening concert, annual arts and crafts sale, and Division I men's ice hockey games.
Sports: There are 9 intercollegiate sports for men and 9 for women, and 17 intramural sports for men and 17 for women. Facilities include a sports center with 2 gyms, weight and exercise rooms, squash, tennis, and racquetball courts, a pool, an ice rink, and playing fields.
Disabled Students: 80% of the campus is accessible. Wheelchair ramps, elevators, special parking, specially equipped rest rooms, lowered drinking fountains, and lowered telephones are available.
Services: Counseling and information services are available, as is tutoring in most subjects. There is a writing center.
Campus Safety and Security: Measures include 24-hour foot and vehicle patrol, self-defense education, escort service, and shuttle buses. There are informal discussions, pamphlets/posters/films, emergency telephones, and lighted pathways/sidewalks.
Programs of Study: CC confers the B.A. degree. Master's degrees are also awarded. Bachelor's degrees are awarded in BIOLOGICAL SCIENCE (biochemistry, biology/biological science, and neurosciences), BUSINESS (international economics), COMMUNICATIONS AND THE ARTS (art history and appreciation, classics, comparative literature, creative writing, dance, dramatic arts, English, film arts, French, German, music, romance languages and literature, Russian, Spanish, and studio art), COMPUTER AND PHYSICAL SCIENCE (chemistry, computer mathematics, geology, mathematics, and physics), ENGINEERING AND ENVIRONMENTAL DESIGN (environmental science), SOCIAL SCIENCE (anthropology, Asian/Oriental studies, economics, history, history of philosophy, liberal arts/general studies, philosophy, political science/government, psychology, religion, sociology, Southwest American studies, and women's studies). Biology, English, and psychology are the largest.
Required: Students must complete 32 units, with at least 9 units outside the division of the major, 18 outside the major department, and 4 in Alternative Perspectives. At least 3 courses in each division are required. Students must take 3 units of natural science with 1 lab science, 3 of social science, and 3 of humanities. Major requirements vary from 8 to 14 units. Students must earn a 2.0 GPA and achieve intermediate-level proficiency in a foreign language. Most majors offer (if not require) a comprehensive exam or a thesis.
Special: CC offers co-op programs with Columbia University School of Law, study abroad in several countries, and 3-2 engineering degrees. There are 3 national honor societies, including Phi Beta Kappa, and 100 departmental honors programs.
Faculty/Classroom: 59% of faculty are male; 41%, female. All both teach and do research. No introductory courses are taught by graduate students. The average class size in an introductory lecture is 20; in a laboratory, 17; and in a regular course, 14.
Admissions: 69% of the 2001-2002 applicants were accepted. The SAT I scores for the 2001-2002 freshman class were: Verbal--7% below 500, 26% between 500 and 599, 48% between 600 and 700, and 19% above 700; Math--5% below 500, 28% between 500 and 599, 51% between 600 and 700, and 16% above 700. The ACT scores were 1% below 18, 14% between 18 and 23, 63% between 24 and 29, and 23% above 29. 87% of the current freshmen were in the top quarter of their class; 99% were in the top half. There were 12 National Merit finalists. 31 freshmen graduated first in their class.
Requirements: The SAT I or ACT is required. In addition, applicants should have completed at least 16 (18 to 20 recommended) high school academic credits. The GED is accepted. An essay is required. AP credits are accepted. Important factors in the admissions decision are advanced placement or honor courses, extracurricular activities record, and evidence of special talent. Applications are accepted on-line via Common App and College Board.
Procedure: Freshmen are admitted fall and spring. Entrance exams should be taken by the fall of the senior year. There are early admissions and deferred admissions plans. Early action applications should be filed by November 15; regular applications, by January 15 for fall entry and November 1 for spring entry. The fall 2001 application fee was $40. Notification of early decision is sent January 1; regular decision, April 15. 14% of all applicants are on a waiting list; 200 were accepted in 2001.
Transfer: 39 transfer students enrolled in 2001-2002. Transfer candidates who are not submitting 3 semesters or 4 quarters of college work must submit their high school record. A letter of recommendation from a professor or teacher and a dean's form are required, as well as an application essay. 8 units of 32 must be completed at CC.
Visiting: There are regularly scheduled orientations for prospective students, including a class visit, an information session with an admissions director, and a student-led tour. There are guides for informal visits and visitors may sit in on classes and stay overnight. To schedule a visit, contact the Admission Office.
Financial Aid: In 2001-2002, 47% of all freshmen and 64% of continuing students received some form of financial aid. 38% of freshmen and 44% of continuing students received need-based aid. The average freshman award was $20,100. Of that total, scholarships or need-based grants averaged $17,930 ($30,736 maximum); loans averaged $2822 ($5175 maximum); and work contracts averaged $1488 ($1600 maximum). 42% of undergraduates work part time. Average annual earnings from campus work are $850. The average financial indebtedness of the 2001 graduate was $14,076. CC is a member of CSS. The CSS/Profile or FAFSA and noncustodial (divorced/separated) parents' statement are required. The fall application deadline is February 15.
International Students: There are 46 international students enrolled. The school actively recruits these students. They must score 550 on the written TOEFL.
Computers: The mainframes are a Data General 8520 and 4605, used for administrative purposes. Academic computing is supported by a distributed network of PCs and Macs. There are 116 machines in public labs and 161 in departmental labs. The local area network is 10/100 Mb with a Gb backbone. All students may access the system. There are no time limits and no fees. It is strongly recommended that all students have a personal computer.
Graduates: In 2001, 507 bachelor's degrees were awarded. In an average class, 6% graduate in 3 years, 71% in 4 years, 79% in 5 years, and 79% in 6 years. 47 companies recruited on campus in 2000-2001. Of the 2000 graduating class, 22% were enrolled in graduate school within 6 months of graduation and 80% were employed.
Admissions Contact: Mark Hatch, Dean of Admission and Financial Aid. A video is available. E-mail: *admission@coloradocollege.edu*
Web: *www.coloradocollege.edu*

COLORADO SCHOOL OF MINES C-2
Golden, CO 80401-1842 (303) 273-3220
(800) 446-9488; Fax: (303) 273-3509

Full-time: 1834 men, 607 women	**Faculty:** 170; I, av$
Part-time: 91 men, 24 women	**Ph.D.s:** 88%
Graduate: 492 men, 207 women	**Student/Faculty:** 14 to 1
Year: semesters, summer session	**Tuition:** $5898 ($17,583)
Application Deadline: June 1	**Room & Board:** $5680

Freshman Class: 1702 applied, 1401 accepted, 604 enrolled
SAT I Verbal/Math: 580/650 **ACT:** 27 **HIGHLY COMPETITIVE**

Colorado School of Mines, founded in 1874, is a public institution offering programs in science, economics, and engineering. In addition to regional accreditation, CSM has baccalaureate program accreditation with ABET. The library contains 356,000 volumes and 236,000 microform items, and subscribes to 2700 periodicals. Computerized library services include the card catalog, interlibrary loans, and database searching. Special learning facilities include a geology museum. The 373-acre campus is in a small town 15 miles west of Denver. Including residence halls, there are 35 buildings.
Student Life: 79% of undergraduates are from Colorado. Others are from 50 states, 62 foreign countries, and Canada. 90% are from public schools. 79% are white. 52% are Protestant; 21%, Catholic; 20% claim no religious affiliation. The average age of freshmen is 18; all undergraduates, 20. 17% do not continue beyond their first year; 60% remain to graduate.
Housing: 620 students can be accommodated in college housing, which includes coed dormitories, on-campus apartments, and married-student housing. On-campus housing is guaranteed for the freshman year only and is available on a first-come, first-served basis. All students may keep cars.
Activities: 19% of men belong to 7 national fraternities; 19% of women belong to 3 national sororities. There are 95 groups on campus, including band, cheerleading, choir, chorus, computers, drama, ethnic, honors, international, literary magazine, marching band, musical theater, newspaper, political, professional, religious, social, social service, student government, and yearbook. Popular campus events include International Day, Winter Carnival, and Parents Day.
Sports: There are 11 intercollegiate sports for men and 6 for women, and 13 intramural sports for men and 12 for women. Facilities include a 10,000-seat stadium, a gym, numerous intramural fields, tennis courts, and a field house.
Disabled Students: All of the campus is accessible. Wheelchair ramps, elevators, special parking, specially equipped rest rooms, special class scheduling, and lowered drinking fountains are available.

Services: Counseling and information services are available, as is tutoring in most subjects. There is remedial math and writing.

Campus Safety and Security: Measures include 24-hour foot and vehicle patrol, informal discussions, emergency telephones, and lighted pathways/sidewalks.

Programs of Study: CSM confers the B.S. degree. Master's and doctoral degrees are also awarded. Bachelor's degrees are awarded in COMPUTER AND PHYSICAL SCIENCE (chemistry, mathematics, and physics), ENGINEERING AND ENVIRONMENTAL DESIGN (chemical engineering, engineering, geological engineering, geophysical engineering, metallurgical engineering, mining and mineral engineering, and petroleum/natural gas engineering), SOCIAL SCIENCE (economics). Chemical engineering, geological engineering, and petroleum engineering are the strongest academically. General engineering, chemical engineering, and mathematical and computing sciences are the largest.

Required: Students must complete 138 to 148 credit hours, with 35 to 40 hours in the major and a GPA of 2.0. Required courses include humanities, calculus, physics, computer science, chemistry, and phys ed.

Special: Co-op programs, internships in the humanities, accelerated degree programs in all majors, dual majors, study abroad in 7 countries, and nondegree study are offered. There is 1 national honor society, a freshman honors program, and 3 departmental honors program.

Faculty/Classroom: 83% of faculty are male; 17%, female. 85% teach undergraduates, 50% do research, and 50% do both. No introductory courses are taught by graduate students. The average class size in an introductory lecture is 75; in a laboratory, 22; and in a regular course, 35.

Admissions: 82% of the 2001-2002 applicants were accepted. The SAT I scores for the 2001-2002 freshman class were: Verbal--13% below 500, 42% between 500 and 599, 36% between 600 and 700, and 9% above 700; Math--2% below 500, 24% between 500 and 599, 56% between 600 and 700, and 18% above 700. The ACT scores were 16% between 21 and 23, 30% between 24 and 26, 35% between 27 and 28, and 19% above 28. 90% of the current freshmen were in the top fifth of their class; 95% were in the top two fifths. In a recent year, 57 freshmen graduated first in their class.

Requirements: The SAT I or ACT is required. In addition, applicants must be graduates of an accredited secondary school. The GED is accepted. Students should have completed 16 high school academic credits, including 4 credits each of English and math, 3 of science, 2 of social studies, and 3 academic electives. AP credits are accepted. Important factors in the admissions decision are advanced placement or honor courses, leadership record, and recommendations by school officials. Applications are accepted on computer disk via CollegeLink, Apply, and Peterson's uniform application, and are accepted on-line via CSM's web site.

Procedure: Freshmen are admitted to all sessions. Entrance exams should be taken late in the junior year or early in the senior year. There is a deferred admissions plan. Applications should be filed by June 1 for fall entry, December 1 for spring entry, and June 10 for summer entry. Notification is sent on a rolling basis. The fall 2001 application fee was $45.

Transfer: 91 transfer students enrolled in 2001-2002. Transfer applicants must have a minimum GPA of 2.75. 30 credits of 138 must be completed at CSM.

Visiting: There are regularly scheduled orientations for prospective students, including a day-long visitation program twice each fall where students may visit departments and talk with faculty. Sessions in admissions and financial aid also are given. There are guides for informal visits and visitors may sit in on classes. To schedule a visit, contact Carmen Brenner at (303) 273-3226 / (800) 446-9488, ext. 3220 or *cbrenner@mines.edu*

Financial Aid: In 2001-2002, 85% of all students received some form of financial aid. 74% of all students received need-based aid. The average freshman award was $12,100. Of that total, scholarships or need-based grants averaged $5700 ($15,000 maximum); loans averaged $5400 ($8600 maximum); and work contracts averaged $1000 ($1400 maximum). 70% of undergraduates work part time. Average annual earnings from campus work are $750. The average financial indebtedness of the 2001 graduate was $17,500. CSM is a member of CSS. The FAFSA is required. The fall application deadline is March 1.

International Students: There are 417 international students enrolled. The school actively recruits these students. They must score 550 on the written TOEFL and also take the SAT I or the ACT.

Computers: The mainframe is an IBM RS/6000 system running AIX. Students can use all public computer systems managed by the CSM Computing Center. This includes central UNIX servers, UNIX workstations, PCs, terminals, and special devices. About 150 systems of various types are available in public (campus) access labs. All students may access the system. Dial-in access and direct network connection is available any time. Computer labs are open 7 A.M. to midnight Monday to Thursday, 7 A.M. to 6 P.M. on Friday, 9 A.M. to 5:30 P.M. on Saturday, and 9 A.M. to midnight on Sunday. There are no time limits and no fees.

Graduates: In 2001, 437 bachelor's degrees were awarded. The most popular majors were general engineering (39%), chemical engineering (20%), and metallurgical and materials engineering (8%). In an average class, 1% graduate in 3 years, 30% in 4 years, 55% in 5 years, and 62% in 6 years. 151 companies recruited on campus in 2000-2001. Of the 2000 graduating class, 10% were enrolled in graduate school within 6 months of graduation and 95% were employed.

Admissions Contact: Bill Young, Director of Enrollment Management. E-mail: *admit@mines.edu* Web: *www.mines.edu*

COLORADO STATE UNIVERSITY — C-1
Fort Collins, CO 80523-0015 — (970) 491-6909 — Fax: (970) 491-7799

Full-time: 8420 men, 9389 women	**Faculty:** 931; I, -$
Part-time: 1056 men, 1034 women	**Ph.D.s:** 99%
Graduate: 1892 men, 2143 women	**Student/Faculty:** 19 to 1
Year: semesters, summer session	**Tuition:** $4002 ($12,444)
Application Deadline: July 1	**Room & Board:** $5670
Freshman Class: 11,806 applied, 9223 accepted, 3654 enrolled	
SAT I Verbal/Math: 540/550	**ACT:** 23 **COMPETITIVE**

Colorado State University, founded in 1870 and part of the Colorado State University system, is a public, land-grant institution, offering 70 undergraduate majors in 56 departments within 8 colleges. There is 1 graduate school. In addition to regional accreditation, Colorado State has baccalaureate program accreditation with AACSB, ABET, ACCE, ACEJMC, ADA, ASLA, CSWE, FIDER, NASM, NCATE, NRPA, and SAF. The 4 libraries contain 1,218,636 volumes, 2,487,207 microform items, and 9226 audiovisual forms/CDs, and subscribe to 21,208 periodicals. Computerized library services include the card catalog, interlibrary loans, and database searching. Special learning facilities include a learning resource center, art gallery, radio station, TV station, an environmental learning center, and a plant environmental research center. The 666-acre campus is in a suburban area in Fort Collins, 65 miles north of Denver. Including residence halls, there are 100 buildings.

Student Life: 80% of undergraduates are from Colorado. Others are from 50 states, 96 foreign countries, and Canada. 82% are white. The average age of freshmen is 18; all undergraduates, 21. 18% do not continue beyond their first year; 60% remain to graduate.

Housing: 4550 students can be accommodated in college housing, which includes coed dormitories, on-campus apartments, married-student housing, fraternity houses, and sorority houses. In addition, there are honors floors and 20 other special-interest floors. On-campus housing is guaranteed for the freshman year only and is available on a first-come, first-served basis. 70% of students commute. All students may keep cars.

Activities: 8% of men belong to 20 national fraternities; 8% of women belong to 15 national sororities. There are 300 groups on campus, including art, band, cheerleading, chess, choir, chorale, chorus, computers, dance, debate, drama, drill team, ethnic, film, forensics, gay, honors, international, jazz band, literary magazine, marching band, musical theater, newspaper, opera, orchestra, pep band, photography, political, professional, radio and TV, religious, social, social service, student government, symphony, and yearbook. Popular campus events include Centertainment, International Poster Exhibition, and Summer Outdoor Theater.

Sports: There are 5 intercollegiate sports for men and 8 for women, and 16 intramural sports for men and 16 for women. Facilities include a 9,000-seat arena, indoor and outdoor tracks, a football stadium, a baseball diamond, intramural fields, indoor swimming pools, a comprehensive student recreation center, and an obstacle course for personal development.

Disabled Students: 90% of the campus is accessible. Wheelchair ramps, elevators, special parking, specially equipped rest rooms, special class scheduling, lowered drinking fountains, lowered telephones, an advocacy office for disabled students, telecommunication devices for the deaf, and special transportation are available.

Services: Counseling and information services are available, as is tutoring in most subjects. There is a reader service for the blind interpreters, and note takers.

Campus Safety and Security: Measures include 24-hour foot and vehicle patrol, self-defense education, escort service, and shuttle buses. There are informal discussions, pamphlets/posters/films, emergency telephones, lighted pathways/sidewalks, and lectures by campus police on a variety of safety issues, a crime victim support unit, and a bike patrol.

Programs of Study: Colorado State confers B.A., B.S., B.F.A., and B.M. degrees. Master's and doctoral degrees are also awarded. Bachelor's degrees are awarded in AGRICULTURE (agricultural business management, agricultural economics, agronomy, animal science, equine science, fishing and fisheries, forestry and related sciences, horticulture, natural resource management, and range/farm management), BIOLOGICAL SCIENCE (biochemistry, biology/biological science, botany, microbiology, nutrition, wildlife biology, and zoology), BUSINESS (accounting, apparel and accessories marketing, banking and finance, business administration and management, hotel/motel and restaurant management, marketing/retailing/merchandising, and recreational facilities management), COMMUNICATIONS AND THE ARTS (art, English, French, German, journalism, music, performing arts, Spanish, speech/debate/rhetoric, and technical and business writing), COMPUTER AND PHYSICAL SCIENCE (chemistry, computer science, geology, information sciences and systems, mathematics, physical sciences, physics, and statistics), EDUCATION (agricultural, home economics, and physical), ENGINEERING AND ENVIRONMENTAL DESIGN (agricultural engineering, chemical engineering, civil engineering, construction management, electrical/electronics engineering, engineering and applied science, industrial engineering technology, interior design, landscape architecture/design, and mechanical engineering), HEALTH PROFESSIONS (environmental health science and occupational therapy), SOCIAL SCIENCE (anthropology, economics, history, home economics, human development, liberal arts/general studies, philosophy, political science/government, psychology, social work, sociology, and water resources). Engineering and applied science, chemistry, and microbiology are the strongest academically. Business, psychology, and biological sciences are the largest.

Required: To graduate, students must complete at least 120 credit hours, 27 of them in the major, with a minimum GPA of 2.0. Students must complete the All University Core described in the catalog.

Special: Colorado State offers co-op programs with Metropolitan State College and Universidad Autonoma in Mexico and participates in cross-registration with AIMS Community College. Study abroad in more than 30 countries, a semester at sea, work-study programs, internships, B.A.-B.S. degrees, and pass/fail options are available. Teaching certification students receive a bachelor's degree in their chosen subject and also complete a certification sequence through the School of Education. There are 43 national honor societies, including Phi Beta Kappa, and a freshman honors program.

Faculty/Classroom: 76% of faculty are male; 24%, female. All both teach and do research. Graduate students teach 10% of introductory courses. The average class size in an introductory lecture is 45; in a laboratory, 22; and in a regular course, 25.

Admissions: 78% of the 2001-2002 applicants were accepted. The SAT I scores for the 2001-2002 freshman class were: Verbal--26% below 500, 48% between 500 and 599, 23% between 600 and 700, and 4% above 700; Math--22% below 500, 47% between 500 and 599, 27% between 600 and 700, and 4% above 700. The ACT scores were 13% below 21, 34% between 21 and 23, 30% between 24 and 26, 12% between 27 and 28, and 12% above 28. 44% of the current freshmen were in the top fifth of their class; 80% were in the top two fifths. There were 14 National Merit finalists and 9 semifinalists. 138 freshmen graduated first in their class.

Requirements: The SAT I or ACT is required. The average freshman has a composite SAT I score of 1114 and an ACT composite of 24. Graduation from secondary school is required. The GED is accepted. Students should have completed 18 high school credits, 15 of which are academic credits, including 4 years of English, 3 of math (algebra I, geometry, algebra II), 2 of natural science, 2 of social science, 1 additional year of natural or social science, and 2 years of the same foreign language. An essay is recommended. AP and CLEP credits are accepted. Important factors in the admissions decision are advanced placement or honor courses, leadership record, and recommendations by school officials. Applications are accepted on-line at the school's web site.

Procedure: Freshmen are admitted to all sessions. Entrance exams should be taken during the junior year or early fall of the senior year. Applications should be filed by July 1 for fall entry and December 1 for spring entry, along with a $30 fee. Notification is sent on a rolling basis.

Transfer: 1789 transfer students enrolled in 2001-2002. Transfer applicants should have at least 12 semester credits of academic classes (not remedial, technical, or applied) completed at accredited institutions and submit transcripts from all universities and colleges attended. Applicants with fewer than 12 credits also must submit high school transcripts and ACT or SAT I scores. A minimum cumulative 2.0 GPA is required. However, applicants with fewer than 30 credits should have at least a 2.5 GPA to be considered a strong candidate for admission. Some programs of study require a higher GPA and completion of specific course work. 32 credits of 120 must be completed at Colorado State.

Visiting: There are regularly scheduled orientations for prospective students, including Visit Days, which provide information about admissions, financial aid, and housing. A presentation on admissions, financial aid, and student life is offered each weekday, followed by a campus tour guided by student volunteers. The presentations start at 9:15 A.M. and 1:15 P.M. There are guides for informal visits and visitors may sit in on classes. To schedule a visit, contact Andrea Moss in the Office of Admissions at (970) 491-6393.

Financial Aid: In 2001-2002, 70% of all freshmen and 65% of continuing students received some form of financial aid. 41% of all students received need-based aid. The average freshman award was $6200. Of that total, scholarships or need-based grants averaged $1000; loans averaged $3000; and work contracts averaged $2000. 47% of undergraduates work part time. Average annual earnings from campus work are $2000. The average financial indebtedness of the 2001 graduate was $15,736. The FAFSA is required. The fall application deadline is March 1.

International Students: There are 243 international students enrolled. The school actively recruits these students. They must score 525 on the written TOEFL or 197 on the electronic version. Scores from other English language proficiency exams may be considered in lieu of the TOEFL. They must also take the SAT I or the ACT.

Computers: The mainframes are an IBM 9672 Model R22 and 4 IBM/6000 servers (production servers) and 4 additional network servers. There are numerous student computer labs on campus, including some in residence halls, dial-up modems, and access to the Internet. Every residence hall room has high-speed Internet access. All students may access the system 24 hours a day. There are no time limits and no fees.

Graduates: In 2001, 3860 bachelor's degrees were awarded. The most popular majors were business general (17%), human development and family studies (5%), and exercise and sport services (4%). In an average class, 31% graduate in 4 years, 59% in 5 years, and 62% in 6 years. 235 companies recruited on campus in 2000-2001.

Admissions Contact: Admissions Counselor. A video is available.
E-mail: *admissions@vines.colostate.edu*
Web: *www.colostate.edu/depts/admission/*

COLORADO TECHNICAL UNIVERSITY D-3
Colorado Springs, CO 80907-3896 (719) 590-6754
Fax: (719) 590-3740

Full-time: 640 men, 200 women	**Faculty:** 30
Part-time: 300 men, 60 women	**Ph.D.s:** 38%
Graduate: 480 men, 70 women	**Student/Faculty:** 28 to 1
Year: quarters, summer session	**Tuition:** $9425
Application Deadline: open	**Room & Board:** n/app
Freshman Class: n/av	
SAT I or ACT: recommended	**LESS COMPETITIVE**

Colorado Technical University, founded in 1965, is a private commuter institution offering programs with technical and management emphasis in computer science, electronic engineering technology, management, computer engineering, and electrical engineering. A large percentage of the students are working adults who have transferred from other colleges. There is a branch campus in Southwest Sioux Falls, South Dakota, which has a student enrollment of about 550. It can be reached at (605) 361-0200. Figures given in the above capsule are approximate. There are 4 undergraduate and 3 graduate schools. In addition to regional accreditation, Colorado Tech has baccalaureate program accreditation with ABET. The library contains 13,000 volumes, 15,000 microform items, and 350 audiovisual forms/CDs, and subscribes to 362 periodicals. Computerized library services include the card catalog, interlibrary loans, and database searching. Special learning facilities include a learning resource center. The 5-acre campus is in a suburban area of Colorado Springs. There are 2 buildings.

Student Life: 95% of students are from Colorado. Others are from 14 foreign countries. 77% are white. The average age of freshmen is 23; all undergraduates, 26. 30% do not continue beyond their first year.

Housing: There are no residence halls. Alcohol is not permitted.

Activities: There are no fraternities or sororities. There are 6 groups on campus, including honors, professional, and student government. Popular campus events include ski activities, a summer picnic, and Artsfest.

Sports: There are 4 intramural sports for men and 4 for women. Facilities include a high-tech workout facility.

Disabled Students: Wheelchair ramps, special parking, specially equipped rest rooms, and lowered drinking fountains are available.

Services: Counseling and information services are available, as is tutoring in most subjects, including including math and computer science. Taped tutorials are offered as well. There is remedial math. Upon entry to Colorado Tech, students are assigned a counselor/mentor who can assist them throughout their academic career.

Campus Safety and Security: Measures include informal discussions, pamphlets/posters/films, emergency telephones, and lighted pathways/sidewalks.

Programs of Study: Colorado Tech confers the B.S. degree. Associate, master's, and doctoral degrees are also awarded. Bachelor's degrees are awarded in BUSINESS (business administration and management, management information systems, and management science), COMMUNICATIONS AND THE ARTS (telecommunications), COMPUTER AND PHYSICAL SCIENCE (computer science), ENGINEERING AND ENVIRONMENTAL DESIGN (computer engineering, electrical/electronics engineering, and electrical/electronics engineering technology). Engineering, computer science, and engineering technology are the strongest academically.

Required: All students must complete 90 quarter hours in general education courses, including math, engineering science, English, and humanities/social sciences. An average of 190 quarter hours, with a cumulative GPA of 2.0, is required to graduate, as is a course in career development.

Special: Internships are possible with several local technology companies. Work-study programs are available with social services, the public library, the Space Foundation, and the university. Nondegree study and credit for life, military, and work experience are possible. There is 1 national honor society.

Faculty/Classroom: 88% of faculty are male; 12%, female. No introductory courses are taught by graduate students. The average class size in an introductory lecture is 30; in a laboratory, 24; and in a regular course, 20.

Requirements: The SAT I or ACT is recommended. In addition, suggested minimum composite scores are 1050 (550 math) on the SAT I or 24 on the ACT. Applicants should be graduates of an accredited high school. The GED is accepted. An essay is required for scholarships. An interview is recommended. Students without transfer of credit or an ACT or SAT I test report must pass Colorado Tech's entrance exams in math and English. AP and CLEP credits are accepted. Important factors in the admissions decision are ability to finance college education, personality/intangible qualities, and recommendations by school officials.

Procedure: Freshmen are admitted to all sessions. Entrance exams should be taken prior to the student's desired entry date. There are early admissions and deferred admissions plans. Application deadlines are open. The fall 2001 application fee was $50.

Transfer: Most new students are transfers. They must meet the same criteria as entering freshmen. The university uses the ACT Asset Placement Evaluation in math and English for acceptance and placement. 60 credits of 190 must be completed at Colorado Tech.

Visiting: There are regularly scheduled orientations for prospective students, consisting of a tour and an admissions overview program. There are guides for informal visits and visitors may sit in on classes. To schedule a visit, contact the Admissions Director.

Financial Aid: 2% of undergraduates work part time. Colorado Tech is a member of CSS. The CSS/Profile and the college's own financial statement are required. Check with the school for current deadlines.

International Students: They must score 550 on the written TOEFL or provide satisfactory evidence of completion of ELS or college-level English and also take the SAT I, ACT, or the college's own entrance exam, scoring 1050 on the SAT I.

Computers: 5 labs with 20 to 24 computers in each are available for student use in structured course labs with professors and unstructured use any other time. 1 lab has 20 DEC 5000 networked workstations; another 3 contain the remaining DEC ALPHA servers for 96 PCs. Printers and plotters are available. All students may access the system 8 A.M. to 11 P.M. Monday through Friday and 8 A.M. to 5 P.M. Saturday. There are no time limits.

Admissions Contact: David L. Porter, Director of Admissions. A video is available. Web: *www.colotechu.edu*

DEVRY UNIVERSITY/COLORADO SPRINGS — D-3
Colorado Springs, CO 80910 — **(719) 632-3000**

Full-time: 67 men, 23 women	**Faculty:** 11
Part-time: 24 men, 14 women	**Ph.D.s:** n/av
Graduate: none	**Student/Faculty:** 8 to 1
Year: semesters, summer session	**Tuition:** $9465
Application Deadline: open	**Room & Board:** n/app
Freshman Class: 163 applied, 141 accepted, 73 enrolled	
SAT I or ACT: recommended	**LESS COMPETITIVE**

DeVry University/Colorado Springs, formerly formerly DeVry Institute of Technology, founded in 2001, is 1 of 23 DeVry schools throughout the United States and Canada. The private institution offers career-oriented degree programs with hands-on training in various fields of business and technology. The library contains 430 volumes and 100 audiovisual forms/CDs, and subscribes to 30 periodicals. Computerized library services include the card catalog, interlibrary loans, and database searching. Special learning facilities include a learning resource center and electronics and other labs.

Student Life: 95% of undergraduates are from Colorado. Others are from 6 states and 1 foreign country. 63% are white; 14% African American; 12% Hispanic. The average age of all undergraduates is 27.

Housing: There are no residence halls. Housing referrals can be obtained through the Student Housing Office. All of students commute. Alcohol is not permitted. All students may keep cars.

Activities: There are no fraternities or sororities. There is 1 professional group on campus. Popular campus events include various food events.

Sports: There is no sports program at DeVry.

Disabled Students: 90% of the campus is accessible. Wheelchair ramps, elevators, special parking, specially equipped rest rooms, and lowered telephones are available.

Services: Counseling and information services are available, as is tutoring in every subject.

Campus Safety and Security: Measures include 24-hour foot and vehicle patrol, escort service, informal discussions, and pamphlets/posters/films. There are emergency telephones and full-time security personnel.

Programs of Study: DeVry confers the B.S. degree. Associate degrees are also awarded. Bachelor's degrees are awarded in BUSINESS (business administration and management), COMMUNICATIONS AND THE ARTS (telecommunications), COMPUTER AND PHYSICAL SCIENCE (computer programming and information sciences and systems), ENGINEERING AND ENVIRONMENTAL DESIGN (computer technology, electrical/electronics engineering technology, and technological management). Computer information systems and business administration are the largest.

Required: To graduate, students must achieve a GPA of at least 2.0 and satisfactorily complete all curriculum requirements. Course requirements vary according to program. All first-semester students take courses in business organization, algebra, psychology, and student success strategies.

Special: Accelerated degree programs are offered in computer information systems and business administration. Co-op programs, nondegree study, and evening and weekend classes are possible.

Faculty/Classroom: All teach undergraduates. The average class size in an introductory lecture is 30; in a laboratory, 30; and in a regular course, 30.

Admissions: 87% of the 2001-2002 applicants were accepted.

Requirements: The SAT I or ACT is recommended. In addition, admissions requirements include graduation from a secondary school; the GED is also accepted. Applicants must pass the DeVry entrance exam or present satisfactory ACT or SAT I scores. An interview is also required. CLEP credit is accepted. Applications are accepted on-line at *Embark.com*.

Procedure: Freshmen are admitted to all sessions. There is a deferred admissions plan. Application deadlines are open. The application fee is $50. Notification is sent on a rolling basis.

Transfer: Applicants must submit official transcripts from all previous colleges attended indicating passing grades in all completed course work, demonstrate language skills proficiency in at least 24 completed semester hours, and present evidence of math proficiency by appropriate college-level credits. 35% of 48 to 154 credits must be completed at DeVry.

Visiting: There are regularly scheduled orientations for prospective students. There are guides for informal visits and visitors may sit in on classes.

Financial Aid: 10% of undergraduates work part time. Average annual earnings from campus work are $8000. The FAFSA is required.

International Students: There is 1 international student enrolled. International students must score 500 on the written TOEFL or 173 on the electronic version and also take the college's own entrance exam.

Admissions Contact: Web: *www.cs.devry.edu*

DEVRY UNIVERSITY/DENVER — C-2
Denver, CO 80221 — **(303) 329-3340; Fax: (303) 329-0955**

Full-time: 142 men, 29 women	**Faculty:** 19
Part-time: 63 men, 35 women	**Ph.D.s:** n/av
Graduate: none	**Student/Faculty:** 9 to 1
Year: semesters, summer session	**Tuition:** $9465
Application Deadline: open	**Room & Board:** n/app
Freshman Class: 307 applied, 273 accepted, 167 enrolled	
SAT I or ACT: recommended	**LESS COMPETITIVE**

DeVry University/Denver, formerly DeVry Institute of Technology, founded in 2001, is a private institution offering hands-on programs in electronics, business administration, computer information systems, information technology, and computer engineering technology. The school is 1 of 23 DeVry schools throughout the United States and Canada. The library contains 500 volumes and 150 audiovisual forms/CDs, and subscribes to 50 periodicals. Computerized library services include the card catalog, interlibrary loans, and database searching. Special learning facilities include a learning resource center and electronics and other labs.

Student Life: 94% of undergraduates are from Colorado. Others are from 9 states and 3 foreign countries. 57% are white; 14% African American; 10% Hispanic. The average age of all undergraduates is 27.

Housing: All students commute. Housing referrals may be obtained through the Student Housing Office. All students may keep cars.

Activities: There are no fraternities or sororities. There are 3 groups on campus, including professional and yearbook. Popular campus events include BBQ and other food events.

Sports: There is no sports program at DeVry University/Denver.

Disabled Students: 90% of the campus is accessible. Wheelchair ramps, elevators, special parking, specially equipped rest rooms, and lowered telephones are available.

Services: Counseling and information services are available, as is tutoring in every subject.

Campus Safety and Security: Measures include escort service, informal discussions, pamphlets/posters/films, and emergency telephones. There are lighted pathways/sidewalks.

Programs of Study: DeVry University/Denver confers the B.S. degree. Associate degrees are also awarded. Bachelor's degrees are awarded in BUSINESS (business administration and management), COMPUTER AND PHYSICAL SCIENCE (computer programming and information sciences and systems), ENGINEERING AND ENVIRONMENTAL DESIGN (electrical/electronics engineering technology). Electronics is the largest.

Required: To graduate, students must complete 48 to 54 credits, achieve a GPA of 2.0, and satisfactorily complete all curriculum requirements. Course requirements vary according to program. All first-semester students take courses in business organization, computer applications, algebra, psychology, and student success strategies.

Special: Accelerated degrees, co-op programs, nondegree study, and evening and weekend classes are possible.

Faculty/Classroom: All teach undergraduates. The average class size in an introductory lecture is 30; in a laboratory, 30; and in a regular course, 30.

Admissions: 89% of the 2001-2002 applicants were accepted.

Requirements: The SAT I or ACT is recommended. In addition, admissions requirements include graduation from a secondary school; the GED is also accepted. Applicants must pass the DeVry entrance exam or present satisfactory ACT or SAT I scores. An interview is required. CLEP credit is accepted. Applications are accepted on-line at *Embark.com*.

Procedure: Freshmen are admitted fall, spring, and summer. There is a deferred admissions plan. Application deadlines are open. The application fee is $50. Notification is sent on a rolling basis.

Transfer: Applicants must present passing grades in all completed college course work, demonstrate language proficiency in at least 24 completed semester hours, and present evidence of math proficiency by appropriate college-level credits. 35% of 48 to 154 credits must be completed at DeVry University/Denver.

Visiting: There are regularly scheduled orientations for prospective students. There are guides for informal visits and visitors may sit in on classes. To schedule a visit, contact Rick Rodman, Director of Admissions at (303) 329-3340.

Financial Aid: 3% of undergraduates work part time. Average annual earnings from campus work are $8000. The average financial indebtedness of the 2001 graduate was $10,344. The FAFSA is required.

International Students: There are 5 international students enrolled. They must score 500 on the written TOEFL or 173 on the electronic version and also take the college's own entrance exam or DeVry's computerized placement test, achieving a minimum score that varies by program.

Admissions Contact: Rick Rodman, Director of Admissions.
Web: *www.den.devry.edu*

FORT LEWIS COLLEGE — B-4
Durango, CO 81301 — (970) 247-7184; Fax: (970) 247-7179

Full-time: 2159 men, 1880 women	**Faculty:** 169; IIB, -$
Part-time: 183 men, 219 women	**Ph.D.s:** 90%
Graduate: none	**Student/Faculty:** 24 to 1
Year: trimesters, summer session	**Tuition:** $2521 ($9603)
Application Deadline: August 1	**Room & Board:** $5138
Freshman Class: 3118 applied, 2623 accepted, 1110 enrolled	
SAT I Verbal/Math: 500/490	**ACT:** 20 **LESS COMPETITIVE**

Fort Lewis College, founded in 1911, is a public institution with undergraduate programs in arts and sciences, business, and education. There are 3 undergraduate schools. In addition to regional accreditation, FLC has baccalaureate program accreditation with AACSB, NASM, and TEAC. The library contains 183,133 volumes and 339,000 microform items, and subscribes to 800 periodicals. Computerized library services include the card catalog, interlibrary loans, and database searching. Special learning facilities include a learning resource center, art gallery, radio station, and a center for Southwest Studies. The 600-acre campus is in a small town 350 miles southwest of Denver and 250 miles northwest of Albuquerque, New Mexico. Including residence halls, there are 43 buildings.

Student Life: 66% of undergraduates are from Colorado. Others are from 50 states, 16 foreign countries, and Canada. 99% are from public schools. 69% are white; 16%, Native American/Eskimo. The average age of freshmen is 18; all undergraduates, 22. 45% do not continue beyond their first year.

Housing: 1540 students can be accommodated in college housing, which includes single-sex and coed dormitories, on-campus apartments, and married-student housing. There is and Hispanic Center, a Native American Center, and an environmental Center. On-campus housing is guaranteed for the freshman year only and is available on a first-come, first-served basis. 66% of students commute. Alcohol is not permitted. All students may keep cars.

Activities: There are no fraternities or sororities. There are 56 groups on campus, including art, band, cheerleading, chess, choir, chorale, chorus, computers, dance, drama, drill team, ethnic, gay, honors, international, jazz band, literary magazine, musical theater, newspaper, orchestra, political, professional, radio and TV, religious, social, social service, student government, and symphony. Popular campus events include Weekend Wipeout, Homecoming Weekend, and Hozhoni Days.

Sports: There are 5 intercollegiate sports for men and 5 for women, and 10 intramural sports for men and 10 for women. Facilities include a field house, outdoor sports complex, indoor swimming pool, and a student life center, which includes a 3-court gym, racquetball court, aerobic/dance studio, track, climbing wall, and a cardio/weight area.

Disabled Students: 80% of the campus is accessible. Wheelchair ramps, elevators, special parking, specially equipped rest rooms, lowered drinking fountains, lowered telephones, and workstations modified for individual needs are available.

Services: Counseling and information services are available, as is tutoring in most subjects. There is a reader service for the blind and remedial math and writing.

Campus Safety and Security: Measures include 24-hour foot and vehicle patrol, self-defense education, escort service, and informal discussions. There are pamphlets/posters/films, emergency telephones, and lighted pathways/sidewalks.

Programs of Study: FLC confers B.A. and B.S. degrees. Associate degrees are also awarded. Bachelor's degrees are awarded in BIOLOGICAL SCIENCE (biology/biological science), BUSINESS (accounting and business administration and management), COMMUNICATIONS AND THE ARTS (art, dramatic arts, English, music, and Spanish), COMPUTER AND PHYSICAL SCIENCE (chemistry, geology, information sciences and systems, mathematics, and physics), HEALTH PROFESSIONS (exercise science), SOCIAL SCIENCE (anthropology, economics, history, humanities, philosophy, political science/government, psychology, sociology, and Southwest American studies). Business, chemistry, and geology are the strongest academically. Business is the largest.

Required: To graduate, students must complete 120 semester hours with 30-40 hours in the major, 50 credits outside the major, and a minimum GPA of 2.0 overall and within the major. A total of 32-44 hours in general distribution courses is required.

Special: The college offers cooperative programs in most majors, numerous internships, a Washington semester for political science majors, study abroad in 23 countries, student-designed majors, a general studies degree, non-degree study, pass/fail option, and B.A.-B.S. degrees. There are 3-2 engineering degrees and a preforestry degree with Colorado State and Northern Arizona Universities. There are 14 national honor societies, and a freshman honors program.

Faculty/Classroom: 53% of faculty are male; 47%, female. 85% both teach and do research. The average class size in an introductory lecture is 27; in a laboratory, 15; and in a regular course, 12.

Admissions: 84% of the 2001-2002 applicants were accepted. The SAT I scores for the 2001-2002 freshman class were: Verbal--54% below 500, 35% between 500 and 599, 10% between 600 and 700, and 1% above 700; Math--50% below 500, 38% between 500 and 599, 11% between 600 and 700, and 1% above 700. The ACT scores were 60% below 21, 24% between 21 and 23, 11% between 24 and 26, 4% between 27 and 28, and 1% above 28. 16% of the current freshmen were in the top fifth of their class; 38% were in the top two fifths. 5 freshmen graduated first in their class.

Requirements: The SAT I or ACT is required with recommended minimum composite scores of 800 and 17 (20 enhanced) respectively. Applicants must be graduates of an accredited secondary school or have a GED certificate. An interview is recommended. A GPA of 2.0 is required. AP and CLEP credits are accepted. Applications are available on-line via the college's web site: *http://www.fortlewis.edu*

Procedure: Freshmen are admitted to all sessions. Entrance exams should be taken in the spring of the junior year in high school. Applications should be filed by August 1 for fall entry, December 1 for winter entry, and April 1 for summer entry. Notification is sent on a rolling basis. The fall 2001 application fee was $20.

Transfer: 352 transfer students enrolled in 2001-2002. Applicants for transfer should have completed a minimum of 12 credit hours and have a GPA of 2.0. Courses completed with a grade of C- or better may transfer. An interview is recommended. 28 credits of 120 must be completed at FLC.

Visiting: There are guides for informal visits and visitors may sit in on classes and stay overnight. To schedule a visit, contact the Office of Admission at *admission@fortlewis.edu*

Financial Aid: In 2001-2002, 61% of all freshmen and 66% of continuing students received some form of financial aid. 49% of all students received need-based aid. The average freshman award was $5755. Of that total, scholarships or need-based grants averaged $1795 ($20,732 maximum); loans averaged $2110 ($20,732 maximum); and work contracts averaged $1850 ($2500 maximum). 20% of undergraduates work part time. Average annual earnings from campus work are $1650. The average financial indebtedness of the 2001 graduate was $14,102. The FAFSA is required. The fall application deadline is February 15.

International Students: There are 45 international students enrolled. They must score 500 on the written TOEFL or 173 on the electronic version.

Computers: The mainframes are a DEC VAX 11/750 and an AT&T 3B2/500. There are also some 175 Macintosh and AT&T PCs available with software provided. All students may access the system Monday through Friday, 7 A.M. to 11 P.M., Saturday and Sunday, noon to 10 P.M. There are no time limits and no fees.

Graduates: In 2001, 621 bachelor's degrees were awarded. The most popular majors were business/marketing (24%), social science and history (14%), and psychology (10%). In an average class, 2% graduate in 3 years, 12% in 4 years, 28% in 5 years, and 31% in 6 years. 75 companies recruited on campus in 2000-2001. Of the 2000 graduating class, 20% were enrolled in graduate school within 6 months of graduation and 80% were employed.

Admissions Contact: Sheri Rochford, Dean, Admission and Development. A video is available. E-mail: *admission@fortlewis.edu*
Web: *www.fortlewis.edu*

MESA STATE COLLEGE — A-2

Grand Junction, CO 81501 (970) 248-1698
(800) 982-MESA; Fax: (970) 248-1973

Full-time: 1749 men, 2232 women	**Faculty:** 204; IIB, --$
Part-time: 488 men, 828 women	**Ph.D.s:** 72%
Graduate: 25 men, 24 women	**Student/Faculty:** 20 to 1
Year: semesters, summer session	**Tuition:** $2288 ($7115)
Application Deadline: July 31	**Room & Board:** $5763
Freshman Class: 1104 applied, 1096 accepted, 1080 enrolled	
ACT: 20	**COMPETITIVE**

Mesa State College, founded in 1925, is a public institution offering undergraduate programs in liberal arts, sciences, business, and preprofessional areas. There are 3 undergraduate schools and 1 graduate school. In addition to regional accreditation, Mesa State has baccalaureate program accreditation with CAHEA and NLN. The library contains 189,000 volumes, 803,012 microform items, and 25,578 audiovisual forms/CDs, and subscribes to 1035 periodicals. Computerized library services include the card catalog, interlibrary loans, and database searching. Special learning facilities include a learning resource center, art gallery, radio station, and TV studio. The 42-acre campus is in a small town 250 miles west of Denver. Including residence halls, there are 26 buildings.

Student Life: 90% of undergraduates are from Colorado. Others are from 30 states, 43 foreign countries, and Canada. 86% are white. The average age of freshmen is 20; all undergraduates, 25. 39% do not continue beyond their first year; 53% remain to graduate.

Housing: 918 students can be accommodated in college housing, which includes coed dormitories and on-campus apartments. On-campus housing is available on a first-come, first-served basis. 81% of students commute. Alcohol is not permitted. All students may keep cars.

Activities: There are no fraternities or sororities. There are 50 groups on campus, including art, cheerleading, choir, chorus, computers, dance, ethnic, honors, international, jazz band, literary magazine, musical theater, newspaper, outdoors, political, professional, radio and TV, religious, social, social service, and student government. Popular campus events include Unity Fest, spring series, and art shows.

Sports: There are 4 intercollegiate sports for men and 7 for women, and 18 intramural sports for men and 18 for women. Facilities include a weight room, tennis courts, a swimming pool, and a recreation center with climbing walls, racquetball courts, an elevated running track, and workout facilities.

Disabled Students: 98% of the campus is accessible. Wheelchair ramps, elevators, special parking, specially equipped rest rooms, special class scheduling, lowered drinking fountains, and lowered telephones are available.

Services: Counseling and information services are available, as is tutoring in every subject, except accounting. There is a reader service for the blind, and remedial math, reading, and writing.

Campus Safety and Security: Measures include 24-hour foot and vehicle patrol, self-defense education, escort service, and informal discussions. There are pamphlets/posters/films, lighted pathways/sidewalks, a crime watch program, an emergency contact service, and first-aid and CPR courses.

Programs of Study: Mesa State confers B.A., B.S., B.B.A., and B.S.N. degrees. Associate and master's degrees are also awarded. Bachelor's degrees are awarded in BIOLOGICAL SCIENCE (biology/biological science), BUSINESS (accounting and business administration and management), COMMUNICATIONS AND THE ARTS (communications, English, and fine arts), COMPUTER AND PHYSICAL SCIENCE (computer science, mathematics, and physical sciences), ENGINEERING AND ENVIRONMENTAL DESIGN (environmental engineering technology), HEALTH PROFESSIONS (nursing), SOCIAL SCIENCE (history, liberal arts/general studies, physical fitness/movement, political science/government, psychology, social science, and sociology). Nursing and allied health, natural science, and math are the strongest academically. Business, natural science, and math are the largest.

Required: To graduate, students must complete a minimum of 123 credits, with 40 hours in upper-level courses in the emphasis area and a minimum GPA of 2.0. All students must take English 111 and 112 as well as 33 hours of general education courses and 3 hours of phys ed. A comprehensive exam is required.

Special: Mesa State offers internships in many of its programs, including one in the state legislature, a Washington semester, work-study programs, student-designed majors in selected studies, and the B.A.-B.S. degree in several majors. Nondegree study for students over 20 years of age and credit for life, military, and work experience are available. There are 10 national honor societies, a freshman honors program, and 5 departmental honors programs.

Faculty/Classroom: 62% of faculty are male; 38%, female. All teach undergraduates. No introductory courses are taught by graduate students. The average class size in an introductory lecture is 30; in a laboratory, 20; and in a regular course, 30.

Admissions: 99% of the 2001-2002 applicants were accepted. The SAT I scores for the 2001-2002 freshman class were: Verbal--54% below 500, 34% between 500 and 599, and 11% between 600 and 700; Math--53% below 500, 36% between 500 and 599, 11% between 600 and 700, and 1% above 700. The ACT scores were 54% below 21, 26% between 21 and 23, 14% between 24 and 26, 4% between 27 and 28, and 2% above 28. 7% of the current freshmen were in the top fifth of their class; 14% were in the top two fifths.

Requirements: The SAT I or ACT is required with a minimum composite score of 940 on the SAT I or 21 on the ACT. Applicants must be graduates of an accredited secondary school or hold the GED. The college prefers that students complete 4 years of high school English, 3 each of math, science, and social studies, 2 of foreign language, and 1 of history. An essay, an interview, and an audition for some classes are recommended. Mesa State accepts applications on disk and on-line. Mesa State requires applicants to be in the upper 75% of their class. A GPA of 2.6 is required. AP and CLEP credits are accepted. Important factors in the admissions decision are recommendations by school officials, personality/intangible qualities, and evidence of special talent.

Procedure: Freshmen are admitted to all sessions. Entrance exams should be taken late in the junior year or early in the senior year. There is a deferred admissions plan. Applications should be filed by July 31 for fall entry and December 1 for spring entry. Notification is sent on a rolling basis.

Transfer: Applicants must have a minimum GPA of 2.0 with 30 semester hours; otherwise, they must meet the criteria for entering freshmen.

Visiting: There are regularly scheduled orientations for prospective students, including advising sessions. There are guides for informal visits and visitors may sit in on classes. To schedule a visit, contact the Admissions Office.

Financial Aid: In a recent year, 75% of all freshmen and 65% of continuing students received some form of financial aid. 70% of freshmen and 50% of continuing students received need-based aid. The average freshman award was $5667. Of that total, scholarships or need-based grants averaged $1904 ($3213 maximum); loans averaged $3763 ($11,873 maximum); and work contracts averaged $2400. 40% of undergraduates work part time. Average annual earnings from campus work are $2400. The average financial indebtedness of a recent year's graduate was $12,900. The FAFSA is required. The fall application deadline is March 1.

International Students: They must score 525 on the written TOEFL or take the MELAB or the Comprehensive English Language Test. The SAT I or the ACT is also required.

Computers: The mainframe is a DEC VAX. All enrolled students have access to the network and to more than 260 computers in 6 labs plus other locations. There are no time limits. The fee is $27 per semester. It is strongly recommended that all students have a personal computer.

Graduates: In a recent year, 514 bachelor's degrees were awarded. The most popular majors were business administration (27%), psychology (14%), and biology (12%). 35 companies recruited on campus in a recent year.

Admissions Contact: Tyre Bush, Director of Admissions and Recruitment. A video is available. E-mail: *tbush@mesastate.edu*
Web: *www.mesastate.edu*

METROPOLITAN STATE COLLEGE OF DENVER — C-2

Denver, CO 80217-3362 (303) 556-3058; Fax: (303) 556-6345

Full-time: 4539 men, 5817 women	**Faculty:** 446
Part-time: 3324 men, 4765 women	**Ph.D.s:** n/av
Graduate: none	**Student/Faculty:** 23 to 1
Year: semesters, summer session	**Tuition:** $2338 ($8186)
Application Deadline: August 12	**Room & Board:** n/app
Freshman Class: 4034 applied, 3475 accepted, 2054 enrolled	
SAT I Verbal/Math: 470/460	**ACT:** 19 **LESS COMPETITIVE**

Metropolitan State College of Denver, founded in 1963, is a public commuter institution offering degree programs in the liberal arts and sciences, business, and professional studies, as well as individualized degree programs. There are 3 undergraduate schools. In addition to regional accreditation, Metro State has baccalaureate program accreditation with ABET, CSWE, NASM, NCATE, NLN, and NRPA. The library contains 692,677 volumes, 1,053,419 microform items, and 16,975 audiovisual forms/CDs, and subscribes to 4150 periodicals. Computerized library services include the card catalog, interlibrary loans, and database searching. Special learning facilities include a learning resource center, art gallery, radio station, a world indoor airport, a writing center, and student support services. The 175-acre campus is in an urban area in Denver. There are 38 buildings.

Student Life: 99% of undergraduates are from Colorado. Others are from 40 states, 66 foreign countries, and Canada. 96% are from public schools. 71% are white; 12% Hispanic. The average age of freshmen is 22; all undergraduates, 26. 38% do not continue beyond their first year.

Housing: There are no residence halls. All students commute. All students may keep cars.

Activities: There are no fraternities or sororities. There are 100 groups on campus, including art, band, cheerleading, chess, choir, chorale, chorus, computers, debate, drama, ethnic, gay, honors, international, jazz band, literary magazine, musical theater, newspaper, orchestra, political, professional, radio and TV, religious, social, social service, student government, and symphony. Popular campus events include Club Day, World Friendship Festival, and Family Night.

Sports: There are 5 intercollegiate sports for men and 5 for women, and 10 intramural sports for men and 6 for women. Facilities include playing fields, volleyball, basketball, badminton, racquetball, handball, squash, and tennis courts, a swimming pool, a dance studio, a weight room, a fitness center and green room, a 3500-seat events center, an auxiliary gym, and a three-quarter-mile jogging path.

Disabled Students: 90% of the campus is accessible. Wheelchair ramps, elevators, special parking, specially equipped rest rooms, special class scheduling, lowered drinking fountains, lowered telephones, and telephones, tapes, and classroom aids for the hearing impaired, an adaptive computer lab, testing accommodations, sign-language and oral interpreters, priority registration, and a resource and referral library are available.

Services: Counseling and information services are available, as is tutoring in most subjects. ESL services and an adult learning services office are available.

Campus Safety and Security: Measures include 24-hour foot and vehicle patrol, self-defense education, escort service, and shuttle buses. There are informal discussions, pamphlets/posters/films, emergency telephones, lighted pathways/sidewalks, and bicycle registration, and date/acquaintance rape education seminars.

Programs of Study: Metro State confers B.A., B.S., and B.F.A. degrees. Bachelor's degrees are awarded in BIOLOGICAL SCIENCE (biology/biological science), BUSINESS (accounting, banking and finance, hospitality management services, management science, marketing/retailing/merchandising, and recreation and leisure services), COMMUNICATIONS AND THE ARTS (art, communications, English, fine arts, industrial design, journalism, modern language, music performance, Spanish, and speech/debate/rhetoric), COMPUTER AND PHYSICAL SCIENCE (atmospheric sciences and meteorology, chemistry, computer management, computer science, information sciences and systems, mathematics, and physics), EDUCATION (music and physical), ENGINEERING AND ENVIRONMENTAL DESIGN (airline piloting and navigation, aviation administration/management, aviation computer technology, civil engineering technology, electrical/electronics engineering technology, environmental science, industrial administration/management, industrial engineering technology, land use management and reclamation, mechanical engineering technology, survey and mapping technology, and surveying engineering), HEALTH PROFESSIONS (health care administration and nursing), SOCIAL SCIENCE (African American studies, anthropology, behavioral science, criminal justice, economics, history, human services, Mexican-American/Chicano studies, philosophy, physical fitness/movement, political science/government, psychology, social work, sociology, and urban studies). Criminal justice, psychology, and computer information systems are the largest.

Required: To graduate, students must complete at least 120 credit hours, 40 of which must be upper division, and 30 in the major, with a minimum overall GPA of 2.0. There are 3 levels of general studies requirements, totaling 33 hours and including a multicultural requirement and a senior experience.

Special: Metro State offers co-op and service-learning programs in most majors, and cross-registration with a consortium of state colleges and the University of Colorado at Denver. Internships, study abroad, work-study programs, dual majors, student-designed majors, nondegree study, and pass/fail options are available. There are 9 national honor societies, a freshman honors program, and 10 departmental honors programs.

Faculty/Classroom: 56% of faculty are male; 44%, female. All teach undergraduates. The average class size in an introductory lecture is 25; in a laboratory, 14; and in a regular course, 19.

Admissions: 86% of the 2001-2002 applicants were accepted. The SAT I scores for the 2001-2002 freshman class were: Verbal--57% below 500, 32% between 500 and 599, 10% between 600 and 700, and 1% above 700; Math--65% below 500, 25% between 500 and 599, and 10% between 600 and 700. The ACT scores were 65% below 21, 21% between 21 and 23, 10% between 24 and 26, 2% between 27 and 28, and 2% above 28. 14% of the current freshmen were in the top fifth of their class; 35% were in the top two fifths. 3 freshmen graduated first in their class.

Requirements: The SAT I or ACT is required. In addition, applicants should be graduates of an accredited secondary school, with 15 Carnegie units. The GED is accepted. Applications are accepted on-line. AP and CLEP credits are accepted. Important factors in the admissions decision are recommendations by school officials, extracurricular activities record, and evidence of special talent.

Procedure: Freshmen are admitted to all sessions. Entrance exams should be taken prior to application. Applications should be filed by August 12 for fall entry, along with a $25 fee. Notification is sent on a rolling basis.

Transfer: 2126 transfer students enrolled in 2001-2002. Applicants must have a 2.0 GPA and be in good standing at their previous school. Some probationary transfers are considered. 30 credits of 120 must be completed at Metro State.

Visiting: There are regularly scheduled orientations for prospective students, including class scheduling and registration, college services and resources, transfer of credit, academic advising, choice of major, career counseling, and assessment testing if needed. There are guides for informal visits and visitors may sit in on classes. To schedule a visit, contact the Office of Admissions.

Financial Aid: 47% of undergraduates work part time. Average annual earnings from campus work are $5000. The average financial indebtedness of the 2001 graduate was $18,222. Metro State is a member of CSS. The FAFSA is required. The fall application deadline is March 1.

International Students: There are 128 international students enrolled. They must score 500 on the written TOEFL. The SAT I or ACT is required if the applicant is under 20 and has graduated from a U.S. high school.

Computers: The mainframe is a Hitachi EX027. There is a DEC ALPHA mini computer along with about 450 PCs housed in 24 different labs. NeXT, Pentium II, and Mac systems are available. All students may access the system. Labs are open 96 hours a week, and 64 dial-up lines are available 24 hours a day. There are no time limits. The fee $4 to $21 depending upon the number of credits a student is taking.

Graduates: In 2001, 2050 bachelor's degrees were awarded. The most popular majors were behavioral science (9%), computer information systems (7%), and criminal justice (7%). In an average class, 4% graduate in 4 years, 13% in 5 years, and 20% in 6 years. 181 companies recruited on campus in 2000-2001. Of the 2000 graduating class, 72% were employed within 6 months of graduation.

Admissions Contact: Office of Admissions. A video is available.
Web: *www.mscd.edu or gopher://mscdgopher*

NAROPA UNIVERSITY

Boulder, CO 80302-6697 — **C-2**

(303) 546-5295
(800) 772-6951; Fax: (303) 546-3572

Full-time: 121 men, 217 women	**Faculty:** 28
Part-time: 22 men, 42 women	**Ph.D.s:** 33%
Graduate: 171 men, 436 women	**Student/Faculty:** 12 to 1
Year: semesters	**Tuition:** $14,092
Application Deadline: February 15	**Room & Board:** $8324
Freshman Class: 166 applied, 162 accepted, 77 enrolled	
SAT I or ACT: not required	**SPECIAL**

Naropa University, founded in 1974, is a private nonprofit, nonsectarian Buddhist-inspired, experiential liberal arts institution. It offers undergraduate and graduate degrees in the arts, social sciences, and the humanities. The library contains 26,000 volumes and 3200 audiovisual forms/CDs, and subscribes to 150 periodicals. Computerized library services include the card catalog, interlibrary loans, and database searching. Special learning facilities include an art gallery, 2 meditation halls, a writing center, a volunteer center, and a career center. The 4-acre campus is in an urban area in Boulder. Including residence halls, there are 16 buildings.

Student Life: 65% of undergraduates are from out of state, mostly the West. Others are from 39 states, 9 foreign countries, and Canada. 79% are white. The average age of freshmen is 20; all undergraduates, 25. 25% do not continue beyond their first year.

Housing: 27 students can be accommodated in college housing, which is a coed dormitory. On-campus housing is guaranteed for the freshman year only and is available on a first-come, first-served basis. 99% of students commute. Alcohol is not permitted. All students may keep cars.

Activities: There are no fraternities or sororities. There are 13 groups on campus, including chorus, dance, drama, ethnic, gay, international, literary magazine, newspaper, political, professional, religious, social, social service, and student government. Popular campus events include African dance and drumming practice days, poetry readings, and cultural festivals.

Sports: There is 1 intramural sports, coed soccer.

Disabled Students: 70% of the campus is accessible. Wheelchair ramps, elevators, special parking, specially equipped rest rooms, special

class scheduling, lowered drinking fountains, and lowered telephones are available.

Services: Counseling and information services are available, as is tutoring in some subjects, including writing. There is a reader service for the blind.

Campus Safety and Security: Measures include informal discussions, pamphlets/posters/films, and lighted pathways/sidewalks.

Programs of Study: Naropa confers the B.A. degree. Master's degrees are also awarded. Bachelor's degrees are awarded in COMMUNICATIONS AND THE ARTS (creative writing, literature, performing arts, and visual and performing arts), EDUCATION (early childhood), ENGINEERING AND ENVIRONMENTAL DESIGN (environmental science), SOCIAL SCIENCE (East Asian studies, interdisciplinary studies, psychology, and religion). Psychology is the largest.

Required: Students must complete 120 credits, 24 to 36 in the major, with a 2.5 average GPA. An extensive core curriculum includes courses in contemplative practices, world wisdom studies, cultural and historical studies, artistic process, leadership and service, healing arts, communication arts, and complex systems.

Special: Work-study programs, internships, dual majors, and student-designed majors are available, as well as study abroad in Bali, Nepal, India, and the Czech Republic. Volunteer opportunities are also available.

Faculty/Classroom: 35% of faculty are male; 65%, female. 60% teach undergraduates. No introductory courses are taught by graduate students. The average class size in an introductory lecture is 20 and in a regular course, 15.

Admissions: 98% of the 2001-2002 applicants were accepted.

Requirements: A high school transcript, an interview, 2 recommendations, and an essay are required. The GED is accepted. A GPA of 2.5 is required. AP and CLEP credits are accepted. Important factors in the admissions decision are personality/intangible qualities, evidence of special talent, and recommendations by school officials. Applications are accepted on-line at the school's web site.

Procedure: Freshmen are admitted fall and spring. There is a deferred admissions plan. Applications should be filed by February 15 for fall entry and October 15 for spring entry, along with a $35 fee. Notification is sent on a rolling basis.

Transfer: 77 transfer students enrolled in 2001-2002. Requirements for transfer students are unique to each academic department. 60 credits of 120 must be completed at Naropa.

Visiting: There are regularly scheduled orientations for prospective students, including daily tours, class visitation, and meetings with counselors. There are guides for informal visits and visitors may sit in on classes. To schedule a visit, contact the Visitation Coordinator at (303) 546-3548 or *admissions@naropa.edu*

Financial Aid: In 2001-2002, 61% of all freshmen and 48% of continuing students received some form of financial aid. 57% of freshmen and 54% of continuing students received need-based aid. The average freshman award was $5500. Of that total, scholarships or need-based grants averaged $7061 ($12,000 maximum); loans averaged $5321 ($8625 maximum); and work contracts averaged $3905 ($4200 maximum). 20% of undergraduates work part time. Average annual earnings from campus work are $1646. The average financial indebtedness of the 2001 graduate was $19,000. The FAFSA is required. The fall application deadline is March 1.

International Students: There are 17 international students enrolled. They must score 550 on the written TOEFL.

Computers: Macs and PCs at the library are available for student use. All students may access the system. There are no time limits and no fees. It is strongly recommended that all students have a personal computer.

Graduates: In 2001, 63 bachelor's degrees were awarded. The most popular majors were psychology (35%), writing and literature (13%), and visual arts (11%). In an average class, 36% graduate in 4 years, 41% in 5 years, and 41% in 6 years.

Admissions Contact: Susan Boyle, Admissions Director.
E-mail: *admissions@naropa.edu* Web: *www.naropa.edu*

REGIS UNIVERSITY C-2

Denver, CO 80221-1099 (303) 458-4900
(800) 388-2366, ext. 4900; Fax: (303) 964-5534

Full-time: 424 men, 674 women	**Faculty:** 68; IIA, -$
Part-time: none	**Ph.D.s:** 95%
Graduate: none	**Student/Faculty:** 16 to 1
Year: semesters, summer session	**Tuition:** $18,590
Application Deadline: open	**Room & Board:** $7150
Freshman Class: 1344 applied, 1160 accepted, 309 enrolled	
SAT I Verbal/Math: 535/528	**ACT:** 24 **COMPETITIVE+**

Regis University, founded in 1877, is a private, Roman Catholic liberal arts institution operated by the Jesuits. Some information in this profile is approximate. There are 3 undergraduate schools. In addition to regional accreditation, Regis has baccalaureate program accreditation with CAHEA, NCATE, and NLN. The library contains 420,799 volumes, 136,379 microform items, and 104,698 audiovisual forms/CDs, and subscribes to 3979 periodicals. Computerized library services include the card catalog, interlibrary loans, and database searching. Special learning facilities include a learning resource center and radio station. The 90-acre campus is in a suburban area in north Denver. Including residence halls, there are 12 buildings.

Student Life: 57% of undergraduates are from Colorado. Others are from 40 states, 23 foreign countries, and Canada. 77% are white. 56% are Catholic. The average age of freshmen is 18; all undergraduates, 21. 50% of freshmen remain to graduate.

Housing: 600 students can be accommodated in college housing, which includes coed dormitories. On-campus housing is guaranteed for all 4 years and is available on a first-come, first-served basis. 63% of students commute. All students may keep cars.

Activities: There are no fraternities or sororities. There are 30 groups on campus, including cheerleading, choir, chorus, dance, ethnic, forensics, gay, honors, international, literary magazine, newspaper, political, professional, radio and TV, religious, social, social service, student government, and yearbook. Popular campus events include Mistletoe Madness, Ranger Week, and Hall Olympics.

Sports: There are 6 intercollegiate sports for men and 6 for women, and 8 intramural sports for men and 8 for women. Facilities include a 2800-seat gym, a pool, tennis courts, and playing fields.

Disabled Students: 80% of the campus is accessible. Wheelchair ramps, elevators, special parking, specially equipped rest rooms, special class scheduling, lowered drinking fountains, and lowered telephones are available.

Services: Counseling and information services are available, as is tutoring in every subject. There is a reader service for the blind.

Campus Safety and Security: Measures include 24-hour foot and vehicle patrol, self-defense education, escort service, and pamphlets/posters/films. There are emergency telephones and lighted pathways/sidewalks.

Programs of Study: Regis confers B.A., B.S., and B.S.N. degrees. Master's degrees are also awarded. Bachelor's degrees are awarded in BIOLOGICAL SCIENCE (biochemistry, biology/biological science, and neurosciences), BUSINESS (accounting, business administration and management, business economics, international business management, and marketing/retailing/merchandising), COMMUNICATIONS AND THE ARTS (communications, English, French, and Spanish), COMPUTER AND PHYSICAL SCIENCE (chemistry, computer science, and mathematics), ENGINEERING AND ENVIRONMENTAL DESIGN (engineering), HEALTH PROFESSIONS (medical records administration/services and nursing), SOCIAL SCIENCE (economics, history, philosophy, political science/government, prelaw, psychology, religion, and sociology). Business is the largest.

Required: To graduate, students must complete 128 credit hours with a minimum GPA of 2.0. The 58-credit core curriculum includes 12 credits of seminars, 7 to 8 of math and natural science, 6 of literature/humanities, social science, religious studies, and philosophy, and 3 each of economics, communication arts, and fine arts.

Special: Cross-registration is possible with Denver University and Metropolitan State. Regis offers internships, study abroad, work-study programs, B.A.-B.S. degrees, dual majors, student-designed majors, a 3-2 engineering degree with Washington University, and pass/fail options. There is 1 national honor society and a freshman honors program.

Faculty/Classroom: 57% of faculty are male; 43%, female. All both teach and do research. The average class size in an introductory lecture is 30; in a laboratory, 15; and in a regular course, 30.

Admissions: 86% of the 2001-2002 applicants were accepted. The SAT I scores for the 2001-2002 freshman class were: Verbal--31% below 500, 46% between 500 and 599, 20% between 600 and 700, and 3% above 700; Math--34% below 500, 42% between 500 and 599, 20% between 600 and 700, and 4% above 700. The ACT scores were 28% below 21, 24% between 21 and 23, 24% between 24 and 26, 13% between 27 and 28, and 11% above 28. 39% of the current freshmen were in the top fifth of their class; 60% were in the top two fifths. In a recent year, 8 freshmen graduated first in their class.

Requirements: The SAT I or ACT is required. In addition, applicants should be graduates of an accredited secondary school. The GED is accepted. Students should have completed 16 high school academic credits, including 4 years of English, 3 each of math, science, and history, 2 of a foreign language, and 1 to 2 of social studies. A recommendation from the high school counselor and an essay are required. An interview is recommended. A GPA of 2.3 is required. AP and CLEP credits are accepted. Important factors in the admissions decision are recommendations by school officials, leadership record, and extracurricular activities record. Applications are accepted on-line or on computer disk.

Procedure: Freshmen are admitted fall and spring. Entrance exams should be taken in the fall. There is a deferred admissions plan. Application deadlines are open. The application fee is $40. Notification is sent on a rolling basis. In a recent year, 3% of applicants were on a waiting list.

Transfer: 115 transfer students enrolled in a recent year. Applicants must have a GPA of 2.5. All previous college work is considered. Regis reviews each applicant individually. 30 credits of 128 must be completed at Regis.

Visiting: There are guides for informal visits and visitors may sit in on classes and stay overnight. To schedule a visit, contact the Admissions Office.

Financial Aid: In 2001-2002, 90% of all students received some form of financial aid. In a recent year, 63% of freshmen and 65% of continuing students received need-based aid. 51% of undergraduates work part time. Average annual earnings from campus work are $1750. The average financial indebtedness of a recent graduate was $15,500. The FAFSA and the college's own financial statement are required. Check with the school for current deadlines.

International Students: In a recent year, there were 31 international students enrolled. The school actively recruits these students. They must score 550 on the written TOEFL or 213 on the electronic version or take the MELAB and the ELS/ALA.

Computers: The mainframe is a DEC VAX 11/785. The mainframe and PCs systems are available 24 hours a day in the computer labs. All students may access the system. There are no time limits and no fees. It is strongly recommended that all students have a personal computer.

Graduates: In a recent class, 161 bachelor's degrees were awarded. The most popular majors were nursing (37%), business (14%), and math (9%). In an average class, 9% graduate in 3 years, 83% in 4 years, and all in 5 years. 41 companies recruited on campus in a recent year.

Admissions Contact: Vic Davolt, Director of Admissions. A CD is available. E-mail: *regisadm@regis.edu* Web: *www.regis.edu*

UNITED STATES AIR FORCE ACADEMY D-3
USAFA, CO 80840-5025 (719) 333-2520
(800) 443-9266; Fax: (719) 333-3012

Full-time: 3682 men, 683 women	**Faculty:** 577
Part-time: none	**Ph.D.s:** 50%
Graduate: none	**Student/Faculty:** 8 to 1
Year: semesters, summer session	**Tuition:** 0
Application Deadline: January 31	**Room & Board:** 0
Freshman Class: n/av	
SAT I or ACT: required	**MOST COMPETITIVE**

The United States Air Force Academy, the newest of the United States service academies, was founded in 1954 and is a public institution. Some information in this profile is approximate. Graduates of the academy receive the B.S. degree and a second lieutenant's commission in the regular Air Force. All graduates are obligated to serve at least 5 years of active duty military service. Tuition, room, board, medical, and dental expenses are paid by the U.S. government. Each cadet receives a monthly salary from which to pay for uniforms, supplies, and personal expenses. Entering freshmen are required to deposit $2500 to defray the initial costs of uniforms and personal expenses incurred upon entry. Students who are unable to submit the full deposit will receive a reduced monthly cash allotment until prescribed levels are reached. Figures in above capsule are approximate. In addition to regional accreditation, USAFA has baccalaureate program accreditation with ABET and CSAB. The 3 libraries contain 688,801 volumes, 621,792 microform items, and 4860 audiovisual forms/CDs, and subscribe to 2106 periodicals. Computerized library services include the card catalog, interlibrary loans, and database searching. Special learning facilities include a learning resource center, art gallery, planetarium, radio station, TV station, field engineering and readiness lab, and aeronautics lab/aeronautical research center. The 18,000-acre campus is in a suburban area 8 miles north of downtown Colorado Springs.

Student Life: 95% of undergraduates are from out of state. Students are from 50 states and 26 foreign countries. 83% are white. 57% are Protestant; 30%, Catholic; 12% claim no religious affiliation. The average age of freshmen is 18; all undergraduates, 20. 18% do not continue beyond their first year; 71% remain to graduate.

Housing: 4400 students can be accommodated in college housing, which includes coed dormitories. On-campus housing is guaranteed for all 4 years. All students live on campus. Alcohol is not permitted. Upperclassmen may keep cars.

Activities: There are no fraternities or sororities. There are 87 groups on campus, including Chamber music, cheerleading, chess, choir, chorale, chorus, computers, drama, drill team, drum and bugle corps, ethnic, film, forensics, honors, literary magazine, marching band, musical theater, newspaper, professional, radio and TV, religious, show choir, social, social service, student government, and yearbook. Popular campus events include Acceptance Parade, Christmas "Messiah" program, and Graduation Week.

Sports: There are 17 intercollegiate sports for men and 10 for women, and 13 intramural sports for men and 12 for women. Facilities include a 47,000-seat stadium, a cadet gym, a field house, 143 acres of athletic facilities and recreational areas, 3 basketball gyms, 4 indoor tennis courts, an Olympic-size swimming pool, a water polo pool, 3 squash and 19 racquetball/handball courts, and 2 weight training rooms.

Services: Counseling and information services are available, as is tutoring in every subject, including studying techniques and English as a second language. There is remedial math, reading, and writing.

Campus Safety and Security: Measures include 24-hour foot and vehicle patrol, self-defense education, escort service, and informal discussions. There are pamphlets/posters/films, emergency telephones, and lighted pathways/sidewalks.

Programs of Study: USAFA confers the B.S. degree. Bachelor's degrees are awarded in BIOLOGICAL SCIENCE (biology/biological science), BUSINESS (management science and operations research), COMMUNICATIONS AND THE ARTS (English), COMPUTER AND PHYSICAL SCIENCE (atmospheric sciences and meteorology, chemistry, computer science, mathematics, physics, and science), ENGINEERING AND ENVIRONMENTAL DESIGN (aeronautical engineering, aerospace studies, civil engineering, computer engineering, electrical/electronics engineering, engineering, engineering and applied science, engineering mechanics, environmental engineering, mechanical engineering, and military science), SOCIAL SCIENCE (behavioral science, economics, geography, history, humanities, international studies, law, political science/government, psychology, and social science). Engineering and basic sciences are the strongest academically. Management, biology, and operations research are the largest.

Required: A total of 145 to 161 semester hours is required, with a minimum GPA of 2.0, to graduate. Cadets must complete the requirements for the core curriculum and for an academic major or the B.S. program. They must be proficient in phys ed and military training, and demonstrate an aptitude for commissioned service and leadership. Required curriculum includes 9 hours of military arts and sciences, 6 of phys ed, and 1 of aviation.

Special: All cadets receive orientation flights in Air Force aircraft and take aviation science courses. A semester exchange program is available with the French Air Force Academy and U.S. Army, Naval, and Coast Guard academies. Freshman classes start in June, and basic cadet training must be completed before academics begin in August. Work-study programs are available, and dual majors are possible in all areas. There is an interdisciplinary space operations major. There are 2 national honor societies.

Faculty/Classroom: 85% of faculty are male; 15%, female. All teach undergraduates and 10% also do research. The average class size in an introductory lecture is 17; in a laboratory, 17; and in a regular course, 17.

Admissions: 17% of the 2001-2002 applicants were accepted. The SAT I scores for the 2001-2002 freshman class were: Verbal--2% below 500, 32% between 500 and 599, 55% between 600 and 700, and 11% above 700; Math--1% below 500, 20% between 500 and 599, 59% between 600 and 700, and 20% above 700. 80% of the current freshmen were in the top fifth of their class; 87% were in the top two fifths. In a recent year, there were 36 National Merit finalists and 35 semifinalists. 121 freshmen graduated first in their class.

Requirements: The SAT I or ACT is required. In addition, candidates must be U.S. citizens between 17 and 22 years of age, unmarried and with no dependents, and nominated from a legal source. Students should have completed 4 years each of English, math, and lab sciences, and 2 years each of social sciences and foreign languages. A computer course is recommended. A personal interview is required, as is an essay and a drug and alcohol abuse certificate. A GPA of 2.0 is required, but 3.0 is recommended. AP credits are accepted. Important factors in the admissions decision are personality/intangible qualities, advanced placement or honor courses, and leadership record.

Procedure: Freshmen are admitted in the summer. Entrance exams should be taken in the spring of the junior year. Check with the school for current application deadlines and fee.

Transfer: All students must enter as freshmen and attend 4 years. All 145 to 161 credits must be completed at USAFA.

Visiting: There are regularly scheduled orientations for prospective students, consisting of a 2-day orientation held in March and April. Students are given briefings by the superintendent, the commandant of cadets, the dean of cadets, and the director of athletics. Students stay overnight in the dorms and shadow their escort cadets the second day, attending classes, training, and meals. Check with the school for current fees. There is also a daily tour. There are guides for informal visits. To schedule a visit, contact the Minority Enrollment Office at (800) 443-3864.

International Students: In a recent year, there were 40 international students enrolled in a recent year. They must take the SAT I or the ACT.

Computers: The mainframes are a Unisys and an HP. All cadets reimburse the academy for a PC upon entry. These PCs are all networked to a 10,000 drop fiber optic LAN called USAFANET. Gateways to the Internet are provided as well, and cadets have limited access to the Unisys. All students may access the system 24 hours a day. There are no time limits and no fees.

Graduates: In a recent class, 954 bachelor's degrees were awarded. The most popular majors were social sciences (31%), engineering (27%), and humanities (19%). In an average class, 71% graduate in 4

years. Of a recent graduating class, 8% were enrolled in graduate school within 6 months of graduation and all were employed.
Admissions Contact: Rolland Stoneman, Associate Director, Admissions/Selections. Web: *www.usafa.edu/rr/*

UNIVERSITY OF COLORADO SYSTEM

The University of Colorado System, established in 1876, is a public system. It is governed by a board of regents and the chief administrator is the president. The primary goal of the system is comprehensive research, instruction, and public service. The total enrollment of all campuses is usually about 41,000, with 4500 faculty members. The University of Colorado at Boulder ranks second among public universities and colleges in overall research expenditures per faculty member. 1 of only 34 public universities belonging to the prestigious Association of American Universities, the University of Colorado at Boulder is the only member institution in the Rocky Mountain area. Profiles of the 4-year campuses in Boulder, Colorado Springs, and Denver are included in this section.

UNIVERSITY OF COLORADO AT BOULDER C-2

Boulder, CO 80309-0552 (303) 492-6301; Fax: (303) 492-7115

Full-time: 11,175 men, 10,207 women	**Faculty:** 1263; 1, -$
Part-time: 1421 men, 1195 women	**Ph.D.s:** 93%
Graduate: 3027 men, 2584 women	**Student/Faculty:** 17 to 1
Year: semesters, summer session	**Tuition:** $3357 ($17,367)
Application Deadline: February 15	**Room & Board:** $5898
Freshman Class: 18,487 applied, 14,637 accepted, 5021 enrolled	
SAT I Verbal/Math: required	**VERY COMPETITIVE**

The University of Colorado at Boulder, established in 1876, is a public institution offering undergraduate and graduate programs in arts and sciences, business, engineering, architecture and planning, music, education, and journalism. There are 7 undergraduate and 3 graduate schools. In addition to regional accreditation, CU-Boulder has baccalaureate program accreditation with AACSB, ABET, ACEJMC, NASM, and NCATE. The 5 libraries contain 2,920,335 volumes, 5,915,785 microform items, and 60,202 audiovisual forms/CDs, and subscribe to 14,772 periodicals. Computerized library services include the card catalog, interlibrary loans, and database searching. Special learning facilities include a learning resource center, art gallery, natural history museum, planetarium, radio station, TV station, an interactive foreign language video center, a mountain research station, and an integrated teaching and learning lab in engineering. The 600-acre campus is in a suburban area 30 miles northwest of Denver. Including residence halls, there are 155 buildings.
Student Life: 67% of undergraduates are from Colorado. Others are from 50 states, 99 foreign countries, and Canada. 80% are white. The average age of freshmen is 19; all undergraduates, 21. 18% do not continue beyond their first year; 64% remain to graduate.
Housing: 6000 students can be accommodated in college housing, which includes coed dormitories, on-campus apartments, and married-student housing. In addition, there are honors houses, special-interest houses, and 5 residential academic programs that include housing. On-campus housing is guaranteed for the freshman year only and is available on a first-come, first-served basis. 75% of students commute. All students may keep cars.
Activities: 8% of men belong to 19 national fraternities; 12% of women belong to 1 local and 10 national sorority. There are more than 150 groups on campus, including art, band, cheerleading, chess, choir, chorale, chorus, computers, dance, drama, drill team, environmental, ethnic, film, gay, honors, international, jazz band, literary magazine, marching band, musical theater, opera, orchestra, pep band, photography, political, professional, radio and TV, religious, social, social service, special interest, student government, symphony, and yearbook. Popular campus events include World Affairs Conference, International Women's Week, and Trivia Bowl.
Sports: There are 7 intercollegiate sports for men and 8 for women, and 16 intramural sports for men and 15 for women. Facilities include a 52,000-seat stadium and an 8700-seat events center, a recreation center that includes an 8-lane swimming pool, diving pool, ice rink, handball and racquetball courts, basketball and squash courts, outdoor tennis courts, weight-training rooms, an indoor running track, and an indoor climbing wall.
Disabled Students: 71% of the campus is accessible. Wheelchair ramps, elevators, special parking, specially equipped rest rooms, special class scheduling, lowered drinking fountains, lowered telephones, assisted classroom listening devices, and TTY, TDD, and TT phone support systems are available.
Services: Counseling and information services are available, as is tutoring in most subjects, a learning disabilities program, and an interpreter for the deaf (curricular and non-curricular). There is a reader service for the blind and remedial writing. There is also a Multicultural Center for Counseling and Community Development, which includes counselors for individuals and groups.
Campus Safety and Security: Measures include 24-hour foot and vehicle patrol, self-defense education, escort service, and shuttle buses. There are informal discussions, pamphlets/posters/films, emergency telephones, and lighted pathways/sidewalks. Campus police are academy-trained and commissioned officers of the Boulder police force. Additional safety programs and services are detailed on the CU-Boulder police home page: *http//www.colorado.edu/police/*
Programs of Study: CU-Boulder confers B.A., B.S., B.Env.D., B.F.A., B.Mus., and B.Mus.Ed. degrees. Master's and doctoral degrees are also awarded. Bachelor's degrees are awarded in BIOLOGICAL SCIENCE (biochemistry, cell biology, environmental biology, and molecular biology), BUSINESS (accounting, banking and finance, business administration and management, human resources, international business management, management science, marketing management, small business management, and tourism), COMMUNICATIONS AND THE ARTS (advertising, art history and appreciation, broadcasting, Chinese, classics, communications, dance, dramatic arts, English, film arts, fine arts, French, Germanic languages and literature, Italian, Japanese, journalism, linguistics, music, Spanish, and telecommunications), COMPUTER AND PHYSICAL SCIENCE (applied mathematics, astronomy, chemistry, computer science, geology, information sciences and systems, mathematics, and physics), EDUCATION (music), ENGINEERING AND ENVIRONMENTAL DESIGN (aeronautical engineering, architectural engineering, chemical engineering, civil engineering, computer engineering, electrical/electronics engineering, engineering, engineering physics, environmental design, environmental engineering, environmental science, and mechanical engineering), HEALTH PROFESSIONS (exercise science and speech pathology/audiology), SOCIAL SCIENCE (American studies, anthropology, Asian/Oriental studies, economics, ethnic studies, geography, German area studies, history, humanities, international relations, philosophy, political science/government, psychology, religion, Russian and Slavic studies, sociology, and women's studies). Engineering, biological sciences, and chemistry are the strongest academically. Psychology, biology, and finance are the largest.
Required: For graduation, students must complete at least 120 credits, including a minimum of 30 in the major. A GPA of at least 2.0 is required. Other requirements vary by undergraduate college and program.
Special: Sewall, Farrand, and other residential programs for freshmen and sophomores offer a small liberal arts college atmosphere while taking advantage of the resources of a major university. A residential program in Baker Hall Village offers courses in the environmental sciences. Student-designed and dual majors, internships, 5-year B.A.-B.S. degrees, 5-year B.A.- M.A. degrees, and cooperative programs in business and engineering are available. Study abroad in more than 60 countries, work-study programs in federal labs, internships, a 3-2 engineering degree, and cross-registration with other University of Colorado campuses are offered. There are 19 national honor societies, including Phi Beta Kappa, a freshman honors program, and 47 departmental honors programs.
Faculty/Classroom: 69% of faculty are male; 31%, female. All both teach and do research. Graduate students teach 19% of introductory courses. The average class size in an introductory lecture is 43; in a laboratory, 16; and in a regular course, 25.
Admissions: 79% of the 2001-2002 applicants were accepted. The SAT I scores for the 2001-2002 freshman class were: Verbal--13% below 500, 49% between 500 and 599, 32% between 600 and 700, and 5% above 700; Math--10% below 500, 42% between 500 and 599, 39% between 600 and 700, and 8% above 700. The ACT scores were 10% below 21, 25% between 21 and 23, 33% between 24 and 26, 16% between 27 and 28, and 16% above 28. There were 13 National Merit finalists. 151 freshmen graduated first in their class.
Requirements: The SAT I or ACT is required. In addition, applicants must have completed 16 credits of high school work as identified by the University of Colorado minimum Academic Preparation Standards. Students are asked to write a personal statement. Interviews are not used in the decision-making process. Auditions are required for consideration to the College of Music. Portfolios are discouraged. Students with a GED are considered on an individual basis. A GPA of 2.0 is required. AP and CLEP credits are accepted. Important factors in the admissions decision are advanced placement or honor courses, geographic diversity, and leadership record. Applications are accepted on-line at *http//www.colorado.edu/admissions/app/appintro.html.*
Procedure: Freshmen are admitted to all sessions. Entrance exams should be taken no later than December of the senior year. There is a deferred admissions plan. Applications should be filed by February 15 for fall entry, October 1 for spring entry, and February 15 for summer entry. The fall 2001 application fee was $40. Notification is sent on a rolling basis. 6% of all applicants are on a waiting list; 29% were accepted in 2001.
Transfer: 1327 transfer students enrolled in 2001-2002. All applicants must submit official high school and college transcripts. Students who have completed fewer than 30 semester hours must also submit SAT I or ACT results. 30 credits of 120 must be completed at CU-Boulder.
Visiting: There are regularly scheduled orientations for prospective students, including advising, placement testing, registration, social and cam-

pus orientation, and meetings with college deans and faculty. Parents are invited also. There are guides for informal visits and visitors may sit in on classes. To schedule a visit, contact the Admissions/Campus Visit Programs or make a reservation on-line at *www.colorado.edu/admissions/calendar/daylong.html*

Financial Aid: In 2001-2002, 53% of all freshmen and 45% of continuing students received some form of financial aid. 28% of freshmen and 29% of continuing students received need-based aid. The average freshman award was $5903. Of that total, scholarships or need-based grants averaged $2875 ($37,300 maximum); loans averaged $2842 ($28,620 maximum); and work contracts averaged $186 ($4084 maximum). 61% of undergraduates work part time. Average annual earnings from campus work are $1789. The average financial indebtedness of the 2001 graduate was $16,737. The FAFSA and tax returns are required. The fall application deadline is March 1.

International Students: There are 315 international students enrolled. They must score 500 on the written TOEFL or 173 (220 for engineering) on the electronic version or take the MELAB. Other tests or verification of proficiency will be considered on an individual basis.

Computers: The mainframe is an Hitachi Data Systems 3090. More than 1200 public access PCs are available in the computer labs, classroom buildings, dormitories, and libraries. All have Internet, Web,and Personal Lookup access. All students have e-mail and Internet accounts on the academic mainframe. All students may access the system 24 hours per day. There are no time limits and no fees. It is strongly recommended that all students have a personal computer.

Graduates: In 2001, 4578 bachelor's degrees were awarded. The most popular majors were psychology (8%), biology (6%), and finance (5%). In an average class, 35% graduate in 4 years, 60% in 5 years, and 65% in 6 years. 400 companies recruited on campus in 2000-2001. Of the 2000 graduating class, 27% were enrolled in graduate school within 6 months of graduation and 79% were employed.

Admissions Contact: Barbara Schneider, Executive Director of Admissions. E-mail: *apply@colorado.edu*
Web: *www.colorado.edu/admissions/apply.html*

UNIVERSITY OF COLORADO AT COLORADO SPRINGS — D-3

Colorado Springs, CO 80933-7150 — (719) 262-3383, (800) 990-8227

Full-time: 1484 men, 2388 women	**Faculty:** 240; IIA, av$
Part-time: 581 men, 791 women	**Ph.D.s:** 94%
Graduate: 721 men, 870 women	**Student/Faculty:** 16 to 1
Year: semesters, summer session	**Tuition:** $3510 ($13,974)
Application Deadline: July 1	**Room & Board:** $5893
Freshman Class: 2288 applied, 1683 accepted, 793 enrolled	
SAT I Verbal/Math: 531/540	**ACT:** 23 — **COMPETITIVE**

The University of Colorado at Colorado Springs, established in 1965, is a public institution, with programs in liberal arts, business, engineering, education, and nursing. There are 4 undergraduate and 5 graduate schools. In addition to regional accreditation, UCCS has baccalaureate program accreditation with AACSB, ABET, CSAB, NCATE, and NLN. The library contains 632,724 volumes, 402,834 microform items, and 5234 audiovisual forms/CDs, and subscribes to 2201 periodicals. Computerized library services include the card catalog, interlibrary loans, and database searching. Special learning facilities include a learning resource center, art gallery, and and a center for excellence in oral communication, a math learning center, a science learning center, a writing center, and a language technology center. The 504-acre campus is in an urban area 70 miles south of Denver. Including residence halls, there are 24 buildings.

Student Life: 93% of undergraduates are from Colorado. Others are from 48 states, 35 foreign countries, and Canada. 75% are white. The average age of freshmen is 19; all undergraduates, 24. 35% do not continue beyond their first year; 40% remain to graduate.

Housing: 600 students can be accommodated in college housing, which includes single-sex and coed dormitories. On-campus housing is available on a first-come, first-served basis. 91% of students commute. All students may keep cars.

Activities: 1% of men and about 1% of women belong to 1 national fraternity; 1% of women belong to 1 local sorority. There are 50 groups on campus, including art, choir, computers, dance, drama, drill team, ethnic, film, gay, honors, international, literary magazine, newspaper, photography, political, professional, radio and TV, religious, social, and student government. Popular campus events include Winter Holiday Festival and Comedy Night.

Sports: There are 5 intercollegiate sports for men and 5 for women, and 13 intramural sports for men and 12 for women. Facilities include a gym, softball and soccer fields, a multipurpose field, tennis and volleyball courts, and a fitness center.

Disabled Students: 95% of the campus is accessible. Wheelchair ramps, elevators, special parking, specially equipped rest rooms, lowered drinking fountains, and lowered telephones are available.

Services: Counseling and information services are available, as is tutoring in most subjects. There is a reader service for the blind.

Campus Safety and Security: Measures include 24-hour foot and vehicle patrol, self-defense education, escort service, and shuttle buses. There are informal discussions, pamphlets/posters/films, emergency telephones, and lighted pathways/sidewalks.

Programs of Study: UCCS confers B.A. and B.S. degrees. Master's and doctoral degrees are also awarded. Bachelor's degrees are awarded in BIOLOGICAL SCIENCE (biology/biological science), BUSINESS (business administration and management), COMMUNICATIONS AND THE ARTS (communications, English, fine arts, and Spanish), COMPUTER AND PHYSICAL SCIENCE (chemistry, computer science, mathematics, and physics), ENGINEERING AND ENVIRONMENTAL DESIGN (electrical/electronics engineering), HEALTH PROFESSIONS (health care administration and nursing), SOCIAL SCIENCE (anthropology, economics, geography, history, philosophy, political science/government, psychology, and sociology). Business, engineering, and psychology are the strongest academically and have the largest enrollments.

Required: To graduate, students must complete 124 credit hours, with at least 30 of them in the major, with a minimum GPA of 2.0. All students must take English and a computer literacy course. Other requirements vary with the program.

Special: The university offers work-study, dual majors, nondegree study, and pass/fail options. There are 3 national honor societies, including Phi Beta Kappa.

Faculty/Classroom: 55% of faculty are male; 45%, female. 93% teach undergraduates, 80% do research, and 80% do both. Graduate students teach 1% of introductory courses. The average class size in an introductory lecture is 32; in a laboratory, 45; and in a regular course, 22.

Admissions: 74% of the 2001-2002 applicants were accepted. The SAT I scores for the 2001-2002 freshman class were: Verbal--29% below 500, 50% between 500 and 599, 18% between 600 and 700, and 3% above 700; Math--29% below 500, 46% between 500 and 599, 23% between 600 and 700, and 2% above 700. The ACT scores were 23% below 21, 23% between 21 and 23, 38% between 24 and 26, 8% between 27 and 28, and 8% above 28. 31% of the current freshmen were in the top fifth of their class; 60% were in the top two fifths.

Requirements: The SAT I or ACT is required, with recommended minimum composite scores of 850 and 18, respectively. Applicants must be graduates of an accredited secondary school. The GED is accepted. Secondary school courses must include 15 high school credits, including 4 years of English, 3 years each of math and science, 2 years each of foreign language and social studies, and 1 academic elective. AP and CLEP credits are accepted. Important factors in the admissions decision are advanced placement or honor courses, evidence of special talent, and recommendations by school officials. Applications are accepted on-line at *www.uccs.edu*

Procedure: Freshmen are admitted to all sessions. Entrance exams should be taken during the senior year. There is a deferred admissions plan. Early decision application should be filed by April 1; regular applications, by July 1 for fall entry, December 1 for spring entry, and May 1 for summer entry. Notification is sent on a rolling basis. The fall 2001 application fee was $45.

Transfer: 668 transfer students enrolled in 2001-2002. Applicants must have a minimum GPA of 2.5 and a minimum of 12 credit hours earned. The school recommends minimum composite scores of 850 on the SAT I or 18 on the ACT. 30 credits of 124 must be completed at UCCS.

Visiting: There are regularly scheduled orientations for prospective students. There are guides for informal visits and visitors may sit in on classes. To schedule a visit, contact the Marketing Office at (719) 262-3072 or *visitcu@uccs.edu*

Financial Aid: In 2001-2002, 56% of all freshmen and 46% of continuing students received some form of financial aid. 35% of freshmen and 37% of continuing students received need-based aid. The average freshman award was $6000. Of that total, scholarships or need-based grants averaged $3426 ($16,452 maximum); loans averaged $5341 ($21,055 maximum); and work contracts averaged $3943 ($9999 maximum). 13% of undergraduates work part time. Average annual earnings from campus work are $4028. The average financial indebtedness of the 2001 graduate was $9423. UCCS is a member of CSS. The FAFSA is required. The fall application deadline is April 1.

International Students: There are 21 international students enrolled. They must score 550 on the written TOEFL and also take the SAT I or the ACT.

Computers: The mainframes are a DEC VAX 4000, 2 DEC VAX Station 3100s, 4 DEC ALPHA, 4 DEC Stations, and 6 HP servers running NT/3 UNIX servers. There are 4 labs with a total of 111 PCs and 3 labs with a total of 30 Macs. There are 7 technology classrooms with a total of 240 PCs. All labs and classrooms can access the Web and the campus network. All students may access the system 8 A.M. to 10 P.M. daily. There are no time limits and no fees. It is strongly recommended that all students have a personal computer.

Graduates: In 2001, 905 bachelor's degrees were awarded. The most popular majors were business (17%), psychology (14%), and communications (13%). In an average class, 12% graduate in 4 years, 20% in 5 years, and 29% in 6 years. 120 companies recruited on campus in 2000-2001.

Admissions Contact: Admissions Office. E-mail: *admrec@uccs.edu* Web: *www.uccs.edu*

UNIVERSITY OF COLORADO AT DENVER C-2

Denver, CO 80217-3364 **(303) 556-3287; Fax: (303) 556-4838**

Full-time: 1950 men, 2520 women
Part-time: 1690 men, 2190 women
Graduate: 2570 men, 3150 women
Year: semesters, summer session
Application Deadline: July 22
Freshman Class: n/av
SAT I or ACT: required
Faculty: 479; IIA, av$
Ph.D.s: n/av
Student/Faculty: 9 to 1
Tuition: $3673 ($12,017)
Room & Board: n/app
COMPETITIVE

The University of Colorado at Denver, established in 1912, is a public, commuter institution with programs in the liberal arts and sciences, business, engineering and applied sciences, music, architecture and planning, and education. Figures in above capsule are approximate. There are 3 undergraduate and 6 graduate schools. In addition to regional accreditation, CU-Denver has baccalaureate program accreditation with AACSB, ABET, NAAB, NASM, and NCATE. The library contains 533,821 volumes, 911,831 microform items, and 18,718 audiovisual forms/CDs, and subscribes to 4719 periodicals. Computerized library services include the card catalog, interlibrary loans, and database searching. Special learning facilities include a learning resource center, art gallery, TV station, and a writing center. The 127-acre campus is in an urban area in downtown Denver. There are 30 buildings.

Student Life: 95% of undergraduates are from Colorado. Others are from 34 states, 45 foreign countries, and Canada. 90% are from public schools. 45% are white. The average age of freshmen is 18; all undergraduates, 26. 27% do not continue beyond their first year; 29% remain to graduate.

Housing: There are no residence halls; there are off-campus apartments. All students commute. Alcohol is not permitted. All students may keep cars.

Activities: There are no fraternities or sororities. There are 50 groups on campus, including art, chorale, computers, dance, drama, ethnic, gay, honors, international, jazz band, musical theater, newspaper, political, professional, religious, social, social service, and student government. Popular campus events include Fall Festival.

Sports: There are 7 intramural sports for men and 7 for women. Facilities include a phys ed building with a pool including a diving well, a weight room, squash, racquetball/handball, and tennis courts and a basketball half-court, a dance studio, 3 gym arenas, a fitness center and a green room, a 400-meter track, a football/rugby/lacrosse field, softball fields, a baseball field, a soccer field, and a sand volleyball court.

Disabled Students: All of the campus is accessible. Wheelchair ramps, elevators, special parking, specially equipped rest rooms, special class scheduling, lowered drinking fountains, lowered telephones, a transit system, and an adaptive computer lab are available.

Services: Counseling and information services are available, as is tutoring in most subjects. There is a reader service for the blind. There are ESL classes and study skills courses.

Campus Safety and Security: Measures include 24-hour foot and vehicle patrol, self-defense education, escort service, and shuttle buses. There are informal discussions, pamphlets/posters/films, emergency telephones, lighted pathways/sidewalks, crime prevention programs, and emergency response.

Programs of Study: CU-Denver confers B.A., B.S., and B.F.A degrees. Master's and doctoral degrees are also awarded. Bachelor's degrees are awarded in BIOLOGICAL SCIENCE (biology/biological science), BUSINESS (business administration and management), COMMUNICATIONS AND THE ARTS (communications, creative writing, dramatic arts, English, fine arts, French, music, and Spanish), COMPUTER AND PHYSICAL SCIENCE (applied mathematics, chemistry, computer science, geology, mathematics, and physics), ENGINEERING AND ENVIRONMENTAL DESIGN (civil engineering, electrical/electronics engineering, and mechanical engineering), SOCIAL SCIENCE (anthropology, economics, geography, history, interdisciplinary studies, philosophy, political science/government, psychology, and sociology). Business, engineering, and psychology are the strongest academically. Business administration, biology, and psychology are the largest.

Required: To graduate, students must complete 120 credit hours with a minimum GPA of 2.0. All students must complete the core curriculum courses in addition to the requirements for the major.

Special: Cross-registration is possible with Metropolitan State College and Community College of Denver. Concurrent enrollment with any University of Colorado campus is possible. Cooperative programs, 1-semester internships, study abroad in 12 countries, work-study programs, an accelerated degree program in business, and B.A.-B.S. degrees are available. The university offers dual majors, a general studies degree, nondegree study, and pass/fail options. Student-designed majors and a 3-2 engineering degree are available. There are small individualized classes, peer advocates, and workshops. There are 8 national honor societies.

Faculty/Classroom: 59% of faculty are male; 41%, female. The average class size in an introductory lecture is 35; in a laboratory, 16; and in a regular course, 24.

Requirements: The SAT I or ACT is required. In addition, preference for admission is given to applicants who rank in the top 30% of their high school graduating class and present a composite score of 21 or higher on the ACT or a combined score of 950 or higher on the SAT I. A GPA of 2.5 is required. AP and CLEP credits are accepted. Important factors in the admissions decision are advanced placement or honor courses, evidence of special talent, and extracurricular activities record. Applications are accepted on-line via Entrata.

Procedure: Freshmen are admitted to all sessions. Entrance exams should be taken in the junior or senior year of high school. There is a deferred admissions plan. Applications should be filed by July 22 for fall entry, December 1 for spring entry, and May 3 for summer entry, along with a $40 fee. Notification is sent on a rolling basis.

Transfer: 959 transfer students enrolled in a recent year. Applicants for transfer must have earned at least 12 credit hours for admission to liberal arts and sciences and music programs, and 24 credit hours for admission to business and engineering. A minimum GPA of 2.5 is required, or 2.0 if transferring from Colorado School of Mines, Colorado State University, or the University of Colorado at Boulder and Colorado Springs. 30 credits of 120 must be completed at CU-Denver.

Visiting: There are regularly scheduled orientations for prospective students, including a mini-lecture, a tour of campus, and financial aid and academic advising. There are guides for informal visits and visitors may sit in on classes. To schedule a visit, contact the Office of Admissions.

Financial Aid: In a recent year, 36% of all freshmen and 44% of continuing students received some form of financial aid. 23% of freshmen and 26% of continuing students received need-based aid. The average freshman award was $3514. 80% of undergraduates work part time. Average annual earnings from campus work are $2000. The average financial indebtedness of a recent graduate was $15,275. CU-Denver is a member of CSS. The FAFSA, the college's own financial statement and tax returns are required. The fall application deadline is March 31.

International Students: There were 230 international students enrolled in a recent year. The school actively recruits these students. They must score 525 on the written TOEFL.

Computers: The mainframe is a Hitachi Model EX-90. There are computer labs with more than 100 PCs and Macs available. Internet access, word processing, spreadsheet, and graphics applications are provided. Remote access is available, as is a fully staffed help center. All students may access the system any time. There are no time limits and no fees.

Graduates: In a recent year, 1164 bachelor's degrees were awarded. The most popular majors were business/marketing (25%), social sciences/history (16%), and psychology (11%). In an average class, 9% graduate in 3 years, 6% in 4 years, 17% in 5 years, and 34% in 6 years.

Admissions Contact: Barbara Edwards, Director of Admissions.
E-mail: *admissions@cudenver.edu*
Web: *www.cudenver.edu/home/main/admissions*

UNIVERSITY OF DENVER C-2

Denver, CO 80208 **(303) 871-2036**
(800) 525-9495; Fax: (303) 871-3301

Full-time: 1598 men, 1836 women
Part-time: 100 men, 458 women
Graduate: 1911 men, 2379 women
Year: quarters, summer session
Application Deadline: February 1
Faculty: 408; I, -$
Ph.D.s: 92%
Student/Faculty: 8 to 1
Tuition: $22,035
Room & Board: $6748
Freshman Class: 3813 applied, 2972 accepted, 930 enrolled
SAT I Verbal/Math: 554/563 **ACT:** 24 **VERY COMPETITIVE**

The University of Denver, established in 1864, is a private institution offering degrees in arts and sciences, fine arts, music, business, engineering, and education. There are 7 undergraduate and 6 graduate schools. In addition to regional accreditation, DU has baccalaureate program accreditation with AACSB, ABET, CSWE, NASAD, and NASM. The 2 libraries contain 1,155,981 volumes, 970,022 microform items, and 1736 audiovisual forms/CDs, and subscribe to 5788 periodicals. Computerized library services include the card catalog, interlibrary loans, and database searching. Special learning facilities include a learning resource center, art gallery, radio station, a high-altitude research field station, an observatory, and elementary, middle, and high schools. The 123-acre campus is in a suburban area 8 miles southeast of the Denver business district. Including residence halls, there are 90 buildings.

Student Life: 56% of undergraduates are from out of state, mostly the Southwest and West. Others are from 50 states, 94 foreign countries, and Canada. 67% are from public schools. 76% are white. The average age of freshmen is 18; all undergraduates, 20. 14% do not continue beyond their first year; 86% remain to graduate.

Housing: 1511 students can be accommodated in college housing, which includes single-sex and coed dormitories, on-campus apartments, married-student housing, fraternity houses, and sorority houses. In addition, there are honors and special-interest floors. On-campus housing is guaranteed for all 4 years. 57% of students commute. All students may keep cars.

Activities: 28% of men belong to 9 national fraternities; 21% of women belong to 5 national sororities. There are 120 groups on campus, including art, band, cheerleading, chess, choir, chorale, chorus, computers, dance, drama, ethnic, film, gay, honors, international, jazz band, literary magazine, musical theater, newspaper, opera, orchestra, pep band, photography, political, professional, radio and TV, religious, social, social service, student government, symphony, and yearbook. Popular campus events include Winter Carnival, Festival of Nations Celebration, and Pioneers in the Rockies Freshman Camp.

Sports: There are 10 intercollegiate sports for men and 11 for women, and 33 intramural sports for men and 32 for women. Facilities include a sports and wellness center with an ice arena, community skating rink, gym, multipurpose field house, Olympic-size swimming pool, exercise facilities, health clinic, yoga studio, tennis courts, and playing field.

Disabled Students: Wheelchair ramps, elevators, special parking, specially equipped rest rooms, special class scheduling, lowered drinking fountains, and lowered telephones are available.

Services: Counseling and information services are available, as is tutoring in most subjects. There is a reader service for the blind and remedial math and writing.

Campus Safety and Security: Measures include 24-hour foot and vehicle patrol, escort service, shuttle buses, and informal discussions. There are pamphlets/posters/films, emergency telephones, lighted pathways/sidewalks, and a bicycle patrol.

Programs of Study: DU confers B.A., B.S., B.F.A., B.M., B.S.Acc., B.S.A.T., B.S.B.A., B.S.Ch., B.S.Comp.E., B.S.E., B.S.E.E., and B.S.M.E. degrees. Master's and doctoral degrees are also awarded. Bachelor's degrees are awarded in AGRICULTURE (animal science), BIOLOGICAL SCIENCE (biochemistry and biology/biological science), BUSINESS (accounting, banking and finance, business administration and management, business economics, hospitality management services, international business management, marketing/retailing/merchandising, and real estate), COMMUNICATIONS AND THE ARTS (art, art history and appreciation, communications, dramatic arts, English, French, German, Italian, jazz, journalism, languages, music, music performance, and Spanish), COMPUTER AND PHYSICAL SCIENCE (astronomy, chemistry, computer science, digital arts/technology, mathematics, physics, science, and statistics), ENGINEERING AND ENVIRONMENTAL DESIGN (computer engineering, construction management, electrical/electronics engineering, environmental science, and mechanical engineering), SOCIAL SCIENCE (anthropology, Asian/Oriental studies, cognitive science, economics, geography, history, international studies, philosophy, political science/government, psychology, public affairs, religion, Russian and Slavic studies, social science, sociology, and women's studies). Communications, psychology, and business are the strongest academically. Communications, accounting, and political science are the largest.

Required: For graduation, students must complete 183 to 204 quarter hours, including 42 to 135 in the major, with a minimum GPA of 2.0. All students must take 12 quarter hours each of English, natural sciences, arts and humanities, and social sciences, 8 of math and computer science, and 4 of oral communication.

Special: DU offers co-op programs, study abroad in more than 45 countries, internships, a Washington quarter, work-study programs, accelerated degree programs, dual majors, a 3-2 engineering program, a 3-2 business program, and B.A.-B.S. programs in psychology, environmental science, and math. Nondegree study and pass/fail options are also available. There are 13 national honor societies, including Phi Beta Kappa, a freshman honors program, and 13 departmental honors program.

Faculty/Classroom: 68% of faculty are male; 32%, female. Graduate students teach 5% of introductory courses. The average class size in an introductory lecture is 40; in a laboratory, 17; and in a regular course, 20.

Admissions: 78% of the 2001-2002 applicants were accepted. 64% of the current freshmen were in the top fifth of their class; 78% were in the top two fifths.

Requirements: The SAT I or ACT is required. In addition, applicants must be graduates of an accredited secondary school. The GED is accepted. The university recommends that applicants have 15 to 20 high school academic credits, including 4 in English, 3 to 4 in math, and 2 to 4 each in foreign language, social science, and natural sciences (2 with lab). Course work in the arts is encouraged. An essay is required of all students. A Hyde interview is required of early action applicants only. An audition is required for music applicants, and a portfolio is recommended for art students. AP and CLEP credits are accepted. Important factors in the admissions decision are advanced placement or honor courses, personality/intangible qualities, and evidence of special talent. Students may apply on-line using Common App, CollegeLink, or CollegeView.

Procedure: Freshmen are admitted to all sessions. Entrance exams should be taken by January of the senior year. There are early admissions and deferred admissions plans. Applications should be filed by February 1 for fall entry, December 1 for winter entry, February 15 for spring entry, and May 15 for summer entry. Notification of early action is sent January 15; regular decision, on a rolling basis. The fall 2001 application fee was $50.

Transfer: 229 transfer students enrolled in 2001-2002. Applicants must submit a transcript from all colleges attended. Those students with fewer than 30 semester hours of college credit must submit a high school record as well. A minimum GPA of 2.0 is required, but a GPA of 3.0 is recommended. 45 credits of 183 to 204 must be completed at DU.

Visiting: There are regularly scheduled orientations for prospective students, including an information session and campus tour. Visitors may sit in on classes and students who have been accepted may stay overnight. To schedule a visit, contact the Appointment Desk in Undergraduate Admission.

Financial Aid: In 2001-2002, 74% of all freshmen and 60% of continuing students received some form of financial aid. 38% of freshmen received need-based aid. The average freshman award was $16,314. Of that total, scholarships or need-based grants averaged $8425 ($17,768 maximum); loans averaged $3295 ($4125 maximum); and work contracts averaged $1500 ($1800 maximum). 26% of undergraduates work part time. Average annual earnings from campus work are $1400. The average financial indebtedness of the 2001 graduate was $9700. The FAFSA is required. The fall application deadline is February 15.

International Students: There are 526 international students enrolled. The school actively recruits these students. They must score 500 on the written TOEFL or 173 on the electronic version and also take the university's own test. The university offers conditional admission.

Computers: The mainframes are a DEC ALPHA 4000 and 4100 servers running both VMS and Digitial UNIX. There are more than 500 PCs available in dormitories, computer labs, the library, and most classrooms, Internet access in all residence rooms, and a laptop computing program for undergraduates. Access to the Internet and the Web, is available on and off campus. All students may access the system 24 hours a day. There are no time limits and no fees. All students are required to have personal computers.

Graduates: In 2001, 660 bachelor's degrees were awarded. The most popular majors were communication (8%), biology (7%), and marketing (6%). In an average class, 2% graduate in 3 years, 58% in 4 years, 68% in 5 years, and 69% in 6 years. 165 companies recruited on campus in 2000-2001. Of the 2000 graduating class, 33% were enrolled in graduate school within 6 months of graduation and 40% were employed.

Admissions Contact: Office of Admission.
E-mail: *admission@du.edu* Web: *www.du.edu*

UNIVERSITY OF NORTHERN COLORADO D-1
Greeley, CO 80639 **(970) 351-2881**
(888) 700-4UNC; Fax: (970) 351-2984

Full-time: 3759 men, 5450 women	**Faculty:** 425; I, --$
Part-time: 373 men, 631 women	**Ph.D.s:** 81%
Graduate: 542 men, 1479 women	**Student/Faculty:** 22 to 1
Year: semesters, summer session	**Tuition:** $2842 ($10,512)
Application Deadline: August 1	**Room & Board:** $5240
Freshman Class: 6709 applied, 5229 accepted, 2140 enrolled	
SAT I Verbal/Math: 520/520	**ACT:** 22 **COMPETITIVE+**

The University of Northern Colorado, founded in 1890, is a state-supported institution offering undergraduate and graduate programs in liberal arts and sciences, business, education, health and human sciences, and performing and visual arts. The enrollment and financial aid figures are from 2000. There are 4 undergraduate schools and 1 graduate school. In addition to regional accreditation, UNC has baccalaureate program accreditation with AACSB, ADA, NASM, NCATE, and NLN. The 3 libraries contain 765,241 volumes, 1,174,796 microform items, and 35,233 audiovisual forms/CDs, and subscribe to 3672 periodicals. Computerized library services include the card catalog, interlibrary loans, and database searching. Special learning facilities include a learning resource center, art gallery, radio station, TV station, and more than 30 partner schools. The 240-acre campus is in a suburban area 50 miles north of Denver. Including residence halls, there are 46 buildings.

Student Life: 88% of undergraduates are from Colorado. Others are from 47 states, 52 foreign countries, and Canada. 95% are from public schools. 82% are white. The average age of freshmen is 18; all undergraduates, 21. 30% do not continue beyond their first year.

Housing: 3029 students can be accommodated in college housing, which includes single-sex and coed dormitories, on-campus apartments, off-campus apartments, married-student housing, fraternity houses, and sorority houses. In addition, there are off-campus houses, graduate women's houses, and special interest floors. On-campus housing is guaranteed for the freshman year only, is available on a first-come, first-served basis, and is available on a lottery system for upperclassmen. 70% of students commute. All students may keep cars.

Activities: 5% of men belong to 11 national fraternities; 5% of women belong to 8 national sororities. There are 114 groups on campus, including art, band, cheerleading, chess, choir, chorale, computers, dance, drama, drill team, ethnic, film, gay, honors, international, jazz band, literary magazine, marching band, musical theater, opera, orchestra, pep band, photography, political, professional, radio and TV, religious, social, social service, student government, symphony, and yearbook. Popular campus events include Hawaiian Luau, Academic Excellence Week, and International Dinner.

Sports: There are 7 intercollegiate sports for men and 9 for women, and 12 intramural sports for men and 10 for women. Facilities include a stadium and a recreation center with 5 gyms, 3 racquetball courts, a weight room and aerobics room, and an indoor track.

Disabled Students: All of the campus is accessible. Wheelchair ramps, elevators, special parking, specially equipped rest rooms, special class scheduling, lowered drinking fountains, lowered telephones, and academic support services such as note taking, transportation, interpreters, adaptive computer instruction, and library assistance are available.

Services: Counseling and information services are available, as is tutoring in most subjects. There is a reader service for the blind, and remedial math, reading, and writing.

Campus Safety and Security: Measures include 24-hour foot and vehicle patrol, escort service, shuttle buses, and pamphlets/posters/films. There are emergency telephones and lighted pathways/sidewalks.

Programs of Study: UNC confers B.A., B.S., B.A.S., B.A.T., B.Mus., and B.Mus.Ed. degrees. Master's and doctoral degrees are also awarded. Bachelor's degrees are awarded in AGRICULTURE (natural resource management), BIOLOGICAL SCIENCE (biochemistry and biology/biological science), BUSINESS (accounting, business administration and management, management science, and marketing/retailing/merchandising), COMMUNICATIONS AND THE ARTS (advertising, art, communications, dance, dramatic arts, English, fine arts, French, German, graphic design, journalism, music, public relations, Spanish, and telecommunications), COMPUTER AND PHYSICAL SCIENCE (actuarial science, atmospheric sciences and meteorology, chemistry, computer science, earth science, geology, information sciences and systems, mathematics, physics, and statistics), EDUCATION (physical and science), HEALTH PROFESSIONS (allied health, community health work, nursing, rehabilitation therapy, and speech pathology/audiology), SOCIAL SCIENCE (African American studies, criminal justice, dietetics, economics, geography, gerontology, history, interdisciplinary studies, international relations, Mexican-American/Chicano studies, philosophy, physical fitness/movement, political science/government, psychology, social science, and sociology). Business, music, and nursing are the strongest academically. Business, interdisciplinary studies, and psychology are the largest.

Required: Students must earn a minimum of 120 semester hours (some majors require additional hours) with a minimum GPA of 2.0. All students must complete 40 semester hours in required general education courses and meet all degree requirements in the major.

Special: UNC offers internships and co-op programs in many majors and study abroad in England, Australia, Spain, France, and Germany or through the International Student Exchange Program. Dual majors, student-designed majors, credit by exam, and pass/fail options are also available. Cross-registration is available with Aims Community College, and there are accelerated degree programs in nursing and business. There are 14 national honor societies and a freshman honors program.

Faculty/Classroom: 52% of faculty are male; 48%, female. All both teach and do research. Graduate students teach 13% of introductory courses. The average class size in an introductory lecture is 41; in a laboratory, 21; and in a regular course, 27.

Admissions: 78% of the 2001-2002 applicants were accepted. The SAT I scores for the 2001-2002 freshman class were: Verbal--39% below 500, 42% between 500 and 599, 17% between 600 and 700, and 2% above 700; Math--38% below 500, 44% between 500 and 599, 16% between 600 and 700, and 2% above 700. The ACT scores were 36% below 21, 30% between 21 and 23, 23% between 24 and 26, 7% between 27 and 28, and 5% above 28. 27% of the current freshmen were in the top fifth of their class; 58% were in the top two fifths. 13 freshmen graduated first in their class.

Requirements: The SAT I or ACT is required. Admission standards are set by the Colorado Commission on Higher Education, but each applicant is evaluated on an individual basis. In general, an ACT score of 22, or an SAT I composite score of 1000, and a cumulative GPA of 2.9, are required. Graduation from an accredited high school is required. AP and CLEP credits are accepted. Important factors in the admissions decision are recommendations by school officials, evidence of special talent, and advanced placement or honor courses. Applications are accepted on-line via Netscape and UNC's web site.

Procedure: Freshmen are admitted fall, spring, and summer. Entrance exams should be taken as early as possible. There is a deferred admissions plan. Applications should be filed by August 1 for fall entry, December 20 for spring entry, and May 1 for summer entry. Notification is sent on a rolling basis. The fall 2001 application fee was $30.

Transfer: 868 transfer students enrolled in 2001-2002. Applicants with 30 or more credit hours must have a minimum college GPA of 2.0. Transfer students who have completed fewer than 12 credit hours of college must meet the same criteria for admission as entering freshmen. 30 credits of 120 must be completed at UNC.

Visiting: There are regularly scheduled orientations for prospective students, including academic advising, registration, tours, and special activities. There are guides for informal visits and visitors may sit in on classes. To schedule a visit, contact the UNC Visitors Center at (970) 351-2097.

Financial Aid: In 2000, 72% of all freshmen and 70% of continuing students received some form of financial aid. 57% of freshmen and 58% of continuing students received need-based aid. The average freshman award was $5928. Of that total, scholarships or need-based grants averaged $3045 ($19,000 maximum); loans averaged $6093 ($19,618 maximum); and work contracts averaged $974 ($5705 maximum). 24% of undergraduates worked part time. Average annual earnings from campus work were $1688. The FAFSA is required. The fall application deadline is March 1.

International Students: There are 31 international students enrolled. They must score 520 on the written TOEFL or take the MELAB, and also take the SAT I or the ACT.

Computers: The mainframe is an IBM Multiprise 2000/2003-106. Students may access the mainframe from a variety of computer labs, including those in academic buildings, the library, the student center, and residence halls. UNC's 15 computer labs (most with access to networks) include terminals with Macs and PCs. All students may access the system. There are no time limits. The fee is $4.50 per credit hour.

Graduates: In 2001, 1747 bachelor's degrees were awarded. The most popular majors were business management (15%), health sciences (12%), and psychology (8%). In an average class, 1% graduate in 3 years, 26% in 4 years, 43% in 5 years, and 45% in 6 years. 458 companies recruited on campus in 2000-2001. Of the 2000 graduating class, 10% were enrolled in graduate school within 6 months of graduation and 85% were employed.

Admissions Contact: Gary Gullickson, Director of Admissions. A video is available. E-mail: *unc@mail.unco.edu* Web: *http://www.unco.edu*

UNIVERSITY OF SOUTHERN COLORADO D-3

Pueblo, CO 81001-4901 **(719) 549-2462**
(877) 872-9653; Fax: (719) 549-2419

Full-time: 1507 men, 1847 women	**Faculty:** 159; IIA, --$
Part-time: 767 men, 1203 women	**Ph.D.s:** 70%
Graduate: 51 men, 112 women	**Student/Faculty:** 21 to 1
Year: semesters, summer session	**Tuition:** $2449 ($9729)
Application Deadline: July 28	**Room & Board:** $5372
Freshman Class: n/av	
SAT I Verbal/Math: 504/507	**LESS COMPETITIVE**

The University of Southern Colorado, founded in 1933, is part of the Colorado State University System. The public institution offers undergraduate programs in humanities and social sciences, business administration, nursing, applied science, technology, engineering, and education. There are 5 undergraduate and 3 graduate schools. In addition to regional accreditation, USC has baccalaureate program accreditation with ABET, ACS, CSWE, NASM, and NLN. The library contains 180,000 volumes, 10,000 microform items, and 16,862 audiovisual forms/CDs, and subscribes to 1327 periodicals. Computerized library services include the card catalog, interlibrary loans, and database searching. Special learning facilities include a learning resource center, art gallery, radio station, TV station, and nature center. The 275-acre campus is in an urban area 100 miles south of Denver. Including residence halls, there are 15 buildings.

Student Life: 87% of undergraduates are from Colorado. Others are from 41 states, 32 foreign countries, and Canada. 59% are white; 26%, Hispanic. The average age of freshmen is 19; all undergraduates, 26. 39% do not continue beyond their first year; 27% remain to graduate.

Housing: 652 students can be accommodated in college housing, which includes coed dormitories and on-campus apartments. On-campus housing is guaranteed for the freshman year only and is available on a first-come, first-served basis. 81% of students commute. Alcohol is not permitted. All students may keep cars.

Activities: 1% of men belong to 2 national fraternities; 1% of women belong to 1 local sorority. There are 68 groups on campus, including art, cheerleading, choir, chorale, computers, drama, ethnic, gay, honors, international, jazz band, literary magazine, newspaper, pep band, political, professional, radio and TV, religious, social, social service, student government, and symphony. Popular campus events include the Town and Gown series, Teacher Career Fair, and departmental lecture series.

Sports: There are 5 intercollegiate sports for men and 5 for women, and 5 intramural sports for men and 3 for women. Facilities include an arena with an indoor swimming pool, a weight room, a rock climbing wall, and racquetball, basketball, and volleyball courts; a sports complex with tennis courts and baseball, softball, and soccer fields; bike trails; a rope course; and a nature center.

Disabled Students: All of the campus is accessible. Wheelchair ramps, elevators, special parking, specially equipped rest rooms, special class scheduling, lowered drinking fountains, and lowered telephones are available.

Services: Counseling and information services are available, as is tutoring in most subjects. Remedial math and English are available on-campus from a local community college.

Campus Safety and Security: Measures include 24-hour foot and vehicle patrol, self-defense education, escort service, and informal discussions. There are pamphlets/posters/films, emergency telephones, and lighted pathways/sidewalks.

Programs of Study: USC confers B.A., B.S., B.S.B.A., B.S.C.E.T., B.S.E.E.T., B.S.I.En., B.S.M.E.T., B.S.N., and B.S.W. degrees. Master's degrees are also awarded. Bachelor's degrees are awarded in BIOLOGICAL SCIENCE (biochemistry, biology/biological science, and biotechnology), BUSINESS (accounting, business administration and management, and recreation and leisure services), COMMUNICATIONS AND THE ARTS (art, broadcasting, communications, English, journalism, music performance, music theory and composition, and Spanish), COMPUTER AND PHYSICAL SCIENCE (chemistry, information sciences and systems, mathematics, and physics), EDUCATION (music), ENGINEERING AND ENVIRONMENTAL DESIGN (automotive technology, civil engineering technology, electrical/electronics engineering technology, industrial administration/management, industrial engineering, mechanical engineering technology, and preengineering), HEALTH PROFESSIONS (chiropractic, environmental health science, exercise science, medical technology, nursing, occupational therapy, physician's assistant, predentistry, premedicine, preoptometry, preosteopathy, prepharmacy, prepodiatry, preveterinary science, and speech pathology/audiology), SOCIAL SCIENCE (criminology, economics, history, political science/government, prelaw, psychology, social science, social work, and sociology). Business, engineering technology, and nursing are the strongest academically. Accounting, biology, and management are the largest.

Required: To graduate, all students must complete at least 120 semester hours, including 40 in upper-division courses and 30 to 48 in the major, with a minimum GPA of 2.0. General education requirements include a 14-credit skills component of courses in communication, computer literacy, and quantitative skills, as well as a 19-credit knowledge component of courses in humanities, social sciences, and science and technology. Other requirements vary with the major.

Special: USC offers co-op programs, internships, study abroad in 8 countries, and on-campus work-study programs. Also available are 5-year combined B.S.B.A./M.B.A. degrees, a 3-2 engineering degree with Colorado State University, dual majors, nondegree study, and preprofessional programs in forestry, physical therapy, and wildlife management. USC is a member of the National Student Exchange. There are 10 national honor societies, including Phi Beta Kappa, a freshman honors program, and 10 departmental honors programs.

Faculty/Classroom: 60% of faculty are male; 39%, female. 99% teach undergraduates, 10% do research, and 4% do both. No introductory courses are taught by graduate students. The average class size in an introductory lecture is 70; in a laboratory, 24; and in a regular course, 22.

Admissions: The SAT I scores for the 2001-2002 freshman class were: Verbal--49% below 500, 37% between 500 and 599, 12% between 600 and 700, and 2% above 700; Math--48% below 500, 37% between 500 and 599, 14% between 600 and 700, and 1% above 700. 22% of the current freshmen were in the top fifth of their class; 49% were in the top two fifths. 14 freshmen graduated first in their class in a recent year.

Requirements: The SAT I or ACT is required. In addition, applicants must be graduates of an accredited secondary school or have a GED certificate with a minimum score of 45. USC computes a CCHE admission index, comprised of the high school GPA and SAT I or ACT scores. Students scoring below 80 will still be considered by an admissions committee. Academic preparation should consist of 4 years of English, 3 of math including algebra and geometry, 2 of natural science including physical science, 2 of social studies including American government, and 2 of a foreign language. AP and CLEP credits are accepted. Important factors in the admissions decision are advanced placement or honor courses, leadership record, and recommendations by school officials.

Procedure: Freshmen are admitted to all sessions. Entrance exams should be taken during the spring of the junior year or the fall of the senior year. Applications should be filed by July 28 for fall entry, December 15 for spring entry, and April 26 for summer entry, along with a $25 fee. Notification is sent on a rolling basis.

Transfer: 367 transfer students enrolled in a recent year. A minimum GPA of 2.0 and official transcripts of previous college work are required. Applicants with fewer than 30 credit hours must submit ACT or SAT I scores and high school transcripts. 30 credits of 120 must be completed at USC.

Visiting: There are regularly scheduled orientations for prospective students, including a tour, lunch, and mini-sessions on financial aid, athletics, scholarships, and student services. There are guides for informal visits and visitors may sit in on classes. To schedule a visit, contact the Admissions Office.

Financial Aid: The FAFSA is required. The fall application deadline is March 1.

International Students: In a recent year there were 174 international students enrolled. The school actively recruits these students. They must score 500 on the written TOEFL or 173 on the electronic version or take the MELAB.

Computers: The mainframes are a Prime 850 with a DOS-based local area network and 12 macrocomputers. 400 PCs and Macs are available for student use in the library, the administration and technology buildings, and several departments. All students may access the system 24 hours a day. There are no time limits. In a recent year, the fee was $2 per credit hour.

Graduates: In a recent class, 661 bachelor's degrees were awarded. The most popular majors were business administration (13%), biology (9%), and social science (9%). In an average class, 10% graduate in 4 years, 23% in 5 years, and 30% in 6 years. 95 companies recruited on campus in a recent year.

Admissions Contact: Pam Anastassiou, Director of Admissions and Records. E-mail: *info@uscolo.edu* Web: *www.uscolo.edu*

WESTERN STATE COLLEGE OF COLORADO B-3

Gunnison, CO 81231 **(970) 943-2119**
(800) 876-5309; Fax: (970) 943-2212

Full-time: 1235 men, 868 women	**Faculty:** 107; IIB, --$
Part-time: 107 men, 92 women	**Ph.D.s:** 76%
Graduate: none	**Student/Faculty:** 20 to 1
Year: semesters, summer session	**Tuition:** $2413 ($8453)
Application Deadline: open	**Room & Board:** $5172
Freshman Class: 1811 applied, 1540 accepted, 589 enrolled	
SAT I Verbal/Math: 500/490	**ACT:** 20 **LESS COMPETITIVE**

Western State College of Colorado, founded in 1901, is a public institution offering undergraduate programs in liberal arts and sciences. There are 7 undergraduate schools. In addition to regional accreditation, Western has baccalaureate program accreditation with NASM. The library contains 156,000 volumes, 1 million microform items, and 5000 audiovisual forms/CDs, and subscribes to 650 periodicals. Computerized library services include the card catalog, interlibrary loans, and database searching. Special learning facilities include a learning resource center, art gallery, radio station, TV station, and botanical gardens. The 228-acre campus is in a rural area 210 miles southwest of Denver. Including residence halls, there are 30 buildings.

Student Life: 72% of undergraduates are from Colorado. Others are from 49 states, 12 foreign countries, and Canada. 85% are from public schools. 90% are white. Most claim no religious affiliation. The average age of freshmen is 18; all undergraduates, 21. 48% do not continue beyond their first year.

Housing: 1200 students can be accommodated in college housing, which includes single-sex and coed dormitories, on-campus apartments, and married-student housing. In addition, there are special interest houses and theme floors in art, science and outdoor pursuits. On-campus housing is guaranteed for the freshman year only and is available on a first-come, first-served basis. 55% of students commute. All students may keep cars.

Activities: 3% of men belong to 1 local fraternity and 2 national fraternities; 2% of women belong to 2 local sororities and 1 national sorority. There are 60 groups on campus, including art, band, cheerleading, choir, chorale, chorus, dance, drama, ethnic, gay, honors, international, jazz band, literary magazine, marching band, musical theater, newspaper, opera, orchestra, outdoors/wilderness, pep band, photography, political, professional, radio and TV, religious, social, social service, student government, and symphony. Popular campus events include Parents Weekend, Spring Carnival, and weekly entertainment programs.

Sports: There are 6 intercollegiate sports for men and 5 for women, and 10 intramural sports for men and 10 for women. Facilities include a fitness center, 2 gyms, a 5000-seat football stadium, an all-weather track, a number of playing fields, a weight room, an indoor swimming pool, a par course, a games/pool area with a bowling alley, and racquetball, tennis, and volleyball courts.

Disabled Students: 75% of the campus is accessible. Wheelchair ramps, elevators, special parking, specially equipped rest rooms, lowered drinking fountains, lowered telephones, and an audio device to increase telephone volume are available.

Services: Counseling and information services are available, as is tutoring in most subjects. There is a reader service for the blind and remedial math and writing.

Campus Safety and Security: Measures include escort service, informal discussions, pamphlets/posters/films, and emergency telephones. There are lighted pathways/sidewalks and van shuttle service during special events to prevent students' drinking and driving.

Programs of Study: Western confers B.A. and B.F.A. degrees. Bachelor's degrees are awarded in BIOLOGICAL SCIENCE (biology/biological science), BUSINESS (accounting, business administration and management, and recreation and leisure services), COMMUNICATIONS AND

THE ARTS (art, communications, dramatic arts, English, fine arts, music, and Spanish), COMPUTER AND PHYSICAL SCIENCE (chemistry, geology, mathematics, and physics), EDUCATION (art, elementary, foreign languages, music, science, and secondary), ENGINEERING AND ENVIRONMENTAL DESIGN (preengineering), HEALTH PROFESSIONS (physical therapy and predentistry), SOCIAL SCIENCE (anthropology, economics, history, physical fitness/movement, political science/government, prelaw, psychology, and sociology). Business, biological sciences, and communications are the strongest academically.

Required: For graduation, students must complete 120 credit hours with a minimum GPA of 2.0. There are liberal arts requirements of 27 credits in human relationships, natural sciences, and creative arts, as well as competencies in written expression, oral communication, and math.

Special: The Department of Business and Accounting offers a co-op program. Students may cross-register with Mesa, Adams, and Metro State colleges. Study abroad, internships, work-study programs, an accelerated degree program in teacher education, dual and student-designed majors, and credit for military and work experience are available. There are 9 national honor societies and a freshman honors program.

Faculty/Classroom: 58% of faculty are male; 42%, female. All both teach and do research. The average class size in an introductory lecture is 22; in a laboratory, 15; and in a regular course, 19.

Admissions: 85% of the 2001-2002 applicants were accepted. The SAT I scores for the 2001-2002 freshman class were: Verbal--48% below 500, 40% between 500 and 599, and 12% between 600 and 700; Math--52% below 500, 38% between 500 and 599, and 10% between 600 and 700. The ACT scores were 55% below 21, 28% between 21 and 23, 14% between 24 and 26, 3% between 27 and 28, and 1% above 28. 17% of the current freshmen were in the top fifth of their class; 43% were in the top two fifths. 10 freshmen graduated first in their class.

Requirements: The SAT I or ACT is required. A minimum composite score of 950 on the SAT I or 20 on the ACT is recommended, as are an essay and an interview. Applicants must be graduates of an accredited secondary school. The GED is accepted with an overall score of 50 or above and a minimum score of 40 in each area. Western recommends that in high school students complete 4 years of English, 3 of math, and 2 each of natural and social science. Coursework in a foreign language and computer science is strongly recommended. Western requires applicants to be in the upper 67% of their class. A GPA of 2.5 is required. AP and CLEP credits are accepted. Important factors in the admissions decision are advanced placement or honor courses, leadership record, and extracurricular activities record.

Procedure: Freshmen are admitted to all sessions. There is a deferred admissions plan. Application deadlines are open. The fall 2001 application fee was $25.

Transfer: 231 transfer students enrolled in a recent year. Applicants for transfer must have a minimum GPA of 2.0 and may be asked to submit the SAT I or ACT test scores. 30 credits of 120 must be completed at Western.

Visiting: There are regularly scheduled orientations for prospective students. There are guides for informal visits and visitors may sit in on classes. To schedule a visit, contact the Admissions Office at (800) 876-5309 or *discover@western.edu*

Financial Aid: 35% of undergraduates work part time. The FAFSA is required. The fall application deadline is April 1.

International Students: There are 38 international students enrolled. They must score 525 on the written TOEFL or 213 on the electronic version.

Computers: The mainframes are a DEC Alpha cluster, consisting of an Alpha 1000, an Alpha Server 3600, an Alpha Server 2100, and a VAX ALPHA 3600. There are more than 150 PCs and terminals available to students in labs and the library. Students have access to word-processing, database, spreadsheet software, and the Internet. All students may access the system at all times. There are no time limits. The fee is $25 per year.

Graduates: In a recent year, 334 bachelor's degrees were awarded. The most popular majors were business/accounting (20%), biology (10%), and history (9%). 15 companies recruited on campus in 2000-2001. Of the 2000 graduating class, 4% were enrolled in graduate school within 6 months of graduation and 95% were employed.

Admissions Contact: Tonya Van Hee, Assistant Director. A video is available. E-mail: *tvanhee@western.edu* Web: *www.western.edu*

CONNECTICUT

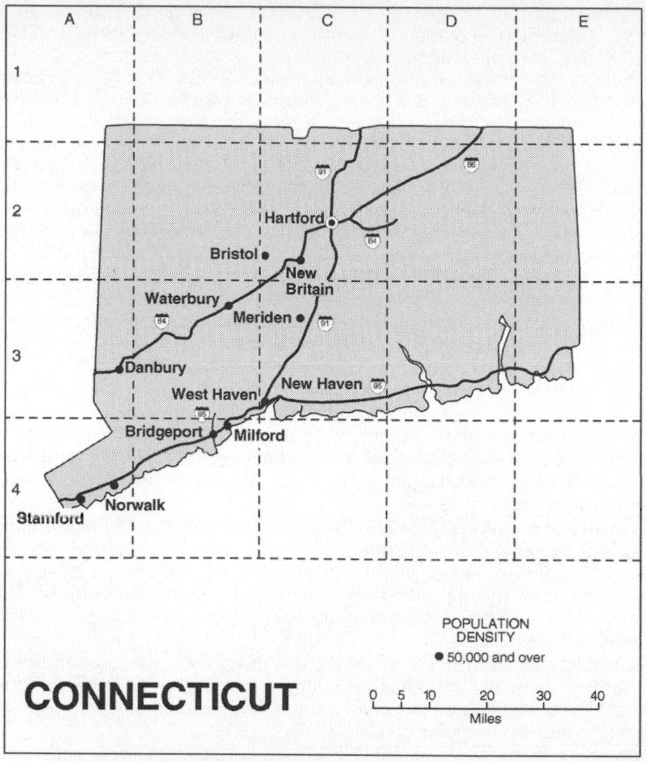

ALBERTUS MAGNUS COLLEGE C-3

New Haven, CT 06511-1189 (203) 773-8501
(800) 578-9160; Fax: (203) 773-9539

Full-time: 606 men, 1121 women	**Faculty:** 38; IIB, -$
Part-time: 31 men, 114 women	**Ph.D.s:** 90%
Graduate: 224 men, 173 women	**Student/Faculty:** 45 to 1
Year: semesters, summer session	**Tuition:** $15,246
Application Deadline: open	**Room & Board:** $6908

Freshman Class: 362 applied, 356 accepted, 114 enrolled
SAT I Verbal/Math: 473/448 **COMPETITIVE**

Albertus Magnus College, founded in 1925, is affiliated with the Roman Catholic Church and operated by the Dominican Sisters of St. Mary of the Springs. The college offers undergraduate and graduate degrees in the liberal arts and sciences and in business. In addition to regional accreditation, Albertus Magnus has baccalaureate program accreditation with IACBE. The library contains 120,000 volumes, 7000 microform items, and 1200 audiovisual forms/CDs, and subscribes to 720 periodicals. Computerized library services include the card catalog, interlibrary loans, and database searching. Special learning facilities include a learning resource center, art gallery, theater, and academic skill center. The 55-acre campus is in a suburban area 80 miles from New York City. Including residence halls, there are 16 buildings.

Student Life: 95% of undergraduates are from Connecticut. Others are from 10 states and 6 foreign countries. 50% are from public schools. 66% are white; 19%, African American. Most are Catholic. The average age of freshmen is 19; all undergraduates, 22. 10% do not continue beyond their first year; 70% remain to graduate.

Housing: 250 students can be accommodated in college housing, which includes single-sex and coed dormitories. Residence halls are mainly old mansions that have been converted into student housing. Each building houses 15 to 65 students. On-campus housing is guaranteed for all 4 years. 60% of students live on campus; of those, 70% remain on campus on weekends. All students may keep cars.

Activities: There are no fraternities or sororities. There are 20 groups on campus, including art, computers, dance, debate, drama, ethnic, film, honors, international, literary magazine, musical theater, photography, political, professional, religious, social, social service, student government, and yearbook. Popular campus events include Fall Candlelight Ceremony, Christmas events, and Laurel Day.

Sports: There are 5 intercollegiate sports for men and 5 for women. Facilities include an Olympic-size pool, a gym, indoor and outdoor tracks, racquetball and volleyball courts, weight and dance rooms, 4 tennis courts, a game room, and soccer and softball fields.

Disabled Students: All of the campus is accessible. Wheelchair ramps, elevators, special parking, specially equipped rest rooms, special class scheduling, lowered drinking fountains, and lowered telephones are available.

Services: Counseling and information services are available, as is tutoring in every subject. There is remedial math, reading, and writing.

Campus Safety and Security: Measures include 24-hour foot and vehicle patrol, escort service, shuttle buses, and informal discussions. There are pamphlets/posters/films and lighted pathways/sidewalks.

Programs of Study: Albertus Magnus confers B.A., B.S., and B.F.A. degrees. Associate and master's degrees are also awarded. Bachelor's degrees are awarded in BIOLOGICAL SCIENCE (biology/biological science), BUSINESS (accounting, business economics, and management information systems), COMMUNICATIONS AND THE ARTS (classics, communications, dramatic arts, English, fine arts, French, romance languages and literature, and Spanish), COMPUTER AND PHYSICAL SCIENCE (mathematics), ENGINEERING AND ENVIRONMENTAL DESIGN (computer technology), HEALTH PROFESSIONS (art therapy, health care administration, predentistry, premedicine, and preveterinary science), SOCIAL SCIENCE (criminology, economics, history, human services, humanities, industrial and organizational psychology, liberal arts/general studies, philosophy, political science/government, prelaw, psychology, religion, sociology, and urban studies). Liberal arts, business, and computer technology are the strongest academically. Business/economics, English, and psychology are the largest.

Required: To graduate, all students must complete at least 120 credit hours, including 60 outside the major and at least 30 in the major. General education requirements, including 6 credits each in English, humanities, and foreign language and 3 each of fine arts, math, science, and senior humanities, must be fulfilled. Courses in phys ed are also required, as are service learning or career exploration. A minimum 2.0 GPA is required.

Special: The college offers junior- and senior-year internships allowing up to 12 credits, study abroad, a Washington semester, work-study programs, and accelerated degree programs in business and economics, communications, English, humanities, and general studies. Also available are dual and student-designed majors, nondegree study, pass/fail options, independent study, and preprofessional programs. Students may take accelerated degree programs in the evening or take weekend courses. There are 5 national honor societies, a freshman honors program, and 12 departmental honors program.

Faculty/Classroom: 46% of faculty are male; 54%, female. All both teach and do research. The average class size in an introductory lecture is 20; in a laboratory, 10; and in a regular course, 15.

Admissions: 98% of the 2001-2002 applicants were accepted. The SAT I scores for the 2001-2002 freshman class were: Verbal--50% below 500, 35% between 500 and 599, 10% between 600 and 700, and 5% above 700; Math--56% below 500, 35% between 500 and 599, and 9% between 600 and 700. 35% of the current freshmen were in the top fifth of their class; 63% were in the top two fifths. There were 7 National Merit semifinalists. 4 freshmen graduated first in their class.

Requirements: The SAT I is required, with a minimum recommended composite score of 800. Applicants must be graduates of an accredited secondary school or have a GED certificate and have completed 16 academic credits, including 4 years of English, 2 or 3 years each of foreign language, math, and science, 2 years of history, and 1 year of social studies. High school transcripts, rank, and 2 letters of recommendation are required. The SAT II: Subject test in writing and an interview are recommended. Albertus Magnus requires applicants to be in the upper 50% of their class. A GPA of 2.5 is required. AP and CLEP credits are accepted. Important factors in the admissions decision are advanced placement or honor courses, recommendations by school officials, and leadership record. Applications are accepted on-line via CollegeNET.

Procedure: Freshmen are admitted to all sessions. Entrance exams should be taken between April of the junior year and November of the senior year. There is a deferred admissions plan. Application deadlines are open. The fall 2001 application fee was $35.

Transfer: 46 transfer students enrolled in 2001-2002. Transfer students must present a minimum 2.0 overall GPA and a 2.0 GPA for all transferable, compatible course work. 30 credits of 120 must be completed at Albertus Magnus.

Visiting: There are regularly scheduled orientations for prospective students, consisting of registration, a general introduction, a financial aid/major introduction, lunch, a campus tour, and an interview. There are guides for informal visits and visitors may sit in on classes and stay overnight. To schedule a visit, contact the Admissions Office.

Financial Aid: In 2001-2002, 83% of all freshmen and 87% of continuing students received some form of financial aid. 83% of freshmen and 87% of continuing students received need-based aid. The average fresh-

man award was $8500. Of that total, scholarships or need-based grants averaged $3500; loans averaged $350; work contracts averaged $1500; and non-need-based aid averaged $1000. 10% of undergraduates work part time. Average annual earnings from campus work are $1000. The average financial indebtedness of the 2001 graduate was $13,000. Albertus Magnus is a member of CSS. The CSS/Profile or FAFSA and the college's own financial statement are required. The fall application deadline is March 15.

International Students: The school actively recruits these students. They must score 550 on the written TOEFL.

Computers: The mainframe is a Prime 2450. There are also 25 terminals and 10 PCs available for student use in the computer center and the library. All students may access the system 9 A.M. to 5 P.M. There are no time limits and no fees. It is strongly recommended that all students have a personal computer.

Graduates: In 2001, 515 bachelor's degrees were awarded. The most popular majors were management (65%), psychology (11%), and sociology (10%). In an average class, 80% graduate in 4 years, and 100% in 5 years. 10 companies recruited on campus in 2000-2001. Of the 2000 graduating class, 25% were enrolled in graduate school within 6 months of graduation and 70% were employed.

Admissions Contact: Richard Lolatte, Dean of Admissions and Financial Aid. E-mail: *admissions@albertus.edu* Web: *www.albertus.edu*

CENTRAL CONNECTICUT STATE UNIVERSITY — C-2

New Britain, CT 06050 — (860) 832-2278; (888) 733-2278; Fax: (860) 832-2522

Full-time: 3246 men, 3390 women	**Faculty:** 391; IIA, +$
Part-time: 1369 men, 1546 women	**Ph.D.s:** 75%
Graduate: 956 men, 1861 women	**Student/Faculty:** 17 to 1
Year: semesters, summer session	**Tuition:** $4374 ($10,356)
Application Deadline: May 1	**Room & Board:** $6030
Freshman Class: 4660 applied, 3013 accepted, 1272 enrolled	
SAT I Verbal/Math: 488/492	**COMPETITIVE**

Central Connecticut State University, founded in 1849, offers degree programs in liberal arts, engineering technology, business, and education. It is part of the Connecticut State University system. There are 4 undergraduate schools and 1 graduate school. In addition to regional accreditation, CCSU has baccalaureate program accreditation with ABET, ACS, CSAB, CSWE, NAIT, NCATE, and NLN. The library contains 620,958 volumes, 542,101 microform items, and 5224 audiovisual forms/CDs, and subscribes to 2813 periodicals. Computerized library services include the card catalog, interlibrary loans, and database searching. Special learning facilities include a learning resource center, art gallery, planetarium, radio station, and writing and math centers. The 294-acre campus is in a suburban area 10 miles west of Hartford. Including residence halls, there are 39 buildings.

Student Life: 98% of undergraduates are from Connecticut. Others are from 26 states, 50 foreign countries, and Canada. 73% are white. 56% claim no religious affiliation; 30% are Catholic. The average age of freshmen is 20; all undergraduates, 23. 28% do not continue beyond their first year; 47% remain to graduate.

Housing: 1900 students can be accommodated in college housing, which includes single-sex and coed dormitories. On-campus housing is guaranteed for all 4 years. 72% of students commute. All students may keep cars.

Activities: 1% of men belong to 2 national fraternities; 1% of women belong to 1 national sorority. There are 100 groups on campus, including art, band, cheerleading, choir, chorale, chorus, computers, dance, drama, ethnic, gay, honors, international, literary magazine, marching band, newspaper, orchestra, pep band, photography, political, professional, radio and TV, religious, social, social service, student government, and yearbook. Popular campus events include Winter and Spring Weekends, First Week, and Vance Lectures.

Sports: There are 10 intercollegiate sports for men and 11 for women, and 8 intramural sports for men and 8 for women. Facilities include a 3800-seat gym, 8 tennis courts, a 6000-seat football stadium, a 37,000-square-foot air-supported recreation facility, a natatorium, weight training rooms, and softball, baseball, touch football, and soccer fields.

Disabled Students: 90% of the campus is accessible. Wheelchair ramps, elevators, special parking, specially equipped rest rooms, special class scheduling, lowered drinking fountains, and lowered telephones are available. Personal care attendants serve as roommates for physically disabled resident students.

Services: Counseling and information services are available, as is tutoring in some subjects. There is a reader service for the blind, and remedial math, reading, and writing.

Campus Safety and Security: Measures include 24-hour foot and vehicle patrol, self-defense education, escort service, and shuttle buses. There are informal discussions, pamphlets/posters/films, emergency telephones, and lighted pathways/sidewalks.

Programs of Study: CCSU confers B.A., B.S., B.F.A., B.S.Ed., B.S.E.T., B.S.I.T., and B.S.N. degrees. Master's degrees are also awarded. Bachelor's degrees are awarded in BIOLOGICAL SCIENCE (biology/biological science), BUSINESS (accounting, banking and finance, business administration and management, entrepreneurial studies, hospitality management services, international business management, management information systems, marketing/retailing/merchandising, and office supervision and management), COMMUNICATIONS AND THE ARTS (art, communications, dramatic arts, English, French, German, graphic design, Italian, music, and Spanish), COMPUTER AND PHYSICAL SCIENCE (actuarial science, chemistry, computer science, earth science, mathematics, physical sciences, physics, and polymer science), EDUCATION (art, athletic training, early childhood, elementary, music, physical, special, technical, and vocational), ENGINEERING AND ENVIRONMENTAL DESIGN (civil engineering technology, construction technology, electrical/electronics engineering technology, engineering technology, industrial engineering technology, manufacturing technology, and mechanical engineering technology), HEALTH PROFESSIONS (medical technology and nursing), SOCIAL SCIENCE (anthropology, criminology, economics, geography, history, international studies, philosophy, political science/government, psychology, social work, and sociology). Business and education are the largest.

Required: To graduate, all students must complete at least 122 to 130 credit hours, depending on the major, with a minimum GPA of 2.0. General education requirements total 44 to 46 credits in arts and humanities, sciences, math, communications, and fitness/wellness studies. Students must also demonstrate foreign language proficiency, complete 6 credits in courses with a global context, and satisfy a First-Year Experience requirement.

Special: The university offers co-op programs and cross-registration with several other Connecticut educational institutions, study abroad in more than 45 countries, internships in most departments, work-study programs, dual majors, and student-designed majors. There are 7 national honor societies, a freshman honors program, and 1 departmental honors program.

Faculty/Classroom: 61% of faculty are male; 39%, female. All teach undergraduates. No introductory courses are taught by graduate students. The average class size in an introductory lecture is 35; in a laboratory, 20; and in a regular course, 25.

Admissions: 65% of the 2001-2002 applicants were accepted. The SAT I scores for the 2001-2002 freshman class were: Verbal--55% below 500, 38% between 500 and 599, 6% between 600 and 700, and 1% above 700; Math--54% below 500, 39% between 500 and 599, 6% between 600 and 700, and 1% above 700. 13% of the current freshmen were in the top fifth of their class; 37% were in the top two fifths.

Requirements: The SAT I is required, with recommended minimum scores of 480 verbal and 440 math. Applicants must be graduates of an accredited secondary school or have earned a GED. An interview is recommended. CCSU also recommends that applicants have 14 academic credits: 4 in English, 3 each in math and a foreign language, and 2 each in science and social sciences, including 1 in U.S. history. AP and CLEP credits are accepted. Important factors in the admissions decision are extracurricular activities record, recommendations by school officials, and advanced placement or honor courses.

Procedure: Freshmen are admitted fall and spring. Entrance exams should be taken in May of the junior year or November of the senior year. There is a deferred admissions plan. Applications should be filed by May 1 for fall entry and November 1 for spring entry. Notification is sent on a rolling basis. The fall 2001 application fee was $40.

Transfer: 624 transfer students enrolled in 2001-2002. Applicants must have a minimum of 12 transferable credits and a GPA of 2.0 and must submit official transcripts from previous schools attended. 45 credits of 122 to 130 must be completed at CCSU.

Visiting: There are regularly scheduled orientations for prospective students, including a fall open house in October and daily and select Saturday visits throughout the fall and spring. There are guides for informal visits and visitors may sit in on classes. To schedule a visit, contact the Admissions Office.

Financial Aid: In 2001-2002, 37% of all freshmen and 36% of continuing students received some form of financial aid. 36% of freshmen and 32% of continuing students received need-based aid. The average freshman award was $4500. Of that total, scholarships or need-based grants averaged $2993 ($7000 maximum); loans averaged $2749 ($6625 maximum); and work contracts averaged $400 ($1600 maximum). 40% of undergraduates work part time. Average annual earnings from campus work are $1000. The average financial indebtedness of the 2001 graduate was $13,524. CCSU is a member of CSS. The FAFSA and federal income tax returns are required. The fall application deadline is April 19.

International Students: They must score 500 on the written TOEFL.

Computers: The mainframe is a DEC VAX 7000/640. The PC lab provides numerous networked PCs as well as terminals connected to the mainframe. Additional terminals are located in other buildings. Another lab provides a variety of Mac PCs for general student use. All students may access the system 8:30 A.M. to 12 P.M., Monday to Thursday; 8:30 A.M. to 6 P.M., Friday; 9 A.M. to 6 P.M., Saturday; and 1 P.M. to 10 P.M., Sunday. There are no time limits and no fees.

Graduates: In 2001, 1167 bachelor's degrees were awarded. The most popular majors were education (16%), psychology (10%), and industrial technology (7%). In an average class, 10% graduate in 4 years, 39% in 5 years, and 45% in 6 years. 63 companies recruited on campus in 2000-2001. Of the 2000 graduating class, 23% were enrolled in graduate school within 6 months of graduation and 80% were employed.
Admissions Contact: Myrna Garcia-Bowen, Director of Admissions. E-mail: *admissions@ccsu.edu* Web: *www.ccsu.edu*

CHARTER OAK STATE COLLEGE

New Britain, CT 06053-2142 — C-2
(860) 832-3800
Fax: (860) 832-3999

Full-time: none	**Faculty:** 69 part-time
Part-time: 754 men, 742 women	**Ph.D.s:** 78%
Graduate: none	**Student/Faculty:** n/av
Year: see profile	**Tuition:** $517 (720)
Application Deadline: open	**Room & Board:** n/app
Freshman Class: n/av	
SAT I or ACT: not required	**SPECIAL**

Charter Oak State College, founded in 1973, is a public liberal arts institution offering an external degree program for adult students who cannot complete a college degree by conventional means because of family, job, or financial considerations. Tuition and fees are $517 ($720 out-of-state) for the first year; tuition is $325 ($467 out-of-state) for continuing students. Credits may be earned by transfer, testing, portfolio review, and contract learning. The offices are in a suburban area 7 miles south of Hartford.
Student Life: 70% of undergraduates are from Connecticut. Others are from 45 states, 2 foreign countries, and Canada. 78% are white. The average age of all undergraduates is 40.
Housing: There are no residence halls.
Activities: There are no fraternities or sororities.
Sports: There is no sports program at Charter Oak.
Disabled Students: Wheelchair ramps, elevators, special parking, specially equipped rest rooms, and lowered drinking fountains are available.The program is a distance-learning one that does not require students to come to the facility. They can obtain services by phone, fax, and e-mail.
Services: Tutoring is available for a fee.
Campus Safety and Security: Measures include 24-hour foot and vehicle patrol.
Programs of Study: Charter Oak confers B.A. and B.S. degrees. Associate degrees are also awarded. Bachelor's degrees are awarded in SOCIAL SCIENCE (liberal arts/general studies).
Required: All baccalaureate students must complete 120 total credits, at least 60 of which must be in liberal arts for the B.S. and 90 for the B.A.; 36 credits must be in the field of concentration.
Special: Student-designed concentrations are available.
Faculty/Classroom: 50% of faculty are male; 50%, female.
Requirements: Charter Oak State College requires applicants to have earned at least 9 college credits. AP and CLEP credits are accepted. Applications are accepted on computer disk.
Procedure: Application deadlines are open. The application fee is $45.
Transfer: Most students who enroll in Charter Oak State College have attended college previously. A minimum of 120 credits is required for the bachelor's degree.
Financial Aid: Some college fees may be waived to help students who demonstrate financial need and show academic promise. The average financial indebtedness of the 2001 graduate was $4555. Charter Oak is a member of CSS. The FAFSA and the college's own financial statement are required. The fall application deadline is June 30.
Graduates: In 2001, 316 bachelor's degrees were awarded.
Admissions Contact: Lori Gagne, Director of Admissions. E-mail: *info@charteroak.edu* Web: *www.charteroak.edu*

CONNECTICUT COLLEGE

New London, CT 06320-4196 — E-3
(860) 439-2200
Fax: (860) 439-4301

Full-time: 730 men, 1025 women	**Faculty:** 155; IIB, +$
Part-time: 18 men, 62 women	**Ph.D.s:** 90%
Graduate: 12 men, 32 women	**Student/Faculty:** 11 to 1
Year: semesters	**Tuition:** $33,585
Application Deadline: January 1	**Room & Board:** see profile
Freshman Class: 4318 applied, 1482 accepted, 472 enrolled	
SAT I Verbal/Math: 660/650	**ACT:** 27 **MOST COMPETITIVE**

Connecticut College, founded in 1911, is a private institution offering degree programs in the liberal arts and sciences. Tuition and room and board are combined in a comprehensive fee. The library contains 652,509 volumes, 151,979 microform items, and 153,156 audiovisual forms/CDs, and subscribes to 3458 periodicals. Computerized library services include the card catalog, interlibrary loans, and database searching. Special learning facilities include a radio station, an observatory, and an arboretum. The 702-acre campus is in a small town midway between Boston and New York City. Including residence halls, there are 51 buildings.
Student Life: 77% of undergraduates are from out of state, mostly the Northeast. Others are from 50 states, 57 foreign countries, and Canada. 36% are from public schools. 78% are white. 27% are Protestant; 26%, Catholic; 17% claim no religious affiliation; 14%, Jewish. The average age of freshmen is 18; all undergraduates, 21. 8% do not continue beyond their first year; 80% remain to graduate.
Housing: 1647 students can be accommodated in college housing, which includes coed dormitories. In addition, there are language houses and special-interest houses. On-campus housing is guaranteed for all 4 years. 98% of students live on campus; of those, 85% remain on campus on weekends. All students may keep cars.
Activities: There are no fraternities or sororities. There are 55 groups on campus, including a cappella, art, band, chess, choir, chorale, chorus, computers, dance, drama, ethnic, film, gay, honors, international, jazz band, literary magazine, newspaper, opera, orchestra, photography, political, radio and TV, religious, social, social service, student government, symphony, and yearbook. Popular campus events include Eclipse Weekend, Harvestfest, and Floralia.
Sports: There are 12 intercollegiate sports for men and 14 for women, and 12 intramural sports for men and 10 for women. Facilities include an 800-seat gym, playing fields, an ice rink, a boat house, a weight training room, an indoor pool, a dance studio, 12 tennis courts, and courts for squash, racquetball, badminton, basketball, and volleyball. There is also a new track and field facility with an all-weather, 8-lane, 400-meter track, facilities for all field events, and a game field.
Disabled Students: 25% of the campus is accessible. Wheelchair ramps, elevators, special parking, specially equipped rest rooms, special class scheduling, lowered drinking fountains, and lowered telephones are available.
Services: Counseling and information services are available, as is tutoring in most subjects.
Campus Safety and Security: Measures include 24-hour foot and vehicle patrol, escort service, informal discussions, and pamphlets/posters/films. There are emergency telephones, lighted pathways/sidewalks, and an electronic access system in student residences.
Programs of Study: Connecticut College confers the B.A. degree. Master's degrees are also awarded. Bachelor's degrees are awarded in BIOLOGICAL SCIENCE (biochemistry, biology/biological science, botany, neurosciences, and zoology), COMMUNICATIONS AND THE ARTS (art, art history and appreciation, Chinese, classics, comparative literature, dance, dramatic arts, English, French, German, Italian, Japanese, music, and music technology), COMPUTER AND PHYSICAL SCIENCE (astrophysics, chemistry, mathematics, and physics), EDUCATION (foreign languages, music, and science), ENGINEERING AND ENVIRONMENTAL DESIGN (architecture, engineering physics, and environmental science), SOCIAL SCIENCE (African studies, American studies, anthropology, East Asian studies, economics, gender studies, Hispanic American studies, history, human development, humanities and social science, international relations, Italian studies, Latin American studies, medieval studies, philosophy, political science/government, psychology, religion, Russian and Slavic studies, sociology, and urban studies). Government, history, and psychology are the largest.
Required: To graduate, students must complete at least 128 credit hours with a minimum GPA of 2.0. Distribution requirements cover 7 courses from 7 academic areas, plus a foreign language. Students must also complete 2 courses designated as Writing Intensive or Writing Enhanced.
Special: Cross-registration with 12 area colleges, internships in government, human services, and other fields, a Washington semester at American University, dual majors, student-designed majors, a 3-2 engineering degree with Washington University in St. Louis and Boston University, nondegree study, and satisfactory/unsatisfactory options are available. One third of the junior class studies abroad. An international studies certificate program is available, which combines competency in a foreign language, an internship, and study abroad. There are also certificate programs in museum studies, community action and public policy, conservation biology and environmental studies, arts and technology, and education. There are 4 national honor societies, including Phi Beta Kappa.
Faculty/Classroom: 55% of faculty are male; 45%, female. All teach undergraduates. No introductory courses are taught by graduate students. The average class size in an introductory lecture is 27; in a laboratory, 15; and in a regular course, 20.
Admissions: 34% of the 2001-2002 applicants were accepted. The SAT I scores for the 2001-2002 freshman class were: Verbal--13% between 500 and 599, 55% between 600 and 700, and 32% above 700; Math--1% below 500, 16% between 500 and 599, 66% between 600 and 700, and 18% above 700. The ACT scores were 3% below 21, 5% between 21 and 23, 28% between 24 and 26, 36% between 27 and 28, and 28% above 28. 83% of the current freshmen were in the top fifth of their class; 99% were in the top two fifths. There were 2 National Merit semifinalists. 6 freshmen graduated first in their class.

Requirements: Any 3 SAT II: Subject tests or the ACT is required. In addition, applicants must be graduates of an accredited secondary school. An essay is required and an interview is recommended. AP credits are accepted. Important factors in the admissions decision are advanced placement or honor courses, leadership record, and evidence of special talent. Applications are accepted on-line.

Procedure: Freshmen are admitted fall and spring. Entrance exams should be taken by January of the senior year. There are early decision, early admissions, and deferred admissions plans. Early decision application should be filed by November 15 or December 15; regular applications, by January 1 for fall entry and December 1 for spring entry. Notification of early decision is sent December 15 or February 15; regular decision, April 1. 187 early decision candidates were accepted for the 2001-2002 class. 25% of recent applicants were on a waiting list; 16 were accepted. The fall 2001 application fee was $55.

Transfer: 25 transfer students enrolled in 2001-2002. Applicants must have a minimum college GPA of 3.0 and be in good standing at the previous school attended. SAT I or ACT scores are required and an interview is recommended. 64 credits of 128 must be completed at Connecticut College.

Visiting: There are regularly scheduled orientations for prospective students, including an introduction to the college, student perspectives, academic programs, a luncheon for parents and students, tours, and a reception. There are guides for informal visits and visitors may sit in on classes and stay overnight. To schedule a visit, contact the Admissions Office.

Financial Aid: In 2001-2002, 44% of all freshmen and 50% of continuing students received some form of financial aid, need-based aid. The average freshman award was $20,737. Of that total, scholarships or need-based grants averaged $19,378 ($34,494 maximum); loans averaged $2751 ($3125 maximum); and work contracts averaged $991 ($1000 maximum). 63% of undergraduates work part time. Average annual earnings from campus work are $693. The average financial indebtedness of the 2001 graduate was $18,602. Connecticut College is a member of CSS. The CSS/Profile or FAFSA and parent and student tax forms, including noncustodial parent's statement or business supplement when applicable, are required. The fall application deadline is January 15.

International Students: There are 140 international students enrolled. The school actively recruits these students. They must score 600 on the written TOEFL or 250 on the electronic version and also take the SAT I or the ACT. Students must also take SAT II: Subject tests in in any 3 subjects.

Computers: The mainframes are a DEC MicroVAX 3900, a DEC System 5500, and a DEC ALPHA Server. There are 3 public terminal rooms for the mainframe system. Macs and IBM PCs are available for student use in computer labs and individual departments. Laser printers, plotters, and scanners are also available. A campuswide network links computer clusters, classrooms, labs, dorm rooms, and the library with voice data and video transmission capabilities. All students may access the system 24 hours a day. There are no time limits and no fees. It is strongly recommended that all students have personal computers.

Graduates: In 2001, 427 bachelor's degrees were awarded. The most popular majors were government (10%), psychology (9%), and economics (8%). In an average class, 75% graduate in 4 years, 81% in 5 years, and 82% in 6 years. 266 companies recruited on campus in 2000-2001. Of the 2000 graduating class, 18% were enrolled in graduate school within 6 months of graduation and 81% were employed.

Admissions Contact: Martha Merrill, Acting Dean of Admissions.
Web: *www.connecticutcollege.edu\admissions*

CONNECTICUT STATE UNIVERSITY SYSTEM

The Connecticut State University System is the largest public system in the state. CSU consists of 4 comprehensive universities and a system office, serving nearly 36,000 students. The CSU universities are located in urban areas: Central Connecticut State University in New Britain, Eastern Connecticut State University in Willimantic, Southern Connecticut State University in New Haven, and Western Connecticut State University in Danbury. The system is governed by a 16-member board of trustees. CSU offers 130 academic programs at the bachelor's, master's, and 6th-year levels. Courses are taught by approximately 2100 faculty members. Students may enroll on a full- or part-time basis in fall, spring, and summer terms. The primary goal of the system is teaching. The main priorities are access to education with emphasis on a multicultural experience, quality within a context of curriculum diversity and a range of delivery systems, and public service including linkages with schools, state government, and private enterprise.

EASTERN CONNECTICUT STATE UNIVERSITY D-2

Willimantic, CT 06226 **(860) 465-5286; Fax: (860) 465-4382**

Full-time: 1559 men, 2015 women | **Faculty:** IIA, av$
Part-time: 569 men, 874 women | **Ph.D.s:** 87%
Graduate: 68 men, 251 women | **Student/Faculty:** 18 to 1
Year: semesters, summer session | **Tuition:** $4092 ($9948)
Application Deadline: May 1 | **Room & Board:** $6270
Freshman Class: 3575 applied, 2256 accepted, 1184 enrolled
SAT I Verbal/Math: 500/500 **COMPETITIVE**

Eastern Connecticut State University, founded in 1889, is the state's public liberal arts institution. There are 3 undergraduate schools and 1 graduate school. The library contains 287,040 volumes, 60,373 microform items, and 3657 audiovisual forms/CDs, and subscribes to 2068 periodicals. Computerized library services include the card catalog, interlibrary loans, and database searching. Special learning facilities include a learning resource center, art gallery, planetarium, radio station, and TV station. The 177-acre campus is in a suburban area 29 miles east of Hartford and 90 miles southwest of Boston. Including residence halls, there are 47 buildings.

Student Life: 92% of undergraduates are from Connecticut. Others are from 29 states and 28 foreign countries. 82% are white. The average age of freshmen is 19; all undergraduates, 26.

Housing: 1966 students can be accommodated in college housing, which includes single-sex and coed dormitories and on-campus apartments. In addition, there are special-interest houses. On-campus housing is available on a first-come, first-served basis and is available on a lottery system for upperclassmen. Priority is given to out-of-town students. 65% of students live on campus. Alcohol is not permitted. Upperclassmen may keep cars.

Activities: There are no fraternities or sororities. There are 48 groups on campus, including art, band, cheerleading, choir, chorus, computers, dance, drama, ethnic, gay, honors, international, jazz band, literary magazine, musical theater, newspaper, orchestra, photography, political, professional, radio and TV, religious, social, social service, student government, and yearbook. Popular campus events include Spring Weekend, Parents Day, and International Festival.

Sports: There are 6 intercollegiate sports for men and 9 for women, and 17 intramural sports for men and 14 for women. Facilities include a 2800-seat field house, a 6-lane swimming pool, a soccer field, a baseball complex, a softball stadium, and tennis, basketball, racquetball, and squash courts.

Disabled Students: 90% of the campus is accessible. Wheelchair ramps, elevators, special parking, specially equipped rest rooms, special class scheduling, lowered drinking fountains, and lowered telephones are available.

Services: Counseling and information services are available, as is tutoring in most subjects. There is a reader service for the blind, and remedial math, reading, and writing.

Campus Safety and Security: Measures include 24-hour foot and vehicle patrol, self-defense education, escort service, and shuttle buses. There are informal discussions, pamphlets/posters/films, emergency telephones, and lighted pathways/sidewalks.

Programs of Study: ECSU confers B.A., B.S. and B.G.S. degrees. Associate and master's degrees are also awarded. Bachelor's degrees are awarded in BIOLOGICAL SCIENCE (biology/biological science), BUSINESS (accounting, business administration and management, and recreation and leisure services), COMMUNICATIONS AND THE ARTS (communications, English, fine arts, and Spanish), COMPUTER AND PHYSICAL SCIENCE (computer science and mathematics), EDUCATION (early childhood, library science, middle school, and physical), ENGINEERING AND ENVIRONMENTAL DESIGN (environmental science), SOCIAL SCIENCE (American studies, economics, history, liberal arts/general studies, political science/government, psychology, social science, social work, and sociology). Biology, Spanish, and math are the strongest academically. Psychology, business administration, and sociology and applied social relations are the largest.

Required: To graduate, students must complete 120 credit hours, including 30 to 48 hours in the major, with a GPA of 2.0. General education requirements include 12 credits in interdisciplinary studies, 9 in social sciences, 7 in natural sciences, and 3 each in math, fine arts, literature, writing, health and phys ed, and computer literacy. Students must also fulfill a foreign language requirement.

Special: ECSU offers co-op programs in all majors, cross-registration with the University of Connecticut, internships, study abroad in 22 countries, a Washington semester, work-study programs, accelerated degree programs, dual majors, a general studies degree, nondegree study, pass/fail options, and credit for military experience. In addition to the B.S./certification programs for early childhood and elementary education, teacher certification is available for middle school and secondary education studies. There are 5 national honor societies, a freshman honors program, and 4 departmental honors program.

Faculty/Classroom: All faculty teach undergraduates. No introductory courses are taught by graduate students. The average class size in a laboratory is 18 and in a regular course, 25.

Admissions: 63% of the 2001-2002 applicants were accepted. The SAT I scores for the 2001-2002 freshman class were: Verbal--47% below 500, 43% between 500 and 599, 9% between 600 and 700, and 1% above 700; Math--47% below 500, 43% between 500 and 599, 9% between 600 and 700, and 1% above 700. 16% of the current freshmen were in the top fifth of their class; 49% were in the top two fifths.

Requirements: The SAT I or ACT is required. In addition, applicants must be graduates of an accredited secondary school or have a GED. They should have completed 13 high school academic credits, including 4 years of English, 3 of math, and 2 each of foreign language, social studies, and science (including 1 of lab science). An interview is recommended. ECSU requires applicants to be in the upper 50% of their class. A GPA of 2.5 is required. AP and CLEP credits are accepted. Important factors in the admissions decision are recommendations by school officials, advanced placement or honor courses, and leadership record.

Procedure: Freshmen are admitted fall and spring. Entrance exams should be taken in November or December of the senior year. There are early admissions and deferred admissions plans. Applications should be filed by May 1 for fall entry and are open for spring entry. The application fee is $40. Notification of early decision is sent November 1; regular decision, on a rolling basis. 8% of all applicants are on a waiting list; 20 were accepted in 2001.

Transfer: 274 transfer students enrolled in 2001-2002. Applicants should have completed a minimum of 12 credit hours with a GPA of 2.5. Official college and high school transcripts are required, and an associate degree and an interview are recommended. 30 credits of 120 must be completed at ECSU.

Visiting: There are regularly scheduled orientations for prospective students, including small group discussions, a tour of the campus, and a personal interview. There are guides for informal visits and visitors may sit in on classes. To schedule a visit, contact the Office of Admissions at (860) 465-5286 or *www.admissions@easternct.edu*

Financial Aid: In a recent year, 87% of all freshmen and 90% of continuing students received some form of financial aid. 85% of continuing students received need-based aid. The average freshman award was $6900. Of that total, scholarships or need-based grants averaged $4800 ($10,500 maximum); loans averaged $1200 ($2625 maximum); and work contracts averaged $1500. 61% of undergraduates work part time. Average annual earnings from campus work were $1500. The average financial indebtedness of the recent graduate was $7700. The FAFSA is required. The fall application deadline is March 15.

International Students: There are 71 international students enrolled. The school actively recruits these students. They must score 550 on the written TOEFL or 213 on the electronic version and also take the SAT I or the ACT, scoring 1020 on the SAT I or 21 on the ACT.

Computers: The mainframe is a DEC VAX 7620 minicomputer. The main lab houses approximately 100 PC stations, comprised of IBM, Mac, and Zenith equipment. Other computer labs are located in the Media Center Building and in the Learning Center. All systems are connected to the campus Ethernet network. All students may access the system. There are no time limits and no fees.

Graduates: In a recent year, 734 bachelor's degrees were awarded. The most popular majors were psychology (15%), sociology and applied social relations (9%), and business/communications (7%). 176 companies recruited on campus.

Admissions Contact: A video is available.
E-mail: *admissions@ecsu.ctstateu.edu* Web: *ecsu.ctstateu.edu*

FAIRFIELD UNIVERSITY

Fairfield, CT 06430-5195 — B-4 — **(203) 254-4100; Fax: (203) 254-4199**

Full-time: 1506 men, 1893 women — **Faculty:** 209; IIA, +$
Part-time: 378 men, 387 women — **Ph.D.s:** 93%
Graduate: 415 men, 575 women — **Student/Faculty:** 16 to 1
Year: semesters, summer session — **Tuition:** $22,885
Application Deadline: February 1 — **Room & Board:** $8000
Freshman Class: 7128 applied, 3504 accepted, 832 enrolled
SAT I Verbal/Math: 584/596 — **HIGHLY COMPETITIVE**

Fairfield University, founded by the Jesuits in 1942, is an independent, Roman Catholic Jesuit institution. There are 5 undergraduate and 5 graduate schools. In addition to regional accreditation, Fairfield has baccalaureate program accreditation with AACSB, AAMFT, ABET, ACS, GACREP, and NLN. The library contains 301,413 volumes, 814,520 microform items, and 11,128 audiovisual forms/CDs, and subscribes to 2609 periodicals. Computerized library services include the card catalog, interlibrary loans, and database searching. Special learning facilities include an art gallery, radio station, TV station, a media center, a 750-seat concert hall/theater, and a rehearsal and improvisation theater. The 200-acre campus is in a suburban area 60 miles northeast of New York City. Including residence halls, there are 30 buildings.

Student Life: 74% of undergraduates are from out of state, mostly the Northeast. Others are from 33 states, 43 foreign countries, and Canada. 64% are from public schools. 88% are white. Most are Catholic. The average age of freshmen is 18; all undergraduates, 20. 10% do not continue beyond their first year; 82% remain to graduate.

Housing: 2539 students can be accommodated in college housing, which includes coed dormitories and on-campus apartments. In addition, there are special-interest houses and a substance-free floor. On-campus housing is guaranteed for all 4 years. 80% of students live on campus; of those, 80% remain on campus on weekends. Upperclassmen may keep cars.

Activities: There are no fraternities or sororities. There are 100 groups on campus, including art, band, cheerleading, chorale, computers, dance, debate, drama, ethnic, film, gay, honors, international, jazz band, literary magazine, musical theater, newspaper, orchestra, pep band, political, professional, radio and TV, religious, social, social service, student government, and yearbook. Popular campus events include Dogwood Festival, Martin Luther King Week, and Harvest Weekend.

Sports: There are 10 intercollegiate sports for men and 11 for women, and 15 intramural sports for men and 15 for women. Facilities include a gym, a 25-meter swimming pool, weight rooms, indoor and outdoor tennis courts, racquetball and volleyball courts, indoor and outdoor tracks, a sauna, and a whirlpool.

Disabled Students: All of the campus is accessible. Wheelchair ramps, elevators, special parking, specially equipped rest rooms, special class scheduling, lowered drinking fountains, and lowered telephones are available. Single rooms are available for disabled students. Accommodations for seeing-eye dogs and a library computer station for physically challenged students are also available.

Services: Counseling and information services are available, as is tutoring in every subject. There is a reader service for the blind.

Campus Safety and Security: Measures include 24-hour foot and vehicle patrol, self-defense education, escort service, and shuttle buses. There are informal discussions, pamphlets/posters/films, emergency telephones, lighted pathways/sidewalks, EMT security officers, and bike patrol.

Programs of Study: Fairfield confers B.A. and B.S. degrees. Master's degrees are also awarded. Bachelor's degrees are awarded in BIOLOGICAL SCIENCE (biology/biological science and neurosciences), BUSINESS (accounting, banking and finance, business administration and management, international business management, and marketing/retailing/merchandising), COMMUNICATIONS AND THE ARTS (communications, English, fine arts, French, German, Italian, and Spanish), COMPUTER AND PHYSICAL SCIENCE (chemistry, computer science, information sciences and systems, mathematics, and physics), HEALTH PROFESSIONS (nursing), SOCIAL SCIENCE (economics, history, philosophy, political science/government, psychology, religion, and sociology). Finance and biology are the strongest academically. Biology, psychology, and communications are the largest.

Required: To graduate, students must complete 120 credits, 60 of them in general education core requirements, with a minimum GPA of 2.0. Distribution requirements include 12 credits in math and natural sciences, 12 credits in history and social sciences, 15 credits in philosophy, religious studies, and ethics, 15 credits in English and fine arts, and 6 credits in foreign languages. First-year students are required to take a course in multiculturalism.

Special: Fairfield participates in CIEE, offers study abroad in 5 countries, a Washington semester, a federal work-study program, B.A.-B.S. degrees in economics, international studies, and psychology, student-designed majors, and dual majors in all subjects. A 3-2 engineering degree is offered with the University of Connecticut, Rensselaer Polytechnic Institute, Columbia University, and Steven Institute of Technology. A general studies degree and credit for life, military, and work experience are available through the School of Continuing Education. Internships, both credit and noncredit, are offered at area corporations, publications, banks, and other businesses. Minors include women's studies, marine science, black studies, environmental studies, jazz, classical studies, Russian and Eastern studies, biochemistry, and Judaic studies. There are 14 national honor societies, including Phi Beta Kappa, and a freshman honors program.

Faculty/Classroom: 56% of faculty are male; 44%, female. All both teach and do research. No introductory courses are taught by graduate students. The average class size in an introductory lecture is 29; in a laboratory, 14; and in a regular course, 24.

Admissions: 49% of the 2001-2002 applicants were accepted. The SAT I scores for the 2001-2002 freshman class were: Verbal--9% below 500, 46% between 500 and 599, 39% between 600 and 700, and 6% above 700; Math--7% below 500, 41% between 500 and 599, 47% between 600 and 700, and 5% above 700. 64% of the current freshmen were in the top fifth of their class; 90% were in the top two fifths. 5 freshmen graduated first in their class.

Requirements: The SAT I is required. In addition, applicants must be graduates of an accredited secondary school. A B average is required. Students should have completed 15 academic credits, including 4 credits of English, 3 credits each of history and math, and 2 credits each of a foreign language, and lab science. The school recommends SAT II: Subject tests in writing, literature, language, and math, and, for nursing and science majors, in the sciences. An interview is recommended. AP and CLEP credits are accepted. Important factors in the admissions decision are advanced placement or honor courses, leadership record, and evidence of special talent. Application forms are available on-line.

Procedure: Freshmen are admitted in the fall. Entrance exams should be taken in the spring of the junior year or fall of the senior year. There are early decision and deferred admissions plans. Early decision application should be filed by November 15; regular applications, by February 1 for fall entry. Notification of early decision is sent January 1; regular decision, April 1. 101 early decision candidates were accepted for the 2001-2002 class. 3% of all applicants are on a waiting list; 73 were accepted in 2001. The fall 2001 application fee was $55.

Transfer: 52 transfer students enrolled in 2001-2002. The SAT I and a college GPA of 2.5 are required (2.8 in business). 60 credits of 120 must be completed at Fairfield.

Visiting: There are regularly scheduled orientations for prospective students, consisting of a summer orientation the third week in June and a fall program 2 days before classes begin. There are guides for informal visits and visitors may sit in on classes and stay overnight. To schedule a visit, contact the Admissions Office.

Financial Aid: In 2001-2002, 89% of all freshmen and 79% of continuing students received some form of financial aid. 52% of all students received need-based aid. The average freshman award was $16,970. Of that total, scholarships or need-based grants averaged $10,303 ($30,615 maximum); loans averaged $3884 ($5625 maximum); and work contracts averaged $1500 (maximum). 39% of undergraduates work part time. Average annual earnings from campus work are $838. The average financial indebtedness of the 2001 graduate was $19,873. Fairfield is a member of CSS. The CSS/Profile or FAFSA, parent and student tax returns, and a verification statement from first-time applicants are required. The fall application deadline is February 15.

International Students: There are 75 international students enrolled. The school actively recruits these students. They must score 550 on the written TOEFL and also take the SAT I, scoring 1150, or the ACT.

Computers: The mainframe is a VAX 6430. Staffed computer labs are maintained in all academic buildings. Mac and IBM PS/2 PCs are available. Terminals are networked throughout campus for access to Netscape and the mainframe. All students may access the system daily until midnight. There are no time limits. The fee is $45 for computer science courses. It is strongly recommended that all students have a personal computer.

Graduates: In 2001, 828 bachelor's degrees were awarded. The most popular majors were marketing (11%), English (10%), and communications (9%). In an average class, 74% graduate in 4 years, 76% in 5 years, and 80% in 6 years. 130 companies recruited on campus in 2000-2001. Of the 2000 graduating class, 18% were enrolled in graduate school within 6 months of graduation and 76% were employed.

Admissions Contact: Judy Dobai, Director. A video is available. E-mail: *admis@mail.fairfield.edu* Web: *www.fairfield.edu*

MITCHELL COLLEGE
New London, CT 06320 (860) 701-5000
(800) 443-2811; Fax: (860) 444-1209

Full-time: 307 men, 281 women | **Faculty:** 20
Part-time: 41 men, 79 women | **Ph.D.s:** 23%
Graduate: none | **Student/Faculty:** 29 to 1
Year: semesters, summer session | **Tuition:** $16,450
Application Deadline: August 30 | **Room & Board:** $7500
Freshman Class: 1024 applied, 641 accepted, 349 enrolled
SAT I Verbal/Math: 470/430 | **ACT:** 18 | **COMPETITIVE**

Mitchell College, founded in 1938, is a private institution offering associate and bachelor degree programs in the liberal arts and professional areas. The library contains 45,000 volumes, 38,928 microform items, and 50 audiovisual forms/CDs, and subscribes to 90 periodicals. Computerized library services include the card catalog, interlibrary loans, and database searching. Special learning facilities include a learning resource center. The 65-acre campus is in a suburban area on the shore of the Thames River where it meets Long Island Sound. Including residence halls, there are 19 buildings.

Student Life: 60% of undergraduates are from Connecticut. Others are from 19 states, 12 foreign countries, and Canada. 50% are from public schools. 61% are white. The average age of freshmen is 18; all undergraduates, 19. 35% do not continue beyond their first year; 65% remain to graduate.

Housing: All students can be accommodated in college housing, which includes single-sex and coed dormitories. On-campus housing is guaranteed for all 4 years. 90% of students live on campus; of those, 68% remain on campus on weekends. Alcohol is not permitted. All students may keep cars.

Activities: There are no fraternities or sororities. There are 35 groups on campus, including art, cheerleading, chorus, computers, drama, ethnic, gay, international, newspaper, professional, religious, social service, student government, and yearbook.

Sports: There are 9 intercollegiate sports for men and 9 for women, and 15 intramural sports for men and 15 for women. Facilities include a basketball court, a fitness center, and a dance studio.

Disabled Students: 50% of the campus is accessible. Elevators, special parking, and specially equipped rest rooms are available.

Services: Counseling and information services are available, as is tutoring in every subject. There is a reader service for the blind.

Campus Safety and Security: Measures include 24-hour foot and vehicle patrol, escort service, shuttle buses, and lighted pathways/sidewalks.

Programs of Study: Mitchell College confers B.A. and B.S. degrees. Associate degrees are also awarded. Bachelor's degrees are awarded in EDUCATION (early childhood), SOCIAL SCIENCE (criminal justice, family/consumer studies, human development, and liberal arts/general studies). General engineering and human development are the strongest academically. Liberal arts and human development are the largest.

Required: To graduate, students must complete 120 credits with a minimum GPA of 2.0.

Special: Numerous internships are available through department heads. Work-study programs and B.A.-B.S. degrees are available. A 3-2 engineering degree with the University of New Haven is offered. There are 2 national honor societies, including Phi Beta Kappa, and 1 departmental honors program.

Faculty/Classroom: 50% of faculty are male; 50%, female. The average class size in an introductory lecture is 12; in a laboratory, 10; and in a regular course, 12.

Admissions: 63% of the 2001-2002 applicants were accepted. 7% of the current freshmen were in the top fifth of their class; 26% were in the top two fifths.

Requirements: The SAT I or ACT is required. The GED is accepted. A recommendation and a personal statement are required. A GPA of 2.0 is required. AP and CLEP credits are accepted. Important factors in the admissions decision are extracurricular activities record, recommendations by school officials, and personality/intangible qualities. Applications are accepted on computer disk and on-line.

Procedure: Freshmen are admitted fall and spring. Entrance exams should be taken during summer orientation. There are early decision and deferred admissions plans. Early decision application should be filed by November 15; regular applications, by August 30 for fall entry and December 15 for spring entry. Notification of early decision is sent December 15; regular decision, on a rolling basis. 20 early decision candidates were accepted for the 2001-2002 class. The fall 2001 application fee was $30.

Transfer: 38 transfer students enrolled in 2001-2002. Applicants must submit college transcripts and a letter of good standing. 30 credits of 120 must be completed at Mitchell College.

Visiting: There are regularly scheduled orientations for prospective students. There are guides for informal visits and visitors may sit in on classes. To schedule a visit, contact the Admissions Office at *admissions@mitchell.edu*

Financial Aid: In 2001-2002, 80% of all students received some form of financial aid. 70% of all students received need-based aid. The average freshman award was $9000. The fall application deadline is May 1.

International Students: The school actively recruits these students. They must score 500 on the written TOEFL or 173 on the electronic version.

Computers: There is ample computer availability. All students may access the system. There are no time limits and no fees. It is strongly recommended that all students have a personal computer.

Graduates: In 2001, 6 bachelor's degrees were awarded. The most popular major was human development and family studies. In an average class, 60% graduate in 4 years. 20 companies recruited on campus in 2000-2001.

Admissions Contact: Robert Creutz, Assistant Director. A video is available. E-mail: *creutz_r@mitchell.edu* Web: *www,mitchell.edu*

QUINNIPIAC UNIVERSITY
C-3
Hamden, CT 06518 (203) 582-8600
(800) 462-1944; Fax: (203) 582-8906

Full-time: 1708 men, 2877 women | **Faculty:** 225; IIA, ++$
Part-time: 156 men, 315 women | **Ph.D.s:** 78%
Graduate: 692 men, 927 women | **Student/Faculty:** 17 to 1
Year: semesters, summer session | **Tuition:** $18,840
Application Deadline: February 15 | **Room & Board:** $8530
Freshman Class: 7281 applied, 5025 accepted, 1187 enrolled
SAT I or ACT: required | **COMPETITIVE**

Quinnipiac University, founded in 1929, is a private institution offering undergraduate and graduate degrees in health sciences, business, communications, liberal arts, education, and law. There are 4 undergraduate and 2 graduate schools. In addition to regional accreditation, Quinnipiac has baccalaureate program accreditation with AACSB, ABA, AOTA, APTA, CAHEA, and NLN. The 2 libraries contain 304,875 volumes,

9100 microform items, and 1890 audiovisual forms/CDs, and subscribe to 3900 periodicals. Computerized library services include interlibrary loans and database searching. Special learning facilities include a learning resource center, radio station, TV station, and a critical care nursing lab. The 200-acre campus is in a suburban area 10 miles north of New Haven and 35 miles south of Hartford. Including residence halls, there are 35 buildings.

Student Life: 69% of undergraduates are from out of state, mostly the Northeast. Others are from 29 states, 14 foreign countries, and Canada. 75% are from public schools. 89% are white. 60% are Catholic; 20% Protestant; 12% claim no religious affiliation. The average age of freshmen is 19; all undergraduates, 21. 12% do not continue beyond their first year; 70% remain to graduate.

Housing: 3450 students can be accommodated in college housing, which includes coed dormitories, on-campus apartments, and off-campus apartments. 75% of students live on campus; of those, 70% remain on campus on weekends. Upperclassmen may keep cars.

Activities: 5% of men belong to 1 local fraternity and 3 national fraternities; 6% of women belong to 1 local sorority and 2 national sororities. There are 65 groups on campus, including cheerleading, chorale, dance, debate, drama, ethnic, film, gay, honors, international, literary magazine, music society, musical theater, newspaper, pep band, photography, political, professional, radio and TV, religious, science, social, social service, student government, women's, and yearbook. Popular campus events include May Weekend, Lip Sync Contest, and Parents Weekend.

Sports: There are 9 intercollegiate sports for men and 10 for women, and 9 intramural sports for men and 10 for women. Facilities include more than 20 acres of playing fields, a 1500-seat gym, 2 basketball courts, a weight training room, a steam room, and a state-of-the-art fitness facility with a large multipurpose room for indoor tennis, basketball, volleyball, track, and aerobics.

Disabled Students: All of the campus is accessible. Wheelchair ramps, elevators, special parking, specially equipped rest rooms, special class scheduling, lowered drinking fountains, lowered telephones, and residence rooms designed for students with wheelchairs are available.

Services: Counseling and information services are available, as is tutoring in most subjects, including all freshman-level courses and others by request. Special workshops on work study skills, library resources, and time management are available.

Campus Safety and Security: Measures include 24-hour foot and vehicle patrol, self-defense education, escort service, and informal discussions. There are pamphlets/posters/films, lighted pathways/sidewalks, and perimeter security in the form of contract security officers at all entrances, and vehicle and occupant check-in identification.

Programs of Study: Quinnipiac confers B.A., B.S., and B.H.S. degrees. Master's degrees are also awarded. Bachelor's degrees are awarded in BIOLOGICAL SCIENCE (biochemistry, biology/biological science, biotechnology, and microbiology), BUSINESS (accounting, banking and finance, business administration and management, business economics, entrepreneurial studies, international business management, management science, and marketing/retailing/merchandising), COMMUNICATIONS AND THE ARTS (advertising, communications, English, journalism, public relations, and Spanish), COMPUTER AND PHYSICAL SCIENCE (chemistry, computer science, digital arts/technology, and mathematics), HEALTH PROFESSIONS (health care administration, health science, nursing, occupational therapy, predentistry, premedicine, radiological science, respiratory therapy, and veterinary science), SOCIAL SCIENCE (criminal justice, economics, gerontology, history, liberal arts/general studies, paralegal studies, political science/government, prelaw, psychobiology, psychology, social science, and sociology). Psychology and mass communications are the strongest academically. Mass communications, physical therapy, and accounting are the largest.

Required: All students must complete 50 semester hours of the core curriculum, which includes competency in English, math, foreign languages, oral communications, and computer information systems. Courses in arts, behavioral and social sciences, humanities, physical and biological sciences, economics, and management are also part of the core. To graduate, students must maintain a minimum GPA of 2.0 over 120 total semester hours.

Special: Internships in all majors, study abroad in more than 25 countries, a Washington semester with American University, work-study programs, dual and student-designed majors, B.A.-B.S. degrees, credit for life experience, and nondegree study are available. A 5 1/2-year freshman entry-level master's in physical therapy and occupational therapy is offered, as well as a 6-year freshman entry-level, physician assistant master's program, and a 5-year master of arts in education for those interested in teaching at the elementary, middle, or high school level. There are 8 national honor societies, and 9 departmental honors programs.

Faculty/Classroom: 58% of faculty are male; 42%, female. 85% teach undergraduates, 58% do research, and 53% do both. No introductory courses are taught by graduate students. The average class size in an introductory lecture is 24; in a laboratory, 15; and in a regular course, 22.

Admissions: 69% of the 2001-2002 applicants were accepted. The SAT I scores for the 2001-2002 freshman class were: Verbal--29% below 500, 56% between 500 and 599, 13% between 600 and 700, and 2% above 700; Math--23% below 500, 56% between 500 and 599, 19% between 600 and 700, and 2% above 700. The ACT scores were 15% below 21, 29% between 21 and 23, 25% between 24 and 26, 25% between 27 and 28, and 6% above 28. 42% of the current freshmen were in the top fifth of their class; 78% were in the top two fifths. 35 freshmen graduated first in their class.

Requirements: The SAT I or ACT is required. A minimum composite score of 1000 on the SAT I or 23 on the ACT is recommended. All students must have completed 16 academic credits, including 4 in English, 3 in math, 2 each in science and social studies, and 5 in electives. The GED is accepted. An interview is recommended, and an essay is required. Quinnipiac requires applicants to be in the upper 50% of their class. A GPA of 2.5 is required. AP and CLEP credits are accepted. Important factors in the admissions decision are advanced placement or honor courses, extracurricular activities record, and leadership record. Quinnipiac accepts applications on-line via the school's web site or through Apply, CollegeLink, or CollegeNET.

Procedure: Freshmen are admitted fall and spring. Entrance exams should be taken in the junior year and early in the senior year. There is a deferred admissions plan. Applications should be filed by February 15 for fall entry and December 15 for spring entry, along with a $45 fee. Notification is sent on a rolling basis. 15% of all applicants are on a waiting list; 150 were accepted in 2001.

Transfer: 148 transfer students enrolled in 2001-2002. Transfer students must have a minimum college GPA of 2.0 and must submit SAT I scores and high school or college transcripts. An interview is recommended. 45 credits of 120 must be completed at Quinnipiac.

Visiting: There are regularly scheduled orientations for prospective students, consisting of interviews, a group information session, student-guided tours, financial aid sessions, an opportunity to speak with faculty, and open houses. There are guides for informal visits and visitors may sit in on classes and stay overnight. To schedule a visit, contact the Admissions Office.

Financial Aid: In 2001-2002, 73% of all students received some form of financial aid. 55% of all students received need-based aid. The average freshman award was $11,801. Of that total, scholarships or need-based grants averaged $7112 ($18,000 maximum); loans averaged $2772 ($4000 maximum); and work contracts averaged $1659 ($1700 maximum). 28% of undergraduates work part time. Average annual earnings from campus work are $1800. The average financial indebtedness of the 2001 graduate was $17,170. The FAFSA and the college's own financial statement are required. The fall application deadline is March 1.

International Students: There are 35 international students enrolled. The school actively recruits these students. They must score 550 on the written TOEFL and also take the SAT I or the ACT.

Computers: The mainframe is a DEC ALPHA 2100. 45 networked PCs are available to all students in the computer center, with an additional 90 PCs in various labs and classrooms for students in specific majors. Residence halls are networked to the central system, and all students have access to e-mail, the Internet, and support software. All students may access the system Monday to Thursday, 8 A.M. to midnight; Friday, 8 A.M. to 10 P.M.; Saturday, 10 A.M. to 6 P.M.; and Sunday, 1 P.M. to midnight. There are no time limits and no fees. It is strongly recommended that all students have a personal computer.

Graduates: In 2001, 747 bachelor's degrees were awarded. The most popular majors were mass communications (11%), occupational therapy (10%), and physical therapy (9%). In an average class, 65% graduate in 4 years, 68% in 5 years, and 72% in 6 years. 75 companies recruited on campus in 2000-2001. Of the 2000 graduating class, 15% were enrolled in graduate school within 6 months of graduation and 88% were employed.

Admissions Contact: Joan Isaac Mohr, Dean of Admissions.
E-mail: *admissions@quinnipiac.edu* Web: *www.quinnipiac.edu*

SACRED HEART UNIVERSITY — B-4

Fairfield, CT 06432-1000 — **(203) 371-7880; Fax: (203) 365-7607**

Full-time: 1133 men, 1704 women	**Faculty:** 144; IIA, av$
Part-time: 395 men, 899 women	**Ph.D.s:** 85%
Graduate: 623 men, 1199 women	**Student/Faculty:** 20 to 1
Year: semesters, summer session	**Tuition:** $18,590
Application Deadline: December 1	**Room & Board:** $7998
Freshman Class: 4300 applied, 3118 accepted, 766 enrolled	
SAT I Verbal/Math: 523/524	**VERY COMPETITIVE**

Sacred Heart University, founded in 1963, is a private Catholic institution that offers majors within health sciences, liberal arts and sciences, business, education, and information technology. Some information in this profile is approximate. There are 3 undergraduate and 3 graduate schools. In addition to regional accreditation, SHU has baccalaureate program accreditation with APTA, CSWE, and NLN. The library contains 263,146 volumes, 82,839 microform items, and 11,577 audiovisual forms/CDs, and subscribes to 2157 periodicals. Computerized library services include the card catalog, interlibrary loans, and database searching. Special learning facilities include a learning resource center, art gallery, radio station, and theater. The 56-acre campus is in a suburban area in southwestern Connecticut, 55 miles northeast of New York City. Including residence halls, there are 19 buildings.

Student Life: 63% of undergraduates are from out of state, mostly the Northeast. Students are from 27 states, 50 foreign countries, and Canada. 51% are from public schools. 81% are white. 75% are Catholic; 17%, Protestant. The average age of freshmen is 18; all undergraduates, 20. 20% do not continue beyond their first year; 80% remain to graduate.

Housing: 1700 students can be accommodated in college housing, which includes coed dormitories, on-campus apartments, and off-campus apartments. In addition, there are honors floors. On-campus housing is guaranteed for all 4 years and is available on a first-come, first-served basis. 68% of students live on campus; of those, 75% remain on campus on weekends. Alcohol is not permitted. Upperclassmen may keep cars.

Activities: 9% of men belong to 4 local fraternities; 11% of women belong to 5 local sororities. There are 70 groups on campus, including art, band, cheerleading, choir, chorale, chorus, computers, dance, debate, drama, drill team, ethnic, film, honors, international, jazz band, literary magazine, marching band, musical theater, newspaper, orchestra, pep band, photography, political, professional, radio and TV, religious, social, social service, student government, and yearbook. Popular campus events include Harvest Weekend, Black History Month, and Latino Month.

Sports: There are 16 intercollegiate sports for men and 17 for women, and 11 intramural sports for men and 11 for women. Facilities include 6 championship tennis courts, an artificial turf field and an all-weather track, a 2100-seat arena, and soccer and softball fields.

Disabled Students: 90% of the campus is accessible. Wheelchair ramps, elevators, special parking, specially equipped rest rooms, special class scheduling, lowered drinking fountains, lowered telephones, and room nameplates are available.

Services: There is a reader service for the blind, and remedial math, reading, and writing.

Campus Safety and Security: Measures include 24-hour foot and vehicle patrol, self-defense education, escort service, and shuttle buses. There are informal discussions, pamphlets/posters/films, emergency telephones, and lighted pathways/sidewalks. All campus-owned residence halls have sprinklers and alarms and are designated nonsmoking.

Programs of Study: SHU confers B.A. and B.S. degrees. Associate and master's degrees are also awarded. Bachelor's degrees are awarded in BIOLOGICAL SCIENCE (biology/biological science), BUSINESS (accounting, banking and finance, business administration and management, international business management, and management science), COMMUNICATIONS AND THE ARTS (art, English, media arts, and Spanish), COMPUTER AND PHYSICAL SCIENCE (chemistry, computer science, and mathematics), ENGINEERING AND ENVIRONMENTAL DESIGN (environmental science), HEALTH PROFESSIONS (medical technology and nursing), SOCIAL SCIENCE (criminal justice, economics, history, international studies, liberal arts/general studies, philosophy, physical fitness/movement, political science/government, psychology, religion, social work, and sociology). Business, biology, and psychology are the strongest academically. Business, computer science, and psychology are the largest.

Required: To graduate, all students must complete 120 credit hours, including 30 to 58 in the major, while maintaining a minimum 2.0 GPA. Distribution requirements include an 18-credit required core consisting of freshman writing, oral communication, college math, and literature and civilizations, and a 30- to 32-credit elective core consisting of 9 credits of social science, 9 of philosophy and religious studies, 6 of arts and humanities, and 6 of science and math. B.S. candidates need an additional course each of math and science; B.A. candidates, an additional 6 credits of foreign language.

Special: SHU offers co-op programs in all majors, paid and unpaid internships at area corporations, including Fortune 500 companies, hospitals, newspapers, and social service agencies, study abroad worldwide, legislative internships, and on-campus work-study. There are 11 national honor societies, a freshman honors program, and 1 departmental honors program.

Faculty/Classroom: 53% of faculty are male; 47%, female. All teach undergraduates and 80% also do research. No introductory courses are taught by graduate students. The average class size in an introductory lecture is 20; in a laboratory, 10; and in a regular course, 20.

Admissions: 73% of the 2001-2002 applicants were accepted. The SAT I scores for the 2001-2002 freshman class were: Verbal--37% below 500, 49% between 500 and 599, 12% between 600 and 700, and 1% above 700; Math--28% below 500, 57% between 500 and 599, 14% between 600 and 700, and 1% above 700. 43% of the current freshmen were in the top fifth of their class; 76% were in the top two fifths.

Requirements: The SAT I is required, with a recommended score ranging from 530 to 710 for verbal and 480 to 650 for math; the ACT is recommended. In addition, applicants must have 16 academic credits and 16 Carnegie units, including 4 years in English, 3 each in math and science, and 2 each in foreign language, social studies, and history. An essay is required and an interview recommended. SHU requires applicants to be in the upper 40% of their class. A GPA of 3.0 is required. AP and CLEP credits are accepted. Important factors in the admissions decision are advanced placement or honor courses, leadership record, and recommendations by school officials. Applications may be submitted on computer disk and on-line using CollegeLink or Apply.

Procedure: Freshmen are admitted fall and spring. Entrance exams should be taken in May of the junior year and/or November of the senior year. There are early decision, early admissions, and deferred admissions plans. Early decision applications should be filed by October 1; regular applications, by December 1 for fall entry. The fall 2001 application fee was $50. Notification of early decision is sent October 15; regular decision, on a rolling basis. 165 early decision candidates were accepted for a recent class. 4% of applicants were on a waiting list; 33 were accepted.

Transfer: 231 transfer students enrolled in a recent year. Applicants must submit 2 letters of recommendation and high school and college transcripts and must have a college GPA of at least 2.5. 30 credits of 120 must be completed at SHU.

Visiting: There are regularly scheduled orientations for prospective students, including open houses on weekends and daily tours. There are guides for informal visits and visitors may sit in on classes and stay overnight. To schedule a visit, contact the Admissions Office.

Financial Aid: In 2001-2002, 80% of all freshmen and 70% of continuing students received some form of financial aid. In a recent year, 66% of freshmen and 64% of continuing students received need-based aid. The average freshman award was $10,595. Of that total, scholarships or need-based grants averaged $6466 ($22,500 maximum); loans averaged $3638; and work contracts averaged $808 ($2000 maximum). 26% of undergraduates work part time. Average annual earnings from campus work are $808. The average financial indebtedness of a recent graduate was $16,880. SHU is a member of CSS. The CSS/Profile or FAFSA is required. Check with the school for current deadlines.

International Students: There are 59 international students enrolled. The school actively recruits these students. They must score 550 on the written TOEFL or take the MELAB, the Comprehensive English Language Test, or the college's own test. They must also take the SAT I or the ACT.

Computers: The mainframe is a DEC 5500. There are 6 labs with nearly 150 PCs available to all students. The campuswide DEC fiber-optic network and academic computing technology serves the entire university, with every residence hall room wired to a port for the network. All students have access to the Internet, and all full-time undergraduate students have a notebook computer. All students may access the system 7 days per week. There are no time limits and no fees.

Graduates: In a recent class, 613 bachelor's degrees were awarded. The most popular majors were business (37%), psychology (18%), and biology (7%). In an average class, 46% graduate in 4 years, 53% in 5 years, and 57% in 6 years. 80 companies recruited on campus in a recent year. Of a recent graduating class, 33% were enrolled in graduate school within 6 months of graduation and 61% were employed.

Admissions Contact: Karen N. Guastelle, Dean of Undergraduate Admissions. E-mail: *enroll@sacredheart.edu* Web: *www.sacredheart.edu*

SAINT JOSEPH COLLEGE
West Hartford, CT 06117

C-2
(860) 231-5216
(800) 285-6565; Fax: (860) 233-5695

Full-time: 705 women
Part-time: 51 men, 531 women
Graduate: 70 men, 582 women
Year: semesters, summer session
Application Deadline: May 1
Freshman Class: 478 applied, 381 accepted, 175 enrolled
SAT I: required
Faculty: 67; IIA, av$
Ph.D.s: 90%
Student/Faculty: 10 to 1
Tuition: $18,360
Room & Board: $7600
ACT: n/av **LESS COMPETITIVE**

Saint Joseph College, founded in 1932 and affiliated with the Roman Catholic Church, is a private primarily women's college offering a liberal arts education with preprofessional programs in nursing, education, and business at the undergraduate level. The Weekend College and graduate school offer coeducational studies. There is 1 undergraduate and 1 graduate school. In addition to regional accreditation, SJC has baccalaureate program accreditation with ADA, CSWE, and NLN. The library contains 134,500 volumes, 52,529 microform items, and 3000 audiovisual forms/CDs, and subscribes to 623 periodicals. Computerized library services include the card catalog, interlibrary loans, and database searching. Special learning facilities include a learning resource center, art gallery, academic resources center, and 2 lab schools: the Gengras Center for Exceptional Children and the School for Young Children. The 84-acre campus is in a suburban area 3 miles west of Hartford. Including residence halls, there are 13 buildings.

Student Life: 95% of undergraduates are from Connecticut. Others are from 9 states. 85% are from public schools. 88% are white. 28% are Catholic. The average age of freshmen is 18; all undergraduates, 21. 20% do not continue beyond their first year; 65% remain to graduate.

Housing: 333 students can be accommodated in college housing, which includes single-sex dormitories. On-campus housing is guaranteed for all 4 years. 55% of students commute. Alcohol is not permitted. All students may keep cars.

Activities: There are no fraternities or sororities. There are 20 groups on campus, including art, choir, chorale, chorus, dance, drama, ethnic, honors, international, literary magazine, musical theater, political, professional, religious, social, social service, student government, and yearbook. Popular campus events include Convocation Cultural Awareness Day, and Winter Weekend.

Sports: There are 7 intercollegiate sports for women and 8 intramural sports for women. Facilities include an all-weather track, a gym, an exercise room, tennis and platform tennis courts, a dance studio, and a pool.

Disabled Students: 75% of the campus is accessible. Wheelchair ramps, elevators, special parking, specially equipped rest rooms, special class scheduling, lowered drinking fountains, and lowered telephones are available. Other needs are met on a case-by-case basis.

Services: Counseling and information services are available, as is tutoring in most subjects, including ESL. There is remedial math, reading, and writing. Other services are arranged as needed through the Academic Resource Center.

Campus Safety and Security: Measures include 24-hour foot and vehicle patrol, self-defense education, escort service, and shuttle buses. There are informal discussions, pamphlets/posters/films, emergency telephones, and lighted pathways/sidewalks.

Programs of Study: SJC confers B.A., B.S., and B.S.N. degrees. Master's degrees are also awarded. Bachelor's degrees are awarded in BIOLOGICAL SCIENCE (biology/biological science), BUSINESS (business economics and management science), COMMUNICATIONS AND THE ARTS (art history and appreciation, English, and Spanish), COMPUTER AND PHYSICAL SCIENCE (chemistry, mathematics, and natural sciences), EDUCATION (special), ENGINEERING AND ENVIRONMENTAL DESIGN (environmental science), HEALTH PROFESSIONS (nursing), SOCIAL SCIENCE (American studies, child psychology/development, dietetics, family/consumer studies, history, humanities, international studies, philosophy, political science/government, psychology, religion, social science, social work, and sociology). Psychology, education, and sciences are the strongest academically. Education, psychology, and English are the largest.

Required: All students must maintain a minimum GPA of 2.0, pass a written or oral comprehensive exam, and take 120 total credit hours including a minimum of 30 in the major and liberal arts requirements of 12 credits in 4 core areas, plus 6 credits in religion, 9 in humanities, 9 in social studies, 7 to 8 in natural science/math, and 1 in phys ed.

Special: The college offers cross-registration through the Hartford consortium, numerous internships, study abroad in Great Britain, Europe, Japan, and Spain, accelerated degree programs in business administration, interdisciplinary majors, student-designed majors, and a dual major in biology-chemistry. Credit for life experience, nondegree study, and pass/fail options is available. There is 1 national honor society, and a freshman honors program.

Faculty/Classroom: 27% of faculty are male; 73%, female. No introductory courses are taught by graduate students. The average class size in an introductory lecture is 30; in a laboratory, 20; and in a regular course, 20.

Admissions: 80% of the 2001-2002 applicants were accepted.

Requirements: The SAT I is required. In addition, applicants need 16 academic credits distributed among English, foreign language, history, math, science, and social studies. The GED is accepted, and an interview is recommended. Applications are accepted on-line. A GPA of 3.0 is required. AP and CLEP credits are accepted. Important factors in the admissions decision are advanced placement or honor courses, recommendations by school officials, and evidence of special talent.

Procedure: Freshmen are admitted fall and spring. There are early decision and deferred admissions plans. Early decision application should be filed by December 1; regular applications, by May 1 for fall entry and December 1 for spring entry. The fall application fee was $35. Notification is sent on a rolling basis. 15 early decision candidates were accepted for the 2001-2002 class.

Transfer: 72 transfer students enrolled in 2001-2002. Saint Joseph accepts transfers up to the beginning of the junior year. Applicants need a minimum college GPA of 2.7 in addition to an interview. 60 credits of 120 must be completed at SJC.

Visiting: There are regularly scheduled orientations for prospective students, including open houses, junior preview days, overnights, and individual appointments. There are guides for informal visits and visitors may sit in on classes and stay overnight. To schedule a visit, contact Kelly Crowley, Director of Admission.

Financial Aid: In 2001-2002, 93% of all freshmen and 86% of continuing students received some form of financial aid. 85% of freshmen and 80% of continuing students received need-based aid. The average freshman award was $13,536. Of that total, scholarships or need-based grants averaged $9343 ($17,500 maximum); loans averaged $5621 ($10,500 maximum); and work contracts averaged $1500. 30% of undergraduates work part time. Average annual earnings from campus work are $1500 (maximum). The average financial indebtedness of the 2001 graduate was $14,600. SJC is a member of CSS. The FAFSA is required. The fall application deadline is February 15.

International Students: They must score 530 on the written TOEFL and also take the SAT I or the ACT.

Computers: The mainframe is a Microsoft NT 4.0 network. The McDonough network center houses 92 Dell Pentium PCs and 12 Power Macs. Access to the Internet, e-mail, and various software packages and educational tools available. All students may access the system during scheduled lab hours. There are no time limits and no fees.

Graduates: In 2001, 210 bachelor's degrees were awarded. The most popular majors were nursing (25%), special education (12%), and psychology (10%). In an average class, 1% graduate in 3 years, 60% in 4 years, 5% in 5 years, and 5% in 6 years. 150 companies recruited on campus in 2000-2001. Of the 2000 graduating class, 21% were enrolled in graduate school within 6 months of graduation and 79% were employed.

Admissions Contact: Mary Yuskis, Director of Admissions. A video is available. E-mail: *admissions@mercy.syc.edu* Web: *www.sjc.edu*

SOUTHERN CONNECTICUT STATE UNIVERSITY C-3

New Haven, CT 06515 **(203) 392-5649; Fax: (203) 392-5727**

Full-time: 2481 men, 3814 women	**Faculty:** 328; IIA,
Part-time: 883 men, 1188 women	**Ph.D.s:** 83%
Graduate: 1012 men, 2926 women	**Student/Faculty:** 17 to 1
Year: semesters, summer session	**Tuition:** $4026 ($9999)
Application Deadline: see profile	**Room & Board:** $6284
Freshman Class: 4551 applied, 3125 accepted, 1429 enrolled	
SAT I Verbal/Math: 480/470	**COMPETITIVE**

Southern Connecticut State University, founded in 1893, is part of the Connecticut State University System and provides undergraduate and graduate liberal arts programs in the arts, business, education, professional studies, and the sciences. Some of the information in this profile is approximate. There are 5 undergraduate and 6 graduate schools. In addition to regional accreditation, SCSU has baccalaureate program accreditation with CSWE and NLN. The library contains 495,660 volumes, 753,033 microform items, and 4689 audiovisual forms/CDs, and subscribes to 3549 periodicals. Computerized library services include the card catalog, interlibrary loans, and database searching. Special learning facilities include a learning resource center, art gallery, planetarium, radio station, and TV station. The 168-acre campus is in an urban area 35 miles south of Hartford. Including residence halls, there are 28 buildings.

Student Life: 92% of undergraduates are from Connecticut. Others are from 20 states, 36 foreign countries, and Canada. 90% are from public schools. 77% are white. 64% are Catholic; 18%, Protestant. The average age of freshmen is 19; all undergraduates, 22. 25% do not continue beyond their first year; 48% remain to graduate.

Housing: 2100 students can be accommodated in college housing, which includes single-sex dormitories and on-campus apartments. On-campus housing is guaranteed for all 4 years. 72% of students commute. Upperclassmen may keep cars.

Activities: 1% of men belong to 3 local and 3 national fraternities; 1% of women belong to 1 local and 2 national sororities. There are 70 groups on campus, including art, band, cheerleading, choir, chorale, chorus, computers, dance, drama, drill team, ethnic, gay, honors, international, jazz band, literary magazine, marching band, musical theater, newspaper, pep band, photography, political, professional, radio and TV, religious, social, social service, student government, and yearbook. Popular campus events include Springfest, Parents Day, and Octoberfest.

Sports: There are 8 intercollegiate sports for men and 9 for women. Facilities include a 6000-seat artificial-surface playing complex for football, soccer, field hockey, and track; a field house and gym facilities for basketball, gymnastics, badminton, tennis, track and field, volleyball, and indoor baseball; and an 8-lane swimming pool.

Disabled Students: 80% of the campus is accessible. Wheelchair ramps, elevators, special parking, specially equipped rest rooms, special class scheduling, lowered drinking fountains, lowered telephones, and special computer facilities are available.

Services: Counseling and information services are available, as is tutoring in every subject. There is a reader service for the blind, and remedial math, reading, and writing.

Campus Safety and Security: Measures include 24-hour foot and vehicle patrol, self-defense education, escort service, and shuttle buses. There are informal discussions, pamphlets/posters/films, emergency telephones, and lighted pathways/sidewalks. Campus security is provided by a campus-based police force.

Programs of Study: SCSU confers B.A., B.S., B.S.Bus.Adm., and B.S.Ed. degrees. Associate and master's degrees are also awarded.

Bachelor's degrees are awarded in BIOLOGICAL SCIENCE (biochemistry and biology/biological science), BUSINESS (accounting, banking and finance, business administration and management, business economics, marketing/retailing/merchandising, and recreation and leisure services), COMMUNICATIONS AND THE ARTS (art history and appreciation, communications, dramatic arts, English, fine arts, French, German, Italian, journalism, Spanish, and studio art), COMPUTER AND PHYSICAL SCIENCE (chemistry, computer science, earth science, mathematics, and physics), EDUCATION (art, early childhood, elementary, foreign languages, health, library science, physical, science, secondary, and special), HEALTH PROFESSIONS (nursing and public health), SOCIAL SCIENCE (economics, geography, history, philosophy, political science/government, psychology, social work, and sociology). Psychology, communications, and elementary education are the largest.

Required: All students must complete distribution requirements that include 6 credits each in English composition and speech, natural sciences, and social sciences, 3 each in American politics, fine arts, foreign languages, math, literature, philosophy, and Western civilization, and 1 each in phys ed and health. To graduate, students must complete 122 total credits, including at least 30 in the major, with a minimum GPA of 2.0.

Special: SCSU offers co-op programs in all academic majors, internships in many departments, study abroad in a variety of countries, a combined B.A.-B.S. degree, dual majors, a general studies degree, student-designed majors in liberal studies, and pass/fail options. There are 2 national honor societies, a freshman honors program, and 1 departmental honors program.

Faculty/Classroom: 61% of faculty are male; 39%, female. 96% teach undergraduates. No introductory courses are taught by graduate students. The average class size in an introductory lecture is 30; in a laboratory, 25; and in a regular course, 22.

Admissions: 69% of the 2001-2002 applicants were accepted. The SAT I scores for the 2001-2002 freshman class were: Math--66% below 500, 29% between 500 and 599, and 6% between 600 and 700. 12% of the current freshmen were in the top fifth of their class; 38% were in the top two fifths.

Requirements: The SAT I, with a minimum composite score of 900 (at least 450 each in verbal and math), or the ACT, with a composite score of 15, is required. In addition, applicants should graduate with 4 years in English, 3 in math, and 2 each in natural sciences and social sciences, including American history; 2 years of foreign language are recommended. The GED is accepted. An essay also is needed. SCSU requires applicants to be in the upper 50% of their class. A GPA of 2.5 is required. AP and CLEP credits are accepted. Important factors in the admissions decision are advanced placement or honor courses, recommendations by school officials, and leadership record.

Procedure: Freshmen are admitted fall and spring. There is an early admissions plan. Recommended application deadlines are May 1 for fall entry and December 1 for spring entry. The application fee is $40. Notification is sent within 3 to 4 weeks after receipt of the completed application.

Transfer: Applicants must have a minimum of 6 college credits with a grade of C or better and an overall GPA of 2.0. The SAT I is required for applicants with fewer than 24 college credits. 30 credits of 122 must be completed at SCSU.

Visiting: There are regularly scheduled orientations for prospective students. Visitors may sit in on classes. To schedule a visit, contact the Admissions Office.

Financial Aid: In 2001-2002, 70% of all freshmen and 60% of continuing students received some form of financial aid. SCSU is a member of CSS. The FAFSA and the college's own financial statement are required. Check with the school for current deadlines.

International Students: These setudents must score 525 on the written TOEFL or 200 on the electronic version, or they must take the SAT I or the ACT.

Computers: The mainframe is a DEC VAX 8650. More than 300 PCs are available for student use in various campus locations. All are networkable. All students may access the system. There are no time limits and no fees.

Graduates: In an average class, 13% graduate in 4 years, 29% in 5 years, and 34% in 6 years.

Admissions Contact: Heather Stearns, Assistant Director of Admissions. Web: *http://www.southernct.edu*

TEIKYO POST UNIVERSITY — B-3

Waterbury, CT 06723-2540 — (203) 596-4520
(800) 345-2562; Fax: (203) 756-5810

Full-time: 242 men, 372 women	**Faculty:** 30
Part-time: 231 men, 505 women	**Ph.D.s:** 63%
Graduate: none	**Student/Faculty:** 20 to 1
Year: semesters, summer session	**Tuition:** $15,200
Application Deadline: open	**Room & Board:** $6600
Freshman Class: 838 applied, 654 accepted, 202 enrolled	
SAT I Verbal/Math: recommended	**COMPETITIVE**

Teikyo Post University, founded in 1890, is a private institution offering liberal arts and business programs with an international focus. There are 2 undergraduate schools. The library contains 84,066 volumes, 75,158 microform items, and 600 audiovisual forms/CDs, and subscribes to 566 periodicals. Computerized library services include the card catalog, interlibrary loans, and database searching. Special learning facilities include a learning resource center and a tutorial center. The 70-acre campus is in an urban area 1 mile west of Waterbury. Including residence halls, there are 13 buildings.

Student Life: 80% of undergraduates are from Connecticut. Others are from 13 states, 19 foreign countries, and Canada. 70% are from public schools. 59% are white; 16% African American. The average age of freshmen is 19; all undergraduates, 26. 23% do not continue beyond their first year; 38% remain to graduate.

Housing: 330 students can be accommodated in college housing, which includes coed dormitories and off-campus apartments. On-campus housing is available on a first-come, first-served basis. 54% of students live on campus; of those, 42% remain on campus on weekends. All students may keep cars.

Activities: There are no fraternities or sororities. There are 25 groups on campus, including chorale, chorus, drama, ethnic, gay, honors, international, literary magazine, social, social service, student government, and yearbook. Popular campus events include dances, concerts, and international food festivals.

Sports: There are 5 intercollegiate sports for men and 6 for women, and 10 intramural sports for men and 10 for women. Facilities include a soccer field, a fitness center, a weight room, a racquetball court, a swimming pool, and tennis courts.

Disabled Students: 70% of the campus is accessible. Wheelchair ramps, elevators, special parking, specially equipped rest rooms, and special class scheduling are available.

Services: Counseling and information services are available, as is tutoring in most subjects. There is a reader service for the blind, and remedial math, reading, and writing.

Campus Safety and Security: Measures include 24-hour foot and vehicle patrol, self-defense education, escort service, and shuttle buses. There are informal discussions, pamphlets/posters/films, and lighted pathways/sidewalks.

Programs of Study: TPU confers B.A. and B.S. degrees. Associate degrees are also awarded. Bachelor's degrees are awarded in BUSINESS (accounting, banking and finance, business administration and management, management science, and marketing/retailing/merchandising), COMMUNICATIONS AND THE ARTS (English), SOCIAL SCIENCE (criminal justice, history, liberal arts/general studies, psychology, and sociology). Biology is the strongest academically. Management and general studies are the largest.

Required: To graduate, all students must maintain a minimum GPA of 2.0 and earn a total of 120 credits, including at least 33 in the major.

Special: Co-op programs in all majors, cross-registration with Naugatuck Valley Community College, study abroad in England, the Netherlands, and Japan, internships with area businesses, general studies degrees, accelerated degree programs, B.A.-B.S. degrees, and credit for life experience are available. There are 2 national honor societies, and 1 departmental honors program.

Faculty/Classroom: 57% of faculty are male; 43%, female. All teach undergraduates. The average class size in an introductory lecture is 25; in a laboratory, 15; and in a regular course, 35.

Admissions: 78% of the 2001-2002 applicants were accepted.

Requirements: The SAT I or ACT is recommended. In addition, applicants must be graduates of an accredited secondary school, with 4 years of English and at least 16 total academic credits. The GED is accepted. TPU requires applicants to be in the upper 50% of their class. A GPA of 2.0 is required. AP and CLEP credits are accepted. Important factors in the admissions decision are personality/intangible qualities, extracurricular activities record, and recommendations by school officials. Applications are accepted on-line.

Procedure: Freshmen are admitted to all sessions. Entrance exams should be taken as early as possible. There are early decision, early admissions, and deferred admissions plans. Early decision applications should be filed by November 1; regular applications, by open for fall entry, along with a $40 fee. Notification of early decision is sent December 15; regular decision, on a rolling basis.

Transfer: 65 transfer students enrolled in 2001-2002. Applicants must have a minimum college GPA of 2.0. The SAT I is recommended. 30 credits of 120 must be completed at TPU.

Visiting: There are regularly scheduled orientations for prospective students, including tours, interviews with admissions counselors, and meetings with faculty and students. There are guides for informal visits and visitors may sit in on classes and stay overnight. To schedule a visit, contact the Admissions Office.

Financial Aid: In 2001-2002, 94% of all freshmen and 90% of continuing students received some form of financial aid. 85% of freshmen and 86% of continuing students received need-based aid. The average freshman award was $16,386. Of that total, scholarships or need-based grants averaged $8665 ($11,750 maximum); loans averaged $2625; work contracts averaged $1096 ($1500 maximum); and PLUS loans average $6547 ($18,000 maximum). 63% of undergraduates work part time. Average annual earnings from campus work are $1108. The average financial indebtedness of the 2001 graduate was $19,875. TPU is a member of CSS. The FAFSA, the college's own financial statement, and parent and student federal tax returns are required. The fall application deadline is March 15.

International Students: There are 65 international students enrolled. The school actively recruits these students. They must score 550 on the written TOEFL and also take the ACT or the college's own entrance exam.

Computers: The mainframe is a DEC. PCs are available for student use in the computer lab, the library, and the tutorial center. All have Internet capabilities. Residence halls are also connected to the Internet for students who have their own computers. All students may access the system. There are no time limits and no fees.

Graduates: In 2001, 198 bachelor's degrees were awarded. The most popular majors were management (30%), general studies (16%), and accounting (12%). In an average class, 36% graduate in 4 years, 31% in 5 years, and 5% in 6 years. 43 companies recruited on campus in 2000-2001. Of the 2000 graduating class, 6% were enrolled in graduate school within 6 months of graduation and 85% were employed.

Admissions Contact: Aline Rossiter, Dean of Admissions. A video is available. E-mail: *tpuadmis@teikyopost.edu* Web: *http://teikopost.edu*

TRINITY COLLEGE — C-2
Hartford, CT 06106 — **(860) 297-2180; Fax: (860) 297-2287**

Full-time: 937 men, 945 women	**Faculty:** 194; IIB, ++$
Part-time: 74 men, 118 women	**Ph.D.s:** 95%
Graduate: 92 men, 90 women	**Student/Faculty:** 10 to 1
Year: semesters	**Tuition:** $26,786
Application Deadline: January 15	**Room & Board:** $7514
Freshman Class: 5476 applied, 1668 accepted, 493 enrolled	
SAT I Verbal/Math: 630/640	**ACT:** 27 **HIGHLY COMPETITIVE**

Founded in 1823, Trinity College in Hartford is an independent, nonsectarian liberal arts college of the highest quality. Its rigorous curriculum is firmly grounded in the traditional liberal arts disciplines and marked by an array of interdisciplinary studies, exceptional offerings in science and engineering, and distinctive educational connections with Connecticut's capital city and cities around the world. In addition to regional accreditation, Trinity has baccalaureate program accreditation with ABET. The library contains 965,316 volumes, 428,857 microform items, and 229,250 audiovisual forms/CDs, and subscribes to 2425 periodicals. Computerized library services include the card catalog, interlibrary loans, and database searching. Special learning facilities include an art gallery, radio station, TV station, and Connecticut Public Television and Radio. The 100-acre campus is in an urban area southwest of downtown Hartford. Including residence halls, there are 78 buildings.

Student Life: 80% of undergraduates are from out of state, mostly the Northeast. Others are from 47 states, 41 foreign countries, and Canada. 43% are from public schools. 75% are white. 32% are Protestant; 30% Catholic; 25% claim no religious affiliation. The average age of freshmen is 18; all undergraduates, 20. 9% do not continue beyond their first year; 85% remain to graduate.

Housing: 1848 students can be accommodated in college housing, which includes coed dormitories, on-campus apartments, and fraternity houses. In addition, there are special-interest houses. On-campus housing is guaranteed for all 4 years. 94% of students live on campus; of those, 70% remain on campus on weekends. Upperclassmen may keep cars.

Activities: There are 3 local and 4 national fraternities. There are no sororities. There are 112 groups on campus, including art, bagpipe band, band, cheerleading, chess, choir, chorale, chorus, dance, debate, drama, ethnic, film, gay, honors, international, jazz band, literary magazine, musical theater, newspaper, pep band, photography, political, professional, radio and TV, religious, social, social service, student government, and yearbook. Popular campus events include Human Rights Lecture Series, Black History Month, and Latino Heritage Week.

Sports: There are 15 intercollegiate sports for men and 13 for women, and 14 intramural sports for men and 14 for women. Facilities include a pool, outdoor and indoor tracks, playing fields, a weight room, a fitness center, and tennis, squash, and basketball courts.

Disabled Students: 60% of the campus is accessible. Wheelchair ramps, elevators, special parking, specially equipped rest rooms, special class scheduling, lowered drinking fountains, and lowered telephones are available.

Services: Counseling and information services are available, as is tutoring in every subject. There is a reader service for the blind. The writing center offers instruction in all forms of writing, and the math center provides individual tutoring on topics related to math and other courses involving quantitative reasoning.

Campus Safety and Security: Measures include 24-hour foot and vehicle patrol, self-defense education, escort service, and shuttle buses. There are informal discussions, pamphlets/posters/films, emergency telephones, and lighted pathways/sidewalks.

Programs of Study: Trinity confers B.A. and B.S. degrees. Master's degrees are also awarded. Bachelor's degrees are awarded in BIOLOGICAL SCIENCE (biochemistry, biology/biological science, and neurosciences), COMMUNICATIONS AND THE ARTS (art history and appreciation, classics, comparative literature, dance, dramatic arts, English, fine arts, French, German, Italian, modern language, music, Russian, Spanish, studio art, and theater management), COMPUTER AND PHYSICAL SCIENCE (chemistry, computer science, mathematics, and physics), EDUCATION (education), ENGINEERING AND ENVIRONMENTAL DESIGN (engineering), SOCIAL SCIENCE (American studies, anthropology, classical/ancient civilization, economics, history, interdisciplinary studies, international studies, Judaic studies, philosophy, political science/government, psychology, public affairs, religion, sociology, and women's studies). History, economics, and political science are the largest.

Required: All students must complete 36 course credits, including 10 to 15 in the major and 1 from each of 5 distribution areas: arts, humanities, natural sciences, numerical and symbolic reasoning, and social sciences. Students must maintain at least a C average overall.

Special: Trinity offers special freshman programs for exceptional students, including interdisciplinary programs in the sciences and the humanities. There is an intensive study program under which students can devote a semester to 1 subject. Cross-registration through such programs as the Hartford Consortium and the Twelve-College Exchange Program, hundreds of internships (some with Connecticut Public Radio and TV on campus), study abroad virtually worldwide, including San Francisco, Rome, South Africa, Trinidad, Russia, and Nepal, a Washington semester, dual majors in all disciplines, student-designed majors, nondegree study, and pass/fail options also are offered. A 5-year advanced degree in electrical or mechanical engineering with Rensselaer Polytechnic Institute also is available. There are 4 national honor societies, including Phi Beta Kappa.

Faculty/Classroom: 58% of faculty are male; 42%, female. All both teach and do research. No introductory courses are taught by graduate students. The average class size in an introductory lecture is 19; in a laboratory, 13; and in a regular course, 13.

Admissions: 30% of the 2001-2002 applicants were accepted. The SAT I scores for the 2001 2002 freshman class were: Verbal--3% below 500, 23% between 500 and 599, 57% between 600 and 700, and 16% above 700; Math--3% below 500, 22% between 500 and 599, 60% between 600 and 700, and 15% above 700. The ACT scores were 4% below 21, 17% between 21 and 23, 26% between 24 and 26, 19% between 27 and 28, and 33% above 28. 73% of the current freshmen were in the top fifth of their class; 94% were in the top two fifths.

Requirements: The SAT I or ACT is required, along with the SAT II: Subject test in writing. Trinity strongly emphasizes individual character and personal qualities in admission. Consequently, an interview and essay are recommended. The college requires 4 years of English, 2 years each in foreign language and algebra, and 1 year each in geometry, history, and lab science. AP credits are accepted. Important factors in the admissions decision are advanced placement or honor courses, extracurricular activities record, and evidence of special talent. Applications are accepted on computer disk and on-line via EXPAN, CollegeLink, and Apply.

Procedure: Freshmen are admitted in the fall. Entrance exams should be taken in the fall of the senior year. There are early decision and deferred admissions plans. Early decision applications should be filed by November 15; regular applications, by January 15 for fall entry. The fall 2001 application fee was $50. Notification of early decision is sent December 15; regular decision, April 1. 198 early decision candidates were accepted for the 2001-2002 class. 26% of all applicants are on a waiting list; 82 were accepted in 2001.

Transfer: 32 transfer students enrolled in 2001-2002. Transfer applicants must take the SAT I or ACT. A minimum college GPA of 3.0 is recommended. 18 credits of 36 must be completed at Trinity.

Visiting: There are regularly scheduled orientations for prospective students. There are guides for informal visits and visitors may sit in on classes and stay overnight. To schedule a visit, contact the Admissions Office.

Financial Aid: In 2001-2002, 40% of all freshmen and 41% of continuing students received some form of financial aid, including need-based aid. The average freshman award was $20,014. Of that total, scholarships or need-based grants averaged $19,407 ($35,900 maximum); loans averaged $3547 ($5163 maximum); work contracts averaged $1447 ($1500 maximum); and Plus and other unsubsidized loans not included in total aid averaged $11,852 ($37,578 maximum). 35% of undergraduates work part time. Average annual earnings from campus work are $1213. The average financial indebtedness of the 2001 graduate was $10,524. Trinity is a member of CSS. The CSS/Profile or FAFSA is required. The fall application deadline is February 1 for regular decision and November for early decision.

International Students: There are 67 international students enrolled. The school actively recruits these students. They must score 550 on the written TOEFL and also take the SAT I or the ACT.

Computers: The mainframe is Peoplesoft on Microsoft NT servers. All dorm rooms are equipped with Ethernet connections. In addition, more than 200 public workstations of various types are available for student use; all can access the Internet and campus-based network resources. The campus network supports UNIX, Windows, and Mac workstations. All students have e-mail accounts, and all are entitled to a personal home page on a campus server. All students may access the system 24 hours daily. There are no time limits and no fees. It is strongly recommended that all students have personal computers.

Graduates: In 2001, 493 bachelor's degrees were awarded. The most popular majors were political science (14%), economics (12%), and history (11%). In an average class, 78% graduate in 4 years, 84% in 5 years, and 86% in 6 years.

Admissions Contact: Larry R. Dow, Dean of Admissions/Financial Aid. E-mail: *admissions.office@mail.trincoll.edu*
Web: *http://www.trincoll.edu*

UNITED STATES COAST GUARD ACADEMY — E-3

New London, CT 06320-8103 (860) 444-8500
(800) 883-8724; Fax: (860) 701-6700

Full-time: 641 men, 256 women	**Faculty:** 112
Part-time: none	**Ph.D.s:** 30%
Graduate: none	**Student/Faculty:** 8 to 1
Year: semesters, summer session	**Tuition:** 0
Application Deadline: December 15	**Room & Board:** n/app
Freshman Class: 2085 applied, 399 accepted, 279 enrolled	
SAT I Verbal/Math: 620/640	**ACT:** 27 **MOST COMPETITIVE**

The U.S. Coast Guard Academy, founded in 1876, is an Armed Forces Service Academy for men and women. Appointments are made solely on the basis of an annual nationwide competition. Except for an entrance fee of $3,000, the federal government covers all cadet expenses by providing a monthly allowance of $600 plus a daily food allowance. In addition to regional accreditation, the academy has baccalaureate program accreditation with ABET. The library contains 150,000 volumes, 60,000 microform items, and 1500 audiovisual forms/CDs, and subscribes to 850 periodicals. Computerized library services include the card catalog, interlibrary loans, and database searching. Special learning facilities include the Coast Guard Museum, a $5 million bridge simulator, and the Leadership Development Center for the Coast Guard. The 110-acre campus is in a suburban area 45 miles southeast of Hartford. Including residence halls, there are 25 buildings.

Student Life: 93% of undergraduates are from out of state, mostly the Northeast. Others are from 50 states and 14 foreign countries. 79% are white. 33% are Catholic; 30% claim no religious affiliation; 29% Protestant. The average age of freshmen is 18; all undergraduates, 21. 21% do not continue beyond their first year; 67% remain to graduate.

Housing: 900 students can be accommodated in college housing, which includes coed dormitories. On-campus housing is guaranteed for all 4 years. All of students live on campus. Alcohol is not permitted. Upperclassmen may keep cars.

Activities: There are no fraternities or sororities. There are many groups and organizations on campus, including bagpipe band, band, cheerleading, choir, chorale, chorus, drill team, drum and bugle corps, ethnic, international, jazz band, marching band, musical theater, newspaper, pep band, political, professional, religious, social, social service, and student government. Popular campus events include Parents Weekend, Coast Guard Day, and Hispanic Heritage and Black History months.

Sports: There are 13 intercollegiate sports for men and 11 for women, and 13 intramural sports for men and 13 for women. Facilities include a field house with 3 basketball courts, a 6-lane swimming pool, 5 racquetball courts, and facilities for track meets, tennis matches, and baseball and softball games; an additional athletic facility with wrestling and weight rooms, basketball courts, gymnastics areas, a swimming pool, and saunas; a 4500-seat stadium; and practice and playing fields, outdoor tennis courts, and rowing and seamanship-sailing centers.

Disabled Students: 24% of the campus is accessible. Wheelchair ramps, elevators, special parking, and specially equipped rest rooms are available.

Services: Counseling and information services are available, as is tutoring in every subject.

Campus Safety and Security: Measures include 24-hour foot and vehicle patrol, self-defense education, and lighted pathways/sidewalks.

Programs of Study: The academy confers the B.S. degree. Bachelor's degrees are awarded in BIOLOGICAL SCIENCE (marine science), BUSINESS (management science and operations research), ENGINEERING AND ENVIRONMENTAL DESIGN (civil engineering, electrical/electronics engineering, mechanical engineering, and naval architecture and marine engineering), SOCIAL SCIENCE (political science/government). Political science/government is the largest.

Required: To graduate, cadets must pass at least 37 courses, of which 25 are core; accumulate a minimum of 126 credit hours, with at least 90 credits of C or better, exclusive of phys ed; complete the academic requirements for 1 of the approved majors and attain a minimum GPA of 2.0 in all required upper-division courses in the major; successfully complete all professional development and phys ed requirements; and maintain a high sense of integrity.

Special: Cross-registration with Connecticut College, summer cruises to foreign ports, 6-week internships with various government agencies, and a 1-semester exchange program with the 3 other military academies are available. All graduates are commissioned in the U.S. Coast Guard. There are 2 national honor societies, a freshman honors program, and 3 departmental honors programs.

Faculty/Classroom: 90% of faculty are male; 10%, female. The average class size in an introductory lecture is 28; in a laboratory, 18; and in a regular course, 20.

Admissions: 19% of the 2001-2002 applicants were accepted. The SAT I scores for the 2001-2002 freshman class were: Verbal--2% below 500, 35% between 500 and 599, 51% between 600 and 700, and 12% above 700; Math--1% below 500, 22% between 500 and 599, 57% between 600 and 700, and 20% above 700. 80% of the current freshmen were in the top fifth of their class; 95% were in the top two fifths. 9 freshmen graduated first in their class in a recent year.

Requirements: The SAT I or ACT is required. In addition, applicants must have reached the age of 17 but not the age of 22 by July 1 of the year of admission, be citizens of the United States, and be single at the time of appointment and remain single while attending the academy. Required secondary school courses include 4 years each of English and math. AP credits are accepted. Important factors in the admissions decision are leadership record, recommendations by school officials, and advanced placement or honor courses. Applications are accepted on-line.

Procedure: Freshmen are admitted in the summer. Entrance exams should be taken by December 15. There is an early admissions plan. Applications should be filed by December 15 for fall entry. Notification is sent on a rolling basis. 5% of all applicants are on a waiting list; 50 were accepted in 2001.

Transfer: All transfer students must meet the same standards as incoming freshmen and must begin as freshmen no matter how many semesters or years of college they have completed. 126 credits of 126 must be completed at the academy.

Visiting: There are regularly scheduled orientations for prospective students, including an admissions briefing and tour of the academy every Friday. To schedule a visit, contact the Director of Admissions.

International Students: There were 18 international students enrolled in a recent year. They must score 550 on the written TOEFL and also take the SAT I or the ACT, scoring 1100 on the SAT I.

Computers: Students may use computer rooms in the dormitories and academic building. All students receive a laptop computer upon entering the academy. All rooms are wired for Internet access. All students may access the system 24 hours a day. There are no time limits and no fees.

Graduates: In 2001, 165 bachelor's degrees were awarded. The most popular majors were management (21%), marine science (19%), and government (17%). In an average class, 60% graduate in 4 years, and 1% in 5 years.

Admissions Contact: Susan D. Bibeau, Director of Admissions. A video is available. E-mail: *admissions@cga.uscg.mil* Web: *www.cga.edu*

UNIVERSITY OF BRIDGEPORT — B-4

Bridgeport, CT 06602 (203) 576-4552
(800) EXCEL-UB; Fax: (203) 576-4941

Full-time: 420 men, 450 women	**Faculty:** 64
Part-time: 104 men, 207 women	**Ph.D.s:** 90%
Graduate: 978 men, 1003 women	**Student/Faculty:** 14 to 1
Year: semesters, summer session	**Tuition:** $15,520
Application Deadline: April 1	**Room & Board:** $7500
Freshman Class: 1355 applied, 1131 accepted, 195 enrolled	
SAT I Verbal/Math: 430/460	**COMPETITIVE**

The University of Bridgeport, founded in 1927, is a private, independent, nonsectarian university offering programs in the arts, humanities, and social sciences, business, engineering and design, natural sciences, human services, dental hygiene, chiropractic and naturopathic medicine, and teacher preparation. There are 10 undergraduate and 7 graduate schools. In addition to regional accreditation, UB has baccalaureate program accreditation with ABET, ADA, and NASAD. The library contains 275,000 volumes, 1 million microform items, and 5000 audiovisual forms/CDs, and subscribes to 1700 periodicals. Computerized library services include interlibrary loans and database searching. Special learning facilities include a learning resource center and art gallery. The 86-acre campus is in an urban area 60 miles northeast of New York City. Including residence halls, there are 30 buildings.

Student Life: 60% of undergraduates are from out of state, mostly the Middle Atlantic. Students are from 31 states, 65 foreign countries, and Canada. 89% are from public schools. 34% are foreign nationals; 27% white; 21% African American; 10% Hispanic. 69% are claim no religious affiliation; 14% Catholic. The average age of freshmen is 20; all undergraduates, 25. 24% do not continue beyond their first year.

Housing: 1014 students can be accommodated in college housing, which includes coed dormitories. In addition, there are special-interest houses and alcohol- and tobacco-free buildings. On-campus housing is guaranteed for all 4 years. 53% of students commute. All students may keep cars.

Activities: 1% of men belong to 2 local fraternities; 2% of women belong to 1 local sorority. There are 44 groups on campus, including art, cheerleading, computers, debate, ethnic, honors, international, literary magazine, newspaper, photography, political, professional, radio and TV, religious, social, social service, student government, and yearbook. Popular campus events include International Festival, Winter Prelude, and Wisteria Ball.

Sports: There are 4 intercollegiate sports for men and 6 for women, and 8 intramural sports for men and 8 for women. Facilities include a gym, athletic fields, tennis and racquetball courts, and a recreation center with an indoor pool.

Disabled Students: 75% of the campus is accessible. Wheelchair ramps, elevators, special parking, specially equipped rest rooms, and special class scheduling are available.

Services: Counseling and information services are available, as is tutoring in every subject. There is a reader service for the blind, and remedial math, reading, and writing.

Campus Safety and Security: Measures include 24-hour foot and vehicle patrol, escort service, informal discussions, and pamphlets/posters/films. There are emergency telephones, lighted pathways/sidewalks, and campus security systems.

Programs of Study: UB confers B.A., B.S., B.E.S., B.F.A., and B.M. degrees. Associate, master's, and doctoral degrees are also awarded. Bachelor's degrees are awarded in BIOLOGICAL SCIENCE (biology/biological science), BUSINESS (accounting, banking and finance, business administration and management, fashion merchandising, international business management, management information systems, management science, and marketing/retailing/merchandising), COMMUNICATIONS AND THE ARTS (communications, English, fine arts, graphic design, illustration, industrial design, journalism, literature, and music), COMPUTER AND PHYSICAL SCIENCE (computer science and mathematics), ENGINEERING AND ENVIRONMENTAL DESIGN (computer engineering and interior design), HEALTH PROFESSIONS (dental hygiene, medical laboratory technology, predentistry, premedicine, and respiratory therapy), SOCIAL SCIENCE (economics, human services, interdisciplinary studies, international studies, prelaw, religion, and social science). Computer science/engineering, business, and dental hygiene are the strongest academically. Dental hygiene, business administration, and computer science/engineering are the largest.

Required: All students are required to complete at least 120 credit hours, including at least 30 in the major field. A minimum GPA of 2.0 is necessary. Distribution requirements cover 33 core credits and are composed of skills, heritage, and capstone sections, including 3 hours each in English composition and quantitative skills, and 24 semester hours consisting of 6 hours each in humanities, natural science, and social science and 3 each in integrated studies and fine arts.

Special: UB offers co-op programs with several local institutions, cross-registration with Sacred Heart and Fairfield Universities, internships in many degree programs, study abroad in England, Switzerland, or Spain, a Washington semester, and work-study programs. In addition, an elective studies accelerated degree program, dual majors, student-designed majors, and B.A.-B.S. degrees are available. Credit for life experience, nondegree study, and pass/fail options are offered. There are 11 national honor societies and 1 departmental honors program.

Faculty/Classroom: 82% of faculty are male; 18%, female. All both teach and do research. No introductory courses are taught by graduate students. The average class size in an introductory lecture is 16; in a laboratory, 10; and in a regular course, 16.

Admissions: 83% of the 2001-2002 applicants were accepted. The SAT I scores for the 2001-2002 freshman class were: Verbal--67% below 500, 24% between 500 and 599, 7% between 600 and 700, and 2% above 700; Math--65% below 500, 20% between 500 and 599, 11% between 600 and 700, and 4% above 700. 25% of the current freshmen were in the top fifth of their class; 48% were in the top two fifths. 2 freshmen graduated first in their class in a recent year.

Requirements: The SAT I or ACT is required. In addition, applicants are required to have 16 academic credits or Carnegie units, including 4 units of English, 3 of math, 2 in social studies, 2 in a lab science, and 5 electives. A portfolio is required for B.F.A. students and an audition for B.M. candidates. UB requires applicants to be in the upper 50% of their class. A GPA of 2.0 is required. AP and CLEP credits are accepted. Important factors in the admissions decision are advanced placement or honor courses, extracurricular activities record, and recommendations by school officials. Applications are accepted on computer disk and on-line.

Procedure: Freshmen are admitted fall and spring. Entrance exams should be taken during the senior year. There are early decision, early admissions, and deferred admissions plans. Applications should be filed by April 1 for fall entry and December 1 for spring entry. The fall 2001 application fee was $40. Notification is sent on a rolling basis.

Transfer: 82 transfer students enrolled in 2001-2002. Transfer applicants need a minimum GPA of 2.5 and at least 12 earned credit hours. The SAT I or ACT and an interview are recommended. 30 credits of 120 must be completed at UB.

Visiting: There are regularly scheduled orientations for prospective students. There are guides for informal visits and visitors may sit in on classes and stay overnight. To schedule a visit, contact the Admissions Office.

Financial Aid: The FAFSA and the college's own financial statement are required. The fall application deadline is April 15.

International Students: There are 349 international students enrolled. The school actively recruits these students. They must score 500 on the written TOEFL or take the MELAB, the Comprehensive English Language Test, or the college's own test.

Computers: The mainframe is a Prime 6350. Computer systems available to students throughout campus include Sun Microsystems workstations, Apollo workstations, 7 all-purpose PC labs, and a specialized microprocessor lab. All students may access the system 8 A.M. to 11 P.M. daily. UBnet is available 24 hours a day from dorm rooms or dial-ups. There are no time limits and no fees.

Graduates: In 2001, 151 bachelor's degrees were awarded. The most popular majors were elective studies (26%), finance (14%), and human services (9%). In an average class, 40% graduate in 4 years, 45% in 5 years, and 50% in 6 years. Of the 2000 graduating class, 10% were enrolled in graduate school within 6 months of graduation and 60% were employed.

Admissions Contact: Barbara L. Maryak, Dean of Admissions. A video is available. E-mail: *admit@bridgeport.edu*
Web: *www.bridgeport.edu*

UNIVERSITY OF CONNECTICUT — D-2

Storrs, CT 06269-3088 — **(860) 486-3137; Fax: (860) 486-1476**

Full-time: 6176 men, 6841 women	**Faculty:** 1036; I, +$
Part-time: 315 men, 256 women	**Ph.D.s:** 94%
Graduate: 2318 men, 2436 women	**Student/Faculty:** 13 to 1
Year: semesters, summer session	**Tuition:** $5824 ($14,942)
Application Deadline: March 1	**Room & Board:** $6298
Freshman Class: 12,351 applied, 8791 accepted, 3149 enrolled	
SAT I Verbal/Math: 560/580	**VERY COMPETITIVE**

The University of Connecticut, founded in 1881, is a public, land-grant, sea-grant, multicampus research institution offering degree programs in liberal arts and sciences and professional studies. There are 10 undergraduate and 5 graduate schools. In addition to regional accreditation, UConn has baccalaureate program accreditation with AACSB, ABET, ACPE, ADA, APTA, ASLA, CAAHEP, CCNE, CSAB, NAACLS, NASAD, NASM, NCATE, and NLN. The library contains 1,766,935 volumes, 3,303,212 microform items, and 53,079 audiovisual forms/CDs, and subscribes to 21,328 periodicals. Computerized library services include the card catalog, interlibrary loans, and database searching. Special learning facilities include a learning resource center, art gallery, natural history museum, planetarium, radio station, and TV station. The 4104-acre campus is in a rural area 25 miles east of Hartford. Including residence halls, there are 150 buildings.

Student Life: 77% of undergraduates are from Connecticut. Others are from 48 states, 43 foreign countries, and Canada. 83% are white. The average age of freshmen is 18; all undergraduates, 20. 12% do not continue beyond their first year.

Housing: 8618 students can be accommodated in college housing, which includes single-sex and coed dormitories, on-campus apartments, married-student housing, fraternity houses, and sorority houses. In addition, there are honors houses, language houses, special-interest houses, substance-free dorms, a floor for older students, and a living/learning center, as well as facilities for international, engineering, and disabled students. On-campus housing is guaranteed for the freshman year only. 70% of students live on campus; of those, 70% remain on campus on weekends. Upperclassmen may keep cars.

Activities: 7% of men belong to 18 national fraternities; 6% of women belong to 9 national sororities. There are 226 groups on campus, including art, band, cheerleading, chess, choir, chorale, chorus, computers, dance, drama, drill team, ethnic, film, gay, honors, international, jazz band, literary magazine, marching band, musical theater, newspaper, opera, orchestra, pep band, photography, political, professional, radio and TV, religious, social, social service, student government, symphony, and yearbook. Popular campus events include Spring Weekend, "UConn Do It" campus clean-up day, and Winter Weekend.

Sports: There are 11 intercollegiate sports for men and 13 for women, and 28 intramural sports for men and 28 for women. Facilities include a sports center, a field house, a 16,000-seat football stadium, a 10,000-seat basketball stadium, and a student, faculty, and staff workout center.

Disabled Students: 80% of the campus is accessible. Wheelchair ramps, elevators, special parking, specially equipped rest rooms, special class scheduling, lowered drinking fountains, lowered telephones, a tactile map, and 4 specially equipped transportation vans are available.

Services: Counseling and information services are available, as is tutoring in most subjects. There is a reader service for the blind. Also available are a Braille printer, a Kurzweil reading machine and Mac computer with voice synthesizer, a machine to enlarge printed material, a talking calculator, and a TDD.

Campus Safety and Security: Measures include 24-hour foot and vehicle patrol, self-defense education, escort service, and shuttle buses. There are informal discussions, pamphlets/posters/films, emergency telephones, and lighted pathways/sidewalks.

Programs of Study: UConn confers B.A., B.S., B.F.A., B.G.S., B.Mus., B.S.E., and B.S.Pharm. degrees. Associate, master's, and doctoral degrees are also awarded. Bachelor's degrees are awarded in AGRICULTURE (agricultural economics, agriculture, agronomy, animal science, horticulture, and natural resource management), BIOLOGICAL SCIENCE (biology/biological science, biophysics, evolutionary biology, genetics, marine science, molecular biology, nutrition, and physiology), BUSINESS (accounting, banking and finance, business administration and management, insurance and risk management, management information systems, marketing/retailing/merchandising, and real estate), COMMUNICATIONS AND THE ARTS (art, art history and appreciation, classics, communications, dramatic arts, English, French, German, journalism, linguistics, music, Portuguese, Spanish, theater design, and visual and performing arts), COMPUTER AND PHYSICAL SCIENCE (chemistry, computer science, geology, mathematics, physics, and statistics), EDUCATION (agricultural, athletic training, education, elementary, English, foreign languages, mathematics, music, recreation, science, social studies, and special), ENGINEERING AND ENVIRONMENTAL DESIGN (biomedical engineering, chemical engineering, civil engineering, computer engineering, electrical/electronics engineering, environmental engineering, environmental science, landscape architecture/design, manufacturing engineering, materials engineering, and mechanical engineering), HEALTH PROFESSIONS (cytotechnology, exercise science, health care administration, medical laboratory technology, nursing, pharmacy, and physical therapy), SOCIAL SCIENCE (anthropology, dietetics, Eastern European studies, economics, geography, history, human development, Italian studies, Latin American studies, Middle Eastern studies, philosophy, political science/government, psychology, sociology, urban studies, and women's studies). Psychology, pre-teaching, and communication sciences are the largest.

Required: To graduate, students must complete 120 credits with a GPA of 2.0. There are general education requirements in foreign language, expository writing, math, literature and the arts, culture and modern society, philosophical and ethical analysis, social scientific and comparative analysis, and science and technology. Students must complete a course that provides hands-on experience in a major computer application.

Special: UConn offers co-op programs in most majors, internships, study abroad in 28 countries, dual majors, general studies degrees, student-designed majors, work-study programs, nondegree study, and pass/fail options. There are 24 national honor societies, including Phi Beta Kappa, and a freshman honors program.

Faculty/Classroom: 69% of faculty are male; 31%, female. The average class size in an introductory lecture is 43; in a laboratory, 16; and in a regular course, 33.

Admissions: 71% of the 2001-2002 applicants were accepted. The SAT I scores for the 2001-2002 freshman class were: Verbal--18% below 500, 52% between 500 and 599, 27% between 600 and 700, and 4% above 700; Math--13% below 500, 48% between 500 and 599, 33% between 600 and 700, and 7% above 700. 48% of the current freshmen were in the top fifth of their class; 87% were in the top two fifths. There were 8 National Merit semifinalists. 26 freshmen graduated first in their class in a recent year.

Requirements: The SAT I or ACT is required. In addition, applicants must be graduates of an approved secondary school and should rank in the upper range of their class. The GED is accepted. Students must complete 16 high school academic units, including 4 years of English, 3 of math, 2 each of foreign language, science, and social studies, and 3 of electives. An essay is required. An audition is required for music and theater students and a portfolio for art students. AP credits are accepted. Important factors in the admissions decision are advanced placement or honor courses, evidence of special talent, and leadership record. Applications are accepted on-line via CollegeLink, Apply, and CollegeView.

Procedure: Freshmen are admitted fall and spring. Entrance exams should be taken in the spring of the junior year or the fall of the senior year. There are early admissions and deferred admissions plans. Applications should be filed by March 1 for fall entry and October 15 for spring entry. The fall application fee was $50. Notification is sent on a rolling basis.

Transfer: 556 transfer students enrolled in 2001-2002. Applicants should have a minimum GPA of 2.5 and submit official transcripts from all colleges previously attended, the high school transcript, and SAT I or ACT scores as needed. An associate degree or a minimum of 54 credit hours is recommended. 30 credits of 120 must be completed at UConn.

Visiting: There are regularly scheduled orientations for prospective students, including daily tours and information sessions. Visitors may sit in on classes with prior permission. To schedule a visit, contact the Lodewick Visitors Center at (860) 486-4900.

Financial Aid: In 2001-2002, 94% of all freshmen and 78% of continuing students received some form of financial aid. 74% of freshmen and 66% of continuing students received need-based aid. The average freshman award was $8415. Of that total, scholarships or need-based grants averaged $5414 ($12,500 maximum); loans averaged $2619 ($5500 maximum); and work contracts averaged $1190 ($1800 maximum). Average annual earnings from campus work are $2100. The average financial indebtedness of the 2001 graduate was $14,394. The FAFSA is required. The fall application deadline is March 1.

International Students: There are 110 international students enrolled. The school actively recruits these students. They must score 550 on the written TOEFL or 213 on the electronic version and also take the college's own test and either the SAT I or the ACT.

Computers: The mainframes are IBM 3090s, Models 150E and 180E. There are more than 1800 terminals on campus located in the computer center, the library, the various schools and colleges, and some residence halls. All students may access the system 24 hours weekdays and from 8 A.M. to noon weekends. There are no time limits and no fees.

Graduates: In 2001, 2837 bachelor's degrees were awarded. The most popular majors were general studies (8%), human development and family studies (7%), and communication sciences (7%). In an average class, 38% graduate in 4 years, 64% in 5 years, and 68% in 6 years. 200 companies recruited on campus in 2000-2001. Of the 2000 graduating class, 29% were enrolled in graduate school within 6 months of graduation and 84% were employed.

Admissions Contact: James D. Morales, Director of Admissions.
E-mail: *beahusky@uconnvm.uconn.edu* Web: *www.uconn.edu*

UNIVERSITY OF HARTFORD
West Hartford, CT 06117

C-2	(860) 243-4296
(800) 947-4303; Fax: (860) 768-4961	
Full-time: 2127 men, 2157 women	**Faculty:** 305; IIA, -$
Part-time: 455 men, 686 women	**Ph.D.s:** 80%
Graduate: 564 men, 855 women	**Student/Faculty:** 14 to 1
Year: semesters, summer session	**Tuition:** $20,810
Application Deadline: open	**Room & Board:** $8074
Freshman Class: 9051 applied, 6495 accepted, 1434 enrolled	
SAT I Verbal/Math: 520/530	**ACT:** 23 **COMPETITIVE**

The University of Hartford, founded in 1877, is an independent, nonsectarian institution offering extensive undergraduate and graduate programs ranging from liberal arts to business. There are 9 undergraduate and 7 graduate schools. In addition to regional accreditation, the university has baccalaureate program accreditation with ABET, APTA, CAHEA, NASAD, NASM, and NCATE. The 3 libraries contain 578,672 volumes and 336,304 microform items, and subscribe to 3447 periodicals. Computerized library services include the card catalog, interlibrary loans, and database searching. Special learning facilities include a learning resource center, art gallery, radio station, TV station, and the Museum of American Political Life. The 320-acre campus is in a suburban area 4 miles northwest of Hartford. Including residence halls, there are 35 buildings.

Student Life: 71% of undergraduates are from out of state, mostly the Northeast. Others are from 45 states, 74 foreign countries, and Canada. 74% are from public schools. 72% are white. 45% are claim no religious affiliation; 25% Islamic, Greek Orthodox; 17% Catholic. The average age of freshmen is 18; all undergraduates, 22. 29% do not continue beyond their first year; 51% remain to graduate.

Housing: 3495 students can be accommodated in college housing, which includes coed dormitories and on-campus apartments. In addition, there are honors houses and special-interest houses, the Residential College for the Arts, and the International Residential College. On-campus housing is guaranteed for all 4 years. 66% of students live on campus; of those, 85% remain on campus on weekends. All students may keep cars.

Activities: 17% of men belong to 7 national fraternities; 21% of women belong to 7 national sororities. There are 45 groups on campus, including art, band, cheerleading, choir, chorale, chorus, computers, drama, ethnic, gay, honors, international, jazz band, literary magazine, musical theater, newspaper, opera, orchestra, pep band, political, professional, radio and TV, religious, social, social service, student government, symphony, and yearbook. Popular campus events include Welcome Weekend, Spring Weekend, and Winter Carnival.

Sports: There are 9 intercollegiate sports for men and 9 for women, and 16 intramural sports for men and 16 for women. Facilities include playing fields, a 25-meter outdoor pool, tennis courts, golf practice cages, a fitness trail, and a sports center with a 4600-seat multipurpose court, an 8-lane swimming pool, a weight room, racquetball courts, a squash court, and saunas.

Disabled Students: Wheelchair ramps, elevators, special parking, specially equipped rest rooms, lowered drinking fountains, and lowered telephones are available.

Services: Counseling and information services are available, as is tutoring in most subjects. There is a reader service for the blind, and remedial math, reading, and writing. The health education office offers peer counseling and workshops on health-related topics. Professional counseling is available.

Campus Safety and Security: Measures include 24-hour foot and vehicle patrol, self-defense education, escort service, and shuttle buses. There are informal discussions, pamphlets/posters/films, emergency telephones, lighted pathways/sidewalks, and bicycle patrol.

Programs of Study: The university confers B.A., B.F.A., B.Mus., B.S.A.E.T., B.S.B.A., B.S.C.E., B.S.Comp.E., B.S.Ed., B.S.E.E., B.S.E.E.T., B.S.M.E., and B.S.N. degrees. Associate, master's, and doctoral degrees are also awarded. Bachelor's degrees are awarded in BIOLOGICAL SCIENCE (biology/biological science), BUSINESS (accounting, banking and finance, entrepreneurial studies, insurance, management information systems, management science, and marketing/retailing/merchandising), COMMUNICATIONS AND THE ARTS (art history and appreciation, arts administration/management, audio technology, communications, dance, dramatic arts, drawing, English, film arts, fine arts, graphic design, illustration, jazz, languages, music, music business management, music history and appreciation, music performance, music theory and composition, musical theater, painting, performing arts, photography, printmaking, sculpture, technical and business writing, theater management, and video), COMPUTER AND PHYSICAL SCIENCE (chemistry, computer science, mathematics, physics, and radiological technology), EDUCATION (early childhood, elementary, music, secondary, and special), ENGINEERING AND ENVIRONMENTAL DESIGN (architectural engineering, biomedical engineering, ceramic science, chemical engineering technology, civil engineering, computer engineering, electrical/electronics engineering, electrical/electronics engineering technology, engineering, environmental engineering, manufacturing engineering, mechanical engineering, and mechanical engineering technology), HEALTH PROFESSIONS (chiropractic, health science, medical laboratory technology, nursing, occupational therapy, physical therapy, predentistry, premedicine, preoptometry, and respiratory therapy), SOCIAL SCIENCE (criminal justice, economics, history, human services, interdisciplinary studies, international studies, Judaic studies, philosophy, political science/government, psychology, sociology, and women's studies). Computer science, engineering, and physical therapy are the strongest academically. Communication, psychology, and elementary education are the largest.

Required: To graduate, students must complete at least 120 credit hours, fulfill the university's core curriculum requirements, and maintain an overall GPA of 2.0. Specific core and course requirements vary with the major.

Special: Cross-registration with the Greater Hartford Consortium, internships in all majors, study abroad, a Washington semester, work-study programs, credit for life experience, nondegree study, and pass/fail options are available. In addition, students may pursue accelerated degrees, B.A.-B.S. degrees, dual majors, or their own individually designed majors. There are interdisciplinary majors in acoustics and music and in experimental studio combining performing, literary, and visual arts. Also available are preprofessional programs in biology/preoptometry with the New England College of Optometry, predentistry with the New York University School of Dentistry, and prechiropractic with the New York Chiropractic College. There are 19 national honor societies, a freshman honors program, and 9 departmental honors programs.

Faculty/Classroom: 59% of faculty are male; 41%, female. All teach undergraduates, 97% do research, and 97% do both. No introductory courses are taught by graduate students. The average class size in an introductory lecture is 21; in a laboratory, 14; and in a regular course, 18.

Admissions: 72% of the 2001-2002 applicants were accepted. The SAT I scores for the 2001-2002 freshman class were: Verbal--38% below 500, 46% between 500 and 599, 14% between 600 and 700, and 2% above 700; Math--34% below 500, 47% between 500 and 599, 17% between 600 and 700, and 2% above 700. The ACT scores were 29% below 21, 35% between 21 and 23, 18% between 24 and 26, 6% between 27 and 28, and 12% above 28. 19% of the current freshmen were in the top fifth of their class; 48% were in the top two fifths.

Requirements: The SAT I is required. In addition, applicants should have 16 academic high school credits and 16 Carnegie units, including 4 units in English, 3 in math (3.5 for B.S. candidates), and 2 each in foreign language, science, and social studies. A portfolio and an audition are required for B.F.A. and B.Mus. candidates, respectively. A personal statement is required and an interview is recommended for all students. AP and CLEP credits are accepted. Important factors in the admissions decision are advanced placement or honor courses, recommendations by school officials, and leadership record.

Procedure: Freshmen are admitted fall and spring. Entrance exams should be taken in the spring of the junior year or the fall of the senior year. There are early admissions and deferred admissions plans. Application deadlines are open. The fall 2001 application fee was $35. Notification is sent on a rolling basis.

Transfer: 242 transfer students enrolled in 2001-2002. Transfer students must have a minimum college GPA of 2.0, with 2.5 recommended, and must submit the SAT I or ACT scores if they have fewer than 30 transferable college-level credits. An interview is also recommended. 30 credits of 120 must be completed at the university.

Visiting: There are regularly scheduled orientations for prospective students. There are guides for informal visits and visitors may sit in on classes and stay overnight. To schedule a visit, contact the Office of Admissions.

Financial Aid: In 2001-2002, 92% of all freshmen and 96% of continuing students received some form of financial aid. 74% of freshmen and 77% of continuing students received need-based aid. The average freshman award was $15,867. Of that total, scholarships or need-based grants averaged $6135 ($20,170 maximum); loans averaged $5710 ($30,000 maximum); and work contracts averaged $1304 ($2839 maximum). 22% of undergraduates work part time. Average annual earnings from campus work are $1100. The average financial indebtedness of the 2001 graduate was $13,500. The FAFSA is required. The fall application deadline is February 1.

International Students: There are 185 international students enrolled. The school actively recruits these students. They must score 550 on the written TOEFL.

Computers: The mainframe is a DEC VAX 6610. Approximately 400 PCs, terminals, and workstations are available for student use in a variety of university locations, some of which are open 8 A.M. to midnight. All students may access the system. There are no time limits and no fees. It is strongly recommended that all students have a personal computer.

Graduates: In 2001, 810 bachelor's degrees were awarded. The most popular majors were communications (9%), occupational therapy (5%), and elementary education (5%). In an average class, 1% graduate in 3 years, 36% in 4 years, 50% in 5 years, and 51% in 6 years. 55 companies recruited on campus in 2000-2001. Of the 2000 graduating class, 23% were enrolled in graduate school within 6 months of graduation and 89% were employed.

Admissions Contact: Richard A. Zeiser, Dean of Admissions.
E-mail: *admission@uhavax.hartford.edu*

UNIVERSITY OF NEW HAVEN — C-3

West Haven, CT 06516 — (203) 932-7319
(800) DIAL-UNH; Fax: (203) 931-6093

Full-time: 971 men, 725 women	**Faculty:** 172; IIA, av$
Part-time: 503 men, 333 women	**Ph.D.s:** 87%
Graduate: 834 men, 863 women	**Student/Faculty:** 10 to 1
Year: semesters, summer session	**Tuition:** $16,560
Application Deadline: open	**Room & Board:** $7300
Freshman Class: 2467 applied, 1871 accepted, 554 enrolled	
SAT I Verbal/Math: 480/480	**LESS COMPETITIVE**

The University of New Haven, founded in 1920, is an independent institution offering undergraduate programs in arts and sciences, business, engineering, public safety and professional studies, and hotel, restaurant, and tourism administration. There are 5 undergraduate schools and 1 graduate school. In addition to regional accreditation, UNH has baccalaureate program accreditation with AACSB and ABET. The library contains 383,969 volumes, 511,144 microform items, and 1066 audiovisual forms/CDs, and subscribes to 1321 periodicals. Computerized library services include the card catalog, interlibrary loans, and database searching. Special learning facilities include a learning resource center, art gallery, radio station, and TV station. The 78-acre campus is in a suburban area 5 miles west of New Haven. Including residence halls, there are 25 buildings.

Student Life: 70% of undergraduates are from Connecticut. Others are from 28 states, 52 foreign countries, and Canada. 85% are from public schools. 70% are white; 11% African American; 11% foreign nationals. The average age of all undergraduates is 26. 25% do not continue beyond their first year.

Housing: 1060 students can be accommodated in college housing, which includes coed dormitories and on-campus apartments. On-campus housing is available on a first-come, first-served basis and is available on a lottery system for upperclassmen. Priority is given to out-of-town students. 64% of students live on campus; of those, 65% remain on campus on weekends. All students may keep cars.

Activities: 4% of men belong to 2 local fraternities and 1 national fraternity; 4% of women belong to 3 local sororities. There are 39 groups on campus, including cheerleading, chorus, dance, drama, ethnic, forensics, gay, honors, international, newspaper, pep band, photography, political, professional, radio and TV, religious, social, social service, student government, and yearbook. Popular campus events include Family Day and Snow Ball Formal.

Sports: There are 10 intercollegiate sports for men and 10 for women, and 10 intramural sports for men and 9 for women. Facilities include baseball, softball, and intramural playing fields; tennis courts; a gym with basketball courts, weight training room, racquetball court, and gymnastics area; and a stadium for football, soccer, and lacrosse.

Disabled Students: 82% of the campus is accessible. Wheelchair ramps, elevators, special parking, specially equipped rest rooms, special class scheduling, lowered drinking fountains, lowered telephones, and special door handles are available.

Services: Counseling and information services are available, as is tutoring in most subjects. There is a reader service for the blind, and remedial math, reading, and writing.

Campus Safety and Security: Measures include 24-hour foot and vehicle patrol, escort service, shuttle buses, and informal discussions. There are pamphlets/posters/films, emergency telephones, lighted pathways/sidewalks, required programs during orientation for new students, and vehicle, bicycle, and foot patrol.

Programs of Study: UNH confers B.A. and B.S. degrees. Associate and master's degrees are also awarded. Bachelor's degrees are awarded in BIOLOGICAL SCIENCE (biology/biological science, biotechnology, and marine biology), BUSINESS (accounting, banking and finance, business administration and management, business economics, hotel/motel and restaurant management, international business management, marketing/retailing/merchandising, sports management, and tourism), COMMUNICATIONS AND THE ARTS (art, audio technology, communications, creative writing, English, graphic design, literature, music, and music business management), COMPUTER AND PHYSICAL SCIENCE (applied mathematics, chemistry, computer management, computer science, mathematics, and natural sciences), ENGINEERING AND ENVIRONMENTAL DESIGN (aviation administration/management, chemical engineering, civil engineering, computer engineering, electrical/electronics engineering, engineering, environmental science, fire protection engineering, industrial engineering, industrial engineering technology, interior design, materials science, mechanical engineering, and occupational safety and health), HEALTH PROFESSIONS (dental hygiene, predentistry, premedicine, and preveterinary science), SOCIAL SCIENCE (clinical psychology, community psychology, corrections, criminal justice, dietetics, fire control and safety technology, fire science, forensic studies, history, law enforcement and corrections, liberal arts/general studies, political science/government, and psychology). Criminal justice, business administration, and fire protection are the strongest academically. Business and marketing, criminal justice, and engineering are the largest.

Required: To graduate, all students must maintain a GPA of 2.0, pass a writing proficiency exam, and complete a total of 120 to 136 credits, depending on the major. Students must complete the Freshman Experience Seminar and take at least 34 credits from the university core curriculum, including a total of 19 in lab science, social sciences, history, literature or philosophy, and art, music, or theater, 6 in communication skills, and 3 each in quantitative skills, computers, and scientific methodology.

Special: UNH offers co-op programs in most majors, internships, work-study programs, student-designed majors in the School of Professional Studies, interdisciplinary majors including biomedical computing, B.A.-B.S. degrees, a 5-year B.S.-M.S. program in environmental science, and nondegree study. Study-abroad programs are available. There are 5 national honor societies, a freshman honors program, and all departments have honors programs.

Faculty/Classroom: 71% of faculty are male; 29%, female. 84% teach undergraduates. No introductory courses are taught by graduate students.

Admissions: 76% of the 2001-2002 applicants were accepted. The SAT I scores for the 2001-2002 freshman class were: Verbal--55% below 500, 35% between 500 and 599, 9% between 600 and 700, and 1% above 700; Math--57% below 500, 35% between 500 and 599, 7% between 600 and 700, and 1% above 700. 22% of the current freshmen were in the top fifth of their class; 44% were in the top two fifths. 3 freshmen graduated first in their class in a recent year.

Requirements: The SAT I or ACT is required. The SAT I is preferred, with a minimum combined score of 900. The GED is accepted. In addition, applicants should be graduates of an accredited secondary school. An interview is recommended. A letter of recommendation is required along with a personal essay. A GPA of 2.0 is required. AP and CLEP credits are accepted. Applications are accepted on-line.

Procedure: Freshmen are admitted fall and spring. Entrance exams should be taken in the fall or winter of the senior year. There is a deferred admissions plan. Application deadlines are open. The fall 2001 application fee was $25. Notification is sent on a rolling basis.

Transfer: 142 transfer students enrolled in 2001-2002. Applicants should have a minimum college GPA of 2.0 and should submit all official transcripts. An interview is recommended, and the SAT I is required for students with fewer than 30 college credits. 30 credits of 120 to 136 must be completed at UNH.

Visiting: There are regularly scheduled orientations for prospective students, including daily information sessions, Open House, Accepted Student Days, and Junior Open House. There are guides for informal visits and visitors may sit in on classes and stay overnight. To schedule a visit, contact the Admissions Office at (800) 342-5864, ext. 7319.

Financial Aid: In 2001-2002, 81% of all freshmen and 73% of continuing students received some form of financial aid. 76% of freshmen and 68% of continuing students received need-based aid. The average freshman award was $12,315. Of that total, scholarships or need-based grants averaged $6716 ($24,407 maximum); loans averaged $6023 ($6625 maximum); and work contracts averaged $270 ($1500 maximum). 15% of undergraduates work part time. Average annual earnings from campus work are $882. The average financial indebtedness of the 2001 graduate was $16,868. UNH is a member of CSS. The FAFSA, the college's own financial statement, and the student's and parents' 1040 tax forms are required. The fall application deadline is March 15.

International Students: The school actively recruits these students. They must score 520 on the written TOEFL or 190 on the electronic version. English-speaking students may submit the SAT I or ACT scores instead.

Computers: The mainframe is a DEC ALPHA. There are 600 PCs located in the computer center, the library, and academic and administrative buildings. All students may access the system 24 hours a day. There are no time limits and no fees.

Graduates: In 2001, 388 bachelor's degrees were awarded. The most popular majors were criminal justice/law enforcement (19%), business administration (10%), and fire science (9%). In an average class, 40% graduate in 6 years. Of the 2000 graduating class, 5% were enrolled in graduate school within 6 months of graduation and 94% were employed.

Admissions Contact: Jane Sangeloty, Director of Undergraduate Admissions and Financial Aid. E-mail: *adminfo@charger.newhaven.edu*
Web: *http://www.newhaven.edu*

WESLEYAN UNIVERSITY
Middletown, CT 06459-4890

C-3
(860) 685-3000
Fax: (860) 685-3001

Full-time: 1312 men, 1464 women	**Faculty:** 313; IIA, ++$
Part-time: 10 men, 6 women	**Ph.D.s:** 93%
Graduate: 166 men, 279 women	**Student/Faculty:** 9 to 1
Year: semesters	**Tuition:** $27,100
Application Deadline: January 1	**Room & Board:** $6950
Freshman Class: 7014 applied, 1796 accepted, 725 enrolled	
SAT I Verbal/Math: 690/690	**ACT:** 29 **MOST COMPETITIVE**

Wesleyan University, founded in 1831, is an independent institution offering programs in the liberal arts and sciences. The 4 libraries contain 1,161,832 volumes, 271,721 microform items, and 18,655 audiovisual forms/CDs, and subscribe to 3167 periodicals. Computerized library services include the card catalog, interlibrary loans, and database searching. Special learning facilities include a learning resource center, art gallery, radio station, and an observatory. The 120-acre campus is in a suburban area 15 miles south of Hartford, and 2 hours from both Boston and New York City. Including residence halls, there are 90 buildings.

Student Life: 84% of undergraduates are from out of state, mostly the Northeast. Others are from 49 states, 46 foreign countries, and Canada. 56% are from public schools. 64% are white. 20% are Jewish; 15% Catholic. The average age of freshmen is 19; all undergraduates, 20. 3% do not continue beyond their first year; 88% remain to graduate.

Housing: 2600 students can be accommodated in college housing, which includes single-sex and coed dormitories, on-campus apartments, off-campus apartments, married-student housing, and fraternity houses. In addition, there are language houses and special-interest houses. On-campus housing is guaranteed for all 4 years. 93% of students live on campus; of those, 95% remain on campus on weekends. All students may keep cars.

Activities: 5% of men and about 3% of women belong to 2 local and 5 national fraternities; 1% of women belong to 2 local sororities. There are 150 groups on campus, including art, band, cheerleading, chess, choir, chorale, chorus, computers, dance, debate, drama, ethnic, film, gay, honors, international, jazz band, literary magazine, musical theater, newspaper, opera, orchestra, pep band, photography, political, professional, radio and TV, religious, social, social service, student government, symphony, and yearbook. Popular campus events include Fall Ball and Spring Fling.

Sports: There are 15 intercollegiate sports for men and 14 for women, and 16 intramural sports for men and 16 for women. Facilities include a 5000-seat stadium, a 3000-seat gym, a 50-meter Olympic-size pool, a 400-meter outdoor track, a 200-meter indoor track, a hockey arena, a strength and fitness center, 16 tennis courts, 14 squash courts, 4 soccer fields, 2 football practice fields, 2 rugby pitches, a boat house, and field hockey, ultimate Frisbee, baseball, and softball fields.

Disabled Students: 25% of the campus is accessible. Wheelchair ramps, elevators, special parking, specially equipped rest rooms, special class scheduling, lowered drinking fountains, and lowered telephones are available.

Services: Counseling and information services are available, as is tutoring in most subjects. There is remedial math and writing.

Campus Safety and Security: Measures include 24-hour foot and vehicle patrol, self-defense education, escort service, and shuttle buses. There are informal discussions, pamphlets/posters/films, emergency telephones, and lighted pathways/sidewalks.

Programs of Study: Wesleyan confers the B.A. degree. Master's and doctoral degrees are also awarded. Bachelor's degrees are awarded in BIOLOGICAL SCIENCE (biochemistry, biology/biological science, molecular biology, and neurosciences), COMMUNICATIONS AND THE ARTS (art history and appreciation, classics, dance, dramatic arts, English, film arts, French, German, Italian, music, romance languages and literature, Russian, Spanish, and studio art), COMPUTER AND PHYSICAL SCIENCE (astronomy, chemistry, computer science, earth science, mathematics, physics, and science technology), SOCIAL SCIENCE (African American studies, American studies, anthropology, archeology, Asian/Oriental studies, classical/ancient civilization, economics, French studies, history, Latin American studies, medieval studies, philosophy, political science/government, psychology, religion, Russian and Slavic studies, sociology, and women's studies). Sciences, economics, and history are the strongest academically. English, government, and history are the largest.

Required: To graduate, all students must complete 128 credit hours. Distribution requirements include 3 courses each in humanities and arts, social and behavioral sciences, and natural science and math. A minimum academic average of 74 must be maintained, with at least 6 semesters of full-time residency.

Special: Wesleyan offers exchange programs with 11 northeastern colleges, cross-registration with 2 area colleges, study abroad in 41 countries on 6 continents, internships, a Washington semester, dual and student-designed majors, and pass/fail options. 3-2 engineering programs with Cal Tech and Columbia University are also available. There are 2 national honor societies, including Phi Beta Kappa, and 40 departmental honors programs.

Faculty/Classroom: 60% of faculty are male; 40%, female. All both teach undergraduates and do research. No introductory courses are taught by graduate students. The average class size in an introductory lecture is 40; in a laboratory, 15; and in a regular course, 24.

Admissions: 26% of the 2001-2002 applicants were accepted. The SAT I scores for the 2001-2002 freshman class were: Verbal--2% below 500, 13% between 500 and 599, 37% between 600 and 700, and 48% above 700; Math--2% below 500, 9% between 500 and 599, 45% between 600 and 700, and 44% above 700. 91% of the current freshmen were in the top fifth of their class; 97% were in the top two fifths. There were 67 National Merit semifinalists. 44 freshmen graduated first in their class.

Requirements: The SAT I or ACT is required, as are SAT II: Subject tests in writing and 2 other subjects. In addition, applicants should have 20 academic credits, including 4 years each of English, foreign language, math, science, and social studies. An essay is necessary. AP credits are accepted. Important factors in the admissions decision are advanced placement or honor courses, recommendations by school officials, and leadership record. Applications are accepted on-line via *Commonapp.org*, Next Stop College, *Embark.com*, Apply!, or CollegeLink.

Procedure: Freshmen are admitted in the fall. Entrance exams should be taken in the spring of the junior year and fall of the senior year. There are early decision and deferred admissions plans. Early decision applications should be filed by November 15; regular applications, by January 1 for fall entry. Notification of early decision is sent December 15; regular decision, April 1. The fall 2001 application fee was $35. 285 early decision candidates were accepted for the 2001-2002 class. A waiting list is an active part of the admissions procedure.

Transfer: 67 transfer students enrolled in 2001-2002. Applicants need a strong academic record and scores submitted from either the SAT I or ACT. An interview is recommended.

Visiting: There are regularly scheduled orientations for prospective students, including 1-hour long campus tours and group information sessions. There are guides for informal visits and visitors may sit in on classes and stay overnight. To schedule a visit, contact the Admissions Office.

Financial Aid: In 2001-2002, 44% of all freshmen and 47% of continuing students received some form of financial aid, including need-based aid. The average freshman award was $23,741. Of that total, scholarships or need-based grants averaged $19,258; loans averaged $2774; and work contracts averaged $1709. 85% of undergraduates work part time. Average annual earnings from campus work are $1100. The average financial indebtedness of the 2001 graduate was $23,323. Wesleyan is a member of CSS. The CSS/Profile or FAFSA is required. The fall application deadline is February 1.

International Students: The school actively recruits these students. They must score 600 on the written TOEFL and also take the SAT I or the ACT. Students must take SAT II: Subject tests in writing and 2 other areas.

Computers: The mainframes are a DEC ALPHA and a Sun UltraSPARC. More than 150 PCs and Macs are connected to the mainframe at various campus locations. Students use a variety of public servers for e-mail, web access, and other applications. Software for word processing and statistical analysis is also available. All students may access the system. There are no time limits. The fee is $10 per month for dorm connectivity. It is strongly recommended that all students have a personal computer.

Graduates: In 2001, 724 bachelor's degrees were awarded. The most popular majors were social sciences/history (31%), visual and performing arts (13%), and area and ethnic studies (12%). In an average class, 1% graduate in 3 years, 82% in 4 years, 87% in 5 years, and 88% in 6 years. 60 companies recruited on campus in 2000-2001.

Admissions Contact: Nancy Hargrave-Meislahn, Dean of Admissions and Financial Aid. E-mail: *admissions@wesleyan.edu*

WESTERN CONNECTICUT STATE UNIVERSITY — A-3

Danbury, CT 06810-6855 — **(203) 837-9000; (877) 837-9278**

Full-time: 1713 men, 1870 women	**Faculty:** 189; IIA, +$
Part-time: 653 men, 844 women	**Ph.D.s:** 80%
Graduate: 264 men, 574 women	**Student/Faculty:** 19 to 1
Year: semesters, summer session	**Tuition:** $4116 ($10,089)
Application Deadline: open	**Room & Board:** $5958
Freshman Class: 2856 applied, 1907 accepted, 848 enrolled	
SAT I Verbal/Math: 480/480	**COMPETITIVE**

Western Connecticut State University, founded in 1903, is a public institution offering programs in business, arts and sciences, and professional studies. It is part of the Connecticut State University system. There are 3 undergraduate schools and 1 graduate school. In addition to regional accreditation, West Conn has baccalaureate program accreditation with CSWE and NLN. The 2 libraries contain 182,915 volumes, 471,099 microform items, and 8654 audiovisual forms/CDs, and subscribe to 1273 periodicals. Computerized library services include the card catalog, interlibrary loans, and database searching. Special learning facilities include a learning resource center, art gallery, radio station, observatory, electron microscope, and photography studio. The 346-acre campus is in a suburban area 65 miles north of New York City. Including residence halls, there are 19 buildings.

Student Life: 89% of undergraduates are from Connecticut. Others are from 22 states, 21 foreign countries, and Canada. 91% are from public schools. 82% are white. The average age of freshmen is 19; all undergraduates, 23. 30% do not continue beyond their first year.

Housing: 1264 students can be accommodated in college housing, which includes single-sex and coed dormitories and on-campus apartments. On-campus housing is guaranteed for all 4 years. 68% of students commute. All students may keep cars.

Activities: 3% of men belong to 3 national fraternities; 2% of women belong to 3 local and 2 national sororities. There are 50 groups on campus, including art, band, cheerleading, chess, choir, chorale, chorus, computers, dance, drama, ethnic, film, gay, honors, international, jazz band, literary magazine, musical theater, newspaper, opera, orchestra, photography, political, professional, radio and TV, religious, social, social service, student government, and yearbook. Popular campus events include West Fest, Midnight Breakfast, and Student Leadership Banquet.

Sports: There are 5 intercollegiate sports for men and 8 for women, and 6 intramural sports for men and 5 for women. Facilities include 2 gyms, a weight training area, 4 tennis courts, 5 playing fields, an indoor swimming pool, and a field house with an indoor running track.

Disabled Students: 95% of the campus is accessible. Wheelchair ramps, elevators, special parking, specially equipped rest rooms, special class scheduling, lowered drinking fountains, and lowered telephones are available.

Services: Counseling and information services are available, as is tutoring in some subjects. There is a reader service for the blind, and remedial math, reading, and writing, and a computer science clinic.

Campus Safety and Security: Measures include 24-hour foot and vehicle patrol, escort service, shuttle buses, and informal discussions. There are pamphlets/posters/films, emergency telephones, and lighted pathways/sidewalks.

Programs of Study: West Conn confers B.A., B.S., B.B.A., and B. Music degrees. Associate and master's degrees are also awarded. Bachelor's degrees are awarded in BIOLOGICAL SCIENCE (biology/biological science), BUSINESS (accounting, banking and finance, business administration and management, management information systems, and marketing management), COMMUNICATIONS AND THE ARTS (art, communications, dramatic arts, English, graphic design, illustration, music, music performance, photography, Spanish, and studio art), COMPUTER AND PHYSICAL SCIENCE (atmospheric sciences and meteorology, chemistry, computer mathematics, computer science, earth science, and mathematics), EDUCATION (elementary, health, music, and secondary), ENGINEERING AND ENVIRONMENTAL DESIGN (environmental science), HEALTH PROFESSIONS (community health work, medical laboratory technology, and nursing), SOCIAL SCIENCE (American studies, anthropology, criminal justice, economics, history, law enforcement and corrections, paralegal studies, political science/government, psychology, social science, social work, and sociology). Education, business, and justice and law administration are the largest.

Required: To graduate, students must complete 122 credit hours, with a minimum GPA of 2.0 or higher for some programs. All students must also fulfill the general education distribution requirements, including phys ed, and the foreign language requirement.

Special: The university offers co-op programs with local corporations and the New England Regional Student Program. Student-designed majors, dual majors, study abroad, and pass/fail options are available. Nondegree study is offered at the University Center for Adult Education. There are 7 national honor societies, a freshman honors program, and 2 departmental honors programs.

Faculty/Classroom: 61% of faculty are male; 39%, female. All teach undergraduates, 25% do research, and 25% do both. No introductory courses are taught by graduate students. The average class size in an introductory lecture is 38; in a laboratory, 17; and in a regular course, 23.

Admissions: 67% of the 2001-2002 applicants were accepted. The SAT I scores for the 2001-2002 freshman class were: Verbal--60% below 500, 34% between 500 and 599, and 6% between 600 and 700; Math--60% below 500, 32% between 500 and 599, 7% between 600 and 700, and 1% above 700. 9% of the current freshmen were in the top fifth of their class; 35% were in the top two fifths.

Requirements: The SAT I is required. The ACT is accepted in lieu of SAT I scores. Applicants must be graduates of an accredited secondary school. The GED is accepted. Students should have completed 13 high school academic credits, including 4 in English, 3 in math, 2 to 3 in foreign language, 2 in science, and 1 each in history and social studies. Additional credits in art, music, and computer science are highly recommended. An essay and an interview are recommended. A GPA of 2.5 is required. AP and CLEP credits are accepted. Important factors in the admissions decision are advanced placement or honor courses, evidence of special talent, and recommendations by school officials. Applications are accepted on-line at *www.wcsu.edu/admissions/ugrad.asp*

Procedure: Freshmen are admitted fall and spring. Entrance exams should be taken by December of the senior year. There is a deferred admissions plan. Application deadlines are open. The application fee is $40. Notification is sent December 15.

Transfer: 358 transfer students enrolled in 2001-2002. Transfers must have a minimum of 12 college credits. Applicants must have a cumulative GPA of 2.0 for all college course work. A higher GPA is required for some programs. 30 credits of 122 must be completed at West Conn.

Visiting: There are regularly scheduled orientations for prospective students, including campus tours on weekdays when classes are in session. There is an Open House on a Sunday in early November. There are guides for informal visits and visitors may sit in on classes. To schedule a visit, contact the Office of Admissions.

Financial Aid: In 2001-2002, 56% of all freshmen and 55% of continuing students received some form of financial aid. 44% of freshmen and 40% of continuing students received need-based aid. The average freshman award was $6255. Of that total, scholarships or need-based grants averaged $2886 ($11,850 maximum); loans averaged $3109 ($15,042 maximum); work contracts averaged $230 ($9168 maximum); and tuition waivers averaged $30 ($2142 maximum). 93% of undergraduates work part time. Average annual earnings from campus work are $2345. The FAFSA and the college's own financial statement are required. The fall application deadline is March 15.

International Students: There are 32 international students enrolled. They must score 550 on the written TOEFL or 213 on the electronic version and also take the SAT I or the ACT.

Computers: 400 IBM and Mac PCs are available for student use in various campus locations. All students may access the system at any time. There are no time limits and no fees.

Graduates: In 2001, 605 bachelor's degrees were awarded. The most popular majors were business (28%), education (11%), and justice and law (9%). In an average class, 1% graduate in 3 years, 19% in 4 years, 36% in 5 years, and 41% in 6 years. 108 companies recruited on campus in 2000-2001. Of the 2000 graduating class, 24% were enrolled in graduate school within 6 months of graduation and 92% were employed.

Admissions Contact: William Hawkins, Director of University Admissions/Enrollment Planning. A video is available.
Web: *www.wcsu.edu/admissions*

YALE UNIVERSITY C-3

New Haven, CT 06520-8234 **(203) 432-9316**
Fax: (203) 432-9392

Full-time: 2661 men, 2592 women | **Faculty:** 1792; I, +$
Part-time: none | **Ph.D.s:** 96%
Graduate: 2267 men, 2218 women | **Student/Faculty:** 3 to 1
Year: semesters, summer session | **Tuition:** $26,100
Application Deadline: December 31 | **Room & Board:** $7930
Freshman Class: 14,809 applied, 2038 accepted, 1297 enrolled
SAT I or ACT: required **MOST COMPETITIVE**

Yale University, founded in 1701, is a private liberal arts institution. In addition to regional accreditation, Yale has baccalaureate program accreditation with ABET, CAHEA, NAAB, NASM, NLN, and SAF. The 43 libraries contain 182,263 audiovisual forms/CDs, and subscribe to 57,377 periodicals. Computerized library services include the card catalog, interlibrary loans, and database searching. Special learning facilities include an art gallery, natural history museum, planetarium, radio station, Beinecke Rare Books and Manuscript Library, Marsh Botanical Gardens and Yale Natural Preserves, and several research centers. The 200-acre campus is in an urban area 75 miles northeast of New York City. Including residence halls, there are 200 buildings.

Student Life: 90% of undergraduates are from out of state, mostly the Middle Atlantic. Others are from 49 states, 74 foreign countries, and Canada. 60% are from public schools. 67% are white; 16% Asian American. The average age of freshmen is 18; all undergraduates, 20. 2% do not continue beyond their first year; 98% remain to graduate.

Housing: 4690 students can be accommodated in college housing, which includes coed dormitories and on-campus apartments. On-campus housing is guaranteed for the freshman year only and is available on a lottery system for upperclassmen. 84% of students live on campus. All students may keep cars.

Activities: There are 300 groups on campus, including art, band, cheerleading, chess, choir, chorale, chorus, computers, dance, debate, drama, ethnic, film, gay, honors, international, jazz band, literary magazine, marching band, musical theater, newspaper, opera, orchestra, pep band, photography, political, professional, radio and TV, religious, social, social service, student government, symphony, and yearbook. Popular campus events include Communiversity Day, fall and spring concerts, and the East/West Film Festival.

Sports: There are 16 intercollegiate sports for men and 17 for women, and 25 intramural sports for men and 21 for women. Facilities include the 71000-seat Yale Bowl, a sports complex, a gym, a swimming pool, a skating rink, a sailing center, an equestrian center, and golf courses.

Disabled Students: Wheelchair ramps, elevators, special parking, specially equipped rest rooms, special class scheduling, lowered drinking fountains, lowered telephones, and door-to-door lift-van service are available.

Services: Counseling and information services are available, as is tutoring in every subject. There is a reader service for the blind.

Campus Safety and Security: Measures include 24-hour foot and vehicle patrol, self-defense education, escort service, and shuttle buses. There are informal discussions, pamphlets/posters/films, emergency telephones, and lighted pathways/sidewalks.

Programs of Study: Yale confers B.A., B.S., and B.L.S. degrees. Master's and doctoral degrees are also awarded. Bachelor's degrees are awarded in BIOLOGICAL SCIENCE (biochemistry, biology/biological science, and biophysics), COMMUNICATIONS AND THE ARTS (art, art history and appreciation, Chinese, classics, comparative literature, dramatic arts, English, film arts, French, German, Italian, Japanese, linguistics, literature, music, Portuguese, Russian, Spanish, and theater management), COMPUTER AND PHYSICAL SCIENCE (applied mathematics, astronomy, chemistry, computer science, geology, mathematics, and physics), ENGINEERING AND ENVIRONMENTAL DESIGN (architecture, biomedical engineering, chemical engineering, electrical/electronics engineering, engineering, engineering and applied science, and mechanical engineering), SOCIAL SCIENCE (African American studies, American studies, anthropology, archeology, classical/ancient civilization, East Asian studies, Eastern European studies, economics, ethics, politics, and social policy, ethnic studies, German area studies, history, history of science, humanities, Judaic studies, Latin American studies, Near Eastern studies, philosophy, political science/government, psychology, religion, sociology, and women's studies). History, biology, and English are the largest.

Required: To graduate, students must complete 36 semester courses, including at least 3 courses in each of 4 distributional groups and at least 12 courses from outside the distributional group that includes their major. Foreign language proficiency must be demonstrated.

Special: The university offers study abroad in several countries including England, Russia, Germany, and Japan, an accelerated degree program, B.A.-B.S. degrees, dual majors, and student-designed majors. Directed Studies, a special freshman program in the humanities, offers outstanding students the opportunity to survey the Western cultural tradition. Programs in the residential colleges allow students with special interests to pursue them in a more informal atmosphere. There is a chapter of Phi Beta Kappa.

Faculty/Classroom: 69% of faculty are male; 31%, female.

Admissions: 14% of the 2001-2002 applicants were accepted.

Requirements: The SAT I or ACT is required. Only those applicants submitting SAT I scores must also take any 3 SAT II: Subject tests. Most successful applicants rank in the top 10% of their high school class. All students must have completed a rigorous high school program encompassing all academic disciplines. 2 essays are required and an interview is recommended. AP credits are accepted. Important factors in the admissions decision are advanced placement or honor courses, leadership record, and extracurricular activities record. Applications are accepted on-line through the College Board's ExPAN program only.

Procedure: Freshmen are admitted in the fall. Entrance exams should be taken any time up to and including the January test date in the year of application. There are early decision, early admissions, and deferred admissions plans. Early decision applications should be filed by November 1; regular applications, by December 31 for fall entry. Notification of early decision is sent mid-December; regular decision, April 1. 7% of all applicants are on a waiting list.

Transfer: 27 transfer students enrolled in 2001-2002. Applicants must take either the SAT I or ACT and have 1 full year of credit. An essay and 3 letters of recommendation are required. 18 courses of 36 must be completed at Yale.

Visiting: There are regularly scheduled orientations for prospective students. There are guides for informal visits and visitors may sit in on classes and stay overnight. To schedule a visit, contact the Admissions Office.

Financial Aid: In 2001-2002, 55% of all students received some form of financial aid. 38% of all students received need-based aid. The average freshman award was $17,430. Of that total, scholarships or need-based grants averaged $17,430; loans averaged $2870; and work contracts averaged $2000. Yale is a member of CSS. The CSS/Profile or FAFSA and student and parent tax returns, as well as the CSS Divorced/Separated Parents Statement and Business/Farm Supplement if applicable, are required. The fall application deadline is February 1.

International Students: The school actively recruits these students. They must score 600 on the written TOEFL and also take the SAT I and 3 SAT II: Subject tests, or the ACT.

Computers: The mainframes are a 2 IBM 4341s, 5 DEC 11/750s, and a DEC VAX 8600. There are also IBM PCs and Macs available in dorms, libraries, classrooms, and the computer center. All students may access the system 24 hours a day. There are no time limits and no fees. It is strongly recommended that all students have a personal computer.

Admissions Contact: Michael May, Assistant Director.
E-mail: *michael.may@yale.edu* Web: *www.yale.edu/admit*

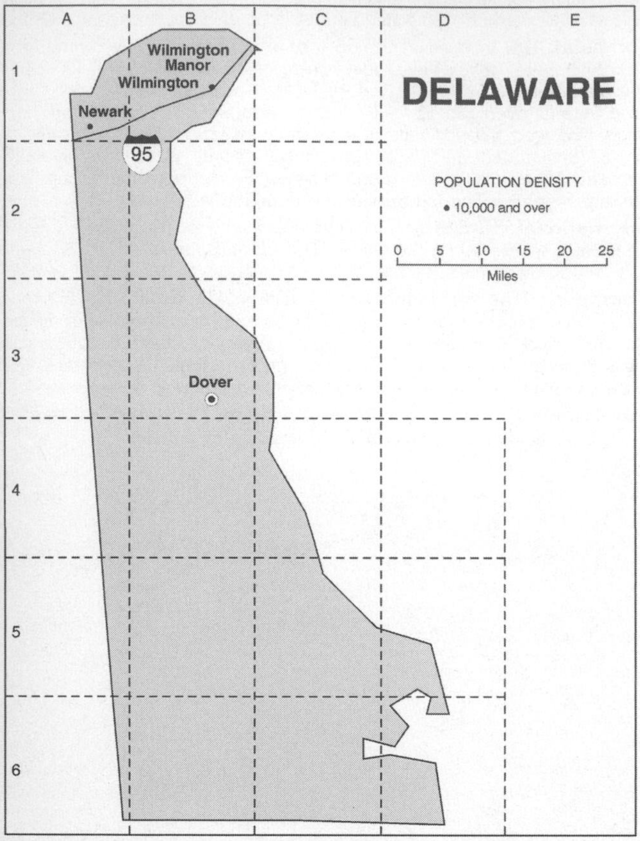

DELAWARE STATE UNIVERSITY

Dover, DE 19901 B-3 (302) 739-4917

Full-time: 970 men, 1300 women
Part-time: 240 men, 400 women
Graduate: 80 men, 170 women
Year: semesters, summer session
Application Deadline: June 1
Freshman Class: 1765 applied, 684 enrolled
SAT I or ACT: required
Faculty: 184; IIA, av$
Ph.D.s: 74%
Student/Faculty: 12 to 1
Tuition: $3414 ($7162)
Room & Board: $4690
LESS COMPETITIVE

Delaware State University, founded in 1891, is a publicly assisted institution offering programs in agricultural and technical fields, business, engineering, liberal and fine arts, health science, professional training, and teacher preparation. Figures in above capsule are approximate. There are 4 undergraduate schools and 1 graduate school. In addition to regional accreditation, DSU has baccalaureate program accreditation with ACBSP and NCATE. The library contains 201,550 volumes, 76,096 microform items, and 13,652 audiovisual forms/CDs, and subscribes to 3058 periodicals. Computerized library services include the card catalog, interlibrary loans, and database searching. Special learning facilities include a learning resource center, art gallery, planetarium, and radio station. The 400-acre campus is in a suburban area 45 miles south of Wilmington. Including residence halls, there are 31 buildings.

Student Life: 56% of undergraduates are from Delaware. Others are from 29 states, 40 foreign countries, and Canada. 90% are from public schools. 64% are African American; 32% white. 18% are claim no religious affiliation. The average age of freshmen is 18; all undergraduates, 21. 32% do not continue beyond their first year; 28% remain to graduate.

Housing: 1334 students can be accommodated in college housing, which includes single-sex dormitories. In addition, there are honors houses and an honors dorm. On-campus housing is available on a first-come, first-served basis. 54% of students commute. Alcohol is not permitted. All students may keep cars.

Activities: 50% of men belong to 4 national fraternities; 50% of women belong to 4 national sororities. There are 53 groups on campus, including cheerleading, choir, drama, ethnic, honors, international, jazz band, marching band, newspaper, pep band, radio and TV, religious, social service, student government, and yearbook. Popular campus events include Parent's Day, Annual Career Fair, and Annual Pride Day.

Sports: There are 8 intercollegiate sports for men and 7 for women, and 20 intramural sports for men and 20 for women. Facilities include an indoor swimming pool, a dance studio, racquetball and handball courts, 2 gyms, a football stadium, a baseball field, an outdoor track, and tennis courts.

Disabled Students: Wheelchair ramps, elevators, special parking, specially equipped rest rooms, and The Office of Disabilities Services provides assistance to students with all types of disabilities.

Services: Counseling and information services are available, as is tutoring in every subject, including remedial math, reading, and writing. A university tutoring program is available with a tutoring lab and tutorial service available in residence halls. A supplemental instruction program is available for challenging courses.

Campus Safety and Security: Measures include 24-hour foot and vehicle patrol, shuttle buses, informal discussions, and pamphlets/posters/films. There are emergency telephones and lighted pathways/sidewalks.

Programs of Study: DSU confers B.A., B.S., B.S.W., and B.Tech. degrees. Master's degrees are also awarded. Bachelor's degrees are awarded in AGRICULTURE (agricultural business management, fish and game management, and natural resource management), BIOLOGICAL SCIENCE (biology/biological science and botany), BUSINESS (accounting, business administration and management, fashion merchandising, hotel/motel and restaurant management, and marketing/retailing/merchandising), COMMUNICATIONS AND THE ARTS (English, French, journalism, music, and Spanish), COMPUTER AND PHYSICAL SCIENCE (chemistry, computer science, mathematics, and physics), EDUCATION (agricultural, art, business, early childhood, elementary, health, home economics, music, physical, science, and special), ENGINEERING AND ENVIRONMENTAL DESIGN (chemical engineering, civil engineering, electrical/electronics engineering, and mechanical engineering), HEALTH PROFESSIONS (community health work, environmental health science, and nursing), SOCIAL SCIENCE (economics, history, parks and recreation management, political science/government, psychology, social work, and sociology). Education is the strongest academically. Business administration, education, and English and mass communications are the largest.

Required: 52 hours of general education requirements must be completed, distributed as follows: 16 hours of core courses, 3 hours of arts and humanities, 6 hours of foreign languages, 6 hours of literature, 6 hours of math, 6 hours of natural sciences, and a minimum 3-hour Senior Capstone Experience course. A total of 121 credit hours and a minimum GPA of 2.0 are required.

Special: The university offers accelerated degrees, combined B.A.-B.S. degrees, student-designed majors, and a 3-2 engineering program with the University of Delaware. Work-study is available on campus. There are assisted internships in airway science and nursing, and co-op programs in business, education, home economics, social work, and agriculture. There are 6 national honor societies, including Phi Beta Kappa, and a freshman honors program.

Faculty/Classroom: 61% of faculty are male; 39%, female. No introductory courses are taught by graduate students. The average class size in a regular course is 16.

Admissions: 6 freshmen graduated first in their class in a recent year.

Requirements: The SAT I or ACT is required. In addition, applicants should graduate from an accredited secondary school or have a GED. 16 academic credits are required, including 4 units of English and 3 of math, of which 2 must be in algebra and 1 must be in geometry, 3 of science courses with a lab, 2 of history and/or social studies, and 4 of electives, including foreign language or computer science courses. A GPA of 2.0 is required. CLEP credit is accepted. Important factors in the admissions decision are extracurricular activities record, advanced placement or honor courses, and recommendations by school officials.

Procedure: Freshmen are admitted fall and spring. Entrance exams should be taken in December or January of the senior year. There is an early admissions plan. Applications should be filed by June 1 for fall entry and December 1 for spring entry, along with a $10 fee. Notification is sent on a rolling basis.

Transfer: 145 transfer students enrolled in a recent year. Applicants must submit a statement of honorable withdrawal and high school and college transcripts. 30 credits of 121 must be completed at DSU.

Visiting: There are regularly scheduled orientations for prospective students, including a High School Day Program. There are guides for informal visits. To schedule a visit, contact Jethro Williams.

Financial Aid: In 2001-2002, 77% of all freshmen and 75% of continuing students received some form of financial aid. 72% of freshmen and 71% of continuing students received need-based aid. The average freshman award was $7047. Of that total, scholarships or need-based grants averaged $3713 ($17,278 maximum); loans averaged $7831 ($17,707 maximum); and work contracts averaged $2806 ($3640 maximum). 4% of undergraduates work part time. Average annual earnings from cam-

pus work are $2376. DSU is a member of CSS. The CSS/Profile or FFS is required. The fall application deadline is February 1.
International Students: They must score 500 on the written TOEFL and also take the SAT I or the ACT.
Computers: The mainframe is an IBM RS/6000. There are computer labs specifically for students, and students may also use terminals in the library. Students may access the university network from their own PC from residence halls. Applications include e-mail, Internet access, word processing, spreadsheets, graphics packages, and others. All students may access the system 24 hours a day. There are no time limits and no fees.
Graduates: In a recent year, 405 bachelor's degrees were awarded. The most popular majors were business administration (17%), education (14%), and accounting and finance (10%). In an average class, 10% graduate in 4 years, 24% in 5 years, and 28% in 6 years. Of the 2000 graduating class, 13% were enrolled in graduate school within 6 months of graduation and 62% were employed.
Admissions Contact: Jethro Williams, Admissions Director.
E-mail: *jwilliam@dsc.edu* Web: *www.dsc.edu*

GOLDEY-BEACOM COLLEGE — B-1
Wilmington, DE 19808 — (302) 998-8814
(800) 833-4877; Fax: (302) 996-5408

Full-time: 300 men, 440 women	**Faculty:** 24
Part-time: 230 men, 340 women	**Ph.D.s:** 49%
Graduate: 70 men, 70 women	**Student/Faculty:** 30 to 1
Year: semesters, summer session	**Tuition:** $7950
Application Deadline: open	**Room & Board:** $3490
Freshman Class: n/av	
SAT I: required	**COMPETITIVE**

Goldey-Beacom College, founded in 1886, is a private business college that provides undergraduate training and education for careers in business, industry, and government. There is 1 graduate school. Figures in the above capsule are approximate. In addition to regional accreditation, Goldey-Beacom College has baccalaureate program accreditation with AACSB and ACBSP. The library contains 48,000 volumes, 27,283 microform items, and 693 audiovisual forms/CDs, and subscribes to 800 periodicals. Computerized library services include interlibrary loans and database searching. Special learning facilities include a learning resource center. The 28-acre campus is in a suburban area 10 miles west of Wilmington. Including residence halls, there are 8 buildings.
Student Life: 60% of undergraduates are from Delaware. Others are from 22 states, 50 foreign countries, and Canada. 75% are from public schools. 81% are white; 10% African American. The average age of freshmen is 19; all undergraduates, 21. 30% do not continue beyond their first year; 70% remain to graduate.
Housing: 300 students can be accommodated in college housing, which includes coed on-campus apartments. In addition, there are special-interest houses. On-campus housing is guaranteed for all 4 years. 80% of students commute. All students may keep cars.
Activities: 10% of men belong to 2 national fraternities; 10% of women belong to 2 national sororities. There are 23 groups on campus, including cheerleading, chorus, computers, drama, ethnic, honors, international, literary magazine, newspaper, professional, religious, social service, and student government. Popular campus events include Goldey-Beacom Follies, Spring Fest, and International Night.
Sports: Facilities include soccer and softball fields, and tennis, basketball, and handball courts.
Disabled Students: All of the campus is accessible. Wheelchair ramps, elevators, special parking, specially equipped rest rooms, lowered drinking fountains, and lowered telephones are available.
Services: Counseling and information services are available, as is tutoring in most subjects. There is a reader service for the blind, and remedial math, reading, and writing. and computer-based tutorials.
Campus Safety and Security: Measures include 24-hour foot and vehicle patrol, self-defense education, informal discussions, and pamphlets/posters/films. There are lighted pathways/sidewalks and security from 6 P.M. to 6 A.M. on the small campus.
Programs of Study: Goldey-Beacom College confers the B.S. degree. Associate and master's degrees are also awarded. Bachelor's degrees are awarded in BUSINESS (accounting, banking and finance, international business management, and marketing/retailing/merchandising), COMPUTER AND PHYSICAL SCIENCE (computer programming). Accounting and computer science are the strongest academically. Accounting and management are the largest.
Required: To graduate, students must complete a minimum of 136 credit hours with an overall GPA of 2.0. Students must also fulfill the college's core requirements in English, math, and computer science.
Special: Co-op programs in all majors, an accelerated degree program, a 5-year advanced business degree, dual majors, internships, study abroad, and work-study programs are available. There is 1 national honor society, a freshman honors program, and 3 departmental honors programs.
Faculty/Classroom: 66% of faculty are male; 34%, female. All teach undergraduates. No introductory courses are taught by graduate students. The average class size in an introductory lecture is 35 and in a regular course, 25.
Requirements: The SAT I is required. In addition, applicants must be high school graduates or have a GED. A GPA of 2.0 is required. AP and CLEP credits are accepted. Important factors in the admissions decision are leadership record, evidence of special talent, and recommendations by school officials.
Procedure: Freshmen are admitted to all sessions. There are early admissions and deferred admissions plans. Application deadlines are open. The application fee is $30.
Transfer: 67 transfer students enrolled in a recent year. Transfer applicants must submit high school and college transcripts. 65 credits of 136 must be completed at Goldey-Beacom College.
Visiting: There are regularly scheduled orientations for prospective students, including an open house. There are guides for informal visits and visitors may sit in on classes and stay overnight. To schedule a visit, contact the Admissions Office.
Financial Aid: In a recent year, 70% of all students received some form of financial aid. 80% of freshmen and 60% of continuing students received need-based aid. The average freshman award was $4180. Of that total, scholarships or need-based grants averaged $1580 ($5875 maximum); and loans averaged $2600 ($6625 maximum). 90% of undergraduates work part time. Average annual earnings from campus work are $1200. Goldey-Beacom College is a member of CSS. The FAFSA is required. Check with the school for current deadlines.
International Students: There are 145 international students enrolled. The school actively recruits these students. They must score 500 on the written TOEFL.
Computers: The mainframes are an IBM Series 4361 and a VM/SP Release 5. The college's 4 computer labs contain more than 160 IBM PS/2 Model 50 terminals. Modems may access the mainframe from off campus 24 hours a day. There are no fees.
Graduates: In a recent year, 180 bachelor's degrees were awarded. The most popular majors were management (33%) and accounting (17%). In an average class, 30% graduate in 3 years, 40% in 4 years, 20% in 5 years, and 10% in 6 years. 70 companies recruited on campus in 2000-2001. Of the 2000 graduating class, 100% were employed within 6 months of graduation.
Admissions Contact: Kevin M. McIntyre, Director of Admissions and Associate Dean. A video is available.
E-mail: *mcintyrk@goldey.gbc.edu* Web: *www.goldey.gbc.edu*

UNIVERSITY OF DELAWARE — A-1
Newark, DE 19716 — (302) 831-8123; Fax: (302) 831-6905

Full-time: 6089 men, 8605 women	**Faculty:** 1098; I, av$
Part-time: 1170 men, 1567 women	**Ph.D.s:** 85%
Graduate: 1478 men, 1464 women	**Student/Faculty:** 13 to 1
Year: 4-1-4, summer session	**Tuition:** $5290 ($14,380)
Application Deadline: February 15	**Room & Board:** $5534
Freshman Class: 18,209 applied, 9581 accepted, 3379 enrolled	
SAT I Verbal/Math: 570/590	**VERY COMPETITIVE**

The University of Delaware, founded in 1743 and chartered in 1833, is a privately controlled, state-assisted institution, offering programs in agricultural and natural resources, liberal arts and sciences, business, education, human services, health and nursing sciences, and engineering. There are 6 undergraduate and 7 graduate schools. In addition to regional accreditation, Delaware has baccalaureate program accreditation with AACSB, ABET, ADA, APTA, CAHEA, NASDTEC, NASM, NCATE, and NLN. The 5 libraries contain 2,492,013 volumes, 3,251,844 microform items, and 13,856 audiovisual forms/CDs, and subscribe to 13,592 periodicals. Computerized library services include the card catalog, interlibrary loans, and database searching. Special learning facilities include a learning resource center, art gallery, radio station, TV station, preschool lab, development ice skating science center, computer-controlled greenhouse, nursing practice labs, physical therapy clinic, 400-acre agricultural research complex, exercise physiology biomechanics labs, foreign language media center, and composite materials center. The 1000-acre campus is in a small town 12 miles southwest of Wilmington; centered on the east coast between New York City and Washington, D.C., and Philadelphia and Baltimore. Including residence halls, there are 400 buildings.
Student Life: 59% of undergraduates are from out of state, mostly the Middle Atlantic. Others are from 50 states, 100 foreign countries, and Canada. 79% are from public schools. 87% are white. 34% are Catholic; 30% claim no religious affiliation; 23% Protestant; 10% Jewish. The average age of freshmen is 18; all undergraduates, 20. 12% do not continue beyond their first year; 70% remain to graduate.
Housing: 7100 students can be accommodated in college housing, which includes single-sex and coed dormitories, on-campus apartments, married-student housing, fraternity houses, and sorority houses. In addition, there are honors houses, language houses, and special-interest

houses, alcohol/smoke-free residence halls, and suites. On-campus housing is guaranteed for all 4 years. 50% of students live on campus; of those, 75% remain on campus on weekends. All students may keep cars.

Activities: 15% of men belong to 1 local fraternity and 17 national fraternities; 15% of women belong to 2 local and 14 national sororities. There are 203 groups on campus, including art, band, cheerleading, chess, choir, chorale, chorus, computers, dance, drama, drill team, ethnic, film, gay, honors, international, jazz band, literary magazine, marching band, musical theater, opera, orchestra, pep band, political, professional, radio and TV, religious, social, social service, student government, symphony, and yearbook. Popular campus events include Greek Week and Convocation Commencement, and Parents and Family Day.

Sports: There are 11 intercollegiate sports for men and 12 for women, and 15 intramural sports for men and 15 for women. Facilities include a 23,000-seat football stadium, 3 multipurpose gyms, 6 outdoor multipurpose fields, 8 outdoor basketball courts, 2 squash courts, 15 racquetball courts, 21 outdoor tennis courts, indoor and outdoor pools, a universal weight room, a 6000-seat basketball arena, a rock climbing wall, a high-ropes challenge course, 4 student fitness centers, a strength and conditioning room with free weights, outdoor and indoor tracks, softball, baseball, lacrosse, and soccer fields, 2 ice arenas, an outdoor hockey rink, and 4 wallyball courts.

Disabled Students: 95% of the campus is accessible. Wheelchair ramps, elevators, special parking, specially equipped rest rooms, special class scheduling, lowered drinking fountains, lowered telephones, and specially equipped residence hall rooms are available.

Services: Counseling and information services are available, as is tutoring in every subject. There is a reader service for the blind, and remedial math, reading, and writing. There is also a writing center, a math center, and an academic services center for assistance with academic self-management development, critical thinking, and problem solving and for individual assistance for students with learning-disabilities.

Campus Safety and Security: Measures include 24-hour foot and vehicle patrol, self-defense education, escort service, and shuttle buses. There are informal discussions, pamphlets/posters/films, emergency telephones, lighted pathways/sidewalks, ongoing student-awareness programs in the residence halls, community policing, and keycard access to residence halls.

Programs of Study: Delaware confers B.A., B.S., B.A. Liberal Studies, B.A.S., B.C.E., B.Ch.E., B.C.P.E., B.E.E., B.E.N.E., B.F.A., B.M.E., B.Mus., B.S.Acc., B.S.Ag., B.S.A.T., B.S.B.A., B.S.Ed., B.S.N., and B.S.P.E. degrees. Associate, master's, and doctoral degrees are also awarded. Bachelor's degrees are awarded in AGRICULTURE (agricultural business management, agricultural economics, agriculture, animal science, natural resource management, plant science, and soil science), BIOLOGICAL SCIENCE (biochemistry, biology/biological science, biotechnology, entomology, nutrition, and plant pathology), BUSINESS (accounting, banking and finance, business administration and management, hotel/motel and restaurant management, management science, marketing/retailing/merchandising, and recreation and leisure services), COMMUNICATIONS AND THE ARTS (art, art history and appreciation, communications, comparative literature, English, fine arts, historic preservation, Italian, journalism, languages, music, music theory and composition, and theater management), COMPUTER AND PHYSICAL SCIENCE (astronomy, chemistry, computer science, geology, geophysics and seismology, information sciences and systems, mathematics, and physics), EDUCATION (agricultural, athletic training, early childhood, education, elementary, English, foreign languages, mathematics, music, physical, psychology, science, secondary, and special), ENGINEERING AND ENVIRONMENTAL DESIGN (bioengineering, chemical engineering, civil engineering, computer engineering, electrical/electronics engineering, engineering technology, environmental engineering, environmental science, landscape architecture/design, and mechanical engineering), HEALTH PROFESSIONS (medical laboratory technology, and nursing), SOCIAL SCIENCE (anthropology, community services, consumer services, criminal justice, dietetics, economics, family and community services, fashion design and technology, food science, geography, history, human development, interdisciplinary studies, international relations, Latin American studies, parks and recreation management, philosophy, physical fitness/movement, political science/government, psychology, sociology, textiles and clothing, and women's studies). Engineering, all sciences, and business are the strongest academically. Biological sciences, elementary teacher education, engineering, psychology, and business are the largest.

Required: For graduation, students must complete at least 120 credits with a minimum GPA of 2.0. All students must take freshman English and 3 credits of course work with multicultural or multiethnic content. Most majors require more than 120 credits. Most degree programs require that half of the courses be in the major field of study.

Special: Students may participate in cooperative programs, internships, study abroad in 25 countries, a Washington semester, and work-study programs. The university offers accelerated degree programs, B.A.-B.S. degrees, dual majors, 68 minors, student-designed majors (Bachelor of Arts in Liberal Studies), and pass/fail options. There are 4-1 degree programs in engineering, and hotel and restaurant management. Nondegree study is available through the Division of Continuing Education. There is an extensive undergraduate research program. Students may earn an enriched degree through the University Honors Program. There are 37 national honor societies, including Phi Beta Kappa, a freshman honors program, and all departments have honors programs.

Faculty/Classroom: 63% of faculty are male; 37%, female. All teach undergraduates. Graduate students teach 5% of introductory courses. The average class size in a laboratory is 18 and in a regular course, 35.

Admissions: 53% of the 2001-2002 applicants were accepted. The SAT I scores for the 2001-2002 freshman class were: Verbal--13% below 500, 53% between 500 and 599, 30% between 600 and 700, and 4% above 700; Math--10% below 500, 43% between 500 and 599, 40% between 600 and 700, and 7% above 700. 50% of the current freshmen were in the top fifth of their class; 86% were in the top two fifths.

Requirements: The SAT I or ACT is required. In addition, applicants should be graduates of an accredited secondary school. The GED is accepted. Students should have completed a minimum of 16 high school academic credits, including 4 years of English, 2 years each of math, science, foreign language, and history, 1 year of social studies, and 3 years of academic course electives. SAT II: Subject tests are recommended, especially for honors program applicants. A writing sample and at least 1 letter of recommendation are required for all applicants. AP credits are accepted. Important factors in the admissions decision are advanced placement or honor courses, recommendations by school officials, and personality/intangible qualities. Applicants may apply on-line at *www.udel.edu/apply/*.

Procedure: Freshmen are admitted fall and spring. Entrance exams should be taken at the end of the junior year or the beginning of the senior year. There are early decision and deferred admissions plans. Early decision applications should be filed by November 15; regular applications, by February 15 for fall entry and November 15 for spring entry, along with a $55 fee. Notification of early decision is sent December 15; regular decision, mid-March. 491 early decision candidates were accepted for the 2001-2002 class. 6% of all applicants are on a waiting list; 45 were accepted in 2001.

Transfer: 602 transfer students enrolled in 2001-2002. Applicants for transfer should have completed at least 24 credits with a minimum GPA of 2.5 for most majors; some majors require a GPA of 3.0 or better and/or specific course work. 30 credits of a minimum of 120 must be completed at Delaware.

Visiting: There are regularly scheduled orientations for prospective students, consisting of a 30-minute admissions information session and a 90-minute walking tour of campus. There are guides for informal visits and visitors may sit in on classes. To schedule a visit, contact the Admissions Office.

Financial Aid: In 2001-2002, 70% of all freshmen and 64% of continuing students received some form of financial aid. 42% of freshmen and 35% of continuing students received need-based aid. The average freshman award was $5500. Of that total, scholarships or need-based grants averaged $4500 ($19,916 maximum); loans averaged $2625 ($4000 maximum); and work contracts averaged $1400 ($2500 maximum). 20% of undergraduates work part time. Average annual earnings from campus work are $1000. The average financial indebtedness of the 2001 graduate was $13,967. The FAFSA is required. The fall application deadline is March 15.

International Students: There are 140 international students enrolled. The school actively recruits these students. They must score 550 on the written TOEFL or 213 on the electronic version and also take the ELPT. The SAT I is recommended.

Computers: The mainframes consist of 2 IBM RS/6000-990, 1 Silicon Graphics Power Challenge, 1 Cray Research J916/8-1024, 2 Sun Microsystems Ultra Enterprise 4,000, and 1 Sun Microsystems Ultra Enterprise 5,000. 35 computing sites are available to students, offering more than 900 terminals, IBMs, PCs, and Macs. All residence hall rooms and many classrooms are equipped with data outlets for network connection. Those registered in computer courses or doing research that requires it may access the system 24 hours a day. There are no time limits and no fees.

Graduates: In 2001, 3192 bachelor's degrees were awarded. The most popular majors were elementary teacher education (6%), psychology (6%), and finance (5%). In an average class, 1% graduate in 3 years, 55% in 4 years, 70% in 5 years, and 72% in 6 years. More than 500 companies recruited on campus in 2000-2001. Of the 2000 graduating class, 20% were enrolled in graduate school within 6 months of graduation and 79% were employed.

Admissions Contact: Larry Griffith, Director of Admissions.
E-mail: *admissions@udel.edu* Web: *www.udel.edu*

WESLEY COLLEGE
B-3
Dover, DE 19901-3875
(302) 736-2400
(800) 937-5398; Fax: (302) 736-2301

Full-time: 497 men, 611 women
Faculty: 57; IIB, -$
Part-time: 138 men, 150 women
Ph.D.s: 75%
Graduate: 28 men, 58 women
Student/Faculty: 19 to 1
Year: semesters, summer session
Tuition: $12,419
Application Deadline: open
Room & Board: $5450
Freshman Class: 1628 applied, 1185 accepted, 447 enrolled
SAT I Verbal/Math: 464/461
COMPETITIVE

Wesley College, founded in 1873, is a private liberal arts institution affiliated with the United Methodist Church. In addition to regional accreditation, Wesley has baccalaureate program accreditation with ABA and NLN. The library contains 96,000 volumes, 15,103 microform items, and 3450 audiovisual forms/CDs, and subscribes to 450 periodicals. Computerized library services include interlibrary loans and database searching. Special learning facilities include a learning resource center and radio station. The 20-acre campus is in a small town 75 miles south of Philadelphia. Including residence halls, there are 20 buildings.

Student Life: 59% of undergraduates are from out of state, mostly the Middle Atlantic. Others are from 18 states and 9 foreign countries. 85% are from public schools. 77% are white; 18% African American. 61% are Protestant; 35% Catholic. The average age of freshmen is 18; all undergraduates, 20. 23% do not continue beyond their first year.

Housing: 620 students can be accommodated in college housing, which includes single-sex dormitories. On-campus housing is guaranteed for all 4 years and is available on a first-come, first-served basis. Priority is given to out-of-town students. 56% of students live on campus; of those, 30% remain on campus on weekends. Alcohol is not permitted. All students may keep cars.

Activities: 15% of men belong to 3 national fraternities; 15% of women belong to 3 local sororities. There are 25 groups on campus, including band, cheerleading, choir, chorale, chorus, computers, drama, ethnic, film, honors, international, jazz band, literary magazine, newspaper, photography, political, professional, radio and TV, religious, social, social service, student government, and yearbook. Popular campus events include Family Day, International Fair, and Spring Fling.

Sports: There are 7 intercollegiate sports for men and 7 for women, and 4 intramural sports for men and 4 for women. Facilities include a swimming pool, tennis courts, a football stadium, athletic fields, a gym, a game room, and an exercise room.

Disabled Students: 80% of the campus is accessible. Wheelchair ramps, elevators, special parking, specially equipped rest rooms, special class scheduling, and lowered drinking fountains are available.

Services: Counseling and information services are available, as is tutoring in every subject. There is remedial math, reading, and writing.

Campus Safety and Security: Measures include 24-hour foot and vehicle patrol, escort service, informal discussions, and pamphlets/posters/films. There are emergency telephones and lighted pathways/sidewalks.

Programs of Study: Wesley confers B.A. and B.S. degrees. Associate and master's degrees are also awarded. Bachelor's degrees are awarded in BIOLOGICAL SCIENCE (biology/biological science), BUSINESS (accounting, business administration and management, management science, and marketing/retailing/merchandising), COMMUNICATIONS AND THE ARTS (communications and English), EDUCATION (elementary, English, physical, secondary, and social studies), ENGINEERING AND ENVIRONMENTAL DESIGN (environmental science), HEALTH PROFESSIONS (medical laboratory technology), SOCIAL SCIENCE (American studies, history, liberal arts/general studies, paralegal studies, political science/government, and psychology). Biological science and accounting are the strongest academically. Management science, education, and psychology are the largest.

Required: For graduation, students must complete 124 credit hours, with at least 15 hours in the major and a minimum GPA of 2.0. 50 hours of core courses, including English, religion, science, math, American culture, non-American culture, and phys ed are required.

Special: Wesley offers internships in business and industry, nursing, environmental science, medical technology, and government agencies. Study abroad in 5 countries, work-study programs, dual majors, pass/fail options, and credit for life, military, and work experience are available. There are 2 national honor societies, and 1 departmental honors program.

Faculty/Classroom: 58% of faculty are male; 42%, female. All teach undergraduates, 3% do research, and 3% do both. No introductory courses are taught by graduate students. The average class size in an introductory lecture is 25; in a laboratory, 15; and in a regular course, 20.

Admissions: 73% of the 2001-2002 applicants were accepted. The SAT I scores for the 2001-2002 freshman class were: Verbal--69% below 500, 26% between 500 and 599, 4% between 600 and 700, and 1% above 700; Math--73% below 500, 23% between 500 and 599, and 4% between 600 and 700. 5 freshmen graduated first in their class.

Requirements: The SAT I is required. In addition, applicants must be graduates of an accredited secondary school; the GED is accepted. Students should have completed 12 academic credits or 16 Carnegie units, including 4 units of English and 2 units each of math, history, science, and social studies. An interview is recommended. Wesley requires applicants to be in the upper 80% of their class. A GPA of 2.0 is required. AP and CLEP credits are accepted. Important factors in the admissions decision are recommendations by school officials, extracurricular activities record, and leadership record. Applications are accepted on-line.

Procedure: Freshmen are admitted fall and winter. Entrance exams should be taken in the junior year. There are early decision and deferred admissions plans. Application deadlines are open. The application fee is $20. 20 early decision candidates were accepted for the 2001-2002 class. 10% of all applicants are on a waiting list; 2 were accepted in 2001.

Transfer: 35 transfer students enrolled in 2001-2002. Applicants must have a minimum GPA of 2.0 and a minimum composite SAT I score of 800. 36 credits of 124 must be completed at Wesley.

Visiting: There are regularly scheduled orientations for prospective students. There are guides for informal visits and visitors may sit in on classes and stay overnight. To schedule a visit, contact the Office of Admissions.

Financial Aid: In 2001-2002, 80% of all freshmen and 78% of continuing students received some form of financial aid. 80% of freshmen and 78% of continuing students received need-based aid. The average freshman award was $6500. Of that total, scholarships or need-based grants averaged $2500 ($4000 maximum); loans averaged $3000 ($6000 maximum); and work contracts averaged $1000 ($2000 maximum). 24% of undergraduates work part time. Average annual earnings from campus work are $1000. The average financial indebtedness of the 2001 graduate was $16,000. The FAFSA or SFS, and the college's own financial statement are required. The fall application deadline is April 15.

International Students: There are 20 international students enrolled. The school actively recruits these students. They must score 550 on the written TOEFL and also take the SAT I.

Computers: The mainframe may be accessed from more than 100 terminals across campus for use in word processing, programming, accounting, and statistics. PCs are available for student use in the writing center, computer center, and accounting lab. All students may access the system 24 hours a day, 7 days a week. There are no time limits and no fees. It is strongly recommended that all students have a personal computer.

Graduates: In 2001, 127 bachelor's degrees were awarded. The most popular majors were management (28%), education (20%), and psychology (17%). In an average class, 1% graduate in 3 years, 39% in 4 years, 48% in 5 years, and 48% in 6 years. 30 companies recruited on campus in 2000-2001. Of the 2000 graduating class, 16% were enrolled in graduate school within 6 months of graduation and 62% were employed.

Admissions Contact: Arthur Jacobs, Director of Admissions. A video is available. E-mail: *jacobsar@mail.wesley.edu* Web: *www.wesley.edu*

WILMINGTON COLLEGE
B-1
New Castle, DE 19720
(302) 328-9407
(877) 967-5464; Fax: (302) 328-5902

Full-time: 579 men, 1049 women
Faculty: 35; IIA, --$
Part-time: 586 men, 1258 women
Ph.D.s: 55%
Graduate: 632 men, 1513 women
Student/Faculty: 47 to 1
Year: semesters, summer session
Tuition: $6530
Application Deadline: open
Room & Board: n/app
Freshman Class: 551 applied, 545 accepted
SAT I Verbal/Math: 450/400
NONCOMPETITIVE

Wilmington College, founded in 1967, is a private, liberal arts commuter college offering admission to students from varied academic backgrounds. There are 5 undergraduate and 6 graduate schools. In addition to regional accreditation, Wilmington has baccalaureate program accreditation with NASDTEC and NLN. The library contains 112,000 volumes, 28,500 microform items, and 7000 audiovisual forms/CDs, and subscribes to 450 periodicals. Computerized library services include the card catalog, interlibrary loans, and database searching. Special learning facilities include a learning resource center, radio station, and TV station. The 18-acre campus is in an urban area 7 miles south of Wilmington. There are 18 buildings.

Student Life: 85% of undergraduates are from Delaware. Others are from 7 states, 5 foreign countries, and Canada. 85% are from public schools. 80% are white; 16% African American. The average age of freshmen is 21; all undergraduates, 27. 6% do not continue beyond their first year; 88% remain to graduate.

Housing: There are no residence halls. All of students commute. The college provides a list of housing accommodations in the community and makes recommendations for off-campus apartments. Alcohol is not permitted. All students may keep cars.

Activities: There are 1 national fraternity. There are no sororities. There are 11 groups on campus, including aviation, Business Professionals of America, cheerleading, film, honors, newspaper, photography, psychology, radio and TV, student government, and yearbook.

Sports: There are 2 intercollegiate sports for men and 3 for women, and 2 intramural sports for men and 3 for women. Facilities include a 1000-seat gym and a recreation room.

Disabled Students: All of the campus is accessible. Wheelchair ramps, elevators, special parking, specially equipped rest rooms, lowered drinking fountains, and lowered telephones are available.

Services: Counseling and information services are available, as is tutoring in some subjects, including math and English. There is remedial math and reading. Staff members also are available to assist students with study skills such as test taking, reading, concentration development, and time management.

Campus Safety and Security: Measures include 24-hour foot and vehicle patrol, escort service, emergency telephones, and lighted pathways/sidewalks.

Programs of Study: Wilmington confers B.A., B.S., and B.S.N. degrees. Associate, master's, and doctoral degrees are also awarded. Bachelor's degrees are awarded in BUSINESS (accounting, banking and finance, business administration and management, personnel management, and sports management), COMMUNICATIONS AND THE ARTS (media arts, multimedia, and video), EDUCATION (early childhood and elementary), ENGINEERING AND ENVIRONMENTAL DESIGN (aviation administration/management), HEALTH PROFESSIONS (nursing), SOCIAL SCIENCE (behavioral science and criminal justice). Nursing and elementary education are the strongest academically. Business, nursing, and elementary education are the largest.

Required: To graduate, students must complete a total of 120 hours with a minimum GPA of 2.0. 54 hours are required in the major. The 36-hour general studies core requirement includes 12 hours of social science, 9 each of English and humanities, and 3 each of math and science. At least 45 credit hours of upper-division course work are required, as is demonstrated competence in verbal and written communication and computational skills. At least 3 credits must be taken in computer operations. Nursing students must also submit official transcripts verifying graduation from a diploma or associate degree nursing program. Candidates for the B.S.N. degree must possess an R.N. license.

Special: The school offers practicums for education students, co-op programs, work-study programs with area employers, internships, a general studies degree, an accelerated degree program, dual majors, pass/fail options, credit for life experience, and by-challenge exam. There is 1 national honor society, and 2 departmental honors programs.

Faculty/Classroom: 70% of faculty are male; 30%, female. 66% teach undergraduates. The average class size in an introductory lecture is 25; in a laboratory, 10; and in a regular course, 17.

Admissions: 99% of the 2001-2002 applicants were accepted.

Requirements: Graduation from an accredited secondary school or satisfactory scores on the GED are required for admission. An interview may be required of some students, and an essay is recommended. A GPA of 2.0 is required. AP and CLEP credits are accepted. Important factors in the admissions decision are recommendations by school officials, advanced placement or honor courses, and ability to finance college education.

Procedure: Freshmen are admitted to all sessions. There is a deferred admissions plan. Application deadlines are open. The application fee is $25. Notification is sent on a rolling basis.

Transfer: 450 transfer students enrolled in a recent year. Applicants must have a 2.0 GPA; those with a lower GPA must have an interview. Some applicants may be required to submit SAT I or ACT scores. Those with fewer than 15 semester credits must submit high school transcripts. No more than 75 semester credits will be accepted for transfer credit. 45 credits of 120 must be completed at Wilmington.

Visiting: There are guides for informal visits and visitors may sit in on classes. To schedule a visit, contact the Admissions Office.

Financial Aid: The CSS/Profile or FFS is required. The fall application deadline is August 15.

International Students: There were 10 international students enrolled in a recent year. They must score 500 on the written TOEFL or they may submit a transcript of successful completion of at least 12 credit hours from a U.S. institution of higher education.

Computers: The mainframe is a DEC MicroVAX 3300. Macs, IBM models 25, PC, XT, and AT are available in the library and in the faculty study. Only students matriculated in communications technology majors may access the system during designated class/lab time. There are no time limits and no fees.

Graduates: In a recent year, 513 bachelor's degrees were awarded. The most popular majors were nursing (22%), human resources management (17%), and business management (17%). 10 companies recruited on campus in 2000-2001.

Admissions Contact: JoAnn Ciuffetelli, Assistant Director of Admissions. E-mail: *jciuf@wilmcoll.edu* Web: *www.wilmcoll.edu*

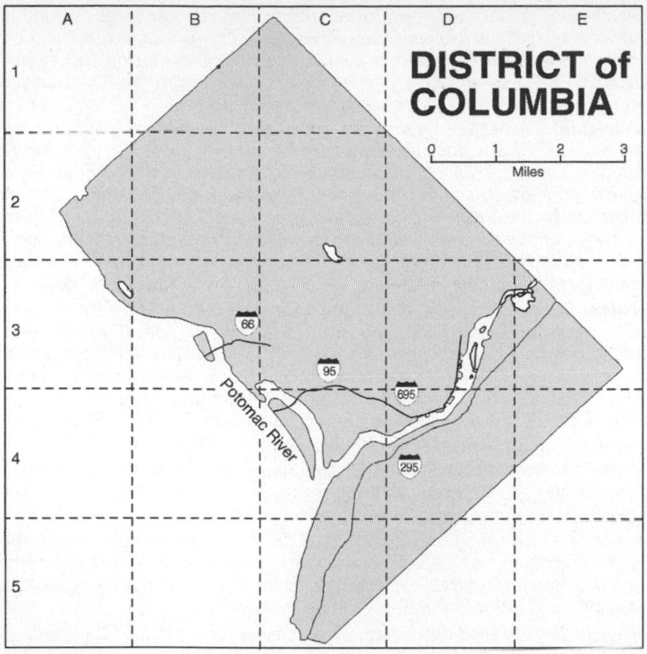

AMERICAN UNIVERSITY
Washington, DC 20016-8001

A-2
(202) 885-6000
Fax: (202) 885-1025

Full-time: 1952 men, 3203 women
Part-time: 125 men, 194 women
Graduate: 1850 men, 2867 women
Year: semesters, summer session
Application Deadline: February 1
Freshman Class: 10,177 applied, 7051 accepted, 1432 enrolled
SAT I Verbal/Math: 609/597
Faculty: 523; I, av$
Ph.D.s: 93%
Student/Faculty: 10 to 1
Tuition: $22,481
Room & Board: $9063
ACT: 26 **VERY COMPETITIVE+**

American University, founded in 1893, is an independent liberal arts institution affiliated with the United Methodist Church. There are 5 undergraduate and 6 graduate schools. In addition to regional accreditation, AU has baccalaureate program accreditation with AACSB, ACEJMC, ACS, NASDTEC, NASM, and NCATE. The library contains 743,000 volumes, 1,043,000 microform items, and 43,000 audiovisual forms/CDs, and subscribes to 3100 periodicals. Computerized library services include the card catalog, interlibrary loans, and database searching. Special learning facilities include a learning resource center, art gallery, radio station, TV station, language resource center, multimedia design and development lab, national center for health fitness, audiotechnology lab, broadcast newsroom, journalism center, and UNIX, intelligent systems, and Oracle development labs. The 78-acre campus is in a suburban area 5 miles northwest of downtown Washington D.C. Including residence halls, there are 37 buildings.

Student Life: 83% of undergraduates are from out of state, mostly the Middle Atlantic. Others are from 50 states, 153 foreign countries, and Canada. 61% are white; 11% foreign nationals. The average age of freshmen is 18; all undergraduates, 19. 14% do not continue beyond their first year; 66% remain to graduate.

Housing: 3500 students can be accommodated in college housing, which includes single-sex and coed dormitories and off-campus apartments. In addition, there is an international/intercultural hall, honors floors, special-interest floors, a wellness floor, and a community service floor. On-campus housing is guaranteed for the freshman year only, is available on a first-come, first-served basis, and is available on a lottery system for upperclassmen. 75% of students live on campus. Alcohol is not permitted. Upperclassmen may keep cars.

Activities: 14% of men belong to 11 national fraternities; 16% of women belong to 13 national sororities. There are more than 150 groups on campus, including art, band, cheerleading, chess, choir, chorale, chorus, computers, dance, drama, ethnic, film, forensics, gay, honors, international, jazz band, literary magazine, musical theater, newspaper, orchestra, pep band, photography, political, professional, radio and TV, religious, social, social service, student government, symphony, and yearbook. Popular campus events include Spring Concert, Family Weekend, and Founders Day Ball.

Sports: There are 9 intercollegiate sports for men and 10 for women, and 14 intramural sports for men and 12 for women. Facilities include a 6000-seat gym, 2 swimming pools, hockey and soccer fields, a softball diamond, an all-purpose field, cardiovascular and strength training equipment, weight rooms, courts for tennis, basketball, and volleyball, an aerobics studio, an indoor jogging track, and an outdoor, 6-lane tartan track.

Disabled Students: 94% of the campus is accessible. Wheelchair ramps, elevators, special parking, specially equipped rest rooms, special class scheduling, lowered drinking fountains, lowered telephones, and a university shuttle equipped to accommodate students in wheelchairs are available.

Services: Counseling and information services are available, as is tutoring in every subject. There is a reader service for the blind, and remedial math, reading, and writing. A math and statistics tutoring lab, a writing center, and a writing lab are available.

Campus Safety and Security: Measures include 24-hour foot and vehicle patrol, self-defense education, escort service, and shuttle buses. There are informal discussions, pamphlets/posters/films, emergency telephones, lighted pathways/sidewalks, safety orientation programs, alarms and closed-circuit cameras, and posted crime alerts.

Programs of Study: AU confers B.A., B.S., B.F.A., and B.S.B.A. degrees. Associate, master's, and doctoral degrees are also awarded. Bachelor's degrees are awarded in BIOLOGICAL SCIENCE (biochemistry and biology/biological science), BUSINESS (accounting, banking and finance, business administration and management, human resources, international business management, management information systems, and marketing management), COMMUNICATIONS AND THE ARTS (art history and appreciation, audio technology, communications, dramatic arts, film arts, fine arts, graphic design, journalism, literature, music, performing arts, public relations, and studio art), COMPUTER AND PHYSICAL SCIENCE (applied mathematics, chemistry, computer science, information sciences and systems, mathematics, physics, and statistics), EDUCATION (elementary and secondary), ENGINEERING AND ENVIRONMENTAL DESIGN (computer graphics, environmental science, and graphic arts technology), HEALTH PROFESSIONS (health science), SOCIAL SCIENCE (American studies, anthropology, area studies, criminal justice, economics, French studies, German area studies, history, interdisciplinary studies, international studies, Judaic studies, Latin American studies, law, liberal arts/general studies, philosophy, political science/government, psychology, religion, Russian and Slavic studies, sociology, Spanish studies, and women's studies). Political science, international studies, and communication are the strongest academically. International studies, political science, and business administration are the largest.

Required: To graduate, students must complete 120 credit hours with a minimum GPA of 2.0. In addition, students must complete 30 credit hours of general education requirements in 5 curricular areas and fulfill the school's competency requirements in English composition and math by either passing an exam or taking a course in each area.

Special: AU offers internships in all majors, study abroad in 16 countries, and a Washington semester program. Work-study is available on campus and with local community service agencies. Dual majors, a liberal studies degree, interdisciplinary programs, student-designed majors, 3-2 engineering degrees, and B.A.-B.S. degrees are also available. Combined bachelor's/master's programs are available in most majors. Cross-registration may be arranged through the Consortium of Universities of the Washington Metropolitan Area. Credit for life experience, nondegree study, and pass/fail options are available. There are preprofessional programs in dentistry, engineering, law, medicine, optometry, osteopathy, pharmacy, and veterinary medicine. There are 16 national honor societies, including Phi Beta Kappa, a freshman honors program, and all departments have honors programs.

Faculty/Classroom: 60% of faculty are male; 40%, female. 93% teach undergraduates and 93% both teach and do research. No introductory courses are taught by graduate students. The average class size in an introductory lecture is 26 and in a regular course, 20.

Admissions: 69% of the 2001-2002 applicants were accepted. The SAT I scores for the 2001-2002 freshman class were: Verbal--4% below 500, 37% between 500 and 599, 46% between 600 and 700, and 13% above 700; Math--6% below 500, 43% between 500 and 599, 43% between 600 and 700, and 8% above 700. 53% of the current freshmen were in the top fifth of their class. There were 5 National Merit finalists.

Requirements: The SAT I or ACT is required. In addition, students must have graduated from an accredited secondary school with at least 16 Carnegie units, including at least 4 units in English, 3 units in college preparatory math (including the equivalent of 2 units in algebra), 3 units in social sciences/history, 2 units in foreign language(s), and 2 units in natural or lab science. Applicants who have satisfactory scores on the GED may also apply. Students may apply using the institutional application, the Common Application, or the on-line application through Apply

Yourself. All students must submit an essay and 2 letters of recommendation. Interviews are recommended. A GPA of 2.0 is required. AP and CLEP credits are accepted. Important factors in the admissions decision are advanced placement or honor courses, extracurricular activities record, and recommendations by school officials.

Procedure: Freshmen are admitted to all sessions. Entrance exams should be taken in the spring of the junior year or the fall of the senior year. There are early decision and deferred admissions plans. Early decision applications should be filed by November 15; regular applications, by February 1 for fall entry, December 1 for spring entry, and April 1 for summer entry, along with a $45 fee. Notification of early decision is sent December 31; regular decision, April 1. 6% of all applicants are on a waiting list.

Transfer: 431 transfer students enrolled in 2001-2002. Transfer applicants must be in good academic and social standing at the school previously attended and have a minimum GPA of 2.5 to be considered competitive for admission. 45 credits of 120 must be completed at AU.

Visiting: There are regularly scheduled orientations for prospective students, including daily tours and information sessions, open houses, and overnight programs. There are guides for informal visits and visitors may sit in on classes and stay overnight. To schedule a visit, contact the Manager, On-Campus Events and Programs.

Financial Aid: In 2001-2002, 67% of all freshmen and 56% of continuing students received some form of financial aid. 43% of freshmen and 39% of continuing students received need-based aid. The average freshman award was $20,232. Of that total, scholarships or need-based grants averaged $13,395; loans averaged $8849; work contracts averaged $1844. 15% of undergraduates work part time. Average annual earnings from campus work are $6489. The average financial indebtedness of the 2001 graduate was $18,764. AU is a member of CSS. The FAFSA and the college's own financial statement are required. The fall application deadline is March 1; November 15 for early decision students.

International Students: There are 4 international students enrolled. The school actively recruits these students. They must take the college's own test and also take the SAT I or ACT if the applicant attends a school with a U.S.-patterned system. It is strongly recommended, but not required, that students take SAT II Subject tests, especially home-schooled students.

Computers: The mainframe is an IBM 3090. More than 200 IBM, Mac, and other PCs are available for student use in various campus locations. All residence hall rooms are fully networked. All students may access the system. There are no time limits and no fees. It is strongly recommended that all students have a personal computer.

Graduates: In 2001, 1082 bachelor's degrees were awarded. The most popular majors were international studies (18%), business administration (17%), and political science (9%). In an average class, 3% graduate in 3 years, 64% in 4 years, 70% in 5 years, and 71% in 6 years. Of the 2000 graduating class, 39% were enrolled in graduate school within 6 months of graduation and 85% were employed.

Admissions Contact: Dr. Sharon Alston, Director of Admissions. A video is available. E-mail: *afa@american.edu*
Web: *www.admissions.american.edu*

CATHOLIC UNIVERSITY OF AMERICA

Washington, DC 20064 — C-2
(202) 319-5305
(800) 673-2772; Fax: (202) 319-6533

Full-time: 1095 men, 1289 women	**Faculty:** 291; I, --$
Part-time: 86 men, 117 women	**Ph.D.s:** 97%
Graduate: 1472 men, 1471 women	**Student/Faculty:** 8 to 1
Year: semesters, summer session	**Tuition:** $20,950
Application Deadline: February 15	**Room & Board:** $8382

Freshman Class: 2191 applied, 1854 accepted, 614 enrolled
SAT I or ACT: required — **VERY COMPETITIVE**

Catholic University of America, founded in 1887 and affiliated with the Roman Catholic Church, offers undergraduate programs through the schools of arts and sciences, engineering, architecture, nursing, philosophy, the Benjamin T. Rome School of Music, and the Metropolitan College. Some information in this profile is approximate. There are 7 undergraduate and 10 graduate schools. In addition to regional accreditation, CUA has baccalaureate program accreditation with ABET, ACPE, CSWE, NAAB, NASDTEC, NASM, NCATE, and NLN. The 8 libraries contain 1,450,190 volumes, 1,473,449 microform items, and 35,080 audiovisual forms/CDs, and subscribe to 10,925 periodicals. Computerized library services include the card catalog, interlibrary loans, and database searching. Special learning facilities include a learning resource center, art gallery, radio station, archeology lab, rare book collection, and electronic/computer classrooms. The 144-acre campus is in an urban area in Washington, D.C. Including residence halls, there are 50 buildings.

Student Life: 93% of undergraduates are from out of state, mostly the Middle Atlantic. Students are from 48 states, 69 foreign countries, and Canada. 37% are from public schools. 75% are white. 88% are Catholic; 10%, Protestant. The average age of freshmen is 19; all undergraduates, 21. 15% do not continue beyond their first year; 69% remain to graduate.

Housing: 1703 students can be accommodated in college housing, which includes single-sex and coed dormitories. In addition, there are special-interest houses, a freshman residential college, and an upperclassmen residential college. On-campus housing is available on a first-come, first-served basis and is available on a lottery system for upperclassmen. 59% of students live on campus; of those, 50% remain on campus on weekends. Upperclassmen may keep cars.

Activities: 1% of men belong to 1 national fraternity; 1% of women belong to 2 national sororities. There are 84 groups on campus, including art, cheerleading, choir, chorale, chorus, computers, dance, debate, drama, ethnic, film, forensics, gay, honors, international, jazz band, literary magazine, musical theater, newspaper, opera, orchestra, pep band, photography, political, professional, radio and TV, religious, social, social service, student government, symphony, and yearbook. Popular campus events include Family Weekend, Oktoberfest, and Beaux Arts Ball.

Sports: There are 10 intercollegiate sports for men and 11 for women, and 6 intramural sports for men and 5 for women. Facilities include an athletic center that houses 4 basketball and 5 handball/racquetball courts, a 6-lane, 25-meter swimming pool, tennis plaza, weight training room, aerobics room, men's and women's saunas, adjoining playing fields, 2 dance studios, indoor jogging track, and 3 volleyball courts.

Disabled Students: 65% of the campus is accessible. Wheelchair ramps, elevators, special parking, specially equipped rest rooms, special class scheduling, lowered drinking fountains, lowered telephones, and accessible classrooms and housing are available.

Services: Counseling and information services are available, as is tutoring in most subjects. Taped books, readers, test accommodations, and sign language interpreters are also available. There is a reader service for the blind, and remedial math, reading, and writing.

Campus Safety and Security: Measures include 24-hour foot and vehicle patrol, self-defense education, escort service, and shuttle buses. There are informal discussions, pamphlets/posters/films, emergency telephones, lighted pathways/sidewalks, fixed security posts, emergency whistles, watch captains in every building, and an access control system.

Programs of Study: CUA confers B.A., B.S., B.A.G.S., B.Arch., B.B.E., B.C.E., B.E.E., B.M., B.M.E., B.Ph., B.S.Arch., B.S.C.S., and B.S.N. degrees. Master's and doctoral degrees are also awarded. Bachelor's degrees are awarded in BIOLOGICAL SCIENCE (biochemistry and biology/biological science), BUSINESS (accounting, banking and finance, business administration and management, human resources, international economics, and management science), COMMUNICATIONS AND THE ARTS (art, art history and appreciation, classics, communications, dramatic arts, English, French, German, Latin, music, music history and appreciation, music performance, music theory and composition, musical theater, painting, piano/organ, sculpture, Spanish, and voice), COMPUTER AND PHYSICAL SCIENCE (chemistry, computer science, elementary particle physics, mathematics, and physics), EDUCATION (art, drama, early childhood, education, elementary, English, mathematics, music, and secondary), ENGINEERING AND ENVIRONMENTAL DESIGN (architecture, biomedical engineering, civil engineering, electrical/electronics engineering, engineering, environmental science, and mechanical engineering), HEALTH PROFESSIONS (medical laboratory technology and nursing), SOCIAL SCIENCE (anthropology, economics, history, liberal arts/general studies, medieval studies, philosophy, political science/government, psychology, religion, social work, and sociology). Politics is the strongest academically. Architecture is the largest.

Required: To graduate, students must complete 120 credit hours, including 42 hours in the major, with a minimum GPA of 2.0. Courses must meet distribution requirements in English composition, philosophy, religion and religious study, language and literature, humanities, math and natural sciences, and social and behavioral sciences. A comprehensive exam is required in most majors.

Special: Cross-registration is available with the Consortium of Universities of the Washington Metropolitan Area. Opportunities are also provided for internships, accelerated degree programs, dual majors, pass/fail options, and study abroad in 10 countries. There are 14 national honor societies, including Phi Beta Kappa, and a freshman honors program.

Faculty/Classroom: 67% of faculty are male; 33%, female. 80% teach undergraduates and all do research. Graduate students teach 20% of introductory courses. The average class size in an introductory lecture is 21; in a laboratory, 20; and in a regular course, 19.

Admissions: 85% of the 2001-2002 applicants were accepted. The SAT I scores for the 2001-2002 freshman class were: Verbal--15% below 500, 42% between 500 and 599, 34% between 600 and 700, and 9% above 700; Math--16% below 500, 47% between 500 and 599, 32% between 600 and 700, and 5% above 700. The ACT scores were 18% below 21, 29% between 21 and 23, 20% between 24 and 26, 19% between 27 and 28, and 14% above 28. 40% of the current freshmen were in the top fifth of their class; 75% were in the top two fifths.

Requirements: The SAT I or ACT is required. In addition,the SAT II: Writing test is required for placement, and the SAT II: Foreign Language test is recommended. Applicants must be graduates of an accredited secondary school. The GED is accepted. Students should present 17 academic credits, including 4 each in English and social studies, 3 each in math and science, 2 in foreign languages, and 1 in fine arts or humanities. An essay is required. An audition is required for music applicants and a portfolio for architecture applicants is recommended. AP and CLEP credits are accepted. Important factors in the admissions decision are extracurricular activities record, leadership record, and advanced placement or honor courses. Applications are accepted on-line via Apply.

Procedure: Freshmen are admitted fall and spring. Entrance exams should be taken by February of the senior year of high school. There are early decision, early admissions, and deferred admissions plans. Early decision applications should be filed by November 15; regular applications, by February 15 for fall entry and December 1 for spring entry, along with a $55 fee. Notification of early decision is sent December 15; regular decision, April 1.

Transfer: 103 transfer students enrolled in a recent year. Applicants must submit a high school transcript, the SAT I or ACT scores, and a college transcript. A letter of recommendation and an essay are required. Terms of admission are finalized by the dean of the appropriate school. 30 credits of 120 must be completed at CUA.

Visiting: There are regularly scheduled orientations for prospective students, including an information session with an admissions counselor and a guided campus tour. There are guides for informal visits and visitors may sit in on classes. To schedule a visit, contact the Admissions Office.

Financial Aid: In 2001-2002, 91% of all freshmen and 86% of continuing students received some form of financial aid. In a recent year, 67% of freshmen and 59% of continuing students received need-based aid. The average freshman award was $14,000. Of that total, scholarships or need-based grants averaged $10,986 ($16,638 maximum); loans averaged $3982 ($20,000 maximum); and work contracts averaged $1500 ($2000 maximum). 45% of undergraduates work part time. Average annual earnings from campus work are $1500. CUA is a member of CSS. The CSS/Profile or FAFSA is required. Check with the school for current deadlines.

International Students: In a recent year, there were 156 international students enrolled. The school actively recruits these students. They must score 550 on the written TOEFL or 213 on the electronic version.

Computers: The mainframes are a Sun E4500, Sun E450, DEC ALPHA 4100 and 2100, and a Compaq 1850. There are 400 networked PCs spread across the campus for student use. All dorms are wired and students have access to the Internet and Web. All students may access the system 24 hours a day. There are no time limits and no fees.

Graduates: In a recent class, 491 bachelor's degrees were awarded. The most popular majors were architecture (15%), business and economics (10%), and nursing (8%). In an average class, 1% graduate in 3 years, 61% in 4 years, 69% in 5 years, and 70% in 6 years. 122 companies recruited on campus in a recent year. Of a recent graduating class, 34% were enrolled in graduate school within 6 months of graduation and 91% were employed.

Admissions Contact: Dale Herold, Dean of Enrollment Services. A video is available. E-mail: *cua-admissions@cua.edu*
Web: *http://www.cua.edu*

CORCORAN SCHOOL OF ART AND DESIGN C-3
Washington, DC 20006 (202) 639-1814
(888) CORCORAN; Fax: (202) 639-1830

Full-time: 110 men, 180 women	**Faculty:** 34
Part-time: 10 men, 20 women	**Ph.D.s:** 63%
Graduate: none	**Student/Faculty:** 8 to 1
Year: semesters, summer session	**Tuition:** $15,520
Application Deadline: open	**Room & Board:** $5515
Freshman Class: n/av	
SAT I or ACT: required	**SPECIAL**

Established in 1890, the Corcoran School of Art and Design is a private professional art college offering undergraduate programs in fine art, design, and photography. Figures in above capsule are approximate. In addition to regional accreditation, Corcoran has baccalaureate program accreditation with NASAD. The library contains 19,000 volumes, and subscribes to 130 periodicals. Computerized library services include interlibrary loans. Special learning facilities include a learning resource center and art gallery. The 7-acre campus is in an urban area in Washington, D.C. There are 3 buildings.

Student Life: 72% of undergraduates are from out of state, mostly the Middle Atlantic. Others are from 24 states, 32 foreign countries, and Canada. 75% are from public schools. 55% are white; 21% foreign nationals; 10% African American. The average age of freshmen is 19; all undergraduates, 23. 3% do not continue beyond their first year; 60% remain to graduate.

Housing: There are no residence halls; housing includes coed off-campus apartments. Housing is guaranteed for the freshman year only and is available on a first-come, first-served basis. Priority is given to out-of-town students. 84% of students commute. Alcohol is not permitted. No one may keep cars.

Activities: There are no fraternities or sororities. There are 4 groups on campus, including art, literary magazine, newspaper, and student government. Popular campus events include student art openings, museum and gallery openings, and visiting artists' lectures.

Sports: There is no sports program at Corcoran.

Disabled Students: 70% of the campus is accessible. Wheelchair ramps, elevators, special parking, specially equipped rest rooms, lowered drinking fountains, and lowered telephones are available.

Services: Counseling and information services are available, as is tutoring in most subjects, including art history, writing, humanities, and general academic subjects. There is remedial writing.

Campus Safety and Security: Measures include 24-hour foot and vehicle patrol, informal discussions, and pamphlets/posters/films.

Programs of Study: Corcoran confers the B.F.A. degree. Associate degrees are also awarded. Bachelor's degrees are awarded in COMMUNICATIONS AND THE ARTS (fine arts, graphic design, and photography). Fine arts is the largest.

Required: Students must complete 126 credits, with 65 to 70 of these in the major, and 23 in the core curriculum, and must maintain a minimum GPA of 2.0. Course distribution must involve the disciplines of art history, humanities, liberal arts, and writing. Curricula will include courses in drawing, design, idea resources, and media. Seniors must present thesis exhibitions.

Special: Cooperative programs are permitted with the ACE and AICA art college consortiums. Opportunities are provided for internships in graphic design and photography, credit by exam, work-study programs with the Corcoran Gallery of Art, and nondegree study.

Faculty/Classroom: 50% of faculty are male; 50%, female. All teach undergraduates. The average class size in an introductory lecture is 23; in a laboratory, 10; and in a regular course, 10.

Requirements: The SAT I or ACT is required. Applicants must have graduated from an approved secondary school; a GED will be accepted. A portfolio is required, and an interview is recommended. A GPA of 2.5 is required. AP credits are accepted. Important factors in the admissions decision are evidence of special talent, personality/intangible qualities, and advanced placement or honor courses.

Procedure: Freshmen are admitted fall and spring. Entrance exams should be taken prior to January 30 of the senior year. There is a deferred admissions plan. Application deadlines are open. The application fee is $30.

Transfer: 53 transfer students enrolled in a recent year. A review of studio art transcripts will be considered for the level of entry of transfer students. A portfolio review will be the final determining factor. 63 credits of 126 must be completed at Corcoran.

Visiting: There are regularly scheduled orientations for prospective students, consisting of personal visit with admissions staff. There are guides for informal visits and visitors may sit in on classes. To schedule a visit, contact the Admissions Department.

Financial Aid: In a recent year, 83% of all freshmen and 69% of continuing students received some form of financial aid. 56% of freshmen and 55% of continuing students received need-based aid. The average freshman award was $12,891. Of that total, scholarships or need-based grants averaged $3976 ($4250 maximum); loans averaged $3550 ($4000 maximum); and alternative loans offered on a credit basis averaged $8119 ($12,300 maximum). 12% of undergraduates work part time. Average annual earnings from campus work are $1849. The average financial indebtedness of a recent graduate was $35,000. Corcoran is a member of CSS. The CSS/Profile and the college's own financial statement are required. The fall application deadline is May 1.

International Students: There were 18 international students enrolled in a recent year. The school actively recruits these students. They must score 550 on the written TOEFL and also take the SAT I or the ACT.

Computers: In labs, the student lounge, and the library there are Macs, Power Macs, and PCs as well as workstations and servers. Internet access is available. All students may access the system. Students may access the system during lab hours in Computer Graphics. There are no fees.

Graduates: In a recent, 74 bachelor's degrees were awarded. The most popular majors were fine arts (48%), graphic design (34%), and photography (19%). In an average class, 60% graduate in 4 years.

Admissions Contact: Anne Bowman, Director of Admissions.
E-mail: *admofc.corcoran.org* Web: *www.corcoran.edu*

GALLAUDET UNIVERSITY
C-3

Washington, DC 20002-3695

(202) 651-5114 (TTY) or (202) 651-5750
(800) 995-0550 (TTY/V); Fax: (202) 651-5744

Full-time: 480 men, 570 women	**Faculty:** 300; IIA, +$
Part-time: 100 men, 100 women	**Ph.D.s:** 66%
Graduate: 90 men, 330 women	**Student/Faculty:** 4 to 1
Year: semesters, summer session	**Tuition:** $8990
Application Deadline: open	**Room & Board:** $7564
Freshman Class: n/av	
SAT I or ACT: not required	**SPECIAL**

Gallaudet University, founded in 1864 as a university designed exclusively for deaf and hard-of-hearing students, offers programs in liberal and fine arts, teacher preparation, and professional training. Figures in above capsule are approximate. There are 4 undergraduate and 4 graduate schools. In addition to regional accreditation, Gallaudet has baccalaureate program accreditation with CSWE and NCATE. The library contains 215,500 volumes, 371,000 microform items, and 4530 audiovisual forms/CDs, and subscribes to 1415 periodicals. Computerized library services include the card catalog, interlibrary loans, and database searching. Special learning facilities include a learning resource center, TV station, child development center, national and international centers on deafness, and a research institute on deafness. The 99-acre campus is in an urban area in Washington, D.C. Including residence halls, there are 30 buildings.

Student Life: 95% of undergraduates are from out of state, mostly the Northeast. Others are from 49 states and Canada. 74% are white; 14% foreign nationals.

Housing: Campus housing includes single-sex and coed dormitories. On-campus housing is guaranteed for the freshman year only and is available on a first-come, first-served basis. 51% of students live on campus; of those, 51% remain on campus on weekends. Alcohol is not permitted. All students may keep cars.

Activities: 15% of men belong to 1 local and 3 national fraternities; 20% of women belong to 2 local and 3 national sororities. There are 32 groups on campus, including art, cheerleading, computers, dance, drama, ethnic, gay, honors, international, literary magazine, newspaper, political, religious, social, social service, student government, and yearbook. Popular campus events include rock festival, drama productions, and lecture series.

Sports: There are 9 intercollegiate sports for men and 8 for women, and 12 intramural sports for men and 12 for women. Facilities include a field house, a gym, a swimming pool, tennis and racquetball courts, weight training rooms, playing fields, and bowling alleys.

Disabled Students: Wheelchair ramps, elevators, special parking, specially equipped rest rooms, special class scheduling, lowered drinking fountains, lowered telephones, and phones with TTY. Sign language skills are required of all faculty and professional staff.

Services: Counseling and information services are available. Tutoring in every subject throughout the tutorial, English, and writing centers is also available. There is remedial math, reading, and writing. An information-on-deafness center is also available.

Campus Safety and Security: Measures include 24-hour foot and vehicle patrol, escort service, shuttle buses, and informal discussions. There are pamphlets/posters/films and lighted pathways/sidewalks.

Programs of Study: Gallaudet confers B.A. and B.S. degrees. Associate, master's, and doctoral degrees are also awarded. Bachelor's degrees are awarded in BIOLOGICAL SCIENCE (biology/biological science), BUSINESS (accounting, business administration and management, entrepreneurial studies, management science, and recreation and leisure services), COMMUNICATIONS AND THE ARTS (apparel design, art history and appreciation, communications, dramatic arts, English, French, German, graphic design, media arts, Russian, Spanish, and studio art), COMPUTER AND PHYSICAL SCIENCE (chemical technology, chemistry, computer science, mathematics, and physics), EDUCATION (art, early childhood, elementary, home economics, physical, and secondary), ENGINEERING AND ENVIRONMENTAL DESIGN (engineering technology), HEALTH PROFESSIONS (recreation therapy), SOCIAL SCIENCE (child care/child and family studies, economics, family/consumer studies, history, interpreter for the deaf, parks and recreation management, philosophy, political science/government, psychology, religion, and social work).

Required: The core curriculum requires 12 hours each of social science and English, 9 of literature and humanities, 8 of lab science, 5 of communication arts, 4 of phys ed, and 3 of philosophy, plus demonstrated proficiency in a foreign language. A total of 124 credits, with 30 to 60 in the major, and a minimum 2.0 GPA are required for graduation.

Special: Gallaudet offers co-op programs with Oberlin College in Ohio and Western Maryland College, cross-registration with the Consortium of Universities of the Washington Metropolitan Area, and a 3-2 engineering degree with George Washington University. Internships, study abroad, dual majors, work-study programs, and B.A.-B.S. degrees are available. There is a chapter of Phi Beta Kappa and a freshman honors program.

Faculty/Classroom: No introductory courses are taught by graduate students.

Requirements: Applicants must submit a recent audiogram and results of the most recent edition of the Stanford Achievement Test. SAT I or ACT scores may be submitted. High school transcripts, letters of recommendation, and writing samples are also required. The GED is accepted. AP and CLEP credits are accepted. Important factors in the admissions decision are advanced placement or honor courses, recommendations by school officials, and leadership record.

Procedure: Freshmen are admitted fall and spring. Entrance exams should be taken in October or November of the senior year. There is a deferred admissions plan. Application deadlines are open. The application fee is $35.

Transfer: Deaf and hard-of-hearing transfer applicants must submit a recent audiogram, official college transcripts from all schools attended, and at least 2 letters of recommendation. Students should have completed 12 or more credit hours with at least a 2.0 GPA; those who do not meet these requirements must submit recent SAT I or ACT scores and a final high school transcript.

Visiting: There are regularly scheduled orientations for prospective students, including a tour of campus, classroom observations, and interviews with selected offices and programs. There are guides for informal visits and visitors may sit in on classes. To schedule a visit, contact the Gallaudet University Visitor's Center at (202) 651-5050.

Financial Aid: The FAFSA and the college's own financial statement are required. Check with the school for current deadlines.

International Students: They must take the MELAB, the Comprehensive English Language Test, or the college's own test and also take the college's own entrance exam or and the most recent edition of the Stanford Achievement Test; SAT I or ACT scores may be submitted.

Computers: The mainframes are a 2 DEC VAX 6250s and 2 DEC VAX 8650s. There are about 1100 PCs, including 145 in public user areas. All residence halls have VT terminals, with Benson Hall housing a computer lab. There is national network access via BITnet, NSFnet, and the Internet. All students may access the system 24 hours a day. There are no time limits and no fees.

Admissions Contact: Director of Admissions.
E-mail: *admission@gallua.gallaudet.edu*

GEORGE WASHINGTON UNIVERSITY
B-3

Washington, DC 20052

(202) 994-6040
(800) 447-3765; Fax: (202) 994-0325

Full-time: 3170 men, 4260 women	**Faculty:** 567; I, +$
Part-time: 670 men, 600 women	**Ph.D.s:** 92%
Graduate: 5810 men, 5840 women	**Student/Faculty:** 13 to 1
Year: semesters, summer session	**Tuition:** $26,170
Application Deadline: December 1	**Room & Board:** $8210
Freshman Class: n/av	
SAT I Verbal/Math: required	**HIGHLY COMPETITIVE**

George Washington University, founded in 1821, is a private institution providing degree programs in arts and sciences, business, engineering, international affairs, health sciences, education, law, and public health. There are 6 undergraduate and 8 graduate schools. Figures in the above capsule are approximate. In addition to regional accreditation, GW has baccalaureate program accreditation with AACSB, ABET, CAHEA, CSAB, NASAD, NASM, and NCATE. The 3 libraries contain 1,841,842 volumes, 2,468,719 microform items, and 17,246 audiovisual forms/CDs, and subscribe to 14,729 periodicals. Computerized library services include the card catalog, interlibrary loans, and database searching. Special learning facilities include a learning resource center, art gallery, radio station, and TV station. The 37-acre campus is in an urban area 3 blocks west of the White House. Including residence halls, there are 123 buildings.

Student Life: 92% of undergraduates are from out of state, mostly the Middle Atlantic. Others are from 49 states, 137 foreign countries, and Canada. 70% are from public schools. 58% are white; 11% foreign nationals. The average age of freshmen is 19; all undergraduates, 20. 8% do not continue beyond their first year; 69% remain to graduate.

Housing: 4243 students can be accommodated in college housing, which includes single-sex and coed dormitories, on-campus apartments, fraternity houses, and sorority floors. In addition, there are special-interest houses. On-campus housing is available on a lottery system for upperclassmen. 58% of students live on campus. All students may keep cars.

Activities: 19% of men belong to 11 national fraternities; 12% of women belong to 7 national sororities. There are 257 groups on campus, including art, band, cheerleading, chess, choir, chorale, chorus, computers, dance, debate, drama, ethnic, film, folk life, forensics, gay, geology, honors, international, jazz band, literary magazine, marching band, musical theater, newspaper, opera, orchestra, pep band, photography, political, professional, radio and TV, religious, social, social service, student government, symphony, and yearbook. Popular campus events include a yearly benefit auction, Spring Fling, and Fall Fest.

Sports: There are 9 intercollegiate sports for men and 8 for women, and 16 intramural sports for men and 16 for women. Facilities include a 5000-seat gym with 2 auxiliary gyms, an AAU swimming pool, weight rooms, a jogging track, squash and racquetball courts, and soccer and baseball fields.
Disabled Students: 95% of the campus is accessible. Wheelchair ramps, elevators, special parking, specially equipped rest rooms, special class scheduling, lowered drinking fountains, and lowered telephones are available.
Services: Counseling and information services are available, as is tutoring in every subject. There is a reader service for the blind.
Campus Safety and Security: Measures include 24-hour foot and vehicle patrol, self-defense education, escort service, and informal discussions. There are pamphlets/posters/films, emergency telephones, lighted pathways/sidewalks, and a bike patrol.
Programs of Study: GW confers B.A., B.S., B.Accy., B.B.A., B.Mus., B.S.C.E., B.S.C.Eng., B.S.C.S., B.S.E.E., B.S.H.S., B.S.M.E., and B.S.S.A. degrees. Associate, master's, and doctoral degrees are also awarded. Bachelor's degrees are awarded in BIOLOGICAL SCIENCE (biology/biological science), BUSINESS (accounting, banking and finance, business administration and management, business economics, human resources, international business management, marketing management, and tourism), COMMUNICATIONS AND THE ARTS (art history and appreciation, broadcasting, Chinese, classics, communications, dance, dramatic arts, English, fine arts, French, German, Japanese, journalism, literature, multimedia, music, music performance, public relations, Russian, and Spanish), COMPUTER AND PHYSICAL SCIENCE (applied mathematics, chemistry, computer science, geology, information sciences and systems, mathematics, physics, statistics, and systems analysis), ENGINEERING AND ENVIRONMENTAL DESIGN (civil engineering, computer engineering, electrical/electronics engineering, engineering, environmental science, and mechanical engineering), HEALTH PROFESSIONS (clinical science, emergency medical technologies, medical laboratory technology, nuclear medical technology, physician's assistant, premedicine, radiological science, and speech pathology/audiology), SOCIAL SCIENCE (American studies, anthropology, archeology, criminal justice, East Asian studies, economics, European studies, geography, history, human services, humanities, interdisciplinary studies, international relations, Judaic studies, Latin American studies, liberal arts/general studies, Middle Eastern studies, philosophy, physical fitness/movement, political science/government, psychology, religion, and sociology). Political communication, international affairs, and biological sciences are the strongest academically. Psychology, political science, and international affairs are the largest.
Required: Students must complete 120 semester hours with a minimum GPA of 2.0 for most majors. Arts and sciences majors must meet general curriculum requirements that include literacy, quantitative and logical reasoning, natural sciences, social and behavioral sciences, creative and performing arts, literature, Western civilization, and foreign languages or culture. Other specific course requirements vary with the different divisions of the university.
Special: Cross-registration is available through the Consortium of Colleges and Universities. There are co-op programs in education, business, engineering, arts and sciences, and international affairs, and internships throughout the Washington metropolitan area. Study abroad in locations throughout the world, work-study programs, dual majors, student-designed majors, and a 3-2 engineering degree program with 8 colleges are also available. Nondegree study, a general studies degree, credit by exam, and pass/fail options are possible. There are 12 national honor societies, including Phi Beta Kappa, a freshman honors program, and 21 departmental honors programs.
Faculty/Classroom: 70% of faculty are male; 30%, female. Graduate students teach 2% of introductory courses. The average class size in an introductory lecture is 32 and in a regular course, 22.
Requirements: The SAT I or ACT is required. In addition, students must have successfully completed a strong academic program in high school. SAT II: Subject tests are strongly recommended. An essay, 1 teacher recommendation, and 1 counselor recommendation are required. An interview is encouraged. AP and CLEP credits are accepted. Important factors in the admissions decision are advanced placement or honor courses, recommendations by school officials, and leadership record. Common App applications are accepted on disk and on-line, and applications may also be submitted on-line via CollegeLink.
Procedure: Freshmen are admitted to all sessions. Entrance exams should be taken in the junior year and the fall semester of the senior year. There are early decision, early admissions, and deferred admissions plans. Early decision applications should be filed by November 1; regular applications, by December 1 for fall entry, October 1 for spring. Notification of early decision is sent December 15; regular decision, March 15. 403 early decision candidates were accepted for the 2001-2002 class. A waiting list is an active part of the admissions procedure. Application fee is $60.
Transfer: 279 transfer students enrolled in a recent year. In addition to a record of high marks and exam scores, applicants must submit official transcripts of all postsecondary work. Minimum GPA requirements vary from 2.5 to 3.0, depending on the major. The SAT I or ACT is required, and an interview is encouraged. 30 credits of 120 must be completed at GW.
Visiting: There are regularly scheduled orientations for prospective students, including group information sessions and campus tours. Class visitation, lunch with current students, and other activities can be arranged, if requested in advance. There are guides for informal visits and visitors may sit in on classes and stay overnight. To schedule a visit, contact the University Visitor Center at (202) 994-6602.
Financial Aid: In a recent year, 70% of all freshmen and 60% of continuing students received some form of financial aid. 48% of freshmen and 39% of continuing students received need-based aid. The average freshman award was $15,064. Of that total, scholarships or need-based grants averaged $10,954; loans averaged $6240; and work contracts averaged $824. The average financial indebtedness of the 2001 graduate was $18,953. GW is a member of CSS. The CSS/Profile or FAFSA and the college's own financial statement are required. Check with the school for current deadlines.
International Students: There were 521 international students enrolled in a recent year. The school actively recruits these students. They must score 550 on the written TOEFL and also take the college's own test and the SAT I or the ACT.
Computers: The mainframes are an IBM 4381/R14, a Sun SPARC Station 2000, and 7 Citrix servers. All residence halls have computer rooms, and the campus computer center is open 24 hours a day. In addition, 7 computer classrooms are available as walk-in labs when classes are not scheduled. Modems are available on the campus network. There is a 24-hour computer lab in the library. All dorm rooms are networked fiber-optically. All students may access the system all the time. There are no time limits and no fees. It is strongly recommended that all students have a personal computer.
Graduates: In a recent year, 1415 bachelor's degrees were awarded. The most popular majors were international affairs (14%), psychology (8%), and political science (7%). In an average class, 2% graduate in 3 years, 60% in 4 years, 68% in 5 years, and 69% in 6 years.
Admissions Contact: Dr. Kathryn M. Napper, Director of Admissions.
E-mail: *gwadm@gwu.edu* Web: *gwired.gwu.edu/adm/*

GEORGETOWN UNIVERSITY — B-3
Washington, DC 20057 (202) 687-3600; Fax: (202) 687-5084

Full-time: 2947 men, 3244 women	**Faculty:** 665; I, +$
Part-time: 100 men, 131 women	**Ph.D.s:** 93%
Graduate: 3150 men, 3116 women	**Student/Faculty:** 6 to 1
Year: semesters, summer session	**Tuition:** $25,425
Application Deadline: January 10	**Room & Board:** $9422
Freshman Class: 15,327 applied, 3194 accepted, 1515 enrolled	
SAT I or ACT: required	**MOST COMPETITIVE**

Georgetown University, founded in 1789, is a private institution affiliated with the Roman Catholic Church and offers programs in arts and sciences, business administration, foreign service, languages and linguistics, and nursing. There are 4 undergraduate and 3 graduate schools. In addition to regional accreditation, Georgetown has baccalaureate program accreditation with AACSB and NLN. The 6 libraries contain 2,363,799 volumes, 3,665,068 microform items, and 65,248 audiovisual forms/CDs, and subscribe to 27,379 periodicals. Computerized library services include the card catalog, interlibrary loans, and database searching. Special learning facilities include a learning resource center, art gallery, planetarium, radio station, and TV station. The 110-acre campus is in an urban area 1.5 miles northwest of downtown Washington D.C. Including residence halls, there are 60 buildings.
Student Life: 99% of undergraduates are from out of state, mostly the Middle Atlantic. Others are from 50 states, 86 foreign countries, and Canada. 44% are from public schools. 68% are white. 54% are Catholic; 24% Protestant. The average age of freshmen is 18; all undergraduates, 20. 2% do not continue beyond their first year; 91% remain to graduate.
Housing: 4293 students can be accommodated in college housing, which includes coed dormitories, on-campus apartments, and special housing for the disabled. Special interest floors are available in some residence halls. On-campus housing is available on a lottery system for upperclassmen. 66% of students live on campus; of those, 95% remain on campus on weekends. No one may keep cars.
Activities: There are no fraternities or sororities. There are 125 groups on campus, including art, band, cheerleading, chess, choir, chorale, chorus, computers, dance, debate, drama, ethnic, gay, honors, international, jazz band, literary magazine, musical theater, newspaper, orchestra, pep band, photography, political, professional, radio and TV, religious, social, social service, student government, symphony, and yearbook. Popular campus events include GU Day and Career Week.
Sports: There are 11 intercollegiate sports for men and 11 for women, and 14 intramural sports for men and 14 for women. Facilities include a field house, a 150,000-square-foot underground facility with a swimming pool, handball/racquetball/squash courts, a jogging track, and weight training equipment, and multipurpose courts for basketball, volleyball, and tennis.

Disabled Students: 92% of the campus is accessible. Wheelchair ramps, elevators, special parking, specially equipped rest rooms, special class scheduling, lowered drinking fountains, lowered telephones, a special map of the campus with accessibility routes, a tactile map of the campus for visually disabled students, and a paratransit vehicle for mobility on the main campus are available.

Services: Counseling and information services are available, as is tutoring in every subject. There is a reader service for the blind.

Campus Safety and Security: Measures include 24-hour foot and vehicle patrol, escort service, shuttle buses, and informal discussions. There are pamphlets/posters/films, emergency telephones, and lighted pathways/sidewalks.

Programs of Study: Georgetown confers B.A.B., B.S., B.A.L.S., B.L.S., B.S.B.A., B.S.F.S., B.S.L.A., B.S.L.I., and B.S.N. degrees. Master's and doctoral degrees are also awarded. Bachelor's degrees are awarded in BIOLOGICAL SCIENCE (biochemistry and biology/biological science), BUSINESS (accounting, banking and finance, business administration and management, international business management, and marketing/retailing/merchandising), COMMUNICATIONS AND THE ARTS (Arabic, Chinese, classics, comparative literature, English, fine arts, French, German, Italian, Japanese, linguistics, Portuguese, Russian, and Spanish), COMPUTER AND PHYSICAL SCIENCE (chemistry, computer science, mathematics, and physics), HEALTH PROFESSIONS (health and nursing), SOCIAL SCIENCE (American studies, economics, history, interdisciplinary studies, international relations, philosophy, political science/government, psychology, religion, and sociology). International affairs, business, and government are the strongest academically. Government, finance, and international affairs are the largest.

Required: Students must complete 120 credits and maintain a minimum GPA of 2.0. A core of liberal arts courses is required, consisting of 2 courses each in philosophy and theology. Computer science is required of students majoring in math and computer science.

Special: Cross-registration is available with a consortium of universities in the Washington metropolitan area. Opportunities are provided for internships, study abroad in 38 countries, work-study programs, student-designed majors, and dual majors. A general studies degree, B.A.-B.S. degrees, nondegree study, credit by examination, and pass/fail options are also offered. There are 15 national honor societies, including Phi Beta Kappa, a freshman honors program, and 9 departmental honors programs.

Faculty/Classroom: 59% of faculty are male; 41%, female. Graduate students teach 9% of introductory courses. The average class size in an introductory lecture is 34; in a laboratory, 18; and in a regular course, 29.

Admissions: 21% of the 2001-2002 applicants were accepted. 91% of the current freshmen were in the top fifth of their class; 99% were in the top two fifths. 149 freshmen graduated first in their class.

Requirements: The SAT I or ACT is required. In addition, graduation from an accredited secondary school is required, including 4 years of English, a minimum of 2 each of a foreign language, math, and social studies, and 1 of natural science. An additional 2 years each of math and science is required for students intending to major in math, science, nursing, or business. SAT II: Subject tests are strongly recommended. Applicants to the Walsh School of Foreign Service and the Faculty of Languages and Linguistics are required to submit results of an SAT II: Subject test in a modern foreign language. A disk application is available from the Office of Undergraduate Admissions. MacApply may also be used, but the application must also be submitted in paper form. AP credits are accepted. Important factors in the admissions decision are evidence of special talent and leadership record.

Procedure: Freshmen are admitted in the fall. Entrance exams should be taken in the junior year and again at the beginning of the senior year. There are early admissions and deferred admissions plans. Early decision applications should be filed by November 1; regular applications, by January 10 for fall entry. The 2001 fall application fee was $60. Notification of early decision is sent December 15; regular decision, April 1. 12% of all applicants are on a waiting list; 149 were accepted in 2001.

Transfer: 219 transfer students enrolled in 2001-2002. Transfer students must have successfully completed a minimum of 12 credit hours with a minimum GPA of 3.0. Either the SAT I or the ACT is required. An interview is recommended. Transfers must complete their last 2 years at Georgetown. 60 credits of 120 must be completed at Georgetown.

Visiting: There are regularly scheduled orientations for prospective students throughout the year, including a question and answer period led by an admissions officer, followed by a campus tour led by a student guide. There are guides for informal visits and visitors may sit in on classes. To schedule a visit, contact the Office of Undergraduate Admissions at Student Financial Services: (202) 687-4547.

Financial Aid: In 2001-2002, 55% of all freshmen and 52% of continuing students received some form of financial aid. 47% of freshmen and 45% of continuing students received need-based aid. The average freshman award was $21,000. Of that total, scholarships or need-based grants averaged $17,000 ($27,000 maximum); loans averaged $2000; and work contracts averaged $2000. 55% of undergraduates work part time. Average annual earnings from campus work are $3000. The average financial indebtedness of the 2001 graduate was $17,900. Georgetown is a member of CSS. The CSS/Profile or FAFSA is required. The fall application deadline is February 1.

International Students: There are 477 international students enrolled. The school actively recruits these students. They must score 550 on the written TOEFL or 213 on the electronic version and also take the SAT I or the ACT. Students must take SAT II: Subject tests in writing and 2 others of the student's choice.

Computers: The mainframes are an IBM ES/9000-320 and a DEC VAX 4000-200, 4000-300, and 8700. In addition, there are about 360 terminals and PCs in the library, computer labs, and the School of Business. All students may access the system. There are no time limits and no fees.

Graduates: In 2001, 1619 bachelor's degrees were awarded. The most popular majors were international affairs (15%), English (10%), and finance (10%). In an average class, 2% graduate in 3 years, 86% in 4 years, 90% in 5 years, and 91% in 6 years. 627 companies recruited on campus in 2000-2001. Of the 2000 graduating class, 28% were enrolled in graduate school within 6 months of graduation and 68% were employed.

Admissions Contact: Charles A. Deacon, Dean of Admissions.
Web: *www.georgetown.edu/undergrad/admissions/*

HOWARD UNIVERSITY — C-3
Washington, DC 20059 — **(202) 806-2763; (800) 822-6363**

Full-time: 2220 men, 3850 women	**Faculty:** 1292; I, --$
Part-time: 200 men, 300 women	**Ph.D.s:** 77%
Graduate: 1560 men, 2130 women	**Student/Faculty:** 5 to 1
Year: semesters, summer session	**Tuition:** $10,222
Application Deadline: see profile	**Room & Board:** $5300
Freshman Class: n/av	
SAT I or ACT: required	**LESS COMPETITIVE**

Howard University, founded in 1867, is a private, nonsectarian institution and the largest predominantly black university in the United States. Figures in above capsule are approximate. There are 5 undergraduate and 7 graduate schools. In addition to regional accreditation, Howard has baccalaureate program accreditation with AACSB, ABET, ACEJMC, ACPE, ADA, AHEA, APTA, CAHEA, CSAB, CSWE, NAAB, NASAD, NASDTEC, NASM, NCATE, and NLN. The 7 libraries contain 2.2 million volumes and 3.4 million microform items, and subscribe to 26,280 periodicals. Computerized library services include the card catalog, interlibrary loans, and database searching. Special learning facilities include a learning resource center, art gallery, radio station, TV station, history and culture research center. The 241-acre campus is in an urban area in Washington, D.C. Including residence halls, there are 72 buildings.

Student Life: 79% of undergraduates are from out of state, mostly the Middle Atlantic. Others are from 48 states, 90 foreign countries, and Canada. 75% are from public schools. 85% are African American. The average age of freshmen is 18; all undergraduates, 21. 20% do not continue beyond their first year; 45% remain to graduate.

Housing: 4453 students can be accommodated in college housing, which includes single-sex and coed dormitories, on-campus apartments, off-campus apartments, and married-student housing. On-campus housing is guaranteed for the freshman year only, is available on a first-come, first-served basis, and is available on a lottery system for upperclassmen. Priority is given to out-of-town students. 51% of students commute. All students may keep cars.

Activities: 3% of men and about 1% of women belong to 4 national fraternities; 3% of women belong to 4 national sororities. There are 150 groups on campus, including bagpipe band, band, cheerleading, chess, choir, chorale, chorus, computers, dance, debate, drama, drill team, drum and bugle corps, honors, international, jazz band, literary magazine, marching band, newspaper, orchestra, political, professional, radio and TV, religious, social, social service, student government, and yearbook. Popular campus events include Spring Festival, Opening Convocation, and Charter Day.

Sports: There are 15 intercollegiate sports for men and 15 for women, and 5 intramural sports for men and 5 for women. Facilities include a sports center, a gym, and practice fields.

Disabled Students: All of the campus is accessible. Wheelchair ramps, elevators, special parking, specially equipped rest rooms, special class scheduling, lowered drinking fountains, and lowered telephones are available.

Services: Counseling and information services are available, as is tutoring in most subjects. There is a reader service for the blind, and remedial math, reading, and writing.

Campus Safety and Security: Measures include 24-hour foot and vehicle patrol, escort service, shuttle buses, and informal discussions. There are pamphlets/posters/films, emergency telephones, and lighted pathways/sidewalks.

Programs of Study: Howard confers B.A., B.S., B.Arch., B.B.A., B.F.A., B.M., B.M.E., B.S.N., B.S.N.S., B.S.O.T., B.S.P.T., B.S. in P.A.,

B.S. in R.T.T. degrees. Master's and doctoral degrees are also awarded. Bachelor's degrees are awarded in BIOLOGICAL SCIENCE (biology/biological science, botany, microbiology, and zoology), BUSINESS (accounting, banking and finance, business administration and management, hospitality management services, hotel/motel and restaurant management, insurance, international business management, and marketing/retailing/merchandising), COMMUNICATIONS AND THE ARTS (art history and appreciation, broadcasting, ceramic art and design, classics, communications, dance, design, dramatic arts, English, film arts, fine arts, French, German, Greek, jazz, journalism, Latin, music, music business management, music history and appreciation, musical theater, photography, printmaking, Russian, and Spanish), COMPUTER AND PHYSICAL SCIENCE (astrophysics, chemistry, computer programming, computer science, information sciences and systems, mathematics, and physics), EDUCATION (art, early childhood, elementary, health, music, physical, recreation, and secondary), ENGINEERING AND ENVIRONMENTAL DESIGN (architecture, chemical engineering, civil engineering, computer engineering, electrical/electronics engineering, and mechanical engineering), HEALTH PROFESSIONS (medical laboratory technology, music therapy, nursing, occupational therapy, pharmacy, physical therapy, physician's assistant, predentistry, premedicine, radiograph medical technology, and speech pathology/audiology), SOCIAL SCIENCE (African American studies, African studies, anthropology, criminal justice, dietetics, economics, history, human development, international relations, philosophy, political science/government, psychology, and sociology). Psychology, business, and engineering are the strongest academically. Accounting, finance, and electrical engineering are the largest.

Required: To graduate, students must complete 121 to 171 credit hours, including 21 to 78 in a major and 12 to 39 in a minor, with a minimum GPA of 2.0. General requirements include 4 courses in phys ed, 2 in freshman English, 1 in writing, and 1 in Afro-American studies; 1 year of college-level math; demonstrated proficiency in a foreign language; and successful completion of a comprehensive exam in the major.

Special: Cross-registration is available with the Consortium of Universities in the Washington Metropolitan Area. Opportunities are also provided for internships, work-study, and co-op programs, study abroad in 5 countries in Europe and Africa, B.A.-B.S. degrees in engineering and business, pass/fail options, and accelerated degree programs in medicine and dentistry. There is a chapter of Phi Beta Kappa and a freshman honors program.

Faculty/Classroom: 68% of faculty are male; 32%, female. The average class size in an introductory lecture is 40; in a laboratory, 20; and in a regular course, 20.

Requirements: The SAT I or ACT is required, with a minimum composite score of 800 on the SAT I (400 verbal, 400 math) or 21 on the ACT. Graduation from an accredited secondary school is required. The GED is accepted. Students must have a minimum of 16 academic credits, including 4 in English, 2 each in foreign language, math, science, and either history or social studies, and 4 in electives. Students must submit letters of recommendation from 2 high school teachers and 1 high school counselor. Other requirements vary by college. Engineering majors must take the SAT II: Subject test in math I. Art majors must submit a portfolio, and music and theater majors must audition. AP credits are accepted. Important factors in the admissions decision are recommendations by school officials and advanced placement or honor courses.

Procedure: Freshmen are admitted to all sessions. Entrance exams should be taken in the fall of the senior year. There are early admissions and deferred admissions plans. Check with school for current deadlines. Notification is sent on a rolling basis. The fall 2001 application fee was $45.

Transfer: All applicants must submit 2 official transcripts from each college or university attended. Students transferring to the School of Business must have successfully completed 18 semester hours or 23 quarter hours of courses, with a minimum GPA of 2.5. For many other majors, the requirement is 12 semester hours or 18 quarter hours, with a minimum GPA of 2.0. Applicants to the College of Arts and Sciences need 3 credits each in English composition and college-level algebra. 30 credits of 121 must be completed at Howard.

Visiting: There are regularly scheduled orientations for prospective students, including an admissions interview, classroom and dorm visits, and conversations with faculty and students. There are guides for informal visits and visitors may sit in on classes and stay overnight. To schedule a visit, contact the Office of Enrollment Management/Recruitment at (202) 806-2900.

Financial Aid: 9% of undergraduates work part time. Average annual earnings from campus work are $3500. Howard is a member of CSS. The FAFSA is required. Check with the school for current deadlines.

International Students: They must score 500 on the written TOEFL and also take the SAT I or the ACT. Students must take SAT II: Subject tests in Writing.

Computers: The mainframes are an IBM ES 9121/440 and an RS 6000 VAX. The main computer center houses PCs and Macs in 3 labs. There are 630 student workstations, 1220 faculty workstations, and 500 for general use. Specialized labs include a multimedia center, a CAM lab, and a virtual classroom. All students may access the system. There are no time limits and no fees.

Admissions Contact: Office of Enrollment Management/ Admissions. E-mail: *admission@howard.edu* Web: *www.howard.edu*

SOUTHEASTERN UNIVERSITY — D-4

Washington, DC 20024 — **(202) 265-5343; Fax: (202) 488-8093**

Full-time: 51 men, 75 women	**Faculty:** 13
Part-time: 106 men, 281 women	**Ph.D.s:** 62%
Graduate: 184 men, 285 women	**Student/Faculty:** 11 to 1
Year: quarters, summer session	**Tuition:** $8505
Application Deadline: open	**Room & Board:** n/app
Freshman Class: 926 applied, 367 accepted, 280 enrolled	
SAT I or ACT: recommended	**LESS COMPETITIVE**

Southeastern University, founded as Washington School for Accountancy in 1879, is a private, commuter college offering programs in business administration, accounting, computer information systems, finance, banking, and marketing to a student body comprised primarily of working adults. There is 1 undergraduate school and 1 graduate school. The library contains 40,000 volumes, and subscribes to 1200 periodicals. Computerized library services include the card catalog and database searching. Special learning facilities include a learning resource center. The 3-acre campus is in an urban area in a residential part of southwest Washington, D.C. There is 1 building.

Student Life: 56% of undergraduates are from District of Columbia. Others are from 4 states, 40 foreign countries, and Canada. 58% are African American; 35% foreign nationals. The average age of freshmen is 29; all undergraduates, 30.

Housing: There are no residence halls. Alcohol is not permitted. Referral listings of long- and short-term housing are available. No one may keep cars.

Activities: There is 1 local fraternity. There are some groups and organizations on campus, including chess, computers, newspaper, and student government. Popular campus events include Annual Awards Ceremony, a chess tournament, and International Week.

Sports: There is no sports program at Southeastern.

Disabled Students: All of the campus is accessible. Wheelchair ramps, special parking, specially equipped rest rooms, special class scheduling, and lowered telephones are available.

Services: Counseling and information services are available, as is tutoring in most subjects. There is remedial math, reading, and writing. There are also individualized learning programs for students in upper level courses.

Campus Safety and Security: Measures include 24-hour foot and vehicle patrol, escort service, shuttle buses, and lighted pathways/sidewalks.

Programs of Study: Southeastern confers the B.S. degree. Associate and master's degrees are also awarded. Bachelor's degrees are awarded in BUSINESS (accounting, banking and finance, business administration and management, and marketing/retailing/merchandising), COMPUTER AND PHYSICAL SCIENCE (information sciences and systems), SOCIAL SCIENCE (law, liberal arts/general studies, and public administration). Business and computer science are the strongest academically. Business and computer science/information systems are the largest.

Required: To graduate, students must complete 120 credit hours, maintaining a 2.0 GPA, including the general studies core curriculum, which consists of 30 hours in the fields of English, information systems, math, humanities, and social science. Also required are 24 hours in the general studies electives, 27 hours of major requirements, 27 hours in the professional core, 6 hours of professional electives, and 6 hours of general electives. All students must take an orientation course and a computer course.

Special: Southeastern offers extensive co-op programs, internships, work-study, accelerated degree programs, B.A.-B.S.degrees, dual majors, and credit by exam and for life/military/work experience. The Add-a-Degree program allows any student with a bachelor's degree to add a second area of expertise, add professional qualifications, or prepare for graduate study by completing necessary foundation courses. There is 1 national honor society.

Faculty/Classroom: 81% of faculty are male; 19%, female. All teach undergraduates. No introductory courses are taught by graduate students. The average class size in a regular course is 11.

Admissions: 40% of the 2001-2002 applicants were accepted.

Requirements: The SAT I or ACT is recommended. In addition, students must be graduates of an accredited secondary school or have a GED and must pass Southeastern's placement test for regular admission. CLEP credit is accepted.

Procedure: Freshmen are admitted to all sessions. Application deadlines are open. The application fee is $45. Notification is sent on a rolling basis.

Transfer: 23 transfer students enrolled in 2001-2002. All transfer applicants must submit transcripts. Up to 60 credits, with a grade of C or better, may be transferred. 60 credits of 120 must be completed at Southeastern.

Visiting: To schedule a visit, contact Jack Flinter at (202) 488-8162.

Financial Aid: In 2001-2002, 54% of all freshmen and 63% of continuing students received some form of financial aid. 43% of freshmen and 54% of continuing students received need-based aid. Scholarships or need-based grants averaged $3000 ($4000 maximum); and loans averaged $3500 ($4000 maximum). 3% of undergraduates work part time. Average annual earnings from campus work are $2900. The average financial indebtedness of the 2001 graduate was $17,125. The FAFSA and the college's own financial statement are required. The fall application deadline is August 15.

International Students: There are 70 international students enrolled. They must take the TOEFL. Applicants scoring below 550 are required to take 2 English courses. Those scoring below 500 are required to enroll in the university's Language Institute.

Computers: Southeastern's computer center has an IBM mainframe. The PC network is fully available to students. Those students required to use computing in their major may access the system. There are no time limits and no fees.

Graduates: In 2001, 69 bachelor's degrees were awarded. The most popular majors were liberal studies (28%), information systems management (23%), and management (17%). In an average class, 20% graduate in 4 years, 40% in 5 years, and 40% in 6 years. 24 companies recruited on campus in 2000-2001.

Admissions Contact: Jack Flinter, Director of Admissions.
E-mail: *jflinter@admin.seu.edu*

STRAYER UNIVERSITY C-3
Washington, DC 20005

(202) 408-2400
(888) 4-STRAYER; Fax: (202) 289-1831

Full-time: 1239 men, 1269 women	**Faculty:** 117
Part-time: 3821 men, 5456 women	**Ph.D.s:** 51%
Graduate: 1061 men, 1163 women	**Student/Faculty:** 22 to 1
Year: quarters, summer session	**Tuition:** $8789
Application Deadline: open	**Room & Board:** n/app
Freshman Class: n/av	
SAT I or ACT: recommended	**SPECIAL**

Strayer University, founded in 1892, is an independent commuter institution with 17 campuses in Washington, D.C., Maryland, and Virginia, as well as a distance learning program via the Internet. All programs are computer or business related.There is 1 graduate school. The library contains 35,000 volumes and 2813 audiovisual forms/CDs, and subscribes to 550 periodicals. Computerized library services include the card catalog, interlibrary loans, and database searching. Special learning facilities include a learning resource center. 2 of the campuses are located in Washington, D.C., 5 are in Maryland, and 10 are in Virginia; campuses vary between urban and suburban.

Student Life: 97% of undergraduates are from District of Columbia. Others are from 26 states, 124 foreign countries, and Canada. 42% are African American; 32%, white. The average age of all undergraduates is 33.

Housing: There are no residence halls. All students commute. Alcohol is not permitted. All students may keep cars.

Activities: There are no fraternities or sororities. There are 13 groups on campus, including computers, debate, ethnic, honors, international, newspaper, professional, and religious.

Sports: The sports program is an athletic club, which uses intercollegiate athletic participation to promote education and student development.

Disabled Students: All of the campus is accessible. Wheelchair ramps, elevators, special parking, specially equipped rest rooms, lowered drinking fountains, and lowered telephones are available.

Services: Counseling and information services are available, as is tutoring in some subjects, including accounting, computer information systems, English, and math at the introductory course level. There is remedial reading and writing.

Campus Safety and Security: Measures include escort service, informal discussions, pamphlets/posters/films, and lighted pathways/sidewalks. There are security guards at all the urban campuses and during evening hours at other campuses, crime seminars held regularly for students and employees, and a campus crime awareness booklet published annually or available via the school's website.

Programs of Study: Strayer confers the B.S. degree. Associate and master's degrees are also awarded. Bachelor's degrees are awarded in BUSINESS (accounting, business administration and management, and international business management), COMPUTER AND PHYSICAL SCIENCE (information sciences and systems and web technology), SOCIAL SCIENCE (economics). Computer information systems, business administration, and accounting are the strongest academically. Computer information systems and business administration are the largest.

Required: To graduate, students must complete 180 quarter hours, including 54 in the major, with a minimum GPA of 2.0. There is a core general studies component to each undergraduate degree, as well as a general business component.

Special: Strayer offers co-op programs in all majors, dual majors, internships with area businesses, accelerated diploma programs in computer information systems and accounting, and credit for military and work experience. There are 2 national honor societies.

Faculty/Classroom: 71% of faculty are male; 29%, female. All teach undergraduates. No introductory courses are taught by graduate students.

Requirements: The SAT I or ACT is recommended. In addition, applicants must either submit SAT I scores of at least 400 verbal and/or 400 math or take Strayer's placement tests. Students must have earned a high school diploma or a GED. AP and CLEP credits are accepted. Applications are accepted on-line via the school's web site.

Procedure: Freshmen are admitted to all sessions. Entrance exams should be taken by the beginning of the first quarter of attendance. There is a deferred admissions plan. Application deadlines are open. The fall 2001 application fee was $35. Notification is sent on a rolling basis.

Transfer: Requirements are the same as for freshmen. 54 quarter credits of 180 must be completed at Strayer.

Visiting: Scheduled orientations for prospective students rotate among the campuses. There are guides for informal visits. To schedule a visit, contact the Campus Manager.

Financial Aid: The FAFSA is required.

International Students: There are 585 international students enrolled. The school actively recruits these students. They must score 500 on the written TOEFL or 173 on the electronic version.

Computers: The mainframe is a Sun SPARC 1000. There are 750 PCs available for student use, some located in the library and learning resource centers. Students have access to the Internet and other on-line services through these terminals. Additionally, each campus has at least 1 PC lab and 1 networking UNIX lab. All students may access the system. There are no time limits and no fees.

Graduates: In 2001, 1379 bachelor's degrees were awarded. The most popular majors were computer information systems (36%), business administration (26%), and computer networking (25%). 200 companies recruited on campus in 2000-2001. Of the 2000 graduating class, 14% were enrolled in graduate school within 6 months of graduation and 86% were employed.

Admissions Contact: Melvin Menns, Washington Campus Manager.
E-mail: *info45@strayer.edu* Web: *http://www.strayer.edu*

TRINITY COLLEGE C-2
Washington, DC 20017

(202) 884-9400
(800) 492-6882; Fax: (202) 884-9403

Full-time: 570 women	**Faculty:** 55; IIB, -$
Part-time: 470 women	**Ph.D.s:** 95%
Graduate: 80 men, 410 women	**Student/Faculty:** 9 to 1
Year: n/app	**Tuition:** $14,870
Application Deadline: open	**Room & Board:** $6500
Freshman Class: n/av	
SAT I or ACT: required	**LESS COMPETITIVE**

Trinity College, founded in 1897, is a private, women's liberal arts college affiliated with the Roman Catholic Church. The school year consists of traditional semesters plus 1-week courses during January and May. Figures in above capsule are approximate. There are 2 undergraduate and 2 graduate schools. In addition to regional accreditation, Trinity has baccalaureate program accreditation with NASDTEC and NCATE. The library contains 178,232 volumes, 5392 microform items, and 2922 audiovisual forms/CDs, and subscribes to 620 periodicals. Computerized library services include the card catalog, interlibrary loans, and database searching. Special learning facilities include a learning resource center, art gallery, computer center, writing center, and career and counseling center. The 26-acre campus is in an urban area 2 1/2 miles north of the U.S. Capitol. Including residence halls, there are 7 buildings.

Student Life: Students com from 35 states, 15 foreign countries, and Canada. 40% are from public schools. 48% are white; 38% African American; 10% Hispanic. 60% are Catholic; 37% Protestant. The average age of freshmen is 18; all undergraduates, 20. 11% do not continue beyond their first year; 87% remain to graduate.

Housing: 500 students can be accommodated in college housing, which includes dormitories. On-campus housing is guaranteed for all 4 years. 95% of students live on campus; of those, 95% remain on campus on weekends. All students may keep cars.

Activities: There are no fraternities. There are 28 groups on campus, including choir, chorale, computers, dance, drama, ethnic, gay, honors, international, jazz band, literary magazine, newspaper, orchestra, photography, political, professional, religious, social, social service, student government, and yearbook. Popular campus events include Founders Day, Class Days, and Junior Ring Day.

Sports: Facilities include 2 athletic fields for soccer and field hockey, a fitness center, 6 tennis courts, and an outdoor sand volleyball court.

Disabled Students: Wheelchair ramps, elevators, special parking, specially equipped rest rooms, and lowered telephones are available.
Services: Counseling and information services are available, as is tutoring in every subject. There is a reader service for the blind and signing for hearing-impaired students.
Campus Safety and Security: Measures include 24-hour foot and vehicle patrol, self-defense education, escort service, and shuttle buses. There are informal discussions, pamphlets/posters/films, emergency telephones, and lighted pathways/sidewalks.
Programs of Study: Trinity confers B.A. and B.S. degrees. Master's degrees are also awarded. Bachelor's degrees are awarded in BIOLOGICAL SCIENCE (biochemistry and biology/biological science), BUSINESS (business administration and management), COMMUNICATIONS AND THE ARTS (communications, English, French, and Spanish), COMPUTER AND PHYSICAL SCIENCE (chemistry), EDUCATION (early childhood and elementary), ENGINEERING AND ENVIRONMENTAL DESIGN (environmental science), HEALTH PROFESSIONS (premedicine), SOCIAL SCIENCE (American studies, economics, history, international studies, political science/government, prelaw, and psychology). English, history, and political science are the strongest academically. Business administration, political science, and psychology are the largest.
Required: To graduate, students must complete a total of 128 credit hours with a minimum GPA of 2.0. Between 42 and 50 hours are required in the major. All students must take the courses required in the Foundation for Leadership curriculum and must complete a senior seminar.
Special: Cross-registration and the Mentor Program are offered through the Consortium of Universities of the Washington Area. Trinity offers internships in all majors and minors, as well as work-study programs. Students may study in France, Italy, and various other countries by arrangement with their faculty adviser. B.A.-B.S. degrees, a 5-year accelerated degree in teaching, a 3-2 engineering degree with George Washington University, dual and student-designed majors, a general studies degree, credit for life experience, nondegree study, and pass/fail options are also available. There are 2 national honor societies, including Phi Beta Kappa, and a freshman honors program.
Faculty/Classroom: 25% of faculty are male; 75%, female. All both teach and do research. No introductory courses are taught by graduate students. The average class size in an introductory lecture is 20; in a laboratory, 10; and in a regular course, 17.
Requirements: The SAT I or ACT is required, in addition, graduation from an accredited secondary school or satisfactory scores on the GED are required for admission. A total of 16 academic credits is required, including 4 years of English and 3 to 4 years each of a foreign language, history, math, and science. AP examinations and SAT II: Subject tests are recommended. An interview and an essay or graded writing sample are required. Trinity accepts applications on computer disk. Instructions will be sent to students upon request. A GPA of 2.0 is required. AP and CLEP credits are accepted. Important factors in the admissions decision are leadership record, extracurricular activities record, and recommendations by school officials.
Procedure: Freshmen are admitted fall, spring, and summer. Entrance exams should be taken in the junior year. There are early admissions and deferred admissions plans. Application deadlines are open. The fall 2001 application fee was $35.
Transfer: Transfer applicants must have a GPA of 2.0. An interview is required. 30 credits of 128 must be completed at Trinity.
Visiting: There are regularly scheduled orientations for prospective students, consisting of a full-day program on the third Friday of each month: an overview of the college, the curriculum, financing, and student life, and a trolley tour of Washington, D.C. There are guides for informal visits and visitors may sit in on classes and stay overnight. To schedule a visit, contact the Office of Admissions at (202) 939-5040 or (800) 492-6882.
Financial Aid: In a recent year, 85% of all freshmen and 83% of continuing students received some form of financial aid. 81% of freshmen and 70% of continuing students received need-based aid. The average freshman award was $14,654. Of that total, scholarships or need-based grants averaged $6000 ($8500 maximum); loans averaged $5130; and work contracts averaged $1000. 55% of undergraduates work part time. Average annual earnings from campus work are $1000. The average financial indebtedness of a recent graduate was $27,643. Trinity is a member of CSS. The CSS/Profile is required. Check with the school for current deadlines.
International Students: The school actively recruits these students. They must score 550 on the written TOEFL and also take the SAT I or the ACT.
Computers: Students may use the 31 IBM and 9 Apple PCs located in the computer center and in residence halls. All have printer access. All students may access the system. There are no time limits and no fees. It is strongly recommended that all students have a personal computer.
Admissions Contact: Gretchen Reinhardt/ Wendy Kares, Associate Director of Admissions. E-mail: *admissions@trinitydc.edu*
Web: *www.consortium.org/~trinity*

UNIVERSITY OF THE DISTRICT OF COLUMBIA C-2

Washington, DC 20008 **(202) 274-5010; Fax: (202) 274-6067**

Full-time: 1525 men, 1800 women	**Faculty:** 343
Part-time: 2425 men, 3500 women	**Ph.D.s:** 52%
Graduate: 220 men, 280 women	**Student/Faculty:** 10 to 1
Year: semesters, summer session	**Tuition:** $2250($5550)
Application Deadline: open	**Room & Board:** n/app
Freshman Class: n/av	
SAT I: n/av	**ACT:** required

NONCOMPETITIVE

The University of the District of Columbia, founded in 1977, is a publicly funded, land grant commuter institution offering programs in liberal arts, business, education, and technical fields. Figures given in above capsule are approximate. There are 5 undergraduate schools and 1 graduate school. In addition to regional accreditation, UDC has baccalaureate program accreditation with ABET, CAHEA, CSWE, NASDTEC, NASM, and NLN. The 4 libraries contain 470,330 volumes, 623,991 microform items, and 21,207 audiovisual forms/CDs, and subscribe to 2787 periodicals. Computerized library services include database searching. Special learning facilities include a learning resource center, art gallery, radio station, TV station, and early childhood learning center. The 22-acre campus is in a suburban area in northwest Washington, D.C. There are 26 buildings.
Student Life: 87% of undergraduates are from District of Columbia. Others are from 49 states and 55 foreign countries. 85% are from public schools. 72% are African American. The average age of freshmen is 18; all undergraduates, 27. 35% do not continue beyond their first year; 65% remain to graduate.
Housing: There are no residence halls. All students commute. Alcohol is not permitted.
Activities: 2% of men belong to 7 national fraternities; 2% of women belong to 5 national sororities. There are 139 groups on campus, including art, band, cheerleading, chess, choir, chorale, computers, dance, drama, drum and bugle corps, ethnic, film, honors, international, jazz band, marching band, newspaper, orchestra, pep band, photography, political, professional, radio and TV, religious, social, social service, student government, and yearbook. Popular campus events include the Cross-Cultural Extended Family Program and International Multicultural Recognition Day.
Sports: There are 6 intercollegiate sports for men and 6 for women, and 8 intramural sports for men and 6 for women. Facilities include a 3000-seat gym, a swimming pool, a weight room, and racquetball and tennis courts.
Disabled Students: All of the campus is accessible. Wheelchair ramps, elevators, special parking, specially equipped rest rooms, lowered drinking fountains, and lowered telephones are available.
Services: Counseling and information services are available, as is tutoring in every subject. There is a reader service for the blind and remedial math and reading.
Campus Safety and Security: Measures include 24-hour foot and vehicle patrol, emergency telephones, and lighted pathways/sidewalks.
Programs of Study: UDC confers B.A., and B.S. degrees. Associate and master's degrees are also awarded. Bachelor's degrees are awarded in BIOLOGICAL SCIENCE (biology/biological science), BUSINESS (accounting, banking and finance, business administration and management, marketing/retailing/merchandising, and office supervision and management), COMMUNICATIONS AND THE ARTS (dramatic arts, English, fine arts, French, media arts, music, and Spanish), COMPUTER AND PHYSICAL SCIENCE (chemistry, computer science, mathematics, and physics), EDUCATION (early childhood, elementary, health, and physical), ENGINEERING AND ENVIRONMENTAL DESIGN (architecture, aviation administration/management, civil engineering, construction engineering, electrical/electronics engineering, electromechanical technology, environmental science, and mechanical engineering), HEALTH PROFESSIONS (nursing and speech pathology/audiology), SOCIAL SCIENCE (criminal justice, economics, fire science, food science, geography, history, philosophy, political science/government, psychology, public administration, social work, sociology, and urban studies). Business is the strongest academically. Fine arts is the largest.
Required: To graduate, students must complete 120 to 130 semester hours with a minimum GPA of 2.0. All students must take 6 hours each of English composition, literature and advanced writing, foreign language, social science, math, and natural sciences, 4 of personal and community health, and 3 each of philosophy and fine arts.
Special: Cross-registration may be arranged through the Consortium of Universities of the Washington Metropolitan Area. Co-op programs with the federal government, internships, study abroad in 4 countries, work-study programs, and B.A.-B.S. degrees in administration of justice, chemistry, and physics are offered. Nondegree study and credit for life experience are also available. There are 4 national honor societies and a freshman honors program.
Faculty/Classroom: 66% of faculty are male; 34%, female. 89% teach undergraduates, 3% do research, and 20% do both. No introductory

courses are taught by graduate students. The average class size in an introductory lecture is 23; in a laboratory, 23; and in a regular course, 23.

Requirements: The ACT is required. In addition, a high school diploma or GED is required for admission, along with an interview. High school courses must include 4 years of English and 2 each of foreign language, social science, lab science, and math (algebra and geometry). AP and CLEP credits are accepted. Important factors in the admissions decision are ability to finance college education, advanced placement or honor courses, and recommendations by school officials.

Procedure: Freshmen are admitted to all sessions. Check with the school for current deadlines. The application fee is $20.

Transfer: Applicants must have a minimum GPA of 2.0. Those with fewer than 30 hours of college credit must submit a high school transcript along with college records. 30 credits of 120 must be completed at UDC.

Visiting: There are guides for informal visits and visitors may sit in on classes. To schedule a visit, contact the Office of Student Recruitment at (202) 282-3350.

Financial Aid: UDC is a member of CSS. The CSS/Profile or FFS is required.

International Students: They must score 550 on the written TOEFL and also take the university's own English, math, and reading tests.

Computers: The mainframes are an IBM 4381 and a DEC VAX 8650. PCs are also available. All students may access the system 24 hours a day. There are no time limits and no fees.

Admissions Contact: Director of Recruitment and Admissions.
Web: *udc2.org*

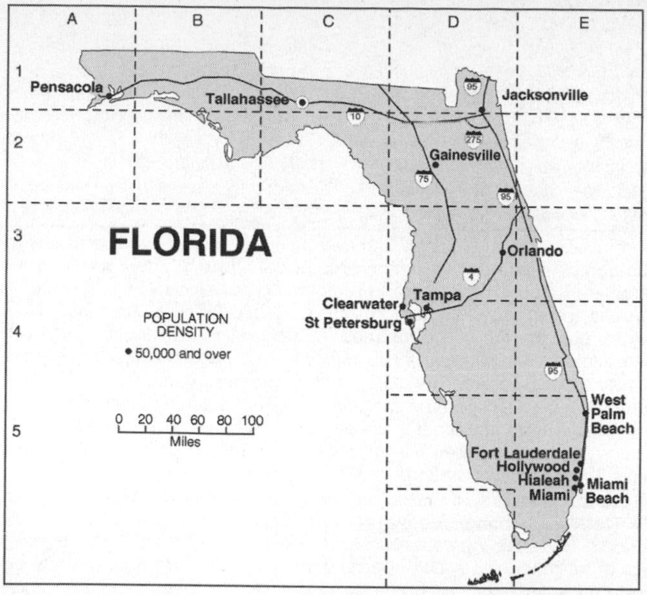

BARRY UNIVERSITY
Miami Shores, FL 33161

E-5
(305) 899-3100
(800) 695-2279; Fax: (305) 899-2971

Full-time: 1008 men, 2268 women
Part-time: 1033 men, 1598 women
Graduate: 853 men, 1931 women
Year: semesters, summer session
Application Deadline: open
Freshman Class: n/av
SAT I or ACT: required

Faculty: 167; IIA, -$
Ph.D.s: 80%
Student/Faculty: 15 to 1
Tuition: $17,500
Room & Board: $6600

LESS COMPETITIVE

Barry University is an independent Roman Catholic institution of liberal arts and professional studies. Figures in the above capsule are approximate. There are 6 undergraduate and 10 graduate schools. In addition to regional accreditation, Barry has baccalaureate program accreditation with CAHEA and NLN. The library contains 290,590 volumes, 512,192 microform items, and 3593 audiovisual forms/CDs, and subscribes to 1851 periodicals. Computerized library services include the card catalog, interlibrary loans, and database searching. Special learning facilities include a learning resource center, radio station, human performance lab, biotechnology lab, photography studios, TV studio, theater, biomechanics lab, and multimedia business classrooms. The 122-acre campus is in a suburban area 14 miles from Fort Lauderdale and 7 miles north of downtown Miami. Including residence halls, there are 26 buildings.

Student Life: 67% of undergraduates are from Florida. Others are from 46 states, 70 foreign countries, and Canada. 75% are from public schools. 39% are white; 30% Hispanic; 17% African American. 24% are Catholic. The average age of freshmen is 19; all undergraduates, 25. 28% do not continue beyond their first year; 48% remain to graduate.

Housing: 715 students can be accommodated in college housing, which includes single-sex and coed dormitories and off-campus apartments. In addition, there are special-interest houses. On-campus housing is guaranteed for the freshman year only, is available on a first-come, first-served basis, and is available on a lottery system for upperclassmen. Priority is given to out-of-town students. 71% of students commute. All students may keep cars.

Activities: 13% of men belong to 3 national fraternities; 4% of women belong to 2 national sororities. There are 82 groups on campus, including cheerleading, chorale, computers, dance, drama, ethnic, honors, international, literary magazine, musical theater, newspaper, photography, political, professional, radio and TV, religious, social, social service, and student government. Popular campus events include Halloween Dance, Festival of Nations, and World AIDS Day.

Sports: There are 5 intercollegiate sports for men and 7 for women. Facilities include baseball, softball, and soccer fields, a health and sports center with an indoor gym, outdoor basketball courts, and racquetball and tennis courts, an outdoor swimming pool, a strength and conditioning center, an athletic training room, a human performance lab, and a biomechanics lab.

Disabled Students: 85% of the campus is accessible. Wheelchair ramps, elevators, special parking, specially equipped rest rooms, special class scheduling, lowered drinking fountains, and lowered telephones are available.

Services: Counseling and information services are available, as is tutoring in most subjects. There is remedial math, reading, and writing.

Campus Safety and Security: Measures include 24-hour foot and vehicle patrol, self-defense education, escort service, and shuttle buses. There are informal discussions, pamphlets/posters/films, emergency telephones, and lighted pathways/sidewalks.

Programs of Study: Barry confers B.A., B.S., B.F.A., B.L.S., B.P.A., B.P.S., B.S.L.S., B.S.N., B.S.T., and B.S.W. degrees. Master's and doctoral degrees are also awarded. Bachelor's degrees are awarded in BIOLOGICAL SCIENCE (biology/biological science and marine biology), BUSINESS (accounting, international business management, management information systems, management science, marketing/retailing/merchandising, and sports management), COMMUNICATIONS AND THE ARTS (advertising, art, broadcasting, communications, dramatic arts, English, French, music performance, photography, public relations, Spanish, and theater management), COMPUTER AND PHYSICAL SCIENCE (chemistry, computer science, and mathematics), EDUCATION (early childhood and physical), ENGINEERING AND ENVIRONMENTAL DESIGN (preengineering), HEALTH PROFESSIONS (cytotechnology, medical technology, nuclear medical technology, nursing, occupational therapy, predentistry, premedicine, prepharmacy, and ultrasound technology), SOCIAL SCIENCE (criminology, economics, history, international studies, liberal arts/general studies, philosophy, political science/government, prelaw, psychology, sociology, and theological studies). Biology, chemistry, and elementary and early childhood education are the strongest academically. Nursing, elementary and early childhood education, and biology are the largest.

Required: To graduate, students must complete 120 credit hours, including at least 48 in upper-division courses, 40 to 60 in the major, and 45 distributed in these curricular divisions: theology and philosophy, written and oral communication, physical or natural science and math, social and behavior sciences, and humanities and the arts. A minimum GPA of 2.0 must be maintained.

Special: Barry offers junior- or senior-year internships, a Washington semester for prelaw/political science students, on-campus work-study programs in all departments, dual majors, a liberal studies degree, an accelerated degree program in nursing, nondegree study, and pass/fail options. Students may study in 5 European countries. Barry is a member of the College Consortium for International Studies; students can participate in more than 50 programs offered by members. There are 15 national honor societies and a freshman honors program.

Faculty/Classroom: 44% of faculty are male; 56%, female. 69% teach undergraduates. No introductory courses are taught by graduate students. The average class size in an introductory lecture is 17; in a laboratory, 14; and in a regular course, 17.

Requirements: The SAT I or ACT is required. In addition, graduation from an accredited secondary school or satisfactory scores on the GED are required for admission. A GPA of 2.0 is required. AP and CLEP credits are accepted. Applications are accepted on computer disk and on-line at the school's web site.

Procedure: Freshmen are admitted to all sessions. Entrance exams should be taken as early as possible. There is an early admissions plan. Check with the school for current application deadlines and fee.

Transfer: 563 transfer students enrolled in a recent year. Applicants must have earned at least 12 acceptable credit hours with a minimum GPA of 2.0. 30 credits of 120 must be completed at Barry.

Visiting: There are guides for informal visits and visitors may sit in on classes. To schedule a visit, contact Undergraduate Admissions at (305) 899-3113 or (800) 695-2279.

Financial Aid: In a recent year, 85% of all freshmen and 87% of continuing students received some form of financial aid. 67% of freshmen and 68% of continuing students received need-based aid. The average freshman award was $16,883. Of that total, scholarships or need-based grants averaged $8907 ($15,425 maximum); loans averaged $4121 ($16,946 maximum); work contracts averaged $2431 ($2500 maximum); and athletic grants and family discounts ($500) averaged $6015 ($12,000 maximum). 19% of undergraduates work part time. Average annual earnings from campus work are $2431. The average financial indebtedness of the 2001 graduate was $17,469. Barry is a member of CSS. The FAFSA is required.

International Students: There were 321 international students enrolled in a recent year. The school actively recruits these students. They must score 550 on the written TOEFL.

Computers: The mainframe is a DEC ALPHA 2100. The system may be accessed via dial-up modems or networked PCs in labs and residence halls. All students may access the system 24 hours a day. There are no time limits and no fees. It is strongly recommended that all students have a personal computer. It is recommended that students in the anesthesiology program (graduate degree) have personal computers. IBM ThinkPad or Dell is recommended.

Graduates: In 2001, 951 bachelor's degrees were awarded. The most popular majors were biology (21%), education (13%), and nursing (9%). In an average class, 49% graduate in 4 years, 48% in 5 years, and 48% in 6 years. 125 companies recruited on campus in 2000-2001.

Admissions Contact: Tracy Fontaine, Director of Admissions. E-mail: *admissions@mail.barry.edu* Web: *www.barry.edu*

BEACON COLLEGE D-3
Leesburg, FL 34748 (352) 787-7660; Fax: (352) 787-0721

Full-time: 43 men, 26 women	**Faculty:** 9
Part-time: none	**Ph.D.s:** 45%
Graduate: none	**Student/Faculty:** 8 to 1
Year: semesters, summer session	**Tuition:** $19,000
Application Deadline: open	**Room & Board:** $5900

Freshman Class: 49 applied, 32 accepted, 28 enrolled
SAT I or ACT: not required **COMPETITIVE**

Beacon College, founded in 1989, is a private institution that offers undergraduate degrees in liberal studies and human services exclusively for students with learning disabilities. The library contains 20,000 volumes and 219 audiovisual forms/CDs, and subscribes to 17 periodicals. Computerized library services include the card catalog, interlibrary loans, and database searching. Special learning facilities include a learning resource center and art gallery. The 2-acre campus is in a small town. Including residence halls, there are 7 buildings.

Student Life: 80% of undergraduates are from out of state, mostly the Northeast. Others are from 21 states and 1 foreign countrY. 40% are from public schools. 79% are white. The average age of freshmen is 19; all undergraduates, 20. 10% do not continue beyond their first year; 77% remain to graduate.

Housing: 70 students can be accommodated in college housing, which includes coed off-campus apartments. On-campus housing is guaranteed for all 4 years. All students live on campus; of those, 97% remain on campus on weekends. Alcohol is not permitted. All students may keep cars.

Activities: There are no fraternities or sororities. There are some groups and organizations on campus, including arts and music, computers, literary magazine, newspaper, student government, and yearbook.

Disabled Students: 90% of the campus is accessible. Wheelchair ramps, special parking, and specially equipped rest rooms are available.

Services: Counseling and information services are available, as is tutoring in every subject. There is remedial math, reading, and writing, and an Academic Mentoring Program.

Campus Safety and Security: Measures include school van transportation.

Programs of Study: Beacon College confers the B.A. degree. Associate degrees are also awarded. Bachelor's degrees are awarded in SOCIAL SCIENCE (human services,and liberal arts/general studies).

Required: To graduate, students must have 123 credit hours, including 45 credit hours of general education and at least 63 credit hours in their major, and a 2.0 GPA. 4 credit hours of phys. ed. are also required, and students in the liberal studies program must write a thesis and take a comprehensive exam.

Special: Internships, B.A.- B.S. degrees, dual majors, and study abroad are possible.

Faculty/Classroom: 47% of faculty are male; 55%, female. All teach undergraduates, 15% do research, and 15% do both. The average class size in an introductory lecture is 8; in a laboratory, 10-12; and in a regular course, 8.

Admissions: 65% of the 2001-2002 applicants were accepted.

Requirements: CLEP credit is accepted.

Procedure: Freshmen are admitted fall and spring. Entrance exams should be taken within 3 years prior to application. There are early decision and deferred admissions plans. Application deadlines are open. The application fee is $50.

Transfer: 3 transfer students enrolled in 2001-2002. 78 credits of 123 must be completed at Beacon College.

Visiting: There are regularly scheduled orientations for prospective students. There are guides for informal visits and visitors may sit in on classes and stay overnight. To schedule a visit, contact Betsy StoutMorrill.

Financial Aid: 10% of all students received some form of financial aid, including need-based aid. 12% of undergraduates work part time. The average financial indebtedness of the 2001 graduate was $350. The FAFSA is required.

International Students: There is 1 international studen enrolled. They must take the TOEFL and the college's own entrance exam, scoring 9.

Computers: All students may access the system during school hours. It is strongly recommended that all students have a personal computer.

Graduates: In 2001, 5 bachelor's degrees were awarded. The most popular majors were liberal studies (80%) and human services (20%). In an average class, 50% graduate in 4 years, 40% in 5 years, and 10% in 6 years.

Admissions Contact: Betsy StoutMorrill, Director of Admissions. E-mail: *admissions@beaconcollege.edu* Web: *www.beaconcollege.edu*

BETHUNE-COOKMAN COLLEGE D-2
Daytona Beach, FL 32114-3099 (386) 238-3803
(800) 448-0228; Fax: (386) 257-5338

Full-time: 1090 men, 1439 women	**Faculty:** 138; IIB, --$
Part-time: 62 men, 133 women	**Ph.D.s:** 57%
Graduate: none	**Student/Faculty:** 18 to 1
Year: semesters, summer session	**Tuition:** $9617
Application Deadline: July 30	**Room & Board:** $6129

Freshman Class: 3329 applied, 1874 accepted, 726 enrolled
SAT I Verbal/Math: 410/410 **COMPETITIVE**

Bethune-Cookman College, founded in 1904, is a private liberal arts institution affiliated with the United Methodist Church. There are 6 undergraduate schools. In addition to regional accreditation, B-CC has baccalaureate program accreditation with CAHEA, NCATE, and NLN. The library contains 163,645 volumes, 45,065 microform items, and 4025 audiovisual forms/CDs, and subscribes to 770 periodicals. Computerized library services include the card catalog, interlibrary loans, and database searching. Special learning facilities include a learning resource center, art gallery, radio station, TV studio, and observatory. The 60-acre campus is in an urban area 65 miles east of Orlando. Including residence halls, there are 35 buildings.

Student Life: 65% of undergraduates are from Florida. Others are from 37 states, 30 foreign countries, and Canada. 90% are from public schools. 90% are African American. Most are Protestant. The average age of freshmen is 18; all undergraduates, 20. 24% do not continue beyond their first year.

Housing: 1772 students can be accommodated in college housing, which includes single-sex dormitories. On-campus housing is guaranteed for the freshman year only and is available on a first-come, first-served basis. Priority is given to out-of-town students. 61% of students live on campus; of those, 88% remain on campus on weekends. Alcohol is not permitted. Upperclassmen may keep cars.

Activities: 10% of men belong to 5 national fraternities; 15% of women belong to 4 national sororities. There are 40 groups on campus, including band, cheerleading, choir, chorale, computers, dance, drama, drill team, honors, international, literary magazine, marching band, newspaper, political, professional, radio and TV, religious, social, student government, and yearbook. Popular campus events include Religious Outreach, Career Day, and Futurism Seminar.

Sports: There are 7 intercollegiate sports for men and 7 for women, and 6 intramural sports for men and 6 for women. Facilities include a gym, a weight room, a practice field, and tennis and racquetball courts.

Disabled Students: 10% of the campus is accessible. Wheelchair ramps, elevators, special parking, specially equipped rest rooms, lowered drinking fountains, and lowered telephones are available.

Services: Counseling and information services are available, as is tutoring in most subjects. There is remedial math, reading, and writing.

Campus Safety and Security: Measures include 24-hour foot and vehicle patrol, escort service, informal discussions, and pamphlets/posters/films. There are lighted pathways/sidewalks.

Programs of Study: B-CC confers B.A. and B.S. degrees. Bachelor's degrees are awarded in BIOLOGICAL SCIENCE (biology/biological science), BUSINESS (accounting, business administration and management, hotel/motel and restaurant management, international business management, and recreation and leisure services), COMMUNICATIONS AND THE ARTS (communications, English, modern language, and music), COMPUTER AND PHYSICAL SCIENCE (chemistry, computer science, information sciences and systems, mathematics, and physics), EDUCATION (business, education of the exceptional child, elementary, English, foreign languages, mathematics, music, physical, science, and social science), HEALTH PROFESSIONS (medical laboratory science and nursing), SOCIAL SCIENCE (criminal justice, gerontology, history, international studies, liberal arts/general studies, philosophy, political science/government, psychology, religion, and sociology). Business administration, elementary education, and nursing are the strongest academically. Business administration, elementary education, and criminal justice are the largest.

Required: To graduate, students must have a total of 124 credit hours with a minimum GPA of 2.0. All students must complete a total of 49 hours in general education requirements, pass all parts of the College-Level Academic Skills Test (CLAST), and pass at a specified level 9 senior exit exams that may include a standardized exam and/or senior area comprehensive exam. They must also complete a senior seminar and senior research paper.

Special: Students may take courses at other institutions with the approval of the area adviser or registrar. B-CC offers cooperative courses in all divisions, internships related to the student's major, work-study programs, nondegree-study, and 3-2 engineering degrees with the Universities of Florida and Central Florida, Tuskegee and Florida Atlantic Universities, and Florida Agriculture and Mechanical University-Florida

State University. Study abroad is available in Spain, France, and Germany. There are 6 national honor societies, including Phi Beta Kappa, a freshman honors program, and 2 departmental honors programs.

Faculty/Classroom: 54% of faculty are male; 46%, female. 95% teach undergraduates and 5% both teach and do research. The average class size in an introductory lecture is 20; in a laboratory, 20; and in a regular course, 18.

Admissions: 56% of the 2001-2002 applicants were accepted. The SAT I scores for the 2001-2002 freshman class were: Verbal--86% below 500, 11% between 500 and 599, and 3% between 600 and 700; Math--88% below 500, 9% between 500 and 599, and 3% between 600 and 700. 18% of the recent freshmen were in the top fifth of their class; 36% were in the top two fifths.

Requirements: The SAT I or ACT is required. In addition, graduation from an accredited secondary school or satisfactory scores on the GED are required for admission. High school courses must include 24 credits with 4 of English, 3 each of math and science, 2 of history, 1/2 each of government, economics, vocational ed, art, management skills, and phys ed, and 9 of electives; 2 years of a modern language are strongly recommended. Students must submit an essay and a letter of recommendation. A GPA of 2.25 is required. AP and CLEP credits are accepted. Important factors in the admissions decision are extracurricular activities record, leadership record, and geographic diversity.

Procedure: Freshmen are admitted to all sessions. Entrance exams should be taken during the fall prior to application. There is a deferred admissions plan. Applications should be filed by July 30 for fall entry, November 30 for spring entry, and April 30 for summer entry. The fall 2001 application fee was $25. Notification is sent on a rolling basis.

Transfer: 87 transfer students enrolled in 2001-2002. Applicants must submit transcripts from previous institutions attended and a statement of good standing and eligibility to return. A minimum GPA of 2.0 is required. Students having fewer than 12 credit hours must meet the requirements for entering freshmen. 30 credits of 124 must be completed at B-CC.

Visiting: There are guides for informal visits and visitors may sit in on classes. To schedule a visit, contact the Admissions Office at (386) 255-1401, ext. 206/303/358 or *coffiee@cookman.edu*

Financial Aid: In 2001-2002, 95% of all freshmen and 96% of continuing students received some form of financial aid. 75% of freshmen and 76% of continuing students received need-based aid. The average freshman award was $13,000. Of that total, scholarships or need-based grants averaged $7900 ($15,800 maximum); loans averaged $4400 ($6650 maximum); and work contracts averaged $500 ($1440 maximum). 75% of undergraduates work part time. Average annual earnings from campus work are $1400. The average financial indebtedness of the 2001 graduate was $22,800. B-CC is a member of CSS. The FAFSA is required. The fall application deadline is March 1.

International Students: There are 172 international students enrolled. The school actively recruits these students. They must score 500 on the written TOEFL and also take the SAT I or the ACT.

Computers: The mainframe is a Sun Enterprise 3000. Each academic building is equipped with computer facilities. More than 250 computer keyboards are available for student use. All students may access the system. There are no time limits and no fees.

Graduates: In 2001, 206 bachelor's degrees were awarded. The most popular majors were elementary education (11%), criminal justice (10%), and business administration (10%). In an average class, 4% graduate in 3 years, 14% in 4 years, 28% in 5 years, and 32% in 6 years. 166 companies recruited on campus in 2000-2001. Of the 2000 graduating class, 25% were enrolled in graduate school within 6 months of graduation and 80% were employed.

Admissions Contact: Edwin Coffie, Director of Admissions. A video is available. E-mail: *coffiee@cookman.edu*
Web: *www.bethune.cookman.edu*

CARLOS ALBIZU UNIVERSITY

Miami, FL 33172-2209 — E-5

(305) 593-1223 ext 137
(800) 672-3246; Fax: (305) 593-1854

Full-time: 14 men, 58 women	**Faculty:** 3
Part-time: 16 men, 56 women	**Ph.D.s:** 90%
Graduate: 121 men, 345 women	**Student/Faculty:** 24 to 1
Year: trimesters, summer session	**Tuition:** $9309
Application Deadline: open	**Room & Board:** n/app
Freshman Class: 26 applied, 20 accepted, 14 enrolled	
SAT I or ACT: not required	**COMPETITIVE**

Carlos Albizu University is a private, non-profit, specialized institution of higher learning offering degrees at the undergraduate, graduate, and doctoral levels. CAU has campuses in San Juan, Puerto Rico, and Miami, Florida, founded in 1966 and 1980 respectively. There is 1 undergraduate and 2 graduate schools. The library contains 21,000 volumes and 733 audiovisual forms/CDs, and subscribes to 350 periodicals. Computerized library services include the card catalog, interlibrary loans, and database searching. Special learning facilities include a learning resource center and an ESOL lab. The 18-acre campus is in an urban area. There are 2 buildings.

Student Life: All undergraduates are from Florida. 75% are Hispanic; 17% African American. The average age of freshmen is 27; all undergraduates, 29. 1% do not continue beyond their first year.

Housing: There are no residence halls. All students commute. Alcohol is not permitted. All students may keep cars.

Activities: There are no fraternities or sororities. There are 2 groups on campus, including newsletter and student government. Popular campus events include the Distinguished Student Award Banquet and the Student Council Initiation Event.

Disabled Students: All of the campus is accessible. Wheelchair ramps, special parking, specially equipped rest rooms, and lowered drinking fountains are available.

Services: Counseling and information services are available, as is tutoring in most subjects. There is a mentoring program and student support services center.

Campus Safety and Security: Measures include 24-hour foot and vehicle patrol, escort service, emergency telephones, and lighted pathways/sidewalks. There is an annual report on crime statistics.

Programs of Study: CAU confers B.A., B.S., and B.B.A. degrees. Master's and doctoral degrees are also awarded. Bachelor's degrees are awarded in BUSINESS (business administration and management), EDUCATION (elementary), SOCIAL SCIENCE (psychology). Psychology is the largest.

Required: To graduate, students must earn 120 to 124 credits, with 30 to 48 in the major. Foundation courses include English composition, oral communication, math, behaviorial life, physical sciences, humanities, cross-cultural studies, literature, liberal arts, and computing, for a total of 48 credits.

Special: CAU offers cross-registration with other area colleges, internships or practicums in psychology and elementary education, federal work-study, and an accelerated degree program in business administration. There is 1 national honor society.

Faculty/Classroom: 40% of faculty are male; 60%, female. All both teach and do research. Graduate students teach 15% of introductory courses. The average class size in an introductory lecture is 10; in a laboratory, 10; and in a regular course, 15.

Admissions: 77% of the 2001-2002 applicants were accepted.

Requirements: A GPA of 2.0 is required. AP and CLEP credits are accepted. Important factors in the admissions decision are advanced placement or honor courses and ability to finance college education.

Procedure: Freshmen are admitted fall, spring, and summer. Application deadlines are open. Notification is sent on a rolling basis. The application fee is $25.

Transfer: 28 transfer students enrolled in 2001-2002. Transfer applicants must have an overall GPA of 2.0 and must submit official transcripts from all colleges previously attended. 30 credits of 120 to 124 must be completed at CAU.

Visiting: There are regularly scheduled orientations for prospective students, consisting of 2 open houses per session. There are guides for informal visits and visitors may sit in on classes. To schedule a visit, contact Dr. Mary-Angie Salva-Ramirez.

Financial Aid: In 2001-2002, 75% of all freshmen and 79% of continuing students received some form of financial aid. 73% of freshmen and 76% of continuing students received need-based aid. The average freshman award was $6710. Of that total, scholarships or need-based grants averaged $2146 ($4350 maximum); loans averaged $3994 ($6424 maximum); and work contracts averaged $570 ($1620 maximum). 9% of undergraduates work part time. Average annual earnings from campus work are $3130. The average financial indebtedness of the 2001 graduate was $13,293. The FAFSA and the college's own financial statement are required. The fall application deadline is June 1.

Computers: The mainframe is an HP 9000 Model L2000. There are 12 computers in the library, 24 in a computer lab, and 9 in an educational technology lab, all available for student use. All students may access the system from 10 A.M. to 11 P.M. Monday through Friday, and from 9 A.M. to 3 P.M. Saturdays. There are no time limits and no fees. It is strongly recommended that all students have a personal computer.

Graduates: In 2001, 32 bachelor's degrees were awarded. Of the 2000 graduating class, 70% were enrolled in graduate school within 6 months of graduation.

Admissions Contact: Dr. Mary-Angie Salva-Ramirez, Recruitment, Admissions, and Outreach. E-mail: *msalva@albizu.edu*
Web: *www.albizu.edu*

CLEARWATER CHRISTIAN COLLEGE D-4

Clearwater, FL 33759 (727) 726-1153, ext. 228
(800) 348-4463; Fax: (727) 726-8597

Full-time: 270 men, 350 women	**Faculty:** 34
Part-time: 10 men, 10 women	**Ph.D.s:** 56%
Graduate: none	**Student/Faculty:** 18 to 1
Year: semesters, summer session	**Tuition:** $9110
Application Deadline: n/av	**Room & Board:** $4050
Freshman Class: n/av	
SAT I or ACT: recommended	**LESS COMPETITIVE**

Clearwater Christian College, founded in 1966, is a private, fundamentalist, nonsectarian institution offering programs in Bible, liberal arts, business, and teacher preparation. Figures in the above capsule are approximate. The library contains 103,000 volumes, 198,000 microform items, and 2100 audiovisual forms/CDs, and subscribes to 1050 periodicals. Computerized library services include the card catalog, interlibrary loans, and database searching. Special learning facilities include a learning resource center. The 130-acre campus is in a small town 10 miles west of Tampa. Including residence halls, there are 7 buildings.

Student Life: 47% of undergraduates are from Florida. Others are from 37 states, 14 foreign countries, and Canada. 27% are from public schools. 89% are white. Most are Protestant. The average age of freshmen is 18; all undergraduates, 20. 39% do not continue beyond their first year; 41% remain to graduate.

Housing: 600 students can be accommodated in college housing, which includes single-sex dormitories. On-campus housing is guaranteed for all 4 years. 81% of students live on campus; of those, all remain on campus on weekends. Alcohol is not permitted. All students may keep cars.

Activities: There are no fraternities or sororities. There are 8 groups on campus, including band, cheerleading, choir, chorale, drama, honors, newspaper, orchestra, pep band, political, professional, religious, student government, and yearbook.

Sports: There are 3 intercollegiate sports for men and 3 for women, and 3 intramural sports for men and 3 for women. Facilities include a gym and a playing field.

Disabled Students: All of the campus is accessible. Wheelchair ramps, elevators, special parking, specially equipped rest rooms, lowered drinking fountains, and lowered telephones are available.

Services: There is a reader service for the blind as needed.

Campus Safety and Security: Measures include 24-hour foot and vehicle patrol, self-defense education, informal discussions, and pamphlets/posters/films. There are emergency telephones and lighted pathways/sidewalks.

Programs of Study: CCC confers B.A. and B.S. degrees. Associate degrees are also awarded. Bachelor's degrees are awarded in BIOLOGICAL SCIENCE (biology/biological science), BUSINESS (accounting and business administration and management), COMMUNICATIONS AND THE ARTS (communications, English, and music), COMPUTER AND PHYSICAL SCIENCE (mathematics), EDUCATION (elementary, music, physical, secondary, social studies, and special), HEALTH PROFESSIONS (premedicine), SOCIAL SCIENCE (biblical studies, history, humanities, ministries, pastoral studies, prelaw, psychology, religious education, and religious music). Education and business are the largest.

Required: General education requirements include 25 hours of human adjustment, 19 each of social science and humanities, 12 of arts and communication, and 10 of science and math. Computer science courses are required. A total of 128 credit hours is required, including more than 60 in the major, with a minimum GPA of 2.0. Students must have no grade lower than a C- in any major requirement and maintain satisfactory Christian service involvement throughout the college career.

Special: On occasion, credit from an approved correspondence school may be accepted, or registration at another school for a course to complete degree requirements at CCC may be permitted. Internships are offered in teacher education, business, and psychology. Work-study programs and nondegree study are possible. There is 1 national honor society.

Faculty/Classroom: 68% of faculty are male; 32%, female. All teach undergraduates. The average class size in an introductory lecture is 50; in a laboratory, 20; and in a regular course, 25.

Admissions: In a recent year, there was 1 National Merit finalist and 2 semifinalists. 20 freshmen graduated first in their class.

Requirements: The SAT I or ACT is recommended, with a minimum score of 870 on the SAT I or 18 on the ACT. Applicants must be high school graduates or have a GED certificate. An essay is required, and an interview is recommended. A GPA of 2.0 is required. AP and CLEP credits are accepted.

Procedure: Freshmen are admitted to all sessions. Entrance exams should be taken in the fall of the senior year. There is a deferred admissions plan. Notification is sent on a rolling basis. Check with the school for current deadlines. The application fee is $35.

Transfer: 59 transfer students enrolled in a recent year. Transfer applicants must submit transcripts from all postsecondary schools attended. Grades of C or better transfer. Applicants must have a minimum cumulative postsecondary GPA of 2.0. 32 credits of 128 must be completed at CCC.

Visiting: There are regularly scheduled orientations for prospective students. There are guides for informal visits and visitors may sit in on classes and stay overnight. To schedule a visit, contact the Admissions Office.

Financial Aid: In a recent year, 75% of all freshmen and 66% of continuing students received some form of financial aid. 34% of freshmen and 41% of continuing students received need-based aid. The average freshman award was $5025. Of that total, scholarships or need-based grants averaged $3337 ($12,934 maximum); and loans averaged $1688 ($14,308 maximum). 90% of undergraduates work part time. Average annual earnings from campus work are $1600. The average financial indebtedness of a recent graduate was $13,051. The CSS/Profile, FAFSA, or FFS are required. The FFS is preferred. Check with the school for current deadlines.

International Students: There were 21 international students enrolled in a recent year. They must score 500 on the written TOEFL and also submit a Foreign Student Data Form. They must also take the SAT I or the ACT, scoring 18 on the ACT.

Computers: The mainframe is an IBM AS/400. Internet access through an on-campus server is available through residence hall rooms, the library, public terminals in residence halls, and the computer lab. All students may access the system. There are no time limits. The fee is $30 annually. It is strongly recommended that all students have a personal computer.

Graduates: In a recent year, 108 bachelor's degrees were awarded. The most popular majors were elementary English (20%), business administration (16%), and psychology (12%). In an average class, 3% graduate in 3 years, 32% in 4 years, 38% in 5 years, and 41% in 6 years. 60 companies recruited on campus in 2000-2001. Of the 2000 graduating class, 16% were enrolled in graduate school within 6 months of graduation and 94% were employed.

Admissions Contact: Benjamin J. Puckett, Dean of Enrollment Services. A video is available. E-mail: *benpuckett@clearwater.edu*
Web: *clearwater.edu*

DEVRY UNIVERSITY/ORLANDO D-3

Orlando, FL 32839 (407) 355-3131
(888) FL-DEVRY; Fax: (407) 370-3198

Full-time: 477 men, 134 women	**Faculty:** 35
Part-time: 141 men, 51 women	**Ph.D.s:** n/av
Graduate: none	**Student/Faculty:** 17 to 1
Year: semesters, summer session	**Tuition:** $9865
Application Deadline: open	**Room & Board:** n/app
Freshman Class: 801 applied, 613 accepted, 306 enrolled	
SAT I or ACT: recommended	**LESS COMPETITIVE**

DeVry University/Orlando, founded in 2000, is a private institution offering hands-on programs in electronics, business administration, computer information systems, telecommunications management, information technology, and computer engineering technology. The school is 1 of 23 information technology DeVry schools throughout the United States and Canada. The library contains 6000 volumes and 611 audiovisual forms/CDs, and subscribes to 2000 periodicals. Computerized library services include the card catalog, interlibrary loans, and database searching. Special learning facilities include a learning resource center and electronics and other labs. .

Student Life: 92% of undergraduates are from Florida. Others are from 23 states and 8 foreign countries. 38% are white; 28% African American; 15% Hispanic. The average age of all undergraduates is 25. 57% do not continue beyond their first year.

Housing: There are no residence halls. All students commute. Housing referrals may be obtained through the Student Housing Office. Alcohol is not permitted. All students may keep cars.

Activities: There are no fraternities or sororities. There are 11 groups on campus, including professional, social, and yearbook. Popular campus events include Model Car Competition, Fun Flicks, and Welcome Picnic.

Sports: There is no sports program at DeVry.

Disabled Students: 98% of the campus is accessible. Special parking, specially equipped rest rooms, lowered drinking fountains, and lowered telephones are available.

Services: Counseling and information services are available, as is tutoring in every subject.

Campus Safety and Security: Measures include escort service, informal discussions, pamphlets/posters/films, and emergency telephones. There are lighted pathways/sidewalks and off-duty police as security.

Programs of Study: DeVry confers the B.S. degree. Associate degrees are also awarded. Bachelor's degrees are awarded in BUSINESS (business administration and management), COMMUNICATIONS AND THE ARTS (telecommunications), COMPUTER AND PHYSICAL SCIENCE (computer programming and information sciences and systems), ENGINEERING AND ENVIRONMENTAL DESIGN (electrical/electronics engi-

neering technology and technological management). Electronics, computer information systems, and telecommunications are the largest.
Required: To graduate, students must complete 48 to 54 credits, achieve a GPA of at least 2.0, and satisfactorily complete all curriculum requirements. Course requirements vary according to program. All first-semester students take courses in business organization, computer applications, algebra, psychology, and student success strategies.
Special: Accelerated degrees, co-op programs, nondegree study, and evening and weekend classes are possible.
Faculty/Classroom: All teach undergraduates. The average class size in an introductory lecture is 30; in a laboratory, 30; and in a regular course, 30.
Admissions: 77% of the 2001-2002 applicants were accepted.
Requirements: The SAT I or ACT is recommended. In addition, admissions requirements include graduation from a secondary school; the GED is also accepted. Applicants must pass the DeVry entrance exam or present satisfactory ACT or SAT I scores. An interview is required. CLEP credit is accepted. Applications are accepted on-line at *Embark.com*.
Procedure: Freshmen are admitted fall, spring, and summer. There is a deferred admissions plan. Application deadlines are open. The application fee is $50. Notification is sent on a rolling basis.
Transfer: 3 transfer students enrolled in 2001-2002. Applicants must present passing grades in all completed college course work, demonstrate language skills proficiency in at least 24 completed semester hours, and present evidence of math proficiency by appropriate college-level credits. 35% of 48 to 154 credits must be completed at DeVry.
Visiting: There are regularly scheduled orientations for prospective students. There are guides for informal visits and visitors may sit in on classes. To schedule a visit, contact Laura Dorsey, New Student Coordinator at (407) 345-2800.
Financial Aid: In 2001-2002, 20% of all freshmen and 74% of continuing students received some form of financial aid. 10% of freshmen and 45% of continuing students received need-based aid. 3% of undergraduates work part time. Average annual earnings from campus work are $6000. The average financial indebtedness of the 2001 graduate was $10,344. The FAFSA is required.
International Students: They must score 500 on the written TOEFL or 173 on the electronic version and also take the college's own entrance exam or DeVry's computerized placement test, achieving a minimum score that varies by program.
Admissions Contact: Aaron McCardell, Dean of Admissions.
Web: *www.orl.devry.edu*

ECKERD COLLEGE

St. Petersburg, FL 33711 D-4
(727) 864-8331
(800) 456-9009; Fax: (727) 866-2304

Full-time: 692 men, 864 women	**Faculty:** 97; IIB, av$
Part-time: 10 men, 15 women	**Ph.D.s:** 95%
Graduate: none	**Student/Faculty:** 14 to 1
Year: 4-1-4, summer session	**Tuition:** $20,085
Application Deadline: April 1	**Room & Board:** $5415
Freshman Class: 1930 applied, 1496 accepted, 424 enrolled	
SAT I Verbal/Math: 574/563	**ACT:** 25 **COMPETITIVE+**

Eckerd College, founded in 1958, is a private liberal arts institution affiliated with the Presbyterian Church (U.S.A.). Interdisciplinary programs are an important part of the school's curriculum. This is reflected in the organization of the faculty into collegia, rather than into traditional departments. The library contains 113,850 volumes, 14,606 microform items, and 1941 audiovisual forms/CDs, and subscribes to 3009 periodicals. Computerized library services include the card catalog, interlibrary loans, and database searching. Special learning facilities include an art gallery, a radio station, a TV station, and a sea mammal necropsy lab. The 267-acre campus is in a suburban area on 1 1/4 miles of waterfront, 5 miles south of St. Petersburg. Including residence halls, there are 67 buildings.
Student Life: 73% of undergraduates are from out of state, mostly the Middle Atlantic. Others are from 45 states, 49 foreign countries, and Canada. 75% are from public schools. 78% are white; 10%, foreign nationals. 37% are no religious affiliation; 26% are Protestant; 25%, Catholic. The average age of freshmen is 18; all undergraduates, 20. 23% do not continue beyond their first year; 60% remain to graduate.
Housing: 1209 students can be accommodated in college housing, which includes single-sex and coed dormitories and on-campus apartments. In addition, there are language houses. On-campus housing is guaranteed for the freshman year only, is available on a first-come, first-served basis, and is available on a lottery system for upperclassmen. 68% of students live on campus; of those, 95% remain on campus on weekends. All students may keep cars.
Activities: There are no fraternities or sororities. There are 74 groups on campus, including cheerleading, chess, choir, chorale, chorus, computers, drama, ethnic, film, gay, honors, international, literary magazine, musical theater, newspaper, photography, political, professional, radio and TV, religious, social, social service, student government, water search and rescue, and yearbook. Popular campus events include the Festival of Cultures, Kon Tiki, and the Festival of Hope.
Sports: There are 6 intercollegiate sports for men and 7 for women, and 11 intramural sports for men and 10 for women. Facilities include a gym, a baseball and softball complex, soccer fields, tennis courts, a weight room, a fitness room, a swimming pool, and waterfront facilities.
Disabled Students: 90% of the campus is accessible. Wheelchair ramps, elevators, special parking, specially equipped rest rooms, special class scheduling, lowered drinking fountains, and owered telephones are available. Readers are available for the visually impaired, as are magnifiers in the library.
Services: Counseling and information services are available, as is tutoring in some subjects, including math, sciences, and foreign languages.
Campus Safety and Security: Measures include 24-hour foot and vehicle patrol, escort service, informal discussions, and pamphlets/posters/films. There are emergency telephones, lighted pathways/sidewalks, and a security gate at the entrance to the campus.
Programs of Study: Eckerd confers B.A. and B.S. degrees. Bachelor's degrees are awarded in BIOLOGICAL SCIENCE (biology/biological science and marine science), BUSINESS (business administration and management, international business management, and management science), COMMUNICATIONS AND THE ARTS (communications, comparative literature, creative writing, dramatic arts, English, French, German, music, Russian, Spanish, and visual and performing arts), COMPUTER AND PHYSICAL SCIENCE (chemistry, computer science, mathematics, and physics), ENGINEERING AND ENVIRONMENTAL DESIGN (environmental science), HEALTH PROFESSIONS (predentistry and premedicine), SOCIAL SCIENCE (American studies, anthropology, economics, history, human development, humanities, international relations, philosophy, political science/government, prelaw, psychology, religion, sociology, and women's studies). Marine science, management, and environmental studies are the largest.
Required: To graduate, students must complete a total of 126 semester hours (36 courses) with a minimum GPA of 2.0. 35 semester hours are required in the major, and a writing portfolio must be submitted before the end of the sophomore year. All students must fulfill core requirements in Western civilization (Western Heritage in a Global Context), aesthetics, cross-cultural and environmental studies, and social relations. In addition, courses in math, foreign languages, and the Judeo-Christian perspective (Quest for Meaning) on contemporary issues are required. All students must take a senior seminar.
Special: Eckerd offers internships in management and human development. Work-study programs, dual majors in all subjects, interdisciplinary majors in international relations and environmental studies, student-designed majors, nondegree study, and pass/fail options are also available. Study-abroad programs are available in a number of countries. Students may earn B.A.-B.S. degrees in biology, chemistry, and marine science. A 3-2 engineering degree is offered with Auburn, Washington, and Columbia Universities and the University of Miami. The Program for Experienced Learners (students 25 and older) offers independent study, weekend courses, and credit for experiential learning. There are 7 national honor societies, a freshman honors program, and 30 departmental honors programs.
Faculty/Classroom: 67% of faculty are male; 33%, female. All both teach undergraduates and do research. The average class size in an introductory lecture is 20; in a laboratory, 15; and in a regular course, 20.
Admissions: 78% of the 2001-2002 applicants were accepted. The SAT I scores for the 2001-2002 freshman class were: Verbal--20% below 500, 48% between 500 and 599, 24% between 600 and 700, and 8% above 700; Math--21% below 500, 50% between 500 and 599, 24% between 600 and 700, and 5% above 700. The ACT scores were 13% below 21, 36% between 21 and 23, 30% between 24 and 26, 9% between 27 and 28, and 12% above 28. 40% of the current freshmen were in the top fifth of their class; 73% were in the top two fifths. There were 3 National Merit finalists and 5 semifinalists. 15 freshmen graduated first in their class.
Requirements: The SAT I or ACT is required. In addition, graduation from an accredited secondary school or satisfactory scores on the GED are required. High school courses must include 4 years of English, 3 each of math and science, 2 each of a foreign language and social studies, and 1 of history. SAT II: Subject tests in writing, literature, and math are recommended. An essay is required and an interview is recommended. A GPA of 2.0 is required. AP and CLEP credits are accepted. Important factors in the admissions decision are advanced placement or honor courses, leadership record, and personality/intangible qualities.
Procedure: Freshmen are admitted fall, winter, and spring. Entrance exams should be taken in October, November, or December. There is a deferred admissions plan. Applications should be filed by April 1 for fall entry, December 1 for winter entry, and December 1 for spring entry. The fall 2001 application fee was $25. Notification is sent on a rolling basis. 8% of all applicants are on a waiting list.
Transfer: 77 transfer students enrolled in a recent year. Applicants must have a minimum GPA of 2.5. The SAT I or ACT is required. An interview is recommended. A faculty recommendation is required. 63 credits of 126 must be completed at Eckerd.

Visiting: There are regularly scheduled orientations for prospective students, consisting of an interview and a tour. There are guides for informal visits and visitors may sit in on classes and stay overnight. To schedule a visit, contact the Admissions Office.

Financial Aid: In 2001-2002, 85% of all students received some form of financial aid. 65% of freshmen and 64% of continuing students received need-based aid. The average freshman award was $17,200. Of that total, scholarships or need-based grants averaged $11,400 ($22,000 maximum); loans averaged $3700 ($4500 maximum); and work contracts averaged $2100 ($2500 maximum). 75% of undergraduates work part time. Average annual earnings from campus work are $1100. The average financial indebtedness of the 2001 graduate was $17,500. The FAFSA is required. The fall application deadline is March 15.

International Students: There were 203 international students enrolled in a recent year. The school actively recruits these students. They must score 550 on the written TOEFL.

Computers: The mainframe consists of 2 Sun SPARC computers. There are 20 PCs in a Novell Network in the computer lab and 40 PCs in the science lab through which students may access the mainframe. Students with their own personal computers may access the mainframe through modems or Ethernet from their dormitory rooms. Each dormitory has a lab with 3 computers connected to the network. All students may access the system at any time. There are no time limits and no fees. It is strongly recommended that all students have a personal computer.

Graduates: In 2001, 304 bachelor's degrees were awarded. The most popular majors were marine science (17%), management (9%), and biology (8%). In an average class, 1% graduate in 3 years, 60% in 4 years, 65% in 5 years, and 66% in 6 years. 110 companies recruited on campus in 2000-2001. Of the 2000 graduating class, 27% were enrolled in graduate school within 6 months of graduation and 66% were employed.

Admissions Contact: Richard Hallin, Dean of Admissions.
E-mail: *hallinrr@eckerd.edu* Web: *http://www.eckerd.edu*

EDWARD WATERS COLLEGE — D-1
Jacksonville, FL 32209 (904) 366-2715
(888) 898-3191; Fax: (904) 366-2706

Full-time: 230 men, 200 women	**Faculty:** 30
Part-time: 10 men, 40 women	**Ph.D.s:** n/av
Graduate: 5 men, 15 women	**Student/Faculty:** 14 to 1
Year: semesters, summer session	**Tuition:** $8724
Application Deadline: see profile	**Room & Board:** $4400
Freshman Class: n/av	
SAT I or ACT: not required	**LESS COMPETITIVE**

Edward Waters College, founded in 1866, is the oldest independent institution of higher learning in Florida. Affiliated with the African Methodist Episcopal Church, the college offers programs in the arts and sciences, business, and education. Figures given in above capsule are approximate. There are 3 undergraduate schools. The library contains 132,000 volumes and 25,000 microform items, and subscribes to 231 periodicals. Computerized library services include the card catalog and database searching. Special learning facilities include a learning resource center, art gallery, radio station, and an African American collection. The 21-acre campus is in an urban area in Jacksonville. Including residence halls, there are 12 buildings.

Student Life: 90% of undergraduates are from Florida. Others are from 12 states, 4 foreign countries, and Canada. All are from public schools. 95% are African American. The average age of freshmen is 18; all undergraduates, 20. 40% do not continue beyond their first year; 60% remain to graduate.

Housing: 200 students can be accommodated in college housing, which includes single-sex dormitories. 55% of students commute. Alcohol is not permitted. All students may keep cars.

Activities: There are 4 national fraternities; 35% of women belong to 4 national sororities. There are 20 groups on campus, including band, cheerleading, choir, chorus, drama, honors, international, jazz band, newspaper, pep band, professional, radio and TV, religious, student government, and yearbook. Popular campus events include Fall and Spring Convocations, Religious Emphasis Week, and African American History Celebration.

Sports: There are 5 intercollegiate sports for men and 5 for women, and 6 intramural sports for men and 6 for women.

Disabled Students: 75% of the campus is accessible. Elevators and specially equipped rest rooms are available.

Services: Counseling and information services are available, as is tutoring in every subject. There is remedial math, reading, and writing. There is a student support services program for students who have potential but have an academically disadvantaged background.

Campus Safety and Security: Measures include 24-hour foot and vehicle patrol, escort service, informal discussions, and emergency telephones. There are lighted pathways/sidewalks.

Programs of Study: EWC confers B.A., B.S., and B.B.A. degrees. Bachelor's degrees are awarded in BIOLOGICAL SCIENCE (biology/biological science), BUSINESS (accounting and business administration and management), COMMUNICATIONS AND THE ARTS (communications and English), COMPUTER AND PHYSICAL SCIENCE (computer science and mathematics), EDUCATION (early childhood, elementary, and physical), SOCIAL SCIENCE (criminal justice, history, philosophy, political science/government, psychology, religion, and sociology). Education is the strongest academically.

Required: To graduate, all students must complete at least 120 credit hours, including 30 in the major, with a 2.0 GPA overall and in the major. Weekly chapel service attendance is required.

Special: EWC offers co-op programs, internships in communications and criminal justice, an engineering program with the University of Miami, dual and student-designed majors, and work-study programs. A joint degree in business administration and organizational management is offered through continuing education to adults with work experience. There is a freshman honors program.

Faculty/Classroom: All teach undergraduates.

Requirements: SAT I or ACT scores are necessary for unconditional admission. Applicants must be graduates of an accredited secondary school or have a GED certificate, and have taken the California Achievement Test. A GPA of 1.5 is required. AP and CLEP credits are accepted. Important factors in the admissions decision are advanced placement or honor courses, ability to finance college education, and recommendations by school officials.

Procedure: Freshmen are admitted fall and spring. Check with the school for current application deadlines and fee. Notification is sent on a rolling basis.

Transfer: 36 credits of 120 must be completed at EWC.

Visiting: To schedule a visit, contact the Admissions Office.

Financial Aid: 15% of undergraduates work part time. EWC is a member of CSS. The FAFSA is required. Check with the school for current deadlines.

International Students: International students are encouraged to take the TOEFL.

Computers: There are computer labs in 1 academic building and in the library. There are no time limits and no fees.

Graduates: In an average class, 20% graduate in 4 years, 23% in 5 years, and 25% in 6 years.

Admissions Contact: Director of Admissions. Web: *www.ewc.edu*

EMBRY-RIDDLE AERONAUTICAL UNIVERSITY — D-2
Daytona Beach, FL 32114 (386) 226-6112
(800) 862-2416; Fax: (386) 226-7070

Full-time: 3476 men, 680 women	**Faculty:** 193; IIA, -$
Part-time: 406 men, 79 women	**Ph.D.s:** 62%
Graduate: 203 men, 77 women	**Student/Faculty:** 22 to 1
Year: semesters, summer session	**Tuition:** $18,400
Application Deadline: July 1	**Room & Board:** $6390
Freshman Class: 2631 applied, 2119 accepted, 1022 enrolled	
SAT I Verbal/Math: 530/560	**ACT:** 23 **COMPETITIVE**

Embry-Riddle Aeronautical University, founded in 1926, is a private institution offering undergraduate programs in aviation, engineering, and business on 2 campuses: one in Daytona Beach and the other, founded in 1978, in Prescott, Arizona. There are 2 undergraduate schools and 1 graduate school. In addition to regional accreditation, ERAU has baccalaureate program accreditation with ABET and ACBSP. The library contains 68,923 volumes, 295,987 microform items, and 6809 audiovisual forms/CDs, and subscribes to 1679 periodicals. Computerized library services include the card catalog, interlibrary loans, and database searching. Special learning facilities include a learning resource center, a radio station, an airway science simulation lab, and the College of Aviation Building. The 164-acre campus is in an urban area 48 miles northeast of Orlando. Including residence halls, there are 40 buildings.

Student Life: 70% of undergraduates are from out of state, mostly the South. Others are from 38 states, 99 foreign countries, and Canada. 68% are white; 16%, foreign nationals. The average age of freshmen is 18; all undergraduates, 21. 22% do not continue beyond their first year.

Housing: 1847 students can be accommodated in college housing, which includes coed dormitories, on-campus apartments, off-campus apartments, and married-student housing. On-campus housing is guaranteed for the freshman year only, is available on a first-come, first-served basis, and is available on a lottery system for upperclassmen. 58% of students commute. All students may keep cars.

Activities: 4% of men belong to 11 national fraternities; 2% of women belong to 3 national sororities. There are 103 groups on campus, including cheerleading, chess, choir, computers, dance, debate, drama, drill team, ethnic, film, gay, honors, international, literary magazine, musical theater, newspaper, pep band, photography, political, professional, radio and TV, religious, social, social service, student government, and yearbook. Popular campus events include Spring Concert and Hypnotist.

Sports: There are 6 intercollegiate sports for men and 4 for women, and 21 intramural sports for men and 19 for women. Facilities include

a field house with a full-size basketball court and 2 practice courts, a fitness center, and a weight room, softball and soccer fields, a swimming pool, a Nautilus/weight room, racquetball and tennis courts, and a fitness trail.

Disabled Students: 95% of the campus is accessible. Wheelchair ramps, elevators, special parking, specially equipped rest rooms, lowered drinking fountains, lowered telephones, and ADA-compliant signage and reception counters are available.

Services: Counseling and information services are available, as is tutoring in most subjects. There is remedial math, reading, and writing.

Campus Safety and Security: Measures include 24-hour foot and vehicle patrol, self-defense education, escort service, and shuttle buses. There are informal discussions, pamphlets/posters/films, emergency telephones, lighted pathways/sidewalks, and "Call A Ride And Live" (CARAL).

Programs of Study: ERAU confers the B.S. degree. Associate and master's degrees are also awarded. Bachelor's degrees are awarded in BUSINESS (business administration and management and transportation management), COMMUNICATIONS AND THE ARTS (communications), COMPUTER AND PHYSICAL SCIENCE (computer science), ENGINEERING AND ENVIRONMENTAL DESIGN (aeronautical engineering, aeronautical science, aeronautical technology, aerospace studies, computer engineering, computer graphics, electrical/electronics engineering, engineering physics, and engineering technology). Engineering is the strongest academically. Aeronautical science (flight) is the largest.

Required: To graduate, students must complete a total of 120 to 136 credit hours, including 60 in the major, with a minimum GPA of 2.0. All students must complete 36 credits of general education requirements, including courses in communication skills, technical report writing, humanities/social sciences, math, physical science, economics, and computer science.

Special: ERAU offers co-op programs and internships in all majors, study abroad in 14 countries, work-study programs, credit for life experience, and nondegree study. There are 7 national honor societies.

Faculty/Classroom: 77% of faculty are male; 23%, female. All teach undergraduates and 8% do research. No introductory courses are taught by graduate students. The average class size in an introductory lecture is 28; in a laboratory, 16; and in a regular course, 28.

Admissions: 81% of the 2001-2002 applicants were accepted. The SAT I scores for the 2001-2002 freshman class were: Verbal--31% below 500, 46% between 500 and 599, 20% between 600 and 700, and 3% above 700; Math--19% below 500, 46% between 500 and 599, 29% between 600 and 700, and 6% above 700. The ACT scores were 20% below 21, 33% between 21 and 23, 26% between 24 and 26, 9% between 27 and 28, and 12% above 28. 41% of the current freshmen were in the top fifth of their class; 72% were in the top two fifths.

Requirements: The SAT I or ACT is required. In addition, students should complete a competitive academic program in high school, including 16 Carnegie units with at least 3 years of math. Admissions decisions are based on the strength of the academic record, rank in class, standardized test scores, recommendations, and the written statement. AP and CLEP credits are accepted. Important factors in the admissions decision are advanced placement or honor courses, recommendations by school officials, and evidence of special talent. Applications are accepted on computer disk and on-line at *www.db.erau.edu/application.html*

Procedure: Freshmen are admitted to all sessions. Entrance exams should be taken during spring of the junior year or fall of the senior year. There is an early decision plan. Early decision applications should be filed by December 1; regular applications, by July 1 for fall entry, November 1 for spring entry, and April 1 for summer entry. The fall 2001 application fee was $30. Notification of early decision is sent in December; regular decision, on a rolling basis. 295 early decision candidates were accepted for the 2001-2002 class.

Transfer: 257 transfer students enrolled in 2001-2002. A GPA of 2.5 is preferred. 30 credits of 120 to 136 must be completed at ERAU.

Visiting: There are regularly scheduled orientations for prospective students. There are guides for informal visits and visitors may sit in on classes and stay overnight. To schedule a visit, contact the Admissions Office.

Financial Aid: In 2001-2002, 78% of all freshmen and 79% of continuing students received some form of financial aid. 76% of freshmen and 75% of continuing students received need-based aid. The average freshman award was $15,784. Of that total, scholarships or need-based grants averaged $3508 ($7500 maximum); and loans averaged $2982 ($6500 maximum). 26% of undergraduates work part time. Average annual earnings from campus work are $2355. The average financial indebtedness of the 2001 graduate was $23,087. The FAFSA is required. The fall application deadline is April 15.

International Students: There are 506 international students enrolled. The school actively recruits these students. They must score 500 on the written TOEFL and also take the SAT I or the ACT.

Computers: The mainframe is an IBM RS/6000 Model F50. Academic computing provides open access computing labs for students. Labs are equipped with 110 high-end PCs, 2 Macs, 35 Sun workstations, and 1 SGI workstation. All students may access the system at any time. There are no time limits and no fees.

Graduates: In 2001, 737 bachelor's degrees were awarded. The most popular majors were aeronautical science (40%), aerospace engineering (13%), and aviation business administration (11%). In an average class, 20% graduate in 4 years, 43% in 5 years, and 48% in 6 years. 175 companies recruited on campus in 2000-2001. Of the 2000 graduating class, 14% were enrolled in graduate school within 6 months of graduation and 92% were employed.

Admissions Contact: Michael Novak, Director of Admissions. A video is available. E-mail: *admit@db.erau.edu* Web: *www.embryriddle.edu*

FLAGLER COLLEGE — D-2

St. Augustine, FL 32085-1027 — (904) 829-6481
(800) 304-4208; Fax: (904) 826-0094

Full-time: 664 men, 1141 women	**Faculty:** 62
Part-time: 19 men, 28 women	**Ph.D.s:** 65%
Graduate: none	**Student/Faculty:** 29 to 1
Year: semesters, summer session	**Tuition:** $6550
Application Deadline: March 1	**Room & Board:** $4000
Freshman Class: 1757 applied, 496 accepted, 407 enrolled	
SAT I Verbal/Math: 560/550	**ACT:** 23 **VERY COMPETITIVE+**

Flagler College, founded in 1968, is an independent liberal arts college. The library contains 80,522 volumes, 70,020 microform items, and 2880 audiovisual forms/CDs, and subscribes to 458 periodicals. Computerized library services include the card catalog, interlibrary loans, and database searching. Special learning facilities include a learning resource center, art gallery, and radio station. The 35-acre campus is in a small town 35 miles south of Jacksonville and 45 miles north of Daytona Beach. Including residence halls, there are 13 buildings.

Student Life: 67% of undergraduates are from Florida. Others are from 46 states, 23 foreign countries, and Canada. 93% are white. The average age of freshmen is 18; all undergraduates, 21. 32% do not continue beyond their first year.

Housing: 720 students can be accommodated in college housing, which includes single-sex dormitories. On-campus housing is guaranteed for the freshman year only and is available on a first-come, first-served basis. 62% of students commute. Alcohol is not permitted. All students may keep cars.

Activities: There are no fraternities or sororities. There are 25 groups on campus, including art, cheerleading, choir, chorus, dance, drama, film, honors, literary magazine, newspaper, photography, professional, radio and TV, religious, social service, and student government. Popular campus events include Flagler Forum; Fall, Spring, Parents, and Luau Weekends; and Spirit Week.

Sports: There are 6 intercollegiate sports for men and 6 for women, and 9 intramural sports for men and 10 for women. Facilities include a 17-acre complex for baseball and soccer, 8 tennis courts, a swimming pool, and a multipurpose gym.

Disabled Students: 80% of the campus is accessible. Wheelchair ramps, elevators, special parking, specially equipped rest rooms, lowered drinking fountains, lowered telephones, and specially equipped residence hall rooms are available.

Services: Counseling and information services are available. Tutoring is available only by referral and based upon private contract between tutor and student. There is a reader service for the blind, and remedial math, reading, and writing.

Campus Safety and Security: Measures include 24-hour foot and vehicle patrol, self-defense education, informal discussions, and pamphlets/posters/films. There are emergency telephones and lighted pathways/sidewalks.

Programs of Study: Flagler confers the B.A. degree. Bachelor's degrees are awarded in BUSINESS (accounting, business administration and management, and sports management), COMMUNICATIONS AND THE ARTS (art, communications, dramatic arts, English, fine arts, graphic design, and Spanish), EDUCATION (art, education of the deaf and hearing impaired, elementary, and secondary), SOCIAL SCIENCE (history, Latin American studies, philosophy, political science/government, psychology, religion, and social science). Business, education, and Latin American studies are the strongest academically. Business, education, and communications are the largest.

Required: To graduate, students must complete a minimum of 120 semester hours, including 30 to 90 hours in the major, with a minimum GPA of 2.0. All students must take 6 hours in English composition, 6 hours in math, and 3 hours in speech communication. In addition, students must take 15 hours of courses required by the general education program in humanities, social sciences, and math/natural sciences. Students must demonstrate basic computer skills, complete a career planning program, and pass all subtests of the College Level Academic Skills Test (CLAST).

Special: The school offers internships, work-study, and dual majors. Students may participate in study-abroad programs in almost any country. Students majoring in deaf education can work directly with students at the Florida State School for the Deaf and Blind. Students in the fashion buying, merchandising, or design programs participate in the visiting student program at the Fashion Institute of Technology in New York City. There are 4 national honor societies, and 2 departmental honors programs.

Faculty/Classroom: 63% of faculty are male; 37%, female. All teach undergraduates. The average class size in an introductory lecture is 30; in a laboratory, 12; and in a regular course, 22.

Admissions: 28% of the 2001-2002 applicants were accepted. The SAT I scores for the 2001-2002 freshman class were: Verbal--13% below 500, 60% between 500 and 599, 23% between 600 and 700, and 4% above 700; Math--18% below 500, 56% between 500 and 599, 25% between 600 and 700, and 1% above 700. The ACT scores were 11% below 21, 46% between 21 and 23, 23% between 24 and 26, 15% between 27 and 28, and 5% above 28. 50% of the current freshmen were in the top fifth of their class; 84% were in the top two fifths. 3 freshmen graduated first in their class.

Requirements: The SAT I or ACT is required. In addition, graduation from an accredited secondary school, or a satisfactory score on the GED, is required for admission. Students must have a total of 19 academic credits. High school courses must include 4 credits of English, 3 credits each of math and science, and 2 credits of a foreign language. An essay is required, and an interview is recommended. Flagler requires applicants to be in the upper 50% of their class. A GPA of 2.75 is required. AP and CLEP credits are accepted. Important factors in the admissions decision are advanced placement or honor courses, leadership record, and extracurricular activities record. Applications are accepted on computer disk and on-line via CollegeNET.

Procedure: Freshmen are admitted fall and spring. Entrance exams should be taken during the fall of the senior year at the latest. There are early decision and deferred admissions plans. Early decision applications should be filed by January 15; regular applications, by March 1 for fall entry and October 15 for spring entry, along with a $20 fee. Notification of early decision is sent February 1; regular decision, March 15. 347 early decision candidates were accepted for the 2001-2002 class. 17% of all applicants are on a waiting list; 34 were accepted in 2001.

Transfer: 100 transfer students enrolled in 2001-2002. Transfer students must have a minimum of 24 semester hours with a minimum GPA of 2.5. Transfers must also score at least 1010 on the SAT I or 21 on the ACT. 45 credits of 120 must be completed at Flagler.

Visiting: There are guides for informal visits and visitors may sit in on classes and stay overnight. To schedule a visit, contact the Office of Admissions.

Financial Aid: In 2001-2002, 85% of all freshmen and 86% of continuing students received some form of financial aid. 35% of freshmen and 37% of continuing students received need-based aid. The average freshman award was $7352. Of that total, scholarships or need-based grants averaged $4935 ($10,750 maximum); loans averaged $2237 ($2625 maximum); and work contracts averaged $180 ($800 maximum). 60% of undergraduates work part time. Average annual earnings from campus work are $487. The average financial indebtedness of the 2001 graduate was $15,988. The FAFSA and the college's own financial statement are required. The fall application deadline is April 1.

International Students: There are 58 international students enrolled. They must score 550 on the written TOEFL.

Computers: The mainframe is a DEC PDP 11/34A.The college has a ratio of 1 computer to every 8 students. All have access to the Internet and the Web. All students may access the system during library hours. There are no time limits and no fees.

Graduates: In 2001, 361 bachelor's degrees were awarded. The most popular majors were business administration (24%), education (19%), and communication (14%). In an average class, 41% graduate in 4 years, and 54% in 5 years. 2 companies recruited on campus in 2000-2001. Of the 2000 graduating class, 12% were enrolled in graduate school within 6 months of graduation and 24% were employed.

Admissions Contact: Marc G. Williar, Director of Admissions. A video is available. E-mail: *admiss@flagler.edu* Web: *www.flagler.edu*

FLORIDA AGRICULTURAL AND MECHANICAL UNIVERSITY C-1

Tallahassee, FL 32307-3200 (850) 599-3796
Fax: (850) 599-3069

Full-time: 4128 men, 5710 women	**Faculty:** n/av
Part-time: 686 men, 742 women	**Ph.D.s:** n/av
Graduate: 288 men, 616 women	**Student/Faculty:** n/av
Year: semesters, summer session	**Tuition:** $2692 ($10,579)
Application Deadline: May 15	**Room & Board:** $4256

Freshman Class: 5838 applied, 4088 accepted, 1964 enrolled
SAT I or ACT: required **COMPETITIVE**

Florida Agricultural and Mechanical University, founded in 1887 and a public institution within the state university system of Florida, offers undergraduate programs in agriculture, allied health science, architecture, the arts and sciences, business and industry, education, engineering, journalism, pharmacy and pharmaceutical sciences, upper-level nursing, and technology. There are 11 undergraduate schools and 1 graduate school. In addition to regional accreditation, Florida A&M has baccalaureate program accreditation with AACSB, ABET, ACEJMC, ACPE, APTA, CSWE, NAAB, NCATE, and NLN. The 8 libraries contain 485,985 volumes, 82,000 microform items, and 62,610 audiovisual forms/CDs, and subscribe to 3639 periodicals. Computerized library services include the card catalog and database searching. Special learning facilities include a learning resource center, art gallery, radio station, TV station, black archives, and observatory. The 419-acre campus is in an urban area 169 miles east of Jacksonville. Including residence halls, there are 111 buildings.

Student Life: 70% of undergraduates are from Florida. Others are from 46 states, 49 foreign countries, and Canada. 95% are from public schools. 94% are African American. The average age of freshmen is 19; all undergraduates, 22. 20% do not continue beyond their first year.

Housing: 2942 students can be accommodated in college housing, which includes single-sex dormitories, on-campus apartments, and married-student housing. On-campus housing is guaranteed for the freshman year only and is available on a first-come, first-served basis. Priority is given to out-of-town students. 51% of students commute. Alcohol is not permitted. Upperclassmen may keep cars.

Activities: There are 4 national fraternities and 4 national sororities. There are 126 groups on campus, including cheerleading, choir, chorus, dance, drama, drill team, ethnic, honors, international, jazz band, marching band, newspaper, orchestra, pep band, political, professional, radio and TV, religious, social, social service, student government, symphony, and yearbook. Popular campus events include FAMU Essen-Theater, FAMU Orchesis Dance Theater, and Ebony Fashion Fair.

Sports: There are 9 intercollegiate sports for men and 8 for women, and 7 intramural sports for men and 5 for women. Facilities include a 3300-seat gym, a 1600-seat auditorium, a 25,559-seat football stadium, swimming pools, baseball diamonds, softball and track fields, tennis courts, a bowling alley, a pool hall, a student activities center, and a fitness center.

Disabled Students: 90% of the campus is accessible. Wheelchair ramps, elevators, special parking, and specially equipped rest rooms are available.

Services: Counseling and information services are available, as is tutoring in some subjects, including math, English, and reading. There is remedial math, reading, and writing.

Campus Safety and Security: Measures include 24-hour foot and vehicle patrol, self-defense education, escort service, and informal discussions. There are pamphlets/posters/films and lighted pathways/sidewalks.

Programs of Study: Florida A&M confers B.A., B.S., B.Arch., B.C.J., B.S.Arch. and Constr.E.T., B.S.Arch.Studies, B.S.Arch.E.T., B.S.C.E., B.S.C.E.T., B.S.Ch.E., B.S.Constr.E.T., B.S.E.E., B.S.Elect.E.T., B.S.H.C.M., B.S.I.E., B.S.J., B.S.M.E., B.S.M.R.A., B.S.N., B.S.Pharm., B.S.P.T., B.S.R.T., B.S.T., and B.S.W. degrees. Associate, master's, and doctoral degrees are also awarded. Bachelor's degrees are awarded in AGRICULTURE (animal science and horticulture), BIOLOGICAL SCIENCE (biology/biological science), BUSINESS (accounting, banking and finance, business administration and management, and business economics), COMMUNICATIONS AND THE ARTS (dramatic arts, English, fine arts, journalism, and music), COMPUTER AND PHYSICAL SCIENCE (actuarial science, chemistry, computer science, mathematics, and physics), EDUCATION (art, business, early childhood, elementary, industrial arts, music, and science), ENGINEERING AND ENVIRONMENTAL DESIGN (chemical engineering, civil engineering, electrical/electronics engineering, engineering technology, industrial engineering, and mechanical engineering), HEALTH PROFESSIONS (nursing, occupational therapy, pharmacy, physical therapy, predentistry, and premedicine), SOCIAL SCIENCE (criminal justice, economics, history, political science/government, psychology, public administration, social science, social work, and sociology). Business, engineering, and pharmacy are the strongest academically. Business, pharmacy, and arts and sciences are the largest.

Required: General education requirements include 36 credit hours in English, humanities, social science, natural science, American history, foreign language, and math at the college algebra level or above. In order to graduate, students must complete at least 120 credit hours, including 30 in a major field, with a minimum GPA of 2.0.

Special: Cooperative programs and cross-registration are offered in conjunction with Florida State University. Internships are available either on or off campus. Florida A&M also offers a Washington semester for architecture majors, a B.A.-B.S. degree, credit for life experience, and pass/fail options. Nondegree study is possible. There are 10 national honor societies and a freshman honors program.

Faculty/Classroom: All teach undergraduates. No introductory courses are taught by graduate students. The average class size in an introductory lecture is 40; in a laboratory, 15; and in a regular course, 40.

Admissions: 70% of the 2001-2002 applicants were accepted. The SAT I scores for the 2001-2002 freshman class were: Verbal and math com--1% between 600 and 700, and 99% above 700. The ACT scores were 64% below 21, 23% between 21 and 24, 10% between 25 and 28, and 3% between 29 and 32.

Requirements: The SAT I or ACT is required, with a minimum composite score of 900 on the SAT I, or 450 on each part, or 19 on the ACT. Applicants must be graduates of accredited secondary schools or have earned a GED. The university requires 19 academic credits, including 4 each in English and academic electives, 3 each in math, science, and social studies, and 2 in foreign language. A GPA of 3.2 is required. AP and CLEP credits are accepted. Important factors in the admissions decision are recommendations by school officials, extracurricular activities record, and evidence of special talent.

Procedure: Freshmen are admitted to all sessions. Entrance exams should be taken by the fall of the senior year. There is a deferred admissions plan. Applications should be filed by May 15 for fall entry, November 15 for spring entry, and April 1 for summer entry. The fall 2001 application fee was $20. Notification is sent on a rolling basis.

Transfer: Applicants must present a minimum GPA of 2.0 in at least 60 semester hours or 90 quarter hours earned. 30 credits of 120 must be completed at Florida A&M.

Visiting: There are regularly scheduled orientations for prospective students. There are guides for informal visits and visitors may sit in on classes. To schedule a visit, contact Dr. Sharon Deunard at (850) 599-3869.

Financial Aid: The university prefers the FFS but will accept the CSS Profile. The fall application deadline is April 1.

International Students: There are 110 international students enrolled. They must score 500 on the written TOEFL and also take the SAT I or the ACT.

Computers: The mainframe is an IBM 4381 Model 13. The school provides more than 100 Apple, Mac, and IBM PCs for academic use. All students may access the system. There are no time limits and no fees.

Graduates: 600 companies recruited on campus in 2000-2001.

Admissions Contact: Barbara Cox, Admissions Officer.
E-mail: *barbara.cox@famu.edu* Web: *www.famu.edu*

FLORIDA ATLANTIC UNIVERSITY — E-5

Boca Raton, FL 33431-0991 — (561) 297-3040
(800) 299-4FAU; Fax: (561) 297-2758

Full-time: 4026 men, 5732 women	**Faculty:** 931; I, --$
Part-time: 3275 men, 5724 women	**Ph.D.s:** 96%
Graduate: 1696 men, 3084 women	**Student/Faculty:** 10 to 1
Year: semesters, summer session	**Tuition:** $2698 ($10,586)
Application Deadline: June 1	**Room & Board:** $6134
Freshman Class: 6289 applied, 4495 accepted, 2031 enrolled	
SAT I Verbal/Math: 514/523	**ACT:** 22 **COMPETITIVE**

Florida Atlantic University, founded in 1961, is a publicly funded liberal arts institution in the State University System of Florida. There are 9 undergraduate and 8 graduate schools. In addition to regional accreditation, FAU has baccalaureate program accreditation with AACSB, ABET, ASHA, CSAB, CSWE, NAAB,NAACLS, NASM, NCATE, and NLN. The 4 libraries contain 1,088,058 volumes, 2,850,824 microform items, and 5761 audiovisual forms/CDs, and subscribe to 7401 periodicals. Computerized library services include the card catalog, interlibrary loans, and database searching. Special learning facilities include a learning resource center, art gallery, radio station, TV station, engineering research labs, marine sciences research center, K–8 developmental research school, nonnative fish research lab, and environmental sciences center. The 860-acre campus is in a suburban area 17 miles north of Ft. Lauderdale and 22 miles south of Palm Beach. Including residence halls, there are 46 buildings.

Student Life: 91% of undergraduates are from Florida. Others are from 49 states, 140 foreign countries, and Canada. 62% are white; 16%, African American; 12%, Hispanic. The average age of freshmen is 19; all undergraduates, 26. 27% do not continue beyond their first year.

Housing: 2100 students can be accommodated in college housing, which includes single-sex and coed dormitories, on-campus apartments, and married-student housing. In addition, there are honors houses. On-campus housing is guaranteed for the freshman year only and is available on a first-come, first-served basis. 92% of students commute. All students may keep cars.

Activities: 1% of men belong to 10 national fraternities; 1% of women belong to 7 national sororities. There are 150 groups on campus, including art, band, cheerleading, chess, choir, chorale, chorus, computers, dance, drama, ethnic, film, gay, honors, international, jazz band, literary magazine, musical theater, newspaper, opera, orchestra, pep band, political, professional, radio and TV, religious, social, social service, student government, and yearbook. Popular campus events include Luau, African American Festival, and Earth Day.

Sports: There are 8 intercollegiate sports for men and 9 for women, and 5 intramural sports for men and 5 for women. Facilities include an athletic center, a gym, a weight room, baseball and softball stadiums, a lighted soccer field, a 25-meter swimming pool with 1- and 10-meter diving boards, lighted outdoor jai alai, a dance area, and 8 tennis, 5 racquetball, 4 badminton, 3 volleyball, and 2 basketball courts.

Disabled Students: All of the campus is accessible. Wheelchair ramps, elevators, special parking, specially equipped rest rooms, lowered drinking fountains, and lowered telephones are available.

Services: Counseling and information services are available, as is tutoring in most subjects. There is a reader service for the blind. Remedial work must be taken at the community college level.

Campus Safety and Security: Measures include 24-hour foot and vehicle patrol, escort service, shuttle buses, and informal discussions. There are pamphlets/posters/films, emergency telephones, and lighted pathways/sidewalks.

Programs of Study: FAU confers B.A., B.S., B.A.E., B.Arch., B.B.A., B.F.A., B.H.S., B.Mus., B.P.M., B.S.C.E., B.S.E., B.S.E.E., B.S.H.S., B.S.M.E., B.S.M.T., B.S.N., B.S.O.E., B.S.W., and B.U.R.P. degrees. Associate, master's, and doctoral degrees are also awarded. Bachelor's degrees are awarded in BIOLOGICAL SCIENCE (biology/biological science and marine biology), BUSINESS (accounting, banking and finance, business administration and management, international business management, marketing/retailing/merchandising, real estate, and small business management), COMMUNICATIONS AND THE ARTS (art, communications, dramatic arts, English, fine arts, French, German, graphic design, Italian, Japanese, journalism, linguistics, music, and Spanish), COMPUTER AND PHYSICAL SCIENCE (chemistry, computer science, geology, information sciences and systems, mathematics, and physics), EDUCATION (elementary, English, foreign languages, physical, and special), ENGINEERING AND ENVIRONMENTAL DESIGN (architecture, computer engineering, electrical/electronics engineering, mechanical engineering, ocean engineering, and urban planning technology), HEALTH PROFESSIONS (health care administration, health science, medical laboratory technology, and nursing), SOCIAL SCIENCE (anthropology, criminal justice, economics, geography, history, interdisciplinary studies, Judaic studies, Latin American studies, liberal arts/general studies, philosophy, political science/government, psychobiology, psychology, public administration, social psychology, social science, social work, and sociology). Engineering, education, and business are the strongest academically. Elementary education, biological sciences, and management are the largest.

Required: All students must take the College Level Academic Skills Test (CLAST) required by the state. To graduate, students must complete a total of 120 credit hours, with a minimum GPA of 2.0. All students must take the required courses in the core curriculum, including 9 credits each of humanities and social sciences and 6 each of math, communication, and natural sciences, and must demonstrate proficiency in a foreign language.

Special: FAU offers cooperative creative programs and internships in most majors. Work-study programs, dual and student-designed majors, a general studies degree, credit for military experience, nondegree study, and pass/fail options are available. The school offers study abroad through all state university system of Florida programs, and an exchange program in ocean engineering with the Polytechnic University of Madrid, Spain; there is also a study abroad center in Salamanca, Spain. Cross-registration is available with all Florida State universities, in science/engineering with Palm Beach and Broward Community Colleges, and in military science with the University of Miami. Students may earn a second baccalaureate degree with 30 additional hours in a number of subjects. There are 15 national honor societies, a freshman honors program, and 9 departmental honors programs.

Faculty/Classroom: 57% of faculty are male; 43%, female. All both teach and do research. Graduate students teach 5% of introductory courses. The average class size in an introductory lecture is 50; in a laboratory, 20; and in a regular course, 30.

Admissions: 71% of the 2001-2002 applicants were accepted. The SAT I scores for the 2001-2002 freshman class were: Verbal--41% below 500, 43% between 500 and 599, 13% between 600 and 700, and 3% above 700; Math--36% below 500, 46% between 500 and 599, 16% between 600 and 700, and 2% above 700. The ACT scores were 40% below 21, 30% between 21 and 23, 17% between 24 and 26, 8% between 27 and 28, and 5% above 28. There were 4 National Merit finalists and 1 semifinalist.

Requirements: The SAT I or ACT is required, with a minimum composite score of 1000 on the SAT I or 23 on the ACT. In addition, graduation from an accredited secondary school or satisfactory scores on the GED are required. Students must have 19 academic credits, including 4 units of English, 3 each of math (algebra I and higher), science (including 2 with substantial lab work), and social studies, and 2 of a foreign language, plus 4 of electives in computer science, fine arts, or humanities. A portfolio or an audition may be requested by individual departments. An essay and an interview are required. A GPA of 2.0 is required. AP and CLEP credits are accepted. Important factors in the admissions decision are advanced placement or honor courses, evidence of special talent, and recommendations by school officials. Applications are accepted on-line.

Procedure: Freshmen are admitted to all sessions. Entrance exams should be taken by June. There are early decision, early admissions, and deferred admissions plans. Applications should be filed by June 1 for fall entry, October 15 for spring entry, and March 15 for summer entry. The fall 2001 application fee was $20. Notification is sent on a rolling basis 2 weeks after receipt of the application. 11 early decision candidates were accepted for the 2001-2002 class.

Transfer: 2871 transfer students enrolled in 2001-2002. Students must have a minimum GPA of 2.0, submit official transcripts from the previous schools attended, and be in good standing at those institutions. Applicants from a community or junior college in Florida with an associate degree are automatically admitted. Students with fewer than 60 transferable hours must meet the same criteria as entering freshmen. 30 credits of 120 must be completed at FAU.

Visiting: There are regularly scheduled orientations for prospective students, consisting of a group tour. There are guides for informal visits. To schedule a visit, contact the Admissions Office.

Financial Aid: In 2000-2001, 61% of all freshmen and 34% of continuing students received some form of financial aid. 52% of freshmen and 29% of continuing students received need-based aid. The average freshman award was $1731. Of that total, scholarships or need-based grants averaged $1683; loans averaged $1853; work contracts averaged $2329; and parent loans (PLUS program) averaged $5333. 5% of undergraduates work part time. Average annual earnings from campus work are $3200. FAU is a member of CSS. The FAFSA is required. The fall application deadline is March 1.

International Students: There are 747 international students enrolled. The school actively recruits these students. They must score 550 on the written TOEFL or 213 on the electronic version and also take the SAT I or the ACT.

Computers: The mainframe is a DEC VAX 6320. There are more than 250 on-campus PCs available for student use. Students may access the mainframe at various sites on campus or via modem. In addition, there is an on-campus network, including e-mail, Bitnet, and common software. All students may access the system. Labs are open from 8 A.M. to 11 P.M. weekdays and various hours on weekends; there is modem access 24 hours daily. There are no time limits and no fees.

Graduates: In 2001, 3233 bachelor's degrees were awarded. The most popular majors were elementary education (11%), finance (5%), and accounting (5%). In an average class, 15% graduate in 4 years, 28% in 5 years, and 35% in 6 years. 200 companies recruited on campus in 2000-2001.

Admissions Contact: Albert Colom, Director of Admissions. A video is available. E-mail: *admisweb@fau.edu* Web: *www.fau.edu*

FLORIDA GULF COAST UNIVERSITY — H-6

Fort Myers, FL 33965-6565 — (941) 590-7878
(888) 889-1095; Fax: (941) 590-7894

Full-time: 751 men, 1288 women	**Faculty:** 157; IIB, av$
Part-time: 430 men, 934 women	**Ph.D.s:** 85%
Graduate: 278 men, 533 women	**Student/Faculty:** 13 to 1
Year: semesters, summer session	**Tuition:** $2201 ($14,659)
Application Deadline: open	**Room & Board:** $7000
Freshman Class: 1615 applied, 1178 accepted, 547 enrolled	
SAT I Verbal/Math: 510/500	**ACT:** 21 **COMPETITIVE**

Florida Gulf Coast University, founded in 1991, is part of the State University System of Florida. There are 5 undergraduate and 15 graduate schools. The library contains 148,382 volumes, 175,000 microform items, and 2295 audiovisual forms/CDs, and subscribes to 1325 periodicals. Computerized library services include the card catalog, interlibrary loans, and database searching. Special learning facilities include a learning resource center, art gallery, radio station, TV station, chickee huts, computer labs, and family resource center. The 760-acre campus is in a rural area in southwest Florida in southern Lee County. Including residence halls, there are 18 buildings.

Student Life: 95% of undergraduates are from Florida. Others are from 23 states, 60 foreign countries, and Canada. 84% are white. The average age of freshmen is 18; all undergraduates, 25. 37% do not continue beyond their first year.

Housing: 800 students can be accommodated in college housing, which includes coed on-campus apartments. 76% of students commute. Alcohol is not permitted. All students may keep cars.

Activities: There is 1 national fraternity and 1 national sorority. There are 53 groups on campus, including dance, debate, ethnic, honors, international, newspaper, professional, religious, social service, and student government.

Sports: There are 4 intercollegiate sports for men and 4 for women, and 3 intramural sports for men and 3 for women. Facilities include a fitness center and a lakefront.

Disabled Students: All of the campus is accessible. Wheelchair ramps, elevators, special parking, specially equipped rest rooms, special class scheduling, lowered drinking fountains, and lowered telephones are available.

Services: Counseling and information services are available, as is tutoring in most subjects.

Campus Safety and Security: Measures include 24-hour foot and vehicle patrol, self-defense education, escort service, and shuttle buses. There are informal discussions, pamphlets/posters/films, emergency telephones, and lighted pathways/sidewalks.

Programs of Study: FGCU confers B.A.and B.S. degrees. Master's degrees are also awarded. Bachelor's degrees are awarded in BUSINESS (accounting, banking and finance, management science, and marketing and distribution), COMPUTER AND PHYSICAL SCIENCE (information sciences and systems), EDUCATION (early childhood, elementary, and special), HEALTH PROFESSIONS (clinical science, health science, nursing, and physical therapy), SOCIAL SCIENCE (criminal justice, human services, and liberal arts/general studies). Management and elementary education are the largest.

Required: To graduate, students must have a 2.0 minimum GPA and 120 credit hours that include courses in phys ed, computer science, general education, service learning, and university colloquium.

Special: The university offers cross-registration with the University of Central Florida, study abroad in China, a Washington semester, and work-study programs. There is 1 national honor society, Phi Beta Kappa, a freshman honors program, and 1 departmental honors program.

Faculty/Classroom: 48% of faculty are male; 52%, female. All teach undergraduates. No introductory courses are taught by graduate students. The average class size in an introductory lecture is 30; in a laboratory, 25; and in a regular course, 30.

Admissions: 73% of the 2001-2002 applicants were accepted. The SAT I scores for the 2001-2002 freshman class were: Verbal--43% below 500, 42% between 500 and 599, 14% between 600 and 700, and 1% above 700; Math--42% below 500, 44% between 500 and 599, 13% between 600 and 700, and 1% above 700. The ACT scores were 30% below 21, 48% between 21 and 23, 9% between 24 and 26, 12% between 27 and 28, and 1% above 28. 40% of the current freshmen were in the top fifth of their class; 74% were in the top two fifths.

Requirements: The SAT I or ACT is recommended. A GPA of 2.0 is required. AP and CLEP credits are accepted. Important factors in the admissions decision are recommendations by school officials, leadership record, and evidence of special talent.

Procedure: Freshmen are admitted to all sessions. Entrance exams should be taken in the junior year. Application deadlines are open. The application fee is $20. Notification is sent on a rolling basis.

Transfer: 615 transfer students enrolled in 2001-2002. 30 credits of 120 must be completed at FGCU.

Visiting: There are regularly scheduled orientations for prospective students. There are guides for informal visits and visitors may sit in on classes. To schedule a visit, contact the Admissions Office.

Financial Aid: In 2001-2002, 82% of all freshmen and 33% of continuing students received some form of financial aid. 33% of freshmen and 38% of continuing students received need-based aid. The average freshman award was $5760. Of that total, scholarships or need-based grants averaged $3253 ($10,017 maximum); loans averaged $2339 ($9560 maximum); and work contracts averaged $475 ($4500 maximum). Average annual earnings from campus work are $6000. The average financial indebtedness of the 2001 graduate was $13,530. The FAFSA is required.

International Students: There are 45 international students enrolled. The school actively recruits these students. They must score 550 on the written TOEFL and also take the SAT I or the ACT, scoring 880 on the SAT I with a 3.0 GPA.

Computers: 8 computer labs/classrooms and 235 university-owned computers are available for classroom and personal use and for on-line admissions and course schedules. All students may access the system any time. There are no time limits and no fees.

Graduates: In 2001, 437 bachelor's degrees were awarded.

Admissions Contact: Michelle Yoranorich, Director of Admissions. E-mail: *oar@fgcu.edu* Web: *http://www.fgcu.edu*

FLORIDA HOSPITAL COLLEGE OF HEALTH SCIENCES — D-3

Orlando, FL 32803 — (407) 303-5548
(800) 500-7747; (407) 303-9408

Full-time: 72 men, 336 women	**Faculty:** 33
Part-time: 79 men, 259 women	**Ph.D.s:** n/av
Graduate: none	**Student/Faculty:** 12 to 1
Year: semesters, summer session	**Tuition:** $4390
Application Deadline: see profile	**Room & Board:** $1400
Freshman Class: 269 applied, 139 accepted, 90 enrolled	
ACT: 19	**COMPETITIVE**

Florida Hospital College of Health Sciences, founded in 1992, is a private institution offering programs in allied health and nursing. There is 1 undergraduate school. In addition to regional accreditation, Florida Hospital College of Health Sciences has baccalaureate program accreditation with NLN, ACOTE, CAAHEP, and JRCERT. The library contains 13,136 volumes and 1000 audiovisual forms/CDs, and subscribes to 171 periodicals. Computerized library services include the card catalog and interlibrary loans. Special learning facilities include a learning resource center. The 9-acre campus is in an urban area in Orlando. Including residence halls, there are 6 buildings.

Student Life: 90% of undergraduates are from Florida. Others are from 29 states. 78% are from public schools. 53% are white; 18% Hispanic; 14% African American. 21% are Protestant; 11% Catholic. The average age of freshmen is 25; all undergraduates, 25.

Housing: 141 students can be accommodated in college housing, which includes single-sex dormitories and on-campus apartments. On-campus housing is available on a first-come, first-served basis. Priority is given to out-of-town students. 84% of students commute. Alcohol is not permitted. Residence hall students may keep cars on campus.

Activities: There are no fraternities or sororities. There are 12 groups on campus, including drama, newspaper, religious, student government, and yearbook. Popular campus events include Fall Festival, International Food Festival, and Spring Picnic.

Sports: There are 3 intramural sports for men and 3 for women. Facilities include an outdoor sports court, canoes, a game room, and billiards.

Disabled Students: All of the campus is accessible. Wheelchair ramps, elevators, special parking, specially equipped rest rooms, and lowered drinking fountains are available.

Campus Safety and Security: Measures include 24-hour foot and vehicle patrol, escort service, informal discussions, and pamphlets/posters/films. There are lighted pathways/sidewalks.

Programs of Study: Florida Hospital College of Health Sciences confers B.S., B.S.N. degrees. Associate degrees are also awarded. Bachelor's degrees are awarded in HEALTH PROFESSIONS (nursing and radiograph medical technology). Sonography, radiology, and nursing are the strongest academically. Nursing and nuclear medicine are the largest.

Required: Students must take at least 127 credits with 64 in the major and maintain a GPA of 2.5.

Faculty/Classroom: 36% of faculty are male; 64%, female. All teach undergraduates. The average class size in an introductory lecture is 27; in a laboratory, 22; and in a regular course, 22.

Admissions: 52% of the 2001-2002 applicants were accepted.

Requirements: The SAT I or ACT is required. A GPA of 2.5 is required. CLEP credit is accepted.

Procedure: Freshmen are admitted to all sessions. A waiting list is an active part of the admissions procedure. Application deadlines and notification dates vary by department. Check with the school. The fee is $20.

Transfer: 187 transfer students enrolled in 2001-2002. Applicants must submit the completed application, the application fee, all previous transcripts, and ACT scores, if applicable. 50 credits of 127 must be completed at Florida Hospital College of Health Sciences.

Visiting: There are regularly scheduled orientations for prospective students, during the fall open house or the spring open house. There are guides for informal visits and visitors may sit in on classes. To schedule a visit, contact Rebekah Barney at (407) 303-9798 or *rebekah_barney@fhchs.edu*.

Financial Aid: In 2001-2002, 59% of all freshmen and 70% of continuing students received some form of financial aid. 23% of freshmen and 39% of continuing students received need-based aid. The average freshman award was $2759. Of that total, scholarships or need-based grants averaged $752 ($1606 maximum); loans averaged $2165 ($6000 maximum); and other sources averaged $1867 ($1875 maximum). 7% of undergraduates work part time. Average annual earnings from campus work are $2000. The average financial indebtedness of the 2001 graduate was $11,619. The FAFSA and the college's own financial statement are required. The fall application deadline is April 12.

International Students: They must score 550 on the written TOEFL or 213 on the electronic version and also take the SAT I or the ACT, scoring 19 on the ACT.

Computers: The mainframe is an IBM AS400. Students have access to 50 PCs in the learning resource center, computer lab, and library. All students may access the system. It is strongly recommended that all students have a personal computer. There are no time limits and no fees.

Graduates: In 2001, 19 bachelor's degrees were awarded. The most popular majors were nursing (47%), radiography (20%), and sonography (13%). In an average class, 36% graduate in 3 years, and 3% in 4 years.

Admissions Contact: Joe Forton, Director of Admissions.
E-mail: *joe_forton@fhchs.edu* Web: *www.fhchs.edu*

FLORIDA INSTITUTE OF TECHNOLOGY — E-3

Melbourne, FL 32901-6975 (321) 674-8030
(800) 888-4348; Fax: (321) 723-9468

Full-time: 1424 men, 608 women	**Faculty:** 149
Part-time: 109 men, 50 women	**Ph.D.s:** 88%
Graduate: 1385 men, 833 women	**Student/Faculty:** 14 to 1
Year: semesters, summer session	**Tuition:** $19,700
Application Deadline: open	**Room & Board:** $5550
Freshman Class: 2630 applied, 2105 accepted, 545 enrolled	
SAT I Verbal/Math: 560/610	**ACT:** 25 **VERY COMPETITIVE**

Florida Institute of Technology, founded in 1958, offers undergraduate degrees in engineering and science, liberal arts, business, psychology, and aeronautics. There are 5 undergraduate and 6 graduate schools. In addition to regional accreditation, Florida Tech has baccalaureate program accreditation with ABET, ACS, APA, CAA, and CSAB. The library contains 390,619 volumes, 297,881 microform items, and 1219 audiovisual forms/CDs, and subscribes to 6906 periodicals. Computerized library services include the card catalog, interlibrary loans, and database searching. Special learning facilities include a learning resource center, radio station, and TV station. The 130-acre campus is in a small town 70 miles east of Orlando. Including residence halls, there are 64 buildings.

Student Life: 59% of undergraduates are from out of state, mostly the Northeast. Others are from 44 states, 82 foreign countries, and Canada. 83% are from public schools. 56% are white; 26%, foreign nationals. The average age of freshmen is 19; all undergraduates, 21. 23% do not continue beyond their first year; 55% remain to graduate.

Housing: 1000 students can be accommodated in college housing, which includes single-sex and coed dormitories and on-campus apartments. On-campus housing is guaranteed for the freshman year only and is available on a first-come, first-served basis. 60% of students commute. All students may keep cars.

Activities: 17% of men belong to 6 national fraternities; 11% of women belong to 2 national sororities. There are 102 groups on campus, including band, cheerleading, chess, chorus, computers, dance, drama, drill team, environmental, ethnic, gay, honors, international, jazz band, literary magazine, newspaper, pep band, political, professional, radio and TV, religious, science fiction, social, social service, student government, and yearbook. Popular campus events include basketball games, Poor Man's Mardi Gras, and Big Man on Campus.

Sports: There are 5 intercollegiate sports for men and 5 for women, and 25 intramural sports for men and 25 for women. Facilities include a sports and recreation facility with 2 basketball courts, a racquetball court, and a 5000-square-foot weight and fitness area with cardiovascular machines, free weights, and specialized weight equipment.

Disabled Students: 90% of the campus is accessible. Wheelchair ramps, elevators, special parking, specially equipped rest rooms, special class scheduling, lowered drinking fountains, and lowered telephones are available.

Services: Counseling and information services are available, as is tutoring in every subject. There is a reader service for the blind, and remedial math, reading, and writing.

Campus Safety and Security: Measures include 24-hour foot and vehicle patrol, self-defense education, escort service, and informal discussions. There are pamphlets/posters/films, emergency telephones, and lighted pathways/sidewalks, and formal "Personal Safety and Security" sessions are given to all University Experience classes by security staff.

Programs of Study: Florida Tech confers B.A., B.S., and B.S.B.A. degrees. Associate, master's, and doctoral degrees are also awarded. Bachelor's degrees are awarded in BIOLOGICAL SCIENCE (biochemistry, biology/biological science, and marine biology), BUSINESS (business administration and management), COMMUNICATIONS AND THE ARTS (communications), COMPUTER AND PHYSICAL SCIENCE (applied mathematics, astrophysics, atmospheric sciences and meteorology, chemistry, computer science, information sciences and systems, oceanography, physics, and planetary and space science), EDUCATION (science), ENGINEERING AND ENVIRONMENTAL DESIGN (aeronautical engineering, aeronautical science, aerospace studies, aviation administration/management, aviation computer technology, chemical engineering, civil engineering, computer engineering, electrical/electronics engineering, environmental science, mechanical engineering, and ocean engineering), HEALTH PROFESSIONS (premedicine), SOCIAL SCIENCE (humanities, interdisciplinary studies, and psychology). Engineering, science, and aeronautics are the strongest academically. Computer engineering, marine biology, and aviation management are the largest.

Required: To graduate, students must have a minimum 2.0 GPA and 120 to 135 credit hours. The required number of hours in the major varies. All students must take 9 hours in communication and humanities and 3 in English composition. The core curriculum also requires 6 credit hours each in physical or life sciences and math, and 3 hours in computer science and social sciences.

Special: Florida Tech offers co-op programs in all majors, and double programs in environmental and chemical engineering, physics and space science, and math and computer science. Internships are available in the senior year for various majors, including psychology and aeronautics. Study-abroad programs, B.A.-B.S. degrees in several majors, and work-study programs are available. There are 9 national honor societies.

Faculty/Classroom: 78% of faculty are male; 22%, female. 94% both teach undergraduates and do research.. Graduate students teach 8% of introductory courses. The average class size in an introductory lecture is 27; in a laboratory, 17; and in a regular course, 18.

Admissions: 80% of the 2001-2002 applicants were accepted. The SAT I scores for the 2001-2002 freshman class were: Verbal--9% below 500, 38% between 500 and 599, 42% between 600 and 700, and 11% above 700; Math--19% below 500, 47% between 500 and 599, 31% between 600 and 700, and 4% above 700. The ACT scores were 11% below 21, 25% between 21 and 23, 27% between 24 and 26, 19% between 27 and 28, and 18% above 28. 52% of the current freshmen were in the top fifth of their class; 80% were in the top two fifths. 4 freshmen graduated first in their class.

Requirements: The SAT I or ACT is required. In addition, applicants must be graduates of an accredited secondary school or have a GED certificate. At least 18 academic credits or Carnegie units are required, including 4 years each of English, math, and science. An experiential essay is required and an interview is recommended. A GPA of 2.8 is required. AP and CLEP credits are accepted. Important factors in the admissions decision are advanced placement or honor courses, recommendations by school officials, and extracurricular activities record. Applications are accepted on-line at *www.fit.edu/ugrad/apply.htm*

Procedure: Freshmen are admitted fall and spring. Entrance exams should be taken during the junior year or the beginning of the senior year of high school. There are early admissions and deferred admissions plans. Application deadlines are open. The application fee is $40. Notification is sent on a rolling basis. 5% of all applicants are on a waiting list.

Transfer: 148 transfer students enrolled in 2001-2002. Applicants must have a minimum 2.5 GPA. If transfer students have fewer than 30 semester hours, high school transcripts and SAT I or ACT scores are required. A personal statement is recommended. 30 credits of 120 to 135 must be completed at Florida Tech.

Visiting: There are regularly scheduled orientations for prospective students, including tours and interviews with admissions staff, faculty, or department heads upon request. There are guides for informal visits and visitors may sit in on classes. To schedule a visit, contact the Admissions Office at *admission@fit.edu*

Financial Aid: In 2001-2002, 95% of all freshmen and 84% of continuing students received some form of financial aid. 77% of freshmen and 65% of continuing students received need-based aid. Scholarships or need-based grants averaged $12,650 ($28,695 maximum); loans averaged $3867 ($9625 maximum); and work contracts averaged $1483 ($1500 maximum). 24% of undergraduates work part time. Average annual earnings from campus work are $1485. The average financial indebtedness of the 2001 graduate was $25,174. Florida Tech is a member of CSS. The FAFSA is required. The fall application deadline is March 15.

International Students: There are 515 international students enrolled. The school actively recruits these students. They must score 550 on the written TOEFL or 213 on the electronic version. If students score below 550 or 213 on the TOEFL, they take language courses on campus. They must also take a math entrance qualifying exam and the SAT I or the ACT, scoring 950 on the SAT I.

Computers: The mainframe is a Sun Enterprise 3000. Students may access the system through more than 250 workstations located in general public or department labs, and through dial-up lines. All student residence halls on the central campus have direct network access in their rooms. Students have access internally to the Florida Tech web-based intranet and externally to the Internet. All students may access the system 24 hours per day. There are no time limits and no fees.

Graduates: In 2001, 391 bachelor's degrees were awarded. The most popular majors were electrical engineering (11%), computer engineering (9%), and marine biology (8%). In an average class, 31% graduate in 4 years, 53% in 5 years, and 56% in 6 years. 110 companies recruited on campus in 2000-2001. Of the 2000 graduating class, 17% were enrolled in graduate school within 6 months of graduation and 80% were employed.

Admissions Contact: Judi Marino, Director, Undergraduate Admissions. A video is available. E-mail: *jmarino@fit.edu*
Web: *http://www.fit.edu*

FLORIDA INTERNATIONAL UNIVERSITY E-5

Miami, FL 33199 **(305) 348-2363; Fax: (305) 348-3648**

Full-time: 6388 men, 8756 women	**Faculty:** 869
Part-time: 4914 men, 5913 women	**Ph.D.s:** 96%
Graduate: 2402 men, 3354 women	**Student/Faculty:** 17 to 1
Year: semesters, summer session	**Tuition:** $2562 ($10,450)
Application Deadline: open	**Room & Board:** $6924
Freshman Class: 6561 applied, 3059 accepted, 1499 enrolled	
SAT I Verbal/Math: 560/550	**ACT:** 25 **VERY COMPETITIVE**

Florida International University, founded in 1965, is part of the State University System of Florida. Some information in this profile is approximate. Undergraduate degrees are offered through the Colleges of Arts and Sciences, Business Administration, Education, Engineering, Health, Science, and Urban and Public Affairs; and the Schools of Accounting, Computer Science, Architecture, Hospitality Management, Music, and Journalism and Mass Communication. The North and University Park campuses are in Miami, and there are 2 educational centers in Fort Lauderdale. There are 12 undergraduate and 12 graduate schools. In addition to regional accreditation, FIU has baccalaureate program accreditation with AACSB, ABET, ACCE, ACEJMC, ADA, APTA, ASLA, CSWE, NAAB, NASM, NCATE, and NLN. The 2 libraries contain 1,397,808 volumes, 3,236,347 microform items, and 115,550 audiovisual forms/CDs, and subscribe to 9910 periodicals. Computerized library services include the card catalog, interlibrary loans, and database searching. Special learning facilities include a learning resource center, radio station, and art museum. The 573-acre campus is in an urban area 10 miles west of downtown Miami. Including residence halls, there are 24 buildings.

Student Life: 90% of undergraduates are from Florida. Others are from 49 states, 115 foreign countries, and Canada. 61% are from public schools. 53% are Hispanic; 22%, white; 14%, African American. The average age of freshmen is 19; all undergraduates, 24. 5% do not continue beyond their first year; 63% remain to graduate.

Housing: 1585 students can be accommodated in college housing, which includes coed dormitories, on-campus apartments, and married-student housing. On-campus housing is available on a first-come, first-served basis. 95% of students commute. All students may keep cars.

Activities: 9% of men belong to 10 national fraternities; 10% of women belong to 1 local and 9 national sororities. There are 150 groups on campus, including band, cheerleading, chorus, ethnic, gay, honors, international, newspaper, political, professional, radio and TV, religious, social, social service, student government, and yearbook.

Sports: There are 6 intercollegiate sports for men and 9 for women, and 14 intramural sports for men and 10 for women. Facilities include a 5000-seat arena with basketball and racquetball courts, an aquatic center, baseball and soccer fields, a fitness center with Nautilus machines, and a racquet sports center with lighted tennis and racquetball courts.

Disabled Students: 96% of the campus is accessible. Wheelchair ramps, elevators, special parking, specially equipped rest rooms, special class scheduling, lowered drinking fountains, land owered telephones are available. There is also accessible computer equipment for visually impaired students, including talking and large-print computers.

Services: Counseling and information services are available, as is tutoring in most subjects. There is a reader service for the blind, and remedial math, reading, and writing. Note taking, adapted testing, and special registration may be arranged for disabled students.

Campus Safety and Security: Measures include 24-hour foot and vehicle patrol, escort service, informal discussions, and pamphlets/posters/films. There are emergency telephones and lighted pathways/sidewalks.

Programs of Study: FIU confers B.A., B.S., B.Ac., B.B.A., B.F.A., B.H.S.A., B.M., B.P.A., and B.S.N. degrees. Associate, master's, and doctoral degrees are also awarded. Bachelor's degrees are awarded in BIOLOGICAL SCIENCE (biology/biological science), BUSINESS (accounting, banking and finance, business administration and management, hospitality management services, international business management, management information systems, management science, marketing/retailing/merchandising, personnel management, real estate, and transportation management), COMMUNICATIONS AND THE ARTS (art, communications, dance, dramatic arts, English, French, German, music, Portuguese, and Spanish), COMPUTER AND PHYSICAL SCIENCE (applied mathematics, chemistry, computer science, geology, mathematics, physics, and statistics), EDUCATION (art, education of the emotionally handicapped, education of the mentally handicapped, elementary, English, foreign languages, health, home economics, mathematics, music, physical, science, social studies, special, specific learning disabilities, and vocational), ENGINEERING AND ENVIRONMENTAL DESIGN (architectural technology, chemical engineering, civil engineering, computer engineering, construction management, electrical/electronics engineering, environmental science, industrial engineering, interior design, and mechanical engineering), HEALTH PROFESSIONS (health care administration, medical laboratory technology, nursing, occupational therapy, and rehabilitation therapy), SOCIAL SCIENCE (criminal justice, dietetics, economics, history, humanities, international relations, Italian studies, liberal arts/general studies, parks and recreation management, philosophy, political science/government, psychology, public administration, religion, social work, sociology, urban studies, and women's studies). Accounting, engineering, and biology are the strongest academically. Accounting, hospitality management, and elementary education are the largest.

Required: To graduate, students must complete between 120 and 152 hours with a 2.0 GPA. There are also general education and writing requirements. Students admitted with fewer than 48 hours must complete the core curriculum.

Special: FIU offers co-op and work-study programs, study abroad in 6 countries, accelerated degree programs, nondegree study, dual majors, and B.A.-B.S. degrees in chemistry, enviromental studies, and geology. There are 25 national honor societies, a freshman honors program, and 18 departmental honors programs.

Faculty/Classroom: 60% of faculty are male; 40%, female. All both teach and do research. Graduate students teach 32% of introductory courses. The average class size in an introductory lecture is 41; in a laboratory, 15; and in a regular course, 23.

Admissions: 47% of the 2001-2002 applicants were accepted. The SAT I scores for the 2001-2002 freshman class were: Verbal--12% below 500, 57% between 500 and 599, 24% between 600 and 700, and 4% above 700; Math--10% below 500, 62% between 500 and 599, 25% between 600 and 700, and 3% above 700. The ACT scores were 1% below 21, 16% between 21 and 23, 57% between 24 and 26, 17% between 27 and 28, and 9% above 28.

Requirements: The SAT I or ACT is required. In addition, applicants must be graduates of an accredited secondary school or have a GED certificate. The required academic courses include 4 units in English, 3 each in math, natural science, and social studies, 2 in a foreign language, and 4 in academic electives. The university's placement tests must be taken the semester before attending. An interview may be required. A GPA of 2.0 is required. AP and CLEP credits are accepted. Important factors in the admissions decision are advanced placement or honor courses, evidence of special talent, and recommendations by school officials. Admissions diskettes are available upon request. A printable online application is available.

Procedure: Freshmen are admitted to all sessions. Entrance exams should be taken during the spring of the junior year. There are early admissions and deferred admissions plans. Application deadlines are open. The application fee is $20. Notification is sent on a rolling basis.

Transfer: 2360 transfer students enrolled in a recent year. Applicants with fewer than 60 semester credits must meet regular freshman admissions requirements. All students must pass the CLAST or take the pre-CLAST testing program during the first term of enrollment, fulfill core curriculum or general education requirements, and have a 2.0 GPA. 30 credits of 120 to 152 must be completed at FIU.

Visiting: There are regularly scheduled orientations for prospective students, including placement tests, advising, a tour, and student activities. There are guides for informal visits and visitors may sit in on classes. To schedule a visit, contact the Office of Admissions.

Financial Aid: In 2001-2002, 52% of all freshmen and 40% of continuing students received some form of financial aid. In a recent year, 72% of freshmen and 73% of continuing students received need-based aid. The average freshman award was $4191. Of that total, scholarships or need-based grants averaged $3521 ($7799 maximum); loans averaged $2636 ($10,500 maximum); and work contracts averaged $2451 ($2500 maximum). 6% of undergraduates work part time. Average annual earnings from campus work are $2000. The average financial indebtedness of a recent graduate was $4650. FIU is a member of CSS. The FAFSA is required. Check with the school for current deadlines.

International Students: In a recent year, there were 1474 international students enrolled. The school actively recruits these students. They must score 500 on the written TOEFL or 173 on the electronic version and also take the SAT I or the ACT.

Computers: The mainframes are a DEC VAX 8800 and a Sun 4/280. Students may access the campus Ethernet network through terminals and PCs and through dial-up access from home. All students may access the system. There are no time limits and no fees.

Graduates: In a recent class, 4071 bachelor's degrees were awarded. The most popular majors were international business (9%), psychology (8%), and elementary education (7%). In an average class, 1% graduate in 3 years, 19% in 4 years, 39% in 5 years, and 50% in 6 years. 180 companies recruited on campus in a recent year. Of a recent graduating class, 37% were enrolled in graduate school within 6 months of graduation and 70% were employed.

Admissions Contact: Carmen Brown, Admissions Director.
E-mail: *brownc@fiu.edu* Web: *http://www.fiu.edu*

FLORIDA MEMORIAL COLLEGE

Miami, FL 33054 — **E-5**
(305) 626-3750
(800) 822-1362; Fax: (305) 626-3769

Full-time: 580 men, 825 women	**Faculty:** 80
Part-time: 50 men, 70 women	**Ph.D.s:** 40%
Graduate: none	**Student/Faculty:** 18 to 1
Year: terms, summer session	**Tuition:** $6000
Application Deadline: open	**Room & Board:** n/app
Freshman Class: n/av	
SAT I or ACT: required	**LESS COMPETITIVE**

Florida Memorial College, founded in 1879, is a private liberal arts institution affiliated with the American Baptist Church. Figures given in the above capsule, and in this profile, are approximate. There are 6 undergraduate schools. The library contains 88,000 volumes, and subscribes to 400 periodicals. Special learning facilities include an aviation center. The 77-acre campus is in an urban area in northwestern Miami. There are 12 buildings.

Student Life: All are from public schools. 38% do not continue beyond their first year; 25% remain to graduate.

Housing: 835 students can be accommodated in college housing, which includes single-sex dorms and off campus apartments. On campus housing is guaranteed for all 4 years. Alcohol is not permitted.

Activities: There are 4 national fraternities and 4 national sororities. There are some groups and organizations on campus, including band, choir, jazz band, religious, and student government. Popular campus event include concerts, drama productions and Sunday services.

Sports: There are 6 intercollegiate sports for men and 6 for women, and 7 intramural sports for men and 7 for women. Facilities include a gym, a pool and a track.

Services: There is remedial math, reading, and writing.

Programs of Study: Florida Memorial confers B.A., and B.S. degrees. Bachelor's degrees are awarded in BIOLOGICAL SCIENCE (biology/biological science), BUSINESS (accounting, business administration and management, and transportation management), COMMUNICATIONS AND THE ARTS (English, fine arts, and music), COMPUTER AND PHYSICAL SCIENCE (chemistry, computer science, and mathematics), EDUCATION (elementary, physical, and secondary), ENGINEERING AND ENVIRONMENTAL DESIGN (air traffic control, aviation administration/management, and aviation computer technology), SOCIAL SCIENCE (criminal justice, philosophy, political science/government, psychology, public administration, religion, and sociology).

Required: To graduate, all students must complete at least 124 credit hours, including 62 hours of general education requirements, with a minimum overall GPA of 2.0. Students must successfully complete all 4 subtests of the Florida College-Level Academic Skills Test by junior year.

Special: Private sector and college internships, work-study, and a 3-2 engineering program with the University of Miami are available. Pass/fail credit and nondegree options are possible. There is a freshman honors program.

Requirements: The SAT I or ACT is required with a minimum composite score of 840 on the SAT I or 17 on the ACT for education majors. Applicants must be graduates of an accredited secondary school or have a GED certificate. 1 faculty and 2 personal recommendations, an autobiography, and a health certificate are required. Up to 20% of a freshman class may be admitted for 1 semester on a conditional basis to demonstrate their abilities. A GPA of 2.0 is required.

Procedure: Freshmen are admitted fall and spring. Check with the school for current application deadlines and fee.

Transfer: Transcripts must be submitted for all previous college work, as well as high school transcripts for students with fewer than 3 credits. The SAT I or ACT is recommended. 30 credits of 124 must be completed at Florida Memorial.

Financial Aid: The CSS/Profile or FFS is required. Check with the school for current deadlines.

International Students: They must take the TOEFL.

Computers: The mainframes are an IBM 9375 Model 60 and a DEC VAX 6210. There is an IBM PS/2 microcomputer lab in the aviation center, and another computer lab in the classroom building. All students may access the system. There are no time limits and no fees.

Admissions Contact: Peggy Kelly, Director of Admissions.
Web: *http://www.fmc.edu*

FLORIDA SOUTHERN COLLEGE D-4
Lakeland, FL 33801-5698 (863) 680-3909
(800) 274-4131; Fax: (863) 680-4120

Full-time: 684 men, 1068 women	**Faculty:** 107; IIB, -$
Part-time: 26 men, 49 women	**Ph.D.s:** 84%
Graduate: 23 men, 25 women	**Student/Faculty:** 16 to 1
Year: semesters, summer session	**Tuition:** $13,930
Application Deadline: August 1	**Room & Board:** $5500
Freshman Class: 1538 applied, 1181 accepted, 515 enrolled	
SAT I Verbal/Math: 490/490	**ACT:** 23 **COMPETITIVE**

Florida Southern College, founded in 1885, is a private institution affiliated with the United Methodist Church offering undergraduate programs through the divisions of humanities, social sciences, and natural sciences. The library contains 171,644 volumes, 432,167 microform items, and 10,366 audiovisual forms/CDs, and subscribes to 641 periodicals. Computerized library services include the card catalog, interlibrary loans, and database searching. Special learning facilities include a learning resource center, art gallery, and planetarium. The 100-acre campus is in a suburban area 30 miles east of Tampa. Including residence halls, there are 40 buildings.

Student Life: 75% of undergraduates are from Florida. Others are from 41 states, 31 foreign countries, and Canada. 75% are from public schools. 84% are white. 45% are Protestant; 19%, Catholic; 18% claim no religious affiliation. The average age of freshmen is 18; all undergraduates, 20. 28% do not continue beyond their first year; 54% remain to graduate.

Housing: 1256 students can be accommodated in college housing, which includes single-sex dormitories, married-student housing, fraternity houses, and sorority houses. On-campus housing is guaranteed for all 4 years. 66% of students live on campus; of those, 60% remain on campus on weekends. Alcohol is not permitted. All students may keep cars.

Activities: 18% of men belong to 5 national fraternities; 17% of women belong to 5 national sororities. There are 44 groups on campus, including art, band, cheerleading, choir, chorale, chorus, drama, ethnic, film, honors, international, jazz band, literary magazine, musical theater, newspaper, opera, orchestra, pep band, photography, political, professional, religious, social, student government, volunteer, and yearbook. Popular campus events include theater productions, a jazz festival, and the Festival of Fine Art series.

Sports: There are 6 intercollegiate sports for men and 6 for women, and 6 intramural sports for men and 6 for women. Facilities include a 2500-seat air-conditioned field house; fields for soccer, softball, and intramurals; 9 lighted tennis courts; aerobics, weight, and fitness facilities; an intramural gym; a heated competitive-size pool; a boathouse for sailboats, sculls, kayaks, and canoes; and a sand volleyball court.

Disabled Students: 20% of the campus is accessible. Wheelchair ramps, elevators, special parking, specially equipped rest rooms, special class scheduling, lowered drinking fountains, and lowered telephones are available.

Services: Counseling and information services are available, as is tutoring in some subjects, including math and English.

Campus Safety and Security: Measures include 24-hour foot and vehicle patrol, escort service, informal discussions, and pamphlets/posters/films. There are emergency telephones and lighted pathways/sidewalks.

Programs of Study: Florida Southern confers B.A., B.S., B.M.E., and R.S.M. degrees. Master's degrees are also awarded. Bachelor's degrees are awarded in AGRICULTURE (horticulture), BIOLOGICAL SCIENCE (biology/biological science), BUSINESS (accounting, banking and finance, business administration and management, business economics, hotel/motel and restaurant management, international business management, marketing/retailing/merchandising, and personnel management), COMMUNICATIONS AND THE ARTS (advertising, communications, dramatic arts, English, journalism, music, public relations, and Spanish), COMPUTER AND PHYSICAL SCIENCE (chemistry, information sciences and systems, mathematics, and physics), EDUCATION (art, athletic training, early childhood, elementary, foreign languages, middle school, music, science, secondary, and special), ENGINEERING AND ENVIRONMENTAL DESIGN (environmental science), SOCIAL SCIENCE (criminal justice, economics, history, humanities, political science/government, psychology, religion, social science, and sociology). Biology, music, and business/economics are the strongest academically. Business, education, and biology are the largest.

Required: To graduate, all students must have completed 124 semester hours of credit, with no more than 42 hours in the major for most programs and a minimum 2.0 GPA. Core requirements include 9 hours of humanities, 8 of natural science, 6 each of English, social sciences, and math, 3 each of history and fine arts, 2 of phys ed, and attendance at faith and life convocation.

Special: Florida Southern offers study abroad in 8 countries, a Washington semester with American University, and a 3-2 engineering degree with Washington University/St. Louis and the Universities of Florida and Miami. Students may choose the United Nations semester in cooperation with Drew University in New Jersey, or the May Option Program, which combines study and travel in England for course credit. Internships with corporations in Tampa, Lakeland, and Orlando are offered through most academic departments and are required by many. Credit for military experience and pass/fail options are available. There are 20 national honor societies and a freshman honors program.

Faculty/Classroom: 64% of faculty are male; 36%, female. All teach undergraduates. No introductory courses are taught by graduate students. The average class size in an introductory lecture is 20; in a laboratory, 15; and in a regular course, 19.

Admissions: 77% of the 2001-2002 applicants were accepted. The SAT I scores for the 2001-2002 freshman class were: Verbal--37% below 500, 45% between 500 and 599, 16% between 600 and 700, and 2% above 700; Math--37% below 500, 44% between 500 and 599, 16% between 600 and 700, and 2% above 700. The ACT scores were 30% below 21, 29% between 21 and 23, 23% between 24 and 26, 9% between 27 and 28, and 9% above 28. 53% of the current freshmen were in the top fifth of their class; 77% were in the top two fifths. 6 freshmen graduated first in their class.

Requirements: The SAT I or ACT is required, with a minimum composite score of 950 on the SAT I or 20 on the ACT. Applicants must be graduates of an accredited secondary school or have a GED certificate. An essay is required and an interview is recommended. A GPA of 2.5 is required. AP and CLEP credits are accepted. Applications are accepted on disk and on-line CollegeView and the Internet.

Procedure: Freshmen are admitted to all sessions. Entrance exams should be taken starting in the junior year of high school. There is a deferred admissions plan. Applications should be filed by August 1 for fall entry and December 1 for spring entry. The fall 2001 application fee was $30. Notification is sent on a rolling basis.

Transfer: 134 transfer students enrolled in 2001-2002. Transfer students must have a minimum 2.5 GPA and must submit SAT I or ACT scores. An associate degree and an interview are recommended. 31 credits of 124 must be completed at Florida Southern.

Visiting: There are regularly scheduled orientations for prospective students, including campuswide open houses. There are guides for informal visits and visitors may sit in on classes and stay overnight. To schedule a visit, contact the Admissions Office at *fscadm@flsouthern.edu*

Financial Aid: In 2001-2002, 96% of all freshmen and 91% of continuing students received some form of financial aid. 70% of freshmen and 80% of continuing students received need-based aid. The average freshman award was $13,517. Of that total, scholarships or need-based grants averaged $8937 ($46,646 maximum); loans averaged $4654 ($19,400 maximum); and work contracts averaged $1561 ($4775 maximum). 78% of undergraduates work part time. Average annual earnings from campus work are $1200. The average financial indebtedness of the 2001 graduate was $12,100. The FAFSA, the college's own financial statement, and parents' and student's tax returns are required. The fall application deadline is March 1.

International Students: There were 88 international students enrolled in a recent year. The school actively recruits these students. They must score 550 on the written TOEFL.

Computers: The mainframe is an IBM AS/400 ESO. 15 IBM PCs are available in the library for students' academic and word processing needs, and there are 5 specialized computer labs for the courses that require computer use. In addition, a central computer lab has been established with 24 computers and extended hours for campuswide use. All students may access the system during lab hours. There are no time limits and no fees. It is strongly recommended that all students have a personal computer.

Graduates: In 2001, 342 bachelor's degrees were awarded. The most popular majors were business (24%), education (15%), and biology (9%). In an average class, 7% graduate in 3 years, 46% in 4 years, 55% in 5 years, and 56% in 6 years. 68 companies recruited on campus in 2000-2001. Of the 2000 graduating class, 15% were enrolled in graduate school within 6 months of graduation and 74% were employed.

Admissions Contact: Barry Connors, Director of Admissions. A video is available. E-mail: *fscadm@flsouthern.edu*
Web: *http://www.flsouthern.edu*

FLORIDA STATE UNIVERSITY C-1
Tallahassee, FL 32306-2400 (850) 644-6200
Fax: (850) 644-0197

Full-time: 10,428 men, 13,568 women	**Faculty:** 1052; I, --$
Part-time: 1814 men, 2421 women	**Ph.D.s:** 91%
Graduate: 2972 men, 3779 women	**Student/Faculty:** 23 to 1
Year: semesters, summer session	**Tuition:** $2513 ($10,402)
Application Deadline: March 1	**Room & Board:** $5322
Freshman Class: 23,770 applied, 15,406 accepted, 5821 enrolled	
SAT I Verbal/Math: 580/580	**ACT:** 25 **HIGHLY COMPETITIVE**

Florida State University, a public institution founded in 1851, is a residential university designated as a Doctoral Research University by the Carnegie Foundation for the Advancement of Teaching. There are 15 undergraduate and 16 graduate schools. In addition to regional accreditation, FSU has baccalaureate program accreditation with AACSB, ABET, ADA, AHEA, ASLA, CSWE, FIDER, NASM, NCATE, NLN, and NRPA. The 6 libraries contain 2,380,757 volumes, 6,758,785 microform items, and 43,275 audiovisual forms/CDs, and subscribe to 16,449 periodicals. Computerized library services include the card catalog, interlibrary loans, and database searching. Special learning facilities include a learning resource center, art gallery, planetarium, radio station, TV station, nuclear accelerator, x-ray emission lab, marine lab, supercomputers, the National High Magnetic Field Laboratory, and the Oak Ridge National Laboratory. The 463-acre campus is in a suburban area 163 miles west of Jacksonville. Including residence halls, there are 213 buildings.

Student Life: 81% of undergraduates are from Florida. Others are from 49 states, 120 foreign countries, and Canada. 89% are from public schools. 74% are white; 12%, African American. The average age of freshmen is 19; all undergraduates, 21. 16% do not continue beyond their first year.

Housing: 5270 students can be accommodated in college housing, which includes single-sex and coed dormitories, on-campus apartments, married-student housing, fraternity houses, and sorority houses. In addition, there are honors houses and special-interest houses. On-campus housing is available on a first-come, first-served basis. All students may keep cars.

Activities: 11% of men belong to 25 national fraternities; 11% of women belong to 22 national sororities. There are 245 groups on campus, including art, band, cheerleading, chess, choir, chorale, chorus, computers, dance, debate, drama, drill team, ethnic, forensics, gay, honors, international, jazz band, literary magazine, marching band, musical theater, newspaper, opera, orchestra, pep band, political, professional, radio and TV, religious, social, social service, student government, symphony, and yearbook. Popular campus events include Twelve Days of Dance, Parents Weekend, and Seven Days of Opening Nights.

Sports: There are 9 intercollegiate sports for men and 10 for women, and 27 intramural sports for men and 27 for women. Facilities include an 80,000-seat stadium, an aquatic center with a heated outdoor swimming pool, a golf course, a track, courts for basketball, tennis, racquetball, and handball, a student recreation center with an indoor Olympic-size swimming pool, 2 Jacuzzis, a steam room, a sauna, 10 racquetball courts, a squash court, a multipurpose gym, a 3-lane jogging track, aerobic rooms, aerobic exercise machines, and free and fixed weights, and a lakefront recreation area for outdoor water sports.

Disabled Students: 99% of the campus is accessible. Wheelchair ramps, elevators, special parking, specially equipped rest rooms, special class scheduling, lowered drinking fountains, and lowered telephones are available.

Services: Counseling and information services are available, as is tutoring in most subjects. There is a reader service for the blind, and remedial math, reading, and writing.

Campus Safety and Security: Measures include 24-hour foot and vehicle patrol, self-defense education, escort service, and shuttle buses. There are informal discussions, pamphlets/posters/films, emergency telephones, and lighted pathways/sidewalks.

Programs of Study: FSU confers B.A., B.S., B.F.A., B.M., B.M.Ed., and B.S.N. degrees. Associate, master's, and doctoral degrees are also awarded. Bachelor's degrees are awarded in AGRICULTURE (environmental studies and plant science), BIOLOGICAL SCIENCE (biochemistry, biology/biological science, cell biology, ecology, evolutionary biology, genetics, marine biology, molecular biology, nutrition, physiology, and zoology), BUSINESS (accounting, banking and finance, business administration and management, entrepreneurial studies, fashion merchandising, hotel/motel and restaurant management, insurance and risk management, international business management, management information systems, management science, marketing/retailing/merchandising, personnel management, recreation and leisure services, small business management, and sports management), COMMUNICATIONS AND THE ARTS (advertising, American literature, apparel design, art history and appreciation, broadcasting, classics, communications, creative writing, dance, dramatic arts, English, fiber/textiles/weaving, film arts, French, German, Greek, Italian, jazz, Latin, linguistics, music, music history and appreciation, music performance, music theory and composition, musical theater, piano/organ, public relations, Russian, Spanish, speech/debate/rhetoric, strings, studio art, theater design, voice, and winds), COMPUTER AND PHYSICAL SCIENCE (actuarial science, applied mathematics, atmospheric sciences and meteorology, chemical technology, chemistry, computer science, geology, information sciences and systems, mathematics, physics, and statistics), EDUCATION (art, early childhood, education of the emotionally handicapped, education of the mentally handicapped, education of the visually handicapped, elementary, English, foreign languages, health, home economics, mathematics, music, physical, reading, science, social science, and specific learning disabilities), ENGINEERING AND ENVIRONMENTAL DESIGN (bioengineering, biomedical engineering, chemical engineering, civil engineering, computer engineering, electrical/electronics engineering, environmental engineering, environmental science, graphic arts technology, industrial engineering, interior design, materials engineering, and mechanical engineering), HEALTH PROFESSIONS (community health work, music therapy, nursing, predentistry, premedicine, preoptometry, prepharmacy, preveterinary science, rehabilitation therapy, and speech pathology/audiology), SOCIAL SCIENCE (American studies, anthropology, Asian/Oriental studies, Caribbean studies, child care/child and family studies, classical/ancient civilization, clothing and textiles management/production/services, criminology, dietetics, Eastern European studies, economics, family/consumer studies, fashion design and technology, food science, geography, history, home economics, humanities, international relations, Latin American studies, philosophy, political science/government, prelaw, psychology, religion, Russian and Slavic studies, social science, social work, sociology, and women's studies). Computer science and natural science are the strongest academically. Business, communication, and criminology are the largest.

Required: Students must take the Florida College-Level Academic Skills Test (CLAST) for admission to upper-division status. The required core curriculum includes 6 semester hours in English composition, 6 to 12 in history/social science, 5 to 11 in humanities/fine arts, and 7 in natural sciences. Most academic areas require at least 120 semester hours for graduation.

Special: Cross-registration with Florida Agricultural and Mechanical University and Tallahassee Community College is possible, as is study at FSU centers in London or Florence and in programs in Costa Rica, France, Russia, Spain, Switzerland, and Vietnam, among other countries. FSU offers cooperative programs in engineering, computer science, business, and communication, work-study programs, general studies and combined B.A.-B.S. degrees, and accelerated degree programs. Internships are required in criminology, human science, and social work. There are preprofessional programs in health and law. There are 49 national honor societies, including Phi Beta Kappa, a freshman honors program, and 60 departmental honors programs.

Faculty/Classroom: 64% of faculty are male; 36%, female. Graduate students teach 47% of introductory courses. The average class size in an introductory lecture is 41; in a laboratory, 18; and in a regular course, 35.

Admissions: 65% of the 2001-2002 applicants were accepted. The SAT I scores for the 2001-2002 freshman class were: Verbal--13% below 500, 47% between 500 and 599, 35% between 600 and 700, and 5% above 700; Math--11% below 500, 46% between 500 and 599, 38% between 600 and 700, and 5% above 700. The ACT scores were 9% below 21, 31% between 21 and 23, 30% between 24 and 26, 15% between 27 and 28, and 14% above 28. 77% of the current freshmen were in the top fifth of their class; 96% were in the top two fifths. There were 68 National Merit finalists.

Requirements: The SAT I or ACT is required. It is recommended that in-state students have at least an A-/B+ weighted average and a minimum composite SAT I score of 1100, or 25 on the ACT. Out-of-state students must meet higher standards. Applicants should have the following high school units: 4 in English, 3 each in math, natural science, and social science, and 2 in a foreign language. Other factors include the number of honors, AP, and IB classes, strength of the academic curriculum, class rank, evidence of special talent, and recommendations by school officials. AP and CLEP credits are accepted. Applications are accepted on-line at the school's web site.

Procedure: Freshmen are admitted fall, spring, and summer. Entrance exams should be taken beginning in the second semester of the junior year. There is an early admissions plan. Applications should be filed by March 1 for fall entry, November 1 for spring entry, and March 1 for summer entry, along with a $20 fee. Notification is sent on a rolling basis.

Transfer: 2203 transfer students enrolled in 2001-2002. Transfer applicants should present at least a 2.5 cumulative college GPA unless transferring from a Florida public community college with an associate in arts degree, in which case the minimum college GPA needed varies according to major. Applicants with less than 60 semester hours of transferable credit must also meet freshman admission requirements. All transfers must have completed 2 years of the same foreign language in high school or have 8 semester hours at the college level. Students must pass the Florida CLAST Examination. 30 credits of 120 must be completed at FSU.

Visiting: There are regularly scheduled orientations for prospective students, including campus tours several times daily on weekdays. Walking and riding tours are available and are coordinated around an 11:00 A.M. admissions information session. There are guides for informal visits and visitors may sit in on classes. To schedule a visit, contact Visitor Services at (850) 644-3246 or *visitorservices@admin.fsu.edu*

Financial Aid: In a recent year, 74% of all freshmen and 60% of continuing students received some form of financial aid. 27% of freshmen and 33% of continuing students received need-based aid. The average freshman award was $7957. Of that total, scholarships or need-based grants averaged $2541 ($3500 maximum); loans averaged $2682 ($3000 maximum); and work contracts averaged $1811 ($2990 maximum). 2% of undergraduates work part time. Average annual earnings from campus work are $1778. The average financial indebtedness of the

2001 graduate was $15,458. The FAFSA and the college's own financial statement are required. The fall application deadline is March 1.

International Students: There are 238 international students enrolled. The school actively recruits these students. They must score 550 on the written TOEFL or 213 on the electronic version and also take the SAT I or the ACT.

Computers: The mainframes are an IBM RS/6000 and 9076 SP2, a Cray Y-MP and CM-2, a CDC CYBER 850, and a DEC VAX 6210. There is also a supercomputer on campus. All students may access the system, although use of some machines is restricted to particular majors or graduate students. There are no time limits and no fees. It is recommended that students in engineering programs have personal computers.

Graduates: In 2001, 5467 bachelor's degrees were awarded. The most popular majors were communication (7%), criminology (6%), and finance (6%). In an average class, 3% graduate in 3 years, 39% in 4 years, 56% in 5 years, and 60% in 6 years.

Admissions Contact: Admissions.
E-mail: *admissions@admin.fsu.edu*
Web: *http://www.admissions.fsu.edu*

INTERNATIONAL COLLEGE — D-5

Naples, FL 34119-7932 — (941) 513-1122
(800) 466-8017; Fax: (941) 513-9054

Full-time: 190 men, 440 women — **Faculty:** 39
Part-time: 50 men, 115 women — **Ph.D.s:** 70%
Graduate: 5 men, 10 women — **Student/Faculty:** 24 to 1
Year: trimesters, summer session — **Tuition:** $7230
Application Deadline: open — **Room & Board:** n/app
Freshman Class: 190 applied, 187 accepted, 125 enrolled
SAT I or ACT: not required — **NONCOMPETITIVE**

International College is a private institution offering a master's degree in business administration, public administration, and criminal justice, a bachelor's degree in accounting, business administration, criminal justice, interdisciplinary studies, management, computer technology, and paralegal studies, and associate degrees in accounting, business administration, computer technology, allied health, and paralegal studes. Enrollment figures in the above capsule are approximate. There are 4 undergraduate schools and 1 graduate school. The library contains 22,233 volumes and 400 audiovisual forms/CDs, and subscribes to 212 periodicals. Computerized library services include the card catalog, interlibrary loans, and database searching. Special learning facilities include an art gallery. The campus is in a suburban area 100 miles west of Fort Lauderdale.

Student Life: 12% are Hispanic; 10% African American.

Housing: There are no residence halls. All of students commute.

Activities: There are no fraternities or sororities. There are some groups and organizations on campus, including student government and yearbook.

Services: Counseling and information services are available, as is tutoring in every subject, career counseling, and placement services for graduates.

Programs of Study: International College confers the B.S. degree. Associate and master's degrees are also awarded. Bachelor's degrees are awarded in BUSINESS (accounting and business administration and management), COMPUTER AND PHYSICAL SCIENCE (information sciences and systems), SOCIAL SCIENCE (criminal justice, interdisciplinary studies, and paralegal studies). Computer information technology is the largest.

Required: To graduate, students must complete a minimum of 120 semester hours, with at least 64 in the major and with a minimum GPA of 2.0. At least 48 hours must be upper-division courses. A comprehensive exam is required.

Special: Dual majors, internships, work study, an accelerated degree in management, on-line classes, and credit for life experience are possible.

Faculty/Classroom: 63% of faculty are male; 38%, female. All teach undergraduates. No introductory courses are taught by graduate students. The average class size in an introductory lecture is 20; in a laboratory, 20; and in a regular course, 20.

Admissions: 98% of the 2001-2002 applicants were accepted.

Requirements: An essay and interview are required. Applications may be submitted on-line at the school's web site, *www.internationalcollege.edu.*. The Common Application is accepted. AP and CLEP credits are accepted.

Procedure: Freshmen are admitted to all sessions. Entrance exams should be taken any time. Application deadlines are open. The fall 2001 application fee was $20. Notification is sent on a rolling basis.

Transfer: 227 transfer students enrolled in 2001-2002. Applicants must submit previous transcripts. Only credits completed with a C or better will transfer. 32 credits of 120 must be completed at International College.

Visiting: There are regularly scheduled orientations for prospective students.

Financial Aid: In 2001-2002, 92% of all freshmen and 93% of continuing students received some form of financial aid. 86% of freshmen and 84% of continuing students received need-based aid. The average freshman award was $7500. Of that total, scholarships or need-based grants averaged $6000 ($7436 maximum); loans averaged $5000 ($10,500 maximum); and work contracts averaged $4760 ($5440 maximum). 2% of undergraduates work part time. Average annual earnings from campus work are $4760. The average financial indebtedness of the 2001 graduate was $15,000. The FAFSA is required. The fall application deadline is September 10.

International Students: The school actively recruits these students. They must score 500 on the written TOEFL or 173 on the electronic version.

Computers: There are 4 classrooms and 2 labs networked with access to the Internet and Web. There are 150 workstations in the library and computer center. E-mail accounts are available. All students may access the system. There are no time limits and no fees.

Graduates: In 2001, 100 bachelor's degrees were awarded. The most popular majors were management/business (77%), criminal justice (13%), and legal studies (5%). 15 companies recruited on campus in 2000-2001. Of the 2000 graduating class, 5% were enrolled in graduate school within 6 months of graduation and 93% were employed.

Admissions Contact: Rita Lampus, Director of Admissions.
E-mail: *rlampus@internationalcollege.edu*
Web: *internationalcollege.edu*

JACKSONVILLE UNIVERSITY — D-1

Jacksonville, FL 32211 — (904) 745-7000
(800) 225-2027; Fax: (904) 745-7012

Full-time: 760 men, 750 women — **Faculty:** 113; IIA, --$
Part-time: 130 men, 200 women — **Ph.D.s:** 69%
Graduate: 130 men, 140 women — **Student/Faculty:** 13 to 1
Year: semesters, summer session — **Tuition:** $15,900
Application Deadline: open — **Room & Board:** $5210
Freshman Class: n/av
SAT I or ACT: required — **LESS COMPETITIVE**

Jacksonville University, founded in 1934, is an independent institution offering bachelor's degrees through the colleges of arts and sciences, fine arts, business, and lifelong learning. Figures in above capsule are approximate. There are 4 undergraduate and 2 graduate schools. In addition to regional accreditation, JU has baccalaureate program accreditation with NASM and NLN. The library contains 274,175 volumes, 147,270 microform items, and 11,357 audiovisual forms/CDs, and subscribes to 715 periodicals. Computerized library services include the card catalog, interlibrary loans, and database searching. Special learning facilities include a learning resource center, art gallery, planetarium, radio station, TV station, and a TV studio, a chemistry research lab, and a marine science center. The 260-acre campus is in a suburban area 10 minutes from downtown Jacksonville, near the St. Johns River. Including residence halls, there are 33 buildings.

Student Life: 67% of undergraduates are from Florida. Others are from 47 states, 44 foreign countries, and Canada. 63% are white; 14% African American. 30% claim no religious affiliation. The average age of freshmen is 19; all undergraduates, 26. 30% do not continue beyond their first year; 45% remain to graduate.

Housing: 1000 students can be accommodated in college housing, which includes single-sex dormitories and on-campus apartments. On-campus housing is guaranteed for all 4 years. 54% of students live on campus. All students may keep cars.

Activities: 20% of men belong to 6 national fraternities; 20% of women belong to 4 national sororities. There are 70 groups on campus, including art, band, cheerleading, choir, chorale, chorus, dance, debate, drama, drill team, ethnic, film, honors, international, jazz band, literary magazine, musical theater, newspaper, opera, orchestra, pep band, photography, political, professional, radio and TV, religious, social, social service, student government, symphony, and yearbook.

Sports: There are 10 intercollegiate sports for men and 9 for women. Facilities include a 1500-seat stadium, a gym, a swimming pool, a boat house, baseball and softball diamonds, a 9-hole golf course, soccer and football fields, and an archery range. There are also tennis, basketball, handball/racquetball, volleyball, and shuffleboard courts, an all-purpose playing field, a 440-yard track, a 540-seat auditorium, a 220-seat recital hall, and a dance pavilion.

Disabled Students: Wheelchair ramps, elevators, special parking, specially equipped rest rooms, special class scheduling, and lowered drinking fountains. Accommodation is made for all students regardless of disability.

Services: Counseling and information services are available, as is tutoring in most subjects. There is a reader service for the blind, remedial math, reading, and writing, and a writer service for note taking in class.

Campus Safety and Security: Measures include 24-hour foot and vehicle patrol, self-defense education, escort service, and informal discus-

sions. There are pamphlets/posters/films, emergency telephones, and lighted pathways/sidewalks.

Programs of Study: JU confers B.A., B.S., B.F.A., B.G.S., B.Mus., B.Mus.Ed., and B.S.N. degrees. Master's degrees are also awarded. Bachelor's degrees are awarded in BIOLOGICAL SCIENCE (biology/biological science and marine science), BUSINESS (accounting, banking and finance, business administration and management, international business management, and marketing/retailing/merchandising), COMMUNICATIONS AND THE ARTS (art, art history and appreciation, communications, dance, dramatic arts, English, French, music, music business management, music performance, music theory and composition, musical theater, Spanish, speech/debate/rhetoric, and studio art), COMPUTER AND PHYSICAL SCIENCE (chemistry, information sciences and systems, mathematics, and physics), EDUCATION (art, dance, education of the exceptional child, elementary, music, physical, and secondary), ENGINEERING AND ENVIRONMENTAL DESIGN (aviation administration/management, computer graphics, electrical/electronics engineering, engineering physics, environmental science, and mechanical engineering), HEALTH PROFESSIONS (nursing), SOCIAL SCIENCE (economics, geography, history, humanities, international studies, philosophy, political science/government, psychology, and sociology). Business administration, nursing, and biology are the largest.

Required: All students must complete a core curriculum, including English 111 and 112, 9 hours of humanities/fine arts, 7 hours of natural science, 6 hours each of English, math, sociopolitical science, and Western civilization, 3 hours each of intensive writing, economics, and computer information systems, and 2 hours of phys ed. A total of 128 hours, with a minimum GPA of 2.0, is needed to graduate.

Special: Internships and work-study are available, as are student-designed majors, and a dual major in music and business. There is a co-op program in art, and a 3-2 engineering degree is available with 7 other universities and technological instititutes. Credit for military experience and study abroad are also possible. There are 12 national honor societies and a freshman honors program.

Faculty/Classroom: 65% of faculty are male; 35%, female. No introductory courses are taught by graduate students. The average class size in an introductory lecture is 18.

Requirements: The SAT I or ACT is required. In addition, applicants must be graduates of an accredited secondary school and provide an official copy of their secondary school transcript, or have a GED. At least 18 academic credits are required, including 4 in English, 3 each in math, natural science, and social sciences, and 2 of the same foreign language. Art students must submit a portfolio. Music, theater, and dance students must audition. A GPA of 2.0 is required. AP and CLEP credits are accepted. Important factors in the admissions decision are advanced placement or honor courses, extracurricular activities record, and leadership record.

Procedure: Freshmen are admitted to all sessions. Entrance exams should be taken in the spring of the junior or senior year and/or fall of the senior year. There is an early admissions plan. Application deadlines are open. The fall 2001 application fee was $25.

Transfer: 190 transfer students enrolled in 2001-2002. Transfer students must submit official transcripts from all colleges attended. Art students must submit a portfolio; music and dance students must audition. Transfer applicants must have completed at least one semester at an accredited college or university, be in good standing at the last institution attended, and have a minimum GPA of 2.0. 32 credits of 128 must be completed at JU.

Visiting: There are regularly scheduled orientations for prospective students, consisting of an interview, a campus tour, advisement, area presentations, registration, and a parents program. There are guides for informal visits and visitors may sit in on classes and stay overnight. To schedule a visit, contact the Admissions office.

Financial Aid: In 2001-2002, 91% of all freshmen and 89% of continuing students received some form of financial aid. 65% of freshmen and 64% of continuing students received need-based aid. The average freshman award was $14,144. Of that total, scholarships or need-based grants averaged $11,011 ($20,760 maximum); loans averaged $3852 ($5625 maximum); and work contracts averaged $1500. 28% of undergraduates work part time. JU is a member of CSS. The FAFSA, the college's own financial statement and a federal tax return and W-2 are required. Check with the school for current deadlines.

International Students: There were 95 international students enrolled in a recent year. The school actively recruits these students. They must score 550 on the written TOEFL and also take the SAT I or the ACT.

Computers: The mainframes are an HP 3000 Series 957 and a Harris NightHawk HN4808. There are 320 IBM PCs and 30 Macs available for student use. These are contained in 9 computer labs and 3 computerized classrooms. Access to the Internet is provided. All students may access the system during lab hours, 7 days a week. There are no time limits and no fees. It is strongly recommended that all students have a personal computer.

Graduates: In a recent year, 396 bachelor's degrees were awarded. The most popular majors were business (21%), nursing (10%), and education (9%). In an average class, 27% graduate in 4 years, 42% in 5 years, and 45% in 6 years. 60 companies recruited on campus in a recent year.

Admissions Contact: David Lesesne, Director of Admissions. A video is available. E-mail: *aroche@ju.edu* Web: *www.ju.edu*

LYNN UNIVERSITY — E-5

Boca Raton, FL 33431 — (561) 237-7080
(800) 888-LYNN; Fax: (561) 237-7100

Full-time: 792 men, 730 women	**Faculty:** 56
Part-time: 81 men, 218 women	**Ph.D.s:** 80%
Graduate: 81 men, 104 women	**Student/Faculty:** 20 to 1
Year: semesters, summer session	**Tuition:** $21,750
Application Deadline: open	**Room & Board:** $7650
Freshman Class: 2562 applied, 1906 accepted, 466 enrolled	
ACT: 22	**COMPETITIVE**

Lynn University, founded in 1962, is a private, nonsectarian liberal arts college offering graduate and undergraduate programs in the arts and sciences, business, education, hospitality, and preprofessional studies. There are 4 undergraduate and 2 graduate schools. In addition to regional accreditation, LU has baccalaureate program accreditation with ABFSE. The library contains 75,000 volumes, 8600 microform items, and 1800 audiovisual forms/CDs, and subscribes to 630 periodicals. Computerized library services include interlibrary loans and database searching. Special learning facilities include a learning resource center, art gallery, radio station, and an academic resource center. The 123-acre campus is in a suburban area midway between Fort Lauderdale and Palm Beach. Including residence halls, there are 16 buildings.

Student Life: 70% of undergraduates are from out of state, mostly the Northeast. Others are from 35 states, 70 foreign countries, and Canada. 34% are from public schools. 38% are Protestant; 36% Catholic; 26% Jewish. The average age of freshmen is 19; all undergraduates, 20. 15% do not continue beyond their first year; 61% remain to graduate.

Housing: 680 students can be accommodated in college housing, which includes single-sex and coed dormitories. On-campus housing is guaranteed for all 4 years. 65% of students live on campus; of those, 74% remain on campus on weekends. All students may keep cars.

Activities: There are 2 local fraternities. There are no sororities. There are 26 groups on campus, including cheerleading, choir, ethnic, film, honors, international, literary magazine, newspaper, photography, political, radio and TV, religious, social, social service, student government, and yearbook. Popular campus events include Holiday Formal.

Sports: There are 5 intercollegiate sports for men and 5 for women, and 10 intramural sports for men and 6 for women. Facilities include baseball and soccer fields, tennis courts, indoor and outdoor basketball courts, an outdoor pool, and a weight facility.

Disabled Students: 90% of the campus is accessible. Wheelchair ramps, elevators, special parking, specially equipped rest rooms, special class scheduling, and lowered drinking fountains are available.

Services: Counseling and information services are available, as is tutoring in some subjects. There are services for learning disabled students. There is remedial math, reading, and writing.

Campus Safety and Security: Measures include 24-hour foot and vehicle patrol, self-defense education, escort service, and informal discussions. There are pamphlets/posters/films and lighted pathways/sidewalks.

Programs of Study: LU confers B.A. and B.S. degrees. Associate and master's degrees are also awarded. Bachelor's degrees are awarded in BUSINESS (accounting, business administration and management, fashion merchandising, hotel/motel and restaurant management, marketing/retailing/merchandising, recreational facilities management, sports management, and tourism), COMMUNICATIONS AND THE ARTS (communications, design, fine arts, and graphic design), EDUCATION (early childhood, education, elementary, and secondary), ENGINEERING AND ENVIRONMENTAL DESIGN (aviation administration/management), HEALTH PROFESSIONS (health care administration), SOCIAL SCIENCE (history, human services, humanities, political science/government, prelaw, psychology, and sociology). Accounting, international management, and education are the strongest academically. Business administration and hotel restaurant management are the largest.

Required: Students are required to complete 120 to 128 credits, with 45 to 50 in the major, and must maintain a minimum GPA of 2.0. In addition, all students must complete a core curriculum of 39 semester hours.

Special: Opportunities are provided for internships, which are required in many majors. There is study abroad in Ireland, Japan, and France. Credit by exam, credit for life experience, and pass/fail options are available.

Faculty/Classroom: 60% of faculty are male; 40%, female. All teach undergraduates. No introductory courses are taught by graduate students. The average class size in an introductory lecture is 26; in a laboratory, 20; and in a regular course, 22.

Admissions: 74% of the 2001-2002 applicants were accepted. The SAT I scores for the 2001-2002 freshman class were: Verbal--56% below 500, 40% between 500 and 599, 3% between 600 and 700, and 1% above 700; Math--58% below 500, 35% between 500 and 599, 6% between 600 and 700, and 1% above 700. 24% of the current freshmen were in the top fifth of their class; 54% were in the top two fifths. 4 freshmen graduated first in their class in a recent year.
Requirements: The SAT I or ACT is required. In addition, graduation from an accredited secondary school is required; a GED will be accepted. An essay and an interview are recommended. A GPA of 2.5 is required. AP and CLEP credits are accepted. Important factors in the admissions decision are recommendations by school officials, personality/intangible qualities, and extracurricular activities record.
Procedure: Freshmen are admitted fall and spring. Entrance exams should be taken during the junior or senior year. There are early admissions and deferred admissions plans. Application deadlines are open. The application fee is $25. Notification is sent on a rolling basis.
Transfer: Transfer students must submit an official transcript from each previous college attended, plus a recommendation from the dean of students. The student must have maintained a minimum GPA of 2.0. An interview is recommended. 30 credits of 120 must be completed at LU.
Visiting: There are guides for informal visits and visitors may sit in on classes. To schedule a visit, contact the Office of Admissions.
Financial Aid: In a recent year, 35% of all freshmen and 25% of continuing students received some form of financial aid. 28% of freshmen and 31% of continuing students received need-based aid. The average freshman award was $13,100. The average financial indebtedness of a recent year's graduate was $12,300. LU is a member of CSS. The FFS is required. Check with the school for current deadlines.
International Students: The school actively recruits these students. They must score 500 on the written TOEFL.
Computers: The mainframe is an AS/400. Mac and IBM PCs are available in the library and computer classroom. All students may access the system. There are no time limits and no fees.
Admissions Contact: Melanie J. Glines, Director of Admission. A video is available. E-mail: *admission@lynn.edu* Web: *www.lynn.edu*

NEW COLLEGE OF FLORIDA — D-4

Sarasota, FL 34243-2197 — **(941) 359-4269; Fax: (941) 359-4435**

Full-time: 223 men, 411 women	**Faculty:** 58
Part-time: none	**Ph.D.s:** 98%
Graduate: none	**Student/Faculty:** 11 to 1
Year: 4-1-4	**Tuition:** $3010 ($12,475)
Application Deadline: May 1	**Room & Board:** $5120
Freshman Class: n/av	
SAT I Verbal/Math: required	**HIGHLY COMPETITIVE+**

New College of Florida (formerly New College of the University of South Florida), established in 1964, is the honors college of the State University System of Florida. The library contains 251,000 volumes, 494,000 microform items, and 4100 audiovisual forms/CDs, and subscribes to 1850 periodicals. Computerized library services include the card catalog, interlibrary loans, and database searching. Special learning facilities include an art gallery, radio station, media and technology center, and writing center. The 144-acre campus is in a suburban area 50 miles south of Tampa. Including residence halls, there are 46 buildings.
Student Life: 70% of undergraduates are from Florida. Others are from 7 foreign countries. 82% are from public schools. 85% are white. The average age of freshmen is 18; all undergraduates, 20. 19% do not continue beyond their first year.
Housing: 387 students can be accommodated in college housing, which includes single-sex and coed dormitories. On-campus housing is guaranteed for the freshman year only and is available on a lottery system for upperclassmen. 97% of students live on campus; of those, 90% remain on campus on weekends. All students may keep cars.
Activities: There are no fraternities or sororities. There are 42 groups on campus, including choir, dance, drama, ethnic, gay, international, literary magazine, newspaper, opera, political, religious, social, social service, student government, and yearbook. Popular campus events include Halloween and graduation parties, a student/faculty softball game, and an AIDS benefit dance marathon.
Sports: There are 8 intramural sports for men and 8 for women. Facilities include a soccer field, a softball diamond, a fitness path, outdoor racquetball, tennis, and basketball courts, a volleyball pit, playground equipment, a swimming pool, and a fitness center with Nautilus equipment and indoor facilities for racquetball, aerobics, and dance.
Disabled Students: 80% of the campus is accessible. Wheelchair ramps, elevators, special parking, specially equipped rest rooms, special class scheduling, lowered drinking fountains, and lowered telephones are available.
Services: Counseling and information services are available, as is tutoring in most subjects. There is a reader service for the blind and remedial writing.
Campus Safety and Security: Measures include 24-hour foot and vehicle patrol, self-defense education, escort service, and informal discussions. There are pamphlets/posters/films, emergency telephones, lighted pathways/sidewalks, 24-hour dispatch/information services, and fire/smoke alarm systems in all dormitories.
Programs of Study: New College confers the B.A. degree. Bachelor's degrees are awarded in BIOLOGICAL SCIENCE (biology/biological science), COMMUNICATIONS AND THE ARTS (classics, fine arts, Germanic languages and literature, languages, literature, music, and Russian languages and literature), COMPUTER AND PHYSICAL SCIENCE (chemistry, mathematics, natural sciences, and physics), ENGINEERING AND ENVIRONMENTAL DESIGN (environmental science), SOCIAL SCIENCE (anthropology, economics, French studies, history, humanities, international studies, medieval studies, philosophy, political science/government, psychology, public administration, religion, social science, sociology, Spanish studies, urban studies, and women's studies). Biology, literature, and psychology are the largest.
Required: An academic credit system is not used. To qualify for graduation, students must complete 7 semester contracts, which are designed by the student in consultation with faculty; 3 independent study projects completed during January each year, between the fall and spring semesters; a senior thesis, which involves original research or creative work and includes working closely with a faculty committee of the student's choice; and an oral baccalaureate exam, which is primarily a defense of the senior thesis.
Special: Cross-registration, domestic and international internships, study abroad in 11 countries at 24 universities, accelerated degree programs, student-designed and interdisciplinary majors, and independent study are available.
Faculty/Classroom: 55% of faculty are male; 45%, female. All teach undergraduates and 95% do research. The average class size in an introductory lecture is 27; in a laboratory, 20; and in a regular course, 18.
Admissions: 61% of the 2001-2002 applicants were accepted. 76% of the current freshmen were in the top fifth of their class; 93% were in the top two fifths. There were 12 National Merit finalists. 4 freshmen graduated first in their class.
Requirements: The SAT I or ACT is required. In addition, graduation from an accredited secondary school (preferred) or the GED is required. High school students should pursue at least 5 academic courses each year, at the most rigorous level available, with a minimum distribution of 4 years of English, 3 years each of math, sciences, and social sciences, 2 consecutive years of the same foreign language, and 4 other academic courses. Application essays must be submitted. A formal interview is recommended for all applicants. A GPA of 3.0 is required. Important factors in the admissions decision are advanced placement or honor courses, evidence of special talent, and ability to finance college education. Applications may be accessed and submitted via CollegeLink, Peterson's, the College Board, and Embark.
Procedure: Freshmen are admitted in the fall. Entrance exams should be taken in time for the scores to be reported as part of the application. There are early admissions and deferred admissions plans. Applications should be filed by May 1 for fall entry. The fall 2001 application fee was $20. Notification is sent on a rolling basis. 6% of all applicants are on a waiting list; 28 were accepted in 2001.
Transfer: 39 transfer students enrolled in 2001-2002. Transfers must be in good academic and financial standing with their previous college(s). Transfers may receive credit for up to 3 semester contracts and 1 independent study project. While at New College, transfers receiving maximum credit must successfully complete at least 4 semester contracts, 2 independent study projects, and the senior thesis with baccalaureate exam.
Visiting: There are regularly scheduled orientations for prospective students, including a campus tour, admissions information session, and/or class visits, which must be scheduled individually by the student through Admissions. Visitors may sit in on classes and stay overnight. To schedule a visit, contact the Office of Admissions at *admissions@ncf.edu*
Financial Aid: In 2001-2002, 97% of all freshmen and 98% of continuing students received some form of financial aid. 34% of freshmen and 36% of continuing students received need-based aid. The average freshman award was $9538. Of that total, scholarships or need-based grants averaged $1823; and loans averaged $1460. The FAFSA is required.
International Students: There are 10 international students enrolled. The school actively recruits these students. They must score 560 on the written TOEFL or take the Test of Written English (TWE)(preferred), and must also take the SAT I or the ACT.
Computers: 4 open-use computer labs exist on campus. All PCs are 486 or better, directly connected to the Internet, and 16MB RAM minimum with Windows 95, some with mulitmedia capabilities. Each lab has a laser printer. 2 open-use Mac facilities are operated by the student government. All students have Internet accounts. All students may access the system 8 A.M. to 11 P.M. Monday through Thursday, and 8 A.M. to 9 P.M. Friday to Sunday. There are no time limits and no fees.
Graduates: In 2001, 173 bachelor's degrees were awarded. The most popular majors were biology (14%), literature (13%), and psychology (10%). In an average class, 49% graduate in 4 years, 59% in 5 years, and 60% in 6 years.

Admissions Contact: Joel Bauman, Dean of Admissions and Financial Aid. E-mail: *admissions@ncf.edu* Web: *www.ncf.edu*

NORTHWOOD UNIVERSITY E-5
West Palm Beach, FL 33409-2911 (561) 478-5500
(800) 458-8325; Fax: (561) 640-3328

Full-time: 416 men, 359 women | **Faculty:** 15
Part-time: 81 men, 107 women | **Ph.D.s:** 23%
Graduate: none | **Student/Faculty:** 52 to 1
Year: terms, summer session | **Tuition:** $12,531
Application Deadline: August 1 | **Room & Board:** $6648
Freshman Class: 557 applied, 399 accepted, 137 enrolled
SAT I Verbal/Math: 480/470 | **ACT:** 20 **LESS COMPETITIVE**

Northwood University, founded in 1959, is a private institution offering undergraduate degrees in business administration and management. Campuses are located in Florida, Michigan, and Texas. The library contains 26,000 volumes, and subscribes to 360 periodicals. Computerized library services include the card catalog, interlibrary loans, and database searching. Special learning facilities include an art gallery, TV station, and the Ethics Center for Business. The 84-acre campus is in a suburban area 70 miles north of Miami. Including residence halls, there are 5 buildings.

Student Life: 70% of undergraduates are from out of state, mostly the Middle Atlantic. Others are from 30 states, 62 foreign countries, and Canada. 78% are from public schools. 56% are white; 22% foreign nationals; 10% African American. The average age of freshmen is 19; all undergraduates, 20. 39% do not continue beyond their first year; 62% remain to graduate.

Housing: 410 students can be accommodated in college housing, which includes single-sex on-campus apartments. On-campus housing is guaranteed for all 4 years. 60% of students live on campus; of those, 65% remain on campus on weekends. All students may keep cars.

Activities: There are no fraternities or sororities. There are 15 groups on campus, including art, computers, debate, drama, ethnic, honors, international, newspaper, photography, political, professional, social, social service, student government, and yearbook. Popular campus events include Automotive Industry Show, Diversity Month, and carnival.

Sports: There are 5 intercollegiate sports for men and 5 for women, and 6 intramural sports for men and 6 for women. Facilities include baseball, softball, and soccer fields, a student center, and a recreation center with an outdoor swimming pool and basketball, tennis, and handball/racquetball courts.

Disabled Students: 80% of the campus is accessible. Wheelchair ramps, elevators, special parking, specially equipped rest rooms, special class scheduling, lowered drinking fountains, and lowered telephones are available.

Services: Counseling and information services are available, as is tutoring in every subject, including accounting, math, English, and computers. There is remedial math and writing.

Campus Safety and Security: Measures include 24-hour foot and vehicle patrol, informal discussions, pamphlets/posters/films, and emergency telephones. There are lighted pathways/sidewalks.

Programs of Study: Northwood University confers the B.B.A. degree. Associate degrees are also awarded. Bachelor's degrees are awarded in BUSINESS (accounting, banking and finance, business administration and management, hospitality management services, international business management, management information systems, marketing management, and transportation and travel marketing), COMMUNICATIONS AND THE ARTS (advertising). Accounting and management information systems are the strongest academically. Business management and automotive marketing are the largest.

Required: To graduate, all students must complete a minimum of 180 credit hours, with 36 credit hours in the major. A minimum GPA of 2.0 must be maintained, and 6 credits of computer science management and 2 credits of executive fitness must be completed. Internships for 1 to 6 credits are required in some majors.

Special: Northwood offers cooperative programs and cross-registration with Georgian College in Canada, internships with various automotive and fashion marketing corporations, a term in Europe with study in 5 countries, and various work-study programs. Also available are an accelerated degree program in all majors, dual majors, credit for military experience, and nondegree study. There is a freshman honors program.

Faculty/Classroom: 23% of faculty are male; 27%, female. All teach undergraduates. The average class size in an introductory lecture is 20; in a laboratory, 19; and in a regular course, 15.

Admissions: 72% of the 2001-2002 applicants were accepted. The SAT I scores for the 2001-2002 freshman class were: Verbal--64% below 500, 32% between 500 and 599, and 4% between 600 and 700; Math--61% below 500, 36% between 500 and 599, and 4% between 600 and 700. The ACT scores were 57% below 21, 23% between 21 and 23, and 20% between 24 and 26. 15% of the current freshmen were in the top fifth of their class; 44% were in the top two fifths.

Requirements: The SAT I or ACT is required. In addition, applicants must be graduates of an accredited secondary school or have a GED certificate. An interview is recommended. Applications are accepted online. A GPA of 2.0 is required. AP and CLEP credits are accepted. Important factors in the admissions decision are advanced placement or honor courses, evidence of special talent, and leadership record.

Procedure: Freshmen are admitted to all sessions. Entrance exams should be taken in the fall of the senior year. There are early admissions and deferred admissions plans. Applications should be filed by August 1 for fall entry, November 1 for winter entry, February 15 for spring entry, and June 1 for summer entry, along with a $25 fee. Notification is sent on a rolling basis.

Transfer: 126 transfer students enrolled in 2001-2002. Applicants must have a minimum 2.0 GPA, with at least 15 credit hours earned and official transcripts of all completed college-level work. Good academic and social standing are required. An interview is recommended. 45 credits of 180 must be completed at Northwood University.

Visiting: There are regularly scheduled orientations for prospective students, including a fall and spring open house, campus tours, and meetings with students and financial aid and academic staff. There are guides for informal visits and visitors may sit in on classes and stay overnight. To schedule a visit, contact the Admissions Office.

Financial Aid: In 2001-2002, 90% of all freshmen and 85% of continuing students received some form of financial aid, including need-based aid. The average freshman award was $14,322. Of that total, scholarships or need-based grants averaged $9131; loans averaged $2575; and work contracts averaged $2981. The average financial indebtedness of the 2001 graduate was $17,125. The FAFSA is required. The fall application deadline is March 15.

International Students: There are 135 international students enrolled. The school actively recruits these students. They must score 500 on the written TOEFL or 173 on the electronic version. They must also take the SAT I or ACT, scoring 16 on the ACT.

Computers: The mainframe is an IBM RS/6000. There are 42 PCs in computer classrooms available to all students when classes are not in session, plus 6 in the student center, 14 in the library, and 13 tied to special automotive software for those academic majors. All students may access the system. There are no time limits. The fee is $35 per year.

Graduates: In 2001, 130 bachelor's degrees were awarded. Of the 2000 graduating class, 99% were employed within 6 months of graduation.

Admissions Contact: Jack Letvinchuk, Admissions Director. A video is available. E-mail: *fladmit@northwood.edu*
Web: *www.northwood.edu*

NOVA SOUTHEASTERN UNIVERSITY E-5
Fort Lauderdale, FL 33314 (954) 262-8000
(800) 338-4723, ext. 8000

Full-time: 637 men, 1722 women | **Faculty:** 67
Part-time: 419 men, 1236 women | **Ph.D.s:** 87%
Graduate: 5268 men, 9747 women | **Student/Faculty:** 35 to 1
Year: trimesters, summer session | **Tuition:** $13,620
Application Deadline: open | **Room & Board:** $6484
Freshman Class: n/av
SAT I or ACT: required **LESS COMPETITIVE**

Nova Southeastern University, founded in 1964, is a private institution offering degree programs in liberal arts, sciences, business, health sciences, and education, and preprofessional studies. There are 2 undergraduate and 8 graduate schools. The 3 libraries contain 425,000 volumes, 150,000 microform items, and 2591 audiovisual forms/CDs, and subscribe to 8791 periodicals. Computerized library services include the card catalog, interlibrary loans, and database searching. Special learning facilities include a learning resource center, art gallery, and radio station. The 232-acre campus is in a suburban area 10 miles west of Fort Lauderdale. Including residence halls, there are 39 buildings.

Student Life: 80% of undergraduates are from Florida. Others are from 30 states, 20 foreign countries, and Canada. 75% are from public schools. 49% are white; 22% African American; 15% Hispanic. The average age of freshmen is 21; all undergraduates, 26. 25% do not continue beyond their first year.

Housing: 500 students can be accommodated in college housing, which includes coed dormitories, on-campus apartments, and married-student housing. On-campus housing is available on a first-come, first-served basis. 94% of students commute. Alcohol is not permitted. All students may keep cars.

Activities: 5% of men belong to 4 national fraternities; 7% of women belong to 2 national sororities. There are 14 groups on campus, including dance, drama, environmental, ethnic, honors, international, musical theater, newspaper, political, professional, radio and TV, religious, social, and student government. Popular campus events include Spring Fest, Raft Race, and Celebrate Diversity.

Sports: There are 4 intercollegiate sports for men and 6 for women, and 11 intramural sports for men and 11 for women. Facilities include

baseball and soccer fields, and a recreational complex with a swimming pool and outdoor basketball and tennis courts.

Disabled Students: All of the campus is accessible. Wheelchair ramps, elevators, special parking, specially equipped rest rooms, lowered drinking fountains, and wheelchair lifts in some buildings are available.

Services: Counseling and information services are available, as is tutoring in most subjects. There is remedial math, reading, and writing.

Campus Safety and Security: Measures include 24-hour foot and vehicle patrol, shuttle buses, informal discussions, and pamphlets/posters/films. There are emergency telephones and lighted pathways/sidewalks.

Programs of Study: NSU confers B.A. and B.S. degrees. Associate, master's, and doctoral degrees are also awarded. Bachelor's degrees are awarded in BIOLOGICAL SCIENCE (life science), BUSINESS (accounting, business administration and management, and hospitality management services), COMPUTER AND PHYSICAL SCIENCE (computer science, information sciences and systems, oceanography, and science and management), EDUCATION (early childhood, education of the exceptional child, elementary, science, and secondary), ENGINEERING AND ENVIRONMENTAL DESIGN (environmental science), HEALTH PROFESSIONS (physician's assistant and premedicine), SOCIAL SCIENCE (humanities, liberal arts/general studies, paralegal studies, prelaw, and psychology). Ocean studies and computer science are the strongest academically. Business and education are the largest.

Required: To graduate, all students must complete at least 120 credit hours, including courses in computer literacy and macroeconomics. A minimum 2.25 GPA is needed for courses in the major, and a 2.0 for all other courses.

Special: NSU offers internships, study abroad, work-study and accelerated degree programs, a general studies degree, and nondegree study. Combined bachelor-professional degree programs and a dual admission program are also available. There is 1 national honor society.

Faculty/Classroom: 61% of faculty are male; 39%, female. No introductory courses are taught by graduate students. The average class size in an introductory lecture is 20 and in a regular course, 17.

Requirements: The SAT I or ACT is required. In addition, applicants must be graduates of an accredited secondary school or have a GED certificate and have completed at least 16 academic credits, including 4 years of English. An essay is required, and an interview is recommended. AP and CLEP credits are accepted. Important factors in the admissions decision are recommendations by school officials, recommendations by alumni, and extracurricular activities record. Applications are accepted on-line at the university's web site.

Procedure: Freshmen are admitted to all sessions. Entrance exams should be taken by March 1 of the senior year. Application deadlines are open. The fall 2001 application fee was $35.

Transfer: 117 transfer students enrolled in 2001-2002. Applicants must have a minimum 2.8 GPA from a regionally accredited institution. An interview is recommended. 30 credits of 120 must be completed at NSU.

Visiting: There are regularly scheduled orientations for prospective students. There are guides for informal visits and visitors may sit in on classes. To schedule a visit, contact the Admissions Office.

Financial Aid: In 2001-2002, 86% of all freshmen and 71% of continuing students received some form of financial aid. 82% of freshmen and 71% of continuing students received need-based aid. The average freshman award was $12,940. Of that total, scholarships or need-based grants averaged $5909; loans averaged $7748; work contracts averaged $4586; and the Florida Resident Access Grant and the Florida Student Assistance Grant averaged $2348. The average financial indebtedness of the 2001 graduate was $21,816. NSU is a member of CSS. The FAFSA and the college's own financial statement are required. The fall application deadline is April 1.

International Students: The school actively recruits these students. They must score 550 on the written TOEFL or take the MELAB.

Computers: The mainframe is a Sun Microsystems Enterprise 5000. There are several PC labs available, including in the dormitories. Internet access is available. All students may access the system. There are no time limits. It is strongly recommended that all students have a personal computer.

Graduates: In 2001, 1058 bachelor's degrees were awarded. The most popular majors were business (47%), education (27%), and health professions (8%). 90 companies recruited on campus in a recent year.

Admissions Contact: Acting Director of Undergraduate Admissions. E-mail: *ncsinfo@nova.edu* Web: *www.nova.edu*

PALM BEACH ATLANTIC COLLEGE — E-5

West Palm Beach, FL 33401-6505 — (561) 803-2100
(800) GO TO PBA; Fax: (561) 803-2186

Full-time: 710 men, 1257 women	**Faculty:** 93; IIA, --$
Part-time: 80 men, 169 women	**Ph.D.s:** 52%
Graduate: 108 men, 208 women	**Student/Faculty:** 21 to 1
Year: semesters, summer session	**Tuition:** $13,170
Application Deadline: open	**Room & Board:** $10,140
Freshman Class: 2319 applied, 1167 accepted, 433 enrolled	
SAT I or ACT: required	**COMPETITIVE**

Palm Beach Atlantic College, founded in 1968 by Baptist Church leaders, is a private, liberal arts institution with a Christian emphasis. There are 5 undergraduate and 4 graduate schools. In addition to regional accreditation, PBA has baccalaureate program accreditation with NASM. The library contains 410,438 volumes, 24,628 microform items, and 3685 audiovisual forms/CDs, and subscribes to 2137 periodicals. Computerized library services include the card catalog, interlibrary loans, and database searching. The 25-acre campus is in an urban area 60 miles north of Miami. Including residence halls, there are 15 buildings.

Student Life: Others are from 40 states, 37 foreign countries, and Canada. 75% are white; 10% African American. 85% are Protestant; 14% Catholic. 34% of freshmen remain to graduate.

Housing: 800 students can be accommodated in college housing, which includes single-sex and coed dormitories, on-campus apartments, and married-student housing. On-campus housing is guaranteed for all 4 years. 56% of students commute. Alcohol is not permitted. All students may keep cars.

Activities: There are no fraternities or sororities. There are 38 groups on campus, including art, cheerleading, chess, choir, chorale, chorus, computers, concert band, dance, drama, ethnic, film, honors, international, jazz band, literary magazine, music ensembles, musical theater, orchestra, pep band, photography, political, professional, radio and TV, religious, social, student government, symphony, and yearbook. Popular campus events include American Free Enterprise Day and Christian Awareness Week.

Sports: There are 5 intercollegiate sports for men and 5 for women, and 18 intramural sports for men and 19 for women. Facilities include a 60,000-square-foot sports and recreation center, a 1750-seat main arena, and an auxiliary gym for basketball, volleyball, and badminton. Racquetball courts, a weight room, a fitness room, a dance room, and an indoor jogging track are also available.

Disabled Students: 80% of the campus is accessible. Wheelchair ramps, elevators, special parking, and specially equipped rest rooms are available.

Services: Counseling and information services are available, as is tutoring in most subjects. There is remedial math, reading, and writing.

Campus Safety and Security: Measures include 24-hour foot and vehicle patrol, self-defense education, escort service, and informal discussions. There are pamphlets/posters/films, emergency telephones, and lighted pathways/sidewalks.

Programs of Study: PBA confers B.A., B.S., and B.Mus. degrees. Associate and master's degrees are also awarded. Bachelor's degrees are awarded in BIOLOGICAL SCIENCE (biology/biological science, and marine biology), BUSINESS (accounting, banking and finance, business administration and management, business economics, international business management, management information systems, management science, and marketing management), COMMUNICATIONS AND THE ARTS (art, communications, dramatic arts, English, music, music performance, music theory and composition, speech/debate/rhetoric, and voice), COMPUTER AND PHYSICAL SCIENCE (computer science, and mathematics), EDUCATION (art, drama, early childhood, education, elementary, English, mathematics, middle school, music, physical, science, secondary, social science, special, and specific learning disabilities), HEALTH PROFESSIONS (predentistry, premedicine, and preveterinary science), SOCIAL SCIENCE (history, interdisciplinary studies, political science/government, psychology, religion, religious music, social science, and theological studies). Business, psychology, and education are the strongest academically. Business, education, and psychology are the largest.

Required: Students must complete core requirements and 120 credit hours, with a minimum of 30 credit hours in the major and 42 upper-level hours. A minimum 2.0 GPA is required.

Special: PBA offers a London semester, internships, an interdisciplinary major, dual majors, student-designed majors, accelerated degree programs in organizational management and ministry, and study abroad through the Coalition of Christian Colleges and Universities. There is a freshman honors program.

Faculty/Classroom: 95% teach undergraduates. No introductory courses are taught by graduate students. The average class size in an introductory lecture is 30; in a laboratory, 24; and in a regular course, 20.

Admissions: 50% of the 2001-2002 applicants were accepted. The SAT I scores for the 2001-2002 freshman class were: Verbal--23% below

500, 52% between 500 and 599, 22% between 600 and 700, and 3% above 700; Math--34% below 500, 44% between 500 and 599, 19% between 600 and 700, and 3% above 700. The ACT scores were 4% below 21, 51% between 21 and 23, 41% between 24 and 26, and 4% above 28. 50% of the current freshmen were in the top quarter of their class; 78% were in the top half.

Requirements: The SAT I or ACT is required. In addition, applicants must be graduates of an accredited secondary school or have a GED certificate, and have completed 18 academic credits-4 in English, 3 in math, science, social studies, and history, and 2 in a foreign language. A minimum composite score of 960 on the SAT I or 21 on the ACT, an essay, and an interview are required. A portfolio is recommended for art students. A GPA of 2.0 is required. AP and CLEP credits are accepted. Important factors in the admissions decision are advanced placement or honor courses, leadership record, and personality/intangible qualities.

Procedure: Freshmen are admitted to all sessions. Entrance exams should be taken in the junior year of high school. There are early decision, early admissions, rolling admissions, and deferred admissions plans. Application deadlines are open. The fall 2001 application fee was $15.

Transfer: 176 transfer students enrolled in 2001-2002. Transfer students must have a minimum 2.0 GPA a minimum of 12 credit hours, 2 letters of recommendation, and an interview is encouraged. 32 credits of 120 must be completed at PBA.

Visiting: There are regularly scheduled orientations for prospective students, including a general open house and a school-specific open house. There are guides for informal visits and visitors may sit in on classes and stay overnight. To schedule a visit, contact the Admissions Office.

Financial Aid: In 2001-2002, 75% of all freshmen and 72% of continuing students received some form of financial aid. 58% of freshmen and 39% of continuing students received need-based aid. The average freshman award was $2392. 15% of undergraduates work part time. Average annual earnings from campus work are $1000. The average financial indebtedness of the 2001 graduate was $16,600. PBA is a member of CSS. The FAFSA, the college's own financial statement and the and state aid form are required. The fall application deadline is April 1.

International Students: The school actively recruits these students. They must score 500 on the written TOEFL.

Computers: The mainframe is a Compaq Proliant 7000. Computer labs are available and there is 1 computer per dorm room. All campus computers are networked to the central student and web servers. No mainframe access is available, although all students have drive space and server space just for web pages. Dial-up connections provide off-campus access. All students may access the system. There are no time limits and no fees. It is strongly recommended that all students have a personal computer.

Graduates: In 2001, 388 bachelor's degrees were awarded. The most popular majors were business/marketing (49%), education (12%), and psychology (10%).

Admissions Contact: Buck James, Vice President of Enrollment Services. E-mail: *admit@pbac.edu* Web: *www.pbac.edu*

RINGLING SCHOOL OF ART AND DESIGN — D-4

Sarasota, FL 34234-5896 (941) 351-5100
(800) 255-7695; Fax: (941) 359-7517

Full-time: 511 men, 440 women	**Faculty:** 55
Part-time: 6 men, 12 women	**Ph.D.s:** 11%
Graduate: none	**Student/Faculty:** 17 to 1
Year: semesters	**Tuition:** $15,420
Application Deadline: open	**Room & Board:** $7080
Freshman Class: 1190 applied, 701 accepted, 279 enrolled	
SAT I Verbal/Math: 510/500	**ACT:** 27 **SPECIAL**

Ringling School of Art and Design, founded in 1931, is a private art college. In addition to regional accreditation, the Ringling School has baccalaureate program accreditation with FIDER and NASAD. The library contains 36,636 volumes and 2482 audiovisual forms/CDs, and subscribes to 325 periodicals. Computerized library services include the card catalog, interlibrary loans, and database searching. Special learning facilities include a learning resource center, an art gallery, and a total of 85,000 slides. The 32-acre campus is in an urban area 50 miles south of Tampa. Including residence halls, there are 51 buildings.

Student Life: 54% of undergraduates are from out of state, mostly the Middle Atlantic. Others are from 45 states, 45 foreign countries, and Canada. 81% are white. The average age of freshmen is 19; all undergraduates, 21. 19% do not continue beyond their first year; 68% remain to graduate.

Housing: 456 students can be accommodated in college housing, which includes single-sex and coed dormitories, on-campus apartments, and married-student housing. On-campus housing is available on a first-come, first-served basis and is available on a lottery system for upperclassmen. Priority is given to out-of-town students. 52% of students commute. Alcohol is not permitted. All students may keep cars.

Activities: 3% of men belong to 1 national fraternity; 2% of women belong to 1 national sorority. There are many groups and organizations on campus, including art, computers, drama, ethnic, gay, international, literary magazine, professional, religious, social, social service, and student government. Popular campus events include Art in the Park, Founders Day, and Goombay Festival.

Sports: There are 3 intramural sports for men and 3 for women. Facilities include a basketball court, a volleyball court, and a weight room.

Disabled Students: 80% of the campus is accessible. Wheelchair ramps, elevators, special parking, specially equipped rest rooms, special class scheduling, and lowered telephones are available.

Services: Counseling and information services are available, as is tutoring in some subjects, including English and math. There is remedial math and writing.

Campus Safety and Security: Measures include 24-hour foot and vehicle patrol, escort service, informal discussions, and emergency telephones. There are lighted pathways/sidewalks.

Programs of Study: The Ringling School confers the B.F.A. degree. Bachelor's degrees are awarded in COMMUNICATIONS AND THE ARTS (fine arts, graphic design, illustration, and photography), ENGINEERING AND ENVIRONMENTAL DESIGN (computer graphics and interior design). Illustration is the largest.

Required: To graduate, all students must complete 123 semester hours, including 75 hours of studio art, 31 hours of liberal arts, and 12 hours of art history, with 75 hours in the major. A minimum 2.0 GPA and courses in drawing, 2- and 3-dimensional design, art history, and written communication are required.

Special: The school offers cross-registration with the Art College Exchange, internships with Walt Disney animation and Home Box Office, and study abroad in France, England, and Ireland. Also available are credit by portfolio, an accelerated degree program in interior design, and a nondegree, continuing education program.

Faculty/Classroom: 60% of faculty are male; 40%, female. All teach undergraduates. The average class size in an introductory lecture is 24 and in a regular course, 17.

Admissions: 59% of the 2001-2002 applicants were accepted. The SAT I scores for the 2001-2002 freshman class were: Verbal--41% below 500, 39% between 500 and 599, 15% between 600 and 700, and 4% above 700; Math--49% below 500, 34% between 500 and 599, 16% between 600 and 700, and 2% above 700.

Requirements: The SAT I or ACT is recommended. In addition, applicants must be graduates of an accredited secondary school or have a GED. Admission is based on the academic record and a portfolio. An essay is required, and an interview is recommended. A GPA of 2.0 is required. AP and CLEP credits are accepted. Important factors in the admissions decision are evidence of special talent, advanced placement or honor courses, and recommendations by school officials. Applications are accepted on-line.

Procedure: Freshmen are admitted in the fall. Application deadlines are open. The application fee is $35. Notification is sent on a rolling basis. A waiting list is an active part of the admissions procedure.

Transfer: 121 transfer students enrolled in 2001-2002. Transfer students must meet the same criteria as freshmen and must also submit college transcripts. 45 credits of 123 must be completed at the Ringling School.

Visiting: There are guides for informal visits and visitors may sit in on classes. To schedule a visit, contact the Admissions Office.

Financial Aid: In 2001-2002, 73% of all freshmen and 72% of continuing students received some form of financial aid. 66% of freshmen and 61% of continuing students received need-based aid. The average freshman award was $14,224. Of that total, scholarships or need-based grants averaged $4896 ($5000 maximum); loans averaged $3621 ($6625 maximum); and non-need-based state tuition differential grants (FRAG) and state merit scholarships averaged $2949 ($5898 maximum). 35% of undergraduates work part time. Average annual earnings from campus work are $2500. The average financial indebtedness of the 2001 graduate was $16,500. The FAFSA and the college's own financial statement are required. The fall application deadline is March 1.

International Students: There are 70 international students enrolled. The school actively recruits these students. They must score 500 on the written TOEFL or 173 on the electronic version.

Computers: PCs are available in the computer center. All students may access the system. There are no time limits and no fees.

Graduates: In 2001, 200 bachelor's degrees were awarded. The most popular majors were illustration (48%), computer animation (21%), and graphic and interactive communication (14%). In an average class, 60% graduate in 4 years, 63% in 5 years, and 64% in 6 years. 40 companies recruited on campus in 2000-2001. Of the 2000 graduating class, 5% were enrolled in graduate school within 6 months of graduation and 90% were employed.

Admissions Contact: James H. Dean, Dean of Admissions.
E-mail: *admissions@rsad.edu* Web: *www.ringling.edu*

ROLLINS COLLEGE
D-3

Winter Park, FL 32789 (407) 646-2161; Fax: (407) 646-1502

Full-time: 655 men, 1015 women
Part-time: 4 men, 2 women
Graduate: 310 men, 435 women
Year: semesters
Application Deadline: February 15
Freshman Class: 2138 applied, 1390 accepted, 472 enrolled
SAT I Verbal/Math: 595/595
Faculty: 148; IIA, av$
Ph.D.s: 89%
Student/Faculty: 11 to 1
Tuition: $23,882
Room & Board: $7341
HIGHLY COMPETITIVE

Rollins College, founded in 1885, is a private, liberal arts institution. In addition to regional accreditation, Rollins has baccalaureate program accreditation with NASM. The library contains 280,000 volumes, 34,000 microform items, and 3800 audiovisual forms/CDs, and subscribes to 2200 periodicals. Computerized library services include the card catalog, interlibrary loans, and database searching. Special learning facilities include a learning resource center, art gallery, radio station, TV station, art museum, theaters, writing center, and math lab. The 67-acre campus is in a suburban area 5 miles north of Orlando. Including residence halls, there are 54 buildings.

Student Life: 47% of undergraduates are from out of state, mostly the Middle Atlantic. Others are from 46 states, 26 foreign countries, and Canada. 57% are from public schools. 76% are white. 48% are Protestant; 28% Catholic; 12% Jewish. The average age of freshmen is 18; all undergraduates, 20. 16% do not continue beyond their first year; 70% remain to graduate.

Housing: 1250 students can be accommodated in college housing, which includes coed dormitories, on-campus apartments, fraternity houses, and sorority houses. In addition, there are honors houses and special-interest houses. On-campus housing is guaranteed for all 4 years. 80% of students live on campus; of those, 80% remain on campus on weekends. Upperclassmen may keep cars.

Activities: 33% of men belong to 4 national fraternities; 33% of women belong to 1 local sorority and 4 national sororities. There are 68 groups on campus, including art, brass ensemble, cheerleading, choir, chorale, chorus, computers, dance, drama, ethnic, film, gay, honors, international, jazz band, literary magazine, musical theater, newspaper, photography, political, professional, radio and TV, religious, social, social service, student government, and yearbook. Popular campus events include Rollins Autumn Art Festival, World Hunger Concert, and the Bach Festival.

Sports: There are 10 intercollegiate sports for men and 11 for women, and 12 intramural sports for men and 12 for women. Facilities include a 2500-seat auditorium, a 600-seat stadium, tennis courts, baseball and soccer fields, a field house with a gym that seats 2500, a weight room, a boat house, and a swimming pool.

Disabled Students: 55% of the campus is accessible. Wheelchair ramps, elevators, special parking, specially equipped rest rooms, special class scheduling, lowered drinking fountains, and lowered telephones are available.

Services: Counseling and information services are available, as is tutoring in every subject. There is a reader service for the blind, and remedial math, reading, and writing.

Campus Safety and Security: Measures include 24-hour foot and vehicle patrol, self-defense education, escort service, and informal discussions. There are pamphlets/posters/films, emergency telephones, lighted pathways/sidewalks, and 24-hour locked residential units.

Programs of Study: Rollins confers the B.A. degree. Master's degrees are also awarded. Bachelor's degrees are awarded in BIOLOGICAL SCIENCE (biology/biological science), BUSINESS (international business management), COMMUNICATIONS AND THE ARTS (art history and appreciation, dramatic arts, English, French, music history and appreciation, music performance, Spanish, studio art, and voice), COMPUTER AND PHYSICAL SCIENCE (chemistry, computer science, mathematics, and physics), EDUCATION (elementary), ENGINEERING AND ENVIRONMENTAL DESIGN (environmental science), SOCIAL SCIENCE (anthropology, classical/ancient civilization, economics, European studies, history, international relations, Latin American studies, philosophy, political science/government, psychology, religion, and sociology). English, biology, and chemistry are the strongest academically. Psychology, English, and international business are the largest.

Required: All students must complete at least 6 skills, including at least 4 cognitive, and at least 2 affective courses, a values requirement, and 4 phys ed courses. A minimum of 35 course units, with 12 to 16 in the course major, and a minimum GPA of 2.0 are required to graduate.

Special: Rollins offers cross-registration with the evening studies division, co-op programs with American University in Washington, D.C., and Paris and the Duke University School of Forestry and Environmental Studies, departmental and professional internships, study abroad in 8 countries, and a Washington semester. Also available are work-study programs, an accelerated degree program in management, a B.A.-B.S. degree in preengineering, an interdepartmental biochemistry/molecular biology major, dual majors in any combination, and student-designed majors in area studies. A 3-2 engineering degree with Washington University in St. Louis and Auburn, Case Western Reserve, Columbia, and Boston Universities is offered. Nondegree study and pass/fail options are possible. There are 3 national honor societies and a freshman honors program.

Faculty/Classroom: 65% of faculty are male; 35%, female. No introductory courses are taught by graduate students. The average class size in an introductory lecture is 25; in a laboratory, 20; and in a regular course, 15.

Admissions: 65% of the 2001-2002 applicants were accepted. The SAT I scores for the 2001-2002 freshman class were: Verbal--12% below 500, 48% between 500 and 599, 35% between 600 and 700, and 5% above 700; Math--13% below 500, 47% between 500 and 599, 35% between 600 and 700, and 5% above 700. The ACT scores were 15% below 21, 25% between 21 and 23, 25% between 24 and 26, 20% between 27 and 28, and 15% above 28. 67% of the current freshmen were in the top quarter of their class; 87% were in the top half. 18 freshmen graduated first in their class.

Requirements: The SAT I or ACT is required. In addition, applicants must be graduates of an accredited secondary school or have a GED certificate, and have completed 4 years of English, 3 of math, and 2 each of foreign language, science, and social studies. An essay is required. SAT II: Subject tests in writing, math, and foreign language and an interview are recommended. Applications are accepted on computer disk by contacting Admissions and specifying PC or Mac. AP credits are accepted. Important factors in the admissions decision are advanced placement or honor courses, evidence of special talent, and extracurricular activities record.

Procedure: Freshmen are admitted fall and spring. Entrance exams should be taken by the first semester of the senior year. There are early decision, early admissions, and deferred admissions plans. Early decision applications should be filed by January 15; regular applications, by February 15 for fall entry and December 1 for spring entry. The fall 2001 application fee was $40. Notification of early decision is sent February 1; regular decision, April 1. 75 early decision candidates were accepted for a recent class. 10% of all applicants are on a waiting list.

Transfer: Transfer students must satisfy all regular admission requirements and submit official transcripts of college and high school work and SAT I or ACT scores. A recommended 2.5 GPA and a year's worth of credit hours earned are required. An interview is recommended. 16 course units of 35 must be completed at Rollins.

Visiting: There are regularly scheduled orientations for prospective students, including 2 all-campus previews in the fall. There are guides for informal visits and visitors may sit in on classes and stay overnight. To schedule a visit, contact the Office of Admissions at *admission@rollins.edu*.

Financial Aid: In 2001-2002, 61% of all freshmen and 67% of continuing students received some form of financial aid. 38% of freshmen and 43% of continuing students received need-based aid. The average freshman award was $22,847. 15% of undergraduates work part time. Average annual earnings from campus work are $891. The average financial indebtedness of the 2001 graduate was $14,500. Rollins is a member of CSS. The CSS/Profile or FAFSA and the college's own financial statement are required. The fall application deadline is March 1.

International Students: The school actively recruits these students. They must score 550 on the written TOEFL and also take the SAT I or the ACT.

Computers: The mainframe is a MicroVAX 3100. The student computing center is open 24 hours. More than 150 terminals and PCs for student use are located in the writing center, residence halls, the library, and departmental lounges. Students may bring their own PC and, with a modem, access the mainframe 24 hours per day. All students may access the system. There are no time limits and no fees.

Graduates: In 2001, 309 bachelor's degrees were awarded. The most popular majors were psychology (10%), English (9%), and international business (8%). In an average class, 60% graduate in 4 years, 64% in 5 years, and 67% in 6 years. 25 companies recruited on campus in 2000-2001. Of the 2000 graduating class, 20% were enrolled in graduate school within 6 months of graduation and 61% were employed.

Admissions Contact: David G. Erdmann, Dean of Admission and Student Financial Planning.

SAINT LEO UNIVERSITY
D-3

Saint Leo, FL 33574-6665 (352) 588-8283
(800) 334-5532; Fax: (352) 588-8257

Full-time: 379 men, 475 women
Part-time: 28 men, 30 women
Graduate: 106 men, 141 women
Year: semesters, summer session
Application Deadline: August 1
Freshman Class: 236 enrolled
SAT I Verbal/Math: 470/480
Faculty: 55; IIB, --$
Ph.D.s: 77%
Student/Faculty: 16 to 1
Tuition: $12,770
Room & Board: $6480
ACT: 20 **LESS COMPETITIVE**

Saint Leo University, a private institution founded in 1889, is affiliated with the Catholic Church. The university offers undergraduate programs in business administration, the humanities, natural sciences, social sciences, education, and preprofessional studies There are 3 undergraduate and 2 graduate schools. In addition to regional accreditation, Saint Leo has baccalaureate program accreditation with CSWE and IACBE. The library contains 122,942 volumes, 27,965 microform items, and 5193 audiovisual forms/CDs, and subscribes to 709 periodicals. Computerized library services include the card catalog, interlibrary loans, and database searching. Special learning facilities include a learning resource center and TV station. The 153-acre campus is in a rural area 40 miles north of Tampa. Including residence halls, there are 20 buildings.

Student Life: 73% of undergraduates are from Florida. Others are from 35 states, 22 foreign countries, and Canada. 70% are from public schools. 65% are white. 73%, claim no religious affiliation; 20% are Catholic. The average age of freshmen is 18; all undergraduates, 23. 29% do not continue beyond their first year.

Housing: 645 students can be accommodated in college housing, which includes single-sex and coed dormitories. On-campus housing is guaranteed for the freshman year only, is available on a first-come, first-served basis, and is available on a lottery system for upperclassmen. 66% of students commute. All students may keep cars.

Activities: 9% of men belong to 4 local and 3 national fraternities; 3% of women belong to 4 local and 2 national sororities. There are 26 groups on campus, including cheerleading, chess, chorus, dance, drama, ethnic, honors, international, literary magazine, newspaper, political, professional, radio and TV, religious, social, social service, student government, and yearbook. Popular campus events include Fall Festival, Spring Fling, and Winter Formal.

Sports: There are 6 intercollegiate sports for men and 7 for women, and 8 intramural sports for men and 8 for women. Facilities include a 2750-seat indoor gym, a weight training room, an outdoor swimming pool, a golf course, soccer, softball, baseball, and track fields, basketball, volleyball, lighted tennis, racquetball, and handball courts, and sailing and canoeing.

Disabled Students: 95% of the campus is accessible. Wheelchair ramps, elevators, special parking, specially equipped rest rooms, lowered drinking fountains are available. Accomodations for persons with disabilities are available on a case-by-case basis with proper documentation.

Services: Counseling and information services are available, as is tutoring in most subjects. There is remedial math and writing.

Campus Safety and Security: Measures include 24-hour foot and vehicle patrol, escort service, informal discussions, and pamphlets/posters/films. There are emergency telephones and lighted pathways/sidewalks.

Programs of Study: Saint Leo confers B.A., B.S., and B.S.W. degrees. Associate and master's degrees are also awarded. Bachelor's degrees are awarded in BIOLOGICAL SCIENCE (biology/biological science), BUSINESS (accounting, business administration and management, human resources, and sports management), COMMUNICATIONS AND THE ARTS (English), COMPUTER AND PHYSICAL SCIENCE (information sciences and systems), EDUCATION (education of the exceptional child, elementary, physical, and secondary), ENGINEERING AND ENVIRONMENTAL DESIGN (environmental science), HEALTH PROFESSIONS (health care administration and medical technology), SOCIAL SCIENCE (criminology, history, human services, international studies, political science/government, psychology, public administration, religion, social work, and sociology). Biological science, English, and environmental science are the strongest academically. Business administration, elementary education, and sport management are the largest.

Required: To graduate, all students must complete a minimum of 120 academic credits, with 30 to 60 hours in the major, all the requirements of their division and major, and 53 to 56 hours in the general education program. The honors program may be substituted for general education requirements. A minimum 2.0 GPA and a capstone course are required, and there is a 30-hour residency requirement.

Special: Saint Leo offers internships in most majors, study abroad in 5 countries, work-study programs on campus, dual majors, and credit for military experience. There is a prelaw program, as well as preprofessional programs in medicine, dentistry, and veterinary science. There are 5 national honor societies and a freshman honors program.

Faculty/Classroom: 58% of faculty are male; 42%, female. All teach undergraduates. No introductory courses are taught by graduate students. The average class size in an introductory lecture is 25; in a laboratory, 10; and in a regular course, 15.

Admissions: The SAT I scores for the 2001-2002 freshman class were: Verbal--59% below 500, 32% between 500 and 599, and 9% between 600 and 700; Math--56% below 500, 37% between 500 and 599, and 7% between 600 and 700. The ACT scores were 61% below 21, 22% between 21 and 23, 12% between 24 and 26, and 5% between 27 and 28. 19% of the current freshmen were in the top fifth of their class; 53% were in the top two fifths.

Requirements: The SAT I or ACT is required. In addition, applicants must be graduates of an accredited secondary school or have a GED certificate, and have completed 4 credits each in English and electives, 3 each in math and social studies, and 2 in science. A GPA of 2.3 is required. AP and CLEP credits are accepted. Important factors in the admissions decision are advanced placement or honor courses, personality/intangible qualities, and recommendations by school officials. Applications are accepted on-line via CollegeLink and Catholic College Application, and at *www.slu4u.net*.

Procedure: Freshmen are admitted in the fall. Entrance exams should be taken by the fall of the senior year. There are early decision and deferred admissions plans. Early decision applications should be filed by November 30; regular applications, by August 1 for fall entry and December 1 for spring entry. The fall 2001 application fee was $35. Notification of early decision is sent December 15; regular decision, on a rolling basis.

Transfer: 113 transfer students enrolled in 2001-2002. Applicants must submit an official transcript from each previously attended college and a recommendation from the dean of students of the last institution attended. A minimum 2.5 GPA is required. 30 credits of 120 must be completed at Saint Leo.

Visiting: There are regularly scheduled orientations for prospective students, consisting of daylong open houses in the fall and spring. There are guides for informal visits and visitors may sit in on classes and stay overnight. To schedule a visit, contact the Office of Admission.

Financial Aid: In 2001-2002, 97% of all freshmen and 85% of continuing students received some form of financial aid. 78% of freshmen and 65% of continuing students received need-based aid. The average freshman award was $11,276. Of that total, scholarships or need-based grants averaged $9110 ($20,800 maximum); loans averaged $2625 ($6625 maximum); work contracts averaged $750 ($2500 maximum); and outside scholarships averaged $450 ($15,000 maximum). 32% of undergraduates work part time. Average annual earnings from campus work are $1545. The average financial indebtedness of the 2001 graduate was $15,000. The FAFSA is required. The fall application deadline is March 1.

International Students: There are 38 international students enrolled. The school actively recruits these students. They must score 550 on the written TOEFL or 213 on the electronic version and also take the SAT I or the ACT.

Computers: The mainframe is a DEC 4100. All students may use the 50 PCs that are located in the library, with 89 computers in all on campus available for student use. In addition, students have been provided notebooks in every residence hall room. All students may access the system. There are no time limits and no fees.

Graduates: In 2001, 163 bachelor's degrees were awarded. The most popular majors were elementary education (17%), criminology (14%), and business (12%). In an average class, 1% graduate in 3 years, 23% in 4 years, 35% in 5 years, and 37% in 6 years. 18 companies recruited on campus in 2000-2001. Of the 2000 graduating class, 27% were enrolled in graduate school within 6 months of graduation and 73% were employed.

Admissions Contact: Gary Bracken, Vice President for Enrollment. E-mail: *admission@saintleo.edu* Web: *www.slu4u.net*

SAINT THOMAS UNIVERSITY — E-5
Miami, FL 33054 — (305) 628-6546
(800) 367-9010; Fax: (305) 628-6591

Full-time: 450 men, 550 women	**Faculty:** 77
Part-time: 120 men, 180 women	**Ph.D.s:** 65%
Graduate: none	**Student/Faculty:** 10 to 1
Year: semesters, summer session	**Tuition:** $14,700
Application Deadline: open	**Room & Board:** $4800
Freshman Class: n/av	
SAT I: recommended	**ACT:** n/av **LESS COMPETITIVE**

Saint Thomas University, founded in 1961, is a private, liberal arts university affiliated with the Roman Catholic Church and sponsored by the Archdiocese of Miami. Figures in above capsule are approximate. There are 2 undergraduate and 2 graduate schools. The 2 libraries contain 200,000 volumes, and subscribe to 1000 periodicals. Computerized library services include the card catalog, interlibrary loans, and database searching. Special learning facilities include a learning resource center and TV station. The 140-acre campus is in a suburban area 10 miles from Miami and Fort Lauderdale. Including residence halls, there are 15 buildings.

Student Life: 85% of undergraduates are from Florida. Others are from 23 states, 45 foreign countries, and Canada. 40% are Hispanic; 23% white; 18% African American; 18% foreign nationals. 62% are Catholic; 20% claim no religious affiliation. The average age of freshmen is 19; all undergraduates, 25. 35% do not continue beyond their first year; 42% remain to graduate.

Housing: 350 students can be accommodated in college housing, which includes coed dormitories. In addition, there are special-interest houses. On-campus housing is guaranteed for all 4 years. Priority is given to out-of-town students. 80% of students commute. All students may keep cars.

Activities: 10% of men and about 2% of women belong to 1 local and 1 national fraternity; 5% of women belong to 1 national sorority. There are 20 groups on campus, including art, cheerleading, choir, computers, drama, ethnic, honors, international, literary magazine, newspaper, photography, political, professional, radio and TV, religious, social, social service, student government, and yearbook. Popular campus events include Senior Capping Ceremony, Freshman Investiture Ceremony, and Land and Water Olympics.

Sports: There are 5 intercollegiate sports for men and 4 for women, and 12 intramural sports for men and 12 for women. Facilities include basketball, soccer, and softball fields, tennis courts, a weight room, and a swimming pool.

Disabled Students: 90% of the campus is accessible. Wheelchair ramps, elevators, special parking, specially equipped rest rooms, and special class scheduling are available.

Services: Counseling and information services are available, as is tutoring in most subjects. There is remedial math, reading, and writing. Computer-assisted instruction is available.

Campus Safety and Security: Measures include 24-hour foot and vehicle patrol, self-defense education, escort service, and informal discussions. There are pamphlets/posters/films, emergency telephones, and lighted pathways/sidewalks.

Programs of Study: STU confers B.A. and B.B.A. degrees. Master's degrees are also awarded. Bachelor's degrees are awarded in BIOLOGICAL SCIENCE (biology/biological science), BUSINESS (accounting, banking and finance, business administration and management, hospitality management services, hotel/motel and restaurant management, human resources, international business management, marketing/retailing/merchandising, sports management, and tourism), COMMUNICATIONS AND THE ARTS (communications, English, and Spanish), COMPUTER AND PHYSICAL SCIENCE (chemistry, computer programming, and computer science), EDUCATION (elementary, secondary, and social studies), HEALTH PROFESSIONS (predentistry and premedicine), SOCIAL SCIENCE (American studies, criminal justice, economics, history, human services, international relations, liberal arts/general studies, political science/government, prelaw, psychology, public administration, religion, and sociology). Sports administration and accounting are the strongest academically. Business management, psychology, and communications are the largest.

Required: All students must complete at least 120 semester credits (126 for business), with 30 to 60 in the major, and specific courses, including 12 credits in English, 9 each in math/physical science, philosophy, and religion, 6 each in history, social science, and humanities. Students must maintain a 2.0 overall GPA and a 2.25 GPA in the major subject.

Special: Communication arts, hospitality management, and sports administration internships, study abroad in Italy and Spain, and a general studies degree are available. The university grants credit for life, military, and work experience via the Life Experience Portfolio. There are 2 national honor societies, a freshman honors program, and 1 departmental honors program.

Faculty/Classroom: 63% of faculty are male; 37%, female. All teach undergraduates and 3% do research. The average class size in an introductory lecture is 25; in a laboratory, 12; and in a regular course, 17.

Requirements: The SAT I is recommended. In addition, applicants should have completed 18 high school units, including 4 units in English, 3 each in math and social science, and 2 in science. A GPA of 2.0 is required. AP and CLEP credits are accepted. Important factors in the admissions decision are recommendations by school officials, advanced placement or honor courses, and evidence of special talent.

Procedure: Freshmen are admitted to all sessions. Entrance exams should be taken in December of the senior year of high school. There is a deferred admissions plan. Application deadlines are open. The application fee is $40.

Transfer: Maximum credit hours accepted are 60 from a junior college and 90 from a 4-year institution. No grade of D is acceptable in courses beyond sophomore level or in the major. Students with fewer than 30 credits must submit a high school transcript and SAT I or ACT scores. 30 credits of 120 must be completed at STU.

Visiting: There are guides for informal visits and visitors may sit in on classes and stay overnight. To schedule a visit, contact the Admissions Office.

Financial Aid: In a recent year, 90% of all students received some form of financial aid. 65% of students received need-based aid. The average freshman award was $7000. Of that total, scholarships or need-based grants averaged $1660 ($11,500 maximum); loans averaged $2360 ($3250 maximum); work contracts averaged $1555 ($2400 maximum); and need-based grants averaged $840 ($2500 maximum). 21% of undergraduates work part time. Average annual earnings from campus work are $2000. The average financial indebtedness of a graduate in a recent year was $9935. The CSS/Profile, FAFSA, or the college's own financial statement are required.

International Students: There were 200 international students enrolled in a recent year. The school actively recruits these students. They must score 525 on the written TOEFL and also take the college's own test.

Computers: The mainframe is a Prime 9755. There are also 30 IBM PS/2 Model 30-286 and 55SX PCs available for academic use in the computer lab. All students may access the system anytime it is available. There are no time limits and no fees.

Graduates: In a recent year, 284 bachelor's degrees were awarded. The most popular majors were human services (15%), business management (12%), and accounting (9%). In an average class, 22% graduate in 4 years, 35% in 5 years, and 42% in 6 years.

Admissions Contact: Assistant Director of Admissions.
E-mail: *kmoeller@stu.edu*

SOUTHEASTERN COLLEGE D-3
Lakeland, FL 33801 (863) 667-5018
(800) 500-8760; Fax: (863) 667-5200

Full-time: 597 men, 649 women	**Faculty:** 43
Part-time: 48 men, 69 women	**Ph.D.s:** 48%
Graduate: none	**Student/Faculty:** 29 to 1
Year: semesters, summer session	**Tuition:** $7542
Application Deadline: August 1	**Room & Board:** $4106
Freshman Class: n/av	
SAT I or ACT: required	**LESS COMPETITIVE**

Southeastern College, founded in 1935 is a Christian liberal arts institution offering 25 degree programs that equip students to serve in both professional careers and ministry-related fields. The 2 libraries contain 94,000 volumes, 1658 microform items, and 2850 audiovisual forms/CDs, and subscribe to 431 periodicals. Computerized library services include the card catalog, interlibrary loans, and database searching. Special learning facilities include a learning resource center, radio station, TV station, and Pentecostal Research Library. The 56-acre campus is in a small town 30 miles east of Tampa and 45 miles west of Orlando. Including residence halls, there are 32 buildings.

Student Life: 58% of undergraduates are from Florida. Others are from 40 states, 8 foreign countries, and Canada. 79% are white; 10% Hispanic. All are Protestant. The average age of freshmen is 18; all undergraduates, 21. 19% do not continue beyond their first year; 35% remain to graduate.

Housing: 910 students can be accommodated in college housing, which includes single-sex dormitories and on-campus apartments. On-campus housing is guaranteed for all 4 years. 60% of students live on campus. Alcohol is not permitted. All students may keep cars.

Activities: There are no fraternities or sororities. There are 20 groups on campus, including band, cheerleading, choir, chorale, chorus, computers, drama, ethnic, honors, international, jazz band, newspaper, radio and TV, religious, social service, student government, and yearbook. Popular campus events include Fall Festival, Christmas Social, and Junior-Senior Banquet.

Sports: There are 4 intercollegiate sports for men and 4 for women, and 8 intramural sports for men and 6 for women. Facilities include a gym, baseball and soccer fields, tennis, racquetball, and beach volleyball courts, a weight room, and intramural fields.

Disabled Students: 90% of the campus is accessible. Wheelchair ramps, elevators, special parking, specially equipped rest rooms, special class scheduling, and lowered drinking fountains are available.

Services: Counseling and information services are available, as is tutoring in some subjects, including math, reading, and English. There is remedial math, reading, and writing.

Campus Safety and Security: Measures include 24-hour foot and vehicle patrol, informal discussions, pamphlets/posters/films, and lighted pathways/sidewalks, and a main entrance security booth attendant.

Programs of Study: Southeastern College confers B.A., B.S., B.M., and B.S.W. degrees. Bachelor's degrees are awarded in BIOLOGICAL SCIENCE (biology/biological science), BUSINESS (accounting, business administration and management, and marketing/retailing/merchandising), COMMUNICATIONS AND THE ARTS (communications, English, and music), EDUCATION (Christian, education of the exceptional child, elementary, middle school, music, and secondary), SOCIAL SCIENCE (biblical studies, interdisciplinary studies, ministries, pastoral studies, psychology, religion, religious music, social work, and youth ministry). Religion, education, and psychology are the strongest academically. Religion is the largest.

Required: Every degree student must complete 125 to 130 hours, including 36 hours of general education and at least 20 hours of religion. Distribution requirements include 6 to 12 hours each in arts and communications, human adjustment, science and math, social sciences, and humanities and fine arts. A minimum GPA of 2.0 must be maintained.

Special: Internships are available in communications, education, ministry, psychology, pastoral studies, Christian education, and business. There are accelerated degree programs in Church leadership and in business and professional leadership. There are 2 national honor societies, and 2 departmental honors program.

Faculty/Classroom: 66% of faculty are male; 34%, female. 96% teach undergraduates. The average class size in an introductory lecture is 60; in a laboratory, 20; and in a regular course, 28.

Requirements: The SAT I or ACT is required. In addition, the GED is accepted. A GPA of 1.5 is required. AP and CLEP credits are accepted. Southeastern accepts applications on-line.

Procedure: Freshmen are admitted to all sessions. Entrance exams should be taken prior to enrollment. There is an early admissions plan. Applications should be filed by August 1 for fall entry and November 15 for spring entry. The fall 2001 fee was $40. Notification is sent on a rolling basis.

Transfer: 137 transfer students enrolled in 2001-2002. Admission requirements for transfer applicants are the same as for first-time students. 30 credits of 130 must be completed at Southeastern College.

Visiting: There are regularly scheduled orientations for prospective students, including College Days (fall and spring), which consist of a 24 hour overview of campus life with class visits, faculty reception, admission/financial aid workshops, a student panel discussion, and a worship service. There are guides for informal visits and visitors may sit in on classes and stay overnight. To schedule a visit, contact the Admission Office.

Financial Aid: In 2001-2002, 58% of all freshmen and 71% of continuing students received some form of financial aid. 51% of freshmen and 62% of continuing students received need-based aid. The average freshman award was $6961. Of that total, scholarships or need-based grants averaged $4986; and loans averaged $2531. 20% of undergraduates work part time. Average annual earnings from campus work are $1500. The FAFSA and the college's own financial statement are required. The fall application deadline is April 15.

International Students: There are 8 international students enrolled. The school actively recruits these students. They must score 500 on the written TOEFL and also take the SAT I or the ACT.

Computers: The mainframe is an IBM AS/400. PCs and Macs are available for student use in the computer lab. E-mail, Internet access, voice mail, and cable are available from each dormitory room. All students may access the system during designated lab hours or from their residence hall. There are no time limits and no fees.

Graduates: In 2001, 222 bachelor's degrees were awarded. In an average class, 30% graduate in 6 years.

Admissions Contact: Omar Rashed, Director of Admission.
E-mail: *admission@secollege.edu* Web: *http://www.secollege.edu*

STATE UNIVERSITY SYSTEM OF FLORIDA

The state university system, established in 1906, is a public system. It is governed by a board of regents whose chief administrator is the chancellor. The primary goals of the system are teaching, research, and public service. The main priorities are to improve the quality of undergraduate education, to solve critical state problems, to forge public-private partnerships, and to increase the efficiency of the system. The total enrollment of all 10 campuses is about 215,000; there are more than 12,000 faculty members. Altogether there are 636 baccalaureate, 590 master's, and 230 doctoral programs offered in the system. 4-year campuses are located in Gainesville, Tallahassee, Tampa, Boca Raton, Pensacola, Orlando, Jacksonville, Miami, and Fort Myers. Profiles of the 4-year campuses are included in this section.

STETSON UNIVERSITY D-2

Deland, FL 32723 **(386) 822-7100**
(800) 688-0101; Fax: (386) 822-7112

Full-time: 882 men, 1181 women	**Faculty:** 191; IIA, av$
Part-time: 49 men, 62 women	**Ph.D.s:** 89%
Graduate: 116 men, 215 women	**Student/Faculty:** 11 to 1
Year: semesters, summer session	**Tuition:** $19,310
Application Deadline: March 1	**Room & Board:** $6330
Freshman Class: 1942 applied, 1545 accepted, 559 enrolled	
SAT I Verbal/Math: 562/559	**ACT:** 24 **VERY COMPETITIVE**

Stetson University, founded in 1883, is an independent institution offering undergraduate programs in liberal arts and sciences, music, and business administration and graduate programs. There are 3 undergraduate and 2 graduate schools. In addition to regional accreditation, Stetson has baccalaureate program accreditation with AACSB, NASM, and NCATE. Computerized library services include the card catalog, interlibrary loans, and database searching. Special learning facilities include an art gallery and a museum of minerals. The 162-acre campus is in a small town 35 miles north of Orlando and 25 miles west of Daytona Beach. Including residence halls, there are 62 buildings.

Student Life: 76% of undergraduates are from Florida. Others are from 43 states, 47 foreign countries, and Canada. 82% are white. 42% are Protestant; 40% claim no religious affiliation; 18% Catholic. The average age of freshmen is 19; all undergraduates, 21. 21% do not continue beyond their first year.

Housing: 1532 students can be accommodated in college housing, which includes single-sex and coed dormitories, fraternity houses, and sorority houses. In addition, there are honors houses, language houses, and special-interest houses. On-campus housing is guaranteed for all 4 years. 70% of students live on campus; of those, 60% remain on campus on weekends. All students may keep cars.

Activities: 33% of men belong to 7 national fraternities; 29% of women belong to 6 national sororities. There are 95 groups on campus, including band, cheerleading, chess, choir, chorale, chorus, computers, dance, drama, ethnic, gay, honors, international, jazz band, literary magazine, musical theater, newspaper, opera, orchestra, political, professional, radio and TV, religious, social, social service, student government, symphony, and yearbook. Popular campus events include Caribbean Week, Asian Week, and Black History Month.

Sports: There are 7 intercollegiate sports for men and 8 for women, and 12 intramural sports for men and 12 for women. Facilities include 4 racquetball, 6 volleyball, and 8 tennis courts, basketball courts, weight and training rooms, baseball and soccer fields, 2 softball fields, a multipurpose field, a training and exercise science facility, a swimming pool, and a 5000-seat auditorium.

Disabled Students: 80% of the campus is accessible. Wheelchair ramps, elevators, special parking, specially equipped rest rooms, special class scheduling, lowered drinking fountains, and lowered telephones are available.

Services: Counseling and information services are available, as is tutoring in most subjects. There is a reader service for the blind.

Campus Safety and Security: Measures include 24-hour foot and vehicle patrol, self-defense education, escort service, and informal discussions. There are pamphlets/posters/films, emergency telephones, and lighted pathways/sidewalks.

Programs of Study: Stetson confers B.A., B.S., B.B.A., B.M., and B.M.E. degrees. Master's degrees are also awarded. Bachelor's degrees are awarded in BIOLOGICAL SCIENCE (biochemistry, biology/biological science, marine biology, and molecular biology), BUSINESS (accounting, banking and finance, business administration and management, business economics, international business management, management science, and marketing/retailing/merchandising), COMMUNICATIONS AND THE ARTS (art, communications, dramatic arts, English, French, German, guitar, music, music performance, music theory and composition, piano/organ, Spanish, and voice), COMPUTER AND PHYSICAL SCIENCE (chemistry, computer science, information sciences and systems, mathematics, and physics), EDUCATION (athletic training, elementary, music, secondary, and social science), ENGINEERING AND ENVIRONMENTAL DESIGN (environmental science and graphic arts technology), HEALTH PROFESSIONS (exercise science, medical technology, and sports medicine), SOCIAL SCIENCE (American studies, economics, geography, history, humanities, international studies, Latin American studies, philosophy, physical fitness/movement, political science/government, prelaw, psychology, religion, Russian and Slavic studies, social science, and sociology). Business, psychology, and education are the largest.

Required: To graduate, all students must complete 120 total credit hours, including 30 to 40 in the major, with a minimum GPA of 2.0. A freshman English sequence and courses in religious studies or philosophy, humanities, natural sciences, and social sciences are required.

Special: Stetson offers co-op programs in preengineering, prelaw, premedicine, and medical technolgoy, internships in many disciplines, study abroad in France, Germany, Spain, Russia, Mexico, Hong Kong, and England, and a Washington semester at American University. B.A.-B.S. degrees, dual majors, student-designed majors through the Honors Programs, 3-2 engineering degrees, a 3-3 law degree with Stetson College of Law, and pass/fail options are also offered. There is also the Leadership Development Program, the Roland George investments Program, in which students manage an actual investment portfolio exceeding $1.7 million, and the Family Business Center. There are 6 national honor societies, including Phi Beta Kappa, and a freshman honors program.

Faculty/Classroom: 60% of faculty are male; 40%, female. 97% teach undergraduates and 50% do research. No introductory courses are taught by graduate students. The average class size in an introductory lecture is 22; in a laboratory, 18; and in a regular course, 17.

Admissions: 80% of the 2001-2002 applicants were accepted. The SAT I scores for the 2001-2002 freshman class were: Verbal--20% below 500, 48% between 500 and 599, 26% between 600 and 700, and 6% above 700; Math--24% below 500, 43% between 500 and 599, 29% between 600 and 700, and 4% above 700. The ACT scores were 23% below 21, 27% between 21 and 23, 29% between 24 and 26, 12% between 27 and 28, and 9% above 28. 57% of the current freshmen were in the top fifth of their class; 82% were in the top two fifths. 15 freshmen graduated first in their class.

Requirements: The SAT I or ACT is required. In addition, applicants must be graduates of an accredited secondary school or have a GED, and have completed 4 years of English, 3 of math and science, and 2 each of foreign language, social sciences, and electives. Auditions are required for music students. A GPA of 2.0 is required. AP and CLEP credits are accepted. Important factors in the admissions decision are advanced placement or honor courses, leadership record, and evidence of special talent. Applications are accepted on-line and on computer disk.

Procedure: Freshmen are admitted to all sessions. Entrance exams should be taken in the spring of the junior year or the fall of the senior year. There are early decision, early admissions, and deferred admissions plans. Early decision applications should be filed by November 1; regular applications, by March 1 for fall entry. Notification is sent on a rolling basis. The fall 2001 application fee was $35.

Transfer: 128 transfer students enrolled in 2001-2002. Transfer students must have completed a semester of academic work in good standing at an accredited college with a minimum 2.0 GPA. A 2.6 GPA and an interview are recommended. 45 credits of 120 must be completed at Stetson.

Visiting: There are regularly scheduled orientations for prospective students, consisting of a campus tour and orientation, interviews, class visits, and presentations. There are guides for informal visits and visitors may sit in on classes and stay overnight. To schedule a visit, contact the Admissions Office.

Financial Aid: In 2001-2002, 97% of all freshmen and 93% of continuing students received some form of financial aid. 59% of freshmen and 58% of continuing students received need-based aid. The average freshman award was $15,726. Of that total, scholarships or need-based grants averaged $11,118 ($27,590 maximum); loans averaged $3781 ($13,938 maximum); work contracts averaged $2250 ($2900 maximum); and Florida Resident Access Grant averaged $2683 ($2686 maximum). 29% of undergraduates work part time. Average annual earnings from campus work are $2233. The average financial indebtedness of the 2001 graduate was $17,000. Stetson is a member of CSS. The FAFSA is required.

International Students: There are 80 international students enrolled. The school actively recruits these students. They must score 550 on the written TOEFL and also take the SAT I or the ACT.

Computers: The mainframe is an HP 9000. There are several general-access computer labs with PCs and Macs networked to each other and to the mainframe. All students may access the system. There are no time limits and no fees.

Graduates: In 2001, 436 bachelor's degrees were awarded. The most popular majors were business (37%), psychology (7%), and education (6%). In an average class, 50% graduate in 4 years, 61% in 5 years, and 63% in 6 years. 90 companies recruited on campus in 2000-2001.

Admissions Contact: Deborah Thompson, Vice President for Enrollment Management. E-mail: *admissions@stetson.edu*
Web: *www.stetson.edu/admissions*

UNIVERSITY OF CENTRAL FLORIDA D-3

Orlando, FL 32816-0111 (407) 823-3000; Fax: (407) 823-3419

Full-time: 9920 men, 12,119 women	**Faculty:** 976; I, --$
Part-time: 3665 men, 4332 women	**Ph.D.s:** 81%
Graduate: 2486 men, 3405 women	**Student/Faculty:** 23 to 1
Year: semesters, summer session	**Tuition:** $2581 ($10,469)
Application Deadline: May 15	**Room & Board:** $5670
Freshman Class: 13,601 applied, 8741 accepted, 3956 enrolled	
SAT I Verbal/Math: 572/580	**ACT:** 25 **VERY COMPETITIVE**

The University of Central Florida, founded in 1963 and part of the State University System of Florida, offers programs in liberal and fine arts, business, engineering, health science, professional training, and teacher preparation. There are 6 undergraduate and 6 graduate schools. In addition to regional accreditation, UCF has baccalaureate program accreditation with AACSB, ABET, CSAB, CSWE, NASM, NCATE, and NLN. The library contains 1,378,025 volumes, 2,309,536 microform items, and 32,967 audiovisual forms/CDs, and subscribes to 7916 periodicals. Computerized library services include the card catalog, interlibrary loans, and database searching. Special learning facilities include a learning resource center, an art gallery, FM and AM radio stations, an observatory, an arboretum, a center for research and education in optics and lasers, an institute for simulation and training, and the Florida Solar Energy Center. The 1445-acre campus is in an urban area 13 miles northeast of downtown Orlando. Including residence halls, there are 79 buildings.

Student Life: 93% of undergraduates are from Florida. Others are from 49 states, 107 foreign countries, and Canada. 71% are white; 10%, Hispanic. The average age of freshmen is 18; all undergraduates, 23. 21% do not continue beyond their first year.

Housing: 6553 students can be accommodated in college housing, which includes single-sex and coed dormitories, on-campus apartments, off-campus apartments, fraternity houses, and sorority houses. In addition, there are honors houses and special-interest houses. On-campus housing is available on a first-come, first-served basis. 82% of students commute. All students may keep cars.

Activities: 14% of men belong to 17 national fraternities; 13% of women belong to 9 national sororities. There are 221 groups on campus, including art, band, cheerleading, choir, chorus, computers, dance, drama, drill team, ethnic, film, forensics, gay, honors, international, jazz band, literary magazine, marching band, medical, musical theater, newspaper, orchestra, photography, political, professional, radio and TV, religious, social, social service, student government, volunteer, and yearbook. Popular campus events include Student Showcase Week, Wellness Fair, and ethnic awareness festivals.

Sports: There are 7 intercollegiate sports for men and 8 for women, and 17 intramural sports for men and 17 for women. Facilities include basketball, racquetball, tennis, disc golf, and badminton courts, a softball field, a swimming pool, a golf driving range, a 400-meter track, a dance/exercise studio, weight rooms, and a 92,000-square-foot arena.

Disabled Students: 95% of the campus is accessible. Wheelchair ramps, elevators, special parking, specially equipped rest rooms, special class scheduling, lowered drinking fountains, and lowered telephones are available.

Services: Counseling and information services are available, as is tutoring in most subjects, including math, physics, statistics, Spanish, biology, chemistry, and economics. There is a reader service for the blind, and remedial math, reading, and writing. A review program for the College-Level Academic Skills Test (CLAST) is also available.

Campus Safety and Security: Measures include 24-hour foot and vehicle patrol, self-defense education, escort service, and shuttle buses. There are informal discussions, pamphlets/posters/films, emergency telephones, and lighted pathways/sidewalks. There is also a college-sponsored transportation system that buses students to and from apartment complexes within a 2- or 3-mile radius of the campus.

Programs of Study: UCF confers B.A., B.S., B.F.A., B.M., B.M.E., B.S.A.E., B.S.B.A., B.S.C.E., B.S.Cp.E., B.S.E.E., B.S.E.E.T., B.S.Env.E., B.S.E.T., B.S.I.E., B.S.M.E., B.S.N., and B.S.W. degrees. Associate, master's, and doctoral degrees are also awarded. Bachelor's degrees are awarded in BIOLOGICAL SCIENCE (biology/biological science and microbiology), BUSINESS (accounting, banking and finance, business administration and management, hospitality management services, management information systems, management science, and marketing/retailing/merchandising), COMMUNICATIONS AND THE ARTS (advertising, art, broadcasting, communications, dramatic arts, English, film arts, fine arts, French, journalism, languages, music, public relations, and Spanish), COMPUTER AND PHYSICAL SCIENCE (chemistry, computer science, digital arts/technology, mathematics, physics, and statistics), EDUCATION (art, business, early childhood, education of the exceptional child, elementary, English, foreign languages, mathematics, music, physical, science, social science, special, and vocational), ENGINEERING AND ENVIRONMENTAL DESIGN (aeronautical engineering, aerospace studies, civil engineering, computer engineering, electrical/electronics engineering, electrical/electronics engineering technology, engineering technology, environmental engineering, industrial engineering technology, and mechanical engineering), HEALTH PROFESSIONS (health care administration, health science, medical laboratory technology, nursing, radiological science, respiratory therapy, and speech pathology/audiology), SOCIAL SCIENCE (anthropology, criminal justice, economics, forensic studies, history, humanities, law, liberal arts/general studies, philosophy, political science/government, psychology, public administration, social science, social work, and sociology). Engineering, business administration, and computer science are the strongest academically. Business, education, and psychology are the largest.

Required: To graduate, students must complete at least 120 semester hours, with 36 hours in general education program courses, including 9 each in communication foundations and cultural and historical foundations, and 6 each in math foundations, science foundations, and social foundations. Students must maintain a minimum GPA of 2.0.

Special: Internships are available in most majors through UCF's extensive partnerships with area businesses and industries such as NASA, Disney, Universal Studios, and AT&T. Students may participate in study-abroad and co-op and work-study programs, earn B.A.-B.S. degrees or a liberal studies degree, or pursue dual majors. Nondegree study and pass/fail options are available. There are 2 national honor societies, including Phi Beta Kappa, and a freshman honors program.

Faculty/Classroom: 63% of faculty are male; 37%, female. All teach undergraduates and 95% do research. No introductory courses are taught by graduate students. The average class size in an introductory lecture is 53; in a laboratory, 30; and in a regular course, 35.

Admissions: 64% of the 2001-2002 applicants were accepted. The SAT I scores for the 2001-2002 freshman class were: Verbal--11% below 500, 54% between 500 and 599, 32% between 600 and 700, and 3% above 700; Math--10% below 500, 49% between 500 and 599, 36% between 600 and 700, and 5% above 700. The ACT scores were 9% below 21, 26% between 21 and 23, 36% between 24 and 26, 17% between 27 and 28, and 12% above 28. 80% of the current freshmen were in the top fifth of their class; 86% were in the top two fifths. There were 26 National Merit finalists and 6 semifinalists. 30 freshmen graduated first in their class.

Requirements: The SAT I or ACT is required. GPA and standardized test scores are rated on a sliding scale. A high school diploma or GED is required. Applicants should have completed 4 units of English, 3 each of math, science (2 with labs), and social studies, and 2 of a foreign language, plus 4 of academic electives. A GPA of 2.0 is required. AP and CLEP credits are accepted. Important factors in the admissions decision are advanced placement or honor courses, evidence of special talent, and leadership record. Applications are accepted on-line at the UCF web site.

Procedure: Freshmen are admitted to all sessions. Entrance exams should be taken during the junior year or the first semester of the senior year. Applications should be filed by May 15 for fall entry, November 15 for spring entry, and April 15 for summer entry, along with a $20 fee. Notification is sent on a rolling basis. 3% of all applicants are on a waiting list.

Transfer: 5273 transfer students enrolled in 2001-2002. A minimum GPA of 2.0 is required in all college work. Either the SAT I or the ACT is required of applicants with fewer than 60 credit hours. Other transfer requirements vary widely depending on credits already earned. 30 credits of 120 must be completed at UCF.

Visiting: There are regularly scheduled orientations for prospective students, including tours offered twice a day, Monday through Friday, followed by a group information session or personal interview. There are guides for informal visits and visitors may sit in on classes. To schedule a visit, contact the Undergraduate Admissions Office.

Financial Aid: In 2001-2002, 33% of all freshmen and 44% of continuing students received some form of financial aid. 27% of freshmen and 40% of continuing students received need-based aid. The average freshman award was $6096. Of that total, scholarships or need-based grants averaged $3259 ($9000 maximum); loans averaged $2531 ($2625 maximum); work contracts averaged $3000 ($4000 maximum); and other sources averaged $1208 ($6038 maximum). 50% of undergraduates work part time. Average annual earnings from campus work are $3086. The average financial indebtedness of the 2001 graduate was $14,395. UCF is a member of CSS. The FAFSA is required. The fall application deadline is March 1.

International Students: There are 411 international students enrolled. They must score 550 on the written TOEFL or 213 on the electronic version.

Computers: The mainframes are a Sun Enterprise 450, an IBM ES/9000 Model 170, and several Novell LAN file servers. 5 public-access computer labs with 500 terminals are available. Students use e-mail to communicate with faculty and classmates, and have free Internet access. All students may access the system at all times. There are no time limits and no fees.

Graduates: In 2001, 5804 bachelor's degrees were awarded. The most popular majors were business (25%), education (12%), and health (10%). In an average class, 2% graduate in 3 years, 27% in 4 years, 45% in 5 years, and 50% in 6 years. 525 companies recruited on campus in 2000-2001.

Admissions Contact: Dr. Gordon Chavis Jr., Executive Director.
E-mail: *admission@mail.ucf.edu* Web: *www.ucf.edu*

UNIVERSITY OF FLORIDA D-2

Gainesville, FL 32611-4000 **(352) 392-1365; n/av**

Full-time, Part-time, and Graduate: 46,221 men and women	**Faculty:** 3844; I, -$
	Ph.D.s: 97%
Year: semesters, summer session	**Student/Faculty:** 18 to 1
Application Deadline: January 29	**Tuition:** $2444 ($10,332)
	Room & Board: $5430
Freshman Class: 12,862 applied, 6881 accepted, 3838 enrolled	
SAT I Verbal/Math: 625/642	**ACT:** 27 **HIGHLY COMPETITIVE**

The University of Florida, founded in 1853, is a public liberal arts institution that is part of the state university system of Florida. There are 14 undergraduate and 17 graduate schools. In addition to regional accreditation, UF has baccalaureate program accreditation with AACSB, ABET, ACCE, ACEJMC, ACPE, ADA, AHEA, APTA, ASLA, FIDER, NAAB, NASAD, NASM, NCATE, NLN, and SAF. The 15 libraries contain 3,401,279 volumes, 6,340,498 microform items, and 30,864 audiovisual forms/CDs, and subscribe to 25,213 periodicals. Computerized library services include the card catalog, interlibrary loans, and database searching. Special learning facilities include a learning resource center, art gallery, natural history museum, radio station, TV station, a performing arts center, and a teaching hospital. The 2000-acre campus is in a suburban area 75 miles from Jacksonville. Including residence halls, there are 850 buildings.

Student Life: 93% of undergraduates are from Florida. Others are from 50 states, 114 foreign countries, and Canada. 76% are white; 10% Hispanic. The average age of freshmen is 18; all undergraduates, 21. 9% do not continue beyond their first year; 64% remain to graduate.

Housing: 6779 students can be accommodated in college housing, which includes single-sex and coed dormitories, on-campus apartments, off-campus apartments, married-student housing, fraternity houses, and sorority houses. In addition, there are honors houses and special-interest houses. On-campus housing is available on a first-come, first-served basis and is available on a lottery system for upperclassmen. 79% of students commute. All students may keep cars.

Activities: 15% of men belong to 29 national fraternities; 15% of women belong to 18 national sororities. There are 450 groups on campus, including art, band, cheerleading, chess, choir, chorale, chorus, computers, dance, drama, drill team, ethnic, film, gay, honors, international, jazz band, literary magazine, marching band, musical theater, newspaper, orchestra, pep band, photography, political, professional, radio and TV, religious, social, social service, student government, symphony, and yearbook. Popular campus events include Madrigal dinners, student-sponsored cultural programs, and Gator Growl, a student-produced variety show.

Sports: There are 8 intercollegiate sports for men and 10 for women. Facilities include tennis, volleyball, and basketball courts, a 12,000-seat athletic center, a 60,000-square-foot fitness park, an Olympic-size swimming pool, a running track, weight rooms, intramural fields, an 85,000-seat stadium, and lakefront facilities.

Disabled Students: 95% of the campus is accessible. Wheelchair ramps, elevators, special parking, specially equipped rest rooms, special class scheduling, lowered drinking fountains, and lowered telephones are available. There is computer access for blind and visually impaired students.

Services: Counseling and information services are available, as is tutoring in every subject. There is a reader service for the blind and a counseling center.

Campus Safety and Security: Measures include 24-hour foot and vehicle patrol, self-defense education, escort service, and shuttle buses. There are informal discussions, pamphlets/posters/films, emergency telephones, lighted pathways/sidewalks, and an apartment safety program in cooperation with local law enforcement.

Programs of Study: UF confers B.A., B.S., B.A.E., B.F.A., B.H.S., B.M.E., B.Mus., B.S.A., B.S.B.A., B.S.F., B.S.N., and B.S.P. degrees. Master's and doctoral degrees are also awarded. Bachelor's degrees are awarded in AGRICULTURE (agricultural business management, agronomy, animal science, dairy science, forestry and related sciences, horticulture, natural resource management, plant science, poultry science, and soil science), BIOLOGICAL SCIENCE (botany, entomology, microbiology, plant pathology, wildlife biology, and zoology), BUSINESS (accounting, banking and finance, insurance, management science, marketing/retailing/merchandising, real estate, and recreation and leisure services), COMMUNICATIONS AND THE ARTS (advertising, art, art history and appreciation, English, French, German, graphic design, journalism, linguistics, music, music history and appreciation, performing arts, photography, Portuguese, public relations, Russian, Spanish, speech/debate/rhetoric, telecommunications, and theater design), COMPUTER AND PHYSICAL SCIENCE (astronomy, chemistry, computer science, geology, mathematics, physics, and statistics), EDUCATION (agricultural, art, elementary, health, music, and special), ENGINEERING AND ENVIRONMENTAL DESIGN (aeronautical engineering, agricultural engineering, architecture, chemical engineering, civil engineering, computer engineering, construction engineering, electrical/electronics engineering, engineering and applied science, environmental engineering, industrial engineering technology, interior design, landscape architecture/design, materials engineering, mechanical engineering, nuclear engineering, nuclear engineering technology, and surveying engineering), HEALTH PROFESSIONS (allied health, nursing, occupational therapy, pharmacy, physical therapy, physician's assistant, and speech pathology/audiology), SOCIAL SCIENCE (American studies, anthropology, Asian/Oriental studies, classical/ancient civilization, criminal justice, East Asian studies, economics, food science, geography, history, home economics, interdisciplinary studies, Judaic studies, philosophy, physical fitness/movement, political science/government, psychology, religion, and sociology). Engineering, pharmacy, and tax law are the strongest academically. Business, engineering, and liberal arts are the largest.

Required: Requirements for graduation vary depending on the major elected, but all students are required to complete a minimum of 120 credits and maintain a minimum 2.0 GPA.

Special: UF offers many internships, dual and student-designed majors, and study abroad in 32 countries. Cross-registration is possible through the Undergraduate Inter-institutional Registration program. Work-study programs, accelerated degree programs, co-op programs, and B.A.-B.S. degrees are available. There are 53 national honor societies, including Phi Beta Kappa, a freshman honors program.

Faculty/Classroom: 79% of faculty are male; 21%, female. Graduate students teach 10% of introductory courses.

Admissions: 53% of the 2001-2002 applicants were accepted. The SAT I scores for the 2001-2002 freshman class were: Verbal--4% below 500, 30% between 500 and 599, 53% between 600 and 700, and 13% above 700; Math--2% below 500, 23% between 500 and 599, 58% between 600 and 700, and 17% above 700. The ACT scores were 1% below 21, 11% between 21 and 23, 24% between 24 and 26, 30% between 27 and 28, and 34% above 28. 84% of the current freshmen were in the top fifth of their class; 97% were in the top two fifths. There were 147 National Merit finalists.

Requirements: The SAT I or ACT is required. The SAT I is preferred. Minimum composite scores are 950 on the SAT I and 19 on the ACT. Candidates should have graduated from an accredited secondary school or have a GED, and have completed 4 years of English, 3 years each of math, science, and social studies, 2 years of a foreign language, and 4 units of academic electives. AP and CLEP credits are accepted. Important factors in the admissions decision are advanced placement or honor courses, parents or siblings attending the school, and recommendations by school officials. Applications are accepted on-line at *www.reg.ufl.edu*.

Procedure: Freshmen are admitted to all sessions. Entrance exams should be taken in the junior year. There is an early decision plan. Early decision applications should be filed by September 26; regular applications, by January 29 for fall entry, October 1 for spring entry, and January 29 for summer entry. The fall 2001 application fee was $20. Notification of early decision is sent October 31; regular decision, March 20.

Transfer: 1934 transfer students enrolled in a recent year. Admission requirements for transfer students vary by college. The lower division is highly competitive; applicants are encouraged to apply at the upper-division level. 30 credits of 120 must be completed at UF.

Visiting: There are regularly scheduled orientations for prospective students, consisting of general information sessions at 10 A.M. and 2 P.M., Monday through Friday (excluding holidays), and a student-guided walking tour of the central campus. There are guides for informal visits and visitors may sit in on classes and stay overnight. To schedule a visit, contact the Admissions Office.

Financial Aid: The average freshman award in a recent year was $6376. Of that total, scholarships or need-based grants averaged $3082; loans averaged $2222; and work contracts averaged $2087. 17% of undergraduates work part time. Average annual earnings from campus work were $1800. The average financial indebtedness of a recent graduate was $13,968. The FAFSA and the college's own financial statement are required. The fall application deadline is April 15.

International Students: In a recent year, there were 142 international students enrolled. They must score 550 on the written TOEFL. Freshmen and lower-division transfers must take the SAT I or ACT.

Computers: The mainframes are an IBM ES9000-831/3VF, an IBM RS6000/SP(9 nodes), and a DEC ALPHA cluster. There are also 353 PCs and 100 Macs available for general student use. Upper-division teaching labs restricted to department majors add several hundred more. All students may access the system via 151 terminals for general student use. There is a limit on the IBM systems, but no limit on the DEC cluster. There are no fees. All students are required to have personal computers.

Graduates: In a recent year, 7429 bachelor's degrees were awarded. In an average class, 67% graduate in 6 years.

Admissions Contact: Bill Kolb, Director of Admissions.
Web: *www.reg.ufl.edu/regadmi.htm*

UNIVERSITY OF MIAMI — E-5

Coral Gables, FL 33124 — (305) 284-4323; Fax: (305) 284-2507

Full-time: 3818 men, 4800 women	**Faculty:** 655; I, av$
Part-time: 251 men, 490 women	**Ph.D.s:** 96%
Graduate: 2482 men, 2595 women	**Student/Faculty:** 13 to 1
Year: semesters, summer session	**Tuition:** $23,228
Application Deadline: February 15	**Room & Board:** $7902
Freshman Class: 14,715 applied, 6804 accepted, 2159 enrolled	
SAT I or ACT: required	**HIGHLY COMPETITIVE**

The University of Miami, founded in 1925, is a private university that offers degrees in more than 130 majors and areas of study. There are 9 undergraduate and 14 graduate schools. In addition to regional accreditation, UM has baccalaureate program accreditation with AACSB, ABET, ACEJMC, APTA, NAAB, NASM, NCATE, and NLN. The 3 libraries contain 2,228,233 volumes, 3,541,773 microform items, and 47,753 audiovisual forms/CDs, and subscribe to 16,305 periodicals. Computerized library services include the card catalog, interlibrary loans, and database searching. Special learning facilities include a learning resource center, art gallery, radio station, TV station, a state-of-the-art research vessel, a sound stage and film studios, a film theater, a performing arts theater, a concert hall, a wellness center, an arboretum, and a palmetum. The 260-acre campus is in a suburban area 6 miles south of Miami. Including residence halls, there are 101 buildings.

Student Life: 57% of undergraduates are from Florida. Others are from 48 states, 99 foreign countries, and Canada. 50% are white; 26% Hispanic; 10% African American. 48% are Catholic; 30% Protestant; 14% Jewish. The average age of freshmen is 18; all undergraduates, 21. 18% do not continue beyond their first year; 61% remain to graduate.

Housing: 3877 students can be accommodated in college housing, which includes single-sex and coed dormitories, on-campus apartments, and fraternity houses. On-campus housing is guaranteed for all 4 years. 60% of students commute. All students may keep cars.

Activities: 13% of men belong to 17 national fraternities; 12% of women belong to 11 national sororities. There are 175 groups on campus, including band, cheerleading, choir, chorale, chorus, dance, debate, drama, ethnic, film, gay, honors, international, jazz band, literary magazine, marching band, musical theater, newspaper, opera, orchestra, pep band, political, professional, radio and TV, religious, social, social service, student government, symphony, and yearbook. Popular campus events include International Week, Cinematic Arts Commission (CAC) Film Festival, and Gusman Concert Hall – Festivale Miami.

Sports: There are 7 intercollegiate sports for men and 10 for women, and 20 intramural sports for men and 20 for women. Facilities include a baseball stadium seating 6000, a soccer stadium, a sports complex, a tennis center, a track and field facility, an athletic center, lighted tennis courts, 4 sports fields, and an Olympic-size swimming pool. A 149,000-square foot indoor/outdoor recreational facility includes a multipurpose room, a courtyard, 4 basketball/volleyball courts, an aerobics room, an atrium/fitness room, a floor hockey/indoor soccer gym, a swimming pool, an elevated jogging track, 6 racquetball and 2 squash courts, a spa, and 2 saunas.

Disabled Students: 95% of the campus is accessible. Wheelchair ramps, elevators, special parking, specially equipped rest rooms, special class scheduling, lowered drinking fountains, lowered telephones, and lowered elevator controls are available.

Services: Counseling and information services are available, as is tutoring in most subjects. There is a reader service for the blind, and remedial math, reading, and writing.

Campus Safety and Security: Measures include 24-hour foot and vehicle patrol, self-defense education, escort service, and shuttle buses. There are informal discussions, pamphlets/posters/films, emergency telephones, lighted pathways/sidewalks. There has been a comprehensive crime prevention program since 1981, including security card access to all residential colleges, office crimewatch, and residence halls crimewatch.

Programs of Study: UM confers B.A., B.S., B.Arch., B.B.A., B.C.S., B.F.A., B.G.S., B.H.S., B. M., B.S.A.E., B.S.B.E., B.S.C., B.S.C.E., B.S.Cp.E., B.S.E.E., B.S.E.S., B.S.I.E., B.S.I.T., B.S.M.E., B.S.N., and B.S.S.A. degrees. Master's and doctoral degrees are also awarded. Bachelor's degrees are awarded in AGRICULTURE (wildlife management), BIOLOGICAL SCIENCE (biochemistry, biology/biological science, marine science, microbiology, and toxicology), BUSINESS (accounting, banking and finance, business administration and management, business economics, business law, entrepreneurial studies, human resources, international business management, management information systems, marketing management, real estate, and sports management), COMMUNICATIONS AND THE ARTS (advertising, art, art history and appreciation, audio technology, broadcasting, ceramic art and design, communications, creative writing, dramatic arts, English, film arts, fine arts, French, German, graphic design, guitar, Italian, jazz, journalism, music, music business management, music performance, music theory and composition, musical theater, painting, percussion, photography, piano/organ, printmaking, public relations, sculpture, Spanish, speech/debate/rhetoric, studio art, telecommunications, theater design, theater management, video, and voice), COMPUTER AND PHYSICAL SCIENCE (applied mathematics, chemistry, computer science, geology, mathematics, physics, and systems analysis), EDUCATION (athletic training, elementary, music, secondary, and special), ENGINEERING AND ENVIRONMENTAL DESIGN (aeronautical engineering, architectural engineering, architecture, biomedical engineering, civil engineering, computer engineering, computer technology, electrical/electronics engineering, engineering, engineering technology, environmental engineering, environmental science, industrial engineering, manufacturing engineering, and mechanical engineering), HEALTH PROFESSIONS (cytotechnology, environmental health science, health care administration, health science, medical technology, music therapy, nursing, physical therapy, predentistry, premedicine, prepharmacy, and preveterinary science), SOCIAL SCIENCE (African American studies, American studies, anthropology, Caribbean studies, criminology, economics, geography, history, international studies, Judaic studies, Latin American studies, philosophy, political science/government, prelaw, psychobiology, psychology, religion, social science, sociology, and women's studies). Marine science, international finance and marketing, and music are the strongest academically. Biology, psychology, and business management are the largest.

Required: Requirements for each degree vary, but all students must complete at least 120 credit hours. All students must fufill general education requirements in English composition, math, writing across the curriculum, natural sciences, social sciences, and arts and humanities. Students must complete 24 to 36 hours in the major and maintain a minimum GPA of 2.0.

Special: UM offers co-op programs in engineering and internships in communications, business, engineering, architecture, and science. There is on- and off-campus work-study, and study abroad in 18 countries. There are 44 national honor societies, including Phi Beta Kappa, and a freshman honors program. All departments have honors program.

Faculty/Classroom: 66% of faculty are male; 34%, female. 78% teach undergraduates. Graduate students teach 23% of introductory courses. The average class size in an introductory lecture is 31; in a laboratory, 16; and in a regular course, 20.

Admissions: 46% of the 2001-2002 applicants were accepted. The SAT I scores for the 2001-2002 freshman class were: Verbal--8% below 500, 42% between 500 and 599, 41% between 600 and 700, and 9% above 700; Math--8% below 500, 38% between 500 and 599, 43% between 600 and 700, and 11% above 700. The ACT scores were 20% between 17 and 22, 31% between 23 and 25, 19% between 26 and 27,

17% between 28 an 29, and 13% 30 and above. 75% of the current freshmen were in the top fifth of their class; 94% were in the top two fifths.

Requirements: The SAT I or ACT is required. In addition, it is recommended that applicants have completed 4 years of English, 3 each of math, science, and social sciences, and 2 of foreign language. Also considered in the admissions decision are a recommendation from a high school counselor and an essay. The GED is accepted. AP and CLEP credits are accepted. Important factors in the admissions decision are advanced placement or honor courses, recommendations by school officials, and evidence of special talent. Students may use the Common App, or the university's application forms, available on paper and on the university's web site at *www.miami.edu/apply*.

Procedure: Freshmen are admitted fall, spring, and summer. Entrance exams should be taken in the fall of the senior year or earlier. There are early decision and deferred admissions plans. Early decision applications should be filed by November 15; regular applications, by February 15 for fall entry, November 15 for spring entry, and March 1 for summer entry, along with a $50 fee. Notification of early decision is sent December 15; regular decision, April 1. 5% of all applicants are on a waiting list.

Transfer: 573 transfer students enrolled in 2001-2002. Transfer applicants must have a GPA of at least 2.5; higher admission standards are in effect for most programs. College transcripts and a statement of good standing from previous institutions attended are required. Courses with grades of C or higher may transfer for credit. 45 credits of 120 must be completed at UM.

Visiting: There are regularly scheduled orientations for prospective students, consisting of several open house programs that enable students to tour the campus and meet with representatives from admission, financial aid, and various university departments. Daily information sessions are offered on campus. There are guides for informal visits and visitors may sit in on classes. To schedule a visit, contact the Admission Office or the specific school or college.

Financial Aid: In 2001-2002, 89% of all freshmen and 84% of continuing students received some form of financial aid. 44% of freshmen and 45% of continuing students received need-based aid. The average freshman award was $21,414. Of that total, scholarships or need-based grants averaged $15,835 ($40,306 maximum); loans averaged $8245 ($35,720 maximum); and work contracts averaged $2051 ($6125 maximum). 27% of undergraduates work part time. Average annual earnings from campus work are $2000. The average financial indebtedness of the 2001 graduate was $28,352. The FAFSA and the state aid form are required. The fall application deadline is February 15.

International Students: There are 750 international students enrolled. The school actively recruits these students. They must take the TOEFL if English is not their native language and score 550 on the written TOEFL or 213 on the electronic version. Students from American schools or IB curriculums must also take the SAT I or ACT.

Computers: The mainframes are an IBM ES/9021 model 580, a DEC VAX cluster, with 2 VAX 4000-600 systems, and 2 VAX 3000 systems. Numerous DEC workstations and more than 40 computer labs are located in residential colleges, libraries, and schools across campus. More than 1000 PCs, workstations, and terminals are available to students. Each residential college has a computer lab with IBM PS/2 and Mac systems, laser printers, and connections to the campuswide network. E-mail access is available. All students may access the system 24 hours a day. There are no time limits and no fees.

Graduates: In 2001, 1750 bachelor's degrees were awarded. The most popular majors were biology (9%), psychology (6%), and finance and international finance and marketing (5%). In an average class, 4% graduate in 3 years, 49% in 4 years, 61% in 5 years, and 63% in 6 years. 99 companies recruited on campus in 2000-2001. Of the 2000 graduating class, 27% were enrolled in graduate school within 6 months of graduation and 38% were employed.

Admissions Contact: Edward M. Gillis, Associate Dean, Enrollments/Director, Admission. An on-line video is available.
E-mail: *admission@miami.edu* Web: *www.miami.edu/admission*

UNIVERSITY OF NORTH FLORIDA D-1

Jacksonville, FL 32224 **(904) 620-2624; Fax: (904) 620-2414**

Full-time: 2976 men, 4199 women	**Faculty:** 366
Part-time: 1783 men, 2641 women	**Ph.D.s:** 95%
Graduate: 559 men, 979 women	**Student/Faculty:** 20 to 1
Year: semesters, summer session	**Tuition:** $2669 ($10,556)
Application Deadline: July 2	**Room & Board:** $5420
Freshman Class: 5181 applied, 3631 accepted, 1518 enrolled	
SAT I Verbal/Math: 566/560	**ACT:** 21 **VERY COMPETITIVE**

The University of North Florida, founded in 1965, is a public university that is part of the state university system. There are 5 undergraduate and 5 graduate schools. In addition to regional accreditation, UNF has baccalaureate program accreditation with AACSB, ABET, ACCE, NASM, NCATE, and NLN. The library contains 746,604 volumes, 1.3 million microform items, and 67,208 audiovisual forms/CDs, and subscribes to 3466 periodicals. Computerized library services include the card catalog, interlibrary loans, and database searching. Special learning facilities include a learning resource center, art gallery, radio station, TV station, theater, auditorium, and nature preserve. The 1300-acre campus is in an urban area 12 miles southeast of downtown Jacksonville. Including residence halls, there are 44 buildings.

Student Life: 91% of undergraduates are from Florida. Others are from 46 states, 102 foreign countries, and Canada. 77% are white; 10% African American. Most claim no religious affiliation. The average age of freshmen is 19; all undergraduates, 25. 7% do not continue beyond their first year.

Housing: 2100 students can be accommodated in college housing, which includes coed dormitories, on-campus apartments, and married-student housing. In addition, there are honors houses. On-campus housing is available on a first-come, first-served basis. 83% of students commute. All students may keep cars.

Activities: 4% of men belong to 7 national fraternities; 4% of women belong to 5 national sororities. There are 141 groups on campus, including art, band, cheerleading, choir, chorale, chorus, computers, dance, drama, ethnic, film, gay, honors, international, jazz band, literary magazine, newspaper, orchestra, pep band, photography, political, professional, radio and TV, religious, social, social service, and student government. Popular campus events include Clubfest, Spring Bash, and Earth Music Fest.

Sports: There are 7 intercollegiate sports for men and 8 for women, and 18 intramural sports for men and 18 for women. Facilities include a baseball stadium, softball, soccer, and multipurpose fields, an aquatic center, a fitness center, jogging trails, racquetball, basketball, volleyball, and tennis courts, a 6,000-seat multipurpose arena, and lakes for canoeing and fishing.

Disabled Students: Wheelchair ramps, elevators, special parking, specially equipped rest rooms, special class scheduling, lowered drinking fountains, and lowered telephones are available. The Disabled Services Office provides specialized assistance and equipment, including priority registration, interpreters for the hearing impaired, and proctored testing.

Services: Counseling and information services are available, as is tutoring in some subjects, including reading, writing, math, business, accounting, physics, biology, chemistry, Spanish, French, and English as a second language.

Campus Safety and Security: Measures include 24-hour foot and vehicle patrol, self-defense education, escort service, and informal discussions. There are pamphlets/posters/films, emergency telephones, lighted pathways/sidewalks, and university police presentations at new student orientation.

Programs of Study: UNF confers B.A., B.S., B.A.E., B.B.A., B.F.A., B.M., B.S.E.E., B.S.H., and B.S.N. degrees. Associate, master's, and doctoral degrees are also awarded. Bachelor's degrees are awarded in BIOLOGICAL SCIENCE (biology/biological science), BUSINESS (accounting, banking and finance, business administration and management, business economics, marketing management, and transportation management), COMMUNICATIONS AND THE ARTS (art, communications, English, fine arts, jazz, music, music performance, and Spanish), COMPUTER AND PHYSICAL SCIENCE (chemistry, computer science, information sciences and systems, mathematics, physics, and statistics), EDUCATION (art, athletic training, elementary, mathematics, middle school, music, physical, science, secondary, and special), ENGINEERING AND ENVIRONMENTAL DESIGN (civil engineering, construction management, electrical/electronics engineering, and mechanical engineering), HEALTH PROFESSIONS (health science, nursing, and predentistry), SOCIAL SCIENCE (anthropology, criminal justice, economics, history, philosophy, political science/government, prelaw, psychology, and sociology). Nursing, special education, and elementary education are the strongest academically. Computer science, psychology, and health science are the largest.

Required: Students are required to take general education distribution requirements, including 9 hours of composition and humanities, and 6 each of natural science, math, and social science. A minimum 2.0 GPA and 120 credit hours, with a minimum of 60 hours in the major, are needed for graduation. All students must take the state-required college-level academic skills test unless exempt.

Special: There are cooperative programs and internships in most majors, and work-study programs with several Jacksonville businesses. Study abroad, a Washington semester, B.A.-B.S. degrees in math, statistics, and psychology, dual majors, and student-designed majors also are available. Credit is given for military experience. There are 5 national honor societies, a freshman honors program, and 19 departmental honors program.

Faculty/Classroom: 61% of faculty are male; 39%, female. 94% teach undergraduates, 80% do research, and 74% do both. No introductory courses are taught by graduate students. The average class size in an introductory lecture is 40; in a laboratory, 17; and in a regular course, 33.

Admissions: 70% of the 2001-2002 applicants were accepted. The SAT I scores for the 2001-2002 freshman class were: Verbal--15% below 500, 54% between 500 and 599, 27% between 600 and 700, and 4%

above 700; Math--16% below 500, 55% between 500 and 599, 27% between 600 and 700, and 2% above 700. The ACT scores were 37% below 21, 47% between 21 and 23, 12% between 24 and 26, 2% between 27 and 28, and 2% above 28. 42% of the current freshmen were in the top fifth of their class; 77% were in the top two fifths. There were 5 National Merit finalists and 2 semifinalists. 4 freshmen graduated first in their class.

Requirements: The SAT I or ACT is required, with minimum acceptable composite scores of 970 on the SAT I, or 20 on the ACT. In addition, applicants must be graduates of an accredited secondary school or have a GED. A total of 15 academic credits plus 4 additional academic electives or 19 Carnegie units is required. Secondary school course work must include 4 years of English, 3 each of math, science, and social studies, and 2 of foreign language. A GPA of 2.5 is required. AP and CLEP credits are accepted. Important factors in the admissions decision are advanced placement or honor courses, recommendations by school officials, and evidence of special talent. Applications are accepted on-line.

Procedure: Freshmen are admitted to all sessions. Entrance exams should be taken during the spring of the junior year or the fall of the senior year. There are early admissions and deferred admissions plans. Applications should be filed by July 2 for fall entry, November 2 for spring entry, and April 8 for summer entry. The fall 2001 application fee was $20. Notification is sent on a rolling basis.

Transfer: 4958 transfer students enrolled in 2001-2002. Transfer applicants with fewer than 60 credit hours must take either the SAT I or the ACT and achieve a minimum composite score of 970 on the SAT I or 20 on the ACT, and must meet all high school unit requirements. The minimum college GPA for transfers is 2.0. Some programs require 2.5. 30 credits of 120 must be completed at UNF.

Visiting: There are regularly scheduled orientations for prospective students, consisting of open houses which include tours of the campus and housing, a general information session, financial aid sessions, academic advising, and personal interviews by request. There are guides for informal visits and visitors may sit in on classes. To schedule a visit, contact the Admissions Office at (904) 620-2625.

Financial Aid: In 2001-2002, 81% of all freshmen and 63% of continuing students received some form of financial aid. 29% of freshmen and 36% of continuing students received need-based aid. The average freshman award was $1985. Of that total, scholarships or need-based grants averaged $1577 ($10,802 maximum); loans averaged $3025 ($18,735 maximum); and work contracts averaged $3579 ($4000 maximum). 6% of undergraduates work part time. Average annual earnings from campus work are $5882. The average financial indebtedness of the 2001 graduate was $12,278. The FAFSA is required. The fall application deadline is April 1.

International Students: There are 87 international students enrolled. The school actively recruits these students. They must score 500 on the written TOEFL and also take the SAT I or the ACT.

Computers: The mainframes are 3 UNIX DEC ALPHA 2100s. The Unix systems, as well as Internet access and e-mail, are accessible via dial-up and network connections in labs and residence halls. There are approximately 600 pentium level PCs in general purpose and distributed labs with 2 application software, including statistics and graphics packages. All students may access the system. The general purpose labs are open 8 A.M. to 1 A.M. Monday to Thursday, 8 A.M. to 9 P.M. Friday, 9 A.M. to 8 P.M., Saturday, and 12 P.M. to 12 A.M. Sunday. The UNIX systems are available 24 hours a day. There are no time limits and no fees. It is recommended that students in building construction management have personal computers. A Pentium 200 notebook with 128 MB RAM and a 6 GB hard drive is recommended.

Graduates: In 2001, 1799 bachelor's degrees were awarded. The most popular majors were health science (11%), elementary teacher education (9%), and communications (9%). In an average class, 1% graduate in 3 years, 12% in 4 years, 27% in 5 years, and 36% in 6 years. 265 companies recruited on campus in 2000-2001.

Admissions Contact: Sherry David, Director of Admissions. A video is available. E-mail: *osprey@unf.edu* Web: *www.unf.edu*

UNIVERSITY OF SOUTH FLORIDA — D-1

Tampa, FL 33620 — **(813) 974-3350; Fax: (813) 974-9689**

Full-time: 7403 men, 10,598 women	**Faculty:** 1510; I, --$
Part-time: 4443 men, 6325 women	**Ph.D.s:** 93%
Graduate: 3249 men, 5214 women	**Student/Faculty:** 12 to 1
Year: semesters, summer session	**Tuition:** $2554 ($10,444)
Application Deadline: May 1	**Room & Board:** $5600
Freshman Class: 12,403 applied, 8294 accepted, 4037 enrolled	
SAT I Verbal/Math: 520/520	**ACT:** 21 **COMPETITIVE**

The University of South Florida, founded in 1956, is a comprehensive public institution, part of the Florida Division of Colleges and Universities, offering programs in liberal and fine arts, business, engineering, health science, and education. USF also maintains campuses at Lakeland, Sarasota, and St. Petersburg. There are 6 undergraduate and 9 graduate schools. In addition to regional accreditation, USF has baccalaureate program accreditation with AACSB, ABET, ACEJMC, ASLA, CSAB, CSWE, NAAB, NASAD, NASM, NCATE, and NLN. The 5 libraries contain 2.3 million volumes, 3.8 million microform items, and 148,986 audiovisual forms/CDs, and subscribe to 10,155 periodicals. Computerized library services include the card catalog, interlibrary loans, and database searching. Special learning facilities include a learning resource center, art gallery, radio station, TV station, mock broadcasting studio, anthropology museum, and botanical gardens. The 1913-acre campus is in an urban area 10 miles northeast of downtown Tampa. Including residence halls, there are 382 buildings.

Student Life: 95% of undergraduates are from Florida. Others are from 50 states, 116 foreign countries, and Canada. 91% are from public schools. 69% are white; 12% African American; 10% Hispanic. The average age of freshmen is 19; all undergraduates, 22. 20% do not continue beyond their first year.

Housing: 3724 students can be accommodated in college housing, which includes single-sex and coed dormitories, on-campus apartments, and married-student housing. In addition, there are honors houses and special-interest houses. On-campus housing is available on a first-come, first-served basis. 87% of students commute. All students may keep cars.

Activities: 6% of men belong to 19 national fraternities; 4% of women belong to 11 national sororities. There are 200 groups on campus, including art, band, cheerleading, chess, choir, chorale, chorus, computers, dance, drama, drill team, ethnic, film, gay, honors, international, jazz band, literary magazine, marching band, musical theater, newspaper, opera, orchestra, pep band, photography, political, professional, radio and TV, religious, social, social service, student government, and symphony. Popular campus events include Women's Awareness Week, Bull Blast, and Week of Welcome.

Sports: There are 8 intercollegiate sports for men and 8 for women, and 14 intramural sports for men and 13 for women. Facilities include a 10000-seat multipurpose arena, 4 pools, tennis and indoor racquetball courts, a track, a jogging course, an indoor recreation center with weight training and aerobics rooms, a soccer stadium, a softball complex, a baseball stadium, and an 18-hole golf course.

Disabled Students: All of the campus is accessible. Wheelchair ramps, elevators, special parking, specially equipped rest rooms, special class scheduling, lowered drinking fountains, and lowered telephones are available.

Services: Counseling and information services are available, as is tutoring in most subjects. There is a reader service for the blind.

Campus Safety and Security: Measures include 24-hour foot and vehicle patrol, self-defense education, escort service, and shuttle buses. There are informal discussions, pamphlets/posters/films, emergency telephones, lighted pathways/sidewalks, and university police.

Programs of Study: USF confers B.A., B.S., B.F.A., B.I.S., B.M., B.S.W., and several engineering degrees. degrees. Associate, master's, and doctoral degrees are also awarded. Bachelor's degrees are awarded in BIOLOGICAL SCIENCE (biology/biological science, and microbiology), BUSINESS (accounting, banking and finance, business administration and management, business economics, management information systems, management science, and marketing/retailing/merchandising), COMMUNICATIONS AND THE ARTS (art, classics, communications, dance, dramatic arts, English literature, French, German, Italian, languages, music, Russian, Spanish, and speech/debate/rhetoric), COMPUTER AND PHYSICAL SCIENCE (chemistry, geology, mathematics, physical sciences, and physics), EDUCATION (art, business, education, education of the emotionally handicapped, education of the mentally handicapped, elementary, English, foreign languages, mathematics, music, physical, science, social studies, special, specific learning disabilities, and vocational), ENGINEERING AND ENVIRONMENTAL DESIGN (chemical engineering, civil engineering, computer engineering, electrical/electronics engineering, engineering, environmental science, industrial engineering, and mechanical engineering), HEALTH PROFESSIONS (medical technology, and nursing), SOCIAL SCIENCE (African American studies, American studies, anthropology, criminology, economics, geography, gerontology, history, humanities, international relations, liberal arts/general studies, philosophy, political science/government, psychology, religion, social science, social work, sociology, and women's studies). Education, fine arts, and sciences are the strongest academically. Business and education are the largest.

Required: To graduate, all students are required to complete at least 120 credit hours, including 36 distributed among English, math, science, social science, historical perspectives, fine arts, and humanities, and 9 of exit requirements in major works/major issues and literature/writing. The number of hours required for each major varies. Students must maintain a minimum GPA of 2.0.

Special: USF offers co-op programs in business and engineering, study abroad, work-study programs, accelerated degree programs in public health and medicine, internships, a Washington semester, dual and student-designed majors, a liberal arts degree, nondegree study, and pass/fail options for some courses. There are 21 national honor societies, a freshman honors program, and 18 departmental honors program.

Faculty/Classroom: 48% teach undergraduates and 16% do research. The average class size in an introductory lecture is 24, in a laboratory, 19; and in a regular course, 20.

Admissions: 67% of the 2001-2002 applicants were accepted. The SAT I scores for the 2001-2002 freshman class were: Verbal--40% below 500, 42% between 500 and 599, 16% between 600 and 700, and 2% above 700; Math--36% below 500, 44% between 500 and 599, 18% between 600 and 700, and 2% above 700. The ACT scores were 13% below 18, 59% between 18 and 23, 26% between 24 and 29, and 2% 30 and above. 44% of the current freshmen were in the top fifth of their class. There were 11 National Merit finalists.

Requirements: The SAT I or ACT is required. In addition, candidates for admission should have completed 4 units each of English and academic electives, 3 each of math, science, and social studies, and 2 of a foreign language. The GED is accepted. Applicants who do not meet minimum requirements but have important attributes, special talents, or unique circumstances are considered for admission by an academic faculty committee. AP and CLEP credits are accepted. Important factors in the admissions decision are advanced placement or honor courses, evidence of special talent, and recommendations by school officials. Applications are accepted on-line. A GPA of 2.0 is required.

Procedure: Freshmen are admitted to all sessions. Entrance exams should be taken at the end of the junior year or the beginning of the senior year. Applications should be filed by May 1 for fall entry, October 25 for spring entry, and March 1 for summer entry, along with a $20 fee. Notification is sent on a rolling basis.

Transfer: 3918 transfer students enrolled in 2001-2002. Students with fewer than 60 transferable hours must meet freshman requirements. Additionally, applicants must have a cumulative college GPA of 2.0 and be in good standing at their last institution. 30 credits of 120 must be completed at USF.

Visiting: There are regularly scheduled orientations for prospective students, including a 2-day program. There are guides for informal visits and visitors may sit in on classes. To schedule a visit, contact the Admissions Office/New Student Orientation at (813) 974-3060 or *orassist@admin.usf.edu*.

Financial Aid: 23% of undergraduates work part time. The FAFSA is required. The fall application deadline is March 1.

International Students: There are 836 international students enrolled. The school actively recruits these students. They must score 550 on the written TOEFL and also take the SAT I or the ACT.

Computers: The mainframe is an IBM 9672-R32 Enterpriser server MVS OS/390. Student computer labs exist throughout campus. All students may access the system. There are no time limits and no fees.

Graduates: In 2001, 4813 bachelor's degrees were awarded. The most popular majors were business (27%), education (14%), and social science (12%). In an average class, 1% graduate in 3 years, 20% in 4 years, 40% in 5 years, and 47% in 6 years. 692 companies recruited on campus in 2000-2001. Of the 2000 graduating class, 21% were enrolled in graduate school within 6 months of graduation and 71% were employed.

Admissions Contact: Dewey Holleman, Director of Admissions.
E-mail: *cleslie@admin.usf.edu*
Web: *http://usfweb.usf.edu/enroll/admiss/admiss.htm*

UNIVERSITY OF TAMPA
Tampa, FL 33606-1490 — D-4 — (813) 253-6211 — (888) 646-2738; Fax: (813) 258--7398

Full-time: 1095 men, 1767 women	**Faculty:** 147; IIB, av$
Part-time: 188 men, 277 women	**Ph.D.s:** 91%
Graduate: 221 men, 275 women	**Student/Faculty:** 19 to 1
Year: semesters, summer session	**Tuition:** $16,722
Application Deadline: open	**Room & Board:** $5890
Freshman Class: 3335 applied, 2713 accepted, 878 enrolled	
SAT I Verbal/Math: 539/534	**ACT:** 23 **COMPETITIVE**

The University of Tampa, founded in 1931, is a comprehensive, independent institution that offers degree programs in more than 60 undergraduate and preprofessional areas of study, and graduate and evening programs. There are 2 undergraduate and 2 graduate schools. In addition to regional accreditation, UT has baccalaureate program accreditation with AACSB, NASM, and NLN. The library contains 220,560 volumes, 10,015 microform items, and 3745 audiovisual forms/CDs, and subscribes to 13,841 periodicals. Computerized library services include the card catalog, interlibrary loans, and database searching. Special learning facilities include a learning resource center, art gallery, radio station, TV station, and fully equipped research vessel for marine science studies, music facility, writing and language labs, academic center for excellence, graphic design studio, and marine science lab. The campus is in an urban area in Tampa. Including residence halls, there are 39 buildings.

Student Life: 50% of undergraduates are from out of state, mostly the Northeast. Others are from 50 states, 85 foreign countries, and Canada. 75% are from public schools. 66% are white. The average age of freshmen is 19; all undergraduates, 22. 24% do not continue beyond their first year; 49% remain to graduate.

Housing: 1996 students can be accommodated in college housing, which includes single-sex and coed dormitories and on-campus apartments. On-campus housing is guaranteed for all 4 years. 57% of students live on campus; of those, 85% remain on campus on weekends. Upperclassmen may keep cars.

Activities: 17% of men belong to 5 national fraternities; 12% of women belong to 7 national sororities. There are 95 groups on campus, including academic, art, band, cheerleading, chess, chorale, chorus, computers, dance, debate, drama, ethnic, gay, honors, international, jazz band, leadership, literary magazine, musical theater, newspaper, opera, orchestra, pep band, political, professional, radio and TV, religious, social, social service, special interest, student government, symphony, and yearbook. Popular campus events include Family Weekend, Plant Park Art Festival, and Global Village Day.

Sports: There are 6 intercollegiate sports for men and 8 for women, and 12 intramural sports for men and 12 for women. Facilities include a sports center, a stadium, baseball, softball, practice, and intramural fields, a boat house, an Olympic-size pool, 6 lighted tennis courts, volleyball, basketball, and racquetball courts, activity and fitness centers, a dance studio, the student union, and recreation rooms in each residence hall.

Disabled Students: All of the campus is accessible. Wheelchair ramps, elevators, special parking, specially equipped rest rooms, lowered drinking fountains, and lowered telephones are available.

Services: Counseling and information services are available, as is tutoring in every subject. There is remedial math, reading, and writing.

Campus Safety and Security: Measures include 24-hour foot and vehicle patrol, self-defense education, escort service, and shuttle buses. There are informal discussions, pamphlets/posters/films, emergency telephones, lighted pathways/sidewalks, and and a full-service, on-campus security office.

Programs of Study: UT confers B.A., B.S., B.F.A., B.L.S., B.M., and B.S.N. degrees. Associate and master's degrees are also awarded. Bachelor's degrees are awarded in BIOLOGICAL SCIENCE (biochemistry, biology/biological science, and marine science), BUSINESS (accounting, banking and finance, business administration and management, business economics, international business management, and marketing/retailing/merchandising), COMMUNICATIONS AND THE ARTS (art, communications, creative writing, English, fine arts, graphic design, music, performing arts, and Spanish), COMPUTER AND PHYSICAL SCIENCE (chemistry, information sciences and systems, and mathematics), EDUCATION (elementary, and secondary), ENGINEERING AND ENVIRONMENTAL DESIGN (computer graphics, and environmental science), HEALTH PROFESSIONS (exercise science, and nursing), SOCIAL SCIENCE (criminology, economics, history, international studies, liberal arts/general studies, political science/government, psychology, social science, sociology, and urban studies). Marine biology and chemistry are the strongest academically. Management, marine science, and communication are the largest.

Required: To graduate, students must maintain a minimum GPA of 2.0 in at least 124 credit hours, including the 2-year Learning Community, 11 each in humanities/fine arts and social science, 6 in natural science, global issues, non-Western studies, and writing-intensive course work. The requirements for individual majors vary.

Special: Students may participate in internships, work-study programs on campus, study abroad in 7 countries, a Washington semester, and an Oxford semester program. UT also offers summer marine science courses at the Gulf Coast Research Laboratory, nondegree study, pass/fail options, and credit for life, military, and work experience. There are 15 national honor societies, a freshman honors program, and 11 departmental honors program.

Faculty/Classroom: 66% of faculty are male; 34%, female. All teach undergraduates. No introductory courses are taught by graduate students. The average class size in an introductory lecture is 19; in a laboratory, 19; and in a regular course, 19.

Admissions: 81% of the 2001-2002 applicants were accepted. The SAT I scores for the 2001-2002 freshman class were: Math--37% below 500, 48% between 500 and 599, 14% between 600 and 700, and 1% above 700. The ACT scores for the 2001-2002 freshman class were: 3% below 17, 48% between 18 and 23, 45% between 24 and 29, and 4% between 30 and 36. 55% of the current freshmen were in the top fifth of their class; 82% were in the top two fifths.

Requirements: The SAT I or ACT is required. In addition, candidates for admission should have completed 4 credits in English, 2 each in math, science, and social studies, and 5 in college-preparatory electives. The GED is accepted. A portfolio or an audition is required for specific art and music programs. UT requires applicants to be in the upper 60% of their class. A GPA of 2.5 is required. AP and CLEP credits are accepted. UT accepts applications on computer disk and on-line.

Procedure: Freshmen are admitted fall, spring, and summer. Entrance exams should be taken by the end of the junior year or early in the senior year. There is a deferred admissions plan. Application deadlines are open. The application fee is $35.

Transfer: 259 transfer students enrolled in 2001-2002. Applicants should have earned 17 college credits with a minimum GPA of 2.0. 31 credits of 124 must be completed at UT.

Visiting: There are regularly scheduled orientations for prospective students, including a campus tour and an interview with an admissions counselor, faculty, and others as requested. There are guides for informal visits and visitors may sit in on classes and stay overnight. To schedule a visit, contact the Admissions Office.

Financial Aid: In 2001-2002, 86% of all students received some form of financial aid. 78% of freshmen and 80% of continuing students received need-based aid. The average freshman award was $13,100. Of that total, scholarships or need-based grants averaged $6512 ($8200 maximum); loans averaged $2717 ($5125 maximum); and work contracts averaged $2000 (maximum). 26% of undergraduates work part time. Average annual earnings from campus work are $1500. The average financial indebtedness of the 2001 graduate was $18,500. UT is a member of CSS. The FAFSA is required. The fall application deadline is open.

International Students: There are 275 international students enrolled. The school actively recruits these students. They must score 550 on the written TOEFL.

Computers: The mainframe is an HP 3000. Students may use 160 Macs and PCs in the computer labs in the computer center, student union, and classroom buildings. There is also a Sun lab with workstations and a multimedia decision support center. All students may access the system. There are no time limits and no fees.

Graduates: In 2001, 535 bachelor's degrees were awarded. The most popular majors were business (32%), education (11%), and communication (8%). In an average class, 44% graduate in 4 years, 52% in 5 years, and 53% in 6 years. 174 companies recruited on campus in 2000-2001. Of the 2000 graduating class, 14% were enrolled in graduate school within 6 months of graduation and all were employed.

Admissions Contact: Barbara P. Strickler, Vice President, Enrollment.
E-mail: *admissions@ut.edu* Web: *www.ut.edu*

UNIVERSITY OF WEST FLORIDA — A-1
Pensacola, FL 32514-5750 — (850) 474-2230
(800) 263-1074; Fax: (850) 474-3360

Full-time: 2099 men, 2903 women	**Faculty:** 381; IIA, --$
Part-time: 1057 men, 1363 women	**Ph.D.s:** 83%
Graduate: 603 men, 1027 women	**Student/Faculty:** 13 to 1
Year: semesters, summer session	**Tuition:** $2078 ($8438)
Application Deadline: June 30	**Room & Board:** $5440
Freshman Class: 2400 applied, 2018 accepted, 870 enrolled	
SAT I Verbal/Math: 540/530	**ACT:** 23 **COMPETITIVE**

The University of West Florida, founded in 1963, is a public, liberal arts institution that is part of the State University system of Florida. There are 3 undergraduate and 3 graduate schools. In addition to regional accreditation, UWF has baccalaureate program accreditation with AACSB, ABET, CSWE, NCATE, and NLN. The library contains 416,380 volumes, 1,635,474 microform items, and 7311 audiovisual forms/CDs, and subscribes to 5032 periodicals. Computerized library services include the card catalog, interlibrary loans, and database searching. Special learning facilities include a learning resource center, art gallery, radio station, TV station, and and an archeology museum. The 1600-acre campus is in a suburban area 10 miles north of downtown Pensacola. Including residence halls, there are 71 buildings.

Student Life: 87% of undergraduates are from Florida. Others are from 49 states, 82 foreign countries, and Canada. 78% are white; 10% African American. The average age of freshmen is 19; all undergraduates, 25.

Housing: 1250 students can be accommodated in college housing, which includes coed dormitories and on-campus apartments. In addition, there are honors houses. On-campus housing is available on a first-come, first-served basis. 85% of students commute. All students may keep cars.

Activities: There are 6 national fraternities and 5 national sororities. There are 85 groups on campus, including art, band, cheerleading, choir, chorale, chorus, debate, drama, ethnic, film, forensics, gay, honors, international, jazz band, literary magazine, newspaper, orchestra, political, professional, radio and TV, religious, social, social service, sports, student government, and symphony.

Sports: There are 6 intercollegiate sports for men and 6 for women, and 16 intramural sports for men and 16 for women. Facilities include facilities for baseball, track, tennis, racquetball, handball, softball, soccer, swimming, diving, weight lifting, and aerobics.

Disabled Students: All of the campus is accessible. Wheelchair ramps, elevators, special parking, specially equipped rest rooms, special class scheduling, and lowered drinking fountains are available.

Services: Counseling and information services are available, as is tutoring in most subjects. There is remedial math, reading, and writing. Remedial courses are offered on campus by the local community college.

Campus Safety and Security: Measures include 24-hour foot and vehicle patrol, escort service, informal discussions, and pamphlets/posters/films. There are emergency telephones and lighted pathways/sidewalks.

Programs of Study: UWF confers B.A., B.S., B.F.A., B.S.B.A., B.S.C.E., B.S.E.E., and B.S.N degrees. Associate, master's, and doctoral degrees are also awarded. Bachelor's degrees are awarded in BIOLOGICAL SCIENCE (biology/biological science, and marine biology), BUSINESS (accounting, banking and finance, business administration and management, business economics, and marketing/retailing/merchandising), COMMUNICATIONS AND THE ARTS (communications, English, music, and studio art), COMPUTER AND PHYSICAL SCIENCE (chemistry, computer science, mathematics, physics, and statistics), EDUCATION (art, early childhood, elementary, health, middle school, music, and secondary), ENGINEERING AND ENVIRONMENTAL DESIGN (computer engineering, and electrical/electronics engineering), HEALTH PROFESSIONS (medical laboratory technology, nursing, predentistry, and premedicine), SOCIAL SCIENCE (criminal justice, history, philosophy, political science/government, prelaw, psychology, religion, social science, social work, and sociology). Accounting, communication arts, and management are the strongest academically. Communication arts, psychology, and business are the largest.

Required: To graduate, students must maintain a 2.0 GPA and complete 120 semester hours with a minimum of 24 hours in the major and 24 hours in upper-division courses.

Special: Internships are arranged on an individual basis through a student's major department. The college offers pass/fail options and credit for military experience. A 3-2 engineering degree is also offered. There are 5 national honor societies and a freshman honors program.

Faculty/Classroom: 68% of faculty are male; 32%, female. All teach undergraduates. The average class size in an introductory lecture is 30; in a laboratory, 21; and in a regular course, 21.

Admissions: 84% of the 2001-2002 applicants were accepted. The SAT I scores for the 2001-2002 freshman class were: Verbal--25% below 500, 50% between 500 and 599, and 25% between 600 and 700; Math--25% below 500, 50% between 500 and 599, and 25% between 600 and 700.

Requirements: The SAT I or ACT is required. In addition, students must have completed 4 years of English, 3 each of math, science, and social studies, and 2 of a foreign language. A GPA of 2.0 is required. AP and CLEP credits are accepted. Important factors in the admissions decision are advanced placement or honor courses, evidence of special talent, and geographic diversity. Applications are accepted on-line at the school's web site.

Procedure: Freshmen are admitted to all sessions. Entrance exams should be taken by the fall of the senior year. There are early admissions and deferred admissions plans. Applications should be filed by June 30 for fall entry, December 1 for spring entry, and April 1 for summer entry, along with a $20 fee. Notification is sent on a rolling basis.

Transfer: 1054 transfer students enrolled in 2001-2002. Applicants must have a 2.0 GPA and a 2.0 at their last institution. Transfer students with fewer than 60 semester hours of transferable credit must meet freshman admission requirements. 30 credits of 120 must be completed at UWF.

Visiting: There are regularly scheduled orientations for prospective students, including 5 Open House Programs per year. There are guides for informal visits and visitors may sit in on classes. To schedule a visit, contact the Admissions Office.

Financial Aid: The CSS/Profile and University of West Florida Request for Financial Aid Consideration form, and SAR are required.

International Students: There are 271 international students enrolled. They must score 525 on the written TOEFL or 193 on the electronic version or take the MELAB. They must and also take the SAT I or the ACT, scoring 970 or 20, respectively.

Computers: The mainframe is an IBM 4381. All students may access the system. There are no time limits and no fees.

Graduates: In 2001, 1286 bachelor's degrees were awarded. The most popular majors were business (22%), education (19%), and psychology (9%).

Admissions Contact: Susie Neeley, Director of Admissions.
E-mail: *admissions@uwf.edu* Web: *www.uwf.edu*

WEBBER COLLEGE
(See Webber International University)

WEBBER INTERNATIONAL UNIVERSITY D-3
(Formerly Webber College)

Babson Park, FL 33827 (863) 638-1431
(800) 741-1844; Fax: (863) 638-1591

Full-time: 219 men, 167 women	**Faculty:** 16
Part-time: 21 men, 44 women	**Ph.D.s:** 54%
Graduate: 19 men, 27 women	**Student/Faculty:** 24 to 1
Year: semesters, summer session	**Tuition:** $10,815
Application Deadline: August 1	**Room & Board:** $3880
Freshman Class: 213 applied, 101 enrolled	
SAT I Verbal/Math: 480/490	**ACT:** 18 **LESS COMPETITIVE**

Webber International University, formerly Webber College, is a privately endowed, nonprofit institution founded in 1927, and offering undergraduate and graduate degrees in business. In addition to regional accreditation, Webber has baccalaureate program accreditation with IACBE. The library contains 28,000 volumes, 105 microform items, and 529 audiovisual forms/CDs, and subscribes to 63 periodicals. Computerized library services include the card catalog, interlibrary loans, and database searching. Special learning facilities include a learning resource center and and Audubon Society museum. The 110-acre campus is in a small town 50 miles east of Tampa and 50 miles south of Orlando. Including residence halls, there are 10 buildings.

Student Life: 64% of undergraduates are from Florida. Others are from 12 states, 36 foreign countries, and Canada. 76% are from public schools. 57% are white; 26% foreign nationals; 10% African American. The average age of freshmen is 19; all undergraduates, 21. 42% do not continue beyond their first year.

Housing: 210 students can be accommodated in college housing, which includes single-sex dormitories. On-campus housing is guaranteed for the freshman year only and is available on a first-come, first-served basis. 55% of students commute. All students may keep cars.

Activities: There are no fraternities or sororities. There are 11 groups on campus, including debate, honors, international, newspaper, political, professional, religious, social, social service, and student government. Popular campus events include Webber Weekend, Christmas Party, and Beach Party.

Sports: There are 7 intercollegiate sports for men and 8 for women, and 4 intramural sports for men and 4 for women. Facilities include 2 gyms, a weight room, tennis courts, 2 racquetball courts, a swimming pool, softball, baseball, and soccer fields, beach volleyball courts, and a lake for water sports.

Disabled Students: 72% of the campus is accessible. Wheelchair ramps, special parking, specially equipped rest rooms, special class scheduling, lowered drinking fountains, and lowered telephones are available.

Services: Counseling and information services are available, as is tutoring in most subjects. There is remedial math, reading, and writing.

Campus Safety and Security: Measures include escort service, informal discussions, pamphlets/posters/films, and lighted pathways/sidewalks. There is a security patrol at night and all weekend.

Programs of Study: Webber confers the B.S. degree. Associate and master's degrees are also awarded. Bachelor's degrees are awarded in BUSINESS (accounting, banking and finance, business administration and management, hotel/motel and restaurant management, international business management, marketing/retailing/merchandising, recreational facilities management, and tourism), and SOCIAL SCIENCE (prelaw). Business administration is the strongest academically and has the largest enrollment.

Required: To graduate, all students must complete 120 credit hours, including courses in their major, a 40-credit general curriculum, and a 30-credit business core. A GPA of 2.0 or better must be maintained. Students must pass the college's required English courses and meet its writing requirements. All students must take at least 3 computer courses.

Special: Cross-registration with other schools may be arranged. Internships are required for international tourism, hospitality management, and sport management majors. Study abroad is available in 2 countries. There is 1 national honor society and 1 departmental honors program.

Faculty/Classroom: 77% of faculty are male; 23%, female. All teach undergraduates, 15% do research, and 15% do both. The average class size in an introductory lecture is 35; in a laboratory, 10; and in a regular course, 21.

Admissions: The SAT I scores for the 2001-2002 freshman class were: Verbal--82% below 500, 16% between 500 and 599, and 2% between 600 and 700; Math--64% below 500, 34% between 500 and 599, and 2% above 700. The ACT scores were 45% below 21, 49% between 21 and 23, 5% between 24 and 26, and 1% between 27 and 28.

Requirements: The SAT I or ACT is required with a minimum composite score of 860 on the SAT I or 18 on the ACT. Applicants should be graduates of accredited secondary schools and have completed 3 years each of English, math, and science and 2 years of social studies. An essay is also required. The GED is accepted. A GPA of 2.0 is required. AP and CLEP credits are accepted. Important factors in the admissions decision are personality/intangible qualities, recommendations by school officials, and leadership record. Applications are accepted on-line at the school's web site.

Procedure: Freshmen are admitted to all sessions. Entrance exams should be taken during the senior year. There are early decision, early admissions, and deferred admissions plans. Applications should be filed by August 1 for fall entry and December 1 for spring entry, along with a $35 fee. Notification is sent on a rolling basis.

Transfer: Applicants must have a minimum GPA of 2.0 with 15 credit hours, leave their previous institution in good academic standing, and submit a letter of recommendation and a student essay. Students with fewer than 15 credits must meet freshman requirements. 30 credits of 120 must be completed at Webber.

Visiting: There are guides for informal visits and visitors may sit in on classes and stay overnight. To schedule a visit, contact the Director of Admissions at (863) 638-2911.

Financial Aid: In 2001-2002, 98% of all students received some form of financial aid. 61% of freshmen and 51% of continuing students received need-based aid. The average freshman award was $12,585. Of that total, scholarships or need-based grants averaged $10,523 ($11,692 maximum); loans averaged $2617; and work contracts averaged $600 ($1000 maximum). 46% of undergraduates work part time. Average annual earnings from campus work are $1000. The average financial indebtedness of the 2001 graduate was $11,813. Webber is a member of CSS. The FAFSA is required. The fall application deadline is August 1.

International Students: There are 115 international students enrolled. The school actively recruits these students. They must score 500 on the written TOEFL or 173 on the electronic version and also take the SAT I or the ACT, scoring 860 on the SAT I or 18 on the ACT.

Computers: There are 35 PCs located at the computer center with direct connections to the Internet. All students may access the system. There are no time limits and no fees. It is strongly recommended that all students have a personal computer.

Graduates: In 2001, 125 bachelor's degrees were awarded.

Admissions Contact: Dr. Deb Miliken, Executive Vice President. A video is available. E-mail: *admissions@webber.edu*
Web: *www.webber.edu*

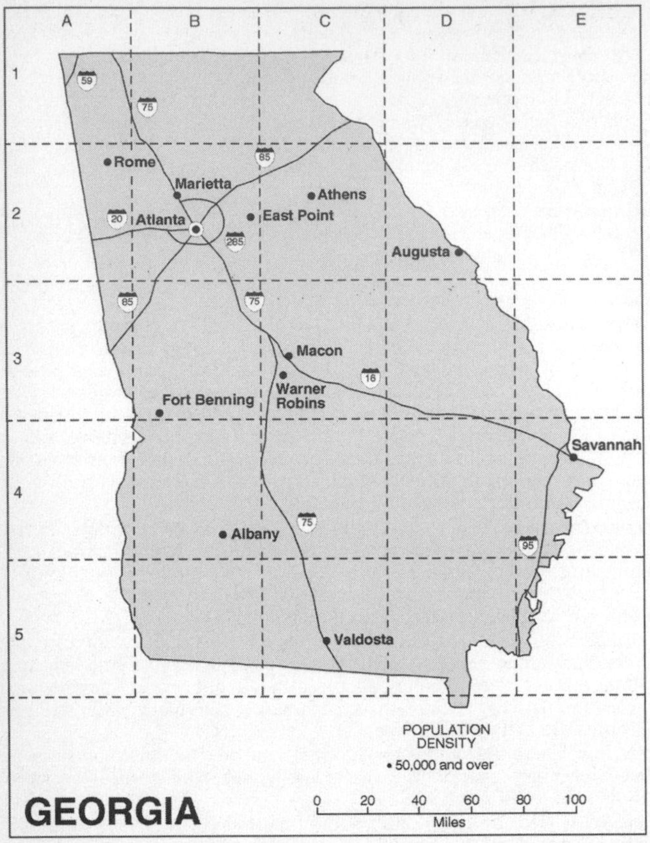

AGNES SCOTT COLLEGE
B-2

Atlanta/Decatur, GA 30030

(404) 471-6285
(800) 868-8602; Fax: (404) 471-6414

Full-time: 822 women	**Faculty:** 81; IIB, +$
Part-time: 1 man, 31 women	**Ph.D.s:** 100%
Graduate: 2 men, 14 women	**Student/Faculty:** 10 to 1
Year: semesters	**Tuition:** $17,670
Application Deadline: March 1	**Room & Board:** $7280

Freshman Class: 709 applied, 525 accepted, 223 enrolled

SAT I or ACT: required **VERY COMPETITIVE**

Agnes Scott College, founded in 1889, is an independent liberal arts college for women, and is affiliated with the Presbyterian Church (U.S.A.). The library contains 211,025 volumes, 31,979 microform items, and 14,334 audiovisual forms/CDs, and subscribes to 1111 periodicals. Computerized library services include the card catalog, interlibrary loans, and database searching. Special learning facilities include a learning resource center, art gallery, planetarium, interactive learning center, multimedia classroom, and center for writing and speaking. The 100-acre campus is in an urban area 6 miles from downtown Atlanta. Including residence halls, there are 24 buildings.

Student Life: 52% of undergraduates are from Georgia. Others are from 39 states, 24 foreign countries, and Canada. 76% are from public schools. 59% are white; 22% African American. 69% are Protestant; 18% Catholic. The average age of freshmen is 18; all undergraduates, 21. 20% do not continue beyond their first year.

Housing: 800 students can be accommodated in college housing, which includes dormitories and on-campus apartments. In addition, there are speial interest houses. On-campus housing is guaranteed for all 4 years. 91% of students live on campus. All students may keep cars.

Activities: There are no fraternities. There are 70 groups on campus, including choir, chorale, dance, drama, ethnic, gay, honors, international, jazz singing, literary magazine, musical theater, newspaper, orchestra, political, professional, religious, social, social service, student government, and yearbook. Popular campus events include Black Cat, street dances, holiday parties, and Senior Investiture.

Sports: Facilities include a gym with a regulation basketball court, an 8-lane indoor pool, a soccer field, tennis courts, a weight room, a track, an aerobics room, and dance studios.

Disabled Students: 90% of the campus is accessible. Wheelchair ramps, elevators, special parking, specially equipped rest rooms, special class scheduling, lowered drinking fountains, lowered telephones, and lifts are available.

Services: Counseling and information services are available, as is tutoring in some subjects, including classical languages, English, math, physics, biology, psychology, chemistry, astronomy, French, German, Spanish, and Japanese. There is a reader service for the blind and centers for writing and speaking.

Campus Safety and Security: Measures include 24-hour foot and vehicle patrol, self-defense education, escort service, and shuttle buses. There are informal discussions, pamphlets/posters/films, emergency telephones, lighted pathways/sidewalks, and reimbursement for taxi service for cross-registration students, and evening shuttle buses.

Programs of Study: Agnes Scott confers the B.A. degree. Master's degrees are also awarded. Bachelor's degrees are awarded in BIOLOGICAL SCIENCE (biochemistry, and biology/biological science), COMMUNICATIONS AND THE ARTS (classical languages, classics, creative writing, dramatic arts, English, fine arts, French, German, music, and Spanish), COMPUTER AND PHYSICAL SCIENCE (astrophysics, chemistry, mathematics, and physics), SOCIAL SCIENCE (anthropology, classical/ancient civilization, economics, history, international relations, philosophy, political science/government, psychology, religion, sociology, and women's studies). Biology, English, and psychology are the largest.

Required: Requirements for graduation include first-year seminar and courses in English composition and reading, foreign language, and phys ed, as well as courses in literature and fine arts, religious or philosophical thought, historical studies or classical civilization, natural science, math, social science, and social and cultural analysis. Students must complete 130 credit hours, including 32 to 52 in the major, with a 2.0 GPA.

Special: There is cross-registration through ARCHE (a 21-member consortium), and more than 300 credit and noncredit internships are available. There is a 3-2 engineering program with the Georgia Institute of Technology, and the college offers dual, student-designed, and interdisciplinary majors, including anthropology/sociology, creative writing/ English literature, math/economics, math/physics, astrophysics, women's studies, and international relations. Pass/fail options are also available. Opportunities for study abroad include exchange programs, a Global Awareness program, which combines fall and spring semester class work with a January travel experience, and Global Connections, a component added to a regular course offering that includes a 2- to 3-week travel and intercultural experience. Also offered are a Washington semester, an Atlanta semester, the PLEN Public Policy Semester, the Mills College Exchange, and a 3-4 architecture degree with Washington University. Teacher certification and Language Across the Curriculum programs are offered. B.A. degree requirements may be completed in 3 years. There are 9 national honor societies, including Phi Beta Kappa.

Faculty/Classroom: 40% of faculty are male; 60%, female. All both teach and do research. No introductory courses are taught by graduate students. The average class size in an introductory lecture is 20; in a laboratory, 13; and in a regular course, 15.

Admissions: 74% of the 2001-2002 applicants were accepted. 68% of the current freshmen were in the top fifth of their class; 9% were in the top two fifths. 3 freshmen graduated first in their class.

Requirements: The SAT I or ACT is required. In addition, applicants (except early admission) must graduate from an accredited secondary school or have a GED. A total of 16 academic credits is recommended, including 4 years of English, 3 of math, and 2 each of a foreign language, science, and social studies. An essay is required, and an interview is recommended. An audition is required for those seeking a music scholarship. AP credits are accepted. Important factors in the admissions decision are advanced placement or honor courses, recommendations by school officials, and leadership record. Applications are accepted online via CollegeLink, Apply, Common Application, Peterson's, EXPAN. Next Stop College, CollegeNET, and Georgia Mentor.

Procedure: Freshmen are admitted fall and spring. Entrance exams should be taken late in the junior year or by January of the senior year. There are early decision, early admissions, and deferred admissions plans. Early decision applications should be filed by November 15; regular applications, by March 1 for fall entry, and November 1 for spring entry, along with a $35 fee. Notification of early decision is sent December 15; regular decision, March 1. 30 early decision candidates were accepted for the 2001-2002 class. 6% of all applicants are on a waiting list; 9 were accepted in 2001.

Transfer: 17 transfer students enrolled in 2001-2002. A minimum GPA of 3.0 is recommended, as is an interview and a letter of recommendation from a professor. 64 credits of 130 must be completed at Agnes Scott.

Visiting: There are regularly scheduled orientations for prospective students, consisting of classes, tours, interviews, residence hall experiences, and informational sessions. There are guides for informal visits and visitors may sit in on classes and stay overnight. To schedule a visit, contact the Office of Admission at (800) 868-8602, ext. 6285.

Financial Aid: In 2000-2001, 97% of all freshmen and 92% of continuing students received some form of financial aid. 68% of freshmen and 66% of continuing students received need-based aid. The average freshman award was $17,850. Of that total, scholarships or need-based grants averaged $13,095; loans averaged $2451 ($2625 maximum); and work contracts averaged $781 ($1600 maximum). 50% of undergraduates work part time. Average annual earnings from campus work are $1600. The average financial indebtedness of the 2001 graduate was $16,891. Agnes Scott is a member of CSS. The FAFSA and the college's own financial statement are required. The CSS/Profile is required for early decision financial aid applicants. The fall application deadline is February 15.

International Students: There are 40 international students enrolled. The school actively recruits these students. They must also take the TOEFL with a score of 600 recommended, and also take the SAT I or the ACT.

Computers: The mainframe is an IBM RS/6000. There are more than 120 computers on campus for student use, with more than 60 PCs located in 4 computer centers and 3 satellite centers in the residence halls, and 8 Macs located in the fine arts building, and 5 in the language lab. All computers on campus are a part of the campus network, which provides Internet access to all students. Residence hall rooms have 1 port per student. All students may access the system. There are no time limits and no fees.

Graduates: In 2001, 152 bachelor's degrees were awarded. The most popular majors were economics/business (16%), psychology (12%), and English (11%). In an average class, 5% graduate in 3 years, 69% in 4 years, 70% in 5 years, and 71% in 6 years. 33 companies recruited on campus in 2000-2001. Of the 2000 graduating class, 26% were enrolled in graduate school within 6 months of graduation and 52% were employed.

Admissions Contact: Stephanie Balmer, Associate VP for Enrollment/Director of Admission. A video is available.
E-mail: *admission@agnesscott.edu* Web: *http://www.agnesscott.edu*

ALBANY STATE UNIVERSITY B-4

Albany, GA 31705-2796 **(229) 430-7862**
(800) 822-RAMS; Fax: (229) 430-3936

Full-time: 851 men, 1608 women	Faculty: 128
Part-time: 150 men, 406 women	Ph.D.s: 52%
Graduate: 114 men, 327 women	Student/Faculty: 19 to 1
Year: semesters, summer session	Tuition: $2398 ($8026)
Application Deadline: July 1	Room & Board: $3366
Freshman Class: 2663 applied, 1310 accepted, 417 enrolled	
SAT I Verbal/Math: 450/450	ACT: 17 COMPETITIVE+

Albany State University, founded in 1903, is a state-supported institution within the University System of Georgia, offering programs in liberal arts, business, health fields, and teacher education. There are 4 undergraduate schools and 1 graduate school. In addition to regional accreditation, Albany State has baccalaureate program accreditation with ACBSP, NCATE, and NLN. The library contains 351,467 volumes, 743,621 microform items, and 3431 audiovisual forms/CDs, and subscribes to 169,097 periodicals. Computerized library services include the card catalog, interlibrary loans, and database searching. Special learning facilities include a radio station. The 144-acre campus is in an urban area 175 miles south of Atlanta. Including residence halls, there are 28 buildings.

Student Life: 98% of undergraduates are from Georgia. 91% are African American. The average age of all undergraduates is 24.

Housing: More than 1000 students can be accommodated in college housing which includes single-sex dormitories. On-campus housing is available on a first-come, first-served basis and is available on a lottery system for upperclassmen. Alcohol is not permitted. All students may keep cars.

Activities: There are 3 national fraternities and 3 national sororities. There are many groups and organizations on campus, including art, band, cheerleading, choir, chorale, computers, dance, debate, drama, drill team, honors, jazz band, marching band, musical theater, pep band, political, professional, religious, social, social service, and student government. Popular campus events include Honors Day and Founders Day.

Sports: There are 5 intercollegiate sports for men and 6 for women, and 2 intramural sports for men and 1 for women. Facilities include tennis courts, baseball and softball fields, an Olympic-size pool, a recreation room, and an all-weather track.

Disabled Students: 90% of the campus is accessible. Wheelchair ramps, elevators, special parking, specially equipped rest rooms, lowered drinking fountains, and lowered telephones are available.

Services: There is remedial math, reading, and writing.

Campus Safety and Security: Measures include 24-hour foot and vehicle patrol, escort service, pamphlets/posters/films, and emergency telephones. There are lighted pathways/sidewalks.

Programs of Study: Albany Stat confers B.A., B.S., B.S.N., and B.S.W. degrees. Associate and master's degrees are also awarded. Bachelor's degrees are awarded in BIOLOGICAL SCIENCE (biology/biological science), BUSINESS (accounting, marketing/retailing/merchandising, and office supervision and management), COMMUNICATIONS AND THE ARTS (art, dramatic arts, English, fine arts, French, music, Spanish, and speech/debate/rhetoric), COMPUTER AND PHYSICAL SCIENCE (chemistry, computer science, information sciences and systems, and mathematics), EDUCATION (early childhood, health, middle school, music, physical, science, and special), HEALTH PROFESSIONS (allied health and nursing), SOCIAL SCIENCE (criminal justice, forensic studies, history, political science/government, psychology, social work, and sociology).

Required: To graduate, all students must complete 120 semester hours, including 30 in the major. The core curriculum includes 12 hours of social science, 10 to 11 of science/math/technology, 9 of essential composition and math skills, 6 of humanities/fine arts, 5 of leadership and global awareness, and 3 of phys ed. Most majors require a minimum GPA of 2.25. Students must take a Regents exam to assess English language skills competency, pass a comprehensive exam in their major, and/or score satisfactorily on the aptitude section of the GRE.

Special: The university offers co-op programs in all majors, 2+2 programs with Darton College, dual majors in social sciences, and 3-2 engineering degrees with the Georgia Institute of Technology. Several work-study programs and a gerontology training program are available. Albany State participates in the Georgian Intern Programs. All language majors are eligible to study abroad. There are 5 national honor societies, a freshman honors program, and 4 departmental honors programs.

Faculty/Classroom: 56% of faculty are male; 44%, female.

Admissions: 49% of the 2001-2002 applicants were accepted. The SAT I scores for the 2001-2002 freshman class were: Verbal--79% below 500, 20% between 500 and 599, and 1% between 600 and 700; Math--78% below 500, 19% between 500 and 599, and 3% between 600 and 700. The ACT scores were 86% below 21, 9% between 21 and 23, 4% between 24 and 26, and 1% between 27 and 28.

Requirements: The SAT I or ACT is required; the student must have a minimum verbal score of 430 and a math score of 400 on the SAT I, or an English score of 17 and a math score of 16 on the ACT. Applicants must be graduates of an accredited secondary school and have completed 4 years each of English and math, 3 each of science and social sciences, and 2 of a foreign language. A GED is accepted; however, GED students must take and pass SAT II: Subject tests in areas where college-preparatory courses are deficient. A GPA of 2.0 is required. AP and CLEP credits are accepted.

Procedure: Freshmen are admitted to all sessions. Entrance exams should be taken by December of the senior year. There is an early admissions plan. Applications should be filed by July 1 for fall entry, November 15 for spring entry, and April 15 for summer entry. The fall application fee was $20.

Transfer: Applicants must provide official transcripts of all previous college work. Students with fewer than 30 transferable semester hours must meet freshman requirements. 30 credits of 120 must be completed at Albany State.

Visiting: There are regularly scheduled orientations for prospective students, consisting of summer and fall orientations and planned campus visitations. There are guides for informal visits and visitors may sit in on classes. To schedule a visit, contact the Office of Student Affairs at (229) 430-4742.

Financial Aid: The FAFSA is required. The priority fall application deadline is April 15.

International Students: Students must score 500 on the written TOEFL and also take the SAT I (scoring 830), the ACT, or the college's own entrance exam.

Computers: The mainframe is an HP 1500. 4 computer labs are available to students, including a 24-hour lab. Students can access the Internet and World Wide Web. All students may access the system. There are no time limits and no fees.

Graduates: In 2001, 485 bachelor's degrees were awarded. The most popular majors were criminal justice (9%), sociology (7%), and allied health science (6%).

Admissions Contact: Fred Suttles, Assistant Director of Recruitment. A video is available. E-mail: *fsuttles@asurams.edu*
Web: *www.asurams.edu*

AMERICAN COLLEGE
(See American InterContinental University)

AMERICAN INTERCONTINENTAL UNIVERSITY (Formerly American College) B-2

Atlanta, GA 30326 (404) 965-5721
(800) 999-4248; Fax: (404) 965-5701

Full-time: 280 men, 710 women	**Faculty:** 37
Part-time: none	**Ph.D.s:** 99%
Graduate: none	**Student/Faculty:** 15 to 1
Year: quarters, summer session	**Tuition:** $12,000
Application Deadline: open	**Room & Board:** n/app
Freshman Class: n/av	
SAT I or ACT: not required	**NONCOMPETITIVE**

American InterContinental University, formerly The American College, is a private institution founded in 1977. AIU offers undergraduate programs in interior design, visual communication, fashion design, fashion marketing, business, video production, and information technology. Figures in above capsule are approximate. In addition to regional accreditation, AIU has baccalaureate program accreditation with FIDER. The library contains 23,000 volumes, 17 microform items, and 600 audiovisual forms/CDs, and subscribes to 300 periodicals. Computerized library services include the card catalog, interlibrary loans, and database searching. Special learning facilities include a learning resource center and art gallery. The 1-acre campus is in an urban area in north Atlanta. Including residence halls, there is 1 building.

Student Life: 62% of undergraduates are from out of state, mostly the South. Others are from 40 states, 54 foreign countries, and Canada. 45% are white; 25% African American; 25% foreign nationals. The average age of freshmen is 19; all undergraduates, 24.

Housing: 200 students can be accommodated in college housing, which includes single-sex off-campus apartments. On-campus housing is available on a first-come, first-served basis. Alcohol is not permitted. All students may keep cars.

Activities: There are no fraternities or sororities. There are 6 groups on campus, including newspaper, professional, social, and student government. Popular campus events include International Day, Career Days, and Fashion Association Bazaar.

Sports: There is no sports program at AIU.

Disabled Students: Wheelchair ramps, elevators, special parking, specially equipped rest rooms, special class scheduling, and lowered telephones are available.

Services: There is remedial math, reading, and writing.

Campus Safety and Security: Measures include 24-hour foot and vehicle patrol, escort service, informal discussions, and pamphlets/posters/films. There are emergency telephones and lighted pathways/sidewalks.

Programs of Study: AIU confers B.B.A. and B.F.A. degrees. Associate degrees are also awarded. Bachelor's degrees are awarded in BUSINESS (business administration and management and fashion merchandising), COMMUNICATIONS AND THE ARTS (video), COMPUTER AND PHYSICAL SCIENCE (information sciences and systems), ENGINEERING AND ENVIRONMENTAL DESIGN (commercial art and interior design), SOCIAL SCIENCE (fashion design and technology). Interior design and visual communication are the strongest academically. Interior design and visual communication are the largest.

Required: In addition to specific requirements for individual programs of study, all students must complete 25 credit hours each in humanities and social sciences and 5 credit hours in math. Students may substitute 10 hours of a foreign language for 10 hours of social science. 190 quarter credit hours are required to graduate, with 140 in the major and a minimum GPA of 2.0.

Special: Students may earn up to 20 credit hours in internships. Study abroad in London and Dubai is offered. All majors offer accelerated degree opportunities. A dual major in fashion marketing and design is available. There is a freshman honors program.

Faculty/Classroom: 39% of faculty are male; 61%, female. All teach undergraduates. The average class size in an introductory lecture is 25; in a laboratory, 16; and in a regular course, 18.

Requirements: Applicants should be graduates of a secondary school and should submit 2 personal references. The GED is accepted. Applications may be made on-line. A GPA of 2.0 is required. AP and CLEP credits are accepted. Important factors in the admissions decision are personality/intangible qualities, leadership record, and evidence of special talent.

Procedure: Freshmen are admitted to all sessions. There is an early admissions plan. Application deadlines are open. The fall 2001 application fee was $35.

Transfer: Transfer students must have a minimum 2.0. GPA. 2 personal references must be submitted. 60 credits of 190 must be completed at AIU.

Visiting: There are regularly scheduled orientations for prospective students. There are guides for informal visits and visitors may sit in on classes. To schedule a visit, contact Suzanne McBride in Admissions.

Financial Aid: 76% of undergraduates work part time. Average annual earnings from campus work are $900. AIU is a member of CSS. The CSS/Profile or FAFSA and the college's own financial statement are required. Check with the school for current deadlines.

International Students: The school actively recruits these students. They must score 500 on the written TOEFL and also take the college's own test.

Computers: There are 76 PCs available to students, 40 in a classroom setting and 36 in a computer lab. All students may access the system. There are no time limits and no fees.

Admissions Contact: Marita Carey, Director of Admissions.
E-mail: *mcarey@aiuniv.edu*

ARMSTRONG ATLANTIC STATE UNIVERSITY E-4

Savannah, GA 31419-1997 (912) 927-5277
(800) 633-2349; Fax: (912) 921-5462

Full-time: 992 men, 1921 women	**Faculty:** 241; IIA, --$
Part-time: 649 men, 1499 women	**Ph.D.s:** 69%
Graduate: 143 men, 543 women	**Student/Faculty:** 12 to 1
Year: semesters, summer session	**Tuition:** $2314 ($8110)
Application Deadline: July 10	**Room & Board:** $4770
Freshman Class: n/av	
SAT I Verbal/Math: 510/500	**COMPETITIVE**

Armstrong Atlantic State University, founded in 1935, is a public institution within the University System of Georgia, offering programs in the arts and sciences, education, and the health professions. There are 3 undergraduate and 3 graduate schools. In addition to regional accreditation, AASU has baccalaureate program accreditation with CAHEA, NASM, NCATE, and NLN. The library contains 206,204 volumes, 651,657 microform items, and 13,145 audiovisual forms/CDs, and subscribes to 1166 periodicals. Computerized library services include the card catalog, interlibrary loans, and database searching. Special learning facilities include a learning resource center and art gallery. The 250-acre campus is in an urban area. Including residence halls, there are 21 buildings.

Student Life: 90% of undergraduates are from Georgia. Others are from 48 states, 51 foreign countries, and Canada. 70% are white; 22% African American. The average age of all undergraduates is 26. 35% do not continue beyond their first year.

Housing: 192 students can be accommodated in college housing, which includes single-sex on-campus apartments. On-campus housing is available on a first-come, first-served basis. 96% of students commute. Alcohol is not permitted. All students may keep cars.

Activities: Tthere are 2 national sororities. There are no fraternities. There are 49 groups on campus, including band, cheerleading, choir, chorus, computers, dance, drama, ethnic, gay, honors, international, jazz band, literary magazine, newspaper, pep band, political, professional, religious, student government, and yearbook. Popular campus events include AASU Celebrates and International Culture Day.

Sports: There are 4 intercollegiate sports for men and 4 for women. Facilities include an indoor pool, a gym, a weight room, an indoor running track, tennis courts, and playing fields.

Disabled Students: 80% of the campus is accessible. Wheelchair ramps, elevators, special parking, specially equipped rest rooms, special class scheduling, and specially equipped living facilities are available.

Services: There is remedial math, reading, and writing.

Campus Safety and Security: Measures include 24-hour foot and vehicle patrol, escort service, pamphlets/posters/films, and emergency telephones. There are lighted pathways/sidewalks.

Programs of Study: AASU confers B.A., B.S., B.G.S., B.Health Science, B.Mus.Ed., B.S.D.H., B.S.Ed., B.S.M.T., and B.S.N. degrees. Associate and master's degrees are also awarded. Bachelor's degrees are awarded in BIOLOGICAL SCIENCE (biology/biological science), COMMUNICATIONS AND THE ARTS (art, dramatic arts, English, music, and Spanish), COMPUTER AND PHYSICAL SCIENCE (applied physics, chemistry, computer science, mathematics, and physical sciences), EDUCATION (art, business, elementary, middle school, music, physical, secondary, and social science), HEALTH PROFESSIONS (dental hygiene, health science, medical laboratory technology, medical technology, nursing, physical therapy, radiological science, respiratory therapy, and speech pathology/audiology), SOCIAL SCIENCE (criminal justice, economics, history, liberal arts/general studies, political science/government, and psychology). Nursing and education are the largest.

Required: The core curriculum consists of 60 hours in humanities, math, natural sciences, and social sciences, and 3 in phys ed. A minimum GPA of 2.0 overall and a grade of C or better in each major course is required. Each student must complete 123 hours, with 29 hours in the major, and must take a comprehensive exam.

Special: AASU offers co-op programs in chemistry, computer science, and engineering, study abroad in 18 countries, many dual-degree programs, including a 3-2 degree in forestry and environmental science with Duke University, and 3-2 engineering programs with several colleges, including Georgia Tech. A general studies degree, cross-registration with Savannah State University, on-campus work-study, and credit for mili-

tary experience are also offered. There are 8 national honor societies, a freshman honors program, and 6 departmental honors programs.
Faculty/Classroom: 52% of faculty are male; 48%, female. No introductory courses are taught by graduate students. The average class size in an introductory lecture is 22; in a laboratory, 18; and in a regular course, 19.
Admissions: The SAT I scores for the 2001-2002 freshman class were: Verbal--43% below 500, 35% between 500 and 599, 20% between 600 and 700, and 2% above 700; Math--49% below 500, 32% between 500 and 599, 17% between 600 and 700, and 2% above 700.
Requirements: The SAT I is required with a minimum score of 420 on each section. Art students must submit a portfolio. Applicants should graduate from an accredited secondary school. A GED may be accepted. College preparatory work should include 4 units of English, 3 each of math, science, and social studies, and 2 of foreign language. Applications are accepted on-line. A GPA of 2.0 is required. AP and CLEP credits are accepted.
Procedure: Freshmen are admitted to all sessions. Applications should be filed by July 10 for fall entry, November 1 for spring entry, and May 1 for summer entry, along with a $20 fee.
Transfer: 511 transfer students enrolled in 2001-2002. Transfer applicants must submit all transcripts and must be in good standing at the last college attended. 30 credits of 123 must be completed at AASU.
Visiting: There are regularly scheduled orientations for prospective students. There are guides for informal visits. To schedule a visit, contact Melanie Mirande at (912) 921-5424.
Financial Aid: The FAFSA and the college's own financial statement are required. The fall application deadline is May 1.
International Students: There were 55 international students enrolled in a recent year. The school actively recruits these students. They must score 500 on the written TOEFL and also take the SAT I or the ACT.
Computers: The mainframe is a DEC VAX 4/750. There are AT&T, Zenith, and Mac PCs for student use in the library and a central computer lab. All students may access the system. There are no time limits and no fees.
Graduates: In 2001, 479 bachelor's degrees were awarded. The most popular majors were nursing (20%), elementary education (13%), and general studies (13%). 71 companies recruited on campus in 2000-2001. Of the 2000 graduating class, 50% were enrolled in graduate school within 6 months of graduation and 95% were employed.
Admissions Contact: Melanie Mirande, Admissions Officer.
E-mail: *melanie_mirande@mailgate.armstrong.edu*
Web: *www.armstrong.edu*

ART INSTITUTE OF ATLANTA

Atlanta, GA 30328 — **B-2**
(770) 394-8300
(800) 275-4242; Fax: (770) 394-0008

Full-time: 1136 men, 996 women	**Faculty:** 72
Part-time: 143 men, 162 women	**Ph.D.s:** 17%
Graduate: none	**Student/Faculty:** 30 to 1
Year: quarters, summer session	**Tuition:** $15,134
Application Deadline: September 1	**Room & Board:** $5490
Freshman Class: n/av	
SAT I or ACT: not required	**SPECIAL**

The Art Institute of Atlanta, founded in 1949, seeks to educate creative professionals. It offers bachelor's degree programs in media arts and animation, digital media production, graphic design, interior design, multimedia and web design, and photographic imaging and associate degree programs in culinary arts, graphic design, multimedia and web design, photographic imaging, and video production. In addition to regional accreditation, the Art Institute has baccalaureate program accreditation with FIDER. The library contains 30,460 volumes and 2428 audiovisual forms/CDs, and subscribes to 159 periodicals. Computerized library services include the card catalog, interlibrary loans, and database searching. Special learning facilities include a learning resource center, art gallery, and an academic support center. The 2-acre campus is in a suburban area in the Metro-Atlanta community of Dunwoody, approximately 5 miles north of the city limits. There is 1 building.
Student Life: 78% of undergraduates are from Georgia. Others are from 39 states and 43 foreign countries. 49% are white; 30% African American. The average age of all undergraduates is 19.
Housing: 268 students can be accommodated in college-sponsored coed off-campus apartments. On-campus housing is available on a first-come, first-served basis. 45-50% of students remain on campus on weekends. All students may keep cars.
Activities: There are no fraternities or sororities. There are 20 groups on campus, including art, dance, gay, international, literary magazine, professional, social service, student government, and yearbook. Popular campus events include gallery openings, Quarterly Welcome Week, and Quarterly Portfolio Show.
Sports: There is 1 intramural sport for men and 1 for women. Facilities include basketball courts and fields for touch football, a swimming pool, and a weight room.
Disabled Students: All of the campus is accessible. Wheelchair ramps, elevators, special parking, specially equipped rest rooms, lowered drinking fountains, and lowered telephones are available.
Services: Counseling and information services are available, as is tutoring in most subjects. There is remedial math, reading, and writing. Tutoring is available in computer classes.
Campus Safety and Security: Measures include 24-hour foot and vehicle patrol, shuttle buses, informal discussions, and pamphlets/posters/films. There are lighted pathways/sidewalks.
Programs of Study: The Art Institute confers the B.F.A. degree. Associate degrees are also awarded. Bachelor's degrees are awarded in COMMUNICATIONS AND THE ARTS (graphic design, multimedia, and photography), ENGINEERING AND ENVIRONMENTAL DESIGN (computer graphics and interior design). Culinary arts, media arts and animation, and graphic design are the largest.
Required: The Art Institute requires 192 credit hours for the B.F.A., with a minimum GPA of 2.0. Students in design-based majors complete a portfolio of work prior to graduation. The core curriculum includes foundation art, English, art history, humanties, math, and science courses.
Special: There is cross-registration with English Language Centers. Internships in all majors, independent study, and study abroad in 2 countries are possible.
Faculty/Classroom: 58% of faculty are male; 42%, female. All teach undergraduates. The average class size in an introductory lecture is 18 and in a regular course, 16.
Requirements: Students must submit SAT I, ACT, ASSET, or COMPASS test scores. (COMPASS testing is offered free at the college to any applicant needing it.) Preference is given to applicants with GPAs of 3.0 or above; a minimum GPA of 2.5 for bachelor's degree applicants is highly recommended. An official transcript showing high school GPA is required; the GED is accepted. An essay and an interview are required. Applications are accepted on-line at the school's web site. AP and CLEP credits are accepted.
Procedure: Freshmen are admitted to all sessions. Entrance exams should be taken prior to the application closing date. There are early admissions and deferred admissions plans. Early decision applications should be filed by September 1, along with a $50 fee. Notification is sent on a rolling basis.
Transfer: In addition to fulfilling general admission requirements, transfer students must also submit all previous college transcripts. 96 credits of 192 must be completed at the Art Institute.
Visiting: There are regularly scheduled orientations for prospective students. There are guides for informal visits and visitors may sit in on classes. To schedule a visit, contact the Office of Admissions.
Financial Aid: 86% of undergraduates work part time. The FAFSA is required.
International Students: There are 104 international students enrolled. The school actively recruits these students. They must score 480 on the written TOEFL.
Computers: Students are allowed full Internet access in each of the college's 12 computer labs. There are 200 microcomputers for student use. All students may access the system. There are no time limits and no fees.
Graduates: In 2001, 40 bachelor's degrees were awarded. 248 companies recruited on campus in 2000-2001.
Admissions Contact: Dr. John Dietrich, Director of Admissions. A video is available. E-mail: *aiaadm@aii.edu* Web: *www.aia.artinstitute.edu*

ATLANTA COLLEGE OF ART

Atlanta, GA 30309 — **B-2**
(404) 733-5100
(800) 832-2104; Fax: (404) 733-5107

Full-time: 220 men, 200 women	**Faculty:** 23
Part-time: 10 men, 10 women	**Ph.D.s:** 87%
Graduate: none	**Student/Faculty:** 18 to 1
Year: semesters, summer session	**Tuition:** $13,000
Application Deadline: open	**Room & Board:** $5600
Freshman Class: n/av	
SAT I or ACT: required	**SPECIAL**

The Atlanta College of Art, founded in 1928, is a private professional art college offering programs in the fine arts, design, and electronic arts. Figures given in above capsule are approximate. In addition to regional accreditation, ACA has baccalaureate program accreditation with NASAD. The library contains 29,000 volumes and 100 audiovisual forms/CDs, and subscribes to 200 periodicals. Computerized library services include interlibrary loans and database searching. Special learning facilities include a learning resource center, art gallery, and printmaking studio, photography darkrooms, computer labs, and experimental sound lab. There is also a sculpture building with a foundry, forge, and woodworking shop. The 6-acre campus is in an urban area in Atlanta. Including residence halls, there are 3 buildings.
Student Life: 52% of undergraduates are from out of state, mostly the South. Others are from 21 states and 6 foreign countries. 80% are from

public schools. 62% are white; 18% African American. 62% are Muslim and Russian Orthodox; 26% Protestant. The average age of freshmen is 18; all undergraduates, 21. 30% do not continue beyond their first year; 55% remain to graduate.

Housing: 120 students can be accommodated in college housing, which includes coed on-campus apartments. On-campus housing is guaranteed for the freshman year only and is available on a first-come, first-served basis. Priority is given to out-of-town students. 70% of students commute. Alcohol is not permitted. All students may keep cars.

Activities: There are no fraternities or sororities. There are 15 groups on campus, including art, ethnic, film, gay, international, photography, social, social service, student government, and yearbook. Popular campus events include Welcome Week, student gallery openings, and Thanksgiving Feast.

Sports: There is no sports program at ACA.

Disabled Students: 95% of the campus is accessible. Wheelchair ramps, elevators, special parking, specially equipped rest rooms, lowered drinking fountains, and lowered telephones are available.

Services: Counseling and information services are available, as is tutoring in some subjects, including liberal arts subjects. A writing lab is available.

Campus Safety and Security: Measures include 24-hour foot and vehicle patrol, self-defense education, escort service, and informal discussions. There are pamphlets/posters/films, emergency telephones, and lighted pathways/sidewalks.

Programs of Study: ACA confers the B.F.A. degree. Bachelor's degrees are awarded in COMMUNICATIONS AND THE ARTS (advertising, design, drawing, fine arts, graphic design, illustration, painting, photography, printmaking, sculpture, and video), ENGINEERING AND ENVIRONMENTAL DESIGN (computer graphics and interior design). Communication design and electronic arts are the largest.

Required: To graduate, the student must complete 42 credits in liberal arts and 78 in studio art for a total of 120 credit hours. Of the 78 studio credits, 33 to 36 must be in the major. The student must also complete 12 credits each in world cultures and art history, 6 in composition, and 3 each in math, science, social science, and humanities. A GPA of 2.0 in the major and overall and a senior exit review are required.

Special: Students may design their own majors, combining 2 or 3 areas of the arts. Special academic programs include cross-registration with the colleges of the University Center of Georgia and other art schools, highly supervised internships, and a dual degree program with Oglethorpe University.

Faculty/Classroom: 65% of faculty are male; 35%, female. All both teach and do research. The average class size in an introductory lecture is 25 and in a regular course, 12.

Requirements: The SAT I or ACT is required. In addition, applicants must have graduated from an accredited secondary school and must submit an essay and portfolio; Either 2 letters of recommendation or 1 letter and an on-campus interview are required. The GED is accepted. Applications are accepted on-line via ACA's web site. ACA requires applicants to be in the upper 50% of their class. A GPA of 2.0 is required. AP credits are accepted. Important factors in the admissions decision are evidence of special talent, personality/intangible qualities, and recommendations by alumni.

Procedure: Freshmen are admitted fall and spring. Entrance exams should be taken during the senior year. There are early admissions and deferred admissions plans. Application deadlines are open. The application fee is $30.

Transfer: Applicants must have a GPA of at least 2.0 and must submit a portfolio and transcripts from previously attended colleges from which credit was earned. Either 2 letters of recommendation or 1 letter and an on-campus interview are required. 39 credits of 120 must be completed at ACA.

Visiting: There are regularly scheduled orientations for prospective students, including open houses, general information sessions, workshops, and special events for prospective students. There are guides for informal visits and visitors may sit in on classes. To schedule a visit, contact the Admissions Office.

Financial Aid: 20% of undergraduates work part time. Average annual earnings from campus work are $1700. ACA is a member of CSS. The FAFSA and the college's own financial statement are required. Check with the school for current deadlines.

International Students: The school actively recruits these students. They must score 500 on the written TOEFL.

Computers: There are 24 computers for student use in the computer center and the electronic arts studio. All students may access the system during scheduled hours. There are no time limits and no fees.

Admissions Contact: Carol Lee Conchar, Director of Enrollment Management. E-mail: *acainfo@woodruff-arts.org* Web: *www.aca.edu*

AUGUSTA STATE UNIVERSITY D-2

Augusta, GA 30904-2200 **(706) 737-1632; Fax: (706) 667-4355**

Full-time: 1176 men, 1893 women
Part-time: 528 men, 1083 women
Graduate: 195 men, 507 women
Year: semesters, summer session
Application Deadline: July 21
Faculty: 195; IIA, --$
Ph.D.s: 71%
Student/Faculty: 16 to 1
Tuition: $2282 ($8078)
Room & Board: n/app
Freshman Class: 1653 applied, 1123 accepted, 802 enrolled
SAT I or ACT: required **COMPETITIVE**

Augusta State University, founded in 1925, is a liberal arts commuter institution within the University System of Georgia. There are 3 undergraduate and 3 graduate schools. In addition to regional accreditation, Augusta State University has baccalaureate program accreditation with AACSB, NASM, NCATE, and NLN. The library contains 430,520 volumes, 946,913 microform items, and 2238 audiovisual forms/CDs, and subscribes to 1030 periodicals. Computerized library services include the card catalog, interlibrary loans, and database searching. Special learning facilities include a learning resource center, art gallery, and radio station. The 72-acre campus is in an urban area 140 miles east of Atlanta on the Georgia-South Carolina border. There are 35 buildings.

Student Life: 89% of undergraduates are from Georgia. Others are from 35 states, 54 foreign countries, and Canada. 95% are from public schools. 63% are white; 22% African American. The average age of freshmen is 19; all undergraduates, 24. 49% do not continue beyond their first year.

Housing: There are no residence halls. All students commute. Alcohol is not permitted. All students may keep cars.

Activities: 2% of men belong to 1 national fraternity; 2% of women belong to 3 national sororities. There are 60 groups on campus, including art, band, cheerleading, choir, chorus, drama, ethnic, honors, international, jazz band, literary magazine, newspaper, orchestra, pep band, photography, political, professional, religious, social, social service, and student government. Popular campus events include Lyceum, Midnight Madness, and SOS.

Sports: There are 6 intercollegiate sports for men and 5 for women, and 5 intramural sports for men and 3 for women. Facilities include a 2000-seat gym, baseball, soccer, and softball fields, a tennis center, and an 18-hole golf course.

Disabled Students: 90% of the campus is accessible. Wheelchair ramps, elevators, special parking, specially equipped rest rooms, special class scheduling, lowered drinking fountains, and lowered telephones are available.

Services: Counseling and information services are available, as is tutoring in most subjects. There is a reader service for the blind, and remedial math, reading, and writing.

Campus Safety and Security: Measures include 24-hour foot and vehicle patrol, escort service, shuttle buses, and informal discussions. There are pamphlets/posters/films and lighted pathways/sidewalks.

Programs of Study: Augusta State University confers B.A., B.S., B.B.A., B.F.A., B.M., and B.S.Ed. degrees. Associate and master's degrees are also awarded. Bachelor's degrees are awarded in BIOLOGICAL SCIENCE (biology/biological science), BUSINESS (accounting, banking and finance, business administration and management, and marketing/retailing/merchandising), COMMUNICATIONS AND THE ARTS (art, communications, English, French, music, Spanish, and studio art), COMPUTER AND PHYSICAL SCIENCE (chemistry, computer science, mathematics, physical sciences, and physics), EDUCATION (early childhood, education of the mentally handicapped, elementary, health, middle school, music, and special), SOCIAL SCIENCE (criminal justice, history, political science/government, psychology, and sociology). Biology, early childhood education, and computer science are the largest.

Required: Students must complete 125 hours, with a minimum GPA of 2.0. All students are required to take 6 courses in phys ed; pass the Regents test in reading and composition; and demonstrate, through course completion or exam, a knowledge of U.S. and Georgia history and their constitutions.

Special: A Washington semester and study abroad may be arranged. The school offers co-op programs with area companies, internships, work-study programs, dual majors, nondegree study, and cross-registration with Paine College. There are 5 national honor societies, a freshman honors program, and 7 departmental honors programs.

Faculty/Classroom: 55% of faculty are male; 45%, female. All teach undergraduates. No introductory courses are taught by graduate students. The average class size in an introductory lecture is 30; in a laboratory, 19; and in a regular course, 27.

Admissions: 68% of the 2001-2002 applicants were accepted. The SAT I scores for the 2001-2002 freshman class were: Verbal--53% below 500, 35% between 500 and 599, 11% between 600 and 700, and 1% above 700; Math--59% below 500, 34% between 500 and 599, and 7% between 600 and 700.

Requirements: The SAT I or ACT is required, with a verbal score of 430 and math score of 400 on the SAT I or a comparable score on the

ACT. Applicants must be graduates of an accredited secondary school. The GED is accepted. Secondary school courses must include 4 units each of English and math, 3 each of science and social science, and 2 of a foreign language. Applications are accepted on-line. A GPA of 2.0 is required. AP and CLEP credits are accepted.
Procedure: Freshmen are admitted fall, spring, and summer. There is a deferred admissions plan. Applications should be filed by July 21 for fall entry and December 6 for spring entry, along with a $20 fee. Notification is sent on a rolling basis.
Transfer: 456 transfer students enrolled in a recent year. Applicants must have completed 30 semester or 45 quarter hours. If fewer than 15 semester hours have been completed, students are considered as entering freshmen and are required to submit appropriate paperwork. 30 credits of 125 must be completed at Augusta State University.
Visiting: There are regularly scheduled orientations for prospective students. There are guides for informal visits and visitors may sit in on classes. To schedule a visit, contact the Admissions Office.
Financial Aid: 89% of undergraduates work part time. Average annual earnings from campus work are $3000. The average financial indebtedness of a recent year's graduate was $14,124. The FAFSA is required. Check with school for current deadlines.
International Students: There were 162 international students enrolled. They must score 540 on the written TOEFL and also take the SAT I.
Computers: The mainframe is a DEC VAX 4200. Access to the Internet and the Web is available from 160 computers in 6 campus labs, plus remote dial-in access from off-campus locations. All students may access the system. There are no time limits and no fees.
Graduates: In 2001, 485 bachelor's degrees were awarded. The most popular majors were psychology (10%), sociology (9%), and early childhood education (7%). In an average class, 1% graduate in 3 years, 8% in 4 years, 17% in 5 years, and 21% in 6 years. 100 companies recruited on campus in 2000-2001.
Admissions Contact: Katherine Sweeney, Registrar and Director of Admissions. E-mail: *admissions@aug.edu*
Web: *www.aug.edu/admissions*

BERRY COLLEGE
Mount Berry, GA 30149-0159 — A-2
(706) 236-2215
(800) BERRYGA; Fax: (706) 290-2178

Full-time: 663 men, 1145 women
Part-time: 18 men, 20 women
Graduate: 56 men, 136 women
Year: semesters, summer session
Application Deadline: February 1
Freshman Class: 1948 applied, 1592 accepted, 539 enrolled
SAT I or ACT: required
Faculty: 96; IIA, -$
Ph.D.s: 94%
Student/Faculty: 19 to 1
Tuition: $13,450
Room & Board: $5400
COMPETITIVE

Berry College, founded in 1902, is a private nonsectarian Christian college offering programs in fine and liberal arts, agriculture, business, teacher preparation, and religion. There are 4 undergraduate schools and 1 graduate school. In addition to regional accreditation, Berry has baccalaureate program accreditation with NASM and NCATE. The library contains 591,807 volumes, 432,967 microform items, and 500 audiovisual forms/CDs, and subscribes to 1414 periodicals. Computerized library services include the card catalog, interlibrary loans, and database searching. Special learning facilities include an art gallery, radio station, TV station, equine center, forestry center, and beef- and dairy-cattle operations. The 28,000-acre campus is in a rural area 65 miles northwest of Atlanta. Including residence halls, there are 37 buildings.
Student Life: 81% of undergraduates are from Georgia. Others are from 35 states, 22 foreign countries, and Canada. 89% are from public schools. 94% are white. 74% are Protestant; 10% Catholic. The average age of all undergraduates is 22. 24% do not continue beyond their first year; 57% remain to graduate.
Housing: 1300 students can be accommodated in college housing, which includes single-sex dormitories and on-campus apartments. On-campus housing is guaranteed for the freshman year only and is available on a first-come, first-served basis. 83% of students live on campus; of those, 57% remain on campus on weekends. Alcohol is not permitted. All students may keep cars.
Activities: There are no fraternities or sororities. There are 67 groups on campus, including cheerleading, chess, choir, computers, dance, drama, ethnic, forensics, honors, international, literary magazine, newspaper, orchestra, pep band, political, professional, radio and TV, religious, social, social service, student government, and yearbook. Popular campus events include Mountain Day and Founders Day.
Sports: There are 7 intercollegiate sports for men and 5 for women, and 13 intramural sports for men and 13 for women. Facilities include running and biking trails, 10 tennis courts, intramural fields, 2 gyms, a weight-training room, an indoor swimming pool, and 3 sand volleyball courts.
Disabled Students: Wheelchair ramps, elevators, special parking, specially equipped rest rooms, and lowered drinking fountains are available.
Services: Counseling and information services are available, as is tutoring in most subjects. There is a reader service for the blind.
Campus Safety and Security: Measures include 24-hour foot and vehicle patrol, shuttle buses, informal discussions, and pamphlets/posters/films. There are lighted pathways/sidewalks.
Programs of Study: Berry confers B.A., B.S., and B.Mu. degrees. Master's degrees are also awarded. Bachelor's degrees are awarded in AGRICULTURE (animal science and horticulture), BIOLOGICAL SCIENCE (biology/biological science), BUSINESS (accounting, business administration and management, and sports management), COMMUNICATIONS AND THE ARTS (art, communications, dramatic arts, English, French, German, music, music performance, Spanish, and studio art), COMPUTER AND PHYSICAL SCIENCE (applied mathematics, chemistry, computer science, mathematics, and physics), EDUCATION (art, athletic training, early childhood, mathematics, middle school, music, and physical), ENGINEERING AND ENVIRONMENTAL DESIGN (environmental science and preengineering), HEALTH PROFESSIONS (predentistry, premedicine, preoptometry, prepharmacy, and preveterinary science), SOCIAL SCIENCE (economics, family/consumer studies, history, interdisciplinary studies, international studies, philosophy, physical fitness/movement, political science/government, prelaw, psychology, religion, social science, sociology, and theological studies). Business and education are the largest.
Required: General education requirements include 5 courses in the humanities and fine arts, 3 each in behavioral science, math and natural sciences, communication, and health and phys ed, and 2 in electives. A 2.0 GPA and a total of 124 credits, including at least 30 hours in the major, are required for graduation. All students are also required to attend at least 3 approved cultural events per semester and pass a comprehensive exam in the major.
Special: The college offers internships, a Washington semester, study abroad in 6 countries, work-study programs, student-designed majors, credit by exam, and nondegree study. There are 3-2 engineering degrees and dual degree programs in several fields with the Georgia Institute of Technology and Mercer University. There is also a dual degree program in nursing with Emory University. There are 15 national honor societies, a freshman honors program, and 2 departmental honors programs.
Faculty/Classroom: 99% teach undergraduates, 33% do research, and 33% do both. No introductory courses are taught by graduate students. The average class size in an introductory lecture is 29; in a laboratory, 22; and in a regular course, 21.
Admissions: 82% of the 2001-2002 applicants were accepted. The SAT I scores for the 2001-2002 freshman class were: Verbal--15% below 500, 42% between 500 and 599, 33% between 600 and 700, and 10% above 700; Math--17% below 500, 48% between 500 and 599, 30% between 600 and 700, and 5% above 700. The ACT scores were 19% below 21, 28% between 21 and 23, 21% between 24 and 26, 14% between 27 and 28, and 17% above 28. 54% of the current freshmen were in the top fifth of their class; 86% were in the top two fifths.
Requirements: The SAT I or ACT is required. In addition, applicants should be graduates of an accredited high school or have a GED. 20 academic credits are required, including 4 units each of English and math (to include algebra I, algebra II, and either geometry or trigonometry), 3 each of science and social studies, and 2 of a foreign language. A GPA of 2.0 is required. AP and CLEP credits are accepted. Important factors in the admissions decision are advanced placement or honor courses, leadership record, and recommendations by school officials. Applications may be submitted on disk using Apply or on-line via Peterson's or College Board.
Procedure: Freshmen are admitted to all sessions. Entrance exams should be taken by the fall of the senior year. There are early decision and early admissions plans. Applications should be filed by February 1 for fall entry, along with a $25 fee. Notification is sent on a rolling basis. A waiting list is an active part of the admissions procedure.
Transfer: 101 transfer students enrolled in a recent year. Applicants must submit official transcripts from all colleges previously attended, have a minimum GPA of 2.4, and be in good standing at the last school attended. 30 credits of 124 must be completed at Berry.
Visiting: There are regularly scheduled orientations for prospective students, on weekdays and Saturday mornings. Students should schedule their campus visit in advance. There are guides for informal visits and visitors may sit in on classes and stay overnight. To schedule a visit, contact the Admissions Office.
Financial Aid: In 2001-2002, 100% of all freshmen and 99% of continuing students received some form of financial aid. 78% of undergraduates work part time. Berry is a member of CSS. The FAFSA and the college's own financial statement are required. Check with the school for current deadlines.
International Students: The school actively recruits these students. They must score 550 on the written TOEFL or 213 on the electronic version and also take the SAT I or the ACT if the student is from an English-speaking country.
Computers: The mainframe is a DEC PDP 11/44. PCs and Macs are located in 4 computer labs and in the library. Internet access is provided. All students may access the system. There are no time limits and no fees.

Admissions Contact: George Gaddie, Dean of Admissions. A video is available. E-mail: *admissions@berry.edu* Web: *www.berry.edu*

BRENAU UNIVERSITY WOMEN'S COLLEGE (Formerly Women's College of Brenau University) B-2

Gainesville, GA 30501 (770) 534-6100
(800) 252-5119; Fax: (770) 538-4306

Full-time: 505 women	**Faculty:** 80; IIA, --$
Part-time: 67 women	**Ph.D.s:** 96%
Graduate: 28 women	**Student/Faculty:** 6 to 1
Year: semesters, summer session	**Tuition:** $12,780
Application Deadline: open	**Room & Board:** $7320
Freshman Class: 375 applied, 303 accepted, 133 enrolled	
SAT I Verbal/Math: 540/510	**COMPETITIVE**

Brenau University Women's College, founded in 1878, is a private undergraduate and graduate liberal arts institution for women. Coeducational programs are offered as part of the university, in an evening and weekend format. There are 4 undergraduate schools. In addition to regional accreditation, Brenau has baccalaureate program accreditation with FIDER and NLN. The library contains 103,740 volumes, 350,328 microform items, and 16,023 audiovisual forms/CDs, and subscribes to 2000 periodicals. Computerized library services include the card catalog, interlibrary loans, and database searching. Special learning facilities include a learning resource center, art gallery, radio station, TV station, and a TV studio. The 57-acre campus is in a small town 50 miles northeast of Atlanta. Including residence halls, there are 50 buildings.

Student Life: 89% of undergraduates are from Georgia. Others are from 19 states and 19 foreign countries. 89% are from public schools. 79% are white; 10% African American. The average age of freshmen is 18; all undergraduates, 22. 39% do not continue beyond their first year.

Housing: 448 students can be accommodated in college housing, which includes single-sex dormitories, on-campus apartments, off-campus apartments, and sorority houses. On-campus housing is guaranteed for all 4 years, is available on a first-come, first-served basis, and is available on a lottery system for upperclassmen. 55% of students commute. Alcohol is not permitted. All students may keep cars.

Activities: 34% of women belong to 9 national sororities. There are no fraternities. There are 46 groups on campus, including art, choir, chorale, chorus, dance, drama, film, honors, international, literary magazine, musical theater, newspaper, opera, photography, political, professional, radio and TV, religious, social, social service, student government, symphony, and yearbook. Popular campus events include Remember All the Traditions Week, May Day, and Spade Hunt.

Sports: Facilities include a tennis center, a recreation field, a gym, and a natatorium.

Disabled Students: 90% of the campus is accessible. Wheelchair ramps, elevators, special parking, specially equipped rest rooms, special class scheduling, lowered drinking fountains, and lowered telephones are available.

Services: There is remedial math, reading, and writing, and professional degreed tutors for diagnosed learning-disabled students.

Campus Safety and Security: Measures include 24-hour foot and vehicle patrol, self-defense education, escort service, and informal discussions. There are pamphlets/posters/films and lighted pathways/sidewalks.

Programs of Study: Brenau confers B.A., B.S., B.B.A., B.F.A., B.M., and B.S.N. degrees. Master's degrees are also awarded. Bachelor's degrees are awarded in BIOLOGICAL SCIENCE (biology/biological science), BUSINESS (accounting, business administration and management, fashion merchandising, and marketing/retailing/merchandising), COMMUNICATIONS AND THE ARTS (arts administration/ management, communications, dance, dramatic arts, English, fine arts, music performance, musical theater, and studio art), EDUCATION (art, dance, early childhood, middle school, music, and special), ENGINEERING AND ENVIRONMENTAL DESIGN (commercial art, environmental science, and interior design), HEALTH PROFESSIONS (nursing and occupational therapy), SOCIAL SCIENCE (history, human ecology, international studies, liberal arts/general studies, paralegal studies, political science/government, and psychology). Occupational therapy, fine arts, and performing arts are the strongest academically. Nursing, occupational therapy, and performing arts are the largest.

Required: To graduate, all students must complete at least 120 semester hours of work including 48 to 69 hours in the major. Requirements for each degree vary, but students must maintain a 2.0 GPA overall and a 2.5 GPA in course work required by the major. Most majors either require or encourage internships. In addition to specific requirements, students must take phys ed courses and demonstrate computer as well as oral and written communication proficiency. Courses in women's health and leisure studies are also required.

Special: Cross-registration is possible with the Atlanta Regional Consortium for Higher Education. Students may study abroad in 10 foreign countries. Brenau offers B.A.-B.S. degrees, work study programs, internships, a Washington semester, a general studies degree, and student-designed majors. Students may receive credit for life, military, and work experience. There are 8 national honor societies, a freshman honors program, and 4 departmental honors programs.

Faculty/Classroom: 37% of faculty are male; 63%, female. All teach undergraduates. No introductory courses are taught by graduate students. The average class size in an introductory lecture is 19; in a laboratory, 12; and in a regular course, 14.

Admissions: 81% of the 2001-2002 applicants were accepted. The SAT I scores for the 2001-2002 freshman class were: Verbal--36% below 500, 41% between 500 and 599, 21% between 600 and 700, and 2% above 700; Math--40% below 500, 44% between 500 and 599, and 16% between 600 and 700. 9 freshmen graduated first in their class.

Requirements: The SAT I or ACT is required. In addition, candidates for admission should have completed 4 units of English, 3 of math, 2 of science, 2 to 3 of social studies, and 7 to 9 of electives. A GPA of 2.5 is required. AP and CLEP credits are accepted. Important factors in the admissions decision are advanced placement or honor courses, recommendations by school officials, and evidence of special talent. The university accepts applications on-line through its web site at *www.brenau.edu/admissions*.

Procedure: Freshmen are admitted fall and spring. Entrance exams should be taken in the fall of the senior year or the spring of the junior year. There are early admissions and deferred admissions plans. Application deadlines are open. The fall application fee was $35. Notification is sent on a rolling basis.

Transfer: 87 transfer students enrolled in 2001-2002. A minimum GPA of 2.5 on transfer credits is required, and transfer students must submit high school transcripts and SAT I scores if fewer than 30 hours were earned. The last 45 semester hours, including at least 30 in the major, must be taken at Brenau. Students must maintain a minimum GPA of 2.0 and 2.5 in the major. 45 credits of 120 must be completed at Brenau.

Visiting: There are regularly scheduled orientations for prospective students, consisting of a campus tour, information sessions, and an interview. There are guides for informal visits and visitors may sit in on classes and stay overnight. To schedule a visit, contact the Admissions Office at *wcadmissions@lib.brenau.edu*.

Financial Aid: In 2001-2002, 97% of all freshmen and 93% of continuing students received some form of financial aid. 58% of freshmen and 57% of continuing students received need-based aid. The average freshman award was $14,279. Of that total, scholarships or need-based grants averaged $12,441 ($20,850 maximum); loans averaged $1201 ($2625 maximum); and work contracts averaged $637 ($2000 maximum). 9% of undergraduates work part time. Average annual earnings from campus work are $1850. The average financial indebtedness of the 2001 graduate was $10,999. The FAFSA is required. The fall application deadline is July 15.

International Students: There are 24 international students enrolled. The school actively recruits these students. They must score 500 on the written TOEFL or 173 on the electronic version or take Level 109 at an ELS Language Center. and also take the SAT I or ACT, or only if the TOEFL is not taken, scoring 900 on the SAT I or 18 on the ACT.

Computers: There is no academic mainframe available to students. There are 112 Pentium and 486 PCs located in labs and residence halls around campus. All are attached to the campuswide network for use of library resources, the Internet (via a T-1 connection), and e-mail. All students may access the system 24 hours per day. There are no time limits and no fees.

Graduates: In 2001, 130 bachelor's degrees were awarded. The most popular majors were occupational therapy (21%), nursing (16%), and teacher education (13%). In an average class, 30% graduate in 4 years, 35% in 5 years, and 40% in 6 years. 20 companies recruited on campus in 2000-2001.

Admissions Contact: Christina Cochran, Coordinator of Women's College Admissions.
E-mail: *ccochran@lib.brenau.edu* or *wcadmissions*
Web: *www.brenau.edu*

BREWTON-PARKER COLLEGE C-4

Mt. Vernon, GA 30445-0197 (912) 583-2241
(800) 342-1087; Fax: (912) 583-4498

Full-time: 310 men, 495 women	**Faculty:** 58
Part-time: 90 men, 235 women	**Ph.D.s:** 60%
Graduate: none	**Student/Faculty:** 14 to 1
Year: semesters, summer session	**Tuition:** $7960
Application Deadline: see profile	**Room & Board:** $2850
Freshman Class: n/av	
SAT I or ACT: recommended	**LESS COMPETITIVE**

Brewton-Parker College, founded in 1904, is a private institution offering instruction in the liberal arts and sciences. It is affiliated with the Georgia Baptist Convention. Figures in above capsule are approximate. The library contains 52,000 volumes, 1307 microform items, and 36,589 audiovisual forms/CDs, and subscribes to 411 periodicals. Computerized library services include the card catalog, interlibrary loans, and database searching. Special learning facilities include a learning resource center, art gallery, and a living history museum. The 275-acre campus is in a rural area 90 miles west of Savannah. Including residence halls, there are 32 buildings.

Student Life: 94% of undergraduates are from Georgia. Others are from 18 states, 10 foreign countries, and Canada. 90% are from public schools. 80% are white; 18% African American. Most are Protestant. The average age of freshmen is 19; all undergraduates, 23. 11% do not continue beyond their first year; 46% remain to graduate.

Housing: 550 students can be accommodated in college housing, which includes single-sex dormitories. On-campus housing is guaranteed for all 4 years. Alcohol is not permitted. All students may keep cars.

Activities: 21% of men belong to 4 local fraternities; 24% of women belong to 4 local sororities. There are 19 groups on campus, including band, cheerleading, choir, chorus, dance, drama, ethnic, honors, international, jazz band, musical theater, newspaper, pep band, professional, religious, social, social service, student government, and yearbook. Popular campus events include Road Rally, Fun Flicks, and the Fine Arts Series.

Sports: There are 5 intercollegiate sports for men and 5 for women, and 5 intramural sports for men and 5 for women. Facilities include softball, baseball, and soccer fields, tennis courts, a swimming pool, a gym, a track, an outdoor volleyball court, a physical fitness building, and a campus lake.

Disabled Students: Wheelchair ramps, special parking, specially equipped rest rooms, and lowered drinking fountains are available.

Services: Counseling and information services are available, as is tutoring in most subjects. There is remedial math, reading, and writing. Tutoring in Spanish is available.

Campus Safety and Security: Measures include 24-hour foot and vehicle patrol, self-defense education, shuttle buses, and informal discussions. There are pamphlets/posters/films and lighted pathways/sidewalks.

Programs of Study: BPC confers B.A., B.S., B.Min., and B.Mu. Degrees. Associate degrees are also awarded. Bachelor's degrees are awarded in BIOLOGICAL SCIENCE (biology/biological science), BUSINESS (business administration and management), COMMUNICATIONS AND THE ARTS (English and music), EDUCATION (business, early childhood, education of the exceptional child, English, mathematics, middle school, and science), HEALTH PROFESSIONS (health), SOCIAL SCIENCE (Christian studies, history, liberal arts/general studies, psychology, and sociology). Education degree programs have the largest enrollments.

Required: The required core curriculum consists of humanities, math and natural science, social science, phys ed, and foreign language. Students must maintain a minimum 2.0 GPA and must complete 120 hours, with half in the major.

Special: The college offers internships, work-study programs, a general studies degree, and nondegree study. There are 2 national honor societies and a freshman honors program.

Faculty/Classroom: All teach undergraduates. The average class size in an introductory lecture is 28; in a laboratory, 15; and in a regular course, 14.

Requirements: The SAT I or ACT is recommended. In addition, a GED is accepted. Students should prepare with 4 years of English, 3 of social studies, and 2 each of foreign language, math, and science. AP credits are accepted. Important factors in the admissions decision are ability to finance college education, personality/intangible qualities, and advanced placement or honor courses.

Procedure: Freshmen are admitted to all sessions. Entrance exams should be taken during the senior year of high school. There are early decision and early admissions plans. Check with the school for current application deadlines. The application fee is $25.

Transfer: Applicants must submit transcripts from previously attended institutions, along with high school transcripts, if they have completed fewer than 30 semester hours. 60 credits of 120 must be completed at BPC.

Visiting: There are regularly scheduled orientations for prospective students, consisting of a campus tour and academic and financial aid sessions. There are guides for informal visits and visitors may sit in on classes and stay overnight. To schedule a visit, contact Jim Beall, Director of Admissions.

Financial Aid: In a recent year, 51% of all freshmen and 60% of continuing students received some form of financial aid. 50% of freshmen and 57% of continuing students received need-based aid. The average freshman award was $3995. Of that total, scholarships or need-based grants averaged $1782 ($5310 maximum); loans averaged $2722 ($6000 maximum); and work contracts averaged $1140 ($1500 maximum). 18% of undergraduates work part time. Average annual earnings from campus work are $1000. The average financial indebtedness of a graduate in a recent year was $5000. BPC is a member of CSS. The FAFSA and the college's own financial statement are required. The fall application deadline is April 3.

International Students: They must score 500 on the written TOEFL or take the MELAB.

Computers: The mainframe is an HP 9000. PCs are available in computer labs, which are accessible to all students. There are no time limits and no fees.

Graduates: In a recent year, 1841 bachelor's degrees were awarded. The most popular majors were teacher education (30%), business administration (15%), and early childhood education (15%). 38 companies recruited on campus in a recent year.

Admissions Contact: Jim Beall, Director of Admissions.
Web: *bpc.edu*

CLARK ATLANTA UNIVERSITY

Atlanta, GA 30314 **B-2**

(404) 880-8918
(800) 668-3228; Fax: (404) 880-6174

Full-time: 1088 men, 2707 women	**Faculty:** 304
Part-time: 47 men, 81 women	**Ph.D.s:** 75%
Graduate: 310 men, 649 women	**Student/Faculty:** 12 to 1
Year: semesters, summer session	**Tuition:** $11,120
Application Deadline: July 1	**Room & Board:** $6054
Freshman Class: 3228 accepted, 1028 enrolled	
SAT I Verbal/Math: 450/450	**ACT:** 18 **COMPETITIVE**

Clark Atlanta University was formed in 1988 from the union of Clark College (1869) and Atlanta University (1865). A private, predominantly black college affiliated with the United Methodist Church, CAU offers programs in arts and sciences, business administration, education, and social work. There are 4 undergraduate and 5 graduate schools. In addition to regional accreditation, CAU has baccalaureate program accreditation with AACSB, CAHEA, CSWE, and NCATE. The library contains 742,257 volumes, 836,593 microform items, and 10,555 audiovisual forms/CDs, and subscribes to 1410 periodicals. Computerized library services include interlibrary loans and database searching. Special learning facilities include a learning resource center, art gallery, radio station, TV station, and a distance learning instructional technology education center. The 113-acre campus is in an urban area 3 miles southwest of Atlanta. Including residence halls, there are 30 buildings.

Student Life: 60% of undergraduates are from out of state, mostly the South. Others are from 41 states, 31 foreign countries, and Canada. 97% are African American. Most are Protestant. The average age of freshmen is 19; all undergraduates, 20. 22% do not continue beyond their first year; 50% remain to graduate.

Housing: 1966 students can be accommodated in college housing, which includes single-sex and coed dormitories and off-campus apartments. On-campus housing is available on a first-come, first-served basis. 63% of students live on campus. Alcohol is not permitted. All students may keep cars.

Activities: 20% of men belong to 4 national fraternities; 30% of women belong to 4 national sororities. There are 75 groups on campus, including art, band, cheerleading, choir, chorale, chorus, computers, dance, drama, drill team, ethnic, film, honors, international, jazz band, marching band, musical theater, newspaper, orchestra, pep band, photography, political, professional, radio and TV, religious, social, social service, student government, symphony, and yearbook. Popular campus events include Commencement and Alumni Weekend, Founders Week, and convocations.

Sports: Facilities include a gym, stadium, and student center.

Disabled Students: 70% of the campus is accessible. Wheelchair ramps, elevators, special parking, and specially equipped rest rooms are available.

Services: Counseling and information services are available, as is tutoring in every subject. There is remedial math, reading, and writing.

Campus Safety and Security: Measures include 24-hour foot and vehicle patrol, escort service, shuttle buses, and informal discussions. There are pamphlets/posters/films, emergency telephones, and lighted pathways/sidewalks.

Programs of Study: CAU confers B.A. and B.S. degrees. Master's and doctoral degrees are also awarded. Bachelor's degrees are awarded in BIOLOGICAL SCIENCE (biology/biological science), BUSINESS (accounting, and business administration and management), COMMUNICATIONS AND THE ARTS (art, communications, English, languages, music, and speech/debate/rhetoric), COMPUTER AND PHYSICAL SCIENCE (chemistry, computer science, mathematics, and physics), EDUCATION (business), ENGINEERING AND ENVIRONMENTAL DESIGN (engineering), HEALTH PROFESSIONS (allied health), SOCIAL SCIENCE (economics, history, philosophy, political science/government, psychology, religion, social work, and sociology). Business administration, physical and biological sciences, and communications are the strongest academically. Biology, business, and communications are the largest.

Required: To graduate, students must complete a minimum of 122 hours of course work, including a prescribed major sequence, with a minimum 2.0 GPA. Beyond the general education core requirements, at least 60% of courses must represent work at or above the 300 level.

Special: Clark Atlanta offers co-op programs, internships, study abroad in 12 countries, accelerated degree programs, and a Washington semester. There is cross-registration with Atlanta University Center, Georgia Institute of Technology, and Georgia State University. B.A.-B.S. degrees may be obtained in business and management, education, and social and natural sciences. Dual majors in allied health and engineering and a 3-2 engineering degree with 7 universities are also available. There are 10 national honor societies, and 8 departmental honors program.

Faculty/Classroom: 64% of faculty are male; 36%, female. The average class size in an introductory lecture is 40; in a laboratory, 20; and in a regular course, 25.

Admissions: The SAT I scores for the 2001-2002 freshman class were: Verbal--76% below 500, 21% between 500 and 599, and 2% between 600 and 700; Math--81% below 500, 16% between 500 and 599, and 3% between 600 and 700. The ACT scores were 77% below 21, 14% between 21 and 23, 7% between 24 and 26, and 2% between 27 and 28.

Requirements: The SAT I or ACT is required. In addition, applicants must be high school graduates or hold the GED. A letter of recommendation is required. A GPA of 2.5 is required. AP and CLEP credits are accepted. Important factors in the admissions decision are ability to finance college education, advanced placement or honor courses, and evidence of special talent. Applications are accepted on-line at the CAU web site, *www.cau.edu*.

Procedure: Freshmen are admitted to all sessions. Entrance exams should be taken by January. There are early admissions and deferred admissions plans. Applications should be filed by July 1 for fall entry and October 1 for spring entry. Notification of early decision is sent January 1; regular decision, on a rolling basis.

Transfer: 215 transfer students enrolled in 2001-2002. 30 credits of 122 must be completed at CAU.

Visiting: There are regularly scheduled orientations for prospective students. There are guides for informal visits and visitors may sit in on classes. To schedule a visit, contact Robin Reid, Admission Counselor at (404) 880-8782.

Financial Aid: In 2001-2002, 92% of all freshmen and 80% of continuing students received some form of financial aid, including need-based aid. The average freshman award was $7838. 5% of undergraduates work part time. Average annual earnings from campus work are $3200. The average financial indebtedness of the 2001 graduate was $50,000. CAU is a member of CSS. The FAFSA is required. The fall application deadline is March 1.

International Students: There are 40 international students enrolled. The school actively recruits these students. They must score 500 on the written TOEFL.

Computers: The mainframe is a DEC VAX 8550. Students may access the mainframe through the academic student computer lab. Those students with assigned user identification codes may access the system during assigned times. There are no time limits and no fees.

Graduates: In 2001, 534 bachelor's degrees were awarded. The most popular majors were business administration (63%), mass media arts (14%), and social work (11%). In an average class, 28% graduate in 4 years, 42% in 5 years, and 50% in 6 years. 300 companies recruited on campus in 2000-2001.

Admissions Contact: Julius Dodds, Director of Admissions.
E-mail: *jdodds@cau.edu* Web: *www.cau.edu*

CLAYTON COLLEGE AND STATE UNIVERSITY B-2
Morrow, GA 30260-0285 (770) 961-3500; (770) 961-3752

Full-time: 749 men, 1344 women	**Faculty:** 143
Part-time: 874 men, 1708 women	**Ph.D.s:** 54%
Graduate: none	**Student/Faculty:** 16 to 1
Year: semesters, summer session	**Tuition:** $2322 ($8118)
Application Deadline: July 1	**Room & Board:** n/app

Freshman Class: 1454 applied, 689 accepted, 452 enrolled
SAT I or ACT: required **COMPETITIVE+**

Clayton College & State University, founded in 1969 as a public junior college, has been a 4-year undergraduate college in the University System of Georgia since 1985. The first baccalaureate degrees were awarded in 1989. There are 4 undergraduate schools. In addition to regional accreditation, Clayton State has baccalaureate program accreditation with ADA, NCATE, and NLN. The library contains 79,324 volumes, 221,576 microform items, and 6414 audiovisual forms/CDs, and subscribes to 750 periodicals. Computerized library services include the card catalog, interlibrary loans, and database searching. Special learning facilities include a learning resource center and a concert facility. The 160-acre campus is in a suburban area 17 miles south of downtown Atlanta near Hartsfield International Airport. There are 10 buildings.

Student Life: 98% of undergraduates are from Georgia. Others are from 18 states, 44 foreign countries, and Canada. The average age of all undergraduates is 28. 43% do not continue beyond their first year.

Housing: There are no residence halls. All students commute. Alcohol is not permitted. All students may keep cars.

Activities: There are no fraternities or sororities. There are 20 groups on campus, including art, band, cheerleading, choir, chorale, chorus, computers, drama, ethnic, gay, honors, international, jazz band, musical theater, newspaper, professional, religious, social, social service, and student government. Popular campus events include Southern Crescent Festival and Spring Fling.

Sports: There are 4 intercollegiate sports for men and 4 for women. Facilities include a gym, jogging trails, a circuit training facility, a weight room, soccer fields, and tennis, badminton, volleyball, and basketball courts.

Disabled Students: All of the campus is accessible. Wheelchair ramps, elevators, special parking, specially equipped rest rooms, special class scheduling, lowered drinking fountains, and lowered telephones are available.

Services: Counseling and information services are available, as is tutoring in most subjects. There is remedial math, reading, and writing.

Campus Safety and Security: Measures include 24-hour foot and vehicle patrol, self-defense education, escort service, and pamphlets/posters/films. There are emergency telephones and lighted pathways/sidewalks.

Programs of Study: Clayton State confers B.A., B.S., B.A.S., B.B.A., B.M., and B.S.N. degrees. Associate degrees are also awarded. Bachelor's degrees are awarded in BUSINESS (accounting, business administration and management, and marketing and distribution), COMMUNICATIONS AND THE ARTS (music, music performance, and music theory and composition), COMPUTER AND PHYSICAL SCIENCE (information sciences and systems), EDUCATION (middle school), ENGINEERING AND ENVIRONMENTAL DESIGN (technological management), HEALTH PROFESSIONS (allied health, dental hygiene, health care administration, and nursing), SOCIAL SCIENCE (interdisciplinary studies). Nursing, middle school education, music performance, and composition are the strongest academically. Management is the largest.

Required: Students in the baccalaureate program must complete 120 to 126 semester hours, including a 60-hour core curriculum in English and humanities, math or sciences, and social sciences. A 2.0 minimum GPA is required for graduation.

Special: Co-op programs and internships can be arranged in all majors except middle school education. The B.A.S. career program enables associate degree holders to complete the baccalaureate degree. Cross-registration is offered through the University Center Consortium. Dual majors, B.A.-B.S. degrees, study abroad, student-designed majors, and work-study programs are offered. Distance learning opportunities are possible. There are 2 national honor societies and a freshman honors program.

Faculty/Classroom: 50% of faculty are male; 50%, female. All teach undergraduates.

Admissions: 47% of the 2001-2002 applicants were accepted. The SAT I scores for the 2001-2002 freshman class were: Verbal--49% below 500, 41% between 500 and 599, and 11% between 600 and 700; Math--50% below 500, 42% between 500 and 599, and 8% between 600 and 700. The ACT scores were 86% below 23, and 14% between 24 and 29.

Requirements: The SAT I or ACT is required, with minimum SAT I scores of 430 verbal and 400 math, or a minimum composite ACT score of 34. Applicants should be graduates of accredited secondary schools. High school preparation should include 4 courses each in English and math, 3 each in science, history, and social studies, and 2 in a foreign language. Students may also be admitted on the strength of their high school academic records. A GPA of 2.0 is required. AP and CLEP credits are accepted. On-line applications must be followed by signed documents and the application fee.

Procedure: Freshmen are admitted to all sessions. Entrance exams should be taken before registration. There are early admissions and deferred admissions plans. Applications should be filed by July 1 for fall entry, December 1 for spring entry, and May 1 for summer entry, along with a $20 fee. Notification is sent on a rolling basis.

Transfer: 468 transfer students enrolled in 2001-2002. Applicants with fewer than 30 semester hours or 45 quarter credits must meet the same criteria as entering freshmen. 39 credits of 120 to 126 must be completed at Clayton State.

Visiting: There are regularly scheduled orientations for prospective students, including tours of the campus and the opportunity to meet faculty and staff and learn about the athletic programs, the notebook computers, and campus life. There are guides for informal visits and visitors may sit in on classes. To schedule a visit, contact the Office of Admissions.

Financial Aid: Clayton State is a member of CSS. The FAFSA and the college's own financial statement are required. The fall application deadline is April 1.

International Students: They must score 550 on the written TOEFL and also take the Georgia State Test for English Proficiency (G-STEP) and the SAT I or the ACT.

Computers: The mainframe is an HP 9000. Universal Personal Information Technology Access is a program to provide each CCSU student with a Microquest notebook computer and Internet access. All students may access the system. All students are required to have personal computers.

Graduates: In 2001, 307 bachelor's degrees were awarded. The most popular majors were business/marketing (47%), nursing/health (29%),

and computer information science (8%). 213 companies recruited on campus in a recent year.
Admissions Contact: Diane Burns, Director of Admissions.
E-mail: *ccsu-info@mail.clayton.edu* Web: *www.clayton.edu*

COLUMBUS STATE UNIVERSITY
Columbus, GA 31907-5645 A-3
(706) 568-2035
(866) 264-2035; Fax: (706) 568-2462

Full-time: 1127 men, 1865 women	**Faculty:** 219; IIA, --$
Part-time: 621 men, 1011 women	**Ph.D.s:** 70%
Graduate: 387 men, 511 women	**Student/Faculty:** 14 to 1
Year: semesters, summer session	**Tuition:** $2352 ($8148)
Application Deadline: August 1	**Room & Board:** $4876
Freshman Class: 1230 accepted, 828 enrolled	
SAT I Verbal/Math: 494/479	**ACT:** 20 LESS COMPETITIVE

Columbus State University, established in 1958, is a public liberal arts institution within the University System of Georgia. There are 4 undergraduate schools and 1 graduate school. In addition to regional accreditation, Columbus State has baccalaureate program accreditation with NASM, NCATE, and NLN. The library contains 250,000 volumes, 692,000 microform items, and 8308 audiovisual forms/CDs, and subscribes to 1389 periodicals. Computerized library services include the card catalog and database searching. Special learning facilities include a learning resource center and and archives. The 132-acre campus is in a suburban area 100 miles south of Atlanta. Including residence halls, there are 26 buildings.
Student Life: 84% of undergraduates are from Georgia. Others are from 30 states and 29 foreign countries. 97% are from public schools. 67% are white; 26% African American. The average age of all undergraduates is 25. 33% do not continue beyond their first year.
Housing: 500 students can be accommodated in college housing, which includes single-sex on-campus apartments and off-campus apartments. On-campus housing is available on a first-come, first-served basis. Priority is given to out-of-town students. 91% of students commute. Alcohol is not permitted. All students may keep cars.
Activities: 2% of men belong to 5 national fraternities; 3% of women belong to 2 local and 3 national sororities. There are 50 groups on campus, including art, band, cheerleading, choir, chorale, chorus, dance, drama, ethnic, honors, international, jazz band, musical theater, newspaper, opera, orchestra, pep band, photography, political, professional, religious, social, social service, student government, and symphony. Popular campus events include Black History Month, Halloween, and Greek Week.
Sports: There are 5 intercollegiate sports for men and 4 for women, and 16 intramural sports for men and 16 for women. Facilities include a gym, a weight room, tennis courts, baseball, soccer, softball, and intramural multipurpose fields, and a walking trail.
Disabled Students: All of the campus is accessible. Wheelchair ramps, elevators, special parking, specially equipped rest rooms, lowered drinking fountains, lowered telephones, and specially equipped electronic doors are available.
Services: Counseling and information services are available, as is tutoring in most subjects. There is a reader service for the blind, and remedial math, reading, and writing.
Campus Safety and Security: Measures include 24-hour foot and vehicle patrol, self-defense education, escort service, and shuttle buses. There are informal discussions, pamphlets/posters/films, emergency telephones, lighted pathways/sidewalks, and and shuttles for evening students.
Programs of Study: Columbus State confers B.A., B.S. B.B.A., B.F.A., B.M., B.S.Ed. and B.S.N. degrees. Associate and master's degrees are also awarded. Bachelor's degrees are awarded in BIOLOGICAL SCIENCE (biology/biological science), BUSINESS (accounting, banking and finance, business administration and management, management information systems, and marketing/retailing/merchandising), COMMUNICATIONS AND THE ARTS (art, communications, dramatic arts, English, music, and music performance), COMPUTER AND PHYSICAL SCIENCE (chemistry, computer science, geology, and mathematics), EDUCATION (art, early childhood, middle school, music, secondary, and special), HEALTH PROFESSIONS (exercise science, health science, nursing, and respiratory therapy), SOCIAL SCIENCE (criminal justice, history, liberal arts/general studies, parks and recreation management, political science/government, psychology, and sociology). Business, education, and music are the strongest academically. Business, computer science, and criminal justice are the largest.
Required: To graduate, all students must maintain a 2.0 GPA and complete a minimum of 123 semester hours, 45 of them in a core curriculum. 3 semester hours of phys ed are required. All students must pass the Georgia Regents Test for competency in reading and writing, complete English 101 and 102 with a C or better, and satisfy the Georgia History and Constitution requirement by taking specified courses at a University System of Georgia institution or, for transfers from outside the system, by passing an exemption test. Some majors require a comprehensive exam.
Special: Cooperative programs in computer programming and engineering, internships, a Washington semester, and study abroad in Asia, Africa, Europe, and the Americas are possible. A 3-2 engineering degree with the Georgia Institute of Technology, an accelerated degree program, and a B.A.-B.S. degree in political science, biology, chemistry, math, or psychology are also available. There are 13 national honor societies, a freshman honors program.
Faculty/Classroom: 67% of faculty are male; 33%, female. Graduate students teach 1% of introductory courses. The average class size in an introductory lecture is 24; in a laboratory, 17; and in a regular course, 20.
Requirements: The SAT I or ACT is required. In addition, the SAT is preferred, with minimum verbal score of 430 and math score of 400. A minimum ACT score of 17 English and 17 math is accepted. Applicants must be graduates of accredited secondary schools. 16 academic credits are required, including 4 each in English and math, 3 each in science and social studies, and 2 in a foreign language. Applications are accepted on-line via CollegeNET. AP and CLEP credits are accepted.
Procedure: Freshmen are admitted to all sessions. Entrance exams should be taken in the fall of the senior year. There are early decision and early admissions plans. Early decision application should be filed by July 6; regular applications, by August 1 for fall entry, December 14 for spring entry, and May 23 for summer entry. Notification is sent on a rolling basis.
Transfer: 331 transfer students enrolled in 2001-2002. Transfer students with fewer than 30 hours of credit must meet the same requirements as entering freshmen. 30 credits of 123 must be completed at Columbus State.
Visiting: There are regularly scheduled orientations for prospective students, During the fall and spring semesters, there are college visitation programs. Prospective students may arrange a tour on any weekday. There are guides for informal visits and visitors may sit in on classes. To schedule a visit, contact the Admissions Office.
Financial Aid: The CSS/Profile or FAFSA is required. The fall application deadline is June 1.
International Students: They must score 550 on the written TOEFL or 213 on the electronic version or take the MELAB. The SAT I or the ACT is also required, with a minimum composite score of 830 on the SAT I.
Computers: The mainframe is an IBM 4361. Computers are available in the computer center, library, business and education departments, and learning labs. All students may access the system. There are no time limits.
Admissions Contact: Susan Lovell, Associate Director of Admissions. A video is available. E-mail: *lovell_susan@colstate.edu*
Web: *www.colstate.edu*

COVENANT COLLEGE
Lookout Mountain, GA 30750 D-4
(706) 820-2398
(888(451-2683; Fax: (706) 820-0893

Full-time: 349 men, 521 women	**Faculty:** 55; IIB, av$
Part-time: 16 men, 15 women	**Ph.D.s:** 81%
Graduate: 24 men, 42 women	**Student/Faculty:** 16 to 1
Year: semesters, summer session	**Tuition:** $16,970
Application Deadline: May 1	**Room & Board:** $5000
Freshman Class: 544 applied, 520 accepted, 242 enrolled	
SAT I Verbal/Math: 590/560	**ACT:** 25 COMPETITIVE+

Covenant College, founded in 1955, is a private liberal arts college affiliated with the Presbyterian Church in America (P.C.A.) The library contains 78,972 volumes, 27,483 microform items, and 11,923 audiovisual forms/CDs, and subscribes to 450 periodicals. Computerized library services include interlibrary loans and database searching. The 310-acre campus is in a suburban area 12 miles southwest of Chattanooga, Tennessee. Including residence halls, there are 10 buildings.
Student Life: 77% of undergraduates are from out of state, mostly the South. Others are from 46 states, 20 foreign countries, and Canada. 91% are white. Most are Protestant. The average age of freshmen is 18; all undergraduates, 20. 20% do not continue beyond their first year.
Housing: 766 students can be accommodated in college housing, which includes single-sex dormitories and on-campus apartments. On-campus housing is guaranteed for all 4 years. 81% of students live on campus; of those, 98% remain on campus on weekends. Alcohol is not permitted. All students may keep cars.
Activities: There are no fraternities or sororities. There are 48 groups on campus, including cheerleading, choir, chorale, dance, drama, honors, international, literary magazine, newspaper, photography, professional, religious, social, social service, student government, symphony, and yearbook. Popular campus events include Madrigal Dinner, Spring Banquet, and Kilter Night.
Sports: There are 3 intercollegiate sports for men and 4 for women, and 7 intramural sports for men and 7 for women. Facilities include a gym, a weight room, a swimming pool, tennis courts, 3 soccer fields, running trails, an aerobics room, and a wellness room equipped with a variety of fitness machines.

Disabled Students: All of the campus is accessible. Wheelchair ramps, elevators, special parking, specially equipped rest rooms, lowered drinking fountains, lowered telephones, and special doors for wheelchair access are available.

Services: Counseling and information services are available, as is tutoring in some subjects, including math and writing.

Campus Safety and Security: Measures include lighted pathways/sidewalks and a watchman who maintains campus security at night.

Programs of Study: Covenant confers B.A., B.S., and B.Mus. degrees. Associate and master's degrees are also awarded. Bachelor's degrees are awarded in BIOLOGICAL SCIENCE (biology/biological science), BUSINESS (business administration and management, and management science), COMMUNICATIONS AND THE ARTS (applied music, English, and music), COMPUTER AND PHYSICAL SCIENCE (chemistry, information sciences and systems, mathematics, natural sciences, and physics), EDUCATION (elementary), SOCIAL SCIENCE (biblical studies, economics, history, interdisciplinary studies, missions, philosophy, psychology, religion, and sociology). Education, business, and biology are the strongest academically. Business, English, and education are the largest.

Required: All students must complete 55 to 63 hours of core and distribution requirements, including course work in Bible studies, interdisciplinary studies, English composition, cross-cultural experience, speech, language, phys ed, computers, lab science, social science, and history. A minimum total of 126 credits and a GPA of 2.0 are required for graduation. All students must also complete an oral interview and a senior integration project, in which they explore a problem in their major field in light of Christian philosophy.

Special: Cross-registration is possible with the Council for Christian Colleges and Universities (CCCU) as are internships in business, psychology, and biology. Students may study abroad in 9 countries or spend a semester in Washington. There is a 3-2 engineering program with Georgia Tech and other universities and technical institutes, and a 13-month degree-completion program for students with 2 years of previous college experience. Juniors and seniors may take classes on a pass/fail basis. There are 2 national honor societies, a freshman honors program, and 2 departmental honors program.

Faculty/Classroom: 92% of faculty are male; 8%, female. All teach undergraduates. No introductory courses are taught by graduate students. The average class size in an introductory lecture is 27; in a laboratory, 17; and in a regular course, 18.

Admissions: 96% of the 2001-2002 applicants were accepted. The SAT I scores for the 2001-2002 freshman class were: Verbal--8% below 500, 43% between 500 and 599, 32% between 600 and 700, and 17% above 700; Math--19% below 500, 44% between 500 and 599, 29% between 600 and 700, and 8% above 700. The ACT scores were 13% below 21, 31% between 21 and 23, 21% between 24 and 26, 15% between 27 and 28, and 20% above 28. 44% of the current freshmen were in the top fifth of their class; 71% were in the top two fifths. 9 freshmen graduated first in their class.

Requirements: The SAT I or ACT is required, with a minimum composite score of 1000 on the SAT I or 21 on the ACT. Applicants must graduate from an accredited high school or have a GED. A minimum GPA of 2.5 is required. Applicants should have 4 years of high school English, 3 years of math, and 2 years each of foreign language, history, science, and social studies. An essay and an interview are required. A GPA of 2.5 is required. AP and CLEP credits are accepted. Important factors in the admissions decision are advanced placement or honor courses, extracurricular activities record, and leadership record.

Procedure: Freshmen are admitted fall and spring. Entrance exams should be taken by January of the senior year. Applications should be filed by May 1 for fall entry and November 1 for spring entry, along with a $25 fee. Notification is sent on a rolling basis.

Transfer: 58 transfer students enrolled in 2001-2002. Transfer applicants must take either the SAT I, with a minimum composite score of 1000, or the ACT, with a minimum composite of 21. Courses with a grade of C or better that apply toward the selected Covenant program will receive transfer credit. 30 credits of 126 must be completed at Covenant.

Visiting: There are regularly scheduled orientations for prospective students, consisting of a campus preview weekend during which high school students stay in dorms and attend classes, seminars, and other college activities. There are guides for informal visits and visitors may sit in on classes and stay overnight. To schedule a visit, contact Kristen Musselman, Admissions Visitor Coordinator at (706) 419-1140.

Financial Aid: In 2001-2002, 87% of all freshmen and 92% of continuing students received some form of financial aid. 71% of freshmen and 66% of continuing students received need-based aid. The average freshman award was $11,678. Of that total, scholarships or need-based grants averaged $9790 ($16,590 maximum); loans averaged $3465 ($10,500 maximum); and work contracts averaged $1979 ($2343 maximum). 38% of undergraduates work part time. Average annual earnings from campus work are $1854. The FAFSA and the college's own financial statement are required. The fall application deadline is March 1.

International Students: There are 14 international students enrolled. The school actively recruits these students. They must score 540 on the written TOEFL or 207 on the electronic version. Entrance exams are not required, but applicants are encouraged to take the SAT I or ACT if it is available in their country.

Computers: 135 PCs are available for student use in 3 computer labs, the library, and dorm clusters. All students may access the system 8 A.M. to 12 A.M., Monday through Thursday and Saturday; 8 A.M. to 6 P.M. on Friday. There are no time limits. The fee is $60 per semester.

Graduates: In 2001, 160 bachelor's degrees were awarded. The most popular majors were history (14%), elementary education (13%), and biology and business (9%). In an average class, 1% graduate in 3 years, 49% in 4 years, 58% in 5 years, and 60% in 6 years. 25 companies recruited on campus in 2000-2001.

Admissions Contact: Bryan Pierce, Director, Student Recruitment. E-mail: *admissions@covenant.edu* Web: *covenant.edu*

DEVRY UNIVERSITY/ALPHARETTA B-2

Alpharetta, GA 30004 **(770) 521-4900; Fax: (770) 664-8824**

Full-time: 814 men, 363 women	**Faculty:** 42
Part-time: 243 men, 128 women	**Ph.D.s:** n/av
Graduate: none	**Student/Faculty:** 28 to 1
Year: semesters, summer session	**Tuition:** $8805
Application Deadline: open	**Room & Board:** n/app

Freshman Class: 759 applied, 630 accepted, 322 enrolled

SAT I or ACT: recommended **LESS COMPETITIVE**

DeVry University/Alpharetta, formerly DeVry Institute of Technology, founded in 1997, is a private institution offering hands-on programs in electronics, business administration, computer information systems, telecommunications management, technical management, information technology, and computer engineering technology. The school is 1 of 23 DeVry schools throughout the United States and Canada. In addition to regional accreditation, DeVry has baccalaureate program accreditation with ABET. The library contains 3517 volumes and 221 audiovisual forms/CDs, and subscribes to 75 periodicals. Computerized library services include the card catalog, interlibrary loans, and database searching. Special learning facilities include a learning resource center and electronics and other labs. The 9-acre campus is in a suburban area. There is 1 building.

Student Life: 82% of undergraduates are from Georgia. Others are from 28 states and 13 foreign countries. 41% are white; 30% African American. The average age of all undergraduates is 27. 60% do not continue beyond their first year.

Housing: There are no residence halls. Housing referrals may be obtained through the Student Housing Office. All students commute. Alcohol is not permitted. All students may keep cars.

Activities: There are no fraternities or sororities. There are 12 groups on campus, including international, newspaper, professional, programming, social, and toastmasters. Popular campus events include Fall Festival, Spring Fling, and Thanksgiving Dinner.

Sports: There are 4 intramural sports for men and 4 for women.

Disabled Students: 98% of the campus is accessible. Wheelchair ramps, elevators, special parking, specially equipped rest rooms, lowered drinking fountains, and lowered telephones are available.

Services: Counseling and information services are available, as is tutoring in every subject.

Campus Safety and Security: Measures include escort service, informal discussions, pamphlets/posters/films, and emergency telephones. There is CCTV and video recording.

Programs of Study: DeVry confers the B.S. degree. Associate degrees are also awarded. Bachelor's degrees are awarded in BUSINESS (business administration and management), COMMUNICATIONS AND THE ARTS (telecommunications), COMPUTER AND PHYSICAL SCIENCE (information sciences and systems), ENGINEERING AND ENVIRONMENTAL DESIGN (computer engineering, electrical/electronics engineering technology, and technological management). Telecommunications, computer information systems, and business administration are the largest.

Required: To graduate, students must achieve a cumulative GPA of at least 2.0 and satisfactorily complete all curriculum requirements. Course requirements vary according to program. All first-semester students take courses in business organization, computer applications, algebra, psychology, and student success strategies.

Special: Accelerated degrees, co-op programs, nondegree study, and evening classes are possible. There are 5 national honor societies.

Faculty/Classroom: All teach undergraduates. The average class size in an introductory lecture is 30; in a laboratory, 30; and in a regular course, 30.

Admissions: 83% of the 2001-2002 applicants were accepted.

Requirements: The SAT I or ACT is recommended. Admissions requirements include graduation from a secondary school; the GED is also accepted. Applicants must pass the DeVry entrance exam or present sat-

isfactory ACT or SAT I scores. An interview is required. CLEP credit is accepted. Applications are accepted on-line at Embark.com.
Procedure: Freshmen are admitted fall, spring, and summer. There is a deferred admissions plan. Application deadlines are open. The application fee is $50. Notification is sent on a rolling basis.
Transfer: 133 transfer students enrolled in 2001-2002. Applicants must present passing grades in all completed college course work, demonstrate language skills proficiency with at least 24 completed semester hours, and present evidence of math proficiency by appropriate college-level credits. 35% of 48 to 154 credits must be completed at DeVry.
Visiting: There are regularly scheduled orientations for prospective students. There are guides for informal visits and visitors may sit in on classes. To schedule a visit, contact Kristi Franklin, New Student Coordinator.
Financial Aid: In a recent year, 41% of all freshmen and 83% of continuing students received some form of financial aid. 35% of freshmen and 69% of continuing students received need-based aid. 4% of undergraduates work part time. Average annual earnings from campus work are $3000. The FAFSA is required.
International Students: There are 39 international students enrolled. They must score 500 on the written TOEFL or 173 on the electronic version and also take the college's own entrance exam.
Computers: Lab facilities include PCs in stand-alone and network configurations with access to the mainframe. LANs provide access to a wide range of applications software. Hard copy from the mainframe is provided through a local minicomputer and medium- and high-speed printers. All students may access the system. Students may access the system during lab hours. There are no fees. It is strongly recommended that all students have personal computers.
Graduates: In 2001, 167 bachelor's degrees were awarded. The most popular majors were business (50%), computer information systems (40%), and electronics engineering technology (10%). 65 companies recruited on campus in 2000-2001.
Admissions Contact: Gerry Purcell, Director of Admissions.
Web: *www.atl.devry.edu/alpharetta/*

DEVRY UNIVERSITY/DECATUR

Decatur, GA 30030-2198 B-2
(404) 292-2645; (800) 221-4771

Full-time: 1418 men, 913 women	**Faculty:** 71
Part-time: 318 men, 276 women	**Ph.D.s:** n/av
Graduate: none	**Student/Faculty:** 33 to 1
Year: semesters, summer session	**Tuition:** $8805
Application Deadline: open	**Room & Board:** n/app

Freshman Class: 1840 applied, 1464 accepted, 759 enrolled
SAT I or ACT: recommended **LESS COMPETITIVE**

The DeVry University/Decatur, formerly DeVry Institute of Technology, a private institution, was established in 1969; there are 22 other DeVry schools in the United States and Canada owned by DeVry University, Inc. The school offers technology-based undergraduate programs in business administration, electronics, computer information systems, telecommunications management, technical management, information technology, and computer engineering technology. In addition to regional accreditation, DeVry has baccalaureate program accreditation with ABET. The library contains 18,929 volumes, 21,024 microform items, and 800 audiovisual forms/CDs, and subscribes to 80 periodicals. Computerized library services include the card catalog, interlibrary loans, and database searching. Special learning facilities include a learning resource center and electronics and other labs. The 18-acre campus is in a suburban area 6 miles from downtown Atlanta. There is 1 building.
Student Life: 82% of undergraduates are from Georgia. Others are from 32 states and 2 foreign countries. 80% are African American. The average age of all undergraduates is 27. 57% do not continue beyond their first year.
Housing: There are no residence halls. Housing referrals may be obtained through the Student Housing Office. All students commute. Alcohol is not permitted. All students may keep cars.
Activities: There are no fraternities or sororities. There are 12 groups on campus, including electronics, environmental, ethnic, film, fitness, ham radio, honors, international, newspaper, professional, social, and toastmasters (speech). Popular campus events include Fall Festival, Spring Fling, and Thanksgiving Dinner.
Sports: There is 1 intercollegiate sport for men, and 4 intramural sports for men and 4 for women.
Disabled Students: 98% of the campus is accessible. Wheelchair ramps, elevators, special parking, specially equipped rest rooms, lowered drinking fountains, and lowered telephones are available.
Services: Counseling and information services are available, as is tutoring in every subject.
Campus Safety and Security: Measures include escort service, informal discussions, pamphlets/posters/films, and emergency telephones. There are lighted pathways/sidewalks. The campus is patrolled by county police 7:30 A.M. to 8 P.M. Monday through Friday and by DeVry security 6:30 A.M. to 11:30 P.M. Monday through Friday and 8 A.M. to 5 P.M. Saturday.
Programs of Study: DeVry confers the B.S. degree. Associate degrees are also awarded. Bachelor's degrees are awarded in BUSINESS (business administration and management), COMMUNICATIONS AND THE ARTS (telecommunications), COMPUTER AND PHYSICAL SCIENCE (information sciences and systems), ENGINEERING AND ENVIRONMENTAL DESIGN (computer engineering, electrical/electronics engineering technology, and technological management). Computer information systems and telecommunications are the largest.
Required: To graduate, students must achieve a cumulative GPA of at least 2.0 and satisfactorily complete all curriculum requirements. Course requirements vary according to program. All first-semester students take courses in business organization, computer applications, algebra, psychology, and student success strategies.
Special: Evening and weekend classes, co-op programs, an accelerated degree program, and nondegree study are possible. There are 4 national honor societies and 3 departmental honors programs.
Faculty/Classroom: All teach undergraduates. The average class size in an introductory lecture is 30; in a laboratory, 30; and in a regular course, 30.
Admissions: 80% of the 2001-2002 applicants were accepted.
Requirements: The SAT I or ACT is recommended. Admissions requirements include graduation from a secondary school; the GED is also accepted. Applicants from accredited postsecondary schools must pass the DeVry entrance exam or present satisfactory ACT or SAT I scores. An interview is required. CLEP credit is accepted. Applications are accepted on-line at Embark.com
Procedure: Freshmen are admitted fall, spring, and summer. There is a deferred admissions plan. Application deadlines are open. The application fee is $50. Notification is sent on a rolling basis.
Transfer: 746 transfer students enrolled in 2001-2002. Applicants must present passing grades in all completed college course work, demonstrate language skills proficiency with at least 24 completed semester hours, and evidence math proficiency by appropriate college-level credits. 35% of 48 to 154 credits must be completed at DeVry.
Visiting: There are regularly scheduled orientations for prospective students. There are guides for informal visits and visitors may sit in on classes. To schedule a visit, contact Karen Krumenaker, New Student Coordinator at (404) 292-7900.
Financial Aid: In a recent year, 63% of all freshmen and 91% of continuing students received some form of financial aid. 55% of freshmen and 79% of continuing students received need-based aid. 4% of undergraduates work part time. Average annual earnings from campus work are $6800. The FAFSA is required.
International Students: There are 68 international students enrolled. They must score 500 on the written TOEFL or 173 on the electronic version and also take the college's own entrance exam.
Computers: The mainframe is an IBM 3081K. Lab facilities include PCs in stand-alone and network configurations, with access to the mainframe. LANs provide access to a wide range of applications software. Hard copy from the mainframe is provided through a local minicomputer and medium- and high-speed printers. Students in the computer information systems program may access the system during published lab hours. There are no fees.
Graduates: In 2001, 412 bachelor's degrees were awarded. The most popular majors were business (48%), computer information systems (44%), and electronics ehgineering technology (8%). 49 companies recruited on campus in 2000-2001.
Admissions Contact: George Ollennu, Director of Admissions.
Web: *www.atl.devry.edu*

EMORY UNIVERSITY

Atlanta, GA 30322 B-2
(800) 727-6036

Full-time: 2821 men, 3427 women	**Faculty:** 583; I, +$
Part-time: 42 men, 84 women	**Ph.D.s:** 98%
Graduate: 2197 men, 2872 women	**Student/Faculty:** 11 to 1
Year: semesters, summer session	**Tuition:** $25,552
Application Deadline: January 15	**Room & Board:** $8240

Freshman Class: 9607 applied, 4096 accepted, 1281 enrolled
SAT I or ACT: required **MOST COMPETITIVE**

Emory University, founded in 1836, is a private institution affiliated with the United Methodist Church. There are 4 undergraduate and 7 graduate schools. The 7 libraries contain 2.7 million volumes, 3,580,981 microform items, and 32,603 audiovisual forms/CDs, and subscribe to 27,426 periodicals. Computerized library services include the card catalog, interlibrary loans, and database searching. Special learning facilities include a learning resource center, art gallery, radio station, TV station, the Michael C. Carlos Museum, the Carter Center, and facilities for direct monitoring of Russian domestic television. The 674-acre campus is in a suburban area 5 miles northeast of downtown Atlanta. Including residence halls, there are 121 buildings.
Student Life: 81% of undergraduates are from out of state, mostly the South. Others are from 50 states, 59 foreign countries, and Canada. 65% are from public schools. 65% are white; 11% African American;

11% Asian American. 35% are Protestant; 30% Jewish; 17% Catholic; 15% claim no religious affiliation. The average age of freshmen is 18; all undergraduates, 20. 6% do not continue beyond their first year.

Housing: 3440 students can be accommodated in college housing, which includes single-sex and coed dormitories, on-campus apartments, married-student housing, fraternity houses, and sorority houses. In addition, there are honors houses, language houses, and special-interest houses. On-campus housing is guaranteed for all 4 years. 63% of students live on campus; of those, 95% remain on campus on weekends. Upperclassmen may keep cars.

Activities: 35% of men belong to 13 national fraternities; 35% of women belong to 9 national sororities. There are 200 groups on campus, including art, bagpipe band, band, cheerleading, chess, choir, chorale, chorus, computers, dance, debate, drama, ethnic, film, gay, honors, international, jazz band, literary magazine, musical theater, newspaper, orchestra, pep band, photography, political, professional, radio and TV, religious, social, social service, student government, symphony, and yearbook. Popular campus events include Heritage Ball, Festival of Nine Lessons, and Martin Luther King Week.

Sports: There are 9 intercollegiate sports for men and 9 for women, and 40 intramural sports for men and 40 for women. Facilities include a phys ed center, which contains a 3000-seat gym with 4 basketball courts, an Olympic-size swimming pool, 2 Nautilus weight rooms, and tennis, racquetball, and squash courts. In addition, there is a soccer field and a 400-meter track, with seating for 2000 spectators.

Disabled Students: 90% of the campus is accessible. Wheelchair ramps, elevators, special parking, specially equipped rest rooms, special class scheduling, lowered drinking fountains, and lowered telephones are available.

Services: Counseling and information services are available, as is tutoring in most subjects. There is a reader service for the blind.

Campus Safety and Security: Measures include 24-hour foot and vehicle patrol, self-defense education, escort service, and shuttle buses. There are informal discussions, pamphlets/posters/films, emergency telephones, and lighted pathways/sidewalks. The campus patrol is a fully accredited police department.

Programs of Study: Emory confers B.A., B.S., B.B.A., and B.S.N. degrees. Associate, master's, and doctoral degrees are also awarded. Bachelor's degrees are awarded in BIOLOGICAL SCIENCE (biology/biological science and neurosciences), BUSINESS (accounting, banking and finance, business administration and management, business economics, and marketing/retailing/merchandising), COMMUNICATIONS AND THE ARTS (art history and appreciation, classics, comparative literature, creative writing, dance, dramatic arts, English, film arts, French, Latin, modern language, music, and Spanish), COMPUTER AND PHYSICAL SCIENCE (chemistry, computer science, mathematics, and physics), EDUCATION (educational statistics and research), HEALTH PROFESSIONS (nursing), SOCIAL SCIENCE (African studies, anthropology, Asian/Oriental studies, classical/ancient civilization, economics, European studies, French studies, German area studies, history, international studies, Judaic studies, Latin American studies, medieval studies, Middle Eastern studies, philosophy, political science/government, psychology, religion, Russian and Slavic studies, sociology, and women's studies). Sciences, English, and psychology are the strongest academically. Business administration, psychology, and economics are the largest.

Required: To graduate, students must complete 132 semester hours, including courses during the first 2 years in English, science, math, history, the social sciences, health, and phys ed. Students must have a GPA of 1.9 for the first 3 years and 2.0 in the senior year. The number of hours required for the major varies by department. A thesis is required for students in honors or dual B.A./M.A. or B.S./M.S. programs.

Special: Special academic programs include cross-registration with Atlanta area colleges and universities, departmental internships, work-study programs, dual majors, 3-2 and 4-2 engineering degrees with Georgia Tech, and pass/fail options. A Washington semester and B.A.-B.S. degrees are available, and students may study abroad in many countries. There are accelerated degree programs offered in biology, chemistry, math, physics, English, history, philosophy, political science, sociology, and computer science. There are 25 national honor societies, including Phi Beta Kappa.

Faculty/Classroom: 70% of faculty are male; 30%, female. All both teach and do research. Graduate students teach 10% of introductory courses. The average class size in an introductory lecture is 25; in a laboratory, 10; and in a regular course, 20.

Admissions: 43% of the 2001-2002 applicants were accepted. The SAT I scores for the 2001-2002 freshman class were: Verbal--17% between 500 and 599, 62% between 600 and 700, and 21% above 700; Math--9% between 500 and 599, 60% between 600 and 700, and 31% above 700. The ACT scores were 1% between 21 and 23, 15% between 24 and 26, 32% between 27 and 28, and 52% above 28. 87% of the current freshmen were in the top fifth of their class; 95% were in the top two fifths. There were 53 National Merit finalists.

Requirements: The SAT I or ACT is required, and 1 SAT II: Subject test is recommended. The student must have acquired 16 academic credits in secondary school, including 4 years of English, 3 of math, and 2 each of history and science. The university requires the student to submit an essay. Important factors in the admissions decision are advanced placement or honor courses, recommendations by school officials, and extracurricular activities record. Applications are accepted on computer disk via CollegeLink and on-line. AP credits are accepted.

Procedure: Freshmen are admitted in the fall. Entrance exams should be taken prior to applying. There are early decision, early admissions, and deferred admissions plans. Early decision applications should be filed by November 1 for round I, January 1 for round II; regular applications, by January 15 for fall entry. Notification of early decision is sent December 15 for round I, February 1 for round II; regular decision, April 1. 470 early decision candidates were accepted for the 2001-2002 class. 5% of all applicants are on a waiting list; 20 were accepted in 2001.

Transfer: 80 transfer students enrolled in 2001-2002. Applicants must have taken the SAT I or ACT and completed at least 1 year of college, with a GPA of 3.0. 64 credits of 132 must be completed at Emory.

Visiting: There are regularly scheduled orientations for prospective students, including a group information session and a campus tour. There are guides for informal visits and visitors may sit in on classes and stay overnight. To schedule a visit, contact the Admission Office.

Financial Aid: In 2001-2002, 55% of all freshmen and 63% of continuing students received some form of financial aid. 38% of freshmen and 42% of continuing students received need-based aid. The average freshman award was $20,070. Of that total, scholarships or need-based grants averaged $15,845; loans averaged $2625; and work contracts averaged $1600. 70% of undergraduates work part time. Average annual earnings from campus work are $1500. The average financial indebtedness of the 2001 graduate was $18,350. Emory is a member of CSS. The CSS/Profile or FAFSA is required. The fall application deadline is February 15.

International Students: There were 141 international students enrolled in a recent year. The school actively recruits these students. They must take the TOEFL and also take the SAT I or the ACT.

Computers: The mainframes are an IBM 9672-E01 and Sun SPARC 20J. There are about 600 PCs located in the library, dorms, computing centers, and some academic departments. All students may access the system 24 hours a day. There are no time limits and no fees.

Graduates: In 2001, 1422 bachelor's degrees were awarded. The most popular majors were business (16%), psychology (10%), and economics (9%). In an average class, 2% graduate in 3 years, 79% in 4 years, 84% in 5 years, and 86% in 6 years. 210 companies recruited on campus in 2000-2001. Of the 2000 graduating class, 55% were enrolled in graduate school within 6 months of graduation.

Admissions Contact: Daniel C. Walls, Dean of Admission. A video is available. E-mail: *admiss@emory.edu*
Web: *www.emory.edu/admissions*

FORT VALLEY STATE UNIVERSITY — B-3

Fort Valley, GA 31030-3298 — (478) 825-6307
(877) 462-3878; Fax: (478) 825-6169

Full-time: 955 men, 1155 women	**Faculty:** 133
Part-time: 85 men, 140 women	**Ph.D.s:** 60%
Graduate: 60 men, 265 women	**Student/Faculty:** 16 to 1
Year: semesters, summer session	**Tuition:** $2412 ($8052)
Application Deadline: see profile	**Room & Board:** $3602
Freshman Class: n/av	
SAT I or ACT: required	**LESS COMPETITIVE**

Fort Valley State University, founded in 1895, is a public land-grant member of the University System of Georgia. The university offers undergraduate programs in the arts and sciences, business, education, agriculture, engineering, and other vocational and technical fields. Graduate programs are offered in early childhood, middle grades education, mental health and rehabilitation counseling, and guidance and counseling. Figures in above capsule are approximate. There are 3 undergraduate schools and 1 graduate school. In addition to regional accreditation, FVSU has baccalaureate program accreditation with NCATE. The library contains 250,000 volumes and 172,000 microform items, and subscribes to 1168 periodicals. Computerized library services include the card catalog, interlibrary loans, and database searching. Special learning facilities include a learning resource center, radio station, TV station, experimental agricultural plots, animal research centers, and greenhouse complex. The 1375-acre campus is in a rural area 30 miles southwest of Macon. Including residence halls, there are 35 buildings.

Student Life: 92% of undergraduates are from Georgia. Others are from 29 states and 5 foreign countries. 92% are African American. 50% of freshmen remain to graduate.

Housing: 982 students can be accommodated in college housing, which includes single-sex dormitories and on-campus apartments. On-campus housing is guaranteed for the freshman year only and is available on a first-come, first-served basis. 65% of students live on campus. Alcohol is not permitted. All students may keep cars.

Activities: There are 4 national fraternities and 5 national sororities. There are 73 groups on campus, including cheerleading, choir, chorus, dance, drama, honors, international, jazz band, marching band, newspaper, opera, orchestra, political, radio and TV, religious, social service, student government, and yearbook. Popular campus events include Black History month.

Sports: There are 8 intercollegiate sports for men, and 3 intramural sports for men and 3 for women. Facilities include a stadium, a gym, a baseball field, lighted tennis courts, an indoor swimming pool, indoor and outdoor tracks, and shuffleboard courts.

Disabled Students: Wheelchair ramps, elevators, special parking, and specially equipped rest rooms are available.

Services: Counseling and information services are available, as is tutoring in most subjects. There is remedial math, reading, and writing.

Campus Safety and Security: Measures include 24-hour foot and vehicle patrol, informal discussions, and pamphlets/posters/films.

Programs of Study: FVSU confers B.A., B.S., B.B.A., and B.S.W. degrees. Associate and master's degrees are also awarded. Bachelor's degrees are awarded in AGRICULTURE (agricultural economics, animal science, horticulture, and plant science), BIOLOGICAL SCIENCE (biology/biological science, nutrition, and zoology), BUSINESS (accounting, business administration and management, marketing/retailing/merchandising, and office supervision and management), COMMUNICATIONS AND THE ARTS (communications and English), COMPUTER AND PHYSICAL SCIENCE (chemistry, computer science, information sciences and systems, and mathematics), EDUCATION (agricultural, early childhood, home economics, mathematics, middle school, physical, and secondary), ENGINEERING AND ENVIRONMENTAL DESIGN (agricultural engineering technology, commercial art, and electrical/electronics engineering technology), HEALTH PROFESSIONS (veterinary science), SOCIAL SCIENCE (child psychology/development, criminal justice, economics, political science/government, psychology, social work, and sociology).

Required: Students must complete general education requirements, including courses in humanities, social science, and math/science, and courses in the major. The bachelor's degree requires a minimum GPA of 2.0 and no grade below C in the major.

Special: Students may participate in cooperative work-study programs with local industries, cross-register for courses at Robins Residence Center, and study abroad. FVSU also offers a 3-2 dual degree program in chemistry/geosciences with the University of Oklahoma, in engineering or other technical fields with Georgia Institute of Technology, and a 3-2 engineering degree with the University of Nevada, Las Vegas. There are 5 national honor societies, and a freshman honors program.

Faculty/Classroom: 60% of faculty are male; 40%, female. The average class size in a regular course is 25.

Requirements: The SAT I or ACT is required. In addition, applicants must be graduates of an accredited secondary school or have earned a GED. The university requires at least 17 academic units of study, including 4 in English, 3 in social science, 3 each in math and science, and 2 of foreign language. A GPA of 2.2 is required. AP and CLEP credits are accepted. Applications are accepted on-line at the FVSU web site.

Procedure: Freshmen are admitted to all sessions. There is an early admissions plan. Check with the school for current applicatio deadlines. There is a $20 fee. Notification is sent on a rolling basis.

Transfer: In addition to meeting standard admission requirements, transfers must submit transcripts from all colleges previously attended. Transfer credit is accepted based on a 2.0 minimum GPA, and only courses with a C or better will be accepted. 45 credits of 180 must be completed at FVSU.

Visiting: There are regularly scheduled orientations for prospective students, including an overview, an introduction of administration and faculty, and a tour. There are guides for informal visits and visitors may sit in on classes. To schedule a visit, contact the Office of Enrollment Management.

Financial Aid: In a recent year, 93% of all students received some form of financial aid including need-based aid. The FAFSA is required. Check with the school for current deadlines.

International Students: There were 38 international students enrolled in a recent year. They must take the college's own test and also take the SAT I or the ACT.

Computers: There are no time limits and no fees. It is strongly recommended that all students have a personal computer.

Admissions Contact: Gerri McCord, Dean of Admissions and Enrollment Management. E-mail: *mccordg@mail.fvsu.edu*
Web: *www.fvsu.edu*

GEORGIA BAPTIST COLLEGE OF NURSING
(See Mercer University)

GEORGIA COLLEGE AND STATE UNIVERSITY C-3

Milledgeville, GA 31061 (478) 445-5004
(800) 342-0471; Fax: (478) 445-1914

Full-time: 1295 men, 2071 women	**Faculty:** 260; IIA, --$
Part-time: 271 men, 446 women	**Ph.D.s:** 73%
Graduate: 320 men, 676 women	**Student/Faculty:** 13 to 1
Year: semesters, summer session	**Tuition:** $3032 ($10,628)
Application Deadline: July 15	**Room & Board:** $4312
Freshman Class: 2517 applied, 1765 accepted, 764 enrolled	
SAT I Verbal/Math: 520/510	**ACT:** 20 **COMPETITIVE**

Georgia College and State University, founded in 1889, is the public liberal arts university of Georgia. There are 4 undergraduate schools and 1 graduate school. In addition to regional accreditation, GC&SU has baccalaureate program accreditation with AACSB, NASM, NCATE, and NLN. The library contains 182,759 volumes, 616,418 microform items, and 4474 audiovisual forms/CDs, and subscribes to 970 periodicals. Computerized library services include the card catalog, interlibrary loans, and database searching. Special learning facilities include a learning resource center, art gallery, radio station, TV station, and museum. The 666-acre campus is in an urban area 30 miles from Macon. Including residence halls, there are 57 buildings.

Student Life: 99% of undergraduates are from Georgia. Others are from 26 states, 45 foreign countries, and Canada. 82% are white; 13%, African American. The average age of freshmen is 19; all undergraduates, 22. 28% do not continue beyond their first year.

Housing: 1100 students can be accommodated in college housing, which includes single-sex and coed dormitories. In addition, there are honors houses, and a Freshman Experience house. On-campus housing is available on a first-come, first-served basis. 70% of students commute. Alcohol is not permitted. All students may keep cars.

Activities: 8% of men belong to 7 national fraternities; 8% of women belong to 6 national sororities. There are 100 groups on campus, including band, Big Brother/Sister, cheerleading, choir, chorale, chorus, dance, debate, drama, ethnic, honors, international, jazz band, literary magazine, musical theater, photography, political, professional, radio and TV, religious, residence hall council, social, social service, and student government. Popular campus events include Week of Welcome, Progressive Dinner, and International Week.

Sports: There are 5 intercollegiate sports for men and 4 for women, and 17 intramural sports for men and 17 for women. Facilities include a basketball arena, a gym, a track, racquetball courts, a weight room, aerobics facilities, an indoor rock-climbing wall, a 70-acre phys ed complex, a soccer field, a ball park, a golf course, tennis courts, an indoor and an outdoor pool, a rope/challenge course, and nearby lakes for canoeing, sailing, and skiing.

Disabled Students: Up to 90% of the campus is accessible. Wheelchair ramps, elevators, special parking, specially equipped rest rooms, lowered drinking fountains, lowered telephones, and disabled student housing are available.

Services: Counseling and information services are available, as is tutoring in most subjects. There is a reader service for the blind, and remedial math, reading, and writing.

Campus Safety and Security: Measures include 24-hour foot and vehicle patrol, self-defense education, escort service, and shuttle buses. There are informal discussions, pamphlets/posters/films, emergency telephones, and lighted pathways/sidewalks.

Programs of Study: GC&SU confers B.A., B.S., B.B.A., B.G.S., B.M.E., B.M.T., and B.S.N. degrees. Master's degrees are also awarded. Bachelor's degrees are awarded in BIOLOGICAL SCIENCE (biology/biological science), BUSINESS (accounting, business administration and management, management science, marketing and distribution, and office supervision and management), COMMUNICATIONS AND THE ARTS (art, communications, dramatic arts, English, French, music, music performance, Spanish, and voice), COMPUTER AND PHYSICAL SCIENCE (chemistry, computer science, information sciences and systems, and mathematics), EDUCATION (athletic training, early childhood, middle school, music, physical, recreation, and special), HEALTH PROFESSIONS (exercise science, music therapy, and nursing), SOCIAL SCIENCE (criminal justice, economics, history, human services, liberal arts/general studies, political science/government, psychology, religious music, and sociology). Education is the strongest academically. Education and nursing are the largest.

Required: To graduate, students must complete at least 120 semester hours, including 60 in the major and 39 in upper-level courses, with a minimum GPA of 2.0. Core curriculum requirements include 12 hours of social science, 11 of math/science, 9 of essential skills, 6 of humanities/fine arts, 4 of global and arts awareness, and 18 of courses related to the major. All B.A. candidates and some B.S. candidates must take foreign language. All students must pass an exam on the history and Constitution of both the U.S. and Georgia, the reading and writing sections of the Regents exam, and a senior exit exam in the major.

Special: GC&SU has study-abroad agreements with institutions worldwide, co-op programs, internships, work-study programs, dual majors, independent study, and student-designed majors. There is a 3-2 engineering degree program with the Georgia Institute of Technology. There are 10 national honor societies and a freshman honors program.

Faculty/Classroom: 52% of faculty are male; 48%, female. All teach undergraduates. No introductory courses are taught by graduate students. The average class size in an introductory lecture is 21 and in a laboratory, 16.

Admissions: 70% of the 2001-2002 applicants were accepted. The SAT I scores for the 2001-2002 freshman class were: Verbal--33% below 500, 56% between 500 and 599, and 11% between 600 and 700; Math--39% below 500, 51% between 500 and 599, and 10% between 600 and 700. The ACT scores were 55% below 21, 35% between 21 and 23, 9% between 24 and 26, and 1% between 27 and 28.

Requirements: The SAT I, with a composite score of 940 (minimum 440 verbal and 400 math), or the ACT, with a score of 20 (minimum 17 English and 18 math), is required. Applicants must be graduates of an accredited or recognized secondary school and must complete the Georgia college-preparatory curriculum requirements, including 4 units each of English and math, 3 each of social science and science, and 2 of a foreign language. A GPA of 2.22 is required. AP and CLEP credits are accepted. Information about applying on-line can be found on the school's web site.

Procedure: Freshmen are admitted to all sessions. Entrance exams should be taken by January of the senior year. Applications should be filed by July 15 for fall entry, December 1 for spring entry, and May 1 for summer entry, along with a $25 fee. Notification is sent on a rolling basis.

Transfer: 301 transfer students enrolled in 2001-2002. Applicants must have at least a 2.0 GPA, submit official transcripts from all colleges attended, and be eligible to return to their previous institution. Those who have completed fewer than 30 semester hours must meet all freshman admissions requirements. 40 credits of 120 must be completed at GC&SU.

Visiting: There are regularly scheduled orientations for prospective students, including receptions, tours, school meetings, information sessions, and academic and cocurricular advising and registration. There are guides for informal visits and visitors may sit in on classes. To schedule a visit, contact the Office of Admissions.

Financial Aid: In a recent year, 60% of all freshmen received some form of financial aid, including need-based aid. The average freshman award was $4407. Of that total, scholarships or need-based grants averaged $3019 ($5000 maximum); loans averaged $2683 ($6427 maximum); and work contracts averaged $1034 ($2301 maximum). 4% of undergraduates work part time. Average annual earnings from campus work are $1338. The average financial indebtedness of the 2001 graduate was $12,572. GC&SU is a member of CSS. The FAFSA and the college's own financial statement are required. The fall application deadline is March 1.

International Students: There are 104 international students enrolled. The school actively recruits these students. They must score 500 on the written TOEFL or 173 on the electronic version or take the IELTS or Cambridge Exam, or they must complete the highest level of an ESL course. They must also take the college's own entrance exam.

Computers: The mainframe is an HP 9000. A VAX PC, with Peachnet, Telnet, and LAN access and access to the HP mainframe, is available for student use, as are other PCs. All students may access the system. Lab hours vary. There are no time limits and no fees.

Graduates: In 2001, 707 bachelor's degrees were awarded. The most popular majors were nursing (14%), psychology (10%), and computer-based information systems (8%). In an average class, 24% graduate in 4 years and 38% in 5 years.

Admissions Contact: Maryllis Wolfgang, Director of Admissions. E-mail: *mwolfgan@mail.gcsu.edu* Web: *www.gcsu.edu*

GEORGIA INSTITUTE OF TECHNOLOGY B-2
Atlanta, GA 30332 **(404) 894-4154; Fax: (404) 894-9511**

Full-time: 7248 men, 2916 women	**Faculty:** 756; I, +$
Part-time: 624 men, 255 women	**Ph.D.s:** 94%
Graduate: 3412 men, 1121 women	**Student/Faculty:** 13 to 1
Year: semesters, summer session	**Tuition:** $3454 ($12,350)
Application Deadline: January 15	**Room & Board:** $5574
Freshman Class: 9476 applied, 5157 accepted, 2225 enrolled	
SAT I Verbal/Math: 642/689	**HIGHLY COMPETITIVE+**

Georgia Institute of Technology, founded in 1885, is a public technological institution offering programs in architecture, management, policy, and international affairs, engineering, computing, and science. There are 6 undergraduate and 6 graduate schools. In addition to regional accreditation, Georgia Tech has baccalaureate program accreditation with AACSB, ABET, CSAB, and NAAB. The 2 libraries contain 3,939,093 volumes, 4,233,606 microform items, and 15,254 audiovisual forms/CDs, and subscribe to 17,000 periodicals. Computerized library services include the card catalog, interlibrary loans, and database searching. Special learning facilities include a learning resource center, art gallery, and radio station. The 365-acre campus is in an urban area. Including residence halls, there are 165 buildings.

Student Life: 65% of undergraduates are from Georgia. Others are from 50 states, 87 foreign countries, and Canada. 85% are from public schools. 70% are white; 14% Asian American. The average age of freshmen is 18; all undergraduates, 20. 10% do not continue beyond their first year.

Housing: 7848 students can be accommodated in college housing, which includes single-sex and coed dormitories, on-campus apartments, married-student housing, fraternity houses, and sorority houses. In addition, there are language houses and special-interest houses. On-campus housing is guaranteed for the freshman year only, is available on a first-come, first-served basis, and is available on a lottery system for upperclassmen. 58% of students live on campus. Alcohol is not permitted. All students, except first-year freshman, may keep cars.

Activities: 29% of men belong to 32 national fraternities; 20% of women belong to 10 national sororities. There are 281 groups on campus, including athletic, band, cheerleading, chess, chorale, chorus, computers, dance, departmental, drama, drill team, ethnic, gay, honors, international, jazz band, literary magazine, marching band, musical theater, newspaper, orchestra, outdoor, pep band, photography, political, professional, radio and TV, religious, social, social service, student government, symphony, and yearbook. Popular campus events include Greek Week and the Ramblin' Wreck Parade.

Sports: There are 9 intercollegiate sports for men and 8 for women, and 12 intramural sports for men and 9 for women. Facilities include indoor and outdoor tennis and track facilities, baseball and softball fields, a 46,000-seat football stadium, a 10,000-seat basketball arena, an Olympic aquatic center for swimming and diving, a golf practice facility, and a student athletic complex that includes 6 multipurpose indoor courts, strength training and cardiofitness facilities, and racquetball and squash courts.

Disabled Students: 60% of the campus is accessible. Wheelchair ramps, elevators, special parking, specially equipped rest rooms, special class scheduling, lowered drinking fountains, lowered telephones, visual alarms in housing, assistive listening devices, adapted furniture in computer labs, adaptable living space, and a paid TDD telephone booth are available.

Services: Counseling and information services are available, as is tutoring in most subjects. There is a reader service for the blind.

Campus Safety and Security: Measures include 24-hour foot and vehicle patrol, self-defense education, escort service, and shuttle buses. There are informal discussions, pamphlets/posters/films, emergency telephones, and lighted pathways/sidewalks.

Programs of Study: Georgia Tech confers B.S. and many specialized bachelor's degrees in science, engineering, and computing fields. Master's and doctoral degrees are also awarded. Bachelor's degrees are awarded in BIOLOGICAL SCIENCE (biology/biological science), BUSINESS (business administration and management, and management science), COMMUNICATIONS AND THE ARTS (industrial design), COMPUTER AND PHYSICAL SCIENCE (applied mathematics, chemistry, computer science, earth science, mathematics, physics, and polymer science), ENGINEERING AND ENVIRONMENTAL DESIGN (aeronautical engineering, architecture, chemical engineering, civil engineering, computer engineering, construction management, electrical/electronics engineering, industrial engineering, materials engineering, materials science, mechanical engineering, nuclear engineering, technology and public affairs, and textile engineering), SOCIAL SCIENCE (economics, history, international relations, psychology, public affairs, and textiles and clothing). Engineering, computer science, and sciences are the strongest academically. Computer science, mechanical and industrial engineering are the largest.

Required: All students must take English, calculus, computer science, social science, and a health science course selected from 2 options. Distribution requirements include 12 hours of humanities, 12 of social science, including specific course work in U.S. and Georgia history and government, 8 of math, 8 of science, 3 of computer science, and 2 of wellness. Students must maintain a 1.95 GPA in 125 hours, and must pass a reading and writing competency exam.

Special: Extensive co-op programs, cross-registration with other Atlanta-area colleges, and internships are available. Study abroad in numerous countries is possible. An engineering transfer program is offered within the university system, and a liberal arts-engineering dual degree program serves area colleges and institutions nationwide. Students have access to multidisciplinary and certificate programs outside their major field of study. The Georgia Tech Regional Engineering Program (GTREP) offers undergraduate and graduate degrees in collaboration with Armstrong Atlantic State University, Georgia Southern University, and Savannah State University. There are 12 national honor societies.

Faculty/Classroom: 84% of faculty are male; 16%, female. All teach undergraduates. Graduate students teach 17% of introductory courses. The average class size in an introductory lecture is 30 and in a laboratory, 19.

Admissions: 54% of the 2001-2002 applicants were accepted. The SAT I scores for the 2001-2002 freshman class were: Verbal--2% below

500, 23% between 500 and 599, 54% between 600 and 700, and 22% above 700; Math--1% below 500, 5% between 500 and 599, 47% between 600 and 700, and 47% above 700. 80% of the current freshmen were in the top fifth of their class; 96% were in the top two fifths. There were 126 National Merit finalists.

Requirements: The SAT I or ACT is required. In addition, candidates for admission must have completed 4 years each of English and math, 3 of science, 2 each of history and the same foreign language, and 1 of social studies. AP credits are accepted. Important factors in the admissions decision are leadership record, extracurricular activities record, and evidence of special talent. To apply on-line, applicants may contact the Office of Undergraduate Admissions or locate Georgia Tech on the World Wide Web at *www.enrollment.gatech.edu*.

Procedure: Freshmen are admitted fall and spring. Entrance exams should be taken by the end of the junior year. Applications should be filed by January 15 for fall and summer entry. Notification is sent March 15.

Transfer: 436 transfer students enrolled in 2001-2002. Transfer applicants must have completed a minimum of 30 semester hours of course work. Grades and academic standing must be satisfactory for the last term of enrollment at the prior college. Competitive GPAs are determined according to the projected major. 36 credits of 120 must be completed at Georgia Tech.

Visiting: There are regularly scheduled orientations for prospective students, consisting of the Connect with Tech program, which includes a Sunday-Monday overnight stay with a current student, class the next morning, and the opportunity to meet with students, faculty, and staff. There are guides for informal visits and visitors may sit in on classes. To schedule a visit, contact the Office of Undergraduate Admissions at (404) 894-6809.

Financial Aid: In 2001-2002, 82% of all freshmen and 46% of continuing students received some form of financial aid. 22% of freshmen and 17% of continuing students received need-based aid. The average freshman award was $8737. Of that total, scholarships or need-based grants averaged $5482 ($14,000 maximum); and loans averaged $8246 ($22,300 maximum). 2% of undergraduates work part time. Average annual earnings from campus work are $2400. The average financial indebtedness of the 2001 graduate was $16,500. The FAFSA and the college's own financial statement are required. The fall application deadline is March 1.

International Students: There are 520 international students enrolled. They must score 600 on the written TOEFL or 250 on the electronic version and also take the SAT I.

Computers: The mainframes are a CDC CYBER Model 990, a CRAY Y/MP-EL, a DEC ALPHA 3000/400, an IBM ES/9000-260, a Sun 4/490, a Sun SPARC Center 2000, a Sun SPARC 20, a Sun VitraEnterprise 4000, an SGI Origin 2000, and an SGI Origin 200. Students have access to 330 public seats in computer clusters at 9 locations on campus. Off campus, students may access one of more than 300 dial-in lines or use the service provided through MCI to access the computer network; on campus, students may use the ethernet connection from any residence hall. All students may access the system. There are no time limits and no fees. All students are required to have personal computers.

Graduates: In 2001, 2035 bachelor's degrees were awarded. The most popular majors were management (15%), industrial engineering (14%), and computer science (13%). In an average class, 24% graduate in 4 years, 59% in 5 years, and 68% in 6 years. 800 companies recruited on campus in 2000-2001.

Admissions Contact: Deborah Smith, Director of Undergraduate Admissions. E-mail: *admissions@success.gatech.edu*
Web: *www.enrollment.gatech.edu*

GEORGIA SOUTHERN UNIVERSITY D-3

Statesboro, GA 30460 **(912) 681-5391; Fax: (912) 486-7240**

Full-time: 5509 men, 5872 women	**Faculty:** 549; IIA, --$
Part-time: 684 men, 733 women	**Ph.D.s:** 78%
Graduate: 456 men, 1117 women	**Student/Faculty:** 21 to 1
Year: semesters, summer session	**Tuition:** $2576 ($8372)
Application Deadline: July 1	**Room & Board:** $4382

Freshman Class: 8146 applied, 5000 accepted, 2665 enrolled
SAT I Verbal/Math: 510/510 **COMPETITIVE**

Georgia Southern University, founded in 1906, is a member of the public university system of Georgia and offers undergraduate degree programs in education, business, liberal arts and social sciences, science and technology, and health and professional studies. There are 5 undergraduate schools and 1 graduate school. In addition to regional accreditation, Georgia Southern has baccalaureate program accreditation with AACSB, ABET, ACCE, CCNE, CSAB, FIDER, NASAD, NASM, NCATE, NLN, and NRPA. The library contains 541,535 volumes, 848,869 microform items, and 29,003 audiovisual forms/CDs, and subscribes to 3470 periodicals. Computerized library services include the card catalog, interlibrary loans, and database searching. Special learning facilities include a learning resource center, art gallery, natural history museum, planetarium, radio station, wildlife center, and botanical gardens. The 600-acre campus is in a small town 50 miles northwest of Savannah. Including residence halls, there are 88 buildings.

Student Life: 94% of undergraduates are from Georgia. Others are from 46 states, 66 foreign countries, and Canada. 68% are white; 27% African American. The average age of freshmen is 18; all undergraduates, 21. 26% do not continue beyond their first year.

Housing: 2750 students can be accommodated in college housing, which includes single-sex and coed dormitories, on-campus apartments, fraternity houses, and sorority houses. In addition, there are honors houses and special-interest houses. On-campus housing is available on a first-come, first-served basis and is available on a lottery system for upperclassmen. 78% of students commute. Alcohol is not permitted. All students may keep cars.

Activities: 10% of men belong to 13 national fraternities; 11% of women belong to 9 national sororities. There are more than 150 groups on campus, including art, band, cheerleading, choir, chorale, chorus, computers, dance, debate, drama, drill team, ethnic, forensics, gay, honors, international, jazz band, literary magazine, marching band, multicultural, newspaper, opera, orchestra, pep band, photography, political, professional, radio, religious, social, social service, student government, symphony, and yearbook. Popular campus events include Eagle Expo Career Fairs, Welcome Week Activities, and Black History Month.

Sports: There are 6 intercollegiate sports for men and 9 for women, and 12 intramural sports for men and 12 for women. Facilities include football, soccer, and softball fields, basketball, handball, racquetball, tennis, and volleyball courts, a weight training area, golf ranges, an exercise trail, football and baseball stadiums, a field house, swimming pools, a challenge course, an activity center, circuit training and cardiovascular equipment, an indoor walking track, and other facilities.

Disabled Students: 90% of the campus is accessible. Wheelchair ramps, elevators, special parking, specially equipped rest rooms, special class scheduling, lowered drinking fountains, and lowered telephones are available.

Services: Counseling and information services are available, as is tutoring in most subjects. There is a reader service for the blind, and remedial math, reading, and writing.

Campus Safety and Security: Measures include 24-hour foot and vehicle patrol, self-defense education, escort service, and informal discussions. There are pamphlets/posters/films, emergency telephones, lighted pathways/sidewalks, and bike police and environmental safety services.

Programs of Study: Georgia Southern confers B.A., B.S., B.A.S., B.B.A., B.F.A., B.G.S., B.M., B.S.B., B.S.C.E.T., B.S.Chem., B.S.Cons., B.S.Ed., B.S.E.E.T., B.S.H.S., B.S.I.E.T., B.S.J.S., B.S.K., B.S.Manu., B.S.Mat., B.S.M.E.T., B.S.M.T., B.S.N., B.S.P., and B.S.P.Mgt. degrees. Master's and doctoral degrees are also awarded. Bachelor's degrees are awarded in BIOLOGICAL SCIENCE (biology/biological science, and nutrition), BUSINESS (accounting, banking and finance, business administration and management, business economics, fashion merchandising, hotel/motel and restaurant management, international economics, marketing/retailing/merchandising, recreation and leisure services, sports management, and transportation management), COMMUNICATIONS AND THE ARTS (art, broadcasting, communications, dramatic arts, English, French, German, journalism, music, music performance, music theory and composition, public relations, and Spanish), COMPUTER AND PHYSICAL SCIENCE (chemistry, computer science, geology, information sciences and systems, mathematics, and physics), EDUCATION (art, business, early childhood, health, mathematics, middle school, music, physical, secondary, special, and technical), ENGINEERING AND ENVIRONMENTAL DESIGN (construction management, electrical/electronics engineering technology, engineering technology, industrial administration/management, industrial engineering technology, interior design, mechanical engineering technology, printing technology, and technological management), HEALTH PROFESSIONS (community health work, exercise science, health, medical technology, nursing, and sports medicine), SOCIAL SCIENCE (anthropology, child care/child and family studies, criminal justice, economics, family/consumer studies, fashion design and technology, food production/management/services, food science, geography, history, international studies, liberal arts/general studies, philosophy, physical fitness/movement, political science/government, psychology, and sociology). Business, nursing, and biology are the largest.

Required: All students must complete a total of 126 semester credit hours, including at least 30 in the major, with a minimum GPA of 2.0. Specific courses must be completed in English, math, history, humanities, science and technology, and social sciences.

Special: GSU offers opportunities for study abroad, internships, work-study programs, B.A.-B.S. degrees, cooperative programs, a general studies degree, cross-registration with Georgia Tech and East Georgia College, and a 3-2 engineering degree with Georgia Institute of Technology, pass/fail options, credit for military service, and nondegree study. There are 14 national honor societies, a freshman honors program.

Faculty/Classroom: 56% of faculty are male; 44%, female. 87% teach undergraduates. No introductory courses are taught by graduate students.

Admissions: 61% of the 2001-2002 applicants were accepted. The SAT I scores for the 2001-2002 freshman class were: Verbal--42% below 500, 48% between 500 and 599, 9% between 600 and 700, and 1% above 700; Math--42% below 500, 46% between 500 and 599, and 12% between 600 and 700.

Requirements: The SAT I or ACT is required. In addition, a high school diploma or the equivalent and satisfactory SAT I or ACT scores and GPA are required. A minimum of 18 credits in college preparatory courses should include 4 each in English and math, 3 each in social studies and science, 2 in a foreign language, and 2 additional courses. A GPA of 2.0 is required. AP and CLEP credits are accepted. Applications are accepted on-line at *www.gasou.edu*.

Procedure: Freshmen are admitted to all sessions. Entrance exams should be taken during the junior year. There is a deferred admissions plan. Applications should be filed by July 1 for fall entry, December 1 for spring entry, and May 1 for summer entry, along with a $20 fee. Notification is sent on a rolling basis.

Transfer: 761 transfer students enrolled in 2001-2002. Applicants must have completed at least 30 semester credit hours of college courses with a minimum GPA of 2.0. Those with fewer than 30 hours must meet freshman requirements. Students transferring with an associate degree must have a minimum GPA of 2.0 in a school with a parallel curriculum. 38 credits of 126 must be completed at Georgia Southern.

Visiting: There are regularly scheduled orientations for prospective students. There are guides for informal visits and visitors may stay overnight. To schedule a visit, contact the Admissions Office.

Financial Aid: In a recent year, 93% of all freshmen and 78% of continuing students received some form of financial aid. 49% of freshmen and 52% of continuing students received need-based aid. The average freshman award was $4829. The average financial indebtedness of a recent graduate was $12,563. The FAFSA is required. The fall application deadline is March 31.

International Students: There are 160 international students enrolled. The school actively recruits these students. They must score 500 on the written TOEFL or 173 on the electronic version or take the MELAB and also take the SAT I or the ACT, scoring 920 on the SAT I.

Computers: The mainframes are IBM, DEC VAX, and HP units. There are 200 IBM PS/2 Model 30, Zenith, Apple, and Mac PCs available in the learning resource center and various labs. Students can obtain VAX and Internet accounts to access the mainframe computers. All students may access the system 24 hours a day. There are no time limits and no fees.

Graduates: In 2001, 1869 bachelor's degrees were awarded. The most popular majors were business/marketing (33%), education (12%), and parks and recreation (9%). In an average class, 12% graduate in 4 years, 28% in 5 years, and 34% in 6 years. 368 companies recruited on campus in 2000-2001.

Admissions Contact: Dr. Teresa Thompson, Director of Admissions. A video is available. E-mail: *admissions@gasou.edu*
Web: *http://www.gasou.edu*

GEORGIA SOUTHWESTERN STATE UNIVERSITY B-4

Americus, GA 31709 (912) 928-1273
(800) 338-0082; Fax: (912) 931-2983

Full-time: 549 men, 900 women	**Faculty:** 128; IIA, --$
Part-time: 165 men, 333 women	**Ph.D.s:** 72%
Graduate: 103 men, 485 women	**Student/Faculty:** 11 to 1
Year: semesters, summer session	**Tuition:** $2223 ($8019)
Application Deadline: August 1	**Room & Board:** $3790
Freshman Class: 979 applied, 672 accepted, 275 enrolled	
SAT I Verbal/Math: 519/499	**ACT:** 21 **COMPETITIVE**

Georgia Southwestern State University, founded in 1906, is a liberal arts, professional and teachers college that is part of the public University System of Georgia. There are 5 undergraduate and 4 graduate schools. In addition to regional accreditation, GSW has baccalaureate program accreditation with NCATE and NLN. The library contains 190,000 volumes, 618,842 microform items, and 1849 audiovisual forms/CDs, and subscribes to 825 periodicals. Computerized library services include the card catalog, interlibrary loans, and database searching. Special learning facilities include a learning resource center, art gallery, and TV station. The 225-acre campus is in a small town 38 miles north of Albany. Including residence halls, there are 37 buildings.

Student Life: 95% of undergraduates are from Georgia. Others are from 18 states, 33 foreign countries, and Canada. 70% are from public schools. 72% are white; 25% African American. The average age of freshmen is 20; all undergraduates, 22. 27% do not continue beyond their first year; 25% remain to graduate.

Housing: 597 students can be accommodated in college housing, which includes single-sex dormitories. In addition, there are special-interest houses and independent fraternity and sorority houses. On-campus housing is guaranteed for all 4 years. 62% of students commute. All students may keep cars.

Activities: 13% of men belong to 7 national fraternities; 15% of women belong to 8 national sororities. There are 55 groups on campus, including art, band, cheerleading, choir, chorale, chorus, computers, dance, drama, ethnic, forensics, Habitat for Humanity, honors, international, jazz band, literary magazine, musical theater, newspaper, nursing, orchestra, photography, political, radio and TV, religious, social, social service, and student government. Popular campus events include Convocation Series.

Sports: There are 3 intercollegiate sports for men and 4 for women, and 9 intramural sports for men and 9 for women. Facilities include 2 gyms, tennis courts, an indoor/outdoor pool, a lake for canoeing, and playing fields for baseball, softball, football, and soccer. The larger gym seats 3000; the smaller seats 500.

Disabled Students: 85% of the campus is accessible. Wheelchair ramps, elevators, special parking, specially equipped rest rooms, special class scheduling, lowered drinking fountains, and accessible dormitories are available.

Services: Counseling and information services are available, as is tutoring in most subjects. There is a reader service for the blind, and remedial math, reading, and writing.

Campus Safety and Security: Measures include 24-hour foot and vehicle patrol, self-defense education, escort service, and informal discussions. There are pamphlets/posters/films, emergency telephones, and lighted pathways/sidewalks.

Programs of Study: GSW confers B.A., B.S., B.A.S., B.B.A., B.F.A., B.S.Ed., and B.S.N. degrees. Associate and master's degrees are also awarded. Bachelor's degrees are awarded in BIOLOGICAL SCIENCE (biology/biological science), BUSINESS (accounting, business administration and management, and marketing/retailing/merchandising), COMMUNICATIONS AND THE ARTS (English, fine arts, and music), COMPUTER AND PHYSICAL SCIENCE (chemistry, computer programming, computer science, geology, and mathematics), EDUCATION (art, business, early childhood, elementary, English, foreign languages, mathematics, middle school, music, recreation, science, secondary, social science, and special), ENGINEERING AND ENVIRONMENTAL DESIGN (computer technology), HEALTH PROFESSIONS (nursing), SOCIAL SCIENCE (history, political science/government, psychology, and sociology). Geology, preprofessional health and nursing, and education are the strongest academically. Business, education, and nursing are the largest.

Required: To graduate, students must complete 120 credit hours, including 18 in the major, with a minimum GPA of 2.0. The core curriculum consists of 12 hours each in English and the humanities, science, math, and social science. The student must also complete 4 courses in health and phys ed, including swimming, and pass tests in reading, writing, and geography.

Special: The college offers a 3-2 engineering degree with the Georgia Institute of Technology, cooperative programs with South Georgia Technical School, a 2-2 degree program in nursing, internships through the Governor's Intern Program, study abroad, and credit for military phys ed and training. There are 15 national honor societies, a freshman honors program, and 1 departmental honors program.

Faculty/Classroom: 56% of faculty are male; 44%, female. All teach undergraduates and 25% do research. No introductory courses are taught by graduate students. The average class size in an introductory lecture is 22; in a laboratory, 19; and in a regular course, 18.

Admissions: 69% of the 2001-2002 applicants were accepted. The SAT I scores for the 2001-2002 freshman class were: Verbal--37% below 500, 48% between 500 and 599, 13% between 600 and 700, and 2% above 700; Math--48% below 500, 39% between 500 and 599, 12% between 600 and 700, and 1% above 700. The ACT scores were 42% below 21, 50% between 21 and 23, and 8% between 24 and 26. 33% of the current freshmen were in the top fifth of their class; 67% were in the top two fifths. 4 freshmen graduated first in their class.

Requirements: The SAT I or ACT is required; the SAT I is preferred. Students must score at least 430 verbal and 400 math on the SAT I, and no lower than 18 on the verbal part and 17 on the math part of the ACT; those with lower scores may gain acceptance through the Developmental Studies Program. Students must be graduates of an accredited secondary school or have a GED certificate. The college requires 16 academic credits and 21 Carnegie units, based on 4 years each of English and math, 3 of science, 2 each of history and a foreign language, and 1 of social studies. An art portfolio and a music audition are recommended for appropriate majors. A GPA of 2.0 is required. AP and CLEP credits are accepted. Important factors in the admissions decision are advanced placement or honor courses, evidence of special talent, and geographic diversity. Applications are accepted on-line at the school's web site.

Procedure: Freshmen are admitted to all sessions. Entrance exams should be taken before the end of the senior year. Applications should be filed by August 1 for fall entry and December 15 for winter entry. The fall 2001 application fee was $20. Notification is sent on a rolling basis. 3% of all applicants are on a waiting list; 8 were accepted in 2001.

Transfer: 188 transfer students enrolled in 2001-2002. Applicants should be in good standing at their former institutions. Those with fewer than 30 hours of transfer credit must meet freshman requirements. 30 credits of 120 must be completed at GSW.

Visiting: There are regularly scheduled orientations for prospective students. There are guides for informal visits and visitors may sit in on classes and stay overnight. To schedule a visit, contact the Admissions Office.

Financial Aid: In 2001-2002, 52% of all freshmen and 68% of continuing students received some form of financial aid. 25% of freshmen and 36% of continuing students received need-based aid. The average freshman award was $4930. Of that total, scholarships or need-based grants averaged $2000 ($3000 maximum); loans averaged $2625 ($6625 maximum); and work contracts averaged $1648. 8% of undergraduates work part time. Average annual earnings from campus work are $1648. The average financial indebtedness of the 2001 graduate was $11,500. The FAFSA is required. The fall application deadline is April 1.

International Students: There are 68 international students enrolled. The school actively recruits these students. They must score 524 on the written TOEFL or 190 on the electronic version.

Computers: The mainframe is an IBM RISC 6000 Model 570. 2 computer labs are equipped with IBM PCs that are connected to the main computer by a token-ring network. All students may access the system 8 A.M. to midnight Monday through Friday and selected hours on weekends. There are no time limits and no fees.

Graduates: In 2001, 294 bachelor's degrees were awarded. The most popular majors were business (24%), education (23%), and psychology/sociology (17%). 108 companies recruited on campus in 2000-2001. Of the 2000 graduating class, 96% were employed within 6 months of graduation.

Admissions Contact: Gary Fallis, Director of Admissions. A video is available. E-mail: *gswapps@canes.gsw.edu* Web: *www.gsw.edu*

GEORGIA STATE UNIVERSITY B-2

Atlanta, GA 30303-3083 (404) 651-2365; Fax: (404) 651-4811

Full-time: 4512 men, 7076 women	**Faculty:** 854; I, av$
Part-time: 2583 men, 4074 women	**Ph.D.s:** 89%
Graduate: 3142 men, 4358 women	**Student/Faculty:** 11 to 1
Year: semesters, summer session	**Tuition:** $3292 ($11,188)
Application Deadline: May 1	**Room & Board:** $4500
Freshman Class: 8134 applied, 4332 accepted, 2200 enrolled	
SAT I Verbal/Math: 530/530	**ACT:** 21 **LESS COMPETITIVE**

Georgia State University, founded in 1913 and a part of the University System of Georgia, is a public residential university offering programs in liberal arts and sciences, business administration, education, law, health sciences, and public policy. There are 5 undergraduate and 6 graduate schools. In addition to regional accreditation, Georgia State has baccalaureate program accreditation with AACSB, ADA, APTA, CAHEA, CSWE, NASAD, NASM, NCATE, and NLN. The 2 libraries contain 1.5 million volumes, 1.6 million microform items, and 60,000 audiovisual forms/CDs, and subscribe to 14,388 periodicals. Computerized library services include interlibrary loans and database searching. Special learning facilities include a learning resource center, art gallery, radio station, TV station, digital arts lab, observatory, instructional technology center, and distance learning classrooms. The 57-acre campus is in an urban area in downtown Atlanta. Including residence halls, there are 45 buildings.

Student Life: 94% of undergraduates are from Georgia. Others are from 49 states, 94 foreign countries, and Canada. 64% are white; 27% African American. The average age of freshmen is 18; all undergraduates, 25.

Housing: 2000 students can be accommodated in college housing, which includes single-sex and coed on-campus apartments. In addition, there are special-interest houses. On-campus housing is available on a first-come, first-served basis. All students may keep cars.

Activities: 8% of men belong to 9 national fraternities; 6% of women belong to 10 national sororities. There are many groups and organizations on campus, including art, band, cheerleading, chess, chorale, chorus, computers, dance, debate, drama, ethnic, film, gay, honors, international, jazz band, literary magazine, musical theater, newspaper, opera, orchestra, pep band, photography, political, professional, radio and TV, religious, social, social service, student government, and yearbook. Popular campus events include International Student Festival, Honors Day, and Greek Week.

Sports: There are 7 intercollegiate sports for men and 7 for women, and 25 intramural sports for men and 25 for women. Facilities include a phys ed complex with 3 gyms, a pool, a diving well, a weight room, indoor and outdoor tennis courts, a climbing wall, a jogging track, exercise rooms, a dance studio, and racquetball courts; the Indian Creek recreation area with a pool, 3 tennis courts, picnic facilities, regular and sand volleyball, basketball courts, and a rope challenge course; and the Panthersville Road athletic fields.

Disabled Students: All of the campus is accessible. Wheelchair ramps, elevators, special parking, specially equipped rest rooms, special class scheduling, lowered drinking fountains, and lowered telephones are available.

Services: Counseling and information services are available, as is tutoring in most subjects. There is a reader service for the blind, and remedial math, reading, and writing. Programs are available in effective studying, reading comprehension, speed reading, test and note taking, test anxiety, fear of public speaking, and organization and planning.

Campus Safety and Security: Measures include 24-hour foot and vehicle patrol, self-defense education, escort service, and shuttle buses. There are informal discussions, pamphlets/posters/films, emergency telephones, lighted pathways/sidewalks, 24-hour security at university housing, and a bicycle patrol.

Programs of Study: Georgia State confers B.A., B.S., B.B.A., B.F.A., B.I.S., B.M., B.S.Ed., and B.S.W. degrees. Master's and doctoral degrees are also awarded. Bachelor's degrees are awarded in BIOLOGICAL SCIENCE (biology/biological science and nutrition), BUSINESS (accounting, banking and finance, business administration and management, business economics, hospitality management services, human resources, insurance and risk management, management information systems, marketing/retailing/merchandising, real estate, and recreation and leisure services), COMMUNICATIONS AND THE ARTS (art, classics, dance, dramatic arts, English, film arts, fine arts, French, German, journalism, music, Spanish, speech/debate/rhetoric, and studio art), COMPUTER AND PHYSICAL SCIENCE (actuarial science, chemistry, computer science, geology, mathematics, and physics), EDUCATION (art, early childhood, health, and middle school), HEALTH PROFESSIONS (medical technology, nursing, physical therapy, and respiratory therapy), SOCIAL SCIENCE (anthropology, criminal justice, economics, geography, history, interdisciplinary studies, philosophy, physical fitness/movement, political science/government, psychology, religion, social work, sociology, and urban studies). Management, computer science, and psychology are the largest.

Required: Students must complete distribution requirements, including courses in humanities, natural science and math, and social science. A minimum of 120 hours must be completed for graduation with a minimum GPA of 2.0.

Special: There is cross-registration with the University Center in Georgia. Internships with numerous employers and government agencies can be arranged. Study abroad is available in Western Europe, Mexico, Israel, the former Soviet Union, and Canada. Work-study, student-designed majors, and pass/fail options are available. The university is also a member of the National Student Exchange. The Summer Scholar program allows high school seniors to take college-level course work. There are 16 national honor societies, a freshman honors program, and 10 departmental honors programs.

Faculty/Classroom: 69% of faculty are male; 31%, female.

Admissions: 53% of the 2001-2002 applicants were accepted. The SAT I scores for the 2001-2002 freshman class were: Verbal--34% below 500, 47% between 500 and 599, 17% between 600 and 700, and 2% above 700; Math--33% below 500, 48% between 500 and 599, 18% between 600 and 700, and 2% above 700. The ACT scores were 13% below 18, 63% between 18 and 23, 23% between 24 and 29, and 1% above 30. 46% of the current freshmen were in the top quarter of their class; 86% were in the top half.

Requirements: The SAT I or ACT is required, with preferred scores on the SAT I of 500 verbal and 500 math; on the ACT 22 English and 22 math. Applicants must graduate from a regionally accredited high school. A total of 15 academic credits is required. Students should prepare with 4 years of high school English, 2 years of the same foreign language, and 3 years each of math, science, and social science. AP and CLEP credits are accepted. Important factors in the admissions decision are evidence of special talent, advanced placement or honor courses, and extracurricular activities record.

Procedure: Freshmen are admitted fall, spring, and summer. Entrance exams should be taken during the first semester of the senior year. There is an early admissions plan. Applications should be filed by May 1 for fall entry, November 15 for spring entry, and April 1 for summer entry, along with a $25 fee. Notification is sent on a rolling basis.

Transfer: Transfer applicants must submit official transcripts of all college-level work, have a minimum GPA of 2.1, have earned 30 semester hours, and be in good academic standing. Those with fewer than 30 semester hours earned must meet freshman requirements.

Visiting: There are guides for informal visits and visitors may sit in on classes. To schedule a visit, contact Susan Goodroe, Welcome Center at (404) 651-3900.

Financial Aid: The average financial indebtedness of a recent year's graduate was $14,580. Georgia State is a member of CSS. The CSS/Profile and the college's own financial statement are required. Check with the school for current deadlines.

International Students: The school actively recruits these students. They must score 550 on the written TOEFL or 213 on the electronic version and also take the college's own test and also take the SAT I scoring 830, or the ACT.

Computers: The mainframes are an Amdahl 5895 and a Unisys 1100/72. There are 300 workstations in 4 PC labs. Internet access is available through an Internet provider at $12 a month for 60 hours of prime time.

In addition, on-campus mainframes can be accessed at no charge through 90 dial-up lines. All students may access the system 24 hours per day. There are no time limits and no fees.

Admissions Contact: Diane M. Weber, Director of Admissions. E-mail: *admissions@gsu.edu* Web: *www.gsu.edu*

KENNESAW STATE UNIVERSITY

Kennesaw, GA 30144-5591 — B-2 — (770) 423-6300; n/av; Fax: (770) 423-6541

Full-time: 2787 men, 4327 women	**Faculty:** 389; IIA, av$
Part-time: 1897 men, 3421 women	**Ph.D.s:** 79%
Graduate: 655 men, 864 women	**Student/Faculty:** 18 to 1
Year: semesters, summer session	**Tuition:** $2306 ($7730)
Application Deadline: see profile	**Room & Board:** n/app
Freshman Class: n/av	
SAT I or ACT: required	LESS COMPETITIVE

Kennesaw State University, founded in 1963, is a 4-year public commuter college in the University System of Georgia. There are 5 undergraduate and 4 graduate schools. In addition to regional accreditation, Kennesaw State has baccalaureate program accreditation with AACSB, NASM, NCATE, and NLN. The library contains 550,000 volumes, 1 million microform items, and 8000 audiovisual forms/CDs, and subscribes to 3300 periodicals. Computerized library services include the card catalog, interlibrary loans, and database searching. Special learning facilities include a learning resource center and art gallery. The 185-acre campus is in a suburban area 25 miles north of Atlanta. There are 18 buildings.

Student Life: 96% of undergraduates are from Georgia. Others are from 31 states, 118 foreign countries, and Canada. 80% are white; 11% African American. The average age of freshmen is 21; all undergraduates, 25. 30% do not continue beyond their first year.

Housing: There are no residence halls. Although all students commute, there are a number of apartments within walking distance of the university. Alcohol is not permitted. All students may keep cars.

Activities: 1% of men belong to 1 local fraternity and 2 national fraternities; 7% of women belong to 1 local sorority and 3 national sororities. There are 87 groups on campus, including art, band, cheerleading, choir, chorale, chorus, computers, drama, ethnic, gay, honors, international, jazz band, literary magazine, newspaper, opera, pep band, political, professional, religious, social, social service, student government, symphony, and yearbook. Popular campus events include KSC Day and Black History Month.

Sports: There are 4 intercollegiate sports for men and 4 for women, and 16 intramural sports for men and 16 for women. Facilities include a gym, a pool, tennis and racquetball courts, and baseball, softball, and soccer fields.

Disabled Students: 90% of the campus is accessible. Wheelchair ramps, elevators, special parking, specially equipped rest rooms, special class scheduling, lowered drinking fountains, lowered telephones, marked crosswalks with curb cuts, adapted computer equipment with voice synthesizer, a voice-activated computer, screen-enlarging programs, a swimming pool lift, microfilm and microfiche facilities for wheelchair-bound and blind students, a brailler, and enlarged-print machines are available.

Services: Counseling and information services are available, as is tutoring in some subjects, including math, foreign languages, and English. There is a reader service for the blind, and remedial math, reading, and writing.

Campus Safety and Security: Measures include 24-hour foot and vehicle patrol, self-defense education, escort service, and informal discussions. There are pamphlets/posters/films, emergency telephones, and lighted pathways/sidewalks.

Programs of Study: Kennesaw State confers B.A., B.S., B.B.A., and B.M. degrees. Master's degrees are also awarded. Bachelor's degrees are awarded in BIOLOGICAL SCIENCE (biology/biological science), BUSINESS (accounting, banking and finance, business economics, management science, and marketing/retailing/merchandising), COMMUNICATIONS AND THE ARTS (art, communications, dramatic arts, English, French, music, music performance, and Spanish), COMPUTER AND PHYSICAL SCIENCE (chemistry, computer science, information sciences and systems, and mathematics), EDUCATION (art, early childhood, elementary, English, foreign languages, health, mathematics, middle school, music, physical, science, and social studies), ENGINEERING AND ENVIRONMENTAL DESIGN (preengineering), HEALTH PROFESSIONS (nursing, predentistry, premedicine, prepharmacy, and preveterinary science), SOCIAL SCIENCE (history, international studies, political science/government, prelaw, and psychology). Business, psychology, and education are the strongest academically. Business and education are the largest.

Required: Requirements vary by degree program. Generally, all students must complete 123 semester hours, including 45 to 47 in core curriculum courses and 39 in upper-level courses, with a minimum GPA of 2.0 and grades of C or better in the major and in required English courses. Students must also successfully complete the University System of Georgia Regents' Testing Program and demonstrate (by course or exam) competency in the history and constitutions of the United States and Georgia.

Special: Students may register for courses with any of the colleges in the University System of Georgia, study abroad in 2 countries, and participate in work-study programs and internships, some with pass/fail options. Dual majors and nondegree programs also are offered. There is a freshman honors program.

Faculty/Classroom: 48% of faculty are male; 52%, female. 10% both teach and do research. No introductory courses are taught by graduate students. The average class size in an introductory lecture is 38; in a laboratory, 32; and in a regular course, 32.

Admissions: The SAT I scores for the 2001-2002 freshman class were: Verbal--29% below 500, 51% between 500 and 599, and 19% between 600 and 700; Math--35% below 500, 48% between 500 and 599, and 15% between 600 and 700.

Requirements: The SAT I or ACT is required, with SAT I scores of at least 510 verbal and 470 math, or ACT scores of at least 22 English and 20 math. Applicants should be graduates of an accredited secondary school or have the GED. Secondary preparation should include 4 units of English, 3 each of math, social science, and science, and economics and government, and 2 of a foreign language. A GPA of 2.0 is required. AP and CLEP credits are accepted. Important factors in the admissions decision are advanced placement or honor courses, ability to finance college education, and recommendations by alumni.

Procedure: Freshmen are admitted fall, spring, and summer. Entrance exams should be taken before June 1. Check with the school for current application deadlines. The fall 2001 application fee was $20. Notification is sent on a rolling basis.

Transfer: 1278 transfer students enrolled in 2001-2002. Applicants should have completed 30 semester hours with a GPA of 2.0 or above; those with a lower GPA may be admitted on probation. Grades of D or better (C or better in English) may be transferred by those with a 2.0 cumulative GPA. Students with fewer than 30 hours of credit must meet freshman requirements. 30 credits of 123 must be completed at Kennesaw State.

Visiting: There are regularly scheduled orientations for prospective students, including Insight Sessions every Tuesday at 4 P.M. and special visits for adult students. There are guides for informal visits. To schedule a visit, contact the Admissions Office at *ksuadmit@kennesaw.edu*.

Financial Aid: The FAFSA is required. The fall application deadline is March 31.

International Students: There are 601 international students enrolled. The school actively recruits these students. They must score 173 on the electronic TOEFL or take ESL level 109.

Computers: The mainframe is a CDC CYBER 850. There are also 78 networked PCs in an open lab that can access mainframes available to all state institutions. Computers may be used for any work associated with instruction. All students may access the system 24 hours a day. There are no time limits and no fees.

Graduates: In 2001, 1646 bachelor's degrees were awarded. The most popular majors were early childhood education (12%), management (10%), and communication (7%).

Admissions Contact: Joe F. Head, Dean of Enrollment Services. A video is available. E-mail: *ksuadmit@ksumail.kennesaw.edu* Web: *www.kennesaw.edu*

LAGRANGE COLLEGE

LaGrange, GA 30240 — A-3 — (706) 880-8253; (800) 593-2885; Fax: (706) 880-8010

Full-time: 279 men, 480 women	**Faculty:** 58; IIB, -$
Part-time: 57 men, 86 women	**Ph.D.s:** 83%
Graduate: 19 men, 21 women	**Student/Faculty:** 13 to 1
Year: 4-1-4, summer session	**Tuition:** $12,360
Application Deadline: open	**Room & Board:** $5136
Freshman Class: 519 applied, 403 accepted, 178 enrolled	
SAT I Verbal/Math: 520/500	**ACT:** 20 — COMPETITIVE

LaGrange College, founded in 1831, is a private liberal arts institution affiliated with the United Methodist Church. Major undergraduate programs include business, art, education, biology, and psychology. In addition to regional accreditation, LaGrange has baccalaureate program accreditation with ACBSP and NLN. The library contains 138,799 volumes, 171,946 microform items, and 3354 audiovisual forms/CDs, and subscribes to 527 periodicals. Computerized library services include the card catalog, interlibrary loans, and database searching. Special learning facilities include a learning resource center, art gallery, 2 music technology labs, and a performing arts theater. The 85-acre campus is in a small town 70 miles southwest of Atlanta. Including residence halls, there are 22 buildings.

Student Life: 87% of undergraduates are from Georgia. Others are from 21 states, 11 foreign countries, and Canada. 60% are from public schools. 80% are white; 13% African American. 54% are Protestant; 33% claim no religious affiliation. The average age of freshmen is 18; all

undergraduates, 21. 12% do not continue beyond their first year; 68% remain to graduate.
Housing: 480 students can be accommodated in college housing, which includes single-sex and coed dormitories. On-campus housing is guaranteed for all 4 years. 52% of students live on campus; of those, 50% remain on campus on weekends. Alcohol is not permitted. All students may keep cars.
Activities: 19% of men belong to 3 national fraternities; 22% of women belong to 3 national sororities. There are 48 groups on campus, including art, cheerleading, choir, chorale, computers, drama, ethnic, gay, honors, international, jazz band, literary magazine, musical theater, newspaper, orchestra, photography, political, professional, religious, social, social service, student government, symphony, and yearbook. Popular campus events include May Day, Greek Week, and International Week.
Sports: There are 6 intercollegiate sports for men and 6 for women, and 7 intramural sports for men and 7 for women. Facilities include a fitness center, West Point Lake, an auditorium, indoor and outdoor pools, 3 gyms, 10 lighted tennis courts, and lighted softball, baseball, and soccer fields.
Disabled Students: 75% of the campus is accessible. Wheelchair ramps, elevators, special parking, specially equipped rest rooms, special class scheduling, and lowered drinking fountains are available.
Services: Counseling and information services are available, as is tutoring in most subjects.
Campus Safety and Security: Measures include 24-hour foot and vehicle patrol, pamphlets/posters/films, lighted pathways/sidewalks, and safety awareness seminars during freshman orientation.
Programs of Study: LaGrange confers B.A, B.S., B.B.A., and B.S.N. degrees. Associate and master's degrees are also awarded. Bachelor's degrees are awarded in BIOLOGICAL SCIENCE (biochemistry and biology/biological science), BUSINESS (accounting, business administration and management, and business economics), COMMUNICATIONS AND THE ARTS (dramatic arts, English, fine arts, music performance, music technology, and Spanish), COMPUTER AND PHYSICAL SCIENCE (chemistry, computer science, and mathematics), EDUCATION (art, early childhood, middle school, and secondary), HEALTH PROFESSIONS (nursing, predentistry, and premedicine), SOCIAL SCIENCE (history, human services, political science/government, prelaw, psychology, religion, religious music, and social work). Business, art, and education are the strongest academically. Business is the largest.
Required: To graduate, all students must complete 108 semester hours, including 60 in the major. The core curriculum includes freshman seminar, English grammar and composition, history, math, computer science, religion, speech, and phys ed. All students must have a minimum GPA of 2.0.
Special: Internships are offered in business, social work, and political science, including positions in a congressional office in Washington. Students may study abroad in Israel and England. A 3-2 engineering degree is offered with Georgia Institute of Technology and Auburn University. There are 12 national honor societies, a freshman honors program, and 8 departmental honors programs.
Faculty/Classroom: 53% of faculty are male; 47%, female. All teach undergraduates and 30% both teach and do research. No introductory courses are taught by graduate students. The average class size in an introductory lecture is 15; in a laboratory, 16; and in a regular course, 11.
Admissions: 78% of the 2001-2002 applicants were accepted. The SAT I scores for the 2001-2002 freshman class were: Verbal--43% below 500, 42% between 500 and 599, 11% between 600 and 700, and 4% above 700; Math--48% below 500, 41% between 500 and 599, and 12% between 600 and 700. The ACT scores were 46% below 21, 22% between 21 and 23, 23% between 24 and 26, 7% between 27 and 28, and 2% above 28. 21% of the current freshmen were in the top fifth of their class; 36% were in the top two fifths. 1 freshman graduated first in the class.
Requirements: The SAT I or ACT is required. In addition, applicants should be graduates of an accredited secondary school or have a GED certificate. They should have completed a minimum of 4 units of English, 3 of social studies, and 2 each of math and science. A GPA of 2.5 is required. AP credits are accepted. Important factors in the admissions decision are extracurricular activities record, personality/intangible qualities, and leadership record.
Procedure: Freshmen are admitted to all sessions. Application deadlines are open. The fall 2001 application fee was $20. Notification is sent on a rolling basis.
Transfer: 63 transfer students were enrolled in a recent year. Transfer students must have a minimum 2.0 GPA and be in good standing with the previous college. 65 credits of 108 must be completed at LaGrange.
Visiting: There are regularly scheduled orientations for prospective students, including admissions workshops, a student panel, and a guided tour of the campus. There are guides for informal visits and visitors may sit in on classes and stay overnight. To schedule a visit, contact the Admission Office at (706) 880-8005 or *lgcadmis@lgc.edu*.
Financial Aid: In 2001-2002, 59% of all freshmen and 62% of continuing students received some form of financial aid, including need-based aid. The average freshman award was $12,906. Of that total, scholarships or need-based grants averaged $8545 ($18,676 maximum); loans averaged $3537 ($18,221 maximum); and work contracts averaged $866 ($1545 maximum). The FAFSA and the college's own financial statement are required. The fall application deadline is May 1.
International Students: There are 26 international students enrolled. The school actively recruits these students. They must score 500 on the written TOEFL.
Computers: The mainframes are an HCX-7 and Sun Microsystems models. Computers are networked via underground fiber-optic cables to dormitory rooms and 5 computer labs, with more than 150 terminals available. All students may access the system 24 hours a day. There are no time limits and no fees.
Graduates: In 2001, 196 bachelor's degrees were awarded. The most popular majors were education (23%), business (17%), and art (7%). In an average class, 25% graduate in 4 years, 38% in 5 years, and 42% in 6 years. 10 companies recruited on campus in 2000-2001.
Admissions Contact: Andy Geeter, Director of Admission.
E-mail: *ageeter@lgc.edu* Web: *www.lgc.edu*

MERCER UNIVERSITY — C-3

Macon, GA 31207-0001 — (478) 301-2650
(800) 840-8577; Fax: (478) 301-2828

Full-time: 1341 men, 2620 women	**Faculty:** 282; IIA, av$
Part-time: 208 men, 571 women	**Ph.D.s:** 92%
Graduate: 982 men, 1593 women	**Student/Faculty:** 14 to 1
Year: semesters, summer session	**Tuition:** $18,290
Application Deadline: July 1	**Room & Board:** $5840
Freshman Class: 2771 applied, 2290 accepted, 660 enrolled	
SAT I Verbal/Math: 580/590	**ACT:** 25 **VERY COMPETITIVE**

Mercer University, founded in 1833, is a private institution affiliated with the Georgia Baptist Convention. The university offers degree programs in liberal arts, business and economics, education, engineering, and professional studies. Mercer also offers a Great Books program as an alternative to the traditional core curriculum. There are 5 undergraduate and 7 graduate schools. In addition to regional accreditation, Mercer has baccalaureate program accreditation with ABET and NASM. The 2 libraries contain 418,865 volumes, 3,055,812 microform items, and 57,166 audiovisual forms/CDs. Computerized library services include the card catalog, interlibrary loans, and database searching. Special learning facilities include a learning resource center. The 130-acre campus is in a suburban area 85 miles south of Atlanta. Including residence halls, there are 58 buildings.
Student Life: 77% of undergraduates are from Georgia. Others are from 35 states, 48 foreign countries, and Canada. 67% are white; 19% African American. 62% are Protestant; 19% claim no religious affiliation. The average age of freshmen is 18; all undergraduates, 20. 24% do not continue beyond their first year.
Housing: 1208 students can be accommodated in college housing, which includes single-sex and coed dormitories, on-campus apartments, married-student housing, fraternity houses, and sorority houses. On-campus housing is guaranteed for the freshman year only, is available on a first-come, first-served basis, and is available on a lottery system for upperclassmen. Priority is given to out-of-town students. 60% of students live on campus; of those, 70% remain on campus on weekends. Alcohol is not permitted. All students may keep cars.
Activities: 15% of men belong to 9 national fraternities; 20% of women belong to 1 local sorority and 7 national sororities. There are 65 groups on campus, including bagpipe band, band, cheerleading, chess, choir, chorale, chorus, computers, dance, debate, drama, ethnic, honors, international, jazz band, literary magazine, musical theater, newspaper, opera, pep band, political, professional, religious, social, social service, student government, and yearbook. Popular campus events include Pilgrimage to Penfield, Spring Concert, and Family Weekend.
Sports: There are 7 intercollegiate sports for men and 7 for women, and 10 intramural sports for men and 10 for women. Facilities include 2 gyms, 3 playing fields, a student center, a swimming pool, a 30-station fitness trail, a lighted intramural complex, and tennis, volleyball, and racquetball courts.
Disabled Students: 85% of the campus is accessible. Wheelchair ramps, elevators, special parking, specially equipped rest rooms, special class scheduling, lowered drinking fountains, lowered telephones, and assistance with registration are available.
Services: Counseling and information services are available, as is tutoring in most subjects. There is a reader service for the blind, and remedial math, reading, and writing.
Campus Safety and Security: Measures include 24-hour foot and vehicle patrol, self-defense education, escort service, and shuttle buses. There are informal discussions, pamphlets/posters/films, emergency telephones, lighted pathways/sidewalks, and external CCTV cameras monitored by the police department.
Programs of Study: Mercer confers B.A., B.S., B.B.A., B.M., B.M.D., B.M.E., B.S.E., B.S.M., and B.S.N. degrees. Master's and doctoral de-

grees are also awarded. Bachelor's degrees are awarded in BIOLOGICAL SCIENCE (biology/biological science), BUSINESS (accounting, banking and finance, business administration and management, and marketing/retailing/merchandising), COMMUNICATIONS AND THE ARTS (English, French, German, Greek, Latin, music, and Spanish), COMPUTER AND PHYSICAL SCIENCE (chemistry, computer science, mathematics, natural sciences, and physics), EDUCATION (early childhood, elementary, music, secondary, and special), ENGINEERING AND ENVIRONMENTAL DESIGN (biomedical engineering, electrical/electronics engineering, environmental engineering, industrial engineering, and mechanical engineering), HEALTH PROFESSIONS (predentistry, premedicine, and prepharmacy), SOCIAL SCIENCE (economics, history, philosophy, political science/government, prelaw, psychology, religion, social science, and sociology). Engineering, chemistry, and English are the strongest academically. Business, English, and engineering are the largest.

Required: To graduate, all students must complete at least 128 semester hours with a minimum GPA of 2.0.

Special: Mercer offers co-op programs in all majors, cross-registration with Wesleyan and Macon State Colleges, B.A.-B.S. degrees in various science and math fields, internships, student-designed majors, work-study programs, and satisfactory-unsatisfactory options for elective courses. Students may study abroad in Spain, France, Great Britain, Australia, Hong Kong, and Morocco. There are 2 national honor societies, a freshman honors program, and 20 departmental honors programs.

Faculty/Classroom: 61% of faculty are male; 39%, female. All teach undergraduates. No introductory courses are taught by graduate students. The average class size in an introductory lecture is 21; in a laboratory, 15; and in a regular course, 17.

Admissions: 83% of the 2001-2002 applicants were accepted. The SAT I scores for the 2001-2002 freshman class were: Verbal--14% below 500, 47% between 500 and 599, 32% between 600 and 699, and 7% above 699; Math--11% below 500, 47% between 500 and 599, 36% between 600 and 699, and 6% above 699. 72% of the current freshmen were in the top quarter of their class; 91% were in the top half. There were 15 National Merit finalists and 25 semifinalists. 50 freshmen graduated first in their class.

Requirements: The SAT I or ACT is required. In addition, applicants must be graduates of an accredited secondary school and have completed 16 academic units. Students should submit their transcript and class rank, a recommendation from a guidance counselor, and a list of extracurricular activities, including employment. A GPA of 3.0 is required. AP and CLEP credits are accepted. Important factors in the admissions decision are advanced placement or honor courses, extracurricular activities record, and evidence of special talent.

Procedure: Freshmen are admitted to all sessions. Entrance exams should be taken in the spring of the junior year or fall of the senior year. There is a deferred admissions plan. Applications should be filed by July 1 for fall entry and November 1 for spring entry. The fall application fee was $40. Notification is sent on a rolling basis.

Transfer: 132 transfer students enrolled in 2001-2002. A minimum GPA of 2.0 is required for all transfer students. Applicants with fewer than 9 semester hours must meet freshman entrance requirements. Those with fewer than 20 semester hours must submit a high school transcript and SAT I or ACT scores, and those with more than 20 semester hours must submit transcripts from all colleges attended and be in good academic standing at their present school, or present evidence of satisfactory work in a previously attended college. 30 credits of 128 must be completed at Mercer.

Visiting: There are regularly scheduled orientations for prospective students, including 26 regional orientation programs in the spring, 3 preorientation sessions during the summer, and a 4-day orientation prior to the beginning of classes. There are guides for informal visits and visitors may sit in on classes and stay overnight. To schedule a visit, contact the Office of Admissions.

Financial Aid: Average annual earnings from campus work are $1600. The FAFSA and the college's own financial statement are required. The fall application deadline is April 1.

International Students: The school actively recruits these students. They must score 550 on the written TOEFL or take Mercer's ELI exit exam. They must also take the SAT I or the ACT, scoring 800 on the SAT I.

Computers: The mainframes are a DEC ALPHA 2100 and VAX 4000 models. Terminals are located in designated public and departmental student computer labs, and they can be accessed from off campus. All students may access the system 24 hours per day if they have dial-in access. There are no time limits and no fees. It is strongly recommended that all students have a personal computer.

Graduates: In 2001, 900 bachelor's degrees were awarded. 168 companies recruited on campus in a recent year. Of a recent graduating class, 35% were enrolled in graduate school within 6 months of graduation and 65% were employed.

Admissions Contact: Allen S. London, Assistant Vice President and Director of Freshman Admissions. A video is available.
E-mail: *admissions@mercer.edu* Web: *www.mercer.edu*

MOREHOUSE COLLEGE

Atlanta, GA 30314 — **B-2**
(404) 215-2632
(800) 851-1254; Fax: (404) 524-5635

Full-time: 2576 men	**Faculty:** 172; IIB, av$
Part-time: 153 men	**Ph.D.s:** 74%
Graduate: none	**Student/Faculty:** 15 to 1
Year: semesters, summer session	**Tuition:** $12,432
Application Deadline: February 15	**Room & Board:** $7382
Freshman Class: 2094 applied, 1588 accepted, 620 enrolled	
SAT I Verbal/Math: 525/535	**ACT:** 22 **COMPETITIVE**

Morehouse College, founded in 1867, is a private men's liberal arts college offering undergraduate programs in the arts and humanities, natural sciences and math, and social sciences and business. In addition to regional accreditation, Morehouse has baccalaureate program accreditation with AACSB. The library contains 550,000 volumes, 15,000 microform items, and 8000 audiovisual forms/CDs, and subscribes to 110 periodicals. Computerized library services include the card catalog, interlibrary loans, and database searching. Special learning facilities include a learning resource center and an academic support center. The 61-acre campus is in an urban area 3 miles southwest of downtown Atlanta. Including residence halls, there are 36 buildings.

Student Life: 76% of undergraduates are from out of state, mostly the South. Students are from 34 states and 23 foreign countries. 80% are from public schools. 95% are African American. The average age of freshmen is 18; all undergraduates, 20. 18% do not continue beyond their first year; 77% remain to graduate.

Housing: 1500 students can be accommodated in college housing, which includes single-sex dormitories. On-campus housing is guaranteed for the freshman year only, is available on a first-come, first-served basis, and is available on a lottery system for upperclassmen. 50% of students live on campus; of those, all remain on campus on weekends. Alcohol is not permitted. Upperclassmen may keep cars.

Activities: 7% of men belong to 5 national fraternities. There are 60 groups on campus, including band, chess, choir, chorus, computers, dance, debate, drama, ethnic, glee club, honors, international, jazz band, literary magazine, marching band, musical theater, newspaper, political, professional, religious, social, social service, speech, student government, and yearbook. Popular campus events include Founders Day, Religious Emphasis Week, and Parents Weekend.

Sports: Facilities include a comprehensive health and phys ed center, a 9000-seat football stadium, a track, and a 5700-seat basketball arena.

Disabled Students: 85% of the campus is accessible. Wheelchair ramps, elevators, special parking, specially equipped rest rooms, lowered drinking fountains, and lowered telephones are available.

Services: Counseling and information services are available, as is tutoring in most subjects. There is remedial math, reading, and writing.

Campus Safety and Security: Measures include 24-hour foot and vehicle patrol, escort service, shuttle buses, and informal discussions. There are pamphlets/posters/films and lighted pathways/sidewalks.

Programs of Study: Morehouse confers B.A. and B.S. degrees. Bachelor's degrees are awarded in BIOLOGICAL SCIENCE (biology/biological science), BUSINESS (accounting, banking and finance, business administration and management, and marketing/retailing/merchandising), COMMUNICATIONS AND THE ARTS (art, English, French, German, music, and Spanish), COMPUTER AND PHYSICAL SCIENCE (chemistry, computer science, mathematics, and physics), EDUCATION (physical), SOCIAL SCIENCE (African American studies, economics, history, international relations, philosophy, political science/government, psychology, religion, sociology, and urban studies). Engineering, business administration, and English are the strongest academically. Business administration, psychology, and computer science are the largest.

Required: Students must complete a minimum of 120 semester hours, including 53 hours in general studies, plus 8 noncredit hours in Freshman Orientation and College Assembly. A 2.0 GPA is required, with no grade below C in the major.

Special: Morehouse is a member of the Atlanta University Center; students may register for courses and even complete a major in any of the 6 member institutions. In addition, students may study abroad in Europe or Africa. A dual-degree program is offered in architecture with the University of Michigan and in engineering with Columbia, Dartmouth, Georgia Tech, Rensselaer, and other schools; students in these programs are offered summer internships. Work study is also available. There are 6 national honor societies, including Phi Beta Kappa, a freshman honors program, and 10 departmental honors programs.

Faculty/Classroom: 71% of faculty are male; 29%, female. All teach undergraduates and 20% do research. The average class size in an introductory lecture is 25; in a laboratory, 30; and in a regular course, 20.

Admissions: 76% of the 2001-2002 applicants were accepted. The SAT I scores for the 2001-2002 freshman class were: Verbal--39% below

500, 40% between 500 and 599, 18% between 600 and 700, and 3% above 700; Math--44% below 500, 36% between 500 and 599, 19% between 600 and 700, and 2% above 700. The ACT scores were 48% below 21, 28% between 21 and 23, 15% between 24 and 26, 6% between 27 and 28, and 3% above 28. 32% of the current freshmen were in the top fifth of their class; 75% were in the top two fifths. 8 freshmen graduated first in their class in a recent year.

Requirements: The SAT I or ACT is required; the minimum SAT I composite score is 1000. In addition, applicants should be graduates of accredited secondary schools or have the GED. Secondary preparation should include 4 units in English, 3 in math, 2 each in natural and social sciences, and 5 in other disciplines. Applicants must write an essay and are urged to seek an interview. A GPA of 2.8 is required. AP and CLEP credits are accepted. Important factors in the admissions decision are advanced placement or honor courses, leadership record, and recommendations by school officials. Application forms are available on-line.

Procedure: Freshmen are admitted fall and spring. Entrance exams should be taken by the fall of the senior year. There are early decision and deferred admissions plans. Early decision application should be filed by November 15; regular applications, by February 15 for fall entry and October 15 for spring entry. The fall 2001 application fee was $45. Notification of early decision is sent December 1; regular decision, March 1. 15% of all applicants are on a waiting list.

Transfer: 66 transfer students were enrolled in a recent year. Transfer applicants must have at least a 2.5 GPA and a minimum of 26 semester hours of credit. 64 credits of 120 must be completed at Morehouse.

Visiting: There are regularly scheduled orientations for prospective students. There are guides for informal visits and visitors may sit in on classes. To schedule a visit, contact the Admissions Office.

Financial Aid: In a recent year, 85% of all students received some form of financial aid. Scholarships or need-based grants averaged $4500 ($8500 maximum). 21% of undergraduates work part time. Average annual earnings from campus work are $1500. The average financial indebtedness of the 2001 graduate was $12,000. The FAFSA and the college's own financial statement are required. The fall application deadline is April 1.

International Students: There were 100 international students enrolled in a recent year. The school actively recruits these students. They must score 500 on the written TOEFL.

Computers: The mainframe is a DEC VAX with multiple PC servers. PCs are available for student use. All students may access the system. There are no time limits and no fees.

Graduates: In a recent year, 465 bachelor's degrees were awarded. The most popular majors were business (32%), psychology (11%), and biology (9%). In an average class, 30% graduate in 4 years, 40% in 5 years, and 50% in 6 years. 60 companies recruited on campus in a recent year.

Admissions Contact: Terrance Dixon, Associate Dean, Admissions and Recruitment. E-mail: *tdixon@morehouse.edu*
Web: *www.morehouse.edu*

MORRIS BROWN COLLEGE — B-2

Atlanta, GA 30314 — **(404) 220-0378; Fax: (404) 220-0371**

Full-time: 2105 men and women	**Faculty:** 97
Part-time: 70 men and women	**Ph.D.s:** 59%
Graduate: none	**Student/Faculty:** 22 to 1
Year: semesters	**Tuition:** $11,243
Application Deadline: see profile	**Room & Board:** $4750
Freshman Class: n/av	
SAT I or ACT: required	**LESS COMPETITIVE**

Morris Brown College, founded in 1881, is a private institution affiliated with the African Methodist Episcopal Church and offering degrees in the arts and sciences, engineering, health science, music, business administration, and education. Figures given in above capsule are approximate. There are 4 undergraduate and 2 graduate schools. The library contains 1,040,391 volumes, and subscribes to 1439 periodicals. Computerized library services include the card catalog, interlibrary loans, and database searching. Special learning facilities include a learning resource center, art gallery, and Herndon Home, a museum. The 18-acre campus is in an urban area 1 mile northwest of downtown Atlanta. Including residence halls, there are 13 buildings.

Student Life: 96% are African American. The average age of freshmen is 18; all undergraduates, 21.

Housing: 900 students can be accommodated in college housing, which includes single-sex dormitories and off-campus apartments. In addition, there are honors houses. On-campus housing is guaranteed for the freshman year only and is available on a first-come, first-served basis. Alcohol is not permitted. All students may keep cars.

Activities: There are 4 national fraternities and 5 local and 4 national sororities. There are 20 groups on campus, including art, band, cheerleading, chess, choir, chorus, computers, dance, drama, ethnic, film, honors, international, jazz band, marching band, newspaper, photography, political, professional, radio and TV, religious, social, social service, student government, and yearbook. Popular campus events include Dr. Martin Luther King Jr.'s birthday, Honors Convocation, and Black History Week.

Sports: There are 2 intercollegiate sports for men and 2 for women, and 7 intramural sports for men and 6 for women. Facilities include a weight room, a swimming pool, a gym, and billiards tables, with use of YWCA facilities available.

Disabled Students: 95% of the campus is accessible. Wheelchair ramps, elevators, special parking, and lowered drinking fountains are available.

Services: Counseling and information services are available, as is tutoring in most subjects, including math and science. There is a reader service for the blind, and remedial math, reading, and writing. Reader equipment is available.

Campus Safety and Security: Measures include 24-hour foot and vehicle patrol, escort service, shuttle buses, and informal discussions. There are pamphlets/posters/films, emergency telephones, and lighted pathways/sidewalks.

Programs of Study: Morris Brown confers B.A. and B.S. degrees. Bachelor's degrees are awarded in BIOLOGICAL SCIENCE (biology/biological science), BUSINESS (accounting, business administration and management, and business economics), COMMUNICATIONS AND THE ARTS (communications, dramatic arts, English, fine arts, French, music, Spanish, and speech/debate/rhetoric), COMPUTER AND PHYSICAL SCIENCE (chemistry, computer science, mathematics, and physics), EDUCATION (business, early childhood, and foreign languages), HEALTH PROFESSIONS (premedicine and recreation therapy), SOCIAL SCIENCE (African studies, criminal justice, economics, history, paralegal studies, philosophy, political science/government, psychology, religion, social science, and sociology). Biology, business administration, and criminal justice are the strongest academically and have the largest enrollments.

Required: Students must complete at least 124 credit hours, including 24 or more in the major, with a minimum GPA of 2.0, and must pass the junior English qualifying writing exam. There are core requirements in humanities, math, natural science, social sciences, and phys ed, as well as a new student seminar.

Special: Students may earn a 3-2 engineering degree with Georgia Institute of Technology. Internships, work-study programs, a general studies degree, and a B.A.-B.S. degree program are available. Morris Brown is part of the Atlanta University Center, which also includes the Interdenominational Theological Center, Clark Atlanta University, and Morehouse and Spelman Colleges, making this the largest consortium of black colleges in the world. Cross-registration is offered with several of these institutions and with members of the University Center in Georgia. The dual degree engineering program earns a B.S. from Morris Brown and a B.S.E. from 1 of 6 institutions: Georgia Tech, Boston University, Auburn University, Rochester Institute of Technology, Rensselaer Polytechnic Institute, University of Alabama, and North Carolina A&T University. Dual degrees are also available in architecture, industrial design, building construction, and landscape architecture with Georgia Tech and the University of Georgia. There is a freshman honors program.

Faculty/Classroom: The average class size in a regular course is 20.

Requirements: The SAT I or ACT is required. In addition, graduation from an accredited secondary school is required; the GED is accepted. Students must have completed 15 Carnegie units, including a total of 12 in English, math, science, and social science. A letter of recommendation from a high school official is required. An essay is recommended. A GPA of 2.0 is required. AP and CLEP credits are accepted. Important factors in the admissions decision are personality/intangible qualities and extracurricular activities record.

Procedure: Freshmen are admitted fall and spring. Entrance exams should be taken by November of the senior year. There is an early admissions plan. Check with the school for current application deadlines. Notification is sent on a rolling basis. The fall 2001 application was $20.

Transfer: Applicants must submit transcripts from high school and colleges attended, a letter of recommendation from a college official, a composite score of 700 on the SAT I or 14 on the ACT, and a minimum GPA of 2.0. A physical exam is also required. 32 credits of 124 must be completed at Morris Brown.

Visiting: There are regularly scheduled orientations for prospective students. There are guides for informal visits and visitors may sit in on classes. To schedule a visit, contact the Office of Admissions at (404) 220-0369.

Financial Aid: 18% of undergraduates work part time. Average annual earnings from campus work are $2310. Morris Brown is a member of CSS. The FAFSA is required. Check with the school for current deadlines.

International Students: The school actively recruits these students. They must also take the TOEFL and the college's own entrance exam.

Computers: The mainframe is a Prime Primos. There are 200 PCs that provide access to the Internet, the World Wide Web, and e-mail. All students may access the system. There are no time limits and no fees.

Admissions Contact: Vory L. Billups, Director of Admissions and Recruitment. A video is available. E-mail: *vbillups@morrisbrown.edu* Web: *www.morrisbrown.edu*

NORTH GEORGIA COLLEGE AND STATE UNIVERSITY B-1
Dahlonega, GA 30597 (706) 864-1754
(800) 498-9581; Fax: (706) 864-1478

Full-time: 1036 men, 1740 women
Part-time: 167 men, 491 women
Graduate: 106 men, 326 women
Year: semesters, summer session
Application Deadline: July 1
Freshman Class: 1926 applied, 646 accepted, 616 enrolled
SAT I Verbal/Math: 530/510
Faculty: 160; IIA, --$
Ph.D.s: 67%
Student/Faculty: 17 to 1
Tuition: $2496 ($8292)
Room & Board: $3826
ACT: 21 **COMPETITIVE+**

North Georgia College and State University, founded in 1873 as a military college, is today a liberal arts college that is part of the public University System of Georgia. One of 4 colleges in the United States classified as military colleges by the Department of the Army, the school requires all male resident students to join its Corps of Cadets; other students are given an option to join. There are 4 undergraduate schools and 1 graduate school. In addition to regional accreditation, NGCSU has baccalaureate program accreditation with ACBSP, APTA, NCATE, and NLN. The library contains 130,881 volumes, 602,789 microform items, and 3289 audiovisual forms/CDs, and subscribes to 2524 periodicals. Computerized library services include the card catalog, interlibrary loans, and database searching. Special learning facilities include an art gallery, planetarium, math lab, language lab, and writing center. The 255-acre campus is in a small town 60 miles north of Atlanta. Including residence halls, there are 25 buildings.

Student Life: 96% of undergraduates are from Georgia. Others are from 15 states, 8 foreign countries, and Canada. 90% are from public schools. 93% are white. The average age of freshmen is 19; all undergraduates, 23. 20% do not continue beyond their first year; 56% remain to graduate.

Housing: 1200 students can be accommodated in college housing, which includes single-sex dormitories. On-campus housing is available on a first-come, first-served basis. 61% of students commute. Alcohol is not permitted. All students may keep cars.

Activities: 13% of men belong to 2 local and 4 national fraternities; 10% of women belong to 4 national sororities. There are 52 groups on campus, including band, cheerleading, choir, chorale, chorus, drama, drill team, ethnic, honors, jazz band, literary magazine, marching band, newspaper, pep band, political, professional, religious, student government, symphony, and yearbook. Popular campus events include Spring Jam, frisbee golf, and Gold Rush.

Sports: There are 5 intercollegiate sports for men and 6 for women, and 7 intramural sports for men and 7 for women. Facilities include a swimming pool, a track, a fully equipped exercise room, a rappeling tower, a confidence course, a picnic area, a 2000-seat gym, and a 250-seat arena.

Disabled Students: 50% of the campus is accessible. Wheelchair ramps, elevators, special parking, and specially equipped rest rooms are available.

Services: Counseling and information services are available, as is tutoring in most subjects. There is a reader service for the blind, and remedial math, reading, and writing.

Campus Safety and Security: Measures include 24-hour foot and vehicle patrol, escort service, informal discussions, and emergency telephones. There are lighted pathways/sidewalks.

Programs of Study: NGCSU confers A.B., B.S., B.B.A., and B.S.N. degrees. Associate and master's degrees are also awarded. Bachelor's degrees are awarded in BIOLOGICAL SCIENCE (biology/biological science), BUSINESS (accounting, banking and finance, business administration and management, business economics, marketing/retailing/merchandising, and recreation and leisure services), COMMUNICATIONS AND THE ARTS (art, arts administration/management, English, French, music, and Spanish), COMPUTER AND PHYSICAL SCIENCE (chemistry, computer science, mathematics, and physics), EDUCATION (art, early childhood, elementary, foreign languages, mathematics, middle school, music, physical, science, secondary, social science, and special), ENGINEERING AND ENVIRONMENTAL DESIGN (preengineering), HEALTH PROFESSIONS (nursing, predentistry, premedicine, prepharmacy, and preveterinary science), SOCIAL SCIENCE (criminal justice, history, political science/government, prelaw, psychology, social science, and sociology). Premedicine, nursing, and preengineering are the strongest academically. Business and teacher education are the largest.

Required: To graduate, students must complete 120 semester credit hours with a minimum GPA of 2.0. English, math, lab sciences, social sciences, and phys ed courses are required.

Special: Special academic programs include a co-op program in business, internships in business and criminal justice, a 3-2 engineering degree with Georgia Institute of Technology, study abroad in Europe, South America, and Canada, dual majors, and credit for life, military, or work experience. There are 9 national honor societies, including Phi Beta Kappa, a freshman honors program, and 8 departmental honors programs.

Faculty/Classroom: 50% of faculty are male; 50%, female. All teach undergraduates. No introductory courses are taught by graduate students. The average class size in an introductory lecture is 30; in a laboratory, 30; and in a regular course, 30.

Admissions: 34% of the 2001-2002 applicants were accepted. The SAT I scores for the 2001-2002 freshman class were: Verbal--27% below 500, 56% between 500 and 599, 15% between 600 and 700, and 2% above 700; Math--38% below 500, 45% between 500 and 599, 15% between 600 and 700, and 1% above 700. The ACT scores were 39% below 21, 39% between 21 and 23, and 20% between 24 and 26.

Requirements: The SAT I is required. In addition, students must have graduated from a secondary school with 4 years of English, 3 each of math, science, and social science, and 2 of a foreign language. The GED is accepted if granted at least 5 years later than the expected high school graduation date. SAT II: Subject tests are required of home-schooled students. A GPA of 2.0 is required. AP and CLEP credits are accepted. Important factors in the admissions decision are leadership record, advanced placement or honor courses, and evidence of special talent. Applications are accepted on-line through the NGCSU web site or Apply.

Procedure: Freshmen are admitted to all sessions. Entrance exams should be taken in the junior year. There is a deferred admissions plan. Applications should be filed by July 1 for fall entry, December 15 for spring entry, and April 15 for summer entry, along with a $25 fee. Notification is sent on a rolling basis. 10% of all applicants are on a waiting list; 30 were accepted in 2001.

Transfer: 270 transfer students enrolled in 2001-2002. Transfer students must have maintained a C average and a clear conduct record, and be in good academic standing. Those who have not completed 90 quarter hours of transferable credit must have completed the approved precollege curriculum and must submit high school transcripts and SAT I or ACT results. 45 credits of 120 must be completed at NGCSU.

Visiting: There are regularly scheduled orientations for prospective students, including an admissions video, a college overview, a tour, and a one-on-one meeting with an admissions counselor. There are guides for informal visits and visitors may stay overnight. To schedule a visit, contact the Admissions Office at *admissions@ngcsu.edu*.

Financial Aid: In a recent year, 95% of all freshmen received some form of financial aid. The CSS/Profile, the college's own financial statement, and tax returns are required. The fall application deadline is May 1.

International Students: There are 52 international students enrolled. They must score 550 on the written TOEFL or 213 on the electronic version and also take the SAT I or the ACT.

Computers: There are 50 Pentium PCs available in the education building and 10 in the library. All students may access the system 8 A.M. to 10 P.M. There are no time limits and no fees.

Graduates: In 2001, 538 bachelor's degrees were awarded. The most popular majors were early childhood education (11%), business management (10%), and biology (9%). In an average class, 1% graduate in 3 years, 28% in 4 years, 45% in 5 years, and 51% in 6 years. 102 companies recruited on campus in 2000-2001. Of the 2000 graduating class, 6% were enrolled in graduate school within 6 months of graduation and 48% were employed.

Admissions Contact: Robert LaVerriere, Director of Undergraduate Admissions and Recruiting. A video is available.
E-mail: *rlaverriere@ngcsu.edu* Web: *www.ngcsu.edu*

OGLETHORPE UNIVERSITY B-2
Atlanta, GA 30319-2797 (404) 364-8307
(800) 428-4484; Fax: (404) 364-8500

Full-time: 315 men, 540 women
Part-time: 60 men, 145 women
Graduate: 35 men, 95 women
Year: semesters, summer session
Application Deadline: open
Freshman Class: n/av
SAT I or ACT: required
Faculty: 56; IIB, av$
Ph.D.s: 96%
Student/Faculty: 15 to 1
Tuition: $19,100
Room & Board: n/app
LESS COMPETITIVE

Oglethorpe University, founded in 1835, is an independent institution offering programs in the liberal arts, business, and teacher preparation. Figures in above capsule are approximate. There are 2 undergraduate and 2 graduate schools. In addition to regional accreditation, Oglethorpe has baccalaureate program accreditation with NCATE. The library contains 119,627 volumes and 3679 audiovisual forms/CDs, and subscribes to 742 periodicals. Computerized library services include the card catalog, interlibrary loans, and database searching. Special learning facilities include a learning resource center, art gallery, and radio station. The

118-acre campus is in a suburban area 10 miles northeast of downtown Atlanta. Including residence halls, there are 25 buildings.

Student Life: 50% of undergraduates are from out of state, mostly the South. Others are from 32 states, 31 foreign countries, and Canada. 74% are from public schools. 68% are white. 44% are Protestant; 31% claim no religious affiliation; 17% Catholic. The average age of freshmen is 18; all undergraduates, 20. 19% do not continue beyond their first year; 63% remain to graduate.

Housing: 575 students can be accommodated in college housing, which includes single-sex and coed dormitories, fraternity houses, and sorority houses. On-campus housing is available on a first-come, first-served basis. Priority is given to out-of-town students. 68% of students live on campus; of those, 60% remain on campus on weekends. All students may keep cars.

Activities: 41% of men belong to 4 national fraternities; 22% of women belong to 2 national sororities. There are 51 groups on campus, including art, cheerleading, choir, chorale, chorus, computers, dance, drama, ethnic, gay, honors, international, literary magazine, newspaper, pep band, photography, political, professional, radio and TV, religious, social, social service, student government, and yearbook. Popular campus events include Boar's Head Ceremony, Oglethorpe Day, and International Night.

Sports: There are 7 intercollegiate sports for men and 6 for women, and 6 intramural sports for men and 6 for women. Facilities include a field house and recreation center, housing basketball and volleyball courts, a running track, handball courts, and a weight room. Outdoor facilities include 6 tennis courts, an all-weather track, an outdoor swimming pool, a sand volleyball court, and soccer, baseball, and intramural fields.

Disabled Students: 90% of the campus is accessible. Wheelchair ramps, elevators, special parking, specially equipped rest rooms, and special class scheduling are available.

Services: Counseling and information services are available, as is tutoring in most subjects, including all core courses, English, writing, accounting, and any subject area by request of professors or students.

Campus Safety and Security: Measures include 24-hour foot and vehicle patrol, self-defense education, informal discussions, and pamphlets/posters/films. There are lighted pathways/sidewalks.

Programs of Study: Oglethorpe confers B.A., B.S., and B.B.A. degrees. Master's degrees are also awarded. Bachelor's degrees are awarded in BIOLOGICAL SCIENCE (biology/biological science), BUSINESS (accounting and business administration and management), COMMUNICATIONS AND THE ARTS (art, communications, and English), COMPUTER AND PHYSICAL SCIENCE (chemistry, computer science, mathematics, and physics), EDUCATION (early childhood, middle school, and secondary), SOCIAL SCIENCE (American studies, behavioral science, economics, history, international studies, philosophy, political science/government, psychology, social work, and sociology). Accounting, biology, and English are the strongest academically. Biology, business administration, and English are the largest.

Required: To graduate, all students must complete at least 120 credit hours, fulfilling a major as well as completing the core curriculum, and achieve a minimum GPA of 2.0. The core curriculum includes course work in writing, literature, Western civilization, math, psychology, philosophy, interdisciplinary social sciences, music or art, physical science, and biological science. All freshmen must complete the first-year experience program.

Special: Oglethorpe offers co-op programs in all majors, cross-registration through the University Center in Georgia, international exchange agreements with several universities in Europe, Asia, and South America, and other study-abroad options. Internships are available in all areas of study, and a Washington semester offers internships with Georgia senators and others. There is a dual-degree program with the Atlanta College of Art and a 3-2 engineering program with Georgia Institute of Technology, the Universities of Florida and Southern California, and Auburn University. Accelerated degrees, dual majors, student-designed majors, federal work-study programs, and nondegree study are offered. There are 7 national honor societies.

Faculty/Classroom: 75% of faculty are male; 25%, female. All teach undergraduates. No introductory courses are taught by graduate students. The average class size in an introductory lecture is 22; in a laboratory, 20; and in a regular course, 16.

Requirements: The SAT I or ACT is required, with a minimum recommended composite score of 950 on the SAT I or 21 on the ACT. Students should graduate from an accredited high school or have a GED certificate. They should have completed 4 courses in English, 3 each in science and social studies, and a math sequence of algebra I and II and geometry. A counselor's or teacher's recommendation is required, and an essay is required for a scholarship. An interview is recommended. AP and CLEP credits are accepted. Important factors in the admissions decision are recommendations by school officials, extracurricular activities record, and advanced placement or honor courses. Applications may be submitted on computer disk using CollegeLink.

Procedure: Freshmen are admitted to all sessions. Entrance exams should be taken late in the junior year or early in the senior year. There are early decision, early admissions, and deferred admissions plans. Early decision applications should be filed by December 5; regular applications, open for fall entry, along with a $35 fee. Notification of early decision is rolling ; regular decision, rolling. 25 early decision candidates were accepted for the 2001-2002 class. The application fee is $35.

Transfer: 104 transfer students enrolled in 2001-2002. Applicants who have completed less than a full year of college work must take the SAT I or ACT. All transfers must be in good academic standing with a minimum GPA of 2.5. An interview is recommended. 48 credits of 120 must be completed at Oglethorpe.

Visiting: There are regularly scheduled orientations for prospective students, including placement tests, class registration, an activities fair, and group activities. There are guides for informal visits and visitors may sit in on classes and stay overnight. To schedule a visit, contact the Admissions Office.

Financial Aid: Oglethorpe is a member of CSS. The FAFSA is required. Check with the school for current deadlines.

International Students: The school actively recruits these students. They must score 500 on the written TOEFL and also take or demonstrate proficiency in English by other means.

Computers: The university is served by a local area network. All students are provided e-mail accounts and may access the network and the Internet on their PCs or through the library or computer labs. All students may access the system. There are no time limits. It is strongly recommended that all students have a personal computer.

Graduates: In an average class, 2% graduate in 3 years, 53% in 4 years, 62% in 5 years, and 65% in 6 years.

Admissions Contact: Dennis T. Matthews, Dean of Enrollment Management. E-mail: *admission@oglethorpe.edu*
Web: *www.oglethorpe.edu*

PAINE COLLEGE — D-2
Augusta, GA 30901-3182 — **(706) 821-8320**
(800) 476-7703; Fax: (706) 821-8691

Full-time: 210 men, 520 women	**Faculty:** 60
Part-time: 40 men, 90 women	**Ph.D.s:** 56%
Graduate: none	**Student/Faculty:** 12 to 1
Year: semesters, summer session	**Tuition:** $8290
Application Deadline: August 1	**Room & Board:** $3606
Freshman Class: n/av	
SAT I: required	**LESS COMPETITIVE**

Paine College, founded in 1882, is a largely African-American private institution affiliated with the Christian Methodist Episcopal Church and the United Methodist Church. It offers programs in liberal arts, business, and teacher preparation. Figures in the above capsule are approximate. The library contains 72,443 volumes, 10,165 microform items, and 1239 audiovisual forms/CDs, and subscribes to 303 periodicals. Computerized library services include interlibrary loans and database searching. Special learning facilities include a learning resource center, art gallery, TV station, and tutorial and enrichment center. The 55-acre campus is in an urban area 150 miles east of Atlanta and 72 miles west of Columbia, South Carolina. Including residence halls, there are 25 buildings.

Student Life: 75% of undergraduates are from Georgia. Others are from 29 states, 2 foreign countries, and Canada. 97% are African American. 80% are Protestant; 10% claim no religious affiliation. The average age of freshmen is 18; all undergraduates, 22. 40% do not continue beyond their first year; 20% remain to graduate.

Housing: 506 students can be accommodated in college housing, which includes single-sex dormitories. On-campus housing is available on a first-come, first-served basis. 58% of students live on campus. Alcohol is not permitted. All students may keep cars.

Activities: 10% of men belong to 4 national fraternities; 10% of women belong to 5 national sororities. There are 15 groups on campus, including cheerleading, choir, chorus, dance, drama, honors, international, NAACP, newspaper, professional, religious, social, student government, and yearbook. Popular campus events include Miss Paine Coronation, Founders Day, and black history activities.

Sports: There are 4 intercollegiate sports for men and 5 for women, and 7 intramural sports for men and 7 for women. Facilities include a gym, a tennis court, a track, and a baseball field.

Disabled Students: 60% of the campus is accessible. Wheelchair ramps, elevators, special parking, specially equipped rest rooms, and lowered drinking fountains are available.

Services: Counseling and information services are available, as is tutoring in most subjects. There is remedial math, reading, and writing.

Campus Safety and Security: Measures include 24-hour foot and vehicle patrol, escort service, informal discussions, and pamphlets/posters/films. There are lighted pathways/sidewalks.

Programs of Study: Paine confers B.A. and B.S. degrees. Bachelor's degrees are awarded in BIOLOGICAL SCIENCE (biology/biological science), BUSINESS (business administration and management), COMMUNICATIONS AND THE ARTS (communications and English), COM-

PUTER AND PHYSICAL SCIENCE (chemistry and mathematics), EDUCATION (early childhood, middle school, music, and secondary), SOCIAL SCIENCE (history, philosophy, psychology, and sociology). Education, natural sciences, and math are the strongest academically. Biology, education, and business are the largest.

Required: Common curriculum requirements include 18 hours in world citizenship/society, 14 in science/technology, 8 to 10 in fundamentals, 9 in spiritual and social values, and 6 in the aesthetic heritage. From 33 to 71 hours are required in the major. A minimum GPA of 2.5 in the major is needed. To graduate, at least 124 credits must be completed. A thesis in most programs and comprehensive exams in some programs may also be required.

Special: Paine has co-op programs in natural and social sciences and business administration, cross-registration with Augusta State University, internships for business administration and sociology majors, and study abroad in France, Africa, and South America. A 3-2 engineering degree is offered with Georgia Institute of Technology and Florida Agricultural and Mechanical University. There are transfer programs with the Medical University of South Carolina at Charleston School of Nursing and Medical College of Georgia. There is 1 national honor society and a freshman honors program.

Faculty/Classroom: 54% of faculty are male; 46%, female. All teach undergraduates. The average class size in an introductory lecture is 25; in a laboratory, 20; and in a regular course, 23.

Requirements: The SAT I is required. In addition, applicants should be graduates of an accredited secondary school or have a GED. A total of 15 academic credits is required, including 4 units of English, 2 each of math and social studies, and 1 of science. A GPA of 2.0 is required. AP and CLEP credits are accepted. Important factors in the admissions decision are recommendations by school officials, advanced placement or honor courses, and evidence of special talent.

Procedure: Freshmen are admitted to all sessions. Entrance exams should be taken during spring and summer testing sessions; they are also offered during each orientation period. There are early decision, early admissions, and deferred admissions plans. Applications should be filed by August 1 for fall entry, December 1 for spring entry, and June 1 for summer entry, along with a $10 fee. Notification is sent on a rolling basis.

Transfer: 46 transfer students enrolled in a recent year. Applicants must meet freshmen criteria except for the SAT I requirement. 30 credits of 124 must be completed at Paine.

Visiting: There are regularly scheduled orientations for prospective students, including meetings with administrators, tours of the city and campus, and placement testing. There are guides for informal visits and visitors may sit in on classes and stay overnight. To schedule a visit, contact Joe Tinsley, Assistant Director of Admissions.

Financial Aid: 50% of undergraduates work part time. Average annual earnings from campus work are $2000. Paine is a member of CSS. The CSS/Profile or FAFSA and the college's own financial statement are required. The fall application deadline is April 15.

International Students: There were 3 international students enrolled in a recent year. The school actively recruits these students. They must score 500 on the written TOEFL and also take the SAT I.

Computers: The mainframes are an IBM AS/400 and 6 servers. There is a Compaq supermicrocomputer on a Novell network available for student use. There are 70 PCs and Macs, and Apple IIes in 3 main labs in the Learning Resource Center, 1 science lab (20 systems), the Tutorial and Enrichment Center (20 systems), 2 business administration division labs (15-20 systems each), and some faculty offices. All students may access the system. There are no time limits and no fees.

Admissions Contact: Joseph Tinsley, Assistant Director of Admissions. E-mail: *tinsley@mail.paine.edu* Web: *www.paine.edu*

PIEDMONT COLLEGE
Demorest, GA 30535 — C-1

(706) 776-0103
(800) 277-7020; Fax: (706) 776-6635

Full-time: 310 men, 529 women	**Faculty:** 89; IIB, -$
Part-time: 55 men, 96 women	**Ph.D.s:** 73%
Graduate: 144 men, 799 women	**Student/Faculty:** 10 to 1
Year: semesters, summer session	**Tuition:** $12,500
Application Deadline: open	**Room & Board:** $4400
Freshman Class: 377 applied, 251 accepted, 206 enrolled	
SAT I Verbal/Math: 500/500	**ACT:** 19 — **COMPETITIVE**

Piedmont College, founded in 1897, is a private, liberal arts institution affiliated with the Congregational Christian Churches of America. There are 4 undergraduate schools and 1 graduate school. The library contains 115,000 volumes, 42,406 microform items, and 402 audiovisual forms/CDs, and subscribes to 449 periodicals. Computerized library services include the card catalog, interlibrary loans, and database searching. Special learning facilities include a learning resource center, art gallery, radio station, a distance learning center, the Georgia Youth Science and Technology Center, and an observatory. The 300-acre campus is in a small town 75 miles northeast of Atlanta. Including residence halls, there are 34 buildings.

Student Life: 96% of undergraduates are from Georgia. Others are from 14 states, 12 foreign countries, and Canada. 93% are from public schools. 90% are white. 63% are Protestant; 30% claim no religious affiliation. The average age of freshmen is 18; all undergraduates, 23. 37% do not continue beyond their first year; 30% remain to graduate.

Housing: 320 students can be accommodated in college housing, which includes single-sex dormitories and on-campus apartments. On-campus housing is guaranteed for all 4 years. 67% of students commute. Alcohol is not permitted. All students may keep cars.

Activities: There are no fraternities or sororities. There are 25 groups on campus, including art, cheerleading, choir, chorale, chorus, computers, drama, honors, literary magazine, musical theater, newspaper, orchestra, professional, radio and TV, religious, social, social service, student government, and yearbook. Popular campus events include Halloween Dance, Spring Formal Dance, and the Lyceum series.

Sports: There are 3 intercollegiate sports for men and 4 for women, and 6 intramural sports for men and 6 for women. Facilities include a gym, 8 tennis courts, beach volleyball courts, and regulation baseball, softball, and soccer fields.

Disabled Students: 85% of the campus is accessible. Wheelchair ramps, elevators, special parking, specially equipped rest rooms, and special class scheduling are available.

Services: Counseling and information services are available, as is tutoring in every subject. There is remedial math, reading, and writing.

Campus Safety and Security: Measures include 24-hour foot and vehicle patrol, self-defense education, escort service, and informal discussions. There are pamphlets/posters/films, emergency telephones, lighted pathways/sidewalks, and campus patrol by the local police department.

Programs of Study: Piedmont confers B.A., B.S., and B.S.N. degrees. Master's degrees are also awarded. Bachelor's degrees are awarded in BIOLOGICAL SCIENCE (biology/biological science), BUSINESS (business administration and management), COMMUNICATIONS AND THE ARTS (art, dramatic arts, English, music, and Spanish), COMPUTER AND PHYSICAL SCIENCE (applied mathematics, chemistry, and mathematics), EDUCATION (art, drama, early childhood, middle school, music, and special), HEALTH PROFESSIONS (nursing), SOCIAL SCIENCE (history, philosophy, psychology, religion, and sociology). Biology, education, and art are the strongest academically. Education, business administration, and social sciences are the largest.

Required: To graduate, a minimum of 120 credit hours is required, with a minimum GPA of 2.0. or higher in some majors. Students must complete 18 to 48 credit hours in their major, 21 in humanities, 14 in math/natural science, 12 in social science, 6 in fine arts, and 3 in computer science.

Special: Piedmont offers internships in business, psychology, education, art management, and political science, and a 2-year completion of a business degree in health care management for those with an associate degree in a health-related area. There are 4 national honor societies, a freshman honors program, and 1 departmental honors program.

Faculty/Classroom: 57% of faculty are male; 43%, female. 93% teach undergraduates. The average class size in an introductory lecture is 17; in a laboratory, 12; and in a regular course, 14.

Admissions: 67% of the 2001-2002 applicants were accepted. The SAT I scores for the 2001-2002 freshman class were: Verbal--45% below 500, 39% between 500 and 599, 14% between 600 and 700, and 2% above 700; Math--48% below 500, 39% between 500 and 599, 11% between 600 and 700, and 2% above 700. The ACT scores were 58% below 21, 19% between 21 and 23, 15% between 24 and 26, and 8% between 27 and 28. 23% of the current freshmen were in the top fifth of their class; 46% were in the top two fifths.

Requirements: The SAT I is required, but the ACT is also accepted. Applicants must be graduates of an accredited secondary school or have a GED certificate. Students must have completed a minimum of 21 academic units. Piedmont Scholars are required to submit an essay. A portfolio is required for art scholarship applicants and an audition for music scholarship applicants. An interview is recommended for all students. A GPA of 2.0 is required. AP and CLEP credits are accepted. Important factors in the admissions decision are leadership record, advanced placement or honor courses, and extracurricular activities record.

Procedure: Freshmen are admitted to all sessions. There is a deferred admissions plan. Application deadlines are open. The fall 2001 application fee was $20. Notification is sent on a rolling basis.

Transfer: 136 transfer students enrolled in a recent year. Applicants must have a GPA of 2.0 at each institution attended. An interview is recommended. 30 credits of 120 must be completed at Piedmont.

Visiting: There are regularly scheduled orientations for prospective students, consisting of student activities, academic assistance and counseling, resident orientation, and a financial aid presentation. There are guides for informal visits and visitors may sit in on classes and stay overnight. To schedule a visit, contact the Admissions Office.

Financial Aid: In 2001-2002, 98% of all freshmen and 92% of continuing students received some form of financial aid. 81% of undergraduates work part time. Average annual earnings from campus work are $1200. The FAFSA is required. Check with the school for current deadlines.

International Students: They must score 550 on the written TOEFL and also take the SAT I or the ACT.

Computers: There are 6 PC labs with 78 computers that connect to the network system, with access to the Internet. All students may access the system more than 90 hours per week. There are no time limits and no fees.

Graduates: In a recent year, 213 bachelor's degrees were awarded. The most popular majors were education (32%), business administration (24%), and psychology (12%). In an average class, 2% graduate in 3 years, 21% in 4 years, and 30% in 5 years.

Admissions Contact: Kathy Edwards-Rarey, Director of Undergraduate Admissions. A video is available. E-mail: *kedwards@piedmont.edu* Web: *www.piedmont.edu*

REINHARDT COLLEGE — B-2

Waleska, GA 30183 — (770) 720-5826; 1-87REINHARDT; Fax: (770) 720-5899

Full-time: 900 men and women	**Faculty:** 40; III, --$
Part-time: 200 men and women	**Ph.D.s:** 47%
Graduate: none	**Student/Faculty:** 11 to 1
Year: semesters, summer session	**Tuition:** $8700
Application Deadline: open	**Room & Board:** $4600
Freshman Class: n/av	
SAT I or ACT: required	**COMPETITIVE**

Reinhardt College, founded in 1883, is an independent institution affiliated with the Methodist Church and offering undergraduate degrees. Figures in the above capsule are approximate. The library contains 40,291 volumes, 1983 microform items, and 3176 audiovisual forms/CDs, and subscribes to 367 periodicals. Computerized library services include the card catalog, interlibrary loans, and database searching. Special learning facilities include an art gallery, natural history museum, and TV station. The 600-acre campus is in a small town 40 miles north of Atlanta. Including residence halls, there are 31 buildings.

Student Life: 97% of undergraduates are from Georgia. 90% are from public schools. 93% are white. 49% are Protestant. The average age of freshmen is 19; all undergraduates, 23. 36% do not continue beyond their first year; 50% remain to graduate.

Housing: 404 students can be accommodated in college housing, which includes single-sex dormitories. On-campus housing is guaranteed for all 4 years. 54% of students commute. Alcohol is not permitted. All students may keep cars.

Activities: There are no fraternities or sororities. There are 14 groups on campus, including cheerleading, honors, newspaper, professional, radio and TV, religious, social, social service, student government, and yearbook. Popular campus events include Spring Day, Spring Formal, and Diversity Days.

Sports: There are 3 intercollegiate sports for men and 2 for women, and 4 intramural sports for men and 4 for women. Facilities include parks, jogging trails, outdoor volleyball, tennis, and basketball courts, soccer and softball fields, pool, weight room, bowling alley, and racquetball courts.

Disabled Students: 90% of the campus is accessible. Wheelchair ramps, elevators, special parking, specially equipped rest rooms, special class scheduling, and lowered drinking fountains are available.

Services: Counseling and information services are available, as is tutoring in every subject.

Campus Safety and Security: Measures include self-defense education, lighted pathways/sidewalks, and a 21-hour patrol.

Programs of Study: Reinhardt confers B.A., B.S., and B.S.B.A. degrees. Associate degrees are also awarded. Bachelor's degrees are awarded in BIOLOGICAL SCIENCE (biology/biological science), BUSINESS (business administration and management), COMMUNICATIONS AND THE ARTS (communications), SOCIAL SCIENCE (liberal arts/general studies). Business and liberal studies are the largest.

Required: To graduate, students must have a core curriculum in the humanities, math and science, social science, lanquage, phys ed, and wellness. A total of 192 quarter hours is required, including 110 in the major. A 2.0 GPA must be maintained.

Special: Internships, study abroad, and work-study programs are available. There is a 3-2 engineering degree offered with Mercer University. There is 1 national honor society and a freshman honors program.

Faculty/Classroom: 45% of faculty are male; 55%, female. 60% teach undergraduates and 40% both teach and do research. The average class size in an introductory lecture is 17; in a laboratory, 17; and in a regular course, 17.

Admissions: There was 1 National Merit finalist. 1 freshman graduated first in the class in a recent year.

Requirements: The SAT I or ACT is required. In addition, the GED is accepted and a placement test may be required. A GPA of 2.25 is required. AP and CLEP credits are accepted. Important factors in the admissions decision are recommendations by alumni, recommendations by school officials, and parents or siblings attending the school. Applications are accepted on-line.

Procedure: Freshmen are admitted to all sessions. Entrance exams should be taken 30 days after acceptance. There is an early admissions plan. Check with the school for current application deadlines.The application fee is $25.

Transfer: 60 transfer students enrolled in 2001-2002. A maximum of 60 quarter hours with a grade of D with a GPA of 2.25 or better may be considered for transfer applicants. 132 credits of 192 must be completed at Reinhardt.

Visiting: There are regularly scheduled orientations for prospective students. There are guides for informal visits and visitors may sit in on classes and stay overnight. To schedule a visit, contact Dana Deas.

Financial Aid: In a recent year, 97% of all freshmen and 90% of continuing students received some form of financial aid. 30% of freshmen and 40% of continuing students received need-based aid. The average freshman award was $3600. Of that total, scholarships or need-based grants averaged $1200 ($5000 maximum); loans averaged $1050 ($2525 maximum); and work contracts averaged $1500 (maximum). 14% of undergraduates work part time. Average annual earnings from campus work are $1485. The average financial indebtedness of the 2001 graduate was $15,000. The FAFSA is required. Check with the school for current deadlines.

International Students: There are 22 international students enrolled. They must score 500 on the written TOEFL.

Computers: There are various computer labs, with network access to each dorm room. All students may access the system. There are no time limits and no fees. It is strongly recommended that all students have a personal computer.

Admissions Contact: Jodi Johnson, Director of Admissions.
E-mail: *admissions@reinhardt.edu* Web: *www.reinhardt.edu*

SAVANNAH COLLEGE OF ART AND DESIGN — E-4

Savannah, GA 31401-3146 — (912) 525-5100; (800) 869-7223; Fax: (912) 525-5995

Full-time: 2251 men, 1970 women	**Faculty:** 243
Part-time: 309 men, 177 women	**Ph.D.s:** 83%
Graduate: 326 men, 305 women	**Student/Faculty:** 17 to 1
Year: quarters, summer session	**Tuition:** $17,825
Application Deadline: open	**Room & Board:** $7250
Freshman Class: 3169 applied, 2664 accepted, 1038 enrolled	
SAT I Verbal/Math: 550/524	**ACT:** 23 — **SPECIAL**

Savannah College of Art and Design, founded in 1978, is a private fine arts university emphasizing career preparation in the visual and performing arts, design, building arts, and the history of art and architecture. There are 4 undergraduate and 4 graduate schools. In addition to regional accreditation, SCAD has baccalaureate program accreditation with NAAB. The library contains 83,017 volumes, 6000 microform items, and 3078 audiovisual forms/CDs, and subscribes to 872 periodicals. Computerized library services include the card catalog, interlibrary loans, and database searching. Special learning facilities include a learning resource center, art gallery, TV station, international center, language lab, writing center, and Internet labs. The campus is in an urban area on the southeast coast of Georgia, midway between Charleston, South Carolina, and Jacksonville, Florida. Including residence halls, there are 41 buildings.

Student Life: 79% of undergraduates are from out of state, mostly the South. Others are from 49 states, 75 foreign countries, and Canada. 48% are white; 10% foreign nationals. The average age of freshmen is 18; all undergraduates, 21. 17% do not continue beyond their first year.

Housing: 1641 students can be accommodated in college housing, which includes single-sex and coed dormitories, on-campus apartments, and theme housing. On-campus housing is available on a first-come, first-served basis. 65% of students commute. Alcohol is not permitted. All students may keep cars.

Activities: There are no fraternities or sororities. There are 45 groups on campus, including art, cheerleading, chess, chorale, computers, dance, drama, ethnic, film, international, literary magazine, musical theater, newspaper, orchestra, photography, professional, radio and TV, religious, social service, and student government. Popular campus events include Sidewalk Arts Festival, Beaux Arts Ball, and International Student Festival.

Sports: There are 9 intercollegiate sports for men and 10 for women, and 8 intramural sports for men and 7 for women. Facilities include an on-campus fitness center, which has an exercise floor and a weight/cardiovascular workout area.

Disabled Students: 74% of the campus is accessible. Wheelchair ramps, elevators, special parking, specially equipped rest rooms, special class scheduling, lowered drinking fountains, and lowered telephones. Facilities vary by building, but individual situations are accommodated.

Services: Counseling and information services are available, as is tutoring in every subject. There is a sign language interpreter for hearing-impaired students and a coordinator of disability services.

Campus Safety and Security: Measures include 24-hour foot and vehicle patrol, self-defense education, escort service, and shuttle buses. There are informal discussions, pamphlets/posters/films, emergency telephones, lighted pathways/sidewalks, and video surveillance cameras.

Programs of Study: SCAD confers the B.F.A. degree. Master's degrees are also awarded. Bachelor's degrees are awarded in COMMUNICATIONS AND THE ARTS (art, art history and appreciation, fiber/textiles/weaving, graphic design, historic preservation, illustration, industrial design, media arts, metal/jewelry, painting, performing arts, photography, and video), ENGINEERING AND ENVIRONMENTAL DESIGN (architecture, computer graphics, furniture design, and interior design), SOCIAL SCIENCE (fashion design and technology). Computer art, graphic design, and photography are the largest.

Required: To graduate, students need 30 to 45 hours of foundation drawing/design. 65 to 70 of liberal arts, 60 to 70 in the major, and 10 to 20 of electives, for a total of 180 quarter hours. All students must earn at least 5 quarter hours in computer courses. Students must maintain a 2.0 GPA overall and a 3.0 in the major.

Special: The college offers study abroad through various programs each summer, on-campus work-study programs, dual majors in all disciplines, sessions for credit in New York and other domestic locations, and internships with artists, designers, museums, agencies, and architectural firms in the United States and abroad. There are 2 national honor societies.

Faculty/Classroom: 53% of faculty are male; 47%, female. All teach undergraduates. No introductory courses are taught by graduate students. The average class size in an introductory lecture is 20 and in a regular course, 11.

Admissions: 84% of the 2001-2002 applicants were accepted. The SAT I scores for the 2001-2002 freshman class were: Verbal--28% below 500, 43% between 500 and 599, 24% between 600 and 700, and 5% above 700; Math--39% below 500, 40% between 500 and 599, 18% between 600 and 700, and 3% above 700. The ACT scores were 24% below 21, 29% between 21 and 23, 22% between 24 and 26, 14% between 27 and 28, and 11% above 28. There was 1 National Merit semifinalist. 1 freshman graduated first in the class.

Requirements: The SAT I or ACT is required. In addition, students must submit a completed application and high school transcript indicating successful completion. Preference is given to students with a 3.0 GPA or above and to students whose SAT I or ACT scores are above the national average. (B.F.A. Architecture candidates with math scores below 540 or 23, respectively, may be admitted to architecture on a conditional basis.) 3 recommendations, an interview, and a portfolio are encouraged. SCAD requires applicants to be in the upper 50% of their class. AP credits are accepted. Important factors in the admissions decision are evidence of special talent, recommendations by school officials, and leadership record. Applications are accepted on-line.

Procedure: Freshmen are admitted to all sessions. Entrance exams should be taken by November of the senior year. There is an early admissions plan. Application deadlines are open. The application fee is $50. Notification is sent on a rolling basis.

Transfer: 428 transfer students enrolled in 2001-2002. Transfer students must submit a completed application and college transcripts. (High school transcripts may be required if the number of college credits is insufficient for evaluating performance.) An official report of SAT I or ACT scores (architecture majors only) and 3 recommendations are required. A portfolio and an interview are encouraged but not required. 45 credits of 180 must be completed at SCAD.

Visiting: There are regularly scheduled orientations for prospective students, including check-in, tours, visits with faculty from areas of interest, portfolio reviews, financial aid counseling, admissions counseling, workshops, and a social event. There are guides for informal visits and visitors may sit in on classes. To schedule a visit, contact the Admission Office.

Financial Aid: In 2001-2002, 76% of all freshmen and 74% of continuing students received some form of financial aid. 40% of freshmen and 66% of continuing students received need-based aid. The average freshman award was $7000. Of that total, scholarships or need-based grants averaged $3800 ($7500 maximum); loans averaged $4500 ($15,000 maximum); and work contracts averaged $2700 ($5500 maximum). 80% of undergraduates work part time. Average annual earnings from campus work are $1200. The average financial indebtedness of the 2001 graduate was $20,000. The FAFSA is required. A customized packet of materials is sent to each applicant interested in financial aid.

International Students: There are 277 international students enrolled. The school actively recruits these students. They must score 500 on the written TOEFL or 177 on the electronic version, and also take the SAT I or the ACT.

Computers: There are approximately 29 computer labs located across the campus, including an Internet lab, a homework lab, a video lab, and 8 computer art labs. All students may access the system. Students may access the system at designated times. There are no fees.

Graduates: In 2001, 555 bachelor's degrees were awarded. The most popular majors were computer art (24%), graphic design (17%), and photography (10%). In an average class, 4% graduate in 3 years, 35% in 4 years, 47% in 5 years, and 59% in 6 years. 45 companies recruited on campus in 2000-2001. Of the 2000 graduating class, 10% were enrolled in graduate school within 6 months of graduation.

Admissions Contact: Pamela Afifi, Vice President for Admission. A video is available. E-mail: *admission@scad.edu* Web: *www.scad.edu*

SAVANNAH STATE UNIVERSITY
Savannah, GA 31404

E-4
(912) 356-2181
(800) 788-0478; Fax: (912) 356-2256

Full-time: 720 men, 780 women	**Faculty:** n/av
Part-time: 230 men, 320 women	**Ph.D.s:** 54%
Graduate: 50 men, 70 women	**Student/Faculty:** n/av
Year: semesters, summer session	**Tuition:** $2550 ($8346)
Application Deadline: see profile	**Room & Board:** n/app
Freshman Class: n/av	
SAT I or ACT: required	**LESS COMPETITIVE**

Savannah State University, founded in 1890, is a liberal arts institution that is part of the University System of Georgia. Undergraduate and graduate degrees are offered through the colleges of business, liberal arts and social sciences, and sciences and technology. Preprofessional programs are available. Figures in the above capsule are approximate. There are 3 undergraduate and 3 graduate schools. In addition to regional accreditation, Savannah State has baccalaureate program accreditation with ABET, CSWE, and NCATE. The library contains 200,000 volumes, 557,690 microform items, and 4173 audiovisual forms/CDs, and subscribes to 832 periodicals. Computerized library services include the card catalog, interlibrary loans, and database searching. Special learning facilities include a learning resource center, radio station, an arts center, and marine science lab. The 165-acre campus is in a suburban area 265 miles southeast of Atlanta. Including residence halls, there are 42 buildings.

Student Life: 80% of undergraduates are from Georgia. Others are from 20 states and 10 foreign countries. 70% are from public schools. 92% are African American. The average age of freshmen is 19; all undergraduates, 23. 62% of freshmen remain to graduate.

Housing: 1260 students can be accommodated in college housing, which includes single-sex dormitories, on-campus apartments, and married-student housing. On-campus housing is available on a first-come, first-served basis. 55% of students commute. Alcohol is not permitted. All students may keep cars.

Activities: 15% of men and about 3% of women belong to 6 national fraternities; 20% of women belong to 4 national sororities. There are 17 groups on campus, including art, band, cheerleading, choir, chorale, computers, dance, debate, drama, drill team, ethnic, international, jazz band, literary magazine, marching band, newspaper, opera, political, professional, radio and TV, religious, student government, and yearbook. Popular campus events include drama presentations, a Fine Arts Festival, and Christmas and spring concerts.

Sports: There are 5 intercollegiate sports for men and 4 for women, and 1 intramural sports for men. Facilities include a student center, gym complex, swimming pool, stadium, field house, tennis court, track, and field.

Disabled Students: 80% of the campus is accessible. Wheelchair ramps, elevators, special parking, specially equipped rest rooms, and lowered drinking fountains are available.

Services: Counseling and information services are available, as is tutoring in every subject. There is remedial math, reading, and writing.

Campus Safety and Security: Measures include 24-hour foot and vehicle patrol, informal discussions, pamphlets/posters/films, and lighted pathways/sidewalks. The campus police department is staffed with public safety officers, building attendants, security guards, safety inspectors, and telephone operators.

Programs of Study: Savannah State confers B.A., B.S., B.B.A., and B.S.W. degrees. Master's degrees are also awarded. Bachelor's degrees are awarded in BIOLOGICAL SCIENCE (biology/biological science and marine biology), BUSINESS (accounting, management information systems, marketing/retailing/merchandising, and recreational facilities management), COMMUNICATIONS AND THE ARTS (broadcasting, communications, English, and music), COMPUTER AND PHYSICAL SCIENCE (chemistry, computer science, mathematics, and physics), ENGINEERING AND ENVIRONMENTAL DESIGN (chemical engineering, civil engineering, electrical/electronics engineering technology, engineering technology, environmental science, mechanical engineering, and petroleum/natural gas engineering), HEALTH PROFESSIONS (predentistry), SOCIAL SCIENCE (criminal justice, history, political science/government, social work, and sociology). Biology, chemistry, and accounting are the strongest academically. Accounting, criminal justice, and management are the largest.

Required: To graduate, all students must fulfill the core curriculum requirements of 30 hours in courses appropriate to the major and 20 hours each of humanities, math and science, and social science. Students must maintain a minimum 2.0 GPA. Students must pass the University System of Georgia Language Skills Exam, 6 hours of phys ed courses, and 3 to 5 hours of a freshman orientation course. Exit competency exams and other requirements may be required.

Special: The college offers co-op programs, cross-registration, study abroad, a student exchange program with Armstrong State College, a dual degree program with Georgia Institute of Technology, the Georgia Legislative Internship Program, on- and off-campus work-study programs, correspondence study, credit for military experience, and nondegree study. There are 7 national honor societies, and a freshman honors program.

Faculty/Classroom: 67% of faculty are male; 32%, female. All teach undergraduates. The average class size in an introductory lecture is 35; in a laboratory, 22; and in a regular course, 33.

Admissions: 5 freshmen graduated first in their class.

Requirements: The SAT I or ACT is required, with a minimum composite score of 880 on SAT I, or 19 on the ACT. In addition, applicants must be graduates of an accredited secondary school. Students should have completed 4 units of English, 3 each of math, science, and social studies, and 2 of 1 foreign language. A GPA of 2.0 is required. AP and CLEP credits are accepted.

Procedure: Freshmen are admitted to all sessions. Entrance exams should be taken early in the senior year. There are early admissions and deferred admissions plans. Check with the school for curret application deadline. The application fee is $20. Notification is sent rolling.

Transfer: Applicants with at least 45 quarter hours or 30 semester hours of core curriculum credit do not need to submit high school transcripts, but must have a 2.0 average. All transfers must submit college transcripts, standardized test scores, and proof of good standing at the previous institution. 30 credits must be completed at Savannah State.

Visiting: There are guides for informal visits and visitors may sit in on classes. To schedule a visit, contact the Office of Admissions.

Financial Aid: In a recent year, 86% of all freshmen received some form of financial aid. The average freshman award was $3200. Grants, loans, and scholarships are available. The average financial indebtedness of a graduate in a recent year was $9000. Savannah State is a member of CSS. The CSS/Profile or FAFSA, the college's own financial statement, and the Scholarship Application Form are required. The fall application deadline is June 1; spring, November 1; summer, April 1.

International Students: They must score 500 on the written TOEFL and also take the SAT I, ACT, the college's own entrance exam, or the Collegiate Placement Exams.

Computers: Students may access Prime systems located in the School of Business and Hubert Technical Sciences Center. All students may access the system 8 A.M. to 10 P.M. There are no time limits and no fees.

Graduates: In a recent year, 312 bachelor's degrees were awarded. In an average class, 29% graduate in 6 years.

Admissions Contact: Roy Jackson, Director of Admissions.
E-mail: *ssuadms@savstate.edu* Web: *http://www.savstate.edu*

SHORTER COLLEGE
Rome, GA 30165-4298 — A-2
(706) 233-7319
(800) 868-6980; Fax: (706) 233-7224

Full-time: 302 men, 618 women	**Faculty:** 64; IIB, --$
Part-time: 16 men, 34 women	**Ph.D.s:** 73%
Graduate: none	**Student/Faculty:** 14 to 1
Year: semesters, summer session	**Tuition:** $9920
Application Deadline: open	**Room & Board:** $5265
Freshman Class: 687 applied, 592 accepted, 258 enrolled	
SAT I Verbal/Math: 530/520	**ACT:** 22 — **COMPETITIVE**

Shorter College, founded in 1873, is a private institution affiliated with the Baptist Church and offering undergraduate degree programs in communications, education, business, fine arts, humanities, social sciences, religion, and natural sciences. There are 4 undergraduate schools. In addition to regional accreditation, Shorter has baccalaureate program accreditation with NASM. The library contains 131,250 volumes, 6818 microform items, and 11,078 audiovisual forms/CDs, and subscribes to 596 periodicals. Computerized library services include the card catalog, interlibrary loans, and database searching. Special learning facilities include a learning resource center, art gallery, natural history museum, and radio station. The 150-acre campus is in a small town 70 miles northwest of Atlanta. Including residence halls, there are 18 buildings.

Student Life: 92% of undergraduates are from Georgia. Others are from 18 states, 18 foreign countries, and Canada. 96% are from public schools. 90% are white. Most are Protestant. The average age of freshmen is 19; all undergraduates, 21. 32% do not continue beyond their first year.

Housing: 618 students can be accommodated in college housing, which includes single-sex dormitories, on-campus apartments, and married-student housing. On-campus housing is guaranteed for the freshman year only and is available on a first-come, first-served basis. 60% of students live on campus; of those, 56% remain on campus on weekends. Alcohol is not permitted. All students may keep cars.

Activities: 20% of men belong to 1 local fraternity; 28% of women belong to 3 local sororities. There are 44 groups on campus, including art, band, cheerleading, choir, chorale, chorus, drama, ethnic, honors, international, literary magazine, musical theater, newspaper, opera, professional, radio and TV, religious, social service, student government, and yearbook. Popular campus events include Parents Weekend and Christmas Dinners.

Sports: There are 5 intercollegiate sports for men and 3 for women, and 12 intramural sports for men and 12 for women. Facilities include a 54,000-square-foot activities complex that houses a basketball arena, dance and aerobics studios, racquetball courts, a weight room, and an indoor jogging track. In addition, there are tennis courts and a swimming pool.

Disabled Students: 50% of the campus is accessible. Wheelchair ramps, elevators, special parking, specially equipped rest rooms, and lowered drinking fountains are available.

Services: Counseling and information services are available, as is tutoring in most subjects. There is a reader service for the blind, and remedial math, reading, and writing. Computerized study skills assessment and training are offered.

Campus Safety and Security: Measures include 24-hour foot and vehicle patrol, self-defense education, escort service, and informal discussions. There are pamphlets/posters/films and lighted pathways/sidewalks. Campus access is controlled via a gatehouse from 6 P.M. to 6 A.M. all weekend and during vacations.

Programs of Study: Shorter confers B.A., B.S., B.B.A., B.C.M., B.F.A., B.M., B.M.Ed., and B.S.E. degrees. Bachelor's degrees are awarded in BIOLOGICAL SCIENCE (biology/biological science), BUSINESS (accounting, business administration and management, and recreational facilities management), COMMUNICATIONS AND THE ARTS (art, communications, dramatic arts, English, French, music, musical theater, piano/organ, public relations, Spanish, and voice), COMPUTER AND PHYSICAL SCIENCE (chemistry, mathematics, and natural sciences), EDUCATION (early childhood, mathematics, middle school, and music), HEALTH PROFESSIONS (medical laboratory technology), SOCIAL SCIENCE (Christian studies, economics, history, parks and recreation management, psychology, religion, religious music, social science, and sociology). Music and natural sciences are the strongest academically. Business, early childhood education, and music are the largest.

Required: To graduate, students must maintain at least a 2.0 overall GPA, or 2.5 for education degrees, in 126 to 138 credits, with grades of C or better in the 27 to 96 credits required for a major. The core curriculum requires 33 hours in English, speech, literature, religion, social science, science, math, phys ed, and the arts. Those seeking B.A. and B.S. degrees will have additional core requirements. In addition, students must complete 42 hours in upper-level courses and pass an English writing exam.

Special: Shorter offers internships in most programs, cross-registration with Berry College, and study abroad in England, China, Austria, and Hong Kong. Dual and student-designed majors and pass/fail options are available. There are 5 national honor societies, a freshman honors program, and 4 departmental honors programs.

Faculty/Classroom: 57% of faculty are male; 43%, female. All teach undergraduates and 30% both teach and do research. The average class size in an introductory lecture is 22; in a laboratory, 20; and in a regular course, 17.

Admissions: 86% of the 2001-2002 applicants were accepted. The SAT I scores for the 2001-2002 freshman class were: Verbal--35% below 500, 43% between 500 and 599, 19% between 600 and 700, and 3% above 700; Math--37% below 500, 47% between 500 and 599, 14% between 600 and 700, and 2% above 700. The ACT scores were 35% below 21, 34% between 21 and 23, 20% between 24 and 26, 10% between 27 and 28, and 1% above 28. 60% of the current freshmen were in the top fifth of their class; 83% were in the top two fifths. 5 freshmen graduated first in their class.

Requirements: The SAT I or ACT is required. In addition, applicants should be graduates of accredited secondary schools or have a GED certificate. Secondary preparation should include 4 units in English, 3 each in history or social sciences, math, and natural sciences, and 2 in foreign language. Prospective music majors must audition and take a theory placement test; prospective theater majors must audition. A GPA of 2.25 is required. AP and CLEP credits are accepted. Important factors in the admissions decision are advanced placement or honor courses, evidence of special talent, and extracurricular activities record.

Procedure: Freshmen are admitted to all sessions. Entrance exams should be taken by the fall of the senior year. Application deadlines are open. The application fee is $25. Notification is sent on a rolling basis.

Transfer: 61 transfer students enrolled in 2001-2002. Applicants must submit transcripts, a character reference, and catalogs from any out-of-state colleges attended. A minimum 2.0 GPA based on transferable credit is required. 30 credits of 126 must be completed at Shorter.

Visiting: There are regularly scheduled orientations for prospective students, consisting of entertainment, financial aid workshops, a student-administration panel discussion, faculty consultations, admissions consultations, and campus/residence hall tours. There are guides for informal visits and visitors may sit in on classes and stay overnight. To schedule a visit, contact the Admissions Office.

Financial Aid: In 2001-2002, all freshmen and 99% of continuing students received some form of financial aid. 72% of freshmen and 73% of continuing students received need-based aid. The average freshman award was $10,674. Of that total, scholarships or need-based grants averaged $8905 ($17,500 maximum); loans averaged $3638 ($11,625 maximum); and work contracts averaged $1400 ($1500 maximum). All in-state students receive a state Tuition Equalization Grant; many in-state students also receive a state HOPE (GA) scholarship. 70% of undergraduates work part time. Average annual earnings from campus work are $1400. The average financial indebtedness of the 2001 graduate was $17,108. The FAFSA and the college's own financial statement are required. The fall application deadline is April 1.

International Students: There are 28 international students enrolled. They must take the TOEFL, scoring 500 on the written version or 173 on the electronic version, or take the MELAB or the ELS English Proficiency Evaluation. They must also take the SAT I or the ACT.

Computers: The mainframe is a DEC 486-33. There are 67 PCs and Macs distributed among 3 networked labs, the library, and the counseling center. All students may access the system. There are no time limits and no fees.

Graduates: In 2001, 175 bachelor's degrees were awarded. The most popular majors were education (29%), biology (15%), and religion (9%). In an average class, 1% graduate in 3 years, 45% in 4 years, 51% in 5 years, and 51% in 6 years. 20 companies recruited on campus in 2000-2001.

Admissions Contact: Wendy B. Sutton, Director of Admissions.
E-mail: *admissions@shorter.edu* Web: *www.shorter.edu*

SOUTH COLLEGE E-4

Savannah, GA 31406 (912) 201-8014; Fax: (912) 201-8072

Full-time: 115 men, 304 women	**Faculty:** 18
Part-time: 40 men, 91 women	**Ph.D.s:** 17%
Graduate: none	**Student/Faculty:** 23 to 1
Year: quarters, summer session	**Tuition:** $8720
Application Deadline: open	**Room & Board:** n/app
Freshman Class: n/av	
SAT I or ACT: recommended	**LESS COMPETITIVE**

South College, a private institution founded in 1899, offers undergraduate programs in business administration and health-related fields. In addition to regional accreditation, South College has baccalaureate program accreditation with APTA and CAHEA. The library contains 15,000 volumes and 148 audiovisual forms/CDs, and subscribes to 64 periodicals. Computerized library services include interlibrary loans and database searching. Special learning facilities include 2 medical labs, 2 computer labs, and a physical therapist assistant lab. The 9-acre campus is in an urban area in Savannah. There are 2 buildings.

Student Life: 98% of undergraduates are from Georgia. Others are from 2 states and 5 foreign countries. 57% are white; 38% African American. The average age of all undergraduates is 30.

Housing: There are no residence halls. All students commute. Alcohol is not permitted. All students may keep cars.

Activities: There are no fraternities or sororities. There are 5 groups on campus, including computers, professional, and student government. Popular campus events include Business Week, Health Professions Month, and Paralegal Week.

Sports: There is no sports program at South College.

Disabled Students: All of the campus is accessible. Wheelchair ramps, elevators, special parking, specially equipped rest rooms, and lowered telephones are available.

Services: Counseling and information services are available, as is tutoring in most subjects. There is remedial math and writing.

Campus Safety and Security: Measures include lighted pathways/sidewalks and a safety patrol during evening class hours.

Programs of Study: South College confers B.B.A., and B.S. in Physician Assistant degrees. Associate degrees are also awarded. Bachelor's degrees are awarded in BUSINESS (business administration and management), HEALTH PROFESSIONS (physician's assistant). Paralegal studies, medical assisting, and business administration are the largest.

Required: Students must earn a 2.0 GPA and take courses in algebra, composition, computers or word processing, personal development, and effective speaking. A total of 183 quarter credits must be completed.

Special: Internships are available in paralegal studies, medical assisting, physical therapist assistant, business administration, and physician assistant. Work-study programs are offered with various employers and South College, and there are dual majors.

Faculty/Classroom: 46% of faculty are male; 54%, female. 98% teach undergraduates. The average class size in an introductory lecture is 18; in a laboratory, 9; and in a regular course, 18.

Requirements: The SAT I or ACT is recommended. In addition, students should score a minimum of 830 on the SAT I or 17 on the ACT; they may also take a test administered by the college. Students must have earned a high school diploma or GED. An interview is required. CLEP credit is accepted.

Procedure: Freshmen are admitted to all sessions. Entrance exams should be taken prior to application. Application deadlines are open. The fall 2001 application fee was $25. Notification is sent on a rolling basis.

Transfer: 14 transfer students enrolled in a recent year. Transfer students must have completed 15 quarter hours or 12 semester hours of academic course work with a minimum 1.5 GPA. 73 credits of 183 must be completed at South College.

Financial Aid: In 2001-2002, 85% of all students received some form of financial aid. 100% of undergraduates work part time. Average annual earnings from campus work are $1410. The FAFSA is required. Check with the school for current deadlines.

International Students: The school actively recruits these students. They must score 550 on the written TOEFL and also take the Computerized Placement Test (CPT).

Computers: 50 PCs are available in 2 labs and in the library. Home access is also available. All students may access the system. There are no time limits and no fees.

Graduates: In a recent year, 7 bachelor's degrees were awarded. The most popular majors were medical assisting (29%), paralegal studies (24%), and accounting (16%). Of a recent graduating class, 97% were employed within 6 months of graduation.

Admissions Contact: Gus Edwards, Director of Admissions.
Web: *southcollege.edu*

SOUTHERN POLYTECHNIC STATE UNIVERSITY B-2

Marietta, GA 30060 (770) 528-7281
(800) 635-3204; Fax: (770) 528-7292

Full-time: 1500 men, 300 women	**Faculty:** 139
Part-time: 1000 men, 215 women	**Ph.D.s:** 57%
Graduate: 340 men, 290 women	**Student/Faculty:** 17 to 1
Year: semesters, summer session	**Tuition:** $2354 ($8150)
Application Deadline: August 1	**Room & Board:** $4308
Freshman Class: 916 applied, 555 accepted, 363 enrolled	
SAT I or ACT: required	**COMPETITIVE**

Southern Polytechnic State University, founded in 1948, is a public institution that is part of the university system of Georgia. The university offers degree programs in arts and sciences, management, technology, and architecture. Enrollment figures in the above capsule are approximate. There are 4 undergraduate schools. In addition to regional accreditation, Southern Polytechnic has baccalaureate program accreditation with ABET, ACCE, and NAAB. The library contains 117,963 volumes, 56,619 microform items, and 60 audiovisual forms/CDs, and subscribes to 1320 periodicals. Computerized library services include the card catalog, interlibrary loans, and database searching. Special learning facilities include a learning resource center and radio station. The 120-acre campus is in a suburban area 15 miles northwest of Atlanta. Including residence halls, there are 23 buildings.

Student Life: 96% of undergraduates are from Georgia. Others are from 22 states, 93 foreign countries, and Canada. The average age of freshmen is 21; all undergraduates, 26. 40% do not continue beyond their first year.

Housing: 476 students can be accommodated in college housing, which includes single-sex and coed dormitories. On-campus housing is available on a first-come, first-served basis. 86% of students commute. All students may keep cars.

Activities: 5% of men belong to 1 local fraternity and 6 national fraternities; 2% of women belong to 3 national sororities. There are 43 groups on campus, including cheerleading, computers, drama, ethnic, honors, international, jazz band, newspaper, political, professional, radio and TV, religious, social service, student government, and yearbook. Popular campus events include Fall Party, Spring Fling, and NSBE Awards Dinner.

Sports: There are 3 intercollegiate sports for men, and 23 intramural sports for men and 23 for women. Facilities include a 1000-seat gym, a baseball field, softball fields, 9 tennis courts, a 500-seat auditorium, outdoor areas for basketball and volleyball, a multipurpose soccer field, an outdoor running track, and an indoor recreational facility with a swimming pool, racquetball courts, exercise and weight training rooms, and basketball courts that are suitable for badminton and volleyball.

Disabled Students: 80% of the campus is accessible. Wheelchair ramps, elevators, special parking, specially equipped rest rooms, special class scheduling, lowered drinking fountains, and lowered telephones are available.

Services: Counseling and information services are available, as is tutoring in some subjects, including English, math, and physics. There is a reader service for the blind.

Campus Safety and Security: Measures include 24-hour foot and vehicle patrol, escort service, informal discussions, and pamphlets/posters/films. There are emergency telephones and lighted pathways/sidewalks.

Programs of Study: Southern Polytechnic confers B.A., B.S., B.Arch., and B.A.S. degrees. Associate and master's degrees are also awarded. Bachelor's degrees are awarded in BUSINESS (business administration and management and marketing and distribution), COMMUNICATIONS AND THE ARTS (communications technology and technical and business writing), COMPUTER AND PHYSICAL SCIENCE (computer science, mathematics, and physics), ENGINEERING AND ENVIRONMENTAL DESIGN (architecture, civil engineering technology, computer technology, construction engineering, electrical/electronics engineering technology, engineering and applied science, industrial engineering technology, manufacturing engineering, mechanical engineering technology, survey and mapping technology, textile engineering, and textile technology). Electrical engineering technology, mechanical engineering technology, and computer science are the strongest academically. Computer science, electrical engineering technology, and mechanical engineering technology are the largest.

Required: All students must complete a core curriculum of 42 semester hours of English composition, college algebra, humanities and fine arts, math and natural sciences, and social sciences. To graduate, students must maintain a minimum 2.0 GPA in 120 to 128 semester hours.

Special: Southern Polytechnic offers cross-registration with the University Center in Georgia, cooperative programs in all majors, dual majors in all disciplines, internships, and study abroad in England, Germany, and France. Credit is given for life experience and by exam. There is 1 national honor society.

Faculty/Classroom: 83% of faculty are male; 17%, female. All teach undergraduates. No introductory courses are taught by graduate students.

Admissions: 61% of the 2001-2002 applicants were accepted. The SAT I scores for the 2001-2002 freshman class were: Verbal--28% below 500, 55% between 500 and 599, 15% between 600 and 700, and 2% above 700; Math--15% below 500, 53% between 500 and 599, 28% between 600 and 700, and 4% above 700. The ACT scores were 69% below 23, 29% between 24 and 29, and 2% above 29.

Requirements: The SAT I or ACT is required. In addition, applicants must be graduates of an accredited secondary school. Students should have completed 21 academic credits, including 4 years of English and math, 3 of science and social studies, and 2 of a foreign language. A GPA of 2.0 is required. AP and CLEP credits are accepted.

Procedure: Freshmen are admitted to all sessions. Entrance exams should be taken at the end of the junior year. There are early admissions and deferred admissions plans. Applications should be filed by August 1 for fall entry, December 1 for spring entry, and May 1 for summer entry, along with a $20 fee. Notification is sent on a rolling basis.

Transfer: 341 transfer students enrolled in 2001-2002. Applicants must have a minimum GPA of 2.0. and must submit college transcripts. SAT I or ACT scores may be required for some students. 30 credits of 120 to 128 must be completed at Southern Polytechnic.

Visiting: There are guides for informal visits. To schedule a visit, contact the Director of Admissions.

Financial Aid: In 2001-2002, 19% of all freshmen and 43% of continuing students received some form of financial aid. 8% of freshmen and 17% of continuing students received need-based aid. The average freshman award was $3460. The average financial indebtedness of the 2001 graduate was $16,585. Southern Polytechnic is a member of CSS. The FAFSA is required. The fall application deadline is March 15.

International Students: There were 201 international students enrolled in a recent year. The school actively recruits these students. They must score 550 on the written TOEFL.

Computers: There are more than 15 servers to run applications. There are 60 PCs available in the student lab and several hundred more in various academic departmental labs for general and specialized uses. All students may access the system. There are no time limits and no fees. It is recommended that students in architecture have personal computers.

Graduates: In 2001, 366 bachelor's degrees were awarded. The most popular majors were engineering/engineering technologies (65%), computer science (17%), and business/marketing (8%). 135 companies recruited on campus in a recent year.

Admissions Contact: Virginia A. Head, Director of Admissions.
E-mail: *admissions@spsu.edu* Web: *www.spsu.edu*

SPELMAN COLLEGE — B-2

Atlanta, GA 30314 — (404) 681-3643
(800) 982-2411; Fax: (404) 215-7788

Full-time: 2081 women	**Faculty:** 145
Part-time: none	**Ph.D.s:** 81%
Graduate: none	**Student/Faculty:** 14 to 1
Year: semesters	**Tuition:** $12,165
Application Deadline: February 1	**Room & Board:** $7050
Freshman Class: 3527 applied, 1744 accepted, 536 enrolled	
SAT I or ACT: required	**COMPETITIVE+**

Spelman College, founded in 1881, is a private, nonsectarian, liberal arts college for black women. In addition to regional accreditation, Spelman has baccalaureate program accreditation with NASM and NCATE. The library contains 500,000 volumes and 385,538 microform items, and subscribes to 1439 periodicals. Special learning facilities include a learning resource center, an art gallery, a language lab, a media center, and music and art studios. The 32-acre campus is in an urban area 3 miles southwest of downtown Atlanta. Including residence halls, there are 24 buildings.

Student Life: 71% of undergraduates are from out of state, mostly the South. Others are from 46 states, 21 foreign countries, and Canada. 86% are from public schools. 96% are African American. The average age of freshmen is 18; all undergraduates, 20. 10% do not continue beyond their first year; 72% remain to graduate.

Housing: 1169 students can be accommodated in college housing, which includes dormitories. In addition, there are honors houses. On-campus housing is guaranteed for the freshman year only, is available on a first-come, first-served basis, and is available on a lottery system for upperclassmen. Priority is given to out-of-town students. 60% of students live on campus; of those, 67% remain on campus on weekends. Alcohol is not permitted. Upperclassmen may keep cars.

Activities: 88% of women belong to 4 local and 4 national sororities.There are 60 groups on campus, including art, band, cheerleading, choir, chorus, dance, drama, gay, honors, international, jazz band, literary magazine, musical theater, newspaper, political, religious, social, student government, and yearbook. Popular campus events include Founders Day and Martin Luther King Jr.'s Birthday.

Sports: Facilities include a gym, tennis courts, a swimming pool, a weight room, dance studios, and bowling lanes.

Disabled Students: 25% of the campus is accessible. Wheelchair ramps, elevators, special parking, and specially equipped rest rooms are available.

Services: Counseling and information services are available, as is tutoring in every subject.

Campus Safety and Security: Measures include 24-hour foot and vehicle patrol, self-defense education, escort service, and shuttle buses. There are informal discussions, pamphlets/posters/films, emergency telephones, and lighted pathways/sidewalks.

Programs of Study: Spelman confers B.A. and B.S. degrees. Bachelor's degrees are awarded in BIOLOGICAL SCIENCE (biochemistry and biology/biological science), COMMUNICATIONS AND THE ARTS (art, dramatic arts, English, fine arts, French, music, and Spanish), COMPUTER AND PHYSICAL SCIENCE (chemistry, computer science, mathematics, natural sciences, and physics), EDUCATION (art), ENGINEERING AND ENVIRONMENTAL DESIGN (engineering), SOCIAL SCIENCE (anthropology, child psychology/development, economics, history, philosophy, political science/government, psychology, religion, sociology, and women's studies). Biology and engineering are the strongest academically. Psychology, biology, and English are the largest.

Required: To graduate, students must complete 120 semester hours, including at least 30 or more in the major, and maintain a GPA of 2.0. Core requirements include 8 credits of African studies, up to 8 of foreign language, 4 of international or women's studies, up to 4 each of English composition, computer literacy, and math, and 2 to 3 of phys ed, plus freshman orientation and sophmore assembly. Students also must complete 4 credits each of divisional requirements in social science, humanities, natural science, and fine arts. A reading course may be required, based on the placement test scores.

Special: Students may cross-register with Atlanta University Center member institutions. Spelman offers internships, study abroad in several countries, student-designed majors, work-study programs at the school, B.A.-B.S. degrees, and dual majors, as well as a 3-2 engineering degree with Georgia Tech, Rochester Institute of Technology, the University of Alabama at Huntsville, Auburn and Boston Universities, and North Carolina Agricultural and Technical State University. The college grants credit for life experience and permits nondegree study. There are 9 national honor societies, including Phi Beta Kappa, and a freshman honors program.

Faculty/Classroom: 36% of faculty are male; 64%, female.

Admissions: 49% of the 2001-2002 applicants were accepted.

Requirements: The SAT I or ACT is required. In addition, applicants should be high school graduates or have a GED certificate. Students should have earned at least 12 academic credits, including 4 in English and 2 each in foreign language, math (algebra and geometry), social studies, and science (including a lab science). Students with additional years in math, science, and language and with AP and honors courses are considered more competitive. An essay is required. An audition or portfolio is recommended for art majors. A GPA of 2.0 is required. AP and CLEP credits are accepted. Important factors in the admissions decision are advanced placement or honor courses, leadership record, and recommendations by school officials.

Procedure: Freshmen are admitted in the fall. Entrance exams should be taken by December of the senior year. There are early acation and deferred admissions plans. Early action applications should be filed by November 15; regular applications, by February 1 for fall entry, along with a $35 fee. Notification of early action is sent December 31; regular decision, April 1. 297 early action candidates were accepted for the 2001-2002 class. 2% of all applicants are on a waiting list; 2 were accepted in 2001.

Transfer: 14 transfer students enrolled in 2001-2002. A 3.0 GPA is recommended, with a minimum 2.0 required. Applicants must submit high school and college transcripts, as well as 2 recommendations from instructors at the last school attended. Students with fewer than 30 semester hours of credit must also submit SAT I or ACT scores. 32 credits of 120 must be completed at Spelman.

Visiting: There are regularly scheduled orientations for prospective students, including a general information session and a campus tour. There are also high school senior days and junior days. There are guides for informal visits. To schedule a visit, contact the Admissions Office at (404) 681-3643, ext. 2188.

Financial Aid: Loans averaged $2625 (maximum); and work contracts averaged $2000 (maximum). 20% of undergraduates work part time. Average annual earnings from campus work are $900. The average financial indebtedness of the 2001 graduate was $18,000. Spelman is a member of CSS. The FAFSA and the college's own financial statement are required. The fall application deadline is April 1.

International Students: The school actively recruits these students. They must score 450 on the written TOEFL and also take the SAT I or the ACT.

Computers: The mainframe is a DEC VAX 11/780. PCs, Macs, and Sun workstations are available. All students may access the system 24 hours a day. There are no time limits. It is strongly recommended that all students have a personal computer.

Graduates: The most popular majors were English (16%), psychology (15%), and economics (10%). In an average class, 2% graduate in 3 years, 81% in 4 years, 88% in 5 years, and 91% in 6 years. Of the 2000 graduating class, 35% were enrolled in graduate school within 6 months of graduation and 51% were employed.

Admissions Contact: Theodora Riley, Interim Director of Admissions and Orientation Services. E-mail: *admiss@spelman.edu*
Web: *www.spelman.edu*

STATE UNIVERSITY OF WEST GEORGIA — A-2

Carrollton, GA 30118 — **(770) 836-6416; Fax: (770) 836-4502**

Full-time: 2389 men, 3596 women	**Faculty:** 314
Part-time: 471 men, 798 women	**Ph.D.s:** 81%
Graduate: 417 men, 1369 women	**Student/Faculty:** 19 to 1
Year: semesters, summer session	**Tuition:** $3004 ($8800)
Application Deadline: July 3	**Room & Board:** $4100
Freshman Class: 4453 applied, 2671 accepted, 1699 enrolled	
SAT I Verbal/Math: 505/500	**ACT:** 20 — **COMPETITIVE**

State University of West Georgia, founded in 1906 as part of the University System of Georgia, is a public institution offering degree programs in liberal arts, business, and teacher preparation. There are 3 undergraduate schools and 1 graduate school. In addition to regional accreditation, West Georgia has baccalaureate program accreditation with AACSB, ACS, CACREP, NASAD, NASM, NASPAA, NCATE, and NLN. The library contains 360,696 volumes, 1,040,266 microform items, and 1289 audiovisual forms/CDs, and subscribes to 1352 periodicals. Computerized library services include the card catalog, interlibrary loans, and database searching. Special learning facilities include a learning resource center, art gallery, radio station, TV station, observatory, state archaeologist office, performing arts center, the Advanced Academy of Georgia, and the Waring Archaeology Laboratory. The 394-acre campus is in a suburban area 50 miles southwest of Atlanta. Including residence halls, there are 65 buildings.

Student Life: 95% of undergraduates are from Georgia. Others are from 36 states, 66 foreign countries, and Canada. 95% are from public schools. 74% are white; 22% African American. The average age of freshmen is 18; all undergraduates, 22. 35% do not continue beyond their first year; 27% remain to graduate.

Housing: 2300 students can be accommodated in college housing, which includes single-sex and coed dormitories and fraternity houses. In addition, there are special-interest houses, a sorority-only residence hall, and housing for the Advanced Academy of Georgia students. On-campus housing is guaranteed for the freshman year only, is available on a first-come, first-served basis, and is available on a lottery system for upperclassmen. Priority is given to out-of-town students. 72% of students commute. All students may keep cars.

Activities: 14% of men belong to 11 national fraternities; 9% of women belong to 9 national sororities. There are 87 groups on campus, including band, cheerleading, choir, chorus, dance, debate, drama, drill team, ethnic, gay, honors, international, jazz band, literary magazine, marching band, musical theater, newspaper, opera, pep band, political, professional, radio and TV, religious, social, social service, student government, and yearbook. Popular campus events include Fine Arts Festival, Spring Fling, and International Student Night.

Sports: There are 4 intercollegiate sports for men and 4 for women, and 15 intramural sports for men and 15 for women. Facilities include 3 gyms, an Olympic-size swimming pool, a weight room, a baseball stadium, an Olympic-size metric track, a football field house, and various intramural and practice fields.

Disabled Students: 65% of the campus is accessible. Wheelchair ramps, elevators, special parking, specially equipped rest rooms, special class scheduling, lowered drinking fountains, and lowered telephones are available.

Services: Counseling and information services are available, as is tutoring in some subjects, including most core subjects. There is a reader service for the blind, remedial math, reading, and writing, braille equipment, and a speech recognition computer.

Campus Safety and Security: Measures include 24-hour foot and vehicle patrol, escort service, shuttle buses, and informal discussions. There are pamphlets/posters/films, emergency telephones, and lighted pathways/sidewalks.

Programs of Study: West Georgia confers B.A., B.S., B.B.A., B.F.A., B.M., B.S.Ed., B.S.E.S., B.S.N., and B.S.Rec. degrees. Master's and doctoral degrees are also awarded. Bachelor's degrees are awarded in AGRICULTURE (environmental studies), BIOLOGICAL SCIENCE (biology/biological science), BUSINESS (accounting, banking and finance, business economics, international economics, management information systems, management science, marketing/retailing/merchandising, and real estate), COMMUNICATIONS AND THE ARTS (art, communications, English, fine arts, French, music, Spanish, and speech/debate/rhetoric), COMPUTER AND PHYSICAL SCIENCE (chemistry, computer science, earth science, geology, mathematics, and physics), EDUCATION (art, business, early childhood, middle school, music, physical, and special), ENGINEERING AND ENVIRONMENTAL DESIGN (environmental science and technological management), HEALTH PROFESSIONS (nursing and speech pathology/audiology), SOCIAL SCIENCE (anthropology, criminology, economics, geography, history, international studies, parks and recreation management, philosophy, political science/government, psychology, sociology, and systems science). Business education and secondary science education are the strongest academically. Computer science, biology, and nursing are the largest.

Required: To graduate, students must have earned 120 semester credit hours with a minimum GPA of 2.0. Distribution requirements include 39 hours in the major, 20 each in the humanities, science, math, and social sciences, and 3 in phys ed.

Special: The university has cooperative and work-study programs with state, regional, national, and international corporations and offers short-term internships and supervised work experience, usually for credit. Cross-registration with the University of Georgia and Dalton College is available. The student may undertake an accelerated-degree program in any major, a dual major in physics/engineering or math/computer science, a 3-2 engineering degree program with Mercer University, Georgia Tech, or Auburn University, nondegree study for teacher certification, and study abroad in Europe, Russia, and China. There are 15 national honor societies, including Phi Beta Kappa, a freshman honors program, and 11 departmental honors programs.

Faculty/Classroom: 53% of faculty are male; 47%, female. 91% teach undergraduates, 60% do research, and 15% do both. No introductory courses are taught by graduate students. The average class size in an introductory lecture is 40; in a laboratory, 24; and in a regular course, 38.

Admissions: 60% of the 2001-2002 applicants were accepted. The SAT I scores for the 2001-2002 freshman class were: Verbal--50% below 500, 39% between 500 and 599, 10% between 600 and 700, and 1% above 700; Math--52% below 500, 39% between 500 and 599, 9% between 600 and 700, and 1% above 700. The ACT scores were 63% below 21, 23% between 21 and 23, 10% between 24 and 26, 2% between 27 and 28, and 2% above 28.

Requirements: The SAT I or ACT is required, with a minimum score of at least 430 on the SAT I verbal section and 400 on the SAT I math section (17 on the ACT English, 17 on the ACT math). Applicants must have completed 16 college preparatory high school units, including 4 each in English and math, 3 each in science and social science, and 2 in foreign language. Applications are accepted on-line at the university's web site. A GPA of 2.5 is required. AP and CLEP credits are accepted.

Procedure: Freshmen are admitted fall, spring, and summer. Entrance exams should be taken by December of the senior year. Early decision

applications should be filed by June 15; regular applications, by July 3 for fall entry. The fall 2001 application fee was $20. Notification is sent on a rolling basis.
Transfer: 510 transfer students enrolled in 2001-2002. Applicants must have a minimum GPA of 2.0 in all work attempted. 30 credits of 120 must be completed at West Georgia.
Visiting: There are regularly scheduled orientations for prospective students. There are guides for informal visits and visitors may sit in on classes. To schedule a visit, contact Dr. Bobby Johnson, Director of Admissions.
Financial Aid: In 2001-2002, 66% of all freshmen and 57% of continuing students received some form of financial aid. 69% of all students received need-based aid. The average freshman award was $3173. Of that total, scholarships or need-based grants averaged $4143; loans averaged $1367; and work contracts averaged $750. Average annual earnings from campus work are $852. The average financial indebtedness of the 2001 graduate was $17,000. West Georgia is a member of CSS. The FAFSA is required.
International Students: There are 77 international students enrolled. The school actively recruits these students. They must score 523 on the written TOEFL or 193 on the electronic version and also take the SAT I or ACT, scoring 430 on the verbal section of the SAT I and 400 on the math section (17 on the ACT English and 17 on the ACT math).
Computers: The mainframes are an IBM RS6000 Model J40, a Sun microsystems 1000, a Sun Enterprise 3000, and an HP 9000 Model G30. More than 1500 PCs support 3 computer labs, as well as the business, arts and sciences, and education departments. All students may access the system. There are no time limits and no fees. It is strongly recommended that all students have a personal computer.
Graduates: In 2001, 935 bachelor's degrees were awarded. The most popular majors were early childhood education (14%), management (8%), and nursing (7%). In an average class, 10% graduate in 4 years, 23% in 5 years, and 26% in 6 years. 250 companies recruited on campus in 2000-2001.
Admissions Contact: Dr. Bobby Johnson, Director of Admissions. E-mail: *rjohnson@westga.edu* Web: *www.westga.edu*

THOMAS UNIVERSITY

Thomasville, GA 31792-7499 — B-5
(229) 226-1621
(800) 538-9784; Fax: (229) 226-1653

Full-time: 144 men, 279 women	**Faculty:** 36
Part-time: 32 men, 106 women	**Ph.D.s:** 65%
Graduate: none	**Student/Faculty:** 12 to 1
Year: semesters, summer session	**Tuition:** $6370
Application Deadline: open	**Room & Board:** $2400
Freshman Class: 132 applied, 132 accepted, 56 enrolled	
SAT I Verbal/Math: 475/455	**ACT:** 18 NONCOMPETITIVE

Thomas University, founded in 1950, is a private liberal arts institution offering 20 undergraduate degrees and masters programs in business administration and rehabilitation counseling. In addition to regional accreditation, Thomas University has baccalaureate program accreditation with NLN. The library contains 43,731 volumes and 823 audiovisual forms/CDs, and subscribes to 412 periodicals. Computerized library services include the card catalog, interlibrary loans, and database searching. Special learning facilities include a learning resource center. The 25-acre campus is in a rural area 28 miles north of Tallahassee. Including residence halls, there are 17 buildings.
Student Life: 90% of undergraduates are from Georgia. Others are from 5 states, 7 foreign countries, and Canada. 99% are from public schools. 64% are white; 24% African American. The average age of freshmen is 26; all undergraduates, 28. 41% do not continue beyond their first year.
Housing: 64 students can be accommodated in college housing, which includes off-campus dormitories and apartments. All students commute. Alcohol is not permitted. All students may keep cars.
Activities: There are no fraternities or sororities. There are 23 groups on campus, including chorus, jazz band, literary magazine, newspaper, religious, social, and student government. Popular campus events include Day on the Green.
Sports: There are 4 intercollegiate sports for men and 4 for women, and 2 intramural sports for men and 2 for women. The university contracts with the city of Thomasville and other groups to use existing public athletic facilities. On-campus facilities include a soccer field, a tennis court, a beach volleyball court, and an outdoor basketball court.
Disabled Students: 90% of the campus is accessible. Wheelchair ramps, special parking, specially equipped rest rooms, and lowered telephones are available.
Services: Counseling and information services are available, as is tutoring in some subjects, including math, biology, and English. There is a reader service for the blind, and remedial math, reading, and writing.
Campus Safety and Security: Measures include informal discussions, pamphlets/posters/films, lighted pathways/sidewalks, an evening vehicle patrol, and sheriff's deputies on-campus.
Programs of Study: Thomas University confers B.A. and B.S. degrees. Associate and master's degrees are also awarded. Bachelor's degrees are awarded in BIOLOGICAL SCIENCE (biology/biological science), BUSINESS (business administration and management and recreational facilities management), COMMUNICATIONS AND THE ARTS (English), EDUCATION (early childhood and middle school), HEALTH PROFESSIONS (nursing and rehabilitation therapy), SOCIAL SCIENCE (criminal justice, humanities, liberal arts/general studies, psychology, social science, and social work). Early childhood education and criminal justice are the largest.
Required: To graduate, students must complete 120 semester hours, including 30 to 60 in the major, with a minimum GPA of 2.0 (2.5 for education majors). Core requirements include 48 to 49 semester hours in English composition, history, biology, math, political science, music or art, and computer science. All students must pass a posttest.
Special: There are 6 national honor societies.
Faculty/Classroom: 56% of faculty are male; 44%, female. 97% teach undergraduates. The average class size in an introductory lecture is 16; in a laboratory, 14; and in a regular course, 9.
Admissions: All of the 2001-2002 applicants were accepted. The SAT I scores for the 2001-2002 freshman class were: Verbal--67% below 500, 23% between 500 and 599, and 10% between 600 and 700; Math--77% below 500, 20% between 500 and 599, and 4% between 600 and 700. The ACT scores were 80% below 21, 10% between 21 and 23, and 10% between 24 and 26.
Requirements: The SAT I or ACT is recommended. In addition, students should be graduates of an accredited high school or its equivalent. A GPA of 2.0 is required. AP and CLEP credits are accepted. Applications are accepted on-line via the school's web site.
Procedure: Freshmen are admitted to all sessions. Entrance exams should be taken prior to enrollment. Application deadlines are open. The fall 2001 application fee was $25. There is a rolling admissions plan.
Transfer: 74 transfer students enrolled in 2001-2002. Applicants should have a minimum college GPA of 2.0 and be in good standing at their current or previous institution. 30 credits of 120 must be completed at Thomas University.
Visiting: There are regularly scheduled orientations for prospective students. There are guides for informal visits. To schedule a visit, contact Julie Tracy at (229) 226-1621 or *jtracy@thomasu.edu*
Financial Aid: In 2001-2002, all freshmen and 96% of continuing students received some form of financial aid. 43% of freshmen and 44% of continuing students received need-based aid. The average freshman award was $5247. Of that total, scholarships or need-based grants averaged $3080; loans averaged $183; and state grants averaged $1984. 2% of undergraduates work part time. Average annual earnings from campus work are $1593. The average financial indebtedness of the 2001 graduate was $3328. Thomas University is a member of CSS. The FAFSA and the college's own financial statement are required. The fall application deadline is open.
International Students: There are 22 international students enrolled. They must score 550 on the written TOEFL or 213 on the electronic version and also take the college's own entrance exam or the MAPS (Multiple Assessment Program/Services).
Computers: There are 48 Gateways in 4 campus labs. All students may access the system 8 A.M. to 9 P.M. Students may access the system for 1 hour. There are no fees. It is strongly recommended that all students have a personal computer.
Graduates: In 2001, 93 bachelor's degrees were awarded. The most popular majors were education (18%), business administration (13%), and nursing (11%). In an average class, 18% graduate in 4 years and 35% in 5 years. 19 companies recruited on campus in 2000-2001.
Admissions Contact: Darla M. Glass, Director of Student Affairs. Web: *thomasu.edu*

TOCCOA FALLS COLLEGE

Toccoa Falls, GA 30598 — C-1
(706) 886-6831
(800) 868-3257; Fax: (706) 282-6012

Full-time: 369 men, 485 women	**Faculty:** 54
Part-time: 24 men, 38 women	**Ph.D.s:** 51%
Graduate: none	**Student/Faculty:** 16 to 1
Year: 4-1-4, summer session	**Tuition:** $10,050
Application Deadline: open	**Room & Board:** $4170
Freshman Class: 986 applied, 689 accepted, 309 enrolled	
SAT I Verbal/Math: 510/488	**ACT:** 22 COMPETITIVE

Toccoa Falls College is an independent, interdenominational Christian college founded in 1907 that offers programs in biblical studies, counseling, Christian education, communications, missions, teacher education, theology, music, business administration, and general studies. In addition to regional accreditation, TFC has baccalaureate program accreditation with NASM. The library contains 106,106 volumes, 22,864 microform items, and 5161 audiovisual forms/CDs, and subscribes to 8294 periodicals. Computerized library services include the card catalog, interlibrary loans, and database searching. Special learning facilities include a learning resource center and a 100,000-watt radio station on campus offering programs 24 hours a day. The 1100-acre campus is in a small town 90 miles northeast of Atlanta. Including residence halls, there are 45 buildings.

Student Life: 61% of undergraduates are from out of state, mostly the South. Others are from 47 states, 16 foreign countries, and Canada. 62% are from public schools. 90% are white. Most are Protestant. The average age of freshmen is 18; all undergraduates, 21. 32% do not continue beyond their first year.

Housing: 629 students can be accommodated in college housing, which includes single-sex dormitories, on-campus apartments, and married-student housing. On-campus housing is guaranteed for all 4 years. 72% of students live on campus; of those, 37% remain on campus on weekends. Alcohol is not permitted. All students may keep cars.

Activities: There are no fraternities or sororities. There are many groups and organizations on campus, including band, cheerleading, choir, chorale, chorus, drama, ethnic, international, jazz band, newspaper, orchestra, outdoor, pep band, photography, radio and TV, religious, social, social service, student government, and yearbook. Popular campus events include Artist Series, Spiritual Emphasis Week, and Lecture Series.

Sports: There are 3 intercollegiate sports for men and 3 for women, and 8 intramural sports for men and 8 for women. Facilities include a gymnatorium with racquetball courts and a weight room, tennis courts, and soccer and baseball fields.

Disabled Students: 70% of the campus is accessible. Wheelchair ramps, elevators, special parking, specially equipped rest rooms, special class scheduling, lowered drinking fountains, and lowered telephones are available.

Services: Counseling and information services are available, as is tutoring in most subjects.

Campus Safety and Security: Measures include 24-hour foot and vehicle patrol, informal discussions, pamphlets/posters/films, and lighted pathways/sidewalks. In addition, the campus is closed at night, with a guard at the entrance.

Programs of Study: TFC confers B.A., B.S., and B.Th. degrees. Associate degrees are also awarded. Bachelor's degrees are awarded in BUSINESS (business administration and management), COMMUNICATIONS AND THE ARTS (broadcasting, communications, English, journalism, music, music performance, music theory and composition, and public relations), EDUCATION (Christian, early childhood, elementary, middle school, music, secondary, and teaching English as a second/foreign language (TESOL/TEFOL)), SOCIAL SCIENCE (biblical languages, biblical studies, counseling/psychology, ministries, missions, pastoral studies, philosophy, religion, religious education, religious music, theological studies, and youth ministry). Biblical studies, missiology, and biblical languages are the strongest academically. Early childhood, counseling, cross-cultural missiology, and youth ministries are the largest.

Required: Students must successfully complete 124 semester hours, with 34 to 70 in their major and a C minus or better in major classes, to earn a bachelor's degree. All students must also complete a core curriculum, which includes 30 hours of Bible and doctrine, an English sequence, phys ed, and math, for a total of 66 hours. A GPA of 2.0 to 2.5 must be maintained. Additional requirements for graduation may include a senior oral comprehensive exam or a thesis and performance of 4 semesters of a student ministry.

Special: The college offers dual majors, and B.A.-B.S. degrees are available. An on-campus work-study program and internships for ministry, teaching, or counseling majors are also provided. There are 2 national honor societies.

Faculty/Classroom: 74% of faculty are male; 26%, female. All teach undergraduates. The average class size in an introductory lecture is 29; in a laboratory, 15; and in a regular course, 25.

Admissions: 70% of the 2001-2002 applicants were accepted. The ACT scores for the 2001-2002 freshman class were 40% below 21, 16% between 21 and 23, 21% between 24 and 26, 16% between 27 and 28, and 7% above 28. 34% of the current freshmen were in the top fifth of their class; 56% were in the top two fifths. 24 freshmen graduated first in their class.

Requirements: The SAT I or ACT is required, with a minimum composite score of 1000 on the SAT I or 21.9 on the ACT. High school graduation or a GED certificate is required. A personal reference from the student's pastor and an essay submitted with the student's application are also required. A GPA of 2.0 is required. AP and CLEP credits are accepted. Important factors in the admissions decision are personality/intangible qualities, extracurricular activities record, and leadership record. Applications are accepted on-line at *www.toccoafalls.edu*

Procedure: Freshmen are admitted to all sessions. Entrance exams should be taken early in the senior year. There is an early decision plan. Application deadlines are open. The fall 2001 application fee was $20. There is a rolling admissions plan and notification is sent on a rolling basis.

Transfer: 61 transfer students enrolled in 2001-2002. Transfer students must have successfully completed 12 semester hours of college credit courses and have maintained a minimum GPA of 2.0. Students must also provide 3 references, and write an essay. 32 credits of 124 or 25% of the degree requirements must be completed at TFC.

Visiting: There are regularly scheduled orientations for prospective students, including visits to the admissions counselor, school directors, and the financial aid office arranged 2 weeks in advance. There are guides for informal visits and visitors may sit in on classes and stay overnight. To schedule a visit, contact the Office of Admissions at *admissions@tfc.edu*

Financial Aid: In a recent year, 88% of all freshmen and 81% of continuing students received some form of financial aid. 59% of freshmen and 52% of continuing students received need-based aid. The average freshman award was $6743. Of that total, scholarships or need-based grants averaged $2400 ($8384 maximum); loans averaged $5085 ($6625 maximum); work contracts averaged $1000 ($2000 maximum); and merit-based aid averaged $2591 ($8384 maximum). 27% of undergraduates work part time. Average annual earnings from campus work are $1784. The average financial indebtedness of a recent graduate was $16,500. The FAFSA and the college's own financial statement are required. The fall application deadline is March 1.

International Students: There are 27 international students enrolled. They must score 500 on the written TOEFL and also take the SAT I or the ACT.

Computers: The mainframe is a DEC ALPHA. The college provides 40 PCs for student use, located in an academic computer lab, all of which are Internet-accessible. The college also provides computers for e-mail and research in the library. All students may access the system. There are no time limits. The fee is $100 for computer classes, $10 per semester for other students. It is strongly recommended that all students have a personal computer.

Graduates: In 2001, 176 bachelor's degrees were awarded. The most popular majors were counseling (22%), world missions (20%), and Bible and theology (20%). In an average class, 4% graduate in 3 years, 24% in 4 years, 38% in 5 years, and 39% in 6 years. 68 companies recruited on campus in 2000-2001.

Admissions Contact: Tommy Campbell, Director of Admissions.
E-mail: *admissions@toccoafalls.edu* Web: *www.toccoafalls.edu*

UNIVERSITY OF GEORGIA C-2
Athens, GA 30602 (706) 542-2112; Fax: (706) 542-1466

Full-time: 9688 men, 12,602 women	**Faculty:** 1809; I, av$
Part-time: 1217 men, 1322 women	**Ph.D.s:** 95%
Graduate: 3002 men, 4486 women	**Student/Faculty:** 12 to 1
Year: semesters, summer session	**Tuition:** $3418 ($11,314)
Application Deadline: January 15	**Room & Board:** $5238
Freshman Class: 13,578 applied, 8470 accepted, 4516 enrolled	
SAT I Verbal/Math: 597/601	**ACT:** 25 **VERY COMPETITIVE**

The University of Georgia, chartered in 1785 and part of the University System of Georgia, offers degree programs in the arts and sciences, marine studies, music, business, agricultural and environmental sciences, education, family and consumer sciences, forest resources, journalism, social work, pharmacy, law, veterinary medicine, and preprofessional studies. There are 12 undergraduate schools and 1 graduate school. In addition to regional accreditation, UGA has baccalaureate program accreditation with AACSB, ABET, ACEJMC, ACPE, ADA, ASLA, CSWE, FIDER, NASAD, NASM, NCATE, NRPA, and SAF. The 3 libraries contain 3,622,094 volumes, 6,001,206 microform items, and 174,967 audiovisual forms/CDs, and subscribe to 39,784 periodicals. Computerized library services include the card catalog, interlibrary loans, and database searching. Special learning facilities include a learning resource center, art gallery, natural history museum, radio station, bioscience learning center, rare book and manuscript library, performing arts center, State Botanical Garden of Georgia, Peabody Awards Archives, and Institute for Newspaper Management Studies. The 605-acre campus is in a small town 80 miles east of Atlanta. Including residence halls, there are 335 buildings.

Student Life: 82% of undergraduates are from Georgia. Others are from 49 states, 131 foreign countries, and Canada. 87% are from public schools. 83% are white. 43% are Protestant; 42% claim no religious affiliation; 10% Catholic. The average age of freshmen is 19; all undergraduates, 21. 10% do not continue beyond their first year; 66% remain to graduate.

Housing: 7933 students can be accommodated in college housing, which includes single-sex and coed dormitories, on-campus apartments, and married-student housing. On-campus housing is available on a first-come, first-served basis. Alcohol is not permitted. All students may keep cars.

Activities: 16% of men belong to 25 national fraternities; 21% of women belong to 22 national sororities. There are 430 groups on campus, including art, band, cheerleading, chess, chorale, chorus, computers, dance, debate, drama, drill team, ethnic, film, gay, honors, international, jazz band, literary magazine, marching band, musical theater, newspaper, orchestra, pep band, photography, political, professional, radio and

TV, religious, social, social service, student government, and yearbook. Popular campus events include UGA Health Fair and dance, music, and art series.

Sports: There are 8 intercollegiate sports for men and 8 for women, and 28 intramural sports for men and 27 for women. Facilities include an 82,122-seat coliseum, a 12,000-seat basketball arena, a 4500-seat tennis stadium, 4 indoor tennis courts, complete football-training facilities, and a sports complex with a lake, a beach, playing fields, and trails. There is also the Ramsey Student Center with 5 gyms, 3 swimming pools, a strength/conditioning room, 10 racquetball courts, an indoor track, and a climbing wall. The Women's Athletic Complex hosts women's soccer and softball programs with 3000-spectator capacity.

Disabled Students: 90% of the campus is accessible. Wheelchair ramps, elevators, special parking, specially equipped rest rooms, special class scheduling, lowered drinking fountains, lowered telephones, wheelchair vans, auxiliary aides, residence hall accommodations, and an adaptive technology lab are available.

Services: Counseling and information services are available, as is tutoring in every subject. There is a reader service for the blind, and remedial math, reading, and writing. Alternate format textbooks and class materials, note takers, modifications for tests and assignments, and counseling and advisement from learning disability specialists are available. There are also sign language interpreters, text type machines, FM/assistive listening devices, and a pilot closed-captioning program.

Campus Safety and Security: Measures include 24-hour foot and vehicle patrol, self-defense education, escort service, and shuttle buses. There are informal discussions, pamphlets/posters/films, emergency telephones, and lighted pathways/sidewalks.

Programs of Study: UGA confers B.A., B.S., B.B.A., B.F.A., B.L.A., B.Mus., B.S.A., B.S.A.E., B.S.BioEng., B.S.Chem., B.S.Ed., B.S.E.H., B.S.F.R., B.S.Family and Consumer Services, B.S.H.E., B.S.P.A., B.S.Pcs., B.S.Phr., and B.S.W., A.B.J. degrees. Associate, master's, and doctoral degrees are also awarded. Bachelor's degrees are awarded in AGRICULTURE (agricultural economics, agriculture, dairy science, fishing and fisheries, forestry and related sciences, horticulture, plant protection (pest management), poultry science, and wildlife management), BIOLOGICAL SCIENCE (biochemistry, biology/biological science, botany, ecology, entomology, genetics, microbiology, nutrition, and zoology), BUSINESS (accounting, business administration and management, fashion merchandising, international business management, management information systems, management science, marketing/retailing/merchandising, real estate, and recreation and leisure services), COMMUNICATIONS AND THE ARTS (advertising, art, broadcasting, communications, comparative literature, design, dramatic arts, English, French, German, Germanic languages and literature, Greek, Italian, journalism, Latin, linguistics, music, music performance, music theory and composition, public relations, romance languages and literature, Spanish, speech/debate/rhetoric, studio art, and telecommunications), COMPUTER AND PHYSICAL SCIENCE (astronomy, chemistry, computer science, geology, mathematics, physics, and statistics), EDUCATION (agricultural, art, business, early childhood, elementary, English, foreign languages, health, marketing and distribution, mathematics, middle school, music, science, social science, special, and trade and industrial), ENGINEERING AND ENVIRONMENTAL DESIGN (agricultural engineering, bioengineering, environmental science, interior design, landscape architecture/design, preengineering, and technology and public affairs), HEALTH PROFESSIONS (environmental health science, music therapy, pharmacy, predentistry, premedicine, preveterinary science, and speech pathology/audiology), SOCIAL SCIENCE (anthropology, child care/child and family studies, classical/ancient civilization, clothing and textiles management/production/services, cognitive science, criminal justice, dietetics, economics, family/consumer studies, food science, geography, history, home furnishings and equipment management/production/services, interdisciplinary studies, Japanese studies, philosophy, political science/government, psychology, religion, social science, social work, and sociology). Business, journalism, and genetics are the strongest academically. Finance, marketing, and psychology are the largest.

Required: Students must have a 2.0 GPA to graduate and must complete a maximum of 120 semester hours, with at least 18 in the major and 42 in general education. Required specific disciplines are grammar, composition, literature, math, biological sciences, history and American government, and environmental literacy. Specific courses include basic phys ed and English 1101 and 1102. UGA also requires all students to pass the Regents Exit Exam, as well as exams on the federal and state constitutions.

Special: UGA offers co-op programs with the Medical College of Georgia and the Georgia Institute of Technology, as well as cross-registration with University Center institutions in urban Atlanta. With the Governor's Intern Program, students may serve a full-time 10-week internship in a state government agency; many other internships are available within the departments, as well as work-study programs within the university and with many area businesses. Students may study abroad in 26 countries. A Washington semester, an accelerated degree program in business, general studies and 3-2 engineering degrees, student-designed majors, dual degrees and double majors, and nondegree study are also available. There are 48 national honor societies, including Phi Beta Kappa, a freshman honors program, and 51 departmental honors programs.

Faculty/Classroom: 67% of faculty are male; 33%, female. 81% teach undergraduates. Graduate students teach 25% of introductory courses. The average class size in an introductory lecture is 75; in a laboratory, 21; and in a regular course, 32.

Admissions: 62% of the 2001-2002 applicants were accepted. The SAT I scores for the 2001-2002 freshman class were: Verbal--6% below 500, 44% between 500 and 599, 41% between 600 and 700, and 9% above 700; Math--5% below 500, 42% between 500 and 599, 45% between 600 and 700, and 8% above 700. There were 65 National Merit finalists in a recent year.

Requirements: The SAT I or ACT is required. In addition, UGA admits freshmen primarily on the basis of high school curriculum, grades earned, and college admissions test scores. The University may consider qualitative information to determine a student's potential for success. Applicants should be high school graduates or present a GED certificate. Students should have taken 4 years of English, 3 each of math, science, and social studies, and 2 of a foreign language. An audition is required for music majors. Applications may be submitted on-line at the UGA web site. AP and CLEP credits are accepted.

Procedure: Freshmen are admitted to all sessions. Entrance exams should be taken in January of the senior year. Applications should be filed by January 15 for fall entry, along with a $50 fee. Notification is sent on a rolling basis.

Transfer: 1962 transfer students enrolled in a recent year. Applicants must have a minimum GPA of 2.3, although transfer GPA requirements vary by program. Students who wish to apply as freshman transfers must meet both transfer GPA admission requirements and the academic requirements for entering freshmen. 40 credits of 120 must be completed at UGA.

Visiting: There are regularly scheduled orientations for prospective students, consisting of campus tours and meetings with faculty, staff, and students. There are guides for informal visits and visitors may sit in on classes and stay overnight. To schedule a visit, contact the Admissions Office.

Financial Aid: In a recent year, 33% of all students received need-based aid. The average freshman award was $4000. Of that total, scholarships or need-based grants averaged $3000; loans averaged $1000 ($2625 maximum); and work contracts averaged $1500 ($3000 maximum). 60% of undergraduates work part time. The average financial indebtedness of a recent year's graduate was $13,600. UGA is a member of CSS. The FAFSA is required. Check with the school for current deadlines.

International Students: There were 246 international students enrolled in a recent year. They must score 550 on the written TOEFL or 213 on the electronic version (or 600 or 250, respectively, if in the College of Business) and also take the SAT I or the ACT, scoring 1000 on the SAT I.

Computers: The mainframes are a comprised of an IBM 3090 Model 400; CDC CYBERs 180/850, 180/845, and 205; and a DEC VAX 11/780. Computers for student use are located at various points across campus, including the library, residence halls, the computer center, academic departments, and computer labs. All students may access the system at designated times for the various locations. There are no time limits and no fees.

Graduates: In a recent year, 5225 bachelor's degrees were awarded. The most popular majors were finance (5%), marketing (5%), and psychology (4%). In an average class, 1% graduate in 3 years, 46% in 4 years, 62% in 5 years, and 66% in 6 years. 687 companies recruited on campus in a recent year.

Admissions Contact: Nancy G. McDuff, Director of Admissions.
E-mail: *undergrad@admissions.uga.edu*
Web: *www.uga.edu/admissions/*

UNIVERSITY SYSTEM OF GEORGIA

The University System of Georgia, established in 1932, is a public system. It is governed by a 16-member board of regents whose chief administrator is the chancellor. The primary goals of the system are teaching, research, and public service. The main priorities are to provide broad access to undergraduate education at a high level of excellence, to provide sound programs of graduate education and research addressing state and national problems and advancing the frontiers of knowledge, and to work cooperatively with all levels and sectors of education to improve the social, cultural, and economic welfare of the state's citizens. The total enrollment of all 34 campuses is more than 200,000, with about 8000 faculty members. There are more than 1000 baccalaureate, 600 master's, and 175 doctoral programs offered through the system.

VALDOSTA STATE UNIVERSITY C-5

Valdosta, GA 31698 (229) 333-5791
(800) 618-1878; Fax: (229) 333-5482

Full-time: 2442 men, 3756 women **Faculty:** 406; IIA, --$
Part-time: 729 men, 1012 women **Ph.D.s:** 70%
Graduate: 264 men, 1036 women **Student/Faculty:** 15 to 1
Year: semesters, summer session **Tuition:** $2526 ($8322)
Application Deadline: August 1 **Room & Board:** $4462
Freshman Class: 4418 applied, 2920 accepted, 1604 enrolled
SAT I Verbal/Math: 515/508 **COMPETITIVE**

Valdosta State University, founded in 1906 and a unit of the University System of Georgia, is a public liberal arts institution offering degrees in arts and sciences, education, business administration, nursing, and fine arts. There are 5 undergraduate and 4 graduate schools. In addition to regional accreditation, VSU has baccalaureate program accreditation with AACSB, ASLHA, CSWE, NASAD, NASM, NCATE, and NLN. The library contains 429,157 volumes, 1,040,368 microform items, and 46,052 audiovisual forms/CDs, and subscribes to 3072 periodicals. Computerized library services include interlibrary loans and database searching. Special learning facilities include a learning resource center, art gallery, planetarium, radio station, TV station, and herbarium. The 200-acre campus is in an urban area of southern Georgia, 3 1/2 hours from Atlanta and from Orlando, Florida. Including residence halls, there are 50 buildings.

Student Life: 92% of undergraduates are from Georgia. Others are from 46 states, 53 foreign countries, and Canada. 70% are from public schools. 73% are white; 21%, African American. The average age of freshmen is 18. 37% do not continue beyond their first year.

Housing: 2000 students can be accommodated in college housing, which includes single-sex and coed dormitories, on-campus apartments, married-student housing, and fraternity houses. In addition, there are honors, wellness, and 24-hour quiet wings in the dorms. On-campus housing is guaranteed for all 4 years. 56% of students live on campus; of those, 65% remain on campus on weekends. Alcohol is not permitted. All students may keep cars.

Activities: 5% of men belong to 10 national fraternities; 3% of women belong to 9 national sororities. There are 111 groups on campus, including art, band, cheerleading, chess, choir, chorale, chorus, computers, dance, debate, drama, drill team, ethnic, gay, honors, international, jazz band, literary magazine, marching band, musical theater, newspaper, orchestra, outdoor, pep band, photography, political, professional, radio and TV, religious, social, social service, student government, and symphony. Popular campus events include Family Day, Beach Trip, and Fall Welcome Back.

Sports: There are 6 intercollegiate sports for men and 5 for women, and 13 intramural sports for men and 13 for women. Facilities include a phys ed complex with a 5500-seat basketball arena, a health fitness center, a weight training room, and a human performance lab; and a gym with a weight room, training room, dance studio, auxiliary gym, and outdoor pool.

Disabled Students: All of the campus is accessible. Wheelchair ramps, elevators, special parking, specially equipped rest rooms, special class scheduling, lowered drinking fountains, lowered telephones, and modified furnishings in dormitory rooms are available.

Services: Counseling and information services are available, as is tutoring in some subjects, including math, reading, and English at no charge. There is a reader service for the blind.

Campus Safety and Security: Measures include 24-hour foot and vehicle patrol, self-defense education, escort service, and shuttle buses. There are pamphlets/posters/films, emergency telephones, lighted pathways/sidewalks, bicycle patrol, security cameras, and electronically operated dormitory entrances.

Programs of Study: VSU confers B.A., B.S., B.A.S., B.B.A., B.F.A., B.G.S., B.M., B.S.Ed., B.S.E.S., and B.S.N. degrees. Associate, master's, and doctoral degrees are also awarded. Bachelor's degrees are awarded in BIOLOGICAL SCIENCE (biology/biological science), BUSINESS (accounting, banking and finance, business administration and management, business economics, and marketing/retailing/merchandising), COMMUNICATIONS AND THE ARTS (art, dramatic arts, English, French, media arts, music, music performance, Spanish, speech/debate/rhetoric, and telecommunications), COMPUTER AND PHYSICAL SCIENCE (applied mathematics, astronomy, chemistry, computer science, information sciences and systems, mathematics, and physics), EDUCATION (art, business, early childhood, health, middle school, music, physical, secondary, special, and trade and industrial), ENGINEERING AND ENVIRONMENTAL DESIGN (environmental science and interior design), HEALTH PROFESSIONS (exercise science, nursing, speech pathology/audiology, and sports medicine), SOCIAL SCIENCE (anthropology, criminal justice, history, liberal arts/general studies, paralegal studies, philosophy, political science/government, psychology, and sociology). Sports medicine, accounting, and nursing are the strongest academically. Education, biology, and nursing are the largest.

Required: To graduate, all students must complete a minimum of 120 semester hours, including 60 in the core curriculum and 20 in a major, with a GPA of 2.0. Reasonable proficiency in written and spoken English is also required.

Special: VSU offers more than 30 dual degrees with the Georgia Institute of Technology and has a co-op program with the Medical College of Georgia. Internships are available, as are work-study programs, study abroad, a general studies degree, and credit for life experience. There are 10 national honor societies, including Phi Beta Kappa, and a freshman honors program.

Faculty/Classroom: 61% of faculty are male; 39%, female. No introductory courses are taught by graduate students. The average class size in an introductory lecture is 27; in a laboratory, 18; and in a regular course, 24.

Admissions: 66% of the 2001-2002 applicants were accepted. The SAT I scores for the 2001-2002 freshman class were: Verbal--46% below 500, 42% between 500 and 599, 11% between 600 and 700, and 1% above 700; Math--46% below 500, 43% between 500 and 599, 10% between 600 and 700, and 1% above 700. The ACT scores were 16% between 21 and 23, 70% between 24 and 26, 13% between 27 and 28, and 1% above 28. 34% of the current freshmen were in the top fifth of their class.

Requirements: The SAT I or ACT is required, with a minimum score of 430 verbal and 400 math on the SAT I or 17 English and 17 math on the ACT. Applicants must be graduates of accredited high schools and have completed the college preparatory curriculum including 4 years each of English and math, 3 each of science and social science, and 2 each of a foreign language and academic or arts electives. A GPA of 2.0 is required. AP and CLEP credits are accepted. Applications are available on-line.

Procedure: Freshmen are admitted to all sessions. Entrance exams should be taken so that the results may be received by VSU at least 20 days prior to registration. Applications should be filed by August 1 for fall entry, December 1 for spring entry, and May 1 for summer entry, along with a $20 fee. There is a rolling admissions pland and notification is sent on a rolling basis.

Transfer: 654 transfer students enrolled in 2001-2002. Applicants with fewer than 30 hours of transferable credit must meet the same qualifications as entering freshmen. Applicants with 30 or more hours must submit transcripts from all previously attended colleges and have earned a minimum GPA of 2.0 in all work attempted. 30 credits of 120 must be completed at VSU.

Visiting: There are regularly scheduled orientations for prospective students, consisting of a Saturday open house 3 times a year, including an academic and activities carousel, campus tour, and lunch. There are guides for informal visits and visitors may sit in on classes. To schedule a visit, contact the Admissions Office at *admissions@valdosta.edu*

Financial Aid: In 2001-2002, 78% of all freshmen and 86% of continuing students received some form of financial aid. 51% of freshmen and 55% of continuing students received need-based aid. The average freshman award was $2000. Of that total, scholarships or need-based grants averaged $2000; and loans averaged $2000 ($18,500 maximum). The HOPE scholarship for Georgia residents pays tution for students wirth a B average. Average annual earnings from campus work are $2000. The average financial indebtedness of the 2001 graduate was $12,725. VSU is a member of CSS. The FAFSA and the college's own financial statement are required. The fall application deadline is June 1.

International Students: There are 214 international students enrolled. They must score 523 on the written TOEFL or 193 on the electronic version.

Computers: The mainframe consists of UNIX-based central servers with Novell netware, an HP 9000 model G70 business server, and a Sun SPARC server 1000. VSU also has access to the CDC CYBER 850, IBM 3090, and other computing facilities of the University System of Georgia. There are 24 PC and terminal labs located in educational buildings and the library. Students have access to the Internet, e-mail, and Galileo. All students may access the system. There are no time limits and no fees.

Graduates: In a recent year, the most popular majors were biology (7%), early childhood education (6%), and nursing (4%).

Admissions Contact: Walter H. Peacock, Director of Admissions. A video is available. E-mail: *admissions@valdosta.edu*
Web: *www.valdosta.edu*

WESLEYAN COLLEGE

Macon, GA 31210 C-3

(912) 757-5206

(800) 447-6610; Fax: (912) 757-4030

Full-time: 529 women	**Faculty:** 46
Part-time: 145 women	**Ph.D.s:** 96%
Graduate: 11 men, 36 women	**Student/Faculty:** 11 to 1
Year: semesters, summer session	**Tuition:** $9800
Application Deadline: March 1	**Room & Board:** $7250

Freshman Class: 500 applied, 368 accepted, 201 enrolled

SAT I or ACT: required **VERY COMPETITIVE**

Wesleyan College, founded in 1836, is a private, liberal arts college for women, affiliated with the United Methodist Church. It is the world's first college chartered to grant degrees to women. In addition to regional accreditation, Wesleyan has baccalaureate program accreditation with NASM. The library contains 142,579 volumes, 33,216 microform items, and 6552 audiovisual forms/CDs, and subscribes to 630 periodicals. Computerized library services include the card catalog, interlibrary loans, and database searching. Special learning facilities include an art gallery, a computerized teaching classroom, language and math labs, collaborative research science labs, and an arboretum. The 200-acre campus is in a suburban area 90 miles south of Atlanta. Including residence halls, there are 18 buildings.

Student Life: 72% of undergraduates are from Georgia. Others are from 23 states and 22 foreign countries. 90% are from public schools. 54% are white; 25%, African American; 11%, foreign nationals. 67% are Protestant; 18% claim no religious affiliation; 11% are Catholic. The average age of freshmen is 22; all undergraduates, 24. 27% do not continue beyond their first year.

Housing: 557 students can be accommodated in college housing, which includes dormitories and on-campus apartments. On-campus housing is guaranteed for all 4 years. 75% of students live on campus; of those, 70% remain on campus on weekends. Alcohol is not permitted. All students may keep cars.

Activities: There are no sororities. There are 40 groups on campus, including art, choir, chorus, computers, dance, debate, drama, ethnic, forensics, gay, honors, international, literary magazine, musical theater, newspaper, political, professional, recreation, religious, social, social service, student government, and yearbook. Popular campus events include Fall Family Weekend, mixers, and class intramurals.

Sports: There are 6 intercollegiate sports for women. Facilities include an equestrian arena, softball and soccer fields, an indoor pool, a gym, a dance studio, a weight room, a lake, a fitness trail, and a fitness center.

Disabled Students: 65% of the campus is accessible. Wheelchair ramps, elevators, special parking, specially equipped rest rooms, special class scheduling, lowered drinking fountains, and lowered telephones are available.

Services: Counseling and information services are available, as is free tutoring, available upon request. In addition, a writing lab, study skills workshops, academic counseling, and sessions with first-year seminar classes conducted by the director of the academic center are available.

Campus Safety and Security: Measures include 24-hour foot and vehicle patrol, self-defense education, escort service, and informal discussions. There are pamphlets/posters/films, emergency telephones, and lighted pathways/sidewalks. Dormitory entrances are kept locked.

Programs of Study: Wesleyan confers the A.B. degree. Master's degrees are also awarded. Bachelor's degrees are awarded in BIOLOGICAL SCIENCE (biology/biological science), BUSINESS (accounting, business administration and management, and international business management), COMMUNICATIONS AND THE ARTS (advertising, art history and appreciation, communications, English, French, music, Spanish, and studio art), COMPUTER AND PHYSICAL SCIENCE (chemistry, mathematics, physical sciences, and physics), EDUCATION (early childhood, middle school, and secondary), SOCIAL SCIENCE (economics, history, humanities, interdisciplinary studies, international relations, philosophy, political science/government, psychology, religion, social science, and sociology). Art, biology, and business are the strongest academically. Business, education, and English are the largest.

Required: Students must complete 120 credit hours with a minimum GPA of 2.0 in order to graduate. Requirements include proficiency in writing, math, and modern foreign language, and 10 courses distributed with 2 but no more than 3 from fine arts, humanities, science and math, and social sciences. A first-year seminar, a speech-intensive course, cross-cultural and workplace experience, and an integrative experience in the major are also required. All classes are seminar based.

Special: Wesleyan offers cross-registration with Mercer University and a 3-2 engineering degree with Georgia Institute of Technology and Auburn and Mercer Universities. More than 150 internships are available, as are interdisciplinary, student-designed, and dual majors, study abroad in 10 countries, a Washington semester, work-study programs, credit for life experience, nondegree study, and pass/fail options. There are 10 national honor societies and a freshman honors program.

Faculty/Classroom: 46% of faculty are male; 54%, female. All teach undergraduates and 75% do research. No introductory courses are taught by graduate students. The average class size in an introductory lecture is 16; in a laboratory, 12; and in a regular course, 13.

Admissions: 74% of the 2001-2002 applicants were accepted. The SAT I scores for the 2001-2002 freshman class were: Verbal--16% below 500, 45% between 500 and 599, 29% between 600 and 700, and 10% above 700; Math--16% below 500, 51% between 500 and 599, 32% between 600 and 700, and 3% above 700. The ACT scores were 13% below 21, 31% between 21 and 23, 24% between 24 and 26, 16% between 27 and 28, and 16% above 28. 52% of the current freshmen were in the top fifth of their class; 84% were in the top two fifths. There were 3 National Merit finalists. 8 freshmen graduated first in their class.

Requirements: The SAT I or ACT is required. In addition, each applicant for admission is reviewed on the following: performance in and quality of a college preparatory curriculum, standardized test score, counselor and teacher recommendation, writing ability, and cocurricular involvement. A minimum of 15 Carnegie units is required, including 4 units of English, 2 units of foreign language, and 3 units each of math, natural sciences, and social sciences. Admitted students must graduate from an accredited secondary school or have a GED certificate. The admission staff does not require but welcomes the opportunity to interview prospective students. Students who wish to be considered for a performance arts scholarship must submit a portfolio or audition. AP and CLEP credits are accepted. Important factors in the admissions decision are advanced placement or honor courses, evidence of special talent, and leadership record. Applications are accepted on-line.

Procedure: Freshmen are admitted fall and spring. Entrance exams should be taken by the fall of the senior year. There are early decision, early admissions, and deferred admissions plans. Early decision applications should be filed by November 15; regular applications, by March 1 for fall entry and December 1 for spring entry. The fall 2001 application fee was $30. Notification of early decision is sent December 15; regular decision, April 1. 20 early decision candidates were accepted for the 2001-2002 class.

Transfer: 43 transfer students enrolled in 2001-2002. Applicants with less than 24 transferable semester hours must submit a final high school transcript and record of standardized test scores in addition to their college transcripts. An interview is recommended. 30 credits of 120 must be completed at Wesleyan.

Visiting: There are regularly scheduled orientations for prospective students, including a campus tour, parent/student panels, class visits, admission and financial aid sessions, and meals in the dining hall. There are guides for informal visits and visitors may sit in on classes and stay overnight. To schedule a visit, contact Betsy Anderberg, Admissions.

Financial Aid: In 2001-2002, all freshmen and 99% of continuing students received some form of financial aid. 77% of freshmen and 78% of continuing students received need-based aid. The average freshman award was $16,953. Of that total, scholarships or need-based grants averaged $11,943 ($17,050 maximum); loans averaged $4094 ($15,525 maximum); and work contracts averaged $916 ($2000 maximum). 48% of undergraduates work part time. Average annual earnings from campus work are $1224. The average financial indebtedness of the 2001 graduate was $19,614. Wesleyan is a member of CSS. The FAFSA and the college's own financial statement are required. The fall application deadline is May 1.

International Students: There are 77 international students enrolled. The school actively recruits these students. They must score 550 on the written TOEFL.

Computers: The campus is fully networked and connected to the Internet. Students have e-mail access. All students may access the system. There are no time limits and no fees. All students are required to have personal computers.

Graduates: In 2001, 91 bachelor's degrees were awarded. The most popular majors were psychology (23%), communication (13%), and business administration (12%). In an average class, 42% graduate in 4 years, 44% in 5 years, and 44% in 6 years.

Admissions Contact: Jonathan M. Stroud, Vice President of Enrollment and Marketing. A video is available.
E-mail: *admissions@wesleyancollege.edu*
Web: *www.wesleyancollege.edu*

WOMEN'S COLLEGE OF BRENAU UNIVERSITY

(See Brenau University Women's College)

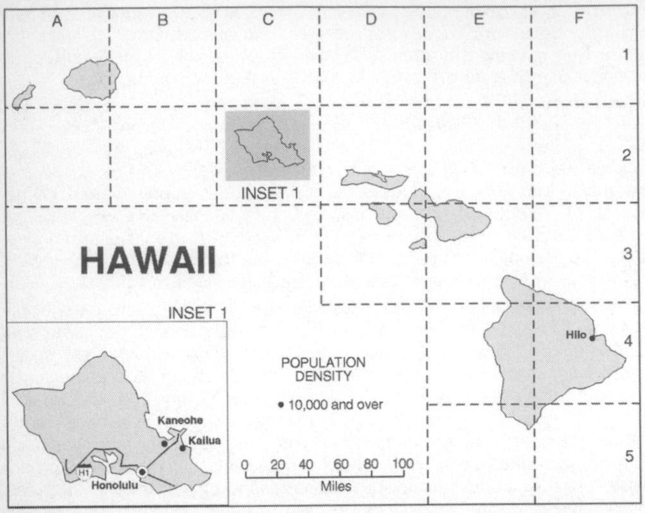

BRIGHAM YOUNG UNIVERSITY/HAWAII C-2
Laie, HI 96762 **(808) 293-3010; Fax: (808) 293-3741**

Full-time: 949 men, 1228 women
Part-time: 40 men, 61 women
Graduate: none
Year: semesters, summer session
Application Deadline: February 15
Freshman Class: 3207 applied, 325 accepted, 178 enrolled
ACT: 22
Faculty: 124
Ph.D.s: 63%
Student/Faculty: 18 to 1
Tuition: $2490 ($3740)
Room & Board: $4400
COMPETITIVE

Brigham Young University/Hawaii, founded in 1955 by the Church of Jesus Christ of Latter-day Saints (LDS), is a private institution offering programs in liberal arts, business, and education. Admissions priority is given to members of the LDS Church. Tuition is $2,490 for LDS students, $3,740 for non-LDS students. There are 3 undergraduate schools. In addition to regional accreditation, BYUH has baccalaureate program accreditation with CSWE. The library contains 317,900 volumes, 948,000 microform items, and 8053 audiovisual forms/CDs, and subscribes to 2100 periodicals. Computerized library services include the card catalog, interlibrary loans, and database searching. Special learning facilities include a learning resource center, art gallery, and natural history museum. The nearby Polynesian Cultural Center houses an art collection and an artifact collection, and provides valuable research opportunities for students in related programs. The 200-acre campus is in a small town 38 miles from Honolulu. Including residence halls, there are 42 buildings.

Student Life: Students are from 43 states, 69 foreign countries, and Canada. 41% are foreign nationals; 38%, white; 12%, Pacific Islander. The average age of freshmen is 20; all undergraduates, 23. 50% do not continue beyond their first year.

Housing: 1374 students can be accommodated in college housing, which includes single-sex dormitories, on-campus apartments, and married-student housing. On-campus housing is guaranteed for the freshman year only and is available on a first-come, first-served basis. 62% of students live on campus; all remain on campus on weekends. Alcohol is not permitted. All students may keep cars.

Activities: There are no fraternities or sororities. There are 41 groups on campus, including art, band, cheerleading, chess, choir, chorale, computers, dance, drama, ethnic, film, honors, international, jazz band, literary magazine, musical theater, newspaper, pep band, political, professional, religious, social, social service, student government, and yearbook. Popular campus events include International Food Fest, International Cultural Night, and Talent Show.

Sports: There are 4 intercollegiate sports for men and 4 for women, and 10 intramural sports for men and 10 for women. Facilities include 3 softball fields, 2 soccer fields, a rugby field, 10 tennis and 4 racquetball courts, a swimming pool, a weight room, a bowling alley, a dance studio, pool tables, a 5000-seat activity center, and 2 basketball gyms, one of which seats 500.

Disabled Students: 95% of the campus is accessible. Wheelchair ramps, elevators, special parking, specially equipped rest rooms, lowered drinking fountains, and lowered telephones are available.

Services: Counseling and information services are available, as is tutoring in most subjects. There is remedial math, reading, and writing.

Campus Safety and Security: Measures include 24-hour foot and vehicle patrol, escort service, informal discussions, and pamphlets/posters/films. There are emergency telephones and lighted pathways/sidewalks.

Programs of Study: BYUH confers B.A., B.S., B.F.A., and B.S.W. degrees. Associate degrees are also awarded. Bachelor's degrees are awarded in BIOLOGICAL SCIENCE (biology/biological science), BUSINESS (accounting, hospitality management services, international business management, and tourism), COMMUNICATIONS AND THE ARTS (art, English, fine arts, and music), COMPUTER AND PHYSICAL SCIENCE (computer science, information sciences and systems, and mathematics), EDUCATION (art, business, elementary, English, mathematics, science, social science, special, and teaching English as a second/foreign language (TESOL/TEFOL)), HEALTH PROFESSIONS (predentistry, and premedicine), SOCIAL SCIENCE (Hawaiian studies, history, interdisciplinary studies, international studies, Pacific area studies, physical fitness/movement, political science/government, psychology, and social work). Biological science, information systems, and education are the strongest academically. International business management, information systems, and psychology are the largest.

Required: Students must complete the 31- to 43-credit general education curriculum, as well as meet English proficiency, religious education, health, and phys ed requirements. A total of 120 credit hours, including 40 in the major, must be earned with a minimum GPA of 2.0 for graduation.

Special: BYUH offers work-study programs with the Polynesian Cultural Center, cooperative programs in most majors, nondegree study, student- designed majors in interdisciplinary studies, dual majors in elementary education and special education, and pass/fail options. There are 5 national honor societies and a freshman honors program.

Faculty/Classroom: 75% of faculty are male; 25%, female. All teach undergraduates and 15% do research.

Admissions: 10% of the 2001-2002 applicants were accepted. The ACT scores for the 2001-2002 freshman class were 38% below 21, 27% between 21 and 23, 23% between 24 and 26, 9% between 27 and 28, and 3% above 28. 15% of the current freshmen were in the top fifth of their class; 50% were in the top two fifths. 4 freshmen graduated first in their class.

Requirements: The SAT I or ACT is required. In addition, the applicant should be a high school graduate. Home-schooled and other nontraditional students should call for more information. A GPA of 3.0 is required. AP and CLEP credits are accepted. Important factors in the admissions decision are geographic diversity, recommendations by alumni, and personality/intangible qualities.

Procedure: Freshmen are admitted to all sessions. Entrance exams should be taken prior to the application deadline. There is a deferred admissions plan. Applications should be filed by February 15 for fall entry, October 31 for winter entry, February 15 for spring entry, and February 15 for summer entry. The fall 2001 application fee was $25. Notification is sent April 1.

Transfer: 214 transfer students enrolled in 2001-2002. Applicants must have 30 hours of college credit, with a minimum GPA of 2.5. 30 credits of 120 must be completed at BYUH.

Visiting: There are guides for informal visits. To schedule a visit, contact the University Relations Office at (808) 293-3660 or *toac@byuh.edu*

Financial Aid: In a recent year, 60% of all freshmen and 82% of continuing students received some form of financial aid. 12% of freshmen and 26% of continuing students received need-based aid. 50% of undergraduates work part time. Average annual earnings from campus work are $6000. The FAFSA is required. The fall application deadline is February 15.

International Students: There are 942 international students enrolled. The school actively recruits these students. They must score 400 on the written TOEFL or 97 on the electronic version or take the MELAB, and must also take the ACT.

Computers: The mainframe is an IBM RS/6000. Students can use the mainframe via the Web for registration and access to student information. Students can also log in to network servers to access their e-mail, and the Internet from any computer on campus. There are approximately 300 computers available to students in campus labs. All students may access the system 18 hours per day. There are no time limits. The fee is $25.

Graduates: In 2001, 357 bachelor's degrees were awarded. The most popular majors were information systems (15%), international business management (10%), and social work (7%). 60 companies recruited on campus in 2000-2001.

Admissions Contact: Jeffrey N. Bunker, Dean for Admissions/Records. A video is available. E-mail: *adm@byuh.edu*
Web: *http://www.byuh.edu*

CHAMINADE UNIVERSITY OF HONOLULU C-2
Honolulu, HI 96816 (808) 735-4735
(800) 735-3733; Fax: (808) 739-4647

Full-time: 410 men, 635 women	**Faculty:** 50
Part-time: 580 men, 410 women	**Ph.D.s:** 67%
Graduate: 240 men, 415 women	**Student/Faculty:** 21 to 1
Year: semesters, summer session	**Tuition:** $12,620
Application Deadline: open	**Room & Board:** $5990
Freshman Class: n/av	
SAT I Verbal/Math: recommended	**COMPETITIVE**

Chaminade University of Honolulu, founded in 1955, is a private institution affiliated with the Roman Catholic Church. The university offers degree programs in business and the arts and sciences. There are 5 undergraduate and 6 graduate schools. The library contains 75,000 volumes, 135,000 microform items, and 1519 audiovisual forms/CDs, and subscribes to 966 periodicals. Computerized library services include interlibrary loans. Special learning facilities include a learning resource center and audiovisual media center. The 62-acre campus is in an urban area 4 miles east of downtown Honolulu. Including residence halls, there are 8 buildings.

Student Life: 72% of undergraduates are from out of state, mostly the West. Others are from 32 states and 30 foreign countries. 45% are from public schools. 40% are white; 34% Asian American; 11% African American. 37% are Catholic. The average age of freshmen is 18; all undergraduates, 22. 30% do not continue beyond their first year; 35% remain to graduate.

Housing: 270 students can be accommodated in college housing, which includes single-sex and coed dormitories and on-campus apartments. On-campus housing is available on a first-come, first-served basis. 70% of students commute. All students may keep cars.

Activities: There are no fraternities or sororities. There are 30 groups on campus, including art, cheerleading, choir, computers, drama, ethnic, honors, international, literary magazine, newspaper, political, professional, religious, social, social service, student government, and yearbook. Popular campus events include Spring Serendipity, International Extravaganza, and Club Fest.

Sports: There are 4 intercollegiate sports for men and 4 for women, and 8 intramural sports for men and 8 for women. Facilities include volleyball, tennis, and basketball courts, fitness and weight-training facilities, cross-country track, flag football, and whiffle golf.

Disabled Students: 5% of the campus is accessible. Special parking and specially equipped rest rooms are available.

Services: Counseling and information services are available, as is tutoring in most subjects. There is remedial math, reading, and writing.

Campus Safety and Security: Measures include 24-hour foot and vehicle patrol, self-defense education, informal discussions, and pamphlets/posters/films. There are emergency telephones and lighted pathways/sidewalks.

Programs of Study: Chaminade confers B.A., B.S., B.B.A., and B.F.A. degrees. Associate and master's degrees are also awarded. Bachelor's degrees are awarded in BIOLOGICAL SCIENCE (biology/biological science), BUSINESS (accounting, business administration and management, business economics, and marketing/retailing/merchandising), COMMUNICATIONS AND THE ARTS (art, communications, and English), COMPUTER AND PHYSICAL SCIENCE (chemistry, and mathematics), EDUCATION (early childhood, elementary, and secondary), ENGINEERING AND ENVIRONMENTAL DESIGN (interior design), SOCIAL SCIENCE (American studies, behavioral science, criminal justice, forensic studies, history, humanities, international relations, philosophy, political science/government, psychology, religion, and social science). Education and communications are the strongest academically. Interior design, business, and education are the largest.

Required: To graduate, students must complete 124 credit hours, including 61 in general education courses and at least 24 in the major at the upper-division level. A 2.0 GPA is required in all majors except criminal justice (2.4), communications (2.5), and education (2.75).

Special: Dual majors are permitted in all programs, and cross-registration is available with 4 other colleges in Hawaii. There are 3-2 engineering degree programs with St. Mary's University in Texas and the University of Dayton. Internships with local companies, work-study programs, study abroad in Japan, and accelerated degree programs are available. Credit by exam, pass/fail options, and nondegree study are also offered. There are 4 national honor societies, and a freshman honors program.

Faculty/Classroom: 54% of faculty are male; 46%, female. All teach undergraduates and 5% do research. No introductory courses are taught by graduate students. The average class size in an introductory lecture is 20; in a laboratory, 13; and in a regular course, 16.

Requirements: The SAT I or ACT is recommended, with a minimum SAT I score of 460 on each part or a composite ACT score of 18. In addition, students must have earned 16 credits, based on 2 years of science, 3 each of math and social studies, and 4 each of English and college preparatory electives. The GED is accepted. An essay is required, and an interview is recommended. A GPA of 2.0 is required. AP and CLEP credits are accepted. Important factors in the admissions decision are leadership record, personality/intangible qualities, and advanced placement or honor courses. Applications are accepted on disk and on-line.

Procedure: Freshmen are admitted to all sessions. Entrance exams should be taken during the first semester of the senior year. There is an early admissions plan. Application deadlines are open. The application fee is $50. Notification is sent on a rolling basis.

Transfer: 100 transfer students enrolled in a recent year. Applicants must have completed at least 12 credit hours with a minimum GPA of 2.0 or better. A minimum composite score of 920 on the SAT or 18 on the ACT is recommended. 30 credits of 124 must be completed at Chaminade.

Visiting: There are guides for informal visits and visitors may sit in on classes. To schedule a visit, contact the Admissions Office.

Financial Aid: In 2001-2002, 89% of all freshmen received some form of financial aid. Chaminade is a member of CSS. The CSS/Profile, FAFSA, FFS, or SFS are required. Check with the school for current deadlines.

International Students: There were 58 international students enrolled in a recent year. The school actively recruits these students. They must score 450 on the written TOEFL or 133 on the electronic version and also take the MELAB, the Comprehensive English Language Test, or the college's own test. The college's own entrance exam or the SAT I or the ACT is also recommended.

Computers: The mainframe is a DEC PDP 11/24. 50 PCs are available in the computer science center and the writing lab. All students may access the system. There are no time limits and no fees.

Graduates: In a recent year, 163 bachelor's degrees were awarded. The most popular majors were criminal justice (22%), psychology (19%), and business administration (12%). In an average class, 2% graduate in 3 years, 17% in 4 years, 31% in 5 years, and 35% in 6 years.

Admissions Contact: Belinda Nagashima, Assistant Director, Admission. A video is available. E-mail: *cuhadm@lava.net*
Web: *chaminade.edu*

HAWAII PACIFIC UNIVERSITY C-2
Honolulu, HI 96813 (808) 544-0238
(800) 669-4724; Fax: (808) 544-1136

Full-time: 1802 men, 2460 women	**Faculty:** 221
Part-time: 1272 men, 1226 women	**Ph.D.s:** 77%
Graduate: 702 men, 572 women	**Student/Faculty:** 19 to 1
Year: 4-1-4, summer session	**Tuition:** $9360
Application Deadline: open	**Room & Board:** $8430
Freshman Class: 2891 applied, 2335 accepted, 625 enrolled	
SAT I Verbal/Math: 550/550	**ACT:** 21 **COMPETITIVE**

Hawaii Pacific University, founded in 1965, is a private institution offering undergraduate and graduate programs in liberal arts, business, computer science, marine science, nursing, and travel industry management. There are 6 undergraduate schools and 1 graduate school. In addition to regional accreditation, HPU has baccalaureate program accreditation with NLN. The 2 libraries contain 160,000 volumes, 310,069 microform items, and 7388 audiovisual forms/CDs, and subscribe to 1969 periodicals. Computerized library services include the card catalog, interlibrary loans, and database searching. Special learning facilities include a learning resource center, an art gallery, and a research vessel (boat). The 135-acre campus is in an urban area. Including residence halls, there are 16 buildings.

Student Life: 68% of undergraduates are from out of state, mostly the West. Others are from 50 states, 106 foreign countries, and Canada. 75% are from public schools. 35% are white; 26%, Asian American; 20%, foreign nationals. The average age of freshmen is 18; all undergraduates, 25. 26% do not continue beyond their first year; 65% remain to graduate.

Housing: 210 students can be accommodated in college housing, which includes single-sex and coed dormitories and off-campus apartments. In addition, there is a home stay program. The housing office assists students in finding apartments and other living arrangements in Honolulu. On-campus housing is available on a first-come, first-served basis. Priority is given to out-of-town students. 97% of students commute. Alcohol is not permitted. All students may keep cars.

Activities: There are no fraternities or sororities. There are 75 groups on campus, including art, band, cheerleading, chorale, computers, dance, debate, drama, ethnic, film, honors, international, literary magazine, musical theater, newspaper, pep band, political, professional, religious, social, social service, and student government. Popular campus events include Intercultural Day, Honors Banquet, and Club Carnival.

Sports: There are 4 intercollegiate sports for men and 4 for women, and 5 intramural sports for men and 5 for women. The university has soccer and softball fields and tennis courts and uses a civic basketball arena.

Disabled Students: 75% of the campus is accessible. Wheelchair ramps, elevators, special parking, specially equipped rest rooms, special class scheduling, lowered drinking fountains, and lowered telephones are available.

Services: Counseling and information services are available, as is tutoring in most subjects. There is remedial math, reading, and writing.

Campus Safety and Security: Measures include 24-hour foot and vehicle patrol, escort service, shuttle buses, and informal discussions. There are pamphlets/posters/films, emergency telephones, and lighted pathways/sidewalks.

Programs of Study: HPU confers B.A., B.S., B.S.B.A., B.S.Comp.Sci., B.S.N., and B.S.W. degrees. Associate and master's degrees are also awarded. Bachelor's degrees are awarded in BIOLOGICAL SCIENCE (marine science), BUSINESS (accounting, business administration and management, business economics, human resources, international business management, management science, marketing management, personnel management, small business management, and tourism), COMMUNICATIONS AND THE ARTS (advertising, communications, English, journalism, and literature), COMPUTER AND PHYSICAL SCIENCE (applied mathematics, computer programming, computer science, oceanography, and science), EDUCATION (teaching English as a second/foreign language (TESOL/TEFOL)), ENGINEERING AND ENVIRONMENTAL DESIGN (environmental science and military science), HEALTH PROFESSIONS (nursing and premedicine), SOCIAL SCIENCE (anthropology, criminal justice, economics, history, human services, humanities, international relations, international studies, Pacific area studies, political science/government, psychology, public administration, social science, social work, and sociology). Marine biology, nursing, and computer science are the strongest academically. Travel industry management, marketing, and communications are the largest.

Required: To graduate, students must complete a minimum of 124 semester hours in most majors, including 21 to 62 in the major, with a minimum GPA of 2.0. The core curriculum includes English, communications, global systems, quantitative skills, economics, humanities, history, and the behavioral and natural sciences; specific courses include an introduction to computers and a career seminar.

Special: Upperclassmen may participate in internships and work-study programs with numerous companies. HPU also offers accelerated degree and co-op programs in all majors, B.A.-B.S. degrees in most majors, student-designed majors, dual majors in all business subjects, a 3-2 engineering degree with Washington University in St. Louis and the University of Southern California, credit for military experience, nondegree study, and pass/fail options. There are 14 national honor societies, a freshman honors program, and 7 departmental honors programs.

Faculty/Classroom: 58% of faculty are male; 42%, female. 87% teach undergraduates, 30% do research, and 30% do both. No introductory courses are taught by graduate students. The average class size in an introductory lecture is 20; in a laboratory, 18; and in a regular course, 19.

Admissions: 81% of the 2001-2002 applicants were accepted. The SAT I scores for the 2001-2002 freshman class were: Verbal--46% below 500, 39% between 500 and 599, 9% between 600 and 700, and 6% above 700; Math--39% below 500, 45% between 500 and 599, 14% between 600 and 700, and 2% above 700. The ACT scores were 31% below 21, 37% between 21 and 23, 20% between 24 and 26, 10% between 27 and 28, and 2% above 28. 36% of the current freshmen were in the top fifth of their class; 65% were in the top two fifths. 20 freshmen graduated first in their class.

Requirements: The SAT I or ACT is required. In addition, applicants must be high school graduates or have a GED certificate. The university prefers completion of 20 credits based on 4 years of English, 2 each of math and social studies, and 2 each of history and science. An essay and an interview are recommended. Certain programs, for example, marine science and nursing, have more specific admissions requirements. A GPA of 2.5 is required. AP and CLEP credits are accepted. Important factors in the admissions decision are recommendations by school officials, advanced placement or honor courses, and evidence of special talent. Applications are accepted on computer disk and on-line via Common App, Apply Now, and the school's web site.

Procedure: Freshmen are admitted to all sessions. Entrance exams should be taken during the spring or summer of the junior year or the fall of the senior year. There is a deferred admissions plan. Application deadlines are open. The fall 2001 application fee was $50. There is a rolling admissions plan.

Transfer: 788 transfer students enrolled in 2001-2002. Applicants must have a GPA of 2.0 in a minimum of 24 credit hours. The SAT I or ACT and an interview are recommended. 30 credits of 124 must be completed at HPU.

Visiting: There are regularly scheduled orientations for prospective students. There are guides for informal visits and visitors may sit in on classes and stay overnight. To schedule a visit, contact Scott Stensrud at the Admissions Office at *admissions@hpu.edu*

Financial Aid: In 2001-2002, 68% of all freshmen and 40% of continuing students received some form of financial aid. 42% of freshmen and 28% of continuing students received need-based aid. The average freshman award was $12,119. Of that total, scholarships or need-based grants averaged $6719 ($24,809 maximum); loans averaged $9103 ($22,147 maximum); and work contracts averaged $2796 ($3000 maximum). 20% of undergraduates work part time. Average annual earnings from campus work are $2224. The average financial indebtedness of the 2001 graduate was $7962. The FAFSA and the college's own financial statement are required. The fall application deadline is March 1.

International Students: There are 1921 international students enrolled. The school actively recruits these students. They must score 550 on the written TOEFL or 213 on the electronic version and also take the college's own test and the SAT I or the ACT.

Computers: There are 376 IBM PCs located in the computer center and tutoring labs equipped with the UNIX system and CD-ROMs. All students may access the system 7 days a week during day and evening hours. There are no time limits and no fees.

Graduates: In 2001, 1263 bachelor's degrees were awarded. The most popular majors were business (35%), nursing (7%), and computer information systems (6%). In an average class, 9% graduate in 3 years, 24% in 4 years, 39% in 5 years, and 43% in 6 years. 886 companies recruited on campus in 2000-2001. Of the 2000 graduating class, 63% were enrolled in graduate school within 6 months of graduation and 69% were employed.

Admissions Contact: Scott Stensrud, Director of Admissions. A video is available. E-mail: *admissions@hpu.edu* Web: *http://www.hpu.edu*

UNIVERSITY OF HAWAII SYSTEM

The University of Hawaii System, established in 1907, is a public system. It is governed by a board of regents, and its chief administrator is the president, who is also the chancellor of the Manoa campus. The mission and purposes of the system are to provide all qualified people in Hawaii an equal opportunity for quality college and university education, to create knowledge and gain insights through research and scholarship, to preserve and contribute to the artistic and cultural heritage of the community, and to provide other public service through the dissemination of current and new ideas and techniques. The main goals are providing access to quality educational experiences and service to the state; implementing differentiated campus missions; championing diversity and respect for differences; strengthening the university's Hawaiian, Asian, Pacific, and international role; and acquiring and mananging resources with accountability and effectiveness. The total enrollment of all ten campuses usually exceeds 45,000, with some 3100 faculty members. Altogether, there are 123 baccalaureate, 88 master's, and 56 doctoral programs offered at the University of Hawaii. The university system includes 4-year campus in Manoa Valley (Honolulu), 1 in Hilo, 1 upper-division campus in Oahu, and 7 community colleges spread across the 4 major islands of Hawaii. Profiles of the 4-year campuses are included in this section.

UNIVERSITY OF HAWAII AT HILO

F-4

Hilo, HI 96720-4091

(808) 974-7414
(800) 897-4456; Fax: (808) 933-0861

Full-time: 870 men, 1327 women	**Faculty:** 162; IIB, av$
Part-time: 234 men, 395 women	**Ph.D.s:** 80%
Graduate: 22 men, 71 women	**Student/Faculty:** 14 to 1
Year: semesters, summer session	**Tuition:** $1658 ($7274)
Application Deadline: July 1	**Room & Board:** $4839
Freshman Class: 1663 applied, 1040 accepted, 415 enrolled	
SAT I Verbal/Math: 480/500	**ACT:** 21 **COMPETITIVE**

The University of Hawaii at Hilo, founded in 1970, is part of the public University of Hawaii and offers degree programs through its Colleges of Agriculture, Arts and Sciences, and Hawaiian language. It has a branch campus at Kealakekua, West Hawaii. Major programs include marine science, volcanology, and astronomy. There are 3 undergraduate and 2 graduate schools. In addition to regional accreditation, UH Hilo has baccalaureate program accreditation with NLN. The library contains 240,000 volumes and 11,000 microform items, and subscribes to 1200 periodicals. Computerized library services include the card catalog, interlibrary loans, and database searching. Special learning facilities include a learning resource center, art gallery, and space science center and marine education center. The 115-acre campus is in a small town 200 miles southeast of Honolulu. Including residence halls, there are 54 buildings.

Student Life: 69% of undergraduates are from Hawaii. Others are from 46 states, 32 foreign countries, and Canada. 76% are from public schools. 31% are white; 27% Asian American; 18% Native American/Eskimo. The average age of all undergraduates is 27. 29% do not continue beyond their first year; 31% remain to graduate.

Housing: 800 students can be accommodated in college housing, which includes coed dormitories, on-campus apartments, off-campus apartments, and married-student housing. In addition, there are honors houses, special-interest houses, and an educational/recreational enrichment hall. On-campus housing is available on a first-come, first-served basis. Priority is given to out-of-town students. 79% of students commute. Alcohol is not permitted. All students may keep cars.

Activities: There are no fraternities or sororities. There are 40 groups on campus, including art, band, cheerleading, chess, choir, chorale, chorus, computers, dance, drama, ethnic, gay, honors, international, jazz band, literary magazine, musical theater, newspaper, pep band, political, professional, religious, social, social service, and student government. Popular campus events include International Night, May Day, and dances.

Sports: There are 5 intercollegiate sports for men and 4 for women, and 10 intramural sports for men and 10 for women. Facilities include a student activities center with billiards and a game room, an athletic complex with basketball courts and a weight room, 8 tennis courts, and baseball, softball, and soccer fields.

Disabled Students: 95% of the campus is accessible. Wheelchair ramps, elevators, special parking, specially equipped rest rooms, special class scheduling, lowered drinking fountains, lowered telephones, and specially designed dorm rooms, cassette recorders, talking calculators, a TDY terminal, a magnifier projector, a large-print typewriter, and taped textbooks are available.

Services: Counseling and information services are available, as is tutoring in most subjects. There is remedial math, reading, and writing.

Campus Safety and Security: Measures include 24-hour foot and vehicle patrol, self-defense education, informal discussions, and emergency telephones. There are lighted pathways/sidewalks.

Programs of Study: UH Hilo confers B.A., B.S., B.B.A., and B.S.N. degrees. Master's degrees are also awarded. Bachelor's degrees are awarded in AGRICULTURE (agriculture), BIOLOGICAL SCIENCE (biology/biological science and marine science), BUSINESS (business administration and management), COMMUNICATIONS AND THE ARTS (art, communications, English, linguistics, and music), COMPUTER AND PHYSICAL SCIENCE (astronomy, chemistry, computer science, geology, mathematics, natural sciences, and physics), HEALTH PROFESSIONS (nursing), SOCIAL SCIENCE (anthropology, criminal justice, economics, geography, Hawaiian studies, history, Japanese studies, liberal arts/general studies, philosophy, political science/government, psychology, and sociology). Business, computer science, and biology are the strongest academically. Business, psychology, and marine science are the largest.

Required: To graduate, students must earn a minimum of 120 semester hours, including at least 30 in the college from which a degree is sought, with a 2.0 GPA overall and in the major. Students also must complete general education requirements, including 10 semester hours of natural sciences with 1 hour of lab, 9 each of humanitites and social sciences, 6 of world cultures, and 3 each of English composition and quantitative reasoning. 3 writing-intensive sourses and 1 Hawaiian/Asian/Pacific course are also required.

Special: UH Hilo offers cross-registration with Hawaii Community College, a political science legislative internship and other internships in business and psychology, and many work-study programs. Students may study abroad through a variety of programs and other internships in business and psychology. The school permits a student-designed liberal studies major, dual degrees, a 3-2 engineering degree with the University of Hawaii at Manoa, nondegree study, pass/fail options, and credit for military experience. There is a freshman honors program.

Faculty/Classroom: 60% of faculty are male; 40%, female. All both teach and do research. The average class size in an introductory lecture is 25; in a laboratory, 25; and in a regular course, 17.

Admissions: 63% of the 2001-2002 applicants were accepted. The SAT I scores for the 2001-2002 freshman class were: Verbal--54% below 500, 34% between 500 and 599, 10% between 600 and 700, and 2% above 700; Math--47% below 500, 37% between 500 and 599, 14% between 600 and 700, and 2% above 700. The ACT scores were 48% below 21, 23% between 21 and 23, 17% between 24 and 26, 6% between 27 and 28, and 4% above 28. 38% of the current freshmen were in the top fifth of their class; 72% were in the top two fifths. 4 freshmen graduated first in their class.

Requirements: The SAT I or ACT is required. In addition, applicants should be high school graduates or present a GED certificate. Students should have earned 22 academic credits, including 4 units of English, 3 of math, 3 of life and physical sciences, and 7 of electives. UH Hilo requires applicants to be in the upper 50% of their class. A GPA of 2.5 is required. AP and CLEP credits are accepted. Important factors in the admissions decision are advanced placement or honor courses, recommendations by school officials, and evidence of special talent. Applications are accepted on-line.

Procedure: Freshmen are admitted fall and spring. Entrance exams should be taken by November of the senior year. There is an early admissions plan. Applications should be filed by July 1 for fall entry and December 1 for spring entry, along with a $25 fee. Notification is sent on a rolling basis.

Transfer: 577 transfer students enrolled in 2001-2002. Applicants must have a GPA of 2.0; those with fewer than 24 college credits must submit their high school transcript and SAT I or ACT results. 30 credits of 120 must be completed at UH Hilo.

Visiting: There are regularly scheduled orientations for prospective students, including a campus tour and a meeting with an admissions counselor. There are guides for informal visits and visitors may sit in on classes. To schedule a visit, contact the Admissions Office at (808) 933-3714.

Financial Aid: In 2001-2002, 55% of all freshmen and 41% of continuing students received some form of financial aid. 55% of freshmen received need-based aid. The average freshman award was $3853. Of that total, scholarships or need-based grants averaged $2390; loans averaged $861; and work contracts averaged $602. 70% of undergraduates work part time. Average annual earnings from campus work are $2600. The average financial indebtedness of the 2001 graduate was $10,698. UH Hilo is a member of CSS. The FAFSA and the college's own financial statement are required. The fall application priority deadline is March 1.

International Students: There are 311 international students enrolled. The school actively recruits these students. They must score 500 on the written TOEFL or 173 on the electronic version and also take the college's own test. The SAT I or ACT is not required, but is recommended.

Computers: The mainframes are a SPARC Center 2000, 2 SPARC Server 690s, and an IBM ES/9000. There are 250 PCs and terminals in various locations on campus. Access to e-mail and the Internet requires a password assignment from the computer center. All students may access the system at posted times in person and any time by modem. There are no time limits and no fees.

Graduates: In 2001, 419 bachelor's degrees were awarded. The most popular majors were psychology (15%), business administration (11%), and marine science (8%). In an average class, 1% graduate in 3 years, 10% in 4 years, 25% in 5 years, and 31% in 6 years. 36 companies recruited on campus in 2000-2001.

Admissions Contact: Admissions Office. A video is available.
E-mail: *uhhadm@hawaii.edu* Web: *www.uhh.hawaii.edu*

UNIVERSITY OF HAWAII AT MANOA C-2

Honolulu, HI 96822 **(808) 956-8975**
(800) 823-9771; Fax: (808) 956-4148

Full-time: 4359 men, 5600 women	**Faculty:** 1132; I, -$
Part-time: 975 men, 1120 women	**Ph.D.s:** 86%
Graduate: 2296 men, 3182 women	**Student/Faculty:** 9 to 1
Year: semesters, summer session	**Tuition:** $3253 ($9733)
Application Deadline: June 1	**Room & Board:** $4609
Freshman Class: 4523 applied, 3204 accepted, 1668 enrolled	
SAT I Verbal/Math: 520/560	**ACT:** 22 **VERY COMPETITIVE**

The University of Hawaii at Manoa, founded in 1907, is the major research institution in the University of Hawaii system. The undergraduate programs offered include liberal arts and sciences, business, education, engineering, nursing, tropical agriculture, architecture, travel industry management, physical science, technology, Hawaiian, Asian-Pacific Studies, social work, and medicine. There are 13 undergraduate and 11 graduate schools. In addition to regional accreditation, UHM has baccalaureate program accreditation with AACSB, ABET, ACEJMC, ACS, ADA, APA, ASLHA, CCNE, CSWE, LCME, NAAB, NAACLS, NASM, and NLN. The 2 libraries contain 3 volumes, 5 microform items, and 50,365 audiovisual forms/CDs, and subscribe to 26,767 periodicals. Computerized library services include the card catalog, interlibrary loans, and database searching. Special learning facilities include a learning resource center, art gallery, radio station, and TV station. The 300-acre campus is in an urban area in Honolulu. Including residence halls, there are 247 buildings.

Student Life: 82% of undergraduates are from Hawaii. Others are from 49 states, 73 foreign countries, and Canada. 67% are from public schools. 63% are Asian American; 23%, white. The average age of freshmen is 18; all undergraduates, 23. 21% do not continue beyond their first year.

Housing: 3065 students can be accommodated in college housing, which includes single-sex and coed dormitories, on-campus apartments, and married-student housing. In addition, there are special-interest houses and substance-free/wellness, first year experience, technology, and 24-hour quiet halls. On-campus housing is available on a lottery system for upperclassmen. 84% of students commute. All students may keep cars.

Activities: 3% of men belong to 2 local fraternities; 8% of women belong to 4 local and 1 national sororities. There are 104 groups on campus, including art, band, cheerleading, chess, choir, chorale, chorus, dance, drama, drill team, ethnic, film, gay, honors, international, literary magazine, marching band, musical theater, newspaper, opera, pep band, photography, political, professional, radio and TV, religious, social, social service, student government, and symphony. Popular campus events include the All Nighters, showcasing the Campus Center, the midnight arena, and the first basketball practice of the season..

Sports: There are 8 intercollegiate sports for men and 10 for women, and 20 intramural sports for men and 20 for women. Facilities include a 10,000-seat arena, a 4400-seat baseball stadium, swimming facilities, 2 weight rooms, a turf field and rubberized track, 2 grass fields, 3 gyms, and an off-campus football stadium.

Disabled Students: 70% of the campus is accessible. Wheelchair ramps, elevators, special parking, specially equipped rest rooms, special class scheduling, lowered drinking fountains, and lowered telephones area available. Disability access information is available on request, and auxiliary aids and program adjustments can be arranged on an individual basis.

Services: Counseling and information services are available, as is tutoring in some subjects, on a limited basis. There is a reader service for the blind.

Campus Safety and Security: Measures include 24-hour foot and vehicle patrol, escort service, shuttle buses, and informal discussions. There are pamphlets/posters/films, emergency telephones, and lighted pathways/sidewalks.

Programs of Study: UHM confers B.A., B.S., B.Arch., B.B.A., B.Ed., B.F.A., B.Mus., and B.S.W. degrees. Master's and doctoral degrees are also awarded. Bachelor's degrees are awarded in AGRICULTURE (agricultural economics, agriculture, agronomy, animal science, and horticulture), BIOLOGICAL SCIENCE (biology/biological science, botany, entomology, microbiology, and zoology), BUSINESS (accounting, banking and finance, business administration and management, business economics, fashion merchandising, human resources, international business management, management information systems, management science, marketing/retailing/merchandising, real estate, recreation and leisure services, and tourism), COMMUNICATIONS AND THE ARTS (art, Chinese, classics, communications, dance, dramatic arts, English, fine arts, French, German, Hawaiian, Japanese, journalism, Korean, music, Russian, Spanish, and speech/debate/rhetoric), COMPUTER AND PHYSICAL SCIENCE (atmospheric sciences and meteorology, chemistry, computer science, geology, geophysics and seismology, information sciences and systems, mathematics, and physics), EDUCATION (athletic training, elementary, physical, recreation, secondary, and special), ENGINEERING AND ENVIRONMENTAL DESIGN (architecture, civil engineering, electrical/electronics engineering, environmental science, and mechanical engineering), HEALTH PROFESSIONS (dental hygiene, health science, medical laboratory technology, nursing, and speech pathology/ audiology), SOCIAL SCIENCE (American studies, anthropology, Asian/ Oriental studies, economics, ethnic studies, family/consumer resource management, food science, geography, Hawaiian studies, history, liberal arts/general studies, philosophy, political science/government, psychology, religion, social work, sociology, and women's studies). Education, business, and medicine are the strongest academically. Information and computer science, psychology, and biology are the largest.

Required: In most disciplines, a minimum GPA of 2.0 and a total of 124 credit hours are required for graduation. The total number of hours required in the major varies according to discipline. All students must fulfill general education core requirements, including 4 semesters of a foreign language or Hawaiian, 3 semesters each of arts and humanities, natural sciences, and social sciences, 2 semesters of world civilization, and 1 semester each of expository writing and math/logic. In addition, 5 of the core courses must be writing intensive.

Special: Internships are available with a variety of employers, including the state legislature, and through 55 different offices as well as academic departments via career services. Co-op and work-study programs are also offered. Dual majors, nondegree study, and pass/fail options are available. The liberal studies program offers student-designed majors. Students may study abroad in any one of 20 countries for a summer, a semester, or a year. There are 5 national honor societies, including Phi Beta Kappa, a freshman honors program, and 2 departmental honors programs.

Faculty/Classroom: 64% of faculty are male; 36%, female.

Admissions: 71% of the 2001-2002 applicants were accepted. The SAT I scores for the 2001-2002 freshman class were: Verbal--35% below 500, 47% between 500 and 599, 16% between 600 and 700, and 2% above 700; Math--19% below 500, 49% between 500 and 599, 27% between 600 and 700, and 5% above 700. The ACT scores were 29% below 21, 35% between 21 and 23, 25% between 24 and 26, 7% between 27 and 28, and 4% above 28.

Requirements: The SAT I or ACT is required, with a minimum score of 550 on both sections of the SAT I, or a minimum composite score of 22 on the ACT. Applicants must be graduates of an accredited secondary school. The GED is accepted. UHM requires 22 Carnegie units or 17 academic credits, including 4 units of English and 3 units each of math, science, and social studies, as well as 4 additional units of college preparatory courses and 5 electives. UHM requires applicants to be in the upper 40% of their class. A GPA of 2.8 is required. AP and CLEP credits are accepted. Important factors in the admissions decision are advanced placement or honor courses, personality/intangible qualities, and leadership record.

Procedure: Freshmen are admitted to all sessions. Entrance exams should be taken by December of the senior year for fall admission. Applications should be filed by June 1 for fall entry and November 1 for spring entry, along with a $40 fee. Notification is sent on a rolling basis.

Transfer: 2088 transfer students enrolled in 2001-2002. Applicants must have a total of 24 semester credits with a minimum GPA of 2.5. 30 credits of 124 must be completed at UHM.

Visiting: There are regularly scheduled orientations for prospective students, including campus tours and information sessions on areas of study, financial aid, and student employment. There are guides for informal visits and visitors may sit in on classes and stay overnight. To schedule a visit, contact School and College Services at (808) 956-7137 or toll free at (877) 447-3233, or at *ireyes@hawaii.edu*

Financial Aid: In 2001-2002, 30% of all freshmen and 38% of continuing students received some form of financial aid. 24% of freshmen and 33% of continuing students received need-based aid. The average freshman award was $6209. Of that total, scholarships or need-based grants averaged $3523 ($7500 maximum); loans averaged $5583 ($18,016 maximum); work contracts averaged $1853 ($2400 maximum); and external scholarships and academic awards overaged $887 ($4456 maximum). 90% of undergraduates work part time. Average annual earnings from campus work are $1800. The average financial indebtedness of the 2001 graduate was $7375. The FAFSA and the college's own financial statement are required. The fall application deadline is March 15.

International Students: There were 554 international students enrolled in a recent year. The school actively recruits these students. They must score 500 on the written TOEFL or 173 on the electronic version and also take the SAT I, or ACT, with the SAT I preferred.

Computers: The mainframe consists of an IBM 9672-RA5 and numerous Sun servers (various models). There are networked IBM and Mac PCs available in labs, academic departments, and offices. Access is also available via dial-up or cable modem from home. All students may access the system. There are no time limits and no fees. It is recommended that students in architecture have personal computers.

Graduates: In 2001, 2316 bachelor's degrees were awarded. The most popular majors were management information systems (6%), psychology (5%), and accounting (5%). In an average class, 10% graduate in 4 years, 39% in 5 years, and 54% in 6 years. 80 companies recruited on campus in 2000-2001.

Admissions Contact: Jan Heu, Interim Director of Admissions and Records. E-mail: *ar-info@hawaii.edu* Web: *www.hawaii.edu/admrec*

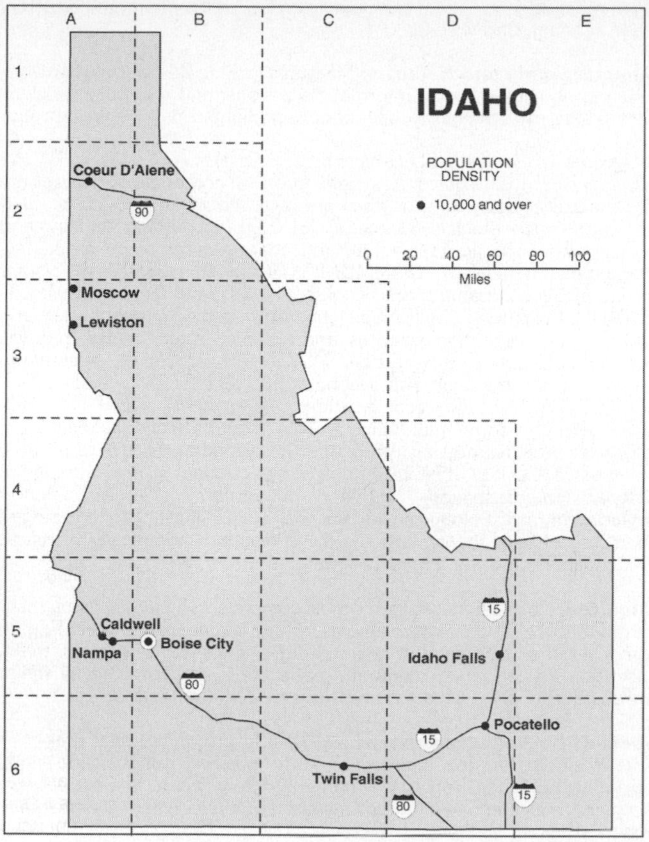

ALBERTSON COLLEGE OF IDAHO
Caldwell, ID 83605-4432 **A-5**
(208) 459-5305
(800) AC-IDAHO; Fax: (208) 459-5757

Full-time: 353 men, 403 women	**Faculty:** 72; III, -$
Part-time: 5 men, 17 women	**Ph.D.s:** 89%
Graduate: none	**Student/Faculty:** 11 to 1
Year: see profile	**Tuition:** $19,500
Application Deadline: June 1	**Room & Board:** $4400
Freshman Class: 631 applied, 616 accepted, 207 enrolled	
SAT I Verbal/Math: 560/565	**ACT:** 25 **VERY COMPETITIVE**

Albertson College of Idaho, founded in 1891, is a private institution offering degree programs in liberal arts education and the sciences. The college runs on a 12-6-12 calendar, with a 6-week intercession. The tuition figure above is for new students. Returning students pay $17,080 in tuition and fees. In addition to regional accreditation, ACI has baccalaureate program accreditation with NASDTEC. The library contains 183,756 volumes, 27,535 microform items, and 1717 audiovisual forms/CDs, and subscribes to 797 periodicals. Computerized library services include the card catalog, interlibrary loans, and database searching. Special learning facilities include an art gallery, natural history museum, planetarium, and rock and mineral collection. The 43-acre campus is in a small town 25 miles west of Boise. Including residence halls, there are 21 buildings.

Student Life: 71% of undergraduates are from Idaho. Others are from 18 states, 11 foreign countries, and Canada. 95% are from public schools. 82% are white. The average age of freshmen is 19; all undergraduates, 21. 30% do not continue beyond their first year; 49% remain to graduate.

Housing: 525 students can be accommodated in college housing, which includes single-sex and coed dormitories. In addition, there is an honors residence hall and special lifestyle floors. On-campus housing is guaranteed for the freshman and sophomore years only, is available on a first-come, first-served basis, and is available on a lottery system for upperclassmen. 56% of students live on campus; of those, 80% remain on campus on weekends. All students may keep cars.

Activities: 19% of men belong to 3 national fraternities; 19% of women belong to 1 local and 3 national sororities. There are 55 groups on campus, including art, band, cheerleading, choir, chorale, chorus, computers, dance, debate, drama, ethnic, film, gay, honors, international, jazz band, jazz choir, literary magazine, musical theater, newspaper, opera, orchestra, pep band, photography, political, professional, religious, social, social service, student government, and yearbook. Popular campus events include Spring Fling, Student-Alumni Career Forum, and Winterfest.

Sports: There are 6 intercollegiate sports for men and 7 for women, and 6 intramural sports for men and 6 for women. Facilities include an activities center with a 3000-seat gym, a weight room, and a swimming pool, as well as a 6500-seat baseball stadium, softball and soccer fields, and an outdoor walking/running path.

Disabled Students: 75% of the campus is accessible. Wheelchair ramps, elevators, special parking, specially equipped rest rooms, and lowered drinking fountains are available.

Services: Counseling and information services are available, as is tutoring in most subjects. There is a reader service for the blind, and remedial math, reading, and writing.

Campus Safety and Security: Measures include 24-hour foot and vehicle patrol, self-defense education, escort service, and informal discussions. There are pamphlets/posters/films, emergency telephones, and lighted pathways/sidewalks.

Programs of Study: ACI confers B.A. and B.S. degrees. Bachelor's degrees are awarded in BIOLOGICAL SCIENCE (biology/biological science), BUSINESS (accounting, business administration and management, international business management, international economics, and sports management), COMMUNICATIONS AND THE ARTS (art, creative writing, dramatic arts, English, music, and Spanish), COMPUTER AND PHYSICAL SCIENCE (chemistry, computer mathematics, mathematics, and physics), EDUCATION (physical), HEALTH PROFESSIONS (exercise science), SOCIAL SCIENCE (anthropology, economics, history, philosophy, political science/government, psychology, and religion). Biology, business, and psychology are the largest.

Required: To graduate, the student must earn 124 credits, including 40 or more in upper-division courses, with a minimum GPA of 2.0. Required disciplines include writing, math, Western civilization, cultural diversity, natural sciences, literature, social sciences, philosophy, religion, fine arts, and phys ed.

Special: ACI offers a 3-2 engineering degree with 4 universities, as well as cross-registration with Northwest Nazarene University. Internships with major corporations, work-study programs on campus, a Washington semester, study abroad, pass/fail options, phys ed credit for military experience, an accelerated degree in business, and nondegree study are also available. The Gipson Scholar Program allows freshmen with superior records to design their own majors. There is 1 national honor society and a freshman honors program. Most departments have honors programs.

Faculty/Classroom: 70% of faculty are male; 30%, female. All both teach and do research. The average class size in an introductory lecture is 18; in a laboratory, 15; and in a regular course, 20.

Admissions: 98% of the 2001-2002 applicants were accepted. The SAT I scores for the 2001-2002 freshman class were: Verbal--18% below 500, 48% between 500 and 599, 28% between 600 and 700, and 6% above 700; Math--20% below 500, 41% between 500 and 599, 37% between 600 and 700, and 2% above 700. The ACT scores were 16% below 21, 23% between 21 and 23, 27% between 24 and 26, 19% between 27 and 28, and 15% above 28. 53% of the current freshmen were in the top fifth of their class; 79% were in the top two fifths. In a recent year, there were 10 National Merit finalists and 1 semifinalist. 27 freshmen graduated first in their class.

Requirements: The SAT I or ACT is required. In addition, applicants must be high school graduates or present a GED certificate. ACI recommends that students have 4 years of English, 3 each of math, history, and social studies, and 2 of science. An essay and a teacher or guidance counselor recommendation are required. AP and CLEP credits are accepted. Important factors in the admissions decision are extracurricular activities record, leadership record, and recommendations by school officials.

Procedure: Freshmen are admitted to all sessions. Entrance exams should be taken by the fall of the senior year. There are early action and deferred admissions plans. Early action applications should be filed by November 15; regular applications, by June 1 for fall entry. The fall 2001 application fee was $40 or $20 on-line. Notification of early action is sent December 15; regular decision, on a rolling basis. 124 early action candidates were accepted for the 2001-2002 class.

Transfer: 29 transfer students enrolled in 2001-2002. Applicants must supply official transcripts and clearance reports from colleges attended, as well as an essay and 1 teacher recommendation. They must also have at least 28 semester hours of college credit. 30 credits of 124 must be completed at ACI.

Visiting: There are regularly scheduled orientations for prospective students, including an overnight stay with student hosts, class visitations, personal appointments with financial aid counselors, professors, and coaches, social events, and a campus tour. Individual tours can also be arranged. There are guides for informal visits and visitors may sit in on classes and stay overnight. To schedule a visit, contact the Admission Office.

Financial Aid: In 2001-2002, 95% of all freshmen and 93% of continuing students received some form of financial aid. 92% of freshmen and 84% of continuing students received need-based aid. The average freshman award was $12,679. Of that total, scholarships or need-based grants averaged $7313 ($19,280 maximum); loans averaged $4125 ($10,500 maximum); work contracts averaged $1170 ($2200 maximum); and athletic and performance scholarships averaged $8100 ($24,200 maximum). 49% of undergraduates work part time. Average annual earnings from campus work are $1192. The average financial indebtedness of the 2001 graduate was $16,699. ACI is a member of CSS. The FAFSA and the college's own financial statement are required. The fall priority deadline is February 15.

International Students: There are 20 international students enrolled. The school actively recruits these students. They must score 550 on the written TOEFL or 213 on the electronic version, or take the MELAB.

Computers: The mainframe is an HP 9000. There are 8 computer lab clusters with 120 PCs, all with access to the Internet. There are also minilabs in residence halls, and every room is wired to provide access to the Internet and other campus computer offerings. All students may access the system at designated times in computer labs; 24 hours in residence halls. There are no time limits and no fees.

Graduates: In 2001, 163 bachelor's degrees were awarded. The most popular majors were biology (18%) and business, history, and psychology (9%). In an average class, 40% graduate in 4 years and 47% in 5 years. 20 companies recruited on campus in 2000-2001. Of the 2000 graduating class, 14% were enrolled in graduate school within 6 months of graduation and 80% were employed.

Admissions Contact: Dennis P. Bergvall, Dean of Enrollment Management. A video is available. E-mail: *admissions@albertson.edu*
Web: *www.albertson.edu*

BOISE STATE UNIVERSITY

Boise, ID 83725 — B-5
(208) 426-1156
(800) 824-7017; Fax: (208) 426-3765

Full-time: 3630 men, 4530 women	**Faculty:** 475; IIA, -$
Part-time: 2125 men, 3005 women	**Ph.D.s:** 78%
Graduate: 715 men, 1440 women	**Student/Faculty:** 17 to 1
Year: semesters, summer session	**Tuition:** $2846 ($8846)
Application Deadline: July 18	**Room & Board:** $3685
Freshman Class: n/av	
SAT I or ACT: required	**LESS COMPETITIVE**

Boise State University, founded in 1932, is part of the Idaho Higher Education System and offers degree programs in the arts and sciences, business, education, health science, public affairs, technology, and vocational technical education. Figures given in above capsule are approximate. There are 7 undergraduate schools and 1 graduate school. In addition to regional accreditation, BSU has baccalaureate program accreditation with AACSB, CAHEA, CSWE, NASM, NCATE, and NLN. The library contains 505,618 volumes, 1,100,000 microform items, and 58,000 audiovisual forms/CDs, and subscribes to 4797 periodicals. Computerized library services include the card catalog, interlibrary loans, and database searching. Special learning facilities include a learning resource center, art gallery, radio station, and technology center. The 110-acre campus is in an urban area in Boise. Including residence halls, there are 60 buildings.

Student Life: 92% of undergraduates are from Idaho. Others are from 49 states, 47 foreign countries, and Canada. 85% are white. The average age of freshmen is 21; all undergraduates, 26. 41% do not continue beyond their first year; 59% remain to graduate.

Housing: 929 students can be accommodated in college housing, which includes single-sex and coed dormitories, on-campus apartments, and married-student housing. On-campus housing is available on a first-come, first-served basis. 93% of students commute. All students may keep cars.

Activities: 1% of men belong to 4 national fraternities; 1% of women belong to 3 national sororities. There are 136 groups on campus, including art, band, cheerleading, chess, choir, chorale, dance, drama, drill team, ethnic, gay, honors, international, jazz band, literary magazine, marching band, newspaper, orchestra, pep band, political, professional, radio and TV, religious, social, social service, and student government. Popular campus events include Spring Fling, Leadership Quest, and Martin Luther King, Jr. Celebration.

Sports: There are 7 intercollegiate sports for men and 7 for women. Facilities include a 30,000-seat stadium, a 12,000-seat indoor arena, a swimming pool, racquetball courts, indoor and outdoor tennis courts, indoor and outdoor tracks, and a weight room.

Disabled Students: 97% of the campus is accessible. Wheelchair ramps, elevators, special parking, specially equipped rest rooms, special class scheduling, lowered drinking fountains, lowered telephones, and electric doors are available.

Services: Counseling and information services are available, as is tutoring in most subjects. There is a reader service for the blind, and remedial math, reading, and writing.

Campus Safety and Security: Measures include 24-hour foot and vehicle patrol, shuttle buses, informal discussions, and pamphlets/posters/films. There are emergency telephones and lighted pathways/sidewalks.

Programs of Study: BSU confers B.A., B.S., B.A.A.S., B.B.A., B.F.A., B.I.S., and B.Mus. degrees. Associate, master's, and doctoral degrees are also awarded. Bachelor's degrees are awarded in BIOLOGICAL SCIENCE (biology/biological science), BUSINESS (accounting, banking and finance, business administration and management, and marketing/retailing/merchandising), COMMUNICATIONS AND THE ARTS (art, communications, dramatic arts, English, fine arts, and music), COMPUTER AND PHYSICAL SCIENCE (chemistry, geology, geophysics and seismology, information sciences and systems, mathematics, physics, and radiological technology), EDUCATION (art, education, elementary, English, music, physical, and secondary), ENGINEERING AND ENVIRONMENTAL DESIGN (construction management), HEALTH PROFESSIONS (environmental health science, health science, medical laboratory technology, nursing, predentistry, premedicine, and respiratory therapy), SOCIAL SCIENCE (anthropology, criminal justice, economics, history, interdisciplinary studies, philosophy, political science/government, psychology, social science, social work, and sociology). Business, art, and theater arts are the strongest academically. Business and education are the largest.

Required: To graduate, students must complete 128 credits with a minimum GPA of 2.0. Core requirements include 6 semester hours in English composition and 12 each in arts and humanities, social sciences, math, and natural sciences. A minimum grade of C is required in all major courses and courses used to meet the core requirements.

Special: BSU offers internships, work-study programs, dual majors, a general studies degree, nondegree study, pass/fail options, and study abroad in England, France, Germany, and Italy. There is a cooperative program in engineering with the University of Idaho. There is a freshman honors program.

Faculty/Classroom: 69% of faculty are male; 31%, female. 94% teach undergraduates. No introductory courses are taught by graduate students. The average class size in an introductory lecture is 30 and in a laboratory, 21.

Requirements: The SAT I or ACT is required. In addition, students must graduate from an accredited high school with a minimum SAT I combined score of 700 or ACT composite score of 17, completed 4 years of English, 3 each of math (algebra I and higher) and natural science, 2 1/2 of social science, 1 of humanities or foreign language, and 1 1/2 in other college-preparatory classes. Students who have not completed all the above classes but meet the other admission requirements will be considered for provisional admission status. AP and CLEP credits are accepted.

Procedure: Freshmen are admitted to all sessions. Applications should be filed by July 18 for fall entry, November 29 for spring entry, one week before classes begin for summer entry, along with a $20 fee. Notification of early and regular decision is sent rolling.

Transfer: A minimum GPA of 2.0 is required for students with at least 14 college credits. Those students with fewer credits must submit SAT I or ACT scores and a high school transcript. 30 credits of 128 must be completed at BSU.

Visiting: There are guides for informal visits and visitors may sit in on classes. To schedule a visit, contact the New Student Information Center at (208) 385-1820 or (800) 824-7017.

Financial Aid: BSU is a member of CSS. The CSS/Profile or FAFSA is required. The deadline for financial application is June 1; need-based aid deadline is February 1; priority deadline, April 1.

International Students: There are 131 international students enrolled. They must score 500 on the written TOEFL.

Computers: The mainframes are an IBM 4341 Model 2 and an HP 3000. There are also 750 PCs and Macs available in labs and faculty offices. All students may access the system. Students may access the system 2 hours at a time in the labs.

Admissions Contact: Mark Wheeler, Dean of Admissions.
E-mail: *mwheeler@bsu.idbsu.edu* Web: *www.boisestate.edu*

IDAHO STATE UNIVERSITY

Pocatello, ID 83209-0009 D-6

(208) 282-2475

n/av; Fax: (208) 282-4231

Full-time: 3542 men, 4151 women	**Faculty:** 577
Part-time: 1451 men, 2023 women	**Ph.D.s:** 68%
Graduate: 1036 men, 1460 women	**Student/Faculty:** 13 to 1
Year: semesters, summer session	**Tuition:** $2800 ($9040)
Application Deadline: August 1	**Room & Board:** $4230
Freshman Class: 4122 applied, 2921 accepted, 2397 enrolled	
SAT I Verbal/Math: 525/530	**ACT:** 20 **COMPETITIVE+**

Idaho State University, founded in 1901, is a public institution offering programs in the liberal arts and sciences, business, education, engineering, and health professions. There are 7 undergraduate schools and 1 graduate school. In addition to regional accreditation, ISU has baccalaureate program accreditation with AACSB, ABET, ACPE, ADA, APTA, CSWE, NASDTEC, NASM, and NCATE. The library contains 462,101 volumes, 1,953,720 microform items, and 622 audiovisual forms/CDs, and subscribes to 3559 periodicals. Computerized library services include the card catalog, interlibrary loans, and database searching. Special learning facilities include a learning resource center, art gallery, natural history museum, planetarium, radio station, and TV station. The 972-acre campus is in a small town 150 miles north of Salt Lake City. Including residence halls, there are 54 buildings.

Student Life: 94% of undergraduates are from Idaho. Others are from 40 states, 52 foreign countries, and Canada. 96% are from public schools. 88% are white. 42% claim no religious affiliation; 38% are Mormon. The average age of freshmen is 20; all undergraduates, 26. 39% do not continue beyond their first year.

Housing: 680 students can be accommodated in college housing, which includes single-sex and coed dormitories, on-campus apartments, and married-student housing. In addition, there are honors houses, special interest houses, and apartments for disabled students. On-campus housing is available on a first-come, first-served basis. Alcohol is not permitted. All students may keep cars.

Activities: 1% of men belong to 3 local fraternities; 1% of women belong to 3 local sororities. There are 140 groups on campus, including band, choir, chorus, computers, dance, debate, drama, ethnic, film, gay, honors, international, jazz band, marching band, newspaper, outdoor, pep band, photography, political, professional, radio and TV, religious, social, student government, and symphony. Popular campus events include movies, concerts, and art displays.

Sports: There are 6 intercollegiate sports for men and 7 for women, and 14 intramural sports for men and 14 for women. Facilities include playing fields, a field house, a gym, a recreation center, tennis courts, an athletic arena, a fitness/wellness center, and facilities for bowling and billiards.

Disabled Students: All of the campus is accessible. Wheelchair ramps, elevators, special parking, specially equipped rest rooms, lowered drinking fountains, lowered telephones, electric doors, and handrails are available.

Services: Counseling and information services are available, as is tutoring in every subject. There is a reader service for the blind, and remedial math, reading, and writing.

Campus Safety and Security: Measures include 24-hour foot and vehicle patrol, self-defense education, escort service, and shuttle buses. There are informal discussions, pamphlets/posters/films, emergency telephones, lighted pathways/sidewalks, and an e-mail bulletin alert service.

Programs of Study: ISU confers B.A., B.S., B.A.G.S., B.A.T., B.B.A., B.F.A., B.M., B.M.E., and B.U.S. degrees. Associate, master's, and doctoral degrees are also awarded. Bachelor's degrees are awarded in BIOLOGICAL SCIENCE (biochemistry, biology/biological science, botany, ecology, microbiology, and zoology), BUSINESS (accounting, banking and finance, business administration and management, human resources, management science, and marketing/retailing/merchandising), COMMUNICATIONS AND THE ARTS (art, communications, dramatic arts, English, fine arts, French, German, music, music performance, Spanish, and speech/debate/rhetoric), COMPUTER AND PHYSICAL SCIENCE (chemistry, computer science, geology, information sciences and systems, mathematics, and physics), EDUCATION (early childhood, elementary, health, music, physical, secondary, special, and vocational), ENGINEERING AND ENVIRONMENTAL DESIGN (computer technology, engineering, and engineering management), HEALTH PROFESSIONS (dental hygiene, health care administration, medical laboratory technology, nursing, physician's assistant, radiological science, and speech pathology/audiology), SOCIAL SCIENCE (American studies, anthropology, dietetics, economics, history, home economics, international studies, liberal arts/general studies, philosophy, political science/government, psychology, social work, and sociology). Biological sciences, business, and eduation are the largest.

Required: Students must satisfy general education requirements in the areas of written and spoken English, math, biological and physical sciences, fine arts, literature, philosophy, U.S. and non-U.S. history, government/economics, foreign language, psychology, anthropology, and sociology. To graduate, students must complete 128 credit hours, including 24 to 50 in the major, with a minimum GPA of 2.0.

Special: ISU participates in the Idaho Dental Education Program and several other medical co-op programs. Students may cross-register through the Western Education Exchange. ISU also offers a work-study program, study abroad in 50 countries, dual and student-designed majors, internships, credit by challenge exam or for life/military/work experience, nondegree study, and a general studies degree. As many as 16 credits of correspondence study may be applied toward the bachelor's degree. There are 11 national honor societies and 6 departmental honors program.

Faculty/Classroom: 58% of faculty are male; 42%, female.

Admissions: 71% of the 2001-2002 applicants were accepted. The SAT I scores for the 2001-2002 freshman class were: Verbal--35% below 500, 43% between 500 and 599, and 21% between 600 and 700; Math--36% below 500, 33% between 500 and 599, 27% between 600 and 700, and 4% above 700. The ACT scores were 52% below 21, 24% between 21 and 23, 16% between 24 and 26, 5% between 27 and 28, and 3% above 28.

Requirements: The SAT I or ACT is required; the ACT is preferred. Applicants must be graduates of an accredited secondary school or have a GED. They should prepare with 4 units of English, 3 each of math and science, 2.5 of social studies, 2 of college preparation, and 1 of foreign language. A GPA of 2.0 is required. AP and CLEP credits are accepted. Important factors in the admissions decision are advanced placement or honor courses, recommendations by school officials, and parents or siblings attending the school. Applications are accepted on-line at the university's web site.

Procedure: Freshmen are admitted to all sessions. Entrance exams should be taken early in the senior year. There are early admissions and deferred admissions plans. Applications should be filed by August 1 for fall entry and December 1 for spring entry, along with a $30 fee. Notification is sent on a rolling basis.

Transfer: 1250 transfer students enrolled in 2001-2002. Applicants must submit a final, official transcript from each college attended. At least 14 credit hours with a minimum GPA of 2.0 is required; students with fewer credit hours are subject to freshman admission requirements. Applicants with fewer than 25 credits must submit high school transcripts. 32 of 128 credits must be completed at ISU.

Visiting: There are regularly scheduled orientations for prospective students. There are guides for informal visits. To schedule a visit, contact Enrollment Planning at (208) 282-3277.

Financial Aid: In a recent year, 56% of all freshmen received some form of financial aid. 70% of freshmen received need-based aid. The average freshman award was $7000. Of that total, loans averaged $7000. 12% of undergraduates work part time. The average financial indebtedness of a recent graduate was $10,827. The FAFSA is required. The fall application deadline is March 15.

International Students: There are 139 international students enrolled. The school actively recruits these students. They must score 500 on the written TOEFL and also take the SAT I or the ACT.

Computers: The mainframe is an HP 3000. Mac and IBM PCs are available to all students in academic buildings. All students may access the system. There are no time limits. The fee is $10 per semester.

Graduates: In 2001, 1105 bachelor's degrees were awarded. The most popular majors were elementary education (8%), social work (7%), and biology (7%). In an average class, 7% graduate in 4 years, 15% in 5 years, and 26% in 6 years. 170 companies recruited on campus in 2000-2001.

Admissions Contact: Mike Echanis, Associate Director for Admissions and Enrollment Programs. E-mail: *echamike@isu.edu*
Web: *www.isu.edu/departments/enroll/*

LEWIS-CLARK STATE COLLEGE

Lewiston, ID 83501-2698 A-3

(208) 792-2210

(800) 933-LCSC; Fax: (208) 792-2876

Full-time: 905 men, 1271 women	**Faculty:** 118; IIB, -$
Part-time: 220 men, 557 women	**Ph.D.s:** 86%
Graduate: none	**Student/Faculty:** 16 to 1
Year: semesters, summer session	**Tuition:** $2550 ($7988)
Application Deadline: open	**Room & Board:** $3946
Freshman Class: 1099 applied, 700 accepted, 519 enrolled	
SAT I Verbal/Math: 482/483	**ACT:** 20 **COMPETITIVE**

Lewis-Clark State College, founded in 1893 and today part of the Idaho Higher Education System, offers programs in the arts and sciences, business, education, nursing, and preprofessional and technical training. It is named for the famed explorers, who once camped near what is now the campus. There are 9 undergraduate schools. In addition to regional accreditation, Lewis-Clark has baccalaureate program accreditation with AACSB, NASDTEC, NCATE, and NLN. The library contains 221,320 volumes, 21,864 microform items, and 6884 audiovisual forms/CDs, and subscribes to 1692 periodicals. Computerized library services include the card catalog, interlibrary loans, and database searching. Special learning facilities include a learning resource center, art gallery, TV station, and an educational technology center. The 44-acre campus is in an urban area 100 miles southeast of Spokane. Including residence halls, there are 29 buildings.

Student Life: 84% of undergraduates are from Idaho. Others are from 18 states, 21 foreign countries, and Canada. 87% are white. The average age of freshmen is 23; all undergraduates, 29. 41% do not continue beyond their first year; 28% remain to graduate.

Housing: 300 students can be accommodated in college housing, which includes single-sex and coed dormitories, off-campus apartments, and married-student housing. In addition, there are honors houses and language houses. On-campus housing is available on a first-come, first-served basis. 91% of students commute. Alcohol is not permitted. All students may keep cars.

Activities: There are no fraternities or sororities. There are 30 groups on campus, including art, chess, choir, chorale, chorus, dance, debate, drama, ethnic, honors, international, jazz band, musical theater, newspaper, orchestra, political, professional, religious, social, and student government. Popular campus events include the World Perspectives Lecture Series, International Exchange Conference, and Artists Series.

Sports: There are 6 intercollegiate sports for men and 6 for women, and 9 intramural sports for men and 9 for women. Facilities include a gym, indoor tennis courts, and a baseball field.

Disabled Students: 95% of the campus is accessible. Wheelchair ramps, elevators, special parking, specially equipped rest rooms, and special class scheduling are available.

Services: Counseling and information services are available, as is tutoring in every subject. There is a reader service for the blind, and remedial math, reading, and writing.

Campus Safety and Security: Measures include 24-hour foot and vehicle patrol, self-defense education, escort service, and shuttle buses. There are lighted pathways/sidewalks.

Programs of Study: Lewis-Clark confers B.A., B.S., B. Applied Sc., B. Applied Tech., B.S.N., and B.S.W. degrees. Associate degrees are also awarded. Bachelor's degrees are awarded in BIOLOGICAL SCIENCE (biology/biological science and environmental biology), BUSINESS (business administration and management), COMMUNICATIONS AND THE ARTS (communications and English), COMPUTER AND PHYSICAL SCIENCE (chemistry, geoscience, mathematics, and natural sciences), EDUCATION (elementary and secondary), HEALTH PROFESSIONS (nursing), SOCIAL SCIENCE (criminal justice, history, liberal arts/general studies, physical fitness/movement, psychology, social science, and social work). Education, business, and nursing are the strongest academically and have the largest enrollments.

Required: Students must earn 128 credit hours, including 43 to 50 in the core curriculum and 48 in their major, with a minimum GPA of 2.0 to graduate.

Special: Lewis-Clark offers cooperative programs and cross-registration with 3 Idaho universities, on-campus internships, work-study programs, a B.A.-B.S. and a general studies degree, student-designed majors, nondegree study, and pass/fail options. The college grants credit for life, military, and work experience through its Portfolio Program. The Individualized Study Center provides instructors and materials for about 50 nonscheduled courses so that students may work at their chosen times. There are also between-semester and weekend academic programs. There is 1 national honor society and a freshman honors program.

Faculty/Classroom: 61% of faculty are male; 39%, female. The average class size in an introductory lecture is 33 and in a laboratory, 25.

Admissions: 64% of the 2001-2002 applicants were accepted.

Requirements: The SAT I or ACT is required, if the applicant is under age 21 at the time of college entrance. Lewis-Clark has a liberal admissions policy, but students must be high school graduates or present a GED certificate. They must have fulfilled requirements in English, math, social and natural sciences, fine arts, foreign language, humanities, and speech, with a minimum GPA of 2.0. An interview is required for students entering technical programs. A GPA of 2.0 is required. AP and CLEP credits are accepted. Recommendations by school officials is an important factor in the admission decision. Lewis-Clark accepts applications on its web site.

Procedure: Freshmen are admitted to all sessions. Entrance exams should be taken before registration. There are early decision, early admissions, and deferred admissions plans. Application deadlines are open. The application fee is $30. Notification is sent on a rolling basis.

Transfer: 257 transfer students enrolled in a recent year. Applicants who do not have a minimum GPA of 2.0 must submit standardized test scores. 32 credits of 128 must be completed at Lewis-Clark.

Visiting: There are regularly scheduled orientations for prospective students, including SOAR (Student Orientation Advising and Registration) sessions and Sneak Preview for high school seniors. Counselors travel to high schools in the northwest. There are guides for informal visits and visitors may sit in on classes and stay overnight. To schedule a visit, contact the Admissions Office.

Financial Aid: In a recent year, 49% of all freshmen and 48% of continuing students received some form of financial aid. 36% of freshmen and 39% of continuing students received need-based aid. The average freshman award was $6795. Of that total, scholarships or need-based grants averaged $1574; loans averaged $2409; and work contracts averaged $2000 (maximum). 6% of undergraduates work part time. Average annual earnings from campus work are $1158. The average financial indebtedness of a recent year's graduate was $13,789. Lewis-Clark is a member of CSS. The FAFSA is required. Check with the school for current deadlines.

International Students: There were 122 international students enrolled in a recent year. The school actively recruits these students. They must score 500 on the written TOEFL or 173 on the electronic version.

Computers: There are 40 PCs and 10 Macs located in computer labs in several buildings on campus and in the library. All students may access the system numerous hours 7 days a week. There are no time limits and no fees.

Graduates: In a recent year, 365 bachelor's degrees were awarded. The most popular majors were business (19%), elementary education (18%), and nursing (18%). In an average class, 3% graduate in 4 years, 12% in 5 years, and 20% in 6 years. 13 companies recruited on campus in a recent year.

Admissions Contact: Steven J. Bussolini, Director of Enrollment Management. E-mail: *admissions@lcsc.edu* Web: *www.lcsc.edu*

NORTHWEST NAZARENE UNIVERSITY — A-5

Nampa, ID 83686 — **(208) 467-8496; (877) NNU-4-YOU**

Full-time: 437 men, 590 women	**Faculty:** 70
Part-time: 30 men, 39 women	**Ph.D.s:** 69%
Graduate: 93 men, 181 women	**Student/Faculty:** 15 to 1
Year: semesters, summer session	**Tuition:** $14,240
Application Deadline: open	**Room & Board:** $4140
Freshman Class: 524 accepted, 269 enrolled	
ACT: 23	**COMPETITIVE**

Northwest Nazarene University, founded in 1913, is a liberal arts college affiliated with the Church of the Nazarene. It offers programs in fine arts, language and literature, math and natural science, philosophy and religion, professional studies, and social science. In addition to regional accreditation, NNU has baccalaureate program accreditation with CSWE, NASM, and NCATE. The library contains 120,000 volumes, 19,500 microform items, and 3500 audiovisual forms/CDs, and subscribes to 830 periodicals. Computerized library services include the card catalog, interlibrary loans, and database searching. Special learning facilities include a learning resource center, art gallery, and an educational media center. The 80-acre campus is in a small town 20 miles west of Boise. Including residence halls, there are 26 buildings.

Student Life: 65% of undergraduates are from out of state, mostly the Northwest. Others are from 23 states and 8 foreign countries. 93% are white. Most are Protestant. The average age of freshmen is 19; all undergraduates, 21. 28% do not continue beyond their first year; 38% remain to graduate.

Housing: 768 students can be accommodated in college housing, which includes single-sex dormitories, off-campus apartments, and married-student housing. On-campus housing is guaranteed for all 4 years. 59% of students live on campus; of those, 80% remain on campus on weekends. Alcohol is not permitted. All students may keep cars.

Activities: There are no fraternities or sororities. There are many groups and organizations on campus, including art, band, cheerleading, chess, choir, chorale, chorus, computers, debate, drama, forensics, honors, international, jazz band, literary magazine, musical theater, newspaper, orchestra, pep band, professional, religious, social service, student government, symphony, and yearbook. Popular campus events include Welcome week, Malibu Days, and Mother-Daughter weekend.

Sports: There are 5 intercollegiate sports for men and 5 for women, and 4 intramural sports for men and 4 for women. Facilities include a lighted baseball field, 2 soccer fields, outdoor basketball, tennis, and sand volleyball courts, a track-and-field facility, a field house, and a park.

Disabled Students: 90% of the campus is accessible. Wheelchair ramps, elevators, special parking, specially equipped rest rooms, special class scheduling, lowered drinking fountains, and alternate testing and evaluation methods are available.

Services: Counseling and information services are available, as is tutoring in every subject. There is remedial math, reading, and writing.

Campus Safety and Security: Measures include 24-hour foot and vehicle patrol, escort service, informal discussions, and emergency telephones. There are lighted pathways/sidewalks, a professional security company, student lock-up-unlock, and walk-around-campus teams.

Programs of Study: NNU confers B.A., B.S., and B.S.N. degrees. Associate and master's degrees are also awarded. Bachelor's degrees are awarded in BIOLOGICAL SCIENCE (biochemistry and biology/biological science), BUSINESS (accounting, business administration and management, international business management, marketing and distribution, and recreation and leisure services), COMMUNICATIONS AND THE ARTS (art, ceramic art and design, communications, English, graphic design, music, painting, sculpture, and Spanish), COMPUTER

AND PHYSICAL SCIENCE (chemistry, computer science, mathematics, natural sciences, and physics), EDUCATION (art, elementary, English, foreign languages, mathematics, music, physical, science, and social science), ENGINEERING AND ENVIRONMENTAL DESIGN (engineering physics), HEALTH PROFESSIONS (nursing and premedicine), SOCIAL SCIENCE (economics, history, international studies, liberal arts/general studies, ministries, philosophy, political science/government, psychology, religion, and social work). Physics, biology, and education are the strongest academically. Biology, education, and social work are the largest.

Required: All students must complete 124 semester credits, of which 43 must be upper division. Students must show competency in communication and language skills, have a 2.0 GPA, demonstrate math proficiency, complete a major field of study, and take a comprehensive exam. In addition, each student must complete general education requirements, which are divided into three categories: English, speech, wellness, math proficiency, and freshman seminar; Bible history and literature, theology, philosophy, and history; and art history/music literature, literature, science, and social science electives.

Special: There is cross-registration with other Nazarene schools and study abroad in 10 countries. The university also offers internships, a work-study program, a general studies degree, dual and student-designed majors, and credit for military experience. There is a 3-2 engineering program with the University of Idaho and Seattle Pacific University. There is 1 national honor society, and a freshman honors program.

Faculty/Classroom: 65% of faculty are male; 35%, female. 97% teach undergraduates, 12% do research, and 12% do both. No introductory courses are taught by graduate students. The average class size in an introductory lecture is 21; in a laboratory, 10; and in a regular course, 16.

Admissions: The ACT scores for the 2001-2002 freshman class were: 35% below 21, 23% between 21 and 23, 21% between 24 and 26, 10% between 27 and 28, and 10% above 28. 45% of the current freshmen were in the top fifth of their class; 70% were in the top two fifths. 14 freshmen graduated first in their class.

Requirements: The ACT is required. In addition, applicants should be graduates of an accredited secondary school; the GED may also be accepted. Applicants should prepare with 4 years of English, 3 each of math, science, and history or social science, and 2 of foreign language. NNU requires applicants to be in the upper 50% of their class. A GPA of 2.5 is required. AP and CLEP credits are accepted. Applications are accepted on-line at the school's web site.

Procedure: Freshmen are admitted to all sessions. Entrance exams should be taken early in the senior year. Application deadlines are open. The fall 2001 application fee was $25. Notification is sent on a rolling basis.

Transfer: 75 transfer students enrolled in 2001-2002. Students who have earned the equivalent of 12 semester credits may be admitted as transfer students. Official transcripts from all colleges previously attended must be submitted. 32 credits of 124 must be completed at NNU.

Visiting: There are regularly scheduled orientations for prospective students, including the opportunity to stay in a dorm and have class visits. There are guides for informal visits and visitors may sit in on classes and stay overnight. To schedule a visit, contact the Campus Visit Coordinator at (208) 467-8640 or *rlkunz@nnu.edu.*

Financial Aid: In 2001-2002, 95% of all freshmen and 96% of continuing students received some form of financial aid. 61% of freshmen and 57% of continuing students received need-based aid. The average freshman award was $9645. Of that total, scholarships or need-based grants averaged $5485 ($18,780 maximum); loans averaged $6031 ($18,625 maximum); work contracts averaged $1703; and institutional, nonneed-based, and nonscholarship averaged $2486 ($9295 maximum). 66% of undergraduates work part time. Average annual earnings from campus work are $827. The average financial indebtedness of the 2001 graduate was $15,560. The FAFSA is required. The fall application deadline is August 25.

International Students: There are 8 international students enrolled. They must score 500 on the written TOEFL or 173 on the electronic version and also take the ACT.

Computers: The mainframe is an HP/3000 Series 58. Mainframe terminals and PCs for student use,including Apple. Languages and software available include APL, BASIC, C++, COBOL, FORTRAN, LOGO, MODSIM II, Paradox, Pascal, Powerhouse 4GL, and RPG. WordPerfect and Quattro are installed in all PCs. All students may access the system. There are no time limits and no fees. It is strongly recommended that all students have a personal computer.

Graduates: In 2001, 198 bachelor's degrees were awarded. The most popular majors were business administration (13%), elementary education (12%), and religion/religious studies (9%). In an average class, 51% graduate in 6 years. 100 companies recruited on campus in 2000-2001.

Admissions Contact: Office of Enrollment Services.
Web: *www.nnu.edu*

UNIVERSITY OF IDAHO

Moscow, ID 83844-2282 A-2
(208) 885-6326
(888) 884-3246; Fax: (208) 885-9119

Full-time: 4284 men, 3620 women	**Faculty:** 740; I, --$
Part-time: 635 men, 542 women	**Ph.D.s:** 70%
Graduate: 1658 men, 1328 women	**Student/Faculty:** 11 to 1
Year: semesters, summer session	**Tuition:** $2720 ($8720)
Application Deadline: August 1	**Room & Board:** $4306
Freshman Class: 3731 applied, 3117 accepted, 1635 enrolled	
SAT I Verbal/Math: 550/550	**ACT:** 23 **COMPETITIVE**

The University of Idaho, founded in 1889 as a land-grant institution, offers programs in art and architecture, agriculture, business and economics, education, engineering, letters and science, mines and earth resources, and natural resources, forestry, wildlife, and range sciences. There are 8 undergraduate and 2 graduate schools. In addition to regional accreditation, UI has baccalaureate program accreditation with AACSB, ABET, ADA, ASLA, CSAB, FIDER, NAAB, NASAD, NASM, NCATE, NRPA, and SAF. The 2 libraries contain 1,556,788 volumes, 189,048 microform items, and 25,405 audiovisual forms/CDs, and subscribe to 8086 periodicals. Computerized library services include the card catalog, interlibrary loans, and database searching. Special learning facilities include a learning resource center, an art gallery, a radio station, a TV station, an electron microscopy center, a lab animal facility, research institutes for water resources and for materials and advanced processing, university farms, and experimental forests. The 800-acre campus is in a small town 90 miles southeast of Spokane, Washington. Including residence halls, there are 147 buildings.

Student Life: 51% of undergraduates are from out of state, mostly the Northwest. Others are from 50 states, 82 foreign countries, and Canada. 98% are from public schools. 83% are white. The average age of freshmen is 19; all undergraduates, 22. 20% do not continue beyond their first year; 48% remain to graduate.

Housing: 2850 students can be accommodated in college housing, which includes single-sex and coed dormitories, on-campus apartments, off-campus apartments, married-student housing, fraternity houses, and sorority houses. In addition, there are honors houses, special-interest houses, cooperative residences, alcohol-and smoke-free, and quiet communities. On-campus housing is guaranteed for all 4 years. 55% of students commute. Alcohol is not permitted. All students may keep cars.

Activities: 16% of men belong to 18 national fraternities; 13% of women belong to 9 national sororities. There are 132 groups on campus, including art, band, cheerleading, chess, choir, chorale, chorus, computers, dance, drama, drill team, ethnic, film, gay, honors, international, jazz band, literary magazine, marching band, musical theater, newspaper, opera, orchestra, pep band, photography, political, professional, radio and TV, religious, social, social service, student government, symphony, and yearbook. Popular campus events include Lionel Hampton Jazz Festival, the Borah Symposium, and Palousafest.

Sports: There are 6 intercollegiate sports for men and 7 for women, and 28 intramural sports for men and 27 for women. Facilities include an activity center, a 17,000-seat domed stadium for basketball and football games, indoor and outdoor tracks, a 2-pool swim center, 3 gyms, a 500-seat auditorium, an 18-hole championship golf course, tennis, racquetball, and handball courts, and a student recreation center with a 55-foot climbing wall.

Disabled Students: 87% of the campus is accessible. Wheelchair ramps, elevators, special parking, specially equipped rest rooms, special class scheduling, lowered drinking fountains, lowered telephones, and 2 motorized wheelchairs, plus readers, note takers, and sign language interpreters, are available.

Services: Counseling and information services are available, as is tutoring in most subjects. There is a reader service for the blind.

Campus Safety and Security: Measures include 24-hour foot and vehicle patrol, self-defense education, informal discussions, and pamphlets/posters/films. There are emergency telephones and lighted pathways/sidewalks.

Programs of Study: UI confers B.A., B.S., B.Arch., B.Dan., B.F.A., B.G.S., B.L.Arch, B.Mus., B.N.S., and B.Tech. degrees. Master's and doctoral degrees are also awarded. Bachelor's degrees are awarded in AGRICULTURE (agricultural business management, agricultural economics, agricultural mechanics, agriculture, animal science, fishing and fisheries, forestry production and processing, horticulture, range/farm management, soil science, and wildlife management), BIOLOGICAL SCIENCE (biology/biological science, botany, entomology, microbiology, molecular biology, and zoology), BUSINESS (accounting, banking and finance, management information systems, marketing/retailing/merchandising, office supervision and management, personnel management, and sports management), COMMUNICATIONS AND THE ARTS (applied music, art, communications, dance, design, dramatic arts, English, fine arts, French, German, journalism, Latin, music, music history and appreciation, music performance, music theory and composition, photography, Spanish, studio art, and telecommunications), COMPUTER AND PHYSICAL SCIENCE (applied mathematics, chemistry, computer science, geology, information sciences and systems, mathematics, and physics), EDUCATION (agricultural, art, business, early childhood, elementary, foreign languages, home economics, industrial arts, marketing and distribution, music, physical, recreation, science, secondary, special, and vocational), ENGINEERING AND ENVIRONMENTAL DESIGN (agricultural engineering, architectural engineering, bioengineering, cartography, chemical engineering, civil engineering, computer engineering, electrical/electronics engineering, geological engineering, interior design, landscape architecture/design, mechanical engineering, metallurgical engineering, and mining and mineral engineering), HEALTH PROFESSIONS (medical laboratory technology and veterinary science), SOCIAL SCIENCE (American studies, anthropology, classical/ancient civilization, criminal justice, dietetics, economics, food science, geography, history, interdisciplinary studies, international relations, Latin American studies, parks and recreation management, philosophy, political science/government, psychology, rural economics, sociology, and textiles and clothing). Electrical engineering, forestry, and business are the strongest academically. Elementary education, business, and electrical and computer engineering are the largest.

Required: To graduate, students must complete at least 128 credit hours, including 36 in upper-division courses and 40 in the major, with a minimum GPA of 2.0. The core curriculum requires a total of 30 credits in communications, math, natural and applied sciences, humanities, and social sciences.

Special: UI offers cooperative programs and cross-registration with Washington State University, internships, extensive study-abroad programs, work-study programs, B.A.-B.S. degrees, dual and student-designed majors, a general studies degree, credit for life and work experience, nondegree study, and pass/fail options. There are 24 national honor societies, including Phi Beta Kappa, and a freshman honors program.

Faculty/Classroom: 69% of faculty are male; 31%, female. Graduate students teach 20% of introductory courses. The average class size in an introductory lecture is 39; in a laboratory, 14; and in a regular course, 16.

Admissions: 84% of the 2001-2002 applicants were accepted. The SAT I scores for the 2001-2002 freshman class were: Verbal--28% below 500, 41% between 500 and 599, 26% between 600 and 700, and 5% above 700; Math--24% below 500, 42% between 500 and 599, 28% between 600 and 700, and 6% above 700. The ACT scores were 25% below 21, 25% between 21 and 23, 24% between 24 and 26, 12% between 27 and 28, and 14% above 28. 44% of the current freshmen were in the top fifth of their class; 70% were in the top two fifths. There were 9 National Merit finalists. 99 freshmen graduated first in their class.

Requirements: The SAT I or ACT is required. In addition, applicants must be graduates of an accredited secondary school. GED certificates are accepted for special admissions only. Students must have completed at least 8 credits in English, 6 each in math and natural science, 5 in social science, 3 in electives, and 2 in humanities/foreign language. A GPA of 3.0 is required. AP and CLEP credits are accepted. Applications are accepted on-line via Netscape.

Procedure: Freshmen are admitted to all sessions. Entrance exams should be taken during the junior or senior year. There are early admissions and deferred admissions plans. Applications should be filed by August 1 for fall entry, December 15 for spring entry, and May 1 for summer entry, along with a $30 fee. Notification is sent on a rolling basis.

Transfer: 690 transfer students enrolled in 2001-2002. Applicants must have completed at least 14 credit hours with a minimum GPA of 2.0, or 2.8 for engineering transfers from outside the state of Idaho. 32 credits of 128 must be completed at UI.

Visiting: There are regularly scheduled orientations for prospective students, including a visit with faculty and financial aid personnel, a tour of the campus, and an overnight stay in the dormitories or Greek houses. There are guides for informal visits and visitors may sit in on classes and stay overnight. To schedule a visit, contact the Office of New Student Services at (208) 885-6163 or *nss@uidaho.edu*

Financial Aid: In 2001-2002, 51% of all freshmen and 43% of continuing students received some form of financial aid. 39% of freshmen and 45% of continuing students received need-based aid. The average freshman award was $6721. Of that total, scholarships or need-based grants averaged $2514 ($9200 maximum); loans averaged $3169 ($6625 maximum); and work contracts averaged $1300 ($1600 maximum). All undergraduates work part time. Average annual earnings from campus work are $1400. The average financial indebtedness of the 2001 graduate was $18,710. The FAFSA is required. The fall application deadline is February 15.

International Students: There are 166 international students enrolled. The school actively recruits these students. They must score 525 on the written TOEFL or 193 on the electronic version and also take the SAT I or the ACT.

Computers: There are more than 600 PCs available in cluster sites across campus and in the PC lab. All students may access the system 23 hours a day in more than 20 labs. There are no time limits and no fees.

Graduates: In 2001, 1477 bachelor's degrees were awarded. The most popular majors were education (22%), engineering (10%), and business (9%). In an average class, 18% graduate in 4 years, 45% in 5 years, and 54% in 6 years. 150 companies recruited on campus in 2000-2001.

Admissions Contact: Daniel D. Davenport, Director, Admissions and Student Financial Aid. A video is available. E-mail: *finaid@uidaho.edu* Web: *www.its.uidaho.edu/admissions/ugrad/*

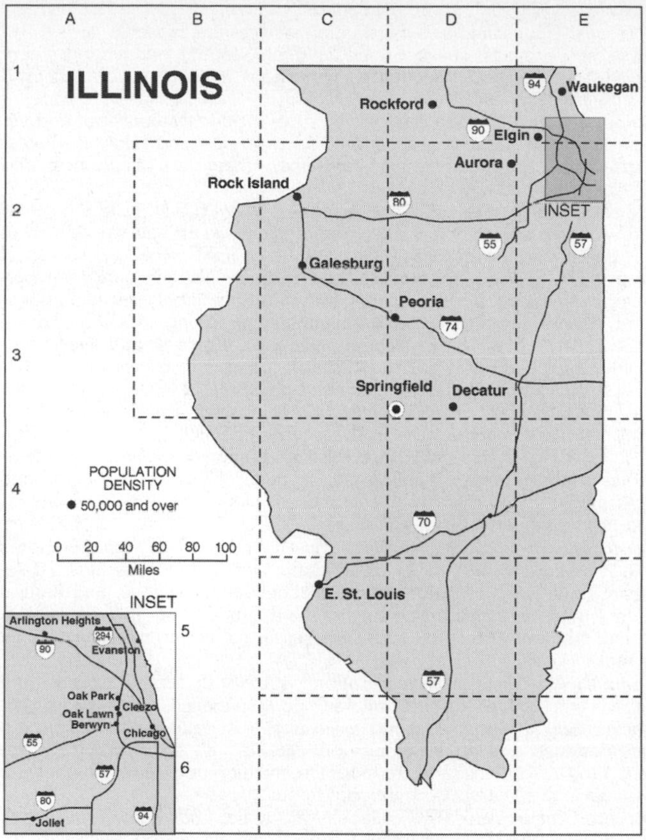

AUGUSTANA COLLEGE C-2

Rock Island, IL 61201-2296 **(309) 794-7341**
(800) 798-8100, ext. 7341; Fax: (309) 794-7422

Full-time: 941 men, 1264 women
Part-time: 15 men, 12 women
Graduate: none
Year: quarters, summer session
Application Deadline: open
Faculty: 142; IIB, av$
Ph.D.s: 91%
Student/Faculty: 16 to 1
Tuition: $18,720
Room & Board: $5397
Freshman Class: 2355 applied, 2026 accepted, 553 enrolled
ACT: 26 **VERY COMPETITIVE+**

Augustana College, founded in 1860, is a private liberal arts institution affiliated with the Evangelical Lutheran Church in America. In addition to regional accreditation, Augustana has baccalaureate program accreditation with NASM and NCATE. The 3 libraries contain 185,026 volumes, 107,037 microform items, and 1741 audiovisual forms/CDs, and subscribe to 1200 periodicals. Computerized library services include the card catalog, interlibrary loans, and database searching. Special learning facilities include a learning resource center, an art gallery,a natural history museum, a planetarium,a radio station, a preschool, a center for communicative disorders, a geology museum, an observatory, a map library, a Swedish immigration research center, 2 outdoor environmental labs, and an educational technology building. The 115-acre campus is in a suburban area 165 miles west of Chicago. Including residence halls, there are 46 buildings.

Student Life: 87% of undergraduates are from Illinois. Others are from 28 states, 19 foreign countries, and Canada. 90% are white. 46% are Protestant; 28%, Catholic; 13% claim no religious affiliation. The average age of freshmen is 18; all undergraduates, 20. 13% do not continue beyond their first year; 73% remain to graduate.

Housing: 1539 students can be accommodated in college housing, which includes single-sex and coed dormitories, on-campus apartments, and off-campus apartments. In addition, there are special-interest houses. On-campus housing is guaranteed for all 4 years. 70% of students live on campus; of those, 75% remain on campus on weekends. Alcohol is not permitted. All students may keep cars.

Activities: 21% of men belong to 7 local fraternities; 28% of women belong to 6 local sororities. There are 110 groups on campus, including alcohol responsibility, band, cheerleading, choir, chorale, chorus, computers, dance, debate, drama, environmental, ethnic, gay, honors, international, jazz band, literary magazine, musical theater, newspaper, opera, orchestra, pep band, political, professional, radio and TV, religious, social, social service, student government, symphony, volunteer, and yearbook. Popular campus events include Messiah performances, Greek Olympics, and Humanities Festival.

Sports: There are 9 intercollegiate sports for men and 8 for women, and 19 intramural sports for men and 18 for women. Facilities include an all-weather track, lighted tennis courts, a phys ed center, an exhibition basketball court, a swimming pool with space for 500 spectators, playing fields, a stadium that seats 3500, and a recreation center with a 200-meter track, court facilities for basketball, volleyball, tennis, and racquetball, and a weight room.

Disabled Students: 75% of the campus is accessible. Wheelchair ramps, elevators, special parking, specially equipped rest rooms, lowered drinking fountains, lowered telephones, adapted college-owned housing, and automatic door openers are available.

Services: Counseling and information services are available, as is tutoring in every subject. There is a reader service for the blind.

Campus Safety and Security: Measures include 24-hour foot and vehicle patrol, self-defense education, escort service, and informal discussions. There are pamphlets/posters/films and lighted pathways/sidewalks.

Programs of Study: Augustana confers the B.A. degree. Bachelor's degrees are awarded in BIOLOGICAL SCIENCE (biology/biological science), BUSINESS (accounting and business administration and management), COMMUNICATIONS AND THE ARTS (art history and appreciation, classics, dramatic arts, English, French, German, music, Scandinavian languages, Spanish, speech/debate/rhetoric, and studio art), COMPUTER AND PHYSICAL SCIENCE (chemistry, computer science, earth science, geology, mathematics, and physics), EDUCATION (art, elementary, music, physical, and secondary), ENGINEERING AND ENVIRONMENTAL DESIGN (engineering physics, environmental science, landscape architecture/design, and preengineering), HEALTH PROFESSIONS (occupational therapy, premedicine, and speech pathology/audiology), SOCIAL SCIENCE (Asian/Oriental studies, economics, geography, history, philosophy, political science/government, psychology, public administration, religion, and sociology). Business administration, biology, and psychology are the largest.

Required: A total of 123 credits with a minimum GPA of 2.0 is required to graduate. Courses in foreign language, religion, writing, phys ed, fine arts, humanities, literature, and the sciences must be completed.

Special: Cooperative degree programs are offered in engineering, environmental management, forestry, landscape architecture, and occupational therapy with Duke, Iowa State, Northwestern, Purdue, and Washington (St. Louis) Universities and the University of Illinois (Urbana-Champaign). Domestic and international internships are offered. Study abroad is possible in 17 countries, including China, Peru, Sweden, Germany, and France, as is fall term study in East Asia, Europe, and Latin America. Interdisciplinary majors are offered in earth science, teaching, Asian studies, and public administration. A B.A.-B.S. degree in occupational therapy is offered, as are 3-2 engineering programs with the University of Illinois and Purdue, Washington (St. Louis), and Iowa State Universities. Work-study programs, double majors, phys ed credits, and pass/fail options are available. There are 13 national honor societies, including Phi Beta Kappa, a freshman honors program, and 12 departmental honors programs.

Faculty/Classroom: 61% of faculty are male; 39%, female. All teach undergraduates and 25% do research. The average class size in an introductory lecture is 23; in a laboratory, 17; and in a regular course, 22.

Admissions: 86% of the 2001-2002 applicants were accepted. The ACT scores for the 2001-2002 freshman class were 10% below 21, 23% between 21 and 23, 24% between 24 and 26, 18% between 27 and 28, and 25% above 28. 58% of the current freshmen were in the top fifth of their class; 85% were in the top two fifths.

Requirements: The SAT I or ACT is required. In addition, applicants should be graduates of an accredited secondary school with 16 academic credits, including 4 in English, 3 in math, 2 each in science and social studies, 1 in foreign language, and other science and math courses for appropriate majors. An audition for music majors and an interview are recommended. The GED is accepted. AP credits are accepted. Important factors in the admissions decision are advanced placement or honor courses, evidence of special talent, and recommendations by school officials. Augustana accepts the Common App on disk. Applications are accepted on-line at *www.collegenet.com*

Procedure: Freshmen are admitted fall, winter, and spring. Entrance exams should be taken by fall of the senior year. There is a deferred admissions plan. Application deadlines are open. The fall 2001 application fee was $25. Notification is sent on a rolling basis. 4% of all applicants are on a waiting list; 8 were accepted in 2001.

Transfer: 79 transfer students enrolled in 2001-2002. A minimum GPA of 2.0 is required. SAT I or ACT scores and an interview are recommended. 60 credits of 123 must be completed at Augustana.

Visiting: There are regularly scheduled orientations for prospective students, including information sessions with speakers, exhibits, campus tours, meetings with faculty, counselors, and students, and social activities. There are guides for informal visits and visitors may sit in on classes and stay overnight. To schedule a visit, contact Martin Sauer, Director of Admissions.

Financial Aid: In 2001-2002, 90% of all freshmen and 96% of continuing students received some form of financial aid. 63% of freshmen and 64% of continuing students received need-based aid. The average freshman award was $15,478. Of that total, scholarships or need-based grants averaged $11,394 and loans averaged $3517. 80% of undergraduates work part time. Average annual earnings from campus work are $900. The average financial indebtedness of the 2001 graduate was $15,923. The FAFSA and the college's own financial statement are required. The fall application deadline is April 5.

International Students: There are 28 international students enrolled. The school actively recruits these students. They must score 550 on the written TOEFL and also take the SAT I or the ACT.

Computers: The mainframes are a DEC ALPHA 3000 and a DEC ALPHA 800. More than 750 college-owned PCs and 650 student-owned PCs are included in a comprehensive network linking academic and administrative buildings and residence halls. Access to the Internet and supercomputers at the University of Illinois is provided. An educational technology building provides extensive facilities for general and multimedia computing. All students may access the system. There are no time limits and no fees. It is strongly recommended that all students have a personal computer.

Graduates: In 2001, 496 bachelor's degrees were awarded. The most popular majors were biology (22%), business administration (16%), and premedicine (8%). In an average class, 69% graduate in 4 years, 73% in 5 years, and 73% in 6 years. 238 companies recruited on campus in 2000-2001. Of the 2000 graduating class, 30% were enrolled in graduate school within 6 months of graduation and 68% were employed.

Admissions Contact: Martin R. Sauer, Director of Admissions.
E-mail: *admissions@augustana.edu* Web: *http://www.augustana.edu*

AURORA UNIVERSITY
Aurora, IL 60506-4892

E-2
(630) 844-5533
(800) 742-5281; Fax: (630) 844-5535

Full-time: 421 men, 614 women	**Faculty:** 63
Part-time: 111 men, 177 women	**Ph.D.s:** 71%
Graduate: 384 men, 1094 women	**Student/Faculty:** 16 to 1
Year: quarters, summer session	**Tuition:** $13,418
Application Deadline: open	**Room & Board:** $5133
Freshman Class: 778 applied, 484 accepted, 223 enrolled	
SAT I Verbal/Math: 485/500	**ACT:** 20 **COMPETITIVE**

Aurora University, founded in 1893, is a private institution that offers graduate and undergraduate degrees in arts and sciences, education, business and information science, communication, nursing and health, recreation, social work, and a professional/staff program. There are 4 undergraduate and 4 graduate schools. In addition to regional accreditation, AU has baccalaureate program accreditation with CSWE, NLN, and NRPA. The library contains 114,144 volumes, 221,286 microform items, and 6791 audiovisual forms/CDs, and subscribes to 627 periodicals. Computerized library services include the card catalog, interlibrary loans, and database searching. Special learning facilities include a learning resource center, art gallery, TV station, a Native American museum, a lake-front campus, and a natural study area in Wisconsin. The 27-acre campus is in a suburban area 40 miles west of Chicago. Including residence halls, there are 19 buildings.

Student Life: 96% of undergraduates are from Illinois. Others are from 17 states. 89% are from public schools. 70% are white; 17% African American; 10% Hispanic. 65% are claim no religious affiliation; 17% Catholic; 17% Protestant. The average age of freshmen is 18; all undergraduates, 26. 24% do not continue beyond their first year.

Housing: 415 students can be accommodated in college housing, which includes single-sex and coed dormitories. On-campus housing is available on a first-come, first-served basis. 69% of students commute. Alcohol is not permitted. All students may keep cars.

Activities: 2% of men belong to 1 local and 3 national fraternities; 3% of women belong to 2 local and 2 national sororities. There are 40 groups on campus, including cheerleading, choir, chorus, computers, dance, drama, ethnic, film, gay, honors, international, literary magazine, musical theater, newspaper, photography, political, professional, radio and TV, religious, social service, student government, and yearbook. Popular campus events include Spring Fling and annual Native American Pow Wow.

Sports: There are 6 intercollegiate sports for men and 5 for women, and 7 intramural sports for men and 6 for women. 35% of men and women participate in sports. Facilities include a fitness center, a weight room, a 2000-seat gym, football and soccer fields, a racquetball court, and a climbing wall.

Disabled Students: 95% of the campus is accessible. Wheelchair ramps, elevators, special parking, specially equipped rest rooms, and special class scheduling are available.

Services: Counseling and information services are available, as is tutoring in most subjects. There is remedial math, reading, and writing. There are professional and peer tutors, workshops in word processing, and computer-based tutorials.

Campus Safety and Security: Measures include 24-hour foot and vehicle patrol, self-defense education, escort service, and informal discussions. There are pamphlets/posters/films, emergency telephones, and lighted pathways/sidewalks.

Programs of Study: AU confers B.A., B.S., B.S.N., B.S.P.S., and B.S.W. degrees. Master's and doctoral degrees are also awarded. Bachelor's degrees are awarded in BIOLOGICAL SCIENCE (biology/biological science), BUSINESS (accounting, business administration and management, business economics, management information systems, management science, and marketing/retailing/merchandising), COMMUNICATIONS AND THE ARTS (communications, English, and literature), COMPUTER AND PHYSICAL SCIENCE (computer science and mathematics), EDUCATION (elementary and physical), ENGINEERING AND ENVIRONMENTAL DESIGN (environmental science and industrial administration/management), HEALTH PROFESSIONS (nursing), SOCIAL SCIENCE (criminal justice, history, humanities, parks and recreation management, philosophy, political science/government, psychology, religion, social work, and sociology). Business, education, and protective services are the largest.

Required: To graduate, students must complete 120 semester hours with a minimum GPA of 2.0. Distribution requirements include 12 semester hours each in humanities, social/behavioral science, and natural science/math, 6 in freshman English, and 3 additional in communication. A minimum of 27 hours is required in the major; most require 36 or more.

Special: AU offers cross-registration with North Central College and Benedictine University, field-related job experience, work-study programs, study abroad in England, Germany, and Mexico, internships, student designed and dual majors, nondegree study, and a B.A.-B.S. degree. Pass/fail options, and credit for life, military, or work experience are also available. There are 3 national honor societies.

Faculty/Classroom: 40% of faculty are male; 60%, female. All teach undergraduates. No introductory courses are taught by graduate students. The average class size in an introductory lecture is 24; in a laboratory, 18; and in a regular course, 16.

Admissions: 62% of the 2001-2002 applicants were accepted. The SAT I scores for the 2001-2002 freshman class were: Verbal--33% below 500, and 66% between 500 and 599; Math--66% below 500, and 33% between 600 and 700. The ACT scores were 54% below 21, 25% between 21 and 23, 11% between 24 and 26, 8% between 27 and 28, and 2% above 28. 27% of the current freshmen were in the top fifth of their class; 51% were in the top two fifths.

Requirements: The SAT I or ACT is recommended. In addition, applicants must be graduates of an accredited secondary school or have earned the GED. AU requires applicants to be in the upper 60% of their class. A GPA of 2.0 is required. AP and CLEP credits are accepted. Important factors in the admissions decision are leadership record, advanced placement or honor courses, and extracurricular activities record. Applications are accepted on-line at *www.aurora.edu*

Procedure: Freshmen are admitted fall, winter, and spring. Entrance exams should be taken by late in the junior year or early in the senior year. There are early decision, early admissions, and deferred admissions plans. Application deadlines are open. 60 early decision candidates were accepted for the 2001-2002 class. The fall 2001 application fee was $25.

Transfer: 260 transfer students enrolled in 2001-2002. Applicants are required to have a minimum GPA of 2.0 and must have completed at least 15 semester hours. 30 credits of 120 must be completed at AU.

Visiting: There are regularly scheduled orientations for prospective students. There are guides for informal visits and visitors may sit in on classes and stay overnight. To schedule a visit, contact the Admissions Office.

Financial Aid: In a recent year, 97% of all freshmen and 73% of continuing students received some form of financial aid. 79% of freshmen and 62% of continuing students received need-based aid. Scholarships or need-based grants averaged $8275 ($15,255 maximum); loans averaged $4125 (maximum); and work contracts averaged $1724 ($1800 maximum). 11% of undergraduates work part time. Average annual earnings from campus work are $849. The average financial indebtedness of the 2001 graduate was $6925. The FAFSA is required. The fall application deadline is May 1.

International Students: In a recent year, there were 8 international students enrolled. They must score 550 on the written TOEFL.

Computers: DEC, HP, IBM, and DELL PCs are available in 4 computer labs. All students may access the system until midnight. There are no time limits and no fees. It is strongly recommended that all students have a personal computer.

Graduates: In 2001, 357 bachelor's degrees were awarded. The most popular majors were business (21%), education (17%), and protective services/public administration (16%). In an average class, 39% graduate in 4 years, 52% in 5 years, and 54% in 6 years. 41 companies recruited on campus in 2000-2001. Of the 2000 graduating class, 15% were enrolled in graduate school within 6 months of graduation and 90% were employed.

Admissions Contact: Office of University Admissions. A video is available. E-mail: *admissions@aurora.edu* Web: *http://www.aurora.edu*

BENEDICTINE UNIVERSITY

Lisle, IL 60532 E-2
(630) 829-4306; Fax: (630) 960-1126

Full-time: 568 men, 795 women	**Faculty:** 67
Part-time: 188 men, 435 women	**Ph.D.s:** 85%
Graduate: 275 men, 439 women	**Student/Faculty:** 20 to 1
Year: semesters, summer session	**Tuition:** $15,630
Application Deadline: open	**Room & Board:** $5700
Freshman Class: 852 applied, 565 accepted, 262 enrolled	
SAT I or ACT: required	**COMPETITIVE**

Benedictine University, founded in 1887, is a private, Roman Catholic liberal arts and sciences institution. There are 3 undergraduate schools. In addition to regional accreditation, Benedictine has baccalaureate program accreditation with ADA and NLN. The library contains 165,907 volumes, 331,148 microform items, and 4224 audiovisual forms/CDs, and subscribes to 7270 periodicals. Computerized library services include the card catalog, interlibrary loans, and database searching. Special learning facilities include a learning resource center, art gallery, natural history museum, and TV station. The 108-acre campus is in a suburban area 25 miles west of Chicago. Including residence halls, there are 9 buildings.

Student Life: 95% of undergraduates are from Illinois. Others are from 22 states and 6 foreign countries. 70% are from public schools. 49% are white; 14% Asian American. The average age of freshmen is 18; all undergraduates, 24. 23% do not continue beyond their first year.

Housing: 618 students can be accommodated in college housing, which includes single-sex and coed dormitories. On-campus housing is available on a first-come, first-served basis. 65% of students commute. All students may keep cars.

Activities: There are no fraternities or sororities. There are 36 groups on campus, including art, band, cheerleading, choir, chorus, computers, dance, debate, ethnic, honors, international, jazz band, literary magazine, musical theater, newspaper, pep band, political, professional, radio and TV, religious, social, social service, and student government. Popular campus events include Family Day, Spring Fest, and Gospel Fest.

Sports: There are 8 intercollegiate sports for men and 8 for women, and 14 intramural sports for men and 13 for women. Facilities include a recreation center housing a main arena, a pool, a weight room, and a dance room; racquetball and tennis courts; and softball, baseball, soccer, and football fields.

Disabled Students: 80% of the campus is accessible. Wheelchair ramps, elevators, special parking, specially equipped rest rooms, and lowered drinking fountains are available.

Services: Counseling and information services are available, as is tutoring in most subjects. There is remedial math, reading, and writing.

Campus Safety and Security: Measures include 24-hour foot and vehicle patrol, self-defense education, escort service, and informal discussions. There are pamphlets/posters/films, emergency telephones, and lighted pathways/sidewalks.

Programs of Study: Benedictine confers B.A., B.S., B.B.A., and B.S.N. degrees. Associate, master's, and doctoral degrees are also awarded. Bachelor's degrees are awarded in BIOLOGICAL SCIENCE (biochemistry, biology/biological science, molecular biology, and nutrition), BUSINESS (accounting, banking and finance, business administration and management, business economics, international business management, management information systems, marketing management, marketing/retailing/merchandising, and organizational behavior), COMMUNICATIONS AND THE ARTS (arts administration/management, communications, literature, music, publishing, Spanish, and studio art), COMPUTER AND PHYSICAL SCIENCE (chemistry, computer science, mathematics, and physics), EDUCATION (elementary and special), ENGINEERING AND ENVIRONMENTAL DESIGN (engineering and applied science and environmental science), HEALTH PROFESSIONS (clinical science, health care administration, health science, nuclear medical technology, and nursing), SOCIAL SCIENCE (economics, history, international studies, philosophy, political science/government, psychology, social science, and sociology). Biology, psychology, and elementary education are the largest.

Required: To graduate students must complete 120 semester hours, including 36 in their major, and maintain a minimum GPA of 2.0. They must complete 12 hours in the arts and humanities, 9 each in social sciences, natural sciences, and cultural heritage, 6 in rhetoric, and 3 each in speech, math, and freshman seminar. A thesis, capstone course or project, or comprehensive exam is required in specific departments.

Special: There is cross-registration with North Central College, Aurora University, and the Illinois Institute of Technology. Benedictine offers study abroad in 3 countries, and exchange programs can be arranged through other colleges. There are 3-2 preengineering degrees with Marquette University and the Universities of Illinois, Detroit, and Notre Dame, and an engineering degree with the Illinois Institute of Technology. Preprofessional programs including prepodiatry, pre-physical therapy, and prenursing are offered. Work-study programs with a number of surrounding firms, internships, an accelerated degree programs in management, credit for work and life experience, and dual majors are also offered. There are 11 national honor societies and a freshman honors program.

Faculty/Classroom: 66% of faculty are male; 34%, female. All both teach and do research. No introductory courses are taught by graduate students. The average class size in an introductory lecture is 22; in a laboratory, 14; and in a regular course, 17.

Admissions: 66% of the 2001-2002 applicants were accepted. The ACT scores for the 2001-2002 freshman class were: 4% below 21, 49% between 21 and 23, 30% between 24 and 26, 10% between 27 and 28, and 5% above 28. 36% of the current freshmen were in the top fifth of their class; 65% were in the top two fifths. 10 freshmen graduated first in their class in a recent year.

Requirements: The SAT I or ACT is required. In addition, to be admitted, students must complete 4 years of English, 3 each of social studies, math, and lab science, and 2 of foreign language. The GED is accepted. AP and CLEP credits are accepted.

Procedure: Freshmen are admitted fall and spring. Application deadlines are open. The fall 2001 application fee was $30.

Transfer: 225 transfer students enrolled in 2001-2002. Applicants must have a C average. A minimum GPA of 2.0 is necessary, and an interview is required in some cases. Students who have completed fewer than 20 semester hours must submit ACTor SAT I scores. 30 credits of 120 must be completed at Benedictine.

Visiting: There are regularly scheduled orientations for prospective students, including a regularly scheduled Visit Day and open houses each semester. There are guides for informal visits and visitors may sit in on classes and stay overnight. To schedule a visit, contact the Admissions Office.

Financial Aid: Benedictine is a member of CSS. The FAFSA, FFS, or SFS and the college's own financial statement are required.

International Students: There are 8 international students enrolled. The school actively recruits these students. They must score 550 on the written TOEFL or 213 on the electronic version and also take the SAT I or the ACT.

Computers: There are 125 PCs available in open labs and classrooms. All students may access the system. Students may use the PC labs from 8 A.M. to 11 P.M. Monday through Friday, 10 A.M. to 3 P.M. Saturday, and 10 A.M. to 11 P.M. Sunday, or 24 hours a day through modems at home, in residence halls, and in the student center. There are no time limits. The fee is $85. It is strongly recommended that all students have a personal computer.

Graduates: In 2001, 411 bachelor's degrees were awarded. The most popular majors were biology (10%), psychology (7%), and elementary education (7%). In an average class, 37% graduate in 4 years, 53% in 5 years, and 55% in 6 years.

Admissions Contact: Kari A. Cranmer, Director of Admissions. A video is available. E-mail: *admissions@ben.edu* Web: *www.ben.edu*

BLACKBURN COLLEGE

Carlinville, IL 62626 C-4
(217) 854-3231
(800) 233-3550; Fax: (217) 854-3713

Full-time: 249 men, 307 women	**Faculty:** 32
Part-time: 5 men, 10 women	**Ph.D.s:** 72%
Graduate: none	**Student/Faculty:** 17 to 1
Year: semesters, summer session	**Tuition:** $9420
Application Deadline: open	**Room & Board:** $4270
Freshman Class: 717 applied, 606 accepted, 230 enrolled	
ACT: 22	**COMPETITIVE**

Blackburn College, founded in 1837, is a private liberal arts institution affiliated with the Presbyterian Church (U.S.A.). The college is noted for its work program, which allows resident students to reduce their education costs and develop useful skills by managing and administering all essential campus services. The library contains 80,000 volumes, and subscribes to 400 periodicals. Computerized library services include interlibrary loans and database searching. Special learning facilities include a learning resource center and art gallery. The 80-acre campus is in a rural area 60 miles north of St. Louis. Including residence halls, there are 13 buildings.

Student Life: 85% of undergraduates are from Illinois. Others are from 12 states and 9 foreign countries. 85% are from public schools. 81% are white; 11% African American. 50% are Protestant; 45% Catholic. The average age of freshmen is 18; all undergraduates, 20. 30% do not continue beyond their first year.

Housing: 480 students can be accommodated in college housing, which includes single-sex and coed dormitories. In addition, there is a quiet residence hall. On-campus housing is guaranteed for all 4 years. 76% of students live on campus; of those, 60% remain on campus on weekends. All students may keep cars.

Activities: There are no fraternities or sororities. There are 15 groups on campus, including band, cheerleading, choir, chorale, chorus, drama, ethnic, international, jazz band, literary magazine, newspaper, religious, social, student government, and yearbook.

Sports: There are 6 intercollegiate sports for men and 6 for women, and 9 intramural sports for men and 9 for women. Facilities include a gym, a swimming pool, racquetball and tennis courts, weight and wrestling rooms, an outdoor track, and lighted playing fields.

Disabled Students: 65% of the campus is accessible. Wheelchair ramps, elevators, special parking, specially equipped rest rooms, special class scheduling, lowered drinking fountains, and lowered telephones are available.

Services: Counseling and information services are available, as is tutoring in most subjects.

Campus Safety and Security: Measures include self-defense education, escort service, lighted pathways/sidewalks, and student-run security through the work program.

Programs of Study: Blackburn confers the B.A. degree. Bachelor's degrees are awarded in BIOLOGICAL SCIENCE (biology/biological science), BUSINESS (accounting, business administration and management, international business management, and international economics), COMMUNICATIONS AND THE ARTS (American literature, art, English literature, music business management, music performance, and Spanish), COMPUTER AND PHYSICAL SCIENCE (chemistry, computer science, and mathematics), EDUCATION (art, elementary, English, music, physical, secondary, and social science), HEALTH PROFESSIONS (medical laboratory technology), SOCIAL SCIENCE (history, political science/government, psychology, and public administration). Life sciences and physical sciences are the strongest academically. Biology, education, and business are the largest.

Required: To graduate, students must complete 122 semester hours with a minimum 2.0 GPA. Requirements include interdisciplinary courses, intercultural courses in foreign languages or English, and foundation courses in writing, literature, math, philosophy or religion, analysis, fine arts, and phys ed. Work program participation is required of resident students. All students must complete their last year in residence.

Special: Blackburn offers supervised off-campus internships related to student majors, co-op programs, work-study programs, and a semester in Mexico, Great Britain, or Washington, D.C. A 3-2 engineering degree with Washington University in St. Louis is offered. Students may design their own majors. There is 1 national honor society.

Faculty/Classroom: 65% of faculty are male; 35%, female. All teach undergraduates. The average class size in an introductory lecture is 25; in a laboratory, 20; and in a regular course, 18.

Admissions: 85% of the 2001-2002 applicants were accepted. The ACT scores for the 2001-2002 freshman class were: 35% below 21, 27% between 21 and 23, 32% between 24 and 26, and 6% between 27 and 28. 38% of the current freshmen were in the top fifth of their class; 68% were in the top two fifths. 4 freshmen graduated first in their class.

Requirements: The SAT I or ACT is required. In addition, applicants should be graduates of an accredited secondary school or have a GED certificate. Blackburn recommends completion of 4 years of English, 2 to 4 of math, and 2 each of lab sciences, social sciences, and foreign language. A personal essay is required. Blackburn requires applicants to be in the upper 60% of their class. A GPA of 2.0 is required. AP and CLEP credits are accepted. Important factors in the admissions decision are leadership record, personality/intangible qualities, and recommendations by school officials. Applications are accepted on-line at the college's web site.

Procedure: Freshmen are admitted fall and spring. Entrance exams should be taken in the junior year or early in the senior year. Application deadlines are open.

Transfer: 37 transfer students enrolled in 2001-2002. Applicants must submit official transcripts of college-level work and be in good standing at the previous institution attended. Students from accredited colleges may receive credit for grades of C or better; those with associate degrees may transfer some D grades. Credit for work at unaccredited institutions may be accepted provisionally. 30 credits of 122 must be completed at Blackburn.

Visiting: There are regularly scheduled orientations for prospective students, including a campus tour and meetings with an admissions representative, the financial aid director, and a department head. There are guides for informal visits and visitors may sit in on classes and stay overnight. To schedule a visit, contact the Admissions Office.

Financial Aid: In 2001-2002, 94% of all students received some form of financial aid. 79% of freshmen and 81% of continuing students received need-based aid. The average freshman award was $7728. Of that total, scholarships or need-based grants averaged $6108 ($13,718 maximum); and loans averaged $1620 ($2625 maximum). All undergraduates work part time. Average annual earnings from campus work are $630. The average financial indebtedness of the 2001 graduate was $11,000. Blackburn is a member of CSS. The FAFSA is required. The fall application deadline is April 1.

International Students: There are 18 international students enrolled. The school actively recruits these students. They must score 525 on the written TOEFL or 200 on the electronic version.

Computers: There are PCs and Macs along with 2 HP workstations available in the computer center. All students may access the system every day during lab hours. There are no time limits and no fees.

Graduates: In 2001, 116 bachelor's degrees were awarded. The most popular majors were business (30%), education (27%), and biology (9%). In an average class, 45% graduate in 4 years, 47% in 5 years, and 48% in 6 years. Of the 2000 graduating class, 10% were enrolled in graduate school within 6 months of graduation and 90% were employed.

Admissions Contact: John C. Malin, Director of Admissions.
E-mail: *jmali@mail.blackburn.edu* Web: *www.blackburn.edu*

BRADLEY UNIVERSITY D-3

Peoria, IL 61625 (309) 677-1000
(800) 447-6460; Fax: (309) 677-2797

Full-time: 2180 men, 2555 women	**Faculty:** 328; IIA, -$
Part-time: 183 men, 249 women	**Ph.D.s:** 82%
Graduate: 477 men, 352 women	**Student/Faculty:** 14 to 1
Year: semesters, summer session	**Tuition:** $15,340
Application Deadline: open	**Room & Board:** $5630
Freshman Class: 4736 applied, 3609 accepted, 1110 enrolled	
SAT I Verbal/Math: 590/610	**ACT:** 25 **VERY COMPETITIVE**

Bradley University, founded in 1897, is an independent, privately endowed institution. Bradley offers a full range of baccalaureate and graduate-level programs, as well as personal attention, from a faculty dedicated to student learning. There are 5 undergraduate schools and 1 graduate school. In addition to regional accreditation, Bradley has baccalaureate program accreditation with AACSB, ABET, ACCE, ADA, NASAD, NASM, NCATE, and NLN. The library contains 508,000 volumes, 784,000 microform items, and 23,400 audiovisual forms/CDs, and subscribes to 1975 periodicals. Computerized library services include the card catalog, interlibrary loans, and database searching. Special learning facilities include a learning resource center, art gallery, radio station, and TV station. The 75-acre campus is in an urban area 160 miles southwest of Chicago. Including residence halls, there are 41 buildings.

Student Life: 84% of undergraduates are from Illinois. Others are from 41 states, 68 foreign countries, and Canada. 76% are from public schools. 82% are white. 36% are Catholic; 20%, Protestant; 12% claim no religious affiliation; 11% are Jewish. The average age of freshmen is 18; all undergraduates, 20. 13% do not continue beyond their first year.

Housing: 2300 students can be accommodated in college housing, which includes single-sex and coed dormitories, on-campus apartments, fraternity houses, and sorority houses. In addition, wellness floors are available in residence halls. On-campus housing is guaranteed for all 4 years. 70% of students live on campus; of those, 99% remain on campus on weekends. Upperclassmen may keep cars.

Activities: 36% of men belong to 19 national fraternities; 33% of women belong to 10 national sororities. There are 223 groups on campus, including art, band, cheerleading, chess, choir, chorale, chorus, computers, dance, drama, forensics, gay, honors, international, jazz band, literary magazine, musical theater, newspaper, orchestra, pep band, photography, political, professional, radio and TV, religious, social, social service, student government, symphony, and yearbook. Popular campus events include Founders Day, Greek Week, and Garret Week.

Sports: There are 6 intercollegiate sports for men and 7 for women, and 24 intramural sports for men and 24 for women. Facilities include tennis courts, a civic center, playing fields, a field house, outdoor lighted basketball courts, and a 6500-seat gym.

Disabled Students: 80% of the campus is accessible. Wheelchair ramps, elevators, special parking, specially equipped rest rooms, and lowered drinking fountains are available.

Services: Counseling and information services are available, as is tutoring in most subjects, including introductory subjects and selected higher-level classes. There is remedial math and writing.

Campus Safety and Security: Measures include 24-hour foot and vehicle patrol, escort service, informal discussions, and pamphlets/posters/films. There are emergency telephones, lighted pathways/sidewalks, engravers for marking personal property, and a medical escort service.

Programs of Study: Bradley confers B.A., B.S., B.F.A., B.M., B.S.C., B.S.C.E., B.S.E.E., B.S.I.E., B.S.M.E., B.S.M.F.E., B.S.M.F.E.T., B.S.N., and B.S.P.T. degrees. Master's degrees are also awarded. Bachelor's degrees are awarded in BIOLOGICAL SCIENCE (biochemistry, biology/biological science, and molecular biology), BUSINESS (accounting, banking and finance, business administration and management, insurance and risk management, international business management, management information systems, and marketing/retailing/merchandising),

COMMUNICATIONS AND THE ARTS (art history and appreciation, communications, dramatic arts, English, French, German, graphic design, multimedia, music, music performance, music theory and composition, photography, printmaking, sculpture, Spanish, and studio art), COMPUTER AND PHYSICAL SCIENCE (actuarial science, chemistry, computer science, geoscience, information sciences and systems, mathematics, and physics), EDUCATION (early childhood, elementary, foreign languages, home economics, music, secondary, and special), ENGINEERING AND ENVIRONMENTAL DESIGN (civil engineering, construction engineering, electrical/electronics engineering, engineering physics, environmental science, industrial engineering, manufacturing engineering, manufacturing technology, and mechanical engineering), HEALTH PROFESSIONS (health science, medical technology, nursing, and physical therapy), SOCIAL SCIENCE (criminal justice, dietetics, economics, family/consumer studies, history, international studies, philosophy, political science/government, psychology, religion, social work, and sociology). Business, engineering, and natural sciences are the strongest academically. Communication, elementary education, and psychology are the largest.

Required: To graduate, the student must complete the school's basic skills and general education curriculum. Overall, the college requires 124 total credit hours, with 32 hours in the student's major and a minimum GPA of 2.0.

Special: Special academic programs include an honors program, co-op programs, internships, a Washington semester, work-study programs, study abroad in 12 countries, B.A.-B.S. degrees in most majors, dual majors, and leadership fellowships. There are 31 national honor societies, and a freshman honors program.

Faculty/Classroom: 68% of faculty are male; 32%, female. All both teach and do research. No introductory courses are taught by graduate students. The average class size in a laboratory is 14 and in a regular course, 20.

Admissions: 76% of the 2001-2002 applicants were accepted. The SAT I scores for the 2001-2002 freshman class were: Verbal--11% below 500, 39% between 500 and 599, 40% between 600 and 700, and 10% above 700; Math--10% below 500, 36% between 500 and 599, 42% between 600 and 700, and 12% above 700. The ACT scores were 8% below 21, 20% between 21 and 23, 32% between 24 and 26, 18% between 27 and 28, and 22% above 28. 56% of the current freshmen were in the top fifth of their class; 82% were in the top two fifths. There were 14 National Merit finalists. 57 freshmen graduated first in their class.

Requirements: The SAT I or ACT is required. A GPA of 2.5 is required. AP and CLEP credits are accepted. Important factors in the admissions decision are advanced placement or honor courses, extracurricular activities record, and evidence of special talent. Applications are accepted on-line.

Procedure: Freshmen are admitted to all sessions. Entrance exams should be taken in the spring of the junior year or the fall of the senior year. There is an early admissions plan. Application deadlines are open. The fall 2001 application fee was $35. Notification is sent on a rolling basis. 4% of all applicants are on a waiting list.

Transfer: 352 transfer students enrolled in 2001-2002. Transfer students must have a minimum GPA of 2.0. Those with fewer than 15 hours of college credit must submit their ACT or SAT I scores and a high school transcript. 30 credits of 124 must be completed at Bradley.

Visiting: There are regularly scheduled orientations for prospective students, including class visits, campus tours, admissions information, financial assistance seminars, lunch, and student and parent meetings. There are guides for informal visits and visitors may sit in on classes and stay overnight. To schedule a visit, contact the Office of Undergraduate Admissions.

Financial Aid: In 2001-2002, 92% of all freshmen and 84% of continuing students received some form of financial aid. 60% of freshmen and 55% of continuing students received need-based aid. The average freshman award was $13,415. Of that total, scholarships or need-based grants averaged $9094 ($14,500 maximum); loans averaged $2886 ($4125 maximum); and work contracts averaged $1435 ($1800 maximum). 26% of undergraduates work part time. Average annual earnings from campus work are $950. The average financial indebtedness of the 2001 graduate was $15,668. Bradley is a member of CSS. The FAFSA is required. The fall application deadline is March 1.

International Students: There are 96 international students enrolled. The school actively recruits these students. They must score 500 on the written TOEFL or 173 on the electronic version. The SAT I or ACT is Recommended.

Computers: The mainframe is a Control Data CYBER 930. There are about 2000 AT&T, Zenith, IBM, and Mac PCs available throughout the campus. All students may access the system 24 hours a day. There are no time limits and no fees.

Graduates: In 2001, 1090 bachelor's degrees were awarded. The most popular majors were communications (13%), elementary education (7%), and psychology (6%). In an average class, 49% graduate in 4 years, 66% in 5 years, and 67% in 6 years. 310 companies recruited on campus in 2000-2001. Of the 2000 graduating class, 17% were enrolled in graduate school within 6 months of graduation and 79% were employed.

Admissions Contact: Angela (Nickie) Roberson, Director of Admissions. A video is available. E-mail: *admissions@bradley.edu*
Web: *www.bradley.edu/admissions/*

CHICAGO STATE UNIVERSITY

Chicago, IL 60628 — **E-2**
(773) 995-2513
(800) 278-3011; Fax: (773) 995-3820

Full-time: 851 men, 2308 women	**Faculty:** 370; IIA, --$
Part-time: 487 men, 1494 women	**Ph.D.s:** 62%
Graduate: 580 men, 1359 women	**Student/Faculty:** 11 to 1
Year: semesters, summer session	**Tuition:** $3151 ($7735)
Application Deadline: November 15	**Room & Board:** $5700

Freshman Class: 1694 applied, 790 accepted, 432 enrolled
ACT: 17 — **COMPETITIVE+**

Chicago State University, founded in 1867, is a public commuter and residential institution controlled by the State of Illinois. It offers day and evening undergraduate programs through the Colleges of Arts and Sciences, Allied Health, Business Administration, Education, and Nursing. There are 5 undergraduate and 2 graduate schools. In addition to regional accreditation, Chicago State has baccalaureate program accreditation with ADA, CAHEA, NCATE, and NLN. The library contains 26,000 volumes and 388,028 microform items, and subscribes to 1734 periodicals. Computerized library services include the card catalog, interlibrary loans, and database searching. Special learning facilities include a learning resource center, art gallery, and radio station. The 161-acre campus is in an urban area 12 miles south of downtown Chicago. Including residence halls, there are 9 buildings.

Student Life: 98% of undergraduates are from Illinois. Others are from 7 foreign countries. 85% are from public schools. 84% are African American; 10% white. The average age of all undergraduates is 31.

Housing: 360 students can be accommodated in college housing, which includes coed dormitories. On-campus housing is available on a first-come, first-served basis. Alcohol is not permitted. All students may keep cars.

Activities: 12% of men and about 15% of women belong to 4 national fraternities and 4 national sororities. There are 17 groups on campus, including cheerleading, choir, drama, drill team, honors, jazz band, literary magazine, musical theater, newspaper, photography, professional, radio and TV, religious, social, student government, and yearbook. Popular campus events include Welcome Week activities, art exhibits, and Black Writers Conference.

Sports: There are 8 intercollegiate sports for men and 3 for women, and 4 intramural sports for men and 2 for women. Facilities include tennis courts, indoor/outdoor tracks, an Olympic-size swimming pool, weight rooms, basketball courts, and a fitness center.

Disabled Students: All of the campus is accessible. Wheelchair ramps, elevators, special parking, specially equipped rest rooms, lowered drinking fountains, and lowered telephones are available.

Services: Counseling and information services are available, as is tutoring in some subjects; including math, science, and accounting. There is remedial math, reading, and writing.

Campus Safety and Security: Measures include 24-hour foot and vehicle patrol, escort service, informal discussions, and pamphlets/posters/films. There are emergency telephones and lighted pathways/sidewalks.

Programs of Study: Chicago State confers B.A., B.S., and B.S.Ed. Degrees. Master's degrees are also awarded. Bachelor's degrees are awarded in BIOLOGICAL SCIENCE (biochemistry and biology/biological science), BUSINESS (accounting, banking and finance, business administration and management, fashion merchandising, hospitality management services, hotel/motel and restaurant management, management science, marketing/retailing/merchandising, and recreation and leisure services), COMMUNICATIONS AND THE ARTS (art, broadcasting, English, music, Spanish, and speech/debate/rhetoric), COMPUTER AND PHYSICAL SCIENCE (chemistry, computer science, data processing, information sciences and systems, mathematics, and physics), EDUCATION (art, bilingual/bicultural, business, early childhood, elementary, industrial arts, music, physical, secondary, special, and vocational), ENGINEERING AND ENVIRONMENTAL DESIGN (industrial engineering technology), HEALTH PROFESSIONS (health, medical records administration/services, nursing, occupational therapy, predentistry, and premedicine), SOCIAL SCIENCE (African American studies, criminal justice, dietetics, economics, geography, history, political science/government, prelaw, psychology, and sociology). Business administration and computer science are the strongest academically and have the largest enrollments.

Required: All students must complete 120 credit hours, including 40 hours in the major, and maintain a 2.0 GPA. They must complete a 39-hour core curriculum as well as examinations in English, math, reading, and the U.S. Constitution.

Special: Chicago State offers a combined B.A.-B.S. degree, a board of governors degree program, a University Without Walls Program, and an

individualized curriculum program. Study abroad in Liberia and life experience credits are also provided. There is a freshman honors program.
Faculty/Classroom: 99% teach undergraduates. The average class size in an introductory lecture is 60; in a laboratory, 26; and in a regular course, 35.
Admissions: 47% of the 2001-2002 applicants were accepted. 1 freshman graduated first in the class in a recent year.
Requirements: The ACT is required, but scores need not be submitted if the applicant is over 23 years of age. Graduation from an accredited secondary school is required; a GED will be accepted. Minimum credits submitted should include 4 units of English, 3 of math, 3 of science, and 3 of social sciences. A GPA of 2.0 is required. AP and CLEP credits are accepted.
Procedure: Freshmen are admitted to all sessions. Applications should be filed by November 15 for fall entry and May 1 for summer entry, along with a $20 fee. Notification is sent on a rolling basis.
Transfer: Transfer students must have a minimum GPA of 2.0, and those with fewer than 30 hours must also meet freshman admission requirements. 30 credits of 120 must be completed at Chicago State.
Visiting: There are regularly scheduled orientations for prospective students. To schedule a visit, contact the Office of Admissions.
Financial Aid: In 2001-2002, 85% of all freshmen and 85% to 90% of continuing students received some form of financial aid. Average annual earnings from campus work are $2700. The FAFSA and the college's own financial statement are required. Check with the school for current deadlines.
International Students: They must score 525 on the written TOEFL or 195 on the electronic version and also take the college's own test.
Computers: The mainframes are a CDC CYBER 180 Model 130A and an IBM 4341. There are 40 Zenith PCs available. All students may access the system 8:30 A.M. to 10 P.M. Monday through Friday, 8:30 A.M. to 5 P.M. Saturday, and l p.m to 8 P.M. Sunday. There are no time limits. The fee is $5.
Admissions Contact: Addie Epps, Director of Admissions.
E-mail: *ug-admissions@csu.edu* Web: *www.csu.edu*

COLUMBIA COLLEGE CHICAGO — E-2
Chicago, IL 60605 (312) 663-1600, ext. 7133
(800) 838-1226; Fax: (312) 344-8024

Full-time: 3674 men, 3698 women — **Faculty:** 261
Part-time: 708 men, 831 women — **Ph.D.s:** 35%
Graduate: 161 men, 344 women — **Student/Faculty:** 28 to 1
Year: semesters, summer session — **Tuition:** $12,844
Application Deadline: August 15 — **Room & Board:** $9219
Freshman Class: 2831 applied, 2548 accepted, 1523 enrolled
ACT: 19 — **LESS COMPETITIVE**

Columbia College Chicago, founded in 1890, is a private liberal arts institution with special emphasis on educating students for creative occupations in the visual, performing, and media and commununication arts. There are 3 undergraduate schools and 1 graduate school. The library contains 205,426 volumes, 128,615 microform items, and 13,772 audiovisual forms/CDs, and subscribes to 1204 periodicals. Computerized library services include the card catalog, interlibrary loans, and database searching. Special learning facilities include a learning resource center, art gallery, radio station, TV station, and contemporary photography museum. The campus is in an urban area in Chicago. Including residence halls, there are 15 buildings.
Student Life: 75% of undergraduates are from Illinois. Others are from 49 states, 51 foreign countries, and Canada. 80% are from public schools. 58% are white; 20%, African American; 11%, Hispanic. The average age of freshmen is 19; all undergraduates, 23.
Housing: 350 students can be accommodated in college housing, which includes coed dormitories. On-campus housing is available on a first-come, first-served basis. Priority is given to out-of-town students. 97% of students commute. Alcohol is not permitted. All students may keep cars.
Activities: There are no fraternities or sororities. There are 27 groups on campus, including art, chorus, computers, dance, drama, ethnic, film, gay, international, jazz band, literary magazine, musical theater, newspaper, photography, political, professional, radio and TV, religious, social service, and student government. Popular campus events include African Heritage, Dr. Martin Luther King Jr.'s Birthday, and Women in the Arts.
Disabled Students: 95% of the campus is accessible. Wheelchair ramps, elevators, specially equipped rest rooms, special class scheduling, and lowered telephones are available.
Services: Counseling and information services are available, as is tutoring in some subjects. There is a reader service for the blind, and remedial math, reading, and writing.
Campus Safety and Security: Measures include self-defense education, escort service, informal discussions, and pamphlets/posters/films. There are emergency telephones and lighted pathways/sidewalks.
Programs of Study: Columbia confers B.A. and B.F.A. degrees. Master's degrees are also awarded. Bachelor's degrees are awarded in BUSINESS (marketing management), COMMUNICATIONS AND THE ARTS (advertising, art, audio technology, creative writing, dance, dramatic arts, film arts, journalism, multimedia, music, music business management, photography, and radio/television technology), EDUCATION (early childhood), ENGINEERING AND ENVIRONMENTAL DESIGN (computer graphics), SOCIAL SCIENCE (interpreter for the deaf). Art, film/video, and management are the largest.
Required: To graduate, all students must complete 124 semester hours of study with a minimum 2.0 GPA. The general studies distribution consists of 9 hours each of literature/humanities and science/math, 6 each of English, history, and social science, and 3 each of computer applications, oral communications, senior seminar, and electives; 1 intensive writing course also is required.
Special: Columbia offers study abroad in 2 countries, independent study, internships, work-study programs, student-designed majors, and a general studies degree.
Faculty/Classroom: 56% of faculty are male; 44%, female. All teach undergraduates. No introductory courses are taught by graduate students. The average class size in a regular course is 16.
Admissions: 90% of the 2001-2002 applicants were accepted.
Requirements: Applicants should be graduates of accredited secondary schools. The GED is also accepted. An interview is recommended. AP and CLEP credits are accepted. Applications are accepted on-line via the school's web site.
Procedure: Freshmen are admitted to all sessions. There is a deferred admissions plan. Applications should be filed by August 15 for fall entry, along with a $25 fee. Notification is sent on a rolling basis.
Transfer: 1351 transfer students enrolled in 2001-2002. Up to 88 credit hours are accepted with a grade of C or better; up to 62 credit hours from 2-year colleges with a grade of C or better are accepted. 36 credits of 124 must be completed at Columbia.
Visiting: There are regularly scheduled orientations for prospective students. There are guides for informal visits and visitors may sit in on classes. To schedule a visit, contact the Undergraduate Admissions Office.
Financial Aid: The FAFSA is required.
International Students: There are 253 international students enrolled. The school actively recruits these students. They must score 500 on the written TOEFL.
Computers: The mainframes are an IBM AS/400 and a P200. PCs are available for student use in the college's computer labs. There are no time limits and no fees.
Graduates: In 2001, 1216 bachelor's degrees were awarded. The most popular majors were film/video (12%), marketing (9%), and art and design (9%).
Admissions Contact: Director of Admissions.
E-mail: *admissions@popmail.colum.edu* Web: *www.colum.edu*

CONCORDIA UNIVERSITY, RIVER FOREST — E-1
River Forest, IL 60305 (708) 209-3100
(800) 285-2668; Fax: (708) 209-3473

Full-time: 390 men, 700 women — **Faculty:** 82; IIB, -$
Part-time: 40 men, 150 women — **Ph.D.s:** 69%
Graduate: 110 men, 500 women — **Student/Faculty:** 13 to 1
Year: semesters, summer session — **Tuition:** $15,100
Application Deadline: see profile — **Room & Board:** $4900
Freshman Class: n/av
SAT I: n/av — **ACT:** required
LESS COMPETITIVE

Concordia University, founded in 1864, is a private liberal arts institution affiliated with the Lutheran Church, Missouri Synod. Figures in the above capsule are approximate. There are 4 undergraduate schools and 1 graduate school. In addition to regional accreditation, Concordia University has baccalaureate program accreditation with NCATE and NLN. The library contains 154,920 volumes, 544,851 microform items, and 3894 audiovisual forms/CDs, and subscribes to 625 periodicals. Computerized library services include the card catalog, interlibrary loans, and database searching. Special learning facilities include a learning resource center, art gallery, natural history museum, radio station, TV station, and early childhood resource center, human performance lab, language lab, computer center, and weather station. The 40-acre campus is in a suburban area 10 miles west of downtown Chicago. Including residence halls, there are 23 buildings.
Student Life: 68% of undergraduates are from Illinois. Others are from 34 states, 15 foreign countries, and Canada. 65% are from public schools. 62% are white; 10% African American. 67% are Protestant; 18% Catholic; 12% Jewish. The average age of freshmen is 18; all undergraduates, 20. 37% do not continue beyond their first year; 60% remain to graduate.
Housing: 750 students can be accommodated in college housing, which includes single-sex and coed dormitories and married-student housing. On-campus housing is guaranteed for all 4 years. 65% of students live on campus; of those, 85% remain on campus on weekends. Alcohol is not permitted. All students may keep cars.

Activities: There are no fraternities or sororities. There are 50 groups on campus, including art, band, cheerleading, choir, chorale, chorus, computers, dance, drama, ethnic, honors, international, jazz band, literary magazine, musical theater, newspaper, pep band, photography, professional, radio and TV, religious, social, social service, student government, symphony, and yearbook. Popular campus events include Orientation Week, Campus Awareness Day, and Family Weekend.
Sports: There are 6 intercollegiate sports for men and 6 for women, and 12 intramural sports for men and 12 for women. Facilities include 2 gyms, an indoor swimming pool, weight training room, human performance lab, football field, tennis courts, baseball and softball fields, track, wrestling room, first aid training room, table tennis, billiards, and table games.
Disabled Students: Wheelchair ramps, elevators, special parking, specially equipped rest rooms, special class scheduling, lowered drinking fountains, and lowered telephones are available.
Services: Counseling and information services are available, as is tutoring in every subject. There is remedial math, reading, and writing.
Campus Safety and Security: Measures include 24-hour foot and vehicle patrol, self-defense education, escort service, and shuttle buses. There are informal discussions, pamphlets/posters/films, emergency telephones, and lighted pathways/sidewalks.
Programs of Study: Concordia University confers B.A., B.Mus., B.Mus.Ed., and B.S.N. degrees. Master's degrees are also awarded. Bachelor's degrees are awarded in BIOLOGICAL SCIENCE (biology/biological science), BUSINESS (accounting and business administration and management), COMMUNICATIONS AND THE ARTS (art, communications, English, and music), COMPUTER AND PHYSICAL SCIENCE (chemistry, computer programming, computer science, mathematics, natural sciences, and physical sciences), EDUCATION (computer, early childhood, elementary, middle school, music, physical, science, and secondary), HEALTH PROFESSIONS (nursing and premedicine), SOCIAL SCIENCE (geography, history, philosophy, physical fitness/movement, political science/government, prelaw, psychology, religion, social science, social work, sociology, and theological studies). Teacher education, music, and computer science are the strongest academically. Teacher education, nursing, and business are the largest.
Required: All students are required to take 2 years of liberal arts, including humanities, English, science, religion, and social science, and 5 quarter hours of phys ed. A 2.0 to 2.25 GPA and a total of 128 to 180 quarter hours are required.
Special: Cross-registration is possible with Dominican University and the Chicago Consortium of Colleges. Concordia also offers internships for liberal arts majors in the Chicago area, study abroad in England, and pass/fail options. There are 3 national honor societies, including Phi Beta Kappa, and a freshman honors program.
Faculty/Classroom: 52% of faculty are male; 48%, female. 94% teach undergraduates, 31% do research, and 31% do both. No introductory courses are taught by graduate students. The average class size in an introductory lecture is 20; in a laboratory, 18; and in a regular course, 25.
Admissions: 7 freshmen graduated first in their class in a recent year.
Requirements: The ACT is required. In addition, applicants should have 15 units of credit, with 11 units in college preparatory courses, including English, math, lab science, and social studies. A letter of recommendation is required, as is a minimum GPA of 2.0 in the college preparatory subjects and a ranking in the top half of their graduating class. Concordia University requires applicants to be in the upper 50% of their class. A GPA of 2.0 is required. AP and CLEP credits are accepted. Important factors in the admissions decision are advanced placement or honor courses, recommendations by school officials, and leadership record. Applications are accepted on-line at the college's web site.
Procedure: Freshmen are admitted to all sessions. Entrance exams should be taken in the spring of the junior year or fall of the senior year. Check with the school for current application deadlines.
Transfer: 94 transfer students enrolled in a recent year. A cumulative GPA of 2.0 or higher at all previous colleges plus letter of recommendation are required. 48 credits of 128 must be completed at Concordia University.
Visiting: There are regularly scheduled orientations for prospective students, consisting of daily planned activities during orientation in the first week of the fall quarter. There are guides for informal visits and visitors may sit in on classes and stay overnight. To schedule a visit, contact the Office of Admission at (708) 209-3100.
Financial Aid: In a recent year, 93% of all freshmen and 87% of continuing students received some form of financial aid. 85% of freshmen and 67% of continuing students received need-based aid. The average freshman award was $12,000. Of that total, scholarships or need-based grants averaged $6300 ($7500 maximum); loans averaged $2625 ($3500 maximum); and work contracts averaged $1200 ($1500 maximum). 35% of undergraduates work part time. Average annual earnings from campus work are $1000. The average financial indebtedness of a graduate in a recent year was $12,000. Concordia University is a member of CSS. The FAFSA, the college's own financial statement and the student and parent 1040 U.S. tax forms are required. Check with school for curret deadlines.
International Students: There were 16 international students enrolled in a recent year. They must score 525 on the written TOEFL or take the MELAB, or successfully complete Level 109 at an ELS language center, and also take the SAT I or the ACT.
Computers: The mainframes are a 3 DEC VAX 6440s, and 1 DEC VAX 6620. There are 20 Macs and 55 PCs. Computers are available in the computer center, the PC lab, and the library. All students may access the system 24 hours per day. There are no time limits and no fees.
Graduates: In a recent year, 241 bachelor's degrees were awarded. The most popular majors were education (35%), nursing (22%), and psychology (6%). In an average class, 67% graduate in 6 years. 40 companies recruited on campus in a recent year. Of the 2000 graduating class, 12% were enrolled in graduate school within 6 months of graduation and 80% were employed.
Admissions Contact: E-mail: *crfadmis@curf.edu*
Web: *www.curf.edu*

DEPAUL UNIVERSITY — E-2
Chicago, IL 60604 — (312) 362-8300
(800) 4-DEPAUL; Fax: (312) 362-5749

Full-time: 4020 men, 5456 women	**Faculty:** 544; I, -$
Part-time: 1330 men, 2214 women	**Ph.D.s:** 73%
Graduate: 4368 men, 3975 women	**Student/Faculty:** 17 to 1
Year: quarters, summer session	**Tuition:** $16,630
Application Deadline: February 1	**Room & Board:** $6960
Freshman Class: 8452 applied, 6113 accepted, 2051 enrolled	
SAT I Verbal/Math: 560/550	**ACT:** 23 **VERY COMPETITIVE**

DePaul University, founded by the Vincentian Order in 1898, is a private Catholic institution with 2 main campuses: the Lincoln Park Campus houses undergraduate programs in liberal arts and sciences, education, theater, and music, and the Loop Campus offers programs in commerce, law, and computer science, telecommunications, and information systems (CTI). There are also 6 suburban campuses. There are 8 undergraduate and 9 graduate schools. In addition to regional accreditation, DePaul has baccalaureate program accreditation with AACSB, NASM, NCATE, and NLN. The 8 libraries contain 1,389,859 volumes, 1,335,256 microform items, and 96,669 audiovisual forms/CDs, and subscribe to 14,585 periodicals. Computerized library services include the card catalog, interlibrary loans, and database searching. Special learning facilities include a learning resource center, art gallery, radio station, a performing arts center, a recording studio, and a marketing research center. The 36-acre campus is in an urban area in Chicago. Including residence halls, there are 39 buildings.
Student Life: 77% of undergraduates are from Illinois. Others are from 50 states, 74 foreign countries, and Canada. 68% are from public schools. 58% are white; 13%, Hispanic; 12%, African American; 10%, Asian American. 33% are Catholic; 12% claim no religious affiliation. The average age of freshmen is 18; all undergraduates, 21.
Housing: 2600 students can be accommodated in college housing, which includes coed dormitories and on-campus apartments. In addition, there are honors houses, limited off-campus apartments, and a condominium complex for upperclassmen. On-campus housing is available on a first-come, first-served basis and on a lottery system for upperclassmen. Priority is given to out-of-town students. 75% of students commute. All students may keep cars.
Activities: 3% of men belong to 9 local fraternities; 3% of women belong to 9 local sororities. There are 140 groups on campus, including cheerleading, choir, chorale, chorus, computers, dance, drama, drill team, ethnic, gay, honors, international, jazz band, marching band, musical theater, opera, pep band, political, professional, radio and TV, religious, social, social service, student government, symphony, and yearbook. Popular campus events include Hispanic Awareness Month, Women's History Month, and Annual Spring Concert (FEST).
Sports: There are 6 intercollegiate sports for men and 7 for women, and 10 intramural sports for men and 8 for women. Facilities include 2 gyms seating 5,308, soccer and softball fields, and a 120,000-square-foot fitness and recreation center with a 4-court gym, a 4-lane track, a 6-lane pool, racquetball courts, a weight and fitness area, a spin studio, and a wellness suite.
Disabled Students: 95% of the campus is accessible. Wheelchair ramps, elevators, special parking, specially equipped rest rooms, lowered drinking fountains, lowered telephones, and a disabled student services department are available.
Services: Counseling and information services are available, as is tutoring in most subjects. There is a reader service for the blind, remedial math, reading, writing, a writing center, a productive learning strategies program, and a student development center.
Campus Safety and Security: Measures include 24-hour foot and vehicle patrol, self-defense education, escort service, and shuttle buses. There are informal discussions, pamphlets/posters/films, emergency telephones, lighted pathways/sidewalks, and a crime prevention office.
Programs of Study: DePaul confers B.A., B.S., B.F.A, B.M., and B.S.C. degrees. Master's and doctoral degrees are also awarded. Bache-

lor's degrees are awarded in BIOLOGICAL SCIENCE (biology/biological science), BUSINESS (accounting, banking and finance, business administration and management, business economics, and marketing/retailing/merchandising), COMMUNICATIONS AND THE ARTS (applied music, art, communications, comparative literature, dramatic arts, English, fine arts, French, German, Italian, jazz, music, music business management, Spanish, and theater design), COMPUTER AND PHYSICAL SCIENCE (chemistry, computer science, information sciences and systems, mathematics, and physics), EDUCATION (early childhood, elementary, foreign languages, music, physical, and secondary), ENGINEERING AND ENVIRONMENTAL DESIGN (environmental science), HEALTH PROFESSIONS (medical laboratory technology), SOCIAL SCIENCE (American studies, economics, geography, history, international studies, Judaic studies, Latin American studies, philosophy, political science/government, psychology, religion, social science, social studies, sociology, urban studies, and women's studies). Commerce, liberal arts and science, and computer science are the largest.

Required: All students must complete general education requirements, including 4 courses in behavioral and social sciences, 3 each in natural sciences and math, 2 each in English composition, world civilization, and philosophy and religion, and 1 each in art, music, and literature. A total of 192 quarter hour credits, including a minimum of 52 in the student's major, and a minimum GPA of 2.0 are required to graduate.

Special: A co-op program in Jewish studies is offered with Spertus College of Judaica. Numerous internships in communications, commerce, computer science, and social sciences are possible. Study abroad is offered in 11 countries, and in a West European Seminar in Comparative Business Practices. Accelerated degree programs, dual majors, a certificate program in acting and costume construction, pass/fail options, and concentrations within the theater major, including acting, costume design, general theater studies, lighting design, playwriting, production theater management, and theater technology, are available. The School for New Learning provides evening and weekend degree programs for adult learners, with credit given for life and work experience. There are 21 national honor societies, a freshman honors program, and 29 departmental honors programs.

Faculty/Classroom: 56% of faculty are male; 44%, female. 36% teach undergraduates. No introductory courses are taught by graduate students. The average class size in an introductory lecture is 18; in a laboratory, 18; and in a regular course, 16.

Admissions: 72% of the 2001-2002 applicants were accepted. The SAT I scores for the 2001-2002 freshman class were: Verbal--22% below 500, 45% between 500 and 599, 29% between 600 and 700, and 4% above 700; Math--27% below 500, 46% between 500 and 599, 24% between 600 and 700, and 3% above 700. The ACT scores were 24% below 21, 30% between 21 and 23, 26% between 24 and 26, 12% between 27 and 28, and 9% above 28. 36% of the current freshmen were in the top fifth of their class; 68% were in the top two fifths. 18 freshmen graduated first in their class.

Requirements: The SAT I or ACT is required. In addition, applicants should have completed 16 Carnegie units or submit the GED. A portfolio is required for theater majors, and an audition for acting and music majors. DePaul requires applicants to be in the upper 50% of their class. A GPA of 2.5 is required. AP and CLEP credits are accepted. Important factors in the admissions decision are advanced placement or honor courses, leadership record, and personality/intangible qualities.

Procedure: Freshmen are admitted to all sessions. Entrance exams should be taken by the spring of the junior year. There are early admissions and deferred admissions plans. Applications should be filed by February 1 for fall entry, December 1 for winter entry, and February 1 for spring entry. The fall 2001 application fee was $35. Notification of early decision is sent January 1; regular decision, on a rolling basis.

Transfer: 1313 transfer students enrolled in 2001-2002. A 2.0 GPA is required for most programs; a 2.5 in commerce. Applicants with fewer than 30 semester hours or 44 quarter hours should submit high school transcripts and SAT I or ACT scores. An audition is required for music and theater majors. 45 credits of 192 must be completed at DePaul.

Visiting: There are regularly scheduled orientations for prospective students, including a 2-day program offered throughout the summer that provides academic advising, assessment testing, and registration, in addition to information on social activities and residence life. There are guides for informal visits and visitors may sit in on classes and stay overnight. To schedule a visit, contact the Admissions Office.

Financial Aid: DePaul is a member of CSS. The FAFSA is required. The fall application deadline is as soon after January 1 as possible.

International Students: They must score 550 on the written TOEFL or 215 on the electronic version and also take the SAT I or the ACT.

Computers: The mainframe is an IBM system/390 Multiprize 2000. There are also 200 mainframe terminals and more than 600 PCs available. All students may access the system 14 hours each day or 24 hours a day by modem. There are no time limits and no fees. It is strongly recommended that all students have personal computers.

Graduates: In a recent year, 1686 bachelor's degrees were awarded. The most popular majors were business/marketing (27%), liberal arts (18%), and computer and information sciences (12%). In an average class, 57% graduate in 5 years, and 57% in 6 years. 100 companies recruited on campus in 2000-2001.

Admissions Contact: Raymond Kennelly, Dean of Admissions.
E-mail: *admitdpu@depaul.edu* Web: *www.depaul.edu*

DEVRY UNIVERSITY/ADDISON (DUPAGE COUNTY) E-2
Addison, IL 60101-6106 (630) 953-1300
(800) 346-5420; Fax: (630) 953-1236

Full-time: 1822 men, 484 women	**Faculty:** 67
Part-time: 900 men, 337 women	**Ph.D.s:** n/av
Graduate: none	**Student/Faculty:** 34 to 1
Year: semesters, summer session	**Tuition:** $8805
Application Deadline: open	**Room & Board:** n/app
Freshman Class: 1181 applied, 1038 accepted, 638 enrolled	
SAT I or ACT: recommended	**LESS COMPETITIVE**

The DeVry University/Addison (DuPage County), formerly DeVry Institute of Technology, a private institution, opened in 1982; there are 22 other DeVry schools in the United States and Canada that are owned by DeVry University, Inc. The school offers hands-on technology-based programs in electronics, business administration, telecommunications management, computer information systems, technical management, information technology, and computer engineering technology. In addition to regional accreditation, DeVry has baccalaureate program accreditation with ABET. The library contains 16,606 volumes and 676 audiovisual forms/CDs, and subscribes to 109 periodicals. Computerized library services include the card catalog, interlibrary loans, and database searching. Special learning facilities include a learning resource center and electronics and other labs. The 15-acre campus is in a suburban area 20 miles west of Chicago. There is 1 building.

Student Life: 94% of undergraduates are from Illinois. Others are from 26 states and 30 foreign countries. 60% are white; 16%, Asian American; 10%, African American. The average age of all undergraduates is 26. 54% do not continue beyond their first year.

Housing: There are no residence halls. Housing referrals can be obtained through the Student Housing Office. All students commute. Alcohol is not permitted. All students may keep cars.

Activities: There are no fraternities or sororities. There are 11 groups on campus, including computers, ethnic, honors, international, literary magazine, newspaper, professional, religious, and social service. Popular campus events include Summer Fest, Casino Night, and Santa Day.

Sports: There are 5 intramural sports for men and 5 for women. Facilities include a weight room, a gym, an indoor and outdoor track, baseball diamonds, and an outdoor pool, all available not far from DeVry.

Disabled Students: 90% of the campus is accessible. Wheelchair ramps, elevators, special parking, specially equipped rest rooms, and lowered drinking fountains are available.

Services: Counseling and information services are available, as is tutoring in every subject.

Campus Safety and Security: Measures include lighted pathways/sidewalks. During business hours, the campus is patrolled by student assistants. An alarm system is in operation during other hours.

Programs of Study: DeVry confers the B.S. degree. Associate degrees are also awarded. Bachelor's degrees are awarded in BUSINESS (business administration and management), COMMUNICATIONS AND THE ARTS (telecommunications), COMPUTER AND PHYSICAL SCIENCE (information sciences and systems), ENGINEERING AND ENVIRONMENTAL DESIGN (computer engineering, electrical/electronics engineering technology, and technological management). Computer information systems, telecommunications, and electronics engineering technology are the largest.

Required: To graduate, students must achieve a cumulative GPA of at least 2.0 and satisfactorily complete all curriculum requirements. Course requirements vary according to program. All first-semester students take courses in business organization, computer applications, algebra, psychology, and student success strategies.

Special: Nondegree study, co-op programs, an accelerated degree program, and evening and weekend classes are available. There are 3 national honor societies and 3 departmental honors programs.

Faculty/Classroom: All teach undergraduates. The average class size in an introductory lecture is 30; in a laboratory, 30; and in a regular course, 30.

Admissions: 88% of the 2001-2002 applicants were accepted.

Requirements: The SAT I or ACT is recommended. Admissions requirements include graduation from a secondary school; the GED is also accepted. Applicants from accredited postsecondary institutions must pass the DeVry entrance exam or present satisfactory ACT or SAT I scores. An interview is required. Applications are accepted on-line at Embark.com. CLEP credit is accepted.

Procedure: Freshmen are admitted fall, spring, and summer. There is a deferred admissions plan. Application deadlines are open. The application fee is $50. Notification is sent on a rolling basis.

Transfer: 60 transfer students enrolled in 2001-2002. Applicants must present passing grades in all completed college course work, demonstrate language skills proficiency with at least 24 completed semester hours, and evidence math proficiency by appropriate college-level credits. 35% of 48 to 154 credits must be completed at DeVry.
Visiting: There are regularly scheduled orientations for prospective students. There are guides for informal visits and visitors may sit in on classes. To schedule a visit, contact Billy Bungert, New Student Coordinator at (708) 953-0610.
Financial Aid: In a recent year, 31% of all freshmen and 73% of continuing students received some form of financial aid. 19% of freshmen and 41% of continuing students received need-based aid. The average freshman award was $5777. Of that total, scholarships or need-based grants averaged $2360 and loans averaged $3417. 3% of undergraduates work part time. Average annual earnings from campus work are $3724. DeVry is a member of CSS. The FAFSA is required. The fall application deadline is November 1.
International Students: There are 75 international students enrolled. They must score 500 on the written TOEFL or 173 on the electronic version or take the MELAB, the Comprehensive English Language Test, or the college's own test.
Computers: The mainframe is an IBM 3081K. Lab facilities include PCs in stand-alone and network configuration, with access to the mainframe. LANs provide access to a wide range of applications software. Hard copy from the mainframe is provided through a local minicomputer and medium- and high-speed printers. Students in computer information systems program may access the system during published lab hours. There are no time limits and no fees.
Graduates: In 2001, 647 bachelor's degrees were awarded. The most popular majors were business (59%), computer information systems (31%), and electronics engineering technology (11%). In an average class, 11% graduate in 3 years, 19% in 4 years, 1% in 5 years, and 1% in 6 years. 55 companies recruited on campus in 2000-2001.
Admissions Contact: Sandra Stack, Director of Admissions.
Web: *www.dpg.devry.edu*

DEVRY UNIVERSITY/CHICAGO E-2
Chicago, IL 60618-5994 (773) 929-6550
(800) 383-3879; Fax: (773) 929-8093

Full-time: 1714 men, 888 women	**Faculty:** 84
Part-time: 848 men, 561 women	**Ph.D.s:** n/av
Graduate: none	**Student/Faculty:** 31 to 1
Year: semesters, summer session	**Tuition:** $8805
Application Deadline: open	**Room & Board:** n/app

Freshman Class: 1360 applied, 1107 accepted, 818 enrolled
SAT I or ACT: recommended **LESS COMPETITIVE**

DeVry University/Chicago, formerly DeVry Institute of Technology, founded in 1931, is a private institution offering hands-on programs in electronics, computer engineering technology, information technology, business administration, telecommunications, technical management, and computer information systems. The school is a part of DeVry University, Inc., an organization administering the 23 DeVry schools throughout the United States and Canada. In addition to regional accreditation, DeVry has baccalaureate program accreditation with ABET. The library contains 17,086 volumes and 1047 audiovisual forms/CDs, and subscribes to 79 periodicals. Computerized library services include the card catalog, interlibrary loans, and database searching. Special learning facilities include a learning resource center and electronics and other labs. The 14-acre campus is in an urban area in northwest Chicago. There is 1 building.
Student Life: 97% of undergraduates are from Illinois. Others are from 20 states and 36 foreign countries. 33% are African American; 25%, Hispanic; 23%, white; 14%, Asian American. The average age of all undergraduates is 26. 55% do not continue beyond their first year.
Housing: There are no residence halls. Housing referrals may be obtained through the Student Housing Office. All students commute. Alcohol is not permitted. All students may keep cars.
Activities: There are no fraternities or sororities. There are 16 groups on campus, including computers, ethnic, honors, international, newspaper, professional, and religious. Popular campus events include Megaflicks and Freaky Photos, Taste of Chicago, and Welcome Week.
Sports: There is no sports program at DeVry.
Disabled Students: 70% of the campus is accessible. Elevators, special parking, specially equipped rest rooms, lowered drinking fountains, and lowered telephones are available.
Services: Counseling and information services are available, as is tutoring in every subject.
Campus Safety and Security: Measures include 24-hour foot and vehicle patrol and lighted pathways/sidewalks. Security guards are on duty Monday through Friday 7 A.M. to midnight. There is 24-hour security on weekends and holidays.
Programs of Study: DeVry confers the B.S. degree. Associate degrees are also awarded. Bachelor's degrees are awarded in BUSINESS (business administration and management), COMMUNICATIONS AND THE ARTS (telecommunications), COMPUTER AND PHYSICAL SCIENCE (information sciences and systems), ENGINEERING AND ENVIRONMENTAL DESIGN (computer engineering, electrical/electronics engineering technology, and technological management). Computer information systems and electronics engineering technology are the largest.
Required: To graduate, students must achieve a cumulative GPA of at least 2.0 and satisfactorily complete all curriculum requirements. Course requirements vary according to program. All first-semester students take courses in business organization, computer applications, algebra, psychology, and student success strategies.
Special: Accelerated degrees, co-op programs, evening and weekend classes, and nondegree study are possible. There are 3 national honor societies and 3 departmental honors programs.
Faculty/Classroom: All teach undergraduates. The average class size in an introductory lecture is 30; in a laboratory, 30; and in a regular course, 30.
Admissions: 81% of the 2001-2002 applicants were accepted.
Requirements: The SAT I or ACT is recommended. Admission requirements include graduation from a secondary school; the GED is also accepted. Applicants must pass the DeVry entrance exam or present satisfactory ACT or SAT I scores. An interview is required. Applications are accepted on-line at Embark.com. CLEP credit is accepted.
Procedure: Freshmen are admitted fall, spring, and summer. There is a deferred admissions plan. Application deadlines are open. The application fee is $50. Notification is sent on a rolling basis.
Transfer: 8 transfer students enrolled in 2001-2002. Applicants must present passing grades in all completed college course work, demonstrate language skills proficiency with at least 24 completed semester hours, and evidence math proficiency by appropriate college-level credits. 35% of 48 to 154 credits must be completed at DeVry.
Visiting: There are regularly scheduled orientations for prospective students. There are guides for informal visits and visitors may sit in on classes. To schedule a visit, contact Marcia Curtis, Enrollment Services Coordinator at (773) 929-8500.
Financial Aid: In 2001-2002, 31% of all freshmen and 82% of continuing students received some form of financial aid. 27% of freshmen and 64% of continuing students received need-based aid. The average freshman award was $6531. 3% of undergraduates work part time. Average annual earnings from campus work are $7200. The FAFSA is required.
International Students: There are 100 international students enrolled. They must score 500 on the written TOEFL or 173 on the electronic version and also take the college's own entrance exam.
Computers: The mainframe is an IBM 3081. Lab facilities include PCs in stand-alone and network configuration, with access to the mainframe. LANs provide access to a wide range of applications software. Hard copy from the mainframe is provided through a local minicomputer and medium- and high-speed printers. Computer information systems students may access the system during lab hours. There are no fees.
Graduates: In 2001, 465 bachelor's degrees were awarded. The most popular majors were computer information systems (46%), business administration (29%), and electronics technology (25%). 115 companies recruited on campus in 2000-2001.
Admissions Contact: Christine Hierl, Director of Admissions.
Web: *www.chi.devry.edu*

DEVRY UNIVERSITY/TINLEY PARK E-2
Tinley Park, IL 60477 (708) 342-3300
(877) 305-8184; Fax: (708) 342-3120

Full-time: 891 men, 266 women	**Faculty:** 30
Part-time: 328 men, 177 women	**Ph.D.s:** n/av
Graduate: none	**Student/Faculty:** 39 to 1
Year: semesters, summer session	**Tuition:** $8805
Application Deadline: open	**Room & Board:** n/app

Freshman Class: 777 applied, 644 accepted, 520 enrolled
SAT I or ACT: recommended **LESS COMPETITIVE**

DeVry University/Tinley Park, DeVry Institute of Technology, founded in 2000, is 1 of 23 DeVry schools throughout the United States and Canada. The private institution offers career-oriented degree programs with hands-on training in various fields of business and technology. The library contains 9919 volumes and 306 audiovisual forms/CDs, and subscribes to 1107 periodicals. Computerized library services include the card catalog, interlibrary loans, and database searching. Special learning facilities include a learning resource center and electronics and other labs. .
Student Life: 93% of undergraduates are from Illinois. Others are from 13 states and 9 foreign countries. 48% are white; 32% African American. The average age of all undergraduates is 26. 44% do not continue beyond their first year.
Housing: There are no residence halls. Housing referrals can be obtained trough the Student Housing Office. All students commute. All students may keep cars.

Activities: There are no fraternities or sororities. There are 6 groups on campus, including computers, professional, and social. Popular campus events include Anniversary Celebration.

Sports: There is no sports program at DeVry.

Disabled Students: All of the campus is accessible. Wheelchair ramps, elevators, special parking, specially equipped rest rooms, special class scheduling, lowered drinking fountains, and lowered telephones are available.

Services: Counseling and information services are available, as is tutoring in every subject.

Campus Safety and Security: Measures include escort service, informal discussions, emergency telephones, and lighted pathways/sidewalks. There are 24-hour emergency telephone/alarm devices and 16-hour patrols by trained security personnel.

Programs of Study: DeVry confers the B.S. degree. Associate degrees are also awarded. Bachelor's degrees are awarded in BUSINESS (business administration and management), COMMUNICATIONS AND THE ARTS (telecommunications), COMPUTER AND PHYSICAL SCIENCE (computer programming and information sciences and systems), ENGINEERING AND ENVIRONMENTAL DESIGN (computer technology, electrical/electronics engineering technology, and technological management). Telecommunications management and computer information systems are the largest.

Required: To graduate, students must achieve a GPA of at least 2.0 and complete all curriculum requirements. Course requirements vary according to program. All first-semester students take courses in business organization, computer applications, algebra, psychology, and student success strategies.

Special: Accelerated degree programs are offered in business administration and telecommunications management. Co-op programs, nondegree study, and evening and weekend classes are possible.

Faculty/Classroom: All teach undergraduates. The average class size in an introductory lecture is 30; in a laboratory, 30; and in a regular course, 30.

Admissions: 83% of the 2001-2002 applicants were accepted.

Requirements: The SAT I or ACT is recommended. In addition, admissions requirements include graduation from a secondary school; the GED is also accepted. Applicants must pass the DeVry entrance exam or present satisfactory ACT or SAT I scores. An interview is required. CLEP credit is accepted. Applications are accepted on-line at *Embark.com*.

Procedure: Freshmen are admitted to all sessions. There is a deferred admissions plan. Application deadlines are open. The application fee is $50. Notification is sent on a rolling basis.

Transfer: 360 transfer students enrolled in 2001-2002. Applicants must submit official transcripts from all previous colleges attended indicating passing grades in all completed course work, demonstrate language skills proficiency in at least 24 completed semester hours, and present evidence of math proficiency by appropriate college-level credits. 35% of 48 to a54 credits must be completed at DeVry.

Visiting: There are regularly scheduled orientations for prospective students. There are guides for informal visits and visitors may sit in on classes. To schedule a visit, contact Jane Miritello, Assistant New Student Coordinator.

Financial Aid: In 2001-2002, 73% of all freshmen received some form of financial aid. 49% of freshmen received need-based aid. 8% of undergraduates work part time. Average annual earnings from campus work are $5000. The average financial indebtedness of the 2001 graduate was $10,344. The FAFSA is required.

International Students: There are 13 international students enrolled. They must score 500 on the written TOEFL or 173 on the electronic version and also take the college's own entrance exam.

Admissions Contact: Bruce Jones, Director of Admissions.
Web: *www.tp.devry.edu*

DOMINICAN UNIVERSITY

River Forest, IL 60305 **E-2**

(708) 524-6800
(800) 828-8475; Fax: (708) 524-5990

Full-time: 323 men, 634 women	**Faculty:** 81; IIA, --$
Part-time: 62 men, 170 women	**Ph.D.s:** 83%
Graduate: 310 men, 1034 women	**Student/Faculty:** 12 to 1
Year: semesters, summer session	**Tuition:** $15,700
Application Deadline: open	**Room & Board:** $5100
Freshman Class: 603 applied, 499 accepted, 223 enrolled	
ACT: 22	**COMPETITIVE**

Dominican University, founded in 1901, is an independent liberal arts institution affiliated with the Roman Catholic Church and sponsored by the Sinsinawa Dominicans. There are 2 undergraduate and 4 graduate schools. In addition to regional accreditation, Dominican University has baccalaureate program accreditation with ACBSP and ADA. The library contains 300,000 volumes, 47,000 microform items, and 4170 audiovisual forms/CDs, and subscribes to 5800 periodicals. Computerized library services include the card catalog, interlibrary loans, and database searching. Special learning facilities include an art gallery, a language lab, and a writing center. The 30-acre campus is in a suburban area 10 miles west of Chicago. Including residence halls, there are 8 buildings.

Student Life: 91% of undergraduates are from Illinois. Others are from 21 states and 15 foreign countries. 55% are from public schools. 73% are white; 14%, Hispanic. 67% are Catholic; 17%, Protestant; 10% claim no religious affiliation. The average age of freshmen is 19; all undergraduates, 23. 15% do not continue beyond their first year.

Housing: 320 students can be accommodated in college housing, which includes single-sex and coed dormitories. On-campus housing is guaranteed for all 4 years. 65% of students commute. All students may keep cars.

Activities: There are no fraternities or sororities. There are 30 groups on campus, including art, cheerleading, choir, computers, dance, drama, ethnic, honors, international, literary magazine, musical theater, newspaper, photography, political, professional, religious, social, social service, and student government. Popular campus events include Founders Day, Spring Fling, and Candle and Rose Ceremony.

Sports: There are 7 intercollegiate sports for men and 7 for women, and 5 intramural sports for men and 5 for women. Facilities include a gym, an indoor running track, an indoor swimming pool, a weight room, a training room, a fitness center, a dance room, racquetball courts, and soccer fields.

Disabled Students: All of the campus is accessible. Wheelchair ramps, elevators, special parking, specially equipped rest rooms, special class scheduling, and lowered drinking fountains are available.

Services: Counseling and information services are available, as is tutoring in most subjects.

Campus Safety and Security: Measures include 24-hour foot and vehicle patrol, escort service, shuttle buses, and informal discussions. There are pamphlets/posters/films, emergency telephones, lighted pathways/sidewalks, and door alarms.

Programs of Study: Dominican University confers B.A., B.S., and B.G.S. degrees. Master's degrees are also awarded. Bachelor's degrees are awarded in AGRICULTURE (natural resource management), BIOLOGICAL SCIENCE (biochemistry, biology/biological science, and nutrition), BUSINESS (accounting, business administration and management, fashion merchandising, and international business management), COMMUNICATIONS AND THE ARTS (art, communications, dramatic arts, English, fine arts, French, graphic design, Italian, journalism, music, performing arts, photography, Spanish, and technical and business writing), COMPUTER AND PHYSICAL SCIENCE (chemistry, computer science, information sciences and systems, and mathematics), ENGINEERING AND ENVIRONMENTAL DESIGN (computer graphics, engineering, and environmental science), SOCIAL SCIENCE (American studies, criminology, dietetics, fashion design and technology, food production/management/services, food science, history, international relations, philosophy, political science/government, psychology, religion, social science, and sociology). English, psychology, and sciences are the strongest academically. Business administration, psychology, and computer science are the largest.

Required: To graduate, students must complete 124 credit hours with a minimum GPA of 2.0. A total of 30 to 56 hours is required in the major. All students must demonstrate proficiency, through a placement exam or the completion of specified courses, in English composition, math, computer competency, and library skills. In addition, students must take 1 interdisciplinary seminar at each academic level and 1 course each in natural sciences, history, fine arts and literature, social sciences, theology, and philosophy. 1 course must meet the multicultural requirement.

Special: Co-op programs in medical technology and nursing with Rush University, cross-registration with Concordia University, internships, study abroad in 4 countries, and a Washington semester are offered. Student-designed majors and interdisciplinary majors, including computer information systems, math and computer science, environmental science, and environmental management, credit for prior learning, and pass/fail options are possible. There is an accelerated degree program in organizational leadership, and a joint B.A.-B.S. in engineering with the Illinios Institute of Technology. There are 11 national honor societies and a freshman honors program.

Faculty/Classroom: 46% of faculty are male; 54%, female. 83% teach undergraduates and all do research. No introductory courses are taught by graduate students. The average class size in an introductory lecture is 25; in a laboratory, 12; and in a regular course, 18.

Admissions: 83% of the 2001-2002 applicants were accepted. The ACT scores for the 2001-2002 freshman class were 33% below 21, 31% between 21 and 23, 20% between 24 and 26, 11% between 27 and 28, and 5% above 28. 40% of the current freshmen were in the top fifth of their class; 70% were in the top two fifths. There were 3 National Merit semifinalists. 2 freshmen graduated first in their class.

Requirements: The SAT I or ACT is required. In addition, graduation from an accredited secondary school or satisfactory scores on the GED are required for admission. The school requires 14 academic credits or 16 Carnegie units. High school courses should include English, math, foreign language, social science, and lab science. An essay is required and an interview is recommended. Dominican University requires applicants to be in the upper 50% of their class. A GPA of 2.5 is required. AP and CLEP credits are accepted. Important factors in the admissions decision are advanced placement or honor courses, recommendations by school officials, and leadership record.

Procedure: Freshmen are admitted to all sessions. Entrance exams should be taken in the junior year. There is a deferred admissions plan. Application deadlines are open. The application fee is $20. There is a rolling admissions plan.

Transfer: 161 transfer students enrolled in 2001-2002. Applicants must have a minimum of 12 credit hours with a GPA of 2.3. An interview is recommended. The high school record will be evaluated if the GPA is below 2.3 at the previous college. The last 34 credits of 124 must be completed at Dominican University.

Visiting: There are regularly scheduled orientations for prospective students, consisting of 5 visiting days and 2 Sunday open house programs per year. Students attend class, tour the campus, and hear faculty and student presentations on visiting days. There are guides for informal visits and visitors may sit in on classes and stay overnight. To schedule a visit, contact the Undergraduate Admissions Office at *domadmis@email.dom.edu*.

Financial Aid: In 2001-2002, 85% of all freshmen and 70% of continuing students received some form of financial aid. 65% of freshmen and 60% of continuing students received need-based aid. The average freshman award was $12,000. Of that total, scholarships or need-based grants averaged $8500 ($15,600 maximum); loans averaged $2000 ($2625 maximum); and work contracts averaged $1800 ($2200 maximum). 90% of undergraduates work part time. Average annual earnings from campus work are $1800. The average financial indebtedness of the 2001 graduate was $14,260. Dominican University is a member of CSS. The FAFSA and tax returns are required. The fall application deadline is open.

International Students: There are 28 international students enrolled. The school actively recruits these students. They must score 550 on the written TOEFL or 213 on the electronic version, or successfully complete ESL level 203.

Computers: The mainframe is a DEC VAX 8400. 105 PCs can access the mainframe, and PCs are available in computer labs and classrooms. All students may access the system 110 hours per week at the computer center or at all times with a modem. There are no time limits and no fees. It is strongly recommended that all students have a personal computer.

Graduates: In 2001, 235 bachelor's degrees were awarded. The most popular majors were business (26%), social sciences/history (18%), and psychology (8%). In an average class, 55% graduate in 4 years, 62% in 5 years, and 63% in 6 years. 4 companies recruited on campus in 2000-2001. Of the 2000 graduating class, 12% were enrolled in graduate school within 6 months of graduation and 95% were employed.

Admissions Contact: Hildegarde Schmidt, Dean of Admissions and Financial Aid. E-mail: *domadmis@email.dom.edu* Web: *www.dom.edu*

EASTERN ILLINOIS UNIVERSITY — E-4

Charleston, IL 61920-3099 — (217) 581-2223
(800) 252-5711; Fax: (217) 581-7060

Full-time: 3552 men, 4653 women	**Faculty:** 573; IIA, --$
Part-time: 336 men, 575 women	**Ph.D.s:** 74%
Graduate: 505 men, 910 women	**Student/Faculty:** 14 to 1
Year: semesters, summer session	**Tuition:** $4301 ($10,306)
Application Deadline: open	**Room & Board:** $5800
Freshman Class: 6133 applied, 4389 accepted, 1434 enrolled	
ACT: 22	**COMPETITIVE**

Eastern Illinois University, founded in 1895, is a state-assisted school offering undergraduate and graduate degrees in arts and sciences and professional studies. There are 4 undergraduate schools and 1 graduate school. In addition to regional accreditation, EIU has baccalaureate program accreditation with AACSB, ACEJMC, ADA, NASAD, NASM, NCATE, and NRPA. The library contains 925,656 volumes, 1,303,163 microform items, and 22,482 audiovisual forms/CDs, and subscribes to 3319 periodicals. Computerized library services include the card catalog, interlibrary loans, and database searching. Special learning facilities include a learning resource center, art gallery, radio station, and TV station. The 320-acre campus is in a small town 50 miles south of Champaign-Urbana. Including residence halls, there are 70 buildings.

Student Life: 98% of undergraduates are from Illinois. Others are from 37 states, 38 foreign countries, and Canada. 98% are from public schools. 89% are white. The average age of freshmen is 18; all undergraduates, 21. 19% do not continue beyond their first year; 69% remain to graduate.

Housing: 5463 students can be accommodated in college housing, which includes single-sex and coed dormitories, on-campus apartments, married-student housing, fraternity houses, and sorority houses. In addition, there are honors houses. On-campus housing is guaranteed for all 4 years. 57% of students commute. Upperclassmen may keep cars.

Activities: 20% of men belong to 13 national fraternities; 21% of women belong to 13 national sororities. There are 155 groups on campus, including art, band, cheerleading, choir, chorale, chorus, computers, dance, debate, drama, drill team, ethnic, forensics, gay, honors, international, jazz band, literary magazine, marching band, musical theater, newspaper, orchestra, pep band, political, professional, radio and TV, religious, social, social service, student government, symphony, and yearbook. Popular campus events include Family Weekend, Greek Week, and an arts festival.

Sports: There are 10 intercollegiate sports for men and 10 for women, and 21 intramural sports for men and 21 for women. Facilities include a swimming pool, a gym, a student recreation center, a track, tennis courts, racquetball courts, and a jogging trail.

Disabled Students: 70% of the campus is accessible. Wheelchair ramps, elevators, special parking, specially equipped rest rooms, special class scheduling, lowered drinking fountains, and lowered telephones are available.

Services: Counseling and information services are available, as is tutoring in most subjects. There is a reader service for the blind, and remedial math, reading, and writing. An academic assistance center advises freshmen and students with undeclared majors. Term paper clinics, study skills seminars, and stress management workshops are also available.

Campus Safety and Security: Measures include 24-hour foot and vehicle patrol, self-defense education, escort service, and shuttle buses. There are informal discussions, pamphlets/posters/films, emergency telephones, and lighted pathways/sidewalks.

Programs of Study: EIU confers B.A., B.S., B.M., B.S.Bus., and B.S.Ed. degrees. Master's degrees are also awarded. Bachelor's degrees are awarded in BIOLOGICAL SCIENCE (biology/biological science), BUSINESS (accounting, banking and finance, business administration and management, marketing/retailing/merchandising, and recreational facilities management), COMMUNICATIONS AND THE ARTS (art, communications, dramatic arts, English, journalism, languages, and music), COMPUTER AND PHYSICAL SCIENCE (chemistry, computer science, geology, information sciences and systems, mathematics, and physics), EDUCATION (early childhood, elementary, health, middle school, physical, secondary, social science, and special), ENGINEERING AND ENVIRONMENTAL DESIGN (engineering and industrial engineering technology), HEALTH PROFESSIONS (medical laboratory science and speech pathology/audiology), SOCIAL SCIENCE (African American studies, economics, family/consumer studies, geography, history, international studies, philosophy, political science/government, psychology, and sociology). Business and education are the strongest academically. Elementary education, family and consumer science, and management are the largest.

Required: A total of 120 credit hours, with a minimum of 40 hours in upper-division courses, must be completed for graduation. The minimum GPA required for graduation is 2.0 (2.5 in education). A core curriculum of 40 to 46 hours includes courses in language, quantitative reasoning and problem solving, scientific awareness, foreign languages, cultural experience, foundations of civilizations, human behavior, social interaction and well-being, the U.S. Constitution, and a senior seminar.

Special: EIU offers a co-op program in clinical laboratory science and an engineering co-op program with the University of Illinois at Champaign-Urbana. Internships, study abroad, dual majors, nondegree study, B.A.-B.S. degrees in athletic training and industrial technology, and pass/fail options are available. Credit for life experience may be granted through the Board of Trustees program and the Career Occupations program. There are 20 national honor societies, a freshman honors program, and 20 departmental honors programs.

Faculty/Classroom: 57% of faculty are male; 43%, female. Graduate students teach 22% of introductory courses. The average class size in an introductory lecture is 29; in a laboratory, 20; and in a regular course, 21.

Admissions: 72% of the 2001-2002 applicants were accepted. The ACT scores for the 2001-2002 freshman class were 48% below 21, 28% between 21 and 23, 18% between 24 and 26, 4% between 27 and 28, and 2% above 28. 26% of the current freshmen were in the top fifth of their class; 60% were in the top two fifths.

Requirements: The SAT I or ACT is required, with required minimum composite scores of 18 on the ACT or 860 on the SAT I for those students who rank in the upper 25% of their class, 19 on the ACT or 900 on the SAT I for those in the upper 50%, and 22 on the ACT or 1020 on the SAT I for those in the upper 75%. SAT II: Subject tests are also accepted. Applicants must be graduates of an accredited secondary school. The GED is accepted. 13 academic credits are required and should include 4 years of English and 3 years each of math, science, and social studies, including 1 year of U.S. history. EIU requires applicants to be in the upper 75% of their class. AP and CLEP credits are accepted. Applications are accepted on-line.

Procedure: Freshmen are admitted to all sessions. Entrance exams should be taken by spring of the junior year. There is an early admissions plan. Application deadlines are open. The application fee is $30. There is a rolling admissions plan.

Transfer: 938 transfer students enrolled in 2001-2002. Transfer students must have earned 30 credit hours with a minimum GPA of 2.0. An associate degree is recommended. 42 credits of 120 must be completed at EIU.

Visiting: There are regularly scheduled orientations for prospective students, including open houses, scheduled several times in the spring and fall, which provide an opportunity to meet with representatives of colleges and academic departments and student services personnel and go on student-led campus tours. There are guides for informal visits and visitors may sit in on classes. To schedule a visit, contact the Office of Orientation.

Financial Aid: 25% of undergraduates work part time. The FAFSA, parent and student income tax forms, and an institutional verification form are required. The fall priority deadline is April 15.

International Students: There were 91 international students enrolled in a recent year. The school actively recruits these students. They must score 500 on the written TOEFL or achieve a proficiency level of 9 from a U.S. ESL center.

Computers: The mainframe is an IBM 9121 model 260. There are also 893 IBM and Mac PCs available to students, of which 556 are networked. All students may access the system. There are no time limits and no fees.

Graduates: In 2001, 2175 bachelor's degrees were awarded. The most popular majors were elementary education (12%), the Board of Trustees program (10%), and speech and psychology (7%). In an average class, 31% graduate in 4 years, 61% in 5 years, and 68% in 6 years. 771 companies recruited on campus in 2000-2001.

Admissions Contact: Dale Wolf, Director of Admissions. A video is available. E-mail: *cdadmit@eiu.edu* Web: *http://www.eiu.edu*

EAST-WEST UNIVERSITY

Chicago, IL 60605 E-2
(312) 939-0111; Fax: (312) 939-0083

Full-time: 255 men, 320 women	**Faculty:** 11
Part-time: 5 men, 10 women	**Ph.D.s:** 8%
Graduate: none	**Student/Faculty:** 52 to 1
Year: quarters, summer session	**Tuition:** $9140
Application Deadline: see profile	**Room & Board:** n/app
Freshman Class: n/av	
SAT I or ACT: not required	**LESS COMPETITIVE**

East-West University, founded in 1978, is a private commuter institution offering undergraduate programs in the arts and sciences, business, computer science, and engineering. Figures given in the above capsule are approximate. The library contains 21,500 volumes and 8500 microform items, and subscribes to 95 periodicals. The campus is in an urban area of Chicago. There is one building.

Student Life: 85% of undergraduates are from Illinois. Others are from 1 state and 9 foreign countries. 97% are from public schools. 75% are African American; 13% Hispanic. The average age of freshmen is 19; all undergraduates, 20.

Housing: There are no residence halls. Alcohol is not permitted.

Activities: There are no fraternities or sororities. There are 3 groups on campus, including drama, international, and student government. Popular campus events include International Day, Mother's Day Banquet, and Black History Celebration.

Sports: There is no sports program at East-West.

Disabled Students: 50% of the campus is accessible. Elevators and specially equipped rest rooms are available.

Services: Counseling and information services are available, as is tutoring in most subjects. There is remedial math, reading, and writing.

Programs of Study: East-West confers B.A. and B.S. degrees. Associate degrees are also awarded. Bachelor's degrees are awarded in BUSINESS (business administration and management), COMMUNICATIONS AND THE ARTS (communications and English), COMPUTER AND PHYSICAL SCIENCE (computer science), ENGINEERING AND ENVIRONMENTAL DESIGN (electrical/electronics engineering technology), SOCIAL SCIENCE (behavioral science). Business administration is the largest.

Required: General education requirements vary according to the degree program. To graduate, students must complete at least 180 quarter hours, including 60 in a major field, with a minimum GPA of 2.0.

Special: East-West offers co-op programs in all majors.

Faculty/Classroom: All teach undergraduates. The average class size in an introductory lecture is 15; in a laboratory, 15; and in a regular course, 15.

Requirements: Applicants must be graduates of accredited secondary schools or have earned a GED. Placement exams are required in math and English. AP and CLEP credits are accepted.

Procedure: Freshmen are admitted to all sessions. Check with school for current application deadlines and fees.

Transfer: East-West accepts only courses with grades of C or better. 48 credits of 180 must be completed at East-West.

Visiting: There are regularly scheduled orientations for prospective students. There are guides for informal visits and visitors may sit in on classes.

Financial Aid: The CSS/Profile is required. Check with the school for current application deadlines.

International Students: The school actively recruits these students. They must take the college's own test, Applicants are encouraged but not required to submit TOEFL scores.

Computers: The mainframe is a Texas Instruments 930. There are 21 IBM PCs available for student use. . There are no time limits.

Admissions Contact: George Carbart, Director of Admissions. E-mail: *george@east-west.edu*

ELMHURST COLLEGE

Elmhurst, IL 60126-3296 E-2
(630) 617-3400
(800) 697-1871; Fax: (630) 617-5501

Full-time: 690 men, 1259 women	**Faculty:** 108; IIB, av$
Part-time: 176 men, 285 women	**Ph.D.s:** 90%
Graduate: 71 men, 59 women	**Student/Faculty:** 18 to 1
Year: 4-1-4, summer session	**Tuition:** $16,200
Application Deadline: April 1	**Room & Board:** $5550
Freshman Class: 1210 applied, 933 accepted, 321 enrolled	
ACT: 22	**COMPETITIVE**

Elmhurst College, founded in 1871, is a private liberal arts college affiliated with the United Church of Christ. In addition to regional accreditation, Elmhurst has baccalaureate program accreditation with NCATE and NLN. The library contains 225,000 volumes, 42,000 microform items, and 3350 audiovisual forms/CDs, and subscribes to 1300 periodicals. Computerized library services include the card catalog, interlibrary loans, and database searching. Special learning facilities include a learning resource center, art gallery, radio station, and a 16-track, 34-channel board recording studio, an electron microscopy lab, and an accelerator lab. The 38-acre campus is in a suburban area 15 miles west of Chicago. Including residence halls, there are 23 buildings.

Student Life: 91% of undergraduates are from Illinois. Others are from 27 states, 17 foreign countries, and Canada. 82% are from public schools. 75% are white. 41% are Catholic; 31% claim no religious affiliation; 13% Protestant; 10% Muslim, Greek Orthodox, Hindu, and Buddhist. The average age of freshmen is 18; all undergraduates, 26. 14% do not continue beyond their first year.

Housing: 745 students can be accommodated in college housing, which includes coed dormitories and off-campus apartments. In addition, there are honors houses. On-campus housing is guaranteed for all 4 years. 70% of students commute. All students may keep cars.

Activities: 5% of men belong to 5 national fraternities; 12% of women belong to 2 local and 3 national sororities. There are 90 groups on campus, including art, band, cheerleading, chess, choir, chorale, chorus, computers, dance, drama, ethnic, film, gay, honors, international, jazz band, literary magazine, musical theater, newspaper, orchestra, pep band, political, professional, radio and TV, religious, social, social service, student government, symphony, and yearbook. Popular campus events include Greek Games, Midwest Jazz Festival, and Spring Fling.

Sports: There are 8 intercollegiate sports for men and 8 for women, and 11 intramural sports for men and 11 for women. Facilities include a phys ed center, weight rooms, and courts for tennis, racquetball, and handball.

Disabled Students: 85% of the campus is accessible. Wheelchair ramps, elevators, special parking, specially equipped rest rooms, special class scheduling, lowered drinking fountains, and lowered telephones are available.

Services: Counseling and information services are available, as is tutoring in most subjects.

Campus Safety and Security: Measures include 24-hour foot and vehicle patrol, escort service, informal discussions, and pamphlets/posters/films. There are emergency telephones and lighted pathways/sidewalks.

Programs of Study: Elmhurst confers B.A., B.S., B.L.S., and B.Mus. degrees. Master's degrees are also awarded. Bachelor's degrees are awarded in BIOLOGICAL SCIENCE (biology/biological science), BUSINESS (accounting, banking and finance, business administration and management, international business management, marketing/retailing/merchandising, recreational facilities management, and transportation management), COMMUNICATIONS AND THE ARTS (art, communications, dramatic arts, English, French, German, music, music business management, and Spanish), COMPUTER AND PHYSICAL SCIENCE (chemistry, computer science, information sciences and systems, mathematics, and physics), EDUCATION (art, athletic training, drama, early childhood, elementary, mathematics, music, physical, secondary, and special), ENGINEERING AND ENVIRONMENTAL DESIGN (environmental science), HEALTH PROFESSIONS (nursing and speech pathology/audiology), SOCIAL SCIENCE (American studies, economics, geography, history, liberal arts/general studies, philosophy, political science/government, psychology, religion, sociology, and urban studies).

Biology, English, and education are the strongest academically. Business administration, nursing, and education-related programs are the largest.
Required: All students are required to take a minimum of 11 general education courses in the following 11 categories: writing and reasoning; Western culture; fine arts; literature; people, power and politics; the natural world; issues and inquiry in science and technology; human behavior; global society; the search for human values; and the Judeo-Christian heritage and religious faith. Students must maintain a 2.0 GPA and complete 128 semester hours. The total number of hours required for the major varies from 32 to 72.
Special: There are cooperative programs in all majors. The Center for Professional Excellence provides internships and mentoring experiences. Internships varying from 1 month to 1 term are available in approximately 20 major fields. Students may study abroad in 10 countries. Elmhurst also offers a Washington semester and a 3-2 engineering degree with the Illinois Institute of Technology, Washington University, and the Universities of Illinois and Southern California. There are accelerated degree programs in business administration and human services administration. Credit for life, military, and work experience, nondegree study and pass/fail options are possible. There are 15 national honor societies, a freshman honors program, and 22 departmental honors programs.
Faculty/Classroom: 56% of faculty are male; 44%, female. All both teach and do research. No introductory courses are taught by graduate students. The average class size in an introductory lecture is 19; in a laboratory, 15; and in a regular course, 16.
Admissions: 77% of the 2001-2002 applicants were accepted. The ACT scores for the 2001-2002 freshman class were: 32% below 21, 34% between 21 and 23, 19% between 24 and 26, 7% between 27 and 28, and 5% above 28. 35% of the current freshmen were in the top fifth of their class; 66% were in the top two fifths. 5 freshmen graduated first in their class in a recent year.
Requirements: The SAT I or ACT is required; the ACT is preferred. In addition, candidates for admission must have completed 16 academic units of credit including at least 3 in English and 2 each of math, social science, and natural science lab courses. 2 years of a foreign language are recommended with the ACT preferred. AP and CLEP credits are accepted. Important factors in the admissions decision are advanced placement or honor courses, leadership record, and extracurricular activities record. Applications are accepted on-line via CollegeNET and the college's web site.
Procedure: Freshmen are admitted fall and spring. Entrance exams should be taken by the spring of the senior year. There are early admissions and deferred admissions plans. Applications should be filed by April 1 for fall entry, January 15 for spring entry, and May 1 for summer entry. Notification is sent on a rolling basis. The fall 2001 applicatioin fee was $25.
Transfer: 258 transfer students enrolled in 2001-2002. Applicants must have a 2.4 GPA and be in good standing at the most recent college attended. A higher GPA is required for nursing, athletic training, and education. 32 credits of 128 must be completed at Elmhurst.
Visiting: There are regularly scheduled orientations for prospective students, including an admissions interview, a campus tour, and faculty meetings if desired. There are guides for informal visits and visitors may sit in on classes and stay overnight. To schedule a visit, contact The Office of Admission.
Financial Aid: In 2001-2002, 90% of all freshmen and 73% of continuing students received some form of financial aid. 77% of freshmen and 65% of continuing students received need-based aid. The average freshman award was $14,923. Of that total, scholarships or need-based grants averaged $10,783 ($17,000 maximum); loans averaged $4190 ($5000 maximum); and work contracts averaged $1131 ($1800 maximum). 63% of undergraduates work part time. Average annual earnings from campus work are $1147. The average financial indebtedness of the 2001 graduate was $14,100. Elmhurst is a member of CSS. The FAFSA and the college's own financial statement are required. The fall application deadline is April 15.
International Students: There were 28 international students enrolled in a recent year. The school actively recruits these students. They must score 525 on the written TOEFL or take the MELAB.
Computers: The mainframes are Dell Power Edge 4200, Unisys HS 6000, IBM 9370, AS400, 9402-EO2, Type 9309, and a Harris Nighthawk. Students may access networked systems via network connections on campus and modem. In addition, 200 PCs and 32 Macs are available for student use in multiple student labs. All students may access the system. Remote access is available 7 days a week, 24 hours a day. Labs are available 98 hours per week. There are no time limits and no fees.
Graduates: In 2001, 658 bachelor's degrees were awarded. The most popular majors were business administration (22%), elementary education (7%), and psychology (6%). In an average class, 1% graduate in 3 years, 53% in 4 years, 67% in 5 years, and 69% in 6 years. 50 companies recruited on campus in a recent year. Of a recent year's graduating class, 19% were enrolled in graduate school within 6 months of graduation and 95% were employed.
Admissions Contact: Andrew B. Sison, Director of Admission.
E-mail: *admit@elmhurst.edu* Web: *www.elmhurst.edu*

EUREKA COLLEGE

Eureka, IL 61530 — **D-3**
(309) 467-6350
(888) 4-EUREKA; Fax: (309) 467-6576

Full-time: 500 men and women	**Faculty:** 44
Part-time: 10 men and women	**Ph.D.s:** 85%
Graduate: none	**Student/Faculty:** 11 to 1
Year: terms, summer session	**Tuition:** $16,900
Application Deadline: open	**Room & Board:** $5300

Freshman Class: 800 applied, 578 accepted, 198 enrolled
ACT: 21 — **COMPETITIVE**

Eureka College, founded in 1855, is a small, private, liberal arts college affiliated with the Christian Church (Disciples of Christ). Figures in the above capsule are approximate. Under the college's intensive study plan, students take only 2 or 3 courses during each of 4 8-week terms. The library contains 85,000 volumes, 4989 microform items, and 977 audiovisual forms/CDs, and subscribes to 343 periodicals. Computerized library services include interlibrary loans and database searching. Special learning facilities include a learning resource center and art gallery. The 112-acre campus is in a small town 18 miles east of Peoria, in central Illinois. Including residence halls, there are 23 buildings.
Student Life: 90% of undergraduates are from Illinois. Others are from 17 states and 1 foreign country. 90% are from public schools. 87% are white. 37% claim no religious affiliation; 31% Protestant; 28% Catholic. The average age of freshmen is 18; all undergraduates, 21. 25% do not continue beyond their first year; 65% remain to graduate.
Housing: 451 students can be accommodated in college housing, which includes single-sex and coed dormitories, fraternity houses, and sorority houses. On-campus housing is guaranteed for all 4 years. 80% of students live on campus; of those, 70% remain on campus on weekends. Alcohol is not permitted. All students may keep cars.
Activities: 35% of men belong to 3 national fraternities; 35% of women belong to 1 local sorority and 2 national sororities. There are 41 groups on campus, including art, cheerleading, choir, chorale, chorus, computers, drama, ethnic, honors, international, literary magazine, newspaper, photography, political, professional, religious, social, social service, student government, and yearbook. Popular campus events include Founders Day and Pride Day.
Sports: There are 8 intercollegiate sports for men and 8 for women, and 6 intramural sports for men and 6 for women. Facilities include a gym, a pool, a weight room, tennis courts, and football, softball, and baseball fields.
Disabled Students: 50% of the campus is accessible. Wheelchair ramps, elevators, special parking, and specially equipped rest rooms are available.
Services: Counseling and information services are available, as is tutoring in most subjects. There is remedial reading and writing, and a writing center.
Campus Safety and Security: Measures include informal discussions, pamphlets/posters/films, and lighted pathways/sidewalks.
Programs of Study: Eureka confers B.A. and B.S. degrees. Bachelor's degrees are awarded in BIOLOGICAL SCIENCE (biology/biological science), BUSINESS (accounting, business administration and management, business economics, and management information systems), COMMUNICATIONS AND THE ARTS (communications, dramatic arts, English, fine arts, and music), COMPUTER AND PHYSICAL SCIENCE (chemistry, computer science, mathematics, and physical sciences), EDUCATION (athletic training, education, elementary, music, physical, science, and secondary), HEALTH PROFESSIONS (medical laboratory technology), SOCIAL SCIENCE (child care/child and family studies, history, liberal arts/general studies, philosophy, physical fitness/movement, political science/government, psychology, religion, social science, and sociology). Chemistry, biology, and education are the strongest academically. Business administration, education, and psychology are the largest.
Required: All students must take English composition, biological and physical sciences, general studies, math, phys ed, Western civilization, 3 humanities courses, and 3 social science courses. A total of at least 124 hours is required for graduation, including 32 hours in the major. A minimum GPA of 2.0 is required.
Special: Cooperative programs include a 3-2 engineering degree with Illinois Institute of Technology, a 2-2 B.S.N. with Mennonite College of Nursing or St. Francis College of Nursing, and a 3-1 clinical lab science degree with St. Francis or St. John's School of Clinical Laboratory Science. Students may study abroad in 5 countries. Professional programs in arts management, art therapy, communications, prelaw, premedicine, preministry, and teacher education are offered. An interdisciplinary major in arts and letters combines visual, performing, and literary arts. Internships and dual majors are offered in various areas. A Washington semester is available. There are 7 national honor societies, a freshman honors program, and 4 departmental honors programs.
Faculty/Classroom: 64% of faculty are male; 36%, female. All teach undergraduates. The average class size in an introductory lecture is 25; in a laboratory, 10; and in a regular course, 20.

Admissions: 72% of the 2001-2002 applicants were accepted. The ACT scores for the 2001-2002 freshman class were: 48% below 21, 21% between 21 and 23, 17% between 24 and 26, 8% between 27 and 28, and 6% above 28. 35% of the current freshmen were in the top fifth of their class; 65% were in the top two fifths.

Requirements: The SAT I or ACT is required. In addition, applicants should be graduates of accredited secondary schools or have the GED. Eureka requires applicants to be in the upper 50% of their class. A GPA of 2.0 is required. AP and CLEP credits are accepted. Important factors in the admissions decision are recommendations by school officials, extracurricular activities record, and leadership record.

Procedure: Freshmen are admitted to all sessions. Entrance exams should be taken by December of the senior year. There is a deferred admissions plan. Application deadlines are open. The application fee is $15. Notification is sent on a rolling basis.

Transfer: Applicants must have at least a 2.0 GPA in previous college work. Those with fewer than 30 hours of transferable credit must submit high school transcripts and ACT scores. Courses with grades below C are not accepted. 30 credits of 124 must be completed at Eureka.

Visiting: There are regularly scheduled orientations for prospective students, including visits with admissions and financial aid advisers, observing student panels, meetings with faculty and coaches, and campus tours. There are guides for informal visits and visitors may sit in on classes and stay overnight. To schedule a visit, contact Tish Guderjan, Office of Admissions.

Financial Aid: In 2001-2002, 98% of all students received some form of financial aid. 49% of undergraduates work part time. Average annual earnings from campus work are $1000. Eureka is a member of CSS. The FAFSA is required. Check with the school for current deadlines.

International Students: The school actively recruits these students. They must score 550 on the written TOEFL.

Computers: The mainframe is a DEC PDP 11/24. There are 50 PCs available in the computer center, library computer lab (with Internet access), and residence halls. All students may access the system. There are no time limits and no fees.

Admissions Contact: John R. Clayton, Dean of Admissions and Financial Aid. E-mail: *admissions@eureka.edu* Web: *www.eureka.edu*

GREENVILLE COLLEGE

D-4

Greenville, IL 62246-0159

(618) 664-2800, ext. 4401
(800) 345-4440; Fax: (618) 664-9841

Full-time: 470 men, 550 women	**Faculty:** 56; IIB, --$
Part-time: 10 men, 10 women	**Ph.D.s:** 61%
Graduate: 20 men, 15 women	**Student/Faculty:** 18 to 1
Year: 4-1-4, summer session	**Tuition:** $14,040
Application Deadline: open	**Room & Board:** $5186
Freshman Class: n/av	
SAT I or ACT: required	**LESS COMPETITIVE**

Greenville College, founded in 1892, is a liberal arts institution affiliated with the Free Methodist Church, and offering degree programs in the humanities, social sciences, education, math, and natural sciences. Figures in the above capsule are approximate. The library contains 124,576 volumes, 2991 microform items, and 1935 audiovisual forms/CDs, and subscribes to 490 periodicals. Computerized library services include the card catalog, interlibrary loans, and database searching. Special learning facilities include a learning resource center, art gallery, radio station, and the Bock Museum. The 12-acre campus is in a small town 50 miles east of St. Louis. Including residence halls, there are 23 buildings.

Student Life: 68% of undergraduates are from Illinois. Others are from 35 states, 14 foreign countries, and Canada. 89% are from public schools. 88% are white. Most are Protestant. The average age of freshmen is 18; all undergraduates, 23. 29% do not continue beyond their first year; 43% remain to graduate.

Housing: 624 students can be accommodated in college housing, which includes single-sex dormitories and on-campus apartments. In addition, there are language houses. On-campus housing is guaranteed for all 4 years. 62% of students live on campus; of those, 45% remain on campus on weekends. Alcohol is not permitted. All students may keep cars.

Activities: There are no fraternities or sororities. There are 20 groups on campus, including art, band, cheerleading, choir, chorale, chorus, computers, drama, ethnic, honors, musical theater, newspaper, orchestra, pep band, professional, radio and TV, religious, social, social service, student government, and yearbook. Popular campus events include Agape Music Festival, All College Hike, and class retreats.

Sports: There are 8 intercollegiate sports for men and 7 for women, and 6 intramural sports for men and 6 for women. Facilities include a gym, a sports training annex, a recreational center, 6 tennis courts, a fitness pool, an all-weather track, and softball, baseball, football, soccer, and practice fields.

Disabled Students: 25% of the campus is accessible. Wheelchair ramps, elevators, special parking, specially equipped rest rooms, special class scheduling, and lowered drinking fountains are available.

Services: Counseling and information services are available, as is tutoring in most subjects, including lower-division general education courses. There is remedial reading and writing. There are also supplemental instruction programs and a program for at-risk freshmen.

Campus Safety and Security: Measures include 24-hour foot and vehicle patrol, escort service, informal discussions, and pamphlets/posters/films. There are emergency telephones, lighted pathways/sidewalks, and alarm systems in some buildings.

Programs of Study: Greenville confers B.A., B.S., and B.Mus.Ed. degrees. Master's degrees are also awarded. Bachelor's degrees are awarded in BIOLOGICAL SCIENCE (biology/biological science and environmental biology), BUSINESS (accounting, business administration and management, management information systems, marketing/retailing/merchandising, and recreation and leisure services), COMMUNICATIONS AND THE ARTS (art, communications, dramatic arts, English, French, modern language, music, public relations, Spanish, and speech/debate/rhetoric), COMPUTER AND PHYSICAL SCIENCE (chemistry, computer science, mathematics, and physics), EDUCATION (art, drama, early childhood, elementary, English, foreign languages, mathematics, music, physical, science, secondary, social studies, and special), SOCIAL SCIENCE (history, liberal arts/general studies, ministries, pastoral studies, philosophy, political science/government, psychology, religion, religious music, social work, sociology, and youth ministry). Biology, chemistry, and math are the strongest academically. Education, communication, and contemporary Christian music are the largest.

Required: All students must successfully complete courses in English composition, a foreign language (for the B.A.), religion, phys ed, humanities, math, natural sciences, social science, and philosophy. A minimum of 132 credit hours and a GPA of 2.0 are required for graduation.

Special: The college provides opportunities for dual majors in such areas as psychology/religion and religion/philosophy, B.A.-B.S. degrees, student-designed and accelerated degree programs in education, work-study programs, study abroad, credit by exam, internships, a general studies degree, pass/fail options, and nondegree study. A 3-2 engineering degree with the University of Illinois, a 2-2 degree with the Illinois State University Mennonite School of Nursing, and an American Studies program in Washington, D.C. are also available. Cross-registration is offered within the Wesleyan Urban Coalition, the Christian College Consortium, and the Council of Christian Colleges and Universities. There are 4 national honor societies, a freshman honors program, and 16 departmental honors programs.

Faculty/Classroom: 75% of faculty are male; 25%, female. All teach undergraduates and 25% do research. The average class size in a regular course is 20.

Admissions: 6 freshmen graduated first in their class in a recent year.

Requirements: The SAT I or ACT is required, with a minimum composite score of 860 on the SAT I or 18 on the ACT. Applicants must have completed a minimum of 16 high school units; recommended are 4 units in English, 2 each in a foreign language and math, and 1 each in a lab science and American history. A GPA of 2.0 is required. A GED certificate will be accepted. An essay is also required. Greenville requires applicants to be in the upper 50% of their class. A GPA of 2.0 is required. AP and CLEP credits are accepted. Important factors in the admissions decision are leadership record, advanced placement or honor courses, and personality/intangible qualities.

Procedure: Freshmen are admitted to all sessions. Entrance exams should be taken in the spring of the junior year. Application deadlines are open. The application fee is $25.

Transfer: 151 transfer students enrolled in a recent year. A minimum average grade of C or better is required. An associate degree will be accepted for transfer. 40 credits of 132 must be completed at Greenville.

Visiting: There are regularly scheduled orientations for prospective students, including campus visits during scheduled preview days. There are guides for informal visits and visitors may sit in on classes and stay overnight. To schedule a visit, contact the Admissions Office.

Financial Aid: The FAFSA is required. Check with school for current deadlines.

International Students: There are 22 international students enrolled in a recent year. They must score 500 on the written TOEFL.

Computers: The mainframe is a Data General MV/9300. There are 100 PCs available in the library and throughout the campus. Database, spreadsheet, and word processing programs are available. A wireless network is available for use anywhere on campus. All students may access the system 24 hours a day. There are no time limits and no fees. It is strongly recommended that all students have a personal computer. It is recommended that students in computer science have personal computers. IBM laptop is recommended.

Graduates: In a recent year, 172 bachelor's degrees were awarded. The most popular majors were education (29%), business/accounting (13%), and biological sciences (8%). In an average class, 43% graduate in 4 years, 46% in 5 years, and 49% in 6 years. 22 companies recruited on campus in a recent year.

Admissions Contact: Randy Comfort, Dean of Admissions.
E-mail: *admissions@greenville.edu* Web: *http://www.greenville.edu*

ILLINOIS COLLEGE

Jacksonville, IL 62650-2299 C-3

(217) 245-3030
(888) 595-3030; Fax: (217) 245-3034

Full-time: 392 men, 466 women	**Faculty:** 62; IIB, -$
Part-time: 3 men, 13 women	**Ph.D.s:** 78%
Graduate: none	**Student/Faculty:** 14 to 1
Year: semesters, summer session	**Tuition:** $11,272
Application Deadline: August 15	**Room & Board:** $4962
Freshman Class: 1061 applied, 705 accepted, 249 enrolled	
SAT I Verbal/Math: 530/590	**ACT:** 23 **COMPETITIVE**

Illinois College, founded in 1829, is a liberal arts institution related to the Presbyterian Church (U.S.A.) and the United Church of Christ. The library contains 143,500 volumes, 127 microform items, and 3000 audiovisual forms/CDs, and subscribes to 620 periodicals. Computerized library services include the card catalog, interlibrary loans, and database searching. Special learning facilities include an art gallery, theater, and television studio. The 62-acre campus is in a small town 35 miles west of Springfield. Including residence halls, there are 26 buildings.

Student Life: 97% of undergraduates are from Illinois. Others are from 11 states and 4 foreign countries. 93% are white. 40% are Catholic; 25% claim no religious affiliation; 20% are Protestant. The average age of freshmen is 18; all undergraduates, 20. 20% do not continue beyond their first year; 50% remain to graduate.

Housing: 750 students can be accommodated in college housing, which includes single-sex and coed dormitories and on-campus apartments. In addition, there are honors houses. On-campus housing is guaranteed for all 4 years. 75% of students live on campus; of those, 70% remain on campus on weekends. All students may keep cars.

Activities: 20% of men belong to 4 local fraternities; 20% of women belong to 3 local sororities. There are 63 groups on campus, including art, band, cheerleading, choir, chorale, computers, debate, drama, ethnic, honors, international, literary magazine, newspaper, photography, political, radio and TV, religious, social, social service, student government, and yearbook. Popular campus events include Osage Orange Picnic, Honors Retreat, and McGaw Fine Arts Series.

Sports: There are 9 intercollegiate sports for men and 8 for women, and 5 intramural sports for men and 5 for women. Facilities include a game room, a gym with 2 basketball and 3 squash and handball courts, volleyball and badminton courts, a swimming pool, a fitness center, playing fields, an all-weather track, and 6 tennis courts.

Disabled Students: 80% of the campus is accessible. Wheelchair ramps, elevators, special parking, specially equipped rest rooms, and lowered drinking fountains are available.

Services: Counseling and information services are available, as is tutoring in some subjects, including accounting, chemistry, computer science, economics, English, French, math, and writing.

Campus Safety and Security: Measures include self-defense education, escort service, shuttle buses, and informal discussions. There are pamphlets/posters/films, emergency telephones, lighted pathways/sidewalks, and 24-hour foot patrol.

Programs of Study: IC confers B.A. and B.S. degrees. Bachelor's degrees are awarded in BIOLOGICAL SCIENCE (biology/biological science), BUSINESS (accounting and business administration and management), COMMUNICATIONS AND THE ARTS (broadcasting, communications, dramatic arts, English, fine arts, French, German, music, Spanish, and speech/debate/rhetoric), COMPUTER AND PHYSICAL SCIENCE (chemistry, computer science, information sciences and systems, mathematics, and physics), EDUCATION (elementary, foreign languages, physical, science, and secondary), ENGINEERING AND ENVIRONMENTAL DESIGN (environmental science), HEALTH PROFESSIONS (medical laboratory technology), SOCIAL SCIENCE (economics, history, international relations, philosophy, political science/government, prelaw, psychology, religion, social work, and sociology). Computer science, math, and history/political science are the strongest academically. Business administration, education, and biology are the largest.

Required: To graduate, all students must fulfill general graduation and convocation requirements and complete at least 120 semester hours. A 2.0 GPA is required. Attendance at graduation is mandatory.

Special: The college offers study abroad in 5 countries, on- and off-campus work-study programs, and internships through the departments of communications and theater, computer science and information systems, economics and business administration, English, and political science. Also available are student-designed and dual majors, B.A.-B.S. degrees, nondegree study, a 3-2 engineering degree with the University of Illinois or Washington University, a 3-2 cooperative program with the Mennonite College of Nursing, and a 3-2 occupational therapy program with Washington University. The Intercultural Exchange Program with Ritsumeikan University in Kyoto, Japan, the Model Illinois Government and Model United Nations simulations, the Urban Studies Program of Associated Colleges of the Midwest in Chicago, and Asian-oriented courses through the Illinois Inter-Institutional Council for Asian and Middle Eastern Studies are offered. There are 9 national honor societies, including Phi Beta Kappa, and 8 departmental honors programs.

Faculty/Classroom: 75% of faculty are male; 25%, female. All teach undergraduates. The average class size in an introductory lecture is 60; in a laboratory, 20; and in a regular course, 20.

Admissions: 66% of the 2001-2002 applicants were accepted. The SAT I scores for the 2001-2002 freshman class were: Verbal--25% below 500, 25% between 500 and 599, and 50% between 600 and 700; Math--20% below 500 and 80% between 500 and 599. The ACT scores were 41% below 21, 31% between 21 and 23, 15% between 24 and 26, 11% between 27 and 28, and 8% above 28. 38% of the current freshmen were in the top fifth of their class; 68% were in the top two fifths. 8 freshmen graduated first in their class.

Requirements: The SAT I or ACT is required. In addition, applicants must be graduates of an accredited secondary school or have a GED certificate. Students should have completed at least 15 academic credits, including 3 in English and 7 from the following: English, foreign language, history, lab science, math, and social studies. Recommendations from high school officials and 2 personal references are required. IC requires applicants to be in the upper 50% of their class. A GPA of 2.0 is required. AP and CLEP credits are accepted. Applications are accepted on-line and on computer disk.

Procedure: Freshmen are admitted to all sessions. Entrance exams should be taken in the spring of the junior year of high school. Application deadlines are open. Applications should be filed by August 15 for fall entry or December 15 for spring, along with a $10 fee. There is a rolling admissions plan and notification is sent on a rolling basis.

Transfer: 45 transfer students enrolled in 2001-2002. Transfer students must have a minimum 2.0 GPA and submit SAT I or ACT scores and transcripts of completed college work. 60 credits of 120 must be completed at IC.

Visiting: There are regularly scheduled orientations for prospective students. There are guides for informal visits and visitors may sit in on classes and stay overnight. To schedule a visit, contact the Admissions Office.

Financial Aid: In 2001-2002, 97% of all students received some form of financial aid. 90% of all students received need-based aid. The average freshman award was $10,148. Of that total, scholarships or need-based grants averaged $4200 ($12,000 maximum); loans averaged $2520 ($5400 maximum); and work contracts averaged $800 ($1200 maximum). 41% of undergraduates work part time. Average annual earnings from campus work are $750. The average financial indebtedness of the 2001 graduate was $13,300. The FAFSA is required. The fall application deadline is May 1.

International Students: There are 4 international students enrolled. They must score 550 on the written TOEFL or 213 on the electronic version.

Computers: The mainframe is a DEC 3000 Model 600S AXP. A computer lab includes 40 PCs that are utilized by the business administration, English, math, and computer science departments. The learning center houses 2 computer labs with 31 486 PCs that are linked together with the Novell local area network. All students may access the system from 7 A.M. to 1 A.M. There are no time limits and no fees.

Graduates: In 2001, 184 bachelor's degrees were awarded. The most popular majors were business administration (20%), education (16%), and biology (11%). In an average class, 1% graduate in 3 years, 44% in 4 years, 50% in 5 years, and 51% in 6 years. 52 companies recruited on campus in 2000-2001. Of the 2000 graduating class, 27% were enrolled in graduate school within 6 months of graduation and 98% were employed.

Admissions Contact: Rick Bystry, Director of Admission.
E-mail: *ribystry@ic.edu* Web: *www.ic.edu*

ILLINOIS INSTITUTE OF TECHNOLOGY

Chicago, IL 60616 E-2

(312) 567-3025
(800) 448-2329; Fax: (312) 567-6939

Full-time: 1080 men, 386 women	**Faculty:** 239; I, -$
Part-time: 300 men, 76 women	**Ph.D.s:** 99%
Graduate: 2813 men, 1395 women	**Student/Faculty:** 6 to 1
Year: semesters, summer session	**Tuition:** $19,300
Application Deadline: open	**Room & Board:** $5882
Freshman Class: 1583 applied, 345 accepted, 293 enrolled	
SAT I Verbal/Math: 650/690	**ACT:** 28
	HIGHLY COMPETITIVE+

Illinois Institute of Technology, founded in 1890, is a private institution offering undergraduate programs in architecture, engineering, applied math, biology, chemistry, physics, computing, political science, and psychology. There are 3 undergraduate and 7 graduate schools. In addition to regional accreditation, IIT has baccalaureate program accreditation with ABET. The library contains 583,271 volumes, 184,296 microform items, and 52,330 audiovisual forms/CDs, and subscribes to 773 periodicals. Computerized library services include the card catalog, interlibrary loans, and database searching. Special learning facilities include a learning resource center and radio station. The 120-acre campus is in an urban area 3 miles south of downtown Chicago. Including residence halls, there are 31 buildings.

Student Life: 54% of undergraduates are from Illinois. Others are from 49 states, 96 foreign countries, and Canada. 70% are from public schools. 49% are white; 18%, foreign nationals; 15%, Asian American. The average age of freshmen is 19; all undergraduates, 23. 14% do not continue beyond their first year; 55% remain to graduate.

Housing: 884 students can be accommodated in college housing, which includes single-sex and coed dormitories, on-campus apartments, married-student housing, fraternity houses, and sorority houses. On-campus housing is guaranteed for all 4 years. 58% of students live on campus; of those, 80% remain on campus on weekends. All students may keep cars.

Activities: 18% of men belong to 7 national fraternities; 9% of women belong to 2 local and 1 national sororities. There are 60 groups on campus, including choir, chorus, commuter, computers, dance, drama, ethnic, gay, honors, international, jazz band, literary magazine, musical theater, photography, professional, radio and TV, religious, social, social service, student government, union, and yearbook. Popular campus events include International Fest, IIT 100 Car Race, and Greek Week.

Sports: There are 4 intercollegiate sports for men and 4 for women. Facilities include tennis, basketball, volleyball, racquetball, and squash courts, soccer and softball fields, a swimming pool, an exercise room, a weight room, a bowling alley, and a game room.

Disabled Students: Wheelchair ramps, elevators, special parking, specially equipped rest rooms, and lowered drinking fountains are available.

Services: Counseling and information services are available, as is tutoring in some subjects, including lower division science, math, engineering, and writing courses. There is a reader service for the blind.

Campus Safety and Security: Measures include 24-hour foot and vehicle patrol, escort service, shuttle buses, and informal discussions. There are pamphlets/posters/films, emergency telephones, and lighted pathways/sidewalks.

Programs of Study: IIT confers B.S. and B.Arch. degrees. Master's and doctoral degrees are also awarded. Bachelor's degrees are awarded in BIOLOGICAL SCIENCE (biochemistry, biology/biological science, biophysics, and molecular biology), COMMUNICATIONS AND THE ARTS (technical and business writing), COMPUTER AND PHYSICAL SCIENCE (applied mathematics, chemistry, computer science, information sciences and systems, physics, and web technology), ENGINEERING AND ENVIRONMENTAL DESIGN (aeronautical engineering, architectural engineering, architecture, chemical engineering, civil engineering, computer engineering, electrical/electronics engineering, manufacturing technology, mechanical engineering, and metallurgical engineering), SOCIAL SCIENCE (political science/government and psychology). All engineering programs are the strongest academically. Architecture and engineering are the largest.

Required: To graduate, students must have completed a total of 126 to 142 credit hours with a minimum cumulative GPA and a minimum major GPA of 2.0. General education requirements include 21 hours of social studies or humanities, 11 hours of science, 5 hours of math, and 1 course in industrial culture.

Special: IIT offers co-op programs in engineering, dual majors, study abroad, and an accelerated degree program in prelaw. There are 2 national honor societies.

Faculty/Classroom: 81% of faculty are male; 19%, female. No introductory courses are taught by graduate students. The average class size in an introductory lecture is 14; in a laboratory, 11; and in a regular course, 14.

Admissions: 22% of the 2001-2002 applicants were accepted. The SAT I scores for the 2001-2002 freshman class were: Verbal--1% below 500, 25% between 500 and 599, 57% between 600 and 700, and 17% above 700; Math--13% between 500 and 599, 50% between 600 and 700, and 37% above 700. The ACT scores were 5% between 21 and 23, 24% between 24 and 26, 21% between 27 and 28, and 50% above 28.

Requirements: The SAT I or ACT is required. In addition, graduation from an accredited secondary school is required for admission. The school requires 16 academic credits, including 4 units each of English and math, 3 of lab science, and 2 of history or social science. A GPA of 3.0 is required. AP credits are accepted. Important factors in the admissions decision are advanced placement or honor courses, leadership record, and recommendations by school officials. Applications are accepted on-line at the school's web site and via CollegeLink and numerous others, including Embark.com.

Procedure: Freshmen are admitted fall and spring. There is a deferred admissions plan. Application deadlines are open. The fall 2001 application fee was $30. There is a rolling admissions plan and notification is sent on a rolling basis.

Transfer: 79 transfer students enrolled in 2001-2002. A minimum 3.0 GPA is required. 45 credits of 126 to 142 must be completed at IIT.

Visiting: There are regularly scheduled orientations for prospective students, including accompanying current students, visiting classes, and attending department receptions. There are guides for informal visits and visitors may sit in on classes and stay overnight. To schedule a visit, contact Amy Ziolkowski.

Financial Aid: In 2001-2002, 98% of all freshmen and 95% of continuing students received some form of financial aid. 43% of freshmen and 47% of continuing students received need-based aid. The average freshman award was $19,117. Of that total, scholarships or need-based grants averaged $11,556 ($24,224 maximum); loans averaged $8062 ($10,500 maximum); work contracts averaged $1847 ($2000 maximum); and Pell, state grants, SEOG, private scholarships and ROTC supplements averaged $5618 ($23,490 maximum). 28% of undergraduates work part time. Average annual earnings from campus work are $2000. The average financial indebtedness of the 2001 graduate was $8661. IIT is a member of CSS. The FAFSA is required. The fall application deadline is April.

International Students: There are 329 international students enrolled. The school actively recruits these students. They must score 550 on the written TOEFL and also take the SAT I or the ACT.

Computers: The mainframes are a DEC VAX 3600 and an SGI Challenge. There are also many Macs and SGI UNIX workstations available in academic buildings. Dormitory rooms are linked to the university network, providing Internet and e-mail access. All students may access the system. There are no time limits and no fees. It is strongly recommended that all students have a personal computer.

Graduates: In 2001, 267 bachelor's degrees were awarded. The most popular majors were architecture (15%), mechanical engineering (13%), and computer science (12%). 58 companies recruited on campus in 2000-2001. Of the 2000 graduating class, 31% were enrolled in graduate school within 6 months of graduation and 58% were employed.

Admissions Contact: Judy Carr, Director of Admissions.
E-mail: *admission@iit.edu* Web: *www.iit.edu*

ILLINOIS STATE UNIVERSITY — D-3

Normal, IL 61761 — (309) 438-2181
(800) 366-2478; Fax: (309) 438-3932

Full-time: 6995 men, 10,037 women	**Faculty:** 865; I, --$
Part-time: 697 men, 743 women	**Ph.D.s:** 82%
Graduate: 1003 men, 1765 women	**Student/Faculty:** 20 to 1
Year: semesters, summer session	**Tuition:** $4477 ($8421)
Application Deadline: March 1	**Room & Board:** $4758
Freshman Class: 10,211 applied, 7905 accepted, 3340 enrolled	
ACT: 23	**COMPETITIVE**

Illinois State University, founded in 1857, is a public institution offering instruction through schools of applied science and technology, arts and sciences, business, education, fine arts, and nursing. There are 6 undergraduate schools and 1 graduate school. In addition to regional accreditation, ISU has baccalaureate program accreditation with AACSB, ADA, AHEA, CSWE, NASAD, NASM, NCATE, NLN, and NRPA. The library contains 1,490,367 volumes, 1,882,332 microform items, and 24,716 audiovisual forms/CDs, and subscribes to 12,119 periodicals. Computerized library services include the card catalog, interlibrary loans, and database searching. Special learning facilities include a learning resource center, art gallery, planetarium, radio station, TV station, and distance-learning classroom. The 850-acre campus is in an urban area 125 miles south of Chicago and 180 miles north of St. Louis. Including residence halls, there are 153 buildings.

Student Life: 96% of undergraduates are from Illinois. Others are from 45 states, 48 foreign countries, and Canada. 89% are from public schools. 88% are white. The average age of freshmen is 18; all undergraduates, 20. 20% do not continue beyond their first year; 54% remain to graduate.

Housing: 7343 students can be accommodated in college housing, which includes single-sex and coed dormitories, on-campus apartments, and married-student housing. In addition, there are honors houses and special-interest houses. On-campus housing is available on a first-come, first-served basis. Alcohol is not permitted. All students may keep cars.

Activities: 10% of men belong to 21 national fraternities; 9% of women belong to 17 national sororities. There are more than 250 groups on campus, including art, band, cheerleading, chess, choir, chorale, chorus, computers, dance, debate, drama, drill team, ethnic, film, forensics, gay, honors, international, jazz band, literary magazine, marching band, musical theater, newspaper, opera, orchestra, pep band, photography, political, professional, radio and TV, religious, social, social service, student government, symphony, and yearbook. Popular campus events include Festival ISU, International Fair, and Madrigal Dinners.

Sports: There are 8 intercollegiate sports for men and 11 for women, and 9 intramural sports for men and 9 for women. Facilities include a student recreational building, a basketball arena, a football stadium, a field house, baseball diamonds, tennis courts, Olympic-size pools, an 18-hole golf course, a soccer and softball field, and a bowling and billiards center.

Disabled Students: All of the campus is accessible. Wheelchair ramps, elevators, special parking, specially equipped rest rooms, special class scheduling, lowered drinking fountains, lowered telephones, a telecommunication device, 2 rooms in the library for visually disabled students,

and a learning lab with a braille thermoform and a variable-speed lexicon are available.
Services: Counseling and information services are available, as is tutoring in every subject. There is a reader service for the blind, and remedial math, reading, and writing. There are also interpreters for the hearing impaired, note takers, taped lectures, and braillists.
Campus Safety and Security: Measures include 24-hour foot and vehicle patrol, self-defense education, escort service, and shuttle buses. There are informal discussions, pamphlets/posters/films, emergency telephones, and lighted pathways/sidewalks.
Programs of Study: ISU confers B.A., B.S., B.F.A., B.Mu., B.Mu.E., and B.S.Ed. degrees. Master's and doctoral degrees are also awarded. Bachelor's degrees are awarded in AGRICULTURE (agriculture), BIOLOGICAL SCIENCE (biochemistry and biology/biological science), BUSINESS (accounting, banking and finance, business administration and management, insurance, international business management, management science, and marketing/retailing/merchandising), COMMUNICATIONS AND THE ARTS (art, communications, dance, dramatic arts, English, French, German, music, music performance, public relations, Spanish, speech/debate/rhetoric, and telecommunications), COMPUTER AND PHYSICAL SCIENCE (chemistry, computer science, digital arts/technology, geology, information sciences and systems, mathematics, and physics), EDUCATION (business, computer, early childhood, elementary, health, middle school, music, physical, and special), ENGINEERING AND ENVIRONMENTAL DESIGN (industrial engineering technology), HEALTH PROFESSIONS (environmental health science, health care administration, medical laboratory technology, nursing, and speech pathology/audiology), SOCIAL SCIENCE (anthropology, criminal justice, economics, fashion design and technology, geography, history, home economics, parks and recreation management, philosophy, political science/government, psychology, safety management, social science, social work, and sociology). Elementary education, business administration, and special education are the largest.
Required: Students must complete 45 hours of general education and a total of 120 credit hours with a minimum GPA of 2.0. In addition, they must pass a writing exam and exams on the Constitutions of the U.S. and the State of Illinois, and one on the proper use of the American flag.
Special: There are numerous cooperative programs and internships, dual majors, study abroad in 11 countries, a general studies degree, student-designed majors, a 3-2 engineering program with the University of Illinois, and work-study programs both on campus and with nonprofit organizations. Pass/fail options are available and credit is given for military experience. ISU is part of the National Student Exchange, enabling qualifying juniors and seniors to study for up to 1 year at one of several hundred colleges around the country. There are 25 national honor societies, including Phi Beta Kappa, a freshman honors program, and 43 departmental honors programs.
Faculty/Classroom: 54% of faculty are male; 46%, female. All teach undergraduates. Graduate students teach 13% of introductory courses. The average class size in an introductory lecture is 37; in a laboratory, 22; and in a regular course, 32.
Admissions: 77% of the 2001-2002 applicants were accepted. The ACT scores for the 2001-2002 freshman class were 25% below 21, 36% between 21 and 23, 27% between 24 and 26, 8% between 27 and 28, and 4% above 28. 28% of the current freshmen were in the top fifth of their class; 64% were in the top two fifths. There were 5 National Merit finalists. 38 freshmen graduated first in their class.
Requirements: The ACT is required. In addition, applicants must be graduates of an accredited secondary school or have a GED. Admission is based on a combination of factors, including class rank and ACT or SAT I score. ISU requires applicants to be in the upper 50% of their class. AP and CLEP credits are accepted. Applications are accepted online.
Procedure: Freshmen are admitted to all sessions. Entrance exams should be taken in the fall of the junior year. Applications should be filed by March 1 for fall entry, along with a $30 fee. There is a rolling admissions plan.
Transfer: 1989 transfer students enrolled in 2001-2002. Graduates of Illinois community colleges holding associate degrees are admitted pending receipt of transcripts. Other students must meet the requirements for beginning freshmen with a minimum 2.0 GPA. 30 credits of 120 must be completed at ISU.
Visiting: There are regularly scheduled orientations for prospective students. There are guides for informal visits and visitors may sit in on classes. To schedule a visit, contact the Admissions Office.
Financial Aid: In 2001-2002, 71% of all freshmen and 63% of continuing students received some form of financial aid. 39% of freshmen and 44% of continuing students received need-based aid. The average freshman award was $5195. Of that total, scholarships or need-based grants averaged $4929 ($15,530 maximum); loans averaged $2761 ($12,396 maximum); and work contracts averaged $1573 ($2150 maximum). 17% of undergraduates work part time. Average annual earnings from campus work are $2415. The average financial indebtedness of the 2001 graduate was $9612. The CSS/Profile, FAFSA, FFS, or SFS is required. The fall application deadline is March 1.
International Students: There are 144 international students enrolled. The school actively recruits these students. They must score 550 on the written TOEFL.
Computers: The mainframe is a Hitachi EX/80. Mainframe terminals are in various locations across campus, and 120 terminals are placed for student access. There are also 1039 PCs in labs and dormitories across campus. All students have an e-mail address and access to the Internet and Web. The mainframe is available to those taking courses involving its use. Students may access the system 24 hours a day. There are no time limits and no fees.
Graduates: In 2001, 4041 bachelor's degrees were awarded. The most popular majors were elementary education (10%), business administration (5%), and marketing (5%). In an average class, 1% graduate in 3 years, 29% in 4 years, 51% in 5 years, and 56% in 6 years. 261 companies recruited on campus in 2000-2001.
Admissions Contact: Steve Adams, Director of Admissions. A video is available. E-mail: *ugradadm@ilstu.edu* Web: *www.ilstu.edu*

ILLINOIS WESLEYAN UNIVERSITY — D-3
Bloomington, IL 61702-2900 — (309) 556-3031
(800) 332-2498; Fax: (309) 556-3411

Full-time: 894 men, 1162 women	**Faculty:** 154; IIB, +$
Part-time: 5 men, 3 women	**Ph.D.s:** 94%
Graduate: none	**Student/Faculty:** 13 to 1
Year: 4-4-1	**Tuition:** $21,640
Application Deadline: March 1	**Room & Board:** $5330
Freshman Class: 2795 applied, 1605 accepted, 578 enrolled	
ACT: required	**HIGHLY COMPETITIVE**

Illinois Wesleyan University, founded in 1850, is a private institution offering programs in liberal arts, fine arts, and nursing. In addition to regional accreditation, Illinois Wesleyan has baccalaureate program accreditation with NASM and NLN. The library contains 254,195 volumes, 13,919 microform items, and 18,500 audiovisual forms/CDs, and subscribes to 1045 periodicals. Computerized library services include the card catalog, interlibrary loans, and database searching. Special learning facilities include a learning resource center, art gallery, radio station, TV station, observatory, multicultural center, and 20-acre tract of virgin timberland. The 72-acre campus is in a suburban area 130 miles from Chicago and 160 miles from St. Louis. Including residence halls, there are 70 buildings.
Student Life: 86% of undergraduates are from Illinois. Others are from 31 states, 27 foreign countries, and Canada. 86% are from public schools. 88% are white. 58% are Protestant; 40% Catholic. The average age of freshmen is 18; all undergraduates, 20. 10% do not continue beyond their first year; 77% remain to graduate.
Housing: 1660 students can be accommodated in college housing, which includes coed dormitories, fraternity houses, and sorority houses. In addition, there are honors houses, language houses, special-interest houses, and an international house. On-campus housing is guaranteed for all 4 years. 80% of students live on campus; of those, 90% remain on campus on weekends. All students may keep cars.
Activities: 38% of men belong to 7 national fraternities; 30% of women belong to 5 national sororities. There are 125 groups on campus, including band, cheerleading, chess, choir, chorale, chorus, computers, dance, drama, ethnic, gay, honors, international, jazz band, literary magazine, marching band, musical theater, newspaper, opera, orchestra, pep band, political, professional, radio and TV, religious, social, social service, student government, symphony, and yearbook. Popular campus events include Parents Days, Blue Moon Coffeehouse, and Fine Arts Festival.
Sports: There are 9 intercollegiate sports for men and 9 for women, and 15 intramural sports for men and 13 for women. Facilities include a fitness center with weight/exercise equipment and racquetball courts; a swimming pool with 1- and 3-meter diving boards; an activity center with a 200-meter, 6-lane indoor track and courts for tennis, recreational basketball, and volleyball; and a separate gym for intercollegiate and other activities.
Disabled Students: 95% of the campus is accessible. Wheelchair ramps, elevators, special parking, specially equipped rest rooms, special class scheduling, lowered drinking fountains, and lowered telephones are available.
Services: Counseling and information services are available, as is tutoring in every subject. There is a reader service for the blind. Assistance in writing and study skills is also available.
Campus Safety and Security: Measures include 24-hour foot and vehicle patrol, self-defense education, escort service, and informal discussions. There are pamphlets/posters/films, emergency telephones, and lighted pathways/sidewalks. A campus safety committee, composed of students, faculty, and staff, meets twice a semester to review security measures and recommend changes.
Programs of Study: Illinois Wesleyan confers B.A., B.S., B.F.A., B.Mus., B.Mus.Ed., and B.S.N. degrees. Bachelor's degrees are awarded in BIOLOGICAL SCIENCE (biology/biological science), BUSINESS (accounting, banking and finance, business administration and manage-

ment, insurance and risk management, and international business management), COMMUNICATIONS AND THE ARTS (dramatic arts, English, fine arts, French, German, music, music theory and composition, musical theater, piano/organ, Russian, Spanish, and voice), COMPUTER AND PHYSICAL SCIENCE (chemistry, computer science, mathematics, natural sciences, and physics), EDUCATION (elementary), HEALTH PROFESSIONS (nursing), SOCIAL SCIENCE (economics, history, international studies, philosophy, political science/government, psychology, religion, and sociology). Business and economics, the fine arts, and the physical sciences are the strongest academically. The physical sciences, music, and business and economics are the largest.

Required: A total of 32 course units is required for the bachelor's degree with a 2.0 GPA. General education requirements include 2 course units in natural sciences and 1 each in literature, intellectual traditions, formal reasoning, cultural and historical change, contemporary social institutions, the arts, analysis of values, and writing colloquium, plus demonstrated proficiency in a foreign language.

Special: There are several co-op programs, including a 3-2 degree in forestry and environmental studies with Duke University, a 2-2 engineering degree with the University of Illinois, and 3-2 engineering programs with a number of universities. Students may study abroad in many locations throughout the world through the Institute for the International Education of Students (IES), Pembroke College, University of Oxford, Beaver College Center for Study Abroad, and many other programs. The university also offers work-study, internships in many areas, Washington and United Nations semesters, dual and student-designed majors, and pass/fail options. There are 23 national honor societies, including Phi Beta Kappa.

Faculty/Classroom: 58% of faculty are male; 42%, female. All both teach and do research. The average class size in an introductory lecture is 21; in a laboratory, 14; and in a regular course, 16.

Admissions: 57% of the 2001-2002 applicants were accepted. The SAT I scores for the 2001-2002 freshman class were: Verbal--3% below 500, 30% between 500 and 599, 46% between 600 and 700, and 21% above 700; Math--2% below 500, 26% between 500 and 599, 53% between 600 and 700, and 19% above 700. The ACT scores were 4% between 21 and 23, 29% between 24 and 26, 27% between 27 and 28, and 40% above 28. 77% of the current freshmen were in the top fifth of their class; 95% were in the top two fifths. There were 8 National Merit finalists and 20 semifinalists. 37 freshmen graduated first in their class.

Requirements: The SAT I or ACT is required. In addition, applicants should graduate from an accredited secondary school, though a GED may be accepted. 15 academic credits are required, including 4 units of English, 3 each of natural science, math, and a foreign language, and 2 of social science. An audition is required for drama and music majors. Applications are accepted on-line and on computer disk. Illinois Wesleyan requires applicants to be in the upper 30% of their class. A GPA of 3.0 is required. AP and CLEP credits are accepted. Important factors in the admissions decision are advanced placement or honor courses, evidence of special talent, and leadership record.

Procedure: Freshmen are admitted fall and spring. Entrance exams should be taken in the spring of the junior year. There are early admissions and deferred admissions plans. Applications should be filed by March 1 for fall entry. Notification is sent on a rolling basis.

Transfer: 8 transfer students enrolled in 2001-2002. Applicants must submit all high school and college transcripts. A GPA of at least 2.5 is required. 13 course units of 32 must be completed at Illinois Wesleyan.

Visiting: There are regularly scheduled orientations for prospective students, The First-Year Experience is a week-long set of activities geared to assist new students in adjusting to campus and academic life. First-year students are housed together to share common challenges and successes in their new enviroment. There are guides for informal visits and visitors may sit in on classes and stay overnight. To schedule a visit, contact the Admissions Office.

Financial Aid: In 2001-2002, 89% of all freshmen and 87% of continuing students received some form of financial aid. 56% of freshmen and 55% of continuing students received need-based aid. The average freshman award was $16,024. Of that total, scholarships or need-based grants averaged $11,228 ($21,504 maximum); loans averaged $3012 ($4400 maximum); and work contracts averaged $1784 ($2060 maximum). 43% of undergraduates work part time. Average annual earnings from campus work are $1882. The average financial indebtedness of the 2001 graduate was $18,103. Illinois Wesleyan is a member of CSS. The CSS/Profile or FAFSA and the college's own financial statement are required. The fall application deadline is March 1.

International Students: There are 54 international students enrolled. The school actively recruits these students. They must score 550 on the written TOEFL.

Computers: The mainframe is an IBM AS/400. There are more than 450 IBM, Mac, and other PC terminals available in various computer labs and dormitories. Access to the Internet and World Wide Web is available through the campus network. All students may access the system. There are no time limits and no fees.

Graduates: The most popular majors were business administration (13%), biology (11%), and psychology (7%). In an average class, 1% graduate in 3 years, 74% in 4 years, 76% in 5 years, and 77% in 6 years. 87 companies recruited on campus in 2000-2001. Of the 2000 graduating class, 25% were enrolled in graduate school within 6 months of graduation and 73% were employed.

Admissions Contact: James R. Ruoti, Dean of Admissions. A video is available. E-mail: *iwuadmit@titan.iwu.edu* Web: *www.iwu.edu*

JUDSON COLLEGE

Elgin, IL 60123-1498 — **E-1**
(847) 695-2500
(800) 879-5376; Fax: (847) 695-0216

Full-time: 375 men, 450 women	**Faculty:** 40; IIB, av$
Part-time: 100 men, 185 women	**Ph.D.s:** 49%
Graduate: none	**Student/Faculty:** 21 to 1
Year: n/av	**Tuition:** $13,790
Application Deadline: open	**Room & Board:** $5190
Freshman Class: n/av	
SAT I or ACT: required	**LESS COMPETITIVE**

Judson College is an evangelical Christian college of the liberal arts, sciences, and professions. The library contains 90,000 volumes, 27,000 microform items, and 17,000 audiovisual forms/CDs, and subscribes to 500 periodicals. Computerized library services include the card catalog, interlibrary loans, and database searching. Special learning facilities include a learning resource center, art gallery, and radio station. The 80-acre campus is in a suburban area 40 miles west of Chicago. Including residence halls, there are 15 buildings.

Student Life: 75% of undergraduates are from Illinois. Others are from 14 states and 18 foreign countries. 81% are white. Most are Protestant. The average age of all undergraduates is 20. 26% do not continue beyond their first year.

Housing: 670 students can be accommodated in college housing, which includes single-sex dormitories, on-campus apartments, and married-student housing. On-campus housing is guaranteed for all 4 years. 58% of students live on campus; of those, 35% remain on campus on weekends. Alcohol is not permitted. All students may keep cars.

Activities: There are no fraternities or sororities. There are many groups and organizations on campus, including art, business, cheerleading, choir, chorale, drama, ethnic, honors, literary magazine, musical theater, newspaper, pep band, political, radio and TV, religious, social, social service, student government, and yearbook. Popular campus events include Spiritual Enrichment Week, Parents Weekend, and Christmas by Candlelight.

Sports: There are 4 intercollegiate sports for men and 5 for women, and 9 intramural sports for men and 8 for women. Facilities include a fitness center, a 1500-seat gym, a soccer field, baseball and softball diamonds, lighted tennis courts, racquetball and handball courts, indoor and outdoor running tracks, and a Nautilus and free-weight facility.

Disabled Students: 80% of the campus is accessible. Wheelchair ramps, elevators, special parking, specially equipped rest rooms, special class scheduling, lowered drinking fountains, and lowered telephones are available.

Services: Counseling and information services are available, as is tutoring in some subjects, including core courses. There is a reader service for the blind, and remedial math, reading, and writing.

Campus Safety and Security: Measures include 24-hour foot and vehicle patrol and lighted pathways/sidewalks.

Programs of Study: Judson confers the B.A. degree. Bachelor's degrees are awarded in BIOLOGICAL SCIENCE (biology/biological science), BUSINESS (accounting, business administration and management, international business management, and sports management), COMMUNICATIONS AND THE ARTS (communications, dramatic arts, English, fine arts, media arts, and music), COMPUTER AND PHYSICAL SCIENCE (chemistry, computer science, and mathematics), EDUCATION (early childhood, elementary, English, mathematics, music, physical, science, and secondary), ENGINEERING AND ENVIRONMENTAL DESIGN (preengineering), HEALTH PROFESSIONS (medical laboratory technology, nursing, predentistry, and premedicine), SOCIAL SCIENCE (anthropology, history, political science/government, prelaw, psychology, sociology, and youth ministry). Chemistry, premedicine, and biology are the strongest academically. Education, art, and business are the largest.

Required: Most students must have a GPA of 2.0; education majors must have a 2.5. Students must complete at least 126 credit hours, including 45 to 66 in the major, and take the college's core courses of Bible study, writing, speech, literature, math, science, history, fine arts, human relations, and phys ed, as well as a course in either anthropology, psychology, or sociology.

Special: The college has co-op programs with North Park College, Rush University, and the Mennonite College of Nursing, cross-registration with the Christian College Coalition, and work-study programs with many businesses. Students may serve internships in art and business, take a Washington semester, a film studies semester in Hollywood, or an ecology studies semester at Sable Institute in Michigan, or study abroad in Russia, Egypt, the Dominican Republic, and Israel. The college allows

dual majors, student-designed majors, and accelerated degrees in business leadership and management. There are pass/fail options for courses outside the major. There is 1 national honor society, and 2 departmental honors programs.
Faculty/Classroom: 90% of faculty are male; 10%, female. 80% teach undergraduates and 20% both teach and do research. The average class size in an introductory lecture is 28; in a laboratory, 9; and in a regular course, 16.
Requirements: The SAT I or ACT is required, with a minimum score of 18 on the ACT; the ACT is preferred. Graduation from secondary school is required. A minimum of 15 academic units is recommended. The college requires submission of an essay and recommends an interview. The GED is accepted. Judson requires applicants to be in the upper 50% of their class. A GPA of 2.0 is required. AP and CLEP credits are accepted. Important factors in the admissions decision are advanced placement or honor courses, recommendations by school officials, and leadership record.
Procedure: Freshmen are admitted to all sessions. Entrance exams should be taken in the spring of the junior year or the fall of the senior year. There is a deferred admissions plan. Application deadlines are open. The application fee is $30.
Transfer: 72 transfer students enrolled in a recent year. Students with fewer than 30 hours of college credit must submit high school transcripts showing a GPA of at least 2.0, as well as ACT results with a composite score of at least 18. Transfer students with more than 30 hours must have a GPA of at least 2.0. 30 credits of 126 must be completed at Judson.
Visiting: There are regularly scheduled orientations for prospective students, including a tour, class visits, a chapel visit, and individual meetings with professors, coaches, and other advisers. There are guides for informal visits and visitors may sit in on classes and stay overnight. To schedule a visit, contact the Enrollment Services Office.
Financial Aid: In a recent year, 80% of all freshmen and 83% of continuing students received some form of financial aid. 78% of freshmen and 79% of continuing students received need-based aid. The average freshman award was $11,884. Of that total, scholarships or need-based grants averaged $8707; and loans averaged $3097. Judson is a member of CSS. The FAFSA and the college's own financial statement are required. Check with the school for current deadlines.
International Students: The school actively recruits these students. They must score 550 on the written TOEFL or take the MELAB.
Computers: There are 30 IBM and 24 Macs available in the computer lab. All students may access the system. There are no time limits and no fees.
Graduates: In a recent year, 147 bachelor's degrees were awarded. In an average class, 5% graduate in 5 years, and 81% in 6 years.
Admissions Contact: Philip G. Guth, Dean for Enrollment Management. E-mail: *admissions@judson-il.edu* Web: *www.judson-il.edu*

KENDALL COLLEGE

Evanston, IL 60201 — E-1

(847) 866-1304
(877) 588-8860; Fax: (847) 733-7450

Recognized candidate for accreditation

Full-time: 120 men, 190 women	**Faculty:** 23
Part-time: 145 men, 75 women	**Ph.D.s:** 33%
Graduate: none	**Student/Faculty:** 13 to 1
Year: quarters, summer session	**Tuition:** $13,590
Application Deadline: open	**Room & Board:** $5529
Freshman Class: n/av	
ACT: required	**LESS COMPETITIVE**

Kendall College, founded in 1934, is a private institution affiliated with the United Methodist Church. It offers programs in liberal arts, business, and professional training, as well as culinary arts. Figures in above capsule are approximate. The library contains 33,000 volumes, 500 microform items, and 50 audiovisual forms/CDs, and subscribes to 210 periodicals. Computerized library services include interlibrary loans and database searching. Special learning facilities include an American Indian museum. The 1-acre campus is in a suburban area 3 miles north of Chicago. Including residence halls, there are 5 buildings.
Student Life: 89% of undergraduates are from Illinois. Others are from 5 states and 5 foreign countries. 70% are from public schools. 78% are white; 16% African American. 18% are Protestant; 15% Catholic; 12% Jewish. The average age of freshmen is 19; all undergraduates, 24. 5% do not continue beyond their first year; 25% remain to graduate.
Housing: 241 students can be accommodated in college housing, which includes single-sex and coed dormitories. On-campus housing is available on a first-come, first-served basis. 55% of students commute. Alcohol is not permitted. No one may keep cars.
Activities: There are no fraternities or sororities. There are 8 groups on campus, including computers, honors, international, literary magazine, newspaper, professional, social service, student government, and yearbook. Popular campus events include Bastille Day, Spring Dance, and May Day.
Sports: There are 4 intercollegiate sports for men and 4 for women. Off-site athletic facilities are rented by the college; there are no campus facilities.
Disabled Students: 75% of the campus is accessible. Wheelchair ramps, elevators, special parking, specially equipped rest rooms, and lowered telephones are available.
Services: Counseling and information services are available, as is tutoring in most subjects, including math, human services, and business. There is remedial math, reading, and writing.
Campus Safety and Security: Measures include 24-hour foot and vehicle patrol and lighted pathways/sidewalks.
Programs of Study: Kendall confers the B.A. degree. Associate degrees are also awarded. Bachelor's degrees are awarded in BUSINESS (business administration and management, hospitality management services, and hotel/motel and restaurant management), EDUCATION (early childhood), SOCIAL SCIENCE (criminal justice, food production/management/services, human services, and social science). Culinary Arts, early childhood education, and hotel and restaurant management are the strongest academically. Culinary arts and hospitality management are the largest.
Required: A 2.0 GPA is required to graduate.
Special: There are internships in culinary arts, hospitality management, human services, and early childhood education. The majority of degrees stress internships. Work-study programs and student-designed majors are also available. Accelerated degree programs are available in business administration and criminal justice. There are 2 national honor societies, including Phi Beta Kappa, and 2 departmental honors programs.
Faculty/Classroom: 61% of faculty are male; 39%, female. 25% do research. The average class size in an introductory lecture is 25; in a laboratory, 15; and in a regular course, 13.
Requirements: The ACT is required. In addition, minimum acceptable score on the SAT I is 425 Verbal, 425 math; on the ACT, the minimum score is 18. However, there is a placement test for students who do not meet the minimum requirement. Applicants should be graduates of an accredited secondary school or have a GED. They should prepare with 4 years of high school math, 2 years each of history, science, and social studies, and 1 year of a foreign language. An interview is recommended. A GPA of 2.0 is required. AP and CLEP credits are accepted.
Procedure: Freshmen are admitted to all sessions. Entrance exams should be taken as soon as requested. There is a deferred admissions plan. Application deadlines are open. The application fee is $30. Notification is sent on a rolling basis.
Transfer: The minimum GPA for transfer applicants is 2.0. An interview is recommended. 84 credits of 184 must be completed at Kendall.
Visiting: There are regularly scheduled orientations for prospective students. There are guides for informal visits and visitors may sit in on classes and stay overnight. To schedule a visit, contact the Admissions Office.
Financial Aid: In a recent year, 80% of all students received some form of financial aid. Average annual earnings from campus work are $1800. Kendall is a member of CSS. The FAFSA is required. Check with the school for current deadlines.
International Students: They must score 500 on the written TOEFL or 173 on the electronic version and also take the college's own test and the SAT I or the ACT.
Computers: IBM PS/2 PCs are available in the computer lab. All students may access the system when there are no computer classes in the lab. There are no time limits.
Graduates: In an average class, 55% graduate in 4 years. Of the 2000 graduating class, 95% were employed within 6 months of graduation.
Admissions Contact: Joy Marks, Director of Admissions.
E-mail: *admissions@kendall.edu* Web: *www.kendall.edu*

KNOX COLLEGE

Galesburg, IL 61401 — C-2

(309) 341-7123
(800) 678-KNOX; Fax: (309) 341-7070

Full-time: 495 men, 622 women	**Faculty:** 92; IIB, av$
Part-time: 13 men, 13 women	**Ph.D.s:** 93%
Graduate: none	**Student/Faculty:** 12 to 1
Year: trimesters	**Tuition:** $22,620
Application Deadline: February 15	**Room & Board:** $5610
Freshman Class: 1428 applied, 1027 accepted, 275 enrolled	
SAT I Verbal/Math: 620/610	**ACT:** 26 **HIGHLY COMPETITIVE**

Knox College, founded in 1837, is an independent liberal arts college. The 3 libraries contain 295,922 volumes, 96,922 microform items, and 5598 audiovisual forms/CDs, and subscribe to 978 periodicals. Computerized library services include the card catalog, interlibrary loans, and database searching. Special learning facilities include a learning resource center, natural history museum, radio station, and 760-acre biological field station near the campus. The 82-acre campus is in a small town 180 miles southwest of Chicago. Including residence halls, there are 42 buildings.
Student Life: 54% of undergraduates are from Illinois. Others are from 48 states and 39 foreign countries. 75% are from public schools. 71%

are white; 10%, foreign nationals. The average age of freshmen is 18; all undergraduates, 20. 12% do not continue beyond their first year; 72% remain to graduate.

Housing: 1114 students can be accommodated in college housing, which includes single-sex and coed dormitories, on-campus apartments, and fraternity houses. In addition, there are special-interest houses. On-campus housing is guaranteed for all 4 years. 96% of students live on campus; of those, 85% remain on campus on weekends. All students may keep cars.

Activities: 33% of men belong to 4 national fraternities; 13% of women belong to 2 national sororities. There are 75 groups on campus, including art, band, chess, choir, chorus, computers, dance, drama, ethnic, gay, honors, international, jazz band, literary magazine, newspaper, orchestra, photography, political, professional, radio and TV, religious, social, social service, student government, symphony, and yearbook. Popular campus events include International Fair, Black Culture Month, Flunk Day, and Pumphandle.

Sports: There are 11 intercollegiate sports for men and 10 for women, and 4 intramural sports for men and 3 for women. Facilities include 6 outdoor playing fields, 2 gyms, a swimming pool, tennis courts, and an outdoor track. The campus stadium seats 5000; the gym, 3000. There are club sports in men's volleyball, lacrosse, and water polo. The field house contains a 200-meter indoor track, tennis and volleyball courts, and multiuse space.

Disabled Students: 60% of the campus is accessible. Wheelchair ramps, elevators, special parking, specially equipped rest rooms, and special class scheduling are available.

Services: There is a reader service for the blind. The Learning Resource Center provides academic support to students in most subjects, particularly development of writing skills.

Campus Safety and Security: Measures include 24-hour foot and vehicle patrol, escort service, informal discussions, and pamphlets/posters/films. There are emergency telephones and lighted pathways/sidewalks.

Programs of Study: Knox confers the B.A. degree. Bachelor's degrees are awarded in BIOLOGICAL SCIENCE (biochemistry and biology/biological science), COMMUNICATIONS AND THE ARTS (art history and appreciation, classics, creative writing, dramatic arts, English literature, French, German, modern language, music, Russian, Spanish, and studio art), COMPUTER AND PHYSICAL SCIENCE (chemistry, computer science, mathematics, and physics), EDUCATION (elementary and secondary), ENGINEERING AND ENVIRONMENTAL DESIGN (environmental science), SOCIAL SCIENCE (African American studies, American studies, anthropology, economics, German area studies, history, international relations, philosophy, political science/government, psychology, Russian and Slavic studies, sociology, and women's studies). Biology, chemistry, and math are the strongest academically. Economics, biology, and education are the largest.

Required: Students must complete a 2-term interdisciplinary preceptorial emphasizing written and oral thinking; 1 unit is taken the freshman year, and the other is completed the junior or senior year. Distribution requirements include 2 courses each in humanities and fine arts, social sciences and history, and math and natural sciences. Foreign language proficiency requirements must also be met. A total of 36 courses, including 9 to 11 in the major, with a minimum GPA of 2.0, is required to graduate.

Special: The normal academic load is 3 courses per term, with 3 terms per year. Cooperative programs are offered with Washington University in St. Louis in architecture and engineering; Columbia University in engineering and law; the University of Illinois at Urbana-Champaign and Rensselaer Polytechnic Institute in engineering; Rush University in medicine, nursing, and medical technology; Duke University in forestry and environmental management; and the University of Chicago in law and social work. Study abroad is available in 20 countries. Other programs include a Washington semester, an urban studies semester, science and library research programs, work-study programs, and numerous internships. Dual majors, student-designed majors, and pass/fail options are available. Early admission to Rush Medical College is possible. Nondegree study is possible. Knox College participates in the Kemper Scholars Program. There are 7 national honor societies, including Phi Beta Kappa. All departments have honors programs.

Faculty/Classroom: 62% of faculty are male; 38%, female. All both teach and do research. The average class size in an introductory lecture is 26; in a laboratory, 16; and in a regular course, 16.

Admissions: 72% of the 2001-2002 applicants were accepted. The SAT I scores for the 2001-2002 freshman class were: Verbal--9% below 500, 32% between 500 and 599, 38% between 600 and 700, and 21% above 700; Math--12% below 500, 30% between 500 and 599, 49% between 600 and 700, and 9% above 700. The ACT scores were 11% below 21, 15% between 21 and 23, 29% between 24 and 26, 14% between 27 and 28, and 31% above 28. 57% of the current freshmen were in the top fifth of their class; 86% were in the top two fifths. There were 5 National Merit finalists and 5 semifinalists. 10 freshmen graduated first in their class.

Requirements: The SAT I or ACT is recommended. In addition, applicants should be graduates of an acccredited secondary school with 15 academic credits, including 4 in English, 3 each in math, science, and history and social studies, and 2 in foreign language. An essay is part of the application process. An interview is recommended. AP and CLEP credits are accepted. Important factors in the admissions decision are advanced placement or honor courses, recommendations by school officials, and extracurricular activities record. Applications are accepted on computer disk and on-line through Apply, CollegeLink, and Common App.

Procedure: Freshmen are admitted to all sessions. Entrance exams should be taken by December 15. There are early action, early admissions, and deferred admissions plans. Early action applications should be filed by December 1; regular applications, by February 15 for fall entry, November 1 for winter entry, and February 1 for spring entry. The fall 2001 application fee was $35. Notification of early action is sent December 15; regular decision, March 31.

Transfer: 43 transfer students enrolled in 2001-2002. A 2.75 GPA is required. An interview is recommended. 13 credits of 36 must be completed at Knox.

Visiting: There are regularly scheduled orientations for prospective students, including 1 late summer and 2 each in fall, winter, and spring, consisting of a personal itinerary for each student that includes a campus tour, class visit, lunch with a student, an interview with a faculty member, and an admissions interview. There are guides for informal visits and visitors may sit in on classes and stay overnight. To schedule a visit, contact the Admission Office at (309) 341-7100.

Financial Aid: In 2001-2002, 96% of all freshmen and 92% of continuing students received some form of financial aid. 76% of freshmen and 73% of continuing students received need-based aid. The average freshman award was $17,739. Of that total, scholarships or need-based grants averaged $14,436 ($22,380 maximum); loans averaged $4202 ($6125 maximum); and work contracts averaged $1392 ($1545 maximum). 68% of undergraduates work part time. Average annual earnings from campus work are $932. The average financial indebtedness of the 2001 graduate was $17,096. Knox is a member of CSS. The FAFSA, the college's own financial statement, and student and parent tax returns are required. The fall application deadline is March 1.

International Students: There are 113 international students enrolled. The school actively recruits these students. They must score 550 on the written TOEFL and also take the SAT I or the ACT.

Computers: The mainframe consists of HP 9000 UNIX servers and NT servers. Virtually every campus building is linked via a fiber optic Ethernet network. There are 5 public networked computer labs equipped with more than 200 Power Macs and Pentiums. Students may connect PCs from their rooms to the library, e-mail services, software applications, and the Internet. All students may access the system. A large student computer lab is open 24 hours. Others are open until midnight. There are no time limits and no fees.

Graduates: In 2001, 313 bachelor's degrees were awarded. The most popular majors were biology (12%), economics (11%), and education (7%). In an average class, 61% graduate in 4 years, 71% in 5 years, and 71% in 6 years. 81 companies recruited on campus in 2000-2001. Of the 2000 graduating class, 35% were enrolled in graduate school within 6 months of graduation and 61% were employed.

Admissions Contact: Paul Steenis, Director of Admission.
E-mail: *admission@knox.edu* Web: *www.knox.edu*

LAKE FOREST COLLEGE — E-1

Lake Forest, IL 60045-2399 — (847) 735-5000
(800) 828-4751; Fax: (847) 735-6271

Full-time: 515 men, 727 women	**Faculty:** 83; IIB, +$
Part-time: 9 men, 9 women	**Ph.D.s:** 98%
Graduate: 5 men, 12 women	**Student/Faculty:** 15 to 1
Year: semesters, summer session	**Tuition:** $22,206
Application Deadline: March 1	**Room & Board:** $5254
Freshman Class: 1607 applied, 1109 accepted, 336 enrolled	
SAT I Verbal/Math: 560/570	**ACT:** 25 **VERY COMPETITIVE**

Lake Forest College, founded in 1857, is a liberal arts institution affiliated by heritage with the Presbyterian Church (U.S.A.). The 2 libraries contain 218,815 volumes, 103,754 microform items, and 11,916 audiovisual forms/CDs, and subscribe to 1397 periodicals. Computerized library services include the card catalog, interlibrary loans, and database searching. Special learning facilities include a learning resource center, art gallery, radio station, multimedia language lab, and an electronic music studio with practice rooms. The 107-acre campus is in a suburban area 30 miles north of Chicago. Including residence halls, there are 30 buildings.

Student Life: 57% of undergraduates are from out of state, mostly the Midwest. Others are from 44 states, 41 foreign countries, and Canada. 68% are from public schools. 80% are white. The average age of freshmen is 18; all undergraduates, 20. 22% do not continue beyond their first year; 63% remain to graduate.

Housing: 900 students can be accommodated in college housing, which includes single-sex and coed dormitories. In addition, there are honors houses, special-interest houses, and options for 24-hour quiet and substance-free housing. On-campus housing is guaranteed for all 4 years. 83% of students live on campus; of those, 98% remain on campus on weekends. Upperclassmen may keep cars.

Activities: 15% of men belong to 2 local fraternities and 1 national fraternity; 22% of women belong to 3 local sororities and 1 national sorority. There are 101 groups on campus, including art, band, cheerleading, chess, choir, chorus, computers, dance, debate, drama, ethnic, film, gay, honors, international, jazz band, literary magazine, newspaper, orchestra, pep band, photography, political, professional, radio and TV, religious, social, social service, student government, and yearbook. Popular campus events include Festival of Ra, Big Chill Weekend, and poet, writer, artist, and scholar-residence programs.

Sports: There are 9 intercollegiate sports for men and 10 for women, and 8 intramural sports for men and 8 for women. Facilities include a gym, tennis courts, indoor and outdoor basketball courts, and racquetball, handball, squash, and outdoor sand volleyball courts. There are also weight and exercise rooms, a pool, an indoor ice rink, and baseball, football, soccer, and intramural fields.

Disabled Students: 80% of the campus is accessible. Wheelchair ramps, elevators, special parking, specially equipped rest rooms, special class scheduling, lowered drinking fountains, and lowered telephones are available.

Services: Counseling and information services are available, as is tutoring in most subjects.

Campus Safety and Security: Measures include 24-hour foot and vehicle patrol, self-defense education, escort service, and shuttle buses. There are informal discussions, pamphlets/posters/films, emergency telephones, and lighted pathways/sidewalks.

Programs of Study: Lake Forest confers the B.A. degree. Master's degrees are also awarded. Bachelor's degrees are awarded in BIOLOGICAL SCIENCE (biology/biological science), BUSINESS (business economics), COMMUNICATIONS AND THE ARTS (art, communications, English, French, German, music, and Spanish), COMPUTER AND PHYSICAL SCIENCE (chemistry, computer science, mathematics, and physics), EDUCATION (education), ENGINEERING AND ENVIRONMENTAL DESIGN (environmental science), SOCIAL SCIENCE (American studies, anthropology, area studies, Asian/Oriental studies, economics, history, international relations, Latin American studies, philosophy, political science/government, psychology, and sociology). Economics, politics, and history are the largest.

Required: All students are required to complete 32 courses with a minimum GPA of 2.0. General education requirements include 2 courses in natural science and math, 2 cultural diversity courses, and 1 course each in freshman studies, freshman writing, humanities, social science, and senior studies.

Special: Lake Forest offers cross-registration with Barat College of De-Paul University and Associated Colleges of the Midwest, an extensive internship program through Chicago Allicance and Outreach Programs, a student-designed Independent Scholar Program, and study abroad in 14 countries. Dual and interdisciplinary majors, including American studies, Asian studies, area studies, art (studio and art history), and environmental studies, are available. There is a Washington semester with American University and a work-study program. A 3-2 engineering degree with Washington University at St. Louis and a 3-2 extended degree program in social service with the University of Chicago School of Social Service Administration are offered. Several minors and a pass/fail option are available. A program in marine biology is offered in the Bahamas. There are 11 national honor societies, including Phi Beta Kappa, and a freshman honors program.

Faculty/Classroom: 57% of faculty are male; 43%, female. All both teach and do research. No introductory courses are taught by graduate students. The average class size in an introductory lecture is 21; in a laboratory, 12; and in a regular course, 16.

Admissions: 69% of the 2001-2002 applicants were accepted. The SAT I scores for the 2001-2002 freshman class were: Verbal--22% below 500, 43% between 500 and 599, 30% between 600 and 700, and 5% above 700; Math--21% below 500, 40% between 500 and 599, 33% between 600 and 700, and 6% above 700. The ACT scores were 9% below 21, 23% between 21 and 23, 29% between 24 and 26, 21% between 27 and 28, and 18% above 28. 46% of the current freshmen were in the top fifth of their class; 71% were in the top two fifths. There were 2 National Merit finalists and 14 semifinalists. 9 freshmen graduated first in their class.

Requirements: The SAT I or ACT is required. In addition, applicants are advised to complete 16 academic credits, including 4 in English, 3 in math, 2 to 4 each in social and natural sciences, and study in 1 or more foreign languages. A GED is accepted. An interview is encouraged. Applications are accepted on computer disk and on-line via CollegeLink, the Common Application, EXPAN, and MacApply. AP credits are accepted. Important factors in the admissions decision are advanced placement or honor courses, evidence of special talent, and extracurricular activities record.

Procedure: Freshmen are admitted fall and winter. Entrance exams should be taken in the junior or senior year. There are early action, early admissions, and deferred admissions plans. Early action applications should be filed by January 1; regular applications, by March 1 for fall entry and December 15 for spring entry. The fall 2001 application fee was $40. Notification of early action is sent January 21; regular decision, March 21. 39 early action candidates were accepted for the 2001-2002 class. 4% of all applicants are on a waiting list; 13 were accepted in 2001.

Transfer: 67 transfer students enrolled in 2001-2002. Transfer applicants should have a minimum C average in all college work and should be in good standing with their previous institution. High school and college transcripts and a letter of recommendation from the academic dean or a teacher at the most recent college attended are required. 16 courses of 32 must be completed at Lake Forest.

Visiting: There are regularly scheduled orientations for prospective students, consisting of class visitation, panel presentations, tours and individual appointments with faculty and/or admission officers. There are guides for informal visits and visitors may sit in on classes and stay overnight. To schedule a visit, contact the Admissions Office.

Financial Aid: In 2001-2002, 84% of all freshmen and 88% of continuing students received some form of financial aid. 64% of freshmen and 72% of continuing students received need-based aid. The average freshman award was $16,465. Of that total, scholarships or need-based grants averaged $15,647 ($24,500 maximum); loans averaged $3432 ($5000 maximum); and work contracts averaged $1600 ($2200 maximum). 79% of undergraduates work part time. Average annual earnings from campus work are $1650. The average financial indebtedness of the 2001 graduate was $15,048. Lake Forest is a member of CSS. The CSS/Profile or FAFSA is required. The fall application deadline is March 1.

International Students: There are 97 international students enrolled. The school actively recruits these students. They must score 550 on the written TOEFL or 220 on the electronic version and also take the SAT I or the ACT.

Computers: There are 190 computers that access the mainframe, the majority of which are available for student use. There are also more than 100 PCs in 11 computer labs in residence halls and academic buildings available for student use. The residence hall PCs have word-processing, database-management, and spreadsheet capabilities. Internet network hookups in residence hall rooms are possible at no charge. All students may access the system 24 hours a day, 7 days a week. There are no time limits and no fees.

Graduates: In 2001, 295 bachelor's degrees were awarded. The most popular majors were business/economics (22%), psychology (7%), and English (7%). In an average class, 62% graduate in 4 years, 63% in 5 years, and 63% in 6 years. 56 companies recruited on campus in 2000-2001. Of the 2000 graduating class, 20% were enrolled in graduate school within 6 months of graduation and 65% were employed.

Admissions Contact: William G. Motzer, Director of Admissions.
E-mail: *admissions@lfc.edu* Web: *http://www.lfc.edu*

LEWIS UNIVERSITY

Romeoville, IL 60446 — E-2

(815) 838-0500, ext. 5250
(800) 897-9000; Fax: (815) 836-5002

Full-time: 1005 men, 1134 women	**Faculty:** 141
Part-time: 429 men, 815 women	**Ph.D.s:** 57%
Graduate: 412 men, 612 women	**Student/Faculty:** 15 to 1
Year: semesters, summer session	**Tuition:** $14,040
Application Deadline: open	**Room & Board:** $6920
Freshman Class: 1339 applied, 873 accepted, 387 enrolled	
SAT I Verbal/Math: 530/570	**ACT:** 22 **COMPETITIVE**

Lewis University, founded in 1932, is a private institution affiliated with the Roman Catholic Church and sponsored by the De La Salle Christian Brothers. A comprehensive liberal arts university, Lewis offers classes at its main campus and at more than 20 satellite locations in the Chicago metropolitan area. There are 3 undergraduate schools and 8 graduate programs. In addition to regional accreditation, Lewis has baccalaureate program accreditation with NCATE and NLN. The library contains 176,200 volumes, 13,100 microform items, and 2609 audiovisual forms/CDs, and subscribes to 1825 periodicals. Computerized library services include the card catalog, interlibrary loans, and database searching. Special learning facilities include a learning resource center, art gallery, radio station, TV station, aviation building, and airport. The 350-acre campus is in a suburban area 35 miles southwest of Chicago. Including residence halls, there are 16 buildings.

Student Life: 97% of undergraduates are from Illinois. Others are from 24 states, 18 foreign countries, and Canada. 68% are white; 16%, African American. Most are Catholic. The average age of freshmen is 19; all undergraduates, 28. 19% do not continue beyond their first year.

Housing: 900 students can be accommodated in college housing, which includes single-sex and coed dormitories. On-campus housing is available on a first-come, first-served basis. 73% of students commute. All students may keep cars.

Activities: 3% of men belong to 4 local and 5 national fraternities; 2% of women belong to 3 national sororities. Lewis also sponsors 3 coed fratorities, to which 2% of men and women belong. There are 27 groups on campus, including band, cheerleading, choir, chorale, chorus, dance, drama, ethnic, flight team, forensics, honors, international, jazz band, literary magazine, musical theater, newspaper, orchestra, pep band, photography, political, professional, radio and TV, religious, social, social service, student government, symphony, and yearbook. Popular campus events include Fall and Spring Formals, Greek Stock, and International Student Food Festival.

Sports: There are 9 intercollegiate sports for men and 9 for women, and 10 intramural sports for men and 10 for women. Facilities include a recreation center containing a field house with 4 multipurpose courts, a fitness center, an aerobics studio, an 8-lane pool, and an indoor track; a tennis complex; an outdoor track; and baseball, softball, and soccer fields.

Disabled Students: 95% of the campus is accessible. Wheelchair ramps, elevators, special parking, specially equipped rest rooms, special class scheduling, lowered drinking fountains, and lowered telephones are available.

Services: Counseling and information services are available, as is tutoring in most subjects. There is remedial math, reading, and writing. The University Success Program provides assistance to those students who do not meet the outright scholastic requirements.

Campus Safety and Security: Measures include 24-hour foot and vehicle patrol, escort service, informal discussions, and pamphlets/posters/films. There are emergency telephones and lighted pathways/sidewalks.

Programs of Study: Lewis confers B.A., B.S., B.E.S., and B.S.N. degrees. Associate and master's degrees are also awarded. Bachelor's degrees are awarded in BIOLOGICAL SCIENCE (biochemistry and biology/biological science), BUSINESS (accounting, banking and finance, business administration and management, human resources, management information systems, marketing/retailing/merchandising, and sports management), COMMUNICATIONS AND THE ARTS (broadcasting, communications, communications technology, dramatic arts, drawing, English, illustration, journalism, multimedia, music, music business management, painting, public relations, radio/television technology, and studio art), COMPUTER AND PHYSICAL SCIENCE (atmospheric sciences and meteorology, chemistry, computer science, mathematics, and physics), EDUCATION (athletic training, elementary, secondary, special, and speech correction), ENGINEERING AND ENVIRONMENTAL DESIGN (aircraft mechanics, airline piloting and navigation, aviation administration/management, computer graphics, environmental science, and pre-engineering), HEALTH PROFESSIONS (community health work, health care administration, nursing, physical therapy, predentistry, premedicine, preoptometry, prepharmacy, and preveterinary science), SOCIAL SCIENCE (Christian studies, criminal justice, economics, history, liberal arts/general studies, philosophy, political science/government, prelaw, psychology, public administration, religion, safety and security technology, social work, and sociology). Aviation, criminal and social justice, and nursing education are the strongest academically and have the largest enrollments.

Required: All students must earn 128 credit hours in courses acceptable for graduation, with one third of these courses in the core curriculum. Students must maintain a minimum GPA of 2.0. At least 4 upper-division courses must be taken in the major. Students must complete the Introduction to the College Experience course and pass a writing proficiency exam.

Special: Lewis offers a general education degree, co-op programs, student-designed majors, B.A.-B.S. degrees, pass/fail options, dual majors, work-study programs, and nondegree study. Internships are required for some majors and optional for all others. There are accelerated-degree programs in business administration, computer network administration, aviation maintenance management, and nursing. The aviation program permits graduates to qualify for the FAA Airframe and Powerplant certificate. There are 10 national honor societies, a freshman honors program, and 10 departmental honors programs.

Faculty/Classroom: 57% of faculty are male; 43%, female. All teach undergraduates. No introductory courses are taught by graduate students. The average class size in an introductory lecture is 14; in a laboratory, 11; and in a regular course, 13.

Admissions: 65% of the 2001-2002 applicants were accepted. The SAT I scores for the 2001-2002 freshman class were: Verbal--36% below 500, 43% between 500 and 599, and 21% between 600 and 700; Math--36% below 500, 36% between 500 and 599, and 29% between 600 and 700. The ACT scores were 42% below 21, 32% between 21 and 23, 16% between 24 and 26, 6% between 27 and 28, and 4% above 28. 19% of the current freshmen were in the top fifth of their class; 43% were in the top two fifths.

Requirements: The SAT I or ACT is required; the ACT is preferred, with a minimum composite score of 20. Applicants should be graduates of an accredited secondary school. The GED is accepted. Students should have 18 units consisting of 3 in English and 15 in other college-preparatory subjects. A GPA of 2.0 is required. AP and CLEP credits are accepted. Applications are accepted on-line, with College Apply software available through the university's web site.

Procedure: Freshmen are admitted to all sessions. Entrance exams should be taken prior to enrollment. Application deadlines are open. The fall 2001 application fee was $35. Notification is sent on a rolling basis.

Transfer: 465 transfer students enrolled in 2001-2002. Applicants must have a 2.0 GPA in transferable course work of at least 12 semester hours, submit official transcripts from all colleges attended, and be in good standing at the previous institution. 32 credits of 128 must be completed at Lewis.

Visiting: There are regularly scheduled orientations for prospective students, consisting of 1- or 2-day sessions (overnight optional) and parent orientation followed by a welcome weekend before the first class day in the fall. There are guides for informal visits and visitors may sit in on classes and stay overnight. To schedule a visit, contact the Admissions Office.

Financial Aid: In 2001-2002, 67% of all freshmen and 66% of continuing students received some form of financial aid. 55% of freshmen and 48% of continuing students received need-based aid. The average freshman award was $16,125. Of that total, scholarships or need-based grants averaged $9103 and loans averaged $6362. 12% of undergraduates work part time through work-stuy programs. Average annual earnings from campus work are $2400. The average financial indebtedness of the 2001 graduate was $15,621. Lewis is a member of CSS. The FAFSA is required. The priority fall application deadline is May 1.

International Students: There are 73 international students enrolled. The school actively recruits these students. They must score 500 on the written TOEFL and also take the SAT I or the ACT.

Computers: The mainframes are 3 IBM RS/6000 units. All students may access the system. There are no time limits. In a recent year the fee was $15.

Graduates: In 2001, 816 bachelor's degrees were awarded. The most popular majors were nursing (12%), criminal and social justice (10%), and business administration (10%). In an average class, 24% graduate in 3 years, 42% in 4 years, 45% in 5 years, and 62% in 6 years.

Admissions Contact: Bill Carter, Director of Enrollment. A video is available. E-mail: *admissions@lewisu.edu* Web: *www.lewisu.edu*

LOYOLA UNIVERSITY OF CHICAGO — E-2

Chicago, IL 60611 — (312) 915-6500
(800) 262-2373; Fax: (312) 915-7216

Full-time: 1861 men, 3585 women	**Faculty:** 479; I, -$
Part-time: 726 men, 1325 women	**Ph.D.s:** 98%
Graduate: 2079 men, 3443 women	**Student/Faculty:** 11 to 1
Year: semesters, summer session	**Tuition:** $18,726
Application Deadline: April 1	**Room & Board:** $7266
Freshman Class: 8746 applied, 6722 accepted, 1424 enrolled	
SAT I Verbal/Math: 580/580	**ACT:** 25 **VERY COMPETITIVE**

Loyola University of Chicago, founded in 1870, is a private Roman Catholic university offering undergraduate curricula in the arts and sciences, business, nursing, social work, and education. There are 5 undergraduate and 9 graduate schools. In addition to regional accreditation, Loyola has baccalaureate program accreditation with AACSB, CSWE, NCATE, and NLN. The 3 libraries contain 983,023 volumes, 1,625,335 microform items, and 32,777 audiovisual forms/CDs, and subscribe to 110,502 periodicals. Computerized library services include the card catalog, interlibrary loans, and database searching. Special learning facilities include a learning resource center, art gallery, radio station, nursing resource center, theater, seismograph station, and an electron microscope. The 105-acre campus is in an urban area in Chicago. Including residence halls, there are 130 buildings.

Student Life: 58% of undergraduates are from Illinois. Others are from 50 states, 78 foreign countries, and Canada. 61% are from public schools. 61% are white. 61% are Catholic; 30% Orthodox (3%), Islam (5%), unknown (11%), other (6%), none (4%). The average age of freshmen is 18; all undergraduates, 21. 15% do not continue beyond their first year; 69% remain to graduate.

Housing: 1985 students can be accommodated in college housing, which includes single-sex and coed dormitories and on-campus apartments. In addition, there are special-interest houses, a 24-hour quiet center, and a living-learning center. On-campus housing is guaranteed for all 4 years. 70% of students commute. All students may keep cars.

Activities: 7% of men belong to 1 local fraternity and 5 national fraternities; 5% of women belong to 8 national sororities. There are 136 groups on campus, including cheerleading, choir, chorus, drama, environmental, ethnic, gay, honors, international, jazz band, literary magazine, musical theater, newspaper, political, professional, radio and TV, religious, social, social service, and student government. Popular campus events include Hunger Week, Harmony Colors Festival, and President's and Valentine's Balls.

Sports: There are 6 intercollegiate sports for men and 7 for women, and 22 intramural sports for men and 22 for women. Facilities include racquetball courts, dance studio, swimming pools, saunas, an elevated jogging track, and weight rooms.

Disabled Students: 95% of the campus is accessible. Wheelchair ramps, elevators, special parking, specially equipped rest rooms, special class scheduling, lowered drinking fountains, and lowered telephones are available.

Services: Counseling and information services are available, as is tutoring in some subjects, including general education courses. There is a reader service for the blind and remedial writing. A writing center is also available for student use.

Campus Safety and Security: Measures include 24-hour foot and vehicle patrol, self-defense education, escort service, and shuttle buses. There are informal discussions, pamphlets/posters/films, emergency telephones, and lighted pathways/sidewalks.

Programs of Study: Loyola confers B.A., B.S., B.A.Classics, B.B.A., B.S.Ed., and B.S.N. degrees. Master's and doctoral degrees are also awarded. Bachelor's degrees are awarded in BIOLOGICAL SCIENCE (biology/biological science), BUSINESS (accounting, banking and finance, business administration and management, business economics, marketing/retailing/merchandising, and personnel management), COMMUNICATIONS AND THE ARTS (communications, dramatic arts, English, fine arts, French, German, Greek, Italian, Latin, and Spanish), COMPUTER AND PHYSICAL SCIENCE (chemistry, computer science, mathematics, and physics), EDUCATION (elementary and special), HEALTH PROFESSIONS (nursing, predentistry, premedicine, and preveterinary science), SOCIAL SCIENCE (anthropology, classical/ancient civilization, criminal justice, economics, history, philosophy, political science/government, psychology, religion, social work, sociology, and theological studies). Biology, psychology, and nursing are the largest.

Required: To graduate, students must have a total of 128 credit hours with a minimum GPA of 2.0. The number of hours required in the major varies. For the core requirement, all students must take 9 hours each of theology, philosophy, and social sciences, and 6 hours each of English composition and humanities.

Special: Sophomores and juniors may study in Italy or Mexico. Dual majors, a Washington semester, nondegree study, and pass/fail options are available. The school also offers a B.A.-B.S. degree in chemistry and a 2-3 engineering degree with the University of Illinois at Urbana-Champaign, and Washington University. For working adults, Mundelein College offers fully accredited programs leading to baccaulaureate degrees in arts and sciences, business and education. There is a chapter of Phi Beta Kappa and a freshman honors program.

Faculty/Classroom: 58% of faculty are male; 42%, female. 93% teach undergraduates and all do research. No introductory courses are taught by graduate students. The average class size in an introductory lecture is 25; in a laboratory, 18; and in a regular course, 15.

Admissions: 77% of the 2001-2002 applicants were accepted. The SAT I scores for the 2001-2002 freshman class were: Verbal--13% below 500, 45% between 500 and 599, 35% between 600 and 700, and 7% above 700; Math--17% below 500, 41% between 500 and 599, 35% between 600 and 700, and 7% above 700. The ACT scores were 16% below 21, 23% between 21 and 23, 26% between 24 and 26, 18% between 27 and 28, and 17% above 28. 55% of the current freshmen were in the top fifth of their class; 85% were in the top two fifths. 12 freshmen graduated first in their class.

Requirements: The SAT I or ACT is required. In addition, graduation from an accredited secondary school or satisfactory scores on the GED are required for admission. 15 academic credits are required. Secondary school courses should include 4 credits of English, 2 of math, and 1 each of science and social studies. An interview is recommended but an essay is not required. AP and CLEP credits are accepted. Important factors in the admissions decision are advanced placement or honor courses, evidence of special talent, and leadership record.

Procedure: Freshmen are admitted to all sessions. Entrance exams should be taken as early as possible, normally in the spring of the junior year. Applications should be filed by April 1 for fall entry and December 1 for spring entry. The fall 2001 application fee was $25. Notification is sent on a rolling basis.

Transfer: 474 transfer students enrolled in 2001-2002. Transfer students must have 20 transferable semester hours of credit, with a minimum GPA of 2.0 for the schools of arts and sciences and education. A minimum GPA of 2.5 is required for the schools of nursing and business administration. If transfers have fewer than 20 hours, students must meet the same requirements as entering freshmen. 45 credits of 128 must be completed at Loyola.

Visiting: There are regularly scheduled orientations for prospective students, including interviews and tours; students may attend classes if previous arrangements have been made. There are guides for informal visits and visitors may sit in on classes and stay overnight. To schedule a visit, contact the Undergraduate Admissions Office at (773) 508-3075.

Financial Aid: In 2001-2002, 93% of all freshmen and 80% of continuing students received some form of financial aid. 72% of freshmen and 66% of continuing students received need-based aid. The average freshman award was $16,633. Of that total, scholarships or need-based grants averaged $13,059 ($18,814 maximum); loans averaged $1786 ($6500 maximum); and work contracts averaged $1788 ($5000 maximum). 65% of undergraduates work part time. Average annual earnings from campus work are $1300. The average financial indebtedness of the 2001 graduate was $16,300. The FAFSA is required. The fall application deadline is March 1.

International Students: There were 55 international students enrolled in a recent year. The school actively recruits these students. They must score 550 on the written TOEFL or 213 on the electronic version.

Computers: The mainframe is an IBM 3081K. More than 190 PCs, networked to commonly used software packages, are available for student use. More than 75 terminals access the mainframe computer for heavy-duty analytical packages. All students may access the system whenever facilities are available. There are no time limits and no fees.

Graduates: In 2001, 1318 bachelor's degrees were awarded. The most popular majors were psychology (12%), biology (10%), and nursing (9%). In an average class, 1% graduate in 3 years, 46% in 4 years, 64% in 5 years, and 67% in 6 years. 360 companies recruited on campus in 2000-2001.

Admissions Contact: April Hansen, Director, Undergraduate Admissions. A video is available. E-mail: *admission@luc.edu*
Web: *http://www.luc.edu*

MACMURRAY COLLEGE
Jacksonville, IL 62650 — C-3
(217) 479-7056
(800) 252-7485; Fax: (217) 245-0405

Full-time: 299 men, 304 women	**Faculty:** 46
Part-time: 10 men, 42 women	**Ph.D.s:** 72%
Graduate: none	**Student/Faculty:** 13 to 1
Year: 4-1-4, summer session	**Tuition:** $13,140
Application Deadline: open	**Room & Board:** $4650
Freshman Class: 722 applied, 665 accepted, 210 enrolled	
SAT I Verbal/Math: 500/510	**ACT:** 22 **LESS COMPETITIVE**

MacMurray College, founded in 1846, is a private liberal arts institution affiliated with the United Methodist Church. In addition to regional accreditation, MacMurray has baccalaureate program accreditation with CCNE and CSWE. The library contains 145,000 volumes and subscribes to 300 periodicals. Computerized library services include the card catalog, interlibrary loans, and database searching. Special learning facilities include a learning resource center and art gallery. The 60-acre campus is in a small town 30 miles west of of Springfield. Including residence halls, there are 16 buildings.

Student Life: 82% of undergraduates are from Illinois. Others are from 25 states and 3 foreign countries. 90% are from public schools. 83% are white; 11%, African American. 42% are Protestant; 23% claim no religious affiliation; 22% are Catholic. The average age of freshmen is 18; all undergraduates, 20. 30% do not continue beyond their first year; 46% remain to graduate.

Housing: 725 students can be accommodated in college housing, which includes single-sex and coed dormitories. On-campus housing is guaranteed for all 4 years. 55% of students live on campus; of those, 70% remain on campus on weekends. Alcohol is not permitted. All students may keep cars.

Activities: 18% of men belong to 1 local and 1 national fraternity; 10% of women belong to 2 local sororities. There are 36 groups on campus, including art, band, cheerleading, choir, chorale, chorus, dance, drama, ethnic, gay, honors, international, literary magazine, musical theater, newspaper, orchestra, pep band, photography, political, professional, religious, social, social service, student government, and yearbook. Popular campus events include spring formal, Sigma Tau Gamma Day, and midnight breakfasts.

Sports: There are 9 intercollegiate sports for men and 8 for women, and 15 intramural sports for men and 15 for women. Facilities include a gym, 3 basketball courts, tennis and outdoor basketball courts, a competition-size swimming pool, a weight room, a wrestling room, dance studios, a game room and TV lounge, and football, soccer, and baseball fields.

Disabled Students: 90% of the campus is accessible. Wheelchair ramps, elevators, special parking, specially equipped rest rooms, special class scheduling, and specially equipped bedrooms with TTD are available.

Services: Counseling and information services are available, as is tutoring in every subject. There is remedial math, reading, and writing. The college provides services to visually and hearing impaired students through interpreters, readers, and note takers.

Campus Safety and Security: Measures include escort service, informal discussions, pamphlets/posters/films, and emergency telephones. There are lighted pathways/sidewalks, evening patrols, and sign-in at dorms.

Programs of Study: MacMurray confers B.A., B.S., B.S.N., and B.S.W. degrees. Associate degrees are also awarded. Bachelor's degrees are awarded in BIOLOGICAL SCIENCE (biology/biological science), BUSINESS (accounting, business administration and management, management information systems, marketing/retailing/merchandising, and sports management), COMMUNICATIONS AND THE ARTS (art, dramatic arts, English, French, journalism, music, and Spanish), COMPUTER AND PHYSICAL SCIENCE (chemistry, computer science, mathematics, and physics), EDUCATION (education of the deaf and hearing impaired, elementary, music, physical, science, secondary, and special), ENGINEERING AND ENVIRONMENTAL DESIGN (preengineering), HEALTH PROFESSIONS (nursing, predentistry, premedicine, and preveterinary science), SOCIAL SCIENCE (criminal justice, history, interpreter for the deaf, liberal arts/general studies, philosophy, political science/government, prelaw, psychology, religion, social work, and youth ministry). Education of the hearing impaired, English, and nursing are the strongest academically. Business, education, and criminal justice are the largest.

Required: To graduate, students must complete 120 semester hours and 2 January term courses, with a minimum GPA of 2.0. All students must take 9 semester hours in rhetorical skills and a 5-course sequence on major ideas in Western civilization and world culture, and satisfy the requirements of the breadth component, a 16-hour distribution of nonmajor courses. Proficiency exams or equivalent courses in math and composition must be taken by all students before the end of the junior year.

Special: The school has co-op programs in modern languages and international studies and cross-registration with 5 colleges through the West Central Illinois Foreign Language Consortium. A 3-2 engineering degree with Washington and Columbia Universities and the University of Missouri (Rolla), a Washington semester, internships in all majors, work-study programs, dual majors, and pass/fail options are available. Students may study abroad in England, Germany, Japan, or Russia. There are 4 national honor societies, a freshman honors program, and 14 departmental honors programs.

Faculty/Classroom: 63% of faculty are male; 37%, female. All teach undergraduates. The average class size in an introductory lecture is 35; in a laboratory, 16; and in a regular course, 15.

Admissions: 92% of the 2001-2002 applicants were accepted. The SAT I scores for the 2001-2002 freshman class were: Verbal--48% below 500, 39% between 500 and 599, and 12% between 600 and 700; Math--53% below 500, 37% between 500 and 599, and 8% between 600 and 700. The ACT scores were 49% below 21, 31% between 21 and 23, 12% between 24 and 26, 4% between 27 and 28, and 3% above 28. 28% of the current freshmen were in the top fifth of their class; 50% were in the top two fifths. In a recent year, 2 freshmen graduated first in their class.

Requirements: The SAT I or ACT is required. In addition, applicants must be graduates of an accredited secondary school. The GED is accepted. Secondary school courses should include 4 years of English, 3 years of math, and 2 years each of science, foreign language, and social studies. MacMurray requires applicants to be in the upper 50% of their class. AP and CLEP credits are accepted. Important factors in the admissions decision are advanced placement or honor courses, extracurricular activities record, and leadership record. Applications are accepted online via Illinois Mentor.

Procedure: Freshmen are admitted fall, winter, spring, and summer. Entrance exams should be taken in the spring of the junior year. There are early admissions and deferred admissions plans. Application deadlines are open. There is a rolling admissions plan and notification is sent on a rolling basis.

Transfer: 49 transfer students enrolled in 2001-2002. Transfer students must have a minimum GPA of 2.0 in at least 28 transferable semester credits. Nursing applicants must have a GPA of 2.75 and a minimum score of 20 on the ACT. 30 credits of 126 must be completed at MacMurray.

Visiting: There are regularly scheduled orientations for prospective students, including a financial aid conference, a tour, and faculty appointments. There are guides for informal visits and visitors may sit in on classes and stay overnight. To schedule a visit, contact the Office of Admissions.

Financial Aid: In 2001-2002, 98% of all freshmen and 92% of continuing students received some form of financial aid. 89% of freshmen and 78% of continuing students received need-based aid. The average freshman award was $12,317. Of that total, scholarships or need-based grants averaged $6055 ($10,000 maximum); loans averaged $4000 ($7100 maximum); and work contracts averaged $843 ($1000 maximum). 66% of undergraduates work part time. Average annual earnings from campus work are $1260. The average financial indebtedness of the 2001 graduate was $15,787. MacMurray is a member of CSS. The FAFSA is required. The fall application deadline is open.

International Students: There are 8 international students enrolled. They must score 550 on the written TOEFL or 213 on the electronic version.

Computers: The mainframe is a DEC ALPHA 2100. There are more than 70 Internet accessible PCs located in student accessible areas in the library or classroom buildings. 24 of these are in a computer classroom in the science building. Additionally, there are PCs in the residence halls. All students may access the system at designated hours throughout the week (8 A.M. to 11 P.M. Monday through Friday, Saturday afternoon, and Sunday afternoon and evening). There are no time limits and no fees.

Graduates: In 2001, 125 bachelor's degrees were awarded. The most popular majors were psychology (13%), criminal justice (10%), and social work (8%). In an average class, 42% graduate in 4 years, 45% in 5 years, and 47% in 6 years. 8 companies recruited on campus in 2000-2001. Of the 2000 graduating class, 14% were enrolled in graduate school within 6 months of graduation and 49% were employed.

Admissions Contact: Tom McGinnis, Dean of Enrollment.
E-mail: *admiss@mac.edu* Web: *www.mac.edu*

MCKENDREE COLLEGE C-5
Lebanon, IL 62254 (618) 537-6835
(800) BEARCAT; Fax: (618) 537-6496

Full-time: 629 men, 910 women	**Faculty:** 64; IIB, -$
Part-time: 182 men, 386 women	**Ph.D.s:** 83%
Graduate: none	**Student/Faculty:** 24 to 1
Year: semesters, summer session	**Tuition:** $13,350
Application Deadline: open	**Room & Board:** $4950

Freshman Class: 1135 applied, 781 accepted, 293 enrolled
ACT: 24 **COMPETITIVE+**

McKendree College, founded in 1828, is the oldest college in Illinois. It is a private liberal arts institution affiliated with the United Methodist Church. In addition to regional accreditation, McKendree has baccalaureate program accreditation with IACBE and NLN. The library contains 140,000 volumes, 40,000 microform items, and 22,000 audiovisual forms/CDs, and subscribes to more than 5000 periodicals. Computerized library services include the card catalog, interlibrary loans, and database searching. Special learning facilities include a learning resource center, greenhouse, and archives. The 80-acre campus is in a small town 23 miles east of St. Louis. Including residence halls, there are 25 buildings.

Student Life: 69% of undergraduates are from Illinois. Others are from 12 states, 12 foreign countries, and Canada. 92% are from public schools. 83% are white; 10%, African American. 30% claim no religious affiliation; 25% are Catholic. The average age of freshmen is 18; all undergraduates, 19. 28% do not continue beyond their first year.

Housing: 637 students can be accommodated in college housing, which includes single-sex and coed dormitories, on-campus apartments, and off-campus apartments. On-campus housing is guaranteed for the freshman year only and is available on a first-come, first-served basis. Priority is given to out-of-town students. 54% of students commute. Alcohol is not permitted. All students may keep cars.

Activities: 8% of men and about 2% of women belong to 3 local and 3 national fraternities; 6% of women belong to 3 local sororities. There are 54 groups on campus, including art, band, cheerleading, choir, chorus, computers, dance, debate, drama, ethnic, forensics, honors, international, jazz band, literary magazine, marching band, musical theater, newspaper, pep band, photography, political, professional, religious, social, social service, student government, and yearbook. Popular campus events include Nightabout Town, Model United Nations, and Family Festival.

Sports: There are 9 intercollegiate sports for men and 9 for women, and 8 intramural sports for men and 8 for women. Facilities include a 1600-seat gym, a fitness center, tennis courts, a student center with table tennis and billiards, an all-weather track, a 3000-seat football stadium, and playing fields.

Disabled Students: 80% of the campus is accessible. Wheelchair ramps, elevators, special parking, specially equipped rest rooms, special class scheduling, and lowered drinking fountains are available.

Services: Counseling and information services are available, as is tutoring in every subject. There is remedial reading.

Campus Safety and Security: Measures include 24-hour foot and vehicle patrol, escort service, shuttle buses, and informal discussions. There are pamphlets/posters/films, emergency telephones, and lighted pathways/sidewalks.

Programs of Study: McKendree confers B.A., B.S., B.B.A., B.F.A., B.S.Ed., and B.S.N. degrees. Bachelor's degrees are awarded in BIOLOGICAL SCIENCE (biology/biological science), BUSINESS (accounting, banking and finance, business administration and management, and marketing/retailing/merchandising), COMMUNICATIONS AND THE ARTS (art, English, music, and speech/debate/rhetoric), COMPUTER AND PHYSICAL SCIENCE (chemistry, computer science, information sciences and systems, and mathematics), EDUCATION (art, athletic training, business, elementary, and physical), HEALTH PROFESSIONS (medical laboratory technology and nursing), SOCIAL SCIENCE (economics, history, international relations, philosophy, political science/government, psychology, religion, social science, and sociology). Biology and computer science are the strongest academically. Business, computer science, and nursing are the largest.

Required: To graduate, students must complete 128 semester hours, with a minimum GPA of 2.0. The 51-credit-hour core curriculum includes 9 credits of social science, 7 of science, 6 of freshman English, 3 each of speech, math, ethics, philosophy or religion, history, cross-cultural studies, literature, fine or performing arts, and computer competency, and 1 to 2 of phys ed. In addition, 2 writing-intensive courses and a writing proficiency exam must be taken. A thesis is required for biology majors seeking a B.S. degree.

Special: McKendree offers internships, work-study programs, study abroad in England, Ireland, and France, a Washington semester, dual and student-designed majors, and nondegree study, as well as a 3-2 program in occupational therapy with Washington University in St. Louis. There are 9 national honor societies, a freshman honors program, and honors programs in all departments.

Faculty/Classroom: 50% of faculty are male; 50%, female. All teach undergraduates and 20% also do research. The average class size in an introductory lecture is 20; in a laboratory, 15; and in a regular course, 15.

Admissions: 69% of the 2001-2002 applicants were accepted. The ACT scores for the 2001-2002 freshman class were: 26% below 21, 29% between 21 and 23, 25% between 24 and 26, 12% between 27 and 28, and 8% above 28. 45% of the current freshmen were in the top fifth of their class; 75% were in the top two fifths. There was 1 National Merit finalist in a recent year. 16 freshmen graduated first in their class.

Requirements: The SAT I or ACT is required. In addition, students must be high school graduates or submit the GED certificate. Completion of at least 15 units of high school work is recommended. A recommendation from the secondary school counselor is required. McKendree requires applicants to be in the upper 50% of their class. A GPA of 2.5 is required. AP and CLEP credits are accepted. Important factors in the admissions decision are advanced placement or honor courses, leadership record, and evidence of special talent. Applications are accepted on-line via the school's web site.

Procedure: Freshmen are admitted to all sessions. Application deadlines are open. Notification is sent on a rolling basis.

Transfer: 195 transfer students enrolled in 2001-2002. Applicants must have a minimum 2.25 GPA from all colleges previously attended. 32 credits of 128 must be completed at McKendree.

Visiting: There are regularly scheduled orientations for prospective students, consisting of Open House Days, where faculty members and personnel from several departments answer questions. Student-led tours of the campus and various other events are also available. There are guides for informal visits and visitors may sit in on classes and stay overnight. To schedule a visit, contact the Admissions Office at (618) 537-4481, ext. 6831 or *mecampbell@mckendree.edu*.

Financial Aid: In 2001-2002, 86% of all freshmen and 82% of continuing students received some form of financial aid. 92% of freshmen and 68% of continuing students received need-based aid. The average freshman award was $11,637. Of that total, scholarships or need-based grants averaged $9862 ($18,300 maximum); loans averaged $2202 ($6625 maximum); and work contracts averaged $1718 ($2000 maximum). 49% of undergraduates work part time. Average annual earnings from campus work are $501. The average financial indebtedness of the 2001 graduate was $13,446. The FAFSA is required. The priority fall application deadline is July 15.

International Students: In a recent year, there were 42 international students enrolled. The school actively recruits these students. They must score 520 on the written TOEFL or 190 on the electronic version and also take the SAT I or the ACT.

Computers: The mainframe is a DEC ALPHA 4000. There are more than 325 terminals on campus and 270 in individual residence rooms. Students may use any of the PCs across 4 labs on campus, another 40 PCs in 2 labs at remote centers, or their own PC in their residence room. All students may access the system. There are no time limits and no fees.

Graduates: In 2001, 505 bachelor's degrees were awarded. The most popular majors were business/marketing (29%), health professions and related sciences (20%), and education (12%). In an average class, 1% graduate in 3 years, 28% in 4 years, 52% in 5 years, and 54% in 6 years. 150 companies recruited on campus in 2000-2001. Of the 2000 graduating class, 14% were enrolled in graduate school within 6 months of graduation and 94% were employed.

Admissions Contact: Mark Campbell, Vice President for Admissions and Financial Aid. A video is available.
E-mail: *mecampbell@mckendree.edu* Web: *www.mckendree.edu*

MILLIKIN UNIVERSITY
Decatur, IL 62522-2084

D-3
(217) 424-6210
(800) 373-7733; Fax: (217) 425-4669

Full-time: 975 men, 1341 women	**Faculty:** 154; IIB, --$
Part-time: 30 men, 43 women	**Ph.D.s:** 88%
Graduate: 16 men, 7 women	**Student/Faculty:** 15 to 1
Year: semesters, summer session	**Tuition:** $18,309
Application Deadline: open	**Room & Board:** $6106
Freshman Class: 2598 applied, 1982 accepted, 647 enrolled	
SAT I Verbal/Math: 550/510	**ACT:** 24 **COMPETITIVE+**

Millikin University, founded in 1901, is a private university affiliated with the Presbyterian Church (U.S.A.) offering undergraduate programs in arts and sciences, nursing, fine arts, and business. There are 4 undergraduate schools. In addition to regional accreditation, Millikin has baccalaureate program accreditation with NASM and NLN. The library contains 172,083 volumes, 20,632 microform items, and 2160 audiovisual forms/CDs, and subscribes to 919 periodicals. Computerized library services include the card catalog, interlibrary loans, and database searching. Special learning facilities include a learning resource center, art gallery, radio station, television lab, computer imaging center, audio/video recording studio, and museum of decorative arts. The 70-acre campus is in a suburban area 180 miles southwest of Chicago and 130 miles northeast of St. Louis, Missouri. Including residence halls, there are 28 buildings.

Student Life: 85% of undergraduates are from Illinois. Others are from 33 states and 13 foreign countries. 85% are from public schools. 84% are white. 53% are Protestant; 24% Catholic; 18% claim no religious affiliation. The average age of freshmen is 18; all undergraduates, 20. 21% do not continue beyond their first year.

Housing: 1425 students can be accommodated in college housing, which includes single-sex and coed dormitories, on-campus apartments, off-campus apartments, fraternity houses, and sorority houses. In addition, there are special-interest houses, Greek houses provided by their own organizations, and smoke-free, academic, and freshmen floors in residence halls. On-campus housing is available on a first-come, first-served basis and is available on a lottery system for upperclassmen. 60% of students live on campus; of those, 80% remain on campus on weekends. Upperclassmen may keep cars.

Activities: 20% of men belong to 9 national fraternities; 25% of women belong to 3 national sororities. There are 91 groups on campus, including art, band, cheerleading, chess, choir, chorale, chorus, computers, dance, drama, ethnic, film, gay, honors, international, jazz band, literary magazine, musical theater, newspaper, opera, orchestra, pep band, photography, political, professional, radio and TV, religious, social, social service, student government, symphony, and yearbook. Popular campus events include Springfest, Fall Family Weekend, and Millipalooza.

Sports: There are 10 intercollegiate sports for men and 9 for women, and 12 intramural sports for men and 12 for women. Facilities include a phys ed center with a 6-lane, 25-yard pool, a fitness/wellness center, a sand volleyball court, a playing field for football and track, and an indoor sports center.

Disabled Students: 65% of the campus is accessible. Wheelchair ramps, elevators, special parking, specially equipped rest rooms, special class scheduling, lowered drinking fountains, and lowered telephones are available.

Services: Counseling and information services are available, as is tutoring in most subjects. A writing center and a basic review course in English fundamentals are available.

Campus Safety and Security: Measures include 24-hour foot and vehicle patrol, self-defense education, escort service, and informal discussions. There are pamphlets/posters/films, emergency telephones, and lighted pathways/sidewalks.

Programs of Study: Millikin confers B.A., B.S., B.F.A., B.M., and B.S.N. degrees. Master's degrees are also awarded. Bachelor's degrees are awarded in BIOLOGICAL SCIENCE (biology/biological science), BUSINESS (accounting, banking and finance, business administration and management, international business management, management information systems, and marketing/retailing/merchandising), COMMUNICATIONS AND THE ARTS (art, arts administration/management, communications, creative writing, dramatic arts, English, French, German, modern language, music, music performance, musical theater, and Spanish), COMPUTER AND PHYSICAL SCIENCE (chemistry, computer science, mathematics, and physics), EDUCATION (art, elementary, foreign languages, middle school, music, physical, science, and secondary), ENGINEERING AND ENVIRONMENTAL DESIGN (commercial art and industrial administration/management), HEALTH PROFESSIONS (art therapy and nursing), SOCIAL SCIENCE (American studies, economics, experimental psychology, history, human services, international studies, philosophy, political science/government, psychology, religion, social science, and sociology). Business, music, and theater are the strongest academically. Accounting, biology, and education are the largest.

Required: Requirements for graduation include courses in critical reading, writing, and research, humanities, fine arts, natural sciences/math, and global and U.S. studies. An off-campus learning experience and a university capstone course are also required. The minimum GPA is 2.0. Students must complete 124 to 136 credit hours, with 33 to 88 in the major.

Special: Millikin offers internships, a Washington semester through American University, study abroad at 22 foreign sites, student-designed majors, a 3-2 engineering degree with Washington University, B.A.-B.S. degrees, credit by exam, and pass/fail options. There are preprofessional programs in engineering, law, optometry, dentistry, medicine, veterinary science, occupational therapy, medical technology, physical therapy, and pharmacy. Students are also offered a United Nations semester at Drew University, affiliate research with the U.S. Department of Energy, affiliate agreements in occupational therapy and medical technology, and an Urban Life Studies Center semester in Chicago. There are 9 national honor societies, a freshman honors program, and 5 departmental honors programs.

Faculty/Classroom: 67% of faculty are male; 33%, female. All both teach and do research. The average class size in an introductory lecture is 25; in a laboratory, 15; and in a regular course, 21.

Admissions: 76% of the 2001-2002 applicants were accepted. The SAT I scores for the 2001-2002 freshman class were: Verbal--44% below 500, 34% between 500 and 599, 18% between 600 and 700, and 4% above 700; Math--29% below 500, 41% between 500 and 599, 27% between 600 and 700, and 3% above 700. The ACT scores were 19% below 21, 27% between 21 and 23, 28% between 24 and 26, 16% between 27 and 28, and 11% above 28. 43% of the current freshmen were in the top fifth of their class; 75% were in the top two fifths. 19 freshmen graduated first in their class.

Requirements: The SAT I or ACT is required. In addition, applicants should be graduates of an accredited secondary school or have a GED. They should prepare with 4 units of high school English, 3 each of history, math, and science, and 2 of foreign language. An audition is required for music-theater, music, or theater majors. A portfolio is required for art majors. Applications are accepted on-line at the school's web site. Millikin requires applicants to be in the upper 50% of their class. A GPA of 2.0 is required. AP and CLEP credits are accepted. Important factors in the admissions decision are recommendations by school officials, personality/intangible qualities, and evidence of special talent.

Procedure: Freshmen are admitted to all sessions. Entrance exams should be taken in April. Application deadlines are open.

Transfer: 110 transfer students enrolled in 2001-2002. Applicants must provide official transcripts from previous institutions, must be in good standing at the previous institution, and must have earned at least a C average in all college study previously attempted. Submission of official high school transcripts and testing is requested. 33 credits of 124 to 136 must be completed at Millikin.

Visiting: There are regularly scheduled orientations for prospective students, consisting of meetings with faculty and coaches, honors, curriculum, housing, and financial aid presentations, and campus tours. There is also an opportunity for students to audition or have portfolios reviewed. There are guides for informal visits and visitors may sit in on classes and stay overnight. To schedule a visit, contact the Admission Office.

Financial Aid: Millikin is a member of CSS. The FAFSA and the college's own financial statement are required. The fall application deadline is June 1.

International Students: The school actively recruits these students. They must score 550 on the written TOEFL.

Computers: The mainframe is a DEC MicroVAX 3800. There are approximately 500 PCs available for student use. Through Novell 4.1.1 servers, these provide access to Microsoft Office software, e-mail, and the Internet. All students may access the system. There are no time limits and no fees.

Graduates: In 2001, 464 bachelor's degrees were awarded. The most popular majors were elementary education (9%), business administration and management (7%), and music performance (7%). In an average class, 60% graduate in 4 years, and 61% in 6 years. 92 companies recruited on campus in 2000-2001. Of the 2000 graduating class, 14% were enrolled in graduate school within 6 months of graduation and 98% were employed.

Admissions Contact: Lin Stoner, Dean of Admission.
E-mail: *admis@mail.millikin.edu* Web: *www.millikin.edu*

MONMOUTH COLLEGE C-2

Monmouth, IL 61462 **(309) 457-2131**
(800) 747-2687; Fax: (309) 457-2141

Full-time: 490 men, 565 women	**Faculty:** 65; IIB, -$
Part-time: 3 men, 14 women	**Ph.D.s:** 75%
Graduate: none	**Student/Faculty:** 16 to 1
Year: semesters	**Tuition:** $17,000
Application Deadline: open	**Room & Board:** $4550

Freshman Class: 1159 applied, 916 accepted, 270 enrolled
ACT: 22 **COMPETITIVE**

Monmouth College, founded in 1853, is a private liberal arts institution affiliated with the Presbyterian Church (U.S.A.). The library contains 230,000 volumes, 75,000 microform items, and 700 audiovisual forms/CDs, and subscribes to 635 periodicals. Computerized library services include the card catalog, interlibrary loans, and database searching. Special learning facilities include a learning resource center, art gallery, radio station, TV station, biology field station on the Mississippi River, and prairie plot of native flora. The 50-acre campus is in a small town 45 miles south of Rock Island and Moline. Including residence halls, there are 26 buildings.

Student Life: 89% of undergraduates are from Illinois. Others are from 20 states, 18 foreign countries, and Canada. 88% are from public schools. 87% are white. 35% are Protestant; 22% Catholic; 20% claim no religious affiliation. The average age of freshmen is 18; all undergraduates, 20. 14% do not continue beyond their first year; 58% remain to graduate.

Housing: 1050 students can be accommodated in college housing, which includes single-sex and coed dormitories and fraternity houses. In addition, there are honors houses and special-interest houses. On-campus housing is guaranteed for all 4 years. 91% of students live on campus; of those, 75% remain on campus on weekends. All students may keep cars.

Activities: 25% of men belong to 3 national fraternities; 30% of women belong to 3 national sororities. There are 60 groups on campus, including art, bagpipe band, band, cheerleading, choir, chorale, chorus, computers, dance, drama, ethnic, gay, honors, international, jazz band, literary magazine, musical theater, newspaper, orchestra, photography, political, professional, radio and TV, religious, social, social service, student government, and yearbook. Popular campus events include Greek Week, Women's Week, and Family Weekend.

Sports: There are 7 intercollegiate sports for men and 7 for women, and 12 intramural sports for men and 12 for women. Facilities include a track, 2 gyms, 2 racquetball courts, weight rooms, a fitness/wellness center, and football, baseball, soccer, and softball fields.

Disabled Students: 20% of the campus is accessible. Wheelchair ramps, elevators, special parking, specially equipped rest rooms, special class scheduling, and lowered drinking fountains are available.

Services: Counseling and information services are available, as is tutoring in most subjects. There is remedial math, reading, and writing.

Campus Safety and Security: Measures include self-defense education, escort service, informal discussions, and pamphlets/posters/films. There are emergency telephones, lighted pathways/sidewalks, and 12-hour foot and vehicle patrols.

Programs of Study: MC confers the B.A. degree. Bachelor's degrees are awarded in BIOLOGICAL SCIENCE (biology/biological science), BUSINESS (accounting, business administration and management, and business economics), COMMUNICATIONS AND THE ARTS (art, classics, communications, dramatic arts, English, French, Greek, Latin, music, and Spanish), COMPUTER AND PHYSICAL SCIENCE (chemistry, computer programming, computer science, mathematics, and physics), EDUCATION (elementary, physical, and secondary), ENGINEERING AND ENVIRONMENTAL DESIGN (environmental science), SOCIAL SCIENCE (anthropology, history, philosophy, political science/government, psychology, religion, and sociology). Education, sciences, and business are the strongest academically. Business and education are the largest.

Required: To graduate, all students must complete 124 credit hours with a minimum GPA of 2.0. A major program must be completed with a minimum of C in all courses. Students must also fulfill 38 hours of the general education program and pass the freshman and senior seminars.

Special: Monmouth offers 3-2 nursing programs with Rush Hospital, and a 3-2 engineering degree with Washington University, Case Western Reserve, and the University of Southern California. Students have the opportunity to study in more than 15 countries in Europe, Asia, and Africa. Internships, a Washington semester, and dual and student-designed synoptic majors are available. There are 12 national honor societies, a freshman honors program, and 8 departmental honors programs.

Faculty/Classroom: 56% of faculty are male; 44%, female. All teach undergraduates. The average class size in an introductory lecture is 22; in a laboratory, 15; and in a regular course, 20.

Admissions: 79% of the 2001-2002 applicants were accepted. 33% of the current freshmen were in the top fifth of their class; 65% were in the top two fifths. 10 freshmen graduated first in their class.

Requirements: The SAT I or ACT is required, with a recommended minimum composite score of 900 on the SAT I, or 19 on the ACT. Applicants must be graduates of accredited high schools and have completed 4 years of English, 3 each of math and social studies, 2 each of science (including 1 of lab), and a foreign language, and 1 of history. A GED is also accepted. MC requires applicants to be in the upper 50% of their class. A GPA of 2.5 is required. AP credits are accepted. Important factors in the admissions decision are advanced placement or honor courses, evidence of special talent, and recommendations by school officials. The general college application is accepted on-line, and through Illinois Mentor.

Procedure: Freshmen are admitted fall and spring. Entrance exams should be taken by the spring of the junior year. Application deadlines are open. Notification is sent on a rolling basis.

Transfer: 71 transfer students enrolled in 2001-2002. Students must have a minimum GPA of 2.5. A minimum composite score of 900 on the SAT I or 19 on the ACT is recommended. 62 credits of 124 must be completed at MC.

Visiting: There are regularly scheduled orientations for prospective students, including tours, admissions and financial aid discussions, faculty appointments, lunch and entertainment, and a talk with the president. There are guides for informal visits and visitors may sit in on classes and stay overnight. To schedule a visit, contact the Admissions Office.

Financial Aid: In 2001-2002, 98% of all students received some form of financial aid. 83% of all students received need-based aid. The average freshman award was $14,854. Of that total, scholarships or need-based grants averaged $10,450; loans averaged $3934; and work contracts averaged $593. 36% of undergraduates work part time. Average annual earnings from campus work are $800. The average financial indebtedness of the 2001 graduate was $16,088. The FAFSA is required. The fall application deadline is May 1.

International Students: There were 45 international students enrolled in a recent year. The school actively recruits these students. They must score 550 on the written TOEFL.

Computers: The mainframe is an HP 9000. There are also more than 150 PCs available, and individual rooms are wired for use. All students may access the system 24 hours a day. There are no time limits and no fees.

Graduates: In 2001, 192 bachelor's degrees were awarded. The most popular majors were business (29%), education (25%), and communication/theater arts (16%). In an average class, 52% graduate in 4 years, 60% in 5 years, and 61% in 6 years. 59 companies recruited on campus in 2000-2001. Of the 2000 graduating class, 28% were enrolled in graduate school within 6 months of graduation and 99% were employed.

Admissions Contact: Marybeth Kemp, Vice President of Admission. A video is available. E-mail: *admit@monm.edu* Web: *www.monm.edu*

NAES COLLEGE E-2

Chicago, IL 60659 **(773) 761-5000; Fax: (773) 761-3808**

Full-time: 65 men and women	**Faculty:** 3
Part-time: 15 men and women	**Ph.D.s:** 20%
Graduate: none	**Student/Faculty:** 22 to 1
Year: semesters, summer session	**Tuition:** $5140
Application Deadline: open	**Room & Board:** n/app
Freshman Class: n/av	
SAT I or ACT: not required	**SPECIAL**

NAES College, founded in 1974, is an independent commuter institution offering a program in community studies for Native Americans employed in Indian programs and agencies. The multicampus college has evening classes. Figures in above capsule are approximate. There are 4 undergraduate schools. The library contains 13,000 volumes, 5 microform items, and 500 audiovisual forms/CDs, and subscribes to 55 periodicals. Computerized library services include the card catalog. The 1-acre campus is in an urban area in Chicago. There is one building.

Student Life: 100% are from public schools. 96% are Native American/Eskimo. The average age of freshmen is 34; all undergraduates, 37. 85% of freshmen remain to graduate.

Housing: There are no residence halls. All of students commute. Alcohol is not permitted. All students may keep cars.

Disabled Students: All of the campus is accessible. Special class scheduling is available.

Services: Counseling and information services are available, as is tutoring in most subjects.

Campus Safety and Security: Measures include pamphlets/posters/films, emergency telephones, and lighted pathways/sidewalks.

Programs of Study: NAES confers the B.A. degree. Bachelor's degrees are awarded in SOCIAL SCIENCE (community services).

Required: To graduate, students must maintain a 2.0 GPA and complete 120 credit hours, including a core curriculum of 6 6-credit courses, with 57 hours in the major. Students are required to complete courses in art, math, science, English literature, tribal language, composition, and speech, and demonstrate computer competence. A field project in the American Indian community is also required.

Special: Cross-registration with Northeastern Illinois University is available and students may receive credit for prior learning.

Faculty/Classroom: 61% of faculty are male; 39%, female. The average class size in an introductory lecture is 10 and in a regular course, 10.

Requirements: The SAT I or ACT is not required. Applicants must be graduates of an accredited secondary school or have a GED certificate and be employed or a volunteer at an Indian organization or agency that serves Indian people in the community where the campus is located or in which the student lives. Applicants must be at least 24 years old or have an associate of art or science degree, or have completed at least 60 semester hours of transferable credit. CLEP credit is accepted. Important factors in the admissions decision are parents or siblings attending the school, advanced placement or honor courses, and personality/intangible qualities.

Procedure: Freshmen are admitted to all sessions. There is an early admissions plan. Application deadlines are open. Notification is sent on a rolling basis.

Transfer: Transfer students must satisfy the same requirements as other applicants. 54 credits of 120 must be completed at NAES.

Visiting: There are regularly scheduled orientations for prospective students. Visitors may sit in on classes. To schedule a visit, contact the campus administrator.

Financial Aid: In a recent year, 80% of all freshmen and 85% of continuing students received some form of financial aid. 80% of freshmen and 85% of continuing students received need-based aid. The average freshman award was $2500. 95% of undergraduates work part time. NAES is a member of CSS. The CSS/Profile, FAFSA, FFS, or SFS is required. Check with the school for current deadlines.

Computers: PCs are available in class and for individual use. All students may access the system 9 A.M. to 8 P.M. There are no time limits and no fees.

Graduates: In a recent year, 20 bachelor's degrees were awarded. In an average class, 70% graduate in 5 years. Recently, 70% were enrolled in graduate school within 6 months of graduation and all were employed.

Admissions Contact: Campus Administrator.
Web: *www.naes.indian.com*

NATIONAL-LOUIS UNIVERSITY E-1

Chicago, IL 60603 **(312) 621-9650; (888) NLU TODAY**

Full-time: 795 men, 2075 women	**Faculty:** IIA, --$
Part-time: 100 men, 375 women	**Ph.D.s:** n/av
Graduate: 610 men, 2590 women	**Student/Faculty:** 12 to 1
Year: quarters, summer session	**Tuition:** $13,995
Application Deadline: open	**Room & Board:** n/app
Freshman Class: n/app	
SAT I or ACT: required	**NONCOMPETITIVE**

National-Louis University, founded in 1886, is an independent institution offering programs in education, liberal arts, health science, business, and human services for the traditional and the adult student. 4 Chicago-area campuses, in Evanston, Wheaton, Wheeling, and the Chicago Loop, accommodate commuters, and academic centers in Elgin, Illinois, Virginia, Missouri, Georgia, Florida, Wisconsin, and Germany offer selected programs for working adults. Figures in above capsule are approximate. There are 3 undergraduate and 3 graduate schools. In addition to regional accreditation, NLU has baccalaureate program accreditation with CAHEA. The library contains 153,000 volumes, 925,978 microform items, and 5043 audiovisual forms/CDs, and subscribes to 3498 periodicals. Computerized library services include the card catalog, interlibrary loans, and database searching. Special learning facilities include a learning resource center and a pre-K through 8 elementary demonstration school. The 12-acre campus is in a suburban area 12 miles north of Chicago. Including residence halls, there are 3 buildings.

Student Life: 95% of undergraduates are from Illinois. Others are from 28 states and 16 foreign countries. 54% are white; 25% African American. The average age of freshmen is 25; all undergraduates, 33. 39% do not continue beyond their first year.

Housing: 200 students can be accommodated in college housing, which includes coed dormitories. On-campus housing is available on a first-come, first-served basis. Priority is given to out-of-town students. 95% of students commute. Upperclassmen may keep cars.

Activities: 11% of women belong to 1 national sorority. There are no fraternities. There are 30 groups on campus, including chorus, drama, ethnic, honors, musical theater, newspaper, professional, religious, student government, and yearbook. Popular campus events include a ski trip and Valentine's Day Dance.

Sports: There is no sports program at NLU. Facilities include a 300-seat gym, a 700-seat auditorium, and a swimming pool.

Disabled Students: 90% of the campus is accessible. Wheelchair ramps, elevators, and special parking are available.

Services: Counseling and information services are available, as is tutoring in most subjects. There is remedial math, reading, and writing. A center for academic development provides services to academically at-risk students.

Campus Safety and Security: Measures include informal discussions, pamphlets/posters/films, lighted pathways/sidewalks, and security guards when campus buildings are open.

Programs of Study: NLU confers B.A. and B.S. degrees. Master's and doctoral degrees are also awarded. Bachelor's degrees are awarded in BIOLOGICAL SCIENCE (biology/biological science), BUSINESS (accounting, business administration and management, and management science), COMMUNICATIONS AND THE ARTS (English and fine arts), COMPUTER AND PHYSICAL SCIENCE (information sciences and systems, mathematics, and science), EDUCATION (early childhood and elementary), HEALTH PROFESSIONS (health care administration, medical laboratory technology, radiation therapy, and respiratory therapy), SOCIAL SCIENCE (anthropology, crosscultural studies, human development, human services, psychology, and social science). Education and business are the strongest academically. Management and education are the largest.

Required: Students must take courses in humanities, natural sciences, and behavioral sciences. Other course requirements vary by program. All students must pass an English competency writing exam. A minimum 2.0 GPA and 180 quarter hours, including 45 in the major, are required to graduate.

Special: NLU offers credit by exam and for experiential learning, and limited nondegree and pass/fail options. There are special completion programs for adults in management, applied behavioral science, and health care leadership. In addition, NLU offers several programs in the field as well as customized programs for working adults. There is 1 national honor society, including Phi Beta Kappa.

Faculty/Classroom: 40% of faculty are male; 60%, female. No introductory courses are taught by graduate students. The average class size in an introductory lecture is 35 and in a regular course, 13.

Requirements: The SAT I or ACT is required of first-time freshmen under 21 years of age. A minimum composite score of 750 on the SAT I or 19 on the ACT is required. Applicants should graduate from an accredited secondary school with 15 academic credits, including 4 in English, 3 in social studies, and 2 each in math and science. The GED is accepted. 2 letters of recommendation, with 1 from the high school counselor recommended, are required; an interview is strongly encouraged. NLU requires applicants to be in the upper 50% of their class. AP and CLEP credits are accepted. Important factors in the admissions decision are recommendations by school officials, leadership record, and evidence of special talent.

Procedure: Freshmen are admitted fall, winter, and spring. Entrance exams should be taken the winter before application. There is a deferred admissions plan. Application deadlines are open. The fall 2001 application fee was $25.

Transfer: 713 transfer students enrolled in a recent year. A minimum GPA of 2.0 is required. Applicants must be in good standing at the college previously attended. Official transcripts from previously attended colleges and letters of recommendation are required. Personal interviews are strongly encouraged. 45 credits of 180 must be completed at NLU.

Visiting: There are regularly scheduled orientations for prospective students, including campus tours, meeting with students and key administrators, attending typical campus entertainment, and visiting classes. There are guides for informal visits and visitors may sit in on classes. To schedule a visit, contact Undergraduate Enrollment Office.

Financial Aid: NLU is a member of CSS. The FAFSA is required. Check with the school for current deadlines.

International Students: They must take the college's own test.

Computers: The mainframe is an IBM AS/400. There are more than 200 Mac and IBM PCs available in computer labs located at the 4 Illinois campuses. Computer access is available at out-of-state campuses. All students may access the system. There are no time limits and no fees.

Graduates: In a recent year, 1013 bachelor's degrees were awarded. In an average class, 46% graduate in 6 years.

Admissions Contact: Pat Patilla, Admissions Director.
E-mail: *nluinfo@wheeling1.nl.edu* Web: *www.nl.edu*

NORTH CENTRAL COLLEGE — E-2

Naperville, IL 60566 — (630) 637-5800
(800) 411-1861; Fax: (630) 637-5121

Full-time: 776 men, 1092 women	**Faculty:** 119; IIA, -$
Part-time: 145 men, 207 women	**Ph.D.s:** 83%
Graduate: 225 men, 223 women	**Student/Faculty:** 16 to 1
Year: terms, summer session	**Tuition:** $17,220
Application Deadline: open	**Room & Board:** $5724
Freshman Class: 1457 applied, 1143 accepted, 444 enrolled	
SAT I Verbal/Math: 550/550	**ACT:** 24 **COMPETITIVE+**

North Central College, founded in 1861, is a private liberal arts institution affiliated with the United Methodist Church. The library contains 141,527 volumes, 187,926 microform items, and 3225 audiovisual forms/CDs, and subscribes to 737 periodicals. Computerized library services include the card catalog, interlibrary loans, and database searching. Special learning facilities include a learning resource center, art gallery, radio station, advising center, foreign language lab, and writing center. The 54-acre campus is in a suburban area 30 miles west of Chicago. Including residence halls, there are 24 buildings.

Student Life: 91% of undergraduates are from Illinois. Others are from 23 states and 18 foreign countries. 88% are white. 41% are Protestant; 32%, Catholic; 25% claim no religious affiliation. The average age of freshmen is 18; all undergraduates, 23. 19% do not continue beyond their first year; 61% remain to graduate.

Housing: 1021 students can be accommodated in college housing, which includes single-sex and coed dormitories and on-campus apartments. In addition, there are special-interest houses. On-campus housing is guaranteed for all 4 years. 58% of students live on campus; of those, 75% remain on campus on weekends. All students may keep cars.

Activities: There are no fraternities or sororities. There are 35 groups on campus, including art, band, cheerleading, choir, chorale, chorus, dance, drama, ethnic, gay, honors, international, jazz band, literary magazine, musical theater, newspaper, pep band, photography, political, professional, radio and TV, religious, social, social service, student government, and yearbook. Popular campus events include Family Weekend, Winter Carnival, and Arts and Letters Festival.

Sports: There are 10 intercollegiate sports for men and 9 for women, and 4 intramural sports for men and 4 for women. Facilities include an indoor track, an outdoor track, a weight room, a football stadium, a baseball stadium, soccer fields, a swimming pool, tennis courts, an athletic training facility, and a human performance lab.

Disabled Students: 54% of the campus is accessible. Wheelchair ramps, elevators, special parking, specially equipped rest rooms, special class scheduling, lowered drinking fountains, and lowered telephones are available.

Services: Counseling and information services are available, as is tutoring in most subjects. There is remedial math, reading, and writing.

Campus Safety and Security: Measures include self-defense education, escort service, informal discussions, and pamphlets/posters/films. There are emergency telephones, lighted pathways/sidewalks, and a 24-hour foot patrol.

Programs of Study: North Central confers B.A. and B.S. degrees. Master's degrees are also awarded. Bachelor's degrees are awarded in BIOLOGICAL SCIENCE (biochemistry, biology/biological science, and zoology), BUSINESS (accounting, banking and finance, business administration and management, international business management, and marketing/retailing/merchandising), COMMUNICATIONS AND THE ARTS (broadcasting, classics, communications, English, fine arts, French, German, Japanese, music, Spanish, and speech/debate/rhetoric), COMPUTER AND PHYSICAL SCIENCE (applied mathematics, chemistry, computer science, mathematics, and physics), EDUCATION (elementary and secondary), ENGINEERING AND ENVIRONMENTAL DESIGN (preengineering), HEALTH PROFESSIONS (nursing, predentistry, premedicine, and preveterinary science), SOCIAL SCIENCE (anthropology, economics, history, philosophy, political science/government, prelaw, psychology, religion, social science, and sociology). Business and education are the largest.

Required: All students must complete a general education core, including 9 hours each in humanities and social sciences, 6.5 hours in life and physical science, 6 hours each in English composition and college integrative seminars, and 3 hours each in speech communication and math. A GPA of 2.0 and a total of 120 credit hours are required for graduation, with 24 to 51 credits taken in the major.

Special: North Central offers co-op programs in medical technology, nursing, and physical therapy, cross-registration with Benedictine University, Elmhurst College, and Aurora University, a Washington semester, and study abroad in more than 60 countries. Internships in all subject areas, work-study programs, a 3-2 engineering degree with Washington, Champaign-Urbana, and Marquette Universities and the Universities of Illinois and Minnesota, credit for life experience, and nondegree study are available. Students may pursue a B.A.-B.S. degree in all business areas and in psychology and physical science. Dual majors, a general studies degree, accelerated degree programs, and student-designed majors are also offered. There are 2 national honor societies, and a freshman honors program.

Faculty/Classroom: 52% of faculty are male; 48%, female. All teach undergraduates and 40% do research. No introductory courses are taught by graduate students. The average class size in an introductory lecture is 21; in a laboratory, 15; and in a regular course, 19.

Admissions: 78% of the 2001-2002 applicants were accepted. The SAT I scores for the 2001-2002 freshman class were: Verbal--25% below 500, 46% between 500 and 599, 28% between 600 and 700, and 1% above 700; Math--20% below 500, 41% between 500 and 599, and 34% between 600 and 700. The ACT scores were 14% below 21, 28% between 21 and 23, 31% between 24 and 26, 14% between 27 and 28, and 14% above 28. 40% of the current freshmen were in the top fifth of their class; 73% were in the top two fifths. 1 freshman graduated first in class.

Requirements: The SAT I or ACT is required, with a minimum composite score of 20 on the ACT or 930 on the SAT I. Applicants must be graduates of an accredited secondary school. The GED is accepted. The recommended secondary school courses are 4 years of English, 3 each of math and science, and 2 each of a foreign language, history, and social studies. The school recommends an interview for all applicants. An essay is required. North Central requires applicants to be in the upper 50% of their class. A GPA of 2.0 is required. AP and CLEP credits are accepted. Important factors in the admissions decision are recommendations by school officials, leadership record, and evidence of special talent. North Central accepts applications on computer disk and on-line.

Procedure: Freshmen are admitted fall, winter, and spring. Entrance exams should be taken in spring of junior year or fall of senior year. There is a deferred admissions plan. Application deadlines are open. The fall 2001 application fee was $25. There is a rolling admissions plan.

Transfer: 179 transfer students enrolled in 2001-2002. Applicants need a 2.25 GPA from the sending school and an interview. 30 credits of 120 must be completed at North Central.

Visiting: There are regularly scheduled orientations for prospective students, including orientation sessions for all freshmen, scheduled during the summer. There are guides for informal visits and visitors may sit in on classes and stay overnight. To schedule a visit, contact the Office of Admissions at *ncadm@noctrl.edu*.

Financial Aid: In 2001-2002, 94% of all freshmen and 80% of continuing students received some form of financial aid. 65% of freshmen and

43% of continuing students received need-based aid. The average freshman award was $14,622. Of that total, scholarships or need-based grants averaged $11,299; loans averaged $2347; and work contracts averaged $703. 33% of undergraduates work part time. Average annual earnings from campus work are $1150. The average financial indebtedness of the 2001 graduate was $13,754. North Central is a member of CSS. The FAFSA and the college's own financial statement are required. The fall application deadline is September 1.

International Students: There are 45 international students enrolled. The school actively recruits these students. They must score 500 on the written TOEFL.

Computers: The mainframes are a Compaq Proliant 1500 and an HP 9000 model K260. Students may use computers located in the on-campus center, computer labs, and the library. There are a total of 110 terminals and PCs available to students. All residence halls are connected to the campus network. All students may access the system 7 A.M. to midnight in the computer center or from a modem or residence hall room at any time. There are no time limits. The fee is $150 per year. It is strongly recommended that all students have a personal computer.

Graduates: In 2001, 515 bachelor's degrees were awarded. The most popular majors were business (23%), elementary education (9%), and speech (9%). In an average class, 1% graduate in 3 years, 59% in 4 years, 67% in 5 years, and 68% in 6 years. 18 companies recruited on campus in 2000-2001. Of the 2000 graduating class, 10% were enrolled in graduate school within 6 months of graduation and 77% were employed.

Admissions Contact: Marguerite Waters, Dean of Admission. A video is available. E-mail: *ncadm@noctrl.edu* Web: *www.noctrl.edu*

NORTH PARK UNIVERSITY

E-2

Chicago, IL 60625-4987 **(312) 583-2700; (800) 888-6728**

Full-time: 495 men, 757 women	**Faculty:** 81
Part-time: 106 men, 215 women	**Ph.D.s:** 41%
Graduate: 270 men, 484 women	**Student/Faculty:** 15 to 1
Year: semesters, summer session	**Tuition:** $17,790
Application Deadline: open	**Room & Board:** $6240

Freshman Class: 1031 applied, 781 accepted, 306 enrolled

ACT: 23 **COMPETITIVE**

North Park University, founded in 1891, is a private liberal arts college affiliated with the Evangelical Covenant Church offering undergraduate programs in the arts and sciences, business, music, and education. There are 5 undergraduate and 3 graduate schools. In addition to regional accreditation, North Park has baccalaureate program accreditation with NLN. The 2 libraries contain 220,000 volumes, 93,000 microform items, and 6500 audiovisual forms/CDs, and subscribe to 950 periodicals. Computerized library services include the card catalog, interlibrary loans, and database searching. Special learning facilities include a learning resource center, an art gallery, and an herbarium. The 30-acre campus is in an urban area 10 miles north of downtown Chicago. Including residence halls, there are 25 buildings.

Student Life: 68% of undergraduates are from Illinois. Others are from 38 states, 38 foreign countries, and Canada. 55% are white. 57% are Protestant; 16% claim no religious affiliation; 13% are Catholic. The average age of freshmen is 18; all undergraduates, 21. 30% do not continue beyond their first year; 65% remain to graduate.

Housing: 943 students can be accommodated in college housing, which includes single-sex dormitories, on-campus apartments, off-campus apartments, and married-student housing. In addition, there are honors houses, language houses, an international living center, and special-interest houses. On-campus housing is guaranteed for all 4 years. 60% of students live on campus; of those, 90% remain on campus on weekends. Alcohol is not permitted. All students may keep cars.

Activities: There are no fraternities or sororities. There are 40 groups on campus, including art, band, cheerleading, choir, chorale, chorus, computers, drama, ethnic, honors, international, jazz band, literary magazine, musical theater, newspaper, opera, orchestra, pep band, photography, political, professional, religious, social, social service, student government, symphony, and yearbook. Popular campus events include dances, concerts, and film festivals.

Sports: There are 8 intercollegiate sports for men and 8 for women, and 5 intramural sports for men and 5 for women. Facilities include football, baseball, track, and soccer fields, tennis courts, a weight room, a gym, a fitness center, and a swimming pool.

Disabled Students: 90% of the campus is accessible. Wheelchair ramps, elevators, specially equipped rest rooms, lowered drinking fountains, and lowered telephones are available.

Services: Counseling and information services are available, as is tutoring in every subject. There is a reader service for the blind, and remedial math, reading, and writing. An extended orientation program is available.

Campus Safety and Security: Measures include 24-hour foot and vehicle patrol, self-defense education, escort service, and informal discussions. There are pamphlets/posters/films, emergency telephones, and lighted pathways/sidewalks.

Programs of Study: North Park confers B.A., B.S., B.Mus., and B.S.Med.Tech. degrees. Master's and doctoral degrees are also awarded. Bachelor's degrees are awarded in BIOLOGICAL SCIENCE (biology/biological science), BUSINESS (accounting, banking and finance, business administration and management, international business management, and marketing/retailing/merchandising), COMMUNICATIONS AND THE ARTS (communications, English, music, and Spanish), COMPUTER AND PHYSICAL SCIENCE (chemistry, mathematics, and physics), EDUCATION (early childhood, elementary, and secondary), HEALTH PROFESSIONS (medical laboratory technology, nursing, occupational therapy, physical therapy, predentistry, and premedicine), SOCIAL SCIENCE (anthropology, economics, history, international relations, philosophy, political science/government, prelaw, psychology, religion, and sociology). Music, sciences, and premedicine are the strongest academically. Nursing, education, and psychology are the largest.

Required: Students must successfully complete 120 semester hours with a minimum 2.0 GPA. The required number of hours in the major varies. Students must meet a general requirement of 17 core courses.

Special: Cross-registration with Christian College Coalition schools is possible. Opportunities are provided for a co-op program in occupational therapy, internships, work-study, a Washington semester, 3-2 engineering degrees, accelerated degree programs in organization management and nursing, credit by examination, dual majors, student-designed majors, B.A.-B.S. degrees, pass/fail options, and study abroad. There are 6 national honor societies, a freshman honors program, and 25 departmental honors programs.

Faculty/Classroom: 50% of faculty are male; 50%, female. All teach undergraduates. The average class size in an introductory lecture is 35; in a laboratory, 20; and in a regular course, 25.

Admissions: 76% of the 2001-2002 applicants were accepted. The ACT scores for the 2001-2002 freshman class were 33% below 21, 26% between 21 and 23, 22% between 24 and 26, 11% between 27 and 28, and 8% above 28. 40% of the current freshmen were in the top fifth of their class; 60% were in the top two fifths. There was 1 National Merit finalist and 1 semifinalist.

Requirements: The SAT I or ACT is recommended. In addition, graduation from an accredited secondary school is required; a GED will be accepted. Students should have completed course work in a foreign language, 4 years of English, and 3 years each of math, science, and social studies. Recommendations from teachers should also be submitted. An essay and an audition are required. An interview is recommended. A GPA of 2.0 is required. AP and CLEP credits are accepted. Important factors in the admissions decision are evidence of special talent, personality/intangible qualities, and parents or siblings attending the school.

Procedure: Freshmen are admitted to all sessions. Entrance exams should be taken during spring of the junior year or fall of the senior year. Application deadlines are open. The fall application fee was $20. There is a rolling admissions plan.

Transfer: 123 transfer students enrolled in 2001-2002. To be eligible for transfer admission, students must submit a reference from a faculty member, counselor, or administrator, and official transcripts from the previous college, and must have maintained a minimum GPA of 2.0. An interview is also recommended. 30 credits of 120 must be completed at North Park.

Visiting: There are regularly scheduled orientations for prospective students. There are guides for informal visits and visitors may sit in on classes and stay overnight. To schedule a visit, contact the Campus Visitation Coordinator at (312) 244-5500.

Financial Aid: In 2001-2002, 98% of all freshmen received some form of financial aid. 77% of freshmen received need-based aid. The average freshman award was $16,100. The average financial indebtedness of the 2001 graduate was $11,800. The CSS/Profile or FFS, the college's own financial statement, and student and parent federal income tax returns are required. The fall application deadline is August 15.

International Students: There are 70 international students enrolled. The school actively recruits these students. They must score 550 on the written TOEFL.

Computers: 120 Mac and IBM PCs are in the computer lab. All dormitory rooms, public areas, classrooms, and the library are wired or have publicly accessible computers. All students may access the system at any time. There are no time limits and no fees.

Graduates: In 2001, 311 bachelor's degrees were awarded. The most popular majors were organization management (13%), biology (9%), and business administration (7%). In an average class, 60% graduate in 4 years, 65% in 5 years, and 65% in 6 years. 300 companies recruited on campus in 2000-2001.

Admissions Contact: John Baworowski, Vice President for Admissions. Web: *http://www.northpark.edu/afao*

NORTHEASTERN ILLINOIS UNIVERSITY

E-2

Chicago, IL 60625 **(773) 442-4046; Fax: (773) 442-4020**

Full-time: 1811 men, 2912 women	**Faculty:** 346; IIA, -$
Part-time: 1375 men, 2226 women	**Ph.D.s:** 79%
Graduate: 823 men, 1794 women	**Student/Faculty:** 14 to 1
Year: semesters, summer session	**Tuition:** $2898 ($7746)
Application Deadline: July 1	**Room & Board:** n/app
Freshman Class: 1812 accepted, 1019 enrolled	
ACT: required	**NONCOMPETITIVE**

Northeastern Illinois University, founded in 1867, is a public liberal arts institution offering degree programs in arts and sciences, business management, and education. There are 4 undergraduate schools and 1 graduate school. In addition to regional accreditation, Northeastern has baccalaureate program accreditation with NCATE. The library contains 459,191 volumes, 749,370 microform items, and 1001 audiovisual forms/CDs, and subscribes to 73,503 periodicals. Computerized library services include interlibrary loans and database searching. Special learning facilities include a learning resource center, art gallery, and radio station. The 63-acre campus is in an urban area in northwest Chicago. There are 10 buildings.

Student Life: 99% of undergraduates are from Illinois. Others are from 22 states and 9 foreign countries. 55% are from public schools. 44% are white; 27% Hispanic, 14% Asian American, 13% African American. The average age of freshmen is 20; all undergraduates, 28. 45% do not continue beyond their first year; 36% remain to graduate.

Housing: There are no residence halls. All students commute. Alcohol is not permitted. All students may keep cars.

Activities: Tthere is 1 local sorority. There are no fraternities. There are 50 groups on campus, including art, band, cheerleading, chess, choir, chorus, computers, dance, drama, ethnic, film, gay, honors, international, jazz band, literary magazine, musical theater, newspaper, opera, orchestra, photography, political, professional, radio and TV, religious, social, social service, and student government. Popular campus events include International Day, fairs, and the Visiting Lecture Series.

Sports: There are 10 intramural sports for men and 10 for women. Facilities include basketball, tennis, and racquetball courts, indoor and outdoor tracks, a pool, a weight room, and baseball and softball fields.

Disabled Students: 94% of the campus is accessible. Wheelchair ramps, elevators, special parking, specially equipped rest rooms, special class scheduling, lowered drinking fountains, lowered telephones, and a Handicap Education Liaison Program (HELP) that allows priority registration are available.

Services: Counseling and information services are available, as is tutoring in most subjects. There is a reader service for the blind, and remedial math, reading, and writing.

Campus Safety and Security: Measures include 24-hour foot and vehicle patrol, escort service, pamphlets/posters/films, and emergency telephones. There are lighted pathways/sidewalks.

Programs of Study: Northeastern confers B.A. and B.S. degrees. Master's degrees are also awarded. Bachelor's degrees are awarded in AGRICULTURE (environmental studies), BIOLOGICAL SCIENCE (biology/biological science), BUSINESS (accounting, business administration and management, and marketing/retailing/merchandising), COMMUNICATIONS AND THE ARTS (English, fine arts, French, music, Spanish, and speech/debate/rhetoric), COMPUTER AND PHYSICAL SCIENCE (chemistry, computer science, earth science, mathematics, and physics), EDUCATION (bilingual/bicultural, early childhood, elementary, physical, secondary, and special), SOCIAL SCIENCE (anthropology, criminal justice, economics, geography, history, philosophy, political science/government, psychology, social work, and sociology). Education, business, and computer science are the strongest academically. Business and education are the largest.

Required: All students are required to take at least 120 semester hours, including 39 hours of foundational general education, 30 to 60 hours in the major, and 12 hours each in social and natural sciences, 9 in humanities, and 6 in fine arts. A 2.0 overall GPA is required for graduation. An overall GPA and college major GPA of 2.5 are required within the College of Business Management and the College of Education.

Special: Alternative degree and nondegree programs are available, as is cross-registration with Governors State University. Some departments offer internships. A dual major in elementary and early childhood or special education is offered. There are pass/fail options. Honors classes are available. There are 12 national honor societies, a freshman honors program, and 18 departmental honors programs.

Faculty/Classroom: 63% of faculty are male; 37%, female. 90% teach undergraduates. No introductory courses are taught by graduate students. The average class size in an introductory lecture is 80; in a laboratory, 20; and in a regular course, 30.

Admissions: 93% of the 2001-2002 applicants were accepted. 23% of the current freshmen were in the top fifth of their class; 53% were in the top two fifths.

Requirements: The ACT is required for freshmen under 21 years of age. A minimum ACT composite score of 19 is required. Applicants must have graduated from a regionally accredited high school or passed the GED. High school preparation should total at least 12 credits, including 4 years in English, 3 each in math, sciences, and social studies, and 2 in foreign language, music, art, fine arts, or vocational education (only 1 vocational course is accepted). Northeastern requires applicants to be in the upper 50% of their class. AP and CLEP credits are accepted. Important factors in the admissions decision are evidence of special talent, advanced placement or honor courses, and recommendations by school officials.

Procedure: Freshmen are admitted to all sessions. There is a deferred admissions plan. Applications should be filed by July 1 for fall entry, November 1 for spring entry, and April 1 for summer entry. The college accepts all applicants. Notification is sent on a rolling basis.

Transfer: Applicants are considered if they have completed at least 30 semester hours of study with a C average. Those with fewer than 30 hours of credit must meet freshman admissions requirements. 30 credits of 120 must be completed at Northeastern.

Visiting: There are guides for informal visits and visitors may sit in on classes. To schedule a visit, contact the School and College Relations Office at (773) 442-4050 or *admrec@neiu.edu*

Financial Aid: The average freshman award was $2835. The FAFSA and the college's own financial statement are required. The fall application deadline is April 1.

International Students: They must score 500 on the written TOEFL or 173 on the electronic version.

Computers: There are 35 IBM terminals in the library and science building, and 100 Macs and PCs in classroom buildings. Those students enrolled in specific courses or doing research may access the system during posted times, which vary from 12 to 15 hours daily. There are no time limits and no fees.

Admissions Contact: Miriam Rivera, Director of Admissions and Records. E-mail: *mrivera@neiu.edu* Web: *www.neiu.edu*

NORTHERN ILLINOIS UNIVERSITY

D-2

DeKalb, IL 60115 **(815) 753-0446**
(800) 892-3050; Fax: (815) 753-1783

Full-time: 7280 men, 8275 women	**Faculty:** 998; I, --$
Part-time: 894 men, 1019 women	**Ph.D.s:** 79%
Graduate: 2502 men, 3808 women	**Student/Faculty:** 16 to 1
Year: semesters, summer session	**Tuition:** $4475 ($7767)
Application Deadline: August 1	**Room & Board:** $5070
Freshman Class: 13,421 applied, 8633 accepted, 2810 enrolled	
ACT: 22	**COMPETITIVE**

Northern Illinois University, founded in 1895, is a publicly funded institution offering undergraduate and graduate programs in a comprehensive range of disciplines. There are 6 undergraduate and 2 graduate schools. In addition to regional accreditation, NIU has baccalaureate program accreditation with AACSB, ABET, ACEJMC, APTA, ASLA, CAHEA, NASAD, NASM, NCATE, and NLN. The 3 libraries contain 1,624,326 volumes, 2,971,571 microform items, and 50,182 audiovisual forms/CDs, and subscribe to 18,394 periodicals. Computerized library services include the card catalog, interlibrary loans, and database searching. Special learning facilities include an art gallery, radio station, TV station, and anthropology museum. The 515-acre campus is in a small town 65 miles west of Chicago. Including residence halls, there are 55 buildings.

Student Life: 95% of undergraduates are from Illinois. Others are from 49 states, 95 foreign countries, and Canada. 84% are from public schools. 73% are white; 13%, African American. 47% are Catholic; 31%, Protestant; 14% claim no religious affiliation. The average age of freshmen is 18; all undergraduates, 22. 23% do not continue beyond their first year; 55% remain to graduate.

Housing: 6000 students can be accommodated in college housing, which includes single-sex and coed dormitories, on-campus apartments, and married-student housing. In addition, there are honors houses, language houses, and special-interest houses in law, computer science, music, political science, and health professions. On-campus housing is guaranteed for the freshman year only and is available on a first-come, first-served basis. All students may keep cars.

Activities: 15% of men belong to 22 national fraternities; 11% of women belong to 15 national sororities. There are 200 groups on campus, including art, band, cheerleading, chess, choir, chorale, chorus, computers, dance, drama, drill team, ethnic, film, gay, honors, international, jazz band, literary magazine, marching band, musical theater, newspaper, orchestra, pep band, photography, political, professional, radio and TV, religious, social, social service, student government, and symphony. Popular campus events include Unity in Diversity Week, Greek Week, and Springfest.

Sports: There are 8 intercollegiate sports for men and 8 for women, and 15 intramural sports for men and 15 for women. Facilities include a sports stadium, a recreation center and field house with facilities for basketball, volleyball, badminton, table tennis, tennis, racquetball/handball, and weight training, and 2 swimming pools.

Disabled Students: 75% of the campus is accessible. Wheelchair ramps, elevators, special parking, specially equipped rest rooms, special class scheduling, lowered drinking fountains, lowered telephones, and special housing and transportation are available.
Services: Formal tutoring is provided for eligible students.
Campus Safety and Security: Measures include 24-hour foot and vehicle patrol, self-defense education, escort service, and shuttle buses. There are informal discussions, pamphlets/posters/films, emergency telephones, lighted pathways/sidewalks, and a bicycle patrol.
Programs of Study: NIU confers B.A., B.S., B.F.A., B.G.S., B.M., and B.S.Ed. degrees. Master's and doctoral degrees are also awarded. Bachelor's degrees are awarded in BIOLOGICAL SCIENCE (biology/biological science), BUSINESS (accounting, banking and finance, business administration and management, marketing/retailing/merchandising, and personnel management), COMMUNICATIONS AND THE ARTS (communications, dramatic arts, English, fine arts, French, German, journalism, music, Russian, and Spanish), COMPUTER AND PHYSICAL SCIENCE (atmospheric sciences and meteorology, chemistry, computer science, geology, mathematics, and physics), EDUCATION (art, early childhood, elementary, home economics, industrial arts, and music), ENGINEERING AND ENVIRONMENTAL DESIGN (electrical/electronics engineering, engineering technology, industrial engineering, and mechanical engineering), HEALTH PROFESSIONS (clinical science, nursing, physical therapy, and speech pathology/audiology), SOCIAL SCIENCE (anthropology, child care/child and family studies, dietetics, economics, geography, history, liberal arts/general studies, philosophy, political science/government, psychology, and sociology). Business, engineering, and sciences are the strongest academically. Business, education, and communications are the largest.
Required: To graduate, students must have a minimum of 124 credit hours and a minimum GPA of 2.0. All students must take English 103 and 104 and Communication Studies 100. In addition, they must take Math 101 or obtain at least a C in Math 155, 201, 206, 210, 211, or 229. The school also requires that students complete 29 hours in distributive studies areas, consisting of 9 to 12 hours in the humanities and arts, 7 to 11 hours in science and math, 6 to 9 hours in social science, and 3 to 6 hours in interdisciplinary studies.
Special: NIU offers internships in several areas. Students may study abroad in 30 countries. A physics/engineering degree is offered in cooperation with the University of Illinois. Either a B.A. or a B.S. may be obtained in the social science programs. Work-study programs, a general studies degree, co-op programs, pass/fail options, and student-designed majors are available. There are 5 national honor societies, a freshman honors program, and 18 departmental honors programs.
Faculty/Classroom: 56% of faculty are male; 44%, female. Graduate students teach 20% of introductory courses. The average class size in an introductory lecture is 37; in a laboratory, 17; and in a regular course, 30.
Admissions: 64% of the 2001-2002 applicants were accepted. The ACT scores for the 2001-2002 freshman class were 30% below 21, 32% between 21 and 23, 22% between 24 and 26, 9% between 27 and 28, and 7% above 28. 11 freshmen graduated first in their class.
Requirements: The ACT is required. In addition, students must have a minimum score of 19 on the ACT and be in the top half of their class, or have an ACT score of 23 and be in the upper two thirds of their class. Graduation from an accredited secondary school or satisfactory scores on the GED are required for admission. Secondary school courses must include 4 years of English and 2 to 3 years each of math, science, and social studies. In addition, students must have completed 1 to 2 years of art, film, foreign language, music, or theater. NIU requires applicants to be in the upper 65% of their class. AP and CLEP credits are accepted. Applications are accepted on-line via the ACT College Connector.
Procedure: Freshmen are admitted to all sessions. Entrance exams should be taken during the junior year. Applications should be filed by August 1 for fall entry, December 15 for spring entry, and May 15 for summer entry. There is a rolling admissions plan.
Transfer: 2008 transfer students enrolled in 2001-2002. Transfer students with 24 or more credit hours must have a minimum GPA of 2.0. The core competency requirements in English, math, and speech must be satisfied by all transfer students. 30 credits of 124 must be completed at NIU.
Visiting: There are regularly scheduled orientations for prospective students, including open house programs, bus tours, faculty meetings, residence hall tours, and department receptions. There are guides for informal visits and visitors may sit in on classes and stay overnight. To schedule a visit, contact the Office of Orientation and Student Assistance at (815) 753-1535.
Financial Aid: 33% of undergraduates work part time. Average annual earnings from campus work are $1200. The FAFSA and the college's own financial statement are required. The fall application deadline is March 1.
International Students: There are 197 international students enrolled. They must score 500 on the written TOEFL.
Computers: The mainframe is an Amdahl 5890/300E. PCs and Macs are available throughout the campus. 57 computer labs on campus provide access for particular colleges and departments. Access to the Internet is free to NIU students from any on-campus lab or residence hall, or through modems. E-mail, a phonebook, a web browser, FTP, and a Newsreader are available. All students may access the system. Computer labs are open more than 150 hours per week. There are no time limits and no fees.
Graduates: In 2001, 3416 bachelor's degrees were awarded. The most popular majors were elementary education (7%), communication studies (7%), and marketing (5%). In an average class, 20% graduate in 4 years, 43% in 5 years, and 49% in 6 years. 800 companies recruited on campus in 2000-2001. Of the 2000 graduating class, 19% were enrolled in graduate school within 6 months of graduation and 89% were employed.
Admissions Contact: Robert Burk, Director of Admissions.
E-mail: *admissionsinfo@niu.edu* Web: *http://www.niu.edu/*

NORTHWESTERN UNIVERSITY — E-1
Evanston, IL 60208 — (847) 491-7271

Full-time: 3647 men, 4031 women	**Faculty:** 918; I, ++$
Part-time: 50 men, 88 women	**Ph.D.s:** 100%
Graduate: 3806 men, 2668 women	**Student/Faculty:** 8 to 1
Year: quarters, summer session	**Tuition:** $25,839
Application Deadline: January 1	**Room & Board:** $7776
Freshman Class: 13,988 applied, 4780 accepted, 1952 enrolled	
SAT I Verbal/Math: 690/710	**ACT:** 31 **MOST COMPETITIVE**

Northwestern University, founded in 1851, is an independent, nonprofit liberal arts institution offering undergraduate study in the arts and sciences, education and social policy, journalism, music, speech, and engineering and applied science. There are 6 undergraduate and 7 graduate schools. In addition to regional accreditation, Northwestern has baccalaureate program accreditation with AACSB, ABET, ACEJMC, APTA, NASM, and NCACS. The 3 libraries contain 4,150,148 volumes, 3,944,195 microform items, and 67,121 audiovisual forms/CDs, and subscribe to 38,257 periodicals. Computerized library services include the card catalog, interlibrary loans, and database searching. Special learning facilities include an art gallery, radio station, TV station, and an observatory. The 231-acre campus is in a suburban area 12 miles north of Chicago on the shores of Lake Michigan. Including residence halls, there are 174 buildings.
Student Life: 78% of undergraduates are from out of state, mostly the Midwest. Others are from 49 states, 98 foreign countries, and Canada. 74% are from public schools. 61% are white; 17% Asian American. 29% are Protestant; 24% Catholic; 18% claim no religious affiliation; 14% Jewish; 11% Buddhist, Islamic, and others. The average age of freshmen is 19; all undergraduates, 20. 4% do not continue beyond their first year; 89% remain to graduate.
Housing: 4174 students can be accommodated in college housing, which includes single-sex and coed dormitories, fraternity houses, and sorority houses. In addition, there are special-interest houses. On-campus housing is guaranteed for the freshman year only. 68% of students live on campus; of those, 95% remain on campus on weekends. Upperclassmen may keep cars.
Activities: 30% of men belong to 18 national fraternities; 39% of women belong to 14 national sororities. There are 250 groups on campus, including band, cheerleading, chess, choir, chorale, chorus, dance, debate, drama, ethnic, film, gay, honors, international, jazz band, literary magazine, marching band, musical theater, newspaper, opera, orchestra, pep band, photography, political, professional, radio and TV, religious, social, social service, student government, symphony, and yearbook. Popular campus events include Waa-Mu Variety Show, Armadillo Day, and Primal Scream.
Sports: There are 8 intercollegiate sports for men and 11 for women, and 30 intramural sports for men and 30 for women. Facilities include a stadium, an arena, a gym, lake-front playing fields for soccer, field hockey, and Frisbee, a boat house, and recreation and sports centers housing basketball, volleyball, tennis, racquetball, swimming, badminton, weight training, jogging, squash, and fitness facilities.
Disabled Students: All of the campus is accessible. Wheelchair ramps, elevators, special parking, specially equipped rest rooms, special class scheduling, lowered drinking fountains, lowered telephones, and accessible dorm rooms are available.
Services: There is a reader service for the blind, one-on-one compensation, remediation, ADHD coaching, note taking, and real-time captioning.
Campus Safety and Security: Measures include 24-hour foot and vehicle patrol, self-defense education for women, escort service, and shuttle buses. There are informal discussions, pamphlets/posters/films, emergency telephones, lighted pathways/sidewalks, and a security keycard system in residence halls.
Programs of Study: Northwestern confers B.A., B.A.M., B.M., B.M.E., B.S.E., B.S.Ed., B.S.J., and B.S.Sp. degrees. Master's and doctoral degrees are also awarded. Bachelor's degrees are awarded in BIOLOGICAL SCIENCE (biology/biological science, molecular biology, and

neurosciences), COMMUNICATIONS AND THE ARTS (art, art history and appreciation, broadcasting, classics, communications, comparative literature, dance, dramatic arts, English, French, German, Italian, journalism, linguistics, music, percussion, performing arts, piano/organ, radio/television technology, Slavic languages, Spanish, voice, and winds), COMPUTER AND PHYSICAL SCIENCE (applied mathematics, astronomy, chemistry, computer science, geology, mathematics, physics, and statistics), EDUCATION (education, music, and secondary), ENGINEERING AND ENVIRONMENTAL DESIGN (biomedical engineering, chemical engineering, civil engineering, computer engineering, electrical/electronics engineering, engineering, environmental engineering, industrial engineering, materials science, and mechanical engineering), HEALTH PROFESSIONS (speech pathology/audiology), SOCIAL SCIENCE (African American studies, American studies, anthropology, cognitive science, economics, Hispanic American studies, history, human development, international studies, philosophy, political science/government, psychology, religion, sociology, and urban studies). Journalism, speech, and physical and life sciences are the strongest academically. Economics, political science, and engineering are the largest.

Required: Requirements for graduation vary by school and degree program. Students must maintain a minimum 2.0 GPA and complete a total of 45 to 48 quarter units.

Special: The university offers cooperative engineering programs throughout the country, many off-campus field studies and research opportunities, internships in the arts, journalism, and teaching, study abroad in 28 countries around the world, a Washington semester, and numerous work-study programs both on and off campus. There is an accelerated degree program in medical education, and B.A.-B.S. degrees in liberal arts and engineering, liberal arts and music, and music and engineering. An integrated science program, an interdisciplinary study in mathematical methods in social sciences, a variety of dual and student-designed majors, pass/fail options, and a teaching media program are also available. There are 25 national honor societies, including Phi Beta Kappa, a freshman honors program, and 40 departmental honors program.

Faculty/Classroom: 72% of faculty are male; 28%, female. All both teach undergraduates and do research. Graduate students teach 4% of introductory courses. The average class size in an introductory lecture is 35; in a laboratory, 14; and in a regular course, 22.

Admissions: 34% of the 2001-2002 applicants were accepted. The SAT I scores for the 2001-2002 freshman class were: Verbal--1% below 500, 9% between 500 and 599, 46% between 600 and 700, and 44% above 700; Math--1% below 500, 6% between 500 and 599, 36% between 600 and 700, and 58% above 700. The ACT scores were 1% below 21, 3% between 21 and 23, 9% between 24 and 26, 13% between 27 and 28, and 75% above 28. 94% of the current freshmen were in the top fifth of their class; 99% were in the top two fifths. 186 freshmen graduated first in their class.

Requirements: The SAT I or ACT is required. In addition, applicants must be graduates of an accredited secondary school or have a GED certificate, and have completed a minimum of 16 units, including 4 units of English, 3 of math, 2 or 3 each of a foreign language and history, and 2 of lab sciences. SAT II: Subject tests are required for the accelerated honors program in medical education and the integrated science program. Auditions are required for applicants to the School of Music. AP credits are accepted. Important factors in the admissions decision are advanced placement or honor courses, recommendations by school officials, and extracurricular activities record. Applications may be submitted on-line via Northwestern's web site.

Procedure: Freshmen are admitted to all sessions. Entrance exams should be taken by December of the senior year. There are early decision and deferred admissions plans. Early decision applications should be filed by November 1; regular applications, by January 1 for fall entry, November 1 for winter entry, February 1 for spring entry, and May 1 for summer entry, along with a $60 fee. Notification of early decision is sent December 15; regular decision, April 15. 421 early decision candidates were accepted for the 2001-2002 class. 3% of all applicants are on a waiting list; 11 were accepted in 2001.

Transfer: 125 transfer students enrolled in 2001-2002. Transfer students need a minimum 3.0 GPA, SAT I or ACT scores, high school record, 1 essay, and the dean's reference form. Applicants are required to have a minimum of 1 year of completed college work to apply to Northwestern. 23 quarter units of 45 to 48 must be completed at Northwestern.

Visiting: There are regularly scheduled orientations for prospective students, including daily information sessions Monday through Friday. There are guides for informal visits and visitors may sit in on classes and stay overnight. To schedule a visit, contact the Admissions Office.

Financial Aid: In 2001-2002, 57% of all freshmen and 60% of continuing students received some form of financial aid. 47% of freshmen and 50% of continuing students received need-based aid. The average freshman award was $21,785. Of that total, scholarships or need-based grants averaged $18,285 ($29,545 maximum); loans averaged $2100 ($5000 maximum); and work contracts averaged $1400 ($2100 maximum). 30% of undergraduates work part time. Average annual earnings from campus work are $2100. The average financial indebtedness of the 2001 graduate was $13,253. Northwestern is a member of CSS. The CSS/Profile, FAFSA, and tax returns under certain conditions are required. The fall application deadline is February 1.

International Students: There are 314 international students enrolled. The school actively recruits these students. They must score 600 on the written TOEFL or 250 on the electronic version and also take the SAT I or the ACT.

Computers: The mainframe is an IBM 3090/180J. All academic and administrative buildings, as well as student residences, are connected to the campus network, through which students have access to e-mail, the campus bulletin board and calendar, and the Internet, as well as the card catalog of the university library. All students may access the system 24 hours per day. There are no time limits and no fees. It is recommended that students in engineering have personal computers.

Graduates: In 2001, 2022 bachelor's degrees were awarded. The most popular majors were social science and history (22%), engineering (14%), and communications (12%). In an average class, 83% graduate in 4 years, 92% in 5 years, and 92% in 6 years. 350 to 400 companies recruited on campus in 2000-2001.

Admissions Contact: Carol Lunkenheimer, Dean of Undergraduate Admission. A video is available.
E-mail: *ug-admission@northwestern.edu*
Web: *http://www.northwesternedu/admissions/*

OLIVET NAZARENE UNIVERSITY — E-2

Bourbonnais, IL 60914 (815) 939-5203
(800) 648-1463; Fax: (815) 935-4998

Full-time: 749 men, 1003 women	**Faculty:** 80; IIA, --$
Part-time: 130 men, 179 women	**Ph.D.s:** 72%
Graduate: 363 men, 926 women	**Student/Faculty:** 22 to 1
Year: semesters, summer session	**Tuition:** $13,464
Application Deadline: August 1	**Room & Board:** $4980
Freshman Class: 1398 applied, 1111 accepted, 548 enrolled	
ACT: 23	**COMPETITIVE**

Olivet Nazarene University, established in 1907, is a nonprofit, private, comprehensive institution affiliated with the Church of the Nazarene. Its undergraduate and graduate programs emphasize the liberal arts, business, communication, health science, art and fine arts, engineering, music, Bible and religious studies, and teacher preparation in an atmosphere of Christian culture. In addition to regional accreditation, Olivet has baccalaureate program accreditation with ABET, ADA, CSWE, IACBE, NASM, NCATE, and NLN. The library contains 165,000 volumes, 38,800 microform items, and 4800 audiovisual forms/CDs, and subscribes to 900 periodicals. Computerized library services include the card catalog, interlibrary loans, and database searching. Special learning facilities include a learning resource center, art gallery, natural history museum, planetarium, radio station, and smart board classrooms. The 190-acre campus is in a small town 60 miles south of Chicago. Including residence halls, there are 34 buildings.

Student Life: 59% of undergraduates are from out of state, mostly the Midwest. Others are from 40 states, 17 foreign countries, and Canada. 88% are white. Most are Protestant. The average age of freshmen is 18; all undergraduates, 20. 32% do not continue beyond their first year; 52% remain to graduate.

Housing: 1550 students can be accommodated in college housing, which includes single-sex dormitories, on-campus apartments, and married-student housing. In addition, there are honors houses. On-campus housing is guaranteed for all 4 years. 75% of students live on campus; of those, 80% remain on campus on weekends. Alcohol is not permitted. All students may keep cars.

Activities: There are no fraternities or sororities. There are 32 groups on campus, including art, athletic booster, band, cheerleading, choir, chorale, chorus, computers, drama, honors, international, jazz band, literary magazine, newspaper, orchestra, pep band, political, professional, radio and TV, religious, social, social service, student government, and yearbook. Popular campus events include Parents Weekend, Halloween Party, and Lipsynch Contest.

Sports: There are 9 intercollegiate sports for men and 9 for women, and 14 intramural sports for men and 14 for women. Facilities include a 3000-seat gym with basketball, volleyball, and racquetball courts, a pool, a weight-lifting room, and an indoor track; a 2500-seat stadium with a track; and an athletic park with softball, baseball, and soccer fields, a jogging track, track and field facilities, an ice rink, and tennis courts.

Disabled Students: 90% of the campus is accessible. Wheelchair ramps, elevators, special parking, specially equipped rest rooms, lowered drinking fountains, and lowered telephones are available.

Services: There is remedial math and writing. In addition to many counseling and information services, tutoring is available in economics, psychology, sociology, chemistry, and Old and New Testament studies. There is a tutoring referral service in all subjects and a learning development center.

Campus Safety and Security: Measures include 24-hour foot and vehicle patrol, self-defense education, escort service, and informal discussions. There are pamphlets/posters/films, lighted pathways/sidewalks, and and an on-campus security service.
Programs of Study: Olivet confers B.A., B.S., B.A.T., and B.S.T. degrees. Associate and master's degrees are also awarded. Bachelor's degrees are awarded in BIOLOGICAL SCIENCE (biology/biological science and zoology), BUSINESS (accounting, business administration and management, and fashion merchandising), COMMUNICATIONS AND THE ARTS (art, English, music, romance languages and literature, and speech/debate/rhetoric), COMPUTER AND PHYSICAL SCIENCE (chemistry, computer science, geology, mathematics, physical sciences, and science technology), EDUCATION (Christian, early childhood, elementary, and physical), ENGINEERING AND ENVIRONMENTAL DESIGN (engineering, environmental design, and environmental science), HEALTH PROFESSIONS (clinical science and nursing), SOCIAL SCIENCE (dietetics, economics, family/consumer studies, history, liberal arts/general studies, philosophy, political science/government, psychology, public affairs, religion, social science, social work, and sociology). Engineering and physical science are the strongest academically. Business administration and education are the largest.
Required: To graduate, students must complete 128 semester hours of credit, with fulfillment of a major and a minimum of 40 hours of credit in upper-division courses, (50 to 64 in the major) and maintain a minimum GPA of 2.0. The required general education studies, 50 to 61 hours, include 12 credit hours of Christianity, 9 to 10 of communication, 7 to 11 of natural science and math, 9 of social sciences, 6 to 8 of international culture, 6 of literature and the arts, and 4 to 5 of personal health. Participation in the Senior Outcomes testing program in general education is required.
Special: Special academic programs include a work-study program, which can be arranged with other institutions, and a general studies degree. A 4-year engineering program (ABET) is available. There are 6 national honor societies, and 5 departmental honors programs.
Faculty/Classroom: 66% of faculty are male; 34%, female.
Admissions: 79% of the 2001-2002 applicants were accepted. The ACT scores for the 2001-2002 freshman class were: 31% below 21, 34% between 21 and 23, 13% between 24 and 26, 12% between 27 and 28, and 10% above 28. 42% of the current freshmen were in the top fifth of their class; 75% were in the top two fifths.
Requirements: The ACT is required, with a minimum score of 16. Other admissions requirements include graduation from an accredited secondary school with 3 units each of English, math, foreign language, and natural science or social science, and an additional 2 of math, foreign language, natural science, or social science. The GED also is accepted. 2 certificates of recommendation must be submitted. Olivet requires applicants to be in the upper 67% of their class. A GPA of 2.0 is required. AP and CLEP credits are accepted. Applications are accepted on-line.
Procedure: Freshmen are admitted to all sessions. Entrance exams should be taken during the spring of the junior year or during the senior year. Applications should be filed by August 1 for fall entry, January 1 for spring entry, and June 1 for summer entry. Notification is sent on a rolling basis.
Transfer: 231 transfer students enrolled in 2001-2002. Transcripts of all college work must be submitted. 30 credits of 128 must be completed at Olivet.
Visiting: There are regularly scheduled orientations for prospective students, including class visits, financial aid, information tour, lunch, professor meetings, and an optional overnight stay. There are guides for informal visits and visitors may sit in on classes and stay overnight. To schedule a visit, contact Jean Milton, the Campus Visit Coordinator in the Admissions Office at *jmilton@olivet.edu*
Financial Aid: In 2001-2002, 95% of all freshmen and 91% of continuing students received some form of financial aid. 54% of freshmen and 58% of continuing students received need-based aid. The average freshman award was $12,834. Of that total, scholarships or need-based grants averaged $5153; loans averaged $3686; work contracts averaged $1000; and leadership or athletic scholarship averaged $3500. 50% of undergraduates work part time. The average financial indebtedness of the 2001 graduate was $13,479. Olivet is a member of CSS. The FAFSA and the college's own financial statement are required. The fall application deadline is March 1.
International Students: There are 15 international students enrolled. They must score 500 on the written TOEFL or 17 on the electronic version or take the MELAB, and also take the ACT, scoring 18.
Computers: There are 30 PCs and IBM PS/2 Model 30s available in the computer lab. There is also a Macintosh lab with 15 machines. 50 PCs are connected to the network with Internet access. All students may access the system. There are no time limits and no fees. It is strongly recommended that all students have personal computers.
Graduates: In 2001, 358 bachelor's degrees were awarded. The most popular majors were education (17%), health professions (17%), and business/marketing (15%). In an average class, 52% graduate in 6 years.
Admissions Contact: Brian Parker, Director of Admissions.
E-mail: *admissions@olivet.edu* Web: *http://www.olivet.edu*

PRINCIPIA COLLEGE

Elsah, IL 62028 — C-4
(618) 374-5181
(800) 277-4648; Fax: (618) 374-4000

Full-time: 235 men, 298 women	**Faculty:** 48; IIB, -$
Part-time: 8 men, 13 women	**Ph.D.s:** 52%
Graduate: none	**Student/Faculty:** 11 to 1
Year: quarters	**Tuition:** $17,670
Application Deadline: March 1	**Room & Board:** $6195
Freshman Class: 252 applied, 225 accepted, 160 enrolled	
SAT I Verbal/Math: 577/564	**ACT:** 25 **COMPETITIVE+**

Principia College, founded in 1910, is a liberal arts and sciences college for Christian Scientists. In addition to regional accreditation, Principia has baccalaureate program accreditation with NCATE. The library contains 206,391 volumes, 188,458 microform items, and 7139 audiovisual forms/CDs, and subscribes to 479 periodicals. Computerized library services include the card catalog, interlibrary loans, and database searching. Special learning facilities include a learning resource center, art gallery, planetarium, radio station, and TV station. The 2600-acre campus is in a rural area 30 miles northeast of St. Louis. Including residence halls, there are 33 buildings.
Student Life: 88% of undergraduates are from out of state, mostly the Midwest. Others are from 46 states, 25 foreign countries, and Canada. 68% are from public schools. 79% are white; 17% foreign nationals. All are Christian Scientists. The average age of freshmen is 18; all undergraduates, 20. 14% do not continue beyond their first year.
Housing: 639 students can be accommodated in college housing, which includes single-sex dormitories, on-campus apartments, and married-student housing. In addition, there are special-interest houses. On-campus housing is guaranteed for all 4 years. 98% of students live on campus; of those, All remain on campus on weekends. Alcohol is not permitted. All students may keep cars.
Activities: There are no fraternities or sororities. There are 34 groups on campus, including art, cheerleading, choir, chorus, computers, dance, drama, ethnic, honors, international, jazz band, literary magazine, musical theater, newspaper, orchestra, photography, political, radio and TV, religious, social, social service, student government, and yearbook. Popular campus events include athletic events, dances, and drama and dance performances.
Sports: There are 9 intercollegiate sports for men and 9 for women, and 6 intramural sports for men and 6 for women. Facilities include 2 gyms, a pool, indoor and outdoor tennis courts, a racquetball court, basketball/volleyball courts, a dance studio, a weight room, baseball, football, soccer, and practice fields, and a 6-lane track.
Disabled Students: Wheelchair ramps, elevators, special parking, specially equipped rest rooms, and lowered drinking fountains are available.
Services: There is remedial reading and writing. Assistance in writing, reading, and study skills is available.
Campus Safety and Security: Measures include 24-hour foot and vehicle patrol, informal discussions, emergency telephones, and lighted pathways/sidewalks.
Programs of Study: Principia confers B.A. and B.S. degrees. Bachelor's degrees are awarded in BIOLOGICAL SCIENCE (biology/biological science), BUSINESS (business administration and management, business economics, and sports management), COMMUNICATIONS AND THE ARTS (communications, dramatic arts, English, fine arts, French, languages, music, Spanish, and studio art), COMPUTER AND PHYSICAL SCIENCE (chemistry, computer science, mathematics, and physics), EDUCATION (elementary and secondary), ENGINEERING AND ENVIRONMENTAL DESIGN (engineering and environmental science), SOCIAL SCIENCE (economics, German area studies, history, international relations, philosophy, political science/government, religion, Russian and Slavic studies, and sociology). Education, studio art, and biology are the strongest academically. Business administration, studio art, and education are the largest.
Required: All students must complete a minimum of 180 quarter hours, with 45 to 93 quarter hours in the major (10 to 15 courses) and at least a 2.0 overall GPA. Courses in foreign language, literature, arts, religion and philosophy, history, social science, math, and natural sciences are required. In addition, students must be certified as proficient in written English, pass a moral reasoning seminar, earn 4 credits in individual and team phys ed activities, and pass a survival swim test.
Special: Students may design their own majors, study abroad or in San Francisco, or pursue a B.A.-B.S. degree. Internships, student-planned with a professor, independent study, a Washington semester, work-study, and an interdisciplinary major, world perspectives, are available. A 3-2 engineering program with Washington University in St. Louis, Southern Illinois University at Carbondale, the University of Southern California, or another university with approval is also possible. A San Francisco field program in business administration is offered. There is 1 national honor society, and a freshman honors program.
Faculty/Classroom: 58% of faculty are male; 42%, female. All teach undergraduates. The average class size in an introductory lecture is 14; in a laboratory, 11; and in a regular course, 11.

Admissions: 89% of the 2001-2002 applicants were accepted. The SAT I scores for the 2001-2002 freshman class were: Verbal--21% below 500, 41% between 500 and 599, 26% between 600 and 700, and 13% above 700; Math--19% below 500, 46% between 500 and 599, 32% between 600 and 700, and 4% above 700. The ACT scores were 27% below 21, 25% between 21 and 23, 22% between 24 and 26, 6% between 27 and 28, and 20% above 28. 35% of the current freshmen were in the top fifth of their class; 51% were in the top two fifths. There were 4 National Merit semifinalists. 3 freshmen graduated first in their class.
Requirements: The SAT I or ACT is required; the SAT I is preferred. An essay is required. SAT II: Subject tests in foreign language and math are recommended. High school preparation should include 4 years of English, 3 of math (including algebra II), 2 to 3 of a foreign language, 2 of natural sciences, history or social sciences, and electives. A GPA of 2.0 is required. AP and CLEP credits are accepted. Important factors in the admissions decision are advanced placement or honor courses, recommendations by school officials, and leadership record.
Procedure: Freshmen are admitted fall, winter, and spring. Entrance exams should be taken in the spring of the junior year and again in the fall of the senior year. There is a deferred admissions plan. Early decision applications should be filed by January 15; regular applications, by March 1 for fall entry, December 1 for winter entry, and March 1 for spring entry. The fall 2001 application fee was $35. Notification is sent on a rolling basis.
Transfer: 25 transfer students enrolled in 2001-2002. Applicants must be in good standing at their previous college or university. 45 credits of 180 must be completed at Principia.
Visiting: There are regularly scheduled orientations for prospective students, including a visit to classes, meeting professors, living in a dormitory, and meeting students (3-day weekend). There are guides for informal visits and visitors may sit in on classes and stay overnight. To schedule a visit, contact Wendie Hosmer.
Financial Aid: In 2001-2002, 87% of all freshmen and 85% of continuing students received some form of financial aid. 65% of freshmen and 62% of continuing students received need-based aid. The average freshman award was $14,196. Of that total, scholarships or need-based grants averaged $7360 ($22,360 maximum); loans averaged $1964 ($7000 maximum); work contracts averaged $479 ($1500 maximum); and staff discounts averaged $850 ($11,404 maximum). 54% of undergraduates work part time. Average annual earnings from campus work are $1705. Principia is a member of CSS. The CSS/Profile and the college's own financial statement are required. The fall application deadline is July 1.
International Students: There are 67 international students enrolled. The school actively recruits these students. They must score 550 on the written TOEFL or 213 on the electronic version.
Computers: The mainframe is an HP 3000. About 200 computer workstations are available to students in 5 academic buildings, as PCs or as remote terminals of the college mainframe computer. PCs and Macs are available to all students on a 24-hour basis. There are no time limits. The fee is $22.
Graduates: In 2001, 121 bachelor's degrees were awarded. The most popular majors were business administration (12%), studio art (12%), and education (12%). In an average class, 66% graduate in 4 years, 73% in 5 years, and 73% in 6 years. 40 companies recruited on campus in 2000-2001. Of the 2000 graduating class, 21% were enrolled in graduate school within 6 months of graduation and 92% were employed.
Admissions Contact: Martha Green Quirk, Dean of Admissions. A video is available. E-mail: *collegeadmissions@prin.edu*
Web: *www.prin.edu/college/admissions*

QUINCY UNIVERSITY

Quincy, IL 62301-2699 — B-3
(217) 228-5210
(800) 688-4295; Fax: (217) 228-5479

Full-time: 449 men, 551 women	**Faculty:** 62; IIB, --$
Part-time: 51 men, 96 women	**Ph.D.s:** 84%
Graduate: 61 men, 111 women	**Student/Faculty:** 16 to 1
Year: semesters, summer session	**Tuition:** $15,430
Application Deadline: open	**Room & Board:** $5020
Freshman Class: 898 applied, 862 accepted, 307 enrolled	
SAT I Verbal/Math: 500/520	**ACT:** 22 — **COMPETITIVE**

Quincy University, established in 1860, is a private liberal arts institution conducted by the Franciscan Friars of the Roman Catholic Church. There are 3 undergraduate and 2 graduate schools. In addition to regional accreditation, Quincy has baccalaureate program accreditation with NASM. The library contains 243166 volumes, 191,217 microform items, and 3951 audiovisual forms/CDs, and subscribes to 680 periodicals. Computerized library services include the card catalog, interlibrary loans, and database searching. Special learning facilities include an art gallery, radio station, TV station, and life science field station. The 75-acre campus is in a small town 120 miles north of St. Louis. Including residence halls, there are 41 buildings.
Student Life: 75% of undergraduates are from Illinois. Others are from 35 states, 14 foreign countries, and Canada. 48% are from public schools. 81% are white. 54% are Catholic; 23% claim no religious affiliation; 20% are Protestant. The average age of freshmen is 18; all undergraduates, 22. 25% do not continue beyond their first year.
Housing: 984 students can be accommodated in college housing, which includes single-sex and coed dormitories, on-campus apartments, married-student housing, fraternity houses, and sorority houses. In addition, there are honors houses and special-interest houses. On-campus housing is guaranteed for all 4 years. 70% of students live on campus; of those, 90% remain on campus on weekends. All students may keep cars.
Activities: 14% of men belong to 2 national fraternities; 11% of women belong to 2 national sororities. There are 43 groups on campus, including bagpipe band, band, cheerleading, chess, choir, chorale, chorus, computers, drama, ethnic, honors, international, jazz band, literary magazine, musical theater, newspaper, opera, orchestra, pep band, political, professional, radio and TV, religious, social, social service, student government, symphony, and yearbook. Popular campus events include Fall Fest/Parents Weekend, Hawk Pride Weekend, and Septemberfest.
Sports: There are 9 intercollegiate sports for men and 8 for women, and 11 intramural sports for men and 11 for women. Facilities include a health and fitness center, 2 gyms, a football/baseball stadium, a soccer stadium, a weight room, a college athletic field, and outdoor basketball/volleyball courts.
Disabled Students: 95% of the campus is accessible. Wheelchair ramps, elevators, special parking, specially equipped rest rooms, special class scheduling, lowered drinking fountains, and lowered telephones are available.
Services: Counseling and information services are available, as is tutoring in every subject. There is a reader service for the blind and remedial writing. Skill development and motivation workshops and courses are available.
Campus Safety and Security: Measures include 24-hour foot and vehicle patrol, self-defense education, escort service, and shuttle buses. There are informal discussions, pamphlets/posters/films, emergency telephones, and lighted pathways/sidewalks.
Programs of Study: Quincy confers B.A., B.S., B.F.A., and B.S.N. degrees. Associate and master's degrees are also awarded. Bachelor's degrees are awarded in BIOLOGICAL SCIENCE (avian sciences and biology/biological science), BUSINESS (accounting, banking and finance, business administration and management, marketing/retailing/merchandising, and sports management), COMMUNICATIONS AND THE ARTS (art, arts administration/management, communications, English, music, and music business management), COMPUTER AND PHYSICAL SCIENCE (chemistry, computer science, information sciences and systems, and mathematics), EDUCATION (art, athletic training, elementary, music, physical, science, secondary, and special), ENGINEERING AND ENVIRONMENTAL DESIGN (aviation administration/management, engineering, and environmental science), HEALTH PROFESSIONS (medical laboratory technology and nursing), SOCIAL SCIENCE (criminal justice, history, human services, humanities, peace studies, philosophy, political science/government, psychology, religious education, social work, sociology, and theological studies). Business, accounting, and science are the strongest academically. Business management, elementary education, and accounting are the largest.
Required: Each student is required to complete a minimum of 124 credit hours, with at least 27 in the major and 39 in upper level courses. In addition, students must complete required courses in rhetoric, science or math, social sciences, humanities, fine arts, theology, and phys ed; complete a senior comprehensive seminar; and maintain a minimum GPA of 2.0.
Special: Dual majors, study abroad in 27 countries, credit by exam, and upper-class and early exploratory internships are available. Pass/fail options, credit for life experience, student-designed majors, a B.A.- B.S. degree in peacemaking studies, and a 3-2 engineering degree with Washington University in St. Louis are also offered. There are 6 national honor societies, and a freshman honors program.
Faculty/Classroom: 69% of faculty are male; 31%, female. All teach undergraduates. No introductory courses are taught by graduate students. The average class size in an introductory lecture is 40; in a laboratory, 20; and in a regular course, 20.
Admissions: 96% of the 2001-2002 applicants were accepted. The SAT I scores for the 2001-2002 freshman class were: Verbal--50% below 500, 30% between 500 and 599, and 20% between 600 and 700. The ACT scores were 35% below 21, 31% between 21 and 23, 21% between 24 and 26, 7% between 27 and 28, and 6% above 28. 29% of the current freshmen were in the top fifth of their class; 55% were in the top two fifths. 4 freshmen graduated first in their class.
Requirements: The SAT I or ACT is required, with a minimum score of 475 verbal and 475 math on the SAT I, or 20 on the ACT. The GED is accepted. College preparatory courses totaling 16 credits should include 4 years of English, 3 each of math and science, and 2 each of a foreign language, history, and social studies. Art students must submit a portfolio, and music students are required to audition. Quincy requires

applicants to be in the upper 50% of their class. A GPA of 2.0 is required. AP and CLEP credits are accepted. Important factors in the admissions decision are leadership record, evidence of special talent, and recommendations by school officials. Students can apply on-line through CollegeView, CollegeLink, and Quincy's web site.

Procedure: Freshmen are admitted fall and spring. Entrance exams should be taken in October of the senior year. There is a deferred admissions plan. Application deadlines are open. The application fee is $25. There is a rolling admissions plan.

Transfer: 127 transfer students enrolled in 2001-2002. Applicants must have a minimum GPA of 2.0. Grades of C or better transfer for credit. 30 credits of 124 must be completed at Quincy.

Visiting: There are regularly scheduled orientations for prospective students, including weekend advising/registration programs throughout the summer. There are guides for informal visits and visitors may sit in on classes and stay overnight. To schedule a visit, contact the Admissions Office at *admissions@quincy.edu*.

Financial Aid: In 2001-2002, 99% of all freshmen and 94% of continuing students received some form of financial aid. 82% of freshmen and 89% of continuing students received need-based aid. The average freshman award was $15,109. Of that total, scholarships or need-based grants averaged $10,356 ($20,450 maximum); loans averaged $3000 ($4625 maximum); and work contracts averaged $1500 (maximum). 43% of undergraduates work part time. Average annual earnings from campus work are $950. The average financial indebtedness of the 2001 graduate was $14,100. The FAFSA is required. The fall application deadline is April 15.

International Students: There are 14 international students enrolled. The school actively recruits these students. They must score 500 on the written TOEFL.

Computers: The mainframe is an HP 9000/K460. More than 300 PCs are available throughout campus. The main academic buildings house 5 computer labs, including a 60-station writing lab and classroom. The library, residence halls, and honors houses also have PC labs. The Internet is available in each computer lab. All students may access the system. There are no time limits and no fees. It is strongly recommended that all students have a personal computer.

Graduates: In 2001, 189 bachelor's degrees were awarded. The most popular majors were elementary education (10%), management (7%), and psychology (6%). 52 companies recruited on campus in 2000-2001. Of the 2000 graduating class, 18% were enrolled in graduate school within 6 months of graduation and 79% were employed.

Admissions Contact: Kevin Brown, Director of Admissions.
E-mail: *brownke@quincy.edu* Web: *http://www.quincy.edu/*

ROCKFORD COLLEGE
Rockford, IL 61108 — D-1
(815) 226-4050
(800) 892-2984; Fax: (815) 226-2822

Full-time: 327 men, 491 women	**Faculty:** 80; IIB, --$
Part-time: 65 men, 173 women	**Ph.D.s:** 45%
Graduate: 105 men, 198 women	**Student/Faculty:** 10 to 1
Year: semesters, summer session	**Tuition:** $18,300
Application Deadline: open	**Room & Board:** $5630
Freshman Class: 637 applied, 386 accepted, 134 enrolled	
SAT I Verbal/Math: 530/520	**ACT:** 22 — **COMPETITIVE**

Rockford College, founded in 1847, is a private institution offering undergraduate and graduate instruction in liberal arts and professional programs. In addition to regional accreditation, Rockford College has baccalaureate program accreditation with NLN. The library contains 167,983 volumes, 7590 microform items, and 9855 audiovisual forms/CDs, and subscribes to 815 periodicals. Computerized library services include the card catalog, interlibrary loans, and database searching. Special learning facilities include a learning resource center and art gallery. The 130-acre campus is in a suburban area 90 miles west of Chicago. Including residence halls, there are 26 buildings.

Student Life: 88% of undergraduates are from Illinois. Others are from 9 states and 2 foreign countries. 75% are from public schools. 83% are white. The average age of freshmen is 18; all undergraduates, 23. 36% do not continue beyond their first year.

Housing: 560 students can be accommodated in college housing, which includes single-sex and coed dormitories. In addition, there are special-interest houses, and intercultural, substance-free, and quiet floors. On-campus housing is guaranteed for all 4 years. 64% of students commute. All students may keep cars.

Activities: There are no fraternities or sororities. There are 28 groups on campus, including art, cheerleading, chorus, computers, dance, drama, ethnic, gay, honors, international, literary magazine, math, musical theater, newspaper, political, professional, religious, scientific, social, social service, and student government. Popular campus events include Snowball Dance, Kids and Sibs Weekend, and Family Weekend.

Sports: There are 6 intercollegiate sports for men and 5 for women, and 12 intramural sports for men and 12 for women. Facilities include a swimming pool, athletic fields, tennis courts, and a fitness center with free weights and Nautilus weight rooms.

Disabled Students: 85% of the campus is accessible. Wheelchair ramps, elevators, special parking, specially equipped rest rooms, special class scheduling, lowered drinking fountains, and lowered telephones are available.

Services: Counseling and information services are available, as is tutoring in most subjects. There is a reader service for the blind, and remedial math, reading, and writing. Diagnostic testing is available.

Campus Safety and Security: Measures include 24-hour foot and vehicle patrol, escort service, informal discussions, and pamphlets/posters/films. There are emergency telephones and lighted pathways/sidewalks.

Programs of Study: Rockford College confers B.A., B.S., B.F.A., and B.S.N. degrees. Master's degrees are also awarded. Bachelor's degrees are awarded in BIOLOGICAL SCIENCE (biology/biological science), BUSINESS (accounting and business administration and management), COMMUNICATIONS AND THE ARTS (art, art history and appreciation, classical languages, dramatic arts, English, fine arts, French, German, music, and Spanish), COMPUTER AND PHYSICAL SCIENCE (chemistry, computer science, mathematics, and science), EDUCATION (athletic training, early childhood, elementary, and physical), ENGINEERING AND ENVIRONMENTAL DESIGN (military science and preengineering), HEALTH PROFESSIONS (nursing, predentistry, premedicine, prepharmacy, and preveterinary science), SOCIAL SCIENCE (anthropology, criminal justice, economics, history, human services, humanities, philosophy, political science/government, prelaw, psychology, religion, social science, social work, sociology, and urban studies). Business, education, and psychology are the largest.

Required: To graduate, students must have a total of at least 124 credit hours and a minimum GPA of 2.0 (nursing 2.5). The required hours for each major varies between 28 and 44. Students are required to take 12 hours of social sciences, 8 to 12 of science, math, and computer science, 8 of language and literature, 6 to 9 of freshman English, 6 of art, and 2 of phys ed. Requirements for some degree programs may vary. All students must complete a senior seminar or project and must demonstrate proficiency in writing or public speaking, either by exam or by enrollment in a course that meets the requirement.

Special: The school offers junior and senior year internships, study abroad in 9 countries, a Washington semester at American University, and work-study programs. Dual majors, student-designed majors, nondegree study, and a 3-2 engineering degree with Washington University in St. Louis, the Universities of Southern California and Illinois, and Illinois Institute of Technology also are available. There are 5 national honor societies, including Phi Beta Kappa, and a freshman honors program.

Faculty/Classroom: 57% of faculty are male; 43%, female. All teach undergraduates. No introductory courses are taught by graduate students. The average class size in an introductory lecture is 25; in a laboratory, 12; and in a regular course, 18.

Admissions: 61% of the 2001-2002 applicants were accepted. The ACT scores for the 2001-2002 freshman class were 47% below 21, 20% between 21 and 23, 15% between 24 and 26, 8% between 27 and 28, and 10% above 28. 23% of the current freshmen were in the top fifth of their class; 45% were in the top two fifths. 4 freshmen graduated first in their class.

Requirements: The ACT is required, with a minimum composite score of 18. Applicants must graduate from an accredited secondary school or demonstrate satisfactory scores on the GED. 16 academic credits are required, including 4 years of English, 2 of math, and 1 each of a foreign language, history, and laboratory science. An essay and an interview are recommended. For performing arts students, an audition is recommended. Rockford College requires applicants to be in the upper 50% of their class. A GPA of 2.5 is required. AP and CLEP credits are accepted. Important factors in the admissions decision are advanced placement or honor courses, recommendations by school officials, and leadership record.

Procedure: Freshmen are admitted to all sessions. Entrance exams should be taken by the fall of the senior year. There is a deferred admissions plan. Application deadlines are open. The application fee is $35. There is a rolling admissions plan.

Transfer: 133 transfer students enrolled in 2001-2002. Applicants must have a minimum GPA of 2.2. Nursing transfer students' minimum GPA is 2.5. 30 credits of 124 must be completed at Rockford College.

Visiting: There are regularly scheduled orientations for prospective students, consisting of a tour, a meeting with faculty members and other students, class visits, and social/athletic programs. A week-long orientation program is required for all freshmen the week before fall classes begin. There are guides for informal visits and visitors may sit in on classes and stay overnight. To schedule a visit, contact the Admissions Office at *admission@rockford.edu*.

Financial Aid: In 2001-2002, 95% of all freshmen and 98% of continuing students received some form of financial aid. Scholarships or need-based grants averaged $3533. 28% of undergraduates work part time. Average annual earnings from campus work are $1500. The FAFSA is required. The fall application deadline is April 1.

International Students: There were 56 international students enrolled in a recent year. The school actively recruits these students. They must score 525 on the written TOEFL, or students can be conditionally admitted, then tested for English proficiency at the school's English Language Study Center.

Computers: The mainframe is an IBM 4341. All students may use the computer lab located in the science building. All students may access the system. There are no time limits and no fees. It is strongly recommended that all students have a personal computer.

Graduates: In 2001, 215 bachelor's degrees were awarded. The most popular majors were education (28%), business (26%), and psychology (8%). 69 companies recruited on campus in 2000-2001.

Admissions Contact: Christopher P. Moderson, Vice President Enrollment Management. A video is available.
E-mail: *chris_moderson@rockford.edu* Web: *www.rockford.edu*

ROOSEVELT UNIVERSITY — E-2
Chicago, IL 60605 — (312) 341-3515
(877) APPLYRU; Fax: (312) 341-3523

Full-time: 733 men, 1149 women	**Faculty:** 190; IIA, av$
Part-time: 954 men, 1792 women	**Ph.D.s:** 85%
Graduate: 960 men, 1902 women	**Student/Faculty:** 10 to 1
Year: semesters, summer session	**Tuition:** $13,970
Application Deadline: open	**Room & Board:** $6270
Freshman Class: n/av	
SAT I or ACT: required	**LESS COMPETITIVE**

Roosevelt University, founded in 1945, is an independent, comprehensive university. There are 5 undergraduate and 5 graduate schools. In addition to regional accreditation, Roosevelt has baccalaureate program accreditation with AACSB, NASM, and NCATE. The 2 libraries contain 405,022 volumes, 130,233 microform items, and 10,000 audiovisual forms/CDs, and subscribe to 1601 periodicals. Computerized library services include the card catalog, interlibrary loans, and database searching. Special learning facilities include a learning resource center and radio station. The campus is in an urban area, in downtown Chicago. Including residence halls, there are 2 buildings.

Student Life: 90% of undergraduates are from Illinois. Others are from 24 states, 70 foreign countries, and Canada. 44% are white; 27% African American, 12% Hispanic, 10% foreign nationals. The average age of freshmen is 21; all undergraduates, 27.

Housing: 300 students can be accommodated in college housing, which includes coed dormitories. On-campus housing is available on a first-come, first-served basis. 94% of students commute.

Activities: 1% of men belong to 1 local fraternity; 1% of women belong to 1 local sorority. There are 45 groups on campus, including band, choir, chorale, chorus, computers, cultural, drama, ethnic, honors, international, jazz band, literary magazine, model U.N., musical theater, newspaper, opera, orchestra, political, professional, radio and TV, religious, social service, student government, and symphony.

Sports: There is 1 intramural sport for men and 1 for women. Facilities include a fitness center and a recreational gym for basketball, volleyball, soccer, and intramural activities.

Disabled Students: All of the campus is accessible. Wheelchair ramps, elevators, specially equipped rest rooms, special class scheduling, and lowered telephones, are available. For special needs, contact the Disabled Student Services Office.

Services: Counseling and information services are available, as is tutoring in most subjects. There is remedial math, reading, and writing, arranged counseling, and testing. Emphasis is placed on individual program planning.

Campus Safety and Security: Measures include shuttle buses and lighted pathways/sidewalks.

Programs of Study: Roosevelt confers B.A., B.S., B.A.Comp.Sci., B.A.Ed., B.F.A.Mus.Theater, B.G.S., B.M., B.S.B.A., B.S. in Hospitality Mgt., and B.S.Telecomm. degrees. Master's and doctoral degrees are also awarded. Bachelor's degrees are awarded in BIOLOGICAL SCIENCE (biology/biological science), BUSINESS (accounting, banking and finance, business administration and management, hotel/motel and restaurant management, insurance, insurance and risk management, management science, marketing/retailing/merchandising, and personnel management), COMMUNICATIONS AND THE ARTS (advertising, art history and appreciation, broadcasting, communications, dramatic arts, English, French, guitar, jazz, journalism, languages, literature, media arts, music, music history and appreciation, music performance, music theory and composition, musical theater, percussion, performing arts, piano/organ, public relations, Spanish, strings, telecommunications, theater design, theater management, voice, and winds), COMPUTER AND PHYSICAL SCIENCE (actuarial science, chemistry, computer science, information sciences and systems, mathematics, and statistics), EDUCATION (early childhood, elementary, music, and secondary), ENGINEERING AND ENVIRONMENTAL DESIGN (electrical/electronics engineering technology and environmental science), HEALTH PROFESSIONS (allied health, medical technology, nuclear medical technology, predentistry, premedicine, prepharmacy, and preveterinary science), SOCIAL SCIENCE (African American studies, American studies, economics, history, international studies, liberal arts/general studies, philosophy, political science/government, prelaw, psychology, public administration, social science, sociology, urban studies, and women's studies). Journalism, accounting, and psychology are the strongest academically.

Required: For graduation, students must complete 120 credit hours, including 54 in the major, with a minimum GPA of 2.0, or 2.5 in the College of Education. The core curriculum consists of courses in the social sciences, natural sciences, and humanities, including English 101 and 102. The last 54 hours must be from a 4-year school.

Special: Roosevelt offers internships in approximately 20 subject areas, on-campus work-study, study abroad in 4 countries, dual and student-designed majors, pass/fail options, and noncredit courses. Adults older than 25 years of age may earn a Bachelor of General Studies through an accelerated degree program. Credit for life, military, and work experience is available in some majors through continuing education. The Roosevelt Scholars Program is offered. There are 4 national honor societies, a freshman honors program, and 20 departmental honors programs.

Faculty/Classroom: All teach undergraduates. No introductory courses are taught by graduate students.

Requirements: The SAT I or ACT is required. In addition, students must have completed 15 academic units, including 4 of English, 3 of math, 2 each of science, social studies, and foreign language, and 1 each of history and electives. An interview is recommended for all applicants, and an audition is required for music and theater candidates. Roosevelt requires applicants to be in the upper 50% of their class. A GPA of 2.0 is required. AP and CLEP credits are accepted. Important factors in the admissions decision are advanced placement or honor courses, evidence of special talent, and extracurricular activities record. Students may apply on-line at the school's web site.

Procedure: Freshmen are admitted to all sessions. There are early decision, early admissions, and deferred admissions plans. Application deadlines are open. The fall 2001 application fee was $25. Notification is sent on a rolling basis.

Transfer: 732 transfer students enrolled in 2001-2002. Applicants must have earned a minimum GPA of 2.0 in all accredited college course work. Offical transcripts must be received from each college where course work was attempted. 30 credits of 120 must be completed at Roosevelt.

Visiting: There are regularly scheduled orientations for prospective students, including open houses and Transfer Days. There are guides for informal visits and visitors may sit in on classes. To schedule a visit, contact the Undergraduate Admissions Office.

Financial Aid: In 2001-2002, 80% of all freshmen and 60% of continuing students received some form of financial aid. Scholarships or need-based grants averaged $1500; loans averaged $2625; and work contracts averaged $1989. The FAFSA and the college's own financial statement are required.

International Students: The school actively recruits these students. They must score 550 on the written TOEFL and also take the college's own test.

Computers: The mainframe is an IBM ES/9000 Model 30. PCs and Mac workstations are available for student use. Services include e-mail, Internet access, and computer-aided instruction in open access computer labs. All students may access the system. Students may access the system 1 hour when demand is great. There are no fees.

Admissions Contact: Gwen Kanelos, Director of Admissions.
E-mail: *applyru@roosevelt.edu* Web: *www.roosevelt.edu*

SAINT XAVIER UNIVERSITY — E-2
Chicago, IL 60655 — (773) 298-3050
(800) 462-9288; Fax: (773) 298-3076

Full-time: 629 men, 1360 women	**Faculty:** 140; IIA, -$
Part-time: 177 men, 649 women	**Ph.D.s:** 81%
Graduate: 425 men, 1676 women	**Student/Faculty:** 14 to 1
Year: semesters, summer session	**Tuition:** $15,130
Application Deadline: August 15	**Room & Board:** $5974
Freshman Class: 1411 applied, 1037 accepted, 365 enrolled	
ACT: 21	**COMPETITIVE**

Saint Xavier University is a private institution founded by the Sisters of Mercy in 1846 and affiliated with the Roman Catholic Church. There are 4 undergraduate and 4 graduate schools. In addition to regional accreditation, Saint Xavier has baccalaureate program accreditation with NASM and NLN. The library contains 172,104 volumes, 10,519 microform items, and 2350 audiovisual forms/CDs, and subscribes to 798 periodicals. Computerized library services include the card catalog, interlibrary loans, and database searching. Special learning facilities include a learning resource center, art gallery, and radio station. The 50-acre campus is in an urban area 15 miles southwest of Chicago's loop. Including residence halls, there are 8 buildings.

Student Life: 97% of undergraduates are from Illinois. Others are from 17 states and 7 foreign countries. 50% are from public schools. 64% are white; 16% African American, 12% Hispanic. 80% are Catholic; 16% Protestant. The average age of freshmen is 18; all undergraduates, 25. 24% do not continue beyond their first year.

Housing: 538 students can be accommodated in college housing, which includes single-sex and coed dormitories. On-campus housing is guaranteed for all 4 years. 81% of students commute. Alcohol is not permitted. All students may keep cars.

Activities: There are no fraternities or sororities. There are 30 groups on campus, including art, band, cheerleading, choir, chorus, computers, drama, ethnic, honors, international, jazz band, literary magazine, marching band, musical theater, newspaper, pep band, political, professional, radio and TV, religious, social service, student government, and yearbook. Popular campus events include Xavierfest, Boat Bash, and Octoberfest.

Sports: There are 4 intercollegiate sports for men and 4 for women, and 4 intramural sports for men and 4 for women. Facilities include baseball and softball diamonds, an outdoor sports facility, and a football field. The convocation and athletic center seats 2200 in the main arena with 4 additional competition courts. It also has racquetball courts, an indoor running track, training rooms, and a health and fitness center.

Disabled Students: 98% of the campus is accessible. Wheelchair ramps, elevators, special parking, specially equipped rest rooms, special class scheduling, lowered drinking fountains, and lowered telephones are available.

Services: Counseling and information services are available, as is tutoring in every subject. There are reading and language clinics and a center for learning disabilities.

Campus Safety and Security: Measures include 24-hour foot and vehicle patrol, self-defense education, escort service, and shuttle buses. There are emergency telephones and lighted pathways/sidewalks.

Programs of Study: Saint Xavier confers B.A., B.S., and B.M. degrees. Master's degrees are also awarded. Bachelor's degrees are awarded in BIOLOGICAL SCIENCE (biology/biological science), BUSINESS (accounting, banking and finance, business administration and management, international business management, and marketing/retailing/merchandising), COMMUNICATIONS AND THE ARTS (communications, English, French, music, and Spanish), COMPUTER AND PHYSICAL SCIENCE (chemistry, computer science, and mathematics), EDUCATION (art, early childhood, elementary, foreign languages, middle school, music, science, and secondary), HEALTH PROFESSIONS (nursing, predentistry, premedicine, prepharmacy, and speech pathology/audiology), SOCIAL SCIENCE (criminal justice, history, philosophy, political science/government, prelaw, psychology, religion, social science, and sociology). Business, nursing, and education are the strongest programs academically and have the largest enrollments.

Required: To graduate, the student must complete 120 credit hours, including the school's 57-semester-hour core curriculum, and earn a GPA of 2.0. The credit hours required in the student's major vary by subject.

Special: The university offers internships, and study abroad in England, Ireland, and Italy. There is a freshman honors program.

Faculty/Classroom: 42% of faculty are male; 50%, female. All teach undergraduates. The average class size in an introductory lecture is 20; in a laboratory, 15; and in a regular course, 16.

Admissions: 73% of the 2001-2002 applicants were accepted. The ACT scores for the 2001-2002 freshman class were: 52% below 21, 25% between 21 and 23, 16% between 24 and 26, 3% between 27 and 28, and 3% above 28. 39% of the current freshmen were in the top fifth of their class; 71% were in the top two fifths.

Requirements: The ACT is required. In addition, students must be graduates of an accredited secondary school and have earned 16 specific academic credits, including 4 years each of English and the natural and social sciences, 3 each of math and academic electives, and 2 years of a foreign language. The GED is accepted. Saint Xavier requires applicants to be in the upper 50% of their class. AP and CLEP credits are accepted. Applications are accepted on-line.

Procedure: Freshmen are admitted fall and spring. Entrance exams should be taken during the spring of the junior year. There is a deferred admissions plan. Applications should be filed by August 15 for fall entry and January 15 for spring entry. Tha fall 2001 application fee was $25. Notification is sent on a rolling basis.

Transfer: 461 transfer students enrolled in 2001-2002. Applicants must have completed 12 semester hours with a GPA of 2.25. An interview is recommended. 30 credits of 120 must be completed at Saint Xavier.

Visiting: There are regularly scheduled orientations for prospective students. There are guides for informal visits and visitors may sit in on classes and stay overnight. To schedule a visit, contact the Director of Admissions.

Financial Aid: In 2001-2002, 77% of all freshmen and 78% of continuing students received some form of financial aid. 64% of freshmen and 65% of continuing students received need-based aid. The average freshman award was $14,568. Of that total, scholarships or need-based grants averaged $8127 ($12,000 maximum); loans averaged $2466 ($16,689 maximum); and work contracts averaged $4246. 12% of undergraduates work part time. The average financial indebtedness of the 2001 graduate was $19,825. The FAFSA is required. The fall application deadline is March 1.

International Students: There are 17 international students enrolled. The school actively recruits these students. They must score 550 on the written TOEFL.

Computers: The mainframes are a DEC VAX 11/750 and an Alpha UNIX. Students are assigned e-mail accounts and have access to the Internet. All students may access the system. There are no time limits and no fees.

Graduates: In 2001, 490 bachelor's degrees were awarded. The most popular majors were nursing (25%), business (21%), and education (19%). In an average class, 30% graduate in 3 years, 74% in 4 years, 49% in 5 years, and 56% in 6 years. Of the 2000 graduating class, 23% were enrolled in graduate school within 6 months of graduation and 98% were employed.

Admissions Contact: Beth Gierach, Director of Enrollment Services. E-mail: *admissions@sxu.edu* Web: *www.sxu.edu.admission*

SCHOOL OF THE ART INSTITUTE OF CHICAGO E-2

Chicago, IL 60603 **(312) 899-5219**
(800) 232-7242; Fax: (312) 899-1840

Full-time: 637 men, 1028 women	**Faculty:** 122
Part-time: 41 men, 96 women	**Ph.D.s:** 87%
Graduate: 160 men, 366 women	**Student/Faculty:** 14 to 1
Year: semesters, summer session	**Tuition:** $21,300
Application Deadline: August 15	**Room & Board:** $6500
Freshman Class: 1183 applied, 933 accepted, 330 enrolled	
SAT I or ACT: required	**SPECIAL**

The School of the Art Institute of Chicago, founded in 1866, is a private institution that is affiliated with the museum of the Art Institute of Chicago. The school offers training in the fine arts and design. There is 1 graduate school. In addition to regional accreditation, SAIC has baccalaureate program accreditation with NASAD. The library contains 71,000 volumes, 157 microform items, and 4000 audiovisual forms/CDs, and subscribes to 350 periodicals. Computerized library services include the card catalog, interlibrary loans, and database searching. Special learning facilities include a learning resource center, an art gallery, a TV station, a film center, a video data bank, a fashion resource center, student galleries, a poetry center, a web-based radio station, the Roger Brown Study Collection, the Joan Flasch Artists Book Collection, the Gene Siskel Film Center, and the collection of the Art Institute of Chicago. The campus is in an urban area in downtown Chicago. Including residence halls, there are 5 buildings.

Student Life: 77% of undergraduates are from out of state, mostly the Midwest. Others are from 48 states, 42 foreign countries, and Canada. 67% are white; 12%, foreign nationals; 10%, Asian American. The average age of freshmen is 19; all undergraduates, 22. 21% do not continue beyond their first year.

Housing: 664 students can be accommodated in college housing, which includes coed dormitories. On-campus housing is available on a first-come, first-served basis and is available on a lottery system for upperclassmen. 65% of students commute. Alcohol is not permitted. All students may keep cars.

Activities: There are no fraternities or sororities. There are 24 groups on campus, including art, ethnic, film, gay, international, literary magazine, newspaper, performance, political, professional, radio and TV, religious, social, social service, and student government. Popular campus events include film center screenings, visiting artist lectures, and exhibitions/openings at galleries.

Sports: There is no sports program at SAIC.

Disabled Students: 98% of the campus is accessible. Wheelchair ramps, elevators, special parking, specially equipped rest rooms, special class scheduling, lowered drinking fountains, and lowered telephones are available. Assistance in other areas is available on an individual basis.

Services: Counseling and information services are available, as is tutoring in every subject. There is remedial reading and writing. Tutoring for students with learning disabilities is provided through the learning center.

Campus Safety and Security: Measures include 24-hour foot and vehicle patrol, self-defense education, shuttle buses, and informal discussions. There are pamphlets/posters/films, emergency telephones, and lighted pathways/sidewalks.

Programs of Study: SAIC confers B.A., B.F.A., and B.Int.Arch. degrees. Master's degrees are also awarded. Bachelor's degrees are awarded in COMMUNICATIONS AND THE ARTS (art history and appreciation, audio technology, ceramic art and design, design, drawing, fiber/textiles/weaving, film arts, painting, photography, printmaking, sculpture, video, and visual and performing arts), COMPUTER AND PHYSICAL SCIENCE (digital arts/technology), EDUCATION (art), ENGINEERING AND ENVIRONMENTAL DESIGN (drafting and design technology and interior design), SOCIAL SCIENCE (fashion design and technology).

Required: All students are required to take 72 credit hours of studio courses, 30 hours of liberal arts, 18 hours of art history, and 12 hours of electives. A total of 132 credit hours must be completed to graduate. All students are required to take English literature and composition, and natural science, social science, and humanities courses, as well as 2-, 3-, and 4-dimensional studio.

Special: The school offers internships, pass/fail options, visual arts co-op programs, cross-registration with Roosevelt University, and many co-operative work-study opportunities. Dual and student-designed majors, a B.A.-B.S. degree, and study abroad in 20 countries with active exchange programs are possible.

Faculty/Classroom: 60% of faculty are male; 40%, female.

Admissions: 79% of the 2001-2002 applicants were accepted.

Requirements: The SAT I or ACT is required, with a minimum score of 500 on the verbal section of the SAT I or a minimum English score of 20 on the ACT. Applicants must be graduates of an accredited secondary school. The GED is accepted. All students must submit a portfolio and an essay. An interview is recommended. AP and CLEP credits are accepted. Important factors in the admissions decision are evidence of special talent, recommendations by school officials, and personality/intangible qualities.

Procedure: Freshmen are admitted fall and spring. There is a deferred admissions plan. For priority consideration, applications should be filed by March 1 for fall or November 15 for spring. Otherwise, applications should be filed by August 15 for fall or January 15 for spring, along with a $55 fee. Notification is sent on a rolling basis.

Transfer: 269 transfer students enrolled in 2001-2002. Transfer students must take the SAT I or ACT. A minimum score of 500 is required on the verbal section of the SAT I and a minimum English score of 20 is required on the ACT. Students must submit a portfolio. 36 credits of 132 must be completed at SAIC.

Visiting: There are guides for informal visits. To schedule a visit, contact the Office of Admissions.

Financial Aid: In 2001-2002, 70% of all freshmen and 74% of continuing students received some form of financial aid. 55% of freshmen and 58% of continuing students received need-based aid. The average freshman award was $16,590. Of that total, scholarships or need-based grants averaged $9329 ($16,850 maximum); loans averaged $3615 ($5625 maximum); work contracts averaged $2925 ($5336 maximum); and other sources averaged $3161 ($14,000 maximum). 31% of undergraduates work part time. Average annual earnings from campus work are $3420. The average financial indebtedness of the 2001 graduate was $10,311. The FAFSA and the college's own financial statement are required. The fall application deadline is April 1.

International Students: There are 216 international students enrolled. The school actively recruits these students. They must score 527 on the written TOEFL or 197 on the electronic version and also take the SAT I or the ACT.

Computers: Students have access to 40 G3 Macs and 29 Power PC Macs in the computer lab. Additionally, there are 75 G3 Macs and 15 Power PC Macs in computer classrooms; 60 G3 Macs, 25 Power PC Macs, 2 IBM/NT workstations, and 15 SGI workstations in departmental labs; 6 IBM workstations in the library; and 8 Power PC Macs in the residence halls. Most are connected to the Web via Ethernet. All students may access the system. There are no time limits and no fees.

Graduates: In 2001, 302 bachelor's degrees were awarded.

Admissions Contact: Pat Lally, Associate Director of Admissions. A video is available. E-mail: *admiss@artic.edu*
Web: *http://www.artic.edu.saic*

SHIMER COLLEGE

Waukegan, IL 60079 C-1
(847) 623-8400
(800) 215-7173; Fax: (847) 249-7171

Full-time: 50 men, 50 women	**Faculty:** 15
Part-time: 5 men, 3 women	**Ph.D.s:** 88%
Graduate: none	**Student/Faculty:** 7 to 1
Year: semesters	**Tuition:** $15,260
Application Deadline: March 1	**Room & Board:** $2300
Freshman Class: n/av	
SAT I or ACT: recommended	**LESS COMPETITIVE**

Shimer College, founded in 1853, is a private liberal arts institution with a curriculum based on original sources and a Socratic teaching method employing discussion classes of 12 or fewer students. The library contains 200,000 volumes. Computerized library services include the card catalog, interlibrary loans, and database searching. The 3-acre campus is in a suburban area 25 miles north of Chicago. Including residence halls, there are 10 buildings.

Student Life: 69% of undergraduates are from out of state, mostly the Northeast. Others are from 19 states and 3 foreign countries. 75% are from public schools. 80% are white. The average age of freshmen is 19; all undergraduates, 24. 20% do not continue beyond their first year.

Housing: 65 students can be accommodated in college housing, which includes coed dormitories, on-campus apartments, and off-campus apartments. On-campus housing is guaranteed for the freshman year only and is available on a first-come, first-served basis. Priority is given to out-of-town students. 50% of students live on campus; of those, 95% remain on campus on weekends. All students may keep cars.

Activities: There are no fraternities or sororities. There are some groups and organizations on campus, including art, chess, computers, drama, literary magazine, newspaper, photography, and student government. Popular campus events include community lunch and poetry reading.

Sports: There is no sports program at Shimer. Facilities include a gym and a pool.

Disabled Students: 20% of the campus is accessible. Wheelchair ramps are available.

Services: Counseling and information services are available, as is tutoring in every subject.

Campus Safety and Security: Measures include escort service and informal discussions.

Programs of Study: Shimer confers B.A. and B.S. degrees. Bachelor's degrees are awarded in COMPUTER AND PHYSICAL SCIENCE (natural sciences), SOCIAL SCIENCE (humanities and social science). Humanities and social science are the strongest academically. Humanities is the largest.

Required: To graduate, students must earn 125 credit hours with a GPA of 2.0, complete 2 comprehensive exams, and submit a thesis. The school requires 60 credit hours in the major for the B.S. degree, 40 for the B.A.; 65 in the core curriculum for the B.S., 85 for the B.A.

Special: Shimer offers internships in all areas of study, study abroad at Oxford in England, and Partnerships in Service Learning in 5 other countries. There is an accelerated degree program, a B.A.-B.S. degree, dual majors in all areas, student-designed majors, and a general studies degree. Nondegree study and pass/fail options are possible.

Faculty/Classroom: 67% of faculty are male; 33%, female. All teach undergraduates. The average class size in a regular course is 7.

Requirements: The SAT I or ACT is recommended. Requirements are highly individualized. Essays and an interview are required. Important factors in the admissions decision are personality/intangible qualities, recommendations by school officials, and leadership record. Applications are accepted on computer disk.

Procedure: Freshmen are admitted fall and spring. There are early decision, early admissions, and deferred admissions plans. Early decision applications should be filed by December 1; regular applications, by March 1 for fall entry and January 1 for spring entry, along with a $10 fee. Notification of early decision is sent December 15; regular decision, on a rolling basis. A waiting list is an active part of the admissions procedure.

Transfer: 11 transfer students enrolled in 2001-2002. Applicants are required to have an interview. 60 credits of 125 must be completed at Shimer.

Visiting: There are regularly scheduled orientations for prospective students, consisting of class visits, lunch, and a financial aid interview. There are guides for informal visits and visitors may sit in on classes and stay overnight. To schedule a visit, contact Bill Paterson.

Financial Aid: In a recent year, 98% of all freshmen and 95% of continuing students received some form of financial aid including need-based aid. The average freshman award was $11,348. Of that total, scholarships or need-based grants averaged $5839 ($20,150 maximum); loans averaged $6134 ($15,400 maximum); and work contracts averaged $674 ($2000 maximum). 70% of undergraduates work part time. Average annual earnings from campus work are $1800. The average financial indebtedness of a recent year's graduate was $15,000. Shimer is a member of CSS. The CSS/Profile is required. The fall application deadline is July 30.

International Students: The school actively recruits these students. They must score 500 on the written TOEFL.

Computers: There are PCs available with Web and Internet access in the computer lab. All students may access the system 24 hours a day. There are no time limits and no fees.

Graduates: In 2001, 14 bachelor's degrees were awarded. The most popular majors were humanities (55%), social sciences (35%), and natural sciences (10%). In an average class, 7% graduate in 3 years, 50% in 4 years, 53% in 5 years, and 58% in 6 years. Of the 2000 graduating class, 20% were enrolled in graduate school within 6 months of graduation and 70% were employed.

Admissions Contact: Bill Paterson, Director of Admissions.
E-mail: *admissions@shimer.edu* Web: *www.shimer.edu*

SOUTHERN ILLINOIS UNIVERSITY SYSTEM

The Southern Illinois University System, established in 1965, is 1 of 2 public senior university systems in Illinois. It has 2 established campuses, Southern Illinois University Carbondale with a School of Medicine in Springfield and a campus in Niigata, Japan, and Southern Illinois University Edwardsville with a school of Dental Medicine in Alton and a center in East St. Louis. The university offers degree programs from the associate through the doctorate, and professional degrees in law, medicine, and dentistry. The SIU Board of Trustees is the legal entity with overall responsibility for the organization and governance of the university and its constituent institutions. The chief executive officer is the president. Dedicated to the traditional academic pursuits of instruction, scholarship, and public service, the university assigns priority to achieving excellence in undergraduate and graduate education, encourages and supports scholarly research and creative achievement, and strives to achieve and maintain cultural diversity. The recent total enrollment of both campuses was 34,745; there were 1,713 full-time instructional faculty members. Altogether there are 4 associate, 127 baccalaureate, 100 master's, and 32 doctoral programs offered at Southern Illinois University.

SOUTHERN ILLINOIS UNIVERSITY AT CARBONDALE D-5

Carbondale, IL 62901 (618) 536-4405; Fax: (618) 453-3250

Full-time: 8478 men, 6566 women	**Faculty:** 912; I, --$
Part-time: 1012 men, 746 women	**Ph.D.s:** 70%
Graduate: 2285 men, 2511 women	**Student/Faculty:** 16 to 1
Year: semesters, summer session	**Tuition:** $4254 ($7356)
Application Deadline: open	**Room & Board:** $4367

Freshman Class: 8112 applied, 5594 accepted, 2163 enrolled

ACT: 22 **COMPETITIVE**

Southern Illinois University at Carbondale, founded in 1869, is a public institution that is part of the Southern Illinois University System. The multicampus university offers undergraduate programs in the Colleges of Applied Sciences and Arts, Agriculture, Business and Administration, Education and Human Services, Engineering, Liberal Arts, Mass Communication and Media Arts, and Science. There are 8 undergraduate and 3 graduate schools. In addition to regional accreditation, SIUC has baccalaureate program accreditation with AACSB, ABET, ABFSE, ACEJMC, ADA, APTA, CAHEA, CSWE, FIDER, NASAD, NASM, NCATE, NRPA, and SAF. The 2 libraries contain 2,429,332 volumes, 4,242,929 microform items, and 317,180 audiovisual forms/CDs, and subscribe to 20,588 periodicals. Computerized library services include the card catalog, interlibrary loans, and database searching. Special learning facilities include a learning resource center, art gallery, natural history museum, radio station, TV station, student-run newspaper, farms and timberlands, greenhouses, livestock facilities, archeological center, aviation program, crime study center, wildlife lab, and international programs and services. The 1133-acre campus is in a small town 96 miles southeast of St. Louis. Including residence halls, there are 256 buildings.

Student Life: 83% of undergraduates are from Illinois. Others are from 49 states, 119 foreign countries, and Canada. 68% are white; 13%, African American. The average age of freshmen is 19; all undergraduates, 24. 28% do not continue beyond their first year; 72% remain to graduate.

Housing: 5349 students can be accommodated in college housing, which includes single-sex and coed dormitories, on-campus apartments, married-student housing, fraternity houses, and sorority houses. In addition, there are honors houses, special-interest houses, family houses, rooms for students with disabilities, over-21 residence halls, and residence halls that stay open during breaks. On-campus housing is guaranteed for the freshman year only and is available on a first-come, first-served basis. 72% of students commute. All students may keep cars.

Activities: 5% of men belong to 13 national fraternities; 4% of women belong to 3 local and 6 national sororities. There are 360 groups on campus, including art, band, cheerleading, chess, choir, chorale, chorus, computers, dance, debate, drama, drill team, drum and bugle corps, ethnic, film, forensics, gay, honors, international, jazz band, literary magazine, marching band, musical theater, newspaper, opera, orchestra, pep band, photography, political, professional, radio and TV, religious, social, social service, student government, symphony, and yearbook. Popular campus events include Cardboard Boat Regatta, International Festival, and Hispanic Month.

Sports: Facilities include a 17,324-seat stadium, a 10,014-seat arena, a women's softball field, a baseball field, a 700-seat gym, boat docks, tennis courts, and a cross-country course. The student recreation center houses an Olympic-size pool, indoor tracks, racquetball, squash, and tennis courts, aerobics equipment, a weight room, and numerous exercise stations. The student recreation center also offers volleyball, basketball, badminton, handball, indoor soccer, a climbing wall, a dance studio, a boxing practice room, and a martial arts practice room.

Disabled Students: 99% of the campus is accessible. Wheelchair ramps, elevators, special parking, specially equipped rest rooms, special class scheduling, lowered drinking fountains, and lowered telephones are available. The university provides classroom and residence hall accommodations and support services for students with physical disabilities.

Services: Counseling and information services are available, as is tutoring in every subject. There is a reader service for the blind and remedial math. Also available are new student orientation, a mentoring program, a writing skills lab, premajor advisement, student development programs, and career counseling. Students often are required to pay for tutorial assistance.

Campus Safety and Security: Measures include 24-hour foot and vehicle patrol, self-defense education, shuttle buses, and informal discussions. There are pamphlets/posters/films, emergency telephones, and lighted pathways/sidewalks. Campus security is operated by law enforcement officers, supplemented with a student patrol program.

Programs of Study: SIUC confers B.A., B.S., B.F.A., and B.Mus. degrees. Associate, master's, and doctoral degrees are also awarded. Bachelor's degrees are awarded in AGRICULTURE (agricultural economics, animal science, forestry and related sciences, and plant science), BIOLOGICAL SCIENCE (avian sciences, biology/biological science, botany, microbiology, physiology, and zoology), BUSINESS (accounting, banking and finance, business administration and management, business economics, business systems analysis, funeral home services, and marketing/retailing/merchandising), COMMUNICATIONS AND THE ARTS (art, broadcasting, classics, design, dramatic arts, English literature, film arts, fine arts, French, German, journalism, linguistics, music, photography, Russian, Spanish, and speech/debate/rhetoric), COMPUTER AND PHYSICAL SCIENCE (chemistry, geology, mathematics, physics, and radiological technology), EDUCATION (business, early childhood, elementary, health, physical, special, and vocational), ENGINEERING AND ENVIRONMENTAL DESIGN (architecture, aviation administration/management, civil engineering, computer engineering, electrical/electronics engineering, engineering management, engineering technology, industrial engineering technology, interior design, mechanical engineering, mining and mineral engineering, and technological management), HEALTH PROFESSIONS (dental hygiene, health care administration, physician's assistant, rehabilitation therapy, and speech pathology/audiology), SOCIAL SCIENCE (anthropology, clothing and textiles management/production/services, criminal justice, dietetics, economics, family/consumer resource management, fire protection, food science, geography, history, international relations, liberal arts/general studies, paralegal studies, parks and recreation management, philosophy, political science/government, psychology, social science, social work, and sociology). Workforce education and development, industrial technology, and radio-television are the strongest academically and have the largest enrollments.

Required: To graduate, all students must meet the university and program requirements, maintain a minimum 2.0 GPA, and complete a minimum of 120 semester hours. The total number of hours in the major varies, and students must complete a university core curriculum.

Special: The university offers internships through the Washington center and study abroad in 40 countries, including Australia, the British Isles, China, the West Bank, and others in Europe, Africa, and Latin America. Also available are a Washington semester, work-study programs, accelerated degree programs, dual majors, and B.A.-B.S. degrees in numerous programs. The College of Applied Sciences and Arts offers technically oriented programs, co-op programs, and work-study. Nondegree study is available through the Community Listeners Permit and Elderhostel. There are 29 national honor societies and a freshman honors program. All departments have honors programs.

Faculty/Classroom: 63% of faculty are male; 37%, female. 80% teach undergraduates, 15% do research, and 50% do both. Graduate students teach 30% of introductory courses. The average class size in an introductory lecture is 195; in a laboratory, 16; and in a regular course, 23.

Admissions: 69% of the 2001-2002 applicants were accepted. The ACT scores for the 2001-2002 freshman class were 27% below 21, 35% between 21 and 23, 22% between 24 and 26, 9% between 27 and 28, and 7% above 28. 20% of the current freshmen were in the top fifth of their class; 43% were in the top two fifths.

Requirements: The ACT is required. In addition, applicants must be graduates of an accredited secondary high school or have a GED certificate, with 4 years of English, 3 years each of math, lab science, and social science, and 2 years of electives, which may include art, music, foreign language, or vocational education. For general admission, a minimum composite score of 20 on the ACT or 18 on the ACT and rank in the top half of the graduating class is required. Some programs require additional materials and/or screening, and higher ACT scores and higher class rank. Applications are accepted on-line at the university's web site. AP and CLEP credits are accepted.

Procedure: Freshmen are admitted to all sessions. Entrance exams should be taken during the spring of the junior year. There is a deferred admissions plan. Application deadlines are open. The application fee is $30. There is a rolling admissions plan.

Transfer: 2670 transfer students enrolled in 2001-2002. All transfer students must have a minimum 2.0 GPA. Students are required to meet freshmen admission requirements if they are under 21 years old and have fewer than 26 credit hours of acceptable transfer work. Some academic programs have higher admission requirements. 30 credits of 120 must be completed at SIUC.

Visiting: There are regularly scheduled orientations for prospective students, including admission counseling, academic program exhibits, student organization exhibits, workshops on financial aid and housing, and tours of the campus and residence halls. There are guides for informal visits and visitors may sit in on classes. To schedule a visit, contact New Student Admission Services.

Financial Aid: In 2001-2002, 78% of all freshmen and 77% of continuing students received some form of financial aid. 55% of all students received need-based aid. The average freshman award was $5987. Of that total, scholarships or need-based grants averaged $2963; loans averaged $2455; and work contracts averaged $569. 51% of undergraduates work part time. Average annual earnings from campus work are $1631. The average financial indebtedness of the 2001 graduate was $12,413. The FAFSA is required. The fall application deadline is April 1.

International Students: There are 540 international students enrolled. The school actively recruits these students. They must score 520 on the written TOEFL or 190 on the electronic version and also take the SAT I, the ACT, or their own country's standardized college entrance exam.

Computers: The mainframe is an IBM 9021-500. Students may use more than 340 PCs that are networked at 4 computing learning centers. Other departments on campus also have labs connected to the mainframe. All students may access the system all the time, all year. There are no time limits and no fees.

Graduates: In 2001, 4609 bachelor's degrees were awarded. The most popular majors were workforce education and development (16%), industrial technology (6%), and health care management (4%). In an average class, 17% graduate in 4 years, 33% in 5 years, and 39% in 6 years. 264 companies recruited on campus in 2000-2001.

Admissions Contact: Walker Allen, Director of Admissions. A video is available. E-mail: *admrec@siu.edu* Web: *www.siuc.edu*

SOUTHERN ILLINOIS UNIVERSITY EDWARDSVILLE C-4

Edwardsville, IL 62026-1600 (618) 650-3705
(800) 447-SIUE; Fax: (618) 650-5013

Full-time: 3427 men, 4605 women	**Faculty:** 483; IIA, -$
Part-time: 759 men, 1008 women	**Ph.D.s:** 84%
Graduate: 1064 men, 1579 women	**Student/Faculty:** 17 to 1
Year: semesters, summer session	**Tuition:** $3291 ($5865)
Application Deadline: May 31	**Room & Board:** $4578

Freshman Class: 4047 applied, 3510 accepted, 1611 enrolled
ACT: required **LESS COMPETITIVE**

Southern Illinois University Edwardsville, founded in 1957, is part of the Southern Illinois University system and offers undergraduate programs in business, education, engineering, arts and sciences, and nursing. Graduate programs also are offered in 34 subject areas. There are 5 undergraduate schools and 1 graduate school. In addition to regional accreditation, SIUE has baccalaureate program accreditation with AACSB, ABET, ADA, CSWE, NASM, NCATE, and NLN. The library contains 775,270 volumes, 1,607,703 microform items, and 28,906 audiovisual forms/CDs, and subscribes to 14,271 periodicals. Computerized library services include the card catalog, interlibrary loans, and database searching. Special learning facilities include a learning resource center, art gallery, radio station, recording studio, engineering labs, anthropology museum, greenhouse, and arboretum. The 2660-acre campus is in a suburban area 18 miles northeast of downtown St. Louis, Missouri. Including residence halls, there are 25 buildings.

Student Life: 86% of undergraduates are from Illinois. Others are from 41 states, 65 foreign countries, and Canada. 82% are white; 11% African American. The average age of all undergraduates is 23. 28% do not continue beyond their first year.

Housing: 3000 students can be accommodated in college housing, which includes coed dormitories, on-campus apartments, married-student housing, fraternity houses, honors, and special-interest wings. On-campus housing is available on a first-come, first-served basis. Priority is given to out-of-town students. 72% of students commute. All students may keep cars.

Activities: 5% of men belong to 10 national fraternities; 4% of women belong to 7 national sororities. There are 140 groups on campus, including academic, art, band, cheerleading, choir, chorale, chorus, dance, drama, ethnic, gay, honors, international, jazz band, literary magazine, musical theater, opera, orchestra, pep band, photography, political, professional, radio and TV, recreational, religious, social, social service, student government, symphony, and yearbook. Popular campus events include Welcome Week, Arts and Issues Series, and International Week.

Sports: There are 7 intercollegiate sports for men and 8 for women, and 11 intramural sports for men and 11 for women. Facilities include the Vadalabene Center and Student Fitness Center, which offer racquetball, basketball, aquatics, volleyball, indoor track, exercise, and weight training; the University Center, which features restaurants, a recreation center, billiards, and a bowling alley; an outdoor swimming pool; a lake for canoeing and sailing; an outdoor track and field and soccer stadium; baseball, softball and soccer fields; extensive walking and biking trails; and a Frisbee course.

Disabled Students: All of the campus is accessible. Wheelchair ramps, elevators, special parking, specially equipped rest rooms, special class scheduling, lowered drinking fountains, lowered telephones, a Visualtek large-screen TV, Kurzweil readers, test-taking facilities, accessible weight-training equipment, and a swimming pool are available.

Services: Counseling and information services are available, as is tutoring in most subjects. There is remedial math, reading, and writing.

Campus Safety and Security: Measures include 24-hour foot and vehicle patrol, self-defense education, escort service, and shuttle buses. There are informal discussions, pamphlets/posters/films, emergency telephones, lighted pathways/sidewalks, and emergency blue lights located throughout campus.

Programs of Study: SIUE confers B.A., B.S., B.F.A., B.L.S., B.M., and B.S.A. degrees. Master's degrees are also awarded. Bachelor's degrees are awarded in BIOLOGICAL SCIENCE (biology/biological science), BUSINESS (accounting, business administration and management, business economics, and management information systems), COMMUNICATIONS AND THE ARTS (art, communications, dance, design, dramatic arts, English, languages, music, and speech/debate/rhetoric), COMPUTER AND PHYSICAL SCIENCE (chemistry, computer science, mathematics, and physics), EDUCATION (early childhood, elementary, health, science, and special), ENGINEERING AND ENVIRONMENTAL DESIGN (civil engineering, computer engineering, construction engineering, electrical/electronics engineering, industrial engineering, manufacturing engineering, and mechanical engineering), HEALTH PROFESSIONS (exercise science, nursing, and speech pathology/audiology), SOCIAL SCIENCE (anthropology, criminal justice, economics, geography, history, liberal arts/general studies, philosophy, political science/government, psychology, social work, and sociology). Business administration, management information systems, and nursing are the largest.

Required: To graduate, students must complete a total of 124 semester hours with a minimum GPA of 2.0. Students must fulfill general education requirements, including 9 hours of math/science, and complete a senior project.

Special: SIUE offers cross-registration with the University of Missouri at St. Louis, co-op programs, internships, which are required by several majors, including mass communications and sociology, work-study programs, dual majors, student-designed majors (available to specific honors students only), study abroad in 5 countries by formal exchange agreements (England, France, Germany, the Netherlands, and Mexico), and in a wide variety of others, a liberal studies degree, and a 5-year (3+2) program in dental medicine and engineering. There are 12 national honor societies, a freshman honors program, and 15 departmental honors programs.

Faculty/Classroom: 58% of faculty are male; 42%, female. Graduate students teach 2% of introductory courses.

Admissions: 87% of the 2001-2002 applicants were accepted. The ACT scores for the 2001-2002 freshman class were: 42% below 21, 26% between 21 and 23, 19% between 24 and 26, 7% between 27 and 28, and 5% above 28. 31% of the current freshmen were in the top fifth of their class; 62% were in the top two fifths.

Requirements: The ACT is required. In addition, applicants must be graduates of an accredited secondary school or have a GED certificate. They must have completed 15 academic credits, based on 4 years of English, 3 each of math and lab science, 2 years of any combination of art, foreign language, music, and vocational education, at least 2 years of government and/or history, plus 1 more year of social studies. AP and CLEP credits are accepted. Applications are accepted on-line at *www.siue.edu*

Procedure: Freshmen are admitted to all sessions. Entrance exams should be taken before high school graduation. Applications should be filed by May 31 for fall entry, December 18 for spring entry, and April 28 for summer entry. Notification is sent on a rolling basis.

Transfer: 1265 transfer students enrolled in 2001-2002. Applicants must have a minimum 2.0 GPA in at least 16 semester hours earned. 30 credits of 124 must be completed at SIUE.

Visiting: There are regularly scheduled orientations for prospective students. There are guides for informal visits and visitors may sit in on classes. To schedule a visit, contact the Admission Counseling Office.

Financial Aid: In a recent year, 64% of all freshmen and 52% of continuing students received some form of financial aid. 55% of freshmen and 44% of continuing students received need-based aid. The average freshman award was $5304. Of that total, scholarships or need-based grants averaged $3994 ($8563 maximum); loans averaged $2654 ($7132 maximum); work contracts averaged $2136 ($2400 maximum); and student work and PLUS loans averaged $9948 ($14,584 maximum). 19% of undergraduates work part time. Average annual earnings from campus work are $1758. The average financial indebtedness of the 2001 graduate was $7472. The FAFSA is required. The fall application deadline is March 1.

International Students: There are 146 international students enrolled. The school actively recruits these students. They must score 550 on the written TOEFL or 213 on the electronic version.

Computers: The mainframe is an IBM 9121/511. There are also 600 PC and Mac workstations located in classrooms and computer labs, including labs at the residence hall and apartment complex. Residence hall rooms and apartments are wired for direct access to the campus network. All students have e-mail accounts and personal web directories.

Adaptive equipment is available for students with disabilities. All students may access the system daily at designated hours with some labs open 24 hours. There are no time limits and no fees.

Graduates: In 2001, 1756 bachelor's degrees were awarded. The most popular majors were business administration (13%), elementary education (11%), and nursing (8%). In an average class, 14% graduate in 4 years, 34% in 5 years, and 41% in 6 years. 494 companies recruited on campus in 2000-2001.

Admissions Contact: Admission Counseling. A video is available. E-mail: *admis@siue.edu* Web: *siue.edu*

TRINITY CHRISTIAN COLLEGE

E-2

Palos Heights, IL 60463

(708) 597-3000
(800) 748-0085; Fax: (708) 385-5665

Full-time: 298 men, 477 women	**Faculty:** 49; IIB, av$
Part-time: 9 men, 10 women	**Ph.D.s:** 62%
Graduate: none	**Student/Faculty:** 16 to 1
Year: semesters	**Tuition:** $13,970
Application Deadline: August 15	**Room & Board:** $5445
Freshman Class: 677 applied, 643 accepted, 313 enrolled	
SAT I Verbal/Math: 518/515	**ACT:** 23 **COMPETITIVE**

Trinity Christian College, founded in 1959, is a private college offering programs in art, business, health science, liberal arts, music, religion, and teacher preparation. In addition to regional accreditation, Trinity has baccalaureate program accreditation with ACBSP and NLN. The library contains 71,816 volumes, 40,450 microform items, and 900 audiovisual forms/CDs, and subscribes to 450 periodicals. Computerized library services include the card catalog, interlibrary loans, and database searching. Special learning facilities include a learning resource center, art gallery, and a Dutch heritage collection. The 53-acre campus is in a suburban area 20 miles southwest of the Chicago Loop. Including residence halls, there are 14 buildings.

Student Life: 53% of undergraduates are from Illinois. Others are from 32 states, 6 foreign countries, and Canada. 37% are from public schools. 88% are white. Most are Protestant. The average age of freshmen is 19; all undergraduates, 31. 27% do not continue beyond their first year.

Housing: 530 students can be accommodated in college housing, which includes coed dormitories, on-campus apartments, and off-campus apartments. On-campus housing is guaranteed for all 4 years. 67% of students live on campus; of those, 45% remain on campus on weekends. Alcohol is not permitted. All students may keep cars.

Activities: There are no fraternities or sororities. There are 21 groups on campus, including art, band, cheerleading, choir, chorale, chorus, drama, ethnic, honors, jazz band, literary magazine, newspaper, pep band, photography, political, professional, religious, social, social service, student government, and yearbook. Popular campus events include the Opus fine arts festival and the Trollstock Concert.

Sports: There are 5 intercollegiate sports for men and 5 for women, and 7 intramural sports for men and 7 for women. Facilities include a gym, a track, a stadium, a baseball diamond, and softball and soccer fields.

Disabled Students: 95% of the campus is accessible. Wheelchair ramps, elevators, special parking, specially equipped rest rooms, and lowered drinking fountains are available.

Services: Counseling and information services are available, as is tutoring in every subject.

Campus Safety and Security: Measures include 24-hour foot and vehicle patrol, self-defense education, escort service, and informal discussions. There are emergency telephones and lighted pathways/sidewalks.

Programs of Study: Trinity confers B.A., B.S., and B.S.N. degrees. Bachelor's degrees are awarded in BIOLOGICAL SCIENCE (biology/biological science), BUSINESS (accounting and business administration and management), COMMUNICATIONS AND THE ARTS (applied music, art, communications, English, music, music performance, Spanish, and studio art), COMPUTER AND PHYSICAL SCIENCE (chemistry, computer science, information sciences and systems, and mathematics), EDUCATION (art, education, elementary, music, and special), HEALTH PROFESSIONS (nursing, predentistry, premedicine, and preoptometry), SOCIAL SCIENCE (biblical studies, history, philosophy, prelaw, psychology, social work, sociology, and theological studies). Business, education, and nursing are the strongest academically and are the largest.

Required: All students must take 9 credits in English and 6 each in philosophy, history, and theology, as well as distribution requirements in cross-cultural studies, natural sciences, social sciences, fine arts, math, and phys ed. Students must complete 125 credit hours and maintain a minimum GPA of 2.0 to graduate.

Special: Students may have various part-time or full-time internships in their major field. There are study-abroad programs in the Netherlands and Spain. Pass/fail options exist. Dual majors are offered. There is 1 national honor society and a freshman honors program.

Faculty/Classroom: 58% of faculty are male; 42%, female. All both teach and do research. The average class size in an introductory lecture is 24; in a laboratory, 17; and in a regular course, 16.

Admissions: 95% of the 2001-2002 applicants were accepted. The ACT scores for the 2001-2002 freshman class were: 32% below 21, 26% between 21 and 23, 20% between 24 and 26, 11% between 27 and 28, and 11% above 28. 25% of the current freshmen were in the top fifth of their class; 31% were in the top two fifths. 4 freshmen graduated first in their class.

Requirements: The ACT is recommended. In addition, applicants should graduate from an accredited high school or have a GED. They should prepare with 3 or 4 years of high school English, 3 years of math, science, and social studies, or 2 years each of a combination of two subject areas chosen among foreign language, math, science, or social studies. An interview is required. Trinity requires applicants to be in the upper 60% of their class. A GPA of 2.3 is required. AP and CLEP credits are accepted. Important factors in the admissions decision are advanced placement or honor courses, leadership record, and recommendations by school officials.

Procedure: Freshmen are admitted fall and spring. Entrance exams should be taken during the last semester of the junior year. Applications should be filed by August 15 for fall entry and January 15 for spring entry. The fall 2001 application fee was $20. Notification is sent on a rolling basis.

Transfer: 73 transfer students enrolled in 2001-2002. Applicants must have 24 hours of acceptable credits and a minimum 2.3 GPA. Associate degrees are recognized for transfer. 30 credits of 120 must be completed at Trinity.

Visiting: There are regularly scheduled orientations for prospective students, including a tour, an interview, a seminar, and class visits. There are guides for informal visits and visitors may sit in on classes and stay overnight. To schedule a visit, contact the Admissions Office.

Financial Aid: In 2001-2002, 96% of all freshmen and 91% of continuing students received some form of financial aid. 71% of freshmen and 63% of continuing students received need-based aid. The average freshman award was $8284. Of that total, scholarships or need-based grants averaged $5706 ($17,740 maximum); loans averaged $2378 ($4525 maximum); and work contracts averaged $651 ($1400 maximum). 50% of undergraduates work part time. Average annual earnings from campus work are $1300. The FAFSA is required. The fall application deadline is February 15.

International Students: There are 17 international students enrolled. They must score 500 on the written TOEFL and also take the SAT I or the ACT, scoring 20 on the ACT.

Computers: There is a PC lab for student use. All students may access the system. There are no time limits and no fees. It is strongly recommended that all students have a personal computer.

Graduates: In 2001, 144 bachelor's degrees were awarded. The most popular majors were education (31%), business (21%), and organizational management (14%). In an average class, 52% graduate in 4 years, 61% in 5 years, and 62% in 6 years. 10 companies recruited on campus in 2000-2001. Of the 2000 graduating class, 4% were enrolled in graduate school within 6 months of graduation and 95% were employed.

Admissions Contact: Peter Hamstra, Vice President for Admissions and Advancement. E-mail: *admissions@trnty.edu* Web: *www.trnty.edu*

TRINITY COLLEGE OF NURSING

C-2

Moline, IL 61265-1216

(309) 779-7812; Fax: (309) 779-7748

Full-time: 2 men, 48 women	**Faculty:** 10
Part-time: 50 women	**Ph.D.s:** 20%
Graduate: none	**Student/Faculty:** 5 to 1
Year: semesters, summer session	**Tuition:** $4300
Application Deadline: open	**Room & Board:** n/app
Freshman Class: n/av	
SAT I or ACT: required	**SPECIAL**

Trinity College of Nursing, founded in 1994, is a private institution offering degrees in nursing. The library contains 4200 volumes and subscribes to 64 periodicals. Computerized library services include the card catalog, interlibrary loans, and database searching. Special learning facilities include a nursing learning lab. The campus is in an urban part of the Illinois/Iowa Quad-Cities on the Mississippi River. There is 1 building.

Student Life: 82% of undergraduates are from Illinois. Others are from 3 states. 95% are white. The average age of freshmen is 25. 14% do not continue beyond their first year; 86% remain to graduate.

Housing: There are no residence halls. All students commute. Alcohol is not permitted.

Activities: There are no fraternities or sororities. There are 5 groups on campus, including honors, social, student government, and Student Nurse Association. Popular campus events include visiting artists' cultural presentations.

Sports: There is no sports program at the college.

Disabled Students: 95% of the campus is accessible. Wheelchair ramps, elevators, special parking, specially equipped rest rooms, and special class scheduling are available.

Services: Counseling and information services are available, as is tutoring in every subject. There is remedial math, reading, and writing.

Campus Safety and Security: Measures include informal discussions, pamphlets/posters/films, emergency telephones, and lighted pathways/sidewalks. There is a safety and security overview during orientation, and a foot and vehicle patrol.

Programs of Study: Trinity confers the B.S.N. degree. Associate degrees are also awarded. Bachelor's degrees are awarded in HEALTH PROFESSIONS (nursing).

Required: Students must complete a minimum of 120 semester hours, including general education courses, and maintain a 2.0 GPA.

Special: There is 1 national honor society and 1 departmental honors program.

Faculty/Classroom: All faculty are female. All teach undergraduates. The average class size in an introductory lecture is 40 and in a laboratory, 25.

Requirements: The SAT I or ACT is required. In addition, applicants should be high school graduates or have the GED. They should have an ACT composite score of 20 or above or an SAT I score of 800 or above. Official transcripts from all high school and postsecondary institutions are required, as is fluency in the English language. Applicants should have the physical ability to provide safe and effective client care and should have CPR certification for health care professionals. A GPA of 2.5 is required. AP and CLEP credits are accepted.

Procedure: Freshmen are admitted in the fall. Entrance exams should be taken in the senior year. There is a deferred admissions plan. Application deadlines are open. The application fee is $50. Notification is sent on a rolling basis. A waiting list is an active part of the admissions procedure.

Transfer: Applicants should have official transcripts, fluency in the English language, confirmed physical/mental ability to provide safe and effective client care, and CPR certification. They should also complete the nursing transition course with a grade of C or higher. 20 credits of 120 must be completed at the college.

Visiting: There are regularly scheduled orientations for prospective students, consisting of a 2-day orientation 2 weeks prior to the start of the fall term. There are guides for informal visits and visitors may sit in on classes and stay overnight. To schedule a visit, contact Barb Kimpe, Admissions Representative, at (309) 779-7700.

Financial Aid: In 2001-2002, 75% of all freshmen and 80% of continuing students received some form of financial aid. 70% of freshmen and 80% of continuing students received need-based aid. The average freshman award was $6375. 55% of undergraduates work part time. The average financial indebtedness of the 2001 graduate was $19,125. The FAFSA is required. The fall application deadline is June 1.

International Students: They must score 600 on the written TOEFL.

Computers: There is a computer lab for student use. All students may access the system. There are no time limits and no fees.

Graduates: In 2001, 8 bachelor's degrees were awarded. 1 company recruited on campus in 2000-2001. Of the 2000 graduating class, all were employed within 6 months of graduation.

Admissions Contact: Barb Kimpe, Admissions Representative.
E-mail: *kimpeb@trinityqc.com* Web: *www.trinityqc.edu*

TRINITY INTERNATIONAL UNIVERSITY E-1

Deerfield, IL 60015 **(847) 317-7000**
(800) 822-3225; Fax: (847) 317-7081

Full-time: 463 men, 636 women	**Faculty:** 37; IIA, --$
Part-time: 38 men, 63 women	**Ph.D.s:** 63%
Graduate: 776 men, 192 women	**Student/Faculty:** 28 to 1
Year: semesters, summer session	**Tuition:** $15,350
Application Deadline: open	**Room & Board:** $5290
Freshman Class: 458 applied, 377 accepted, 194 enrolled	
SAT I Verbal/Math: 565/535	**ACT:** 24 **COMPETITIVE+**

Trinity International University, established in 1897 by the Evangelical Free Church, is a Christian, liberal arts institution offering undergraduate, graduate, and doctoral programs. There are 3 graduate schools. In addition to regional accreditation, Trinity has baccalaureate program accreditation with NCACS. The library contains 241,700 volumes, 147,500 microform items, and 4600 audiovisual forms/CDs, and subscribes to 1400 periodicals. Computerized library services include the card catalog, interlibrary loans, and database searching. The 111-acre campus is in a suburban area 25 miles north of Chicago. Including residence halls, there are 34 buildings.

Student Life: 52% of undergraduates are from out of state, mostly the Midwest. Students are from 33 states, 5 foreign countries, and Canada. 78% are white; 11% African American. Most are Protestant. The average age of freshmen is 18; all undergraduates, 21. 20% do not continue beyond their first year; 50% remain to graduate.

Housing: 700 students can be accommodated in college housing, which includes single-sex dormitories, on-campus apartments, off-campus apartments, and married-student housing. On-campus housing is guaranteed for all 4 years. 80% of students live on campus; of those, 75% remain on campus on weekends. Alcohol is not permitted. Upperclassmen may keep cars.

Activities: There are no fraternities or sororities. There are 20 groups on campus, including art, band, cheerleading, choir, chorale, computers, debate, drama, ethnic, gospel choir, handbell choir, honors, international, jazz band, literary magazine, newspaper, orchestra, pep band, political, religious, social service, student government, symphony, and yearbook. Popular campus events include Santa Lucia Festival, Spring Pops Concert, and Fine Arts Series.

Sports: There are 7 intercollegiate sports for men and 6 for women, and 6 intramural sports for men and 6 for women. Facilities include a student center, a sports complex, and football and soccer fields. Students have access to a nearby indoor tennis and racquetball club.

Disabled Students: 75% of the campus is accessible. Wheelchair ramps, elevators, special parking, specially equipped rest rooms, and special class scheduling are available.

Services: Counseling and information services are available, as is tutoring in every subject. There is a reader service for the blind, and remedial math, reading, and writing.

Campus Safety and Security: Measures include 24-hour foot and vehicle patrol, escort service, informal discussions, and emergency telephones. There are lighted pathways/sidewalks.

Programs of Study: Trinity confers the B.A. degree. Master's and doctoral degrees are also awarded. Bachelor's degrees are awarded in BIOLOGICAL SCIENCE (biology/biological science), BUSINESS (accounting, business administration and management, marketing/retailing/merchandising, and sports management), COMMUNICATIONS AND THE ARTS (communications, English, and music), COMPUTER AND PHYSICAL SCIENCE (chemistry, computer science, and mathematics), EDUCATION (athletic training, elementary, and secondary), HEALTH PROFESSIONS (premedicine and sports medicine), SOCIAL SCIENCE (biblical studies, Christian studies, history, humanities, liberal arts/general studies, philosophy, psychology, religion, social science, and youth ministry). English, Christian studies, and education are the strongest academically. Business, Christian studies, and education are the largest.

Required: To graduate, all students must complete 126 semester hours, including 58 general education hours and a variable 36 to 54 hours in the major. A GPA of 2.0 is required. Chapel attendance, Christian service, Bible study, science, and phys ed are also required.

Special: Students can cross-register with the Christian College Consortium and at Trinity Evangelical Divinity School. Trinity offers 3 levels of internships, study abroad in 7 countries, an opportunity through the American Studies Program to spend a semester in Washington, and work-study programs. Dual majors, a general studies degree, and nondegree study are offered. There is 1 national honor society and a freshman honors program.

Faculty/Classroom: 62% of faculty are male; 38%, female. All teach undergraduates. The average class size in an introductory lecture is 40; in a laboratory, 20; and in a regular course, 15.

Admissions: 82% of the 2001-2002 applicants were accepted. The SAT I scores for the 2001-2002 freshman class were: Verbal--20% below 500, 43% between 500 and 599, 29% between 600 and 700, and 8% above 700; Math--33% below 500, 47% between 500 and 599, and 20% between 600 and 700. The ACT scores were 32% below 21, 31% between 21 and 23, 25% between 24 and 26, 8% between 27 and 28, and 4% above 28. 42% of the current freshmen were in the top fifth of their class; 69% were in the top two fifths. 5 freshmen graduated first in their class in a recent year.

Requirements: The SAT I or ACT is required, with a minimum composite score of 890 on the SAT I or 19 on the ACT. The ACT is preferred. Applicants should be graduates of an accredited high school and have completed 15 academic credits: 2 each in art, a foreign language, math, music, science, and social studies, and 3 in English. A GED is accepted. Recommendations from a pastor must be submitted. Trinity requires applicants to be in the upper 50% of their class. A GPA of 2.5 is required. AP and CLEP credits are accepted. Important factors in the admissions decision are personality/intangible qualities, leadership record, and advanced placement or honor courses. Applications are accepted on-line via the school's web site.

Procedure: Freshmen are admitted fall and spring. Entrance exams should be taken during spring of the junior year or fall of the senior year. Application deadlines are open. Application fee is $25. Notification is sent on a rolling basis.

Transfer: 82 transfer students enrolled in 2001-2002. Applicants must submit college transcripts and have a cumulative college GPA of 2.0 or higher. 30 credits of 126 must be completed at Trinity.

Visiting: There are regularly scheduled orientations for prospective students, including class visits, meetings with professors and admission counselors, and a dorm visit. There are guides for informal visits and visitors may sit in on classes and stay overnight. To schedule a visit, contact the Admissions Office.

Financial Aid: The FAFSA is required. The fall application deadline is April 15.

International Students: There were 19 international students enrolled in a recent year. They must score 530 on the written TOEFL and also take the SAT I or the ACT.

Computers: Trinity provides 100 PCs for academic use. Most dormitory rooms have access to the Internet. All students may access the system. There are no time limits and no fees.
Graduates: In 2001, 158 bachelor's degrees were awarded. The most popular majors were elementary education (10%), youth ministry (9%), and psychology (6%). 20 companies recruited on campus in 2000-2001. Of the 2000 graduating class, 24% were enrolled in graduate school within 6 months of graduation and 50% were employed.
Admissions Contact: Matthew Yoder, Director of Undergraduate Admissions. E-mail: *tcdadm@tiu.edu* Web: *www.tiu.edu*

UNIVERSITY OF CHICAGO E-2

Chicago, IL 60637 (773) 702-8650; Fax: (773) 702-4199

Full-time: 2003 men, 2046 women	**Faculty:** 927; I, ++$
Part-time: 12 men, 11 women	**Ph.D.s:** 99%
Graduate: 5232 men, 3257 women	**Student/Faculty:** 4 to 1
Year: quarters, summer session	**Tuition:** $26,775
Application Deadline: January 1	**Room & Board:** $8312
Freshman Class: 7454 applied, 3261 accepted, 1082 enrolled	
SAT I or ACT: required	**MOST COMPETITIVE**

The University of Chicago, founded in 1891, is a private liberal arts institution offering undergraduate and graduate programs with emphases on the biological and physical sciences, the humanities, and the social sciences. In addition to regional accreditation, Chicago has baccalaureate program accreditation with NCATE. The 8 libraries contain 5.7 million volumes, 2 million microform items, and 15,000 audiovisual forms/CDs, and subscribe to 47,000 periodicals. Computerized library services include the card catalog, interlibrary loans, and database searching. Special learning facilities include a learning resource center, art gallery, radio station, film studies center, language labs, museum of Near Eastern antiquities, and Renaissance Society (contemporary art). The 190-acre campus is in an urban area in Chicago. Including residence halls, there are 200 buildings.
Student Life: 79% of undergraduates are from out of state, mostly the Middle Atlantic. Others are from 49 states, 49 foreign countries, and Canada. 70% are from public schools. 65% are white; 16% Asian American. The average age of freshmen is 18; all undergraduates, 20. 5% do not continue beyond their first year.
Housing: 2700 students can be accommodated in college housing, which includes coed dormitories, on-campus apartments, and married-student housing. In addition, there is an international house. On-campus housing is guaranteed for all 4 years. 66% of students live on campus; of those, 95% remain on campus on weekends. No one may keep cars.
Activities: 12% of men belong to 9 national fraternities; 5% of women belong to 2 national sororities. There are 175 groups on campus, including art, bagpipe band, band, cheerleading, chess, choir, chorale, chorus, college bowl, computers, dance, debate, drama, ethnic, film, gay, honors, international, jazz band, literary magazine, model UN, musical theater, newspaper, orchestra, pep band, photography, political, professional, radio and TV, religious, social, social service, student government, symphony, and yearbook. Popular campus events include Summer Breeze Festival, Kuviasungnerk Winter Festival, and Festival of the Arts.
Sports: There are 10 intercollegiate sports for men and 9 for women, and 18 intramural sports for men and 18 for women. Facilities include a field house, a 1500-seat stadium, a 1500-seat arena, and a student activities center housing a movie theater, TV and pool rooms, and a pub.
Disabled Students: Wheelchair ramps, elevators, special parking, specially equipped rest rooms, special class scheduling, lowered drinking fountains, and lowered telephones are available.
Services: Counseling and information services are available, as is tutoring in some subjects, including math, physics, chemistry, writing, and biology. There is a reader service for the blind.
Campus Safety and Security: Measures include 24-hour foot and vehicle patrol, escort service, shuttle buses, and informal discussions. There are pamphlets/posters/films, emergency telephones, and lighted pathways/sidewalks.
Programs of Study: Chicago confers B.A. and B.S. degrees. Master's and doctoral degrees are also awarded. Bachelor's degrees are awarded in BIOLOGICAL SCIENCE (biochemistry and biology/biological science), COMMUNICATIONS AND THE ARTS (art history and appreciation, classics, comparative literature, English, film arts, fine arts, German, Japanese, Korean, linguistics, music, romance languages and literature, and Russian), COMPUTER AND PHYSICAL SCIENCE (chemistry, computer science, geoscience, mathematics, physics, and statistics), ENGINEERING AND ENVIRONMENTAL DESIGN (environmental science), SOCIAL SCIENCE (African American studies, anthropology, Asian/Oriental studies, Christian studies, classical/ancient civilization, economics, gender studies, geography, history, humanities, international studies, Judaic studies, Latin American studies, medieval studies, Near Eastern studies, philosophy, political science/government, psychology, public affairs, religion, social science, and sociology). Economics, biology, and political science are the largest.
Required: To graduate, students must complete 42 quarter courses, including 9 to 13 courses in the major, with an overall GPA of 1.75 and 2.0 in the major. The core curriculum includes sequences in humanities, social sciences, biological and physical sciences, civilization, and foreign languages. Also required are 2 quarters of math, 1 of art or music, and 1 year of noncredit phys ed.

Special: Special academic programs include cross-registration through the Committee on Institutional Cooperation, international, national, and local internships in most disciplines as well as a summer internship in Washington, study abroad in 12 countries, and work-study in most departments. There are 3-2 programs available through the schools of law, business, social service administration, and public policy. B.A.-B.S. and general studies degrees are offered, as are student-designed majors. Nondegree study and pass/fail options are possible. There are 2 national honor societies, including Phi Beta Kappa.

Faculty/Classroom: 75% of faculty are male; 25%, female. All both teach and do research.

Admissions: 44% of the 2001-2002 applicants were accepted. 93% of the current freshmen were in the top fifth of their class; 98% were in the top two fifths. There were 183 National Merit finalists.

Requirements: The SAT I or ACT is required. In addition, other admissions criteria include a recommended secondary school curriculum of 4 years of English, 3 to 4 years each of history, social studies, math, and science, and 3 years of a foreign language. The GED is accepted. An essay must be submitted, and an interview is recommended. AP credits are accepted. Important factors in the admissions decision are advanced placement or honor courses, personality/intangible qualities, and extracurricular activities record.

Procedure: Freshmen are admitted in the fall. Entrance exams should be taken during the junior or senior year. There are early action, early admissions, and deferred admissions plans. Early action applications should be filed by November 1; regular applications, by January 1 for fall entry, along with a $60 fee. Notification of early action is sent December 15; regular decision, April 1. 18% of all applicants are on a waiting list; 82 were accepted in 2001.

Transfer: 72 transfer students enrolled in 2001-2002. 18 quarter credits of 42 must be completed at Chicago.

Visiting: There are regularly scheduled orientations for prospective students, including meeting with an admissions counselor and students, sitting in on classes, visiting faculty, and staying in a residence hall. There are guides for informal visits and visitors may sit in on classes and stay overnight. To schedule a visit, contact College Admissions.

Financial Aid: In 2001-2002, 65% of all freshmen and 68% of continuing students received some form of financial aid. 55% of freshmen and 56% of continuing students received need-based aid. Chicago is a member of CSS. The CSS/Profile or FAFSA and the college's own financial statement are required. The fall application deadline is February 1.

International Students: There are 294 international students enrolled. The school actively recruits these students. They must score 600 on the written TOEFL or 250 on the electronic version and also take the SAT I or the ACT.

Computers: The mainframes are an Amdahl 5880, 2 Sun minicomputers, and a Silicon Graphics 4D/240 minicomputer. Students are able to access the Amdahl or the Suns through personal user accounts. In addition, there are 7 public computer clusters with IBM PCs and Macs, as well as computer clusters in many of the residence halls. All residence hall rooms are linked to the campus computer network. All students may access the system any time. There are no time limits and no fees.

Graduates: In 2001, 989 bachelor's degrees were awarded. The most popular majors were economics (22%), biological science (12%), and political science (8%). In an average class, 85% graduate in 4 years, and 90% in 6 years.

Admissions Contact: Theodore O'Neill, Dean, College Admissions. Web: *www.uchicago.edu*

UNIVERSITY OF ILLINOIS SYSTEM

The University of Illinois System, established in 1867, is a public system governed by a board of trustees with the president as chief executive. The primary goals of the system are to provide undergraduate and graduate education, to conduct research, and to provide public service. The flagship campus is located in Urbana-Champaign (37,684 students). The 2 other campuses are located in Chicago (24,530) and in the state capital, Springfield (4,288). The Springfield campus, historically an upper-division institution offering course work from the second-semester sophomore level through the graduate level, admitted its first freshman class in fall 2001. The Chicago and Urbana-Champaign campuses offer 4-year, graduate, and doctoral programs. More than 5000 faculty teach at the 3 institutions. Profiles of the 4-year campuses are included in this section.

UNIVERSITY OF ILLINOIS AT CHICAGO E-2

Chicago, IL 60680 (312) 996-4350; Fax: (312) 413-7628

Full-time: 6248 men, 7837 women **Faculty:** 1073; I, av$
Part-time: 906 men, 896 women **Ph.D.s:** 90%
Graduate: 4038 men, 5030 women **Student/Faculty:** 13 to 1
Year: semesters, summer session **Tuition:** $4644 ($10,920)
Application Deadline: February 1 **Room & Board:** $6058
Freshman Class: 9512 applied, 6049 accepted, 2692 enrolled
SAT I or ACT: required **VERY COMPETITIVE**

The University of Illinois at Chicago, founded in 1946, is a public institution with undergraduate and graduate programs in the liberal arts, art and fine arts, business, engineering, architecture, health sciences, music, teacher preparation, and social work, and professional training in dentistry, medicine, and pharmacy. There are 9 undergraduate schools and 1 graduate school. In addition to regional accreditation, UIC has baccalaureate program accreditation with AACSB, ABET, ACPE, ADA, APTA, CSAB, CSWE, NAAB, NASAD, and NLN. The 8 libraries contain 2,072,288 volumes, 3,536,182 microform items, and 25,755 audiovisual forms/CDs, and subscribe to 15,538 periodicals. Computerized library services include the card catalog, interlibrary loans, and database searching. Special learning facilities include a learning resource center, art gallery, radio station, Jane Addams Hull House, which is a restored settlement house, and the James Woodworth Prairie Reserve. The 216-acre campus is in an urban area just west of downtown Chicago. Including residence halls, there are 105 buildings.

Student Life: 95% of undergraduates are from Illinois. Others are from 49 states, 90 foreign countries, and Canada. 78% are from public schools. 46% are white; 20% Asian American; 14% Hispanic. The average age of freshmen is 18; all undergraduates, 22. 22% do not continue beyond their first year.

Housing: 2650 students can be accommodated in college housing, which includes coed dormitories and on-campus apartments. In addition, there are honors houses, the President's Award House, and special-interest floors. On-campus housing is available on a first-come, first-served basis. 89% of students commute. All students may keep cars.

Activities: 4% of men belong to 5 local and 6 national fraternities; 3% of women belong to 1 local and 12 national sororities. There are 202 groups on campus, including art, band, cheerleading, chess, choir, chorus, computers, dance, drama, ethnic, gay, honors, international, jazz band, literary magazine, newspaper, political, professional, religious, social, social service, and student government. Popular campus events include Activities and Services Fair, UIC Fashion Show, and Women's Heritage Month.

Sports: There are 9 intercollegiate sports for men and 9 for women, and 13 intramural sports for men and 13 for women. Facilities include a 12,000-seat sports pavilion, a sports and fitness center, a recreation center, a 1000-seat gym, 3 pools, racquetball and tennis courts, a baseball field, a bowling alley, indoor and outdoor tracks, and weight rooms.

Disabled Students: 80% of the campus is accessible. Wheelchair ramps, elevators, special parking, specially equipped rest rooms, special class scheduling, lowered drinking fountains, and lowered telephones are available.

Services: Counseling and information services are available, as is tutoring in most subjects, including a writing center and academic skills classes. There is a reader service for the blind, and remedial math, reading, and writing.

Campus Safety and Security: Measures include 24-hour foot and vehicle patrol, self-defense education, escort service, and shuttle buses. There are informal discussions, pamphlets/posters/films, emergency telephones, lighted pathways/sidewalks, and emergency call buttons across campus.

Programs of Study: UIC confers B.A., B.S., B.Arch., B.F.A., B.S.C. and E., B.S.C.E., B.S.Ch.E., B.S.E.E., B.S.E.M., B.S.E.M.A.N., B.S.M.E., B.S.N., and B.S.W. degrees. Master's and doctoral degrees are also awarded. Bachelor's degrees are awarded in BIOLOGICAL SCIENCE (biochemistry, biology/biological science, and nutrition), BUSINESS (accounting, banking and finance, business administration and management, business statistics, management science, and marketing/retailing/merchandising), COMMUNICATIONS AND THE ARTS (art history and appreciation, classics, design, dramatic arts, French, graphic design, industrial design, Italian, literature, music, photography, Polish, Russian, Spanish, speech/debate/rhetoric, and studio art), COMPUTER AND PHYSICAL SCIENCE (chemistry, computer science, geology, information sciences and systems, mathematics, physics, and statistics), EDUCATION (art, education, elementary, English, foreign languages, mathematics, physical, science, and secondary), ENGINEERING AND ENVIRONMENTAL DESIGN (architecture, bioengineering, chemical engineering, civil engineering, computer engineering, electrical/electronics engineering, engineering, engineering management, engineering physics, industrial engineering technology, and mechanical engineering), HEALTH PROFESSIONS (medical laboratory science, nursing, occupational therapy, and pharmacy), SOCIAL SCIENCE (African American studies, anthropology, classical/ancient civilization, criminal justice, economics, geography, German area studies, history, Latin American studies, philosophy, political science/government, psychology, social work, and sociology). Math, nursing, and philosophy are the strongest academically. Accounting, engineering, and psychology are the largest.

Required: Students must demonstrate proficiency in written English through either course work or testing, and complete 24 hours of general education, including 6 hours each of humanities, social sciences, and natural sciences. The remaining 6 hours may be spread across the 3 categories. A minimum overall GPA of 3.0 on a 5.0 scale is required. Total number of hours to graduate varies by major but is always at least 120.

Special: Special academic programs include a wide variety of co-op and program internships, work-study with some 70 on-and off-campus employers, and study abroad opportunities at accredited foreign universities, as well as special programs in France, Italy, Canada, Austria, Spain, and Mexico. There is cross-registration with the City Colleges of Chicago. Interdisciplinary majors are offered in architectural studies, communications and theater, French business studies, math and computer science, thermomechanics and energy information and bioengineering, and information and decision sciences. Students may pursue a 3-2 engineering degree with Chicago State, Eastern Illinois, Illinois State, Northeastern Illinois, and Western Illinois Universities. Up to 4 semester hours of credit may be granted for military experience. Dual and student-designed majors, nondegree study, and pass/fail options are available. There are 10 national honor societies, including Phi Beta Kappa, and a freshman honors program.

Faculty/Classroom: 73% of faculty are male; 27%, female. 50% teach undergraduates, all do research, and 50% do both. The average class size in an introductory lecture is 100; in a laboratory, 24; and in a regular course, 32.

Admissions: 64% of the 2001-2002 applicants were accepted.

Requirements: The SAT I or ACT is required. In addition, applicants should be graduates of an accredited secondary school; the GED is accepted. The recommended secondary school curriculum varies according to the college program chosen, but 16 high school credits are required. AP and CLEP credits are accepted. Important factors in the admissions decision are recommendations by school officials, evidence of special talent, and advanced placement or honor courses. Applications are accepted on-line at the university's web site.

Procedure: Freshmen are admitted to all sessions. Entrance exams should be taken in the spring of the junior year or the fall of the senior year. There is an early admissions plan. Applications should be filed by February 1 for fall entry, October 1 for spring entry, and April 1 for summer entry, along with a $40 fee. Notification is sent on a rolling basis.

Transfer: 1589 transfer students enrolled in 2001-2002. Transferable hours and minimum GPA vary according to program. 30 credits of 120 must be completed at UIC.

Visiting: There are regularly scheduled orientations for prospective students, consisting of a general meeting, a college meeting, and campus tours. There are guides for informal visits and visitors may sit in on classes. To schedule a visit, contact the Office of Undergraduate Admissions.

Financial Aid: 58% of freshmen received need-based aid. The FAFSA is required. The fall application deadline is March 1.

International Students: There are 265 international students enrolled. They must score 520 on the written TOEFL or 190 on the electronic version or take the MELAB. They must also take the SAT I or ACT. Minimum required scores depend on the specific college.

Computers: The mainframe is an IBM 3090-300J. Numerous terminals and PCs are located in labs, classrooms, libraries, and residence halls throughout the campus. All students may access the system 24 hours daily. There are no time limits and no fees.

Graduates: In 2001, 3174 bachelor's degrees were awarded. The most popular majors were psychology (11%), information and decision science (7%), and biological science (7%). In an average class, 9% graduate in 4 years, 29% in 5 years, and 37% in 6 years. 175 companies recruited on campus in 2000-2001.

Admissions Contact: Rob Sheinkopf, Executive Director of Admissions and Records. E-mail: *uicadmit@uic.edu*
Web: *http://www.uic.edu/depts/oar*

UNIVERSITY OF ILLINOIS AT URBANA-CHAMPAIGN E-3

Urbana, IL 61801 (217) 333-0302; Fax: (217) 244-0903

Full-time: 14,512 men, 13,112 women **Faculty:** 1894; I, av$
Part-time: 568 men, 554 women **Ph.D.s:** 96%
Graduate: 4954 men, 3998 women **Student/Faculty:** 15 to 1
Year: semesters, summer session **Tuition:** $5226 ($13,046)
Application Deadline: January 1 **Room & Board:** $6090
Freshman Class: n/av
SAT I or ACT: not required **HIGHLY COMPETITIVE+**

The University of Illinois at Urbana-Champaign, founded in 1867, is the oldest and largest campus in the University of Illinois system, offering some 150 undergraduate and more than 100 graduate degree programs. There are 9 undergraduate schools and 1 graduate school. In addition to regional accreditation, Illinois has baccalaureate program accreditation with AACSB, ABET, ACEJMC, ADA, AHEA, ASLA, CSWE, NAAB, NASAD, NASM, NCATE, NRPA, and SAF. The 42 libraries contain 9,647,652 volumes, 8,976,026 microform items, and 159,365 audiovisual forms/CDs, and subscribe to 91,054 periodicals. Computerized library services include the card catalog, interlibrary loans, and database searching. Special learning facilities include a learning resource center, art gallery, natural history museum, radio station, TV station, language learning lab, performing arts center, and graphic technologies lab. The campus is in a small town 130 miles south of Chicago. Including residence halls, there are 200 buildings.

Student Life: 93% of undergraduates are from Illinois. Others are from 49 states, 121 foreign countries, and Canada. 67% are white; 12% Asian American. The average age of freshmen is 19; all undergraduates, 21. 7% do not continue beyond their first year; 80% remain to graduate.

Housing: 8374 students can be accommodated in college housing, which includes single-sex and coed dormitories, on-campus apartments, and married-student housing. In addition, there are language houses, special-interest houses, and privately owned residence halls. On-campus housing is guaranteed for all 4 years. 70% of students commute. All students may keep cars.

Activities: 22% of men belong to 3 local and 52 national fraternities; 22% of women belong to 3 local and 27 national sororities. There are 850 groups on campus, including art, band, cheerleading, choir, chorale, chorus, computers, dance, debate, drama, drill team, ethnic, film, gay, honors, international, jazz band, literary magazine, marching band, musical theater, newspaper, opera, orchestra, pep band, photography, political, professional, radio and TV, religious, social, social service, student government, symphony, and yearbook. Popular campus events include Quad Day to introduce campus organizations, Dad's Weekend, and Mom's Weekend.

Sports: There are 8 intercollegiate sports for men and 9 for women, and 30 intramural sports for men and 30 for women. Facilities include one of the world's largest intramural sports and recreation buildings, numerous student union facilities, and acres of outdoor playing fields. Memorial Football Stadium seats 69,000 and Assembly Hall seats 16,000 for basketball games, concerts, and special events.

Disabled Students: All of the campus is accessible. Wheelchair ramps, elevators, special parking, specially equipped rest rooms, special class scheduling, lowered drinking fountains, lowered telephones, and housing and fitness equipment are available.

Services: Counseling and information services are available, as is tutoring in every subject. There is a reader service for the blind. Transportation and rehabilitation services are offered, as well as interpreters, note taking, taped lectures, and modified test times or formats.

Campus Safety and Security: Measures include 24-hour foot and vehicle patrol, self-defense education, escort service, and shuttle buses. There are informal discussions, pamphlets/posters/films, emergency telephones, lighted pathways/sidewalks, safety presentations, and evaluations by campus police.

Programs of Study: Illinois confers A.B., B.S., B.A.U.P., B.F.A., B.Land.Arch., B.Mus., B.S.Ed., B.S.J., B.S.W., and B.V.M. degrees. Master's and doctoral degrees are also awarded. Bachelor's degrees are awarded in AGRICULTURE (agricultural economics, agricultural mechanics, agronomy, animal science, forestry and related sciences, and horticulture), BIOLOGICAL SCIENCE (biochemistry, biology/biological science, biophysics, microbiology, molecular biology, and physiology), BUSINESS (accounting, banking and finance, business administration and management, marketing/retailing/merchandising, and recreation and leisure services), COMMUNICATIONS AND THE ARTS (advertising, art history and appreciation, broadcasting, classics, comparative literature, crafts, dance, dramatic arts, English, French, Germanic languages and literature, graphic design, industrial design, Italian, journalism, linguistics, media arts, music, music history and appreciation, music theory and composition, painting, photography, Portuguese, Russian languages and literature, sculpture, Spanish, speech/debate/rhetoric, and voice), COMPUTER AND PHYSICAL SCIENCE (actuarial science, astronomy, chemistry, computer science, geology, mathematics, physics, and statistics), EDUCATION (agricultural, art, computer, early childhood, elementary, foreign languages, music, physical, secondary, and special), ENGINEERING AND ENVIRONMENTAL DESIGN (aeronautical engineering, agricultural engineering, airline piloting and navigation, architecture, bioengineering, ceramic engineering, chemical engineering, city/community/regional planning, civil engineering, computer engineering, electrical/electronics engineering, engineering, engineering mechanics, engineering physics, environmental science, industrial engineering, landscape architecture/design, materials science, mechanical engineering, metallurgical engineering, and nuclear engineering), HEALTH PROFESSIONS (public health, speech pathology/audiology, and veterinary science), SOCIAL SCIENCE (anthropology, East Asian studies, economics, family/consumer studies, food science, geography, history, human development, humanities, international studies, Latin American studies, liberal arts/general studies, philosophy, political science/government, psychology, religion, Russian and Slavic studies, and sociology). Advertising, engineering and music are the strongest academically. Psychology, accountancy, and electrical and computer engineering are the largest.

Required: All students must demonstrate proficiency in the use of the English language, complete 6 hours each in humanities, social sciences, and natural sciences, and maintain a minimum GPA of 2.0 on a 4.0 scale. Minimum hours needed to graduate range from 120 to 132, depending on the major.

Special: Illinois offers cooperative engineering programs with 30 midwestern liberal arts colleges; 16 summer, semester, and full-year programs abroad and numerous exchange opportunities; and cross-registration with Parkland Community College. Unusual opportunities include a leisure studies semester in Scotland and a summer parliamentary internship in London. A dual degree in liberal arts and engineering is offered, as well as student-designed majors and a 3-2 engineering program with numerous universities. On-campus work-study and pass/fail options are possible. There are 50 national honor societies, including Phi Beta Kappa, and a freshman honors program.

Faculty/Classroom: 77% of faculty are male; 23%, female. 89% teach undergraduates, all do research, and 89% do both. The average class size in an introductory lecture is 124; in a laboratory, 22; and in a regular course, 29.

Admissions: 62% of the 2001-2002 applicants were accepted. 80% of the current freshmen were in the top fifth of their class; 96% were in the top two fifths.

Requirements: Applicants should be graduates of accredited secondary schools or have the GED. High school preparation must include 4 years of English, 3 or more of math, 2 each of lab science and social studies, and, for most programs, 2 of foreign languages. A personal essay is optional. Visual arts applicants must submit a portfolio; performing arts applicants are required to audition. AP and CLEP credits are accepted. Important factors in the admissions decision are evidence of special talent, advanced placement or honor courses, and geographic diversity.

Procedure: Freshmen are admitted fall and spring. Entrance exams should be taken by spring of the junior year and no later than October of the senior year. There are early admissions and deferred admissions plans. Applications should be filed by January 1 for fall entry and November 1 for spring entry. Notification is sent February 20. The fall 2001 application fee was $40.

Transfer: 1088 transfer students enrolled in 2001-2002. Transfer application requirements differ by degree program. Generally, students transferring should have junior standing of 60 hours; students from other institutions must have at least a C average in previous college work. Admission is also subject to the number of places available. 30 credits of 120 must be completed at Illinois.

Visiting: There are regularly scheduled orientations for prospective students, consisting of presentations given by the admissions staff at 10 A.M. and 1 P.M. daily on weekdays; a videotape of the campus is shown, and tours are provided. There are guides for informal visits and visitors may sit in on classes. To schedule a visit, contact the Campus Visitors Center at (217) 333-0824 or *visits@oar.viuc.edu*

Financial Aid: In 2001-2002, 81% of all freshmen received some form of financial aid. 39% of freshmen and 38% of continuing students received need-based aid. The average freshman award was $5257. Of that total, scholarships or need-based grants averaged $5257 ($7500 maximum); loans averaged $2772 ($4125 maximum); and work contracts averaged $1500 ($2000 maximum). 33% of undergraduates work part time. Average annual earnings from campus work are $1594. The average financial indebtedness of the 2001 graduate was $14,791. The FAFSA and the college's own financial statement are required. The fall application deadline is March 15.

International Students: They must score 550 on the written TOEFL or take the MELAB.

Computers: The mainframes are an IBM RS/6000/540, an IBM 380, a Sequent Symmetry S81, a Convex C240, and an IBM 3801/KX6. About 3000 computer workstations are located in classrooms, labs, and residence halls across campus. All students may access the system 24 hours a day. Students may access the system 20 hours per week on dial-in access only; there is no limit from networked PCs. There are no fees. It is strongly recommended that all students have a personal computer. It is recommended that students in law school have personal computers. Pentium 120 is recommended.

Graduates: In 2001, 6431 bachelor's degrees were awarded. The most popular majors were finance (7%), biological sciences (7%), and English (7%). In an average class, 2% graduate in 3 years, 54% in 4 years, 75% in 5 years, and 78% in 6 years. 999 companies recruited on campus in 2000-2001. Of the 2000 graduating class, 40% were enrolled in graduate school within 6 months of graduation and 85% were employed.

Admissions Contact: Tammie Bouseman, Assistant Director, Undergraduate Admissions. A video is available.
E-mail: *admission@oar.uiuc.edu* Web: *www.oar.uiuc.edu*

UNIVERSITY OF SAINT FRANCIS E-2

Joliet, IL 60435 (815) 740-3400
(800) 735-7500; Fax: (815) 740-4285

Full-time: 380 men, 706 women
Part-time: 78 men, 220 women
Graduate: 233 men, 980 women
Year: semesters, summer session
Application Deadline: open
Freshman Class: 811 applied, 646 accepted, 175 enrolled
ACT: required
Faculty: 67; IIB, --$
Ph.D.s: 55%
Student/Faculty: 16 to 1
Tuition: $14,300
Room & Board: $5350
COMPETITIVE

The University of Saint Francis, founded as a college in 1920, is a private liberal arts and professional institution affiliated with the Roman Catholic Church. There are 4 undergraduate and 3 graduate schools. In addition to regional accreditation, USF has baccalaureate program accreditation with CSWE, NLN, and NRPA. The library contains 110,855 volumes, 2543 microform items, and 3982 audiovisual forms/CDs, and subscribes to 800 periodicals. Computerized library services include the card catalog, interlibrary loans, and database searching. Special learning facilities include a learning resource center, art gallery, radio station, TV station, greenhouse, and wireless education classroom. The 17-acre campus is in a suburban area 35 miles southwest of Chicago. Including residence halls, there are 7 buildings.

Student Life: 97% of undergraduates are from Illinois. Others are from 15 states, 4 foreign countries, and Canada. 70% are from public schools. 77% are white. 70% are Catholic; 28% Protestant. The average age of freshmen is 18; all undergraduates, 25. 23% do not continue beyond their first year; 54% remain to graduate.

Housing: 374 students can be accommodated in college housing, which includes coed dormitories, and a learning and living community for the natural sciences and nursing students (special wing in residence hall). On-campus housing is guaranteed for the freshman year only, is available on a first-come, first-served basis, and is available on a lottery system for upperclassmen. Priority is given to out-of-town students. 74% of students commute. All students may keep cars.

Activities: There are no fraternities or sororities. There are 27 groups on campus, including cheerleading, choir, chorale, chorus, drama, ethnic, honors, literary magazine, newspaper, professional, radio and TV, religious, social, social service, and student government. Popular campus events include artist lecture series, Spring Fling, and Little Sibs Weekend.

Sports: There are 6 intercollegiate sports for men and 8 for women, and 2 intramural sports for men and 2 for women. Facilities include a 10,000-seat lighted football stadium, an indoor arena, a baseball field, a Nautilus center, and basketball, racquetball, volleyball, and badminton courts. A recreation center houses a gym, handball courts, weight room, training room, offices, and classrooms; a campus fitness center has facilities for swimming, weight training, aerobic training, and indoor and outdoor tracks. Baseball, softball, football, and golf facilities are available off campus.

Disabled Students: 90% of the campus is accessible. Wheelchair ramps, elevators, special parking, specially equipped rest rooms, special class scheduling, lowered drinking fountains, and lowered telephones are available.

Services: Counseling and information services are available, as is tutoring in most subjects. The writing center provides help with papers. A math center for tutorial assistance and numerous computerized tutorial programs for courses are also available.

Campus Safety and Security: Measures include 24-hour foot and vehicle patrol, self-defense education, escort service, and shuttle buses. There are informal discussions, pamphlets/posters/films, emergency telephones, lighted pathways/sidewalks, first-response trained security, sexual assault counseling, and routine fire inspection.

Programs of Study: USF confers B.A., B.S., B.B.A., and B.S.W. degrees. Master's degrees are also awarded. Bachelor's degrees are awarded in BIOLOGICAL SCIENCE (biology/biological science), BUSINESS (accounting, banking and finance, business administration and management, marketing/retailing/merchandising, and recreational facilities management), COMMUNICATIONS AND THE ARTS (communications, English, fine arts, and journalism), COMPUTER AND PHYSICAL SCIENCE (computer programming, computer science, information sciences and systems, and mathematics), EDUCATION (elementary), ENGINEERING AND ENVIRONMENTAL DESIGN (computer technology and environmental science), HEALTH PROFESSIONS (allied health, health, medical technology, nuclear medical technology, nursing, predentistry, premedicine, preveterinary science, radiation therapy, and radiograph medical technology), SOCIAL SCIENCE (criminal justice, history, liberal arts/general studies, political science/government, prelaw, psychology, social work, and theological studies). Biology and education are the strongest academically. Business, nursing, and education are the largest.

Required: To graduate, students are required to complete 128 credit hours with a minimum of 36 hours in the major while maintaining a GPA of 2.0. The required liberal education core includes courses in the following areas: literacy, literary inquiry and aesthetic awareness, numerical understanding and scientific inquiry, historical understanding, social awareness, philosophical inquiry, and religious foundations. A thesis or other senior capstone experience is also required.

Special: Internships, on and off campus, paid and unpaid, are available for most majors. The college also offers an accelerated degree program in applied organizational management, dual majors, interdisciplinary majors, a pass/fail option, a Washington semester, study abroad, and credit for life, military, and work experience. There are 10 national honor societies.

Faculty/Classroom: 40% of faculty are male; 60%, female. All teach undergraduates, 20% do research, and 20% do both. No introductory courses are taught by graduate students. The average class size in an introductory lecture is 26; in a laboratory, 16; and in a regular course, 18.

Admissions: 80% of the 2001-2002 applicants were accepted. 35% of the current freshmen were in the top fifth of their class; 70% were in the top two fifths. 2 freshmen graduated first in their class.

Requirements: The ACT is required. In addition, admission requirements also include 4 years of English, 2 of math, including geometry, 2 each of science (1 lab) and social studies, and 3 of either art, music, foreign language, or computer science. USF requires applicants to be in the upper 50% of their class. A GPA of 2.5 is required. AP and CLEP credits are accepted. Important factors in the admissions decision are personality/intangible qualities, advanced placement or honor courses, and leadership record. Applications are accepted on-line and on computer disk.

Procedure: Freshmen are admitted fall and spring. Entrance exams should be taken in the spring of the junior year or the fall of the senior year. There is an early decision plan. Application deadlines are open. The fall application fee was $20. Notification is sent on a rolling basis.

Transfer: 1335 transfer students enrolled in a recent year. Transfer students must have a GPA of 2.0 and must submit transcripts from colleges previously attended; applicants with fewer than 30 semester hours must also submit high school transcripts. 32 credits of 128 must be completed at USF.

Visiting: There are regularly scheduled orientations for prospective students, including orientation, meeting faculty, a tour, and student presentations. There are guides for informal visits and visitors may sit in on classes and stay overnight. To schedule a visit, contact the Admissions Office.

Financial Aid: In 2001-2002, 98% of all freshmen and 89% of continuing students received some form of financial aid. 57% of freshmen and 60% of continuing students received need-based aid. The average freshman award was $13,793. Of that total, scholarships or need-based grants averaged $9579 ($20,570 maximum); loans averaged $3312 ($20,570 maximum); and work contracts averaged $1967 ($2500 maximum). 66% of undergraduates work part time. Average annual earnings from campus work are $1155. The average financial indebtedness of the 2001 graduate was $11,670. The FAFSA and the college's own financial statement are required. The fall application deadline is June 1.

International Students: There are 7 international students enrolled. They must score 550 on the written TOEFL.

Computers: The mainframe is a 2 Digital 6000s. There are about 100 terminals and PCs in 3 student labs, network access from dorm rooms, and 24-hour telephone access to the computer network from off campus. All students may access the system 24 hours a day. There are no time limits and no fees.

Graduates: In a recent year, 270 bachelor's degrees were awarded. The most popular majors were nursing (24%), elementary education (15%), and management (9%). In an average class, 44% graduate in 4 years, 63% in 5 years, and 63% in 6 years. 42 companies recruited on campus in 2000-2001. Of the 2000 graduating class, 6% were enrolled in graduate school within 6 months of graduation and 86% were employed.

Admissions Contact: Sheryl Paul, Director of Admissions. A video is available. E-mail: *spaul@stfrancis.edu* Web: *www.stfrancis.edu*

VANDERCOOK COLLEGE OF MUSIC E-2

Chicago, IL 60616-3731 (312) 225-6288
(800) 448-2655; Fax: (312) 225-5211

Full-time: 48 men, 31 women
Part-time: 1 man, 3 women
Graduate: 30 men, 35 women
Year: semesters
Application Deadline: June 1
Freshman Class: 44 applied, 38 accepted, 24 enrolled
ACT: 23
Faculty: 11
Ph.D.s: 70%
Student/Faculty: 7 to 1
Tuition: $13,810
Room & Board: $5600
SPECIAL

VanderCook College of Music, founded in 1909, is devoted solely to the preparation of music educators. There is 1 graduate school. In addition to regional accreditation, VCM has baccalaureate program accreditation with NASM. The 2 libraries contain 20,000 volumes, 2000 microform items, and 5000 audiovisual forms/CDs, and subscribe to 80 periodicals. Computerized library services include the card catalog, interlibrary loans, and database searching. Special learning facilities include a learning resource center. The 1-acre campus is in an urban area 3 miles from the center of Chicago.

Student Life: 60% of undergraduates are from Illinois. Others are from 11 states, 1 foreign country, and Canada. 80% are from public schools. 63% are white; 32% African American. The average age of freshmen is 19; all undergraduates, 21. 8% do not continue beyond their first year; 80% remain to graduate.

Housing: All students can be accommodated in college housing, which includes single-sex and coed dormitories, on-campus apartments, married-student housing, and fraternity houses. On-campus housing is guaranteed for all 4 years. 60% of students live on campus; of those, 90% remain on campus on weekends. Alcohol is not permitted. All students may keep cars.

Activities: 50% of men belong to 2 local fraternities and 1 national fraternity; 20% of women belong to 2 local sororities and 1 national sorority. There are 10 groups on campus, including band, choir, chorale, chorus, jazz band, musical theater, orchestra, pep band, religious, and student government.

Sports: There is no sports program at VCM. Facilities include a swimming pool, a gym, and tennis courts.

Disabled Students: Special parking and special class scheduling are available.

Campus Safety and Security: Measures include 24-hour foot and vehicle patrol, self-defense education, escort service, and shuttle buses. There are informal discussions, emergency telephones, and lighted pathways/sidewalks.

Programs of Study: VCM confers the B.M.Ed. degree. Master's degrees are also awarded. Bachelor's degrees are awarded in EDUCATION (music).

Required: To graduate, students must complete a total of 134 semester hours distributed in the 5 major categories of general education, professional education, applied music performance, fundamentals and theory, and music education. They must also pass performance proficiency exams on 17 instruments and a vocal proficiency exam.

Faculty/Classroom: 44% of faculty are male; 56%, female. All teach undergraduates. No introductory courses are taught by graduate students. The average class size in an introductory lecture, in a laboratory, and in a regular course is 15.

Admissions: 86% of the 2001-2002 applicants were accepted. The ACT scores for the 2001-2002 freshman class were: 33% below 21, 20% between 21 and 23, 27% between 24 and 26, 7% between 27 and 28, and 13% above 28. 35% of the current freshmen were in the top fifth of their class; 60% were in the top two fifths. There was 1 National Merit semifinalist.

Requirements: The SAT I or ACT is required, with a minimum composite score of 900 on the SAT I or 18 on the ACT. Graduation from an accredited secondary school or a satisfactory score on the GED is required for admission. Secondary school courses must include 3 units each of English and science, 2 each of math, social studies, music, and a foreign language, and 1 each of history and art. An audition and an interview are required. VCM requires applicants to be in the upper 75% of their class. A GPA of 2.0 is required. AP and CLEP credits are accepted. Important factors in the admissions decision are evidence of special talent, recommendations by alumni, and extracurricular activities record.

Procedure: Freshmen are admitted fall and spring. Entrance exams should be taken during the junior year. There are early decision, early admissions, and deferred admissions plans. Early decision applications should be filed by May 1; regular applications, by June 1 for fall entry and October 1 for spring entry, along with a $35 fee. Notification is sent on a rolling basis. 8 early decision candidates were accepted for the 2001-2002 class.

Transfer: 5 transfer students enrolled in 2001-2002. Transfer students must have a minimum GPA of 2.5. An audition and an interview are required. Courses taken at other institutions in performance, theory, and history must be validated.

Visiting: There are regularly scheduled orientations for prospective students, including the opportunity to observe a class, meet students and faculty, and tour the campus. There are guides for informal visits and visitors may sit in on classes and stay overnight. To schedule a visit, contact James Malley, Director of Admission.

Financial Aid: In 2001-2002, 80% of all freshmen and 5% of continuing students received some form of financial aid. 30% of undergraduates work part time. The FAFSA is required. The fall application deadline is June 1.

International Students: There are 3 international students enrolled. They must score 500 on the written TOEFL.

Computers: Macs are available. All students may access the system. There are no time limits and no fees.

Graduates: In 2001, 16 bachelor's degrees were awarded. The most popular major was music education (100%). In an average class, 90% graduate in 4 years, and 10% in 5 years. Of the 2000 graduating class, all were employed within 6 months of graduation.

Admissions Contact: James P. Malley, Jr., Director of Admissions.
E-mail: *jmalley@vandercook.edu*

WEST SUBURBAN COLLEGE OF NURSING E-2

Oak Park, IL 60302 **(708) 763-6530; Fax: (708) 763-1531**

Full-time: 3 men, 127 women	**Faculty:** 9
Part-time: none	**Ph.D.s:** 33%
Graduate: none	**Student/Faculty:** 14 to 1
Year: semesters, summer session	**Tuition:** $15,182
Application Deadline: open	**Room & Board:** $4900

Freshman Class: 30 applied, 22 accepted, 10 enrolled
ACT: required **SPECIAL**

West Suburban College of Nursing, founded in 1982, is a private, nonsectarian college of nursing offering a joint-degree program with Concordia University in River Forest. In addition to regional accreditation, West Sub has baccalaureate program accreditation with NLN. The library contains 3000 volumes and 1000 audiovisual forms/CDs, and subscribes to 350 periodicals. Computerized library services include the card catalog, interlibrary loans, and database searching. The 20-acre campus is in a suburban area 10 miles west of downtown Chicago. There is 1 building.

Student Life: 95% of undergraduates are from Illinois. Others are from 5 states and 2 foreign countries. 60% are from public schools. 73% are white; 15% African American; 10% Asian American. The average age of freshmen is 18; all undergraduates, 25.

Housing: On-campus housing is provided by Concordia University and is guaranteed for all 4 years. 60% of students commute. Alcohol is not permitted. All students may keep cars.

Activities: There are no fraternities or sororities. Concordia University sponsors extracurricular activities, clubs, and organizations.

Sports: There are 4 intercollegiate sports for men and 2 for women, and 1 intramural sport for men. Athletic and recreation facilities are sponsored by Concordia University.

Disabled Students: Lowered drinking fountains are available.

Services: There is tutoring in some subjects, with the subjects varying per semester. There is remedial math, reading, and writing.

Campus Safety and Security: Measures include 24-hour foot and vehicle patrol, escort service, shuttle buses, and lighted pathways/sidewalks.

Programs of Study: West Sub confers the B.S. degree. Bachelor's degrees are awarded in HEALTH PROFESSIONS (nursing).

Required: To graduate, students must have a minimum of 129 semester hours with a minimum GPA of 2.0. 56 semester hours are required in nursing. All students must take courses in nursing, psychology, sociology, chemistry, anatomy, physiology, microbiology, statistics, physical ed, humanities, communications, and theology.

Faculty/Classroom: All faculty members are female. All teach undergraduates. The average class size in an introductory lecture is 20; in a laboratory, 6; and in a regular course, 12.

Admissions: 73% of the 2001-2002 applicants were accepted.

Requirements: The ACT is required, with a minimum composite score of 20 recommended. Graduation from an accredited secondary school or satisfactory scores on the GED are required for admission. Students should have 16 academic credits, including 4 years of English and 1 unit each in chemistry and biology, as well as courses in math, history, and social studies. A personal recommendation and an essay are required. West Sub requires applicants to be in the upper 33% of their class. A GPA of 2.5 is required. AP and CLEP credits are accepted. Important factors in the admissions decision are recommendations by school officials, advanced placement or honor courses, and personality/intangible qualities. Applications are accepted on0lline at the school's web site.

Procedure: Freshmen are admitted to all sessions. Entrance exams should be taken in the spring of the junior year. Application deadlines are open. The application fee is $25. Notification is sent on a rolling basis.

Transfer: 21 transfer students enrolled in 2001-2002. Transfer students must have a minimum GPA of 2.5 in all college courses completed. A letter of recommendation and an essay are required. 56 credits of 129 must be completed at West Sub.

Visiting: There are regularly scheduled orientations for prospective students, including open houses. There are guides for informal visits and visitors may sit in on classes and stay overnight. To schedule a visit, contact the Admissions Office.

Financial Aid: In 2001-2002, 90% of all students received some form of financial aid, including need-based aid. Concordia University handles financial aid. The CSS/Profile or FAFSA is required.

International Students: International students take the TOEFL, scoring 500 on the written version, or take the MELAB. They must also take the ACT, scoring 20.

Computers: PCs are available on the Concordia University campus. There are no fees.

Graduates: In 2001, 31 bachelor's degrees were awarded.

Admissions Contact: Dara Lawyer, Interim Director of Admissions.
Web: *www.wscn.curf.edu*

WESTERN ILLINOIS UNIVERSITY C-3

Macomb, IL 61455-1390 **(309) 298-3157; Fax: (309) 298-3111**

Full-time: 4688 men, 4612 women **Faculty:** 599; IIA, -$
Part-time: 622 men, 833 women **Ph.D.s:** 71%
Graduate: 913 men, 1538 women **Student/Faculty:** 16 to 1
Year: semesters, summer session **Tuition:** $4509 ($1974)
Application Deadline: see profile **Room & Board:** $5062
Freshman Class: 8115 applied, 4952 accepted, 1712 enrolled
ACT: 23 **COMPETITIVE**

Western Illinois University, founded in 1899, is a public institution with 4 colleges and a school of graduate and international studies. There are 4 undergraduate schools and 1 graduate school. In addition to regional accreditation, WIU has baccalaureate program accreditation with AACSB, ADA, NASM, NCATE, and NRPA. The 5 libraries contain 998,041 volumes, 1,342,620 microform items, and 3445 audiovisual forms/CDs, and subscribe to 3200 periodicals. Computerized library services include the card catalog, interlibrary loans, and database searching. Special learning facilities include an art gallery, natural history museum, radio station, and TV station. The 1050-acre campus is in a rural area 76 miles from Peoria and 151 miles from St. Louis. Including residence halls, there are 52 buildings.

Student Life: 93% of undergraduates are from Illinois. Others are from 46 states, 54 foreign countries, and Canada. 89% are from public schools. 87% are white. The average age of freshmen is 18; all undergraduates, 24. 26% do not continue beyond their first year; 46% remain to graduate.

Housing: 4755 students can be accommodated in college housing, which includes single-sex and coed dormitories, on-campus apartments, and married-student housing. In addition, there are honors houses, special-interest houses, academic majors, honors, and wellness floors in residence halls. On-campus housing is guaranteed for all 4 years. 55% of students commute. Alcohol is not permitted. All students may keep cars.

Activities: 8% of men belong to 18 national fraternities; 8% of women belong to 10 national sororities. There are 254 groups on campus, including art, band, cheerleading, chess, choir, chorale, chorus, computers, dance, drama, drill team, ethnic, gay, honors, international, jazz band, literary magazine, marching band, musical theater, newspaper, opera, orchestra, pep band, photography, political, professional, radio and TV, religious, social, social service, student government, symphony, and yearbook. Popular campus events include Family Weekend, Summer Music Theater, and International Bazaar.

Sports: There are 10 intercollegiate sports for men and 9 for women, and 25 intramural sports for men and 25 for women. Facilities include a 9-hole golf course, tennis courts, a football field, a basketball court, a swimming pool, and a recreation center.

Disabled Students: 95% of the campus is accessible. Wheelchair ramps, elevators, special parking, specially equipped rest rooms, special class scheduling, lowered drinking fountains, and lowered telephones are available.

Services: Counseling and information services are available, as is tutoring in some subjects, including English, math, computer science, science, social sciences, and humanitites. There is a reader service for the blind and remedial math and writing.

Campus Safety and Security: Measures include 24-hour foot and vehicle patrol, self-defense education, escort service, and shuttle buses. There are informal discussions, pamphlets/posters/films, emergency telephones, lighted pathways/sidewalks, and a beacon system.

Programs of Study: WIU confers B.A., B.S., B.B., B.F.A., B.S.Ed., and B.S.W. degrees. Master's degrees are also awarded. Bachelor's degrees are awarded in AGRICULTURE (agriculture), BIOLOGICAL SCIENCE (biology/biological science), BUSINESS (accounting, banking and finance, business administration and management, management information systems, marketing/retailing/merchandising, and personnel management), COMMUNICATIONS AND THE ARTS (art, communications, dramatic arts, English, French, journalism, media arts, music, and Spanish), COMPUTER AND PHYSICAL SCIENCE (chemistry, computer science, geology, mathematics, and physics), EDUCATION (bilingual/bicultural, elementary, industrial arts, physical, special, and technical), ENGINEERING AND ENVIRONMENTAL DESIGN (industrial engineering technology and manufacturing technology), HEALTH PROFESSIONS (health science, medical technology, and speech pathology/audiology), SOCIAL SCIENCE (criminal justice, economics, family/consumer studies, geography, history, law enforcement and corrections, parks and recreation management, philosophy, political science/government, psychology, social work, and sociology). Accounting, chemistry, and human resource management are the strongest academically. Communication, law enforcement, and justice administration are the largest.

Required: To graduate, all students must complete at least 120 credit hours and have a minimum 2.0 GPA. Students must take 44 hours in the fields of basic skills, well-being, natural science and math, historical and social foundations, and humanities. A writing exam is also required.

Special: WIU offers internships in business, law enforcement, and physical training, study abroad in 4 countries, and dual programs in engineering, dentistry, medicine, and medical technology. Student-designed majors and independent study are available through the Experimental Studies, Board of Trustees, and Individual Studies programs. The Board of Trustees degree program offers credit for work experience. Also available are a field campus and a life science station on the Mississippi River, a 3-2 engineering program with the University of Illinois, and various preprofessional programs. There are 30 national honor societies, a freshman honors program, and 34 departmental honors programs.

Faculty/Classroom: 62% of faculty are male; 38%, female. 97% teach undergraduates, 90% do research, and 90% do both. Graduate students teach 1% of introductory courses. The average class size in an introductory lecture is 36; in a laboratory, 23; and in a regular course, 25.

Admissions: 61% of the 2001-2002 applicants were accepted. The ACT scores for the 2001-2002 freshman class were: 40% below 21, 32% between 21 and 23, 19% between 24 and 26, 5% between 27 and 28, and 4% above 28. 22% of the current freshmen were in the top fifth of their class; 53% were in the top two fifths. 6 freshmen graduated first in their class in a recent year.

Requirements: The SAT I or ACT is required, with a minimum composite score of 850 on the SAT I, or 18 on the ACT, both for the admissions decision and for placement purposes. Students must have 4 years of English, 3 years each of math, science, and social studies, and 2 electives in art, film, foreign language, music, speech, theater, journalism, religion, philosophy, or vocational education. Academic Services is a multicultural recruitment and supportive admissions program for selected students who do not meet freshman or transfer requirements. WIU requires applicants to be in the upper 50% of their class. A GPA of 2.2 is required. AP and CLEP credits are accepted. Important factors in the admissions decision are ability to finance college education, recommendations by alumni, and recommendations by school officials. Applications are accepted on-line.

Procedure: Freshmen are admitted to all sessions. Check with the school for current application deadlines and fee. Entrance exams should be taken by April of the senior year. There is a deferred admissions plan. Notification is sent on a rolling basis.

Transfer: 1375 transfer students enrolled in 2001-2002. Students transferring fewer than 24 semester credits or 36 quarter credits must submit a high school transcript or GED certificate, have scored at least 22 on the ACT, and be in good standing at their last school. A minimum 2.0 GPA is required. 30 credits of 120 must be completed at WIU.

Visiting: There are regularly scheduled orientations for prospective students. There are guides for informal visits and visitors may sit in on classes and stay overnight. To schedule a visit, contact the Admissions Office at (309) 298-3140.

Financial Aid: In 2001-2002, 52% of all freshmen and 50% of continuing students received some form of financial aid. 44% of freshmen and 45% of continuing students received need-based aid. The average freshman award was $6025. Of that total, scholarships or need-based grants averaged $5003; loans averaged $2362; and work contracts averaged $1099. 20% of undergraduates work part time. Average annual earnings from campus work are $1043. The average financial indebtedness of the 2001 graduate was $12,900. The FAFSA is required. The fall application deadline is March 1.

International Students: There are 187 international students enrolled. The school actively recruits these students. They must score 550 on the written TOEFL or successfully complete WIU's ESL program.

Computers: The mainframe is an IBM Multiprise 2003 Model 126. Computer access is available through the library, various residence halls, and the computer labs. All students may access the system anytime. There are no time limits and no fees.

Graduates: In 2001, 2164 bachelor's degrees were awarded. The most popular majors were law enforcement and justice administration (13%), elementary education (9%), and communication (6%). In an average class, 28% graduate in 4 years, 47% in 5 years, and 49% in 6 years. 105 companies recruited on campus in 2000-2001. Of the 2000 graduating class, 14% were enrolled in graduate school within 6 months of graduation and 78% were employed.

Admissions Contact: Admissions Office. A video is available.
E-mail: *wiuadm@wiu.edu* Web: *www.wiu.edu*

WHEATON COLLEGE
Wheaton, IL 60187-5593 E-2
(630) 752-5005
(800) 222-2419; Fax: (630) 752-5285

Full-time: 1138 men, 1190 women **Faculty:** 181; IIA, av$
Part-time: 26 men, 24 women **Ph.D.s:** 92%
Graduate: 224 men, 234 women **Student/Faculty:** 13 to 1
Year: semesters, summer session **Tuition:** $16,390
Application Deadline: January 15 **Room & Board:** $5544
Freshman Class: 1870 applied, 1057 accepted, 575 enrolled
SAT I or ACT: required **HIGHLY COMPETITIVE**

Wheaton College, founded in 1860, is a nonprofit, private, nondenominational institution committed to providing students with a Christian education. Basically a liberal arts school, it offers undergraduate programs in business, the arts and fine arts, music, teacher preparation, and religious and Bible studies. In addition to regional accreditation, Wheaton has baccalaureate program accreditation with NASM and NCATE. The 2 libraries contain 342,746 volumes, 674,827 microform items, and 32,761 audiovisual forms/CDs, and subscribe to 3264 periodicals. Computerized library services include the card catalog, interlibrary loans, and database searching. Special learning facilities include a radio station and a communications resource center with TV and audio studios, a special collection of British authors' books and papers, an evangelical museum with document archives, and the center for Applied Christian Ethics. The 80-acre campus is in a suburban area 25 miles west of Chicago. Including residence halls, there are 35 buildings.

Student Life: 77% of undergraduates are from out of state, mostly the Midwest. Others are from 49 states, 13 foreign countries, and Canada. 67% are from public schools. 88% are white. Most are Protestant. The average age of freshmen is 18; all undergraduates, 20. 6% do not continue beyond their first year; 83% remain to graduate.

Housing: 2091 students can be accommodated in college housing, which includes single-sex dormitories, on-campus apartments, off-campus apartments, and married-student housing. In addition, the college owns ans rents houses to groups of students. On-campus housing is guaranteed for the freshman year only and is available on a lottery system for upperclassmen. 88% of students live on campus; of those, 95% remain on campus on weekends. Alcohol is not permitted. Upperclassmen may keep cars.

Activities: There are no fraternities or sororities. There are 71 groups on campus, including band, cheerleading, chess, choir, chorale, chorus, dance, debate, drama, drill team, ethnic, forensics, international, jazz band, literary magazine, newspaper, orchestra, pep band, radio and TV, religious, social, social service, student government, symphony, and yearbook. Popular campus events include Air Jam and an artist concert series.

Disabled Students: Wheelchair ramps, elevators, special parking, specially equipped rest rooms, special class scheduling, lowered drinking fountains, lowered telephones, and other provisions as needed are available.

Services: There is a reader service for the blind and a writing center. Other services are provided as needed.

Campus Safety and Security: Measures include 24-hour foot and vehicle patrol, self-defense education, escort service, and informal discussions. There are pamphlets/posters/films, emergency telephones, and lighted pathways/sidewalks.

Programs of Study: Wheaton confers B.A., B.S., B.M., and B.M.E. degrees. Master's and doctoral degrees are also awarded. Bachelor's degrees are awarded in BIOLOGICAL SCIENCE (biology/biological science), BUSINESS (business economics), COMMUNICATIONS AND THE ARTS (art, communications, English, French, German, music, and Spanish), COMPUTER AND PHYSICAL SCIENCE (chemistry, computer science, geology, mathematics, physical sciences, and physics), EDUCATION (elementary, music, science, and secondary), ENGINEERING AND ENVIRONMENTAL DESIGN (environmental science), SOCIAL SCIENCE (anthropology, archeology, biblical studies, economics, history, interdisciplinary studies, philosophy, physical fitness/movement, political science/government, psychology, religion, social science, and sociology).

Required: To graduate, students must complete 124 semester hours, 36 in upper-division courses, with a varying number of hours in a major, and maintain at least a 2.0 GPA. General education requirements include competency in a foreign language, math, speech, writing, and Bible studies; distribution requirements include fine arts, history, literature, sciences, physical sciences, philosophy, social sciences, and sport/fitness.

Special: Special academic programs include internships, study abroad in 8 countries, an urban semester in Chicago and a Washington semester. Dual majors are available in all areas, as are student-designed majors. A 3-2 engineering degree is offered with the Illinois Institute of Technology, University of Illinois, Case Western Reserve University School of Engineering, and Washington University School of Engineering and Applied Science; transfer to other engineering schools is also possible. A 3-2 nursing degree is offered with Emory University, Goshen Nursing School, University of Rochester, and Rush University. Pass/fail options are available. There are 10 national honor societies, and 11 departmental honors programs.

Faculty/Classroom: 68% of faculty are male; 32%, female. No introductory courses are taught by graduate students.

Admissions: 57% of the 2001-2002 applicants were accepted. The SAT I scores for the 2001-2002 freshman class were: Verbal--2% below 500, 17% between 500 and 599, 49% between 600 and 700, and 32% above 700; Math--4% below 500, 16% between 500 and 599, 50% between 600 and 700, and 30% above 700. The ACT scores were 7% between 21 and 23, 16% between 24 and 26, 21% between 27 and 28, and 56% above 28. 74% of the current freshmen were in the top fifth of their class; 94% were in the top two fifths. There were 59 National Merit finalists. In a recent year, 64 freshmen graduated first in their class.

Requirements: The SAT I or ACT is required. In addition, a high school diploma is required and the GED is accepted. Wheaton requires a general college preparatory program of 18 units, including 4 of English, 3 to 4 of math, science, and social studies, and 2 to 3 of a foreign language. AP and CLEP credits are accepted. Personality/intangible qualities is an important factor in the admission decision.

Procedure: Freshmen are admitted in the fall. Entrance exams should be taken November of the senior year. There is a deferred admissions plan. Applications should be filed by January 15 for fall entry. Notification is sent April 1; 31 were accepted in 2001. The fall application fee was $35.

Transfer: 75 transfer students enrolled in 2001-2002. Applicants must have completed 15 semester hours with a 3.0 average and present a high school transcript, college transcript, and an essay or personal statement. An interview is required. 48 credits of 124 must be completed at Wheaton.

Visiting: There are regularly scheduled orientations for prospective students, consisting of presentations by faculty, administrators, students, and financial aid and admissions staff, as well as social activities. There are guides for informal visits and visitors may sit in on classes and stay overnight. To schedule a visit, contact the Admissions Office at (630) 752-5600.

Financial Aid: In 2001-2002, 73% of all freshmen and 64% of continuing students received some form of financial aid. The average freshman award was $10,589. The average financial indebtedness of the 2001 graduate was $14,595. The FAFSA and the college's own financial statement are required. The fall application deadline is February 15.

International Students: There are 22 international students enrolled in a recent year. The school actively recruits these students. They mst take the TOEFL, TSE, and TWE.

Computers: The mainframes are a DEC ALPHA and RISC/Ultrix minicomputers. Also available are 95 IBM PCs and Macs located in 5 student labs with networked print services and file servers, all of which have network access, plus 8 dial-up modem lines. There are 31 PCs and 5 printers located in 5 dorm labs. Students also may access the campus network using their own computers in their dorm rooms. All students may access the system 24 hours a day. Students may access the system 2 hours at one sitting if there is a waiting list; otherwise, there is no limit. There are no fees.

Graduates: In 2001, 584 bachelor's degrees were awarded. The most popular majors were English (18%), social sciences and history (14%), and philosophy, theology, and religion (14%).

Admissions Contact: Director of Admissions.
E-mail: *admissions@wheaton.edu* Web: *http://www.wheaton.edu*

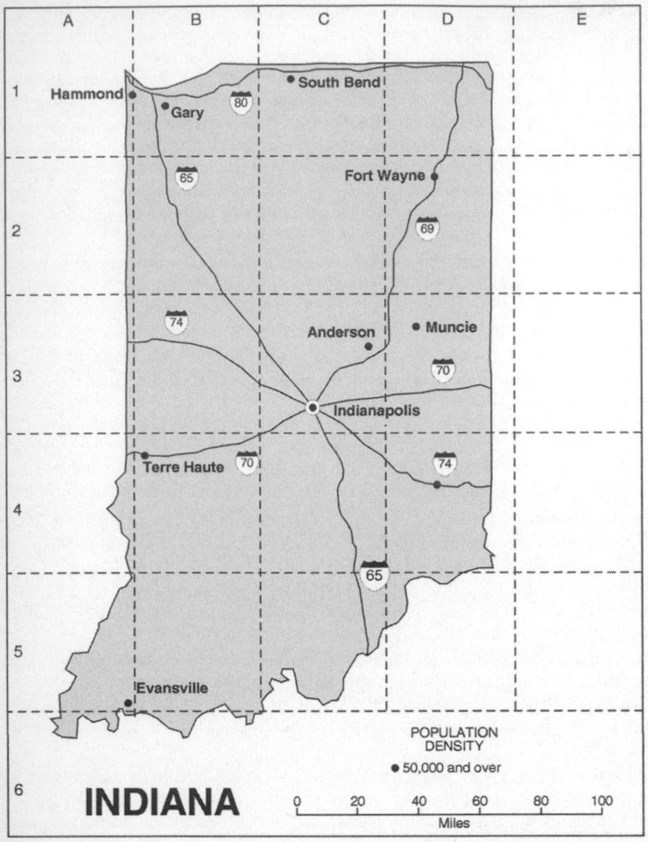

ANDERSON UNIVERSITY

C-3

Anderson, IN 46012

(765) 641-4080
(800) 428-6414; Fax: (765) 641-3851

Full-time: 750 men, 1070 women
Part-time: 75 men, 110 women
Graduate: 140 men, 110 women
Year: semesters, summer session
Application Deadline: open
Freshman Class: n/av
SAT I or ACT: required

Faculty: 123; IIB, --$
Ph.D.s: 70%
Student/Faculty: 14 to 1
Tuition: $14,680
Room & Board: $4750

LESS COMPETITIVE

Anderson University, founded in 1917, is a private liberal arts institution affiliated with the Church of God. The university offers programs in theoretical and applied science, social and professional studies, and arts, culture, and religion. Figures in above capsule are approximate. There are 3 undergraduate and 3 graduate schools. In addition to regional accreditation, Anderson has baccalaureate program accreditation with ACBSP, CSWE, NASM, NCATE, and NLN. The library contains 264,208 volumes, 89,884 microform items, and 12,000 audiovisual forms/CDs, and subscribes to 947 periodicals. Computerized library services include the card catalog, interlibrary loans, and database searching. Special learning facilities include a learning resource center, art gallery, radio station, and the Museum of the Bible and the Ancient Near East. The 100-acre campus is in a suburban area 40 miles northeast of Indianapolis. Including residence halls, there are 26 buildings.

Student Life: 61% of undergraduates are from Indiana. Others are from 42 states, 15 foreign countries, and Canada. 97% are from public schools. 93% are white. 83% are Protestant; 13% claim no religious affiliation. The average age of freshmen is 18; all undergraduates, 21. 25% do not continue beyond their first year; 50% remain to graduate.

Housing: 1243 students can be accommodated in college housing, which includes single-sex dormitories, on-campus apartments, off-campus apartments, and married-student housing. On-campus housing is guaranteed for all 4 years. 61% of students live on campus; of those, 50% remain on campus on weekends. Alcohol is not permitted. All students may keep cars.

Activities: There are no fraternities or sororities. There are 41 groups on campus, including art, band, cheerleading, choir, chorale, drama, ethnic, film, honors, international, jazz band, literary magazine, musical theater, newspaper, opera, orchestra, photography, political, professional, radio and TV, religious, social, social service, student government, symphony, and yearbook. Popular campus events include Christmas Carols, Celebration Weekend, and Black Awareness.

Sports: There are 8 intercollegiate sports for men and 8 for women, and 7 intramural sports for men and 6 for women. Facilities include 2 gyms, football, baseball/softball, and soccer fields, an 8-lane all-weather track, tennis courts, a bowling alley, and a game room. The campus stadium seats 4200 and the indoor gym seats 2400.

Disabled Students: 95% of the campus is accessible. Wheelchair ramps, elevators, special parking, specially equipped rest rooms, special class scheduling, lowered drinking fountains, and lowered telephones are available.

Services: Counseling and information services are available, as is tutoring in most subjects. There is a reader service for the blind, and remedial math, reading, and writing.

Campus Safety and Security: Measures include 24-hour foot and vehicle patrol, self-defense education, escort service, and informal discussions. There are pamphlets/posters/films, emergency telephones, and lighted pathways/sidewalks. Indiana State police academy graduates are security officers.

Programs of Study: Anderson confers B.A. and B.S.N. degrees. Associate, master's, and doctoral degrees are also awarded. Bachelor's degrees are awarded in BIOLOGICAL SCIENCE (biology/biological science), BUSINESS (accounting, banking and finance, business administration and management, management science, marketing/retailing/merchandising, and sports management), COMMUNICATIONS AND THE ARTS (communications, dramatic arts, English, fine arts, French, German, graphic design, music business management, music performance, and Spanish), COMPUTER AND PHYSICAL SCIENCE (chemistry, computer science, mathematics, and physics), EDUCATION (art, Christian, elementary, foreign languages, health, music, physical, science, and social studies), HEALTH PROFESSIONS (medical laboratory technology, and nursing), SOCIAL SCIENCE (criminal justice, economics, family/consumer studies, history, philosophy, political science/government, psychology, religion, social work, and sociology). Physical sciences is the strongest academically. Business, education, and music are the largest.

Required: Requirements for graduation include the general education core, consisting of 55 hours, a minimum 2.0 GPA overall and in the major, 124 total credit hours, and a minimum of 36 hours in the major. All students must complete a liberal arts seminar. The last 24 credit hours must be taken in residence.

Special: Anderson offers co-op programs with Purdue University, internships through the Center for Public Service, study abroad in 25 countries through the International Studies Program, and a Washington semester. Also available are credit for military experience and pass/fail options. Courses in electronic engineering may be taken through the Purdue Anderson campus. Preprofessional programs are offered in medicial, podiatry, dentistry, law, engineering, seminary, and several allied health fields. There are 12 national honor societies, a freshman honors program, and 10 departmental honors programs.

Faculty/Classroom: 57% of faculty are male; 43%, female. 91% teach undergraduates. No introductory courses are taught by graduate students. The average class size in an introductory lecture is 29; in a laboratory, 14; and in a regular course, 17.

Admissions: 24 freshmen graduated first in their class in a recent year.

Requirements: The SAT I or ACT is required. In addition, applicants must be graduates of an accredited secondary school or have a GED certificate, and submit a photograph, references, and a health form. A GPA of 2.0 is required. AP and CLEP credits are accepted. Important factors in the admissions decision are leadership record, parents or siblings attending the school, and personality/intangible qualities. Applications are accepted on-line at the school's web site: *www.anderson.edu.*

Procedure: Freshmen are admitted fall and spring. Entrance exams should be taken in the fall of the junior year. Application deadlines are open. The fall 2001 application fee was $20.

Transfer: 104 transfer students enrolled in 2001-2002. Applicants must have a minimum 2.0 GPA, satisfactory SAT I or ACT scores, and transcripts for all previously attended colleges. 24 credits of 124 must be completed at Anderson.

Visiting: There are regularly scheduled orientations for prospective students, including a campus tour, an academic overview, a financial aid and athletics overview, and appointments with professors and departmental chairs. There are guides for informal visits and visitors may sit in on classes and stay overnight. To schedule a visit, contact the Admissions Office.

Financial Aid: In a recent year, 99% of all freshmen and 88% of continuing students received some form of financial aid. 75% of freshmen and 73% of continuing students received need-based aid. The average

freshman award was $13,049. Of that total, scholarships or need-based grants averaged $7500 ($18,000 maximum); loans averaged $5000 ($5500 maximum); and work contracts averaged $2400 (maximum). 35% of undergraduates work part time. Average annual earnings from campus work are $2000. The average financial indebtedness of a recent graduate was $17,650. Anderson is a member of CSS. The FAFSA is required. Check with the school for current deadlines.

International Students: There were 25 international students enrolled in a recent year. They must score 550 on the written TOEFL and also take the SAT I, scoring 800.

Computers: The mainframes are an HP 3000/948 and an HP 9000/832. The mainframes are accessible throughout the campus either through a local area network or by modem. All students may access the system. There are no time limits and no fees.

Graduates: In a recent year, 328 bachelor's degrees were awarded. The most popular majors were elementary education (13%), mass communication (6%), and social work (5%). In an average class, 1% graduate in 3 years, 32% in 4 years, 47% in 5 years, and 50% in 6 years. 48 companies recruited on campus in 2000-2001. Of the 2000 graduating class, 20% were enrolled in graduate school within 6 months of graduation.

Admissions Contact: Admissions Counselor.
E-mail: *info@anderson.edu* Web: *www.anderson.edu*

BALL STATE UNIVERSITY
Muncie, IN 47306 — B-3
(765) 285-8300
(800) 482-4BSU; Fax: (765) 285-1632

Full-time: 6354 men, 7906 women	**Faculty:** 806; I, --$
Part-time: 611 men, 738 women	**Ph.D.s:** 76%
Graduate: 849 men, 1204 women	**Student/Faculty:** 18 to 1
Year: semesters, summer session	**Tuition:** $3830 ($10,290)
Application Deadline: March 1	**Room & Board:** $4830
Freshman Class: 3513 enrolled	
SAT I Verbal/Math: 520/520	**ACT:** 22 **COMPETITIVE**

Ball State University, founded in 1918, is a public university offering undergraduate and graduate programs through 7 academic colleges in applied sciences and technology; architecture and planning; business; communication, information, and media; fine arts; sciences and humanities; and teacher education. The Honors College and the University College are interdisciplinary colleges. There are 7 undergraduate schools and 1 graduate school. In addition to regional accreditation, Ball State has baccalaureate program accreditation with AACSB, ACEJMC, ADA, AHEA, CAHEA, CSAB, CSWE, NAAB, NASAD, NASM, NCATE, and NLN. The 3 libraries contain 1,108,532 volumes, 1,012,210 microform items, and 509,899 audiovisual forms/CDs, and subscribe to 3077 periodicals. Computerized library services include interlibrary loans and database searching. Special learning facilities include a learning resource center, art gallery, planetarium, radio station, TV station, and research centers in solar energy, human performance, and international programs. The 955-acre campus is in a suburban area 56 miles northwest of Indianapolis. Including residence halls, there are 57 buildings.

Student Life: 91% of undergraduates are from Indiana. Others are from 49 states, 86 foreign countries, and Canada. 90% are white. The average age of freshmen is 18; all undergraduates, 21. 23% do not continue beyond their first year.

Housing: 6400 students can be accommodated in college housing, which includes single-sex and coed dormitories, on-campus apartments, married-student housing, and fraternity houses. In addition, there are honors houses, wellness halls, and special-interest houses. On-campus housing is guaranteed for the freshman year only. 60% of students commute. Alcohol is not permitted. All students may keep cars.

Activities: 10% of men belong to 19 national fraternities; 10% of women belong to 1 local sorority and 15 national sororities. There are 300 groups on campus, including art, band, cheerleading, chess, choir, chorale, chorus, computers, dance, debate, drama, drill team, ethnic, film, forensics, gay, honors, international, jazz band, literary magazine, marching band, musical theater, newspaper, orchestra, pep band, photography, political, professional, radio and TV, religious, social, social service, student government, symphony, and yearbook. Popular campus events include Watermelon Bust, Unity Week, and Family Weekend.

Sports: There are 9 intercollegiate sports for men and 10 for women, and 43 intramural sports for men and 41 for women. Facilities include an 11,500-seat basketball and volleyball arena, 2 gyms, a field sports building, tennis courts, and an aquatic center. The campus stadium seats 16,320.

Disabled Students: All of the campus is accessible. Wheelchair ramps, elevators, special parking, specially equipped rest rooms, special class scheduling, lowered drinking fountains, lowered telephones, a special resource guide, an accessibility map (including tactile), and text telephones (TDD) in all key offices are available.

Services: Counseling and information services are available, as is tutoring in most subjects. There is a reader service for the blind.

Campus Safety and Security: Measures include 24-hour foot and vehicle patrol, self-defense education, escort service, and shuttle buses. There are informal discussions, pamphlets/posters/films, emergency telephones, and lighted pathways/sidewalks.

Programs of Study: Ball State confers B.A., B.S., B.Arch., B.F.A., B.G.S., B.Land.Arch., B.Mus., B.S.W., and B.Urban Planning and Development degrees. Associate, master's, and doctoral degrees are also awarded. Bachelor's degrees are awarded in AGRICULTURE (fishing and fisheries and natural resource management), BIOLOGICAL SCIENCE (biology/biological science, botany, cell biology, genetics, microbiology, molecular biology, wildlife biology, and zoology), BUSINESS (accounting, banking and finance, business administration and management, business economics, insurance, management science, marketing/retailing/merchandising, personnel management, real estate, and sports management), COMMUNICATIONS AND THE ARTS (art, broadcasting, classical languages, classics, communications, dance, dramatic arts, English, film arts, fine arts, French, German, graphic design, guitar, journalism, music, music performance, photography, piano/organ, Spanish, speech/debate/rhetoric, telecommunications, and voice), COMPUTER AND PHYSICAL SCIENCE (actuarial science, chemistry, computer science, geology, mathematics, and physics), EDUCATION (art, business, early childhood, education of the deaf and hearing impaired, educational media, elementary, foreign languages, health, home economics, industrial arts, journalism, middle school, music, science, secondary, social studies, special, and technical), ENGINEERING AND ENVIRONMENTAL DESIGN (architecture, environmental design, graphic arts technology, landscape architecture/design, and urban planning technology), HEALTH PROFESSIONS (health science, medical laboratory technology, nursing, predentistry, premedicine, prepharmacy, and speech pathology/audiology), SOCIAL SCIENCE (anthropology, criminal justice, dietetics, economics, food production/management/services, geography, history, home economics, Latin American studies, liberal arts/general studies, paralegal studies, parks and recreation management, philosophy, physical fitness/movement, political science/government, prelaw, psychology, religion, social work, and sociology). Architecture, business, and education are the strongest academically. Elementary education and business are the largest.

Required: All students must take at least 126 credits and maintain a 2.0 GPA for graduation. Required courses include English composition, math, speech, history, physical sciences, social or behavioral sciences, humanities or fine arts, global studies, and 3 hours of phys ed. In addition, all juniors must pass a writing competency exam.

Special: Nearly all undergraduate disciplines offer internships. Study abroad is possible at the university's London center and in 20 other programs; students may also spend a semester in Washington, D.C., and co-op and work-study programs are available. Most disciplines offer dual majors. There is a 3-2 program in engineering, an award-winning program in entrepreneurship, a general studies degree, nondegree study, and pass/fail options. There are 40 national honor societies, and a freshman honors program.

Faculty/Classroom: 63% of faculty are male; 37%, female. 94% teach undergraduates, 75% do research, and 73% do both. No introductory courses are taught by graduate students. The average class size in an introductory lecture is 50; in a laboratory, 18; and in a regular course, 30.

Admissions: The SAT I scores for the 2001-2002 freshman class were: Verbal--41% below 500, 43% between 500 and 599, 14% between 600 and 700, and 2% above 700; Math--39% below 500, 42% between 500 and 599, 17% between 600 and 700, and 2% above 700. The ACT scores were 35% below 21, 25% between 21 and 23, 23% between 24 and 26, 8% between 27 and 28, and 9% above 28. 34% of the current freshmen were in the top fifth of their class; 67% were in the top two fifths. There were 7 National Merit finalists. 40 freshmen graduated first in their class.

Requirements: The SAT I or ACT is required. In addition, applicants must be graduates of an accredited high school or have a GED diploma. Admission is based on strength of the applicant's curriculum, grades in English, math, lab sciences, social sciences, and foreign language, curricula patterns and grade trends, and the SAT I or ACT scores. For Indiana applicants, Ball State considers completion of Core 40 as the recommended preparation for college-bound students; completion of the Academic Honors Diploma is encouraged. AP and CLEP credits are accepted. Important factors in the admissions decision are advanced placement or honor courses, recommendations by school officials, and personality/intangible qualities.

Procedure: Freshmen are admitted fall, spring, and summer. Entrance exams should be taken during the spring of the junior year or early in the senior year. There is a deferred admissions plan. Applications should be filed by March 1 for fall entry, December 1 for spring entry, and April 1 for summer entry. The fall 2001 application fee was $25. Notification is sent on a rolling basis.

Transfer: 783 transfer students enrolled in 2001-2002. Transfer applicants should have earned a 2.0 GPA on a 4.0 scale (as computed by Ball State) to be considered for admission. An official high school transcript or GED score report and official transcripts from each postsecondary institution are required. 63 credits of 126 must be completed at Ball State.

Visiting: There are regularly scheduled orientations for prospective students. There are guides for informal visits and visitors may sit in on classes and stay overnight. To schedule a visit, contact the University Visitors Center at (765) 285-5683 (out-of-state) or (800) 482-4BSU.

Financial Aid: In 2001-2002, 85% of all freshmen and 70% of continuing students received some form of financial aid. 49% of freshmen and 47% of continuing students received need-based aid. The average freshman award was $5460. Of that total, scholarships or need-based grants averaged $2760; loans averaged $2550; and work contracts averaged $150. 32% of undergraduates work part time. Average annual earnings from campus work are $1200. The average financial indebtedness of the 2001 graduate was $15,689. Ball State is a member of CSS. The FAFSA is required. The fall application deadline is March 1.

International Students: There were 409 international students enrolled in a recent year. The school actively recruits these students. They must score 550 on the written TOEFL.

Computers: The mainframes are an IBM and VAX cluster. The university supports more than 70 computer labs on campus, and there are more than 3000 computer workstations. 2 mainframe computers with about 200 terminals are available to students, as are more than 300 PCs. All students may access the system at any time except from 5 P.M. Friday to 8 A.M. Saturday. There are no time limits and no fees.

Graduates: In a recent year, 3821 bachelor's degrees were awarded. The most popular majors were science and humanities (36%), education (16%), and applied sciences and technology (16%). In an average class, 20% graduate in 4 years, 41% in 5 years, and 52% in 6 years. 300 companies recruited on campus in a recent year.

Admissions Contact: Lawrence Waters, Dean of Admissions and Enrollment Services. E-mail: *askus@wp.bsu.edu* Web: *www.bsu.edu*

BETHEL COLLEGE C-1

Mishawaka, IN 46545 (574) 257-3339

(800) 422-4101; Fax: (574) 257-3335

Full-time: 428 men, 701 women	**Faculty:** 75; IIB, --$
Part-time: 124 men, 288 women	**Ph.D.s:** 63%
Graduate: 63 men, 56 women	**Student/Faculty:** 15 to 1
Year: semesters, summer session	**Tuition:** $13,300
Application Deadline: August 1	**Room & Board:** $4350
Freshman Class: 505 applied, 497 accepted, 307 enrolled	
SAT I Verbal/Math: 540/530	**ACT:** 22 **LESS COMPETITIVE**

Bethel College, founded in 1947, is a private institution affiliated with the Missionary Church, offering a liberal arts education with a Christian perspective. In addition to regional accreditation, Bethel has baccalaureate program accreditation with NCATE and NLN. The library contains 100,981 volumes, 4165 microform items, and 3863 audiovisual forms/CDs, and subscribes to 450 periodicals. Computerized library services include the card catalog, interlibrary loans, and database searching. Special learning facilities include a learning resource center, art gallery, and radio station. The 70-acre campus is in a suburban area 90 miles east of Chicago. Including residence halls, there are 31 buildings.

Student Life: 73% of undergraduates are from Indiana. Others are from 27 states, 14 foreign countries, and Canada. 78% are from public schools. 86% are white. Most are Protestant. The average age of freshmen is 19; all undergraduates, 26. 14% do not continue beyond their first year.

Housing: 780 students can be accommodated in college housing, which includes single-sex dormitories and on-campus apartments. On-campus housing is guaranteed for all 4 years. 51% of students commute. Alcohol is not permitted. Upperclassmen may keep cars.

Activities: There are no fraternities or sororities. There are 18 groups on campus, including art, band, cheerleading, choir, chorale, chorus, computers, drama, honors, international, jazz band, literary magazine, musical theater, newspaper, pep band, professional, radio and TV, religious, social, social service, student government, and yearbook. Popular campus events include Christmas Banquet, Junior-Senior Banquet, and Spiritual Emphasis Week.

Sports: There are 8 intercollegiate sports for men and 8 for women, and 15 intramural sports for men and 15 for women. Facilities include a gym; a weight room; exercise, baseball and training facilites; baseball, softball and soccer fields; tennis courts; and a practice track.

Disabled Students: 78% of the campus is accessible. Wheelchair ramps, elevators, special parking, specially equipped rest rooms, and lowered drinking fountains are available.

Services: Counseling and information services are available, as is tutoring in every subject. There is remedial math, reading, and writing.

Campus Safety and Security: Measures include 24-hour foot and vehicle patrol, escort service, informal discussions, and pamphlets/posters/films. There are emergency telephones and lighted pathways/sidewalks.

Programs of Study: Bethel confers B.A., B.S., and B.S.N. degrees. Associate and master's degrees are also awarded. Bachelor's degrees are awarded in BIOLOGICAL SCIENCE (biology/biological science, and environmental biology), BUSINESS (accounting, business administration and management, and sports management), COMMUNICATIONS AND THE ARTS (art, communications, dramatic arts, English, music, and music performance), COMPUTER AND PHYSICAL SCIENCE (applied physics, chemistry, computer science, digital arts/technology, mathematics, and physics), EDUCATION (business, elementary, English, mathematics, music, physical, science, secondary, and social studies), ENGINEERING AND ENVIRONMENTAL DESIGN (aeronautical engineering, chemical engineering, civil engineering, electrical/electronics engineering, interior design, and mechanical engineering), HEALTH PROFESSIONS (nursing, predentistry, and premedicine), SOCIAL SCIENCE (biblical studies, criminal justice, history, human services, international studies, interpreter for the deaf, liberal arts/general studies, ministries, missions, philosophy, prelaw, psychology, religion, religious music, social science, sociology, and youth ministry). Education, religion, american sign language/english interpreting, psychology, environmental biology and music are the strongest academically and have the largest enrollments are the strongest academically. Business, education, religion and nursing are the largest.

Required: To graduate, students must complete 124 credits, including 24 to 52 in the major, with a minimum 2.0 GPA. Also required are 4 semesters of phys ed, 10 credits in Bible and religion, courses in communication skills, social science and history, fine arts and humanities, and natural sciences and math, and a course called Lifelong Physical Awareness. Computer proficiency is also required.

Special: A cooperative program is offered with the University of Notre Dame, and students may cross-register for courses at various local colleges including Northern Indiana Consortium for Education (NICE). Also available are a B.A.-B.S. degree in engineering, a 3-2 engineering degree with the University of Notre Dame and Tri-State University (Angola), a liberal arts degree, and an accelerated degree in organizational management (for students age 25 and over). Bethel also offers nondegree courses, a pass/fail option, student teaching, some business and computer internships, study in Ecuador, China, Russia, Israel, and Jamaica, double majors, and work-study programs. There is a freshman honors program.

Faculty/Classroom: 51% of faculty are male; 49%, female. All teach undergraduates, 10% do research, and 10% do both. No introductory courses are taught by graduate students. The average class size in an introductory lecture is 50; in a laboratory, 15; and in a regular course, 21.

Admissions: 98% of the 2001-2002 applicants were accepted. The SAT I scores for the 2001-2002 freshman class were: Verbal--37% below 500, 37% between 500 and 599, 22% between 600 and 700, and 4% above 700; Math--35% below 500, 39% between 500 and 599, 24% between 600 and 700, and 2% above 700. 37% of the current freshmen were in the top fifth of their class; 66% were in the top two fifths. 4 freshmen graduated first in their class.

Requirements: The SAT I or ACT is required. In addition, with recommended minimum scores of 450 verbal and 450 math on the SAT I, and 17 on the verbal and 17 on the math sections of the ACT. Applicants should be graduates of accredited secondary schools or have the GED. Required secondary school credits include 8 units in English, 6 each in math, lab science, and social science, and 4 units in a foreign language. Chemistry is required for nursing majors. An interview is recommended. An audition is required of music program applicants. The college accepts applications on computer disk via CollegeLink and at their web site. A GPA of 2.0 is required. AP and CLEP credits are accepted.

Procedure: Freshmen are admitted to all sessions. Entrance exams should be taken as early as possible in the junior or senior year. There are early admissions and deferred admissions plans. Applications should be filed by August 1 for fall entry and December 1 for winter entry, along with a $25 fee. Notification is sent on a rolling basis.

Transfer: 187 transfer students enrolled in 2001-2002. Grades of C or better are eligible for transfer; students without a minimum GPA of 2.0 may be admitted on probation. Other admission requirements are the same as for entering freshmen. 30 credits of 124 must be completed at Bethel.

Visiting: There are regularly scheduled orientations for prospective students, including an interview, chapel visit, tour, lunch, and a class or professor visit as requested. There are guides for informal visits and visitors may sit in on classes and stay overnight. To schedule a visit, contact the Office of Admissions.

Financial Aid: In 2001-2002, 84% of all freshmen and 81% of continuing students received some form of financial aid. 64% of freshmen and 56% of continuing students received need-based aid. The average freshman award was $11,545. Of that total, scholarships or need-based grants averaged $4060; loans averaged $3321; and Average need-based self-help award (excluding PLUS loans, unsubsidized loans and private alternative loans. $4164. 22% of undergraduates work part time. The average financial indebtedness of the 2001 graduate was $14,330. Bethel is a member of CSS. The FAFSA, the college's own financial statement and the SAR are required. The fall application deadline is March 1.

International Students: There are 35 international students enrolled. They must score 540 on the written TOEFL or 207 on the electronic version.

Computers: The mainframe is a Novell Network. There are 66 IBM and Mac PCs. All students may access the system Monday through Friday 8 A.M. to midnight and Saturday 8 A.M. to 7 P.M. in the computer labs. There are no time limits and no fees. It is strongly recommended that all students have a personal computer.

Graduates: In 2001, 357 bachelor's degrees were awarded. The most popular majors were business areas (35%), education (17%), and nursing (14%). In an average class, 70% graduate in 4 years, 26% in 5 years, and 3% in 6 years. 175 companies recruited on campus in 2000-2001.

Admissions Contact: Andrea Helmuth, Director of Admissions. E-mail: *helmuta@bethelcollege.edu* Web: *www.bethelcollege.edu*

BUTLER UNIVERSITY

Indianapolis, IN 46208 C-3

(317) 940-8100

(888) 940-8100; Fax: (317) 940-8150

Full-time: 1274 men, 2209 women	**Faculty:** 237; IIA, -$
Part-time: 34 men, 56 women	**Ph.D.s:** 83%
Graduate: 350 men, 341 women	**Student/Faculty:** 15 to 1
Year: semesters, summer session	**Tuition:** $19,130
Application Deadline: open	**Room & Board:** $6450
Freshman Class: n/av	
SAT I or ACT: required	**VERY COMPETITIVE+**

Butler University, founded in 1855, is an independent institution offering programs in liberal arts and sciences, business administration, fine arts, pharmacy, and health sciences. There are 5 undergraduate and 5 graduate schools. In addition to regional accreditation, Butler has baccalaureate program accreditation with AACSB, ACPE, NASM, and NCATE. The 2 libraries contain 303,080 volumes, 181,381 microform items, and 13,948 audiovisual forms/CDs, and subscribe to 2831 periodicals. Computerized library services include the card catalog, interlibrary loans, and database searching. Special learning facilities include a learning resource center, planetarium, TV station, and observatory. The 290-acre campus is in a suburban area 5 miles from downtown Indianapolis. Including residence halls, there are 19 buildings.

Student Life: 58% of undergraduates are from Indiana. Others are from 40 states, 41 foreign countries, and Canada. 86% are from public schools. 91% are white. 57% are Protestant; 28% Catholic; 11% claim no religious affiliation. The average age of freshmen is 18; all undergraduates, 20. 19% do not continue beyond their first year.

Housing: 1500 students can be accommodated in college housing, which includes single-sex and coed dormitories, on-campus apartments, fraternity houses, and sorority houses. In addition, there are special-interest houses. On-campus housing is guaranteed for all 4 years. 62% of students live on campus; of those, 50% remain on campus on weekends. Alcohol is not permitted. All students may keep cars.

Activities: 25% of men belong to 8 national fraternities; 25% of women belong to 8 national sororities. There are 97 groups on campus, including band, cheerleading, choir, chorale, chorus, dance, debate, drama, drill team, ethnic, gay, honors, international, jazz band, literary magazine, marching band, musical theater, newspaper, opera, orchestra, pep band, photography, political, professional, radio and TV, religious, social, social service, student government, symphony, and yearbook. Popular campus events include Geneva Stunts, Spring Sing, and Spring Sports Spectacular.

Sports: There are 10 intercollegiate sports for men and 9 for women, and 23 intramural sports for men and 23 for women. Facilities include a 10,000-seat field house, a 20,000-seat football stadium, tennis courts, indoor and outdoor tracks, a weight-training room, an indoor pool, an aerobics/exercise room, intramural fields, and baseball, softball, and soccer fields.

Disabled Students: 90% of the campus is accessible. Wheelchair ramps, elevators, special parking, specially equipped rest rooms, special class scheduling, and lowered drinking fountains are available.

Services: Counseling and information services are available, as is tutoring in every subject. There is a reader service for the blind. A writer's studio offers assistance in all areas of the writing process.

Campus Safety and Security: Measures include 24-hour foot and vehicle patrol, self-defense education, escort service, and informal discussions. There are pamphlets/posters/films, emergency telephones, and lighted pathways/sidewalks.

Programs of Study: Butler confers B.A., B.S., B.F.A., B.M., B.S.H.S., and B.S.P. degrees. Master's and doctoral degrees are also awarded. Bachelor's degrees are awarded in BIOLOGICAL SCIENCE (biology/biological science), BUSINESS (accounting, banking and finance, international business management, and marketing/retailing/merchandising), COMMUNICATIONS AND THE ARTS (arts administration/management, communications, dance, dramatic arts, English, French, German, Greek, journalism, Latin, music, music business management, music performance, music theory and composition, performing arts, Spanish, speech/debate/rhetoric, and telecommunications), COMPUTER AND PHYSICAL SCIENCE (actuarial science, chemistry, computer science, mathematics, and physics), EDUCATION (elementary, music, and secondary), HEALTH PROFESSIONS (pharmacy, physician's assistant, and speech pathology/audiology), SOCIAL SCIENCE (anthropology, criminal justice, economics, history, international studies, philosophy, political science/government, psychology, religion, and sociology). Pharmacy, chemistry, and biology are the strongest academically. Business, education, and pharmacy are the largest.

Required: The core curriculum includes specific courses in English, speech, computer literacy, phys ed, and interdisciplinary studies, as well as distribution requirements in humanities, fine arts, social science, natural science, and quantitative reasoning. To graduate, students must complete 126 to 166 semester hours with a minimum GPA of 2.0.

Special: Butler offers cross-registration with the 4 other members of the Consortium for Urban Education, co-op programs in business administration, and internships in pharmacy, arts administration, and business programs. A 3-2 degree program in engineering with Purdue University and in forestry with Duke University, extensive study-abroad programs, and work-study programs are available. There are dual majors including French, German, and Spanish combined with business studies, student-designed majors, a general studies degree, pass/fail options, and nondegree study. There are 5 national honor societies and a freshman honors program.

Faculty/Classroom: 64% of faculty are male; 36%, female. 92% teach undergraduates and 75% both teach and do research. No introductory courses are taught by graduate students. The average class size in an introductory lecture is 24; in a laboratory, 18; and in a regular course, 19.

Admissions: 66% of the current freshmen were in the top fifth of their class; 88% were in the top two fifths. There were 12 National Merit finalists and 26 semifinalists. 67 freshmen graduated first in their class.

Requirements: The SAT I or ACT is required. In addition, applicants should be graduates of an accredited secondary school, but Butler will consider talented or gifted students without a diploma. Students should have earned at least 17 academic units, based on 4 years of English, 3 each of math and lab science, 2 each of a foreign language and history/social science, and the rest in electives. An audition is required for dance, music, and theater majors, and an interview is required for radio/TV majors. Butler requires applicants to be in the upper 50% of their class. A GPA of 2.0 is required. AP and CLEP credits are accepted. Important factors in the admissions decision are advanced placement or honor courses, evidence of special talent, and leadership record. Applications are accepted on-line at the school's web site.

Procedure: Freshmen are admitted to all sessions. Entrance exams should be taken during the junior year. There are early admissions and deferred admissions plans. Early Admission I applications should be filed by December 1 and Early Admission II applications by February 1; the deadlines are open for regular appplications. Application fee is $35. Notification is sent on a rolling basis. 2% of all applicants are on a waiting list; 50 were accepted in 2001.

Transfer: 91 transfer students enrolled in 2001-2002. Applicants who have completed more than 12 hours of college work must present transcripts from all previous colleges attended, indicating good standing and a minimum GPA of 2.0, and an official high school transcript showing a posted date of graduation. Those students with fewer than 12 hours must also submit SAT I or ACT scores. Students wishing to transfer into pharmacy or physician assistant programs should contact the Office of Admission for requirements and deadlines. 45 credits of 126 to 166 must be completed at Butler.

Visiting: There are regularly scheduled orientations for prospective students, including a campus tour, faculty visit, and financial aid interview. There are guides for informal visits and visitors may sit in on classes and stay overnight. To schedule a visit, contact the Office of Admission.

Financial Aid: In 2001-2002, 90% of all freshmen and 89% of continuing students received some form of financial aid. 43% of freshmen and 45% of continuing students received need-based aid. The average freshman award was $13,565. Of that total, scholarships or need-based grants averaged $8735 ($18,940 maximum); and loans averaged $4830 ($21,040 maximum). 40% of undergraduates work part time. Average annual earnings from campus work are $1200. The average financial indebtedness of the 2001 graduate was $10,000. Butler is a member of CSS. The FAFSA and the college's own financial statement are required. The fall application deadline is March 1.

International Students: There are 60 international students enrolled. The school actively recruits these students. They must score 550 on the written TOEFL or 213 on the electronic version or complete level 5 at the American Language Academy on Butler's campus.

Computers: The mainframe is a DEC VAX 6610. Ethernet fiber-optic technology connects all Mac and MS/DOS PCs (150 in labs for students) to the mainframe. All students may access the system 24 hours a day. There are no time limits and no fees. It is strongly recommended that all students have a personal computer.

Graduates: In 2001, 660 bachelor's degrees were awarded. The most popular majors were marketing (9%), pharmacy (9%), and elementary education (7%). In an average class, 56% graduate in 4 years, 66% in

5 years, and 67% in 6 years. 300 companies recruited on campus in 2000-2001. Of the 2000 graduating class, 19% were enrolled in graduate school within 6 months of graduation and 74% were employed.

Admissions Contact: Bill Preble, Director of Admission. A video is available. E-mail: *admission@butler.edu* Web: *www.butler.edu*

CALUMET COLLEGE OF ST. JOSEPH B-1
Whiting, IN 46394 **(219) 473-4215**
(877) 700-9100; Fax: (219) 473-4259

Full-time: 460 men and women	**Faculty:** 30; IIB, --$
Part-time: 560 men and women	**Ph.D.s:** 50%
Graduate: none	**Student/Faculty:** 15 to 1
Year: semesters, summer session	**Tuition:** $7500
Application Deadline: open	**Room & Board:** n/app
Freshman Class: n/av	
SAT I or ACT: not required	**LESS COMPETITIVE**

Calumet College of St. Joseph, founded in 1951, is a private, Catholic institution offering commuting students a liberal arts education in a Christian environment. Figures in above capsule are approximate. The library contains 121,143 volumes, 3761 microform items, and 1958 audiovisual forms/CDs, and subscribes to 213 periodicals. Computerized library services include interlibrary loans and database searching. Special learning facilities include a learning resource center and art gallery. The 256-acre campus is in an urban area 15 miles southeast of Chicago in northwest Indiana. There is one building.

Student Life: 70% of undergraduates are from Indiana. Others are from 2 states. 65% are from public schools. 55% are white; 22% African American; 15% Hispanic. Most are Catholic. The average age of freshmen is 21; all undergraduates, 35. 15% do not continue beyond their first year; 58% remain to graduate.

Housing: There are no residence halls. All students commute. Alcohol is not permitted. All students may keep cars.

Activities: There are no fraternities or sororities. There are 15 groups on campus, including drama, ethnic, literary magazine, musical theater, newspaper, photography, professional, social, social service, and student government. Popular campus events include Thanksgiving Ethnicfest and Student Appreciation Week.

Sports: There are 4 intramural sports for men and 4 for women.

Disabled Students: All of the campus is accessible. Wheelchair ramps, elevators, special parking, and specially equipped rest rooms are available.

Services: Counseling and information services are available, as is tutoring in every subject. There is remedial math, reading, and writing.

Campus Safety and Security: Measures include emergency telephones and lighted pathways/sidewalks.

Programs of Study: Cal College confers B.A., B.S., B.S.Ed., and B.S.M.T. degrees. Associate degrees are also awarded. Bachelor's degrees are awarded in BIOLOGICAL SCIENCE (biology/biological science), BUSINESS (accounting and business administration and management), COMMUNICATIONS AND THE ARTS (communications, English, and fine arts), COMPUTER AND PHYSICAL SCIENCE (information sciences and systems), EDUCATION (art, business, elementary, science, secondary, and social science), ENGINEERING AND ENVIRONMENTAL DESIGN (industrial administration/management), HEALTH PROFESSIONS (medical laboratory technology), SOCIAL SCIENCE (addiction studies, criminal justice, history, liberal arts/general studies, social science, social work, sociology, and theological studies). Management, accounting, and criminal justice are the strongest academically. Management, human services, and education are the largest.

Required: All students must complete 64 semester hours of general education courses, including English composition, economics, speech, theology, philosophy, communication and fine arts, science and math, and social and behavioral science. A total of 124 semester hours with a minimum GPA of 2.0 is required to graduate.

Special: The college offers a cooperative 3-1 baccalaureate degree in medical technology with the schools of St. Margaret-Mercy Hospital in Indiana, where students complete their study and a clinical internship. An accelerated degree completion program in organizational management is possible in 13 months for those with 60 college credits. The LEAP program offers credit for life experience. Study abroad, internships, work-study programs, a general studies degree, pass/fail options, and nondegree study are possible.

Faculty/Classroom: 69% of faculty are male; 31%, female. All teach undergraduates. The average class size in an introductory lecture is 25; in a laboratory, 20; and in a regular course, 20.

Requirements: Applicants should have completed 4 years of high school English, 3 to 4 of math, 2 to 3 of science, and 2 of social studies. The GED is accepted. An essay and an interview are recommended. The Vocabulary and Reading Assessment Test is required. A GPA of 2.0 is required. AP and CLEP credits are accepted. Important factors in the admissions decision are geographic diversity, personality/intangible qualities, and parents or siblings attending the school. Applications may be submitted on computer disk via CollegeLink.

Procedure: Freshmen are admitted to all sessions. Entrance exams should be taken by May of the junior year. There are early decision, early admissions, and deferred admissions plans. Application deadlines are open. 10 early decision candidates were accepted for the 2001-2002 class.

Transfer: A 2.0 GPA is required. An interview is recommended. The Vocabulary and Reading Assessment Test is required. 30 credits of 124 must be completed at Cal College.

Visiting: There are regularly scheduled orientations for prospective students. There are guides for informal visits and visitors may sit in on classes. To schedule a visit, contact Kevin B. Gober in Admissions.

Financial Aid: Cal College is a member of CSS. The CSS/Profile or FAFSA and the college's own financial statement are required. The deadline for financial aid application is the first day of classes.

International Students: They must score 600 on the written TOEFL and also take the college's own entrance exam, scoring 700.

Computers: The mainframe is a Prime 2755. All students may access the system Monday through Friday from 8 A.M. to 10 P.M., except during class lab times. There are no time limits.

Graduates: 50 companies recruited on campus in a recent year.

Admissions Contact: Kevin B. Gober, Director of Admissions. Web: *www.ccsj.edu*

DEPAUW UNIVERSITY B-3
Greencastle, IN 46135 **(765) 658-4006**
(800) 447-2495; Fax: (765) 658-4007

Full-time: 949 men, 1229 women	**Faculty:** 208; IIB, +$
Part-time: 20 men, 21 women	**Ph.D.s:** 92%
Graduate: none	**Student/Faculty:** 10 to 1
Year: semesters	**Tuition:** $21,500
Application Deadline: February 1	**Room & Board:** $6500
Freshman Class: 3044 applied, 1591 accepted, 620 enrolled	
SAT I or ACT: required	**HIGHLY COMPETITIVE**

DePauw University, founded in 1837, is a private institution affiliated with the United Methodist Church offering programs in the fields of liberal arts and music. There are 2 undergraduate schools. In addition to regional accreditation, DePauw has baccalaureate program accreditation with NASM and NCATE. The 3 libraries contain 281,928 volumes, 373,687 microform items, and 14,106 audiovisual forms/CDs, and subscribe to 3423 periodicals. Computerized library services include the card catalog, interlibrary loans, and database searching. Special learning facilities include a learning resource center, art gallery, natural history museum, radio station, TV station, observatory, and nature preserve. The 175-acre campus is in a small town 45 miles west of Indianapolis. Including residence halls, there are 55 buildings.

Student Life: 54% of undergraduates are from Indiana. Others are from 44 states and 15 foreign countries. 85% are from public schools. 87% are white. 51% are Protestant; 22% Catholic. The average age of freshmen is 18; all undergraduates, 20. 8% do not continue beyond their first year; 79% remain to graduate.

Housing: 2253 students can be accommodated in college housing, which includes coed dormitories, on-campus apartments, off-campus apartments, fraternity houses, and sorority houses. In addition, there are special-interest houses. On-campus housing is guaranteed for all 4 years. 94% of students live on campus. All students may keep cars.

Activities: 57% of men belong to 12 national fraternities; 54% of women belong to 1 local sorority and 10 national sororities. There are 65 groups on campus, including art, band, cheerleading, chess, choir, chorale, chorus, computers, dance, debate, drama, ethnic, film, gay, honors, international, jazz band, literary magazine, musical theater, newspaper, opera, orchestra, pep band, political, professional, radio and TV, religious, social, social service, student government, symphony, and yearbook. Popular campus events include Little 5, Monon Bell, and Old Gold Day.

Sports: There are 9 intercollegiate sports for men and 10 for women, and 15 intramural sports for men and 13 for women. Facilities include a recreation center, a 4000-seat stadium, baseball, soccer, and field hockey fields, 3 basketball courts, indoor/outdoor tennis courts and tracks, a pool, a fitness center, volleyball and badminton courts, and a 3200-seat indoor gym.

Disabled Students: 85% of the campus is accessible. Wheelchair ramps, elevators, special parking, specially equipped rest rooms, special class scheduling, lowered drinking fountains, and lowered telephones are available.

Services: Counseling and information services are available, as is tutoring in most subjects. There is a reader service for the blind.

Campus Safety and Security: Measures include 24-hour foot and vehicle patrol, escort service, informal discussions, and pamphlets/posters/films. There are emergency telephones and lighted pathways/sidewalks.

Programs of Study: DePauw confers B.A., B.M.A., B.M.E., and B.Mu. degrees. Bachelor's degrees are awarded in BIOLOGICAL SCIENCE (biology/biological science), COMMUNICATIONS AND THE ARTS (art history and appreciation, classical languages, communications, English, English literature, French, German, Greek, Latin, music, music business management, music performance, music theory and composition, romance languages and literature, Spanish, and studio art), COMPUTER AND PHYSICAL SCIENCE (chemistry, computer science, earth science, geology, mathematics, and physics), EDUCATION (elementary and music), ENGINEERING AND ENVIRONMENTAL DESIGN (preengineering), HEALTH PROFESSIONS (medical technology), SOCIAL SCIENCE (anthropology, classical/ancient civilization, East Asian studies, economics, geography, history, interdisciplinary studies, peace studies, philosophy, physical fitness/movement, political science/government, psychology, religion, Russian and Slavic studies, sociology, and women's studies). English, economics, and communications are the largest.

Required: Students must demonstrate competence in oral communications, quantitative reasoning, and writing. Successful completion of 124 semester hours, including 32 to 40 in the major, is required for graduation. In addition, students must fulfill distribution requirements in natural sciences and math, social and behavioral sciences, literature and the arts, historical and philosophical understanding, foreign language, and self-expression. A comprehensive exam, thesis, or seminar is required for each major.

Special: DePauw offers dual majors in any 2 disciplines, student-designed majors, internships for honors programs and winter-term projects, unlimited study-abroad options through cooperative arrangements with other universities, a Washington semester, pass/fail options, and credit by departmental exam. Also available are 3-2 engineering degrees with Case Western Reserve, Columbia, and Washington Universities and a 3-2 nursing program with Rush University Hospital in Chicago. The Media Fellows, Management Fellows, and Science Research Fellows programs offer majors in any discipline, plus a semester-long internship. There are 13 national honor societies, including Phi Beta Kappa, and a freshman honors program.

Faculty/Classroom: 60% of faculty are male; 40%, female. All teach undergraduates. The average class size in an introductory lecture is 20; in a laboratory, 14; and in a regular course, 15.

Admissions: 52% of the 2001-2002 applicants were accepted. The SAT I scores for the 2001-2002 freshman class were: Verbal--6% below 500, 46% between 500 and 599, 37% between 600 and 700, and 11% above 700; Math--7% below 500, 40% between 500 and 599, 43% between 600 and 700, and 10% above 700. The ACT scores were 4% below 21, 18% between 21 and 23, 30% between 24 and 26, 23% between 27 and 28, and 25% above 28. 75% of the current freshmen were in the top fifth of their class; 95% were in the top two fifths. There were 10 National Merit finalists. 18 freshmen graduated first in their class.

Requirements: The SAT I or ACT is required. In addition, graduation from an accredited secondary school or a GED is required for admission. Course distribution must include 4 in English, 3 to 4 each in math, social studies, and science (2 or more with lab), and 2 to 4 in a foreign language. An essay is required, and an interview is strongly recommended. Applicants for the School of Music must audition. AP and CLEP credits are accepted. Important factors in the admissions decision are advanced placement or honor courses, recommendations by school officials, and personality/intangible qualities. Applications are accepted on computer disk or on-line.

Procedure: Freshmen are admitted fall and spring. Entrance exams should be taken as early as possible. There are early decision, early admissions, and deferred admissions plans. Early decision applications should be filed by November 1; regular applications, by February 1 for fall entry and December 1 for spring entry. The fall 2001 application fee was $40. Notification of early decision is sent December 1; regular decision, April 1. 33 early decision candidates were accepted for a recent class. A waiting list is an active part of the admissions procedure.

Transfer: 14 transfer students enrolled in 2001-2002. Applicants must submit either SAT I or ACT scores. High school and college transcripts are required, and a minimum GPA on previous college work of 3.0 is preferred. 60 credits of 124 must be completed at DePauw.

Visiting: There are regularly scheduled orientations for prospective students, consisting of daylong student/parent programs that include campus tours, faculty viewpoints, conversations with students, admissions information, financial aid and career planning sessions, and a meal in a residence hall. There are guides for informal visits and visitors may sit in on classes and stay overnight. To schedule a visit, contact Anna Logan, Admission Program and Visit Coordinator.

Financial Aid: In a recent year, 99% of all freshmen and 96% of continuing students received some form of financial aid. 55% of freshmen and 47% of continuing students received need-based aid. The average freshman award was $19,671. Of that total, scholarships or need-based grants averaged $15,624 ($21,485 maximum); loans averaged $2512 ($3825 maximum); and work contracts averaged $1535 ($1700 maximum). 39% of undergraduates work part time. Average annual earnings from campus work are $749. The average financial indebtedness of a recent year's graduate was $13,218. DePauw is a member of CSS. The CSS/Profile or FAFSA and the college's own financial statement are required. The fall application deadline is February 15.

International Students: There were 29 international students enrolled in a recent year. The school actively recruits these students. They must score 560 on the written TOEFL or 225 on the electronic version and also take the SAT I or the ACT.

Computers: The mainframe is a DEC ALPHA D520 cluster. 130 PCs are available for student use. Locations include the computer center, the library, residence halls, fraternities, sororities, and all academic offices. All public PCs, student rooms, classrooms, and faculty/staff offices are wired for access to the campuswide network and the Internet. Seminars are taught regularly, and all students have a computer account. All students may access the system 24 hours a day. There are no time limits and no fees.

Graduates: In 2001, 526 bachelor's degrees were awarded. The most popular majors were communications (16%), economics (11%), and creative writing (9%). In an average class, 73% graduate in 4 years, 78% in 5 years, and 79% in 6 years. 50 companies recruited on campus in 2000-2001. Of the 2000 graduating class, 21% were enrolled in graduate school within 6 months of graduation and 79% were employed.

Admissions Contact: Madeleine R. Eagon, Vice President for Admission and Financial Aid. A video is available.
E-mail: *admissions@depauw.edu* Web: *http://www.depauw.edu*

EARLHAM COLLEGE

Richmond, IN 47374 — **D-3**
(765) 983-1600
(800) 327-5426; Fax: (765) 983-1560

Full-time: 473 men, 581 women	**Faculty:** 92; IIB, av$
Part-time: 8 men, 16 women	**Ph.D.s:** 97%
Graduate: 26 men, 41 women	**Student/Faculty:** 11 to 1
Year: semesters	**Tuition:** $22,308
Application Deadline: February 15	**Room & Board:** $5138
Freshman Class: 1153 applied, 923 accepted, 266 enrolled	
SAT I Verbal/Math: 630/590	**ACT:** 26 **VERY COMPETITIVE+**

Earlham College, established in 1847 by the Society of Friends, is a private liberal arts college that emphasizes Quaker values. It offers undergraduate programs in humanities, fine arts, social sciences, languages, music, and natural sciences. The 2 libraries contain 392,100 volumes, 235,400 microform items, and 6590 audiovisual forms/CDs, and subscribe to 1660 periodicals. Computerized library services include the card catalog, interlibrary loans, and database searching. Special learning facilities include a learning resource center, art gallery, natural history museum, planetarium, radio station, observatory, herbarium, and greenhouse. The 800-acre campus is in a small town 70 miles east of Indianapolis and 40 miles west of Dayton, Ohio. Including residence halls, there are 57 buildings.

Student Life: 73% of undergraduates are from out of state, mostly the Midwest. Students are from 48 states and 26 foreign countries. 75% are from public schools. 78% are white. 33% are claim no religious affiliation; 23% Protestant; 13% Buddhist, Islamic, and other non-Protestant. The average age of freshmen is 18; all undergraduates, 20. 16% do not continue beyond their first year.

Housing: 968 students can be accommodated in college housing, which includes single-sex and coed dormitories. In addition, there are language houses and special-interest houses, Jewish student and black student cultural centers, on-campus houses, a peace studies house, a Latino and Asian American cultural center, an international cultural center, an interfaith house, and a small working farm. On-campus housing is guaranteed for all 4 years. 84% of students live on campus; of those, 84% remain on campus on weekends. Alcohol is not permitted. All students may keep cars.

Activities: There are no fraternities or sororities. There are 64 groups on campus, including art, cheerleading, choir, chorale, chorus, computers, dance, drama, ethnic, film, gay, international, jazz band, literary magazine, musical theater, newspaper, photography, political, radio and TV, religious, social, social service, student government, symphony, and yearbook. Popular campus events include Reggae Festival, Japanese Spring Festival, and Women's Spring Festival.

Sports: There are 8 intercollegiate sports for men and 9 for women, and 5 intramural sports for men and 5 for women. A fitness center includes cardiovascular equipment and weights, group fitness and dance rooms, a field house with 4 indoor courts for tennis, volleyball, and basketball, 2 racquetball courts, an indoor climbing wall, an indoor running track, a 25-meter pool, a performance gym, and a massage therapist. Outdoor facilities include a natural grass football field, 10 all-weather tennis courts, basketball courts, a trail for cross-country running and skiing, and baseball, softball, soccer, lacrosse, and field hockey fields.

Disabled Students: 90% of the campus is accessible. Wheelchair ramps, elevators, special parking, specially equipped rest rooms, and lowered drinking fountains are available.

Services: Counseling and information services are available, as is tutoring in some subjects, including humanities sciences, languages, some math, and other subjects on request. There is a reader service for the blind.

Campus Safety and Security: Measures include 24-hour foot and vehicle patrol, self-defense education, escort service, and shuttle buses. There are informal discussions, pamphlets/posters/films, and lighted pathways/sidewalks.

Programs of Study: Earlham confers the B.A. degree. Master's degrees are also awarded. Bachelor's degrees are awarded in BIOLOGICAL SCIENCE (biology/biological science), BUSINESS (management science), COMMUNICATIONS AND THE ARTS (art, dramatic arts, English, French, German, music, and Spanish), COMPUTER AND PHYSICAL SCIENCE (chemistry, computer science, geology, geoscience, mathematics, and physics), EDUCATION (education), ENGINEERING AND ENVIRONMENTAL DESIGN (environmental science), SOCIAL SCIENCE (African American studies, anthropology, classical/ancient civilization, economics, history, Japanese studies, Latin American studies, philosophy, political science/government, psychology, religion, and sociology). Natural sciences, psychology, and English are the strongest academically. Biology, psychology, and history are the largest.

Required: To graduate, all students must complete courses in humanities, foreign language, fine arts, the natural sciences, social sciences, religion and/or philosophy, multicultural and intercultural, and phys ed. Students must also maintain a minimum GPA of 2.0 and complete a total of 120 semester hours, including 32 semester hours in the major and at least 36 in upper-level courses. A comprehensive exam and/or thesis is required, depending on the major.

Special: Opportunities are provided for dual majors, co-op programs in education, nursing, business, and architecture, cross-registration with Indiana University East, internships, work-study programs, accelerated degree programs, nondegree study, and student-designed majors. Study abroad is available through 27 foreign and domestic programs. Preprofessional and professional options are offered in law and medicine. There is a 3-2 engineering degree with Case Western Reserve University, Columbia University, University of Rochester, and Rensselaer Polytechnic Institute. There is 1 national honor society, Phi Beta Kappa.

Faculty/Classroom: 62% of faculty are male; 38%, female. All teach undergraduates, and 75% also do research. No introductory courses are taught by graduate students. The average class size in an introductory lecture is 25; in a laboratory, 15; and in a regular course, 14.

Admissions: 80% of the 2001-2002 applicants were accepted. The SAT I scores for the 2001-2002 freshman class were: Verbal--11% below 500, 23% between 500 and 599, 46% between 600 and 700, and 20% above 700; Math--21% below 500, 33% between 500 and 599, 35% between 600 and 700, and 11% above 700. The ACT scores were 18% below 21, 15% between 21 and 23, 26% between 24 and 26, 20% between 27 and 28, and 21% above 28. 55% of the current freshmen were in the top fifth of their class; 79% were in the top two fifths. There were 6 National Merit finalists. 7 freshmen graduated first in their class.

Requirements: The SAT I is required. In addition, in most cases, graduation from an accredited secondary school is required; a GED will be accepted. Home-schooled students are not required to take the GED or have a high school diploma. Students must have completed at least 15 academic credits, including 4 years of English, 3 of math, and 2 each of science, history or social studies, and a foreign language. Students are required to submit an essay and letters of recommendation from a teacher and guidance counselor. An interview is recommended. A GPA of 3.0 is required. AP credits are accepted. Important factors in the admissions decision are advanced placement or honor courses, evidence of special talent, and extracurricular activities record. Applications are accepted online via the Common Application and CollegeNET.

Procedure: Freshmen are admitted fall and spring. Entrance exams should be taken during the spring of the junior year or early fall of the senior year. There are early decision, early admissions, and deferred admissions plans. Early decision applications should be filed by December 1; regular applications, by February 15 for fall entry, and November 15 for spring entry. The fall 2001 application fee was $30. Notification of early decision is sent December 15; regular decision, March 15. 35 early decision candidates were accepted for the 2001-2002 class.

Transfer: 29 transfer students enrolled in 2001-2002. Applicants must take the SAT I or ACT and have a minimum GPA of 2.3 in college course work. An interview is recommended. High school and college transcripts, an essay, and a statement of good standing from the prior institution are required. 60 credits of 120 must be completed at Earlham.

Visiting: There are regularly scheduled orientations for prospective students, including class visitation, an admissions interview, a tour, and special appointments with faculty. There are guides for informal visits and visitors may sit in on classes and stay overnight. To schedule a visit, contact the Admissions Office (Cindy Parshall) at (765) 983-1591.

Financial Aid: In 2001-2002, 80% of all freshmen and 67% of continuing students received some form of financial aid. 61% of all students received need-based aid. The average freshman award was $19,986. Of that total, scholarships or need-based grants averaged $12,692 ($25,068 maximum); loans averaged $3337 ($5125 maximum); and work contracts averaged $4577. 55% of undergraduates work part time. Average annual earnings from campus work are $790. The average financial indebtedness of the 2001 graduate was $14,918. Earlham is a member of CSS. The FAFSA and the college's own financial statement are required. The fall application deadline is March 1.

International Students: There are 52 international students enrolled. The school actively recruits these students. They must score 550 on the written TOEFL and also take the SAT I or the ACT.

Computers: The mainframes are a DEC Micro Vax 3100-80, 2 DEC ALPHA 1000s, 2 Dell Power Edge 2100/200s, and an Apple Power Mac G3. There are 6 public computer labs containing a total of 120 machines. All lab machines give access to the Internet, the World Wide Web, and e-mail services. In addition, students who have their own computers can connect from dorm rooms to the campus LAN. All students may access the system 24 hours per day. There are no time limits and no fees.

Graduates: In 2001, 201 bachelor's degrees were awarded. The most popular majors were psychology (16%), biology (15%), and history (6%). In an average class, 60% graduate in 4 years, 67% in 5 years, and 69% in 6 years. 86 companies recruited on campus in 2000-2001.

Admissions Contact: Jeff Rickey, Dean of Admissions and Financial Aid. A video is available. E-mail: *admission@earlham.edu*
Web: *http://www.earlham.edu*

FRANKLIN COLLEGE OF INDIANA C-4
Franklin, IN 46131 (317) 738-8062
(800) 852-0232; Fax: (317) 738-8274

Full-time: 437 men, 522 women	**Faculty:** 58
Part-time: 28 men, 41 women	**Ph.D.s:** 84%
Graduate: none	**Student/Faculty:** 17 to 1
Year: 4-1-4, summer session	**Tuition:** $14,885
Application Deadline: open	**Room & Board:** $5020
Freshman Class: 1054 applied, 742 accepted, 311 enrolled	
SAT I Verbal/Math: 525/527	**ACT:** 23 **COMPETITIVE**

Franklin College of Indiana, founded in 1834, is a private liberal arts college affiliated with the American Baptist Churches, U.S.A. In addition to regional accreditation, Franklin College has baccalaureate program accreditation with NCATE. The library contains 103,863 volumes, 277,243 microform items, and 6764 audiovisual forms/CDs, and subscribes to 806 periodicals. Computerized library services include the card catalog, interlibrary loans, and database searching. Special learning facilities include a learning resource center, radio station, and TV station. The 74-acre campus is in a small town 20 miles south of Indianapolis. Including residence halls, there are 20 buildings.

Student Life: 93% of undergraduates are from Indiana. Others are from 19 states and 5 foreign countries. 94% are white. 51% are Protestant; 29% claim no religious affiliation; 16% Catholic. The average age of freshmen is 18; all undergraduates, 20. 24% do not continue beyond their first year.

Housing: 685 students can be accommodated in college housing, which includes single-sex and coed dormitories, substance/alcohol-free residence hall living area, and fraternity houses. On-campus housing is available on a first-come, first-served basis and is available on a lottery system for upperclassmen. 73% of students live on campus. All students may keep cars.

Activities: 54% of men belong to 5 national fraternities; 48% of women belong to 4 national sororities. There are 60 groups on campus, including art, cheerleading, choir, chorus, drama, ethnic, film, honors, international, literary magazine, musical theater, newspaper, pep band, photography, political, professional, radio and TV, religious, social, social service, student government, and yearbook. Popular campus events include Grizzly Grand Prix, Annual Kite Carnival, and Greek Week.

Sports: There are 8 intercollegiate sports for men and 8 for women, and 7 intramural sports for men and 6 for women. Facilities include athletic and soccer fields, tennis courts, a phys ed center, and a fitness center.

Disabled Students: All of the campus is accessible. Wheelchair ramps, elevators, special parking, specially equipped rest rooms, special class scheduling, lowered drinking fountains, and specially equipped dormitory rooms are available.

Services: Counseling and information services are available, as is tutoring in most subjects. There is a reader service for the blind, and remedial math, reading, and writing.

Campus Safety and Security: Measures include 24-hour foot and vehicle patrol, escort service, pamphlets/posters/films, and emergency telephones. There are lighted pathways/sidewalks.

Programs of Study: Franklin College confers the B.A. degree. Bachelor's degrees are awarded in BIOLOGICAL SCIENCE (biology/biological science), BUSINESS (accounting, business administration and management, and recreation and leisure services), COMMUNICATIONS AND THE ARTS (dramatic arts, English, French, journalism, and Spanish), COMPUTER AND PHYSICAL SCIENCE (chemistry, computer science, information sciences and systems, mathematics, and physics), EDUCATION (athletic training, elementary, and physical), SOCIAL SCIENCE (American studies, Canadian studies, economics, history, philosophy, political science/government, psychology, religion, and sociology). Biology, business, and education are the strongest academically. Journalism, education, and business are the largest.

Required: Requirements for graduation include 96 hours outside the major, including general education; winter term and related field and activity courses; a minimum of 24 hours in the major; and 136 total credit hours. Each student must maintain a minimum GPA of 2.0 and must pass the Senior Competency Test, which is administered by the department in which the student completes a major.

Special: Cooperative programs in nursing, political science, Canadian studies, forestry, and engineering are available, as are January and summer internships. Study abroad in 16 countries and cross-registration with 7 Indiana universities and colleges and the Indianapolis Museum of Art are permitted. A 3-2 engineering degree with Washington University at St. Louis is possible. There are 10 national honor societies.

Faculty/Classroom: 67% of faculty are male; 33%, female. All teach undergraduates. The average class size in an introductory lecture is 18; in a laboratory, 15; and in a regular course, 18.

Admissions: 70% of the 2001-2002 applicants were accepted. The SAT I scores for the 2001-2002 freshman class were: Verbal--37% below 500, 42% between 500 and 599, 16% between 600 and 700, and 2% above 700; Math--31% below 500, 49% between 500 and 599, 16% between 600 and 700, and 1% above 700. The ACT scores were 27% below 21, 41% between 21 and 23, 27% between 24 and 28, and 4% above 28. 50% of the current freshmen were in the top fifth of their class; 79% were in the top two fifths. There were 4 National Merit semifinalists. 5 freshmen graduated first in their class.

Requirements: The SAT I or ACT is required. In addition, candidates for admission should have completed 4 years of English, 3 to 4 of math, 2 to 3 of science, 2 each of art and music, social studies, and a foreign language, and typing and basic computing skills courses. The GED is accepted, and an essay is required. AP and CLEP credits are accepted. Important factors in the admissions decision are evidence of special talent, leadership record, and advanced placement or honor courses. Applications are accepted on computer disk and on-line via CollegeView, ExPAN, Apply, and the college web site.

Procedure: Freshmen are admitted to all sessions. Entrance exams should be taken in the spring of the junior year or the fall of the senior year. Application deadlines are open. The fall 2001 application fee was $30. Notification is sent on a rolling basis.

Transfer: 69 transfer students enrolled in 2001-2002. Transfer students must have at least a 2.0 cumulative GPA and submit official transcripts from previously attended colleges. 30 credits of 136 must be completed at Franklin College.

Visiting: There are regularly scheduled orientations for prospective students, including academic presentations, admissions and financial presentations, a student life presentation, campus tours, lunch, and opportunities to talk to professors and sit in on a class. There are guides for informal visits and visitors may sit in on classes and stay overnight. To schedule a visit, contact the Admissions Office.

Financial Aid: In 2001-2002, 98% of all freshmen and 95% of continuing students received some form of financial aid. 83% of freshmen and 78% of continuing students received need-based aid. The average freshman award was $12,314. Of that total, scholarships or need-based grants averaged $8533 ($20,100 maximum); loans averaged $3055 ($5475 maximum); and work contracts averaged $686 ($1500 maximum). 26% of undergraduates work part time. Average annual earnings from campus work are $777. The average financial indebtedness of the 2001 graduate was $15,579. The FAFSA is required. The fall application deadline is March 1.

International Students: There are 6 international students enrolled. The school actively recruits these students. They must score 550 on the written TOEFL. Completion of level 109 in an English language service (ELS) center is necessary.

Computers: There are 105 PCs in labs in the computer center, library, teaching and learning centers, and other campus buildings. All students may access the system 8 A.M. to midnight. There are no time limits and no fees.

Graduates: In 2001, 195 bachelor's degrees were awarded. The most popular majors were journalism (16%), elementary education (12%), and physical education (11%). In an average class, 1% graduate in 3 years, 48% in 4 years, 55% in 5 years, and 56% in 6 years. 5 companies recruited on campus in 2000-2001. Of the 2000 graduating class, 15% were enrolled in graduate school within 6 months of graduation and 70% were employed.

Admissions Contact: Alan Hill, VP for Enrollment and Student Affairs. E-mail: *admissions@franklincollege.edu*
Web: *http://www.franklincollege.edu/admissions_index.htm*

GOSHEN COLLEGE

Goshen, IN 46526 — C-1

(574) 574-7535
(800) 348-7422; Fax: (574) 535-7609

Full-time: 334 men, 517 women	**Faculty:** 74; IIB, --$
Part-time: 54 men, 81 women	**Ph.D.s:** 65%
Graduate: none	**Student/Faculty:** 12 to 1
Year: semesters, summer session	**Tuition:** $13,890
Application Deadline: August 15	**Room & Board:** $5060
Freshman Class: 414 applied, 380 accepted, 178 enrolled	
SAT I Verbal/Math: 575/566	**ACT:** 26 **VERY COMPETITIVE+**

Goshen College, founded in 1894, is a private liberal arts institution affiliated with the Mennonite Church. In addition to regional accreditation, Goshen has baccalaureate program accreditation with CSWE, NCATE, and NLN. The library contains 120,000 volumes, 140,000 microform items, and 1500 audiovisual forms/CDs, and subscribes to 900 periodicals. Computerized library services include the card catalog, interlibrary loans, and database searching. Special learning facilities include a learning resource center, art gallery, and radio station. The 135-acre campus is in a small town 120 miles east of Chicago. Including residence halls, there are 24 buildings.

Student Life: 51% of undergraduates are from out of state, mostly the Midwest. Others are from 38 states and 36 foreign countries. 83% are white; 10% foreign nationals. Most are Protestant. The average age of freshmen is 19; all undergraduates, 20. 23% do not continue beyond their first year.

Housing: 696 students can be accommodated in college housing, which includes single-sex and coed dormitories, off-campus apartments, and married-student housing. In addition, there are small-group special-interest houses. On-campus housing is guaranteed for all 4 years. 60% of students live on campus; of those, 85% remain on campus on weekends. Alcohol is not permitted. All students may keep cars.

Activities: There are no fraternities or sororities. There are 26 groups on campus, including chess, choir, chorale, chorus, drama, ethnic, honors, international, jazz band, literary magazine, musical theater, newspaper, opera, orchestra, photography, professional, radio and TV, religious, social, social service, student government, and yearbook. Popular campus events include Ethnic Fair, February Fest, and Fall Fest.

Sports: There are 7 intercollegiate sports for men and 7 for women, and 8 intramural sports for men and 8 for women. Facilities include a fitness center with an indoor track and swimming pool, 3 basketball courts, a soccer field, tennis courts, a sand volleyball court, and a 400-meter, all-weather track.

Disabled Students: All of the campus is accessible. Wheelchair ramps, elevators, special parking, specially equipped rest rooms, special class scheduling, lowered drinking fountains, and lowered telephones are available.

Services: Counseling and information services are available, as is tutoring in every subject. There is a reader service for the blind, and remedial math, reading, and writing.

Campus Safety and Security: Measures include 24-hour foot and vehicle patrol, self-defense education, escort service, and informal discussions. There are pamphlets/posters/films and lighted pathways/sidewalks.

Programs of Study: Goshen confers B.A. and B.S.N degrees. Bachelor's degrees are awarded in BIOLOGICAL SCIENCE (biology/biological science and molecular biology), BUSINESS (accounting and business administration and management), COMMUNICATIONS AND THE ARTS (American Sign Language, communications, dramatic arts, English, French, German, music, and Spanish), COMPUTER AND PHYSICAL SCIENCE (chemistry, computer programming, mathematics, natural sciences, and physics), EDUCATION (art, business, early childhood, elementary, foreign languages, middle school, music, physical, science, secondary, and teaching English as a second/foreign language (TESOL/TEFOL)), ENGINEERING AND ENVIRONMENTAL DESIGN (environmental science and preengineering), HEALTH PROFESSIONS (nursing, predentistry, premedicine, prepharmacy, and preveterinary science), SOCIAL SCIENCE (biblical studies, economics, history, peace studies, psychology, religion, social work, and sociology). Business, elementary education, and social work are the largest.

Required: All students must complete the general education program, including courses in literature and communication, fine arts, Bible, religion, philosophy, natural science, math, social science, and history, and 12 hours of international education in the Study Service Term and 1 hour of fitness. A total of 120 (B.A.) to 124 (B.S.N.) credit hours with a minimum GPA of 2.0 is required to graduate.

Special: A semester abroad internship in the required Study Service Term is possible in China, Indonesia, Germany, Ivory Coast, Costa Rica, and the Dominican Republic. Cross-registration is offered with member colleges of the Northern Indiana Consortium for Education. A Washington semester, dual majors, student-designed majors, and a 3-2 engineering degree with the University of Illinois, Washington University in St. Louis, Pennsylvania State University, and Case Western Reserve University are available. Credit for life experience, pass/fail options, and nondegree study are possible. There is 1 national honor society, a freshman honors program, and 1 departmental honors program.

Faculty/Classroom: 63% of faculty are male; 37%, female. All both teach and do research. The average class size in an introductory lecture is 28; in a laboratory, 14; and in a regular course, 22.

Admissions: 92% of the 2001-2002 applicants were accepted. The SAT I scores for the 2001-2002 freshman class were: Verbal--23% below 500, 34% between 500 and 599, 30% between 600 and 700, and 13% above 700; Math--26% below 500, 37% between 500 and 599, 24% between 600 and 700, and 13% above 700. The ACT scores were 21% below 21, 12% between 21 and 23, 21% between 24 and 26, 16% between 27 and 28, and 30% above 28. 69% of the current freshmen were in the top fifth of their class; 96% were in the top two fifths.

Requirements: The SAT I or ACT is required. In addition, applicants should be graduates of an accredited secondary school or have a GED equivalent, with 4 years of high school English, 2 to 4 years of math, and 2 years each of foreign language, science, history, and social studies. An interview is recommended. Goshen requires applicants to be in the upper 50% of their class. A GPA of 2.0 is required. AP and CLEP credits are accepted. Important factors in the admissions decision are advanced placement or honor courses, recommendations by school officials, and recommendations by alumni. Applications are accepted on-line at the school's web site.

Procedure: Freshmen are admitted to all sessions. Entrance exams should be taken by fall of the senior year. Applications should be filed by August 15 for fall entry, December 15 for winter entry, and April 15 for spring entry. Notification is sent on a rolling basis. The application fee is $25.

Transfer: 44 transfer students enrolled in 2001-2002. A GPA of 2.0 or higher is required on previous college work. 30 credits of 120 must be completed at Goshen.

Visiting: There are regularly scheduled orientations for prospective students, consisting of a campus tour, parents session, talks with professors, financial aid session, visitation, overnight stay in the dorms, student panel, and a campus interview. There are guides for informal visits and visitors may sit in on classes and stay overnight. To schedule a visit, contact the Admissions Office.

Financial Aid: In a recent year, 99% of all freshmen and 97% of continuing students received some form of financial aid. 69% of freshmen and 66% of continuing students received need-based aid. The average freshman award was $12,205. Of that total, scholarships or need-based grants averaged $8906 ($18,585 maximum); loans averaged $4142 ($17,902 maximum); and work contracts averaged $911 ($1520 maximum). 72% of undergraduates work part time. Average annual earnings from campus work are $1095. The average financial indebtedness of the 2001 graduate was $12,550. The CSS/Profile and the college's own financial statement are required. The fall application deadline is March 1.

International Students: There are 97 international students enrolled. The school actively recruits these students. They must score 550 on the written TOEFL or 213 on the electronic version.

Computers: The mainframe is a DEC MicroVAX 3100. There are 2 computer labs available to all students. Each computer lab has 60 computers. All dorm rooms are wired for Ethernet access to the Internet. All students may access the system Center 1: Monday to Thursday, 8 A.M. to midnight, Friday, 8 A.M. to 8 P.M., Saturday 1 P.M. to 5 P.M., Sunday 1 P.M. to midnight; Center 2: 7 A.M. to 5 A.M. daily. There are no time limits and no fees.

Graduates: In 2001, 237 bachelor's degrees were awarded. The most popular majors were business (14%), elementary education (9%), and social work (8%). In an average class, 58% graduate in 5 years, and 63% in 6 years. 28 companies recruited on campus in 2000-2001. Of the 2000 graduating class, 30% were enrolled in graduate school within 6 months of graduation and 70% were employed.

Admissions Contact: Director of Admissions. A video is available.
E-mail: *admissions@goshen.edu* Web: *http://www.goshen.edu*

GRACE COLLEGE — C-2
Winona Lake, IN 46590 — (219) 372-5100, ext. 6114
(800) 54-GRACE; Fax: (219) 372-5114

Full-time: 350 men, 544 women	**Faculty:** 39; IIA, --$
Part-time: 30 men, 48 women	**Ph.D.s:** 63%
Graduate: 19 men, 25 women	**Student/Faculty:** 23 to 1
Year: semesters, summer session	**Tuition:** $11,760
Application Deadline: August 1	**Room & Board:** $5008
Freshman Class: n/av	
SAT I Verbal/Math: 532/579	**ACT:** 23 **COMPETITIVE**

Grace College, founded in 1948, is a Christian liberal arts institution affiliated with the Fellowship of Grace Brethren Churches. There is 1 graduate school. In addition to regional accreditation, Grace has baccalaureate program accreditation with NASM and NCATE. The library contains 142,000 volumes, 26,000 microform items, and 2400 audiovisual forms/CDs, and subscribes to 360 periodicals. Computerized library services include the card catalog, interlibrary loans, and database searching. Special learning facilities include an art gallery. The 150-acre campus is in a rural area 40 miles west of Fort Wayne. Including residence halls, there are 15 buildings.

Student Life: 53% of undergraduates are from out of state, mostly the Midwest. Students are from 37 states, 7 foreign countries, and Canada. 74% are from public schools. 94% are white. Most are Protestant. The average age of freshmen is 18; all undergraduates, 23. 15% do not continue beyond their first year; 80% remain to graduate.

Housing: 748 students can be accommodated in college housing, which includes single-sex dormitories. On-campus housing is available on a first-come, first-served basis and is available on a lottery system for upperclassmen. Priority is given to out-of-town students. 74% of students live on campus; of those, 80% remain on campus on weekends. Alcohol is not permitted. All students may keep cars.

Activities: There are no fraternities or sororities. There are 12 groups on campus, including band, cheerleading, choir, drama, newspaper, orchestra, pep band, religious, social, student government, and yearbook. Popular campus events include Fall Fest, Heart of the Holidays, and VIP Days.

Sports: There are 7 intercollegiate sports for men and 7 for women, and 4 intramural sports for men and 2 for women. Facilities include a gym, soccer fields, tennis courts, and softball and baseball diamonds.

Disabled Students: 80% of the campus is accessible. Wheelchair ramps, elevators, special parking, and specially equipped rest rooms are available.

Services: Counseling and information services are available, as is tutoring in most subjects. There is remedial writing.

Campus Safety and Security: Measures include 24-hour foot and vehicle patrol, escort service, and lighted pathways/sidewalks.

Programs of Study: Grace confers B.A., B.S., B.M., and B.S.W. degrees. Associate and master's degrees are also awarded. Bachelor's degrees are awarded in BIOLOGICAL SCIENCE (biology/biological science), BUSINESS (accounting, business administration and management, and management information systems), COMMUNICATIONS AND THE ARTS (art, communications, English, French, German, graphic design, music, Russian, and Spanish), COMPUTER AND PHYSICAL SCIENCE (mathematics and science), EDUCATION (art, business, elementary, English, foreign languages, mathematics, music, physical, and science), HEALTH PROFESSIONS (predentistry and premedicine), SOCIAL SCIENCE (biblical studies, counseling/psychology, criminal justice, prelaw, psychology, religion, social work, sociology, and youth ministry). Biology, psychology, and business are the strongest academically. Psychology, elementary education, and biblical studies are the largest.

Required: To graduate, students must complete 124 hours, including 36 to 54 in the major, and have a minimum GPA of 2.0. The required core curriculm of 56 hours consists of languages/literature, religion/philosophy, education, social sciences, natural sciences, and a liberal arts seminar.

Special: Students may study abroad in 5 countries. A B.A.-B.S. degree is available in all majors except languages, English, and biblical studies. Dual majors are offered in psychology, sociology, communication, business, accounting, and youth ministries. There is 1 national honor society and a freshman honors program.

Faculty/Classroom: 75% of faculty are male; 25%, female. 99% teach undergraduates and 10% both teach and do research. No introductory courses are taught by graduate students. The average class size in an introductory lecture is 48; in a laboratory, 14; and in a regular course, 17.

Admissions: The SAT I scores for the 2001-2002 freshman class were: Verbal--34% below 500, 44% between 500 and 599, 20% between 600 and 700, and 2% above 700; Math--39% below 500, 43% between 500 and 599, 16% between 600 and 700, and 2% above 700. The ACT scores were 38% below 21, 23% between 21 and 23, 25% between 24 and 26, 10% between 27 and 28, and 4% above 28. 33% of the current freshmen were in the top fifth of their class; 61% were in the top two fifths. 10 freshmen graduated first in their class.

Requirements: The SAT I or ACT is recommended, with a minimum composite score of 950 on the SAT I or 20 on the ACT. Applicants must have completed 15 Carnegie units, including 4 of English, 3 each of math and science, 2 each of a foreign language and social studies, and 1 of history. A GED is accepted. Grace requires applicants to be in the upper 50% of their class. A GPA of 2.3 is required. AP and CLEP credits are accepted. Important factors in the admissions decision are advanced placement or honor courses, leadership record, and personality/intangible qualities. Applications are accepted on computer disk.

Procedure: Freshmen are admitted to all sessions. Entrance exams should be taken in October, December, or February. There is a deferred admissions plan. Applications should be filed by August 1 for fall entry and December 1 for spring entry. The fall 2001 application fee was $20. Notification is sent on a rolling basis.

Transfer: 59 transfer students enrolled in 2001-2002. Transfer applicants should have a minimum 2.0 GPA in addition to fulfilling freshman entrance requirements. 30 credits of 124 must be completed at Grace.

Visiting: There are regularly scheduled orientations for prospective students, including tours, class visits, and meetings with professors. There are guides for informal visits and visitors may sit in on classes and stay overnight. To schedule a visit, contact the Visitors Center at (219) 372-5100, ext. 6003.

Financial Aid: In 2001-2002, 83% of all freshmen and 78% of continuing students received some form of financial aid. 81% of freshmen and 76% of continuing students received need-based aid. The average freshman award was $10,605. Of that total, scholarships or need-based grants averaged $5000 ($5500 maximum); loans averaged $4915 ($4625 maximum); and work contracts averaged $690 ($1300 maximum). 53% of undergraduates work part time. Average annual earnings from campus work are $1300. The average financial indebtedness of the 2001 graduate was $21,100. The FAFSA is required. The fall application deadline is March 1.

International Students: There are 15 international students enrolled. They must score 500 on the written TOEFL and also take the SAT I or the ACT, scoring 950 on the SAT I.

Computers: The mainframe is an IBM AS/400. There are 2 classroom labs along with satellite labs located in major dormitories. 60 PCs are available to students, and all provide access to the Internet. All students may access the system when the classrooms and labs are open. There are no time limits and no fees. It is strongly recommended that all students have a personal computer.

Graduates: In 2001, 161 bachelor's degrees were awarded. The most popular majors were biblical studies (20%), elementary education (20%), and psychology (19%). In an average class, 10% graduate in 3 years, 47% in 4 years, 7% in 5 years, and 6% in 6 years. 45 companies recruited on campus in 2000-2001. Of the 2000 graduating class, 14% were enrolled in graduate school within 6 months of graduation and 84% were employed.

Admissions Contact: Anecia R. Miller, Director of Admissions.
E-mail: *millerar@grace.edu* Web: *http://www.grace.edu*

HANOVER COLLEGE
Hanover, IN 47243 D-5
(812) 866-7022
(800) 213-2178; Fax: (812) 866-7098

Full-time: 509 men, 591 women	**Faculty:** 94; IIB, av$
Part-time: 4 men, 7 women	**Ph.D.s:** 80%
Graduate: none	**Student/Faculty:** 12 to 1
Year: 4-4-1	**Tuition:** $12,370
Application Deadline: March 1	**Room & Board:** $5190
Freshman Class: 1171 applied, 940 accepted, 306 enrolled	
SAT I Verbal/Math: 560/560	**ACT:** 25 **VERY COMPETITIVE**

Hanover College, founded in 1827 and the oldest private college in Indiana, is a liberal arts school affiliated with the United Presbyterian Church. In addition to regional accreditation, Hanover has baccalaureate program accreditation with NCATE. The library contains 213,659 volumes, 44,583 microform items, and 4413 audiovisual forms/CDs, and subscribes to 1015 periodicals. Computerized library services include the card catalog, interlibrary loans, and database searching. Special learning facilities include a learning resource center, art gallery, planetarium, TV station, and a geology museum. The 650-acre campus is in a rural area 45 miles north of Louisville, Kentucky. Including residence halls, there are 35 buildings.

Student Life: 64% of undergraduates are from Indiana. Others are from 36 states, 18 foreign countries, and Canada. 86% are from public schools. 91% are white. 50% are Protestant; 27% claim no religious affiliation; 22% Catholic. The average age of freshmen is 18; all undergraduates, 19. 22% do not continue beyond their first year.

Housing: 1050 students can be accommodated in college housing, which includes single-sex and coed dormitories, on-campus apartments, fraternity houses, and sorority houses. In addition, there are honors houses and special-interest houses, and a multicultural center. On-campus housing is guaranteed for all 4 years. 92% of students live on campus; of those, 85% remain on campus on weekends. Upperclassmen may keep cars.

Activities: 37% of men belong to 4 national fraternities; 47% of women belong to 4 national sororities. There are 38 groups on campus, including band, cheerleading, choir, chorus, computers, dance, debate, drama, ethnic, film, honors, international, jazz band, literary magazine, musical theater, newspaper, orchestra, pep band, photography, political, professional, radio and TV, religious, social, social service, student government, and yearbook. Popular campus events include a community artist series, a foreign film series, and Spring Fling.

Sports: There are 8 intercollegiate sports for men and 9 for women, and 10 intramural sports for men and 10 for women. Facilities include a health and recreation center consisting of a 2000-seat performance gym, a multisports forum, a suspended running track, racquetball and squash courts, a weight room, a training room, and a physiology lab. There also is an outdoor athletic complex consisting of a 5000-seat stadium and performance and practice fields.

Disabled Students: 75% of the campus is accessible. Wheelchair ramps, elevators, special parking, lowered drinking fountains, and lowered telephones are available.

Services: Counseling and information services are available, as is tutoring in most subjects. There is remedial writing.

Campus Safety and Security: Measures include 24-hour foot and vehicle patrol, self-defense education, escort service, and shuttle buses. There are informal discussions, pamphlets/posters/films, emergency telephones, and lighted pathways/sidewalks.

Programs of Study: Hanover confers the B.A. degree. Bachelor's degrees are awarded in BIOLOGICAL SCIENCE (biology/biological science), BUSINESS (business administration and management), COMMUNICATIONS AND THE ARTS (art, art history and appreciation, classics, communications, dramatic arts, English, French, German, music, and Spanish), COMPUTER AND PHYSICAL SCIENCE (chemistry, computer science, geology, mathematics, and physics), EDUCATION (elementary and physical), SOCIAL SCIENCE (anthropology, economics, history, international studies, Latin American studies, medieval studies, philosophy, political science/government, psychology, sociology, and theological studies). Arts and sciences and interdisciplinary studies are the strongest academically. Business administration is the largest.

Required: The required core curriculum includes foreign language, philosophy, phys ed, fine arts, English, 3 physical or life sciences, 2 social sciences, speech, and history. Students must complete 37 units of credit, including 8 to 12 in the major, maintain a GPA of 2.0, pass a comprehensive exam, and participate in a culminating experience in the major.

Special: Internships, study abroad, a Washington semester, and student-designed majors in international studies and Latin American studies are offered. In addition, there is cross-registration with the Spring Term Consortium, the University of Indianapolis, and Alma, Elmira, Northland, Transylvania, Wartburg, and William Woods Colleges. There are 4 national honor societies and 4 departmental honors programs.

Faculty/Classroom: 60% of faculty are male; 40%, female. All teach undergraduates. The average class size in an introductory lecture is 30; in a laboratory, 20; and in a regular course, 17.

Admissions: 80% of the 2001-2002 applicants were accepted. The SAT I scores for the 2001-2002 freshman class were: Verbal--24% below 500, 43% between 500 and 599, 29% between 600 and 700, and 4% above 700; Math--22% below 500, 41% between 500 and 599, 33% between 600 and 700, and 4% above 700. The ACT scores were 24% below 21, 18% between 21 and 23, 21% between 24 and 26, 14% between 27 and 28, and 23% above 28. 51% of the current freshmen were in the top fifth of their class; 87% were in the top two fifths. 18 freshmen graduated first in their class.

Requirements: The SAT I or ACT is required. Admission is competitive, based on the applicant pool. The college requires 16 academic credits, including 4 years of English and 2 each of a foreign language, math, science, and either history or social studies. The GED is accepted. The college also requires a foreign language achievement test as well as an essay; an interview is recommended. AP credits are accepted. Important factors in the admissions decision are recommendations by school officials, advanced placement or honor courses, and extracurricular activities record. Applications may be submitted on computer disk.

Procedure: Freshmen are admitted fall and winter. Entrance exams should be taken late in the spring of the junior year. There is a deferred admissions plan. Early decision applications should be filed by mid-December 1; regular applications, by March 1 for fall entry, along with a $25 fee. Notification of early decision is sent December ; regular decision, on a rolling basis, after January 20. 12% of all applicants are on a waiting list; 53 were accepted in 2001.

Transfer: 24 transfer students enrolled in 2001-2002. Transfer students must submit transcripts from all colleges attended and must have performed successfully. SAT I or ACT scores and high school record may also be taken into consideration. 17 credits of 37 must be completed at Hanover.

Visiting: There are regularly scheduled orientations for prospective students. There are guides for informal visits and visitors may sit in on classes and stay overnight. To schedule a visit, contact the Office of Admissions.

Financial Aid: In 2001-2002, 51% of all freshmen and 53% of continuing students received some form of financial aid. 50% of freshmen and 49% of continuing students received need-based aid. The average freshman award was $9297. Of that total, scholarships or need-based grants averaged $7719 ($17,560 maximum) and loans averaged $2532 ($2625 maximum). 33% of undergraduates work part time. Average annual earnings from campus work are $825. The average financial indebtedness of the 2001 graduate was $11,735. The FAFSA is required. The fall application deadline is March 1.

International Students: There are 36 international students enrolled. The school actively recruits these students. They must score 550 on the written TOEFL or 213 on the electronic version and also take the SAT I or the ACT.

Computers: The mainframe is a DEC ALPHA Server 2100. Mac and PC networks are available. Students may access the system in computer labs and through ports located in every dorm room. All students may access the system in computer labs, 8 A.M. to 11 P.M. Monday through Thursday, 8 A.M. to 5 P.M. Friday, 8 A.M. to 5 P.M. Saturday, and 8 A.M. to 11 P.M. Sunday. There are no time limits and no fees.

Graduates: In 2001, 232 bachelor's degrees were awarded. The most popular majors were business administration (19%), elemantary education (9%), and communication (7%). In an average class, 65% graduate in 4 years, 67% in 5 years, and 68% in 6 years. 49 companies recruited on campus in 2000-2001. Of the 2000 graduating class, 32% were enrolled in graduate school within 6 months of graduation and 66% were employed.

Admissions Contact: Kenneth P. Moyer, Dean of Admissions. A video is available. E-mail: *admissions@hanover.edu* Web: *www.hanover.edu*

HUNTINGTON COLLEGE D-2
Huntington, IN 46750 (219) 359-4000
(800) 642-6493; Fax: (219) 358-3699

Full-time: 285 men, 470 women	**Faculty:** 51; IIB, -$
Part-time: 35 men, 40 women	**Ph.D.s:** 82%
Graduate: 45 men, 5 women	**Student/Faculty:** 15 to 1
Year: 4-1-4, summer session	**Tuition:** $15,480
Application Deadline: August 1	**Room & Board:** n/app
Freshman Class: 677 applied, 640 accepted, 87 enrolled	
SAT I or ACT: required	**LESS COMPETITIVE**

Huntington College, founded in 1897, is a private Christian liberal arts college affiliated with the Church of the United Brethren in Christ. Figures in above capsule are approximate. In addition to regional accreditation, Huntington has baccalaureate program accreditation with NCATE. The library contains 144,006 volumes, 4177 microform items, and 3661 audiovisual forms/CDs, and subscribes to 487 periodicals. Computerized library services include interlibrary loans and database searching. Special learning facilities include a learning resource center, art gallery, radio station, TV station, a writing center, and an arboretum. The 170-acre campus is in a small town 20 miles southwest of Fort Wayne. Including residence halls, there are 25 buildings.

Student Life: 60% of undergraduates are from Indiana. Others are from 30 states, 10 foreign countries, and Canada. 85% are from public schools. 98% are white. Most are Protestant. The average age of freshmen is 18; all undergraduates, 20. 21% do not continue beyond their first year; 65% remain to graduate.

Housing: 499 students can be accommodated in college housing, which includes single-sex dormitories, on-campus apartments, and married-student housing. On-campus housing is guaranteed for all 4 years. 72% of students live on campus; of those, 60% remain on campus on weekends. Alcohol is not permitted. All students may keep cars.

Activities: There are no fraternities or sororities. There are 30 groups on campus, including art, band, cheerleading, choir, chorale, chorus, computers, drama, ethnic, film, honors, international, jazz band, literary magazine, musical theater, newspaper, opera, orchestra, pep band, photography, professional, radio and TV, religious, social, social service, student government, symphony, and yearbook. Popular campus events include African American Week, the artist-lecture series, and chapel series.

Sports: There are 7 intercollegiate sports for men and 6 for women, and 7 intramural sports for men and 6 for women. Facilities include a field house with an indoor running track, 3 basketball courts, indoor and outdoor tennis courts, a swimming pool, softball and baseball diamonds, an outdoor track, soccer and intramural fields, and rollerblading.

Disabled Students: 90% of the campus is accessible. Wheelchair ramps, elevators, special parking, specially equipped rest rooms, and lowered drinking fountains are available.

Services: Counseling and information services are available, as is tutoring in most subjects, including English and math. There is a reader service for the blind, and remedial math, reading, and writing.

Campus Safety and Security: Measures include 24-hour foot and vehicle patrol and lighted pathways/sidewalks.

Programs of Study: Huntington confers B.A., B.S., and B.Mus. degrees. Associate and master's degrees are also awarded. Bachelor's degrees are awarded in BIOLOGICAL SCIENCE (biology/biological science), BUSINESS (business administration and management and organizational behavior), COMMUNICATIONS AND THE ARTS (art, communications, English, and music performance), COMPUTER AND PHYSICAL SCIENCE (chemistry, information sciences and systems, and mathematics), EDUCATION (art, education, elementary, English, mathematics, music, physical, science, and social studies), HEALTH PROFESSIONS (medical laboratory technology and premedicine), SOCIAL SCIENCE (biblical studies, history, ministries, parks and recreation management, philosophy, prelaw, psychology, sociology, and youth ministry). Education, youth ministries, and theater are the strongest academically. Business and elementary education are the largest.

Required: Students must complete a minimum of 128 credit hours and maintain a GPA of 2.0 overall and in the major. Students must pass an English competency exam, complete a program in general education, and take 36 hours in upper-division courses numbered 300 or above, 3 hours of computers, 2 hours of phys ed, and 3 January term courses in at least 2 departments.

Special: Various companies in the area offer internships, and a work-study program is available. Students may study abroad in England, Costa Rica, Jamaica, and Israel. A Washington semester, a Hollywood semester, dual majors, correspondence courses with other schools, an accelerated degree program in organizational management, and pass/fail options are available. There is 1 national honor society, including Phi Beta Kappa, and a freshman honors program.

Faculty/Classroom: 67% of faculty are male; 33%, female. All teach undergraduates, 30% do research, and 30% do both. No introductory courses are taught by graduate students. The average class size in an introductory lecture is 35; in a laboratory, 15; and in a regular course, 25.

Admissions: 95% of the 2001-2002 applicants were accepted. There was 1 National Merit finalist and 3 semifinalists. 16 freshmen graduated first in their class in a recent year.

Requirements: The SAT I or ACT is required. In addition, secondary school courses should include 4 years of English, 3 of college-preparatory math, and 3 of social studies, including 1 each of American and world history. Huntington requires applicants to be in the upper 50% of their class. A GPA of 2.3 is required. AP and CLEP credits are accepted. Important factors in the admissions decision are recommendations by school officials, recommendations by alumni, and personality/intangible qualities.

Procedure: Freshmen are admitted to all sessions. Entrance exams should be taken before or during the fall semester of the senior year. There are early admissions and deferred admissions plans. Applications should be filed by August 1 for fall entry, along with a $20 fee. Notification is sent on a rolling basis.

Transfer: 51 transfer students enrolled in 2001-2002. Transfer applicants should be in good standing at the college previously attended and have maintained a GPA of 2.0. Courses with a grade of C or better transfer. All transcripts and an essay are required. 30 credits of 128 must be completed at Huntington.

Visiting: There are regularly scheduled orientations for prospective students, available on 3 days notice. There are guides for informal visits and visitors may sit in on classes and stay overnight. To schedule a visit, contact Carlene Peters.

Financial Aid: The average freshman award in a recent year was $9000. Of that total, scholarships or need-based grants averaged $6000 ($18,330 maximum); loans averaged $2400 ($5625 maximum); and work contracts averaged $800 ($1800 maximum). 45% of undergraduates work part time. Average annual earnings from campus work are $800. The average financial indebtedness of a recent graduate was $23,000. The FAFSA and the college's own financial statement are required. Check with the school for current deadlines.

International Students: There are 12 international students enrolled. They must score 525 on the written TOEFL.

Computers: There are 150 IBM and Macs in classroom buildings. Internet access is available, with an on-campus network. All students may access the system The mainframe computer system may be used from 9 A.M. to 11 P.M. Monday through Thursday, 9 A.M. to 5 P.M. Friday, and 9 A.M. to 2 P.M. Saturday. There are no time limits and no fees. It is strongly recommended that all students have a personal computer.

Graduates: In an average class, 2% graduate in 3 years, and 55% in 4 years. 30 companies recruited on campus in a recent year.

Admissions Contact: Jeff Berggren, Dean of Enrollment. A video is available. E-mail: *admissions@huntington.edu*
Web: *norm.huntington.edu*

INDIANA INSTITUTE OF TECHNOLOGY D-2
Fort Wayne, IN 46803-1297 (219) 422-5561, ext. 2251
(800) 937-2448; Fax: (219) 422-7696

Full-time: 587 men, 565 women	**Faculty:** 41
Part-time: 539 men, 779 women	**Ph.D.s:** 50%
Graduate: 162 men, 118 women	**Student/Faculty:** 27 to 1
Year: semesters, summer session	**Tuition:** $13,560
Application Deadline: open	**Room & Board:** $5246
Freshman Class: 1923 applied, 1257 accepted, 225 enrolled	
SAT I Verbal/Math: 455/478	**ACT:** 21 **COMPETITIVE**

Indiana Institute of Technology, established in 1930, is a private institution offering degrees primarily in business, engineering, and computer science. There are 2 undergraduate schools. In addition to regional accreditation, Indiana Tech has baccalaureate program accreditation with ABET. The library contains 33,000 volumes, 1000 microform items, and 150 audiovisual forms/CDs, and subscribes to 160 periodicals. Computerized library services include the card catalog, interlibrary loans, and database searching. Special learning facilities include a learning resource center. The 25-acre campus is in an urban area 150 miles east of Chicago. Including residence halls, there are 10 buildings.

Student Life: 84% of undergraduates are from Indiana. Others are from 36 states and 11 foreign countries. 95% are from public schools. 68% are white; 22% African American. The average age of freshmen is 18; all undergraduates, 26. 30% do not continue beyond their first year; 40% remain to graduate.

Housing: 270 students can be accommodated in college housing, which includes coed dormitories and fraternity houses. On-campus housing is guaranteed for the freshman year only and is available on a first-come, first-served basis. Priority is given to out-of-town students. 60% of students commute. Alcohol is not permitted. All students may keep cars.

Activities: 15% of men belong to 3 national fraternities; 5% of women belong to 1 local sorority. There are 20 groups on campus, including cheerleading, computers, dance, ethnic, honors, international, newspaper, pep band, professional, religious, social, social service, and student government.

Sports: There are 3 intercollegiate sports for men and 3 for women, and 6 intramural sports for men and 6 for women. Facilities include basketball, badminton, and volleyball courts, a weight room, and an indoor field house for soccer, softball, and baseball.

Disabled Students: 25% of the campus is accessible. Wheelchair ramps, elevators, special parking, specially equipped rest rooms, lowered drinking fountains, and lowered telephones are available.

Services: Counseling and information services are available, as is tutoring in most subjects. There is remedial math, reading, and writing.

Campus Safety and Security: Measures include 24-hour foot and vehicle patrol and lighted pathways/sidewalks.

Programs of Study: Indiana Tech confers the B.S. degree. Associate and master's degrees are also awarded. Bachelor's degrees are awarded in BUSINESS (accounting and business administration and management), COMPUTER AND PHYSICAL SCIENCE (computer programming, computer science, and information sciences and systems), ENGINEERING AND ENVIRONMENTAL DESIGN (civil engineering, computer engineering, electrical/electronics engineering, industrial engineering, manufacturing engineering, and mechanical engineering), HEALTH PROFESSIONS (recreation therapy), SOCIAL SCIENCE (human services and parks and recreation management). Engineering and computer science are the strongest academically. Business administration is the largest.

Required: To graduate, students must complete a minimum of 120 credit hours, including at least 35 in the major, with a 2.0 minimum GPA. General education requirements include at least 18 hours in social science/humanities and 9 in English.

Special: The school offers co-op programs in business administration and computer studies, internships, work-study programs, and accelerated degree programs in business administration and human services. Credit for life experience is offered through the Extended Studies Program. Dual majors, nondegree study, and pass/fail options are available. There is 1 national honor society.

Faculty/Classroom: 71% of faculty are male; 29%, female. All teach undergraduates. No introductory courses are taught by graduate students. The average class size in an introductory lecture is 30; in a laboratory, 22; and in a regular course, 21.

Admissions: 65% of the 2001-2002 applicants were accepted. 17% of the current freshmen were in the top fifth of their class; 36% were in the top two fifths. 2 freshmen graduated first in their class.

Requirements: The SAT I or ACT is required. In addition, applicants must be graduates of an accredited secondary school. The GED is accepted. At least 13 academic credits are required, including 4 to 6 units of social studies, 4 units of English, 3 to 6 units of math, and 2 units of a lab science. An interview is recommended. A GPA of 2.0 is required. AP and CLEP credits are accepted. Important factors in the admissions decision are leadership record, parents or siblings attending the school, and recommendations by alumni. Applications are accepted on-line at the school's web site.

Procedure: Freshmen are admitted to all sessions. Entrance exams should be taken by January of the senior year. There are early decision, early admissions, and deferred admissions plans. Early decision applications should be filed by October 1; deadlines are open for regular applications. Application fee is $50. Notification of early decision is sent October 15; regular decision, within 2 weeks of receipt of the completed application. 42 early decision candidates were accepted for the 2001-2002 class.

Transfer: 56 transfer students enrolled in 2001-2002. Applicants must be in good standing and have a minimum GPA of 2.0. The SAT I is recommended. 30 credits of 120 must be completed at Indiana Tech.

Visiting: There are regularly scheduled orientations for prospective students, including a campus tour, classroom visits, and meetings with financial aid personnel, coaches, and current students. There are guides for informal visits and visitors may sit in on classes. To schedule a visit, contact Thomas R. Filus at (800) 937-2448, ext. 2208.

Financial Aid: In 2001-2002, 92% of all freshmen and 95% of continuing students received some form of financial aid. 88% of freshmen and 89% of continuing students received need-based aid. The average freshman award was $12,200. Of that total, scholarships or need-based grants averaged $7800; loans averaged $6272; and work contracts averaged $1550. 34% of undergraduates work part time. Average annual earnings from campus work are $1600. The average financial indebtedness of the 2001 graduate was $18,500. Indiana Tech is a member of CSS. The FAFSA and the college's own financial statement are required. The fall application deadline is March 1.

International Students: There are 25 international students enrolled. The school actively recruits these students. They must score 500 on the written TOEFL and take the college's own test. They must also take the SAT I or the ACT, scoring 700 on the SAT I.

Computers: The mainframes are several Windows NT servers. All students have an e-mail account and access to the Internet and various servers via the 75 Macs and PCs in the library and labs. All students may access the system Monday through Friday, 8 A.M. to 10 P.M. There are no time limits and no fees. All students are required to have personal computers.

Graduates: In 2001, 446 bachelor's degrees were awarded. The most popular majors were business (92%), engineering (5%), and accounting (1%). In an average class, 1% graduate in 3 years, 25% in 4 years, 30% in 5 years, and 35% in 6 years. 2 companies recruited on campus in 2000-2001. Of the 2000 graduating class, 3% were enrolled in graduate school within 6 months of graduation and 90% were employed.

Admissions Contact: Thomas R. Filus, Director of Admissions. A video is available. E-mail: *filus@indtech.edu* Web: *http://www.indtech.edu*

INDIANA STATE UNIVERSITY

B-4

Terre Haute, IN 47809

(812) 237-2121
(800) 742-0891; Fax: (812) 237-8023

Full-time: 3990 men, 4406 women	**Faculty:** I, --$
Part-time: 597 men, 741 women	**Ph.D.s:** n/av
Graduate: 692 men, 895 women	**Student/Faculty:** n/av
Year: semesters, summer session	**Tuition:** $3672 ($9166)
Application Deadline: August 1	**Room & Board:** $4789
Freshman Class: 5555 applied, 4790 accepted, 2211 enrolled	
SAT I Verbal/Math: 460/460	**ACT:** 19 **LESS COMPETITIVE**

Indiana State University, founded in 1865, is a publicly supported institution offering undergraduate and graduate study in liberal arts and sciences, business, health, phys ed and recreation, education, nursing, and technology. There are 6 undergraduate schools and 1 graduate school. In addition to regional accreditation, ISU has baccalaureate program accreditation with AACSB, ADA, AHEA, CAHEA, NASAD, NASM, NCATE, NLN, and NRPA. The 3 libraries contain 800,000 volumes, 850,000 microform items, and 25,000 audiovisual forms/CDs, and subscribe to 5000 periodicals. Computerized library services include the card catalog, interlibrary loans, and database searching. Special learning facilities include a learning resource center, art gallery, planetarium, radio station, TV station, and African American cultural center. The 92-acre campus is in an urban area 75 miles west of Indianapolis. Including residence halls, there are 55 buildings.

Student Life: 91% of undergraduates are from Indiana. Others are from 49 states, 77 foreign countries, and Canada. 95% are from public schools. 82% are white; 10% African American. The average age of freshmen is 19; all undergraduates, 23. 30% do not continue beyond their first year; 40% remain to graduate.

Housing: 3905 students can be accommodated in college housing, which includes single-sex and coed dormitories, married-student housing, special freshman dorms, fraternity houses, and sorority houses. In addition, there are honors houses and special-interest houses. On-campus housing is guaranteed for all 4 years. 63% of students commute. Alcohol is not permitted. All students may keep cars.

Activities: 18% of men belong to 21 national fraternities; 11% of women belong to 13 national sororities. There are 200 groups on campus, including art, band, cheerleading, choir, chorale, chorus, computers, drama, drill team, ethnic, film, gay, honors, international, jazz band, marching band, musical theater, newspaper, opera, orchestra, pep band, political, professional, radio and TV, religious, social, social service, student government, symphony, and yearbook. Popular campus events include a contemporary music festival, Theaterfest, and Black History Month.

Sports: There are 7 intercollegiate sports for men and 7 for women, and 27 intramural sports for men and 25 for women. Facilities include a 20,000-seat football stadium, a 10,000-seat basketball arena, 2 softball diamonds, a baseball field, 2 indoor and outdoor tracks, 2 pools, indoor and outdoor basketball and tennis courts, racquetball, sand volleyball, and volleyball courts, a physical fitness center with weight training facilities, and 3 fitness and wellness facilities located in 2 residence halls and the student union.

Disabled Students: 98% of the campus is accessible. Wheelchair ramps, elevators, special parking, specially equipped rest rooms, special class scheduling, lowered drinking fountains, lowered telephones, and special dining hall facilities are available.

Services: Counseling and information services are available, as is tutoring in most subjects. There is a reader service for the blind. In addition, there is a learning skills center, an academic advisement center, a counseling center, student support services, a math lab, and a writing lab.

Campus Safety and Security: Measures include 24-hour foot and vehicle patrol, self-defense education, escort service, and informal discussions. There are pamphlets/posters/films, emergency telephones, lighted pathways/sidewalks, and bicycle and car registration.

Programs of Study: ISU confers B.A., B.S., B.F.A., B.M., B.M.E., and B.S.W. degrees. Associate, master's, and doctoral degrees are also awarded. Bachelor's degrees are awarded in BIOLOGICAL SCIENCE (biology/biological science), BUSINESS (accounting, banking and finance, business administration and management, hotel/motel and restaurant management, insurance, management information systems, marketing and distribution, marketing/retailing/merchandising, office supervision and management, recreation and leisure services, and sports management), COMMUNICATIONS AND THE ARTS (art history and appreciation, broadcasting, communications, dramatic arts, English, film arts, fine arts, French, German, journalism, Latin, music, Russian, Spanish, and studio art), COMPUTER AND PHYSICAL SCIENCE (chemistry, computer science, geology, mathematics, and physics), EDUCATION (art, business, early childhood, educational media, elementary, foreign languages, health, home economics, industrial arts, middle school, music, physical, science, secondary, social studies, and special), ENGINEERING AND ENVIRONMENTAL DESIGN (aeronautical technology, airline piloting and navigation, computer technology, construction technology, electrical/electronics engineering technology, industrial engineering technology, interior design, manufacturing technology, mechanical engineering technology, and preengineering), HEALTH PROFESSIONS (environmental health science, medical laboratory technology, nursing, predentistry, premedicine, prepharmacy, preveterinary science, and speech pathology/audiology), SOCIAL SCIENCE (African American studies, anthropology, child care/child and family studies, criminology, dietetics, economics, food science, geography, history, home economics, interdisciplinary studies, liberal arts/general studies, parks and recreation management, philosophy, political science/government, prelaw, psychology, religion, safety management, social work, sociology, textiles and clothing, and urban studies). Safety management, criminology, and business are the strongest academically. Criminology, communication, and elementary education are the largest.

Required: All students must complete a minimum of 47 credit hours in the general education program. The program requires 11 to 17 credit hours in basic studies, which includes English composition, communications, math, and phys ed, and 36 hours in liberal studies courses. A minimum GPA of 2.0 and a total of 124 credit hours are required for graduation. In addition, all students must have a distribution of hours in upper-division courses.

Special: The school has cross-registration with the Rose-Hulman Institute of Technology, Saint Mary-of-the-Woods College, and Ivy Tech State College. Internships are available in athletic training, criminology, environmental health, political science, safety management, and sports studies. There is a co-op program, and summer and winter work-study is available. The school offers a general studies degree, credit for life experience, nondegree study, and a 3-2 engineering degree with Purdue University. There is a freshman honors program.

Faculty/Classroom: 90% of faculty members teach undergraduates and 10% both teach and do research. Graduate students teach 5% of introductory courses.

Admissions: 86% of the 2001-2002 applicants were accepted. The SAT I scores for the 2001-2002 freshman class were: Verbal--65% below 500, 27% between 500 and 599, 7% between 600 and 700, and 1% above 700; Math--63% below 500, 29% between 500 and 599, 7% between 600 and 700, and 1% above 700. The ACT scores were 63% below 21, 21% between 21 and 23, 10% between 24 and 26, 3% between 27 and 28, and 2% above 28. 19% of the current freshmen were in the top fifth of their class; 42% were in the top two fifths. 5 freshmen graduated first in their class.

Requirements: The SAT I or ACT is required. In addition, the applicant must be a graduate of an accredited secondary school. The GED is accepted. An essay is not required. Applicants are reviewed based on a combination of class rank, grade point average, strength of curriculum, academic progress, and standardized test scores. Those students who rank in the top 50% of their class are routinely admitted, whereas those in the bottom 50% of their class are reviewed on an individual basis. Routine admission does not guarantee admission to specific majors. A GPA of 2.0 is required. AP and CLEP credits are accepted. Important factors in the admissions decision are advanced placement or honor courses, leadership record, and extracurricular activities record. Applications are available on-line at the school's web site.

Procedure: Freshmen are admitted to all sessions. Entrance exams should be taken before January 1. There is a deferred admissions plan. Applications should be filed by August 1 for fall entry, December 1 for spring entry, and May 1 for summer entry. The fall 2001 application fee was $25. Notification is sent on a rolling basis.

Transfer: 714 transfer students enrolled in 2001-2002. Transfer students must have a minimum GPA of 2.0. 30 credits of 124 must be completed at ISU.

Visiting: There are regularly scheduled orientations for prospective students, consisting of Sycamore Preview Days, which include campus tours, opportunities to meet with academic advisers in the majors students are considering, and formal sessions with representatives from financial aid and the career center. There are guides for informal visits and visitors may sit in on classes and stay overnight. To schedule a visit, contact the Admissions Office.

Financial Aid: The FAFSA and the college's own financial statement are required. The fall application deadline is March 1.

International Students: There are 182 international students enrolled. The school actively recruits these students. They must score 500 on the written TOEFL.

Computers: The mainframes are IBM 4381 Models 23 and 13 and a DEC VAX 8350. Students have 24-hour access to terminals located at the central computer center, most academic buildings, and residence halls. Students may use the mainframe to access university software. Residence hall rooms are wired for students to use their own computers. All students may access the system. There are no time limits and no fees.

Graduates: In an average class, 4% graduate in 3 years, 22% in 4 years, 35% in 5 years, and 36% in 6 years.

Admissions Contact: Ron Brown, Director. A video is available.
E-mail: *admissions@indstate.edu*
Web: *http://web.indstate.edu/admissions/*

INDIANA UNIVERSITY SYSTEM

The Indiana University System, established in 1820, is a public system governed by a board of trustees. The chief administrator is the president. The primary goals of the system are research, graduate education, and economical growth and access to education. Total enrollment of all 8 campuses generally exceeds 93,000, with some 4000 faculty members. There are 313 baccalaureate, 207 master's, and 108 doctoral programs offered within the system. 4-year campuses are located in Bloomington, Kokomo, South Bend, Gary, New Albany, and Richmond. The Indianapolis and Fort Wayne campuses are operated jointly with Purdue University. Profiles of the 6 campuses are included in this section.

INDIANA UNIVERSITY BLOOMINGTON — C-4

Bloomington, IN 47405-1106 — **(812) 855-0661** — **Fax: (812) 855-5102**

Full-time: 13,093 men, 14,786 women	**Faculty:** 1655; I, -$
Part-time: 1075 men, 1203 women	**Ph.D.s:** 87%
Graduate: 3383 men, 3525 women	**Student/Faculty:** 17 to 1
Year: semesters, summer session	**Tuition:** $4734 ($14,469)
Application Deadline: February 1	**Room & Board:** $5978
Freshman Class: 20,228 applied, 16,777 accepted, 6815 enrolled	
SAT I Verbal/Math: 542/554	**ACT:** 24 **COMPETITIVE+**

Indiana University Bloomington, founded in 1820, is a comprehensive institution that is part of the Indiana University system. The university offers undergraduate programs in arts and sciences, allied health sciences, business, dentistry, education, health, physical education, recreation, journalism, music, nursing, optometry, public and environmental affairs, social work and informatics. There are 9 undergraduate and 9 graduate schools. In addition to regional accreditation, IU has baccalaureate program accreditation with AACSB, ACBSP, ACEJMC, ADA, APTA, ASLA, CAHEA, CSWE, FIDER, NASAD, NASM, NCATE, and NLN. The 22 libraries contain 6,384,711 volumes, 4,520,143 microform items, and 545,061 audiovisual forms/CDs, and subscribe to 64,027 periodicals. Computerized library services include the card catalog, interlibrary loans, and database searching. Special learning facilities include a learning resource center, art gallery, natural history museum, radio station, TV station, observatory, arboretum, museum of world cultures, garden and nature center, musical arts center, and more than 70 research centers. The 1878-acre campus is in a small town 50 miles southwest of Indianapolis. Including residence halls, there are 489 buildings.

Student Life: 72% of undergraduates are from Indiana. Others are from 49 states, 135 foreign countries, and Canada. 86% are white. The average age of freshmen is 19; all undergraduates, 21. 13% do not continue beyond their first year.

Housing: 12,000 students can be accommodated in college housing, which includes single-sex and coed dormitories, off-campus apartments, and married-student housing. In addition, there are honors houses, language houses, and special-interest houses, living-learning centers, an international center, a center for women, a wellness center, freshmen interest groups (FIG), and thematic communities. On-campus housing is guaranteed for all 4 years. Alcohol is not permitted. All students may keep cars.

Activities: 16% of men belong to fraternities; 17% of women belong to sororities. There are more than 400 groups on campus, including art, band, cheerleading, chess, choir, chorale, chorus, computers, dance, debate, drama, drill team, ethnic, film, gay, honors, international, jazz band, literary magazine, marching band, musical theater, newspaper, opera, orchestra, pep band, photography, political, professional, radio and TV, religious, social, social service, student government, symphony, and yearbook. Popular campus events include Little 500 and Founder's Day.

Sports: There are 11 intercollegiate sports for men and 13 for women, and 29 intramural sports for men and 28 for women. Facilities include

a 52,000-seat football stadium, an 18,000-seat soccer/bicycle stadium, an 18,000-seat indoor gym, a 2,300-seat auditorium, an assembly hall, indoor/outdoor swimming pools, a tennis pavilion, an indoor practice facility, a golf driving range, and a student recreation and aquatics center.

Disabled Students: 95% of the campus is accessible. Wheelchair ramps, elevators, special parking, specially equipped rest rooms, special class scheduling, lowered drinking fountains, lowered telephones, and scheduled transportation are available.

Services: Counseling and information services are available, as is tutoring in most subjects. There is a reader service for the blind, and remedial math, reading, and writing. Skills workshops are also offered.

Campus Safety and Security: Measures include 24-hour foot and vehicle patrol, self-defense education, escort service, and shuttle buses. There are informal discussions, pamphlets/posters/films, emergency telephones, lighted pathways/sidewalks, and safety awareness education.

Programs of Study: IU confers B.A., B.S., B.F.A., B.M., B.M.E., and B.S.G.S. degrees. Associate, master's, and doctoral degrees are also awarded. Bachelor's degrees are awarded in BIOLOGICAL SCIENCE (biochemistry, biology/biological science, microbiology, and nutrition), BUSINESS (accounting, apparel and accessories marketing, banking and finance, business administration and management, business economics, entrepreneurial studies, insurance, labor studies, management information systems, marketing/retailing/merchandising, real estate, recreation and leisure services, sports management, and tourism), COMMUNICATIONS AND THE ARTS (audio technology, ballet, classics, communications, comparative literature, dance, dramatic arts, East Asian languages and literature, English, fine arts, folklore and mythology, French, German, guitar, Italian, jazz, journalism, Latin, linguistics, music, music performance, music theory and composition, piano/organ, Portuguese, Russian, Spanish, speech/debate/rhetoric, studio art, telecommunications, visual and performing arts, and voice), COMPUTER AND PHYSICAL SCIENCE (astronomy, astrophysics, chemistry, computer science, earth science, geology, information sciences and systems, mathematics, physics, and science), EDUCATION (athletic training, early childhood, educational media, elementary, health, middle school, music, physical, school psychology, secondary, and special), ENGINEERING AND ENVIRONMENTAL DESIGN (aerospace studies, environmental science, interior design, and occupational safety and health), HEALTH PROFESSIONS (health science, optometry, public health, and speech pathology/audiology), SOCIAL SCIENCE (African American studies, anthropology, cognitive science, criminal justice, dietetics, East Asian studies, economics, family/consumer studies, gender studies, geography, history, human development, international studies, Judaic studies, liberal arts/general studies, Near Eastern studies, parks and recreation management, philosophy, physical fitness/movement, political science/government, psychology, public administration, public affairs, religion, Russian and Slavic studies, social studies, sociology, and women's studies). Sciences, music, and business are the strongest academically. Business, education, and arts and sciences are the largest.

Required: The general requirements for graduation include courses in English and writing, math, foreign language, arts and humanities, social and behavioral sciences, natural sciences, and culture studies. Students must complete 122 credit hours, with approximately 36 hours in the major. Many degrees have intensive writing requirements, and the minimum GPA requirement varies by department. Liberal arts requirements are common throughout all degree programs.

Special: IU offers cooperative programs with universities in many countries, including the People's Republic of China, a variety of internships, and study abroad in more than 25 countries. A Washington semester work-study programs, B.A.-B.S. degrees in the sciences and liberal arts, dual majors, and the general studies degree through the School of Continuing Studies are available. Student-designed majors through the Individualized Major Program, credit for military experience, nondegree study through the School of Continuing Studies, and pass/fail options are also available. There are 18 national honor societies, and a freshman honors program.

Faculty/Classroom: 67% of faculty are male; 33%, female.

Admissions: 83% of the 2001-2002 applicants were accepted. The SAT I scores for the 2001-2002 freshman class were: Verbal--29% below 500, 45% between 500 and 599, 22% between 600 and 700, and 4% above 700; Math--25% below 500, 42% between 500 and 599, 27% between 600 and 700, and 5% above 700. The ACT scores were 4% between 12 and 17, 36% between 18 and 23, 51% between 24 and 29, and 9% between 30 and 36. 52% of the current freshmen were in the top quarter of their class; 90% were in the top half. There were 26 National Merit finalists. 121 freshmen graduated first in their class.

Requirements: The SAT I or ACT is required. In addition, applicants must be graduates of an accredited secondary high school or have a GED certificate. SAT II: Subject tests are recommended for credit and placement. Auditions for music majors are required. An interview is recommended for information purposes. IU requires applicants to be in the upper 50% of their class. A GPA of 2.0 is required. AP and CLEP credits are accepted. Important factors in the admissions decision are advanced placement or honor courses, parents or siblings attending the school, and recommendations by school officials. Applications may be submitted on-line via the World Wide Web.

Procedure: Freshmen are admitted to all sessions. Entrance exams should be taken in the late junior year or early senior year. There is a deferred admissions plan. Applications should be filed by February 1 for fall entry, November 1 for spring entry, and February 1 for summer entry. Notification is sent on a rolling basis. The fall 2001 application fee was $40.

Transfer: 816 transfer students enrolled in 2001-2002. Admission for transfers is selective. Most successful applicants have a 2.5 or higher GPA and no grades below C in recent work. Applicants with less than 1 year of transfer work must also meet freshman admission standards. 30 credits of 122 must be completed at IU.

Visiting: There are regularly scheduled orientations for prospective students, including admissions counseling and answers to students' questions about the school. There are guides for informal visits and visitors may sit in on classes and stay overnight. To schedule a visit, contact the scheduling director at (812) 855-3512.

Financial Aid: In 2001-2002, 55% of all freshmen received some form of financial aid. The average freshman award was $5636. The FAFSA is required. The fall application deadline is March 1.

International Students: There were 1375 international students enrolled in a recent year. The school actively recruits these students.

Computers: The mainframe is a DEC system. More than 1500 Macs and PCs are available in more than 55 computing labs across campus. All dormitories are wired to handle student PCs. All students may access the system 24 hours a day. There are no time limits. The fee is $200. It is strongly recommended that all students have a personal computer. It is recommended that students in computer science have personal computers.

Graduates: In 2001, 5204 bachelor's degrees were awarded. The most popular majors were business/marketing (23%), education (15%), and protective services/public administration (8%). 100 companies recruited on campus in 2000-2001.

Admissions Contact: Mary Ellen Anderson, Director of Admissions. E-mail: *iuadmit@indiana.edu* Web: *http://www.indiana.edu/~iuadmit*

INDIANA UNIVERSITY EAST

Richmond, IN 47374-1289 — D-3

(765) 973-8208
(800) 959-4485; Fax: (765) 973-8288

Full-time: 341 men, 785 women	**Faculty:** 69; IIB, --$
Part-time: 368 men, 911 women	**Ph.D.s:** 59%
Graduate: 15 men, 40 women	**Student/Faculty:** 16 to 1
Year: semesters, summer session	**Tuition:** $3415 ($8719)
Application Deadline: open	**Room & Board:** n/app
Freshman Class: 546 applied, 466 accepted, 433 enrolled	
SAT I Verbal/Math: 462/445	**ACT:** 20 **COMPETITIVE**

Indiana University East, established in 1971, is a public institution serving a commuter student body. The university offers undergraduate degree programs in humanities, natural science and math, behavioral and social sciences, education, business and technology, nursing, public and environmental affairs, social work, and continuing studies. There are 9 undergraduate schools. In addition to regional accreditation, IU East has baccalaureate program accreditation with NCATE and NLN. The library contains 65,884 volumes, 52,383 microform items, and 9798 audiovisual forms/CDs, and subscribes to 436 periodicals. Computerized library services include the card catalog, interlibrary loans, and database searching. Special learning facilities include an art gallery. The 194-acre campus is in a small town 40 miles west of Dayton, Ohio, and 70 miles east of Indianapolis. There are 9 buildings.

Student Life: 95% of undergraduates are from Indiana. Others are from 10 states, 8 foreign countries, and Canada. 84% are white. The average age of freshmen is 23; all undergraduates, 28. 44% do not continue beyond their first year.

Housing: There are no residence halls. All students commute. Alcohol is not permitted.

Activities: There is 1 national fraternity and 1 national sorority. There are 20 groups on campus, including art, cheerleading, drama, ethnic, literary magazine, newspaper, photography, political, professional, religious, social, social service, and student government. Popular campus events include fall and spring festivals and a Wednesday lunch program.

Sports: There are 4 intramural sports for men and 4 for women. Facilities include a softball field, tennis courts, a sand volleyball court, and a field house.

Disabled Students: 98% of the campus is accessible. Wheelchair ramps, elevators, special parking, lowered drinking fountains, lowered telephones, special testing accommodations, and note taking are available.

Services: Counseling and information services are available, as is tutoring in some subjects, including for several freshman-level courses. There is a reader service for the blind, and remedial math, reading, and writing.

Campus Safety and Security: Measures include escort service, informal discussions, pamphlets/posters/films, and emergency telephones.

There are lighted pathways/sidewalks and a 14-hour foot and vehicle patrol.

Programs of Study: IU East confers B.A., B.S., B.G.S., B.S.B.A., B.S.Ed., and B.S.N. degrees. Associate degrees are also awarded. Bachelor's degrees are awarded in BIOLOGICAL SCIENCE (biology/biological science), BUSINESS (business administration and management), COMMUNICATIONS AND THE ARTS (communications and English), COMPUTER AND PHYSICAL SCIENCE (information sciences and systems), EDUCATION (elementary and secondary), HEALTH PROFESSIONS (nursing), SOCIAL SCIENCE (behavioral science, liberal arts/general studies, and social work). Nursing, business, and education are the largest.

Required: To graduate, students must satisfactorily complete an English composition course, demonstrate computer literacy, and complete a minimum of 120 semester hours with a GPA of at least 2.0.

Special: IU East offers a cooperative program in criminal justice with Indiana University-Purdue University and an organizational leadership program through Purdue's Statewide Technology program. IU East also offers cross-registration with Earlham College, dual majors, independent study, an internship in social work, pass/fail options, study abroad through Indiana University Bloomington, and credit for life experience. Nondegree study is possible. There is 1 national honor society.

Faculty/Classroom: 47% of faculty are male; 53%, female.

Admissions: 79% of the 2001-2002 applicants were accepted. The SAT I scores for the 2001-2002 freshman class were: Verbal--68% below 500, 27% between 500 and 599, and 5% between 600 and 700; Math--73% below 500, 24% between 500 and 599, 2% between 600 and 700, and 1% above 700. The ACT scores were 32% between 12 and 17, 48% between 18 and 23, and 20% between 24 and 29. 16% of the current freshmen were in the top quarter of their class; 45% were in the top half.

Requirements: The SAT I or ACT is recommended. In addition, a minimum GPA of 2.0 is required for applicants who have graduated from high school in the preceding 3 years. Applicants must be graduates of accredited secondary schools or have earned a GED. They must have completed 15 academic credits, including 4 in English, 2 each in math, social studies, and foreign language, and 1 in science, as well as an additional 4 units of academic study. 4 credits in a foreign language are strongly recommended. IU East requires applicants to be in the upper 50% of their class. AP and CLEP credits are accepted.

Procedure: Freshmen are admitted to all sessions. Entrance exams should be taken during the junior or senior year. There are early admissions and deferred admissions plans. Application deadlines are open. The fall 2001 application fee was $25. Notification is sent on a rolling basis.

Transfer: 134 transfer students enrolled in 2001-2002. Applicants must have a GPA of 2.0 and submit college transcripts. Grades of C or better transfer for credit. 30 credits of 120 must be completed at IU East.

Visiting: There are regularly scheduled orientations for prospective students, including tours, counseling, registration, and financial aid sessions. There are guides for informal visits and visitors may sit in on classes. To schedule a visit, contact the Admissions Office.

Financial Aid: In 2001-2002, 74% of all first-time, full-time freshmen received some form of financial aid. The average freshman award was $4156. The FAFSA and the college's own financial statement are required. The fall application deadline is March 1.

Computers: There are 110 networked PCs in 7 public labs connected to the Internet. All students may access the system during the operating hours of the university. There are no time limits. The fee is $110.

Graduates: In 2001, 150 bachelor's degrees were awarded. The most popular majors were education (27%), health professions (21%), and liberal arts (20%).

Admissions Contact: James Bland, Acting Director of Student Recruitment. E-mail: *admit@indiana.edu*
Web: *http://www.iue.indiana.edu/admissions/*

INDIANA UNIVERSITY KOKOMO — C-2

Kokomo, IN 46904-9003 — **(765) 455-9217; (888) 875-4485**

Full-time: 355 men, 821 women	**Faculty:** 75; IIB, av$
Part-time: 412 men, 931 women	**Ph.D.s:** 62%
Graduate: 84 men, 138 women	**Student/Faculty:** 16 to 1
Year: semesters, summer session	**Tuition:** $3422 ($8721)
Application Deadline: August 3	**Room & Board:** n/app
Freshman Class: 699 applied, 609 accepted, 515 enrolled	
SAT I Verbal/Math: 479/465	**ACT:** 19 **LESS COMPETITIVE**

Indiana University Kokomo, founded in 1945 and part of the Indiana University system, offers a wide range of programs that emphasize liberal arts, business, education, and nursing. There are 8 undergraduate and 2 graduate schools. In addition to regional accreditation, IUK has baccalaureate program accreditation with ABET, NCATE, and NLN. The library contains 133,962 volumes, 439,799 microform items, and 5287 audiovisual forms/CDs, and subscribes to 1598 periodicals. Computerized library services include the card catalog, interlibrary loans, and database searching. Special learning facilities include a learning resource center, art gallery, and observatory. The 54-acre campus is in a small town 45 miles north of Indianapolis. There are 20 buildings.

Student Life: 99% of undergraduates are from Indiana. Others are from 14 states, 9 foreign countries, and Canada. 92% are white. The average age of freshmen is 21; all undergraduates, 26. 47% do not continue beyond their first year.

Housing: There are no residence halls. All students commute. Alcohol is not permitted.

Activities: There are no fraternities or sororities. There are 20 groups on campus, including chorale, computers, drama, ethnic, political, religious, social service, student government, and yearbook.

Sports: There is 1 intramural sport for men and 1 for women.

Disabled Students: All of the campus is accessible. Wheelchair ramps, elevators, special parking, specially equipped rest rooms, special class scheduling, lowered drinking fountains, and lowered telephones are available.

Services: There is remedial math, reading, and writing. Students who do not meet regular admissions standards can be admitted under the Guided Study Program, which includes courses in basic skills as needed, counseling and tutoring, and a seminar on studying.

Campus Safety and Security: Measures include escort service and lighted pathways/sidewalks. Campus police are on duty from 7 A.M. to 10 P.M.

Programs of Study: IUK confers B.A., B.S., B.G.S., B.S.Bus., B.S.Ed., B.S.Med.Tech., and B.S.N. degrees. Associate and master's degrees are also awarded. Bachelor's degrees are awarded in BIOLOGICAL SCIENCE (biology/biological science), BUSINESS (accounting, business administration and management, business economics, labor studies, and marketing management), COMMUNICATIONS AND THE ARTS (communications and English), COMPUTER AND PHYSICAL SCIENCE (information sciences and systems and mathematics), EDUCATION (elementary), HEALTH PROFESSIONS (medical laboratory technology and nursing), SOCIAL SCIENCE (behavioral science, criminal justice, humanities, liberal arts/general studies, psychology, social science, and sociology). Arts and sciences and education are the largest.

Required: All students must maintain a minimum GPA of 2.0 while taking 120 credit hours. All students must demonstrate competency in English.

Special: Student-designed majors, a general studies degree, internships, study abroad, joint programs with other Indiana University campuses and with Purdue University, pass/fail options, nondegree study, and credit for military experience and by exam are available. There is 1 national honor society and a freshman honors program.

Faculty/Classroom: 43% of faculty are male; 57%, female.

Admissions: 87% of the 2001-2002 applicants were accepted. The SAT I scores for the 2001-2002 freshman class were: Verbal--59% below 500, 34% between 500 and 599, 6% between 600 and 700, and 1% above 700; Math--67% below 500, 27% between 500 and 599, and 6% between 600 and 700. The ACT scores were 31% below 18, 58% between 18 and 23, 10% between 24 and 29, and 1% above 29. 23% of the current freshmen were in the top quarter of their class; 56% were in the top half.

Requirements: The SAT I or ACT is required, with a recommended composite score of 900 on the SAT I or 19 on the ACT. Admission requirements include 14 academic credits, including 4 years in English and 10 or more credits in math, social studies, science, and foreign languages. The GED is accepted. IUK requires applicants to be in the upper 50% of their class. AP and CLEP credits are accepted.

Procedure: Freshmen are admitted to all sessions. Entrance exams should be taken prior to registration. There are early admissions and deferred admissions plans. Applications should be filed by August 3 for fall entry, December 1 for spring entry, and April 15 for summer entry. The fall 2001 application fee was $30. Notification is sent on a rolling basis.

Transfer: 161 transfer students enrolled in 2001-2002. Transfer applicants must have a minimum GPA of 2.0 and clear records of conduct from previously attended colleges. 30 credits of 120 must be completed at IUK.

Visiting: There are regularly scheduled orientations for prospective students. There are guides for informal visits and visitors may sit in on classes. To schedule a visit, contact the Admissions Office.

Financial Aid: In 2001-2002, 37% of all freshmen and 40% of continuing students received some form of financial aid. 27% of freshmen and 28% of continuing students received need-based aid. The average freshman award was $4034. The FAFSA and the college's own financial statement are required. The fall application deadline is March 1.

International Students: There were 6 international students enrolled in a recent year. They must score 550 on the written TOEFL.

Computers: Labs are available when they are not reserved for classes. The fee is $125 per academic year.

Graduates: In 2001, 186 bachelor's degrees were awarded. The most popular majors were education (21%), liberal arts (20%), and business/marketing (18%).

Admissions Contact: Patty Young, Director of Admissions.
E-mail: *iuadmis@iuk.edu*
Web: *http://www.iuk.edu/admission/admission/index.html*

INDIANA UNIVERSITY NORTHWEST B-1

Gary, IN 46408 (219) 980-6991
(800) 437-5409; Fax: (219) 981-4219

Full-time: 647 men, 1420 women | **Faculty:** 163; IIA, -$
Part-time: 561 men, 1389 women | **Ph.D.s:** 60%
Graduate: 189 men, 413 women | **Student/Faculty:** 13 to 1
Year: semesters, summer session | **Tuition:** $3447 ($8746)
Application Deadline: August 1 | **Room & Board:** n/app
Freshman Class: 1135 applied, 891 accepted, 657 enrolled
SAT I Verbal/Math: 451/429 | **ACT:** 20 | **COMPETITIVE**

Indiana University Northwest, established in 1948, is one of 8 campuses of the Indiana University system. A public commuter school, it offers liberal arts and professional programs. There are 8 undergraduate and 3 graduate schools. In addition to regional accreditation, IUN has baccalaureate program accreditation with AACSB, ADA, NCATE, and NLN. The library contains 241,735 volumes, 340,519 microform items, and 1212 audiovisual forms/CDs, and subscribes to 1628 periodicals. Computerized library services include interlibrary loans. Special learning facilities include a learning resource center and art gallery. The 38-acre campus is in an urban area 30 miles southeast of Chicago. There are 12 buildings.

Student Life: 99% of undergraduates are from Indiana. Others are from 14 states, 34 foreign countries, and Canada. 61% are white; 25% African American; 10% Hispanic. The average age of freshmen is 21; all undergraduates, 27. 40% do not continue beyond their first year.

Housing: There are no residence halls. All students commute. Alcohol is not permitted. All students may keep cars.

Activities: There are 3 national fraternities and 3 national sororities. There are 70 groups on campus, including chess, chorale, drama, ethnic, honors, literary magazine, musical theater, political, professional, social, student government, and yearbook. Popular campus events include Student/Faculty Dinner Dance and Health Fair.

Sports: There are 3 intercollegiate sports for men and 3 for women, and 8 intramural sports for men and 5 for women.

Disabled Students: 90% of the campus is accessible. Wheelchair ramps, elevators, special parking, specially equipped rest rooms, special class scheduling, lowered drinking fountains, and lowered telephones are available.

Services: Counseling and information services are available, as is tutoring in some subjects, including biology, anatomy and physiology, Spanish I, chemistry, sociology, and math. There is a reader service for the blind, and remedial math, reading, and writing.

Campus Safety and Security: Measures include 24-hour foot and vehicle patrol, escort service, emergency telephones, and lighted pathways/sidewalks.

Programs of Study: IUN confers B.A., B.S., and B.G.S. degrees. Associate and master's degrees are also awarded. Bachelor's degrees are awarded in BIOLOGICAL SCIENCE (biology/biological science), BUSINESS (accounting, business administration and management, and labor studies), COMMUNICATIONS AND THE ARTS (communications, dramatic arts, English, fine arts, French, public relations, and Spanish), COMPUTER AND PHYSICAL SCIENCE (actuarial science, chemistry, geology, information sciences and systems, and mathematics), EDUCATION (elementary and secondary), HEALTH PROFESSIONS (health care administration, hospital administration, and nursing), SOCIAL SCIENCE (African American studies, criminal justice, economics, history, liberal arts/general studies, philosophy, political science/government, psychology, public administration, and sociology). Business and nursing are the strongest academically.

Required: Each division sets its own degree requirements. All students must maintain a minimum GPA of 2.0 and complete at least 120 credit hours to graduate.

Special: IUN offers cross-registration with Purdue University, work-study, dual majors, independent study, internships, study abroad in 25 countries, credit for life, military, and work experience, nondegree study, and pass/fail options. There are 3 national honor societies.

Faculty/Classroom: 53% of faculty are male; 47%, female.

Admissions: 79% of the 2001-2002 applicants were accepted. The SAT I scores for the 2001-2002 freshman class were: Verbal--70% below 500, 25% between 500 and 599, and 5% between 600 and 700; Math--77% below 500, 19% between 500 and 599, and 5% between 600 and 700. The ACT scores were 29% between 12 and 17, 46% between 18 and 23, 24% between 24 and 29, and 2% above 29. 22% of the current freshmen were in the top quarter of their class; 50% were in the top half.

Requirements: The SAT I or ACT is required for students who have graduated in the past 3 years, with a minimum composite SAT I score of 860. Applicants must be graduates of an accredited secondary school, with 16 academic units. The GED is accepted. The university recommends an interview. IUN requires applicants to be in the upper 50% of their class. A GPA of 2.0 is required. AP and CLEP credits are accepted. Important factors in the admissions decision are advanced placement or honor courses, leadership record, and recommendations by school officials.

Procedure: Freshmen are admitted fall and spring. Entrance exams should be taken as early as possible. There are early admissions and deferred admissions plans. Applications should be filed by August 1 for fall entry, December 1 for spring entry, and May 1 for summer entry. The fall 2001 application fee was $25. Notification is sent on a rolling basis.

Transfer: 231 transfer students enrolled in 2001-2002. Residents of Indiana must have a 2.0 GPA. Out-of-state transfers must have a C+ average or higher. The SAT I or ACT is recommended. Grades of C or better transfer for credit. 30 credits of 120 must be completed at IUN.

Visiting: There are regularly scheduled orientations for prospective students. There are guides for informal visits and visitors may sit in on classes. To schedule a visit, contact the Admissions Office.

Financial Aid: In 2001-2002, 51% of all first-time, full-time freshmen received some form of financial aid. The average freshman award was $3665. The FAFSA and the college's own financial statement are required. The fall application deadline is March 1.

International Students: International students must score 550 on the written TOEFL and also take the SAT I or the ACT.

Computers: The mainframe is a Prime 9955 II. PCs and Macs are available in labs and offices. All students may access the system any time. There are no time limits. The fee is $150.

Graduates: In 2001, 405 bachelor's degrees were awarded. The most popular majors were business/marketing (22%), liberal arts (15%), and health professions (14%).

Admissions Contact: Charmaine Connelly, Associate Director of Admissions. E-mail: *cconnelly@iun.indiana.edu*
Web: *http://www.iun.indiana.edu/admissions/undergra.htm*

INDIANA UNIVERSITY SOUTH BEND C-1

South Bend, IN 46634-7111 (219) 237-4480

Full-time: 1228 men, 1929 women | **Faculty:** 251; IIA, --$
Part-time: 984 men, 1929 women | **Ph.D.s:** 69%
Graduate: 477 men, 870 women | **Student/Faculty:** 13 to 1
Year: semesters, summer session | **Tuition:** $3515 ($9384)
Application Deadline: open | **Room & Board:** n/app
Freshman Class: 1600 applied, 1409 accepted, 1029 enrolled
SAT I Verbal/Math: 486/475 | **ACT:** 20 | **COMPETITIVE**

Indiana University South Bend, a commuter institution of the state-supported university system, was founded in 1941 and offers undergraduate programs in arts and sciences, business and economics, dental health, education, music, nursing, and public and environmental affairs. There are 11 undergraduate and 5 graduate schools. In addition to regional accreditation, IUSB has baccalaureate program accreditation with ADA, NCATE, and NLN. The library contains 288,750 volumes, 437,348 microform items, and 29,869 audiovisual forms/CDs, and subscribes to 1968 periodicals. Computerized library services include the card catalog, interlibrary loans, and database searching. Special learning facilities include a learning resource center, art gallery, science labs, studios for fine and performing arts, instructional media services, and an academic resource center. The 80-acre campus is in a suburban area 90 miles east of Chicago. There are 34 buildings.

Student Life: 97% of undergraduates are from Indiana. Others are from 31 states, 71 foreign countries, and Canada. 86% are white. The average age of freshmen is 21; all undergraduates, 26. 36% do not continue beyond their first year.

Housing: There are no residence halls. All students commute. Alcohol is not permitted. No one may keep cars.

Activities: There is 1 national sorority. There are no fraternities. There are 52 groups on campus, including art, cheerleading, chorus, drama, ethnic, film, gay, honors, international, jazz band, literary magazine, musical theater, opera, orchestra, pep band, political, professional, religious, social, social service, student government, symphony, and yearbook. Popular campus events include Job Fair, club days, and New Student Welcome Day.

Sports: There is 1 intercollegiate sport for men and 1 for women, and 5 intramural sports for men and 4 for women. Facilities include a running club for men and women.

Disabled Students: 95% of the campus is accessible. Wheelchair ramps, elevators, special parking, specially equipped rest rooms, special class scheduling, lowered drinking fountains, and lowered telephones are available.

Services: Counseling and information services are available, as is tutoring in every subject. There is remedial math, reading, and writing, taped texts, note takers, and interpreters or transcription services.

Campus Safety and Security: Measures include 24-hour foot and vehicle patrol, escort service, informal discussions, and pamphlets/posters/films. There are emergency telephones and lighted pathways/sidewalks.

Programs of Study: IUSB confers B.S., B.A., B.M., B.M.E., and B.S.Ed. degrees. Associate and master's degrees are also awarded.

Bachelor's degrees are awarded in BIOLOGICAL SCIENCE (biology/biological science), BUSINESS (accounting, business administration and management, labor studies, and marketing/retailing/merchandising), COMMUNICATIONS AND THE ARTS (communications, dramatic arts, English, fine arts, French, German, music, piano/organ, Spanish, and speech/debate/rhetoric), COMPUTER AND PHYSICAL SCIENCE (chemistry, computer science, mathematics, and physics), EDUCATION (elementary, music, science, secondary, social studies, and special), ENGINEERING AND ENVIRONMENTAL DESIGN (industrial administration/management), HEALTH PROFESSIONS (health care administration and nursing), SOCIAL SCIENCE (criminal justice, economics, history, liberal arts/general studies, philosophy, political science/government, psychology, public affairs, sociology, and women's studies). Accounting, management, and marketing are the strongest academically. Business, education, and liberal arts and sciences are the largest.

Required: All students must complete divisional requirements and general education and concentration courses, including English composition. A total of 120 to 123 semester hours, with a minimum GPA of 2.0, is required to graduate.

Special: Cross-registration with the Northern Indiana Consortium for Education (NICE), internships, study abroad, accelerated degree programs, and dual majors are possible. There is a freshman honors program.

Faculty/Classroom: 51% of faculty are male; 49%, female. No introductory courses are taught by graduate students.

Admissions: 88% of the 2001-2002 applicants were accepted. The SAT I scores for the 2001-2002 freshman class were: Verbal--56% below 500, 33% between 500 and 599, and 11% between 600 and 700; Math--61% below 500, 30% between 500 and 599, and 9% between 600 and 700. The ACT scores were 2% below 12, 30% between 12 and 17, 45% between 18 and 23, 20% between 24 and 29, and 4% above 29. 22% of the current freshmen were in the top quarter of their class; 57% were in the top half.

Requirements: The SAT I or ACT is required. In addition, applicants should have completed 13 Carnegie units or GED equivalent with a minimum composite of 52. An interview is recommended. IUSB requires applicants to be in the upper 50% of their class. A GPA of 2.0 is required. CLEP credit is accepted. Important factors in the admissions decision are advanced placement or honor courses, extracurricular activities record, and leadership record.

Procedure: Freshmen are admitted to all sessions. Entrance exams should be taken 1 year to 6 months before entering the university. There is a deferred admissions plan. Application deadlines are open; the priority date is July 1. The fall 2001 application fee was $40. Notification is sent on a rolling basis.

Transfer: 409 transfer students enrolled in 2001-2002. A 2.0 GPA is required. College transcripts must be submitted. 30 credits of 120 must be completed at IUSB.

Visiting: There are regularly scheduled orientations for prospective students, including a visit to the admissions office, a campus tour, professor meetings, and information on financial aid. There are guides for informal visits and visitors may sit in on classes. To schedule a visit, contact the Admissions Office at (219) 237-4839.

Financial Aid: In 2001-2002, 63% of all first-time, full-time freshmen received some form of financial aid. The average freshman award was $3614. The FAFSA is required. The fall application deadline is March 1.

International Students: The school actively recruits these students. They must score 550 on the written TOEFL.

Computers: The mainframe is a Sun system. The mainframe can be accessed through computer labs and networks. More than 800 Macs and PCs are available for student use. Students have e-mail and Web access and can connect to the Indiana University statewide network, which includes IBM mainframes, VAX clusters, and on-line library services. All students may access the system 7 days a week. There are no time limits. The fee is $150.

Graduates: In 2001, 548 bachelor's degrees were awarded. The most popular majors were education (24%), business/marketing (20%), and liberal arts/general studies (13%).

Admissions Contact: Jeff Johnston, Director of Admissions.
E-mail: *iuadmis@iusb.edu*
Web: *http://www.iusb.edu/admission/admission/index.html*

INDIANA UNIVERSITY SOUTHEAST — C-5

New Albany, IN 47150 — (812) 941-2212
(800) 852-8835; Fax: (812) 941-2595

Full-time: 1160 men, 1909 women	**Faculty:** 170; IIA, -$
Part-time: 957 men, 1642 women	**Ph.D.s:** 78%
Graduate: 321 men, 568 women	**Student/Faculty:** 18 to 1
Year: semesters, summer session	**Tuition:** $3459 ($8759)
Application Deadline: July 15	**Room & Board:** n/app
Freshman Class: 1352 applied, 1173 accepted, 915 enrolled	
SAT I Verbal/Math: 480/468	**ACT:** 20 — **COMPETITIVE**

Indiana University Southeast, established in 1941, is a state-supported institution, part of the Indiana University system, and offers undergraduate and graduate programs in humanities, social sciences, natural sciences, business and economics, education, general studies, and nursing. There are 8 undergraduate and 3 graduate schools. In addition to regional accreditation, IUS has baccalaureate program accreditation with AACSB, NCATE, and NLN. The library contains 207,815 volumes, 348,192 microform items, and 7489 audiovisual forms/CDs, and subscribes to 1041 periodicals. Computerized library services include the card catalog, interlibrary loans, and database searching. Special learning facilities include an art gallery. The 177-acre campus is in a suburban area 7 miles northwest of Louisville, Kentucky, and 114 miles south of Indianapolis. There are 18 buildings.

Student Life: 85% of undergraduates are from Indiana. Others are from 9 states, 26 foreign countries, and Canada. 90% are white. The average age of freshmen is 20; all undergraduates, 25. 36% do not continue beyond their first year.

Housing: There are no residence halls. All students commute. Alcohol is not permitted.

Activities: There are 2 national fraternities and 4 national sororities. There are more than 50 groups on campus, including art, band, cheerleading, choir, chorus, computers, drama, ethnic, film, gay, honors, literary magazine, orchestra, political, religious, social, student government, and yearbook.

Sports: There are 2 intercollegiate sports for men and 2 for women, and 4 intramural sports for men and 4 for women. Facilities include a 1600-seat activities building with a basketball court, facilities for jogging, badminton, volleyball, weightlifting, and gymnastics, 6 tennis courts, baseball and softball fields, and playing fields.

Disabled Students: All of the campus is accessible. Wheelchair ramps, elevators, special parking, specially equipped rest rooms, lowered drinking fountains, lowered telephones, and special accommodations as needed are available.

Services: Counseling and information services are available, as is tutoring in every subject. There is a reader service for the blind, and remedial math, reading, and writing. The coordinator for services to students with disabilities provides information and coordination of needed services.

Campus Safety and Security: Measures include 24-hour foot and vehicle patrol, self-defense education, pamphlets/posters/films, and emergency telephones. There are lighted pathways/sidewalks and a police department on campus.

Programs of Study: IUS confers B.A., B.S., and B.G.S. degrees. Associate and master's degrees are also awarded. Bachelor's degrees are awarded in BIOLOGICAL SCIENCE (biology/biological science), BUSINESS (accounting, banking and finance, business administration and management, business economics, labor studies, and marketing/retailing/merchandising), COMMUNICATIONS AND THE ARTS (communications, English, fine arts, French, music, and Spanish), COMPUTER AND PHYSICAL SCIENCE (chemistry, computer science, and mathematics), EDUCATION (elementary, science, secondary, social studies, and special), HEALTH PROFESSIONS (medical technology and nursing), SOCIAL SCIENCE (economics, geography, German area studies, history, liberal arts/general studies, philosophy, political science/government, psychology, and sociology). Education, business, and continuing studies are the largest.

Required: Students must complete 120 credit hours, with 30 in upper-level courses and at least 25 in the major, and must maintain a minimum cumulative GPA of 2.0. In addition, all students must complete a core curriculum that includes courses in English composition, math, computer literacy, arts and humanities, and social and natural sciences.

Special: Cross-registration with Metroversity is possible, and opportunities are provided for study abroad, internships, work-study programs, dual majors, a general studies degree, credit by exam, nondegree study, and pass/fail options.

Faculty/Classroom: 55% of faculty are male; 45%, female.

Admissions: 87% of the 2001-2002 applicants were accepted. The SAT I scores for the 2001-2002 freshman class were: Verbal--59% below 500, 33% between 500 and 599, and 8% between 600 and 700; Math--64% below 500, 30% between 500 and 599, and 6% between 600 and 700. The ACT scores were 24% between 12 and 17, 58% between 18 and 23, and 18% between 24 and 29. 28% of the current freshmen were in the top quarter of their class; 61% were in the top half.

Requirements: The SAT I or ACT is required with minimum scores of 400 verbal and 400 math on the SAT I or 19 on the ACT. These requirements are waived if the applicant has been out of high school for 3 or more years. Graduation from an accredited secondary school is required; the GED is accepted. Applicants must have completed 14 academic units, including 4 in English, 3 in math, 2 in social studies, 1 in lab science, and 4 academic electives. 2 units in foreign language are recommended. IUS requires applicants to be in the upper 50% of their class. A GPA of 2.0 is required. AP and CLEP credits are accepted.

Procedure: Freshmen are admitted to all sessions. Entrance exams should be taken during high school. There are early admissions and deferred admissions plans. Applications should be filed by July 15 for fall entry, December 1 for spring entry, and April 15 for summer entry. The fall 2001 application fee was $30. Notification is sent on a rolling basis.

Transfer: 320 transfer students enrolled in 2001-2002. A GPA of 2.0 is required for Indiana residents, 2.5 for out-of-state applicants. If the student has fewer than 26 transferable semester hours, the high school record should reflect compliance with freshman admission requirements. 30 credits of 120 must be completed at IUS.

Visiting: There are regularly scheduled orientations for prospective students, including an opportunity for students to apply for admission, financial aid, and scholarships, a faculty perspective, a student perspective, and a campus tour. There are guides for informal visits and visitors may sit in on classes. To schedule a visit, contact the Office of Admissions.

Financial Aid: In 2001-2002, 53% of all first-time, full-time freshmen received some form of financial aid. The average freshman award was $3726. The FAFSA and the college's own financial statement are required. The fall application deadline is March 1.

International Students: International students must score 550 on the written TOEFL.

Computers: All students have access to the Indiana University Computing Network, notably the DEC VAX and IBM 3090 series computers. There is a local area network with several general and specialized computing applications on PCs and Macs. All students may access the system. There are no time limits. The fee is $84.

Graduates: In 2001, 500 bachelor's degrees were awarded. The most popular majors were education (25%), business/marketing (20%), and liberal arts (15%).

Admissions Contact: David B. Campbell, Director of Admissions. E-mail: *admissions@ius.edu* Web: *www.indiana.edu*

INDIANA UNIVERSITY-PURDUE UNIVERSITY FORT WAYNE D-2

Fort Wayne, IN 46805-1499 **(219) 481-6812**
(800) 324-4739; Fax: (219) 481-6880

Full-time: 2512 men, 3213 women	**Faculty:** 333; IIA, --$
Part-time: 1924 men, 2633 women	**Ph.D.s:** 85%
Graduate: 333 men, 514 women	**Student/Faculty:** 17 to 1
Year: semesters, summer session	**Tuition:** $3166 ($7169)
Application Deadline: August 1	**Room & Board:** n/app
Freshman Class: 2479 applied, 2393 accepted, 1722 enrolled	
SAT I Verbal/Math: 481/482	**ACT:** 20 **LESS COMPETITIVE**

In 1964, Indiana University at Fort Wayne, founded in 1917, joined Purdue University at Fort Wayne, founded in 1944. The combined school, a state-controlled institution, offers programs in liberal arts, science, business, education, health sciences, engineering, technology, and public affairs. There are 9 undergraduate and 5 graduate schools. In addition to regional accreditation, IPFW has baccalaureate program accreditation with AACSB, ABET, NASM, NCATE, and NLN. The library contains 458,699 volumes, 534,119 microform items, and 1049 audiovisual forms/CDs, and subscribes to 3236 periodicals. Computerized library services include the card catalog, interlibrary loans, and database searching. Special learning facilities include a learning resource center, art gallery, and TV station. The 565-acre campus is in a suburban area 113 miles north of Indianapolis. There are 11 buildings.

Student Life: 94% of undergraduates are from Indiana. Others are from 38 states, 66 foreign countries, and Canada. 80% are from public schools. 88% are white. The average age of freshmen is 23.7; all undergraduates, 25.8. 34% do not continue beyond their first year.

Housing: There are no residence halls. All students commute. Alcohol is not permitted. No one may keep cars.

Activities: 1% of men belong to 2 local fraternities; 1% of women belong to 2 local sororities. There are 61 groups on campus, including art, cheerleading, choir, dance, debate, drama, ethnic, forensics, gay, honors, international, literary magazine, musical theater, newspaper, political, professional, religious, social, and student government.

Sports: There are 7 intercollegiate sports for men and 7 for women, and 11 intramural sports for men and 9 for women. Facilities include a physical fitness center with a gym, 3 basketball courts, an indoor track, a weight room, 4 racquetball courts, 1 Wallyball court, a fencing and dance room, baseball and soccer fields, and an indoor soccer facility.

Disabled Students: All of the campus is accessible. Wheelchair ramps, elevators, special parking, specially equipped rest rooms, lowered drinking fountains, and lowered telephones are available.

Services: Counseling and information services are available, as is tutoring in most subjects. There is a reader service for the blind, and remedial math, reading, and writing.

Campus Safety and Security: Measures include 24-hour foot and vehicle patrol, self-defense education, escort service, and pamphlets/posters/films. There are emergency telephones and lighted pathways/sidewalks.

Programs of Study: IPFW confers B.A., B.S., B.C.L.S., B.F.A., B.G.S., B.M.T.P., B.Mus., B.Mus.Ed., B.S.B., B.S.C., B.S.E., B.S.Ed., B.S.E.E., B.S.G., B.S.H.M., B.S.L.S., B.S.M.E., and B.S.P.A. degrees. Associate and master's degrees are also awarded. Bachelor's degrees are awarded in BIOLOGICAL SCIENCE (biology/biological science), BUSINESS (accounting, banking and finance, business economics, and marketing/retailing/merchandising), COMMUNICATIONS AND THE ARTS (broadcasting, communications, English, fine arts, French, German, Spanish, speech/debate/rhetoric, and telecommunications), COMPUTER AND PHYSICAL SCIENCE (chemistry, computer programming, computer science, earth science, geology, information sciences and systems, mathematics, and physics), EDUCATION (elementary, foreign languages, music, science, and secondary), ENGINEERING AND ENVIRONMENTAL DESIGN (electrical/electronics engineering, engineering, engineering technology, industrial engineering technology, and mechanical engineering), HEALTH PROFESSIONS (nursing, predentistry, premedicine, and speech pathology/audiology), SOCIAL SCIENCE (anthropology, criminal justice, economics, history, philosophy, political science/government, prelaw, psychology, public administration, social science, and sociology). Engineering is the strongest academically. Business and education are the largest.

Required: To graduate, all bachelor's degree students must complete 120 credits, including 36 general education hours, and take English composition, speech communication, and math.

Special: There are continuing education, co-op, and work-study programs, as well as study abroad in France, Spain, Austria, and Germany. An accelerated general studies degree, cross-registration with other Fort Wayne colleges, B.A.-B.S. degrees, dual majors, a Washington semester for Public Affairs students, internships, and credit for military experience are available. Nondegree study and pass/fail options are possible. There are 6 national honor societies, and a freshman honors program.

Faculty/Classroom: 63% of faculty are male; 37%, female. All teach undergraduates, and 92% also do research. Graduate students teach 3% of introductory courses. The average class size in an introductory lecture is 30; in a laboratory, 20; and in a regular course, 25.

Admissions: 97% of the 2001-2002 applicants were accepted. The SAT I scores for the 2001-2002 freshman class were: Verbal--59% below 500, 32% between 500 and 599, 8% between 600 and 700, and 1% above 700; Math--58% below 500, 32% between 500 and 599, 9% between 600 and 700, and 1% above 700. The ACT scores were 24% below 18, 57% between 18 and 23, 18% between 24 and 29, and 2% above 29. 17% of the current freshmen were in the top fifth of their class; 41% were in the top two fifths.

Requirements: The SAT I is required and the ACT is recommended, with a minimum composite score of 950 on the SAT I. Applicants should have 20 academic credits, including 4 years of English, 3 years of math, and 3 years combination of science, social studies, and foreign language. The GED is accepted. An interview is recommended. IPFW requires applicants to be in the upper 20% of their class. AP and CLEP credits are accepted. Important factors in the admissions decision are recommendations by school officials, evidence of special talent, and advanced placement or honor courses. Applications are accepted on-line at the school's web site.

Procedure: Freshmen are admitted fall, spring, and summer. Entrance exams should be taken in the senior year of high school. Applications should be filed by August 1 for fall entry, December 15 for spring entry, and May 1 for summer entry, along with a $30 fee. Notification is sent on a rolling basis.

Transfer: 759 transfer students enrolled in 2001-2002. Transfer applicants must have a minimum GPA of 2.0. Grades of C or better transfer for credit. 32 credits of 120 must be completed at IPFW.

Visiting: There are regularly scheduled orientations for prospective students. There are guides for informal visits and visitors may sit in on classes. To schedule a visit, contact the Admissions Office.

Financial Aid: In 2000-2001, 42% of all freshmen and 56% of continuing students received some form of financial aid. 30% of freshmen and 39% of continuing students received need-based aid. The average freshman award was $4652. 2% of undergraduates work part time. Average annual earnings from campus work are $1237. The average financial indebtedness of the 2001 graduate was $8104. IPFW is a member of CSS. The FAFSA is required. The fall application deadline is March 1.

International Students: There are 162 international students enrolled. The school actively recruits these students. They must take the TOEFL, scoring 550, or take the MELAB; they must also take de SAT I, scoring

750, or the ACT. Students must have an SAT I verbal score of 480 or above; pass level 109 of an ESL program; or receive a B at 0 level of the GCE.

Computers: The mainframe is an IBM 9672-R21. 251 networked PCs are available in various labs; 30 e-mail kiosks are in lobbies of various buildings. All students may access the system. There are no time limits and no fees.

Graduates: In 2001, 713 bachelor's degrees were awarded. The most popular majors were education (20%), business (20%), and general studies (10%). In an average class, 5% graduate in 4 years, 10% in 5 years, and 21% in 6 years. 126 companies recruited on campus in 2000-2001.

Admissions Contact: Carol Isaacs, Director of Admissions.
E-mail: *ipfwadms@ipfw.edu* Web: *www.ipfw.edu*

INDIANA UNIVERSITY-PURDUE UNIVERSITY INDIANAPOLIS C-3

Indianapolis, IN 46202-5143 (317) 274-4591
Fax: (317) 278-1862

Full-time: 4848 men, 7109 women	**Faculty:** 1787; IIA, av$
Part-time: 3631 men, 5107 women	**Ph.D.s:** 91%
Graduate: 2172 men, 3116 women	**Student/Faculty:** 7 to 1
Year: semesters, summer session	**Tuition:** $4171 ($12,273)
Application Deadline: open	**Room & Board:** $5302
Freshman Class: 6060 applied, 4405 accepted, 2978 enrolled	
SAT I Verbal/Math: 492/489	**ACT:** 21 **COMPETITIVE**

The Indianapolis campus, founded in 1946, has offered undergraduate and graduate instruction under the auspices of both Purdue and Indiana Universities since 1969. The state-controlled institution serves a primarily commuter student body and offers degree programs in the arts and sciences, business, education, engineering and technology, health science, religious studies, and professional training. There are 17 undergraduate and 15 graduate schools. In addition to regional accreditation, IUPUI has baccalaureate program accreditation with AACSB, ABET, ACCE, ACEJMC, ADA, APTA, CAHEA, CSWE, NASAD, NASM, NCATE, and NLN. The 4 libraries contain 1,307,346 volumes, 2,346,208 microform items, and 430,127 audiovisual forms/CDs, and subscribe to 14,798 periodicals. Computerized library services include the card catalog and database searching. Special learning facilities include an art gallery, 85-acre medical center, and electronic classroom. The 370-acre campus is in an urban area near downtown Indianapolis. Including residence halls, there are 58 buildings.

Student Life: 97% of undergraduates are from Indiana. Others are from 45 states, 116 foreign countries, and Canada. 83% are white; 11% African American. The average age of freshmen is 19; all undergraduates, 23. 38% do not continue beyond their first year.

Housing: 350 students can be accommodated in college housing, which includes coed dormitories, on-campus apartments, off-campus apartments, and married-student housing. In addition, there are special-interest houses. On-campus housing is available on a first-come, first-served basis. 99% of students commute. Alcohol is not permitted. All students may keep cars.

Activities: There are 3 national fraternities and 2 national sororities. There are more than 200 groups on campus, including cheerleading, chorale, chorus, dance, debate, drama, ethnic, gay, honors, international, jazz band, literary magazine, opera, pep band, political, professional, radio and TV, religious, social, social service, student government, and yearbook. Popular campus events include Career Day, Ice Cream Social, and Activities Fair.

Sports: There are 8 intercollegiate sports for men and 8 for women, and 16 intramural sports for men and 14 for women. Facilities include a 12,000-seat track and field stadium, a 3-pool natatorium, softball fields, a tennis center, and the National Institute for Fitness and Sport.

Disabled Students: All of the campus is accessible. Wheelchair ramps, elevators, special parking, specially equipped rest rooms, special class scheduling, lowered drinking fountains, lowered telephones, classroom aids, and sign language interpreters are available.

Services: Counseling and information services are available, as is tutoring in most subjects. There is a reader service for the blind, and remedial math, reading, and writing.

Campus Safety and Security: Measures include 24-hour foot and vehicle patrol, self-defense education, escort service, and shuttle buses. There are informal discussions, pamphlets/posters/films, emergency telephones, and lighted pathways/sidewalks.

Programs of Study: IUPUI confers B.A., B.S., B.A.E., B.F.A., B.G.S., B.S.E., B.S.E.E., B.S.M.E., and B.S.W. degrees. Associate, master's, and doctoral degrees are also awarded. Bachelor's degrees are awarded in BIOLOGICAL SCIENCE (biology/biological science), BUSINESS (accounting, banking and finance, business administration and management, business economics, human resources, insurance, labor studies, marketing/retailing/merchandising, office supervision and management, real estate, and tourism), COMMUNICATIONS AND THE ARTS (American Sign Language, art history and appreciation, ceramic art and design, communications, English, fine arts, French, German, journalism, media arts, painting, photography, printmaking, sculpture, Spanish, and speech/debate/rhetoric), COMPUTER AND PHYSICAL SCIENCE (chemistry, computer science, geology, information sciences and systems, mathematics, and physics), EDUCATION (art, elementary, health, physical, secondary, and social studies), ENGINEERING AND ENVIRONMENTAL DESIGN (computer engineering, computer technology, construction technology, electrical/electronics engineering, electrical/electronics engineering technology, engineering, engineering technology, environmental science, manufacturing technology, mechanical engineering, mechanical engineering technology, and woodworking), HEALTH PROFESSIONS (cytotechnology, dental hygiene, environmental health science, health care administration, medical laboratory technology, medical technology, nuclear medical technology, nursing, occupational therapy, physical therapy, public health, radiation therapy, and respiratory therapy), SOCIAL SCIENCE (anthropology, criminal justice, economics, geography, history, liberal arts/general studies, philosophy, political science/government, psychology, public affairs, religion, social work, and sociology). Engineering and technology, nursing, and education are the largest.

Required: All students must complete a computer course toward the 122 to 126 credits required for the bachelor's degree.

Special: There is a metropolitan studies program for career work in the city and cross-registration with the Consortium for Urban Education. IUPUI also offers study abroad, combined B.A.-B.S. degree programs, internships, work-study programs, dual majors, student-designed majors, nondegree study, nontraditional programs for adult learners, and interdisciplinary majors such as business economics and public policy, health occupations education, and interdisciplinary engineering. There are 2 national honor societies and a freshman honors program.

Faculty/Classroom: 62% of faculty are male; 38%, female.

Admissions: 73% of the 2001-2002 applicants were accepted. The SAT I scores for the 2001-2002 freshman class were: Verbal--56% below 500, 34% between 500 and 599, 9% between 600 and 700, and 1% above 700; Math--58% below 500, 32% between 500 and 599, 9% between 600 and 700, and 1% above 700. The ACT scores were 25% between 12 and 17, 53% between 18 and 23, 21% between 24 and 29, and 1% above 29. 27% of the current freshmen were in the top quarter of their class; 63% were in the top half.

Requirements: The SAT I or ACT is required for recent high school graduates. Applicants should be graduates of an accredited high school, rank in the upper half of their class, and have completed 14 Carnegie units, including 4 in English, 3 in math, 2 in social studies, and 1 in lab science. A GPA of 2.0 is required. AP and CLEP credits are accepted. Recommendations by school officials is an important factor in the admission decision. The university accepts applications on computer disk.

Procedure: Freshmen are admitted to all sessions. Entrance exams should be taken by the end of junior year or fall of senior year. There are early admissions and deferred admissions plans. Application deadlines are open. The fall 2001 application fee was $35. Notification is sent on a rolling basis.

Transfer: 1725 transfer students enrolled in 2001-2002. Transfers who are Indiana residents must present a minimum GPA of 2.0 in all previous college work; out-of-state residents need a minimum 2.5. All applicants must be in good standing at their former schools. 30 credits of 122 must be completed at IUPUI.

Visiting: There are regularly scheduled orientations for prospective students, consisting of a campus tour and talks with students. There are guides for informal visits and visitors may sit in on classes. To schedule a visit, contact the Enrollment Center.

Financial Aid: In 2001-2002, 70% of all first-time, full-time freshmen received some form of financial aid. The average freshman award was $4060. The FAFSA is required. The fall application deadline is March 1.

International Students: Internatonal students must score 550 on the written TOEFL.

Computers: The mainframe is an IBM 3090. PCs are available for all students. All students may access the system up to 24 hours a day in some clusters. There are no time limits. The fee is $161 per semester.

Graduates: In 2001, 2114 bachelor's degrees were awarded. The most popular majors were health professions (24%), business/marketing (20%), and liberal arts (15%).

Admissions Contact: Mike Donahue, Director of Admissions.
E-mail: *apply@iupui.edu* Web: *www.iupui.edu/~enroll/*

INDIANA WESLEYAN UNIVERSITY

Marion, IN 46953-9980 C 2

(765) 677-2138

(800) 332-6901; Fax: (765) 677-2333

Full-time: 1839 men, 3260 women	**Faculty:** 90; IIB, -$
Part-time: 221 men, 401 women	**Ph.D.s:** 51%
Graduate: 989 men, 1219 women	**Student/Faculty:** 37 to 1
Year: 4-4-1, summer session	**Tuition:** $12,740
Application Deadline: August 1	**Room & Board:** $4940
Freshman Class: 1988 applied, 1515 accepted, 691 enrolled	
SAT I Verbal/Math: 539/543	**ACT:** 23 **COMPETITIVE**

Indiana Wesleyan University, founded in 1920, is a private institution affiliated with the Methodist Church. The university offers undergraduate programs in the arts and sciences, business, education, fine arts, nursing, professional training, and religious studies. There are 8 undergraduate schools and 1 graduate school. In addition to regional accreditation, IWU has baccalaureate program accreditation with CAHEA, CSWE, and NLN. The library contains 89,992 volumes, 123,706 microform items, and 8027 audiovisual forms/CDs, and subscribes to 1185 periodicals. Computerized library services include the card catalog, interlibrary loans, and database searching. Special learning facilities include a learning resource center, art gallery, radio station, and TV station. The 132-acre campus is in an urban area 60 miles north of Indianapolis. Including residence halls, there are 26 buildings.

Student Life: 60% of undergraduates are from Indiana. Others are from 45 states, 14 foreign countries, and Canada. 93% are white. Most are Protestant. 21% do not continue beyond their first year; 22% remain to graduate.

Housing: 1000 students can be accommodated in college housing, which includes single-sex dormitories and on-campus apartments. On-campus housing is guaranteed for all 4 years. 52% of students live on campus; of those, 30% remain on campus on weekends. Alcohol is not permitted. All students may keep cars.

Activities: There are no fraternities or sororities. There are 31 groups on campus, including art, cheerleading, choir, chorale, chorus, drama, honors, international, jazz band, literary magazine, newspaper, orchestra, photography, professional, radio and TV, religious, social service, student government, and yearbook.

Sports: There are 7 intercollegiate sports for men and 7 for women. Facilities include a gym, racquetball courts, a weight room, and a 65-acre outdoor athletic complex featuring a world-class track.

Disabled Students: 60% of the campus is accessible. Wheelchair ramps, elevators, special parking, specially equipped rest rooms, and lowered drinking fountains are available.

Services: Counseling and information services are available, as is tutoring in most subjects. There is remedial reading and writing, external testing, notetaker service, and advocacy.

Campus Safety and Security: Measures include self-defense education, escort service, pamphlets/posters/films, and emergency telephones. There are lighted pathways/sidewalks.

Programs of Study: IWU confers B.A. and B.S. degrees. Associate and master's degrees are also awarded. Bachelor's degrees are awarded in BIOLOGICAL SCIENCE (biology/biological science), BUSINESS (accounting, business administration and management, marketing/retailing/merchandising, and recreational facilities management), COMMUNICATIONS AND THE ARTS (art, communications, creative writing, English, music, Spanish, and studio art), COMPUTER AND PHYSICAL SCIENCE (chemistry, mathematics, and science), EDUCATION (art, elementary, English, music, nursing, physical, science, and social studies), HEALTH PROFESSIONS (medical laboratory technology, predentistry, premedicine, and preveterinary science), SOCIAL SCIENCE (biblical studies, criminal justice, economics, history, ministries, political science/government, psychology, religion, religious music, social studies, social work, and sociology). Nursing, education, and religion are the strongest academically.

Required: Students must attend chapel services 3 times a week. General education requirements include 12 credit hours of humanities, 10 of math and science, 9 each of English and history or social studies, 6 of biblical literature, and 3 each of intercultural experience and phys ed. Foreign language courses are required for the B.A., computer literacy courses for the B.S. To graduate, students must complete at least 124 semester hours, including 40 in a major field of study, with a minimum GPA of 2.0 overall and 2.25 in the major.

Special: Students may study abroad in Europe, Mexico, Israel, and Haiti. IWU also offers internships, co-op programs with the Wesleyan Urban Coalition of Christian colleges, cross-registration with Taylor University, a Washington semester, work-study programs, pass/fail options, and nondegree study. Adult learners may earn credit for life experience toward bachelor's degrees in business through the LEAP program. There are 2 national honor societies, and 2 departmental honors programs.

Faculty/Classroom: 60% of faculty are male; 40%, female. All teach undergraduates.

Admissions: 76% of the 2001-2002 applicants were accepted. The SAT I scores for the 2001-2002 freshman class were: Verbal--38% below 500, 35% between 500 and 599, 24% between 600 and 700, and 4% above 700; Math--28% below 500, 48% between 500 and 599, 21% between 600 and 700, and 4% above 700. 25% of the current freshmen were in the top fifth of their class; 50% were in the top two fifths.

Requirements: The SAT I or ACT is required. In addition, applicants should be graduates of accredited secondary schools or have earned a GED. The university requires 10 units of college preparatory study that includes courses in English, science, social science, math, and foreign language. Recommendations are also required. A GPA of 2.0 is required. AP and CLEP credits are accepted.

Procedure: Freshmen are admitted to all sessions. Entrance exams should be taken in the junior year or early in the senior year. There are early admissions and deferred admissions plans. Applications should be filed by August 1 for fall entry. Notification is sent on a rolling basis.

Transfer: In addition to standard admissions requirements, transfers must submit transcripts of all previous college work and be in good standing at their former school. 60 credits of 124 must be completed at IWU.

Visiting: There are regularly scheduled orientations for prospective students, including appointments with admissions counselors and professors, campus tours, classroom visits, and meals. There are guides for informal visits and visitors may sit in on classes and stay overnight. To schedule a visit, contact the Admissions Office.

Financial Aid: In 2001-2002, 85% of continuing students received some form of financial aid. The FAFSA and the college's own financial statement are required. Check with the school for current deadlines.

International Students: The school actively recruits these students. They must score 550 on the written TOEFL and also take the college's own test and the SAT I or the ACT.

Computers: The mainframe is an HP Apollo 9000/720. PCs and Macs are available in computer labs, dorms, and a few public access sites. There are approximately 70 systems available. All students may access the system from 8 A.M. to 10 P.M. There are no time limits and no fees.

Admissions Contact: Dr. John S. Grady, Vice President for Enrollment Management. E-mail: *admissions@indwes.edu*

MANCHESTER COLLEGE

North Manchester, IN 46962-0365 C-2

(260) 982-5055

(800) 852-3648; Fax: (260) 982-5239

Full-time: 491 men, 611 women	**Faculty:** 68; IIB, --$
Part-time: 17 men, 16 women	**Ph.D.s:** 93%
Graduate: 15 men, 16 women	**Student/Faculty:** 16 to 1
Year: 4-1-4, summer session	**Tuition:** $16,080
Application Deadline: open	**Room & Board:** $5930
Freshman Class: 1103 applied, 896 accepted, 334 enrolled	
SAT I Verbal/Math: 510/520	**ACT:** 23 **COMPETITIVE**

Manchester College, established in 1889, is a private liberal arts college affiliated with the Church of the Brethren offering undergraduate and graduate major programs in accounting, business and economics, premedicine, education, psychology, the social sciences, and the humanities. In addition to regional accreditation, Manchester has baccalaureate program accreditation with CSWE and NCATE. The library contains 174,078 volumes, 23,014 microform items, and 5258 audiovisual forms/CDs, and subscribes to 973 periodicals. Computerized library services include the card catalog, interlibrary loans, and database searching. Special learning facilities include a learning resource center, planetarium, radio station, and a 100-acre nature preserve. The 124-acre campus is in a small town 35 miles west of Fort Wayne in northeastern Indiana. Including residence halls, there are 44 buildings.

Student Life: 89% of undergraduates are from Indiana. Others are from 23 states, 29 foreign countries, and Canada. 99% are from public schools. 87% are white. 65% are Protestant; 21% claim no religious affiliation; 12% Catholic. The average age of freshmen is 18; all undergraduates, 20. 25% do not continue beyond their first year; 55% remain to graduate.

Housing: 979 students can be accommodated in college housing, which includes single-sex and coed dormitories, off-campus apartments, and married-student housing. In addition, there are special-interest houses. The AAFRO House is a special-interest facility providing social, cultural, and educational opportunities to African-American students at the college. Theme units for students interested in science and health are located within the residence hall system. On-campus housing is guaranteed for all 4 years. 77% of students live on campus; of those, 50% remain on campus on weekends. Alcohol is not permitted. All students may keep cars.

Activities: There are no fraternities or sororities. There are 55 groups on campus, including band, cheerleading, choir, chorale, chorus, computers, dance, drama, ethnic, gay, honors, international, jazz band, literary magazine, musical theater, newspaper, orchestra, pep band, photography, political, professional, radio and TV, religious, social, social service, student government, symphony, and yearbook. Popular campus events include Parents Weekend, Sibling Weekend, and International Fair.

Sports: There are 9 intercollegiate sports for men and 8 for women, and 13 intramural sports for men and 12 for women. Facilities include a phys ed and recreation center with an 1800-seat gym, racquetball courts, and tennis courts; facilities for indoor track, a cross-country and an all-weather track, and athletic fields for baseball, softball, soccer, and football.

Disabled Students: 20% of the campus is accessible. Wheelchair ramps, elevators, special parking, specially equipped rest rooms, special class scheduling, lowered drinking fountains, and lowered telephones are available.

Services: Counseling and information services are available, as is tutoring in every subject. There is a reader service for the blind, a learning center with an academic assistance program, and a seminar to enhance study and learning skills and time and project management.

Campus Safety and Security: Measures include 24-hour foot and vehicle patrol, escort service, informal discussions, and pamphlets/posters/films. There are emergency telephones and lighted pathways/sidewalks.

Programs of Study: Manchester confers B.A. and B.S. degrees. Associate and master's degrees are also awarded. Bachelor's degrees are awarded in BIOLOGICAL SCIENCE (biochemistry and biology/biological science), BUSINESS (accounting, banking and finance, business administration and management, and international business management), COMMUNICATIONS AND THE ARTS (art, communications, English, French, German, music, and Spanish), COMPUTER AND PHYSICAL SCIENCE (chemistry, computer science, mathematics, and physics), EDUCATION (art, elementary, health, middle school, and secondary), ENGINEERING AND ENVIRONMENTAL DESIGN (engineering), HEALTH PROFESSIONS (medical laboratory technology), SOCIAL SCIENCE (anthropology, economics, history, interdisciplinary studies, peace studies, philosophy, political science/government, prelaw, psychology, religion, social work, and sociology). Education, accounting, and biology-chemistry are the strongest academically. Education, accounting, and communication studies are the largest.

Required: Students must complete a general studies curriculum, including requirements in humanities, social sciences, and natural sciences, as well as specific courses in English composition, public communication, Western civilization, and physical fitness. To graduate, students must complete a minimum of 128 semester hours, including 26 to 52 hours in a major field, with a GPA of at least 2.0 (2.5 for the education major). A comprehensive exam in the major is also required.

Special: The college offers cooperative programs in nursing and engineering science. The Brethren Colleges Abroad program allows study abroad in Ecuador, China, England, France, Germany, Japan, Mexico, and Spain. Overseas study is also available in Turkey, Indonesia, and Brazil. Manchester also offers B.A.-B.S. degrees, internships, work-study programs, dual majors, student-designed majors, a 3-2 engineering program, pass/fail options, and nondegree study. Other special academic features include independent study, required study in non-Western culture, and interdisciplinary programs in both peace studies and environmental studies. There are 6 national honor societies, a freshman honors program, and 5 departmental honors programs.

Faculty/Classroom: 59% of faculty are male; 41%, female. All teach undergraduates. No introductory courses are taught by graduate students. The average class size in an introductory lecture is 30; in a laboratory, 15; and in a regular course, 20.

Admissions: 81% of the 2001-2002 applicants were accepted. The SAT I scores for the 2001-2002 freshman class were: Verbal--46% below 500, 40% between 500 and 599, 12% between 600 and 700, and 2% above 700; Math--42% below 500, 39% between 500 and 599, 17% between 600 and 700, and 2% above 700. The ACT scores were 14% below 18, 48% between 18 and 23, 30% between 24 and 29, and 5% above 29. 50% of the current freshmen were in the top quarter of their class; 80% were in the top half. 10 freshmen graduated first in their class.

Requirements: The SAT I or ACT is required, with a minimum SAT I composite of 900, with 450 on each part, or an ACT composite of 18. Each application is reviewed on an individual basis. The GED is accepted. For high school students, the college recommends completion of 28 academic credits, based on 4 years each of English, math, and science and 2 years each of foreign language, history, and social studies. Manchester requires applicants to be in the upper 50% of their class. A GPA of 2.3 is required. AP and CLEP credits are accepted. Important factors in the admissions decision are advanced placement or honor courses, leadership record, and recommendations by school officials. The college accepts applications on computer disk.

Procedure: Freshmen are admitted to all sessions. Entrance exams should be taken by November of the senior year. There are early admissions and deferred admissions plans. Application deadlines are open. The application fee is $20. Notification is sent on a rolling basis.

Transfer: 31 transfer students enrolled in 2001-2002. Transfer students must present a minimum GPA of 2.0 in all previous college work. 96 credits of 128 must be completed at Manchester.

Visiting: There are regularly scheduled orientations for prospective students, including meetings about financial aid, meetings with faculty and with admissions, and campus tours. Visitors may also eat meals on campus, sit in on classes, and meet with current students. There are guides for informal visits and visitors may sit in on classes and stay overnight. To schedule a visit, contact Jill Biehl, Campus Visit Coordinator at *jlb@manchester.edu*

Financial Aid: In 2001-2002, all freshmen and 96% of continuing students received some form of financial aid. The average freshman award was $15,678. Of that total, scholarships or need-based grants averaged $11,883; and loans averaged $2954. 40% of undergraduates work part time. The average financial indebtedness of the 2001 graduate was $13,461. The FAFSA is required. The fall application deadline is rolling.

International Students: There are 55 international students enrolled. The school actively recruits these students. They must score 550 on the written TOEFL or 213 on the electronic version.

Computers: The mainframe is an IBM AS/400. PC labs are available in various academic buildings and residence halls; in addition, various departments have computer labs for students. All students may access the system any time. There are no time limits and no fees.

Graduates: In 2001, 171 bachelor's degrees were awarded. The most popular majors were business (28%), education (21%), and communications (8%). In an average class, 44% graduate in 4 years, 50% in 5 years, and 51% in 6 years. 25 companies recruited on campus in 2000-2001. Of the 2000 graduating class, 24% were enrolled in graduate school within 6 months of graduation and 74% were employed.

Admissions Contact: Jolane Rohr, Director of Admissions.
E-mail: *admitinfo@manchester.edu* Web: *www.manchester.edu*

MARIAN COLLEGE — C-3
Indianapolis, IN 46222 — (317) 955-6300
(800) 772-7264; Fax: (317) 955-6401

Full-time: 266 men, 606 women	**Faculty:** 77
Part-time: 52 men, 336 women	**Ph.D.s:** 58%
Graduate: none	**Student/Faculty:** 11 to 1
Year: semesters, summer session	**Tuition:** $15,630
Application Deadline: open	**Room & Board:** $5390
Freshman Class: 700 applied, 560 accepted, 189 enrolled	
SAT I Verbal/Math: 490/490	**ACT:** 20 **COMPETITIVE**

Marian College, an independent institution, was founded in 1851 by the Sisters of St. Francis and is today affiliated with the Roman Catholic Church. The college offers undergraduate programs in the arts and sciences, business, education, fine arts, and the health professions. In addition to regional accreditation, Marian has baccalaureate program accreditation with ADA, AHEA, CAHEA, NCATE, and NLN. The library contains 144,000 volumes and 500 audiovisual forms/CDs, and subscribes to 590 periodicals. Computerized library services include interlibrary loans and database searching. Special learning facilities include a learning resource center, art gallery, and the 35-acre Wetlands Ecology Laboratory. The 114-acre campus is in an urban area 6 miles from downtown Indianapolis. Including residence halls, there are 22 buildings.

Student Life: 95% of undergraduates are from Indiana. Others are from 19 states, 17 foreign countries, and Canada. 69% are from public schools. 69% are white; 16% African American. 44% are Catholic; 43% Protestant. The average age of freshmen is 19; all undergraduates, 24. 30% do not continue beyond their first year; 55% remain to graduate.

Housing: 515 students can be accommodated in college housing, which includes single-sex and coed dormitories, on-campus apartments, and married-student housing. In addition, there are academic houses. On-campus housing is guaranteed for all 4 years. 51% of students commute. Alcohol is not permitted. All students may keep cars.

Activities: There are no fraternities or sororities. There are 33 groups on campus, including art, band, cheerleading, choir, chorale, chorus, computers, departmental, drama, drill team, ethnic, honors, international, jazz band, literary magazine, musical theater, pep band, photography, political, professional, religious, social, social service, student government, and yearbook. Popular campus events include Knightly Music Awards, Mock Rock, and Student Production Theater.

Sports: There are 9 intercollegiate sports for men and 9 for women, and 12 intramural sports for men and 12 for women. Facilities include varsity and intramural gyms, racquetball courts, a weight-training room, and a phys ed assessment lab.

Disabled Students: 90% of the campus is accessible. Wheelchair ramps, elevators, special parking, and special class scheduling are available.

Services: Counseling and information services are available, as is tutoring in most subjects. There is a reader service for the blind, remedial math and writing, study skills training, and peer tutoring.

Campus Safety and Security: Measures include 24-hour foot and vehicle patrol, escort service, shuttle buses, and informal discussions. There are pamphlets/posters/films and lighted pathways/sidewalks.

Programs of Study: Marian confers B.S., B.S., and B.S.N. degrees. Associate degrees are also awarded. Bachelor's degrees are awarded in BIOLOGICAL SCIENCE (biology/biological science), BUSINESS (accounting, banking and finance, business administration and management, and sports management), COMMUNICATIONS AND

THE ARTS (art history and appreciation, communications, dramatic arts, English, French, graphic design, music, Spanish, and studio art), COMPUTER AND PHYSICAL SCIENCE (chemistry and mathematics), EDUCATION (early childhood, elementary, physical, and special), ENGINEERING AND ENVIRONMENTAL DESIGN (environmental science), HEALTH PROFESSIONS (nursing), SOCIAL SCIENCE (economics, history, pastoral studies, philosophy, political science/government, psychology, religious education, sociology, and theological studies). Accounting, finance, and English are the strongest academically. Nursing, business administration, and education are the largest.

Required: To graduate, students must complete 128 semester hours, including 30 to 40 in the major, with a minimum GPA of 2.0 overall and in the major. General education requirements include 14 semester hours in cultural awareness, 10 to 12 in scientific and quantitative reasoning, 9 to 17 in written and oral communication and foreign language, and 9 each in moral reasoning and individual and social awareness.

Special: Co-op programs in accounting, finance, business administration, chemistry, management information systems, and sociology, and cross-registration through the Consortium for Urban Education are offered. A dual degree program in math and computer science and accelerated degrees in nursing, business administration, and management information systems are also offered. Internships, study abroad, independent study, dual and student-designed majors, and pass/fail options are all available. There are 8 national honor societies and a freshman honors program.

Faculty/Classroom: 52% of faculty are male; 48%, female. All teach undergraduates. The average class size in an introductory lecture is 20; in a laboratory, 15; and in a regular course, 15.

Admissions: 80% of the 2001-2002 applicants were accepted. The SAT I scores for the 2001-2002 freshman class were: Verbal--51% below 500, 42% between 500 and 599, 6% between 600 and 700, and 1% above 700; Math--50% below 500, 38% between 500 and 599, 11% between 600 and 700, and 1% above 700. The ACT scores were 56% below 21, 21% between 21 and 23, 15% between 24 and 26, 6% between 27 and 28, and 1% above 28. 29% of the current freshmen were in the top fifth of their class; 60% were in the top two fifths. 2 freshmen graduated first in their class.

Requirements: The SAT I or ACT is required. In addition, applicants must be graduates of an accredited secondary school or have a GED. Marian requires 20 academic units, including 4 units in English, 2 each in a foreign language and math, of which algebra and geometry are recommended, and 2 each in a lab science and social studies. A GPA of 2.0 is required. AP and CLEP credits are accepted. Important factors in the admissions decision are recommendations by school officials, recommendations by alumni, and leadership record. Applications are accepted on-line at the college's web site.

Procedure: Freshmen are admitted to all sessions. Entrance exams should be taken at the end of the junior year or the beginning of the senior year. Application deadlines are open. The application fee is $20. Notification is sent on a rolling basis.

Transfer: 178 transfer students enrolled in 2001-2002. In addition to meeting standard admissions requirements, applicants must submit transcripts of all college work and be in good standing at their former school. Students transferring fewer than 30 credit hours must have a 1.75 GPA; those having more than 30 hours must have a 2.0 GPA. 32 credits of 128 must be completed at Marian.

Visiting: There are regularly scheduled orientations for prospective students, including a campus tour, visits with faculty and coaches, and financial aid information. There are guides for informal visits and visitors may sit in on classes and stay overnight. To schedule a visit, contact the Admissions Office.

Financial Aid: In 2001-2002, 95% of all freshmen and 90% of continuing students received some form of financial aid. 69% of freshmen and 80% of continuing students received need-based aid. The average freshman award was $14,085. Of that total, scholarships or need-based grants averaged $10,706 ($19,258 maximum); loans averaged $2388 ($4125 maximum); and work contracts averaged $991 ($1000 maximum). 69% of undergraduates work part time. Average annual earnings from campus work are $1000. The average financial indebtedness of the 2001 graduate was $12,110. Marian is a member of CSS. The FAFSA and the college's own financial statement are required. The fall application deadline is March 1.

International Students: The school actively recruits these students. They must score 550 on the written TOEFL or 220 on the electronic version.

Computers: More than 150 PCs and Mac computers are available for student use in the library, several computer centers, and a variety of special-purpose classrooms. The entire campus, including all residence hall rooms, is wired for network access, including a high-speed Internet/Web connection. All students may access the system. There are no time limits. The fee is $50 per semester. It is strongly recommended that all students have a personal computer.

Graduates: In a recent year, 213 bachelor's degrees were awarded. The most popular majors were nursing (25%), business (16%), and education (13%). In an average class, 1% graduate in 3 years, 32% in 4 years, 45% in 5 years, and 48% in 6 years. 152 companies recruited on campus in a recent year. Of the 2000 graduating class, 19% were enrolled in graduate school within 6 months of graduation and 79% were employed.

Admissions Contact: Karen Kist, Director of Admissions.
E-mail: *admit@marian.edu* Web: *www.marian.edu*

MARTIN UNIVERSITY — C-3

Indianapolis, IN 46218 — (317) 543-3254; Fax: (317) 543-4790

Full-time: 70 men, 220 women	**Faculty:** 26
Part-time: 90 men, 185 women	**Ph.D.s:** 38%
Graduate: 60 men, 90 women	**Student/Faculty:** 11 to 1
Year: semesters, summer session	**Tuition:** $8370
Application Deadline: open	**Room & Board:** n/app
Freshman Class: n/av	
SAT I or ACT: not required	**SPECIAL**

Martin University, established in 1977, is a private liberal arts institution offering undergraduate programs primarily to low-income minority-group adults. It also offers graduate degrees in community psychology and urban ministry studies. Figures in the above capsule are approximate. Computerized library services include interlibrary loans and database searching. Special learning facilities include a learning resource center and English and math labs. The 8-acre campus is in an urban area in Indianapolis. There are 10 buildings.

Student Life: Students are from 4 foreign countries. 90% are from public schools. 90% are African American. The average age of freshmen is 43; all undergraduates, 40. 10% do not continue beyond their first year; 65% remain to graduate.

Housing: There are no residence halls. Alcohol is not permitted. All students may keep cars.

Activities: There are no fraternities or sororities. There are some groups and organizations on campus, including choir, civil rights, computers, newspaper, opera, and social service. Popular campus events include internal and external conferences, St. Martin de Porres Feast Day, and Fine Arts Festival.

Sports: There is no sports program at Martin U.

Disabled Students: 90% of the campus is accessible. Wheelchair ramps, elevators, special parking, and specially equipped rest rooms are available.

Services: Counseling and information services are available, as is tutoring in most subjects. There is remedial math, reading, and writing. and addiction services.

Campus Safety and Security: Measures include 24-hour foot and vehicle patrol.

Programs of Study: Martin U confers B.A. and B.S. degrees. Master's degrees are also awarded. Bachelor's degrees are awarded in BIOLOGICAL SCIENCE (biology/biological science), BUSINESS (accounting, business administration and management, insurance, and marketing/retailing/merchandising), COMMUNICATIONS AND THE ARTS (communications, English, fine arts, music, and piano/organ), COMPUTER AND PHYSICAL SCIENCE (chemistry and mathematics), EDUCATION (early childhood, education, and vocational), ENGINEERING AND ENVIRONMENTAL DESIGN (computer technology), HEALTH PROFESSIONS (nursing), SOCIAL SCIENCE (African American studies, behavioral science, community services, counseling/psychology, criminal justice, history, humanities, political science/government, psychology, religion, and sociology). Humanities and psychology are the strongest academically. Business is the largest.

Required: Students must successfully complete 134 credits, including 36 in the humanities, 12 in English, 9 in social science, and 6 in math, with at least 36 in the major and a minimum GPA of 2.0. Other required courses include computer science and logic and a foreign language for the B.A. Students must complete a final project in their major.

Special: Cross-registration is permitted with 7 schools in the Consortium of Urban Education in the area. Opportunities are provided for internships, student-designed majors, and credit based on assessment of prior learning. There is 1 departmental honors program.

Faculty/Classroom: All teach undergraduates and 10% do research. No introductory courses are taught by graduate students. The average class size in an introductory lecture is 10 and in a laboratory, 8.

Requirements: Graduation from an accredited secondary school is required; a GED will be accepted. No specific number of academic credits is required. An essay, an interview, and diagnostic testing are required. CLEP credit is accepted.

Procedure: Freshmen are admitted to all sessions. Entrance exams should be taken at the time of admission. Application deadlines are open. The application fee is $25.

Transfer: Transfers are accepted from accredited regional schools. 34 credits of 134 must be completed at Martin U.

Visiting: There are regularly scheduled orientations for prospective students, consisting of four 3-hour sessions. There are guides for informal visits and visitors may sit in on classes. To schedule a visit, contact the Recruitment Office at (317) 543-3865.

Financial Aid: In a recent year, 80% of all freshmen and 70% of continuing students received some form of financial aid. 65% of freshmen and 75% of continuing students received need-based aid. The average freshman award was $11,000. 2% of undergraduates work part time. Average annual earnings from campus work are $1500. The average financial indebtedness of a graduate in a recent year was $26,000. The FAFSA is required. The fall application deadline is March 1.

International Students: They must score 550 on the written TOEFL.

Computers: The mainframe is an IBM/34. There are also 20 IBM PCs available with an assistant on duty. All students may access the system. There are no time limits and no fees.

Admissions Contact: Brenda Shaheed, Director of Admissions. E-mail: *bshaheed@martin.edu*

NOTRE DAME UNIVERSITY
(See University of Notre Dame)

OAKLAND CITY UNIVERSITY — A-5
Oakland City, IN 47660 — (812) 749-1222
(800) 737-5125; Fax: (812) 749-1233

Full-time: 600 men, 400 women	**Faculty:** 30; IIB, --$
Part-time: 30 men, 40 women	**Ph.D.s:** 45%
Graduate: 80 men and women	**Student/Faculty:** 33 to 1
Year: semesters, summer session	**Tuition:** $11,286
Application Deadline: open	**Room & Board:** n/app
Freshman Class: n/av	
SAT I or ACT: required	**LESS COMPETITIVE**

Oakland City University, founded in 1885, is a private liberal arts institution affiliated with the General Association of General Baptists. Figures given in above capsule are approximate. There are 6 undergraduate and 2 graduate schools. In addition to regional accreditation, OCU has baccalaureate program accreditation with NCATE. The library contains 75,000 volumes and 18,000 microform items, and subscribes to 350 periodicals. Computerized library services include the card catalog and interlibrary loans. Special learning facilities include a learning resource center and art gallery. The 20-acre campus is in a small town 30 miles north of Evansville, Illinois. Including residence halls, there are 15 buildings.

Student Life: 88% of undergraduates are from Indiana. Others are from 18 states and 6 foreign countries. 90% are from public schools. 96% are white. 76% are Protestant; 30% claim no religious affiliation; 13% Catholic. The average age of freshmen is 19; all undergraduates, 24. 30% do not continue beyond their first year; 70% remain to graduate.

Housing: 246 students can be accommodated in college housing, which includes single-sex dormitories. In addition, there are special-interest houses. On-campus housing is available on a first-come, first-served basis. 57% of students commute. Alcohol is not permitted. All students may keep cars.

Activities: There are no fraternities or sororities. There are 19 groups on campus, including art, cheerleading, chess, choir, chorus, computers, departmental, drama, honors, international, musical theater, newspaper, pep band, photography, professional, religious, social, social service, student government, and yearbook. Popular campus events include Fall Festival Week, Spring Fling, and Fine Arts Festival.

Sports: There are 4 intercollegiate sports for men and 5 for women, and 25 intramural sports for men and 25 for women. Facilities include a gym, a health and phys ed center with a 1400-seat gym, and a playing field.

Disabled Students: 99% of the campus is accessible. Wheelchair ramps, special parking, specially equipped rest rooms, and lowered drinking fountains are available.

Services: Counseling and information services are available, as is tutoring in every subject. There is a reader service for the blind, and remedial math, reading, and writing.

Campus Safety and Security: Measures include self-defense education, escort service, informal discussions, and pamphlets/posters/films. There are emergency telephones, lighted pathways/sidewalks, and security in the evenings.

Programs of Study: OCU confers B.A. and B.S. degrees. Associate and master's degrees are also awarded. Bachelor's degrees are awarded in BIOLOGICAL SCIENCE (biology/biological science), BUSINESS (accounting and business administration and management), COMMUNICATIONS AND THE ARTS (English, fine arts, and music), COMPUTER AND PHYSICAL SCIENCE (chemistry, computer programming, computer science, and mathematics), EDUCATION (art, business, elementary, middle school, music, science, and secondary), HEALTH PROFESSIONS (premedicine), SOCIAL SCIENCE (prelaw and religion). Education is the strongest academically. Education is the largest.

Required: Liberal arts students must take a general studies core, including 1 computer science course and 2 hours of phys ed. A minimum GPA of 2.0 (2.5 in the major) and 120 total semester hours are needed.

Special: OCU offers campus work-study programs, an accelerated business degree program, business and networking internships, a B.A.-B.S. degree, dual majors, credit for significant work or service experience, nondegree study, pass/fail options, and a general studies degree. There are 3 national honor societies.

Faculty/Classroom: No introductory courses are taught by graduate students. The average class size in an introductory lecture is 20; in a laboratory, 16; and in a regular course, 20.

Requirements: The SAT I or ACT is required, with a minimum SAT I composite score of 700 or ACT composite score of 18. Preparatory programs usually include 4 units of English, 2 each of social science and science, 2 to 4 of a foreign language, and 3 to 4 of math. An interview is recommended. The GED is accepted. A GPA of 2.0 is required. AP and CLEP credits are accepted. Important factors in the admissions decision are personality/intangible qualities, evidence of special talent, and extracurricular activities record.

Procedure: Freshmen are admitted to all sessions. Entrance exams should be taken in the fall of the senior year. There is a deferred admissions plan. Application deadlines are open.

Transfer: Transfer applicants need a minimum GPA of 2.0 and a composite score of 700 on the SAT I or 18 on the ACT. An interview is recommended. 35 credits of 120 must be completed at OCU.

Visiting: There are regularly scheduled orientations for prospective students. There are guides for informal visits and visitors may sit in on classes and stay overnight. To schedule a visit, contact the Admissions Office.

Financial Aid: OCU is a member of CSS. The FAFSA and the college's own financial statement are required. Check with the school for current deadlines.

International Students: They must score 500 on the written TOEFL and also take the SAT I or the ACT.

Computers: All students may access the system. There are no time limits and no fees.

Admissions Contact: Buddy Harris, Director of Admissions.

PURDUE UNIVERSITY SYSTEM

Purdue University was founded in 1869 as a land-grand institution in West Lafayette, Indiana. Since opening its doors to 39 students in 1874, Purdue has grown to a statewide system whose priorities are teaching, research, and service. The total enrollment of all 5 campuses is approximately 66,000 students with more than 37,000 at the main campus in West Lafayette. Purdue offers nearly 6100 courses in more than 200 specializations. Graduate students can work toward a master's or doctoral degree in approximately 60 different departmental programs. Among the 25 largest colleges and universities in the nation, Purdue maintains a tradition of providing students with an excellent, affordable education.

PURDUE UNIVERSITY/CALUMET — B-1
Hammond, IN 46323 — (219) 989-2213
(800) HI PURDUE; Fax: (219) 989-2775

Full-time: 1934 men, 2469 women	**Faculty:** 238; IIA, -$
Part-time: 1627 men, 2056 women	**Ph.D.s:** 56%
Graduate: 313 men, 666 women	**Student/Faculty:** n/av
Year: semesters, summer session	**Tuition:** $3631 ($8257)
Application Deadline: open	**Room & Board:** n/app
Freshman Class: 1776 applied, 1759 accepted, 1200 enrolled	
SAT I Verbal/Math: 460/450	**NONCOMPETITIVE**

Purdue University/Calumet, established in 1946, is a public commuter institution offering undergraduate degrees in general studies, liberal arts, and professional studies. There are 2 undergraduate schools and 1 graduate school. In addition to regional accreditation, Purdue Cal has baccalaureate program accreditation with ABET, NCATE, and NLN. The library contains 200,000 volumes, 460,000 microform items, and 227 audiovisual forms/CDs, and subscribes to 1640 periodicals. Computerized library services include the card catalog and database searching. Special learning facilities include an art gallery, a computer education building, and an educational media laboratory. The 130-acre campus is in an urban area 25 miles southeast of Chicago. There are 11 buildings.

Student Life: 91% of undergraduates are from Indiana. Others are from 7 states, 3 foreign countries, and Canada. 90% are from public schools. 82% are white. The average age of freshmen is 20; all undergraduates, 29.

Housing: There are no residence halls. All students commute. Alcohol is not permitted.

Activities: There are 3 national fraternities and 3 national sororities. There are 45 groups on campus, including cheerleading, chorus, computers, drama, ethnic, honors, literary magazine, musical theater, newspaper, political, professional, religious, social service, and student government. Popular campus events include Orientation, Latin Culture Month, and Black History Month.

Sports: There are 2 intercollegiate sports for men and 2 for women, and 4 intramural sports for men and 4 for women. Facilities include a

1500-seat gym, racquetball courts, a baseball field, a running track, a weight room, and a total fitness center.

Disabled Students: 90% of the campus is accessible. Wheelchair ramps, elevators, special parking, specially equipped rest rooms, special class scheduling, lowered drinking fountains, lowered telephones, and electric door openers on all but 1 student building are available.

Services: Counseling and information services are available, as is tutoring in most subjects. There is a reader service for the blind, and remedial math, reading, and writing.

Campus Safety and Security: Measures include 24-hour foot and vehicle patrol, escort service, informal discussions, and pamphlets/posters/films. There are emergency telephones, lighted pathways/sidewalks, and student patrols.

Programs of Study: Purdue Cal confers B.A., B.S., B.S.Ch., and B.S.E. degrees. Associate and master's degrees are also awarded. Bachelor's degrees are awarded in BIOLOGICAL SCIENCE (biology/biological science, biotechnology, microbiology, and zoology), BUSINESS (accounting, banking and finance, business economics, hotel/motel and restaurant management, and marketing/retailing/merchandising), COMMUNICATIONS AND THE ARTS (broadcasting, communications, English, French, German, and Spanish), COMPUTER AND PHYSICAL SCIENCE (chemistry, computer programming, computer science, information sciences and systems, mathematics, and physics), EDUCATION (early childhood, elementary, foreign languages, science, and secondary), ENGINEERING AND ENVIRONMENTAL DESIGN (computer engineering, computer technology, construction technology, electrical/electronics engineering, electrical/electronics engineering technology, engineering, engineering technology, industrial engineering technology, mechanical engineering, and mechanical engineering technology), HEALTH PROFESSIONS (medical laboratory technology, nursing, optometry, physical therapy, predentistry, premedicine, prepharmacy, and preveterinary science), SOCIAL SCIENCE (criminal justice, history, international relations, philosophy, political science/government, prelaw, psychology, social work, and sociology). Engineering, nursing, and behavioral sciences are the strongest academically. Engineering, business, and nursing are the largest.

Required: Graduation requirements vary depending on the program. The total number of credit hours required for a degree varies from 126 to 136, with 24 to 73 in the major. All students must take English composition and 36 hours of general education courses and maintain a C average.

Special: Some cooperative programs, internships, and work-study programs are available to students. Purdue Cal offers cross-registration in philosophy, study in Spain, and credit for life, military, and work experience, as well as nondegree study and pass/fail options. There is a freshman honors program.

Faculty/Classroom: The average class size in an introductory lecture is 24; in a laboratory, 24; and in a regular course, 24.

Admissions: 99% of the 2001-2002 applicants were accepted. The SAT I scores for the 2001-2002 freshman class were: Verbal--67% below 500, 28% between 500 and 599, 5% between 600 and 700, and 1% above 700, Math--69% below 500, 24% between 500 and 599, 6% between 600 and 700, and 1% above 700. 15% of the current freshmen were in the top fifth of their class; 37% were in the top two fifths.

Requirements: The SAT I or ACT is required. In addition, the SAT II: Subject test in mathematics is required. Applicants must be graduates of an accredited secondary school. The GED is acccepted. 33 Carnegie units are required for admission. Required courses vary, depending on the curriculum, and include 3 or 4 years of English, 2 or 3 years of math, 2 years of foreign language, and 1 year of history or social studies. Purdue Cal requires applicants to be in the upper 66% of their class. AP and CLEP credits are accepted. Important factors in the admissions decision are recommendations by school officials, advanced placement or honor courses, and personality/intangible qualities.

Procedure: Freshmen are admitted to all sessions. Entrance exams should be taken between November and March of the senior year. Application deadlines are open. Notification is sent on a rolling basis.

Transfer: Applicants must have a minimum GPA of 2.0. for transfer credit. 36 credits of 126 must be completed at Purdue Cal.

Visiting: There are regularly scheduled orientations for prospective students. There are guides for informal visits and visitors may sit in on classes. To schedule a visit, contact the Media Service Office, Admissions, or the academic departments at (219) 989-2289.

Financial Aid: Purdue Cal is a member of CSS. The CSS/Profile is required. Check with the school for current deadlines.

International Students: They must score 550 on the written TOEFL or 213 on the electronic version and also take the SAT I or the ACT, scoring 500.

Computers: The mainframes are an IBM 4341/LI, 2 DEC VAX 11/780S, and a DEC VAX 8600. Numerous PCs are available. All students may access the system. There are no time limits and no fees.

Admissions Contact: Paul McGuinness, Admissions Director.
E-mail: *adms.@calumet.purdue.edu* Web: *www.calumet.purdue.edu*

PURDUE UNIVERSITY/WEST LAFAYETTE B-3

West Lafayette, IN 47907 **(765) 494-1776; Fax: (765) 494-0544**

Full-time: 17,066 men, 12,172 women
Part-time: 970 men, 779 women
Graduate: 4257 men, 2916 women
Year: semesters, summer session
Application Deadline: open
Freshman Class: 21,760 applied, 16,727 accepted, 6504 enrolled
SAT I Verbal/Math: 550/584
Faculty: 1849; I, -$
Ph.D.s: 99%
Student/Faculty: 16 to 1
Tuition: $4164 ($13,872)
Room & Board: $6120
ACT: 25 **VERY COMPETITIVE**

Purdue University, founded in 1869, is a publicly supported institution offering degree programs with an emphasis on engineering, business, communications, arts, and social sciences. There are 12 undergraduate schools and 1 graduate school. In addition to regional accreditation, Purdue has baccalaureate program accreditation with AACSB, ABET, ACCE, ACPE, ADA, ASLA, NCATE, NLN, and SAF. The 15 libraries contain 1,173,046 volumes, 2,487,846 microform items, and 11,412 audiovisual forms/CDs, and subscribe to 17,644 periodicals. Computerized library services include the card catalog, interlibrary loans, and database searching. Special learning facilities include a learning resource center, art gallery, and radio station. The 1579-acre campus is in a suburban area 65 miles northwest of Indianapolis. Including residence halls, there are 145 buildings.

Student Life: 69% of undergraduates are from Indiana. Others are from 49 states, 105 foreign countries, and Canada. 84% are white. Most claim no religious affiliation. The average age of freshmen is 18; all undergraduates, 21. 11% do not continue beyond their first year; 67% remain to graduate.

Housing: 11,689 students can be accommodated in college housing, which includes single-sex and coed dormitories, on-campus apartments, married-student housing, fraternity houses, and sorority houses. In addition, there are 3 floors in a women's hall for women in engineering or science. On-campus housing is available on a first-come, first-served basis. 61% of students commute. Alcohol is not permitted. Upperclassmen may keep cars.

Activities: 17% of men belong to 48 national fraternities; 17% of women belong to 26 national sororities. There are 600 groups on campus, including band, cheerleading, chess, choir, chorale, chorus, computers, dance, debate, drama, ethnic, gay, honors, international, jazz band, literary magazine, marching band, newspaper, orchestra, pep band, photography, political, professional, radio and TV, religious, social, social service, student government, symphony, and yearbook. Popular campus events include Grand Prix Race, Old Masters, and Gala week.

Sports: There are 10 intercollegiate sports for men and 10 for women, and 27 intramural sports for men and 26 for women. Facilities include a 14,000-seat arena, a 62,000-seat stadium, an intercollegiate athletic facility, a recreational gym, a field house, an athletic center, intramural playing fields, 2 golf courses, and baseball, softball, track, and women's soccer fields.

Disabled Students: 90% of the campus is accessible. Wheelchair ramps, elevators, special parking, specially equipped rest rooms, special class scheduling, lowered drinking fountains, lowered telephones, and a lab with assistive technology and special computers are available.

Services: Counseling and information services are available, as is tutoring in every subject. There is a reader service for the blind, and remedial math, reading, and writing.

Campus Safety and Security: Measures include 24-hour foot and vehicle patrol, self-defense education, escort service, and informal discussions. There are pamphlets/posters/films, emergency telephones, lighted pathways/sidewalks, and public transportation routes throughout campus.

Programs of Study: Purdue confers B.A., B.S., B.P.E, B.S.A.A.E., B.S.A.B.E., B.S.A.G.E., B.S.C.E., B.S.C.E.E., B.S.C.E.M., B.S.Ch., B.S.Ch.E., B.S.C.M.P.E., B.S.E., B.S.E.E., B.S.E.H., B.S.F., B.S.I.E., B.S.I.E.D., B.S.I.M., B.S.L.A., B.S.L.S., B.S.L.S.E., B.S.M.E., B.S.M.S.E., B.S.N.E., and B.S.Pharm. degrees. Associate, master's, and doctoral degrees are also awarded. Bachelor's degrees are awarded in AGRICULTURE (agricultural business management, agricultural economics, agricultural mechanics, agriculture, agronomy, animal science, conservation and regulation, forestry and related sciences, horticulture, natural resource management, plant protection (pest management), and wildlife management), BIOLOGICAL SCIENCE (biochemistry, biology/biological science, ecology, entomology, and nutrition), BUSINESS (accounting, hotel/motel and restaurant management, management science, marketing management, office supervision and management, recreation and leisure services, and retailing), COMMUNICATIONS AND THE ARTS (apparel design, art history and appreciation, classics, communications, comparative literature, crafts, creative writing, design, dramatic arts, English, film arts, fine arts, French, German, industrial design, Japanese, journalism, languages, Latin, linguistics, media arts, photography, public relations, Russian, Spanish, telecommunications, and theater design), COMPUTER AND PHYSICAL SCIENCE (actuarial science, applied mathematics, applied physics, atmospheric sciences and meteorology, chemistry, computer science, earth science, geology, information sciences and systems, mathematics, physics, science, and statistics), EDUCATION (agricultural, art, athletic training, educational media, elementary, English, foreign languages, health, industrial arts, mathematics, physical, science, secondary, social studies, and special), ENGINEERING AND ENVIRONMENTAL DESIGN (aeronautical engineering, aeronautical technology, agricultural engineering, architectural engineering, biomedical engineering, chemical engineering, civil engineering, computer engineering, computer graphics, computer technology, construction engineering, construction technology, electrical/electronics engineering, electrical/electronics engineering technology, engineering, geological engineering, graphic arts technology, industrial administration/management, industrial engineering, industrial engineering technology, interior design, landscape architecture/design, materials engineering, mechanical engineering, mechanical engineering technology, nuclear engineering, ocean engineering, preengineering, surveying engineering, systems engineering, and transportation engineering), HEALTH PROFESSIONS (community health work, environmental health science, exercise science, health science, medical technology, nursing, pharmacy, predentistry, premedicine, prepharmacy, speech pathology/audiology, and veterinary science), SOCIAL SCIENCE (African American studies, American studies, anthropology, child care/child and family studies, consumer services, dietetics, economics, family and community services, food science, history, Italian studies, Judaic studies, law, liberal arts/general studies, medieval studies, philosophy, political science/government, prelaw, psychology, religion, sociology, and urban studies). Engineering, actuarial science, and industrial management are the strongest academically. Management, preengineering, and mechanical engineering are the largest.

Required: To graduate, students must complete approximately 128 hours and earn a minimum GPA of 2.0. In most majors, students must take courses in English, math, science, computer science, and social sciences.

Special: Cooperative programs are available in engineering, technology, agriculture, management, science, and consumer and family sciences. Cross-registration with Purdue's regional campuses, numerous internships, study abroad in 41 countries, dual majors, student-designed majors, nondegree study, and pass/fail options are also offered. There are 14 national honor societies, including Phi Beta Kappa, a freshman honors program, and 10 departmental honors programs.

Faculty/Classroom: 76% of faculty are male; 24%, female. The average class size in an introductory lecture is 50 and in a laboratory, 22.

Admissions: 77% of the 2001-2002 applicants were accepted. The SAT I scores for the 2001-2002 freshman class were: Verbal--25% below 500, 48% between 500 and 599, 23% between 600 and 700, and 4% above 700; Math--18% below 500, 39% between 500 and 599, 34% between 600 and 700, and 9% above 700. The ACT scores were 1% below 18, 32% between 18 and 23, 54% between 24 and 29, and 13% above 29. 61% of the current freshmen were in the top quarter of their class; 94% were in the top half. 187 freshmen graduated first in their class.

Requirements: The SAT I or ACT is required. In addition, Purdue recommends that most students have 15 semester credits, including 4 years of English, 3 to 4 of math, and 2 to 4 of lab science. The GED is accepted. AP and CLEP credits are accepted. Important factors in the admissions decision are advanced placement or honor courses, recommendations by school officials, and parents or siblings attending the school. Applications are accepted on-line.

Procedure: Freshmen are admitted to all sessions. Entrance exams should be taken at the end of the junior year. Application deadlines are open. The application fee is $30. Notification is sent on a rolling basis.

Transfer: 941 transfer students enrolled in 2001-2002. Transfer students must file a regular application at least 30 days before the start of the semester and submit SAT I/ACT results and high school and college transcripts. Students must be in good academic standing and meet the same subject-matter requirements as a beginning student. A minimum 2.3 GPA is required; many programs require a higher average and have some subject requirements. 32 credits of 128 must be completed at Purdue.

Visiting: There are regularly scheduled orientations for prospective students, including fall and spring preview days, which consist of admission, financial aid, housing, and school sessions, a campus tour, and dormitory visits. The Summer Visit Program consists of a counselors' orientation and campus and residence hall visits. There are guides for informal visits and visitors may sit in on classes. To schedule a visit, contact the Office of Admissions.

Financial Aid: In 2001-2002, 76% of all freshmen and 63% of continuing students received some form of financial aid. 54% of freshmen and 49% of continuing students received need-based aid. The average freshman award was $6293. Of that total, scholarships or need-based grants averaged $4779 ($6300 maximum); loans averaged $3292; and work contracts averaged $1395 ($1600 maximum). 12% of undergraduates work part time. Average annual earnings from campus work are $859. The average financial indebtedness of the 2001 graduate was $15,486. Purdue is a member of CSS. The FAFSA is required. The fall application deadline is March 1.

International Students: There are 2005 international students enrolled. They must score 550 on the written TOEFL or 213 on the electronic version.

Computers: Central computer services are provided on a variety of servers, including about 20 models of the IBM RS/6000 class, about 15 models of the Sun Enterprise 4000 family, an IBM SP2 machine, and an Intel Paragon. Students may access central computing facilities through approximately 80 lab locations containing about 2100 workstations (Windows, Macs, and UNIX). Direct network connections are also available in each residence hall room. Students are granted a career account that provides e-mail and Internet services during their entire time at Purdue. All students may access the system 24 hours daily. There are no time limits and no fees.

Graduates: In 2001, 5579 bachelor's degrees were awarded. The most popular majors were management (7%), electrical and computer engineering (5%), and communications (5%). In an average class, 31% graduate in 4 years, 59% in 5 years, and 65% in 6 years. 800 companies recruited on campus in 2000-2001.

Admissions Contact: Dr. Douglas L. Christiansen, Director, Admissions. E-mail: *admissions@purdue.edu* Web: *www.purdue.edu/*

ROSE-HULMAN INSTITUTE OF TECHNOLOGY B-4

Terre Haute, IN 47803 **(812) 877-1511**
(800) 248-7448; Fax: (812) 877-8941

Full-time: 1260 men, 284 women	**Faculty:** 123; IIB, ++$
Part-time: 23 men, 6 women	**Ph.D.s:** 99%
Graduate: 156 men, 20 women	**Student/Faculty:** 13 to 1
Year: quarters, summer session	**Tuition:** $21,668
Application Deadline: March 1	**Room & Board:** $6039
Freshman Class: 3034 applied, 2040 accepted, 404 enrolled	
SAT I Verbal/Math: 610/680	**ACT:** 28
	HIGHLY COMPETITIVE+

Rose-Hulman Institute of Technology, founded in 1874, is a private college emphasizing engineering, science, and math. In addition to regional accreditation, Rose-Hulman has baccalaureate program accreditation with ABET. The library contains 75,949 volumes, 532 microform items, and 365 audiovisual forms/CDs, and subscribes to 593 periodicals. Computerized library services include the card catalog, interlibrary loans, and database searching. Special learning facilities include a learning resource center, art gallery, planetarium, and radio station. The 200-acre campus is in a suburban area on the east side of Terre Haute. Including residence halls, there are 35 buildings.

Student Life: 51% of undergraduates are from out of state, mostly the Midwest. Students are from 49 states, 4 foreign countries, and Canada. 91% are white. The average age of freshmen is 18; all undergraduates, 20. 7% do not continue beyond their first year; 75% remain to graduate.

Housing: 870 students can be accommodated in college housing, which includes single-sex and coed dormitories, on-campus apartments, fraternity houses, and sorority houses. In addition, there are sophomore residence halls. On-campus housing is guaranteed for the freshman year only, is available on a first-come, first-served basis, and is available on a lottery system for upperclassmen. 55% of students live on campus; of those, 60% remain on campus on weekends. All students may keep cars.

Activities: 45% of men belong to 8 national fraternities; 45% of women belong to 2 national sororities. There are 60 groups on campus, including band, cheerleading, chess, chorus, computers, dance, debate, drama, drill team, ethnic, gay, honors, international, jazz band, literary magazine, newspaper, pep band, photography, political, professional, radio and TV, religious, social, social service, student government, and yearbook. Popular campus events include art shows, concerts, and plays.

Sports: There are 10 intercollegiate sports for men and 9 for women, and 12 intramural sports for men and 11 for women. Facilities include a field house, a recreational center, a swimming pool, tennis courts, and intramural fields.

Disabled Students: 95% of the campus is accessible. Wheelchair ramps, elevators, special parking, specially equipped rest rooms, special class scheduling, and lowered drinking fountains are available.

Services: Counseling and information services are available, as is tutoring in most subjects.

Campus Safety and Security: Measures include 24-hour foot and vehicle patrol, escort service, informal discussions, and pamphlets/posters/films. There are emergency telephones, lighted pathways/sidewalks, medical transports, and free traffic assistance.

Programs of Study: Rose-Hulman confers the B.S. degree. Master's degrees are also awarded. Bachelor's degrees are awarded in BIOLOGICAL SCIENCE (biology/biological science), COMPUTER AND PHYSICAL SCIENCE (chemistry, computer science, mathematics, optics, and physics), ENGINEERING AND ENVIRONMENTAL DESIGN (chemical engineering, civil engineering, computer engineering, electrical/electronics engineering, and mechanical engineering), SOCIAL SCIENCE (economics). Engineering, science, and math are the strongest academically. Electrical and computer engineering, mechanical engineering, and computer science are the largest.

Required: All students must complete at least 196 quarter hours with a minimum GPA of 2.0 and 36 hours in the humanities and social sciences. Freshmen are required to take calculus, biology, chemistry, or physics.

Special: The institute offers co-op programs, independent study, cross-registration with Indiana State University, summer industrial internships, study abroad in 8 countries, and dual majors. Pass/fail options also are available. There are 10 national honor societies.

Faculty/Classroom: 86% of faculty are male; 14%, female. All teach undergraduates and 20% do research. No introductory courses are taught by graduate students. The average class size in an introductory lecture is 30; in a laboratory, 20; and in a regular course, 26.

Admissions: 67% of the 2001-2002 applicants were accepted. The SAT I scores for the 2001-2002 freshman class were: Math--1% below 500, 11% between 500 and 599, 48% between 600 and 700, and 40% above 700. The ACT scores for the 2001-2002 freshman class were: 9% between 24 and 26, 56% between 27 and 28, and 35% above 28. 93% of the current freshmen were in the top fifth of their class; 99% were in the top two fifths. There were 27 National Merit finalists and 40 semifinalists. 45 freshmen graduated first in their class.

Requirements: The SAT I or ACT is required. In addition, candidates should have at least 16 units of credit, including 4 in English, 2 in social sciences, and 1 each in math, chemistry, physics, and electives. An essay and an interview are recommended. Rose-Hulman requires applicants to be in the upper 25% of their class. AP credits are accepted. Important factors in the admissions decision are advanced placement or honor courses, recommendations by school officials, and personality/intangible qualities. Applications are accepted on-line at the Rose-Hulman web site.

Procedure: Freshmen are admitted in the fall. Entrance exams should be taken in the fall of the senior year or spring of the junior year. Applications should be filed by March 1 for fall entry, along with a $40 fee. Notification is sent within 3 weeks of receipt of a completed application.

Transfer: 17 transfer students enrolled in a recent year. Applicants need 1 year each of calculus and chemistry and a minimum GPA of 3.0. An interview is recommended. 60 quarter credits of 196 must be completed at Rose-Hulman.

Visiting: There are regularly scheduled orientations for prospective students, including interviews, campus tours, and academic meetings. There are guides for informal visits and visitors may sit in on classes and stay overnight. To schedule a visit, contact the Admissions Office at (812) 877-8213.

Financial Aid: In 2001-2002, 95% of all freshmen and 92% of continuing students received some form of financial aid. 63% of freshmen and 72% of continuing students received need-based aid. The average freshman award was $15,035. Of that total, scholarships or need-based grants averaged $4600 ($14,000 maximum); loans averaged $5500 ($6500 maximum); and work contracts averaged $1500 ($1750 maximum). 65% of undergraduates work part time. Average annual earnings from campus work are $1500. The average financial indebtedness of the 2001 graduate was $26,000. Rose-Hulman is a member of CSS. The FAFSA is required. The fall application deadline is March 1.

International Students: There are 19 international students enrolled. They must score 550 on the written TOEFL or 210 on the electronic version. They must also take the SAT I or ACT, scoring 500 verbal and 550 math on the SAT I.

Computers: There are network connections in all residence hall rooms and most classrooms and labs. All students may access the system. There are no time limits and no fees. All students are required to have personal computers.

Graduates: In 2001, 356 bachelor's degrees were awarded. The most popular majors were mechanical engineering (26%), electrical engineering (15%), and chemical engineering (14%). In an average class, 3% graduate in 3 years, 65% in 4 years, and 80% in 5 years. 165 companies recruited on campus in 2000-2001. Of the 2000 graduating class, 15% were enrolled in graduate school within 6 months of graduation and 99% were employed.

Admissions Contact: Charles G. Howard, Dean of Admissions.
E-mail: *admis.ofc@rose-hulman.edu* Web: *www.rose-hulman.edu*

SAINT FRANCIS COLLEGE
(See University of Saint Francis)

SAINT JOSEPH'S COLLEGE B 2
Rensselaer, IN 47978 (219) 866-6170
(800) 447-8781; Fax: (219) 866-6122

Full-time: 381 men, 407 women	**Faculty:** 53; IIB, --$
Part-time: 23 men, 103 women	**Ph.D.s:** 85%
Graduate: none	**Student/Faculty:** 19 to 1
Year: semesters, summer session	**Tuition:** $16,040
Application Deadline: open	**Room & Board:** $5600
Freshman Class: 1019 applied, 755 accepted, 213 enrolled	
SAT I Verbal/Math: 499/505	**ACT:** 22 **COMPETITIVE**

St. Joseph's College, founded in 1889, is a private Catholic institution providing a liberal arts core curriculum with an interdisciplinary approach and practical, career-oriented experiences. In addition to regional accreditation, SJC has baccalaureate program accreditation with NCATE. The library contains 157,929 volumes, 62,203 microform items, and 22,392 audiovisual forms/CDs, and subscribes to 556 periodicals. Computerized library services include the card catalog, interlibrary loans, and database searching. Special learning facilities include a learning resource center, radio station, and TV station. The 340-acre campus is in a small town 83 miles south of Chicago and 90 miles north of Indianapolis. Including residence halls, there are 30 buildings.

Student Life: 72% of undergraduates are from Indiana. Others are from 20 states, 3 foreign countries, and Canada. 89% are white. 54% are Catholic; 30% Protestant; 12% claim no religious affiliation. The average age of freshmen is 19; all undergraduates, 21. 31% do not continue beyond their first year; 54% remain to graduate.

Housing: 878 students can be accommodated in college housing, which includes single-sex dormitories and on-campus apartments. In addition, there is housing for nontraditional or adult students and special-interest floors. On-campus housing is guaranteed for all 4 years. 73% of students live on campus; of those, 60% remain on campus on weekends. All students may keep cars.

Activities: There are no fraternities or sororities. There are 28 groups on campus, including art, band, cheerleading, choir, chorale, chorus, computers, debate, drama, ethnic, forensics, honors, jazz band, literary magazine, marching band, musical theater, newspaper, orchestra, pep band, photography, political, professional, radio and TV, religious, social, social service, student government, and yearbook. Popular campus events include the Little 500 Go-Kart Race, Alumni Weekend, and Little Siblings Weekend.

Sports: There are 8 intercollegiate sports for men and 8 for women, and 4 intramural sports for men and 4 for women. Facilities include a field house, a 2500-seat gym, a recreation center, a baseball complex, a lighted soccer field, a football facility, and a lake with a sand beach.

Disabled Students: 40% of the campus is accessible. Wheelchair ramps, elevators, special parking, specially equipped rest rooms, special class scheduling, lowered drinking fountains, and lowered telephones are available.

Services: Counseling and information services are available, as is tutoring in every subject. There is a reader service for the blind, and remedial math, reading, and writing.

Campus Safety and Security: Measures include 24-hour foot and vehicle patrol, escort service, informal discussions, and pamphlets/posters/films. There are lighted pathways/sidewalks.

Programs of Study: SJC confers B.A., B.S., and B.S.N. degrees. Associate and master's degrees are also awarded. Bachelor's degrees are awarded in BIOLOGICAL SCIENCE (biology/biological science), BUSINESS (accounting, banking and finance, business administration and management, international business management, management information systems, and marketing/retailing/merchandising), COMMUNICATIONS AND THE ARTS (art, communications, creative writing, English, and music), COMPUTER AND PHYSICAL SCIENCE (chemistry, computer science, and mathematics), EDUCATION (elementary, middle school, music, physical, science, and secondary), ENGINEERING AND ENVIRONMENTAL DESIGN (environmental science), HEALTH PROFESSIONS (medical technology, nursing, predentistry, and premedicine), SOCIAL SCIENCE (criminal justice, economics, history, human services, international studies, philosophy, political science/government, prelaw, psychology, religion, social work, and sociology). Accounting, biology, and education are the strongest academically. Biology, business administration, and education are the largest.

Required: Students must complete 45 hours in the general education program and 36 hours in the major. A total of 120 credit hours with a minimum GPA of 2.0 is required to graduate.

Special: Internships in all fields, a Washington semester, and study abroad throughout Europe and Latin America are available. Dual majors are offered in business, science, and math/computer science, as well as music/business administration. Credit for life, military, and work experience, nondegree study, student-designed majors, and pass/fail options are offered. The core program consists of lectures and discussions over a 4-year period. There are 3 national honor societies and a freshman honors program.

Faculty/Classroom: 63% of faculty are male; 37%, female. All teach undergraduates. The average class size in an introductory lecture is 15; in a laboratory, 18; and in a regular course, 13.

Admissions: 74% of the 2001-2002 applicants were accepted. The SAT I scores for the 2001-2002 freshman class were: Verbal--51% below 500, 40% between 500 and 599, 7% between 600 and 700, and 2% above 700; Math--52% below 500, 33% between 500 and 599, 14% between 600 and 700, and 1% above 700. The ACT scores were 37% below 21, 27% between 21 and 23, 18% between 24 and 26, 10% between 27 and 28, and 8% above 28. 33% of the current freshmen were in the top fifth of their class; 54% were in the top two fifths. 4 freshmen graduated first in their class.

Requirements: The SAT I or ACT is required, with recommended minimum scores of 500 verbal and 500 math on the SAT I or 18 on the ACT. Applicants should be graduates of an accredited secondary school or have earned the GED. They should have completed 15 academic credits, 10 of which must be from the following academic fields: English, foreign language, social studies, math, and natural sciences. An interview is recommended. SJC requires applicants to be in the upper 50% of their class. A GPA of 2.0 is required. AP and CLEP credits are accepted. Important factors in the admissions decision are advanced placement or honor courses, recommendations by school officials, and recommendations by alumni. Applications are accepted via the school's web site and on computer disk through CollegeView.

Procedure: Freshmen are admitted fall and winter. Entrance exams should be taken by January of the senior year. There are early decision and deferred admissions plans. Application deadlines are open. Application fee is $25. Notification of early decision is sent October 15; regular decision, December 15.

Transfer: 30 transfer students enrolled in 2001-2002. Applicants must have a GPA of 2.0. A minimum composite score of 1000 on the SAT I or 19 on the ACT is recommended. Grades of C or better transfer for credit. 30 credits of 120 must be completed at SJC.

Visiting: There are regularly scheduled orientations for prospective students, consisting of Discover Days, Special Interest Days, and early registration. There are guides for informal visits and visitors may sit in on classes and stay overnight. To schedule a visit, contact the Admissions Office.

Financial Aid: In 2001-2002, 72% of all freshmen and 84% of continuing students received some form of financial aid. 58% of freshmen and 63% of continuing students received need-based aid. The average freshman award was $12,000. Of that total, scholarships or need-based grants averaged $9000 ($21,480 maximum); loans averaged $3000 ($3825 maximum); and work contracts averaged $1000 ($1500 maximum). 32% of undergraduates work part time. Average annual earnings from campus work are $1000. The average financial indebtedness of the 2001 graduate was $18,000. The FAFSA and combined admission and financial aid application are required. The fall application deadline is March 1.

International Students: There are 3 international students enrolled. They must score 550 on the written TOEFL and also take the SAT I or the ACT.

Computers: The mainframe is a Prime. 4 centrally located labs house PCs with Sun workstations, laser printers, image scanners, and a desktop publishing center. 66 computers are available for student use. Network access is also available in dorm rooms for students who have their own computers. All students may access the system from 7:30 A.M. to midnight, or by special request. There are no time limits. The fee is $2 per credit hour.

Graduates: In 2001, 162 bachelor's degrees were awarded. The most popular majors were business (26%), biological science (14%), and education (12%). In an average class, 47% graduate in 4 years, 56% in 5 years, and 57% in 6 years. 41 companies recruited on campus in 2000-2001. Of the 2000 graduating class, 20% were enrolled in graduate school within 6 months of graduation and 94% were employed.

Admissions Contact: Frank P. Bevec, Director of Admissions, Assistant Vice President for Enrollment Management.
E-mail: *admissions@saintjoe.edu* Web: *www.saintjoe.edu*

SAINT MARY-OF-THE-WOODS COLLEGE B-4

St. Mary-of-the-Woods, IN 47876 (812) 535-5106
(800) 926-SMWC; Fax: (812) 535-4900

Full-time: 391 women	**Faculty:** 55; IIB, --$
Part-time: 7 men, 986 women	**Ph.D.s:** 65%
Graduate: 18 men, 100 women	**Student/Faculty:** 7 to 1
Year: semesters, summer session	**Tuition:** $15,570
Application Deadline: July 15	**Room & Board:** $5750
Freshman Class: 273 applied, 233 accepted, 115 enrolled	
SAT I Verbal/Math: 506/475	**ACT:** 23 **LESS COMPETITIVE**

Saint Mary-of-the-Woods, founded in 1840, is a private, liberal arts women's college affiliated with the Roman Catholic Church. In addition to regional accreditation, The Woods has baccalaureate program accreditation with NASM and NCATE. The library contains 142,000 volumes and 1676 microform items, and subscribes to 460 periodicals. Computerized library services include the card catalog, interlibrary loans, and database searching. Special learning facilities include a learning resource center and art gallery. The 200-acre campus is in a rural area 5 miles northwest of Terre Haute. Including residence halls, there are 10 buildings.

Student Life: 65% of undergraduates are from Indiana. Others are from 49 states and 5 foreign countries. 70% are from public schools. 45% are Catholic. The average age of freshmen is 18; all undergraduates, 32. 25% do not continue beyond their first year; 60% remain to graduate.

Housing: 500 students can be accommodated in college housing, which includes single-sex dormitories. Housing for student mothers with young children is available. On-campus housing is guaranteed for all 4 years. 75% of students commute. Alcohol is not permitted. All students may keep cars.

Activities: There are no sororities. There are 30 groups on campus, including band, chorale, chorus, computers, dance, drama, ethnic, honors, international, literary magazine, musical theater, orchestra, professional, religious, social, social service, student government, and yearbook. Popular campus events include Ring Day, Christmas at The Woods, and Pops Concert.

Sports: Facilities include stables, an athletic field, a gym, tennis courts, a pool, a weight room, a fitness course, and a volleyball pit.

Disabled Students: 75% of the campus is accessible. Wheelchair ramps, elevators, special parking, specially equipped rest rooms, and special class scheduling are available.

Services: Counseling and information services are available, as is tutoring in every subject. There is remedial math and writing.

Campus Safety and Security: Measures include 24-hour foot and vehicle patrol, self-defense education, informal discussions, and pamphlets/posters/films. There are emergency telephones and lighted pathways/sidewalks.

Programs of Study: The Woods confers B.A. and B.S. degrees. Associate and master's degrees are also awarded. Bachelor's degrees are awarded in AGRICULTURE (equine science), BIOLOGICAL SCIENCE (biology/biological science), BUSINESS (accounting, business administration and management, human resources, and marketing/retailing/merchandising), COMMUNICATIONS AND THE ARTS (English, fine arts, journalism, languages, and music), COMPUTER AND PHYSICAL SCIENCE (computer science, information sciences and systems, and mathematics), EDUCATION (art, early childhood, elementary, foreign languages, middle school, music, science, secondary, and special), HEALTH PROFESSIONS (medical technology, music therapy, predentistry, and premedicine), SOCIAL SCIENCE (gerontology, human services, humanities, international studies, prelaw, psychology, social science, social work, and theological studies). Paralegal, music therapy, and equine studies are the strongest academically. Education and business are the largest.

Required: All students must complete a 61-credit-hour general studies curriculum, which includes a freshman course in lifelong learning; courses in writing, speech, phys ed, computer science, and math; selected courses in religion, fine arts, philosophy, science, and social sciences; and 2 capstone interdisciplinary integrative courses. Completion of 125 credit hours with a minimum GPA of 2.0 is necessary for graduation.

Special: The college offers cross-registration with Indiana State University and Rose-Hulman Institute of Technology, student-designed majors, study abroad in Spain, Taiwan, and the United Kingdom, a B.A.-B.S. degree, dual majors, internships, pass/fail options, on-campus work-study, and nondegree study. The Women's External Degree program, offering 19 majors, provides educational opportunities to women who study mostly at home.

Faculty/Classroom: 10% of faculty are male; 90%, female. 95% teach undergraduates. No introductory courses are taught by graduate students. The average class size in an introductory lecture is 15; in a laboratory, 15; and in a regular course, 12.

Admissions: 85% of the 2001-2002 applicants were accepted. 22% of the current freshmen were in the top fifth of their class; 58% were in the top two fifths. 5 freshmen graduated first in their class in a recent year.

Requirements: The SAT I or ACT is required. In addition, candidates should be graduates of an accredited secondary school. The GED is accepted. Students should have completed 4 years of English, 3 years each of social sciences, lab science, and math (algebra 1, algebra 2, and geometry), and 2 years of a foreign language. A GPA of 2.0 is required, as is a letter of recommendation. AP and CLEP credits are accepted.

Procedure: Freshmen are admitted fall and spring. Entrance exams should be taken in the fall semester of the senior year. There is a deferred admissions plan. Applications should be filed by July 15 for fall entry and December 1 for spring entry, along with a $30 fee. Notification is sent on a rolling basis.

Transfer: 28 transfer students enrolled in 2001-2002. Transfer students should be in good academic standing at their most recent institution with a minimum 2.0 GPA. 30 credits of 125 must be completed at The Woods.

Visiting: There are regularly scheduled orientations for prospective students, including a campus tour, class visit, and meetings with faculty, financial aid, and admissions staff. There are guides for informal visits and visitors may sit in on classes and stay overnight. To schedule a visit, contact the Office of Admissions at (812) 535-5106.
Financial Aid: In 2001-2002, 90% of all students received some form of financial aid. 60% of freshmen and 70% of continuing students received need-based aid. The average freshman award was $10,500. Of that total, scholarships or need-based grants averaged $7300 ($12,500 maximum); and work contracts averaged $600 ($800 maximum). 70% of undergraduates work part time. Average annual earnings from campus work are $600. The average financial indebtedness of the 2001 graduate was $17,000. The FAFSA is required.
International Students: There are 7 international students enrolled. The school actively recruits these students. They must score 500 on the written TOEFL.
Computers: The mainframe is a Novell PC network. Students have full access to the World Wide Web from several computer labs across campus. All students may access the system during posted lab hours, or access can be made by personal computers at any time. There are no time limits and no fees.
Graduates: In 2001, 132 bachelor's degrees were awarded. The most popular majors were elementary education (24%), business administration (11%), and psychology (11%). In an average class, 3% graduate in 3 years, 53% in 4 years, 54% in 5 years, and 55% in 6 years.
Admissions Contact: Joel Wincowski, Director of Admission. A video is available. E-mail: *smwcadms@smwc.edu* Web: *www.smwc.edu*

SAINT MARY'S COLLEGE
Notre Dame, IN 46556 C-1
(219) 284-4587
(800) 551-7621; Fax: (219) 284-4716

Full-time: 1485 women	**Faculty:** 108; IIB, av$
Part-time: 2 men, 36 women	**Ph.D.s:** 95%
Graduate: none	**Student/Faculty:** 14 to 1
Year: semesters	**Tuition:** $18,300
Application Deadline: March 1	**Room & Board:** $6174
Freshman Class: 1011 applied, 830 accepted, 438 enrolled	
SAT I Verbal/Math: 560/550	**ACT:** 25 **VERY COMPETITIVE**

Saint Mary's College, established in 1844, was founded and sponsored by the Congregation of the Sisters of the Holy Cross. It is a Catholic comprehensive college for women in the liberal arts tradition. In addition to regional accreditation, Saint Mary's has baccalaureate program accreditation with CSWE, NASAD, NASM, NCATE, and NLN. The library contains 209,375 volumes, 13,905 microform items, and 3399 audiovisual forms/CDs, and subscribes to 776 periodicals. Computerized library services include the card catalog and database searching. Special learning facilities include an art gallery. The 275-acre campus is in a suburban area 90 miles east of Chicago. Including residence halls, there are 14 buildings.
Student Life: 72% of undergraduates are from out of state, mostly the Midwest. Others are from 49 states and 5 foreign countries. 45% are from public schools. 91% are white. 88% are Catholic; 10% Protestant. The average age of freshmen is 18; all undergraduates, 20. 16% do not continue beyond their first year.
Housing: 1575 students can be accommodated in college housing, which includes dormitories. In addition, there is an independent living residence floor for seniors. On-campus housing is guaranteed for all 4 years and is available on a first-come, first-served basis. 82% of students live on campus; of those, 80% remain on campus on weekends. All students may keep cars.
Activities: There are no sororities. There are 80 groups on campus, including art, band, cheerleading, choir, chorale, chorus, dance, drama, drill team, ethnic, honors, international, jazz band, literary magazine, marching band, musical theater, newspaper, orchestra, pep band, political, professional, radio and TV, religious, social, social service, student government, and yearbook. Popular campus events include Fall Festival, winter carnival, and spring celebration.
Sports: There are 8 intercollegiate sports for women and 15 intramural sports for women. Facilities include an athletic facility, outdoor tennis and volleyball courts, a soccer field, a softball field, and a swimming pool.
Disabled Students: 99% of the campus is accessible. Wheelchair ramps, elevators, special parking, specially equipped rest rooms, and lowered drinking fountains are available.
Services: Counseling and information services are available, as is tutoring in most subjects. A writing center is available.
Campus Safety and Security: Measures include 24-hour foot and vehicle patrol, self-defense education, escort service, and shuttle buses. There are informal discussions, pamphlets/posters/films, emergency telephones, lighted pathways/sidewalks, and key cards for residence hall entry, and underground tunnels connecting buildings.
Programs of Study: Saint Mary's confers B.A., B.S., B.B.A., B.F.A., and B.Mus. degrees. Bachelor's degrees are awarded in BIOLOGICAL SCIENCE (biology/biological science), BUSINESS (business administration and management), COMMUNICATIONS AND THE ARTS (art, communications, dramatic arts, English, fine arts, French, music, and Spanish), COMPUTER AND PHYSICAL SCIENCE (chemistry and mathematics), EDUCATION (elementary), HEALTH PROFESSIONS (nursing), SOCIAL SCIENCE (economics, history, humanities, philosophy, political science/government, psychology, religion, social work, and sociology). Art, business, and English are the strongest academically. Business, education, and communications are the largest.
Required: Students must successfully complete 128 credits, with at least 24 in the major, and must maintain a minimum GPA of 2.0. Students must also complete distribution requirements in fine arts, history, language, literature, math, philosophy, science, religion, and other selected disciplines. Advanced proficiency in composition within the student's major must also be demonstrated, and a comprehensive exam in the major area is required by the end of the senior year.
Special: Cross-registration is permitted with the University of Notre Dame and a consortium of 6 northern Indiana colleges. Opportunities are provided for internships, a Washington semester, an accelerated degree program in nursing, dual and student-designed majors, a 3-2 engineering degree with the University of Notre Dame, nondegree study, pass/fail options, and study abroad in 18 countries. There are 9 national honor societies, and 2 departmental honors programs.
Faculty/Classroom: 39% of faculty are male; 61%, female. All teach undergraduates. The average class size in an introductory lecture is 22; in a laboratory, 15; and in a regular course, 16.
Admissions: 82% of the 2001-2002 applicants were accepted. The SAT I scores for the 2001-2002 freshman class were: Verbal--18% below 500, 48% between 500 and 599, 30% between 600 and 700, and 4% above 700; Math--20% below 500, 46% between 500 and 599, 30% between 600 and 700, and 4% above 700. The ACT scores were 12% below 21, 23% between 21 and 23, 36% between 24 and 26, 16% between 27 and 28, and 12% above 28. 53% of the current freshmen were in the top fifth of their class; 88% were in the top two fifths. There were 2 National Merit finalists and 4 semifinalists. 12 freshmen graduated first in their class.
Requirements: The SAT I or ACT is required. In addition, SAT II: Subject tests are required in writing, math, and foreign language. Graduation from an accredited secondary school is required; a GED will be accepted. Applicants must have completed 16 academic credits, including 4 in English, 3 in math, 2 in a foreign language, 2 in history or social studies, 1 in science, and the remainder from college preparatory electives in the above areas. An essay is required. St. Mary's has its own on-line application. AP and CLEP credits are accepted. Important factors in the admissions decision are advanced placement or honor courses, evidence of special talent, and recommendations by school officials.
Procedure: Freshmen are admitted fall and spring. Entrance exams should be taken between March of the junior year and December of the senior year. There are early decision and deferred admissions plans. Early decision applications should be filed by November 15; regular applications, by March 1 for fall entry and November 15 for spring entry. Notification of early decision is sent December 15; regular decision, on a rolling basis. 120 early decision candidates were accepted for the 2001-2002 class. The fall 2001 application fee was $30.
Transfer: 52 transfer students enrolled in 2001-2002. Students must submit a transcript from high school and each previous college attended, along with an essay, a recommendation from a college adviser, and SAT I or ACT test scores if the student has fewer than 30 semester hours of transferable credit. All transfer applicants must have maintained a minimum GPA of 3.0. An interview is recommended. 60 credits of 128 must be completed at Saint Mary's.
Visiting: There are regularly scheduled orientations for prospective students, including campus tours and visits with admissions and financial aid counselors and faculty and athletic staff. There are guides for informal visits and visitors may sit in on classes and stay overnight. To schedule a visit, contact the Campus Visit Coordinator.
Financial Aid: In 2001-2002, 89% of all freshmen and 78% of continuing students received some form of financial aid. 61% of freshmen and 57% of continuing students received need-based aid. Scholarships or need-based grants averaged $10,156 ($19,100 maximum); loans averaged $4873 ($12,500 maximum); and work contracts averaged $1239 ($2500 maximum). 45% of undergraduates work part time. Average annual earnings from campus work are $1239. The average financial indebtedness of the 2001 graduate was $16,346. Saint Mary's is a member of CSS. The CSS/Profile or FAFSA is required. The fall application deadline is March 1.
International Students: There are 9 international students enrolled. The school actively recruits these students. They must take the TOEFL and also take the SAT I or the ACT.
Computers: The mainframe is a Sun Ultra Enterprise 450. 162 PCs and Macs are available for student use in the computer labs and at various other locations around campus. All computers are networked and have Internet access. All students have direct access to the campus network from their dorm rooms. The Internet, on-line instructional materials and the library catalog are available for college-related work. All students

may access the system 24 hours a day, 7 days a week. There are no time limits and no fees. It is strongly recommended that all students have a personal computer.

Graduates: In 2001, 312 bachelor's degrees were awarded. The most popular majors were elementary education (17%), business administration (14%), and communications (10%). In an average class, 65% graduate in 4 years, 68% in 5 years, and 70% in 6 years. 36 companies recruited on campus in 2000-2001. Of the 2000 graduating class, 19% were enrolled in graduate school within 6 months of graduation and 74% were employed.

Admissions Contact: Mary Pat Nolan, Director of Admission. A video is available. E-mail: *admission@saintmarys.edu*
Web: *www.saintmarys.edu*

TAYLOR UNIVERSITY — D-3

Upland, IN 46989-1001 (765) 998-5134
(800) 882-3456; Fax: (765) 998-4925

Full-time: 875 men, 952 women	**Faculty:** 118; IIB, --$
Part-time: 13 men, 18 women	**Ph.D.s:** 75%
Graduate: none	**Student/Faculty:** 15 to 1
Year: 4-1-4, summer session	**Tuition:** $16,572
Application Deadline: January 15	**Room & Board:** $4990
Freshman Class: 1512 applied, 1163 accepted, 536 enrolled	
SAT I Verbal/Math: 600/610	**ACT:** 27 **VERY COMPETITIVE+**

Taylor University, founded in 1846, is a Christian interdenominational liberal arts institution. In addition to regional accreditation, Taylor has baccalaureate program accreditation with CSWE, NASM, and NCATE. The library contains 195,351 volumes, 10,842 microform items, and 6846 audiovisual forms/CDs, and subscribes to 688 periodicals. Computerized library services include the card catalog, interlibrary loans, and database searching. Special learning facilities include a learning resource center, art gallery, radio station, TV station, 65-acre arboretum, C. S. Lewis Collection, and observatory. The 250-acre campus is in a rural area 70 miles north of Indianapolis. Including residence halls, there are 26 buildings.

Student Life: 69% of undergraduates are from out of state, mostly the Midwest. Students are from 45 states, 17 foreign countries, and Canada. 79% are from public schools. 93% are white. Most are Protestant. The average age of freshmen is 18; all undergraduates, 19. 11% do not continue beyond their first year; 75% remain to graduate.

Housing: 1532 students can be accommodated in college housing, which includes single-sex dormitories, off-campus apartments, and married-student housing. On-campus housing is guaranteed for all 4 years. 97% of students live on campus; of those, 90% remain on campus on weekends. Alcohol is not permitted. All students may keep cars.

Activities: There are no fraternities or sororities. There are many groups and organizations on campus, including art, band, cheerleading, choir, chorale, chorus, computers, drama, ethnic, film, honors, international, jazz band, literary magazine, musical theater, newspaper, opera, orchestra, pep band, photography, political, professional, radio and TV, religious, social, social service, student government, symphony, and yearbook. Popular campus events include Taylathon, Youth Conference, and Martin Luther King Day observances.

Sports: There are 8 intercollegiate sports for men and 7 for women, and 14 intramural sports for men and 14 for women. Facilities include a gym, a field house, a wellness center, tennis and racquetball courts, a track, and a lake for swimming and ice skating.

Disabled Students: 80% of the campus is accessible. Wheelchair ramps, elevators, special parking, specially equipped rest rooms, special class scheduling, lowered drinking fountains, and lowered telephones are available.

Services: Counseling and information services are available, as is tutoring in most subjects. There is a reader service for the blind, and remedial math, reading, and writing.

Campus Safety and Security: Measures include 24-hour foot and vehicle patrol, escort service, pamphlets/posters/films, and lighted pathways/sidewalks.

Programs of Study: Taylor confers B.A., B.S., and B.Mus. degrees. Associate degrees are also awarded. Bachelor's degrees are awarded in BIOLOGICAL SCIENCE (biology/biological science and environmental biology), BUSINESS (accounting, banking and finance, international business management, management science, marketing and distribution, recreation and leisure services, and sports management), COMMUNICATIONS AND THE ARTS (art, communications, dramatic arts, English, French, journalism, music, and Spanish), COMPUTER AND PHYSICAL SCIENCE (chemistry, computer science, mathematics, natural sciences, and physics), EDUCATION (art, athletic training, Christian, elementary, English, foreign languages, mathematics, music, physical, science, and social studies), ENGINEERING AND ENVIRONMENTAL DESIGN (computer engineering, computer graphics, engineering physics, environmental engineering, and environmental science), HEALTH PROFESSIONS (health science), SOCIAL SCIENCE (biblical studies, economics, geography, history, international studies, philosophy, political science/government, psychology, social work, and sociology). Computer science, environmental science, and engineering physics are the strongest academically. Business, education, and computer science are the largest.

Required: Students must complete 128 credits and maintain a minimum GPA of 2.0 overall and 2.3 in the major. In addition to the requirements of the major, which include a comprehensive exam, each student must complete classes in computer science, fine arts, public speaking, Bible literature, Christian belief, literature, writing, science, history, social science, cross-cultural, phys ed, a senior seminar, fitness for life, and an upper-level philosophy course.

Special: Opportunities are provided for internships, cooperative programs, a Washington semester, study abroad in 12 countries, work-study programs, dual majors, student-designed majors, B.A.-B.S. degrees, and a 3-2 engineering degree. There is cross-registration with the other members of the Council for Christian Colleges and Universities and the Christian College Consortium. There are 7 national honor societies and a freshman honors program.

Faculty/Classroom: 72% of faculty are male; 28%, female. All teach undergraduates. The average class size in an introductory lecture is 25; in a laboratory, 15; and in a regular course, 25.

Admissions: 77% of the 2001-2002 applicants were accepted. The SAT I scores for the 2001-2002 freshman class were: Verbal--13% below 500, 31% between 500 and 599, 47% between 600 and 700, and 9% above 700; Math--10% below 500, 35% between 500 and 599, 44% between 600 and 700, and 11% above 700. The ACT scores were 6% below 21, 16% between 21 and 23, 25% between 24 and 26, 28% between 27 and 28, and 25% above 28. 64% of the current freshmen were in the top fifth of their class; 87% were in the top two fifths. There were 12 National Merit finalists. 42 freshmen graduated first in their class.

Requirements: The SAT I or ACT is required, with composite scores of 1000 on the SAT I and 24 on the ACT recommended. Graduation from an accredited secondary school is required; a GED will be accepted. It is recommended that applicants complete 4 years of English, 3 to 4 each of math and lab science, 2 each of social studies and a foreign language, and course work in computing, typing/keyboarding, and the arts. An interview is recommended for all students, and an audition is required for music majors. Taylor requires applicants to be in the upper 40% of their class. A GPA of 2.8 is required. AP and CLEP credits are accepted. Important factors in the admissions decision are personality/intangible qualities, evidence of special talent, and leadership record. Applications are accepted on-line at the school's web site.

Procedure: Freshmen are admitted fall and spring. Entrance exams should be taken during the spring of the junior year or fall of the senior year. There is a deferred admissions plan. Early decision application should be filed by September 15, October 15, or November 15; regular applications, by January 15 for fall entry, along with a $20 fee. Notification is sent 1 month after the application deadline. A waiting list is an active part of the admissions procedure.

Transfer: 42 transfer students enrolled in 2001-2002. Applicants must have maintained a minimum GPA of 2.5 and have completed at least 12 credit hours at the previous college. An interview is recommended. 48 credits of 128 must be completed at Taylor.

Visiting: There are regularly scheduled orientations for prospective students, including a campus tour, lunch, class meetings, faculty meetings, a financial aid session, and an admissions interview. There are guides for informal visits and visitors may sit in on classes and stay overnight. To schedule a visit, contact the Campus Visit Coordinator.

Financial Aid: In 2001-2002, 89% of all freshmen and 87% of continuing students received some form of financial aid. 55% of freshmen and 54% of continuing students received need-based aid. The average freshman award was $13,000. Of that total, scholarships or need-based grants averaged $8300 ($16,350 maximum); loans averaged $3400 ($4125 maximum); and work contracts averaged $1300 ($1800 maximum). 50% of undergraduates work part time. Average annual earnings from campus work are $1200. The average financial indebtedness of the 2001 graduate was $14,900. Taylor is a member of CSS. The FAFSA and the college's own financial statement are required. The fall application deadline is March 1.

International Students: There are 32 international students enrolled. The school actively recruits these students. They must score 550 on the written TOEFL.

Computers: The mainframes are a DEC PDP 11/70 and MicroVAX 3600 models. There are PCs at sites throughout the campus in a ratio of 1 for each 13 students. All students may access the system. There are no time limits and no fees. It is strongly recommended that all students have a personal computer.

Graduates: In 2001, 470 bachelor's degrees were awarded. The most popular majors were business (10%), psychology (7%), and education (6%). In an average class, 67% graduate in 4 years, 79% in 5 years, and 80% in 6 years. 123 companies recruited on campus in 2000-2001. Of the 2000 graduating class, 13% were enrolled in graduate school within 6 months of graduation and 78% were employed.

Admissions Contact: Stephen Mortland, Director of Admissions.
E-mail: *admissions_u@tayloru.edu* Web: *www.tayloru.edu*

TRI-STATE UNIVERSITY-MAIN CAMPUS D-1

Angola, IN 46703 (219) 665-4365
(800) 347-4878; Fax: (219) 665-4578

Full-time: 778 men, 349 women **Faculty:** 58
Part-time: 65 men, 76 women **Ph.D.s:** 71%
Graduate: none **Student/Faculty:** 19 to 1
Year: semesters, summer session **Tuition:** $15,950
Application Deadline: June 1 **Room & Board:** $5250
Freshman Class: 1433 applied, 1086 accepted, 321 enrolled
SAT I or ACT: required **COMPETITIVE**

Tri-State University, founded in 1884, is a private, independent university with 4 schools: Allen School of Engineering and Technology, Ketner School of Business, School of Education, and School of Arts and Sciences. There are 4 undergraduate schools. In addition to regional accreditation, Tri-State has baccalaureate program accreditation with ABET. The library contains 141,543 volumes, 15,439 microform items, and 6087 audiovisual forms/CDs, and subscribes to 162 periodicals. Computerized library services include the card catalog, interlibrary loans, and database searching. Special learning facilities include a learning resource center and radio station. The 400-acre campus is in a small town 30 miles north of Ft. Wayne. Including residence halls, there are 18 buildings.

Student Life: 60% of undergraduates are from Indiana. Others are from 21 states, 23 foreign countries, and Canada. 80% are from public schools. 87% are white. The average age of freshmen is 19; all undergraduates, 22. 25% do not continue beyond their first year.

Housing: 571 students can be accommodated in college housing, which includes coed dormitories. On-campus housing is guaranteed for all 4 years. 53% of students commute. Alcohol is not permitted. All students may keep cars.

Activities: 25% of men belong to 8 national fraternities; 15% of women belong to 6 local sororities. There are 35 groups on campus, including cheerleading, choir, computers, drama, ethnic, honors, international, newspaper, pep band, professional, radio and TV, religious, social service, student government, and yearbook.

Sports: There are 10 intercollegiate sports for men and 10 for women, and 6 intramural sports for men and 5 for women. Facilities include a gym with a pool, indoor and outdoor tracks, basketball and racquetball courts, an 18-hole golf course, and a football stadium.

Disabled Students: 98% of the campus is accessible. Wheelchair ramps, elevators, special parking, specially equipped rest rooms, special class scheduling, lowered drinking fountains, and lowered telephones are available.

Services: Counseling and information services are available, as is tutoring in some subjects, including math, business, engineering, accounting, and English. There is remedial math.

Campus Safety and Security: Measures include pamphlets/posters/films and lighted pathways/sidewalks.

Programs of Study: Tri-State confers B.A. and B.S. degrees. Associate degrees are also awarded. Bachelor's degrees are awarded in BIOLOGICAL SCIENCE (biology/biological science), BUSINESS (accounting, business administration and management, management science, marketing/retailing/merchandising, and recreation and leisure services), COMMUNICATIONS AND THE ARTS (communications), COMPUTER AND PHYSICAL SCIENCE (chemistry, computer science, information sciences and systems, mathematics, and physical sciences), EDUCATION (elementary, English, mathematics, physical, science, secondary, and social science), ENGINEERING AND ENVIRONMENTAL DESIGN (chemical engineering, civil engineering, drafting and design technology, electrical/electronics engineering, engineering management, environmental science, industrial administration/management, and mechanical engineering), HEALTH PROFESSIONS (premedicine), SOCIAL SCIENCE (criminal justice, psychology, and social science). Engineering, business, and education are the strongest academically and are the largest.

Required: Candidates for graduation must complete 120 to 132 semester hours, satisfying general education, program, and major requirements and maintaining a minimum overall GPA of 2.0. Required courses vary by degree sought. All students must complete a general education curriculum including science, math, American studies, social science, global studies, English composition, humanistics, computer literacy, and oral communication course work. Some majors have senior design projects.

Special: Cooperative education programs are available in engineering, business, and computer science. Opportunities exist for internships and work-study programs with the university and many companies. There are 12 national honor societies.

Faculty/Classroom: 78% of faculty are male; 22%, female. All teach undergraduates and 10% also do research. The average class size in an introductory lecture is 30; in a laboratory, 16; and in a regular course, 18.

Admissions: 76% of the 2001-2002 applicants were accepted. 35% of the current freshmen were in the top fifth of their class; 66% were in the top two fifths. 3 freshmen graduated first in their class.

Requirements: The SAT I or ACT is required. In addition, candidates for admission should be graduates of accredited secondary schools. The GED is accepted. Most students should have 4 years of English and 2 years each of science, social studies, and math. A GPA of 2.0 is required. AP and CLEP credits are accepted. Important factors in the admissions decision are advanced placement or honor courses, recommendations by school officials, and leadership record. Applications are accepted on-line at Tri-State's web site.

Procedure: Freshmen are admitted to all sessions. Entrance exams should be taken in the junior or senior year. There is a deferred admissions plan. Early decision application should be filed by March 1; regular applications, by June 1 for fall entry. The fall 2001 application fee was $20. Notification is sent on a rolling basis.

Transfer: 35 transfer students enrolled in 2001-2002. In addition to meeting the university's requirements for freshmen, applicants must have satisfactory records from previous institutions. 30 credits of 120 must be completed at Tri-State.

Visiting: There are regularly scheduled orientations for prospective students, including meetings with faculty, administrators, and financial aid personnel, a campus tour, and a reception. There are guides for informal visits and visitors may sit in on classes. To schedule a visit, contact the Admissions Office at (219) 665-4132.

Financial Aid: In 2001-2002, 99% of all freshmen and 95% of continuing students received some form of financial aid. 32% of freshmen and 22% of continuing students received need-based aid. The average freshman award was $6035. Of that total, scholarships or need-based grants averaged $2659 ($10,500 maximum); loans averaged $2250 ($2625 maximum); and work contracts averaged $439 ($2500 maximum). 48% of undergraduates work part time. Average annual earnings from campus work are $500. The average financial indebtedness of the 2001 graduate was $11,872. The FAFSA is required. The fall application deadline is March 1.

International Students: There are 52 international students enrolled. The school actively recruits these students. They must take the TOEFL, scoring 550 on the written version, or take the MELAB. Applicants not transferring credits in math or English must be tested in those subjects.

Computers: There are about 150 networked PCs in 8 labs and other campus locations. All residence halls are networked to the campus computing system and the Internet. All students may access the system. There are no time limits and no fees.

Graduates: In 2001, 214 bachelor's degrees were awarded. The most popular majors were engineering (42%), business (26%), and education (11%). In an average class, 26% graduate in 4 years, 45% in 5 years, and 49% in 6 years. 25 companies recruited on campus in 2000-2001. Of the 2000 graduating class, 5% were enrolled in graduate school within 6 months of graduation and 90% were employed.

Admissions Contact: Sara Yarian, Director of Admission.
E-mail: *admit@tristate.edu* Web: *www.tristate.edu*

UNIVERSITY OF EVANSVILLE A-5

Evansville, IN 47722-0329 (812) 479-2468
(800) 423-8633; Fax: (812) 474-4076

Full-time: 887 men, 1412 women **Faculty:** 177; IIA, -$
Part-time: 169 men, 206 women **Ph.D.s:** 86%
Graduate: 2 men, 11 women **Student/Faculty:** 13 to 1
Year: semesters, summer session **Tuition:** $17,395
Application Deadline: December 1 **Room & Board:** $5470
Freshman Class: 1866 applied, 1689 accepted, 513 enrolled
SAT I Verbal/Math: 559/561 **ACT:** 25 **VERY COMPETITIVE+**

The University of Evansville, founded in 1854, is a private institution affiliated with the United Methodist Church. The university offers undergraduate degree programs in arts and sciences, business administration, education, engineering and computing sciences, fine arts, and nursing and health sciences. There are 4 undergraduate schools and 1 graduate school. In addition to regional accreditation, UE has baccalaureate program accreditation with ABET, APTA, NASM, NCATE, and NLN. The library contains 272,405 volumes, 454,088 microform items, and 10,094 audiovisual forms/CDs, and subscribes to 1350 periodicals. Computerized library services include interlibrary loans and database searching. Special learning facilities include a learning resource center and radio station. The 75-acre campus is in an urban area 120 miles west of Louisville. Including residence halls, there are 39 buildings.

Student Life: 61% of undergraduates are from Indiana. Others are from 45 states, 42 foreign countries, and Canada. 94% are from public schools. 88% are white. 41% are claim no religious affiliation; 39% Protestant; 20% Catholic. The average age of freshmen is 19; all undergraduates, 20. 18% do not continue beyond their first year; 63% remain to graduate.

Housing: 1885 students can be accommodated in college housing, which includes single-sex and coed dormitories, on-campus apartments, off-campus apartments, and fraternity houses. In addition, there are special-interest houses and an international house. On-campus housing is guaranteed for all 4 years. 70% of students live on campus; of those,

85% remain on campus on weekends. Alcohol is not permitted. All students may keep cars.

Activities: 21% of men belong to 6 national fraternities; 20% of women belong to 4 national sororities. There are 101 groups on campus, including art, band, cheerleading, choir, chorale, chorus, computers, dance, drama, drill team, ethnic, film, honors, international, jazz band, literary magazine, marching band, musical theater, newspaper, orchestra, pep band, photography, political, professional, radio and TV, religious, social, social service, student government, and yearbook. Popular campus events include Musical Madness, Greek Weekend, and Bike Race.

Sports: There are 8 intercollegiate sports for men and 8 for women, and 15 intramural sports for men and 14 for women. Facilities include an athletic center, a 2000-seat stadium, a 3000-seat playing field, a baseball diamond, and practice facilities.

Disabled Students: 98% of the campus is accessible. Wheelchair ramps, elevators, special parking, and specially equipped rest rooms are available.

Services: Counseling and information services are available, as is tutoring in most subjects. There is a reader service for the blind and remedial writing.

Campus Safety and Security: Measures include 24-hour foot and vehicle patrol, escort service, informal discussions, and pamphlets/posters/films. There are emergency telephones and lighted pathways/sidewalks.

Programs of Study: UE confers B.A., B.S., B.F.A., B.L.S., B.M., B.M.M.E., and B.M.M.T. degrees. Associate and master's degrees are also awarded. Bachelor's degrees are awarded in BIOLOGICAL SCIENCE (biology/biological science), BUSINESS (accounting, banking and finance, business administration and management, international business management, and marketing/retailing/merchandising), COMMUNICATIONS AND THE ARTS (art, art history and appreciation, communications, creative writing, dramatic arts, English, French, German, graphic design, literature, music, music business management, music performance, Spanish, studio art, theater design, and theater management), COMPUTER AND PHYSICAL SCIENCE (chemistry, computer programming, computer science, mathematics, and physics), EDUCATION (art, athletic training, elementary, English, mathematics, middle school, music, physical, science, secondary, social studies, and special), ENGINEERING AND ENVIRONMENTAL DESIGN (civil engineering, computer engineering, electrical/electronics engineering, engineering management, environmental science, and mechanical engineering), HEALTH PROFESSIONS (music therapy, nursing, physical therapy, premedicine, and sports medicine), SOCIAL SCIENCE (anthropology, archeology, behavioral science, biblical studies, classical/ancient civilization, criminal justice, economics, gerontology, history, international studies, liberal arts/general studies, paralegal studies, philosophy, physical fitness/movement, political science/government, prelaw, psychobiology, psychology, religion, sociology, and theological studies). Theater, physical therapy, and engineering are the strongest academically. Health sciences and psychology are the largest.

Required: To graduate, students must complete at least 124 semester hours with a minimum 2.0 GPA overall and in their major, generally with 36 to 40 hours in the major. All students must take a core of 9 hours of world cultures, 7 of natural sciences, 6 each of humanities/fine arts, foreign language, and social sciences, and 3 each of math and senior seminar. 2 years of foreign language are required for the B.A. A demonstration of writing proficiency, a capstone course in the major, and completion of the fitness/wellness course are required for graduation.

Special: Students may study abroad in the United Kingdom and Germany. UE also offers cooperative programs in engineering, chemistry, and business with various industries, internships in such fields as communications and business, credit for life experience through the Center for Continuing Education, student-designed majors, and pass/fail options in elective courses. There are 18 national honor societies, a freshman honors program, and 20 departmental honors programs.

Faculty/Classroom: 69% of faculty are male; 31%, female. All teach undergraduates. No introductory courses are taught by graduate students. The average class size in an introductory lecture is 20.

Admissions: 91% of the 2001-2002 applicants were accepted. The SAT I scores for the 2001-2002 freshman class were: Verbal--22% below 500, 45% between 500 and 599, 27% between 600 and 700, and 6% above 700; Math--18% below 500, 47% between 500 and 599, 30% between 600 and 700, and 5% above 700. The ACT scores were 2% below 21, 28% between 21 and 23, 39% between 24 and 26, 16% between 27 and 28, and 15% above 28. 52% of the current freshmen were in the top fifth of their class; 84% were in the top two fifths. There were 11 National Merit finalists. 18 freshmen graduated first in their class.

Requirements: The SAT I or ACT is required; to be competitive for admission, students should submit a minimum SAT I composite score of 1100 or ACT composite of 24. Applicants must be graduates of accredited secondary schools; applicants who have been home-schooled are also considered. The university recommends completion of 4 years of college-preparatory English, 3 each of math (algebra I and II, geometry) and social science, and 2 of a foreign language. An interview is recommended but not required. UE requires applicants to be in the upper 50% of their class. A GPA of 2.0 is required. AP and CLEP credits are accepted. Important factors in the admissions decision are advanced placement or honor courses, leadership record, and recommendations by school officials.

Procedure: Freshmen are admitted fall and spring. Entrance exams should be taken by December of the senior year. There are early action, early admissions, and deferred admissions plans. Early action applications should be filed by December 1; thereafter applications are accepted as space permits. The fall 2001 application fee was $30. Notification of early decision is sent December 15; regular decision, on a rolling basis.

Transfer: 97 transfer students enrolled in 2001-2002. Applicants must have a minimum GPA of 2.0 in all previous college work. 63 credits of 124 must be completed at UE.

Visiting: There are regularly scheduled orientations for prospective students, including a campus tour, faculty academic sessions, financial aid and admission appointments, and study abroad and honors program sessions. There are guides for informal visits and visitors may sit in on classes and stay overnight. To schedule a visit, contact the Admissions Office.

Financial Aid: In 2001-2002, 99% of all freshmen and 89% of continuing students received some form of financial aid. 66% of freshmen and 70% of continuing students received need-based aid. The average freshman award was $13,833. Of that total, scholarships or need-based grants averaged $10,533 ($23,265 maximum); loans averaged $3577 ($5625 maximum); and work contracts averaged $1259 ($1650 maximum). 20% of undergraduates work part time. Average annual earnings from campus work are $1283. The average financial indebtedness of the 2001 graduate was $16,054. UE is a member of CSS. The FAFSA and the college's own financial statement are required. The fall application deadline is March 1.

International Students: There are 239 international students enrolled. The school actively recruits these students. They must score 500 on the written TOEFL or 173 on the electronic version and also take a writing placement test and the SAT I or the ACT.

Computers: The mainframe is an IBM Multiprise 2003-206. There are 7 public computer labs and several departmental computer clusters connected to a LAN using UNIX, Novell, Windows NT, and Mac servers. Almost every computer on campus has access to the network, including student-owned computers in the residence halls. All students may access the system at any time. There are no time limits and no fees. It is recommended that students in some courses have personal computers.

Graduates: In 2001, 572 bachelor's degrees were awarded. The most popular majors were business (16%), health services (12%), and fine arts (9%). In an average class, 64% graduate in 4 years, 66% in 5 years, and 68% in 6 years. 100 companies recruited on campus in 2000-2001. Of the 2000 graduating class, 15% were enrolled in graduate school within 6 months of graduation and 75% were employed.

Admissions Contact: Cherie Leonhardt, Director of Undergraduate Admissions. A video is available. E-mail: *admissions@evansville.edu*
Web: *http://www.evansville.edu*

UNIVERSITY OF INDIANAPOLIS — C-3
Indianapolis, IN 46227-3697 — **(317) 788-3216**
(800) 232-8634; Fax: (317) 788-3300

Full-time: 742 men, 1278 women	**Faculty:** 138; IIA, --$
Part-time: 239 men, 595 women	**Ph.D.s:** 69%
Graduate: 227 men, 620 women	**Student/Faculty:** 15 to 1
Year: 4-4-1, summer session	**Tuition:** $15,350
Application Deadline: open	**Room & Board:** $5490
Freshman Class: n/av	
SAT I or ACT: required	**COMPETITIVE**

The University of Indianapolis, established in 1902, is a private liberal arts school affiliated with the United Methodist Church. It provides undergraduate and graduate studies with an emphasis on education, business, nursing, and arts and sciences. There are 5 undergraduate and 7 graduate schools. In addition to regional accreditation, U of I has baccalaureate program accreditation with ACBSP, ACEJMC, APTA, CSWE, NASM, NCATE, and NLN. The library contains 171,782 volumes, 15,002 microform items, and 7023 audiovisual forms/CDs, and subscribes to 972 periodicals. Computerized library services include the card catalog, interlibrary loans, and database searching. Special learning facilities include a learning resource center, art gallery, planetarium, radio station, TV station, and archeology lab. The 60-acre campus is in a suburban area on the south side of Indianapolis. Including residence halls, there are 13 buildings.

Student Life: 85% of undergraduates are from Indiana. Others are from 17 states, 60 foreign countries, and Canada. 79% are white. 55% are Protestant; 23% claim no religious affiliation; 21% Catholic. The average age of freshmen is 18; all undergraduates, 22. 21% do not continue beyond their first year; 52% remain to graduate.

Housing: 1150 students can be accommodated in college housing, which includes single-sex and coed dormitories, on-campus apartments, and married-student housing. On-campus housing is guaranteed for all

4 years. 50% of students live on campus. Alcohol is not permitted. All students may keep cars.

Activities: There are no fraternities or sororities. There are 45 groups on campus, including academic, art, cheerleading, chess, choir, chorale, chorus, computers, dance, drama, ethnic, gay, honors, international, jazz band, literary magazine, musical theater, newspaper, orchestra, pep band, photography, political, professional, radio and TV, religious, social, social service, and student government. Popular campus events include Brown County Day, Cyclerama, and winter and spring formals.

Sports: There are 11 intercollegiate sports for men and 10 for women, and 7 intramural sports for men and 7 for women. Facilities include a health and fitness center including a 3500-seat gym, an Olympic-size swimming pool, racquetball courts, a weight room, and a dance studio.

Disabled Students: All of the campus is accessible. Wheelchair ramps, elevators, special parking, specially equipped rest rooms, special class scheduling, lowered drinking fountains, and lowered telephones are available.

Services: Counseling and information services are available, as is tutoring in every subject. There is remedial math and writing.

Campus Safety and Security: Measures include 24-hour foot and vehicle patrol, self-defense education, escort service, and emergency telephones. There are lighted pathways/sidewalks.

Programs of Study: U of I confers B.A., B.S., B.F.A., B.M., B.S.N., and B.S.W. degrees. Associate, master's, and doctoral degrees are also awarded. Bachelor's degrees are awarded in BIOLOGICAL SCIENCE (biology/biological science), BUSINESS (accounting, banking and finance, business administration and management, business economics, international business management, management information systems, marketing/retailing/merchandising, and sports management), COMMUNICATIONS AND THE ARTS (broadcasting, communications, dramatic arts, English, French, German, journalism, music, music performance, musical theater, public relations, Spanish, speech/debate/rhetoric, and studio art), COMPUTER AND PHYSICAL SCIENCE (chemistry, computer science, earth science, mathematics, and physics), EDUCATION (art, athletic training, elementary, foreign languages, mathematics, middle school, physical, science, secondary, and social studies), ENGINEERING AND ENVIRONMENTAL DESIGN (commercial art, electrical/electronics engineering, environmental science, and mechanical engineering), HEALTH PROFESSIONS (art therapy, medical laboratory technology, and nursing), SOCIAL SCIENCE (anthropology, archeology, corrections, economics, history, international relations, law enforcement and corrections, philosophy, political science/government, psychology, religion, social science, social work, and sociology). Business, nursing, and science (biology/chemistry) are the strongest academically. Business is the largest.

Required: All undergraduate students must complete at least 124 hours, including 24 hours or more in the major with a GPA of 2.0 or better. Requirements include a core curriculum in which 8 learning goals must be met. Students must also take a health and phys ed course and 1 spring term, and attend lecture/performance events.

Special: Cross-registration is offered in conjunction with 6 area colleges. Cooperative programs, internships, various work-study programs, study abroad, dual and student-designed majors, accelerated programs in liberal studies and organizational leadership, and pass/fail options are available. A fleximester, which is a 3-week spring term and 2 7-week summer sessions, also is offered. There are 11 national honor societies, a freshman honors program, and 5 departmental honors programs.

Faculty/Classroom: 50% of faculty are male; 50%, female. 96% teach undergraduates. No introductory courses are taught by graduate students. The average class size in an introductory lecture is 17; in a laboratory, 13; and in a regular course, 17.

Admissions: 47% of the current freshmen were in the top fifth of their class; 68% were in the top two fifths. There were 2 National Merit semifinalists. 15 freshmen graduated first in their class.

Requirements: The SAT I or ACT is required, with a minimum SAT I composite of 920 or ACT composite of 20. Each applicant should have at least 24 academic credits, including at least 12 units total from English and literature (not including speech), history, foreign language, math lab science, and social studies. The GED is accdepted. An interview is recommended. U of I requires applicants to be in the upper 50% of their class. A GPA of 2.0 is required. AP and CLEP credits are accepted. The university accepts applications on-line at its web site.

Procedure: Freshmen are admitted to all sessions. There is a deferred admissions plan. Application deadlines are open. The application fee is $20. Notification is sent on a rolling basis.

Transfer: 114 transfer students enrolled in 2001-2002. No ACT or SAT I is needed if applicants have a grade average of C and 20 semester hours of credit. 30 credits of 124 must be completed at U of I.

Visiting: There are regularly scheduled orientations for prospective students, including campus visits and tours. There are guides for informal visits and visitors may sit in on classes and stay overnight. To schedule a visit, contact the Admissions Office at (800) 232-8634, ext. 3441 or *treinhardt@uindy.edu*.

Financial Aid: In 2001-2002, 82% of all freshmen and 87% of continuing students received some form of financial aid. 73% of freshmen and 78% of continuing students received need based aid. The average freshman award was $12,891. Of that total, scholarships or need-based grants averaged $7209 ($12,910 maximum); loans averaged $1082 ($3825 maximum); work contracts averaged $222 ($1500 maximum); and institutional grants and scholarships or unsubsidized Stafford loans averaged $4378. 50% of undergraduates work part time. Average annual earnings from campus work are $1400. The average financial indebtedness of the 2001 graduate was $17,152. U of I is a member of CSS. The FAFSA, the college's own financial statement, and parent and student tax returns are required. The fall application deadline is March 1.

International Students: There are 143 international students enrolled. The school actively recruits these students. They must score 500 on the written TOEFL or 173 on the electronic version.

Computers: The mainframe is a DEC VAX 4300. Students have access from residence halls. There are also both Macs and IBMs available to students in 5 of 7 academic buildings. All students may access the system 7 days per week. There are no time limits and no fees.

Graduates: In 2001, 363 bachelor's degrees were awarded. The most popular majors were business (27%), education (16%), and biology (8%). In an average class, 4% graduate in 3 years, 49% in 4 years, and 51% in 5 years. 112 companies recruited on campus in 2000-2001. Of the 2000 graduating class, 25% were enrolled in graduate school within 6 months of graduation and 68% were employed.

Admissions Contact: Ron Wilks, Director of Admissions.
E-mail: *admissions@uindy.edu* Web: *www.uindy.edu*

UNIVERSITY OF NOTRE DAME — C-1
Notre Dame, IN 46556 — (574) 631-7505

Full-time: 4392 men, 3801 women	**Faculty:** 736; I, +$
Part-time: 14 men, 1 woman	**Ph.D.s:** 88%
Graduate: 1755 men, 1091 women	**Student/Faculty:** 11 to 1
Year: semesters, summer session	**Tuition:** $24,497
Application Deadline: January 7	**Room & Board:** $6210
Freshman Class: 9385 applied, 3338 accepted, 2036 enrolled	
SAT I Verbal/Math: 670/690	**ACT:** 31 **MOST COMPETITIVE**

The University of Notre Dame, founded in 1842, is a private institution affiliated with the Roman Catholic Church offering undergraduate programs in architecture, arts and letters, business administration, engineering, and science. There are 5 undergraduate and 6 graduate schools. In addition to regional accreditation, Notre Dame has baccalaureate program accreditation with AACSB, ABET, and NAAB. The 9 libraries contain 2,601,429 volumes, 2,044,171 microform items, and 21,981 audiovisual forms/CDs, and subscribe to 19,489 periodicals. Computerized library services include the card catalog, interlibrary loans, and database searching. Special learning facilities include a learning resource center, art gallery, radio station, and art museum. The 1250-acre campus is in a suburban area 90 miles east of Chicago. Including residence halls, there are 156 buildings.

Student Life: 91% of undergraduates are from out of state, mostly the Midwest. Students are from 50 states, 104 foreign countries, and Canada. 50% are from public schools. 78% are white. Most are Catholic. The average age of freshmen is 18; all undergraduates, 20. 3% do not continue beyond their first year; 93% remain to graduate.

Housing: 6220 students can be accommodated in college housing, which includes single-sex dormitories. On-campus housing is guaranteed for the freshman year only, is available on a first-come, first-served basis, and is available on a lottery system for upperclassmen. 77% of students live on campus; of those, 92% remain on campus on weekends. Upperclassmen may keep cars.

Activities: There are no fraternities or sororities. There are 269 groups on campus, including art, bagpipe band, band, cheerleading, chess, choir, chorale, chorus, computers, dance, debate, drama, ethnic, film, forensics, honors, international, jazz band, literary magazine, marching band, musical theater, newspaper, orchestra, pep band, photography, political, professional, radio, religious, social, social service, student government, symphony, and yearbook. Popular campus events include a spring festival, home football weekends, and the Collegiate Jazz Festival.

Sports: There are 13 intercollegiate sports for men and 13 for women, and 23 intramural sports for men and 21 for women. Facilities include an athletic and convocation center with an 11,500-seat basketball arena and a hockey arena, a tennis pavilion, a golf course, an indoor sports center, a recreational sports center, and an aquatic center. The campus football stadium seats 80,225. There are general-purpose playing fields, stadiums for track, lacrosse, and baseball, and soccer and softball fields.

Disabled Students: 85% of the campus is accessible. Wheelchair ramps, elevators, special parking, specially equipped rest rooms, special class scheduling, lowered drinking fountains, and lowered telephones are available.

Services: There is a reader service for the blind.

Campus Safety and Security: Measures include 24-hour foot and vehicle patrol, self-defense education, escort service, and shuttle buses. There are informal discussions, pamphlets/posters/films, emergency telephones, and lighted pathways/sidewalks.

Programs of Study: Notre Dame confers B.A., B.S., B.Arch., B.B.A., and B.F.A. degrees. Master's and doctoral degrees are also awarded. Bachelor's degrees are awarded in BIOLOGICAL SCIENCE (biochemistry and biology/biological science), BUSINESS (accounting, banking and finance, management information systems, management science, and marketing/retailing/merchandising), COMMUNICATIONS AND THE ARTS (art history and appreciation, Chinese, English, film arts, French, German, Greek, Italian, Japanese, Latin, music, Russian, Spanish, and studio art), COMPUTER AND PHYSICAL SCIENCE (chemistry, computer science, mathematics, and physics), EDUCATION (science), ENGINEERING AND ENVIRONMENTAL DESIGN (aeronautical engineering, chemical engineering, civil engineering, computer engineering, electrical/electronics engineering, environmental engineering, environmental science, and mechanical engineering), HEALTH PROFESSIONS (predentistry and premedicine), SOCIAL SCIENCE (American studies, classical/ancient civilization, economics, history, liberal arts/general studies, medieval studies, philosophy, political science/government, psychology, sociology, and theological studies). Engineering, theology, and business are the strongest academically. Accounting, government, and English are the largest.

Required: All students must complete courses in English, philosophy, science, history, theology, math, social science, and phys ed. A total of 120 semester hours with a minimum GPA of 2.0 is required to graduate.

Special: Cross-registration is offered with Saint Mary's College. Study abroad is possible in 17 countries. A 5-year arts and letters/engineering B.A.-B.S. degree is offered. There is a program of liberal studies, centered on the discussion of great books. Internships, an accelerated degree program, a Washington semester, dual majors, 3-2 engineering degrees, and pass/fail options are available. There are 12 national honor societies, including Phi Beta Kappa, and 2 departmental honors programs.

Faculty/Classroom: 76% of faculty are male; 24%, female.

Admissions: 36% of the 2001-2002 applicants were accepted. The SAT I scores for the 2001-2002 freshman class were: Verbal--3% below 500, 13% between 500 and 599, 48% between 600 and 700, and 37% above 700; Math--1% below 500, 9% between 500 and 599, 42% between 600 and 700, and 48% above 700. The ACT scores were 1% below 21, 1% between 21 and 23, 6% between 24 and 26, 7% between 27 and 28, and 85% above 28. 94% of the current freshmen were in the top fifth of their class; 99% were in the top two fifths. 291 freshmen graduated first in their class.

Requirements: The SAT I or ACT is required. In addition, applicants should be graduates of an accredited secondary school with 16 Carnegie credits completed, including 4 years of English, 3 of math, and 2 each of science, foreign language, and history. The SAT II: Subject test in a foreign language is recommended. An essay is required. An audition or a portfolio is recommended for some majors. AP credits are accepted. Students can apply on-line through the university's web site or through ExPAN.

Procedure: Freshmen are admitted in the fall. Entrance exams should be taken by the fall of the senior year. There is a deferred admissions plan. Early decision applications should be filed by November 1; regular applications, by January 7 for fall entry. The fall 2001 application fee was $50. Notification of early decision is sent December 15; regular decision, April 1. 4% of all applicants are on a waiting list.

Transfer: 126 transfer students enrolled in 2001-2002. Applicants should have completed at least 27 semester hours of transferable credit and maintained a 3.0 GPA in all courses. Admission depends on openings in each undergraduate college. 60 credits of 120 must be completed at Notre Dame.

Visiting: There are regularly scheduled orientations for prospective students, including small group sessions for students, larger sessions for parents, and tours for all. Visitors may sit in on classes and stay overnight. To schedule a visit, contact the Admissions telephone receptionists.

Financial Aid: In 2001-2002, 81% of all freshmen and 87% of continuing students received some form of financial aid. 50% of freshmen and 57% of continuing students received need-based aid. The average freshman award was $19,000. Of that total, scholarships or need-based grants averaged $14,400 ($33,100 maximum); loans averaged $5000 ($10,000 maximum); and work contracts averaged $1000 ($2100 maximum). 48% of undergraduates work part time. Average annual earnings from campus work are $900. The average financial indebtedness of the 2001 graduate was $14,290. Notre Dame is a member of CSS. The CSS/Profile or FAFSA and federal income tax return are required. The fall application deadline is February 15.

International Students: There are 214 international students enrolled. The school actively recruits these students. They must score 550 on the written TOEFL.

Computers: The mainframes are an HP 3000 and 2 ORIGEN 2000s. There are 880 PCs, Macs, and UNIX computers in open clusters that students can use to complete their course work and access the Internet. All students may access the system 24 hours a day. There are no time limits and no fees. It is strongly recommended that all students have a personal computer.

Graduates: In 2001, 1954 bachelor's degrees were awarded. The most popular majors were finance (13%), government (9%), and accountancy (7%). In an average class, 88% graduate in 4 years, 94% in 5 years, and 94% in 6 years. 351 companies recruited on campus in 2000-2001. Of the 2000 graduating class, 63% were employed within 6 months of graduation.

Admissions Contact: Daniel J. Saracino, Assistant Provost for Enrollment. E-mail: *admissions.admissio.1@nd.edu* Web: *www.nd.edu*

UNIVERSITY OF SAINT FRANCIS (Formerly Saint Francis College) D-2
Fort Wayne, IN 46808 (219) 434-3264
(800) 729-4732; Fax: (219) 434-3183

Full-time: 320 men, 670 women	**Faculty:** 89; IIA, --$
Part-time: 110 men, 455 women	**Ph.D.s:** 60%
Graduate: 65 men, 145 women	**Student/Faculty:** 11 to 1
Year: semesters, summer session	**Tuition:** $13,090
Application Deadline: open	**Room & Board:** $4700
Freshman Class: n/av	
SAT I or ACT: required	**LESS COMPETITIVE**

University of Saint Francis (formerly Saint Francis College) is a Roman Catholic liberal arts college founded in 1890 by the sisters of Saint Francis. Figures in the above capsule are approximate. There is 1 graduate school. In addition to regional accreditation, USF has baccalaureate program accreditation with CAHEA, CSWE, and NLN. The library contains 85,544 volumes, 584,239 microform items, and 3990 audiovisual forms/CDs, and subscribes to 480 periodicals. Computerized library services include the card catalog, interlibrary loans, and database searching. Special learning facilities include a learning resource center, art gallery, planetarium, and TV station. The 75-acre campus is in a suburban area west of Fort Wayne. Including residence halls, there are 19 buildings.

Student Life: 72% of undergraduates are from Indiana. Others are from 9 states. 85% are white. 53% are Protestant; 45% Catholic. The average age of freshmen is 18; all undergraduates, 27. 36% do not continue beyond their first year.

Housing: 240 students can be accommodated in college housing, which includes single-sex dormitories. On-campus housing is guaranteed for the freshman year only and is available on a first-come, first-served basis. 66% of students commute. Alcohol is not permitted. All students may keep cars.

Activities: There are no fraternities or sororities. There are 25 groups on campus, including art, band, cheerleading, dance, drama, ethnic, newspaper, pep band, professional, radio and TV, religious, social, social service, student government, and yearbook. Popular campus events include Little Regatta and Spring Fling.

Sports: There are 8 intercollegiate sports for men and 8 for women, and 4 intramural sports for men and 4 for women. Facilities include a gym with 2 basketball courts or 3 volleyball courts, a weight room, a baseball diamond, a beach volleyball pit, a football stadium, and soccer, baseball, and softball fields.

Disabled Students: 85% of the campus is accessible. Wheelchair ramps, elevators, special parking, specially equipped rest rooms, and lowered drinking fountains are available.

Services: Counseling and information services are available, as is tutoring in most subjects. There is remedial math, reading, and writing, and help for the learning disabled, individual counseling, and peer tutoring.

Campus Safety and Security: Measures include 24-hour foot and vehicle patrol, escort service, pamphlets/posters/films, and emergency telephones. There are lighted pathways/sidewalks.

Programs of Study: USF confers B.A., B.S., B.B.A., B.L.S., B.S.Ed., B.S.N., and B.S.W. degrees. Associate and master's degrees are also awarded. Bachelor's degrees are awarded in BIOLOGICAL SCIENCE (biology/biological science), BUSINESS (accounting, business administration and management, and human resources), COMMUNICATIONS AND THE ARTS (communications, English, and fine arts), COMPUTER AND PHYSICAL SCIENCE (chemistry and science), EDUCATION (art, business, elementary, English, health, science, secondary, social studies, and special), ENGINEERING AND ENVIRONMENTAL DESIGN (commercial art and environmental science), HEALTH PROFESSIONS (allied health, medical laboratory technology, nursing, predentistry, premedicine, and radiograph medical technology), SOCIAL SCIENCE (American studies, history, human services, liberal arts/general studies, ministries, psychology, religion, and social work). Commercial art, nursing, and biological sciences are the strongest academically. Business, art, nursing, and education are the largest.

Required: All students must complete courses in humanities, social and behavioral science, religious studies, life and physical sciences, oral and written communication, phys ed, computer science, and reading. 128 semester hours with a minimum GPA of 2.0 and at least 30 hours in the major are required to graduate.

Special: Internships in commercial art, business, and social work are available, as well as on-campus work-study programs and nondegree study. Students also can receive credit for life experience. There is 1 national honor society, a freshman honors program, and 1 departmental honors program.

Faculty/Classroom: 52% of faculty are male; 48%, female. 95% teach undergraduates. No introductory courses are taught by graduate students. The average class size in an introductory lecture is 25; in a laboratory, 15; and in a regular course, 14.

Requirements: The SAT I or ACT is required, with a minimum composite score of 960 on the SAT I or 19 on the ACT. 4 years of English, 2 each of math and science, and 1 of social studies are suggested. USF requires applicants to be in the upper 50% of their class. A GPA of 2.0 is required. AP and CLEP credits are accepted. Important factors in the admissions decision are advanced placement or honor courses, recommendations by school officials, and extracurricular activities record.

Procedure: Freshmen are admitted to all sessions. Entrance exams should be taken in the spring of the junior year or fall of the senior year. There is a deferred admissions plan. Application deadlines are open. The application fee is $20.

Transfer: Applicants need a minimum GPA of 2.0 and must submit all college transcripts. 32 credits of 128 must be completed at USF.

Visiting: There are regularly scheduled orientations for prospective students, including meetings with faculty and staff and student tours. There are guides for informal visits and visitors may sit in on classes and stay overnight. To schedule a visit, contact the Admissions Office.

Financial Aid: USF is a member of CSS. The FAFSA and the college's own financial statement are required. The fall application deadline is March 1.

International Students: They must score 550 on the written TOEFL.

Computers: The mainframe is an IBM AS/400. More than 25 PCs with links to the World Wide Web are available in classrooms, the library, computer labs, and residence halls. All students may access the system 7 days a week. There are no time limits and no fees.

Admissions Contact: David C. McMahan, Director of Admissions. A video is available. E-mail: *dmcmahan@sf.edu* Web: *www.sf.edu*

UNIVERSITY OF SOUTHERN INDIANA

Evansville, IN 47712 — A-5
(812) 464-1765
(800) 467-1965; Fax: (812) 465-7154

Full-time: 2754 men, 4023 women	**Faculty:** 275; IIA, --$
Part-time: 779 men, 1227 women	**Ph.D.s:** 63%
Graduate: 169 men, 410 women	**Student/Faculty:** 25 to 1
Year: semesters, summer session	**Tuition:** $3143 ($7605)
Application Deadline: August 15	**Room & Board:** $5512
Freshman Class: 4105 applied, 3834 accepted, 2039 enrolled	
SAT I Verbal/Math: 472/474	**ACT:** 19 LESS COMPETITIVE

The University of Southern Indiana, founded in 1965, is a public institution offering undergraduate programs in business, education and human service, liberal arts, nursing and health professions, and science and engineering technology. There are 5 undergraduate schools and 1 graduate school. In addition to regional accreditation, USI has baccalaureate program accreditation with AACSB, ABET, ADA, CSWE, and NCATE. The library contains 222,842 volumes, 609,353 microform items, and 7563 audiovisual forms/CDs, and subscribes to 3283 periodicals. Computerized library services include the card catalog, interlibrary loans, and database searching. Special learning facilities include a learning resource center, radio station, and TV station. The 300-acre campus is in a suburban area 150 miles south of Indianapolis. Including residence halls, there are 48 buildings.

Student Life: 90% of undergraduates are from Indiana. Others are from 28 states, 28 foreign countries, and Canada. 94% are white. The average age of freshmen is 18; all undergraduates, 21. 38% do not continue beyond their first year.

Housing: 2947 students can be accommodated in college housing, which includes single-sex and coed dormitories, on-campus apartments, off-campus apartments, and married-student housing. On-campus housing is available on a first-come, first-served basis. Priority is given to out-of-town students. 69% of students commute. Alcohol is not permitted. All students may keep cars.

Activities: 5% of men belong to 4 national fraternities; 4% of women belong to 5 national sororities. There are 102 groups on campus, including art, cheerleading, choir, chorus, computers, dance, drama, ethnic, film, gay, honors, international, jazz band, literary magazine, musical theater, newspaper, pep band, photography, political, professional, radio and TV, religious, social, social service, student government, and yearbook. Popular campus events include Eagle Gran Prix Bike Race, Spring Fling, and Oksoberfest.

Sports: There are 6 intercollegiate sports for men and 7 for women, and 11 intramural sports for men and 10 for women. Facilities include a physical activities center with a swimming pool, a weight room, 6 tennis courts, and a 3000-seat multipurpose area and a recreation and fitness center with weights, cardiovascular equipment, and exercise programs.

Disabled Students: 90% of the campus is accessible. Wheelchair ramps, elevators, special parking, specially equipped rest rooms, special class scheduling, lowered drinking fountains, lowered telephones, and student assistance through the counseling center are available.

Services: Counseling and information services are available, as is tutoring in most subjects. There is a reader service for the blind, and remedial math, reading, and writing.

Campus Safety and Security: Measures include 24-hour foot and vehicle patrol, escort service, shuttle buses, and pamphlets/posters/films. There are emergency telephones and lighted pathways/sidewalks.

Programs of Study: USI confers B.A., B.S., B.G.S., B.S.N., and B.S.W. degrees. Associate and master's degrees are also awarded. Bachelor's degrees are awarded in BIOLOGICAL SCIENCE (biology/biological science and biophysics), BUSINESS (accounting, banking and finance, business administration and management, business economics, and marketing/retailing/merchandising), COMMUNICATIONS AND THE ARTS (broadcasting, communications, dramatic arts, English, German, journalism, Spanish, and speech/debate/rhetoric), COMPUTER AND PHYSICAL SCIENCE (chemistry and mathematics), EDUCATION (art, business, elementary, middle school, science, and secondary), ENGINEERING AND ENVIRONMENTAL DESIGN (engineering technology), HEALTH PROFESSIONS (nursing, occupational therapy, predentistry, and premedicine), SOCIAL SCIENCE (economics, history, philosophy, political science/government, prelaw, psychology, social work, and sociology). Occupational therapy and math are the strongest academically. Business, education, and liberal arts are the largest.

Required: The university's core curriculum goals focus on four areas: the mind (enhancement of cognitive abilities), the self (enhancement of individual development), the world (enhancement of cultural and natural awareness), and the synthesis (the integration and application of knowledge). These are then subdivided into 13 smaller objectives concerned with critical thinking, oral and written communication, math, information processing, ethics, the arts, health and lifestyle, history, individual development and social behavior, science, Western culture, global communities, and interdisciplinary studies. A total of 50 credit hours is distributed among the objectives with a total of 124 credit hours needed to graduate. A minimum cumulative 2.0 GPA is required.

Special: Students may participate in cooperative programs, internships in business and communications, and work-study programs. Study abroad, dual majors, pass/fail options, and B.A.-B.S. degrees are possible. There are 12 national honor societies.

Faculty/Classroom: 52% of faculty are male; 48%, female. All teach undergraduates. No introductory courses are taught by graduate students. The average class size in an introductory lecture is 100; in a laboratory, 35; and in a regular course, 20.

Admissions: 93% of the 2001-2002 applicants were accepted. The SAT I scores for the 2001-2002 freshman class were: Verbal--63% below 500, 29% between 500 and 599, and 8% between 600 and 700; Math--61% below 500, 30% between 500 and 599, 8% between 600 and 700, and 1% above 700. The ACT scores were 62% below 21, 22% between 21 and 23, 11% between 24 and 26, 3% between 27 and 28, and 2% above 28. 20% of the current freshmen were in the top fifth of their class; 44% were in the top two fifths. 31 freshmen graduated first in their class.

Requirements: The SAT I or ACT is required. In addition, applicants must be graduates of an accredited secondary school, with a minimum GPA of 2.0. The GED is accepted. An interview is recommended if the student is below admissions standards. AP and CLEP credits are accepted. Important factors in the admissions decision are advanced placement or honor courses, evidence of special talent, and leadership record. Applications are accepted on-line at *www.usi.edu/admissn/admit.asp*.

Procedure: Freshmen are admitted fall, spring, and summer. Entrance exams should be taken in the spring term of the junior year. Applications should be filed by August 15 for fall entry, January 1 for spring entry, and June 1 for summer entry, along with a $25 fee. Notification is sent on a rolling basis.

Transfer: 637 transfer students enrolled in 2001-2002. Grades of C- and above will transfer for credit. 30 credits of 124 must be completed at USI.

Visiting: There are regularly scheduled orientations for prospective students, including meetings with counselors and faculty and campus tours. There are guides for informal visits and visitors may sit in on classes and stay overnight. To schedule a visit, contact the Office of Admission at *enroll@usi.edu*.

Financial Aid: In 2001-2002, 73% of all freshmen and 58% of continuing students received some form of financial aid. 48% of freshmen and 37% of continuing students received need-based aid. The average freshman award was $4206. Of that total, scholarships or need-based grants averaged $3290 ($14,083 maximum); loans averaged $2880 ($8578 maximum); and work contracts averaged $1575 ($2000 maximum). 67% of undergraduates work part time. Average annual earnings from campus work are $1370. The average financial indebtedness of the 2001 graduate was $12,611. USI is a member of CSS. The FAFSA and the college's own financial statement are required. The fall application deadline is March 1.

International Students: There are 41 international students enrolled. They must score 525 on the written TOEFL and also take the SAT I or the ACT.

Computers: The mainframes are an IBM 4381 and an IBM 4361. All students may access the system. There are no time limits and no fees.

Graduates: In 2001, 961 bachelor's degrees were awarded. The most popular majors were elementary education (14%), business administration (12%), and health services (6%). In an average class, 12% graduate in 4 years, 26% in 5 years, and 30% in 6 years. 242 companies recruited on campus in 2000-2001.

Admissions Contact: Eric Otto, Director of Admission.
E-mail: *eotto@usi.edu* Web: *www.usi.edu*

VALPARAISO UNIVERSITY B-1

Valparaiso, IN 46383 (219) 464-5011
(888) GO-VALPO; Fax: (219) 464-6898

Full-time: 1295 men, 1392 women	**Faculty:** 190
Part-time: 52 men, 134 women	**Ph.D.s:** 88%
Graduate: 304 men, 356 women	**Student/Faculty:** 14 to 1
Year: semesters, summer session	**Tuition:** $18,700
Application Deadline: August 15	**Room & Board:** $4870
Freshman Class: 2901 applied, 2344 accepted, 668 enrolled	
SAT I Verbal/Math: 580/580	**ACT:** 27 **VERY COMPETITIVE+**

Valparaiso University, founded in 1859, is an independent institution affiliated with the Lutheran Church and offering degree programs in arts and sciences, business administration, engineering, nursing, and law. There are 5 undergraduate and 2 graduate schools. In addition to regional accreditation, Valpo has baccalaureate program accreditation with AACSB, ABET, ACS, CCNE, CSWE, NASM, NCATE, and NLN. The 2 libraries contain 587,333 volumes, 1,805,687 microform items, and 13,082 audiovisual forms/CDs, and subscribe to 5293 periodicals. Computerized library services include the card catalog, interlibrary loans, and database searching. Special learning facilities include a learning resource center, art gallery, planetarium, radio station, TV station, observatory, weather station, center for visual and performing arts, and nuclear physics lab. The 310-acre campus is in a small town 45 miles southeast of Chicago. Including residence halls, there are 53 buildings.

Student Life: 65% of undergraduates are from out of state, mostly the Midwest. Students are from 47 states, 48 foreign countries, and Canada. 80% are from public schools. 87% are white. 60% are Protestant; 21%, Catholic. The average age of freshmen is 19; all undergraduates, 21. 14% do not continue beyond their first year; 72% remain to graduate.

Housing: 1955 students can be accommodated in college housing, which includes single-sex and coed dormitories, on-campus apartments, off-campus apartments, fraternity houses, and sorority houses. In addition, there are language houses, non-smoking halls, and quiet halls. On-campus housing is guaranteed for all 4 years. 62% of students live on campus; of those, 80% remain on campus on weekends. Alcohol is not permitted. Upperclassmen may keep cars.

Activities: 30% of men belong to 8 national fraternities; 30% of women belong to 7 national sororities. There are 100 groups on campus, including art, band, cheerleading, chess, choir, chorale, chorus, computers, dance, drama, ethnic, gay, honors, international, jazz band, literary magazine, musical theater, newspaper, orchestra, pep band, photography, political, professional, radio and TV, religious, social, social service, student government, symphony, and yearbook. Popular campus events include Christmas Concert, Madrigal Dinner, and Jazz Festival.

Sports: There are 8 intercollegiate sports for men and 8 for women, and 20 intramural sports for men and 20 for women. Facilities include an athletics-recreation center that houses a 4800-seat gym, racquetball courts, weight rooms, swimming pools, basketball courts, and an indoor track. Other facilities include a 5000-seat football and soccer stadium, baseball and track fields, a cross-country course, tennis courts, an outdoor recreation center, and game rooms.

Disabled Students: 55% of the campus is accessible. Wheelchair ramps, elevators, special parking, specially equipped rest rooms, and special class scheduling are available.

Services: Counseling and information services are available, as is tutoring in every subject. There is a reader service for the blind. A writing center provides assistance.

Campus Safety and Security: Measures include 24-hour foot and vehicle patrol, self-defense education, escort service, and shuttle buses. There are informal discussions, pamphlets/posters/films, emergency telephones, and lighted pathways/sidewalks.

Programs of Study: Valpo confers B.A., B.S., B.Mus., B.Mus.Ed., B.S.Acc., B.S.Bus.Adm., B.S.C.E., B.S.Ed., B.S.E.E., B.S.F.A., B.S.M.E., B.S.N., B.S.P.E., and B.S.W. degrees. Associate, master's, and doctoral degrees are also awarded. Bachelor's degrees are awarded in BIOLOGICAL SCIENCE (biology/biological science), BUSINESS (accounting, banking and finance, business administration and management, international business management, international economics, marketing/retailing/merchandising, and sports management), COMMUNICATIONS AND THE ARTS (art, broadcasting, classics, communications, dramatic arts, English, French, German, journalism, music, and Spanish), COMPUTER AND PHYSICAL SCIENCE (atmospheric sciences and meteorology, chemistry, computer science, geology, information sciences and systems, mathematics, and physics), EDUCATION (athletic training, elementary, middle school, music, physical, and secondary), ENGINEERING AND ENVIRONMENTAL DESIGN (civil engineering, electrical/electronics engineering, environmental science, and mechanical engineering), HEALTH PROFESSIONS (exercise science and nursing), SOCIAL SCIENCE (American studies, Asian/Oriental studies, criminology, economics, European studies, geography, history, international public service, ministries, philosophy, political science/government, psychology, religion, social work, sociology, and theological studies). Biology, engineering, and English are the strongest academically. Business, engineering, and education are the largest.

Required: General education requirements include the 10-credit Valpo core plus 3 courses in math/natural and behavioral sciences, 2 each of theology, literature/fine arts, and social analysis, and 1 each of philosophy/history, global perspectives, U.S. diversity, and phys ed; requirements may vary by degree program. To graduate, students must complete at least 124 credit hours, including a minimum of 24 in the major, with a GPA of at least 2.0.

Special: There is cross-registration with Indiana University Northwest. Valparaiso maintains cooperative programs in most majors, including urban studies with the Association of Midwest Colleges, as well as a United Nations semester with Drew University and a Washington semester with American University. Students may study abroad in 9 countries. Internships, the B.A.-B.S. degree, work-study programs, dual and student-designed majors, an accelerated degree program in numerous majors, pass/fail options, and nondegree study are also available. Other special academic features include Christ College, which is an autonomous honors college. There are 6 national honor societies, a freshman honors program, and 25 departmental honors programs.

Faculty/Classroom: 60% of faculty are male; 40%, female. 80% teach undergraduates. No introductory courses are taught by graduate students. The average class size in an introductory lecture is 25; in a laboratory, 15; and in a regular course, 20.

Admissions: 81% of the 2001-2002 applicants were accepted. The SAT I scores for the 2001-2002 freshman class were: Verbal--13% below 500, 41% between 500 and 599, 36% between 600 and 700, and 10% above 700; Math--11% below 500, 45% between 500 and 599, 31% between 600 and 700, and 13% above 700. The ACT scores were 5% below 21, 19% between 21 and 23, 27% between 24 and 26, 20% between 27 and 28, and 29% above 28. 61% of the current freshmen were in the top fifth of their class; 85% were in the top two fifths. There were 19 National Merit finalists. 27 freshmen graduated first in their class.

Requirements: The SAT I or ACT is required. In addition, applicants must be graduates of an accredited secondary school or have earned a GED. Valpo requires completion of 4 years of English, 3 to 4 of math, 2 to 3 of lab science, 2 each of history and foreign language, and 3 of additional academic courses. An essay and an interview are recommended for all applicants, and an audition is required for music majors. AP and CLEP credits are accepted. Important factors in the admissions decision are advanced placement or honor courses, extracurricular activities record, and evidence of special talent. Students can apply on-line via the school's web site.

Procedure: Freshmen are admitted to all sessions. Entrance exams should be taken prior to the senior year. There are early admissions and deferred admissions plans. Applications should be filed by August 15 for fall entry. The fall 2001 application fee was $30. Notification is sent on a rolling basis.

Transfer: 93 transfer students enrolled in 2001-2002. Applicants must submit official transcripts from all colleges attended. A minimum GPA of 2.0 (3.0 for nursing majors) is required for all college work. If the applicant has completed fewer than 24 credit hours, entrance exam scores are required. An interview is recommended. 30 credits of 124 must be completed at Valpo.

Visiting: There are regularly scheduled orientations for prospective students, including a campus tour conducted by a current student, an interview with a counselor, and the option to meet with professors, attend a class, and meet with a coach. There are guides for informal visits and visitors may sit in on classes and stay overnight. To schedule a visit, contact the Admissions Office.

Financial Aid: In 2001-2002, 91% of all freshmen and 90% of continuing students received some form of financial aid. 68% of freshmen and 62% of continuing students received need-based aid. The average freshman award was $15,189. Of that total, scholarships or need-based grants averaged $11,678 ($25,570 maximum); loans averaged $5510 ($23,240 maximum); and work contracts averaged $1724 ($2000 maximum). 40% of undergraduates work part time. Average annual earnings from campus work are $1015. The average financial indebtedness of the 2001 graduate was $18,762. Valpo is a member of CSS. The FAFSA is required. The fall application deadline is March 1.

International Students: There are 108 international students enrolled. The school actively recruits these students. They must score 550 on the

written TOEFL or 213 on the electronic version or complete Valparaiso's institutional Intensive English language program.

Computers: The mainframe is a DEC VAX 4000 Model 500A. Services available to students include academic applications, the library bibliographic system and periodic indexes, the Internet and World Wide Web, and E-mail. There are 561 student computers, primarily Pentiums, Power Macs, and 486s, located throughout the campus. UNIX workstations are available in some departments. All residence halls have 24-hour computer clusters. Remote access to university resources includes a high-speed modem pool with PPP capability. All students may access the system 7 days a week. There are no time limits and no fees. It is recommended that students in engineering have a Pentium-level PC.

Graduates: In 2001, 635 bachelor's degrees were awarded. The most popular majors were education (12%), psychology (7%), and nursing (6%). In an average class, 1% graduate in 3 years, 56% in 4 years, 70% in 5 years, and 71% in 6 years. 64 companies recruited on campus in 2000-2001. Of the 2000 graduating class, 23% were enrolled in graduate school within 6 months of graduation and 74% were employed.

Admissions Contact: Office of Admissions. A video is available. E-mail: *undergrad.admissions@valpo.edu* Web: *www.valpo.edu*

WABASH COLLEGE

Crawfordsville, IN 47933-0352 B-3

(765) 361-6253

(800) 345-5385; Fax: (765) 361-6437

Full-time: 840 men	**Faculty:** 79; IIB, +$
Part-time: 9 men	**Ph.D.s:** 99%
Graduate: none	**Student/Faculty:** 11 to 1
Year: semesters	**Tuition:** $19,243
Application Deadline: February 1	**Room & Board:** $6092
Freshman Class: 1165 applied, 626 accepted, 237 enrolled	
SAT I Verbal/Math: 589/603	**ACT:** 26 **HIGHLY COMPETITIVE**

Wabash College, founded in 1832, is a private, liberal arts men's college with a strong emphasis on preprofessional programs. In addition to regional accreditation, Wabash has baccalaureate program accreditation with NCATE. The library contains 263,315 volumes, 8074 microform items, and 8063 audiovisual forms/CDs, and subscribes to 1337 periodicals. Computerized library services include the card catalog, interlibrary loans, and database searching. Special learning facilities include a learning resource center, art gallery, radio station, archival center, and research centers for the study of theology and religion and inquiry in the liberal arts. The 55-acre campus is in a small town 45 miles northwest of Indianapolis. Including residence halls, there are 33 buildings.

Student Life: 73% of undergraduates are from Indiana. Others are from 35 states, 14 foreign countries, and Canada. 93% are from public schools. 80% are white. The average age of freshmen is 18; all undergraduates, 20. 14% do not continue beyond their first year.

Housing: About 820 students can be accommodated in college housing, which includes dorms, off-campus apartments, an international house, and fraternity houses. In addition, there are language houses. On-campus housing is guaranteed for all 4 years. 92% of students live on campus; of those, 65% remain on campus on weekends.

Activities: 75% of men belong to 10 national fraternities. There are 40 groups on campus, including art, band, cheerleading, chess, choir, chorus, computers, debate, drama, drum corps, ethnic, film, foreign language, forensics, gay, honors, international, jazz band, literary magazine, musical theater, newspaper, orchestra, pep band, photography, political, professional, radio, religious, social, social service, student government, symphony, and yearbook. Popular campus events include Pan-Hel Weekend, Fall Bash, and Chapel Sing.

Sports: Facilities include a 4200-seat stadium, indoor and outdoor tennis courts, football, baseball, and soccer fields, a swimming pool, an indoor track, an all-weather track, wrestling and weight rooms, racquetball and handball courts, a ropes challenge course, an 1800-seat basketball arena, a wellness center, and an aerobics studio.

Disabled Students: 60% of the campus is accessible. Wheelchair ramps, elevators, special parking, specially equipped rest rooms, lowered drinking fountains, lowered telephones, and counseling are available.

Services: Tutoring is available in most subjects. There is a typing/reading service for the blind, and remedial math, reading, and writing. There is a quantitative skills center as well as a writing center where, under professional supervision, students help each other.

Campus Safety and Security: Measures include 24-hour foot and vehicle patrol, escort service, pamphlets/posters/films, and emergency telephones. There are lighted pathways/sidewalks.

Programs of Study: Wabash confers the A.B. degree. Bachelor's degrees are awarded in BIOLOGICAL SCIENCE (biology/biological science), COMMUNICATIONS AND THE ARTS (art, classics, dramatic arts, English, French, German, Greek, Latin, music, Spanish, and speech/debate/rhetoric), COMPUTER AND PHYSICAL SCIENCE (chemistry, mathematics, and physics), SOCIAL SCIENCE (economics, history, philosophy, political science/government, psychology, and religion). Preprofessional studies, economics, and religion are the strongest academically. History, psychology, and economics are the largest.

Required: All students must complete at least 3 courses each in literature/fine arts, behavioral science, and natural science/math, 2 in history, philosophy, or religion, and 1 in quantitative skills. To graduate, students must maintain a minimum 2.0 GPA for 136 credit hours (34 courses), which include a freshman tutorial and 2 semesters of cultures and traditions. The student must pass a written comprehensive exam in the major as well as a senior oral exam and must demonstrate proficiency in English and in a foreign language at a level equivalent to 2 college courses.

Special: Wabash offers internships with off-campus organizations, study abroad in an unlimited number of countries, a Washington semester with American University, dual majors, a B.A.-B.S. degree in engineering, and both a 3-2 engineering program and a 3-3 law program with Columbia University and Washington University in St. Louis. A tuition-free Ninth Semester Teacher Education Program is also available. There are 9 national honor societies, including Phi Beta Kappa, and 7 departmental honors programs.

Faculty/Classroom: 84% of faculty are male; 16%, female. All teach undergraduates. The average class size in an introductory lecture is 24; in a laboratory, 16; and in a regular course, 13.

Admissions: 54% of the 2001-2002 applicants were accepted. The SAT I scores for the 2001-2002 freshman class were: Verbal--13% below 500, 40% between 500 and 599, 36% between 600 and 700, and 10% above 700; Math--6% below 500, 36% between 500 and 599, 47% between 600 and 700, and 11% above 700. The ACT scores were 10% below 21, 18% between 21 and 23, 33% between 24 and 26, 20% between 27 and 28, and 19% above 28. 61% of the current freshmen were in the top fifth of their class; 91% were in the top two fifths. There were 2 National Merit finalists. 9 freshmen graduated first in their class.

Requirements: The SAT I or ACT is required. In addition, Wabash recommends that applicants have 4 high school courses in English, 3 to 4 in math, and 2 each in foreign language, lab science, and social studies. An essay is required and an interview is recommended. AP and CLEP credits are accepted. Students can apply on-line via CollegeLink, ExPAN, Common App, or the school's web site.

Procedure: Freshmen are admitted fall and spring. Entrance exams should be taken by the spring of the junior year or fall of the senior year. There are early decision, early action, early admissions, and deferred admissions plans. Early decision application should be filed by November 15; early action, by December 15; regular applications, by February 1 for fall entry and December 1 for spring entry. The fall 2001 application fee was $30. Notification of early decision is sent December 15; early action, January 15; regular decision, on a rolling basis. 37 early decision candidates were accepted for the 2001-2002 class. 10% of all applicants are on a waiting list; 9 were accepted in 2001.

Transfer: 5 transfer students enrolled in 2001-2002. Applicants must submit official transcripts of all college courses attended. Wabash strongly considers the overall high school and college background of applicants. A minimum GPA of 2.5, recommendations from the college adviser and dean of students at the previous college attended, and a personal written statement are required, with an interview strongly recommended. 17 credits of 34 must be completed at Wabash.

Visiting: There are regularly scheduled orientations for prospective students, consisting of a tour, lunch, an opportunity to meet faculty, coaches, and alumni, and panel discussions on academics, extracurricular activities, and financial aid. There are guides for informal visits and visitors may sit in on classes and stay overnight. To schedule a visit, contact Mary Skelton of the Admissions Office at (800) 345-5385 or (765) 361-6276 or *skeltonm@wabash.edu*.

Financial Aid: In 2001-2002, 95% of all freshmen and 96% of continuing students received some form of financial aid. 76% of freshmen and 71% of continuing students received need-based aid. The average freshman award was $17,968. Of that total, scholarships or need-based grants averaged $13,907 ($25,010 maximum); loans averaged $3301 ($7625 maximum); and work contracts averaged $1648 ($1800 maximum). 58% of undergraduates work part time. Average annual earnings from campus work are $900. The average financial indebtedness of the 2001 graduate was $16,504. Wabash is a member of CSS. The CSS/Profile or FAFSA and federal tax form with W-2 statements are required. The fall application deadline is February 15.

International Students: There are 33 international students enrolled. They must take the TOEFL, scoring 213 on a 300 scale on the written version or 240 on the electronic version, or take the MELAB.

Computers: The mainframe is a DEC ALPHA 2100 server. Every student has an account on a Novell server, with a network connection in the student's living unit. There are more than 100 Macs and Power PCs in 6 public classrooms. All students may access the system 24 hours per day or at designated times for specific computers.

Graduates: In 2001, 178 bachelor's degrees were awarded. The most popular majors were history (15%), English (12%), and political science (11%). In an average class, 66% graduate in 4 years, and 69% in 5 years. 61 companies recruited on campus in 2000-2001. Of the 2000 graduating class, 38% were enrolled in graduate school within 6 months of graduation and 60% were employed.

Admissions Contact: Steve Klein, Director of Admissions. A video is available. E-mail: *admissions@wabash.edu* Web: *www.wabash.edu*

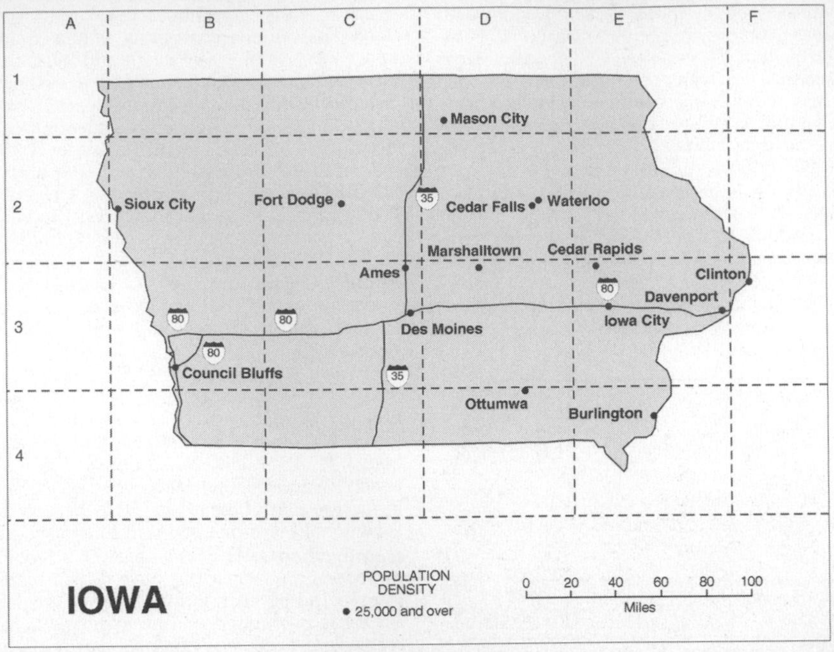

ALLEN COLLEGE — D-2

Waterloo, IA 50703 — (319) 226-2002; Fax: (319) 226-2051

Full-time: 11 men, 171 women
Part-time: 3 men, 48 women
Graduate: 1 man, 23 women
Year: semesters, summer session
Application Deadline: open
Freshman Class: 38 applied, 35 accepted, 20 enrolled
ACT: 20
Faculty: 18
Ph.D.s: 8%
Student/Faculty: 10 to 1
Tuition: $8544
Room & Board: $4410
SPECIAL

Allen College, founded in 1989, is a private institution offering a baccalaureate program in nursing. In addition to regional accreditation, Allen College has baccalaureate program accreditation with NLN. The library contains 3400 volumes and 646 audiovisual forms/CDs, and subscribes to 102 periodicals. Computerized library services include the card catalog, interlibrary loans, and database searching. The 20-acre campus is in a suburban area. There are 2 buildings.

Student Life: 98% of undergraduates are from Iowa. Others are from 4 states. 97% are white. The average age of freshmen is 18; all undergraduates, 25. 33% do not continue beyond their first year; 67% remain to graduate.

Housing: There are no residence halls. All students commute. Alcohol is not permitted. All students may keep cars. There are living facilities available at cooperative colleges.

Activities: There are no fraternities or sororities. There are 6 groups on campus, including newspaper, student government, and yearbook. Popular campus events include Fall Fling and Winter Party.

Sports: There is no sports program at Allen College.

Disabled Students: All of the campus is accessible. Wheelchair ramps, elevators, special parking, specially equipped rest rooms, and lowered drinking fountains are available.

Services: Counseling and information services are available, as is tutoring in most subjects.

Campus Safety and Security: Measures include informal discussions, pamphlets/posters/films, and lighted pathways/sidewalks.

Programs of Study: Allen College confers the B.S.N. degree. Associate and master's degrees are also awarded. Bachelor's degrees are awarded in HEALTH PROFESSIONS (nursing).

Required: To graduate, all students must complete general education courses in humanities, social science, natural science, and electives and maintain a 2.0 GPA. 125 credits are required, with 68 in the major.

Special: Cross-registration is available with the University of Northern Iowa and Wartburg College. Co-op programs in nursing and radiography are also available. There is 1 departmental honors program.

Faculty/Classroom: 4% of faculty are male; 96%, female. 88% teach undergraduates. The average class size in an introductory lecture is 25; in a laboratory, 8; and in a regular course, 25.

Admissions: 92% of the 2001-2002 applicants were accepted. The ACT scores for the 2001-2002 freshman class were: 63% below 21, 26% between 21 and 23, and 11% between 24 and 26. 37% of the current freshmen were in the top fifth of their class; 68% were in the top two fifths.

Requirements: The ACT is required, with a minimum composite score of 18. An essay, a letter of recommendation, and class rank in the upper 50th percentile are required. Core high school courses including 4 years of English, 3 each of math and social studies, and 1 each of chemistry, biology, and 1 other science are required. Students must earn grades of C or better. AP and CLEP credits are accepted. Applications are accepted on-line at the college's web site.

Procedure: Freshmen are admitted fall, spring, and summer. Application deadlines are open. The application fee is $20. Notification is sent on a rolling basis. 5% of all applicants are on a waiting list; 1 was accepted in 2001.

Transfer: 40 transfer students enrolled in 2001-2002. Students must have a college GPA of 2.5 and submit an essay and a letter of recommendation. 30 credits of 125 must be completed at Allen College.

Visiting: There are regularly scheduled orientations for prospective students, including an opportunity to speak to the Director of Admissions, the Director of Financial Aid, and department chairs and to tour campus. There are guides for informal visits and visitors may sit in on classes. To schedule a visit, contact Lois Hagedorn at (319) 226-2000 or *hagedole@ihs.org*.

Financial Aid: In 2001-2002, 67% of all freshmen and 71% of continuing students received some form of financial aid. 67% of all students received need-based aid. The average freshman award was $5088. Of that total, scholarships or need-based grants averaged $3056 ($6976 maximum); and loans averaged $2381 ($6625 maximum). 4% of undergraduates work part time. Average annual earnings from campus work are $2000. The average financial indebtedness of the 2001 graduate was $15,737. The FAFSA and the college's own financial statement are required. The fall application deadline is March 1.

International Students: They must score 550 on the written TOEFL and also take the ACT, scoring 18.

Computers: The mainframe is an IBM. A 24-hour computer lab includes 21 computers and Internet access. All students may access the system 24 hours a day. There are no time limits. The fee is $35 per semester. It is strongly recommended that all students have a personal computer.

Graduates: In 2001, 51 bachelor's degrees were awarded. In an average class, 9% graduate in 4 years, 57% in 5 years, and 7% in 6 years. 40 companies recruited on campus in 2000-2001.

Admissions Contact: Barb Seible, Director of Admissions.
E-mail: *seiblebj@ihs.org* Web: *www.allencollege.edu*

BRIAR CLIFF COLLEGE
(See Briar Cliff University)

BRIAR CLIFF UNIVERSITY
(Formerly Briar Cliff College)
B-2

Sioux City, IA 51104-0100

(712) 279-5200
(800) 662-3303; Fax: (712) 279-5410

Full-time: 289 men, 435 women
Part-time: 84 men, 161 women
Graduate: none
Year: trimesters, summer session
Application Deadline: open
Freshman Class: 918 applied, 668 accepted, 195 enrolled
SAT I or ACT: required

Faculty: 44; IIB, --$
Ph.D.s: 61%
Student/Faculty: 17 to 1
Tuition: $13,890
Room & Board: $4767

LESS COMPETITIVE

Briar Cliff University, formerly Briar Cliff College and founded in 1930, is a private Roman Catholic-Franciscan liberal arts institution. There is 1 undergraduate and 1 graduate school. In addition to regional accreditation, Briar Cliff has baccalaureate program accreditation with AACSB, CSWE, and NLN. The library contains 104,597 volumes, 34,226 microform items, and 14,258 audiovisual forms/CDs, and subscribes to 1000 periodicals. Computerized library services include the card catalog, interlibrary loans, and database searching. Special learning facilities include a learning resource center, art gallery, radio station, TV station, and cadaver lab. The 70-acre campus is in a suburban area minutes from downtown Sioux City. Including residence halls, there are 11 buildings.

Student Life: 73% of undergraduates are from Iowa. Others are from 28 states, 3 foreign countries, and Canada. 73% are white. 40% are Catholic; 40% claim no religious affiliation; 20% Protestant. The average age of freshmen is 18; all undergraduates, 24. 13% do not continue beyond their first year.

Housing: 553 students can be accommodated in college housing, which includes single-sex and coed dormitories. On-campus housing is guaranteed for all 4 years. 57% of students commute. All students may keep cars.

Activities: There are no fraternities or sororities. There are 27 groups on campus, including art, cheerleading, choir, chorus, computers, drama, drill team, ethnic, film, international, jazz band, literary magazine, musical theater, newspaper, pep band, photography, professional, radio and TV, religious, social, social service, student government, and yearbook. Popular campus events include Winterfest, St. Francis Day, and International Dinner.

Sports: There are 7 intercollegiate sports for men and 7 for women, and 15 intramural sports for men and 15 for women. Facilities include baseball, softball, and soccer fields, and a recreation center with 2 racquetball courts, a running track, tennis courts, 2 basketball/volleyball courts, and weight-lifting facilities.

Disabled Students: 90% of the campus is accessible. Wheelchair ramps, elevators, special parking, specially equipped rest rooms, lowered drinking fountains, and lowered telephones are available.

Services: Counseling and information services are available, as is tutoring in most subjects. There is remedial math, reading, and writing.

Campus Safety and Security: Measures include 24-hour foot and vehicle patrol, escort service, informal discussions, and pamphlets/posters/films. There are emergency telephones and lighted pathways/sidewalks.

Programs of Study: Briar Cliff confers B.A., B.S., B.S.N., and B.S.W. degrees. Associate and master's degrees are also awarded. Bachelor's degrees are awarded in BIOLOGICAL SCIENCE (biology/biological science), BUSINESS (accounting, business administration and management, and human resources), COMMUNICATIONS AND THE ARTS (English, fine arts, music, and Spanish), COMPUTER AND PHYSICAL SCIENCE (chemistry, computer science, and mathematics), EDUCATION (elementary, health, and secondary), ENGINEERING AND ENVIRONMENTAL DESIGN (preengineering), HEALTH PROFESSIONS (medical laboratory technology, nursing, predentistry, premedicine, and prepharmacy), SOCIAL SCIENCE (history, psychology, social work, sociology, and theological studies). Accounting, nursing, and psychology are the strongest academically. Business administration and nursing are the largest.

Required: To graduate, students must complete a minimum of 120 semester hours with at least 36 in the major. 10 general education foundation courses and 6 1-hour independent research courses are required. A GPA of 2.0 with no more than 1 D in the major must be maintained, and proficiency in standard English expression and oral communication skills must be demonstrated.

Special: Internships in Chicago and Washington, study abroad, dual majors, work-study programs, student-designed interdisciplinary majors, and pass/fail options are available. Students may earn a 3-2 engineering degree with Iowa State University.

Faculty/Classroom: 53% of faculty are male; 47%, female. All teach undergraduates. The average class size in an introductory lecture is 20; in a laboratory, 15; and in a regular course, 15 to 20.

Admissions: 73% of the 2001-2002 applicants were accepted.

Requirements: The SAT I or ACT is required. The ACT is preferred, and a score of 19 qualifies for automatic acceptance review. Applicants need not be graduates of an accredited secondary school. The GED is accepted. Admission to freshman standing requires 4 years each of English and math, 3 of science, 2 of history, and 1 of social studies. Applications are accepted on-line at the university's web site. Briar Cliff requires applicants to be in the upper 50% of their class. A GPA of 2.0 is required. AP and CLEP credits are accepted. Important factors in the admissions decision are leadership record, extracurricular activities record, and advanced placement or honor courses.

Procedure: Freshmen are admitted to all sessions. Entrance exams should be taken by October for scholarship consideration, by April for admission. Application deadlines are open. Application fee is $20.

Transfer: 47 transfer students enrolled in a recent year. Applicants must have a minimum GPA of 2.0 with at least 10 credit hours earned and satisfactory dismissal from the previous institution. Grades of D or better transfer for credit. 30 credits of 120 must be completed at Briar Cliff.

Visiting: There are regularly scheduled orientations for prospective students, including a presidential welcome, a meeting with faculty and student panels, a luncheon, campus tours, a slide show, and financial aid information. There are guides for informal visits and visitors may sit in on classes and stay overnight. To schedule a visit, contact the Admissions Office at (800) 662-3303, ext. 5201 or *admissions@briar-cliff.edu*

Financial Aid: In 2001-2002, 98% of all freshmen and 94% of continuing students received some form of financial aid. 90% of freshmen and 94% of continuing students received need-based aid. The average freshman award was $11,364. Of that total, scholarships or need-based grants averaged $6000 ($14,220 maximum); loans averaged $4100 ($10,500 maximum); and work contracts averaged $900 ($3500 maximum). 96% of undergraduates work part time. Average annual earnings from campus work are $1100. The average financial indebtedness of the 2001 graduate was $19,700. Briar Cliff is a member of CSS. The CSS/Profile, FAFSA, FFS or SFS is required. The fall application deadline is open.

International Students: There are 5 international students enrolled. The school actively recruits these students. They must score 500 on the written TOEFL or take the MELAB. The TOEFL is preferred.

Computers: There are 55 workstations located in writing labs in residence halls and the computer center. A portable workstation can be attached at 70 locations around campus. There are 12 computers available for student use in the library and 33 computers available to students in the computer labs. There is a total of 100 computers available for student use on a daily basis. All students may access the system 24 hours each day. There are no time limits. A computer usage fee is included in the $12-per-credit-hour student fee.

Graduates: In 2001, 201 bachelor's degrees were awarded. The most popular majors were business administration (18%), nursing (13%), and biology and human resources management (11%). In an average class, 45% graduate in 4 years, 48% in 5 years, and 59% in 6 years.

Admissions Contact: Sharisue Wilcoxon, Vice President/Enrollment Management. Web: *www.briar-cliff.edu*

BUENA VISTA UNIVERSITY
B-2

Storm Lake, IA 50588

(712) 749-2235
(800) 383-9600; Fax: (712) 749-2037

Full-time: 615 men, 637 women
Part-time: 18 men, 22 women
Graduate: 53 men, 47 women
Year: 4-1-4, summer session
Application Deadline: open
Freshman Class: n/av
ACT: 22

Faculty: 82; IIB, av$
Ph.D.s: 55%
Student/Faculty: 15 to 1
Tuition: $17,846
Room & Board: $4982

COMPETITIVE

Buena Vista University, founded in 1891, is a private institution affiliated with the Presbyterian Church (U.S.A.). The university offers undergraduate degree programs in business, education, communication and arts, science, social science, philosophy, and religion, and an accredited master's program in education. Programs emphasize career education with a liberal arts foundation. There are 5 undergraduate schools and 1 graduate school. In addition to regional accreditation, Buena Vista has baccalaureate program accreditation with CSWE. The library contains 154,782 volumes, 40,657 microform items, and 3920 audiovisual forms/CDs, and subscribes to 705 periodicals. Computerized library services include the card catalog, interlibrary loans, and database searching. Special learning facilities include a learning resource center, art gallery, radio station, TV station, and student newspaper desktop production lab. The 60-acre campus is in a small town 65 miles east of Sioux City. Including residence halls, there are 16 buildings.

Student Life: 85% of undergraduates are from Iowa. Others are from 17 states, 6 foreign countries, and Canada. 80% are from public schools. 94% are white. 54% are Protestant; 27% Catholic; 12% claim no religious affiliation. The average age of freshmen is 18; all undergraduates, 20. 21% do not continue beyond their first year; 61% remain to graduate.

Housing: 1127 students can be accommodated in college housing, which includes single-sex and coed dormitories and on-campus apartments. In addition, there are honors houses and special-interest houses. On-campus housing is guaranteed for all 4 years. 86% of students live on campus; of those, 60% remain on campus on weekends. All students may keep cars.

Activities: There are no fraternities or sororities. There are 50 groups on campus, including art, band, cheerleading, choir, chorale, chorus, computers, debate, drama, drill team, environmental, ethnic, gender, honors, international, jazz band, literary magazine, marching band, musical theater, newspaper, orchestra, pep band, photography, political, professional, radio and TV, religious, social, social service, student government, and yearbook. Popular campus events include Winter Olympics, Academic and Cultural Events Series, and Buenafication Day.

Sports: There are 9 intercollegiate sports for men and 8 for women, and 10 intramural sports for men and 10 for women. Facilities include a 380-seat auditorium, a 1000-seat auditorium, a 4000-seat stadium, a field house with a 4000-seat gym, basketball, volleyball, racquetball, and tennis courts, football, softball, and baseball fields, a track, facilities for weight training and other recreational activities, an Olympic-size indoor pool, and a game room.

Disabled Students: 90% of the campus is accessible. Wheelchair ramps, elevators, special parking, specially equipped rest rooms, special class scheduling, lowered drinking fountains, lowered telephones, and automatic/remote-controlled doors are available.

Services: Counseling and information services are available, as is tutoring in most subjects. There is a reader service for the blind, and remedial math, reading, and writing.

Campus Safety and Security: Measures include 24-hour foot and vehicle patrol, self-defense education, escort service, and shuttle buses. There are informal discussions, pamphlets/posters/films, emergency telephones, lighted pathways/sidewalks, and an enhanced 911 system on campus.

Programs of Study: Buena Vista confers B.A. and B.S. degrees. Master's degrees are also awarded. Bachelor's degrees are awarded in BIOLOGICAL SCIENCE (biology/biological science), BUSINESS (accounting, banking and finance, business administration and management, business economics, international business management, marketing/retailing/merchandising, and sports management), COMMUNICATIONS AND THE ARTS (art, arts administration/management, communications, English, graphic design, music, Spanish, and speech/debate/rhetoric), COMPUTER AND PHYSICAL SCIENCE (chemistry, computer science, mathematics, physics, and science), EDUCATION (art, business, elementary, middle school, music, science, secondary, and special), SOCIAL SCIENCE (criminal justice, economics, history, philosophy, physical fitness/movement, political science/government, psychology, public administration, religion, social science, and social work). Biology, mass communication, and business are the strongest academically. Education, biology, and management are the largest.

Required: All students must complete 3 semester hours of fine arts and 6 semester hours each of natural sciences, humanities, social sciences, communication, and writing. In addition, students must successfully complete English 100 and 200, demonstrate proficiency by exam in math and writing, and participate in the Academic and Cultural Events Series, through which they attend lectures and performances by national and world leaders. The bachelor's degree requires a minimum of 128 semester hours, including 30 to 62 hours in the major, with a GPA of at least 2.0, or 2.5 for education majors.

Special: Special academic offerings include a Florida internship for business students, a work-study program with Marriott Foodservice, and a 3-2 engineering degree program with Washington University in St. Louis. Students may study abroad in Japan, Taiwan, Australia, and Europe. Buena Vista offers dual and student-designed majors, credit for life experience, and pass/fail options in courses outside the major field. Nondegree study is possible. Internships are required in many majors and encouraged in most. The J. Leslie Rollins Fellowship allows 1 or 2 students each year to design an internship anywhere in the world. There is 1 national honor society and a freshman honors program.

Faculty/Classroom: 62% of faculty are male; 38%, female. All teach undergraduates. The average class size in an introductory lecture is 30; in a laboratory, 25; and in a regular course, 18.

Admissions: The ACT scores for the 2001-2002 freshman class were: 45% below 21, 19% between 21 and 23, 22% between 24 and 26, 8% between 27 and 28, and 7% above 28. 30% of the current freshmen were in the top fifth of their class; 65% were in the top two fifths. There were 20 National Merit semifinalists. 22 freshmen graduated first in their class.

Requirements: The ACT is recommended, SAT I scores may be submitted instead. Minimum scores should be 21 on the ACT or 950 on SAT I, with 475 on each part. Applicants must be graduates of an accredited secondary school or have earned a GED. The college requires 13 academic credits, including 4 of English and 3 each of math, social studies, and science. Campus visits and an interview are recommended. Buena Vista requires applicants to be in the upper 50% of their class. A GPA of 2.75 is required. AP and CLEP credits are accepted. Important factors in the admissions decision are advanced placement or honor courses, leadership record, and recommendations by school officials. Buena Vista accepts applications on computer disk via the Common App and via CollegeNet, Apply, and the school's web site, *www.bvu.edu.*.

Procedure: Freshmen are admitted fall, winter, and spring. Entrance exams should be taken during the spring of the junior year or October of the senior year. There are early admissions and deferred admissions plans. Application deadlines are open. Notification is sent on a rolling basis. The fall 2001 application fee was $25.

Transfer: 66 transfer students enrolled in 2001-2002. A high school diploma and a minimum GPA of 2.5 from the applicant's college are required. 30 credits of 128 must be completed at Buena Vista.

Visiting: There are regularly scheduled orientations for prospective students, including a campus tour and meetings with an admissions counselor, faculty representatives, coaches, and activity representatives in the student's areas of interest. There are guides for informal visits and visitors may sit in on classes and stay overnight. To schedule a visit, contact the Director of Admissions.

Financial Aid: In 2001-2002, 99% of all students received some form of financial aid. 89% of freshmen and 90% of continuing students received need-based aid. The average freshman award was $16,926. Of that total, scholarships or need-based grants averaged $13,187 ($22,828 maximum); loans averaged $2968 ($5125 maximum); and work contracts averaged $771 ($1600 maximum). 60% of undergraduates work part time. Average annual earnings from campus work are $1074. The average financial indebtedness of the 2001 graduate was $17,046. Buena Vista is a member of CSS. The FAFSA and the college's own financial statement are required. The fall application deadline is June 1.

International Students: There are 23 international students enrolled. The school actively recruits these students. They must score 500 on the written TOEFL and also take the Comprehensive English Language Test.

Computers: The mainframe is a DEC ALPHA AXP. There are IBM and Mac labs located in the main computer center. Some 200 terminals are located in the library, the residence hall lounges, and other locations. Access to the Internet and e-mail is available to all students. All students may access the system. There are no time limits and no fees.

Graduates: In 2001, 255 bachelor's degrees were awarded. The most popular majors were education (12%), management (9%), and marketing (8%). In an average class, 1% graduate in 3 years, 42% in 4 years, 53% in 5 years, and 55% in 6 years. 40 companies recruited on campus in 2000-2001. Of the 2000 graduating class, 15% were enrolled in graduate school within 6 months of graduation and 98% were employed.

Admissions Contact: Louise Cummings-Simmons, Director of Admissions. A video is available. E-mail: *admissions@bvu.edu*
Web: *www.bvu.edu*

CENTRAL COLLEGE
Pella, IA 50219

D-3
(641) 628-5285
(800) 458-5503; Fax: (641) 628-5316

Full-time: 639 men, 934 women	**Faculty:** 89; IIB, -$
Part-time: 23 men, 27 women	**Ph.D.s:** 80%
Graduate: none	**Student/Faculty:** 18 to 1
Year: semesters, summer session	**Tuition:** $15,714
Application Deadline: March 1	**Room & Board:** $5492
Freshman Class: 1438 applied, 1258 accepted, 412 enrolled	
SAT I or ACT: required	**COMPETITIVE**

Central College, founded in 1853, is a private institution affiliated with the Reformed Church in America. The college offers undergraduate degree programs in applied arts, behavioral sciences, cross-cultural studies, fine arts, humanities, and natural sciences. In addition to regional accreditation, Central has baccalaureate program accreditation with NASM and NCATE. The 4 libraries contain 195,000 volumes, 55,000 microform items, and 8500 audiovisual forms/CDs, and subscribe to 925 periodicals. Computerized library services include the card catalog, interlibrary loans, and database searching. Special learning facilities include a learning resource center, art gallery, radio station, and fiber-optic classroom. The 133-acre campus is in a suburban area 45 miles southeast of Des Moines. Including residence halls, there are 45 buildings.

Student Life: 82% of undergraduates are from Iowa. Others are from 33 states, 13 foreign countries, and Canada. 98% are from public schools. 88% are white. 67% are Protestant; 21% Catholic; 11% claim no religious affiliation. The average age of freshmen is 18; all undergraduates, 20. 20% do not continue beyond their first year.

Housing: 1300 students can be accommodated in college housing, which includes single-sex and coed dormitories, on-campus apartments, married-student housing, fraternity houses, and sorority houses. In addition, there are honors houses, language houses, and special-interest houses. On-campus housing is guaranteed for all 4 years. 88% of students live on campus; of those, 70% remain on campus on weekends. Alcohol is not permitted. All students may keep cars.

Activities: 12% of men belong to 4 local fraternities; 5% of women belong to 2 local sororities. There are 71 groups on campus, including art, band, cheerleading, choir, chorus, drama, drill team, ethnic, gay, honors, international, jazz band, literary magazine, marching band, musical theater, newspaper, opera, orchestra, pep band, photography, political, professional, radio and TV, religious, social, social service, student government, symphony, and yearbook. Popular campus events include Career Day, Interdisciplinary Research Symposium, and Academic Seminar.

Sports: There are 9 intercollegiate sports for men and 8 for women, and 12 intramural sports for men and 11 for women. Facilities include an athletic complex with a 7000-seat stadium and 2500-seat gym, a 700-seat auditorium, a golf driving range, several practice and competition fields, tennis courts, and a field house with an indoor track.

Disabled Students: 90% of the campus is accessible. Wheelchair ramps, elevators, special parking, specially equipped rest rooms, special class scheduling, lowered drinking fountains, and lowered telephones are available.

Services: Counseling and information services are available, as is tutoring in every subject. There is a reader service for the blind.

Campus Safety and Security: Measures include 24-hour foot and vehicle patrol, self-defense education, escort service, and informal discussions. There are pamphlets/posters/films, emergency telephones, and lighted pathways/sidewalks.

Programs of Study: Central confers the B.A. degree. Bachelor's degrees are awarded in BIOLOGICAL SCIENCE (biology/biological science), BUSINESS (accounting, business administration and management, and international business management), COMMUNICATIONS AND THE ARTS (communications, dramatic arts, English, fine arts, French, German, languages, linguistics, music, and Spanish), COMPUTER AND PHYSICAL SCIENCE (chemistry, computer science, mathematics, and physics), EDUCATION (elementary, music, and secondary), ENGINEERING AND ENVIRONMENTAL DESIGN (environmental science), HEALTH PROFESSIONS (exercise science), SOCIAL SCIENCE (anthropology, economics, history, international studies, philosophy, political science/government, psychology, religion, and sociology). Business management, elementary education, and exercise science are the largest.

Required: General education requirements include 44 semester hours, including 11 in cultural awareness, 6 each in central foundations and core focus, and 3 each in art, historical perspectives, mathematical reasoning, religion, scientific inquiry, social and behavioral inquiry, and textual interpretation. Each department also establishes a communication skill requirement, and foreign language proficiency must be demonstrated. To graduate, students must complete a minimum of 120 semester hours with a GPA of at least 2.0.

Special: Nearly half the students participate in study abroad programs in London, Paris, Vienna, Mexico, Spain, Wales, and the Netherlands. Central also offers a Washington semester, a Chicago program, numerous internship opportunities, and work-study. A 3-4 program in architecture and a 3-2 degree program in engineering are offered with Washington University in St. Louis. A general studies degree, student-designed majors, and pass/no credit options are possible. There is 1 national honor society and a freshman honors program.

Faculty/Classroom: 60% of faculty are male; 40%, female. All both teach and do research. The average class size in an introductory lecture is 19; in a laboratory, 15; and in a regular course, 20.

Admissions: 87% of the 2001-2002 applicants were accepted. 47% of the current freshmen were in the top fifth of their class; 76% were in the top two fifths. 38 freshmen graduated first in their class.

Requirements: The SAT I or ACT is required. In addition, applicants must be graduates of an accredited secondary school or have earned a GED. Central requires 16 academic credits and recommends that they include 4 years of English, 3 each of lab science, social studies, and math, including 2 in algebra and 1 in geometry, and 2 of foreign language. An interview is required and an essay is recommended. Applications are accepted at the college's web site. Central requires applicants to be in the upper 50% of their class. A GPA of 2.7 is required. AP and CLEP credits are accepted. Important factors in the admissions decision are leadership record, recommendations by school officials, and evidence of special talent.

Procedure: Freshmen are admitted to all sessions. Entrance exams should be taken in the spring of the junior year. There is a deferred admissions plan. Applications should be filed by March 1 for fall entry, November 1 for spring entry, and May 1 for summer entry. Notification is sent on a rolling basis. The fall 2001 application fee was $25.

Transfer: 48 transfer students enrolled in 2001-2002. Each tranfer student is considered individually. Interviews are encouraged. 30 credits of the last 45 must be completed at Central.

Visiting: There are regularly scheduled orientations for prospective students, including a campus tour, a registration session with academic advisers, and presentations by the academic dean, student life dean, financial aid director, and admissions staff. There are guides for informal visits and visitors may sit in on classes and stay overnight. To schedule a visit, contact the Admissions Office at (641) 628-5286 or *admission@central.edu*

Financial Aid. In 2001-2002, all freshmen and 98% of continuing students received some form of financial aid. 82% of all students received need-based aid. The average freshman award was $12,033. Of that total, scholarships or need-based grants averaged $9139 ($16,612 maximum); loans averaged $2759 ($4625 maximum); and work contracts averaged $1213 ($1400 maximum). 90% of undergraduates work part time. Average annual earnings from campus work are $743. The average financial indebtedness of the 2001 graduate was $20,499. Central is a member of CSS. The FAFSA is required. The fall application deadline is April 1.

International Students: There are 23 international students enrolled. The school actively recruits these students. They must score 530 on the written TOEFL or 197 on the electronic version.

Computers: The mainframes are a DEC VAX 3400 and 5500 and an AT&T 382/4000. There are also 5 VAX 3100 workstations, 63 terminals, and 200 PCs located in 9 labs across campus. Languages supported include Pascal, COBOL, C, PROLOG, LISP, BASIC, FORTRAN, Ada, and Modula-2. Statistical packages available are Minitab and SPSS. Microsoft Word is used for word processing and SuperCalc 4 and EXCEL for spreadsheet. All students may access the system. There are no time limits and no fees.

Graduates: In 2001, 269 bachelor's degrees were awarded. The most popular majors were business management (14%), elementary education (12%), and exercise science (11%). In an average class, 60% graduate in 4 years. 80 companies recruited on campus in 2000-2001. Of the 2000 graduating class, 18% were enrolled in graduate school within 6 months of graduation and 90% were employed.

Admissions Contact: Sam Vande Weerd, Director of Admission.
E-mail: *admissions@central.edu* Web: *www.central.edu*

CLARKE COLLEGE
Dubuque, IA 52001 — E-2

(563) 588-6316
(800) 383-2345; Fax: (563) 588-6789

Full-time: 265 men, 506 women	**Faculty:** 92
Part-time: 79 men, 202 women	**Ph.D.s:** 75%
Graduate: 35 men, 114 women	**Student/Faculty:** 8 to 1
Year: semesters, summer session	**Tuition:** $15,120
Application Deadline: open	**Room & Board:** $5505
Freshman Class: 691 applied, 420 accepted, 133 enrolled	
SAT I Verbal/Math: 504/501	**ACT:** 24 — **COMPETITIVE+**

Clarke College, established in 1843, is a nonprofit, private Catholic institution. A strong liberal arts core is integrated into all majors and preprofessional programs. In addition to regional accreditation, Clarke has baccalaureate program accreditation with APTA, CSWE, NASM, NCATE, and NLN. The library contains 109,789 volumes, 9757 microform items, and 1362 audiovisual forms/CDs, and subscribes to 1613 periodicals. Computerized library services include the card catalog, interlibrary loans, and database searching. Special learning facilities include a learning resource center, art gallery, planetarium, art slide library, electronic music studio, and several computer-integrated specialized departmental labs. The 60-acre campus is in an urban area 180 miles west of Chicago. Including residence halls, there are 13 buildings.

Student Life: 62% of undergraduates are from Iowa. Others are from 29 states, 15 foreign countries, and Canada. 80% are from public schools. 94% are white. 51% are Catholic; 30% claim no religious affiliation; 12% Protestant. The average age of freshmen is 23; all undergraduates, 25. 22% do not continue beyond their first year; 65% remain to graduate.

Housing: 585 students can be accommodated in college housing, which includes single-sex and coed dormitories and on-campus apartments. In addition, there is a residence hall and an apartment residence building reserved for juniors and seniors. On-campus housing is guaranteed for all 4 years. 64% of students live on campus; of those, 61% remain on campus on weekends. All students may keep cars.

Activities: There are no fraternities or sororities. There are 50 groups on campus, including art, cheerleading, choir, chorus, computers, drama, ethnic, honors, international, jazz band, literary magazine, newspaper, pep band, photography, political, professional, religious, social, social service, and student government. Popular campus events include Family Weekend, New Year's Dance, and Midnight Pancake Breakfast.

Sports: There are 8 intercollegiate sports for men and 8 for women, and 15 intramural sports for men and 13 for women. Facilities include a 1000-seat gym, a 700-seat arena, an indoor track, a swimming pool, a soccer field, basketball, volleyball, tennis, and racquetball courts, a fitness trail, weight and aerobics rooms, and an indoor batting cage/pitching mound area. There are baseball/softball fields and 2 alpine ski courses nearby, plus a municipal golf course adjacent to the campus.

Disabled Students: 90% of the campus is accessible. Wheelchair ramps, elevators, special parking, specially equipped rest rooms, special class scheduling, lowered drinking fountains, and lowered telephones are available.

Services: Counseling and information services are available, as is tutoring in most subjects. There is remedial math, reading, and writing.

Campus Safety and Security: Measures include 24-hour foot and vehicle patrol, informal discussions, pamphlets/posters/films, and emergency telephones. There are lighted pathways/sidewalks.

Programs of Study: Clarke confers B.A., B.S., and B.F.A. degrees. Associate and master's degrees are also awarded. Bachelor's degrees are awarded in BIOLOGICAL SCIENCE (biology/biological science), BUSINESS (accounting, business administration and management, and marketing management), COMMUNICATIONS AND THE ARTS (advertising, art, art history and appreciation, communications, dramatic arts, English, fine arts, French, music, Spanish, and studio art), COMPUTER AND PHYSICAL SCIENCE (chemistry, computer science, information sciences and systems, and mathematics), EDUCATION (art, early childhood, elementary, music, secondary, and special), HEALTH PROFESSIONS (nursing and physical therapy), SOCIAL SCIENCE (history, philosophy, physical fitness/movement, political science/government, psychology, religion, social work, and sociology). Biology, education, and computer science are the strongest academically. Education, nursing, and computer science are the largest.

Required: To graduate, all students must complete 124 semester hours, with 30 to 70 in the major, and maintain a GPA of 2.0 (2.5 for education majors or 3.25 for physical therapy majors). Students must complete a freshman seminar and courses in logic, composition, speech, research, and thinking skills; demonstrate computer literacy; and take Senior Performance, an integrative studies course in the major. The 51-hour core curriculum also includes 9 hours each of science, social sciences, and humanities and 6 hours each of religious studies, multicultural studies, and philosophy.

Special: There are co-op programs in most majors, cross-registration with Loras College and the University of Dubuque, and study abroad. Clarke also offers internships in chemistry, biology, and communications; an accelerated degree program in many majors for nontraditional, evening students; a B.A.-B.S. degree in biology, chemistry, psychology, business, and computer science; and a B.F.A.-B.A. program in art. There are also on- and off-campus work-study programs, dual majors, student-designed majors, and a freshman-entry 6-year physical therapy program. There are 4 national honor societies, a freshman honors program, and 3 departmental honors program.

Faculty/Classroom: 35% of faculty are male; 65%, female. All both teach and do research. No introductory courses are taught by graduate students. The average class size in an introductory lecture is 24; in a laboratory, 11; and in a regular course, 14.

Admissions: 61% of the 2001-2002 applicants were accepted. The SAT I scores for the 2001-2002 freshman class were: Verbal--55% below 500, 18% between 500 and 599, 18% between 600 and 700, and 9% above 700; Math--45% below 500, 27% between 500 and 599, and 27% between 600 and 700. The ACT scores were 24% below 21, 31% between 21 and 23, 32% between 24 and 26, 8% between 27 and 28, and 4% above 28. 35% of the current freshmen were in the top fifth of their class; 70% were in the top two fifths. 2 freshmen graduated first in their class in a recent year.

Requirements: The SAT I or ACT is required. In addition, the high school transcript should include 4 years of English, 3 each of math, history/social science, and science (4 for human biology and physical therapy majors), 2 of the same foreign language, and 5 of electives. Clarke requires applicants to be in the upper 50% of their class. A GPA of 2.0 is required. AP and CLEP credits are accepted. Advanced placement or honor courses is an important factor in the admission decision. Applications are accepted on-line at Clarke's web site.

Procedure: Freshmen are admitted to all sessions. Entrance exams should be taken in the spring of the junior year or the fall of the senior year. There is a deferred admissions plan. Application deadlines are open. Notification is sent on a rolling basis. The fall 2001 application fee was $25.

Transfer: 75 transfer students enrolled in 2001-2002. Applicants must submit a transcript and a recommendation from the dean of students for each college attended. Students with fewer than 24 completed semester hours must also submit a high school transcript and SAT I or ACT scores. 30 credits of 124 must be completed at Clarke.

Visiting: There are guides for informal visits and visitors may sit in on classes and stay overnight. To schedule a visit, contact the Admissions Office.

Financial Aid: In 2001-2002, all freshmen and 98% of continuing students received some form of financial aid. 83% of freshmen and 77% of continuing students received need-based aid. The average freshman award was $13,637. Of that total, scholarships or need-based grants averaged $10,538 ($16,750 maximum); loans averaged $2918 ($4625 maximum); and work contracts averaged $1422 ($1700 maximum). 75% of undergraduates work part time. Average annual earnings from campus work are $904. The average financial indebtedness of the 2001 graduate was $16,778. The FAFSA is required.

International Students: There are 34 international students enrolled. The school actively recruits these students. They must score 550 on the written TOEFL, or 190 to 220 on the electronic version, and also take the SAT I, scoring 1000, or the ACT, scoring 21.

Computers: The mainframes are 3 IBM RS/6000s, models 43P, 380, and C20. In addition, there are 203 networked PCs located in 17 labs for student use. All of these have mainframe, Internet, and World Wide Web access. On-campus students have access from residence hall rooms; off-campus students may access a modem pool. All students may access the system at any time. There are no time limits. The fee is $150 per year.

Graduates: In 2001, 221 bachelor's degrees were awarded. The most popular majors were human health science (34%), communication (25%), and nursing (21%). In an average class, 51% graduate in 4 years, 63% in 5 years, and 63% in 6 years. 50 companies recruited on campus in 2000-2001. Of the 2000 graduating class, 32% were enrolled in graduate school within 6 months of graduation and 65% were employed.

Admissions Contact: Omar Correa, Director of Admissions.
E-mail: *ocorrea@clarke.edu* Web: *www.clarke.edu*

COE COLLEGE — E-3

Cedar Rapids, IA 52402 — (319) 399-8500
(877) CALL-COE; Fax: (319) 399-8816

Full-time: 508 men, 634 women	**Faculty:** 82; IIB, av$
Part-time: 58 men, 80 women	**Ph.D.s:** 92%
Graduate: 8 men, 23 women	**Student/Faculty:** 14 to 1
Year: 4-1-4, summer session	**Tuition:** $19,340
Application Deadline: March 1	**Room & Board:** $5410
Freshman Class: 1085 applied, 899 accepted, 290 enrolled	
SAT I Verbal/Math: 570/570	**ACT:** 24 **VERY COMPETITIVE**

Coe College, founded in 1851, is a private liberal arts institution affiliated with the Presbyterian Church (U.S.A.). In addition to regional accreditation, Coe has baccalaureate program accreditation with NASM and NLN. The 2 libraries contain 213,385 volumes, 9917 microform items, and 9595 audiovisual forms/CDs, and subscribe to 767 periodicals. Computerized library services include the card catalog, interlibrary loans, and database searching. Special learning facilities include a learning resource center, art gallery, planetarium, radio station, and ornithological wing. The 75-acre campus is in an urban area 225 miles west of Chicago. Including residence halls, there are 19 buildings.

Student Life: 62% of undergraduates are from Iowa. Others are from 40 states, 20 foreign countries, and Canada. 92% are from public schools. 89% are white. The average age of freshmen is 18; all undergraduates, 22. 21% do not continue beyond their first year.

Housing: 970 students can be accommodated in college housing, which includes single-sex and coed dormitories and on-campus apartments. In addition, there are special-interest houses and a substance-free facility. On-campus housing is guaranteed for all 4 years. 85% of students live on campus; of those, 75% remain on campus on weekends. All students may keep cars.

Activities: 27% of men belong to 4 national fraternities; 20% of women belong to 3 national sororities. There are 60 groups on campus, including art, band, cheerleading, choir, chorale, chorus, computers, dance, drama, ethnic, gay, honors, international, jazz band, literary magazine, newspaper, orchestra, pep band, political, professional, religious, social, social service, student government, and yearbook. Popular campus events include Coe Olympics, International Student Banquet and Cultural Show, and Flunk Day.

Sports: There are 11 intercollegiate sports for men and 10 for women, and 8 intramural sports for men and 8 for women. Facilities include a racquet center with 4 indoor and 6 outdoor tennis courts, 4 racquetball courts, 2 squash courts, and a 200-meter indoor track; and a field house with an indoor natatorium, an indoor track, wrestling and weight rooms, a rock-climbing wall, courts for basketball and volleyball, and batting cages for baseball and softball. There also are a 400-meter outdoor track, softball diamond, and 1100-seat football/soccer stadium.

Disabled Students: 35% of the campus is accessible. Wheelchair ramps, elevators, special parking, and specially equipped rest rooms are available.

Services: Counseling and information services are available, as is tutoring in most subjects. There is a reader service for the blind. A writing center and an educational support program are available.

Campus Safety and Security: Measures include 24-hour foot and vehicle patrol, escort service, informal discussions, and pamphlets/posters/films. There are emergency telephones and lighted pathways/sidewalks.

Programs of Study: Coe confers B.A., B.Mus., and B.S.N. degrees. Master's degrees are also awarded. Bachelor's degrees are awarded in BIOLOGICAL SCIENCE (biochemistry, biology/biological science, and molecular biology), BUSINESS (accounting, and business administration and management), COMMUNICATIONS AND THE ARTS (art, dramatic arts, English, French, German, literature, music, public relations, and Spanish), COMPUTER AND PHYSICAL SCIENCE (chemistry, computer science, mathematics, physics, and science), EDUCATION (athletic training, elementary, music, physical, and secondary), ENGINEERING AND ENVIRONMENTAL DESIGN (environmental science and preengineering), HEALTH PROFESSIONS (medical laboratory technology, nursing, physical therapy, predentistry, and premedicine), SOCIAL SCI-

ENCE (African American studies, American studies, Asian/Oriental studies, classical/ancient civilization, economics, history, human services, interdisciplinary studies, philosophy, political science/government, prelaw, psychology, religion, sociology, and women's studies). Chemistry, physics, and athletic training are the strongest academically. Business administration, psychology, and English are the largest.

Required: All students must take 4 writing-emphasis courses, a first-year seminar, and a distribution of courses in fine arts, natural science, social science, and Western and foreign culture. A minimum of 36 course credits, including 8 to 12 in the major, and a 2.0 GPA are required for graduation. Students in an honors program must submit a thesis, and psychology and physics majors must pass a comprehensive examination. All students are required to do an internship, practicum, independent research project, or off-campus study program.

Special: Coe offers cross-registration with nearby Mount Mercy College and the University of Iowa; cooperative programs in architecture and social services administration; Washington and New York semesters; and study abroad in 13 countries. Internships, nondegree study, and dual and student-designed majors also are possible. Core course instructors serve as students' mentors. There are 7 national honor societies, including Phi Beta Kappa and a freshman honors program. All departments have honors programs.

Faculty/Classroom: 57% of faculty are male; 43%, female. 98% teach undergraduates and 95% both teach and do research. No introductory courses are taught by graduate students. The average class size in an introductory lecture is 13; in a laboratory, 14; and in a regular course, 16.

Admissions: 83% of the 2001-2002 applicants were accepted. The SAT I scores for the 2001-2002 freshman class were: Verbal--15% below 500, 49% between 500 and 599, 29% between 600 and 700, and 6% above 700; Math--18% below 500, 41% between 500 and 599, 37% between 600 and 700, and 4% above 700. The ACT scores were 16% below 21, 24% between 21 and 23, 32% between 24 and 26, 15% between 27 and 28, and 13% above 28. 53% of the current freshmen were in the top fifth of their class; 85% were in the top two fifths. 14 freshmen graduated first in their class.

Requirements: The SAT I or ACT is required. In addition, Coe recommends that applicants have 4 years in English, 3 each in math, history, science, and social studies, and 2 in foreign language. All students must submit an essay. In addition, fine arts students need a portfolio or audition. The GED is accepted. Coe requires applicants to be in the upper 40% of their class. A GPA of 2.75 is required. AP and CLEP credits are accepted. Important factors in the admissions decision are advanced placement or honor courses, recommendations by school officials, and leadership record. Coe accepts applications on-line via CollegeLink, Apply, and its own web site.

Procedure: Freshmen are admitted fall and spring. Entrance exams should be taken in the spring of the junior year or the fall of the senior year. There are early action and deferred admissions plans. Early action applications should be filed by December 15; regular applications, by March 1 for fall entry. Notification of early action is sent January 15; regular decision, March 15.

Transfer: 49 transfer students enrolled in 2001-2002. Applicants must be high school graduates, have a minimum GPA of 2.5, and submit either the SAT I or ACT scores. An associate degree and an interview also are recommended. 9 course credits of 36 must be completed at Coe.

Visiting: There are regularly scheduled orientations for prospective students, consisting of tours, a luncheon, and informational sessions on admission, financial aid, and student life. There are guides for informal visits and visitors may sit in on classes and stay overnight. To schedule a visit, contact Sharon Fair, Campus Visit Coordinator at *sfair@coe.edu*.

Financial Aid: In 2001-2002, 96% of all freshmen and 94% of continuing students received some form of financial aid. 84% of all students received need-based aid. The average freshman award was $18,680. Of that total, scholarships or need-based grants averaged $13,170 ($19,140 maximum); loans averaged $4000 ($5625 maximum); and work contracts averaged $1200 ($1600 maximum). 48% of undergraduates work part time. Average annual earnings from campus work are $1200. The average financial indebtedness of the 2001 graduate was $18,901. The FAFSA is required. The fall application deadline is March 1.

International Students: There are 79 international students enrolled. The school actively recruits these students. They must score 500 on the written TOEFL or 173 on the electronic version and also take the SAT I or the ACT.

Computers: The main computer system is a LAN operating under Novell netware. Students may access the campus network from approximately 189 PCs located in 7 labs on campus. All residence hall rooms are networked for student-owned machines. All students may access the system 24 hours a day. There are no time limits and no fees.

Graduates: In 2001, 265 bachelor's degrees were awarded. The most popular majors were economics and business administration (14%), psychology (12%), and English (9%). In an average class, 59% graduate in 4 years, and 61% in 5 years. 73 companies recruited on campus in 2000-2001. Of the 2000 graduating class, 22% were enrolled in graduate school within 6 months of graduation and 76% were employed.

Admissions Contact: Dennis Trotter, Vice President for Admission and Financial Aid. E-mail: *dtrotter@coe.edu* Web: *www.coe.edu*

CORNELL COLLEGE

E-3

Mount Vernon, IA 52314-1098 **(319) 895-4215**
(800) 747-1112; Fax: (319) 895-4451

Full-time: 413 men, 564 women	**Faculty:** 85; IIB, av$
Part-time: 4 men, 5 women	**Ph.D.s:** 91%
Graduate: none	**Student/Faculty:** 11 to 1
Year: terms	**Tuition:** $19,570
Application Deadline: open	**Room & Board:** $5410
Freshman Class: 1182 applied, 826 accepted, 302 enrolled	
SAT I Verbal/Math: 580/580	**ACT:** 24 **VERY COMPETITIVE**

Cornell College, founded in 1853, is an independent institution affiliated with the United Methodist Church. Its emphases are on the liberal arts and on student service and leadership. Cornell has a 1-course-at-a-time calendar in which the year is divided into nine 3 1/2 week terms. In addition to regional accreditation, Cornell has baccalaureate program accreditation with NASM. The library contains 171,523 volumes, 235,000 microform items, and 8016 audiovisual forms/CDs, and subscribes to 774 periodicals. Computerized library services include the card catalog, interlibrary loans, and database searching. Special learning facilities include a learning resource center, art gallery, natural history museum, and radio station. The 129-acre campus is in a small town 15 miles east of Cedar Rapids. Including residence halls, there are 41 buildings.

Student Life: 70% of undergraduates are from out of state, mostly the Midwest. Others are from 38 states and 7 foreign countries. 90% are from public schools. 90% are white. 35% are Protestant; 34% claim no religious affiliation; 20% Catholic. The average age of freshmen is 18; all undergraduates, 20. 21% do not continue beyond their first year.

Housing: 973 students can be accommodated in college housing, which includes single-sex and coed dormitories and on-campus apartments. In addition, there are special-interest houses. On-campus housing is guaranteed for all 4 years. 92% of students live on campus; of those, 70% remain on campus on weekends. All students may keep cars.

Activities: 30% of men belong to 7 local fraternities; 32% of women belong to 7 local sororities. There are 76 groups on campus, including art, band, cheerleading, chess, choir, chorale, chorus, computers, debate, drama, environmental, ethnic, gay, honors, international, jazz band, leadership development, literary magazine, musical theater, newspaper, opera, orchestra, pep band, performing arts, photography, political, professional, radio and TV, religious, social, social service, student government, and yearbook. Popular campus events include Family Weekend and Summer Slam.

Sports: There are 10 intercollegiate sports for men and 9 for women, and 33 intramural sports for men and 33 for women. Facilities include an 1800-seat football stadium with an 8-lane all weather track, lighted baseball stadium and softball facilities, soccer game and practice fields, and 6 outdoor tennis courts. The sports center has a 1500-seat basketball arena and 3 additional basketball courts, 4 racquetball courts, a 200-meter indoor track, 4 indoor tennis courts, 3 volleyball courts, 2 batting cages, weight room, fitness equipment, and indoor practice space for football, baseball, softball, and soccer.

Disabled Students: 43% of the campus is accessible. Wheelchair ramps, elevators, special parking, specially equipped rest rooms, special class scheduling, lowered drinking fountains, and lowered telephones are available.

Services: Counseling and information services are available, as is tutoring in every subject. There is a reader service for the blind.

Campus Safety and Security: Measures include 24-hour foot and vehicle patrol, informal discussions, pamphlets/posters/films, and emergency telephones. There are lighted pathways/sidewalks and a Living and Learning Group that promotes safety on campus.

Programs of Study: Cornell confers B.A., B.Mus., B.Ph., and B.S.S. degrees. Bachelor's degrees are awarded in BIOLOGICAL SCIENCE (biology/biological science), BUSINESS (international business management), COMMUNICATIONS AND THE ARTS (dramatic arts, English, fine arts, French, German, languages, music, Russian, and Spanish), COMPUTER AND PHYSICAL SCIENCE (chemistry, computer science, geology, mathematics, and physics), EDUCATION (art, elementary, foreign languages, music, science, and secondary), ENGINEERING AND ENVIRONMENTAL DESIGN (environmental science), SOCIAL SCIENCE (anthropology, classical/ancient civilization, economics, history, international relations, Latin American studies, medieval studies, philosophy, political science/government, psychology, religion, sociology, and women's studies). Biology, philosophy, and geology are the strongest academically. Psychology, education, and English are the largest.

Required: To graduate, all students must complete 32 course credits (128 semester hours), with 7 to 15 in a faculty-approved major, and maintain at least a 2.0 GPA. B.A. candidates must complete 4 courses in humanities, 2 each in science (1 with a lab) and social science, 1 each in fine arts and math, and 1 to 4 in a foreign language, and complete, but not exceed 11 courses in the major. B.S.S. candidates need not meet all of the above requirements.

Special: Special academic programs include 25 study-abroad opportunities and internships, including a Washington Center internship, cross-registration with Rush University, an accelerated degree program in all majors, work-study programs, dual majors in all areas, student-designed majors toward a B.S.S. degree, and interdepartmental/interdisciplinary majors that include biochemistry and molecular biology and origins of behavior. There is a 3-2 engineering program, a 3-4 architecture program, and a 3-2 occupational therapy program with Washington University in St. Louis; a 3-2 social services program with the University of Chicago; a 3-2 forestry and environmental management program with Duke University; and a 3-2 natural resource management program with the University of Michigan. Nondegree study is possible. There are 9 national honor societies, including Phi Beta Kappa.

Faculty/Classroom: 51% of faculty are male; 49%, female. All teach undergraduates, 75% do research, and 75% do both. The average class size in an introductory lecture is 18; in a laboratory, 13; and in a regular course, 15.

Admissions: 70% of the 2001-2002 applicants were accepted. The SAT I scores for the 2001-2002 freshman class were: Verbal--27% below 500, 26% between 500 and 599, 42% between 600 and 700, and 5% above 700; Math--18% below 500, 36% between 500 and 599, 37% between 600 and 700, and 9% above 700. The ACT scores were 15% below 21, 25% between 21 and 23, 31% between 24 and 26, 14% between 27 and 28, and 15% above 28. 46% of the current freshmen were in the top fifth of their class; 82% were in the top two fifths. There was 1 National Merit finalist. 13 freshmen graduated first in their class.

Requirements: The SAT I or ACT is required. In addition, applicants should must be graduates of an accredited secondary school, with a recommended 4 years each of English and history/social studies, 3 each of math and science, 2 to 4 of a foreign language, and 1 each of art and music. The GED is accepted. An essay is required and an interview is advised. Cornell recommends applicants be in the upper 50% of their class. A GPA of 2.8 is recommended. AP and CLEP credits are accepted. Important factors in the admissions decision are leadership record, evidence of special talent, and advanced placement or honor courses.

Procedure: Freshmen are admitted to all sessions. Entrance exams should be taken in the spring of the junior year. There is a deferred admissions plan. Application deadlines are open. Notification is sent on a rolling basis.

Transfer: 35 transfer students enrolled in 2001-2002. Applicants must submit official college and high school transcripts, along with a statement of good standing from the previous college attended. 8 credits of 32 must be completed at Cornell.

Visiting: There are regularly scheduled orientations for prospective students, including campus tours and meetings with an informational panel, a student panel, financial aid staff, and faculty and or coaches as requested. There are guides for informal visits and visitors may sit in on classes and stay overnight. To schedule a visit, contact Judy Penn, Visit Coordinator at (319) 895-4161 or *jpenn@cornellcollege.edu*.

Financial Aid: In 2001-2002, 99% of all freshmen and 96% of continuing students received some form of financial aid. 65% of freshmen and 71% of continuing students received need-based aid. The average freshman award was $18,190. Of that total, scholarships or need-based grants averaged $14,610 ($20,000 maximum); loans averaged $3940 ($6625 maximum); and work contracts averaged $800 ($1000 maximum). 81% of undergraduates work part time. Average annual earnings from campus work are $1000. The average financial indebtedness of the 2001 graduate was $16,880. The FAFSA, the college's own financial statement, and the student's and parent's tax returns are required. The fall application deadline is March 1.

International Students: There are 33 international students enrolled. The school actively recruits these students. They must score 500 on the written TOEFL and also take the college's own test.

Computers: The mainframes are Intel server class machines. There are also 80 PCs in academic labs, the library, and the commons. All academic computer facilities have access to the Internet system. Students may also access the system by modem. All students may access the system from 7 A.M. to 11 P.M. There are no time limits and no fees.

Graduates: In 2001, 243 bachelor's degrees were awarded. The most popular majors were psychology (13%), economics and business (12%), and biology (10%). In an average class, 3% graduate in 3 years, 54% in 4 years, 61% in 5 years, and 63% in 6 years. 14 companies recruited on campus in 2000-2001. Of the 1999 graduating class, 31% were enrolled in graduate school within 6 months of graduation and 66% were employed.

Admissions Contact: Dean of Admissions and Financial Assistance. A video is available. E-mail: *admissions@cornellcollege.edu*
Web: *www.cornellcollege.edu*

DORDT COLLEGE B-1

Sioux Center, IA 51250 (712) 722-6080
(800) 34-DORDT; Fax: (712) 722-1967

Full-time: 598 men, 733 women
Part-time: 23 men, 42 women
Graduate: 36 men, 80 women
Year: semesters
Application Deadline: July 1
Freshman Class: 793 applied, 742 accepted, 379 enrolled
SAT I Verbal/Math: 580/580
Faculty: 75; IIB, -$
Ph.D.s: 75%
Student/Faculty: 18 to 1
Tuition: $14,100
Room & Board: $4000
ACT: 24 **COMPETITIVE+**

Dordt College, founded in 1955, is a private institution affiliated with the Christian Reformed Church. The curriculum, which is designed to reflect the principles of the Christian faith, leads to degrees in liberal arts, agriculture, art, music, business, engineering, and teaching preparation. In addition to regional accreditation, Dordt has baccalaureate program accreditation with ABET and CSWE. The library contains 185,000 volumes, 14,819 microform items, and 3616 audiovisual forms/CDs, and subscribes to 700 periodicals. Computerized library services include the card catalog and interlibrary loans. Special learning facilities include a learning resource center, planetarium, radio station, and 2 observatories, as well as a 160-acre agriculture stewardship center just north of the campus. The 60-acre campus is in a rural area 42 miles north of Sioux City. Including residence halls, there are 22 buildings.

Student Life: 58% of undergraduates are from out of state, mostly the Midwest. Others are from 37 states, 18 foreign countries, and Canada. 40% are from public schools. 98% are white. Most are Protestant. The average age of freshmen is 18; all undergraduates, 21. 18% do not continue beyond their first year.

Housing: 1250 students can be accommodated in college housing, which includes single-sex and coed dormitories, on-campus apartments, and off-campus apartments. On-campus housing is guaranteed for all 4 years. 90% of students live on campus; of those, 80% remain on campus on weekends. Alcohol is not permitted. All students may keep cars.

Activities: There are no fraternities or sororities. There are 25 groups on campus, including band, choir, chorale, computers, dance, drama, drill team, forensics, international, jazz band, literary magazine, newspaper, opera, orchestra, pep band, professional, radio and TV, religious, social, social service, student government, symphony, and yearbook. Popular campus events include Parents Day in October.

Sports: There are 7 intercollegiate sports for men and 7 for women, and 10 intramural sports for men and 10 for women. Facilities include a 2500-seat gym with 2 courts; an 85,000-square-foot recreation center, which includes a 200-meter indoor track, 3 courts adaptable for basketball, volleyball, and tennis, 3 racquetball courts, weight lifting and exercise equipment rooms, and a golf simulation room; an outdoor track; tennis courts; soccer, softball, and baseball fields; and an indoor pool adjacent to the campus.

Disabled Students: 95% of the campus is accessible. Wheelchair ramps, elevators, special parking, specially equipped rest rooms, special class scheduling, lowered drinking fountains, and lowered telephones are available.

Services: Counseling and information services are available, as is tutoring in most subjects. There is a reader service for the blind, and remedial math, reading, and writing.

Campus Safety and Security: Measures include 24-hour foot and vehicle patrol and lighted pathways/sidewalks.

Programs of Study: Dordt confers B.A., B.S., and B.S.W. degrees. Associate and master's degrees are also awarded. Bachelor's degrees are awarded in BIOLOGICAL SCIENCE (biology/biological science), BUSINESS (accounting and business administration and management), COMMUNICATIONS AND THE ARTS (broadcasting, communications, dramatic arts, Dutch, English, fine arts, German, graphic design, journalism, languages, music, Spanish, and speech/debate/rhetoric), COMPUTER AND PHYSICAL SCIENCE (chemistry, computer programming, computer science, information sciences and systems, mathematics, and physics), EDUCATION (art, business, elementary, foreign languages, music, and secondary), ENGINEERING AND ENVIRONMENTAL DESIGN (chemical engineering, electrical/electronics engineering, engineering, environmental science, and mechanical engineering), HEALTH PROFESSIONS (health science, medical laboratory technology, predentistry, and premedicine), SOCIAL SCIENCE (history, philosophy, political science/government, prelaw, psychology, religion, social science, social work, sociology, and youth ministry). Engineering, business administration, and social work are the strongest academically. Education is the largest.

Required: All students must complete a college introductory course and a distribution of 14 other courses in the various academic disciplines, including General Education 300. Proficiency requirements must be met in English, math, and phys ed. To graduate, students must complete a minimum of 126 credits with a 2.0 GPA.

Special: Students may study abroad in 9 countries. Dordt also offers a Washington semester, a Chicago Metro semester, a joint nursing degree program with St. Luke's School of Nursing, B.A.-B.S. degrees in engineering and agriculture, and numerous internships in all majors. Dual majors, student designed majors, and pass/fail options are available.

Faculty/Classroom: 90% of faculty are male; 10%, female. All teach undergraduates. The average class size in an introductory lecture is 30; in a laboratory, 20; and in a regular course, 25.

Admissions: 94% of the 2001-2002 applicants were accepted. The SAT I scores for the 2001-2002 freshman class were: Verbal--17% below 500, 38% between 500 and 599, 38% between 600 and 700, and 7% above 700; Math--19% below 500, 38% between 500 and 599, 33% between 600 and 700, and 10% above 700. The ACT scores were 18% below 21, 28% between 21 and 23, 24% between 24 and 26, 16% between 27 and 28, and 14% above 28. 34% of the current freshmen were in the top fifth of their class; 64% were in the top two fifths. There were 3 National Merit finalists and 3 semifinalists. 15 freshmen graduated first in their class.

Requirements: The SAT I or ACT is required. In addition, applicants must be graduates of accredited secondary schools or have earned a GED. The college requires 18 academic credits, including 4 in English, and 2 each in foreign language, math, science, and social studies. A GPA of 2.25 is required. AP and CLEP credits are accepted. Important factors in the admissions decision are advanced placement or honor courses, evidence of special talent, and leadership record.

Procedure: Freshmen are admitted fall and spring. Entrance exams should be taken by October of the senior year and no later than April. Applications should be filed by July 1 for fall entry. Notification is sent on a rolling basis. The fall 2001 application fee was $25.

Transfer: 44 transfer students enrolled in 2001-2002. Transfer students must have a GPA of 2.0. 62 credits of 126 must be completed at Dordt.

Visiting: There are regularly scheduled orientations for prospective students, including tours, class visits, personal visits with professors and coaches, and a financial aid session. There are guides for informal visits and visitors may sit in on classes and stay overnight. To schedule a visit, contact the Admissions Office.

Financial Aid: In 2001-2002, 98% of all students received some form of financial aid. The average freshman award was $12,500. Of that total, scholarships or need-based grants averaged $2500 ($5000 maximum); loans averaged $3000 ($6000 maximum); work contracts averaged $1300 (maximum); and grants $1500 ($2000 maximum). 80% of undergraduates work part time. Average annual earnings from campus work are $1300. The average financial indebtedness of the 2001 graduate was $14,500. The FAFSA and the college's own financial statement are required. The fall application deadline is April 15.

International Students: There are 149 international students enrolled. The school actively recruits these students. They must score 550 on the written TOEFL or 213 on the electronic version and also take the SAT I or the ACT, scoring 19 on the ACT.

Computers: Dordt provides 150 IBM, Apple, and Altos PCs for academic use. All students may access the system. There are no time limits and no fees.

Graduates: In 2001, 269 bachelor's degrees were awarded. The most popular majors were education (24%), business (17%), and engineering (7%). In an average class, 68% graduate in 4 years. 50 companies recruited on campus in 2000-2001. Of the 2000 graduating class, 8% were enrolled in graduate school within 6 months of graduation and 97% were employed.

Admissions Contact: Quentin Van Essen, Executive Director of Admissions. E-mail: *admissions@dordt.edu* Web: *www.dordt.edu*

DRAKE UNIVERSITY
Des Moines, IA 50311 C-3

(515) 271-3181
(800) 44-DRAKE; Fax: (515) 271-2831

Full-time: 1279 men, 2016 women	**Faculty:** 231; IIA, av$
Part-time: 114 men, 168 women	**Ph.D.s:** 92%
Graduate: 691 men, 882 women	**Student/Faculty:** 14 to 1
Year: semesters, summer session	**Tuition:** $17,790
Application Deadline: March 1	**Room & Board:** $5040
Freshman Class: 2735 applied, 2392 accepted, 754 enrolled	
SAT I Verbal/Math: 570/590	**ACT:** 25 **VERY COMPETITIVE**

Drake University, founded in 1881, is a private institution offering undergraduate and graduate programs in arts and sciences, business and public administration, pharmacy and health sciences, journalism and mass communication, education, fine arts, and law. There are 6 undergraduate and 2 graduate schools. In addition to regional accreditation, Drake has baccalaureate program accreditation with AACSB, ACEJMC, ACPE, NASAD, NASM, NCATE, and NLN. The 2 libraries contain 472,110 volumes, 848,010 microform items, and 6000 audiovisual forms/CDs, and subscribe to 2000 periodicals. Computerized library services include the card catalog, interlibrary loans, and database searching. Special learning facilities include a learning resource center, art gallery, radio station, TV station, observatory, and the Henry G. Harmon Fine Arts Center. The 120-acre campus is in a suburban area in Des Moines. Including residence halls, there are 48 buildings.

Student Life: 59% of undergraduates are from out of state, mostly the Midwest. Students are from 45 states, 55 foreign countries, and Canada. 85% are from public schools. 86% are white. 23% are Protestant; 17% Catholic. The average age of freshmen is 18; all undergraduates, 21. 19% do not continue beyond their first year; 80% remain to graduate.

Housing: 1850 students can be accommodated in college housing, which includes coed dormitories, married-student housing, fraternity houses, and sorority houses. On-campus housing is guaranteed for all 4 years. 53% of students live on campus; of those, 80% remain on campus on weekends. All students may keep cars.

Activities: 30% of men belong to 10 national fraternities; 28% of women belong to 10 national sororities. There are 130 groups on campus, including art, band, cheerleading, chess, choir, chorale, chorus, computers, dance, drama, drill team, ethnic, gay, honors, international, jazz band, literary magazine, marching band, musical theater, newspaper, opera, orchestra, pep band, photography, political, professional, radio and TV, religious, social, social service, student government, and symphony. Popular campus events include Drake Relays, Supreme Court Days, and Parents Weekend.

Sports: There are 8 intercollegiate sports for men and 8 for women, and 20 intramural sports for men and 20 for women. Facilities include a football stadium, an indoor swimming pool, an aerobics room, 2 weight rooms, basketball, volleyball, and badminton courts, 2 indoor tracks and 1 outdoor track, 4 racquetball courts, and 6 indoor and 6 outdoor tennis courts. There is a recreation and sports facility that seats 7000.

Disabled Students: 80% of the campus is accessible. Wheelchair ramps, elevators, special parking, specially equipped rest rooms, special class scheduling, lowered drinking fountains, lowered telephones, an IBM-compatible computer and scanner that includes a voice and screen enlargement program, closed-caption television, and TDD are available.

Services: There is a reader service for the blind. The Student Disability Service works with Recordings for the Blind and the Iowa Department for the Blind to access books on audiotape and to coordinate volunteer readers.

Campus Safety and Security: Measures include 24-hour foot and vehicle patrol, self-defense education, escort service, and shuttle buses. There are informal discussions, pamphlets/posters/films, emergency telephones, and lighted pathways/sidewalks.

Programs of Study: Drake confers B.A., B.S., B.A.Journ. and Mass Comm., B.Art., B.Art Ed., B.F.A., B.Mus., B.Mus.Ed., B.S.B.A., B.S.Ed, B.S.N., and B.S.Pharm. degrees. Master's and doctoral degrees are also awarded. Bachelor's degrees are awarded in BIOLOGICAL SCIENCE (biology/biological science and neurosciences), BUSINESS (accounting, banking and finance, business administration and management, insurance and risk management, international business management, management science, marketing management, and marketing/retailing/merchandising), COMMUNICATIONS AND THE ARTS (advertising, art history and appreciation, broadcasting, communications, dramatic arts, English, graphic design, journalism, literature, music, music business management, music performance, percussion, performing arts, printmaking, public relations, speech/debate/rhetoric, strings, studio art, and voice), COMPUTER AND PHYSICAL SCIENCE (actuarial science, chemistry, computer science, information sciences and systems, mathematics, and physics), EDUCATION (elementary, mathematics, middle school, music, science, secondary, and social studies), ENGINEERING AND ENVIRONMENTAL DESIGN (environmental science and military science), HEALTH PROFESSIONS (medical technology, pharmacy, predentistry, premedicine, and preveterinary science), SOCIAL SCIENCE (clinical psychology, crosscultural studies, economics, ethics, politics, and social policy, experimental psychology, gerontology, history, international relations, law, philosophy, political science/government, prelaw, psychology, religion, religious music, sociology, and women's studies). Actuarial science, pharmacy, and physics/astronomy are the strongest academically. Pharmacy, accounting, and music peformance are the largest.

Required: Undergraduates must take a first-year seminar and general education courses leading to communication, critical thinking, artistic experience, historical consciousness, information and technical literacy, multicultural experience, scientific and quantitative literacy, and values and ethics. A capstone demonstration is required. For graduation, 124 credit hours are required with 27 to 36 hours in the major. The minimum GPA is 2.0.

Special: Study abroad is available in 67 countries and at sea. The university offers cross-registration, internships, a Washington semester, a United Nations semester, and work-study programs. Dual majors, B.A.-B.S. degrees, a 3-2 engineering degree, student-designed majors, credit for military and work experience, and nondegree study are possible. Students may take a maximum of 12 hours of course work on a credit/no credit basis. There are 25 national honor societies, including Phi Beta Kappa, and a freshman honors program.

Faculty/Classroom: 62% of faculty are male; 38%, female. All teach undergraduates and 90% do research. No introductory courses are taught by graduate students. The average class size in an introductory lecture is 80; in a laboratory, 20; and in a regular course, 45.

Admissions: 87% of the 2001-2002 applicants were accepted. The SAT I scores for the 2001-2002 freshman class were: Verbal--16% below 500, 37% between 500 and 599, 36% between 600 and 700, and 11% above 700; Math--24% below 500, 39% between 500 and 599, 32% between 600 and 700, and 6% above 700. The ACT scores were 9% below 21, 24% between 21 and 23, 29% between 24 and 26, 15% between 27 and 28, and 25% above 28. 56% of the current freshmen were in the top fifth of their class; 86% were in the top two fifths. There were 4 National Merit finalists. 25 freshmen graduated first in their class.

Requirements: The SAT I or ACT is required. In addition, applicants must be graduates of an accredited secondary school. The GED is accepted. Students must have completed 4 years of English, 2 years of math, and 10 other units to be selected from English, foreign languages, social studies, math, lab sciences, and others. A portfolio is required for art majors and for those seeking scholarship consideration. An audition is necessary for admission to the music program. Tapes are accepted. Drake requires applicants to be in the upper 50% of their class. A GPA of 3.0 is required. AP and CLEP credits are accepted. Important factors in the admissions decision are advanced placement or honor courses, extracurricular activities record, and leadership record. Applications are accepted on-line and on computer disk via several programs.

Procedure: Freshmen are admitted to all sessions. Entrance exams should be taken during the spring of the junior year or early fall of the senior year. There is a deferred admissions plan. Early decision applications should be filed by August 1; regular applications, by March 1 for fall entry and December 1 for spring entry, along with a $25 fee. Notification is sent on a rolling basis.

Transfer: 178 transfer students enrolled in 2001-2002. Applicants must have a minimum GPA of 2.0 and have completed 24 credit hours for evaluation. Grades of C or better transfer for credit. There is no assurance that all courses transferred will apply toward the major requirement. The final 30 hours must be completed in residence. Transfer students are admitted in the fall, spring, and summer. 30 credits of 124 must be completed at Drake.

Visiting: There are regularly scheduled orientations for prospective students, including an opportunity for students and parents to confer with professors, meet with current students, and attend information sessions on academic programs, financial aid, housing, and the Drake campus. Also included are a walking tour and lunch. There are guides for informal visits and visitors may sit in on classes and stay overnight. To schedule a visit, contact the Visit Coordinator in the Office of Admissions.

Financial Aid: In 2001-2002, 97% of all freshmen and 96% of continuing students received some form of financial aid. 61% of freshmen and 58% of continuing students received need-based aid. The average freshman award was $15,188. Of that total, scholarships or need-based grants averaged $11,159; loans averaged $4276; and work contracts averaged $1175. 58% of undergraduates work part time. Average annual earnings from campus work are $1031. The average financial indebtedness of the 2001 graduate was $21,422. The FAFSA is required. The fall application deadline is March 1.

International Students: There are 181 international students enrolled. The school actively recruits these students. They must score 530 on the written TOEFL or 197 on the electronic version.

Computers: The mainframes are 2 Digital 4000/600s, 1 Digital 4000/300, and 3 Digital ALPHA Server 2100s with quad processors. Every residence hall room is equipped with a Power Mac 7100 computer, printer, and software. A data network permits students to access a variety of services from their rooms, including the campuswide information system, the on-line library catalog, the Internet, and e-mail. Several additional computer labs are located across campus. All students may access the system. There are no time limits. The fee is $100 (for residence hall residents).

Graduates: In 2001, 654 bachelor's degrees were awarded. The most popular majors were pharmacy (12%), biology (7%), and accounting (4%). In an average class, 50% graduate in 4 years, 60% in 5 years, and 68% in 6 years. 90 companies recruited on campus in 2000-2001. Of the 2000 graduating class, 17% were enrolled in graduate school within 6 months of graduation and 78% were employed.

Admissions Contact: Thomas F. Willoughby, Dean of Admissions and Financial Aid. E-mail: *admission@drake.edu*
Web: *www.choose.drake.edu*

GRACELAND UNIVERSITY — C-4

Lamoni, IA 50140 — (641) 784-5118
(866) 472-2352; Fax: (641) 784-5480

Full-time: 505 men, 598 women — **Faculty:** 85; IIB, --$
Part-time: 101 men, 168 women — **Ph.D.s:** 60%
Graduate: 28 men, 71 women — **Student/Faculty:** 13 to 1
Year: 4-1-4, summer session — **Tuition:** $13,145
Application Deadline: May 1 — **Room & Board:** $2700
Freshman Class: 981 applied, 601 accepted, 251 enrolled
SAT I Verbal/Math: 511/503 — **ACT:** 22 — **COMPETITIVE**

Graceland University, formerly Graceland College, established in 1895, is a private liberal arts college sponsored by the Community of Christ. Graceland also maintains a campus in Independence, MO. There are 4 undergraduate and 3 graduate schools. In addition to regional accreditation, Graceland has baccalaureate program accreditation with CCNE, NCATE, and NLN. The library contains 119,037 volumes, 122,524 microform items, and 3088 audiovisual forms/CDs, and subscribes to 581 periodicals. Computerized library services include the card catalog, interlibrary loans, and database searching. Special learning facilities include a learning resource center, art gallery, and a center for the study of the Korean War. The 167-acre campus is in a small town 80 miles south of Des Moines. Including residence halls, there are 20 buildings.

Student Life: 61% of undergraduates are from out of state, mostly the Midwest. Others are from 41 states, 21 foreign countries, and Canada. 83% are white. 26% are Protestant; 14% claim no religious affiliation; 11% Catholic. The average age of freshmen is 19; all undergraduates, 22. 25% do not continue beyond their first year; 47% remain to graduate.

Housing: 715 students can be accommodated in college housing, which includes single-sex dormitories and married-student housing. On-campus housing is guaranteed for all 4 years. 64% of students live on campus; of those, 42% remain on campus on weekends. Alcohol is not permitted. All students may keep cars.

Activities: There are no fraternities or sororities. There are 54 groups on campus, including art, band, cheerleading, chess, choir, chorale, chorus, computers, dance, drama, drill team, ethnic, gay, honors, international, jazz band, musical theater, newspaper, orchestra, pep band, political, professional, radio and TV, religious, social, social service, student government, symphony, and yearbook. Popular campus events include Renaissance Week, Multi-Cultural Week, and New Year's in November.

Sports: There are 9 intercollegiate sports for men and 8 for women, and 17 intramural sports for men and 17 for women. Facilities include a sports complex with an all-weather track and lighted soccer and football fields; a phys ed center with an indoor junior Olympic-size pool, a 5-court gym, an indoor track, a weight room, and courts for racquetball, basketball, volleyball, and tennis; an intramural sports complex; 8 lighted tennis courts; an 18-hole disc golf course; and 2 small lakes.

Disabled Students: 86% of the campus is accessible. Wheelchair ramps, elevators, special parking, specially equipped rest rooms, special class scheduling, lowered drinking fountains, and lowered telephones are available.

Services: Counseling and information services are available, as is tutoring in most subjects. There is a reader service for the blind, and remedial math, reading, and writing.

Campus Safety and Security: Measures include 24-hour foot and vehicle patrol, escort service, informal discussions, and pamphlets/posters/films. There are emergency telephones, lighted pathways/sidewalks, and night security personnel.

Programs of Study: Graceland confers B.A., B.S., and B.S.N. degrees. Master's degrees are also awarded. Bachelor's degrees are awarded in BIOLOGICAL SCIENCE (biology/biological science), BUSINESS (accounting, business administration and management, international business management, recreation and leisure services, and recreational facilities management), COMMUNICATIONS AND THE ARTS (communications, dramatic arts, English, German, graphic design, literature, modern language, music, Spanish, speech/debate/rhetoric, and studio art), COMPUTER AND PHYSICAL SCIENCE (chemistry, computer science, information sciences and systems, mathematics, and science), EDUCATION (athletic training, elementary, music, and physical), ENGINEERING AND ENVIRONMENTAL DESIGN (commercial art), HEALTH PROFESSIONS (health, medical laboratory technology, nursing, predentistry, premedicine, and preveterinary science), SOCIAL SCIENCE (addiction studies, criminal justice, economics, history, human services, international studies, liberal arts/general studies, philosophy, psychology, religion, social science, and sociology). Business administration, education, and nursing are the largest.

Required: To graduate, students must complete 128 credit hours, including 39 in upper-division courses and an average of 40 in the major, and maintain a minimum GPA of 2.0 overall and in the major. General education requirements include studies in humanities, social sciences, natural sciences, behavioral sciences, ethics, math, computer science, leadership, thinking skills, human diversity, and the arts.

Special: Internships are required in business, education, recreation, communications, and publication design. Graceland offers study abroad, cross-registration, B.A.-B.S. degrees, work-study, dual and student-designed majors, and a general studies degree. Credit for life, military, or work experience is possible. A pass/fail option is available for 2 courses each semester. The university also offers nondegree study, home study in addiction studies and nursing, a program for students with learning disabilities, an accelerated degree program in nursing, and a 3-2 engineering degree with the University of Iowa and the University of Missouri-Rolla. There are 3 national honor societies, a freshman honors program, and 6 departmental honors program.

Faculty/Classroom: 52% of faculty are male; 48%, female. All teach undergraduates and 10% do research. The average class size in an introductory lecture is 24; in a laboratory, 24; and in a regular course, 11.

Admissions: 61% of the 2001-2002 applicants were accepted. The SAT I scores for the 2001-2002 freshman class were: Verbal--48% below 500, 28% between 500 and 599, 15% between 600 and 700, and 9% above 700; Math--52% below 500, 21% between 500 and 599, 24% between 600 and 700, and 3% above 700. The ACT scores were 46% below 21, 22% between 21 and 23, 20% between 24 and 26, 5% between 27 and 28, and 7% above 28. There were 4 National Merit finalists. 5 freshmen graduated first in their class.

Requirements: The SAT I or ACT is required. In addition,Graceland requires applicants to meet 2 of these 3 criteria: rank in the upper 50% of their class, a GPA of 2.0, and a minimum composite score of 960 on the SAT I or 21 on the ACT. Applicants must be graduates of an accredited secondary school. The GED is accepted. An interview is recommended. The university accepts applications on computer disk and on-line via CollegeLink, Apply, College Profile 2000, or the school's web site. AP and CLEP credits are accepted. Important factors in the admissions decision are advanced placement or honor courses, evidence of special talent, and leadership record.

Procedure: Freshmen are admitted to all sessions. Entrance exams should be taken in the junior or senior year. Applications should be filed by May 1 for fall entry and December 1 for spring entry, along with a $50 fee. Notification is sent on a rolling basis.

Transfer: 180 transfer students enrolled in 2001-2002. Applicants must submit official transcripts from all colleges attended and from high school. The required GPA varies by the number of hours of college study completed. Transfer students are admitted every term. 32 credits of 128 must be completed at Graceland.

Visiting: There are regularly scheduled orientations for prospective students, including a campus tour and opportunities to meet students, faculty, and campus personnel. There are guides for informal visits and visitors may sit in on classes and stay overnight. To schedule a visit, contact Helen Caples at (641) 784-5127 or *caples@graceland.edu*

Financial Aid: In 2001-2002, 97% of all freshmen and 88% of continuing students received some form of financial aid. 65% of freshmen and 62% of continuing students received need-based aid. The average freshman award was $14,859. Of that total, scholarships or need-based grants averaged $9785 ($20,487 maximum); loans averaged $4429 ($16,876 maximum); and work contracts averaged $976 ($3400 maximum). 40% of undergraduates work part time. Average annual earnings from campus work are $1104. The average financial indebtedness of the 2001 graduate was $8715. The FAFSA is required. The fall application deadline is March 1.

International Students: There are 88 international students enrolled. The school actively recruits these students. They must score 450 on the written TOEFL or 133 on the electronic version.

Computers: The mainframe is an HP 9000 Model D330. There are workstations in the computer engineering, computer science, chemistry, physics, and music labs, and in the computer center. There are also 3 PC labs and / Mac lab. All residence hall rooms are PC accessible. All students may access the system anytime. There are no time limits and no fees. It is strongly recommended that all students have a personal computer.

Graduates: In 2001, 197 bachelor's degrees were awarded. The most popular majors were nursing (15%), business administration (12%), and elementary education (8%). In an average class, 28% graduate in 4 years, 43% in 5 years, and 47% in 6 years. 7 companies recruited on campus in 2000-2001. Of the 2000 graduating class, 17% were enrolled in graduate school within 6 months of graduation and 80% were employed.

Admissions Contact: Bonita A. Booth, Vice Provost for Enrollment Management and Dean of Admissions.
E-mail: *admissions@graceland.edu* Web: *www.graceland.edu*

GRAND VIEW COLLEGE C-3

Des Moines, IA 50316-1599 (515) 263-2810
(800) 444-6083; Fax: (515) 263-2974

Full-time: 302 men, 669 women	**Faculty:** 66
Part-time: 165 men, 266 women	**Ph.D.s:** 64%
Graduate: none	**Student/Faculty:** 15 to 1
Year: semesters, summer session	**Tuition:** $13,430
Application Deadline: open	**Room & Board:** $4166
Freshman Class: 365 applied, 361 accepted, 193 enrolled	
ACT: 20	**NONCOMPETITIVE**

Grand View College, founded in 1896, is a private liberal arts college affiliated with the Evangelical Lutheran Church in America that focuses on connecting liberal arts with career preparation. In addition to regional accreditation, Grand View has baccalaureate program accreditation with NLN. The library contains 102,406 volumes, 166,681 microform items, and 6162 audiovisual forms/CDs, and subscribes to 3412 periodicals. Computerized library services include interlibrary loans and database searching. Special learning facilities include a learning resource center, radio station, and TV station. The 25-acre campus is in an urban area in a residential area of Des Moines. Including residence halls, there are 22 buildings.

Student Life: 96% of undergraduates are from Iowa. Others are from 17 states, 12 foreign countries, and Canada. 89% are from public schools. 91% are white. 51% are claim no religious affiliation; 28% Protestant; 12% Catholic. The average age of freshmen is 18; all undergraduates, 26. 37% do not continue beyond their first year.

Housing: 258 students can be accommodated in college housing, which includes coed dormitories and on-campus apartments. In addition, there are special-interest houses. On-campus housing is guaranteed for the freshman year only and is available on a first-come, first-served basis. 82% of students commute. All students may keep cars.

Activities: There are no fraternities or sororities. There are 26 groups on campus, including art, cheerleading, choir, chorale, chorus, departmental, drama, ethnic, honors, international, newspaper, professional, radio and TV, religious, social service, and student government. Popular campus events include Stundenterfest.

Sports: There are 3 intercollegiate sports for men and 4 for women, and 8 intramural sports for men and 8 for women. Facilities include a 1200-seat phys ed building with facilities for varsity athletics and recreation programs, tennis courts, and an athletic field.

Disabled Students: 90% of the campus is accessible. Wheelchair ramps, elevators, special parking, specially equipped rest rooms, special class scheduling, lowered drinking fountains, lowered telephones, and support services for the disabled are available.

Services: Counseling and information services are available, as is tutoring in every subject. Support services for the blind and hearing-impaired also are available.

Campus Safety and Security: Measures include escort service, shuttle buses, informal discussions, and pamphlets/posters/films. There are emergency telephones, lighted pathways/sidewalks, and an evening-to-dawn campus security patrol.

Programs of Study: Grand View confers B.A. and B.S.N. degrees. Associate degrees are also awarded. Bachelor's degrees are awarded in BIOLOGICAL SCIENCE (biology/biological science), BUSINESS (accounting and business administration and management), COMMUNICATIONS AND THE ARTS (broadcasting, communications, English, graphic design, journalism, and visual and performing arts), COMPUTER AND PHYSICAL SCIENCE (applied mathematics, computer science, and information sciences and systems), EDUCATION (elementary and secondary), HEALTH PROFESSIONS (nursing), SOCIAL SCIENCE (criminal justice, human services, political science/government, and psychology). Art, nursing, and education are the strongest academically. Business, nursing, and education are the largest.

Required: Students must complete core requirements, including courses in English, public speaking, liberal arts, integrating seminar, other culture encounter, religion or philosophy, history or other humanities, laboratory science, and social science. Students must complete at least 124 hours of work, including 60 hours in courses other than the major and 24 hours in the major. Students must maintain an overall GPA of 2.0 and a 2.2 GPA in the major. Students must also demonstrate computer proficiency.

Special: Co-op programs, cross-registration with Drake University and Des Moines Area Community College, student-designed majors, study abroad, and internships for most majors are available. Dual majors, a B.A.-B.S. degree, a Washington semester, work-study programs, and an accelerated degree program in business administration are offered. Nondegree study, a liberal arts degree, a certificate in art therapy, and pass/fail options are possible. There are 4 national honor societies, and a freshman honors program.

Faculty/Classroom: 45% of faculty are male; 55%, female. All teach undergraduates and 40% both teach and do research. The average class size in an introductory lecture is 25; in a laboratory, 15; and in a regular course, 25.

Admissions: 99% of the 2001-2002 applicants were accepted. The ACT scores for the 2001-2002 freshman class were: 54% below 21, 26% between 21 and 23, 15% between 24 and 26, 4% between 27 and 28, and 1% above 28. 25% of the current freshmen were in the top fifth of their class; 50% were in the top two fifths. 1 freshman graduated first in class.

Requirements: The ACT is required and the SAT I is recommended, with a minimum recommended score of 18 on the ACT, or the equivalent on the SAT I. Students must be graduates of an accredited secondary school. The GED is also accepted. Grand View recommends that students should have completed 4 courses in English, 3 courses each in math, science, and social science, and 2 courses in a foreign language. A GPA of 2.0 is required. AP and CLEP credits are accepted. Applications are accepted on-line.

Procedure: Freshmen are admitted fall, spring, and summer. Entrance exams should be taken during the second semester of the junior year. There is a deferred admissions plan. Application deadlines are open. Notification is sent on a rolling basis.

Transfer: 196 transfer students enrolled in 2001-2002. In addition, applicants must submit transcripts from each college attended. 30 credits of 124 must be completed at Grand View.

Visiting: There are regularly scheduled orientations for prospective students, including placement tests, a financial aid session, lunch, advisor meetings, and a registration session. There are guides for informal visits and visitors may sit in on classes and stay overnight. To schedule a visit, contact the Admissions Office at *admiss@gvc.edu*

Financial Aid: In 2001-2002, 99% of all freshmen and 98% of continuing students received some form of financial aid. 70% of freshmen and 80% of continuing students received need-based aid. The average freshman award was $15,815. Of that total, scholarships or need-based grants averaged $8877; loans averaged $2894; and work contracts averaged $1500. 95% of undergraduates work part time. Average annual earnings from campus work are $1500. The average financial indebtedness of the 2001 graduate was $18,133. Grand View is a member of CSS. The FAFSA is required. The fall application deadline is April 15.

International Students: There are 18 international students enrolled. They must score 550 on the written TOEFL or 210 on the electronic version or take the MELAB and also take the SAT I or the ACT, scoring 18.

Computers: The mainframes are a DEC VAX and a DEC ALPHA. There are also more than 150 terminals and 60 PCs available for student use in classrooms, 3 computer labs, and faculty and administrative offices. All students may access the system. There are no time limits and no fees.

Graduates: In 2001, 285 bachelor's degrees were awarded. The most popular majors were nursing (22%), business administration (20%), and education (13%). In an average class, 25% graduate in 4 years, 35% in 5 years, and 37% in 6 years. 66 companies recruited on campus in 2000-2001. Of the 2000 graduating class, 5% were enrolled in graduate school within 6 months of graduation and 95% were employed.

Admissions Contact: Diane Schafer Johnson, Director of Admissions. E-mail: *djohnson@gvc.edu* Web: *gvc.edu*

GRINNELL COLLEGE
Grinnell, IA 50112

D-3
(641) 269-3600
(800) 247-0113; Fax: (641) 269-4800

Full-time: 610 men, 691 women	**Faculty:** 137; IIB, ++$
Part-time: 12 men, 25 women	**Ph.D.s:** 94%
Graduate: none	**Student/Faculty:** 9 to 1
Year: semesters	**Tuition:** $22,250
Application Deadline: January 20	**Room & Board:** $6050
Freshman Class: 1980 applied, 1281 accepted, 360 enrolled	
SAT I Verbal/Math: 680/660	**ACT:** 30

HIGHLY COMPETITIVE+

Grinnell College, founded in 1846, is a private institution that offers undergraduate degree programs in the arts and sciences. The 3 libraries contain 474,738 volumes, 375,336 microform items, and 27,332 audiovisual forms/CDs, and subscribe to 3032 periodicals. Computerized library services include the card catalog, interlibrary loans, and database searching. Special learning facilities include a learning resource center, art gallery, observatory, physics museum, print and drawing gallery, and student-run radio station. The 95-acre campus is in a small town 55 miles east of Des Moines. Including residence halls, there are 64 buildings.

Student Life: 86% of undergraduates are from out of state, mostly the Midwest. Others are from 50 states, 53 foreign countries, and Canada. 82% are from public schools. 69% are white; 10% foreign nationals. 40% claim no religious affiliation; 30% Protestant; 10% Catholic. The average age of freshmen is 18; all undergraduates, 20. 9% do not continue beyond their first year; 81% remain to graduate.

Housing: 1100 students can be accommodated in college housing, which includes single-sex and coed dormitories. In addition, there are language houses and special-interest houses. On-campus housing is guaranteed for all 4 years. 86% of students live on campus; of those, 96% remain on campus on weekends. All students may keep cars.

Activities: There are no fraternities or sororities. There are 145 groups on campus, including art, chess, choir, chorale, chorus, computers, dance, debate, drama, ethnic, film, forensics, gay, honors, international, jazz band, literary magazine, musical theater, newspaper, orchestra, photography, political, radio and TV, religious, social, social service, student government, and yearbook. Popular campus events include Waltz, Disco, and Mary B. James Ball.

Sports: There are 10 intercollegiate sports for men and 10 for women, and 7 intramural sports for men and 6 for women. Facilities include a phys ed complex, a gym, 5 sports fields, a track, and 3 intramural fields.

Disabled Students: 70% of the campus is accessible. Wheelchair ramps, elevators, special parking, specially equipped rest rooms, special class scheduling, lowered drinking fountains, and lowered telephones are available.

Services: Counseling and information services are available, as is tutoring in every subject. There is a reader service for the blind. and reading, writing, math, and science labs.

Campus Safety and Security: Measures include self-defense education, escort service, informal discussions, and pamphlets/posters/films. There are emergency telephones, lighted pathways/sidewalks, fire drills, and a committee on personal safety education. Security information and reports are released to the entire campus when incidents occur.

Programs of Study: Grinnell confers the B.A. degree. Bachelor's degrees are awarded in BIOLOGICAL SCIENCE (biochemistry and biology/biological science), COMMUNICATIONS AND THE ARTS (art, Chinese, classics, dramatic arts, English, French, German, music, Russian, and Spanish), COMPUTER AND PHYSICAL SCIENCE (chemistry, computer science, mathematics, physics, and science), SOCIAL SCIENCE (anthropology, economics, history, philosophy, political science/government, psychology, religion, and sociology). Math, history, and biology are the largest.

Required: All students are required to take a tutorial in the first semester focusing on writing. All students must also complete a major field, which includes between 32 and 48 credits in most departments. Of the total 124 credits needed for the bachelor's degree, no more than 48 may be earned in any one department or 92 in any one division, and a minimum 2.0 GPA must be maintained.

Special: Students may participate in more than 100 study-abroad programs in 34 countries or in off-campus study at selected locations in the United States. Grinnell offers cooperative programs in architecture with Washington University in St. Louis and a 3-2 engineering program with California Institute of Technology, Columbia University, and Rensselaer Polytechnic Institute. There is also an extensive internship program, a Washington semester, a general studies degree in science, student-designed majors, and S/D/F grading options in selected courses. Grinnell's special "plus-2" option permits students to add 2 credits to a regular course through independent study. Students may pursue one of 10 interdisciplinary concentrations in addition to their major. Accelerated degree programs of 6 to 7 semesters may be approved on an individual basis. There are 2 national honor societies, including Phi Beta Kappa.

Faculty/Classroom: 61% of faculty are male; 39%, female. All both teach and do research. The average class size in an introductory lecture is 19; in a laboratory, 13; and in a regular course, 16.

Admissions: 65% of the 2001-2002 applicants were accepted. The SAT I scores for the 2001-2002 freshman class were: Verbal--1% below 500, 9% between 500 and 599, 43% between 600 and 700, and 47% above 700; Math--15% between 500 and 599, 52% between 600 and 700, and 33% above 700. The ACT scores were 5% below 21, 3% between 21 and 23, 11% between 24 and 26, 14% between 27 and 28, and 67% above 28. 85% of the current freshmen were in the top fifth of their class; 99% were in the top two fifths. There were 21 National Merit semifinalists. 38 freshmen graduated first in their class.

Requirements: The SAT I or ACT is required. In addition, applicants must be graduates of accredited secondary schools. The college recommends 17 Carnegie units, 4 each in English and math, and 3-4 each in lab science, social studies, and a foreign language. An essay is required and an interview is recommended. AP credits are accepted. Important factors in the admissions decision are advanced placement or honor courses, evidence of special talent, and personality/intangible qualities. Applications are accepted on-line via College NET or Common App.

Procedure: Freshmen are admitted in the fall. Entrance exams should be taken during the second semester of the junior year or early in the fall semester of the senior year. There are early decision and deferred admissions plans. Early decision applications should be filed by November 20; regular applications, by January 20 for fall entry. Notification of early decision is sent December 20; regular decision, April 1. The fall 2001 application fee was $30. 43 early decision candidates were accepted for the 2001-2002 class. 8% of all applicants are on a waiting list; 67 were accepted in 2001.

Transfer: 41 transfer students enrolled in 2001-2002. Students must submit all college transcripts and have a 3.0 GPA. 62 credits of 124 must be completed at Grinnell.

Visiting: There are regularly scheduled orientations for prospective students, including a campus tour, an interview with a member of the admissions staff, an opportunity to attend classes, presentations/discussions with students and faculty from a number of academic departments, overnight accommodations, and complimentary meals. There are guides for informal visits and visitors may sit in on classes and stay overnight. To schedule a visit, contact the Admissions Office at *askgrin@grinell.edu*

Financial Aid: In 2001-2002, 93% of all freshmen and 87% of continuing students received some form of financial aid. 64% of freshmen and 56% of continuing students received need-based aid. The average freshman award was $16,582. Of that total, scholarships or need-based grants averaged $13,080; loans averaged $3761; and work contracts averaged $1800 ($2500 maximum). 56% of undergraduates work part time. Average annual earnings from campus work are $1800. The average financial indebtedness of the 2001 graduate was $13,324. The FAFSA and the college's own financial statement are required. The fall application deadline is February 1.

International Students: There are 124 international students enrolled. The school actively recruits these students. They must score 550 on the written TOEFL or 220 on the electronic version and also take the SAT I or the ACT.

Computers: Central servers include 2 Proliant 6000s running Windows NT and a Compaq Alpha Server 4100 running UNIX. There are more than 250 networked computers on campus for the exclusive use of students. All college residences have network connections. All students may access the system 24 hours a day. There are no time limits and no fees.

Graduates: In 2001, 381 bachelor's degrees were awarded. The most popular majors were biology (12%), economics (9%), and English (8%). In an average class, 75% graduate in 4 years, 83% in 5 years, and 84% in 6 years. 113 companies recruited on campus in 2000-2001. Of the 2000 graduating class, 30% were enrolled in graduate school within 6 months of graduation and 50% were employed.

Admissions Contact: James Sumner, Dean for Admission and Financial Aid. A video is available. E-mail: *askgrin@grinnell.edu*
Web: *http://www.grinnell.edu*

IOWA BOARD OF REGENTS

The Iowa Board of Regents, established in 1905, is a public system whose chief administrator is the executive director. The primary goals of the system are teaching, research, and public service. The total enrollment in fall 2001 of all 3 university campuses was 70,661. In fall 2000, there were 6551 faculty members of which 3755 are tenured or on a tenure track. There are also 2 Special Schools, the Iowa School for the Deaf and the Iowa Braille and Sight Saving School. Altogether there are 336 baccalaureate, 311 master's, and 189 doctoral programs offered. Profiles of the University of Iowa, Iowa State University, and the University of Northern Iowa are included in this section.

IOWA STATE UNIVERSITY

C-3

Ames, IA 50011-2011

(515) 294-5836
(800) 262-3810; Fax: (515) 294-2592

Full-time: 11,837 men, 9395 women	**Faculty:** 1272; I, -$
Part-time: 990 men, 838 women	**Ph.D.s:** 87%
Graduate: 2572 men, 1791 women	**Student/Faculty:** 17 to 1
Year: semesters, summer session	**Tuition:** $3442 ($10,776)
Application Deadline: August 21	**Room & Board:** $4666

Freshman Class: 10,658 applied, 9604 accepted, 4654 enrolled
ACT: 24 **VERY COMPETITIVE**

Iowa State University, established in 1858, is a public land-grant institution offering undergraduate and graduate programs in agriculture, business, design, education, engineering, family and consumer sciences, liberal arts and sciences, and veterinary medicine. There are 8 undergraduate schools and 1 graduate school. In addition to regional accreditation, Iowa State has baccalaureate program accreditation with AACSB, ABET, ACEJMC, ACS, ADA, AHEA, APA, ASLA, CSAB, FIDER, NAAB, NASM, and SAF. The library contains 2,314,873 volumes, 3,293,450 microform items, and 926,000 audiovisual forms/CDs, and subscribes to 19,643 periodicals. Computerized library services include the card catalog, interlibrary loans, and database searching. Special learning facilities include a learning resource center, art gallery, natural history museum, planetarium, radio station, and TV station. The 1788-acre campus is in a suburban area 30 miles north of Des Moines. Including residence halls, there are 175 buildings.

Student Life: 77% of undergraduates are from Iowa. Others are from 49 states, 116 foreign countries, and Canada. 94% are from public schools. 88% are white. The average age of freshmen is 18; all undergraduates, 21. 16% do not continue beyond their first year.

Housing: 9900 students can be accommodated in college housing, which includes single-sex and coed dormitories, on-campus apartments, married-student housing, fraternity houses, and sorority houses. In addition, there are honors houses, special-interest houses, nonalcoholic houses, cross cultural houses, no-smoking houses, quiet houses, academic learning communities, and adult undergraduate housing. On-campus housing is guaranteed for all 4 years. 64% of students commute. All students may keep cars.

Activities: 13% of men belong to 1 local fraternity and 30 national fraternities; 12% of women belong to 1 local sorority and 17 national sororities. There are 543 groups on campus, including art, band, cheerleading, chess, choir, chorale, chorus, computers, dance, debate, drama, drum and bugle corps, ethnic, film, forensics, gay, honoraries, honors, international, jazz band, literary magazine, marching band, musical theater, newspaper, opera, orchestra, pep band, photography, political, professional, radio and TV, recreation/sports, religious, social, social service, special interest, student government, and symphony. Popular campus events include VEISHEA, spring festival, and Honors Week.

Sports: There are 7 intercollegiate sports for men and 12 for women, and 43 intramural sports for men and 43 for women. Facilities include a coliseum, a stadium/field, a baseball and softball complex, a track complex, a tennis complex, multipurpose gyms, swimming pools, an ice center, a phys ed building, recreation centers, multipurpose intramural-recreation fields, and a soccer competitive site.

Disabled Students: 93% of the campus is accessible. Wheelchair ramps, elevators, special parking, specially equipped rest rooms, special class scheduling, lowered drinking fountains, lowered telephones, voice-recognition and output computer systems, accessible public transportation, and adaptive recreational equipment are available.

Services: Counseling and information services are available, as is tutoring in most subjects. There is a reader service for the blind and remedial math and writing. Also available are a Kiersweil Reader, an Arkanstone Reader, enlargement services, talking and braille text from the Iowa Commission for the Blind, a braille printer, loaner printer, loaner computers, steno-captioning service, a TTY telecommunications device, FM listeners, and sign interpreters.

Campus Safety and Security: Measures include 24-hour foot and vehicle patrol, self-defense education, escort service, and shuttle buses. There are informal discussions, pamphlets/posters/films, emergency telephones, lighted pathways/sidewalks, and a Help Van for motorists.

Programs of Study: Iowa State confers B.A, B.S., B.Arch., B.B.A., B.F.A., B.L.A., B.L.S., and B.Mus. degrees. Master's and doctoral degrees are also awarded. Bachelor's degrees are awarded in AGRICULTURE (agricultural business management, agriculture, agronomy, animal science, dairy science, forestry and related sciences, horticulture, international agriculture, plant protection (pest management), and plant science), BIOLOGICAL SCIENCE (biochemistry, biology/biological science, biophysics, botany, entomology, genetics, microbiology, nutrition, plant pathology, and zoology), BUSINESS (accounting, banking and finance, business administration and management, fashion merchandising, hotel/motel and restaurant management, international business management, management science, marketing/retailing/merchandising, and transportation management), COMMUNICATIONS AND THE ARTS (advertising, communications, design, English, fine arts, French, German, graphic design, journalism, linguistics, music, Russian, Spanish, and speech/debate/rhetoric), COMPUTER AND PHYSICAL SCIENCE (atmospheric sciences and meteorology, chemistry, computer science, earth science, geology, mathematics, physics, and statistics), EDUCATION (agricultural, early childhood, elementary, health, industrial arts, physical, and secondary), ENGINEERING AND ENVIRONMENTAL DESIGN (aeronautical engineering, agricultural engineering, architecture, chemical engineering, city/community/regional planning, civil engineering, computer engineering, construction engineering, electrical/electronics engineering, engineering, engineering technology, environmental science, industrial engineering technology, interior design, landscape architecture/design, materials engineering, and mechanical engineering), SOCIAL SCIENCE (anthropology, child care/child and family studies, child psychology/development, dietetics, economics, family/consumer resource management, family/consumer studies, fashion design and technology, food science, history, international relations, liberal arts/general studies, philosophy, political science/government, psychology, religion, sociology, and textiles and clothing). Engineering, agriculture, and statistics, are the strongest academically. Engineering, business, and agriculture are the largest.

Required: A minimum of 120 1/2 to 169 1/2 credit hours, depending on the major, and a GPA of 2.0 are required for graduation. The total number of credits required in the major varies. All students must take freshman English, library instruction, 3 credits in U.S. diversity, and 3 credits in internationalization.

Special: Iowa State offers cooperative programs in engineering, forestry, agronomy, chemistry, computer science, economics, agricultural systems technology, business administration, industrial technology, and performing arts, and cross-registration with the Universities of Iowa and Northern Iowa. Internships, study abroad in more than 100 countries, dual majors, the B.A.-B.S. degree, student-designed majors, and accelerated degree programs are available. Interdisciplinary studies include agricultural biochemistry, agricultural systems technology, animal ecology, public service and administration in agriculture, and engineering operations. There are work-study programs, a Washington semester, nondegree study, and pass/no pass options. There are 15 national honor societies, including Phi Beta Kappa, a freshman honors program, and 7 departmental honors programs.

Faculty/Classroom: 71% of faculty are male; 29%, female. 87% teach undergraduates. Graduate students teach 16% of introductory courses. The average class size in an introductory lecture is 63; in a laboratory, 18; and in a regular course, 31.

Admissions: 90% of the 2001-2002 applicants were accepted. The ACT scores for the 2001-2002 freshman class were: 3% between 21 and 23, 40% between 24 and 26, 45% between 27 and 28, and 12% above 28. 56% of the current freshmen were in the top fifth of their class; 91% were in the top two fifths. There were 113 National Merit finalists.

Requirements: The SAT I or ACT is required. In addition, applicants must graduate from an accredited secondary school. The GED is accepted. For admission to freshman standing, students must have completed 4 years of English, 3 each of math and science, and 2 to 3 of social studies. For the College of Liberal Arts and Sciences, 2 years of a single foreign language are also required. Applications are accepted on-line via ExPAN, Apply, CollegeView, and others and at the school's web site. Iowa State requires applicants to be in the upper 50% of their class. AP and CLEP credits are accepted.

Procedure: Freshmen are admitted to all sessions. Entrance exams should be taken during the spring of the junior year or the fall of the senior year. There is a deferred admissions plan. Applications should be filed by August 21 for fall entry and January 10 for spring entry. Notification is sent on a rolling basis. The fall 2001 application fee was $20.

Transfer: 1656 transfer students enrolled in 2001-2002. Applicants must have a minimum GPA of 2.0 and at least 24 semester credits of acceptable transfer course work. They must also submit standardized test scores and provide a statement of good standing from prior institutions. 32 credits of 120½ to 169½ must be completed at Iowa State.

Visiting: There are regularly scheduled orientations for prospective students, including presentations on academics, admissions, residence hall living, fraternity and sorority life, and financial aid. There is also a group session with an adviser and a tour of the campus. There are guides for informal visits and visitors may sit in on classes and stay overnight. To schedule a visit, contact Phil Caffrey, Admissions Office at (515) 294-0821.

Financial Aid: In 2001-2002, 63% of all freshmen and 85% of continuing students received some form of financial aid. 27% of undergraduates work part time. Average annual earnings from campus work are $3400. The average financial indebtedness of the 2001 graduate was $16,979. Iowa State is a member of CSS. The FAFSA is required. The fall application deadline is March 1.

International Students: There are 1131 international students enrolled. The school actively recruits these students. They must score 500 on the written TOEFL or take the college's own test.

Computers: More than 125 instructional computing labs and classrooms are located in campus buildings and residence halls. These sites contain more than 2200 PCs, Macs, and workstations. Almost all machines are connected to the campus network and the Internet. All enrolled students qualify for a network account, which gives them access to e-mail, the web,. All students may access the system. Residence hall labs, Computation Center labs, and a few other sites are open 24 hours a day. Access to labs in academic buildings is restricted to building hours. There are no time limits. The fee is $47 per semester. Engineering, MIS, and computer science students pay a higher fee.

Graduates: In 2001, 4019 bachelor's degrees were awarded. The most popular majors were business (19%), engineering (17%), and agriculture (11%). In an average class, 1% graduate in 3 years, 27% in 4 years, 59% in 5 years, and 64% in 6 years. More than 230 companies recruited on campus in 2000-2001. Of the 2000 graduating class, 16% were enrolled in graduate school within 6 months of graduation and 80% were employed.

Admissions Contact: Phil Caffrey, Associate Director, Admissions. E-mail: *admissions@iastate.edu* Web: *www.iastate.edu*

IOWA WESLEYAN COLLEGE — E-4

Mount Pleasant, IA 52641 — (319) 385-6231
(800) 582-2383; Fax: (319) 385-6296

Full-time: 259 men, 259 women	**Faculty:** 45
Part-time: 63 men, 231 women	**Ph.D.s:** 35%
Graduate: none	**Student/Faculty:** 11 to 1
Year: 4-1-4, summer session	**Tuition:** $14,380
Application Deadline: open	**Room & Board:** $4460
Freshman Class: 530 applied, 337 accepted, 126 enrolled	
ACT: 17	**COMPETITIVE**

Iowa Wesleyan College, founded in 1842, is a private institution affiliated with the United Methodist Church. The college offers undergraduate degree programs in business, education, fine arts, human studies, language and literature, nursing, and science. There are 7 undergraduate schools. In addition to regional accreditation, Wesleyan has baccalaureate program accreditation with NLN. The library contains 106,816 volumes, 26,757 microform items, and 3492 audiovisual forms/CDs, and subscribes to 431 periodicals. Computerized library services include the card catalog, interlibrary loans, and database searching. Special learning facilities include a learning resource center, art gallery, and radio station. The 60-acre campus is in a small town 45 miles south of Iowa City. Including residence halls, there are 16 buildings.

Student Life: 77% of undergraduates are from Iowa. Others are from 24 states and 11 foreign countries. 98% are from public schools. 88% are white. 38% are Protestant; 12% Catholic; 11% claim no religious affiliation. The average age of freshmen is 19; all undergraduates, 28. 32% do not continue beyond their first year; 42% remain to graduate.

Housing: 455 students can be accommodated in college housing, which includes single-sex dormitories. On-campus housing is guaranteed for all 4 years. 58% of students live on campus; of those, 42% remain on campus on weekends. All students may keep cars.

Activities: 8% of men belong to 1 national fraternity; 12% of women belong to 2 national sororities. There are 37 groups on campus, including art, band, cheerleading, choir, chorus, ethnic, film, honors, international, jazz band, literary magazine, newspaper, orchestra, pep band, photography, professional, radio and TV, religious, social, student government, symphony, and yearbook. Popular campus events include Forum, Winterfest, and Spring Thing.

Sports: There are 7 intercollegiate sports for men and 7 for women, and 11 intramural sports for men and 11 for women. Facilities include a 32-acre complex with baseball, softball, and football fields and an all-weather quarter-mile track. There is also a gym, a remodeled swimming pool, and a basketball court.

Disabled Students: 15% of the campus is accessible. Wheelchair ramps, elevators, special parking, and special class scheduling are available.

Services: Counseling and information services are available, as is tutoring in most subjects. There is remedial math, reading, and writing.

Campus Safety and Security: Measures include 24-hour foot and vehicle patrol, self-defense education, escort service, and informal discussions. There are pamphlets/posters/films, emergency telephones, and lighted pathways/sidewalks.

Programs of Study: Wesleyan confers B.A., B.S., B.G.S., B.M.E., and B.S.N. degrees. Bachelor's degrees are awarded in BIOLOGICAL SCIENCE (biology/biological science, life science, and physiology), BUSINESS (accounting, business administration and management, international business management, and sports management), COMMUNICATIONS AND THE ARTS (communications, English, fine arts, and music), COMPUTER AND PHYSICAL SCIENCE (chemistry, computer science, and mathematics), EDUCATION (art, early childhood, elementary, music, physical, science, and secondary), ENGINEERING AND ENVIRONMENTAL DESIGN (preengineering), HEALTH PROFESSIONS (environmental health science, nursing, predentistry, premedicine, preoptometry, and preveterinary science), SOCIAL SCIENCE (criminal justice, history, prelaw, psychology, and sociology). English, communications, and chemistry are the strongest academically. Business, elementary education, and nursing are the largest.

Required: General education requirements include 5 semester hours of computer science/math, 4 semester hours of science, and 3 each of history/political science, religion/philosophy, social science, literature, and fine arts. Students must also demonstrate proficiency in composition, satisfy a safety and survival requirement, and successfully complete English 101 and 102, a life and health course, and a service learning project. A minimum of 124 semester hours is required for the bachelor's degree.

Special: The college maintains a cooperative program with Southeastern Community College. There are also internships in every major, a study-abroad program in Japan and Mexico, a selective studies option, a general studies degree, credit in nursing through challenge examinations, and satisfactory/unsatisfactory grade options. There are 6 national honor societies.

Faculty/Classroom: 51% of faculty are male; 49%, female. All teach undergraduates. The average class size in an introductory lecture is 22; in a laboratory, 24; and in a regular course, 14.

Admissions: 64% of the 2001-2002 applicants were accepted. The ACT scores for the 2001-2002 freshman class were: 80% below 21, 11% between 21 and 23, and 9% between 24 and 26. 14% of the current freshmen were in the top fifth of their class; 35% were in the top two fifths. 2 freshmen graduated first in their class in a recent year.

Requirements: The ACT is required. In addition, applicants must be graduates of accredited secondary schools or have earned a GED. Wesleyan requires applicants to be in the upper 50% of their class. A GPA of 2.0 is required. AP and CLEP credits are accepted. Important factors in the admissions decision are geographic diversity, evidence of special talent, and advanced placement or honor courses. Applications are accepted on computer disk and on-line via CollegeLink and Apply.

Procedure: Freshmen are admitted fall, winter, and spring. Entrance exams should be taken in April of the junior year or in June, October, or December of the senior year. There are early admissions and deferred admissions plans. Application deadlines are open. Notification is sent on a rolling basis.

Transfer: 70 transfer students enrolled in a recent year. A minimum cumulative college GPA of 2.0 is required. 30 credits of 124 must be completed at Wesleyan.

Visiting: There are regularly scheduled orientations for prospective students, including meetings with admissions, financial aid, and academic staff, as well as social activities. There are guides for informal visits and visitors may sit in on classes and stay overnight. To schedule a visit, contact the Admissions Office.

Financial Aid: In 2001-2002, 98% of all freshmen and 95% of continuing students received some form of financial aid. 75% of undergraduates work part time. Average annual earnings from campus work are $1000. Wesleyan is a member of CSS. The FAFSA and the college's own financial statement are required. Check with the school for current deadlines.

International Students: The school actively recruits these students. They must score 500 on the written TOEFL or 173 on the electronic version.

Computers: The mainframe is an HP9000/Model E25. There are 48 PCs available in open computer labs for students to complete class assignments. Access to the Internet is available on 5 PCs. All students may access the system 8 A.M. to 10 P.M. There are no time limits and no fees.

Graduates: In a recent year, 137 bachelor's degrees were awarded. The most popular majors were elementary education (23%), business (22%), and nursing (20%). In an average class, 30% graduate in 4 years, 33% in 5 years, and 33% in 6 years. 20 companies recruited on campus in a recent year.

Admissions Contact: David C. File, Associate VP and Dean. A video is available. E-mail: *admitrwl@iwc.edu* Web: *www.iwc.edu*

LORAS COLLEGE

Dubuque, IA 52004-0178 — E-2

(563) 588-7236
(800) 245-6727; Fax: (563) 588-7119

Full-time: 755 men, 772 women	**Faculty:** 118; IIB, --$
Part-time: 46 men, 63 women	**Ph.D.s:** 96%
Graduate: 45 men, 77 women	**Student/Faculty:** 13 to 1
Year: semesters, summer session	**Tuition:** $17,069
Application Deadline: open	**Room & Board:** $5925
Freshman Class: n/av	
SAT I or ACT: required	**COMPETITIVE+**

Loras College, founded in 1839, is a Roman Catholic liberal arts institution offering degree programs in humanities, social and behavioral studies, natural sciences, philosophy and religious studies, and professional studies. The library contains 431,903 volumes, 74,243 microform items, and 1617 audiovisual forms/CDs, and subscribes to 962 periodicals. Computerized library services include the card catalog, interlibrary loans, and database searching. Special learning facilities include a learning resource center, art gallery, planetarium, radio station, and TV station. The 60-acre campus is in a small town 180 miles west of Chicago and 250 miles south of Minneapolis. Including residence halls, there are 18 buildings.

Student Life: 57% of undergraduates are from Iowa. Others are from 27 states, 13 foreign countries, and Canada. 60% are from public schools. 91% are white. 64% are Catholic; 28% claim no religious affiliation. The average age of freshmen is 19; all undergraduates, 21. 24% do not continue beyond their first year.

Housing: 1119 students can be accommodated in college housing, which includes single-sex and coed dormitories, on-campus apartments, and off-campus apartments. In addition, there are honors houses. On-campus housing is guaranteed for all 4 years. 62% of students live on campus; of those, 65% remain on campus on weekends. All students may keep cars.

Activities: 3% of men belong to 3 national fraternities; 2% of women belong to 2 national sororities. There are 59 groups on campus, including band, cheerleading, choir, chorus, computers, drama, ethnic, forensics, honors, international, jazz band, literary magazine, newspaper, pep band, photography, political, professional, radio and TV, religious, social, social service, student government, and yearbook. Popular campus events include Family Weekend, Tri-College Free Day, and Awareness Week.

Sports: There are 10 intercollegiate sports for men and 9 for women, and 111 intramural sports for men and 111 for women. Facilities include a sports center with 3 gym floors, a swimming pool, 4 racquetball courts, and an 8-lane Olympic indoor/outdoor track. There are also 4 outdoor tennis courts, a field house for basketball games, and a soccer field. The campus stadium seats 3500.

Disabled Students: 70% of the campus is accessible. Wheelchair ramps, elevators, special parking, specially equipped rest rooms, special class scheduling, lowered drinking fountains, and lowered telephones are available.

Services: Counseling and information services are available, as is tutoring in every subject. There is remedial math and writing.

Campus Safety and Security: Measures include 24 hour foot and vehicle patrol, escort service, informal discussions, and pamphlets/posters/films. There are lighted pathways/sidewalks.

Programs of Study: Loras confers B.A., B.S., and B.M. degrees. Associate and master's degrees are also awarded. Bachelor's degrees are awarded in BIOLOGICAL SCIENCE (biochemistry and biology/biological science), BUSINESS (accounting, banking and finance, business administration and management, international business management, management information systems, marketing/retailing/merchandising, personnel management, and sports management), COMMUNICATIONS AND THE ARTS (art history and appreciation, broadcasting, classical languages, creative writing, English literature, French, German, journalism, music, public relations, Spanish, speech/debate/rhetoric, and studio art), COMPUTER AND PHYSICAL SCIENCE (chemistry, computer science, mathematics, physics, and science), EDUCATION (art, early childhood, elementary, foreign languages, music, physical, science, secondary, and special), ENGINEERING AND ENVIRONMENTAL DESIGN (electrical/electronics engineering), HEALTH PROFESSIONS (exercise science, medical technology, nuclear medical technology, and physical therapy), SOCIAL SCIENCE (classical/ancient civilization, criminal justice, economics, history, international studies, liberal arts/general studies, ministries, philosophy, political science/government, psychology, religion, social work, and sociology). Accounting and business, communication arts, and education are the largest.

Required: To graduate, students must complete a total of 120 credits with a minimum GPA of 2.0. The required number of credits in the major varies. The required general education program totals 36 to 37 credit hours and includes courses in critical thinking, writing, oral communication, quantitative reasoning, the scientific method, cultural diversity and cultural traditions, religion and religious traditions, values, self and society, and aesthetics. All students must complete and present 2 1-credit student portfolios for review.

Special: The college offers cross-registration with Clarke College and the University of Dubuque, and study abroad in 11 countries. Also available are various internships, on-campus work-study programs, a 3-2 engineering degree, a Washington semester with American University, pass/fail options, combined liberal arts-preprofessional programs, dual and student-designed majors, and adult degree programs. There are 7 national honor societies and a freshman honors program.

Faculty/Classroom: 67% of faculty are male; 33%, female. All teach undergraduates. No introductory courses are taught by graduate students. The average class size in an introductory lecture is 20; in a laboratory, 23; and in a regular course, 15.

Admissions: 30% of the current freshmen were in the top fifth of their class; 54% were in the top two fifths. 4 freshmen graduated first in their class.

Requirements: The SAT I or ACT is required. In addition, applicants must be graduates of an accredited secondary school or have a GED certificate, and have completed 4 units of English and 3 each of math, science, social studies, and history. An essay and an interview are recommended. Loras requires applicants to be in the upper 50% of their class. A GPA of 2.5 is required. AP and CLEP credits are accepted. Important factors in the admissions decision are evidence of special talent, leadership record, and advanced placement or honor courses. Applications are accepted on-line via the Apply Yourself Application Network and CollegeLink.

Procedure: Freshmen are admitted fall and spring. Entrance exams should be taken in April or June before the senior year or October of the senior year. Application deadlines are open. Notification is sent on a rolling basis. The fall 2001 application fee was $25.

Transfer: 99 transfer students enrolled in 2001-2002. Transfer students must have a minimum 2.0 GPA and submit transcripts of previous college work. Other requirements apply. 30 credits of 120 must be completed at Loras.

Visiting: There are regularly scheduled orientations for prospective students, consisting of 4 visitation days for all students and 7 programs for specific geographic locations. There are guides for informal visits and visitors may sit in on classes. To schedule a visit, contact the Office of Admissions.

Financial Aid: In 2001-2002, 87% of all freshmen and 56% of continuing students received some form of financial aid. 40% of freshmen and 32% of continuing students received need-based aid. The average freshman award was $10,619. Of that total, scholarships or need-based grants averaged $7767 ($17,090 maximum); loans averaged $3470 ($8126 maximum); and work contracts averaged $1780 ($2000 maximum). 35% of undergraduates work part time. Average annual earnings from campus work are $600. The average financial indebtedness of the 2001 graduate was $16,853. The FAFSA is required. The fall application deadline is April 15.

International Students: There are 35 international students enrolled. The school actively recruits these students. They must score 500 on the written TOEFL.

Computers: The mainframes are 2 IBM RISC 6000s. PCs are available throughout the campus. All students may access the system, and all computer equipment is available for student use on most days until 11 P.M. There are no time limits and no fees.

Graduates: In 2001, 315 bachelor's degrees were awarded. The most popular majors were business (30%), education (13%), and communications (10%). In an average class, 51% graduate in 4 years, and 61% in 5 years. 25 companies recruited on campus in 2000-2001. Of the 2000 graduating class, 11% were enrolled in graduate school within 6 months of graduation and 75% were employed.

Admissions Contact: Tim Hauber, Director of Admissions. A video is available. E-mail: *adms@loras.edu* Web: *www.loras.edu*

LUTHER COLLEGE

Decorah, IA 52101 — **E-1**

(563) 387-1287
(800) 458-8437; Fax: (563) 387-2159

Full-time: 988 men, 1507 women	**Faculty:** 181; IIB, av$
Part-time: 31 men, 49 women	**Ph.D.s:** 81%
Graduate: none	**Student/Faculty:** 14 to 1
Year: 4-1-4, summer session	**Tuition:** $19,325
Application Deadline: March 1	**Room & Board:** $3975
Freshman Class: 1911 applied, 1595 accepted, 636 enrolled	
SAT I Verbal/Math: 616/603	**ACT:** 25 **VERY COMPETITIVE+**

Luther College, affiliated with the Evangelical Lutheran Church in America, is a liberal arts institution founded in 1861. In addition to regional accreditation, Luther has baccalaureate program accreditation with CSWE, NASM, NCATE, and NLN. The library contains 355,571 volumes, 25,014 microform items, and 10,432 audiovisual forms/CDs, and subscribes to 1115 periodicals. Computerized library services include the card catalog, interlibrary loans, and database searching. Special learning facilities include a learning resource center, art gallery, natural history museum, planetarium, and radio station. The 800-acre campus is in a small town 70 miles south of Rochester, Minnesota. Including residence halls, there are 23 buildings.

Student Life: 63% of undergraduates are from out of state, mostly the Midwest. Others are from 37 states, 45 foreign countries, and Canada. 90% are from public schools. 87% are white. 70% are Protestant; 15% Catholic; 14% claim no religious affiliation. The average age of freshmen is 18; all undergraduates, 20. 16% do not continue beyond their first year.

Housing: 2168 students can be accommodated in college housing, which includes coed dormitories, on-campus apartments, off-campus apartments, and married-student housing. In addition, there are language houses, dialogue floors, and wellness floors. On-campus housing is guaranteed for all 4 years. 82% of students live on campus; of those, 85% remain on campus on weekends. All students may keep cars.

Activities: 8% of men belong to 4 local fraternities; 9% of women belong to 4 local sororities. There are 116 groups on campus, including art, band, cheerleading, choir, chorale, chorus, computers, dance, drama, ethnic, forensics, gay, honors, international, jazz band, literary magazine, musical theater, newspaper, opera, orchestra, pep band, photography, political, professional, radio and TV, religious, social, social service, student government, symphony, and yearbook. Popular campus events include the annual performance of Handel's Messiah (with 1000-voice choir), the Ethnic Arts Fair, and Parents Weekend.

Sports: There are 10 intercollegiate sports for men and 9 for women, and 47 intramural sports for men and 47 for women. Facilities include 5 hardwood basketball courts, an indoor swimming pool, 4 batting cages, a fitness center, a climbing wall, 3 soccer fields, a golf driving range, a dance studio, 5 downhill ski runs, a 4000-seat stadium and 3500-seat gym, 6 indoor tennis courts, 3 racquetball courts, an indoor 6-lane 200-meter track, an outdoor 8-lane polyurethane 400-meter track, and 9 outdoor tennis courts.

Disabled Students: 95% of the campus is accessible. Wheelchair ramps, elevators, special parking, specially equipped rest rooms, lowered drinking fountains, and lowered telephones are available.

Services: Counseling and information services are available, as is tutoring in every subject. There is a reader service for the blind, and remedial math, reading, and writing.

Campus Safety and Security: Measures include 24-hour foot and vehicle patrol, self-defense education, informal discussions, and pamphlets/posters/films. There are emergency telephones and lighted pathways/sidewalks.

Programs of Study: Luther confers the B.A. degree. Bachelor's degrees are awarded in BIOLOGICAL SCIENCE (biology/biological science), BUSINESS (accounting and management information systems), COMMUNICATIONS AND THE ARTS (art, communications, dance, dramatic arts, English, French, German, Greek, Latin, music, speech/debate/rhetoric, and theater management), COMPUTER AND PHYSICAL SCIENCE (chemistry, computer science, mathematics, and physics), EDUCATION (early childhood, elementary, foreign languages, music, science, secondary, and special), ENGINEERING AND ENVIRONMENTAL DESIGN (preengineering), HEALTH PROFESSIONS (cytotechnology, health, medical laboratory technology, nursing, predentistry, and premedicine), SOCIAL SCIENCE (African American studies, anthropology, biblical languages, economics, history, international relations, political science/government, prelaw, psychology, Scandinavian studies, social work, and sociology). Biology, music, and management are the strongest academically. Biology, management, and psychology are the largest.

Required: Students must complete 11 hours of interdisciplinary English and history, 9 hours of religion/philosophy, 6 to 9 of foreign language, 7 of natural science, 7 of social science, 3 each of fine arts, global studies, and quantitative/symbolic reasoning, and 2 of phys ed. The B.A. requires 128 semester hours with a GPA of at least 2.0 in the major. A senior project and writing course are required. Foreign language proficiency must be demonstrated.

Special: Internships in all disciplines, work-study programs, a Washington semester, study-abroad plans in numerous countries, pass/fail options, student-designed and dual majors, and 3-2 engineering degrees with Washington University in St. Louis and the University of Minnesota are available. There are 10 national honor societies, including Phi Beta Kappa, a freshman honors program, and 2 departmental honors program.

Faculty/Classroom: 58% of faculty are male; 42%, female. All teach undergraduates. The average class size in an introductory lecture is 30; in a laboratory, 13; and in a regular course, 21.

Admissions: 83% of the 2001-2002 applicants were accepted. The SAT I scores for the 2001-2002 freshman class were: Verbal--7% below 500, 31% between 500 and 599, 47% between 600 and 700, and 15% above 700; Math--10% below 500, 32% between 500 and 599, 47% between 600 and 700, and 11% above 700. The ACT scores were 10% below 21, 25% between 21 and 23, 26% between 24 and 26, 17% between 27 and 28, and 22% above 28. 59% of the current freshmen were in the top fifth of their class; 84% were in the top two fifths. There were 11 National Merit finalists and 7 semifinalists. 45 freshmen graduated first in their class.

Requirements: The SAT I or ACT is required, with a minimum composite SAT I score of 990. High school applicants should have 4 years of English, 3 each of math and social studies, and 2 of science. An essay is required, and an interview is recommended. The GED is accepted. Luther requires applicants to be in the upper 50% of their class. A GPA of 2.5 is required. AP and CLEP credits are accepted. Important factors in the admissions decision are advanced placement or honor courses, evidence of special talent, and extracurricular activities record. Applications are accepted on computer disk and on-line at the school's web site.

Procedure: Freshmen are admitted to all sessions. Entrance exams should be taken by the fall of the senior year. There are early admissions and deferred admissions plans. Applications should be filed by March 1 for fall entry, December 1 for winter entry, and January 1 for spring entry, along with a $25 fee. Notification is sent November 1.

Transfer: 70 transfer students enrolled in 2001-2002. Applicants must meet the same high school standards and the SAT I or ACT requirements as entering freshmen, with a minimum GPA of 2.5 in parallel college course work. 32 credits of 128 must be completed at Luther.

Visiting: There are regularly scheduled orientations for prospective students. There are guides for informal visits and visitors may sit in on classes and stay overnight. To schedule a visit, contact the Admissions Office *visit@luther.edu*.

Financial Aid: In 2001-2002, 98% of all freshmen and 95% of continuing students received some form of financial aid. 69% of freshmen and 66% of continuing students received need-based aid. The average freshman award was $16,274. Of that total, scholarships or need-based grants averaged $8466 ($21,100 maximum); loans averaged $3332 ($4625 maximum); work contracts averaged $1452 ($1700 maximum); and outside scholarships averaged $1114 ($14,010 maximum). 70% of undergraduates work part time. Average annual earnings from campus work are $1010. The average financial indebtedness of the 2001 graduate was $16,495. Luther is a member of CSS. The FAFSA, the college's own financial statement, and a family tax return are required. The fall application deadline is March 1.

International Students: There are 161 international students enrolled. The school actively recruits these students. They must score 550 on the written TOEFL or 213 on the electronic version and also take the SAT I or the ACT.

Computers: The mainframes are an HP 3000/957 and an HP 9000. Students have access to computers in several clusters around campus. About 300 computers and 16 terminals are connected to the campus network and to the Internet. All students may access the system 8 A.M. to midnight with provision for extending. There are no time limits and no fees.

Graduates: In 2001, 557 bachelor's degrees were awarded. The most popular majors were biology (16%), management (9%), and psychology (9%). In an average class, 63% graduate in 4 years, 71% in 5 years, and 72% in 6 years. 152 companies recruited on campus in 2000-2001. Of the 2000 graduating class, 22% were enrolled in graduate school within 6 months of graduation and 72% were employed.

Admissions Contact: Jon Lund, Vice President for Enrollment Management. A video is available. E-mail: *admissions@luther.edu*
Web: *www.luther.edu*

MAHARISHI UNIVERSITY OF MANAGEMENT E-4

Fairfield, IA 52557 (641) 472-1110
(800) 369-6480; Fax: (641) 472-1179

Full-time: 103 men, 94 women	**Faculty:** 69
Part-time: 4 men, 9 women	**Ph.D.s:** 67%
Graduate: 384 men, 140 women	**Student/Faculty:** 4 to 1
Year: semesters	**Tuition:** $24,030
Application Deadline: April 15	**Room & Board:** $5200
Freshman Class: n/av	
SAT I Verbal/Math: 585/573	**ACT:** 25 VERY COMPETITIVE

Maharishi University of Management, established in 1971, is a private institution offering undergraduate and graduate programs in a broad range of disciplines. The university provides Consciousness-Based education and incorporates the group practice of the Maharishi Transcendental Meditation technique into a traditional academic program. The 2 libraries contain 145,000 volumes, 59,900 microform items, and 13,276 audiovisual forms/CDs, and subscribe to 850 periodicals. Computerized library services include the card catalog, interlibrary loans, and database searching. Special learning facilities include a learning resource center, art gallery, radio station, psychophysiology, electronic engineering, visual technology, and physics labs, and a scanning electron microscope. The 94-acre campus is in a small town 114 miles southeast of Des Moines. Including residence halls, there are 94 buildings.

Student Life: 67% of undergraduates are from out of state, mostly the Middle Atlantic. Students are from 27 states, 21 foreign countries, and Canada. 50% are white; 36% foreign nationals. 25% are claim no religious affiliation. The average age of freshmen is 19; all undergraduates, 21. 24% do not continue beyond their first year; 57% remain to graduate.

Housing: 1000 students can be accommodated in college housing, which includes single-sex dormitories, on-campus apartments, and married-student housing. In addition, there are special-interest houses and privately owned, on-campus housing for students with families. On-campus housing is guaranteed for all 4 years. 79% of students live on campus; of those, 94% remain on campus on weekends. Alcohol is not permitted. All students may keep cars.

Activities: There are no fraternities or sororities. There are 21 groups on campus, including art, chess, chorale, dance, drama, ecology, entrepreneurial, ethnic, international, musical theater, newspaper, permaculture, photography, political, professional, radio and TV, religious, social, social service, student government, and yearbook. Popular campus events include sports festivals, seasonal celebrations, and International Cultural Exchange Festival.

Sports: There is 1 intercollegiate sport for women, and 15 intramural sports for men and 15 for women. Facilities include indoor tennis, basketball, and volleyball courts, a gym, a weight-training room, a field house, a swimming pool, a table tennis room, an outdoor fitness trail, cross-country ski trails, camping facilities, baseball batting and golf driving cages, a golf putting range, an indoor 4-lane jogging track, a dance studio, and a rock-climbing wall.

Disabled Students: All of the campus is accessible. Wheelchair ramps, special parking, specially equipped rest rooms, and lowered telephones are available.

Services: Counseling and information services are available, as is tutoring in every subject. There is remedial math, reading, and writing.

Campus Safety and Security: Measures include 24-hour foot and vehicle patrol, escort service, informal discussions, and emergency telephones. There are lighted pathways/sidewalks.

Programs of Study: Maharishi University of Management confers B.A., B.S., and B.F.A. degrees. Associate, master's, and doctoral degrees are also awarded. Bachelor's degrees are awarded in AGRICULTURE (environmental studies), BIOLOGICAL SCIENCE (biology/biological science), BUSINESS (management science), COMMUNICATIONS AND THE ARTS (dramatic arts, fine arts, and literature), COMPUTER AND PHYSICAL SCIENCE (chemistry, computer science, mathematics, and web services), EDUCATION (education), ENGINEERING AND ENVIRONMENTAL DESIGN (electrical/electronics engineering and electrical/electronics engineering technology), SOCIAL SCIENCE (psychology). Engineering, math, and computer science are the strongest academically. Fine arts and management are the largest.

Required: Students must complete 175 credit units, with a minimum of 60 credits in the major, and must also complete the Natural Law Seminar program of 40 credit units. All students must maintain a minimum GPA of 2.0 Additional requirements include health and fitness courses, the Science of Creative Intelligence course with its applied aspect, the Transcendental Meditation program, and courses in math and writing proficiency. The 44-week school year and block scheduling system allow students to take 1 course at a time.

Special: Opportunities are provided for internships, B.A.-B.S. degrees in biochemistry, biology, chemistry, computer science, and psychology, study abroad, and nondegree study. Systematic programs are offered in the Science of Creative Intelligence, by which students apply knowledge to practical professional values. There are several 1-month blocks a year during which students may study, for example, art in Italy, literature in Switzerland, or business in Japan. There is a freshman honors program.

Faculty/Classroom: 70% of faculty are male; 30%, female. 53% teach undergraduates, 16% do research, and 50% do both. The average class size in an introductory lecture is 31; in a laboratory, 6; and in a regular course, 11.

Admissions: The SAT I scores for the 2001-2002 freshman class were: Verbal--19% below 500, 23% between 500 and 599, 50% between 600 and 700, and 8% above 700; Math--26% below 500, 27% between 500 and 599, 35% between 600 and 700, and 12% above 700. There were 3 National Merit finalists.

Requirements: The SAT I or ACT is required. In addition, applicants must graduate from an accredited secondary school or have a GED. An essay and 2 personal recommendations are required. An interview is recommended. A GPA of 2.5 is required. AP and CLEP credits are accepted. Important factors in the admissions decision are personality/intangible qualities, recommendations by school officials, and leadership record. Applications are accepted on-line.

Procedure: Freshmen are admitted fall and spring. Entrance exams should be taken in the fall of the senior year or spring of the junior year. Applications should be filed by April 15 for fall entry and January 1 for winter entry. The fall 2001 application fee was $25. Notification is sent on a rolling basis.

Transfer: 20 transfer students enrolled in 2001-2002. Students must have a 2.5 GPA and acceptable recommendations and meet all standards set by the university. 75 credits of 175 must be completed at Maharishi University of Management.

Visiting: There are regularly scheduled orientations for prospective students, including campus tours, visits to classes, interviews, student panels, and informal dinners. There are guides for informal visits and visitors may sit in on classes and stay overnight. To schedule a visit, contact Julie Beaufort, Director of Guest Services at *jbeaufort@mum.edu*.

Financial Aid: In 2001-2002, 93% of all freshmen and 95% of continuing students received some form of financial aid. 89% of freshmen and 81% of continuing students received need-based aid. The average freshman award was $21,454. Of that total, scholarships or need-based grants averaged $12,804 ($15,960 maximum); loans averaged $4946 ($10,500 maximum); and work contracts averaged $1600 ($2400 maximum). 75% of undergraduates work part time. Average annual earnings from campus work are $1600. The average financial indebtedness of the 2001 graduate was $26,477. The FAFSA is required.

International Students: There are 75 international students enrolled. The school actively recruits these students. They must score 550 on the written TOEFL or 213 on the electronic version and also take the college's own test.

Computers: About 130 IBM and Mac PCs are available throughout the campus. All students may access the system daytime and evenings. There are no time limits and no fees. It is strongly recommended that all students have a personal computer.

Graduates: In 2001, 43 bachelor's degrees were awarded. The most popular majors were fine arts (37%), management (16%), and biological/life sciences (12%). In an average class, 28% graduate in 4 years, and 47% in 6 years. 10 companies recruited on campus in 2000-2001. Of the 2000 graduating class, 22% were enrolled in graduate school within 6 months of graduation and 75% were employed.

Admissions Contact: Brad Mylett, Director of Admissions. A video is available. E-mail: *admissions@mum.edu* Web: *www.mum.edu*

MERCY COLLEGE OF HEALTH SCIENCES C-8

Des Moines, IA 50309-1239 (515) 643-6715
(800) 637-2994; Fax: (515) 643-6698

Full-time: 25 men, 335 women	**Faculty:** n/av
Part-time: none	**Ph.D.s:** n/av
Graduate: none	**Student/Faculty:** n/av
Year: semesters, summer session	**Tuition:** $8900
Application Deadline: see profile	**Room & Board:** n/app
Freshman Class: n/av	
SAT I or ACT: n/av	SPECIAL

Mercy College of Health Sciences was founded in 1995 and is affiliated with the Religious Sister of Mercy (RSM), a religious order of Roman Catholic women. Figures in the above capsule are approximate. There are 4 undergraduate schools. The 2 libraries contain 5070 volumes and 1066 audiovisual forms/CDs, and subscribe to 108 periodicals. Computerized library services include the card catalog, interlibrary loans, and database searching. Special learning facilities include clinical labs. The 4-acre campus is in an urban area in Des Moines. There are 3 buildings.

Student Life: 95% of undergraduates are from Iowa. Others are from 3 states and 2 foreign countries. The average age of freshmen is 28; all undergraduates, 28.

Housing: There are no residence halls. All students commute. Alcohol is not permitted. All students may keep cars.

Activities: There are no fraternities or sororities. There are 2 groups on campus, including professional and student government. Popular campus events include Mercy Day.
Sports: There is no sports program at Mercy College of Health Sciences.
Disabled Students: All of the campus is accessible. Wheelchair ramps, elevators, special parking, specially equipped rest rooms, and lowered drinking fountains are available.
Services: Counseling and information services are available, as is tutoring in most subjects. There is remedial math.
Campus Safety and Security: Measures include 24-hour foot and vehicle patrol, escort service, shuttle buses, and informal discussions. There are pamphlets/posters/films and lighted pathways/sidewalks.
Programs of Study: Mercy College of Health Sciences confers the B.S.N. degree. Associate degrees are also awarded. Bachelor's degrees are awarded in HEALTH PROFESSIONS (nursing). Radiologic Technology is the strongest academically. Nursing is the largest.
Required: There is a community service requirement, and a caring course is also required.
Special: Internships are available. There is 1 national honor society.
Faculty/Classroom: All teach undergraduates. The average class size in an introductory lecture is 25.
Procedure: Check with the school for current application deadlines and fee.
Financial Aid: The FAFSA is required. Check with school for deadlines.
Computers: There are no time limits and no fees.
Graduates: In a recent year, 8 bachelor's degrees were awarded. The most popular majors were nursing (65%), radiologic technology (15%), and surgical technology (12%).
Admissions Contact: Admissions officer.
E-mail: *admissions@mchs.edu* Web: *www.mchs.edu*

MORNINGSIDE COLLEGE B-2
Sioux City, IA 51106 (712) 274-5111
(800) 831-0806; Fax: (712) 274-5101

Full-time: 279 men, 465 women	**Faculty:** 65; IIB, --$
Part-time: 33 men, 60 women	**Ph.D.s:** 85%
Graduate: 22 men, 124 women	**Student/Faculty:** 11 to 1
Year: semesters, summer session	**Tuition:** $14,210
Application Deadline: open	**Room & Board:** $4914

Freshman Class: 757 applied, 689 accepted, 182 enrolled
ACT: 22 **COMPETITIVE**

Morningside College, founded in 1894, is a private college affiliated with the United Methodist Church. Its curriculum includes the liberal arts and preprofessional and professional programs of study. In addition to regional accreditation, Morningside has baccalaureate program accreditation with NASM, NCATE, and NLN. The library contains 113,242 volumes, 252,285 microform items, and 5349 audiovisual forms/CDs, and subscribes to 604 periodicals. Computerized library services include the card catalog, interlibrary loans, and database searching. Special learning facilities include a learning resource center, art gallery, radio station, TV station, and observatory. The 41-acre campus is in a suburban area 100 miles north of Omaha on Interstate 29, at the convergence of the states of South Dakota, Nebraska, and Iowa. Including residence halls, there are 17 buildings.
Student Life: 76% of undergraduates are from Iowa. Others are from 21 states and 7 foreign countries. 95% are from public schools. 88% are white. 51% are Protestant; 25% claim no religious affiliation; 24% Catholic. The average age of freshmen is 19; all undergraduates, 21. 37% do not continue beyond their first year.
Housing: 655 students can be accommodated in college housing, which includes coed dormitories and on-campus apartments. In addition, there are freshman halls. On-campus housing is guaranteed for all 4 years. 64% of students live on campus; of those, 60% remain on campus on weekends. All students may keep cars.
Activities: 16% of men belong to 2 national fraternities; 8% of women belong to 2 national sororities. There are 38 groups on campus, including art, band, cheerleading, choir, chorale, chorus, computers, dance, drama, ethnic, honors, international, jazz band, literary magazine, newspaper, orchestra, photography, political, professional, radio and TV, religious, social, student government, and yearbook. Popular campus events include Friday is Writing Day, Academic and Cultural Arts Series, and Christmas at Morningside.
Sports: There are 6 intercollegiate sports for men and 6 for women, and 32 intramural sports for men and 28 for women. Facilities include an 8000-seat stadium, a football field, a campus recreation center with basketball, volleyball, badminton, tennis, and racquetball/handball courts, an elevated track, a weight room, and a 6-lane, 25-meter swimming pool.
Disabled Students: 80% of the campus is accessible. Wheelchair ramps, elevators, special parking, specially equipped rest rooms, and special class scheduling are available.
Services: Counseling and information services are available, as is tutoring in most subjects. There is a reader service for the blind, and remedial math, reading, and writing.
Campus Safety and Security: Measures include self-defense education, escort service, informal discussions, and pamphlets/posters/films. There are emergency telephones and lighted pathways/sidewalks. The college is in compliance with the Crime Awareness and Campus Security Act of 1990.
Programs of Study: Morningside confers B.A., B.S., B.Mus., B.Mus.Ed., and B.S.N. degrees. Master's degrees are also awarded. Bachelor's degrees are awarded in BIOLOGICAL SCIENCE (biology/biological science), BUSINESS (accounting and business administration and management), COMMUNICATIONS AND THE ARTS (art, communications, dramatic arts, English, graphic design, music, photography, and Spanish), COMPUTER AND PHYSICAL SCIENCE (chemistry, computer science, mathematics, and physics), EDUCATION (art, business, elementary, English, mathematics, music, science, social studies, and special), ENGINEERING AND ENVIRONMENTAL DESIGN (engineering), HEALTH PROFESSIONS (nursing), SOCIAL SCIENCE (history, philosophy, political science/government, psychology, and religion). Business administration, education, and biology are the largest.
Required: The total number of credit hours required for graduation is 124, with 44 hours of core curriculum in liberal arts and 30 hours minimum in the major. Students must have a minimum GPA of 2.0 to graduate.
Special: There are co-op programs in engineering and medical technology. Internships are available in all departments. Study abroad in 5 countries, a Washington semester, work-study programs, both on campus and with 20 nonprofit agencies, a dual major in philosophy/religious studies, and student-designed majors are available. Morningside has articulation agreements with engineering schools at Iowa State University, Washington University in St. Louis, and South Dakota State University. There are 15 national honor societies and a freshman honors program. The honors program is interdepartmental.
Faculty/Classroom: 60% of faculty are male; 40%, female. All teach undergraduates, 20% do research, and 20% do both. No introductory courses are taught by graduate students. The average class size in an introductory lecture is 24; in a laboratory, 13; and in a regular course, 16.
Admissions: 91% of the 2001-2002 applicants were accepted. The ACT scores for the 2001-2002 freshman class were: 44% below 21, 25% between 21 and 23, 18% between 24 and 26, 9% between 27 and 28, and 4% above 28. 30% of the current freshmen were in the top fifth of their class; 61% were in the top two fifths. 4 freshmen graduated first in their class.
Requirements: The ACT is required. In addition, applicants must also be graduates of an accredited secondary school. The GED is accepted. A portfolio is required for all studio art majors and an audition for performing music majors. Applicants graduating from high school 5 years or more prior to entering college are exempted from submitting the ACT scores. Those entering from a home-schooled environment must submit a portfolio of writing and 2 letters of recommendation from teachers or tutors. Morningside requires applicants to be in the upper 50% of their class. A GPA of 2.5 is required. AP and CLEP credits are accepted. Important factors in the admissions decision are recommendations by school officials, evidence of special talent, and advanced placement or honor courses. Applications are accepted on-line.
Procedure: Freshmen are admitted to all sessions. Entrance exams should be taken in the junior year. Application deadlines are open. The application fee is $25. Notification is sent on a rolling basis.
Transfer: 62 transfer students enrolled in 2001-2002. Transfer applicants must take the ACT and have an interview. They must have 24 semester hours with a 2.0 or above cumulative average. They must present official transcripts of previous collegiate records. 30 credits of 124 must be completed at Morningside.
Visiting: There are regularly scheduled orientations for prospective students, consisting of a campus tour, appointments with faculty and financial aid, and an interview with an admissions counselor. There are guides for informal visits and visitors may sit in on classes and stay overnight. To schedule a visit, contact the Office of Admissions at (800) 831-0806, ext. 5111.
Financial Aid: In 2001-2002, all freshmen and 99% of continuing students received some form of financial aid. 81% of freshmen and 80% of continuing students received need-based aid. The average freshman award was $16,047. Of that total, scholarships or need-based grants averaged $9873 ($22,004 maximum); loans averaged $3169 ($8125 maximum); and work contracts averaged $1478 ($2000 maximum). All undergraduates work part time. Average annual earnings from campus work are $1037. The average financial indebtedness of the 2001 graduate was $17,046. The FAFSA is required. The fall application deadline is March 1.
International Students: There are 19 international students enrolled. They must score 425 on the written TOEFL or 113 on the electronic version.
Computers: The mainframes is an IBM RISC System 6000, Model 39H. Morningside's computing envioronment includes 4 public labs with

a total of 70 networked workstations; 7 departmental labs with a total of 50 workstations; a networked PC on every resident student's desk; several Window NT and Linus file/application servers; an IBM RS/6000 Model 570 server for e-mail and the library OPAC; an IBM RS/6000 Model 320 for statistical analysis; an IBM RS/6000 Model 39H running the AIMS institutional administration software; and a proxy server/firewall with a T1 connection to the Internet. All students may access the system. Lab workstations may be used 8 A.M. to 11 P.M. Monday through Friday and 2 p.m to 11 P.M. Saturday and Sunday; residence hall workstations may be used 24 hours a day, 7 days a week. There are no time limits and no fees.

Graduates: In 2001, 215 bachelor's degrees were awarded. The most popular majors were business (25%), education (11%), and nursing (10%). In an average class, 1% graduate in 3 years, 38% in 4 years, 49% in 5 years, and 50% in 6 years. 23 companies recruited on campus in 2000-2001. Of the 2000 graduating class, 13% were enrolled in graduate school within 6 months of graduation and 81% were employed.

Admissions Contact: Terri Curry, Vice President of Student Services. E-mail: *mscadm@morningside.edu* Web: *http://www.morningside.edu*

MOUNT MERCY COLLEGE

Cedar Rapids, IA 52402 — E-3

(319) 368-6460

(800) 248-4504; Fax: (319) 363-5270

Full-time: 262 men, 657 women	**Faculty:** 64; IIB, --$
Part-time: 175 men, 293 women	**Ph.D.s:** 66%
Graduate: none	**Student/Faculty:** 14 to 1
Year: 4-1-4, summer session	**Tuition:** $14,560
Application Deadline: December 30	**Room & Board:** $4830
Freshman Class: 448 applied, 386 accepted, 185 enrolled	
ACT: 23	**VERY COMPETITIVE**

Mount Mercy College, founded in 1928, is a private liberal arts institution affiliated with the Roman Catholic Church. In addition to regional accreditation, Mount Mercy has baccalaureate program accreditation with CSWE and NLN. The library contains 116,000 volumes, 1800 microform items, and 4700 audiovisual forms/CDs, and subscribes to 900 periodicals. Computerized library services include the card catalog, interlibrary loans, and database searching. Special learning facilities include a learning resource center, art gallery, and video media room. The 36-acre campus is in an urban area 230 miles west of Chicago. Including residence halls, there are 9 buildings.

Student Life: 93% of undergraduates are from Iowa. Others are from 14 states, 7 foreign countries, and Canada. 86% are from public schools. 96% are white. 41% are Catholic; 38% Protestant. The average age of freshmen is 18; all undergraduates, 24. 14% do not continue beyond their first year.

Housing: 510 students can be accommodated in college housing, which includes coed dormitories and on-campus apartments. In addition, there is returning adult student housing. On-campus housing is guaranteed for all 4 years. 54% of students commute. All students may keep cars.

Activities: There are no fraternities or sororities. There are 30 groups on campus, including academic, art, band, cheerleading, choir, chorale, chorus, computers, drama, drill team, film, honors, international, literary magazine, musical theater, newspaper, pep band, political, professional, religious, social, social service, and student government. Popular campus events include Hillfest, Spring Fling, and family weekend.

Sports: There are 6 intercollegiate sports for men and 7 for women, and 10 intramural sports for men and 10 for women. Facilities include a center, a 2000-seat stadium, an auditorium-gym, an indoor hitting facility, a weight room, an aerobics area, karate facilities, and 2 racquetball courts.

Disabled Students: 95% of the campus is accessible. Wheelchair ramps, elevators, special parking, specially equipped rest rooms, and lowered drinking fountains are available.

Services: Counseling and information services are available, as is tutoring in most subjects, including all communication skills. There is a reader service for the blind, and remedial math, reading, and writing.

Campus Safety and Security: Measures include self-defense education, escort service, informal discussions, and pamphlets/posters/films. There are emergency telephones, lighted pathways/sidewalks, 24-hour safety presence and evening and weekend foot patrol, cameras at residence hall entrances, and a patrol parking area.

Programs of Study: Mount Mercy confers B.A., B.S., B.A.A., B.A.S., and B.B.A. degrees. Bachelor's degrees are awarded in BIOLOGICAL SCIENCE (biology/biological science), BUSINESS (accounting, business administration and management, and marketing/retailing/merchandising), COMMUNICATIONS AND THE ARTS (art, dramatic arts, English, music, public relations, speech/debate/rhetoric, and visual and performing arts), COMPUTER AND PHYSICAL SCIENCE (computer science, information sciences and systems, and mathematics), EDUCATION (elementary and music), HEALTH PROFESSIONS (health care administration, medical laboratory technology, and nursing), SOCIAL SCIENCE (criminal justice, history, international studies, political science/government, psychology, religion, social work, sociology, and urban studies). Nursing, social work, and accounting are the strongest academically. Administrative management, nursing, and education are the largest.

Required: To graduate, students must complete 123 semester hours, with at least 30 hours in the major, and maintain at least a 2.0 GPA. General education requirements include a total of 12 courses in philosophy, religious studies, English, speech, arts, social and natural sciences, history, and multicultural studies.

Special: Mount Mercy offers internships in many majors, work-study programs on campus, cross-registration with Coe College, a general studies degree, an accelerated program in business, and student-designed, interdisciplinary majors. Credit for prior experiential learning may be granted, and pass/fail options are possible. There are 2 national honor societies and a freshman honors program.

Faculty/Classroom: 42% of faculty are male; 58%, female. All teach undergraduates. The average class size in an introductory lecture is 25; in a laboratory, 14; and in a regular course, 25.

Admissions: 86% of the 2001-2002 applicants were accepted. The ACT scores for the 2001-2002 freshman class were: 24% below 21, 24% between 21 and 23, 28% between 24 and 26, 24% between 27 and 28, and 4% above 28. 7 freshmen graduated first in their class.

Requirements: The SAT I or ACT is required, with a recommended minimum score of 400 on each section of the SAT I or a composite score of 19 on the ACT. Other admissions requirements include graduation from an accredited secondary school, with 16 Carnegie units, including 4 of English, 3 of social studies, and 2 each of math, history, and foreign language. A recommendation from a high school teacher or counselor and an essay or personal statement are also required. Mount Mercy requires applicants to be in the upper 50% of their class. A GPA of 2.5 is required. AP and CLEP credits are accepted. Important factors in the admissions decision are recommendations by school officials, extracurricular activities record, and advanced placement or honor courses. Applications are accepted on-line at the school's web site.

Procedure: Freshmen are admitted to all sessions. Entrance exams should be taken in the junior year or the fall of the senior year. There is a deferred admissions plan. Applications should be filed by December 30 for winter entry. Notification is sent on a rolling basis. The fall 2001 application fee was $20.

Transfer: 192 transfer students enrolled in a recent year. Applicants must have at least a 2.0 GPA. Associate degree holders must submit transcripts from all previous colleges attended; students with fewer credits earned must also submit a high school transcript. An interview is recommended. 30 credits of 123 must be completed at Mount Mercy.

Visiting: There are regularly scheduled orientations for prospective students, consisting of a presidential welcome, campus tour, student panel, faculty academic fair, presentations on college selection and admission requirements, and student evaluation. There are guides for informal visits and visitors may sit in on classes and stay overnight. To schedule a visit, contact the Admissions Office at (319) 363-8213, ext. 6460 or *admission@mtmercy.edu*

Financial Aid: In 2001-2002, all freshmen and 79% of continuing students received some form of financial aid. 82% of freshmen and 65% of continuing students received need-based aid. The average freshman award was $15,287. Of that total, scholarships or need-based grants averaged $7335 ($14,560 maximum); loans averaged $2611 ($4625 maximum); work contracts averaged $1402 ($1500 maximum); and in state grants averaged $4000 (maximum). 29% of undergraduates work part time. Average annual earnings from campus work are $1000. The average financial indebtedness of the 2001 graduate was $16,152. The FAFSA is required. The fall application deadline is March 1.

International Students: 13 international students enrolled in a recent year.They must score 500 on the written TOEFL.

Computers: The mainframe is a Sun 4/280. PCs and Sun workstations are networked in the computer center with access to the Internet. The computer ratio is 1 to 13 students, and there are 24-hour computer labs in residence halls. All students may access the system 24 hours a day. There are no time limits and no fees.

Graduates: In 2001, 286 bachelor's degrees were awarded. The most popular majors were business administrative management (15%), nursing (14%), and elementary education/accounting (11%). In an average class, 1% graduate in 3 years, 89% in 4 years, 98% in 5 years, and 99% in 6 years. 60 companies recruited on campus in 2000-2001. Of the 2000 graduating class, 8% were enrolled in graduate school within 6 months of graduation and 90% were employed.

Admissions Contact: Margaret M. Jackson, Interim Dean of Admission. E-mail: *admission@.mtmercy.edu* Web: *www.mtmercy.edu*

MOUNT SAINT CLARE COLLEGE F-3

Clinton, IA 52733-2967 (563) 243-6102
(800) 242-4153; Fax: (563) 242-2003

Full-time: 184 men, 217 women **Faculty:** 23
Part-time: 29 men, 49 women **Ph.D.s:** 39%
Graduate: 4 men, 36 women **Student/Faculty:** 17 to 1
Year: semesters, summer session **Tuition:** $14,050
Application Deadline: August 15 **Room & Board:** $5000
Freshman Class: n/av
SAT I: n/av **ACT:** required
LESS COMPETITIVE

Mount St. Clare College is a Franciscan, liberal arts college founded in 1918 and sponsored by the Sisters of St. Francis. The library contains 80,759 volumes, 73,405 microform items, and 2458 audiovisual forms/CDs, and subscribes to 645 periodicals. Computerized library services include the card catalog, interlibrary loans, and database searching. Special learning facilities include a learning resource center, art gallery, and a living lab adjacent to the campus. The 25-acre campus is in a small town 135 miles west of Chicago. Including residence halls, there are 6 buildings.

Student Life: 59% of undergraduates are from Iowa. Others are from 12 states, 10 foreign countries, and Canada. 70% are from public schools. 86% are white. 44% claim no religious affiliation; 31% Catholic; 24% Protestant. The average age of freshmen is 19; all undergraduates, 22. 40% do not continue beyond their first year; 59% remain to graduate.

Housing: 233 students can be accommodated in college housing, which includes single-sex and coed dormitories. On-campus housing is guaranteed for all 4 years. 64% of students commute. All students may keep cars.

Activities: There are no fraternities or sororities. There are 20 groups on campus, including band, cheerleading, choir, computers, drama, ethnic, gay, honors, international, musical theater, newspaper, pep band, professional, religious, SI SEA (Iowa State Education Association), social, social service, and student government. Popular campus events include Family Weekend, Matriculation Ceremony, and Earth Day.

Sports: There are 7 intercollegiate sports for men and 7 for women, and 6 intramural sports for men and 6 for women. Facilities include an arena with 2 regulation-size basketball courts, a fitness center, a 4-lane perimeter track, 2 locker rooms plus 2 rooms and 1 training room. St. Francis gym is located on campus. There is a soccer field and an indoor swimming pool.

Disabled Students: 95% of the campus is accessible. Wheelchair ramps, elevators, special parking, specially equipped rest rooms, lowered drinking fountains, and special doors for the disabled are available.

Services: Counseling and information services are available, as is tutoring in most subjects. There is a reader service for the blind, remedial math, reading, and writing, voice-activated computer software, exam proctoring, and prep courses for the GRE and MCAT.

Campus Safety and Security: Measures include 24-hour foot and vehicle patrol, self-defense education, escort service, and informal discussions. There are pamphlets/posters/films, emergency telephones, lighted pathways/sidewalks, and a 24-hour campus security department.

Programs of Study: MSC confers B.A., B.S., B.A.S., and B.G.S degrees. Associate degrees are also awarded. Bachelor's degrees are awarded in BIOLOGICAL SCIENCE (biology/biological science), BUSINESS (accounting and business administration and management), COMMUNICATIONS AND THE ARTS (communications, English, and visual and performing arts), COMPUTER AND PHYSICAL SCIENCE (information sciences and systems), EDUCATION (business, elementary, and science), HEALTH PROFESSIONS (cytotechnology), SOCIAL SCIENCE (criminal justice, interdisciplinary studies, liberal arts/general studies, religion, and social science). Accounting, business administration, and elementary education are the strongest academically. Liberal arts, elementary education, and business administration are the largest.

Required: Students must complete 122 semester hours, including 34 semester hours of general education requirements, plus 12 hours of competencies (computer/writing/math), and 30 in a major, with a minimum 2.0 GPA. A final exam, report, or project is required in every course and must be given at a time designated by the Division of Records.

Special: Special academic programs include a co-op program in nursing with Clarke College, internships, study abroad in Italy, a dual major in accounting and business, and a general studies program. There are 2 national honor societies, and 1 departmental honors program.

Faculty/Classroom: 53% of faculty are male; 47%, female. All teach undergraduates. No introductory courses are taught by graduate students. The average class size in an introductory lecture is 32; in a laboratory, 15; and in a regular course, 20.

Admissions: 18% of the current freshmen were in the top fifth of their class; 35% were in the top two fifths. 2 freshmen graduated first in their class.

Requirements: The ACT is required. The SAT I is accepted. Applicants must be graduates of an accredited secondary school or have earned a GED and must meet 2 of the following requirements: a GPA of 2.0 in college preparatory or regular high school courses, rank in the upper half of the graduating class, and a minimum ACT composite score of 18 or SAT I composite score of 750. MSC requires applicants to be in the upper 50% of their class. A GPA of 2.0 is required. AP and CLEP credits are accepted. Applications are accepted on-line at the school's web site.

Procedure: Freshmen are admitted to all sessions. Entrance exams should be taken before enrolling. There are early admissions and deferred admissions plans. Applications should be filed by August 15 for fall entry, January 10 for spring entry, and June 1 for summer entry, along with a $20 fee. Notification is sent on a rolling basis.

Transfer: 88 transfer students enrolled in a recent year. Applicants may have 64 semester hours of 100-level or higher courses from a 2-year school, and up to 90 semester hours maximum. 30 credits of 122 must be completed at MSC.

Visiting: There are regularly scheduled orientations for prospective students, including 2-day orientation sessions held during the summer for students and parents. There are guides for informal visits and visitors may sit in on classes and stay overnight. To schedule a visit, contact the Admissions Office at (563) 242-4023.

Financial Aid: In 2001-2002, 93% of all freshmen and 95% of continuing students received some form of financial aid. 87% of freshmen and 82% of continuing students received need-based aid. The average freshman award was $11,112. Of that total, scholarships or need-based grants averaged $8882 ($12,580 maximum); and work contracts averaged $1200 ($1650 maximum). 36% of undergraduates work part time. Average annual earnings from campus work are $1106. The average financial indebtedness of the 2001 graduate was $15,223. MSC is a member of CSS. The FAFSA and parents' and student's income tax form are required. The fall application deadline is June 1.

International Students: There are 16 international students enrolled. The school actively recruits these students. They must score 420 on the written TOEFL.

Computers: MSC provides 56 PCs in 4 locations for student use. All students may access the system during scheduled times daily. There are no time limits. The fee is $20 per semester.

Graduates: In 2001, 124 bachelor's degrees were awarded. The most popular majors were elementary education (26%), business administration (19%), and social science (17%). In an average class, 18% graduate in 4 years, 16% in 5 years, and 37% in 6 years. 26 companies recruited on campus in 2000-2001. Of the 2000 graduating class, 87% were employed within 6 months of graduation.

Admissions Contact: Waunita M. Sullivan, Director of Enrollment. A video is available. E-mail: *admissns@clare.edu*
Web: *http://www.clare.edu*

NORTHWESTERN COLLEGE OF IOWA B-2

Orange City, IA 51041 (712) 707-7130
(800) 747-4757; Fax: (712) 707-7164

Full-time: 467 men, 776 women **Faculty:** 70; IIB, --$
Part-time: 19 men, 32 women **Ph.D.s:** 90%
Graduate: none **Student/Faculty:** 18 to 1
Year: semesters, summer session **Tuition:** $13,750
Application Deadline: open **Room & Board:** $3880
Freshman Class: 1125 applied, 1020 accepted, 374 enrolled
ACT: 24 **COMPETITIVE+**

Northwestern College, founded in 1882, is affiliated with the Reformed Church in America and offers liberal arts and teacher education programs. In addition to regional accreditation, Northwestern has baccalaureate program accreditation with CSWE and NCATE. The library contains 108,500 volumes, 36,470 microform items, and 5385 audiovisual forms/CDs, and subscribes to 563 periodicals. Computerized library services include the card catalog, interlibrary loans, and database searching. Special learning facilities include a learning resource center, art gallery, radio station, and TV station. The 55-acre campus is in a small town 40 miles northeast of Sioux City, and 75 miles southeast of Sioux Falls. Including residence halls, there are 25 buildings.

Student Life: 57% of undergraduates are from Iowa. Others are from 27 states and 14 foreign countries. 88% are from public schools. 96% are white. Most are Protestant. The average age of freshmen is 18; all undergraduates, 20. 23% do not continue beyond their first year.

Housing: 1025 students can be accommodated in college housing, which includes single-sex dormitories, on-campus apartments, and married-student housing. On-campus housing is guaranteed for all 4 years. 81% of students live on campus; of those, 60% remain on campus on weekends. Alcohol is not permitted. All students may keep cars.

Activities: There are no fraternities or sororities. There are 32 groups on campus, including art, band, cheerleading, choir, chorus, drama, drill team, film, honors, international, jazz band, literary magazine, musical theater, newspaper, orchestra, pep band, photography, political, professional, radio and TV, religious, social, social service, student government, symphony, and yearbook. Popular campus events include Winter Carnival, Spring Fest, and a Model Arab League.

Sports: There are 9 intercollegiate sports for men and 8 for women, and 11 intramural sports for men and 11 for women. Facilities include an athletic field, a 3000-seat stadium, a 2200-seat arena, a 176-meter indoor track, 4 handball/racquetball courts, 4 basketball/volleyball courts, archery, gymnastics rooms, and an outdoor track.

Disabled Students: 90% of the campus is accessible. Wheelchair ramps, elevators, special parking, specially equipped rest rooms, and lowered drinking fountains are available.

Services: Counseling and information services are available, as is tutoring in most subjects. There is remedial math, reading, and writing.

Campus Safety and Security: Measures include informal discussions, pamphlets/posters/films, and lighted pathways/sidewalks.

Programs of Study: Northwestern confers B.A. and B.S.W. degrees. Associate degrees are also awarded. Bachelor's degrees are awarded in AGRICULTURE (agricultural business management), BIOLOGICAL SCIENCE (biology/biological science), BUSINESS (accounting, business administration and management, and business economics), COMMUNICATIONS AND THE ARTS (communications, dramatic arts, English, fine arts, French, music, and Spanish), COMPUTER AND PHYSICAL SCIENCE (actuarial science, chemistry, computer science, and mathematics), EDUCATION (art, business, early childhood, elementary, foreign languages, middle school, music, physical, science, secondary, and special), HEALTH PROFESSIONS (medical laboratory technology, predentistry, and premedicine), SOCIAL SCIENCE (criminal justice, economics, history, philosophy, physical fitness/movement, political science/government, prelaw, psychology, religion, religious music, social work, and sociology). Biology, education, and religion are the strongest academically. Business and education are the largest.

Required: All students are required to take 45-61 credits in the core curriculum, including courses in Bible, language, history, math, literature, writing, philosophy, social and natural sciences, fine arts, and phys ed. Students must maintain a 2.0 GPA for 124 total credits, with 36-42 in the major, and pass both writing and math competency levels.

Special: Northwestern offers co-op programs in nursing and engineering, numerous internships, a Washington semester, student-designed majors, and study abroad in 15 countries, including Spain, France, and the Netherlands. There is a 3-2 engineering degree with Washington University at St. Louis, and a 2-2 nursing program with Trinity College or Briar Cliff College. There are 2 national honor societies, a freshman honors program, and 30 departmental honors programs.

Faculty/Classroom: 65% of faculty are male; 35%, female. All teach undergraduates, 69% do research, and 69% do both. The average class size in an introductory lecture is 30 and in a laboratory, 20.

Admissions: 91% of the 2001-2002 applicants were accepted. The ACT scores for the 2001-2002 freshman class were: 21% below 21, 21% between 21 and 23, 28% between 24 and 26, 14% between 27 and 28, and 16% above 28. 50% of the current freshmen were in the top fifth of their class; 72% were in the top two fifths. There were 6 National Merit semifinalists. 35 freshmen graduated first in their class.

Requirements: The SAT I or ACT is required. In addition, applicants with a minimum ACT composite of 19, in the top half of their high school class, and with a 2.4 GPA are generally accepted. Applicants should be graduates of an accredited secondary school. The suggested distribution of high school courses is 4 years of English, 3 years each of math and social studies, and 2 of natural science. An interview is recommended. The GED is accepted. Northwestern requires applicants to be in the upper 75% of their class. A GPA of 2.0 is required. AP and CLEP credits are accepted. Important factors in the admissions decision are personality/intangible qualities, leadership record, and evidence of special talent. Applications are accepted on computer disk and on-line via the school's home page and Apply.

Procedure: Freshmen are admitted to all sessions. Entrance exams should be taken in the spring of the junior year. Application deadlines are open. Notification is sent on a rolling basis beginning November 1. The fall 2001 application fee was $25.

Transfer: 53 transfer students enrolled in 2001-2002. Transfer applicants must submit a transcript and letter of recommendation. A minimum college GPA of 2.0 is required. 30 credits of 124 must be completed at Northwestern.

Visiting: There are regularly scheduled orientations for prospective students. There are guides for informal visits and visitors may sit in on classes and stay overnight. To schedule a visit, contact Harold Hoftyzer at the Admissions Office at (712) 707-7142 or (800) 747-4757 or *haroldh@nwciowa.edu*.

Financial Aid: In 2001-2002, 99% of all students received some form of financial aid. 91% of freshmen and 92% of continuing students received need-based aid. The average freshman award was $10,500. Of that total, scholarships or need-based grants averaged $4775 ($16,000 maximum); loans averaged $4200 ($5125 maximum); and work contracts averaged $1050 ($1800 maximum). 82% of undergraduates work part time. Average annual earnings from campus work are $1050. The average financial indebtedness of the 2001 graduate was $16,500. Northwestern is a member of CSS. The FAFSA and the college's own financial statement are required. The fall application deadline is April 1.

International Students: There are 34 international students enrolled. The school actively recruits these students. They must score 550 on the written TOEFL.

Computers: The mainframes are an HP9000 Novell Network and a Windows NT server. There are 160 terminals available in residence halls, the learning resource center, and the education and business facilities. All student rooms are wired for PC connection to the network system. All students have access to Internet and World Wide Web. All students may access the system 24 hours a day in residence halls; 7 A.M. to 12 P.M. in academic buildings. There are no time limits and no fees.

Graduates: In 2001, 229 bachelor's degrees were awarded. The most popular majors were business administration (32%), elementary education (14%), and biology (10%). In an average class, 1% graduate in 3 years, 45% in 4 years, 54% in 5 years, and 54% in 6 years. 20 companies recruited on campus in 2000-2001. Of the 2000 graduating class, 12% were enrolled in graduate school within 6 months of graduation and 85% were employed.

Admissions Contact: Ronald K. De Jong, Dean of Admissions. A video is available. E-mail: *rondj@nwciowa.edu*
Web: *admissions@nwciowa.edu*

SAINT AMBROSE UNIVERSITY — E-3

Davenport, IA 52803 — (563) 333-6311
(800) 383-2627; Fax: (563) 333-6297

Full-time: 743 men, 1012 women	**Faculty:** 151; IIB, -$
Part-time: 185 men, 331 women	**Ph.D.s:** 67%
Graduate: 437 men, 583 women	**Student/Faculty:** 12 to 1
Year: 4-1-4, summer session	**Tuition:** $14,654
Application Deadline: open	**Room & Board:** $5340
Freshman Class: 1100 applied, 949 accepted, 414 enrolled	
ACT: 21	**COMPETITIVE**

St. Ambrose University, founded in 1882 in affiliation with the Roman Catholic Church, offers degree programs through the colleges of arts and sciences, business, and human services. There also is a college-level seminary. There are 3 undergraduate and 16 graduate schools. In addition to regional accreditation, St. Ambrose has baccalaureate program accreditation with ABET, ACBSP, ACOTE, AOTA, APTE/APTA, and CSWE. The library contains 95,357 volumes, 6441 microform items, and 2659 audiovisual forms/CDs, and subscribes to 15,900 periodicals. Computerized library services include the card catalog, interlibrary loans, and database searching. Special learning facilities include a learning resource center, art gallery, radio station, TV station, and observatory. The 10-acre campus is in an urban area 180 miles west of Chicago. Including residence halls, there are 21 buildings.

Student Life: 62% of undergraduates are from Iowa. Others are from 22 states, 13 foreign countries, and Canada. 60% are from public schools. 91% are white. 65% are Catholic; 35% Protestant. The average age of freshmen is 18; all undergraduates, 25. 20% do not continue beyond their first year.

Housing: 1089 students can be accommodated in college housing, which includes single-sex and coed dormitories and on-campus apartments. In addition, there are townhouse residences for upper-division students. On-campus housing is guaranteed for all 4 years. 53% of students commute. All students may keep cars.

Activities: There are no fraternities or sororities. There are 24 groups on campus, including art, band, cheerleading, choir, chorale, dance, debate, drama, ethnic, honors, international, jazz band, literary magazine, newspaper, orchestra, pep band, photography, political, professional, radio and TV, religious, social, social service, student government, and symphony. Popular campus events include Multicultural Weeks, Parents Weekend, and Brother/Sister Weekend.

Sports: There are 9 intercollegiate sports for men and 9 for women, and 10 intramural sports for men and 10 for women. Facilities include tennis, handball/racquetball, and volleyball courts, a swimming pool, a golf room, an archery range, a gym, a weight-lifting room, and a running track.

Disabled Students: 95% of the campus is accessible. Wheelchair ramps, elevators, special parking, specially equipped rest rooms, special class scheduling, and lowered drinking fountains are available.

Services: Counseling and information services are available, as is tutoring in most subjects. There is a reader service for the blind, and remedial math, reading, and writing.

Campus Safety and Security: Measures include 24-hour foot and vehicle patrol, self-defense education, escort service, and informal discussions. There are pamphlets/posters/films, emergency telephones, and lighted pathways/sidewalks.

Programs of Study: St. Ambrose confers B.A., B.S., B.A.M.T., B.A.S.S., B.B.A., B.B.A.A., B.E.D., B.E.S., B.M.E., B.S.I.E., and B.S.O.T. degrees. Master's and doctoral degrees are also awarded. Bachelor's degrees are awarded in BIOLOGICAL SCIENCE (biology/biological science), BUSINESS (accounting, business administration and management, business economics, management science, and marketing/ retailing/merchandising), COMMUNICATIONS AND THE ARTS (communications, English, fine arts, French, German, music, Spanish, and speech/debate/rhetoric), COMPUTER AND PHYSICAL SCIENCE (chemistry, computer science, mathematics, and physics), EDUCATION (art, elementary, music, physical, and secondary), ENGINEERING AND ENVIRONMENTAL DESIGN (engineering physics and industrial engineering), HEALTH PROFESSIONS (health science), SOCIAL SCIENCE (criminal justice, economics, history, philosophy, political science/ government, psychology, public administration, and sociology). Business, psychology, and elementary education are the largest.

Required: To graduate, all students must complete at least 120 credit hours, including 45 outside the major and 30 in upper-level courses. A minimum GPA of 2.0 is required. Students must also complete developmental courses and demonstrate proficiency in English composition, math, public speaking, and library skills, among other requirements.

Special: The university offers co-op and work-study programs, study abroad in England, Ireland, Italy, Spain, Austria, and Germany, internships, a 3-2 engineering degree with the University of Iowa and Iowa State University, accelerated degree programs, combined B.A.-B.S. degrees, dual majors, and student-designed majors. Credit for life, military, and work experience, nondegree study, and pass/fail options also are available. There are 3 national honor societies, and 3 departmental honors programs.

Faculty/Classroom: 62% of faculty are male; 38%, female. All both teach and do research. No introductory courses are taught by graduate students. The average class size in an introductory lecture is 21; in a laboratory, 18; and in a regular course, 17.

Admissions: 86% of the 2001-2002 applicants were accepted. The ACT scores for the 2001-2002 freshman class were: 46% below 21, 29% between 21 and 23, 16% between 24 and 26, 5% between 27 and 28, and 4% above 28. 28% of the current freshmen were in the top fifth of their class; 51% were in the top two fifths. 15 freshmen graduated first in their class.

Requirements: The ACT is required. The SAT I, with a minimum composite score of 780, may be substituted. Applicants must be graduates of an accredited secondary school; the GED is accepted. An interview is recommended. St. Ambrose requires applicants to be in the upper 50% of their class. A GPA of 2.5 is required. AP and CLEP credits are accepted. Important factors in the admissions decision are recommendations by school officials, leadership record, and parents or siblings attending the school. Applications are accepted on-line at the St. Ambrose web site.

Procedure: Freshmen are admitted to all sessions. Entrance exams should be taken in the spring of the junior year. There are early decision and deferred admissions plans. Application deadlines are open. The application fee is $25. Notification is sent on a rolling basis.

Transfer: 294 transfer students enrolled in 2001-2002. Applicants must have a college GPA of 2.0. 30 credits of 120 must be completed at St. Ambrose.

Visiting: There are regularly scheduled orientations for prospective students, including breakfast, welcome, testing, panel given by current students, student and parent meeting with faculty mentor, evening meeting and activity; on the next day, there is advising and registration. Parents follow their own agenda (with panels and tours). There are guides for informal visits and visitors may sit in on classes and stay overnight. To schedule a visit, contact the Admissions Office at *admit@sau.edu*.

Financial Aid: In 2001-2002, 92% of all freshmen and 85% of continuing students received some form of financial aid. 76% of freshmen and 74% of continuing students received need-based aid. The average freshman award was $12,598. Of that total, scholarships or need-based grants averaged $4602 ($6136 maximum); loans averaged $2713 ($3032 maximum); work contracts averaged $1508 ($2877 maximum); and the Iowa Tuition Grant (Iowa residents only) averaged $3538. All undergraduates work part time. Average annual earnings from campus work are $1508. The average financial indebtedness of the 2001 graduate was $19,625. St. Ambrose is a member of CSS. The FAFSA is required. The fall application deadline is March 15.

International Students: There are 18 international students enrolled. The school actively recruits these students. They must score 500 on the written TOEFL or 213 (recommended) on the electronic version.

Computers: The mainframe is a DEC ALPHA. There are several PC labs on campus. All residence halls are wired for network connections. All students may access the system 8:30 A.M. to 9 P.M. There are no time limits and no fees.

Graduates: In 2001, 449 bachelor's degrees were awarded. The most popular majors were business (17%), psychology (16%), and elementary education (8%). In an average class, 1% graduate in 3 years, 54% in 4 years, 66% in 5 years, and 67% in 6 years. 50 companies recruited on campus in 2000-2001. Of the 2000 graduating class, 22% were enrolled in graduate school within 6 months of graduation and 85% were employed.

Admissions Contact: Meg Flaherty, Director of Admissions. A video is available. E-mail: *flahertymegf@ambrose.edu*
Web: *www.sau.edu/sau.html*

SIMPSON COLLEGE — C-3
Indianola, IA 50125 — (515) 961-1624
(800) 362-2454; Fax: (515) 961-1870

Full-time: 569 men, 738 women	**Faculty:** 84; IIB, -$
Part-time: 192 men, 317 women	**Ph.D.s:** 90%
Graduate: none	**Student/Faculty:** 16 to 1
Year: 4-4-1, summer session	**Tuition:** $15,908
Application Deadline: open	**Room & Board:** $5292
Freshman Class: 1185 applied, 1024 accepted, 299 enrolled	
SAT I Verbal/Math: 590/580	**ACT:** 24 **COMPETITIVE+**

Simpson College, founded in 1860, is a private liberal arts institution affiliated with the United Methodist Church. In addition to regional accreditation, Simpson has baccalaureate program accreditation with NASM. The 2 libraries contain 151,574 volumes, 12,268 microform items, and 5107 audiovisual forms/CDs, and subscribe to 711 periodicals. Computerized library services include the card catalog, interlibrary loans, and database searching. Special learning facilities include a learning resource center, art gallery, a science reference library, and an extensive collection from the Antebellum era. The 63-acre campus is in a suburban area 12 miles south of Des Moines. Including residence halls, there are 34 buildings.

Student Life: 91% of undergraduates are from Iowa. Others are from 27 states, 11 foreign countries, and Canada. 96% are from public schools. 92% are white. 21% are Catholic; 17% claim no religious affiliation. The average age of freshmen is 18; all undergraduates, 22. 18% do not continue beyond their first year.

Housing: 1032 students can be accommodated in college housing, which includes single-sex and coed dormitories, on-campus apartments, fraternity houses, and sorority houses. In addition, there are honors houses, language houses, special-interest houses, and theme houses. On-campus housing is guaranteed for all 4 years. 82% of students live on campus; of those, 85% remain on campus on weekends. All students may keep cars.

Activities: 32% of men belong to 1 local fraternity and 3 national fraternities; 30% of women belong to 4 national sororities. There are 80 groups on campus, including art, band, cheerleading, choir, chorale, chorus, computers, drama, drill team, ethnic, gay, honors, international, jazz band, literary magazine, musical theater, newspaper, opera, pep band, political, professional, radio and TV, religious, social, social service, student government, and yearbook. Popular campus events include Campus Day, Greek Week, and Minority Emphasis Week.

Sports: There are 9 intercollegiate sports for men and 9 for women, and 23 intramural sports for men and 23 for women. Facilities include a gym and an athletic center with a field house containing 2 racquetball courts, a wrestling practice room, a weight room, indoor batting facilities, a training room, a pool and sauna, 3 indoor tennis courts, and 2 running tracks. Outdoor facilities include a football stadium, an 8-lane track, 6 tennis courts, 2 basketball courts, a sand volleyball court, and football, soccer, baseball, and softball fields.

Disabled Students: 85% of the campus is accessible. Wheelchair ramps, elevators, special parking, specially equipped rest rooms, special class scheduling, and lowered drinking fountains are available.

Services: Counseling and information services are available, as is tutoring in every subject. There is a reader service for the blind.

Campus Safety and Security: Measures include self-defense education, escort service, informal discussions, and pamphlets/posters/films. There are emergency telephones, lighted pathways/sidewalks, and a campus patrol during day and evening hours.

Programs of Study: Simpson confers B.A. and B.Mus. degrees. Bachelor's degrees are awarded in BIOLOGICAL SCIENCE (biochemistry and biology/biological science), BUSINESS (accounting, international business management, marketing/retailing/merchandising, and sports management), COMMUNICATIONS AND THE ARTS (art, communications, dramatic arts, English, French, German, journalism, music, music performance, Spanish, and speech/debate/rhetoric), COMPUTER AND PHYSICAL SCIENCE (chemistry, computer science, information sciences and systems, and mathematics), EDUCATION (athletic training, business, drama, elementary, music, and physical), ENGINEERING AND ENVIRONMENTAL DESIGN (environmental science), SOCIAL SCIENCE (criminal justice, economics, history, international relations, philosophy, political science/government, psychology, religion, and sociology). Natural sciences, management, and visual and performing arts are the strongest academically. Management, education, and biology are the largest.

Required: Graduation requirements include at least 128 credit hours for a B.A. and 132 credit hours for a B.Mus., with a GPA of 2.0. Students must satisfactorily complete the Cornerstone Studies in Liberal Arts, including a senior colloquium; fulfill 84 hours in the major division and 30 to 42 hours in the major department; take a May term course each year; and demonstrate competency in writing, math, and foreign language.

Special: Simpson offers a 3-2 engineering degree with Washington University at St. Louis, cross-registration at American and Drew Universities, internships, a Washington semester, study abroad in 15 to 20 countries, and work-study programs. Also available are dual majors, student-designed majors, nondegree study, credit for life, military, and work experience, and a pass/fail option for 1 course per year. There are preprofessional programs in nursing, optometry, physical therapy, dentistry, medicine, pharmacy, and veterinary medicine. There are 13 national honor societies, a freshman honors program, and 8 departmental honors programs.

Faculty/Classroom: 70% of faculty are male; 30%, female. All teach undergraduates. The average class size in an introductory lecture is 30 and in a laboratory, 12.

Admissions: 86% of the 2001-2002 applicants were accepted. The SAT I scores for the 2001-2002 freshman class were: Verbal--23% below 500, 45% between 500 and 599, 27% between 600 and 700, and 6% above 700; Math--30% below 500, 34% between 500 and 599, 31% between 600 and 700, and 6% above 700. The ACT scores were 18% below 21, 30% between 21 and 23, 27% between 24 and 26, 18% between 27 and 28, and 14% above 28. 44% of the current freshmen were in the top fifth of their class; 70% were in the top two fifths. 18 freshmen graduated first in their class.

Requirements: The SAT I or ACT is required. In addition, applicants must be graduates of an accredited secondary school. The GED is accepted. Test scores, counselor recommendations, GPA, college prep course grades, and class rank are all considered in a selective admissions process. The college strongly recommends that applicants complete 4 years of English and 3 each of math, lab science, social science, and a foreign language. The college requires an audition for music and theater scholarships. A portfolio is required for art scholarships. AP and CLEP credits are accepted. Important factors in the admissions decision are advanced placement or honor courses, recommendations by school officials, and leadership record. Applications are accepted on-line.

Procedure: Freshmen are admitted to all sessions. Entrance exams should be taken in the junior or senior year. There is a deferred admissions plan. Application deadlines are open. Notification is sent on a rolling basis.

Transfer: 69 transfer students enrolled in 2001-2002. In addition to freshman requirements, transfer applicants are considered on the basis of college work taken and grades received. Applicants must take either the SAT I or ACT. The recommended GPA is 2.5, and grades of 2.0 and above transfer for credit. The school admits transfer students every term. 32 of 128 to 132 credits must be completed at Simpson.

Visiting: There are regularly scheduled orientations for prospective students, including a full-day orientation program scheduled 3 times during the summer, when students meet with an academic adviser, register for classes, and participate in activity information sessions. Parents are encouraged to attend. There are guides for informal visits and visitors may sit in on classes and stay overnight. To schedule a visit, contact the Office of Admissions.

Financial Aid: In 2001-2002, 98% of all students received some form of financial aid. 84% of freshmen and 85% of continuing students received need-based aid. The average freshman award was $16,382. Of that total, scholarships or need-based grants averaged $12,115 ($21,400 maximum); loans averaged $3800 ($16,625 maximum); and work contracts averaged $766 ($1655 maximum). 51% of undergraduates work part time. Average annual earnings from campus work are $961. The average financial indebtedness of the 2001 graduate was $19,053. Simpson is a member of CSS. The FAFSA is required. The fall application deadline is July 1.

International Students: The school actively recruits these students. They must score 550 on the written TOEFL or 213 on the electronic version and also take the SAT I or the ACT.

Computers: The mainframe is a DEC ALPHA 2100. All campus-owned buildings are connected to the mainframe network and have Internet access. There are 218 PCs available for student use in the library, Carver Science Center, and McNeill Computer Lab, where computer consultants are available to assist students. PCs are also available in residence halls. All students may access the system 24 hours a day. There are no time limits and no fees.

Graduates: In 2001, 369 bachelor's degrees were awarded. The most popular majors were management (15%), communications (9%), and elementary education (7%). In an average class, 54% graduate in 4 years, and 65% in 5 years. 173 companies recruited on campus in 2000-2001. Of the 2000 graduating class, 11% were enrolled in graduate school within 6 months of graduation and 87% were employed.

Admissions Contact: John Kellogg, Vice President for Enrollment and Institutional Advancement. A video is available.
E-mail: *admiss@simpson.edu* Web: *www.simpson.edu*

UNIVERSITY OF DUBUQUE — E-2
Dubuque, IA 52001 — (319) 589-3200
(800) 722-5583; Fax: (319) 556-3690

Full-time: 450 men, 245 women — **Faculty:** 34
Part-time: 24 men, 37 women — **Ph.D.s:** 80%
Graduate: 187 men, 93 women — **Student/Faculty:** 20 to 1
Year: semesters, summer session — **Tuition:** $14,910
Application Deadline: May 1 — **Room & Board:** $5020
Freshman Class: 551 applied, 451 accepted, 243 enrolled
SAT I Verbal/Math: 500/500 — **ACT:** 23 — **COMPETITIVE**

The University of Dubuque, established in 1852, is a private liberal arts institution affiliated with the Presbyterian Church (U.S.A.). Strengths in the undergraduate curriculum include environmental science, business, aviation, education, and computer graphics/interactive media. There are 4 undergraduate and 2 graduate schools. The library contains 164,859 volumes, 20,739 microform items, and 2180 audiovisual forms/CDs, and subscribes to 801 periodicals. Computerized library services include the card catalog, interlibrary loans, and database searching. Special learning facilities include a learning resource center and art gallery. The 56-acre campus is in a suburban area 180 miles northwest of Chicago. Including residence halls, there are 21 buildings.

Student Life: 60% of undergraduates are from out of state, mostly the Midwest. Others are from 31 states and 21 foreign countries. 90% are from public schools. 73% are white; 11% African American. 50% claim no religious affiliation; 25% Catholic; 24% Protestant. The average age of freshmen is 19; all undergraduates, 24. 22% do not continue beyond their first year.

Housing: 432 students can be accommodated in college housing, which includes single-sex and coed dormitories, on-campus apartments, and married-student housing. In addition, there are special-interest houses. On-campus housing is guaranteed for all 4 years. 50% of students live on campus; of those, 75% remain on campus on weekends. Alcohol is not permitted. All students may keep cars.

Activities: 11% of men belong to 5 local fraternities; 10% of women belong to 3 local sororities. There are 24 groups on campus, including cheerleading, choir, chorale, chorus, computers, dance, drama, ethnic, honors, international, musical theater, newspaper, pep band, political, professional, religious, social, social service, student government, and yearbook. Popular campus events include Founder's Day Ball, Annual Gala, and Family Weekend.

Sports: There are 8 intercollegiate sports for men and 7 for women, and 13 intramural sports for men and 13 for women. Facilities include a sports center with basketball and volleyball courts, 2 racquetball courts, a wrestling room, an athletic training room; a football field and track; baseball and softball fields; a practice football/intramural field; and a cardiovascular workout center.

Disabled Students: 50% of the campus is accessible. Wheelchair ramps, elevators, special parking, specially equipped rest rooms, special class scheduling, and lowered drinking fountains are available.

Services: Counseling and information services are available, as is tutoring in some subjects, including English, math, economics, accounting, and computer literacy. There is remedial math, reading, and writing.

Campus Safety and Security: Measures include 24-hour foot and vehicle patrol, self-defense education, escort service, and shuttle buses. There are informal discussions, pamphlets/posters/films, emergency telephones, lighted pathways/sidewalks, and security-locked residence halls.

Programs of Study: UD confers B.A., B.S., and B.B.A. degrees. Associate and master's degrees are also awarded. Bachelor's degrees are awarded in BIOLOGICAL SCIENCE (biology/biological science), BUSINESS (accounting and business administration and management), COMMUNICATIONS AND THE ARTS (English and speech/debate/rhetoric), COMPUTER AND PHYSICAL SCIENCE (computer science), EDUCATION (education and physical), ENGINEERING AND ENVIRONMENTAL DESIGN (aviation administration/management, computer graphics, and environmental science), SOCIAL SCIENCE (philosophy, psychology, religion, and sociology). Business, environmental science, and education are the strongest academically. Business, aviation management/flight operations, and computer graphics are the largest.

Required: Students must complete 12 hours each in humanities, natural sciences, and social sciences, must fulfill specific requirements in English, literature, world history, science, math, and computer science, and must complete work in a major. A total of 120 credits must be earned, with a minimum GPA of 2.0 (2.5 for education majors), for graduation.

Special: UD offers cross-registration with Loras and Clarke Colleges, internships, study abroad in Europe and South America, a Washington semester, work-study programs, accelerated degree programs, B.A.-B.S. degrees, dual and student-designed majors, credit for life, military, and work experience, nondegree study, and pass/fail options. B.A.-M.A. programs are offered in conjunction with the university's theological seminary. Adult degree programs and an environmental field trip to Colorado and New Mexico are available. There are 8 national honor societies, and 2 departmental honors programs.

Faculty/Classroom: 65% of faculty are male; 35%, female. All teach undergraduates. No introductory courses are taught by graduate students. The average class size in an introductory lecture is 20; in a laboratory, 16; and in a regular course, 17.

Admissions: 82% of the 2001-2002 applicants were accepted. The ACT scores for the 2001-2002 freshman class were: 38% below 21, 34% between 21 and 23, 15% between 24 and 26, 8% between 27 and 28, and 4% above 28. 23% of the current freshmen were in the top fifth of their class; 50% were in the top two fifths. 3 freshmen graduated first in their class in a recent year.

Requirements: The SAT I or ACT is required. In addition, applicants must graduate from an accredited secondary school with a minimum of 4 years in English and 3 each in math, social sciences, and natural sciences. Other academic areas, such as foreign languages, business courses, computer programming, and the fine and performing arts, are also considered. The GED is accepted. Essays and recommendations are encouraged and may be required if the ACT is less than 18 or the SAT I is less than 740. Auditions are required for music scholarship candidates. UD requires applicants to be in the upper 50% of their class. A GPA of 2.0 is required. AP and CLEP credits are accepted. Important factors in the admissions decision are recommendations by school officials, leadership record, and extracurricular activities record. Applications are accepted on-line via the school's web site.

Procedure: Freshmen are admitted fall and spring. Entrance exams should be taken before the senior year. There is a deferred admissions plan. Applications should be filed by May 1 for fall entry. Notification is sent on a rolling basis. The fall 2001 application fee was $25.

Transfer: 132 transfer students enrolled in 2001-2002. A minimum GPA of 2.0 is required. The applicant must be in good standing at all previously attended institutions. 30 credits of 120 must be completed at UD.

Visiting: There are regularly scheduled orientations for prospective students, including a campus tour and visits with coaches, faculty, admissions, and financial aid advisers. There are guides for informal visits and visitors may sit in on classes and stay overnight. To schedule a visit, contact Jesse James, Admission Director.

Financial Aid: In 2001-2002, 95% of all freshmen and 89% of continuing students received some form of financial aid. 93% of freshmen and 85% of continuing students received need-based aid. The average freshman award was $16,280. Of that total, scholarships or need-based grants averaged $8425 ($9000 maximum); loans averaged $3500 ($6625 maximum); and work contracts averaged $1500 ($2000 maximum). 65% of undergraduates work part time. Average annual earnings from campus work are $1500. The average financial indebtedness of the 2001 graduate was $17,250. The FAFSA is required. The fall application deadline is April 1.

International Students: There are 76 international students enrolled. The school actively recruits these students. They must score 500 on the written TOEFL or 270 on the electronic version and also take the college's own test.

Computers: The mainframe is a Compaq Proliant 3000. Students have access to 100 PCs and to Internet and e-mail services. All students may access the system from 8 A.M. to 11 P.M. daily. There are no time limits and no fees.

Graduates: In 2001, 139 bachelor's degrees were awarded. The most popular majors were business administration (31%), education (21%), and aviation (10%). In an average class, 2% graduate in 3 years, 50% in 4 years, 60% in 5 years, and 70% in 6 years. 30 companies recruited on campus in 2000-2001. Of the 2000 graduating class, 98% were employed within 6 months of graduation.

Admissions Contact: Jesse L. James, Admission Director.
E-mail: *jjames@dbq.edu* Web: *www.dbq.edu*

UNIVERSITY OF IOWA

E-3

Iowa City, IA 52242-1396

(319) 335-3847
(800) 553-IOWA; Fax: (319) 335-1535

Full-time: 7896 men, 9412 women	**Faculty:** 1630; I, av$
Part-time: 1002 men, 1293 women	**Ph.D.s:** 99%
Graduate: 4593 men, 4572 women	**Student/Faculty:** 11 to 1
Year: semesters, summer session	**Tuition:** $3522 ($11,950)
Application Deadline: May 15	**Room & Board:** $5085
Freshman Class: 11,836 applied, 10,089 accepted, 4005 enrolled	
SAT I Verbal/Math: 590/605	**ACT:** 24 **COMPETITIVE+**

The University of Iowa, founded in 1847, is a comprehensive, public institution. Its undergraduate and graduate programs emphasize the liberal and fine arts, business, engineering, health science, and the professions. There are 6 undergraduate and 5 graduate schools. In addition to regional accreditation, Iowa has baccalaureate program accreditation with AACSB, ABET, ACEJMC, ACPE, ADA, AHEA, APTA, CAHEA, CSWE, NASM, NCATE, and NLN. The 13 libraries contain 4,027,546 volumes, 6,640,879 microform items, and 267,192 audiovisual forms/CDs, and subscribe to 44,644 periodicals. Computerized library services include the card catalog, interlibrary loans, and database searching. Special learning facilities include an art gallery, natural history museum, radio station, and UI hospitals and clinics, the Iowa Center for the Arts, and a driving simulator. The 1900-acre campus is in a small town 110 miles east of Des Moines and 220 miles west of Chicago. Including residence halls, there are 115 buildings.

Student Life: 68% of undergraduates are from Iowa. Others are from 49 states, 70 foreign countries, and Canada. 89% are from public schools. 86% are white. The average age of freshmen is 18; all undergraduates, 22. 18% do not continue beyond their first year.

Housing: 5546 students can be accommodated in college housing, which includes coed dormitories, on-campus apartments, and married-student housing. In addition, there are honors houses, language houses, and special-interest houses, a quiet house, upperclass floors, and floors for women in science and engineering, men in engineering, health sciences, business, and performing arts. On-campus housing is available on a first-come, first-served basis and is available on a lottery system for upperclassmen. All students may keep cars.

Activities: 11% of men belong to 23 national fraternities; 12% of women belong to 17 national sororities. There are 363 groups on campus, including art, band, cheerleading, chess, choir, chorale, chorus, computers, dance, debate, drama, drill team, ethnic, film, forensics, gay, honors, international, jazz band, literary magazine, marching band, musical theater, newspaper, opera, orchestra, pep band, photography, political, professional, radio and TV, religious, social, social service, student government, symphony, and yearbook. Popular campus events include Riverfest, Greek Week, and Weeks of Welcome.

Sports: There are 10 intercollegiate sports for men and 12 for women, and 30 intramural sports for men and 28 for women. Facilities include a 70,397-seat stadium, a 15,500-seat arena, softball and baseball stadiums, an 18-hole golf course, a pool, basketball courts, racquetball and handball courts, outdoor and indoor tennis courts, weight and fitness rooms, outdoor and indoor running tracks, a 1000-seat field hockey stadium, a field campus for hiking, cross-country skiing, canoeing, and a soccer field.

Disabled Students: 98% of the campus is accessible. Wheelchair ramps, elevators, special parking, specially equipped rest rooms, special class scheduling, lowered drinking fountains, lowered telephones, and a transportation service are available.

Services: Counseling and information services are available, as is tutoring in most subjects. There is a reader service for the blind, and remedial math, reading, and writing.

Campus Safety and Security: Measures include 24-hour foot and vehicle patrol, self-defense education, escort service, and shuttle buses. There are informal discussions, pamphlets/posters/films, emergency telephones, and lighted pathways/sidewalks.

Programs of Study: Iowa confers B.A., B.S., B.B.A., B.F.A., B.L.S., B.M., B.S.E., B.S.M., and B.S.N. degrees. Master's and doctoral degrees are also awarded. Bachelor's degrees are awarded in BIOLOGICAL SCIENCE (biochemistry, biology/biological science, and microbiology), BUSINESS (accounting, banking and finance, business administration and management, business economics, management science, marketing/retailing/merchandising, and recreation and leisure services), COMMUNICATIONS AND THE ARTS (art, art history and appreciation, broadcasting, classics, communications, comparative literature, dance, dramatic arts, English, film arts, fine arts, French, German, Greek, Italian, journalism, Latin, linguistics, music, Portuguese, Russian, Spanish, and speech/debate/rhetoric), COMPUTER AND PHYSICAL SCIENCE (actuarial science, astronomy, chemistry, computer science, geology, information sciences and systems, mathematics, physics, and statistics), EDUCATION (art, elementary, foreign languages, health, middle school, music, science, and secondary), ENGINEERING AND ENVIRONMENTAL DESIGN (biomedical engineering, chemical engineering, civil engineering, computer engineering, electrical/electronics engineering, engineering, environmental science, industrial administration/management, industrial engineering, and mechanical engineering), HEALTH PROFESSIONS (medical laboratory technology, nuclear medical technology, nursing, pharmacy, predentistry, premedicine, and speech pathology/audiology), SOCIAL SCIENCE (African American studies, American studies, anthropology, Asian/Oriental studies, classical/ancient civilization, economics, geography, history, liberal arts/general studies, parks and recreation management, philosophy, political science/government, prelaw, psychology, religion, Russian and Slavic studies, social science, social work, and sociology). Business, engineering, and psychology are the largest.

Required: To graduate, students must complete at least 120 semester hours, with a GPA of 2.0. General education program includes rhetoric, historical perspectives, foreign language, quantitative and formal reasoning, humanities, and natural and social sciences. In addition, students choose 2 of the following to satisfy a distributed general education area: cultural diversity, fine arts, foreign civilization and culture, phys ed, social science, humanities, or historical perspectives.

Special: The University of Iowa offers cooperative education programs and internships in more than 70 academic departments, combined degree programs in liberal arts and engineering; liberal arts and business; liberal arts and nursing; and study abroad in more than 40 countries. Dual and student-designed majors, B.A. and B.S. degrees, certificate programs including Native American studies, global studies, international business, and women's studies, credit for military experience, and pass/nonpass options are also available. There are 21 national honor societies, including Phi Beta Kappa, a freshman honors program, and 52 departmental honors programs.

Faculty/Classroom: 72% of faculty are male; 28%, female.

Admissions: 85% of the 2001-2002 applicants were accepted. The SAT I scores for the 2001-2002 freshman class were: Verbal--14% below 500, 38% between 500 and 599, 36% between 600 and 700, and 13% above 700; Math--14% below 500, 33% between 500 and 599, 39% between 600 and 700, and 15% above 700. The ACT scores were 14% below 21, 28% between 21 and 23, 30% between 24 and 26, 18% between 27 and 28, and 13% above 28. 40% of the current freshmen were in the top fifth of their class; 76% were in the top two fifths. There were 34 National Merit finalists. 183 freshmen graduated first in their class.

Requirements: The SAT I or ACT is required. In addition, Iowa residents must rank in the upper 50% of their high school class (nonresidents in the upper 30%) or must meet an acceptable combination of class rank and test scores. All applicants must have completed 4 years of high school English, 3 years each of social studies and science, 3 years of math (including 2 years of algebra and 1 of geometry), and 2 years of a single foreign language. Music students must audition. Applications are accepted on-line at the university's web site. Iowa requires applicants to be in the upper 50% of their class. AP and CLEP credits are accepted.

Procedure: Freshmen are admitted to all sessions. Entrance exams should be taken in the junior year. There is a deferred admissions plan. Applications should be filed by May 15 for fall entry, November 15 for spring entry, and May 15 for summer entry. Notification is sent on a rolling basis. The fall 2001 application fee was $30.

Transfer: 1274 transfer students enrolled in 2001-2002. For the College of Liberal Arts, a GPA of at least 2.25 is required for applicants with 24 or more semester hours of credit. Those with fewer credits are considered on the same criteria as freshmen. Other colleges have different requirements. 30 credits of 120 must be completed at Iowa.

Visiting: There are regularly scheduled orientations for prospective students, including information sessions, campus tours, and visits to departments, residence halls, and classrooms. There are guides for informal visits and visitors may sit in on classes. To schedule a visit, contact the Admission Visitors Center at (319) 335-1566.

Financial Aid: In 2001-2002, 63% of all freshmen and 58% of continuing students received some form of financial aid. 42% of freshmen and 40% of continuing students received need-based aid. The average freshman award was $5150. Of that total, scholarships or need-based grants averaged $1650 ($11,000 maximum); loans averaged $2250; and work contracts averaged $2000. All undergraduates work part time. Average annual earnings from campus work are $2000. The average financial indebtedness of the 2001 graduate was $11,300. The FAFSA and the college's own financial statement are required.

International Students: There are 355 international students enrolled. The school actively recruits these students. They must score 530 on the written TOEFL or 197 on the electronic version and also take The SATI or SCT. International students must submit TOEFL for admission purposes and may be asked to take a proficiency exam after arriving on campus.

Computers: The mainframes are an IBM 9672, IBM RS6000-SP2, and SG1 Power Challenge XL-16. There are 1100 networked PCs at 26 public computer centers on campus. There are an additional 500 PCs in 33 departmental instructional labs on campus. All students may access the system 24 hours a day, 7 days a week. There are no time limits. The fee varies by college.

Graduates: In 2001, 3696 bachelor's degrees were awarded. In an average class, 1% graduate in 3 years, 35% in 4 years, 61% in 5 years, and 65% in 6 years. 272 companies recruited on campus in 2000-2001.

Admissions Contact: Michael Barron, Director of Admissions.
E-mail: *admission@uiowa.edu* Web: *http://www.uiowa.edu*

UNIVERSITY OF NORTHERN IOWA D-2

Cedar Falls, IA 50614-0018 (319) 273-2281
(800) 772-2037; Fax: (319) 273-2885

Full-time: 4679 men, 6530 women	**Faculty:** 596; IIA, -$
Part-time: 550 men, 715 women	**Ph.D.s:** 73%
Graduate: 549 men, 1047 women	**Student/Faculty:** 19 to 1
Year: semesters, summer session	**Tuition:** $3440 ($8762)
Application Deadline: August 15	**Room & Board:** $4410
Freshman Class: 4688 applied, 3786 accepted, 2104 enrolled	
SAT I Verbal/Math: 529/531	**ACT:** 23 **COMPETITIVE**

The University of Northern Iowa, established in 1876, is a public institution offering degree programs in business administration, education, humanities and fine arts, natural science, and social and behavioral sciences. There are 5 undergraduate schools and 1 graduate school. In addition to regional accreditation, UNI has baccalaureate program accreditation with AACSB, ACS, ADA, ASLA, CSWE, NASAD, NASM, and NRPA. The library contains 742,493 volumes, 1,059,905 microform items, and 22,467 audiovisual forms/CDs, and subscribes to 6976 periodicals. Computerized library services include the card catalog, interlibrary loans, and database searching. Special learning facilities include a learning resource center, art gallery, natural history museum, planetarium, radio station, and observatory. The university also sponsors a laboratory school, a waste reduction center, and several research institutes. The 788-acre campus is in a small town about 100 miles north of Des Moines. Including residence halls, there are 64 buildings.

Student Life: 93% of undergraduates are from Iowa. Others are from 46 states, 76 foreign countries, and Canada. 89% are white. The average age of freshmen is 18; all undergraduates, 21. 18% do not continue beyond their first year; 60% remain to graduate.

Housing: 4939 students can be accommodated in college housing, which includes single-sex and coed dormitories, on-campus apartments, and married-student housing. In addition, there are special-interest houses. On-campus housing is guaranteed for all 4 years. 64% of students commute. All students may keep cars.

Activities: 3% of men belong to 7 national fraternities; 3% of women belong to 4 national sororities. There are 232 groups on campus, including art, band, cheerleading, choir, chorale, chorus, computers, dance, drama, drill team, ethnic, film, gay, honors, international, jazz band, literary magazine, marching band, musical theater, newspaper, nontraditional students, opera, orchestra, pep band, political, professional, radio and TV, religious, social, social service, student government, symphony, and yearbook. Popular campus events include Winterfest, International Food Fair, and Diversity Week.

Sports: There are 9 intercollegiate sports for men and 9 for women, and 25 intramural sports for men and 24 for women. Facilities include a domed stadium, a field house, a basketball facility, and a wellness and recreation center with an 8-lane swimming pool, 6 handball/racquetball courts, a climbing wall, weight rooms, and basketball courts.

Disabled Students: Wheelchair ramps, elevators, special parking, specially equipped rest rooms, special class scheduling, lowered drinking fountains, lowered telephones, personal care attendants, and TDDs are available.

Services: Counseling and information services are available, as is tutoring in some subjects, including macroeconomics, accounting, business statistics, biology, physics, physical science, chemistry, and Spanish. There is a reader service for the blind, remedial math and writing, and a note-taking service.

Campus Safety and Security: Measures include 24-hour foot and vehicle patrol, escort service, informal discussions, and pamphlets/posters/films. There are emergency telephones and lighted pathways/sidewalks.

Programs of Study: UNI confers B.A., B.S., B.F.A., B.L.S., B.Mus., and B.T. degrees. Master's and doctoral degrees are also awarded. Bachelor's degrees are awarded in BIOLOGICAL SCIENCE (biology/biological science, biotechnology, microbiology, and nutrition), BUSINESS (accounting, banking and finance, management information systems, management science, marketing/retailing/merchandising, and recreation and leisure services), COMMUNICATIONS AND THE ARTS (art history and appreciation, broadcasting, communications, dramatic arts, English, fine arts, French, German, graphic design, music, music performance, music theory and composition, public relations, Spanish, speech/debate/rhetoric, studio art, and theater design), COMPUTER AND PHYSICAL SCIENCE (chemistry, computer science, earth science, geology, information sciences and systems, mathematics, physics, and science), EDUCATION (art, athletic training, business, early childhood, elementary, foreign languages, health, middle school, music, physical, science, special, teaching English as a second/foreign language (TESOL/TEFOL), and technical), ENGINEERING AND ENVIRONMENTAL DESIGN (construction management, electromechanical technology, energy management technology, industrial engineering technology, and manufacturing technology), HEALTH PROFESSIONS (speech pathology/audiology), SOCIAL SCIENCE (American studies, anthropology, Asian/Oriental studies, clothing and textiles management/production/services, criminology, dietetics, economics, European studies, family and community services, geography, history, humanities, Latin American studies, liberal arts/general studies, philosophy, political science/government, psychology, public administration, religion, Russian and Slavic studies, social science, social work, and sociology). Accounting, management, and education are the strongest academically. Accounting and elementary education are the largest.

Required: Degree requirements include completion of 124 to 130 credits, with 30 to 60 in the major. Liberal arts majors must maintain a minimum GPA of 2.0 (2.5 for education majors). General education requirements include 11 hours of civilizations and cultures, 9 each of natural science/technology, social science, and communication, 6 of arts/literature/philosophy/religion, and 3 of personal wellness. Students must meet requirements in foreign language and complete a capstone course in environment, technology, and society. Education students must complete a 32-credit professional sequence.

Special: Internships and co-op programs are offered through all colleges of the university. Students may study abroad in 19 countries and may participate in a Washington semester. Interdisciplinary majors include safety education, chemistry/marketing, design/human environment, and natural history interpretation. Cross-registration, work-study programs, a general studies degree, dual and student-designed majors, nondegree study, and pass/fail options are also available. There are 25 national honor societies and a freshman honors program.

Faculty/Classroom: 56% of faculty are male; 44%, female. 97% both teach and do research. Graduate students teach 1% of introductory courses. The average class size in an introductory lecture is 49; in a laboratory, 18; and in a regular course, 26.

Admissions: 81% of the 2001-2002 applicants were accepted. The SAT I scores for the 2001-2002 freshman class were: Verbal--37% below 500, 35% between 500 and 599, 24% between 600 and 700, and 4% above 700; Math--39% below 500, 31% between 500 and 599, 24% between 600 and 700, and 7% above 700. The ACT scores were 27% below 21, 32% between 21 and 23, 24% between 24 and 26, 9% between 27 and 28, and 8% above 28. 40% of the current freshmen were in the top fifth of their class; 76% were in the top two fifths. 80 freshmen graduated first in their class.

Requirements: The ACT is required. In addition, applicants must graduate from an approved secondary school. The GED, with a minimum standard score of 57, is accepted. High school requirements include 4 years of English, 3 years each of math, social studies, and science, and 2 years or more of electives, which may include foreign language and fine arts. UNI requires applicants to be in the upper 50% of their class. AP and CLEP credits are accepted. Important factors in the admissions decision are advanced placement or honor courses, evidence of special talent, and leadership record. An on-line application can be accessed from the school's web site.

Procedure: Freshmen are admitted to all sessions. Entrance exams should be taken by October of the senior year. Applications should be filed by August 15 for fall entry, December 31 for spring entry, and May 15 for summer entry, along with a $20 fee. Notification is sent on a rolling basis.

Transfer: 1221 transfer students enrolled in 2001-2002. Applicants must have a minimum GPA of 2.0 to 2.5, depending on the number of credits they wish to transfer. Other applicants may be admitted on academic probation. 32 credits of 124 to 130 must be completed at UNI.

Visiting: There are regularly scheduled orientations for prospective students, including a student panel, lunch, a campus tour, and presentations by admissions, financial aid, housing, and academic departments. There are guides for informal visits and visitors may sit in on classes and stay overnight. To schedule a visit, contact the Admissions Office.

Financial Aid: In 2001-2002, 82% of all freshmen and 68% of continuing students received some form of financial aid. 54% of freshmen and 55% of continuing students received need-based aid. The average freshman award was $11,425. Of that total, scholarships or need-based grants averaged $2293 ($13,172 maximum); loans averaged $4922 ($6625 maximum); and work contracts averaged $1753 ($3000 maximum). 34% of undergraduates work part time. Average annual earnings from campus work are $1753. The average financial indebtedness of the 2001 graduate was $12,671. The FAFSA is required. The fall application deadline is open.

International Students: There are 191 international students enrolled. The school actively recruits these students. They must score 550 on the written TOEFL or 213 on the electronic version.

Computers: The mainframe consists of a DEC ALPHA 4000-160, a DEC ALPHA server 2000 4/200, a Sun SPARC Station 10, and an IBM ES 9121/210. The network is available to students through 800 PCs located in 7 public access labs and through 87 dial-in ports. All students may have accounts on the VMS system and Internet privileges. All students may access the system 24 hours a day. There are no time limits and no fees.

Graduates: In 2001, 2266 bachelor's degrees were awarded. The most popular majors were elementary education (16%), general studies (5%), and management (4%). In an average class, 1% graduate in 3 years, 29% in 4 years, 62% in 5 years, and 64% in 6 years. 150 companies recruited on campus in 2000-2001.

Admissions Contact: Clark Elmer, Director of Enrollment Management and Admissions. E-mail: *admissions@uni.edu* Web: *www.uni.edu*

UPPER IOWA UNIVERSITY
Fayette, IA 52142-1857 — E-2 — (319) 425-5281 — (800) 553-4150; Fax: (319) 425-5277

Full-time: 418 men, 257 women	**Faculty:** 35; IIB, --$
Part-time: 16 men, 12 women	**Ph.D.s:** 75%
Graduate: 3 men, 12 women	**Student/Faculty:** 19 to 1
Year: terms	**Tuition:** $12,856
Application Deadline: open	**Room & Board:** $4582
Freshman Class: 512 applied, 480 accepted, 170 enrolled	
ACT: 21	**COMPETITIVE**

Upper Iowa University, founded in 1857, is a private institution with a liberal arts focus. The library contains 132,175 volumes, 8895 microform items, and 2040 audiovisual forms/CDs, and subscribes to 287 periodicals. Computerized library services include interlibrary loans and database searching. Special learning facilities include a learning resource center and art gallery. The 75-acre campus is in a rural area 65 miles north of Cedar Rapids. Including residence halls, there are 12 buildings.

Student Life: 60% of undergraduates are from Iowa. Others are from 14 states, 5 foreign countries, and Canada. 90% are from public schools. 75% are white; 13% African American. The average age of freshmen is 18; all undergraduates, 22. 36% do not continue beyond their first year; 64% remain to graduate.

Housing: 515 students can be accommodated in college housing, which includes single-sex dormitories. On-campus housing is guaranteed for all 4 years. 70% of students live on campus; of those, 50% remain on campus on weekends. All students may keep cars.

Activities: 16% of men belong to 5 local fraternities and 1 national fraternity; 35% of women belong to 5 local sororities. There are 31 groups on campus, including art, band, cheerleading, choir, chorus, computers, drama, environmental, international, newspaper, outdoor pursuits, pep band, political, religious, social, social service, student government, and yearbook. Popular campus events include Winterfest, Greek Week, and Springfest.

Sports: There are 9 intercollegiate sports for men and 8 for women, and 4 intramural sports for men and 4 for women. Facilities include a bowling alley, a golf course, an indoor swimming pool, a rock climbing wall, a weight room, and nearby cross-country skiing areas.

Disabled Students: 70% of the campus is accessible. Wheelchair ramps, elevators, special parking, specially equipped rest rooms, special class scheduling, lowered drinking fountains, and lowered telephones are available. The school will make accommodations when necessary.

Services: Counseling and information services are available, as is tutoring in most subjects. There is remedial math, reading, and writing.

Campus Safety and Security: Measures include escort service, informal discussions, pamphlets/posters/films, and emergency telephones. There are lighted pathways/sidewalks and a security officer living in each residence hall.

Programs of Study: Upper Iowa confers B.A. and B.S. degrees. Associate and master's degrees are also awarded. Bachelor's degrees are awarded in AGRICULTURE (conservation and regulation), BIOLOGICAL SCIENCE (biology/biological science), BUSINESS (accounting, banking and finance, business administration and management, management information systems, management science, marketing/retailing/merchandising, and recreation and leisure services), COMMUNICATIONS AND THE ARTS (art, arts administration/management, communications, English, fine arts, graphic design, and music), COMPUTER AND PHYSICAL SCIENCE (chemistry, mathematics, and science), EDUCATION (athletic training, elementary, and physical), HEALTH PROFESSIONS (health and health care administration), SOCIAL SCIENCE (American studies, criminology, human services, physical fitness/movement, psychology, social science, and sociology). Business, education, and preprofessional science are the strongest academically. Conservation management, education, and management information systems are the largest.

Required: All students must complete at least 120 semester hours with a GPA of 2.0 overall and 2.5 in the major. Distribution requirements include 9 hours each in English and speech, 6 each in arts and humanities, natural sciences, and social science, and 3 each in math, computer skills, and cultures.

Special: Internships, a work-study program, study abroad, a 3-year B.A. degree in any major, and student-designed majors are available. There are 3 national honor societies and a freshman honors program.

Faculty/Classroom: 55% of faculty are male; 45%, female. All teach undergraduates, 20% do research, and 20% do both. The average class size in an introductory lecture is 30; in a laboratory, 10; and in a regular course, 15.

Admissions: 94% of the 2001-2002 applicants were accepted. The ACT scores for the 2001-2002 freshman class were: 40% below 21, 20% between 21 and 23, 20% between 24 and 26, 15% between 27 and 28, and 5% above 28. 10% of the current freshmen were in the top fifth of their class; 40% were in the top two fifths. 4 freshmen graduated first in their class.

Requirements: The SAT I or ACT is required. In addition, recommendations from counselors and extracurricular activities in school, church, and community are also considered in the admissions process. A GPA of 2.0 is required. AP and CLEP credits are accepted.

Procedure: Freshmen are admitted to all sessions. Entrance exams should be taken in the spring of junior year. Application deadlines are open. The application fee is $15. Notification is sent on a rolling basis.

Transfer: 128 transfer students enrolled in 2001-2002. The prime consideration for transfer students is continued good standing in an accredited institution. Credit is generally given for all lecture and lab courses. 30 credits of 120 must be completed at Upper Iowa.

Visiting: There are regularly scheduled orientations for prospective students, including campus tours, meals, and visits with faculty and admissions counselors. There are guides for informal visits and visitors may sit in on classes and stay overnight. To schedule a visit, contact the Admissions Administrative Assistant/Office Manager.

Financial Aid: In 2001-2002, 96% of all freshmen and 92% of continuing students received some form of financial aid. 90% of freshmen received need-based aid. The average freshman award was $9125. Of that total, scholarships or need-based grants averaged $3625 ($10,752 maximum); loans averaged $3850 ($7625 maximum); and work contracts averaged $1650. All undergraduates work part time. Average annual earnings from campus work are $1650. The average financial indebtedness of the 2001 graduate was $17,125. The FAFSA and the college's own financial statement are required. The fall application deadline is open.

International Students: There are 34 international students enrolled. The school actively recruits these students. They must score 450 on the written TOEFL.

Computers: The mainframe is an IBM. Macs are also available. All students may access the system. There are no time limits and no fees.

Graduates: In 2001, 986 bachelor's degrees were awarded. The most popular majors were management (34%), social work/human resources (14%), and accounting (10%). In an average class, 90% graduate in 4 years, and 10% in 5 years. Of the 2000 graduating class, 93% were employed within 6 months of graduation.

Admissions Contact: Kent McElvania, Director of Admissions. E-mail: *admissions@uiu.edu* Web: *www.uiu.edu*

WARTBURG COLLEGE
Waverly, IA 50677-0903 D-2
(319) 352-8264
(800) 772-2085; Fax: (319) 352-8579

Full-time: 656 men, 906 women	**Faculty:** 91; IIB, -$
Part-time: 35 men, 52 women	**Ph.D.s:** 92%
Graduate: none	**Student/Faculty:** 17 to 1
Year: 4-4-1, summer session	**Tuition:** $16,565
Application Deadline: August 1	**Room & Board:** $4600
Freshman Class: 1562 applied, 1373 accepted, 470 enrolled	
SAT I Verbal/Math: 580/610	**ACT:** 24 **VERY COMPETITIVE**

Wartburg College, established in 1852, is a private liberal arts institution affiliated with the Evangelical Lutheran Church in America. In addition to regional accreditation, Wartburg has baccalaureate program accreditation with CSWE, NASM, and NCATE. The library contains 138,763 volumes, 7411 microform items, and 2963 audiovisual forms/CDs, and subscribes to 829 periodicals. Computerized library services include the card catalog, interlibrary loans, and database searching. Special learning facilities include a learning resource center, art gallery, natural history museum, planetarium, radio station, TV station, business center, classroom technology center, fine arts center, journalism lab, symbolic computation lab, music computer lab, 6 acres of native grasses and prairie plants, and more than 100 acres of native timber used for field trips and research. The 118-acre campus is in a small town 15 miles north of Waterloo/Cedar Falls. Including residence halls, there are 34 buildings.

Student Life: 76% of undergraduates are from Iowa. Others are from 25 states, 32 foreign countries, and Canada. 95% are from public schools. 89% are white. 73% are Protestant; 23% Catholic. The average age of freshmen is 19; all undergraduates, 20. 25% do not continue beyond their first year; 73% remain to graduate.

Housing: 1286 students can be accommodated in college housing, which includes single-sex and coed dormitories and on-campus townhouses for single senior students. In addition, there are special-interest houses. On-campus housing is guaranteed for all 4 years. 82% of students live on campus; of those, 60% remain on campus on weekends. All students may keep cars.

Activities: There are no fraternities or sororities. There are 94 groups on campus, including art, band, cheerleading, choir, chorale, chorus, computers, dance, debate, drama, ethnic, forensics, gay, honors, international, jazz band, literary magazine, musical theater, newspaper, opera, orchestra, pep band, photography, political, professional, radio and TV, religious, social, social service, student government, symphony, and yearbook. Popular campus events include Artist Series, Convocations, and Family Weekend.

Sports: There are 10 intercollegiate sports for men and 9 for women, and 8 intramural sports for men and 8 for women. Facilities include a phys ed center that includes a field house, handball/racquetball/squash courts, basketball and tennis/badminton/volleyball courts, an indoor track, a weight room, a cardiovascular room, and an aerobics and wrestling room; a 5000-seat stadium with a football field and all-weather track; a 2000-seat gym; a lighted baseball park; football, soccer, and softball fields; and outdoor tennis courts.

Disabled Students: 85% of the campus is accessible. Wheelchair ramps, elevators, special parking, specially equipped rest rooms, special class scheduling, lowered drinking fountains, lowered telephones, and several residence-hall rooms equipped to accommodate physically disabled students are available.

Services: Counseling and information services are available, as is tutoring in most subjects. There is remedial math, a supplemental instruction program, and assistance with speech writing and delivery. A writing and reading center is also available.

Campus Safety and Security: Measures include 24-hour foot and vehicle patrol, self-defense education, escort service, and informal discussions. There are pamphlets/posters/films, emergency telephones, lighted pathways/sidewalks, 24-hour patrol, and student escort service.

Programs of Study: Wartburg confers B.A., B.A.A., B.A.S., B.M., and B.M.E. degrees. Bachelor's degrees are awarded in BIOLOGICAL SCIENCE (biochemistry and biology/biological science), BUSINESS (accounting, banking and finance, business administration and management, international business management, marketing/retailing/merchandising, and recreation and leisure services), COMMUNICATIONS AND THE ARTS (applied music, art, arts administration/management, broadcasting, communications, creative writing, dramatic arts, English, French, German, graphic design, journalism, music, music performance, music theory and composition, public relations, and Spanish), COMPUTER AND PHYSICAL SCIENCE (chemistry, computer science, information sciences and systems, mathematics, and physics), EDUCATION (art, elementary, English, foreign languages, journalism, mathematics, music, physical, science, secondary, and social studies), ENGINEERING AND ENVIRONMENTAL DESIGN (engineering and applied science), HEALTH PROFESSIONS (medical laboratory technology, music therapy, and occupational therapy), SOCIAL SCIENCE (economics, French studies, German area studies, history, international relations, philosophy, political science/government, psychology, religion, religious music, social work, and sociology). Math, biology, and chemistry are the strongest academically. Biology, education, and business are the largest.

Required: Degree requirements include a minimum cumulative and major GPA of 2.0 and completion of 36 course credits (128 semester hours), including 4 May term course credits. All students must complete the Wartburg Plan of Essential Education, an integrative and interdisciplinary program of study, based on course work in thinking strategies, reasoning skills, faith and reflection, health and wellness, and literacy in writing, diversity, and a foreign language. Students must also demonstrate proficiency in information systems and in oral communication and must complete a capstone project.

Special: Special academic programs at Wartburg include those in leadership education and global and multicultural studies. Internships are available in all majors and there are internship programs in Denver, Washington, D.C., and abroad. Study abroad in 15 countries, on-campus work-study, dual majors in any combination, and individualized majors are possible. A 3-2 engineering degree is offered with Iowa State University, the Universities of Iowa and Illinois, and Washington University in St. Louis. Other 3-2 degrees are possible in medical technology and occupational therapy. A deferred Admit program with the University of Iowa College of Dentistry is offered, as is an array of experiential learning opportunities. There are 11 national honor societies.

Faculty/Classroom: 52% of faculty are male; 48%, female. All teach undergraduates and 36% do research. The average class size in an introductory lecture is 38; in a laboratory, 22; and in a regular course, 28.

Admissions: 88% of the 2001-2002 applicants were accepted. The SAT I scores for the 2001-2002 freshman class were: Verbal--21% below 500, 42% between 500 and 599, 18% between 600 and 700, and 18% above 700; Math--18% below 500, 30% between 500 and 599, 36% between 600 and 700, and 15% above 700. The ACT scores were 22% below 21, 21% between 21 and 23, 25% between 24 and 26, 18% between 27 and 28, and 14% above 28. 54% of the current freshmen were in the top fifth of their class; 75% were in the top two fifths. There were 4 National Merit finalists. 43 freshmen graduated first in their class.

Requirements: The SAT I or ACT is required, with a minimum score of 790 on the SAT I or 18 on the ACT expected. Candidates for admission must be graduates of an accredited secondary school, having completed 4 years of English, 3 each of math and science, 2 each of social studies and foreign language, and 1 of introduction to computers. The GED is accepted, with an average of 50 or above expected. Wartburg requires applicants to be in the upper 50% of their class. A GPA of 2.2 is required. AP and CLEP credits are accepted. Important factors in the admissions decision are advanced placement or honor courses, recommendations by school officials, and leadership record.

Procedure: Freshmen are admitted fall and winter. Entrance exams should be taken before the senior year. There is an early action plan. Early action applications should be filed by December 1; regular applications, by August 1 for fall entry and December 30 for winter entry. Notification is sent on a rolling basis. The fall 2001 application fee was $20.

Transfer: 51 transfer students enrolled in 2001-2002. Applicants must have earned an associate degree or have maintained a minimum GPA of 2.0 in previous college work for 1 year. The ACT or the SAT I must be taken; the minimum acceptable ACT score is 19. Students must submit official transcripts from all colleges attended. 7 credits of 36 must be completed at Wartburg.

Visiting: There are regularly scheduled orientations for prospective students, including an introduction to academic and student life conducted by administrators, faculty, and students, and advising and registration. There are guides for informal visits and visitors may sit in on classes and stay overnight. To schedule a visit, contact the Admissions Office.

Financial Aid: In a recent year, 97% of all students received some form af aid. 67% of freshmen and 61% of continuing students received need-based aid. The average freshman award was $14,136. Of that total, scholarships or need-based grants averaged $9305; loans averaged $4010; and work contracts averaged $821 ($1500 maximum). 60% of undergraduates work part time. Average annual earnings from campus work are $1551. The average financial indebtedness of the 2001 graduate was $17,366. The FAFSA is required. The fall application deadline is March 1.
International Students: There are 69 international students enrolled. The school actively recruits these students. They must score 550 on the written TOEFL or take the MELAB. SAT I or ACT scores are not required but are useful in admissions decisions.
Computers: The mainframes are a DEC VAX 4000-300, DEC ALPHA 2000, DEC VAX Station 3100, DEC VAX 3300 l, and two ALPHA 1000A. All students may use the mainframe system, Internet, and World Wide Web. Students are assigned a password and a user ID. More than 200 Macs and PCs are also available. All students may access the system. There are no time limits. The fee is $75.
Graduates: In 2001, 324 bachelor's degrees were awarded. The most popular majors were business adminstration (20%), elementary education (17%), and biology (13%). In an average class, 1% graduate in 3 years, 65% in 4 years, 70% in 5 years, and 71% in 6 years. 50 companies recruited on campus in 2000-2001. Of a recent graduating class, 20% were enrolled in graduate school within 6 months of graduation and 75% were employed.
Admissions Contact: Doug Bowman, Dean of Admissions and Financial Aid. A video is available. E-mail: *admissions@wartburg.edu*
Web: *www.wartburg.edu*

WILLIAM PENN UNIVERSITY — D-3
Oskaloosa, IA 52577 — **(641) 673-1012**
(800) 779-7366; Fax: (641) 673-1396

Full-time: 749 men, 629 women	**Faculty:** 43
Part-time: 63 men, 106 women	**Ph.D.s:** 40%
Graduate: none	**Student/Faculty:** 32 to 1
Year: semesters, summer session	**Tuition:** $13,270
Application Deadline: open	**Room & Board:** $4305
Freshman Class: 756 applied, 544 accepted, 265 enrolled	
ACT: 21	**COMPETITIVE**

William Penn University, founded in 1873, is a private liberal arts institution affiliated with the Society of Friends (Quakers). There are 2 undergraduate schools. In addition to regional accreditation, William Penn has baccalaureate program accreditation with NCATE. The library contains 66,500 volumes, 2879 microform items, and 423 audiovisual forms/CDs, and subscribes to 345 periodicals. Computerized library services include the card catalog, interlibrary loans, and database searching. Special learning facilities include a learning resource center, art gallery, radio station, and Mideast collection. The 40-acre campus is in a rural area 58 miles southeast of Des Moines. Including residence halls, there are 13 buildings.
Student Life: 73% of undergraduates are from Iowa. Others are from 41 states, 10 foreign countries, and Canada. 90% are from public schools. 83% are white; 10% African American. 44% are Protestant; 39% claim no religious affiliation; 13% Catholic. The average age of freshmen is 19; all undergraduates, 25. 35% do not continue beyond their first year; 40% remain to graduate.
Housing: 500 students can be accommodated in college housing, which includes single-sex and coed dormitories. On-campus housing is guaranteed for all 4 years. 60% of students commute. Alcohol is not permitted. All students may keep cars.
Activities: 5% of men belong to 2 local fraternities; 5% of women belong to 3 local sororities. There are 30 groups on campus, including band, cheerleading, choir, chorale, chorus, computers, drama, ethnic, honors, international, jazz band, literary magazine, musical theater, newspaper, pep band, photography, professional, radio, religious, social, social service, student government, and yearbook. Popular campus events include Multicultural Day and Campus Beautification Day.
Sports: There are 8 intercollegiate sports for men and 6 for women, and 6 intramural sports for men and 6 for women. Facilities include include a gym with 2 regulation-size basketball courts and wrestling and weight training rooms, baseball and softball fields, 3 tennis courts, and football and soccer practice fields.
Disabled Students: 70% of the campus is accessible. Wheelchair ramps, elevators, special parking, specially equipped rest rooms, and special class scheduling are available.
Services: Counseling and information services are available, as is tutoring in most subjects. There is remedial math, reading, and writing.
Campus Safety and Security: Measures include 24-hour foot and vehicle patrol, informal discussions, emergency telephones, and lighted pathways/sidewalks.
Programs of Study: William Penn confers the B.A. degree. Associate degrees are also awarded. Bachelor's degrees are awarded in BIOLOGICAL SCIENCE (biology/biological science and biotechnology), BUSINESS (accounting, business administration and management, recreation and leisure services, and sports management), COMMUNICATIONS AND THE ARTS (communications, English, fine arts, journalism, and public relations), COMPUTER AND PHYSICAL SCIENCE (computer science), EDUCATION (elementary, health, physical, science, secondary, and special), ENGINEERING AND ENVIRONMENTAL DESIGN (environmental science, industrial administration/management, and industrial engineering technology), SOCIAL SCIENCE (criminology, history, human services, political science/government, psychology, and sociology). Elementary and secondary education, industrial technology, and business are the strongest academically. Education and business are the largest.
Required: To graduate, students must complete 124 hours, with 30 to 75 hours in the major. A GPA of 2.0 overall and in major and minor courses is required. Leadership core requirements total 47 hours in English/communications, math, natural science, social science, religion, fine arts, and philosophy.
Special: William Penn offers internships, work-study programs with local businesses, dual majors, nondegree study, pass/fail options, and 3-2 engineering degree programs with Iowa State and Washington Universities. Preprofessional studies, driver and safety education, and endorsements in numerous secondary education subjects are also offered. There are 2 national honor societies, including Phi Beta Kappa.
Faculty/Classroom: 57% of faculty are male; 43%, female. All teach undergraduates. The average class size in an introductory lecture is 25.
Admissions: 72% of the 2001-2002 applicants were accepted. The ACT scores for the 2001-2002 freshman class were: 49% below 21, 36% between 21 and 23, 12% between 24 and 26, 2% between 27 and 28, and 1% above 28. 20% of the current freshmen were in the top fifth of their class; 51% were in the top two fifths. 2 freshmen graduated first in their class.
Requirements: The SAT I or ACT is required. In addition, applicants must be graduates of an accredited secondary and should have completed 15 high school units. The GED is accepted. A GPA of 2.0 is required. AP and CLEP credits are accepted. Important factors in the admissions decision are evidence of special talent, extracurricular activities record, and leadership record. Applications are accepted on-line via the school's web site.
Procedure: Freshmen are admitted to all sessions. Entrance exams should be taken late in the junior year or early in the senior year. There are early admissions and deferred admissions plans. Application deadlines are open. The priority deadline for regular applications is March 1. The application fee is $20. Notification is sent on a rolling basis.
Transfer: 164 transfer students enrolled in 2001-2002. Applicants must be in good standing at their previous institution and submit official transcripts from previously attended schools. 30 credits of 124 must be completed at William Penn.
Visiting: There are regularly scheduled orientations for prospective students, including a 1-day visit comprised of meetings with faculty, student services, financial aid, personnel, and people who share students' interests. There are guides for informal visits and visitors may sit in on classes and stay overnight. To schedule a visit, contact the Director of Admissions.
Financial Aid: In 2001-2002, 97% of all students received some form of financial aid. 95% of freshmen and 96% of continuing students received need-based aid. The average freshman award was $18,373. Of that total, scholarships or need-based grants averaged $9537 ($15,575 maximum); loans averaged $2625 (maximum); and work contracts averaged $1825 ($2000 maximum). 70% of undergraduates work part time. Average annual earnings from campus work are $1600. The average financial indebtedness of the 2001 graduate was $18,600. The FAFSA is required. The priority deadline for fall applications is April 1.
International Students: There are 15 international students enrolled. The school actively recruits these students. They must score 500 on the written TOEFL.
Computers: The mainframe is an HP 3000. There are more than 70 terminals and PCs in the computer lab and library, with data access in every dorm room. All students may access the system. There are no time limits and no fees.
Graduates: In 2001, 220 bachelor's degrees were awarded. The most popular majors were business management (61%), elementary education (9%), and psychology (5%). In an average class, 56% graduate in 4 years, 90% in 5 years, and 98% in 6 years. 160 companies recruited on campus in 2000-2001. Of the 2000 graduating class, 15% were enrolled in graduate school within 6 months of graduation and 75% were employed.
Admissions Contact: Mary Boyd, Director of Admissions.
E-mail: *admissions@wmpenn.edu* Web: *www.wmpenn.edu*

KANSAS

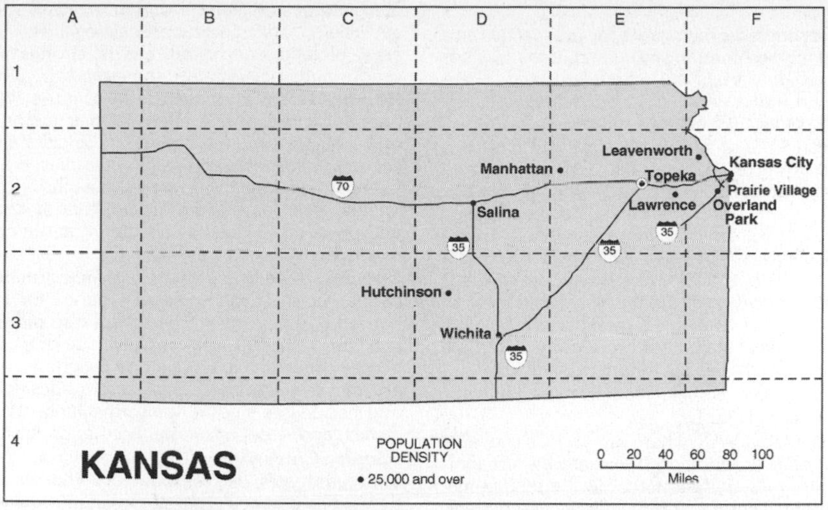

BAKER UNIVERSITY

Baldwin City, KS 66006 — E-2

(785) 594-8307

(800) 873-4282; Fax: (785) 594-8372

Full-time: 340 men, 400 women	**Faculty:** 67; IIB, --$
Part-time: 5 men, 20 women	**Ph.D.s:** 90%
Graduate: none	**Student/Faculty:** 11 to 1
Year: 4-1-4, summer session	**Tuition:** $12,900
Application Deadline: open	**Room & Board:** $4880
Freshman Class: n/av	
ACT: 24	**COMPETITIVE+**

Baker University, founded in 1858, is a private liberal arts institution operated by the United Methodist Church. Figures in the above capsule are approximate. There are 2 undergraduate schools and 1 graduate school. In addition to regional accreditation, Baker has baccalaureate program accreditation with ACBSP, NASM, NCATE, and NLN. The library contains 65,000 volumes, 1000 microform items, and 300 audiovisual forms/CDs, and subscribes to 320 periodicals. Computerized library services include the card catalog, interlibrary loans, and database searching. Special learning facilities include a learning resource center, art gallery, natural history museum, radio station, TV station, greenhouse, and wetlands. The 26-acre campus is in a rural area 35 miles southwest of Kansas City and 15 miles south of Lawrence in a small community. Including residence halls, there are 26 buildings.

Student Life: 67% of undergraduates are from Kansas. Others are from 20 states and 8 foreign countries. 95% are from public schools. 88% are white. 74% are Protestant; 22% claim no religious affiliation; 20% Catholic. The average age of freshmen is 18; all undergraduates, 20. 13% do not continue beyond their first year; 46% remain to graduate.

Housing: 400 students can be accommodated in college housing, which includes single-sex and coed dormitories, on-campus apartments, fraternity houses, and sorority houses. On-campus housing is guaranteed for all 4 years. 80% of students live on campus; of those, 75% remain on campus on weekends. Alcohol is not permitted. All students may keep cars.

Activities: 59% of men belong to 1 local and 3 national fraternities; 61% of women belong to 4 national sororities. There are 42 groups on campus, including art, band, cheerleading, chess, choir, chorale, chorus, dance, debate, drama, drill team, ethnic, forensics, honors, international, jazz band, literary magazine, marching band, musical theater, newspaper, opera, orchestra, pep band, photography, political, professional, radio and TV, religious, social, social service, student government, and yearbook. Popular campus events include Maple Leaf Festival and Alumni Day.

Sports: There are 9 intercollegiate sports for men and 9 for women, and 10 intramural sports for men and 10 for women. Facilities include a 3500-seat stadium, a 2500-seat gym, practice and varsity fields for football, track, soccer, and baseball, 3 basketball courts, racquetball courts, a jogging track, a wellness facility, and a weight room.

Disabled Students: 45% of the campus is accessible. Wheelchair ramps, elevators, special parking, specially equipped rest rooms, special class scheduling, lowered drinking fountains, and lowered telephones are available.

Services: Counseling and information services are available, as is tutoring in most subjects. There is a reader service for the blind, and remedial math, reading, and writing.

Campus Safety and Security: Measures include escort service, informal discussions, lighted pathways/sidewalks, and a patrol from 5 P.M. to 6 A.M.

Programs of Study: Baker confers B.A., B.S., B.M., and B.M.E. degrees. Bachelor's degrees are awarded in BIOLOGICAL SCIENCE (biology/biological science and wildlife biology), BUSINESS (accounting, banking and finance, business administration and management, business economics, and international business management), COMMUNICATIONS AND THE ARTS (art history and appreciation, communications, dramatic arts, English, fine arts, French, German, music, Spanish, and studio art), COMPUTER AND PHYSICAL SCIENCE (chemistry, computer science, information sciences and systems, mathematics, and physics), EDUCATION (art, business, elementary, music, and secondary), ENGINEERING AND ENVIRONMENTAL DESIGN (environmental science), HEALTH PROFESSIONS (nursing, predentistry, and premedicine), SOCIAL SCIENCE (economics, history, philosophy, political science/government, prelaw, psychology, religion, and sociology). Biology, education, and music are the strongest academically. Business, education, and psychology are the largest.

Required: To graduate, all students must complete 132 credit hours, including 24 to 30 hours in the major and 42 hours in 6 basic areas of study, with a minimum GPA of 2.0. Courses in phys ed, computer science, and English composition are required.

Special: Internships are encouraged for students in most majors during the interterm of the sophomore year. Baker also offers study abroad, B.A.-B.S. and accelerated degree programs, dual majors, pass/fail options, and credit for life, military, and work experience. A 3-2 engineering degree may be earned in conjunction with Washington University and the University of Kansas. An interdisciplinary applied environmental sciences program offers majors in environmental chemistry, wildlife biology, and environmental technology and management. There are 13 national honor societies, a freshman honors program, and 9 departmental honors programs.

Faculty/Classroom: 67% of faculty are male; 33%, female. All teach undergraduates and 25% both teach and do research. The average class size in an introductory lecture is 35; in a laboratory, 20; and in a regular course, 24.

Admissions: There were 6 National Merit semifinalists. 10 freshmen graduated first in their class.

Requirements: The SAT I or ACT is required. In addition, candidates for admission must graduate from an accredited secondary school or earn a GED. High school course work in English, a foreign language, social studies, math, and natural science is recommended. Applications of students not meeting these requirements will be reviewed, and students may be admitted on a probationary basis. Students are required to submit ACT or SAT I scores. Applications are available on-line at the school's web site. A GPA of 3.0 is required. AP and CLEP credits are accepted.

Procedure: Freshmen are admitted fall and spring. Entrance exams should be taken in the fall of the senior year. There are early admissions and deferred admissions plans. Application deadlines are open. The application fee is $20.

Transfer: Transfer applicants must supply a recommendation form, available from the Baker Admissions Office. The ACT or the SAT I score, official high school transcript, and official transcripts of all college courses are required. The minimum GPA is 2.7. 31 credits of 132 must be completed at Baker.

Visiting: There are regularly scheduled orientations for prospective students, Preview Days scheduled for freshmen in spring and in fall, and for transfers in spring and fall. Individual visits are scheduled daily. There are guides for informal visits and visitors may sit in on classes and stay overnight. To schedule a visit, contact Admissions Office.

Financial Aid: In a recent year, 98% of all freshmen and 97% of continuing students received some form of financial aid. 59% of freshmen and 56% of continuing students received need-based aid. The average freshman award was $12,066. Of that total, scholarships or need-based grants averaged $5284 ($16,450 maximum); loans averaged $3740 ($5625 maximum); and work contracts averaged $1400 ($2100 maximum). 38% of undergraduates work part time. Average annual earnings from campus work are $1000. The average financial indebtedness of graduates in a recent year was $17,941. Baker is a member of CSS. The FAFSA and the college's own financial statement are required. The fall application deadline is April 15. March 1 is the priority deadline.

International Students: The school actively recruits these students. They must score 525 on the written TOEFL.

Computers: The mainframe is a DEC VAX. There are 45 PCs available for student use in the computer lab. In addition, there are 24 terminals in the lab and 6 in each dormitory for student access to the mainframe. All students may access the system. There are no time limits and no fees.

Admissions Contact: S. Paigeillum, Director of Admissions.
E-mail: *admission@george.bakeru.edu* Web: *www.bakeru.edu*

BENEDICTINE COLLEGE

E-1

Atchison, KS 66002

(913) 367-5340, ext. 2476
(800) 467-5340; Fax: (913) 367-6102

Full-time: 453 men, 426 women	**Faculty:** 57
Part-time: 176 men, 242 women	**Ph.D.s:** 81%
Graduate: 34 men, 17 women	**Student/Faculty:** 15 to 1
Year: semesters, summer session	**Tuition:** $13,215
Application Deadline: open	**Room & Board:** $5270
Freshman Class: 648 applied, 569 accepted, 259 enrolled	
SAT I Verbal/Math: 517/511	**ACT:** 22 **LESS COMPETITIVE**

Benedictine College, established in 1971, is a liberal arts, Catholic, Benedictine institution. In addition to regional accreditation, Benedictine has baccalaureate program accreditation with NASM and NCATE. The library contains 366,212 volumes, 36,431 microform items, and 831 audiovisual forms/CDs, and subscribes to 501 periodicals. Computerized library services include the card catalog, interlibrary loans, and database searching. Special learning facilities include a learning resource center. The 225-acre campus is in a small town 45 miles north of Kansas City. Including residence halls, there are 18 buildings.

Student Life: 53% of undergraduates are from Kansas. Others are from 34 states, 16 foreign countries, and Canada. 55% are from public schools. 83% are white. 68% are Catholic; 14% Protestant; 10% claim no religious affiliation. The average age of freshmen is 18; all undergraduates, 23. 30% do not continue beyond their first year.

Housing: 725 students can be accommodated in college housing, which includes single-sex dormitories. On-campus housing is guaranteed for all 4 years. 82% of students live on campus. All students may keep cars.

Activities: There are no fraternities or sororities. There are 24 groups on campus, including band, cheerleading, choir, chorale, computers, drama, drill team, ethnic, honors, international, jazz band, literary magazine, musical theater, newspaper, orchestra, pep band, photography, political, professional, religious, social, social service, student government, symphony, and yearbook. Popular campus events include Discovery Week, Parents Weekend, and All School Mass.

Sports: There are 7 intercollegiate sports for men and 8 for women, and 7 intramural sports for men and 7 for women. Facilities include a gym, weight rooms, a football and track stadium, baseball, softball, and track fields, and an isometrics training room.

Disabled Students: 80% of the campus is accessible. Wheelchair ramps, elevators, special parking, specially equipped rest rooms, special class scheduling, and lowered drinking fountains are available.

Services: Counseling and information services are available, as is tutoring in most subjects. There is remedial math, reading, and writing.

Campus Safety and Security: Measures include 24-hour foot and vehicle patrol, informal discussions, pamphlets/posters/films, and lighted pathways/sidewalks.

Programs of Study: Benedictine confers B.A., B.S., and B.Mus.Ed. degrees. Associate and master's degrees are also awarded. Bachelor's degrees are awarded in BIOLOGICAL SCIENCE (biochemistry and biology/biological science), BUSINESS (accounting and business administration and management), COMMUNICATIONS AND THE ARTS (dramatic arts, English, French, journalism, music, Spanish, and theater management), COMPUTER AND PHYSICAL SCIENCE (astronomy, chemistry, computer science, mathematics, natural sciences, and physics), EDUCATION (athletic training, elementary, music, physical, secondary, and special), SOCIAL SCIENCE (economics, history, liberal arts/general studies, philosophy, political science/government, psychology, religion, social science, sociology, and youth ministry). Physical science, biology, and history are the strongest academically. Biology, education, and sociology are the largest.

Required: To graduate, students must complete 128 semester hours, pass a comprehensive exam in their major, and earn a minimum GPA of 2.0 overall and in the major. Curriculum requirements include 9 hours each in philosophy and religious studies, 8 hours each in English, natural science, and foreign language, 6 each in Western civilization and social science, 4 in math, 3 in fine arts, and 2 each in speech communication and phys. ed. A dean's colloquium and a comprehensive exam are also required.

Special: Benedictine offers cross-registration with the 14 other members of the Kansas City Regional Council for Higher Education and study abroad in 6 countries. The school also offers a 3-2 occupational therapy program with Washington University of St. Louis and a 3-2 engineering degree. Internships, work-study programs, dual majors, an interdisciplinary music marketing major, student-designed majors, pass/fail options, and nondegree study are also available. There are 4 national honor societies, and 4 departmental honors program.

Faculty/Classroom: 71% of faculty are male; 29%, female. All teach undergraduates. No introductory courses are taught by graduate students. The average class size in an introductory lecture is 25; in a laboratory, 20; and in a regular course, 20.

Admissions: 88% of the 2001-2002 applicants were accepted. The SAT I scores for the 2001-2002 freshman class were: Verbal--49% below 500, 34% between 500 and 599, 12% between 600 and 700, and 5% above 700; Math--46% below 500, 32% between 500 and 599, 20% between 600 and 700, and 2% above 700. The ACT scores were 34% below 21, 28% between 21 and 23, 19% between 24 and 26, 10% between 27 and 28, and 9% above 28. 27% of the current freshmen were in the top fifth of their class; 65% were in the top two fifths. 7 freshmen graduated first in their class.

Requirements: The ACT is required. In addition, applicants should graduate in the upper 50% of their class at an accredited secondary school. Students should have 16 academic units, including 4 in English, 3 to 4 in math, 2 to 4 in foreign language and science, 2 in social science, and 1 in history. An interview is recommended. Counselor recommendations are required. A GPA of 2.5 is required. AP and CLEP credits are accepted. Important factors in the admissions decision are advanced placement or honor courses, recommendations by school officials, and recommendations by alumni. Applications are accepted on-line.

Procedure: Freshmen are admitted to all sessions. Entrance exams should be taken before the July following graduation from high school. There is a deferred admissions plan. Application deadlines are open. The application fee is $25. Notification is sent on a rolling basis.

Transfer: 74 transfer students enrolled in 2001-2002. Applicants must submit transcripts from all colleges attended, a statement of courses in progress, and an adviser recommendation. A minimum GPA of 2.0 is required. 24 credits of 128 must be completed at Benedictine.

Visiting: There are regularly scheduled orientations for prospective students, consisting of an advanced placement exam, preregistration, meetings with the dean, student affairs, and business office and financial aid representatives, and campus tours. The orientations are scheduled for April, June, and July. There are guides for informal visits and visitors may sit in on classes and stay overnight. To schedule a visit, contact the Admissions Office at *bcadmiss@benedictine.edu*.

Financial Aid: In 2001-2002, 86% of all freshmen and 88% of continuing students received some form of financial aid. 74% of freshmen and 75% of continuing students received need-based aid. The average freshman award was $11,308. Of that total, scholarships or need-based grants averaged $8016 ($12,116 maximum); loans averaged $4862 ($14,500 maximum); work contracts averaged $1574 ($2000 maximum); and outside awards averaged $1459 ($4462 maximum). 41% of undergraduates work part time. Average annual earnings from campus work are $900. The average financial indebtedness of the 2001 graduate was $20,822. Benedictine is a member of CSS. The FAFSA and the college's own financial statement are required. The fall application deadline is April 1.

International Students: There are 11 international students enrolled. The school actively recruits these students. They must score 535 on the written TOEFL or take the MELAB and also take the SAT I or the ACT, scoring 18 on the ACT.

Computers: The mainframe is an HP 9000 D 380. A lab contains 18 Macs. Smaller clusters of PCs are available in residence halls and the administration building. Each residence hall room has Ethernet access. All students may access the system 24 hours a day in residence halls, and 7:45 A.M. to 11 P.M. weekdays, with shorter hours on weekends, in PC labs. There are no time limits and no fees.

Graduates: In 2001, 219 bachelor's degrees were awarded. The most popular majors were business/marketing (21%), education (19%), and social sciences and history (16%). In an average class, 1% graduate in 3 years, 40% in 4 years, 45% in 5 years, and 48% in 6 years. 35 companies recruited on campus in 2000-2001. Of the 2000 graduating class, 23% were enrolled in graduate school within 6 months of graduation and 76% were employed.

Admissions Contact: Kelly Vowels, Dean of Enrollment Management.
E-mail: *kvowels@raven.benedictine.edu* Web: *www.benedictine.edu*

BETHANY COLLEGE D-2
Lindsborg, KS 67456 (785) 227-3311
(800) 826-2281; Fax: (785) 227-2004

Full-time: 306 men, 265 women **Faculty:** 42; IIB, --$
Part-time: 23 men, 28 women **Ph.D.s:** 61%
Graduate: none **Student/Faculty:** 14 to 1
Year: 4-1-4, summer session **Tuition:** $12,943
Application Deadline: August 1 **Room & Board:** $3659
Freshman Class: 560 applied, 413 accepted, 220 enrolled
ACT: 26 **COMPETITIVE+**

Bethany College, founded in 1881, is a small liberal arts institution affiliated with the Evangelical Lutheran Church in America. In addition to regional accreditation, Bethany has baccalaureate program accreditation with CSWE, NASM, and NCATE. The 2 libraries contain 120,164 volumes, 44,670 microform items, and 3518 audiovisual forms/CDs, and subscribe to 709 periodicals. Computerized library services include interlibrary loans and database searching. Special learning facilities include a learning resource center and art gallery. The 80-acre campus is in a rural area 65 miles north of Wichita and 20 miles south of Salina. Including residence halls, there are 17 buildings.

Student Life: 61% of undergraduates are from Kansas. Others are from 25 states and 8 foreign countries. 95% are from public schools. 86% are white. 45% are Protestant; 18% no preference, other; 15% Catholic. The average age of freshmen is 18; all undergraduates, 20. 22% do not continue beyond their first year; 45% remain to graduate.

Housing: 608 students can be accommodated in college housing, which includes single-sex and coed dormitories and on-campus apartments. In addition, there are special-interest houses. On-campus housing is available on a first-come, first-served basis. 85% of students live on campus; of those, 80% remain on campus on weekends. All students may keep cars.

Activities: 19% of men belong to 3 local fraternities; 20% of women belong to 3 local sororities. There are 61 groups on campus, including art, band, cheerleading, choir, chorale, chorus, computers, drama, drill team, ethnic, honors, international, jazz band, musical theater, newspaper, orchestra, pep band, photography, political, professional, religious, social, social service, student government, symphony, and yearbook. Popular campus events include the Messiah Festival of Art and Music Holy Week Festival.

Sports: There are 7 intercollegiate sports for men and 7 for women, and 30 intramural sports for men and 30 for women. Facilities include a 1500-seat gym, a 4000-seat stadium, tennis courts, a jogging track, handball/racquetball courts, and a weight training area.

Disabled Students: 98% of the campus is accessible. Wheelchair ramps, elevators, special parking, specially equipped rest rooms, special class scheduling, and lowered drinking fountains are available.

Services: Counseling and information services are available, as is tutoring in every subject. There is a reader service for the blind and remedial writing.

Campus Safety and Security: Measures include self-defense education, informal discussions, pamphlets/posters/films, and emergency telephones. There are lighted pathways/sidewalks and a campus patrol at night; residence halls are locked from midnight to 9 A.M.

Programs of Study: Bethany confers the B.A. degree. Bachelor's degrees are awarded in BIOLOGICAL SCIENCE (biology/biological science), BUSINESS (accounting, business administration and management, and business economics), COMMUNICATIONS AND THE ARTS (art, communications, dramatic arts, English, fine arts, and music), COMPUTER AND PHYSICAL SCIENCE (chemistry and mathematics), EDUCATION (art, athletic training, business, elementary, English, mathematics, middle school, music, physical, science, and secondary), HEALTH PROFESSIONS (medical laboratory technology, predentistry, and premedicine), SOCIAL SCIENCE (economics, history, parks and recreation management, prelaw, psychology, social science, social work, and sociology). Chemistry, English, and history are the strongest academically. Business and education are the largest.

Required: All students must complete 38 to 54 semester hours of general education requirements, 2 semester hours of personal wellness classes, and a junior writing proficiency exam. A total of 128 credit hours with a minimum GPA of 2.0 is required for graduation.

Special: Bethany offers co-op programs and cross-registration through the Associated Colleges of Central Kansas and a 3-2 aerospace engineering degree with Wichita State University. Internships, a Chicago semester, a Washington semester, work-study programs, accelerated degree programs in economics/business and pre-engineering, dual majors, including history-political science and religion-philosophy, student-designed majors, and limited pass/fail options are also available. There are 5 national honor societies.

Faculty/Classroom: 76% of faculty are male; 24%, female. All teach undergraduates. The average class size in an introductory lecture is 30; in a laboratory, 8; and in a regular course, 22.

Admissions: 74% of the 2001-2002 applicants were accepted. The ACT scores for the 2001-2002 freshman class were: 50% below 21, 13% between 21 and 23, 24% between 24 and 26, 6% between 27 and 28, and 7% above 28. 33% of the current freshmen were in the top fifth of their class; 60% were in the top two fifths. 15 freshmen graduated first in their class.

Requirements: The ACT is required. In addition, applicants should be graduates of an accredited secondary school, with 4 years of English, 3 of social studies, 2 each of math and science, and 1 each of foreign language and phys ed. The GED is accepted. An interview is recommended, along with a portfolio or an audition for some majors. Bethany requires applicants to be in the upper 50% of their class. A GPA of 2.5 is required. AP and CLEP credits are accepted. Important factors in the admissions decision are advanced placement or honor courses, leadership record, and evidence of special talent. Applications are accepted on-line.

Procedure: Freshmen are admitted to all sessions. Applications should be filed by August 1 for fall entry, December 15 for winter entry, and January 15 for spring entry, along with a $20 fee. Notification is sent on a rolling basis.

Transfer: 63 transfer students enrolled in 2001-2002. A GPA of 2.3 in 24 credit hours is required. 60 credits of 128 must be completed at Bethany.

Visiting: There are regularly scheduled orientations for prospective students, including campus tours, a faculty visit, class enrollment, and a financial aid visit. There are guides for informal visits and visitors may sit in on classes and stay overnight. To schedule a visit, contact the Office of Admissions at *admissions@bethanylb.edu*.

Financial Aid: In a recent year, 98% of all students received some form of aid. 80% of all students received need-based aid. The average freshman award was $13,577. Of that total, scholarships or need-based grants averaged $5287 ($8000 maximum); loans averaged $3628 ($4625 maximum); and work contracts averaged $1400 ($2000 maximum). 84% of undergraduates work part time. Average annual earnings from campus work are $1056. The average financial indebtedness of the 2001 graduate was $12,636. The CSS/Profile, FAFSA, FFS, or SFS is required. The fall application deadline is August 1.

International Students: There are 9 international students enrolled. The school actively recruits these students. They must score 525 on the written TOEFL.

Computers: The mainframe is an HP 9000. There is a networked computer system with an 8 to 1 computer to student ratio. All students may access the system from 7 A.M. to midnight. There are no time limits. The fee is $10 per semester.

Graduates: In 2001, 115 bachelor's degrees were awarded. The most popular majors were economics and business (25%), education (13%), and elementary education (11%). In an average class, 1% graduate in 3 years, 39% in 4 years, 45% in 5 years, and 47% in 6 years. 7 companies recruited on campus in 2000-2001. Of the 2000 graduating class, 22% were enrolled in graduate school within 6 months of graduation and 70% were employed.

Admissions Contact: Daniel McKinney, Dean of Admissions and Financial Aid. A video is available.
E-mail: *mckinney@bethany.bethanylb.edu* Web: *www.bethanylb.edu*

BETHEL COLLEGE D-3
North Newton, KS 67117 (316) 284-5230
(800) 522-1887, ext. 230; Fax: (316) 284-5870

Full-time: 243 men, 239 women **Faculty:** 50; IIB, --$
Part-time: 20 men, 23 women **Ph.D.s:** 61%
Graduate: none **Student/Faculty:** 10 to 1
Year: 4-1-4, summer session **Tuition:** $12,200
Application Deadline: open **Room & Board:** $5155
Freshman Class: 432 applied, 323 accepted, 126 enrolled
ACT: 24 **COMPETITIVE+**

Bethel College, established in 1887, is a private liberal arts institution affiliated with the Mennonite Church U.S.A. In addition to regional accreditation, Bethel has baccalaureate program accreditation with CCNE and CSWE. The 2 libraries contain 133,600 volumes, 13,425 microform items, and 5798 audiovisual forms/CDs, and subscribe to 560 periodicals. Computerized library services include the card catalog, interlibrary loans, and database searching. Special learning facilities include a learning resource center, art gallery, natural history museum, and radio station. The 60-acre campus is in a suburban area 25 miles north of Wichita. Including residence halls, there are 13 buildings.

Student Life: 65% of undergraduates are from Kansas. Others are from 25 states and 15 foreign countries. 98% are from public schools. 80% are white. 78% are Protestant; 13% claim no religious affiliation. The average age of freshmen is 18; all undergraduates, 21. 28% do not continue beyond their first year.

Housing: 592 students can be accommodated in college housing, which includes single-sex and coed dormitories, off-campus apartments, and married-student housing. On-campus housing is guaranteed for all 4 years. 75% of students live on campus; of those, 60% remain on campus on weekends. Alcohol is not permitted. All students may keep cars.

Activities: There are no fraternities or sororities. There are 40 groups on campus, including art, cheerleading, chess, choir, chorale, chorus, computers, dance, debate, drama, ethnic, forensics, international, jazz band, literary magazine, musical theater, newspaper, opera, orchestra, pep band, radio and TV, religious, social, social service, student government, symphony, and yearbook. Popular campus events include Fall Festival, Winter Frolic, and Spring Fling.

Sports: There are 5 intercollegiate sports for men and 5 for women, and 7 intramural sports for men and 7 for women, and 2 coed intramural sports. Facilities include 2 gyms, a weight room, an exericise room, tennis courts, a soccer field, an all-weather track, football and baseball fields, an outdoor basketball court, an outdoor sand volleyball court, and a nature trail.

Disabled Students: 70% of the campus is accessible. Wheelchair ramps, elevators, special parking, specially equipped rest rooms, and lowered drinking fountains are available.

Services: Counseling and information services are available, as is tutoring in most subjects. There is a reader service for the blind, and remedial math, reading, and writing.

Campus Safety and Security: Measures include escort service, informal discussions, emergency telephones, and lighted pathways/sidewalks.

Programs of Study: Bethel confers B.A., B.S., B.S.N., B.S.S.W. degrees. Bachelor's degrees are awarded in BIOLOGICAL SCIENCE (biology/biological science), BUSINESS (accounting and business administration and management), COMMUNICATIONS AND THE ARTS (art, communications, English, fine arts, German, music, and Spanish), COMPUTER AND PHYSICAL SCIENCE (chemistry, computer science, information sciences and systems, mathematics, natural sciences, and physics), EDUCATION (elementary), HEALTH PROFESSIONS (health science and nursing), SOCIAL SCIENCE (community services, history, peace studies, psychology, religion, social science, and social work). English, biology, and psychology are the strongest academically. Nursing, elementary education, and social work are the largest.

Required: To graduate, students must earn a total of 124 credits, including 24 to 50 in the major, 12 to 50 of those in upper-level courses, with a GPA of 2.0. Students must also meet general education requirements that include demonstrating competency in writing, math, speech, computers, and foreign language. Additional distribution requirements include convocation, religious studies, natural sciences, math or philosophy, cross-cultural learning, social sciences, humanities, fine arts, and health management.

Special: Students may cross-register with Associated Colleges of Central Kansas (ACCK) institutions and Hesston College. Internships are required in many majors. Work-study programs, study abroad in 14 countries, dual majors, student-designed majors, a Washington semester, and pass/fail options are also available. The college offers a 3-2 engineering degree with University of Kansas, Kansas State University, and Wichita State University.

Faculty/Classroom: 63% of faculty are male; 37%, female. All teach undergraduates, 30% do research, and 30% do both. The average class size in an introductory lecture is 30; in a laboratory, 16; and in a regular course, 16.

Admissions: 75% of the 2001-2002 applicants were accepted. 5 freshmen graduated first in their class.

Requirements: The SAT I or ACT is required. Applicants should present a minimum ACT composite of 19 or SAT I total of 890 with a minimum GPA of 2.5 for automatic admission. The GED is accepted. Auditions are required of candidates applying for some scholarships, and interviews are recommended for all applicants. Specific departmental requirements may vary. CLEP, AP, and International Baccalaureate credit may be awarded. Important factors in the admissions decision are evidence of special talent, recommendations by alumni, and parents or siblings attending the school. Applications are accepted on-line via the school's web site.

Procedure: Freshmen are admitted to all sessions. Entrance exams should be taken by the fall of the senior year. Application deadlines are open. The fall 2001 application fee was $20. Notification is sent on a rolling basis.

Transfer: 58 transfer students enrolled in 2001-2002. A high school transcript (or GED), or official college transcript (minimum 2.0 GPA), ACT or SAT I scores (waived if the student has more than 24 hours accepted in transfer to Bethel College), and a transfer recommendation are required. Automatic admission requires a cumulative GPA of 2.0 and a 19 ACT or 890 SAT I score. 30 credits of 124 must be completed at Bethel.

Visiting: There are regularly scheduled orientations for prospective students, including a campus tour, classroom observations, visits with faculty, an interview with an admissions counselor, lunch, and overnight residence hall lodging. There are guides for informal visits and visitors may sit in on classes and stay overnight. To schedule a visit, contact the Admissions Office.

Financial Aid: In 2001-2002, 98% of all freshmen and 93% of continuing students received some form of financial aid. 83% of freshmen and 73% of continuing students received need-based aid. The average freshman award was $13,207. Of that total, scholarships or need-based grants averaged $4054 ($12,200 maximum); loans averaged $3245 ($9625 maximum); and work contracts averaged $1000 ($1500 maximum). 69% of undergraduates work part time. Average annual earnings from campus work are $798. The average financial indebtedness of the 2001 graduate was $11,379. Bethel is a member of CSS. The FAFSA is required. The fall application deadline is March 15.

International Students: There are 21 international students enrolled. The school actively recruits these students. They must score 540 on the written TOEFL or 207 on the electronic version.

Computers: The mainframes are IBM PC servers with NT software. 30 IBM and Mac PCs with printers are available in the campus computer center, library, and music and nursing labs. All students may access the system 18 hours a day. There are no time limits. The fee is $20 per semester.

Graduates: In 2001, 101 bachelor's degrees were awarded. The most popular majors were nursing (17%), history (8%), and English (7%). In an average class, 42% graduate in 4 years, 52% in 5 years, and 52% in 6 years. 58 companies recruited on campus in 2000-2001. Of the 2000 graduating class, 9% were enrolled in graduate school within 6 months of graduation and 98% were employed.

Admissions Contact: Shirley King, Dean of Enrollment Services. A video is available. E-mail: *admissions@bethelks.edu*
Web: *http://www.bethelks.edu*

EMPORIA STATE UNIVERSITY — E-2

Emporia, KS 66801-5087 — **(620) 341-5465**
(877) GO-TO-ESU; Fax: (620) 341-5599

Full-time: 1447 men, 2248 women	**Faculty:** 244; IIA, --$
Part-time: 218 men, 374 women	**Ph.D.s:** 82%
Graduate: 408 men, 1128 women	**Student/Faculty:** 15 to 1
Year: semesters, summer session	**Tuition:** $2284 ($7138)
Application Deadline: open	**Room & Board:** $3914
Freshman Class: 1275 applied, 1152 accepted, 723 enrolled	
ACT: required	**LESS COMPETITIVE**

Emporia State University, founded in 1863, is a state-supported institution that offers degree programs in liberal arts, business, teacher education, and vocational fields, as well as various graduate programs. There are 3 undergraduate and 4 graduate schools. In addition to regional accreditation, ESU has baccalaureate program accreditation with ACS, CAAHEP, CACREP, NASM, NCATE, and NLN. The library contains 555,057 volumes, 1,159,343 microform items, and 7140 audiovisual forms/CDs, and subscribes to 1416 periodicals. Computerized library services include the card catalog, interlibrary loans, and database searching. Special learning facilities include a learning resource center, art gallery, natural history museum, planetarium, theater, geology museum, on-campus elementary school, and Great Plains study center. The 207-acre campus is in a small town 110 miles from Kansas City in the Bluestem Region of the Flint Hills. Including residence halls, there are 22 buildings.

Student Life: 94% of undergraduates are from Kansas. Others are from 42 states, 54 foreign countries, and Canada. 93% are from public schools. 86% are white. The average age of freshmen is 20; all undergraduates, 22. 31% do not continue beyond their first year.

Housing: 1045 students can be accommodated in college housing, which includes single-sex and coed dormitories and on-campus apartments. In addition, there are honors houses, upperclass houses, nonsmoking and alcohol-free living areas and special-interest houses. On-campus housing is available on a first-come, first-served basis and is available on a lottery system for upperclassmen. Priority is given to out-of-town students. 69% of students commute. All students may keep cars.

Activities: 14% of men belong to 6 national fraternities; 8% of women belong to 3 national sororities. There are 117 groups on campus, including art, band, cheerleading, choir, chorale, chorus, computers, drama, drill team, ethnic, film, gay, honors, international, jazz band, literary magazine, marching band, musical theater, newspaper, opera, orchestra, pep band, political, professional, religious, social, social service, student government, symphony, travel, and yearbook. Popular campus events include Campus/Community Festival, Martin Luther King Celebration, and Twin Rivers Festival.

Sports: There are 7 intercollegiate sports for men and 8 for women, and 11 intramural sports for men and 11 for women. Facilities include a 7000-seat stadium, a recreation center, an Olympic-size pool, 5 gyms, 6 handball courts, exercise, physical therapy, and dance rooms, a sports complex with 3 softball fields and 1 baseball diamond, an all-weather 8-

lane track, a soccer field, and 3 additional softball fields separate from the sports complex.

Disabled Students: All of the campus is accessible. Wheelchair ramps, elevators, special parking, specially equipped rest rooms, special class scheduling, lowered drinking fountains, and lowered telephones are available.

Services: There is a reader service for the blind, and remedial math, reading, and writing.

Campus Safety and Security: Measures include 24-hour foot and vehicle patrol, self-defense education, escort service, and informal discussions. There are pamphlets/posters/films, emergency telephones, lighted pathways/sidewalks, motorist-assist programs, safety and self-awareness programs for students and parents, 24-hour residence hall monitoring, and smoke detectors in residence halls.

Programs of Study: ESU confers B.A., B.S., B.F.A., B.I.S., B Mus., B.Mus.Ed., B.S.Bus., B.S.Ed., and B.S.N. degrees. Master's and doctoral degrees are also awarded. Bachelor's degrees are awarded in BIOLOGICAL SCIENCE (biology/biological science), BUSINESS (accounting, business administration and management, management information systems, management science, marketing/retailing/merchandising, and recreation and leisure services), COMMUNICATIONS AND THE ARTS (art, communications, dramatic arts, English, and music), COMPUTER AND PHYSICAL SCIENCE (chemistry, computer science, earth science, information sciences and systems, mathematics, physical sciences, and physics), EDUCATION (art, business, elementary, foreign languages, health, music, physical, and secondary), HEALTH PROFESSIONS (nursing and rehabilitation therapy), SOCIAL SCIENCE (economics, history, liberal arts/general studies, political science/government, psychology, social science, and sociology). Elementary education is the largest.

Required: To graduate, all students must complete at least 124 credit hours, including 40 in upper-division courses, with a minimum GPA of 2.0. Students must also pass competency exams in reading, math, and writing and complete the general education program for their field of study, which includes course in math, physical science, humanities, history, spech, cultural diversity, fitness, and phys ed.

Special: ESU offers co-op programs and internships in many majors, study abroad in 32 countries, work-study programs, on-campus and online general studies degrees, B.A.-B.S. degrees, dual and student-designed majors, 3-2 engineering degrees with Kansas State University, Wichita State University, and the University of Kansas, credit for military experience, nondegree study, independent study, evening and Saturday classes, and pass/no credit options. There are 15 national honor societies, a freshman honors program, and 9 departmental honors programs.

Faculty/Classroom: 66% of faculty are male; 34%, female. The average class size in an introductory lecture is 41; in a laboratory, 21; and in a regular course, 21.

Admissions: 90% of the 2001-2002 applicants were accepted.

Requirements: The ACT is required. In addition, applicants must meet 1 of these 3 criteria: an ACT score of 21 or above, class rank in the top third, or a 2.0 GPA in the Kansas core curriculum. Students should have completed 4 units of English, 3 each of natural science, math, and social science, and 1 of computer technology. Applicants may also be admitted through an exceptions window and are encouraged to apply. AP and CLEP credits are accepted. Applications are accepted on-line.

Procedure: Freshmen are admitted to all sessions. Entrance exams should be taken in October or December of the senior year. There are early admissions and deferred admissions plans. Application deadlines are open, but students are advised to submit applications no later than 10 days before school starts. The fall 2001 application fee was $25. Notification is sent on a rolling basis.

Transfer: 447 transfer students enrolled in 2001-2002. Applicants must submit official transcripts of all previous college work. The minimum GPA depends on the number of semester hours earned. Physical activity requirements must be met. 30 credits of 124 must be completed at ESU.

Visiting: There are regularly scheduled orientations for prospective students, including campus and residence hall tours, meetings with admissions and financial aid personnel, and appointments with academic and extracurriculars personnel if desired. There are guides for informal visits and visitors may sit in on classes and stay overnight. To schedule a visit, contact Susan Brinkman, Director of Admissions.

Financial Aid: In 2000-2001, 52% of all freshmen and 63% of continuing students received some form of financial aid. 40% of freshmen and 49% of continuing students received need-based aid. The average freshman award was $3569. Of that total, scholarships or need-based grants averaged $3569; loans averaged $1784 ($2625 maximum); and work contracts averaged $2025 ($3000 maximum). 22% of undergraduates work part time. Average annual earnings from campus work are $1465. The average financial indebtedness of the 2001 graduate was $12,439. The FAFSA and the State of Kansas Aid form are required. The fall application deadline is March 15.

International Students: There are 118 international students enrolled. The school actively recruits these students. They must score 450 on the written TOEFL or 133 on the electronic version, or take the MELAB, or take the college's own test. Students who score below 520 on the written TOEFL may need to enroll in an intensive English course. They must also take the ACT, scoring 21.

Computers: The mainframe is an IBM 9021 Model 260. For those who have an account on the mainframe, the Internet can be accessed from labs on campus. Students who have accounts may access the system 22 hours per day. There are no time limits and no fees.

Graduates: In 2001, 710 bachelor's degrees were awarded. The most popular majors were elementary education (18%), sociology (8%), and business administration (7%). In an average class, 19% graduate in 4 years, 33% in 5 years, and 39% in 6 years. 230 companies recruited on campus in 2000-2001. Of the 2000 graduating class, 18% were enrolled in graduate school within 6 months of graduation and 81% were employed.

Admissions Contact: Susan Brinkman, Director of Admissions. E-mail: *go2esu@emporia.edu* Web: *www.emporia.edu*

FORT HAYS STATE UNIVERSITY — C-2

Hays, KS 67601-4099 — (785) 628-5666

(800) 628-FHSU; Fax: (785) 628-4014

Full-time: 1756 men, 1954 women	**Faculty:** 254; IIA, --$
Part-time: 340 men, 515 women	**Ph.D.s:** 74%
Graduate: 359 men, 702 women	**Student/Faculty:** 15 to 1
Year: semesters, summer session	**Tuition:** $2217 ($7070)
Application Deadline: open	**Room & Board:** $4077
Freshman Class: 1260 applied, 754 enrolled	
ACT: recommended	**LESS COMPETITIVE**

Fort Hays State University, established in 1902, is a public liberal arts institution offering programs in arts and sciences, business, education, health and life sciences, and preprofessional study. Some information in this profile is approximate. There are 4 undergraduate schools and 1 graduate school. In addition to regional accreditation, FHSU has baccalaureate program accreditation with AACSB, NASM, NCATE, and NLN. The library contains 300,000 volumes, 500,000 microform items, and 1480 audiovisual forms/CDs, and subscribes to 3100 periodicals. Computerized library services include the card catalog, interlibrary loans, and database searching. Special learning facilities include an art gallery, natural history museum, radio station, TV station, and English lab. The 200-acre campus is in a small town 180 miles northwest of Wichita. Including residence halls, there are 44 buildings.

Student Life: 93% of undergraduates are from Kansas. Others are from 36 states, 32 foreign countries, and Canada. 95% are from public schools. 87% are white. The average age of freshmen is 18; all undergraduates, 23. 61% do not continue beyond their first year; 40% remain to graduate.

Housing: 1000 students can be accommodated in college housing, which includes single-sex and coed dormitories, on-campus apartments, married-student housing, fraternity houses, and sorority houses. On-campus housing is guaranteed for all 4 years. 82% of students commute. All students may keep cars.

Activities: 1% of men belong to 3 national fraternities; 1% of women belong to 3 national sororities. There are 85 groups on campus, including art, band, cheerleading, choir, chorale, chorus, computers, dance, debate, drama, drill team, ethnic, film, gay, honors, international, jazz band, literary magazine, marching band, musical theater, newspaper, opera, orchestra, pep band, photography, political, professional, radio and TV, religious, social, social service, student government, symphony, and yearbook. Popular campus events include Octoberfest and Parents Day.

Sports: There are 8 intercollegiate sports for men and 7 for women, and 40 intramural sports for men and 40 for women. Facilities include a 6300-seat stadium, tennis courts, and a coliseum containing a 6800-seat basketball arena, a track, and wrestling and training rooms.

Disabled Students: 75% of the campus is accessible. Wheelchair ramps, elevators, special parking, specially equipped rest rooms, special class scheduling, lowered drinking fountains, lowered telephones, Arkenstone reader, TDD, and voice dictation programs are available.

Services: Counseling and information services are available, as is tutoring in most subjects. There is remedial math and reading.

Campus Safety and Security: Measures include 24-hour foot and vehicle patrol, escort service, informal discussions, and emergency telephones. There are lighted pathways/sidewalks.

Programs of Study: FHSU confers B.A., B.S., B.B.A., B.F.A., B.G.S., B.M., and B.S.W. degrees. Associate and master's degrees are also awarded. Bachelor's degrees are awarded in AGRICULTURE (agricultural business management and agriculture), BIOLOGICAL SCIENCE (biology/biological science), BUSINESS (accounting, banking and finance, business administration and management, management information systems, marketing/retailing/merchandising, and office supervision and management), COMMUNICATIONS AND THE ARTS (art, communications, English, fine arts, French, German, modern language, music, music performance, music theory and composition, Spanish, and telecommunications), COMPUTER AND PHYSICAL SCIENCE (chemistry, computer science, geology, information sciences and systems, mathematics, physical sciences, physics, radiological technology, and science), EDUCATION (art, elementary, music, physical, and technical), HEALTH PROFESSIONS (nursing and speech pathology/audiology), SOCIAL SCIENCE (criminal justice, economics, history, liberal arts/general studies, philosophy, political science/government, psychology, social work, and sociology). Speech pathology is the strongest academically. Teacher education, business administration, and nursing are the largest.

Required: To graduate, students must earn an overall minimum GPA of 2.0 or higher in some departments, for 124 credit hours, including 40 hours in upper-level study and 30 hours minimum in the major. The 55-hour liberal arts general education curriculum includes courses addressing personal wellness, analysis and communication, international studies, humanities, math, and natural, social, and behavioral sciences.

Special: Students may, with approval, earn their degrees through a cooperative program with FHSU and another accredited institution, or a correspondence or extension school. Cross-registration with several community colleges, internships, study abroad, work-study programs, a 3-2 engineering degree with Kansas State University, B.A.-B.S. degrees, a general studies degree, and pass/fail options are available. There are 21 national honor societies and a freshman honors program.

Faculty/Classroom: 64% of faculty are male; 36%, female. All teach undergraduates. The average class size in an introductory lecture is 17; in a laboratory, 17; and in a regular course, 18.

Admissions: The ACT scores for the 2001-2002 freshman class were 47% below 21, 24% between 21 and 23, 18% between 24 and 26, 6% between 27 and 28, and 5% above 28. There were 2 National Merit semifinalists in a recent year.

Requirements: The ACT is recommended. In addition, candidates for admission who are residents of Kansas must graduate from an accredited secondary school or earn a GED. Nonresidents must have earned better than a 2.0 GPA as well. Applications may be submitted on-line via the web site at *www.fhsu.edu*. AP and CLEP credits are accepted.

Procedure: Freshmen are admitted fall, spring, and summer. Entrance exams should be taken in the senior year. Application deadlines are open. The application fee is $25.

Transfer: 480 transfer students enrolled in a recent year. Applicants must have a minimum college GPA of 2.0 and submit official college transcripts from all institutions previously attended. 30 credits of 124 must be completed at FHSU.

Visiting: There are regularly scheduled orientations for prospective students. There are guides for informal visits and visitors may sit in on classes and stay overnight. To schedule a visit, contact the office of Admissions, Campus Tour Coordinator.

Financial Aid: In 2001-2002, 78% of all freshmen and 70% of continuing students received some form of financial aid. 60% of undergraduates work part time. Average annual earnings from campus work are $1200. The average financial indebtedness of a recent graduate was $13,958. The FFS and the college's own financial statement are required. Check with the school for current deadlines.

International Students: In a recent year, there were 47 international students enrolled. The school actively recruits these students. They must score 500 on the written TOEFL or 173 on the electronic version.

Computers: The mainframe is an IBM ES/9000 Model 9121. The system may be accessed by modem and by terminals located in dormitories and in PC labs in each residence hall and each major academic building. Students can dial into the Web using a pool of 48 modems on the campus backbone. There are at least 225 PCs with Web access in student labs. All students may access the system The modem pool may be used 24 hours a day, the labs until 11 P.M. There are no time limits and no fees.

Admissions Contact: Roger Schieferecke, Director of Admissions. A video is available. E-mail: *tigers@fhsu.edu* Web: *www.fhsu.edu*

FRIENDS UNIVERSITY

D-3

Wichita, KS 67213

(316) 295-5100
(800) 577-2233; Fax: (316) 295-5101

Full-time: 396 men, 521 women	**Faculty:** IIA, --$
Part-time: 100 men and women	**Ph.D.s:** n/av
Graduate: 273 men, 288 women	**Student/Faculty:** n/av
Year: semesters, summer session	**Tuition:** $12,250
Application Deadline: open	**Room & Board:** $3712
Freshman Class: 736 accepted, 349 enrolled	
ACT: 21	**LESS COMPETITIVE**

Friends University, established in 1898, is an interdenominational institution offering undergraduate and graduate degrees through the Colleges of Arts and Sciences, Business and Information Technology, and Adult and Professional Studies. There are 3 undergraduate and 3 graduate schools. In addition to regional accreditation, Friends has baccalaureate program accreditation with NASM and NCATE. The library contains 75,540 volumes, 319,861 microform items, and 13,135 audiovisual forms/CDs, and subscribes to 321 periodicals. Computerized library services include the card catalog, interlibrary loans, and database searching. Special learning facilities include a learning resource center, art gallery, and observatory. The 54-acre campus is in an urban area 200 miles southwest of Kansas City. Including residence halls, there are 15 buildings.

Student Life: 71% are white. 86% are Protestant; 10% Catholic. The average age of freshmen is 19; all undergraduates, 21.

Housing: 326 students can be accommodated in college housing, which includes single-sex dormitories, on-campus apartments, and off-campus apartments. In addition, there are upperclassmen floors. On-campus housing is available on a first-come, first-served basis. Alcohol is not permitted. All students may keep cars.

Activities: There is 1 local fraternity and 1 national sorority. There are many groups and organizations on campus, including art, band, cheerleading, choir, chorale, chorus, computers, dance, dance team, drama, ethnic, honors, international, jazz band, musical theater, orchestra, pep band, photography, political, professional, religious, social, social service, student government, symphony, yearbook, and yell-leading. Popular campus events include Christian Emphasis Week, Cherry Carnival, and Symphony of Spring.

Sports: There are 9 intercollegiate sports for men and 8 for women, and 6 intramural sports for men and 6 for women. Facilities include a 2600-seat stadium and athletic field for football and soccer, a phys ed center with basketball and racquetball courts, an intramural gym, and tennis courts.

Disabled Students: 95% of the campus is accessible. Wheelchair ramps, elevators, special parking, specially equipped rest rooms, special class scheduling, lowered drinking fountains, and lowered telephones are available.

Services: Counseling and information services are available, as is tutoring in most subjects.

Campus Safety and Security: Measures include 24-hour foot and vehicle patrol, pamphlets/posters/films, and lighted pathways/sidewalks.

Programs of Study: Friends confers B.A., B.S., B.B.A., B.F.A., and B.Mus. degrees. Associate and master's degrees are also awarded. Bachelor's degrees are awarded in BIOLOGICAL SCIENCE (biology/biological science and zoology), BUSINESS (accounting, business administration and management, international business management, and management information systems), COMMUNICATIONS AND THE ARTS (art, ballet, English, fine arts, music, musical theater, and Spanish), COMPUTER AND PHYSICAL SCIENCE (chemistry, computer science, information sciences and systems, mathematics, and radiological technology), EDUCATION (art, business, elementary, English, foreign languages, health, music, science, secondary, and social science), ENGINEERING AND ENVIRONMENTAL DESIGN (environmental science), HEALTH PROFESSIONS (premedicine), SOCIAL SCIENCE (history, human services, political science/government, psychology, and religion). Science is the strongest academically. Business and education are the largest.

Required: To graduate, students must complete 124 credit hours, including 33 to 54 in general education (varies by degree sought) and 24 to 45 in the major, with a minimum GPA of 2.0. Distribution requirements include course work in humanities, fine arts, religion and philosophy, behavioral science, and natural science.

Special: Students may cross-register with Newman University, and they can pursue internships in their majors. A study-abroad program is available in Cancun, Mexico, and several Asian countries. Friends offers accelerated degree programs in business management, organizational management and leadership, computer information systems, criminal justice, and electronic commerce management, as well as dual majors in accounting/business administration, and math/computer science.There is a 3-2 engineering degree program with Wichita State University. Friends also offers a general studies degree, credit for life, military, and work experience, nondegree study, and pass/fail options. For working adults, the College of Adult and Professional Studies offers undergraduate degrees and certificate programs. There is 1 national honor society, a freshman honors program, and 1 departmental honors program.

Faculty/Classroom: 92% teach undergraduates. No introductory courses are taught by graduate students. The average class size in an introductory lecture is 35; in a laboratory, 18; and in a regular course, 25.

Requirements: The SAT I or ACT is required. In addition, candidates for admission must graduate from an accredited secondary school or earn a GED, having completed 4 courses in English, 2 each in history and math, and 1 each in science and social studies. The composite ACT score or converted SAT I score is multiplied by the high school GPA. A result of 45 is the minimum for full admission; students scoring lower may be admitted provisionally. Interviews are recommended; portfolios and auditions are advised in appropriate instances. A GPA of 2.0 is required. CLEP credit is accepted.

Procedure: Freshmen are admitted fall and spring. Entrance exams should be taken in the spring of the junior year or fall of the senior year. There is an early admissions plan. Application deadlines are open. The fall 2001 application fee was $15. Notification is sent on a rolling basis.

Transfer: 115 transfer students enrolled in 2001-2002. Applicants with fewer than 15 semester hours must submit ACT or SAT I scores and high school and college transcripts. 30 credits of 124 must be completed at Friends.

Visiting: There are regularly scheduled orientations for prospective students, including half-day classroom visits, individual instructor visits, discussion with current students, a tour, lunch, and a financial aid session. There are guides for informal visits and visitors may sit in on classes and stay overnight. To schedule a visit, contact the Admissions Office at *baye@friends.edu*

Financial Aid: Average annual earnings from campus work are $1500. The FAFSA is required. The fall application deadline is May 1.

International Students: The school actively recruits these students. They must score 500 on the written TOEFL or 118 on the electronic version unless they are either native speakers of English or non-native speakers who attended an English-speaking high school. SAT I or ACT scores may be submitted in place of TOEFL scores.

Computers: The mainframe is an NCR Tower. 200 Pentium PCs are available for student use. All students may access the system. There are no time limits and no fees. It is strongly recommended that all students have a personal computer.

Graduates: In 2001, 159 bachelor's degrees were awarded. The most popular majors were business administration (15%), elementary education (12%), and human services/psychology (11%).

Admissions Contact: Tony Myers, Director of Admissions. E-mail: *tmyers@friends.edu* Web: *www.friends.edu*

KANSAS STATE UNIVERSITY

Manhattan, KS 66506 E-2

(785) 532-6250; Fax: (785) 532-6393

Full-time: 8545 men, 7560 women	**Faculty:** I, --$
Part-time: 1311 men, 1354 women	**Ph.D.s:** 88%
Graduate: 1595 men, 2031 women	**Student/Faculty:** 19 to 1
Year: semesters, summer session	**Tuition:** $2835 ($9762)
Application Deadline: open	**Room & Board:** $4160

Freshman Class: 8077 applied, 5006 accepted, 3283 enrolled

ACT: required **COMPETITIVE**

Kansas State University, established in 1863, is a land-grant institution offering degree programs in agriculture, arts and sciences, business, engineering, human ecology, architecture, education, veterinary medicine, and technology. There are 9 undergraduate schools and 1 graduate school. In addition to regional accreditation, K-State has baccalaureate program accreditation with AACSB, ABET, ACCE, AHEA, CSWE, FIDER, NAAB, NASM, NCATE, and NRPA. The 6 libraries contain 1,441,132 volumes, 2,529,194 microform items, and 3469 audiovisual forms/CDs, and subscribe to 13,063 periodicals. Computerized library services include the card catalog, interlibrary loans, and database searching. Special learning facilities include a learning resource center, art gallery, planetarium, radio station, TV station, nuclear reactor, laser center, cancer research center, and telecommunications satellite teaching. The 668-acre campus is in a suburban area 125 miles west of Kansas City. Including residence halls, there are 96 buildings.

Student Life: 89% of undergraduates are from Kansas. Others are from 50 states, 98 foreign countries, and Canada. 86% are white. The average age of freshmen is 18; all undergraduates, 20. 24% do not continue beyond their first year; 48% remain to graduate.

Housing: 4300 students can be accommodated in college housing, which includes single-sex and coed dormitories, on-campus apartments, off-campus apartments, married-student housing, fraternity houses, and sorority houses. In addition, there are honors houses and special-interest houses. On-campus housing is available on a first-come, first-served basis. 74% of students commute. Alcohol is not permitted. All students may keep cars.

Activities: 20% of men belong to 28 national fraternities; 19% of women belong to 16 national sororities. There are 340 groups on campus, including band, cheerleading, chess, choir, chorale, chorus, computers, dance, drama, drill team, ethnic, film, gay, honors, international, jazz band, literary magazine, marching band, musical theater, newspaper, orchestra, pep band, photography, political, professional, radio and TV, religious, social, social service, student government, symphony, and yearbook. Popular campus events include Family Weekend, K-State Open House, and Winterfest.

Sports: There are 7 intercollegiate sports for men and 8 for women, and 45 intramural sports for men and 45 for women. Facilities include indoor and outdoor tracks, baseball fields, tennis courts, basketball courts, swimming pools, a football stadium, and an indoor practice field. A multipurpose recreation facility is open 16 hours a day.

Disabled Students: 85% of the campus is accessible. Wheelchair ramps, elevators, special parking, specially equipped rest rooms, special class scheduling, lowered drinking fountains, lowered telephones, and a campus shuttle service are available.

Services: Counseling and information services are available, as is tutoring in every subject. There is a reader service for the blind, and remedial math, reading, and writing.

Campus Safety and Security: Measures include 24-hour foot and vehicle patrol, self-defense education, escort service, and shuttle buses. There are informal discussions, pamphlets/posters/films, emergency telephones, lighted pathways/sidewalks, televised monitors in parking lots, CPR classes, and vehicle assistance devices.

Programs of Study: K-State confers B.A., B.S., B.Arch., B.F.A., B.Int.Arch., B.L.A., B.M.E., B.S.A., B.S.Arch., B.S.Ag.E., B.S.B.A., B.S.C.E., B.S.Ch.E, B.S.Comp.Eng., B.S.Comp.Sci., B.S.Die., B.S.E.E., B.S.El.Ed., B.S.I.E., B.S.I.S., B.S.M.E., and B.S.Nuc.Eng. degrees. Associate, master's, and doctoral degrees are also awarded. Bachelor's degrees are awarded in AGRICULTURE (agricultural business management, agricultural economics, agronomy, animal science, fish and game management, and horticulture), BIOLOGICAL SCIENCE (biochemistry, biology/biological science, life science, microbiology, and nutrition), BUSINESS (accounting, apparel and accessories marketing, banking and finance, business administration and management, hotel/motel and restaurant management, management information systems, and marketing/retailing/merchandising), COMMUNICATIONS AND THE ARTS (apparel design, applied music, art, communications, dramatic arts, English, journalism, modern language, music, and speech/debate/rhetoric), COMPUTER AND PHYSICAL SCIENCE (chemistry, computer science, geology, geophysics and seismology, information sciences and systems, mathematics, physical sciences, physics, and statistics), EDUCATION (agricultural, art, elementary, music, and secondary), ENGINEERING AND ENVIRONMENTAL DESIGN (aeronautical technology, agricultural engineering, architectural engineering, architecture, chemical engineering, civil engineering, computer engineering, construction management, electrical/electronics engineering, electrical/electronics engineering technology, industrial engineering, interior design, landscape architecture/design, manufacturing engineering, mechanical engineering, mechanical engineering technology, and nuclear engineering), HEALTH PROFESSIONS (medical technology, predentistry, premedicine, and speech pathology/audiology), SOCIAL SCIENCE (anthropology, dietetics, economics, family and community services, family/consumer studies, food production/management/services, food science, geography, history, human ecology, humanities, parks and recreation management, philosophy, physical fitness/movement, political science/government, psychology, social science, social work, sociology, and textiles and clothing). Architecture, engineering, and accounting are the strongest academically. Journalism, animal science, and elementary education are the largest.

Required: To graduate, students must complete 120 to 167 credits with a minimum GPA of 2.0. All students must take expository writing, public speaking, and physical fitness. General education requirements vary by major but include at least 18 hours of approved courses.

Special: K-State offers co-op programs, internships, and dual degrees and majors through most of its colleges. Cross-registration is available with Kansas State at Salina and Kansas Wesleyan University, as is study abroad in more than 100 countries. A 3-2 engineering degree program, nondegree study, and pass/fail options are also available. There are 53 national honor societies, including Phi Beta Kappa, a freshman honors program, and 7 departmental honors programs.

Faculty/Classroom: 70% of faculty are male; 30%, female. The average class size in an introductory lecture is 129; in a laboratory, 22; and in a regular course, 28.

Admissions: 62% of the 2001-2002 applicants were accepted. The ACT scores for the 2001-2002 freshman class were 7% below 18, 46% between 18 and 23, 38% between 24 and 29, and 9% 30 and above. 60% of the current freshmen were in the top fifth of their class; 89% were in the top two fifths.

Requirements: The ACT is required. In addition, applicants must meet 1 of these 3 criteria: an ACT score of 21 or above, class rank in the top third, or a 2.0 GPA in the Kansas core curriculum. It is recommended that students complete 4 units of English, 3 each of natural science, math, and social studies, and 1 of computer technology. The GED is accepted. AP and CLEP credits are accepted. Applications are accepted on-line.

Procedure: Freshmen are admitted to all sessions. Entrance exams should be taken in the junior and senior years. Application deadlines are open. The fall 2001 application fee was $25. Notification is sent on a rolling basis.

Transfer: 1732 transfer students enrolled in 2001-2002. Applicants must have a minimum of 24 credit hours and a college GPA of 2.0 or otherwise meet freshman requirements. Students must submit official transcripts from previous colleges attended. 30 credits of 120 must be completed at K-State.

Visiting: There are regularly scheduled orientations for prospective students, including campus tours and visits with academic advisers and admissions representatives. There are guides for informal visits and visitors may sit in on classes and stay overnight. To schedule a visit, contact New Student Services at (785) 532-6318.

Financial Aid: In 2001-2002, 95% of all freshmen received some form of financial aid. 95% of freshmen and 50% of continuing students received need-based aid. Scholarships or need-based grants averaged $3890; and loans averaged $2840. The average financial indebtedness of the 2001 graduate was $15,927. The FAFSA is required. The fall application deadline is March 15.

International Students: They must score 550 on the written TOEFL or 213 on the electronic version or present acceptable scores on the SAT

I or the ACT and also take an English proficiency test given at the university.

Computers: The mainframe is an IBM 3090/200E. There are 110 PCs in public labs and more than 30 UNIX workstations located at various sites across campus. The Sun UNIX computer has 96 ports. All students may access the system 24 hours a day. There are no time limits. The fee is $100 per semester for students enrolled in engineering programs and computer sciences.

Graduates: In 2001, 3280 bachelor's degrees were awarded. The most popular majors among recent graduates were business/marketing (17%), agriculture (13%), and education (12%). In an average class, 20% graduate in 4 years, 46% in 5 years, and 52% in 6 years.

Admissions Contact: Larry Moeder, Director of Admissions. A video is available. E-mail: *kstate@ksu.edu* Web: *www.ksu.edu*

KANSAS WESLEYAN UNIVERSITY — D-2

Salina, KS 67401-6196 — (785) 827-5541, ext. 1285
(800) 874-1154, ext. 1285; Fax: (785) 827-0927

Full-time: 220 men, 270 women — **Faculty:** 43; IIB, --$
Part-time: 70 men, 150 women — **Ph.D.s:** 51%
Graduate: 20 men, 20 women — **Student/Faculty:** 11 to 1
Year: semesters, summer session — **Tuition:** $13,400
Application Deadline: open — **Room & Board:** $4000
Freshman Class: n/av
SAT I or ACT: required — **COMPETITIVE+**

Kansas Wesleyan, founded in 1886, is affiliated with the United Methodist Church. The college offers undergraduate programs in the arts and sciences, business, and education. Some information in this profile is approximate. There is 1 graduate school. The library contains 82,000 volumes, 33,505 microform items, and 984 audiovisual forms/CDs, and subscribes to 421 periodicals. Computerized library services include the card catalog, interlibrary loans, and database searching. Special learning facilities include a learning resource center, art gallery, planetarium, radio station, greenhouse, and cadaver lab. The 25-acre campus is in an urban area 90 miles north of Wichita. Including residence halls, there are 12 buildings.

Student Life: 75% of undergraduates are from Kansas. Others are from 14 states and 3 foreign countries. 92% are from public schools. 85% are white. 48% are Protestant; 39% claim no religious affiliation; 13% are Catholic. The average age of freshmen is 22; all undergraduates, 25. 33% do not continue beyond their first year.

Housing: 450 students can be accommodated in college housing, which includes single-sex dormitories, on-campus apartments, and married-student housing. On-campus housing is guaranteed for all 4 years. 83% of students commute. Alcohol is not permitted. All students may keep cars.

Activities: 10% of men belong to 1 local and 1 national fraternity; 5% of women belong to 1 local sorority. There are 38 groups on campus, including art, band, cheerleading, choir, chorale, chorus, computers, dance, drama, ethnic, film, honors, international, literary magazine, musical theater, newspaper, pep band, photography, professional, radio and TV, religious, social, social service, student government, and yearbook. Popular campus events include Spring Fling, Sweetheart Dance, and Family Weekend.

Sports: There are 7 intercollegiate sports for men and 7 for women, and 8 intramural sports for men and 6 for women. Facilities include a gym, a sand volleyball court, football practice and game fields, a multipurpose courtyard, a track, and a weight room.

Disabled Students: 90% of the campus is accessible. Wheelchair ramps, elevators, special parking, specially equipped rest rooms, special class scheduling, lowered drinking fountains, and lowered telephones are available.

Services: Counseling and information services are available, as is tutoring in most subjects. There is remedial reading and writing.

Campus Safety and Security: Measures include self-defense education, escort service, informal discussions, and pamphlets/posters/films. There are lighted pathways/sidewalks, random security checks, and private service security guards.

Programs of Study: Kansas Wesleyan confers B.A., B.S., and B.S.N. degrees. Associate and master's degrees are also awarded. Bachelor's degrees are awarded in BIOLOGICAL SCIENCE (biology/biological science), BUSINESS (accounting and business economics), COMMUNICATIONS AND THE ARTS (communications, dramatic arts, English, music, Spanish, speech/debate/rhetoric, and studio art), COMPUTER AND PHYSICAL SCIENCE (chemistry, computer science, mathematics, and physics), EDUCATION (art, music, physical, secondary, and special), HEALTH PROFESSIONS (nursing), SOCIAL SCIENCE (addiction studies, criminal justice, history, prelaw, psychology, religion, religious education, and sociology). Premedicine, nursing, and preengineering are the strongest academically. Education, nursing, and business are the largest.

Required: Students must demonstrate proficiency in English and math and must fulfill distribution requirements in 15 liberal arts components, including environmental awareness, biblical heritage, and lifetime recreation. Courses in phys ed and computers are required. To graduate, students must complete at least 126 credit hours, including 30 to 40 in a major field of study, with a minimum GPA of 2.0.

Special: Cross-registration is available with other members of the Associated Colleges of Central Kansas and the Salina College Consortium. Cooperative degree programs are offered in agriculture, cytotechnology, engineering, environmental studies, and medical technology. Kansas Wesleyan also offers January interterm study trips throughout the United States and abroad, Washington, D.C., and UN semesters, internships, dual majors, student designed-majors, credit for life experience, and nondegree study. A 3-2 engineering degree is offered with Columbia University and Washington University at St. Louis. There are 4 national honor societies.

Faculty/Classroom: 55% of faculty are male; 45%, female. 65% both teach and do research. The average class size in an introductory lecture is 23; in a laboratory, 7; and in a regular course, 13.

Requirements: The SAT I or ACT is required, with minimum composite scores of 850 on the SAT I, or 18 on the ACT. Applicants must be graduates of accredited secondary schools or have earned a GED. An interview is recommended. Kansas Wesleyan requires applicants to be in the upper 50% of their class. A GPA of 2.5 is required. AP and CLEP credits are accepted.

Procedure: Freshmen are admitted to all sessions. Entrance exams should be taken as early as possible. There is a deferred admissions plan. Application deadlines are open. The fall 2001 application fee was $20.

Transfer: 148 transfer students enrolled in a recent year. Transfers must submit transcripts from all colleges previously attended. Those students transferring fewer than 15 credit hours must submit ACT or SAT I scores and a high school transcript. A minimum GPA of 2.0 is recommended. 63 credits of 126 must be completed at Kansas Wesleyan.

Visiting: There are regularly scheduled orientations for prospective students. There are guides for informal visits and visitors may sit in on classes and stay overnight. To schedule a visit, contact the Admissions Office.

Financial Aid: In 2001-2002, 90% of all students received some form of financial aid. Kansas Wesleyan is a member of CSS. The FAFSA and tax forms are required.

International Students: The school actively recruits these students. They must score 500 on the written TOEFL or 173 on the electronic version.

Computers: The mainframe is a Data General MV-8000. PCs are available in the computer science lab and in the library. All students may access the system at any time. There are no time limits and no fees.

Graduates: In an average class, 16% graduate in 6 years.

Admissions Contact: Admissions Office.
E-mail: *admissions@kwu.edu* Web: *www.kwu.edu*

MCPHERSON COLLEGE — D-2

McPherson, KS 67460 — (316) 241-0731, ext. 1270
(800) 365-7402; Fax: (316) 241-8443

Full-time: 198 men, 164 women — **Faculty:** 39; IIB, --$
Part-time: 10 men, 25 women — **Ph.D.s:** 60%
Graduate: none — **Student/Faculty:** 9 to 1
Year: 4-1-4, summer session — **Tuition:** $12,720
Application Deadline: open — **Room & Board:** $4990
Freshman Class: 461 applied, 359 accepted, 121 enrolled
SAT I Verbal/Math: 490/480 — **ACT:** 20 — **COMPETITIVE**

McPherson College, founded in 1887 and affiliated with the Church of the Brethren, is a private, nonprofit institution offering undergraduate programs in the arts and sciences, business, and education. The library contains 90,535 volumes, 59,549 microform items, and 4484 audiovisual forms/CDs, and subscribes to 308 periodicals. Computerized library services include the card catalog, interlibrary loans, and database searching. Special learning facilities include a learning resource center, art gallery, natural history museum, and an automobile restoration center. The 23-acre campus is in a small town 60 miles north of Wichita. Including residence halls, there are 15 buildings.

Student Life: 57% of undergraduates are from out of state, mostly the Midwest. Others are from 30 states and 6 foreign countries. 99% are from public schools. 75% are white; 11% African American, 10% Hispanic. 52% are Protestant; 23% Catholic. The average age of freshmen is 19; all undergraduates, 22. 40% do not continue beyond their first year.

Housing: 392 students can be accommodated in college housing, which includes single-sex and coed dormitories. On-campus housing is guaranteed for all 4 years. 66% of students live on campus; of those, 65% remain on campus on weekends. Alcohol is not permitted. All students may keep cars.

Activities: There are no fraternities or sororities. There are 26 groups on campus, including art, band, cheerleading, choir, chorus, computers, drama, ethnic, honors, international, musical theater, newspaper, orchestra, pep band, professional, religious, social service, student government, and yearbook. Popular campus events include Family Weekend.

Sports: There are 5 intercollegiate sports for men and 6 for women, and 4 intramural sports for men and 4 for women. Facilities include a sports center with 2 full-size courts, a racquetball court, and a fitness center with an open weight-training room.

Disabled Students: 95% of the campus is accessible. Wheelchair ramps, elevators, special parking, specially equipped rest rooms, special class scheduling, and lowered drinking fountains are available.

Services: Counseling and information services are available, as is tutoring in most subjects. There is remedial reading and writing.

Campus Safety and Security: Measures include informal discussions, pamphlets/posters/films, emergency telephones, and lighted pathways/sidewalks.

Programs of Study: McPherson confers B.A. and B.S. degrees. Associate degrees are also awarded. Bachelor's degrees are awarded in AGRICULTURE (agricultural economics, agronomy, and animal science), BIOLOGICAL SCIENCE (biology/biological science), BUSINESS (accounting and business administration and management), COMMUNICATIONS AND THE ARTS (art, English, music, Spanish, and speech/debate/rhetoric), COMPUTER AND PHYSICAL SCIENCE (chemistry, computer science, mathematics, and physics), EDUCATION (elementary, physical, secondary, and special), ENGINEERING AND ENVIRONMENTAL DESIGN (industrial engineering technology), SOCIAL SCIENCE (history, philosophy, psychology, religion, and sociology). Natural/physical science, education, and business are the strongest academically. Business and education are the largest.

Required: To graduate, students must complete 124 credits, including 32 in the major, with a GPA of 2.0. All students must fulfill general education requirements in the following areas: written and oral communication, aesthetics, history, society, natural sciences, technology and culture, and religion/beliefs/values. Students must also participate in an integrative seminar and a service experience, and must complete a global/intercultural experience, which may include intercultural studies courses or modern language courses.

Special: Cross-registration with other colleges is available through the Associated Colleges of Central Kansas. McPherson also offers internships, study abroad in 10 countries, credit by exam, a general studies degree, student-designed majors, and pass/fail options. There are preprofessional programs in health, engineering, law, forestry, veterinary medicine, nursing and medicine, optometry, and dentistry. There are 3 national honor societies, including Phi Beta Kappa, and 3 departmental honors programs.

Faculty/Classroom: 66% of faculty are male; 34%, female. All teach undergraduates. The average class size in an introductory lecture is 30; in a laboratory, 12; and in a regular course, 12.

Admissions: 78% of the 2001-2002 applicants were accepted. The SAT I scores for the 2001-2002 freshman class were: Verbal--54% below 500, 40% between 500 and 599, 3% between 600 and 700, and 3% above 700; Math--63% below 500, 27% between 500 and 599, and 10% between 600 and 700. The ACT scores were 60% below 21, 22% between 21 and 23, 12% between 24 and 26, 4% between 27 and 28, and 1% above 28. 21% of the current freshmen were in the top fifth of their class; 54% were in the top two fifths. 2 freshmen graduated first in their class.

Requirements: The SAT I or ACT is required. In addition, the GED is accepted. A GPA of 2.0 is required. AP and CLEP credits are accepted. Important factors in the admissions decision are recommendations by school officials, evidence of special talent, and parents or siblings attending the school. Applications are accepted on-line at the school's web site.

Procedure: Freshmen are admitted fall, winter, and spring. Entrance exams should be taken in the junior year. There is a deferred admissions plan. Application deadlines are open. The application fee is $25. Notification is sent on a rolling basis.

Transfer: 29 transfer students enrolled in 2001-2002. Applicants must have satisfactorily completed 12 credit hours of college course work covering 3 academic areas with a 2.0 GPA. 32 credits of 124 must be completed at McPherson.

Visiting: There are regularly scheduled orientations for prospective students, consisting of campus tours, meetings with admissions personnel, and class attendance. There are guides for informal visits and visitors may sit in on classes and stay overnight. To schedule a visit, contact Admissions Office.

Financial Aid: In 2001-2002, 99% of all students received some form of financial aid. 94% of freshmen and 92% of continuing students received need-based aid. The average freshman award was $15,773. Of that total, scholarships or need-based grants averaged $4077 ($6000 maximum); loans averaged $3950 ($5625 maximum); and work contracts averaged $1993 ($2500 maximum). 36% of undergraduates work part time. Average annual earnings from campus work are $1098. The average financial indebtedness of the 2001 graduate was $19,996. The FAFSA is required. The fall application deadline is March 15.

International Students: There are 6 international students enrolled. They must score 550 on the written TOEFL.

Computers: The mainframe is an Encore. 2 computer labs provide access to word processing, the Internet, and the Web. Computer hookup is available in dorm rooms as well. All students may access the system. There are no time limits and no fees.

Graduates: In 2001, 72 bachelor's degrees were awarded. The most popular majors were business/marketing (22%), social sciences and history (18%), and elementary education (15%). In an average class, 24% graduate in 4 years, 32% in 5 years, and 35% in 6 years.

Admissions Contact: Fred Schmidt, Director of Admissions.
E-mail: *schmidtf@mcpherson.edu* Web: *www.mcpherson.edu*

MIDAMERICA NAZARENE UNIVERSITY F-2
Olathe, KS 66062-1899 **(913) 791-3380**
(800) 800-8887; Fax: (913) 791-3487

Full-time: 545 men, 609 women	**Faculty:** 73
Part-time: 58 men, 78 women	**Ph.D.s:** 46%
Graduate: 101 men, 293 women	**Student/Faculty:** 16 to 1
Year: semesters, summer session	**Tuition:** $11,638
Application Deadline: August 1	**Room & Board:** $5322
Freshman Class: 504 applied, 255 enrolled	
SAT I Verbal/Math: 550/490	**ACT:** 23 **COMPETITIVE**

MidAmerica Nazarene University was founded in 1966 as a private liberal arts institution affiliated with the Church of the Nazarene. In addition to regional accreditation, MNU has baccalaureate program accreditation with ACBSP, NASM, and NLN. The library contains 410,316 volumes, 282,020 microform items, and 5081 audiovisual forms/CDs, and subscribes to 225 periodicals. Computerized library services include the card catalog, interlibrary loans, and database searching. Special learning facilities include a learning resource center and radio station. The 105-acre campus is in a suburban area 19 miles southwest of downtown Kansas City, Missouri. Including residence halls, there are 21 buildings.

Student Life: 61% of undergraduates are from Kansas. Others are from 33 states, 2 foreign countries, and Canada. 93% are from public schools. 87% are white. 67% are Protestant; 28% claim no religious affiliation. The average age of freshmen is 19; all undergraduates, 21. 25% do not continue beyond their first year.

Housing: 704 students can be accommodated in college housing, which includes single-sex dormitories, on-campus apartments, and off-campus apartments. On-campus housing is guaranteed for all 4 years. 59% of students live on campus; of those, all remain on campus on weekends. Alcohol is not permitted. All students may keep cars.

Activities: There are no fraternities or sororities. There are 28 groups on campus, including cheerleading, choir, chorus, computers, drama, ethnic, honors, international, jazz band, newspaper, orchestra, pep band, political, professional, radio and TV, religious, student government, and yearbook. Popular campus events include Mr. MNU and Welcome Week.

Sports: There are 6 intercollegiate sports for men and 6 for women, and 6 intramural sports for men and 6 for women. Facilities include a weight room, a football stadium, a gym, a track, tennis and sand volleyball courts, and softball, baseball, and soccer fields.

Disabled Students: 90% of the campus is accessible. Wheelchair ramps, elevators, special parking, specially equipped rest rooms, special class scheduling, and lowered drinking fountains are available.

Services: Counseling and information services are available, as is tutoring in most subjects. There is a reader service for the blind, and remedial math, reading, and writing. There are also test-taking accommodations, interpreters for the hearing impaired, and note takers for the blind, hearing impaired, and learning disabled.

Campus Safety and Security: Measures include 24-hour foot and vehicle patrol, self-defense education, escort service, and informal discussions. There are pamphlets/posters/films, emergency telephones, and lighted pathways/sidewalks.

Programs of Study: MNU confers B.A. and B.S.N. degrees. Associate and master's degrees are also awarded. Bachelor's degrees are awarded in AGRICULTURE (international agriculture), BIOLOGICAL SCIENCE (biology/biological science), BUSINESS (accounting and business administration and management), COMMUNICATIONS AND THE ARTS (communications, English, modern language, music, and Spanish), COMPUTER AND PHYSICAL SCIENCE (chemistry, computer science, mathematics, and physics), EDUCATION (athletic training, business, Christian, elementary, English, health, mathematics, music, physical, science, and social studies), HEALTH PROFESSIONS (nursing), SOCIAL SCIENCE (criminal justice, history, psychology, religion, and sociology). Management and human relations, elementary education, and business administration are the largest.

Required: All students must meet core curriculum requirements in humanities-communications, natural sciences-math, social sciences, religion-philosophy, and phys ed. Students must maintain a minimum GPA of 2.0 and complete 126 semester hours to graduate.

Special: MNU offers nondegree study, cross-registration with the Christian College Coalition, study abroad in 4 countries, internships, and a Washington semester. There are accelerated degree programs in management and human relations and in nursing. There is 1 national honor society, and 4 departmental honors programs.

Faculty/Classroom: 63% of faculty are male; 37%, female. All teach undergraduates. No introductory courses are taught by graduate students. The average class size in an introductory lecture is 27; in a laboratory, 14; and in a regular course, 12.

Admissions: The SAT I scores for the 2001-2002 freshman class were: Verbal--17% below 500, 52% between 500 and 599, 27% between 600 and 700, and 4% above 700; Math--26% below 500, 48% between 500 and 599, and 26% between 600 and 700. The ACT scores were 31% below 21, 37% between 21 and 23, 14% between 24 and 26, 9% between 27 and 28, and 9% above 28. 20% of the current freshmen were in the top fifth of their class; 60% were in the top two fifths. There was 1 National Merit finalist and 3 semifinalists. 6 freshmen graduated first in their class.

Requirements: The SAT I or ACT is required, with recommended composite scores of 18 on the ACT and 670 on the SAT I. Candidates for admission should be graduates of an accredited secondary school. The GED is accepted. Students should have completed 15 units of study, including 4 units of English and 3 each of natural science, social studies, and math. An essay is optional. A GPA of 2.0 is required. AP and CLEP credits are accepted.

Procedure: Freshmen are admitted to all sessions. Entrance exams should be taken during the senior year. Applications should be filed by August 1 for fall entry and December 15 for winter entry. The fall 2001 application fee was $15. Notification is sent on a rolling basis. 3 early decision candidates were accepted for the 2001-2002 class.

Transfer: 65 transfer students enrolled in 2001-2002. Transfer applicants should have earned 24 or more hours at an accredited institution and not be on academic or disciplinary probation. ACT or SAT I scores are required. 30 credits of 126 must be completed at MNU.

Visiting: There are regularly scheduled orientations for prospective students, including an academic fair, advising, class visitation, informational meetings, social activities, and experiencing residential life. There are guides for informal visits and visitors may sit in on classes and stay overnight. To schedule a visit, contact the Office of Admissions.

Financial Aid: In 2001-2002, 93% of all freshmen received some form of financial aid. 70% of freshmen received need-based aid. The average freshman award was $10,138. Of that total, scholarships or need-based grants averaged $5197 ($17,950 maximum); loans averaged $4816 ($18,622 maximum); and work contracts averaged $1318 ($2200 maximum). Loans include PLUS and A++ loans and unsubsidized loans. The average financial indebtedness of the 2001 graduate was $13,731. The FAFSA and the college's own financial statement are required. The fall application deadline is March 1.

International Students: There are 6 international students enrolled. They must score 500 on the written TOEFL or take the ACT and/or SAT I if from a world area where English is the offical first language. They must also take the SAT I or ACT, and placement tests for incoming freshmen.

Computers: The mainframes are a DEC Microvax 3100 and DEC Alpha 4000. There are 40 general access PCs in the library, with an additional 35 in the computer lab reserved for business, math, and computer science majors. All students have access to e-mail and the Internet. Dial-up access is available any time from residence halls and off-campus sites. All students may access the system 7:30 A.M. to 11 P.M. Monday to Thursday and to 5 P.M. Friday; 10 A.M. to 5 P.M. Saturday. Students may access the system 30 minutes for Internet access; no limits for Metz lab. There are no fees.

Graduates: In 2001, 318 bachelor's degrees were awarded. The most popular majors were human resources management (38%), elementary education (8%), and business administration (7%). In an average class, 47% graduate in 6 years. 40 companies recruited on campus in 2000-2001.

Admissions Contact: Ann Owens, Applicant Secretary. A video is available. E-mail: *admissions@mnu.edu* Web: *www.mnu.edu*

NEWMAN UNIVERSITY

Wichita, KS 67213 — D-3
(316) 942-4291, ext. 144
(877) NEWMANU; Fax: (316) 942-4483

Full-time: 270 men, 625 women	**Faculty:** 76; IIB, --$
Part-time: 250 men, 375 women	**Ph.D.s:** 44%
Graduate: 120 men, 295 women	**Student/Faculty:** 12 to 1
Year: semesters, summer session	**Tuition:** $10,148
Application Deadline: open	**Room & Board:** $3950
Freshman Class: n/av	
SAT I or ACT: required	**LESS COMPETITIVE**

Newman University, established in 1933, is a private, liberal arts institution affiliated with the Roman Catholic Church. Figures in the above capsule are approximate. There are 5 undergraduate schools and 1 graduate school. In addition to regional accreditation, NU has baccalaureate program accreditation with NLN. The library contains 140,545 volumes, 86,053 microform items, and 2400 audiovisual forms/CDs, and subscribes to 506 periodicals. Computerized library services include the card catalog, interlibrary loans, and database searching. Special learning facilities include a learning resource center, art gallery, planetarium, TV station, and allied health and nursing labs. The 53-acre campus is in an urban area. Including residence halls, there are 11 buildings.

Student Life: 88% of undergraduates are from Kansas. Others are from 25 states and 14 foreign countries. 96% are from public schools. 83% are white. 59% are Protestant; 41% Catholic. The average age of freshmen is 18; all undergraduates, 25. 34% do not continue beyond their first year; 33% remain to graduate.

Housing: 243 students can be accommodated in college housing, which includes single-sex and coed dormitories, on-campus apartments, and married-student housing. On-campus housing is guaranteed for all 4 years. 87% of students commute. Alcohol is not permitted. All students may keep cars.

Activities: There are no fraternities or sororities. There are 30 groups on campus, including cheerleading, choir, chorale, computers, drama, ethnic, forensics, honors, international, literary magazine, newspaper, political, professional, religious, social, social service, and student government. Popular campus events include Family Weekend, Take-off Week, and Midnight Madness.

Sports: There are 4 intercollegiate sports for men and 5 for women, and 6 intramural sports for men and 6 for women. Facilities include baseball, softball, and soccer fields, and a sports complex.

Disabled Students: All of the campus is accessible. Wheelchair ramps, elevators, special parking, specially equipped rest rooms, special class scheduling, lowered drinking fountains, and lowered telephones are available.

Services: Counseling and information services are available, as is tutoring in most subjects. There is remedial math and writing.

Campus Safety and Security: Measures include 24-hour foot and vehicle patrol, escort service, informal discussions, and pamphlets/posters/films. There are lighted pathways/sidewalks.

Programs of Study: NU confers B.A., B.S., and B.S.N. degrees. Associate and master's degrees are also awarded. Bachelor's degrees are awarded in BIOLOGICAL SCIENCE (biology/biological science), BUSINESS (accounting, business administration and management, and marketing/retailing/merchandising), COMMUNICATIONS AND THE ARTS (art, communications, and English), COMPUTER AND PHYSICAL SCIENCE (chemistry, information sciences and systems, and mathematics), EDUCATION (athletic training, elementary, middle school, and secondary), HEALTH PROFESSIONS (nursing, occupational therapy, and ultrasound technology), SOCIAL SCIENCE (addiction studies, counseling/psychology, criminal justice, history, pastoral studies, psychology, religion, and sociology). Nursing, biology, and chemistry are the strongest academically. Nursing, business, and education are the largest.

Required: Degree requirements include completion of 124 credit hours, 30 of which must be upper division. The number of credits required in the major varies. A minimum GPA of 2.0 is required for graduation, and students must fulfill the college's liberal arts requirement, including courses in philosophy and theology.

Special: NU offers cross-registration with Friends University and a 3-2 engineering degree with Kansas State University. Students can earn accelerated degrees in business or education. Work-study programs are available, and credit may be conferred for life, military, and work experience. Students seeking nondegree study may enroll on a space-available basis. Dual majors, student-designed majors in liberal studies, and internships are also possible. There are 3 national honor societies and 1 departmental honors program.

Faculty/Classroom: 38% of faculty are male; 62%, female. 85% teach undergraduates. No introductory courses are taught by graduate students. The average class size in a regular course is 11.

Admissions: 4 freshmen graduated first in their class in a recent year.

Requirements: The SAT I or ACT is required, with a minimum composite score of 18 on the ACT. Candidates for admission must graduate from an accredited secondary school with 23 high school academic credits, including 4 credits of English, and 3 each of math, science, and social studies. 2 credits of a foreign language are recommended. A GPA of 2.0 is required. AP and CLEP credits are accepted.

Procedure: Freshmen are admitted fall, spring, and summer. Entrance exams should be taken during the spring of the junior year or fall of the senior year. There is a deferred admissions plan. Application deadlines are open. The application fee is $15.

Transfer: 232 transfer students enrolled in a recent year. A minimum GPA of 2.0 is required. 30 credits of 124 must be completed at NU.

Visiting: There are regularly scheduled orientations for prospective students, including meetings with faculty, athletic coaches, co-curricular sponsors, financial aid counselors, admissions counselors, and a campus tour. There are guides for informal visits and visitors may sit in on classes and stay overnight. To schedule a visit, contact the Admissions Office.

Financial Aid: In a recent year, 95% of all freshmen and 85% of continuing students received some form of financial aid. 65% of freshmen and 64% of continuing students received need-based aid. The average freshman award was $9425. Of that total, scholarships or need-based grants averaged $7500 ($13,000 maximum); loans averaged $1500 ($7625 maximum); and work contracts averaged $2425 ($3000 maxi-

mum). 96% of undergraduates work part time. Average annual earnings from campus work are $1200. The average financial indebtedness of a recent graduate was $18,000. The FAFSA and the college's own financial statement are required. Check with the school for current deadlines.
International Students: There were 35 international students enrolled in a recent year. The school actively recruits these students. They must score 530 on the written TOEFL.
Computers: The mainframes are a Several Compaq Proliant servers, both 800 and 1600 models. Microcomputers are available in the 3 academic computer labs, library, residence halls, and learning center. There are 80 PCs, all with Internet and T-1 access. All students have computer accounts and e-mail. All students may access the system. There are no time limits and no fees.
Graduates: In a recent year, 306 bachelor's degrees were awarded. The most popular majors were education (30%), health professions (25%), and business (24%). In an average class, 21% graduate in 4 years, 28% in 5 years, and 33% in 6 years. 20 companies recruited on campus in a recent year.
Admissions Contact: Sr. Catherine Shippen, Admissions Secretary/Receptionist. E-mail: *admissions@newmanu.edu*
Web: *www.newmanu.edu*

OTTAWA UNIVERSITY E-2
Ottawa, KS 66067-3399 (785) 242-5200, ext. 5555
(800) 755-5200,; Fax: (785) 229-1008

Full-time: 260 men, 190 women
Part-time: 10 men, 15 women
Graduate: none
Year: semesters, summer session
Application Deadline: open
Freshman Class: n/av
ACT: 20
Faculty: 21; IIB, --$
Ph.D.s: 54%
Student/Faculty: 20 to 1
Tuition: $11,800
Room & Board: n/av
LESS COMPETITIVE

Ottawa University, founded in 1865 and affiliated with the American Baptist Churches, is a private institution offering programs through the divisions of arts and humanities, natural sciences, and social and behavioral sciences. Figures in the above capsule are approximate. The library contains 90,000 volumes, and subscribes to 400 periodicals. Computerized library services include interlibrary loans and database searching. Special learning facilities include a learning resource center, art gallery, and radio station. The 64-acre campus is in a small town 45 miles southwest of Kansas City. Including residence halls, there are 15 buildings.
Student Life: 55% of undergraduates are from Kansas. Others are from 18 states, 5 foreign countries, and Canada. 99% are from public schools. 77% are white; 11% African American. 64% are Protestant; 20% claim no religious affiliation; 13% Catholic. The average age of freshmen is 19; all undergraduates, 22. 25% do not continue beyond their first year; 30% remain to graduate.
Housing: 428 students can be accommodated in college housing, which includes single-sex dormitories, on-campus apartments, and married-student housing. On-campus housing is guaranteed for all 4 years. 58% of students live on campus; of those, 65% remain on campus on weekends. Alcohol is not permitted. All students may keep cars.
Activities: There are no fraternities or sororities. There are 35 groups on campus, including cheerleading, choir, chorale, chorus, computers, dance, debate, drama, ethnic, forensics, honors, international, jazz band, musical theater, newspaper, orchestra, pep band, photography, professional, radio and TV, religious, social, social service, student government, and yearbook. Popular campus events include Family Day, Charter Day, and Christmas Feast.
Sports: There are 7 intercollegiate sports for men and 7 for women, and 12 intramural sports for men and 12 for women. Facilities include a field, a sports complex, an athletic center, and a gym with a wellness center.
Disabled Students: 50% of the campus is accessible. Wheelchair ramps, elevators, special parking, specially equipped rest rooms, and special class scheduling are available.
Services: Counseling and information services are available, as is tutoring in most subjects. There is remedial math, reading, and writing.
Campus Safety and Security: Measures include self-defense education, escort service, pamphlets/posters/films, and lighted pathways/sidewalks. There is a night security guard. In addition, students are issued individual residence hall security and room keys.
Programs of Study: OU confers the B.A. degree. Bachelor's degrees are awarded in BIOLOGICAL SCIENCE (biology/biological science), BUSINESS (accounting, business administration and management, and management information systems), COMMUNICATIONS AND THE ARTS (art, communications, dramatic arts, English, and music), COMPUTER AND PHYSICAL SCIENCE (chemistry, information sciences and systems, and mathematics), EDUCATION (elementary and physical), SOCIAL SCIENCE (history, human services, political science/government, psychology, religion, and sociology). English, business, and math are the strongest academically. Business, teacher education, and human services are the largest.
Required: To graduate, students must complete 9 courses in 8 academic areas with a minimum GPA of 2.0. The university requires students to complete 124 semester hours, with 24 to 40 in the major. Three interdisciplinary general education seminars must be completed. In addition, students must attend 10 University Program events each semester for 6 semesters.
Special: Internships are available, especially in business, human services, and teacher education. Student-designed majors are an option. 3/2 engineering degrees with Kansas State and the University of Kansas, 3 +1 degree in medical technology, and preprofessional programs in premedicine, predentistry, prelaw, and preministry are available. Work-study programs are also offered. There are 2 national honor societies.
Faculty/Classroom: 60% of faculty are male; 40%, female. All teach undergraduates. The average class size in a laboratory is 12.
Requirements: The ACT is required. In addition, the GED is accepted. There are no specific high school courses required, but a sound college preparatory curriculum is highly recommended. OU requires applicants to be in the upper 50% of their class. A GPA of 2.5 is required. AP and CLEP credits are accepted. Important factors in the admissions decision are parents or siblings attending the school, recommendations by alumni, and recommendations by school officials.
Procedure: Freshmen are admitted to all sessions. Entrance exams should be taken as early as possible. Application deadlines are open. The fall 2001 application fee was $15.
Transfer: Transfer applicants must submit transcripts from all colleges attended and must have a 2.0 GPA and 12 hours of college credit, or else they must meet freshman requirements. 30 credits of 124 must be completed at OU.
Visiting: There are regularly scheduled orientations for prospective students, including Discovery Day in the early spring, which gives prospective students a chance to meet faculty, students, and staff and to learn more about Ottawa University, the admissions process, and financial aid. There are guides for informal visits and visitors may sit in on classes and stay overnight. To schedule a visit, contact D'Nette Orr or Marikay Galutia of the Admissions Office at (913) 242-5200, ext. 5541, or (800) 755-5200.
Financial Aid: In a recent year, 99% of all freshmen and 95% of continuing students received some form of financial aid. 88% of freshmen and 90% of continuing students received need-based aid. The average freshman award was $12,800. Of that total, scholarships or need-based grants averaged $4100 ($14,500 maximum); loans averaged $2750 ($4625 maximum); and work contracts averaged $1750 ($2000 maximum). 80% of undergraduates work part time. Average annual earnings from campus work are $1500. The average financial indebtedness of a recent graduate was $12,000. The FAFSA and the college's own financial statement are required. Check with the school for current deadlines.
International Students: The school actively recruits these students. They must score 500 on the written TOEFL or take the MELAB, .
Computers: The mainframe is an IBM AS/400. There are 2 computer labs and there is connectivity in every dorm room with Internet access. All students may access the system. There are no time limits and no fees.
Graduates: In a recent year, 56 bachelor's degrees were awarded. The most popular majors were business administration (30%), elementary education (16%), and biology (12%). In an average class, 13% graduate in 4 years, 28% in 5 years, and 30% in 6 years. 53 companies recruited on campus in a recent year.
Admissions Contact: Tim Albers, Director of Admissions. A video is available. E-mail: *admiss@ottawa.edu* Web: *www.ottawa.edu*

PITTSBURG STATE UNIVERSITY F-3
Pittsburg, KS 66762 (620) 235-4251
(800) 854-PITT; Fax: (620) 235-6003

Full-time: 4856 men and women
Part-time: 614 men and women
Graduate: 1253 men and women
Year: semesters, summer session
Application Deadline: open
Freshman Class: 1061 applied, 1052 accepted, 945 enrolled
ACT: 21
Faculty: 242; IIA, --$
Ph.D.s: 88%
Student/Faculty: 20 to 1
Tuition: $2338 ($7192)
Room & Board: $3890
NONCOMPETITIVE

Pittsburg State University, founded in 1903, is a state-supported institution offering programs in arts and sciences, business, education, and technology. There are 4 undergraduate schools and 1 graduate school. In addition to regional accreditation, Pitt State has baccalaureate program accreditation with AACSB, ABET, CSWE, NASM, NCATE, and NLN. The 2 libraries contain 718,422 volumes, 797,204 microform items, and 1640 audiovisual forms/CDs, and subscribe to 4512 periodicals. Computerized library services include the card catalog, interlibrary loans, and database searching. Special learning facilities include a learning resource center, art gallery, planetarium, radio station, TV station, and dedicated channel on local cable television. The 233-acre campus is in a small town 100 miles south of Kansas City. Including residence halls, there are 34 buildings.

Student Life: 84% of undergraduates are from Kansas. Others are from 46 states, 51 foreign countries, and Canada. 98% are from public schools. 89% are white. The average age of all undergraduates is 27. 22% do not continue beyond their first year; 52% remain to graduate.

Housing: 907 students can be accommodated in college housing, which includes coed dormitories, on-campus apartments, married-student housing, fraternity houses, and sorority houses. On-campus housing is guaranteed for all 4 years. Alcohol is not permitted. All students may keep cars.

Activities: 10% of men belong to 7 national fraternities; 11% of women belong to 3 national sororities. There are 140 groups on campus, including art, band, cheerleading, chess, choir, computers, dance, drill team, ethnic, honors, housing, international, jazz band, literary magazine, marching band, newspaper, pep band, photography, political, professional, radio and TV, recreational, religious, social, social service, student government, and yearbook. Popular campus events include Greek Week, Multicultural Month, and Welcome Week.

Sports: There are 6 intercollegiate sports for men and 5 for women, and 9 intramural sports for men and 9 for women. Facilities include a football stadium, indoor and outdoor tracks, a basketball arena, softball diamonds, a baseball field, a weight room, a dance studio, an Olympic-size pool, volleyball, racquetball, and badminton courts, indoor and outdoor tennis courts, and sand volleyball courts.

Disabled Students: 70% of the campus is accessible. Wheelchair ramps, elevators, special parking, specially equipped rest rooms, special class scheduling, lowered drinking fountains, and lowered telephones are available.

Services: Counseling and information services are available, as is tutoring in some subjects, including accounting, biology, chemistry, foreign language, math, computers, physics, psychology, reading/study, and writing. There is a Student Support Services Office and a counseling center.

Campus Safety and Security: Measures include 24-hour foot and vehicle patrol, escort service, informal discussions, and pamphlets/posters/films. There are emergency telephones and lighted pathways/sidewalks.

Programs of Study: Pitt State confers B.A., B.S., B.B.A., B.F.A., B.Gen.Studies, B.Music, B.M.Ed. B.S. Ed., B.S.E.T., B.S.Med. Tech., B.S.N., B.S.T., and B.Voc.-Tech Ed. degrees. Associate and master's degrees are also awarded. Bachelor's degrees are awarded in BIOLOGICAL SCIENCE (biology/biological science), BUSINESS (accounting, banking and finance, business administration and management, and marketing/retailing/merchandising), COMMUNICATIONS AND THE ARTS (art, communications, English, French, music, and Spanish), COMPUTER AND PHYSICAL SCIENCE (chemistry, computer science, information sciences and systems, mathematics, and physics), EDUCATION (art, elementary, foreign languages, music, and vocational), ENGINEERING AND ENVIRONMENTAL DESIGN (engineering technology, and printing technology), HEALTH PROFESSIONS (medical technology, and nursing), SOCIAL SCIENCE (criminal justice, economics, family/consumer studies, geography, history, political science/government, psychology, social science, social work, and sociology). Business administration, elementary education, and engineering technology are the largest.

Required: To graduate, students must complete 124 semester hours, including 35 to 60 hours in the major, with a minimum GPA of 2.0. General education requirements total 49 hours (up to 54 for education majors) and include courses in English, speech, math, humanities, social and behavioral sciences, natural and physical sciences, producing and consuming, and lifetime fitness are required.

Special: Co-op and work-study programs, internships, a general studies degree, B.A.-B.S. degrees, dual majors, a 3-2 engineering degree with the University of Kansas and Kansas State University, credit by exam, nondegree study, and pass/fail options are available. Pitt State has student exchange programs with 70 countries. There are 22 national honor societies, including Phi Beta Kappa, a freshman honors program, and 23 departmental honors programs.

Faculty/Classroom: 71% of faculty are male; 29%, female. 96% teach undergraduates and 83% do research. Graduate students teach 5% of introductory courses. The average class size in an introductory lecture is 50; in a laboratory, 20; and in a regular course, 35.

Admissions: 99% of the 2001-2002 applicants were accepted. The ACT scores of the 2001-2002 freshmen class were 53% between 18 and 23, 24% between 24 and 29, and 3% 30 and above. 12% of the current freshmen were in the top fifth of their class; 37% were in the top two fifths.

Requirements: The ACT is required. In addition, applicants must meet 1 of these 3 criteria: an ACT score of 21 or above, class rank in the top third, or a 2.0 GPA in the Kansas core curriculum. Candidates may also be accepted through an exceptions window. The GED is accepted. A GPA of 2.0 is required for in-state applicants (2.5 for out-of-state). AP and CLEP credits are accepted. Important factors in the admissions decision are advanced placement or honor courses, geographic diversity, and ability to finance college education.

Procedure: Freshmen are admitted to all sessions. Entrance exams should be taken before or during the first semester of the freshman year of college. Application deadlines are open. The fall 2001 application fee was $25. Notification is sent on a rolling basis.

Transfer: Applicants must have 24 credit hours and a college GPA of 2.0 or else meet freshman admissions requirements. 30 credits of 124 must be completed at Pitt State.

Visiting: There are regularly scheduled orientations for prospective students. There are guides for informal visits and visitors may sit in on classes. To schedule a visit, contact the Admissions Office.

Financial Aid: The FAFSA is required. The fall application deadline is March 15.

International Students: The school actively recruits these students. They must score 520 on the written TOEFL or 190 on the electronic version or submit minimum scores of 980 on the SAT I or 21 on the ACT, or have taken English course work.

Computers: The mainframe is an IBM system. 7 student labs can access the mainframe, e-mail, and university fiber-optic network via PCs. More than 250 workstations and 200 software packages are available. Bitnet and Internet are also available. All students may access the system 7 A.M. to midnight. There are no time limits and no fees.

Admissions Contact: Ange Peterson, Director of Admission and Retention. A video is available. E-mail: *psuadmit@pittstate.edu*
Web: *www.pittstate.edu*

SAINT MARY COLLEGE F-2

Leavenworth, KS 66048 (913) 758-6165
(800) 752-7043; Fax: (913) 758-6140

Full-time: 163 men, 174 women	**Faculty:** 34; IIB, --$
Part-time: 20 men, 127 women	**Ph.D.s:** 61%
Graduate: 56 men, 232 women	**Student/Faculty:** 10 to 1
Year: semesters, summer session	**Tuition:** $12,312
Application Deadline: open	**Room & Board:** $4986
Freshman Class: n/av	
ACT: 22	**COMPETITIVE**

Saint Mary College, founded in 1923, is a private liberal arts institution affiliated with the Roman Catholic Church and sponsored by the Sisters of Charity of Leavenworth. Some information in this profile is approximate. There is 1 graduate school. In addition to regional accreditation, Saint Mary College has baccalaureate program accreditation with NCATE. The library contains 100,820 volumes and 1675 microform items, and subscribes to 301 periodicals. Computerized library services include the card catalog, interlibrary loans, and database searching. Special learning facilities include a learning resource center, art gallery, and several special library collections. The 240-acre campus is in a small town 25 miles northwest of Kansas City, Missouri. Including residence halls, there are 10 buildings.

Student Life: 69% of undergraduates are from Kansas. Others are from 18 states and 6 foreign countries. 75% are white; 12%, African American; 12%, Hispanic. 45% are Baptist, Lutheran, Methodist, and Nazarene; 35%, Catholic; 18% claim no religious affiliation. 64% do not continue beyond their first year; 43% remain to graduate.

Housing: 333 students can be accommodated in college housing, which includes single-sex and coed dormitories. On-campus housing is guaranteed for all 4 years. 56% of students live on campus. All students may keep cars.

Activities: There are no fraternities or sororities. There are 25 groups on campus, including art, cheerleading, choir, chorale, chorus, computers, dance, drama, honors, literary magazine, musical theater, newspaper, opera, political, professional, religious, social, social service, and student government. Popular campus events include Fall Convocation, Founders Day, and Family Weekend.

Sports: There are 6 intercollegiate sports for men and 6 for women, and 10 intramural sports for men and 10 for women. Facilities include a 500-seat sports center, soccer and softball fields, 3 tennis courts, a sandlot volleyball court, 2 racquetball courts, a weight and exercise room, a swimming pool, a dance and aerobics space, a walking trail, and an indoor jogging track.

Disabled Students: 90% of the campus is accessible. Wheelchair ramps, elevators, special parking, and specially equipped rest rooms are available.

Services: Counseling and information services are available, as is tutoring in most subjects.

Campus Safety and Security: Measures include self-defense education, informal discussions, pamphlets/posters/films, and lighted pathways/sidewalks. There are 14-hour foot and vehicle patrols, and controlled access to residence halls.

Programs of Study: Saint Mary College confers B.A. and B.S. degrees. Associate and master's degrees are also awarded. Bachelor's degrees are awarded in BIOLOGICAL SCIENCE (biology/biological science), BUSINESS (accounting, business administration and management, and international business management), COMMUNICATIONS AND THE ARTS (art, dramatic arts, and English), COMPUTER AND PHYSICAL SCIENCE (chemistry, information sciences and systems, and mathematics), EDUCATION (elementary), SOCIAL SCIENCE (history, industrial and organizational psychology, interdisciplinary studies, liberal arts/general studies, pastoral studies, political science/government, psychology, sociology, and theological studies).

Required: To graduate, students must complete all general education requirements and earn at least 128 credits, including 30 to 42 in the major, with a minimum GPA of 2.0. The core curriculum includes freshman humanities, colloquium in human communities, introduction to fine arts, and a senior integration project. Distribution requirements include 3 courses each in English, math, natural science, and social and behavioral sciences, and 2 courses each in theology, philosophy, history, foreign language, and phys ed, plus an additional literature course, a fine arts course, and an elective in arts. Completion of a writing portfolio is also required.

Special: The college offers co-op programs with the University of Kansas, cross-registration with the Kansas City Regional Council for Higher Education Consortium, a student exchange program in Tokyo at Sophia University's summer session, and study abroad in Europe. Internships, work-study programs, and pass/fail options are also available. There are 2 national honor societies.

Faculty/Classroom: 45% of faculty are male; 55%, female. All teach undergraduates. No introductory courses are taught by graduate students. The average class size in an introductory lecture is 20 and in a laboratory, 12.

Admissions: The ACT scores for the 2001-2002 freshman class were 26% below 21, 28% between 21 and 23, 28% between 24 and 26, 13% between 27 and 28, and 5% above 28.

Requirements: The SAT I or ACT is required. In addition, applicants should be graduates of an accredited secondary school. The GED is accepted. A GPA of 2.5 is required. AP and CLEP credits are accepted. Important factors in the admissions decision are parents or siblings attending the school, recommendations by alumni, and recommendations by school officials.

Procedure: Freshmen are admitted fall and spring. Entrance exams should be taken in the spring of the junior year and fall of the senior year. There are early decision and early admissions plans. Application deadlines are open.The application fee is $10.

Transfer: 49 transfer students enrolled in a recent year. A college GPA of 2.0 is required. 30 credits of 128 must be completed at Saint Mary College.

Visiting: There are regularly scheduled orientations for prospective students, consisting of visiting classes, interviewing with faculty and financial aid representatives, and touring the campus. There are guides for informal visits and visitors may sit in on classes and stay overnight. To schedule a visit, contact the Admissions Office.

Financial Aid: In 2001-2002, 95% of all freshmen received some form of financial aid. 59% of undergraduates work part time. The average financial indebtedness of a recent graduate was $7500. Saint Mary College is a member of CSS. The FAFSA is required.

International Students: The school actively recruits these students. They must score 500 on the written TOEFL or 170 on the electronic version.

Computers: The mainframe is an IBM AS/400. Media labs are available for course work, and computer labs are available for homework. There are also some PCs in residence halls. All students may access the system. There are no time limits and no fees.

Graduates: In a recent year, 132 bachelor's degrees were awarded. The most popular major was elementary education (15%).

Admissions Contact: John Wilbur, Director of Admissions. A video is available. E-mail: *admiss@hub.smcks.edu* Web: *www.smcks.edu*

SOUTHWESTERN COLLEGE D-3
Winfield, KS 67156-2499 (620) 229-6236
(800) 846-1543; Fax: (620) 229-6344

Full-time: 269 men, 314 women	**Faculty:** 55; IIB, --$
Part-time: 320 men, 272 women	**Ph.D.s:** 56%
Graduate: 45 men, 56 women	**Student/Faculty:** 11 to 1
Year: semesters, summer session	**Tuition:** $13,076
Application Deadline: August 1	**Room & Board:** $4580
Freshman Class: 398 applied, 285 accepted, 131 enrolled	
SAT I Verbal/Math: 480/480	**ACT:** 23 **COMPETITIVE**

Southwestern College, established in 1885, is a private institution affiliated with the Kansas West Conference of the United Methodist Church. In addition to regional accreditation, Southwestern has baccalaureate program accreditation with CSWE, NASM, and NLN. The 2 libraries contain 70,000 volumes, 1000 microform items, and 20 audiovisual forms/CDs, and subscribe to 300 periodicals. Computerized library services include the card catalog, interlibrary loans, and database searching. Special learning facilities include a learning resource center, art gallery, radio station, TV station, and a biological field station. The 82-acre campus is in a small town 45 miles southeast of Wichita. Including residence halls, there are 20 buildings.

Student Life: 82% of undergraduates are from Kansas. Others are from 18 states and 10 foreign countries. 84% are white. The average age of freshmen is 18; all undergraduates, 29. 33% do not continue beyond their first year; 51% remain to graduate.

Housing: 386 students can be accommodated in college housing, which includes single-sex and coed dormitories, on-campus apartments, and married-student housing. In addition, there are honors houses. On-campus housing is guaranteed for the freshman year only and is available on a first-come, first-served basis. 70% of students commute. Alcohol is not permitted. All students may keep cars.

Activities: 15% of men and about 1% of women belong to 1 local and 1 national fraternity; 12% of women belong to 1 local and 1 national sorority. There are 32 groups on campus, including band, cheerleading, choir, chorus, dance, debate, drama, drill team, ethnic, film, forensics, honors, international, jazz band, literary magazine, musical theater, newspaper, orchestra, pep band, photography, political, professional, radio and TV, religious, social, social service, student government, symphony, and yearbook. Popular campus events include Movie Nights, Spring Formal, and Kickback Day.

Sports: There are 7 intercollegiate sports for men and 7 for women, and 2 intramural sports for men and 2 for women. Facilities include a 2400-seat stadium, tennis and basketball courts, playing floors, exercise rooms, a gym, an indoor swimming pool, a running track, a soccer field, a weight room, and a Frisbee golf course.

Disabled Students: 80% of the campus is accessible. Wheelchair ramps, elevators, special parking, specially equipped rest rooms, special class scheduling, lowered drinking fountains, and lowered telephones are available.

Services: Counseling and information services are available, as is tutoring in every subject. There is remedial math, reading, and writing. Tutoring is available in every subject upon request. A reader service is available for dyslexic students.

Campus Safety and Security: Measures include 24-hour foot and vehicle patrol, self-defense education, escort service, and informal discussions. There are emergency telephones and lighted pathways/sidewalks.

Programs of Study: Southwestern confers B.A., B.S., B.B.A., B.G.S., B.L.S., B.Mus., B.Ph., and B.S.N. degrees. Master's degrees are also awarded. Bachelor's degrees are awarded in BIOLOGICAL SCIENCE (biochemistry, biology/biological science, and marine biology), BUSINESS (business administration and management, human resources, management information systems, management science, purchasing/inventory management, and sports management), COMMUNICATIONS AND THE ARTS (communications, dramatic arts, English, French, music, and Spanish), COMPUTER AND PHYSICAL SCIENCE (chemistry, computer programming, computer science, mathematics, and physics), EDUCATION (drama, early childhood, elementary, English, foreign languages, mathematics, music, physical, and science), ENGINEERING AND ENVIRONMENTAL DESIGN (computer technology and manufacturing technology), HEALTH PROFESSIONS (nursing), SOCIAL SCIENCE (criminal justice, history, liberal arts/general studies, pastoral studies, and psychology). Biology, education, and nursing are the strongest academically and have the largest enrollments.

Required: To graduate, students must earn 124 credits, fulfill all requirements of the major, and maintain a GPA of 2.0. Students must complete the integrative studies requirements.

Special: Southwestern offers internships in industry and social and civic agencies, and study abroad in Japan and Bulgaria. A music and theater dual major is available and other combinations or degrees are possible with approval from the Academic Affairs Committee. There is a 3-2 engineering degree program with Washington University of St. Louis. Work-study programs, an accelerated degree program, credit for life, military, and work experience, nondegree study, and pass/fail options are also available. There are 4 national honor societies, including Phi Beta Kappa, a freshman honors program, and 3 departmental honors programs.

Faculty/Classroom: 60% of faculty are male; 40%, female. All teach undergraduates. No introductory courses are taught by graduate students. The average class size in an introductory lecture is 39; in a laboratory, 10; and in a regular course, 13.

Admissions: 72% of the 2001-2002 applicants were accepted. The SAT I scores for the 2001-2002 freshman class were: Verbal--64% below 500, 25% between 500 and 599, and 11% between 600 and 700. The ACT scores were 12% below 18, 48% between 18 and 23, 38% between 24 and 29, and 2% above 29. 47% of the current freshmen were in the top quarter of their class; 72% were in the top two half.

Requirements: The ACT is required and the SAT I is recommended. In addition, all candidates for admission must graduate from an accredited secondary school with a specified college bound curriculum and a GPA of 2.5. The GED is accepted and an essay is required. Interviews are recommended. AP and CLEP credits are accepted. Applications are accepted on-line at *Embark.com*

Procedure: Freshmen are admitted fall, spring, and summer. There is a deferred admissions plan. Applications should be filed by August 1 for fall entry and January 1 for spring entry. The fall 2001 application fee was $20. Notification is sent on a rolling basis.

Transfer: 72 transfer students enrolled in 2001-2002. Applicants must have a college GPA of 2.0 and must submit an essay. 30 credits of 124 must be completed at Southwestern.

Visiting: There are regularly scheduled orientations for prospective students, including 4 Explore More events. There are guides for informal visits and visitors may sit in on classes and stay overnight. To schedule a visit, contact the Admissions Office.

Financial Aid: In 2001-2002, 70% of all freshmen and 90% of continuing students received some form of financial aid. 73% of freshmen and 65% of continuing students received need-based aid. The average freshman award was $9539. Of that total, scholarships or need-based grants averaged $5539 ($7065 maximum) and loans averaged $4000 ($5625 maximum). Average annual earnings from campus work are $700. The average financial indebtedness of the 2001 graduate was $15,206. The FAFSA and the college's own financial statement are required. The fall application deadline is July 1.

International Students: There are 36 international students enrolled. The school actively recruits these students. They must score 550 on the written TOEFL or 213 on the electronic version.

Computers: The mainframe is an IBM AS/400. Students have access to Internet connections from all dorm rooms. 5 computer labs with a total of 50 computers that also connect to the World Wide Web are also available. The mainframe is accessed by students with permission from computer lab personnel. IBM ThinkPad laptops are issued to all incoming freshmen. There are no time limits and no fees. All students are required to have personal computers.

Graduates: In 2001, 389 bachelor's degrees were awarded. The most popular majors were business (54%), nursing (10%), and computer (9%). In an average class, 2% graduate in 3 years, 38% in 4 years, 46% in 5 years, and 48% in 6 years. 15 companies recruited on campus in 2000-2001. Of the 2000 graduating class, 16% were enrolled in graduate school within 6 months of graduation and 90% were employed.

Admissions Contact: Brenda Hicks, Director of Admission.
E-mail: *scadmit@sckans.edu* Web: *www.sckans.edu*

STERLING COLLEGE
Sterling, KS 67579 — D-3
(316) 278-4275
(800) 346-1017; Fax: (316) 278-4411

Full-time: 210 men, 229 women	**Faculty:** 36; IIB, --$
Part-time: 9 men, 13 women	**Ph.D.s:** 44%
Graduate: none	**Student/Faculty:** 12 to 1
Year: 4-1-4	**Tuition:** $11,582
Application Deadline: open	**Room & Board:** $4788
Freshman Class: 437 applied, 257 accepted, 106 enrolled	
SAT I Verbal/Math: 490/510	**ACT:** 22 **VERY COMPETITIVE**

Sterling College, established in 1887, is a private liberal arts institution affiliated with the Presbyterian Church (U.S.A.), offering undergraduate curricula in 17 majors plus teacher preparation. The library contains 61,430 volumes, 2120 microform items, and 2125 audiovisual forms/CDs, and subscribes to 846 periodicals. Computerized library services include the card catalog and database searching. Special learning facilities include a learning resource center, art gallery, a museum, and a theater. The 43-acre campus is in a small town 70 miles northwest of Wichita. Including residence halls, there are 19 buildings.

Student Life: 63% of undergraduates are from Kansas. Others are from 29 states and 10 foreign countries. 85% are from public schools. 87% are white. Most are Protestant. The average age of freshmen is 18; all undergraduates, 20. 40% do not continue beyond their first year.

Housing: 490 students can be accommodated in college housing, which includes single-sex dormitories. On-campus housing is guaranteed for all 4 years. 79% of students live on campus; of those, 80% remain on campus on weekends. Alcohol is not permitted. All students may keep cars.

Activities: There are no fraternities or sororities. There are 12 groups on campus, including art, band, cheerleading, choir, chorus, debate, drama, ethnic, forensics, honors, international, jazz band, literary magazine, musical theater, newspaper, pep band, photography, political, professional, religious, social service, student government, and yearbook. Popular campus events include Habitat for Humanity Week, community picnic, and Missions and International Peacemaker Convocations/Events.

Sports: There are 7 intercollegiate sports for men and 7 for women, and 6 intramural sports for men and 6 for women. Facilities include a weight-training facility, an exercise deck, a swimming pool, a track and football field and stadium, a baseball diamond, a soccer field, practice fields, and basketball, handball, and tennis courts.

Disabled Students: 88% of the campus is accessible. Wheelchair ramps, special parking, and special class scheduling are available.

Services: Counseling and information services are available, as is tutoring in every subject. There is remedial math, reading, and writing and special accommodations are provided on an as-needed basis.

Campus Safety and Security: Measures include informal discussions, lighted pathways/sidewalks, and evening and nighttime foot and vehicle patrol.

Programs of Study: Sterling confers B.A. and B.S. degrees. Bachelor's degrees are awarded in BIOLOGICAL SCIENCE (biology/biological science), BUSINESS (business administration and management), COMMUNICATIONS AND THE ARTS (art, dramatic arts, English, fine arts, music, and speech/debate/rhetoric), COMPUTER AND PHYSICAL SCIENCE (computer science and mathematics), EDUCATION (elementary, music, and physical), SOCIAL SCIENCE (behavioral science, history, religious education, and theological studies). Biology, behavioral science, and education are the strongest academically. Biology, business administration, and education are the largest.

Required: To graduate, students must complete 52-57 credits in a general education curriculum including writing, math, science, social science, philosophy, computers, fine arts, and religion. They must have an overall GPA of 2.0, with 2.5 in the major. A total of 124 credits must be earned, with 39-48 in the major. Physical fitness and chapel/convocation requirements must also be met.

Special: Sterling offers cross-registration with the Associated Colleges of Central Kansas and the Council of Christian Colleges and Univertsities. Internships are available in most majors, as is study abroad in 5 countries. A Washington semester and work-study programs are offered. Student-designed majors are possible. There are 4 national honor societies, and 1 departmental honors program.

Faculty/Classroom: 67% of faculty are male; 33%, female. All teach undergraduates. The average class size in an introductory lecture is 30; in a laboratory, 24; and in a regular course, 15 to 20.

Admissions: 59% of the 2001-2002 applicants were accepted. The SAT I scores for the 2001-2002 freshman class were: Verbal--56% below 500, 13% between 500 and 599, and 31% between 600 and 700; Math--44% below 500, 44% between 500 and 599, and 12% between 600 and 700. The ACT scores were 41% below 21, 14% between 21 and 23, 26% between 24 and 26, 9% between 27 and 28, and 10% above 28. 9 freshmen graduated first in their class.

Requirements: The SAT I or ACT is required. In addition, applicants must graduate from an accredited secondary school or have a GED. An interview is recommended. A GPA of 2.2 is required. AP and CLEP credits are accepted. Important factors in the admissions decision are personality/intangible qualities, extracurricular activities record, and leadership record. An application is available on the college web site.

Procedure: Freshmen are admitted fall and spring. Entrance exams should be taken in the spring of the junior year. There is an early admissions plan. Regular application deadlines are open. Early decision deadline is November 15. Notification is sent on a rolling basis; early decision notification, December 12. The application fee is $25.

Transfer: 53 transfer students enrolled in 2001-2002. Transfer students must maintain at least a C average. 24 credits of 124 must be completed at Sterling.

Visiting: There are regularly scheduled orientations for prospective students, including visits with admissions, financial aid, and current students. There are guides for informal visits and visitors may sit in on classes and stay overnight. To schedule a visit, contact the Admissions Office at (620) 278-4314 or *admissions@sterling.edu*

Financial Aid: In 2001-2002, all of all freshmen and 98% of continuing students received some form of financial aid. 92% of all students received need-based aid. The average freshman award was $12,485. Of that total, scholarships or need-based grants averaged $8677 ($12,100 maximum); loans averaged $2625 ($6625 maximum); work contracts averaged $1100 ($1600 maximum); and scholarships, grants, loans, awards, employment, state, SEOG, and other college grants averaged $10,183 ($12,100 maximum). 60% of undergraduates work part time. Average annual earnings from campus work are $756. The average financial indebtedness of the 2001 graduate was $14,055. The FAFSA is required. The fall application deadline is March 15.

International Students: There are 10 international students enrolled. They must score 520 on the written TOEFL or 190 on the electronic version and also take the SAT I or the ACT, scoring 18 on the ACT.

Computers: The mainframe is a Novell Network. There are Internet-connected computer labs in the library, in an academic building, and in 2 of the 4 residence halls. All students may access the system 16 hours per day. There are no time limits and no fees.

Graduates: In 2001, 71 bachelor's degrees were awarded. The most popular majors were business administration (15%), elementary education (14%), and biology (12%). In an average class, 1% graduate in 3 years, 73% in 4 years, 92% in 5 years, and 95% in 6 years.

Admissions Contact: Calvin White, VP for Enrollment Services.
E-mail: *admissions@sterling.edu* Web: *www.sterling.edu*

TABOR COLLEGE
Hillsboro, KS 67063 D-2
(620) 947-3121, ext. 1723
(800) TABOR-99; Fax: (620) 947-6276

Full-time: 211 men, 195 women	**Faculty:** 26; IIB, --$
Part-time: 67 men, 99 women	**Ph.D.s:** 69%
Graduate: 6 men, 15 women	**Student/Faculty:** 16 to 1
Year: 4-1-4	**Tuition:** $13,000
Application Deadline: August 1	**Room & Board:** $4600

Freshman Class: 280 applied, 164 accepted, 98 enrolled
ACT: 22 **LESS COMPETITIVE**

Tabor College, established in 1908, is a private liberal arts facility affiliated with the Mennonite Brethren Church. In addition to regional accreditation, Tabor has baccalaureate program accreditation with CSWE and NASM. The library contains 80,754 volumes, 435 microform items, and 795 audiovisual forms/CDs, and subscribes to 265 periodicals. Computerized library services include the card catalog, interlibrary loans, and database searching. Special learning facilities include a learning resource center and a writing center. The 26-acre campus is in a rural area 50 miles north of Wichita. Including residence halls, there are 28 buildings.

Student Life: 67% of undergraduates are from Kansas. Others are from 17 states, 4 foreign countries, and Canada. 90% are from public schools. 88% are white. 82% are Protestant; 14% unspecified. The average age of freshmen is 18; all undergraduates, 20. 10% do not continue beyond their first year; 67% remain to graduate.

Housing: 210 students can be accommodated in college housing, which includes single-sex dormitories and off-campus apartments. On-campus housing is guaranteed for all 4 years. 84% of students live on campus; of those, 85% remain on campus on weekends. Alcohol is not permitted. All students may keep cars.

Activities: There are no fraternities or sororities. There are 18 groups on campus, including art, band, cheerleading, choir, chorale, chorus, computers, drama, drill team, ethnic, honors, international, jazz band, musical theater, newspaper, pep band, photography, political, religious, social service, student government, and yearbook. Popular campus events include Service Emphasis Week and Mission Emphasis Week.

Sports: There are 8 intercollegiate sports for men and 8 for women, and 10 intramural sports for men and 10 for women. Facilities include 4 lighted tennis courts, 2 racquetball courts, lighted football and baseball fields, several practice fields, a soccer field, a curbed metric all-weather track, a gym with 2 playing floors, a practice/intramural gym, an indoor soccer court, and aerobic exercise, athletic training, and weight rooms.

Disabled Students: 75% of the campus is accessible. Wheelchair ramps, elevators, special parking, specially equipped rest rooms, special class scheduling, lowered drinking fountains, and lowered telephones are available.

Services: Counseling and information services are available, as is tutoring in most subjects. Tutoring is available for most learning disabled students and for those on academic probation.

Campus Safety and Security: Measures include lighted pathways/sidewalks.

Programs of Study: Tabor confers B.A. and B.S. degrees. Associate degrees are also awarded. Bachelor's degrees are awarded in BIOLOGICAL SCIENCE (biology/biological science), BUSINESS (accounting, business administration and management, marketing/retailing/merchandising, and office supervision and management), COMMUNICATIONS AND THE ARTS (communications, English, and music), COMPUTER AND PHYSICAL SCIENCE (chemistry, computer science, mathematics, and natural sciences), EDUCATION (athletic training, business, elementary, health, middle school, music, physical, science, secondary, and special), SOCIAL SCIENCE (biblical studies, history, humanities, international studies, ministries, philosophy, psychology, religion, social science, and sociology). The sciences are the strongest academically. Business and education are the largest.

Required: All students must complete 47 to 59 hours of general education courses including biblical and religious studies, history of diverse cultures, creative expression, natural and mathematical systems, values, social sciences, language, communication, computer literacy, physical fitness, and a college success seminar. A total of 124 credits, 16 of which must be in the major, with a minimum GPA of 2.0, is required in order to graduate.

Special: Cross-registration is offered with the Association of Colleges of Central Kansas. Study abroad in 5 countries is possible. Dual majors, student-designed majors, internships, a Washington semester for juniors or seniors, and pass/fail options are available, as is a 3-2 engineering degree with Wichita State University. An accelerated degree program in management organizational development and preprofessional curricula in allied health, law, and medicine are also offered. There is a freshman honors program and 1 departmental honors program.

Faculty/Classroom: 73% of faculty are male; 27%, female. All teach undergraduates. The average class size in an introductory lecture is 32; in a laboratory, 12; and in a regular course, 20.

Admissions: 59% of the 2001-2002 applicants were accepted. 40% of the current freshmen were in the top fifth of their class; 71% were in the top two fifths.

Requirements: The ACT is required. In addition, an essay is required and an interview is recommended. A GPA of 2.0 is required. AP and CLEP credits are accepted. Personality/intangible qualities is an important factor in the admission decision. Tabor is a part of the CollegeLink electronic application system. Applications are also accepted on-line via Tabor's web site: *www.tabor.edu*

Procedure: Freshmen are admitted to all sessions. Entrance exams should be taken in October of the senior year. Early decision applications should be filed by February 1; regular applications, by August 1 for fall entry, along with a $20 fee. Notification is sent on a rolling basis.

Transfer: 26 transfer students enrolled in 2001-2002. A minimum 2.0 GPA is required and an interview is recommended. 33 credits of 124 must be completed at Tabor.

Visiting: There are regularly scheduled orientations for prospective students, including a tour, admissions interview, and faculty, class, and financial aid visits. If requested, an audition or tryout will be scheduled. There are guides for informal visits and visitors may sit in on classes and stay overnight. To schedule a visit, contact Admissions Counselors at *campusvisit@tabor.edu*

Financial Aid: In 2001-2002, all students received some form of financial aid. 85% of freshmen and 77% of continuing students received need-based aid. The average freshman award was $4673. Of that total, scholarships or need-based grants averaged $2909 ($15,315 maximum); loans averaged $2527; and work contracts averaged $1000 ($3200 maximum). 43% of undergraduates work part time. Average annual earnings from campus work are $1000. The average financial indebtedness of the 2001 graduate was $16,813. The FAFSA, a federal income tax form, and W-2 forms are required. The fall application deadline is March 1.

International Students: They must score 525 on the written TOEFL and also take the SAT I or the ACT.

Computers: The mainframe is a Dual 83/80. There are also 60 PCs available in the administration building and labs. All students may access the system. There are no time limits and no fees.

Graduates: In 2001, 122 bachelor's degrees were awarded. The most popular majors were business marketing (38%), philosophy, religion, theology (17%), and education (15%).

Admissions Contact: Glenn L. Lygrisse, Vice President, Enrollment Management. E-mail: *admissions@.tabor.edu* Web: *www.tabor.edu*

UNIVERSITY OF KANSAS
Lawrence, KS 66045 E-2
(785) 864-3911
(888) 686-7323; Fax: (785) 864-5017

Full-time: 8488 men, 9526 women	**Faculty:** 1185; I, -$
Part-time: 974 men, 1074 women	**Ph.D.s:** 95%
Graduate: 3823 men, 4305 women	**Student/Faculty:** 15 to 1
Year: semesters, summer session	**Tuition:** $2884 ($9811)
Application Deadline: April 1	**Room & Board:** $4348

Freshman Class: 8479 applied, 5861 accepted, 4208 enrolled
ACT: 25 **VERY COMPETITIVE**

The University of Kansas, founded in 1866, is a public, comprehensive institution. Its undergraduate and graduate programs emphasize the liberal arts, business, fine arts, music, teacher preparation, journalism, engineering, architecture, social welfare, law, and health science, including pharmacy. Its medical center campus is located in Kansas City. There are 11 undergraduate and 3 graduate schools. In addition to regional accreditation, KU has baccalaureate program accreditation with AACSB, ABET, ACEJMC, ACPE, APTA, CAHEA, CSWE, NAAB, NASAD, NASM, NCATE, NLN, AOTA, CAAHEP, and NAACLS. The 12 libraries contain 3,752,553 volumes, 3,368,126 microform items, and 48,554 audiovisual forms/CDs, and subscribe to 32,722 periodicals. Computerized library services include the card catalog, interlibrary loans, and database searching. Special learning facilities include a learning resource center, art gallery, natural history museum, radio station, TV station, and observatory, film studio, space technology center, state-of-the-art performing arts center, and art, natural history, classics, anthropology, entomology, and invertebrate paleontology museums. The 1000-acre campus is in a suburban area 40 miles west of Kansas City. Including residence halls, there are 185 buildings.

Student Life: 72% of undergraduates are from Kansas. Others are from 50 states, 116 foreign countries, and Canada. 84% are white. The average age of freshmen is 18; all undergraduates, 21. 20% do not continue beyond their first year.

Housing: 5241 students can be accommodated in college housing, which includes single-sex and coed dormitories, on-campus apartments, off-campus apartments, and married-student housing. In addition, there are honors houses. On-campus housing is available on a first-come, first-served basis. Alcohol is not permitted. All students may keep cars.

Activities: 17% of men belong to 22 national fraternities; 18% of women belong to 13 national sororities. There are 350 groups on campus, including art, band, cheerleading, chess, choir, chorale, chorus, dance, debate, drama, environmental, ethnic, film, gay, honors, international, jazz band, literary magazine, marching band, musical theater, newspaper, opera, orchestra, pep band, photography, political, professional, radio and TV, religious, social, social service, student government, symphony, and yearbook. Popular campus events include Holiday Vespers, music and theater presentations, and Rock Chalk Revue.

Sports: There are 7 intercollegiate sports for men and 11 for women, and 20 intramural sports for men and 20 for women. Facilities include a field house with an indoor track and basketball and volleyball courts; a 52000-seat football stadium with an outdoor track; a sports pavilion with an indoor football field; a health and phys ed center housing 2 indoor pools, handball and racquetball courts, an indoor climbing wall, a weight/exercise/gymnastics/combative room, and gyms; baseball, lacrosse, ultimate, cricket, football, soccer, and rugby fields; tennis courts; and a bowling alley.

Disabled Students: 95% of the campus is accessible. Wheelchair ramps, elevators, special parking, specially equipped rest rooms, special class scheduling, lowered drinking fountains, and lowered telephones are available.

Services: Counseling and information services are available, as is tutoring in most subjects, including how-to sessions on study and organizational skills and workshops on note taking. There is a reader service for the blind and remedial math. A writing center is available to students.

Campus Safety and Security: Measures include 24-hour foot and vehicle patrol, shuttle buses, informal discussions, and pamphlets/posters/films. There are emergency telephones and lighted pathways/sidewalks.

Programs of Study: KU confers B.A., B.S., B.A.E., B.Arch., B.F.A., B.G.S., B.M., B.M.E., B.S.B., B.S.E., B.S.J., B.S.N., and B.S.W. degrees. Master's and doctoral degrees are also awarded. Bachelor's degrees are awarded in AGRICULTURE (environmental studies), BIOLOGICAL SCIENCE (biochemistry, biology/biological science, and microbiology), BUSINESS (accounting, and business administration and management), COMMUNICATIONS AND THE ARTS (advertising, art, art history and appreciation, broadcasting, classical languages, dance, design, dramatic arts, East Asian languages and literature, English, French, German, Germanic languages and literature, journalism, linguistics, music history and appreciation, music performance, music theory and composition, painting, printmaking, sculpture, Slavic languages, Spanish, speech/debate/rhetoric, theater design, and voice), COMPUTER AND PHYSICAL SCIENCE (astronomy, atmospheric sciences and meteorology, chemistry, computer science, geology, mathematics, and physics), EDUCATION (art, athletic training, elementary, health, middle school, music, physical, and secondary), ENGINEERING AND ENVIRONMENTAL DESIGN (aeronautical engineering, architectural engineering, architecture, chemical engineering, civil engineering, computer engineering, electrical/electronics engineering, engineering physics, mechanical engineering, and petroleum/natural gas engineering), HEALTH PROFESSIONS (clinical science, cytotechnology, music therapy, nursing, pharmacy, respiratory therapy, and speech pathology/audiology), SOCIAL SCIENCE (African American studies, African studies, American studies, anthropology, archeology, cognitive science, developmental psychology, Eastern European studies, economics, European studies, geography, history, humanities, international studies, Latin American studies, philosophy, political science/government, psychology, social work, sociology, theological studies, Western civilization/culture, and women's studies). Business, pharmacy, and engineering are the strongest academically. Engineering, biological sciences, and psychology are the largest.

Required: To graduate with a B.A., B.S., or B.G.S. degree, all students must complete at least 124 credit hours, including 27 to 50 in the major, and maintain a GPA of at least 2.0. These, as well as curricula and distribution requirements, vary according to the school and the major. English composition and literature must be taken.

Special: Special academic programs include internships, study abroad in more than 55 countries, a Washington semester, and work-study programs with the university. A cooperative program in engineering is offered, as are B.A.-B.S. degrees in many combinations, interdisciplinary majors, and dual majors in any approved combination. General studies degrees are available in many areas, and student-designed majors are possible. Nondegree study and pass/fail options are offered. There are 11 national honor societies, including Phi Beta Kappa, and a freshman honors program. All departments have honors programs.

Faculty/Classroom: 68% of faculty are male; 32%, female. 89% teach undergraduates, all do research, and 89% do both. Graduate students teach 24% of undergraduate courses. The average class size in a laboratory is 20 and in a regular course, 22.

Admissions: 69% of the 2001-2002 applicants were accepted. The ACT scores for the 2001-2002 freshman class were: 17% below 21, 25% between 21 and 23, 27% between 24 and 26, 13% between 27 and 28, and 18% above 28. 58% of the current freshmen were in the top quarter of their class; 89% were in the top half. There were 104 National Merit finalists.

Requirements: The SAT I or ACT is required. In addition, applicants must have at least a 2.0 GPA; must have an ACT composite score of at least 21 or an SAT I score of at least 970 and a minimum 2.0 GPA; or must take the Kansas Regents required college preparatory curriculum and have at least a 2.5 GPA. Regents curriculum includes 4 years each of English, 3 of college preparatory math, science (1 of lab science), and social sciences, 2 years of a foreign language, and 1 year of computer technology. 1 year of fine or performing arts is recommended. The GED is accepted. Music performance students must audition. KU requires applicants to be in the top third of their class. A GPA of 2.0 (2.5 out-of-state) is required. AP and CLEP credits are accepted. Important factors in the admissions decision are advanced placement or honor courses, evidence of special talent, and geographic diversity.

Procedure: Freshmen are admitted to all sessions. Entrance exams should be taken by the end of the junior year. There is a deferred admissions plan. Applications should be filed by April 1 for fall entry, December 1 for spring entry, and February 1 for summer entry along with a $25 fee. Notification is sent on a rolling basis. 2% of all applicants are on a waiting list; 150 were accepted in 2001. Applications are accepted on-line at the university's web site.

Transfer: 1337 transfer students enrolled in 2001-2002. For entrance to the College of Liberal Arts and Sciences, transfer students must have at least 24 credit hours with a minimum GPA of 2.5. The criteria vary widely within the other schools, some of which may also consider the ACT score and course work. 30 credits of 124 must be completed at KU.

Visiting: There are regularly scheduled orientations for prospective students, consisting of a summer orientation program that includes a 1-day campus visit. There are guides for informal visits and visitors may sit in on classes and stay overnight. To schedule a visit, contact the KU Visitor Center at *visitku@ku.edu*

Financial Aid: In 2000-2001, 50% of all freshmen and 47% of continuing students received some form of financial aid. 34% of freshmen and 33% of continuing students received need-based aid. The average freshman award was $5371. 17% of undergraduates work part time. Average annual earnings from campus work are $2000. The average financial indebtedness of the 2001 graduate was $17,002. The FAFSA is required. The fall application deadline is March 1.

International Students: There are 671 international students enrolled. The school actively recruits these students. Students are tested upon arrival at KU; a high TOEFL score may be accepted in place of the university test.

Computers: The mainframe is an Amdahl 5890/300E. There are hundreds of terminals around the campus in labs and at the computer center. Many PCs are also available campuswide. All students may access the system 24 hours a day, 7 days a week. There are no time limits and no fees.

Graduates: In 2001, 3673 bachelor's degrees were awarded. The most popular majors were business (9%), journalism (9%), and biology sciences (7%). In an average class, 1% graduate in 3 years, 26% in 4 years, 51% in 5 years, and 55% in 6 years. More than 200 companies recruited on campus in 2000-2001. Of the 2000 graduating class, 24% were enrolled in graduate school within 6 months of graduation and 56% were employed.

Admissions Contact: Alan Cerveny, Director of Admissions and Scholarships. A video is available. E-mail: *adm@ku.edu*
Web: *www.admissions.ku.edu*

WASHBURN UNIVERSITY OF TOPEKA — E-2

Topeka, KS 66621 — **(785) 231-1010, ext. 1030; (800) 332-0291**

Full-time: 1241 men, 1848 women	**Faculty:** 240; IIA, -$
Part-time: 719 men, 1290 women	**Ph.D.s:** 95%
Graduate: 453 men, 567 women	**Student/Faculty:** 13 to 1
Year: semesters, summer session	**Tuition:** $3356 ($7496)
Application Deadline: August 3	**Room & Board:** $3410 ($3715)
Freshman Class: 995 applied, 995 accepted, 741 enrolled	
ACT: 21	**NONCOMPETITIVE**

Washburn is a publicly funded, independently governed, state-coordinated university. Established in 1865, the school offers more than 190 programs leading to certification, associate, bachelor, master, and juris doctor degrees through the College of Arts and Sciences and the Schools of Law, Business, Nursing, and Applied Studies. There are 4 undergraduate and 4 graduate schools. In addition to regional accreditation, Washburn has baccalaureate program accreditation with ACS, APTA, CAAHEP, CAHEA, CSWE, NASAD, NASM, NCATE, and NLN. The 2 libraries contain 331,435 volumes, 574,490 microform items, and 1784 audiovisual forms/CDs, and subscribe to 2699 periodicals. Computerized library services include interlibrary loans and database searching. Special learning facilities include a learning resource center, art gallery, planetarium, and TV station. The 160-acre campus is in an urban area 60 miles west of Kansas City. Including residence halls, there are 17 buildings.

Student Life: 94% of undergraduates are from Kansas. Others are from 42 states, 44 foreign countries, and Canada. 87% are from public schools. 68% are white. The average age of freshmen is 23; all undergraduates, 25. 39% do not continue beyond their first year; 50% remain to graduate.

Housing: 478 students can be accommodated in college housing, which includes coed dormitories, fraternity houses, and sorority houses. In addition, there are special-interest houses. On-campus housing is available on a first-come, first-served basis. Priority is given to out-of-town students. 80% of students commute. Alcohol is not permitted. All students may keep cars.

Activities: 12% of men belong to 1 local and 3 national fraternities; 11% of women belong to 4 national sororities. There are 90 groups on campus, including art, band, campus activities board, cheerleading, chess, choir, chorus, computers, dance, debate, drama, drill team, drum and bugle corps, ethnic, forensics, gay, honors, international, jazz band, literary magazine, marching band, musical theater, newspaper, orchestra, peer educators, pep band, political, professional, radio and TV, religious, social, social service, student government, and yearbook. Popular campus events include Greek Week, Student Activities Fair, Annual Music Festival.

Sports: There are 5 intercollegiate sports for men and 4 for women, and 8 intramural sports for men and 8 for women.

Disabled Students: 95% of the campus is accessible. Wheelchair ramps, elevators, special parking, specially equipped rest rooms, special class scheduling, lowered drinking fountains, lowered telephones, and specially designed residential suites are available. Note takers, readers, library assistance, recorders, and tapes are also available.

Services: Counseling and information services are available, as is tutoring in most subjects. There is a reader service for the blind and remedial math and writing.

Campus Safety and Security: Measures include 24-hour foot and vehicle patrol, self-defense education, escort service, and informal discussions. There are pamphlets/posters/films, emergency telephones, lighted pathways/sidewalks, whistle campaign, operation ID, textbook ID program, bicycle patrol, and fire safety programs for residential living facilities.

Programs of Study: Washburn confers B.A., B.S., B.A.S., B.B.A., B.Ed., B.F.A., B.I.S., B.M., B.P.A., B.S.C.T., B.S.N., and B.S.W. degrees. Associate, master's, and doctoral degrees are also awarded. Bachelor's degrees are awarded in BIOLOGICAL SCIENCE (biology/biological science), BUSINESS (accounting, banking and finance, business administration and management, business economics, and marketing/retailing/merchandising), COMMUNICATIONS AND THE ARTS (art, art history and appreciation, communications, dramatic arts, English, French, German, media arts, music, music performance, Spanish, speech/debate/rhetoric, and theater design), COMPUTER AND PHYSICAL SCIENCE (chemistry, computer programming, information sciences and systems, mathematics, physics, and science), EDUCATION (art, early childhood, elementary, music, physical, and secondary), ENGINEERING AND ENVIRONMENTAL DESIGN (technological management), HEALTH PROFESSIONS (medical laboratory technology and nursing), SOCIAL SCIENCE (anthropology, corrections, economics, history, human services, law enforcement and corrections, liberal arts/general studies, philosophy, political science/government, psychology, public administration, religion, social work, and sociology). Natural sciences, art, and music are the strongest academically. Business administration, criminal justice, and nursing are the largest.

Required: Students must complete courses in the arts and humanities, English composition, natural sciences, math, social sciences, and phys ed. A minimum GPA of 2.0 is required over 124 credit hours, including 30 to 40 in the major, for graduation.

Special: Washburn offers a co-op program in computer information science, internships in numerous departments, and study abroad in 8 countries. Dual and student-designed majors, an integrated studies degree, credit by examination, nondegree study, and pass/fail options are also available. A 3-2 engineering degree is possible in conjunction with the University of Kansas and Kansas State University. There are 9 national honor societies, a freshman honors program, and 22 departmental honors program.

Faculty/Classroom: 60% of faculty are male; 40%, female. 90% teach undergraduates and 1all do research. No introductory courses are taught by graduate students. The average class size in an introductory lecture is 35; in a laboratory, 20; and in a regular course, 25.

Admissions: All of the 2001-2002 applicants were accepted. The ACT scores for the 2001-2002 freshman class were: 43% below 21, 24% between 21 and 23, 20% between 24 and 26, 7% between 27 and 28, and 6% above 28. 26% of the current freshmen were in the top fifth of their class; 57% were in the top two fifths. 17 freshmen graduated first in their class.

Requirements: The ACT is required. In addition, applicants should be graduates of an accredited secondary school or have the GED. Applications are accepted on-line. AP and CLEP credits are accepted.

Procedure: Freshmen are admitted to all sessions. Applications should be filed by August 3 for fall entry, January 10 for spring entry, and May 1 for summer entry. The college accepts all applicants. Notification is sent on a rolling basis.

Transfer: 543 transfer students enrolled in 2001-2002. Applicants must meet the same requirements as incoming freshmen. 30 credits of 124 must be completed at Washburn.

Visiting: There are regularly scheduled orientations for prospective students, consisting of a campus visit program Mondays through Fridays at 9:30 A.M. or 1:30 P.M. that includes a tour, visits with faculty, financial aid information, and the opportunity to have all questions answered. There are guides for informal visits and visitors may sit in on classes and stay overnight. To schedule a visit, contact April Sutton at *zzdpadm@washburn.edu*

Financial Aid: In 2001-2002, 60% of all freshmen and 67% of continuing students received some form of financial aid. 43% of freshmen and 44% of continuing students received need-based aid. The average freshman award was $870. Of that total, scholarships or need-based grants averaged $982 ($3748 maximum); loans averaged $1601 ($6107 maximum); and work contracts averaged $1330 ($3000 maximum). 7% of undergraduates work part time. Average annual earnings from campus work are $1437. The average financial indebtedness of the 2001 graduate was $11,000. Washburn is a member of CSS. The FAFSA is required. The fall application deadline is March 1.

International Students: There are 160 international students enrolled. The school actively recruits these students. They must score 520 on the written TOEFL.

Computers: The mainframes are a Prime 9755 and an IBM AS/400. Available computers include Sun microsystems workstations, and Macs, IBM, and Zenith PCs. Students in computer classes may access the system during a wide variety of hours. There are no time limits and no fees.

Graduates: In 2001, 594 bachelor's degrees were awarded. The most popular majors were business (20%), nursing (12%), and criminal justice (9%). In an average class, 42% graduate in 4 years, 51% in 5 years, and 60% in 6 years. 215 companies recruited on campus in 2000-2001.

Admissions Contact: April E. Sutton, Director of Admissions.
E-mail: *zzdpadm@washburn.edu* Web: *www.washburn.edu*

WICHITA STATE UNIVERSITY — D-3

Wichita, KS 67260 — (316) 978-3085
(800) 362-2594; Fax: (316) 978-3174

Full-time: 2932 men, 3799 women	**Faculty:** 460; I, --$
Part-time: 2002 men, 2570 women	**Ph.D.s:** 78%
Graduate: 1605 men, 1946 women	**Student/Faculty:** 15 to 1
Year: semesters, summer session	**Tuition:** $2759 ($9374)
Application Deadline: August 1	**Room & Board:** $4120
Freshman Class: 3229 applied, 2385 accepted, 1236 enrolled	
ACT: 21	**COMPETITIVE**

Wichita State University, established in 1895, is a public institution offering programs in the liberal arts and sciences, business, engineering, education, and health professions. There are 6 undergraduate schools and 1 graduate school. In addition to regional accreditation, WSU has baccalaureate program accreditation with AACSB, ABET, ADA, APTA, CAHEA, CSWE, NASM, NCATE, and NLN. The library contains 1,590,705 volumes, 1,102,728 microform items, and 47,558 audiovisual forms/CDs, and subscribes to 15,169 periodicals. Computerized library services include the card catalog, interlibrary loans, and database searching. Special learning facilities include a learning resource center, art gallery, radio station, TV station, and electronic classroom, telecourses, the National Institute for Aviation Research, museum of art, and public observatory. The 330-acre campus is in an urban area in the metropolitan Wichita area. Including residence halls, there are 61 buildings.

Student Life: 90% of undergraduates are from Kansas. Others are from 48 states, 95 foreign countries, and Canada. 73% are white; 10% foreign nationals. The average age of freshmen is 21; all undergraduates, 26. 32% do not continue beyond their first year.

Housing: 1443 students can be accommodated in college housing, which includes coed dormitories, on-campus apartments, married-student housing, fraternity houses, and sorority houses. In addition, there are honors houses. On-campus housing is available on a first-come, first-served basis. 92% of students commute. Alcohol is not permitted. All students may keep cars.

Activities: 7% of men belong to 10 national fraternities; 4% of women belong to 8 national sororities. There are 99 groups on campus, including art, band, cheerleading, chess, choir, chorus, computers, dance, debate, drama, ethnic, film, gay, honors, international, jazz band, literary magazine, musical theater, newspaper, opera, orchestra, pep band, photography, political, professional, radio and TV, religious, social, social service, student government, and symphony. Popular campus events include Hippodrome, International Week, and Renaissance Festival.

Sports: There are 7 intercollegiate sports for men and 8 for women, and 24 intramural sports for men and 24 for women. Facilities include a 10,656-seat arena, 2 stadiums, an 18-hole golf course, a baseball field, a tennis complex, and a recreation and sports center.

Disabled Students: 98% of the campus is accessible. Wheelchair ramps, elevators, special parking, specially equipped rest rooms, special class scheduling, lowered drinking fountains, lowered telephones, wheelchairs, and braille typewriters are available. Interpreters for the hearing impaired, note taking, and typing services are also offered.

Services: Counseling and information services are available, as is tutoring in most subjects. There is a reader service for the blind, and remedial math, reading, and writing. Group and individual psychological services are available for students and their families.

Campus Safety and Security: Measures include 24-hour foot and vehicle patrol, self-defense education, escort service, and shuttle buses. There are informal discussions, pamphlets/posters/films, emergency telephones, lighted pathways/sidewalks, and a bicycle patrol.

Programs of Study: WSU confers B.A., B.S., B.A.E., B.B.A., B.F.A., B.G.S., B.H.S., B.M., B.M.E., B.S.A.E., B.S.E., B.S.E.E., B.S.I.E., B.S.M.E., and B.S.N. degrees. Associate, master's, and doctoral degrees are also awarded. Bachelor's degrees are awarded in BIOLOGICAL SCIENCE (biology/biological science), BUSINESS (accounting, banking and finance, business administration and management, entrepreneurial studies, human resources, international business management, management science, marketing/retailing/merchandising, and sports management), COMMUNICATIONS AND THE ARTS (art, art history and appreciation, communications, English, French, graphic design, Latin, music, Spanish, studio art, and visual and performing arts), COMPUTER AND PHYSICAL SCIENCE (chemistry, computer science, geology, mathematics, and physics), EDUCATION (art, elementary, music, physical, secondary, and special), ENGINEERING AND ENVIRONMENTAL DESIGN (aeronautical engineering, computer engineering, electrical/electronics engineering, industrial engineering, manufacturing engineering, and mechanical engineering), HEALTH PROFESSIONS (health care administration, medical laboratory technology, nursing, physician's assistant, and speech pathology/audiology), SOCIAL SCIENCE (anthropology, criminal justice, economics, ethnic studies, gerontology, history, liberal arts/general studies, philosophy, political science/government, psychology, social work, sociology, and women's studies). Aerospace engineering, engineering, and business are the strongest academically. Management, education, and computer science are the largest.

Required: To graduate, students need at least 124 credit hours, with a GPA of 2.0 to 2.5, depending on the major. Specific distribution requirements, as well as department requirements, must also be met. The core curriculum consists of 14 courses (42 hours) in general education.

Special: WSU offers co-op programs, internships, study abroad, work-study programs, and a Washington semester. Dual and student-designed majors, a general studies degree, credit by exam, nondegree study, and pass/fail options are also available. There are 14 national honor societies, and a freshman honors program.

Faculty/Classroom: 63% of faculty are male; 37%, female. 85% both teach and do research. The average class size in an introductory lecture is 22; in a laboratory, 22; and in a regular course, 28.

Admissions: 74% of the 2001-2002 applicants were accepted. The ACT scores for the 2001-2002 freshman class were: 45% below 21, 27% between 21 and 23, 17% between 24 and 26, 6% between 27 and 28, and 5% above 28. 24% of the current freshmen were in the top fifth of their class; 50% were in the top two fifths.

Requirements: The ACT is recommended. In addition, applicants must submit a minimum composite ACT score of 21 or a combined SAT I score of 990, rank in the top one third of their high school graduating class, and have a 2.0 GPA (nonresidents, 2.5). Requirements include 4 years of English, 3 each of math, natural and social sciences, and 1 of computer technology. AP and CLEP credits are accepted.

Procedure: Freshmen are admitted to all sessions. There are early admissions and deferred admissions plans. Applications should be filed by August 1 for fall entry and January 1 for spring entry, along with a $25 fee. Notification is sent on a rolling basis.

Transfer: 4242 transfer students enrolled in 2001-2002. Applicants must have a minimum GPA of 2.0 to 2.5, depending on the WSU college they wish to enter. 30 credits of 124 must be completed at WSU.

Visiting: There are regularly scheduled orientations for prospective students. Students may schedule their visit on-line through the school's web site. There are guides for informal visits and visitors may sit in on classes and stay overnight. To schedule a visit, contact the Admissions Office at (316) 689-3085.

Financial Aid: 26% of freshmen and 51% of continuing students received need-based aid. The average freshman award was $900. Of that total, scholarships or need-based grants averaged $935 ($40,000 maximum); loans averaged $1350 ($5400 maximum); and work contracts averaged $770 ($7500 maximum). Average annual earnings from campus work are $1408. The average financial indebtedness of the 2001 graduate was $15,980. The FAFSA is required. The fall application deadline is March 15.

International Students: There are 504 international students enrolled. The school actively recruits these students. .

Computers: The mainframes are an IBM ES 9121/440 and a DEC VAX/4000. Computing labs are located throughout the campus. Students have access as needed and required by academic programs and courses. All students may access the system 24 hours a day. Students may access the system based on allocated funds. There are no fees.

Graduates: In 2001, 1725 bachelor's degrees were awarded. The most popular majors were elementary education (6%), business administration (4%), and accounting (4%). In an average class, 8% graduate in 4 years, 24% in 5 years, and 30% in 6 years. 58 companies recruited on campus in 2000-2001. Of the 2000 graduating class, 21% were enrolled in graduate school within 6 months of graduation and 96% were employed.

Admissions Contact: Christine Schneikart-Luebbe, Director of Admissions. A video is available. E-mail: *admissions@wichita.edu*
Web: *http://www.wichita.edu*

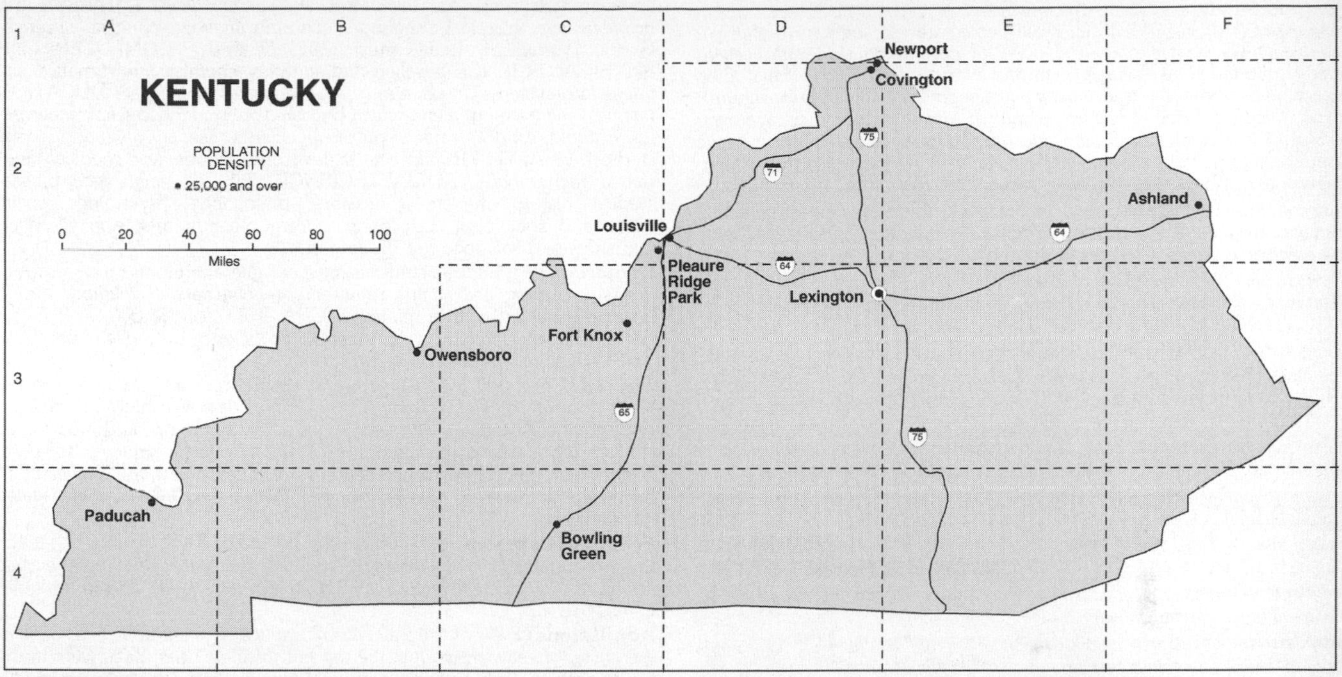

ALICE LLOYD COLLEGE
Pippa Passes, KY 41844

E-4
(606) 368-6036, ext. 6134
(888) 280-4252; Fax: (606) 368-6215

Full-time: 539 men and women	**Faculty:** 27
Part-time: 26 men and women	**Ph.D.s:** 67%
Graduate: none	**Student/Faculty:** 20 to 1
Year: semesters	**Tuition:** $640 ($4560)
Application Deadline: August 1	**Room & Board:** $1465

Freshman Class: 674 applied, 388 accepted, 163 enrolled
ACT: 20 **VERY COMPETITIVE**

Alice Lloyd College, founded in 1923, is a private liberal arts facility emphasizing Christian values and serving the Appalachian community. Within a 108-county area, which includes most of Eastern Kentucky and parts of Ohio, Tennessee, West Virginia, and Virginia, annual fees are $640; outside of this 108-county area, tuition and fees are $4560. In addition to regional accreditation, ALC has baccalaureate program accreditation with NCATE. The library contains 62,000 volumes, 1500 microform items, and 300 audiovisual forms/CDs, and subscribes to 300 periodicals. Computerized library services include the card catalog, interlibrary loans, and database searching. Special learning facilities include a learning resource center, art gallery, radio station, and performing arts center. The 225-acre campus is in a rural area in the eastern part of the state. Including residence halls, there are 35 buildings.

Student Life: 80% of undergraduates are from Kentucky. Others are from 6 states and 5 foreign countries. 99% are from public schools. 99% are white. Most are Protestant. The average age of freshmen is 18; all undergraduates, 23.

Housing: 451 students can be accommodated in college housing, which includes single-sex dormitories and Caney Cottage scholarship program housing. On-campus housing is guaranteed for all 4 years. 77% of students live on campus; of those, 20% remain on campus on weekends. Alcohol is not permitted. All students may keep cars.

Activities: There are no fraternities or sororities. There are 16 groups on campus, including cheerleading, chess, choir, chorus, computers, drama, honors, newspaper, pep band, photography, professional, radio and TV, religious, social, student government, and yearbook. Popular campus events include Religious Emphasis Week, Alcohol Awareness Week, and Appalachia Day.

Sports: There are 4 intercollegiate sports for men and 3 for women, and 11 intramural sports for men and 11 for women. Facilities include an indoor pool, weight rooms, a 1500-seat gym, recreation areas, 2 tennis courts, a baseball/athletic field, and 2 racquetball courts.

Disabled Students: 85% of the campus is accessible. Wheelchair ramps, elevators, special parking, specially equipped rest rooms, and special class scheduling are available.

Services: Counseling and information services are available, as is tutoring in every subject. There is remedial math, reading, and writing.

Campus Safety and Security: Measures include 24-hour foot and vehicle patrol, self-defense education, escort service, and informal discussions. There are pamphlets/posters/films, emergency telephones, and lighted pathways/sidewalks.

Programs of Study: ALC confers B.A. and B.S. degrees. Bachelor's degrees are awarded in BIOLOGICAL SCIENCE (biology/biological science), BUSINESS (business administration and management), COMMUNICATIONS AND THE ARTS (English), EDUCATION (elementary, middle school, physical, secondary, and social studies), ENGINEERING AND ENVIRONMENTAL DESIGN (preengineering), HEALTH PROFESSIONS (prepharmacy), SOCIAL SCIENCE (history). Biology, education and business administration are the strongest academically. Biology is the largest.

Required: To graduate, students must complete a work-study requirement extending through each semester and a 49-semester-hour general education requirement, including phys ed, health, composition, philosophy, and speech. 128 credit hours are required. Students must maintain a 2.0 GPA (2.5 for education majors) to graduate.

Special: Special arrangements include a 2-2 engineering degree with the Universities of Kentucky, Louisville, and West Virginia. Credit by exam and limited work-study are possible. There is 1 national honor society, including Phi Beta Kappa.

Faculty/Classroom: 60% of faculty are male; 40%, female. All teach undergraduates and 30% do research. The average class size in an introductory lecture is 30; in a laboratory, 10; and in a regular course, 17.

Admissions: 58% of the 2001-2002 applicants were accepted. The SAT I scores for the 2001-2002 freshman class were: Verbal--15% below 500, 30% between 500 and 599, and 55% between 600 and 700. The ACT scores were 45% below 21, 34% between 21 and 23, 10% between 24 and 26, 9% between 27 and 28, and 2% above 28. 11 freshmen graduated first in their class.

Requirements: The SAT I or ACT is required. In addition, applicants must be graduates of an accredited secondary school or have a GED, having successfully completed 13 academic credits, including 4 in English and 3 each in math, science, and social studies. A GPA of 2.25 is required. AP and CLEP credits are accepted. Applications are accepted on-line at *www.alc.edu*

Procedure: Freshmen are admitted fall and spring. Entrance exams should be taken in the fall of the senior year. Applications should be filed by August 1 for fall entry and December 15 for spring entry. Notification is sent on a rolling basis.

Transfer: 43 transfer students enrolled in 2001-2002. Applicants must have a minimum 2.0 GPA, 2.5 for some majors, be in good standing at their previous school, and have a minimum ACT score of 17. 30 credits of 128 must be completed at ALC.

Visiting: There are regularly scheduled orientations for prospective students, consisting of summer and fall orientations. There are guides for informal visits and visitors may sit in on classes and stay overnight. To schedule a visit, contact Sean Damron, Director of Admissions at (606) 368-6036.

Financial Aid: In 2001-2002, all students received some form of financial aid. 54% of freshmen and 53% of continuing students received need-based aid. The average freshman award was $7783. Of that total, scholarships or need-based grants averaged $5935 ($7392 maximum); loans averaged $200 ($2000 maximum); and work contracts averaged $1648 ($3616 maximum). All undergraduates work part time. Average annual earnings from campus work are $1648. The average financial indebtedness of the 2001 graduate was $1060. The FAFSA is required.

International Students: In a recent year, there were 7 international students enrolled. They must score 550 on the written TOEFL or 213 on the electronic version and also take the SAT I or the ACT.

Computers: The mainframe is an IBM S/36. There are 70 Gateway PCs available in the computer center. In addition, the science lab has 10 PCs. All students may access the system. There are no fees.

Graduates: In 2001, 66 bachelor's degrees were awarded. In an average class, 20% graduate in 4 years, 21% in 5 years, and 22% in 6 years. Of the 2000 graduating class, 96% were employed within 6 months of graduation.

Admissions Contact: Sean Damron, Director of Admissions. A video is available. E-mail: *admissions@alicelloyd.edu* Web: *www.alc.edu*

ASBURY COLLEGE D-3

Wilmore, KY 40390-1198 (859) 858-3511
(800) 888-1818; Fax: (859) 858-3921

Full-time: 519 men, 754 women	**Faculty:** 91; IIB, --$
Part-time: 25 men, 30 women	**Ph.D.s:** 53%
Graduate: 6 men, 18 women	**Student/Faculty:** 14 to 1
Year: semesters, summer session	**Tuition:** $14,740
Application Deadline: August 1	**Room & Board:** $3800

Freshman Class: 848 applied, 713 accepted, 331 enrolled
SAT I or ACT: required **VERY COMPETITIVE**

Asbury College, founded in 1890, is an independent nondenominational liberal arts institution. In addition to regional accreditation, Asbury has baccalaureate program accreditation with NASM. The library contains 152,048 volumes, 20,918 microform items, and 8551 audiovisual forms/CDs, and subscribes to 6822 periodicals. Computerized library services include the card catalog, interlibrary loans, and database searching. Special learning facilities include a learning resource center, art gallery, radio station, TV station, and media and fine arts centers. The 65-acre campus is in a rural area 20 miles south of Lexington. Including residence halls, there are 30 buildings.

Student Life: 75% of undergraduates are from out of state, mostly the South. Others are from 42 states, 14 foreign countries, and Canada. 75% are from public schools. 96% are white. Most are Protestant. The average age of freshmen is 18; all undergraduates, 21. 18% do not continue beyond their first year; 58% remain to graduate.

Housing: 1231 students can be accommodated in college housing, which includes single-sex dormitories, on-campus apartments, off-campus apartments, and married-student housing. In addition, there are language and leadership development/community service houses. On-campus housing is guaranteed for all 4 years. 88% of students live on campus; of those, 82% remain on campus on weekends. Alcohol is not permitted. Upperclassmen may keep cars.

Activities: There are no fraternities or sororities. There are 50 groups on campus, including art, band, choir, chorale, chorus, computers, debate, drama, ethnic, film, forensics, honors, international, jazz band, literary magazine, missionary, musical theater, newspaper, opera, orchestra, political, radio and TV, religious, social service, student government, and yearbook. Popular campus events include Parents Weekend, Artists Series, and Jym Jamboree.

Sports: There are 6 intercollegiate sports for men and 6 for women, and 6 intramural sports for men and 6 for women. Facilities include a 1,500-seat gym, athletic fields, tennis courts, an indoor swimming pool, and indoor/outdoor basketball courts.

Disabled Students: 80% of the campus is accessible. Wheelchair ramps, elevators, special parking, specially equipped rest rooms, special class scheduling, lowered drinking fountains, and lowered telephones are available.

Services: Counseling and information services are available, as is tutoring in most subjects. There is remedial writing. For students on academic probation, there are mentors who provide help in such areas as time management and test-taking skills. There is some help available for the visually impaired, such as tapes and agencies that offer aid.

Campus Safety and Security: Measures include 24-hour foot and vehicle patrol, escort service, pamphlets/posters/films, and lighted pathways/sidewalks. There are planning forums and a student parking and safety committee.

Programs of Study: Asbury confers B.A. and B.S.Ed. degrees. Master's degrees are also awarded. Bachelor's degrees are awarded in BIOLOGICAL SCIENCE (biochemistry and biology/biological science), BUSINESS (accounting, business administration and management, and recreation and leisure services), COMMUNICATIONS AND THE ARTS (art, broadcasting, classical languages, communications, English, French, Greek, journalism, Latin, music, and Spanish), COMPUTER AND PHYSICAL SCIENCE (applied mathematics, chemistry, information sciences and systems, mathematics, and physical sciences), EDUCATION (art, athletic training, elementary, English, foreign languages, mathematics, middle school, music, physical, science, secondary, and social studies), HEALTH PROFESSIONS (exercise science, and medical laboratory technology), SOCIAL SCIENCE (biblical languages, biblical studies, history, ministries, missions, philosophy, psychology, social work, and sociology). Education, communication arts, and Christian ministries and missions are the largest.

Required: To graduate, students must complete a minimum of semester hours, including liberal arts requirements, 9 hours of religion, and 3 hours of phys ed, with a minimum GPA of 2.0 for the B.A. or 2.75 for the B.S.Ed. Students must demonstrate proficiency in English and math, and take a comprehensive exam.

Special: For-credit internships are available in several academic areas as are opportunities for study abroad. There is a Washington semester through the American Studies Program. Dual majors and nondegree study are possible as are credit/no credit options for seniors. 3-2 engineering and computer science degrees are offfered with the University of Kentucky. There are 6 national honor societies, and 7 departmental honors programs.

Faculty/Classroom: 63% of faculty are male; 37%, female. All teach undergraduates, 1% do research, and 1% do both. The average class size in an introductory lecture is 23; in a laboratory, 18; and in a regular course, 18.

Admissions: 84% of the 2001-2002 applicants were accepted. 58% of the current freshmen were in the top fifth of their class; 87% were in the top two fifths. There were 3 National Merit finalists. 26 freshmen graduated first in their class.

Requirements: The SAT I or ACT is required, with a minimum score of 525 verbal and 505 math on the SAT I or 22 on the ACT. Applicants must be graduates of an accredited secondary school or have the GED. Applicants should complete 15 high school academic credits, including 4 units of English, 3 each of math and social studies, and 2 each of science and a foreign language. Incoming students must take proficiency exams in math and English. A GPA of 2.5 is required. AP and CLEP credits are accepted. Applications are accepted on-line at the school's web site.

Procedure: Freshmen are admitted to all sessions. Entrance exams should be taken in the junior year or in the first semester of the senior year. There is a deferred admissions plan. Applications should be filed by August 1 for fall entry, December 1 for spring entry, and April 1 for summer entry, along with a $30 fee. Notification is sent on a rolling basis.

Transfer: 55 transfer students enrolled in 2001-2002. Transfer applicants should have completed a minimum of 12 quarter hours or 8 semester hours, have an overall minimum GPA of 2.0, and be in good standing at the previous institutions attended. 49 credits of 124 must be completed at Asbury.

Visiting: There are regularly scheduled orientations for prospective students, consisting of visitation weekends in which students stay overnight in dorms, visit classes, attend departmental open houses, participate in meal/question-answer sessions, a financial aid session, chapel, and campus events. There are guides for informal visits and visitors may sit in on classes and stay overnight. To schedule a visit, contact the Admissions Office at (859) 858-3511, ext. 2142.

Financial Aid: In 2001-2002, 81% of all freshmen and 98% of continuing students received some form of financial aid. 57% of freshmen and 44% of continuing students received need-based aid. The average freshman award was $10,591. 43% of undergraduates work part time. Average annual earnings from campus work are $1200. The average financial indebtedness of the 2001 graduate was $15,994. The FAFSA and the college's own financial statement are required. The fall application deadline is March 1.

International Students: There are 14 international students enrolled. They must score 550 on the written TOEFL or 213 on the electronic version and also take the SAT I or the ACT.

Computers: The mainframes are an IBM RS/6000, 4 Novell servers, and 9 Windows NT servers. There are 62 PCs available in the Microcomputer Resource Center and academic departments, as well as 21 PCs in the Mac lab. The science center has a Novell 5.0 network. All students may access the system. There are no time limits and no fees. It is strongly recommended that all students have a personal computer.

Graduates: In 2001, 277 bachelor's degrees were awarded. The most popular majors were psychology (11%), English (9%), and elementary education (9%). In an average class, 1% graduate in 3 years, 41% in 4 years, 55% in 5 years, and 57% in 6 years. 70 companies recruited on campus in 2000-2001.

Admissions Contact: Stan F. Wiggam, Dean of Admissions. A video is available. E-mail: *admissions@asbury.edu* Web: *www.asbury.edu*

BELLARMINE UNIVERSITY D-2

Louisville, KY 40205 (502) 452-8131
(800) 274-4723; Fax: (502) 452-8002

Full-time: 519 men, 941 women	**Faculty:** 98
Part-time: 107 men, 168 women	**Ph.D.s:** 92%
Graduate: 146 men, 367 women	**Student/Faculty:** 15 to 1
Year: semesters, summer session	**Tuition:** $15,560
Application Deadline: August 15	**Room & Board:** $4880
Freshman Class: 1291 applied, 1080 accepted, 375 enrolled	
SAT I Verbal/Math: 530/540	**ACT:** 24 VERY COMPETITIVE

Bellarmine University, formerly know as Bellarmine College and founded in 1950, is a private liberal arts institution affiliated with the Roman Catholic Church. Some information in this profile is approximate. There are 4 undergraduate and 3 graduate schools. In addition to regional accreditation, Bellarmine has baccalaureate program accreditation with NCATE and NLN. The library contains 97,033 volumes, 625,768 microform items, and 4784 audiovisual forms/CDs, and subscribes to 1758 periodicals. Computerized library services include the card catalog, interlibrary loans, and database searching. Special learning facilities include a learning resource center and art gallery. The 120-acre campus is in a suburban area in Louisville. Including residence halls, there are 17 buildings.

Student Life: 71% of undergraduates are from Kentucky. Others are from 24 states, 21 foreign countries, and Canada. 32% are from public schools. 94% are white. 65% are Catholic; 30%, Protestant. The average age of freshmen is 18; all undergraduates, 23. 18% do not continue beyond their first year; 60% remain to graduate.

Housing: 480 students can be accommodated in college housing, which includes single-sex and coed dormitories. On-campus housing is guaranteed for all 4 years. 63% of students commute. Alcohol is not permitted. All students may keep cars.

Activities: 6% of men and about 3% of women belong to 3 national fraternities; 3% of women belong to 1 national sorority. There are 50 groups on campus, including art, band, cheerleading, choir, chorale, chorus, computers, dance, drama, ethnic, honors, international, jazz band, literary magazine, musical theater, newspaper, opera, pep band, photography, political, professional, religious, social, social service, student government, and yearbook. Popular campus events include Hillside Concerts, Midnight Breakfast, and Bellarmine Volunteer Days.

Sports: There are 7 intercollegiate sports for men and 9 for women, and 12 intramural sports for men and 12 for women. Facilities include a basketball arena, weight rooms, indoor and outdoor tennis courts, a par 3 golf course, exercise and aerobics rooms in residence halls, a track, and softball and baseball fields.

Disabled Students: 85% of the campus is accessible. Wheelchair ramps, elevators, special parking, specially equipped rest rooms, special class scheduling, lowered drinking fountains, lowered telephones, and accessible residence hall rooms are available.

Services: Counseling and information services are available, as is tutoring in every subject. The Academic Resource Center provides one-on-one or group tutoring for all 100- and 200-level courses. Disability Services provides note takers, distraction-reduced testing environments, extended time, books on tape, and scribe services.

Campus Safety and Security: Measures include 24-hour foot and vehicle patrol, self-defense education, escort service, and informal discussions. There are pamphlets/posters/films, emergency telephones, lighted pathways/sidewalks, 24-hour locked residence halls, security alert bulletins, CPR-certified security, and security cameras in residence halls and in the parking lot.

Programs of Study: Bellarmine confers B.A. and B.S. degrees. Master's degrees are also awarded. Bachelor's degrees are awarded in BIOLOGICAL SCIENCE (biology/biological science), BUSINESS (accounting, business administration and management, and international business management), COMMUNICATIONS AND THE ARTS (art, arts administration/management, communications, English, and music), COMPUTER AND PHYSICAL SCIENCE (actuarial science, chemistry, computer science, information sciences and systems, and mathematics), EDUCATION (elementary, middle school, secondary, and special), ENGINEERING AND ENVIRONMENTAL DESIGN (computer engineering and preengineering), HEALTH PROFESSIONS (nursing, predentistry, premedicine, prepharmacy, and preveterinary science), SOCIAL SCIENCE (economics, history, liberal arts/general studies, philosophy, political science/government, prelaw, psychology, sociology, and theological studies). Premedicine, accounting, and business are the strongest academically. Accounting, business, and nursing are the largest.

Required: In order to graduate, students must complete a minimum of 126 credit hours with a minimum GPA of 2.0. Between 24 and 45 hours are required in the major. All students must fulfill 60 credit hours of core requirements, including English, philosophy, theology, math, social sciences, natural sciences, fine arts, Western civilization, American experience, transcultural experience, and freshman and senior seminars.

Special: Cross-registration may be arranged through Kentuckiana Metroversity, a consortium of colleges in Kentucky and southern Indiana. Bellarmine also offers study abroad in more than 43 countries, internships in most majors, a Washington semester, a liberal studies degree, dual majors, accelerated degree programs, credit for life experience, pass/fail options during the junior and senior years, and a marine biology program in the Bahamas. There are 5 national honor societies and a freshman honors program.

Faculty/Classroom: 58% of faculty are male; 42%, female. 91% teach undergraduates. No introductory courses are taught by graduate students. The average class size in an introductory lecture is 25; in a laboratory, 18; and in a regular course, 18.

Admissions: 84% of the 2001-2002 applicants were accepted. The SAT I scores for the 2001-2002 freshman class were: Verbal--29% below 500, 47% between 500 and 599, 19% between 600 and 700, and 3% above 700; Math--33% below 500, 43% between 500 and 599, 20% between 600 and 700, and 2% above 700. The ACT scores were 3% below 21, 37% between 21 and 23, 27% between 24 and 26, 27% between 27 and 28, and 6% above 28. 55% of the current freshmen were in the top fifth of their class; 83% were in the top two fifths. 16 freshmen graduated first in their class in a recent year.

Requirements: The SAT I or ACT is required; applicants should have a minimum composite score of 970 on the SAT I or a minimum composite score of 21 on the ACT. The GED is accepted. High school courses should include 4 years of English, 3 years of math, and 2 years each of science and social studies. An essay is required. Bellarmine requires applicants to be in the upper 50% of their class. A GPA of 2.5 is required. AP and CLEP credits are accepted. Important factors in the admissions decision are advanced placement or honor courses, extracurricular activities record, and recommendations by school officials. Applications are accepted on-line at *www.bellarmine.edu*

Procedure: Freshmen are admitted to all sessions. Entrance exams should be taken by December of the senior year. There are early admissions and deferred admissions plans. Applications should be filed by August 15 for fall entry, December 15 for spring entry, and May 15 for summer entry, along with a $25 fee. Notification is sent on a rolling basis.

Transfer: 257 transfer students enrolled in a recent year. Applicants should have a minimum college GPA of 2.0. Most submit transcripts high school and from all postsecondary schools attended. 36 credits of 126 must be completed at Bellarmine.

Visiting: There are regularly scheduled orientations for prospective students, including an admissions and financial aid session, a campus tour, interviews with faculty, and participation in a student panel. There are guides for informal visits and visitors may sit in on classes and stay overnight. To schedule a visit, contact the Office of Admission.

Financial Aid: In 2001-2002, 96% of all freshmen and 85% of continuing students received some form of financial aid. 15% of undergraduates work part time. Average annual earnings from campus work are $1443. The average financial indebtedness of a recent graduate was $13,800. Bellarmine is a member of CSS. The FAFSA is required. Check with the school for current deadlines.

International Students: In a recent year, there were 24 international students enrolled. They must score 550 on the written TOEFL or take or MELAB.

Computers: The mainframe is an HP 9000. All computer labs in the academic buildings are on the campus network, with Internet and Web access, and are available to all students. Approximately 200 PCs are available to students in locations across campus, including residence halls and 24-hour study rooms. All students may access the system. There are no time limits and no fees.

Graduates: In a recent year, 305 bachelor's degrees were awarded. The most popular majors were nursing (19%), business administration (17%), and accounting (13%). In an average class, 1% graduate in 3 years, 53% in 4 years, 59% in 5 years, and 60% in 6 years. 35 companies recruited on campus in a recent year. Of a recent graduating class, 15% were enrolled in graduate school within 6 months of graduation and 90% were employed.

Admissions Contact: Timothy Sturgeon, Dean of Admission.
E-mail: *admissions@bellarmine.edu* Web: *http://www.bellarmine.edu*

BEREA COLLEGE D-3

Berea, KY 40404 (859) 985-3500; Fax: (859) 985-3512

Full-time: 706 men, 913 women	**Faculty:** 131; IIB, av$
Part-time: 23 men, 32 women	**Ph.D.s:** 88%
Graduate: none	**Student/Faculty:** 12 to 1
Year: 4-1-4, summer session	**Tuition:** $199
Application Deadline: open	**Room & Board:** $3871
Freshman Class: 1871 applied, 603 accepted, 425 enrolled	
SAT I Verbal/Math: 555/540	**ACT:** 23 VERY COMPETITIVE

Berea College, founded in 1855, is a private liberal arts institution. Berea combines college, federal, and state grants, as well as outside scholarships earned by students, to provide every admitted student with a 4-year, full tuition scholarship. Therefore, no student pays tuition at Berea college. In addition, for a nominal fee, the college provides a laptop for every student. As part of these scholarship agreements, each student is expected to perform some of the labor required in maintaining the institution while carrying a normal academic load. For participation in the student labor program, each student is credited with a labor grant that is incorporated into the full tuition scholarship. Room, board, and fees are assessed on a sliding scale according to how much each family can afford. In addition to regional accreditation, Berea has baccalaureate program accreditation with ADA, NCATE, and NLN. The library contains 340,665 volumes, 123,152 microform items, and 5829 audiovisual forms/CDs, and subscribes to 1527 periodicals. Computerized library services include the card catalog, interlibrary loans, and database searching. Special learning facilities include a learning resource center, art gallery, planetarium, and a geology museum. The 140-acre campus is in a small town 40 miles south of Lexington. Including residence halls, there are 58 buildings.

Student Life: 57% of undergraduates are from out of state, mostly the South. Others are from 45 states and 64 foreign countries. 74% are white; 14% African American. The average age of freshmen is 18; all undergraduates, 20. 17% do not continue beyond their first year.

Housing: 1287 students can be accommodated in college housing, which includes single-sex dormitories and married-student housing. In addition, there are special-interest houses and a single-parent house. On-campus housing is guaranteed for all 4 years. 79% of students live on campus. Alcohol is not permitted.

Activities: There are no fraternities or sororities. There are 70 groups on campus, including art, band, cheerleading, chess, choir, chorus, dance, debate, drama, ethnic, gay, honors, international, jazz band, literary magazine, newspaper, orchestra, pep band, photography, political, professional, religious, social, social service, student government, and yearbook. Popular campus events include Mountain Day and Labor Day.

Sports: There are 9 intercollegiate sports for men and 8 for women, and 7 intramural sports for men and 7 for women. Facilities include 2 gyms, an indoor swimming pool, 5 racquetball courts, 15 tennis courts, playing fields, a dance studio, a 3-lane indoor walking track, an 8-lane all-weather track, and weight training and cardiovascular exercise rooms.

Disabled Students: 50% of the campus is accessible. Wheelchair ramps, elevators, special parking, specially equipped rest rooms, special class scheduling, lowered drinking fountains, lowered telephones, and electronic doors, and a lift chair for the indoor pool are available.

Services: Counseling and information services are available, as is tutoring in some subjects. There is a reader service for the blind, and remedial math, reading, and writing. The Center for Effective Communication offers individual consultation in writing, reading, listening, speaking, learning strategies and styles, and study skills. Berea's 9 tutorial labs assist with study skills, project development, homework assignments, clarification of concepts, skills development, and software application.

Campus Safety and Security: Measures include 24-hour foot and vehicle patrol, self-defense education, escort service, and informal discussions. There are pamphlets/posters/films, emergency telephones, lighted pathways/sidewalks. Berea has ongoing programs on campus safety, theft prevention, assault and rape prevention, fire prevention, defensive driving, and occupational safety, including work with hazardous materials.

Programs of Study: Berea confers B.A. and B.S. degrees. Bachelor's degrees are awarded in AGRICULTURE (agriculture), BIOLOGICAL SCIENCE (biology/biological science), BUSINESS (business administration and management), COMMUNICATIONS AND THE ARTS (art, classical languages, dramatic arts, English, French, German, industrial design, music, and Spanish), COMPUTER AND PHYSICAL SCIENCE (chemistry, mathematics, and physics), EDUCATION (art, elementary, foreign languages, home economics, middle school, music, physical, and secondary), ENGINEERING AND ENVIRONMENTAL DESIGN (industrial engineering technology), HEALTH PROFESSIONS (nursing), SOCIAL SCIENCE (child care/child and family studies, dietetics, economics, history, philosophy, political science/government, psychology, religion, sociology, and women's studies). Business administration is the largest.

Required: Students must complete a 15-course general education program, including courses in wellness, cultural studies, the arts, Western traditions, recent world issues, contemporary Christianity, quantitative reasoning, and natural and social sciences, and courses emphasizing reading and written communication. 1 short-term (January) course for each full academic year in residence and attendance at convocations are also required. To graduate, students must complete 33 courses, including 8 to 12 in the major, with a minimum GPA of 2.0 overall and in the major. Nursing majors must complete 35 courses.

Special: Students may study abroad in Italy, Austria, Spain, France, Germany, and Japan. Internships, work-study programs, dual degrees, independent and team-initiated studies, and dual and student-designed majors are available. A 3-2 engineering degree is offered with Washington University and the University of Kentucky. All students participate in an on-campus work program 10 to 15 hours per week. There are 17 national honor societies.

Faculty/Classroom: 59% of faculty are male; 41%, female. All teach undergraduates. The average class size in a laboratory is 20 and in a regular course, 20.

Admissions: 32% of the 2001-2002 applicants were accepted. The SAT I scores for the 2001-2002 freshman class were: Verbal--24% below 500, 44% between 500 and 599, 27% between 600 and 700, and 5% above 700; Math--29% below 500, 44% between 500 and 599, 24% between 600 and 700, and 3% above 700. The ACT scores were 21% below 21, 30% between 21 and 23, 29% between 24 and 26, 11% between 27 and 28, and 9% above 28. 53% of the current freshmen were in the top fifth of their class; 83% were in the top two fifths. 11 freshmen graduated first in their class in a recent year.

Requirements: The SAT I or ACT is required. In addition, applicants should be graduates of an accredited secondary school. The GED is accepted. Home-schooled students are also encouraged to apply. Financial need is a requirement for admission. Berea recommends that applicants present as part of their high school record 4 units in English, 3 in math, and 2 each in science and social studies. Work in a foreign language is highly desirable. AP and CLEP credits are accepted. Important factors in the admissions decision are ability to finance college education, geographic diversity, and advanced placement or honor courses.

Procedure: Freshmen are admitted fall and spring. Entrance exams should be taken late in the junior year or early in the senior year. Application deadlines are open. Notification is sent on a rolling basis.

Transfer: 29 transfer students enrolled in 2001-2002. Applicants must be in good standing at the last college attended and have a minimum GPA of 2.4. 8 credits of 33 (35 for nursing) must be completed at Berea.

Visiting: There are regularly scheduled orientations for prospective students, consisting of welcome, admissions, and student and residence life sessions, departmental visits, a campus tour, a musical performance, and lunch. There are guides for informal visits and visitors may sit in on classes and stay overnight. To schedule a visit, contact Nancy Bolin, Campus Visit Coordinator at *nancy_bolin@berea.edu*.

Financial Aid: In 2001-2002, all students received some form of financial aid, including need-based aid. The average freshman award was $21,787. Of that total, scholarships or need-based grants averaged $20,742; loans averaged $85; and work contracts averaged $960. All of undergraduates work part time. Average annual earnings from campus work are $1390. The average financial indebtedness of the 2001 graduate was $3567. The FAFSA is required. The fall application deadline is April 1.

International Students: There are 102 international students enrolled. They must score 500 on the written TOEFL.

Computers: The mainframe is an HP 9000. Approximately 190 networked PCs for student use are located in the computer center lab, residence halls, library, and departmental labs. For a nominal fee, the college provides a laptop for each student. All students may access the system 24 hours a day, 7 days a week. There are no time limits.

Graduates: In 2001, 236 bachelor's degrees were awarded. The most popular majors were business administration (15%), child and family studies (11%), and industrial/manufacturing (10%). In an average class, 29% graduate in 4 years, 47% in 5 years, and 52% in 6 years. 80 to 100 companies recruited on campus in 2000-2001.

Admissions Contact: Joseph Bagnoli, Director of Admissions.
E-mail: *joe_bagnoli@berea.edu* Web: *www.berea.edu*

BRESCIA UNIVERSITY — B-3

Owensboro, KY 42301 — **(270) 686-4241; Fax: (270) 686-4314**

Full-time: 198 men, 336 women	**Faculty:** 43; IIB, --$
Part-time: 103 men, 165 women	**Ph.D.s:** 70%
Graduate: 14 men, 21 women	**Student/Faculty:** 12 to 1
Year: semesters, summer session	**Tuition:** $9845
Application Deadline: open	**Room & Board:** $4380
Freshman Class: 264 applied, 210 accepted, 117 enrolled	
ACT: 22	**COMPETITIVE**

Brescia University, founded in 1925 as a women's junior college, became a 4-year, coeducational liberal arts institution in 1950. It is a private school affiliated with the Roman Catholic Church. The university offers certificates, associate, baccalaureate, and master's degrees through semester and weekend classes. The library contains 183,406 volumes, 364,553 microform items, and 6580 audiovisual forms/CDs, and subscribes to 5334 periodicals. Computerized library services include the card catalog, interlibrary loans, and database searching. Special learning facilities include a learning resource center and art gallery. The 6-acre campus is in an urban area 32 miles southeast of Evansville, Indiana, and 125 miles from both Louisville and Nashville. Including residence halls, there are 14 buildings.

Student Life: 78% of undergraduates are from Kentucky. Others are from 18 states, 18 foreign countries, and Canada. 89% are white. 39% are Catholic; 32% Protestant; 27% claim no religious affiliation. The average age of freshmen is 20; all undergraduates, 30. 33% do not continue beyond their first year.

Housing: 224 students can be accommodated in college housing, which includes single-sex and coed dormitories and on-campus apartments. On-campus housing is available on a first-come, first-served basis. 73% of students commute. Alcohol is not permitted. All students may keep cars.

Activities: There are no fraternities or sororities. There are 23 groups on campus, including choir, chorus, computers, creative writing, drama, honors, international, literary magazine, newspaper, philosophy, professional, religious, social, social service, student government, and yearbook. Popular campus events include Family Weekend, Opening Year Mass, and Inaugural Ball.

Sports: There are 4 intercollegiate sports for men and 5 for women, and 11 intramural sports for men and 11 for women. Facilities include 2 tennis courts, a gym, a weight room, a game room, a cardiovascular workout room, a racquetball court, a batting cage, and a baseball field.

Disabled Students: 95% of the campus is accessible. Wheelchair ramps, elevators, special parking, specially equipped rest rooms, lowered drinking fountains, and lowered telephones are available.

Services: Counseling and information services are available, as is tutoring in most subjects. There is remedial math, reading, and writing.

Campus Safety and Security: Measures include escort service, informal discussions, emergency telephones, and lighted pathways/sidewalks. There is night security.

Programs of Study: Brescia confers B.A., B.S., and B.S.W. degrees. Associate and master's degrees are also awarded. Bachelor's degrees are awarded in BIOLOGICAL SCIENCE (biology/biological science), BUSINESS (accounting, banking and finance, business administration and management, business economics, and human resources), COMMUNICATIONS AND THE ARTS (art, English, and graphic design), COMPUTER AND PHYSICAL SCIENCE (chemistry, computer science, mathematics, and physical sciences), EDUCATION (art, elementary, and special), HEALTH PROFESSIONS (art therapy, medical technology, and speech pathology/audiology), SOCIAL SCIENCE (history, human development, liberal arts/general studies, pastoral studies, psychology, religion, social studies, and social work). Education, business, and English are the strongest academically. Business, social work, and education are the largest.

Required: All students must earn 128 credit hours, including 42 upper-division hours, and 30 or more hours in the major, while maintaining an overall GPA of 2.0 and 2.5 in the major. Distribution requirements include 18 hours in aesthetics, language, and literature, 12 in social science, 9 each in fine arts, science, and math, 6 in religious studies, and 3 in philosophy. Students must also demonstrate computer competency.

Special: Brescia offers a combined engineering degree with the University of Kentucky and the University of Louisville. Work-study programs, student-designed majors, nondegree study, dual majors, study abroad in Mexico, an internship in professional writing, pass/fail options and cross-registration with Kentucky Wesleyan are available. The Weekend College offers four 9-week modules of study. There are 2 national honor societies and a freshman honors program.

Faculty/Classroom: 47% of faculty are male; 53%, female. All teach undergraduates. No introductory courses are taught by graduate students. The average class size in an introductory lecture is 14; in a laboratory, 10; and in a regular course, 12.

Admissions: 80% of the 2001-2002 applicants were accepted. The ACT scores for the 2001-2002 freshman class were: 36% below 21, 30% between 21 and 23, 16% between 24 and 26, 11% between 27 and 28, and 7% above 28. 45% of the current freshmen were in the top fifth of their class; 63% were in the top two fifths.

Requirements: The SAT I or ACT is required. In addition, essays and recommendations are helpful. High school units should include 4 of English, 3 of math, and 2 each in social studies, science, foreign language, fine arts, and computer science. Brescia requires applicants to be in the upper 50% of their class. A GPA of 2.5 is required. AP and CLEP credits are accepted. Important factors in the admissions decision are advanced placement or honor courses and recommendations by school officials. Applications are accepted on-line at the university's web site.

Procedure: Freshmen are admitted to all sessions. Entrance exams should be taken at the end of the junior year. Application deadlines are open. The fall 2001 application fee was $25.

Transfer: 80 transfer students enrolled in 2001-2002. Transfer students must have a minimum GPA of 2.0. 42 credits of 128 must be completed at Brescia.

Visiting: There are regularly scheduled orientations for prospective students, including spring and fall open houses for freshmen and a spring transfer open house. There are guides for informal visits and visitors may sit in on classes and stay overnight. To schedule a visit, contact the Admissions Director.

Financial Aid: In 2001-2002, 85% of all freshmen and 80% of continuing students received some form of financial aid. 68% of freshmen and 51% of continuing students received need-based aid. The average freshman award was $9690. Of that total, scholarships or need-based grants averaged $5604 ($12,998 maximum); loans averaged $2438 ($5500 maximum); work contracts averaged $618 ($1236 maximum); and other sources averaged $341 ($8000 maximum). All undergraduates work part time. Average annual earnings from campus work are $1236. The average financial indebtedness of the 2001 graduate was $12,777. Brescia is a member of CSS. The FAFSA is required. The fall application deadline is March 1.

International Students: There are 35 international students enrolled. The school actively recruits these students. They must score 550 on the written TOEFL or 213 on the electronic version and also take the SAT I or the ACT.

Computers: 45 PCs are available for student use at various locations on campus. There is a computer lab in each academic building. Student PCs are connected to the campus network, with Internet access. All students may access the system. There are no time limits. The fee was $10 per semester in a recent year.

Graduates: In 2001, 93 bachelor's degrees were awarded. The most popular majors were business (26%), social work (15%), and communication sciences and disorders (10%). In an average class, 2% graduate in 3 years, 30% in 4 years, 47% in 5 years, and 43% in 6 years. 21 companies recruited on campus in 2000-2001. Of the 2000 graduating class, 19% were enrolled in graduate school within 6 months of graduation and 80% were employed.

Admissions Contact: Sister Mary Austin Blank, Director of Admissions. A video is available. E-mail: *admissions@brescia.edu*
Web: *www.brescia.edu*

CAMPBELLSVILLE UNIVERSITY — D-3
Campbellsville, KY 42718-2799 (270) 789-5220
(800) 264-6014; Fax: (270) 789-5071

Full-time: 536 men, 615 women	**Faculty:** 74
Part-time: 139 men, 338 women	**Ph.D.s:** 68%
Graduate: 70 men, 78 women	**Student/Faculty:** 16 to 1
Year: semesters, summer session	**Tuition:** $9940
Application Deadline: July 1	**Room & Board:** $4400
Freshman Class: 1005 applied, 774 accepted, 334 enrolled	
ACT: 21	**COMPETITIVE**

Campbellsville University, founded in 1906, is a private, comprehensive institution affiliated with the Kentucky Baptist Convention. There are 6 undergraduate and 5 graduate schools. In addition to regional accreditation, Campbellsville has baccalaureate program accreditation with NASM. The 2 libraries contain 108,000 volumes, 24,000 microform items, and 8000 audiovisual forms/CDs, and subscribe to 360 periodicals. Computerized library services include the card catalog, interlibrary loans, and database searching. Special learning facilities include a learning resource center, art gallery, radio station, TV station, a teacher resource center, the Kentuckiana Collection, Clay Hill Memorial Forest, and The American Civil War Institute. The 72-acre campus is in a small town 85 miles southwest of Lexington and 85 miles southeast of Louisville. Including residence halls, there are 46 buildings.

Student Life: 84% of undergraduates are from Kentucky. Others are from 26 states and 24 foreign countries. 96% are from public schools. 86% are white. The average age of freshmen is 18; all undergraduates, 21.

Housing: 750 students can be accommodated in college housing, which includes single-sex dormitories and on-campus apartments. In addition, there are honors houses and special-interest houses. On-campus housing is guaranteed for all 4 years. 56% of students commute. Alcohol is not permitted. All students may keep cars.

Activities: There are no fraternities or sororities. There are 45 groups on campus, including art, band, cheerleading, choir, chorale, chorus, computers, drama, ethnic, honors, international, jazz band, literary magazine, marching band, musical theater, newspaper, opera, orchestra, pep band, photography, political, professional, radio and TV, religious, social, social service, student government, symphony, and yearbook. Popular campus events include Valentine Banquet, a Christmas celebration, and Heritage Day.

Sports: There are 7 intercollegiate sports for men and 7 for women, and 10 intramural sports for men and 10 for women. Facilities include a swimming pool, a 1700-seat gym, a football stadium, a baseball field, an intramural activities center with skating facilities and large game rooms, and softball and soccer fields.

Disabled Students: 85% of the campus is accessible. Wheelchair ramps, elevators, special parking, specially equipped rest rooms, special class scheduling, lowered drinking fountains, lowered telephones, and widened doorways are available.

Services: Counseling and information services are available, as is tutoring in most subjects. There is remedial math, reading, and writing. There is also an AIDS education program and a study skills program.

Campus Safety and Security: Measures include 24-hour foot and vehicle patrol, self-defense education, escort service, and informal discussions. There are pamphlets/posters/films, emergency telephones, and lighted pathways/sidewalks.

Programs of Study: Campbellsville confers B.A., B.S., B.M., B.S.B.A., B.S.Med.Tech, and B.S.W. degrees. Associate and master's degrees are also awarded. Bachelor's degrees are awarded in BIOLOGICAL SCIENCE (biology/biological science), BUSINESS (accounting, business administration and management, and office supervision and management), COMMUNICATIONS AND THE ARTS (art, communications, English, and music), COMPUTER AND PHYSICAL SCIENCE (chemistry, information sciences and systems, and mathematics), EDUCATION (athletic training, elementary, middle school, physical, and recreation), HEALTH PROFESSIONS (medical laboratory technology and sports medicine), SOCIAL SCIENCE (Christian studies, economics, history, political science/government, psychology, religious education, religious music, social work, and sociology). Biology, chemistry, and music are the strongest academically. Elementary education, business administration, and music are the largest.

Required: All candidates must be of good moral character. All students must complete a minimum of 128 semester hours, including 30 in the major, 21 in the minor, and 51 in general education courses. The minimum GPA is 2.5 for education majors, 2.1 for all others. All students must fulfill an English composition requirement.

Special: Legislative and public administration internships, a Washington semester, and federal work-study programs are available. The university also offers a semester in London program, 3-2 engineering degree with the University of Kentucky, dual majors, credit by exam, credit for life, military, and work experience, nondegree study, and pass/fail options. There is a freshman honors program.

Faculty/Classroom: 64% of faculty are male; 36%, female. 98% teach undergraduates and 2% do research. No introductory courses are taught by graduate students. The average class size in an introductory lecture is 25; in a laboratory, 13; and in a regular course, 18.

Admissions: 77% of the 2001-2002 applicants were accepted. The ACT scores for the 2001-2002 freshman class were: 47% below 21, 30% between 21 and 23, 17% between 24 and 26, 3% between 27 and 28, and 3% above 28. 45% of the current freshmen were in the top fifth of their class; 75% were in the top two fifths. In a recent year, there were 2 National Merit semifinalists. 11 freshmen graduated first in their class.

Requirements: The ACT is required and the SAT I is recommended; the SAT I may be substituted for the ACT. Applicants must be graduates of an accredited secondary school with a GPA of 2.0. The GED is accepted. An interview is recommended. A GPA of 2.0 is required. AP and CLEP credits are accepted. Important factors in the admissions decision are evidence of special talent, leadership record, and advanced placement or honor courses. Applications are accepted on computer disk and on-line via the university's web site or CollegeLink.

Procedure: Freshmen are admitted to all sessions. Entrance exams should be taken no later than February of the senior year. There is a deferred admissions plan. Applications should be filed by July 1 for fall entry and November 1 for spring entry. Notification is sent on a rolling basis. The fall 2001 application fee was $20.

Transfer: 119 transfer students enrolled in 2001-2002. Of the 128 credits needed to graduate, all students must complete one third of the credits required for the major and the minor at the university; the last year must be completed in residence. 32 credits of 128 must be completed at Campbellsville.

Visiting: There are regularly scheduled orientations for prospective students, consisting of visitation days held in October, February, and April. There are guides for informal visits and visitors may sit in on classes and stay overnight. To schedule a visit, contact Admissions.

Financial Aid: In 2001-2002, 94% of all students received some form of financial aid. 70% of freshmen and 68% of continuing students received need-based aid. Scholarships or need-based grants averaged $3500 ($12,230 maximum); loans averaged $2625 ($5500 maximum); and work contracts averaged $1700. 48% of undergraduates work part time. Average annual earnings from campus work are $1700. Campbellsville is a member of CSS. The FAFSA is required. The fall application deadline is April 1.

International Students: There are 79 international students enrolled. The school actively recruits these students. They must score 500 on the written TOEFL or take the MELAB and also take the SAT I or the ACT, scoring 19 on the ACT.

Computers: The mainframe consists of more than 12 client-server systems. There are 4 labs with Pentium-class computers. 102 PCs are available in labs for student use and 2 residence halls are wired for the Internet from individual rooms. All other students have dial-in access for the Internet both on and off campus. All students may access the system 24 hours a day or during lab hours. Students may access the system 45 hours monthly on dial-in access only. The fee is $120.

Graduates: In 2001, 166 bachelor's degrees were awarded. In an average class, 35% graduate in 6 years.

Admissions Contact: Trent Argo, Director of Admissions. A video is available. E-mail: *admissions@campbellsvil.edu*
Web: *www.campbellsvil.edu*

CENTRE COLLEGE D-3

Danville, KY 40422 (859) 238-5350
(800) 423-6236; Fax: (859) 238-5373

Full-time: 477 men, 580 women | **Faculty:** 88; IIB, +$
Part-time: 5 men, 8 women | **Ph.D.s:** 88%
Graduate: none | **Student/Faculty:** 12 to 1
Year: 4-1-4 | **Tuition:** $18,000
Application Deadline: February 1 | **Room & Board:** $6000
Freshman Class: 1265 applied, 1041 accepted, 299 enrolled
SAT I Verbal/Math: 631/618 | **ACT:** 27 **HIGHLY COMPETITIVE**

Centre College, founded in 1819 by the Presbyterian Church (U.S.A.), is an independent liberal arts and sciences institution. The library contains 152,721 volumes, 3946 microform items, and 3500 audiovisual forms/CDs, and subscribes to 2076 periodicals. Computerized library services include the card catalog, interlibrary loans, and database searching. Special learning facilities include an art gallery and a performing arts center. The 100-acre campus is in a small town 35 miles southwest of Lexington and 80 miles southeast of Louisville. Including residence halls, there are 54 buildings.

Student Life: 65% of undergraduates are from Kentucky. Others are from 38 states, 7 foreign countries, and Canada. 69% are from public schools. 95% are white. 61% are Protestant; 19% claim no religious affiliation; 18% Catholic. The average age of freshmen is 18; all undergraduates, 20. 13% do not continue beyond their first year; 73% remain to graduate.

Housing: 970 students can be accommodated in college housing, which includes single-sex and coed dormitories, on-campus apartments, fraternity houses, and sorority houses. On-campus housing is guaranteed for all 4 years. 95% of students live on campus; of those, 90% remain on campus on weekends. All students may keep cars.

Activities: 58% of men belong to 6 national fraternities; 65% of women belong to 4 national sororities. There are 77 groups on campus, including art, band ensembles, cheerleading, choir, chorus, computers, dance, debate, drama, ethnic, film, forensics, gay, honors, international, jazz band, literary magazine, musical theater, newspaper, orchestra, pep band, photography, political, professional, religious, social, social service, student government, and yearbook. Popular campus events include Carnival, Honors Convocation, and Spring Sing.

Sports: There are 9 intercollegiate sports for men and 10 for women, and 15 intramural sports for men and 15 for women. Facilities include a complex with a 1500-seat gym, 3 basketball courts, 2 volleyball courts, training room, game room, sauna, weight room, fitness center, and racquetball/handball courts. There is also a 2500-seat stadium, tennis courts, and playing fields for football, track, baseball, softball, soccer, field hockey, and other sports. The natatorium has a 25-yard, 6-lane swimming pool. Golf teams compete at the local country club.

Disabled Students: 65% of the campus is accessible. Wheelchair ramps, elevators, special parking, specially equipped rest rooms, special class scheduling, and electronic doors are available.

Services: Counseling and information services are available, as is tutoring in most subjects. There is a reader service for the blind.

Campus Safety and Security: Measures include 24-hour foot and vehicle patrol, self-defense education, escort service, and informal discussions. There are pamphlets/posters/films, emergency telephones, lighted pathways/sidewalks, and a crime prevention program through notices and publications, and a working relationship with outside agencies.

Programs of Study: Centre confers B.A. and B.S. degrees. Bachelor's degrees are awarded in BIOLOGICAL SCIENCE (biochemistry, biology/biological science, and molecular biology), COMMUNICATIONS AND THE ARTS (dramatic arts, English, fine arts, French, German, music, and Spanish), COMPUTER AND PHYSICAL SCIENCE (chemistry, computer science, mathematics, physical chemistry, and physics), EDUCATION (elementary), SOCIAL SCIENCE (anthropology, classical/ancient civilization, economics, history, international relations, philosophy, political science/government, psychobiology, psychology, religion, and sociology). English, economics, and biology are the strongest academically and have the largest enrollments.

Required: All students must earn an overall GPA of 2.0 and complete a minimum of 111 credit hours. Students also must demonstrate competency in writing, foreign language, and math plus 1 course beyond basic skills in 1 of these areas. A freshman humanities program and a freshman seminar must be completed. Core curriculum requirements include 2 courses each in the humanities or art from the aesthetic context; the scientific/technological context; the social context, and the fundamental questions context. 2 phys ed courses must be completed by the end of sophomore year.

Special: Centre offers internships, study abroad in 9 countries, work-study, and a 3-2 engineering degree with Vanderbilt University, Washington University at St. Louis, Columbia University, and the University of Kentucky. Student-designed majors, interdisciplinary majors including chemical physics, secondary education certification, and prelaw, prebusiness, and premedicine programs are available. Pass/fail options also are available. There are 8 national honor societies, including Phi Beta Kappa.

Faculty/Classroom: 66% of faculty are male; 34%, female. All both teach and do research. The average class size in an introductory lecture is 20; in a laboratory, 14; and in a regular course, 17.

Admissions: 82% of the 2001-2002 applicants were accepted. The SAT I scores for the 2001-2002 freshman class were: Verbal--5% below 500, 33% between 500 and 599, 49% between 600 and 700, and 13% above 700; Math--6% below 500, 39% between 500 and 599, 48% between 600 and 700, and 7% above 700. The ACT scores were 11% between 21 and 23, 33% between 24 and 26, 25% between 27 and 28, and 30% above 28. 77% of the current freshmen were in the top fifth of their class; 98% were in the top two fifths. There were 7 National Merit semifinalists. 31 freshmen graduated first in their class.

Requirements: The SAT I or ACT is required, but no minimum test scores are required. Students should have completed a minimum of 15 academic credits, including 4 years each in English and math, 3 years each in science and social studies, 2 years in foreign language, and 1 year in an art- or music-related course. An essay is required and an interview is strongly recommended. AP credits are accepted. Important factors in the admissions decision are advanced placement or honor courses, extracurricular activities record, and recommendations by school officials. Applications are accepted on computer disk and on-line via Common Application On-line, Apply!, and the school's web site.

Procedure: Freshmen are admitted in the fall. Entrance exams should be taken by November of the senior year. There are early decision, early admissions, and deferred admissions plans. Early decision applications should be filed by November 15; regular applications, by February 1 for fall entry. Notification of early decision is sent December 15; regular decision, March 1. 75 early decision candidates were accepted for the 2001-2002 class. 10% of all applicants are on a waiting list; 25 were accepted in 2001.

Transfer: 16 transfer students enrolled in 2001-2002. Applicants for transfer must have all previous college transcripts on file and a recommendation from the dean of the most recent college attended. If the student has completed fewer than 2 years of college work, high school records must also be submitted. 45 credits of 111 must be completed at Centre.

Visiting: There are regularly scheduled orientations for prospective students, including a campus tour, an interview, class visits, faculty appointments, and an overnight stay, if requested. There are guides for informal visits and visitors may sit in on classes and stay overnight. To schedule a visit, contact the Office of Admission at (800) 423-6236 or *admission@centre.edu.*

Financial Aid: In 2001-2002, 90% of all students received some form of financial aid. 67% of freshmen and 54% of continuing students received need-based aid. The average freshman award was $17,208. 49% of undergraduates work part time. Average annual earnings from campus work are $1312. The average financial indebtedness of the 2001 graduate was $14,100. Centre is a member of CSS. The FAFSA and the college's own financial statement are required. The fall application deadline is March 1.

International Students: There are 13 international students enrolled. They must score 580 on the written TOEFL or may submit SAT I or ACT scores.

Computers: There are 150 PCs available for network use in the residence halls, various classroom buildings, and the library. Residence hall rooms are connected to the network. All students may access the system. There are no time limits and no fees.

Graduates: In 2001, 236 bachelor's degrees were awarded. The most popular majors were history/social science (42%), biology (15%), and English (11%). In an average class, 65% graduate in 4 years, and 68% in 6 years. 25 companies recruited on campus in 2000-2001. Of the 2000 graduating class, 35% were enrolled in graduate school within 6 months of graduation and 90% were employed.

Admissions Contact: J. Carey Thompson, Dean of Admission and Student Financial Planning. A video is available.
E-mail: *admission@centre.edu* Web: *http://www.centre.edu*

CUMBERLAND COLLEGE — E-4
Williamsburg, KY 40769 — (606) 539-4241
(800) 343-1609; Fax: (606) 539-4303

Full-time: 644 men, 700 women	**Faculty:** 94
Part-time: 98 men, 127 women	**Ph.D.s:** 67%
Graduate: 37 men, 101 women	**Student/Faculty:** 14 to 1
Year: semesters, summer session	**Tuition:** $10,388
Application Deadline: open	**Room & Board:** $4476
Freshman Class: 1074 applied, 754 accepted, 416 enrolled	
SAT I Verbal/Math: 491/509	**ACT:** 21 — **COMPETITIVE**

Cumberland College, founded in 1889, is a private liberal arts institution affiliated with the Kentucky Baptist Convention. The library contains 189,861 volumes, 769,342 microform items, and 3660 audiovisual forms/CDs, and subscribes to 653 periodicals. Computerized library services include the card catalog, interlibrary loans, and database searching. Special learning facilities include a learning resource center, art gallery, natural history museum, TV station, and a distance learning lab. The 50-acre campus is in a small town 100 miles south of Lexington and 65 miles north of Knoxville. Including residence halls, there are 30 buildings.

Student Life: 64% of undergraduates are from Kentucky. Others are from 39 states, 16 foreign countries, and Canada. 94% are from public schools. 93% are white. Most are Protestant. The average age of freshmen is 18; all undergraduates, 20. 37% do not continue beyond their first year; 59% remain to graduate.

Housing: 1100 students can be accommodated in college housing, which includes single-sex dormitories. On-campus housing is guaranteed for all 4 years. 63% of students live on campus; of those, 60% remain on campus on weekends. Alcohol is not permitted. All students may keep cars.

Activities: There are no fraternities or sororities. There are 45 groups on campus, including art, band, cheerleading, choir, chorale, chorus, dance, debate, drama, drill team, ethnic, forensics, honors, international, jazz band, literary magazine, marching band, musical theater, pep band, political, professional, religious, social, social service, student government, TV, and yearbook. Popular campus events include Madrigal Dinner, Hanging of the Greens, and Valentine's Dance.

Sports: There are 12 intercollegiate sports for men and 12 for women, and 6 intramural sports for men and 6 for women. Facilities include a gym, an athletic/convocation complex, a game room, tennis courts, a field house, baseball/softball and practice football fields, a swimming pool, a sauna and weight room located in the housing area, and a football, track, and soccer complex.

Disabled Students: 75% of the campus is accessible. Wheelchair ramps, special parking, specially equipped rest rooms, special class scheduling, and lowered drinking fountains are available.

Services: Counseling and information services are available, as is tutoring in every subject.

Campus Safety and Security: Measures include 24-hour foot and vehicle patrol, self-defense education, escort service, and informal discussions. There are pamphlets/posters/films and lighted pathways/sidewalks.

Programs of Study: CC confers B.A., B.S., B.G.S., and B.M. degrees. Master's degrees are also awarded. Bachelor's degrees are awarded in BIOLOGICAL SCIENCE (biology/biological science), BUSINESS (accounting, business administration and management, and office supervision and management), COMMUNICATIONS AND THE ARTS (art, communications, dramatic arts, English, and music), COMPUTER AND PHYSICAL SCIENCE (chemistry, information sciences and systems, mathematics, and physics), EDUCATION (art, business, elementary, English, health, mathematics, middle school, music, physical, science, social studies, and special), HEALTH PROFESSIONS (health, medical laboratory technology, and public health), SOCIAL SCIENCE (history, political science/government, psychology, religion, religious music, and social work). Biology, business, and chemistry are the strongest academically. Biology, psychology, and education are the largest.

Required: All students must complete 128 semester hours, including 49 hours of liberal arts courses and an average of 36 hours in a major, while maintaining an overall GPA of 2.0 (2.5 for those seeking teacher certification). General education requirements include courses from the areas of physical fitness, art, music, theater, speech, religion, English composition, literature, history, math, natural and social sciences, community service, and fine arts or philosophy. A comprehensive exam may be required. Programs presented for graduation must include 2 majors, 1 major and 1 minor, 1 major with 15 hours of restricted electives, or 3 minors.

Special: Internships, study abroad in England and China, a Washington semester, and work-study programs with the college, local businesses, and other educational institutions are available. CC offers B.A.-B.S. degrees in all majors except music, dual majors in all major fields, a general studies degree, and nondegree study. There are 11 national honor societies, a freshman honors program, and 12 departmental honors program.

Faculty/Classroom: 67% of faculty are male; 32%, female. 96% teach undergraduates and 8% do research. No introductory courses are taught by graduate students. The average class size in an introductory lecture is 20; in a laboratory, 15; and in a regular course, 15.

Admissions: 70% of the 2001-2002 applicants were accepted. The SAT I scores for the 2001-2002 freshman class were: Verbal--53% below 500, 42% between 500 and 599, and 5% between 600 and 700; Math--47% below 500, 38% between 500 and 599, 14% between 600 and 700, and 1% above 700. The ACT scores were 40% below 21, 35% between 21 and 23, 13% between 24 and 26, 7% between 27 and 28, and 5% above 28. 38% of the current freshmen were in the top fifth of their class; 64% were in the top two fifths. 16 freshmen graduated first in their class.

Requirements: The SAT I or ACT is required, with composite scores of better than 17 for the ACT or 780 for the SAT I required. Consideration is given to those with ACT scores of 16 and 17, provided the high school GPA is 2.5 or above in college prep classes. Although each application is considered individually, students must have fulfilled general high school requirements of 4 years of English, 3 each of math and science, and 2 of social studies. A completed Teacher Recommendation Form from a current teacher, a completed High School Information Form signed by the guidance counselor, and a high school transcript are required. The college also recommends an interview. The GED is accepted. A GPA of 2.0 is required. AP and CLEP credits are accepted. Important factors in the admissions decision are leadership record, recommendations by school officials, and advanced placement or honor courses. Applications are accepted on computer disk and on-line.

Procedure: Freshmen are admitted to all sessions. Entrance exams should be taken prior to admission consideration. Application deadlines are open. The application fee is $25.

Transfer: 68 transfer students enrolled in 2001-2002. Applicants must have verification from their previous school that they are eligible to return. Students with fewer than 30 semester or 45 quarter hours must meet freshman admissions requirements. 30 credits of 128 must be completed at CC.

Visiting: There are regularly scheduled orientations for prospective students, consisting of a tour, a departmental conference, an advising session, adjustment information, and general information. There are guides for informal visits and visitors may sit in on classes and stay overnight. To schedule a visit, contact the Admissions Office.

Financial Aid: In 2001-2002, 97% of all freshmen and 90% of continuing students received some form of financial aid. 75% of freshmen and 74% of continuing students received need-based aid. The average freshman award was $11,553. Of that total, scholarships or need-based grants averaged $7485 ($14,864 maximum); loans averaged $3292 ($4000 maximum); and work contracts averaged $776 ($2000 maximum). 60% of undergraduates work part time. Average annual earnings from campus work are $1700. The average financial indebtedness of the 2001 graduate was $14,275. CC is a member of CSS. The FAFSA is required. The fall application deadline is March 1.

International Students: There are 26 international students enrolled. They must score 550 on the written TOEFL or 213 on the electronic version or take the MELAB. They must also take the SAT I, ACT, or the English Placement Examination, scoring 18 on the ACT.

Computers: The mainframes are a UNIX Sperry UNIVAC and an IBM AS/400. There are more than 200 Pentium, Pentium-2, Gateway, and AT&T PCs available throughout the campus, with several dedicated departmental and dorm labs. For those with their own computers, access to the system is available in all dorm rooms. All students may access the system 8 A.M. to 9 P.M. daily for the main lab; hours vary for other labs. There are no time limits. The fee was $75 in a recent year.

Graduates: In 2001, 260 bachelor's degrees were awarded. The most popular majors were education (24%), business (11%), and psychology (9%). In an average class, 1% graduate in 3 years, 24% in 4 years, 36% in 5 years, and 45% in 6 years. 10 companies recruited on campus in 2000-2001. Of the 2000 graduating class, 20% were enrolled in graduate school within 6 months of graduation and 75% were employed.

Admissions Contact: Erica Harris, Senior Admissions Counselor. A video is available. E-mail: *admiss@cc.cumber.edu*
Web: *www.cumber.edu*

EASTERN KENTUCKY UNIVERSITY — E-3
Richmond, KY 40475 — **(606) 622-2106**
(800) 465-9191; Fax: (606) 622-3024

Full-time: 3949 men, 5693 women	**Faculty:** 574; IIA, -$
Part-time: 1291 men, 1871 women	**Ph.D.s:** 70%
Graduate: 570 men, 1323 women	**Student/Faculty:** 17 to 1
Year: semesters, summer session	**Tuition:** $2706 ($7374)
Application Deadline: August 1	**Room & Board:** $2924

Freshman Class: 4762 applied, 3760 accepted, 2151 enrolled
ACT: 21 — **COMPETITIVE**

Eastern Kentucky University, established in 1906, is a public, state-supported institution offering degree programs in the arts and sciences, business, environmental studies, health fields, education, and public service occupations. There are 5 undergraduate schools and 1 graduate school. In addition to regional accreditation, EKU has baccalaureate program accreditation with ADA, AHEA, CSWE, FIDER, NASM, NCATE, NLN, and NRPA. The 3 libraries contain 837,945 volumes, 1,410,522 microform items, and 4221 audiovisual forms/CDs, and subscribe to 3565 periodicals. Computerized library services include the card catalog, interlibrary loans, and database searching. Special learning facilities include a learning resource center, art gallery, natural history museum, planetarium, radio station, TV station, and law enforcement complex that includes a training tank for underwater rescue and recovery. The 628-acre campus is in a small town 20 miles south of Lexington. Including residence halls, there are 98 buildings.

Student Life: 92% of undergraduates are from Kentucky. Others are from 45 states, 49 foreign countries, and Canada. 90% are from public schools. 89% are white. The average age of freshmen is 18; all undergraduates, 21. 35% do not continue beyond their first year.

Housing: 5646 students can be accommodated in college housing, which includes single-sex and coed dormitories, on-campus apartments, and married-student housing. In addition, there are honors houses, special-interest houses, and special accommodations for senior home economics sudents. On-campus housing is guaranteed for all 4 years. 67% of students commute. Alcohol is not permitted. All students may keep cars.

Activities: 4% of men belong to 12 national fraternities; 4% of women belong to 10 national sororities. There are 151 groups on campus, including art, band, cheerleading, choir, chorale, chorus, computers, dance, debate, drama, drill team, ethnic, film, gay, honors, international, jazz band, marching band, musical theater, newspaper, orchestra, pep band, photography, political, professional, radio and TV, religious, social service, student government, symphony, and yearbook. Popular campus events include Hanging of the Greens at Christmas, International Month, and fraternity/sorority competitions.

Sports: There are 8 intercollegiate sports for men and 8 for women, and 12 intramural sports for men and 12 for women. Facilities include 5 gyms, 1 outdoor and 2 indoor swimming pools, 19 outdoor hard-court and 4 indoor tennis courts, handball and racquetball courts, training rooms, a dance studio, a martial arts room, a wellness center, weight facilities, a conditioning center, a 7000-seat basketball arena, a 20,000-seat stadium, an 8-lane outdoor track, a field hockey area, an 18-hole golf course, and fields for baseball, softball, and soccer,

Disabled Students: 85% of the campus is accessible. Wheelchair ramps, elevators, special parking, specially equipped rest rooms, special class scheduling, lowered drinking fountains, and lowered telephones are available.

Services: Counseling and information services are available, as is tutoring in some subjects, including math, English, and reading, and in other fields upon request. There is a reader service for the blind, and remedial math, reading, and writing.

Campus Safety and Security: Measures include 24-hour foot and vehicle patrol, self-defense education, escort service, and shuttle buses. There are informal discussions, pamphlets/posters/films, emergency telephones, lighted pathways/sidewalks, and 16 crime-prevention programs.

Programs of Study: EKU confers B.A., B.S., B.B.A., B.F.A., B.I.S., B.M., B.M.Ed., B.S.N., and B.S.W. degrees. Associate and master's degrees are also awarded. Bachelor's degrees are awarded in AGRICULTURE (agriculture, horticulture, and wildlife management), BIOLOGICAL SCIENCE (biology/biological science and microbiology), BUSINESS (accounting, banking and finance, business administration and management, and marketing/retailing/merchandising), COMMUNICATIONS AND THE ARTS (art, broadcasting, dramatic arts, English, French, journalism, music, performing arts, public relations, Spanish, and speech/debate/rhetoric), COMPUTER AND PHYSICAL SCIENCE (chemistry, computer programming, computer science, geology, mathematics, and statistics), EDUCATION (art, business, education of the deaf and hearing impaired, elementary, foreign languages, health, home economics, industrial arts, middle school, music, physical, secondary, special, and technical), ENGINEERING AND ENVIRONMENTAL DESIGN (airline piloting and navigation, construction technology, environmental science, interior design, and manufacturing technology), HEALTH PROFESSIONS (environmental health science, health care administration, nursing, and occupational therapy), SOCIAL SCIENCE (anthropology, child care/child and family studies, corrections, dietetics, economics, fire protection, forensic studies, geography, history, paralegal studies, philosophy, political science/government, psychology, social work, and sociology). Occupational therapy, psychology, and nursing are the strongest academically. Education, nursing, and law enforcement are the largest.

Required: All students must complete 51 credit hours of general education requirements, including courses in phys ed, health, English, natural science, social science, math, and the humanities. To graduate, students must complete a total of 128 credit hours, including 45 to 60 in the major, with a minimum GPA of 2.0.

Special: EKU offers cooperative programs with all academic colleges, internships, and study abroad in various European countries. Students may opt for credit by exam, nondegree study, pass/fail options, student-designed and dual majors, and a general studies degree. There are 30 national honor societies, including Phi Beta Kappa, a freshman honors program, and 1 departmental honors program.

Faculty/Classroom: 55% of faculty are male; 45%, female. 98% teach undergraduates and 25% both teach and do research. Graduate students teach 1% of introductory courses. The average class size in an introductory lecture is 30; in a laboratory, 15; and in a regular course, 25.

Admissions: 79% of the 2001-2002 applicants were accepted.

Requirements: The ACT is required. EKU requires applicants to be in the upper 50% of their class. A GPA of 2.0 is required. AP and CLEP credits are accepted. Important factors in the admissions decision are evidence of special talent, extracurricular activities record, and leadership record. Applications can be downloaded from the school's web site.

Procedure: Freshmen are admitted to all sessions. Entrance exams should be taken prior to enrollment. Applications should be filed by August 1 for fall entry, along with a $25 fee. Notification is sent on a rolling basis.

Transfer: 4058 transfer students enrolled in a recent year. Applicants must have a 2.0 cumulative GPA from all accredited institutions previously attended and must not have been dismissed. 30 credits of 128 must be completed at EKU.

Visiting: There are regularly scheduled orientations for prospective students, consisting of a 1-day program during the summer prior to fall enrollment. There are guides for informal visits and visitors may sit in on classes and stay overnight. To schedule a visit, contact the Admissions Office by phone or at *donna.queen@eku.edu*.

Financial Aid: In a recent year, 57% of all freshmen and 48% of continuing students received some form of financial aid. 37% of freshmen and 33% of continuing students received need-based aid. The average freshman award was $5711. Of that total, scholarships or need-based grants averaged $2983; loans averaged $1991; and work contracts averaged $2983. 92% of undergraduates work part time. Average annual earnings from campus work are $2000. The average financial indebtedness of a recent graduate was $15,100. EKU is a member of CSS. The CSS/Profile and the college's own financial statement are required. The fall application deadline is April 15.

International Students: In a recent year, there were 161 international students enrolled. The school actively recruits these students. They must score 500 on the written TOEFL and also take the ACT, scoring 21, or the SAT I for those applicants from states where the SAT I is dominant.

Computers: The mainframe is a DEC VAX. About 300 networked PCs with Internet access are located in various academic buildings, the library, and the student center. Internet service is also available in residence halls. All students may access the system. There are no time limits and no fees.

Graduates: In a recent class, 1762 bachelor's degrees were awarded. The most popular majors were liberal and fine arts (40%), education (20%), and nursing, occupational therapy (15%). In an average class, 7% graduate in 4 years, 20% in 5 years, and 27% in 6 years. 409 companies recruited on campus in a recent year. Of a recent graduating class, 61% were enrolled in graduate school within 6 months of graduation and 84% were employed.

Admissions Contact: Stephen A. Byrn, Director of Admissions. E-mail: *admissions@eku.edu* Web: *http://www.eku.edu/admissions/*

GEORGETOWN COLLEGE

Georgetown, KY 40324-1696 D-2
(502) 863-8009
(800) 788-9985; Fax: (502) 868-7733

Full-time: 556 men, 749 women	**Faculty:** 90; IIB, --$
Part-time: 34 men, 23 women	**Ph.D.s:** 90%
Graduate: 37 men, 305 women	**Student/Faculty:** 15 to 1
Year: semesters, summer session	**Tuition:** $13,580
Application Deadline: February 15	**Room & Board:** $4820
Freshman Class: 827 applied, 782 accepted, 357 enrolled	
ACT: 25	**VERY COMPETITIVE**

Georgetown College, founded in 1829, is a private liberal arts college affiliated with the Kentucky Baptist Convention. The library contains 145,794 volumes, 170,069 microform items, and 3009 audiovisual forms/CDs, and subscribes to 833 periodicals. Computerized library services include the card catalog, interlibrary loans, and database searching. Special learning facilities include a learning resource center, art gallery, planetarium, and radio station. The 104-acre campus is in a suburban area 12 miles north of Lexington. Including residence halls, there are 40 buildings.

Student Life: 83% of undergraduates are from Kentucky. Others are from 26 states, 16 foreign countries, and Canada. 90% are from public schools. 96% are white. 83% are Protestant; 13% Catholic. The average age of freshmen is 18; all undergraduates, 20. 20% do not continue beyond their first year; 53% remain to graduate.

Housing: 1242 students can be accommodated in college housing, which includes single-sex dormitories, on-campus apartments, married-student housing, fraternity houses, and sorority houses. On-campus housing is guaranteed for all 4 years. 92% of students live on campus; of those, 78% remain on campus on weekends. Alcohol is not permitted. All students may keep cars.

Activities: 28% of men belong to 1 local and 4 national fraternities; 40% of women belong to 4 national sororities. There are 97 groups on campus, including academic, art, band, cheerleading, choir, chorale, chorus, computers, dance, drama, ethnic, forensics, honors, international, jazz band, literary magazine, musical theater, newspaper, pep band, photography, political, professional, radio and TV, religious, social, social service, student government, and yearbook. Popular campus events include Festival of Song, Parents Day, and Hanging of the Green (Christmas).

Sports: There are 7 intercollegiate sports for men and 7 for women, and 11 intramural sports for men and 11 for women. Facilities include a 3000-seat stadium, 8 tennis courts, soccer, baseball/football, and intramural fields, and a 1550-seat gym housing a Nautilus room, a weight-lifting area, racquetball courts, and a training room.

Disabled Students: 70% of the campus is accessible. Wheelchair ramps, elevators, special parking, specially equipped rest rooms, and special class scheduling are available.

Services: Counseling and information services are available, as is tutoring in every subject.

Campus Safety and Security: Measures include 24-hour foot and vehicle patrol, self-defense education, escort service, and shuttle buses. There are informal discussions, pamphlets/posters/films, emergency telephones, and lighted pathways/sidewalks.

Programs of Study: Georgetown confers B.A., B.S., B.M., and B.M.E. degrees. Master's degrees are also awarded. Bachelor's degrees are awarded in BIOLOGICAL SCIENCE (biology/biological science), BUSINESS (accounting, banking and finance, business economics, international business management, management information systems, management science, marketing/retailing/merchandising, and recreation and leisure services), COMMUNICATIONS AND THE ARTS (art, communications, English, French, German, music, and Spanish), COMPUTER AND PHYSICAL SCIENCE (chemistry, computer science, mathematics, and physics), EDUCATION (elementary, foreign languages, music, and physical), ENGINEERING AND ENVIRONMENTAL DESIGN (environmental science), HEALTH PROFESSIONS (medical laboratory technology and nursing), SOCIAL SCIENCE (American studies, child care/child and family studies, European studies, history, human services, philosophy, political science/government, psychology, religion, religious music, sociology, and youth ministry). Biology and English are the strongest academically. Business and psychology are the largest.

Required: All students are required to complete 56 semester hours of general education courses, including 16 in fine arts and humanities, 9 in foreign language and culture (or otherwise demonstrate proficiency), 8 in communication, 6 each in religion, natural sciences, and social sciences, 3 in math, and 2 in phys ed. A total of 128 semester hours, including 33 to 60 in the major, with a minimum GPA of 2.0, is required to graduate, as is successful completion of a comprehensive exam in the major.

Special: Georgetown offers cross-registration with the University of Kentucky Air Force ROTC for aerospace studies. A 3-2 engineering degree is available with the University of Kentucky and Washington University in St. Louis. Internships, co-op programs in math and computer science, study abroad in 5 countries, work-study programs, dual and student-designed majors, and pass/fail options are available. Interdisciplinary majors include business administration/communication arts and business administration/ethics. A dual degree is offered in engineering arts. Nondegree study is possible. There are 19 national honor societies and a freshman honors program.

Faculty/Classroom: 65% of faculty are male; 35%, female. All teach undergraduates. No introductory courses are taught by graduate students. The average class size in an introductory lecture is 21 and in a regular course, 18.

Admissions: 95% of the 2001-2002 applicants were accepted. The ACT scores for the 2001-2002 freshman class were: 13% below 21, 31% between 21 and 23, 26% between 24 and 26, 16% between 27 and 28, and 14% above 28. 61% of the current freshmen were in the top fifth of their class; 82% were in the top two fifths. 28 freshmen graduated first in their class.

Requirements: The SAT I or ACT is required. In addition, applicants should have completed 4 high school credits in English, 3 each in math and science, 2 in a foreign language, and 1 each in social studies and history, with additional credits in electives strongly encouraged. A student essay is required; Kentucky high school applicants may substitute a writing portfolio entry. Georgetown requires applicants to be in the upper 50% of their class. A GPA of 2.0 is required. AP and CLEP credits are accepted. Important factors in the admissions decision are advanced placement or honor courses, evidence of special talent, and leadership record. Applications are accepted on-line.

Procedure: Freshmen are admitted to all sessions. Entrance exams should be taken from December of the junior year through October of the senior year. There is an early decision plan. Early decision application should be filed by December 1. For best consideration, students should apply before February 15 of their senior year of high school. Notification is sent on a rolling basis. The fall 2001 application fee was $25. 15 early decision candidates were accepted for the 2001-2002 class.

Transfer: 41 transfer students enrolled in 2001-2002. Applicants must be in good standing at the school most recently attended and must submit official college and high school transcripts. 30 credits of 128 must be completed at Georgetown.

Visiting: There are regularly scheduled orientations for prospective students, consisting of campus tours and information on admissions, financial assistance, student life, and academic programs. There are guides for informal visits and visitors may sit in on classes and stay overnight. To schedule a visit, contact Brian Taylor, Director of Admissions.

Financial Aid: In 2001-2002, 98% of all freshmen and 97% of continuing students received some form of financial aid. 58% of freshmen and 68% of continuing students received need-based aid. The average freshman award was $13,339. Of that total, scholarships or need-based grants averaged $10,376 ($19,050 maximum); loans averaged $2367 ($6625 maximum); and work contracts averaged $596 ($1800 maximum). 33% of undergraduates work part time. Average annual earnings from campus work are $968. The average financial indebtedness of the 2001 graduate was $9569. The FAFSA is required. The fall application deadline is March 1.

International Students: There are 19 international students enrolled. They must score 520 on the written TOEFL or 190 on the electronic version.

Computers: The mainframe is an HP 9000/K2 60 D320. There are about 200 PCs with word processing, statistical analysis, spreadsheets, programming languages, ERIC, and other databases, available in the library and departmental labs. Students may access academic computing via the Ethernet network connection. All students may access the system. There are no time limits. The fee is $150.

Graduates: In 2001, 204 bachelor's degrees were awarded. The most popular majors were psychology (19%), business (15%), and communication arts (14%). In an average class, 44% graduate in 4 years, 59% in 5 years, and 61% in 6 years. 28 companies recruited on campus in 2000-2001. Of the 2000 graduating class, 45% were enrolled in graduate school within 6 months of graduation. Of those who did not go to graduate school, 88% were employed.

Admissions Contact: Brian Taylor, Director of Admissions.
E-mail: *admissions@georgetowncollege.edu*
Web: *http://www.georgetowncollege.edu*

KENTUCKY CHRISTIAN COLLEGE F-2
Grayson, KY 41143 (606) 474-6613
(800) KCC-3181; Fax: (606) 474-3155

Full-time: 268 men, 290 women	**Faculty:** 27; IIB, --$
Part-time: 8 men, 12 women	**Ph.D.s:** 92%
Graduate: 15 men, 1 woman	**Student/Faculty:** 21 to 1
Year: semesters, summer session	**Tuition:** $8544
Application Deadline: open	**Room & Board:** $4128
Freshman Class: 273 applied, 226 accepted, 159 enrolled	
SAT I or ACT: required	**COMPETITIVE**

Kentucky Christian College, established in 1919, is a private Christian college affiliated with the Church of Christ and offering undergraduate programs in Bible studies along with Christian ministry, psychology, social work, business administration, teacher education, music, history, and intercultural studies. In addition to regional accreditation, KCC has baccalaureate program accreditation with CSWE. The library contains 101,859 volumes, 738 microform items, and 3547 audiovisual forms/CDs, and subscribes to 439 periodicals. Computerized library services include interlibrary loans and database searching. Special learning facilities include a learning resource center and radio station. The 121-acre campus is in a small town 20 miles from Ashland and 90 miles east of Lexington. Including residence halls, there are 16 buildings.

Student Life: 69% of undergraduates are from out of state, mostly the Midwest. Others are from 24 states, 8 foreign countries, and Canada. 94% are white. Most are Protestant. The average age of freshmen is 18; all undergraduates, 20. 34% do not continue beyond their first year.

Housing: 556 students can be accommodated in college housing, which includes single-sex dormitories, on-campus apartments, and married-student housing. On-campus housing is guaranteed for all 4 years. 91% of students live on campus. Alcohol is not permitted. All students may keep cars.

Activities: There are no fraternities or sororities. There are 14 groups on campus, including cheerleading, choir, chorale, drama, jazz band, musical theater, newspaper, pep band, professional, radio and TV, religious, social service, student government, and yearbook. Popular campus events include Feast of Christmas, Days of Future Knights, and Summer in the Son.

Sports: There are 4 intercollegiate sports for men and 4 for women, and 16 intramural sports for men and 16 for women. Facilities include a gym, soccer and recreational fields, a baseball diamond, a student life recreational center, and racquetball and tennis courts.

Disabled Students: 95% of the campus is accessible. Wheelchair ramps, elevators, special parking, specially equipped rest rooms, lowered drinking fountains, and lowered telephones are available.

Services: Counseling and information services are available, as is tutoring in some subjects. RAs on campus serve as dorm tutors in various subjects. There is a reader service for the blind, and remedial math, reading, and writing.

Campus Safety and Security: Measures include escort service, informal discussions, emergency telephones, and lighted pathways/sidewalks. There is a full-time security guard.

Programs of Study: KCC confers B.A. and B.S. degrees. Associate and master's degrees are also awarded. Bachelor's degrees are awarded in BUSINESS (business administration and management), COMMUNICATIONS AND THE ARTS (literature, music, and music performance), COMPUTER AND PHYSICAL SCIENCE (mathematics and science), EDUCATION (elementary, middle school, and music), SOCIAL SCIENCE (biblical studies, counseling/psychology, history, ministries, philosophy, psychology, religious music, social work, and youth ministry). Teacher education and ministry are the largest.

Required: To graduate, students must complete 132 semester hours with at least 30 hours in the major and a minimum GPA of 2.0. Required courses include freshman orientation, phys ed, English, history, Introduction to Christian Doctrine, and Survey of Biblical Literature. Candidates for the B.A. degree must fulfill a 14-hour language requirement. All students complete a 30-hour Bible studies concentration along with their chosen field of study. Students must also participate in a Christian service program.

Special: Internships, work-study programs, B.A.-B.S. degrees, and dual majors are offered. Internships are required in business, education, ministry, and social work. Nondegree study is available. There is a chapter of Phi Beta Kappa.

Faculty/Classroom: 81% of faculty are male; 19%, female. All teach undergraduates and 25% also do research. The average class size in an introductory lecture is 30; in a laboratory, 15; and in a regular course, 17.

Admissions: 83% of the 2001-2002 applicants were accepted. The SAT I scores for the 2001-2002 freshman class were: Verbal--68% below 500, 16% between 500 and 599, and 16% between 600 and 700; Math--52% below 500, 44% between 500 and 599, and 4% between 600 and 700. The ACT scores were 43% below 21, 23% between 21 and 23, 19% between 24 and 26, 5% between 27 and 28, and 9% above 28. 3 freshmen graduated first in their class.

Requirements: The SAT I or ACT is required, with a minimum composite score of 830 on the SAT I or 17 on the ACT. Applicants with lower test scores who have a high school GPA of 2.5 or higher will be considered. Applicants must graduate from an accredited secondary school or have a GED. Essays are required. A GPA of 2.0 is required. AP and CLEP credits are accepted. Applications are accepted on-line at the school's web site.

Procedure: Freshmen are admitted to all sessions. There are early decision and deferred admissions plans. Application deadlines are open. The fall 2001 application fee was $25. Notification is sent on a rolling basis.

Transfer: 37 transfer students enrolled in 2001-2002. Applicants must have a cumulative GPA of 2.0. They must submit transcripts from all previous institutions and must be in good standing at the last college attended. 32 credits of 132 must be completed at KCC.

Visiting: There are regularly scheduled orientations for prospective students, consisting of an interview, a campus tour, lunch, and class attendance. Also, a semester-long orientation class is offered for all first-time freshmen. There are guides for informal visits and visitors may sit in on classes and stay overnight. To schedule a visit, contact Leslie Arnold, Assistant to the Director of Admissions.

Financial Aid: In 2001-2002, 76% of all freshmen and 71% of continuing students received some form of financial aid. 41% of freshmen and 49% of continuing students received need-based aid. The average freshman award was $6621. Of that total, scholarships or need-based grants averaged $2864 ($8837 maximum); loans averaged $3137 ($7125 maximum); and work contracts averaged $1000 ($3300 maximum). 54% of undergraduates work part time. Average annual earnings from campus work are $1586. The average financial indebtedness of the 2001 graduate was $19,497. The FAFSA and the college's own financial statement are required. The fall application deadline is April 1.

International Students: There are 13 international students enrolled. They must score 500 on the written TOEFL and also take the SAT I or the ACT.

Computers: The mainframe is an IBM RS/6000. There is a Novell Network with connections provided in dorm rooms. Computers are located in the library, academic building labs, and student life center. All students may access the system. There are no time limits. In a recent year, the fee was $100.

Graduates: In 2001, 76 bachelor's degrees were awarded. The most popular majors were Christian ministry (29%), teacher education (24%), and business administration (17%). In an average class, 45% graduate in 4 years and 50% in 6 years.

Admissions Contact: Sandra Deakins, Director of Admissions.
E-mail: *knights@email.kcc.edu* Web: *www.kcc.edu*

KENTUCKY STATE UNIVERSITY D-2
Frankfort, KY 40601 (502) 227-6322
(800) 633-9415; Fax: (502) 227-6239

Full-time: 765 men, 920 women	**Faculty:** n/av
Part-time: 190 men, 405 women	**Ph.D.s:** n/av
Graduate: 50 men, 65 women	**Student/Faculty:** n/av
Year: n/av	**Tuition:** $2546 ($6958)
Application Deadline: open	**Room & Board:** $3600
Freshman Class: n/av	**ACT:** required
	NONCOMPETITIVE

Kentucky State University, founded in 1886, is a public liberal arts institution that emphasizes student involvement in seminars and course planning. Figures in the above capsule are approximate. There are 4 undergraduate schools and 1 graduate school. In addition to regional accreditation, KSU has baccalaureate program accreditation with AACSB, ADA, AHEA, CSWE, NASM, NCATE, and NLN. The library contains 350,000 volumes, 309,606 microform items, and 12,477 audiovisual forms/CDs, and subscribes to 1116 periodicals. Computerized library services include the card catalog, interlibrary loans, and database searching. Special learning facilities include a learning resource center, art gallery, and and a 167-acre agricultural research farm. The 475-acre campus is in a small town 25 miles west of Lexington. Including residence halls, there are 34 buildings.

Student Life: 71% of undergraduates are from Kentucky. Others are from 28 states, 28 foreign countries, and Canada. 99% are from public schools. 59% are African American; 36% white. The average age of freshmen is 19; all undergraduates, 25. 30% do not continue beyond their first year; 35% remain to graduate.

Housing: 887 students can be accommodated in college housing, which includes single-sex dormitories and on-campus apartments. In addition, there are special-interest houses. On-campus housing is guaranteed for the freshman year only and is available on a first-come, first-served basis. 67% of students commute. Alcohol is not permitted. All students may keep cars.

Activities: 10% of men belong to 1 local and 5 national fraternities; 9% of women belong to 1 local and 4 national sororities. There are 70 groups on campus, including art, band, cheerleading, chess, choir, chorale, computers, dance, honors, international, literary magazine, marching band, musical theater, newspaper, political, religious, social, social service, student government, and yearbook. Popular campus events include plays, concerts, and talent shows.

Sports: There are 7 intercollegiate sports for men and 6 for women, and 10 intramural sports for men and 7 for women. Facilities include a 6500-seat football stadium, an indoor swimming pool, tennis courts, a bowling alley, training and weight rooms, a field house, baseball, track, and field complexes.

Disabled Students: Wheelchair ramps, elevators, special parking, specially equipped rest rooms, lowered drinking fountains, lowered telephones, and electric doors are available.

Services: Counseling and information services are available, as is tutoring in every subject. There is a reader service for the blind, and remedial math, reading, and writing.

Campus Safety and Security: Measures include 24-hour foot and vehicle patrol, self-defense education, and lighted pathways/sidewalks.

Programs of Study: Bachelor's degrees are awarded in BIOLOGICAL SCIENCE (biology/biological science), BUSINESS (accounting, apparel and accessories marketing, business administration and management, business economics, management science, and marketing/retailing/merchandising), COMMUNICATIONS AND THE ARTS (English, fine arts, music performance, and studio art), COMPUTER AND PHYSICAL SCIENCE (applied mathematics, chemistry, computer science, and mathematics), EDUCATION (art, early childhood, elementary, mathematics, music, physical, secondary, and social studies), HEALTH PROFESSIONS (medical laboratory technology), SOCIAL SCIENCE (child psychology/development, criminal justice, economics, history, liberal arts/general studies, political science/government, psychology, public administration, social work, sociology, and textiles and clothing).

Requirements: The ACT is required. In addition, a composite score of 19 in-state and 20 out-of-state on the ACT is needed. Applicants are required to have 4 years in English, 3 in math, 2 each in science and history, and 9 additional precollege curriculum classes. The GED is accepted. AP and CLEP credits are accepted.

Procedure: Freshmen are admitted to all sessions. Entrance exams should be taken from October to April. There are early admissions and deferred admissions plans. Application deadlines are open. The fall 2001 application fee was $15. Notification is sent on a rolling basis.

Transfer: Transfer applicants must have a 2.0 minimum GPA at previous colleges. Only C grades transfer. If fewer than 30 semester credits are transferable, applicants must meet freshman criteria. 32 credits of 128 must be completed at KSU.

Visiting: There are regularly scheduled orientations for prospective students, including tours and meetings with faculty and financial aid officers. There are guides for informal visits and visitors may sit in on classes. To schedule a visit, contact Admissions.

Financial Aid: In a recent year, 80% of all freshmen and 85% of continuing students received some form of financial aid. 65% of freshmen and 60% of continuing students received need-based aid. The average freshman award was $6500. Of that total, scholarships or need-based grants averaged $1500 ($3125 maximum); loans averaged $2625 ($6500 maximum); work contracts averaged $800 ($1000 maximum); and $500 to $1000 per academic year comes from external scholarship sources. 55% of undergraduates work part time. Average annual earnings from campus work are $1000. The average financial indebtedness of a recent graduate was $12,000. KSU is a member of CSS. The FAFSA and the college's own financial statement are required. Check with the school for current deadlines.

International Students: They must score 525 on the written TOEFL and also take the SAT I or the ACT.

Computers: The mainframes are an IBM 4361 and an IBM 9375. Many IBM and Mac PCs are available in various departmental computer labs; some are connected to a LAN. A PC lab is in the library for any student to use for homework or word processing applications. All students may access the system 13 hours a day. There are no time limits. The fee is $15 per semester.

Graduates: In a recent year, 193 bachelor's degrees were awarded. The most popular majors were public administration (12%), nursing (10%), and elementary education (9%).

Admissions Contact: Mr. Jimmy Arrington, Director of Admissions. A video is available. E-mail: *webmaster/gymail.kysu.edu*
Web: *www.kysu.edu.*

KENTUCKY WESLEYAN COLLEGE — B-3

Owensboro, KY 42302-1039 — (270) 852-3242
(800) 999-0592; Fax: (270) 926-3196

Full-time: 342 men, 289 women	**Faculty:** 38; IIB, --$
Part-time: 19 men, 21 women	**Ph.D.s:** 82%
Graduate: none	**Student/Faculty:** 17 to 1
Year: semesters, summer session	**Tuition:** $10,820
Application Deadline: open	**Room & Board:** $4980
Freshman Class: 554 applied, 450 accepted, 164 enrolled	
SAT I Verbal/Math: 480/495	**ACT:** 22 **COMPETITIVE**

Kentucky Wesleyan College, founded in 1858, is a private liberal arts institution affiliated with the United Methodist Church. KWC offers undergraduate programs in natural sciences, humanities and fine arts, and social sciences. Additionally, academic programs are offered in criminal justice, nursing, human resources administration, mass communication, and computer science. In addition to regional accreditation, KWC has baccalaureate program accreditation with NLN. The library contains 96,000 volumes, 65,000 microform items, and 3500 audiovisual forms/CDs, and subscribes to 400 periodicals. Computerized library services include the card catalog, interlibrary loans, and database searching. Special learning facilities include a learning resource center, art gallery, and radio station. The 55-acre campus is in an urban area 95 miles southwest of Louisville and 120 miles north of Nashville, Tennessee. Including residence halls, there are 15 buildings.

Student Life: 71% of undergraduates are from Kentucky. Others are from 16 states, 1 foreign country, and Canada. 93% are from public schools. 91% are white. 81% are Protestant; 18% Catholic. The average age of freshmen is 18; all undergraduates, 20. 31% do not continue beyond their first year.

Housing: 392 students can be accommodated in college housing, which includes single-sex and coed dormitories, on-campus apartments, fraternity houses, and sorority houses. On-campus housing is guaranteed for all 4 years. 53% of students commute. Alcohol is not permitted. All students may keep cars.

Activities: 19% of men belong to 3 national fraternities; 23% of women belong to 2 national sororities. There are 43 groups on campus, including art, cheerleading, choir, chorale, chorus, computers, drama, ethnic, literary magazine, musical theater, newspaper, pep band, professional, radio and TV, religious, social, social service, student government, and yearbook. Popular campus events include Family Weekend, Student Appreciation Week, and theater productions.

Sports: There are 6 intercollegiate sports for men and 6 for women, and 7 intramural sports for men and 7 for women. Facilities include a health and recreation center, which houses an 800-seat gym, a fully equipped weight training center, racquetball courts, batting and pitching facilities for softball and baseball, and a multipurpose auxiliary gym. Outdoor facilities include a baseball park, a softball park, a soccer field, and additional practice fields for football and soccer. Varsity basketball games are played in the 5,000-seat Owensboro Sports Center.

Disabled Students: 64% of the campus is accessible. Wheelchair ramps, elevators, special parking, specially equipped rest rooms, special class scheduling, and lowered drinking fountains are available.

Services: Counseling and information services are available, as is tutoring in most subjects.

Campus Safety and Security: Measures include 24-hour foot and vehicle patrol, escort service, informal discussions, and pamphlets/posters/films. There are lighted pathways/sidewalks.

Programs of Study: KWC confers B.A., B.S., B.M., B.M.E., and B.S.N. degrees. Bachelor's degrees are awarded in BIOLOGICAL SCIENCE (biology/biological science), BUSINESS (accounting, business administration and management, business economics, and human resources), COMMUNICATIONS AND THE ARTS (art, communications, dramatic arts, English, and music), COMPUTER AND PHYSICAL SCIENCE (chemistry, computer science, and physics), EDUCATION (art, elementary, middle school, music, physical, and secondary), ENGINEERING AND ENVIRONMENTAL DESIGN (preengineering), HEALTH PROFESSIONS (nursing, predentistry, and premedicine), SOCIAL SCIENCE (criminal justice, early childhood studies, history, political science/

government, prelaw, psychology, and sociology). Natural sciences, education, and business are the strongest academically. Business, accounting, and general education are the largest.

Required: All students are required to complete the following general education program of skills and content requirements: 9 hours each in humanities and social sciences, 8 hours in natural science, 6 hours in history, 3 hours each in religion, integrated studies, and multicultural studies, and 2 hours in phys ed. Students must demonstrate proficiency in math, computing, oral and written communication, and foreign language. To graduate, students must complete a total of 128 credits, including 36 in the major, with a 2.0 GPA.

Special: A cooperative program in early childhood development with Brescia University is available. Internships and student-designed majors are available in many programs and are established on an individual basis. A dual degree in engineering is offered with Auburn University and the University of Kentucky. A Washington semester and study abroad in 5 countries are also available. There are 8 national honor societies, and 7 departmental honors program.

Faculty/Classroom: 66% of faculty are male; 34%, female. All teach undergraduates and 30% do research. The average class size in an introductory lecture is 25; in a laboratory, 17; and in a regular course, 18.

Admissions: 81% of the 2001-2002 applicants were accepted. The SAT I scores for the 2001-2002 freshman class were: Verbal--57% below 500, 30% between 500 and 599, and 13% between 600 and 700; Math--65% below 500, 17% between 500 and 599, and 17% between 600 and 700. 7 freshmen graduated first in their class. 37% of the current freshmen were in the top quarter of their class; 67% were in the top half.

Requirements: The SAT I or ACT is required. In addition, applicants should have completed 13 high school units in college preparatory English, math, science, social studies, and a foreign language, or the GED equivalent. Applicants are considered individually. Students must take the SAT I or ACT and submit the scores if they have been out of high school fewer than 5 years. A GPA of 2.25 is required. AP and CLEP credits are accepted. Important factors in the admissions decision are advanced placement or honor courses, evidence of special talent, and leadership record. Applications are accepted on computer disk and via CollegeLink and other computer applications.

Procedure: Freshmen are admitted to all sessions. Entrance exams should be taken during the spring of the junior year or the fall of the senior year. The fall 2001 application fee was $20. There is a deferred admissions plan. Application deadlines are open. Notification is on a rolling basis.

Transfer: 40 transfer students enrolled in 2001-2002. Transfer applicants should have a minimum GPA of 2.0 in all course work and be in good standing at the previously attended institution. 30 credits of 128 must be completed at KWC.

Visiting: There are regularly scheduled orientations for prospective students, including a campus tour, meetings with faculty and students, and dining on campus. There are guides for informal visits and visitors may sit in on classes and stay overnight. To schedule a visit, contact the Admissions Office at (207) 850-3120 or *krasp@kwc.edu*.

Financial Aid: In 2001-2002, 93% of all freshmen and 90% of continuing students received some form of financial aid. 84% of freshmen and 77% of continuing students received need-based aid. The average freshman award was $9967. Of that total, scholarships or need-based grants averaged $8240; loans averaged $2164; and work contracts averaged $2696. 51% of undergraduates work part time. KWC is a member of CSS. The FAFSA and the college's own financial statement are required. The fall application deadline is August 1.

International Students: They must score 500 on the written TOEFL. SAT I or ACT scores are required of international students who do not have a TOEFL score or who want to play NCAA sports.

Computers: The mainframe is an IBM AS/400 minicomputer. The campus computer network links all residential and academic buildings to a central unit. Software includes Harvard Graphics, Lotus 1-2-3, dBASE IV, WordPerfect, WordStar, E-mail, Pagemaker, Corel Draw, PC Globe, PC USA, and Printshop. The system is available 24 hours a day through in-room network stations or residence hall study rooms. All students may access the system from 8 A.M. to 11 P.M. There are no time limits and no fees.

Graduates: In 2001, 150 bachelor's degrees were awarded. The most popular majors were accounting (20%), communication arts (16%), and general education (13%). In an average class, 41% graduate in 5 years. 17 companies recruited on campus in 2000-2001. Of the 2000 graduating class, 21% were enrolled in graduate school within 6 months of graduation and 84% were employed.

Admissions Contact: Mark Dartt, Director of Institutional Research. A video is available. E-mail: *mdartt@kwc.edu* Web: *www.kwc.edu*

LINDSEY WILSON COLLEGE — D-3
Columbia, KY 42728
(270) 384-8504
(800) 264-0138; Fax: (270) 384-8591

Full-time: 475 men, 760 women
Part-time: 30 men, 105 women
Graduate: 10 men, 30 women
Year: semesters, summer session
Application Deadline: open
Freshman Class: n/av
SAT I or ACT: recommended
Faculty: 44; IIB, --$
Ph.D.s: 57%
Student/Faculty: 27 to 1
Tuition: $11,592
Room & Board: $4800
LESS COMPETITIVE

Lindsey Wilson College, founded in 1903, is a private liberal arts college affiliated with the United Methodist Church, offering undergraduate programs in arts and sciences, business administration, education, human services, and pre-health. Figures in the above capsule are approximate. In addition to regional accreditation, Lindsey has baccalaureate program accreditation with NCATE. The library contains 350,000 volumes, 200,000 microform items, and 5220 audiovisual forms/CDs, and subscribes to 1300 periodicals. Computerized library services include the card catalog, interlibrary loans, and database searching. Special learning facilities include a learning resource center and art gallery. The 40-acre campus is in a small town 100 miles southeast of Louisville. Including residence halls, there are 35 buildings.

Student Life: 89% of undergraduates are from Kentucky. Others are from 15 states, 23 foreign countries, and Canada. 90% are from public schools. 89% are white. 78% are Protestant; 16% claim no religious affiliation. The average age of freshmen is 19; all undergraduates, 24. 46% do not continue beyond their first year.

Housing: 650 students can be accommodated in college housing, which includes single-sex dormitories, on-campus apartments, and married-student housing. In addition, there are honors houses. On-campus housing is guaranteed for all 4 years. 51% of students commute. Alcohol is not permitted. All students may keep cars.

Activities: There are no fraternities or sororities. There are 30 groups on campus, including art, cheerleading, choir, chorale, chorus, computers, dance, drama, film, honors, international, literary magazine, musical theater, newspaper, pep band, photography, political, professional, religious, social, social service, student government, and yearbook. Popular campus events include Hanging of the Greens, Parent Day, Tradition Day, and Founders Day.

Sports: There are 8 intercollegiate sports for men and 8 for women, and 15 intramural sports for men and 15 for women. Facilities include a sports center with a 1000-seat gym and a weight-training room, a sand volleyball court, and the student union building.

Disabled Students: 80% of the campus is accessible. Wheelchair ramps, elevators, special parking, specially equipped rest rooms, special class scheduling, and lowered drinking fountains are available.

Services: Counseling and information services are available, as is tutoring in every subject. There is remedial math, reading, and writing.

Campus Safety and Security: Measures include escort service, informal discussions, pamphlets/posters/films, and lighted pathways/sidewalks. There are and 12-hour foot and vehicle patrol.

Programs of Study: Lindsey confers the B.A. degree. Associate and master's degrees are also awarded. Bachelor's degrees are awarded in BIOLOGICAL SCIENCE (biology/biological science), BUSINESS (accounting and business administration and management), COMMUNICATIONS AND THE ARTS (art, communications and English), EDUCATION (elementary, and secondary), SOCIAL SCIENCE (American studies, criminal justice, history, human services, liberal arts/general studies, and social science). Business, elementary education, and human services are the strongest academically. Business, elementary education, and human services are the largest.

Required: All students must complete general education core requirements, including courses in communication of ideas, math, natural science, religion, humanities, fine arts, social behavioral science, and phys ed, as well as a 1-hour personal development career seminar. A total of 128 semester hours, with a minimum GPA of 2.0, is required to graduate.

Special: Human services majors are offered a social services practicum in their field of study. Internships, work-study programs, a general studies degree, and pass/fail options in some courses are available. Study abroad is possible through Lindsey in London and the Northern Ireland Exchange. There is a freshman honors program.

Faculty/Classroom: 47% of faculty are male; 53%, female. All teach undergraduates. No introductory courses are taught by graduate students. The average class size in an introductory lecture is 26; in a laboratory, 20; and in a regular course, 26.

Admissions: 3 freshmen graduated first in their class in a recent year.

Requirements: The SAT I or ACT is recommended. In addition, applicants should have completed 20 academic high school credits or the GED equivalent. A GPA of 2.8 is required. AP and CLEP credits are accepted. Important factors in the admissions decision are geographic diversity, recommendations by alumni, and recommendations by school officials.

Procedure: Freshmen are admitted fall and spring. Entrance exams should be taken during the junior year. There is an early decision plan. Application deadlines are open. Notification is sent on a rolling basis.
Transfer: Transfer applicants are required to submit an official transcript from schools previously attended. An interview is recommended. 30 credits of 128 must be completed at Lindsey.
Visiting: There are regularly scheduled orientations for prospective students. There are guides for informal visits and visitors may sit in on classes and stay overnight. To schedule a visit, contact the Admissions Office.
Financial Aid: In a recent year, 96% of all freshmen received some form of financial aid. 31% of undergraduates work part time. Average annual earnings from campus work are $800. Lindsey is a member of CSS. The CSS/Profile and the college's own financial statement are required. Check with the school for current deadlines.
International Students: The school actively recruits these students. They must score 490 on the written TOEFL or take the MELAB.
Computers: The mainframe is a Data General MV/15000. There are 40 IBM PC/XT-compatibles in the main computing lab and 40 PCs in the English composition classroom/lab for word processing purposes. Mainly those enrolled in computing courses may access the system. There are no time limits and no fees.
Admissions Contact: Claude Bacon. E-mail: *bacon@lindsey.edu* Web: *www.lindsey.edu*

MIDWAY COLLEGE

Midway, KY 40347-1120 — D-3
(859) 846-5767
(800) 755-0031; Fax: (859) 846-5823

Full-time: 87 men, 552 women	**Faculty:** 38; III, --$
Part-time: 31 men, 204 women	**Ph.D.s:** 40%
Graduate: none	**Student/Faculty:** 17 to 1
Year: semesters, summer session	**Tuition:** $10,275
Application Deadline: open	**Room & Board:** $5540
Freshman Class: 358 applied, 255 accepted, 197 enrolled	
SAT I Verbal/Math: 520/471	**ACT:** 19 **COMPETITIVE**

Midway College, founded in 1847, is a private institution affiliated with the Disciples of Christ. The day college is for women only and the evening program is an accelerated coeducational program. The library contains 52,000 volumes, 57,000 microform items, and 8900 audiovisual forms/CDs, and subscribes to 450 periodicals. Computerized library services include the card catalog, interlibrary loans, and database searching. Special learning facilities include a learning resource center. The 105-acre campus is in a rural area in Woodford County, 15 minutes from Lexington. Including residence halls, there are 10 buildings.
Student Life: 88% of undergraduates are from Kentucky. Others are from 31 states, 5 foreign countries, and Canada. 90% are white. 32% are Protestant. The average age of freshmen is 26; all undergraduates, 30. 36% do not continue beyond their first year.
Housing: 250 students can be accommodated in college housing, which includes dormitories. On-campus housing is available on a first-come, first-served basis. 79% of students commute. Alcohol is not permitted. All students may keep cars.
Activities: There are no fraternities or sororities. There are 25 groups on campus, including art, choir, chorale, dance, honors, newspaper, professional, religious, social, social service, student government, and yearbook.
Sports: There are 7 intercollegiate sports for women. Facilities include a full service gym, a weight room, tennis courts, soccer and softball fields, and an equine arena.
Disabled Students: 45% of the campus is accessible. Wheelchair ramps, elevators, special parking, specially equipped rest rooms, special class scheduling, lowered drinking fountains, and lowered telephones are available.
Services: Counseling and information services are available, as is tutoring in every subject. There are writing and math labs.
Campus Safety and Security: Measures include 24-hour foot and vehicle patrol, emergency telephones, and lighted pathways/sidewalks.
Programs of Study: Midway College confers B.A. and B.S. degrees. Associate degrees are also awarded. Bachelor's degrees are awarded in AGRICULTURE (equine science), BIOLOGICAL SCIENCE (biology/biological science), BUSINESS (business administration and management), COMMUNICATIONS AND THE ARTS (English), COMPUTER AND PHYSICAL SCIENCE (chemistry and mathematics), EDUCATION (education), ENGINEERING AND ENVIRONMENTAL DESIGN (environmental science), HEALTH PROFESSIONS (nursing), SOCIAL SCIENCE (liberal arts/general studies and psychology). Biology, nursing, and equine science are the strongest academically. Nursing, equine science, and business are the largest.
Required: All students must complete 130 credits including 82 to 91 major and elective credits and 39 to 48 general education credits. Core requirements include courses in math, computing, science, communication, and composition. A 2.0 GPA must be maintained.
Special: A cooperative program in teacher education, study abroad in 11 countries, and an accelerated degree program in organizational management are offered. There are 2 national honor societies, including Phi Beta Kappa, and a freshman honors program.
Faculty/Classroom: 29% of faculty are male; 71%, female. All both teach undergraduates and do research. The average class size in an introductory lecture is 16; in a laboratory, 12; and in a regular course, 11.
Admissions: 71% of the 2001-2002 applicants were accepted. The SAT I scores for the 2001-2002 freshman class were: Verbal--42% below 500, 29% between 500 and 599, and 29% between 600 and 700; Math--57% below 500, and 43% between 500 and 599. The ACT scores were 63% below 21, 29% between 21 and 23, and 8% between 24 and 26. 21% of the current freshmen were in the top fifth of their class; 48% were in the top two fifths. 2 freshmen graduated first in their class.
Requirements: The SAT I or ACT is required. In addition, a score of 50 or better on the GED is required for acceptance. A GPA of 2.2 is required. AP and CLEP credits are accepted. Important factors in the admissions decision are leadership record, extracurricular activities record, and recommendations by school officials.
Procedure: Freshmen are admitted fall, spring, and summer. SAT I or ACT scores must be received by the school by August 1. Application deadlines are open. The fall 2001 application fee was $25. Notification is sent on a rolling basis.
Transfer: 65 transfer students enrolled in 2001-2002. Applicants must have a minimum college GPA of 2.0. 39 credits of 130 must be completed at Midway College.
Visiting: There are regularly scheduled orientations for prospective students, including campus tours, faculty and student conferences, and the president's address. There are guides for informal visits and visitors may sit in on classes. To schedule a visit, contact Kim Bryan in Admissions at (859) 846-5786 or *kbryan@midway.edu*.
Financial Aid: In 2001-2002, 84% of all freshmen and 73% of continuing students received some form of financial aid. 88% of freshmen and 90% of continuing students received need-based aid. The average freshman award was $10,981. Of that total, scholarships or need-based grants averaged $7369 ($16,122 maximum); and loans averaged $4999 ($11,625 maximum). 18% of undergraduates work part time. Average annual earnings from campus work are $1573. The average financial indebtedness of the 2001 graduate was $11,427. Midway College is a member of CSS. The FAFSA is required. The fall application deadline is April 15.
International Students: There are 5 international students enrolled. They must score 500 on the written TOEFL and also take the SAT I or the ACT.
Computers: The mainframe is a midrange IBM AS400. Via a Windows network, students have full access to the Internet, e-mail and Web on 60 PCs located in labs, classrooms, dorms, and the library. All students may access the system. There are no time limits and no fees.
Graduates: In 2001, 195 bachelor's degrees were awarded. The most popular majors were organizational management and business (32%), nursing (28%), and equine studies/science (9%). In an average class, 22% graduate in 4 years, and 32% in 5 years. 15 companies recruited on campus in 2000-2001.
Admissions Contact: Kim Bryan, Director of Admissions. A video is available. E-mail: *kbryan@midway.edu* Web: *www.midway.edu*

MOREHEAD STATE UNIVERSITY

Morehead, KY 40351 — E-2
(606) 783-2000
(800) 354-2090; Fax: (606) 783-5038

Full-time: 2617 men, 3517 women	**Faculty:** 346; IIA, --$
Part-time: 216 men, 849 women	**Ph.D.s:** 62%
Graduate: 559 men, 1269 women	**Student/Faculty:** 18 to 1
Year: semesters, summer session	**Tuition:** $2710 ($7204)
Application Deadline: open	**Room & Board:** $3800
Freshman Class: 5180 applied, 3772 accepted, 1590 enrolled	
ACT: 20	**COMPETITIVE**

Morehead State University, founded in 1922, is a public institution offering degree programs in applied science and technology, humanities, educational and behavioral sciences, and business. There are 4 undergraduate schools and 1 graduate school. In addition to regional accreditation, MSU has baccalaureate program accreditation with ACBSP, CSWE, NASM, NCATE, and NLN. The library contains 299,290 volumes, 771,044 microform items, and 21,033 audiovisual forms/CDs, and subscribes to 13,570 periodicals. Computerized library services include the card catalog and database searching. Special learning facilities include a learning resource center, art gallery, planetarium, radio station, TV station, 320-acre farm complex, and robotics lab. The 1044-acre campus is in a small town 60 miles east of Lexington. Including residence halls, there are 148 buildings.
Student Life: 88% of undergraduates are from Kentucky. Others are from 40 states, 40 foreign countries, and Canada. 95% are from public schools. 94% are white. The average age of freshmen is 19; all undergraduates, 24. 37% do not continue beyond their first year.
Housing: 3801 students can be accommodated in college housing, which includes single-sex and coed dormitories, on-campus apartments,

married-student housing, and fraternity houses. In addition, there are honors houses, a cross-cultural house, and housing for farm students. On-campus housing is guaranteed for all 4 years. 57% of students commute. Alcohol is not permitted. All students may keep cars.

Activities: 20% of men belong to 1 local fraternity and 13 national fraternities; 20% of women belong to 7 national sororities. There are 95 groups on campus, including art, band, cheerleading, choir, chorale, chorus, computers, dance, drama, drill team, drum and bugle corps, ethnic, honors, international, jazz band, marching band, musical theater, newspaper, orchestra, pep band, photography, political, professional, radio and TV, religious, social, social service, student government, symphony, and yearbook. Popular campus events include Greek Week, Parents Weekend, and Black History Month.

Sports: There are 11 intercollegiate sports for men and 9 for women, and 24 intramural sports for men and 24 for women. Facilities include an athletic complex, a 6500-seat gym, a 10000-seat stadium, a pool, bowling lanes, and a wellness/fitness center.

Disabled Students: 85% of the campus is accessible. Wheelchair ramps, elevators, special parking, specially equipped rest rooms, special class scheduling, lowered drinking fountains, and lowered telephones are available.

Services: Counseling and information services are available, as is tutoring in most subjects. There is a reader service for the blind, and remedial math, reading, and writing.

Campus Safety and Security: Measures include 24-hour foot and vehicle patrol, escort service, shuttle buses, and informal discussions. There are emergency telephones and lighted pathways/sidewalks.

Programs of Study: MSU confers A.B., B.S., B.B.A., B.M., B.M.Ed., B.S.N., B.S.W., and B.U.S. degrees. Associate and master's degrees are also awarded. Bachelor's degrees are awarded in AGRICULTURE (agriculture), BIOLOGICAL SCIENCE (biology/biological science, ecology, and life science), BUSINESS (accounting, banking and finance, business economics, management science, marketing management, and real estate), COMMUNICATIONS AND THE ARTS (communications, dramatic arts, English, music, and speech/debate/rhetoric), COMPUTER AND PHYSICAL SCIENCE (chemistry, earth science, geology, mathematics, and physics), EDUCATION (agricultural, business, elementary, health, home economics, industrial arts, middle school, music, physical, and special), ENGINEERING AND ENVIRONMENTAL DESIGN (industrial engineering technology), HEALTH PROFESSIONS (medical laboratory technology and nursing), SOCIAL SCIENCE (geography, history, liberal arts/general studies, paralegal studies, philosophy, political science/government, psychology, social science, social work, and sociology). Biological sciences is the strongest academically. Elementary education is the largest.

Required: All students must complete 42 semester hours (45 for teacher certification) of general education courses, including 15 hours in communications and humanities, 12 in natural and mathematical sciences, 12 in social and behavioral sciences, and 3 in health or phys ed. A total of 128 semester hours, with a minimum GPA of 2.0, is required in order to graduate.

Special: Cross-registration is offered with the University of Kentucky. Students may earn specialist certification in education. Study abroad in 3 countries, a Washington semester, a 3-2 engineering degree, dual and student-designed majors, a general studies degree, credit for life experience, pass/fail options and nondegree study are available. There are 9 national honor societies and a freshman honors program.

Faculty/Classroom: 62% of faculty are male; 38%, female. All teach undergraduates. No introductory courses are taught by graduate students.

Admissions: 73% of the 2001-2002 applicants were accepted.

Requirements: The SAT I or ACT is required. In addition, applicants should have completed the Kentucky Pre-College Curriculum requirement. An interview is recommended. A GPA of 2.0 is required. AP and CLEP credits are accepted. Applications are accepted on-line at MSU's web site.

Procedure: Freshmen are admitted to all sessions. Entrance exams should be taken in the spring of the junior year. Application deadlines are open. Notification is sent on a rolling basis.

Transfer: 468 transfer students enrolled in 2001-2002. Applicants should have a minimum GPA of 2.0 with at least 12 credit hours earned and be in good standing at their previous institution. They must have completed a precollege curriculum or meet any deficiencies. 32 credits of 128 must be completed at MSU.

Visiting: There are regularly scheduled orientations for prospective students, consisting of registration for classes, advisement, and an overview of MSU. There are guides for informal visits and visitors may sit in on classes and stay overnight. To schedule a visit, contact the Office of Admissions.

Financial Aid: In 2001-2002, 70% of all freshmen received some form of financial aid, including need-based aid. The average freshman award was $5569. 24% of undergraduates work part time. Average annual earnings from campus work are $1400. The average financial indebtedness of the 2001 graduate was $12,604. MSU is a member of CSS. The FAFSA and the college's own financial statement are required. The fall application deadline is April 1.

International Students: There are 59 international students enrolled. They must score 500 on the written TOEFL or take the MELAB. They must also take the SAT I or ACT exam, with the ACT preferred.

Computers: The mainframes are 2 HP G-50s. Teaching labs have networked computers. All students may access the system days and evenings. There are no time limits. The fee is $10 per semester.

Graduates: In 2001, 921 bachelor's degrees were awarded. The most popular majors were elementary education (8%), general studies (7%), and communications (6%). In an average class, 40% graduate in 6 years. 500 companies recruited on campus in a recent year.

Admissions Contact: Joel Pace, Associate Director, Admissions.
E-mail: *admissions@morehead-st.edu* Web: *www.morehead.st.edu*

MURRAY STATE UNIVERSITY — B-4

Murray, KY 42071 — (270) 762-3741
(800) 272-4678; Fax: (270) 762-3050

Full-time: 2847 men, 3775 women	**Faculty:** 376; IIA, --$
Part-time: 415 men, 738 women	**Ph.D.s:** 77%
Graduate: 634 men, 1239 women	**Student/Faculty:** 18 to 1
Year: semesters, summer session	**Tuition:** $2754 ($7422)
Application Deadline: August 1	**Room & Board:** $3918
Freshman Class: 2743 applied, 2411 accepted, 1310 enrolled	
ACT: 23	**COMPETITIVE**

Murray State University, founded in 1922, is a public institution offering degree programs in business and public affairs, education, health sciences and human services, humanities and fine arts, engineering, technology and science, and agriculture. There are 5 undergraduate and 6 graduate schools. In addition to regional accreditation, MSU has baccalaureate program accreditation with AACSB, ABET, ACEJMC, ACS, ADA, ASLA, AVMA, CSWE, NASAD, NASM, NCATE,and NLN. The library contains 385,000 volumes, 194,800 microform items, and 18,700 audiovisual forms/CDs, and subscribes to 109,600 periodicals. Computerized library services include the card catalog, interlibrary loans, and database searching. Special learning facilities include a learning resource center, art gallery, natural history museum, radio station, TV station, biological station, interactive telecommunications network, and web-based courses. The 236-acre campus is in a small town 130 miles northwest of Nashville. Including residence halls, there are 94 buildings.

Student Life: 71% of undergraduates are from Kentucky. Others are from 46 states, 66 foreign countries, and Canada. 80% are from public schools. 87% are white. The average age of freshmen is 19; all undergraduates, 22. 27% do not continue beyond their first year; 45% remain to graduate.

Housing: 3000 students can be accommodated in college housing, which includes single-sex and coed dormitories, on-campus apartments, married-student housing, and sorority houses. In addition, there are residential colleges. On-campus housing is guaranteed for all 4 years. 62% of students commute. Alcohol is not permitted. All students may keep cars.

Activities: 19% of men belong to 13 national fraternities; 11% of women belong to 7 national sororities. There are 226 groups on campus, including art, band, cheerleading, chess, choir, chorale, chorus, computers, dance, debate, drama, drill team, ethnic, forensics, honors, international, jazz band, literary magazine, marching band, musical theater, newspaper, orchestra, pep band, photography, political, professional, radio and TV, religious, social, social service, student government, symphony, and yearbook.

Sports: There are 10 intercollegiate sports for men and 11 for women, and 30 intramural sports for men and 30 for women. Facilities include a physical fitness center, a 16,500-seat stadium, 2 gyms seating 6000, gymnastics and weight rooms, an indoor jogging track, racquetball courts, a swimming pool, outdoor tennis, basketball, and volleyball courts, a Parcourse physical fitness trail, and the 8500-seat Regional Special Events Center.

Disabled Students: 96% of the campus is accessible. Wheelchair ramps, elevators, special parking, specially equipped rest rooms, special class scheduling, and lowered drinking fountains are available.

Services: Counseling and information services are available, as is tutoring in most subjects. There is remedial math, reading, and writing.

Campus Safety and Security: Measures include 24-hour foot and vehicle patrol, self-defense education, escort service, and informal discussions. There are pamphlets/posters/films, emergency telephones, and lighted pathways/sidewalks.

Programs of Study: MSU confers B.A., B.S., B.F.A., B.I.S., B.M., B.M.E., B.S.A., B.S.B., B.S.N., B.S.V.T.E., and B.S.W. degrees. Associate and master's degrees are also awarded. Bachelor's degrees are awarded in AGRICULTURE (agricultural mechanics, agriculture, animal science, fishing and fisheries, and horticulture), BIOLOGICAL SCIENCE (biochemistry, biology/biological science, and wildlife biology), BUSINESS (accounting, banking and finance, business administration and management, business economics, marketing/retailing/merchandising, and personnel management), COMMUNICATIONS AND THE ARTS (advertising, broadcasting, communications, dramatic arts, English, fine arts, French, German, journalism, languages, music, Spanish, speech/debate/rhetoric, and telecommunications), COMPUTER AND PHYSICAL SCIENCE (chemistry, computer programming, computer science, earth science, geology, mathematics, and physics), EDUCATION (agricultural, art, business, early childhood, elementary, foreign languages, health, home economics, industrial arts, middle school, music, and secondary), ENGINEERING AND ENVIRONMENTAL DESIGN (civil engineering technology, computer technology, construction technology, electrical/electronics engineering technology, engineering technology, occupational safety and health, and technological management), HEALTH PROFESSIONS (nursing, predentistry, premedicine, speech pathology/audiology, and veterinary science), SOCIAL SCIENCE (criminal justice, crosscultural studies, dietetics, economics, geography, history, liberal arts/general studies, parks and recreation management, philosophy, political science/government, prelaw, psychology, social work, and sociology). Premedicine, engineering, and physics are the strongest academically. Business, nursing, and education are the largest.

Required: All students must complete University Studies requirements, including courses in communications and basic skills, lab sciences and math, humanities and fine arts, social sciences, and foreign language. A total of 128 semester hours, including at least 30 in the major, with a minimum GPA of 2.0 are required to graduate.

Special: MSU offers cooperative programs in all majors, cross-registration through the National Student Exchange, internships, study abroad in 23 countries, work-study, dual majors, B.A.-B.S. degrees, and 3-2 engineering degrees with the University of Louisville and the University of Kentucky. Credit for life experience and a degree in independent studies are also offered. Nondegree study is possible. There are 25 national honor societies, including Phi Beta Kappa, a freshman honors program, and 20 departmental honors program.

Faculty/Classroom: 60% of faculty are male; 40%, female. All teach undergraduates. The average class size in an introductory lecture is 30 and in a laboratory, 25.

Admissions: 88% of the 2001-2002 applicants were accepted. The ACT scores for the 2001-2002 freshman class were: 20% below 21, 30% between 21 and 23, 30% between 24 and 26, 12% between 27 and 28, and 8% above 28. 60% of the current freshmen were in the top fifth of their class; 88% were in the top two fifths. There were 9 National Merit finalists and 11 semifinalists in a recent year. 61 freshmen graduated first in their class.

Requirements: The ACT is required, with a minimum composite score of 18 in-state. In-state residents must rank in the top half of their class; out-of-state applicants must rank in the top half of their class and have a 22 on the ACT or be in the top third and have an 18 on the ACT. Applicants should have completed 22 high school academic credits, including 4 units in English, 3 in math, 2 each in science and social studies, and 9 in electives; in addition, MSU strongly recommends a fourth year of math, 2 of foreign language, and 1 of fine arts. A portfolio or audition is required for art and music majors. An interview is recommended. AP and CLEP credits are accepted. Important factors in the admissions decision are advanced placement or honor courses and leadership record. Applications are available on-line at the school's web site.

Procedure: Freshmen are admitted to all sessions. Entrance exams should be taken before January of the enrollment year. There is an early admissions plan. Applications should be filed by August 1 for fall entry, December 1 for spring entry, and May 1 for summer entry, along with a $25 fee. Notification is sent on a rolling basis.

Transfer: 695 transfer students enrolled in 2001-2002. Applicants must have a minimum GPA of 2.0 in at least 12 hours of degree credit. 24 credits of 128 must be completed at MSU.

Visiting: There are regularly scheduled orientations for prospective students, in the fall and spring. There are guides for informal visits and visitors may sit in on classes and stay overnight. To schedule a visit, contact the School Relations Office at (270) 762-2896 or *paul.radke@murraystate.edu*

Financial Aid: In 2001-2002, 70% of all students received some form of financial aid. 45% of all students received need-based aid. The average freshman award was $4510. Of that total, scholarships or need-based grants averaged $2400 ($6672 maximum); loans averaged $2500 ($2625 maximum); and work contracts averaged $1450 ($2500 maximum). 30% of undergraduates work part time. Average annual earnings from campus work are $1450. The average financial indebtedness of the 2001 graduate was $6900. The FAFSA is required. The fall application deadline is April 1.

International Students: There are 234 international students enrolled. The school actively recruits these students. They must score 500 on the written TOEFL and also take or complete level five in MSU's English Language Institute; they must also take the ACT.

Computers: The mainframe is an IBM. Students may access the mainframe through computer labs in each of 6 colleges and the student center. PCs are available at these locations and throughout the campus, including the residential colleges. All students may access the system. There are no time limits and no fees. It is strongly recommended that all students have a personal computer.

Graduates: In 2001, 1225 bachelor's degrees were awarded. The most popular majors were early elementary education (8%), business administration (6%), and agriculture (5%). In an average class, 32% graduate in 4 years, 40% in 5 years, and 40% in 6 years. 715 companies recruited on campus in 2000-2001.

Admissions Contact: Jim Vaughan, Acting Dean of Admissions and Registrar. E-mail: *jim.vaughan@murraystate.edu*
Web: *http://www.murraystate.edu*

NORTHERN KENTUCKY UNIVERSITY — D-1
Highland Heights, KY 41099 — (859) 572-5220
(800) 637-9948; Fax: (859) 572-6665

Full-time: 7673 men and women	**Faculty:** IIA, --$
Part-time: 3165 men and women	**Ph.D.s:** 82%
Graduate: 871 men and women	**Student/Faculty:** n/av
Year: semesters, summer session	**Tuition:** $2460 ($6708)
Application Deadline: August 1	**Room & Board:** $3892
Freshman Class: n/av	
SAT I or ACT: required	**NONCOMPETITIVE**

Northern Kentucky University, founded in 1968, is a publicly controlled institution offering programs in arts and sciences, business, and professional studies. There are 4 undergraduate and 4 graduate schools. In addition to regional accreditation, NKU has baccalaureate program accreditation with CAHEA, CSWE, NASM, and NLN. The 3 libraries contain 267,257 volumes, 135,257 microform items, and 2133 audiovisual forms/CDs, and subscribe to 4423 periodicals. Computerized library services include the card catalog, interlibrary loans, and database searching. Special learning facilities include a learning resource center, art gallery, radio station, TV station, and a biology and geology museum. The 300-acre campus is in a suburban area 7 miles southeast of Cincinnati, Ohio. Including residence halls, there are 42 buildings.

Student Life: 77% of undergraduates are from Kentucky. Others are from 35 states, 40 foreign countries, and Canada. 80% are white. The average age of freshmen is 20; all undergraduates, 26. 35% do not continue beyond their first year.

Housing: 1140 students can be accommodated in college housing, which includes single-sex and coed dormitories and on-campus apartments. On-campus housing is available on a first-come, first-served basis. Priority is given to out-of-town students. 91% of students commute. Alcohol is not permitted. All students may keep cars.

Activities: 4% of men belong to 6 national fraternities; 4% of women belong to 7 national sororities. There are 80 groups on campus, including art, cheerleading, chorale, chorus, computers, dance, drama, drill team, ethnic, film, gay, honors, international, jazz band, literary magazine, musical theater, newspaper, pep band, photography, political, professional, radio and TV, religious, social, social service, and student government. Popular campus events include Northern Noel, Musicfest, and Kentucky Awareness Week.

Sports: There are 6 intercollegiate sports for men and 5 for women, and 15 intramural sports for men and 13 for women. Facilities include a 2000-seat gym, baseball and soccer fields, tennis and racquetball courts, a track, a weight room, and a swimming pool.

Disabled Students: All of the campus is accessible. Elevators, special parking, specially equipped rest rooms, special class scheduling, lowered drinking fountains, and lowered telephones are available.

Services: Counseling and information services are available, as is tutoring in most subjects. There is a reader service for the blind, and remedial math, reading, and writing. There are also developmental education courses.

Campus Safety and Security: Measures include 24-hour foot and vehicle patrol, escort service, informal discussions, and pamphlets/posters/films. There are emergency telephones and lighted pathways/sidewalks.

Programs of Study: NKU confers B.A., B.S., B.Mus., B.Mus.Ed., B.S.N., and B.S.W. degrees. Associate and master's degrees are also awarded. Bachelor's degrees are awarded in BIOLOGICAL SCIENCE (biology/biological science), BUSINESS (accounting, labor studies, management science, marketing/retailing/merchandising, and organizational behavior), COMMUNICATIONS AND THE ARTS (art, dramatic arts, English, French, graphic design, journalism, music, performing arts, radio/television technology, Spanish, and speech/debate/rhetoric), COMPUTER AND PHYSICAL SCIENCE (chemistry, computer science, geology, information sciences and systems, mathematics, and physics), EDUCATION (art, business, elementary, industrial arts, middle school, physical, science, and secondary), ENGINEERING AND ENVIRONMENTAL DESIGN (construction technology, industrial engineering technology, manufacturing engineering, manufacturing technology, and pre-engineering), HEALTH PROFESSIONS (mental health/human services, nursing, predentistry, premedicine, prepharmacy, and preveterinary science), SOCIAL SCIENCE (anthropology, economics, geography, history, international studies, philosophy, physical fitness/movement, political science/government, prelaw, psychology, public administration, social science, social work, and sociology). Education, nursing, and biology are the largest.

Required: All students must complete 54 semester hours of general studies, including English composition and speech, the arts, computer literacy, history, humanities, math, philosophy, sciences, and social sciences, along with major and minor requirements. A total of 128 semester hours, with a minimum GPA of 2.0, is required to graduate.

Special: A 3-2 engineering degree is offered with the University of Kentucky. Cross-registration is possible through the Greater Cincinnati Area Consortium of colleges and universities. Study abroad in 6 countries, a Washington semester, internships for communication majors, on-campus work-study programs, an accelerated degree program, an interdisciplinary honors program, B.A.-B.S. degrees, dual majors, and pass/fail options are offered. There are co-op programs in most majors. Student-designed majors and credit for work experience are available. Nondegree study is possible. There are 8 national honor societies, and a freshman honors program.

Faculty/Classroom: 52% of faculty are male; 48%, female. All teach undergraduates. No introductory courses are taught by graduate students. The average class size in a regular course is 26.

Requirements: The SAT I or ACT is required. In addition, students who score at least a 20 on the English and math portions of the ACT and who meet all precollege curriculum requirements, including 4 units of English, 3 of math (algebra I, geometry, algebra II), 2 of U.S. history, world civilization (for Kentucky residents only), and 2 of science (biology and chemistry or physics), are granted regular admission. Others may be admitted with a stipulation or restriction on their admission. A high school diploma is required; the GED is accepted. Applications are accepted on-line. AP and CLEP credits are accepted.

Procedure: Freshmen are admitted to all sessions. Entrance exams should be taken prior to enrollment. There are early action, early admissions, and deferred admissions plans. Early action applications should be filed by February 1; regular applications, by August 1 for fall entry, along with a $25 fee. The college accepts all applicants. Notification is sent on a rolling basis.

Transfer: Students must be eligible to return to their previous institution. College transcripts from previous institutions are required. 30 credits of 128 must be completed at NKU.

Visiting: There are regularly scheduled orientations for prospective students, consisting of a 1-day program with sessions on student services and financial aid, activities, a campus tour, and academic information, advising, and registration. There are guides for informal visits and visitors may sit in on classes and stay overnight. To schedule a visit, contact the Office of Admissions at *admit@nku.edu*.

Financial Aid: The average freshman award was $4830. Of that total, scholarships or need-based grants averaged $3000; and loans averaged $2625. 13% of undergraduates work part time. Average annual earnings from campus work are $2423. The average financial indebtedness of the 2001 graduate was $5130. The FAFSA and the college's own financial statement are required. The fall application deadline is April 1.

International Students: The school actively recruits these students. They must score 500 on the written TOEFL or take the MELAB.

Computers: The mainframes are a DEC VAX 4600 and an AXP 4600. Students can access the mainframes via 24 terminals in central computing labs and 10 in specific departments. There are 185 PCs in central labs and 30 dial-in modem lines available. All students may access the system 7 days a week. There are no time limits. The fee $15 per semester.

Graduates: In 2001, 1142 bachelor's degrees were awarded. The most popular majors were marketing/business (21%), education (18%), and social science/history (9%). In an average class, 36% graduate in 6 years. 102 companies recruited on campus in 2000-2001.

Admissions Contact: Melissa Gorbrandt, Admissions Director of Admissions. E-mail: *gorbrandt@nku.edu* Web: *www.nku.edu*

PIKEVILLE COLLEGE

Pikeville, KY 41501 F-3

(606) 218-5251

(866) 232-7700; Fax: (606) 218-5255

Full-time: 376 men, 515 women	**Faculty:** 61; IIB, --$
Part-time: 15 men, 42 women	**Ph.D.s:** 44%
Graduate: 162 men, 84 women	**Student/Faculty:** 15 to 1
Year: semesters, summer session	**Tuition:** $8200
Application Deadline: August 23	**Room & Board:** $3800
Freshman Class: 794 applied, 794 accepted, 360 enrolled	
SAT I Verbal/Math: 360/360	**ACT:** 18 **NONCOMPETITIVE**

Pikeville College, established as a boarding school in 1889, is a private liberal arts institution affiliated with the Presbyterian Church (U.S.A.). The 2 libraries contain 77,795 volumes, 31,451 microform items, and 1598 audiovisual forms/CDs, and subscribe to 309 periodicals. Computerized library services include the card catalog, interlibrary loans, and database searching. Special learning facilities include an art gallery. The 27-acre campus is in a small town 20 miles from the Virginia border in the eastern Kentucky hills. Including residence halls, there are 10 buildings.

Student Life: 82% of undergraduates are from Kentucky. Others are from 18 states and 14 foreign countries. 99% are from public schools. 89% are white. 85% are Protestant; 10% claim no religious affiliation. The average age of freshmen is 20; all undergraduates, 22. 39% do not continue beyond their first year; 25% remain to graduate.

Housing: 495 students can be accommodated in college housing, which includes single-sex and coed dormitories, on-campus apartments, and married-student housing. On-campus housing is guaranteed for all 4 years. 50% of students live on campus; of those, 10% remain on campus on weekends. Alcohol is not permitted. All students may keep cars.

Activities: There are no fraternities or sororities. There are 25 groups on campus, including band, cheerleading, choir, chorus, computers, dance, debate, drama, honors, jazz band, literary magazine, newspaper, pep band, political, professional, religious, social service, student government, and yearbook. Popular campus events include Founders Day.

Sports: There are 7 intercollegiate sports for men and 7 for women, and 10 intramural sports for men and 10 for women. Facilities include a gym, basketball and volleyball courts, tennis courts, and softball and baseball fields.

Disabled Students: 90% of the campus is accessible. Wheelchair ramps, elevators, special parking, specially equipped rest rooms, lowered drinking fountains, and an elevator from the main parking lot to the upper campus are available.

Services: Counseling and information services are available, as is tutoring in most subjects, including math, English, biology, all physical sciences, and computers. There is remedial math, reading, and writing.

Campus Safety and Security: Measures include 24-hour foot and vehicle patrol, self-defense education, escort service, and shuttle buses. There are informal discussions, pamphlets/posters/films, lighted pathways/sidewalks, and night security guards.

Programs of Study: PC confers B.A., B.S., and B.B.A. degrees. Associate and doctoral degrees are also awarded. Bachelor's degrees are awarded in BIOLOGICAL SCIENCE (biology/biological science), BUSINESS (business administration and management), COMMUNICATIONS AND THE ARTS (art and English), COMPUTER AND PHYSICAL SCIENCE (chemistry, computer science, and mathematics), EDUCATION (elementary, middle school, and secondary), HEALTH PROFESSIONS (medical technology), SOCIAL SCIENCE (criminal justice, history, human services, psychology, religion, social science, and sociology). Business, psychology, and education are the largest.

Required: All students must complete core courses in humanities, English, social sciences, natural sciences, and math, as well as 2 courses each in religion, phys ed, and history, and 1 course in computer science. Additional requirements include 6 hours in a foreign language for the B.A. degree and 2 lab science courses for the B.S. degree. An overall GPA of 2.0 is required. To graduate, students must complete 128 semester hours, with 30 to 60 hours in the major.

Special: Students may earn up to 6 credits at other institutions while enrolled at the college. A 3-1 degree in medical technology is available in conjunction with the Pikeville College School of Osteopathic Medicine. Internships, B.A.-B.S. degrees, credit for life, military, and work experience, and pass/fail options are offered. Nondegree study is possible. There are 3 national honor societies, a freshman honors program, and 1 departmental honors program.

Faculty/Classroom: 48% of faculty are male; 52%, female. All teach undergraduates and 10% both teach and do research. No introductory courses are taught by graduate students. The average class size in an introductory lecture is 25; in a laboratory, 20; and in a regular course, 15.

Admissions: 100% of the 2001-2002 applicants were accepted. The SAT I scores for the 2001-2002 freshman class were: Verbal--92% below 500, and 8% between 500 and 599; Math--100% below 500. The ACT scores were 67% below 21, 17% between 21 and 23, 10% between 24 and 26, 5% between 27 and 28, and 1% above 28. 22 freshmen graduated first in their class.

Requirements: The ACT is required. In addition, applicants must graduate from an accredited secondary school or have a GED. An interview is recommended. AP and CLEP credits are accepted. Applications are accepted on-line at the college's web site.

Procedure: Freshmen are admitted to all sessions. Entrance exams should be taken in October of the year preceding entry. There are early admissions and deferred admissions plans. Applications should be filed by August 23 for fall entry, January 17 for spring entry, and June for summer entry. The college accepts all applicants. Notification is sent on a rolling basis.

Transfer: 97 transfer students enrolled in 2001-2002. All college transcripts and a review of students on suspension and probation are required. 30 credits of 128 must be completed at PC.

Visiting: There are regularly scheduled orientations for prospective students, consisting of a campus tour and lunch. There are guides for informal visits and visitors may sit in on classes and stay overnight. To schedule a visit, contact Melinda Lynch.

Financial Aid: In a recent year, 98% of all freshmen and 91% of continuing students received some form of financial aid. 93% of freshmen and 89% of continuing students received need-based aid. The average

freshman award was $2500. Of that total, scholarships or need-based grants averaged $3500 ($7000 maximum); loans averaged $2850 ($5500 maximum); and work contracts averaged $800 ($1600 maximum). 87% of undergraduates work part time. Average annual earnings from campus work are $800. The average financial indebtedness of the 2001 graduate was $10,000. The FAFSA and the college's own financial statement are required. The fall application deadline is March 15.

International Students: There are 24 international students enrolled. They must score 500 on the written TOEFL and also take the SAT I or ACT for placement purposes only.

Computers: The mainframe is an IBM AS/400. There are 72 PCs available on campus, all with access to the Internet and World Wide Web through a campus network. All students may access the system 8 A.M. to 11 P.M. There are no time limits and no fees.

Graduates: In 2001, 96 bachelor's degrees were awarded. The most popular majors were business (19%), biology (17%), and psychology/human services (14%). In an average class, 3% graduate in 3 years, 20% in 4 years, 33% in 5 years, and 35% in 6 years. 150 companies recruited on campus in 2000-2001. Of the 2000 graduating class, 5% were enrolled in graduate school within 6 months of graduation and 75% were employed.

Admissions Contact: Melinda Lynch, Director of Admissions. E-mail: *wewantyou@pc.edu* Web: *http://www.pc.edu*

SPALDING UNIVERSITY

Louisville, KY 40203-2188 — D-2 — (502) 585-7111
(800) 896-8941, ext. 2111; Fax: (502) 992-2418

Full-time: 629 men and women	**Faculty:** 58
Part-time: 157 men and women	**Ph.D.s:** 67%
Graduate: 531 men and women	**Student/Faculty:** 11 to 1
Year: terms, summer session	**Tuition:** $12,096
Application Deadline: August 1	**Room & Board:** $3100
Freshman Class: 521 applied, 491 accepted, 258 enrolled	
ACT: 21	**COMPETITIVE**

Spalding University, established in 1814, is a private institution affiliated with the Roman Catholic Church and offers undergraduate degrees in the arts, business, health sciences, professional training, religious studies, and teacher preparation. Some information in this profile is approximate. There are 5 undergraduate and 4 graduate schools. In addition to regional accreditation, Spalding has baccalaureate program accreditation with CSWE, NCATE, and NLN. The library contains 220,232 volumes, 16,246 microform items, and 8669 audiovisual forms/CDs, and subscribes to 601 periodicals. Computerized library services include the card catalog, interlibrary loans, and database searching. Special learning facilities include a learning resource center, an art gallery, video production facilities, an audio recording studio, and a digital media center. The 5-acre campus is in an urban area in downtown Louisville. Including residence halls, there are 8 buildings.

Student Life: 80% of undergraduates are from Kentucky. Others are from 33 states, 25 foreign countries, and Canada. 85% are from public schools. 78% are white; 13%, African American. 34% are Catholic; 33%, Protestant; 30% claim no religious affiliation. The average age of freshmen is 22; all undergraduates, 26. 35% do not continue beyond their first year; 65% remain to graduate.

Housing: 276 students can be accommodated in college housing, which includes coed dormitories. On-campus housing is guaranteed for all 4 years. 84% of students commute. Alcohol is not permitted. All students may keep cars.

Activities: There are no fraternities or sororities. There are 20 groups on campus, including art, cheerleading, choir, chorus, drama, ethnic, honors, international, literary magazine, newspaper, photography, political, professional, religious, social, social service, and student government. Popular campus events include Halloween Dance, the Rat Race, and Moonlight in the Mansion.

Sports: There are 3 intercollegiate sports for men and 4 for women, and 2 intramural sports for men and 2 for women. Facilities include a gym and an exercise room.

Disabled Students: 95% of the campus is accessible. Wheelchair ramps, elevators, special parking, specially equipped rest rooms, special class scheduling, lowered drinking fountains, note takers, extended test-taking time, oral testing, and special classroom accommodations are available.

Services: Counseling and information services are available, as is tutoring in every subject. There is a reader service for the blind.

Campus Safety and Security: Measures include self-defense education, escort service, informal discussions, and pamphlets/posters/films. There are emergency telephones, lighted pathways/sidewalks, and direct access to campus security via "2180" number from campus phones.

Programs of Study: Spalding confers B.A., B.S., B.S.B.A., B.S.C.S., B.S.Ed., B.S.El.Ed., B.S.N., B.S.O.T., and B.S.S.W. degrees. Associate, master's, and doctoral degrees are also awarded. Bachelor's degrees are awarded in BIOLOGICAL SCIENCE (biology/biological science), BUSINESS (accounting and business administration and management), COMMUNICATIONS AND THE ARTS (art, communications, and English), COMPUTER AND PHYSICAL SCIENCE (chemistry, computer science, and mathematics), EDUCATION (early childhood, education, elementary, middle school, and secondary), HEALTH PROFESSIONS (clinical science, nursing, and occupational therapy), SOCIAL SCIENCE (history, liberal arts/general studies, ministries, pastoral studies, philosophy, psychology, religion, social studies, social work, and sociology). Nursing, education, and psychology are the strongest academically. Nursing, education, business, and occupational therapy are the largest.

Required: To graduate, students must earn 128 credits, with a maximum of 40 credits in the major for the B.A. degree and 50 credits for the B.S. degree, and a minimum overall GPA of 2.0. All students must complete a university studies requirement of 15 credits in humanities, 15 credits in social sciences, 12 credits in commnication, 9 credits in natural sciences and math, 6 credits in religious studies, and a 1-credit general introduction to the college.

Special: Cross-registration is offered with the Kentuckiana Metroversity consortium. Internships, primarily in communications and education, and work-study programs are available. Study abroad, B.A.-B.S. degrees, dual and student-designed majors, and a liberal studies degree are offered. Credit is given for life, military, or work experience, and pass/fail options are available. Weekend College enables students to earn a bachelor's degree by attending classes only on weekends. There are 6 national honor societies.

Faculty/Classroom: 38% of faculty are male; 62%, female. 83% teach undergraduates. No introductory courses are taught by graduate students. The average class size in an introductory lecture is 20; in a laboratory, 10; and in a regular course, 20.

Admissions: 94% of the 2001-2002 applicants were accepted. 2 freshmen graduated first in their class in a recent year.

Requirements: The SAT I or ACT is required. In addition, applicants must be graduates of an accredited secondary school and should have completed 4 years of high school English and 2 years each of a foreign language, math, science, and social studies. A GED may be substituted for the high school degree. A GPA of 2.5 is required. AP and CLEP credits are accepted. Important factors in the admissions decision are advanced placement or honor courses, recommendations by school officials, and evidence of special talent. Applications are accepted on-line.

Procedure: Freshmen are admitted to all sessions. Entrance exams should be taken by August 1. There is an early admissions plan. Applications should be filed by August 1 for fall entry and December 1 for spring entry, along with a $20 fee. Notification is sent on a rolling basis.

Transfer: 96 transfer students enrolled in a recent year. It is preferred that applicants have a 2.5 GPA, but special circumstances will be considered. 32 credits of 128 must be completed at Spalding.

Visiting: There are regularly scheduled orientations for prospective students. There are guides for informal visits and visitors may sit in on classes and stay overnight. To schedule a visit, contact Gayle Milam.

Financial Aid: In a recent year, 86% of all freshmen and 94% of continuing students received some form of financial aid. 48% of freshmen and 58% of continuing students received need-based aid. The average freshman award was $10,485. Of that total, scholarships or need-based grants averaged $5768 ($13,090 maximum); loans averaged $3660 ($6625 maximum); and work contracts averaged $1613 ($2475 maximum). 13% of undergraduates work part time. Average annual earnings from campus work are $1663. The average financial indebtedness of a recent graduate was $15,106. Spalding is a member of CSS. The FAFSA and the college's own financial statement are required. Check with the school for current deadlines.

International Students: In a recent year, there were 88 international students enrolled. The school actively recruits these students. They must score 535 on the written TOEFL or 203 on the electronic version and also take the SAT I or the ACT, scoring 19 on the ACT.

Computers: The mainframe is an HP 3000. 106 PCs are available for student use. Spalding maintains 6 computer labs and a digital media center, as well as computer access in the library. Most computers have access to the Internet and a variety of network software applications. All students may access the system. There are no time limits and no fees. It is strongly recommended that all students have a personal computer.

Graduates: In a recent year, 174 bachelor's degrees were awarded. The most popular majors were nursing/ occupational therapy (40%), education (16%), and business communication (11%). In an average class, 34% graduate in 4 years, 45% in 5 years, and 47% in 6 years. 10 companies recruited on campus in a recent year.

Admissions Contact: Kate Harrison, Executive Director of Admission. E-mail: *admissions@spalding.edu* Web: *www.spalding.edu*

THOMAS MORE COLLEGE D-1
Crestview Hills, KY 41017-3495 (606) 344-3332
(800) 825-4557; Fax: (606) 344-3638

Full-time: 540 men, 440 women	**Faculty:** 77; IIB, --$
Part-time: 125 men, 307 women	**Ph.D.s:** 68%
Graduate: 76 men, 57 women	**Student/Faculty:** 13 to 1
Year: semesters, summer session	**Tuition:** $13,550
Application Deadline: August 15	**Room & Board:** $4150

Freshman Class: 1288 applied, 981 accepted, 306 enrolled
SAT I or ACT: required **LESS COMPETITIVE**

Thomas More College, founded in 1921 as Villa Madonna College, is a private Catholic institution offering undergraduate programs in liberal arts and sciences, and an MBA in business administration. In addition to regional accreditation, Thomas More has baccalaureate program accreditation with NLN. The library contains 126,923 volumes, 49,145 microform items, and 2136 audiovisual forms/CDs, and subscribes to 606 periodicals. Computerized library services include the card catalog, interlibrary loans, and database searching. Special learning facilities include a learning resource center and art gallery. The 100-acre campus is in a suburban area 8 miles south of Cincinnati. Including residence halls, there are 8 buildings.

Student Life: 66% of undergraduates are from Kentucky. Others are from 12 states and 9 foreign countries. 71% are from public schools. 90% are white. 37% are Catholic; 19%, Protestant. The average age of freshmen is 18; all undergraduates, 26. 32% do not continue beyond their first year; 51% remain to graduate.

Housing: 250 students can be accommodated in college housing, which includes single-sex and coed dormitories. On-campus housing is available on a first-come, first-served basis. Priority is given to out-of-town students. 80% of students commute. All students may keep cars.

Activities: There are no fraternities or sororities. There are 29 groups on campus, including art, cheerleading, computers, debate, drama, ethnic, honors, international, literary magazine, newspaper, political, professional, religious, social, social service, and student government. Popular campus events include fall and spring formals, Spring Pig Roast, and International Awareness Week.

Sports: There are 6 intercollegiate sports for men and 6 for women, and 6 intramural sports for men and 6 for women. Facilities include an athletic/convocation center with a 1,500-seat indoor gym and a 2,100-seat arena, plus baseball, football, softball, and soccer fields, 16 tennis courts (8 indoor), 4 racquetball courts, an indoor pool, a track, and weight and exercise rooms.

Disabled Students: 99% of the campus is accessible. Wheelchair ramps, elevators, special parking, and specially equipped rest rooms are available.

Services: Counseling and information services are available, as is tutoring in every subject. There is a reader service for the blind, remedial math, reading, and writing, and signing for the hearing impaired.

Campus Safety and Security: Measures include 24-hour foot and vehicle patrol, self-defense education, escort service, and informal discussions. There are pamphlets/posters/films and lighted pathways/sidewalks.

Programs of Study: Thomas More confers B.A., B.S., B.B.A., B.E.S., and B.S.N. degrees. Associate and master's degrees are also awarded. Bachelor's degrees are awarded in BIOLOGICAL SCIENCE (biology/biological science), BUSINESS (accounting and business administration and management), COMMUNICATIONS AND THE ARTS (art, communications, dramatic arts, English, fine arts, and speech/debate/rhetoric), COMPUTER AND PHYSICAL SCIENCE (chemistry, computer science, mathematics, and physics), EDUCATION (elementary, middle school, and secondary), HEALTH PROFESSIONS (medical laboratory technology and nursing), SOCIAL SCIENCE (criminal justice, economics, history, international studies, liberal arts/general studies, philosophy, psychology, sociology, and theological studies). Business, biology, and information systems are the largest.

Required: All students must complete 56 to 61 hours of core requirements, including 6 credits each in English, theology, social sciences, global history, fine arts, philosophy, and natural sciences, and 3 each in foreign language, speech, and math. A total of 128 credit hours, including 36 to 76 in the major, with a minimum GPA of 2.0 is required to graduate.

Special: There are co-op programs in all majors but nursing and education and 3-2 engineering degrees with the universities of Cincinnati, Dayton, Detroit, Kentucky, and Notre Dame. Cross-registration is possible through the Greater Cincinnati Consortium. The college offers dual majors in international studies with a second major of the student's choice. There are also internships, study abroad in 10 countries, B.A.-B.S. degrees, student-designed majors, work-study programs, credit for life experience, and pass/fail options. The Bachelor of Elected Studies degree provides adult learners with an individualized program. Nondegree study is possible. There are 6 national honor societies, a freshman honors program, and departmental honors programs.

Faculty/Classroom: 54% of faculty are male; 46%, female. All teach undergraduates. No introductory courses are taught by graduate students. The average class size in an introductory lecture is 20; in a laboratory, 10; and in a regular course, 13.

Admissions: 76% of the 2001-2002 applicants were accepted. 22% of the current freshmen were in the top fifth of their class; 45% were in the top two fifths. 1 freshman graduated first in class.

Requirements: The SAT I or ACT is required, and the minimum composite score needed is 1010 on the SAT I or 20 on the ACT. Applicants should have completed 16 high school academic credits, including 4 years of English and 2 each of math, science, social studies, and foreign language. Thomas More requires applicants to be in the upper 50% of their class. A GPA of 2.0 is required. AP and CLEP credits are accepted. Important factors in the admissions decision are advanced placement or honor courses, leadership record, and personality/intangible qualities. The registration fee is waived for students who apply on-lilne through the school's web site.

Procedure: Freshmen are admitted to all sessions. Entrance exams should be taken in the spring of the junior year or in the fall of the senior year. There are early admissions and deferred admissions plans. Applications should be filed by August 15 for fall entry and January 5 for spring entry, along with a $25 fee. Notification is sent on a rolling basis.

Transfer: 32 transfer students enrolled in 2001-2002. Applicants should be in good academic standing and have a minimum GPA of 2.0 in 24 semester hours earned. 38 credits of 128 must be completed at Thomas More.

Visiting: There are regularly scheduled orientations for prospective students, including a campus tour and meetings with an admissions counselor, a professor in one's major field (if decided), and financial aid staff. There are guides for informal visits and visitors may sit in on classes and stay overnight. To schedule a visit, contact the Admissions Office.

Financial Aid: In 2001-2002, 100% of all freshmen and 90% of continuing students received some form of financial aid. 85% of all students received need-based aid. The average freshman award was $9500. Of that total, scholarships or need-based grants averaged $2970 ($13,200 maximum); loans averaged $3400 ($6625 maximum); work contracts averaged $1700; and Kentucky State funds $1430 ($3060 maximum). 90% of undergraduates work part time. Average annual earnings from campus work are $1700. The average financial indebtedness of the 2001 graduate was $21,000. Thomas More is a member of CSS. The FAFSA and the college's own financial statement are required. The fall application deadline is March 15.

International Students: There are 13 international students enrolled. The school actively recruits these students. They must score 515 on the written TOEFL.

Computers: The mainframe is an HP K-9000. There are also 105 PCs available in labs and classrooms, and ports available in dorms. All students may access the system anytime. There are no time limits. The fee is $125 per semester. It is recommended that students in accelerated degree programs for BBA and MBA degrees have personal computers.

Graduates: In 2001, 245 bachelor's degrees were awarded. The most popular majors were business (49%), biology (8%), and nursing (7%). In an average class, 1% graduate in 3 years, 37% in 4 years, 51% in 5 years, and 53% in 6 years. 84 companies recruited on campus in 2000-2001. Of the 2000 graduating class, 22% were enrolled in graduate school within 6 months of graduation and 78% were employed.

Admissions Contact: Bob McDermott, Director of Admissions. A video is available. E-mail: *robert.mcdermott@thomasmore.edu*
Web: *www.thomasmore.edu*

TRANSYLVANIA UNIVERSITY D-3
Lexington, KY 40508-1797 (859) 233-8242
(800) 872-6798; Fax: (859) 233-8797

Full-time: 453 men, 592 women	**Faculty:** 76; IIB, av$
Part-time: 4 men, 3 women	**Ph.D.s:** 97%
Graduate: none	**Student/Faculty:** 14 to 1
Year: 4-4-1, summer session	**Tuition:** $16,010
Application Deadline: March 1	**Room & Board:** $5770

Freshman Class: 1092 applied, 964 accepted, 306 enrolled
SAT I Verbal/Math: 610/600 **ACT:** 26 **VERY COMPETITIVE+**

Transylvania University, founded in 1780, is an independent liberal arts institution affiliated with the Christian Church (Disciples of Christ). In addition to regional accreditation, Transylvania has baccalaureate program accreditation with NCATE. The library contains 118,000 volumes, 65 microform items, and 1768 audiovisual forms/CDs, and subscribes to 540 periodicals. Computerized library services include the card catalog, interlibrary loans, and database searching. Special learning facilities include a learning resource center, art gallery, natural history museum, and radio station. The 48-acre campus is in an urban area 80 miles east of Louisville and 80 miles south of Cincinnati, Ohio. Including residence halls, there are 23 buildings.

Student Life: 82% of undergraduates are from Kentucky. Others are from 31 states and 3 foreign countries. 84% are from public schools. 93% are white. 63% are Protestant; 20% claim no religious affiliation; 15%, Catholic. The average age of freshmen is 17; all undergraduates,

20. 20% do not continue beyond their first year; 70% remain to graduate.

Housing: 900 students can be accommodated in college housing, which includes single-sex and coed dormitories and on-campus apartments. In addition, there are language houses. On-campus housing is guaranteed for all 4 years. 80% of students live on campus; of those, 85% remain on campus on weekends. All students may keep cars.

Activities: 60% of men belong to 4 national fraternities; 60% of women belong to 4 national sororities. There are 51 groups on campus, including art, band, cheerleading, choir, chorus, computers, dance, debate, drama, ethnic, forensics, gay, honors, international, jazz band, literary magazine, musical theater, newspaper, orchestra, pep band, political, professional, radio and TV, religious, social, social service, student government, and yearbook. Popular campus events include the Presentation Ball, Madrigal Dinner, and the Kenan Lecture Series.

Sports: There are 7 intercollegiate sports for men and 9 for women, and 10 intramural sports for men and 10 for women. Facilities include a 1300-seat performance gym, 2 recreation gyms, a dance/aerobics room, an indoor jogging track, a swimming pool, basketball and racquetball/handball courts, 6 tennis courts, 3 athletic fields (baseball, men's soccer/field hockey, and women's soccer/softball), and weight and fitness rooms.

Disabled Students: 90% of the campus is accessible. Wheelchair ramps, elevators, special parking, specially equipped rest rooms, special class scheduling, and lowered drinking fountains are available. Arrangements are made according to individual needs.

Services: Counseling and information services are available, as is tutoring in every subject.

Campus Safety and Security: Measures include 24-hour foot and vehicle patrol, self-defense education, escort service, and shuttle buses. There are informal discussions, pamphlets/posters/films, emergency telephones, lighted pathways/sidewalks, and a security presentation during freshman orientation.

Programs of Study: Transylvania confers the B.A. degree. Bachelor's degrees are awarded in BIOLOGICAL SCIENCE (biology/biological science), BUSINESS (accounting and business administration and management), COMMUNICATIONS AND THE ARTS (dramatic arts, English, French, music, Spanish, and studio art), COMPUTER AND PHYSICAL SCIENCE (chemistry, computer science, mathematics, and physics), EDUCATION (elementary and middle school), HEALTH PROFESSIONS (exercise science), SOCIAL SCIENCE (economics, history, philosophy, political science/government, psychology, religion, and sociology). Business, biology, and psychology are the largest.

Required: All students must complete general education requirements in foundations of the liberal arts, academic career skills, humanities, lifetime fitness, fine arts, natural sciences, math, Western and non-Western cultural traditions, social sciences, and foreign language. 4 upper-level liberal arts classes are also required. A total of 36 course units, including 10 to 14 in the major, with a minimum GPA of 2.0, is required to graduate.

Special: 3-2 engineering degrees with the University of Kentucky, Vanderbilt University, and Washington University in St. Louis are offered. Cross-registration with May Term Consortium schools, internships, study abroad in many countries, work-study programs, a Washington semester, dual majors, and student-designed majors are available. There are 9 national honor societies.

Faculty/Classroom: 62% of faculty are male; 38%, female. All teach undergraduates. The average class size in an introductory lecture is 20; in a laboratory, 12; and in a regular course, 18.

Admissions: 88% of the 2001-2002 applicants were accepted. The SAT I scores for the 2001-2002 freshman class were: Verbal--15% below 500, 36% between 500 and 599, 34% between 600 and 700, and 15% above 700; Math--17% below 500, 32% between 500 and 599, 40% between 600 and 700, and 11% above 700. The ACT scores were 7% below 21, 14% between 21 and 23, 27% between 24 and 26, 23% between 27 and 28, and 29% above 28. 76% of the current freshmen were in the top fifth of their class; 94% were in the top two fifths. There were 4 National Merit finalists and 1 semifinalist. 40 freshmen graduated first in their class.

Requirements: The SAT I or ACT is required. In addition, 1 essay and 2 recommendations are required. An interview is strongly recommended. Transylvania requires applicants to be in the upper 50% of their class. A GPA of 2.75 is required. AP credits are accepted. Important factors in the admissions decision are advanced placement or honor courses, recommendations by school officials, and extracurricular activities record. Applications are available on-line at the university's web site.

Procedure: Freshmen are admitted fall and winter. Entrance exams should be taken during the junior year; no later than December of the senior year for scholarship consideration or February for general admission. There are early admissions and deferred admissions plans. Applications should be filed by March 1 for fall entry and December 5 for winter entry. Notification is sent on a rolling basis. A waiting list is an active part of the admissions procedure. The fall 2001 application fee was $20.

Transfer: 18 transfer students enrolled in 2001-2002. Applicants must have a minimum GPA of 2.75 and should submit official copies of all college transcripts, 2 recommendations, and 1 essay. A high school transcript or GED is required. 18 credits of 36 must be completed at Transylvania.

Visiting: There are regularly scheduled orientations for prospective students, consisting of campus open houses in fall and winter for high school juniors and seniors, including a welcome program, an academic information fair, campus tours, a luncheon, and a financial aid session. There are guides for informal visits and visitors may sit in on classes and stay overnight. To schedule a visit, contact Amy Drake at *adrake@transy.edu*

Financial Aid: In 2001-2002, 99% of all freshmen and 97% of continuing students received some form of financial aid. 57% of freshmen and 59% of continuing students received need-based aid. The average freshman award was $13,766. Of that total, scholarships or need-based grants averaged $10,811 ($21,780 maximum); loans averaged $1902 ($4625 maximum); and work contracts averaged $1153 ($2000 maximum). 45% of undergraduates work part time. Average annual earnings from campus work are $1210. The average financial indebtedness of the 2001 graduate was $13,910. Transylvania is a member of CSS. The FAFSA is required. The fall application deadline is March 1.

International Students: There are 4 international students enrolled. They must score 550 on the written TOEFL or 213 on the electronic version. They must also take the TWE and the SAT I or the ACT, scoring 1030 on the SAT I or 21 on the ACT.

Computers: The mainframe is an IBM 4381. There are about 60 terminals accessing the mainframe and 220 PCs in 8 computer labs available for student use. Word processing, programming languages, statistical software packages, e-mail, and the Internet are available. Computing facilities are available in all academic buildings and residence halls. Students can also access the campus network and the Internet from their dorm rooms. All students may access the system 24 hours a day. There are no time limits and no fees. It is strongly recommended that all students have a personal computer.

Graduates: In 2001, 237 bachelor's degrees were awarded. The most popular majors were business administration (26%), biology (12%), and psychology (10%). In an average class, 1% graduate in 3 years, 60% in 4 years, 65% in 5 years, and 67% in 6 years. 13 companies recruited on campus in 2000-2001. Of the 2000 graduating class, 44% were enrolled in graduate school within 6 months of graduation and 52% were employed.

Admissions Contact: Sarah Coen, Director of Admissions. A video is available. E-mail: *admissions@transy.edu* Web: *www.transy.edu*

UNION COLLEGE
Barbourville, KY 40906-9989 — E-4

(606) 546-4151, ext. 1229
(800) 489-8646; Fax: (606) 546-1667

Full-time: 263 men, 262 women	**Faculty:** 46
Part-time: 11 men, 40 women	**Ph.D.s:** 63%
Graduate: 108 men, 163 women	**Student/Faculty:** 11 to 1
Year: semesters, summer session	**Tuition:** $11,770
Application Deadline: open	**Room & Board:** $4150
Freshman Class: n/av	
SAT I or ACT: required	**COMPETITIVE**

Union College, founded in 1879, is a private liberal arts institution affiliated with the United Methodist Church. The library contains 107,707 volumes, 418,730 microform items, and 5131 audiovisual forms/CDs, and subscribes to 2451 periodicals. Computerized library services include the card catalog, interlibrary loans, and database searching. Special learning facilities include a learning resource center. The 100-acre campus is in a small town 95 miles south of Lexington and 85 north of Knoxville, Tennessee. Including residence halls, there are 20 buildings.

Student Life: 69% of undergraduates are from Kentucky. Others are from 26 states and 12 foreign countries. 93% are from public schools. 80% are white; 13%, African American. 65% are Protestant; 11%, Catholic. The average age of freshmen is 19; all undergraduates, 24. 30% do not continue beyond their first year; 47% remain to graduate.

Housing: 415 students can be accommodated in college housing, which includes single-sex and coed dormitories, on-campus apartments, and married-student housing. On-campus housing is guaranteed for all 4 years. 53% of students commute. Alcohol is not permitted. All students may keep cars.

Activities: There are no fraternities or sororities. There are 20 groups on campus, including band, cheerleading, chess, choir, chorale, chorus, computers, drama, ethnic, honors, international, literary magazine, newspaper, orchestra, pep band, professional, religious, social, social service, and student government. Popular campus events include Daniel Boone Festival, Halloween and Valentine dances, and Wilson-Gross lecture series.

Sports: There are 6 intercollegiate sports for men and 6 for women, and 5 intramural sports for men and 3 for women. Facilities include a 2800-seat campus stadium, a 3000-seat gym, an indoor pool, tennis courts, a weight training center, an athletic training center, a baseball stadium, and fields for football, soccer, and softball.

Disabled Students: 80% of the campus is accessible. Wheelchair ramps, elevators, special parking, specially equipped rest rooms, special class scheduling, lowered drinking fountains, and lowered telephones are available.
Services: Counseling and information services are available, as is tutoring in most subjects. There is a tutoring lab with computer support.
Campus Safety and Security: Measures include 24-hour foot and vehicle patrol, self-defense education, escort service, and informal discussions. There are pamphlets/posters/films, emergency telephones, and lighted pathways/sidewalks.
Programs of Study: Union confers B.A., B.S., and B.Mus. degrees. Associate and master's degrees are also awarded. Bachelor's degrees are awarded in BIOLOGICAL SCIENCE (biology/biological science), BUSINESS (accounting, business administration and management, and sports management), COMMUNICATIONS AND THE ARTS (dramatic arts, English, and music), COMPUTER AND PHYSICAL SCIENCE (physics), EDUCATION (business, elementary, middle school, music, secondary, and special), SOCIAL SCIENCE (criminal justice, history, and psychology). Education, sciences, and social sciences are the strongest academically. Education, business, and social sciences are the largest.
Required: All students are required to complete a 46-credit liberal education core, including 12 to 13 hours each in basic competencies and humanities, 9 in history/behavioral sciences, and 7 to 8 in natural sciences. English composition and 3 hours of phys ed also are required. A total of 128 semester hours, including 30 in the major, with a minimum GPA of 2.0 is required to graduate.
Special: A 3-2 engineering degree is offered with the University of Kentucky, and Auburn University. Work-study programs, study abroad in 6 countries, and internships in business, sociology, and psychology are available. A 16-credit Appalachian studies semester, dual majors, a general studies degree, and credit for life and work experience are also offered.
Faculty/Classroom: 59% of faculty are male; 41%, female. 94% teach undergraduates and 2% both teach and do research. No introductory courses are taught by graduate students. The average class size in an introductory lecture is 25; in a laboratory, 16; and in a regular course, 15.
Admissions: 16% of the current freshmen were in the top fifth of their class; 37% were in the top two fifths. 3 freshmen graduated first in their class.
Requirements: The SAT I or ACT is required. In addition, applicants should present 20 academic credits, including 4 years in English, 3 in math, and 2 each in science, social studies, and history, as well as electives. An interview or audition is recommended. Union requires applicants to be in the upper 50% of their class. A GPA of 2.0 is required. AP and CLEP credits are accepted. Important factors in the admissions decision are evidence of special talent, geographic diversity, and advanced placement or honor courses. Applications are accepted on-line.
Procedure: Freshmen are admitted to all sessions. Entrance exams should be taken by January of the senior year. There is a deferred admissions plan. Application deadlines are open. The application fee is $20. Notification is sent on a rolling basis.
Transfer: 88 transfer students enrolled in 2001-2002. Applicants should have a minimum GPA of 2.0. 30 credits of 128 must be completed at Union.
Visiting: There are regularly scheduled orientations for prospective students, consisting of advising and registration, parents sessions, and break-out sessions. There are guides for informal visits and visitors may sit in on classes and stay overnight. To schedule a visit, contact Admissions at *www.unionky.edu*
Financial Aid: In 2001-2002, 95% of all freshmen and 90% of continuing students received some form of financial aid. 90% of freshmen and 81% of continuing students received need-based aid. The average freshman award was $12,061. Of that total, scholarships or need-based grants averaged $9052 ($15,970 maximum); loans averaged $2552 ($2625 maximum); and work contracts averaged $955 ($1000 maximum). 45% of undergraduates work part time. Average annual earnings from campus work are $760. The average financial indebtedness of the 2001 graduate was $11,283. Union is a member of CSS. The CSS/Profile or FAFSA is required. The fall application deadline is March 15.
International Students: There are 32 international students enrolled. The school actively recruits these students. They must score 550 on the written TOEFL or 219 on the electronic version or take the MELAB or the college's own test, and also complete an ELS program at level 109.
Computers: The mainframes are an HP3000, an AT&T, and a UNIX-based super micro. There are 55 terminals in the science center and main classroom buildings, 20 Macs in English writing labs, and 25 Internet workstations in the library. All students may access the system. There are no time limits and no fees.
Graduates: In 2001, 108 bachelor's degrees were awarded. The most popular majors were education (30%), business (19%), and psychology (10%). In an average class, 16% graduate in 4 years, 27% in 5 years, and 30% in 6 years. 6 companies recruited on campus in 2000-2001.
Admissions Contact: Andre Washington, Assistant Director of Admissions. A video is available. E-mail: *contact@unionky.edu*
Web: *www.unionky.edu*

UNIVERSITY OF KENTUCKY — D-3
Lexington, KY 40506-0032 — **(606) 257-2000; Fax: (606) 257-3823**

Full-time: 7140 men, 7715 women	**Faculty:** 1239; I, -$
Part-time: 970 men, 1020 women	**Ph.D.s:** 98%
Graduate: 2870 men, 3350 women	**Student/Faculty:** 12 to 1
Year: semesters, summer session	**Tuition:** $3735 ($10,275)
Application Deadline: February 15	**Room & Board:** $4030
Freshman Class: n/av	
SAT I or ACT: required	**COMPETITIVE**

The University of Kentucky, founded in 1865, is a public land-grant institution offering undergraduate and graduate programs in a variety of areas. Figures in the above capsule are approximate. There are 13 undergraduate schools and 1 graduate school. In addition to regional accreditation, UK has baccalaureate program accreditation with AACSB, ABET, ACEJMC, ACPE, ADA, AHEA, APTA, ASLA, CAHEA, CSWE, FIDER, NAAB, NASAD, NASM, NCATE, NLN, NRPA, and SAF. The 13 libraries contain 2,792,293 volumes, 5,872,795 microform items, and 73,600 audiovisual forms/CDs, and subscribe to 26,539 periodicals. Computerized library services include the card catalog and database searching. Special learning facilities include a learning resource center, art gallery, natural history museum, radio station, and TV station. The 764-acre campus is in a suburban area 75 miles south of Cincinnati. Including residence halls, there are 335 buildings.
Student Life: 83% of undergraduates are from Kentucky. Others are from 49 states, 114 foreign countries, and Canada. 85% are from public schools. 87% are white. The average age of freshmen is 18; all undergraduates, 22. 20% do not continue beyond their first year; 50% remain to graduate.
Housing: 6166 students can be accommodated in college housing, which includes single-sex and coed dormitories, on-campus apartments, married-student housing, fraternity houses, and sorority houses. In addition, there are honors houses, language houses, and special-interest houses. On-campus housing is available on a first-come, first-served basis. 69% of students commute. Alcohol is not permitted. All students may keep cars.
Activities: 15% of men belong to 22 national fraternities; 17% of women belong to 16 national sororities. There are 272 groups on campus, including band, cheerleading, chess, choir, chorale, chorus, computers, dance, debate, drama, drill team, ethnic, gay, honors, international, jazz band, literary magazine, marching band, musical theater, newspaper, orchestra, pep band, photography, political, professional, radio and TV, religious, social, social service, student government, symphony, and yearbook. Popular campus events include Little Kentucky Derby, Cultural Diversity Week, and Spotlight Jazz Series.
Sports: There are 11 intercollegiate sports for men and 12 for women, and 22 intramural sports for men and 22 for women. Facilities include a 58,000-seat football stadium, a 24,500-seat arena for basketball and other activities, an aquatic center and swimming pool, baseball fields, a training center, indoor tennis courts, and a field house.
Disabled Students: 90% of the campus is accessible. Wheelchair ramps, elevators, special parking, specially equipped rest rooms, special class scheduling, lowered drinking fountains, and lowered telephones are available.
Services: There is a reader service for the blind and remedial math.
Campus Safety and Security: Measures include 24-hour foot and vehicle patrol, self-defense education, escort service, and shuttle buses. There are informal discussions, pamphlets/posters/films, emergency telephones, and lighted pathways/sidewalks.
Programs of Study: UK confers B.A., B.S., B.Arch., B.B.A., B.F.A., B.H.S., and B.M. degrees. Master's and doctoral degrees are also awarded. Bachelor's degrees are awarded in AGRICULTURE (agricultural economics, agriculture, animal science, and forestry and related sciences), BIOLOGICAL SCIENCE (biology/biological science, botany, and zoology), BUSINESS (accounting, banking and finance, business economics, hotel/motel and restaurant management, and marketing/retailing/merchandising), COMMUNICATIONS AND THE ARTS (advertising, art history and appreciation, arts administration/management, communications, dramatic arts, English, French, German, Italian, journalism, linguistics, music, music performance, Russian, Spanish, and telecommunications), COMPUTER AND PHYSICAL SCIENCE (chemistry, computer science, geology, mathematics, and physics), EDUCATION (agricultural, art, business, early childhood, elementary, foreign languages, health, mathematics, middle school, music, physical, science, secondary, social studies, and special), ENGINEERING AND ENVIRONMENTAL DESIGN (chemical engineering, civil engineering, electrical/electronics engineering, landscape architecture/design, materials engineering, mechanical engineering, and mining and mineral engineering), HEALTH PROFESSIONS (nursing, physical therapy, and physician's assistant), SOCIAL SCIENCE (anthropology, economics, food science, geography, history, Latin American studies, philosophy, political science/government, psychology, social work, sociology, and textiles and clothing). Pharmacy, architecture, and allied health are the strongest academically. Finance, accounting, and marketing are the largest.

Required: All students must maintain a minimum 2.0 GPA and complete at least 120 credit hours. Students must demonstrate competency in math, foreign language, writing, and oral communications. Required studies include courses in basic skills, inference, and communicative skills, along with disciplinary and cross-disciplinary studies.
Special: Co-op programs are offered in engineering, business, computer science, math, and agriculture. The Academic Common Market allows students in 14 southern states to study outside the university. Internships in a variety of fields, study abroad in 36 countries, work-study programs with the university and local businesses, and credit for life experience are also available. An accelerated degree program, B.A.-B.S. degrees, dual and double majors, a general studies degree, student-designed majors, a 3-2 engineering degree with several smaller schools in Kentucky, nondegree study, and pass/fail options are also offered. There are 12 national honor societies, including Phi Beta Kappa, and a freshman honors program.
Faculty/Classroom: 70% of faculty are male; 30%, female. 66% teach undergraduates.
Admissions: There were 65 National Merit finalists. 106 freshmen graduated first in their class in a recent year.
Requirements: The SAT I or ACT is required. In addition, minimum scores vary with the GPA. Applicants must complete 20 Carnegie units, including 4 years of English, 3 of math, and 2 each of science and social studies. A fourth year of math, 2 years of foreign language, and 1 year of fine arts also are recommended. A portfolio is required for art studio courses, and an audition is required for music performance. A GPA of 2.0 is required. AP and CLEP credits are accepted.
Procedure: Freshmen are admitted to all sessions. Entrance exams should be taken before Christmas of the senior year. Applications should be filed by February 15 for fall entry, October 15 for spring entry, and April 15 for summer entry, along with a $20 fee. Notification of early decision is sent rolling; regular decision, on a rolling basis.
Transfer: 1443 transfer students enrolled in a recent year. Transfer students need a minimum GPA of 2.0. If they have fewer than 24 credit hours, they must meet freshmen admission standards. With 24 credits or more, the SAT I or ACT is not required. 30 credits of 120 must be completed at UK.
Visiting: There are regularly scheduled orientations for prospective students, including a campus tour and information on admissions, housing, financial aid, and campus activities. There are guides for informal visits and visitors may sit in on classes. To schedule a visit, contact the UK Visitor Center at (606) 257-3595.
Financial Aid: 32% of freshmen and 34% of continuing students received need-based aid in a recent year. The average freshman award was $6007. Of that total, scholarships or need-based grants averaged $2967; loans averaged $2765; and work contracts averaged $2893. UK is a member of CSS. The FAFSA is required. The fall application deadline is February 15. The scholarship deadline is January 15.
International Students: There were 366 international students enrolled in a recent year. The school actively recruits these students. They must score 525 on the written TOEFL.
Computers: The mainframes are an IBM 3090/6055 and a Convex/HP Meta Series System. 21 terminals access the mainframe in the UK computing center. There are 831 PCs in 13 public computer labs, and students may access the university system via phone modem. Several colleges also operate computer labs and classrooms for their students. All students may access the system 24 hours daily in the computing center, and various hours in labs. There are no time limits and no fees.
Graduates: In a recent, 3285 bachelor's degrees were awarded. The most popular majors were business (20%), engineering (10%), and health professions (9%). In an average class, 21% graduate in 4 years, 43% in 5 years, and 51% in 6 years.
Admissions Contact: Randy Mills, Associate Director for Recruitment.
E-mail: *admissio@uky.edu* Web: *www.uky.edu*

UNIVERSITY OF LOUISVILLE
Louisville, KY 40292 D-2
(502) 852-6531
(800) 334-8635; Fax: (502) 852-4476

Full-time: 4481 men, 5361 women | **Faculty:** 720; I, --$
Part-time: 2045 men, 2244 women | **Ph.D.s:** 90%
Graduate: 2951 men, 3312 women | **Student/Faculty:** 14 to 1
Year: semesters, summer session | **Tuition:** $3794 ($10,472)
Application Deadline: open | **Room & Board:** $3608
Freshman Class: 5201 applied, 3924 accepted, 2261 enrolled
SAT I or ACT: required — **LESS COMPETITIVE**

The University of Louisville, founded in 1798, is a public institution offering a wide range of undergraduate and academic graduate programs. There are 8 undergraduate and 4 graduate schools. In addition to regional accreditation, U of L has baccalaureate program accreditation with AACSB, ABET, ACEJMC, ASLA, CAHEA, NAAB, NASM, NCATE, and NLN. The 6 libraries contain 1,700,846 volumes, 1,958,749 microform items, and 24,593 audiovisual forms/CDs, and subscribe to 15,000 periodicals. Computerized library services include the card catalog, interlibrary loans, and database searching. Special learning facilities include a learning resource center, art gallery, planetarium, and radio station. The campus is in an urban area.
Student Life: 87% of undergraduates are from Kentucky. Others are from 49 states, 80 foreign countries, and Canada. 90% are from public schools. 80% are white; 11% African American. The average age of freshmen is 19; all undergraduates, 26. 29% do not continue beyond their first year.
Housing: 2400 students can be accommodated in college housing, which includes coed dormitories, on-campus apartments, off-campus apartments, married-student housing, fraternity houses, and sorority houses. In addition, there are honors houses and special-interest houses. On-campus housing is available on a first-come, first-served basis. Priority is given to out-of-town students. 84% of students commute. All students may keep cars.
Activities: 5% of men belong to 14 national fraternities; 3% of women belong to 1 local sorority and 9 national sororities. There are 49 groups on campus, including art, band, cheerleading, chess, choir, chorale, chorus, computers, dance, drama, ethnic, film, gay, honors, international, jazz band, literary magazine, marching band, musical theater, newspaper, opera, orchestra, pep band, photography, political, professional, radio and TV, religious, social, social service, student government, and symphony.
Sports: There are 9 intercollegiate sports for men and 11 for women, and 43 intramural sports for men and 43 for women. Facilities include a 19,400-seat gym and a football stadium.
Disabled Students: 90% of the campus is accessible. Wheelchair ramps, elevators, special parking, specially equipped rest rooms, special class scheduling, lowered drinking fountains, and lowered telephones are available.
Services: Counseling and information services are available, as is tutoring in every subject.
Campus Safety and Security: Measures include 24-hour foot and vehicle patrol, escort service, shuttle buses, and informal discussions. There are pamphlets/posters/films, emergency telephones, and lighted pathways/sidewalks.
Programs of Study: U of L confers B.A., B.S., and B.F.A. degrees. Associate, master's, and doctoral degrees are also awarded. Bachelor's degrees are awarded in AGRICULTURE (equine science), BIOLOGICAL SCIENCE (biology/biological science), BUSINESS (accounting, banking and finance, business administration and management, business economics, management science, marketing/retailing/merchandising, and sports management), COMMUNICATIONS AND THE ARTS (art, art history and appreciation, communications, dramatic arts, English, French, linguistics, music, and Spanish), COMPUTER AND PHYSICAL SCIENCE (chemistry, computer science, information sciences and systems, mathematics, and physics), EDUCATION (art, business, early childhood, elementary, foreign languages, middle school, music, physical, science, secondary, and teaching English as a second/foreign language (TESOL/TEFOL)), ENGINEERING AND ENVIRONMENTAL DESIGN (airline piloting and navigation, chemical engineering, civil engineering, computer engineering, electrical/electronics engineering, engineering, engineering management, industrial engineering, and mechanical engineering), HEALTH PROFESSIONS (health, medical laboratory technology, medical science, and nursing), SOCIAL SCIENCE (African studies, anthropology, criminal justice, geography, history, humanities, liberal arts/general studies, paralegal studies, philosophy, political science/government, psychology, sociology, and women's studies). Engineering, health professional, and business management are the strongest academically. The arts and sciences, business, and education are the largest.
Required: Distribution requirements include at least 6 hours each in social sciences, natural sciences, the history of world civilizations, and humanities. Freshmen are required to take college writing or advanced composition, and 2 phys ed courses. A total of 123 semester hours, including 46 to 60 hours in the major, with a minimum GPA of 2.5 (2.0 in education, 2.75 in engineering) is required in order to graduate.
Special: Cross-registration with other schools, study abroad in 5 countries, work-study programs, and B.A.-B.S. degrees are offered. A general studies degree, nondegree study, and pass/fail options are available. Co-op programs in engineering and business and internships are also possible. There is a freshman honors program.
Faculty/Classroom: 51% of faculty are male; 39%, female. The average class size in an introductory lecture is 31 and in a regular course, 29.
Admissions: 75% of the 2001-2002 applicants were accepted. The ACT scores for the 2001-2002 freshman class were: 36% below 21, 26% between 21 and 23, 20% between 24 and 26, 9% between 27 and 28, and 9% above 28. There were 4 National Merit finalists and 5 semifinalists.
Requirements: The SAT I or ACT is required, with a minimum composite score of 20 on the ACT, or a minimum score of 450 on each section of the SAT I. Applicants must have 20 academic credits, including 4 units of English, 3 in math, and 2 each in history, science, and social studies. A GPA of 2.5 is required. Applications are accepted on-line. AP and CLEP credits are accepted.

Procedure: Freshmen are admitted fall, spring, and summer. Entrance exams should be taken in spring or summer of junior year. There are early decision and early admissions plans. Application deadlines are open. The fall 2001 application fee was $25. Notification is sent on a rolling basis.

Transfer: 1053 transfer students enrolled in 2001-2002. Transfer students must have a minimum GPA of 2.0. 30 credits of 123 must be completed at U of L.

Visiting: There are regularly scheduled orientations for prospective students. There are guides for informal visits and visitors may sit in on classes. To schedule a visit, contact Admissions.

Financial Aid: The CSS/Profile or FAFSA and the college's own financial statement are required.

International Students: There are 221 international students enrolled. They must score 550 on the written TOEFL.

Computers: All students may access the system. Check with the school for current fees.

Graduates: In 2001, 1819 bachelor's degrees were awarded. The most popular majors were business (20%), engineering (11%), and social sciences and history (11%).

Admissions Contact: Jenny Sawyer, Director of Admissions.
E-mail: *admitme@gwise.louisville.edu* Web: *http://www.louisville.edu*

WESTERN KENTUCKY UNIVERSITY

C-4

Bowling Green, KY 42101-3576 **(270) 745-2551**
(800) 495-8463; Fax: (270) 745-6133

Full-time: 4566 men, 6135 women	**Faculty:** 599; IIA, -$
Part-time: 1244 men, 2190 women	**Ph.D.s:** 81%
Graduate: 773 men, 1671 women	**Student/Faculty:** 18 to 1
Year: semesters, summer session	**Tuition:** $2844 ($7424)
Application Deadline: August 1	**Room & Board:** $3990
Freshman Class: n/av	
SAT I or ACT: required	**COMPETITIVE**

Western Kentucky University, founded in 1906, is a public institution with undergraduate and graduate programs in liberal arts, health science, business, agricultural and technical studies, art and fine arts, professional training, music, and teacher preparation. There are 6 undergraduate schools and 1 graduate school. In addition to regional accreditation, Western has baccalaureate program accreditation with AACSB, ABET, ACEJMC, ADA, CSAB, CSWE, NASAD, NASM, NCATE, NLN, and NRPA. The 3 libraries contain 591,912 volumes, 2,651,784 microform items, and 93,955 audiovisual forms/CDs, and subscribe to 4564 periodicals. Computerized library services include the card catalog, interlibrary loans, and database searching. Special learning facilities include a learning resource center, art gallery, planetarium, radio station, TV station, and the Kentucky Museum. The 200-acre campus is in a suburban area 65 miles north of Nashville, Tennessee. Including residence halls, there are 48 buildings.

Student Life: 84% of undergraduates are from Kentucky. Others are from 45 states, 53 foreign countries, and Canada. 88% are white. The average age of freshmen is 19; all undergraduates, 25. 9% do not continue beyond their first year; 41% remain to graduate.

Housing: 4568 students can be accommodated in college housing, which includes single-sex and coed dormitories and sorority houses. In addition, there are honors houses. On-campus housing is available on a first-come, first-served basis. Alcohol is not permitted. All students may keep cars.

Activities: 10% of men belong to 14 national fraternities; 10% of women belong to 11 national sororities. There are 215 groups on campus, including band, cheerleading, chess, choir, chorale, chorus, computers, dance, debate, drama, drill team, ethnic, forensics, gay, honors, international, jazz band, literary magazine, marching band, musical theater, newspaper, opera, orchestra, pep band, political, professional, radio and TV, religious, social, social service, student government, symphony, and yearbook. Popular campus events include Spring Tug of War, Spring Sing, and Organizational Fair.

Sports: There are 11 intercollegiate sports for men and 10 for women, and 17 intramural sports for men and 16 for women. Facilities include a 17,500-seat stadium, gyms, a pool, a track, an 11,300-seat arena, basketball and tennis courts, baseball and softball fields, facilities for bowling, billiards, and table tennis, a movie theater, and a night spot. There is also a student health and activities center with an indoor track, a weight room, an aerobics studio, racquetball courts, an Olympic-size pool, and 4 more gyms.

Disabled Students: 60% of the campus is accessible. Wheelchair ramps, elevators, special parking, specially equipped rest rooms, special class scheduling, and lowered telephones are available. Services are available for students with special needs through the Equal Opportunity/504 ADA Compliance Office.

Services: Counseling and information services are available, as is tutoring in some subjects, with both departmental and freelance tutoring offered. The Student Support Services program offers tutoring in general education courses. There is a reader service for the blind, and remedial math, reading, and writing.

Campus Safety and Security: Measures include 24-hour foot and vehicle patrol, escort service, shuttle buses, and informal discussions. There are pamphlets/posters/films, emergency telephones, and lighted pathways/sidewalks.

Programs of Study: Western confers A.B., B.S., B.F.A., B.G.S., B.M., and B.S.N. degrees. Associate and master's degrees are also awarded. Bachelor's degrees are awarded in AGRICULTURE (agriculture), BIOLOGICAL SCIENCE (biochemistry, biology/biological science, and genetics), BUSINESS (accounting, banking and finance, business administration and management, business economics, hotel/motel and restaurant management, marketing/retailing/merchandising, and recreation and leisure services), COMMUNICATIONS AND THE ARTS (advertising, broadcasting, communications, dramatic arts, English, fine arts, French, German, journalism, music, music performance, performing arts, public relations, Spanish, speech/debate/rhetoric, and studio art), COMPUTER AND PHYSICAL SCIENCE (chemistry, computer science, geology, information sciences and systems, mathematics, and physics), EDUCATION (art, business, elementary, health, home economics, library science, middle school, physical, science, special, and trade and industrial), ENGINEERING AND ENVIRONMENTAL DESIGN (civil engineering, civil engineering technology, electrical/electronics engineering, electrical/electronics engineering technology, electromechanical technology, environmental science, industrial engineering technology, interior design, mechanical engineering, and mechanical engineering technology), HEALTH PROFESSIONS (dental hygiene, health care administration, medical technology, nursing, public health, and speech pathology/audiology), SOCIAL SCIENCE (anthropology, dietetics, economics, geography, history, parks and recreation management, philosophy, political science/government, psychology, religion, social studies, social work, sociology, and textiles and clothing). Teacher education, journalism, and biology are the strongest academically. Accounting, elementary education, and psychology are the largest.

Required: To graduate, all students must complete at least 128 semester hours, with a varying number of hours in the major, and maintain a minimum GPA of 2.0. Curricula must include 44 semester hours of general education requirements and 42 semester hours in upper-division courses, and includes 6 semester hours of English composition and 3 semester hours each of Western civilization, foreign language, speech, and literature.

Special: Internships in many areas, study abroad in 20 countries, work-study programs, and cooperative programs with the Universities of Louisville and Kentucky and Eastern Kentucky University are offered. Accelerated degree programs are available in some majors. Dual majors include math and physical science, and physics and engineering. A general studies degree, student-designed majors, a Washington semester, and a 3-2 engineering degree are offered. Credit for life, military, or work experience may be granted, and nondegree study is possible. There are 35 national honor societies, and a freshman honors program.

Faculty/Classroom: 57% of faculty are male; 43%, female.

Admissions: 34% of the current freshmen were in the top fifth of their class; 60% were in the top two fifths. There were 4 National Merit semifinalists. 86 freshmen graduated first in their class.

Requirements: The SAT I or ACT is required, with a minimum composite ACT score of 20 or SAT I of 930. Other admissions requirements include graduation from an accredited secondary school with 22 academic credits, including 4 years of English, and courses in algebra 1 and 2, geometry, 3 years of social studies and 3 years of science including 1 lab. The GED also is accepted. A GPA of 2.5 is required. AP and CLEP credits are accepted. Important factors in the admissions decision are advanced placement or honor courses, recommendations by school officials, and recommendations by alumni. Applications are accepted on-line via CollegeNET.

Procedure: Freshmen are admitted to all sessions. Entrance exams should be taken by fall of the senior year. There are early admissions and deferred admissions plans. Applications should be filed by August 1 for fall entry, January 1 for spring entry, and May 1 for summer entry, along with a $30 fee. Notification is sent on a rolling basis.

Transfer: 823 transfer students enrolled in 2001-2002. Applicants must have a minimum GPA of 2.0, including a 2.0 in the last term before transfer, and be in good standing. 1 official transcript from each college is required. Applicants with fewer than 24 semester hours toward a degree must submit a high school transcript. 32 credits of 128 must be completed at Western.

Visiting: There are regularly scheduled orientations for prospective students, including campus tours, informational sessions, presentations, and a video. There are guides for informal visits and visitors may sit in on classes and stay overnight. To schedule a visit, contact the Office of Admissions at *tours@wku.edu*

Financial Aid: In 2001-2002, 97% of all freshmen and 67% of continuing students received some form of financial aid. 47% of freshmen and 41% of continuing students received need-based aid. The average freshman award was $4412. Of that total, scholarships or need-based grants averaged $3124 ($11,180 maximum); loans averaged $3231 ($10,594 maximum); work contracts averaged $1967 ($5254 maximum); and Veteran benefits, alumni waiver, residence hall waiver, institutional work, and Kentucky work study averaged $3216 ($11,050 maximum). 8% of undergraduates work part time. Average annual earnings from campus work are $2098. The average financial indebtedness of the 2001 graduate was $14,438. Western is a member of CSS. The FAFSA is required. The fall application deadline is April 1.

International Students: There are 90 international students enrolled. They must score 525 on the written TOEFL or 197 on the electronic version or take the MELAB and also take the SAT I or the ACT, scoring 20 on the ACT.

Computers: The mainframes are a DEC ALPHA 4100 and an IBM 9121-260. Approximately 400 PCs in 7 on-campus and 3 off-campus labs are served by LANs for software and Internet access. All students may use these facilities and have e-mail accounts. In addition, students who live in the residence halls may have their computers connected to the campus LAN for all services available in the computing labs. All students may access the system 8 A.M. to midnight Monday to Thursday, 8 A.M. to 5 P.M. on Saturday, and 1 P.M. to midnight on Sunday. There are no time limits. The fee is $35 per semester.

Graduates: In 2001, 1695 bachelor's degrees were awarded. The most popular majors were general studies (9%), elementary education (9%), and psychology (4%). 202 companies recruited on campus in 2000-2001.

Admissions Contact: Sharon Dyrsen, Admissions and Academic Services Director. A video is available. E-mail: *admission@wku.edu*
Web: *www.wku.edu*

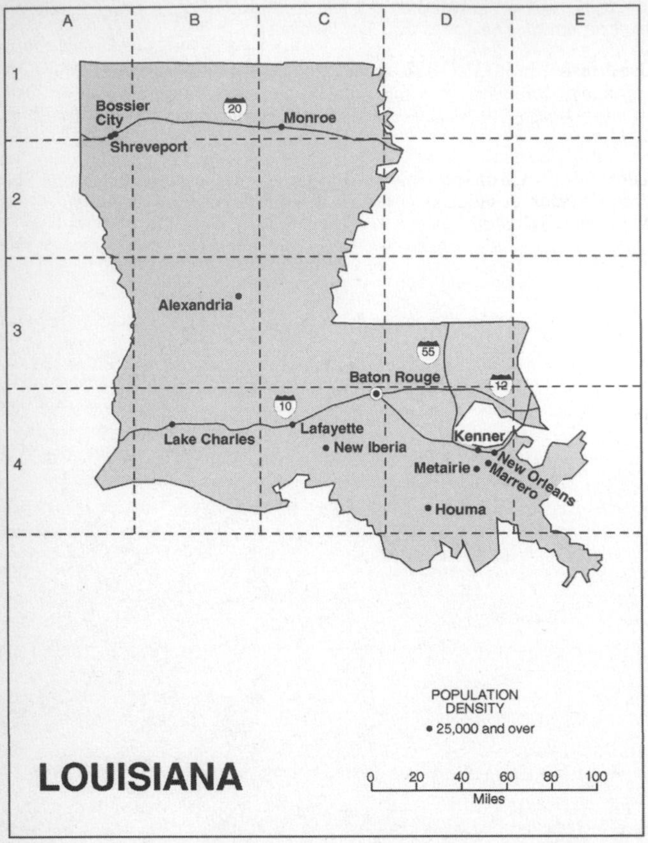

CENTENARY COLLEGE OF LOUISIANA

CENTENARY COLLEGE OF LOUISIANA	**A-1**
Shreveport, LA 71104	**(318) 869-5131; Fax: (318) 869-5005**
Full-time: 351 men, 537 women	**Faculty:** 74; IIB, av$
Part-time: 9 men, 13 women	**Ph.D.s:** 91%
Graduate: 56 men, 83 women	**Student/Faculty:** 12 to 1
Year: semesters, summer session	**Tuition:** $15,800
Application Deadline: February 15	**Room & Board:** $5800
Freshman Class: 737 applied, 634 accepted, 259 enrolled	
SAT I Verbal/Math: 580/580	**ACT:** 26 **COMPETITIVE+**

Centenary College of Louisiana, founded in 1825, is a private institution affiliated with the United Methodist Church, offering degrees in the liberal arts, music, business, sciences, and education. There are 2 graduate schools. In addition to regional accreditation, Centenary has baccalaureate program accreditation with NASM. The 2 libraries contain 180,000 volumes, 310,671 microform items, and 425 audiovisual forms/CDs, and subscribe to 942 periodicals. Computerized library services include the card catalog, interlibrary loans, and database searching. Special learning facilities include a radio station, a theater, and an art museum. The 65-acre campus is in a suburban area in the northwest corner of Louisana, 180 miles east of Dallas, Texas. Including residence halls, there are 20 buildings.

Student Life: 60% of undergraduates are from Louisiana. Others are from 38 states, 18 foreign countries, and Canada. 85% are white. 57% are Protestant; 23% claim no religious affiliation; 18%, Catholic. The average age of freshmen is 18; all undergraduates, 20. 24% do not continue beyond their first year; 55% remain to graduate.

Housing: 672 students can be accommodated in college housing, which includes single-sex and coed dormitories and on-campus apartments. In addition, there is a women's honors house and cold housing for eligible upperclasmen. On-campus housing is guaranteed for all 4 years and is available on a first-come, first-served basis. 60% of students live on campus. Alcohol is not permitted. All students may keep cars.

Activities: 25% of men belong to 4 national fraternities; 20% of women belong to 2 national sororities. There are 55 groups on campus, including band, cheerleading, choir, chorale, chorus, dance, drama,environmental, film, forensics, gay, honors, jazz band, literary magazine, musical theater, newspaper, opera, orchestra, pep band, photography, political, professional, radio and TV, religious, social, social service, student government, symphony, and yearbook. Popular campus events include Fall Fest, Spring Fling, and President's Convocation.

Sports: There are 7 intercollegiate sports for men and 9 for women, and 10 intramural sports for men and 10 for women. Facilities include a 3000-seat gym, 2 weight rooms, basketball, racquetball, and tennis courts, and baseball, soccer, and softball fields. There is a fitness center with aerobic exercise and strengthening equipment, a natatorium, and basketball/volleyball/raquetball courts.

Disabled Students: 90% of the campus is accessible. Wheelchair ramps, elevators, special parking, specially equipped rest rooms, special class scheduling, lowered drinking fountains, lowered telephones, and lowered security phones are available.

Services: Counseling and information services are available, as is tutoring in some subjects, including biology, physics, chemistry, math, and English.

Campus Safety and Security: Measures include 24-hour foot and vehicle patrol, escort service, informal discussions, and pamphlets/posters/films. There are emergency telephones and lighted pathways/sidewalks.

Programs of Study: Centenary confers B.A., B.S., and B.M. degrees. Master's degrees are also awarded. Bachelor's degrees are awarded in BIOLOGICAL SCIENCE (biochemistry, biology/biological science, biophysics, and neurosciences), BUSINESS (accounting and business administration and management), COMMUNICATIONS AND THE ARTS (art, communications, dance, English, French, German, music, music performance, Spanish, and speech/debate/rhetoric), COMPUTER AND PHYSICAL SCIENCE (chemistry, geology, mathematics, and physics), EDUCATION (elementary, foreign languages, music, science, and social studies), ENGINEERING AND ENVIRONMENTAL DESIGN (environmental science), HEALTH PROFESSIONS (health science and premedicine), SOCIAL SCIENCE (economics, history, liberal arts/general studies, philosophy, political science/government, prelaw, psychology, religion, religious music, and sociology). Physical sciences, life sciences, and foreign languages are the strongest academically. Business, biology, and psychology are the largest.

Required: To graduate, all students must complete 124 semester hours, with a maximum of 45 in the major and minimum of 30 at the upper-division level, including a writing and speaking class in the major at the junior level, and maintain a minimum GPA of 2.0. Core curriculum requirements include courses in the humanities and social sciences. In addition, freshmen must take a liberal arts orientation, and all students must complete a community service project, study or live in a different culture, study abroad, and fulfill career explorations.

Special: Centenary offers study abroad in 7 countries, cross-registration with Associated Colleges of the South, internships in all majors, a Washington semester, and a work-study program with the college itself. A 3-1 communication disorders degree with Louisiana State University Medical Center is possible, as is a 3-2 engineering degree with Washington University in St. Louis, University of Southern California, and Southern Methodist, Louisiana Tech, and Case Western Reserve Universities. A 3-2 applied science preprofessional degree combines with health administration or medical school. Preveterinary studies, general studies and interdisciplinary degrees, and student-designed majors are available. There are 7 national honor societies, and 10 departmental honors program.

Faculty/Classroom: 58% of faculty are male; 42%, female. 98% teach undergraduates. No introductory courses are taught by graduate students. The average class size in an introductory lecture is 25; in a laboratory, 24; and in a regular course, 25.

Admissions: 86% of the 2001-2002 applicants were accepted. The SAT I scores for the 2001-2002 freshman class were: Verbal--21% below 500, 34% between 500 and 599, 36% between 600 and 700, and 9% above 700; Math--15% below 500, 40% between 500 and 599, 35% between 600 and 700, and 10% above 700. The ACT scores were 9% below 21, 23% between 21 and 23, 27% between 24 and 26, 19% between 27 and 28, and 22% above 28. 49% of the current freshmen were in the top fifth of their class; 78% were in the top two fifths.

Requirements: The SAT I or ACT is required, with a minimum composite score of 950 on the SAT I or 20 on the ACT, although accepted students average 1100 and 24 respectively. Applicants should be high school graduates. Secondary school preparation should include 15 academic credits, including 4 of English, 3 each of math and science, 2 each of a foreign language and history, 1 of social studies, and electives. Music students must audition; art students are advised to present a portfolio. A GPA of 2.0 is required. AP and CLEP credits are accepted. Important factors in the admissions decision are advanced placement or honor courses, leadership record, and ability to finance college education. Applications are accepted on-line via Common App and at the school's web site.

Procedure: Freshmen are admitted to all sessions. Entrance exams should be taken by the fall of the senior year. There are early decision, early admissions, and deferred admissions plans. Early decision applications should be filed by December 1; regular applications, by February

15 for fall entry and December 1 for spring entry. Notification of early decision is sent January 1; regular decision, March 15. The fall 2001 application fee was $30.

Transfer: 37 transfer students enrolled in 2001-2002. Transfer applicants must have a minimum GPA of 2.0 and demonstrate good performance in a liberal arts curriculum. 45 credits of 124 must be completed at Centenary.

Visiting: There are regularly scheduled orientations for prospective students, consisting of information sessions with a counselor, a tour of the campus, a visit to a class or with faculty, and lunch. There are guides for informal visits and visitors may sit in on classes and stay overnight. To schedule a visit, contact the Admissions Office at *tcrowley@centenary.edu*

Financial Aid: In 2001-2002, 97% of all freshmen and 91% of continuing students received some form of financial aid. 62% of freshmen and 61% of continuing students received need-based aid. The average freshman award was $15,299. Of that total, scholarships or need-based grants averaged $12,667 ($20,600 maximum); loans averaged $2761 ($6625 maximum); work contracts averaged $1476 ($1500 maximum); and tuition remission and athletic scholarships averaged $12,240 ($20,600 maximum). 25% of undergraduates work part time. Average annual earnings from campus work are $1430. The average financial indebtedness of the 2001 graduate was $14,700. Centenary is a member of CSS. The FAFSA is required. The FAF is accepted, as well as College Estimator for Early Decision candidacy. The fall application deadline is March 15.

International Students: There are 34 international students enrolled. The school actively recruits these students. They must score 550 on the written TOEFL.

Computers: The mainframe is an IBM System 36. All students may access the system. There are no time limits. The fee is $50. It is strongly recommended that all students have a personal computer.

Graduates: In 2001, 142 bachelor's degrees were awarded. The most popular majors were business (22%), biology (11%), and English (7%). In an average class, 37% graduate in 4 years, 50% in 5 years, and 52% in 6 years.

Admissions Contact: Eugene Gregory, Vice President of College Relations. E-mail: *egregory@centenary.edu* Web: *www.centenary.edu*

DILLARD UNIVERSITY

New Orleans, LA 70122-3097 — D-4

(504) 816-4670
(800) 216-6637; Fax: (504) 816-4895

Full-time: 2137 men and women	**Faculty:** 127
Part-time: none	**Ph.D.s:** 49%
Graduate: none	**Student/Faculty:** 17 to 1
Year: semesters, summer session	**Tuition:** $10,210
Application Deadline: open	**Room & Board:** $5836

Freshman Class: 3033 applied, 1969 accepted, 653 enrolled
ACT: 22 — **VERY COMPETITIVE**

Dillard University, established in 1930, is an independent, nonsectarian, liberal arts institution, affiliated with the United Church of Christ and the United Methodist Church. It offers undergraduate programs in business, education, humanities, natural sciences, nursing, and social sciences. There are 6 undergraduate divisions. In addition to regional accreditation, Dillard has baccalaureate program accreditation with NLN. The library contains 101,358 volumes, 1150 microform items, and 320 audiovisual forms/CDs, and subscribes to 323 periodicals. Computerized library services include the card catalog, interlibrary loans, and database searching. Special learning facilities include a learning resource center, art gallery, and radio station. The 35-acre campus is in an urban area in New Orleans. Including residence halls, there are 19 buildings.

Student Life: 50% of undergraduates are from out of state, mostly the South. Others are from 37 states and 9 foreign countries. 98% are African American. 28% do not continue beyond their first year.

Housing: 1058 students can be accommodated in college housing, which includes single-sex dormitories, on-campus apartments, and off-campus apartments. On-campus housing is guaranteed for all 4 years, is available on a first-come, first-served basis, and is available on a lottery system for upperclassmen. Priority is given to out-of-town students. Alcohol is not permitted. All students may keep cars.

Activities: There are 4 national fraternities and 4 national sororities. There are 64 groups on campus, including art, cheerleading, chess, choir, chorus, dance, drama, ethnic, honors, professional, religious, social service, student government, and yearbook. Popular campus events include Coronation, Avenue of the Oaks Gala, and Founder's Day.

Sports: There are 3 intercollegiate sports for men and 3 for women. Facilities include a gym, a swimming pool, and a Nautilus room.

Disabled Students: 70% of the campus is accessible. Wheelchair ramps, elevators, special parking, specially equipped rest rooms, and special class scheduling are available.

Services: Counseling and information services are available, as is tutoring in every subject. There is remedial math, reading, and writing.

Campus Safety and Security: Measures include 24-hour foot and vehicle patrol, informal discussions, pamphlets/posters/films, and lighted pathways/sidewalks.

Programs of Study: Dillard confers B.A., B.S., and B.S.N. degrees. Bachelor's degrees are awarded in BIOLOGICAL SCIENCE (biology/biological science), BUSINESS (accounting and business administration and management), COMMUNICATIONS AND THE ARTS (art, communications, dramatic arts, English, French, languages, music, music business management, music performance, Spanish, and speech/debate/rhetoric), COMPUTER AND PHYSICAL SCIENCE (chemistry, computer science, mathematics, and physics), EDUCATION (elementary, physical, secondary, and special), ENGINEERING AND ENVIRONMENTAL DESIGN (engineering), HEALTH PROFESSIONS (nursing, premedicine, and public health), SOCIAL SCIENCE (African studies, criminal justice, economics, history, Japanese studies, philosophy, political science/government, psychology, religion, social work, sociology, and urban studies). Biological sciences is the largest.

Required: Students must successfully complete 125 semester hours and maintain a minimum overall GPA of 2.0 and a GPA of 2.0 or better in all courses in the major. In addition, all students must complete 46 semester hours in the core curriculum, which includes courses in English composition, world literature, English literature, math, natural sciences, world history, political science, economics, university assembly, phys ed, and academic orientation. Additionally, each student must engage in a minimum of 120 clock hours of volunteer service in the community.

Special: Opportunities are provided for internships, work-study programs, credit by exam, nondegree study, and pass/fail options. All social science majors are encouraged to pursue a double major. There is a 4-year co-op degree in music therapy with Loyola University, a clinical public health curriculum with Howard University, a 5-year joint degree in urban studies with Columbia University, and preengineering dual degree programs with the Georgia Institute of Technology and Auburn and Columbia Universities. There are 3 national honor societies.

Faculty/Classroom: 46% of faculty are male; 54%, female. All teach undergraduates. The average class size in an introductory lecture is 25.

Admissions: 65% of the 2001-2002 applicants were accepted. 18 freshmen graduated first in their class.

Requirements: The SAT I or ACT is recommended. In addition, graduation from an accredited secondary school is required; a GED will be accepted. Applicants must submit an academic record of 20 units, distributed as follows: 4 units in English, 3 each in math and natural sciences, 2 in social studies, and 8 in other academic electives. Recommendations from a high school teacher and the principal or a student counselor are required. A GPA of 2.2 is required. AP credits are accepted. Important factors in the admissions decision are recommendations by school officials, leadership record, and personality/intangible qualities. Applications are available on-line at the school's web site.

Procedure: Freshmen are admitted to all sessions. Entrance exams should be taken between April of the junior year and December of the senior year. There are early admissions and deferred admissions plans. The priority deadline is December 1. Notification is sent on a rolling basis. The fall 2001 application fee was $20.

Transfer: 47 transfer students enrolled in 2001-2002. Applicants for transfer must submit a secondary school record or equivalent, transcripts from previous colleges showing an average grade of C, and personal recommendations. No more than 60 semester hours may be submitted for transfer credit. 65 credits of 125 must be completed at Dillard.

Visiting: Orientations for prospective students are scheduled on an individual basis. There are guides for informal visits and visitors may sit in on classes and stay overnight. To schedule a visit, contact Campus Visit Coordinator.

Financial Aid: In 2001-2002, 98% of all students received some form of financial aid. 85% of freshmen and 97% of continuing students received need-based aid. Scholarships or need-based grants averaged $3085; and loans averaged $4222. 14% of undergraduates work part time. Average annual earnings from campus work are $2000. The average financial indebtedness of the 2001 graduate was $18,000. Dillard is a member of CSS. The FAFSA and the college's own financial statement are required. The fall application deadline is March 1.

International Students: They must score 500 on the written TOEFL and also take the SAT I or the ACT.

Computers: The mainframe is an IBM AS/400. It is strongly recommended that all students have a personal computer.

Graduates: In 2001, 216 bachelor's degrees were awarded. The most popular majors were public health (16%), biology (13%), and mass communications (9%). Of the 2000 graduating class, 45% were enrolled in graduate school within 6 months of graduation and 45% were employed.

Admissions Contact: Linda G. Nash, Director of Admissions.
Web: *www.dillard.edu*

GRAMBLING STATE UNIVERSITY

Grambling, LA 71245 B-1

(318) 274-6423
(888) 863-3655; Fax: (318) 274-3292

Full-time: 1627 men, 2103 women
Part-time: 121 men, 201 women
Graduate: 129 men, 319 women
Year: semesters, summer session
Application Deadline: July 15
Freshman Class: 2661 applied, 1549 accepted, 996 enrolled
ACT: 17
Faculty: 227; IIA, --$
Ph.D.s: 55%
Student/Faculty: 16 to 1
Tuition: $2589
Room & Board: $2736
NONCOMPETITIVE

Grambling State University, founded in 1901, is a constituent member of the University of Louisiana System. A historically and predominantly black comprehensive university, GSU offers degrees ranging from associate to doctorate. There are 6 undergraduate schools and 1 graduate school. In addition to regional accreditation, GSU has baccalaureate program accreditation with AACSB, ACEJMC, CSWE, NASM, NASPAA, NAST, NCATE, NLN, and NRPA. The library contains 306,990 volumes, 121,954 microform items, and 6282 audiovisual forms/CDs, and subscribes to 109,517 periodicals. Computerized library services include the card catalog, interlibrary loans, and database searching. Special learning facilities include a learning resource center, radio station, and TV station. The 340-acre campus is in a small town 60 miles from Shreveport. Including residence halls, there are 67 buildings.

Student Life: 66% of undergraduates are from Louisiana. Others are from 41 states, 14 foreign countries, and Canada. 95% are African American. 80% are Protestant; 15%, Catholic. The average age of freshmen is 18; all undergraduates, 20.

Housing: 2611 students can be accommodated in college housing, which includes single-sex dormitories. In addition, there are honors houses, and floors with private rooms. 55% of students commute. Alcohol is not permitted. All students may keep cars.

Activities: 2% of men belong to 4 national fraternities; 7% of women belong to 4 national sororities. There are 81 groups on campus, including art, band, cheerleading, choir, computers, dance, drama, honors, international, jazz band, marching band, newspaper, orchestra, political, professional, radio and TV, religious, social, social service, student government, symphony, and yearbook. Popular campus events include Founders Day, Black History Month, and Springfest.

Sports: There are 8 intercollegiate sports for men and 9 for women, and 6 intramural sports for men and 3 for women. Facilities include a gym, tennis courts, a 20,000-seat football stadium, an intramural center, a baseball field, a softball field, and an 1850-seat basketball gym.

Disabled Students: 80% of the campus is accessible. Wheelchair ramps, elevators, special parking, specially equipped rest rooms, special class scheduling, lowered drinking fountains, and lowered telephones are available.

Services: Counseling and information services are available, as is tutoring in some subjects, including biology, English, chemistry, history, math, and physics. There is remedial math, reading, and writing.

Campus Safety and Security: Measures include 24-hour foot and vehicle patrol, escort service, pamphlets/posters/films, and emergency telephones. There are lighted pathways/sidewalks.

Programs of Study: GSU confers B.A., B.S., B.A.S.W., B.P.A., and B.S.N. degrees. Associate, master's, and doctoral degrees are also awarded. Bachelor's degrees are awarded in BIOLOGICAL SCIENCE (biology/biological science), BUSINESS (accounting, business administration and management, business economics, hotel/motel and restaurant management, marketing/retailing/merchandising, and recreation and leisure services), COMMUNICATIONS AND THE ARTS (art, communications, dramatic arts, English, French, music, and Spanish), COMPUTER AND PHYSICAL SCIENCE (chemistry, computer science, information sciences and systems, mathematics, and physics), EDUCATION (art, business, drama, early childhood, elementary, English, foreign languages, home economics, industrial arts, mathematics, music, physical, science, and special), ENGINEERING AND ENVIRONMENTAL DESIGN (engineering technology), HEALTH PROFESSIONS (nursing and speech pathology/audiology), SOCIAL SCIENCE (criminal justice, food production/management/services, history, political science/government, prelaw, psychology, public administration, social work, and sociology). Nursing, education, and computer science are the strongest academically. Business management is the largest.

Required: To graduate, students must complete at least 125 semester hours, with a minimum GPA of 2.0. Students also must earn a passing grade in each part of the general education integration seminar and pass the senior comprehensive competency exam. An exam is also required in the sophomore year. General education requirements include courses in English, math, computer literacy, natural sciences, arts, humanities, and social studies for a total of 42 semester hours.

Special: B.A.-B.S. degrees in some subjects, work-study programs, nondegree study, and cross-registration with Louisiana Tech University are offered. GSU sponsors Project Rescue for disadvantaged students. Internships, study abroad, accelerated degree programs, dual majors, and student-designed majors are also possible. There are 15 national honor societies, and a freshman honors program.

Faculty/Classroom: 60% of faculty are male; 40%, female. 83% teach undergraduates and 3% do research. Graduate students teach 2% of introductory courses. The average class size in an introductory lecture is 25; in a laboratory, 20; and in a regular course, 30.

Admissions: 58% of the 2001-2002 applicants were accepted. There were 2 National Merit finalists. 5 freshmen graduated first in their class.

Requirements: The SAT I or ACT is required. In addition, applicants must be graduates of an accredited high school. The GED is accepted. AP and CLEP credits are accepted. Important factors in the admissions decision are ability to finance college education, parents or siblings attending the school, and personality/intangible qualities. Applications are accepted on-line.

Procedure: Freshmen are admitted to all sessions. There is an early admissions plan. Applications should be filed by July 15 for fall entry, December 15 for spring entry, and May 15 for summer entry. The application fee is $20. Notification is sent on a rolling basis.

Transfer: 162 transfer students enrolled in 2001-2002. Applicants must submit official transcripts from all previously attended colleges and must be in good standing at the school most recently attended. 30 credits of 128 must be completed at GSU.

Visiting: There are regularly scheduled orientations for prospective students. There are guides for informal visits and visitors may sit in on classes and stay overnight. To schedule a visit, contact Nora D. Bingaman Taylor, Director of Admissions.

Financial Aid: In 2001-2002, 85% of all freshmen received some form of financial aid, including need-based aid. The average freshman award was $7405. Of that total, scholarships or need-based grants averaged $3750 ($6688 maximum); loans averaged $2625 ($6625 maximum); work contracts averaged $1030 (maximum); and the maximum out-of-state waiver was $5350. All undergraduates work part time. Average annual earnings from campus work are $1030. The average financial indebtedness of the 2001 graduate was $35,000. The FAFSA, the college's own financial statement, and the Singlefile Form are required. The fall application deadline is June 1.

International Students: There are 21 international students enrolled. The school actively recruits these students. They must score 450 on the written TOEFL and also take the SAT I or the ACT.

Graduates: In 2001, 663 bachelor's degrees were awarded. The most popular majors were criminal justice (10%), leisure studies (10%), and computer information systems (9%). In an average class, 31% graduate in 6 years. 167 companies recruited on campus in 2000-2001.

Admissions Contact: Nora D. Bingaman Taylor, Director of Admissions. E-mail: *bingamann@alpha0.gram.edu* Web: *www.gram.edu*

LOUISIANA COLLEGE

Pineville, LA 71359-0560 B-3

(318) 487-7259
(800) 487-1906; Fax: (318) 487-7550

Full-time: 463 men, 592 women
Part-time: 43 men, 106 women
Graduate: none
Year: semesters, summer session
Application Deadline: open
Freshman Class: 907 applied, 688 accepted, 292 enrolled
ACT: 23
Faculty: 68; IIB, --$
Ph.D.s: 69%
Student/Faculty: 16 to 1
Tuition: $8200
Room & Board: $3316
COMPETITIVE

Louisiana College, founded in 1906, is a private liberal arts college affiliated with the Southern Baptist Churches of Louisiana. In addition to regional accreditation, LC has baccalaureate program accreditation with AACSB, CSWE, NASM, and NLN. The library contains 133,405 volumes, 104,654 microform items, and 900 audiovisual forms/CDs, and subscribes to 424 periodicals. Computerized library services include the card catalog, interlibrary loans, and database searching. Special learning facilities include a learning resource center, art gallery, radio station, and a performing arts center. The 81-acre campus is in a small town 1 mile northeast of Alexandria. Including residence halls, there are 16 buildings.

Student Life: 92% of undergraduates are from Louisiana. Others are from 18 states, 7 foreign countries, and Canada. 87% are white. The average age of freshmen is 18; all undergraduates, 22. 33% do not continue beyond their first year.

Housing: 682 students can be accommodated in college housing, which includes single-sex dormitories, on-campus apartments, and married-student housing. On-campus housing is guaranteed for all 4 years. 52% of students live on campus. Alcohol is not permitted. All students may keep cars.

Activities: 20% of men belong to 4 local fraternities; 35% of women belong to 3 local sororities. There are 44 groups on campus, including art, band, cheerleading, choir, chorale, chorus, debate, drama, honors, international, jazz band, literary magazine, musical theater, newspaper, opera, pep band, political, religious, social, social service, student government, symphony, and yearbook. Popular campus events include Gala Christmas, Sanders Lecture Series, and Miss LC Pageant.

Sports: There are 6 intercollegiate sports for men and 6 for women, and 11 intramural sports for men and 11 for women. Facilities include a field house for basketball, a baseball field, a fitness/wellness center, a jogging trail, tennis courts, an intramural/soccer/football field, an outdoor beach volleyball court, softball field, and a practice football field.
Disabled Students: 95% of the campus is accessible. Wheelchair ramps, elevators, special parking, specially equipped rest rooms, and lowered telephones are available.
Services: Counseling and information services are available, as is tutoring in most subjects. There is a reader service for the blind and remedial math and writing. PASS (Program to Assist Student Success) offers services for students with learning disabilities.
Campus Safety and Security: Measures include 24-hour foot and vehicle patrol, self-defense education, escort service, and informal discussions. There are pamphlets/posters/films and lighted pathways/sidewalks.
Programs of Study: LC confers B.A., B.S., B.G.S., B.M., B.S.N., and B.S.W. degrees. Bachelor's degrees are awarded in BIOLOGICAL SCIENCE (biology/biological science), BUSINESS (business administration and management), COMMUNICATIONS AND THE ARTS (communications, dramatic arts, English, French, graphic design, journalism, languages, multimedia, music, speech/debate/rhetoric, and studio art), COMPUTER AND PHYSICAL SCIENCE (chemistry and mathematics), EDUCATION (art, athletic training, business, elementary, English, health, mathematics, music, science, secondary, social studies, and special), HEALTH PROFESSIONS (exercise science, medical laboratory technology, music therapy, nursing, predentistry, premedicine, preoptometry, preveterinary science, and speech pathology/audiology), SOCIAL SCIENCE (criminal justice, economics, history, philosophy, prelaw, psychology, public administration, religion, religious education, religious music, social work, and sociology). Education, biology, and business are the largest.
Required: To graduate, students must complete 127 total credit hours, including a central core of 56 hours in all degree programs, and maintain a minimum GPA of 2.0. The must also complete Cultural/Intellectural and Spiritual Enrichment requirements and earn at least 25% of credit applied toward degree through instruction offered by LC.
Special: Study abroad in London and Hong Kong, interdisciplinary studies, work-study programs, nondegree study, internships, and pass/fail options are offered. There are 13 national honor societies, and a freshman honors program.
Faculty/Classroom: 50% of faculty are male; 50%, female. All teach undergraduates. The average class size in an introductory lecture is 30; in a laboratory, 20; and in a regular course, 18.
Admissions: 76% of the 2001-2002 applicants were accepted. The ACT scores for the 2001-2002 freshman class were: 27% below 21, 33% between 21 and 23, 22% between 24 and 26, 12% between 27 and 28, and 6% above 28. There was 1 National Merit finalist. 28 freshmen graduated first in their class.
Requirements: The SAT I or ACT is required. In addition, candidates for admission must have completed 17 units, including 4 in high school English and 3 each in math, science, and social studies, and have a minimum ACT score of 20 (SAT I 930). LC requires applicants to be in the upper 50% of their class. A GPA of 2.0 is required. AP and CLEP credits are accepted. Important factors in the admissions decision are advanced placement or honor courses, extracurricular activities record, and leadership record. Applications are accepted on-line via CollegeNET.
Procedure: Freshmen are admitted fall, spring, and summer. Entrance exams should be taken during the junior or senior year. Application deadlines are open. The application fee is $25. Notification is sent on a rolling basis.
Transfer: 136 transfer students enrolled in 2001-2002. Applicants must have an overall minimum GPA of 2.0. 30 credits of 127 must be completed at LC.
Visiting: There are regularly scheduled orientations for prospective students, consisting of spring and fall campus preview days and a 2-day orientation and pre-registration in June. There are guides for informal visits and visitors may sit in on classes and stay overnight. To schedule a visit, contact the Office of Admissions.
Financial Aid: In a recent year, 90% of all freshmen and 80% of continuing students received some form of financial aid. 40% of all students received need-based aid. Scholarships or need-based grants averaged $3800 ($6200 maximum); loans averaged $2200 ($2625 maximum); and work contracts averaged $1000 ($1400 maximum). 19% of undergraduates work part time. The average financial indebtedness of the 2001 graduate was $18,000. The FAFSA or FFS and the college's own financial statement are required.
International Students: They must score 550 on the written TOEFL or 213 on the electronic version.
Computers: The mainframe is a DEC VAX. There are PC labs for Mac and IBM-compatible PCs. All students may access the system. There are no time limits and no fees.
Graduates: In 2001, 158 bachelor's degrees were awarded. The most popular majors were biology (13%), management/marketing (9%), and psychology (8%). In an average class, 1% graduate in 3 years, 23% in 4 years, 39% in 5 years, and 42% in 6 years. 65 companies recruited on campus in 2000-2001.
Admissions Contact: Mary Wagner, Director of Admissions.
E-mail: *admissions@lacollege.edu* Web: *lacollege.edu*

LOUISIANA STATE UNIVERSITY SYSTEM

The Louisiana State University System, established in 1860, is a public system governed by a board of supervisors. The chief administrator is the president. The primary goal of the system is to foster excellence in learning (teaching), discovery (research), engagement (service), and health/care (training). The main priority is effectively preparing citizens for an increasingly complex world, using its expertise in the generation, preservation, application, and dissemination of knowledge, healthcare, and the development of new technologies. Each of the ten system campuses, along with its Healthcare Service Division, will serve a vital role by preparing its stakeholders to incorporate new knowledge and technologies into their daily lives, thereby improving their productivity and health while enhancing their quality of life and opportunities for future success. Total enrollment in the LSU System is more than 61,400 with 5396 faculty, 1,556 other academic employees, 3284 professional employees, and 16,774 classified employees. Profiles of the 4-year campuses located in Baton Rouge, Shreveport, and New Orleans are included in this section. For a tour of the Louisiana State University System and its campuses, visit our website at *http://www.lsusystem.lsu.edu/*.

LOUISIANA STATE UNIVERSITY AND AGRICULTURAL AND MECHANICAL COLLEGE — C-4

Baton Rouge, LA 70803 — **(225) 578-1175; Fax: (225) 578-4433**

Full-time: 11,394 men, 12,479 women	**Faculty:** 1126; I, --$
Part-time: 1164 men, 1491 women	**Ph.D.s:** 80%
Graduate: 2241 men, 2633 women	**Student/Faculty:** 21 to 1
Year: semesters, summer session	**Tuition:** $3468 ($8768)
Application Deadline: April 15	**Room & Board:** $4546
Freshman Class: 10,183 applied, 8078 accepted, 5039 enrolled	
ACT: 24	**VERY COMPETITIVE**

Louisiana State University and Agricultural and Mechanical College, a public institution founded in 1860, and part of the Louisiana State University System, offers programs in agriculture, arts and sciences, basic sciences, business administration, art and design, education, engineering, music and dramatic arts, and mass communication. There are 12 undergraduate and 4 graduate schools. In addition to regional accreditation, LSU has baccalaureate program accreditation with AACSB, ABET, ACCE, ACEJMC, ADA, ASLA, CSWE, FIDER, NAAB, NASAD, NASM, NCATE, and SAF. The 2 libraries contain 3,133,626 volumes, 5,279,855 microform items, and 23,170 audiovisual forms/CDs, and subscribe to 24,838 periodicals. Computerized library services include the card catalog, interlibrary loans, and database searching. Special learning facilities include a learning resource center, art gallery, natural history museum, radio station, TV station, 3 herbariums, and museums of natural science, natural history, geoscience, rural life, and art. The 2000-acre campus is in an urban area. Including residence halls, there are 250 buildings.
Student Life: 89% of undergraduates are from Louisiana. Others are from 49 states, 125 foreign countries, and Canada. 77% are white; 10% African American. 41% are Catholic; 28% Protestant; 27% claim no religious affiliation. The average age of freshmen is 19; all undergraduates, 22. 17% do not continue beyond their first year.
Housing: 7497 students can be accommodated in college housing, which includes single-sex and coed dormitories, on-campus apartments, married-student housing, fraternity houses, and sorority houses. In addition, there are honors houses and special-interest houses. 77% of students commute. All students may keep cars.
Activities: 12% of men belong to 23 national fraternities; 16% of women belong to 15 national sororities. There are 304 groups on campus, including art, band, cheerleading, choir, chorus, computers, dance, debate, drama, ethnic, gay, honors, international, jazz band, literary magazine, marching band, musical theater, newspaper, opera, orchestra, pep band, political, professional, radio and TV, religious, social, social service, student government, symphony, and yearbook. Popular campus events include Rush Week, Martin Luther King Day Celebration, and LSU Union Ice Cream/Watermelon Giveaways.
Sports: There are 8 intercollegiate sports for men and 10 for women, and 20 intramural sports for men and 20 for women. Facilities include a 91,600-seat stadium, a 14,237-seat domed sports center, a 7700-seat baseball stadium, a 400-meter track with seating for 5600, a natatorium with an 8-lane Olympic pool and diving well, an indoor track, and courts for handball, badminton, volleyball, and tennis. The recreational sports facility provides a multifaceted program that includes aquatics, sports clubs, informal recreation, instructional sports, intramural sports, outdoor recreation, special-events activities, and sports medicine. There is also an indoor practice facility for football, a soccer field that seats 1500, and a softball stadium that seats 1500.

Disabled Students: 60% of the campus is accessible. Wheelchair ramps, elevators, special parking, specially equipped rest rooms, special class scheduling, lowered drinking fountains, lowered telephones, telecommunication devices for the deaf, and power doors are available.

Services: Counseling and information services are available, as is tutoring in some subjects, including English, math, foreign languages, and sciences. There is remedial reading and writing. There are designated sections of math and Latin for students with learning disabilities.

Campus Safety and Security: Measures include 24-hour foot and vehicle patrol, self-defense education, escort service, and shuttle buses. There are informal discussions, pamphlets/posters/films, emergency telephones, lighted pathways/sidewalks, and specialized crime prevention programs.

Programs of Study: LSU confers B.A., B.S., B.A. in M.C., B.Arch., B.F.A., B.G.S., B.Int.Design, B.Land.Arch., B.M., B.M.Ed., B.S.B.E., B.S.C.E., B.S.Ch.E., B.S.Cons.M., B.S.E.E., B.S.Env.Engineering, B.S.F., B.S.I.E., B.S. in Geol., B.S.M.E., and B.S.P.E. degrees. Master's and doctoral degrees are also awarded. Bachelor's degrees are awarded in AGRICULTURE (agricultural business management, animal science, forestry and related sciences, natural resource management, and plant science), BIOLOGICAL SCIENCE (biochemistry, biology/biological science, nutrition, and wildlife biology), BUSINESS (accounting, banking and finance, business administration and management, business economics, international economics, management information systems, management science, and marketing/retailing/merchandising), COMMUNICATIONS AND THE ARTS (communications, dramatic arts, English, fine arts, French, German, Latin, music, Spanish, and speech/debate/rhetoric), COMPUTER AND PHYSICAL SCIENCE (chemistry, computer science, geology, mathematics, and physics), EDUCATION (elementary, music, secondary, and vocational), ENGINEERING AND ENVIRONMENTAL DESIGN (architecture, bioengineering, chemical engineering, civil engineering, computer engineering, construction management, electrical/electronics engineering, environmental engineering, industrial engineering, interior design, landscape architecture/design, mechanical engineering, and petroleum/natural gas engineering), HEALTH PROFESSIONS (speech pathology/audiology), SOCIAL SCIENCE (anthropology, dietetics, economics, family/consumer studies, food science, geography, history, international studies, liberal arts/general studies, philosophy, physical fitness/movement, political science/government, psychology, Russian and Slavic studies, sociology, and textiles and clothing). Biological sciences, chemical engineering, and chemistry are the strongest academically. Biological sciences, mass communication, and general business are the largest.

Required: To graduate, all students must have a minimum overall 2.0 GPA in at least 127 credit hours, with 50 to 69 in the major. They must complete a general education component of 38 to 39 semester hours in approved courses in 6 major areas, including 9 hours in humanities, 8 to 9 in natural sciences, 6 each in English composition, analytical reasoning, and social sciences, and 3 in the arts.

Special: Co-op programs in numerous majors, cross-registration with Southern University and Baton Rouge Community College, study abroad, and work-study programs are offered. B.A.-B.S. degrees, dual majors, a general studies degree, nondegree study, an evening school, a program of study for adult learners, and pass/fail options are available. There are 40 national honor societies, including Phi Beta Kappa, a freshman honors program, and 17 departmental honors programs.

Faculty/Classroom: 68% of faculty are male; 32%, female. 86% teach undergraduates, 60% do research, and 60% do both. Graduate students teach 24% of introductory courses. The average class size in an introductory lecture is 44; in a laboratory, 20; and in a regular course, 38.

Admissions: 79% of the 2001-2002 applicants were accepted. The ACT scores for the 2001-2002 freshman class were: 17% below 21, 35% between 21 and 23, 24% between 24 and 26, 13% between 27 and 28, and 10% above 28. 47% of the current freshmen were in the top fifth of their class; 75% were in the top two fifths. There were 39 National Merit finalists and 39 semifinalists. 122 freshmen graduated first in their class.

Requirements: The ACT is required and the SAT I is recommended. In addition, applicants must be graduates of an accredited secondary school. GED certificates may be accepted in unusual circumstances. Students must have completed 4 credits in English, 3 each in specific math, science, and social studies courses, 2 credits in a foreign language, 1/2 credit in computer skills, and 2 additional credits from the above categories or certain courses in the visual and performing arts. A GPA of 2.8 is required. AP and CLEP credits are accepted. Important factors in the admissions decision are advanced placement or honor courses, evidence of special talent, and recommendations by school officials. Applications may be submitted on-line at *http://web.srr.lsu.edu/admissions*

Procedure: Freshmen are admitted to all sessions. Entrance exams should be taken in the fall of the senior year. There is an early admissions plan. Applications should be filed by April 15 for fall entry, December 1 for spring entry, and April 15 for summer entry, along with a $25 fee. Notification is sent on a rolling basis.

Transfer: 858 transfer students enrolled in 2001-2002. Transfer students must submit an official transcript from each previously attended school. Requirements are 30 or more semester hours with a minimum 2.5 GPA, and a college level English and math course. 30 credits of 120 to 160 must be completed at LSU.

Visiting: There are regularly scheduled orientations for prospective students, including an information session and a tour of campus. Department appointments can be arranged. There are guides for informal visits and visitors may sit in on classes and stay overnight. To schedule a visit, contact the Office of Recruitment and Tours at (225) 578-6652.

Financial Aid: In 2000-2001, 95% of all freshmen and 75% of all undergraduates received some form of financial aid. 22% of freshmen and 29% of all undergraduates received need-based aid. The average freshman award was $5080. Of that total, scholarships or need-based grants averaged $3200 ($10,900 maximum); loans averaged $3800 ($16,000 maximum); and work contracts averaged $1500 ($9400 maximum). 23% of undergraduates work part time. Average annual earnings from campus work are $2000. The average financial indebtedness of the 2001 graduate was $17,818. The FAFSA is required. The fall application deadline is February 1.

International Students: There are 658 international students enrolled. The school actively recruits these students. They must score 500 on the written TOEFL or 173 on the electronic version.

Computers: The mainframes are an IBM 4672/RX3, and an IBM SP. Public labs contain more than 800 networked PCs. All students may access the system up to 16 hours per day, 7 days per week (public facilities). There are no time limits and no fees. It is recommended that students in College of Design have personal computers.

Graduates: In 2001, 4025 bachelor's degrees were awarded. The most popular majors were general studies (6%), informations systems and decision sciences (6%), and mass communication (5%). In an average class, 22% graduate in 4 years, 48% in 5 years, and 56% in 6 years. 513 companies recruited on campus in 2000-2001.

Admissions Contact: Clare Brooks, Admissions Director. A video is available. E-mail: *admissions@lsu.edu* Web: *www.lsu.edu*

LOUISIANA STATE UNIVERSITY IN SHREVEPORT — A-1
Shreveport, LA 71115 (318) 797-5061
(800) 229-5957; Fax: (318) 797-5286

Full-time: 905 men, 1365 women	**Faculty:** 139; IIA, --$
Part-time: 485 men, 800 women	**Ph.D.s:** 83%
Graduate: 220 men, 465 women	**Student/Faculty:** 16 to 1
Year: semesters, summer session	**Tuition:** $2480 ($6810)
Application Deadline: see profile	**Room & Board:** n/av
Freshman Class: n/av	
ACT: required	**NONCOMPETITIVE**

Louisiana State University in Shreveport, established in 1965, is a state-supported, primarily commuter institution offering undergraduate and graduate programs through the colleges of liberal arts, business, education, and sciences. Figures in the above capsule are approximate. There are 4 undergraduate and 4 graduate schools. In addition to regional accreditation, LSUS has baccalaureate program accreditation with AACSB, CSAB, and NCATE. The library contains 279,821 volumes, 364,744 microform items, and 1914 audiovisual forms/CDs, and subscribes to 1190 periodicals. Computerized library services include the card catalog, interlibrary loans, and database searching. Special learning facilities include an art gallery, radio station, heritage center, and museum of life sciences. The 200-acre campus is in an urban area 7 miles south of downtown Shreveport. Including residence halls, there are 18 buildings.

Student Life: 98% of undergraduates are from Louisiana. Others are from 49 states, 10 foreign countries, and Canada. 95% are from public schools. 75% are white; 20% African American. The average age of freshmen is 20; all undergraduates, 25. 21% do not continue beyond their first year; 30% remain to graduate.

Housing: 480 students can be accommodated in college housing, which includes single-sex and coed on-campus apartments. On-campus housing is available on a first-come, first-served basis. 94% of students commute. Alcohol is not permitted. All students may keep cars.

Activities: 5% of men belong to 3 national fraternities; 3% of women belong to 2 national sororities. There are 50 groups on campus, including art, chess, choir, computers, debate, drama, ethnic, honors, literary magazine, newspaper, photography, political, professional, radio and TV, religious, social, social service, and student government. Popular campus events include Fall Fest, Spring Fling, and Welcome Back Bash.

Sports: There is 1 intercollegiate sport for men. Facilities include tennis and racquetball courts, sand or volleyball courts, a swimming pool, gym, weight room, dance studio, football fields, softball diamonds, and a soccer field.

Disabled Students: All of the campus is accessible. Wheelchair ramps, elevators, special parking, specially equipped rest rooms, lowered drinking fountains, and lowered telephones are available.

Services: Counseling and information services are available, as is tutoring in some subjects, including math and English. There is a reader service for the blind and remedial math and writing.

Campus Safety and Security: Measures include 24-hour foot and vehicle patrol, escort service, emergency telephones, and lighted pathways/sidewalks, and commissioned University police officers.

Programs of Study: LSUS confers B.A., B.S., B.C.J., B.G.S. degrees. Master's degrees are also awarded. Bachelor's degrees are awarded in BIOLOGICAL SCIENCE (biochemistry and biology/biological science), BUSINESS (accounting, banking and finance, business administration and management, business economics, management science, and marketing/retailing/merchandising), COMMUNICATIONS AND THE ARTS (communications, English, fine arts, French, journalism, Spanish, and speech/debate/rhetoric), COMPUTER AND PHYSICAL SCIENCE (chemistry, computer science, mathematics, and physics), EDUCATION (art, elementary, and secondary), ENGINEERING AND ENVIRONMENTAL DESIGN (environmental science), SOCIAL SCIENCE (economics, geography, history, liberal arts/general studies, political science/government, psychology, and sociology). Elementary education and psychology are the largest.

Required: All students must take a computer course. A minimum of 128 semester hours, with a minimum GPA of 2.0, is required for the bachelor's degree.

Special: Opportunities are provided for cross-registration with Southern University/Shreveport, internships, a Washington semester, a general studies degree, a 3-2 engineering degree with Louisiana Tech University, credit for military service schools, nondegree study, and pass/fail options. There are 5 national honor societies.

Faculty/Classroom: 65% of faculty are male; 35%, female. 70% do research and 70% both teach and do research. No introductory courses are taught by graduate students. The average class size in an introductory lecture is 29; in a laboratory, 25; and in a regular course, 26.

Requirements: The ACT is required, with a minimum composite score of 18. Graduation from an accredited secondary school is required. The GED will be accepted. Conditional admission is granted to those who do not meet minimum requirements. AP and CLEP credits are accepted.

Procedure: Freshmen are admitted to all sessions. Entrance exams should be taken by the ACT national date. The college accepts all in-state residents. Notification is sent on a rolling basis. Check with the school for current deadlines. The fall 2001 application fee was $10.

Transfer: 502 transfer students enrolled in a recent year. Transfers must be in good academic standing, with a GPA of 2.0, or they may enter on probation. They must be eligible to continue at the last institution attended. 30 credits of 128 must be completed at LSUS.

Visiting: There are regularly scheduled orientations for prospective students, including a preview program during the spring semester for high school juniors and seniors. There are guides for informal visits. To schedule a visit, contact Michael Valentine, Kelli Stevens, or Nicole Shelby at (318) 797-5119.

Financial Aid: In a recent year, 40% of all freshmen and 30% of continuing students received some form of financial aid. 25% of all students received need-based aid. 90% of undergraduates work part time. Average annual earnings from campus work are $1800. The FAFSA and FSAR are required. Check with the school for current deadlines.

International Students: There were 10 international students enrolled in a recent year. They must score 500 on the written TOEFL and also take the SAT I or the ACT, scoring 18 on the ACT.

Computers: The mainframe is an IBM ES/9000 Model 120. PCs are available for academic use in student labs and faculty offices. PCs with Internet and Web access are located throughout the campus. All students may access the system. There are no time limits and no fees.

Graduates: In a recent year, 449 bachelor's degrees were awarded. The most popular majors were elementary education (12%), management (12%), and accounting (8%). In an average class, 18% graduate in 6 years. 75 companies recruited on campus in a recent year.

Admissions Contact: Kelli Stevens, Admission Counselor.
E-mail: *kstevens@pilot.lsus.edu* Web: *www.lsus.edu*

LOUISIANA TECH UNIVERSITY

Ruston, LA 71272 — B-3
(318) 257-3036
(800) LATECH-1; Fax: (318) 257-2499

Full-time: 4012 men, 3473 women	**Faculty:** 373; IIA, --$
Part-time: 655 men, 920 women	**Ph.D.s:** 80%
Graduate: 661 men, 973 women	**Student/Faculty:** 20 to 1
Year: quarters, summer session	**Tuition:** $3041 ($7946)
Application Deadline: August 4	**Room & Board:** $3465
Freshman Class: 3289 applied, 3007 accepted, 1929 enrolled	
SAT I: n/av	**ACT:** required **COMPETITIVE**

Louisiana Tech University, founded in 1894, is a public institution offering programs in arts and sciences, business, agriculture, engineering, health science, education, fine and liberal arts, and human ecology. There are 5 undergraduate and 5 graduate schools. In addition to regional accreditation, Tech has baccalaureate program accreditation with AACSB, ABET, ADA, AHEA, ASLA, CAHEA, FIDER, NAAB, NASAD, NASM, NCATE, NLN, and SAF. The library contains 1,108,260 volumes and 1,891,666 microform items, and subscribes to 2469 periodicals. Computerized library services include the card catalog, interlibrary loans, and database searching. Special learning facilities include a learning resource center, art gallery, natural history museum, planetarium, and radio station. The 235-acre campus is in a small town 30 miles west of Monroe and 70 miles east of Shreveport. Including residence halls, there are 134 buildings.

Student Life: 87% of undergraduates are from Louisiana. Others are from 49 states, 51 foreign countries, and Canada. 80% are from public schools. 73% are white; 15%, African American. 51% are Protestant; 12%, Catholic. The average age of freshmen is 19; all undergraduates, 20. 22% do not continue beyond their first year; 43% remain to graduate.

Housing: 3250 students can be accommodated in college housing, which includes single-sex and coed dormitories and married-student housing. In addition, there are honors houses. On-campus housing is guaranteed for all 4 years. 70% of students commute. Alcohol is not permitted. All students may keep cars.

Activities: 10% of men belong to 9 national fraternities; 12% of women belong to 5 national sororities. There are 121 groups on campus, including art, band, cheerleading, choir, chorale, chorus, computers, dance, debate, drama, drill team, drum and bugle corps, ethnic, film, honors, international, jazz band, marching band, musical theater, newspaper, opera, orchestra, pep band, photography, political, professional, radio and TV, religious, social, social service, student government, symphony, and yearbook. Popular campus events include International Student Festival, Spring Fling, and Little Theater concerts.

Sports: There are 5 intercollegiate sports for men and 5 for women, and 10 intramural sports for men and 10 for women. Facilities include a football stadium, a coliseum, an intramural complex, a natatorium, a 9-hole golf course, and 10 lighted tennis courts.

Disabled Students: 95% of the campus is accessible. Wheelchair ramps, elevators, special parking, specially equipped rest rooms, lowered drinking fountains, and lowered telephones are available.

Services: Counseling and information services are available, as is tutoring in some subjects. There is a reader service for the blind, and remedial math, reading, and writing.

Campus Safety and Security: Measures include 24-hour foot and vehicle patrol, self-defense education, escort service, and informal discussions. There are emergency telephones and lighted pathways/sidewalks.

Programs of Study: Tech confers B.A., B.S., B. Arch., B.F.A., and B.G.S. degrees. Associate, master's, and doctoral degrees are also awarded. Bachelor's degrees are awarded in AGRICULTURE (agricultural business management, animal science, forestry and related sciences, and wildlife management), BIOLOGICAL SCIENCE (biology/biological science), BUSINESS (accounting, banking and finance, business administration and management, business economics, business systems analysis, management science, marketing/retailing/merchandising, and personnel management), COMMUNICATIONS AND THE ARTS (English, fine arts, French, journalism, music, music performance, Spanish, and speech/debate/rhetoric), COMPUTER AND PHYSICAL SCIENCE (chemistry, computer science, geology, mathematics, and physics), EDUCATION (art, early childhood, elementary, foreign languages, music, physical, secondary, and special), ENGINEERING AND ENVIRONMENTAL DESIGN (airline piloting and navigation, architecture, aviation administration/management, biomedical engineering, chemical engineering, civil engineering, construction engineering, electrical/electronics engineering technology, environmental science, industrial engineering, and mechanical engineering), HEALTH PROFESSIONS (medical laboratory technology, medical records administration/services, and speech pathology/audiology), SOCIAL SCIENCE (dietetics, geography, history, liberal arts/general studies, political science/government, psychology, and sociology). Business and engineering are the strongest academically and have the largest enrollments.

Required: All students must complete 45 quarter hours of general education courses, including 12 hours in humanities, 9 each in natural and social sciences, 6 each in English and math, and 3 in arts or computer literacy. A total of 120 to 142 quarter hours, with a minimum GPA of 2.0, is required to graduate.

Special: Co-op programs are available in engineering and applied and natural sciences, and cross-registration with Grambling State University is offered. Internships in agriculture, engineering, dietetics, and human ecology are offered. Study abroad, work-study programs, dual majors, a general studies degree, nondegree study, and pass/fail options are available. There is a chapter of Phi Beta Kappa and a freshman honors program.

Faculty/Classroom: 67% of faculty are male; 33%, female. 95% teach undergraduates and 75% both teach and do research. Graduate students teach 2% of introductory courses. The average class size in an introductory lecture is 40; in a laboratory, 20; and in a regular course, 26.

Admissions: 93% of the 2001-2002 applicants were accepted. The ACT scores for the 2001-2002 freshman class were: 36% below 21, 28% between 21 and 23, 21% between 24 and 26, 9% between 27 and 28, and 6% above 28. There were 2 National Merit finalists.

Requirements: The ACT is required. In addition, applicants must be graduates of an accredited secondary school or have a GED. Tech requires applicants to be in the upper 35% of their class. A GPA of 2.2 is required. AP credits are accepted.

Procedure: Freshmen are admitted to all sessions. Applications should be filed by August 4 for fall entry, October 24 for winter entry, January 30 for spring entry, and May 9 for summer entry. Notification is sent on a rolling basis. The fall 2001 application fee was $20.

Transfer: 524 transfer students enrolled in 2001-2002. Transfer applicants should have a 2.0 GPA and be eligible to enroll in the school from which they are transferring. 30 credits of 120 to 142 must be completed at Tech.

Visiting: There are regularly scheduled orientations for prospective students. There are guides for informal visits and visitors may stay overnight. To schedule a visit, contact the Admissions Office.

Financial Aid: In a recent year, 82% of all freshmen and 87% of continuing students received some form of financial aid. 68% of freshmen and 80% of continuing students received need-based aid. The average freshman award was $4915. Of that total, scholarships or need-based grants averaged $3076 ($7000 maximum); loans averaged $1532 ($4700 maximum); and work contracts averaged $338. 27% of undergraduates worked part time. Average annual earnings from campus work were $2283. The average financial indebtedness of a recent graduate was $11,802. The FAFSA is required. The fall application deadline is July 16.

International Students: There are 139 international students enrolled. The school actively recruits these students. They must score 500 on the written TOEFL.

Computers: The mainframe is an IBM 9121-210. Computer labs are located within each college, with PCs and terminals networked to the mainframe, as well as specialized local network workstations. There are also computer labs located in dormitories in the central computing center, and in the library. All students may access the system 24 hours a day, 7 days a week. There are no time limits.

Graduates: In 2001, 1267 bachelor's degrees were awarded. The most popular majors were business (20%), engineering (14%), and education (9%). In an average class, 22% graduate in 4 years, 46% in 5 years, and 51% in 6 years. 740 companies recruited on campus in 2000-2001.

Admissions Contact: Jan Albritton, Admissions Office. A video is available. E-mail: *bulldog@latech.edu* Web: *http://www.latech.edu*

LOYOLA UNIVERSITY NEW ORLEANS — D-4

New Orleans, LA 70118-6195 — **(504) 865-3240**
(800) 4-LOYOLA; Fax: (504) 865-3383

Full-time: 1195 men, 2040 women	**Faculty:** 234; IIA, av$
Part-time: 154 men, 403 women	**Ph.D.s:** 92%
Graduate: 671 men, 1046 women	**Student/Faculty:** 14 to 1
Year: semesters, summer session	**Tuition:** $16,700
Application Deadline: February 15	**Room & Board:** $6806
Freshman Class: 3419 applied, 2373 accepted, 866 enrolled	
SAT I or ACT: required	**VERY COMPETITIVE+**

Loyola University New Orleans, founded in 1912, is a private institution operated by the Society of Jesus and affiliated with the Roman Catholic Church. There are 4 undergraduate schools and 1 graduate school. In addition to regional accreditation, Loyola has baccalaureate program accreditation with AACSB, ACS, NASM, and NLN. The 2 libraries contain 401,548 volumes, 1,304,300 microform items, and 15,484 audiovisual forms/CDs, and subscribe to 4545 periodicals. Computerized library services include the card catalog, interlibrary loans, and database searching. Special learning facilities include a learning resource center, art gallery, TV station, and theater. The 20-acre campus is in an urban area 5 miles from downtown New Orleans. Including residence halls, there are 24 buildings.

Student Life: 53% of undergraduates are from Louisiana. Others are from 50 states, 61 foreign countries, and Canada. 37% are from public schools. 64% are white; 11%, African American; 10%, Hispanic. Most are Catholic. The average age of freshmen is 18; all undergraduates, 20. 19% do not continue beyond their first year; 55% remain to graduate.

Housing: 1381 students can be accommodated in college housing, which includes single-sex and coed dormitories and on-campus apartments. In addition, there are special-interest houses. On-campus housing is available on a first-come, first-served basis. Priority is given to out-of-town students. 61% of students commute. Upperclassmen may keep cars.

Activities: 16% of men belong to 1 local fraternity and 5 national fraternities; 17% of women belong to 6 national sororities. There are 120 groups on campus, including art, band, cheerleading, choir, chorale, chorus, computers, dance, drama, ethnic, film, gay, honors, international, jazz band, literary magazine, musical theater, newspaper, opera, orchestra, photography, political, professional, radio and TV, religious, social, social service, student government, symphony, and yearbook. Popular campus events include Riverboat Party Charity Dance, Loyolapalooza, and Spring Music Festival.

Sports: There are 5 intercollegiate sports for men and 6 for women, and 10 intramural sports for men and 10 for women. Facilities include a sports complex with an arena, 6 multipurpose courts for basketball, tennis, volleyball, badminton, and floor hockey, 3 racquetball courts, an Olympic-style natatorium, a jogging track, a weight-lifting and conditioning area, and a baseball stadium.

Disabled Students: 99% of the campus is accessible. Wheelchair ramps, elevators, special parking, specially equipped rest rooms, lowered drinking fountains, lowered telephones, and special housing, special class relocation to provide accessibility are available.

Services: Counseling and information services are available, as is tutoring in most subjects. There is remedial math and writing. Peer tutoring is available in all introductory common curriculum courses. A reader service for the blind is provided for all exams and for course work if books on tape are not sufficient.

Campus Safety and Security: Measures include 24-hour foot and vehicle patrol, self-defense education, escort service, and shuttle buses. There are informal discussions, pamphlets/posters/films, emergency telephones, lighted pathways/sidewalks, CCTV coverage, card access control, intrusion alarm monitoring, first aid medical assistance, motor vehicle assistance, bicycle registration, finger printing services, and crime prevention services.

Programs of Study: Loyola confers B.A., B.S., B.Acc., B.A.S., B.B.A., B.C.J., B.F.A., B.L.S., B.Mus., B.Mus.Ed., B.Mus. Therapy, and B.S.N. degrees. Master's and doctoral degrees are also awarded. Bachelor's degrees are awarded in BIOLOGICAL SCIENCE (biology/biological science), BUSINESS (accounting, banking and finance, business administration and management, international business management, management science, marketing/retailing/merchandising, and organizational behavior), COMMUNICATIONS AND THE ARTS (communications, communications technology, creative writing, dramatic arts, English, fine arts, French, German, graphic design, jazz, music business management, music performance, music theory and composition, piano/organ, Russian, Spanish, studio art, and visual and performing arts), COMPUTER AND PHYSICAL SCIENCE (chemistry, computer science, information sciences and systems, mathematics, and physics), EDUCATION (elementary and music), HEALTH PROFESSIONS (music therapy and nursing), SOCIAL SCIENCE (classical/ancient civilization, criminal justice, economics, history, philosophy, political science/government, psychology, religion, religious education, social science, and sociology). Biology, chemistry, and English are the strongest academically. Communications, psychology, and biology are the largest.

Required: All students must complete a core curriculum that includes courses in English composition and literature, math, philosophy, science, world civilization, and religious studies; the number of credit hours varies by college. At least 120 credit hours, with at least 30 in the major, and a minimum GPA of 2.0 are required to graduate.

Special: Cross-registration is available with Xavier University, Notre Dame Seminary, the University of New Orleans, Tulane University, and Southern University of New Orleans. Internships with the New Orleans business community are also available. Study abroad in 7 countries, dual and student-designed majors, nondegree studies, and a general studies degree are offered. A Washington semester through American University and a 3-2 engineering degree with Tulane University are also offered. There are 16 national honor societies, a freshman honors program, and 7 departmental honors program.

Faculty/Classroom: 61% of faculty are male; 39%, female. 89% teach undergraduates and 90% do research. No introductory courses are taught by graduate students. The average class size in an introductory lecture is 30; in a laboratory, 34; and in a regular course, 18.

Admissions: 69% of the 2001-2002 applicants were accepted. 48% of the current freshmen were in the top fifth of their class; 78% were in the top two fifths. 11 freshmen graduated first in their class.

Requirements: The SAT I or ACT is required. In addition, candidates for admission must be graduates of an accredited secondary school or have a GED. They should have completed 4 units in high school English and 3 each in math, science, and social sciences, along with 4 academic electives; 2 units in a foreign language are recommended. A portfolio is required for fine arts students; an audition for music majors. An interview is recommended for scholarship consideration. AP and CLEP credits are accepted. Important factors in the admissions decision are advanced placement or honor courses, recommendations by school officials, and evidence of special talent. Applications are accepted on disk, or on-line via the university's web site or Next Step College, Common App, Catholic Common App, EXPAN, or CollegeLink.

Procedure: Freshmen are admitted to all sessions. Entrance exams should be taken during the junior or senior year. There are early admissions and deferred admissions plans. Applications should be filed by February 15 for fall entry and November 1 for spring entry, along with a $20 fee. Notification is sent on a rolling basis.

Transfer: 241 transfer students enrolled in 2001-2002. Applicants must have a minimum 2.25 GPA on all attempted college-level work; 12 credit hours are needed for consideration. 30 credits of 120 must be completed at Loyola.

Visiting: There are regularly scheduled orientations for prospective students, including class and department visits, a student panel, a tour, a financial aid session, a campus support panel, meetings with faculty members, and an overnight stay. There are guides for informal visits and visitors may sit in on classes and stay overnight. To schedule a visit, contact the Admissions Office.

Financial Aid: In 2001-2002, 57% of all freshmen and 54% of continuing students received some form of financial aid including need-based aid. The average freshman award was $13,633. Of that total, scholarships or need-based grants averaged $10,729 ($16,187 maximum); and loans averaged $2547 ($2625 maximum). The average financial indebtedness of the 2001 graduate was $17,981. The FAFSA is required. The fall priority deadline is February 1.

International Students: There are 186 international students enrolled. The school actively recruits these students. They must score 550 on the written TOEFL or 213 on the electronic version and also take the college's own test and the SAT I or the ACT.

Computers: The mainframes are an IBM SP/2, IBM ES/9000, a DEC VAX 3100-80, and 2 DEC ALPHA 3000 Model 300s. Students may connect to the system via 2500 campuswide Internet ports, 48 modem lines, 75 public workstations, and Internet-ready residence hall rooms. All students may access the system at any time. There are no time limits. The fee is $50 per semester. It is strongly recommended that all students have a personal computer.

Graduates: In 2001, 647 bachelor's degrees were awarded. The most popular majors were communications (18%), psychology (5%), and marketing and management (4%). In an average class, 34% graduate in 4 years, 51% in 5 years, and 53% in 6 years. 168 companies recruited on campus in 2000-2001. Of the 2000 graduating class, 24% were enrolled in graduate school within 6 months of graduation and 52% were employed.

Admissions Contact: Deborah C. Stieffel, Dean of Admissions and Enrollment Management. A video is available.
E-mail: *admit@loyno.edu* Web: *http://www.loyno.edu*

MCNEESE STATE UNIVERSITY B-4

Lake Charles, LA 70609-2495 (337) 475-5148
(800) 622-3352; Fax: (337) 475-5189

Full-time: 2389 men, 3308 women	**Faculty:** 262; IIA, --$
Part-time: 427 men, 721 women	**Ph.D.s:** 64%
Graduate: 283 men, 652 women	**Student/Faculty:** 22 to 1
Year: semesters, summer session	**Tuition:** $2511 ($8851)
Application Deadline: open	**Room & Board:** $2748
Freshman Class: 2031 applied, 1740 accepted, 1383 enrolled	
SAT I: n/av	**ACT:** required

LESS COMPETITIVE

McNeese State University, founded in 1939, and part of the University of Louisiana System, is a public institution offering programs in business, agriculture, engineering, education, film arts, science, liberal arts, and nursing. There are 6 undergraduate schools and 1 graduate school. In addition to regional accreditation, MSU has baccalaureate program accreditation with AACSB, AAFCS, ABET, ACS, ADA, CAHEA, CSAB, NAACLS, NASM, NCATE, and NLN. The library contains 546,183 volumes, 1,437,496 microform items, and 1382 audiovisual forms/CDs, and subscribes to 1808 periodicals. Computerized library services include the card catalog, interlibrary loans, and database searching. Special learning facilities include a learning resource center, art gallery, planetarium, a farm, a vertebrate museum, and a community health care clinic. The 580-acre campus is in a suburban area 120 miles west of Baton Rouge and 60 miles east of Beaumont, Texas. Including residence halls, there are 95 buildings.

Student Life: 92% of undergraduates are from Louisiana. Others are from 33 states, 51 foreign countries, and Canada. 78% are white; 17% African American. The average age of freshmen is 22; all undergraduates, 24. 34% do not continue beyond their first year.

Housing: 850 students can be accommodated in college housing, which includes single-sex and coed dormitories, on-campus apartments, and married-student housing. In addition, there are honors houses and a 12-month hall for out-of-state and international students who cannot go home. On-campus housing is guaranteed for all 4 years. 90% of students commute. Alcohol is not permitted. All students may keep cars.

Activities: 5% of men belong to 7 national fraternities; 5% of women belong to 6 national sororities. There are 93 groups on campus, including art, band, cheerleading, choir, chorale, chorus, computers, dance, debate, drama, drill team, ethnic, honors, international, jazz band, marching band, musical theater, newspaper, orchestra, pep band, political, professional, religious, social, social service, student government, symphony, and yearbook. Popular campus events include Spring Fling.

Sports: There are 7 intercollegiate sports for men and 9 for women, and 15 intramural sports for men and 15 for women. Facilities include a football stadium, softball and intramural fields, an indoor/outdoor track, a 50-meter pool, a coliseum, a baseball complex, outdoor tennis courts, an 8,000-square-foot weight room, racquetball courts, and 3 regulation basketball courts.

Disabled Students: 94% of the campus is accessible. Wheelchair ramps, elevators, special parking, specially equipped rest rooms, lowered drinking fountains, academic planning and registration assistance, and classroom and testing accommodations are available.

Services: Counseling and information services are available, as is tutoring in some subjects, including English, math, chemistry, physics, and biology. There is remedial math, reading, and writing, and a study skills course.

Campus Safety and Security: Measures include 24-hour foot and vehicle patrol, escort service, informal discussions, and pamphlets/posters/films. There are lighted pathways/sidewalks, security guards posted at the residence halls from 11 P.M. until 7 A.M., and a crime stoppers program.

Programs of Study: MSU confers B.A., B.S., B.Mus., B.Mus.Ed., and B.S.N. degrees. Associate and master's degrees are also awarded. Bachelor's degrees are awarded in AGRICULTURE (agricultural business management, agriculture, animal science, and wildlife management), BIOLOGICAL SCIENCE (biology/biological science), BUSINESS (accounting, banking and finance, business administration and management, and marketing/retailing/merchandising), COMMUNICATIONS AND THE ARTS (broadcasting, communications, dramatic arts, English, fine arts, languages, music, speech/debate/rhetoric, and visual and performing arts), COMPUTER AND PHYSICAL SCIENCE (chemistry, computer science, geology, information sciences and systems, mathematics, physics, and radiological technology), EDUCATION (business, early childhood, elementary, foreign languages, guidance, health, home economics, science, and special), ENGINEERING AND ENVIRONMENTAL DESIGN (chemical engineering, civil engineering, electrical/electronics engineering, environmental science, and mechanical engineering), HEALTH PROFESSIONS (medical laboratory technology, and nursing), SOCIAL SCIENCE (criminal justice, economics, family/consumer studies, history, liberal arts/general studies, psychology, and sociology). Education, nursing, and engineering are the largest.

Required: The general requirements for graduation include 9 hours each in the humanities and natural sciences, 6 each in English, math, and social sciences, 3 in arts and computer literacy, and 1 in orientation, for a total of 43 core hours. A total of 120 credit hours with a minimum GPA equivalent of C is needed.

Special: MSU offers co-op programs in engineering, internships in medical technology, radiologic technology, and education, dual majors, a general studies degree, nondegree study, and credit for military experience. There are 13 national honor societies, and a freshman honors program.

Faculty/Classroom: 58% of faculty are male; 42%, female. 94% teach undergraduates and 11% both teach and do research. The average class size in an introductory lecture is 38; in a laboratory, 25; and in a regular course, 27.

Admissions: 86% of the 2001-2002 applicants were accepted.

Requirements: The ACT is required. In addition, applicants must have a high school GPA of at least 3.0 or an ACT score of at least 20 (SAT I 940). Applications are accepted on-line. AP and CLEP credits are accepted.

Procedure: Freshmen are admitted to all sessions. Entrance exams should be taken prior to enrolling. There is an early admissions plan. Application deadlines are open. The application fee is $20. Notification is sent on a rolling basis.

Transfer: 355 transfer students enrolled in 2001-2002. Transferees must be eligible for readmission to the last collegiate institution attended. 30 credits of 120 must be completed at MSU.

Visiting: There are regularly scheduled orientations for prospective students. There are guides for informal visits and visitors may sit in on classes and stay overnight. To schedule a visit, contact John Martin, Enrollment Information Center at (377) 475-5504 or *jmartin@mail.mcneese.edu*

Financial Aid: The FAFSA or FFS and the college's own financial statement are required. The fall application deadline is May 1.

International Students: There are 78 international students enrolled. The school actively recruits these students. They must score 525 on the written TOEFL or 195 on the electronic version and also take the SAT I or the ACT.

Computers: The mainframe is an IBM 9121-190. There are numerous Macs and PCs available in labs. The library houses terminals linked to MSU's computing services. The College of Science's academic computer center, the primary facility for computer science students, houses an IBM System/34, a PC lab, and terminals to access the mainframe as well as a VAX 3800-Utrix operating system. All students may access the system during lab operating hours. There are no time limits and no fees.

Graduates: In 2001, 815 bachelor's degrees were awarded. The most popular majors were education (30%), business (19%), and nursing (6%). 33 companies recruited on campus in 2000-2001.

Admissions Contact: Tammie Pettis, Director of Admissions.
E-mail: *tpettis@mail.mcneese.edu* Web: *mcneese.edu*

NICHOLLS STATE UNIVERSITY D-4

Thibodaux, LA 70301 (504) 448-4507
(877) 642-4655; Fax: (504) 448-4929

Full-time: 2041 men, 3354 women | **Faculty:** 246; IIB, --$
Part-time: 379 men, 769 women | **Ph.D.s:** 53%
Graduate: 173 men, 490 women | **Student/Faculty:** 22 to 1
Year: semesters, summer session | **Tuition:** $2440
Application Deadline: open | **Room & Board:** $2850
Freshman Class: 2838 applied, 2810 accepted, 1451 enrolled
SAT I Verbal/Math: 482/483 | **ACT:** 19 | **NONCOMPETITIVE**

Nicholls State University, established in 1948, and part of the University of Louisiana System, is a public liberal arts institution offering instruction in health sciences, fine arts, business, teacher preparation, and agricultural and technical disciplines. There are 6 undergraduate and 4 graduate schools. In addition to regional accreditation, Nicholls has baccalaureate program accreditation with AACSB, AAFCS, ACEJMC, ADA, AHEA, CAAHEP, CSAB, IAME, NASM, NCATE, and NLN. The library contains 544,677 volumes, 396,049 microform items, and 3374 audiovisual forms/CDs, and subscribes to 1341 periodicals. Computerized library services include the card catalog, interlibrary loans, and database searching. Special learning facilities include a learning resource center, art gallery, radio station, TV station, and a culinary institute, a rural development institute, and centers for the study of dyslexia, women and government, and economic education. The 210-acre campus is in a small town 50 miles southwest of New Orleans and 60 miles southeast of Baton Rouge. Including residence halls, there are 47 buildings.

Student Life: 97% of undergraduates are from Louisiana. Others are from 31 states, 29 foreign countries, and Canada. 79% are white; 16%, African American. 45% are Catholic; 38% claim no religious affiliation; 13%, Protestant. The average age of freshmen is 20; all undergraduates, 23. 45% do not continue beyond their first year.

Housing: 1056 students can be accommodated in college housing, which includes single-sex and coed dormitories and married-student housing. On-campus housing is guaranteed for the freshman year only and is available on a first-come, first-served basis. 86% of students commute. Alcohol is not permitted. All students may keep cars.

Activities: 5% of men belong to 7 national fraternities; 5% of women belong to 7 national sororities. There are 73 groups on campus, including art, band, cheerleading, chess, choir, chorale, chorus, computers, dance, debate, drama, drill team, ethnic, gay, honors, international, jazz band, literary magazine, marching band, musical theater, newspaper, pep band, photography, political, professional, radio and TV, religious, social, social service, student government, symphony, and yearbook. Popular campus events include Midterm Exam Week Breakfast, Family Day, and Crawfish Boil.

Sports: There are 7 intercollegiate sports for men and 8 for women, and 4 intramural sports for men and 4 for women. Facilities include a stadium, 2 gyms, tennis and raquetball courts, a soccer field, a swimming pool, baseball and softball fields, and a weight room.

Disabled Students: Wheelchair ramps, elevators, special parking, specially equipped rest rooms, special class scheduling, lowered drinking fountains, and lowered telephones are available.

Services: Counseling and information services are available, as is tutoring in most subjects. There is a reader service for the blind and remedial math and writing.

Campus Safety and Security: Measures include 24-hour foot and vehicle patrol, self-defense education, escort service, and informal discussions. There are pamphlets/posters/films, emergency telephones, and lighted pathways/sidewalks.

Programs of Study: Nicholls confers B.A., B.S., B.M.E., B.S.N., and B.G.S. degrees. Associate and master's degrees are also awarded. Bachelor's degrees are awarded in AGRICULTURE (agricultural business management), BIOLOGICAL SCIENCE (biology/biological science), BUSINESS (accounting, banking and finance, business administration and management, marketing/retailing/merchandising, and personnel management), COMMUNICATIONS AND THE ARTS (art, communications, English, French, journalism, and music), COMPUTER AND PHYSICAL SCIENCE (chemistry, computer science, information sciences and systems, and mathematics), EDUCATION (business, elementary, music, secondary, and special), HEALTH PROFESSIONS (health science, nursing, and speech pathology/audiology), SOCIAL SCIENCE (dietetics, family/consumer studies, food production/management/services, history, political science/government, psychology, and sociology). Language and literature, art, and economics and finance are the strongest academically. Teacher education, general studies, and nursing are the largest.

Required: All students must complete general education requirements, including 9 hours each in English, natural sciences, and humanities, 6 hours each in social sciences and math, 3 hours each in the arts and student development, 2 semesters of health and phys ed, and a computer literacy course. At least 125 total credit hours, plus a minimum of 24 hours in the major, with a minimum GPA of 2.0, are required to graduate.

Special: Internships are offered in business areas, government, home economics, computer science, and psychology. A Washington semester congressional internship, dual majors in education, and student-designed majors in general studies are available. Nondegree study and credit for military experience are possible. There is a seven-on/seven-off degree program for offshore oil field workers. There are 12 national honor societies, a freshman honors program, and 1 departmental honors program.

Faculty/Classroom: 55% of faculty are male; 45%, female. 98% teach undergraduates, 12% do research, and 12% do both. Graduate students teach 2% of introductory courses. The average class size in an introductory lecture is 61; in a laboratory, 21; and in a regular course, 26.

Admissions: 99% of the 2001-2002 applicants were accepted. The SAT I scores for the 2001-2002 freshman class were: Verbal--46% below 500, 34% between 500 and 599, and 20% between 600 and 700; Math--56% below 500, 29% between 500 and 599, and 15% between 600 and 700. The ACT scores were 66% below 21, 23% between 21 and 23, 8% between 24 and 26, 2% between 27 and 28, and 1% above 28. 26% of the current freshmen were in the top fifth of their class; 50% were in the top two fifths. 8 freshmen graduated first in their class.

Requirements: The ACT is recommended. In addition, applicants must be graduates of an accredited secondary school or have the GED. Institutional placement tests are given for English, math, and reading. Nicholls requires applicants to be in the upper 50% of their class. A GPA of 2.5 is required. AP and CLEP credits are accepted. Applications are accepted on-line.

Procedure: Freshmen are admitted to all sessions. Entrance exams should be taken as early as possible. There is an early admissions plan. Applications deadlines are open. The university accepts all applicants. Notification is sent on a rolling basis. The fall 2001 application fee was $20.

Transfer: 321 transfer students enrolled in 2001-2002. Transfer applicants must be eligible to return to the institution from which they are transferring. 31 credits of 125 must be completed at Nicholls.

Visiting: There are regularly scheduled orientations for prospective students. There are guides for informal visits and visitors may sit in on classes and stay overnight. To schedule a visit, contact Admissions Information.

Financial Aid: In 2001-2002, 76% of all freshmen and 58% of continuing students received some form of financial aid. 50% of freshmen received need-based aid. The average freshman award was $2489. Of that total, scholarships or need-based grants averaged $2700 ($11,044 maximum); loans averaged $2503 ($9374 maximum); and student employment averaged $1202 ($5216 maximum). 9% of undergraduates work part time. Average annual earnings from campus work are $1234. The FAFSA or FFS are required. The fall application deadline is April 15.

International Students: There are 44 international students enrolled. The school actively recruits these students. They must score 500 on the written TOEFL or 173 on the electronic version.

Computers: The mainframe is an IBM 9221 Model 170. There are 290 Zenith, Dell, and Mac PCs (386 or above) available in 9 buildings. All students may access the system 24 hours a day. There are no time limits and no fees.

Graduates: In 2001, 746 bachelor's degrees were awarded. The most popular majors were education (24%), general studies (12%), and nursing (8%). In an average class, 22% graduate in 6 years. 124 companies recruited on campus in 2000-2001.

Admissions Contact: Becky L. Durocher, Director of Admissions.
E-mail: *esai-bl@nicholls.edu* Web: *www.nicholls.edu*

NORTHWESTERN STATE UNIVERSITY OF LOUISIANA B-2

Natchitoches, LA 71497 (318) 357-4503
(800) 327-1903; Fax: (318) 357-5567

Full-time: 2491 men, 4093 women | **Faculty:** 252; IIA, --$
Part-time: 452 men, 1337 women | **Ph.D.s:** 53%
Graduate: 243 men, 799 women | **Student/Faculty:** 26 to 1
Year: semesters, summer session | **Tuition:** $2613 ($8283)
Application Deadline: August 15 | **Room & Board:** $3132
Freshman Class: 3576 applied, 3576 accepted, 1685 enrolled
ACT: 21 | **NONCOMPETITIVE**

Northwestern State University of Louisiana, founded in 1884, offers undergraduate programs in business, education, liberal arts, nursing, and science and technology. There are 7 undergraduate schools and 1 graduate school. In addition to regional accreditation, NSU has baccalaureate program accreditation with AACSB, CAHEA, CSWE, NASM, NCATE, and NLN. The library contains 677,866 volumes, 126,460 microform items, and 2754 audiovisual forms/CDs, and subscribes to 1749 periodicals. Computerized library services include the card catalog, interlibrary loans, and database searching. Special learning facilities include an art gallery, natural history museum, planetarium, radio station, and TV station. The 1000-acre campus is in a small town 50 miles northwest of Alexandria. Including residence halls, there are 36 buildings.

Student Life: 94% of undergraduates are from Louisiana. Others are from 40 states, 26 foreign countries, and Canada. 83% are from public schools. 65% are white; 26%, African American. The average age of freshmen is 21; all undergraduates, 24. 35% do not continue beyond their first year; 28% remain to graduate.

Housing: 2000 students can be accommodated in college housing, which includes single-sex and coed dormitories, on-campus apartments, married-student housing, fraternity houses, and sorority houses. In addition, there are honors houses. On-campus housing is available on a first-come, first-served basis. 72% of students commute. Alcohol is not permitted. All students may keep cars.

Activities: 12% of men belong to 11 national fraternities; 8% of women belong to 1 local sorority and 7 national sororities. There are 90 groups on campus, including art, band, cheerleading, chess, choir, chorale, chorus, computers, dance, debate, drama, drill team, ethnic, film, gay, honors, international, jazz band, literary magazine, marching band, musical theater, newspaper, orchestra, pep band, photography, political, professional, radio and TV, religious, social, social service, student government, symphony, and yearbook. Popular campus events include Mardi Gras.

Sports: There are 7 intercollegiate sports for men and 7 for women, and 13 intramural sports for men and 14 for women. Facilities include a 16,000-seat football stadium, a 5000-seat indoor gym, sports training and basketball centers, a track, and a coliseum. The largest auditorium/arena seats 1500.

Disabled Students: Wheelchair ramps, elevators, special parking, specially equipped rest rooms, special class scheduling, lowered drinking fountains, and lowered telephones are available.

Services: Counseling and information services are available, as is tutoring in most subjects. There is remedial math, reading, and writing.

Campus Safety and Security: Measures include 24-hour foot and vehicle patrol, escort service, shuttle buses, and pamphlets/posters/films. There are emergency telephones, lighted pathways/sidewalks, call telephones, and safety entrances.

Programs of Study: NSU confers B.A., B.S., B.M., and B.S.N. degrees. Associate and master's degrees are also awarded. Bachelor's degrees are awarded in BIOLOGICAL SCIENCE (biology/biological science), BUSINESS (accounting, business administration and management, and hospitality management services), COMMUNICATIONS AND THE ARTS (art, dramatic arts, English, journalism, and music), COMPUTER AND PHYSICAL SCIENCE (chemistry, information sciences and systems, mathematics, physics, and radiological technology), EDUCATION (early childhood, elementary, music, physical, secondary, and special), ENGINEERING AND ENVIRONMENTAL DESIGN (electrical/electronics engineering technology, graphic arts technology, and industrial engineering technology), HEALTH PROFESSIONS (medical technology and nursing), SOCIAL SCIENCE (anthropology, criminal justice, family/consumer studies, history, liberal arts/general studies, political science/government, psychology, social science, social work, and sociology). Business administration, nursing, and Liberal arts/general studies are the largest.

Required: To graduate, all students must complete their senior year in residence, plus an approved curriculum, the university education requirement, and a minimum of 120 semester hours, with at least 30 semester hours in the major field. Distribution requirements include 12 credits each of communications and social sciences, 9 of natural sciences, 6 each of fine arts and math, and 4 of personal fitness. A minimum 2.0 GPA is needed for all hours taken at NSU.

Special: NSU offers cooperative programs with local businesses, internships, study abroad on 5 continents, and work-study programs. A general studies degree, credit for experience, nondegree study, and pass/fail options are available. There are 8 national honor societies, including Phi Beta Kappa and a freshman honors program.

Faculty/Classroom: 51% of faculty are male; 49%, female. 91% teach undergraduates, 17% do research, and 83% do both. Graduate students teach 4% of introductory courses. The average class size in an introductory lecture is 20.

Admissions: 100% of the 2001-2002 applicants were accepted. The ACT scores for the 2001-2002 freshman class were: 61% below 21, 21% between 21 and 23, 11% between 24 and 26, 4% between 27 and 28, and 3% above 28.

Requirements: The ACT is required. In addition, applicants must be graduates of an accredited secondary school or have a GED certificate. Students must have completed 4 units of English, 3 units each of history and math, and 2 units each of science and social studies. AP and CLEP credits are accepted. Applications are accepted on-line via CollegeNET.

Procedure: Freshmen are admitted to all sessions. Entrance exams should be taken before the semester begins. Applications should be filed by August 15 for fall entry, January 10 for spring entry, and May 10 for summer entry. The university accepts all applicants. Notification is sent on a rolling basis. The fall 2001 application fee was $20.

Transfer: 468 transfer students enrolled in 2001-2002. Transfer students must be eligible for readmission to their former university or college in order to enter NSU. 30 credits of 120 must be completed at NSU.

Visiting: There are regularly scheduled orientations for prospective students, consisting of a campus tour with special focus on financial aid, housing and board, academic requirements and selecting a major, registration, campus organizations, and adapting to the college. There are guides for informal visits and visitors may sit in on classes and stay overnight. To schedule a visit, contact Director of Admissions.

Financial Aid: The CSS/Profile or FFS is required. The fall application deadline is April 1.

International Students: There are 36 international students enrolled. They must score 550 on the written TOEFL and also take the SAT I or the ACT.

Computers: The mainframes are a DEC VAX 11/785 and 11/750. PCs are available for academic use in the department of business administration, in the computer center, and in the department of math and physical sciences. All students may access the system at all times. There are no time limits and no fees.

Graduates: In 2001, 959 bachelor's degrees were awarded. The most popular majors were general studies (20%), nursing (14%), and business administration (9%). In an average class, 9% graduate in 3 years, 23% in 4 years, 32% in 5 years, and 34% in 6 years.

Admissions Contact: Jana Lucky, Director of Admissions.
E-mail: *luckyj@nsula.edu* Web: *www.nsula.edu*

OUR LADY OF HOLY CROSS COLLEGE — D-4

New Orleans, LA 70131-7399 — (504) 394-7744
(800) 259-7744; Fax: (504) 391-2421

Full-time: 188 men, 600 women	**Faculty:** 20
Part-time: 118 men, 344 women	**Ph.D.s:** 70%
Graduate: 26 men, 71 women	**Student/Faculty:** 39 to 1
Year: semesters, summer session	**Tuition:** $5140
Application Deadline: July 20	**Room & Board:** n/app
Freshman Class: 820 applied, 809 accepted, 437 enrolled	
ACT: 20	**NONCOMPETITIVE**

Our Lady of Holy Cross College, founded in 1916, is a private commuter college affiliated with the Roman Catholic Church. In addition to regional accreditation, OLHCC has baccalaureate program accreditation with NLN. The library contains 56,700 volumes, 136,015 microform items, and 13,598 audiovisual forms/CDs, and subscribes to 601 periodicals. Computerized library services include the card catalog, interlibrary loans, and database searching. The 40-acre campus is in an urban area in New Orleans. There is one building.

Student Life: 99% of undergraduates are from Louisiana. Others are from 4 states. 39% are from public schools. 74% are white; 15%, African American. 74% are Catholic; 14%, Protestant. The average age of freshmen is 23; all undergraduates, 26. 10% do not continue beyond their first year; 70% remain to graduate.

Housing: There are no residence halls. All students commute. Alcohol is not permitted. All students may keep cars.

Activities: There are no fraternities or sororities. There are 11 groups on campus, including choir, chorus, computers, drama, ethnic, honors, international, literary magazine, professional, social, social service, student government, and yearbook. Popular campus events include Fall Fest, Crawfish Boil, and Christmas dances.

Sports: There are 5 intramural sports for men and 4 for women.

Disabled Students: All of the campus is accessible. Wheelchair ramps, elevators, special parking, specially equipped rest rooms, lowered drinking fountains, and lowered telephones are available.

Services: There is remedial math, reading, and writing.

Campus Safety and Security: Measures include self-defense education, escort service, pamphlets/posters/films, emergency telephones, and lighted pathways/sidewalks. There is a foot patrol inside and outside of the building from 7:30 A.M. to 10 P.M.

Programs of Study: OLHCC confers B.A. and B.S. degrees. Associate and master's degrees are also awarded. Bachelor's degrees are awarded in BIOLOGICAL SCIENCE (biology/biological science), BUSINESS (accounting, business administration and management, and marketing and distribution), COMMUNICATIONS AND THE ARTS (English), EDUCATION (elementary and secondary), HEALTH PROFESSIONS (health science and nursing), SOCIAL SCIENCE (behavioral science, history, liberal arts/general studies, social psychology, and social science). Nursing is the strongest academically and the largest.

Required: A total of 128 credit hours, with 33 to 36 hours in the major, and a minimum GPA of 2.0 are required to graduate. All students must take courses in theology, philosophy, literature, English composition, math, natural sciences, library orientation, social sciences, speech, fine arts, and computer science.

Special: Co-op programs in business, internships with the Navy Civilian Personnel Office, study abroad in France, and credit for life, military, and work experience are offered.

Faculty/Classroom: 20% of faculty are male; 80%, female. 98% teach undergraduates and 2% do research. The average class size in an introductory lecture is 25; in a laboratory, 24; and in a regular course, 20.

Admissions: 99% of the 2001-2002 applicants were accepted.

Requirements: The ACT is required. In addition, the GED is accepted. A GPA of 2.5 is required. AP and CLEP credits are accepted. Important factors in the admissions decision are leadership record, recommendations by school officials, and recommendations by alumni.
Procedure: Freshmen are admitted to all sessions. Entrance exams should be taken a week before registration. Applications should be filed by July 20 for fall entry, December 20 for spring entry, and May 1 for summer entry. The fall 2001 application fee was $15.
Transfer: Transfer applicants must have an overall 2.0 GPA for unconditional admission. 30 credits of 128 must be completed at OLHCC.
Visiting: There are regularly scheduled orientations for prospective students. There are guides for informal visits and visitors may sit in on classes. To schedule a visit, contact the Office of Student Affairs and Admissions.
Financial Aid: 3% of undergraduates work part time. Average annual earnings from campus work are $1000. OLHCC is a member of CSS. The FAFSA and the college's own financial statement are required. The fall application deadline is April 15.
International Students: They must score 500 on the written TOEFL and also take the SAT I or the ACT.
Computers: There are 30 PCs available in a computer lab and 40 in the academic skills center. All students may access the system. There are no time limits and no fees.
Admissions Contact: Kristine H. Kopecky, V.P. for Student Affairs. A video is available. E-mail: *kkopecky@olhcc.edu* Web: *www.olhcc.edu*

SOUTHEASTERN LOUISIANA UNIVERSITY D-3
Hammond, LA 70402 (985) 549-2066
(800) 222-7358; Fax: (985) 549-5632

Full-time: 4100 men, 6724 women
Part-time: 634 men, 363 women
Graduate: 412 men, 1289 women
Year: semesters, summer session
Application Deadline: July 15
Faculty: 470; IIA, --$
Ph.D.s: 55%
Student/Faculty: 23 to 1
Tuition: $2607 ($7935)
Room & Board: $3440
Freshman Class: 3421 applied, 2963 accepted, 2092 enrolled
ACT: 20 **LESS COMPETITIVE**

Southeastern Louisiana University, founded in 1925, is a public university offering courses in liberal arts, fine arts, and professional studies. There are 5 undergraduate schools and 1 graduate school. In addition to regional accreditation, Southeastern has baccalaureate program accreditation with AACSB, ACS, ASLA, CSWE, NASM, NCATE, and NLN. The library contains 367,250 volumes, 772,432 microform items, and 48,456 audiovisual forms/CDs, and subscribes to 2089 periodicals. Computerized library services include the card catalog, interlibrary loans, and database searching. Special learning facilities include a learning resource center, art gallery, and radio station. The 375-acre campus is in a small town 57 miles northwest of New Orleans and 49 miles east of Baton Rouge. Including residence halls, there are 87 buildings.
Student Life: 98% of undergraduates are from Louisiana. Others are from 35 states, 39 foreign countries, and Canada. 82% are white; 14% African American. The average age of freshmen is 21; all undergraduates, 23. 34% do not continue beyond their first year.
Housing: 2454 students can be accommodated in college housing, which includes single-sex and coed dormitories, on-campus apartments, fraternity houses, and sorority houses. On-campus housing is available on a first-come, first-served basis. 88% of students commute. Alcohol is not permitted. All students may keep cars.
Activities: 5% of men belong to 1 local fraternity and 9 national fraternities; 3% of women belong to 9 national sororities. There are 89 groups on campus, including art, band, cheerleading, choir, chorale, chorus, computers, dance, debate, drama, ethnic, gay, honors, international, jazz band, literary magazine, newspaper, orchestra, professional, radio and TV, religious, social, social service, student government, symphony, and yearbook. Popular campus events include Fanfare (cultural events month).
Sports: There are 7 intercollegiate sports for men and 8 for women, and 10 intramural sports for men and 8 for women. Facilities include a recreation center with a pool, weightlifting, aerobics facilities, a fitness gym, 4 indoor basketball courts, 4 flag football fields, 4 softball fields, and 12 tennis courts.
Disabled Students: 90% of the campus is accessible. Wheelchair ramps, elevators, special parking, specially equipped rest rooms, special class scheduling, lowered drinking fountains, and lowered telephones are available.
Services: Counseling and information services are available, as is tutoring in some subjects, including math, writing, English, and science. There is remedial math, reading, and writing.
Campus Safety and Security: Measures include 24-hour foot and vehicle patrol, self-defense education, escort service, and informal discussions. There are pamphlets/posters/films, emergency telephones, lighted pathways/sidewalks, community policing, and bicycle patrols.
Programs of Study: Southeastern confers B.A., B.S., B.G.S., B.M., and B.M.E. degrees. Associate and master's degrees are also awarded. Bachelor's degrees are awarded in AGRICULTURE (horticulture), BIOLOGICAL SCIENCE (biology/biological science), BUSINESS (accounting, banking and finance, business administration and management, and marketing/retailing/merchandising), COMMUNICATIONS AND THE ARTS (art, communications, English, French, music, and Spanish), COMPUTER AND PHYSICAL SCIENCE (chemistry, computer science, mathematics, and physics), EDUCATION (art, elementary, English, foreign languages, mathematics, music, science, social studies, and special), ENGINEERING AND ENVIRONMENTAL DESIGN (industrial engineering technology), HEALTH PROFESSIONS (nursing and speech pathology/audiology), SOCIAL SCIENCE (criminal justice, family/consumer studies, history, liberal arts/general studies, political science/government, psychology, social work, and sociology). Teacher education, nursing, and biological sciences are the largest.
Required: To graduate, students must complete a core curriculum in English, math, computer literacy, social and natural sciences, arts, foreign languages, and humanities and maintain a 2.0 (2.5 in some majors) cumulative GPA.
Special: Southeastern offers a general studies degree, co-op programs, study abroad in Mexico, Canada, England, Italy, Austria, and the Caribbean, nondegree study, and pass/fail options. There are 6 national honor societies and a freshman honors program.
Faculty/Classroom: 45% of faculty are male; 55%, female. Graduate students teach 1% of introductory courses. The average class size in an introductory lecture is 30.
Admissions: 87% of the 2001-2002 applicants were accepted. The ACT scores for the 2001-2002 freshman class were: 62% below 21, 26% between 21 and 23, 8% between 24 and 26, 2% between 27 and 28, and 1% above 28.
Requirements: The ACT is required. In addition, applicants should have an ACT score of 20 or rank in the upper 50% of their class or have a GPA of 2.0 in a core of courses including English, math, science, and social studies. Applications are accepted on-line at the school's web site. AP and CLEP credits are accepted.
Procedure: Freshmen are admitted to all sessions. Entrance exams should be taken prior to registering for classes. There is a deferred admissions plan. Applications should be filed by July 15 for fall entry, December 1 for spring entry, and May 1 for summer entry. The fall 2001 application fee was $20. Notification is sent on a rolling basis.
Transfer: 604 transfer students enrolled in 2001-2002. Applicants with less than 12 hours must meet freshman entrance requirements. Those with more must have a GPA of 2.0. All must be eligible to attend the last institution. 30 credits of 125 must be completed at Southeastern.
Visiting: There are regularly scheduled orientations for prospective students. There are guides for informal visits and visitors may stay overnight. To schedule a visit, contact Office of Admission and Financial Aid at (985) 549-5629.
Financial Aid: The average freshman award was $3648. The FAFSA and the college's own financial statement are required. The fall application deadline is May 1.
International Students: There are 89 international students enrolled. They must score 500 on the written TOEFL or 173 on the electronic version.
Computers: The mainframes are 2 DEC VAX 6330s and 1 DEC AXP. There are PC and mainframe terminals for student use throughout the campus. Dial-in access is also available. All students may access the system. There are no time limits and no fees.
Graduates: In 2001, 1520 bachelor's degrees were awarded. The most popular majors were elementary education (11%), management (10%), and nursing (7%). In an average class, 3% graduate in 4 years, 13% in 5 years, and 20% in 6 years. 123 companies recruited on campus in 2000-2001.
Admissions Contact: Josie Mercante, Interim Associate Director of Admissions. A video is available. E-mail: *jmercante@selu.edu*
Web: *www.selu.edu/ENROLL*

SOUTHERN UNIVERSITY SYSTEM

The Southern University System, established in 1975, is the only historically black university system in the United States. It is a Louisiana public system governed by the Southern University Board of Supervisors, with the president serving as chief administrator. The system consists of 2 4-year institutions at Baton Rouge and New Orleans, a 2-year institution at Shreveport, and a law center. The system's major land grant programs are primarily conducted through the Cooperative Extension and Agricultural Program dating to 1890. The priorities of the system are teaching, public service, international outreach, and research. Student population totals 16,000, representing 41 states and 57 nations, with a faculty and staff of more than 2400. The institutions of the Southern University System offer 152 degree programs ranging from certificates to doctorates. Collectively, 8 certificate, 43 associate, 76 bachelor, 22 master, 1 law, and 5 doctoral degrees are awarded.

SOUTHERN UNIVERSITY AND A&M COLLEGE C-4

Baton Rouge, LA 70813 (504) 771-2430
(800) 256-1531; Fax: (504) 772-2500

Full-time: 2806 men, 3922 women	**Faculty:** 465; IIA, --$
Part-time: 285 men, 459 women	**Ph.D.s:** 60%
Graduate: 323 men, 924 women	**Student/Faculty:** 14 to 1
Year: semesters, summer session	**Tuition:** $2682 ($8474)
Application Deadline: July 1	**Room & Board:** $3683
Freshman Class: 3336 applied, 1460 accepted, 1221 enrolled	
ACT: 17	**COMPETITIVE+**

Southern University and A&M College, founded in 1880, is a publicly supported, nonsectarian, land-grant institution offering degree programs in agriculture, family and consumer science, arts and humanities, architecture, business, education, engineering, nursing, public policy and urban affairs, and sciences. There are 9 undergraduate schools and 1 graduate school. In addition to regional accreditation, Southern has baccalaureate program accreditation with AACSB, ABET, ACEJMC, ADA, AHEA, CSAB, CSWE, NAAB, NASM, NCATE, and NLN. The 2 libraries contain 107,886 volumes, 614,291 microform items, and 42,116 audiovisual forms/CDs, and subscribe to 1960 periodicals. Computerized library services include interlibrary loans and database searching. Special learning facilities include a learning resource center, art gallery, and the Black Heritage Collection. The 884-acre campus is in an urban area of Baton Rouge.

Student Life: 80% of undergraduates are from Louisiana. Others are from 38 states and 49 foreign countries. 75% are from public schools. 94% are African American. The average age of freshmen is 18; all undergraduates, 22. 36% do not continue beyond their first year; 60% remain to graduate.

Housing: 2641 students can be accommodated in college housing, which includes single-sex and coed dormitories. 65% of students commute. Alcohol is not permitted. Upperclassmen may keep cars.

Activities: 8% of men belong to 4 national fraternities; 3% of women belong to 4 national sororities. There are 83 groups on campus, including art, band, cheerleading, chess, choir, chorale, computers, drama, ethnic, honors, international, jazz band, marching band, newspaper, political, professional, religious, social, student government, and yearbook. Popular campus events include Founder's Day and Bayou Classic football game at the New Orleans Super Dome.

Sports: There are 9 intercollegiate sports for men and 8 for women, and 8 intramural sports for men and 8 for women. Facilities center around the main activity complex, which accommodates theater, convocations, and athletic contests.

Disabled Students: All of the campus is accessible. Wheelchair ramps, elevators, special parking, specially equipped rest rooms, special class scheduling, and special housing are available.

Services: Counseling and information services are available, as is tutoring in every subject. There is a reader service for the blind, and remedial math, reading, and writing.

Campus Safety and Security: Measures include 24-hour foot and vehicle patrol, informal discussions, pamphlets/posters/films, and emergency telephones. There are lighted pathways/sidewalks.

Programs of Study: Southern confers B.A., B.S., B.Arch., B.Mus., B.Mus.Ed., and B.S.N. degrees. Associate, master's, and doctoral degrees are also awarded. Bachelor's degrees are awarded in AGRICULTURE (agricultural economics, agriculture, and forestry and related sciences), BIOLOGICAL SCIENCE (biology/biological science), BUSINESS (accounting, business administration and management, business economics, and marketing/retailing/merchandising), COMMUNICATIONS AND THE ARTS (communications, dramatic arts, English, fine arts, French, music, and Spanish), COMPUTER AND PHYSICAL SCIENCE (chemistry, computer science, mathematics, and physics), EDUCATION (early childhood, elementary, mathematics, music, secondary, and special), ENGINEERING AND ENVIRONMENTAL DESIGN (architecture, civil engineering, electrical/electronics engineering, engineering technology, mechanical engineering, and mechanical engineering technology), HEALTH PROFESSIONS (nursing, rehabilitation therapy, and speech pathology/audiology), SOCIAL SCIENCE (family/consumer studies, history, political science/government, psychology, social work, and sociology). Nursing, business management, and biology are the largest.

Required: All students must pass a general competency exam measuring proficiency in communication, computation, logical thinking, and general knowledge. Courses in English composition and literature, math, natural sciences, arts, humanities, social sciences, health, and phys ed are required, as well as 60 hours of community service and 3 hours of African-American studies. All students also must take the GRE at the end of the junior year. To graduate, they must complete 124 semester hours (at least 31 in the major) with a minimum GPA of 2.0 overall and in the major.

Special: Cross-registration, nondegree study, credit for military experience, accelerated degrees, co-op education, study abroad, internships, work-study, and an exchange program and dual majors in chemistry/chemical engineering with Louisiana State University are available. There are 9 national honor societies, a freshman honors program, and 1 departmental honors program.

Faculty/Classroom: 54% of faculty are male; 46%, female. 93% teach undergraduates. No introductory courses are taught by graduate students. The average class size in a regular course is 30.

Admissions: 44% of the fall 2002 applicants were accepted. There was 1 National Merit finalist and 2 semifinalists. 8 freshmen graduated first in their class.

Requirements: The SAT I or ACT is required. In addition, the school recommends that applicants have 15 Carnegie units, including 4 of English, 3 each of math, social studies, science, and foreign language, and 1 of fine arts. The GED is accepted. A GPA of 2.3 is required. AP and CLEP credits are accepted. Applications are accepted on-line at the school's web site.

Procedure: Freshmen are admitted to all sessions. Entrance exams should be taken in 11th grade. There is an early admissions plan. Applications should be filed by July 1 for fall entry, December 1 for spring entry, and April 1 for summer entry. Notification is sent on a rolling basis. The fall 2001 application fee was $5.

Transfer: 201 transfer students enrolled in 2001-2002. Transfer students must complete at least 1 year at Southern and must be in good standing. 31 credits of 124 must be completed at Southern.

Visiting: There are regularly scheduled orientations for prospective students, consisting of summer and fall orientation programs. There are guides for informal visits. To schedule a visit, contact Office of Admissions at (225) 771-2430 or *admit@subr.edu*

Financial Aid: In 2001-2002, 25% of all freshmen and 75% of continuing students received some form of financial aid. The average freshman award was $6375. Of that total, loans averaged $2625 (maximum) and work contracts averaged $1600 (maximum). 12% of undergraduates work part time. Average annual earnings from campus work are $1050. The average financial indebtedness of the 2001 graduate was $23,500. The FAFSA is required. The fall application deadline is May 31.

International Students: There are 189 international students enrolled. The school actively recruits these students. They must score 500 on the written TOEFL and also take the SAT I or the ACT, scoring 17 on the ACT.

Computers: The mainframe is an IBM. Students have access to the Internet in departmental labs, the library, and the computer science labs. All students may access the system. There are no fees.

Graduates: In 2001, 1029 bachelor's degrees were awarded. The most popular majors were nursing (9%), rehabilitation services (7%), and psychology (5%). In an average class, 22% graduate in 6 years. 295 companies recruited on campus in 2000-2001. Of the 2000 graduating class, 16% were enrolled in graduate school within 6 months of graduation and 19% were employed.

Admissions Contact: Velva Thomas, Director of Admissions.
E-mail: *admit@subr.edu* Web: *www.subr.edu*

SOUTHERN UNIVERSITY AT NEW ORLEANS D-4

New Orleans, LA 70126 (504) 286-5314

Full-time: 450 men and women	**Faculty:** n/av
Part-time: none	**Ph.D.s:** n/av
Graduate: 70 men and women	**Student/Faculty:** n/av
Year: semester	**Tuition:** $995 ($1869)
Application Deadline: July 1	**Room & Board:** n/av
Freshman Class: n/av	**ACT:** required
	NONCOMPETITIVE

Southern University at New Orleans, established in 1956, is a public commuter institution offering programs in liberal arts and sciences, business, education, and the technologies. Figures given in the above capsule are approximate. In addition to regional accreditation, SUNO has baccalaureate program accreditation with CSWE. The library contains 300,000 volumes. The 22-acre campus is in a suburban area. There are 10 buildings.

Programs of Study: Bachelor's degrees are awarded in BIOLOGICAL SCIENCE (biology/biological science), BUSINESS (accounting, business administration and management, secretarial studies/office management, and transportation management), COMMUNICATIONS AND THE ARTS (English, fine arts, journalism, Spanish, and speech/debate/rhetoric), COMPUTER AND PHYSICAL SCIENCE (chemistry, computer science, mathematics, and physics), EDUCATION (art, business, education of the deaf and hearing impaired, elementary, English, foreign languages, mathematics, music, physical, recreation, science, secondary, and social studies), ENGINEERING AND ENVIRONMENTAL DESIGN (technological management), HEALTH PROFESSIONS (health care administration), SOCIAL SCIENCE (addiction studies, criminal justice, economics, history, political science/government, psychology, social work, and sociology).

Requirements: The ACT is required.

Procedure: Applications should be filed by July 1 for fall entry, December 1 for spring entry, and May 1 for summer entry, along with a $5 fee. Notification of both early decision and regular decision is sent on a rolling basis.

Financial Aid: The SAR financial statement is required. The fall application deadline is April 15.

International Students: They must score 500 on the written TOEFL.

Computers: All students may access the system. There are no time limits and no fees.

Admissions Contact: Director of Admissions and Registrar.

TULANE UNIVERSITY

New Orleans, LA 70118 — D-4

(504) 865-5731

(800) 873-9283; Fax: (504) 862-8715

Full-time: 2825 men, 2916 women	**Faculty:** 514; I, av$
Part-time: 697 men, 1084 women	**Ph.D.s:** n/av
Graduate: 1271 men, 1416 women	**Student/Faculty:** 11 to 1
Year: semesters, summer session	**Tuition:** $26,885
Application Deadline: January 15	**Room & Board:** $7128

Freshman Class: 10,868 applied, 6638 accepted, 1527 enrolled

SAT I Verbal/Math: 659/644 — **HIGHLY COMPETITIVE+**

Tulane University, founded in 1834, is a private institution offering degree programs in liberal arts and sciences, business, architecture, and engineering. There are 6 undergraduate and 8 graduate schools. In addition to regional accreditation, Tulane has baccalaureate program accreditation with AACSB, ABET, ACS,CSAB, CSWE, and NAAB. The 9 libraries contain 2.2 million volumes, 1,253,648 microform items, and 83,774 audiovisual forms/CDs, and subscribe to 14,986 periodicals. Computerized library services include the card catalog, interlibrary loans, and database searching. Special learning facilities include a learning resource center, art gallery, planetarium, radio station, and TV station. The 110-acre campus is in an urban area in uptown New Orleans. Including residence halls, there are 70 buildings.

Student Life: 64% of undergraduates are from out of state, mostly the Northeast. Others are from 49 states, 100 foreign countries, and Canada. 50% are from public schools. 78% are white; 11% African American. 38% are Catholic; 28% Jewish; 28% Protestant. The average age of freshmen is 18; all undergraduates, 20. 17% do not continue beyond their first year.

Housing: 3447 students can be accommodated in college housing, which includes single-sex and coed dormitories, on-campus apartments, and married-student housing. In addition, there are honors houses, special-interest floors, and substance-free, urban issues, and leadership halls. On-campus housing is guaranteed for the freshman year only and is available on a lottery system for upperclassmen. 59% of students commute. Upperclassmen may keep cars.

Activities: 19% of men belong to 15 national fraternities; 33% of women belong to 9 national sororities. There are 200 groups on campus, including art, band, cheerleading, chess, choir, chorale, chorus, computers, dance, drama, drill team, ethnic, film, gay, honors, international, jazz band, literary magazine, marching band, musical theater, newspaper, opera, orchestra, pep band, photography, political, professional, radio and TV, religious, social, social service, student government, symphony, and yearbook. Popular campus events include Newcomb College Spring Arts Festival, International Festival, and Outreach Tulane Land.

Sports: There are 8 intercollegiate sports for men and 8 for women, and 30 intramural sports for men and 30 for women. Facilities include a baseball diamond, track complex, tennis facility, a recreation center with indoor and outdoor pools, indoor track, gymnastics area, weight room, and squash and racquetball courts.

Disabled Students: 60% of the campus is accessible. Wheelchair ramps, elevators, special parking, specially equipped rest rooms, lowered drinking fountains, and lowered telephones are available.

Services: Counseling and information services are available, as is tutoring in some subjects, including high-demand math and science classes and some languages.

Campus Safety and Security: Measures include 24-hour foot and vehicle patrol, self-defense education, escort service, and shuttle buses. There are informal discussions, pamphlets/posters/films, emergency telephones, lighted pathways/sidewalks, trained student patrols, and programs about living safely off campus. Victim resources include academic assistance, legal counseling, emergency housing, and security review of home and personal security habits.

Programs of Study: Tulane confers B.A., B.S., B. Arch., B.F.A., B.G.S., B.S.E., and B.S.M. degrees. Associate, master's, and doctoral degrees are also awarded. Bachelor's degrees are awarded in BIOLOGICAL SCIENCE (biochemistry, cell biology, ecology, and evolutionary biology), BUSINESS (accounting, business administration and management, management science, and marketing management), COMMUNICATIONS AND THE ARTS (art history and appreciation, classics, communications, dance, dramatic arts, English, French, German, Italian, linguistics, media arts, music, Portuguese, Russian, Spanish, and studio art), COMPUTER AND PHYSICAL SCIENCE (chemistry, computer science, earth science, geology, information sciences and systems, mathematics, and physics), ENGINEERING AND ENVIRONMENTAL DESIGN (architecture, biomedical engineering, chemical engineering, civil engineering, computer engineering, electrical/electronics engineering, engineering, environmental engineering, environmental science, and mechanical engineering), HEALTH PROFESSIONS (exercise science), SOCIAL SCIENCE (African studies, American studies, anthropology, Asian/Oriental studies, cognitive science, economics, history, Judaic studies, Latin American studies, medieval studies, philosophy, political science/government, psychology, religion, Russian and Slavic studies, sociology, and women's studies). Environmental sciences, political economy, and preprofessional programs are the strongest academically. English, psychology, and biology are the largest.

Required: All students in the liberal arts and sciences must meet proficiency requirements in English, foreign language, and math. They must take a distribution component including courses in humanities and fine arts, social sciences, and sciences and math. A total of 120 credits, including at least 24 in the major, with a minimum cumulative GPA of 2.0, is required to graduate.

Special: Students may pursue cross-registration with Loyola and Xavier Universities, numerous internships, study abroad in 15 countries, work-study programs, a Washington semester, and B.A.-B.S. degrees in liberal arts, engineering, and architecture. Tulane also offers accelerated joint degrees with its schools of medicine, law, business, and public health; student-designed, dual, and interdisciplinary majors, including art and biology, Greek and Latin, mathematical economics, political economy, and cognitive studies; and a 3-2 engineering degree with Loyola University in New Orleans. There are 32 national honor societies, including Phi Beta Kappa, and a freshman honors program.

Faculty/Classroom: 71% of faculty are male; 29%, female. All both teach and do research. The average class size in an introductory lecture is 30; in a laboratory, 20; and in a regular course, 25.

Admissions: 61% of the 2001-2002 applicants were accepted. The SAT I scores for the 2001-2002 freshman class were: Verbal--3% below 500, 12% between 500 and 599, 52% between 600 and 700, and 33% above 700; Math--3% below 500, 18% between 500 and 599, 55% between 600 and 700, and 24% above 700. 78% of the current freshmen were in the top fifth of their class; 96% were in the top two fifths.

Requirements: The SAT I or ACT is required. In addition, applicants must be graduates of an accredited secondary school or have a GED certificate. It is recommended that students have completed 4 years each of high school English and math, and 3 each of foreign language, social studies, and the sciences. SAT II: Subject tests in writing, math, and foreign language are recommended for placement purposes and are required for home-schooled applicants. An essay is required. A portfolio is recommended for architecture applicants only. AP credits are accepted. Important factors in the admissions decision are advanced placement or honor courses, recommendations by school officials, and extracurricular activities record. The application form is available on-line via *Embark.com*, Apply, or Common App.

Procedure: Freshmen are admitted fall and spring. Entrance exams should be taken during the spring of the junior year or the fall of the senior year. There are early decision, early admissions, and deferred admissions plans. Early decision applications should be filed by November 1; regular applications, by January 15 for fall entry and November 1 for spring entry, along with a $55 fee. Notification of early decision is sent December 15; regular decision, by April 1. 2483 early decision candidates were accepted for the 2001-2002 class. A waiting list is an active part of the admissions procedure.

Transfer: 118 transfer students enrolled in 2001-2002. Applicants must submit SAT I or ACT scores, high school transcripts, proof of good standing at previously attended institutions, and transcripts (with course descriptions) from all colleges or universities attended. A minimum 3.0 GPA is recommended. 60 credits of 120 must be completed at Tulane.

Visiting: There are regularly scheduled orientations for prospective students, including 3 on-campus Saturday programs in the fall, daily information sessions, and tours Monday through Friday and Saturday mornings during the academic year. Also, selected classes are open to visitors. In the spring semester, more structured programs are available daily. There are guides for informal visits and visitors may sit in on classes and stay overnight. To schedule a visit, contact the Office of Undergraduate Admission.

Financial Aid: In 2001-2002, 80% of all freshmen and 71% of continuing students received some form of financial aid. 33% of freshmen and 35% of continuing students received need-based aid. The average freshman award was $20,549. Of that total, scholarships or need-based grants averaged $18,025 ($35,000 maximum); loans averaged $1924 ($5625 maximum); and work contracts averaged $600 ($2000 maximum). 26% of undergraduates work part time. Average annual earnings from campus work are $1090. The average financial indebtedness of the 2001 graduate was $19,915. Tulane is a member of CSS. The CSS/Profile or FAFSA, the Noncustodial Parents Statement, and the Business/Farm Supplement as applicable are required. The fall application deadline is December 15.

International Students: There are 184 international students enrolled. The school actively recruits these students. They must take the TOEFL and the SAT I or ACT.

Computers: The mainframe is a cluster of 8 IBM RS/6000s. There are 22 computer labs on campus housing more than 250 workstations, all are connected to the university network. Access to the mainframe is possible from any terminal PC/workstation, and from residence hall rooms if students have their own PCs. The university network extends to all campus buildings. Each residence hall room has a data connection for. All students may access the system 24 hours a day. There are no time limits and no fees. It is strongly recommended that all students have a personal computer.

Graduates: In 2001, 1302 bachelor's degrees were awarded. The most popular majors were business (23%), social sciences (20%), and engineering (9%). In an average class, 64% graduate in 4 years, 75% in 5 years, and 77% in 6 years.

Admissions Contact: Richard Whiteside, VP for Enrollment Management and Institutional Research. A video is available.
E-mail: *undergrad.admission@tulane.edu* Web: *www.tulane.edu*

UNIVERSITY OF LOUISIANA AT LAFAYETTE C-4

Lafayette, LA 70504 (337) 482-6473; Fax: (337) 482-6195

Full-time: 5057 men, 6429 women	**Faculty:** 522; I, --$
Part-time: 859 men, 1568 women	**Ph.D.s:** 79%
Graduate: 710 men, 866 women	**Student/Faculty:** 22 to 1
Year: semesters, summer session	**Tuition:** $2314 ($9264)
Application Deadline: open	**Room & Board:** $2886
Freshman Class: 4373 applied, 3604 accepted, 2287 enrolled	
ACT: 21	**COMPETITIVE**

University of Louisiana at Lafayette, founded in 1898, is a public institution offering degree programs in liberal arts, fine arts, business, agriculture, technical disciplines, health science, engineering, and teacher preparation. There are 9 undergraduate schools and 1 graduate school. In addition to regional accreditation, UL Lafayette has baccalaureate program accreditation with AACSB, ABET, ACEJMC, ADA, AHEA, ASLA, CAHEA, CSAB, FIDER, NAAB, NASM, NCATE, and NLN. The library contains 873,173 volumes, 1,768,368 microform items, and 255,992 audiovisual forms/CDs, and subscribes to 4965 periodicals. Computerized library services include the card catalog, interlibrary loans, and database searching. Special learning facilities include a learning resource center, art gallery, radio station, and numerous research centers for environmental, business, science, computer, and business studies. The 1375-acre campus is in an urban area 129 miles west of New Orleans. Including residence halls, there are 239 buildings.

Student Life: 94% of undergraduates are from Louisiana. Others are from 47 states, 95 foreign countries, and Canada. 74% are white; 16%, African American. 54% are Catholic; 25% claim no religious affiliation; 18%, Protestant. The average age of freshmen is 18; all undergraduates, 23. 28% do not continue beyond their first year; 30% remain to graduate.

Housing: 1611 students can be accommodated in college housing, which includes single-sex dormitories, married-student housing, and fraternity houses. In addition, there are honors houses, special-interest houses, residence halls for athletes, and for Pan-Hellenic groups. On-campus housing is guaranteed for all 4 years. 89% of students commute. All students may keep cars.

Activities: 3% of men and about 3% of women belong to 14 national fraternities; 5% of women belong to 8 national sororities. There are 200 groups on campus, including band, cheerleading, choir, chorus, computers, dance, drama, drum and bugle corps, ethnic, gay, honors, international, jazz band, marching band, newspaper, opera, orchestra, photography, political, professional, radio and TV, religious, social, social service, student government, and yearbook. Popular campus events include Rajun Roar, Black Expo Week, and Entertainment Week.

Sports: There are 8 intercollegiate sports for men and 7 for women, and 16 intramural sports for men and 16 for women. Facilities include a 31,000-seat stadium, a 12,000-seat basketball arena, a gym, a track, a softball park, tennis courts, various playing fields, and a health and phys ed complex.

Disabled Students: 90% of the campus is accessible. Wheelchair ramps, elevators, special parking, specially equipped rest rooms, special class scheduling, TDDs, and an adaptive computer lab with voice synthesizer, visual-tech, and brailler are available.

Services: Counseling and information services are available, as is tutoring in most subjects. There is remedial math, reading, and writing; an entering freshman can only be in 1 remedial course.

Campus Safety and Security: Measures include 24-hour foot and vehicle patrol, escort service, shuttle buses, and informal discussions. There are pamphlets/posters/films, emergency telephones, and lighted pathways/sidewalks.

Programs of Study: UL Lafayette confers B.A., B.S., B.A.M., B.F.A., B.G.S., B.M.E., B.M.P., B.M.P.P., B.S.A., B.S.A.E., B.S.B.A., B.S.C.E., B.S.C.I.E., B.S.E.E., B.S.I.T., B.S.M.E., B.S.N., and B.S.P.E. degrees. Associate, master's, and doctoral degrees are also awarded. Bachelor's degrees are awarded in BUSINESS (accounting, banking and finance, business administration and management, fashion merchandising, hotel/motel and restaurant management, management science, marketing/retailing/merchandising, and personnel management), COMMUNICATIONS AND THE ARTS (advertising, broadcasting, communications, dance, dramatic arts, English, fine arts, French, music, public relations, Spanish, and telecommunications), COMPUTER AND PHYSICAL SCIENCE (chemistry, computer science, geology, mathematics, physics, and statistics), EDUCATION (agricultural, art, elementary, English, foreign languages, health, home economics, industrial arts, mathematics, music, science, secondary, social studies, and special), ENGINEERING AND ENVIRONMENTAL DESIGN (chemical engineering, civil engineering, computer engineering, electrical/electronics engineering, industrial engineering, interior design, land use management and reclamation, mechanical engineering, and petroleum/natural gas engineering), HEALTH PROFESSIONS (nursing and speech pathology/audiology), SOCIAL SCIENCE (anthropology, criminal justice, dietetics, economics, history, philosophy, political science/government, psychology, and sociology). Computer science, engineering, and math/statistics/physical sciences are the strongest academically. Nursing, elementary education, and business administration are the largest.

Required: Students are required to complete 42 semester hours of general education courses in the arts, literature, history, math, sciences, behavioral sciences, and composition. Phys ed is required in all but engineering and nursing programs. A minimum of 124 semester hours, with at least 33 in the major, is required for graduation. A minimum GPA of 2.0 is needed; some majors require higher GPAs.

Special: Various internships are available, including a Washington semester. Students may study in France, Canada, Belgium, Japan, and Mexico. UL Lafeyette also offers an accelerated degree program in nursing, B.A.-B.S. degrees, and dual majors. There are 6 national honor societies and a freshman honors program.

Faculty/Classroom: 59% of faculty are male; 41%, female.

Admissions: 82% of the 2001-2002 applicants were accepted. The ACT scores for the 2001-2002 freshman class were: 49% below 21, 31% between 21 and 23, 13% between 24 and 26, 5% between 27 and 28, and 3% above 28.

Requirements: The SAT I or ACT is required. In addition, admissions criteria are based on a sliding scale of standardized test scores and GPA. Students should be graduates of accredited secondary schools or have the GED. UL Lafayette requires that students have at least 4 units in English, 3 each in math, science, and social studies, and 4 1/2 in electives, recommended to include 2 in foreign language, 1 each in fine arts and speech, and 1/2 in computer studies. AP and CLEP credits are accepted.

Procedure: Freshmen are admitted to all sessions. There are early admissions and deferred admissions plans. Application deadlines are open. Notification is on a rolling basis. The application fee is $20.

Transfer: 574 transfer students enrolled in 2001-2002. A cumulative GPA of 2.0 is required. 30 credits of 124 must be completed at UL Lafayette.

Visiting: There are regularly scheduled orientations for prospective students, including campus tours. There are guides for informal visits. To schedule a visit, contact the Secretary of High School Relations at (337) 482-6553 or *enroll@louisiana.edu*

Financial Aid: In a recent year, 65% of all freshmen and 70% of continuing students received some form of financial aid. 58% of freshmen and 53% of continuing students received need-based aid. The average freshman award was $3490. Of that total, scholarships or need-based grants averaged $400 ($6000 maximum); loans averaged $1900 ($6625 maximum); and work contracts averaged $1250 ($2100 maximum). 30% of undergraduates work part time. Average annual earnings from campus work are $1250. The average financial indebtedness of the 2001 graduate was $15,000. UL Lafayette is a member of CSS. The FAFSA is required. The fall application deadline is March 1.

International Students: There are 313 international students enrolled. The school actively recruits these students. They must score 550 on the written TOEFL or 213 on the electronic version and also take the SAT I or the ACT, scoring 15 on the ACT. Students must take SAT II: Subject tests in math and English.

Computers: The mainframes are an IBM 9672 and 3 Sun 4/490 servers. About 450 terminals and Sun workstations are located in public terminal rooms and dorms. The Sun facility provides e-mail and various network services. All students may access the system anytime. There are no time limits and no fees.

Graduates: In 2001, 1866 bachelor's degrees were awarded. The most popular majors were business (18%), general studies (15%), and education (14%). In an average class, 7% graduate in 4 years, 21% in 5 years, and 29% in 6 years. 114 companies recruited on campus in 2000-2001.

Admissions Contact: Leroy Broussard, Director of Admissions.
E-mail: *admissions@louisiana.edu* Web: *www.louisiana.edu*

UNIVERSITY OF LOUISIANA AT MONROE C-1

Monroe, LA 71209 (318) 362-4661
(800) 372-5127; Fax: (318) 342-1049

Full-time: 2915 men, 445 women	**Faculty:** 467; IIA, --$
Part-time: 40 men, 955 women	**Ph.D.s:** 50%
Graduate: 240 men, 810 women	**Student/Faculty:** 16 to 1
Year: semesters, summer session	**Tuition:** $2307 ($4129)
Application Deadline: open	**Room & Board:** $2900
Freshman Class: n/av	**ACT:** required
	NONCOMPETITIVE

The University of Louisiana at Monroe, founded in 1931, is a public institution offering programs in business, education, liberal arts, pharmacy and health sciences, and pure and applied science. Figures in the above capsule are approximate. There are 5 undergraduate schools and 1 graduate school. In addition to regional accreditation, ULM has baccalaureate program accreditation with AACSB, ACCE, ACEJMC, ACPE, ADA, AHEA, ASLA, CAHEA, CSAB, CSWE, NASM, NCATE, and NLN. The library contains 605,064 volumes, 550,963 microform items, and 49 audiovisual forms/CDs, and subscribes to 2912 periodicals. Computerized library services include the card catalog, interlibrary loans, and database searching. Special learning facilities include a learning resource center, art gallery, planetarium, radio station, herbarium, state poison control center, and state tumor registry. The 238-acre campus is in an urban area 90 miles east of Shreveport on I-20. Including residence halls, there are 75 buildings.

Student Life: 93% of undergraduates are from Louisiana. Others are from 40 states, 54 foreign countries, and Canada. 77% are from public schools. 69% are white; 26% African American. The average age of freshmen is 18; all undergraduates, 23. 37% do not continue beyond their first year; 25% remain to graduate.

Housing: 3685 students can be accommodated in college housing, which includes single-sex and coed dormitories and a scholastic residence hall. On-campus housing is available on a first-come, first-served basis. 74% of students commute. Alcohol is not permitted. All students may keep cars.

Activities: 3% of men belong to 7 national fraternities; 2% of women belong to 8 national sororities. There are 126 groups on campus, including art, band, cheerleading, choir, chorale, chorus, computers, dance, drama, drill team, ethnic, film, gay, honors, international, jazz band, literary magazine, marching band, musical theater, newspaper, opera, orchestra, pep band, photography, political, professional, radio and TV, religious, social, social service, student government, symphony, and yearbook. Popular campus events include Honors Day Assembly, "Miss Northeast" Pageant, and Spring Fever.

Sports: There are 9 intercollegiate sports for men and 9 for women, and 44 intramural sports for men and 31 for women. Facilities include 2 stadiums, a natatorium, a coliseum, tennis courts, a softball complex, an activity center, a baseball complex, an archery range, bowling lanes, and a bayou.

Disabled Students: 98% of the campus is accessible. Wheelchair ramps, elevators, special parking, specially equipped rest rooms, special class scheduling, lowered drinking fountains, and specially equipped dorm rooms are available.

Services: Counseling and information services are available, as is tutoring in most subjects. There is remedial math, reading, and writing.

Campus Safety and Security: Measures include 24-hour foot and vehicle patrol, escort service, shuttle buses, and lighted pathways/sidewalks.

Programs of Study: ULM confers B.A., B.S., B.B.A., B.F.A., B.G.S., B.M., and B.M.E. degrees. Associate, master's, and doctoral degrees are also awarded. Bachelor's degrees are awarded in AGRICULTURE (agricultural business management), BIOLOGICAL SCIENCE (biology/biological science, and toxicology), BUSINESS (accounting, banking and finance, business administration and management, insurance, management information systems, management science, and marketing/retailing/merchandising), COMMUNICATIONS AND THE ARTS (art, English, film arts, French, journalism, music, photography, radio/television technology, Spanish, and speech/debate/rhetoric), COMPUTER AND PHYSICAL SCIENCE (atmospheric sciences and meteorology, chemistry, computer science, geology, mathematics, physics, and radiological technology), EDUCATION (art, early childhood, elementary, English, foreign languages, mathematics, music, physical, science, social studies, and special), ENGINEERING AND ENVIRONMENTAL DESIGN (aviation administration/management and construction engineering), HEALTH PROFESSIONS (clinical science, dental hygiene, health, nursing, occupational therapy, pharmacy, premedicine, and speech pathology/audiology), SOCIAL SCIENCE (child care/child and family studies, criminal justice, economics, family/consumer studies, geography, history, liberal arts/general studies, political science/government, prelaw, psychology, social work, and sociology). Pharmacy, occupational therapy, and dental hygiene are the strongest academically. Pharmacy, nursing, and general studies are the largest.

Required: Students are required to take 9 hours each of natural sciences and humanities, 6 each of English, social sciences, and math, and 3 of the arts. An overall minimum GPA of 2.0 is required for graduation along with a total number of credits that varies by degree.

Special: A co-op program in business, an internship in pharmacy, a general studies degree, nondegree study, and credit for life, military, and work experience are offered. There are 22 national honor societies, a freshman honors program, and 2 departmental honors programs.

Faculty/Classroom: 58% of faculty are male; 42%, female. The average class size in a laboratory is 24.

Requirements: The ACT is required. In addition, applicants must be graduates of an accredited high school or have a GED. CLEP credit is accepted.

Procedure: Freshmen are admitted to all sessions. Entrance exams should be taken by April 1. Application deadlines are open. The fall 2001 application fee was $15.

Transfer: 673 transfer students enrolled in 2001-2002. Applicants must submit transcripts from previously attended institutions and should be eligible to return to the school from which they are transferring. 30 credits must be completed at ULM.

Visiting: There are regularly scheduled orientations for prospective students, consisting of the mandatory PREP program, which includes campus tours, meetings with deans/advisers, class registration, and placement examinations. There are guides for informal visits and visitors may sit in on classes. To schedule a visit, contact Jeff Hood.

Financial Aid: The FAFSA is required. Check with the school for current deadlines.

International Students: The school actively recruits these students. They must score 600 on the written TOEFL and also take the ACT.

Computers: The mainframes are an IBM system/390 multipurpose 2003/105, a DEC ALPHA 2100, and a Sunspace Server 1000. The DEC ALPHA serves as the primary mail server on the campus academic network that connects 17 academic buildings and supports 150 terminals and 1400 PCs. The IBM system supports the Business Affairs and Enrollment Management Divisions. The Sunspace supports the school's web server. There are 27 computer labs on campus. All students may access the system 24 hours a day. There are no time limits.

Graduates: In a recent year, 1263 bachelor's degrees were awarded. The most popular majors were pharmacy (13%), general studies (8%), and psychology (7%). In an average class, 1% graduate in 3 years, 20% in 5 years, and 30% in 6 years. 392 companies recruited on campus in 2000-2001.

Admissions Contact: Carletta Brouder, Associate Director of Admissions. E-mail: *rebrower@ulm.edu* Web: *www.ulm.edu*

UNIVERSITY OF NEW ORLEANS D-4

New Orleans, LA 70148 (504) 280-6595
(800) 256-5866; Fax: (504) 280-5522

Full-time: 4095 men, 5274 women	**Faculty:** 515
Part-time: 1518 men, 2080 women	**Ph.D.s:** 75%
Graduate: 1562 men, 2485 women	**Student/Faculty:** 18 to 1
Year: semesters, summer session	**Tuition:** $3552 ($11,146)
Application Deadline: July 1	**Room & Board:** $6608
Freshman Class: 4508 applied, 3611 accepted, 2204 enrolled	
SAT I Verbal/Math: 520/514	**ACT:** 20 **COMPETITIVE**

University of New Orleans, founded in 1958, is a public liberal arts institution. There are 6 undergraduate schools and 1 graduate school. In addition to regional accreditation, UNO has baccalaureate program accreditation with AACSB, ABET, ABFSE, NASM, and NCATE. The library contains 822,000 volumes, 2,368,000 microform items, and 124,000 audiovisual forms/CDs, and subscribes to 4900 periodicals. Computerized library services include interlibrary loans and database searching. Special learning facilities include a learning resource center, art gallery, and radio station. The 345-acre campus is in an urban area in a residential area of New Orleans. Including residence halls, there are 30 buildings.

Student Life: 71% of undergraduates are from Louisiana. Others are from 47 states, 89 foreign countries, and Canada. 67% are from public schools. 56% are white; 22%, African American. 39% are Catholic; 38% claim no religious affiliation; 18%, Protestant. The average age of freshmen is 18; all undergraduates, 23. 31% do not continue beyond their first year.

Housing: 1425 students can be accommodated in college housing, which includes coed dormitories and married-student housing. On-campus housing is available on a first-come, first-served basis. 91% of students commute. All students may keep cars.

Activities: 1% of men belong to 7 national fraternities; 1% of women belong to 5 national sororities. There are 125 groups on campus, including art, band, cheerleading, chess, choir, chorale, chorus, computers, dance, drama, ethnic, film, gay, honors, international, jazz band, literary magazine, newspaper, opera, orchestra, pep band, photography, political, professional, radio and TV, religious, social, social service, student government, and yearbook. Popular campus events include Fall Fest, April Fest, and Ambassadors Fishing Rodeo.

Sports: There are 5 intercollegiate sports for men and 5 for women, and 7 intramural sports for men and 4 for women. Facilities include the UNO Lakefront Arena, Privateer Park, 12 tennis courts, a swimming pool, and a health and phys ed center. A recreation and fitness center has free weights, cardiovascular equipment, an indoor track, exercise classes, 2 dry saunas, racquetball courts, basketball courts, a lap pool (indoor), an outdoor pool, and equipment accessible to the disabled.

Disabled Students: 96% of the campus is accessible. Wheelchair ramps, elevators, special parking, specially equipped rest rooms, special class scheduling, lowered drinking fountains, and lowered telephones are available.

Services: Counseling and information services are available, as is tutoring in most subjects. There is a reader service for the blind, and remedial math, reading, and writing.

Campus Safety and Security: Measures include 24-hour foot and vehicle patrol, escort service, informal discussions, and pamphlets/posters/films. There are emergency telephones, lighted pathways/sidewalks, and monitored parking.

Programs of Study: UNO confers B.A., B.S., and B.G.S. degrees. Master's and doctoral degrees are also awarded. Bachelor's degrees are awarded in BIOLOGICAL SCIENCE (biology/biological science), BUSINESS (accounting, banking and finance, business administration and management, business economics, hotel/motel and restaurant management, marketing/retailing/merchandising, and tourism), COMMUNICATIONS AND THE ARTS (art, communications, dramatic arts, English, fine arts, French, music, and Spanish), COMPUTER AND PHYSICAL SCIENCE (chemistry, computer science, geology, geophysics and seismology, mathematics, and physics), EDUCATION (business, elementary, English, foreign languages, mathematics, music, physical, science, and secondary), ENGINEERING AND ENVIRONMENTAL DESIGN (civil engineering, electrical/electronics engineering, marine engineering, mechanical engineering, and naval architecture and marine engineering), HEALTH PROFESSIONS (medical technology, premedicine, and preveterinary science), SOCIAL SCIENCE (anthropology, economics, geography, history, philosophy, political science/government, psychology, sociology, and urban studies). Business administration, accounting, and general studies are the largest.

Required: Requirements for graduation include 12 hours in social science and the humanities, 11 hours in science, and 6 hours each in English composition and literature, and in math. To graduate, students must complete 128 hours with a minimum GPA of 2.0.

Special: Students may participate in co-op programs with LSU Medical Center and may cross-register with Southern University in New Orleans, Elaine P. Nunez Community College, and Delgado Community College. Internships are required in most professional programs and work-study programs are available with various federal agencies and private companies. Students may study abroad in Austria and France or participate in a Washington semester. UNO also offers dual and student-designed majors, B.A.-B.S. degrees, preprofessional programs in nursing and physical therapy, and nondegree study. Pass/fail options and limited credit for life, military, and work experience are available. There are 4 national honor societies, a freshman honors program, and 26 departmental honors programs.

Faculty/Classroom: 63% of faculty are male; 37%, female. 96% teach undergraduates and 87% do research. Graduate students teach 16% of introductory courses. The average class size in an introductory lecture is 35; in a laboratory, 23; and in a regular course, 24.

Admissions: 80% of the 2001-2002 applicants were accepted. The SAT I scores for the 2001-2002 freshman class were: Verbal--44% below 500, 34% between 500 and 599, 18% between 600 and 700, and 4% above 700; Math--44% below 500, 34% between 500 and 599, 19% between 600 and 700, and 3% above 700. The ACT scores were 52% below 21, 29% between 21 and 23, 12% between 24 and 26, 4% between 27 and 28, and 3% above 28. 30% of the current freshmen were in the top fifth of their class; 65% were in the top two fifths.

Requirements: The SAT I or ACT is required. In addition, applicants must be high school graduates with a college preparatory program of 4 units in English, 3 each in math and science, 2 each in foreign language, history, and academic social studies, and 1/2 in computer science. A GPA of 2.0 is required. AP and CLEP credits are accepted. Important factors in the admissions decision are advanced placement or honor courses, recommendations by school officials, and evidence of special talent. Applications are accepted on-line via CollegeView and Apply.

Procedure: Freshmen are admitted to all sessions. Entrance exams should be taken at least 6 months prior to enrollment. There is an early admissions plan. Applications should be filed by July 1 for fall entry, November 15 for spring entry, and May 1 for summer entry. Notification is sent on a rolling basis. The fall 2001 application fee was $20.

Transfer: A minimum college GPA of 2.0 is required. Applicants with fewer than 24 semester hours of credit must take the SAT I or the ACT. 30 credits of 128 must be completed at UNO.

Visiting: There are guides for informal visits and visitors may sit in on classes and stay overnight. To schedule a visit, contact the Office of Admissions.

Financial Aid: In 2000-2001, 73% of all freshmen and 79% of continuing students received some form of financial aid. 37% of freshmen and 41% of continuing students received need-based aid. The average freshman award was $4257. Of that total, scholarships or need-based grants averaged $3600 ($5200 maximum); loans averaged $2990 ($5200 maximum); and work contracts averaged $1650 ($2900 maximum). 8% of undergraduates work part time. Average annual earnings from campus work are $2700. The average financial indebtedness of the 2001 graduate was $21,000. UNO is a member of CSS. The FAFSA is required. The fall application deadline is May 1.

International Students: There are 319 international students enrolled. The school actively recruits these students. They must score 550 on the written TOEFL and also take the university's own test, the SAT I, or the ACT.

Computers: The mainframes are a DEC VAX 7620, an IBM 9672, and a Cray-YMP. There are 850 PCs connected to the mainframe via the Ethernet network that provide access to word processing, spreadsheets, and database systems. All students may access the system for class assignments and course research. There are no time limits and no fees.

Graduates: In 2001, 1352 bachelor's degrees were awarded. The most popular majors were general studies (14%), general business (9%), and elementary education (7%). In an average class, 4% graduate in 4 years, 10% in 5 years, and 22% in 6 years. 200 companies recruited on campus in 2000-2001.

Admissions Contact: Office of Admissions.
E-mail: *admissions@uno.edu* Web: *www.uno.edu*

XAVIER UNIVERSITY OF LOUISIANA D-4

New Orleans, LA 70125 **(504) 483-7388; Fax: (504) 485-7941**

Full-time: 807 men, 2158 women	**Faculty:** IIA, --$
Part-time: 42 men, 89 women	**Ph.D.s:** 88%
Graduate: 68 men, 275 women	**Student/Faculty:** 15 to 1
Year: semesters, summer session	**Tuition:** $11,000
Application Deadline: March 1	**Room & Board:** $6000
Freshman Class: 3970 applied, 3399 accepted, 894 enrolled	
SAT I or ACT: required	**LESS COMPETITIVE**

Xavier University of Louisiana, founded in 1925, is a private liberal arts university affiliated with the Roman Catholic Church. There are 2 graduate schools. In addition to regional accreditation, Xavier has baccalaureate program accreditation with ACPE and NASM. The 2 libraries contain more than 130,000 volumes, 744,591 microform items, and 5000 audiovisual forms/CDs, and subscribe to 2350 periodicals. Computerized library services include the card catalog, interlibrary loans, and database searching. Special learning facilities include a learning resource center, TV station, and electronic classrooms. The 29-acre campus is in an urban area 2 miles from downtown New Orleans. Including residence halls, there are 34 buildings.

Student Life: 62% of undergraduates are from out of state, mostly the South. 80% are from public schools. 92% are African American. The average age of freshmen is 18; all undergraduates, 20. 27% do not continue beyond their first year.

Housing: 1071 students can be accommodated in college housing, which includes single-sex and coed dormitories and on-campus apartments. In addition, there are honors houses. On-campus housing is available on a first-come, first-served basis. Priority is given to out-of-town students. 70% of students live on campus. Alcohol is not permitted. All students may keep cars.

Activities: 2% of men belong to 4 national fraternities; 6% of women belong to 4 national sororities. There are 66 groups on campus, including art, band, cheerleading, chess, choir, chorus, computers, dance, drama, drill team, ethnic, honors, international, jazz band, literary magazine, newspaper, opera, pep band, political, professional, radio and TV, religious, social, social service, student government, and yearbook. Popular campus events include Wellness Week, OctoberFest, and Culturefest.

Sports: There are 3 intercollegiate sports for men and 3 for women, and 22 intramural sports for men and 22 for women. Facilities include a gym, a swimming pool, tennis courts, and a recreation room.

Disabled Students: 98% of the campus is accessible. Wheelchair ramps, elevators, special parking, specially equipped rest rooms, special class scheduling, lowered drinking fountains, and lowered telephones are available.

Services: Counseling and information services are available, as is tutoring in every subject. There is a reader service for the blind, and remedial math, reading, and writing.

Campus Safety and Security: Measures include 24-hour foot and vehicle patrol, escort service, shuttle buses, and informal discussions. There are pamphlets/posters/films, emergency telephones, and lighted pathways/sidewalks.

Programs of Study: Xavier confers B.A., B.S., and B.M. degrees. Master's and doctoral degrees are also awarded. Bachelor's degrees are awarded in BIOLOGICAL SCIENCE (biochemistry, biology/biological science, microbiology, and toxicology), BUSINESS (accounting, banking and finance, business administration and management, business economics, marketing/retailing/merchandising, and personnel management), COMMUNICATIONS AND THE ARTS (communications, English, fine arts, French, music, and Spanish), COMPUTER AND PHYSICAL SCIENCE (chemistry, computer science, mathematics, physics, and statistics), EDUCATION (art, early childhood, elementary, English, mathematics, music, physical, science, secondary, and social studies), HEALTH PROFESSIONS (predentistry, premedicine, and speech pathology/audiology), SOCIAL SCIENCE (history, philosophy, political science/government, prelaw, psychology, sociology, and theological studies). Science, education, and English are the strongest academically. Pharmacy, biology, and business are the largest.

Required: Requirements for graduation include 9 semester hours in English, 6 each in history, social science, language, theology, philosophy, and natural sciences, 3 each in speech, math, and the arts, and 1 in health and phys ed. Students must complete 128 to 132 total credit hours, including 24 to 54 total hours in the major. Students must maintain a minimum GPA of 2.0, take Introduction to African American History/Culture, pass a comprehensive exam, and by the beginning of the junior year declare a minor in an academic discipline other than the major.

Special: The university offers cooperative programs in any major and 3-2 engineering degrees with Tulane, Louisiana State, Morgan State, and Southern Universities as well as the Universities of Wisconsin, Maryland, New Orleans, and Detroit, and Georgia Institute of Technology. In addition, students may cross-register at colleges of the New Orleans Consortium. Internships are available in legal, political, and pharmaceutical areas. Students may earn an accelerated degree in biology, chemistry, psychology, or political science, pursue dual majors in engineering and biostatistics, opt for nondegree study, and earn a B.A.-B.S. degree in almost any combination. Students may study abroad in 6 countries or participate in an exchange program with Notre Dame University and Saint Michael's College. There are 7 national honor societies, a freshman honors program, and 5 departmental honors programs.

Faculty/Classroom: 55% of faculty are male; 45%, female. No introductory courses are taught by graduate students. The average class size in an introductory lecture is 25; in a laboratory, 21; and in a regular course, 21.

Admissions: 86% of the 2001-2002 applicants were accepted. The SAT I scores for the 2001-2002 freshman class were: Verbal--52% below 500, 36% between 500 and 599, 11% between 600 and 700, and 2% above 700; Math--53% below 500, 35% between 500 and 599, 10% between 600 and 700, and 1% above 700. The ACT scores were 79% below 23, 20% between 24 and 29, and 1% above 29. 53% of the current freshmen were in the top quarter of their class; 81% were in the top half.

Requirements: The SAT I or ACT is required. In addition, candidates for admission must have completed 4 units of English, 2 of math, 1 each of science and social studies, and 8 of academic electives. A GPA of 2.0 is required. AP and CLEP credits are accepted. Important factors in the admissions decision are advanced placement or honor courses, recommendations by school officials, and evidence of special talent. Applications are accepted on-line at *www.xula.edu/admapplication.html*

Procedure: Freshmen are admitted fall, spring, and summer. Entrance exams should be taken in the spring of the junior year or the fall of the senior year. Applications should be filed by March 1 for fall entry, December 1 for spring entry, and April 15 for summer entry, along with a $25 fee. Notification is sent April 15. A waiting list is an active part of the admissions procedure.

Transfer: 155 transfer students enrolled in 2001-2002. Applicants must submit college transcripts; high school transcripts are required of applicants with fewer than 30 transferable credits. 30 credits of 128 to 132 must be completed at Xavier.

Visiting: There are guides for informal visits and visitors may sit in on classes and stay overnight. To schedule a visit, contact the Admissions Office at (504) 483-7578.

Financial Aid: In 2001-2002, 82% of all freshmen and 79% of continuing students received some form of financial aid. 53% of freshmen and 48% of continuing students received need-based aid. The average freshman award was $8033. Xavier is a member of CSS. The FAFSA is required. The fall application deadline is January 1.

International Students: They must score 550 on the written TOEFL and also take the SAT I or the ACT.

Computers: The mainframes are an HP 3000 and an HP 9000. An open lab in the science building has 25 terminals from which students can log on to the mainframe. In addition, computer labs in other buildings contain PCs for student use. All students may access the system. There are no time limits and no fees.

Graduates: In 2001, 468 bachelor's degrees were awarded. The most popular majors were biology (37%), physical sciences (15%), and psychology (13%).

Admissions Contact: Winston D. Brown, Dean of Admissions.
E-mail: *apply@xula.edu* Web: *www.xula.edu*

MAINE

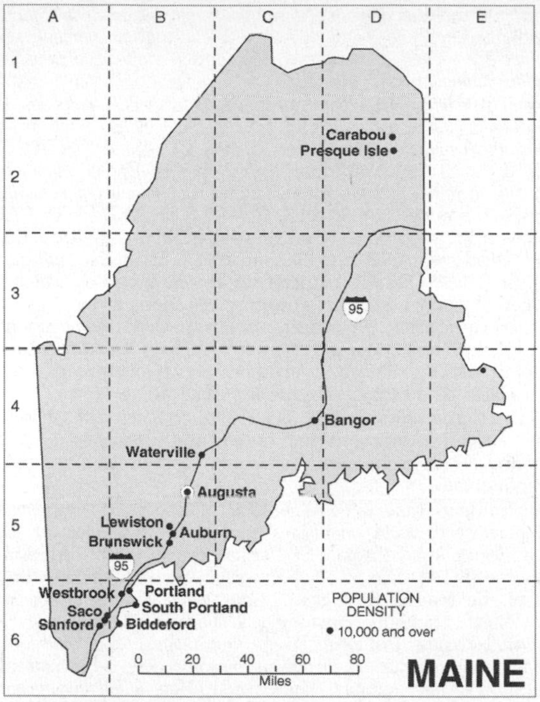

BATES COLLEGE — B-5

Lewiston, ME 04240 — **(207) 786-6000; Fax: (207) 786-6025**

Full-time: 871 men, 896 women — **Faculty:** 163; IIB, +$
Part-time: none — **Ph.D.s:** 97%
Graduate: none — **Student/Faculty:** 11 to 1
Year: 4-4-1 (5-week spring short term) — **Tuition:** $34,100
Application Deadline: January 15 — **Room & Board:** n/app
Freshman Class: 4264 applied, 1397 accepted, 582 enrolled
SAT I Verbal/Math: 670/670 — **MOST COMPETITIVE**

Bates College, founded in 1855, is a private liberal arts institution. A comprehensive fee of $34,100 (shown in above capsule) includes tuition and room and board. In addition to regional accreditation, Bates has baccalaureate program accreditation with ACS. The library contains 547,449 volumes, 297,276 microform items, and 27,479 audiovisual forms/CDs, and subscribes to 2491 periodicals. Computerized library services include the card catalog, interlibrary loans, and database searching. Special learning facilities include a learning resource center, art gallery, planetarium, radio station, TV station, 654-acre mountain conservation area, observatory, language resource center, and the Edmund S. Muskie archives. The 109-acre campus is in a suburban area 140 miles north of Boston. Including residence halls, there are 70 buildings.

Student Life: 89% of undergraduates are from out of state, mostly the Northeast. Others are from 50 states, 57 foreign countries, and Canada. 60% are from public schools. 87% are white. The average age of freshmen is 18; all undergraduates, 20. 6% do not continue beyond their first year; 87% remain to graduate.

Housing: 1604 students can be accommodated in college housing, which includes single-sex and coed dormitories. In addition, there are special-interest houses, and drug-free, and quiet/study housing. On-campus housing is guaranteed for all 4 years. 90% of students live on campus; of those, 75% remain on campus on weekends. All students may keep cars.

Activities: There are no fraternities or sororities. There are 80 groups on campus, including art, chess, choir, chorale, chorus, computers, dance, debate, drama, ethnic, film, gay, honors, international, jazz band, literary magazine, musical theater, newspaper, orchestra, outdoor recreation, pep band, photography, political, professional, radio and TV, religious, social, social service, student government, and yearbook. Popular campus events include Winter Carnival, international dinners, and ocean clambakes.

Sports: There are 15 intercollegiate sports for men and 15 for women, and 8 intramural sports for men and 8 for women. Facilities include a pool, a field house, indoor and outdoor tracks, indoor and outdoor tennis courts, 3 basketball courts, 3 volleyball courts, dance and fencing space, squash and racquetball courts, training rooms, a rock-climbing wall, a boat house, a winter sports arena, a weight room, and football, soccer, baseball, softball, and lacrosse fields.

Disabled Students: 60% of the campus is accessible. Wheelchair ramps, elevators, special parking, specially equipped rest rooms, special class scheduling, and lowered telephones are available.

Services: Counseling and information services are available, as is tutoring in every subject. There is a reader service for the blind and remedial math and writing.

Campus Safety and Security: Measures include 24-hour foot and vehicle patrol, self-defense education, escort service, and shuttle buses. There are informal discussions, pamphlets/posters/films, emergency telephones, and lighted pathways/sidewalks.

Programs of Study: Bates confers B.A. and B.S. degrees. Bachelor's degrees are awarded in BIOLOGICAL SCIENCE (biochemistry, biology/biological science, and neurosciences), COMMUNICATIONS AND THE ARTS (art, Chinese, dramatic arts, East Asian languages and literature, English, French, German, Japanese, music, Russian, Spanish, and speech/debate/rhetoric), COMPUTER AND PHYSICAL SCIENCE (chemistry, geology, mathematics, and physics), ENGINEERING AND ENVIRONMENTAL DESIGN (environmental science), SOCIAL SCIENCE (African American studies, American studies, anthropology, classical/ancient civilization, economics, history, philosophy, political science/government, psychology, religion, sociology, and women's studies). Political science, psychology, economics and English are the largest.

Required: Requirements for graduation include 5 courses in humanities, 3 each in natural science and social science, and 1 each in quantitative techniques and phys ed. The total number of hours in the major varies by department, but students should take at least 32 courses, plus 2 short terms, and maintain a minimum GPA of 2.0. A senior thesis is required.

Special: Internships, research apprenticeships, study abroad, and a Washington semester are possible. Dual, student-designed, and interdisciplinary majors, and a 3-2 engineering degree with Columbia University, Dartmouth College, Case Western Reserve University, Rensselaer Polytechnic Institute, and Washington University in St. Louis are available. Students in any major may graduate in 3 years, and a B.A.-B.S. is possible in all majors. Students may also participate in the Williams-Mystic Seaport program in marine biology and maritime history, and exchanges with Spelman College, Morehouse College, Washington and Lee University, and McGill University are possible. There are 2 national honor societies, including Phi Beta Kappa, and 30 departmental honors programs.

Faculty/Classroom: 59% of faculty are male; 41%, female. All both teach and do research. The average class size in an introductory lecture is 21; in a laboratory, 16; and in a regular course, 17.

Admissions: 33% of the 2001-2002 applicants were accepted. The SAT I scores for the 2001-2002 freshman class were: Verbal--1% below 500, 8% between 500 and 599, 61% between 600 and 700, and 30% above 700; Math--6% between 500 and 599, 63% between 600 and 700, and 31% above 700. 89% of the current freshmen were in the top fifth of their class; 99% were in the top two fifths.

Requirements: Candidates for admission should have completed 4 years of English, 3 each of math, social science, and a foreign language, and 2 of lab science. Essays are required and an interview on or off campus is strongly recommended. The submission of test scores is optional. AP credits are accepted. Important factors in the admissions decision are advanced placement or honor courses, evidence of special talent, and leadership record. Bates accepts applications electronically via Common App.

Procedure: Freshmen are admitted fall and winter. There are early decision, early admissions, and deferred admissions plans. Early decision applications should be filed by November 15 or January 1; regular applications, by January 15 for fall entry and November 1 for winter entry. Notification of early decision is sent December 16 or February 1; regular decision, by March 31. 219 early decision candidates were accepted for the 2001-2002 class. 7% of all applicants are on a waiting list. The fall 2001 application fee was $50.

Transfer: 5 transfer students enrolled in a recent year. More weight is given to the student's college record than to high school credentials. Applicants must submit official college and high school transcripts, a statement of good standing, 3 letters of recommendation, and an essay. An interview is strongly recommended. 16 credits of 32 must be completed at Bates.

Visiting: There are guides for informal visits and visitors may sit in on classes and stay overnight. To schedule a visit, contact the Admissions Office.

Financial Aid: In 2001-2002, 43% of all freshmen and 41% of continuing students received some form of financial aid. 35% of freshmen and 36% of continuing students received need-based aid. The average freshman award was $22,455. Of that total, scholarships or need-based grants averaged $18,728; loans averaged $2327; and work contracts averaged $1400. 50% of undergraduates work part time. Average annual earnings from campus work are $1400. Bates is a member of CSS. The CSS/Profile or FAFSA and parent and student tax returns and W-2 forms are required. The fall application deadline is January 15.

International Students: There are 90 international students enrolled. The school actively recruits these students. The TOEFL is preferred, but Bates will consider other parallel forms of exams.

Computers: The mainframes are a DEC ALPHA 2100, a Dual Processor RISC, and a DEC 1000 RISC. All students are assigned a user ID, which provides access to academic software, e-mail and the Internet. There are 785 college desktop computers and workstations. More than 1300 computers are connected to the system in dorm rooms. All students may access the system. There are no time limits and no fees.

Graduates: In 2001, 435 bachelor's degrees were awarded. The most popular majors were political science (11%), psychology (9%), English (8%), and economics (8%). In an average class, 2% graduate in 3 years, 84% in 4 years, 86% in 5 years, and 87% in 6 years. 70 companies recruited on campus in 2000-2001.

Admissions Contact: Wylie L. Mitchell, Dean of Admissions.
E-mail: *admissions@bates.edu* Web: *www.bates.edu*

BOWDOIN COLLEGE

B-5

Brunswick, ME 04011 **(207) 725-3100; Fax: (207) 725-3101**

Full-time: 824 men, 797 women	**Faculty:** 151; IIB, ++$
Part-time: 3 men, 11 women	**Ph.D.s:** 93%
Graduate: none	**Student/Faculty:** 11 to 1
Year: semesters	**Tuition:** $25,890
Application Deadline: January 1	**Room & Board:** $6760
Freshman Class: 4536 applied, 1080 accepted, 452 enrolled	
SAT I Verbal/Math: 690/680	**MOST COMPETITIVE**

Bowdoin College, established in 1794, is a private liberal arts institution. The 5 libraries contain 931,983 volumes, 102,514 microform items, and 19,042 audiovisual forms/CDs, and subscribe to 2708 periodicals. Computerized library services include the card catalog, interlibrary loans, and database searching. Special learning facilities include a learning resource center, art gallery, radio station, TV station, museum of art, arctic museum, language media center, women's resource center, electronic classroom, coastal studies center, the John Brown Russwurm African American Center, and the Craft Center ceramics studio and photography darkroom. The Bowdoin Scientific Station, located in the Bay of Fundy, New Brunswick, Canada, is a 200-acre island for scientific study by Bowdoin students. The 110-acre campus is in a small town 25 miles northeast of Portland. Including residence halls, there are 92 buildings.

Student Life: 86% of undergraduates are from out of state, mostly the Northeast. Others are from 49 states, 29 foreign countries, and Canada. 53% are from public schools. 79% are white. The average age of freshmen is 18; all undergraduates, 20. 6% do not continue beyond their first year; 91% remain to graduate.

Housing: 1525 students can be accommodated in college housing, which includes single-sex and coed dormitories, on-campus apartments, and off-campus apartments. In addition, there are special-interest houses. All first-year students participate in the College House System. Their residence hall is associated with 1 of 6 campus houses. All upperclass students are also eligible to participate. All first-year students and sophomores are required to live on campus. On-campus housing is available on a lottery system for upperclassmen. 88% of students live on campus; of those, 99% remain on campus on weekends. All students may keep cars.

Activities: There are no fraternities or sororities. There are 75 groups on campus, including a capella singing, art, choir, chorale, chorus, computers, dance, debate, drama, ethnic, film, gay, honors, improvisational comedy, international, jazz band, literary magazine, musical theater, newspaper, orchestra, outing, photography, political, professional, radio and TV, religious, social, social service, student government, volunteer, and yearbook. Popular campus events include Sara and James Bowdoin Day, Parents Weekend, and Ivies Weekend.

Sports: There are 14 intercollegiate sports for men and 15 for women, and 12 intramural sports for men and 11 for women. Facilities include an ice arena, a field house, a swimming pool, 2 gyms, indoor and outdoor track facilities, tennis and squash courts, a climbing wall, a boathouse, outing club cabin, and cross-country ski trails. There are also weight and aerobics rooms and 35 acres of playing fields for football, baseball, softball, lacrosse, field hockey, and soccer. The fitness center includes Cybex ergonometric equipment, free weights, and various fitness machines.

Disabled Students: 40% of the campus is accessible. Wheelchair ramps, elevators, special parking, specially equipped rest rooms, lowered drinking fountains, and lowered telephonesare available. All new buildings and renovations to old buildings are built to ADA compliance standards.

Services: Counseling and information services are available, as is tutoring in most subjects. There is a reader service for the blind. A counselor is available to assist students with accommodations as needed. Tutoring is available through the Quantitative Skills Program and the Writing Skills Project.

Campus Safety and Security: Measures include 24-hour foot and vehicle patrol, self-defense education, escort service, and shuttle buses. There are informal discussions, pamphlets/posters/films, emergency telephones, lighted pathways/sidewalks, and emergency warning whistles. Residences are locked 24 hours a day, and a staffed communications center is available around the clock.

Programs of Study: Bowdoin confers A.B. and B.A. degrees. Bachelor's degrees are awarded in BIOLOGICAL SCIENCE (biochemistry, biology/biological science, and neurosciences), COMMUNICATIONS AND THE ARTS (art history and appreciation, classics, English, French, German, music, romance languages and literature, Russian, Spanish, studio art, and visual and performing arts), COMPUTER AND PHYSICAL SCIENCE (chemistry, computer science, geology, mathematics, and physics), ENGINEERING AND ENVIRONMENTAL DESIGN (environmental science), SOCIAL SCIENCE (African studies, anthropology, archeology, Asian/Oriental studies, classical/ancient civilization, economics, history, Latin American studies, philosophy, political science/government, psychology, religion, sociology, and women's studies). Biology, economics, and English are the strongest academically. Government and legal studies, English, and biology are the largest.

Required: Degree requirements include 32 courses, with at least 2 semesters in natural science and math, social and behavioral sciences, humanities and fine arts, and non-Eurocentric studies, and completion of major requirements.

Special: Students may take advantage of about 100 approved programs all over the world, including Intercollegiate Center for Classical Studies in Rome, Intercollegiate Sri Lanka Education (ISLE), South India Term Abroad (SITA), The Swedish Program, Semester in Environmental Science at the Marine Biological Laboratory, Woods Hole, and the Twelve College Exchange (including Williams College-Mystic Seaport and National Theater Institute). Dual majors in any combination, interdisciplinary majors, student-designed majors, B.A.-B.S. degrees, and pass/fail options are available. The college offers a 3-2 engineering degree with the California Institute of Technology and Columbia University and 3-3 legal studies with Columbia University Law School. There is a chapter of Phi Beta Kappa.

Faculty/Classroom: 57% of faculty are male; 43%, female. All both teach and do research. The average class size in an introductory lecture is 30; in a laboratory, 6; and in a regular course, 16.

Admissions: 24% of the 2001-2002 applicants were accepted. The SAT I scores for the 2001-2002 freshman class were: Verbal--2% below 500, 8% between 500 and 599, 43% between 600 and 700, and 47% above 700; Math--2% below 500, 8% between 500 and 599, 52% between 600 and 700, and 38% above 700. 93% of the current freshmen were in the top fifth of their class; 7% were in the top two fifths. There were 20 National Merit finalists. 40 freshmen graduated first in their class.

Requirements: There are no specific academic requirements, but typical applicants for admission will have 4 years each of English, social studies, foreign language, and math, 3 1/2 years of science, and 1 course each in art, music, and history. A high school record, 2 teacher recommendations, and an essay are required. AP credits are accepted. Important factors in the admissions decision are advanced placement or honor courses, recommendations by school officials, and personality/intangible qualities. Applications are accepted on-line at *www.bowdoin.edu/admissions/applying/*.

Procedure: Freshmen are admitted in the fall. Entrance exams are required for counseling and placement only and should be submitted by the late summer before the freshman year. There are early decision and deferred admissions plans. Early decision applications should be filed by November 15; regular applications, by January 1 for fall entry, along with a $60 fee. Notification of early decision is sent December 15; regular decision, April 15. 184 early decision candidates were accepted for the 2001-2002 class. 1% of all applicants are on a waiting list.

Transfer: 2 transfer students enrolled in 2001-2002. College grades of B or better are required to transfer. Applicants should submit high school and college transcripts, a dean's or adviser's statement from the most recent college attended, and 2 recommendations from recent professors. 16 credits of 32 must be completed at Bowdoin.

Visiting: There are regularly scheduled orientations for prospective students, in which students should be prepared to talk informally about their academic record, interests, talents, and goals. There are guides for informal visits and visitors may sit in on classes and stay overnight. To schedule a visit, contact the Admissions Office at *admissions@bowdoin.edu*

Financial Aid: In 2001-2002, 44% of all freshmen and 39% of continuing students received some form of financial aid. 46% of freshmen and 40% of continuing students received need-based aid. The average freshman award was $23,745. Of that total, scholarships or need-based grants averaged $17,583 ($33,600 maximum); loans averaged $4832 ($5100 maximum); and work contracts averaged $1007 ($1400 maximum). 65% of undergraduates work part time. Average annual earnings from campus work are $1075. The average financial indebtedness of the

2001 graduate was $14,682. Bowdoin is a member of CSS. The CSS/Profile or FAFSA and the college's own financial statement are required. The fall application deadline is February 15.

International Students: There are 55 international students enrolled. The school actively recruits these students. They must score 600 on the written TOEFL or 250 on the electronic version. SAT I scores must be submitted at matriculation for counseling and placement.

Computers: The mainframes are 2 DEC ALPHA 1000 servers; 2 ALPHAServer 1200s, and 1 Compaq DS 20. Students access servers from 165 public PCs and terminals. Network access, including the Internet and the Web, is available from all dorm rooms. More than 1000 students access the network from their dorm rooms. Almost all students use e-mail. All students may access the system 24 hours a day. There are no time limits and no fees. It is strongly recommended that all students have a personal computer.

Graduates: In 2001, 429 bachelor's degrees were awarded. The most popular majors were government and legal studies (17%), English (13%), and economics (11%). In an average class, 1% graduate in 3 years, 83% in 4 years, 90% in 5 years, and 91% in 6 years. 325 companies recruited on campus in 2000-2001. Of the 2000 graduating class, 13% were enrolled in graduate school within 6 months of graduation and 86% were employed.

Admissions Contact: James Miller, Dean of Admissions/Student Aid. A video is available. E-mail: *admissions@bowdoin.edu*
Web: *www.bowdoin.edu*

COLBY COLLEGE

Waterville, ME 04901-8841 — **B-4** — **(207) 872-3168** — **(800) 723-3032; Fax: (207) 872-3474**

Full-time: 866 men, 942 women	**Faculty:** 157; IIB, ++$
Part-time: 1	**Ph.D.s:** 96%
Graduate: none	**Student/Faculty:** 12 to 1
Year: 4-1-4	**Tuition:** $34,290
Application Deadline: January 1	**Room & Board:** n/app
Freshman Class: 3909 applied, 1323 accepted, 488 enrolled	
SAT I Verbal/Math: 660/670	**ACT:** 28 **MOST COMPETITIVE**

Colby College, founded in 1813, is a private liberal arts college. Students are charged a comprehensive fee of $34,290 annually (shown in the above capsule), which includes tuition, room and board, and required fees. In addition to regional accreditation, Colby has baccalaureate program accreditation with ACS. The 3 libraries contain 953,160 volumes, 303,050 microform items, and 21,915 audiovisual forms/CDs, and subscribe to 2230 periodicals. Computerized library services include the card catalog, interlibrary loans, and database searching. Special learning facilities include a learning resource center, art gallery, radio station, observatory, astronomy classroom, satellite dishes, arboretum, and state wildlife management area. The 714-acre campus is in a small town 75 miles north of Portland. Including residence halls, there are 58 buildings.

Student Life: 89% of undergraduates are from out of state, mostly the Northeast. Others are from 48 states, 63 foreign countries, and Canada. 58% are from public schools. 87% are white. The average age of freshmen is 18; all undergraduates, 20. 6% do not continue beyond their first year; 88% remain to graduate.

Housing: 1729 students can be accommodated in college housing, which includes coed dormitories and on-campus apartments. In addition, there are substance-free halls, quiet residence halls, and apartments for seniors. On-campus housing is guaranteed for all 4 years. 94% of students live on campus. All students may keep cars.

Activities: There are no fraternities or sororities. There are 90 groups on campus, including art, band, choir, chorale, chorus, coed woodsman team, computers, dance, debate, drama, environment, ethnic, film, gay, honors, human rights, international, jazz band, literary magazine, musical theater, newspaper, orchestra, photography, political, professional, radio and TV, religious, social, social service, student government, symphony, women's, and yearbook. Popular campus events include Family Weekend, Foss Arts Festival, and International Extravaganza.

Sports: There are 16 intercollegiate sports for men and 17 for women, and 10 intramural sports for men and 9 for women. Facilities include an athletic center with fitness, weight training, and exercise areas; a gym with badminton, volleyball, and basketball courts; a hockey and skating rink; a field house for track, baseball, softball, tennis, lacrosse, and golf; a swimming pool and saunas; and squash and handball courts. There are also outdoor playing fields, tennis courts, an all-weather track, cross-country skiing and running trails, and a climbing wall.

Disabled Students: 90% of the campus is accessible. Wheelchair ramps, elevators, special parking, specially equipped rest rooms, special class scheduling, lowered drinking fountains, and lowered telephones are available.

Services: Counseling and information services are available, as is tutoring in every subject. There is a reader service for the blind, a writing center, and a support program for learning-disabled students.

Campus Safety and Security: Measures include 24-hour foot and vehicle patrol, self-defense education, escort service, and shuttle buses. There are informal discussions, pamphlets/posters/films, emergency telephones, lighted pathways/sidewalks, a women's safety program, a property identification program, party monitors (security officers), a student emergency response team, courtesy rides, and keycard dorm access.

Programs of Study: Colby confers the A.B. degree. Bachelor's degrees are awarded in BIOLOGICAL SCIENCE (biology/biological science), COMMUNICATIONS AND THE ARTS (art, classics, creative writing, English, German, Germanic languages and literature, music, performing arts, and Spanish), COMPUTER AND PHYSICAL SCIENCE (applied mathematics, chemistry, computer science, geology, mathematics, physics, and science technology), ENGINEERING AND ENVIRONMENTAL DESIGN (environmental science), SOCIAL SCIENCE (American studies, anthropology, classical/ancient civilization, East Asian studies, economics, French studies, history, international studies, Latin American studies, philosophy, political science/government, psychology, religion, sociology, and women's studies). Biology, chemistry, and physics are the strongest academically. Biology, English, and government are the largest.

Required: To graduate, all students must take English composition and fulfill a foreign language requirement. They must also take 2 courses in the natural sciences and 1 course each in the arts, historical studies, literature, quantitative reasoning, the social sciences, and human or cultural diversity, and meet Colby's wellness requirement by attending 8 lectures. Students must complete a total of 128 credit hours, including 3 January term courses, and maintain a GPA of 2.0.

Special: Colby offers study abroad in numerous countries, and the Colby-Bates-Bowdoin consortium has centers in London; Quito, Ecuador; and CapeTown, South Africa. Colby also offers Washington semester programs through American University and the Washington Center, on-campus work-study, exchange programs with various colleges and universities, a 3-2 engineering degree with Dartmouth College, the University of Rochester, and Case Western Reserve University, and maritime and oceanographic studies programs. Dual and student-designed majors are possible. There are 9 national honor societies, including Phi Beta Kappa, and 22 departmental honors programs.

Faculty/Classroom: 59% of faculty are male; 41%, female. All both teach and do research. The average class size in a regular course is 17.

Admissions: 34% of the 2001-2002 applicants were accepted. The SAT I scores for the 2001-2002 freshman class were: Verbal--2% below 500, 14% between 500 and 599, 53% between 600 and 700, and 31% above 700; Math--10% between 500 and 599, 55% between 600 and 700, and 35% above 700. The ACT scores were 7% between 18 and 23, 65% between 24 and 29, and 28% between 30 and 36. 89% of the current freshmen were in the top fifth of their class; 100% were in the top two fifths. 18 freshmen graduated first in their class.

Requirements: The SAT I or ACT is required. In addition, candidates should be high school graduates with a recommended academic program of 4 years of English, 3 each of foreign language and math, and 2 each of science (including lab work), social studies/history, and other college-preparatory courses. AP credits are accepted. Important factors in the admissions decision are leadership record, advanced placement or honor courses, and extracurricular activities record. Applications are accepted on-line via Common App (with a Colby supplement), Apply, and via the web site at *www.colby.edu/admissions*.

Procedure: Freshmen are admitted fall and winter. Entrance exams should be taken by January of the senior year. There are early decision, early admissions, and deferred admissions plans. Applications should be filed by January 1 for fall entry. Notification is sent April 1. 201 early decision candidates were accepted for the 2001-2002 class. 13% of all applicants are on a waiting list; 6% were accepted in 2001. The fall 2001 application fee was $55.

Transfer: 13 transfer students enrolled in 2001-2002. Applicants must have a minimum GPA of 3.0 and, as a rule, have earned enough credit hours to qualify for at least sophomore standing. They must be in good academic and social standing and should submit references from a faculty member and a dean of their current school. If the SAT I or ACT has been taken, the results must be submitted as well. 64 credits of 128 must be completed at Colby.

Visiting: There are regularly scheduled orientations for prospective students, including panel discussions, tours, class visits, complimentary meals, interviews, and information sessions. There are guides for informal visits and visitors may sit in on classes and stay overnight. To schedule a visit, contact Overnight Host Hotline at (207) 872-3377 or *admvol@colby.edu*

Financial Aid: In 2001-2002, 66% of all students received some form of financial aid. 43% of freshmen and 36% of continuing students received need-based aid. The average freshman award was $22,603. Of that total, scholarships or need-based grants averaged $21,851 ($36,800 maximum); loans averaged $1590 ($3300 maximum); and work contracts averaged $860 ($1700 maximum). 68% of undergraduates work part time. Average annual earnings from campus work are $800. The average financial indebtedness of the 2001 graduate was $17,400. The CSS/Profile or FAFSA and the college's own financial statement are required. The fall application deadline is February 1.

International Students: There are 88 international students enrolled. The school actively recruits these students. They must score 600 on the written TOEFL or 240 on the electronic version.

Computers: The mainframes are three HP806/E25, an HP820/D280, an HP871/D270, an HP770/J210, and an HP867/G40. Access to the campus network, local resources, and the Internet is available in all classrooms, labs, offices, and library study areas, as well as from each residence hall, where there is a port for every student and additional ports in lounges. 280 computers are available for student use in open clusters, departmental clusters, and labs. Laser printers are available for student use in all clusters. Students are provided with an e-mail account and storage space for personal web pages. All students may access the system 24 hours a day. There are no time limits and no fees. It is strongly recommended that students have their own PCs.

Graduates: In 2001, 468 bachelor's degrees were awarded. The most popular majors were biology (15%), English (12%), and government (11%). In an average class, 84% graduate in 4 years, 87% in 5 years, and 88% in 6 years. 96 companies recruited on campus in 2000-2001. Of the 2000 graduating class, 19% were enrolled in graduate school within 6 months of graduation and 80% were employed.

Admissions Contact: Parker J. Beverage, Dean of Admissions and Financial Aid. E-mail: *admissions@colby.edu* Web: *www.colby.edu*

COLLEGE OF THE ATLANTIC — D-5
Bar Harbor, ME 04609 — (207) 288-5015
(800) 528-0025; Fax: (207) 288-4126

Full-time: 107 men, 153 women	**Faculty:** 19
Part-time: 4 men, 5 women	**Ph.D.s:** 86%
Graduate: 2 women	**Student/Faculty:** 14 to 1
Year: terms	**Tuition:** $21,384
Application Deadline: March 1	**Room & Board:** $5610
Freshman Class: 233 applied, 174 accepted, 69 enrolled	
SAT I Verbal/Math: 628/593	**ACT:** 26 **VERY COMPETITIVE+**

College of the Atlantic, founded in 1969, is a private liberal arts college dedicated to the study of human ecology. The library contains 35,000 volumes, 274 microform items, and 1484 audiovisual forms/CDs, and subscribes to 475 periodicals. Computerized library services include the card catalog, interlibrary loans, and database searching. Special learning facilities include a learning resource center, art gallery, natural history museum, writing center, taxidermy lab, photography lab, marine mammal research center, 2 greenhouses, 80-acre organic farm, and 2 offshore research stations. The 29-acre campus is in a small town 45 miles southeast of Bangor, along the Atlantic Ocean shoreline. Including residence halls, there are 13 buildings.

Student Life: 74% of undergraduates are from out of state, mostly the Northeast. Others are from 38 states, 20 foreign countries, and Canada. 74% are from public schools. 93% are white. The average age of freshmen is 19; all undergraduates, 21. 7% do not continue beyond their first year; 67% remain to graduate.

Housing: 100 students can be accommodated in college housing, which includes coed dormitories. In addition, there is a substance-free house. On-campus housing is guaranteed for the freshman year only, is available on a first-come, first-served basis, and is available on a lottery system for upperclassmen. Priority is given to out-of-town students. 60% of students commute. Alcohol is not permitted. All students may keep cars.

Activities: There are no fraternities or sororities. There are 25 groups on campus, including art, chess, choir, chorus, computers, dance, drama, environmental, gay, international, jazz band, literary magazine, musical theater, newspaper, orchestra, photography, political, social, social service, and student government. Popular campus events include the annual Bar Island swim, contra dances, and Halloween party.

Sports: There is 1 intercollegiate sport for men and 1 for women, and 3 intramural sports for men and 3 for women. All students are members of the local YMCA and may use its pool, Nautilus equipment, and volleyball and basketball facilities, as well as nearby tennis courts. Acadia National Park offers seasonal outdoor activities. The college has camping and outdoor equipment and canoes, sea kayaks, and sailboats for student use, and offers a sailing class.

Disabled Students: 80% of the campus is accessible. Wheelchair ramps, elevators, special parking, specially equipped rest rooms, lowered drinking fountains, lowered telephones, and specially equipped residence hall rooms are available.

Services: Counseling and information services are available, as is tutoring in some subjects, including writing, math, language, photography, and computer use. There is remedial math and writing.

Campus Safety and Security: Measures include 24-hour foot and vehicle patrol, escort service, shuttle buses, and informal discussions. There are pamphlets/posters/films, emergency telephones, and lighted pathways/sidewalks.

Programs of Study: COA confers the B.A. degree. Master's degrees are also awarded. Bachelor's degrees are awarded in SOCIAL SCIENCE (human ecology).

Required: Students design their own program. They must complete a total of 36 COA credits, including 2 interdisciplinary core courses and 2 courses each in environmental science, human studies, and arts and design. Also required are group study, a 3-credit internship, a human ecology essay, participation in a 3-credit senior project, and community service.

Special: Teacher certification is offered in elementary, and secondary, science, English, and social studies education. Students may cross-register with the University of Maine and other local nautical schools. Study abroad is available in Uruguay, Mexico, and the Czech Republic. Students arrange internships with a broad range of employers. Pass/ fail grading options are available.

Faculty/Classroom: 63% of faculty are male; 37%, female. All teach undergraduates, 60% do research, and 60% do both. The average class size in an introductory lecture is 20; in a laboratory, 14; and in a regular course, 14.

Admissions: 75% of the 2001-2002 applicants were accepted. The SAT I scores for the 2001-2002 freshman class were: Verbal--39% between 500 and 599, 43% between 600 and 700, and 18% above 700; Math--10% below 500, 39% between 500 and 599, 47% between 600 and 700, and 4% above 700. The ACT scores were 40% between 24 and 26, and 60% above 28. 39% of the current freshmen were in the top fifth of their class; 75% were in the top two fifths. There were 2 National Merit finalists and 7 semifinalists.

Requirements: The SAT I or ACT is recommended. In addition, candidates for admission must be high school graduates who have completed 4 years of English, 3 to 4 of math, 2 to 3 of science, 2 of a foreign language, and 1 of history. AP and CLEP credits are accepted. Important factors in the admissions decision are advanced placement or honor courses, leadership record, and personality/intangible qualities. Applications are accepted on computer disk and on-line.

Procedure: Freshmen are admitted fall, winter, and spring. Entrance exams should be taken in the junior or senior year. There are early decision and deferred admissions plans. Early decision applications should be filed by December 1; regular applications, by March 1 for fall entry, November 15 for winter entry, and February 15 for spring entry, along with a $45 fee. Notification of early decision is sent December 15; regular decision, April 1. 28 early decision candidates were accepted for the 2001-2002 class. A waiting list is an active part of the admissions procedure.

Transfer: 22 transfer students enrolled in 2001-2002. 18 credits of 36 must be completed at COA.

Visiting: There are regularly scheduled orientations for prospective students, including an annual fall tour for high school seniors on Columbus Day. There are guides for informal visits and visitors may sit in on classes and stay overnight. To schedule a visit, contact Donna McFarland.

Financial Aid: In a recent year, 78% of all freshmen and 74% of continuing students received some form of financial aid. 72% of freshmen and 70% of continuing students received need-based aid. The average freshman award was $17,479. Of that total, scholarships or need-based grants averaged $10,895 ($16,500 maximum); loans averaged $3137 ($8125 maximum); and work contracts averaged $1917 ($2100 maximum). 86% of undergraduates work part time. Average annual earnings from campus work are $1000. The average financial indebtedness of the 2001 graduate was $17,125. COA is a member of CSS. The FAFSA and the college's own financial statement are required. The fall application deadline is February 15.

International Students: There are 28 international students enrolled. The school actively recruits these students. They must score 550 on the written TOEFL or 217 on the electronic version and also take the IB English exam.

Computers: More than 40 PCs, including Dell System 220/325, IBM XT and AT, and Mac, are available in 2 computer centers and a science lab. The graphics lab contains 7 workstations and peripherals. There is Internet access in each dorm room, with worldwide e-mail capability. All students may access the system 24 hours a day. There are no time limits and no fees. It is strongly recommended that all students have a personal computer.

Graduates: In 2001, 69 bachelor's degrees were awarded. In an average class, 59% graduate in 4 years, 66% in 5 years, and 67% in 6 years. Of the 2000 graduating class, 2% were enrolled in graduate school within 6 months of graduation and 75% were employed.

Admissions Contact: Sarah G. Baker, Director of Admission.
E-mail: *inquiry@ecology.coa.edu* Web: *www.coa.edu*

HUSSON COLLEGE
Bangor, ME 04401-2999 C-4
(207) 941-7100
(800) 4-HUSSON; Fax: (207) 941-7935

Full-time: 325 men, 585 women	**Faculty:** 44
Part-time: 196 men, 430 women	**Ph.D.s:** 54%
Graduate: 89 men, 172 women	**Student/Faculty:** 21 to 1
Year: semesters, summer session	**Tuition:** $10,010
Application Deadline: open	**Room & Board:** $5350
Freshman Class: 753 applied, 743 accepted, 351 enrolled	
SAT I Verbal/Math: 450/458	**ACT:** 22 LESS COMPETITIVE

Husson College, founded in 1898, is a private institution offering business, health careers, teaching, and other professional training. There are 4 undergraduate and 2 graduate schools. In addition to regional accreditation, Husson has baccalaureate program accreditation with CAPTE and NLN. The library contains 35,748 volumes, 12,308 microform items, and 247 audiovisual forms/CDs, and subscribes to 500 periodicals. Computerized library services include the card catalog, interlibrary loans, and database searching. Special learning facilities include a learning resource center, art gallery, and radio station. The 200-acre campus is in an urban area in the city of Bangor. Including residence halls, there are 7 buildings.

Student Life: 79% of undergraduates are from Maine. Others are from 23 states, 6 foreign countries, and Canada. 98% are from public schools. 89% are white. The average age of freshmen is 20; all undergraduates, 22. 32% do not continue beyond their first year.

Housing: 800 students can be accommodated in college housing, which includes coed dormitories. In addition, there are honors houses. On-campus housing is guaranteed for all 4 years. 59% of students commute. All students may keep cars.

Activities: 2% of men belong to 1 local fraternity and 2 national fraternities; 4% of women belong to 3 local sororities. There are 32 groups on campus, including cheerleading, choir, computers, drama, ethnic, international, literary magazine, newspaper, pep band, professional, radio and TV, social, social service, student government, and yearbook. Popular campus events include Spring Fling, Winter Carnival, and Greek Alumni Weekend.

Sports: There are 5 intercollegiate sports for men and 6 for women, and 8 intramural sports for men and 8 for women. Facilities include a gym, an Olympic-size swimming pool, weight training and mat rooms, a health and fitness center, and basketball and tennis courts.

Disabled Students: 80% of the campus is accessible. Wheelchair ramps, elevators, special parking, specially equipped rest rooms, lowered drinking fountains, and lowered telephones are available.

Services: Counseling and information services are available, as is tutoring in most subjects. There is remedial math and writing.

Campus Safety and Security: Measures include informal discussions, pamphlets/posters/films, and lighted pathways/sidewalks.

Programs of Study: Husson confers the B.S. degree. Associate and master's degrees are also awarded. Bachelor's degrees are awarded in BIOLOGICAL SCIENCE (biology/biological science and life science), BUSINESS (accounting, banking and finance, business administration and management, business systems analysis, hospitality management services, marketing/retailing/merchandising, and sports management), COMPUTER AND PHYSICAL SCIENCE (computer programming), EDUCATION (business and physical), HEALTH PROFESSIONS (nursing), SOCIAL SCIENCE (criminal justice, paralegal studies, and psychology). Accounting, nursing, and physical therapy are the strongest academically. Business administration is the largest.

Required: Requirements for graduation vary by program, but a total of 120 credit hours with a minimum GPA of 2.0 is necessary. A course in computer information systems is required in the first year for most programs.

Special: Experiential learning is part of the core curriculum in all majors. Internships are incorporated in accounting, computer information systems, sports management, hospitality management, international business, and family business. Co-op programs, externships, and clinicals are included in the curriculum in all other majors. Students can go a fifth year and obtain a master's in business in accounting, business administration, or CIS, and in phys ed with a concentration in sports management. An accelerated degree program, dual majors, and student-designed majors are also available.

Faculty/Classroom: 49% of faculty are male; 51%, female. All teach undergraduates. No introductory courses are taught by graduate students. The average class size in an introductory lecture is 20; in a laboratory, 16; and in a regular course, 19.

Admissions: 99% of the 2001-2002 applicants were accepted. The SAT I scores for the 2001-2002 freshman class were: Verbal--76% below 500, 22% between 500 and 599, 2% between 600 and 700, and 1% above 700; Math--70% below 500, 25% between 500 and 599, and 5% between 600 and 700. The ACT scores were 40% below 21, 20% between 21 and 23, and 40% between 24 and 26. 16% of the current freshmen were in the top fifth of their class; 46% were in the top two fifths.

Requirements: The SAT I is required. In addition, applicants must be graduates of an accredited secondary school or have earned a GED. A recommendation from a high school counselor is required. Husson requires applicants to be in the upper 50% of their class. A GPA of 2.0 is required. AP and CLEP credits are accepted. Important factors in the admissions decision are advanced placement or honor courses, recommendations by school officials, and leadership record.

Procedure: Freshmen are admitted to all sessions. Entrance exams should be taken prior to enrollment. There are early admissions and deferred admissions plans. Application deadlines are open. Notification is on a rolling basis. The application fee is $25. 3% of all applicants are on a waiting list; 3 were accepted in 2001.

Transfer: 113 transfer students enrolled in 2001-2002. Applicants must have a 2.0 GPA. Courses with a C grade or better transfer. 30 credits of 120 must be completed at Husson.

Visiting: There are regularly scheduled orientations for prospective students, including an interview and campus tour. There are guides for informal visits and visitors may sit in on classes and stay overnight. To schedule a visit, contact the Admissions Office at (800) 448-7766.

Financial Aid: In 2001-2002, 92% of all freshmen and 83% of continuing students received some form of financial aid. 92% of freshmen and 86% of continuing students received need-based aid. The average freshman award was $11,000. Of that total, scholarships or need-based grants averaged $4250 ($13,412 maximum); loans averaged $2625 ($5625 maximum); and work contracts averaged $1500. 80% of undergraduates work part time. Average annual earnings from campus work are $1337. The average financial indebtedness of the 2001 graduate was $17,500. Husson is a member of CSS. The FAFSA is required. The fall application deadline is open.

International Students: There are 52 international students enrolled. The school actively recruits these students. They must score 500 on the written TOEFL or 173 on the electronic version and also take the SAT I or ACT. Students who score less than 500 on the TOEFL may be accepted conditionally and must enroll in a full-time intensive English program.

Computers: Computer labs with a total of 115 workstations are available exclusively for student use. All students may access the system 24 hours a day. There are no time limits and no fees.

Graduates: In 2001, 260 bachelor's degrees were awarded. The most popular majors were business administration (43%), nursing (22%), and accounting (18%). In an average class, 62% graduate in 4 years, and 76% in 5 years. 35 companies recruited on campus in 2000-2001. Of the 2000 graduating class, 2% were enrolled in graduate school within 6 months of graduation and 95% were employed.

Admissions Contact: Jane Goodwin, Director of Admissions. A video is available. E-mail: *admit@husson.edu* Web: *www.husson.edu*

MAINE COLLEGE OF ART
Portland, ME 04101 B-6
(207) 775-3052
(800) 639-4808; Fax: (207) 772-5069

Full-time: 165 men, 212 women	**Faculty:** 30
Part-time: 10 men, 23 women	**Ph.D.s:** 93%
Graduate: 8 men, 18 women	**Student/Faculty:** 13 to 1
Year: semesters	**Tuition:** $18,825
Application Deadline: open	**Room & Board:** $7542
Freshman Class: 408 applied, 368 accepted, 155 enrolled	
SAT I Verbal/Math: 530/480	**ACT:** 21 SPECIAL

Maine College of Art, established in 1882, is a private, independent visual art college. In addition to regional accreditation, MECA has baccalaureate program accreditation with NASAD. The library contains 18,500 volumes and 150 audiovisual forms/CDs, and subscribes to 100 periodicals. Computerized library services include the card catalog, interlibrary loans, and database searching. Special learning facilities include an art gallery. The campus is in an urban area 100 miles north of Boston in downtown Portland. Including residence halls, there are 6 buildings.

Student Life: 52% of undergraduates are from out of state, mostly the Northeast. Others are from 21 states and 4 foreign countries. 97% are white. The average age of freshmen is 21; all undergraduates, 24. 30% do not continue beyond their first year.

Housing: 100 students can be accommodated in college housing, which includes coed dormitories and on-campus apartments. On-campus housing is available on a first-come, first-served basis. 75% of students commute. Alcohol is not permitted. All students may keep cars.

Activities: There are no fraternities or sororities. There are 9 groups on campus, including art, computers, dance, drama, international, newspaper, photography, social, and student government. Popular campus events include annual art sale, art auction, and Earth Day celebration.

Sports: There is no sports program at MECA.

Disabled Students: 65% of the campus is accessible. Wheelchair ramps, elevators, specially equipped rest rooms, and lowered drinking fountains are available.

Services: Counseling and information services are available, as is tutoring in every subject. There is remedial math, reading, and writing. Academic support for writing papers, study skills, and time management is available, as is help for students with learning disabilities.

Campus Safety and Security: Measures include self-defense education, informal discussions, pamphlets/posters/films, and safety training by local police.

Programs of Study: MECA confers the B.F.A. degree. Master's degrees are also awarded. Bachelor's degrees are awarded in COMMUNICATIONS AND THE ARTS (graphic design, metal/jewelry, painting, photography, printmaking, and sculpture), ENGINEERING AND ENVIRONMENTAL DESIGN (ceramic science). Graphic design, ceramics, painting are the largest.

Required: All students must take 2 years of studio foundation courses (drawing and design), 5 semesters of art history, 3 of humanities/social science, and 2 each in the studio major, English compostion, and natural science. A semester in critical issues and 2 in Western civilization are also required. 134 total credit hours are necessary, with 36 class credits in the major. Students must maintain a minimum GPA of 2.0. A senior thesis is required.

Special: Cross-registration with Bowdoin College, the Greater Portland Alliance of Colleges and Universities, and ACAD Mobility is available, as are internships utilizing professional artists and design and photography studios. An internship coordinator supervises the formal program for elective credit. There are also Art in Service internships. The continuing studies program provides for nondegree study. A minor in art history is also offered, as are dual and student-designed majors.

Faculty/Classroom: 55% of faculty are male; 45%, female. All teach undergraduates. No introductory courses are taught by graduate students. The average class size in an introductory lecture is 136; in a laboratory, 18; and in a regular course, 20.

Admissions: 90% of the 2001-2002 applicants were accepted. The SAT I scores for the 2001-2002 freshman class were: Verbal--38% below 500, 41% between 500 and 599, 19% between 600 and 700, and 2% above 700; Math--61% below 500, 33% between 500 and 599, and 6% between 600 and 700. The ACT scores were 50% below 21, 17% between 21 and 23, 17% between 24 and 26, and 17% between 27 and 28. 5% of the current freshmen were in the top fifth of their class; 29% were in the top two fifths.

Requirements: The SAT I or ACT is required. In addition, it is recommended that candidates for admission complete 4 years of English, 3 years each of art and math, and 2 years each of foreign language, science, and social studies. AP credits are accepted. Important factors in the admissions decision are evidence of special talent, recommendations by school officials, and advanced placement or honor courses. Applications are accepted on computer disk.

Procedure: Freshmen are admitted fall and spring. Entrance exams should be taken in the fall of the senior year. There are early admissions and deferred admissions plans. Application deadlines are open. Notification is sent within 4 weeks of completing application requirements. The application fee is $40.

Transfer: 50 transfer students enrolled in 2001-2002. Transfers must submit an official copy of their college transcripts. 67 credits of 134 must be completed at MECA.

Visiting: There are regularly scheduled orientations for prospective students, including a tour and a portfolio review and/or chat with an admissions counselor. There are guides for informal visits and visitors may sit in on classes. To schedule a visit, contact Kate Quin-Easter in the Admissions Office at (800) 639-4808, ext. 226.

Financial Aid: In 2001-2002, 78% of all freshmen and 99% of continuing students received some form of financial aid. 78% of freshmen and 99% of continuing students received need-based aid. The average freshman award was $14,464. Of that total, scholarships or need-based grants averaged $7629 ($18,360 maximum); loans averaged $8090 ($20,500 maximum); and work contracts averaged $455 ($1440 maximum). 21% of undergraduates work part time. Average annual earnings from campus work are $1341. The average financial indebtedness of the 2001 graduate was $23,634. MECA is a member of CSS. The FAFSA is required. The fall application deadline is March 1.

International Students: There were 6 international students enrolled in a recent year. The school actively recruits these students. They must score 500 on the written TOEFL.

Computers: Technology allowing digital imaging, animation, web site design, and Internet access is available to students through the Imaging Center. General computer access is available in the student center. All students may access the system Time is scheduled around classroom use. There are no time limits and no fees.

Graduates: In 2001, 55 bachelor's degrees were awarded. The most popular majors were graphic design (29%), ceramics (18%), and painting (18%). In an average class, 33% graduate in 4 years, 38% in 5 years, and 48% in 6 years.

Admissions Contact: Jodie Lane, Director of Admissions. A video is available. E-mail: *admissions@meca.edu* Web: *www.meca.edu*

MAINE MARITIME ACADEMY — C-5

Castine, ME 04420 — (207) 326-2206
(800) 227-8465; Fax: (207) 326-2515

Full-time: 595 men, 105 women	**Faculty:** 65
Part-time: 12 men, 1 woman	**Ph.D.s:** 37%
Graduate: 12 men, 2 women	**Student/Faculty:** 11 to 1
Year: semesters	**Tuition:** $5584 ($9619)
Application Deadline: July 1	**Room & Board:** $5327
Freshman Class: 473 applied, 380 accepted, 201 enrolled	
SAT I Verbal/Math: 513/524	**COMPETITIVE**

Maine Maritime Academy, founded in 1941, is a public institution offering degree programs in ocean and marine-oriented studies with emphasis on engineering, transportation, business management, and ocean sciences, as well as preparing graduates for the merchant marine and uniformed services of the United States. The academic calendar consists of 2 semesters plus a 2- to 3-month annual training cruise. Students from the New England region pay $7953 in tuition and fees. There are 4 undergraduate schools and 1 graduate school. In addition to regional accreditation, MMA has baccalaureate program accreditation with ABET. The library contains 75,381 volumes and 600 audiovisual forms/CDs, and subscribes to 950 periodicals. Computerized library services include the card catalog, interlibrary loans, and database searching. Special learning facilities include a planetarium and more than 60 vessels, and bridge, radar, power plant, and cargo system simulators. The 50-acre campus is in a small town 38 miles south of Bangor on the east coast of Penobscot Bay. Including residence halls, there are 14 buildings.

Student Life: 65% of undergraduates are from Maine. Others are from 35 states, 7 foreign countries, and Canada. 90% are from public schools. 97% are white. The average age of freshmen is 19; all undergraduates, 24. 12% do not continue beyond their first year; 70% remain to graduate.

Housing: 600 students can be accommodated in college housing, which includes coed dormitories and on-campus apartments. On-campus housing is guaranteed for all 4 years. 80% of students live on campus; of those, 25% remain on campus on weekends. Alcohol is not permitted. All students may keep cars.

Activities: 6% of men and about 25% of women belong to 1 national fraternity. There are no sororities. There are 30 groups on campus, including amateur radio, bagpipe band, band, drama, drill team, engineering, ethnic, international, marching band, newspaper, outing, pep band, photography, professional, social, social service, student government, and yearbook. Popular campus events include Daisy Day, Klondike Derby, and Family Weekend.

Sports: There are 6 intercollegiate sports for men and 6 for women, and 10 intramural sports for men and 10 for women. Facilities include 2 weight rooms, an Olympic pool, a field house, a gym, racquetball and squash courts, an aerobics room, and a multisports athletic field.

Disabled Students: All of the campus is accessible. Wheelchair ramps, elevators, special parking, and specially equipped rest rooms are available.

Services: Counseling and information services are available, as is tutoring in most subjects. There is remedial math, reading, and writing.

Campus Safety and Security: Measures include 24-hour foot and vehicle patrol, informal discussions, pamphlets/posters/films, and lighted pathways/sidewalks. There are medical and counseling services.

Programs of Study: MMA confers the B.S. degree. Associate and master's degrees are also awarded. Bachelor's degrees are awarded in BUSINESS (international business management), COMPUTER AND PHYSICAL SCIENCE (oceanography), ENGINEERING AND ENVIRONMENTAL DESIGN (engineering, engineering technology, marine engineering, maritime science, and transportation technology). Marine systems engineering is the strongest academically. Marine engineering technology is the largest.

Required: A minimum GPA of 2.0 in an average of 140 total credit hours is required for graduation. A comprehensive exam is required for USCG license candidates.

Special: The annual training cruise gives students practical experience aboard the academy's 500-foot ship or on assigned merchant ships. Co-op programs are encouraged in every major. Internships are highly recommended.

Faculty/Classroom: 76% of faculty are male; 24%, female. All teach undergraduates. No introductory courses are taught by graduate students. The average class size in an introductory lecture is 30; in a laboratory, 15; and in a regular course, 25.

Admissions: 80% of the 2001-2002 applicants were accepted. The SAT I scores for the 2001-2002 freshman class were: Math--33% below 500, 49% between 500 and 599, 16% between 600 and 700, and 1% above 700. 37% of the current freshmen were in the top fifth of their class; 62% were in the top two fifths.

Requirements: The SAT I or ACT is required. In addition, candidates for admission must have completed 4 years of English, 3 years of math, and 2 years of lab science. Courses must include algebra I, algebra II/

trigonometry, geometry, and either chemistry or physics with a lab. In addition, the academy recommends 1 year of a foreign language. MMA requires applicants to be in the upper 50% of their class. A GPA of 2.0 is required. AP and CLEP credits are accepted. Important factors in the admissions decision are advanced placement or honor courses, evidence of special talent, and leadership record. Applications are accepted on-line via CollegeLink.

Procedure: Freshmen are admitted fall and spring. Entrance exams should be taken as early as possible in the senior year. There are early decision and deferred admissions plans. Early decision application should be filed by December 20; regular applications, by July 1 for fall entry and November 1 for spring entry. Notification is sent on a rolling basis. 15 early decision candidates were accepted for the 2001-2002 class. The fall 2001 application fee was $15.

Transfer: 5 transfer students enrolled in 2001-2002. Applicants must have a minimum 2.0 GPA in previous college work and meet the same prerequisites as entering freshmen.

Visiting: There are regularly scheduled orientations for prospective students, consisting of 3 open houses per year; campus visits are available weekdays throughout the year. There are guides for informal visits and visitors may sit in on classes and stay overnight. To schedule a visit, contact the Admissions Office at (207) 326-4311.

Financial Aid: In 2001-2002, 74% of all freshmen and 76% of continuing students received some form of financial aid. 84% of freshmen and 68% of continuing students received need-based aid. The average freshman award was $8100. Of that total, scholarships or need-based grants averaged $2700 ($7000 maximum); loans averaged $4600 ($6600 maximum); and work contracts averaged $800 ($2000 maximum). 38% of undergraduates work part time. Average annual earnings from campus work are $460. The average financial indebtedness of the 2001 graduate was $15,650. MMA is a member of CSS. The FAFSA, student and parent tax returns, and verification worksheet are required. The fall application deadline is March 1.

International Students: There are 30 international students enrolled. They must score 550 on the written TOEFL and also take the SAT I or the ACT.

Computers: PCs are available. All students may access the system. There are no time limits. The fee $100. All students are required to have personal computers.

Graduates: In 2001, 121 bachelor's degrees were awarded. The most popular majors were marine engineering (40%), marine transportation (18%), and power engineering (10%). In an average class, 48% graduate in 4 years, and 52% in 5 years. 60 companies recruited on campus in 2000-2001. Of the 2000 graduating class, 4% were enrolled in graduate school within 6 months of graduation and 95% were employed.

Admissions Contact: Jeff Wright, Director of Admissions. A video is available. E-mail: *admissions@mma.edu*
Web: *www.mainemaritime.edu*

SAINT JOSEPH'S COLLEGE OF MAINE

Standish, ME 04084-5203 — **A-6**
(207) 893-7746
(800) 338 7057; Fax: (207) 893-7862

Full-time: 297 men, 564 women	**Faculty:** 55; IIB, --$
Part-time: 10 men, 22 women	**Ph.D.s:** 98%
Graduate: none	**Student/Faculty:** 16 to 1
Year: semesters, summer session	**Tuition:** $15,850
Application Deadline: open	**Room & Board:** $6650
Freshman Class: 1110 applied, 970 accepted, 316 enrolled	
SAT I or ACT: required	**LESS COMPETITIVE**

Saint Joseph's College of Maine, formerly Saint Joseph's College, founded in 1912, is a private, Roman Catholic institution offering liberal arts and preprofessional programs. In addition to regional accreditation, Saint Joseph's College of Maine has baccalaureate program accreditation with CCNE, NEASC, and NLN. The library contains 95,000 volumes, 5000 microform items, and 3350 audiovisual forms/CDs, and subscribes to 400 periodicals. Computerized library services include the card catalog, interlibrary loans, and database searching. Special learning facilities include a learning resource center, radio station, and TV station. The 331-acre campus is in a rural area 16 miles west of Portland. Including residence halls, there are 18 buildings.

Student Life: 63% of undergraduates are from Maine. Others are from 15 states and 3 foreign countries. 90% are white. 65% are Catholic; 30%, Protestant. The average age of freshmen is 18; all undergraduates, 20. 25% do not continue beyond their first year.

Housing: 700 students can be accommodated in college housing, which includes single-sex and coed dorms, and substance-free housing. On-campus housing is guaranteed for all 4 years. 81% of students live on campus; of those, 70% remain on campus on weekends. All students may keep cars.

Activities: There are no fraternities or sororities. There are 30 groups on campus, including Americorp for Literacy, Best Buddies, cheerleading, choir, computers, drama, ethnic, Habitat for Humanity, honors, international, literary magazine, musical theater, newspaper, photography, political, professional, radio and TV, religious, social, social service, sports, student government, Superkids, and yearbook. Popular campus events include Family Weekend, Christmas Benefit Concert, and Spring Fling.

Sports: There are 5 intercollegiate sports for men and 6 for women, and 12 intramural sports for men and 12 for women. Facilities include a multipurpose facility housing a gym, a workout room with free weights, Nautilus and other weight-training equipment, a cardiovascular workout room, dance aerobics rooms, a climbing wall, a 25-meter pool, saunas, and an elevated jogging track. There are also soccer and field hockey fields, a private beach on a lake, lighted athletic fields for baseball and softball, cross-country running and ski trails, and a low ropes course.

Disabled Students: 40% of the campus is accessible. Wheelchair ramps, elevators, special parking, specially equipped rest rooms, special class scheduling, and lowered drinking fountains are available.

Services: Counseling and information services are available, as is tutoring in most subjects. There is remedial math, reading, and writing.

Campus Safety and Security: Measures include 24-hour foot and vehicle patrol, self-defense education, escort service, and informal discussions. There are pamphlets/posters/films, lighted pathways/sidewalks, and round-the-clock security officers.

Programs of Study: Saint Joseph's College of Maine confers B.A., B.S., B.S.B.A., and B.S.N. degrees. Associate and master's degrees are also awarded. Bachelor's degrees are awarded in BIOLOGICAL SCIENCE (biology/biological science), BUSINESS (business administration and management), COMMUNICATIONS AND THE ARTS (communications and English), COMPUTER AND PHYSICAL SCIENCE (chemistry and mathematics), EDUCATION (elementary and physical), ENGINEERING AND ENVIRONMENTAL DESIGN (environmental science), HEALTH PROFESSIONS (nursing and prepharmacy), SOCIAL SCIENCE (criminal justice, history, philosophy, psychology, sociology, and theological studies). Business, nursing, and biology are the strongest academically. Elementary education, business, and nursing are the largest.

Required: To graduate, students must complete 128 credit hours with a minimum GPA of 2.0, including 8 hours of English, history, theology, and a foreign language, 4 each of science and math, and 8 of electives.

Special: Saint Joseph's offers internships, cross-registration with 4 southern Maine colleges, study abroad in Nova Scotia and Ireland, a semester at sea, dual majors, work-study programs, and non-degree study. There are 2 national honor societies, a freshman honors program, and 6 departmental honors programs.

Faculty/Classroom: 42% of faculty are male; 58%, female. All teach undergraduates. The average class size in an introductory lecture is 25; in a laboratory, 12; and in a regular course, 19.

Admissions: 87% of the 2001-2002 applicants were accepted. 21% of the current freshmen were in the top fifth of their class; 51% were in the top two fifths. 4 freshmen graduated first in their class.

Requirements: The SAT I or ACT is required. In addition, candidates for admission must be high school graduates who have completed 4 units in English, 3 to 4 in math, 2 in foreign language, and 1 to 3 each in history, science, and social studies. A GPA of 2.0 is required. AP and CLEP credits are accepted. Important factors in the admissions decision are advanced placement or honor courses, recommendations by school officials, and extracurricular activities record. Applications are accepted on-line at the school's web site.

Procedure: Freshmen are admitted fall and spring. Entrance exams should be taken by January of the senior year. There are early decision, early admissions, and deferred admissions plans. Early decision applications should be filed by November 9; regular application deadlines are open. Notification is sent on a rolling basis. 179 early decision candidates were accepted for the 2001-2002 class.

Transfer: 33 transfer students enrolled in 2001-2002. Transfer students should have a minimum GPA of 2.0. 32 credits of 128 must be completed at Saint Joseph's College of Maine.

Visiting: There are regularly scheduled orientations for prospective students, including Application and Acceptance Day programs, visits on 5 fall Saturdays, and summer visits. There are guides for informal visits and visitors may sit in on classes and stay overnight. To schedule a visit, contact the Office of Admission at *admissions@sjcme.edu*

Financial Aid: In 2001-2002, 98% of all students received some form of financial aid. 90% of freshmen and 89% of continuing students received need-based aid. The average freshman award was $12,880. Of that total, scholarships or need-based grants averaged $9165 ($15,260 maximum); loans averaged $3100 ($8125 maximum); and work contracts averaged $615 ($1200 maximum). 35% of undergraduates work part time. Average annual earnings from campus work are $608. The average financial indebtedness of the 2001 graduate was $16,950. Saint Joseph's College of Maine is a member of CSS. The college's own financial statement is required. The fall application deadline is March 1.

International Students: There are 3 international students enrolled. They must score 500 on the written TOEFL and also take the SAT I and the SAT II ESL Test.

Computers: The mainframes are an AT&T 3430 Server and a Pyramid Mis-Z. There are 71 PC terminals available to students in the computer room, the library, the resource center, and most academic departments. All students may access the system 24 hours a day in all labs and until 10 P.M. in the library. There are no time limits and no fees. It is strongly recommended that all students have a personal computer.

Graduates: In 2001, 148 bachelor's degrees were awarded. The most popular majors were education (18%), business (16%), and nursing (13%). In an average class, 50% graduate in 4 years, and 55% in 6 years. 18 companies recruited on campus in 2000-2001. Of the 2000 graduating class, 11% were enrolled in graduate school within 6 months of graduation and 92% were employed.

Admissions Contact: Nancy Griffin, Director of Admissions.
E-mail: *admissions@sjcme.edu* Web: *www.sjcme.edu*

THOMAS COLLEGE
Waterville, ME 04901 — B-4
(207) 877-0101
(800) 339-7001; Fax: (207) 877-0114

Full-time: 240 men, 240 women	**Faculty:** 22; IIB, --$
Part-time: 80 men, 200 women	**Ph.D.s:** 45%
Graduate: 80 men, 100 women	**Student/Faculty:** 22 to 1
Year: semesters, summer session	**Tuition:** $13,290
Application Deadline: open	**Room & Board:** $5625
Freshman Class: n/av	
SAT I: required	**LESS COMPETITIVE**

Founded in 1894, Thomas College's mission is to develop intelligent, responsible, and competent citizens who have the capacity and desire for personal success and professional growth in business, social services, and related organizations. Figures in above capsule are approximate. The library contains 28,000 volumes, 2 microform items, and 100 audiovisual forms/CDs, and subscribes to 100 periodicals. Computerized library services include the card catalog, interlibrary loans, and database searching. Special learning facilities include a learning resource center and art gallery. The 70-acre campus is in a rural area 75 miles north of Portland. Including residence halls, there are 5 buildings.

Student Life: 96% of undergraduates are from Maine. Others are from 9 states and 3 foreign countries. 85% are from public schools. 96% are white. The average age of freshmen is 23; all undergraduates, 25.

Housing: 275 students can be accommodated in college housing, which includes coed dormitories and off-campus apartments. On-campus housing is guaranteed for the freshman year only, is available on a first-come, first-served basis, and is available on a lottery system for upperclassmen. 57% of students live on campus; of those, 55% remain on campus on weekends. All students may keep cars.

Activities: 3% of men belong to 1 local and 1 national fraternity; 5% of women belong to 2 local sororities and 1 national sorority. There are 26 groups on campus, including cheerleading, chorus, computers, drama, honors, international, professional, religious, social, social service, student government, and yearbook. Popular campus events include Winter Carnival, Spring Fling, and Olympic Day.

Sports: There are 4 intercollegiate sports for men and 5 for women, and 6 intramural sports for men and 6 for women. Facilities include a gym, a basketball court, a weight and fitness room, soccer and softball fields, a training area, a baseball field, a field hockey field, an intramural field, and cross-country skiing and snowshoe trails. Facilities for swimming, indoor tennis, racquetball, and hockey are available locally.

Disabled Students: 80% of the campus is accessible. Wheelchair ramps, special parking, specially equipped rest rooms, and special class scheduling are available.

Services: Counseling and information services are available, as is tutoring in most subjects. There is remedial math, reading, and writing.

Campus Safety and Security: Measures include 24-hour foot and vehicle patrol, informal discussions, pamphlets/posters/films, and lighted pathways/sidewalks.

Programs of Study: Thomas confers the B.S. degree. Associate and master's degrees are also awarded. Bachelor's degrees are awarded in BUSINESS (accounting, business administration and management, business economics, management information systems, management science, marketing management, and sports management), COMPUTER AND PHYSICAL SCIENCE (information sciences and systems), EDUCATION (business), SOCIAL SCIENCE (international studies). Accounting and management information systems are the strongest academically. Accounting, management, and computer information systems are the largest.

Required: To graduate, students must achieve a minimum GPA of 2.0, fulfill all course requirements, and complete a minimum of 120 total credit hours of study including 30 hours in the major.

Special: Students may cross-register with Colby College and Kennebec Valley Technical College. There are co-op programs and internships available in most majors. The college also offers study in Canada through the New England-Quebec Exchange and in France. 5-year degrees are offered in most majors where a B.S. is available. There are 2 national honor societies.

Faculty/Classroom: 60% of faculty are male; 40%, female. All teach undergraduates. The average class size in an introductory lecture is 22 and in a regular course, 14.

Admissions: 1 freshman graduated first in the class in a recent year.

Requirements: The SAT I is required. In addition, candidates for admission must be high school graduates with an academic program that includes 4 years of English and 2 years of math. A letter of recommendation from a secondary school counselor is required. An interview is highly recommended. A GPA of 2.0 is required. AP and CLEP credits are accepted. Important factors in the admissions decision are advanced placement or honor courses, recommendations by school officials, and personality/intangible qualities. Applications are accepted on-line at the school's web site.

Procedure: Freshmen are admitted to all sessions. Entrance exams should be taken by the fall of the senior year. There are early admissions and deferred admissions plans. Application deadlines are open. Application fee is $25.

Transfer: 30 transfer students enrolled in a recent year. Applicants should have a minimum college GPA of 2.0. The school recommends the SAT I (with a minimum score of 860) as well as an interview. Official transcripts from all previously attended postsecondary institutions are required. 60 credits of 120 must be completed at Thomas.

Visiting: There are guides for informal visits and visitors may sit in on classes. To schedule a visit, contact the Admissions Office at (207) 859-1101 or (800) 339-7001.

Financial Aid: In a recent year, 94% of all freshmen and 91% of continuing students received some form of financial aid. 90% of freshmen and 87% of continuing students received need-based aid. The average freshman award was $13,743. Of that total, scholarships or need-based grants averaged $8660 ($16,375 maximum); loans averaged $4812 ($5100 maximum); and work contracts averaged $271 ($1600 maximum). All undergraduates work part time. Average annual earnings from campus work are $1300. The average financial indebtedness of a graduate in a recent year was $19,000. The FAFSA is required. The fall application deadline is open.

International Students: The school actively recruits these students. They must score 530 on the written TOEFL and also take the SAT I.

Computers: 70 networked PCs are available to students at various locations. Desktop publishing, spreadsheet, database, word processing, graphics, presentation, web browsing, and e-mail software are available. All students may access the system 24 hours a day. There are no time limits and no fees. It is strongly recommended that all students have a personal computer.

Graduates: In a recent year, 79 bachelor's degrees were awarded. The most popular majors were accounting (28%), computer information systems (20%), and sports management (14%). In an average class, 40% graduate in 4 years, 57% in 5 years, and 60% in 6 years. 58 companies recruited on campus in a recent year.

Admissions Contact: Robert Callahan, Dean of Admissions.
E-mail: *admiss@thomas.edu* Web: *www.thomas.edu*

UNITY COLLEGE
Unity, ME 04988-0532 — C-4
(207) 948-3131; Fax: (207) 948-6277

Full-time: 329 men, 163 women	**Faculty:** 34
Part-time: 11 men, 9 women	**Ph.D.s:** 61%
Graduate: none	**Student/Faculty:** 15 to 1
Year: semesters, summer session	**Tuition:** $14,345
Application Deadline: open	**Room & Board:** $5500
Freshman Class: 488 applied, 458 accepted, 172 enrolled	
SAT I Verbal/Math: 490/490	**LESS COMPETITIVE**

Unity College, founded in 1965, is a private, independent institution offering undergraduate programs in environmental science, natural resource management, and wilderness-based outdoor recreation. Some information in this profile may be approximate. In addition to regional accreditation, Unity has baccalaureate program accreditation with SAF. The library contains 46,000 volumes and 750 audiovisual forms/CDs, and subscribes to 651 periodicals. Computerized library services include the card catalog, interlibrary loans, and database searching. Special learning facilities include a learning resource center and art gallery. The 205-acre campus is in a rural area 18 miles east of Waterville. Including residence halls, there are 18 buildings.

Student Life: 72% of undergraduates are from out of state, mostly the Northeast. Others are from 23 states and 2 foreign countries. 97% are from public schools. 99% are white. 57% are Catholic; 30%, Protestant. The average age of freshmen is 18; all undergraduates, 20. 18% do not continue beyond their first year; 82% remain to graduate.

Housing: 306 students can be accommodated in college housing, which includes coed dormitories and off-campus apartments. On-campus housing is guaranteed for all 4 years. 80% of students live on campus; of those, 80% remain on campus on weekends. All students may keep cars.

Activities: There are no fraternities or sororities. There are 34 groups on campus, including art, drama, literary magazine, newspaper, photography, student government, and yearbook. Popular campus events include Regional Woodsman's Meet in October.

Sports: There are 3 intercollegiate sports for men and 2 for women, and 10 intramural sports for men and 8 for women. Facilities include a gym, a weight training room, playing fields, a nature trail, and game rooms.

Disabled Students: 80% of the campus is accessible. Wheelchair ramps, special parking, and special class scheduling are available.

Services: Counseling and information services are available, as is tutoring in every subject. There is remedial math, reading, and writing. A full-time learning disability specialist is on staff.

Campus Safety and Security: Measures include 24-hour foot and vehicle patrol, informal discussions, and emergency telephones.

Programs of Study: Unity confers B.A. and B.S. degrees. Associate degrees are also awarded. Bachelor's degrees are awarded in AGRICULTURE (conservation and regulation, and fishing and fisheries), BIOLOGICAL SCIENCE (ecology, environmental biology, and wildlife biology), EDUCATION (environmental), ENGINEERING AND ENVIRONMENTAL DESIGN (environmental science), HEALTH PROFESSIONS (environmental health science), SOCIAL SCIENCE (human ecology, interdisciplinary studies, and parks and recreation management). Aquaculture, fisheries, and ecology are the strongest academically. Conservation law enforcement, wilderness-based recreation, and wildlife are the largest.

Required: General education requirements include 38 credits in English composition, oral communication, math, computer science, life science, physical science, and electives, as well as 9 credits in a specialization outside the major field. Students must complete at least 120 credit hours with a minimum GPA of 2.0. An internship, thesis, or seminar is required in all bachelor degree programs.

Special: The college offers co-op programs, credit-bearing internships, study abroad, a Washington semester, work-study programs, accelerated degree programs, dual and student-designed majors, and credit for life experience. A mentor program, in which a faculty member assists a student with research, is available to those students who earn a minimum GPA of 3.33 in their first 30 credit hours. There is 1 national honor society and a freshman honors program.

Faculty/Classroom: 66% of faculty are male; 33%, female. All teach undergraduates.

Admissions: 94% of the 2001-2002 applicants were accepted. The SAT I scores for the 2001-2002 freshman class were: Verbal--75% below 500 and 25% between 500 and 599; Math--75% below 500 and 25% between 500 and 599. 20% of the current freshmen were in the top fifth of their class; 44% were in the top two fifths.

Requirements: Applicants must be graduates of an accredited secondary school with a minimum GPA of 2.0. The GED is accepted. SAT I or ACT scores, though not required, should be submitted, if available, for placement purposes. An essay is required and an interview is recommended. A GPA of 2.0 is required. AP and CLEP credits are accepted. Important factors in the admissions decision are advanced placement or honor courses, recommendations by alumni, and leadership record.

Procedure: Freshmen are admitted fall and spring. Entrance exams should be taken in the junior or senior year. There are early admissions and deferred admissions plans. Application deadlines are open. The application fee is $25. A waiting list is an active part of the admissions procedure.

Transfer: Applicants must present a minimum college GPA of 2.0 and are encouraged to submit SAT I scores. 60 credits of 120 must be completed at Unity.

Visiting: There are regularly scheduled orientations for prospective students. There are guides for informal visits and visitors may sit in on classes and stay overnight. To schedule a visit, contact the Admissions Office.

Financial Aid: In a recent year, 88% of all freshmen and 79% of continuing students received some form of financial aid. 77% of freshmen and 72% of continuing students received need-based aid. The average freshman award was $7705. Of that total, scholarships or need-based grants averaged $5763 ($10,000 maximum); loans averaged $4235 ($10,500 maximum); and work contracts averaged $1475 ($2448 maximum). 57% of undergraduates work part time. Average annual earnings from campus work are $1322. Unity is a member of CSS. The CSS/Profile or FAFSA and the college's own financial statement are required. Check with the school for current deadlines.

International Students: The school actively recruits these students. They must score 500 on the written TOEFL or 173 on the electronic version.

Computers: A network of IBM-compatible PCs is available in the environmental science building. Macs are available in a number of locations on campus. All residence hall systems are hard-wired for Internet access. All students may access the system. There are no time limits and no fees.

Graduates: In a recent year, 119 bachelor's degrees were awarded. 76 companies recruited on campus in a recent year. Of a recent graduating class, 13% were enrolled in graduate school within 6 months of graduation and 90% were employed.

Admissions Contact: Kay Fiedler, Director of Admissions.
E-mail: *admissions@unity.unity.edu* Web: *www.unity.edu*

UNIVERSITY OF MAINE SYSTEM

The University of Maine System, established in 1968, is a public system. It is governed by a board of trustees whose chief administrator is the chancellor. The primary goals of the system are teaching, research, and public service. The main priorities are to strengthen human services through programs in education, health, and social services; to provide international exchange and foreign language programs; and to conduct science and technology education and basic and applied research. The total enrollment of all 7 campuses is about 30,000, with nearly 1500 faculty members. There are 208 baccalaureate, 75 master's, and 23 doctoral programs offered in the system. Profiles of the 4-year campuses, located in Augusta, Farmington, Fort Kent, Machias, Orono, and Presque Isle, are included in this section.

UNIVERSITY OF MAINE

Orono, ME 04469-5713 — C-4
(207) 581-1561
(877) 4UM-ADMIT; Fax: (207) 581-1213

Full-time: 3491 men, 3384 women	**Faculty:** 519; I, +$
Part-time: 546 men, 1090 women	**Ph.D.s:** 86%
Graduate: 731 men, 1456 women	**Student/Faculty:** 13 to 1
Year: semesters, summer session	**Tuition:** $5070 ($12,840)
Application Deadline: open	**Room & Board:** $5728
Freshman Class: 4811 applied, 3854 accepted, 1620 enrolled	
SAT I Verbal/Math: 540/540	**ACT:** 23 **COMPETITIVE**

The University of Maine, established in 1865, is a publicly funded, land-grant institution in the University of Maine system. The university offers degree programs in the arts and sciences, business, public policy, health fields, engineering, education, forestry, and agriculture. There are 5 undergraduate schools and 1 graduate school. In addition to regional accreditation, U Maine has baccalaureate program accreditation with AACSB, ABET, ACS, ADA, AHEA, ASLHA, CAHEA, CSAB, CSWE, NASAD, NASM, NASPAA, NCATE, NLN, and SAF. The library contains 1,199,529 volumes, 2,265,375 microform items, and 89,092 audiovisual forms/CDs, and subscribes to 5400 periodicals. Computerized library services include the card catalog, interlibrary loans, and database searching. Special learning facilities include an art gallery, planetarium, radio station, TV station, concert hall and other music facilities, 2 theaters, a digital media lab, and an anthropology museum. The 3300-acre campus is in a small town 8 miles north of Bangor. Including residence halls, there are 158 buildings.

Student Life: 85% of undergraduates are from Maine. Others are from 45 states, 74 foreign countries, and Canada. 92% are white. The average age of freshmen is 18; all undergraduates, 23. 21% do not continue beyond their first year; 54% remain to graduate.

Housing: 3628 students can be accommodated in college housing, which includes single-sex and coed dormitories, on-campus apartments, off-campus apartments, and married-student housing. In addition, there are honors houses, language houses, and special-interest houses, substance-free housing, quiet sections, and graduate family and academic wings. On-campus housing is guaranteed for the freshman year only and is available on a first-come, first-served basis. 55% of students commute. All students may keep cars.

Activities: There is 1 local fraternity and 12 national fraternities, and 6 national sororities. There are 128 groups on campus, including art, band, cheerleading, chess, choir, chorale, chorus, computers, dance, drama, drill team, ethnic, film, gay, honors, international, jazz band, literary magazine, marching band, musical theater, newspaper, opera, orchestra, pep band, photography, political, professional, radio and TV, religious, social, social service, student government, symphony, and yearbook. Popular campus events include Maine Day, Family and Friends Weekend, and International Week.

Sports: There are 9 intercollegiate sports for men and 10 for women, and 33 intramural sports for men and 33 for women. Facilities include a sports arena for hockey and basketball, a field house, an indoor climbing center, a fitness center, a swimming pool, a weight room, an indoor track, a dance studio, basketball, volleyball, badminton, squash, tennis, and racquetball courts, and baseball, softball, soccer, field hockey, and football fields.

Disabled Students: 90% of the campus is accessible. Wheelchair ramps, elevators, special parking, specially equipped rest rooms, special class scheduling, lowered drinking fountains, lowered telephones, and a transport van are available.

Services: Counseling and information services are available, as is tutoring in some subjects, including lower-level courses. There is a reader service for the blind. Developmental courses are offered in remedial math, reading, and writing.

Campus Safety and Security: Measures include 24-hour foot and vehicle patrol, self-defense education, escort service, and informal discussions. There are pamphlets/posters/films, emergency telephones, and lighted pathways/sidewalks.

Programs of Study: U Maine confers B.A. and B.S. degrees. Master's and doctoral degrees are also awarded. Bachelor's degrees are awarded in AGRICULTURE (agriculture, animal science, fishing and fisheries, forest engineering, forestry and related sciences, horticulture, natural resource management, wildlife management, and wood science), BIOLOGICAL SCIENCE (biochemistry, biology/biological science, biotechnology, botany, cell biology, marine science, microbiology, molecular biology, nutrition, and zoology), BUSINESS (business administration and management and business economics), COMMUNICATIONS AND THE ARTS (art, communications, dramatic arts, English, French, German, journalism, Latin, modern language, music, music performance, romance languages and literature, Spanish, and speech/debate/rhetoric), COMPUTER AND PHYSICAL SCIENCE (chemistry, computer science, geology, mathematics, and physics), EDUCATION (art, elementary, health, music, physical, recreation, and secondary), ENGINEERING AND ENVIRONMENTAL DESIGN (bioengineering, chemical engineering, civil engineering, computer engineering, construction technology, electrical/electronics engineering, electrical/electronics engineering technology, engineering physics, environmental science, mechanical engineering, mechanical engineering technology, paper and pulp science, and surveying engineering), HEALTH PROFESSIONS (clinical science, medical laboratory technology, nursing, and speech pathology/audiology), SOCIAL SCIENCE (anthropology, child care/child and family studies, economics, food science, history, international studies, parks and recreation management, philosophy, political science/government, psychology, public administration, social work, sociology, and women's studies). Engineering and technology, business administration, and forest resources are the strongest academically. Education, business administration, and psychology are the largest.

Required: To graduate, students must complete a minimum of 120 credit hours, including a minimum of 48 in the major, with a minimum GPA of 2.0. 40 credits in approved courses must be taken. General education requirements include 18 credits in human values and social context, 6 credits in math/statistics/computer science, 2 courses in science, and at least 1 course in ethics. English composition is required. Students must demonstrate writing competency and complete a capstone experience.

Special: A Professional Preparation Team program is offered by the College of Education. Cross-registration through the National Student Exchange and at other University of Maine campuses, internships at the upper level, a Washington semester, work-study programs both on- and off-campus, a B.A.-B.S. degree, dual majors, a general studies degree, and pass/fail options are available. Students may study abroad in more than 40 countries. Cooperative programs are available in most majors, and accelerated degree programs may be arranged. There are 28 national honor societies, including Phi Beta Kappa, a freshman honors program, and 5 departmental honors programs.

Faculty/Classroom: 60% of faculty are male; 40%, female. All full-time faculty teach undergraduates. Graduate students teach 5% of introductory courses. The average class size in an introductory lecture is 36; in a laboratory, 20; and in a regular course, 36.

Admissions: 80% of the 2001-2002 applicants were accepted. The SAT I scores for the 2001-2002 freshman class were: Verbal--29% below 500, 47% between 500 and 599, 21% between 600 and 700, and 3% above 700; Math--31% below 500, 43% between 500 and 599, 22% between 600 and 700, and 4% above 700. The ACT scores were 28% below 21, 29% between 21 and 23, 24% between 24 and 26, 12% between 27 and 28, and 7% above 28. 41% of the current freshmen were in the top fifth of their class; 75% were in the top two fifths. There were 5 National Merit finalists. 31 freshmen graduated first in their class.

Requirements: The SAT I or ACT is required; the GED is accepted. The number of academic or Carnegie credits required varies according to the program. The required secondary school courses also vary with each program but should include 4 credits of English, 3 of math, 2 each of lab science, social studies, and a foreign language, and 3 of electives. Guidance counselor recommendation is required for high school students. The school recommends that students submit an essay. An audition is required for music majors. AP and CLEP credits are accepted. Important factors in the admissions decision are advanced placement or honor courses, recommendations by school officials, and evidence of special talent. Applications are accepted on-line via the school's web site and via Next Stop College.

Procedure: Freshmen are admitted fall and spring. Entrance exams should be taken by January of the senior year. There is a deferred admissions plan. Application deadlines are open. Notification is on a rolling basis, beginning December 1. The fall 2001 application fee was $25.

Transfer: 479 transfer students enrolled in 2001-2002. Applicants must submit transcripts of all college and high school records. A minimum GPA of 2.0 is required. 30 credits of 120 must be completed at U Maine.

Visiting: There are regularly scheduled orientations for prospective students, including an opening welcome, campus tours, registration, department tours, student panel, admissions, financial aid, and student life sessions, performing arts presentation, and auditions. There are guides for informal visits and visitors may sit in on classes. To schedule a visit, contact the Visitors' Center at (207) 581-3740.

Financial Aid: In 2001-2002, 70% of all freshmen and 74% of continuing students received some form of financial aid. 62% of freshmen and 70% of continuing students received need-based aid. The average freshman award was $6969. Of that total, scholarships or need-based grants averaged $5395; loans averaged $3308; and work contracts averaged $1650. 60% of undergraduates work part time. Average annual earnings from campus work are $1700. The average financial indebtedness of the 2001 graduate was $17,816. The FAFSA is required. The fall application deadline is March 1.

International Students: There are 172 international students enrolled. The school actively recruits these students. They must score 530 on the written TOEFL or 197 on the electronic version and also take the SAT I or ACT; SAT I is preferred.

Computers: The mainframe is an IBM 3090 UM/CMS. There are 3 computer clusters on campus, and PCs are available in the residence halls. All students may access the system 24 hours a day. There are no time limits and no fees.

Graduates: In 2001, 1258 bachelor's degrees were awarded. The most popular majors were engineering (16%), education (15%), and business (10%). In an average class, 29% graduate in 4 years, 52% in 5 years, and 56% in 6 years. 143 companies recruited on campus in 2000-2001. Of the 2000 graduating class, 23% were enrolled in graduate school within 6 months of graduation and 92% were employed.

Admissions Contact: Jonathan H. Henry, Director of Admissions. A video is available. E-mail: *um-admit@maine.edu*
Web: *www.umaine.edu*

UNIVERSITY OF MAINE AT AUGUSTA — B-5

Augusta, ME 04430 — (207) 621-3447
(877) UMA-1234; Fax: (207) 621-3116

Full-time: 400 men, 1076 women	**Faculty:** 102; IIB, --$
Part-time: 978 men, 3121 women	**Ph.D.s:** 38%
Graduate: none	**Student/Faculty:** 14 to 1
Year: semesters, summer session	**Tuition:** $3928 ($8638)
Application Deadline: June 15	**Room & Board:** n/app
Freshman Class: 2491 applied, 1479 accepted, 1286 enrolled	
SAT I or ACT: not required	**COMPETITIVE**

The University of Maine at Augusta, founded in 1965, offers both associate and baccalaureate degrees and is part of the University of Maine System. There are 3 undergraduate schools. In addition to regional accreditation, UMA has baccalaureate program accreditation with ADA and NLN. The 3 libraries contain 85,015 volumes, 11,694 microform items, and 7082 audiovisual forms/CDs, and subscribe to 862 periodicals. Computerized library services include the card catalog, interlibrary loans, and database searching. Special learning facilities include a learning resource center, art gallery, and an interactive television system. The 165-acre campus is in a small town 50 miles north of Portland. There are 14 buildings.

Student Life: 99% of undergraduates are from Maine. Others are from 15 states, 9 foreign countries, and Canada. 99% are from public schools. The average age of freshmen is 27; all undergraduates, 32. 40% do not continue beyond their first year; 30% remain to graduate.

Housing: There are no residence halls. All students commute. Alcohol is not permitted. All students may keep cars.

Activities: There are no fraternities or sororities. There are 10 groups on campus, including art, computers, honors, international, jazz band, literary magazine, pep band, professional, student government, and yearbook. Popular campus events include UMA Day, community lunches, and the Annual Leadership Conference.

Sports: There are 2 intercollegiate sports for men and 3 for women, and 3 intramural sports for men and 3 for women. Facilities include the UMA Community Outdoor Leisure Center, which is also open to the public. Facilities provide for seasonal activities and feature a running and cross-country skiing trail, tennis courts, a soccer field, and a softball field. Indoor facilities include a small gym, a racquetball court, and a fitness center.

Disabled Students: 95% of the campus is accessible. Wheelchair ramps, elevators, special parking, specially equipped rest rooms, special class scheduling, lowered drinking fountains, and lowered telephones are available.

Services: Counseling and information services are available, as is tutoring in most subjects. There is a reader service for the blind, and remedial math, reading, and writing.

Campus Safety and Security: Measures include pamphlets/posters/films, lighted pathways/sidewalks, and an evening vehicle patrol.

Programs of Study: UMA confers B.A., B.S., and B.Mus. degrees. Associate degrees are also awarded. Bachelor's degrees are awarded in BIOLOGICAL SCIENCE (biology/biological science), BUSINESS (accounting, banking and finance, and business administration and management), COMMUNICATIONS AND THE ARTS (art, English, and jazz), COMPUTER AND PHYSICAL SCIENCE (information sciences and systems), EDUCATION (library science), HEALTH PROFESSIONS (dental hygiene and mental health/human services), SOCIAL SCIENCE (interdisciplinary studies, public administration, and social science). Business administration is the largest.

Required: All students must complete at least 120 hours, including 30 to 40 in the major, with a minimum GPA of 2.0. All degree programs require courses in English and communications, humanities, math and computer sciences, and social sciences. Specific course requirements differ by degree program.

Special: Work-study and internship programs with local employers, study abroad, a general studies degree, nondegree study, and pass/fail options are available. UMA administers a displaced homemakers project, offering personal and professional development training and counseling.

Faculty/Classroom: 57% of faculty are male; 43%, female. All teach undergraduates. The average class size in an introductory lecture is 30; in a laboratory, 15; and in a regular course, 30.

Admissions: 59% of the 2001-2002 applicants were accepted. 12% of the current freshmen were in the top fifth of their class; 63% were in the top two fifths.

Requirements: Applicants should have a high school diploma or the GED. Recommended secondary preparation varies according to the degree program. Students are encouraged to submit SAT I scores for placement only. Applicants for the B.M. program must audition. AP and CLEP credits are accepted. Applications are available on-line at the UMA web site.

Procedure: Freshmen are admitted to all sessions. Entrance exams should be taken in November or January of the senior year. There are early decision, early admissions, and deferred admissions plans. Early decision applications should be filed by November 1; regular applications, by June 15 for fall entry and October 15 for spring entry. Notification of early decision is sent December 1; regular decision, on a rolling basis. A waiting list is an active part of the admissions procedure. The fall 2001 application fee was $25.

Transfer: 457 transfer students enrolled in 2001-2002. 30 credits of 120 must be completed at UMA.

Visiting: There are regularly scheduled orientations for prospective students, during the month before the beginning of a semester. There are guides for informal visits and visitors may sit in on classes. To schedule a visit, contact the Admissions and Records Office.

Financial Aid: In 2001-2002, 77% of all freshmen and 73% of continuing students received some form of financial aid. 58% of freshmen and 64% of continuing students received need-based aid. The average freshman award was $3098. Of that total, scholarships or need-based grants averaged $2066 ($7974 maximum); and loans averaged $1778 ($7000 maximum). 3% of undergraduates work part time. Average annual earnings from campus work are $1491. The average financial indebtedness of the 2001 graduate was $10,533. The FAFSA is required. The fall application deadline is March 1.

International Students: There are 14 international students enrolled. They must score 500 on the written TOEFL.

Computers: The mainframes are a comprised of an IBM 3033 and an IBM 4381. Terminals are available at the Student Computer Center on the main campus and at off-campus locations. All students may access the system 24 hours a day at home, 8 A.M. to 8:30 P.M. in a shared lab. There are no time limits and no fees.

Graduates: In a recent year, 77 bachelor's degrees were awarded. The most popular majors were mental health/human services (22%), business administration (16%), and nursing (15%). In an average class, 24% graduate in 3 years, 45% in 4 years, 59% in 5 years, and 67% in 6 years. 84 companies recruited on campus in a recent year.

Admissions Contact: Wm. Clark Ketcham, Director of Enrollment Services. A video is available. E-mail: *ketcham@maine.edu*
Web: *www.uma.maine.edu*

UNIVERSITY OF MAINE AT FARMINGTON B-4
Farmington, ME 04938-1990 **(207) 778-7050**
Fax: (207) 778-8182

Full-time: 690 men, 1403 women	**Faculty:** 116; IIB, --$
Part-time: 103 men, 223 women	**Ph.D.s:** 86%
Graduate: none	**Student/Faculty:** 18 to 1
Year: semesters, summer session	**Tuition:** $4317 ($9702)
Application Deadline: open	**Room & Board:** $4846

Freshman Class: 1772 applied, 1279 accepted, 641 enrolled
SAT I Verbal/Math: 530/515 **COMPETITIVE**

The University of Maine at Farmington, part of the University of Maine System, is a public liberal arts institution offering programs in arts and sciences, teacher education, and human services. There are 2 undergraduate schools. In addition to regional accreditation, UMF has baccalaureate program accreditation with NCATE. The library contains 104,313 volumes, 78,903 microform items, and 8572 audiovisual forms/CDs, and subscribes to 1581 periodicals. Computerized library services include the card catalog, interlibrary loans, and database searching. Special learning facilities include a learning resource center, art gallery, radio station, instructional media center, archeology research center, and 20-workstation electronic classroom. The 50-acre campus is in a small town 38 miles northwest of Augusta. Including residence halls, there are 35 buildings.

Student Life: 82% of undergraduates are from Maine. Others are from 32 states, 16 foreign countries, and Canada. 88% are from public schools. 95% are white. The average age of all undergraduates is 23. 20% do not continue beyond their first year; 52% remain to graduate.

Housing: 834 students can be accommodated in college housing, which includes single-sex and coed dormitories and on-campus apartments. In addition, there are wellness floors and an international guest house. On-campus housing is guaranteed for all 4 years. 60% of students commute. All students may keep cars.

Activities: There are no fraternities or sororities. There are 51 groups on campus, including band, chamber choir, cheerleading, choir, chorus, commuter, dance, drama, environmental, film, gay, honors, international, language, literary magazine, musical theater, newspaper, orchestra, outing, pep band, photography, political, professional, radio and TV, religious, social, social service, student government, and yearbook. Popular campus events include Parents and Alumni weekends, Winter Carnival Weekend, and Student Symposium Day.

Sports: There are 5 intercollegiate sports for men and 6 for women, and 12 intramural sports for men and 12 for women. Facilities include a 500-seat gym, baseball, softball, and soccer fields, a field house with an indoor jogging track, 4 multipurpose courts, a swimming pool, and a weight-training center. A ski area, mountain climbing, canoeing, and white water rafting opportunities are nearby.

Disabled Students: 50% of the campus is accessible. Wheelchair ramps, elevators, special parking, specially equipped rest rooms, special class scheduling, lowered drinking fountains, lowered telephones, an accessible van, a swimming pool, and TDD are available.

Services: Counseling and information services are available, as is tutoring in every subject. There is a reader service for the blind, and remedial math, reading, and writing.

Campus Safety and Security: Measures include 24-hour foot and vehicle patrol, self-defense education, escort service, and informal discussions. There are pamphlets/posters/films, emergency telephones, lighted pathways/sidewalks, and safety whistles.

Programs of Study: UMF confers B.A., B.S., B.F.A., and B.G.S. degrees. Bachelor's degrees are awarded in BIOLOGICAL SCIENCE (biology/biological science), BUSINESS (business economics), COMMUNICATIONS AND THE ARTS (art, creative writing, dramatic arts, English, language arts, music, and visual and performing arts), COMPUTER AND PHYSICAL SCIENCE (computer mathematics, computer science, geochemistry, geology, and mathematics), EDUCATION (early childhood, education of the emotionally handicapped, education of the exceptional child, education of the mentally handicapped, elementary, English, health, mathematics, science, secondary, social science, and special), ENGINEERING AND ENVIRONMENTAL DESIGN (environmental science), HEALTH PROFESSIONS (community health work and rehabilitation therapy), SOCIAL SCIENCE (geography, history, interdisciplinary studies, international studies, liberal arts/general studies, philosophy, political science/government, psychology, sociology, and women's studies). Education, environmental science, and creative writing are the strongest academically. Elementary education, secondary education, and interdisciplinary studies are the largest.

Required: All students must maintain a minimum GPA of 2.0 while earning 120 semester hours, including 30 in their major. Core requirements include 9 hours each in social and behavioral sciences and the humanities, 8 in science, 4 in English composition, 3 each in math, health, and phys ed, and a foreign language.

Special: Study abroad in 4 countries, as well as numerous opportunities through the National Student Exchange program, work-study with UMF, and student-designed majors are available. Internships are required in rehabilitation and health and are available in all disciplines. Also possible is interdisciplinary field study in many disciplines, a ski industry certificate, nondegree study, and pass/fail options. There are 2 national honor societies, a freshman honors program, and 10 departmental honors programs.

Faculty/Classroom: 54% of faculty are male; 46%, female. All teach undergraduates. The average class size in an introductory lecture is 45; in a laboratory, 20; and in a regular course, 19.

Admissions: 72% of the 2001-2002 applicants were accepted. The SAT I scores for the 2001-2002 freshman class were: Verbal--38% below 500, 43% between 500 and 599, 16% between 600 and 700, and 3% above 700; Math--43% below 500, 39% between 500 and 599, 17% between 600 and 700, and 1% above 700. 33% of the current freshmen were in the top fifth of their class; 65% were in the top two fifths. 3 freshmen graduated first in their class.

Requirements: Applicants are required to have 16 to 19 college preparatory courses, including 4 in English, 3 to 5 in math, 3 electives, 2 to 3 in lab science, and 2 each in social science and foreign language. An essay is required, and an interview recommended. A counselor recommendation is required. The GED is accepted for older, highly motivated students. UMF requires applicants to be in the upper 50% of their class. A GPA of 2.4 is required. AP and CLEP credits are accepted. Important factors in the admissions decision are advanced placement or honor courses, recommendations by school officials, and leadership record. Applications are accepted on-line via Apply and CollegeLink.

Procedure: Freshmen are admitted fall and spring. There are early decision, early admissions, and deferred admissions plans. Application deadlines are open. Notification is sent on a rolling basis. 104 early decision candidates were accepted for a recent class. 2% of all applicants are on a waiting list; 4 were accepted in 2001. The fall 2001 application fee was $25.

Transfer: 140 transfer students enrolled in 2001-2002. Applicants must have a minimum GPA of 2.0 (2.5 for some majors). 30 credits of 120 must be completed at UMF.

Visiting: There are regularly scheduled orientations for prospective students, including sessions on financial aid, majors, student life, the admissions process, and special opportunities such as study abroad, and tours of the campus. There are guides for informal visits and visitors may sit in on classes. To schedule a visit, contact the Admissions Office.

Financial Aid: In 2001-2002, 59% of all freshmen and 63% of continuing students received some form of financial aid. 16% of freshmen received need-based aid. The average freshman award was $8497. Of that total, scholarships or need-based grants averaged $4000; loans averaged $2751; and work contracts averaged $1746. The average financial indebtedness of the 2001 graduate was $14,435. UMF is a member of CSS. The FAFSA is required. The fall application deadline is March 1.

International Students: The school actively recruits these students. They must score 530 on the written TOEFL or 190 on the electronic version. The SAT I is optional but recommended for placement.

Computers: The mainframes are an IBM 3090, IBM PC-RT, and Sun SPARC station 1+. There are 145 workstations of Pentium PCs and 68040 Macs for general student use. All are at the Academic Computer Center, except 34 in departmental student labs. All have Internet and Web access through the campus T-1 link. All students have access to networked applications, personal network disk space, web publishing space, and free Internet dial-in. All students may access the system. 35 stations are available 24 hours a day, the rest 80 hours per week. There are no time limits. The fee is $90 per year, on average.

Graduates: In 2001, 428 bachelor's degrees were awarded. The most popular majors were interdisciplinary (33%), elementary education (30%), and rehabilitation services (11%). In an average class, 43% graduate in 4 years, and 59% in 5 years. 25 companies recruited on campus in 2000-2001. Of the 2000 graduating class, 18% were enrolled in graduate school within 6 months of graduation and 92% were employed.

Admissions Contact: Sharon Oliver, Director of Admissions.
E-mail: *umfadmit@maine.edu* Web: *www.umf.maine.edu*

UNIVERSITY OF MAINE AT FORT KENT — D-1

Fort Kent, ME 04743-1292 — (207) 834-7600
(888) TRY-UMFK; Fax: (207) 834-7609

Full-time: 247 men, 345 women	**Faculty:** 35; IIB, --$
Part-time: 79 men, 226 women	**Ph.D.s:** 70%
Graduate: none	**Student/Faculty:** 17 to 1
Year: semesters, summer session	**Tuition:** $3590 ($8280)
Application Deadline: open	**Room & Board:** $4224

Freshman Class: 626 applied, 539 accepted, 290 enrolled
SAT I: 444/465 — **LESS COMPETITIVE**

The University of Maine at Fort Kent, founded in 1878, is a publicly funded liberal arts institution within the University of Maine system. Figures in above capsule are approximate. In addition to regional accreditation, UMFK has baccalaureate program accreditation with NLN. The library contains 66,371 volumes, 90 microform items, and 1310 audiovisual forms/CDs, and subscribes to 390 periodicals. Computerized library services include the card catalog, interlibrary loans, and database searching. Special learning facilities include a learning resource center, radio station, greenhouse, and biological park. The 52-acre campus is in a small town 200 miles north of Bangor. Including residence halls, there are 14 buildings.

Student Life: 68% of undergraduates are from Maine. Others are from 10 states, 2 foreign countries, and Canada. 72% are white; 29% Hispanic. The average age of freshmen is 20; all undergraduates, 26. 22% do not continue beyond their first year; 78% remain to graduate.

Housing: 175 students can be accommodated in college housing, which includes coed dormitories. On-campus housing is guaranteed for all 4 years. 87% of students commute. Alcohol is not permitted. All students may keep cars.

Activities: 5% of men belong to 1 national fraternity; 2% of women belong to 1 national sorority. There are 25 groups on campus, including cheerleading, chorale, chorus, computers, dance, drama, environmental, international, literature, literary magazine, musical theater, newspaper, outing, professional, radio and TV, religious, and student government. Popular campus events include French Heritage Festival, Spring Meltdown, and Winter Carnival.

Sports: There are 5 intercollegiate sports for men and 4 for women, and 8 intramural sports for men and 8 for women. Facilities include an 11,500-square-foot gym, racquetball courts, soccer field, weight room, cardiovascular room, intramural fields, and game rooms in the residence halls.

Disabled Students: 80% of the campus is accessible. Wheelchair ramps, elevators, special parking, specially equipped rest rooms, special class scheduling, lowered drinking fountains, and lowered telephones are available.

Services: Counseling and information services are available, as is tutoring in every subject. There is a reader service for the blind, and remedial math, reading, and writing.

Campus Safety and Security: Measures include informal discussions, pamphlets/posters/films, and lighted pathways/sidewalks.

Programs of Study: UMFK confers B.A., B.S., B.S.E.S, B.S.N., and B.U.S. degrees. Associate degrees are also awarded. Bachelor's degrees are awarded in BIOLOGICAL SCIENCE (biology/biological science), BUSINESS (business administration and management), COMMUNICATIONS AND THE ARTS (English and French), COMPUTER AND PHYSICAL SCIENCE (computer science), EDUCATION (elementary, secondary), ENGINEERING AND ENVIRONMENTAL DESIGN (environmental science), HEALTH PROFESSIONS (nursing), SOCIAL SCIENCE (behavioral science, liberal arts/general studies, and social science). Environmental studies, nursing, and biology are the strongest academically. Education, nursing, and behavioral science are the largest.

Required: A minimum GPA of 2.0 and a total of 120 credit hours (2.5 GPA and 126 credit hours for business, 127 credit hours for nursing, and 128 for education) are required for graduation. Curricula and distribution requirements vary by major.

Special: Internships are required for business majors. A general studies degree, a B.A.-B.S. degree in bilingual-bicultural studies, credit for life experience, and nondegree study are available. Students may cross-register with the College Universitaire Saint Louis Maillet in New Brunswick. Study abroad may be arranged in Canada, France, and Mexico through the University of Maine at Farmington. Interactive TV courses broadcast from other universities are available on campus. There is 1 national honor society.

Faculty/Classroom: 61% of faculty are male; 39%, female. All teach undergraduates. The average class size in an introductory lecture is 20; in a laboratory, 15; and in a regular course, 25.

Admissions: 86% of the 2001-2002 applicants were accepted. The SAT I scores for the 2001-2002 freshman class were: Math--74% below 500; 22% between 500 and 599; 3% between 600 and 700; and 1% above 700. 16% of the current freshmen were in the top fifth of their class; 37% were in the top two fifths.

Requirements: The SAT I is recommended. In addition, applicants should be graduates of an accredited secondary school. The GED is accepted. Required secondary school courses include 4 years of English and 2 each of social studies, math, and lab science. A foreign language is suggested. An essay and an interview are recommended. AP and CLEP credits are accepted. Important factors in the admissions decision are recommendations by school officials, advanced placement or honor courses, and evidence of special talent. Applications are accepted on-line at the school's web site.

Procedure: Freshmen are admitted fall and spring. Entrance exams should be taken before March of the senior year. There are early decision, early admissions, and deferred admissions plans. Application deadlines are open. The application fee is $25.

Transfer: 164 transfer students enrolled in 2001-2002. Applicants must submit transcripts from each college and secondary school attended. The SAT I and an interview are recommended. 30 credits of 120 must be completed at UMFK.

Visiting: There are regularly scheduled orientations for prospective students, including placement testing, meetings with advisers, campus tours, and get-aquainted activities. There are guides for informal visits and visitors may sit in on classes and stay overnight. To schedule a visit, contact the Admissions Office at (207) 834-7601.

Financial Aid: In a recente year, 80% of all students received some form of financial aid. 70% of all students received need-based aid. The average freshman award was $3780. Of that total, scholarships or need-based grants averaged $3475; loans averaged $2923; and work contracts averaged $1000. 54% of undergraduates work part time. Average annual earnings from campus work are $1000. The average financial indebtedness of a graduate in a recent year was $3789. UMFK is a member of CSS. The FAFSA and income tax forms are required. The fall application deadline is March 15.

International Students: There are 239 international students enrolled. The school actively recruits these students. They must score 500 on the written TOEFL and also take the college's own test. The SAT I scores may be submitted in place of the TOEFL.

Computers: The mainframes include a Novell 311 and Novell 3.12 serving a Dell 2100/200 Power Edge CPU and Dell Power Edge 4100. PCs are available in the dormitories, the library, and 2 computer centers. All students may access the system from 8 A.M. to 11 P.M. in the library and computer centers, and 24 hours a day in the dormitories. There are no time limits. The fee is $5.

Graduates: In a recent year, 155 bachelor's degrees were awarded. The most popular majors were education (18%), business (11%), and computer (9%). In an average class, 30% graduate in 3 years, and 33% in 5 years. 2 companies recruited on campus in a recent year.

Admissions Contact: Melik Peter Khoury, Director of Admissions. E-mail: *umfkadm@maine.edu* Web: *www.umfk.maine.edu*

UNIVERSITY OF MAINE AT MACHIAS E-4
Machias, ME 04654 (207) 255-1318
(888) GO-TO-UMM; Fax: (207) 255-1363

Full-time: 190 men, 310 women	**Faculty:** 42; IIB, --$
Part-time: 120 men, 290 women	**Ph.D.s:** 61%
Graduate: none	**Student/Faculty:** 12 to 1
Year: semesters, summer session	**Tuition:** $3614 ($8324)
Application Deadline: open	**Room & Board:** $4075
Freshman Class: n/av	
SAT I or ACT: required	**LESS COMPETITIVE**

The University of Maine at Machias, founded in 1909, is a publicly funded liberal arts institution in the University of Maine system. Figures in above capsule are approximate. In addition to regional accreditation, UMM has baccalaureate program accreditation with NRPA. The library contains 79,507 volumes, 4653 microform items, and 2136 audiovisual forms/CDs, and subscribes to 461 periodicals. Computerized library services include the card catalog, interlibrary loans, and database searching. Special learning facilities include a learning resource center, art gallery, radio station, and aquariums for marine and aquaculture studies. The 42-acre campus is in a rural area 85 miles east of Bangor. Including residence halls, there are 8 buildings.

Student Life: 85% of undergraduates are from Maine. Others are from 20 states, 12 foreign countries, and Canada. 98% are from public schools. 92% are white. The average age of freshmen is 19; all undergraduates, 28. 39% do not continue beyond their first year; 46% remain to graduate.

Housing: 300 students can be accommodated in college housing, which includes single-sex and coed dormitories. On-campus housing is guaranteed for all 4 years. 70% of students commute. All students may keep cars.

Activities: 3% of men belong to 2 local and 2 national fraternities; 2% of women belong to 3 local sororities and 1 national sorority. There are 25 groups on campus, including art, cheerleading, chorale, chorus, computers, dance, drama, gay, honors, international, literary magazine, musical theater, newspaper, outing, pep band, photography, pop band, professional, religious, social service, student government, and yearbook. Popular campus events include Winter Carnival, Spring Weekend, and Family Weekend.

Sports: There are 3 intercollegiate sports for men and 4 for women, and 10 intramural sports for men and 10 for women. Facilities include 2 gyms, weight/exercise rooms, handball/raquetball courts, a pool, and a 64-acre recreational center with a lodge and cabins on the lake.

Disabled Students: 85% of the campus is accessible. Wheelchair ramps, elevators, special parking, specially equipped rest rooms, lowered drinking fountains, and automatic doors are available.

Services: Counseling and information services are available, as is tutoring in every subject. There is remedial math, reading, and writing. The Student Resource Coordinator provides one-on-one services, including learning strategies, study skills, and assistance with papers and learning styles.

Campus Safety and Security: Measures include informal discussions, pamphlets/posters/films, lighted pathways/sidewalks, a keyless entry system for residence halls, and security patrol from 5 P.M. to 1 A.M. Sunday to Wednesday and from 5 P.M. to 5 A.M. Thursday to Saturday.

Programs of Study: UMM confers B.A., B.S., B.C.S., and B.S.E.S. degrees. Associate degrees are also awarded. Bachelor's degrees are awarded in BIOLOGICAL SCIENCE (biology/biological science and marine biology), BUSINESS (accounting, business administration and management, marketing/retailing/merchandising, and recreation and leisure services), COMMUNICATIONS AND THE ARTS (English and fine arts), EDUCATION (business, elementary, and middle school), ENGINEERING AND ENVIRONMENTAL DESIGN (environmental science), SOCIAL SCIENCE (behavioral science, history, human services, and liberal arts/general studies). Elementary education, marine biology, and environmental studies are the strongest academically. Biology, behavioral science, and business administration are the largest.

Required: To graduate, students must complete a minimum of 120 credit hours with a GPA of 2.0. The core curriculum consists of 40-43 hours in the areas of communication skills, science and math, humans in social context, fine arts, historical and cultural perspectives, and lifetime fitness.

Special: Co-op programs in all majors except education, cross-registration, internships, work-study programs, an accelerated degree program, a B.A.-B.S. degree, study abroad in England and Wales, and a student designed concentration in environmental science are available. UMM also offers credit for prior learning, nondegree study, and a pass/fail option in certain courses. There is a freshman honors program.

Faculty/Classroom: 68% of faculty are male; 32%, female. All teach undergraduates. The average class size in an introductory lecture is 21; in a laboratory, 16; and in a regular course, 17.

Requirements: The SAT I or ACT is required, with a minimum composite SAT I score of 1000. All candidates must be graduates of an accredited secondary school. The GED is accepted. UMM strongly recommends completion of 4 units of English, 3 of math, 2 each of lab science, social science/history, and fine arts or foreign language, 3 of electives, and a computer course. An essay and an interview are also strongly recommended. UMM requires applicants to be in the upper 50% of their class. A GPA of 2.84 is required. AP and CLEP credits are accepted. Important factors in the admissions decision are advanced placement or honor courses, evidence of special talent, and leadership record.

Procedure: Freshmen are admitted fall and spring. There are early admissions and deferred admissions plans. Application deadlines are open. The application fee is $25.

Transfer: 47 transfer students enrolled in a recent year. A minimum college GPA of 2.0 and evidence of good standing are required of transfer applicants. 30 credits of 120 must be completed at UMM.

Visiting: There are regularly scheduled orientations for prospective students, consisting of programs just prior to fall and spring semester. There are guides for informal visits and visitors may sit in on classes and stay overnight. To schedule a visit, contact the Admissions Office.

Financial Aid: 70% of undergraduates work part time. Average annual earnings from campus work are $800. The FAFSA is required. Check with the school for current deadlines.

International Students: There were 31 international students enrolled in a recent year. The school actively recruits these students. They must score 500 on the written TOEFL and also take the college's own test.

Computers: The mainframes are an IBM RS/6000, a 3033U, and a 4381 Model 3. Students have access to 3 major labs and 2 clusters of MS-DOS PCs as well as 1 lab of Macs, providing access to the mainframe as well as to Internet resources. Machines are all on interconnected lines for file servers and mail servers. All students have access to the mainframe as well as to Internet resources. All students may access the system from 8 a.m to midnight and by request; there is also a 24-hour study room available. There are no time limits and no fees.

Graduates: In a recent year, 83 bachelor's degrees were awarded. The most popular majors were environmental science (19%), elementary education (17%), and English (13%). In an average class, 19% graduate in 4 years, 42% in 5 years, and 46% in 6 years. 10 companies recruited on campus in a recent year.

Admissions Contact: David P. Baldwin, Director of Admissions. A video is available. E-mail: *admissions@acad.umm.maine.edu*
Web: *www.umm.maine.edu*

UNIVERSITY OF MAINE AT PRESQUE ISLE D-2
Presque Isle, ME 04769-2888 (207) 768-9532
Fax: (207) 768-9608

Full-time: 376 men, 577 women	**Faculty:** 61; IIB, --$
Part-time: 118 men, 296 women	**Ph.D.s:** 56%
Graduate: none	**Student/Faculty:** 16 to 1
Year: semesters, summer session	**Tuition:** $3700 ($8410)
Application Deadline: open	**Room & Board:** $4264
Freshman Class: 300 applied, 270 accepted, 236 enrolled	
SAT I or ACT: not required	**LESS COMPETITIVE**

The University of Maine at Presque Isle, founded in 1903, is a public institution within the University of Maine system offering liberal arts, teacher education, and professional programs leading to postsecondary certificates and associate and bachelor's degrees. There are 2 undergraduate schools. In addition to regional accreditation, UM-Presque Isle has baccalaureate program accreditation with CSWE and NRPA. The library contains 126,316 volumes, 295,852 microform items, and 1281 audiovisual forms/CDs, and subscribes to 416 periodicals. Computerized library services include the card catalog, interlibrary loans, and database searching. Special learning facilities include a learning resource center, art gallery, natural history museum, radio station, and theater. The 150-acre campus is in a rural area 150 miles north of Bangor. Including residence halls, there are 11 buildings.

Student Life: 80% of undergraduates are from Maine. Others are from 20 states, 6 foreign countries, and Canada. 81% are white; 14% foreign nationals. The average age of freshmen is 19; all undergraduates, 24. 35% do not continue beyond their first year.

Housing: 400 students can be accommodated in college housing, which includes single-sex and coed dormitories, on-campus apartments, off-campus apartments, and married-student housing. On-campus housing is guaranteed for all 4 years. 73% of students commute. All students may keep cars.

Activities: 2% of men belong to 1 national fraternity; 1% of women belong to 1 national sorority. There are 27 groups on campus, including band, choir, chorus, drama, ethnic, gay, honors, international, musical theater, physical education, political, professional, radio and TV, religious, social, social service, student government, and yearbook. Popular campus events include Spring Ball, Winter Blast, and Spring Fest.

Sports: There are 5 intercollegiate sports for men and 5 for women, and 15 intramural sports for men and 15 for women. Facilities include a multifunctional structure that houses a gym, a weight room, phys ed labs, a sports medicine facility, Athletic Hall of Fame, and an auditorium. A large playing field contains baseball, soccer, and tennis courts. There are also hiking trails, a bike path, and a ropes course.

Disabled Students: All of the campus is accessible. Wheelchair ramps, elevators, special parking, specially equipped rest rooms, special class scheduling, lowered drinking fountains, and lowered telephones are available.

Services: Counseling and information services are available, as is tutoring in most subjects. There is remedial math, reading, and writing.

Campus Safety and Security: Measures include informal discussions, pamphlets/posters/films, lighted pathways/sidewalks, and an escort service, available to those students who request it.

Programs of Study: UM-Presque Isle confers B.A., B.S., B.F.A., B.L.S., and B.S.W. degrees. Associate degrees are also awarded. Bachelor's degrees are awarded in BIOLOGICAL SCIENCE (biology/biological science), BUSINESS (accounting, business administration and management, and recreation and leisure services), COMMUNICATIONS AND THE ARTS (art, communications, and English), COMPUTER AND PHYSICAL SCIENCE (mathematics), EDUCATION (elementary, health, physical, and secondary), ENGINEERING AND ENVIRONMENTAL DESIGN (environmental science), SOCIAL SCIENCE (behavioral science, criminal justice, international studies, liberal arts/general studies, and social work). Education, social work, and criminal justice are the largest.

Required: Core requirements for the B.A. degrees include 18 credits in humanities, 12 in social science, 11 in math/science, and 4 in phys ed/health. The student must complete a minimum number of credits, which varies according to major, with a cumulative GPA of 2.0 in 120 to 128 credit hours. Requirements for the B.S. and other degrees vary considerably with each major.

Special: The university participates in transfer programs in agriculture, nutrition science, animal and veterinary science, and a 3-2 engineering degree with the University of Maine at Orono. There is a nursing program with the University of Maine at Fort Kent. There are study-abroad programs in France, Ireland, and Canada (other countries are available) and internships in many majors. UM-Presque Isle offers work-study programs, dual and student-designed majors, a B.A.-B.S. degree, and nondegree study. Students can apply for credit by exam and credit for life, military, and work experience. A credit/no credit option is available. There is 1 national honor society, a freshman honors program, and 5 departmental honors programs.

Faculty/Classroom: 57% of faculty are male; 43%, female. All teach undergraduates. The average class size in an introductory lecture is 20; in a laboratory, 12; and in a regular course, 15.

Admissions: 90% of the 2001-2002 applicants were accepted. 15% of the current freshmen were in the top fifth of their class; 39% were in the top two fifths. 3 freshmen graduated first in their class.

Requirements: Applicants should have completed 16 academic credits at an accredited secondary school, including 4 in English, 3 each in math and social studies, and 2 each in science with a lab, foreign language, and electives. A GED certificate may be substituted. The university recommends an essay and an interview for all candidates. Art majors must submit a portfolio. AP and CLEP credits are accepted. Important factors in the admissions decision are advanced placement or honor courses, ability to finance college education, and evidence of special talent. Applications are accepted on-line at the school's web site.

Procedure: Freshmen are admitted to all sessions. Entrance exams should be taken by January 1. There are early decision and deferred admissions plans. Application deadlines are open. The fall 2001 application fee was $25. Notification is sent on a rolling basis.

Transfer: 120 transfer students enrolled in 2001-2002. A GPA of 2.0 from an accredited college or university is required. It is recommended that applicants submit SAT I scores and arrange an interview. Transfer applicants must also submit official transcripts from all colleges attended along with an official high school transcript. 30 credits of 120 must be completed at UM-Presque Isle.

Visiting: There are regularly scheduled orientations for prospective students, including advisement, a campus tour, and meetings with faculty and coaches. There are guides for informal visits and visitors may sit in on classes and stay overnight. To schedule a visit, contact Beverly A. McAvaddy at *mcavaddy@umpi.maine.edu*.

Financial Aid: 77% of all students received some form of financial aid. 91% of freshmen and 88% of continuing students received need-based aid. The average freshman award was $6758. Of that total, scholarships or need-based grants averaged $5065; loans averaged $2109; and work contracts averaged $1700. The average financial indebtedness of the 2001 graduate was $5193. The FAFSA is required. The fall application deadline is April 1.

International Students: There are 276 international students enrolled. The school actively recruits these students. They must score 550 on the written TOEFL or 230 on the electronic version.

Computers: Mac and IBM PCs are available in the computer lab. 90 stations are available for student access. All students may access the system. There are no time limits. The fee applies to any hours in excess of 50 hours per month.

Graduates: In 2001, 240 bachelor's degrees were awarded. The most popular majors were liberal arts/general studies (39%), education (15%), and interdisciplinary studies (11%). In an average class, 10% graduate in 4 years, 19% in 5 years, and 5% in 6 years. 35 companies recruited on campus in 2000-2001. Of the 2000 graduating class, 7% were enrolled in graduate school within 6 months of graduation.

Admissions Contact: Brian Manter, Director of Admissions. A video is available. E-mail: *manter@polaris.umpi.maine.edu*
Web: *www.umpi.maine.edu*

UNIVERSITY OF NEW ENGLAND — A-6
Biddeford, ME 04005 — (207) 283-0171
(800) 477-4UNE; Fax: (207) 286-3678

Full-time: 269 men, 831 women	**Faculty:** 109; IIA, --$
Part-time: 67 men, 222 women	**Ph.D.s:** 96%
Graduate: 459 men, 1014 women	**Student/Faculty:** 10 to 1
Year: semesters, summer session	**Tuition:** $17,340
Application Deadline: open	**Room & Board:** $6770
Freshman Class: 993 accepted, 403 enrolled	
SAT I Verbal/Math: 530/540	**LESS COMPETITIVE**

University of New England, founded in 1831, offers undergraduate degrees in the health sciences, natural sciences, social sciences, liberal arts, education, and management; graduate degrees in professional and occupational programs; teacher education; doctor of osteopathic medicine; continuing education; and cooperative education. There are 2 undergraduate and 6 graduate schools. In addition to regional accreditation, UNE has baccalaureate program accreditation with APTA, CSWE, and NLN. The library contains 139,783 volumes, 7416 microform items, and 9674 audiovisual forms/CDs, and subscribes to 1032 periodicals. Computerized library services include the card catalog, interlibrary loans, and database searching. Special learning facilities include a learning resource center, art gallery, and video studio. The 550-acre campus is in a rural area 16 miles south of Portland. Including residence halls, there are 27 buildings.

Student Life: 53% of undergraduates are from out of state, mostly the Northeast. Students are from 34 states and 1 foreign country. 86% are white. The average age of freshmen is 21. 22% do not continue beyond their first year.

Housing: 575 students can be accommodated in college housing, which includes single-sex and coed dormitories, on-campus apartments, and married-student housing. In addition, there are special-interest houses and a wellness house. On-campus housing is guaranteed for the freshman year only. 56% of students commute. Upperclassmen may keep cars.

Activities: There are no fraternities or sororities. There are 44 groups on campus, including band, cheerleading, choir, chorale, dance, environmental, gay, honors, international, newspaper, professional, religious, sailing, social, social service, student government, and yearbook. Popular campus events include Welcome Back Week, Family and Friends Weekend, and fall leadership retreat.

Sports: There are 5 intercollegiate sports for men and 6 for women, and 8 intramural sports for men and 8 for women. Facilities include a 1500-seat gym, a fitness center, a pool, racquetball courts, soccer and softball fields, outdoor volleyball facilities, and a multipurpose recreational field.

Disabled Students: 85% of the campus is accessible. Wheelchair ramps, elevators, special parking, specially equipped rest rooms, special class scheduling, lowered drinking fountains, lowered telephones, and stair climbers are available.

Services: Counseling and information services are available, as is tutoring in every subject. There is a reader service for the blind, and remedial math, reading, and writing.

Campus Safety and Security: Measures include 24-hour foot and vehicle patrol, self-defense education, escort service, and shuttle buses. There are informal discussions, pamphlets/posters/films, emergency telephones, and lighted pathways/sidewalks. A safe-ride program provides drivers for students.

Programs of Study: UNE confers B.A., B.S., and B.S.N. degrees. Associate, master's, and doctoral degrees are also awarded. Bachelor's degrees are awarded in BIOLOGICAL SCIENCE (biology/biological science, environmental biology, and marine biology), BUSINESS (business administration and management and sports management), COMMUNICATIONS AND THE ARTS (English), EDUCATION (early childhood, elementary, science, and secondary), ENGINEERING AND ENVIRONMENTAL DESIGN (environmental science), HEALTH PROFESSIONS (biomedical science, dental hygiene, health care administration, medical laboratory technology, nursing, occupational therapy, physical therapy, predentistry, premedicine, and prepharmacy), SOCIAL SCIENCE (American studies, human development, prelaw, and psychology).

Required: A total of 120 credits with a minimum GPA of 2.0 is required for graduation. Some programs require more than 120 credits. Students must take 43 credits in a liberal arts core curriculum of humanities, sciences, and social sciences. Most majors require 1-semester internships. Courses in English composition, computer science, Western traditions, human development, and math are required.

Special: UNE offers cross-registration with the Greater Portland Alliance of Colleges and Universities, internships in all majors, work-study programs, study abroad, student-designed and dual majors in all departments, a 3-4 medical program, and a 3-2 physician assistant program. The Freshmen Biology Learning Community provides combined studies in English and life sciences. There is 1 national honor society.

Faculty/Classroom: 45% of faculty are male; 55%, female. 73% teach undergraduates. No introductory courses are taught by graduate students. The average class size in an introductory lecture is 21; in a laboratory, 16; and in a regular course, 20.

Admissions: The SAT I scores for the 2001-2002 freshman class were: Verbal--34% below 500, 48% between 500 and 599, 16% between 600 and 700, and 1% above 700; Math--35% below 500, 46% between 500 and 599, and 19% between 600 and 700. 36% of the current freshmen were in the top fifth of their class; 70% were in the top two fifths. 4 freshmen graduated first in their class.

Requirements: The SAT I or ACT is required. In addition, applicants should be high school graduates with 4 years of English, 3 years each of math and science, and 2 years each of history and social studies. The GED is accepted. A personal interview is recommended. AP and CLEP credits are accepted. Important factors in the admissions decision are advanced placement or honor courses, recommendations by school officials, and leadership record. Applications are accepted on-line at the school's web site.

Procedure: Freshmen are admitted fall and spring. Entrance exams should be taken in the spring of the junior year or the fall of the senior year. There are early decision, early admissions, and deferred admissions plans. Early decision applications should be filed by November 15; regular application deadlines are open. The fee is $40. Notification of early decision is sent December 15; regular decision, on a rolling basis.

Transfer: Transfer applicants should present a GPA of at least 2.5 in college work. An interview is recommended. 30 credits of 120 must be completed at UNE.

Visiting: There are regularly scheduled orientations for prospective students, including a tour and information session, and an interview if the student has formally applied. There are guides for informal visits and visitors may sit in on classes. To schedule a visit, contact the Admissions Office at (207) 283-0171, ext. 2102.

Financial Aid: In 2001-2002, 95% of continuing students received some form of financial aid. 92% of continuing students received need-based aid. Scholarships or need-based grants averaged $7946 ($21,550 maximum); loans averaged $10,157 ($25,500 maximum); and work contracts averaged $1000 ($1250 maximum). The average financial indebtedness of the 2001 graduate was $19,851. The FAFSA is required. The fall application deadline is May 1.

International Students: There are 6 international students enrolled. They must score 550 on the written TOEFL.

Computers: The mainframe is a Novell network. There are 32 PCs available in the main academic building and the library. There are no time limits and no fees.

Graduates: In 2001, 206 bachelor's degrees were awarded. 80 companies recruited on campus in 2000-2001.

Admissions Contact: Patricia T. Cribby, Dean of Admissions.
E-mail: *jshea@mailbox.une.edu* Web: *www.une.edu*

UNIVERSITY OF SOUTHERN MAINE

Gorham, ME 04038-1088 — **B-6** — **(207) 780-5670**
(800) 800-4876; Fax: (207) 780-5640

Full-time: 1762 men, 2662 women	**Faculty:** 396; IIA, -$
Part-time: 1686 men, 2721 women	**Ph.D.s:** 73%
Graduate: 679 men, 1456 women	**Student/Faculty:** 11 to 1
Year: semesters, summer session	**Tuition:** $4696 ($11,611)
Application Deadline: February 15	**Room & Board:** $5873

Freshman Class: 2926 applied, 2410 accepted, 1069 enrolled
SAT I Verbal/Math: 522/519 — **COMPETITIVE**

The University of Southern Maine, founded in 1878, is a publicly funded, multicampus, comprehensive, residential, liberal arts institution serving the University of Maine system. There are 5 undergraduate and 8 graduate schools. In addition to regional accreditation, USM has baccalaureate program accreditation with AACSB, ABET, CSWE, NCATE, and NLN. The 3 libraries contain 521,000 volumes, 1,133,000 microform items, and 2250 audiovisual forms/CDs, and subscribe to 3850 periodicals. Computerized library services include the card catalog, interlibrary loans, and database searching. Special learning facilities include a learning resource center, art gallery, planetarium, radio station, TV station, and cartography collections. The 144-acre campus is in an urban area 110 miles north of Boston and 10 miles west of the urban Portland campus. Including residence halls, there are 66 buildings.

Student Life: 93% of undergraduates are from Maine. Others are from 23 states, 7 foreign countries, and Canada. 97% are white. The average age of freshmen is 20; all undergraduates, 26. 31% do not continue beyond their first year.

Housing: 1500 students can be accommodated in college housing, which includes coed dormitories, on-campus apartments, and married-student housing. In addition, there are honors houses, special-interest houses, and a fine arts house. The Russell Scholars Program is a selected small community in which students live and attend class together. A chemical-free floor and a 24-hour quiet floor are also available. On-campus housing is guaranteed for all 4 years. 79% of students commute. All students may keep cars.

Activities: 4% of men belong to 1 local and 3 national fraternity; 4% of women belong to 2 local and 2 national sororities. There are 100 groups on campus, including art, band, cheerleading, chess, choir, chorale, chorus, commuter, computers, dance, drama, environmental, ethnic, film, gay, honors, international, jazz band, literary magazine, musical theater, newspaper, opera, orchestra, outing, photography, political, professional, radio and TV, religious, ski, social, social service, student government, and yearbook. Popular campus events include Winter Weekend, Spring Fling, and comedy nights.

Sports: There are 14 intercollegiate sports for men and 14 for women, and 19 intramural sports for men and 19 for women. Facilities include gyms, tennis courts, athletic fields, racquetball and squash courts, cross-country ski trails, two weight-training and fitness facilities, an ice arena, a field house, and an indoor track.

Disabled Students: All of the campus is accessible. Wheelchair ramps, elevators, special parking, specially equipped rest rooms, special class scheduling, lowered drinking fountains, and lowered telephones are available.

Services: Counseling and information services are available, as is tutoring in most subjects. There is a reader service for the blind, and remedial math, reading, and writing.

Campus Safety and Security: Measures include 24-hour foot and vehicle patrol, self-defense education, escort service, and shuttle buses. There are informal discussions, pamphlets/posters/films, emergency telephones, lighted pathways/sidewalks, and preventive programs within residence halls.

Programs of Study: USM confers B.A., B.S., and B.F.A. degrees. Associate and master's degrees are also awarded. Bachelor's degrees are awarded in BIOLOGICAL SCIENCE (biology/biological science), BUSINESS (accounting and business administration and management), COMMUNICATIONS AND THE ARTS (communications, dramatic arts, English, fine arts, French, music, and music performance), COMPUTER AND PHYSICAL SCIENCE (chemistry, computer science, geology, geoscience, mathematics, and physics), EDUCATION (music and technical), ENGINEERING AND ENVIRONMENTAL DESIGN (electrical/electronics engineering, environmental science, and industrial engineering technology), HEALTH PROFESSIONS (environmental health science, health science, nursing, recreation therapy, and sports medicine), SOCIAL SCIENCE (anthropology, economics, geography, history, philosophy, political science/government, psychology, social work, sociology, and women's studies). Electrical engineering, computer science, and nursing are the strongest academically. Business administration, nursing, and English are the largest.

Required: A total of 120 hours, of which 36 to 94 are in the major, and a minimum GPA of 2.0 are required for graduation. All students must fulfill the distribution requirements of the 3-part core curriculum: basic competence, methods of inquiry/ways of knowing, and interdisciplinary studies.

Special: Cross-registration within the University of Maine system and 4 Greater Portland colleges, a Washington semester, and study abroad in more than 12 countries are offered. Internships, co-op and work-study programs, a B.A.-B.S. degree, dual and student-designed majors, a 2-2 engineering program with the University of Maine, credit for life experience, nondegree study, and pass/fail options are also available. There is a January intersession. There are 2 national honor societies, a freshman honors program, and 1 departmental honors program.

Faculty/Classroom: 55% of faculty are male; 45%, female. 80% teach undergraduates, all do research, and 80% do both. No introductory courses are taught by graduate students. The average class size in an introductory lecture is 50; in a laboratory, 20; and in a regular course, 22.

Admissions: 82% of the 2001-2002 applicants were accepted. The SAT I scores for the 2001-2002 freshman class were: Verbal--39% below 500, 44% between 500 and 599, 15% between 600 and 700, and 2% above 700; Math--41% below 500, 45% between 500 and 599, 13% between 600 and 700, and 1% above 700. The ACT scores were 43% below 21, 40% between 21 and 23, 14% between 24 and 26, and 3% above 28. 24% of the current freshmen were in the top fifth of their class; 63% were in the top two fifths. 1 freshman graduated first in the class.

Requirements: The SAT I or ACT is required. In addition, applicants must be graduates of an accredited secondary school. The GED is accepted. Either 41 academic credits or 20 1/2 Carnegie units are required. Secondary school courses should include 4 years of English, 3 of math, 2 each of a foreign language and lab science, and 1 each of history and social studies. An essay is required, as are auditions for music applicants and interviews for applicants to the School of Applied Science. Guidance counselor recommendations are required for those students applying during their senior year. USM requires applicants to be in the upper 50% of their class. A GPA of 2.0 is required. AP and CLEP credits are accepted. Important factors in the admissions decision are advanced placement or honor courses, recommendations by school officials, and extracurricular activities record. Students can apply on-line through the USM web site or via Apply/Peterson's, Next Step College, The Princeton Review, and CollegeLink.

Procedure: Freshmen are admitted fall and spring. Entrance exams should be taken between May of the junior year and January of the senior year. There is a deferred admissions plan. Applications should be filed by February 15 (priority deadline) for fall entry and December 1 for spring entry. Notification is sent on a rolling basis. The fall 2001 application fee was $25.

Transfer: 715 transfer students enrolled in 2001-2002. Applicants must have a minimum GPA of 2.0 or 2.75 for those from nonregionally accredited institutions. Students who have been out of high school for less than 3 years must submit SAT I scores. 30 credits of 120 must be completed at USM.

Visiting: There are regularly scheduled orientations for prospective students, including campus tours and group information sessions, as well as special events such as fall open houses. Interviews are also available on request. There are guides for informal visits and visitors may sit in on classes. To schedule a visit, contact the Office of Admission.

Financial Aid: In 2001-2002, 80% of all freshmen and 70% of continuing students received some form of financial aid. 68% of freshmen and 71% of continuing students received need-based aid. The average freshman award was $7290. Of that total, scholarships or need-based grants averaged $3762 ($4000 maximum); loans averaged $2866 ($4875 maximum); work contracts averaged $818 ($2200 maximum); and non need-based gift aid averaged $2968. 80% of undergraduates work part time. Average annual earnings from campus work are $1500. The average financial indebtedness of the 2001 graduate was $18,296. USM is a member of CSS. The FAFSA is required. The FAT is required for students transferring from another college or vocational school for the spring semester. The fall application deadline is February 15.

International Students: There are 38 international students enrolled. They must score 500 on the written TOEFL or 175 on the electronic version and also take the SAT I or the ACT.

Computers: The mainframe is an IBM 4341. The mainframe is linked to the Bitnet, Internet, and Gopher networks. There are about 1000 terminals and microcomputers, of which 283 are available for student use. Most residence hall rooms have computer hook ups. All students may access the system 16 hours per day. There are no time limits and no fees.

Graduates: In 2001, 934 bachelor's degrees were awarded. The most popular majors were social science and history (23%), business (13%), and nursing (11%). 50 companies recruited on campus in 2000-2001.

Admissions Contact: David M. Pirani, Director of Admission.
E-mail: *usmadm@maine.maine.edu* Web: *www.usm.maine.edu*

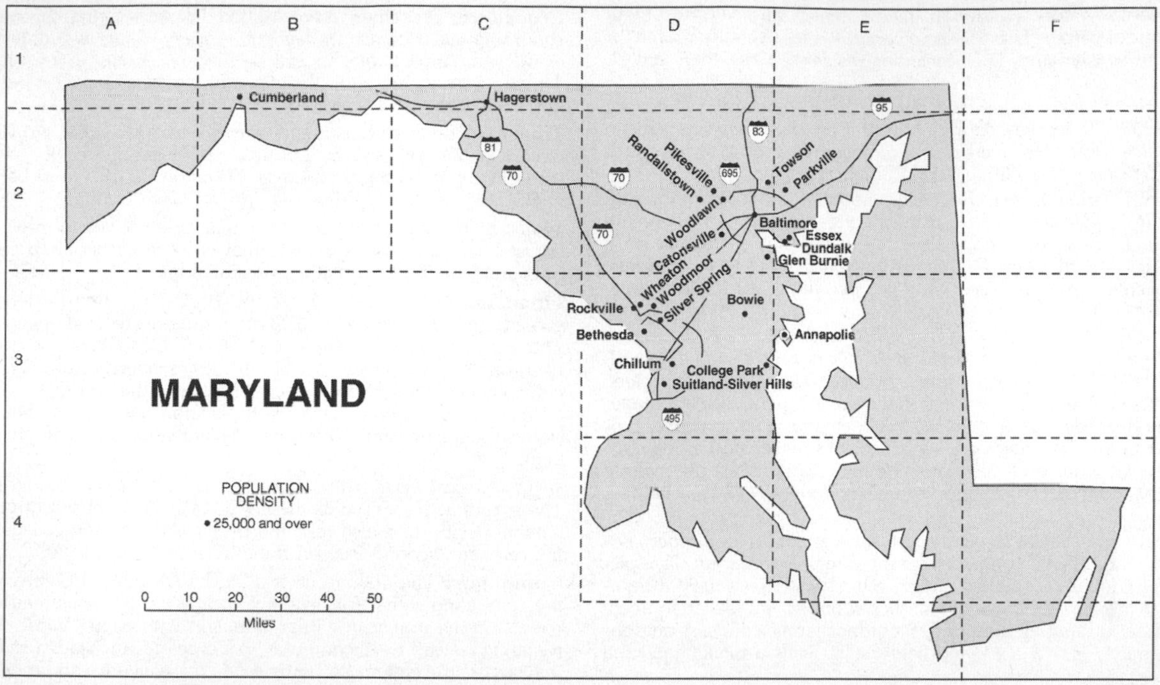

BALTIMORE HEBREW UNIVERSITY D-2

Baltimore, MD 21215-3996 (410) 578-6903; Fax: (410) 578-6940

Full-time: 30 men, 60 women
Part-time: 35 men, 85 women
Graduate: 15 men, 45 women
Year: semesters, summer session
Application Deadline: open
Freshman Class: n/av
SAT I or ACT: not required
Faculty: 10
Ph.D.s: 90%
Student/Faculty: 9 to 1
Tuition: $8030
Room & Board: n/app
SPECIAL

Baltimore Hebrew University, founded in 1919, is a private nonsectarian commuter institution of Jewish higher education and a major center of advanced Jewish study in the United States. Figures in above capsule are approximate. The library contains 100,000 volumes, 7500 microform items, and 1100 audiovisual forms/CDs, and subscribes to 225 periodicals. Computerized library services include the card catalog and interlibrary loans. Special learning facilities include a language lab. The 2-acre campus is in an urban area in residential northwest Baltimore. There is one building.

Student Life: 96% of undergraduates are from Maryland. Others are from 3 states and 4 foreign countries. 98% are white. Most are Jewish. The average age of freshmen is 30; all undergraduates, 44.

Housing: There are no residence halls. All students commute. Alcohol is not permitted. All students may keep cars.

Activities: There are no fraternities or sororities. There are some groups and organizations on campus, including dance, Hebrew, and Yiddish. Popular campus events include film series, singles brunches, and concerts.

Sports: There is no sports program at BHU.

Disabled Students: 50% of the campus is accessible. Wheelchair ramps and special parking are available.

Services: Counseling and information services are available, as is tutoring in some subjects, including Hebrew, Yiddish, and Russian.

Campus Safety and Security: Measures include escort service, pamphlets/posters/films, lighted pathways/sidewalks, lighted parking lot, and guards during class hours.

Programs of Study: BHU confers the B.A. degree. Associate, master's, and doctoral degrees are also awarded. Bachelor's degrees are awarded in SOCIAL SCIENCE (Judaic studies).

Required: To graduate, students must earn a minimum GPA of 2.0 in a total of 120 credits, including 78 of Jewish studies in literature, philosophy, and history, and 42 of general studies in social and behavioral sciences, arts and humanities, literature, physical or biological science, math, and English composition.

Special: BHU offers study abroad in Israel, cross-registration with Johns Hopkins and Towson Universities and Goucher College, and co-op programs with Johns Hopkins University, University of Maryland/Baltimore County, and University of Maryland School of Social Work.

Faculty/Classroom: 64% of faculty are male; 36%, female. All teach undergraduates and 90% do research. No introductory courses are taught by graduate students. The average class size in an introductory lecture is 10 and in a regular course, 10.

Requirements: A candidate's high school record is reviewed by the dean, who also conducts a personal interview. BHU requires applicants to be in the upper 25% of their class. A GPA of 3.0 is required. AP and CLEP credits are accepted. Important factors in the admissions decision are recommendations by school officials, personality/intangible qualities, and evidence of special talent.

Procedure: Freshmen are admitted to all sessions. There are early decision and early admissions plans. Application deadlines are open. The fall 2001 application fee was $20.

Transfer: Applicants must meet freshman requirements. 30 credits of 120 must be completed at BHU.

Visiting: There are guides for informal visits and visitors may sit in on classes. To schedule a visit, contact Dr. George Berlin, Dean at (410) 578-6900.

Financial Aid: The FAFSA and the college's own financial statement are required.

International Students: They must score 500 on the written TOEFL and also take the college's own test.

Computers: PCs in the computer room, with Hebrew language software, are available for word processing and computer course assignments. All students may access the system. There are no time limits and no fees. All students may access the system. There are no time limits and no fees.

Admissions Contact: Dr. George Berlin, Dean.
E-mail: *bhu@bhu.edu* Web: *www.bhu.edu*

BOWIE STATE UNIVERSITY D-3

Bowie, MD 20715 (301) 860-3421; Fax: (301)860-3438

Full-time: 1079 men, 1556 women
Part-time: 266 men, 641 women
Graduate: 435 men, 1204 women
Year: semesters, summer session
Application Deadline: August 1
Freshman Class: 2274 applied, 1080 accepted, 616 enrolled
SAT I Verbal/Math: 448/435
Faculty: 131; IIA, -$
Ph.D.s: 68%
Student/Faculty: 20 to 1
Tuition: $3802 ($9884)
Room & Board: $5498
COMPETITIVE+

Bowie State University, founded in 1865, is a historically black, publicly supported comprehensive liberal arts institution within the University System of Maryland. There are 3 undergraduate schools and 1 graduate school. In addition to regional accreditation, BSU has baccalaureate program accreditation with ACBSP, CSAB, CSWE, NCATE, and NLN. The library contains 233,527 volumes, 394,883 microform items, and 2946 audiovisual forms/CDs, and subscribes to 672 periodicals. Computerized library services include the card catalog, interlibrary loans, and database searching. Special learning facilities include a learning resource center, art gallery, radio station, TV station, media center, and satellite operations and control center. The 312-acre campus is in a suburban area 18 miles north of Washington, D.C. Including residence halls, there are 20 buildings.

Student Life: 90% of undergraduates are from Maryland. Others are from 33 states, 39 foreign countries, and Canada. 83% are African American; 13% white. The average age of freshmen is 21; all undergraduates, 25. 27% do not continue beyond their first year.

Housing: 885 students can be accommodated in college housing, which includes single-sex and coed dormitories. In addition, there are honors sections of residence halls. On-campus housing is available on a first-come, first-served basis. Priority is given to out-of-town students. 75% of students commute. Alcohol is not permitted. All students may keep cars.

Activities: 2% of men belong to 6 national fraternities; 2% of women belong to 4 national sororities. There are 52 groups on campus, including art, band, cheerleading, choir, chorale, commuter, computers, dance, drama, drill team, honors, international, jazz band, literary magazine, marching band, musical theater, NAACP, pep band, political, professional, radio and TV, religious, social, social service, student government, Urban League, and yearbook. Popular campus events include Black History Month Convocation, Parents/Founders Day, and Honors Convocation.

Sports: There are 4 intercollegiate sports for men and 6 for women. Facilities include an athletic complex with a basketball arena, an Olympic-size pool, 8 handball/racquetball courts, a wrestling room, weight training rooms, a dance studio, a gymnastics room, a 4500-seat football/soccer stadium, a baseball diamond, 6 outdoor tennis courts, 4 outdoor basketball courts, and a track-and-field facility with a walking/jogging lane.

Disabled Students: All of the campus is accessible. Wheelchair ramps, elevators, special parking, specially equipped rest rooms, lowered drinking fountains, lowered telephones, and wide doors are available.

Services: Counseling and information services are available, as is tutoring in most subjects. There is a reader service for the blind, and remedial math, reading, and writing.

Campus Safety and Security: Measures include 24-hour foot and vehicle patrol, self-defense education, escort service, and shuttle buses. There are informal discussions, pamphlets/posters/films, emergency telephones, and lighted pathways/sidewalks.

Programs of Study: BSU confers B.A. and B.S. degrees. Master's and doctoral degrees are also awarded. Bachelor's degrees are awarded in BIOLOGICAL SCIENCE (biology/biological science), BUSINESS (business administration and management), COMMUNICATIONS AND THE ARTS (broadcasting, English, and fine arts), COMPUTER AND PHYSICAL SCIENCE (computer science and mathematics), EDUCATION (early childhood, elementary, English, and science), ENGINEERING AND ENVIRONMENTAL DESIGN (computer technology), HEALTH PROFESSIONS (nursing), SOCIAL SCIENCE (criminal justice, history, interdisciplinary studies, political science/government, psychology, social work, and sociology). Business administration, computer science, and elementary education are the largest.

Required: A total of 120 credit hours with a minimum GPA of 2.0 is required for graduation. The number of hours that must be taken in a student's major varies. General education requirements include 12 credits in social science, 9 in arts and humanities, 7 to 8 in sciences, 6 in English compositions and 3 each in math, computer literacy, health and wellness, and freshman seminar.

Special: BSU offers cooperative programs, internships in communications and practice teaching, work-study programs, B.A.-B.S. degrees, dual majors, credit for life experience, and a 3-2 engineering degree. Dual-degree programs in engineering and dentistry are available at the University of Maryland. Cross-registration is offered with other members of the University System of Maryland. There are 16 national honor societies and a freshman honors program. All departments have honors programs.

Faculty/Classroom: 57% of faculty are male; 43%, female. 76% teach undergraduates. No introductory courses are taught by graduate students. The average class size in an introductory lecture is 25; in a laboratory, 10; and in a regular course, 19.

Admissions: 47% of the 2001-2002 applicants were accepted. The SAT I scores for the 2001-2002 freshman class were: Verbal--77% below 500, 20% between 500 and 599, 2% between 600 and 700, and 1% above 700; Math--82% below 500, 16% between 500 and 599, and 2% between 600 and 700.

Requirements: The SAT I or ACT is required, with a minimum composite score of 900. Applicants should be graduates of an accredited secondary school. The GED is accepted. Students should have completed 15 academic units, including 4 of English, 3 each of math, science, and social science/history, and 2 of a foreign language or advanced technology. Applications are accepted on-line. A GPA of 2.2 is required. AP and CLEP credits are accepted. Important factors in the admissions decision are advanced placement or honor courses, extracurricular activities record, and leadership record.

Procedure: Freshmen are admitted fall and spring. Entrance exams should be taken before the end of January. There is a deferred admissions plan. Applications should be filed by August 1 for fall entry and January 1 for spring entry. Notification is sent on a rolling basis. The fall 2001 application fee was $40.

Transfer: 488 transfer students enrolled in 2001-2002. Applicants must have a minimum GPA of 2.0. The SAT I is required if fewer than 25 credit hours are being transferred. 30 credits of 120 must be completed at BSU.

Visiting: There are regularly scheduled orientations for prospective students. There are guides for informal visits. To schedule a visit, contact Shingiral Chanaiwa, Director of Admissions.

Financial Aid: In 2001-2002, 60% of continuing students received some form of financial aid. 50% of all students received need-based aid. The average freshman award was $6189. Of that total, scholarships or need-based grants averaged $3942; loans averaged $2517; and work contracts averaged $2688. The FAFSA and the college's own financial statement are required. The fall application deadline is March 1 for in-state students or April 15 for out-of-state students for priority consideration.

International Students: There are 31 international students enrolled. The school actively recruits these students. They must score 500 on the written TOEFL and also take the SAT I, ACT, or the college's own entrance exam, scoring 900 on the SAT I or 19 on the ACT.

Computers: The mainframe is a DEC VAX 6210. PCs are available in the computing center for academic purposes. Students may request accounts on the mainframe in conjunction with course work. All students requiring access to a computer to complete an academic assignment may access the system 24 hours a day on weekdays and modified hours on weekends. There are no time limits. There is a $6 per credit hour fee to use the system.

Graduates: In 2001, 533 bachelor's degrees were awarded. The most popular majors were business administration (26%), computer technology (14%), and social science/history (14%). In an average class, 14% graduate in 4 years, 32% in 5 years, and 39% in 6 years. 171 companies recruited on campus in 2000-2001. Of the 2000 graduating class, 34% were enrolled in graduate school within 6 months of graduation and 60% were employed.

Admissions Contact: Shingiral Chanaiwa, Director of Admissions.
E-mail: *schanaiwa@bowiestate.edu* Web: *www.bowiestate.edu*

CAPITOL COLLEGE

Laurel, MD 20708 | **D-3**
(301) 953-3200
(800) 950-1992; Fax: (301) 953-1442

Full-time: 241 men, 78 women	**Faculty:** 19
Part-time: 242 men, 69 women	**Ph.D.s:** 2%
Graduate: 121 men, 50 women	**Student/Faculty:** 17 to 1
Year: semesters, summer session	**Tuition:** $15,022
Application Deadline: open	**Room & Board:** $3440
Freshman Class: 213 applied, 191 accepted, 48 enrolled	
SAT I Verbal/Math: 475/505	**LESS COMPETITIVE**

Capitol College was founded in 1927 as the Capitol Radio Engineering Institute, a correspondence school. Today it is a private college offering undergraduate programs in engineering and computer technology, as well as graduate programs in management and electronic commerce. Some information in this profile is approximate. There is 1 graduate school. In addition to regional accreditation, Capitol has baccalaureate program accreditation with ABET. The library contains 10,000 volumes and subscribes to 100 periodicals. Computerized library services include the card catalog, interlibrary loans, and database searching. Special learning facilities include a learning resource center and state-of-the-art labs. The 52-acre campus is in a rural area 19 miles north of Washington, D.C. Including residence halls, there are 9 buildings.

Student Life: 72% of undergraduates are from Maryland. Others are from 16 states and 21 foreign countries. 43% are white; 39%, African American. The average age of freshmen is 23; all undergraduates, 28. 41% do not continue beyond their first year.

Housing: 100 students can be accommodated in college housing, which includes coed on-campus apartments. On-campus housing is available on a first-come, first-served basis. Priority is given to out-of-town students. 87% of students commute. All students may keep cars.

Activities: There are no fraternities or sororities. There are 17 groups on campus, including chess, computers, literary magazine, newspaper, professional, and student government. Popular campus events include Octoberfest and Spring Bash.

Sports: Facilities include an off-campus gym, a basketball court, a student center, and an athletic field.

Disabled Students: All of the campus is accessible. Wheelchair ramps, elevators, special parking, specially equipped rest rooms, and lowered drinking fountains are available.
Services: Counseling and information services are available, as is tutoring in most subjects, including math, electronics, English, and developmental English.
Campus Safety and Security: Measures include lighted pathways/sidewalks.
Programs of Study: Capitol confers the B.S. degree. Associate and master's degrees are also awarded. Bachelor's degrees are awarded in COMMUNICATIONS AND THE ARTS (telecommunications), COMPUTER AND PHYSICAL SCIENCE (optics), ENGINEERING AND ENVIRONMENTAL DESIGN (computer engineering, electrical/electronics engineering, and engineering technology). Electrical/electronics engineering is the strongest academically and has the largest enrollment.
Required: A minimum GPA of 2.0 and 130 to 137 credit hours are required for graduation. Additional curriculum requirements vary with the major.
Special: Internships and work-study programs are offered through the school's cooperative education program. There are 2 national honor societies.
Faculty/Classroom: 71% of faculty are male; 29%, female. All teach undergraduates. No introductory courses are taught by graduate students. The average class size in an introductory lecture is 20 and in a regular course, 22.
Admissions: 90% of the 2001-2002 applicants were accepted. The SAT I scores for the 2001-2002 freshman class were: Verbal--67% below 500, 31% between 500 and 599, 1% between 600 and 700, and 1% above 700; Math--44% below 500, 43% between 500 and 599, 12% between 600 and 700, and 1% above 700.
Requirements: The SAT I is required, with a minimum composite score of 860. Applicants should be graduates of an accredited secondary school. The GED is accepted. 20 academic credits or 20 Carnegie units are required. Secondary school courses must include 4 units of English, 3 of math, and 2 each of science and social studies. An essay and an interview are recommended. A GPA of 2.2 is required. AP and CLEP credits are accepted. Important factors in the admissions decision are advanced placement or honor courses, recommendations by school officials, and extracurricular activities record. Applications are accepted on-line at the school's web site.
Procedure: Freshmen are admitted to all sessions. Entrance exams should be taken by March 1. Application deadlines are open. The fall 2001 application fee was $25.
Transfer: 39 transfer students enrolled in a recent year. Transfer students must have earned 15 college credits and a minimum GPA of 2.0. 40 credits of 130 to 137 must be completed at Capitol.
Visiting: There are regularly scheduled orientations for prospective students. There are guides for informal visits and visitors may sit in on classes and stay overnight. To schedule a visit, contact the Admissions Office.
Financial Aid: Capitol is a member of CSS. The CSS/Profile is required. Check with the school for current deadlines.
International Students: The school actively recruits these students. They must score 500 on the written TOEFL.
Computers: The mainframe is a DEC VAX 11/750. There are also 25 Tandy, IBM, and TRS80 PCs available in labs. All students may access the system. There are no time limits and no fees. It is recommended that students in computer engineering technology have personal computers.
Admissions Contact: Anthony Miller, Dean of Admissions.
E-mail: *admissions@capitol-college.edu*
Web: *http://www.capitol-college.edu*

COLLEGE OF NOTRE DAME OF MARYLAND D-2
Baltimore, MD 21210 **(410) 532-5330**
(800) 435-0300; Fax: (410) 532-6287

Full-time: 670 men and women	**Faculty:** 74; IIB, -$
Part-time: 1700 men and women	**Ph.D.s:** 65%
Graduate: none	**Student/Faculty:** 9 to 1
Year: 4-1-4, summer session	**Tuition:** $16,900
Application Deadline: open	**Room & Board:** $6200
Freshman Class: n/av	
SAT I or ACT: required	**LESS COMPETITIVE**

The College of Notre Dame of Maryland, founded in 1873, is a private liberal arts institution primarily for women and affiliated with the Catholic Church. Figures given in the above capsule are approximate. In addition to regional accreditation, Notre Dame has baccalaureate program accreditation with NLN. The library contains 290,000 volumes, 378,138 microform items, and 24,000 audiovisual forms/CDs, and subscribes to 2000 periodicals. Computerized library services include the card catalog and database searching. Special learning facilities include a learning resource center, art gallery, planetarium, radio station, TV station, graphic arts studio, roof-top greenhouse, and cultural center. The 58-acre campus is in a suburban area 10 miles north of Baltimore. Including residence halls, there are 11 buildings.
Student Life: 70% of undergraduates are from Maryland. Others are from 21 states.
Housing: 450 students can be accommodated in college housing, which includes single-sex dormitories. On-campus housing is guaranteed for all 4 years. 65% of students live on campus; of those, 60% remain on campus on weekends. Alcohol is not permitted. All students may keep cars.
Activities: There are no fraternities or sororities. There are 24 groups on campus, including art, choir, dance, drama, ethnic, honors, international, literary magazine, newspaper, political, professional, radio and TV, religious, social, social service, student government, and yearbook. Popular campus events include Honors Convocation, Antostal Day, and Multicultural Awareness Week.
Sports: Facilities include a sports/activities complex that houses racquetball courts, a dance studio, a fitness center, an indoor walking track, a game room, an activities resource center, and a basketball court.
Disabled Students: 98% of the campus is accessible. Wheelchair ramps, elevators, special parking, specially equipped rest rooms, and lowered drinking fountains are available.
Services: Counseling and information services are available, as is tutoring in most subjects.
Campus Safety and Security: Measures include 24-hour foot and vehicle patrol, self-defense education, escort service, and informal discussions. There are pamphlets/posters/films and lighted pathways/sidewalks.
Programs of Study: Notre Dame confers B.A. and B.S. degrees. Master's degrees are also awarded. Bachelor's degrees are awarded in BIOLOGICAL SCIENCE (biology/biological science), BUSINESS (accounting, banking and finance, business administration and management, international business management, and marketing/retailing/merchandising), COMMUNICATIONS AND THE ARTS (art history and appreciation, classics, communications, English, graphic design, modern language, music, photography, and studio art), COMPUTER AND PHYSICAL SCIENCE (chemistry, computer science, information sciences and systems, mathematics, and physics), EDUCATION (art, early childhood, elementary, foreign languages, music, science, secondary, and special), ENGINEERING AND ENVIRONMENTAL DESIGN (preengineering), HEALTH PROFESSIONS (nursing, predentistry, premedicine, and prepharmacy), SOCIAL SCIENCE (economics, history, interdisciplinary studies, international relations, liberal arts/general studies, political science/government, prelaw, psychology, and religion). Business, education, and communication arts are the strongest academically.
Required: To graduate, students must complete a total of 128 credit hours with a minimum GPA of 2.0 (2.5 in many majors). All students must fulfill the distribution requirements in the general education core, the major, and electives, and must demonstrate proficiency in writing, public speaking, computer literacy, and library research. In most majors, a minimum of 42 hours is required. All students must take a speech course and 2 courses in phys ed, and some majors require senior practicums.
Special: The college offers cross-registration with Johns Hopkins, Towson State, and Morgan State universities; Coppin State, Goucher, and Loyola colleges; and the Maryland Institute College of Art. Study abroad, internships, dual bachelor's degrees in nursing and engineering, 3-2 engineering degrees with Johns Hopkins University and the University of Maryland, and pass/fail options are available. Notre Dame's Weekend College offers bachelor's degree programs for employed adults. There are 8 national honor societies, a freshman honors program, and 4 departmental honors programs.
Faculty/Classroom: 30% of faculty are male; 70%, female. All teach undergraduates. The average class size in an introductory lecture is 30; in a laboratory, 20; and in a regular course, 20.
Requirements: The SAT I or ACT is required. In addition, the SAT I is required for scholarship purposes. Applicants should be graduates of an accredited secondary school. 18 academic credits are required, including 4 units of English, 3 each of math and a foreign language, and 2 each of history and science, plus 4 electives. An essay is required and an interview is recommended. Notre Dame offers its viewbook and application on disk; recommendations and essays can also be submitted through this option. A GPA of 2.5 is required. AP credits are accepted. Important factors in the admissions decision are recommendations by school officials, advanced placement or honor courses, and leadership record.
Procedure: Freshmen are admitted fall and spring. Entrance exams should be taken no later than January of the senior year. There are early decision, early admissions, and deferred admissions plans. Application deadlines are open. Check with the school for current application fee.
Transfer: Notre Dame requires a minimum GPA of 2.5 for transfer students but recommends a GPA of 3.0. A combined score of 800 is required for the SAT I and 18 for the ACT. Students must also submit a letter of recommendation and an essay. 60 credits of 128 must be completed at Notre Dame.
Visiting: There are regularly scheduled orientations for prospective students, consisting of programs in June and January, each of which includes a stay in the dormitory, registration, and advisement. There are

guides for informal visits and visitors may sit in on classes. To schedule a visit, contact the Office of Admissions.

Financial Aid: Notre Dame is a member of CSS. The CSS/Profile or FAFSA is required. Check with the school for current deadlines.

International Students: The school actively recruits these students. They must take the TOEFL and college's own entrance exam for placement purposes.

Computers: The mainframe is a DEC MicroVAX II. There are 80 PC and Mac workstations located in academic and administrative buildings. Access to the Internet is possible. All students may access the system 7 days a week. There are no time limits and no fees.

Admissions Contact: Karen Stakem Hornig, Director of Admissions. E-mail: *admiss@ndm.edu* Web: *www.ndm.edu*

COLUMBIA UNION COLLEGE D-3
Takoma Park, MD 20912 (301) 891-4080
(800) 835-4212; Fax: (301) 891-4230

Full-time: 259 men, 382 women	**Faculty:** 50; IIB, --$
Part-time: 161 men, 267 women	**Ph.D.s:** 48%
Graduate: 1 man, 3 women	**Student/Faculty:** 13 to 1
Year: semesters, summer session	**Tuition:** $14,178
Application Deadline: August 15	**Room & Board:** $4849
Freshman Class: 712 applied, 329 accepted, 160 enrolled	
SAT I Verbal/Math: 500/395	**ACT:** 20 **COMPETITIVE+**

Columbia Union College, founded in 1904, is a private liberal arts institution affiliated with the Seventh-day Adventist Church. In addition to regional accreditation, CUC has baccalaureate program accreditation with CAHEA and NLN. The library contains 131,166 volumes and 7500 audiovisual forms/CDs, and subscribes to 5358 periodicals. Computerized library services include the card catalog, interlibrary loans, and database searching. Special learning facilities include a learning resource center and radio station. The 19-acre campus is in a suburban area 7 miles north of Washington, D.C. Including residence halls, there are 10 buildings.

Student Life: 53% of undergraduates are from Maryland. Others are from 36 states, 41 foreign countries, and Canada. 31% are from public schools. 45% are African American; 29% white. The average age of freshmen is 18; all undergraduates, 28. 48% do not continue beyond their first year.

Housing: 440 students can be accommodated in college housing, which includes single-sex dormitories and married-student housing. On-campus housing is guaranteed for all 4 years. 62% of students commute. Alcohol is not permitted. All students may keep cars.

Activities: There are no fraternities or sororities. There are 10 groups on campus, including band, choir, chorale, honors, newspaper, orchestra, radio and TV, religious, student government, and yearbook.

Sports: There are 6 intercollegiate sports for men and 5 for women, and 5 intramural sports for men and 4 for women. Facilities include a swimming pool, a gym, racquetball and tennis courts, a sports field, a student lounge, and a weight room.

Disabled Students: 1% of the campus is accessible. Elevators and specially equipped rest rooms are available.

Services: Counseling and information services are available, as is tutoring in some subjects, including all English, math, accounting, and chemistry courses. There is remedial math and writing.

Campus Safety and Security: Measures include 24-hour foot and vehicle patrol, escort service, informal discussions, and pamphlets/posters/films. There are lighted pathways/sidewalks.

Programs of Study: CUC confers B.A., B.S., and B.M. degrees. Associate and master's degrees are also awarded. Bachelor's degrees are awarded in BIOLOGICAL SCIENCE (biochemistry), BUSINESS (accounting, business administration and management, management science, and personnel management), COMMUNICATIONS AND THE ARTS (communications, English, journalism, and music), COMPUTER AND PHYSICAL SCIENCE (chemistry, computer science, information sciences and systems, and mathematics), EDUCATION (elementary, English, and mathematics), HEALTH PROFESSIONS (health care administration, nursing, predentistry, premedicine, and respiratory therapy), SOCIAL SCIENCE (history, liberal arts/general studies, prelaw, psychology, and religion). Nursing, business, and music are the strongest academically. Communications, business, and nursing are the largest.

Required: To graduate, students must earn 120 to 128 credit hours, including 36 upper division, with a minimum GPA of 2.0 overall and 2.5 in the major. Students must take 12 hours of religion, 9 of social sciences, 8 of physical sciences, natural sciences, and math, 6 of humanities and practical and applied arts, and 3 of phys ed and health. Courses in English, communication, and computer science are also required.

Special: CUC offers co-op programs in business communication, computer science, English, math, and nursing, internships in counseling psychology, work-study programs, a general studies degree, student-designed majors, credit for life experience, nondegree study, and pass/fail options. Dual majors are available in engineering/chemistry, and math with the University of Maryland. Students may study abroad in France, Spain, and Austria. There is an adult evening program for degree completion as well as an external (correspondence) degree. There are 6 national honor societies, a freshman honors program, and 1 departmental honors program.

Faculty/Classroom: 58% of faculty are male; 42%, female. All teach undergraduates and 10% both teach and do research. No introductory courses are taught by graduate students. The average class size in an introductory lecture is 30; in a laboratory, 16; and in a regular course, 12.

Admissions: 46% of the 2001-2002 applicants were accepted. The SAT I scores for the 2001-2002 freshman class were: Verbal--61% below 500, 27% between 500 and 599, 11% between 600 and 700, and 1% above 700; Math--68% below 500, 25% between 500 and 599, and 7% between 600 and 700. The ACT scores were 59% below 21, 21% between 21 and 23, 10% between 24 and 26, 7% between 27 and 28, and 2% above 28.

Requirements: The SAT I or ACT is required, with a minimum composite score of 800, or at least 400 in each section, on the SAT I or 18 on the ACT. Applicants must be graduates of an accredited secondary school. The GED is accepted. 21 Carnegie units are required, including 4 years of high school English and 2 years each of history, math, and lab science. An essay is recommended. CUC requires applicants to be in the upper 50% of their class. A GPA of 2.5 is required. AP and CLEP credits are accepted. Important factors in the admissions decision are advanced placement or honor courses, leadership record, and recommendations by school officials. Applications are accepted on-line.

Procedure: Freshmen are admitted to all sessions. Entrance exams should be taken in the fall semester of the senior year. There is a deferred admissions plan. Applications should be filed by August 15 for fall entry, December 1 for spring entry, and May 1 for summer entry, along with a $25 fee. Notification is sent on a rolling basis.

Transfer: 164 transfer students enrolled in 2001-2002. Transfer students must have at least 12 hours of college credit and a minimum GPA of 2.0. 30 credits of 120 to 128 must be completed at CUC.

Visiting: There are regularly scheduled orientations for prospective students. There are guides for informal visits and visitors may sit in on classes and stay overnight. To schedule a visit, contact the Office of College Advancement.

Financial Aid: The FAFSA and the college's own financial statement are required. The fall application deadline is March 1.

International Students: There are 28 international students enrolled. They must take the TOEFL scoring 550 on the written version or 213 on the electronic version, or take the MELAB or the college's own test. They must also take the SAT I or ACT.

Computers: The mainframes are an AT&T 3B2/400 and an HP 932. There are 40 PCs available in the computer lab and in academic departments. Students in computer classes may access the system 8 A.M. to midnight. There are no time limits and no fees. It is strongly recommended that all students have a personal computer.

Graduates: In 2001, 244 bachelor's degrees were awarded. The most popular majors were business/marketing (34%), psychology (22%), and computer and information sciences (12%). In an average class, 28% graduate in 6 years.

Admissions Contact: Emile John, Director of Admissions. E-mail: *enroll@cuc.edu* Web: *www.cuc.edu*

COPPIN STATE COLLEGE D-2
Baltimore, MD 21216 (410) 951-3600
(800) 635-3674; Fax: (410) 523-7351

Full-time: 601 men, 1750 women	**Faculty:** 110
Part-time: 207 men, 681 women	**Ph.D.s:** 64%
Graduate: 173 men, 591 women	**Student/Faculty:** 21 to 1
Year: semesters, summer session	**Tuition:** $3477 ($8604)
Application Deadline: July 15	**Room & Board:** $5656
Freshman Class: n/av	
SAT I or ACT: required	**LESS COMPETITIVE**

Coppin State College, founded in 1900 and part of the University System of Maryland, offers undergraduate programs in liberal arts, teacher education, and nursing. Some of the information in this profile is approximate. There are 3 undergraduate schools and 1 graduate school. In addition to regional accreditation, Coppin has baccalaureate program accreditation with NCATE and NLN. The library contains 200,000 volumes and 233,000 microform items, and subscribes to 715 periodicals. Computerized library services include the card catalog and interlibrary loans. Special learning facilities include a learning resource center, a TV station, and an on-campus video production company. The 38-acre campus is in an urban area in Baltimore. Including residence halls, there are 9 buildings.

Student Life: 90% of undergraduates are from Maryland. Others are from 10 states and 5 foreign countries. 90% are from public schools. 80% are African American; 10%, white. The average age of freshmen is 19; all undergraduates, 23.

Housing: 315 students can be accommodated in college housing, which includes coed dormitories. On-campus housing is guaranteed for all 4 years. 93% of students commute. Alcohol is not permitted. All students may keep cars.

Activities: 20% of men and about 30% of women belong to 4 national fraternities; 27% of women belong to 4 national sororities. There are 40 groups on campus, including art, cheerleading, choir, chorus, computers, dance, drama, ethnic, film, honors, international, musical theater, newspaper, political, professional, radio and TV, religious, social, social service, student government, and yearbook. Popular campus events include the Lyceum Series, the Honors Program, and Christmas and Black History Month programs.

Sports: There are 7 intercollegiate sports for men and 7 for women, and 5 intramural sports for men and 5 for women. Facilities include a 2500-seat gym, an indoor swimming pool, handball and racquetball courts, a soccer field, a dance studio, a weight room, a track, and a baseball field.

Disabled Students: 90% of the campus is accessible. Wheelchair ramps, elevators, special parking, specially equipped rest rooms, lowered drinking fountains, lowered telephones, and individual attention for students requiring specialized materials, equipment, or instructional style accommodation are available.

Services: Counseling and information services are available, as is tutoring in every subject. There is remedial math, reading, and writing.

Campus Safety and Security: Measures include 24-hour foot and vehicle patrol, escort service, shuttle buses, and pamphlets/posters/films. There are emergency telephones and lighted pathways/sidewalks.

Programs of Study: Coppin confers B.A., B.S., and B.S.N. degrees. Master's degrees are also awarded. Bachelor's degrees are awarded in BIOLOGICAL SCIENCE (biology/biological science), BUSINESS (business administration and management and marketing management), COMMUNICATIONS AND THE ARTS (English), COMPUTER AND PHYSICAL SCIENCE (chemistry, computer science, and mathematics), EDUCATION (elementary, and special), ENGINEERING AND ENVIRONMENTAL DESIGN (preengineering), HEALTH PROFESSIONS (nursing, predentistry, and prepharmacy), SOCIAL SCIENCE (criminal justice, history, psychology, social science, and social work). Management science and education are the strongest academically and are the largest.

Required: To graduate, all students must have a minimum 2.0 GPA and a minimum of 120 credit hours, with 36 to 40 hours in the major. Students must complete about 50 hours of liberal arts courses in English, math, speech, history, health, phys ed, natural and social sciences, and philosophy. All seniors must take a standardized exit exam relevant to their major.

Special: The college offers co-op programs with Dundalk Community College and Morgan University, internships in criminal justice, management science, and sociology, dual majors in engineering, pharmacy, physical therapy, and dentistry, and B.A.-B.S. degrees in all majors. Work-study is also available. There are 3 national honor societies, including Phi Beta Kappa, and a freshman honors program.

Faculty/Classroom: 54% of faculty are male; 46%, female. The average class size in a regular course is 25.

Requirements: The SAT I or ACT is required. In addition, applicants must be graduates of an accredited secondary school or have a GED certificate. Students must have completed 4 courses in English, 2 courses each in history, math, science, and social studies, and 1 course in foreign language. A GPA of 2.5 is required. Up to 15% of a freshman class may be admitted conditionally without these requirements, and those students who graduated high school more than 5 years ago will be reviewed individually. CLEP credit is accepted. Important factors in the admissions decision are advanced placement or honor courses, extracurricular activities record, and evidence of special talent. Applications are accepted on-line through Coppin's web site.

Procedure: Freshmen are admitted to all sessions. There are early decision and early admissions plans. Applications should be filed by July 15 for fall entry and December 15 for spring entry, along with a $35 fee. Notification is sent on a rolling basis.

Transfer: Transfer students must have a minimum 2.0 GPA and be in good academic standing at the former institution. Applicants with fewer than 25 credits must meet freshman requirements. 30 credits of 120 must be completed at Coppin.

Visiting: There are regularly scheduled orientations for prospective students, consisting of open house's. There are guides for informal visits and visitors may sit in on classes. To schedule a visit, contact Admissions.

Financial Aid: In a recent year, 90% of all freshmen and 85% of continuing students received some form of financial aid. 90% of freshmen and 85% of continuing students received need-based aid. Coppin is a member of CSS. The FAFSA and the college's own financial statement are required. Check with the school for current deadlines.

International Students: They must score 500 on the written TOEFL or 173 on the electronic version.

Computers: The mainframe is a DEC VAX 11/780. There are more than 200 PCs available for students. All students may access the system. There are no time limits and no fees.

Admissions Contact: Admissions Counselors.
E-mail: *admissions@coppin.edu* Web: *http://www.coppin.edu/*

FROSTBURG STATE UNIVERSITY — B-1

Frostburg, MD 21532 (301) 687-4201; Fax: (301) 687-7074

Full-time: 1945 men, 2082 women	**Faculty:** 249; IIA, av$
Part-time: 129 men, 198 women	**Ph.D.s:** 85%
Graduate: 391 men, 538 women	**Student/Faculty:** 16 to 1
Year: semesters, summer session	**Tuition:** $4256 ($9754)
Application Deadline: open	**Room & Board:** $5424
Freshman Class: 2872 applied, 2161 accepted, 920 enrolled	
SAT I: required	**COMPETITIVE**

Frostburg State University, founded in 1898, is a part of the University System of Maryland. The university offers programs through the colleges of liberal arts and sciences, business, and education. There are 3 undergraduate and 10 graduate schools. In addition to regional accreditation, FSU has baccalaureate program accreditation with CSWE and NRPA. The library contains 356,200 volumes, 300,203 microform items, and 71,985 audiovisual forms/CDs, and subscribes to 3390 periodicals. Computerized library services include the card catalog, interlibrary loans, and database searching. Special learning facilities include a learning resource center, art gallery, planetarium, radio station, TV station, environmental lab, and distance education labs. The 260-acre campus is in a small town about 150 miles west of Baltimore and northwest of Washington D.C. Including residence halls, there are 31 buildings.

Student Life: 88% of undergraduates are from Maryland. Others are from 27 states, 16 foreign countries, and Canada. 81% are white; 13% African American. The average age of freshmen is 19; all undergraduates, 22. 30% do not continue beyond their first year.

Housing: 1700 students can be accommodated in college housing, which includes single-sex and coed dormitories. In addition, there are honors houses, special interest houses, international houses, and disabled student housing. On-campus housing is guaranteed for all 4 years. 60% of students commute. All students may keep cars.

Activities: 10% of men belong to 5 national fraternities; 10% of women belong to 5 national sororities. There are 150 groups on campus, including art, band, cheerleading, choir, chorale, chorus, computers, dance, drama, drill team, ethnic, gay, honors, international, jazz band, literary magazine, marching band, musical theater, newspaper, orchestra, pep band, photography, political, professional, radio and TV, religious, social, social service, student government, symphony, and yearbook. Popular campus events include Parents Weekend, cultural events series, and Welcome Week.

Sports: There are 9 intercollegiate sports for men and 11 for women, and 5 intramural sports for men and 4 for women. Facilities include a game room, a 3600-seat main arena, a practice gym, 5 athletic fields, 2 intramural fields, an indoor swimming pool, a dance studio, a wellness room, 6 lighted tennis courts, weight rooms, a dance lab, a football stadium, an 8-lane 400-meter track, training rooms, team rooms, and baseball, racquetball, squash, and archery rooms.

Disabled Students: All of the campus is accessible. Wheelchair ramps, elevators, special parking, specially equipped rest rooms, special class scheduling, lowered drinking fountains, and lowered telephones are available.

Services: Counseling and information services are available, as is tutoring in every subject. There is a reader service for the blind, and remedial math, reading, and writing.

Campus Safety and Security: Measures include 24-hour foot and vehicle patrol, self-defense education, escort service, and shuttle buses. There are informal discussions, pamphlets/posters/films, emergency telephones, lighted pathways/sidewalks, and bicycle patrol.

Programs of Study: FSU confers B.A., B.S., B.F.A., and B.T.P. degrees. Master's degrees are also awarded. Bachelor's degrees are awarded in AGRICULTURE (fish and game management and wildlife management), BIOLOGICAL SCIENCE (biology/biological science), BUSINESS (accounting, business administration and management, and recreation and leisure services), COMMUNICATIONS AND THE ARTS (communications, design, dramatic arts, English, languages, music, and speech/debate/rhetoric), COMPUTER AND PHYSICAL SCIENCE (actuarial science, chemistry, computer science, mathematics, physics, and science), EDUCATION (business, early childhood, elementary, middle school, and physical), ENGINEERING AND ENVIRONMENTAL DESIGN (environmental science), SOCIAL SCIENCE (criminal justice, economics, geography, history, international studies, law enforcement and corrections, liberal arts/general studies, philosophy, political science/government, psychology, social science, social work, and sociology). Business, education, and the natural sciences are the strongest academically. Education, business, and computer science are the largest.

Required: A minimum GPA of 2.0 and 120 credit hours are required to graduate. All students must complete 7 to 14 credits in natural science, 6 to 9 credits in humanities and social sciences, and 3 to 6 credits in creative and performing arts. Courses in computer science, speech and composition, personalized health fitness, and math are also required.

Special: FSU offers co-op programs in applied physics, electrical engineering, and mechanical engineering with the University of Maryland, internships through individual departments, study abroad in Ireland, England, Germany, Denmark, and Ecuador through the International Student Exchange Program, work-study and accelerated degree programs, B.A.-B.S. degrees in all majors, and a dual major in engineering. The 3-2 engineering degree is coordinated with the University of Maryland at College Park. Cross-registration, nondegree study, and pass/fail options are also available. Distance learning, an advanced degree program, and honors programs are available. There are 18 national honor societies, a freshman honors program, and 15 departmental honors programs.

Faculty/Classroom: 59% of faculty are male; 41%, female. All teach undergraduates. No introductory courses are taught by graduate students. The average class size in an introductory lecture is 25; in a laboratory, 9; and in a regular course, 20.

Admissions: 75% of the 2001-2002 applicants were accepted. The SAT I scores for the 2001-2002 freshman class were: Verbal--50% below 500, 39% between 500 and 599, 10% between 600 and 700, and 1% above 700; Math--46% below 500, 41% between 500 and 599, 12% between 600 and 700, and 1% above 700. The ACT scores were 66% below 21, 27% between 21 and 23, 5% between 24 and 26, and 2% between 27 and 28. 25% of the current freshmen were in the top fifth of their class; 59% were in the top two fifths.

Requirements: The SAT I is required. In addition, applicants must be graduates of an accredited secondary school or have the GED. Secondary preparation should include 4 units of English, 3 each of math and social studies, and 2 of a foreign language and science. An interview is recommended. A GPA of 2.0 is required. AP and CLEP credits are accepted. Important factors in the admissions decision are recommendations by school officials, extracurricular activities record, and advanced placement or honor courses. Applications are accepted on-line via the FSU home page and the University System of Maryland on-line application.

Procedure: Freshmen are admitted to all sessions. Entrance exams should be taken in the junior or senior year. There is an early admissions plan. Application deadlines are open. The application fee is $30. Notification is sent on a rolling basis.

Transfer: 372 transfer students enrolled in 2001-2002. Transfer students with 12 to 23 credits must have a minimum GPA of 2.5 and provide an official high school transcript and SAT I scores. Students with 24 or more credits must have a minimum GPA of 2.0. 30 credits of 120 must be completed at FSU.

Visiting: There are regularly scheduled orientations for prospective students, including tours Monday through Friday at 11 A.M. and 2 P.M. There are guides for informal visits and visitors may sit in on classes. To schedule a visit, contact the Office of Admissions.

Financial Aid: In 2001-2002, 75% of all freshmen and 65% of continuing students received some form of financial aid. 45% of freshmen and 46% of continuing students received need-based aid. The average freshman award was $4676. Of that total, scholarships or need-based grants averaged $1898 ($5500 maximum); loans averaged $2262 ($4600 maximum); and work contracts averaged $939 ($1000 maximum). 35% of undergraduates work part time. Average annual earnings from campus work are $750. The average financial indebtedness of the 2001 graduate was $13,700. The FAFSA and the college's own financial statement are required. The fall application deadline is March 1.

International Students: There are 21 international students enrolled. The school actively recruits these students. They must score 560 on the written TOEFL or 220 on the electronic version and also take the SAT I or the ACT.

Computers: The mainframe is a VAX/VMS 4300. There are 668 computers in open and specialized labs throughout the campus. All students may access the system 8 A.M. to midnight. There are no time limits and no fees. It is strongly recommended that all students have a personal computer.

Graduates: In 2001, 812 bachelor's degrees were awarded. The most popular majors were education (16%), business administration (14%), and psychology (8%). In an average class, 28% graduate in 4 years, 57% in 5 years, and 63% in 6 years. 61 companies recruited on campus in 2000-2001.

Admissions Contact: Trisha Gregory, Associate Director of Admissions. E-mail: *fsuadmissions@frostburg.edu* Web: *www.frostburg.edu*

GOUCHER COLLEGE

Baltimore, MD 21204 — D-2

(410) 337-6100
(800) 468-2437; Fax: (410) 337-6354

Full-time: 334 men, 839 women	**Faculty:** 86; IIB, +$
Part-time: 17 men, 42 women	**Ph.D.s:** 94%
Graduate: 199 men, 576 women	**Student/Faculty:** 14 to 1
Year: semesters	**Tuition:** $22,300
Application Deadline: February 1	**Room & Board:** $8350

Freshman Class: 2146 applied, 1557 accepted, 364 enrolled
SAT I Verbal/Math: 620/570 — **VERY COMPETITIVE+**

Goucher College, founded in 1885, is a private liberal arts college. In addition to regional accreditation, Goucher has baccalaureate program accreditation with NCATE. The library contains 300,000 volumes, 65,077 microform items, and 10,000 audiovisual forms/CDs, and subscribes to 6100 periodicals. Computerized library services include the card catalog, interlibrary loans, and database searching. Special learning facilities include a learning resource center, art gallery, TV studio, theater, technology/learning center, international technology and media center, and centers for writing, math, and politics. The 287-acre campus is in a suburban area 8 miles north of Baltimore. Including residence halls, there are 18 buildings.

Student Life: 60% of undergraduates are from out of state, mostly the Middle Atlantic. Students are from 42 states and 20 foreign countries. 70% are from public schools. 66% are white. The average age of freshmen is 19; all undergraduates, 22. 18% do not continue beyond their first year.

Housing: 875 students can be accommodated in college housing, which includes single-sex and coed dormitories and on-campus apartments. In addition, there are language houses and special-interest houses. On-campus housing is guaranteed for all 4 years. 70% of students live on campus. All students may keep cars.

Activities: There are no fraternities or sororities. There are 40 groups on campus, including art, chorale, chorus, dance, drama, environmental, ethnic, film, gay, honors, international, jazz band, literary magazine, martial arts, newspaper, orchestra, political, professional, religious, social, social service, student government, symphony, and yearbook. Popular campus events include Get into Goucher Day, Spring Gala, and Blind Date Ball.

Sports: There are 7 intercollegiate sports for men and 9 for women, and 12 intramural sports for men and 12 for women. Facilities include 2 gyms, an indoor swimming pool, a weight room, a dance studio, a training room, racquetball and squash courts, tennis courts, and indoor and outdoor equestrian facilities.

Disabled Students: All of the campus is accessible. Wheelchair ramps, elevators, special parking, specially equipped rest rooms, special class scheduling, and an auditorium loop for the hearing impaired are available.

Services: Counseling and information services are available, as is tutoring in most subjects. There is a reader service for the blind. Many academic support options are available through the college's Academic Center for Excellence (ACE).

Campus Safety and Security: Measures include 24-hour foot and vehicle patrol, self-defense education, escort service, and shuttle buses. There are informal discussions, pamphlets/posters/films, emergency telephones, lighted pathways/sidewalks, a whistle-alert program, a student safety and security committee, and a manned guard/gatehouse during evening hours.

Programs of Study: Goucher confers the B.A. degree. Master's degrees are also awarded. Bachelor's degrees are awarded in BIOLOGICAL SCIENCE (biology/biological science), BUSINESS (management science), COMMUNICATIONS AND THE ARTS (art history and appreciation, arts administration/management, communications, dance, dramatic arts, English, French, historic preservation, music, Russian, Spanish, and studio art), COMPUTER AND PHYSICAL SCIENCE (applied physics, chemistry, computer science, mathematics, and physics), EDUCATION (elementary and special), SOCIAL SCIENCE (American studies, economics, history, interdisciplinary studies, international relations, international studies, philosophy, political science/government, psychology, social science, sociology, and women's studies). Biology, chemistry, and history are the strongest academically. English, management, and psychology are the largest.

Required: To graduate, all students must complete 120 hours, with a minimum GPA of 2.0. Requirements include 1 lab-related course in the natural sciences, 1 course each in the humanities, social sciences, math, and the arts, and the first-year colloquium course for freshmen. Students are also required to demonstrate proficiency in computers, writing, and a foreign language. Other requirements include a 4-class distribution requirement in phys ed and at least 3 semester hours of an off-campus experience.

Special: Goucher offers internships, study abroad in 11 countries, and other off-campus experiences. The college also collaborates with many of the 22 other colleges in the Baltimore Collegetown Network (*www.colltown.org*). Students may cross-register with Johns Hopkins

University, Towson University, Loyola College, Morgan State University, College of Notre Dame, Baltimore Hebrew University, and Maryland Institute, College of Art. An advanced degree program with the Monterey Institute for International Studies, B.A.-B.S. degrees, and a 3-2 engineering degree with Johns Hopkins are offered. Dual majors are an option, and student-designed majors and pass/no pass options are also available. There is 1 national honor society, Phi Beta Kappa, a freshman honors program, and 18 departmental honors programs.

Faculty/Classroom: 39% of faculty are male; 61%, female. All teach undergraduates, and 90% also do research. The average class size in an introductory lecture is 16; in a laboratory, 9; and in a regular course, 12.

Admissions: 73% of the 2001-2002 applicants were accepted. The SAT I scores for the 2001-2002 freshman class were: Verbal--8% below 500, 32% between 500 and 599, 50% between 600 and 700, and 10% above 700; Math--13% below 500, 48% between 500 and 599, 37% between 600 and 700, and 2% above 700. 55% of the current freshmen were in the top fifth of their class; 80% were in the top two fifths. 5 freshmen graduated first in their class.

Requirements: The SAT I or ACT is required. In addition, applicants should be graduates of an accredited high school or have earned the GED. Secondary preparation should include at least 14 academic units, preferably 4 in English, 3 in math (algebra I and II and geometry), 2 each in the same foreign language and in lab science, and 2 or 3 in social studies. A personal essay is required, and an interview is recommended. Prospective arts majors are urged to seek an audition or submit a portfolio. AP credits are accepted. Important factors in the admissions decision are extracurricular activities record, recommendations by school officials, and advanced placement or honor courses. Applications are accepted on computer disk.

Procedure: Freshmen are admitted fall and spring. Entrance exams should be taken in spring of the junior year or fall of the senior year. There are early decision, early admissions, and deferred admissions plans. Early decision applications should be filed by December 1; regular applications, by February 1 for fall entry and December 1 for spring entry. Notification of early decision is sent January 15; regular decision, April 1. 25 early decision candidates were accepted for the 2001-2002 class. 7% of all applicants are on a waiting list; 4 were accepted in 2001.

Transfer: 46 transfer students enrolled in 2001-2002. Applicants must present a GPA of at least 2.5 in 30 hours of college work. An interview, a personal essay, and recommendations from college teachers or counselors are also required, as is a graded paper. 60 credits of 120 must be completed at Goucher.

Visiting: There are regularly scheduled orientations for prospective students, including an academic presentation, a student panel, discussions, a campus tour, an interview, and an opportunity to sit in on classes and to meet with faculty, coaches, and other staff. There are guides for informal visits and visitors may sit in on classes and stay overnight. To schedule a visit, contact the Office of Admissions.

Financial Aid: In 2001-2002, 79% of all freshmen and 80% of continuing students received some form of financial aid. 77% of all students received need-based aid. The average freshman award was $15,509. Of that total, scholarships or need-based grants averaged $8500 ($22,000 maximum); loans averaged $4625 ($5500 maximum); and work contracts averaged $1200 ($1500 maximum). 46% of undergraduates work part time. Average annual earnings from campus work are $1200. The average financial indebtedness of the 2001 graduate was $14,500. Goucher is a member of CSS. The CSS/Profile or FAFSA and the college's own financial statement are required. The fall application deadline is February 15.

International Students: The school actively recruits these students. They must score 550 on the written TOEFL and also take the SAT I.

Computers: The mainframe is an HP 9000, Series 800. PCs are available in academic labs, dorms, and the library. All dorm rooms are wired for direct access to the Internet and the Web. An intracampus network is in place. All students may access the system. Some facilities are available around the clock. There are no time limits and no fees.

Graduates: In 2001, 271 bachelor's degrees were awarded. The most popular majors were psychology (14%), communication (12%), and biological science (8%). In an average class, 56% graduate in 4 years, 64% in 5 years, and 68% in 6 years. 25 companies recruited on campus in 2000-2001. Of the 2000 graduating class, 22% were enrolled in graduate school within 6 months of graduation and 76% were employed.

Admissions Contact: Carlton E. Surbeck, Director of Admissions. A video is available. E-mail: *admission@goucher.edu*
Web: *www.goucher.edu*

HOOD COLLEGE

C-2

Frederick, MD 21701-8575

(301) 696-3400
(800) 922-1599; Fax: (301) 696-3819

Full-time: 38 men, 557 women	**Faculty:** 72; IIA, --$
Part-time: 59 men, 130 women	**Ph.D.s:** 92%
Graduate: 281 men, 542 women	**Student/Faculty:** 9 to 1
Year: semesters, summer session	**Tuition:** $19,120
Application Deadline: February 15	**Room & Board:** $6900
Freshman Class: 502 applied, 372 accepted, 113 enrolled	
SAT I Verbal/Math: 577/557	**ACT:** 23 **VERY COMPETITIVE**

Hood College, founded in 1893, is an independent, comprehensive college primarily for women that offers an integration of the liberal arts and professional preparation, as well as undergraduate majors in the natural sciences. In addition to regional accreditation, Hood has baccalaureate program accreditation with ADA and CSWE. The library contains 163,864 volumes, 588,015 microform items, and 3864 audiovisual forms/CDs, and subscribes to 5080 periodicals. Computerized library services include the card catalog, interlibrary loans, and database searching. Special learning facilities include a learning resource center, art gallery, aquatic center, child development lab, observatory, and Whitaker Campus Center, a library and information technology center that forms the hub of the campus computing network. The 50-acre campus is in a suburban area 45 miles northwest of Washington, D.C., and 45 miles west of Baltimore. Including residence halls, there are 31 buildings.

Student Life: 77% of undergraduates are from Maryland. Others are from 20 states, 22 foreign countries, and Canada. 82% are from public schools. 60% are white; 11% African American. 79% are claim no religious affiliation; 12% Protestant. The average age of freshmen is 18; all undergraduates, 24. 15% do not continue beyond their first year.

Housing: 552 students can be accommodated in college housing, which includes single-sex dormitories. In addition, there are language houses. Special-interest floors in the residence halls include a living/learning floor and a community service floor. On-campus housing is guaranteed for all 4 years. 52% of students live on campus; of those, 60% remain on campus on weekends. All students may keep cars.

Activities: There are no fraternities or sororities. There are 53 groups on campus, including art, choir, chorale, chorus, computers, dance, drama, environmental, ethnic, gay, honors, international, literary magazine, musical theater, newspaper, opera, political, professional, religious, social, social service, student government, and yearbook. Popular campus events include Ring Formal, performance of "The Messiah" with the U.S. Naval Academy, and Spirit Week.

Sports: There are 8 intercollegiate sports for women and 3 intramural sports for women. Facilities include a gym with regulation basketball and volleyball courts, a weight room, an aerobics room, indoor and outdoor swimming pools, a 1-mile par course, a softball diamond, 6 tennis courts, an outdoor volleyball court, and 3 multiuse fields (field hockey, soccer, and lacrosse).

Disabled Students: 37% of the campus is accessible. Wheelchair ramps, elevators, special parking, specially equipped rest rooms, and special class scheduling are available.

Services: Counseling and information services are available, as is tutoring in some subjects. Services such as readers for the blind and interpreters for the hearing impaired are arranged for individual students. There are also services for students with learning disabilities, a writing lab, a language lab, and courses in time management and study skills.

Campus Safety and Security: Measures include 24-hour foot and vehicle patrol, self-defense education, escort service, and informal discussions. There are pamphlets/posters/films, emergency telephones, lighted pathways/sidewalks, and an electronic access control system with 24-hour monitoring in all residence halls.

Programs of Study: Hood confers B.A. and B.S. degrees. Master's degrees are also awarded. Bachelor's degrees are awarded in BIOLOGICAL SCIENCE (biochemistry and biology/biological science), BUSINESS (business administration and management and management science), COMMUNICATIONS AND THE ARTS (art, communications, English, French, German, music, and Spanish), COMPUTER AND PHYSICAL SCIENCE (chemistry, computer science, information sciences and systems, and mathematics), EDUCATION (early childhood, English, foreign languages, mathematics, science, secondary, and special), ENGINEERING AND ENVIRONMENTAL DESIGN (environmental science), SOCIAL SCIENCE (economics, history, Latin American studies, law, philosophy, political science/government, psychology, religion, social work, and sociology). Biology, math, and computer science are the strongest academically. Early childhood education, biology, and psychology are the largest.

Required: To graduate, students must complete a total of 124 credit hours, with a minimum GPA of 2.0 overall and in the major. 24 to 57 credits are required in a student's major. All students must complete 32 to 41 credits in the core curriculum, which includes English, math, and language courses, courses in methods of inquiry, and interdisciplinary courses in Western civilization, non-Western civilization and society, science, and technology. Enrollment in the final 30 credits must be on the Hood Campus as a degree candidate.

Special: The college offers a Washington semester with American University, dual majors, student-designed majors, credit for life experience, nondegree study, pass/fail options, and cross-registration with area colleges and the Duke University Marine Sciences Education Consortium. Internships of up to 15 credits are available in all majors at more than 100 sites throughout the United States and abroad. Students may study abroad in the Dominican Republic, Japan, Spain, France, and other countries. There are 11 national honor societies and a freshman honors program.

Faculty/Classroom: 42% of faculty are male; 58%, female. All teach undergraduates and do research. The average class size in an introductory lecture is 13; in a laboratory, 8; and in a regular course, 13.

Admissions: 74% of the 2001-2002 applicants were accepted. The SAT I scores for the 2001-2002 freshman class were: Verbal--17% below 500, 41% between 500 and 599, 35% between 600 and 700, and 7% above 700; Math--20% below 500, 49% between 500 and 599, 25% between 600 and 700, and 7% above 700. The ACT scores were 22% below 21, 33% between 21 and 23, 22% between 24 and 26, 17% between 27 and 28, and 6% above 28. 66% of the current freshmen were in the top fifth of their class; 93% were in the top two fifths. There was 1 National Merit finalist and 1 semifinalist. 4 freshmen graduated first in their class.

Requirements: The SAT I or ACT is required. In addition, applicants should be graduates of an accredited secondary school. The GED is accepted. Hood recommends the completion of at least 16 academic credits in high school, including courses in English, social sciences, natural sciences, foreign languages, and math. An essay is required and an interview is recommended. A GPA of 2.5 is required. AP and CLEP credits are accepted. Important factors in the admissions decision are advanced placement or honor courses, leadership record, and personality/intangible qualities. Hood accepts applications on-line.

Procedure: Freshmen are admitted fall and spring. Entrance exams should be taken in spring of the junior year or fall of the senior year. There are early admissions and deferred admissions plans. Applications should be filed by February 15 for fall entry and December 31 for spring entry. The fall 2001 application fee was $35. Notification is sent March 15.

Transfer: 64 transfer students enrolled in 2001-2002. Applicants must have at least 12 college credits and a minimum GPA of 2.5. A total of 70 credits may be transferred. 30 credits of 124 must be completed at Hood.

Visiting: There are regularly scheduled orientations for prospective students, including tours and meetings with faculty, students, and administrators and admissions interviews. There are guides for informal visits and visitors may sit in on classes and stay overnight. To schedule a visit, contact the Admissions Office.

Financial Aid: In 2001-2002, 98% of all freshmen and 78% of continuing students received some form of financial aid. 76% of freshmen and 55% of continuing students received need-based aid. The average freshman award was $19,338. Of that total, scholarships or need-based grants averaged $14,232 ($26,695 maximum); loans averaged $3930 ($10,027 maximum); work contracts averaged $1800; and Parent Plus Loans averaged $7170 ($14,820 maximum). 42% of undergraduates work part time. Average annual earnings from campus work are $1800. The average financial indebtedness of the 2001 graduate was $15,642. The FAFSA is required. The fall application deadline is February 15.

International Students: There are 40 international students enrolled. The school actively recruits these students. They must score 550 on the written TOEFL or 215 on the electronic version and also take the Comprehensive English Language Test or the college's own test. SAT I scores may be substituted for the TOEFL.

Computers: The mainframes include Compaq Alpha 800, 2100a, and 4000 servers. Students may use the 10 PCs in a 24-hour computing lab or dial in from off campus. There are 150 PCs in 6 student labs, and 28 Macs in other labs, and 3 to 4 computers in each residence hall. All students may access the system 24 hours per day from a PC in the 24-hour computing lab, from a student's PC in a residence hall, or from the student's home if there is a modem. Otherwise, the system may be accessed weekdays 8:30 A.M. to midnight in the PC lab. There are no time limits and no fees. It is strongly recommended that all students have a personal computer.

Graduates: In 2001, 226 bachelor's degrees were awarded. The most popular majors were early childhood education (12%), management (11%), and psychology (10%). In an average class, 2% graduate in 3 years, 58% in 4 years, 62% in 5 years, and 62% in 6 years. 50 companies recruited on campus in 2000-2001. Of the 2000 graduating class, 25% were enrolled in graduate school within 6 months of graduation and 61% were employed.

Admissions Contact: Dr. Susan Hallenbeck, Dean of Admissions.
E-mail: *admissions@hood.edu* Web: *www.hood.edu*

JOHNS HOPKINS UNIVERSITY — D-2

Baltimore, MD 21218 — **(410) 516-8341; Fax: (410) 516-6025**

Full-time: 2319 men, 1614 women	**Faculty:** n/av
Part-time: 23 men, 5 women	**Ph.D.s:** n/av
Graduate: 838 men, 559 women	**Student/Faculty:** n/av
Year: 4-1-4, summer session	**Tuition:** $26,720
Application Deadline: January 1	**Room & Board:** $8506
Freshman Class: 9127 applied, 3132 accepted, 1016 enrolled	
SAT I Verbal/Math: 690/720	**ACT:** 31 **MOST COMPETITIVE**

Johns Hopkins University, founded in 1876, is a private multicampus institution offering undergraduate degrees through the Schools of Arts and Sciences and Engineering, and graduate degrees through those and the Schools of International Studies, Nursing, Medicine, and Hygiene and Public Health, and the Peabody Institute (music). There are 5 undergraduate and 8 graduate schools. In addition to regional accreditation, Johns Hopkins has baccalaureate program accreditation with ABET. The 6 libraries contain 3,380,206 volumes, 3,990,862 microform items, and 295,952 audiovisual forms/CDs, and subscribe to 23,043 periodicals. Computerized library services include the card catalog, interlibrary loans, and database searching. Special learning facilities include an art gallery and radio station. The 140-acre campus is in an urban area 3 miles north of downtown Baltimore. Including residence halls, there are 36 buildings.

Student Life: 78% of undergraduates are from out of state, mostly the Middle Atlantic. Others are from 50 states, 53 foreign countries, and Canada. 68% are from public schools. 66% are white; 19% Asian American. The average age of freshmen is 18; all undergraduates, 20. 5% do not continue beyond their first year; 88% remain to graduate.

Housing: 2107 students can be accommodated in college housing, which includes single-sex and coed dormitories, on-campus apartments, off-campus apartments, and married-student housing. In addition, there are special-interest houses. On-campus housing is available on a lottery system for upperclassmen. 54% of students live on campus; of those, 90% remain on campus on weekends. Upperclassmen may keep cars.

Activities: 18% of men belong to 12 national fraternities; 19% of women belong to 7 national sororities. There are 183 groups on campus, including art, band, cheerleading, chess, choir, chorale, chorus, computers, dance, debate, drama, ethnic, film, gay, honors, international, jazz band, literary magazine, marching band, musical theater, newspaper, opera, orchestra, pep band, photography, political, professional, radio and TV, religious, social, social service, student government, symphony, and yearbook. Popular campus events include Spring Fair, Fiji Islander, and MSE Symposium.

Sports: There are 14 intercollegiate sports for men and 12 for women, and 24 intramural sports for men and 24 for women. Facilities include a 4000-seat stadium, outdoor playing fields, a swimming pool and diving board, wrestling and fencing rooms, a weight room, saunas, a climbing wall, and courts for basketball, volleyball, badminton, squash, and handball.

Disabled Students: 80% of the campus is accessible. Wheelchair ramps, elevators, special parking, specially equipped rest rooms, special class scheduling, lowered drinking fountains, and lowered telephones are available.

Services: Counseling and information services are available, as is tutoring in most subjects. There is a reader service for the blind.

Campus Safety and Security: Measures include 24-hour foot and vehicle patrol, self-defense education, escort service, and shuttle buses. There are informal discussions, pamphlets/posters/films, emergency telephones, and lighted pathways/sidewalks.

Programs of Study: Johns Hopkins confers B.A. and B.S. degrees. Master's and doctoral degrees are also awarded. Bachelor's degrees are awarded in BIOLOGICAL SCIENCE (biology/biological science, biophysics, cell biology, ecology, life science, molecular biology, and neurosciences), BUSINESS (banking and finance, business administration and management, human resources, management science, and marketing management), COMMUNICATIONS AND THE ARTS (art history and appreciation, classics, English, French, German, Italian, media arts, music, music performance, music theory and composition, performing arts, romance languages and literature, and Spanish), COMPUTER AND PHYSICAL SCIENCE (applied mathematics, chemistry, computer science, earth science, geology, geophysics and seismology, information sciences and systems, mathematics, natural sciences, oceanography, physics, and quantitative methods), EDUCATION (music), ENGINEERING AND ENVIRONMENTAL DESIGN (biomedical engineering, chemical engineering, civil engineering, computer engineering, electrical/electronics engineering, engineering, engineering mechanics, environmental engineering, environmental science, industrial engineering, materials engineering, materials science, and mechanical engineering), HEALTH PROFESSIONS (nursing, premedicine, and public health), SOCIAL SCIENCE (American studies, anthropology, cognitive science, crosscultural studies, East Asian studies, economics, geography, history, history of science, humanities, interdisciplinary studies, international studies, Latin American studies, Near Eastern studies, philosophy, political science/government, prelaw, psychology, public affairs, social science, sociology, and urban studies). Biology, international studies, and biomedical engineering are the largest.

Required: Although there is no required core curriculum, all students must take 40 hours in the major and 30 hours outside their major field. The B.A. requires a total of 120 hours; the B.S. in engineering requires 120 to 128 hours, depending on the major. A GPA of at least 2.0 is required for graduation. All students must take at least 4 courses (2 for engineers) with a writing-intensive component to graduate.

Special: Johns Hopkins offers an extensive array of special programs, including internships, dual majors in music and arts, and sciences and engineering, cross-registration with all Baltimore-area colleges and all Johns Hopkins divisions, a cooperative 5-year civil engineering program, a student-designed semester at the Johns Hopkins School of International Studies in Washington, D.C., and various multidisciplinary programs. Students may enroll at Johns Hopkins in Bologna, Italy, or Nanjing, China, or arrange programs in Europe, South America, the Far East, or Australia. Accelerated degrees are available in 21 fields. Students may earn combined B.A.-B.S. degrees in biomedical, computer, or mathematical engineering or a combined B.A.-B.M. through the Peabody Institute. Pass/fail options are available in nonmajor courses. There are 4 national honor societies, including Phi Beta Kappa, and 25 departmental honors programs.

Admissions: 34% of the 2001-2002 applicants were accepted. The SAT I scores for the 2001-2002 freshman class were: Verbal--1% below 500, 8% between 500 and 599, 44% between 600 and 700, and 47% above 700; Math--3% between 500 and 599, 30% between 600 and 700, and 67% above 700. The ACT scores were 3% between 21 and 23, 9% between 24 and 26, 14% between 27 and 28, and 75% above 28. 89% of the current freshmen were in the top fifth of their class; 98% were in the top two fifths. There were 31 National Merit finalists. 87 freshmen graduated first in their class.

Requirements: The SAT I or ACT is required. In addition, applicants should be graduates of an accredited secondary school or have the GED. The university recommends that secondary preparation include 4 years each of English and math, 2 or 3 of social science or history, at least 2, preferably 3, of lab science, and 2 of a foreign language. Applicants must submit SAT II: Subject tests in writing and literature and 2 others of their choice. 2 personal essays are required, and an interview is recommended. Common App, CollegeLink, and Mac Apply computer disk applications are accepted. Applications are also accepted on-line via the university's own service at *apply.jhu.edu*. AP credits are accepted. Important factors in the admissions decision are advanced placement or honor courses, leadership record, and evidence of special talent.

Procedure: Freshmen are admitted in the fall. Entrance exams should be taken by January for regular decision, or November for early decision. There are early decision and deferred admissions plans. Early decision applications should be filed by November 15; regular applications, by January 1 for fall entry. The fall 2001 application fee was $60. Notification of early decision is sent December 15; regular decision, by April 15. 262 early decision candidates were accepted for the 2001-2002 class. 17% of all applicants are on a waiting list; 55 were accepted in 2001.

Transfer: 21 transfer students enrolled in 2001-2002. Applicants should have sophomore or junior standing and at least a B average in previous college work. Applications must include a written essay and at least 1 letter of recommendation. High school records and standardized test scores are also required. 60 credits of 120 must be completed at Johns Hopkins.

Visiting: There are regularly scheduled orientations for prospective students, including campus tours, group information sessions, and panel discussions with students and faculty offered weekday mornings and afternoons. There are guides for informal visits and visitors may sit in on classes and stay overnight. To schedule a visit, contact the Office of Undergraduate Admissions.

Financial Aid: In 2001-2002, 49% of all freshmen and 50% of continuing students received some form of financial aid. 43% of freshmen and 37% of continuing students received need-based aid. The average freshman award was $24,532. Of that total, scholarships or need-based grants averaged $20,032; loans averaged $2500 ($4000 maximum); and work contracts averaged $2000 (maximum). 50% of undergraduates work part time. Average annual earnings from campus work are $1000. The average financial indebtedness of the 2001 graduate was $16,600. The FAFSA and the college's own financial statement are required. The fall application deadline is February 1.

International Students: There are 306 international students enrolled. The school actively recruits these students. They must score 600 on the written TOEFL or 250 on the electronic version and also take the SAT I or the ACT. Students must take SAT II: Subject tests in writing.

Computers: The mainframes are an AT&T 3B4000, a DEC VAX 6410, an IBM 3081, and a UNIX O/S. PC labs are available for student use in academic buildings and in some residence halls, with 1 lab open 24 hours a day. Residence halls are Internet ready. All students may access the system 24 hours a day, 7 days a week. There are no time limits. The fee is $60.

Graduates: In 2001, 890 bachelor's degrees were awarded. The most popular majors were biomedical engineering (13%), international studies (10%), and economics (6%). In an average class, 5% graduate in 3 years, 78% in 4 years, 84% in 5 years, and 87% in 6 years. 268 companies recruited on campus in 2000-2001. Of the 2000 graduating class, 42% were enrolled in graduate school within 6 months of graduation and 43% were employed.

Admissions Contact: John Latting, Director of Undergraduate Admissions. A video is available. E-mail: *jlatting1@jhuadiq.admin.jhu.edu* Web: *www.apply.jhu.edu*

LOYOLA COLLEGE IN MARYLAND D-2

Baltimore, MD 21210 **(410) 617-5012**
(800) 221-9107; Fax: (410) 617-2176

Full-time: 1445 men, 1940 women	**Faculty:** 234; IIA, av$
Part-time: 23 men, 35 women	**Ph.D.s:** 93%
Graduate: 1002 men, 1519 women	**Student/Faculty:** 14 to 1
Year: semesters, summer session	**Tuition:** $23,500
Application Deadline: January 15	**Room & Board:** $7400
Freshman Class: 6577 applied, 4012 accepted, 886 enrolled	
SAT I Verbal/Math: 600/610	**HIGHLY COMPETITIVE**

Loyola College, founded in 1852, is a private liberal arts college affiliated with the Roman Catholic Church and the Jesuit tradition. It offers degree programs in arts and sciences, and business and management. There are 2 undergraduate and 2 graduate schools. In addition to regional accreditation, Loyola has baccalaureate program accreditation with AACSB, ABET, CSAB, and NASDTEC. The library contains 424,685 volumes, 326,236 microform items, and 9245 audiovisual forms/CDs, and subscribes to 2163 periodicals. Computerized library services include the card catalog, interlibrary loans, and database searching. Special learning facilities include an art gallery. The 89-acre campus is in an urban area 3 miles from downtown Baltimore. Including residence halls, there are 29 buildings.

Student Life: 23% of undergraduates are from Maryland. Others are from 42 states, 18 foreign countries, and Canada. 55% are from public schools. 87% are white. Most are Catholic. The average age of freshmen is 18; all undergraduates, 20. 8% do not continue beyond their first year; 78% remain to graduate.

Housing: 2474 students can be accommodated in college housing, which includes coed dormitories and on-campus apartments. In addition, there are honors houses and special-interest houses. On-campus housing is guaranteed for the freshman year only and is available on a first-come, first-served basis. 77% of students live on campus; of those, 77% remain on campus on weekends. Alcohol is not permitted. Upperclassmen may keep cars.

Activities: There are no fraternities or sororities. There are 101 groups on campus, including art, band, cheerleading, chess, choir, chorale, chorus, computers, dance, drama, ethnic, honors, international, jazz band, literary magazine, musical theater, newspaper, orchestra, pep band, photography, political, professional, religious, social, social service, student government, symphony, and yearbook. Popular campus events include International Festival, Maryland Day, and Fall Rock Concert.

Sports: There are 7 intercollegiate sports for men and 7 for women, and 15 intramural sports for men. Facilities include a pool, a sauna, a weight room, racquetball, tennis, and squash courts, a 3000-seat arena, a 2000-seat multipurpose outdoor facility, and a fitness center.

Disabled Students: 99% of the campus is accessible. Wheelchair ramps, elevators, special parking, specially equipped rest rooms, special class scheduling, lowered drinking fountains, and lowered telephones are available.

Services: Counseling and information services are available, as is tutoring in most subjects. There is a reader service for the blind and remedial math.

Campus Safety and Security: Measures include 24-hour foot and vehicle patrol, self-defense education, escort service, and shuttle buses. There are informal discussions, pamphlets/posters/films, emergency telephones, and lighted pathways/sidewalks.

Programs of Study: Loyola confers B.A., B.S., B.B.A., B.S.E.E., and B.S.E.S. degrees. Master's and doctoral degrees are also awarded. Bachelor's degrees are awarded in BIOLOGICAL SCIENCE (biology/biological science), BUSINESS (accounting and business administration and management), COMMUNICATIONS AND THE ARTS (communications, creative writing, English, fine arts, French, German, Latin, and Spanish), COMPUTER AND PHYSICAL SCIENCE (chemistry, computer science, mathematics, and physics), EDUCATION (elementary), ENGINEERING AND ENVIRONMENTAL DESIGN (electrical/electronics engineering and engineering), HEALTH PROFESSIONS (speech pathology/audiology), SOCIAL SCIENCE (classical/ancient civilization, economics, history, philosophy, political science/government, psychology, sociology, and theological studies). General business, psychology, and biology are the largest.

Required: All students must complete 120 hours, including 36 in the major, with at least a 2.0 GPA. The required core curriculum includes 2 courses each in history, language (at the second-year level), literature, philosophy, social sciences, and theology; 1 course each in composition, ethics, fine arts, math, and natural sciences; and 1 additional course in math, natural science, or computer science.

Special: Loyola offers cross-registration with Johns Hopkins, Towson State, and Morgan State Universities, Goucher College, the College of Notre Dame, Maryland Art Institute, and Peabody Conservatory. Credit-bearing internships are available in most majors, and there are study-abroad programs in Thailand, Belgium, and England. Work-study programs and dual majors are also offered. There are 23 national honor societies, including Phi Beta Kappa, a freshman honors program, and 1 departmental honors program.

Faculty/Classroom: 64% of faculty are male; 36%, female. 90% teach undergraduates, 98% do research, and 87% do both. No introductory courses are taught by graduate students. The average class size in an introductory lecture is 25; in a laboratory, 16; and in a regular course, 21.

Admissions: 61% of the 2001-2002 applicants were accepted. The SAT I scores for the 2001-2002 freshman class were: Verbal--5% below 500, 43% between 500 and 599, 47% between 600 and 700, and 6% above 700; Math--3% below 500, 36% between 500 and 599, 54% between 600 and 700, and 6% above 700. 64% of the current freshmen were in the top fifth of their class; 91% were in the top two fifths. 10 freshmen graduated first in their class in a recent year.

Requirements: The SAT I is required. In addition, applicants should have graduated from an accredited secondary school or have earned the GED. Secondary preparation should include 4 years of English, 3 to 4 each of math, foreign language, natural science, and classical or modern foreign language, and 2 to 3 of history. A personal essay is required; an interview is recommended. AP and CLEP credits are accepted. Important factors in the admissions decision are advanced placement or honor courses, recommendations by school officials, and extracurricular activities record.

Procedure: Freshmen are admitted fall and spring. Entrance exams should be taken by December of the senior year. There are early admissions and deferred admissions plans. Applications should be filed by January 15 for fall entry and December 15 for spring entry. Notification is sent April 15. 8% of all applicants were on a waiting list in a recent year.

Transfer: 53 transfer students enrolled in 2001-2002. Transfer applicants should have at least a 2.5 GPA in previous college work and should submit SAT I scores. Other factors considered include types of college courses taken and the secondary school record. 60 credits of 120 must be completed at Loyola.

Visiting: There are regularly scheduled orientations for prospective students, including a general information session, an interview, and a campus tour. There are guides for informal visits and visitors may sit in on classes. To schedule a visit, contact the Admissions Office.

Financial Aid: In a recent year, 68% of all freshmen and 63% of continuing students received some form of financial aid. 57% of freshmen and 52% of continuing students received need-based aid. The average freshman award was $14,020. Of that total, scholarships or need-based grants averaged $9260 ($17,700 maximum); loans averaged $3010 ($3625 maximum); and work contracts averaged $1750 (maximum). 14% of undergraduates work part time. Average annual earnings from campus work are $1450. The average financial indebtedness of a recent year's graduate was $15,210. Loyola is a member of CSS. The CSS/Profile or FAFSA and, if applicable, noncustodial parent's statement and business/farm supplement are required. The fall application deadline is February 10.

International Students: The school actively recruits these students. They must score 550 on the written TOEFL and also take the SAT I.

Computers: The mainframe are 2 DEC VAX 11/785 computers. There are more than 200 PCs and Macs available. All students may access the system. There are no time limits and no fees.

Graduates: In a recent year, 782 bachelor's degrees were awarded. The most popular majors were business/marketing (35%), social sciences and history (12%), and communications/communications technology (11%). In an average class, 71% graduate in 4 years, 77% in 5 years, and 78% in 6 years. Of a recent year's graduating class, 19% were enrolled in graduate school within 6 months of graduation and 69% were employed.

Admissions Contact: William Bossemeyer, Dean of Admissions. A video is available. Web: *www.loyola.edu*

MARYLAND INSTITUTE COLLEGE OF ART — D-2

Baltimore, MD 21217 — **(410) 225-2222; Fax: (410) 225-2337**

Full-time: 459 men, 719 women	**Faculty:** 102
Part-time: 5 men, 12 women	**Ph.D.s:** 74%
Graduate: 51 men, 87 women	**Student/Faculty:** 12 to 1
Year: semesters, summer session	**Tuition:** $21,080
Application Deadline: January 15	**Room & Board:** $6640
Freshman Class: 1693 applied, 775 accepted, 320 enrolled	
SAT I Verbal/Math: 570/550	**SPECIAL**

Maryland Institute College of Art, founded in 1826, is a private accredited institution offering undergraduate and graduate degrees in the fine arts. In addition to regional accreditation, MICA has baccalaureate program accreditation with FIDER and NASAD. The library contains 54,000 volumes and 5000 audiovisual forms/CDs, and subscribes to 300 periodicals. Computerized library services include the card catalog, interlibrary loans, and database searching. Special learning facilities include a learning resource center and 7 large art galleries, open to the public year-round, featuring work by MICA faculty, students, and nationally and internationally known artists, a slide library containing 200,000 slides; 3 guest-curated major art galleries; 5 other galleries for undergraduate and graduate exhibitons. The 12-acre campus is in an urban area in the Mt. Royal cultural center of Baltimore. Including residence halls, there are 20 buildings.

Student Life: 78% of undergraduates are from out of state, mostly the Northeast. Others are from 46 states, 50 foreign countries, and Canada. 80% are from public schools. 71% are white. The average age of freshmen is 18; all undergraduates, 20. 18% do not continue beyond their first year; 61% remain to graduate.

Housing: 400 students can be accommodated in college housing, which includes coed dormitories, on-campus apartments, off-campus apartments, and married-student housing. Residence halls include rooms where students can do artwork 24 hours a day. On-campus housing is guaranteed for the freshman year only, is available on a first-come, first-served basis, and is available on a lottery system for upperclassmen. 88% of students live on campus; of those, 95% remain on campus on weekends. Alcohol is not permitted. All students may keep cars.

Activities: There are no fraternities or sororities. There are 18 groups on campus, including art, chess, drama, ethnic, film, international, literary magazine, photography, political, professional, religious, social, social service, student government, and yearbook. Popular campus events include regular bus trips to galleries and museums in New York and Washington, D.C., dances, and exhibition openings.

Sports: There is 1 intramural sport for men and 1 for women. Facilities include a nearby recreation center with volleyball, basketball, weight-training facilities, and aerobics.

Disabled Students: 85% of the campus is accessible. Wheelchair ramps, elevators, special parking, specially equipped rest rooms, special class scheduling, lowered drinking fountains, lowered telephones, and lowered fire extinguishers are available.

Services: Counseling and information services are available, as is tutoring in some subjects, including writing and study skills.

Campus Safety and Security: Measures include 24-hour foot and vehicle patrol, self-defense education, escort service, and shuttle buses. There are informal discussions, pamphlets/posters/films, emergency telephones, building monitors in most buildings, and periodic discussions and seminars on safety.

Programs of Study: MICA confers the B.F.A. degree. Master's degrees are also awarded. Bachelor's degrees are awarded in COMMUNICATIONS AND THE ARTS (ceramic art and design, drawing, fiber/textiles/weaving, fine arts, graphic design, illustration, painting, photography, printmaking, and sculpture), ENGINEERING AND ENVIRONMENTAL DESIGN (interior design). Fine arts, painting, and graphic design are the strongest academically and have the largest enrollments.

Required: All students complete a foundation program in their first year, including courses in painting, drawing, two- and three-dimensional design, and liberal arts. Of a total 126 credits, students must take one third of the courses in liberal arts and two thirds in studio arts, with 63 credits in the major and a minimum 2.0 GPA. Seniors must complete a focused, professionally oriented body of work.

Special: Exchange programs are offered with Goucher College, Loyola and Notre Dame Colleges, Johns Hopkins University, the Peabody Conservatory of Music, and the University of Baltimore. Cross-registration is possible with any member schools in the Alliance of Independent Colleges of Art and the East Coast Art Schools Consortium. A New York studio semester is available. Study abroad is possible in the junior year in any of 12 countries including the Maryland Institute's Center for Advanced Art and Culture in Aix-en-Provence, France. Dual and student-designed majors are available, and there are work-study programs. Juniors and seniors who meet prerequisites are eligible for credit-earning internships locally and nationally.

Faculty/Classroom: 55% of faculty are male; 45%, female. 94% teach undergraduates. No introductory courses are taught by graduate students. The average class size in an introductory lecture is 17 and in a regular course, 14.

Admissions: 46% of the 2001-2002 applicants were accepted. The SAT I scores for the 2001-2002 freshman class were: Verbal--18% below 500, 41% between 500 and 599, 33% between 600 and 700, and 8% above 700; Math--27% below 500, 42% between 500 and 599, 20% between 600 and 700, and 3% above 700. 76% of the current freshmen were in the top two fifths of their class. There were 3 National Merit semifinalists. 4 freshmen graduated first in their class.

Requirements: The SAT I is required. In addition, emphasis is primarily on the applicant's portfolio, which is reviewed as part of the admissions process. Applicants submit 12 to 20 pieces of their best current work in and out of school, including samples of drawing from observation. Academic history including grades and course level is also seriously considered. AP credits are accepted. Important factors in the admissions decision are evidence of special talent, advanced placement or honor courses, and personality/intangible qualities.

Procedure: Freshmen are admitted fall and spring. Entrance exams should be taken in the spring of the junior year. There are early decision, early admissions, and deferred admissions plans. Early decision applications should be filed by November 15; regular applications, by January 15 for fall entry and December 1 for spring entry. The fall 2001 application fee was $45. Notification of early decision is sent December 15; regular decision, March 1. 23 early decision candidates were accepted for the 2001-2002 class.

Transfer: 58 transfer students enrolled in 2001-2002. Transfer applicants must submit high school and college transcripts, a personal essay, a portfolio, and letters of recommendation. 62 credits of 126 must be completed at MICA.

Visiting: There are regularly scheduled orientations for prospective students, including campus tours, portfolio reviews, personal interviews, discussions about careers in art and financing one's education, and opportunities to sit in on classes. There are guides for informal visits. To schedule a visit, contact the Admissions Office at (410) 225-2294.

Financial Aid: In 2001-2002, 81% of all freshmen and 74% of continuing students received some form of financial aid. 59% of freshmen and 68% of continuing students received need-based aid. The average freshman award was $10,569. Of that total, scholarships or need-based grants averaged $7571 ($21,250 maximum); loans averaged $2257 ($8625 maximum); and work contracts averaged $742 ($2300 maximum). 60% of undergraduates work part time. Average annual earnings from campus work are $1100. The average financial indebtedness of the 2001 graduate was $12,500. MICA is a member of CSS. The FAFSA and the college's own financial statement are required. The fall application deadline is March 1.

International Students: There are 66 international students enrolled. The school actively recruits these students. They must score 550 on the written TOEFL and also take or take the SAT I or the Cambridge Exam.

Computers: The mainframes are an IBM AS/400, an IBM Netfinity 7000, and an IBM Netfinity 5500 M10. There are 226 IBM PCs and Macs available for student use, throughout the campus with Internet access. Every student has an e-mail address, and residence halls are wired for Internet access. Also available are high-end peripherals such as scanners, digital video editing equipment, and state-of-the-art software for 2-D and 3-D applications. All students may access the system 24 hours a day. There are no time limits and no fees.

Graduates: In 2001, 238 bachelor's degrees were awarded. The most popular majors were general fine arts (29%), illustration and graphic design (16%), and painting (12%). In an average class, 1% graduate in 3 years, 51% in 4 years, 61% in 5 years, and 63% in 6 years. 30 companies recruited on campus in 2000-2001. Of the 2000 graduating class, 23% were enrolled in graduate school within 6 months of graduation and 75% were employed.

Admissions Contact: Theresa Lynch Bedoya, Vice President Dean of Admissions/Financial Aid. E-mail: *admissions@mica.edu*
Web: *www.mica.edu*

MORGAN STATE UNIVERSITY — D-2
Baltimore, MD 21251 — (410) 319-3000
(800) 332-6674; Fax: (410) 319-3684

Full-time: 2070 men, 2940 women	**Faculty:** 243; IIA, av$
Part-time: 350 men, 440 women	**Ph.D.s:** 80%
Graduate: 200 men, 290 women	**Student/Faculty:** 21 to 1
Year: semesters, summer session	**Tuition:** $4508 ($10,718)
Application Deadline: see profile	**Room & Board:** $5570
Freshman Class: n/av	
SAT I or ACT: required	**LESS COMPETITIVE**

Morgan State University, founded in 1867, is a comprehensive public institution offering undergraduate and graduate programs leading to liberal arts, preprofessional, and professional degrees. Figures given in the above capsule are approximate. There are 5 undergraduate schools and 1 graduate school. In addition to regional accreditation, Morgan State has baccalaureate program accreditation with AACSB, ABET, ADA, ASLA, CSWE, NAAB, NASAD, NASM, and NCATE. The library contains 389,516 volumes, 738,311 microform items, and 45,855 audiovisual forms/CDs, and subscribes to 3011 periodicals. Computerized library services include the card catalog, interlibrary loans, and database searching. Special learning facilities include a learning resource center, art gallery, radio station, and TV station. The 140-acre campus is in a suburban area in the northeast corner of Baltimore. Including residence halls, there are 30 buildings.

Student Life: 60% of undergraduates are from Maryland. Others are from 40 states, 20 foreign countries, and Canada. 91% are from public schools. 92% are African American. The average age of freshmen is 19; all undergraduates, 25. 24% do not continue beyond their first year; 36% remain to graduate.

Housing: 1800 students can be accommodated in college housing, which includes single-sex and coed dormitories and on-campus apartments. In addition, there are honors houses. On-campus housing is available on a first-come, first-served basis. 70% of students commute. Alcohol is not permitted. All students may keep cars.

Activities: 4% of men belong to 4 national fraternities; 3% of women belong to 4 national sororities. There are 100 groups on campus, including art, band, cheerleading, chess, choir, chorale, chorus, computers, dance, debate, drama, drill team, ethnic, film, forensics, honors, international, jazz band, literary magazine, marching band, musical theater, newspaper, orchestra, pep band, photography, political, professional, radio and TV, religious, social, social service, student government, and yearbook. Popular campus events include Kwanzaa and I Love Morgan Day.

Sports: There are 6 intercollegiate sports for men and 6 for women, and 17 intramural sports for men and 16 for women. Facilities include a field house, a gym, a weight room, a swimming pool, tennis and racquetball courts, and various playing fields.

Disabled Students: 90% of the campus is accessible. Wheelchair ramps, elevators, special parking, specially equipped rest rooms, special class scheduling, and lowered drinking fountains are available.

Services: Counseling and information services are available, as is tutoring in every subject. There is a reader service for the blind, and remedial math, reading, and writing. There are also note takers and sign language interpreters for disabled students.

Campus Safety and Security: Measures include 24-hour foot and vehicle patrol, self-defense education, escort service, and shuttle buses. There are informal discussions, pamphlets/posters/films, emergency telephones, and lighted pathways/sidewalks.

Programs of Study: Morgan State confers A.B., B.S., and B.S.Ed. degrees. Master's and doctoral degrees are also awarded. Bachelor's degrees are awarded in BIOLOGICAL SCIENCE (biology/biological science), BUSINESS (accounting, business administration and management, hospitality management services, and marketing/retailing/merchandising), COMMUNICATIONS AND THE ARTS (dramatic arts, English, fine arts, music, speech/debate/rhetoric, and telecommunications), COMPUTER AND PHYSICAL SCIENCE (chemistry, computer science, information sciences and systems, mathematics, and physics), EDUCATION (elementary, health, and physical), ENGINEERING AND ENVIRONMENTAL DESIGN (civil engineering, electrical/electronics engineering, engineering physics, and industrial engineering technology), HEALTH PROFESSIONS (medical laboratory technology, and mental health/human services), SOCIAL SCIENCE (African American studies, economics, history, home economics, philosophy, political science/government, psychology, religion, social work, and sociology). Engineering, chemistry, and social work are the strongest academically. Business administration, accounting, electrical engineering, and telecommunications are the largest.

Required: To graduate, students must complete at least 120 credit hours, including 74 in the major, with a 2.0 GPA. All students must pass speech and writing proficiency exams prior to their senior year. The 46-credit general education requirement includes courses in English, humanities, logic, history, behavioral science, science, math, African American history, and health and phys ed. Seniors must pass a proficiency exam in their major.

Special: Co-op programs in public and private institutions may be arranged for pharmacy honors, predentistry, premedicine, and special education students. The university also offers internships for juniors and seniors, work-study programs, and preprofessional physical therapy and prelaw programs. Dual majors may be pursued, but do not lead to a dual degree. There are 28 national honor societies, including Phi Beta Kappa, and a freshman honors program.

Faculty/Classroom: 67% of faculty are male; 33%, female. All teach undergraduates and 76% do research. No introductory courses are taught by graduate students. The average class size in an introductory lecture is 31; in a laboratory, 26; and in a regular course, 21.

Requirements: The SAT I or ACT is required, with a minimum composite score of 900 on the SAT I. In addition, applicants should be high school graduates, or have earned the GED, and are encouraged to have 4 years of English, 3 of math, 2 each of science, social studies, and history, and 1 of a foreign language. A personal essay is recommended and, when appropriate, an audition. A GPA of 2.0 is required. AP and CLEP credits are accepted. Important factors in the admissions decision are recommendations by school officials, evidence of special talent, and parents or siblings attending the school.

Procedure: Freshmen are admitted fall and spring. Entrance exams should be taken during the fall semester of the junior or senior year. There is an early admissions plan. Notification is sent on a rolling basis. Check with the school for current deadlines. The fall 2001 application fee was $25.

Transfer: Applicants with fewer than 24 credits must submit high school transcripts; those with fewer than 12 credits must also submit SAT I scores. Applicants are expected to have at least a 2.0 GPA in all college work attempted and be in good standing at the last institution attended. 30 credits of 120 must be completed at Morgan State.

Visiting: There are regularly scheduled orientations for prospective students, including placement testing and academic advising. There are guides for informal visits and visitors may sit in on classes. To schedule a visit, contact Delores Norris.

Financial Aid: Morgan State is a member of CSS. The FAFSA and the college's own financial statement are required.

International Students: They must score 550 on the written TOEFL or take ALIGU and the SAT I or ACT. Students who have not attended any school during the preceding 3 years are not required to submit standardized test scores.

Computers: The mainframes are a DEC VAX 11/780 and an 8300. There are also IBM and Mac PCs available. All students may access the system. There are no time limits and no fees.

Graduates: In an average class, 12% graduate in 4 years, and 12% in 5 years.

Admissions Contact: Delores Norris, Acting Director of Admission and Recruitment. Web: *www.morgan.edu*

MOUNT SAINT MARY'S COLLEGE D-1

Emmitsburg, MD 21727 (301) 447-5214
(800) 448-4347; Fax: (301) 447-5860

Full-time: 580 men, 749 women	**Faculty:** 93; IIB, -$
Part-time: 57 men, 156 women	**Ph.D.s:** 91%
Graduate: 274 men, 153 women	**Student/Faculty:** 14 to 1
Year: semesters, summer session	**Tuition:** $18,680
Application Deadline: March 1	**Room & Board:** $7060
Freshman Class: 1946 applied, 1541 accepted, 355 enrolled	
SAT I Verbal/Math: 542/541	**COMPETITIVE**

Mount Saint Mary's College, founded in 1808, is a private liberal arts institution affiliated with the Roman Catholic Church. In addition to regional accreditation, The Mount has baccalaureate program accreditation with NASDTEC. The library contains 201,757 volumes, 20,000 microform items, and 4440 audiovisual forms/CDs, and subscribes to 928 periodicals. Computerized library services include the card catalog, interlibrary loans, and database searching. Special learning facilities include a learning resource center, art gallery, radio station, TV station, and archives. The 1400-acre campus is in a rural area 60 miles northwest of Washington, D.C., and 50 miles west of Baltimore. Including residence halls, there are 25 buildings.

Student Life: 53% of undergraduates are from Maryland. Others are from 30 states, 10 foreign countries, and Canada. 57% are from public schools. 89% are white. 83% are Catholic; 16% Protestant. The average age of freshmen is 18; all undergraduates, 21. 20% do not continue beyond their first year; 66% remain to graduate.

Housing: 1179 students can be accommodated in college housing, which includes coed dormitories and on-campus apartments. In addition, there are special-interest houses, wellness floors, and quiet floors. On-campus housing is guaranteed for all 4 years. 83% of students live on campus; of those, 80% remain on campus on weekends. All students may keep cars.

Activities: There are no fraternities or sororities. There are 49 groups on campus, including cheerleading, chess, choir, chorale, dance, drama, ethnic, honors, international, literary magazine, musical theater, newspaper, photography, political, professional, radio and TV, religious, social, social service, student government, and yearbook. Popular campus events include Spring Fling, Founders Day, and Mountapalooza.

Sports: There are 9 intercollegiate sports for men and 9 for women, and 20 intramural sports for men and 20 for women. Facilities include multipurpose indoor courts, a track, a pool, aerobics facilities, a sauna, a weight room, a basketball arena, lighted tennis courts, and playing fields.

Disabled Students: 60% of the campus is accessible. Wheelchair ramps, elevators, special parking, specially equipped rest rooms, special class scheduling, lowered drinking fountains, and lowered telephones are available.

Services: Counseling and information services are available, as is tutoring in every subject. There is a reader service for the blind, remedial math, study skills and language lab, and a writing center. Closed-caption TV and software for sight-impaired students are also available.

Campus Safety and Security: Measures include 24-hour foot and vehicle patrol, escort service, informal discussions, and pamphlets/posters/films. There are emergency telephones, lighted pathways/sidewalks, and access control.

Programs of Study: The Mount confers B.A. and B.S. degrees. Master's degrees are also awarded. Bachelor's degrees are awarded in BIOLOGICAL SCIENCE (biochemistry and biology/biological science), BUSINESS (accounting and business administration and management), COMMUNICATIONS AND THE ARTS (communications, English, fine arts, French, German, and Spanish), COMPUTER AND PHYSICAL SCIENCE (chemistry, computer science, and mathematics), EDUCATION (elementary and secondary), SOCIAL SCIENCE (economics, history, interdisciplinary studies, international studies, philosophy, political science/government, psychology, social studies, sociology, and theological studies). Business and finance, sociology, and elementary education are the largest.

Required: Students are required to take a 4-year, 52-credit core curriculum (with an additional foreign language proficiency requirement) in liberal arts, which includes a freshman seminar, a 4-course Western civilization sequence including art and literature, and courses in science and math, American culture, philosophy, theology, non-Western culture, and ethics. Graduation requirements include 120 credits, with most majors requiring 36 credits (30 to 36 in the major) and a minimum GPA of 2.0.

Special: Mount Saint Mary's offers cross-registration with an area community college, study abroad in the U.K., Europe, and South America, and secondary teacher certification in biology, business education, English, foreign languages, math, and social science. Dual majors, interdisciplinary majors in biopsychology, American culture, and classical studies, a general studies degree, a 3-2 nursing degree, and nondegree and accelerated study are possible. A number of independently designed internships, work-study programs, and pass/fail options are available. There also is an integrated freshman year program. There are 16 national honor societies, a freshman honors program, and 14 departmental honors programs.

Faculty/Classroom: 67% of faculty are male; 33%, female. 97% teach undergraduates, 97% do research, and 97% do both. No introductory courses are taught by graduate students. The average class size in an introductory lecture is 23; in a laboratory, 17; and in a regular course, 20.

Admissions: 79% of the 2001-2002 applicants were accepted. The SAT I scores for the 2001-2002 freshman class were: Verbal--27% below 500, 51% between 500 and 599, 20% between 600 and 700, and 2% above 700; Math--28% below 500, 51% between 500 and 599, 19% between 600 and 700, and 2% above 700. 32% of the current freshmen were in the top fifth of their class; 63% were in the top two fifths. 3 freshmen graduated first in their class.

Requirements: The SAT I is required. In addition, applicants should be graduates of an accredited secondary school or hold the GED. Secondary preparation should include 4 years of English, 3 each of math, history, natural science, and social sciences, and 2 of a foreign language. An interview is recommended. AP and CLEP credits are accepted. Important factors in the admissions decision are recommendations by school officials, advanced placement or honor courses, and extracurricular activities record. Applications are accepted on-line at the school's web site or at *www.embark.com*.

Procedure: Freshmen are admitted fall and spring. Entrance exams should be taken by January of the senior year. There are early action and deferred admissions plans. Applications should be filed by March 1 for fall entry and December 1 for spring entry. The fall 2001 application fee $35. Notification is sent on a rolling basis.

Transfer: 46 transfer students enrolled in 2001-2002. Transfer applicants should have at least a 2.5 GPA in previous college work, be in good academic and disciplinary standing, and account for all time elapsed since graduation from high school. 30 credits of 120 must be completed at The Mount.

Visiting: There are regularly scheduled orientations for prospective students, including campus tours and information sessions on academic programs, community life, admissions, and financial aid. There are guides for informal visits and visitors may sit in on classes and stay overnight. To schedule a visit, contact the Admissions Office.

Financial Aid: In 2001-2002, 97% of all freshmen and 92% of continuing students received some form of financial aid. 66% of all students received need-based aid. The average freshman award was $16,090. Of that total, scholarships or need-based grants averaged $10,716 ($25,740 maximum); loans averaged $3923 ($4125 maximum); and work contracts averaged $1451 ($1500 maximum). 35% of undergraduates work part time. Average annual earnings from campus work are $1200. The average financial indebtedness of the 2001 graduate was $8716. The Mount is a member of CSS. The CSS/Profile or FAFSA is required. The fall application deadline is March 15.

International Students: There are 11 international students enrolled. They must score 550 on the written TOEFL and also take the SAT I or the ACT.

Computers: The mainframes are comprised of an IBM AS/400, a Sun 20 SPARC Station IPX, and a SPARC server 1000. There are 100 PCs located in 6 computer labs across campus; students have access to the SPARC Server via Telnet. All students may access the system 24 hours per day. There are no time limits and no fees. It is strongly recommended that all students have a personal computer.

Graduates: In 2001, 289 bachelor's degrees were awarded. The most popular majors were business and finance (26%), sociology (13%), and elementary education (12%). In an average class, 1% graduate in 3 years, 68% in 4 years, 70% in 5 years, and 71% in 6 years. 150 companies recruited on campus in 2000-2001. Of the 2000 graduating class, 33% were enrolled in graduate school within 6 months of graduation and 98% were employed.

Admissions Contact: Stephen Neitz, Executive Director of Admissions and Financial Aid. A video is available.
E-mail: *admissions@msmary.edu* Web: *www.msmary.edu*

SAINT JOHN'S COLLEGE — E-3
Annapolis, MD 21404 (410) 626-2523
(800) 727-9238; Fax: (410) 269-7916

Full-time: 260 men, 214 women	**Faculty:** 69; IIB
Part-time: 1 man, 2 women	**Ph.D.s:** 72%
Graduate: 39 men, 28 women	**Student/Faculty:** 7 to 1
Year: semesters, summer session	**Tuition:** $25,990
Application Deadline: open	**Room & Board:** $6770

Freshman Class: 464 applied, 363 accepted, 113 enrolled
SAT I or ACT: not required — **HIGHLY COMPETITIVE+**

St. John's College, founded as King William's School in 1696 and chartered as St. John's in 1784, is a private institution that offers a single all-required curriculum sometimes called the Great Books Program. Students and faculty work together in small discussion classes without lecture courses, written finals, or emphasis on grades. The program is a rigorous interdisciplinary curriculum based on the great works of literature, math, philosophy, theology, sciences, political theory, music, history, and economics. There is also a campus in Santa Fe, New Mexico. The 2 libraries contain 98,016 volumes, 412 microform items, and 1873 audiovisual forms/CDs, and subscribe to 114 periodicals. Computerized library services include the card catalog, interlibrary loans, and database searching. Special learning facilities include an art gallery and planetarium. The 36-acre campus is in a small town 35 miles east of Washington, D.C., and 32 miles south of Baltimore. Including residence halls, there are 16 buildings.

Student Life: 85% of undergraduates are from out of state, mostly the Middle Atlantic. Students are from 47 states, 9 foreign countries, and Canada. 65% are from public schools. 89% are white. The average age of freshmen is 19; all undergraduates, 20. 20% do not continue beyond their first year; 75% remain to graduate.

Housing: 291 students can be accommodated in college housing, which includes coed dormitories. On-campus housing is guaranteed for the freshman year only and is available on a lottery system for upperclassmen. 65% of students live on campus; of those, 95% remain on campus on weekends. Upperclassmen may keep cars.

Activities: There are no fraternities or sororities. There are 32 groups on campus, including art, chorus, computers, dance, drama, film, gay, literary magazine, newspaper, photography, political, religious, social service, student government, and yearbook. Popular campus events include Reality Weekend, Senior Prank, and College Navy Croquet Match.

Sports: There are 2 intercollegiate sports for men and 2 for women, and 19 intramural sports for men and 19 for women. Facilities include a gym with a weight room, cardio room, and indoor running track, tennis courts, a boat house, and playing fields.

Disabled Students: 70% of the campus is accessible. Wheelchair ramps, elevators, special parking, specially equipped rest rooms, special class scheduling, lowered drinking fountains, lowered telephones, and ground floor dorm rooms are available.

Services: Counseling and information services are available, as is tutoring in most subjects. There is remedial math and writing.

Campus Safety and Security: Measures include 24-hour foot and vehicle patrol, escort service, informal discussions, and pamphlets/posters/films. There are emergency telephones and lighted pathways/sidewalks.

Programs of Study: St. John's confers the B.A. degree. Master's degrees are also awarded. Bachelor's degrees are awarded in SOCIAL SCIENCE (liberal arts/general studies, Western civilization/culture, and Western European studies).

Required: The common curriculum, equivalent to 132 credits, covers a range of classic to modern works. Students attend small seminars; 9-week preceptorials on specific works or topics; language, music, and math tutorials; and a 3-year natural sciences lab. Active learning occurs through discussion, translations, writing, experiments, mathematical demonstration, and musical analysis. Students take oral exams each semester and submit annual essays. Sophomores also take a math exam and seniors an oral exam that admits them to degree candidacy. Seniors also present a final essay to the faculty and take a 1-hour public oral exam.

Faculty/Classroom: 76% of faculty are male; 24%, female. All teach undergraduates. No introductory courses are taught by graduate students. The average class size in a laboratory is 15 and in a regular course, 15.

Admissions: 78% of the 2001-2002 applicants were accepted. 67% of the current freshmen were in the top fifth of their class; 87% were in the top two fifths. There were 7 National Merit finalists and 7 semifinalists.

Requirements: Applicants need not be high school graduates; some students are admitted before they complete high school. Test scores may be submitted but are not required. Secondary preparation should include 4 years of English, 3 of math, and 2 each of foreign language, science, and history. Applicants must submit written essays, which are critical to the admissions decision, and are strongly urged to schedule an interview. Important factors in the admissions decision are recommendations by school officials, advanced placement or honor courses, and personality/intangible qualities.

Procedure: Freshmen are admitted fall and spring. There are early admissions and deferred admissions plans. The preferred application deadlines are March 1 for fall entry and December 15 for spring entry. Notification is sent on a rolling basis.

Transfer: 20 transfer students enrolled in 2001-2002. Transfer students may enter only as freshmen and must complete the entire program at St. John's. The admissions criteria are the same as for regular students. Students in good academic standing may transfer to the Santa Fe campus at the beginning of any academic year. 132 credits of 132 must be completed at St. John's.

Visiting: There are regularly scheduled orientations for prospective students, consisting of an overnight stay on campus, class visits, and a tour. There are guides for informal visits and visitors may sit in on classes and stay overnight. To schedule a visit, contact the Admission Office at (410) 626-2522.

Financial Aid: In 2001-2002, 54% of all freshmen and 58% of continuing students received some form of financial aid. 54% of freshmen and 55% of continuing students received need-based aid. The average freshman award was $19,826. Of that total, scholarships or need-based grants averaged $15,475 ($21,000 maximum); loans averaged $2625 ($5500 maximum); and work contracts averaged $2200 (maximum). 75% of undergraduates work part time. Average annual earnings from campus work are $2410. The average financial indebtedness of the 2001 graduate was $17,525. The CSS/Profile or FAFSA is required. The fall application deadline is February 15.

International Students: There are 11 international students enrolled. The school actively recruits these students. They must take the TOEFL and the SAT I.

Computers: The mainframe is an IBM AS/400. There is a network of 8 Macs available for student use in a computer room, as well as 1 Mac and 10 PCs in the library. They are equipped with word-processing programs and a variety of other software. All student dormatories are connected to the network. All students may access the system 24 hours a day. There are no time limits and no fees.

Graduates: In 2001, 95 bachelor's degrees were awarded. The most popular major was liberal arts (100%). In an average class, 57% graduate in 4 years, 66% in 5 years, and 70% in 6 years. 11 companies recruited on campus in 2000-2001. Of the 2000 graduating class, 18% were enrolled in graduate school within 6 months of graduation and 40% were employed.

Admissions Contact: John Christensen, Director of Admissions.
E-mail: *admissions@sjca.edu* Web: *www.sjca.edu*

SAINT MARY'S COLLEGE OF MARYLAND — E-4
St. Mary's City, MD 20686 (240) 895-5000
(800) 492-7181; Fax: (240) 895-5001

Full-time: 605 men, 919 women	**Faculty:** 120; IIB, +$
Part-time: 51 men, 113 women	**Ph.D.s:** 94%
Graduate: none	**Student/Faculty:** 13 to 1
Year: semesters, summer session	**Tuition:** $7549 ($12,534)
Application Deadline: January 15	**Room & Board:** $6555

Freshman Class: 1447 applied, 1027 accepted, 456 enrolled
SAT I Verbal/Math: 620/610 — **HIGHLY COMPETITIVE**

St. Mary's College of Maryland, founded in 1840, is a small public liberal arts college in the Maryland State College and University System. In addition to regional accreditation, Saint Mary's has baccalaureate program accreditation with NASM. The library contains 176,748 volumes, 44,665 microform items, and 10,437 audiovisual forms/CDs, and subscribes to 2141 periodicals. Computerized library services include the card catalog, interlibrary loans, and database searching. Special learning facilities include a learning resource center, art gallery, radio station, TV station, historic archeological site, and estuarine research facilities. The 275-acre campus is in a rural area 70 miles south of Washington, D.C. Including residence halls, there are 34 buildings.

Student Life: 87% of undergraduates are from Maryland. Others are from 31 states and 24 foreign countries. 80% are from public schools. 85% are white. 40% are Protestant; 27% Catholic; 25% claim no religious affiliation. The average age of freshmen is 19; all undergraduates, 21. 13% do not continue beyond their first year; 72% remain to graduate.

Housing: 1267 students can be accommodated in college housing, which includes single-sex and coed dormitories and on-campus apartments. In addition, there are language houses and speial interest houses. On-campus housing is guaranteed for the freshman year only, is available on a first-come, first-served basis, and is available on a lottery system for upperclassmen. 74% of students live on campus; of those, 60% remain on campus on weekends. All students may keep cars.

Activities: There are no fraternities or sororities. There are 73 groups on campus, including academic, art, band, cheerleading, chess, choir, chorale, chorus, dance, drama, ethnic, film, gay, honors, international, jazz band, literary magazine, musical theater, newspaper, orchestra, outdoors, photography, political, professional, radio and TV, religious, social, social service, student government, symphony, and yearbook. Popular campus events include Parents Weekend, World Carnival, and concerts.

Sports: There are 7 intercollegiate sports for men and 8 for women, and 8 intramural sports for men and 8 for women. Facilities include an athletic track, a pool, basketball, volleyball, and tennis courts, training, weight, and exercise rooms, a boat house, pier, and sailing fleet, and baseball, soccer, and lacrosse fields.

Disabled Students: 86% of the campus is accessible. Wheelchair ramps, elevators, special parking, specially equipped rest rooms, special class scheduling, lowered drinking fountains, lowered telephones, and living suites that meet ADA standards are available.

Services: Counseling and information services are available, as is tutoring in some subjects, including math, writing, physics, foreign languages, biology, chemistry, and economics. There is a reader service for the blind.

Campus Safety and Security: Measures include 24-hour foot and vehicle patrol, self-defense education, escort service, and informal discussions. There are pamphlets/posters/films, emergency telephones, lighted pathways/sidewalks, and student security assistant foot patrols.

Programs of Study: Saint Mary's confers the B.A. degree. Bachelor's degrees are awarded in BIOLOGICAL SCIENCE (biology/biological science), COMMUNICATIONS AND THE ARTS (dramatic arts, English, fine arts, languages, and music), COMPUTER AND PHYSICAL SCIENCE (chemistry, computer science, mathematics, natural sciences, and physics), SOCIAL SCIENCE (anthropology, economics, history, human development, philosophy, political science/government, psychology, public affairs, religion, and sociology). Biology, psychology, and English are the strongest academically. Economics, psychology, and biology are the largest.

Required: Students must complete general education requirements in writing, math, foreign language, history, the arts, literature, physical, biological, behavioral, and policy sciences, philosophy, and an interdisciplinary seminar. There is a senior project. Students must meet additional requirements in their major fields and complete 128 semester hours with at least a 2.0 GPA.

Special: St. Mary's offers exchange programs with Johns Hopkins University and the National Student Exchange, study abroad, dual and student-designed majors, and nondegree study. There are pass/fail options for some courses. Unpaid internships for credit, with placement worldwide, are also permitted. There are 6 national honor societies, including Phi Beta Kappa, a freshman honors program, and 4 departmental honors programs.

Faculty/Classroom: 57% of faculty are male; 43%, female. All both teach and do research. The average class size in an introductory lecture is 24; in a laboratory, 16; and in a regular course, 14.

Admissions: 71% of the 2001-2002 applicants were accepted. The SAT I scores for the 2001-2002 freshman class were: Verbal--6% below 500, 29% between 500 and 599, 47% between 600 and 700, and 18% above 700; Math--7% below 500, 39% between 500 and 599, 48% between 600 and 700, and 6% above 700. 73% of the current freshmen were in the top fifth of their class; 91% were in the top two fifths. There were 5 National Merit semifinalists. 25 freshmen graduated first in their class.

Requirements: The SAT I or ACT is required. In addition, applicants should have graduated from an accredited secondary school or earned the GED. Minimum high school preparation should include 4 units of English, 3 each of math, social studies, and science, and 7 electives. An essay, a resume of cocurricular activities, and 2 letters of recommendation are required. A GPA of 2.0 is required. AP and CLEP credits are accepted. Important factors in the admissions decision are advanced placement or honor courses, recommendations by school officials, and extracurricular activities record. Applications are accepted on-line at the school's website.

Procedure: Freshmen are admitted fall and spring. Entrance exams should be taken in May of the junior year or November of the senior year. There is an early decision plan. Early decision applications should be filed by December 1; regular applications, by January 15 for fall entry and October 15 for spring entry, along with a $25 fee. Notification of early decision is sent January 1; regular decision, April 1. 108 early decision candidates were accepted for the 2001-2002 class. 9% of all applicants are on a waiting list; 18 were accepted in 2001.

Transfer: 71 transfer students enrolled in 2001-2002. Transfer applicants with a minimum of 24 credits should have at least a 2.0 GPA. Those with fewer credits should have at least a 2.5 GPA. 38 credits of 128 must be completed at Saint Mary's.

Visiting: There are regularly scheduled orientations for prospective students, including group presentations, interaction with faculty and students, and campus tours. There are guides for informal visits and visitors may sit in on classes and stay overnight. To schedule a visit, contact the Admissions Office.

Financial Aid: In 2001-2002, 86% of all freshmen and 70% of continuing students received some form of financial aid. 30% of freshmen and 51% of continuing students received need-based aid. The average freshman award was $8817. Of that total, scholarships or need-based grants averaged $3850 ($8500 maximum); loans averaged $2625 ($19,840 maximum); work contracts averaged $1100 ($1500 maximum); and nonneed-based grants and waivers averaged $1242 ($10,000 maximum). 25% of undergraduates work part time. Average annual earnings from campus work are $1250. The average financial indebtedness of the 2001 graduate was $15,100. Saint Mary's is a member of CSS. The FAFSA is required. The fall application deadline is March 1.

International Students: There are 34 international students enrolled. They must score 550 on the written TOEFL and also take the SAT I or the ACT.

Computers: The mainframes are DEC MicroVAX 3100 and a DEC 6520. Students can use any of the 140 Pentium systems, 3 Mac workstations, or multimedia stand-alone workstations. Access to the Internet and e-mail is available. There are several computer labs on campus. All students may access the system during all lab hours. There are no time limits and no fees.

Graduates: In 2001, 357 bachelor's degrees were awarded. The most popular majors were biology (17%), economics (16%), and political science (10%). In an average class, 1% graduate in 3 years, 67% in 4 years, 81% in 5 years, and 72% in 6 years. 78 companies recruited on campus in 2000-2001. Of the 2000 graduating class, 29% were enrolled in graduate school within 6 months of graduation and 96% were employed.

Admissions Contact: Richard Edgar, Director of Admissions. A video is available. E-mail: *admissions@smcm.edu*
Web: *http://www.smcm.edu*

SALISBURY UNIVERSITY — F-4
Salisbury, MD 21801 — **(410) 543-6161; Fax: (410) 546-6016**

Full-time: 2295 men, 2985 women	**Faculty:** 291; IIA, -$
Part-time: 333 men, 447 women	**Ph.D.s:** 75%
Graduate: 174 men, 448 women	**Student/Faculty:** 18 to 1
Year: 4-1-4, summer session	**Tuition:** $4486 ($9942)
Application Deadline: January 15	**Room & Board:** $6090
Freshman Class: 4978 applied, 2598 accepted, 942 enrolled	
SAT I Verbal/Math: 550/570	**VERY COMPETITIVE**

Salisbury University, formerly Salisbury State University, founded in 1925, is a public comprehensive university providing undergraduate programs in the liberal arts, sciences, preprofessional and professional programs, and select, mostly applied, graduate programs in business, education, nursing, psychology, English, and history. There are 4 undergraduate schools and 1 graduate school. In addition to regional accreditation, SU has baccalaureate program accreditation with AACSB, ACS, CAAHEP, CSWE, NAACLS, NCATE, NEHSPAC, and NLN. The library contains 251,991 volumes, 720,426 microform items, and 10,638 audiovisual forms/CDs, and subscribes to 1678 periodicals. Computerized library services include the card catalog, interlibrary loans, and database searching. Special learning facilities include a learning resource center, art gallery, radio station, TV station, Research Center for Delmarva History and Culture, Enterprise Development Group, Shorecan Small Business Resources Center, and Scarborough Leadership Center. The 140-acre campus is in a small town 110 miles southeast of Baltimore and 100 miles east of Washington, D.C. Including residence halls, there are 43 buildings.

Student Life: 82% of undergraduates are from Maryland. Others are from 38 states, 37 foreign countries, and Canada. 80% are from public schools. 88% are white. The average age of freshmen is 18; all undergraduates, 23. 18% do not continue beyond their first year.

Housing: 1701 students can be accommodated in college housing, which includes single-sex and coed dormitories and off-campus apartments. In addition, there are 2 international houses. On-campus housing is available on a first-come, first-served basis and is available on a lottery system for upperclassmen. 68% of students commute. Upperclassmen may keep cars.

Activities: 5% of men belong to 4 national fraternities; 6% of women belong to 4 national sororities. There are 104 groups on campus, including art, band, cheerleading, chess, choir, chorale, chorus, computers, dance, drama, ethnic, film, gay, honors, international, jazz band, literary magazine, musical theater, newspaper, orchestra, pep band, political, professional, radio and TV, religious, social, social service, student government, symphony, and yearbook. Popular campus events include October Fest, Spring Fling, and Festival of Culture.

Sports: There are 9 intercollegiate sports for men and 10 for women, and 22 intramural sports for men and 22 for women. Facilities include a 3000-seat stadium, a 2000-seat gym, a multipurpose gym, a 25-meter, 6-lane swimming pool, indoor climbing walls, a dance studio, racquetball and indoor and outdoor tennis courts, a baseball diamond, varsity and practice fields, an all-weather track, a Nautilus center, a strength room, lighted intramural fields, outdoor sand volleyball courts, and soccer fields.

Disabled Students: 90% of the campus is accessible. Wheelchair ramps, elevators, special parking, specially equipped rest rooms, special class scheduling, lowered drinking fountains, and lowered telephones are available. All emergency phones meet ADA standards.

Services: Counseling and information services are available, as is tutoring in some subjects. There is a reader service for the blind, remedial math, reading, and writing, and extended test-taking time.

Campus Safety and Security: Measures include 24-hour foot and vehicle patrol, self-defense education, escort service, and shuttle buses. There are informal discussions, pamphlets/posters/films, emergency telephones, and lighted pathways/sidewalks.

Programs of Study: SU confers B.A., B.S., B.A.S.W., and B.F.A. degrees. Master's degrees are also awarded. Bachelor's degrees are awarded in BIOLOGICAL SCIENCE (biology/biological science), BUSINESS (accounting, business administration and management, and management information systems), COMMUNICATIONS AND THE ARTS (art, communications, English, fine arts, French, music, Spanish, and theater management), COMPUTER AND PHYSICAL SCIENCE (chemistry, computer science, mathematics, and physics), EDUCATION (athletic training, elementary, health, and physical), HEALTH PROFESSIONS (environmental health science, nursing, and respiratory therapy), SOCIAL SCIENCE (economics, geography, history, interdisciplinary studies, peace studies, philosophy, political science/government, psychology, social work, and sociology). Chemistry, business, and social work are the strongest academically. Business administration, elementary education, and biology are the largest.

Required: Students must complete 45 semester hours of general education requirements, including specific courses in English composition and literature, world civilization, math, and phys ed. The bachelor's degree requires completion of at least 120 semester hours, including 30 or more in the major field, with a minimum GPA of 2.0. Some majors may have higher requirements. 30 of the last 37 credit hours must be completed at SU, except for special co-op programs.

Special: Cross-registration with schools in the University System of Maryland and study abroad in numerous countries are offered. SU also offers an Annapolis semester, a Washington semester, internships, work-study programs, accelerated degree programs in dentistry, optometry, podiatric medicine, and pharmacy, dual majors in biology/environmental marine science, social work/sociology, and engineering, interdisciplinary and student-designed majors including physics/microelectronics, a 3-2 engineering degree with the University of Maryland at College Park, Old Dominion University, and Widener University, a co-op program in electrical engineering, and pass/fail options. There are 20 national honor societies, a freshman honors program, and 15 departmental honors programs.

Faculty/Classroom: 62% of faculty are male; 38%, female. All teach undergraduates and 16% both teach and do research. No introductory courses are taught by graduate students. The average class size in an introductory lecture is 29 and in a laboratory, 23.

Admissions: 52% of the 2001-2002 applicants were accepted. The SAT I scores for the 2001-2002 freshman class were: Verbal--23% below 500, 54% between 500 and 599, 21% between 600 and 700, and 2% above 700; Math--16% below 500, 53% between 500 and 599, 29% between 600 and 700, and 2% above 700. 46% of the current freshmen were in the top fifth of their class; 96% were in the top two fifths. There were 3 National Merit finalists. 10 freshmen graduated first in their class.

Requirements: The SAT I is required. In addition, applicants must be graduates of accredited secondary schools or have earned a GED. The university requires 14 academic credits or 20 Carnegie units, including 4 in English, 3 each in math and social studies, 3 in science (2 with labs), and 2 in foreign language. Auditions are required for admission into the music and B.F.A. programs once admission to the university is granted. Essays are recommended but are not required. A campus visit is recommended for all students. A GPA of 2.0 is required. AP and CLEP credits are accepted. Important factors in the admissions decision are advanced placement or honor courses, leadership record, and extracurricular activities record. Applications are accepted on-line at the school's web site.

Procedure: Freshmen are admitted to all sessions. Entrance exams should be taken by November of the senior year. There are early decision and early admissions plans. Early decision applications should be filed by December 15; regular applications, by January 15 for fall entry and January 1 for spring entry. The fall 2001 application fee was $30. Notification of early decision is sent January 15; regular decision, March 15. 270 early decision candidates were accepted for the 2001-2002 class. 34% of all applicants are on a waiting list; 24 were accepted in 2001.

Transfer: 577 transfer students enrolled in 2001-2002. Applicants must present a minimum GPA of 2.0 in at least 24 transferable credit hours earned. Students with fewer than 24 credit hours must be eligible for freshman admission in addition to maintaining at least a 2.0 GPA in college courses. 30 credits of 120 to 125 must be completed at SU.

Visiting: There are regularly scheduled orientations for prospective students, including presentations, tours, meetings with faculty and staff, and Saturday open house programs. There are guides for informal visits and visitors may sit in on classes. To schedule a visit, contact the Admissions Office at (888) 543-0148.

Financial Aid: In 2001-2002, 63% of all freshmen and 65% of continuing students received some form of financial aid. 45% of freshmen and 60% of continuing students received need-based aid. The average freshman award was $4722. Of that total, scholarships or need-based grants averaged $3663; and loans averaged $2646. 30% of undergraduates work part time. Average annual earnings from campus work are $1500. The average financial indebtedness of the 2001 graduate was $15,206. The FAFSA is required. The fall application deadline is March 1.

International Students: There are 44 international students enrolled. They must score 550 on the written TOEFL or 213 on the electronic version and also take the SAT I.

Computers: The mainframes are a DEC VAX 4000-705A, a DEC ALPHA 2100-4/275, a cluster DEC VAX 8350, and a DEC VAX 6310. There are 24 VAX graphics-capable terminals connected to the mainframe that are available for student use. The University Center has 30 PCs networked to a server. In addition, there are 6 computer labs, each containing approximately 30 PCs using the Novell network with a MicroVAX as a server; a 19-station, networked Mac lab; 1850 residence hall ports; and an academic help room. 9 out of 12 dorms have ResNet services, which allow 2 computers and the phone to be used at the same time. In the general academic lab, scanning and color printing are available to all students. All students may access the system 24 hours daily via modem or in residence halls. There are no time limits and no fees. It is strongly recommended that all students have a personal computer.

Graduates: In 2001, 1285 bachelor's degrees were awarded. The most popular majors were business administration (14%), elementary education (12%), and communication arts (10%). In an average class, 50% graduate in 4 years, 67% in 5 years, and 71% in 6 years. 250 companies recruited on campus in 2000-2001. Of the 2000 graduating class, 27% were enrolled in graduate school within 6 months of graduation and 93% were employed.

Admissions Contact: Jane H. Dane, Dean of Enrollment Management. E-mail: *admissions@salisbury.edu*
Web: *http://www.salisbury.edu/admissions*

SOJOURNER-DOUGLASS COLLEGE — D-2
Baltimore, MD 21201 — **(410) 276-0306; Fax: (410) 675-1810**

Full-time: 40 men, 145 women	**Faculty:** 14
Part-time: 15 men, 40 women	**Ph.D.s:** 18%
Graduate: none	**Student/Faculty:** 13 to 1
Year: trimesters	**Tuition:** $4170
Application Deadline: open	**Room & Board:** n/app
Freshman Class: n/av	
SAT I or ACT: not required	**LESS COMPETITIVE**

Sojourner-Douglas College, established in 1980, is a private institution offering undergraduate programs in administration, human and social resources, and human growth and development to a predominantly black student body. Figures given in the above capsule are approximate. The library contains 20,000 volumes. Special learning facilities include a learning resource center. The campus is in an urban area in Baltimore.

Housing: There are no residence halls. All students commute. Alcohol is not permitted.

Activities: There are no fraternities or sororities. There are 5 groups on campus, including student government and yearbook.

Sports: There is no sports program at Sojourner-Douglass.

Disabled Students: Wheelchair ramps, elevators, and special parking are available.

Services: Counseling and information services are available, as is tutoring in some subjects, including reading, writing, math, and study skills.

Programs of Study: Sojourner-Douglass confers the B.A. degree. Bachelor's degrees are awarded in BUSINESS (business administration and management, and tourism), COMMUNICATIONS AND THE ARTS (broadcasting), EDUCATION (early childhood), HEALTH PROFESSIONS (health care administration), SOCIAL SCIENCE (criminal justice, gerontology, psychology, public administration, and social work).

Required: In order to graduate, students must earn 63 to 66 general education credits, with 15 credits in English literature and composition; 15 credits in political science, history, economics, sociology, geography, psychology, and anthropology; 12 credits in the humanities; 9 credits in natural science and math; and 3 credits each in career planning and personal development, psychology of the black family in America, and psychology of racism. 12 credits must be earned in a project that demonstrates competence in the major. 6 credits must be earned in the sociology of work. There is also a 3-credit education seminar requirement. A total of 132 credits is needed to graduate, with 54 to 69 in the major.

Special: Credit may be granted for life, military, and work experience. Faculty supervised independent study is possible for adult students.

Requirements: The SAT I or ACT is not required. Applicants must be graduates of an accredited secondary school or have a GED certificate. They must have completed 4 years of English and 2 years each of math, history, and social studies. Autobiographical essays, resumes, and interviews are required.

Procedure: Freshmen are admitted to all sessions. Application deadlines are open.

Transfer: Transfer criteria are the same as for entering freshmen; however, transfers are not accepted to all classes.

Visiting: There are regularly scheduled orientations for prospective students. To schedule a visit, contact the Office of Admissions at (410) 276-0306.

Financial Aid: The CSS/Profile, FAFSA, FFS, or SFS and Federal income tax form are required. Check with the school for current deadlines.

Computers: There are no time limits and no fees.

Admissions Contact: LaVerne B. Cawthorne, Coordinator of Admissions.

TOWSON UNIVERSITY
D-2

Towson, MD 21252-0001
(410) 704-2113
(888) 4-TOWSON; Fax: (410) 704-3030

Full-time: 4591 men, 7166 women
Faculty: 559; IIA, -$
Part-time: 965 men, 1237 women
Ph.D.s: n/av
Graduate: 763 men, 2258 women
Student/Faculty: 21 to 1
Year: semesters, summer session
Tuition: $4984 ($11,870)
Application Deadline: May 1
Room & Board: $6104
Freshman Class: 9402 applied, 5507 accepted, 1957 enrolled
SAT I: required
ACT: recommended
VERY COMPETITIVE

Towson University, founded in 1866, is part of the University System of Maryland and offers undergraduate and graduate programs in liberal arts and sciences, allied health sciences, education, fine arts, communication, and business and economics. There are 6 undergraduate schools and 1 graduate school. In addition to regional accreditation, Towson has baccalaureate program accreditation with AACSB, CAHEA, NASDTEC, NASM, and NLN. The library contains 547,072 volumes, 843,881 microform items, and 14,722 audiovisual forms/CDs, and subscribes to 3066 periodicals. Computerized library services include the card catalog, interlibrary loans, and database searching. Special learning facilities include a learning resource center, art gallery, planetarium, radio station, TV station, curriculum center, herbarium, animal museum, observatory, and greenhouse. The 321-acre campus is in a suburban area 2 miles north of Baltimore. Including residence halls, there are 40 buildings.

Student Life: 81% of undergraduates are from Maryland. Others are from 44 states, 95 foreign countries, and Canada. 65% are from public schools. 76% are white; 11% African American. The average age of freshmen is 18; all undergraduates, 22. 18% do not continue beyond their first year; 54% remain to graduate.

Housing: 3310 students can be accommodated in college housing, which includes coed dormitories, on-campus apartments, and married-student housing. In addition, there are honors houses, an international house, and separate alcohol-free, smoke-free, substance-free, quiet, leadership, or coed floors. On-campus housing is available on a first-come, first-served basis and is available on a lottery system for upperclassmen. Priority is given to out-of-town students. 75% of students commute. Upperclassmen may keep cars.

Activities: 7% of men belong to 18 national fraternities; 6% of women belong to 13 national sororities. There are 105 groups on campus, including art, band, cheerleading, choir, chorale, chorus, computers, dance, debate, drama, ethnic, forensics, gay, honors, international, jazz band, literary magazine, marching band, musical theater, newspaper, orchestra, pep band, political, professional, radio and TV, religious, social, social service, student government, symphony, and yearbook. Popular campus events include fraternity and sorority dances, Ethics Forum, and Tiger Fest.

Sports: There are 10 intercollegiate sports for men and 11 for women, and 10 intramural sports for men and 10 for women. Facilities include an athletic center, a stadium with artificial turf, baseball and softball fields, tennis courts, a pool, a soccer field, and 3 practice fields. Recreation facilities include 3 gyms, a weight room, a pool, lighted playing fields, and an indoor climbing wall.

Disabled Students: 85% of the campus is accessible. Wheelchair ramps, elevators, special parking, specially equipped rest rooms, special class scheduling, lowered drinking fountains, lowered telephones, automatic doors, specially equipped apartments and dormitory rooms, assistive listening devices in theaters and concert halls, and interior and exterior signage are available.

Services: Counseling and information services are available, as is tutoring in most subjects. There is a reader service for the blind, and remedial math, reading, and writing. There are also note takers, English language and tutorial services centers, a writing lab, and signers for the hearing impaired.

Campus Safety and Security: Measures include 24-hour foot and vehicle patrol, self-defense education, escort service, and shuttle buses. There are informal discussions, pamphlets/posters/films, emergency telephones, lighted pathways/sidewalks, Operation ID, and a police dog on campus.

Programs of Study: Towson confers B.A., B.S., B.F.A., and B.M. degrees. Master's and doctoral degrees are also awarded. Bachelor's degrees are awarded in BIOLOGICAL SCIENCE (biology/biological science and molecular biology), BUSINESS (accounting, business administration and management, electronic business, and sports management), COMMUNICATIONS AND THE ARTS (art, communications, dance, English, French, German, media arts, music, Spanish, and theater design), COMPUTER AND PHYSICAL SCIENCE (chemistry, computer science, earth science, geology, geoscience, information sciences and systems, mathematics, and physics), EDUCATION (art, athletic training, dance, early childhood, education, education of the deaf and hearing impaired, elementary, music, physical, and special), ENGINEERING AND ENVIRONMENTAL DESIGN (environmental science), HEALTH PROFESSIONS (exercise science, health care administration, health science, medical laboratory technology, nursing, occupational therapy, speech pathology/audiology, and sports medicine), SOCIAL SCIENCE (anthropology, crosscultural studies, economics, family/consumer studies, geography, gerontology, history, interdisciplinary studies, international studies, law, philosophy, political science/government, psychology, religion, social science, sociology, and women's studies). Fine arts, business, and education are the strongest academically. Business disciplines, mass communications, and psychology are the largest.

Required: Students must complete course work in the arts, English, humanities, math, biological or physical science, social science, information technology, and global awareness.

Special: Towson University offers cooperative programs with other institutions in the University System of Maryland and at Loyola College, the College of Notre Dame, or Johns Hopkins University, cross-registration at more than 80 colleges through the National Student Exchange, and study abroad. Students may pursue a dual major in physics and engineering, an interdisciplinary studies degree, which allows them to design their own majors, a 3-2 engineering program with the University of Maryland at College Park, or nondegree study. There are pass/fail options, extensive evening offerings, and opportunities to earn credits between semesters. Internships are available in most majors, and work-study programs are offered both on and off campus. There are 20 national honor societies, a freshman honors program, and 12 departmental honors programs.

Faculty/Classroom: 56% of faculty are male; 44%, female. The average class size in an introductory lecture is 25; in a laboratory, 24; and in a regular course, 25.

Admissions: 59% of the 2001-2002 applicants were accepted. The SAT I scores for the 2001-2002 freshman class were: Verbal--25% below 500, 55% between 500 and 599, 19% between 600 and 700, and 2% above 700; Math--20% below 500, 57% between 500 and 599, 22% between 600 and 700, and 2% above 700.

Requirements: The SAT I is required, generally with a composite score of 1100. The ACT is recommended and will be accepted in lieu of the SAT I. Applicants should have graduated from an accredited secondary school or earned the GED. Secondary preparation should include 4 years of English, 3 each of math, lab science, and social studies, and 2 of foreign language. Prospective music and dance majors must audition. AP and CLEP credits are accepted. Important factors in the admissions decision are advanced placement or honor courses, recommendations by school officials, and leadership record. Applications are accepted on-line via Towson's web site

Procedure: Freshmen are admitted fall and spring. Entrance exams should be taken in the junior and senior year. There is a deferred admissions plan. Applications should be filed by May 1 for fall entry and December 1 for spring entry. The fall 2001 application fee was $35. Notification is sent on a rolling basis.

Transfer: 1864 transfer students enrolled in 2001-2002. Transfer applicants should have earned at least 30 academic credits. For those with less than 30 attempted, freshman requirements must be met. Minimum GPA requirements range from 2.0 to 2.5, depending on the number of credits completed. 30 credits of 120 must be completed at Towson.

Visiting: There are regularly scheduled orientations for prospective students, including campus tours, a session for parents, a session on the admissions process for transfers and freshmen, and a roundtable discussion. There are guides for informal visits. To schedule a visit, contact the Admissions Office.

Financial Aid: In 2001-2002, 73% of all freshmen and 69% of continuing students received some form of financial aid. 41% of freshmen and 39% of continuing students received need-based aid. The average freshman award was $5439. Of that total, scholarships or need-based grants averaged $2834; and loans averaged $4408. 72% of undergraduates work part time. Average annual earnings from campus work are $1185. The average financial indebtedness of the 2001 graduate was $15,836. Towson is a member of CSS. The FAFSA is required. The fall application deadline is February 15.

International Students: There are 430 international students enrolled. The school actively recruits these students. The TOEFL is required at preadmission, with a minimum score of 500; a college test is required at postadmission. The SAT I or ACT is also required, but the school accepts the TOEFL as a substitute for the verbal SAT I (the minimum score on the math portion of te SAT I is 550). Graduates of the campus English language center are not required to take the TOEFL.

Computers: The mainframes are a 3 SGI Challenge/IRIX systems, 2 DEC VAX/VMS systems, and 2 DEC 5200/Ultrix systems. Each student receives a computer account that provides e-mail, personal web pages, and access to UNIX System software. There are 65 labs on campus with 1208 total workstations, including 1009 PCs, 133 Macs, and 22 UNIX workstations. Systems are accessible 24 hours daily except 5 P.M. to 9 P.M. Fridays. There are no time limits and no fees.

Graduates: In 2001, 2608 bachelor's degrees were awarded. The most popular majors were business administration (16%), mass communication (14%), and psychology (9%). In an average class, 27% graduate in 4 years, and 56% in 6 years. 115 companies recruited on campus in 2000-2001.

Admissions Contact: Louise Shulack, Director of Admissions. A video is available. E-mail: *admissions@towson.edu* Web: *www.towson.edu*

UNITED STATES NAVAL ACADEMY E-3
Annapolis, MD 21402-5018 (410) 293-4361
(800) 638-9156; Fax: (410) 293-4348

Full-time: 3500 men, 600 women	**Faculty:** 600; IIB, ++$
Part-time: none	**Ph.D.s:** 90%
Graduate: none	**Student/Faculty:** 7 to 1
Year: semesters, summer session	**Tuition:** 0
Application Deadline: open	**Room & Board:** 0
Freshman Class: n/av	
SAT I or ACT: required	**MOST COMPETITIVE**

The United States Naval Academy, founded in 1845, is a national military service college offering undergraduate degree programs and professional training in aviation, surface ships, submarines, and various military, maritime, and technical fields. The U.S. Navy pays tuition, room and board, medical and dental care, and a monthly stipend to all Naval Academy students. Figures given the above capsule are approximate. In addition to regional accreditation, Annapolis has baccalaureate program accreditation with ABET and CSAB. The library contains 530,000 volumes, and subscribes to 2000 periodicals. Computerized library services include the card catalog, interlibrary loans, and database searching. Special learning facilities include a learning resource center, art gallery, planetarium, radio station, TV station, a propulsion laboratory, a nuclear reactor, an oceanographic research vessel, towing tanks, a flight simulator, and a naval history museum. The 329-acre campus is in a small town 30 miles southeast of Baltimore and 35 miles east of Washington, D.C. Including residence halls, there are 25 buildings.

Student Life: 97% of undergraduates are from out of state, mostly the Northeast. Others are from 49 states and 21 foreign countries. 80% are white. 50% are Protestant; 49% Catholic. The average age of freshmen is 18; all undergraduates, 20. 11% do not continue beyond their first year; 77% remain to graduate.

Housing: 4100 students can be accommodated in college housing, which includes coed dormitories. On-campus housing is guaranteed for all 4 years. All students live on campus; of those, 75% remain on campus on weekends. Alcohol is not permitted. Upperclassmen may keep cars.

Activities: There are no fraternities or sororities. There are 75 groups on campus, including bagpipe band, cheerleading, chess, choir, chorus, computers, debate, drama, drill team, drum and bugle corps, ethnic, honors, international, jazz band, literary magazine, musical theater, pep band, photography, professional, radio and TV, religious, social, social service, student government, and yearbook. Popular campus events include Commissioning Week, which includes the Plebe Recognition Ceremony, Ring Dance, and graduation.

Sports: There are 20 intercollegiate sports for men and 9 for women, and 23 intramural sports for men and 10 for women. Facilities include a 30,000-seat stadium, a 5000-seat basketball arena, an Olympic pool with a diving well for 10-meter diving boards, a wrestling arena, a 200-meter indoor track, a 400-meter outdoor track, an indoor ice rink, 6 Nautilus and weight rooms, and facilities for gymnastics, boxing, fencing, and other sports.

Disabled Students: All of the campus is accessible. Wheelchair ramps, elevators, special parking, and specially equipped rest rooms are available.

Services: Counseling and information services are available, as is tutoring in most subjects. There is remedial math, reading, and writing.

Campus Safety and Security: Measures include 24-hour foot and vehicle patrol, self-defense education, shuttle buses, and emergency telephones. There are lighted pathways/sidewalks and gate guards.

Programs of Study: Annapolis confers the B.S. degree. Bachelor's degrees are awarded in COMMUNICATIONS AND THE ARTS (English), COMPUTER AND PHYSICAL SCIENCE (chemistry, computer science, mathematics, oceanography, physics, and science), ENGINEERING AND ENVIRONMENTAL DESIGN (aeronautical engineering, electrical/electronics engineering, engineering, marine engineering, mechanical engineering, naval architecture and marine engineering, ocean engineering, and systems engineering), SOCIAL SCIENCE (economics, history, and political science/government). Chemistry, aeronautical engineering, and systems engineering are the strongest academically. Mechanical engineering, math, and oceanography are the largest.

Required: Students must complete 140 semester hours, including core requirements in engineering, natural sciences, humanities, and social sciences. Phys ed is required during all 4 years. Physical readiness testing must be passed. During required summer training sessions, students train aboard U.S. ships, submarines, and aircraft. Graduates serve at least 5 years on active duty as commissioned officers of the Navy or Marine Corps.

Special: Study in Washington, D.C., is available during 1 semester of the senior year. A voluntary graduate program is available for those who complete requirements early and wish to begin master's work at nearby institutions, such as Georgetown or Johns Hopkins universities. Trident Scholars may spend their senior year in independent research. There are 10 national honor societies, and 5 departmental honors programs.

Faculty/Classroom: 80% of faculty are male; 20%, female. All teach undergraduates. The average class size in an introductory lecture is 23; in a laboratory, 10; and in a regular course, 15.

Requirements: The SAT I or ACT is required. In addition, candidates must be unmarried with no dependents, U.S. citizens of good moral character, and between 17 and 23 years of age. Candidates should have a sound secondary school background, including 4 years each of English and math, 2 years of a foreign language, and 1 year each of U.S. history, world or European history, chemistry, physics, and computer literacy. Candidates must obtain an official nomination from congressional or military sources. An interview is conducted, and medical and physical examinations must be passed in order to qualify for admission. AP credits are accepted. Important factors in the admissions decision are advanced placement or honor courses, recommendations by school officials, and leadership record.

Procedure: Freshmen are admitted in the summer. Entrance exams should be taken after December of the junior year. Application deadlines are open.

Transfer: All students enter as freshmen. All of the required 140 credits must be completed at Annapolis.

Visiting: There are regularly scheduled orientations for prospective students, including visitation weekends for candidates likely to be accepted, summer seminars, and Admissions Day. Visitors may sit in on classes.

International Students: Students must take the TOEFL and also take the SAT I or the ACT.

Computers: The mainframe is a Honeywell DPS8. There are also 1500 PCs available in the dorm, library, computer center, and computer lab. All students may access the system. There are no time limits and no fees.

Admissions Contact: Candidate Guidance Office.
Web: *www.nadn.navy.mil*

UNIVERSITY OF MARYLAND/BALTIMORE COUNTY D-2
Baltimore, MD 21250 (410) 455-2291
(800) UMBC-4U2; Fax: (410) 455-1094

Full-time: 3806 men, 3766 women	**Faculty:** 446; I, --$
Part-time: 888 men, 868 women	**Ph.D.s:** 85%
Graduate: 811 men, 1098 women	**Student/Faculty:** 17 to 1
Year: 4-1-4, summer session	**Tuition:** $5910 ($11,290)
Application Deadline: March 15	**Room & Board:** $6280
Freshman Class: 5282 applied, 3460 accepted, 1360 enrolled	
SAT I Verbal/Math: 590/610	**ACT:** 23 **VERY COMPETITIVE**

University of Maryland/Baltimore County, founded in 1966, is a public research university offering programs in liberal arts and sciences and engineering. There are 3 undergraduate and 2 graduate schools. In addition to regional accreditation, UMBC has baccalaureate program accreditation with ABET, CSWE, and NCATE. The library contains 749,618 volumes, 1,036,790 microform items, and 39,007 audiovisual forms/CDs, and subscribes to 4282 periodicals. Computerized library services include the card catalog, interlibrary loans, and database searching. Special learning facilities include a learning resource center, art gallery, radio station, centers for imaging research, earth systems technology, and telecommunications research, and institutes for medicine and policy analysis and research. The 530-acre campus is in a suburban area 5 miles southwest of Baltimore. Including residence halls, there are 50 buildings.

Student Life: 87% of undergraduates are from Maryland. Others are from 39 states, 80 foreign countries, and Canada. 84% are from public schools. 56% are white; 16% African American; 16% Asian American. The average age of freshmen is 18; all undergraduates, 23. 18% do not continue beyond their first year; 50% remain to graduate.

Housing: 2906 students can be accommodated in college housing, which includes single-sex and coed dormitories and on-campus apartments. In addition, there are honors houses, language houses, wellness and quiet-study floors, and same-sex floors. On-campus housing is guaranteed for the freshman year only and is available on a first-come, first-served basis. 62% of students commute. Alcohol is not permitted. All students may keep cars.

Activities: 3% of men belong to 11 national fraternities; 3% of women belong to 8 national sororities. There are 167 groups on campus, including band, cheerleading, chess, choir, chorus, computers, Council of Majors, dance, debate, drama, ethnic, film, gay, honors, Intellectual Sports Council, international, jazz band, literary magazine, Model United Nations, musical theater, newspaper, opera, orchestra, pep band, political, professional, radio and TV, religious, social, social service, student government, and symphony. Popular campus events include Quadmania, Greek Week, and Gospel Extravaganza.

Sports: There are 10 intercollegiate sports for men and 12 for women, and 16 intramural sports for men and 16 for women. Facilities include a multipurpose arena, an aquatic center, a fitness center, tennis courts, a 4500-seat stadium, playing and practice fields, an indoor track, an outdoor cross-country course, a golf driving range, a track and field complex, and a soccer stadium.

Disabled Students: 95% of the campus is accessible. Wheelchair ramps, elevators, special parking, specially equipped rest rooms, special class scheduling, lowered drinking fountains, lowered telephones, a braille writer, tape recorders, talking book machines, TTY, talking calculators, Optacon, and information on the talking computer are available.

Services: Counseling and information services are available, as is tutoring in most subjects. There is a reader service for the blind, and remedial math, reading, and writing. Other services include note takers, readers, mobility training, American Sign Language interpreters, and scribes for students who have a need based on a manual or learning disability.

Campus Safety and Security: Measures include self-defense education, escort service, shuttle buses, and pamphlets/posters/films. There are emergency telephones, lighted pathways/sidewalks, a 24-hour police department, and a campus risk management department.

Programs of Study: UMBC confers B.A., B.S., and B.S.E. degrees. Master's and doctoral degrees are also awarded. Bachelor's degrees are awarded in BIOLOGICAL SCIENCE (biochemistry and biology/biological science), COMMUNICATIONS AND THE ARTS (dance, dramatic arts, English, fine arts, French, German, linguistics, modern language, music, Russian, Spanish, theater design, and visual and performing arts), COMPUTER AND PHYSICAL SCIENCE (chemistry, computer science, information sciences and systems, mathematics, and physics), ENGINEERING AND ENVIRONMENTAL DESIGN (chemical engineering, computer engineering, and mechanical engineering), HEALTH PROFESSIONS (emergency medical technologies and health science), SOCIAL SCIENCE (African American studies, American studies, anthropology, classical/ancient civilization, crosscultural studies, economics, geography, history, interdisciplinary studies, philosophy, political science/government, psychology, social work, and sociology). Chemistry, biology, and engineering are the strongest academically. Information systems, computer science, and biological sciences are the largest.

Required: To graduate, students are required to complete at least 120 credits, including 45 at the upper-division level, with a minimum GPA of 2.0. The core curriculum includes courses in arts and humanities, social sciences, math and natural sciences, phys ed, and modern or classical language and culture. Students must pass an English composition course with a C or better.

Special: Dual and student-designed majors, cooperative education programs in all majors, a Washington semester, the Public Affairs Scholars Program, cross-registration with University of Maryland schools and Johns Hopkins University, internships, both paid and nonpaid, in public, private, and nonprofit organizations, study abroad in 19 countries, work-study programs, B.A.-B.S. degrees, pass/fail options, and nondegree study are available. UMBC also offers various opportunities in interdisciplinary studies and in such fields as artificial intelligence and optical communications. There are 15 national honor societies, including Phi Beta Kappa, a freshman honors program, and 17 departmental honors programs.

Faculty/Classroom: 63% of faculty are male; 37%, female. The average class size in an introductory lecture is 39; in a laboratory, 18; and in a regular course, 26.

Admissions: 66% of the 2001-2002 applicants were accepted. The SAT I scores for the 2001-2002 freshman class were: Verbal--11% below 500, 43% between 500 and 599, 37% between 600 and 700, and 9% above 700; Math--4% below 500, 38% between 500 and 599, 44% between 600 and 700, and 14% above 700. The ACT scores were 16% below 21, 34% between 21 and 23, 23% between 24 and 26, 10% between 27 and 28, and 17% above 28. 53% of the current freshmen were in the top fifth of their class; 79% were in the top two fifths. There were 4 National Merit finalists.

Requirements: The SAT I or ACT is required. In addition, minimum high school preparation should include 4 years of English, 3 each of social science/history and math, including algebra I and II and geometry, 3 of lab sciences, and 2 of a foreign language. An essay is required of all freshman applicants. A GPA of 2.5 is required. AP and CLEP credits are accepted. Important factors in the admissions decision are advanced placement or honor courses, recommendations by school officials, and leadership record. Applications are accepted on-line at the school's web site through CollegeNET.

Procedure: Freshmen are admitted to all sessions. Entrance exams should be taken by the fall of the senior year. Applications should be filed by March 15 for fall entry, December 1 for winter entry, December 15 for spring entry, and May 15 for summer entry, along with a $45 fee. Notification is sent beginning in February. 8% of all applicants are on a waiting list; 25 were accepted in 2001.

Transfer: 1139 transfer students enrolled in 2001-2002. A 2.5 cumulative GPA for all previous college work is recommended. Applicants with fewer than 30 semester hours should submit SAT I scores and the high school transcript; they must also meet freshman admission requirements. 30 credits of 120 must be completed at UMBC.

Visiting: There are regularly scheduled orientations for prospective students, including a group information session with an admissions counselor followed by a student-guided walking tour of campus. Saturday information sessions and 4 campus open houses are also scheduled each fall. There are guides for informal visits and visitors may sit in on classes and stay overnight. To schedule a visit, contact the Admissions Office.

Financial Aid: In a recent year, 68% of all freshmen and 64% of continuing students received some form of financial aid. 49% of freshmen and 42% of continuing students received need-based aid. The average freshman award was $6000. Of that total, scholarships or need-based grants averaged $3000 ($16,000 maximum); loans averaged $2500 ($10,500 maximum); and work contracts averaged $500 ($1600 maximum). 7% of undergraduates work part time. Average annual earnings from campus work are $820. The average financial indebtedness of a recent year's graduate was $12,000. The FAFSA is required. The fall application deadline is March 1.

International Students: There are 393 international students enrolled. They must score 213 on the electronic TOEFL.

Computers: UMBC's network consists of 10 Sun and SGI Unix servers. Many of UMBC's research projects rely on high-end computers such as the Silicon Graphics. Challenge XL 20-processor supercomputer. UMBC has approximately 3,000 computers on campus, all of which have access to the Internet and the Web. Roughly 700 of these are available to students. These include more than 140 Silicon Graphics machines, 220 Macs, 20 Sun Workstations, and 300 PCs. The campus also has 120 modems for resident students and 300 modems for off-campus access. All students may access the system. There are no time limits and no fees.

Graduates: In 2001, 1606 bachelor's degrees were awarded. The most popular majors were information systems (20%), psychology (11%), and computer science (9%). In an average class, 31% graduate in 4 years, 48% in 5 years, and 52% in 6 years. 997 companies recruited on campus in 2000-2001. Of the 1999 graduating class, 35% were enrolled in graduate school within 1 year of graduation and 93% were employed.

Admissions Contact: Yvette Mozie-Ross, Director of Admissions.
E-mail: *admissions@umbc.edu* Web: *http://www.umbc.edu*

UNIVERSITY OF MARYLAND/COLLEGE PARK — D-3

College Park, MD 20742 (301) 314-8385
(800) 422-5867; Fax: (301) 314-9693

Full-time: 11,375 men, 10,919 women	**Faculty:** 1537; I, av$
Part-time: 1200 men, 955 women	**Ph.D.s:** 88%
Graduate: 4317 men, 3981 women	**Student/Faculty:** 15 to 1
Year: semesters, summer session	**Tuition:** $5341 ($13,413)
Application Deadline: February 15	**Room & Board:** $6618
Freshman Class: 19,668 applied, 10,819 accepted, 4380 enrolled	
SAT I or ACT: required	**COMPETITIVE**

University of Maryland/College Park, founded in 1856, is a land-grant institution, the flagship campus of the state's university system, offering undergraduate and graduate degrees. There are 11 undergraduate and 13 graduate schools. In addition to regional accreditation, Maryland has baccalaureate program accreditation with AACSB, ABET, ACEJMC, ASLA, CACREP, CSWE, NAAB, NASM, and NCATE. The 7 libraries contain 2,897,466 volumes, 5,423,534 microform items, and 249,076 audiovisual forms/CDs, and subscribe to 33,310 periodicals. Computerized library services include the card catalog, interlibrary loans, and database searching. Special learning facilities include a learning resource center, art gallery, radio station, TV station, and an observatory. The 1203-

acre campus is in a suburban area 3 miles northeast of Washington, D.C., and 35 miles south of Baltimore. Including residence halls, there are 340 buildings.

Student Life: 74% of undergraduates are from Maryland. Others are from 49 states, 154 foreign countries, and Canada. 60% are white; 14% Asian American; 13% African American. 37% are Catholic; 30% Protestant; 20% Jewish; 13% Protestant including Baptist, United Methodist, Presbyterian, Lutheran, Espiscopal. The average age of freshmen is 18; all undergraduates, 21. 9% do not continue beyond their first year; 66% remain to graduate.

Housing: 8541 students can be accommodated in college housing, which includes single-sex and coed dormitories, on-campus apartments, fraternity houses, and sorority houses. In addition, there are honors houses, language houses, special-interest houses, an international house, a Civicus house, and a College Park Scholars house. On-campus housing is guaranteed for all 4 years. Alcohol is not permitted. Upperclassmen may keep cars.

Activities: 9% of men belong to 28 national fraternities; 9% of women belong to 21 national sororities. There are 364 groups on campus, including art, band, cheerleading, chess, choir, chorale, chorus, computers, dance, debate, drama, drill team, ethnic, film, forensics, gay, honors, international, jazz band, literary magazine, marching band, musical theater, newspaper, opera, orchestra, pep band, photography, political, professional, radio and TV, religious, social, social service, student government, symphony, and yearbook. Popular campus events include Panhellenic Council Step Show, Handel Festival, and Art Attack.

Sports: There are 12 intercollegiate sports for men and 13 for women, and 60 intramural sports for men and 16 for women. Facilities include 2 indoor and 2 outdoor swimming pools, intramural fields, tennis, squash, racquetball, and basketball courts, a fitness center, a track, a bowling alley, a 50,000-seat stadium, a 14,500-seat gym, and a golf course.

Disabled Students: 95% of the campus is accessible. Wheelchair ramps, elevators, special parking, specially equipped rest rooms, special class scheduling, lowered drinking fountains, lowered telephones, a special shuttle service, and electronic doors are available.

Services: Counseling and information services are available, as is tutoring in most subjects, including all 100- and 200-level courses. There is a reader service for the blind and remedial math.

Campus Safety and Security: Measures include 24-hour foot and vehicle patrol, self-defense education, escort service, and shuttle buses. There are informal discussions, pamphlets/posters/films, emergency telephones, lighted pathways/sidewalks, and video surveillance.

Programs of Study: Maryland confers B.A., B.S., B.L.A., and B.M. degrees. Master's and doctoral degrees are also awarded. Bachelor's degrees are awarded in AGRICULTURE (agricultural business management, agricultural economics, agriculture, agronomy, animal science, conservation and regulation, horticulture, natural resource management, and plant science), BIOLOGICAL SCIENCE (biochemistry, biology/biological science, cell biology, genetics, marine biology, microbiology, nutrition, and zoology), BUSINESS (accounting, banking and finance, business administration and management, human resources, international business management, international economics, management information systems, marketing management, and operations research), COMMUNICATIONS AND THE ARTS (art history and appreciation, Chinese, classics, communications, dance, dramatic arts, English, French, Germanic languages and literature, Japanese, journalism, linguistics, music, music performance, romance languages and literature, Russian, Spanish, and studio art), COMPUTER AND PHYSICAL SCIENCE (astronomy, chemistry, computer science, geology, information sciences and systems, mathematics, physical sciences, and physics), EDUCATION (art, drama, early childhood, elementary, English, foreign languages, health, mathematics, music, physical, science, secondary, and special), ENGINEERING AND ENVIRONMENTAL DESIGN (aeronautical engineering, architecture, bioengineering, chemical engineering, civil engineering, computer engineering, electrical/electronics engineering, engineering, environmental science, fire protection engineering, landscape architecture/design, materials engineering, mechanical engineering, and nuclear engineering), HEALTH PROFESSIONS (preveterinary science), SOCIAL SCIENCE (African American studies, American studies, anthropology, criminal justice, criminology, dietetics, economics, family/consumer studies, food science, geography, history, Italian studies, Judaic studies, philosophy, physical fitness/movement, political science/government, psychology, Russian and Slavic studies, sociology, and women's studies). Engineering, computer science, and business are the strongest academically. Computer science, communication, and criminology and criminal justice are the largest.

Required: Most programs require a minimum of 120 credits for graduation; the number of hours required in the major varies. All students must take 43 to 46 credits in a multidisciplinary core curriculum, including 10 in math and science, 9 each in social sciences, and humanities and the arts, 6 in advanced studies, and 3 diversity credits. Freshman and junior composition are also required, and students must maintain a 2.0 GPA.

Special: Each of the 11 undergraduate schools offers special programs, and there is a campuswide cooperative education program offering engineering and other majors. In addition, the university offers cross-registration with other colleges in the Consortium of Universities of the Washington Metropolitan Area, the MD-VA Veterans Program, the B.A.-B.S. degree in most majors, dual and student-designed majors, nondegree study, an accelerated veterinary medicine program, study abroad in 20 countries, work-study programs with government and non-profit organizations, and internship opportunities with members of Congress and the Maryland State House, the local media, and various federal agencies. There are 51 national honor societies, including Phi Beta Kappa, a freshman honors program, and 39 departmental honors programs.

Faculty/Classroom: 65% of faculty are male; 35%, female. 59% teach undergraduates and 41% do research. Graduate students teach 19% of introductory courses. The average class size in an introductory lecture is 41; in a laboratory, 18; and in a regular course, 35.

Admissions: 55% of the 2001-2002 applicants were accepted. The SAT I scores for the 2001-2002 freshman class were: Verbal--7% below 500, 34% between 500 and 599, 45% between 600 and 700, and 14% above 700; Math--5% below 500, 22% between 500 and 599, 51% between 600 and 700, and 22% above 700. 83% of the current freshmen were in the top quarter of their class.

Requirements: The SAT I or ACT is required. In addition, the university evaluates exam scores along with GPA, curriculum, and other criteria. Applicants should be graduates of accredited secondary schools or have the GED. Secondary preparation should include 4 years of English, 3 of history or social sciences, 2 of algebra and 1 of plane geometry, and 2 of lab sciences. An essay and counselor recommendation are required. Music majors must also audition. AP and CLEP credits are accepted. Important factors in the admissions decision are advanced placement or honor courses, recommendations by school officials, and evidence of special talent. Applications may be submitted on-line.

Procedure: Freshmen are admitted fall, spring, and summer. Entrance exams should be taken at the end of the junior year or the beginning of the senior year. There are early decision and early admissions plans. Early decision applications should be filed by December 1; regular applications, by February 15 for fall entry and December 15 for spring entry. The fall 2001 application fee was $45. Notification of early decision is sent February 1; regular decision, on a rolling basis. 16% of all applicants are on a waiting list.

Transfer: 2123 transfer students enrolled in 2001-2002. Transfer applicants from regionally accredited institutions should have attempted at least 12 credits and have earned at least a 2.5 GPA, although this requirement varies depending on space available. Applicants from Maryland community colleges may be given special consideration. 30 credits of 120 must be completed at Maryland.

Visiting: There are regularly scheduled orientations for prospective students, consisting of an information session followed by a tour. There are guides for informal visits and visitors may sit in on classes and stay overnight. To schedule a visit, contact the Office of Undergraduate Admissions.

Financial Aid: In 2001-2002, 73% of all freshmen and 66% of continuing students received some form of financial aid. 35% of freshmen and 40% of continuing students received need-based aid. The average freshman award was $7016. Of that total, scholarships or need-based grants averaged $5344 ($19,799 maximum); loans averaged $3449 ($13,750 maximum); and federal work-study averaged $1280 ($4200 maximum). 5% of undergraduates work part time. Average annual earnings from campus work are $1280. The average financial indebtedness of the 2001 graduate was $14,076. The FAFSA is required. The fall application deadline is February 15.

International Students: There are 582 international students enrolled. They must score 575 on the written TOEFL or take the APIEL or ELPT.

Computers: The mainframe is an IBM 9672/RC4. There are 1600 PCs available for student use in academic buildings, computer centers and libraries, and residence halls are wired for PCs. IBM and Mac word-processing programs are available to all registered students. The Computer Science Center supports advanced workstation and PC labs across campus for day and evening self-study and class projects. All students may access the system 24 hours a day, 7 days a week. There are no time limits and no fees.

Graduates: In 2001, 5304 bachelor's degrees were awarded. The most popular majors were criminology and criminal justice (7%), computer science (5%), and finance (5%). In an average class, 33% graduate in 4 years, 59% in 5 years, and 64% in 6 years. 331 companies recruited on campus in 2000-2001.

Admissions Contact: Admissions Officer. A video is available.
E-mail: *um-admit@uga.umd.edu* Web: *www.maryland.edu*

UNIVERSITY OF MARYLAND/EASTERN SHORE F-4

Princess Anne, MD 21853 (410) 651-6410; Fax: (410) 651-7922

Full-time: 1145 men, 1436 women | **Faculty:** 90; IIA, --$
Part-time: 164 men, 389 women | **Ph.D.s:** 80%
Graduate: 152 men, 140 women | **Student/Faculty:** 29 to 1
Year: semesters, summer session | **Tuition:** $4128 ($8612)
Application Deadline: see profile | **Room & Board:** $5130
Freshman Class: 2498 applied, 1954 accepted, 787 enrolled
SAT I: required **COMPETITIVE**

University of Maryland/Eastern Shore, founded in 1886, is a public university, part of the University of Maryland System, offering undergraduate and graduate programs in the arts and sciences, professional studies, and agricultural sciences. Some information in this profile is approximate. There are 3 undergraduate schools and 1 graduate school. The library contains 150,000 volumes. Computerized library services include the card catalog, interlibrary loans, and database searching. Special learning facilities include a learning resource center, art gallery, and radio station. The 600-acre campus is in a rural area 15 miles south of Salisbury. Including residence halls, there are 40 buildings.

Student Life: 71% of undergraduates are from Maryland. Others are from 32 states, 48 foreign countries, and Canada. 85% are from public schools. 76% are African American; 18%, white. 90% are Protestant; 10% claim no religious affiliation. The average age of freshmen is 18; all undergraduates, 24. 25% do not continue beyond their first year; 36% remain to graduate.

Housing: 1530 students can be accommodated in college housing, which includes single-sex dormitories, on-campus apartments, and off-campus apartments. In addition, there are honors houses. On-campus housing is available on a first-come, first-served basis and is available on a lottery system for upperclassmen. 50% of students live on campus; of those, 30% remain on campus on weekends. All students may keep cars.

Activities: 20% of men belong to 4 national fraternities; 20% of women belong to 4 national sororities. There are 25 groups on campus, including art, band, cheerleading, choir, chorale, chorus, computers, dance, drama, drill team, ethnic, honors, international, jazz band, literary magazine, musical theater, newspaper, pep band, photography, political, professional, radio and TV, religious, social, social service, student government, and yearbook. Popular campus events include Parents Day, Spring Festival, and Ethnic Festival.

Sports: There are 5 intercollegiate sports for men and 5 for women, and 4 intramural sports for men and 4 for women. Facilities include an indoor swimming pool and a 3000-seat stadium.

Disabled Students: 20% of the campus is accessible. Wheelchair ramps, elevators, special parking, specially equipped rest rooms, special class scheduling, lowered drinking fountains, and lowered telephones are available.

Services: Counseling and information services are available, as is tutoring in every subject. There is remedial math, reading, and writing.

Campus Safety and Security: Measures include 24-hour foot and vehicle patrol, escort service, shuttle buses, and informal discussions. There are pamphlets/posters/films, emergency telephones, lighted pathways/sidewalks, and a student security team.

Programs of Study: UMES confers B.A., B.S., B.G.S., and B.M. degrees. Master's and doctoral degrees are also awarded. Bachelor's degrees are awarded in AGRICULTURE (agriculture and poultry science), BIOLOGICAL SCIENCE (biology/biological science), BUSINESS (accounting, business administration and management, and hotel/motel and restaurant management), COMMUNICATIONS AND THE ARTS (English), COMPUTER AND PHYSICAL SCIENCE (chemistry, computer science, and mathematics), EDUCATION (agricultural, art, business, elementary, health, home economics, industrial arts, mathematics, music, physical, science, secondary, and social science), ENGINEERING AND ENVIRONMENTAL DESIGN (aeronautical science, construction technology, engineering technology, and environmental science), HEALTH PROFESSIONS (physical therapy and rehabilitation therapy), SOCIAL SCIENCE (criminal justice, history, home economics, liberal arts/general studies, and sociology). Physical therapy, engineering, and environmental science are the strongest academically. Business, hotel and restaurant management, and biology are the largest.

Required: Students must complete 122 hours, including 36 hours in the major, 15 in communicative and quantitative skills, 9 in humanities, 7 in natural sciences, 6 in social sciences, and 4 in health and phys ed. A minimum 2.0 overall GPA is required.

Special: Students may cross-register at Salisbury State University. A cooperative education program, internships, a winter term, work-study programs, a general studies degree, and dual and student-designed majors are offered. Also available are an accelerated degree program and a 3-2 engineering degree with the University of Maryland/College Park. There are pass/fail options. There is 1 national honor society, a freshman honors program, and 10 departmental honors program.

Faculty/Classroom: 45% of faculty are male; 55%, female. 85% teach undergraduates and 15% do research. Graduate students teach 1% of introductory courses. The average class size in an introductory lecture is 75; in a laboratory, 18; and in a regular course, 30.

Admissions: 78% of the 2001-2002 applicants were accepted.

Requirements: The SAT I is required. In addition, applicants should be graduates of accredited secondary schools or have the GED. A GPA of 2.5 is required. High school preparation should include 4 years of English, 3 each of social science or history and math, including 2 of algebra and 1 of geometry, and 2 of laboratory science. An essay and interview are recommended. UMES recommends that prospective art education majors submit a portfolio. Students may earn credit by examination. AP and CLEP credits are accepted. Important factors in the admissions decision are advanced placement or honor courses, leadership record, and recommendations by school officials.

Procedure: Freshmen are admitted to all sessions. Entrance exams should be taken by April. There are early decision, early admissions, and deferred admissions plans. Check with the school for current application deadlines. The fall 2001 application fee was $25. Notification is sent on a rolling basis.

Transfer: Transfer applicants must have attempted at least 9 credits at another institution and have at least a cumulative GPA of 2.0, or have earned an associate degree or completed 56 hours of community college work. 75 credits of 122 must be completed at UMES.

Visiting: There are regularly scheduled orientations for prospective students, including 2 formal orientation sessions and 9 visitation/open house days. There are guides for informal visits and visitors may sit in on classes and stay overnight. To schedule a visit, contact the Office of Recruitment.

Financial Aid: In 2001-2002, 85% of all freshmen received some form of financial aid. UMES is a member of CSS. The college's own financial statement is required.

International Students: They must score 500 on the written TOEFL and also take the SAT I, scoring 800.

Computers: The mainframe is an IBM 4341. About 80 microcomputers are available in the library and various departments. There are no fees. It is strongly recommended that all students have a personal computer.

Admissions Contact: Cheryll Collier-Mills, Director of Admissions and Recruitment. E-mail: *ccmills@mail.umes.edu* Web: *www.umes.edu*

UNIVERSITY OF MARYLAND/UNIVERSITY COLLEGE D-3

Adelphi, MD 20783 (301) 985-7000
(800) 285-6832; Fax: (301) 985-7364

Full-time: 851 men, 1330 women | **Faculty:** 77
Part-time: 5870 men, 8011 women | **Ph.D.s:** 81%
Graduate: 3111 men, 3060 women | **Student/Faculty:** 28 to 1
Year: semesters, summer session | **Tuition:** $5910 ($10,920)
Application Deadline: open | **Room & Board:** n/app
Freshman Class: 3768 applied, 3768 accepted, 3717 enrolled
SAT I or ACT: not required **SPECIAL**

University of Maryland/University College was founded in 1947 to serve the needs of the adult continuing education student. It offers evening and weekend courses in the liberal arts and sciences and in business at more than 20 locations throughout the Washington, D.C.-Baltimore area and the state of Maryland. The library subscribes to 22 periodicals. Computerized library services include the card catalog, interlibrary loans, and database searching. Special learning facilities include an art gallery and TV station. The campus is in an urban area.

Student Life: 83% of undergraduates are from Maryland. Others are from 49 states, 65 foreign countries, and Canada. 48% are white; 31% African American. The average age of all undergraduates is 34.

Housing: There are no residence halls. All students commute. Alcohol is not permitted. All students may keep cars.

Activities: There are no fraternities or sororities.

Sports: There is no sports program at UMUC.

Services: Counseling and information services are available, as is tutoring in some subjects, including math, writing, accounting, and computing. Referrals are available for tutoring in other subjects. There are fees for tutoring. There is a reader service for the blind.

Campus Safety and Security: Measures include 24-hour foot and vehicle patrol and emergency telephones.

Programs of Study: UMUC confers B.A. and B.S. degrees. Associate and master's degrees are also awarded. Bachelor's degrees are awarded in BUSINESS (accounting, business administration and management, human resources, management science, and marketing management), COMMUNICATIONS AND THE ARTS (communications and English), COMPUTER AND PHYSICAL SCIENCE (computer science and information sciences and systems), ENGINEERING AND ENVIRONMENTAL DESIGN (computer technology and environmental science), SOCIAL SCIENCE (criminal justice, fire science, history, humanities, liberal arts/general studies, paralegal studies, psychology, and social science). Business has the largest enrollment.

Required: A general education requirement of 30 semester hours includes courses in communications, humanities, social sciences, and math/science. The B.A. degree requires 12 semester hours of a foreign language. A minimum 2.0 GPA and 120 credit hours are required to graduate.

Special: UMUC offers cooperative programs in interdisciplinary studies. There are a number of work-study programs with local employers. Credit by exam, credit for life/work experience, nondegree study, and pass/fail options are available. Through UMUC's open learning program, a number of independent learning courses, including telecourses, are available. There are 4 national honor societies.

Faculty/Classroom: 67% of faculty are male; 33%, female. All teach undergraduates. The average class size in a regular course is 24.

Admissions: All 2001-2002 applicants were accepted.

Requirements: Students should be graduates of an accredited secondary school or have a GED equivalent. AP and CLEP credits are accepted. Applications are accepted on-line via UMUC's home page.

Procedure: Freshmen are admitted to all sessions. Application deadlines are open. Application fee is $30. The college accepts all applicants. Notification is sent on a rolling basis.

Transfer: 2562 transfer students enrolled in 2001-2002. 30 credits of 120 must be completed at UMUC.

Financial Aid: The average financial indebtedness of the 2001 graduate was $1846. The FAFSA and SAR (for Pell grants) are required.

International Students: There are 92 international students enrolled. They must score 550 on the written TOEFL or 213 on the electronic version and also take the college's own test.

Computers: All students may access the system. There are no time limits and no fees.

Graduates: In 2001, 2157 bachelor's degrees were awarded. The most popular majors were business and management (21%), information systems management (14%), and computer and information science (13%).

Admissions Contact: Technical Director, Admission and Information. E-mail: *umucinfo@nova.umuc.edu* Web: *http://www.umuc.edu*

UNIVERSITY SYSTEM OF MARYLAND

The University System of Maryland, established in 1807, is a public system. It is governed by a board of regents whose chief administrator is the chancellor. The primary goals of the system are research, teaching, and public service, while each campus serves a special mission. The flagship institution is the University of Maryland, College Park, which holds the distinctive mission of enrolling the most academically talented students from the state and across the nation. The combined enrollment of all campuses in the USM is about 128,000; the total faculty for all campuses in nearly 10,000. Altogether the 13 USM institutions offer more than 600 academic programs leading to 31 undergraduate, master's, doctoral, and preprofessional degrees. More specific profiles for each campus are included in this section.

VILLA JULIE COLLEGE

Stevenson, MD 21153 D-2

(410) 486-7001

(877) 468-6852; Fax: (410) 602-6600

Full-time: 547 men, 1234 women	**Faculty:** 85
Part-time: 130 men, 465 women	**Ph.D.s:** 61%
Graduate: 46 men, 25 women	**Student/Faculty:** 21 to 1
Year: semesters, summer session	**Tuition:** $12,076
Application Deadline: March 1	**Room & Board:** $3950
Freshman Class: 1430 applied, 1202 accepted, 521 enrolled	
SAT I Verbal/Math: 518/517	**COMPETITIVE**

Villa Julie College, founded in 1947, is an independent, comprehensive college offering a liberal arts education combined with career preparation. In addition to regional accreditation, VJC has baccalaureate program accreditation with ABA, CAHEA, and NLN. The library contains 124,417 volumes, 141,646 microform items, and 2288 audiovisual forms/CDs, and subscribes to 720 periodicals. Computerized library services include the card catalog, interlibrary loans, and database searching. Special learning facilities include a learning resource center, art gallery, a theater, and video studio. The 60-acre campus is in a suburban area 10 miles northwest of Baltimore. There are 15 buildings.

Student Life: 97% of undergraduates are from Maryland. Others are from 7 states and 4 foreign countries. 76% are from public schools. 82% are white; 10% African American. 41% are claim no religious affiliation; 29% Catholic; 25% Protestant. The average age of freshmen is 18; all undergraduates, 24. 24% do not continue beyond their first year.

Housing: There are no residence halls. 301 students can be accommodated in college housing, which includes coed off-campus apartments. 83% of students commute. Alcohol is not permitted. All students may keep cars.

Activities: 22% of women belong to 1 national sorority. There are no fraternities. There are 30 groups on campus, including academic, art, band, cheerleading, chess, chorus, computers, drama, environmental, ethnic, gay, honors, jazz band, literary magazine, newspaper, pep band, political, professional, religious, service learning, social, social service, student government, and wilderness. Popular campus events include Welcome Picnic, art receptions, and BSU Latin Dance.

Sports: There are 9 intercollegiate sports for men and 10 for women, and 8 intramural sports for men and 8 for women. Facilities include tennis courts and an athletic field, a 1000-seat gym, a fitness center, a NATA-certified training room, and an aerobics room.

Disabled Students: 95% of the campus is accessible. Wheelchair ramps, elevators, special parking, specially equipped rest rooms, special class scheduling, lowered drinking fountains, and lowered telephones are available.

Services: Counseling and information services are available, as is tutoring in most subjects, including free individual tutoring as well as study groups led by a tutor, peer tutoring, paraprofessional tutoring, and faculty tutoring. There is remedial math, reading, and writing.

Campus Safety and Security: Measures include self-defense education, escort service, shuttle buses, and informal discussions. There are pamphlets/posters/films, emergency telephones, and lighted pathways/sidewalks. There are also 15-hour foot and vehicle patrols during VJC's operating hours.

Programs of Study: VJC confers B.A. and B.S. degrees. Associate and master's degrees are also awarded. Bachelor's degrees are awarded in BIOLOGICAL SCIENCE (biology/biological science and biotechnology), BUSINESS (business administration and management, and business systems analysis), COMMUNICATIONS AND THE ARTS (design and English), COMPUTER AND PHYSICAL SCIENCE (chemistry and information sciences and systems), HEALTH PROFESSIONS (nursing), SOCIAL SCIENCE (family/consumer studies, interdisciplinary studies, liberal arts/general studies, paralegal studies, and psychology). Liberal arts and technology, nursing, and paralegal are both the strongest academically and the largest.

Required: General college requirements include courses in writing and literature, history, communication and fine arts, philosophy and religion, social sciences, math, natural science, computer information systems, phys ed, and interdisciplinary patterns of thought. Students must complete a minimum of 120 hours, including 45 hours in upper-level courses, with at least a 2.0 overall GPA. The number of hours required per major varies. Many majors require a capstone course and an internship.

Special: A general studies program is offered, as is an interdisciplinary bachelor degree major. There are cooperative education programs in several majors as well as internships and independent study opportunities. A supervised working/learning experience offered to second-year students requires a minimum of 120 hours per semester. Students may earn credit by exam. Study abroad in 4 countries through programs offered at other colleges, a work-study program, student-designed majors, interdisciplinary majors, including liberal arts and technology, computer accounting, and business information systems, and education courses for state certification are available. Cross-registration with the Baltimore Student Exchange Program is available. B.A.-B.S. degrees are offered in biology, chemistry, psychology, and visual communication design. There are 6 national honor societies, a freshman honors program, and 7 departmental honors programs.

Faculty/Classroom: 48% of faculty are male; 52%, female. 99% teach undergraduates and 5% both teach and do research. No introductory courses are taught by graduate students. The average class size in an introductory lecture is 15; in a laboratory, 12; and in a regular course, 15.

Admissions: 84% of the 2001-2002 applicants were accepted. The SAT I scores for the 2001-2002 freshman class were: Verbal--39% below 500, 45% between 500 and 599, 15% between 600 and 700, and 1% above 700; Math--40% below 500, 43% between 500 and 599, 16% between 600 and 700, and 1% above 700. 42% of the current freshmen were in the top fifth of their class; 71% were in the top two fifths.

Requirements: The SAT I or ACT is required. Applicants must be graduates of an accredited secondary school. Although a secondary transcript is required, particular secondary preparation is not stipulated for all programs. An essay is required and an interview is recommended. AP and CLEP credits are accepted. Important factors in the admissions decision are advanced placement or honor courses, recommendations by school officials, and leadership record.

Procedure: Freshmen are admitted fall, spring, and summer. Entrance exams should be taken between September and November of the senior year. There is a deferred admissions plan. Applications should be filed by March 1 for fall entry, December 1 for spring entry, and May 15 for summer entry. The fall 2001 application fee was $25. Notification is sent on a rolling basis.

Transfer: 201 transfer students enrolled in 2001-2002. Transfer applicants must have an admissions interview, provide both college and secondary school transcripts, and have a minimum 2.5 GPA. Grades earned at other institutions are not included in calculating the GPA required for graduation. 30 credits of 120 must be completed at VJC.

Visiting: There are regularly scheduled orientations for prospective students, including a general overview, information on how to apply and how to finance a college education, special academic presentations, tours, meetings with faculty and students, and lunch. There are guides for informal visits and visitors may sit in on classes. To schedule a visit, contact the Admissions Office.

Financial Aid: In 2001-2002, 65% of all freshmen and 52% of continuing students received some form of financial aid. 43% of freshmen and 40% of continuing students received need-based aid. The average freshman award was $16,681. Of that total, scholarships or need-based grants averaged $5147 ($11,300 maximum); loans averaged $2460 ($6625 maximum); and work contracts averaged $1200 ($2500 maximum). 5% of undergraduates work part time. Average annual earnings from campus work are $1400. The average financial indebtedness of the 2001 graduate was $14,562. VJC is a member of CSS. The FAFSA and the college's own financial statement are required. The fall application deadline is March 1.

International Students: There are 7 international students enrolled. They must score 550 on the written TOEFL.

Computers: The mainframe is an IBM. More than 200 networked PCs are available for student use in classrooms and labs. The campuswide fiber-optic backbone provides an SNA gateway to the IBM mainframe, library card catalog access via a CD-ROM server, student dial-in from home, Mac connectivity, electromic mail, and hundreds of software applications in all disciplines. All students may access the system at all times. There are no time limits and no fees.

Graduates: In 2001, 353 bachelor's degrees were awarded. The most popular majors were computer and information systems (42%), nursing (17%), and liberal arts and technology (17%). In an average class, 31% graduate in 4 years, 45% in 5 years, and 46% in 6 years. 60 companies recruited on campus in 2000-2001. Of the 2000 graduating class, 8% were enrolled in graduate school within 6 months of graduation and 99% were employed.

Admissions Contact: Mark J. Hergan, Dean of Admissions. A video is available. E-mail: *admissions@vjc.edu* Web: *www.vjc.edu*

WASHINGTON COLLEGE

Chestertown, MD 21620-1197 — E-2

(410) 778-7700
(800) 422-1782; Fax: (410) 778-7287

Full-time: 447 men, 712 women	**Faculty:** 77; IIB, +$
Part-time: 19 men, 45 women	**Ph.D.s:** 92%
Graduate: 27 men, 25 women	**Student/Faculty:** 15 to 1
Year: semesters	**Tuition:** $22,300
Application Deadline: February 15	**Room & Board:** $5740
Freshman Class: 1914 applied, 1391 accepted, 338 enrolled	
SAT I Verbal/Math: 578/567	**ACT:** 23 **VERY COMPETITIVE**

Washington College, founded in 1782, is an independent college offering programs in the liberal arts and sciences, business management, and teacher preparation. The library contains 237,072 volumes, 243,622 microform items, and 5807 audiovisual forms/CDs, and subscribes to 863 periodicals. Computerized library services include the card catalog, interlibrary loans, and database searching. Special learning facilities include a learning resource center, the Center for the American Experience, and the Center for Environment and Society. The 112-acre campus is in a small town 75 miles from Baltimore. Including residence halls, there are 39 buildings.

Student Life: 53% of undergraduates are from Maryland. Others are from 37 states, 37 foreign countries, and Canada. 66% are from public schools. 84% are white. The average age of freshmen is 19; all undergraduates, 21. 18% do not continue beyond their first year; 64% remain to graduate.

Housing: 1130 students can be accommodated in college housing, which includes single-sex and coed dormitories and on-campus apartments. In addition, there are special-interest houses, an international house, a science house, and substance-free housing. On-campus housing is guaranteed for the freshman year only and is available on a lottery system for upperclassmen. 78% of students live on campus; of those, 65% remain on campus on weekends. All students may keep cars.

Activities: 25% of men belong to 3 national fraternities; 25% of women belong to 3 national sororities. There are 52 groups on campus, including cheerleading, chorale, chorus, dance, debate, drama, education, ethnic, gay, honors, international, jazz band, leadership, literary magazine, minority and human rights, newspaper, opera, orchestra, photography, political, professional, religious, social, social service, student government, and yearbook. Popular campus events include fall and spring convocations, George Washington Birthday Ball, and May Day.

Sports: There are 7 intercollegiate sports for men and 9 for women, and 7 intramural sports for men and 6 for women. Facilities include a swim center, a gym, a field house, squash and racquetball courts, a fitness center, playing and practice fields, and a boat house. There are riding facilities nearby.

Disabled Students: 80% of the campus is accessible. Wheelchair ramps, elevators, special parking, specially equipped rest rooms, special class scheduling, lowered drinking fountains, lowered telephones, motorized carts, and curb cuts are available.

Services: Counseling and information services are available, as is tutoring in every subject. There is remedial math and writing, a writing center, a math lab, a study skills tutor, and peer tutors.

Campus Safety and Security: Measures include 24-hour foot and vehicle patrol, escort service, informal discussions, and pamphlets/posters/films. There are emergency telephones, lighted pathways/sidewalks, and peer education through student groups.

Programs of Study: WC confers B.A. and B.S. degrees. Master's degrees are also awarded. Bachelor's degrees are awarded in BIOLOGICAL SCIENCE (biology/biological science), BUSINESS (business administration and management), COMMUNICATIONS AND THE ARTS (art, dramatic arts, English, fine arts, French, German, music, and Spanish), COMPUTER AND PHYSICAL SCIENCE (chemistry, computer science, mathematics, and physics), ENGINEERING AND ENVIRONMENTAL DESIGN (environmental science), SOCIAL SCIENCE (American studies, anthropology, economics, history, humanities, international studies, philosophy, political science/government, psychology, and sociology). Psychology, English, and chemistry are the strongest academically. Biology, English, and psychology are the largest.

Required: All students are required to take 2 freshman seminars and 11 courses distributed among the social sciences, natural sciences, humanities, quantitative studies, foreign langauges, and a writing requirement. The senior obligation consists of a comprehensive exam, thesis, or independent project. Students must complete 128 credit hours, including at least 32 in the major, to graduate. A minimum GPA of 2.0 is required.

Special: Internships are available in all majors. There is study abroad in 20 countries and a Washington semester at American University. The college offers a 3-2 engineering degree with the University of Maryland at College Park, as well as a 3-2 nursing program with Johns Hopkins University, credit by exam, pass/fail options, and student-designed majors. There are 7 national honor societies.

Faculty/Classroom: 63% of faculty are male; 37%, female. 97% teach undergraduates. No introductory courses are taught by graduate students. The average class size in an introductory lecture is 24; in a laboratory, 16; and in a regular course, 16.

Admissions: 73% of the 2001-2002 applicants were accepted. The SAT I scores for the 2001-2002 freshman class were: Verbal--16% below 500, 44% between 500 and 599, 33% between 600 and 700, and 7% above 700; Math--16% below 500, 51% between 500 and 599, 30% between 600 and 700, and 4% above 700. The ACT scores were 27% below 21, 19% between 21 and 23, 35% between 24 and 26, 5% between 27 and 28, and 14% above 28. 63% of the current freshmen were in the top fifth of their class; 88% were in the top two fifths. 10 freshmen graduated first in their class.

Requirements: The SAT I or ACT is required. In addition, applicants must be graduates of an accredited secondary school or have a GED. 16 Carnegie units are required. Applicants should take high school courses in English, foreign language, history, math, science, and social studies. An essay is required, and an interview is recommended. A GPA of 2.5 is required. AP and CLEP credits are accepted. Important factors in the admissions decision are advanced placement or honor courses, recommendations by school officials, and leadership record. Applications are accepted on-line via the Common Application.

Procedure: Freshmen are admitted fall and spring. Entrance exams should be taken in the spring of the junior year or fall of the senior year. There is an early decision plan. Early decision applications should be filed by November 15; regular applications, by February 15 for fall entry and December 1 for spring entry, along with a $40 fee. Notification of early decision is sent December 15; regular decision, March 1. 19 early decision candidates were accepted for the 2001-2002 class. A waiting list is an active part of the admissions procedure.

Transfer: 46 transfer students enrolled in 2001-2002. A minimum GPA of 2.5 is required. An associate degree and interview are recommended. 56 credits of 128 must be completed at WC.

Visiting: There are regularly scheduled orientations for prospective students, consisting of weekday visits. There are guides for informal visits and visitors may sit in on classes and stay overnight. To schedule a visit, contact the Admissions Office.

Financial Aid: In 2001-2002, 86% of all freshmen and 85% of continuing students received some form of financial aid. 50% of freshmen received need-based aid. The average freshman award was $13,914. Of that total, scholarships or need-based grants averaged $10,000 ($15,000 maximum); loans averaged $2625 ($3800 maximum); and work contracts averaged $1200 ($1500 maximum). 50% of undergraduates work part time. Average annual earnings from campus work are $760. The average financial indebtedness of the 2001 graduate was $17,711. WC is a member of CSS. The FAFSA, the college's own financial statement, and parents' and students' federal income tax returns are required. The fall application deadline is February 15.

International Students: There are 79 international students enrolled. The school actively recruits these students. They must score 550 on the written TOEFL.

Computers: The mainframe is a Data General Aviion 5500. Students may access the mainframe, the library collection, and the Internet via a campus network of more than 130 Macs in the library, academic buildings, and dormitories. All students may access the system. There are no time limits and no fees. It is strongly recommended that all students have a personal computer.

Graduates: In 2001, 235 bachelor's degrees were awarded. The most popular majors were business management (13%), economics (11%), and English (11%). In an average class, 62% graduate in 4 years, 65% in 5 years, and 66% in 6 years. 35 companies recruited on campus in 2000-2001. Of the 2000 graduating class, 38% were enrolled in graduate school within 6 months of graduation.

Admissions Contact: Kevin Coveney, Vice President of Admissions. A video is available. E-mail: *adm-off@washcoll.edu*
Web: *www.washcoll.edu*

WESTERN MARYLAND COLLEGE

Westminster, MD 21157-4390 — D-1

(410) 857-2230
(800) 638-5005; Fax: (410) 857-2757

Full-time: 694 men, 875 women	**Faculty:** 92; IIB, +$
Part-time: 27 men, 45 women	**Ph.D.s:** 92%
Graduate: 338 men, 1145 women	**Student/Faculty:** 17 to 1
Year: 4-1-4	**Tuition:** $20,550
Application Deadline: March 15	**Room & Board:** $5450
Freshman Class: 1614 applied, 1293 accepted, 369 enrolled	
SAT I Verbal/Math: 563/560	**VERY COMPETITIVE**

Western Maryland College, founded in 1867, is a private college offering programs in the liberal arts. In addition to regional accreditation, Western Maryland has baccalaureate program accreditation with CSWE and NASM. The library contains 207,207 volumes, 1,405,556 microform items, and 10,126 audiovisual forms/CDs, and subscribes to 3842 periodicals. Computerized library services include the card catalog, interlibrary loans, and database searching. Special learning facilities include an art gallery, radio station, TV station, and physics observatory. The 160-acre campus is in a small town 30 miles northwest of Baltimore. Including residence halls, there are 60 buildings. In May 2002, the school was renamed McDaniel College.

Student Life: 68% of undergraduates are from Maryland. Others are from 27 states and 23 foreign countries. 79% are white. 45% are Protestant; 24% Catholic. The average age of freshmen is 18; all undergraduates, 20. 14% do not continue beyond their first year.

Housing: 1200 students can be accommodated in college housing, which includes single-sex and coed dormitories and on-campus apartments. In addition, there are honors houses, language houses, special-interest houses, fraternity and sorority floors, academic clusters, and substance-free floors. On-campus housing is guaranteed for all 4 years. 77% of students live on campus; of those, 85% remain on campus on weekends. Upperclassmen may keep cars.

Activities: 15% of men belong to 2 local and 3 national fraternities; 16% of women belong to 2 local and 2 national sororities. There are 125 groups on campus, including art, band, cheerleading, choir, chorale, chorus, computers, debate, drama, ethnic, film, gay, honors, international, jazz band, literary magazine, musical theater, newspaper, orchestra, pep band, photography, political, professional, radio and TV, religious, social, social service, student government, and yearbook. Popular campus events include Spring Fling, Senior Week, and Families Weekend.

Sports: There are 11 intercollegiate sports for men and 11 for women, and 9 intramural sports for men and 9 for women. Facilities include a 9-hole golf course, tennis courts, a swimming pool, a football stadium with a track, a squash/racquetball court, a weight training center, basketball and volleyball courts, and soccer, softball, and lacrosse fields.

Disabled Students: 75% of the campus is accessible. Wheelchair ramps, elevators, special parking, specially equipped rest rooms, special class scheduling, lowered drinking fountains, lowered telephones, and interpreting and TTY are available.

Services: Counseling and information services are available, as is tutoring in most subjects. There is a reader service for the blind and remedial math.

Campus Safety and Security: Measures include 24-hour foot and vehicle patrol, escort service, informal discussions, and pamphlets/posters/films. There are emergency telephones and lighted pathways/sidewalks.

Programs of Study: Western Maryland confers the B.A. degree. Master's degrees are also awarded. Bachelor's degrees are awarded in BIOLOGICAL SCIENCE (biology/biological science), BUSINESS (business administration and management), COMMUNICATIONS AND THE ARTS (communications, dramatic arts, English, fine arts, French, German, music, and Spanish), COMPUTER AND PHYSICAL SCIENCE (chemistry, mathematics, and physics), EDUCATION (physical), SOCIAL SCIENCE (economics, history, philosophy, political science/government, psychology, religion, social work, and sociology). Physics, English, and social work are the strongest academically. Biology, English, and foreign languages are the largest.

Required: Distribution requirements for all students include cross-cultural studies, literature and fine arts, humanities, natural sciences, quantitative analysis, and social sciences. All students must take English composition, foreign language, and phys ed (4 courses) and pass a math proficiency exam. A total of 128 credit hours is required for graduation, including 38 to 50 in the major. The college uses a 4-course system, with most courses 4 credits. The minimum GPA for graduation is 2.0.

Special: Internships are available in all majors. Study abroad is available around the world. There is a Washington semester in conjunction with American University and 3-2 engineering programs with Washington University and the University of Maryland. The college offers work-study programs, dual and student-designed majors, credit by exam (in foreign languages), and pass/fail options. Western Maryland has a 5-year deaf education program and offers certification in elementary and secondary education. The college also offers advanced standing for international baccalaureate recipients. There are 12 national honor societies, including Phi Beta Kappa, a freshman honors program, and 19 departmental honors programs.

Faculty/Classroom: 59% of faculty are male; 41%, female. All teach undergraduates. No introductory courses are taught by graduate students. The average class size in an introductory lecture is 18; in a laboratory, 19; and in a regular course, 15.

Admissions: 80% of the 2001-2002 applicants were accepted. The SAT I scores for the 2001-2002 freshman class were: Verbal--18% below 500, 53% between 500 and 599, 23% between 600 and 700, and 6% above 700; Math--19% below 500, 51% between 500 and 599, 27% between 600 and 700, and 3% above 700. 65% of the current freshmen were in the top fifth of their class; 87% were in the top two fifths. There was 1 National Merit finalist. 27 freshmen graduated first in their class.

Requirements: The SAT I is required, with a minimum composite score of 900. Applicants must be graduates of an accredited secondary school or have a GED. 16 academic credits are required, including 4 years of English, 3 each of foreign language, math, and social studies, and 2 of a lab science. SAT II: Subject tests and an interview are recommended. An essay is required. Western Maryland requires applicants to be in the upper 50% of their class. A GPA of 2.5 is required. AP and CLEP credits are accepted. Important factors in the admissions decision are advanced placement or honor courses, leadership record, and evidence of special talent. Applications are accepted on computer disk and on-line via CollegeLink and Common App.

Procedure: Freshmen are admitted fall and spring. Entrance exams should be taken at the end of the junior year. There is a deferred admissions plan. Applications should be filed by March 15 for fall entry and January 15 for spring entry, along with a $40 fee. Notification is sent April 1.

Transfer: 54 transfer students enrolled in 2001-2002. A minimum college GPA of 2.5 is required. If fewer than 30 credits transfer, a minimum composite SAT I score of 900 is required to transfer. An interview is recommended. 30 credits of 128 must be completed at Western Maryland.

Visiting: There are regularly scheduled orientations for prospective students, including meeting the president, a panel of faculty, and a panel of students. Tours of the campus for parents are conducted by faculty members; students tour with current students. There are guides for informal visits and visitors may sit in on classes and stay overnight. To schedule a visit, contact the Admissions Office.

Financial Aid: In 2001-2002, 89% of all students received some form of financial aid. 62% of freshmen and 59% of continuing students received need-based aid. The average freshman award was $16,819. Of that total, scholarships or need-based grants averaged $7690 ($24,000 maximum); loans averaged $3300 ($7825 maximum); and work contracts averaged $1392 ($1600 maximum). 21% of undergraduates work part time. Average annual earnings from campus work are $663. The average financial indebtedness of the 2001 graduate was $9687. The CSS/Profile, FAFSA, FFS or SFS and the college's own financial statement are required. The fall application deadline is March 1.

International Students: There are 70 international students enrolled. The school actively recruits these students. They must score 213 on the electronic TOEFL.

Computers: The mainframe is an IBM RISC 6000. 7 labs provide access to 132 PCs, all with access to the Internet and the World Wide Web. All students may access the system. One lab is open 24 hours per day; other labs are open 8:30 A.M. to midnight daily. The network is available 24 hours per day. There are no time limits and no fees.

Graduates: In 2001, 392 bachelor's degrees were awarded. The most popular majors were sociology (18%), economics and business administration (14%), and communication (8%). In an average class, 2% graduate in 3 years, 64% in 4 years, 70% in 5 years, and 71% in 6 years. 49 companies recruited on campus in 2000-2001. Of the 2000 graduating class, 36% were enrolled in graduate school within 6 months of graduation and 91% were employed.

Admissions Contact: Martha O'Connell, Dean of Admissions.
E-mail: *admissio@wmdc.edu* Web: *www.wmdc.edu*

MASSACHUSETTS

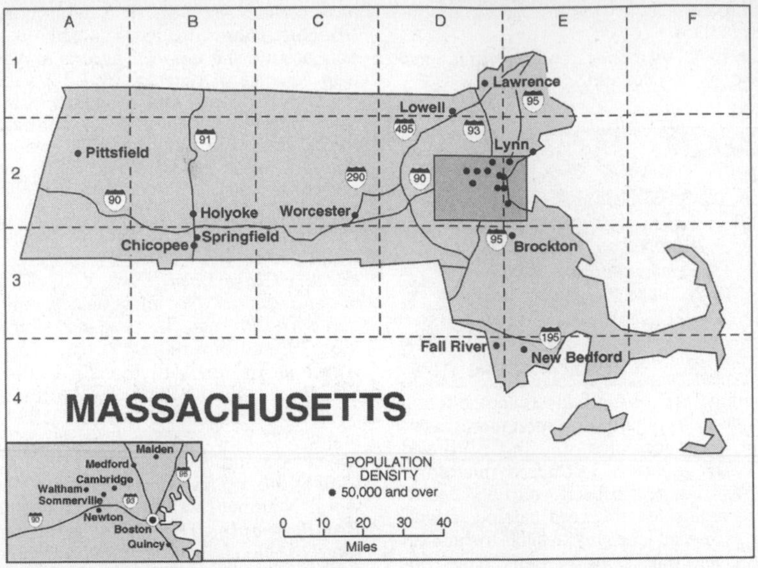

AMERICAN INTERNATIONAL COLLEGE — B-3

Springfield, MA 01109 — (413) 205-3201
(800) 242-3142; Fax: (413) 205-3943

Full-time: 441 men, 444 women — **Faculty:** 75
Part-time: 57 men, 126 women — **Ph.D.s:** 63%
Graduate: 129 men, 312 women — **Student/Faculty:** 12 to 1
Year: semesters, summer session — **Tuition:** $14,800
Application Deadline: open — **Room & Board:** $7468
Freshman Class: 1025 applied, 790 accepted, 259 enrolled
SAT I Verbal/Math: 476/484 — **LESS COMPETITIVE**

American International College, founded in 1885, is an independent institution offering programs in liberal arts, business, health science, and teacher preparation. In addition to regional accreditation, AIC has baccalaureate program accreditation with ACOTE, APTA, NASDTEC, and NLN. The library contains 118,000 volumes, 450,000 microform items, and 1380 audiovisual forms/CDs, and subscribes to 425 periodicals. Computerized library services include the card catalog, interlibrary loans, and database searching. Special learning facilities include a learning resource center, art gallery, radio station, and TV station. The 58-acre campus is in an urban area 75 miles west of Boston. Including residence halls, there are 22 buildings.

Student Life: 59% of undergraduates are from Massachusetts. Others are from 30 states, 15 foreign countries, and Canada. 83% are from public schools. 64% are white; 22% African American. 66% are Catholic; 26% Protestant. The average age of freshmen is 19; all undergraduates, 23. 18% do not continue beyond their first year; 56% remain to graduate.

Housing: 720 students can be accommodated in college housing, which includes single-sex and coed dormitories. On-campus housing is guaranteed for all 4 years. 53% of students commute. Alcohol is not permitted. All students may keep cars.

Activities: 3% of men belong to 1 local fraternity and 2 national fraternities; 4% of women belong to 2 local sororities. There are 40 groups on campus, including cheerleading, chorale, computers, dance, drama, ethnic, honors, international, literary magazine, musical theater, newspaper, political, professional, radio and TV, religious, social, social service, student government, women's and yearbook. Popular campus events include holiday semi-formals and international festival.

Sports: There are 9 intercollegiate sports for men and 7 for women, and 9 intramural sports for men and 8 for women. Facilities include 2 gyms, a football stadium, tennis courts, playing fields, and a health and fitness center.

Disabled Students: 75% of the campus is accessible. Wheelchair ramps, elevators, special parking, specially equipped rest rooms, special class scheduling, and lowered drinking fountains are available.

Services: Counseling and information services are available, as is tutoring in every subject. There is remedial math and writing.

Campus Safety and Security: Measures include 24-hour foot and vehicle patrol, escort service, shuttle buses, and informal discussions. There are pamphlets/posters/films and lighted pathways/sidewalks.

Programs of Study: AIC confers B.A., B.S., B.B.A., B.S.B.A., B.S.N., and B.S.O.T. degrees. Associate, master's, and doctoral degrees are also awarded. Bachelor's degrees are awarded in BIOLOGICAL SCIENCE (biochemistry and biology/biological science), BUSINESS (accounting, business administration and management, business economics, entrepreneurial studies, human resources, international business management, and marketing/retailing/merchandising), COMMUNICATIONS AND THE ARTS (advertising, communications, English, and Spanish), COMPUTER AND PHYSICAL SCIENCE (chemistry, mathematics, and science), EDUCATION (early childhood, elementary, foreign languages, middle school, science, secondary, and special), HEALTH PROFESSIONS (medical laboratory technology, nursing, occupational therapy, physical therapy, predentistry, and premedicine), SOCIAL SCIENCE (criminal justice, economics, history, international relations, liberal arts/general studies, philosophy, political science/government, prelaw, psychology, public administration, and sociology). Psychology, preprofessional, and health sciences are the strongest academically. Criminal justice, physical therapy, and nursing are the largest.

Required: Distribution requirements include 12 credits of social sciences, 9 of English, 8 of laboratory science, 6 of humanities, 3 of math, and 3 computer-oriented. A total of 120 credit hours is required for graduation, with 30 to 36 hours in the major. A minimum 2.0 GPA is required for graduation. Students must take 4 credits of phys ed.

Special: Cross-registration with other colleges in the area is permitted. Internships are available in all programs, and study abroad is offered, as is a Washington semester. AIC also offers dual majors, credit by examination, credit for life/military/work experience, nondegree study, and for lower-division students, pass/fail options. There are 2 national honor societies, a freshman honors program, and 9 departmental honors programs.

Faculty/Classroom: 54% of faculty are male; 46%, female. All teach undergraduates, 15% do research, and 15% do both. No introductory courses are taught by graduate students. The average class size in an introductory lecture is 27; in a laboratory, 16; and in a regular course, 19.

Admissions: 77% of the 2001-2002 applicants were accepted. The SAT I scores for the 2001-2002 freshman class were: Verbal--59% below 500, 32% between 500 and 599, 7% between 600 and 700, and 2% above 700; Math--54% below 500, 34% between 500 and 599, 9% between 600 and 700, and 3% above 700. 20% of the current freshmen were in the top fifth of their class; 45% were in the top two fifths. 4 freshmen graduated first in their class.

Requirements: The SAT I is required. In addition, students must be graduates of an accredited secondary school or have a GED. They must have completed 16 academic credits of secondary school work with a minimum of 4 years of English, 2 each of history, math, and science, and 1 of social studies. An interview is recommended. A GPA of 2.0 is required. AP and CLEP credits are accepted. Important factors in the admissions decision are recommendations by school officials, advanced placement or honor courses, and personality/intangible qualities. Applications are accepted on-line.

Procedure: Freshmen are admitted to all sessions. Entrance exams should be taken by March of the senior year. There are early decision, early admissions, and deferred admissions plans. Application deadlines are open. The application fee is $20. Notification of early decision is sent December 15; regular decision, on a rolling basis. 35 early decision candidates were accepted for the 2001-2002 class.

Transfer: 132 transfer students enrolled in 2001-2002. Transfer applicants must have at least a 2.0 GPA. 45 credits of 120 must be completed at AIC.

Visiting: There are regularly scheduled orientations for prospective students, including open houses with faculty, a student life panel, departmental faculty presentations, a financial aid presentation, a tour, and brunch. There are guides for informal visits and visitors may sit in on classes and stay overnight. To schedule a visit, contact the Admissions Office.

Financial Aid: In 2001-2002, 89% of all freshmen and 85% of continuing students received some form of financial aid. 70% of freshmen and 73% of continuing students received need-based aid. The average freshman award was $16,559. Of that total, scholarships or need-based grants averaged $7022 ($14,000 maximum); loans averaged $4614 ($5500 maximum); and work contracts averaged $1200 ($1600 maximum). 62% of undergraduates work part time. Average annual earnings from campus work are $1150. The average financial indebtedness of the 2001 graduate was $17,125. The FAFSA is required. The fall application deadline is May 1.

International Students: There are 58 international students enrolled. The school actively recruits these students. They must score 500 on the written TOEFL or 173 on the electronic version and also take the SAT I or the ACT if English is the first language.

Computers: The mainframe is an IBM ALPHA. The college network is accessible by PCs located in computer labs throughout campus, all with Internet access. Free Internet access is also provided in all residence hall rooms. All students may access the system 7 days per week for a total of 80 hours. There are no time limits and no fees.

Graduates: The most popular majors were occupational therapy (12%), psychology (12%), and criminal justice (11%). In an average class, 50% graduate in 4 years, 58% in 5 years, and 59% in 6 years. 42 companies recruited on campus in a recent year. Of the 2000 graduating class, 21% were enrolled in graduate school within 6 months of graduation and 85% were employed.

Admissions Contact: Peter Miller, Dean of Admissions. A video is available. E-mail: *inquiry@www.aic.edu* Web: *www.aic.edu*

AMHERST COLLEGE B-2

Amherst, MA 01002-5000 **(413) 542-2328; Fax: (413) 542-2040**

Full-time: 835 men, 790 women	**Faculty:** 179; IIB, ++$
Part-time: none	**Ph.D.s:** 93%
Graduate: none	**Student/Faculty:** 9 to 1
Year: semesters	**Tuition:** $27,240
Application Deadline: December 31	**Room & Board:** $7100
Freshman Class: 5175 applied, 973 accepted, 430 enrolled	
SAT I Verbal/Math: 705/697	**ACT:** 29 **MOST COMPETITIVE**

Amherst College, founded in 1821, is a private liberal arts institution. The 5 libraries contain 938,983 volumes, 159,822 microform items, and 58,141 audiovisual forms/CDs, and subscribe to 5340 periodicals. Computerized library services include the card catalog, interlibrary loans, and database searching. Special learning facilities include an art gallery, natural history museum, planetarium, radio station, observatory, the Emily Dickinson Homestead, and the Amherst Center for Russian Culture. The 964-acre campus is in a small town 90 miles west of Boston. Including residence halls, there are 67 buildings.

Student Life: 84% of undergraduates are from out of state, mostly the Middle Atlantic. Students are from 50 states, 30 foreign countries, and Canada. 60% are from public schools. 51% are white; 11% Asian American. The average age of freshmen is 18; all undergraduates, 19. 3% do not continue beyond their first year; 96% remain to graduate.

Housing: 1650 students can be accommodated in college housing, which includes single-sex and coed dormitories. In addition, there are language houses, special-interest houses, and 1 cooperative house. On-campus housing is guaranteed for all 4 years. 98% of students live on campus; of those, 95% remain on campus on weekends. Upperclassmen may keep cars.

Activities: There are no fraternities or sororities. There are more than 100 groups on campus, including art, band, chess, choir, chorale, chorus, computers, dance, debate, drama, ethnic, film, gay, honors, international, jazz band, literary magazine, newspaper, opera, orchestra, photography, political, professional, radio and TV, religious, social, social service, student government, symphony, and yearbook. Popular campus events include Newport Jazz, Harlem Renaissance, and Casino Night.

Sports: There are 13 intercollegiate sports for men and 14 for women, and 6 intramural sports for men and 6 for women. Facilities include 2 gyms, a pool, a field house, a hockey rink, an outdoor track, a fitness center, 10 international squash courts, an indoor jogging track, 3 indoor and 30 outdoor tennis courts, baseball and softball diamonds, a 9-hole golf course, and playing fields.

Disabled Students: Wheelchair ramps, elevators, special parking, specially equipped rest rooms, special class scheduling, lowered drinking fountains, and lowered telephones are available.

Services: Counseling and information services are available, as is tutoring in every subject. There is a reader service for the blind, a quantitative skills center, and a writing center.

Campus Safety and Security: Measures include 24-hour foot and vehicle patrol, self-defense education, escort service, and shuttle buses. There are informal discussions, pamphlets/posters/films, lighted pathways/sidewalks, ACEMS (Amherst College Emergency Medical Service), and access code pad security to dorms, plus "blue light" emergency telephones placed in 19 locations around campus.

Programs of Study: Amherst confers the B.A. degree. Bachelor's degrees are awarded in BIOLOGICAL SCIENCE (biology/biological science and neurosciences), COMMUNICATIONS AND THE ARTS (classics, dance, dramatic arts, English, fine arts, French, German, Greek, Latin, music, Russian, and Spanish), COMPUTER AND PHYSICAL SCIENCE (astronomy, chemistry, computer science, geology, mathematics, and physics), SOCIAL SCIENCE (African American studies, American studies, anthropology, Asian/Oriental studies, economics, European studies, history, interdisciplinary studies, law, philosophy, political science/government, psychology, religion, sociology, and women's studies). English, psychology, and biology are the largest.

Required: To earn the B.A., all students must complete 32 courses, equivalent to 128 credits, 8 to 14 of which are in the major, with at least a C average. Other than a 1-semester freshman seminar in liberal studies, there are no specific course requirements. A thesis or comparable work is required for honors candidates.

Special: Students may cross-register through the Five College Consortium, the other members of which are all within 10 miles of Amherst, or through the Twelve College Exchange Program. A number of interterm and summer internships are available, as is study abroad in 36 countries. Dual majors, student-designed interdisciplinary majors based on independent study as of the junior or senior year, and work-study programs are possible. There are limited pass/fail options. There are 2 national honor societies, including Phi Beta Kappa. All departments have honors programs.

Faculty/Classroom: 63% of faculty are male; 37%, female. All both teach and do research. The average class size in a regular course is 18.

Admissions: 19% of the 2001-2002 applicants were accepted. The SAT I scores for the 2001-2002 freshman class were: Verbal--8% between 500 and 599, 31% between 600 and 700, and 61% above 700; Math--8% between 500 and 599, 34% between 600 and 700, and 57% above 700. The ACT scores were 4% below 21, 5% between 21 and 23, 12% between 24 and 26, 12% between 27 and 28, and 67% above 28. 95% of the current freshmen were in the top fifth of their class; 3% were in the top two fifths. There were 80 National Merit semifinalists. 37 freshmen graduated first in their class.

Requirements: The SAT I or ACT is required, as well as 3 SAT II: Subject tests. Amherst strongly recommends that applicants take 4 years of English, math through precalculus, 3 or 4 years of a foreign language, 2 years of history and social science, and at least 2 years of natural science, including a lab science. 2 essays are required. Important factors in the admissions decision are advanced placement or honor courses, recommendations by school officials, and evidence of special talent. Students may apply on-line through the school's web site.

Procedure: Freshmen are admitted in the fall. Entrance exams should be taken no later than December of the senior year. There are early decision and deferred admissions plans. Early decision applications should be filed by November 15; regular applications, by December 31 for fall entry. The fall 2001 application fee was $55. Notification of early decision is sent December 15; regular decision, April 1. 131 early decision candidates were accepted for the 2001-2002 class. 15% of all applicants are on a waiting list.

Transfer: 5 transfer students enrolled in 2001-2002. Applicants must have full sophomore standing and a minimum 3.0 GPA in previous college work. Transfers are accepted for the sophomore and junior classes only, and Amherst recommends that they submit SAT I or ACT scores, plus high school and college transcripts, and seek a personal interview. 64 credits of 128 must be completed at Amherst.

Visiting: There are regularly scheduled orientations for prospective students, consisting of information sessions led by a dean and student-led tours. There are guides for informal visits and visitors may sit in on classes and stay overnight. To schedule a visit, contact the Admission Office.

Financial Aid: In 2001-2002, 45% of all freshmen and 47% of continuing students received some form of financial aid. 45% of all students received need-based aid. The average freshman award was $26,473. Of that total, scholarships or need-based grants averaged $23,496 ($35,770 maximum); loans averaged $1870 ($4850 maximum); and work contracts averaged $1109 ($2250 maximum). 40% of undergraduates work part time. Average annual earnings from campus work are $1330. The average financial indebtedness of the 2001 graduate was $12,270. Amherst is a member of CSS. The CSS/Profile or FAFSA is required. The fall application deadline is February 1.

International Students: There are 69 international students enrolled. The school actively recruits these students. They must score 600 on the written TOEFL or 250 on the electronic version or take the MELAB. Students must also take the SAT I or ACT and any 3 SAT II: Subject tests.

Computers: The mainframes are a DEC VMS and a DEC UNIX. There are more than 160 PCs around campus. Most are located in the computer center, library, campus center, and labs. In addition, each student has a hard-wired point of access from each dorm room with Ethernet, Internet, and e-mail accounts. All students may access the system 24 hours a day. There are no time limits and no fees.

Graduates: In 2001, 454 bachelor's degrees were awarded. The most popular majors were English (11%), psychology (7%), and biology (6%). In an average class, 84% graduate in 4 years, 92% in 5 years, and 94% in 6 years. 51 companies recruited on campus in 2000-2001. Of the 2000 graduating class, 29% were enrolled in graduate school within 6 months of graduation and 62% were employed.

Admissions Contact: Katherine L. Fretwell, Director of Admissions. E-mail: *admission@amherst.edu* Web: *http://www.amherst.edu*

ANNA MARIA COLLEGE C-2

Paxton, MA 01612-1198 **(508) 849-3367**
(800) 344-4586, ext. 367; Fax: (508) 849-3362

Full-time: 192 men, 384 women	**Faculty:** 35
Part-time: 115 men, 141 women	**Ph.D.s:** 51%
Graduate: 205 men, 227 women	**Student/Faculty:** 16 to 1
Year: semesters, summer session	**Tuition:** $16,500
Application Deadline: March 1	**Room & Board:** $6300
Freshman Class: 508 applied, 440 accepted, 139 enrolled	
SAT I Verbal/Math: 480/470	**ACT:** 18 **LESS COMPETITIVE**

Anna Maria College, founded in 1946, is a small, comprehensive Catholic college offering career-oriented programs in liberal and fine arts, business, and teacher preparation. In addition to regional accreditation, AMC has baccalaureate program accreditation with CSWE and NLN. The library contains 77,264 volumes, 1673 microform items, and 1258 audiovisual forms/CDs, and subscribes to 302 periodicals. Computerized library services include the card catalog and database searching. Special learning facilities include a learning resource center and an audiovisual center. The 180-acre campus is in a rural area 8 miles northwest of Worcester. Including residence halls, there are 13 buildings.

Student Life: 81% of undergraduates are from Massachusetts. Others are from 13 states and 6 foreign countries. 72% are from public schools. 86% are white. The average age of freshmen is 21; all undergraduates, 25. 21% do not continue beyond their first year; 74% remain to graduate.

Housing: 394 students can be accommodated in college housing, which includes coed dormitories. On-campus housing is guaranteed for the freshman year only, is available on a first-come, first-served basis, and is available on a lottery system for upperclassmen. 59% of students live on campus. All students may keep cars.

Activities: There are no fraternities or sororities. There are 23 groups on campus, including art, cheerleading, choir, chorus, computers, drama, ethnic, gay, honors, international, jazz band, musical theater, pep band, political, professional, religious, social, social service, student government, and yearbook. Popular campus events include Harvest Weekend, Winter Semi-Formal, and Spring Weekend.

Sports: There are 5 intercollegiate sports for men and 6 for women, and 2 intramural sports for men and 2 for women. Facilities include an activities center with a basketball court, locker rooms, and weight and fitness equipment; soccer, baseball, and softball fields; a sand volleyball court; an outdoor basketball court; and a fitness trail.

Disabled Students: 93% of the campus is accessible. Wheelchair ramps, elevators, special parking, specially equipped rest rooms, and special class scheduling are available.

Services: Counseling and information services are available, as is tutoring in every subject, including through a tutoring lab. There is a reader service for the blind, and remedial math, reading, and writing.

Campus Safety and Security: Measures include 24-hour foot and vehicle patrol, escort service, shuttle buses, and informal discussions. There are pamphlets/posters/films, emergency telephones, and lighted pathways/sidewalks.

Programs of Study: AMC confers B.A., B.S., B.B.A., B.F.A., B.M., and B.S.N. degrees. Associate and master's degrees are also awarded. Bachelor's degrees are awarded in BIOLOGICAL SCIENCE (biology/biological science), BUSINESS (business administration and management), COMMUNICATIONS AND THE ARTS (art, English, music, music performance, and studio art), EDUCATION (art, early childhood, elementary, and music), HEALTH PROFESSIONS (art therapy, music therapy, and nursing), SOCIAL SCIENCE (criminal justice, fire science, history, human development, liberal arts/general studies, paralegal studies, political science/government, psychology, social science, and social work). Criminal justice, education, and music are the largest.

Required: The 60-credit core curriculum consists of classes in English, literature, math, computers, natural science, foreign language, fine arts, history, philosophy, social/behavioral sciences, and religious studies. A total of 120 credits is required for graduation, with a minimum of 30 in the major, and a 2.0 GPA.

Special: Cross-registration with the Colleges of the Worcester Consortium, internships in all majors, and a 3-2 engineering degree in conjunction with the Worcester Polytechnic Institute are available. The art and business major results in a B.F.A. degree. There are preprofessional concentrations in law, dentistry, medicine, and veterinary science. The college offers study abroad, a Washington semester, accelerated degree programs, a general studies degree, credit by exam, work-study programs, and 5-year advanced degree programs in business, counseling psychology, and criminal justice. There are 5 national honor societies and 2 departmental honors programs.

Faculty/Classroom: 43% of faculty are male; 57%, female. All teach undergraduates. No introductory courses are taught by graduate students. The average class size in an introductory lecture is 20; in a laboratory, 20; and in a regular course, 13.

Admissions: 87% of the 2001-2002 applicants were accepted. The SAT I scores for the 2001-2002 freshman class were: Verbal--59% below 500, 34% between 500 and 599, 6% between 600 and 700, and 1% above 700; Math--64% below 500, 29% between 500 and 599, and 7% between 600 and 700. The ACT scores were 71% below 21, and 29% between 21 and 23. 14% of the current freshmen were in the top fifth of their class; 42% were in the top two fifths.

Requirements: The SAT I is required; the ACT is accepted. A GED is accepted. 16 academic units are recommended, including 4 years of English, 2 years each of foreign language, history, math, and sciences, and 1 year of social studies. An interview is recommended. When applicable, an audition and portfolio are required. Students who have been out of high school for 3 or more years, or transfer students with 10 or more college-level courses, do not need to submit standardized test scores. An essay is required. A GPA of 2.0 is required. AP and CLEP credits are accepted. Important factors in the admissions decision are advanced placement or honor courses, evidence of special talent, and leadership record.

Procedure: Freshmen are admitted fall and spring. Entrance exams should be taken in the spring of the junior year and in the fall of the senior year. There is a deferred admissions plan. Priiority application dates are March 1 for fall entry and January 1 for spring entry. The fall 2001 application fee was $30. Notification is sent on a rolling basis.

Transfer: 31 transfer students enrolled in 2001-2002. Transfers with a minimum GPA of 2.0 are accepted for upper-division work. 45 credits of 120 must be completed at AMC.

Visiting: There are regularly scheduled orientations for prospective students, including on-campus interviews, campus tours, a day visitation program by appointment, and a fall open house. There are guides for informal visits and visitors may sit in on classes and stay overnight. To schedule a visit, contact the Undergraduate Admission Office at (508) 849-3360.

Financial Aid: In 2001-2002, 89% of all freshmen and 75% of continuing students received some form of financial aid. 84% of freshmen and 74% of continuing students received need-based aid. The average freshman award was $13,441. Of that total, scholarships or need-based grants averaged $9562 ($15,250 maximum); loans averaged $4473 ($14,996 maximum); and work contracts averaged $947 ($2000 maximum). 19% of undergraduates work part time. Average annual earnings from campus work are $534. The average financial indebtedness of the 2001 graduate was $17,500. The FAFSA is required. The fall application deadline is March 1.

International Students: There are 7 international students enrolled. The school actively recruits these students. They must score 500 on the written TOEFL. Students who score below 500 on the TOEFL may be admitted to the college's ESL program.

Computers: The mainframe is an IBM AS/400 Windows NT Network. There is a main computer lab in the library with more than 21 computers, a mini lab in the learning center, and access to the network in every dorm room along with a mini lab in the dorm. Available programs include e-mail, the Internet, MS Office, CD-ROM, accounting software, and an on-line legal database. Students do not have access to the IBM AS/400. All students may access the system. There are no time limits and no fees. It is strongly recommended that all students have a personal computer.

Graduates: In 2001, 140 bachelor's degrees were awarded. The most popular majors were criminal justice (32%), business (16%), and education (9%). In an average class, 93% graduate in 4 years, and 7% in 5 years.

Admissions Contact: Laurie Peltier, Director of Admission. E-mail: *admission@annamaria.edu* Web: *www.annamaria.edu*

ART INSTITUTE OF BOSTON AT LESLEY UNIVERSITY E-2

Boston, MA 02215-2598 (617) 585-6700
(800) 773-0494; Fax: (617) 437-1226

Full-time: 191 men, 276 women **Faculty:** 22
Part-time: 139 men, 185 women **Ph.D.s:** 65%
Graduate: none **Student/Faculty:** 21 to 1
Year: semesters, summer session **Tuition:** $15,085
Application Deadline: see profile **Room & Board:** $8600
Freshman Class: 698 applied, 343 accepted, 114 enrolled
SAT I Verbal/Math: 513/489 **SPECIAL**

The Art Institute of Boston at Lesley University, founded in 1912, is a private institution offering undergraduate visual art programs leading to the baccalaureate degree, 3 year diplomas, and Advanced Professional Certificates. In addition to regional accreditation, AIB has baccalaureate program accreditation with NASAD. The library contains 9000 volumes and 450 audiovisual forms/CDs, and subscribes to 80 periodicals. Computerized library services include interlibrary loans and database searching. Special learning facilities include an art gallery. The campus is in an urban area in the Kenmore Square area of Boston. Including residence halls, there are 2 buildings.

Student Life: 52% of undergraduates are from out of state, mostly the Northeast. Students are from 28 states, 19 foreign countries, and Canada. 55% are white. The average age of freshmen is 18; all undergraduates, 20. 17% do not continue beyond their first year.

Housing: 100 students can be accommodated in college housing, which includes coed dormitories. On-campus housing is available on a first-come, first-served basis. 85% of students commute. Alcohol is not permitted. No one may keep cars.

Activities: There are no fraternities or sororities. There are 9 groups on campus, including art, chess, chorale, drama, ethnic, gay, international, literary magazine, and musical theater. Popular campus events include New York City museum trips, DuPont Lecture series, and animation festivals.

Sports: A discounted health club membership is available.

Disabled Students: 75% of the campus is accessible. Wheelchair ramps, elevators, specially equipped rest rooms, special class scheduling, and lowered drinking fountains are available.

Services: Counseling and information services are available, as is tutoring in some subjects, including art history, computers, and ESL. There is remedial reading and writing.

Campus Safety and Security: Measures include shuttle buses, pamphlets/posters/films, and security guards.

Programs of Study: AIB confers the B.F.A. degree. Bachelor's degrees are awarded in COMMUNICATIONS AND THE ARTS (design, fine arts, illustration, and photography).

Required: All students must complete 124 to 128 credits, including 31 credits in the foundation program and 82 or more in the major. Juniors and seniors must maintaina minimum GPA of 2.3; freshmen and sophomores, 2.0. Senior juries are required.

Special: There is cross-registration with Boston Architectural Center and Lesley University. Internships are required for design majors and encouraged for all other majors. Accelerated degree programs in all majors, study abroad in Italy, and dual majors in fine art/illustration, design/illustration, and illustration/animation are offered. There is a freshman honors program and 1 departmental honors program.

Faculty/Classroom: 56% of faculty are male; 44%, female. All teach undergraduates. The average class size in an introductory lecture is 25; in a laboratory, 12; and in a regular course, 15.

Admissions: 49% of the 2001-2002 applicants were accepted. The SAT I scores for the 2001-2002 freshman class were: Verbal--29% below 500, 49% between 500 and 599, 20% between 600 and 700, and 2% above 700; Math--49% below 500, 44% between 500 and 599, 6% between 600 and 700, and 1% above 700.

Requirements: The SAT I or ACT is required. In addition, applicants must submit official high school transcripts; a portfolio review is required. Letters of recommendation and a campus tour are encouraged. AP and CLEP credits are accepted. Important factors in the admissions decision are evidence of special talent, advanced placement or honor courses, and leadership record.

Procedure: Freshmen are admitted to all sessions. There is a deferred admissions plan. The priority application deadline is February 15 for fall entry an November 15 for spring entry. After these dates, applications are considered on a rolling basis, as space allows. The fall 2001 application fee was $40. Notification is sent on a rolling basis. A waiting list is an active part of the admissions procedure.

Transfer: 48 transfer students enrolled in 2001-2002. High school and college transcripts, a portfolio review, and SAT I/ACT scores (if graduated since 1995) are required. 36 credits of 124 must be completed at AIB.

Visiting: There are regularly scheduled orientations for prospective students, including an open house offering demonstrations of course work, tours of the school, portfolio reviews, and showings of student and faculty work. There are guides for informal visits and visitors may sit in on classes. To schedule a visit, contact the Office of Admissions.

Financial Aid: In 2001-2002, 66% of all freshmen and 69% of continuing students received some form of financial aid. 68% of freshmen and 66% of continuing students received need-based aid. The average freshman award was $7558. Of that total, scholarships or need-based grants averaged $3705; loans averaged $7558 ($23,070 maximum); and work contracts averaged $1435 ($2000 maximum). 8% of undergraduates work part time. Average annual earnings from campus work are $1709. The average financial indebtedness of the 2001 graduate was $17,125. The FAFSA and the college's own financial statement are required. The fall application deadline is March 15.

International Students: There were 73 international students enrolled in a recent year. The school actively recruits these students. They must score 500 on the written TOEFL.

Computers: Computers are available for digital imaging, desktop publishing, animation, scanning, word processing, and Internet access. There are 3 labs of 50 Macs, and satellite computers are distributed in groups throughout the college for specialized uses. All students may access the system. There are no time limits and no fees.

Graduates: In 2001, 68 bachelor's degrees were awarded. The most popular majors were illustration (33%), design (24%), and photography (21%).

Admissions Contact: Bradford White, Director of Admissions.
E-mail: *admissions@aiboston.edu* Web: *www.aiboston.edu*

ASSUMPTION COLLEGE C-2

Worcester, MA 01609 (888) 882-7786; Fax: (508) 799-4412

Full-time: 799 men, 1261 women **Faculty:** 136
Part-time: 3 men, 3 women **Ph.D.s:** 93%
Graduate: 92 men, 236 women **Student/Faculty:** 15 to 1
Year: semesters, summer session **Tuition:** $18,945
Application Deadline: March 1 **Room & Board:** $7375
Freshman Class: 2804 applied, 2113 accepted, 606 enrolled
SAT I Verbal/Math: 530/540 **ACT:** 22 **COMPETITIVE**

Assumption College, founded in 1904 by Augustinians of the Assumption, offers a Catholic, liberal arts and sciences education to undergraduates, along with programs for graduate and continuing education students. The library contains 184,639 volumes, 17,690 microform items, and 1450 audiovisual forms/CDs, and subscribes to 1119 periodicals. Computerized library services include the card catalog, interlibrary loans, and database searching. Special learning facilities include a learning resource center and TV station. The 150-acre campus is in an urban area 45 miles west of Boston. Including residence halls, there are 38 buildings.

Student Life: 68% of undergraduates are from Massachusetts. Others are from 23 states, 17 foreign countries, and Canada. 69% are from public schools. 95% are white. The average age of freshmen is 18; all undergraduates, 20. 18% do not continue beyond their first year; 71% remain to graduate.

Housing: 1939 students can be accommodated in college housing, which includes single-sex dormitories and on-campus apartments. In addition, there are special-interest houses, freshman dorms, substance-free housing, and a living/learning center. On-campus housing is guaranteed for all 4 years. 88% of students live on campus; of those, 75% remain on campus on weekends. Upperclassmen may keep cars.

Activities: There are no fraternities or sororities. There are 40 groups on campus, including art, band, cheerleading, choir, chorale, chorus, computers, dance, drama, ethnic, film, honors, international, literary magazine, musical theater, newspaper, pep band, photography, political, professional, radio and TV, religious, social, social service, student government, and yearbook. Popular campus events include Pup Cup Weekend, Christmas Ball, and Sibling Weekend.

Sports: There are 10 intercollegiate sports for men and 9 for women, and 12 intramural sports for men and 12 for women. Facilities include a 3000-seat gym, baseball and softball diamonds, a field hockey area, a soccer field, and tennis courts. A recreation center houses a 6-lane swimming pool, a jogging/walking track, 4 racquetball courts, an aerobics/dance studio, fully equipped Bodymaster and free-weight rooms, a fitness center, and a field house with 3 multipurpose courts for basketball, volleyball, and floor hockey.

Disabled Students: 69% of the campus is accessible. Wheelchair ramps, elevators, special parking, specially equipped rest rooms, special class scheduling, lowered drinking fountains, and lowered telephones are available.

Services: Counseling and information services are available, as is tutoring in most subjects, including math, reading, and writing. There is a reader service for the blind, and signing for the deaf.

Campus Safety and Security: Measures include 24-hour foot and vehicle patrol, self-defense education, escort service, and shuttle buses. There are informal discussions, pamphlets/posters/films, emergency telephones, and lighted pathways/sidewalks.

Programs of Study: Assumption confers the B.A. degree. Associate and master's degrees are also awarded. Bachelor's degrees are awarded in BIOLOGICAL SCIENCE (biology/biological science), BUSINESS (accounting, business administration and management, international business management, international economics, marketing management, and marketing/retailing/merchandising), COMMUNICATIONS AND THE ARTS (classics, communications, English, French, languages, Spanish, and visual and performing arts), COMPUTER AND PHYSICAL SCIENCE (chemistry, computer science, and mathematics), ENGINEERING AND ENVIRONMENTAL DESIGN (environmental science), HEALTH PROFESSIONS (rehabilitation therapy), SOCIAL SCIENCE (economics, French studies, history, international studies, Latin American studies, philosophy, political science/government, psychology, sociology, Spanish studies, and theological studies). Business, natural sciences, and political science are the strongest academically. English, theology, and psychology are the largest.

Required: Students must complete a core curriculum of 3 courses from different disciplines in social science: 2 courses in 1 and 1 course in another of the 3 areas of math, natural science, and foreign languages; 2 courses each of English composition, philosophy, and theology; 1 each of literature, history, and either art, music, or theater arts, and 1 additional course in 2 of the 3 areas of philosophy and theology, literature, and history. A minimum of 120 semester credit hours, with a minimum of 38 semester courses, must be completed; 9 to 12 courses must be in the upper division of the major. A minimum 2.0 GPA is required.

Special: There are co-op programs in gerontology studies and marine studies. Cross-registration with the Worcester Consortium and a 3-2 engineering program with Worcester Polytechnic Institute are permitted. The college offers internships, study abroad, a Washington semester, a general studies degree, student-designed and dual majors, credit by examination, and credit for military experience. There are 8 national honor societies, a freshman honors program, and 2 departmental honors programs.

Faculty/Classroom: 56% of faculty are male; 44%, female. All teach undergraduates. No introductory courses are taught by graduate students. The average class size in an introductory lecture is 21; in a laboratory, 15; and in a regular course, 21.

Admissions: 75% of the 2001-2002 applicants were accepted. The SAT I scores for the 2001-2002 freshman class were: Verbal--27% below 500, 54% between 500 and 599, 18% between 600 and 700, and 1% above 700; Math--29% below 500, 52% between 500 and 599, 18% between 600 and 700, and 1% above 700. The ACT scores were 35% below 21, 35% between 21 and 23, 23% between 24 and 26, 6% between 27 and 28, and 2% above 28. 31% of the current freshmen were in the top fifth of their class; 64% were in the top two fifths. 3 freshmen graduated first in their class.

Requirements: The SAT I is required. In addition, all applicants must graduate from an accredited secondary school or have a GED. 18 academic units are required, including 4 years of English, 3 of math, and 2 each of history, science, and foreign language. An essay and an interview are recommended. AP and CLEP credits are accepted. Important factors in the admissions decision are advanced placement or honor courses, recommendations by school officials, and evidence of special talent. Applications are accepted on-line via ExPan, Apply, Embark, College Link, the Common Application, and the school's web site.

Procedure: Freshmen are admitted fall and spring. Entrance exams should be taken in May of the junior year or November of the senior year. There are early decision and deferred admissions plans. Early decision applications should be filed by November 15; regular applications, by March 1 for fall entry and December 1 for spring entry, along with a $40 fee. Notification of early decision is sent December 15; regular decision, on a rolling basis. 27 early decision candidates were accepted for the 2001-2002 class. 7% of all applicants are on a waiting list; 37 were accepted in 2001.

Transfer: 36 transfer students enrolled in 2001-2002. Transfer students must have maintained a minimum 2.5 GPA at their previous college. SAT I scores and high school and college transcripts are required. 60 credits of 120 must be completed at Assumption.

Visiting: There are regularly scheduled orientations for prospective students, consisting of new student orientation, meetings with future classmates, choosing roommates, registration, testing, conferences with academic advisers, and discussions of aspects of college life. There are guides for informal visits and visitors may sit in on classes. To schedule a visit, contact the Admissions Office.

Financial Aid: In 2001-2002, 91% of all freshmen and 89% of continuing students received some form of financial aid. 69% of freshmen and 68% of continuing students received need-based aid. The average freshman award was $11,907. Of that total, scholarships or need-based grants averaged $9804 ($22,250 maximum); loans averaged $3432 ($8625 maximum); and work contracts averaged $1482 ($1500 maximum). 23% of undergraduates work part time. Average annual earnings from campus work are $1482. The average financial indebtedness of the 2001 graduate was $18,523. Assumption is a member of CSS. The FAFSA is required. The fall application deadline is March 1.

International Students: There are 21 international students enrolled. The school actively recruits these students.

Computers: There are 27 servers, most powerful of which is a DEC 4100. Students have full Ethernet access to the Internet and campus networked information systems in all classrooms, dorm rooms, the computer center, and the library. There are some 1700 computers connected to the network. Roughly 160 of these are public cluster machines spread throughout the campus. All access the Web and e-mail as well as a full suite of other applications. All students may access the system. There are no time limits and no fees.

Graduates: In 2001, 443 bachelor's degrees were awarded. The most popular majors were social and rehabilitation services (16%), communications (11%), and psychology (10%). In an average class, 66% graduate in 4 years, 67% in 5 years, and 68% in 6 years. Of the 2000 graduating class, 22% were enrolled in graduate school within 6 months of graduation and 89% were employed.

Admissions Contact: Mary Bresnahan, Dean of Admissions. A video is available. E-mail: *admiss@assumption.edu*
Web: *http://www.assumption.edu*

ATLANTIC UNION COLLEGE
South Lancaster, MA 01561

C-2
(978) 368-2235
(800) 282-2030; Fax: (978) 368-2517

Full-time: 184 men, 287 women	**Faculty:** 41
Part-time: 41 men, 90 women	**Ph.D.s:** 59%
Graduate: 60 men, 59 women	**Student/Faculty:** 11 to 1
Year: semesters, summer session	**Tuition:** $26,858
Application Deadline: August 1	**Room & Board:** $7176
Freshman Class: 242 applied, 223 accepted, 145 enrolled	
SAT I Verbal/Math: 430/410	**ACT:** 17 **LESS COMPETITIVE**

Atlantic Union College, founded in 1882, is a private institution affiliated with the Seventh-day Adventist Church, offering undergraduate programs in the arts and sciences, business, education, health science, nursing, and religious studies. In addition to regional accreditation, AUC has baccalaureate program accreditation with CSWE, NASM, and NLN. The library contains 136,744 volumes, 11,029 microform items, and 4069 audiovisual forms/CDs, and subscribes to 535 periodicals. Computerized library services include the card catalog, interlibrary loans, and database searching. Special learning facilities include a learning resource center, art gallery, model elementary and secondary schools, and music conservatory. The 314-acre campus is in a small town 50 miles west of Boston. Including residence halls, there are 35 buildings.

Student Life: 57% of undergraduates are from out of state, mostly the Northeast. Others are from 15 states, 21 foreign countries, and Canada. 49% are African American; 21% Hispanic; 18% white; 10% foreign nationals. 14% do not continue beyond their first year.

Housing: Student housing includes single-sex dormitories, on-campus apartments, off-campus apartments, and married-student housing. On-campus housing is guaranteed for all 4 years. Alcohol is not permitted. All students may keep cars.

Activities: There are no fraternities or sororities. There are 13 groups on campus, including art, band, choir, chorale, drama, ethnic, honors, literary magazine, newspaper, orchestra, religious, student government, and yearbook. Popular campus events include Fall Picnic, Cultural Heritage Weeks, and Fine Arts Week.

Sports: There are 5 intramural sports for men and 5 for women. Facilities include a gym, a field house, a swimming pool, tennis courts, a racquetball court, and softball and soccer fields.

Disabled Students: Wheelchair ramps, elevators, special parking, and specially equipped rest rooms are available.

Services: Counseling and information services are available, as is tutoring in most subjects. There is remedial math, reading, and writing.

Campus Safety and Security: Measures include self-defense education, informal discussions, and lighted pathways/sidewalks.

Programs of Study: AUC confers B.A., B.S., and B.M. degrees. Associate and master's degrees are also awarded. Bachelor's degrees are awarded in BIOLOGICAL SCIENCE (biochemistry, biology/biological science, and life science), BUSINESS (accounting and business administration and management), COMMUNICATIONS AND THE ARTS (art, English, French, music, and Spanish), COMPUTER AND PHYSICAL SCIENCE (computer science, information sciences and systems, and mathematics), EDUCATION (early childhood, elementary, and music), HEALTH PROFESSIONS (nursing), SOCIAL SCIENCE (history, liberal arts/general studies, ministries, psychology, religion, social work, and theological studies). Nursing, English, and business are the strongest academically. Business, education, and nursing are the largest.

Required: Students must complete 9 hours each in humanities, religion/ethics, science, and social science. Foreign language proficiency, a phys ed requirement, 40 hours of community service, and a course in college writing must also be completed. AUC requires 128 to 143 credit hours for the bachelor's degree, with 30 to 60 in the major, and a 2.0 GPA.

Special: There is cross-registration with Mount Wachusett Community College and the Colleges of Worcester Consortium. Students may study abroad in 6 countries. AUC also offers newspaper and biology research internships, cooperative programs in several majors, pass/fail options, and nondegree study. The Summer Advantage in New England program offers precollege credit to high school honor students. There is also an adult degree program, in which most study is done at home, and in which student-designed majors are permited. Dual majors, an accelerated degree in management and professional studies, a 1-3 engineering degree with Walla Walla College, and preprofessional curricula in dentistry, dental hygiene, medicine, respiratory therapy, radiologic technology, and veterinary medicine in conjunction with Loma Linda University are offered. There are 2 national honor societies, a freshman honors program, and 2 departmental honors programs.

Faculty/Classroom: 41% of faculty are male; 17%, female. All teach undergraduates and 10% both teach and do research. The average class size in an introductory lecture is 20; in a laboratory, 10; and in a regular course, 20.

Admissions: 92% of the 2001-2002 applicants were accepted. The SAT I scores for the 2001-2002 freshman class were: Verbal--69% below 500, 26% between 500 and 599, and 8% between 600 and 700; Math--72% below 500, 23% between 500 and 599, and 5% between 600 and 700. The ACT scores were 71% below 21, 15% between 21 and 23, 8% between 24 and 26, and 6% between 27 and 28.

Requirements: The SAT I or ACT is required. In addition, applicants should be graduates of an accredited secondary school. The GED is accepted with a minimum score of 250. Required academic credits include 4 years of high school English and 2 years each of a foreign language, math, history, and science. A GPA of 2.0 is required. AP and CLEP credits are accepted. Important factors in the admissions decision are recommendations by school officials, recommendations by alumni, and personality/intangible qualities. Applications are accepted on disk and on-line through CollegeLink and the AUC web page.

Procedure: Freshmen are admitted fall and spring. Entrance exams should be taken during the senior year of high school. Applications should be filed by August 1 for fall entry and January 2 for spring entry, along with a $25 fee. Notification is sent on a rolling basis.

Transfer: 35 transfer students enrolled in 2001-2002. Applicants who have completed at least 24 semester hours are not required to submit SAT I or ACT scores. Applicants from junior colleges may receive credit for up to 72 semester hours. Only a grade of C or better transfers for credit. 30 credits of 128 must be completed at AUC.

Visiting: There are regularly scheduled orientations for prospective students, including campus tours, class visits, and financial aid and admissions information sessions. There are guides for informal visits and visitors may sit in on classes and stay overnight. To schedule a visit, contact Maureen Moncrieffe at (978) 368-2255 or *mhmoncrieffe@atlanticuc.edu*

Financial Aid: In 2001-2002, 88% of all freshmen and 84% of continuing students received some form of financial aid. 75% of freshmen and 77% of continuing students received need-based aid. The average freshman award was $6500. Of that total, scholarships or need-based grants averaged $1200 ($3000 maximum) and loans averaged $2500 ($2625 maximum). 80% of undergraduates work part time. Average annual earnings from campus work are $1200. The average financial indebtedness of the 2001 graduate was $18,000. The FAFSA and the college's own financial statement are required. The fall application deadline is May 1.

International Students: There are 70 international students enrolled. The school actively recruits these students. They must score 525 on the written TOEFL.

Computers: The mainframe is a DEC MicroVAX II on a Novell Network. 40 PCs and terminals are available for student use in the computer lab. All students may access the system. There are no time limits and no fees. It is strongly recommended that all students have personal computers.

Graduates: In 2001, 123 bachelor's degrees were awarded. The most popular majors were nursing (25%) and business administration (16%).

Admissions Contact: Rosita Lashley, Director of Admissions. A video is available. E-mail: *enroll@atlanticuc.edu* Web: *www.atlanticuc.edu*

BABSON COLLEGE

Babson Park, MA 02457 — D-2

(781) 239-5522
(800) 488-3696; Fax: (781) 239-4135

Full-time: 1080 men, 639 women	**Faculty:** 146; IIB, +$
Part-time: none	**Ph.D.s:** 90%
Graduate: 1116 men, 493 women	**Student/Faculty:** 12 to 1
Year: semesters, summer session	**Tuition:** $24,544
Application Deadline: February 1	**Room & Board:** $8746

Freshman Class: 3127 applied, 1081 accepted, 398 enrolled
SAT I Verbal/Math: 600/640 — **HIGHLY COMPETITIVE**

Babson College, founded in 1919, is a private business school. All students start their own businesses during their freshman year with money loaned by the college. In addition to regional accreditation, Babson has baccalaureate program accreditation with AACSB. The library contains 130,961 volumes, 346,785 microform items, and 4310 audiovisual forms/CDs, and subscribes to 1062 periodicals. Computerized library services include the card catalog, interlibrary loans, and database searching. Special learning facilities include a learning resource center, art gallery, radio station, performing arts theater, center for entrepreneurial studies, management center, language and culture center, writing center, math center, visual arts center, and center for executive education. The 380-acre campus is in a suburban area 14 miles west of Boston. Including residence halls, there are 65 buildings.

Student Life: 53% of undergraduates are from out of state, mostly the Northeast. Others are from 40 states, 64 foreign countries, and Canada. 55% are from public schools. 47% are white; 19% foreign nationals. The average age of freshmen is 18; all undergraduates, 20. 11% do not continue beyond their first year; 81% remain to graduate.

Housing: 1399 students can be accommodated in college housing, which includes single-sex and coed dormitories, on-campus apartments, and married-student housing. In addition, there are special-interest houses, substance-free living, fraternity and sorority towers, and a cultural house. On-campus housing is guaranteed for all 4 years. 85% of students live on campus; of those, 70% remain on campus on weekends. All students may keep cars.

Activities: 8% of men belong to 3 national fraternities; 13% of women belong to 2 national sororities. There are 47 groups on campus, including a capella group, art, dance, drama, ethnic, gay, honors, international, jazz band, literary magazine, musical theater, newspaper, photography, political, professional, radio and TV, religious, social, social service, student government, and yearbook. Popular campus events include Family Weekend, Founders Day, and Multicultural Week.

Sports: There are 11 intercollegiate sports for men and 11 for women, and 8 intramural sports for men and 8 for women. Facilities include a sports complex with an indoor pool, a 200-meter, 6-lane indoor track, a 1500-square-foot field house, a 600-seat gym with 3 basketball courts, 5 squash and 2 racquetball courts, a fitness center, a dance aerobics studio, locker rooms with saunas, and a sports medicine facility.

Disabled Students: 75% of the campus is accessible. Wheelchair ramps, elevators, special parking, specially equipped rest rooms, special class scheduling, and lowered drinking fountains are available.

Services: Counseling and information services are available, as is tutoring in most subjects. There are writing/speech skills and math/science skills centers.

Campus Safety and Security: Measures include 24-hour foot and vehicle patrol, self-defense education, escort service, and shuttle buses. There are informal discussions, pamphlets/posters/films, emergency telephones, lighted pathways/sidewalks, shuttle buses on Saturdays, and a motorist assist program, a transportation service for the cross-registration program, vans available to students for school activities, and crime prevention programs.

Programs of Study: Babson confers the B.S.M. degree. Master's degrees are also awarded. Bachelor's degrees are awarded in BUSINESS (business administration and management).

Required: Students must complete a curriculum of general management and liberal arts, with 50% in management and 50% in liberal arts. A total of 128 semester hours is required for graduation. A minimum GPA of 2.0 is required. The curriculum focuses on rhetoric, numeracy, ethics/social responsibility, international/multicultural perspectives, and leadership/teamwork/creativity competencies. Students specialize in certain aspects of business.

Special: There is cross-registration with Brandeis University, Pine Manor, Wellesley, and Regis Colleges, and F.W. Olin College of Engineering. Internships and study abroad in 20 countries are available. All concentrations are self-designed. There are 7 national honor societies, a freshman honors program, and 1 departmental honors program.

Faculty/Classroom: 67% of faculty are male; 33%, female. 90% teach undergraduates, 85% do research, and 80% do both. No introductory courses are taught by graduate students. The average class size in an introductory lecture is 34; in a laboratory, 20; and in a regular course, 26.

Admissions: 35% of the 2001-2002 applicants were accepted. The SAT I scores for the 2001-2002 freshman class were: Verbal--3% below 500, 44% between 500 and 599, 48% between 600 and 700, and 5% above 700; Math--19% between 500 and 599, 63% between 600 and 700, and 17% above 700. 80% of the current freshmen were in the top fifth of their class.

Requirements: The SAT I or ACT is required. In addition, applicants must be graduates of an accredited secondary school or have a GED. 16 academic courses are required, including 4 credits of English, 3 of math, 2 of social studies, and 1 of science. A fourth year of math is strongly recommended. Essays are required. An interview is recommended. SAT II: Subject tests in writing and math (either IC or IIC) are recommended. AP and CLEP credits are accepted. Important factors in the admissions decision are advanced placement or honor courses, evidence of special talent, and leadership record. Applications are accepted on computer disk and on-line via CollegeLink, ExPAN, CollegeView, and College Edge.

Procedure: Freshmen are admitted in the fall. Entrance exams should be taken prior to application (SAT I or ACT). There are early decision, early admissions, and deferred admissions plans. Early decision applications should be filed by December 1; regular applications, by February 1 for fall entry and November 1 for spring entry. Notification of early decision is sent January 1; regular decision, April 1. 36 early decision candidates were accepted for a recent year's class. The application fee is $50; $100 for international students.

Transfer: 48 transfer students enrolled in 2001-2002. Transfer applicants are expected to demonstrate solid academic performance at their prior institution and must submit 1 essay and 1 recommendation from a college teacher or administrator, in addition to a high school transcript and SAT I scores. 64 credits of 128 must be completed at Babson.

Visiting: There are regularly scheduled orientations for prospective students, including 3 open houses each year. Personal interviews, campus tours, and group information sessions are also available. There are guides for informal visits and visitors may sit in on classes and stay overnight. To schedule a visit, contact the Admission Office at at least 2 weeks in advance.

Financial Aid: In 2001-2002, 46% of all freshmen and 41% of continuing students received some form of financial aid. 43% of freshmen received need-based aid. Scholarships or need-based grants averaged $19,648. 34% of undergraduates work part time. Average annual earnings from campus work are $2484. The average financial indebtedness of the 2001 graduate was $23,000. Babson is a member of CSS. The CSS/Profile or FAFSA and tax returns are required. The fall application deadline is February 15.

International Students: There are 329 international students enrolled. The school actively recruits these students. They must score 550 on the written TOEFL or 213 on the electronic version or take the English Language Proficiency Test and also take the SAT I or the ACT. Students must take SAT II: Subject tests in math (IC or IIC) and writing.

Computers: Residence hall rooms have access to GlobeNet through a 10-Base-T Ethernet connection. Access to the Internet, including Netscape for browsing the World Wide Web, and e-mail are also provided. All students may access the system. There are no time limits and no fees. It is strongly recommended that all students have a personal computer.

Graduates: In a recent year, 415 bachelor's degrees were awarded. In an average class, 77% graduate in 4 years, 78% in 5 years, and 81% in 6 years. 301 companies recruited on campus in a recent year. Of a recent year's graduating class, 3% were enrolled in graduate school within 6 months of graduation and 92% were employed.

Admissions Contact: Monica Inzer, Dean of Undergraduate Admission and Financial Services. A video is available.
E-mail: *ugradadmission@babson.edu* Web: *www.babson.edu*

BAY PATH COLLEGE
Longmeadow, MA 01106 (413) 565-1331
(800) 782-7284; Fax: (413) 565-1105

Full-time: 669 women	**Faculty:** 33
Part-time: 249 women	**Ph.D.s:** 54%
Graduate: 54 women	**Student/Faculty:** 20 to 1
Year: semesters	**Tuition:** $14,754
Application Deadline: open	**Room & Board:** $7554
Freshman Class: n/av	
SAT I or ACT: required	**COMPETITIVE**

Bay Path College, founded in 1897, is a private liberal arts institution offering innovative undergraduate programs for women only and graduate programs for men and women. In addition to regional accreditation, Bay Path has baccalaureate program accreditation with AOTA. The library contains 44,000 volumes, 4019 microform items, and 2153 audiovisual forms/CDs, and subscribes to 150 periodicals. Computerized library services include the card catalog, interlibrary loans, and database searching. Special learning facilities include a learning resource center and an art center. The 44-acre campus is in a suburban area 3 miles south of Springfield. Including residence halls, there are 17 buildings.

Student Life: 60% of undergraduates are from Massachusetts. Others are from 15 states and 17 foreign countries. 67% are white; 10% African American. The average age of freshmen is 18; all undergraduates, 35.

Housing: On-campus housing includes single-sex dormitories and is guaranteed for all 4 years. Alcohol is not permitted. All students may keep cars.

Activities: There are no fraternities. There are 31 groups on campus, including cheerleading, chorale, computers, dance, ethnic, honors, international, literary magazine, musical theater, newspaper, professional, religious, social, social service, and student government. Popular campus events include Fall and Spring Campus Days, Family and Friends Weekend, and Six Flags New England Day.

Sports: Facilities include a fitness center that houses a weight training room, a dance studio, and an aerobics room; and a nearby 12-acre playing field with soccer and softball fields, a walking/jogging track, and a field house.

Disabled Students: Wheelchair ramps, elevators, special parking, and specially equipped rest rooms are available.

Services: Counseling and information services are available, as is tutoring in every subject.

Campus Safety and Security: Measures include 24-hour foot and vehicle patrol, escort service, informal discussions, and emergency telephones. There are lighted pathways/sidewalks.

Programs of Study: Bay Path confers B.A. and B.S. degrees. Associate and master's degrees are also awarded. Bachelor's degrees are awarded in BIOLOGICAL SCIENCE (biology/biological science), BUSINESS (business administration and management, electronic business, hospitality management services, international business management, management information systems, and marketing/retailing/merchandising), COMMUNICATIONS AND THE ARTS (communications, fine arts, graphic design, and performing arts), COMPUTER AND PHYSICAL SCIENCE (information sciences and systems), EDUCATION (early childhood, education administration, and elementary), ENGINEERING AND ENVIRONMENTAL DESIGN (interior design), HEALTH PROFESSIONS (occupational therapy), SOCIAL SCIENCE (American studies, child psychology/development, criminal justice, forensic studies, gerontology, industrial and organizational psychology, international studies, law, liberal arts/general studies, and psychology).

Required: To graduate, students must complete at least 120 credits with a minimum GPA of 2.0. The 46-hour core curriculum included course work in communication, science, social science, math and fine and performing arts.

Special: Cross-registration is possible with other member schools of the Cooperating Colleges of Greater Springfield Consortium. Bay Path's capital of the world program allows students to visit a different world center during each spring break.

Faculty/Classroom: 44% of faculty are male; 56%, female. All teach undergraduates. No introductory courses are taught by graduate students.

Admissions: The SAT I scores for the 2001-2002 freshman class were: Verbal--53% below 500, 36% between 500 and 599, 10% between 600 and 700, and 1% above 700; Math--62% below 500, 35% between 500 and 599, 4% between 600 and 700, and 1% above 700. The ACT scores were 33% below 21 and 67% between 21 and 23.

Requirements: The SAT I or ACT is required. In addition, applicants should have completed at least 4 academic courses each year, including 4 years of English, 3 of math, at least 2 each of social studies and lab sciences, and 2 of a foreign language. An essay is required, as are letters of recommendation from a guidance counselor and a teacher. An interview is strongly recommended. Applications are accepted on-line. AP and CLEP credits are accepted.

Procedure: Freshmen are admitted fall and spring. Entrance exams should be taken in the spring of the junior year or by December of the senior year. There are early admissions and rolling admissions plans. Application deadlines are open. The fall 2001 application fee was $25.

Transfer: 28 transfer students enrolled in 2001-2002. Applicants must be in good standing at their previous school and are encouraged to arrange for an interview at Bay Path. Students who have earned fewer than 12 credits must submit SAT I or ACT scores. 30 credits of 120 must be completed at Bay Path.

Visiting: There are regularly scheduled orientations for prospective students. There are guides for informal visits and visitors may sit in on classes. To schedule a visit, contact Brenda Wishart, Director of Enrollment Services.

Financial Aid: In 2001-2002, 92% of all freshmen received some form of financial aid. The FAFSA, the college's own financial statement, and parent and student income tax forms are required. The fall application deadline is April 1.

International Students: There are 42 international students enrolled. The school actively recruits these students. They must score 500 on the written TOEFL.

Computers: The mainframe is an IBM AS/400. There are 200 PCs distributed throughout the campus. All provide Internet and e-mail access. All students may access the system. There are no time limits and no fees.

Graduates: In 2001, 108 bachelor's degrees were awarded. The most popular majors were business (34%), computer and information sciences (16%), and liberal arts (12%).

Admissions Contact: Brenda Wishart, Director of Enrollment Services. E-mail: *admiss@baypath.edu* Web: *www.baypath.edu*

BECKER COLLEGE C-2
Worcester, MA 01615-0071 (508) 791-9241, ext. 245
(877) 5BECKER; Fax: (508) 890-1500

Full-time: 177 men, 563 women	**Faculty:** 39
Part-time: 100 men, 458 women	**Ph.D.s:** 20%
Graduate: none	**Student/Faculty:** 19 to 1
Year: semesters, summer session	**Tuition:** $14,050
Application Deadline: open	**Room & Board:** $7180
Freshman Class: 1309 applied, 1181 accepted, 352 enrolled	
SAT I: required	**ACT:** recommended
	LESS COMPETITIVE

Becker College, founded in 1887, is an independent undergraduate liberal arts and sciences institution offering baccalaureate degrees in various programs. In addition to regional accreditation, Becker College has baccalaureate program accreditation with NLN. The 2 libraries contain 60,000 volumes, and subscribe to 200 periodicals. Computerized library services include the card catalog, interlibrary loans, and database searching. Special learning facilities include a learning resource center, radio station, day care centers, a veterinary clinic, and a preschool facility. The Worcester campus is in a suburban area 40 miles west of Boston. Including residence halls, there are 27 buildings.

Student Life: 70% of undergraduates are from Massachusetts. Others are from 18 states, 6 foreign countries, and Canada. 77% are white. The average age of all undergraduates is 22.

Housing: Students can be accommodated in college housing, which includes single-sex and coed dormitories. In addition, there is 21 and over housing. On-campus housing is guaranteed for all 4 years. 65% of students live on campus. Alcohol is not permitted. All students may keep cars.

Activities: There are no fraternities or sororities. There are 22 groups on campus, including animal, art, cheerleading, chorus, dance, drama, ethnic, gay, honors, international, newspaper, outdoors, photography, professional, radio and TV, social, social service, student government, and yearbook. Popular campus events include Family Day, Class Day, and Spree Day.

Sports: There are 8 intercollegiate sports for men and 7 for women, and 7 intramural sports for men and 7 for women.

Disabled Students: 80% of the campus is accessible. Wheelchair ramps, elevators, special parking, specially equipped rest rooms, lowered drinking fountains, and lowered telephones are available. All classes and most dorms are accessible.

Services: Counseling and information services are available, as is tutoring in most subjects. There is remedial math and writing. There is also an academic support center for students.

Campus Safety and Security: Measures include self-defense education, escort service, shuttle buses, and informal discussions. There are pamphlets/posters/films, emergency telephones, and lighted pathways/sidewalks.

Programs of Study: Becker College confers B.A. and B.S. degrees. Associate degrees are also awarded. Bachelor's degrees are awarded in BUSINESS (accounting, banking and finance, business administration and management, hospitality management services, human resources, marketing and distribution, and sports management), COMMUNICATIONS AND THE ARTS (communications, design, and graphic design), EDUCATION (early childhood and elementary), ENGINEERING AND ENVIRONMENTAL DESIGN (interior design), HEALTH PROFESSIONS (exercise science, health, and veterinary science), SOCIAL SCIENCE (child care/child and family studies, criminal justice, human development, law, and psychology).

Required: To graduate, baccalaureate students must complete 122 semester hours and maintain a 2.0 minimum GPA. Distribution requirements vary with the program of study.

Special: Cross-registration is offered through the Worcester Consortium of Higher Education. There are co-op programs, internships, study abroad, student-designed majors, work-study programs, and B.A.-B.S. degrees. There is 1 national honor society, Phi Beta Kappa, and a freshman honors program.

Faculty/Classroom: 41% of faculty are male; 59%, female. All teach undergraduates. The average class size in an introductory lecture is 20; in a laboratory, 15; and in a regular course, 15.

Admissions: 90% of the 2001-2002 applicants were accepted.

Requirements: The SAT I is required and the ACT is recommended. In addition, a high school transcript is required. An interview is optional. A GPA of 2.0 is required. AP and CLEP credits are accepted. Important factors in the admissions decision are recommendations by school officials, extracurricular activities record, and evidence of special talent. Applications are available on-line at the Becker web site and via Common App.

Procedure: Freshmen are admitted to all sessions. Application deadlines are open. The fall 2001 application fee was $25. Notification is sent on a rolling basis.

Transfer: 80 transfer students enrolled in 2001-2002. Requirements for transfer students depend on the program. 62 credits of 122 must be completed at Becker College.

Visiting: There are regularly scheduled orientations for prospective students. There are guides for informal visits and visitors may sit in on classes. To schedule a visit, contact the Admissions Receptionist.

Financial Aid: In 2001-2002, 90% of all students received some form of financial aid, including need-based aid. The average freshman award was $5910. Average annual earnings from campus work are $1000. The FAFSA and the college's own financial statement are required. The fall application deadline is April 1.

International Students: The school actively recruits these students. They must score 500 on the written TOEFL or 173 on the electronic version and also take the SAT I or the ACT.

Computers: Any vacant computer is available for student use. Internet access is available in libraries. All dorms are wired for Internet access. All students may access the system. There are no time limits and no fees.

Graduates: In 2001, 41 bachelor's degrees were awarded. 30 companies recruited on campus in 2000-2001.

Admissions Contact: Elaine Lapomardo, Vice President of Enrollment Management. E-mail: *admissions@beckercollege.edu*
Web: *www.beckercollege.edu*

BENJAMIN FRANKLIN INSTITUTE OF TECHNOLOGY

Boston, MA 02116 **(617) 423-4630; Fax: (617) 482-3706**

Full-time: 268 men, 35 women	**Faculty:** 32
Part-time: 11 men	**Ph.D.s:** 3%
Graduate: none	**Student/Faculty:** 10 to 1
Year: semesters, summer session	**Tuition:** $10,990
Application Deadline: August 15	**Room & Board:** $9660
Freshman Class: 574 applied, 545 accepted, 177 enrolled	
SAT I or ACT: recommended	**SPECIAL**

Benjamin Franklin Institute of Technology, founded in 1908, is a private technical college offering degree programs in industrial and engineering technologies. In addition to regional accreditation, Benjamin Franklin Institute of Technology has baccalaureate program accreditation with ABET. The library contains 10,000 volumes, and subscribes to 70 periodicals. Computerized library services include the card catalog, interlibrary loans, and database searching. Special learning facilities include a learning resource center. The 3-acre campus is in an urban area. There are 3 buildings.

Student Life: 95% of undergraduates are from Massachusetts. Others are from 7 states and 7 foreign countries. 35% are African American; 35% white; 14% Hispanic; 12% Asian American. The average age of freshmen is 22; all undergraduates, 22.

Housing: Housing is available through Boston University on a first-come, first-served basis. Priority is given to out-of-town students

Activities: There are no fraternities or sororities. There are some groups and organizations on campus, including newspaper, student government, and women's. Popular campus events include Technology Olympics and International Culture Day.

Sports: There are 1 intercollegiate sport for men, and 2 intramural sports for men.

Disabled Students: 50% of the campus is accessible. Elevators and specially equipped rest rooms are available.

Services: Counseling and information services are available, as is tutoring in every subject. There is remedial math, reading, and writing.

Programs of Study: Benjamin Franklin Institute of Technology confers the B.S. degree. Associate degrees are also awarded. Bachelor's degrees are awarded in ENGINEERING AND ENVIRONMENTAL DESIGN (automotive technology).

Required: To graduate, students must earn a minimum cumulative GPA of 2.0.

Special: If qualified, 2-year Franklin graduates may transfer to Northeastern University. Automotive technology management students have access to Northeastern's facilities and resources.

Faculty/Classroom: 74% of faculty are male; 26%, female. All teach undergraduates. The average class size in an introductory lecture is 30; in a laboratory, 12; and in a regular course, 25.

Admissions: 95% of the 2001-2002 applicants were accepted.

Requirements: The SAT I or ACT is recommended. In addition, applicants should be high school graduates or have the GED. A GPA of 2.0 is required.

Procedure: Freshmen are admitted fall and spring. Applications should be filed by August 15 for fall entry and January 1 for spring entry, along with a $20 fee. Notification is sent on a rolling basis.

Visiting: Visitors may sit in on classes. To schedule a visit, contact the Office of Admission.

Financial Aid: In 2001-2002, 94% of all freshmen and 90% of continuing students received some form of financial aid. Benjamin Franklin Institute of Technology is a member of CSS. The FAFSA is required. The fall priority application deadline is April 15.

International Students: They must score 500 on the written TOEFL or 173 on the electronic version or take the college's own test or another recognized ESL program.

Computers: There are more than 130 networked computers in labs, the library, and electronic classrooms. All have access to the system and to the Internet via a T-1 line. There are no time limits and no fees. It is strongly recommended that all students have a personal computer.

Graduates: 34 companies recruited on campus in 2000-2001. Of the 2000 graduating class, 98% were employed within 6 months of graduation.

Admissions Contact: Will Arvelo, Dean of Enrollment Services.
E-mail: *warvelo@bfit.edu* Web: *www.bfit.edu*

BENTLEY COLLEGE

Waltham, MA 02452-4705 D-2
(781) 891-2244
(800) 523-2354; Fax: (781) 891-3414

Full-time: 2169 men, 1541 women **Faculty:** 243; IIA, ++$
Part-time: 248 men, 298 women **Ph.D.s:** 82%
Graduate: 721 men, 610 women **Student/Faculty:** 15 to 1
Year: semesters, summer session **Tuition:** $22,050
Application Deadline: February 1 **Room & Board:** $9010
Freshman Class: 5906 applied, 2250 accepted, 855 enrolled
SAT I Verbal/Math: 560/600 **HIGHLY COMPETITIVE**

Bentley College is a independent institution that offers advanced business education along with a strong foundation in the arts and sciences. In addition to regional accreditation, Bentley has baccalaureate program accreditation with AACSB. The library contains 212,573 volumes, 1320 microform items, and 4705 audiovisual forms/CDs, and subscribes to 650 periodicals. Computerized library services include the card catalog, interlibrary loans, and database searching. Special learning facilities include a learning resource center, art gallery, planetarium, radio station, the Accounting Center for Electronic Learning and Business Management, the Center for Languages and International Collaboration, the Center for Marketing Technology, the Design and Usability Testing Center, an academic technology center, and a trading room. The 163-acre campus is in a suburban area 10 miles west of Boston. Including residence halls, there are 43 buildings.

Student Life: 57% of undergraduates are from Massachusetts. Others are from 42 states, 66 foreign countries, and Canada. 75% are from public schools. 73% are white. The average age of freshmen is 18; all undergraduates, 21. 6% do not continue beyond their first year.

Housing: 2968 students can be accommodated in college housing, which includes single-sex and coed dormitories, on-campus apartments, and off-campus apartments. In addition, there are special-interest houses, substance-free, intensive study, and smoke-free housing. On-campus housing is guaranteed for all 4 years. 78% of students live on campus. Upperclassmen may keep cars.

Activities: 12% of men and women belong to 4 local and 2 national fraternities; 12% of women belong to 5 national sororities. There are 90 groups on campus, including alcohol awareness, art, band, cheerleading, choir, chorale, computers, dance, debate, drama, ethnic, film, forensics, gay, honors, international, jazz band, literary magazine, musical theater, newspaper, pep band, photography, political, professional, radio and TV, religious, social, social service, student government, and yearbook. Popular campus events include Monte Carlo Night, a film series, and Spring Weekend.

Sports: There are 11 intercollegiate sports for men and 10 for women, and 8 intramural sports for men and 8 for women. Facilities include a basketball court; a competition-size swimming pool with a diving tank; saunas and a steam bath; volleyball courts; baseball batting and golf cages; racquetball/handball courts; an indoor track; a dance studio; a 7000-square-foot exercise room with fitness equipment that includes treadmills, stationary bikes, StairMaster and Nautilus equipment, and free weights; 2 lighted playing fields, one natural grass and one synthetic, for football, soccer, lacrosse, and other sports; 6 lighted tennis courts; a baseball field with seating for 1700; and an outdoor track.

Disabled Students: 95% of the campus is accessible. Wheelchair ramps, elevators, special parking, specially equipped rest rooms, and lowered telephones are available.

Services: Counseling and information services are available, as is tutoring in most subjects. There is remedial math, reading, and writing, and a Kurzweil reading machine.

Campus Safety and Security: Measures include 24-hour foot and vehicle patrol, self-defense education, escort service, and shuttle buses. There are informal discussions, pamphlets/posters/films, emergency telephones, and lighted pathways/sidewalks.

Programs of Study: Bentley confers B.A. and B.S. degrees. Associate and master's degrees are also awarded. Bachelor's degrees are awarded in BUSINESS (accounting, banking and finance, business administration and management, business economics, management information systems, and marketing management), COMMUNICATIONS AND THE ARTS (communications and English), COMPUTER AND PHYSICAL SCIENCE (mathematics), SOCIAL SCIENCE (history, interdisciplinary studies, international studies, liberal arts/general studies, paralegal studies, philosophy, and public affairs). Accountancy and finance are the strongest academically.

Required: All undergraduate students complete general education courses in areas such as expository writing, mathematical sciences, natural sciences, humanities, behavioral sciences, information technology, political science, history, philosophy, and economics. Students in B.S. programs take a common core of 10 courses covering major business areas such as accounting, business law, and marketing. All students take elective courses that fulfill a diversity, international, and communication intensive requirement. A total of 120 to 122 credit hours is required for graduation, with a minimum GPA of 2.0. All students must take phys ed, and first-year students complete a first-year seminar course.

Special: There is cross-registration with Regis College and Brandeis University, and internships are available in business and public service. The college offers study abroad in 11 countries, a Washington semester, work-study programs, accelerated degree programs, student-designed majors, credit by exam, and nondegree study. There is also a minor concentration program through which business majors can broaden their exposure to the arts and sciences, and arts and science majors can minor in business or interdisciplinary topics. There is 1 national honor society and 3 departmental honors programs.

Faculty/Classroom: 67% of faculty are male; 33%, female. All teach undergraduates. No introductory courses are taught by graduate students. The average class size in a regular course is 30.

Admissions: 38% of the 2001-2002 applicants were accepted. The SAT I scores for the 2001-2002 freshman class were: Verbal--12% below 500, 62% between 500 and 599, 24% between 600 and 700, and 1% above 700; Math--4% below 500, 45% between 500 and 599, 46% between 600 and 700, and 5% above 700. 57% of the current freshmen were in the top fifth of their class; 88% were in the top two fifths. 4 freshmen graduated first in their class.

Requirements: The SAT I or ACT is required. In addition, applicants must be graduates of an accredited high school or have a GED. Recommended high school preparation is 4 units each in English and math, including algebra I and II, geometry, and a senior-year math course; 3 units in lab science; 2 to 3 units in a foreign language; 2 units in social science; and 2 additional units in English, math, social science or lab science, foreign langauage, or speech. AP and CLEP credits are accepted. Important factors in the admissions decision are advanced placement or honor courses and recommendations by school officials. Applications are accepted on-line via CollegeNET, Common App, Mass Mentor, NextStop College, and College Quest.

Procedure: Freshmen are admitted fall and spring. Entrance exams should be taken before the January test date. There are early decision and deferred admissions plans. Early decision applications should be filed by December 1; regular applications, by February 1 for fall entry and November 15 for spring entry. The fall 2001 application fee was $50. Notification of early decision is sent December 28; regular decision, April 1. 103 early decision candidates were accepted for the 2001-2002 class. 21% of all applicants are on a waiting list; 131 were accepted in 2001.

Transfer: 126 transfer students were enrolled in a recent year. The SAT I or the ACT is required of all applicants who have completed fewer than 30 college credits. All official college transcripts must be submitted. 45 credits of 120 to 122 must be completed at Bentley.

Visiting: There are regularly scheduled orientations for prospective students, including fall, spring, and summer open house programs. Interviews are arranged by appointment; campus tours take place at regularly scheduled times each weekday. There are fall Fridays information sessions. There are guides for informal visits and visitors may sit in on classes. To schedule a visit, contact the Office of Undergraduate Admission at (781) 891-2455.

Financial Aid: In 2001-2002, 72% of all freshmen and 63% of continuing students received some form of financial aid. 51% of freshmen and 49% of continuing students received need-based aid. The average freshman award was $19,156. Of that total, scholarships or need-based grants averaged $13,828 ($24,960 maximum); loans averaged $3340 ($4925 maximum); and work contracts averaged $1988 ($2200 maximum). 26% of undergraduates work part time. Average annual earnings from campus work are $1330. The average financial indebtedness of the 2001 graduate was $17,811. Bentley is a member of CSS. The CSS/Profile or FAFSA is required. The fall application deadline is February 1.

International Students: There are 309 international students enrolled. The school actively recruits these students. They must score 551 on the written TOEFL and also take the SAT I or the ACT.

Computers: The mainframes are a DEC VAX 6620 and a DEC VAX 6510. With one "port-per-pillow" in residence halls, students have individual access from their dorm room to the campus computing system and the Internet. A growing number of Bentley classrooms feature port-per-seat network connections as well. The college also provides more than 100 PCs and Macs in centralized labs. All have network access. All students may access the system during lab hours, 7 days a week. There are no time limits and no fees. All students are required to have laptop computers.

Graduates: In 2001, 814 bachelor's degrees were awarded. The most popular majors were finance (29%), accountancy (16%), and marketing (15%). In an average class, 66% graduate in 4 years, and 73% in 5 years. 250 companies recruited on campus in 2000-2001. Of the 2000 graduating class, 11% were enrolled in graduate school within 6 months of graduation.

Admissions Contact: Judith Pearson, Director of Undergraduate Admission. E-mail: *ugadmission@bentley.edu* Web: *www.bentley.edu*

BERKLEE COLLEGE OF MUSIC

E-2

Boston, MA 02215-3693 (617) 266-1400, ext. 2222
(800) BERKLEE; Fax: (617) 747-2047

Full-time: 3043 men and women	**Faculty:** 210; IIB, +$
Part-time: 372 men and women	**Ph.D.s:** n/av
Graduate: none	**Student/Faculty:** 14 to 1
Year: semesters, summer session	**Tuition:** $17,715
Application Deadline: open	**Room & Board:** $9290

Freshman Class: 2582 applied, 1873 accepted, 916 enrolled
SAT I or ACT: required **SPECIAL**

Berklee College of Music, founded in 1945, is a private institution offering programs in music production and engineering, film scoring, music business/management, composition, music synthesis, music education, music therapy, performance, contemporary writing and production, jazz composition, songwriting, and professional music. The library contains 31,274 volumes and 22,974 audiovisual forms/CDs, and subscribes to 122 periodicals. Computerized library services include the card catalog and database searching. Special learning facilities include a learning resource center and 10 recording studios, 5 performance venues, and film scoring, music synthesis, and songwriting labs. The campus is in an urban area in the Fenway Cultural District, Back Bay, Boston. Including residence halls, there are 14 buildings.

Student Life: 80% of undergraduates are from out of state, mostly the Northeast. Others are from 55 states, 81 foreign countries, and Canada. 71% are white; 30% foreign nationals. The average age of freshmen is 22; all undergraduates, 23. 35% do not continue beyond their first year; 60% remain to graduate.

Housing: 800 students can be accommodated in college housing, which includes coed dormitories. On-campus housing is available on a first-come, first-served basis and is available on a lottery system for upperclassmen. 88% of students commute. Alcohol is not permitted. No one may keep cars.

Activities: There are no fraternities or sororities. There are 62 groups on campus, including art, band, choir, chorale, chorus, computers, drama, ethnic, gay, international, jazz band, musical theater, newspaper, orchestra, professional, religious, social, social service, and student government. Popular campus events include International Students Fair and Concert, daily recitals and concerts, and Singer Showcase.

Sports: There are 4 intramural sports for men and 4 for women. Facilities include discount memberships at the YMCA, a student rate at the Massachusetts College of Art fitness room, and memberships at the Sheraton Fitness Center and the Tennis and Racquet Club of Boston are available.

Disabled Students: All of the campus is accessible. Wheelchair ramps, elevators, special class scheduling, lowered drinking fountains, and lowered telephones are available.

Services: Counseling and information services are available, as is tutoring in every subject. There is a reader service for the blind. tape recorders, untimed testing, and learning center resources.

Campus Safety and Security: Measures include 24-hour foot and vehicle patrol, escort service, informal discussions, and pamphlets/posters/films. There are emergency telephones and lighted pathways/sidewalks.

Programs of Study: Berklee confers the B.M. degree. Master's degrees are also awarded. Bachelor's degrees are awarded in COMMUNICATIONS AND THE ARTS (audio technology, jazz, music, music business management, music performance, and music theory and composition), EDUCATION (music), HEALTH PROFESSIONS (music therapy). Performance, professional music, and music production and engineering are the largest.

Required: Students working toward a degree must take general education courses in English composition/literature, history, physical science, and social sciences. Music course programs vary by specialization. A total of 120 credits must be completed with a minimum GPA of 2.0.

Special: Berklee offers cross-registration with the Pro-Arts Consortium, study abroad in the Netherlands, internships in music education and music production and engineering, 5-year dual majors, and a 4-year professional (nondegree) diploma program. Work-study programs, an accelerated degree program, student-designed majors, and credit by exam are available.

Faculty/Classroom: 82% of faculty are male; 18%, female. All teach undergraduates. The average class size in an introductory lecture is 30; in a laboratory, 8; and in a regular course, 14.

Admissions: 73% of the 2001-2002 applicants were accepted.

Requirements: The SAT I or ACT is required. In addition, applicants must be graduates of an accredited secondary school that has a college preparatory program or have their GED. An audition and interview are recommended. Applicants must also submit a detailed reference letter regarding their training and experience in music, a letter from a private instructor, school music director, or professional musician. A GPA of 2.0 is required. AP credits are accepted. Important factors in the admissions decision are evidence of special talent, extracurricular activities record, and recommendations by alumni. Applications are accepted on-line at *www.embark.com*

Procedure: Freshmen are admitted to all sessions. Entrance exams should be taken in the fall of the senior year of high school. There are early admissions and deferred admissions plans. Application deadlines are open. Application fee is $75. A waiting list is an active part of the admissions procedure. Notification is sent on a rolling basis.

Transfer: 268 transfer students enrolled in 2001-2002. Applicants must go through the same application procedures as entering freshmen, as well as submit all previous college records. 60 credits of 120 must be completed at Berklee.

Visiting: There are regularly scheduled orientations for prospective students, consisting of 2 tours scheduled daily during semesters, with the morning tour followed by an information session given by an admissions counselor. There are guides for informal visits. To schedule a visit, contact the Admissions Office.

Financial Aid: 13% of undergraduates work part time. The CSS/Profile or FFS and the college's own financial statement are required.

International Students: There are 1030 international students enrolled. The school actively recruits these students. They must take the college's own test and also the SAT I or the ACT.

Computers: The mainframe is an IBM RS/6000 operating under AIX Version 4.32. There are more than 45 networked Macs in the learning center. All students may access the system. There are no time limits and no fees.

Graduates: In 2001, 638 bachelor's degrees were awarded.

Admissions Contact: Marsha Ginn, Director of Admissions. A video is available. E-mail: *admissions@berklee.edu* Web: *www.berklee.edu*

BOSTON ARCHITECTURAL CENTER

E-2

Boston, MA 02115 (617) 262-5000; Fax: (617) 585-0121

Full-time: 310 men, 110 women	**Faculty:** n/av
Part-time: 60 men, 10 women	**Ph.D.s:** 80%
Graduate: 110 men, 80 women	**Student/Faculty:** n/av
Year: semesters, summer session	**Tuition:** $7236
Application Deadline: open	**Room & Board:** n/app

Freshman Class: 370 applied, 280 accepted, 180 enrolled
SAT I or ACT: not required **SPECIAL**

Boston Architectural Center, founded in 1889 as the Boston Architectural Club, is an independent commuter institution offering professional programs in architecture and interior design. Some information in this profile is approximate. Students work in architectural and interior design offices during the day and attend classes at night. There are 2 undergraduate and 2 graduate schools. In addition to regional accreditation, BAC has baccalaureate program accreditation with NAAB. The library contains 25,000 volumes and subscribes to 140 periodicals. Computerized library services include the card catalog and database searching. Special learning facilities include an art gallery. The campus is in an urban area in Boston. There are 2 buildings.

Student Life: 53% of undergraduates are from Massachusetts. Others are from 43 states and 1 foreign country. 88% are white. The average age of freshmen is 26; all undergraduates, 26. 47% do not continue beyond their first year; 25% remain to graduate.

Housing: There are no residence halls. All students commute. Alcohol is not permitted.

Activities: There are no fraternities or sororities. There are 4 groups on campus, including newspaper, professional, student government, and yearbook.

Sports: There is no sports program at BAC.

Disabled Students: All of the campus is accessible. Wheelchair ramps, elevators, special parking, and specially equipped rest rooms are available.

Services: Counseling and information services are available, as is tutoring in most subjects. The writing center provides one-on-one writing assistence and special services for ESL students.

Campus Safety and Security: Measures include pamphlets/posters/films, lighted pathways/sidewalks, and full-time building security during operating hours.

Programs of Study: BAC confers B.Arch. and B.Int.Design. degrees. Master's degrees are also awarded. Bachelor's degrees are awarded in ENGINEERING AND ENVIRONMENTAL DESIGN (architecture and interior design).

Required: To graduate, all students must complete 123 academic credits, 93 of which must be in professional subjects and 30 in general education courses; 21 credits must be earned in liberal arts courses. Students must earn 54 additional credits by working in architectural or interior-design offices or related fields. Academic study is divided into 3 segments, the final segment being the thesis year, which consists of 2 semesters of student-designed study under the guidance of a faculty adviser. A minimum 2.5 GPA is required.

Special: BAC offers study abroad and cross-registration with the Art Institute of Boston and schools in the Professional Arts Consortium in Boston for studio and professional courses. The participating schools are BAC, Berklee College of Music, the Boston Conservatory, Emerson College, Massachusetts College of Art, and the School of the MFA.

Faculty/Classroom: 86% of faculty are male; 14%, female. All teach undergraduates. The average class size in an introductory lecture is 33 and in a laboratory, 8.

Admissions: 76% of recent applicants were accepted.

Requirements: All applicants who have graduated from high school or have a college degree are admitted on a first-come, first-served basis. Official transcripts from previously attended secondary schools and colleges must be submitted to determine qualification for admission and advanced placement. AP credits are accepted. Applications are accepted on-line at BAC's web site.

Procedure: Freshmen are admitted fall and spring. There is a deferred admissions plan. Application deadlines are open. The fall 2001 application fee was $50.

Transfer: 78 transfer students enrolled in a recent year. Applicants for transfer must have a 2.0 GPA to receive transfer credit in most courses; 3.0 in math and physics. 47 credits of 123 must be completed at BAC.

Visiting: There are regularly scheduled orientations for prospective students, consisting of monthly presentations. There are guides for informal visits and visitors may sit in on classes. To schedule a visit, contact the Admissions Office.

Financial Aid: In a recent year, 37% of all freshmen and 63% of continuing students received some form of financial aid. 38% of freshmen and 62% of continuing students received need-based aid. The average freshman award was $6457. Of that total, scholarships or need-based grants averaged $1440 ($3125 maximum); and loans averaged $5830 ($6625 maximum). The average financial indebtedness of a recent graduate was $40,000. BAC is a member of CSS. The FAFSA and the college's own financial statement are required. Check with the school for current deadlines.

International Students: They must score 550 on the written TOEFL.

Computers: There are 50 Macs and IBM PCs available for student use, all with Internet access. All students may access the system. There are no time limits.

Graduates: In a recent year, 53 bachelor's degrees were awarded.

Admissions Contact: William Dunfey, Director of Admissions.
E-mail: *admissions@the-bac.edu* Web: *www.the-bac.edu*

BOSTON COLLEGE

Chestnut Hill, MA 02467 — E-2
(617) 552-3100
(800) 360-2522; Fax: (617) 552-0798

Full-time: 4260 men, 4740 women	**Faculty:** 631; I, +$
Part-time: none	**Ph.D.s:** 98%
Graduate: 1924 men, 2586 women	**Student/Faculty:** 14 to 1
Year: semesters, summer session	**Tuition:** $25026
Application Deadline: January 2	**Room & Board:** $8860)

Freshman Class: 19,059 applied, 6401 accepted, 2108 enrolled
SAT I Verbal/Math: 600-690/620-700 — **MOST COMPETITIVE**

Boston College, founded in 1863, is an independent institution affiliated with the Roman Catholic Church and the Jesuit Order. It offers undergraduate programs in the arts and sciences, business, nursing, and education, and graduate and professional programs. Some information in this profile is approximate. There are 4 undergraduate and 7 graduate schools. In addition to regional accreditation, BC has baccalaureate program accreditation with AACSB, CSWE, NCATE, and NLN. The 6 libraries contain 1,737,880 volumes, 3,249,601 microform items, and 118,054 audiovisual forms/CDs, and subscribe to 20,910 periodicals. Computerized library services include the card catalog, interlibrary loans, and database searching. Special learning facilities include a learning resource center, art gallery, radio station, and TV station. The 240-acre campus is in a suburban area 6 miles west of Boston. Including residence halls, there are 90 buildings.

Student Life: 73% of undergraduates are from out of state, mostly the Northeast. Others are from 49 states, 63 foreign countries, and Canada. 61% are from public schools. 75% are white. 76% are Catholic; 11% claim no religious affiliation; 11%, Protestant. The average age of freshmen is 19; all undergraduates, 20. 6% do not continue beyond their first year; 85% remain to graduate.

Housing: 6475 students can be accommodated in college housing, which includes single-sex and coed dormitories and on-campus apartments. In addition, there are honors houses, language houses, and special-interest houses. On-campus housing is guaranteed for the freshman year only and is available on a lottery system for upperclassmen. 74% of students live on campus; of those, 75% remain on campus on weekends. Upperclassmen may keep cars.

Activities: There are no fraternities or sororities. There are 100 groups on campus, including art, band, cheerleading, chess, choir, chorale, chorus, computers, dance, debate, drama, ethnic, film, honors, international, jazz band, literary magazine, marching band, musical theater, newspaper, orchestra, pep band, photography, political, professional, radio and TV, religious, social, social service, student government, symphony, and yearbook. Popular campus events include Middlemarch Ball, Christmas Chorale, and Senior Week.

Sports: There are 17 intercollegiate sports for men and 16 for women, and 8 intramural sports for men and 7 for women. Facilities include a 44,500-seat stadium, a forum that seats 8500 for basketball and 7600 for ice hockey, a field, a track, and a student recreation complex.

Disabled Students: All of the campus is accessible. Wheelchair ramps, elevators, special parking, specially equipped rest rooms, special class scheduling, lowered drinking fountains, and lowered telephones are available.

Services: Counseling and information services are available, as is tutoring in most subjects. There is a reader service for the blind, and an academic development center that serves all students.

Campus Safety and Security: Measures include 24-hour foot and vehicle patrol, self-defense education, escort service, and shuttle buses. There are informal discussions, pamphlets/posters/films, emergency telephones, lighted pathways/sidewalks, safety seminars and safety walking tours, and whistles distributed to incoming students.

Programs of Study: BC confers B.A. and B.S. degrees. Master's and doctoral degrees are also awarded. Bachelor's degrees are awarded in BIOLOGICAL SCIENCE (biochemistry and biology/biological science), BUSINESS (accounting, banking and finance, business administration and management, business economics, human resources, management science, marketing/retailing/merchandising, and operations research), COMMUNICATIONS AND THE ARTS (art history and appreciation, classics, communications, dramatic arts, English, film arts, French, Italian, linguistics, music, romance languages and literature, and studio art), COMPUTER AND PHYSICAL SCIENCE (chemistry, computer science, geology, geophysics and seismology, information sciences and systems, mathematics, and physics), EDUCATION (early childhood, elementary, secondary, and special), ENGINEERING AND ENVIRONMENTAL DESIGN (environmental science), HEALTH PROFESSIONS (nursing), SOCIAL SCIENCE (classical/ancient civilization, economics, German area studies, Hispanic American studies, history, human development, philosophy, political science/government, psychology, Russian and Slavic studies, sociology, and theological studies). Humanities and social sciences are the strongest academically. English, finance, psychology, and communication are the largest.

Required: Core requirements include 2 courses each in natural science, social science, history, philosophy, and theology, and 1 course each in literature, writing, math, cultural diversity, and the arts. To graduate, students must complete 114 credits (121 in nursing), including at least 30 in the major, with a minimum 1.667 GPA (1.5 in management). Computer science is required for management majors, intermediate-level foreign language proficiency for arts and sciences and management students, and a freshman writing seminar for all students except honors and AP students.

Special: There are internship programs in arts and sciences. Students may cross-register with Boston University, Brandeis University, Hebrew College, Pine Manor College, Regis College, and Tufts University. BC also offers a Washington semester with American University, work-study programs with nonprofit agencies, study abroad, dual and student-designed majors, credit by exam, and pass/fail options. Students may pursue a 3-2 engineering program with Boston University and accelerated programs in business, social work, and education. There are also special programs in social work and philosophy/theology, in language immersion, capstone courses, and in exploring fundamental questions of faith, peace, and justice. There are 12 national honor societies, including Phi Beta Kappa, a freshman honors program, and 8 departmental honors programs.

Faculty/Classroom: 67% of faculty are male; 33%, female. All both teach and do research. Graduate students teach 12% of introductory courses. The average class size in a laboratory is 15 and in a regular course, 30.

Admissions: 34% of the 2001-2002 applicants were accepted. The SAT I scores for the 2001-2002 freshman class were: Verbal--4% below 500, 18% between 500 and 599, 56% between 600 and 700, and 22% above 700; Math--2% below 500, 13% between 500 and 599, 55% between 600 and 700, and 30% above 700. 89% of the current freshmen were in the top fifth of their class; 98% were in the top two fifths. There were 7 National Merit finalists in a recent year.

Requirements: The SAT I or ACT is required. In addition, students must also take SAT II: Subject tests in writing, mathematics level I or II, and any third test. Applicants must be graduates of an accredited high school completing 4 units each of English, foreign language, math, and science. Those students applying to the School of Nursing must complete at least 2 years of a lab science, including 1 unit of chemistry. Applicants to the School of Management are strongly encouraged to take 4 years of college preparatory math. An essay is required. AP credits are accepted. Important factors in the admissions decision are evidence of special talent, leadership record, and advanced placement or honor courses. Electronic application materials are available through *www.apply.embark.com/ugrad/bc*, *www.commonapp.org*, and *www.nextstopcollege.org*

Procedure: Freshmen are admitted fall and spring. Entrance exams should be taken no later than January of the senior year. There are early action, early and deferred admissions plans. Early action applications should be filed by November 1; regular applications, by January 2 for fall entry and November 1 for spring entry. The fall 2001 application fee was $55. Notification of early action is sent December 15; regular decision, April 15. A waiting list is an active part of the admissions procedure.

Transfer: 225 transfer students enrolled in a recent year. Applicants must have a current GPA of at least 2.5 and must have earned a minimum of 9 semester hours. High school transcripts, letters of recommendation, and SAT I or ACT scores are required. 54 credits of 114 must be completed at BC.

Visiting: There are regularly scheduled orientations for prospective students, consisting of group information sessions and campus tours Monday through Friday. There are guides for informal visits and visitors may sit in on classes. To schedule a visit, contact the Office of Undergraduate Admission.

Financial Aid: In a recent year, 49% of all freshmen and 48% of continuing students received some form of financial aid. 47% of freshmen and 46% of continuing students received need-based aid. The average freshman award was $18,793. Of that total, scholarships or need-based grants averaged $13,934 ($21,760 maximum); loans averaged $3459; and work contracts averaged $1400 ($1500 maximum). 19% of undergraduates work part time. Average annual earnings from campus work are $1500. The average financial indebtedness of a recent graduate was $16,417. BC is a member of CSS. The CSS/Profile or FAFSA and the federal income tax form, W-2's, and Divorced/Separated Statement (when applicable) are required. Check with the school for current deadlines.

International Students: In a recent year, there were 252 international students enrolled. They must score 600 on the written TOEFL or 250 on the electronic version and also take the SAT I or ACT and SAT II: Subject tests in writing, mathematics level I or II, and any third test.

Computers: The mainframes are an IBM 3270 and DEC VAX 11/785 and 8700 units. More than 200 PCs are available, providing database searches, optical disk references, and on-line access to catalog services. Software includes word processing, programming languages, statistical analysis, graphics production, and database management packages. Printers include high-speed line printers, high-resolution dot-matrix printers, and laser printers. All students may access the system at all times. There are no time limits and no fees.

Graduates: In a recent year, 2141 bachelor's degrees were awarded. The most popular majors were finance (11%), English (9%), and economics (8%). In an average class, 81% graduate in 4 years and 85% in 6 years. 300 companies recruited on campus in a recent year. Of a recent graduating class, 16% were enrolled in graduate school within 6 months of graduation and 69% were employed.

Admissions Contact: John L. Mahoney, Jr., Director of Undergraduate Admission. A video is available.
E-mail: *undergraduate.admission@bc.edu* Web: *www.bc.edu*

BOSTON CONSERVATORY

Boston, MA 02215 E-2
(617) 536-6340; Fax: (617) 536-3176

Full-time: 100 men, 240 women	**Faculty:** 17
Part-time: 10 men, 15 women	**Ph.D.s:** 1%
Graduate: 130 men and women	**Student/Faculty:** 15 to 1
Year: semesters, summer session	**Tuition:** $20,200
Application Deadline: open	**Room & Board:** $6800
Freshman Class: n/av	
SAT I or ACT: recommended	**SPECIAL**

The Boston Conservatory, founded in 1867, is a private, coeducational college providing degree programs in music, musical theater, and dance. Figures given in the above capsule are approximate. In addition to regional accreditation, the conservatory has baccalaureate program accreditation with NASM. The library contains 40,000 volumes, and subscribes to 120 periodicals. Computerized library services include interlibrary loans and database searching. The campus is in an urban area in Boston's Back Bay. Including residence halls, there are 7 buildings.

Student Life: 20% of students are from Massachusetts. Others are from 36 states, 29 foreign countries, and Canada. 90% are white. The average age of freshmen is 18. 23% do not continue beyond their first year; 44% remain to graduate.

Housing: 164 students can be accommodated in college housing, which includes single-sex and coed dormitories. In addition, there are special-interest houses and international housing. On-campus housing is guaranteed for all 4 years. 67% of students commute. Alcohol is not permitted. All students may keep cars.

Activities: There is 1 national fraternity and there are 2 national sororities. There are 19 groups on campus, including band, choir, chorale, chorus, dance, drama, ethnic, gay, international, musical theater, newspaper, opera, orchestra, political, professional, religious, social service, student government, and yearbook. Popular campus events include Parents Weekend.

Sports: There is no sports program at the conservatory.

Disabled Students: 20% of the campus is accessible. Elevators are available.

Services: Counseling and information services are available, as is tutoring in every subject. A fee is required.

Campus Safety and Security: Measures include 24-hour foot and vehicle patrol, self-defense education, and informal discussions.

Programs of Study: The conservatory confers B.F.A. and B.Mus. degrees. Bachelor's degrees are awarded in COMMUNICATIONS AND THE ARTS (dance, guitar, music, music performance, music theory and composition, musical theater, opera, and piano/organ), EDUCATION (music). Music is the largest.

Required: All students must successfully complete the curriculum with no more than 12 credit hours of D-grade work. In addition, music performance majors must present recitals, music education majors must present a recital from memory, and composition majors must pass an exam on their primary instrument, present a portfolio of original composition, and perform a recital.

Special: There are 3 national honor societies, and 1 departmental honors program.

Faculty/Classroom: All teach undergraduates. No introductory courses are taught by graduate students. The average class size in an introductory lecture is 15; in a laboratory, 5; and in a regular course, 15.

Requirements: The SAT I or ACT is recommended and scores are reviewed. An audition is required. An academic high school diploma or GED also is required. A GPA of 2.0 is required. AP and CLEP credits are accepted. Important factors in the admissions decision are evidence of special talent, extracurricular activities record, and personality/intangible qualities.

Procedure: Freshmen are admitted in the fall. Entrance exams should be taken as early as possible. There is a deferred admissions plan. Application deadlines are open.

Transfer: A successful audition and a 2.0 GPA are required. Transfer credits are determined by exam or review by the division head and the dean. The high school transcript is required if fewer than 30 college credits have been earned.

Visiting: Visitors may sit in on classes. To schedule a visit, contact the Admissions Office at (617) 536-6340.

Financial Aid: The conservatory is a member of CSS. The CSS/Profile and the college's own financial statement are required. Check with the school for current deadlines.

International Students: The school actively recruits these students. They must take the TOEFL or the MELAB or the college's own test, or the SAT I, scoring 950 on the SAT I. An audition also is required.

Computers: Mac PCs are available to all students. Students may access the system when the library is open. There are no time limits and no fees.

Admissions Contact: Halley Shefler, Director of Enrollment Management.

BOSTON UNIVERSITY

Boston, MA 02215 E-2
(617) 353-2300; Fax: (617) 353-9695

Full-time: 5983 men, 9617 women	**Faculty:** 1283; I, +$
Part-time: 1117 men, 885 women	**Ph.D.s:** 80%
Graduate: 4783 men, 5371 women	**Student/Faculty:** 12 to 1
Year: semesters, summer session	**Tuition:** $26,228
Application Deadline: January 1	**Room & Board:** $8750
Freshman Class: 27,562 applied, 13,270 accepted, 3601 enrolled	
SAT I Verbal/Math: 640/650	**ACT:** 28 **MOST COMPETITIVE**

Boston University, founded in 1839, is a private institution offering undergraduate and graduate programs in basic studies, liberal arts, communication, hotel and food administration, allied health education management, and fine arts. There are 10 undergraduate and 16 graduate schools. In addition to regional accreditation, BU has baccalaureate program accreditation with AACSB, ABET, NASM, and NCATE. The 23 libraries contain 1.7 million volumes, 2.6 million microform items, and 50,788 audiovisual forms/CDs, and subscribe to 20,129 periodicals. Computerized library services include the card catalog, interlibrary loans, and database searching. Special learning facilities include a learning resource center, art gallery, planetarium, radio station, TV station, astronomy observatory, 20th century archives, theater and theater company in residence, scientific computing and visualization lab, hotel/food administration culinary center, performance center, multimedia center, center for photonics research, center for remote sensing, the Metcalf Center for Science and Engineering, the Geddes language lab, and a speech, language, and hearing clinic. The 133-acre campus is in an urban area on the Charles River in Boston's Back Bay. Including residence halls, there are 337 buildings.

Student Life: 76% of undergraduates are from out of state, mostly the Middle Atlantic. Others are from 49 states, 105 foreign countries, and Canada. 72% are from public schools. 63% are white; 12%, Asian American. 38% are Catholic; 21%, Protestant; 18% claim no religious affiliation; 12%, Jewish; 11%, Buddhist, Hindu, Islamic, and Eastern

Rite Orthodox. The average age of freshmen is 19; all undergraduates, 21. 12% do not continue beyond their first year; 71% remain to graduate.

Housing: 9539 students can be accommodated in college housing, which includes single-sex and coed dormitories, on-campus apartments, off-campus apartments, and married-student housing. In addition, there are honors houses, language houses, and special-interest houses, and international floors and houses.. On-campus housing is guaranteed for all 4 years. 68% of students live on campus; of those, 80% remain on campus on weekends. All students may keep cars.

Activities: 5% of men belong to 9 national fraternities; 7% of women belong to 9 national sororities. There are 380 groups on campus, including art, band, cheerleading, chess, choir, chorale, chorus, computers, dance, drama, ethnic, film, gay, honors, international, jazz band, literary magazine, marching band, musical theater, newspaper, opera, orchestra, pep band, photography, political, professional, radio and TV, religious, social, social service, student government, symphony, and yearbook. Popular campus events include World Fair, Head of the Charles River Regatta, and the Boston Marathon.

Sports: There are 12 intercollegiate sports for men and 13 for women, and 15 intramural sports for men and 14 for women. Facilities include 2 gyms, an ice-skating rink, saunas, a pool, a dance studio, a crew tank, a weight room, indoor and outdoor tracks, tennis and volleyball courts, multipurpose playing fields, and a boathouse.

Disabled Students: 90% of the campus is accessible. Wheelchair ramps, elevators, special parking, specially equipped rest rooms, special class scheduling, lowered drinking fountains, lowered telephones, tactile and access maps, visual fire alarms for the deaf, adaptive computers, and ASL interpreters are available.

Services: Counseling and information services are available, as is tutoring in most subjects, including liberal arts, science, engineering, and management. There is a reader service for the blind.

Campus Safety and Security: Measures include 24-hour foot and vehicle patrol, self-defense education, escort service, and shuttle buses. There are informal discussions, pamphlets/posters/films, emergency telephones, lighted pathways/sidewalks, and a mountain bicycle patrol system. There is a uniformed safety/security assistant on duty 24 hours a day in large residence halls and there are 60 academy-trained officers in the university police department.

Programs of Study: BU confers B.A., B.S., B.F.A., B.L.S., B.Mus., and B.S.B.A. degrees. Master's and doctoral degrees are also awarded. Bachelor's degrees are awarded in BIOLOGICAL SCIENCE (biochemistry, biology/biological science, ecology, marine biology, neurosciences, nutrition, and physiology), BUSINESS (accounting, banking and finance, business administration and management, hotel/motel and restaurant management, international business management, management information systems, marketing/retailing/merchandising, operations research, and organizational behavior), COMMUNICATIONS AND THE ARTS (advertising, art history and appreciation, broadcasting, classics, communications, dramatic arts, English, film arts, French, German, graphic design, Greek (classical), Greek (modern), Italian, journalism, Latin, linguistics, music, music history and appreciation, music performance, music theory and composition, painting, public relations, Russian, sculpture, Spanish, theater design, and theater management), COMPUTER AND PHYSICAL SCIENCE (applied mathematics, astronomy, astrophysics, chemistry, computer science, earth science, information sciences and systems, mathematics, physics, and planetary and space science), EDUCATION (art, athletic training, bilingual/bicultural, drama, early childhood, education of the deaf and hearing impaired, elementary, English, foreign languages, mathematics, music, physical, science, social studies, and special), ENGINEERING AND ENVIRONMENTAL DESIGN (aeronautical engineering, biomedical engineering, computer engineering, electrical/electronics engineering, engineering, environmental science, industrial engineering, manufacturing engineering, and mechanical engineering), HEALTH PROFESSIONS (exercise science, health science, occupational therapy, physical therapy, predentistry, premedicine, rehabilitation therapy, and speech pathology/audiology), SOCIAL SCIENCE (American studies, anthropology, archeology, classical/ancient civilization, East Asian studies, economics, geography, history, interdisciplinary studies, international relations, Latin American studies, philosophy, physical fitness/movement, political science/government, psychology, religion, Russian and Slavic studies, sociology, and urban studies). The University Professors Program, accelerated medical and dental programs, and the management honors program are the strongest academically. Communication/journalism, business administration and management, and engineering are the largest.

Required: Most students are required to complete 128 credit hours to qualify for graduation. Hours in the major, specific disciplines, curricula, distribution requirements, and minimum GPA vary, depending on the school or college of BU attended. All freshmen must take an English composition course unless exempted by their SAT I verbal or AP scores.

Special: Cross-registration is permitted with Brandeis University, Tufts University, Boston College, and Hebrew College in Massachusetts. Opportunities are provided for internships, co-op programs in engineering, a Washington semester, on- and off-campus work-study, accelerated degrees in medicine and dentistry, B.A.-B.S. degrees, dual majors, student-designed majors, credit by exam, nondegree studies, pass/fail options, and study abroad in 14 countries. A 3-2 engineering degree is offered with 16 schools, and 2-2 engineering agreements with 6 schools, plus 107 other 2-2 agreements. The University Professors Program offers a creative cross-disciplinary approach, and the College of Basic Studies offers team teaching. There are 12 national honor societies, including Phi Beta Kappa, and a freshman honors program.

Faculty/Classroom: 64% of faculty are male; 36%, female. 57% teach undergraduates. The average class size in an introductory lecture is 57; in a laboratory, 22; and in a regular course, 20.

Admissions: 48% of the 2001-2002 applicants were accepted. The SAT I scores for the 2001-2002 freshman class were: Verbal--25% between 500 and 599, 55% between 600 and 700, and 20% above 700; Math--17% between 500 and 599, 61% between 600 and 700, and 22% above 700. The ACT scores were 9% between 18 and 23, 62% between 24 and 29, and 29% above 29. 87% of the current freshmen were in the top fifth of their class; 99% were in the top two fifths. There were 38 National Merit finalists. 101 freshmen graduated first in their class.

Requirements: The SAT I or ACT is required. Applicants are evaluated on an individual basis. Evidence of strong academic performance in a college-prep curriculum, including 4 years of English, math, science, and social studies/history with at least 3 years of a foreign language, will be the most important aspect of a student's application review. SAT II: Subject tests are required for the accelerated medical and dental programs and recommended for the College of Communication, the University Professors Program, and the College of Arts and Sciences. Candidates for the School for the Arts must present a portfolio or participate in an audition. AP and CLEP credits are accepted. Applications are accepted on-line via CollegeView, ExPAN, and the school's web site.

Procedure: Freshmen are admitted fall and spring. Entrance exams should be taken in the junior year or early in the senior year. There are early decision, early admissions, and deferred admissions plans. Early decision applications should be filed by November 1; regular applications, by January 1 for fall entry and November 1 for spring entry. The fall 2001 application fee was $60. Notification of early decision is sent December 31; regular decision, March 15. 123 early decision candidates were accepted for the 2001-2002 class. 9% of all applicants are on a waiting list; 1075 were accepted in 2001.

Transfer: 304 transfer students enrolled in 2001-2002. College transcripts, SAT I or ACT scores, and a complete high school transcript (or GED) should be submitted. Recommendations and an essay are also recommended.

Visiting: There are regularly scheduled orientations for prospective students, consisting of personal interviews, class visits, lunch with current students, campus tours, and information sessions. Appointments must be made in advance. There are guides for informal visits and visitors may sit in on classes and stay overnight. To schedule a visit, contact the Admissions Reception Center at (617) 353-2318 or *www.bu.edu/admissions/visit/ca*.

Financial Aid: In 2001-2002, 69% of all freshmen and 63% of continuing students received some form of financial aid. The average freshman award was $22,916. Of that total, scholarships or need-based grants averaged $16,200 ($32,000 maximum); loans averaged $3189 ($5000 maximum); and work contracts averaged $1954 ($2000 maximum). 75% of undergraduates work part time. Average annual earnings from campus work are $1543. The average financial indebtedness of the 2001 graduate was $17,808. BU is a member of CSS. The CSS/Profile or FAFSA is required. The fall application deadline is February 15.

International Students: There are 1523 international students enrolled. The school actively recruits these students. They must score 550 on the written TOEFL or 213 on the electronic version and also take the SAT I or the ACT.

Computers: The mainframe is an IBM RS/6000 cluster. The campus network provides the entire university community with high-speed access to e-mail, the Internet, the World Wide Web, and other resources. Facilities include a supercomputer cluster of SGI/Cray Origin 2000 systems, an SGI Power Challenge Array, several SGI workstations, and a computer graphics lab. All students may access the system 24 hours a day. There are no time limits and no fees.

Graduates: In 2001, 3484 bachelor's degrees were awarded. The most popular majors were social sciences (16%), communications (16%), and business and management (15%). In an average class, 2% graduate in 3 years, 58% in 4 years, 70% in 5 years, and 72% in 6 years. 500 companies recruited on campus in 2000-2001.

Admissions Contact: Kelly Walter, Interim Director, Undergraduate Admissions. A video is available. E-mail: *admissions@bu.edu or intadmis@bu.edu* Web: *www.bu.edu*

BRANDEIS UNIVERSITY

Waltham, MA 02454 | D-2
(781) 736-3500
(800) 622-0622; Fax: (781) 736-3536

Full-time: 1330 men, 1721 women | **Faculty:** 326; I, -$
Part-time: 14 men, 16 women | **Ph.D.s:** 95%
Graduate: 927 men, 874 women | **Student/Faculty:** 9 to 1
Year: semesters, summer session | **Tuition:** $27,076
Application Deadline: January 31 | **Room & Board:** $7405
Freshman Class: 6653 applied, 2708 accepted, 736 enrolled
SAT I Verbal/Math: 660/670 | **MOST COMPETITIVE**

Brandeis University, founded in 1948, is a private liberal arts institution. The 3 libraries contain 918,385 volumes, 900,009 microform items, and 34,404 audiovisual forms/CDs, and subscribe to 21,857 periodicals. Computerized library services include the card catalog, interlibrary loans, and database searching. Special learning facilities include a learning resource center, art gallery, radio station, TV station, astronomical observatory, cultural center, treasure hall, art museum, and audiovisual center. The 235-acre campus is in a suburban area 10 miles west of Boston. Including residence halls, there are 98 buildings.

Student Life: 75% of undergraduates are from out of state, mostly the Northeast. Others are from 50 states, 54 foreign countries, and Canada. 70% are from public schools. 70% are white; 10% Asian American. The average age of freshmen is 18; all undergraduates, 20. 7% do not continue beyond their first year; 78% remain to graduate.

Housing: 2542 students can be accommodated in college housing, which includes coed dormitories, on-campus apartments, and off-campus apartments. In addition, there are special-interest houses. On-campus housing is guaranteed for the freshman year only, is available on a first-come, first-served basis, and is available on a lottery system for upperclassmen. 82% of students live on campus; of those, 90% remain on campus on weekends. All students may keep cars.

Activities: There are no fraternities or sororities. There are 184 groups on campus, including art, cheerleading, chess, choir, chorale, chorus, computers, dance, debate, drama, ethnic, film, gay, honors, international, jazz band, literary magazine, musical theater, newspaper, orchestra, pep band, photography, political, professional, radio and TV, religious, social, social service, student government, symphony, and yearbook. Popular campus events include Community Service Day, Intercultural Center Open House, and Midnight Madness.

Sports: There are 11 intercollegiate sports for men and 11 for women, and 6 intramural sports for men and 5 for women. Facilities include a 7000-seat field house, a basketball arena, an indoor swimming pool, 3 indoor tennis courts, 10 squash and racquetball courts, an indoor track, several multipurpose rooms for fencing, aerobics, dance, and wrestling, sauna and steam rooms, Nautilus and free weight rooms, soccer and practice fields, baseball and softball diamonds, a cross-country and fitness trail, and 10 outdoor tennis courts.

Disabled Students: 78% of the campus is accessible. Wheelchair ramps, elevators, special parking, specially equipped rest rooms, special class scheduling, lowered drinking fountains, and lowered telephones are available. Libraries, student centers, several other buildings, sports facilities, and the majority of residence halls are fully accessible.

Services: Counseling and information services are available, as is tutoring in most subjects.

Campus Safety and Security: Measures include 24-hour foot and vehicle patrol, self-defense education, escort service, and shuttle buses. There are informal discussions, pamphlets/posters/films, emergency telephones, and lighted pathways/sidewalks.

Programs of Study: Brandeis confers B.A. and B.S. degrees. Master's and doctoral degrees are also awarded. Bachelor's degrees are awarded in BIOLOGICAL SCIENCE (biochemistry, biology/biological science, and neurosciences), COMMUNICATIONS AND THE ARTS (American literature, art history and appreciation, classics, comparative literature, dramatic arts, English, English literature, fine arts, French, German, linguistics, music, performing arts, Russian, and Spanish), COMPUTER AND PHYSICAL SCIENCE (chemistry, computer science, mathematics, physics, and science), SOCIAL SCIENCE (African American studies, African studies, American studies, anthropology, economics, European studies, history, Islamic studies, Judaic studies, Latin American studies, Middle Eastern studies, Near Eastern studies, philosophy, political science/government, psychology, and sociology). Sciences, history, and English are the strongest academically. Economics, biology, and politics are the largest.

Required: For the bachelor's degree, all students must complete 3 interrelated semester courses from an approved cluster, including selections from at least 2 different schools of the university. They must also complete 1 course from the University Seminar in Humanistic Inquiries and 1 in non-Western or cross-cultural studies, as well as a 1-semester course in each of the university's schools of creative arts, humanities, science, and social science. Writing, quantitative reasoning, and foreign language requirements also must be met. A total of 32 semester courses must be completed to graduate.

Special: Students may pursue interdepartmental programs in 18 different fields. Students may cross-register with Boston, Wellesley, Babson, and Bentley Colleges, and Boston and Tufts Universities. Study abroad is possible in 48 countries. Internships are available in virtually every field, and a work-study program is also provided. Dual and student-designed majors can be arranged. The university also offers credit by exam, nondegree study, and pass/fail options. Opportunities for early acceptance to area medical schools are offered to Brandeis students. There are 4 national honor societies, including Phi Beta Kappa, a freshman honors program, and 99 departmental honors program.

Faculty/Classroom: 61% of faculty are male; 39%, female. All both teach and do research. Graduate students teach 10% of introductory courses. The average class size in a regular course is 21.

Admissions: 41% of the 2001-2002 applicants were accepted. The SAT I scores for the 2001-2002 freshman class were: Verbal--1% below 500, 12% between 500 and 599, 55% between 600 and 700, and 32% above 700; Math--1% below 500, 14% between 500 and 599, 48% between 600 and 700, and 37% above 700. 86% of the current freshmen were in the top fifth of their class; 99% were in the top two fifths.

Requirements: The SAT I or ACT is required. In addition, students submitting the SAT I score must also take 3 SAT II: Subject tests, including writing. The ACT may be submitted instead of the SAT I and II. Applicants should prepare with 4 years of high school English, 3 each of foreign language and math, and at least 1 each of science and social studies. An essay is required, and an interview is recommended. AP credits are accepted. Important factors in the admissions decision are advanced placement or honor courses, recommendations by school officials, and extracurricular activities record. Brandeis accepts applications on-line and on computer disk via Common App, CollegeLink, Apply, and their web site.

Procedure: Freshmen are admitted fall and spring. Entrance exams should be taken by the fall of the senior year. There are early decision and deferred admissions plans. Early decision application should be filed by January 1; regular applications, by January 31 for fall entry and December 1 for spring entry along with a $55 fee. Notification of early decision is sent within 4 weeks of receipt of a completed application; regular notification is sent April 15. 159 early decision candidates were accepted for the 2001-2002 class. 7% of all applicants are on a waiting list; 105 were accepted in 2001.

Transfer: 44 transfer students enrolled in 2001-2002. Major consideration is given to the quality of college-level work completed, the secondary school record, testing, professors' and deans' evaluations, and the impression made by the candidate. Because there is a 2-year residence requirement, students should apply before entering their junior year. 16 courses of 32 must be completed at Brandeis.

Visiting: There are regularly scheduled orientations for prospective students, including year-round student-led campus tours and, in the summer, information sessions given by the admissions staff. There are guides for informal visits and visitors may sit in on classes and stay overnight. To schedule a visit, contact the Office of Admissions.

Financial Aid: In 2001-2002, 42% of all freshmen and 45% of continuing students received some form of financial aid. 37% of freshmen and 40% of continuing students received need-based aid. The average freshman award was $19,659. Of that total, scholarships or need-based grants averaged $15,012; and loans averaged $4647. 42% of undergraduates work part time. Average annual earnings from campus work are $1326. Brandeis is a member of CSS. The CSS/Profile or FAFSA and copies of student and parent income tax returns for matriculating students are required. The fall application deadline is January 31.

International Students: There are 188 international students enrolled. The school actively recruits these students. They must score 600 on the written TOEFL or 250 on the electronic version. Applicants whose native language is English must take the SAT I and SAT II: Subject tests.

Computers: The mainframe is a DEC VAX cluster for undergraduate network services. There are three clusters located throughout the campus containing more than 100 Mac and IBM-compatible computers and printers for both. All Macs and some IBMs are connected to the campus network via an Ethernet Gateway, giving students access to Student Network Services accounts. Access to the mainframe is also available from students' rooms. All students may access the system. There are no time limits and no fees.

Graduates: In 2001, 753 bachelor's degrees were awarded. The most popular majors were social science and history (38%), biological/life sciences (15%), and psychology (11%). In an average class, 80% graduate in 4 years, 83% in 5 years, and 84% in 6 years. 60 companies recruited on campus in a recent year.

Admissions Contact: Deena Whitfield, Director of Enrollment.
E-mail: *sendinfo@brandeis.edu* Web: *http://www.brandeis.edu*

BRIDGEWATER STATE COLLEGE E-3

Bridgewater, MA 02325 (508) 531-1237; Fax: (508) 531-1746

Full-time: 2164 men, 3440 women	**Faculty:** 263; IIA, --$
Part-time: 619 men, 976 women	**Ph.D.s:** 87%
Graduate: 458 men, 1381 women	**Student/Faculty:** 21 to 1
Year: semesters, summer session	**Tuition:** $2823 ($8963)
Application Deadline: March 1	**Room & Board:** $4766
Freshman Class: 4681 applied, 3485 accepted, 1148 enrolled	
SAT I Verbal/Math: 500/500	**ACT:** 20 **COMPETITIVE+**

Bridgewater State College, founded in 1840, is a state-supported college offering undergraduate and graduate programs in liberal arts, education, business, aviation science, and preprofessional studies. There are 3 undergraduate schools and 1 graduate school. In addition to regional accreditation, The college has baccalaureate program accreditation with CSWE and NCATE. The library contains 294,271 volumes, 721,639 microform items, and 10,113 audiovisual forms/CDs, and subscribes to 2220 periodicals. Computerized library services include the card catalog, interlibrary loans, and database searching. Special learning facilities include a learning resource center, art gallery, radio station, astronomical observatory, human performance lab and flight simulators, electronic classrooms, teleconferencing facility with a satellite dish, and children's developmental clinic. The 235-acre campus is in a suburban area 28 miles south of Boston. Including residence halls, there are 37 buildings.

Student Life: 97% of undergraduates are from Massachusetts. Others are from 22 states, 13 foreign countries, and Canada. 75% are white. 55% are Catholic; 16% claim no religious affiliation. The average age of freshmen is 19; all undergraduates, 23. 27% do not continue beyond their first year.

Housing: 1745 students can be accommodated in college housing, which includes single-sex and coed dormitories and on-campus apartments. On-campus housing is guaranteed for all 4 years. 72% of students commute. All students may keep cars.

Activities: 2% of men and about 2% of women belong to 2 local and 3 national fraternities; 2% of women belong to 3 national sororities. There are 74 groups on campus, including adult student, band, cheerleading, choir, chorale, computers, dance, drama, ethnic, gay, honors, interfraternal, international, jazz band, literary magazine, newspaper, pep band, photography, political, professional, radio and TV, religious, social, social service, student government, women's and yearbook. Popular campus events include Convocation, Multiculture Day, and Christmas and Spring balls.

Sports: There are 10 intercollegiate sports for men and 11 for women, and 6 intramural sports for men and 4 for women. Facilities include 2 gyms, an Olympic-size swimming pool, tennis courts, a football stadium, a 9-lane track, soccer, lacrosse, and field hockey fields, and a baseball and softball complex.

Disabled Students: 95% of the campus is accessible. Wheelchair ramps, elevators, special parking, specially equipped rest rooms, special class scheduling, lowered drinking fountains, lowered telephones, handicapped van service, and a college-operated transit system are available.

Services: Counseling and information services are available, as is tutoring in most subjects. There is a reader service for the blind, and remedial math, reading, and writing. There are taped texts, classroom interpreters, scribes/note takers, testing accommodations, and a speech/hearing/language center.

Campus Safety and Security: Measures include 24-hour foot and vehicle patrol, self-defense education, escort service, and shuttle buses. There are informal discussions, pamphlets/posters/films, emergency telephones, lighted pathways/sidewalks, and a college-operated transit system that runs from 7 A.M. to midnight, Monday through Friday, and a safety-escort van that runs from 6 P.M. to 3 A.M.

Programs of Study: The college confers B.A., B.S., and B.S.Ed. degrees. Master's degrees are also awarded. Bachelor's degrees are awarded in BIOLOGICAL SCIENCE (biology/biological science), BUSINESS (management science), COMMUNICATIONS AND THE ARTS (art, communications, English, music, and Spanish), COMPUTER AND PHYSICAL SCIENCE (chemistry, computer science, earth science, geology, mathematics, and physics), EDUCATION (early childhood, elementary, physical, and special), ENGINEERING AND ENVIRONMENTAL DESIGN (aviation administration/management), SOCIAL SCIENCE (anthropology, criminal justice, economics, geography, history, philosophy, political science/government, psychology, social work, and sociology). Management science, aviation science, and education are the strongest academically. Management science, psychology, and education are the largest.

Required: Students are required to complete a minimum of 120 semester hours, with 24 to 36 hours in the major and 52 to 55 hours in general education courses. Students must maintain a minimum GPA of 2.0 and must complete an introduction to information resources course.

Special: Opportunities are provided for cross-registration with other Massachusetts schools, internships in most majors, dual majors in any subjects, core requirement credit for military service and work experience, nondegree study, and study abroad in England and Canada. A Washington semester offers possible internship experience in political science. There are 11 national honor societies, a freshman honors program, and 14 departmental honors program.

Faculty/Classroom: 59% of faculty are male; 41%, female. All teach undergraduates. No introductory courses are taught by graduate students. The average class size in an introductory lecture is 32; in a laboratory, 18; and in a regular course, 24.

Admissions: 74% of the 2001-2002 applicants were accepted. 18% of the current freshmen were in the top fifth of their class; 52% were in the top two fifths.

Requirements: The SAT I or ACT is required. In addition, graduation from an accredited secondary school is required; a GED will be accepted. Applicants must have successfully completed 16 Carnegie units, including 4 years of English, 3 of math, 3 of science with 1 lab science, 2 of a foreign language, 1 each of history and social studies, and 3 in other college preparatory electives. An essay is recommended. A GPA of 3.0 is required. AP and CLEP credits are accepted. Important factors in the admissions decision are advanced placement or honor courses, leadership record, and evidence of special talent. Applications are accepted on-line via CollegeLine and EXPAN.

Procedure: Freshmen are admitted fall and spring. Entrance exams should be taken no later than January. There are early action and deferred admissions plans. Early action applications should be filed by November 16; regular applications, by March 1 for fall entry and December 1 for spring entry along with a $20 application fee. Notification of early action is sent December 15; regular decision, by April 15. 8% of all applicants are on a waiting list; 5 were accepted in 2001.

Transfer: 670 transfer students enrolled in 2001-2002. Transfer students must have maintained a minimum GPA of 2.0 at the previous college, although this alone does not guarantee admission. Priority is given to community college graduates. 30 credits of 120 must be completed at Bridgewater.

Visiting: There are regularly scheduled orientations for prospective students, including tours Monday through Friday at 11 A.M. and 3 P.M. and information sessions on Fridays at 10 A.M. when college is in session. Visitations are available on a limited basis Saturdays during the fall. Campus tours are available year round. There are guides for informal visits and visitors may sit in on classes. To schedule a visit, contact the Office of Admissions.

Financial Aid: In 2001-2002, 45% of all freshmen and 33% of continuing students received some form of financial aid. 72% of freshmen and 52% of continuing students received need-based aid. The average freshman award was $6512. Of that total, scholarships or need-based grants averaged $2877 ($7050 maximum); loans averaged $2731 ($13,500 maximum); work contracts averaged $1795 ($2000 maximum); and merit aid averaged $2678 ($5023 maximum). 22% of undergraduates work part time. Average annual earnings from campus work are $4000. The average financial indebtedness of the 2001 graduate was $9348. The college is a member of CSS. The FAFSA, the college's own financial statement and the parents' tax returns are required. The fall application priority deadline is March 1.

International Students: There are 157 international students enrolled. They must score 500 on the written TOEFL.

Computers: The mainframes are a DEC 3000-300LX, a DEC ALPHA server 1000 4/200, a DEC 300-600, an ALPHA server 4000 5/400, a VAX 4000-300, a DEC ALPHA server 2100 4/233, and a DEC VAXstation 4000/600. In addition to the computer facilities for instructional purposes, the college provides general access to about 400 PCs. The college also provides connectivity to hosts and the home page via SLIP/PPP connection from off-campus using a modem. Residential students' PCs may be connected to the campus network and the Internet. All students may access the system 7 days a week. There are no time limits and no fees.

Graduates: In 2001, 1097 bachelor's degrees were awarded. The most popular majors were education (15%), psychology (14%), and management (12%). In an average class, 1% graduate in 3 years. 83 companies recruited on campus in 2000-2001. Of the 2000 graduating class, 16% were enrolled in graduate school within 6 months of graduation and 92% were employed.

Admissions Contact: Steven King, Jr., Director of Admissions.
E-mail: *admission@bridgew.edu* Web: *www.bridgew.edu*

CAMBRIDGE COLLEGE D-2
Cambridge, MA 02138-5304 (617) 868-1000
(800) 877-4723; Fax: (617) 868-1124

Full-time: 49 men and women	**Faculty:** n/av
Part-time: 348 men and women	**Ph.D.s:** n/av
Graduate: 2336 men and women	**Student/Faculty:** n/av
Year: semesters, summer session	**Tuition:** $10,800
Application Deadline: open	**Room & Board:** n/app
Freshman Class: n/av	
SAT I or ACT: not required	**SPECIAL**

Cambridge College offers undergraduate and graduate programs for working adults in the fields of education, management, human services, and counseling.
Student Life: 40% of students are African American. The average age of all students is 40.
Programs of Study: Cambridge confers B.A. and B.S. degrees in management, human services, and psychology.
Requirements: Applicants must have 3 or more years of work experience, as well as a high school diploma or GED.
Procedure: Application deadlines are open. Check with the school for the current application fee.
International Students: They must score 550 on the written TOEFL or 213 on the electronic version.
Admissions Contact: Dr. Ezat Parnia, Vice President for Enrollment and Marketing. Web: *www.cambridge.edu*

CLARK UNIVERSITY C-2
Worcester, MA 01610-1477 (508) 793-7431
(800) 462-5275; Fax: (508) 793-8821

Full-time: 749 men, 1147 women	**Faculty:** 164; IIA, +$
Part-time: 97 men, 145 women	**Ph.D.s:** 99%
Graduate: 376 men, 441 women	**Student/Faculty:** 12 to 1
Year: semesters, summer session	**Tuition:** $24,620
Application Deadline: February 1	**Room & Board:** $4550
Freshman Class: 3704 applied, 2536 accepted, 515 enrolled	
SAT I Verbal/Math: 500/580	**ACT:** 25 **HIGHLY COMPETITIVE**

Clark University, founded in 1887, is an independent liberal arts and research institution. There are 2 undergraduate and 3 graduate schools. In addition to regional accreditation, Clark has baccalaureate program accreditation with AACSB and NASDTEC. The 4 libraries contain 592,159 volumes, 59,953 microform items, and 984 audiovisual forms/CDs, and subscribe to 1303 periodicals. Computerized library services include the card catalog, interlibrary loans, and database searching. Special learning facilities include a learning resource center, art gallery, radio station, TV studio, campus cable network, center for music with 2 studios for electronic music, 2 theaters, magnetic resonance imaging facility, and arboretum. The 50-acre campus is in an urban area 50 miles west of Boston. Including residence halls, there are 56 buildings.
Student Life: 60% of undergraduates are from out of state, mostly the Northeast. Others are from 42 states, 57 foreign countries, and Canada. 70% are from public schools. 65% are white. 33% are claim no religious affiliation; 22% Catholic; 16% Protestant; 14% Jewish. The average age of freshmen is 19; all undergraduates, 20. 15% do not continue beyond their first year; 70% remain to graduate.
Housing: 1452 students can be accommodated in college housing, which includes single-sex and coed dormitories and on-campus apartments. In addition, there are special-interest, nonsmoking, quiet, substance awareness, and year-round houses. On-campus housing is guaranteed for the freshman and sophomore years only and is available on a lottery system for upperclassmen. 75% of students live on campus. All students may keep cars.
Activities: There are no fraternities or sororities. There are 80 groups on campus, including art, band, chess, choir, chorale, chorus, dance, debate, drama, ethnic, film, gay, honors, international, jazz band, literary magazine, musical theater, newspaper, pep band, photography, political, professional, radio and TV, religious, social, social service, student government, and yearbook. Popular campus events include Fall Fest, Martin Luther King Commemoration, and Academic Spree Day.
Sports: There are 8 intercollegiate sports for men and 9 for women, and 13 intramural sports for men and 13 for women. Facilities include an athletic center with a 2000-seat gym, a pool, a fitness center, tennis courts, outdoor fields, baseball and softball diamonds, and a boathouse.
Disabled Students: 90% of the campus is accessible. Wheelchair ramps, elevators, special parking, specially equipped rest rooms, special class scheduling, lowered drinking fountains, lowered telephones, and specially equipped residence rooms are available.
Services: Counseling and information services are available, as is tutoring in some subjects, including math, biology, chemistry, economics, and psychology. For learning-disabled students, the university provides early orientation, alternative test-taking accommodations, a learning specialist, and compensatory skill training in written expression, math application, and learning strategies. A writing center provides assistance to all students.
Campus Safety and Security: Measures include 24-hour foot and vehicle patrol, self-defense education, escort service, and shuttle buses. There are informal discussions, pamphlets/posters/films, emergency telephones, and lighted pathways/sidewalks.
Programs of Study: Clark confers the B.A. degree. Master's and doctoral degrees are also awarded. Bachelor's degrees are awarded in BIOLOGICAL SCIENCE (biochemistry and biology/biological science), BUSINESS (business administration and management), COMMUNICATIONS AND THE ARTS (art history and appreciation, communications, comparative literature, dramatic arts, English, film arts, fine arts, French, languages, music, romance languages and literature, Spanish, studio art, and visual and performing arts), COMPUTER AND PHYSICAL SCIENCE (chemistry, computer science, mathematics, and physics), ENGINEERING AND ENVIRONMENTAL DESIGN (environmental science), HEALTH PROFESSIONS (predentistry and premedicine), SOCIAL SCIENCE (classical/ancient civilization, economics, geography, history, international relations, international studies, philosophy, political science/government, prelaw, psychology, and sociology). Psychology, biology, and government and international relations are the strongest academically. Psychology, government and international relations, and business management are the largest.
Required: Each student is required to complete 2 critical thinking courses in 2 categories of verbal expression and formal analysis, and 6 perspectives courses, representing the categories of aesthetics, comparative, historical, language and culture, science, and values. A student must receive passing grades in a minimum of 32 full courses, with a C- or better in at least 24 of these courses, and maintain a minimum 2.0 GPA to graduate.
Special: For-credit internships are available in all disciplines with private corporations and small businesses, medical centers, and government agencies. There is cross-registration with members of the Worcester Consortium, including Holy Cross and Worcester Polytechnic Institute. Clark also offers study abroad in 10 countries, a Washington semester with American University, work-study programs, dual and student-designed majors, pass/no record options, and a 3-2 engineering degree with Columbia University, Washington University, and Worcester Polytechnic Institute. A gerontology certificate is offered with the Worcester Consortium for Higher Education. There are 6 national honor societies, including Phi Beta Kappa.
Faculty/Classroom: 65% of faculty are male; 35%, female. All both teach and do research. No introductory courses are taught by graduate students. The average class size in an introductory lecture is 34; in a laboratory, 14; and in a regular course, 21.
Admissions: 69% of the 2001-2002 applicants were accepted. The SAT I scores for the 2001-2002 freshman class were: Verbal--10% below 500, 39% between 500 and 599, 41% between 600 and 700, and 10% above 700; Math--11% below 500, 48% between 500 and 599, 36% between 600 and 700, and 5% above 700. The ACT scores were 14% below 21, 21% between 21 and 23, 30% between 24 and 26, 16% between 27 and 28, and 19% above 28. 58% of the current freshmen were in the top fifth of their class; 90% were in the top two fifths. 7 freshmen graduated first in their class.
Requirements: The SAT I or ACT is required. In addition, the SAT II: Writing test is also recommended. Applicants must graduate from an accredited secondary school or have a GED. 16 Carnegie units are required, including 4 years of English, 3 each of math and science, and 2 each of foreign language and social studies, including history. An interview is recommended. AP credits are accepted. Important factors in the admissions decision are advanced placement or honor courses, recommendations by alumni, and recommendations by school officials.
Procedure: Freshmen are admitted fall and spring. Entrance exams should be taken by November of the senior year. There are early decision and deferred admissions plans. Early decision application should be filed by November 15; regular applications, by February 1 for fall entry and November 15 for spring entry, along with a $50 fee. Notification of early decision is sent January 1; regular decision, April 1. 57 early decision candidates were accepted for the 2001-2002 class. 1% of all applicants are on a waiting list; 8 were accepted in 2001.
Transfer: 51 transfer students enrolled in 2001-2002. Applicants should have a minimum GPA of about 2.8. At least one full semester of college course work is required. High school and college transcripts, recent SAT I or ACT test scores, a staement of good standing from previous institutions attended, and a transfer statement are required. Grades of C or better in comparable course work transfer for credit. 16 courses of 32 must be completed at Clark.
Visiting: There are regularly scheduled orientations for prospective students. Open houses during fall and spring semesters include tours, information sessions, and talks with faculty, administration, and coaches. There are guides for informal visits and visitors may sit in on classes and stay overnight. To schedule a visit, contact the Admissions Office.
Financial Aid: In 2001-2002, 94% of all freshmen and 80% of continuing students received some form of financial aid. 65% of all students received need-based aid. The average freshman award was $18,662. Of

that total, scholarships or need-based grants averaged $14,335 ($22,400 maximum); loans averaged $2812 ($5625 maximum); and work contracts averaged $1800 ($2000 maximum). 55% of undergraduates work part time. Average annual earnings from campus work are $1500. The average financial indebtedness of the 2001 graduate was $17,650. Clark is a member of CSS. The CSS/Profile or FAFSA is required. The fall application deadline is February 1.

International Students: There are 151 international students enrolled. The school actively recruits these students. They must score 550 on the written TOEFL or 213 on the electronic version and also take the SAT I or the ACT, scoring 400 on the verbal and 400 on the math SAT I.

Computers: The mainframes are a cluster including the DEC VAX 6420, and 6410, the VAX Station 3100/76, and the DEC ALPHA Systems 3000/400, 2000/233, 4000/710 and ALPHA Server 4000. There are networked departmental systems in various buildings throughout campus and PC and Mac computers in 2 public computer labs, plus campuswide access to the Internet. All students may access the system 7 days per week via direct connections from the campus network (including residence halls) and through modems. There are no time limits and no fees.

Graduates: In 2001, 430 bachelor's degrees were awarded. The most popular majors were psychology (15%), biology (8%), and government and international relations (8%). In an average class, 1% graduate in 3 years, 60% in 4 years, 69% in 5 years, and 72% in 6 years. 100 companies recruited on campus in 2000-2001. Of the 2000 graduating class, 27% were enrolled in graduate school within 6 months of graduation.

Admissions Contact: Harold M. Wingood, Dean of Admissions.
E-mail: *admissions@clarku.edu*

COLLEGE OF OUR LADY OF THE ELMS — B-3

Chicopee, MA 01013 — (413) 592-3189
(800) 255-ELMS; Fax: (413) 594-2781

Full-time: 62 men, 356 women	**Faculty:** 38
Part-time: 25 men, 187 women	**Ph.D.s:** 76%
Graduate: 11 men, 78 women	**Student/Faculty:** 11 to 1
Year: semesters	**Tuition:** $14,744
Application Deadline: open	**Room & Board:** $5900
Freshman Class: 323 applied, 226 accepted, 68 enrolled	
SAT I Verbal/Math: 491/475	**COMPETITIVE**

College of Our Lady of the Elms, founded in 1928, is a Roman Catholic institution offering undergraduate degrees in liberal arts and sciences and graduate degrees in liberal arts, education, and theology. In addition to regional accreditation, Elms College has baccalaureate program accreditation with CSWE and NLN. The library contains 103,136 volumes, 77,784 microform items, and 2208 audiovisual forms/CDs, and subscribes to 695 periodicals. Computerized library services include the card catalog, interlibrary loans, and database searching. Special learning facilities include a learning resource center, art gallery, radio station, TV station, and rare books collection. The 32-acre campus is in a suburban area 2 miles north of Springfield and 90 miles west of Boston. Including residence halls, there are 11 buildings.

Student Life: 85% of undergraduates are from Massachusetts. Others are from 9 states and 10 foreign countries. 74% are from public schools. 80% are white. Most are Catholic. The average age of freshmen is 20; all undergraduates, 22. 11% do not continue beyond their first year.

Housing: 315 students can be accommodated in college housing, which includes single-sex and coed dormitories. On-campus housing is guaranteed for all 4 years. 60% of students commute. All students may keep cars.

Activities: There are no fraternities or sororities. There are 41 groups on campus, including art, choir, chorale, chorus, computers, dance, drama, ethnic, honors, international, literary magazine, musical theater, newspaper, photography, professional, radio and TV, religious, social, social service, student government, and yearbook. Popular campus events include Soph Show, Cap and Gown, and Ring Ceremony.

Sports: There are 6 intercollegiate sports for men and 9 for women, and 6 intramural sports for men and 6 for women. Facilities include fitness and athletic center housing a suspended indoor track, a 25-meter, 6-lane pool, a weight and aerobics room, a multipurpose arena, a basketball court, and a volleyball court.

Disabled Students: 40% of the campus is accessible. Wheelchair ramps, elevators, special parking, specially equipped rest rooms, special class scheduling, lowered drinking fountains, lowered telephones, and automated doors are available.

Services: Counseling and information services are available, as is tutoring in every subject. There is a reader service for the blind, and remedial math, reading, and writing. There also is an academic advising and resource center, a counseling service office, career services, wellness services, student activities, a campus ministry office, and resident advisers.

Campus Safety and Security: Measures include 24-hour foot and vehicle patrol, self-defense education, escort service, and informal discussions. There are pamphlets/posters/films, emergency telephones, and lighted pathways/sidewalks. A safety and security manual is published each year, and there is a safety and security committee of administrators, students, faculty, and staff.

Programs of Study: Elms College confers B.A. and B.S. degrees. Associate and master's degrees are also awarded. Bachelor's degrees are awarded in BIOLOGICAL SCIENCE (biology/biological science), BUSINESS (accounting, business administration and management, international business management, and marketing/retailing/merchandising), COMMUNICATIONS AND THE ARTS (English, fine arts, and Spanish), COMPUTER AND PHYSICAL SCIENCE (chemistry, computer science, mathematics, and natural sciences), EDUCATION (bilingual/bicultural, early childhood, elementary, foreign languages, middle school, science, secondary, special, and teaching English as a second/foreign language (TESOL/TEFOL)), HEALTH PROFESSIONS (health science, medical laboratory technology, nursing, predentistry, premedicine, and speech pathology/audiology), SOCIAL SCIENCE (American studies, international studies, paralegal studies, prelaw, psychology, religion, social work, and sociology). Nursing, education, and biology are the strongest academically. Education, business, and nursing are the largest.

Required: To graduate, all students must complete 120 hours with a 2.0 GPA. 54 hours are required in courses in rhetoric, computer science, history, religion, phys ed, philosophy, sociology, fine arts, humanities, foreign language, math, senior seminar, and service learning experience.

Special: Students may cross-register at any of the Cooperating Colleges of Greater Springfield or Consortium of Sisters of St. Joseph Colleges. Internships are available with local hospitals, businesses, and schools. Study abroad, student-designed interdepartmental majors, accelerated degree programs, work-study, dual majors, nondegree study, and pass/fail options are offered. There are 5 national honor societies, including Phi Beta Kappa, and a freshman honors program.

Faculty/Classroom: 35% of faculty are male; 65%, female. 90% teach undergraduates, 93% do research, and 92% do both. No introductory courses are taught by graduate students. The average class size in an introductory lecture is 13; in a laboratory, 8; and in a regular course, 11.

Admissions: 70% of the 2001-2002 applicants were accepted. The SAT I scores for the 2001-2002 freshman class were: Verbal--51% below 500, 41% between 500 and 599, and 8% between 600 and 700; Math--56% below 500, 37% between 500 and 599, 5% between 600 and 700, and 2% above 700. 28% of the current freshmen were in the top fifth of their class; 62% were in the top two fifths.

Requirements: The SAT I or ACT is required. The college prefers SAT I composite scores of at least 900. Applicants should be graduates of accredited high schools or have earned the GED. Secondary preparation should include 4 units of English, 3 each of math and science, and 2 each of foreign language, history, and social studies. A personal essay is required; an interview is recommended. Elms College accepts applications on-line via CollegeLink, Common App, and National Catholic College Common Application. Elms College requires applicants to be in the upper 50% of their class. A GPA of 2.5 is required. AP and CLEP credits are accepted. Important factors in the admissions decision are advanced placement or honor courses, recommendations by school officials, and extracurricular activities record.

Procedure: Freshmen are admitted fall and spring. Entrance exams should be taken no later than November of the senior year. There are early admissions and deferred admissions plans. Application deadlines are open. The fall 2001 application fee was $30.

Transfer: 68 transfer students enrolled in a recent year. Applicants must have a minimum 2.0 GPA. 45 credits of 120 must be completed at Elms College.

Visiting: There are regularly scheduled orientations for prospective students, including tours and interviews scheduled weekdays between 9 A.M. and 4 P.M. as well as 2 open houses in the fall and 1 in the spring. There are guides for informal visits and visitors may sit in on classes and stay overnight. To schedule a visit, contact the Admission Office.

Financial Aid: In 2001-2002, 75% of all freshmen and 89% of continuing students received some form of financial aid. 75% of freshmen and 88% of continuing students received need-based aid. The average freshman award was $11,618. Of that total, scholarships or need-based grants averaged $8168; and loans averaged $3442. 30% of undergraduates work part time. Average annual earnings from campus work are $1200. The average financial indebtedness of the 2001 graduate was $18,600. Elms College is a member of CSS. The FAFSA and the college's own financial statement are required. The fall application deadline is March 1.

International Students: The school actively recruits these students. The college requires either the TOEFL, with a minimum score of 500, or the SAT I.

Computers: The mainframe is a DEC ALPHA 2100 4/275. Computer labs consist of 1 in the library, 3 in the main building, 2 in residence halls, and 1 in the college center. 4 of the labs offer World Wide Web access, 6 offer Internet access. All students have e-mail accounts. All students may access the system 8 A.M. to 10 P.M. Monday through Friday, 12 noon to 9 P.M. Saturday and Sunday, and residence hall labs are open 24 hours. There are no time limits and no fees.

Graduates: In 2001, 134 bachelor's degrees were awarded. The most popular majors were nursing (17%), social work (13%), and education

(10%). In an average class, 1% graduate in 3 years, 54% in 4 years, and 56% in 5 years.

Admissions Contact: Joseph P. Wagner, Director of Admission. E-mail: *admissions@elms.edu* Web: *www.elms.edu*

COLLEGE OF THE HOLY CROSS C-2
Worcester, MA 01610 **(508) 793-2443**
(800) 442-2421; Fax: (508) 793-3888

Full-time: 1326 men, 1456 women	**Faculty:** 222; IIB, ++$
Part-time: 13 men, 16 women	**Ph.D.s:** 97%
Graduate: none	**Student/Faculty:** 13 to 1
Year: semesters	**Tuition:** $25,020
Application Deadline: January 15	**Room & Board:** $7760
Freshman Class: 4753 applied, 2021 accepted, 694 enrolled	
SAT I Verbal/Math: 630/628	**MOST COMPETITIVE**

College of the Holy Cross, founded in 1843, is a private liberal arts college affiliated with the Roman Catholic Church and the Jesuit Order. The 3 libraries contain 575,420 volumes, 15,244 microform items, and 24,337 audiovisual forms/CDs, and subscribe to 1869 periodicals. Computerized library services include the card catalog, interlibrary loans, and database searching. Special learning facilities include an art gallery, radio station, greenhouses, facilities for aquatic research, and multimedia resource center. The 174-acre campus is in a suburban area 45 miles west of Boston. Including residence halls, there are 27 buildings.

Student Life: 66% of undergraduates are from out of state, mostly the Northeast. Others are from 47 states, 17 foreign countries, and Canada. 46% are from public schools. 78% are white. The average age of freshmen is 18; all undergraduates, 20. 5% do not continue beyond their first year; 93% remain to graduate.

Housing: 2114 students can be accommodated in college housing, which includes coed dormitories and off-campus apartments. In addition, there are special-interest houses, a fit-for-life program house, and a first-year program house. On-campus housing is guaranteed for all 4 years. 78% of students live on campus; of those, 90% remain on campus on weekends. Upperclassmen may keep cars.

Activities: There are no fraternities or sororities. There are 101 groups on campus, including art, band, cheerleading, choir, chorale, chorus, computers, dance, debate, drama, drill team, ethnic, film, gay, honors, international, jazz band, literary magazine, marching band, musical theater, newspaper, orchestra, pep band, photography, political, professional, radio, religious, social, social service, student government, and yearbook. Popular campus events include Spring Weekend, Family Weekend, and Senior Weekend.

Sports: There are 13 intercollegiate sports for men and 14 for women, and 5 intramural sports for men and 4 for women. Facilities include an Astroturf playing field, baseball and football fields, indoor and outdoor running tracks, a swimming pool, an ice rink, indoor crew tanks, a basketball arena, weight and exercise rooms, a wellness center and tennis, squash, and racquetball courts.

Disabled Students: 85% of the campus is accessible. Wheelchair ramps, elevators, special parking, specially equipped rest rooms, special class scheduling, lowered drinking fountains, and lowered telephones are available.

Services: Counseling and information services are available, as is tutoring in every subject, and math and writing workshops. Language labs are also available.

Campus Safety and Security: Measures include 24-hour foot and vehicle patrol, self-defense education, escort service, and shuttle buses. There are informal discussions, pamphlets/posters/films, emergency telephones, and lighted pathways/sidewalks.

Programs of Study: Holy Cross confers the A.B. degree. Bachelor's degrees are awarded in BIOLOGICAL SCIENCE (biochemistry and biology/biological science), COMMUNICATIONS AND THE ARTS (art history and appreciation, classics, dramatic arts, English, French, German, Italian, music, Russian, Spanish, and studio art), COMPUTER AND PHYSICAL SCIENCE (chemistry, mathematics, and physics), SOCIAL SCIENCE (African American studies, African studies, anthropology, Asian/Oriental studies, economics, gerontology, history, international studies, Latin American studies, Middle Eastern studies, peace studies, philosophy, political science/government, psychology, religion, and sociology). English, psychology, and political science are the largest.

Required: Distribution requirements include social science, natural and mathematical science, cross-cultural studies, religious and philosophical studies, historical studies and the arts, and literature. In addition, students must demonstrate competence in a classical or modern language or American sign language. A total of 32 courses worth at least 1 unit each is required for graduation, with 10 to 14 courses in the major. The minimum GPA for graduation is 2.0.

Special: Local internships are available through the Center for Interdisciplinary and Special Studies in health and education, law and business, journalism, social service, state and local government, scientific research, and cultural affairs. Student-designed majors, dual majors including economics-accounting, a Washington semester, and study abroad are possible. There is a 3-2 engineering program with Columbia University or Dartmouth College, and premedicine and predentistry programs are available. Students may cross-register with other universities in the Colleges of Worcester Consortium. Nondegree study is possible. There are 17 national honor societies, including Phi Beta Kappa, and 5 departmental honors program.

Faculty/Classroom: 57% of faculty are male; 43%, female. All both teach and do research. The average class size in an introductory lecture is 23; in a laboratory, 20; and in a regular course, 17.

Admissions: 43% of the 2001-2002 applicants were accepted. The SAT I scores for the 2001-2002 freshman class were: Verbal--3% below 500, 26% between 500 and 599, 54% between 600 and 700, and 17% above 700; Math--2% below 500, 24% between 500 and 599, 60% between 600 and 700, and 14% above 700. 85% of the current freshmen were in the top fifth of their class; 99% were in the top two fifths. 17 freshmen graduated first in their class.

Requirements: The SAT I or ACT is required. In addition, applicants should be graduates of an accredited secondary school or hold the GED. Recommended preparatory courses include English, foreign language, history, math, and science. An essay and the SAT II: Subject tests in writing and 2 other areas are required. An interview is recommended. AP credits are accepted. Important factors in the admissions decision are advanced placement or honor courses, recommendations by school officials, and evidence of special talent.

Procedure: Freshmen are admitted in the fall. Entrance exams should be taken by December of the senior year. There are early decision, early admissions, and deferred admissions plans. Early decision applications should be filed by December 15; regular applications, by January 15 for fall entry. Notification of early decision is sent on a rolling basis; regular decision, April 1. 246 early decision candidates were accepted for the 2001-2002 class. 8% of all applicants are on a waiting list; 16 were accepted in 2001.

Transfer: 20 transfer students enrolled in 2001-2002. Transfer students must have a minimum GPA of 3.2. The SAT I is required, as are transcripts and 2 teacher recommendations. Personal interviews are highly recommended. 16 credits of 32 must be completed at Holy Cross.

Visiting: There are regularly scheduled orientations for prospective students, including fall open houses in October and November consisting of informational panels on academics, admissions, financial aid, and student life, as well as tours of the facilities. There are guides for informal visits and visitors may sit in on classes and stay overnight. To schedule a visit, contact the Admissions Office.

Financial Aid: In 2001-2002, 65% of all freshmen and 59% of continuing students received some form of financial aid. 60% of freshmen and 53% of continuing students received need-based aid. The average freshman award was $16,556. Of that total, scholarships or need-based grants averaged $13,925 ($24,600 maximum); loans averaged $4552 ($4725 maximum); work contracts averaged $1208 ($1300 maximum); and outside sources $4324. 32% of undergraduates work part time. Average annual earnings from campus work are $1340. The average financial indebtedness of the 2001 graduate was $16,063. Holy Cross is a member of CSS. The CSS/Profile or FAFSA is required. The fall application deadline is February 1.

International Students: There are 21 international students enrolled. The school actively recruits these students. They must score 550 on the written TOEFL or 213 on the electronic version and also take the SAT I or the ACT. Students must take SAT II: Subject tests in writing and 2 others of the student's choice.

Computers: The mainframe is a DEC ALPHA 3100. There are 4 public labs and a dozen departmental labs on campus housing more than 200 Intel PCs and 50 Macs. Every residence hall room has access to the college computer network. All students may access the system 24 hours per day. There are no time limits and no fees.

Graduates: In 2001, 664 bachelor's degrees were awarded. The most popular majors were economics (16%), English (15%), and psychology (14%). In an average class, 87% graduate in 4 years, 91% in 5 years, and 90% in 6 years.

Admissions Contact: Admissions Office. A video is available. E-mail: *admissions@holycross.edu* Web: *www.holycross.edu*

CURRY COLLEGE E-2
Milton, MA 02186-9984 **(617) 333-2210**
(800) 669-0686; Fax: (617) 333-2114

Full-time: 615 men, 610 women	**Faculty:** 80; IIB, av$
Part-time: 500 men, 590 women	**Ph.D.s:** 53%
Graduate: 65 men, 60 women	**Student/Faculty:** 15 to 1
Year: semesters, summer session	**Tuition:** $18,815
Application Deadline: see profile	**Room & Board:** $7210
Freshman Class: n/av	
SAT I or ACT: required	**LESS COMPETITIVE**

Curry College, founded in 1879, is a private liberal arts institution. Figures in the above capsule are approximate. In addition to regional accreditation, Curry has baccalaureate program accreditation with NLN.

The library contains 90,000 volumes, 14,000 microform items, and 190 audiovisual forms/CDs, and subscribes to 625 periodicals. Computerized library services include the card catalog, interlibrary loans, and database searching. Special learning facilities include a learning resource center and radio station. The 131-acre campus is in a suburban area 7 miles southwest of Boston. Including residence halls, there are 36 buildings.

Student Life: 79% of undergraduates are from Massachusetts. Others are from 31 states, 12 foreign countries, and Canada. 68% are from public schools. 71% are white. The average age of freshmen is 18; all undergraduates, 20. 30% do not continue beyond their first year; 51% remain to graduate.

Housing: 826 students can be accommodated in college housing, which includes single-sex and coed dormitories. In addition, there are honors houses, special-interest houses, and a 9-month house for international students. On-campus housing is available on a first-come, first-served basis and is available on a lottery system for upperclassmen. 66% of students live on campus; of those, 80% remain on campus on weekends. All students may keep cars.

Activities: There are no fraternities or sororities. There are 20 groups on campus, including cheerleading, chorale, dance, drama, ethnic, film, honors, international, literary magazine, musical theater, newspaper, photography, political, professional, radio and TV, religious, social, social service, student government, and yearbook. Popular campus events include formal dances, a concert series, and Career Day.

Sports: There are 7 intercollegiate sports for men and 6 for women, and 5 intramural sports for men and 5 for women. Facilities include a 500-seat gym, a dance studio, 13 outdoor tennis courts, an outdoor pool, 5 athletic fields, a 1000-seat stadium, a 500-seat auditorium, and a 5000-meter cross-country trail.

Disabled Students: 60% of the campus is accessible. Wheelchair ramps, elevators, special parking, specially equipped rest rooms, and special class scheduling are available.

Services: Counseling and information services are available, as is tutoring in most subjects. There is a reader service for the blind, and remedial math, reading, and writing. General development courses in writing, reading, and math are designed to develop the student's basic skills. LD tutoring, an Essential Skills Center, and the Program for Advancement of Learning are also available.

Campus Safety and Security: Measures include 24-hour foot and vehicle patrol, escort service, shuttle buses, and informal discussions. There are pamphlets/posters/films, emergency telephones,and lighted pathways/sidewalks. A campus safety office offers security services.

Programs of Study: Curry confers B.A. and B.S.N. degrees. Master's degrees are also awarded. Bachelor's degrees are awarded in BIOLOGICAL SCIENCE (biology/biological science), BUSINESS (business administration and management), COMMUNICATIONS AND THE ARTS (communications, English, and visual and performing arts), COMPUTER AND PHYSICAL SCIENCE (chemistry and physics), EDUCATION (early childhood, elementary, health, and special), ENGINEERING AND ENVIRONMENTAL DESIGN (environmental science), HEALTH PROFESSIONS (nursing), SOCIAL SCIENCE (criminal justice, history, philosophy, psychology, and sociology). Nursing is the strongest academically. Business, communications, and criminal justice are the largest.

Required: Successful completion of the liberal arts core curriculum and a total of 120 semester hours (121 for nursing), with at least 30 in the major, and a minimum 2.0 GPA, are required for graduation. Nursing students must pass a comprehensive exam.

Special: Curry offers internships in all majors, an accelerated degree with approval of the dean, study abroad, work-study programs, dual and student-designed majors, credit by exam and for life, work, and military experience, nondegree study, and pass/fail options. There are 2 national honor societies.

Faculty/Classroom: 43% of faculty are male; 57%, female. All teach undergraduates. No introductory courses are taught by graduate students. The average class size in an introductory lecture is 20; in a laboratory, 12; and in a regular course, 20.

Requirements: The SAT I or ACT is required, with average scores of 450 verbal and 430 math on the SAT I. Applicants must be graduates of an accredited secondary school or have a GED. 16 credits are required, including 4 years of English, 2 each of foreign language, history, science, and social studies, and 3 of math. An essay is required, and an interview recommended. A portfolio where appropriate is also advised. Applications are available at the Curry web site. A GPA of 2.0 is required. AP and CLEP credits are accepted. Important factors in the admissions decision are recommendations by school officials, extracurricular activities record, and evidence of special talent.

Procedure: Freshmen are admitted fall and spring. Entrance exams should be taken in the junior year or in November of the senior year. There are early decision, early admissions, and deferred admissions plans. Notification of early decision is sent rolling; regular decision, on a rolling basis. Check with the school for current deadlines. The fee is $40.

Transfer: 81 transfer students enrolled in 2001-2002. Transfer applicants must be in good academic standing at their previous college with a minimum GPA of 2.0. An interview is recommended. 30 credits of 120 must be completed at Curry.

Visiting: There are regularly scheduled orientations for prospective students, consisting of interviews with an admissions counselor and tours with a student. There are guides for informal visits and visitors may sit in on classes and stay overnight. To schedule a visit, contact the Admissions Office.

Financial Aid: In a recent year, 70% of all freshmen and 65% of continuing students received some form of financial aid. 56% of freshmen and 53% of continuing students received need-based aid. The average freshman award was $12,500. Of that total, scholarships or need-based grants averaged $5000; loans averaged $2625; work contracts averaged $1200; and need-based self-help averaged $3825. 40% of undergraduates work part time. Average annual earnings from campus work are $1200. The average financial indebtedness of a recent year's graduate was $18,000. Curry is a member of CSS. The FAFSA and the college's own financial statement are required. The fall application deadline is March 1.

International Students: The school actively recruits these students. They must score 500 on the written TOEFL and also take the SAT I or the ACT.

Computers: The mainframe is a DEC 2100/400 AXP. All students have access to the Internet from residence hall rooms. More than 100 PCs are available for student use in various campus locations. All students may access the system. There are no time limits and no fees. It is strongly recommended that all students have a personal computer.

Graduates: In a recent year, 335 bachelor's degrees were awarded. The most popular majors were criminal justice (22%), nursing (21%), and business management (20%). In an average class, 47% graduate in 4 years, and 50% in 5 years.

Admissions Contact: Michael Poll, Dean of Admissions and Financial Aid. E-mail: *curryadm@curry.edu* Web: *www.curry.edu*

EASTERN NAZARENE COLLEGE — E-2

Quincy, MA 02170 — (617) 745-3711
(800) 883-6288; Fax: (617) 745-3980

Full-time: 245 men, 355 women	**Faculty:** 52
Part-time: 15 men, 25 women	**Ph.D.s:** 57%
Graduate: 30 men, 140 women	**Student/Faculty:** 13 to 1
Year: 4-1-4, summer session	**Tuition:** $14,458
Application Deadline: see profile	**Room & Board:** $4975
Freshman Class: n/av	
SAT I or ACT: required	**LESS COMPETITIVE**

Eastern Nazarene College, founded in 1918, is a private college affiliated with the Church of the Nazarene. It offers a program in the liberal arts. Figures in the above capsule are approximate. In addition to regional accreditation, ENC has baccalaureate program accreditation with CSWE. The library contains 115,000 volumes, and subscribes to 600 periodicals. Computerized library services include interlibrary loans and database searching. Special learning facilities include a learning resource center and radio station. The 15-acre campus is in a suburban area 6 miles south of Boston. Including residence halls, there are 16 buildings.

Student Life: 55% of undergraduates are from out of state, mostly the Northeast. Others are from 27 states, 24 foreign countries, and Canada. 88% are white. Most are Protestant. The average age of freshmen is 18; all undergraduates, 20. 25% do not continue beyond their first year; 60% remain to graduate.

Housing: 638 students can be accommodated in college housing, which includes single-sex dormitories and married-student housing. On-campus housing is guaranteed for all 4 years. 75% of students live on campus; of those, 75% remain on campus on weekends. Alcohol is not permitted. All students may keep cars.

Activities: There are no fraternities or sororities. There are 34 groups on campus, including band, cheerleading, choir, chorale, chorus, drama, jazz band, literary magazine, musical theater, newspaper, pep band, photography, professional, radio and TV, religious, social service, student government, and yearbook. Popular campus events include Freshmen Breakout, All-School Outing, and Junior/Senior Banquet.

Sports: There are 5 intercollegiate sports for men and 5 for women, and 4 intramural sports for men and 5 for women. Facilities include a phys ed center equipped with a basketball area, batting cage, and playing courts.

Disabled Students: 65% of the campus is accessible. Wheelchair ramps, elevators, special parking, and specially equipped rest rooms are available.

Services: Counseling and information services are available, as is tutoring in most subjects. There is remedial math, reading, and writing.

Campus Safety and Security: Measures include 24-hour foot and vehicle patrol, self-defense education, escort service, and informal discussions. There are pamphlets/posters/films, emergency telephones, and lighted pathways/sidewalks.

Programs of Study: ENC confers B.A. and B.S. degrees. Associate and master's degrees are also awarded. Bachelor's degrees are awarded in

BIOLOGICAL SCIENCE (biology/biological science and marine biology), BUSINESS (accounting and business administration and management), COMMUNICATIONS AND THE ARTS (advertising, broadcasting, communications, dramatic arts, English, French, journalism, literature, music, music performance, Spanish, and speech/debate/rhetoric), COMPUTER AND PHYSICAL SCIENCE (chemistry, computer science, mathematics, physics, and science), EDUCATION (athletic training, education, elementary, music, science, and social science), ENGINEERING AND ENVIRONMENTAL DESIGN (computer engineering, engineering physics, and environmental science), HEALTH PROFESSIONS (sports medicine), SOCIAL SCIENCE (child psychology/development, Christian studies, clinical psychology, history, ministries, physical fitness/movement, psychology, religion, religious music, social studies, social work, and sociology). Chemistry, physics, and history are the strongest academically. Education, business, and psychology are the largest.

Required: All students must complete the core curriculum of writing and rhetoric, biblical history, social science, science or math, symbolic systems and intercultural awareness, philosophy and religion, and phy ed. A total of 130 credits is required for the B.A. or B.S., with 32 to 40 in the major. Minimum GPA for graduation is 2.0.

Special: Internships are available in the metropolitan Boston area. Study abroad in Costa Rica, a Washington semester, a 3-2 engineering degree with Boston University, and a cooperative program with the Massachusetts College of Pharmacy are offered. Work-study programs, dual majors, credit for life/military/work experience, and pass/fail options are available. An off-campus degree-completion program for adults in business administration is offered. There is 1 national honor society.

Faculty/Classroom: 72% of faculty are male; 28%, female. 83% teach undergraduates. No introductory courses are taught by graduate students. The average class size in an introductory lecture is 75; in a laboratory, 20; and in a regular course, 22.

Requirements: The SAT I or ACT is required. In addition, applicants must be graduates of an accredited secondary school or have a GED. They must have a minimum of 16 academic credits, including 4 of English, 2 to 4 each of math and foreign language, 1 to 4 of science, and 1 to 2 each of history and social studies. Music students must audition. An essay and interview are recommended. A GPA of 2.3 is required. AP and CLEP credits are accepted. Important factors in the admissions decision are advanced placement or honor courses, recommendations by school officials, and leadership record.

Procedure: Freshmen are admitted to all sessions. Entrance exams should be taken in the spring of the junior year. There is a deferred admissions plan. Check with the school for current deadlines. Notification is sent on a rolling basis. The fall 2001 application fee was $25.

Transfer: A minimum 2.0 GPA is required. An interview is recommended. 60 credits of 130 must be completed at ENC.

Visiting: There are regularly scheduled orientations for prospective students. There are guides for informal visits and visitors may sit in on classes and stay overnight. To schedule a visit, contact the Office of Admissions.

Financial Aid: In a recent year, 98% of all freshmen and 95% of continuing students received some form of financial aid. 92% of freshmen and 89% of continuing students received need-based aid. The average freshman award was $11,179. Average annual earnings from campus work are $2000. ENC is a member of CSS. The FAFSA and the college's own financial statement are required. Check with the school for current deadlines.

International Students: They must score 500 on the written TOEFL.

Computers: The mainframes are a DEC VAX 11/750 and a Plexus P/60. There are more than 30 microcomputers available for student use in the library. Access to the mainframe computers is gained by assigned password, and terminals are plentiful. All students may access the system. There are no time limits. The fee is $5.

Graduates: In an average class, 44% graduate in 4 years, and 51% in 5 years.

Admissions Contact: James Heyward, Director of Admission.
E-mail: *admissio@enc.edu* Web: *www.enc.edu*

EMERSON COLLEGE E-2

Boston, MA 02116 **(617) 824-8600; Fax: (617) 824-8609**

Full-time: 1195 men, 1662 women	**Faculty:** 100; IIA, av$
Part-time: 167 men, 388 women	**Ph.D.s:** 79%
Graduate: 221 men, 706 women	**Student/Faculty:** 29 to 1
Year: semesters, summer session	**Tuition:** $20,718
Application Deadline: February 1	**Room & Board:** $9260
Freshman Class: 4071 applied, 1914 accepted, 639 enrolled	
SAT I Verbal/Math: 617/584	**ACT:** 26 **HIGHLY COMPETITIVE**

Emerson College, founded in 1880, is a private, independent college for the study of commmunication and performing arts. There are 2 undergraduate and 3 graduate schools. The library contains 197,000 volumes, 11,000 microform items, and 8800 audiovisual forms/CDs, and subscribes to 7600 periodicals. Computerized library services include the card catalog, interlibrary loans, and database searching. Special learning facilities include a learning resource center, radio station, TV station, film production facilities, DVD authoring and digital production labs, speech-language-hearing clinics, and proscenium stage theater. The campus is in an urban area in the Back Bay and Theatre District of Boston. Including residence halls, there are 15 buildings.

Student Life: 65% of undergraduates are from out of state, mostly the Middle Atlantic. Others are from 45 states, 40 foreign countries, and Canada. 76% are from public schools. 86% are white. The average age of freshmen is 18; all undergraduates, 20. 16% do not continue beyond their first year.

Housing: 1207 students can be accommodated in college housing, which includes coed dormitories. In addition, there are special-interest houses and theme floors: digital culture and writer's block. On-campus housing is available on a first-come, first-served basis and is available on a lottery system for upperclassmen. 51% of students live on campus; of those, 75% remain on campus on weekends. No one may keep cars.

Activities: 4% of men belong to 2 local and 1 national fraternities; 4% of women belong to 2 local and 2 national sororities. There are 55 groups on campus, including computers, dance, debate, drama, ethnic, film, forensics, gay, honors, international, literary magazine, musical theater, newspaper, photography, political, professional, radio and TV, religious, social, social service, student government, and yearbook. Popular campus events include Live Music Week, Cultural Awareness and Holiday Celebration, and Hand Me Down Night.

Sports: There are 6 intercollegiate sports for men and 6 for women and 1 intramural sport for women. Facilities include a 10,000-square-foot fitness center. Transportation is provided to athletic fields and gym.

Disabled Students: 50% of the campus is accessible. Wheelchair ramps, elevators, specially equipped rest rooms, special class scheduling, and residence hall accommodations are available.

Services: Counseling and information services are available, as is tutoring in most subjects. There is remedial math, reading, and writing.

Campus Safety and Security: Measures include 24-hour foot and vehicle patrol, self-defense education, escort service, and shuttle buses. There are informal discussions, pamphlets/posters/films, emergency telephones, and lighted pathways/sidewalks.

Programs of Study: Emerson confers B.A., B.S., B.F.A., and B.S.Sp. degrees. Master's and doctoral degrees are also awarded. Bachelor's degrees are awarded in BUSINESS (marketing management), COMMUNICATIONS AND THE ARTS (advertising, broadcasting, communications, creative writing, dramatic arts, film arts, journalism, media arts, musical theater, performing arts, public relations, publishing, radio/television technology, speech/debate/rhetoric, theater design, and theater management), HEALTH PROFESSIONS (speech pathology/audiology), SOCIAL SCIENCE (interdisciplinary studies). Visual and media arts, writing, and literature and publishing are the strongest academically. Visual and media arts, performing arts, and communication are the largest.

Required: All students must complete 128 credit hours, with 40 to 64 in their major, with a minimum GPA of 2.0. The required general education curriculum consists of communications, liberal arts, and global multicultural perspectives course work, for a total of 56 credits. A course in voice and articulation is required.

Special: Student-designed, interdisciplinary, and dual majors are available. Cross-registration is offered with the 6-member Boston Pro Arts Consortium, Sufflok University, and Wheelock College. 700 internships are possible in Boston and 250 in Los Angeles. Internships bear credit and are graded. Emerson has nondegree study and pass/fail options, as well as study abroad in the Netherlands and a summer film program in Prague. There is 1 national honor society, a freshman honors program, and 6 departmental honors program.

Faculty/Classroom: 56% of faculty are male; 44%, female. 93% teach undergraduates. Graduate students teach 5% of introductory courses. The average class size in an introductory lecture is 40; in a laboratory, 14; and in a regular course, 20.

Admissions: 47% of the 2001-2002 applicants were accepted. The SAT I scores for the 2001-2002 freshman class were: Verbal--3% below 500, 36% between 500 and 599, 47% between 600 and 700, and 14% above 700; Math--8% below 500, 50% between 500 and 599, 36% between 600 and 700, and 5% above 700. The ACT scores were 6% below 21, 20% between 21 and 23, 31% between 24 and 26, 31% between 27 and 28, and 12% above 28. 45% of the current freshmen were in the top fifth of their class; 85% were in the top two fifths. 5 freshmen graduated first in their class.

Requirements: The SAT I or ACT is required. In addition, candidates must be graduates of an accredited secondary school or hold a GED certificate. They must have completed 16 Carnegie units, including 4 in English and 3 each in science, social studies, foreign language, and math. An essay is required. Candidates for performing arts programs may be required to audition or interview, or submit a portfolio or resume. AP and CLEP credits are accepted. Important factors in the admissions decision are advanced placement or honor courses, evidence of special talent, and recommendations by school officials.

Procedure: Freshmen are admitted fall and spring. Entrance exams should be taken before January of the senior year. There are early action, early admissions, and deferred admissions plans. Early action applications should be filed by November 15; regular applications, by February 1 for fall entry and November 1 for spring entry along with a $55 fee. Notification of early decision is sent December 15; regular decision, April 1. 396 early decision candidates were accepted for the 2001-2002 class. 16% of all applicants are on a waiting list; 54 were accepted in 2001.

Transfer: 239 transfer students enrolled in 2001-2002. Official transcripts from high school (or a GED), all college course work, plus 2 letters of recommendation are required. SAT I or ACT scores must be submitted, unless the candidate possesses an associate degree or has been out of school 3 or more years. 32 credits of 128 must be completed at Emerson.

Visiting: There are regularly scheduled orientations for prospective students, including an information session with an admissions representative and tour lead by a currently enrolled student. There are guides for informal visits and visitors may sit in on classes with advance notice. To schedule a visit, contact the Office of Undergraduate Admission.

Financial Aid: In 2001-2002, 56% of all freshmen and 48% of continuing students received some form of financial aid. 54% of freshmen and 46% of continuing students received need-based aid. The average freshman award was $13,000. Of that total, scholarships or need-based grants averaged $10,600 ($20,224 maximum); loans averaged $3300 ($4125 maximum); and work contracts averaged $1600 ($1700 maximum). 56% of undergraduates work part time. Average annual earnings from campus work are $1600. The average financial indebtedness of the 2001 graduate was $17,125. The CSS/Profile or FAFSA and the college's own financial statement are required. The fall application deadline is March 1.

International Students: There are 158 international students enrolled. The school actively recruits these students. They must score 550 on the written TOEFL or 213 on the electronic version and also take the SAT I or the ACT.

Computers: The mainframe is a DEC VAX 4500. Many PCs are available in the academic computing center and new media center. All campus buildings, including residence halls, are networked and have direct access to the college server. All students may access the system 24 hours a day. There are no time limits and no fees. It is strongly recommended that all students have a personal computer.

Graduates: In 2001, 647 bachelor's degrees were awarded. The most popular majors were visual and media arts (30%), communication (25%), and performing arts (25%). In an average class, 1% graduate in 3 years, 58% in 4 years, 61% in 5 years, and 63% in 6 years. 100 companies recruited on campus in 2000-2001. Of the 2000 graduating class, 3% were enrolled in graduate school within 6 months of graduation and 87% were employed.

Admissions Contact: Sara S. Ramirez, Director of Undergraduate Admission. E-mail: *admission@emerson.edu* Web: *www.emerson.edu*

EMMANUEL COLLEGE

Boston, MA 02115 — **E-2** — **(617) 735-9715; Fax: (617) 735-9801**

Full-time: 138 men, 745 women	**Faculty:** 44; IIB, av$
Part-time: 84 men, 342 women	**Ph.D.s:** 76%
Graduate: 31 men, 109 women	**Student/Faculty:** 20 to 1
Year: semesters, summer session	**Tuition:** $16,412
Application Deadline: open	**Room & Board:** $7390
Freshman Class: 1050 applied, 922 accepted, 259 enrolled	
SAT I Verbal/Math: 510/490	**ACT:** 24 — **COMPETITIVE+**

Emmanuel College, founded in 1919 by the Sisters of Notre Dame de Namar, is a Catholic college offering a liberal arts and sciences curriculum that emphasizes career development. In addition to regional accreditation, the college has baccalaureate program accreditation with ACPE and NLN. The library contains 96,111 volumes, 2005 microform items, and 531 audiovisual forms/CDs, and subscribes to 414 periodicals. Computerized library services include the card catalog, interlibrary loans, and database searching. Special learning facilities include a learning resource center and art gallery. The 16-acre campus is in an urban area in Boston. Including residence halls, there are 8 buildings.

Student Life: 78% of undergraduates are from Massachusetts. Others are from 23 states and 40 foreign countries. 72% are from public schools. 60% are white. 44% are Catholic; 43% claim no religious affiliation. The average age of freshmen is 18; all undergraduates, 20. 21% do not continue beyond their first year.

Housing: 855 students can be accommodated in college housing, which includes single-sex and coed dormitories. On-campus housing is guaranteed for all 4 years. 75% of students live on campus; of those, 50% remain on campus on weekends. Alcohol is not permitted. Upperclassmen may keep cars.

Activities: There are no fraternities or sororities. There are 20 groups on campus, including art, chorus, dance, drama, ethnic, honors, international, literary magazine, musical theater, newspaper, orchestra, political, professional, religious, social, social service, student government, and yearbook. Popular campus events include Spring Weekend, Clam Bake, and Tap Off Tournament.

Sports: There are 6 intercollegiate sports for men and 8 for women, and 2 intramural sports for men and 2 for women. Facilities include a 500-seat gym, a training room/locker room, a fitness center, and a 500-seat auditorium. Students have access to a swimming pool, aerobic facilities, and 2 tennis courts.

Disabled Students: 75% of the campus is accessible. Wheelchair ramps, elevators, special parking, specially equipped rest rooms, special class scheduling, and lowered telephones are available.

Services: Counseling and information services are available, as is tutoring in every subject. There is remedial math, reading, and writing.

Campus Safety and Security: Measures include 24-hour foot and vehicle patrol, shuttle buses, informal discussions, and pamphlets/posters/films. There are emergency telephones, lighted pathways/sidewalks, and 24-hour staffed residence hall desks.

Programs of Study: the college confers B.A., B.S., and B.F.A. degrees. Master's degrees are also awarded. Bachelor's degrees are awarded in BIOLOGICAL SCIENCE (biochemistry and biology/biological science), BUSINESS (business administration and management), COMMUNICATIONS AND THE ARTS (art history and appreciation, communications, English, fine arts, Spanish, and studio art), COMPUTER AND PHYSICAL SCIENCE (chemistry, and mathematics), EDUCATION (art, elementary, and secondary), ENGINEERING AND ENVIRONMENTAL DESIGN (preengineering), HEALTH PROFESSIONS (art therapy, health care administration, medical laboratory technology, nursing, predentistry, premedicine, and preveterinary science), SOCIAL SCIENCE (political science/government, prelaw, psychology, and sociology). Liberal arts is the strongest academically. Business administration, psychology, and biology are the largest.

Required: Students must complete a broad range of distribution requirements including fine arts, math, writing, humanities, foreign language, philosophy, science, social science, and religious studies. Computer literacy is required. The core curriculum includes 2 interdisciplinary courses. A total of 128 credit hours is required, with 10 to 17 courses in the major, 15 general requirements, 5 to 7 elective or minor courses, and a minimum GPA of 2.0 for graduation.

Special: There is cross-registration with Wheelock College, Simmons College, Massachusetts College of Art, Massachusetts College of Pharmacy, Wentworth Institute of Technology, and Andover-Newton Theological School. The college offers internships, study abroad, a Washington semester, work-study programs on campus and in Boston-area organizations, an accelerated degree program in business administration, a B.A.-B.S. degree in biology, dual and student-designed majors, a general studies degree, a 3-2 engineering degree with Wentworth Institute of Technology, and pass/fail options. The adult learner degree program offers learning opportunities at off-campus sites for men and women age 23 and older. There are 4 national honor societies, and a freshman honors program. All departments have honors programs.

Faculty/Classroom: 29% of faculty are male; 71%, female. All both teach and do research. No introductory courses are taught by graduate students. The average class size in an introductory lecture is 16; in a laboratory, 11; and in a regular course, 15.

Admissions: 88% of the 2001-2002 applicants were accepted. The SAT I scores for the 2001-2002 freshman class were: Verbal--43% below 500, 38% between 500 and 599, and 19% between 600 and 700; Math--52% below 500, 37% between 500 and 599, and 11% between 600 and 700. The ACT scores were 30% below 21, 20% between 21 and 23, 25% between 24 and 26, 15% between 27 and 28, and 10% above 28. 34% of the current freshmen were in the top fifth of their class; 70% were in the top two fifths. 1 freshman graduated first in the class.

Requirements: The SAT I or ACT is required. In addition, applicants must be graduates of an accredited secondary school or have a GED. 16 academic credits are required, including 4 years of English, 3 years of math, and 2 years each of foreign language, lab science, and social studies. An essay and an interview are required. Applications are accepted on-line at the school's web site. AP and CLEP credits are accepted. Important factors in the admissions decision are advanced placement or honor courses, recommendations by school officials, and leadership record.

Procedure: Freshmen are admitted fall and spring. Entrance exams should be taken by November of the senior year. There are early decision, early admissions, and deferred admissions plans. Early decision applications should be filed by November 1; regular application deadlines are open for fall and spring entry. The fee is $40. Notification of early decision is sent December 1; regular decision, on a rolling basis.

Transfer: 33 transfer students enrolled in 2001-2002. Students must submit essays, college and high school transcripts, and 2 letters of recommendation. They must be financially and academically eligible to return to the previously attended institution. 64 credits of 128 must be completed at the college.

Visiting: There are regularly scheduled orientations for prospective students. There are guides for informal visits and visitors may sit in on classes and stay overnight. To schedule a visit, contact the Admissions Office.

Financial Aid: In 2001-2002, 87% of all freshmen and 92% of continuing students received some form of financial aid. 75% of freshmen and

86% of continuing students received need-based aid. The average freshman award was $15,602. Of that total, scholarships or need-based grants averaged $11,016 ($24,750 maximum); loans averaged $3664 ($8625 maximum); and work contracts averaged $2000 (maximum). 31% of undergraduates work part time. Average annual earnings from campus work are $1274. The average financial indebtedness of the 2001 graduate was $14,072. The FAFSA, the college's own financial statement and the parents' and students' income tax forms are required. The fall application deadline is April 1.

International Students: There are 69 international students enrolled. The school actively recruits these students. They must score 500 on the written TOEFL or take ESL level 109 or the equivalent, and also take the SAT I or the ACT.

Computers: The mainframe is an IBM RS/6000 Model 390. IBM PCs and Macs are available in the computer and academic resource centers. A campus-wide network permits access to the Internet and other services from the library, dorm rooms, and other locations. All students may access the system. There are no time limits and no fees.

Graduates: In 2001, 329 bachelor's degrees were awarded. The most popular majors were business administration (50%), nursing (11%), and psychology/English (5%). In an average class, 52% graduate in 4 years, 52% in 5 years, and 54% in 6 years.

Admissions Contact: Sandra Robbins, Dean of Admissions. E-mail: *enroll@emmanuel.edu* Web: *www.emmanuel.edu*

ENDICOTT COLLEGE

E-2

Beverly, MA 01915

(978) 921-1000
(800) 325-1114; Fax: (978) 232-2520

Full-time: 468 men, 939 women	**Faculty:** 51; IIB, -$
Part-time: n/av	**Ph.D.s:** 44%
Graduate: n/av	**Student/Faculty:** 28 to 1
Year: semesters, summer session	**Tuition:** $15,704
Application Deadline: open	**Room & Board:** $8000
Freshman Class: 2115 applied, 1282 accepted, 423 enrolled	
SAT I Verbal/Math: 514/508	**ACT:** 21 **COMPETITIVE**

Endicott College, founded in 1939, is a private institution offering programs in arts and sciences, business and communications, health sciences, sports science and hospitality, education, art and design, criminal justice, and computer and information technology. In addition to regional accreditation, Endicott College has baccalaureate program accreditation with FIDER and NLN. The library contains 118,000 volumes, 23,500 microform items, and 475 audiovisual forms/CDs, and subscribes to 3500 periodicals. Computerized library services include the card catalog, interlibrary loans, and database searching. Special learning facilities include a learning resource center, art gallery, radio station, and TV station. The 200-acre campus is in a suburban area 20 miles north of Boston. Including residence halls, there are 32 buildings.

Student Life: 50% of undergraduates are from out of state, mostly the Northeast. Others are from 30 states and 26 foreign countries. 81% are white. The average age of freshmen is 18; all undergraduates, 19. 30% do not continue beyond their first year.

Housing: 1184 students can be accommodated in college housing, which includes single-sex and coed dormitories, on-campus apartments, and off-campus apartments. In addition, there is substance-free housing. On-campus housing is available on a first-come, first-served basis and is available on a lottery system for upperclassmen. 84% of students live on campus. All students may keep cars.

Activities: There are no fraternities or sororities. There are 36 groups on campus, including adventure, art, cheerleading, chorus, dance, drama, ethnic, film, fitness, gay, honors, international, investment, literary magazine, newspaper, professional, radio and TV, religious, sailing, social, social service, student government, and yearbook.

Sports: There are 7 intercollegiate sports for men and 9 for women, and 6 intramural sports for men and 6 for women. Facilities include a 1400-seat gym with racquetball and basketball courts, weight, fitness, and aerobics rooms, indoor track, and field house. Outdoor facilities include 6 tennis courts, and field hockey, softball, lighted baseball, lacrosse, and soccer fields.

Disabled Students: 90% of the campus is accessible. Wheelchair ramps, elevators, special parking, specially equipped rest rooms, special class scheduling, and lowered drinking fountains are available.

Services: Counseling and information services are available, as is tutoring in every subject. There is a reader service for the blind, remedial math, reading, and writing, and an interpreter service for hearing-impaired students.

Campus Safety and Security: Measures include 24-hour foot and vehicle patrol, self-defense education, escort service, and shuttle buses. There are informal discussions, pamphlets/posters/films, emergency telephones, and lighted pathways/sidewalks.

Programs of Study: Endicott College confers B.A., B.S., and B.F.A. degrees. Associate and master's degrees are also awarded. Bachelor's degrees are awarded in BUSINESS (business administration and management and hotel/motel and restaurant management), COMMUNICATIONS AND THE ARTS (communications and fine arts), EDUCATION (physical), ENGINEERING AND ENVIRONMENTAL DESIGN (computer technology and interior design), HEALTH PROFESSIONS (nursing), SOCIAL SCIENCE (criminal justice, liberal arts/general studies, and psychology). Business is the largest.

Required: To graduate, students must complete 128 credit hours with a minimum GPA of 2.0 (2.5 in education and nursing). Core requirements include 9 credits in science, humanities, social sciences, math, and writing courses, 12 upper-division electives, 3 credits in first-year seminar, senior seminar, and capstone.

Special: Cross-registration is available with NECCUM and internships are required in every major. Students may study abroad, and there are accelerated degree programs in business administration and psychology. Student-designed majors are available in liberal studies. There are 2 national honor societies, a freshman honors program, and 1 departmental honors program.

Faculty/Classroom: 48% of faculty are male; 52%, female. All teach undergraduates. The average class size in an introductory lecture is 19; in a laboratory, 19; and in a regular course, 19.

Admissions: 61% of the 2001-2002 applicants were accepted. The SAT I scores for the 2001-2002 freshman class were: Verbal--40% below 500, 51% between 500 and 599, and 9% between 600 and 700; Math--42% below 500, 52% between 500 and 599, and 5% between 600 and 700. The ACT scores were 38% below 21, 58% between 21 and 23, and 4% between 24 and 26. 20% of the current freshmen were in the top fifth of their class; 58% were in the top two fifths.

Requirements: The SAT I is required. In addition, essays and 2 science and math recommendations are required for nursing (including chemistry), physical therapist assistant, and athletic training majors. AP and CLEP credits are accepted. Important factors in the admissions decision are leadership record, recommendations by school officials, and extracurricular activities record. Applications are available on-line via The Princeton Review, at *www.review.com*, and Massachusetts Mentor, at *www.massmentor.edu*

Procedure: Freshmen are admitted fall and spring. Entrance exams should be taken in fall of the senior year. There is a deferred admissions plan. Application deadlines are open. Notification is sent on a rolling basis. The fall 2001 application fee was $25.

Transfer: 61 transfer students enrolled in 2001-2002. The SAT I or ACT is required, as are official high school and college transcripts, and a letter of recommendation. 24 credits of 128 must be completed at Endicott College.

Visiting: There are regularly scheduled orientations for prospective students, including testing, preregistration, and an introduction to general student life. There are guides for informal visits and visitors may sit in on classes and stay overnight. To schedule a visit, contact the Admission Office.

Financial Aid: In 2001-2002, 54% of all freshmen and 60% of continuing students received some form of financial aid. 53% of freshmen and 58% of continuing students received need-based aid. The average freshman award was $11,106. Of that total, scholarships or need-based grants averaged $7925 ($10,000 maximum); loans averaged $3677 ($4125 maximum); and work contracts averaged $1400. 30% of undergraduates work part time. Average annual earnings from campus work are $1400 (maximum). The average financial indebtedness of the 2001 graduate was $17,125. Endicott College is a member of CSS. The FAFSA and the college's own financial statement are required. The fall application deadline is March 15.

International Students: There are 131 international students enrolled. The school actively recruits these students. They must score 525 on the written TOEFL.

Computers: The mainframe is a Digital ALPHA. There are 5 academic computer labs that house Mac and Pentium computers. Students have access to the Internet and e-mail. All students may access the system Monday to Thursday, 7:45 A.M. to midnight; Friday, 7:45 A.M. to 5 P.M.; Saturday, 9 A.M. to 5 P.M.; and Sunday, 1 P.M. to midnight. There are no time limits. The fee $306 for residents, $132 for commuters. It is strongly recommended that all students have a personal computer.

Graduates: In 2001, 259 bachelor's degrees were awarded. The most popular majors were business administration (25%), hospitality studies (11%), and psychology (9%). In an average class, 50% graduate in 6 years. 50 companies recruited on campus in 2000-2001. Of the 2000 graduating class, 19% were enrolled in graduate school within 6 months of graduation and 96% were employed.

Admissions Contact: Thomas J. Redman, VP, Admissions. A video is available. E-mail: *admissio@endicott.edu* Web: *www.endicott.edu*

FISHER COLLEGE
Boston, MA 02116-1500

D-13
(617) 236-8818
(800) 446-1226; Fax: (617) 236-5473

Full-time: 161 men, 363 women	**Faculty:** 28
Part-time: 10 men and women	**Ph.D.s:** 22%
Graduate: none	**Student/Faculty:** 19 to 1
Year: semesters, summer session	**Tuition:** $15,200
Application Deadline: open	**Room & Board:** $7900
Freshman Class: n/av	
ACT: not required	**COMPETITIVE**

Fisher College, founded in 1903 is an independent institution offering a bachelor's degree in management. The 2 libraries contain 32,000 volumes and 1500 audiovisual forms/CDs, and subscribe to 150 periodicals. Computerized library services include the card catalog, interlibrary loans, and database searching. Special learning facilities include a learning resource center. The 1-acre campus is in an urban area in Boston. Including residence halls, there are 12 buildings.

Student Life: 60% of undergraduates are from Massachusetts. Others are from 15 states, 87 foreign countries, and Canada. 80% are from public schools. 37% are white; 21% African American; 10% Hispanic. The average age of freshmen is 17; all undergraduates, 17.

Housing: 292 students can be accommodated in college housing, which includes single-sex and coed dormitories. On-campus housing is available on a first-come, first-served basis and is available on a lottery system for upperclassmen. Priority is given to out-of-town students. 50% of students live on campus. Alcohol is not permitted. No one may keep cars.

Activities: There are no fraternities or sororities. There are 13 groups on campus, including cheerleading, chess, computers, ethnic, gay, honors, international, photography, political, professional, religious, social, social service, student government, and yearbook. Popular campus events include ski trips, dances, and horseback riding.

Sports: There are 2 intercollegiate sports for men and 2 for women.

Disabled Students: 85% of the campus is accessible. Wheelchair ramps, elevators, special parking, and specially equipped rest rooms are available.

Services: Counseling and information services are available, as is tutoring in every subject. There is remedial math, reading, and writing.

Campus Safety and Security: Measures include 24-hour foot and vehicle patrol, shuttle buses, pamphlets/posters/films, and lighted pathways/sidewalks.

Programs of Study: Fisher College confers the B.S. degree. Associate degrees are also awarded. Bachelor's degrees are awarded in BUSINESS (business administration and management). Management is the largest.

Required: Students must complete a minimum of 120 hours, with at least 36 in the major and a minimum GPA of 2.0. Students must also take English I, English II, and a freshman seminar. Distribution requirements include 6 hours each in humanities, social science, and math/science.

Special: Internships, work-study, and dual majors are available. There is 1 national honor society, including Phi Beta Kappa, a freshman honors program, and 1 departmental honors program.

Faculty/Classroom: 45% of faculty are male; 55%, female. All teach undergraduates, 10% do research, and 10% do both. The average class size in an introductory lecture is 17; in a laboratory, 12; and in a regular course, 19.

Requirements: AP and CLEP credits are accepted. Important factors in the admissions decision are recommendations by school officials, leadership record, and advanced placement or honor courses.

Procedure: Freshmen are admitted fall and spring. Application deadlines are open. The application fee is $25 and applications are accepted at the college's web site.

Transfer: 60 transfer students enrolled in 2001-2002. Transfer requirements are the same as for all students, including submission of college transcript. 30 credits of 120 must be completed at Fisher College.

Visiting: There are regularly scheduled orientations for prospective students. There are guides for informal visits and visitors may sit in on classes. To schedule a visit, contact the Office of Admissions at *admissions@fisher.edu*

Financial Aid: In 2001-2002, 83% of all freshmen and 51% of continuing students received some form of financial aid. 75% of freshmen received need-based aid. The average freshman award was $10,611. Of that total, scholarships or need-based grants averaged $11,125 ($15,625 maximum); loans averaged $4625 ($8625 maximum); and work contracts averaged $1800 ($2500 maximum). 38% of undergraduates work part time. Average annual earnings from campus work are $479. The average financial indebtedness of the 2001 graduate was $14,125. The FAFSA is required.

International Students: There are 87 international students enrolled. The school actively recruits these students. They must score 450 on the written TOEFL or 133 on the electronic version and also take the college's own test.

Computers: All students may access the system. There are no time limits and no fees.

Graduates: In 2001, 5 bachelor's degrees were awarded. Management was the most popular major.

Admissions Contact: Marietta Baier, Associate Director Admissions. E-mail: *admissions@fisher.edu* Web: *www.fisher.edu*

FITCHBURG STATE COLLEGE
Fitchburg, MA 01420-2697

C-2
(978) 665-3144
(800) 705-9692; Fax: (978) 665-4540

Full-time: 921 men, 1324 women	**Faculty:** 204; IIA, -$
Part-time: 472 men, 502 women	**Ph.D.s:** 75%
Graduate: 404 men, 1410 women	**Student/Faculty:** 11 to 1
Year: semesters, summer session	**Tuition:** $2988 ($9068)
Application Deadline: April 1	**Room & Board:** $4848
Freshman Class: 2094 applied, 1273 accepted, 431 enrolled	
SAT I Verbal/Math: 510/500	**COMPETITIVE**

Fitchburg State College, founded in 1894, is a public college offering programs in liberal arts, business, communications, health sciences, and education. In addition to regional accreditation, Fitchburg State has baccalaureate program accreditation with CCNE, IACBE, NAACLS, and NCATE. The library contains 232,825 volumes, 476,829 microform items, and 2381 audiovisual forms/CDs, and subscribes to 2164 periodicals. Computerized library services include the card catalog, interlibrary loans, and database searching. Special learning facilities include a learning resource center, art gallery, radio station, a campus school, a graphics center, and a TV studio. The 45-acre campus is in a small town 45 miles west of Boston. Including residence halls, there are 33 buildings.

Student Life: 92% of undergraduates are from Massachusetts. Others are from 14 states and 10 foreign countries. 80% are from public schools. 90% are white. The average age of freshmen is 18; all undergraduates, 20. 25% do not continue beyond their first year.

Housing: 1374 students can be accommodated in college housing, which includes coed dormitories and on-campus apartments. In addition, there are speial interest houses. On-campus housing is guaranteed for all 4 years. 60% of students commute. All students may keep cars.

Activities: 3% of men belong to 4 national fraternities; 3% of women belong to 1 local sorority and 2 national sororities. There are 65 groups on campus, including band, cheerleading, chorus, computers, dance, drama, ethnic, film, gay, honors, international, jazz band, literary magazine, newspaper, photography, political, professional, radio and TV, religious, social, social service, student government, and yearbook. Popular campus events include the Visiting Artists and Lecturers Series, Americulture Arts Festival, and Falcon Fest.

Sports: There are 8 intercollegiate sports for men and 8 for women, and 8 intramural sports for men and 8 for women. Facilities include a 1000-seat gym, an indoor/outdoor track, a weight room, intramural fields, the student union, volleyball, basketball, racquetball, and tennis courts, a swimming pool, and a dance studio.

Disabled Students: 80% of the campus is accessible. Wheelchair ramps, elevators, special parking, specially equipped rest rooms, special class scheduling, lowered drinking fountains, lowered telephones, and an adaptive computer lab are available.

Services: Counseling and information services are available, as is tutoring in most subjects. There is a reader service for the blind, and remedial math, reading, and writing.

Campus Safety and Security: Measures include 24-hour foot and vehicle patrol, self-defense education, escort service, and shuttle buses. There are informal discussions, pamphlets/posters/films, emergency telephones, and lighted pathways/sidewalks.

Programs of Study: Fitchburg State confers B.A., B.S., and B.S.Ed. Degrees. Master's degrees are also awarded. Bachelor's degrees are awarded in BIOLOGICAL SCIENCE (biology/biological science), BUSINESS (business administration and management), COMMUNICATIONS AND THE ARTS (communications and English), COMPUTER AND PHYSICAL SCIENCE (computer science, earth science, and mathematics), EDUCATION (early childhood, elementary, industrial arts, middle school, secondary, and special), ENGINEERING AND ENVIRONMENTAL DESIGN (industrial engineering technology), HEALTH PROFESSIONS (medical laboratory technology and nursing), SOCIAL SCIENCE (criminal justice, economics, geography, history, human services, liberal arts/general studies, political science/government, psychology, and sociology). Computer science, clinical laboratory sciences, and nursing are the strongest academically. Business administration, communications, and nursing are the largest.

Required: All students must complete a minimum of 120 credit hours with a GPA of at least 2.0 overall and in the major. Distribution requirements include courses from the categories of ideas and events, human behavior, literature/language/arts, and the quantitative/scientific area. Two introductory semesters of writing plus junior/senior writing in the major, 1 semester of health and fitness, and a computer literacy course are also required.

Special: Students may cross-register at any other Massachusetts state college and may take courses at institutions in the Worcester Consortium. Internships in a variety of fields, accelerated degree programs, B.A.-B.S. degrees, dual majors, and a student-designed general studies major are offered. There are 6 national honor societies, a freshman honors program, and 7 departmental honors programs.

Faculty/Classroom: 55% of faculty are male; 45%, female. All teach undergraduates and 20% both teach and do research. No introductory courses are taught by graduate students. The average class size in an introductory lecture is 20; in a laboratory, 15; and in a regular course, 20.

Admissions: 61% of the 2001-2002 applicants were accepted. The SAT I scores for the 2001-2002 freshman class were: Verbal--43% below 500, 44% between 500 and 599, 12% between 600 and 700, and 1% above 700; Math--46% below 500, 44% between 500 and 599, and 10% between 600 and 700.

Requirements: The SAT I is recommended. In addition, applicants should be graduates of accredited high schools or have the GED. Secondary preparation should include 4 years of English, 3 years each of math and liberal arts or phys ed, and 2 years each of a foreign language, social studies including U.S. history, and science. A personal interview is recommended. A GPA of 2.0 is required. AP and CLEP credits are accepted. Important factors in the admissions decision are advanced placement or honor courses, leadership record, and extracurricular activities record.

Procedure: Freshmen are admitted fall and spring. Entrance exams should be taken in the junior or senior year. There are early admissions and deferred admissions plans. Applications should be filed by April 1 for fall entry and December 1 for spring entry, along with a $10 fee. Notification is sent on a rolling basis. 2% of all applicants are on a waiting list; 1% were accepted in 2001.

Transfer: 331 transfer students enrolled in 2001-2002. Applicants should present a minimum GPA of 2.0 in at least 12 credits of transferable college work. An associate degree and personal interview are recommended. 45 credits of 120 must be completed at Fitchburg State.

Visiting: There are regularly scheduled orientations for prospective students, including tours of the campus and residence halls, admissions/financial aid information, and academic program advising. There are guides for informal visits and visitors may sit in on classes. To schedule a visit, contact the Admissions Office.

Financial Aid: The FAFSA and the college's own financial statement are required. The fall application deadline is March 1.

International Students: There are 30 international students enrolled. The school actively recruits these students. They must score 550 on the written TOEFL or 213 on the electronic version.

Computers: The mainframe is a Tricord ES8000. Some 250 PCs are available for student use in the residence halls and in various labs throughout the campus. All residence hall rooms have full Internet access. All students may access the system 24 hours per day. There are no time limits and no fees.

Graduates: In 2001, 477 bachelor's degrees were awarded. The most popular majors were business administration (13%), communications (13%), and nursing (10%). In an average class, 21% graduate in 4 years, 40% in 5 years, and 41% in 6 years. 30 companies recruited on campus in 2000-2001. Of the 2000 graduating class, 10% were enrolled in graduate school within 6 months of graduation and 94% were employed.

Admissions Contact: Robert McGann, Dean of Enrollment Management. A video is available. E-mail: *admissions@fsc.edu*
Web: *www.fsc.edu*

FRAMINGHAM STATE COLLEGE D-2
Framingham, MA 01701-9101 **(508) 626-4500**
Fax: (508) 626-4017

Full-time: 1078 men, 2047 women	**Faculty:** 168
Part-time: 384 men, 534 women	**Ph.D.s:** 73%
Graduate: 411 men, 1461 women	**Student/Faculty:** 19 to 1
Year: semesters, summer session	**Tuition:** $2856 ($8936)
Application Deadline: March 1	**Room & Board:** $4403
Freshman Class: 3731 applied, 2252 accepted, 660 enrolled	
SAT I Verbal/Math: 528/513	**COMPETITIVE**

Framingham State College, founded in 1839, is a comprehensive public institution offering degree programs based on a liberal arts foundation that includes distinctive career opportunities. In addition to regional accreditation, FSC has baccalaureate program accreditation with ADA, AHEA, and NLN. The library contains 183,171 volumes, 572,088 microform items, and 767 audiovisual forms/CDs, and subscribes to 1490 periodicals. Computerized library services include the card catalog, interlibrary loans, and database searching. Special learning facilities include a learning resource center, art gallery, planetarium, radio station, greenhouse, TV studio, early childhood demonstration lab, and Christa Corrigan McAuliffe Challenger Center for Education and Teaching Excellence. The 73-acre campus is in a suburban area 20 miles west of Boston. Including residence halls, there are 19 buildings.

Student Life: 91% of undergraduates are from Massachusetts. Others are from 19 states, 26 foreign countries, and Canada. 80% are from public schools. 90% are white. The average age of freshmen is 19; all undergraduates, 21. 27% do not continue beyond their first year.

Housing: 1450 students can be accommodated in college housing, which includes single-sex and coed dormitories. 55% of students commute. Alcohol is not permitted. Upperclassmen may keep cars.

Activities: There are no fraternities or sororities. There are 35 groups on campus, including art, cheerleading, chorale, chorus, computers, dance, drama, ethnic, gay, honors, international, literary magazine, newspaper, professional, radio and TV, religious, social, social service, student government, and yearbook. Popular campus events include the Sandbox Festival and performances by the Hilltop Players.

Sports: There are 6 intercollegiate sports for men and 6 for women, and 6 intramural sports for men and 6 for women. Facilities include an athletic and recreation center, a gym, and a student center. A football field, soccer field, tennis courts, and basketball courts are available on lower campus fields.

Disabled Students: 90% of the campus is accessible. Wheelchair ramps, elevators, special parking, specially equipped rest rooms, special class scheduling, lowered drinking fountains, and lowered telephones are available.

Services: Counseling and information services are available, as is tutoring in most subjects. There is a reader service for the blind, and remedial math, reading, and writing. The College Skills Center offers free tutoring in writing, math, and reading. Subject tutoring may be arranged for an hourly fee.

Campus Safety and Security: Measures include 24-hour foot and vehicle patrol, self-defense education, escort service, and shuttle buses. There are informal discussions, pamphlets/posters/films, emergency telephones, and lighted pathways/sidewalks.

Programs of Study: FSC confers B.A. and B.S. degrees. Master's degrees are also awarded. Bachelor's degrees are awarded in BIOLOGICAL SCIENCE (biology/biological science and nutrition), BUSINESS (business administration and management), COMMUNICATIONS AND THE ARTS (art history and appreciation, communications, English, fine arts, French, and Spanish), COMPUTER AND PHYSICAL SCIENCE (chemistry, computer science, and mathematics), EDUCATION (early childhood and elementary), ENGINEERING AND ENVIRONMENTAL DESIGN (preengineering), SOCIAL SCIENCE (clothing and textiles management/production/services, economics, family/consumer studies, food science, geography, history, political science/government, psychology, sociology, and textiles and clothing). Business administration, elementary/early childhood education, and food and nutrition are the largest.

Required: The college's goal-based General Education model includes: writing; math; language (optional), literature or philosophy; visual or performing arts; physical science; life science; historical studies; social and behavioral sciences; forces in the United States; study of Constitutions, gender, class, and race; non-Western studies; contemporary issues and trends; integrative studies; and professional studies (optional). Every student must take 12 General Education courses and fulfill all required goals. A total of 128 credits (32 courses), including 40 to 68 credits in the major, and a 2.0 GPA, are required to graduate.

Special: The college offers a 2-3 preengineering program in cooperation with the University of Massachusetts at Amherst, Lowell, and Dartmouth. Cross-registration is possible at any of the state colleges. Study abroad in 6 countries, a Washington semester, and various internships are available. Pass/fail options are limited to 2 courses. There are 6 national honor societies, a freshman honors program, and 6 departmental honors program.

Faculty/Classroom: 55% of faculty are male; 45%, female. All teach undergraduates. No introductory courses are taught by graduate students. The average class size in an introductory lecture is 25 and in a laboratory, 25.

Admissions: 60% of the 2001-2002 applicants were accepted. The SAT I scores for the 2001-2002 freshman class were: Verbal--32% below 500, 55% between 500 and 599, 12% between 600 and 700, and 1% above 700; Math--41% below 500, 50% between 500 and 599, 8% between 600 and 700, and 1% above 700. 17% of the current freshmen were in the top fifth of their class; 53% were in the top two fifths. 2 freshmen graduated first in their class.

Requirements: The SAT I is required. In addition, applicants must have a high school diploma or the GED. Secondary preparation must total 16 college-preparatory credits, including 4 years of English, 3 each of math and science (2 with lab), and 2 each of foreign language and social science. The required 2 years of electives may include additional academic subjects or art, music, or computer courses. Prospective art majors must submit a portfolio. A GPA of 3.0 is required. AP and CLEP credits are accepted. Important factors in the admissions decision are advanced placement or honor courses, leadership record, and recommendations by school officials. The college accepts applications on-line.

Procedure: Freshmen are admitted fall and spring. Entrance exams should be taken in the spring of the junior year or fall of the senior year.

There are early admissions and deferred admissions plans. Applications should be filed by March 1 for fall entry and December 1 for spring entry, along with a $25 fee. Notification is sent in December.

Transfer: 363 transfer students enrolled in 2001-2002. Applicants with more than 24 college credits must present a college GPA of at least 2.5; those with fewer than 24 credits must also meet freshman admission requirements. Official transcripts must be submitted from all colleges previously attended. 32 credits of 128 must be completed at FSC.

Visiting: There are regularly scheduled orientations for prospective students, including campus tours and information sessions. There are guides for informal visits and visitors may sit in on classes and stay overnight. Overnight visits must be arranged at least 3 weeks in advance. To schedule a visit, contact the Admissions Office.

Financial Aid: In 2001-2002, 61% of all freshmen and 55% of continuing students received some form of financial aid. 55% of freshmen and 37% of continuing students received need-based aid. The average freshman award was $5430. Of that total, scholarships or need-based grants averaged $1920 ($7420 maximum); loans averaged $3400 ($5500 maximum); and work contracts averaged $250 ($1600 maximum). 45% of undergraduates work part time. Average annual earnings from campus work are $1000. The average financial indebtedness of the 2001 graduate was $10,875. The FAFSA is required. The fall application deadline is March 1.

International Students: There are 103 international students enrolled. They must score 550 on the written TOEFL.

Computers: The mainframe is a Compaq Proliant 1500 server running Windows NT/Novell 3.12. There are more than 160 network connections to the student server filtered throughout 7 computer labs that all have access to the Internet using Netscape. There are also many departmental LANs that consist of Macs and PCs. The student residence halls also have a network connection to the student server for students who bring their own PCs to the college. All students may access the system at any time. There are no time limits and no fees. It is strongly recommended that all students have personal computers.

Graduates: In 2001, 575 bachelor's degrees were awarded. The most popular majors were business and management (13%), psychology (12%), and sociology (12%). In an average class, 40% graduate in 4 years, 42% in 5 years, and 45% in 6 years. 45 companies recruited on campus in 2000-2001. Of the 2000 graduating class, 15% were enrolled in graduate school within 6 months of graduation and 95% were employed.

Admissions Contact: Dr. Phillip M. Dooher, Vice President, Enrollment Management and Dean of Admissions.
E-mail: *admiss@frc.mass.edu* Web: *http://www.framingham.edu*

GORDON COLLEGE
Wenham, MA 01984 — E-2
(978) 927-2300, ext.4217
(800) 343-1379; Fax: (978) 524-3722

Full-time: 524 men, 1048 women	**Faculty:** 84; IIB, av$
Part-time: 21 men, 31 women	**Ph.D.s:** 97%
Graduate: 12 men, 58 women	**Student/Faculty:** 19 to 1
Year: semesters	**Tuition:** $18,134
Application Deadline: March 1	**Room & Board:** $5460
Freshman Class: 1027 applied, 850 accepted, 441 enrolled	
SAT I Verbal/Math: 600/580	**ACT:** 26 **VERY COMPETITIVE+**

Gordon College, founded in 1889, is an independent Christian college emphasizing a Christian approach to the liberal arts and sciences. In addition to regional accreditation, Gordon has baccalaureate program accreditation with CSWE and NASM. The library contains 180,588 volumes, 31,162 microform items, and 8922 audiovisual forms/CDs, and subscribes to 563 periodicals. Computerized library services include the card catalog, interlibrary loans, and database searching. Special learning facilities include a learning resource center and art gallery. The 500-acre campus is in a small town 25 miles north of Boston. Including residence halls, there are 28 buildings.

Student Life: 73% of undergraduates are from out of state, mostly the Northeast. Others are from 42 states, 21 foreign countries, and Canada. 92% are white. Most are Protestant. The average age of freshmen is 18; all undergraduates, 19. 12% do not continue beyond their first year.

Housing: 1390 students can be accommodated in college housing, which includes single-sex dormitories and on-campus apartments. In addition, there are special-interest houses. On-campus housing is available on a lottery system for upperclassmen. 88% of students live on campus; of those, 70% remain on campus on weekends. Alcohol is not permitted. All students may keep cars.

Activities: There are no fraternities or sororities. There are 35 groups on campus, including art, band, cheerleading, chess, choir, chorus, computers, drama, ethnic, honors, international, jazz band, literary magazine, musical theater, newspaper, off-campus ministries, orchestra, pep band, photography, political, professional, religious, social, social service, student government, student outreach, symphony, and yearbook. Popular campus events include Genesis Week, International Week, and an artists series.

Sports: There are 7 intercollegiate sports for men and 9 for women, and 12 intramural sports for men and 12 for women. Facilities include a gym, weight rooms, tennis courts, athletic fields, a training room, a swimming pool, a climbing wall, racquetball courts, an aerobics room, ski/running trails, an outdoor ropes course, a sauna, and a walking track.

Disabled Students: 90% of the campus is accessible. Wheelchair ramps, elevators, special parking, specially equipped rest rooms, special class scheduling, lowered drinking fountains, and electric doors are available.

Services: Counseling and information services are available, as is tutoring in some subjects, including math, writing, and core science. There is remedial math, reading, and writing. There are writing and academic support centers. Gordon also provides special advising, study skills help, support groups for some liberal arts core courses, walk-in help, and assistance finding volunteer note takers.

Campus Safety and Security: Measures include 24-hour foot and vehicle patrol, escort service, informal discussions, and pamphlets/posters/films. There are emergency telephones and lighted pathways/sidewalks.

Programs of Study: Gordon confers B.A., B.S., and B.Mu. degrees. Master's degrees are also awarded. Bachelor's degrees are awarded in BIOLOGICAL SCIENCE (biology/biological science), BUSINESS (accounting, business administration and management, and recreation and leisure services), COMMUNICATIONS AND THE ARTS (art, communications, English, French, German, languages, music, music performance, and Spanish), COMPUTER AND PHYSICAL SCIENCE (chemistry, computer science, mathematics, and physics), EDUCATION (early childhood, elementary, music, and special), SOCIAL SCIENCE (biblical studies, economics, history, international studies, philosophy, physical fitness/movement, political science/government, psychology, social work, sociology, and youth ministry). English, biology, and psychology are the strongest academically. English, communications, and biblical studies are the largest.

Required: All students must demonstrate competency in writing, speech, and foreign language. The core curriculum consists of 8 credits in biblical studies, 8 in social and behavioral sciences, 8 in natural sciences, math, and computer science, 6 in humanities, and 4 each in fine arts and freshman seminar. A total of 124 credits is required for graduation, with 18 or more in the major and a minimum GPA of 2.0.

Special: Gordon offers cooperative education, internships, and cross-registration with other institutions in the Northeast Consortium of Colleges and Universities in Massachusetts. There is a 3-2 engineering program with the University of Massachusetts at Lowell and a 2-2 program in allied health with the Thomas Jefferson College of Allied Health Science in Philadelphia. B.A.-B.S. degrees, dual majors, student-designed majors, nondegree study, and pass/fail options are all available. Off-campus study opportunities include a Washington semester, the Christian College Consortium Visitor Program, the LaVida Wilderness Expedition, the Nova Scotia Student Exchange Program, and study abroad in Europe, the Middle East, China, the Philippines, and Latin America. There are 2 national honor societies, and 11 departmental honors programs.

Faculty/Classroom: 71% of faculty are male; 29%, female. All teach undergraduates. No introductory courses are taught by graduate students. The average class size in an introductory lecture is 29; in a laboratory, 14; and in a regular course, 26.

Admissions: 83% of the 2001-2002 applicants were accepted. The SAT I scores for the 2001-2002 freshman class were: Verbal--6% below 500, 40% between 500 and 599, 43% between 600 and 700, and 11% above 700; Math--10% below 500, 45% between 500 and 599, 41% between 600 and 700, and 4% above 700. The ACT scores were 3% below 21, 15% between 21 and 23, 37% between 24 and 26, 23% between 27 and 28, and 22% above 28. 48% of the current freshmen were in the top fifth of their class; 70% were in the top two fifths. There were 6 National Merit finalists. 6 freshmen graduated first in their class.

Requirements: The SAT I or ACT is required. In addition, applicants must graduate from an accredited secondary school or have a GED. A minimum of 17 Carnegie units is required, including 4 English courses and 2 courses each in math, science, and social studies. Foreign language is a recommended elective. An essay, a personal reference, and an interview are required. Music majors must audition. AP and CLEP credits are accepted. Important factors in the admissions decision are advanced placement or honor courses, leadership record, and personality/intangible qualities. Applications are accepted on-line through CollegeLink at the school's web site.

Procedure: Freshmen are admitted in the fall. Entrance exams should be taken in the spring of the junior year and the fall of the senior year. There are early decision and deferred admissions plans. Early decision applications should be filed by December 1; regular applications, by March 1 for fall entry and October 15 for spring entry, along with a $40 fee. Notification of early decision is sent January 1; regular decision, on a rolling basis. 61 early decision candidates were accepted for the 2001-2002 class. 4% of all applicants are on a waiting list; 2% were accepted in 2001.

Transfer: 69 transfer students enrolled in 2001-2002. Applicants must have a minimum GPA of 2.5. College transcripts, high school transcripts, and SAT I or ACT scores if the applicant has completed less than 1 year of full-time study, an essay, an interview, and personal and academic references are required. 32 credits of 124 must be completed at Gordon.

Visiting: There are regularly scheduled orientations for prospective students, consisting of 5 open house programs throughout the fall, winter, and spring. There are guides for informal visits and visitors may sit in on classes and stay overnight. To schedule a visit, contact Cheryl Ellis, Visitation Coordinator.

Financial Aid: In 2001-2002, 78% of all freshmen and 75% of continuing students received some form of financial aid. 63% of freshmen and 66% of continuing students received need-based aid. The average freshman award was $12,707. Of that total, scholarships or need-based grants averaged $9599 ($17,378 maximum); loans averaged $2794 ($5500 maximum); and work contracts averaged $1500 ($1700 maximum). 90% of undergraduates work part time. Average annual earnings from campus work are $1200. The average financial indebtedness of the 2001 graduate was $7880. Gordon is a member of CSS. The CSS/Profile or FAFSA is required. The fall application deadline is March 1.

International Students: There are 53 international students enrolled. The school actively recruits these students. They must score 550 on the written TOEFL or 213 on the electronic version or take the SAT I or ACT.

Computers: The mainframe is a 4 DEC/Compaq Alpha. There are also 75 Macs and IBM PCs available in student labs and the computer center. The campus network may be accessed from residence halls, and there is access to the Internet and the World Wide Web. All students may access the system at any time. There are no time limits and no fees.

Graduates: In 2001, 312 bachelor's degrees were awarded. The most popular majors were communications (9%), English (9%), and biblical studies (7%). In an average class, 53% graduate in 4 years, 66% in 5 years, and 68% in 6 years.

Admissions Contact: Silvio Vazquez, Dean of Admissions.
E-mail: *vazquez@hope.gordon.edu* Web: *www.gordon.edu*

HAMPSHIRE COLLEGE B-2

Amherst, MA 01002 (413) 559-5471; Fax: (413) 559-5631

Full-time: 513 men, 706 women	**Faculty:** 103; IIB,
Part-time: none	**Ph.D.s:** 89%
Graduate: none	**Student/Faculty:** 12 to 1
Year: 4-1-4	**Tuition:** $26,871
Application Deadline: February 1	**Room & Board:** $7010
Freshman Class: 1971 applied, 1158 accepted, 355 enrolled	
SAT I Verbal/Math: 650/600	**ACT:** 28

HIGHLY COMPETITIVE+

Hampshire College, founded in 1965, is a private institution offering a liberal arts education with an emphasis on independent research, creative work, and multidisciplinary study. The library contains 124,710 volumes, 4534 microform items, and 8727 audiovisual forms/CDs, and subscribes to 731 periodicals. Computerized library services include the card catalog, interlibrary loans, and database searching. Special learning facilities include an art gallery, TV station, multimedia center, farm center, music and dance studios, optics lab, electronics shop, integrated greenhouse and aquaculture facility, fabrication shop, and performing arts center. The 800-acre campus is in a rural area 20 miles north of Springfield. Including residence halls, there are 28 buildings.

Student Life: 82% of undergraduates are from out of state, mostly the Northeast. Others are from 46 states, 25 foreign countries, and Canada. 76% are white. The average age of freshmen is 19; all undergraduates, 20.

Housing: 1100 students can be accommodated in college housing, which includes single-sex and coed dormitories and on-campus apartments. In addition, there are special-interest halls and apartments. On-campus housing is guaranteed for all 4 years. 95% of students live on campus. All students may keep cars.

Activities: There are no fraternities or sororities. There are 80 groups on campus, including art, chorus, computers, dance, drama, ethnic, film, gay, international, literary magazine, musical theater, orchestra, photography, political, radio and TV, religious, social, social service, and student government. Popular campus events include Southern Exposure, Spring Jam, and Casino Night.

Sports: There are 3 intercollegiate sports for men and 2 for women, and 18 intramural sports for men and 18 for women. Facilities include 2 multipurpose sports centers housing a glass-enclosed swimming pool, a 12,000-square-foot playing floor, a 30-foot climbing wall, a weight lifting area, 4 indoor tennis courts, and a jogging track. Other facilities include soccer fields, 10 outdoor tennis courts, 2 softball diamonds, and a 2-mile nature trail.

Disabled Students: 90% of the campus is accessible. Wheelchair ramps, elevators, special parking, specially equipped rest rooms, special class scheduling, lowered drinking fountains, and lowered telephones are available. The college provides a variety of support services to meet individual special needs.

Services: Counseling and information services are available, as is tutoring in most subjects. There is a reader service for the blind, an advising center, a writing and reading program, and a lab quantitative skills program.

Campus Safety and Security: Measures include 24-hour foot and vehicle patrol, escort service, informal discussions, and pamphlets/posters/films. There are lighted pathways/sidewalks, an EMT on-call program, and dormitory doors accessible by students only.

Programs of Study: Hampshire confers the B.A. degree. Bachelor's degrees are awarded in AGRICULTURE (agriculture and animal science), BIOLOGICAL SCIENCE (biology/biological science, botany, ecology, marine biology, nutrition, and physiology), COMMUNICATIONS AND THE ARTS (art history and appreciation, communications, comparative literature, creative writing, dance, dramatic arts, film arts, fine arts, journalism, linguistics, literature, media arts, music, performing arts, photography, and video), COMPUTER AND PHYSICAL SCIENCE (chemistry, computer science, geology, mathematics, physics, and science), EDUCATION (education), ENGINEERING AND ENVIRONMENTAL DESIGN (architecture, environmental design, and environmental science), HEALTH PROFESSIONS (health science and premedicine), SOCIAL SCIENCE (African American studies, African studies, American studies, anthropology, Asian/Oriental studies, cognitive science, crosscultural studies, economics, family/consumer studies, geography, history, humanities, international relations, international studies, Judaic studies, Latin American studies, law, Middle Eastern studies, peace studies, philosophy, political science/government, psychology, religion, sociology, urban studies, and women's studies). Film/photography/video is the strongest academically. Social sciences is the largest.

Required: All students must complete 3 divisions of study. In Division I, Basic Studies, students work in each of Hampshire's 5 schools: Cognitive Science; Humanities, Arts and Cultural Studies; Natural Science; Interdisciplinary Arts; and Social Science, and must complete 2 courses or the Division I exam project. In Division II, the Concentration, students explore their field or fields of emphasis through individually designed internships or field studies. In Division III, Advanced Studies, students complete a major independent study project, centered on a specific topic, question, or idea. Students must also include service to the college or the surrounding community and consider some aspect of their work from a non-Western perspective.

Special: Cross-registration is possible with other members of the Five-College Consortium (Amherst College, the University of Massachusetts, Smith College, and Mount Holyoke). Internships, multidisciplinary dual majors, and study abroad (in the ISEP program, Tibetan Center, or a Costa Rica semester) are offered. All majors are student-designed. Students may complete their programs in fewer than 4 years.

Faculty/Classroom: 52% of faculty are male; 48%, female. All teach undergraduates. The average class size in a regular course is 17.

Admissions: 59% of the 2001-2002 applicants were accepted. The SAT I scores for the 2001-2002 freshman class were: Verbal--3% below 500, 21% between 500 and 599, 46% between 600 and 700, and 30% above 700; Math--11% below 500, 40% between 500 and 599, 42% between 600 and 700, and 7% above 700. The ACT scores were 2% below 21, 10% between 21 and 23, 26% between 24 and 26, 28% between 27 and 28, and 34% above 28. 54% of the current freshmen were in the top fifth of their class; 81% were in the top two fifths. There were 7 National Merit semifinalists.

Requirements: In addition, applicants must submit all transcripts from 9th grade on or GED/state equivalency exam results. Students are required to submit a personal statement and an analytic essay or academic paper. An interview is recommended. AP credits are accepted. Important factors in the admissions decision are personality/intangible qualities, evidence of special talent, and extracurricular activities record.

Procedure: Freshmen are admitted fall and spring. There are early decision, early admissions, and deferred admissions plans. Early decision application should be filed by November 15; regular applications, by February 1 for fall entry and November 15 for spring entry. The fall 2001 application fee was $50. Notification of early decision is sent December 15; regular decision, April 1. 56 early decision candidates were accepted for the 2001-2002 class. 5% of all applicants are on a waiting list; 4 were accepted in 2001. The Common Application is accepted on-line as is the school's version at *www.hampshire.edu*

Transfer: 52 transfer students enrolled in 2001-2002. A proposed program of study, high school and college transcripts, and 1 recommendation must be submitted.

Visiting: There are regularly scheduled orientations for prospective students, including interviews, information sessions, campus tours, Discover Hampshire Days, Campus Visitation Days, and an overnight program. There are guides for informal visits and visitors may sit in on classes and stay overnight. To schedule a visit, contact the Admissions Office.

Financial Aid: In 2001-2002, 52% of all students received some form of financial aid including need-based aid. The average freshman award was $20,385. Of that total, scholarships or need-based grants averaged $15,660; loans averaged $2625; and work contracts averaged $2300. Average annual earnings from campus work are $2300. The CSS/Profile or FAFSA and the college's own financial statement are required. The fall application deadline is February 1.

International Students: There are 40 international students enrolled. The school actively recruits these students. They must score 577 on the written TOEFL or 233 on the electronic version.

Computers: The mainframe is a Sun SPARC Station 20 model 50. Hampshire uses a variety of computers as file servers. Several computing labs on campus allow students access to PCs and networked systems. In addition, all student rooms are networked and many students own PCs. All students may access the system 24 hours per day via their own PCs or at designated hours in the labs, generally 8 A.M. to midnight, but up to 24 hours at the end of each semester. There are no time limits and no fees.

Graduates: In 2001, 261 bachelor's degrees were awarded. The most popular majors were art (9%), film/photo (9%), and theater (6%).

Admissions Contact: Karen S. Parker, Director of Admissions. E-mail: *admissions@hampshire.edu* Web: *www.hampshire.edu*

HARVARD UNIVERSITY/HARVARD COLLEGE (Formerly Harvard and Radcliff Colleges) D-2

Cambridge, MA 02138 (617) 495-1551; Fax: (617) 495-8821

Full-time: 3526 men, 3120 women	**Faculty:** 837; I, ++$
Part-time: 6 men, 6 women	**Ph.D.s:** 99%
Graduate: 5547 men, 4804 women	**Student/Faculty:** 8 to 1
Year: semesters, summer session	**Tuition:** $26,019
Application Deadline: January 1	**Room & Board:** $8250
Freshman Class: 19,014 applied, 2110 accepted, 1637 enrolled	
SAT I or ACT: required	**MOST COMPETITIVE**

Harvard College is the undergraduate college of Harvard University. Some information in this profile is approximate. Harvard College was founded in 1636. There are 10 graduate schools. In addition to regional accreditation, Harvard has baccalaureate program accreditation with ABET. The 97 libraries contain 13 million volumes and subscribe to 100,000 periodicals. Computerized library services include the card catalog, interlibrary loans, and database searching. Special learning facilities include a learning resource center, art gallery, natural history museum, planetarium, and radio station. The 380-acre campus is in an urban area across the Charles River from Boston. Including residence halls, there are 400 buildings.

Student Life: 81% of undergraduates are from out of state, mostly the Middle Atlantic. Others are from 50 states, 118 foreign countries, and Canada. 67% are from public schools. 43% are white; 17%, Asian American. The average age of freshmen is 18; all undergraduates, 20. 96% of freshmen remain to graduate.

Housing: 6325 students can be accommodated in college housing, which includes coed dormitories and on-campus apartments. On-campus housing is guaranteed for all 4 years. 97% of students live on campus. All students may keep cars.

Activities: There are no fraternities or sororities. There are 250 groups on campus, including art, band, cheerleading, chess, choir, chorale, chorus, computers, dance, debate, drama, ethnic, film, gay, honors, international, jazz band, literary magazine, marching band, musical theater, newspaper, opera, orchestra, pep band, photography, political, professional, radio and TV, religious, social, social service, student government, symphony, and yearbook. Popular campus events include Harvard/Yale football, Head of the Charles crew regatta, and Cultural Rhythms Festival.

Sports: There are 21 intercollegiate sports for men and 20 for women, and 16 intramural sports for men and 16 for women. Facilities include several gyms and athletic centers, pools, a track, boat houses, a sailing center, a hockey rink, and various courts and playing fields.

Disabled Students: Wheelchair ramps, elevators, special parking, specially equipped rest rooms, special class scheduling, lowered drinking fountains, lowered telephones, tutors, adaptive equipment in the field of information technology, TDD/TTY, shuttle van service, a student support organization called ABLE, and an adaptive technology lab are available.

Services: Counseling and information services are available, as is tutoring in every subject. There is a reader service for the blind.

Campus Safety and Security: Measures include 24-hour foot and vehicle patrol, self-defense education, escort service, and shuttle buses. There are informal discussions, pamphlets/posters/films, emergency telephones, and lighted pathways/sidewalks.

Programs of Study: Harvard confers A.B. and S.B. degrees. Master's and doctoral degrees are also awarded. Bachelor's degrees are awarded in BIOLOGICAL SCIENCE (biochemistry, biology/biological science, and biophysics), COMMUNICATIONS AND THE ARTS (art history and appreciation, Chinese, classics, creative writing, English, fine arts, folklore and mythology, French, German, Greek, Hebrew, Italian, Japanese, Latin, linguistics, literature, music, Portuguese, Russian, and Spanish), COMPUTER AND PHYSICAL SCIENCE (applied mathematics, astronomy, chemistry, computer science, geology, geophysics and seismology, mathematics, physical sciences, physics, and statistics), ENGINEERING AND ENVIRONMENTAL DESIGN (engineering, environmental design, environmental science, and preengineering), SOCIAL SCIENCE (African American studies, American studies, anthropology, Asian/Oriental studies, economics, European studies, history, humanities, Middle Eastern studies, philosophy, political science/government, psychology, religion, Russian and Slavic studies, Sanskrit and Indian studies, social science, social studies, sociology, and women's studies). Economics, government, and biology are the largest.

Required: In 8 semesters, students must pass a minimum of 32 1-semester courses. The average course load is 4 courses per semester, but the course rate may be varied for special reasons. A typical balanced program devotes about one fourth of its courses to core curriculum requirements, one half to the concentration (or major field), and the remaining one fourth to electives.

Special: Students may cross-register with MIT and with other schools within the university, and may design their own concentrations or enroll for nondegree study. Internships and study abroad may be arranged. Accelerated degree programs, dual majors, a 3-2 engineering degree, and a combined A.B.-S.B. in engineering are offered. There are pass/fail options. There is a chapter of Phi Beta Kappa.

Faculty/Classroom: 98% teach undergraduates, 97% do research, and 95% do both. No introductory courses are taught by graduate students. The average class size in a regular course is 25.

Admissions: 11% of the 2001-2002 applicants were accepted. 98% of the current freshmen were in the top fifth of their class; all were in the top two fifths.

Requirements: The SAT I or ACT is required, as well as 3 SAT II: Subject tests. Applicants need not be high school graduates but are expected to be well prepared academically. An essay and an interview are required, in addition to a transcript, counselor report, and 2 teacher recommendations from academic disciplines. AP credits are accepted. Important factors in the admissions decision are evidence of special talent, personality/intangible qualities, and recommendations by school officials.

Procedure: Freshmen are admitted in the fall. Entrance exams should be taken by January of the senior year. There are early action, early admissions and deferred admissions plans. Early action applications should be filed by November 1; regular applications, by January 1 for fall entry. The fall 2001 application fee was $60. Notification is sent April 3. A waiting list is an active part of the admissions procedure.

Transfer: Transfer applicants must have completed at least 1 full year of daytime study in a degree-granting program at 1 institution. Students are required to submit the SAT I or ACT, 2 letters of recommendation, high school and college transcripts with a dean's report, and several essays. 16 courses of 32 must be completed at Harvard.

Visiting: There are regularly scheduled orientations for prospective students, consisting of group information sessions and tours. There are guides for informal visits and visitors may sit in on classes and stay overnight. To schedule a visit, contact the Undergraduate Admissions Office.

Financial Aid: In a recent year, 80% of all freshmen and 69% of continuing students received some form of financial aid. 48% of freshmen and 46% of continuing students received need-based aid. The average freshman award was $21,229. 70% of undergraduates work part time. Harvard is a member of CSS. The CSS/Profile or FAFSA, the college's own financial statement, and federal tax forms are required. Check with the school for current deadlines.

International Students: In a recent year, there were 472 international students enrolled. The school actively recruits these students.

Computers: All residences have Internet access. There are also PCs available for use in the science center and all residence halls. All students may access the system 24 hours per day. There are no time limits and no fees.

Graduates: In a recent year, 1663 bachelor's degrees were awarded. The most popular majors were economics (12%), government (9%), and biology (8%). In an average class, 97% graduate in 5 years. 373 companies recruited on campus in a recent year.

Admissions Contact: Marlyn McGrath Lewis, Director of Admissions. A video is available. E-mail: *college@harvard.edu*
Web: *www.college.harvard.edu*

HELLENIC COLLEGE/HOLY CROSS GREEK ORTHODOX SCHOOL OF THEOLOGY D-2
Brookline, MA 02445 (617) 731-3500, ext.1260
Fax: (617) 850-1460

Full-time: 36 men, 20 women
Part-time: 2 men
Graduate: 105 men, 13 women
Year: semesters
Application Deadline: August 15
Freshman Class: 40 applied, 34 accepted, 24 enrolled
SAT I Verbal/Math: 501/507
Faculty: 8
Ph.D.s: 100%
Student/Faculty: 7 to 1
Tuition: $9865
Room & Board: $7350
ACT: 17 **COMPETITIVE**

Hellenic College, founded in 1937, is a private college affiliated with the Greek Orthodox Church. It offers programs in the classics, elementary education, religious studies, and human development. In addition to regional accreditation, Hellenic College/Holy Cross Greek Orthodox School of Theology has baccalaureate program accreditation with NASDTEC. The library contains 109,000 volumes, 510 microform items, and 1340 audiovisual forms/CDs, and subscribes to 770 periodicals. Computerized library services include the card catalog, interlibrary loans, and database searching. Special learning facilities include archives, rare books, a Greek cultural center, and a language lab. The 52-acre campus is in an urban area 4 miles southwest of Boston. Including residence halls, there are 7 buildings.

Student Life: 90% of undergraduates are from out of state, mostly the Midwest. Others are from 29 states, 8 foreign countries, and Canada. 98% are from public schools. 98% are white; 10% foreign nationals. Most are Most are Greek or Eastern Orthodox. The average age of freshmen is 20; all undergraduates, 25. 3% do not continue beyond their first year; 93% remain to graduate.

Housing: 220 students can be accommodated in college housing, which includes single-sex dormitories, on-campus apartments, and married-student housing. On-campus housing is guaranteed for all 4 years. 95% of students live on campus; of those, 95% remain on campus on weekends. Alcohol is not permitted. All students may keep cars.

Activities: There are 9 groups on campus, including choir, ethnic, photography, religious, social, social service, student government, and yearbook. Popular campus events include Feast of the Holy Cross, Matriculation Day, and Campus Christmas Party.

Sports: Facilities include a gym, tennis and racquetball courts, and a football field.

Disabled Students: 10% of the campus is accessible. Wheelchair ramps and special parking are available.

Services: Counseling and information services are available, as is tutoring in some subjects, including Greek and music writing and composition. There is remedial math, reading, and writing.

Campus Safety and Security: Measures include a shuttle bus, informal discussions, pamphlets/posters/films, and lighted pathways/sidewalks. There is a 16-hour security patrol.

Programs of Study: Hellenic College/Holy Cross Greek Orthodox School of Theology confers the B.A. degree. Master's degrees are also awarded. Bachelor's degrees are awarded in COMMUNICATIONS AND THE ARTS (classics), EDUCATION (elementary), SOCIAL SCIENCE (human development and religion). Religious studies is the strongest academically.

Required: To graduate, students must complete 129 credits, with 39 in the major, and maintain a minimum overall GPA of 2.0. General education requirements include 72 credits, with courses in English language and literature, music, history, science, philosophy, and social science.

Special: The college offers cross-registration with Boston Theological Institute and with Newbury College, and credit by examination.

Faculty/Classroom: 80% of faculty are male; 20%, female. All teach undergraduates. No introductory courses are taught by graduate students. The average class size in an introductory lecture is 75; in a laboratory, 20; and in a regular course, 22.

Admissions: 85% of the 2001-2002 applicants were accepted. The SAT I scores for the 2001-2002 freshman class were: Verbal--34% below 500, 33% between 500 and 599, and 33% between 600 and 700; Math--55% below 500, 25% between 500 and 599, and 20% between 600 and 700. The ACT scores were 50% below 21, and 50% between 21 and 23.

Requirements: In addition, applicants should graduate from an accredited secondary school or have a GED. 15 academic credits are required, including 4 units of English, 2 each of math, foreign language, and social studies, and 1 of science. An essay is required. A GPA of 2.5 is required. AP and CLEP credits are accepted. Important factors in the admissions decision are recommendations by school officials, advanced placement or honor courses, and recommendations by alumni.

Procedure: Freshmen are admitted fall and spring. There is a deferred admissions plan. Applications should be filed by August 15 for fall entry and January 1 for spring entry. The fall 2001 application fee was $35.

Transfer: 11 transfer students enrolled in 2001-2002. The SAT I, an autobiographical statement, recommendation letters, high school transcripts, and a health certificate are required. 60 credits of 129 must be completed at Hellenic College/Holy Cross Greek Orthodox School of Theology.

Visiting: There are regularly scheduled orientations for prospective students, including observation of classroom and student life. There are guides for informal visits and visitors may sit in on classes and stay overnight. To schedule a visit, contact Agnes Desses, Office of Admissions at (617) 850-1260.

Financial Aid: The CSS/Profile or FAFSA and the college's own financial statement are required. The fall application deadline is May 1.

International Students: There are 21 international students enrolled. They must score 500 on the written TOEFL or 173 on the electronic version.

Computers: The mainframe is an IBM AS/400 Model F20. 10 PCs are available for student use in the computer lab, and Internet access is provided through the library computers. The library is on an integrated network with 13 other libraries. All students may access the system. There are no time limits and no fees.

Graduates: In 2001, 10 bachelor's degrees were awarded. The most popular majors were religious studies (60%), elementary education (30%), and human development (10%). In an average class, 97% graduate in 4 years, and 3% in 5 years.

Admissions Contact: Agnes Desses, Assistant Director, Admissions. A video is available. E-mail: *admissions@hchc.edu* Web: *www.hchc.edu*

HOLY CROSS
(See College of the Holy Cross)

LASELL COLLEGE D-2
Newton, MA 02466 (617) 243-2225
(888) LASELL-4; Fax: (617) 976-4343

Full-time: 211 men, 640 women
Part-time: 2 men, 6 women
Graduate: none
Year: semesters
Application Deadline: open
Freshman Class: 1502 applied, 1289 accepted, 327 enrolled
SAT I Verbal/Math: 460/450
Faculty: 43
Ph.D.s: 38%
Student/Faculty: 20 to 1
Tuition: $16,100
Room & Board: $8000
COMPETITIVE

Lasell College, founded in 1851, is a private nonsecular institution whose curriculum combines classroom study with practical experience in the sciences, business, education, and health fields. There are 3 undergraduate schools. The library contains 55,335 volumes, 47,488 microform items, and 2560 audiovisual forms/CDs, and subscribes to 489 periodicals. Computerized library services include the card catalog, interlibrary loans, and database searching. Special learning facilities include a learning resource center, art gallery, an early childhood curriculum library, Lasell Inn (bed and breakfast), Lasell Village (retirement community), a nursery school, and a daycare center. The 50-acre campus is in a suburban area 8 miles west of Boston. Including residence halls, there are 42 buildings.

Student Life: 66% of undergraduates are from Massachusetts. Others are from 20 states, 8 foreign countries, and Canada. 95% are from public schools. 73% are white; 10% African American. The average age of freshmen is 18; all undergraduates, 21. 25% do not continue beyond their first year.

Housing: 720 students can be accommodated in college housing, which includes single-sex and coed dormitories and on-campus apartments. In addition, there are special-interest houses. On-campus housing is guaranteed for all 4 years. 80% of students live on campus; of those, 90% remain on campus on weekends. All students may keep cars.

Activities: There are no fraternities or sororities. There are 20 groups on campus, including cheerleading, chorale, dance, drama, ethnic, gay, honors, international, literary magazine, newspaper, political, professional, social, social service, and student government. Popular campus events include River Day, Torchlight Parade, and Awards Night.

Sports: There are 5 intercollegiate sports for men and 7 for women, and 3 intramural sports for men and 3 for women. Facilities include an athletic center with a basketball court, a volleyball court, an indoor track, a dance studio, an exercise room, and locker rooms, plus 2 athletic fields.

Disabled Students: 50% of the campus is accessible. Wheelchair ramps, elevators, special parking, specially equipped rest rooms, lowered drinking fountains, and lowered telephones are available.

Services: Counseling and information services are available, as is tutoring in every subject. There is remedial math, reading, and writing, and books on tape.

Campus Safety and Security: Measures include 24-hour foot and vehicle patrol, self-defense education, escort service, and shuttle buses. There are informal discussions, pamphlets/posters/films, emergency telephones, and lighted pathways/sidewalks.

Programs of Study: Lasell confers B.A. and B.S. degrees. Associate degrees are also awarded. Bachelor's degrees are awarded in BUSI-

NESS (accounting, banking and finance, business administration and management, fashion merchandising, hospitality management services, hotel/motel and restaurant management, international business management, management information systems, marketing/retailing/merchandising, and tourism), EDUCATION (athletic training, early childhood, elementary, secondary, and special), HEALTH PROFESSIONS (exercise science, and health care administration), SOCIAL SCIENCE (child care/child and family studies, criminal justice, fashion design and technology, human services, law, liberal arts/general studies, paralegal studies, physical fitness/movement, psychology, and sociology). Allied health is the strongest academically. Business, education, and allied health are the largest.

Required: To graduate, students must complete 124 credit hours with a minimum GPA of 2.0. Requirements include 2 courses in writing and math, 1 course in literature, art, music, or drama, 1 in history, philosophy, or language, 1 in social science, one in science, and a computer literacy course. An internship is also required.

Special: Internships are built into the curriculum, and work-study programs are available on campus. Student-designed majors and student-arranged study-abroad programs are possible. All programs feature connected learning, which is an ongoing practical application of classroom theory. There is a freshman honors program.

Faculty/Classroom: 33% of faculty are male; 67%, female. All teach undergraduates. The average class size in an introductory lecture is 20; in a laboratory, 11; and in a regular course, 14.

Admissions: 86% of the 2001-2002 applicants were accepted. The SAT I scores for the 2001-2002 freshman class were: Verbal--60% below 500, 36% between 500 and 599, and 4% between 600 and 700; Math--60% below 500, 35% between 500 and 599, and 5% between 600 and 700.

Requirements: The SAT I is required. In addition, applicants should have completed 16 Carnegie units of high school study. The GED is accepted. A letter of recommendation is required and an interview is recommended. A GPA of 2.0 is required. AP and CLEP credits are accepted. Important factors in the admissions decision are advanced placement or honor courses, personality/intangible qualities, and leadership record. Applications are accepted on-line.

Procedure: Freshmen are admitted fall and spring. Application deadlines are open. The priority deadline is March 15. The application fee is $25.

Transfer: 42 transfer students enrolled in 2001-2002. Applicants must have a minimum of 2.0 GPA. 45 credits of 125 must be completed at Lasell.

Visiting: There are regularly scheduled orientations for prospective students, consisting of the president's welcome, faculty presentations, tours, and student panels. There are guides for informal visits and visitors may sit in on classes and stay overnight. To schedule a visit, contact the Admissions Office/Sally Carola at *scarola@lasell.edu*

Financial Aid: In 2001-2002, 93% of all freshmen and 94% of continuing students received some form of financial aid. 82% of freshmen and 86% of continuing students received need-based aid. The average freshman award was $15,793. Of that total, scholarships or need-based grants averaged $12,000 ($15,000 maximum); loans averaged $3736 ($7625 maximum); and work contracts averaged $1000 ($1500 maximum). 32% of undergraduates work part time. Average annual earnings from campus work are $800. The average financial indebtedness of the 2001 graduate was $19,500. Lasell is a member of CSS. The FAFSA and the college's own financial statement are required. The fall application deadline is March 1.

International Students: There are 30 international students enrolled. They must score 500 on the written TOEFL.

Computers: The mainframe is a Windows NT network. The college is served by a local area network, with computer equipment available in the main lab, the business lab, and the CAD labs. There are 75 units in class and lab space. Residence halls are wired and additional PCs are available in study areas within residence halls. All students may access the system during regularly scheduled lab hours. There are no time limits and no fees.

Graduates: In 2001, 67 bachelor's degrees were awarded. The most popular majors were education (26%), business (23%), and fashion (9%). In an average class, 71% graduate in 4 years. Of the 2000 graduating class, 8% were enrolled in graduate school within 6 months of graduation and 90% were employed.

Admissions Contact: Darryl Tiggle, Director of Admission.
E-mail: *info@lasell.edu* Web: *www.lasell.edu*

LESLEY COLLEGE

D-2

Cambridge, MA 02138-2790 **(617) 349-8800**
(800) 999-1959 ext. 8800; Fax: (617) 349-8150

Full-time: 528 women	**Faculty:** 37
Part-time: 25 women	**Ph.D.s:** 70%
Graduate: 753 men, 4324 women	**Student/Faculty:** 14 to 1
Year: semesters, summer session	**Tuition:** $17,425
Application Deadline: March 15	**Room & Board:** $7900
Freshman Class: n/av	
SAT I or ACT: required	**LESS COMPETITIVE**

Lesley College, founded in 1909, is a private, primarily women's institution. Within Lesley's School of Undergraduate Studies, the Women's College offers degree programs in education, human services, management, liberal arts, and interdisciplinary studies. Bachelor's programs in alternative formats are offered to returning students through the coeducational Baccalaureate College and the School of Management. Students may also elect to take courses at the Art Institute of Boston at Lesley College. The library contains 100,992 volumes, 784,632 microform items, and 855 audiovisual forms/CDs, and subscribes to 717 periodicals. Computerized library services include the card catalog, interlibrary loans, and database searching. Special learning facilities include a learning resource center and center for teaching resources, media production facility, and full-text databases. The 5-acre campus is in an urban area 3 miles northwest of Boston. Including residence halls, there are 45 buildings.

Student Life: 69% of undergraduates are from Massachusetts. Others are from 36 states, 12 foreign countries, and Canada. 70% are from public schools. 72% are white. The average age of freshmen is 18. 20% do not continue beyond their first year; 60% remain to graduate.

Housing: 425 students can be accommodated in college housing, which includes single-sex dormitories. In addition, there are speial interest houses. On-campus housing is guaranteed for all 4 years. 84% of students live on campus. No one may keep cars.

Activities: There are no fraternities or sororities. There are 20 groups on campus, including cheerleading, choir, chorus, drama, ethnic, feminist, gay, international, literary magazine, professional, religious, social, social service, student government, and yearbook. Popular campus events include Family and Friends Weekend, School Spirit Days, and various awareness days.

Sports: There are 6 intercollegiate sports for women and 3 intramural sports for women. Facilities include a gym, outdoor tennis courts, and a fitness center with Nautilus circuit, free weights, and cardiovascular equipment. Students may also use an Olympic-size swimming pool at a nearby school and local playing field facilities.

Disabled Students: 80% of the campus is accessible. Wheelchair ramps, elevators, special parking, specially equipped rest rooms, special class scheduling, and lowered drinking fountains. The Disability Services office provides document review and arranges for reasonable accommodations for special needs students.

Services: Counseling and information services are available, as is tutoring in most subjects. There is a reader service for the blind, remedial math, reading, and writing, and study skills and interpreter services.

Campus Safety and Security: Measures include 24-hour foot and vehicle patrol, self-defense education, escort service, and shuttle buses. There are informal discussions, pamphlets/posters/films, emergency telephones, and lighted pathways/sidewalks.

Programs of Study: Lesley confers the B.S. degree. Associate, master's, and doctoral degrees are also awarded. Bachelor's degrees are awarded in BUSINESS (management science), COMPUTER AND PHYSICAL SCIENCE (natural sciences), EDUCATION (early childhood, elementary, middle school, and special), SOCIAL SCIENCE (human services, humanities, and social science). Education is the largest.

Required: Students must complete 45 hours of general education requirements, including 15 of humanities, 12 of natural science, 9 of social science, 6 of multicultural perspectives, and 3 of first-year seminar; emphasis is given to cross-curriculum components in writing, critical and quantitative reasoning, global perspectives, and leadership and ethics. To graduate, students need 128 total credit hours, including 27 in the liberal arts majors or 41 to 43 in professional majors, with a minimum 2.0 GPA.

Special: Study abroad in England and Sweden, a Washington Justice semester, and on-campus work-study programs are offered. All students participate in at least 3 field placement experiences. There are combined accelerated degree programs in management, counseling, and education majors. Accelerated and weekend course programs are offered for Adult Baccalaureate College and School of Management degree programs.

Faculty/Classroom: 24% of faculty are male; 76%, female. All both teach and do research. No introductory courses are taught by graduate students. The average class size in an introductory lecture is 15 and in a regular course, 16.

Admissions: The SAT I scores for the 2001-2002 freshman class were: Verbal--42% below 500, 48% between 500 and 599, 9% between 600 and 700, and 1% above 700; Math--53% below 500, 39% between 500 and 599, 6% between 600 and 700, and 2% above 700. 34% of the current freshmen were in the top fifth of their class; 81% were in the top two fifths.

Requirements: The SAT I or ACT is required. In addition, applicants must be graduates of an accredited secondary school or have a GED. Students must have completed 15 academic units, including 4 in English, 2 to 3 in science with a lab course, 2 to 3 in math, and 1 in U.S. history. A writing sample and 2 recommendations are required; an interview is recommended. AP and CLEP credits are accepted. Important factors in the admissions decision are extracurricular activities record, recommendations by school officials, and advanced placement or honor courses. Applications are accepted on computer disk using Apply or CollegeLink.

Procedure: Freshmen are admitted fall and spring. Entrance exams should be taken by November of the senior year. There are early decision and deferred admissions plans. Early decision applications should be filed by December 1; regular applications, by March 15 for fall entry and December 15 for spring entry. Notification of early decision is sent December 15; regular decision, on a rolling basis. The fall 2001 application fee was $35.

Transfer: 50 transfer students enrolled in a recent year. Applicants must have earned at least 12 credit hours and a minimum 2.0 GPA. Recommendations are required and an interview is recommended. 68 credits of 128 must be completed at Lesley.

Visiting: There are regularly scheduled orientations for prospective students, including personal interviews with professional staff and student campus tours. There are guides for informal visits and visitors may sit in on classes and stay overnight. To schedule a visit, contact Lori Coutu, Assistant Director of Admissions.

Financial Aid: In 2001-2002, 87% of all freshmen and 81% of continuing students received some form of financial aid. 74% of freshmen and 73% of continuing students received need-based aid. The average freshman award was $15,025. Of that total, scholarships or need-based grants averaged $9965 ($15,170 maximum); loans averaged $4395 ($5500 maximum); and work contracts averaged $1552 ($2000 maximum). 47% of undergraduates work part time. Average annual earnings from campus work are $1191. The average financial indebtedness of the 2001 graduate was $21,680. The FAFSA, the college's own financial statement, and parent and student federal tax returns are required. The fall application deadline is February 1.

International Students: 30 international students enrolled in a recent year. The school actively recruits these students. They must score 500 on the written TOEFL.

Computers: The mainframe is an IBM. More than 120 Apple IIs, Macs and IBM PCs are available in computer labs, the learning center, the library, classrooms, and some dorms. There is also a word processing center. The library is part of an on-line Internet network and OCLC. All students may access the system during library hours primarily; the word processing center is available 24 hours a day. There are no time limits and no fees.

Admissions Contact: Jane A. Raley, Director, Women's College Admissions. E-mail: *ugadm@mail.lesley.edu* Web: *http://www.lesley.edu*

MASSACHUSETTS BOARD OF HIGHER EDUCATION

The Massachusetts Board of Higher Education was established in 1991. It is governed by an 11-member board appointed by the governor, whose chief administrator is the chancellor. The board is the central coordinating authority for the state's public higher education system of 15 community colleges, 9 state colleges, and 5 campuses of the U of Mass. The total enrollment of all 29 campuses is approximately 177,000. Profiles of the 4-year campuses, located in Amherst, Boston, Buzzard's Bay, Bridgewater, Fitchburg, Framingham, Lowell, North Adams, Salem, North Dartmouth, Westfield, and Worcester, are included in this section.

MASSACHUSETTS COLLEGE OF ART E-2

Boston, MA 02115 **(617) 879-7222**
n/av; Fax: (617) 879-7250

Full-time: 469 men, 783 women	**Faculty:** 71
Part-time: 63 men, 143 women	**Ph.D.s:** 71%
Graduate: 30 men, 74 women	**Student/Faculty:** 18 to 1
Year: semesters, summer session	**Tuition:** $4068 ($13,198)
Application Deadline: March 1	**Room & Board:** $9632
Freshman Class: 1137 applied, 526 accepted, 236 enrolled	
SAT I Verbal/Math: 567/535	**SPECIAL**

Massachusetts College of Art, founded in 1873, is a public institution offering undergraduate and graduate programs in art, design, and education. There is 1 undergraduate and 1 graduate school. There is 1 undergraduate school. In addition to regional accreditation, MassArt has baccalaureate program accreditation with NASAD. The library contains 232,900 volumes and 8700 microform items, and subscribes to 757 periodicals. Computerized library services include the card catalog and interlibrary loans. Special learning facilities include an art gallery, a computer arts center, performance spaces, and film viewing rooms. The 5-acre campus is in an urban area in Boston. Including residence halls, there are 6 buildings.

Student Life: 73% of undergraduates are from Massachusetts. Others are from 27 states, 60 foreign countries, and Canada. 85% are from public schools. 71% are white. The average age of freshmen is 18; all undergraduates, 23. 10% do not continue beyond their first year; 50% remain to graduate.

Housing: 203 students can be accommodated in college housing, which includes single-sex and coed dormitories. In addition, there is a visual art college residence hall with ventilated workrooms, a visiting artist suite, and gallery space. On-campus housing is available on a first-come, first-served basis and is available on a lottery system for upperclassmen. Priority is given to out-of-town students. 86% of students commute. Alcohol is not permitted. No one may keep cars.

Activities: There are no fraternities or sororities. There are 30 groups on campus, including art, computers, ethnic, film, gay, international, literary magazine, newspaper, photography, political, professional, radio and TV, social, social service, student government, and yearbook. Popular campus events include Eventworks, First Night Ice Sculpture, and gallery exhibitions and openings.

Sports: There are 7 intercollegiate sports for men and 6 for women, and 8 intramural sports for men and 6 for women. Facilities include a gym, a fitness center, and courts for squash, volleyball, and basketball.

Disabled Students: 95% of the campus is accessible. Wheelchair ramps, elevators, special parking, specially equipped rest rooms, special class scheduling, lowered drinking fountains, and lowered telephones are available.

Services: There is remedial reading and writing.

Campus Safety and Security: Measures include 24-hour foot and vehicle patrol, self-defense education, escort service, and shuttle buses. There are informal discussions, pamphlets/posters/films, emergency telephones, and lighted pathways/sidewalks.

Programs of Study: MassArt confers the B.F.A. degree. Master's degrees are also awarded. Bachelor's degrees are awarded in COMMUNICATIONS AND THE ARTS (art history and appreciation, ceramic art and design, fiber/textiles/weaving, film arts, fine arts, glass, graphic design, illustration, industrial design, media arts, metal/jewelry, painting, photography, printmaking, sculpture, and studio art), EDUCATION (art), ENGINEERING AND ENVIRONMENTAL DESIGN (architecture), SOCIAL SCIENCE (fashion design and technology). Painting, illustration, and graphic design are the largest.

Required: A total of 120 semester credits is required for graduation; the minimum GPA varies by major. Typically, students take 42 credits in liberal arts, 18 in studio foundations, 36 in the major, and 24 in electives. Beginning in the sophomore year, the student's work is reviewed by panels of faculty and visiting artists.

Special: MassArt offers cross-registration with several consortiums, internships for advanced students, on- and off-campus work-study programs, study-abroad and foreign-exchange programs, an open major for exceptional students, and dual majors in most combinations of concentrations.

Faculty/Classroom: 46% of faculty are male; 54%, female. All teach undergraduates. No introductory courses are taught by graduate students. The average class size in an introductory lecture is 23; in a laboratory, 12; and in a regular course, 14.

Admissions: 46% of the 2001-2002 applicants were accepted. The SAT I scores for the 2001-2002 freshman class were: Verbal--15% below 500, 50% between 500 and 599, 28% between 600 and 700, and 8% above 700; Math--30% below 500, 47% between 500 and 599, 21% between 600 and 700, and 2% above 700. 46% of the current freshmen were in the top fifth of their class; 85% were in the top two fifths.

Requirements: The SAT I is required. In addition, applicants should be graduates of an accredited secondary school or have earned the GED. College-preparatory studies should include as a minimum 4 years of English, 3 each of math and science, 2 each of social studies and a foreign language, plus 2 academic electives. A personal essay and portfolio are required, and an interview and letters of reference are recommended. A GPA of 3.0 is required. AP and CLEP credits are accepted. Important factors in the admissions decision are evidence of special talent, recommendations by school officials, and personality/intangible qualities.

Procedure: Freshmen are admitted fall and spring. Entrance exams should be taken in the early fall of the senior year. There are early decision and deferred admissions plans. Early decision applications should be filed by December 1; regular applications, by March 1 for fall entry and November 1 for spring entry. The fall 2001 application fee was $25. Notification of early decision is sent December 20; regular decision, on a rolling basis. 13 early decision candidates were accepted for the 2001-2002 class. 10% of all applicants are on a waiting list.

Transfer: 161 transfer students enrolled in 2001-2002. Applicants must submit secondary school and postsecondary school transcripts, a statement of purpose, and a portfolio of at least 15 pieces, preferably in slides. An interview is recommended. 60 credits of 120 must be completed at MassArt.

Visiting: There are regularly scheduled orientations for prospective students, including an information session and a campus tour. There are guides for informal visits and visitors may sit in on classes. To schedule a visit, contact the Admissions Office.

Financial Aid: In a recent year, 75% of all freshmen and 65% of continuing students received some form of financial aid. 54% of freshmen and 46% of continuing students received need-based aid. The average freshman award was $7356. Of that total, scholarships or need-based grants averaged $3200 ($10,700 maximum); loans averaged $2650 ($6235 maximum); and work contracts averaged $1300 ($2000 maximum). 84% of undergraduates work part time. Average annual earnings from campus work are $800. The average financial indebtedness of the 2001 graduate was $14,500. The CSS/Profile, FAFSA, FFS, or SFS is required. The fall application deadline is May 1.

International Students: There are 68 international students enrolled. They must score 530 on the written TOEFL.

Computers: The mainframe is an IBM. MassArt provides Amiga, Mac, IBM, and NEC PCs for academic use. They are located in the computer center. All students may access the system. There are no time limits. The fee is $100 for students using the computer arts center who are not enrolled in a computer design course. There are computers available in the library for all students at no fee.

Graduates: In 2001, 258 bachelor's degrees were awarded. The most popular majors were design (24%), painting (17%), and illustration (10%). In an average class, 1% graduate in 3 years, 25% in 4 years, 45% in 5 years, and 53% in 6 years. 8 companies recruited on campus in 2000-2001. Of the 2000 graduating class, 1% were enrolled in graduate school within 6 months of graduation and 95% were employed.

Admissions Contact: Kay Ransdell, Dean of Admissions. A video is available. E-mail: *admissions@massart.edu*
Web: *http://www.massart.edu*

MASSACHUSETTS COLLEGE OF LIBERAL ARTS A-1
North Adams, MA 01247-4100 (413) 662-5410
(800) 292-6632; Fax: (413) 662-5179

Full-time: 445 men, 640 women	**Faculty:** 84
Part-time: 100 men, 210 women	**Ph.D.s:** 73%
Graduate: 45 men, 80 women	**Student/Faculty:** 13 to 1
Year: semesters, summer session	**Tuition:** $3497 ($11,857)
Application Deadline: open	**Room & Board:** $5220
Freshman Class: n/av	
SAT I or ACT: required	**LESS COMPETITIVE**

Massachusetts College of Liberal Arts, founded in 1894, is a liberal arts institution emphasizing business and education courses. Figures in the above capsule are approximate. In addition to regional accreditation, MCLA has baccalaureate program accreditation with NCATE. The library contains 168,225 volumes, 312,298 microform items, and 6645 audiovisual forms/CDs, and subscribes to 583 periodicals. Computerized library services include the card catalog, interlibrary loans, and database searching. Special learning facilities include a learning resource center, art gallery, radio station, and TV station. The 80-acre campus is in a rural area 45 miles east of Albany. Including residence halls, there are 19 buildings.

Student Life: 84% of undergraduates are from Massachusetts. Others are from 20 states, 5 foreign countries, and Canada. 80% are from public schools. 91% are white. The average age of freshmen is 19; all undergraduates, 24. 28% do not continue beyond their first year; 35% remain to graduate.

Housing: 1100 students can be accommodated in college housing, which includes single-sex and coed dormitories and on-campus apartments. On-campus housing is guaranteed for all 4 years. Upperclassmen may keep cars.

Activities: 4% of men belong to 2 local fraternities and 1 national fraternity; 9% of women belong to 2 local and 3 national sororities. There are 50 groups on campus, including band, cheerleading, choir, chorus, computers, dance, drama, ethnic, gay, honors, international, jazz band, literary magazine, musical theater, newspaper, photography, political, professional, radio and TV, religious, social, social service, student government, and yearbook. Popular campus events include Parents Weekend and Winter Carnival.

Sports: There are 6 intercollegiate sports for men and 6 for women, and 10 intramural sports for men and 10 for women. Facilities include a campus center with a swimming pool, weight rooms, a fitness center, and handball, squash, and racquetball courts; an outdoor complex with tennis courts and soccer, baseball, and softball fields; a 1750-seat gym; and a 5-mile cross-country running trail.

Disabled Students: 80% of the campus is accessible. Wheelchair ramps, elevators, special parking, specially equipped rest rooms, and special class scheduling are available.

Services: Counseling and information services are available, as is tutoring in some subjects, including most general education requirements. There is remedial math, reading, and writing. The Tutoring Exchange Network has qualified peers tutoring small groups.

Campus Safety and Security: Measures include 24-hour foot and vehicle patrol, self-defense education, escort service, and informal discussions. There are pamphlets/posters/films, emergency telephones, and lighted pathways/sidewalks.

Programs of Study: MCLA confers B.A. and B.S. degrees. Master's degrees are also awarded. Bachelor's degrees are awarded in BIOLOGICAL SCIENCE (biology/biological science), BUSINESS (business administration and management), COMMUNICATIONS AND THE ARTS (English and fine arts), COMPUTER AND PHYSICAL SCIENCE (computer science, mathematics, and physics), EDUCATION (education), SOCIAL SCIENCE (history, interdisciplinary studies, philosophy, psychology, and sociology). English, education, and biology are the strongest academically. Business and education are the largest.

Required: All students must complete at least 120 credits, including 50 in a core curriculum, and maintain a GPA of at least 2.0. Phys ed and computer science courses are required.

Special: MCLA offers cross-registration with Williams College and Berkshire Community College, dual majors, internships in all majors, and study abroad in many countries within the International College Program. Student-designed majors, pass/fail options, nondegree study, and independent study also are available. There are 8 national honor societies, a freshman honors program, and 6 departmental honors programs.

Faculty/Classroom: 69% of faculty are male; 31%, female. All teach undergraduates. No introductory courses are taught by graduate students. The average class size in an introductory lecture is 20; in a laboratory, 9; and in a regular course, 19.

Requirements: The SAT I or ACT is required. In addition, an eligibility index is used to determine a minimum SAT I score. Applicants should have completed 16 Carnegie units, including 4 courses in English, 3 each in science and math, and 2 each in foreign language, history/social science, and electives. The GED is accepted. A GPA of 2.0 is required. AP and CLEP credits are accepted. Important factors in the admissions decision are advanced placement or honor courses, evidence of special talent, and parents or siblings attending the school.

Procedure: Freshmen are admitted fall and spring. Entrance exams should be taken by January of the senior year. There are early decision and deferred admissions plans. Application deadlines are open. The application fee is $25.

Transfer: 113 transfer students enrolled in a recent year. Applicants who have a minimum of 12 semester hours from an accredited college are eligible. Students are evaluated on the basis of past college records, which must include a GPA of at least 2.5 with fewer than 25 credits or a 2.0 with 25 credits or more. 30 credits of 120 must be completed at MCLA.

Visiting: There are regularly scheduled orientations for prospective students, including a 2-day, overnight program for students who have been accepted. There are guides for informal visits and visitors may sit in on classes. To schedule a visit, contact the Admissions Office.

Financial Aid: In a recent year, 69% of all freshmen and 64% of continuing students received some form of financial aid. 54% of all students received need-based aid. The average freshman award was $6842. Of that total, scholarships or need-based grants averaged $3778 ($7050 maximum); loans averaged $3081 ($13,000 maximum); and work contracts averaged $1337 ($1600 maximum). 27% of undergraduates work part time. Average annual earnings from campus work are $2503. The average financial indebtedness of a graduate in a recent year was $15,524. MCLA is a member of CSS. The FAFSA and the college's own financial statement are required. Check with the school for current deadlines.

International Students: There were 6 international students enrolled in a recent year. The school actively recruits these students. They must score 550 on the written TOEFL and also take the SAT I.

Computers: The mainframes are a CDC CYBER 815 and a DEC VAX 1850. There are 5 general-use computer labs, 3 with Gateway PCs and 2 with Apple G3 computers. All are connected to the campus network, the e-mail server, and Internet. Special-purpose labs are available in the sciences, social sciences, and computer science. All students may access the system. Limits on student access to the system vary with the time of year.

Graduates: In a recent year, 310 bachelor's degrees were awarded. The most popular majors were business (21%), sociology (20%), and English communications (16%). In an average class, 1% graduate in 3 years, 27% in 4 years, 32% in 5 years, and 37% in 6 years.

Admissions Contact: Denise C. Richardello, Dean of Enrollment Management. A video is available. E-mail: *admissions@mcla.mass.edu*
Web: *www.mcla.mass.edu*

MASSACHUSETTS COLLEGE OF PHARMACY AND HEALTH SCIENCES E-2

Boston, MA 02115 (617) 732-2850
(800) 225-5506; Fax: (617) 732-2118

Full-time: 507 men, 1046 women	**Faculty:** 118
Part-time: 83 men, 181 women	**Ph.D.s:** 97%
Graduate: 38 men, 67 women	**Student/Faculty:** 13 to 1
Year: semesters, summer session	**Tuition:** $18,221
Application Deadline: February 1	**Room & Board:** $8910

Freshman Class: 346 applied, 233 accepted, 115 enrolled
SAT I Verbal/Math: 508/542 **SPECIAL**

The Massachusetts College of Pharmacy and Health Sciences, established in 1823, is a private, independent institution offering undergraduate and graduate programs in chemistry, pharmacy, nursing, and health sciences. There are 4 undergraduate schools and 1 graduate school. In addition to regional accreditation, MCPHS has baccalaureate program accreditation with ACPE, CAHEA, and NLN. The library contains 70,000 volumes and 80,000 microform items, and subscribes to 800 periodicals. Computerized library services include the card catalog, interlibrary loans, and database searching. Special learning facilities include a learning resource center and radio station. The 2-acre campus is in an urban area 1 mile from Boston's center. Including residence halls, there are 2 buildings.

Student Life: 68% of undergraduates are from Massachusetts. Others are from 32 states, 31 foreign countries, and Canada. 52% are white; 33% Asian American. The average age of freshmen is 18; all undergraduates, 21. 10% do not continue beyond their first year.

Housing: 176 students can be accommodated in college housing, which includes single-sex and coed dormitories. On-campus housing is guaranteed for the freshman year only, is available on a first-come, first-served basis, and is available on a lottery system for upperclassmen. 85% of students commute. Alcohol is not permitted. No one may keep cars.

Activities: 5% of men belong to 6 national fraternities; 5% of women belong to 2 national sororities. There are 20 groups on campus, including drama, ethnic, international, newspaper, professional, religious, social service, student government, and yearbook.

Sports: There are 10 intramural sports for men and 10 for women. MCPHS shares facilities with the Massachusetts College of Art, which include a wellness center with weight training equipment and a gym with court space for basketball, volleyball, and badminton.

Disabled Students: 90% of the campus is accessible. Wheelchair ramps, elevators, special parking, specially equipped rest rooms, and lowered drinking fountains are available.

Services: In addition to some personal counseling services, tutoring is provided free of charge, including group and individual peer tutoring.

Campus Safety and Security: Measures include informal discussions, pamphlets/posters/films, lighted pathways/sidewalks, security guards at all entrances, and admission to labs by means of a security pass worn by all students, faculty, and staff.

Programs of Study: MCPHS confers B.S., B.S.Ch., B.S.H., B.S.Nuc.T., B.S.P., and B.S.Rad.Tech. degrees. Associate, master's, and doctoral degrees are also awarded. Bachelor's degrees are awarded in COMPUTER AND PHYSICAL SCIENCE (chemistry and radiological technology), HEALTH PROFESSIONS (allied health, health, nuclear medical technology, pharmacy, and premedicine), SOCIAL SCIENCE (psychology). Pharmacy is the largest.

Required: Graduation requirements vary by program. Students must complete course work in expository writing, history and politics, psychology, sociology, interpersonal communications in the health professions, evolution of the health professions, biomedical ethics, and humanities. Quarter hours required for graduation range from 190 to 274, depending on the degree. Students must maintain a minimum GPA of 2.0.

Special: MCPHS offers cross-registration with the other colleges of the Fenway Consortium, cooperative programs with Simmons College and Western New England College, an externship program in radiopharmacy in conjunction with Massachusetts General Hospital, internships, and work-study programs. There are 2 national honor societies.

Faculty/Classroom: 51% of faculty are male; 49%, female. All both teach and do research. No introductory courses are taught by graduate students. The average class size in a regular course is 14.

Admissions: 67% of the 2001-2002 applicants were accepted. The SAT I scores for the 2001-2002 freshman class were: Verbal--41% below 500, 44% between 500 and 599, 10% between 600 and 700, and 2% above 700; Math--20% below 500, 62% between 500 and 599, 14% between 600 and 700, and 3% above 700. 36% of the current freshmen were in the top fifth of their class; 68% were in the top two fifths. 1 freshman graduated first in the class.

Requirements: The SAT I is required. In addition, applicants must graduate from an accredited secondary school with 16 units, including 4 of English, 3 of math, 2 of lab science, 1 of history, and 6 of other college-preparatory subjects. The college also advises advanced chemistry or physics with lab and an extra unit of math. Interviews are recommended. Letters of reference from a guidance counselor and a science or math teacher and 2 student essays are required. AP and CLEP credits are accepted. Important factors in the admissions decision are advanced placement or honor courses and recommendations by school officials. Applications are accepted on-line via the school's web site.

Procedure: Freshmen are admitted in the fall. Entrance exams should be taken by December of the senior year. There are early decision and deferred admissions plans. Early decision applications should be filed by November 1; regular applications, by February 1 for fall entry. Notification of early decision is sent December 1; regular decision, on a rolling basis. The fall 2001 application fee was $70. 10 early decision candidates were accepted for the 2001-2002 class.

Transfer: 340 transfer students enrolled in 2001-2002. Applicants must complete 190 to 274 credits to graduate and have a minimum GPA of 2.5. Those with 1 year or less of college credit must submit secondary school transcripts.

Visiting: There are regularly scheduled orientations for prospective students, including a campus tour and information sessions. There are guides for informal visits. To schedule a visit, contact the Admissions Office.

Financial Aid: In 2001-2002, 90% of all students received some form of financial aid. 85% of all students received need-based aid. The average freshman award was $14,895. Of that total, scholarships or need-based grants averaged $8680 ($21,650 maximum); loans averaged $5170 ($9625 maximum); and work contracts averaged $1500 (maximum). The FAFSA and the college's own financial statement are required. The fall application deadline is March 15.

International Students: The school actively recruits these students. They must score 550 on the written TOEFL or 213 on the electronic version and also take the college's own test and the SAT I or the ACT.

Computers: The college provides IBM and Leading Edge PCs for academic use by all students. They are available in the library and the lab and research facility. All students may access the system. There are no time limits and no fees. It is strongly recommended that all students have a personal computer.

Graduates: In 2001, 280 bachelor's degrees were awarded. The most popular major was pharmacy (86%).

Admissions Contact: Kathleen Houghton, Director of Admission.
E-mail: *admissions@mcp.edu* Web: *www.mcp.edu*

MASSACHUSETTS INSTITUTE OF TECHNOLOGY D-2

Cambridge, MA 02139 (617) 253-4791
n/av; Fax: (617) 258-8304

Full-time: 2413 men, 1741 women	**Faculty:** 945; I, ++$
Part-time: 42 men, 24 women	**Ph.D.s:** 99%
Graduate: 4292 men, 1692 women	**Student/Faculty:** 4 to 1
Year: 4-1-4	**Tuition:** $27,728
Application Deadline: January 1	**Room & Board:** $7500

Freshman Class: 10,490 applied, 1787 accepted, 1030 enrolled
SAT I Verbal/Math: 720/770 **ACT:** 32 **MOST COMPETITIVE**

Massachusetts Institute of Technology, founded in 1861, is a private, independent, land-grant institution offering programs in architecture and planning, engineering, humanities and social science, science, health sciences, technology, and management. There are 5 undergraduate and 6 graduate schools. In addition to regional accreditation, MIT has baccalaureate program accreditation with AACSB, ABET, CSAB, and NAAB. The 10 libraries contain 2,623,154 volumes, 2,337,598 microform items, and 27,366 audiovisual forms/CDs, and subscribe to 21,794 periodicals. Computerized library services include the card catalog, interlibrary loans, and database searching. Special learning facilities include an art gallery, radio station, and TV station. The 155-acre campus is in an urban area 1 mile north of Boston. Including residence halls, there are 158 buildings.

Student Life: 90% of undergraduates are from out of state, mostly the Northeast. Others are from 50 states, 88 foreign countries, and Canada. 76% are from public schools. 34% are white; 28% Asian American; 11% Hispanic. The average age of freshmen is 19; all undergraduates, 20. 3% do not continue beyond their first year; 92% remain to graduate.

Housing: 4000 students can be accommodated in college housing, which includes single-sex and coed dormitories, on-campus apartments, married-student housing, fraternity houses, and sorority houses. In addition, there are language houses, special-interest houses, off-campus independent living groups, and non-Greek cooperative houses. On-campus housing is guaranteed for all 4 years. 97% of students live on campus. Upperclassmen may keep cars.

Activities: 40% of men belong to 3 local and 25 national fraternities; 20% of women belong to 5 national sororities. There are 332 groups on campus, including art, band, cheerleading, chess, choir, chorale, chorus, computers, dance, debate, drama, ethnic, film, gay, honors, international, jazz band, literary magazine, marching band, musical theater, newspaper, orchestra, photography, political, professional, radio and TV, religious, social, social service, student government, symphony, and yearbook. Popular campus events include Rush/Orientation Week, Senior Week, and Spring Weekend.

Sports: There are 21 intercollegiate sports for men and 17 for women, and 19 intramural sports for men and 19 for women. Facilities include an athletic center housing an ice rink and a 6-lane 200-meter indoor track. Other facilities include a pool, a sailing pavilion with sailboats for use on the Charles River, a boathouse with rowing shells, basketball/volleyball/badminton gyms, softball, football, soccer, and lacrosse fields, tennis courts, a running track, a fitness center with Nautilus equipment, and an Astroturf field.

Disabled Students: 85% of the campus is accessible. Wheelchair ramps, elevators, special parking, specially equipped rest rooms, special class scheduling, lowered drinking fountains, lowered telephones, wheelchair lifts, and automatic doors are available. An adaptive technology lab and special library services are also in place.

Services: Counseling and information services are available, as is tutoring in every subject. There is a reader service for the blind. Accommodations for students with documented disabilities include exam time extensions, exams on tape, readers, scribes, textbooks on tape, enlarged materials, braille materials, and notetakers.

Campus Safety and Security: Measures include 24-hour foot and vehicle patrol, self-defense education, escort service, and shuttle buses. There are informal discussions, pamphlets/posters/films, emergency telephones, and lighted pathways/sidewalks.

Programs of Study: MIT confers the S.B. degree. Master's and doctoral degrees are also awarded. Bachelor's degrees are awarded in BIOLOGICAL SCIENCE (biology/biological science), BUSINESS (management science), COMMUNICATIONS AND THE ARTS (art, creative writing, dramatic arts, German, literature, media arts, and music), COMPUTER AND PHYSICAL SCIENCE (chemistry, computer science, earth science, mathematics, and physics), ENGINEERING AND ENVIRONMENTAL DESIGN (aeronautical engineering, aerospace studies, chemical engineering, civil engineering, computer engineering, electrical/electronics engineering, environmental engineering, materials engineering, materials science, mechanical engineering, nuclear engineering, ocean engineering, and urban planning technology), SOCIAL SCIENCE (American studies, anthropology, archeology, cognitive science, East Asian studies, economics, history, Latin American studies, medieval studies, philosophy, political science/government, psychology, Russian and Slavic studies, and women's studies). Engineering, science, and management are the strongest academically. Engineering is the largest.

Required: To graduate, students must fulfill the General Institute Requirements, as well as writing and phys ed requirements, and earn an additional 180 to 198 credit units, while fulfilling departmental program requirements. A GPA of 3.0 on a scale of 5.0 should be maintained. The General Institute Requirements consist of 8 courses in humanities, arts, and social sciences, 6 in science, including chemistry, physics, calculus, and biology, 2 in restricted science and technology electives, and 1 lab, for a total of 17 courses.

Special: MIT offers cross-registration with Harvard, Wellesley, the Massachusetts College of Art, and the School of the Museum of the Museum of Fine Arts. Internships are offered including a summer freshman/alumni program, an engineering internship, and an electrical engineering and computer science internship. Study abroad is offered in the Cambridge-MIT Institute in England, departmental exchange programs in Europe and the Netherlands, and through programs administered by other schools. A Washington semester, on-and off-campus work-study, and accelerated degree and dual major programs in all majors are offered. There is also the Undergraduate Research Opportunities Program (UROP), offering students research work with faculty, the undergraduate Practice Opportunities Program (UPOP), real-world, for-credit placements in industry or government for sophomores, and the Second Summer Program, which places minority students in paid engineering-aide jobs the summer before their sophomore year. There are 10 national honor societies and 7 departmental honors programs.

Faculty/Classroom: 84% of faculty are male; 16%, female. All both teach and do research. No introductory courses are taught by graduate students.

Admissions: 17% of the 2001-2002 applicants were accepted. The SAT I scores for the 2001-2002 freshman class were: Verbal--4% between 500 and 599, 32% between 600 and 700, and 63% above 700; Math--1% between 500 and 599, 11% between 600 and 700, and 89% above 700. The ACT scores were 5% between 24 and 26, 7% between 27 and 28, and 87% above 28. 99% of the current freshmen were in the top fifth of their class; 100% were in the top two fifths. 251 freshmen graduated first in their class.

Requirements: The SAT I or ACT is required. In addition, 3 SAT II: Subject tests, including math, science, and writing, literature, or history are required. 14 academic units are recommended, including 4 of each English and math, 3 of lab science, 2 of social studies, and 1 of foreign language. The GED is accepted. Essays, 2 teacher evaluations, and an interview are required. AP credits are accepted. Important factors in the admissions decision are evidence of special talent, extracurricular activities record, and leadership record. Applications are accepted at *http://www.mit.edu/admissions/www/applications/index.html*

Procedure: Freshmen are admitted in the fall. Entrance exams should be taken by the January test date. There are early action and deferred admissions plans. Early action application should be filed by November 1; regular applications, by January 1 for fall entry along with a $60 fee. Notification of early action is sent December 15; regular decision, March 22. 585 early action candidates were accepted for the 2001-2002 class. 5% of all applicants are on a waiting list; 156 were accepted in 2001.

Transfer: 31 transfer students enrolled in 2001-2002. Transfer applicants must have completed 2 or more terms at an accredited college, university, technical institute, military academy, or community college and be in good standing there. They must have taken 1 year of college-level calculus and calculus-based physics and 1 semester each of biology and chemistry. They must also submit scores for 3 SAT II: Subject tests in math, science, and English or history. Non-native-English speakers may substitute the TOEFL for the SAT II: Subject test in English or history. Competitive applicants have a 3.5 GPA or higher. At least 3 semesters must be completed at MIT.

Visiting: There are regularly scheduled orientations for prospective students, including daily tours followed by an information session with an admissions officer. Visitors may sit in on classes and stay overnight. To schedule a visit, contact the Admissions office at (617) 258-5515.

Financial Aid: In 2001-2002, 83% of all freshmen and 59% of continuing students received some form of financial aid. 55% of freshmen and 53% of continuing students received need-based aid. The average freshman award was $24,788. Of that total, scholarships or need-based grants averaged $18,026 ($36,310 maximum); loans averaged $3260 ($6625 maximum); and work contracts averaged $832 ($5600 maximum). 61% of undergraduates work part time. Average annual earnings from campus work are $2086. The average financial indebtedness of the 2001 graduate was $20,484. The CSS/Profile or FAFSA, the college's own financial statement, the Parent W2s, Parent 1040s, documentation of family trusts, and parent business tax forms are required. The fall application deadline is February 8.

International Students: There are 345 international students enrolled. They must score 577 on the written TOEFL or 233 on the electronic version. Students may opt to take the TOEFL and 2 SAT II: Subject tests in math and science. Applicants who have been using English for less than 5 years or who do not speak it at home are encouraged to take the TOEFL as a supplement to the required tests. They must also take the SAT I or ACT and 3 SAT II: Subject tests in math, science, and writing, literature, or history.

Computers: The mainframe is an IBM ES/9000 Model 570. An Athena Computing Environment provides approximately 700 public workstations distributed across campus. Specialized departmental computing facilities are also available. Digital-network connections are provided to dorm rooms and living groups. All students may access the system at all times. There are no time limits and no fees.

Graduates: In 2001, 1183 bachelor's degrees were awarded. The most popular majors were electrical engineering (18%), computer science (13%), and mechanical engineering/biology (9%). In an average class, 4% graduate in 3 years, 83% in 4 years, 89% in 5 years, and 92% in 6 years. 950 companies recruited on campus in 2000-2001. Of the 2000 graduating class, 37% were enrolled in graduate school within 6 months of graduation.

Admissions Contact: Admissions Officers.
Web: *http://web.mit.edu/admissions/www/*

MASSACHUSETTS MARITIME ACADEMY — E-4
Buzzards Bay, MA 02532-1803 (508) 830-5000; (800) 544-3411

Full-time: 676 men, 105 women	**Faculty:** 60
Part-time: 45 men, 5 women	**Ph.D.s:** 70%
Graduate: none	**Student/Faculty:** 13 to 1
Year: semesters	**Tuition:** $4206 ($12,346)
Application Deadline: open	**Room & Board:** $5763
Freshman Class: 650 applied, 435 accepted, 261 enrolled	
SAT I Verbal/Math: 510/530	**COMPETITIVE**

Massachusetts Maritime Academy, founded in 1891, is the oldest continuously operating maritime academy in the country. Some information in this profile is approximate. Cooperative educational learning and leadership training opportunities prepare graduates for professional positions within private industry or, if opted, military commissions. The library contains 40,171 volumes, 11,674 microform items, and 1113 audiovisual forms/CDs, and subscribes to 505 periodicals. Computerized library services include interlibrary loans and database searching. Special learning facilities include a learning resource center, a planetarium, a full bridge-training simulator, an oil-spill management simulator, a liquid cargo-handling simulator, and a computer-aided design lab. The 55-acre campus is in a small town 60 miles south of Boston. Including residence halls, there are 9 buildings.

Student Life: 72% of undergraduates are from Massachusetts. Others are from 26 states and 11 foreign countries. 73% are from public schools. 90% are white. The average age of freshmen is 18; all undergraduates, 21. 15% do not continue beyond their first year; 70% remain to graduate.

Housing: 800 students can be accommodated in college housing, which includes coed dormitories. On-campus housing is guaranteed for all 4 years. 97% of students live on campus; of those, 35% remain on campus on weekends. Alcohol is not permitted. All students may keep cars.

Activities: There are no fraternities or sororities. There are 15 groups on campus, including band, choir, chorus, computers, drill team, jazz band, marching band, newspaper, photography, professional, religious, social service, student government, and yearbook. Popular campus events include Homecoming and Ring Dance.

Sports: There are 8 intercollegiate sports for men and 6 for women, and 13 intramural sports for men and 5 for women. Facilities include football and baseball fields, a pistol range, outdoor tennis and basketball courts, a sailing center, an Olympic-size swimming pool, 2 weight rooms, 3 multipurpose handball courts, wrestling courts, and fitness rooms. An indoor gym/auditorium seats 2500.

Disabled Students: 90% of the campus is accessible. Wheelchair ramps, elevators, special parking, and specially equipped rest rooms are available.

Services: Counseling and information services are available, as is tutoring in most subjects.

Campus Safety and Security: Measures include 24-hour foot and vehicle patrol and lighted pathways/sidewalks.

Programs of Study: MMA confers the B.S. degree. Bachelor's degrees are awarded in BUSINESS (international business management and transportation management), ENGINEERING AND ENVIRONMENTAL DESIGN (environmental engineering, industrial engineering, and marine engineering). Marine engineering is the strongest academically and is the largest.

Required: All students must complete 164 credit hours with a minimum of 60 hours in the major and a GPA of 2.0. Requirements include 4 courses in phys ed, 2 each in chemistry and naval science, and 1 each in algebra/trigonometry, introduction to computers, English composition, American literature, Western civilization, economics, analysis, American government, first aid, admiralty law, introduction to marine transportation, introduction to marine engineering, sea term/deck, sea term/engine, and calculus.

Special: MMA offers a junior-year internship in a commercial shipping program. Educational experience includes a minimum of 120 days aboard a training ship, with visits to foreign ports. There are cooperative programs in facilities and environmental engineering and in marine safety and environmental protection. A dual major is available in marine engineering and marine transportaton.

Faculty/Classroom: 96% of faculty are male; 4%, female. All teach undergraduates and 3% do research. The average class size in an introductory lecture is 25; in a laboratory, 12; and in a regular course, 22.

Admissions: 67% of the 2001-2002 applicants were accepted. The SAT I scores for the 2001-2002 freshman class were: Verbal--48% below 500, 42% between 500 and 599, 9% between 600 and 700, and 1% above 700; Math--36% below 500, 47% between 500 and 599, 16% between 600 and 700, and 1% above 700. 15% of the current freshmen were in the top fifth of their class; 70% were in the top two fifths.

Requirements: The SAT I or ACT is required. In addition, applicants must have graduated from an accredited secondary school or hold a GED certificate. They should have completed 16 Carnegie units, including 4 in English, 3 in math, and 2 each in a foreign language, science, and social science. An essay is required, and an interview is strongly recommended. A GPA of 2.0 is required. AP and CLEP credits are accepted. Important factors in the admissions decision are advanced placement or honor courses, recommendations by school officials, and extracurricular activities record.

Procedure: Freshmen are admitted in the fall. There are early decision and deferred admissions plans. Early decision applications should be filed by November 1; for regular application deadlines are open. The fall 2001 application fee was $40.

Transfer: Students must have a minimum GPA of 2.0. 30 credits of 164 must be completed at MMA.

Visiting: There are regularly scheduled orientations for prospective students, including a campus tour and an admissions interview. There are guides for informal visits and visitors may sit in on classes and stay overnight.

Financial Aid: In a recent year, 71% of all freshmen and 66% of continuing students received some form of financial aid. 42% of freshmen and 43% of continuing students received need-based aid. The average freshman award was $7205. Of that total, scholarships or need-based grants averaged $3100 ($5000 maximum); loans averaged $2700 ($4125 maximum); and work contracts averaged $1500. 16% of undergraduates work part time. Average annual earnings from campus work are $1000. The average financial indebtedness of a recent graduate was $13,000. MMA is a member of CSS. The CSS/Profile or FAFSA and the college's own financial statement are required. Check with the school for current deadlines.

International Students: They must score 500 on the written TOEFL and also take the SAT I or the ACT.

Computers: The mainframe is a CDC Cyber 172. PCs are provided for student use in the computer lab and dormitory. All students may access the system 8 A.M. to 11 P.M. There are no time limits and no fees. It is strongly recommended that all students have a personal computer.

Graduates: In an average class, 70% graduate in 4 years. 60 companies recruited on campus in a recent year.

Admissions Contact: Francis McDonald, Dean of Enrollment Services. A video is available. E-mail: *admissions@mma.mass.edu*
Web: *http://www.mma.mass.edu*

MERRIMACK COLLEGE — E-2
North Andover, MA 01845 — (978) 837-5100
n/av; Fax: (978) 837-5133

Full-time: 1003 men, 1096 women	**Faculty:** 142; IIB, av$
Part-time: 206 men, 263 women	**Ph.D.s:** 80%
Graduate: 2 men, 23 women	**Student/Faculty:** 15 to 1
Year: semesters, summer session	**Tuition:** $17,645
Application Deadline: February 15	**Room & Board:** $8080
Freshman Class: 3407 applied, 2078 accepted, 533 enrolled	
SAT I Verbal/Math: 540/560	**ACT:** 24 **VERY COMPETITIVE**

Merrimack College, founded in 1947 by the Augustinian clergy of the Roman Catholic Church, offers undergraduate programs in science, engineering, business administration, and liberal arts. In addition to regional accreditation, Merrimack has baccalaureate program accreditation with ABET and CAAHEP. The library contains 113,520 volumes, 10,632 microform items, and 1970 audiovisual forms/CDs, and subscribes to 1104 periodicals. Computerized library services include the card catalog, interlibrary loans, and database searching. Special learning facilities include a learning resource center, art gallery, planetarium, TV station, the National Microscale Chemistry Center, the Urban Resource Institute, Rogers Center for the Arts, and Stevens Service Learning Center. The 220-acre campus is in a suburban area 25 miles north of Boston. Including residence halls, there are 33 buildings.

Student Life: 72% of undergraduates are from Massachusetts. Others are from 27 states, 17 foreign countries, and Canada. 60% are from public schools. 94% are white. 80% are Catholic; 12% Protestant. The average age of freshmen is 18; all undergraduates, 20. 14% do not continue beyond their first year.

Housing: 1380 students can be accommodated in college housing, which includes coed dormitories and on-campus apartments. In addition, there are special-interest, international, wellness, engineeering, and theme houses. On-campus housing is guaranteed for all 4 years. 70% of students live on campus; of those, 90% remain on campus on weekends. Upperclassmen may keep cars.

Activities: 15% of men belong to 3 local fraternities; 5% of women belong to 3 local sororities. There are 47 groups on campus, including art, cheerleading, choir, chorale, chorus, computers, dance, drama, ethnic, gay, honors, international, literary magazine, musical theater, newspaper, pep band, photography, political, professional, radio and TV, religious, social, social service, student government, and yearbook. Popular campus events include Springfest, Peace and Social Justice Awareness Week, and Family Weekend.

Sports: There are 8 intercollegiate sports for men and 8 for women, and 6 intramural sports for men and 6 for women. Facilities include an athletic complex including an ice rink, basketball court, an aerobics studio, and a well-equipped exercise room, and outdoor facilities including 2 sets of tennis courts and baseball, football, softball, soccer, lacrosse, and field hockey fields.

Disabled Students: All of the campus is accessible. Wheelchair ramps, elevators, special parking, specially equipped rest rooms, special class scheduling, lowered drinking fountains, and lowered telephones are available.

Services: Counseling and information services are available, as is tutoring in every subject. Math, science, and writing resource centers are available to all students.

Campus Safety and Security: Measures include 24-hour foot and vehicle patrol, escort service, shuttle buses, and informal discussions. There are pamphlets/posters/films, emergency telephones, and lighted pathways/sidewalks.

Programs of Study: Merrimack confers B.A. and B.S. degrees. Associate and master's degrees are also awarded. Bachelor's degrees are awarded in BIOLOGICAL SCIENCE (biochemistry and biology/biological science), BUSINESS (accounting, business administration and management, business economics, international business management, and marketing/retailing/merchandising), COMMUNICATIONS AND THE ARTS (communications, English, and modern language), COMPUTER AND PHYSICAL SCIENCE (chemistry, computer science, mathematics, and physics), EDUCATION (elementary and secondary), ENGINEERING AND ENVIRONMENTAL DESIGN (civil engineering, electrical/electronics engineering, and environmental science), HEALTH PROFESSIONS (allied health, predentistry, premedicine, and sports medicine), SOCIAL SCIENCE (economics, history, philosophy, political science/government, prelaw, psychology, religion, and sociology). Science, engineering, and business are the strongest academically. Business, psychology, and liberal arts are the largest.

Required: All students are required to emphasize liberal arts with a variety of courses that must include 3 each in humanities, social science, and math and science, 2 each in theology and philosophy, and 1 each in English composition and freshman seminar. Students also must maintain a minimum GPA of 2.0 while taking a total of 120 credit hours, including 30 in the major.

Special: Merrimack offers cooperative programs in business, engineering, liberal arts, and computer science, cross-registration through the Northeast Consortium, internships in all arts and science programs, study abroad in 6 countries, and a Washington semester at American University. Work-study programs, a 5-year combined B.A.-B.S. degree in many major fields, and dual and self-designed majors are available. General studies, nondegree study, and pass/fail options are possible. There are 2 national honor societies.

Faculty/Classroom: 72% of faculty are male; 28%, female. All teach undergraduates, 60% do research, and 60% do both. No introductory courses are taught by graduate students. The average class size in an introductory lecture is 25; in a laboratory, 20; and in a regular course, 15.

Admissions: 61% of the 2001-2002 applicants were accepted. The SAT I scores for the 2001-2002 freshman class were: Verbal--6% below 500, 67% between 500 and 599, 25% between 600 and 700, and 2% above 700; Math--7% below 500, 69% between 500 and 599, 19% between 600 and 700, and 5% above 700. The ACT scores were 2% below 21, 70% between 21 and 23, 25% between 24 and 26, and 3% between 27 and 28. 27% of the current freshmen were in the top fifth of their class; 68% were in the top two fifths. 4 freshmen graduated first in their class.

Requirements: The SAT I or ACT is required. In addition, for business administration, humanities, and social science majors, Merrimack recommends that applicants complete 4 units of English, 3 each of math and science, and 2 of social studies. For other majors, an additional math course and 1 additional course in science are needed. An essay is required, and an interview is recommended. Applicants should have completed 16 Carnegie units. Merrimack requires applicants to be in the upper 50% of their class. A GPA of 2.7 is required. AP and CLEP credits are accepted. Important factors in the admissions decision are advanced placement or honor courses, recommendations by school officials, and leadership record. Applications are accepted on-line via Apply and CollegeLink.

Procedure: Freshmen are admitted fall and spring. Entrance exams should be taken during the spring of the junior year and the fall of the senior year. There are early action and deferred admissions plans. Early action applications should be filed by November 30; regular applications, by February 15 for fall entry and December 15 for spring entry, along with a $40 fee. Notification of early action is sent December 15; regular decision, March 1. 12% of all applicants are on a waiting list.

Transfer: 93 transfer students enrolled in 2001-2002. Applicants must have maintained a minimum 2.0 GPA while accumulating 30 credits. The SAT I, an interview, and a letter of recommendation are recommended. 45 credits of 120 must be completed at Merrimack.

Visiting: There are regularly scheduled orientations for prospective students, including 10 information sessions on Saturdays in the fall and 4 financial aid information sessions throughout the year. There are guides for informal visits and visitors may sit in on classes and stay overnight. To schedule a visit, contact the Office of Admissions *admission@merrimack.edu*

Financial Aid: In 2001-2002, 75% of all freshmen and 70% of continuing students received some form of financial aid. 70% of freshmen and 52% of continuing students received need-based aid. The average freshman award was $12,125. Of that total, scholarships or need-based grants averaged $7500 ($25,525 maximum); loans averaged $3625 (maximum); and work contracts averaged $1000 ($2000 maximum). 75% of undergraduates work part time. Average annual earnings from campus work are $2000. The average financial indebtedness of the 2001 graduate was $18,000. Merrimack is a member of CSS. The CSS/Profile or FAFSA is required. The fall application deadline is February 15.

International Students: There are 40 international students enrolled. The school actively recruits these students. They must score 550 on the written TOEFL or 213 on the electronic version and also take the Comprehensive English Language Test.

Computers: The mainframe is a DEC VAX 11/785. PCs for academic use are available in the library, classrooms, and residence halls. All students may access the system. There are no time limits and no fees. It is strongly recommended that all students have a personal computer.

Graduates: In 2001, 472 bachelor's degrees were awarded. The most popular majors were management (15%), accounting (12%), and psychology (7%). In an average class, 49% graduate in 4 years, 65% in 5 years, and 67% in 6 years. 154 companies recruited on campus in 2000-2001. Of the 2000 graduating class, 9% were enrolled in graduate school within 6 months of graduation and 92% were employed.

Admissions Contact: Mary Lou Retelle, Dean of Admission and Financial Aid. E-mail: *mretelle@merrimack.edu*
Web: *www.merrimack.edu*

MONTSERRAT COLLEGE OF ART — E-2

Beverly, MA 01915 — (978) 921-4242
(800) 836-0487; Fax: (978) 921-4241

Full-time: 151 men, 213 women	**Faculty:** 20
Part-time: 9 men, 9 women	**Ph.D.s:** 65%
Graduate: none	**Student/Faculty:** 18 to 1
Year: semesters	**Tuition:** $13,855
Application Deadline: open	**Room & Board:** $6480
Freshman Class: 365 applied, 305 accepted, 92 enrolled	
SAT I Verbal/Math: 514/477	**SPECIAL**

Montserrat College of Art, founded in 1970, is an independent residential professional institution offering degrees in painting and drawing, fine arts, printmaking, graphic design, illustration, photography, and sculpture, with a complementary program in art education. In addition to regional accreditation, Montserrat has baccalaureate program accreditation with ACBSP and NASAD. The library contains 13,000 volumes and 100 audiovisual forms/CDs, and subscribes to 65 periodicals. Computerized library services include the card catalog, interlibrary loans, and database searching. Special learning facilities include a learning resource center and art gallery. The 10-acre campus is in a suburban area 26 miles north of Boston. Including residence halls, there are 12 buildings.

Student Life: 50% of undergraduates are from out of state, mostly the Northeast. Others are from 19 states, 3 foreign countries, and Canada. 79% are white. The average age of freshmen is 18; all undergraduates, 21. 19% do not continue beyond their first year.

Housing: 262 students can be accommodated in college housing, which includes single-sex and coed on-campus apartments. In addition, there are special-interest houses and quiet houses. All housing is smoke free. On-campus housing is available on a first-come, first-served basis and is available on a lottery system for upperclassmen. 63% of students live on campus. Alcohol is not permitted. All students may keep cars.

Activities: There are no fraternities or sororities. There are 9 groups on campus, including art, gay, international, literary magazine, newspaper, radio and TV, religious, social, and student government. Popular campus events include Forum Days, Halloween and Christmas parties, and gallery openings.

Sports: There is no sports program at Montserrat.

Disabled Students: 50% of the campus is accessible. Wheelchair ramps, elevators, special parking, specially equipped rest rooms, and special class scheduling are available. All rooms are accessible to people in wheelchairs.

Services: Counseling and information services are available, as is tutoring in every subject. There is remedial writing and study skills. There is also a reader service for students with dyslexia.

Campus Safety and Security: Measures include self-defense education, informal discussions, pamphlets/posters/films, and emergency telephones. There are lighted pathways/sidewalks. In addition, resident assistants, who are trained in first aid and CPR, patrol the buildings.

Programs of Study: Montserrat confers the B.F.A. degree. Bachelor's degrees are awarded in COMMUNICATIONS AND THE ARTS (fine arts, graphic design, illustration, painting, photography, printmaking, and sculpture), EDUCATION (art).

Required: To graduate, all students are required to complete 120 credits, including 78 in studio courses and 42 in liberal arts courses. To enter the senior program, Montserrat students must have a portfolio. During semester-end evaluations, each student displays work from all courses and is evaluated by a faculty panel.

Special: Montserrat is a member of the Northeast Consortium of Colleges and Universities in Massachusetts, which allows students to take classes at any member college for the same cost. Credit study is available through the continuing education department. Montserrat also offers internships, summer study in New York City or Italy, dual and student-designed majors in fine arts and in art education, and a mobility program that allows students to spend a semester at another school within the Association of Independent Colleges of Art and Design.

Faculty/Classroom: 40% of faculty are male; 60%, female. All teach undergraduates. The average class size in an introductory lecture is 20 and in a regular course, 18.

Admissions: The SAT I scores for the 2001-2002 freshman class were: Verbal--40% below 500, 44% between 500 and 599, 13% between 600 and 700, and 3% above 700; Math--72% below 500, 24% between 500 and 599, and 4% between 600 and 700.

Requirements: The SAT I or ACT is required. In addition, students must submit an artist's statement, a portfolio, 2 letters of recommendation, and a high school transcript, although no specific program of study is required. A portfolio interview is strongly recommended. A GPA of 2.25 is required. AP and CLEP credits are accepted. Important factors in the admissions decision are evidence of special talent, advanced placement or honor courses, and personality/intangible qualities.

Procedure: Freshmen are admitted fall and spring. There is a deferred admissions plan. Application deadlines are open. The application fee is $40.

Transfer: 22 transfer students enrolled in a recent year. Applicants are required to submit a portfolio, transcripts from a previous college, and an artist's statement. They should also be interviewed. 60 credits of 120 must be completed at Montserrat.

Visiting: There are regularly scheduled orientations for prospective students, including tours of college studios, observation of classes, and portfolio consultations. There are guides for informal visits and visitors may sit in on classes. To schedule a visit, contact Lena Hill, Administrative Assistant.

Financial Aid: In 2001-2002, 72% of all freshmen and 74% of continuing students received some form of financial aid. 64% of freshmen and 70% of continuing students received need-based aid. The average freshman award was $9536. Of that total, scholarships or need-based grants averaged $2800 ($11,304 maximum); loans averaged $7000 ($2100 maximum); and work contracts averaged $1000. 15% of undergraduates work part time. Average annual earnings from campus work are $1500. The average financial indebtedness of the 2001 graduate was $12,500. Montserrat is a member of CSS. The FAFSA is required. The fall application deadline is March 1.

International Students: There are 5 international students enrolled. The school actively recruits these students. They must score 550 on the written TOEFL or 213 on the electronic version and also take the SAT I or the ACT.

Computers: The graphic design department provides 27 Macs, digital photography capabilities, and CD-ROM. Access to the Internet and the World Wide Web is available in the library. All students may access the system 8 A.M. to 11 P.M. daily. There are no time limits and no fees.

Graduates: In 2001, 54 bachelor's degrees were awarded. The most popular majors were fine arts (61%), illustration (22%), and graphic design (17%). In an average class, 1% graduate in 3 years, 79% in 4 years, 97% in 5 years, and 98% in 6 years.

Admissions Contact: Stephen M. Negron, Director of Admissions. E-mail: *admiss@montserrat.edu* Web: *www.montserrat.edu*

MOUNT HOLYOKE COLLEGE — B-3

South Hadley, MA 01075 — **(413) 538-2023; Fax: (413) 538-2409**

Full-time: 1 man, 1965 women	**Faculty:** 190; IIB, ++$
Part-time: 3 men, 68 women	**Ph.D.s:** 95%
Graduate: 1 woman	**Student/Faculty:** 10 to 1
Year: semesters	**Tuition:** $26,408
Application Deadline: January 15	**Room & Board:** $7720
Freshman Class: 2881 applied, 1424 accepted, 506 enrolled	
SAT I Verbal/Math: 645/615 (mean)	**ACT:** 27 **HIGHLY COMPETITIVE**

Mount Holyoke, founded in 1837, is the oldest institution of higher learning for women in the United States. An independent, liberal arts college, it affords students great freedom in selecting course studies. The library contains 702,086 volumes, 26,000 microform items, and 3200 audiovisual forms/CDs, and subscribes to 3152 periodicals. Computerized library services include the card catalog, interlibrary loans, and database searching. Special learning facilities include a learning resource center, art gallery, radio station, observatory, child study and language centers, an arboretum, and a leadership center housing the college's speaking, arguing, and writing program. The 800-acre campus is in a small town 90 miles west of Boston and 160 miles north of New York City. Including residence halls, there are 40 buildings.

Student Life: 75% of undergraduates are from out of state, mostly New England. Others are from 47 states, 77 foreign countries, and Canada. 61% of first-year students are from public schools. 58% are white; 17% foreign nationals; 10% Asian American. The average age of freshmen is 18; all undergraduates, 21. 3% do not continue beyond their first year; 90% remain to graduate.

Housing: 1928 students can be accommodated in college housing, which includes single-sex dormitories and on-campus apartments. On-campus housing is guaranteed for all 4 years. 89% of students live on campus. All students may keep cars.

Activities: There are no fraternities. There are 125 groups on campus, including art, band, cheerleading, choir, chorale, chorus, computers, dance, debate, drama, ethnic, film, gay, honors, international, jazz band, literary magazine, musical theater, newspaper, orchestra, photography, political, radio and TV, religious, social, social service, student government, symphony, and yearbook. Popular campus events include Festival of Diversity, Glascock Intercollegiate Poetry Contest, and the Founders Day Ceremony.

Sports: A sports and dance complex houses 2 rehearsal dance studios, a performance dance studio, and classroom; gym with basketball, volleyball, and badminton courts; 8 lane, 25-meter pool and separate diving tank; 3,100 square-foot weight room; and field house with 1/8 mile 4-lane track, indoor pole vault pit, indoor long jump pit, 6 tennis courts, cardiovascular area, 5 international squash courts, and 2 racquetball courts. Outdoor facilities include 12 tennis cours, 1/4 mile 6-lane track, field hockey, soccer, lacrosse, rugby, and softball fields, rowing tank, a cross-country course, an equestrian center with 2 indoor arenas, and a golf course.

Disabled Students: 87% of the campus is accessible. Wheelchair ramps, elevators, special parking, specially equipped rest rooms, and special class scheduling are available.

Services: Counseling and information services are available, as is tutoring in every subject. The writing center is available to all students at all levels. There is a reader service for the blind.

Campus Safety and Security: Measures include 24-hour foot and vehicle patrol, self-defense education, escort service, and shuttle buses. There are pamphlets/posters/films, emergency telephones, and lighted pathways/sidewalks.

Programs of Study: Mount Holyoke confers the A.B. degree. Master's degrees are also awarded. Bachelor's degrees are awarded in BIOLOGICAL SCIENCE (biochemistry and biology/biological science), COMMUNICATIONS AND THE ARTS (art history and appreciation, classical languages, dance, dramatic arts, English, French, German, Greek, Italian, Latin, music, romance languages and literature, Russian, Spanish, and studio art), COMPUTER AND PHYSICAL SCIENCE (astronomy, chemistry, computer science, geology, mathematics, physics, and statistics), EDUCATION (early childhood, elementary, mathematics, science, and social science), SOCIAL SCIENCE (African American studies, American studies, anthropology, Asian/Oriental studies, classical/ancient civilization, economics, European studies, geography, history, international relations, Judaic studies, Latin American studies, medieval studies, philosophy, political science/government, psychobiology, psychology, religion, sociology, and women's studies). Sciences and mathematics are the strongest academically. English, psychology, and biology are the largest.

Required: Students must maintain a minimum GPA of 2.0 while taking 128 total credits, with 32 to 56 in the major. Students must complete 3 courses in the humanities, 2 courses each in science/math and social studies, a foreign language, a multicultural perspective course, and 6 credits in phys ed. A minor field of study is necessary for those not pursuing a double major, or an interdisciplinary major.

Special: Mount Holyoke offers students cross-registration through the Five-College Consortium. The college also offers dual-degree opportunities, including a 3-2 engineering program and a 3-2 program in public health, both with the University of Massachusets at Amherst, and 3-2 programs in engineering with Dartmouth College and Caltech. Other opportunities include the 12-College Exchange Program, science and international studies internships, study-abroad programs (semester or full-year), a Washington semester, work-study, student-designed majors, dual majors, a January program, accelerated degrees, non-degree study, and pass/fail options. There are 2 national honor societies, including Phi Beta Kappa, and a freshman honors program. All departments have honors programs.

Faculty/Classroom: 46% of faculty are male; 54%, female. All teach undergraduates. No introductory courses are taught by graduate students. The average class size in an introductory lecture is 15; in a laboratory, 12; and in a regular course, 15.

Admissions: 49% of the 2001-2002 applicants were accepted. The SAT I scores for the 2001-2002 freshman class were: Verbal--2% below 500, 21% between 500 and 599, 55% between 600 and 700, and 22% above 700; Math--3% below 500, 32% between 500 and 599, 52% between 600 and 700, and 13% above 700. The ACT scores were 1% below 18, 13% between 18 and 23, 60% between 24 and 29, and 26% between 30 and 36. 82% of the current freshmen were in the top quarter of their class; 98% were in the top half.

Requirements: The SAT I and ACT are considered if submitted, but are not required. In addition, the school recommends that applicants have 4 years each of English and foreign language, 3 each of math and science, and 2 of social studies. An essay is required and an interview is strongly recommended. AP credits are accepted. Important factors in the admissions decision are recommendations by school officials, leadership record, and advanced placement or honor courses. Applications are accepted on-line via the college's web site and Embark.

Procedure: Freshmen are admitted in the fall. Entrance exams should be taken before the application deadline. There are early admissions and deferred admissions plans. Early decision applications should be filed by November 15 (early decision 2 by January 1); regular applications, by January 15 for fall entry. The fall 2001 application fee was $55. Notification of early decision is sent December 31; regular decision, April 1. 184 early decision candidates were accepted for the 2001-2002 class. 12% of all applicants are on a waiting list; 49 were accepted in 2001.

Transfer: 60 transfer students enrolled in 2001-2002. A statement of good standing, transcripts of secondary school or college-level work, and an essay are required of transfer applicants. An interview is recommended. SAT I scores will be considered if submitted, but are not required. 64 credits of 128 must be completed at Mount Holyoke.

Visiting: There are regularly scheduled orientations for prospective students. There are guides for informal visits and visitors may sit in on classes and stay overnight. To schedule a visit, contact the Admission Office.

Financial Aid: In 2001-2002, 63% of all freshmen and 70% of continuing students received some form of financial aid. 60% of freshmen and

70% of continuing students received need-based aid. The average freshman award was $21,398. Of that total, scholarships or need-based grants averaged $20,300 ($31,479 maximum); loans averaged $3050 ($4625 maximum); and work contracts averaged $1500 ($1900 maximum). 70% of undergraduates work part time. Average annual earnings from campus work are $1245. The average financial indebtedness of the 2001 graduate was $13,000. The CSS/Profile or FAFSA and parent and student tax returns are required. The fall application deadline is January 15.

International Students: There are 348 international students enrolled. The school actively recruits these students. They must take the TOEFL if English is not the first language and score 600 on the written TOEFL or 250 on the electronic version.

Computers: The mainframes are a DEC MicroVAX and a Sun system. A computer center houses several labs containing various PCs and workstations. There are 4 other labs distributed elsewhere. Most residence halls contain word-processing facilities with 3 to 6 computers. The mainframes may be accessed via PCs connected to Ethernet or by modem. Network connections beyond the campus are through a DECnet to neighbor. All students may access the system. There are no time limits and no fees.

Graduates: In 2001, 491 bachelor's degrees were awarded. The most popular majors were social sciences and history (33%), psychology (14%), and English (10%). In an average class, 73% graduate in 4 years, 78% in 5 years, and 79% in 6 years. 50 companies recruited on campus in 2000-2001. Of the 2000 graduating class, 27% were enrolled in graduate school within 2 months of graduation and 99% were employed.

Admissions Contact: Diane C. Anci, Dean of Admission. A video is available. E-mail: *admissions@mtholyoke.edu* Web: *mtholyoke.edu*

MOUNT IDA COLLEGE — D-2

Newton Centre, MA 02459 — **(617) 928-4735; Fax: (617) 928-4507**

Full-time: 396 men, 594 women	**Faculty:** 53
Part-time: 61 men, 114 women	**Ph.D.s:** n/av
Graduate: none	**Student/Faculty:** 19 to 1
Year: semesters, summer session	**Tuition:** $16,425
Application Deadline: open	**Room & Board:** $8950
Freshman Class: 550 enrolled	
SAT I or ACT: required	**LESS COMPETITIVE**

Mount Ida College, founded in 1899, is a private institution offering primarily baccalaureate programs that prepare students for a profession through a curriculum that emphasizes career studies integrated with liberal learning. There are 4 undergraduate schools. In addition to regional accreditation, Mount Ida has baccalaureate program accreditation with ABFSE, ADA, FIDER, and NASAD. The library contains 62,500 volumes, 68 microform items, and 2000 audiovisual forms/CDs, and subscribes to 530 periodicals. Computerized library services include the card catalog, interlibrary loans, and database searching. Special learning facilities include a learning resource center, art gallery, radio station, TV station, communication lab, darkroom, sewing rooms, blueprint-making facility, and dental labs. The 85-acre campus is in a suburban area 8 miles west of Boston. Including residence halls, there are 18 buildings.

Student Life: 50% of undergraduates are from out of state, mostly the Northeast. Others are from 27 states, 41 foreign countries, and Canada. 80% are from public schools. 60% are white; 19% African American. The average age of freshmen is 18; all undergraduates, 19.

Housing: 700 students can be accommodated in college housing, which includes single-sex and coed dormitories. In addition, there are honors houses, and housing for students over age 21. On-campus housing is guaranteed for all 4 years. 60% of students live on campus; of those, 60% remain on campus on weekends. All students may keep cars.

Activities: There are no fraternities or sororities. There are 25 groups on campus, including cheerleading, chess, choir, commuter, drama, equestrian, ethnic, fashion, gay, honors, international, literary magazine, newspaper, pep band, photography, professional, radio and TV, religious, social, social service, student government, travel, and yearbook. Popular campus events include a fashion show, 2 formal dances, and sporting events.

Sports: There are 7 intercollegiate sports for men and 6 for women, and 8 intramural sports for men and 10 for women. Facilities include a gym, playing fields, a fitness center, tennis courts, an outdoor swimming pool, athletic fields, and an athletic center.

Disabled Students: 75% of the campus is accessible. Wheelchair ramps, elevators, special parking, specially equipped rest rooms, and special class scheduling are available.

Services: Counseling and information services are available, as is tutoring in most subjects. There is a program for learning disabled students, for which a fee is charged. Studies skills courses are also available. The Learning Circle is an innovative campuswide initiative that provides a professional learning specialist to assist students and monitor their academic progress.

Campus Safety and Security: Measures include 24-hour foot and vehicle patrol, self-defense education, escort service, and shuttle buses. There are informal discussions, pamphlets/posters/films, emergency telephones, and lighted pathways/sidewalks.

Programs of Study: Mount Ida confers B.A., B.S., and B.L.S. degrees. Associate degrees are also awarded. Bachelor's degrees are awarded in AGRICULTURE (equine science), BUSINESS (business administration and management, fashion merchandising, funeral home services, hospitality management services, marketing/retailing/merchandising, retailing, and small business management), COMMUNICATIONS AND THE ARTS (communications, graphic design, journalism, media arts, and radio/television technology), EDUCATION (early childhood), ENGINEERING AND ENVIRONMENTAL DESIGN (interior design), HEALTH PROFESSIONS (veterinary science), SOCIAL SCIENCE (child psychology/development, criminal justice, fashion design and technology, law, liberal arts/general studies, ministries, and public administration). Veterinary technology is the strongest academically. Liberal arts studies is the largest.

Required: Candidates for a bachelor's degree require 128 credits with a 2.0 GPA. All students in the junior college must complete a freshman core and phys ed requirement.

Special: Internships in the form of work experience are available in each department. Work-study provided by the college, student-designed majors, study abroad in England and France, a general studies degree, an interdisciplinary major in legal studies, nondegree study, and a combined B.A.-B.S. degree also are available. There are 2 national honor societies, including Phi Beta Kappa, a freshman honors program, and 5 departmental honors programs.

Faculty/Classroom: 46% of faculty are male; 54%, female. The average class size in an introductory lecture is 25; in a laboratory, 16; and in a regular course, 20.

Requirements: The SAT I or ACT is required. In addition, applicants are required to have 4 units of English, 3 of social studies, and 2 each of math and science. A portfolio is recommended for certain programs, while an interview is recommended for all applicants. The GED is accepted. A GPA of 2.0 is required. CLEP credit is accepted. Important factors in the admissions decision are recommendations by school officials, evidence of special talent, and extracurricular activities record.

Procedure: Freshmen are admitted fall and spring. Entrance exams should be taken as early as possible. There are early admissions and deferred admissions plans. Application deadlines are open. The application fee is $35.

Transfer: Applicants need a minimum GPA of C and must submit college and high school transcripts. 32 credits of 128 must be completed at Mount Ida.

Visiting: There are regularly scheduled orientations for prospective students, consisting of fall and spring open houses. There are guides for informal visits and visitors may sit in on classes. To schedule a visit, contact the Admissions Office at (617) 928-4506.

Financial Aid: In a recent year, 82% of all freshmen and 78% of continuing students received some form of financial aid. 80% of freshmen and 70% of continuing students received need-based aid. The average freshman award was $8200. Of that total, scholarships or need-based grants averaged $5000 ($7000 maximum); loans averaged $3500 ($5500 maximum); work contracts averaged $1500 ($2000 maximum); and private/merit-based awards averaged $1500 ($2500 maximum). 70% of undergraduates work part time. Average annual earnings from campus work are $1500. The average financial indebtedness of a recent year's graduate was $6000. Mount Ida is a member of CSS. The FAFSA, the college's own financial statement and the and tax returns are required. The fall application priority deadline is May 1.

International Students: There are 115 international students enrolled. The school actively recruits these students.

Computers: The mainframe is an IBM AS/400. There are 80 computers for student use, including IBM and Mac. Web access is available. All students may access the system. There are no time limits and no fees. It is strongly recommended that all students have a personal computer.

Admissions Contact: Judith A. Kaufman. E-mail: *micglobe@tiac.net* Web: *www.mountida.edu*

NEW ENGLAND CONSERVATORY OF MUSIC — E-2

Boston, MA 02115 — **(617) 585-1101; Fax: (617) 585-1115**

Full-time: 188 men, 168 women	**Faculty:** 54; IIA, --$
Part-time: 14 men, 11 women	**Ph.D.s:** 22%
Graduate: 152 men, 239 women	**Student/Faculty:** 7 to 1
Year: semesters	**Tuition:** $21,800
Application Deadline: December 1	**Room & Board:** $9400
Freshman Class: n/av	
SAT I or ACT: required	**SPECIAL**

The New England Conservatory of Music, founded in 1867, is the oldest private school of its kind in the United States. It combines classroom study of music with an emphasis on performance for talented young musicians. There is 1 graduate school. In addition to regional accreditation, NEC has baccalaureate program accreditation with NASM. The 3 libraries contain 70,000 volumes, 500 microform items, and 20,000 audiovisual forms/CDs, and subscribe to 250 periodicals. Computerized library services include interlibrary loans. Special learning facilities include an electronic music studio. The 8-acre campus is in an urban area 2 miles south of downtown Boston. Including residence halls, there are 4 buildings.

Student Life: 71% of undergraduates are from out of state, mostly the Northeast. Others are from 45 states, 35 foreign countries, and Canada. 75% are from public schools. 60% are white; 24% Asian American; 10% foreign nationals. The average age of freshmen is 18; all undergraduates, 21.

Housing: 168 students can be accommodated in college housing, which includes coed dormitories. On-campus housing is guaranteed for the freshman year only. Alcohol is not permitted. All students may keep cars.

Activities: 3% of men belong to fraternities; 2% of women belong to 1 national sorority. There are 12 groups on campus, including band, choir, chorale, chorus, computers, gay, international, jazz band, opera, orchestra, political, religious, student government, and symphony. Popular campus events include visits of guest performers, 600 NEC concerts per year, and Halloween Dance.

Sports: There is no sports program at NEC.

Disabled Students: All of the campus is accessible. Elevators, special parking, specially equipped rest rooms, and lowered drinking fountains are available.

Services: Counseling and information services are available, as is tutoring in most subjects. There is remedial writing.

Campus Safety and Security: Measures include escort service, informal discussions, pamphlets/posters/films, and 24-hour security at the residence hall.

Programs of Study: NEC confers the B.Mus. degree. Master's and doctoral degrees are also awarded. Bachelor's degrees are awarded in COMMUNICATIONS AND THE ARTS (applied music, jazz, music, music history and appreciation, music performance, music theory and composition, and visual and performing arts), EDUCATION (music).

Required: Requirements for graduation include a minimum 2.0 GPA, an average of 120 total credits, and a senior recital.

Special: NEC offers cross-registration with Northeastern, Brandeis, and Tufts Universities, and Simmons College, as well as a 5-year double major degree program with Tufts University. There is a freshman honors program.

Faculty/Classroom: 72% of faculty are male; 28%, female. The average class size in an introductory lecture is 30 and in a regular course, 15.

Requirements: The SAT I or ACT is required. In addition, the applicant must be a graduate of an accredited secondary school or have a GED. An essay is required, as is an audition after submitting the formal application. In some cases, taped auditions are accepted; these must be submitted with the admissions application. Applicants are expected to have reached an advanced level of performance accomplishment. A GPA of 2.75 is required. AP and CLEP credits are accepted. Important factors in the admissions decision are evidence of special talent, recommendations by school officials, and parents or siblings attending the school.

Procedure: Freshmen are admitted in the fall. Entrance exams should be taken by March 1. There is a deferred admissions plan. Applications should be filed by December 1 for fall entry, along with a $100 fee. Notification is sent by April 1. 5% of all applicants are on a waiting list.

Transfer: 23 transfer students enrolled in a recent year. Transfer students must audition and submit all college-level transcripts and a transfer statement. 60 credits of 120 must be completed at NEC.

Visiting: There are regularly scheduled orientations for prospective students, consisting of a full range of scheduled events on audition days. Visitors may sit in on classes. To schedule a visit, contact the Admissions Office.

Financial Aid: In a recent year, 90% of all students received some form of financial aid. 80% of freshmen and 85% of continuing students received need-based aid. The average freshman award was $17,500. Of that total, scholarships or need-based grants averaged $8700 ($19,650 maximum); loans averaged $7500 (maximum); and work contracts averaged $1500 ($2500 maximum). 80% of undergraduates work part time. Average annual earnings from campus work are $1500. The average financial indebtedness of a recent graduate was $15,000. NEC is a member of CSS. The FAFSA and the college's own financial statement are required. The fall application deadline is December 1.

International Students: There were 35 international students enrolled in a recent year. The school actively recruits these students. They must score 500 on the written TOEFL and also take the SAT I or the ACT, scoring 1000 on the SAT I.

Computers: Macs, a library of music software, and synthesizers are available in the computer studio. All students may access the system. There are no time limits and no fees.

Graduates: In a recent year, 100 bachelor's degrees were awarded. The most popular majors were performance (90%) and composition (10%). In an average class, 100% graduate in 5 years. 50 companies recruited on campus in a recent year. Of a recent graduating class, 85% were enrolled in graduate school within 6 months of graduation.

Admissions Contact: Thomas Novak, Acting Director of Admissions.
E-mail: *admissions@newenglandconservatory.edu*
Web: *www.newenglandconservatory.edu*

NEWBURY COLLEGE

Brookline, MA 02445-5796 — D-2 — (617) 730-7007
(800) NEWBURY; Fax: (617) 731-9618

Full-time: 390 men, 410 women	**Faculty:** 47
Part-time: 2500 men and women	**Ph.D.s:** 17%
Graduate: none	**Student/Faculty:** 17 to 1
Year: semesters, summer session	**Tuition:** $14,090
Application Deadline: March 1	**Room & Board:** $7400
Freshman Class: 1084 applied, 815 accepted, 323 enrolled	
SAT I Verbal/Math: recommended **ACT:** 19	**COMPETITIVE**

Newbury College, founded in 1962, is a private institution offering degree programs in business, legal studies, computer science, design, communications, and culinary arts There are 3 undergraduate schools. In addition to regional accreditation, Newbury has baccalaureate program accreditation with FIDER. The library contains 32,459 volumes, 74,000 microform items, and 1900 audiovisual forms/CDs, and subscribes to 1109 periodicals. Computerized library services include the card catalog, interlibrary loans, and database searching. Special learning facilities include a learning resource center, radio station, and TV station. The 10-acre campus is in a suburban area 3 miles west of Boston. Including residence halls, there are 12 buildings.

Student Life: 59% of undergraduates are from Massachusetts. Others are from 20 states, 42 foreign countries, and Canada. 52% are white; 24% foreign nationals; 14% African American. The average age of freshmen is 19; all undergraduates, 21.

Housing: 202 students can be accommodated in college housing, which includes single-sex and coed dormitories. In addition, there are special-interest houses a multicultural house, and quiet dorms. Priority for on-campus housing is given to out-of-town students. 67% of students commute. Alcohol is not permitted. Upperclassmen may keep cars.

Activities: There are no fraternities or sororities. There are 20 groups on campus, including debate, drama, ethnic, honors, international, literary magazine, professional, radio and TV, social, social service, student government, and yearbook. Popular campus events include Multicultural Week, Spring Fling, and Fall Fest.

Sports: There are 6 intercollegiate sports for men and 6 for women, and 9 intramural sports for men and 9 for women. Facilities include an off-site gym and a cardiovascular/weight room.

Disabled Students: 71% of the campus is accessible. Wheelchair ramps, elevators, special parking, and specially equipped rest rooms are available.

Services: Counseling and information services are available, as is tutoring in every subject. There is a reader service for the blind, and remedial math, reading, and writing.

Campus Safety and Security: Measures include 24-hour foot and vehicle patrol, escort service, shuttle buses, and pamphlets/posters/films. There are lighted pathways/sidewalks.

Programs of Study: Newbury confers the B.S. degree. Associate degrees are also awarded. Bachelor's degrees are awarded in BUSINESS (accounting, business administration and management, hotel/motel and restaurant management, and international business management), COMMUNICATIONS AND THE ARTS (communications), COMPUTER AND PHYSICAL SCIENCE (computer programming, and computer science), ENGINEERING AND ENVIRONMENTAL DESIGN (interior design), HEALTH PROFESSIONS (health care administration), SOCIAL SCIENCE (criminal justice, food production/management/services, paralegal studies, prelaw, and psychology). Legal studies is the strongest academically. Business administration is the largest.

Required: Candidates for a bachelor's degree must earn 120 credits or 60 credits beyond the associate degree, with a 2.0 GPA. Distribution requirements include courses in math, lab science, literature, and social science, as well as 3 additional credits in arts and sciences.

Special: Internships are part of the bachelor degree program. Dual majors are available. Credits earned for associate degrees in professional areas can be applied toward the college's bachelor degree programs. There is a 3-3 law program with Massachusetts School of Law and study abroad in many countries. There is a freshman honors program.

Faculty/Classroom: 51% of faculty are male; 49%, female. All teach undergraduates. The average class size in an introductory lecture is 20; in a laboratory, 10; and in a regular course, 16.

Requirements: The SAT I or ACT is recommended. In addition, applicants must submit 2 letters of recommendation and high school transcripts. A personal interview is strongly recommended. A GPA of 2.0 is required. AP and CLEP credits are accepted. Important factors in the admissions decision are leadership record, recommendations by alumni, and extracurricular activities record. Applications are accepted on-line at the school's web site, and through *embark.com*.

Procedure: Freshmen are admitted fall and spring. Entrance exams should be taken following acceptance. There are early decision and deferred admissions plans. Early decision applications should be filed by December 1; regular applications, by March 1 for fall entry and November 1 for spring entry, along with a $50 fee. Notification of early decision is sent January 1; regular decision, April 1.

Transfer: 35 transfer students enrolled in 2001-2002. Transfer students must submit 2 recommendations and high school and college transcripts. 30 credits of 120 must be completed at Newbury.

Visiting: There are regularly scheduled orientations for prospective students, including fall and spring open houses, daily interviews, and campus tours. There are guides for informal visits and visitors may sit in on classes. To schedule a visit, contact the Office of Admission.

Financial Aid: In 2001-2002, 78% of all students received some form of financial aid. 75% of all students received need-based aid. 35% of undergraduates work part time. Average annual earnings from campus work are $1250. The FAFSA and the college's own financial statement are required. The fall application deadline is March 1.

International Students: There are 233 international students enrolled. The school actively recruits these students. They must score 450 on the written TOEFL and also take the college's own test.

Computers: The mainframes are a DEC VAX 4000-100 and 3600. Students have access to Mac and PCs in the computer labs, all with Internet access. All students may access the system. There are no time limits and no fees.

Graduates: In 2001, 115 bachelor's degrees were awarded. The most popular majors were hotel and restaurant management (25%), business management (18%), and computer information systems (10%). 60 companies recruited on campus in 2000-2001. Of the 2000 graduating class, 12% were enrolled in graduate school within 6 months of graduation and 96% were employed.

Admissions Contact: Jacqueline Giordano, Dean of Admission. E-mail: *info@newbury.edu* Web: *www.newbury.edu*

NICHOLS COLLEGE
Dudley, MA 01571 — C-3

(508) 943-2055
(800) 470-3379; Fax: (508) 943-9885

Full-time: 562 men, 237 women	**Faculty:** 40
Part-time: 162 men, 336 women	**Ph.D.s:** 76%
Graduate: 130 men, 118 women	**Student/Faculty:** 20 to 1
Year: semesters, summer session	**Tuition:** $16,800
Application Deadline: open	**Room & Board:** $7810
Freshman Class: 843 applied, 749 accepted, 283 enrolled	
SAT I Verbal/Math: 450/460	**LESS COMPETITIVE**

Nichols College, founded in 1931, is a private institution emphasizing business and liberal arts. There are campuses in Dudley, Auburn, Franklin, Marlborough, and Whitinsville. The library contains 62,000 volumes, 8000 microform items, and 544 audiovisual forms/CDs, and subscribes to 450 periodicals. Computerized library services include the card catalog, interlibrary loans, and database searching. Special learning facilities include a learning resource center, radio station, and the Robert C. Fischer Policy and Cultural Institute. The 210-acre campus is in a rural area 20 miles south of Worcester. Including residence halls, there are 43 buildings.

Student Life: 59% of undergraduates are from Massachusetts. Others are from 17 states and 5 foreign countries. 79% are from public schools. 91% are white. Most are Catholic. The average age of freshmen is 18; all undergraduates, 20. 36% do not continue beyond their first year; 45% remain to graduate.

Housing: 532 students can be accommodated in college housing, which includes single-sex and coed dormitories. In addition, there is substance-free housing. On-campus housing is guaranteed for all 4 years. 75% of students live on campus; of those, 55% remain on campus on weekends. All students may keep cars.

Activities: There are no fraternities or sororities. There are 26 groups on campus, including cheerleading, chess, computers, departmental, drama, honors, international, literary magazine, newspaper, political, professional, radio and TV, religious, student government, and yearbook. Popular campus events include Parents Weekend, Spring Weekend, and 100 Days Social.

Sports: There are 8 intercollegiate sports for men and 6 for women, and 7 intramural sports for men and 3 for women. Facilities include a field house with basketball courts, a swimming pool, a sauna, aerobics and weight training rooms, and athletic training facilities. There is also an athletic complex with a gym, a suspended jogging track, 2 racquetball courts, a squash court, an indoor climbing wall, and 2 fitness rooms. Outdoor facilities include 6 tennis courts, a volleyball court, a basketball court, and a 9-hole golf course.

Disabled Students: 67% of the campus is accessible. Wheelchair ramps, elevators, special parking, specially equipped rest rooms, special class scheduling, and lowered drinking fountains are available. The college makes every effort to accommodate students with special needs.

Services: Counseling and information services are available, as is tutoring in most subjects. There is remedial math and ESL assistance by appointment.

Campus Safety and Security: Measures include 24-hour foot and vehicle patrol, self-defense education, escort service, and informal discussions. There are pamphlets/posters/films and lighted pathways/sidewalks.

Programs of Study: Nichols confers B.A. and B.S. degrees. Associate and master's degrees are also awarded. Bachelor's degrees are awarded in BUSINESS (accounting, banking and finance, business administration and management, business economics, management information systems, marketing/retailing/merchandising, personnel management, and sports management), COMMUNICATIONS AND THE ARTS (English), COMPUTER AND PHYSICAL SCIENCE (mathematics), SOCIAL SCIENCE (economics, history, industrial and organizational psychology, and psychology). Accounting, management, and marketing are the strongest academically. Sports management and accounting are the largest.

Required: All students must complete a program of study within 10 semesters and maintain a GPA of 2.0 overall and in their major. Business students need 33 hours of business core classes out of the total 122 hours required of all students for graduation. Students must complete 2 writing-intensive upper-level courses, and they must attend 28 events within the Cultural Experience: The Arts, Sciences, and Public Policy Program.

Special: Nichols offers internships designed with departmental approval, study abroad at Regents College in London and at the University of Nova Scotia, a Washington semester, a general business degree, a teacher certification program, and nondegree study. There are 2 national honor societies, and 8 departmental honors programs.

Faculty/Classroom: 77% of faculty are male; 23%, female. All teach undergraduates, 34% do research, and 34% do both. No introductory courses are taught by graduate students. The average class size in a laboratory is 18 and in a regular course, 23.

Admissions: 89% of the 2001-2002 applicants were accepted. The SAT I scores for the 2001-2002 freshman class were: Verbal--70% below 500, 26% between 500 and 599, and 4% between 600 and 700; Math--68% below 500, 29% between 500 and 599, and 4% between 600 and 700. 7% of the current freshmen were in the top fifth of their class; 26% were in the top two fifths. 1 freshman graduated first in the class in a recent year.

Requirements: The SAT I or ACT is required. In addition, applicants must be graduates of accredited secondary schools or have earned a GED. Recommended preparation includes 4 years of high school English, 3 of math, 2 each of science and social studies, and 5 of academic electives. A GPA of 2.0 is required. AP and CLEP credits are accepted. Important factors in the admissions decision are advanced placement or honor courses, recommendations by school officials, and personality/intangible qualities. Applications are accepted on-line through the school's web site.

Procedure: Freshmen are admitted fall and spring. Entrance exams should be taken by November of the senior year. There are early decision, early admissions, and deferred admissions plans. Application deadlines are open. The application fee is $25. Notification is sent on a rolling basis.

Transfer: 43 transfer students enrolled in 2001-2002. Applicants need a minimum GPA of 1.75 in courses to be transferred and must submit official transcripts of all previous college study. 30 credits of 122 must be completed at Nichols.

Visiting: There are regularly scheduled orientations for prospective students, including meetings with faculty members and preregistration; separate orientation programs are tailored for transfers only. There are guides for informal visits and visitors may sit in on classes and stay overnight. To schedule a visit, contact the Admissions Office.

Financial Aid: In a recent year, 95% of all freshmen and 90% of continuing students received some form of financial aid. 80% of freshmen and 75% of continuing students received need-based aid. The average freshman award was $12,668. 33% of undergraduates work part time. Average annual earnings from campus work are $800. The average financial indebtedness of a recent graduate was $17,500. The FAFSA is required. The fall application deadline is March 1.

International Students: The school actively recruits these students. They must score 500 on the written TOEFL or 173 on the electronic version or have acceptable scores on the SAT I or ACT.

Computers: There are 246 connections to the central network in the academic center and 1 or 2 connections in every dorm room. A laptop PC with printer, software, and hardware is included in the tuition for each incoming student. All students may access the system 24 hours a day. There are no time limits and no fees. All students are required to have personal computers.

Graduates: In 2001, 142 bachelor's degrees were awarded. The most popular majors were general business (25%), general management (16%), and marketing (11%). In an average class, 1% graduate in 3 years, 33% in 4 years, 41% in 5 years, and 43% in 6 years. Of the 2000 graduating class, 1% were enrolled in graduate school within 6 months of graduation and 96% were employed.

Admissions Contact: R. Joseph Bellavance, Dean of Admissions. A CD-ROM is available. E-mail: *admissions@nichols.edu*
Web: *www.nichols.edu*

NORTHEASTERN UNIVERSITY

E-2

Boston, MA 02115 (617) 373-2200; Fax: (617) 373-8780

Full-time: 7063 men, 6900 women	**Faculty:** 774; I, -$
Part-time: none	**Ph.D.s:** n/av
Graduate: 2061 men, 2156 women	**Student/Faculty:** 18 to 1
Year: quarters, summer session	**Tuition:** $20,733
Application Deadline: open	**Room & Board:** $9345

Freshman Class: 16,173 applied, 10,155 accepted, 2933 enrolled

SAT I Verbal/Math: 570/590 **ACT:** 25 **VERY COMPETITIVE**

Northeastern University, founded in 1898, is a private, nonsectarian institution offering programs that include an experiential learning component and that integrate professional work experience with classroom study. The academic program usually requires 5 years to complete. There are 6 undergraduate and 8 graduate schools. In addition to regional accreditation, Northeastern has baccalaureate program accreditation with AACSB, ABET, ACPE, ADA, APTA, CAHEA, CSAB, and NLN. The 7 libraries contain 694,499 volumes, 2,194,794 microform items, and 17,113 audiovisual forms/CDs, and subscribe to 7825 periodicals. Computerized library services include the card catalog, interlibrary loans, and database searching. Special learning facilities include a learning resource center, art gallery, and radio station. The 60-acre campus is in an urban area in the heart of the Back Bay section of Boston. Including residence halls, there are 55 buildings.

Student Life: 60% of undergraduates are from out of state, mostly the Northeast. Others are from 49 states, 119 foreign countries, and Canada. 74% are white. The average age of freshmen is 18; all undergraduates, 21. 17% do not continue beyond their first year.

Housing: 6267 students can be accommodated in college housing, which includes single-sex and coed dormitories, on-campus apartments, and fraternity houses. In addition, there are honors houses, special-interest houses, and quiet, engineering, living and learning, international, and wellness halls. On-campus housing is guaranteed for the freshman year only, is available on a first-come, first-served basis, and is available on a lottery system for upperclassmen. 91% of freshmen live on campus. Upperclassmen may keep cars.

Activities: 4% of men belong to 4 local and 10 national fraternities; 4% of women belong to 8 national sororities. There are 190 groups on campus, including art, band, cheerleading, chess, chorale, chorus, computers, dance, debate, disabled student, drama, ethnic, gay, honors, international, jazz band, literary magazine, musical theater, newspaper, orchestra, outing, pep band, photography, political, professional, radio and TV, religious, social, social service, student government, symphony, and yearbook. Popular campus events include NUAlive!, International Week, and Parents Weekend.

Sports: There are 9 intercollegiate sports for men and 11 for women, and 14 intramural sports for men and 14 for women. Facilities include outdoor and indoor tracks, a football stadium, an indoor hockey arena, a swimming pool, indoor and outdoor tennis courts, racquetball, volleyball, and basketball courts, and exercise and weight machines.

Disabled Students: 95% of the campus is accessible. Wheelchair ramps, elevators, special parking, specially equipped rest rooms, special class scheduling, lowered drinking fountains, and lowered telephones are available.

Services: Counseling and information services are available, as is tutoring in most subjects. The Academic Assistance Center offers tutoring services in reading, language, vocabulary, note taking, test preparation, and related study skills. Individualized computer instruction is provided through the Computer-Aided Instruction Lab.

Campus Safety and Security: Measures include 24-hour foot and vehicle patrol, self-defense education, escort service, and pamphlets/posters/films. There are emergency telephones, lighted pathways/sidewalks, and awareness programs on rape prevention, alcohol abuse, personal safety, and crime prevention. A state-of-the-art fire and security alarm center monitors residence halls, academic buildings, and athletic facilities.

Programs of Study: Northeastern confers B.A., B.S., and B.Ed. degrees. Associate, master's, and doctoral degrees are also awarded. Bachelor's degrees are awarded in BIOLOGICAL SCIENCE (biochemistry, biology/biological science, neurosciences, and toxicology), BUSINESS (accounting, business administration and management, human resources, insurance, international business management, management information systems, marketing/retailing/merchandising, small business management, and transportation management), COMMUNICATIONS AND THE ARTS (advertising, art, communications, dramatic arts, English, French, journalism, languages, linguistics, music, performing arts, public relations, and Spanish), COMPUTER AND PHYSICAL SCIENCE (applied physics, chemistry, computer programming, computer science, geology, information sciences and systems, mathematics, and physics), EDUCATION (athletic training, early childhood, and elementary), ENGINEERING AND ENVIRONMENTAL DESIGN (chemical engineering, civil engineering, computer engineering, computer technology, electrical/electronics engineering, electrical/electronics engineering technology, engineering, engineering technology, industrial engineering, mechanical engineering, and mechanical engineering technology), HEALTH PROFESSIONS (dental hygiene, health science, medical laboratory science, nursing, pharmacy, physical therapy, rehabilitation therapy, and speech pathology/audiology), SOCIAL SCIENCE (African American studies, anthropology, criminal justice, economics, history, human services, interdisciplinary studies, international relations, interpreter for the deaf, philosophy, physical fitness/movement, political science/government, psychology, and sociology). Engineering, computer science, and business administration are the strongest academically. Arts and sciences and business administration are the largest.

Required: Although each college has its own requirements, students must generally complete an upper-division writing proficiency requirement in addition to at least 176 quarter hours with a minimum GPA of 2.0.

Special: Northeastern offers paid professional internships with area companies in Boston, around the country, and throughout the world to integrate classroom instruction with professional experience. Cross-registration with the New England Conservatory of Music and Hebrew College, among other universities and colleges, study abroad in dozens of countries, a Washington semester, work-study through the university and in neighboring public and private agencies, and dual majors, and student-designed majors in the arts and sciences are also offered. Nondegree adult and continuing education are available, as are programs and scholarships for racial minorities and women, and accelerated degrees in engineering, nursing, the arts and sciences, pharmacy, and business. There are 26 national honor societies, a freshman honors program, and 10 departmental honors programs.

Faculty/Classroom: 61% of faculty are male; 39%, female.

Admissions: 63% of the 2001-2002 applicants were accepted. The SAT I scores for the 2001-2002 freshman class were: Verbal--16% below 500, 49% between 500 and 599, 31% between 600 and 700, and 5% above 700; Math--9% below 500, 45% between 500 and 599, 39% between 600 and 700, and 8% above 700.

Requirements: The SAT I or ACT is required. In addition, Northeastern recommends that applicants have 17 academic units, including 4 in English, 3 each in math, science, and social studies, and 2 each in foreign language and history. An essay is required and an interview is recommended. AP and CLEP credits are accepted. Important factors in the admissions decision are recommendations by school officials, advanced placement or honor courses, and leadership record. Applications are accepted on-line at the school's web site.

Procedure: Freshmen are admitted fall and winter. Entrance exams should be taken from October of the junior year through December of the senior year. There are early admissions and deferred admissions plans. Application deadlines are open. The fall 2001 application fee was $50. Pllications received by February 15 receive a repose by April 1. 13% of all applicants are on a waiting list; 95 were accepted in 2001.

Transfer: 655 transfer students enrolled in 2001-2002. Candidates applying for transfer must have a satisfactory college record. Credit is generally granted for a grade of C or better in any reasonably equivalent course. Candidates must be in good standing and must be eligible to continue in the institution they are currently attending. Emphasis is placed on the college record, but the high school record will be considered. SAT I or ACT scores are required of transfer applicants who have completed less than 48 quarter hours of college work. 48 credits of 176 must be completed at Northeastern.

Visiting: There are regularly scheduled orientations for prospective students. There are guides for informal visits. To schedule a visit, contact the Office of Undergraduate Admissions.

Financial Aid: In 2001-2002, 84% of all freshmen and 72% of continuing students received some form of financial aid. 77% of freshmen and 71% of continuing students received need-based aid. The average freshman award was $13,024. Of that total, scholarships or need-based grants averaged $10,461; loans averaged $3240; and work contracts averaged $1062. 30% of undergraduates work part time. Average annual earnings from campus work are $1806. Northeastern is a member of CSS. The CSS/Profile and FAFSA are required. Upperclassmen must submit the university's own financial statement. The fall application deadline is February 15.

International Students: There are 989 international students enrolled. The school actively recruits these students. They must score 550 on the written TOEFL and also take the SAT I or the ACT. Minimum scores vary by and within program.

Computers: The mainframe is a Super-miniVAX cluster consisting of 2 DEC VAX 6000-440 computers. Students may gain access to the mainframe systems from on-campus computer labs or off-campus dial-in modems. The computers accessed are utilized for various computer courses, e-mail, computer conferencing, and bulletin board purposes. All students may access the system 24 hours daily. There are no time limits and no fees.

Graduates: In 2001, 2207 bachelor's degrees were awarded. The most popular majors were business (24%), health sciences (17%), and engineering (12%). In an average class, 45% graduate in 5 years, and 50% in 6 years. 200 companies recruited on campus in a recent year. Of the

2000 graduating class, 12% were enrolled in graduate school within 6 months of graduation and 95% were employed.

Admissions Contact: Ronne A. Patrick, Director of Admissions. A video is available. E-mail: *admissions@neu.edu* Web: *http://www.neu.edu*

PINE MANOR COLLEGE
E-2

Chestnut Hill, MA 02467
(617) 731-7104
(800) 762-1357; Fax: (617) 731-7199

Full-time: 390 women	**Faculty:** 28; IIB, --$
Part-time: 16 women	**Ph.D.s:** 81%
Graduate: none	**Student/Faculty:** 14 to 1
Year: semesters, summer session	**Tuition:** $11,894
Application Deadline: open	**Room & Board:** $7450
Freshman Class: 423 applied, 308 accepted, 138 enrolled	
SAT I Verbal/Math: 440/420	**ACT:** 17 **LESS COMPETITIVE**

Pine Manor College, established in 1911, is a private liberal arts college for women. The library contains 68,154 volumes, 65,824 microform items, and 1644 audiovisual forms/CDs, and subscribes to 1757 periodicals. Computerized library services include the card catalog, interlibrary loans, and database searching. Special learning facilities include a learning resource center, art gallery, radio station, TV station, and a language lab. The 60-acre campus is in a suburban area 5 miles west of Boston. Including residence halls, there are 28 buildings.

Student Life: 59% of undergraduates are from Massachusetts. Others are from 25 states and 27 foreign countries. 45% are from public schools. 45% are white; 22% African American; 14% Hispanic; 11% foreign nationals. The average age of freshmen is 19; all undergraduates, 21. 30% do not continue beyond their first year.

Housing: 510 students can be accommodated in college housing. In addition, there are special-interest houses, nonsmoking dorms, and a wellness floor (no alcohol allowed). On-campus housing is guaranteed for all 4 years. 76% of students live on campus; of those, 80% remain on campus on weekends. All students may keep cars.

Activities: There are no fraternities or sororities. There are 25 groups on campus, including chorus, dance, diversity drama, ethnic, gay, honors, international, interior design, literary magazine, minority, musical theater, newspaper, political, professional, psychology, radio and TV, religious, social, social service, student government, student health, and yearbook. Popular campus events include Late Night Breakfast during finals, Stressbusters, and Halloween Party.

Sports: Facilities include a modern gym, softball and soccer fields, cross-country trails, tennis courts, a dance studio, and a weight room.

Disabled Students: 40% of the campus is accessible. Wheelchair ramps, elevators, special parking, specially equipped rest rooms, and lowered drinking fountains are available.

Services: Counseling and information services are available, as is tutoring in every subject. There is remedial math, reading, and writing. The learning resource center has professional and peer tutoring and workshops.

Campus Safety and Security: Measures include 24-hour foot and vehicle patrol, self-defense education, escort service, and shuttle buses. There are informal discussions, pamphlets/posters/films, emergency telephones, and lighted pathways/sidewalks.

Programs of Study: PMC confers the B.A. degree. Associate degrees are also awarded. Bachelor's degrees are awarded in BIOLOGICAL SCIENCE (biology/biological science), BUSINESS (business administration and management), COMMUNICATIONS AND THE ARTS (art, communications, and English), SOCIAL SCIENCE (ethics, politics, and social policy, history, and psychology). Psychology, visual arts, and business administration are the largest.

Required: An outcomes-based general education program, with portfolio assessment, is a college requirement. A 4-year leadership program complements the portfolio program. This assists students in exploring inclusive and socially responsible leadership. In addition, students must maintain a minimum GPA of 2.0 and take a total of 132 semester hours.

Special: Pine Manor offers cross-registration with area colleges, internships at more than 1000 sites, and study abroad throughout the world and at sea. A Washington semester, work-study programs, dual majors, student-designed majors, a B.A.-B.S. degree, nondegree study within continuing education, and pass/fail options for 1 course each semester also are available as is the English Language Institute for students whose native language is not English. There is 1 national honor society, and a freshman honors program.

Faculty/Classroom: 40% of faculty are male; 60%, female. All teach undergraduates. The average class size in an introductory lecture is 16; in a laboratory, 16; and in a regular course, 13.

Admissions: 73% of the 2001-2002 applicants were accepted. The SAT I scores for the 2001-2002 freshman class were: Verbal--69% below 500, 24% between 500 and 599, and 7% between 600 and 700; Math--77% below 500, 19% between 500 and 599, and 4% between 600 and 700. The ACT scores were 79% below 21, 14% between 21 and 23, and 7% between 24 and 26. 9% of the current freshmen were in the top fifth of their class; 27% were in the top two fifths.

Requirements: The SAT I or ACT is required. In addition, applicants are required to have taken 4 courses in English and 2 in math. Additional courses in foreign language, social science, natural science, and elective areas are recommended. An essay is also required. An interview is recommended. The GED is accepted, and the number of Carnegie units required is 16. AP and CLEP credits are accepted. Important factors in the admissions decision are recommendations by school officials, leadership record, and advanced placement or honor courses. Applications are accepted on-line at *www.pmc.edu* and via Next Stop College.

Procedure: Freshmen are admitted fall and spring. There is a deferred admissions plan. Application deadlines are open. The fall 2001 application fee was $25. Notification is sent on a rolling basis.

Transfer: 29 transfer students enrolled in 2001-2002. Pine Manor requires transfer students to submit 2 letters of recommendation (1 from a professor) and college and high school transcripts. The SAT I or ACT also is recommended. 32 credits of 132 must be completed at PMC.

Visiting: There are regularly scheduled orientations for prospective students, including a campus tour and interview. There are guides for informal visits and visitors may sit in on classes and stay overnight. To schedule a visit, contact the Admissions Office.

Financial Aid: In 2001-2002, 76% of all freshmen and 72% of continuing students received some form of financial aid. 72% of freshmen and 70% of continuing students received need-based aid. The average freshman award was $14,840. Of that total, scholarships or need-based grants averaged $11,585 ($12,300 maximum); loans averaged $2489 ($2625 maximum); and work contracts averaged $1317 ($1500 maximum). Average annual earnings from campus work are $1500. The average financial indebtedness of the 2001 graduate was $14,711. PMC is a member of CSS. The FAFSA and the college's own financial statement are required. The fall application deadline is March 15.

International Students: There are 43 international students enrolled. The school actively recruits these students. They must score 475 on the written TOEFL or 153 on the electronic version.

Computers: PCs and Macs are available for student use in computer centers in the library and in the science, management, and art buildings. The communications center houses a computerized print media room. All students may access the system. There are no time limits and no fees.

Graduates: In 2001, 43 bachelor's degrees were awarded. The most popular majors were business administration (23%), biology (16%), and psychology/education and communication (14%). In an average class, 50% graduate in 5 years.

Admissions Contact: Bill Nichols, Dean of Admissions.
E-mail: *admissions@pmc.edu* Web: *www.pmc.edu*

REGIS COLLEGE
D-2

Weston, MA 02493-1571
(781) 768-7100
(800) 456-1820; Fax: (781) 768-7071

Full-time: 643 women	**Faculty:** 56; IIB, -$
Part-time: 11 men, 197 women	**Ph.D.s:** 86%
Graduate: 9 men, 221 women	**Student/Faculty:** 11 to 1
Year: semesters, summer session	**Tuition:** $18,400
Application Deadline: see profile	**Room & Board:** $8350
Freshman Class: 731 applied, 596 accepted, 183 enrolled	
SAT I Verbal/Math: 510/490	**COMPETITIVE**

Regis College, founded in 1927, is a private liberal arts institution for women, affiliated with the Roman Catholic Church. In addition to regional accreditation, Regis has baccalaureate program accreditation with CSWE, NASDTEC, and NLN. The library contains 135,594 volumes, 41,536 microform items, and 5076 audiovisual forms/CDs, and subscribes to 1078 periodicals. Computerized library services include the card catalog, interlibrary loans, and database searching. Special learning facilities include a learning resource center, art gallery, radio station, and museum of stamps and postal history, and fine arts center. The 168-acre campus is in a suburban area 12 miles west of Boston. Including residence halls, there are 15 buildings.

Student Life: 84% of undergraduates are from Massachusetts. Others are from 23 states and 4 foreign countries. 74% are from public schools. 48% are white. The average age of freshmen is 18; all undergraduates, 22. 24% do not continue beyond their first year; 68% remain to graduate.

Housing: 619 students can be accommodated in college housing, which includes single-sex dormitories and quiet floors. On-campus housing is guaranteed for all 4 years. 71% of students live on campus; of those, 50% remain on campus on weekends. All students may keep cars.

Activities: There are no fraternities. There are 30 groups on campus, including art, choir, chorale, chorus, commuter, computers, dance, drama, ethnic, honors, international, literary magazine, musical theater, photography, political, professional, radio and TV, religious, social, social service, student government, and yearbook. Popular campus events include Father/Daughter Dance, Women's History Month, and Mother/Daughter Luncheon.

Sports: Facilities include a softball diamond, a soccer field, 4 tennis courts, and an athletic facility with a gym, an aerobics and dance studio, squash courts, a pool, and a sauna and Jacuzzi. A fitness center provides a full range of cardiovascular machines as well as free weights and Nautilus equipment.

Disabled Students: 87% of the campus is accessible. Wheelchair ramps, elevators, special parking, specially equipped rest rooms, special class scheduling, lowered drinking fountains, and lowered telephones are available.

Services: Counseling and information services are available, as is tutoring in every subject. There is a reader service for the blind and remedial math and writing. There are academic support services for learning-disabled students.

Campus Safety and Security: Measures include 24-hour foot and vehicle patrol, self-defense education, escort service, and shuttle buses. There are informal discussions, pamphlets/posters/films, emergency telephones, and lighted pathways/sidewalks.

Programs of Study: Regis confers B.A., B.S.N., and B.S.W. degrees. Associate and master's degrees are also awarded. Bachelor's degrees are awarded in BIOLOGICAL SCIENCE (biochemistry, and biology/biological science), BUSINESS (management science), COMMUNICATIONS AND THE ARTS (art, communications, dramatic arts, English, French, and Spanish), COMPUTER AND PHYSICAL SCIENCE (chemistry, computer science, and mathematics), EDUCATION (museum studies), HEALTH PROFESSIONS (nursing), SOCIAL SCIENCE (economics, history, political science/government, psychology, social work, and sociology). Communication, English, and management are the largest.

Required: To graduate, students must complete a total of 38 4-credit courses, including 8 to 12 in the major, with a minimum GPA of 2.0.

Special: Cross-registration with Boston, Babson, and Bentley Colleges and through the Sisters of St. Joseph Consortium is offered. Students may study abroad at Regis affiliates in London and in Kyoto, Japan, Ireland, or through programs of other American colleges. Regis also offers internships, study abroad, a Washington semester at American University, dual and self-designed majors, work-study, nondegree study, and pass/fail options. There are special programs in American studies; communication; computer science; graphics; Greek, international, legal, and women's studies; and teacher-training. A 3-2 engineering degree is available with Worcester Polytechnic Institute. There are 8 national honor societies, a freshman honors program, and 20 departmental honors program.

Faculty/Classroom: 23% of faculty are male; 77%, female. 86% teach undergraduates. No introductory courses are taught by graduate students. The average class size in an introductory lecture is 18; in a laboratory, 18; and in a regular course, 16.

Admissions: 82% of the 2001-2002 applicants were accepted. The SAT I scores for the 2001-2002 freshman class were: Verbal--43% below 500, 37% between 500 and 599, 16% between 600 and 700, and 4% above 700; Math--52% below 500, 40% between 500 and 599, 8% between 600 and 700, and 1% above 700. 33% of the current freshmen were in the top fifth of their class; 69% were in the top two fifths.

Requirements: The SAT I is required. In addition, the minimum score needed is 800, 400 each on verbal and math. Applicants should have 4 years of English, 3 or 4 electives, 3 of math, and 2 each of foreign language, social studies, and natural science, including a lab science. An essay and 2 letters of recommendation are required. An interview is strongly encouraged. The GED is accepted. Application may be made via Mac-compatible disk, which must be accompanied by the transcript, letters of recommendation, and signed copy of the college's paper application. Regis requires applicants to be in the upper 50% of their class. A GPA of 2.5 is required. AP and CLEP credits are accepted. Important factors in the admissions decision are recommendations by school officials, ability to finance college education, and extracurricular activities record. Applications are accepted on-lilne via Common App, CollegeLink, and Mass Mentor.

Procedure: Freshmen are admitted fall and spring. Entrance exams should be taken during the fall before enrollment. There is a deferred admissions plan. Applications should be filed by December 1 for spring entry. The fall 2001 application fee was $30. Notification is sent on a rolling basis.

Transfer: 26 transfer students enrolled in 2001-2002. Transfer students need an admission application and fee; an official high school transcript if fewer than 9 college courses have been completed; an official college transcript; 1 letter of recommendation from a professor at the previous college attended; the academic catalog of the previous college; an essay; the SAT I scores if fewer than 16 courses have been completed; and health records. 72 credits of 152 must be completed at Regis.

Visiting: There are regularly scheduled orientations for prospective students, consisting of programs hosted 3 times during the summer prior to fall enrollment and once during January before second semester enrollment. There are guides for informal visits and visitors may sit in on classes and stay overnight. To schedule a visit, contact the Admissions Office at E-Mail: *admission@regiscollege.edu*

Financial Aid: In 2001-2002, 95% of all freshmen received some form of financial aid. 88% of freshmen and 87% of continuing students received need-based aid. The average freshman award was $17,543. Of that total, scholarships or need-based grants averaged $10,000 ($16,000 maximum); loans averaged $4625 ($29,330 maximum); and work contracts averaged $1500 ($2500 maximum). 50% of undergraduates work part time. Average annual earnings from campus work are $1110. The average financial indebtedness of the 2001 graduate was $22,741. Regis is a member of CSS. The FAFSA and the college's own financial statement are required. The fall application deadline is March 1.

International Students: 27 international students enrolled in a recen year. The school actively recruits these students. They must score 500 on the written TOEFL or 173 on the electronic version and also take the SAT I, scoring 400.

Computers: The mainframe is an HP 9000/K360. There are 155 IBM PCs and Macs available in the academic computer center and in various departments. All computers have access to the Internet and Web. Students have access to a Web server, NT servers for printing, and AppleShare servers for file sharing. All students may access the system daily at posted hours in the academic computing center or by permission in the individual departments. There are no time limits and no fees.

Graduates: In 2001, 193 bachelor's degrees were awarded. The most popular majors were nursing (13%), sociology (11%), and communications (9%). In an average class, 62% graduate in 4 years, 66% in 5 years, and 68% in 6 years. 25 companies recruited on campus in 2000-2001. Of the 2000 graduating class, 11% were enrolled in graduate school within 6 months of graduation and 34% were employed.

Admissions Contact: Leona McCaughey-Dreszak, Director of Admission. E-mail: *admission@regiscollege.edu* Web: *www.regiscollege.edu*

SALEM STATE COLLEGE — E-2

Salem, MA 01970 — **(978) 542-6200; Fax: (978) 542-6893**

Full-time: 1740 men, 2685 women	**Faculty:** 320
Part-time: 855 men, 1560 women	**Ph.D.s:** 77%
Graduate: 335 men, 910 women	**Student/Faculty:** 14 to 1
Year: semesters, summer session	**Tuition:** $3095 ($9175)
Application Deadline: open	**Room & Board:** $4386
Freshman Class: n/av	
SAT I or ACT: required	**LESS COMPETITIVE**

Salem State College, founded in 1854, is a public institution offering programs in liberal arts, business, education, and nursing. Figures given in the above capsule are approximate. There are 5 undergraduate schools and 1 graduate school. In addition to regional accreditation, Salem State has baccalaureate program accreditation with CSWE, NASAD, NCATE, and NLN. The library contains 225,000 volumes and 300,000 microform items, and subscribes to 1340 periodicals. Computerized library services include the card catalog, interlibrary loans, and database searching. Special learning facilities include a learning resource center, art gallery, radio station, TV station, and observatory. The 62-acre campus is in an urban area 18 miles northeast of Boston. Including residence halls, there are 19 buildings.

Student Life: 85% of undergraduates are from Massachusetts. Others are from 18 states, 12 foreign countries, and Canada. 98% are from public schools. 89% are white. 75% are Catholic; 15% Protestant. The average age of freshmen is 19; all undergraduates, 25. 14% do not continue beyond their first year; 29% remain to graduate.

Housing: 950 students can be accommodated in college housing, which includes single-sex and coed dormitories and on-campus apartments. On-campus housing is available on a first-come, first-served basis. Priority is given to out-of-town students. 79% of students commute. Upperclassmen may keep cars.

Activities: There are no fraternities or sororities. There are 44 groups on campus, including art, band, cheerleading, choir, chorale, chorus, computers, dance, drama, ethnic, gay, honors, international, jazz band, literary magazine, musical theater, newspaper, photography, political, radio and TV, religious, social, social service, student government, and yearbook. Popular campus events include Welcome Week, Arts Festival, and Senior Week.

Sports: There are 10 intercollegiate sports for men and 10 for women, and 15 intramural sports for men and 15 for women. There is an athletic center with 27 facilities, including a 1600-seat gym, a 2800-seat ice rink, an 8-lane swimming pool, 4 tennis courts, a weight room, a dance studio, and a wellness fitness center.

Disabled Students: 90% of the campus is accessible. Wheelchair ramps, elevators, special parking, specially equipped rest rooms, lowered drinking fountains, and lowered telephones are available.

Services: Counseling and information services are available, as is tutoring in every subject. There is a reader service for the blind, and remedial math, reading, and writing.

Campus Safety and Security: Measures include 24-hour foot and vehicle patrol, self-defense education, escort service, and shuttle buses. There are informal discussions, pamphlets/posters/films, emergency telephones, and lighted pathways/sidewalks.

Programs of Study: Salem State confers B.A., B.S., B.S.B.A., B.F.A., B.S.Ed., B.G.S., B.S.N., and B.S.W. degrees. Master's degrees are also awarded. Bachelor's degrees are awarded in BIOLOGICAL SCIENCE (biology/biological science), BUSINESS (accounting, banking and finance, business administration and management, and marketing/retailing/merchandising), COMMUNICATIONS AND THE ARTS (advertising, communications, design, dramatic arts, English, fine arts, and photography), COMPUTER AND PHYSICAL SCIENCE (chemistry, computer programming, earth science, geology, and mathematics), EDUCATION (art, business, education, science, and secondary), ENGINEERING AND ENVIRONMENTAL DESIGN (cartography), HEALTH PROFESSIONS (medical laboratory technology and nursing), SOCIAL SCIENCE (criminal justice, economics, geography, history, psychology, social work, and sociology). Sciences is the strongest academically. Business administration is the largest.

Required: All students must demonstrate basic competence in reading, math, and computer literacy, and are required to take a distribution of classes that includes 36 to 38 credits in humanities, sciences, and social sciences. Specific courses required are English composition, speech, phys ed, and the first-year seminar. All core and distribution requirements may be waived if the student passes a departmentally prescribed exemption exam. A minimum GPA of 2.0 and a total of 127 credits, with 36 in the major, are needed to graduate.

Special: Study abroad is available in 3 countries. Cross-registration through a consortium, internships, work-study programs, student-designed and dual majors, B.A.-B.S. degrees, and a general studies degree are offered. Life experience credit, nondegree study, and pass/fail options also are possible. There are 13 national honor societies, a freshman honors program, and 9 departmental honors programs.

Faculty/Classroom: 52% of faculty are male; 48%, female. All teach undergraduates. The average class size in an introductory lecture is 28; in a laboratory, 15; and in a regular course, 22.

Requirements: The SAT I or ACT is required. In addition, Salem State requires that applicants earn 16 credits, including 4 years of English, 3 years each of math and science, and 2 years each of foreign language and history. Courses in music, art, drama, computer science, and psychology are suggested. Art majors must provide a portfolio. A GED is acceptable. Students with a GED, those out of school more than 3 years, and the learning disabled do not need the SAT I. A GPA of 2.9 is required. AP and CLEP credits are accepted. Important factors in the admissions decision are advanced placement or honor courses, evidence of special talent, and recommendations by school officials. Application forms are available on-line at the Salem web site.

Procedure: Freshmen are admitted in the fall. Entrance exams should be taken November and December of the senior year. There is a deferred admissions plan. Application deadlines are open. The application fee is $10 ($40 out-of-state). A waiting list is an active part of the admissions procedure.

Transfer: 580 transfer students enrolled in a recent year. Transfer students are required to have a minimum GPA of 2.0 with more than 24 credits; 2.5 with fewer than 24 credits. 30 credits of 127 must be completed at Salem State.

Visiting: There are regularly scheduled orientations for prospective students. There are guides for informal visits and visitors may sit in on classes. To schedule a visit, contact the Admissions Office.

Financial Aid: In a recent year, 41% of all freshmen and 63% of continuing students received some form of financial aid. 45% of freshmen and 40% of continuing students received need-based aid. The average freshman award was $7276. Of that total, scholarships or need-based grants averaged $2396 ($7729 maximum); loans averaged $4139 ($6625 maximum); work contracts averaged $640 ($1500 maximum); and grants $101 ($3130 maximum). 86% of undergraduates work part time. Average annual earnings from campus work are $1600. The average financial indebtedness of a graduate in a recent year was $22,851. Salem State is a member of CSS. The FAFSA is required. Check with the school for current deadlines.

International Students: There were 161 international students enrolled in a recent year. The school actively recruits these students. They must score 500 on the written TOEFL.

Computers: The mainframe is a SUN 3500 with an Enterprise server. More than 500 networked PCs are available throughout the campus. All students may access the system. There are no time limits and no fees.

Admissions Contact: Nate Bryant, Director of Admissions.
E-mail: *nate.bryant@salem.mass.edu* Web: *www.salem.mass.edu*

SIMMONS COLLEGE
Boston, MA 02115 — **E-2**
(617) 521-2051
(800) 345-8468; Fax: (617) 521-3190

Full-time: 1090 women	**Faculty:** 175; IIA, av$
Part-time: 77 women	**Ph.D.s:** 65%
Graduate: 234 men, 1498 women	**Student/Faculty:** 6 to 1
Year: semesters, summer session	**Tuition:** $21,668
Application Deadline: February 1	**Room & Board:** $8750
Freshman Class: 1708 applied, 1185 accepted, 298 enrolled	
SAT I Verbal/Math: 566/539	**ACT:** 23 **VERY COMPETITIVE**

Simmons College, founded in 1899, is a private institution primarily for women that offers a comprehensive education combining the arts, sciences, and humanities with preprofessional training. In addition to regional accreditation, Simmons has baccalaureate program accreditation with ADA, APTA, CSWE, and NLN. The 5 libraries contain 235,431 volumes, 9599 microform items, and 2873 audiovisual forms/CDs, and subscribe to 1675 periodicals. Computerized library services include the card catalog, interlibrary loans, and database searching. Special learning facilities include an art gallery and TV studio, foreign language lab, physical therapy motion lab, nursing lab, and library science technology center. The 12-acre campus is in an urban area in Boston. Including residence halls, there are 26 buildings.

Student Life: 60% of undergraduates are from Massachusetts. Others are from 38 states and 26 foreign countries. 78% are from public schools. 70% are white. 38% are claim no religious affiliation; 30% Catholic; 16% Jewish; 16% Protestant. The average age of freshmen is 18; all undergraduates, 20. 15% do not continue beyond their first year; 69% remain to graduate.

Housing: 1049 students can be accommodated in college housing, which includes single-sex and coed dormitories and off-campus apartments. In addition, there are special-interest houses. On-campus housing is guaranteed for all 4 years. 70% of students live on campus; of those, 75% remain on campus on weekends. No one may keep cars.

Activities: There are no fraternities or sororities. There are 70 groups on campus, including chorale, dance, debate, drama, ethnic, film, gay, honors, international, literary magazine, newspaper, political, professional, religious, social, social service, student government, and yearbook. Popular campus events include Spring Spree, May Day Breakfast, and Culture Shock.

Sports: There are 8 intercollegiate sports for women and 4 intramural sports for women. Facilities include an 8-lane pool, a spa and sauna, 2 racquetball and 2 squash courts, 2 rowing tanks, 3 fitness rooms, a dance studio, an indoor track, and a gym with 3 badminton courts, 2 volleyball courts, and a basketball court.

Disabled Students: All of the campus is accessible. Wheelchair ramps, elevators, special parking, specially equipped rest rooms, special class scheduling, lowered drinking fountains, and lowered telephones are available.

Services: Counseling and information services are available, as is tutoring in some subjects, including basic freshman courses, languages, biology, chemistry, psychology, and math. There is a reader service for the blind and remedial math and writing. The school also provides study groups, individual tutoring, help with study skills and time management, and assistance for students with learning disabilities and special needs.

Campus Safety and Security: Measures include 24-hour foot and vehicle patrol, self-defense education, escort service, and shuttle buses. There are informal discussions, pamphlets/posters/films, emergency telephones, lighted pathways/sidewalks, and closed-circuit TV, ID card access, and security training in first response and crisis intervention.

Programs of Study: Simmons confers B.A. and B.S. degrees. Master's and doctoral degrees are also awarded. Bachelor's degrees are awarded in BIOLOGICAL SCIENCE (biochemistry, biology/biological science, and nutrition), BUSINESS (accounting, banking and finance, management information systems, and marketing/retailing/merchandising), COMMUNICATIONS AND THE ARTS (advertising, art, arts administration/management, communications, English, English as a second/foreign language, French, graphic design, music, music history and appreciation, public relations, and Spanish), COMPUTER AND PHYSICAL SCIENCE (chemistry, computer science, and mathematics), EDUCATION (early childhood, elementary, secondary, social studies, and special), ENGINEERING AND ENVIRONMENTAL DESIGN (environmental science), HEALTH PROFESSIONS (community health work, nursing, physical therapy, premedicine, and public health), SOCIAL SCIENCE (African American studies, dietetics, East Asian studies, economics, food science, history, human services, international relations, philosophy, political science/government, prelaw, psychobiology, psychology, public affairs, sociology, and women's studies). Physical therapy and education are the strongest academically. Physical therapy and psychology are the largest.

Required: To graduate, students must complete 128 semester hours, including 20 to 40 in the major, and maintain a minimum GPA of 2.0. 8 semester hours in a supervised independent learning experience or an internship are also required. They must also fulfill foreign language and math competency requirements. In addition to completing the multidisciplinary core course, students must complete 1 course from each of the following categories: creative and performing arts; language, literature, and culture; quantitative analysis and reasoning; social and historical perspectives; and psychological and ethical development.

Special: Cross-registration is available with Hebrew, Emmanuel, and Wheelock colleges, the New England Conservatory of Music, Massachusetts College of Art, and Wentworth Institute of Technology. Simmons offers study abroad in Europe through the Institute of European Studies. A Washington semester at American University, internship programs, a B.A.-B.S. degree, dual majors, interdisciplinary majors, student-designed majors, work-study programs, and pass/fail options are also offered. There is a dual-degree program in chemistry and pharmacy with Massachusetts College of Pharmacy and Health Sciences. There is a freshman honors program.

Faculty/Classroom: 25% of faculty are male; 75%, female. 100% both teach and do research. No introductory courses are taught by graduate students. The average class size in an introductory lecture is 50; in a laboratory, 12; and in a regular course, 16.

Admissions: 69% of the 2001-2002 applicants were accepted. The SAT I scores for the 2001-2002 freshman class were: Verbal--16% below 500, 48% between 500 and 599, 31% between 600 and 700, and 5% above 700; Math--29% below 500, 47% between 500 and 599, 23% between 600 and 700, and 1% above 700. 48% of the current freshmen were in the top fifth of their class; 82% were in the top two fifths. There were 7 National Merit semifinalists. 2 freshmen graduated first in their class.

Requirements: The SAT I or ACT is required. In addition, Simmons recommends that applicants have 4 years of English, 3 each of math, science, and social studies, and 2 of a foreign language. An essay is required, and an interview is strongly recommended. A GPA of 3.0 is required. AP and CLEP credits are accepted. Important factors in the admissions decision are advanced placement or honor courses, recommendations by school officials, and extracurricular activities record. Applications are accepted on disk and on-line via the school's web site and Common App.

Procedure: Freshmen are admitted fall and spring. Entrance exams should be taken by February 1 of the senior year. There are early admissions and deferred admissions plans. Early action applications should be filed by December 1; regular applications, by February 1 for fall entry and December 1 for spring entry, along with a $35 fee. Notification of early action is sent January 20; regular decision, April 15. 660 early action candidates were accepted for the 2001-2002 class. 3% of all applicants are on a waiting list.

Transfer: 39 transfer students enrolled in 2001-2002. Applicants should have a GPA of 2.8, at least 9 college-level credit hours, official transcripts from all colleges attended, and a faculty recommendation and dean's report from the previous college attended. 48 credits of 128 must be completed at Simmons.

Visiting: There are regularly scheduled orientations for prospective students, including a campus tour, class attendance, an interview, and meetings with faculty and students. There are guides for informal visits and visitors may sit in on classes and stay overnight. To schedule a visit, contact the Admissions Office.

Financial Aid: In a recent year, 80% of all students received some form of financial aid. 74% of freshmen and 73% of continuing students received need-based aid. The average freshman award was $19,618. Of that total, scholarships or need-based grants averaged $12,441 ($23,135 maximum); loans averaged $3675 ($4125 maximum); and work contracts averaged $1900 ($2100 maximum). 75% of undergraduates work part time. Average annual earnings from campus work are $1500. The average financial indebtedness of the 2001 graduate was $21,125. Simmons is a member of CSS. The CSS/Profile or FAFSA, the college's own financial statement and federal tax returns or W2 forms are required. The fall application deadline is February 1.

International Students: There were 46 international students enrolled in a recent year. The school actively recruits these students. They must score 560 on the written TOEFL or 220 on the electronic version and also take the SAT I or the ACT.

Computers: The mainframe is a DEC ALPHA server with an ATM network. There are 93 Macs and 91 PCs on the academic network, including public-access machines in the library and residence halls. These are available for course-related web access, general web access and e-mail, with Minitab and SAS statistics packages and personal productivity applications. All students may access the system. There are no time limits and no fees. It is strongly recommended that all students have a personal computer.

Graduates: In a recent year, 290 bachelor's degrees were awarded. The most popular majors were nursing (18%), physical therapy (11%), and sociology (6%). In an average class, 61% graduate in 4 years, 65% in 5 years, and 66% in 6 years. 25 companies recruited on campus in 2000-2001. Of the 2000 graduating class, 75% were employed within 6 months of graduation.

Admissions Contact: Jennifer O'Laughlin Hieber, Interim Director of Undergraduate Admissions. E-mail: *ugadm@simmons.edu*
Web: *www.simmons.edu*

SIMON'S ROCK COLLEGE OF BARD — A-2
Great Barrington, MA 01230-9702 — (413) 528-7313
(800) 235-7186; Fax: (413) 528-7334

Full-time: 172 men, 224 women	**Faculty:** 36
Part-time: 6 men, 12 women	**Ph.D.s:** 94%
Graduate: none	**Student/Faculty:** 11 to 1
Year: semesters	**Tuition:** $25,610
Application Deadline: June 30	**Room & Board:** $6840
Freshman Class: 556 applied, 234 accepted, 162 enrolled	
SAT I Verbal/Math: 635/580	**ACT:** 25 **HIGHLY COMPETITIVE**

Simon's Rock College of Bard, founded in 1964, is a private liberal arts school especially designed to permit students who have completed the 10th or 11th grades to enroll for collegiate studies in 8 interdisciplinary majors. The library contains 63,000 volumes, 7140 microform items, and 3450 audiovisual forms/CDs, and subscribes to 440 periodicals. Computerized library services include the card catalog, interlibrary loans, and database searching. Special learning facilities include a learning resource center, art gallery, radio station, language lab, greenhouse, and community garden. The 275-acre campus is in a small town 50 miles west of Springfield. Including residence halls, there are 38 buildings.

Student Life: 85% of undergraduates are from out of state, mostly the Middle Atlantic. Others are from 28 states and 3 foreign countries. 74% are from public schools. 73% are white. The average age of freshmen is 17; all undergraduates, 18. 19% do not continue beyond their first year.

Housing: 349 students can be accommodated in college housing, which includes single-sex and coed dormitories and on-campus apartments. In addition, there are special-interest houses. On-campus housing is guaranteed for all 4 years. 78% of students live on campus; of those, 85% remain on campus on weekends. Alcohol is not permitted. Upperclassmen may keep cars.

Activities: There are no fraternities or sororities. There are 24 groups on campus, including art, chorus, computers, dance, debate, drama, ethnic, film, gay, jazz band, literary magazine, multicultural, newspaper, orchestra, photography, political, radio and TV, religious, social, social service, student government, women's center, and yearbook. Popular campus events include Winter Solstice, May Fest, and Prom Nite.

Sports: There are 3 intercollegiate sports for men and 3 for women, and 6 intramural sports for men and 6 for women. Facilities include an 8-lane swimming pool, a multicourt gym, 3 racquetball courts, an elevated running track, a fitness and weight-training center, a rock-climbing wall, a soccer field, 4 tennis courts, and hiking trails.

Disabled Students: 80% of the campus is accessible. Wheelchair ramps, elevators, special parking, specially equipped rest rooms, special class scheduling, and lowered drinking fountains are available.

Services: Counseling and information services are available, as is tutoring in most subjects. Study skills instruction is available upon request; there is a library study skills class.

Campus Safety and Security: Measures include self-defense education, escort service, informal discussions, and pamphlets/posters/films. There are emergency telephones, lighted pathways/sidewalks, and security officers from 4 P.M. to 8 P.M. weekdays and 24 hours a day on weekends.

Programs of Study: Simon's Rock confers the B.A. degree. Associate degrees are also awarded. Bachelor's degrees are awarded in BIOLOGICAL SCIENCE (biology/biological science and ecology), COMMUNICATIONS AND THE ARTS (art, art history and appreciation, creative writing, dance, dramatic arts, drawing, English literature, fine arts, French, German, Germanic languages and literature, literature, modern language, music history and appreciation, music performance, music theory and composition, painting, performing arts, photography, Spanish, studio art, and visual and performing arts), COMPUTER AND PHYSICAL SCIENCE (applied mathematics, chemistry, mathematics, natural sciences, physics, quantitative methods, and science), HEALTH PROFESSIONS (premedicine), SOCIAL SCIENCE (African American studies, American studies, Asian/Oriental studies, crosscultural studies, East Asian studies, Eastern European studies, ethics, politics, and social policy, European studies, French studies, German area studies, interdisciplinary studies, Latin American studies, philosophy, political science/government, psychology, and Russian and Slavic studies). Cross-cultural relations, psychology, and music are the strongest academically. Literary studies; politics, law, and society; and psychology are the largest.

Required: All students must complete a writing and thinking workshop, a 2-semester freshman seminar, a sophomore seminar, and a cultural perspectives seminar. The core curriculum also includes distribution requirements in the arts, math, natural sciences, and foreign languages, and phys ed. A total of 120 credits, including at least 32 in the major, plus an interdisciplinary B.A. seminar, an 8-credit senior thesis, and a minimum 2.0 GPA are needed for the B.A. in liberal arts.

Special: A major consists of selecting 2 concentrations from the 36 available; 1 concentration may be self-designed. Independent study internships in many fields, study abroad, a cooperative program with Bard College, and pass/fail options are also available.

Faculty/Classroom: 60% of faculty are male; 40%, female. All both teach and do research. The average class size in an introductory lecture is 14; in a laboratory, 13; and in a regular course, 10.

Admissions: 42% of the 2001-2002 applicants were accepted. The SAT I scores for the 2001-2002 freshman class were: Verbal--4% below 500, 33% between 500 and 599, 39% between 600 and 700, and 24% above 700; Math--26% below 500, 34% between 500 and 599, 30% between 600 and 700, and 10% above 700. The ACT scores were 50% between 21 and 23, 20% between 24 and 26, 20% between 27 and 28, and 10% above 28.

Requirements: The SAT I is required and the ACT is recommended. The admissions committee looks more toward the required interview, essay, recommendations, and special talent. The school recommends that prospective students finish 2 years each of English, foreign languages, history, math, science, and social studies. A GPA of 2.0 is required. AP credits are accepted. Important factors in the admissions decision are advanced placement or honor courses, recommendations by school officials, and evidence of special talent.

Procedure: Freshmen are admitted fall and spring. Entrance exams should be taken prior to June 10. There are early admissions and deferred admissions plans. Applications should be filed by June 30 for fall entry, along with a $40 fee. Notification is sent on a rolling basis. 7% of all applicants are on a waiting list; 16 were accepted in 2001.

Transfer: One 1 transfer student enrolled in 2001-2002. Transfer students must be evaluated by the dean of academic affairs and registrar. 72 credits of 120 must be completed at Simon's Rock.

Visiting: There are regularly scheduled orientations for prospective students, including attending a class, a campus tour, and an interview. There are guides for informal visits and visitors may sit in on classes. To schedule a visit, contact Barbara Shultis, Receptionist, Office of Admission at (413) 528-7312 or (800) 235-7186.

Financial Aid: In 2001-2002, 85% of all freshmen and 92% of continuing students received some form of financial aid. 54% of all students received need-based aid. The average freshman award was $11,290. Of that total, scholarships or need-based grants averaged $6635 ($15,000 maximum); loans averaged $3648 ($8625 maximum); and work contracts averaged $1200 ($1500 maximum). 40 full merit scholarships are given each year through the Acceleration to Excellence Program. 37% of undergraduates work part time. Average annual earnings from campus work are $1500. The average financial indebtedness of the 2001 graduate was $10,500. Simon's Rock is a member of CSS. The CSS/Profile or FAFSA is required. The fall application deadline is June 15.

International Students: There are 3 international students enrolled. They must score 550 on the written TOEFL.

Computers: Students may access the central servers from PCs in their dorm rooms or from 2 computer labs. A network connection is available in each dorm room. All students may access the system. There are no time limits and no fees. It is strongly recommended that all students have a personal computer.

Graduates: In 2001, 41 bachelor's degrees were awarded. The most popular majors were literary studies (17%), politics, law, and society (13%), and psychology (12%). In an average class, 70% graduate in 4 years, 89% in 5 years, and 94% in 6 years.

Admissions Contact: Mary-King Austin, Dean of Admission. A video is available. Web: *http://www.simons-rock.edu/*

SMITH COLLEGE — B-2

Northampton, MA 01063 — **(413) 585-2500; Fax: (413) 585-2527**

Full-time: 2623 women	**Faculty:** 280; IIA, ++$
Part-time: 42 women	**Ph.D.s:** 98%
Graduate: 49 men, 399 women	**Student/Faculty:** 9 to 1
Year: semesters	**Tuition:** $24,742
Application Deadline: January 15	**Room & Board:** $8560
Freshman Class: 2869 applied, 1559 accepted, 660 enrolled	
SAT I Verbal/Math: 650/610	**ACT:** 28

HIGHLY COMPETITIVE+

Smith College, founded in 1871, is the largest independent women's college in the United States and offers a liberal arts education. The 4 libraries contain 1,268,443 volumes, 139,674 microform items, and 64,126 audiovisual forms/CDs, and subscribe to 2775 periodicals. Computerized library services include the card catalog, interlibrary loans, and database searching. Special learning facilities include a learning resource center, art gallery, radio station, TV station, astronomy observatories, a center for foreign languages and culture, a digital design studio, plant and horticultural labs, art studios with casting, printmaking, and darkroom facilities, and specialized libraries for science, music, and art. The 125-acre campus is in a small town 90 miles west of Boston. Including residence halls, there are 105 buildings.

Student Life: 77% of undergraduates are from out of state, mostly the Middle Atlantic. Others are from 50 states, 53 foreign countries, and Canada. 65% are from public schools. 71% are white. 21% are claim no religious affiliation; 17% Protestant; 14% Catholic; 13% including Bahai, Buddhist, Eastern Orthodox, Hindu, Mormon, Musl; 10% Jewish. The average age of freshmen is 18; all undergraduates, 21. 9% do not continue beyond their first year; 83% remain to graduate.

Housing: 2453 students can be accommodated in college housing, which includes single-sex dormitories and on-campus apartments. In addition, there are language houses, special-interest houses, nonsmoking houses, 2 cooperative houses, housing for nontraditional-age students, an apartment complex for a limited number of juniors and seniors, a senior house, and a French-speaking house. On-campus housing is guaranteed for all 4 years. 96% of students live on campus. Upperclassmen may keep cars.

Activities: There are no fraternities or sororities. There are 102 groups on campus, including art, chess, choir, chorale, chorus, computers, dance, debate, drama, ethnic, film, gay, honors, international, literary magazine, musical theater, newspaper, orchestra, pep band, photography, political, professional, radio and TV, religious, social, social service, student government, symphony, and yearbook. Popular campus events include International Student Day, Spring and Winter Weekends, and Rally Day.

Sports: There are 14 intercollegiate sports for women and 12 intramural sports for women. Facilities include indoor and outdoor tracks and tennis courts, riding rings, 2 gyms, a climbing wall, an indoor swimming pool with 1- and 3-meter diving boards, 2 weight-training rooms, a dance studio, 2 athletic training rooms, a human performance lab, squash courts, and field hockey, soccer, lacrosse, and softball fields. There is a performing arts center and a concert hall.

Disabled Students: 75% of the campus is accessible. Wheelchair ramps, elevators, special parking, specially equipped rest rooms, special class scheduling, lowered drinking fountains, lowered telephones, communications-accessible rooms, and accessible van service are available.

Services: Counseling and information services are available, as is tutoring in every subject. There is a reader service for the blind. Numerous services are provided for learning-disabled students, including note taking, oral tests, readers, tutors, books on tape, reading software, voice recognition, tape recorders, extended-timed tests, and writing counselors.

Campus Safety and Security: Measures include 24-hour foot and vehicle patrol, self-defense education, escort service, and shuttle buses. There are informal discussions, pamphlets/posters/films, emergency telephones,and lighted pathways/sidewalks. First-year students are required to attend panel discussions on campus safety. Specialized personal safety presentations, including self-defense and sexual assault information, are provided to various houses and organizations. There are crime prevention programs including operation identification bicycle registration.

Programs of Study: Smith confers A.B. and B.S. Engineering degrees. Master's and doctoral degrees are also awarded. Bachelor's degrees are awarded in BIOLOGICAL SCIENCE (biochemistry, biology/biological science, and neurosciences), COMMUNICATIONS AND THE ARTS (art history and appreciation, classics, comparative literature, dance, dramatic arts, East Asian languages and literature, English, French, Germanic languages and literature, Greek, Italian, Latin, music, Russian, Spanish, and studio art), COMPUTER AND PHYSICAL SCIENCE (astronomy, chemistry, computer science, geology, mathematics, and physics), EDUCATION (early childhood and elementary), ENGINEERING AND ENVIRONMENTAL DESIGN (engineering), SOCIAL SCIENCE (African American studies, American studies, anthropology, classical/ancient civilization, economics, French studies, history, Latin American studies, Luso-Brazilian studies, medieval studies, philosophy, political science/government, psychology, religion, Russian and Slavic studies, sociology, and women's studies). Government, psychology, and art are the largest.

Required: All students plan individual programs in consultation with faculty advisers and take 64 credits outside their major and 36 to 64 credits in the major. Students must maintain a minimum 2.0 GPA in all academic work and during the senior year. A total of 128 credits is needed to graduate.

Special: Smith offers study abroad in more than 50 countries, including the Smith College programs in Italy, France, Germany, and Switzerland, and affiliated programs in India, Japan, Russia, China, South Africa, Peru, Brazil, and Spain. Other opportunities include cross-registration with 5 area colleges, a Washington semester, Smithsonian internships, exchanges with historically black colleges and other liberal arts colleges, and at BioSphere2. Support for nontraditional-age students and for international students is provided, and funding for a summer internship is available for every undergraduate. Accelerated degree programs, student-designed majors, dual majors, and non-degree study are offered. There are 3 national honor societies, including Phi Beta Kappa.

Faculty/Classroom: 54% of faculty are male; 46%, female. All both teach and do research. No introductory courses are taught by graduate students. The average class size in an introductory lecture is 23; in a laboratory, 15; and in a regular course, 17.

Admissions: 54% of the 2001-2002 applicants were accepted. The SAT I scores for the 2001-2002 freshman class were: Verbal--4% below 500, 20% between 500 and 599, 45% between 600 and 700, and 28% above 700; Math--4% below 500, 33% between 500 and 599, 45% between 600 and 700, and 15% above 700. The ACT scores were 5% below 21, 7% between 21 and 23, 30% between 24 and 26, 15% between 27 and 28, and 43% above 28. 83% of the current freshmen were in the top fifth of their class; 96% were in the top two fifths. 19 freshmen graduated first in their class.

Requirements: The SAT I or ACT is required. In addition, Smith highly recommends that applicants have 4 years of English, 3 years each of math, science, and a foreign language, and 2 years of history. SAT II: Subject tests, especially in writing, are strongly recommended, as are personal interviews. The GED is accepted. Applications are accepted on-line via Embark and Common App. AP credits are accepted. Important factors in the admissions decision are advanced placement or honor courses, leadership record, and recommendations by school officials.

Procedure: Freshmen are admitted in the fall. Entrance exams should be taken before January of the senior year. There are early decision, early admissions, and deferred admissions plans. Early decision applications should be filed by November 15 (early decision winter: January 1); regular applications, by January 15 for fall entry, along with a $50 fee. Notification of early decision is sent December 15 and January 25; regular decision, early April. 154 early decision candidates were accepted for the 2001-2002 class. 9% of all applicants are on a waiting list.

Transfer: 93 transfer students enrolled in 2001-2002. Criteria for transfer students are similar to those for entering freshmen, with more emphasis on the college record. 64 credits of 128 must be completed at Smith.

Visiting: There are regularly scheduled orientations for prospective students, including student-guided tours available 5 times a day, Monday through Friday, when school is in full session and on Saturday mornings from September to January. Interviews may also be scheduled during these times. Information sessions are offered twice daily most of the year. There are guides for informal visits and visitors may sit in on classes and stay overnight. To schedule a visit, contact the admissions receptionist.

Financial Aid: In 2001-2002, 69% of all students received some form of financial aid. 57% of freshmen and 59% of continuing students received need-based aid. The average freshman award was $23,676. Of that total, scholarships or need-based grants averaged $19,962 ($34,362 maximum); loans averaged $2199 ($3625 maximum); and work contracts averaged $1515 ($1800 maximum). 51% of undergraduates work part time. Average annual earnings from campus work are $1143. The average financial indebtedness of the 2001 graduate was $19,546. Smith is a member of CSS. The CSS/Profile or FAFSA and the college's own financial statement are required. The fall application deadline is February 1.

International Students: There are 170 international students enrolled. The school actively recruits these students. If the language of instruction in school is English, the SAT I is required. Otherwise, the TOEFL is required with a recommended minimum score of 600.

Computers: The mainframe consists of 1 DEC VAX, 5 DEC ALPHAs, 4 Sun, 11 other UNIX systems, and more than 40 Novell and NT servers. Computing facilities include more than 550 PCs and Mac computers in public labs, classrooms, the libraries, and the foreign language center. All dorm rooms have high-speed Ethernet connections and offer unlimited Internet access at no cost. Computing resources are connected by a campuswide fiber-optic network. All students may access the system. There are no time limits and no fees.

Graduates: In 2001, 701 bachelor's degrees were awarded. The most popular majors were psychology (10%), government (10%), and art (7%). In an average class, 2% graduate in 3 years, 80% in 4 years, 83% in 5 years, and 83% in 6 years. 58 companies recruited on campus in 2000-2001. Of the 2000 graduating class, 13% were enrolled in graduate school within 6 months of graduation and 73% were employed.

Admissions Contact: Audrey Smith, Director of Admission.
E-mail: *admission@smith.edu* Web: *smith.edu*

SPRINGFIELD COLLEGE
Springfield, MA 01109 — B-3

(413) 748-3136
(800) 343-1257; Fax: (413) 748-3694

Full-time: 2077 men and women	**Faculty:** 210; IIA, --$
Part-time: 105 men and women	**Ph.D.s:** 62%
Graduate: 862 men and women	**Student/Faculty:** 10 to 1
Year: semesters, summer session	**Tuition:** $18,000
Application Deadline: April 1	**Room & Board:** $6520
Freshman Class: 2337 applied, 1671 accepted, 567 enrolled	
SAT I Verbal/Math: 500/510	**COMPETITIVE**

Springfield College, established in 1885, is a private liberal arts and sciences institution. There are 3 undergraduate schools and 1 graduate school. In addition to regional accreditation, S.C. has baccalaureate program accreditation with APTA, CAHEA, and NRPA. The library contains 168,332 volumes, 736,056 microform items, and 3200 audiovisual forms/CDs, and subscribes to 831 periodicals. Computerized library services include the card catalog, interlibrary loans, and database searching. Special learning facilities include an art gallery, radio station, and an outdoor center. The 160-acre campus is in a suburban area 26 miles north of Hartford, Connecticut. Including residence halls, there are 38 buildings.

Student Life: Students are from 30 states, 12 foreign countries, and Canada. 83% are from public schools. 93% are white. The average age of freshmen is 18; all undergraduates, 21. 12% do not continue beyond their first year.

Housing: 1980 students can be accommodated in college housing, which includes single-sex and coed dormitories, on-campus apartments, off-campus apartments, and married-student housing. In addition, there are special-interest houses, and a wellness dorm. On-campus housing is guaranteed for all 4 years. 85% of students live on campus; of those, 70% remain on campus on weekends. Alcohol is not permitted. Upperclassmen may keep cars.

Activities: There are no fraternities or sororities. There are 58 groups on campus, including art, band, cheerleading, choir, chorus, club sports, computers, dance, drama, ethnic, film, gay, honors, international, jazz band, literary magazine, musical theater, newspaper, pep band, professional, radio and TV, religious, social, social service, student government, and yearbook. Popular campus events include Parents Weekend and Stepping Up Day.

Sports: There are 13 intercollegiate sports for men and 11 for women, and 10 intramural sports for men and 10 for women, and 10 coed. Facilities include a 2000-seat stadium, a 2000-seat gym, a superturf football/soccer/lacrosse/field hockey field, 8 tennis courts, baseball and softball fields, and free weight and Nautilus rooms.

Disabled Students: 75% of the campus is accessible. Wheelchair ramps, elevators, special parking, specially equipped rest rooms, special class scheduling, and lowered drinking fountains are available.

Services: Counseling and information services are available, as is tutoring in every subject. There is remedial math and writing.

Campus Safety and Security: Measures include 24-hour foot and vehicle patrol, self-defense education, escort service, and shuttle buses. There are informal discussions, pamphlets/posters/films, emergency telephones, and lighted pathways/sidewalks.

Programs of Study: S.C. confers B.A. and B.S. degrees. Master's and doctoral degrees are also awarded. Bachelor's degrees are awarded in BIOLOGICAL SCIENCE (biochemistry, biology/biological science, and biotechnology), BUSINESS (business administration and management and sports management), COMMUNICATIONS AND THE ARTS (English and fine arts), COMPUTER AND PHYSICAL SCIENCE (chemistry, information sciences and systems, and mathematics), EDUCATION (early childhood, elementary, health, middle school, physical, science, and secondary), ENGINEERING AND ENVIRONMENTAL DESIGN (computer graphics), HEALTH PROFESSIONS (art therapy, emergency medical technologies, environmental health science, health care administration, predentistry, premedicine, recreation therapy, and rehabilitation therapy), SOCIAL SCIENCE (gerontology, history, human services, parks and recreation management, physical fitness/movement, political science/government, prelaw, psychology, and sociology). Physical therapy and athletic training are the strongest academically. Physical education is the largest.

Required: To graduate, students must complete a total of 130 credits with a 2.0 GPA. Core requirements include 50 semester hours in English, social and natural sciences, health, religion, philosophy, and art, and 4 credits in phys ed.

Special: There is a co-op program and cross-registration with cooperating colleges in the greater Springfield area. Internships are required in most majors, and there is limited study abroad. There are 2 national honor societies.

Faculty/Classroom: 52% of faculty are male; 48%, female. No introductory courses are taught by graduate students. The average class size in an introductory lecture is 125; in a laboratory, 20; and in a regular course, 30.

Admissions: 72% of the 2001-2002 applicants were accepted. The SAT I scores for the 2001-2002 freshman class were: Verbal--49% below 500, 43% between 500 and 599, and 7% between 600 and 700; Math--41% below 500, 42% between 500 and 599, 16% between 600 and 700, and 1% above 700. 26% of the current freshmen were in the top fifth of their class; 54% were in the top two fifths.

Requirements: The SAT I or ACT is required. In addition, applicants must be graduates of an accredited secondary school and have completed 4 years of English and 3 years each of history, math, and science. The school accepts the GED. An essay is required and an interview is recommended. AP and CLEP credits are accepted. Important factors in the admissions decision are advanced placement or honor courses, leadership record, and extracurricular activities record. Applications are accepted on-line.

Procedure: Freshmen are admitted fall and spring. Entrance exams should be taken by November of the senior year. There are early decision, early admissions, and deferred admissions plans. Early decision applications should be filed by December 1; regular applications, by April 1 for fall entry and December 1 for spring entry, along with a $40 fee. Notification of early decision is sent February 1; regular decision, on a rolling basis. A waiting list is an active part of the admissions procedure.

Transfer: Grades of 2.0 transfer for credit. Transfer students are admitted in the fall and spring.

Visiting: There are guides for informal visits and visitors may sit in on classes and stay overnight. To schedule a visit, contact the Admissions Office.

Financial Aid: The CSS/Profile or FAFSA and tax returns for parents and the student are required. The fall application deadline is March 15.

International Students: There are 20 international students enrolled. The school actively recruits these students. They must score 525 on the written TOEFL and also take the SAT I or the ACT.

Computers: The mainframe is an IBM AS/400. There are also 30 Apple IIe, IBM PS/2 Model 30, and IBM PS/2 Model 25 PCs available for academic use. All students may access the system. There are no time limits and no fees.

Graduates: Of the 2000 graduating class, 19% were enrolled in graduate school within 6 months of graduation and 78% were employed.

Admissions Contact: Mary N. DeAngelo, Director of Admissions. A video is available. E-mail: *admissions@spfldcol.edu*
Web: *www.springfieldcollege.edu*

STONEHILL COLLEGE E-3

Easton, MA 02357 (508) 565-1373; Fax: (508) 565-1545

Full-time: 914 men, 1233 women	**Faculty:** 127; IIB, av$
Part-time: 7 men, 8 women	**Ph.D.s:** 76%
Graduate: 1 man, 8 women	**Student/Faculty:** 17 to 1
Year: semesters, summer session	**Tuition:** $18,360
Application Deadline: January 15	**Room & Board:** $8492
Freshman Class: 4936 applied, 2120 accepted, 588 enrolled	
SAT I Verbal/Math: 580/590	**ACT:** 25 **HIGHLY COMPETITIVE**

Stonehill College, founded in 1948 by the Holy Cross Fathers, is a private Roman Catholic college offering undergraduate degrees in business administration, liberal arts, and the sciences. The library contains 188,000 volumes, 79,973 microform items, and 3738 audiovisual forms/CDs, and subscribes to 1110 periodicals. Computerized library services include the card catalog, interlibrary loans, and database searching. Special learning facilities include a learning resource center, radio station, an observatory, and an institute for the study of law and society. The 375-acre campus is in a suburban area 20 miles south of Boston. Including residence halls, there are 26 buildings.

Student Life: 59% of undergraduates are from Massachusetts. Others are from 30 states, 11 foreign countries, and Canada. 74% are of freshmen from public schools. 92% are white. 76% are Catholic; 11% claim no religious affiliation; 11% Protestant. The average age of freshmen is 18; all undergraduates, 20. 10% do not continue beyond their first year; 81% remain to graduate.

Housing: 1810 students can be accommodated in college housing, which includes single-sex and coed dormitories. In addition, there are special-interest houses, substance-free/wellness housing, and community service housing. On-campus housing is guaranteed for all 4 years. 85% of students live on campus; of those, 75% remain on campus on weekends. All students may keep cars.

Activities: There are no fraternities or sororities. There are 58 groups on campus, including academic, band, cheerleading, chess, choir, chorus, computers, dance, drama, environmental, ethnic, gay, honors, international, literary magazine, musical theater, newspaper, pep band, political, professional, radio and TV, religious, social, social service, student government, and yearbook. Popular campus events include Fall Concert, Spring Weekend, and Halloween Mixer.

Sports: There are 9 intercollegiate sports for men and 11 for women, and 17 intramural sports for men and 17 for women. Facilities include a 2000-seat stadium for football, soccer, and lacrosse, a gym with basketball and volleyball courts, a recreational and intramural sports complex, tennis courts, and baseball, softball, and field hockey fields.

Disabled Students: 85% of the campus is accessible. Wheelchair ramps, elevators, special parking, specially equipped rest rooms, special class scheduling, lowered drinking fountains, lowered telephones, telecommunication devices for the deaf, and 10 dormitory rooms designed specifically for disabled students are available.

Services: Counseling and information services are available, as is tutoring in most subjects, an LD specialist, and free diagnostic testing. There is a reader service for the blind and remedial writing.

Campus Safety and Security: Measures include 24-hour foot and vehicle patrol, self-defense education, escort service, and informal discussions. There are pamphlets/posters/films, emergency telephones, lighted pathways/sidewalks, bicycle patrols, and a weekend guest sign-in policy.

Programs of Study: Stonehill confers B.A., B.S., and B.S.B.A. degrees. Master's degrees are also awarded. Bachelor's degrees are awarded in BIOLOGICAL SCIENCE (biochemistry and biology/biological science), BUSINESS (accounting, banking and finance, business administration and management, business economics, and marketing/retailing/merchandising), COMMUNICATIONS AND THE ARTS (communications, English, fine arts, and languages), COMPUTER AND PHYSICAL SCIENCE (chemistry, computer science, and mathematics), EDUCATION (education), ENGINEERING AND ENVIRONMENTAL DESIGN (computer engineering), HEALTH PROFESSIONS (health care administration and medical technology), SOCIAL SCIENCE (American studies, criminal justice, economics, history, interdisciplinary studies, international studies, philosophy, political science/government, psychology, public administration, religion, and sociology). Biology, chemistry, and accounting are the strongest academically. Education studies, psychology, and communication are the largest.

Required: All students must complete a cornerstone program, which consists of 4 common courses within history/literature and philosophy/religious studies, 2 linked courses and a third tutorial course, a moral reasoning course, and a senior capstone experience. Distribution requirements include 1 course each in natural science, social science, and statistical reasoning. Students must complete 40 3- to 4-credit courses while maintaining a minimum GPA of 2.0.

Special: On-campus work-study, international and domestic internships, and a Washington semester through the Washington Center are available. Cross-registration with 8 other Massachusetts schools in the SACHEM consortium is also available. A 3-2 computer engineering degree is offered with the University of Notre Dame. Opportunities for study abroad include the Stonehill Program in France, a Stonehill-Quebec Exchange, a semester in Irish studies at the National University of Ireland Dublin, and a worldwide Foreign Studies Program. Nondegree, directed, and field study are available as well as a pass/fail option for upperclassmen. Programs in early childhood, elementary, and secondary education lead to the state's provisional teacher certification. Stonehill is also a member of the Marine Studies Consortium. Preprofessional preparation is available in medicine, dentistry, veterinary science, law, and theology. There are 12 national honor societies, a freshman honors program, and 7 departmental honors programs.

Faculty/Classroom: 64% of faculty are male; 36%, female. All teach undergraduates. No introductory courses are taught by graduate students. The average class size in an introductory lecture is 23; in a laboratory, 17; and in a regular course, 21.

Admissions: 43% of the 2001-2002 applicants were accepted. The SAT I scores for the 2001-2002 freshman class were: Verbal--8% below 500, 51% between 500 and 599, 39% between 600 and 700, and 2% above 700; Math--6% below 500, 48% between 500 and 599, 42% between 600 and 700, and 4% above 700. 76% of the current freshmen were in the top fifth of their class; 96% were in the top two fifths. There was 1 National Merit semifinalist. 6 freshmen graduated first in their class.

Requirements: The SAT I or ACT is required. In addition, applicants should be graduates of an accredited high school or have earned the GED. Secondary preparation should include 4 units of English; 2 units of the same foreign language; 1 unit of a lab science; 2 units of algebra; and 1 unit of geometry; 3 combined units of history, political science, and social sciences. To these units elective subjects are to be added. Additional units in math are generally suggested, and especially suggested for business and science majors. An essay, school report, and teacher evaluations are also required. AP and CLEP credits are accepted. Important factors in the admissions decision are advanced placement or honor courses, evidence of special talent, and leadership record. Applications are accepted on-line at *Emark.com* and via Common App.

Procedure: Freshmen are admitted fall and spring. Entrance exams should be taken in October. There are early decision and deferred admissions plans. Early decision applications should be filed by November 1; regular applications, by January 15 for fall entry and November 1 for spring entry, along with a $50 fee. Notification of early decision is sent December 31; regular decision, by April 1. 67 early decision candidates were accepted for the 2001-2002 class. 18% of all applicants are on a waiting list; 7 were accepted in 2001.

Transfer: 13 transfer students enrolled in 2001-2002. Applicants must have a minimum GPA of 2.0, with 3.0-4.0 recommended. Official high school transcripts and college transcripts, along with catalogs with course descriptions from all colleges attended, are required. SAT I or ACT scores are required and an interview is recommended. 60 credits of 120 must be completed at Stonehill.

Visiting: There are regularly scheduled orientations for prospective students, consisting of group information sessions and guided campus tours available by appointment throughout the year. Visitors may sit in on classes. To schedule a visit, contact the Admissions Office.

Financial Aid: In 2001-2002, 90% of all freshmen and 85% of continuing students received some form of financial aid. 62% of freshmen and 63% of continuing students received need-based aid. The average freshman award was $11,585. Of that total, scholarships or need-based grants averaged $10,660 ($26,852 maximum); loans averaged $3472 ($6625 maximum); and work contracts averaged $1675 ($1800 maximum). 35% of undergraduates work part time. Average annual earnings from campus work are $889. The average financial indebtedness of the 2001 graduate was $11,142. Stonehill is a member of CSS. The CSS/Profile or FAFSA is required. The fall application deadline is February 1.

International Students: There are 24 international students enrolled. The school actively recruits these students. They must score 550 on the written TOEFL or 213 on the electronic version and also take the SAT I or the ACT.

Computers: The mainframe is an IBM AS/400. More than 200 PCs are available in public labs throughout the campus. Available software includes instructional packages, web page development tools, graphics tools, programming languages, and database tools for student use. Every resident has a direct network connection, and laptop connections are available in many common areas and the library. Students are provided e-mail accounts, personal web pages, and central data storage. All students may access the system 7 days a week, 24 hours a day. There are no time limits and no fees. It is strongly recommended that all students have personal computers.

Graduates: In 2001, 559 bachelor's degrees were awarded. The most popular majors were education studies (11%), communication (10%), and accounting (8%). In an average class, 81% graduate in 4 years, 83% in 5 years, and 84% in 6 years. 90 companies recruited on campus in 2000-2001. Of the 2000 graduating class, 17% were enrolled in graduate school within 6 months of graduation and 82% were employed.

Admissions Contact: Brian P. Murphy, Dean of Admissions and Enrollment. E-mail: *admissions@stonehill.edu* Web: *www.stonehill.edu*

SUFFOLK UNIVERSITY E-2

Boston, MA 02108-2770 (617) 573-8460
(800) 6SUFFOL; Fax: (617) 742-4291

Full-time: 1200 men, 1540 women **Faculty:** 227; IIA, ++$
Part-time: 262 men, 435 women **Ph.D.s:** 91%
Graduate: 825 men, 957 women **Student/Faculty:** 12 to 1
Year: semesters, summer session **Tuition:** $16,616
Application Deadline: open **Room & Board:** $9990
Freshman Class: 3283 applied, 2738 accepted, 721 enrolled
SAT I Verbal/Math: 500/490 **COMPETITIVE**

Suffolk University, founded in 1906, is a private institution offering undergraduate and graduate degrees in the arts and sciences, business, and law. There are 2 undergraduate and 3 graduate schools. In addition to regional accreditation, Suffolk has baccalaureate program accreditation with AACSB and FIDER. The 3 libraries contain 300,894 volumes, 262,078 microform items, and 319 audiovisual forms/CDs, and subscribe to 5334 periodicals. Computerized library services include the card catalog, interlibrary loans, and database searching. Special learning facilities include a learning resource center, art gallery, radio station, and TV station. The 2-acre campus is in an urban area in the Beacon Hill area of downtown Boston. Including residence halls, there are 14 buildings.

Student Life: 69% of undergraduates are from Massachusetts. Others are from 34 states, 97 foreign countries, and Canada. 68% are from public schools. 60% are white; 14% foreign nationals. The average age of freshmen is 18; all undergraduates, 22. 25% do not continue beyond their first year.

Housing: 506 students can be accommodated in college housing, which includes coed dormitories. On-campus housing is available on a first-come, first-served basis and is available on a lottery system for upperclassmen. 84% of students commute. Alcohol is not permitted. No one may keep cars.

Activities: 1% of men and about 1% of women belong to 1 local and 1 national fraternity. There are no sororities. There are 40 groups on campus, including art, cheerleading, choir, chorale, chorus, computers, debate, drama, ethnic, evening students, film, forensics, gay, graduate students, honors, international, literary magazine, musical theater, newspaper, orientation, photography, political, professional, radio and TV, recycle, religious, social, social service, student government, transfer, women's community service, and yearbook. Popular campus events include Hispanic Fiesta, Fallfest Talent Show, and Temple Street Fair.

Sports: There are 7 intercollegiate sports for men and 5 for women, and 2 intramural sports for men and 2 for women. A gym for basketball, volleyball, aerobics, intramurals, and indoor baseball/softball practice, and a fully equipped fitness center are available to the university community.

Disabled Students: 95% of the campus is accessible. Wheelchair ramps, elevators, specially equipped rest rooms, special class scheduling, lowered drinking fountains, and lowered telephones are available.

Services: Counseling and information services are available, as is tutoring in most subjects. There is a reader service for the blind, and remedial math, reading, and writing.

Campus Safety and Security: Measures include 24-hour foot and vehicle patrol, self-defense education, escort service, and informal discussions. There are pamphlets/posters/films, emergency telephones, and lighted pathways/sidewalks.

Programs of Study: Suffolk confers B.A., B.S., B.F.A., B.S.B.A., B.S.G.S., and B.S.J. degrees. Associate, master's, and doctoral degrees are also awarded. Bachelor's degrees are awarded in BIOLOGICAL SCIENCE (biochemistry, biology/biological science, and marine science), BUSINESS (accounting, banking and finance, entrepreneurial studies, international business management, international economics, management science, and marketing/retailing/merchandising), COMMUNICATIONS AND THE ARTS (broadcasting, communications, dramatic arts, English, fine arts, French, graphic design, journalism, performing arts, public relations, Spanish, and speech/debate/rhetoric), COMPUTER AND PHYSICAL SCIENCE (chemistry, computer programming, computer science, information sciences and systems, mathematics, and physics), EDUCATION (business and elementary), ENGINEERING AND ENVIRONMENTAL DESIGN (computer engineering, electrical/electronics engineering, environmental engineering, environmental engineering technology, environmental science, and interior design), HEALTH PROFESSIONS (cytotechnology, medical laboratory technology, medical science, and radiological science), SOCIAL SCIENCE (criminal justice, economics, history, human development, human services, humanities, industrial and organizational psychology, paralegal studies, philosophy, political science/government, psychology, public administration, social science, and sociology). Business, sociology, and criminal justice are the strongest academically. Business subjects, sociology, and communications are the largest.

Required: All students must complete 122 semester hours with at least a 2.0 GPA. Distribution requirements vary by degree program.

Special: Numerous cooperative education and work-study programs are available in the Boston area. Cross-registration is offered with Emerson College. Study abroad in 25 countries and a semester internship in Washington, D.C., as well as local and international internships, are possible. Majors in medical biophysics and radiation biology taught in collaboration with Massachusetts General Hospital, dual and student-designed majors, and a lawyer's assistant certificate program are also available. Also, Suffolk has opened new campuses in Spain and Senegal. There are 19 national honor societies, a freshman honors program, and 9 departmental honors programs.

Faculty/Classroom: 58% of faculty are male; 42%, female. 96% teach undergraduates, 90% do research, and 90% do both. The average class size in an introductory lecture is 20; in a laboratory, 12; and in a regular course, 17.

Admissions: 83% of the 2001-2002 applicants were accepted. The SAT I scores for the 2001-2002 freshman class were: Verbal--47% below 500, 42% between 500 and 599, 11% between 600 and 700, and 1% above 700; Math--52% below 500, 39% between 500 and 599, and 9% between 600 and 700. 19% of the current freshmen were in the top fifth of their class; 46% were in the top two fifths.

Requirements: The SAT I is required. In addition, applicants should have a high school diploma or the GED. Recommended secondary preparation includes 4 years of English, 3 years of math, 2 years each of a foreign language and science, and 1 year of American history. Exact requirements differ by degree program. A personal essay is required, and an interview is recommended. A GPA of 2.0 is required. AP and CLEP credits are accepted. Important factors in the admissions decision are advanced placement or honor courses, recommendations by school officials, and leadership record. Applications are accepted on computer disk and/or on-line via Common App. Application forms are also available at the school's web site.

Procedure: Freshmen are admitted to all sessions. Entrance exams should be taken by December of the senior year. There are early admissions and deferred admissions plans. Application deadlines are open. The fall 2001 application fee was $40. Notification is sent on a rolling basis.

Transfer: 245 transfer students enrolled in 2001-2002. Applicants should have a minimum 2.5 GPA from an accredited college. Those with fewer than 15 college credits must submit a high school transcript. 30 credits of 122 must be completed at Suffolk.

Visiting: There are regularly scheduled orientations for prospective students, including a general presentation and an overview panel presentation of student life, career and co-op opportunities, learning center services, and athletics, academic department meetings, and campus tours. There are guides for informal visits and visitors may sit in on classes. To schedule a visit, contact the Admissions Office.

Financial Aid: In 2001-2002, 76% of all freshmen and 65% of continuing students received some form of financial aid. 65% of freshmen and 54% of continuing students received need-based aid. The average freshman award was $13,382. Of that total, scholarships or need-based grants averaged $6787 ($22,300 maximum); loans averaged $7130 ($29,798 maximum); and work contracts averaged $1863 ($3000 maximum). 77% of undergraduates work part time. Average annual earnings from campus work are $1500. Suffolk is a member of CSS. The FAFSA, the college's own financial statement, and verification of income are required. The fall application deadline is March 1.

International Students: There are 500 international students enrolled. The school actively recruits these students. They must score 525 on the written TOEFL or 197 on the electronic version and also take the college's own test and the SAT I or the ACT.

Computers: The mainframe is an IBM RS/6000. Various computer labs on campus house more than 200 PCs with access to the mainframe. Students have access to the Internet, LEXIS/NEXIS database, the Suffolk on-line library system, CD-ROM library and information systems, as well as Sun and DEC UNIX workstations. All students may access the system. There are no time limits and no fees.

Graduates: In 2001, 643 bachelor's degrees were awarded. The most popular majors were sociology (11%), finance (9%), and communications (9%). In an average class, 1% graduate in 3 years, 38% in 4 years, 50% in 5 years, and 54% in 6 years. More than 50 companies recruited on campus in 2000-2001. Of the 2000 graduating class, 27% were enrolled in graduate school within 6 months of graduation and 85% were employed.

Admissions Contact: Walter Caffey, Dean of Enrollment Management. A video is available. E-mail: *admission@admin.suffolk.edu*
Web: *www.suffolk.edu*

TUFTS UNIVERSITY D-2

Medford, MA 02155 **(617) 627-3170; Fax: (617) 627-3860**

Full-time: 2153 men, 2526 women	**Faculty:** 371; I, av$
Part-time: 34 men, 42 women	**Ph.D.s:** 99%
Graduate: 1861 men, 2415 women	**Student/Faculty:** 13 to 1
Year: semesters, summer session	**Tuition:** $26,892
Application Deadline: January 1	**Room & Board:** $7982

Freshman Class: 13,700 applied, 3178 accepted, 1163 enrolled
SAT I or ACT: required **MOST COMPETITIVE**

Tufts University, founded in 1852, is a private institution offering undergraduate programs in liberal arts and sciences and engineering. There are 2 undergraduate and 8 graduate schools. In addition to regional accreditation, Tufts has baccalaureate program accreditation with ABET, ADA, and CAHEA. The 2 libraries contain 1,018,000 volumes, 1,158,000 microform items, and 33,800 audiovisual forms/CDs, and subscribe to 4895 periodicals. Computerized library services include the card catalog, interlibrary loans, and database searching. Special learning facilities include a learning resource center, art gallery, radio station, TV station, and theater. The 140-acre campus is in a suburban area 5 miles northwest of Boston. Including residence halls, there are 167 buildings.

Student Life: 77% of undergraduates are from out of state, mostly the Middle Atlantic. Others are from 50 states, 70 foreign countries, and Canada. 60% are from public schools. 54% are white; 13% Asian American. The average age of freshmen is 18; all undergraduates, 20. 4% do not continue beyond their first year.

Housing: 3550 students can be accommodated in college housing, which includes single-sex and coed dormitories, on-campus apartments, fraternity houses, and sorority houses. In addition, there are language houses, cooperative houses, and special-interest houses. Freshmen and sophomores are required to live on campus. On-campus housing is available on a lottery system for upperclassmen. 75% of students live on campus. Upperclassmen may keep cars.

Activities: 15% of men belong to 9 national fraternities; 3% of women belong to 3 national sororities. There are 160 groups on campus, including art, band, cheerleading, chess, choir, chorale, chorus, computers, dance, debate, drama, environmental, ethnic, forensics, gay, honors, international, jazz band, literary magazine, marching band, musical theater, newspaper, orchestra, outdoors, pep band, photography, political, professional, radio and TV, religious, social, social service, student government, symphony, and yearbook. Popular campus events include a dramatic arts series, national and international forums, and an international affairs symposium.

Sports: There are 17 intercollegiate sports for men and 16 for women, and 10 intramural sports for men and 6 for women. Facilities include a football stadium, 2 gyms, an 8-lane all-weather track, 9 tennis courts, a field house, an indoor cage, an indoor track, 7 squash courts, a swimming pool, a dance room, a weight room, a sauna, a sailing center, an exercise center, and baseball, softball, and playing fields.

Disabled Students: 90% of the campus is accessible. Wheelchair ramps, elevators, special parking, specially equipped rest rooms, special class scheduling, lowered drinking fountains, lowered telephones, and other special services as needed are available.

Services: Counseling and information services are available, as is tutoring in some subjects, as needed through the Academic Resources Center. There is a reader service for the blind. Services are also available through women's, African American, Hispanic American, Asian American, international, and lesbian-gay-bisexual centers, and through the Counseling Center and Career Planning Center.

Campus Safety and Security: Measures include 24-hour foot and vehicle patrol, escort service, shuttle buses, and informal discussions. There are pamphlets/posters/films, emergency telephones, and lighted pathways/sidewalks.

Programs of Study: Tufts confers B.A., B.S., B.S.C.E., B.S.Ch.E., B.S. Comp. Eng., B.S.E., B.S.E.E., B.S.E.S., B.S. Environmental Eng., and B.S.M.E. degrees. Master's and doctoral degrees are also awarded. Bachelor's degrees are awarded in BIOLOGICAL SCIENCE (biochemistry, biology/biological science, and biotechnology), COMMUNICATIONS AND THE ARTS (art history and appreciation, Chinese, classics, dramatic arts, English, French, German, Greek, Japanese, Latin, music, Russian, and Spanish), COMPUTER AND PHYSICAL SCIENCE (applied physics, astrophysics, chemistry, computer science, geology, mathematics, and physics), EDUCATION (early childhood), ENGINEERING AND ENVIRONMENTAL DESIGN (architecture, biomedical engineering, chemical engineering, civil engineering, computer engineering, electrical/electronics engineering, engineering, engineering and applied science, engineering physics, environmental science, and mechanical engineering), SOCIAL SCIENCE (American studies, anthropology, archeology, Asian/Oriental studies, biopsychology, child psychology/development, clinical psychology, economics, experimental psychology, German area studies, history, international relations, Judaic studies, Middle Eastern studies, peace studies, philosophy, political science/government, psychology, religion, Russian and Slavic studies, sociology, and women's studies). International relations, biology, and English are the largest.

Required: Liberal arts students must complete 34 courses, 10 of them in the area of concentration. Requirements include foundation courses in writing and foreign language or culture and courses in humanities, arts, social sciences, math, and natural sciences. Requirements for engineering students include a total of 38 courses, 12 of them in the area of concentration, and distribution requirements in English, math and science, humanities, and social sciences.

Special: The university offers cross-registration at Swarthmore College, Boston University, Boston College, and Brandeis University, a Washington semester, and study abroad in England, Spain, France, Moscow, Chile, Japan, Ghana, and Germany. Many internships are available. Double majors in the liberal arts are common; student-designed majors are possible. There is a 5-year B.A./M.A. or B.S./M.S. program in engineering or liberal arts, a B.A.-B.F.A. program with the Museum School of Fine Arts, and a B.A.-B.M. program with the New England Conservatory of Music. Pass/fail options are offered. There are 4 national honor societies, including Phi Beta Kappa.

Faculty/Classroom: 60% of faculty are male; 40%, female. All both teach and do research. No introductory courses are taught by graduate students. The average class size in a regular course is 20.

Admissions: 23% of the 2001-2002 applicants were accepted. 87% of the current freshmen were in the top fifth of their class; 97% were in the top two fifths.

Requirements: The university accepts either the SAT I and the results of 3 SAT II: Subject tests, or the ACT. Liberal arts applicants should take the SAT II: Subject test in writing and 2 others; engineering applicants should take writing, math level I or II, and either physics or chemistry. In addition, all applicants should be high school graduates or hold the GED. Academic preparation is expected to include 4 years of English, 3 years each of humanities and a foreign language, 2 years each of social and natural sciences, and 1 year of history. A personal essay is required. AP credits are accepted. Important factors in the admissions decision are advanced placement or honor courses, recommendations by school officials, and extracurricular activities record. Tufts provides an on-line Embark application via its web site.

Procedure: Freshmen are admitted in the fall. Entrance exams should be taken by January of the senior year. There are early decision, early admissions, and deferred admissions plans. Early decision applications should be filed by November 15; regular applications, by January 1 for fall entry, along with a $60 fee. Notification of early decision is sent December 15; regular decision, April 1. 503 early decision candidates were accepted for the 2001-2002 class. A waiting list is an active part of the admissions procedure.

Transfer: 56 transfer students enrolled in 2001-2002. Admission is competitive. Primary consideration is given to college and secondary school achievement and record of personal involvement. 17 courses of 34 must be completed at Tufts.

Visiting: There are regularly scheduled orientations for prospective students, including orientation sessions twice a day, Monday through Friday, April 1 to December 10, followed by campus tours. There are additional orientation sessions and tours on selected Saturday mornings during the fall. There are guides for informal visits and visitors may sit in on classes and stay overnight. To schedule a visit, contact the Admissions Office.

Financial Aid: In 2001-2002, 41% of all freshmen and 39% of continuing students received some form of financial aid. 39% of freshmen and 37% of continuing students received need-based aid. The average freshman award was $22,028. Of that total, scholarships or need-based grants averaged $19,209; loans averaged $3477; and work contracts averaged $1671. 40% of undergraduates work part time. The average financial indebtedness of the 2001 graduate was $15,169. Tufts is a member of CSS. The CSS/Profile or FAFSA and parent and student federal income tax forms are required. The fall application deadline is February 15.

International Students: There are 325 international students enrolled. The school actively recruits these students. They must take the TOEFL if English is not their first language. The student must also take the ACT, or the SAT I and 3 SAT II: Subject tests, including writing.

Computers: The mainframes are a DEC Alpha Server 8200 with 4 Alpha processors and a DEC MicroVAX 3600 processors; the machines operate on VMS and UNIX. Mainframes and PC labs are networked on a universitywide computer network called Jumbonet. There are 254 terminals and PCs in 5 locations across campus, supported by 45 printers in various locations. A special computer-aided design (CAD) lab is available to undergraduates. All campus residence rooms are hard-wired for access to the university computer. All students may access the system 24 hours a day. There are no time limits and no fees.

Graduates: In 2001, 1330 bachelor's degrees were awarded. The most popular majors were international relations (11%), biology (10%), and English (8%). In an average class, 90% graduate in 6 years. 150 companies recruited on campus in 2000-2001.

Admissions Contact: David Cuttino, Dean of Admissions.
E-mail: *admissions.inquiry@ase.tufts.edu* Web: *www.tufts.edu*

UNIVERSITY OF MASSACHUSETTS AMHERST B-2

Amherst, MA 01003 **(413) 545-0222; Fax: (413) 545-4312**

Full-time: 8706 men, 9179 women	**Faculty:** 1155; I, av$
Part-time: 699 men, 784 women	**Ph.D.s:** 94%
Graduate: 2593 men, 2717 women	**Student/Faculty:** 16 to 1
Year: semesters, summer session	**Tuition:** $5880 ($14,433)
Application Deadline: February 1	**Room & Board:** $5115
Freshman Class: 18,625 applied, 13,518 accepted, 4203 enrolled	
SAT I or ACT: required	**VERY COMPETITIVE**

Established in 1863, University of Massachusetts Amherst is a major public, research land-grant institution offering nearly 100 academic majors. There are 9 undergraduate and 9 graduate schools. In addition to regional accreditation, UMass has baccalaureate program accreditation with AACSB, ABET, ASLA, FIDER, NASM, NCATE, NLN, and SAF. The 4 libraries contain 3,048,106 volumes, 2,452,070 microform items, and 16,990 audiovisual forms/CDs, and subscribe to 15,231 periodicals. Computerized library services include the card catalog, interlibrary loans, and database searching. Special learning facilities include a learning resource center, art gallery, radio station, TV station, and botanical gardens. The 1463-acre campus is in a small town 90 miles west of Boston and 60 miles north of Hartford, Connecticut. Including residence halls, there are 200 buildings.

Student Life: 75% of undergraduates are from Massachusetts. 71% are white. The average age of freshmen is 18; all undergraduates, 21. 16% do not continue beyond their first year.

Housing: Housing includes single-sex and coed dormitories, on-campus apartments, married-student housing, fraternity houses, and sorority houses. In addition, there are honors houses, language houses, and special interest houses, language corridors, a multicultural dorm, and family housing. On-campus housing is guaranteed for the freshman and sophomore years only and is available on a lottery system for upperclassmen. 59% of students live on campus. All students may keep cars.

Activities: 6% of men belong to fraternities; 5% of women belong to sororities. There are 200 groups on campus, including art, band, cheerleading, chess, choir, chorale, chorus, computers, dance, debate, drama, ethnic, film, gay, honors, international, jazz band, literary magazine, marching band, musical theater, newspaper, opera, orchestra, pep band, photography, political, professional, radio and TV, religious, social, social service, student government, student-owned businesses, symphony, and yearbook. Popular campus events include Midnight Madness (first basketball practice), Spring Pond Concert, and Asian and Caribbean cultural nights.

Sports: Facilities include 120 acres of multipurpose fields, a track, and 22 tennis courts. Indoor facilities include 3 pools, 3 handball/squash courts, weight rooms, fitness centers, basketball/volleyball/badminton courts, and a track.

Disabled Students: Wheelchair ramps, elevators, special parking, specially equipped rest rooms, special class scheduling, lowered drinking fountains, and lowered telephones are available. All programs are made accessible through accommodations.

Services: Counseling and information services are available, as is tutoring in most subjects. There is a reader service for the blind and remedial math and reading.

Campus Safety and Security: Measures include 24-hour foot and vehicle patrol, self-defense education, escort service, and shuttle buses. There are informal discussions, pamphlets/posters/films, emergency telephones, lighted pathways/sidewalks, and tight restrictions on residence hall access.

Programs of Study: UMass confers B.A., B.S., B.B.A., B.F.A., B.G.S., and B.Mus. degrees. Associate, master's, and doctoral degrees are also awarded. Bachelor's degrees are awarded in AGRICULTURE (animal science, forestry and related sciences, natural resource management, plant science, soil science, and wildlife management), BIOLOGICAL SCIENCE (biochemistry, biology/biological science, microbiology, and nutrition), BUSINESS (accounting, banking and finance, business administration and management, hotel/motel and restaurant management, marketing management, and sports management), COMMUNICATIONS AND THE ARTS (art history and appreciation, Chinese, classics, communications, comparative literature, dance, design, dramatic arts, English, French, German, Japanese, journalism, linguistics, music, Portuguese, Spanish, and studio art), COMPUTER AND PHYSICAL SCIENCE (astronomy, chemistry, computer science, earth science, geology, mathematics, physics, and science), EDUCATION (early childhood, elementary, physical, and secondary), ENGINEERING AND ENVIRONMENTAL DESIGN (chemical engineering, civil engineering, computer engineering, construction technology, electrical/electronics engineering, environmental design, environmental science, industrial engineering, landscape architecture/design, and mechanical engineering), HEALTH PROFESSIONS (exercise science, medical laboratory technology, nursing, predentistry, premedicine, preveterinary science, and speech pathology/audiology), SOCIAL SCIENCE (African American studies, anthropology, economics, ethics, politics, and social policy, food science, geography, history, interdisciplinary studies, Italian studies, Judaic studies, law, liberal arts/general studies, Middle Eastern studies, philosophy, political science/government, prelaw, psychology, Russian and Slavic studies, sociology, and women's studies). Chemical engineering, computer science, and electrical engineering are the strongest academically. Psychology, communication, and English are the largest.

Required: For graduation, students must complete 120 credit hours and maintain a minimum GPA of 2.0 overall and in the major, with at least 2 courses fulfilling a diversity requirement. The general education requirements for all students include courses in writing, the social world, the biological and physical world, math, and analytic reasoning.

Special: Cross-registration is possible through the Five-College Consortium (Smith, Mt. Holyoke, Hampshire, and Amherst) and with other University of Massachusetts campuses. Students may participate in co-op programs, internships in every major, study abroad in more than 30 countries, a Washington semester, work-study programs in various university departments, dual majors in most subjects, and student-designed majors. The University Without Walls program gives credit for life, military, and work experience. Other special academic features include the Commonwealth Honors College, the National Student Exchange Program, Learning Support Services, the Native American Student Support Program, the Minority and Women in Engineering Programs, the Bilingual Collegiate Program, the Committee for the College Education of Black and Other Minority Students, the United Asian Learning Resource Center, and Residential Academic Programs. There are more than 25 national honor societies, including Phi Beta Kappa, and a freshman honors program.

Faculty/Classroom: 70% of faculty are male; 30%, female. All both teach and do research. No introductory courses are taught by graduate students. The average class size in an introductory lecture is 47; in a laboratory, 24; and in a regular course, 34.

Admissions: 73% of the 2001-2002 applicants were accepted. The SAT I scores for the 2001-2002 freshman class were: Verbal--24% below 500, 45% between 500 and 599, 26% between 600 and 700, and 5% above 700; Math--19% below 500, 45% between 500 and 599, 29% between 600 and 700, and 7% above 700. 51% of the current freshmen were in the top quarter of their class; 89% were in the top half. 52 freshmen graduated first in their class.

Requirements: The SAT I or ACT is required. In addition, applicants must be graduates of an accredited secondary school, or have the GED. The university recommends that students complete 16 Carnegie units, including 4 years of English, 3 years of math, 3 years of natural sciences (including 2 years lab), 2 years of electives, 2 years of foreign language, and 2 years of social sciences. 4 years of math are required for business, computer science, and engineering majors. Students must present a portfolio for admission to the art program and must audition for admission to music and dance. UMass requires applicants to be in the upper 89% of their class. A GPA of 2.0 is required. AP and CLEP credits are accepted. Important factors in the admissions decision are extracurricular activities record, evidence of special talent, and personality/intangible qualities. Applications are accepted on-line at the school's web site.

Procedure: Freshmen are admitted fall and spring. Entrance exams should be taken before February 1. There is a deferred admissions plan. Applications should be filed by February 1 for fall entry and October 15 for spring entry. The application fee is $40 in-state and $50 out-of-state. Notification is sent on a rolling basis, beginning December 15.

Transfer: 1109 transfer students enrolled in 2001-2002. Transfer applicants must submit transcripts from all colleges or universities attended, and an essay. Those with fewer than 30 credits must submit high school transcripts and SAT I scores. Priority is given to students with an associate degree. Grades of C- or better transfer for credit. 45 credits of 120 must be completed at UMass.

Visiting: There are regularly scheduled orientations for prospective students, including twice-daily guided tours and daily information sessions. There are guides for informal visits and visitors may sit in on classes and stay overnight. To schedule a visit, contact the University Tour Service at (413) 545-4237 or the Admissions Office at (413) 545-0222.

Financial Aid: In 2001-2002, 51% of all freshmen and 55% of continuing students received some form of financial aid. The average freshman award was $5526. The average financial indebtedness of the 2001 graduate was $15,256. UMass is a member of CSS. The FAFSA is required. The fall application deadline is March 1.

International Students: There are 359 international students enrolled. They must score 550 on the written TOEFL.

Computers: The mainframe consists of central host computers running on UNIX. There are approximately 325 computers, both PCs and Macs, in 13 computer labs and classrooms throughout the campus. Nearly all residence hall rooms have direct, high-speed connections to the campus network. Students have access to e-mail, the Internet, and the Web. All

students may access the system. There are no time limits. The fee is $30 per semester.
Graduates: In 2001, 4054 bachelor's degrees were awarded. In an average class, 59% graduate in 6 years.
Admissions Contact: Joseph C. Marshall, Assistant Vice Chairman for Enrollment Services. A video is available.
E-mail: *mail@admissions.umass.edu* Web: *www.umass.edu*

UNIVERSITY OF MASSACHUSETTS BOSTON E-2

Boston, MA 02125-3393 (617) 287-6100; Fax: (617) 287-6242

Full-time: 2555 men, 3375 women	**Faculty:** 468; I, -$
Part-time: 2077 men, 2558 women	**Ph.D.s:** 93%
Graduate: 858 men, 1925 women	**Student/Faculty:** 13 to 1
Year: semesters, summer session	**Tuition:** $4227 ($12,357)
Application Deadline: January 11	**Room & Board:** n/app
Freshman Class: 2652 applied, 1539 accepted, 701 enrolled	
SAT I Verbal/Math: 523/535	**COMPETITIVE**

The University of Massachusetts Boston, established in 1964, is a public commuter institution offering undergraduate studies in arts and sciences and in preprofessional training. There are 4 undergraduate and 5 graduate schools. In addition to regional accreditation, UMass Boston has baccalaureate program accreditation with NLN. The library contains 461,078 volumes, 827,117 microform items, and 1885 audiovisual forms/CDs, and subscribes to 2784 periodicals. Computerized library services include the card catalog, interlibrary loans, and database searching. Special learning facilities include a learning resource center, art gallery, radio station, tropical greenhouse, observatory, adaptive computer lab, languages lab, and applied language and math center. The 177-acre campus is in an urban area 5 miles south of downtown Boston. There are 10 buildings.
Student Life: 94% of undergraduates are from Massachusetts. Others are from 37 states, 99 foreign countries, and Canada. 48% are white; 11% African American. The average age of freshmen is 19; all undergraduates, 27. 31% do not continue beyond their first year.
Housing: There are no residence halls. All of students commute. Alcohol is not permitted. All students may keep cars.
Activities: There are no fraternities or sororities. There are 70 groups on campus, including art, band, cheerleading, chess, choir, chorale, chorus, computers, dance, drama, ethnic, film, gay, honors, international, jazz band, literary magazine, musical theater, newspaper, orchestra, photography, political, professional, radio and TV, religious, social, social service, student government, and yearbook. Popular campus events include Convocation Day, seasonal festivals, and lecture series.
Sports: There are 8 intercollegiate sports for men and 7 for women, and 15 intramural sports for men and 13 for women. Facilities include an athletic center with a 3500-seat gym with 4 basketball and 2 volleyball courts, an ice rink that seats 1000, an Olympic-size swimming pool with high-dive area, a multipurpose weight room, and a sports medicine area; an 8-lane, 400-meter track; 8 tennis courts; a softball diamond, 3 multipurpose fields primarily used for soccer and lacrosse, and several other recreational fields; a boat house, dock, and fleet of sailboats and rowing dories; and a fitness center with strength-training equipment, cardiovascular machines, and racquetball and squash courts.
Disabled Students: All of the campus is accessible. Wheelchair ramps, elevators, special parking, specially equipped rest rooms, special class scheduling, lowered drinking fountains, lowered telephones, amplified phones, powered doors, indoor-connected building access, an accessible shuttle bus, an adaptive computer lab, and a center for students with disabilities are available.
Services: Counseling and information services are available, as is tutoring in every subject. There is a reader service for the blind, and remedial math, reading, and writing. There are also reading study skills workshops and a math resource center available.
Campus Safety and Security: Measures include 24-hour foot and vehicle patrol, self-defense education, escort service, and shuttle buses. There are informal discussions, pamphlets/posters/films, emergency telephones, lighted pathways/sidewalks, Operation ID, motorist assistance, and crime prevention programs.
Programs of Study: UMass Boston confers B.A. and B.S. degrees. Master's and doctoral degrees are also awarded. Bachelor's degrees are awarded in BIOLOGICAL SCIENCE (biochemistry and biology/biological science), BUSINESS (management science), COMMUNICATIONS AND THE ARTS (art, classical languages, classics, dramatic arts, English, French, Greek (classical), Italian, Latin, music, Russian, and Spanish), COMPUTER AND PHYSICAL SCIENCE (applied mathematics, chemistry, computer science, mathematics, and physics), EDUCATION (physical), ENGINEERING AND ENVIRONMENTAL DESIGN (engineering physics), HEALTH PROFESSIONS (medical technology and nursing), SOCIAL SCIENCE (African American studies, American studies, anthropology, community services, criminal justice, economics, ethics, politics, and social policy, geography, German area studies, gerontology, history, human services, philosophy, political science/government, psychology, sociology, and women's studies). Management, nursing, and psychology are the largest.

Required: For graduation, students must complete 120 credit hours (123 hours in the College of Nursing) and maintain a minimum GPA of 2.0. Distribution requirements vary by college. All students must demonstrate writing proficiency.

Special: Students may cross-register with Massachusetts College of Art, Bunker Hill Community College, Roxbury Community College, and Hebrew College. Umass Boston also offers cooperative programs, internships, study abroad, work-study programs, student-designed majors, B.A.-B.S. degrees, nondegree study, pass/fail options, and dual and interdisciplinary majors, including anthropology/history, biology/medical technology, philosophy/public policy, and psychology/sociology. Also available are 3-1 and 2-2 engineering programs with various area institutions. The College of Public and Community Service provides social-oriented education, generally to older students. There are 3 national honor societies, and a freshman honors program.

Faculty/Classroom: 53% of faculty are male; 47%, female. All both teach and do research. No introductory courses are taught by graduate students. The average class size in an introductory lecture is 19; in a laboratory, 14; and in a regular course, 20.

Admissions: 58% of the 2001-2002 applicants were accepted. The SAT I scores for the 2001-2002 freshman class were: Verbal--54% below 500, 30% between 500 and 599, 14% between 600 and 700, and 2% above 700; Math--48% below 500, 34% between 500 and 599, 17% between 600 and 700, and 2% above 700. 19% of the current freshmen were in the top fifth of their class; 54% were in the top two fifths.

Requirements: The SAT I or ACT is required. In addition, with a minimum composite score of 890 on the SAT I; test scores are not required of students who have been out of high school for 3 or more years. Applicants should be graduates of an accredited secondary school. The GED is accepted. The university requires the completion of 16 Carnegie units, including 4 years of English, 3 of college preparatory math and science, 2 each of a foreign language and social studies, and 2 electives in the above academic areas or in humanities, arts, or computer science. An essay is recommended. A GPA of 3.0 is required. AP and CLEP credits are accepted. Important factors in the admissions decision are advanced placement or honor courses, recommendations by school officials, and personality/intangible qualities. Applications are accepted on-line via ExPAN and the school's web site.

Procedure: Freshmen are admitted fall and spring. Entrance exams should be taken by the fall of the senior year. There is a deferred admissions plan. Applications should be filed by January 11 for fall entry and August 16 for spring entry. The fall 2001 application fee was $40. Notification is sent on a rolling basis.

Transfer: 1542 transfer students enrolled in 2001-2002. Applicants with fewer than 24 credits must meet freshman requirements. To transfer, students must have a minimum GPA of 2.0 (2.75 for management, nursing, and engineering). Grades of C or better transfer for credit. 30 credits of 120 to 123 must be completed at UMass Boston.

Visiting: There are regularly scheduled orientations for prospective students, including general information sessions about the university and the admissions process and a tour of the campus. There are guides for informal visits and visitors may sit in on classes. To schedule a visit, contact Marketing and Information Services at (617) 287-6000 or *enrollment.information@umb.edu*

Financial Aid: The FAFSA and the college's own financial statement are required. The fall application deadline is March 1.

International Students: There are 615 international students enrolled. The school actively recruits these students. They must score 550 on the written TOEFL or 213 on the electronic version and also take the SAT I if the language of instruction is English, scoring 900.

Computers: The mainframes are DEC VAX models 8800, 6000-410, and 6000-510. Students may access the mainframe through terminals located in the terminal room. There are also a number of PC labs containing Macs, IBMs, and other PCs. Most of the 390 terminals and PCs are located in the library, with the remainder in classroom buildings. All students may access the system 24 hours a day. There are no time limits and no fees.

Graduates: In 2001, 1475 bachelor's degrees were awarded. The most popular majors were management (21%), social science (17%), and psychology (13%). In an average class, 1% graduate in 3 years, 7% in 4 years, 20% in 5 years, and 27% in 6 years.

Admissions Contact: Liliana Mickle, Director, Undergraduate Admissions. E-mail: *undergrad@umb.edu* Web: *www.umb.edu*

UNIVERSITY OF MASSACHUSETTS DARTMOUTH E-4

North Dartmouth, MA 02747-2300 (508) 999-8605
Fax: (508) 999-8755

Full-time: 2594 men, 2750 women	**Faculty:** 352; IIA, +$
Part-time: 523 men, 771 women	**Ph.D.s:** 87%
Graduate: 373 men, 449 women	**Student/Faculty:** 15 to 1
Year: semesters, summer session	**Tuition:** $4129 ($12,283)
Application Deadline: open	**Room & Board:** $5723
Freshman Class: 5070 applied, 3400 accepted, 1197 enrolled	
SAT I Verbal/Math: 520/530	**COMPETITIVE**

University of Massachusetts Dartmouth, founded in 1895, is a public institution that provides undergraduate and graduate programs in the liberal and creative arts and sciences and in professional training. There are 5 undergraduate schools and 1 graduate school. In addition to regional accreditation, UMass Dartmouth has baccalaureate program accreditation with AACSB, ABET, ACS, CSAB, NAACLS, NASAD, NASDTEC, and NLN. The library contains 455,323 volumes, 810,127 microform items, and 12,980 audiovisual forms/CDs, and subscribes to 2925 periodicals. Computerized library services include the card catalog, interlibrary loans, and database searching. Special learning facilities include a learning resource center, art gallery, radio station, TV station, observatory, marine research vessels, and a number of cultural and research centers. The 710-acre campus is in a suburban area approximately 60 miles south of Boston, 35 miles east of Providence, Rhode Island, and 3 miles west of Cape Cod. Including residence halls, there are 20 buildings.

Student Life: 94% of undergraduates are from Massachusetts. Others are from 26 states and 28 foreign countries. 85% are from public schools. 87% are white. The average age of freshmen is 18; all undergraduates, 22. 21% do not continue beyond their first year.

Housing: 2258 students can be accommodated in college housing, which includes coed dormitories and on-campus apartments. In addition, there are honors houses, a quiet house, and apartments for upperclassmen. On-campus housing is guaranteed for all 4 years. 60% of students commute. All students may keep cars.

Activities: 1% of men belong to 1 local and 2 national fraternities; 1% of women belong to 1 national sorority. There are 90 groups on campus, including art, band, cheerleading, choir, chorale, chorus, computers, drama, ethnic, gay, honors, international, jazz band, literary magazine, musical theater, newspaper, orchestra, pep band, political, professional, radio and TV, religious, social, social service, student government, symphony, and yearbook. Popular campus events include Welcome Back Week, Winterfest, and Spring Fling Week.

Sports: There are 11 intercollegiate sports for men and 12 for women, and 10 intramural sports for men and 10 for women. Facilities include a 3000-seat gym, an 1850-seat football stadium, an aquatic sports center, 13 tennis courts, a weight room, a running track, and soccer, softball, and intramural fields.

Disabled Students: 90% of the campus is accessible. Wheelchair ramps, elevators, special parking, specially equipped rest rooms, special class scheduling, lowered drinking fountains, lowered telephones, and mobility assistance, note takers/readers, alternative testing, and an office of disabled student services are available.

Services: Counseling and information services are available, as is tutoring in most subjects, including through the writing/reading, science/engineering, math/business, and academic resource centers. There is a reader service for the blind, and remedial math, reading, and writing.

Campus Safety and Security: Measures include 24-hour foot and vehicle patrol, self-defense education, escort service, and shuttle buses. There are pamphlets/posters/films, emergency telephones, lighted pathways/sidewalks, and bicycle patrol.

Programs of Study: UMass Dartmouth confers B.A., B.S., and B.F.A. degrees. Master's and doctoral degrees are also awarded. Bachelor's degrees are awarded in BIOLOGICAL SCIENCE (biochemistry, biology/biological science, and marine biology), BUSINESS (accounting, banking and finance, business administration and management, management information systems, and marketing/retailing/merchandising), COMMUNICATIONS AND THE ARTS (art history and appreciation, ceramic art and design, design, English, fiber/textiles/weaving, French, graphic design, illustration, metal/jewelry, music, painting, photography, Portuguese, sculpture, Spanish, and technical and business writing), COMPUTER AND PHYSICAL SCIENCE (chemistry, computer science, mathematics, and physics), EDUCATION (art), ENGINEERING AND ENVIRONMENTAL DESIGN (civil engineering, computer engineering, electrical/electronics engineering, materials science, mechanical engineering, and textile technology), HEALTH PROFESSIONS (medical laboratory science and nursing), SOCIAL SCIENCE (anthropology, criminal justice, economics, history, humanities and social science, interdisciplinary studies, philosophy, political science/government, psychology, and sociology). Engineering, physical/life sciences, and design/fine arts are the strongest academically. Design, psychology, and biology are the largest.

Required: The core curriculum requires 9 credits each of communication skills, cultural and artistic literacy, and math/science/technology, 6 each of global awareness and information/computer literacy, and 3 of ethics. Colleges set some additional distribution course requirements. The B.A. requires foreign language study. To graduate, students must complete 120 to 132 credit hours and maintain a 2.0 GPA.

Special: The university permits cross-registration through the SACHEM Consortium of 9 schools in Massachusetts. Study abroad in 9 countries, an engineering or business co-op program, a Washington semester, internships, numerous work-study programs, dual majors, and student-designed majors are available. Teacher certification in elementary and secondary education is available. Nondegree study, pass/fail options, and credit for life experience are possible. There are 5 national honor societies and a freshman honors program.

Faculty/Classroom: 68% of faculty are male; 32%, female. All teach undergraduates and 60% also do research. Graduate students teach 3% of introductory courses. The average class size in an introductory lecture is 28; in a laboratory, 11; and in a regular course, 15.

Admissions: 67% of the 2001-2002 applicants were accepted. The SAT I scores for the 2001-2002 freshman class were: Verbal--35% below 500, 45% between 500 and 599, 17% between 600 and 700, and 2% above 700; Math--32% below 500, 47% between 500 and 599, 19% between 600 and 700, and 2% above 700. 28% of the current freshmen were in the top fifth of their class; 65% were in the top two fifths. In a recent year, 3 freshmen graduated first in their class.

Requirements: The SAT I is required. In addition, applicants should have 4 years of English, 3 each of science and math, 2 of the same foreign language, 1 each of social studies and U.S. history, and 2 of college-preparatory electives. The GED is accepted. An audition is necessary for music majors, and a portfolio is recommended for studio arts and design applicants. All applicants must submit an essay. A GPA of 3.0 is required. AP and CLEP credits are accepted. Important factors in the admissions decision are recommendations by school officials, advanced placement or honor courses, and evidence of special talent.

Procedure: Freshmen are admitted fall and spring. Entrance exams should be taken during the spring of the junior year or early fall of the senior year. There are early decision, early admissions, rolling admissions, and deferred admissions plans. Application deadlines are open. 43 early decision candidates were accepted for the 2001-2002 class. The fall 2001 application fee was $25 (in-state) or $45 (out-of-state).

Transfer: 446 transfer students enrolled in 2001-2002. Applicants must submit all official college transcripts and must take the SAT I unless they graduated from high school more than 3 years prior to applying. Those with fewer than 30 transferable credits must submit high school records. 45 credits of 120 to 132 must be completed at UMass Dartmouth.

Visiting: There are regularly scheduled orientations for prospective students, including scheduled campus tours Monday through Friday and most Saturdays. There are guides for informal visits and visitors may sit in on classes. To schedule a visit, contact the Admissions Office, or sign up through the school's web site.

Financial Aid: The FAFSA is required. The fall application priority deadline is March 1.

International Students: There are 71 international students enrolled. They must score 500 on the written TOEFL and also take the SAT I.

Computers: The mainframe is a DEC ALPHA 2100 cluster. There are several computer labs on campus that have more than 368 PCs available, and computer ports are in every dorm room for students with their own terminal to hook into the university mainframe. All students may access the system during the day and evening as well as on weekends. There are no time limits and no fees. It is strongly recommended that all students have a personal computer.

Graduates: In 2001, 850 bachelor's degrees were awarded. The most popular majors were psychology (8%), sociology (8%), and visual design (8%). In an average class, 25% graduate in 4 years, 39% in 5 years, and 43% in 6 years. 400 companies recruited on campus in 2000-2001.

Admissions Contact: Steve Briggs, Director of Admissions.
E-mail: *admissions@umassd.edu* Web: *www.umassd.edu*

UNIVERSITY OF MASSACHUSETTS LOWELL D-1

Lowell, MA 01854 (978) 934-3931 or (978) 934-3931
(800) 410-4607; Fax: (978) 934-3086

Full-time: 3021 men, 2247 women	**Faculty:** 405; I, av$
Part-time: 2719 men, 1556 women	**Ph.D.s:** 89%
Graduate: 1443 men, 1203 women	**Student/Faculty:** 13 to 1
Year: semesters, summer session	**Tuition:** $4255 ($11,892)
Application Deadline: open	**Room & Board:** $5215
Freshman Class: 3286 applied, 2284 accepted, 979 enrolled	
SAT I Verbal/Math: 519/537	**VERY COMPETITIVE**

The University of Massachussets Lowell, founded in 1895, is a public institution offering undergraduate programs through the schools of arts and sciences, engineering, health professions, management science, and music, and graduate programs in education. There are 5 undergraduate schools and 1 graduate school. In addition to regional accreditation, UMass Lowell has baccalaureate program accreditation with AACSB, ABET, APTA, CAHEA, CSAB, NASAD, NASM, NCATE, and NLN. The

3 libraries contain 810,849 volumes, 1,701,316 microform items, and 7205 audiovisual forms/CDs, and subscribe to 1865 periodicals. Computerized library services include the card catalog, interlibrary loans, and database searching. Special learning facilities include a learning resource center, art gallery, radio station, many experimental and investigative labs, and the Research Foundation, which includes a materials testing division and centers for atmospheric research and tropical disease. The 100-acre campus is in an urban area 30 miles northwest of Boston. Including residence halls, there are 37 buildings.

Student Life: 85% of undergraduates are from Massachusetts. Others are from 42 states, 69 foreign countries, and Canada. 75% are white. The average age of freshmen is 18; all undergraduates, 23. 25% do not continue beyond their first year; 43% remain to graduate.

Housing: 2536 students can be accommodated in college housing, which includes single-sex and coed dormitories, off-campus apartments, and married-student housing. In addition, there are special-interest houses. On-campus housing is available on a first-come, first-served basis. 67% of students commute. All students may keep cars.

Activities: There are no fraternities or sororities. There are 100 groups on campus, including art, band, cheerleading, computers, drama, ethnic, gay, honors, international, marching band, newspaper, pep band, photography, political, professional, radio and TV, religious, social, social service, student government, and yearbook.

Sports: There are 15 intercollegiate sports for men and 10 for women, and 34 intramural sports for men and 34 for women. Facilities include a 2000-seat gym, a pool, weight-training facilities, and areas for gymnastics, wrestling, and judo. There are also courts for handball, squash, and tennis, and various playing fields.

Disabled Students: 70% of the campus is accessible. Wheelchair ramps, elevators, special parking, specially equipped rest rooms, special class scheduling, lowered drinking fountains, and lowered telephones are available.

Services: Counseling and information services are available, as is tutoring in most subjects. There is a reader service for the blind and remedial writing.

Campus Safety and Security: Measures include 24-hour foot and vehicle patrol, escort service, shuttle buses, and informal discussions. There are pamphlets/posters/films, emergency telephones, and lighted pathways/sidewalks.

Programs of Study: UMass Lowell confers B.A., B.S., B.F.A., B.L.A., B.M., B.S.B.A., B.S.E., B.S.E.T., B.S.I.M., and B.S.I.T. degrees. Associate, master's, and doctoral degrees are also awarded. Bachelor's degrees are awarded in BIOLOGICAL SCIENCE (biology/biological science), BUSINESS (business administration and management), COMMUNICATIONS AND THE ARTS (English, fine arts, modern language, and music performance), COMPUTER AND PHYSICAL SCIENCE (applied mathematics, chemistry, computer science, information sciences and systems, mathematics, and physics), ENGINEERING AND ENVIRONMENTAL DESIGN (chemical engineering, civil engineering, electrical/electronics engineering, engineering technology, environmental science, industrial administration/management, industrial engineering technology, mechanical engineering, and plastics engineering), HEALTH PROFESSIONS (clinical science, community health work, exercise science, and nursing), SOCIAL SCIENCE (American studies, criminal justice, economics, history, liberal arts/general studies, philosophy, political science/government, psychology, and sociology). Engineering and management are the largest.

Required: All students must complete a minimum of 120 credits with a 2.0 GPA. Core requirements include 6 credits of English composition, 3 credits of human values, and an area distribution requirement of 27 to 29 credits outside the major in behavioral and social science, fine arts and the humanities, and math and the sciences.

Special: Cross-registration, coop, and work-study programs are available, as are opportunities for study abroad. The university offers a combined B.A.-B.S. degree in engineering, and dual majors and nondegree study, as well as pass/fail options. There are 2 national honor societies, and a freshman honors program.

Faculty/Classroom: 72% of faculty are male; 28%, female. All teach undergraduates.

Admissions: 70% of the 2001-2002 applicants were accepted. The SAT I scores for the 2001-2002 freshman class were: Verbal--38% below 500, 46% between 500 and 599, 14% between 600 and 700, and 2% above 700; Math--28% below 500, 50% between 500 and 599, 19% between 600 and 700, and 3% above 700.

Requirements: The SAT I or ACT is required. The SAT I is preferred. In addition, applicants should have a high school diploma or the GED. The university recommends that secondary preparation include 4 courses in English, 3 each in social science/history and math, 2 each in science and a foreign language, and 2 academic electives. Prospective music majors must audition, and an interview is recommended for all students. A GPA of 3.0 is required. AP and CLEP credits are accepted.

Procedure: Freshmen are admitted fall and spring. Entrance exams should be taken by January of the senior year. There is a deferred admissions plan. Application deadlines are open. The application fee is $20.

Transfer: 781 transfer students enrolled in 2001-2002. Transfer applicants must present at least a 2.0 GPA in previous college work, and must complete at least 30 credits in residence for a bachelor's degree. Those with fewer than 30 credits must meet freshman admission requirements. 30 credits of 120 must be completed at UMass Lowell.

Visiting: There are regularly scheduled orientations for prospective students. To schedule a visit, contact the Office of Student Services at (978) 934-2105.

Financial Aid: In 2001-2002, 44% of all freshmen and 58% of continuing students received some form of financial aid. 39% of freshmen and 49% of continuing students received need-based aid. The average freshman award was $6500. The average financial indebtedness of the 2001 graduate was $15,569. The FAFSA is required. The fall application deadline is March 1.

International Students: There are 177 international students enrolled. They must score 500 on the written TOEFL and also take the SAT I or the ACT.

Computers: The mainframes are a cluster of DEC VAX 6420s, 8700s, and 8800s. 2500 terminals, PCs, and workstations are linked to more than 150 multiuser systems in a campuswide communications network. All students may access the system. There are no time limits and no fees.

Graduates: In 2001, 1113 bachelor's degrees were awarded. The most popular majors were business administration (21%), criminal justice (11%), and psychology (8%). In an average class, 21% graduate in 4 years, 35% in 5 years, and 37% in 6 years.

Admissions Contact: Lisa Johnson, Director, Admissions.
Web: *admissions@uml.edu*

WELLESLEY COLLEGE — D-2

Wellesley, MA 02481 — **(781) 283-2270; Fax: (781) 283-3678**

Full-time: 2201 women	**Faculty:** 223; IIB, ++$
Part-time: 12 men, 60 women	**Ph.D.s:** 97%
Graduate: none	**Student/Faculty:** 10 to 1
Year: semesters	**Tuition:** $25,504
Application Deadline: January 15	**Room & Board:** $7890
Freshman Class: 3047 applied, 1299 accepted, 582 enrolled	
SAT I Verbal/Math: 679/666	**ACT:** 29 **MOST COMPETITIVE**

Wellesley College, established in 1870, is a small, private, diverse liberal arts and sciences college for women. The 5 libraries contain more than 1 million volumes, 488,721 microform items, and 22,777 audiovisual forms/CDs, and subscribe to 4945 periodicals. Computerized library services include the card catalog, interlibrary loans, and database searching. Special learning facilities include a learning resource center, art gallery, radio station, science center, botanic greenhouse, observatory, center for developmental studies and services, centers for research on women and child study, and media and technology center. The 500-acre campus is in a suburban area 12 miles west of Boston. Including residence halls, there are 64 buildings.

Student Life: 80% of undergraduates are from out of state, mostly the Middle Atlantic. Others are from 50 states, 60 foreign countries, and Canada. 63% are from public schools. 48% are white; 25% Asian American. The average age of freshmen is 18; all undergraduates, 20. 5% do not continue beyond their first year; 87% remain to graduate.

Housing: 2120 students can be accommodated in college housing, which includes single-sex dormitories. In addition, there are language houses, language corridors, co-ops, and special-interest houses. On-campus housing is guaranteed for all 4 years. 97% of students live on campus. Upperclassmen may keep cars.

Activities: There are no fraternities or sororities. There are 160 groups on campus, including art, choir, chorus, computers, dance, debate, drama, ethnic, film, gay, honors, international, jazz band, literary magazine, musical theater, newspaper, orchestra, photography, political, professional, radio and TV, religious, social, social service, student government, symphony, and yearbook. Popular campus events include Parents Weekend, Step-Singing, and Hoop-Rolling.

Sports: Facilities include an indoor pool, dance studios, a weight room, an indoor track, a golf course, and courts for racquetball, squash, tennis, and volleyball.

Disabled Students: All of the campus is accessible. Wheelchair ramps, elevators, special parking, specially equipped rest rooms, special class scheduling, lowered drinking fountains, lowered telephones, specially equipped dormitories, and signage in Braille are available.

Services: Counseling and information services are available, as is tutoring in every subject. There is a reader service for the blind.

Campus Safety and Security: Measures include 24-hour foot and vehicle patrol, self-defense education, escort service, and shuttle buses. There are informal discussions, pamphlets/posters/films, emergency telephones, and lighted pathways/sidewalks.

Programs of Study: Wellesley confers the B.A. degree. Bachelor's degrees are awarded in BIOLOGICAL SCIENCE (biochemistry, biology/biological science, biophysics, and neurosciences), COMMUNICATIONS AND THE ARTS (art history and appreciation, Chinese, comparative literature, dramatic arts, English, fine arts, French, German, Greek, Italian,

Japanese, languages, Latin, music, Russian, Spanish, and studio art), COMPUTER AND PHYSICAL SCIENCE (astronomy, chemistry, computer science, geology, mathematics, and physics), EDUCATION (elementary and secondary), ENGINEERING AND ENVIRONMENTAL DESIGN (architecture), SOCIAL SCIENCE (African American studies, American studies, anthropology, Asian/Oriental studies, classical/ancient civilization, cognitive science, economics, European studies, history, international relations, Judaic studies, Latin American studies, medieval studies, peace studies, philosophy, political science/government, psychobiology, psychology, religion, sociology, and women's studies). Psychology, English, and economics are the largest.

Required: All students must complete 32 units, at least 8 of which are in the major field, with a minimum 2.0 GPA. Requirements include 3 courses each in humanities, social science, and natural science and math; 1 multicultural course; 1 semester of expository writing in any department; and 8 credits in phys ed. Students must also possess proficiency in a modern or ancient foreign language. A thesis is required for departmental honors. A quantitative reasoning requirement must be satisfied by all students.

Special: Students may cross-register at MIT, Brandeis University, or Babson College. Exchange programs are available with Spelman College in Georgia and Mills College in California, with members of the 12-College Exchange, with Williams College in Maritime Studies, and with the National Theatre Institute. Study abroad is possible in Wellesley-administered programs in various countries, in exchange programs in Russia and Japan, and at Cambridge and Oxford in England. There are summer internship programs in Boston and Washington, D.C. Dual majors, student-designed majors, nondegree study, and pass/fail options are possible. A 3-2 program with MIT awards a B.A.-B.S. degree. There are 2 national honor societies, including Phi Beta Kappa, and 51 departmental honors programs.

Faculty/Classroom: 40% of faculty are male; 60%, female. All both teach and do research. The average class size in an introductory lecture is 25; in a laboratory, 15; and in a regular course, 21.

Admissions: 43% of the 2001-2002 applicants were accepted. The SAT I scores for the 2001-2002 freshman class were: Verbal--1% below 500, 11% between 500 and 599, 42% between 600 and 700, and 46% above 700; Math--2% below 500, 13% between 500 and 599, 52% between 600 and 700, and 33% above 700. The ACT scores were 47% above 29. 87% of the current freshmen were in the top fifth of their class; 99% were in the top two fifths.

Requirements: The SAT I and 3 SAT IIs (including the writing test), or the ACT, are required. Wellesley College does not require a fixed plan of secondary school course preparation. Entering students normally have completed 4 years of college preparatory studies in secondary school that include training in clear and coherent writing and interpreting literature; history; principles of math (typically 4 years); competence in at least 1 foreign language, ancient or modern (usually 4 years of study); and experience in at least 2 lab sciences. An essay is required, and an interview is recommended. AP credits are accepted. Important factors in the admissions decision are advanced placement or honor courses and extracurricular activities record. Applications are accepted on-line at the college's web site or via Common App.

Procedure: Freshmen are admitted in the fall. Entrance exams should be taken during the spring of the junior year or fall of the senior year (no later than December). There are early decision and deferred admissions plans. Early decision applications should be filed by November 1; regular applications, by January 15 for fall entry. The fall 2001 application fee was $50. Notification of early decision is sent December 15; regular decision, April 1. 125 early decision candidates were accepted for the 2001-2002 class. 17% of all applicants are on a waiting list.

Transfer: 29 transfer students enrolled in 2001-2002. Applicants must provide high school and college transcripts and SAT I scores. An interview is required. 16 credits of 32 must be completed at Wellesley.

Visiting: There are guides for informal visits and visitors may sit in on classes and stay overnight. To schedule a visit, contact the Admissions Office.

Financial Aid: In 2001-2002, 56% of all freshmen and 54% of continuing students received some form of financial aid, including need-based aid. The average freshman award was $19,686. Average annual earnings from campus work are $1800. The average financial indebtedness of the 2001 graduate was $15,467. Wellesley is a member of CSS. The CSS/Profile or FAFSA, the college's own financial statement, and the most recent income tax returns of parents and student are required. The fall application deadline is January 15.

International Students: There are 162 international students enrolled. The school actively recruits these students. They must score 600 on the written TOEFL or 250 on the electronic version or take the ELPT or the APIEL and also take the SAT I or the ACT. Students must take SAT II: Subject tests in writing and 2 other areas.

Computers: The mainframes are comprised of a DEC VAX 8550 and a Digital AXP. Students may access the mainframe through more than 200 PCs located in the science center, library, and dormitories. All students may access the system. There are no time limits and no fees.

Graduates: In 2001, 601 bachelor's degrees were awarded. The most popular majors were economics (9%), psychology (9%), and English (9%). In an average class, 86% graduate in 4 years, 89% in 5 years, and 90% in 6 years. 124 companies recruited on campus in 2000-2001. Of the 2000 graduating class, 19% were enrolled in graduate school within 6 months of graduation and 77% were employed.

Admissions Contact: Janet Lavin Rapelye, Dean of Admission. A video is available. E-mail: *admission@wellesley.edu*
Web: *www.wellesley.edu*

WENTWORTH INSTITUTE OF TECHNOLOGY E-2

Boston, MA 02115 **(617) 989-4000**
(800) 556-0610; Fax: (617) 989-4010

Full-time: 2045 men, 490 women	**Faculty:** 122
Part-time: 624 men, 114 women	**Ph.D.s:** 30%
Graduate: none	**Student/Faculty:** 21 to 1
Year: semesters, summer session	**Tuition:** $13,650
Application Deadline: May 1	**Room & Board:** $6800
Freshman Class: 3623 applied, 2548 accepted, 1018 enrolled	
SAT I Verbal/Math: 483/519	**COMPETITIVE**

Wentworth Institute of Technology, founded in 1904, is a private college specializing in architecture, design, engineering, technology, and management. In addition to regional accreditation, WIT has baccalaureate program accreditation with ABET, ACCE, FIDER, IACBE, and NAAB. The library contains 77,000 volumes, 90 microform items, and 750 audiovisual forms/CDs, and subscribes to 500 periodicals. Computerized library services include the card catalog, interlibrary loans, and database searching. Special learning facilities include a learning resource center, radio station, printed-circuit lab, CAD/CAM/CAE labs, design studios, and numerically controlled manufacturing systems. The 30-acre campus is in an urban area in Boston. Including residence halls, there are 27 buildings.

Student Life: 65% are white. The average age of freshmen is 20; all undergraduates, 22. 33% do not continue beyond their first year.

Housing: 1665 students can be accommodated in college housing, which includes coed dormitories and on-campus apartments. On-campus housing is available on a first-come, first-served basis and is available on a lottery system for upperclassmen. Priority is given to out-of-town students. Upperclassmen may keep cars.

Activities: There are no fraternities or sororities. There are 40 groups on campus, including computers, dance, drama, ethnic, gay, honors, international, literary magazine, musical theater, newspaper, orchestra, professional, radio and TV, religious, social, social service, student government, and yearbook. Popular campus events include Design Lecture Series, Beaux Arts Ball, and Women's History Month.

Sports: There are 9 intercollegiate sports for men and 6 for women, and 5 intramural sports for men and 5 for women. Facilities include gyms, tennis courts, a riflery range, a fitness center, an outdoor basketball court, and softball, soccer, and lacrosse playing fields.

Disabled Students: 30% of the campus is accessible. Wheelchair ramps, elevators, special parking, specially equipped rest rooms, special class scheduling, lowered drinking fountains, and lowered telephones are available.

Services: Counseling and information services are available, as is tutoring in every subject. There is remedial math and writing. Free tutoring is available to all students through the learning center.

Campus Safety and Security: Measures include 24-hour foot and vehicle patrol, self-defense education, escort service, and shuttle buses. There are pamphlets/posters/films, emergency telephones, and lighted pathways/sidewalks. All campus police officers have emergency medical training.

Programs of Study: WIT confers B.S. and B.Arch. degrees. Associate degrees are also awarded. Bachelor's degrees are awarded in COMMUNICATIONS AND THE ARTS (industrial design), COMPUTER AND PHYSICAL SCIENCE (computer science), ENGINEERING AND ENVIRONMENTAL DESIGN (architectural technology, architecture, civil engineering technology, computer technology, construction management, construction technology, electrical/electronics engineering technology, electromechanical technology, environmental engineering, industrial administration/management, interior design, mechanical engineering technology, and technological management). Architectural engineering technology, computer science, and electronic engineering technology are the largest.

Required: For a bachelor's degree, students must complete a total of 136 to 176 hours, depending on the major, with a minimum GPA of 2.0 overall and 2.5 in the major. An introductory computer course is required of all students.

Special: WIT offers extensive cooperative programs; cross-registration with other members of the Colleges of the Fenway Consortium; study abroad, including study in France for third-year architecture students; interdisciplinary majors, including engineering technology and facilities planning and management; a dual major in technical management; and nondegree study. Most students at the bachelor's level attend school in the summer, as most cooperative work occurs during the academic year. There is 1 national honor society.

Faculty/Classroom: 76% of faculty are male; 24%, female. All teach undergraduates. The average class size in an introductory lecture is 28; in a laboratory, 28; and in a regular course, 25.

Admissions: 70% of the 2001-2002 applicants were accepted. The SAT I scores for the 2001-2002 freshman class were: Verbal--58% below 500, 32% between 500 and 599, 9% between 600 and 700, and 1% above 700; Math--39% below 500, 44% between 500 and 599, 15% between 600 and 700, and 2% above 700.

Requirements: The SAT I or ACT is required. In addition, applicants must be graduates of an accredited secondary school or have the GED. High school course requirements vary by major. AP and CLEP credits are accepted. Important factors in the admissions decision are advanced placement or honor courses, leadership record, and extracurricular activities record. Applications are accepted on computer disk and on-line via CollegeLink and through WIT's web site.

Procedure: Freshmen are admitted fall and spring. Entrance exams should be taken in the spring of the junior year or the fall of the senior year. There is a deferred admissions plan. Applications should be filed by May 1 for fall entry and December 1 for spring entry. The fall 2001 application fee was $30. Notification is sent on a rolling basis. A waiting list is an active part of the admissions procedure.

Transfer: 144 transfer students enrolled in 2001-2002. Requirements for transfer students vary by program. All applicants must submit official college and high school transcripts. Portfolios and faculty reviews are recommended of applicants to industrial design, interior design, and architecture programs. Grades of C or better transfer for credit. Transfer students must take 50% of the course work in their degree program at Wentworth in order to graduate.

Visiting: There are regularly scheduled orientations for prospective students, including a 2-day orientation with an optional overnight stay. There are guides for informal visits and visitors may sit in on classes and stay overnight. To schedule a visit, contact the Admissions Office.

Financial Aid: In 2001-2002, 76% of all freshmen and 43% of continuing students received some form of financial aid. 57% of freshmen and 43% of continuing students received need-based aid. The average freshman award was $6725. Of that total, scholarships or need-based grants averaged $1000; loans averaged $2625; work contracts averaged $1600; and Gate Loans averaged $1500. 29% of undergraduates work part time. Average annual earnings from campus work are $1600. The average financial indebtedness of the 2001 graduate was $10,199. The FAFSA is required. The fall application deadline is March 1.

International Students: There are 225 international students enrolled. The school actively recruits these students. They must score 525 on the written TOEFL or 197 on the electronic version or take the MELAB. They must also take the SAT I or the ACT, with the SAT I recommended.

Computers: The mainframe is a DEC VAX 400/300. The academic VAX may be accessed via 30 terminals and several modems, as well as from 115 networked PCs in various student labs. In addition, 122 Pentium systems and 47 Mac and Power Mac systems, all networked, are available in student labs throughout the institute. All students may access the system. There are no time limits and no fees. It is strongly recommended that all students have a personal computer.

Graduates: In a recent class, the most popular majors were architecture/architectural engineering (16%), construction management (12%), and electronic engineering (9%). In an average class, 48% graduate in 4 years. 42 companies recruited on campus in a recent year. Of a recent graduating class, 2% were enrolled in graduate school within 6 months of graduation and 81% were employed.

Admissions Contact: Keiko Broomhead, Director of Financial Aid. E-mail: *admissions@wit.edu* Web: *http://www.wit.edu*

WESTERN NEW ENGLAND COLLEGE B-3

Springfield, MA 01119 **(413) 782-1321**
(800) 325-1122; Fax: (413) 782-1777

Full-time: 1167 men, 893 women	**Faculty:** 122; IIA, +$
Part-time: 808 men, 223 women	**Ph.D.s:** 88%
Graduate: 894 men, 555 women	**Student/Faculty:** 17 to 1
Year: semesters, summer session	**Tuition:** $16,494
Application Deadline: open	**Room & Board:** $7388

Freshman Class: 4068 applied, 3028 accepted, 663 enrolled
SAT I Verbal/Math: 510/530 **COMPETITIVE**

Western New England College, founded in 1919, is a private institution offering undergraduate programs in business, engineering, and liberal arts. There are 3 undergraduate and 2 graduate schools. In addition to regional accreditation, WNEC has baccalaureate program accreditation with ABET and CSWE. The library contains 119,000 volumes, 363,142 microform items, and 5815 audiovisual forms/CDs, and subscribes to 266 periodicals. Computerized library services include the card catalog, interlibrary loans, and database searching. Special learning facilities include an art gallery and radio station. The 215-acre campus is in a suburban area 90 miles west of Boston. Including residence halls, there are 33 buildings.

Student Life: 56% of undergraduates are from out of state, mostly the Northeast. Others are from 27 states and 14 foreign countries. 87% are white. 11% are Catholic. 25% do not continue beyond their first year; 51% remain to graduate.

Housing: 1600 students can be accommodated in college housing, which includes single-sex and coed dormitories and on-campus apartments. In addition, students are often grouped by academic interest areas or in theme housing. On-campus housing is guaranteed for all 4 years. 79% of students live on campus. All students may keep cars.

Activities: There are no fraternities or sororities. There are 60 groups on campus, including art, cheerleading, chorus, computers, dance, drama, ethnic, honors, international, jazz band, literary magazine, newspaper, pep band, photography, political, professional, radio and TV, religious, social, social service, student government, and yearbook. Popular campus events include Spring Week, Family and Friends Weekend, and Winter Week.

Sports: There are 10 intercollegiate sports for men and 9 for women, and 9 intramural sports for men and 9 for women. Facilities include a healthful living center equipped for basketball (2000 seats), wrestling, racquetball, squash, aerobics, fitness, and volleyball, as well as a weight room, an 8-lane pool, and a track. There is also a 1200-seat football stadium.

Disabled Students: 90% of the campus is accessible. Wheelchair ramps, elevators, special parking, specially equipped rest rooms, special class scheduling, lowered drinking fountains, and lowered telephones are available.

Services: Counseling and information services are available, as is tutoring in most subjects.

Campus Safety and Security: Measures include 24-hour foot and vehicle patrol, self-defense education, escort service, and shuttle buses. There are informal discussions, pamphlets/posters/films, emergency telephones, lighted pathways/sidewalks, security cameras, medical response, fire response, and a comprehensive public safety awareness program.

Programs of Study: WNEC confers B.A., B.S., B.S.B.A., B.S.E., B.S.E.E., B.S.I.E., B.S.M.E., and B.S.W. degrees. Associate, master's, and doctoral degrees are also awarded. Bachelor's degrees are awarded in BIOLOGICAL SCIENCE (biology/biological science), BUSINESS (accounting, banking and finance, business administration and management, management science, marketing/retailing/merchandising, and sports management), COMMUNICATIONS AND THE ARTS (advertising and English), COMPUTER AND PHYSICAL SCIENCE (chemistry, computer science, information sciences and systems, and mathematics), EDUCATION (elementary and secondary), ENGINEERING AND ENVIRONMENTAL DESIGN (bioengineering, electrical/electronics engineering, environmental science, industrial engineering, and mechanical engineering), SOCIAL SCIENCE (criminal justice, economics, history, international studies, law enforcement and corrections, political science/government, psychology, social work, and sociology). Engineering is the strongest academically. Criminal justice, management, and sports management are the largest.

Required: To graduate, students must complete 122 credit hours, with a minimum GPA of 2.0. Requirements include 2 courses each in English, math, lab science, and phys ed, and 1 course each in history, culture, and computers. A first-year seminar is also required for freshmen. Other requirements vary according to the major.

Special: Students may cross-register with cooperating colleges of Greater Springfield. The college offers internships, study abroad, a Washington semester, work-study programs, B.A.-B.S. degrees, an accelerated degree program, and dual and student-designed majors. The 3+3 law program offers qualified students the opportunity to earn a J.D. in 6 years. Pharmacy and physician assistant programs are offered in association with the Massachusetts College of Pharmacy and Health Sciences. There are 6 national honor societies, and a freshman honors program.

Faculty/Classroom: 75% of faculty are male; 25%, female. No introductory courses are taught by graduate students. The average class size in an introductory lecture is 23; in a laboratory, 20; and in a regular course, 20.

Admissions: 74% of the 2001-2002 applicants were accepted. The SAT I scores for the 2001-2002 freshman class were: Verbal--43% below 500, 45% between 500 and 599, 11% between 600 and 700, and 1% above 700; Math--34% below 500, 47% between 500 and 599, 18% between 600 and 700, and 1% above 700. 28% of the current freshmen were in the top fifth of their class; 59% were in the top two fifths. 1 freshman graduated first in the class.

Requirements: The SAT I or ACT is required. In addition, applicants must be graduates of an approved secondary school and must have completed 4 years of high school English, 2 or more years of math, 1 or more years of science, and 1 year of history. An interview is recommended. The preferred service is *massmentor.edu*. A GPA of 2.2 is required. AP and CLEP credits are accepted. Important factors in the admissions decision are advanced placement or honor courses, extracurricular activities record, and recommendations by school officials. Applications are accepted on-line.

Procedure: Freshmen are admitted fall and spring. Entrance exams should be taken in the spring of the junior year or fall of the senior year. There are early admissions and deferred admissions plans. Application deadlines are open. The application fee is $30. Notification is sent on a rolling basis.

Transfer: 109 transfer students enrolled in a recent year. Applicants must have a minimum GPA of 2.3. Grades of C or better transfer for credit. The college admits transfer students in the fall and spring. 30 credits of 122 must be completed at WNEC.

Visiting: There are regularly scheduled orientations for prospective students, including 7 open houses. There are guides for informal visits and visitors may sit in on classes and stay overnight. To schedule a visit, contact the Undergraduate Admissions Office.

Financial Aid: In 2000-2001, 83% of all freshmen and 61% of continuing students received some form of financial aid. 73% of freshmen and 53% of continuing students received need-based aid. The average freshman award was $10,896. Of that total, scholarships or need-based grants averaged $7193 ($24,650 maximum); loans averaged $2801 ($10,625 maximum); and work contracts averaged $2137 ($2400 maximum). 31% of undergraduates work part time. Average annual earnings from campus work are $1067. WNEC is a member of CSS. The FAFSA and federal tax returns are required. The fall application deadline is rolling.

International Students: There are 17 international students enrolled. They must score 500 on the written TOEFL or 173 on the electronic version.

Computers: The mainframe is a Data General MV/40000 HAII. There are 300 PCs/terminals in 6 labs in various locations on campus. All students have e-mail and Internet access from residence hall rooms. All students may access the system at varying hours from campus labs; 24 hours a day from residence halls. There are no time limits and no fees.

Graduates: In 2001, 693 bachelor's degrees were awarded. The most popular majors were accounting (7%), criminal justice (7%), and psychology (4%). In an average class, 42% graduate in 4 years, 50% in 5 years, and 53% in 6 years. 32 companies recruited on campus in 2000-2001. Of the 2000 graduating class, 8% were enrolled in graduate school within 6 months of graduation and 87% were employed.

Admissions Contact: Dr. Charles R. Pollock, Dean of Enrollment Management. A video is available. E-mail: *ugradmis@wnec.edu*
Web: *www.wnec.edu*

WESTFIELD STATE COLLEGE — B-3

Westfield, MA 01086-1630 — (413) 572-5218
(800) 322-8401; Fax: (413) 572-0520

Full-time: 1592 men, 1985 women — **Faculty:** 171; IIA, --$
Part-time: 207 men, 278 women — **Ph.D.s:** 81%
Graduate: 113 men, 241 women — **Student/Faculty:** 21 to 1
Year: semesters, summer session — **Tuition:** $3556 ($9636)
Application Deadline: March 1 — **Room & Board:** $4838
Freshman Class: 3528 applied, 2354 accepted, 968 enrolled
SAT I: required — **COMPETITIVE**

Westfield State College, founded in 1838, is a public college with liberal arts and teacher preparation programs and professional training. There is 1 undergraduate and 1 graduate school. In addition to regional accreditation, 577 Westfield State has baccalaureate program accreditation with CAAHEP and CSWE. The library contains 124,363 volumes, 547,002 microform items, and 2379 audiovisual forms/CDs, and subscribes to 819 periodicals. Computerized library services include the card catalog, interlibrary loans, and database searching. Special learning facilities include a learning resource center, art gallery, radio station, TV station, and a geology museum. The 257-acre campus is in a rural area 15 miles west of Springfield. Including residence halls, there are 14 buildings.

Student Life: 93% of undergraduates are from Massachusetts. Others are from 20 states, 1 foreign countries, and Canada. 78% are white. The average age of freshmen is 18; all undergraduates, 20. 26% do not continue beyond their first year.

Housing: 2114 students can be accommodated in college housing, which includes coed dormitories and on-campus apartments. In addition, there is a living-learning unit, special housing for disabled students, and international student housing. On-campus housing is guaranteed for all 4 years. 59% of students live on campus; of those, 70% remain on campus on weekends. Upperclassmen may keep cars.

Activities: There are no fraternities or sororities. There are 50 groups on campus, including art, band, chess, choir, chorale, chorus, drama, ethnic, gay, honors, jazz band, literary magazine, musical theater, newspaper, orchestra, pep band, photography, political, professional, radio and TV, religious, social service, student government, and yearbook. Popular campus events include Halloween Dance, Spring Weekend, and Comedy Night.

Sports: There are 6 intercollegiate sports for men and 8 for women, and 11 intramural sports for men and 11 for women. Facilities include a track, baseball and softball fields, tennis courts, a 400-seat gym, and a 5000-seat stadium.

Disabled Students: 60% of the campus is accessible. Wheelchair ramps, elevators, special parking, specially equipped rest rooms, special class scheduling, and lowered telephones are available.

Services: Counseling and information services are available, as is tutoring in every subject. There is a reader service for the blind, and remedial math, reading, and writing.

Campus Safety and Security: Measures include 24-hour foot and vehicle patrol, escort service, shuttle buses, and pamphlets/posters/films. There are emergency telephones and lighted pathways/sidewalks.

Programs of Study: 577 Westfield State confers B.A., B.S., and B.S.E degrees. Master's degrees are also awarded. Bachelor's degrees are awarded in BIOLOGICAL SCIENCE (biology/biological science), BUSINESS (business administration and management), COMMUNICATIONS AND THE ARTS (communications, dramatic arts, English, fine arts, and music), COMPUTER AND PHYSICAL SCIENCE (computer science, information sciences and systems, and mathematics), EDUCATION (art, business, early childhood, elementary, middle school, music, science, secondary, and special), ENGINEERING AND ENVIRONMENTAL DESIGN (environmental science), SOCIAL SCIENCE (criminal justice, economics, history, interdisciplinary studies, physical fitness/movement, political science/government, psychology, social work, sociology, and urban studies). Computer science, English, and psychology are the strongest academically. Criminal justice, education, and business are the largest.

Required: Students must complete a total of 120 credit hours, with 43 or more credits in 8 specified areas and 30 to 40 hours in the major. The college requires a 2.0 GPA overall and 2.0 in major courses. U.S. history or government and diversity awareness courses are required.

Special: Students may cross-register through College Academic Program Sharing, National Student Exchange, and Cooperating Colleges of Greater Springfield. Internships are for credit only in conjunction with all major programs. The college offers study abroad in 36 countries, a Washington semester for political science, criminal justice, and psychology majors, dual majors, student-designed majors, and some credit for military experience. There are 8 national honor societies and a freshman honors program.

Faculty/Classroom: 63% of faculty are male; 37%, female. All teach undergraduates. No introductory courses are taught by graduate students. The average class size in an introductory lecture is 28; in a laboratory, 15; and in a regular course, 25.

Admissions: 67% of the 2001-2002 applicants were accepted. The SAT I scores for the 2001-2002 freshman class were: Verbal--40% below 500, 48% between 500 and 599, and 12% between 600 and 700; Math--41% below 500, 48% between 500 and 599, and 11% between 600 and 700.

Requirements: The SAT I is required. In addition, applicants must achieve between a 2.0 and 3.0 cumulative average in academic subjects, contingent upon the SAT I scores. They must be graduates of an accredited secondary school and must have completed 4 years of college preparatory level English, 3 years of math (algebra I and II and geometry), 2 years of social sciences (including 1 year of U.S history), 3 sciences, including 2 with lab, 2 foreign language, and 2 years of electives. The GED is accepted. A portfolio is required for admission to the art program, and an audition is necessary for admission to the music program. Applications are accepted on-line at *http://infowise.wsc.ma.edu*. A GPA of 2.0 is required. AP and CLEP credits are accepted. Important factors in the admissions decision are advanced placement or honor courses, leadership record, and evidence of special talent.

Procedure: Freshmen are admitted fall and spring. Entrance exams should be taken in the spring of the junior year and fall of the senior year. There is a deferred admissions plan. Applications should be filed by March 1 for fall entry and November 15 for spring entry along with an application fee of $25 for in-state applicants and $40 for all others. Notification is sent on a rolling basis.

Transfer: 224 transfer students enrolled in 2001-2002. Transfer students must have 24 transferable credits with a minimum cumulative GPA of 2.0 (higher for some majors). A grade of C- or better with a 2.0 GPA will transfer for credit. Of the 120 credits required for a bachelor's degree, a minimum of 30 credits must be completed at the college. Transfer students are admitted in the fall and spring. 30 credits of 120 must be completed at Westfield State.

Visiting: There are regularly scheduled orientations for prospective students, including a campus tour, classroom observation, academic department presentations, lunch with faculty, staff, and students, and a question-and-answer session moderated by a panel of administrators. There are guides for informal visits. To schedule a visit, contact the Admission Office.

Financial Aid: In a recent year, 69% of all freshmen and 68% of continuing students received some form of financial aid. 45% of freshmen and 42% of continuing students received need-based aid. The average freshman award was $5044. Of that total, scholarships or need-based grants averaged $2949 ($9015 maximum); loans averaged $3358

($14,625 maximum); work contracts averaged $1195 ($1750 maximum); and supplemental nonneed-based loans $1202 ($3312 maximum). 21% of undergraduates work part time. The average financial indebtedness of a recent year's graduate was $9370. 577 Westfield State is a member of CSS. The FAFSA is required. The fall application deadline is March 1.

International Students: They must score 550 on the written TOEFL and also take the SAT I.

Computers: The mainframe is a DEC ALPHA. There are 200 public access PCs in 9 campus labs supporting both Mac and PC platforms. The campus network has 650 nodes. Residence halls are fully wired for Internet access and about a quarter of resident students are connected. All students may access the system. There are no time limits and no fees.

Graduates: In 2001, 840 bachelor's degrees were awarded. The most popular majors were criminal justice (20%), elementary education (15%), and business management (13%). In an average class, 37% graduate in 4 years, 52% in 5 years, and 53% in 6 years. 80 companies recruited on campus in 2000-2001.

Admissions Contact: Michelle Mattie, Director of Student Admin. Service Center. A video is available. E-mail: *admission@wsc.ma.edu* Web: *www.wsc.ma.edu*

WHEATON COLLEGE

Norton, MA 02766 — **D-3**
(508) 286-8251
(800) 394-6003; Fax: (508) 286-8271

Full-time: 533 men, 999 women	**Faculty:** 96; IIB, +$
Part-time: 4 men, 15 women	**Ph.D.s:** 97%
Graduate: none	**Student/Faculty:** 13 to 1
Year: semesters	**Tuition:** $25,790
Application Deadline: January 15	**Room & Board:** $7150
Freshman Class: 3249 applied, 1974 accepted, 494 enrolled	
SAT I Verbal/Math: 610/590	**ACT:** 25 **VERY COMPETITIVE**

Wheaton College, established in 1834, is an independent liberal arts institution. The library contains 667,930 volumes, 78,388 microform items, and 12,164 audiovisual forms/CDs, and subscribes to 2139 periodicals. Computerized library services include the card catalog, interlibrary loans, and database searching. Special learning facilities include an art gallery, planetarium, radio station, and TV station. The 385-acre campus is in a suburban area 35 miles southeast of Boston and 15 miles north of Providence. Including residence halls, there are 84 buildings.

Student Life: 62% of undergraduates are from out of state, mostly the Northeast. Others are from 40 states and 29 foreign countries. 61% are from public schools. 82% are white. The average age of freshmen is 18; all undergraduates, 19. 15% do not continue beyond their first year; 72% remain to graduate.

Housing: 1420 students can be accommodated in college housing, which includes single-sex and coed dormitories. In addition, there are language houses, substance awareness, multicultural awareness, international understanding, wellness, and quiet houses. On-campus housing is guaranteed for all 4 years. 98% of students live on campus; of those, 87% remain on campus on weekends. All students may keep cars.

Activities: There are no fraternities or sororities. There are 65 groups on campus, including art, BACCHUS (nonalcoholic events), choir, chorale, chorus, dance, drama, ethnic, film, gay, honors, international, jazz band, literary magazine, musical theater, newspaper, photography, political, radio and TV, religious, social, social service, student government, symphony, and yearbook. Popular campus events include Otis Social Justice Symposium and Award, AutumnFest, and Spring Weekend.

Sports: There are 9 intercollegiate sports for men and 13 for women. Facilities include an 8-lane stretch pool, a field house with 5 tennis courts, 1 outdoor and 3 indoor basketball courts, a 200-meter track, a golf/archery range and batting cage, an 850-seat gym, 7 lighted outdoor tennis courts, a running course, a baseball stadium, 2 athletic fields, an aerobics/dance studio, and a fitness center.

Disabled Students: 50% of the campus is accessible. Wheelchair ramps, elevators, special parking, specially equipped rest rooms, special class scheduling, and lowered telephones are available.

Services: Counseling and information services are available, as is tutoring in most subjects. There is a reader service for the blind and remedial writing. Peer tutoring and note takers for hearing-impaired students are available.

Campus Safety and Security: Measures include 24-hour foot and vehicle patrol, self-defense education, escort service, and informal discussions. There are pamphlets/posters/films, emergency telephones, and lighted pathways/sidewalks.

Programs of Study: Wheaton confers the A.B. degree. Bachelor's degrees are awarded in BIOLOGICAL SCIENCE (biochemistry and biology/biological science), COMMUNICATIONS AND THE ARTS (art history and appreciation, classics, creative writing, English, fine arts, French, German, literature, music, and Russian), COMPUTER AND PHYSICAL SCIENCE (astronomy, chemistry, computer mathematics, computer science, mathematics, and physics), ENGINEERING AND ENVIRONMENTAL DESIGN (environmental science), SOCIAL SCIENCE (American studies, anthropology, Asian/Oriental studies, classical/ancient civilization, economics, Hispanic American studies, history, international relations, Italian studies, philosophy, political science/government, psychology, religion, Russian and Slavic studies, social psychology, sociology, and women's studies). Arts and sciences are the strongest academically. Psychology, economics, and sociology are the largest.

Required: Among the requirements for graduation are 32 course credits (4 semester hours each), with a minimum of 10 credits in the major, at least 3 of which are at the 300 level or above. Students must also fulfill general education requirements, complete 2 phys ed courses, and maintain a minimum GPA of 2.0 (C-) in all courses to remain in good academic standing.

Special: Students may cross-register with Brown University as well as with colleges in the Southeastern Association for Cooperation in Higher Education in Massachusetts and with schools participating in the 12 College Exchange Program. Wheaton offers study abroad in 23 countries, internship programs, nondegree study, dual majors, student-designed majors, a Washington semester at American University, and interdisciplinary majors, including math and economics, math and computer science, physics and astronomy, and theater and English dramatic literature. A 3-2 engineering degree is offered with George Washington University, Dartmouth College, and Worcester Polytechnic Institute. Pass/fail options are possible. There are 8 national honor societies, including Phi Beta Kappa, and a freshman honors program.

Faculty/Classroom: 50% of faculty are male; 50%, female. All both teach and do research. The average class size in an introductory lecture is 40; in a laboratory, 20; and in a regular course, 19.

Admissions: 61% of the 2001-2002 applicants were accepted. The SAT I scores for the 2001-2002 freshman class were: Verbal--5% below 500, 34% between 500 and 599, 51% between 600 and 700, and 10% above 700; Math--6% below 500, 45% between 500 and 599, 45% between 600 and 700, and 4% above 700. The ACT scores were 4% between 12 and 17, 19% between 18 and 23, 69% between 24 and 29, and 8% between 30 and 36. 57% of the current freshmen were in the top fifth of their class; 87% were in the top two fifths. There were 10 National Merit semifinalists in a recent year. 3 freshmen graduated first in their class in a recent year.

Requirements: In addition, submission of SAT I or ACT scores is optional. Applicants must be graduates of an accredited secondary school. Recommended courses include English with emphasis on composition skills, 4 years; foreign language and math, 3 to 4 years each; social studies, 3 years; and lab science, 2 to 3 years. The GED is accepted. Wheaton requires an essay and strongly recommends an interview. Applications can be submitted on-line or computer disk via Apply or CollegeLink. AP credits are accepted. Important factors in the admissions decision are advanced placement or honor courses, extracurricular activities record, and leadership record.

Procedure: Freshmen are admitted to all sessions. Entrance exams should be taken in October and/or November. There are early decision, early admissions, and deferred admissions plans. Early decision application should be filed by November 15; regular applications, by January 15 for fall entry. Notification of early decision is sent December 15; regular decision, April 1. 98 early decision candidates were accepted for the 2001-2002 class. 11% of all applicants were on a waiting list in a recent year; 29 were accepted.

Transfer: 8 transfer students enrolled in 2001-2002. Transfer students are encouraged to present a strong B average in their college work to date. Preference will be given to college over high school work. The college transcript is evaluated individually for transfer of credit. 16 credits of 32 must be completed at Wheaton.

Visiting: There are regularly scheduled orientations for prospective students, including class visits, tours, panels on financial aid, student life, and athletics, lunch with faculty, and department open houses. There are guides for informal visits and visitors may sit in on classes and stay overnight. To schedule a visit, contact the Admissions Office.

Financial Aid: In 2001-2002, 67% of all freshmen and 69% of continuing students received some form of financial aid. In a recent year, 56% of freshmen and 59% of continuing students received need-based aid. The average freshman award was $16,908. The average financial indebtedness of the 2001 graduate was $16,903. Wheaton is a member of CSS. The CSS/Profile or FAFSA and if applicable, noncustodial parent's statement and business/farm supplement are required. The fall application deadline is February 1.

International Students: There were 33 international students enrolled in a recent year. The school actively recruits these students. They must score 550 on the written TOEFL.

Computers: 100 public-access PCs are available on campus. All buildings and residence halls are networked, and arriving students are given access to e-mail, the Web, the Internet, and the campus network. All students may access the system 24 hours a day, 7 days a week. There are no time limits and no fees. It is strongly recommended that all students have a personal computer.

Graduates: In a recent year, 337 bachelor's degrees were awarded. The most popular majors were social sciences and history (32%), psychology (20%), and English (12%). In an average class, 70% graduate in 4 years, 71% in 5 years, and 72% in 6 years. 23 companies recruited on campus in a recent year. Of a recent year's graduating class, 28% were enrolled in graduate school within 6 months of graduation and 63% were employed.

Admissions Contact: Gail Berson, Dean of Admission and Student Aid. A video is available. E-mail: *admission@wheatoncollege.edu*
Web: *www.wheatoncollege.edu*

WHEELOCK COLLEGE

Boston, MA 02215-4176 — E-2
(617) 879-2206
(800) 734-5212; Fax: (617) 566-4453

Full-time: 36 men, 571 women	**Faculty:** 52; IIA, -$
Part-time: 9 women	**Ph.D.s:** 78%
Graduate: 31 men, 361 women	**Student/Faculty:** 12 to 1
Year: semesters	**Tuition:** $18,195
Application Deadline: March 1	**Room & Board:** $7325
Freshman Class: 447 applied, 361 accepted, 139 enrolled	
SAT I Verbal/Math: 519/499	**COMPETITIVE**

Wheelock College, established in 1888, is a private institution with programs in education, child life and family studies, social work, and human services. In addition to regional accreditation, Wheelock College has baccalaureate program accreditation with CSWE and NCATE. The library contains 96,273 volumes, 415,264 microform items, and 3756 audiovisual forms/CDs, and subscribes to 547 periodicals. Computerized library services include the card catalog, interlibrary loans, and database searching. Special learning facilities include a learning resource center, art gallery, and the Wheelock Family Theater. The 7-acre campus is in an urban area in Boston. Including residence halls, there are 10 buildings.

Student Life: 65% of undergraduates are from Massachusetts. Others are from 20 states, 6 foreign countries, and Canada. 90% are from public schools. 81% are white. The average age of freshmen is 18; all undergraduates, 20. 15% do not continue beyond their first year; 66% remain to graduate.

Housing: 500 students can be accommodated in college housing, which includes single-sex and coed dormitories. In addition, there is a cooperative living house, and nonsmoking and wellness floors. On-campus housing is guaranteed for all 4 years and is available on a lottery system for upperclassmen. 73% of students live on campus; of those, 50% remain on campus on weekends. Upperclassmen may keep cars.

Activities: There are no fraternities or sororities. There are 25 groups on campus, including choir, chorale, drama, ethnic, gay, honors, international, newspaper, professional, religious, social, social service, and student government. Popular campus events include Kids Day, Family Weekend, and Senior/Sophomore Banquet.

Sports: There are 5 intercollegiate sports for women, and 7 intramural sports for men and 7 for women. Facilities include a sports complex at a neighboring college with a pool and diving board, racquetball courts, a weight room, an indoor track, a basketball court, crew tanks, and cardiovascular equipment.

Disabled Students: 67% of the campus is accessible. Wheelchair ramps, elevators, special parking, specially equipped rest rooms, special class scheduling, lowered drinking fountains, and lowered telephones are available.

Services: Counseling and information services are available, as is tutoring in every subject. There is a reader service for the blind, and remedial math, reading, and writing. Academic support services provide individualized programs upon request.

Campus Safety and Security: Measures include escort service, informal discussions, lighted pathways/sidewalks, and 24-hour foot patrol.

Programs of Study: Wheelock College confers B.A., B.S., and B.S.W. degrees. Master's degrees are also awarded. Bachelor's degrees are awarded in EDUCATION (early childhood, elementary, and special), SOCIAL SCIENCE (child care/child and family studies, human development, and social work). Teaching, social work, and child life are the strongest academically and have the largest enrollments.

Required: To graduate, students must complete between 134 and 140 credit hours, with a minimum GPA of 2.0. Wheelock requires at least a 32-credit major combined with a 36-credit professional studies program. Students must earn 26 credits in English composition, math, human growth and development, children and their environments, first-year seminar, visual and performing arts, and 1 course in first aid.

Special: Wheelock offers cross-registration with all colleges in the Colleges of the Fenway and internships that include student teaching and social work practice. Dual majors, study-abroad programs, and pass/fail options are available. Students may receive credit for life and work experience. Students begin practical field work their freshman year and continue for all 4 years. There is 1 national honor society, and a freshman honors program.

Faculty/Classroom: 17% of faculty are male; 83%, female. 61% teach undergraduates. No introductory courses are taught by graduate students. The average class size in an introductory lecture is 20; in a laboratory, 17; and in a regular course, 15.

Admissions: 81% of the 2001-2002 applicants were accepted. The SAT I scores for the 2001-2002 freshman class were: Verbal--38% below 500, 43% between 500 and 599, 15% between 600 and 700, and 4% above 700; Math--47% below 500, 37% between 500 and 599, 12% between 600 and 700, and 4% above 700. 17% of the current freshmen were in the top fifth of their class; 42% were in the top two fifths. 1 freshman graduated first in their class.

Requirements: The SAT I is required. In addition, applicants must be graduates of an accredited secondary school and must have completed 4 years of English, 3 years of math, and 2 years each of science and history. The GED is accepted. The college requires an essay and recommends an interview. A GPA of 2.0 is required. AP and CLEP credits are accepted. Important factors in the admissions decision are advanced placement or honor courses, evidence of special talent, and personality/intangible qualities. Wheelock subscribes to CollegeLink, CollegeView, and other electronic application services, but requires hard copies of all applications.

Procedure: Freshmen are admitted fall and spring. Entrance exams should be taken in the spring of the junior year and/or fall of the senior year. There are early decision and deferred admissions plans. Early decision applications should be filed by December 1; regular applications, by March 1 for fall entry and December 1 for spring entry. The fall 2001 application fee was $30. Notification of early decision is sent January 1; regular decision, on a rolling basis. 37 early decision candidates were accepted for the 2001-2002 class.

Transfer: 46 transfer students enrolled in 2001-2002. Transfer students must have a minimum GPA of 2.0 and must present 2 letters of recommendation. Grades of C- or better transfer for credit. 67 credits of 134 must be completed at Wheelock College.

Visiting: There are guides for informal visits and visitors may sit in on classes and stay overnight. To schedule a visit, contact the Undergraduate Admissions Office.

Financial Aid: In 2001-2002, 92% of all freshmen and 80% of continuing students received some form of financial aid. 80% of all students received need-based aid. The average freshman award was $13,000. Of that total, scholarships or need-based grants averaged $6900 ($10,000 maximum); loans averaged $5140 ($5625 maximum); and work contracts averaged $1253 ($1300 maximum). 33% of undergraduates work part time. Average annual earnings from campus work are $540. The average financial indebtedness of the 2001 graduate was $19,445. The FAFSA and the college's own financial statement are required. The fall application deadline is March 1.

International Students: There are 3 international students enrolled. They must score 500 on the written TOEFL.

Computers: Students have port-per-pillow access to the Internet through an ATM-backbone campuswide network. All classrooms are equipped with dataports integrating technology into the curriculum. All students may access the system 24 hours a day any time school is in session. There are no time limits and no fees.

Graduates: In 2001, 127 bachelor's degrees were awarded. The most popular majors were teacher education (69%), child life (17%), and social work (14%). In an average class, 63% graduate in 4 years, 65% in 5 years, and 66% in 6 years. 50 companies recruited on campus in 2000-2001. Of the 2000 graduating class, 12% were enrolled in graduate school within 6 months of graduation and 95% were employed.

Admissions Contact: Lynne E. Dailey, Dean of Admissions. A video is available. E-mail: *undergrad@wheelock.edu*
Web: *www.wheelock.edu*

WILLIAMS COLLEGE

Williamstown, MA 01267- — A-1
(413) 597-2211

Full-time: 1060 men, 1020 women	**Faculty:** 211; IIB, ++$
Part-time: 20 men, 20 women	**Ph.D.s:** 97%
Graduate: 20 men, 30 women	**Student/Faculty:** 10 to 1
Year: 4-1-4	**Tuition:** $25,540
Application Deadline: see profile	**Room & Board:** $6830
Freshman Class: n/av	
SAT I or ACT: required	**MOST COMPETITIVE**

Williams College, founded in 1793, is a private institution offering undergraduate degrees in liberal arts and graduate degrees in art history and development economics. Figures in the above capsule are approximate. The 11 libraries contain 834,755 volumes, 484,405 microform items, and 32,729 audiovisual forms/CDs, and subscribe to 2865 periodicals. Computerized library services include the card catalog, interlibrary loans, and database searching. Special learning facilities include a learning resource center, art gallery, planetarium, radio station, a 2500-acre experimental forest, an environmental studies center, a center for foreign languages, literatures, and cultures, a rare book library, and a studio art center. The 450-acre campus is in a small town 150 miles north of New York City and west of Boston. Including residence halls, there are 97 buildings.

Student Life: 86% of undergraduates are from out of state, mostly the Northeast. Others are from 48 states, 32 foreign countries, and Canada. 55% are from public schools. 71% are white. 31% are Protestant; 28% claim no religious affiliation; 22% Catholic; 10% Jewish; 8% other (Buddhist, Islamic, Mormon, Quaker, Seventh Day Adventist). The average age of freshmen is 18; all undergraduates, 20. 3% do not continue beyond their first year; 94% remain to graduate.

Housing: 2001 students can be accommodated in college housing, which includes single-sex and coed dormitories, on-campus apartments, and cooperative housing, in which students prepare their own meals. On-campus housing is guaranteed for all 4 years. 96% of students live on campus. Upperclassmen may keep cars.

Activities: There are no fraternities or sororities. There are 115 groups on campus, including art, band, a capella singing groups, chess, choir, chorale, chorus, comedy group, computers, dance, debate, drama, ethnic, film, gay, handball choir, honors, international, jazz band, literary magazine, marching band, musical theater, newspaper, orchestra, pep band, photography, political, radio and TV, religious, social service, student government, symphony, and yearbook. Popular campus events include Winter Carnival, Mountain Day, and Multicultural Center-sponsored activities.

Sports: There are 16 intercollegiate sports for men and 15 for women, and 17 intramural sports for men and 17 for women. Facilities include 2 gyms, a 50-meter pool, a dance studio, a weight room, rowing tanks, a boathouse, a golf course, playing fields, and courts for tennis, squash, and paddle tennis. The campus stadium seats 6795.

Disabled Students: Wheelchair ramps, elevators, special parking, specially equipped rest rooms, special class scheduling, lowered drinking fountains, lowered telephones, wheelchair lifts, and special laundry and kitchen facilities are available.

Services: Counseling and information services are available, as is tutoring in every subject. There is a reader service for the blind, and remedial math, reading, and writing. Other services include a peer health program, rape and sexual assault hotline, and 10-1 counseling service.

Campus Safety and Security: Measures include 24-hour foot and vehicle patrol, self-defense education, escort service, and informal discussions. There are pamphlets/posters/films, emergency telephones, and lighted pathways/sidewalks.

Programs of Study: Williams confers the B.A. degree. Master's degrees are also awarded. Bachelor's degrees are awarded in BIOLOGICAL SCIENCE (biology/biological science), COMMUNICATIONS AND THE ARTS (art, art history and appreciation, classics, dramatic arts, English, fine arts, French, German, literature, music, Russian, and Spanish), COMPUTER AND PHYSICAL SCIENCE (astronomy, astrophysics, chemistry, computer science, geology, mathematics, and physics), SOCIAL SCIENCE (American studies, anthropology, Asian/Oriental studies, economics, history, philosophy, political science/government, psychology, religion, and sociology). English, psychology, and economics are the largest.

Required: All students must complete 4 winter studies and 32 courses, 9 of which are in the major field, with a C- or higher. Requirements include 3 semester-long courses in each of 3 academic divisions: languages and arts, social sciences, and science and math. Also required are 1 course in cultural pluralism and 4 semesters of phys ed.

Special: Students may cross-register at Bennington or Massachusetts College of Liberal Arts and study abroad in Madrid, Oxford, Cairo, Beijing, and Kyoto, or any approved program with another college or university. Teaching and medical field experiences, dual and student-designed majors, internships, and a 3-2 engineering program with Columbia University and Washington University are offered. There are pass/fail options during the winter term. Each department offers at least one Oxford-model tutorial every year. There are 2 national honor societies, including Phi Beta Kappa.

Faculty/Classroom: 60% of faculty are male; 40%, female. All both teach and do research. No introductory courses are taught by graduate students. The average class size in an introductory lecture is 31; in a laboratory, 14; and in a regular course, 22.

Requirements: The SAT I or ACT is required. In addition, SAT II: Subject tests in 3 subjects are required. Secondary preparation should include 4 years each of English and math, 3 to 4 years of foreign language, and at least 2 years each of science and social studies. A personal essay must be submitted. AP credits are accepted. Important factors in the admissions decision are advanced placement or honor courses, recommendations by school officials, and evidence of special talent. Williams accepts the Common Application and applications via EXPAN, Apply, and College Link.

Procedure: Freshmen are admitted in the fall. There are early decision and deferred admissions plans. A waiting list is an active part of the admissions procedure. Check with the school for current deadlines. The fall 2001 application fee was $50.

Transfer: 9 transfer students enrolled in a recent year. Transfer applicants should present a 3.5 GPA in previous college work and must submit either the SAT I or ACT scores. 2 years must be completed at Williams.

Visiting: There are regularly scheduled orientations for prospective students, consisting of panels, forums, class visits, and campus tours. There are guides for informal visits and visitors may sit in on classes and stay overnight. To schedule a visit, contact the Purple Key Society office at (413) 597-3148.

Financial Aid: In a recent year, 44% of all freshmen and 40% of continuing students received some form of financial aid, including need-based aid. The average freshman award was $22,216. Of that total, scholarships or need-based grants averaged $19,901; loans averaged $2186; work contracts averaged $1462; and summer work averaged $1250. 60% of undergraduates work part time. Average annual earnings from campus work are $800. The average financial indebtedness of the 2001 graduate was $15,625. Williams is a member of CSS. The CSS/Profile or FAFSA and the college's own financial statement are required. Check with the school for current deadlines.

International Students: There were 116 international students enrolled in a recent year. The school actively recruits these students. They must score 600 on the written TOEFL if English is not the applicant's first language, and also take the SAT I or the ACT. Students must take SAT II: Subject tests in English and 2 other subjects.

Computers: The mainframe is a DEC VAX 11/785. The Computer Center houses the mainframe, which has 40 ports, as well as 7 Sun Microsystems workstations and 100 assorted PCs, Macs, and graphics terminals. Additional PCs are located in the library and other academic buildings. All public-access DEC terminals and PCs are networked. All students may access the system. There are no time limits and no fees.

Graduates: In a recent year, 497 bachelor's degrees were awarded. The most popular majors were economics (15%), biology (12%), and English (11%). In an average class, 89% graduate in 4 years, 93% in 5 years, and 94% in 6 years. 100 companies recruited on campus in a recent year.

Admissions Contact: Richard Nesbitt, Director of Admission.
E-mail: *admission@williams.edu* Web: *www.williams.edu/admissions/*

WORCESTER POLYTECHNIC INSTITUTE — C-2

Worcester, MA 01609-2280 **(508) 831-5286; Fax: (508) 831-5875**

Full-time: 2098 men, 610 women	**Faculty:** 212; IIA, ++$
Part-time: 53 men, 10 women	**Ph.D.s:** 98%
Graduate: 798 men, 266 women	**Student/Faculty:** 13 to 1
Year: quarters, summer session	**Tuition:** $24,890
Application Deadline: February 1	**Room & Board:** $7900
Freshman Class: 3146 applied, 2460 accepted, 700 enrolled	
SAT I Verbal/Math: 620/680	**ACT:** 29
	HIGHLY COMPETITIVE+

Worcester Polytechnic Institute, founded in 1865, is a private institution with a unique, project-oriented program of study primarily in engineering and other technical fields. In addition to regional accreditation, WPI has baccalaureate program accreditation with ABET. The library contains 277,844 volumes, 109,648 microform items, and 2500 audiovisual forms/CDs, and subscribes to 4698 periodicals. Computerized library services include the card catalog, interlibrary loans, and database searching. Special learning facilities include a learning resource center, radio station, TV station, a robotics lab, a wind tunnel, and a greenhouse. The 80-acre campus is in a suburban area 40 miles west of Boston. Including residence halls, there are 30 buildings.

Student Life: 53% of undergraduates are from Massachusetts. Others are from 44 states, 47 foreign countries, and Canada. 74% are from public schools. 82% are white. The average age of freshmen is 18; all undergraduates, 20. 6% do not continue beyond their first year; 80% remain to graduate.

Housing: 1247 students can be accommodated in college housing, which includes coed dormitories and on-campus apartments. In addition, there are special-interest houses. On-campus housing is guaranteed for the freshman year only and is available on a lottery system for upperclassmen. Upperclassmen may keep cars.

Activities: 32% of men belong to 12 national fraternities; 34% of women belong to 2 national sororities. There are 100 groups on campus, including art, band, cheerleading, chess, choir, chorale, chorus, computers, dance, drama, ethnic, gay, honors, international, jazz band, literary magazine, musical theater, newspaper, orchestra, pep band, photography, political, professional, radio and TV, religious, social, social service, student government, symphony, and yearbook. Popular campus events include Traditions Day, New Voices Festival, and Winter Carnival.

Sports: There are 11 intercollegiate sports for men and 10 for women, and 15 intramural sports for men and 9 for women. Facilities include an aerobics area, baseball and softball fields, bowling alleys, an 8-lane synthetic surface track, a fitness center, a crew center, a playing field with artificial turf, a pool, basketball, tennis, racquetball and squash courts, and a 2,800-seat gym.

Disabled Students: 90% of the campus is accessible. Wheelchair ramps, elevators, special parking, specially equipped rest rooms, special class scheduling, and lowered drinking fountains are available.

Services: Counseling and information services are available, as is tutoring in every subject.
Campus Safety and Security: Measures include 24-hour foot and vehicle patrol, self-defense education, escort service, and shuttle buses. There are informal discussions, pamphlets/posters/films, emergency telephones, lighted pathways/sidewalks, and a student-run emergency medical service supervised by the campus police department.
Programs of Study: WPI confers the B.S. degree. Master's and doctoral degrees are also awarded. Bachelor's degrees are awarded in BIOLOGICAL SCIENCE (biochemistry, biology/biological science, and biotechnology), BUSINESS (management engineering, management information systems, and management science), COMPUTER AND PHYSICAL SCIENCE (chemistry, computer science, mathematics, and physics), ENGINEERING AND ENVIRONMENTAL DESIGN (biomedical engineering, chemical engineering, civil engineering, electrical/electronics engineering, engineering physics, industrial engineering, manufacturing engineering, and mechanical engineering), SOCIAL SCIENCE (economics, humanities, interdisciplinary studies, and social science). Engineering is the largest.
Required: For a B.S. degree, WPI requires that students in science and engineering complete a individual project in the humanities. Students must also complete 2 major team projects. Distribution requirements vary according to the major, and all students must take courses in social sciences and phys ed.
Special: Students may cross-register with 9 other colleges in the Colleges of Worcester Consortium. Co-op programs in all majors, internships, work-study programs, dual majors in every subject, student-designed majors, 3-2 engineering degrees, nondegree study, and pass/fail options are all available. There is a 7-year veterinary medicine program with Tufts Veterinary School and an accelerated degree program in fire protection engineering. There are special project centers in Europe, Latin America, Asia, Australia, Africa, and the U.S. There are 10 national honor societies.
Faculty/Classroom: 82% of faculty are male; 18%, female. 96% teach undergraduates and 50% do research. No introductory courses are taught by graduate students. The average class size in an introductory lecture is 35; in a laboratory, 20; and in a regular course, 25.
Admissions: 78% of the 2001-2002 applicants were accepted. The SAT I scores for the 2001-2002 freshman class were: Verbal--7% below 500, 43% between 500 and 599, 40% between 600 and 700, and 10% above 700; Math--21% below 500, 19% between 500 and 599, 55% between 600 and 700, and 25% above 700. 70% of the current freshmen were in the top fifth of their class; 95% were in the top two fifths.
Requirements: The SAT I or ACT is required. In addition, SAT II: Subject tests in writing, math I or II, and a science are also required. Applicants must have completed 4 years of math precalculus and 2 lab sciences. An essay is optional. Students may apply at the school's web site or through EXPAN or CollegeLink. AP credits are accepted. Important factors in the admissions decision are advanced placement or honor courses, recommendations by school officials, and extracurricular activities record.
Procedure: Freshmen are admitted fall and spring. Entrance exams should be taken between April and December. There are early action, early admissions, and deferred admissions plans. Early action applications should be filed by November 15; regular applications, by February 1 for fall entry and November 15 for spring entry. The fall 2001 application fee was $60. Notification of early action is sent December 15; regular decision, April 1. 173 early decision candidates were accepted for the 2001-2002 class. A waiting list is an active part of the admissions procedure.
Transfer: 57 transfer students enrolled in 2001-2002. Grades of C or better transfer for credit. 8 units of 45 must be completed at WPI.
Visiting: There are regularly scheduled orientations for prospective students, consisting of meetings and presentations from various academic and extracurricular groups. There are guides for informal visits and visitors may sit in on classes and stay overnight. To schedule a visit, contact the Admissions Office.
Financial Aid: In 2001-2002, 86% of all freshmen and 83% of continuing students received some form of financial aid. 79% of freshmen and 77% of continuing students received need-based aid. The average freshman award was $19,970. Of that total, scholarships or need-based grants averaged $14,065 ($27,560 maximum); loans averaged $2345 ($5375 maximum); work contracts averaged $1330 ($1400 maximum); and outside scholarships averaged $2230 ($13,000 maximum). 59% of undergraduates work part time. Average annual earnings from campus work are $1000. The average financial indebtedness of the 2001 graduate was $18,321. WPI is a member of CSS. The CSS/Profile or FAFSA and CSS Non-Custodial Parent Statement are required. The fall application deadline is March 1.
International Students: The school actively recruits these students. They must score 550 on the written TOEFL and also take the SAT I or the ACT. Students must take SAT II: Subject tests in writing, math, and science.
Computers: The UNIX-based mainframe is accessible via 8 parallel processors and a campuswide data network available in many locations, including the College Computer Center. The center also features 56 X terminals. More than 1,000 IBM PC-6300 computers are available throughout the campus in general-access and specialized labs and computer classrooms. All students may access the system 24 hours daily. There are no time limits and no fees.
Graduates: In 2001, 586 bachelor's degrees were awarded. The most popular majors were mechanical engineering (20%), electrical engineering (17%), and computer science (16%). In an average class, 1% graduate in 3 years, 66% in 4 years, 75% in 5 years, and 80% in 6 years. 200 companies recruited on campus in 2000-2001. Of the 2000 graduating class, 15% were enrolled in graduate school within 6 months of graduation and 75% were employed.
Admissions Contact: Kristin R. Tichenor, Director of Admissions.
E-mail: *admissions@wpi.edu* Web: *www.wpi.edu*

WORCESTER STATE COLLEGE — C-2
Worcester, MA 01602-2597 — **(508) 929-8040; Fax: (508) 929-8131**

Full-time: 1190 men, 1918 women	**Faculty:** 165
Part-time: 696 men, 1111 women	**Ph.D.s:** 71%
Graduate: 241 men, 612 women	**Student/Faculty:** 19 to 1
Year: semesters, summer session	**Tuition:** $2573 ($8653)
Application Deadline: open	**Room & Board:** $5328
Freshman Class: n/av	
SAT I Verbal/Math: 500/490	**ACT:** 20 **LESS COMPETITIVE**

Worcester State College, established in 1874, is part of the Massachusetts public higher education system and offers undergraduate and graduate programs. A liberal arts core is emphasized, as are selected areas of science, the health professions, education, and business and management. There is 1 graduate school. The library contains 143,887 volumes, 15,149 microform items, and 11,963 audiovisual forms/CDs, and subscribes to 1130 periodicals. Computerized library services include the card catalog, interlibrary loans, and database searching. Special learning facilities include a learning resource center, radio station, TV station, photographic labs, audiovisual center, multimedia classrooms with satellite connectivity, discipline-specific computer labs, and speech, language, and hearing clinic. The 53-acre campus is in an urban area 40 miles west of Boston. Including residence halls, there are 8 buildings.
Student Life: 95% of undergraduates are from Massachusetts. Others are from 19 states, 84 foreign countries, and Canada. 81% are white. The average age of freshmen is 26; all undergraduates, 27. 25% do not continue beyond their first year; 37% remain to graduate.
Housing: 688 students can be accommodated in college housing, which includes coed dormitories and on-campus apartments. On-campus housing is available on a first-come, first-served basis. Priority is given to out-of-town students. 84% of students commute. Alcohol is not permitted. Upperclassmen may keep cars.
Activities: There are no fraternities or sororities. There are 44 groups on campus, including cheerleading, chorale, drama, ethnic, gay, honors, international, jazz band, newspaper, professional, radio and TV, religious, social, social service, student government, and yearbook. Popular campus events include Winter Carnival, Senior Week, and a lecture series.
Sports: There are 9 intercollegiate sports for men and 7 for women, and 2 intramural sports for men and 2 for women. Facilities include an auditorium, a gym, a fitness center, tennis courts, a track, baseball and softball diamonds, and football, field hockey, and all-purpose fields.
Disabled Students: 75% of the campus is accessible. Wheelchair ramps, elevators, special parking, specially equipped rest rooms, lowered drinking fountains, lowered telephones, and priority registration are available.
Services: Counseling and information services are available, as is tutoring in most subjects in conjunction with Quinsigamond Community College courses and WSC instructors. There is a reader service for the blind, and remedial math, reading, and writing.
Campus Safety and Security: Measures include 24-hour foot and vehicle patrol, self-defense education, and informal discussions. There are pamphlets/posters/films, emergency telephones, and lighted pathways/sidewalks. The dormitory is protected by a state-of-the-art security system. An escort service is available on request.
Programs of Study: WSC confers B.A. and B.S. degrees. Master's degrees are also awarded. Bachelor's degrees are awarded in BIOLOGICAL SCIENCE (biology/biological science and biotechnology), BUSINESS (business administration and management), COMMUNICATIONS AND THE ARTS (communications, English, and Spanish), COMPUTER AND PHYSICAL SCIENCE (chemistry, computer science, mathematics, and natural sciences), EDUCATION (early childhood and elementary), HEALTH PROFESSIONS (health, health science, nursing, occupational therapy, and speech pathology/audiology), SOCIAL SCIENCE (criminal justice, economics, geography, history, psychology, sociology, and urban studies). Occupational therapy and nursing are the strongest academically. Business administration, psychology, and education are the largest.
Required: Students must complete a foundation requirement, including English composition, math, and the study of the U.S. and Massachusetts

constitutions. Distribution requirements include 12 credits each in humanities, behavioral and social sciences, and natural sciences and math; 9 in fine arts; and 3 in health or phys ed. To graduate students must complete 120 credits, including 30 to 48 in the major, with a minimum 2.0 GPA overall and in the major.

Special: Cross-registration with the Worcester Consortium for Higher Education is available, as are co-op programs, internships, work-study, B.A.-B.S. degrees, dual majors, a 3-2 engineering degree with Worcester Polytechnic Institute and the Universities of Massachusetts at Dartmouth and Lowell, nondegree study, and a pass/fail option. There is 1 national honor society, a freshman honors program, and 15 departmental honors programs.

Faculty/Classroom: 55% of faculty are male; 45%, female. All teach undergraduates. No introductory courses are taught by graduate students.

Admissions: The SAT I scores for the 2001-2002 freshman class were: Verbal--49% below 500, 43% between 500 and 599, 7% between 600 and 700, and 1% above 700; Math--52% below 500, 40% between 500 and 599, 7% between 600 and 700, and 1% above 700. The ACT scores were 50% below 21, 31% between 21 and 23, 15% between 24 and 26, and 4% between 27 and 28.

Requirements: The SAT I is required. For students with a GPA of 2.9 or above, a minimum SAT I or ACT score may be required. For students whose GPA is below 2.9, a minimum SAT I or ACT score is applied according to a scale established by WSC. Applicants must graduate from an accredited secondary school. They should have completed 4 years of English, 3 of math, 2 each of a foreign language, a lab science, and social studies, including 1 year of U.S. history and government, and 2 electives. The College Board Student Descriptive questionnaire must be submitted. A GPA of 2.0 is required. AP and CLEP credits are accepted. Applications are accepted on-line via WSC's web site; processing is provided by Apply.

Procedure: Freshmen are admitted to all sessions. Entrance exams should be taken in the spring of the junior year or the fall of the senior year. There is a deferred admissions plan. Application deadlines are open. The fall 2001 application fee was $10. Notification is sent on a rolling basis.

Transfer: 374 transfer students enrolled in a recent year. Transfer applicants must have earned 12 college credits with a minimum 2.5 GPA or 13 to 23 credits with a minimum 2.0 GPA. Students with fewer than 23 transfer credits may be admitted under the same criteria as first-time freshmen. 30 credits of 120 must be completed at WSC.

Visiting: There are regularly scheduled orientations for prospective students, including a campus tour and review of campus life and organizations, success in college, special opportunities, and available services. There are guides for informal visits and visitors may sit in on classes and stay overnight. To schedule a visit, contact the Dean of Enrollment Management.

Financial Aid: In a recent year, 74% of all freshmen received some form of financial aid. 58% of freshmen and 51% of continuing students received need-based aid. The average freshman award was $3817. Of that total, scholarships or need-based grants averaged $1710; loans averaged $1916; and work contracts averaged $191. The average financial indebtedness of the 2001 graduate was $10,973. WSC is a member of CSS. The FAFSA is required. The fall application deadline is March 1.

International Students: In a recent year, there were 81 international students enrolled. They must score 550 on the written TOEFL and also take the SAT I or the ACT.

Computers: The mainframe is a DEC ALPHA 4100. Students apply for a user ID or enroll in courses requiring use of discipline-specific labs. Students work at PC workstations on the collegewide network. There are 449 PC workstations at various campus locations. Students with user IDs may access e-mail and the Internet. All students may access the system. There are no time limits and no fees.

Graduates: In a recent class, 642 bachelor's degrees were awarded. The most popular majors were business administration (19%), psychology (14%), and early childhood and elementary education (10%). In an average class, 1% graduate in 3 years, 16% in 4 years, 31% in 5 years, and 37% in 6 years.

Admissions Contact: Michael Backes, Dean of Enrollment Management. A video is available. E-mail: *admissions@worcester.edu*
Web: *http://www.worcester.edu/*

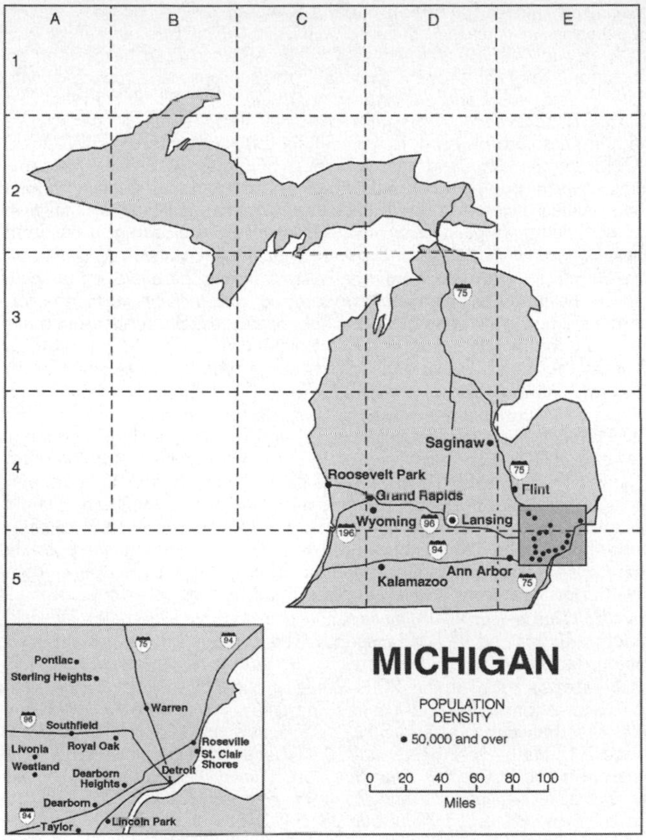

ADRIAN COLLEGE
Adrian, MI 49221-2575 — E-5
(517) 265-5161, ext. 4326
(800) 877-2246; Fax: (517) 264-3331

Full-time: 443 men, 559 women
Part-time: 15 men, 38 women
Graduate: none
Year: semesters, summer session
Application Deadline: March 15
Faculty: 66; IIB, -$
Ph.D.s: 88%
Student/Faculty: 15 to 1
Tuition: $14,850
Room & Board: $4820
Freshman Class: 1215 applied, 1096 accepted, 275 enrolled
ACT: 22 — **COMPETITIVE**

Adrian College, founded in 1859, is a private liberal arts institution affiliated with the United Methodist Church. The library contains 143,269 volumes, 45,911 microform items, and 1144 audiovisual forms/CDs, and subscribes to 595 periodicals. Computerized library services include the card catalog, interlibrary loans, and database searching. Special learning facilities include a learning resource center, art gallery, planetarium, radio station, a solar greenhouse, and an observatory. The 100-acre campus is in a small town 35 miles southwest of Ann Arbor. Including residence halls, there are 30 buildings.

Student Life: 76% of undergraduates are from Michigan. Others are from 18 states, 9 foreign countries, and Canada. 92% are white. 42% are claim no religious affiliation; 27% Protestant; 21% Catholic. The average age of freshmen is 18; all undergraduates, 19. 30% do not continue beyond their first year; 49% remain to graduate.

Housing: 1117 students can be accommodated in college housing, which includes single-sex and coed dormitories and fraternity houses. In addition, there are substance-free, smoke-free, extended quiet hours, and upperclassmen only residence halls. On-campus housing is guaranteed for all 4 years. 75% of students live on campus; of those, 50% remain on campus on weekends. All students may keep cars.

Activities: 30% of men belong to 4 national fraternities; 30% of women belong to 3 national sororities. There are more than 60 groups on campus, including art, band, cheerleading, choir, chorale, chorus, computers, dance, drama, drill team, ethnic, gay, honors, international, jazz band, literary magazine, musical theater, newspaper, orchestra, pep band, photography, political, professional, radio and TV, religious, social, social service, student government, symphony, and yearbook. Popular campus events include Greek Week, Family Weekend, and International Week.

Sports: There are 8 intercollegiate sports for men and 8 for women, and 10 intramural sports for men and 10 for women. Facilities include a sport and fitness center featuring a multipurpose forum with 3 courts for basketball, volleyball, and tennis, and an indoor track, racquetball courts, a weight room, and a 1350-seat performance gym; a 5000-seat football stadium; baseball and softball fields; 2 soccer fields; 6 tennis courts; a 400-meter track; and numerous intramural fields.

Disabled Students: 80% of the campus is accessible. Wheelchair ramps, elevators, special parking, specially equipped rest rooms, lowered drinking fountains, lowered telephones, and readers, note takers, and test accommodations are available.

Services: Counseling and information services are available, as is tutoring in most subjects. There is a reader service for the blind, and remedial math, reading, and writing, including scribes, and note takers.

Campus Safety and Security: Measures include self-defense education, escort service, informal discussions, and pamphlets/posters/films. There are emergency telephones and lighted pathways/sidewalks.

Programs of Study: Adrian confers B.A., B.S., B.B.A., B.F.A., B.M., and B.M.E. degrees. Associate degrees are also awarded. Bachelor's degrees are awarded in BIOLOGICAL SCIENCE (biology/biological science), BUSINESS (accounting, business administration and management, fashion merchandising, international business management, and management information systems), COMMUNICATIONS AND THE ARTS (art, arts administration/management, communications, dramatic arts, English, French, German, music, and Spanish), COMPUTER AND PHYSICAL SCIENCE (chemistry, earth science, mathematics, and physics), EDUCATION (music, physical, and secondary), ENGINEERING AND ENVIRONMENTAL DESIGN (environmental science and interior design), SOCIAL SCIENCE (criminal justice, economics, history, human services, international studies, physical fitness/movement, political science/government, psychology, religion, and sociology). Business, social sciences, and art and design are the largest.

Required: To graduate, students must maintain a 2.0 average over 124 credit hours, 30 of which must be in upper-division courses. 19 hours of distribution requirements and 25 of basic educational proficiency are required, including 2 semesters of foreign language and 1 each of communication, English, fine arts, fitness, humanities, math, natural or physical science, religion or philosophy, and social science.

Special: Adrian offers preprofessional programs in engineering, health sciences, law, ministry, and art therapy; study abroad and a Washington semester; student-designed majors and a dual philosophy/religion program; internships in more than 600 locations, and a 3-2 engineering degree with Washington University in St. Louis and the University of Detroit Mercy. There are 14 national honor societies, and a freshman honors program.

Faculty/Classroom: 56% of faculty are male; 44%, female. All teach undergraduates. The average class size in an introductory lecture is 20; in a laboratory, 13; and in a regular course, 15.

Admissions: 90% of the 2001-2002 applicants were accepted. The ACT scores for the 2001-2002 freshman class were: 39% below 21, 27% between 21 and 23, 21% between 24 and 26, 8% between 27 and 28, and 5% above 28. 44% of the current freshmen were in the top fifth of their class; 74% were in the top two fifths.

Requirements: The SAT I or ACT is required. In addition, applicants must be graduates of an accredited secondary school. The GED is accepted. Each student is reviewed individually based on several criteria. An interview is recommended. Adrian requires applicants to be in the upper 50% of their class. A GPA of 2.5 is required. AP and CLEP credits are accepted. Important factors in the admissions decision are advanced placement or honor courses, leadership record, and extracurricular activities record. Applications are accepted on-line and are available via the college's web site.

Procedure: Freshmen are admitted in the fall. Entrance exams should be taken during the spring of the junior year or fall of the senior year. There is a deferred admissions plan. Applications should be filed by March 15 for fall entry. The fall 2001 application fee was $20. Notification is sent on a rolling basis.

Transfer: 38 transfer students enrolled in 2001-2002. Applicants must have an above-average GPA and provide final high school transcripts. If the student has completed fewer than 24 semester hours, ACT or SAT I test scores are also required. Grades of 2.0 and above transfer for credit. The college admits transfer students every semester. 34 credits of 124 must be completed at Adrian.

Visiting: There are regularly scheduled orientations for prospective students, including a student-guided campus tour and visits with an admissions counselor, professors from the student's area of interest, and an athletics coach, if applicable. Visitors may sit in on classes and stay overnight. To schedule a visit, contact the Admissions Office.

Financial Aid: In 2001-2002, 78% of all freshmen and 71% of continuing students received some form of financial aid. 78% of freshmen and 75% of continuing students received need-based aid. The average fresh-

man award was $14,552. Of that total, scholarships or need-based grants averaged $9411 ($12,335 maximum); loans and work contracts averaged $4023. 43% of undergraduates work part time. Average annual earnings from campus work are $812. The average financial indebtedness of the 2001 graduate was $15,326. The FAFSA is required. The fall application deadline is March 15.

International Students: There are 20 international students enrolled. The school actively recruits these students. They must score 500 on the written TOEFL and also take the SAT I or the ACT.

Computers: The mainframes are a DEC VAX and a DEC ALPHA. Networked labs with 82 PCs are located in academic buildings. Every residence hall room has a network connection. All students may access the system weekdays from 9 A.M. to 11 p.m; Saturday from noon to 5 P.M.; and Sunday from noon to 11 P.M. There are no time limits and no fees. It is strongly recommended that all students have a personal computer.

Graduates: In 2001, 173 bachelor's degrees were awarded. The most popular majors were business (24%), social sciences/history (18%), and English (13%). In an average class, 34% graduate in 4 years, 48% in 5 years, and 50% in 6 years. 50 companies recruited on campus in 2000-2001.

Admissions Contact: Janel Sutkus, Director of Admissions.
E-mail: *admissions@adrian.edu* Web: *www.adrian.edu*

ALBION COLLEGE — D-5
Albion, MI 49224 (517) 629-0321
(800) 858-6770; Fax: (517) 629-0569

Full-time: 686 men, 857 women	**Faculty:** 121; IIB, av$
Part-time: 1 man, 4 women	**Ph.D.s:** 92%
Graduate: none	**Student/Faculty:** 13 to 1
Year: semesters, summer session	**Tuition:** $19,578
Application Deadline: open	**Room & Board:** $5604
Freshman Class: 1297 applied, 1127 accepted, 451 enrolled	
SAT I Verbal/Math: 580/580	**ACT:** 25 **VERY COMPETITIVE**

Albion College, established in 1835, is a private institution affiliated with the United Methodist Church and offering undergraduate degrees in liberal arts curricula. In addition to regional accreditation, Albion has baccalaureate program accreditation with NASM. The library contains 355,040 volumes, 67,188 microform items, and 6040 audiovisual forms/CDs, and subscribes to 986 periodicals. Computerized library services include the card catalog, interlibrary loans, and database searching. Special learning facilities include a learning resource center, art gallery, radio station, nature center, women's center, observatory, and honors program center. The 225-acre campus is in a small town 90 miles west of Detroit and 175 miles east of Chicago. Including residence halls, there are 30 buildings.

Student Life: 89% of undergraduates are from Michigan. Others are from 28 states, 19 foreign countries, and Canada. 84% are from public schools. 86% are white. 28% are Catholic; 26% claim no religious affiliation. The average age of freshmen is 18; all undergraduates, 20. 15% do not continue beyond their first year.

Housing: 1600 students can be accommodated in college housing, which includes single-sex and coed dormitories, on-campus apartments, off-campus apartments, married-student housing, and fraternity houses. In addition, there are language houses, special-interest houses, and special-interest annexes. On-campus housing is guaranteed for all 4 years. 99% of students live on campus; of those, 70% remain on campus on weekends. All students may keep cars.

Activities: 40% of men belong to 5 national fraternities; 40% of women belong to 6 national sororities. There are 122 groups on campus, including art, band, cheerleading, chess, choir, chorale, chorus, computers, dance, drama, ethnic, film, gay, honors, international, jazz band, literary magazine, marching band, a medieval society, musical theater, newspaper, opera, orchestra, pep band, political, professional, radio and TV, religious, social, social service, a sports club association, student government, symphony, and yearbook. Popular campus events include International Week, Briton Bash, and Albion Performing Arts and Lecture Series.

Sports: There are 9 intercollegiate sports for men and 9 for women, and 19 intramural sports for men and 18 for women. Facilities include a stadium, an aquatic center, a gym, baseball, soccer, and football fields, tennis courts, an archery range, a surfaced track, a field events area, outdoor basketball courts, practice fields, and a canoeing facility. There is also a recreation and wellness center with intramural basketball, volleyball, badminton, racquetball, and tennis courts, a track, a weight training room, a human performance lab, and a training/rehabilitation unit.

Disabled Students: 90% of the campus is accessible. Wheelchair ramps, elevators, special parking, specially equipped rest rooms, special class scheduling, lowered drinking fountains, and lowered telephones are available.

Services: Counseling and information services are available, as is tutoring in most subjects, and assistance for the deaf. There is a reader service for the blind. The Developing Skills Center offers individual assistance to students for study skills enhancement.

Campus Safety and Security: Measures include 24-hour foot and vehicle patrol, self-defense education, escort service, and shuttle buses. There are informal discussions, pamphlets/posters/films, emergency telephones, and lighted pathways/sidewalks.

Programs of Study: Albion confers B.A. and B.F.A. degrees. Bachelor's degrees are awarded in BIOLOGICAL SCIENCE (biology/biological science), COMMUNICATIONS AND THE ARTS (art, art history and appreciation, English, French, German, music, Spanish, speech/debate/rhetoric, and visual and performing arts), COMPUTER AND PHYSICAL SCIENCE (chemistry, computer science, earth science, geoscience, mathematics, and physics), EDUCATION (physical), HEALTH PROFESSIONS (predentistry and premedicine), SOCIAL SCIENCE (American studies, anthropology, economics, history, international studies, philosophy, political science/government, psychology, public affairs, religion, and sociology). English, economics, biology are the strongest academically. Economics, English, and psychology are the largest.

Required: To graduate, students must complete 2 units each in social science, humanities, and math and science, and 1 in fine arts, environmental studies, gender studies, and ethnic studies. Students must maintain a minimum GPA of 2.0 and complete 124 semester hours with 32 hours in the major. All students must pass a writing competence exam.

Special: Albion offers work-study and internship programs, study abroad in 19 countries, a Washington semester, and study in New York City,Philadelphia, Oak Ridge, Chicago, and the Virgin Islands. Students may earn a 3-2 engineering degree in conjunction with Columbia, Case Western, or Michigan Technological Universities, or the University of Michigan. Student-designed majors, dual and interdisciplinary majors, including computational math, speech communication and theater, math/physics, and math/economics, and pass/fail grading are possible. There are 4 national honor societies, including Phi Beta Kappa, a freshman honors program, and 18 departmental honors programs.

Faculty/Classroom: 70% of faculty are male; 30%, female. All teach undergraduates and 94% do research. The average class size in an introductory lecture is 27; in a laboratory, 16; and in a regular course, 17.

Admissions: 87% of the 2001-2002 applicants were accepted. The SAT I scores for the 2001-2002 freshman class were: Verbal--13% below 500, 44% between 500 and 599, 37% between 600 and 700, and 6% above 700; Math--15% below 500, 43% between 500 and 599, 35% between 600 and 700, and 7% above 700. The ACT scores were 13% below 21, 22% between 21 and 23, 29% between 24 and 26, 17% between 27 and 28, and 19% above 28. 53% of the current freshmen were in the top fifth of their class; 88% were in the top two fifths. There were 7 National Merit finalists and 5 semifinalists in a recent year. 15 freshmen graduated first in their class.

Requirements: The SAT I or ACT is required. In addition, applicants must graduate from an accredited secondary school or earn a GED. Completion of 15 Carnegie credits is required. A strong background in English, math, and the lab and social sciences is recommended. Albion requires applicants to be in the upper 50% of their class. A GPA of 2.5 is required. AP and CLEP credits are accepted. Important factors in the admissions decision are advanced placement or honor courses, extracurricular activities record, and personality/intangible qualities. Applications are accepted on-line at the Albion web site via CollegeNet and Common App.

Procedure: Freshmen are admitted fall and spring. Entrance exams should be taken in April or June of the junior year. There are early decision, early admissions, and deferred admissions plans. Early decision applications should be filed by November 15; regular applications deadlines are open for fall entry. The fall 2001 application fee was $20. Notification of early decision is sent December 1; regular decision, on a rolling basis. 35 early decision candidates were accepted for the 2001-2002 class.

Transfer: 24 transfer students enrolled in 2001-2002. Transfer applicants must submit official college transcripts. Grades of 2.0 or better are considered for transfer credit. Albion evaluates the applicant's course work before conferring transfer credit. 12 credits of 124 must be completed at Albion.

Visiting: There are regularly scheduled orientations for prospective students, consisting of 5 SOAR programs for students and parents: 1 1/2-day events held from early May to late August. There are guides for informal visits and visitors may sit in on classes and stay overnight. To schedule a visit, contact the Admissions Office.

Financial Aid: In 2001-2002, 98% of all freshmen and 96% of continuing students received some form of financial aid. 66% of freshmen and 60% of continuing students received need-based aid. The average freshman award was $16,823. Of that total, scholarships or need-based grants averaged $14,660 ($27,794 maximum); loans averaged $2610 ($5125 maximum); and work contracts averaged $1238 ($1525 maximum). 57% of undergraduates work part time. Average annual earnings from campus work are $989. The average financial indebtedness of the 2001 graduate was $16,244. Albion is a member of CSS. The FAFSA is required. The fall application deadline is March 1.

International Students: There are 23 international students enrolled. The school actively recruits these students. They must score 550 on the written TOEFL and also take the SAT I or the ACT.

Computers: The mainframe is a DEC ALPHA 2100/400. Suites of Macs and PCs are available in locations across campus. They operate as on-line terminals and are connected to the campus network. All students may access the system most days and evening hours. There are no time limits and no fees. It is strongly recommended that all students have personal computers.

Graduates: In 2001, 334 bachelor's degrees were awarded. The most popular majors were economics/management (32%), English (14%), and biology (10%). In an average class, 1% graduate in 3 years, 71% in 4 years, 74% in 5 years, and 77% in 6 years. 205 companies recruited on campus in 2000-2001. Of the 2000 graduating class, 38% were enrolled in graduate school within 6 months of graduation and 92% were employed.

Admissions Contact: Doug Kellar, Associate Vice President for Enrollment. A video is available. E-mail: *dkellar@albion.edu*
Web: *www.albion.edu*

ALMA COLLEGE

Alma, MI 48801-1599 D-4
(989) 463-7139
(800) 321-ALMA; Fax: (989) 463-7057

Full-time: 542 men, 783 women	**Faculty:** 86; IIB,
Part-time: 21 men, 25 women	**Ph.D.s:** 89%
Graduate: none	**Student/Faculty:** 15 to 1
Year: terms	**Tuition:** $16,602
Application Deadline: open	**Room & Board:** $5984

Freshman Class: 1237 applied, 1010 accepted, 320 enrolled
ACT: 25 **VERY COMPETITIVE**

Alma College, established in 1886, is a private, liberal arts institution affiliated with the Presbyterian Church (U.S.A.). In addition to regional accreditation, Alma has baccalaureate program accreditation with NASM. The library contains 241,168 volumes, 242,159 microform items, and 6986 audiovisual forms/CDs, and subscribes to 1029 periodicals. Computerized library services include the card catalog, interlibrary loans, and database searching. Special learning facilities include a learning resource center, art gallery, planetarium, radio station, an audio-visual center, and a language lab. The 100-acre campus is in a small town 50 miles north of Lansing. Including residence halls, there are 24 buildings.

Student Life: 95% of undergraduates are from Michigan. Others are from 21 states, 19 foreign countries, and Canada. 93% are from public schools. 93% are white. 30% are claim no religious affiliation; 28% Protestant; 24% Catholic; 17% are from more than 15 other denominations. The average age of freshmen is 18; all undergraduates, 20. 15% do not continue beyond their first year; 72% remain to graduate.

Housing: 1195 students can be accommodated in college housing, which includes single-sex and coed dormitories, on-campus apartments, fraternity houses, and sorority houses. In addition, there are language houses, special-interest houses, and an international house for students who live or have traveled overseas. 85% of students live on campus; of those, 60% remain on campus on weekends. All students may keep cars.

Activities: 33% of men belong to 1 local and 4 national fraternities; 22% of women belong to 1 local and 4 national sororities. There are 123 groups on campus, including art, bagpipe band, band, cheerleading, chess, choir, chorale, computers, dance, drama, ethnic, gay, honors, international, jazz band, literary magazine, marching band, musical theater, newspaper, orchestra, photography, political, professional, radio and TV, religious, social, social service, student government, symphony, and yearbook. Popular campus events include All Nighter and Song Fest.

Sports: There are 9 intercollegiate sports for men and 9 for women, and 14 intramural sports for men and 14 for women. Facilities include a recreation center with a climbing wall, fitness center, 4 courts, and suspended 3-lane track; an indoor gym and pool; an outdoor sports complex with an artificial turf playing field, an 8-lane track, and baseball and softball fields; a weight training room; and racquetball and tennis courts.

Disabled Students: 90% of the campus is accessible. Wheelchair ramps, elevators, special parking, specially equipped rest rooms, special class scheduling, lowered drinking fountains, 2 residence halls with private baths, and several small housing units are available.

Services: Counseling and information services are available, as is tutoring in every subject. Both individual and group tutoring are available. There is a reader service for the blind, and remedial math, reading, and writing.

Campus Safety and Security: Measures include informal discussions, pamphlets/posters/films, emergency telephones, and lighted pathways/sidewalks. There is a 24-hour foot patrol.

Programs of Study: Alma confers B.A., B.S., B.F.A., and B.M. degrees. Bachelor's degrees are awarded in BIOLOGICAL SCIENCE (biology/biological science), BUSINESS (business administration and management and international business management), COMMUNICATIONS AND THE ARTS (communications, design, dramatic arts, English, French, German, music, and Spanish), COMPUTER AND PHYSICAL SCIENCE (chemistry, computer science, mathematics, and physics), EDUCATION (elementary and secondary), HEALTH PROFESSIONS (health science), SOCIAL SCIENCE (economics, history, philosophy, political science/government, psychology, religion, and sociology). Education, business administration, and exercise and health science are the strongest academically. Business administration, biology, and education are the largest.

Required: Degree requirements include completion of a minimum of 136 credit hours; 148 hours are required for the B.F.A. degree, 136 to 156 for the B.M. degree. Students must attain a minimum GPA of 2.0, or 3.0 for fine arts majors. All students must demonstrate proficiency in English, communication, and computation, and they must complete distribution requirements, which include 16 fine arts and humanities credits (4 credits in each of creative or performing arts, literature, philosophy, religious studies, or humanities), and 16 each of social science and life and physical science credits. The total number of program credits is 36 for a departmental major, 56 for an interdepartmental major, and 56 to 58 for self-designed majors.

Special: Alma offers internships in many fields, study abroad in 12 countries, and a Washington semester at American University. There are work-study programs, dual majors, B.A.-B.S. degrees, and student-designed majors in a wide variety of subjects. The college confers 3-2 engineering degrees in conjunction with the University of Michigan, Michigan Technological University, and Washington University in St. Louis. Nondegree study may be pursued, and students have a pass/fail grading option. A 4-week spring term provides intensive study in 1 course, often combined with travel. There are 4 national honor societies, including Phi Beta Kappa, a freshman honors program, and 16 departmental honors programs.

Faculty/Classroom: 65% of faculty are male; 35%, female. All teach undergraduates and 63% do research. The average class size in an introductory lecture is 20; in a laboratory, 16; and in a regular course, 21.

Admissions: 82% of the 2001-2002 applicants were accepted. The ACT scores for the 2001-2002 freshman class were: 13% below 21, 27% between 21 and 23, 30% between 24 and 26, 16% between 27 and 28, and 14% above 28. 62% of the current freshmen were in the top fifth of their class; 92% were in the top two fifths. There were 4 National Merit finalists. 11 freshmen graduated first in their class.

Requirements: The SAT I or ACT is required; the ACT is preferred. Applicants must have graduated from an accredited secondary school and have earned 16 Carnegie units, including 4 years of English and 3 each of math, science, and social studies, with 2 of a foreign language recommended. Alma prefers applicants in the upper 25% of their class. An essay is recommended and a portfolio and audition are required for performing arts scholarships. A GPA of 3.0 is required. AP credits are accepted. Important factors in the admissions decision are advanced placement or honor courses, leadership record, and recommendations by school officials. Application forms are available on-line at the school's web site.

Procedure: Freshmen are admitted fall, winter, and spring. Entrance exams should be taken in the spring of the junior year or as late as the winter of the senior year. There are early action and deferred admissions plans. Early action applications should be filed by November 1; regular applications are open for fall entry. There is a $25 fee. Notification of early action is sent November 15; regular decision, on a rolling basis.

Transfer: 29 transfer students enrolled in 2001-2002. Students wishing to transfer to Alma must have a minimum GPA of 3.0 from other colleges attended. 34 credits of 136 must be completed at Alma.

Visiting: There are regularly scheduled orientations for prospective students, consisting of faculty talks, tours, a meal on campus, financial aid information, and admissions sessions. There are guides for informal visits and visitors may sit in on classes and stay overnight. To schedule a visit, contact the Admissions Office.

Financial Aid: In 2001-2002, 98% of all students received some form of financial aid. 39% of freshmen and 78% of continuing students received need-based aid. The average freshman award was $15,897. Of that total, scholarships or need-based grants averaged $13,036 ($18,942 maximum); loans averaged $3193 ($4125 maximum); work contracts averaged $500 ($1500 maximum); and external and restricted awards plus employee dependent tuition grants averaged $2001. 45% of undergraduates work part time. Average annual earnings from campus work are $800. The average financial indebtedness of the 2001 graduate was $10,125. Alma is a member of CSS. The FAFSA is required. The fall application deadline is March 1.

International Students: There are 28 international students enrolled. The school actively recruits these students. They must score 525 on the written TOEFL. The SAT I or ACT is required if the TOEFL is not submitted.

Computers: The mainframes are 2 DEC Alpha 2100 4/275, and 1 DEC Alpha 200. The on-campus VAX network links 600 terminals, printers, and PCs across campus. Macs are available in 6 residence halls, department labs, the Colina Library classroom, and the Academic Center. All residence halls are wired for Internet access for a user fee. All students may access the system all hours. There are no time limits. It is strongly recommended that all students have personal computers.

Graduates: In 2001, 277 bachelor's degrees were awarded. The most popular majors were business administration (17%), education (14%), and biology (9%). In an average class, 1% graduate in 3 years, 54% in 4 years, 66% in 5 years, and 75% in 6 years. 38 companies recruited on campus in 2000-2001. Of the 2000 graduating class, 40% were enrolled in graduate school within 6 months of graduation and 96% were employed.

Admissions Contact: Paul Pollatz, Director of Admissions. E-mail: *admissions@alma.edu* Web: *www.alma.edu*

ANDREWS UNIVERSITY C-5
Berrien Springs, MI 49104-0740 (616) 471-3834
(800) 253-2874; Fax: (616) 471-3228

Full-time: 660 men, 830 women
Part-time: 100 men, 195 women
Graduate: 650 men, 520 women
Year: quarters
Application Deadline: open
Freshman Class: n/av
SAT I: recommended
Faculty: 174
Ph.D.s: 65%
Student/Faculty: 9 to 1
Tuition: $13,676
Room & Board: $4020
ACT: required
LESS COMPETITIVE

Andrews University, established in 1874, is a private institution, affiliated with the Seventh-day Adventist Church, that offers undergraduate degrees in business, education, arts and sciences, and technology. Figures in above capsule are approximate. There are 4 undergraduate and 5 graduate schools. In addition to regional accreditation, Andrews has baccalaureate program accreditation with ADA, AHEA, APTA, CAHEA, NASM, NCATE, and NLN. The library contains 781,965 volumes, 269,385 microform items, and 44,316 audiovisual forms/CDs, and subscribes to 3004 periodicals. Special learning facilities include a natural history museum, radio station, and archeological museum. The 1600-acre campus is in a rural area 15 miles south of Benton Harbor. Including residence halls, there are 57 buildings.

Student Life: 64% of undergraduates are from out of state, mostly the Midwest. Others are from 48 states, 87 foreign countries, and Canada. 39% are from public schools. The average age of freshmen is 19; all undergraduates, 24. 35% do not continue beyond their first year; 47% remain to graduate.

Housing: 1705 students can be accommodated in college housing, which includes dormitories, on-campus apartments, off-campus apartments, and married-student housing. On-campus housing is available on a first-come, first-served basis. Alcohol is not permitted. All students may keep cars.

Activities: There is 1 national fraternity and 1 national sorority. There are many groups and organizations on campus, including band, choir, chorale, chorus, computers, drama, ethnic, honors, international, newspaper, professional, religious, social, social service, student government, and yearbook.

Sports: Facilities include a gym, a pool, racquetball courts, and health clubs in 2 of 3 dorms.

Disabled Students: Wheelchair ramps, special parking, and specially equipped rest rooms are available.

Services: Counseling and information services are available, as is tutoring in every subject. There is remedial math, reading, and writing.

Programs of Study: Andrews confers B.A., B.S., B.B.A., B.F.A., B.Mus., B.S.D., B.S.Educ., B.S.El.Ed., B.S.W., and B.T. degrees. Associate, master's, and doctoral degrees are also awarded. Bachelor's degrees are awarded in AGRICULTURE (agriculture, animal science, and horticulture), BIOLOGICAL SCIENCE (anatomy, biochemistry, biology/biological science, biophysics, botany, molecular biology, nutrition, physiology, and zoology), BUSINESS (accounting, banking and finance, business administration and management, business economics, management information systems, and marketing/retailing/merchandising), COMMUNICATIONS AND THE ARTS (art, ceramic art and design, communications, creative writing, design, English, French, graphic design, journalism, literature, music, music performance, painting, photography, public relations, Spanish, and visual and performing arts), COMPUTER AND PHYSICAL SCIENCE (applied mathematics, chemistry, computer science, information sciences and systems, mathematics, and physics), EDUCATION (art, elementary, English, mathematics, music, physical, science, secondary, social studies, teaching English as a second/foreign language (TESOL/TEFOL), and technical), ENGINEERING AND ENVIRONMENTAL DESIGN (aeronautical technology, aircraft mechanics, architecture, automotive technology, aviation administration/management, aviation computer technology, biomedical equipment technology, computer graphics, computer technology, construction management, electrical/electronics engineering, electrical/electronics engineering technology, engineering, environmental science, graphic arts technology, industrial engineering, landscape architecture/design, and mechanical engineering technology), HEALTH PROFESSIONS (allied health, art therapy, biomedical science, exercise science, medical laboratory technology, nursing, preveterinary science, public health, and speech pathology/audiology), SOCIAL SCIENCE (anthropology, behavioral science, crosscultural studies, dietetics, economics, family/consumer studies, history, human development, interdisciplinary studies, pastoral studies, political science/government, psychology, religion, religious education, social studies, social work, sociology, theological studies, and youth ministry). Nursing, physical therapy, and education are the largest.

Required: Students must complete 190 quarter credits, with a minimum of 45 credits in upper-division work. Specific course requirements include religion, English, behavioral sciences, fine arts, and phys ed.

Special: Students may pursue a second major in business administration. Study abroad, student-designed majors, nondegree study, and pass/fail options are available. There is a freshman honors program.

Requirements: The ACT is required and the SAT I is recommended. In addition, candidates for admission must graduate from an accredited secondary school or earn a GED. Ten Carnegie units are required, and students must have completed 4 courses in English and 2 courses each in history, math, and science. Interviews are recommended for all applicants. A GPA of 2.0 is required. CLEP credit is accepted. Important factors in the admissions decision are advanced placement or honor courses, leadership record, and evidence of special talent.

Procedure: Entrance exams should be taken as early as possible. Application deadlines are open. The application fee is $30.

Transfer: Transfer applicants must submit a high school transcript and transcripts from all colleges attended. A maximum of 70 hours or 105 quarter credits may be transferred from a junior college toward a bachelor's degree. Credits should be relevant to the student's major at Andrews University. The minimum GPA is 2.0, and the ACT is recommended. Students must meet freshman entrance requirements if they are tranferring with less than sophomore standing from an accredited college. 45 credits of 190 must be completed at Andrews.

Visiting: There are regularly scheduled orientations for prospective students. There are guides for informal visits and visitors may sit in on classes and stay overnight. To schedule a visit, contact the Admissions Office.

Financial Aid: Andrews is a member of CSS. The CSS/Profile is required. Check with the school for current deadlines.

International Students: The school actively recruits these students. They must score 450 on the written TOEFL.

Computers: The mainframe is a Xerox Sigma 9. All students may access the system. There are no time limits and no fees.

Admissions Contact: Lois Zygowiec, Assistant Director, Enrollment Services. E-mail: *loisz@andrews.edu* Web: *www.andrews.edu*

AQUINAS COLLEGE D-4
Grand Rapids, MI 49506-1799 (616) 732-4460
(800) 678-9593; Fax: (616) 732-4469

Full-time: 507 men, 1071 women
Part-time: 136 men, 302 women
Graduate: 175 men, 380 women
Year: semesters, summer session
Application Deadline: open
Freshman Class: 1308 applied, 1073 accepted, 321 enrolled
ACT: 24
Faculty: 100; IIB, --$
Ph.D.s: 71%
Student/Faculty: 16 to 1
Tuition: $14,876
Room & Board: $5176
COMPETITIVE+

Aquinas College, established in 1866, is a private liberal arts institution affiliated with the Roman Catholic Church that offers undergraduate and graduate degrees through day and evening programs. The library contains 112,458 volumes, 223,804 microform items, and 4907 audiovisual forms/CDs, and subscribes to 725 periodicals. Computerized library services include the card catalog, interlibrary loans, and database searching. Special learning facilities include a learning resource center, art gallery, radio station, greenhouses, and an observatory. The campus is in a suburban area.

Student Life: 93% of undergraduates are from Michigan. Others are from 23 states, 10 foreign countries, and Canada. 75% are from public schools. 92% are white. 48% are Catholic; 21% Protestant. The average age of freshmen is 18; all undergraduates, 20. 25% do not continue beyond their first year; 51% remain to graduate.

Housing: 700 students can be accommodated in college housing, which includes single-sex and coed dormitories and on-campus apartments. In addition, there are special-interest houses and service learning houses. On-campus housing is guaranteed for all 4 years. 66% of students live on campus; of those, 35% remain on campus on weekends. All students may keep cars.

Activities: There are no fraternities or sororities. There are 45 groups on campus, including cheerleading, choir, chorus, computers, dance, drama, ethnic, honors, international, jazz band, literary magazine, photography, political, radio and TV, religious, social, social service, student government, and yearbook. Popular campus events include Spring Fling, Activities @ Moose Cafe, and a jazz festival.

Sports: There are 9 intercollegiate sports for men and 10 for women, and 13 intramural sports for men and 13 for women. Facilities include a gym, a weight room, a recreation room, an indoor track, softball and soccer fields, and indoor tennis courts.

Disabled Students: 95% of the campus is accessible. Wheelchair ramps, elevators, special parking, specially equipped rest rooms, special class scheduling, lowered drinking fountains, and lowered telephones are available.

Services: Counseling and information services are available, as is tutoring in most subjects. There is a reader service for the blind, and remedial math, reading, and writing.
Campus Safety and Security: Measures include 24-hour foot and vehicle patrol, escort service, informal discussions, and pamphlets/posters/films. There are emergency telephones and lighted pathways/sidewalks.
Programs of Study: Aquinas confers B.A., B.S., B.A.G.E., B.F.A., B.S.B.A., and B.S.I.B. degrees. Associate and master's degrees are also awarded. Bachelor's degrees are awarded in BIOLOGICAL SCIENCE (biology/biological science), BUSINESS (business administration and management and international business management), COMMUNICATIONS AND THE ARTS (art, art history and appreciation, communications, drawing, English, fine arts, French, German, music, painting, photography, printmaking, sculpture, and Spanish), COMPUTER AND PHYSICAL SCIENCE (chemistry, information sciences and systems, and mathematics), EDUCATION (education and physical), ENGINEERING AND ENVIRONMENTAL DESIGN (environmental science), HEALTH PROFESSIONS (health, medical technology, and nuclear medical technology), SOCIAL SCIENCE (economics, geography, history, interdisciplinary studies, international studies, philosophy, political science/government, psychology, sociology, and theological studies). Business administration and education are the strongest academically and have the largest enrollments.
Required: To graduate, students must complete 124 semester hours, with 30 to 48 in the major, and maintain a minimum GPA of 2.0. The general education program consists of a core of 18 to 30 hours, which includes, from the first to the fourth year, foreign language and a year-long integrated skills course, and courses in the humanities, religion, and global perspectives; and distribution requirements of 30 to 33 hours, which include courses in cultural diversity, mythology and spirituality, natural sciences, the fine arts, and quantitative reasoning and technology.
Special: Students may cross-register with the Dominican Consortium and may study abroad in Ireland, Germany, France, Spain, Costa Rica, Peru, or Japan. Co-op programs and internships are available in all majors, and work-study programs are also available. Students may pursue dual majors in business administration and accounting, sports management, communication arts, or art, and student-designed majors can be arranged. There is a 3-1 program in nuclear medicine technology with St. Louis University, as well as preengineering, prehealth, and teacher certification programs. Aquinas offers a general studies degree and may confer credit for life, military, and work experience. A pass/fail grading option is available. There are 5 national honor societies, a freshman honors program, and 5 departmental honors programs.
Faculty/Classroom: 57% of faculty are male; 43%, female. All teach undergraduates. No introductory courses are taught by graduate students. The average class size in an introductory lecture is 20; in a laboratory, 20; and in a regular course, 18.
Admissions: 82% of the 2001-2002 applicants were accepted. The ACT scores for the 2001-2002 freshman class were: 31% below 21, 25% between 21 and 23, 25% between 24 and 26, 9% between 27 and 28, and 9% above 28. 40% of the current freshmen were in the top fifth of their class; 69% were in the top two fifths. There was 1 National Merit semifinalist in a recent year. 10 freshmen graduated first in their class.
Requirements: The SAT I or ACT is recommended; the minimum composite score acceptable for the ACT is 18. Candidates for admission must graduate from an accredited secondary school. Students must have completed 15 Carnegie units, 4 years of English and social studies, and 3 to 4 years each of math and science. Interviews are recommended for all applicants, and auditions are recommended in appropriate instances. A GPA of 2.5 is required. AP and CLEP credits are accepted. Important factors in the admissions decision are advanced placement or honor courses, leadership record, and extracurricular activities record. Applications are accepted on-line at the school's web site.
Procedure: Freshmen are admitted fall and winter. Entrance exams should be taken during the spring of the junior year. Application deadlines are open. The application fee is $25. Notification is sent on a rolling basis.
Transfer: 85 transfer students enrolled in 2001-2002. Transfer applicants must have earned at least 12 credits in academic course work from an accredited junior or 4-year college with a minimum GPA of 2.0. Interviews are recommended. 30 credits of 124 must be completed at Aquinas.
Visiting: There are regularly scheduled orientations for prospective students, consisting of a tour of the campus and presentations by financial aid personnel, program directors, coaches, and faculty. There are guides for informal visits and visitors may sit in on classes and stay overnight. To schedule a visit, contact Thomas Mikowski, Director of Admissions at (616) 459-8281, ext. 5193 or *admissions@aquinas.edu*
Financial Aid: In 2001-2002, 99% of all freshmen and 98% of continuing students received some form of financial aid. 78% of freshmen and 73% of continuing students received need-based aid. The average freshman award was $14,840. Of that total, scholarships or need-based grants averaged $12,583 ($14,876 maximum) and loans averaged $2257 ($2625 maximum). 51% of undergraduates work part time. Average annual earnings from campus work are $1025. The average financial indebtedness of the 2001 graduate was $12,200. The FAFSA is required. The fall application deadline is June 1.
International Students: There are 14 international students enrolled. They must score 550 on the written TOEFL or take the MELAB.
Computers: The mainframe is a Digital ALPHA 2100. There are 85 terminals available in classrooms, computer labs, dorms, and the residence halls. All students may access the system 91 hours per week during open lab times. There are no time limits and no fees. It is strongly recommended that all students have personal computers.
Graduates: In 2001, 297 bachelor's degrees were awarded. The most popular majors were business administration (26%), social science (16%), and communication arts (5%). In an average class, 1% graduate in 3 years, 29% in 4 years, 48% in 5 years, and 53% in 6 years. 30 companies recruited on campus in 2000-2001. Of the 2000 graduating class, 11% were enrolled in graduate school within 6 months of graduation and 86% were employed.
Admissions Contact: Thomas Mikowski, Director of Admissions. A video is available. E-mail: *mikowtho@aquinas.edu*
Web: *www.aquinas.edu/admissions*

BAKER COLLEGE OF FLINT

Flint, MI 48507-5508 — **E-4**
(810) 766-4000
(800) 822-2537; 4049

Full-time: 774 men, 1614 women	**Faculty:** 23
Part-time: 648 men, 1363 women	**Ph.D.s:** 13%
Graduate: none	**Student/Faculty:** 41 to 1
Year: quarters, summer session	**Tuition:** $6995
Application Deadline: open	**Room & Board:** $725 (room only)

Freshman Class: 2127 applied, 2127 accepted, 1598 enrolled
SAT I or ACT: not required — **NONCOMPETITIVE**

Baker College, established in 1911, is an independent institution offering undergraduate degrees in business, health science, and technical curricula. It is part of the Baker College System. In addition to regional accreditation, Baker has baccalaureate program accreditation with CAHEA. The library contains 60,000 volumes, 1200 microform items, and 475 audiovisual forms/CDs, and subscribes to 190 periodicals. Computerized library services include the card catalog, interlibrary loans, and database searching. Special learning facilities include a learning resource center. The 30-acre campus is in an urban area 60 miles northwest of Detroit. Including residence halls, there are 6 buildings.
Student Life: 92% of undergraduates are from Michigan. Others are from 4 foreign countries and Canada. 72% are white; 22% African American. The average age of all undergraduates is 28.
Housing: 189 students can be accommodated in college housing, which includes single-sex and coed dormitories, on-campus apartments, and off-campus apartments. On-campus housing is available on a first-come, first-served basis. Priority is given to out-of-town students. 98% of students commute. Alcohol is not permitted. All students may keep cars.
Activities: There are no fraternities or sororities. There are 15 groups on campus, including computers, literary magazine, professional, and social. Popular campus events include Baker College Spirit Day and Martin Luther King Jr. Day.
Sports: There is no sports program at Baker. Facilities include a gym and a weight room.
Disabled Students: All of the campus is accessible. Wheelchair ramps, elevators, special parking, specially equipped rest rooms, lowered drinking fountains, and lowered telephones are available.
Services: Counseling and information services are available, as is tutoring in most subjects.
Campus Safety and Security: Measures include 24-hour foot and vehicle patrol, self-defense education, escort service, and informal discussions. There are pamphlets/posters/films and lighted pathways/sidewalks. High-traffic areas of the college re monitored by video camera.
Programs of Study: Baker confers B.B.A., B.B.L., and B.I.M. degrees. Associate degrees are also awarded. Bachelor's degrees are awarded in BUSINESS (accounting, business administration and management, marketing management, and office supervision and management), COMPUTER AND PHYSICAL SCIENCE (computer programming), ENGINEERING AND ENVIRONMENTAL DESIGN (aviation administration/management, drafting and design technology, electrical/electronics engineering technology, and interior design), HEALTH PROFESSIONS (health care administration and occupational therapy). Business administration and health information management are the largest.
Required: Degree requirements include completion of 180 to 208 quarter hours with a minimum GPA of 2.0. All students must complete math and computer courses and an employment course.
Special: Co-op programs, work-study, internships, and dual and interdisciplinary majors are available. An accelerated degree program is possible in business administration.
Faculty/Classroom: 46% of faculty are male; 54%, female. All teach undergraduates.

Admissions: All of the 2001-2002 applicants were accepted.

Requirements: Baker College has no entrance requirements. Students without either a high school diploma or a GED may still be admitted on the basis of Baker College test results.

Procedure: Freshmen are admitted to all sessions. Application deadlines are open. Application fee is $20.

Transfer: 527 transfer students enrolled in 2001-2002. Transcripts from all previous colleges must be submitted. Grades of C or better are eligible for transfer credit. 48 quarter hours of 180 to 208 must be completed at Baker.

Visiting: There are regularly scheduled orientations for prospective students, including orientation and testing. There are guides for informal visits and visitors may sit in on classes. To schedule a visit, contact the Admissions Office.

Financial Aid: The FAFSA and the college's own financial statement are required.

Computers: The mainframe is an IBM System 36 Model B24. There are 220 networked PCs available for student use. All students may access the system during school hours. There are no time limits and no fees.

Graduates: In 2001, 227 bachelor's degrees were awarded. The most popular majors were business/marketing (63%), health (23%), and information science (6%).

Admissions Contact: Mark Heaton, Vice President of Admissions. E-mail: *heaton_m@flint.baker.edu*

CALVIN COLLEGE D-4

Grand Rapids, MI 49546 (616) 957-6106
(800) 688-0122; Fax: (616) 957-8551

Full-time: 1784 men, 2260 women	**Faculty:** 284; IIB, av$
Part-time: 110 men, 103 women	**Ph.D.s:** 83%
Graduate: 5 men, 32 women	**Student/Faculty:** 14 to 1
Year: 4-1-4, summer session	**Tuition:** $14,870
Application Deadline: August 15	**Room & Board:** $5180
Freshman Class: 1920 applied, 1891 accepted, 1031 enrolled	
SAT I Verbal/Math: 580/600	**ACT:** 26 **NONCOMPETITIVE**

Calvin College, established in 1876, is a private institution affiliated with the Christian Reformed Church, offering undergraduate and graduate degrees in liberal arts. In addition to regional accreditation, Calvin has baccalaureate program accreditation with ABET, ACCE, CSWE, NASM, NCATE, and NLN. The library contains 802,000 volumes, 785,000 microform items, and 22,400 audiovisual forms/CDs, and subscribes to 2700 periodicals. Computerized library services include the card catalog, interlibrary loans, and database searching. Special learning facilities include a learning resource center, art gallery, radio station, TV station, ecosystem preserve, electron microscope lav, an observatory with a 16-inch telescope, and a greenhouse. The 370-acre campus is in a suburban area 7 miles southeast of downtown Grand Rapids. Including residence halls, there are 40 buildings.

Student Life: 54% of undergraduates are from Michigan. Others are from 46 states, 34 foreign countries, and Canada. 43% are from public schools. 84% are white. Most are Protestant. The average age of freshmen is 18; all undergraduates, 20. 14% do not continue beyond their first year; 66% remain to graduate.

Housing: 2500 students can be accommodated in college housing, which includes single-sex dormitories and on-campus apartments. In addition, there are language houses, a residence hall wing designated as a multicultural community, and 3 urban houses designated as residential living with a community/urban focus. On-campus housing is guaranteed for the freshman year only. 58% of students live on campus; of those, 90% remain on campus on weekends. Alcohol is not permitted. All students may keep cars.

Activities: There are no fraternities or sororities. There are 40 groups on campus, including art, band, cheerleading, chess, choir, chorale, chorus, computers, dance, drama, ethnic, film, honors, international, literary magazine, musical theater, newspaper, orchestra, pep band, political, professional, radio and TV, religious, social, social service, student government, symphony, and yearbook. Popular campus events include Parents Weekend, the spring and fall music and art festivals, and the January lecture series.

Sports: There are 8 intercollegiate sports for men and 9 for women, and 29 intramural sports for men and 22 for women. Facilities include a 4500-seat field house, a soccer facility, baseball and softball diamonds, an 8-lane, 400-meter polyurethane track, a weight-training/exercise room, a natatorium that contains a diving pool, 6 tennis courts, 2 sand beach volleyball courts, a paved recreational trail around campus, and multiple playing/practice fields.

Disabled Students: 85% of the campus is accessible. Wheelchair ramps, elevators, special parking, specially equipped rest rooms, special class scheduling, lowered drinking fountains, lowered telephones, dedicated accessible suites in residence halls, electric door openers, and reserved classroom seating are available.

Services: Counseling and information services are available, as is tutoring in most subjects. There is a reader service for the blind, and remedial math, reading, and writing. A Braille print service for the blind, books on tape, note taking, interpreting, diagnostic testing, special advising, and early registration are available.

Campus Safety and Security: Measures include 24-hour foot and vehicle patrol, self-defense education, escort service, and informal discussions. There are pamphlets/posters/films, emergency telephones, lighted pathways/sidewalks, a crime alert bulletin, and reports in the school newspaper.

Programs of Study: Calvin confers B.A., B.S., B.F.A., B.M.E., B.S.A., B.S.C.D., B.S.E., B.S.N., B.S.R., and B.S.W. degrees. Master's degrees are also awarded. Bachelor's degrees are awarded in BIOLOGICAL SCIENCE (biochemistry, biology/biological science, and biotechnology), BUSINESS (accounting, business administration and management, and recreation and leisure services), COMMUNICATIONS AND THE ARTS (art history and appreciation, classical languages, classics, communications, Dutch, English, French, German, Greek, Latin, music, and Spanish), COMPUTER AND PHYSICAL SCIENCE (chemistry, computer science, geology, mathematics, and physics), EDUCATION (art, elementary, physical, secondary, and special), ENGINEERING AND ENVIRONMENTAL DESIGN (civil engineering, electrical/electronics engineering, engineering, environmental science, and mechanical engineering), HEALTH PROFESSIONS (nursing and predentistry), SOCIAL SCIENCE (criminal justice, economics, geography, history, philosophy, political science/government, prelaw, psychology, religion, social work, and sociology). Natural sciences, history, and English are the strongest academically. Education, engineering, and business are the largest.

Required: Degree requirements include completion of 124 credit hours, with 28 credits in the major. All students must complete specific course work in English, religion, history, science, math, communication, fine arts, psychology or sociology, economics or political science, philosophy, phys ed, information technology, and cross-cultural engagement. A minimum GPA of 2.0 is required.

Special: A variety of dual majors and student-designed majors is available, as well as combined curriculum programs in occupational therapy and speech pathology. Students may study abroad in 16 countries and enroll in a Washington semester. Cooperative programs include Los Angeles film studies, the Au Sable Institute, the Chicago Metropolitan program, Oregon extension, Latin American, Middle East, and Russian studies, and in business. Internships, work-study programs, and cross-registration at Grand Valley State University, in special education, at Michigan State, in communications disorders, in occupational therapy at Washington University, and at Reformed Bible College, in religion, are also available. There are 6 national honor societies, a freshman honors program, and all departments have honors programs.

Faculty/Classroom: 68% of faculty are male; 32%, female. All both teach and do research. No introductory courses are taught by graduate students. The average class size in an introductory lecture is 26; in a laboratory, 17; and in a regular course, 20.

Admissions: 98% of the 2001-2002 applicants were accepted. The SAT I scores for the 2001-2002 freshman class were: Verbal--14% below 500, 43% between 500 and 599, 30% between 600 and 700, and 13% above 700. The ACT scores were 10% below 21, 19% between 21 and 23, 29% between 24 and 26, 21% between 27 and 28, and 21% above 28. 38% of the current freshmen were in the top fifth of their class; 64% were in the top two fifths. There were 25 National Merit finalists and 25 semifinalists. 41 freshmen graduated first in their class.

Requirements: The ACT is required. In selecting students for admission, Calvin College looks for evidence of Christian commitment and for the capacity and desire to learn. Students who are interested in the Christian perspective and curriculum of Calvin, and who show interest in its aims, are eligible for consideration. Although the prospect of academic success is of primary consideration, the aspirations of the applicant, the recommendation of a high school counselor, teacher, or principal, and the ability of Calvin to be of service, will also be considered in admission decisions. A GPA of 2.5 is required. AP and CLEP credits are accepted. Important factors in the admissions decision are recommendations by school officials, leadership record, and extracurricular activities record. Applications are accepted on-line at the school's web site.

Procedure: Freshmen are admitted to all sessions. Entrance exams should be taken during the spring of the junior year or fall of the senior year. There is a deferred admissions plan. Applications should be filed by August 15 for fall entry, December 15 for winter entry, January 15 for spring entry, and are open for summer entry. The fall 2001 application fee was $35. Notification is sent on a rolling basis.

Transfer: 124 transfer students enrolled in 2001-2002. Applicants from 4-year colleges are required to have a minimum GPA of 2.0; from 2-year colleges, 2.5. The SAT I minimum requirements are 390 on the verbal section and 420 on the math section. A minimum score of 20 is required on the ACT. 31 credits of 124 must be completed at Calvin.

Visiting: There are regularly scheduled orientations for prospective students. Prospective students and their families are invited to explore Calvin firsthand by scheduling an individual visit or through the "Fridays at Calvin" campus visitation program, which offers sectionals, class visits, lunch with professors, campus tours, and an overnight stay at the residence halls. There are guides for informal visits and visitors may sit in on classes and stay overnight. To schedule a visit, contact the Admissions Office.

Financial Aid: In 2001-2002, 96% of all freshmen and 94% of continuing students received some form of financial aid. 65% of freshmen and 62% of continuing students received need-based aid. The average freshman award was $10,200. Of that total, scholarships or need-based grants averaged $7400 ($14,800 maximum); loans averaged $4400 ($6625 maximum); and work contracts averaged $1500 ($2000 maximum). 80% of undergraduates work part time. Average annual earnings from campus work are $1200. The average financial indebtedness of the 2001 graduate was $14,000. The FAFSA and the college's own financial statement are required. The fall application deadline is August 1.

International Students: There are 292 international students enrolled. The school actively recruits these students. They must score 550 on the written TOEFL or take the MELAB if the student scored low on the TOEFL.

Computers: The mainframe is an IBM RS/6000. There are 1500 PCs on campus with access to the network/Internet, and more than 900 are available to students. All students may access the system at any time. There are no time limits and no fees.

Graduates: In 2001, 918 bachelor's degrees were awarded. The most popular majors were English (7%), business (7%), and elementary education (7%). In an average class, 1% graduate in 3 years, 50% in 4 years, 68% in 5 years, and 70% in 6 years. 85 companies recruited on campus in 2000-2001. Of the 2000 graduating class, 19% were enrolled in graduate school within 6 months of graduation and 80% were employed.

Admissions Contact: Dale D. Kuiper, Director of Admissions.
E-mail: *admissions@calvin.edu* Web: *www.calvin.edu*

CENTER FOR CREATIVE STUDIES (See College For Creative Studies)

CENTRAL MICHIGAN UNIVERSITY D-4

Mount Pleasant, MI 48859 (989) 774-3076; Fax: (989) 774-7267

Full-time: 6629 men, 9971 women	**Faculty:** 756; IIA, av$
Part-time: 1251 men, 1679 women	**Ph.D.s:** 82%
Graduate: 3341 men, 4926 women	**Student/Faculty:** 22 to 1
Year: semesters, summer session	**Tuition:** $3735 ($8928)
Application Deadline: open	**Room & Board:** $4620
Freshman Class: 11,769 applied, 8203 accepted, 3607 enrolled	
SAT I Verbal/Math: 520/530	**ACT:** 22 **COMPETITIVE**

Central Michigan University, founded in 1892, is a public university offering programs in liberal arts, business, and health, education, and human services. There are 6 undergraduate schools and 1 graduate school. In addition to regional accreditation, CMU has baccalaureate program accreditation with AACSB, NASM, NCATE, and NRPA. The library contains 826,744 volumes, 1,260,223 microform items, and 23,575 audio visual forms/CDs, and subscribes to 4346 periodicals. Computerized library services include the card catalog, interlibrary loans, and database searching. Special learning facilities include a learning resource center, art gallery, natural history museum, radio station, TV station, an observatory, and a student newspaper. The 854-acre campus is in a small town 70 miles north of Lansing. Including residence halls, there are 54 buildings.

Student Life: 96% of undergraduates are from Michigan. Others are from 49 states, 81 foreign countries, and Canada. 89% are from public schools. 82% are white; 11% African American. The average age of freshmen is 18; all undergraduates, 22. 21% do not continue beyond their first year.

Housing: 6000 students can be accommodated in college housing, which includes single-sex and coed dormitories, on-campus apartments, and married-student housing. In addition, there are honors houses, a science and technology residential college, and a health professions residential college. On-campus housing is guaranteed for all 4 years. Alcohol is not permitted. All students may keep cars.

Activities: 7% of men belong to 13 national fraternities; 7% of women belong to 11 national sororities. There are 250 groups on campus, including art, cheerleading, choir, chorus, computers, dance, drama, ethnic, gay, honors, international, jazz band, literary magazine, marching band, musical theater, newspaper, orchestra, pep band, photography, political, professional, radio and TV, religious, social, social service, student government, symphony, and yearbook. Popular campus events include Student Activities Fair, CMU and You Day, and Big/Little Sister/Brother Weekend.

Sports: There are 6 intercollegiate sports for men and 7 for women, and 27 intramural sports for men and 26 for women. Facilities include 9 flag football/soccer and 4 lighted softball fields; 6 outdoor tennis, 12 racquetball, 11 basketball, 10 volleyball, and 16 badminton courts; 3 swimming pools; 2 saunas; an indoor track; indoor turf and tennis courts, weight rooms, an aerobics area, an archery range, 2 auxiliary gyms for floor hockey, basketball, and indoor soccer; a 12-lane bowling alley; and 8 pool/billiard tables. The campus football stadium seats 20086, the baseball stadium 4200, and the basketball gym 6050.

Disabled Students: 95% of the campus is accessible. Wheelchair ramps, elevators, special parking, specially equipped rest rooms, special class scheduling, lowered drinking fountains, and lowered telephones are available.

Services: Counseling and information services are available, as is tutoring in most subjects. There is a reader service for the blind, and remedial math, reading, and writing. Tutoring is provided free of charge to students with a GPA below 2.0.

Campus Safety and Security: Measures include escort service, shuttle buses, informal discussions, and pamphlets/posters/films. There are emergency telephones and lighted pathways/sidewalks.

Programs of Study: CMU confers B.A., B.S., B.A.A., B.F.A., B.Indiv.S., B.Mus., B.S.B.A., B.S.E., and B.S.E.T. degrees. Master's and doctoral degrees are also awarded. Bachelor's degrees are awarded in BIOLOGICAL SCIENCE (biology/biological science), BUSINESS (accounting, banking and finance, business administration and management, court reporting, management science, marketing/retailing/merchandising, and retailing), COMMUNICATIONS AND THE ARTS (broadcasting, communications, dramatic arts, English, fine arts, French, German, journalism, languages, music, and Spanish), COMPUTER AND PHYSICAL SCIENCE (actuarial science, chemistry, computer science, earth science, geology, mathematics, physical sciences, physics, and statistics), EDUCATION (art, bilingual/bicultural, business, early childhood, education, elementary, foreign languages, guidance, health, home economics, industrial arts, middle school, music, science, secondary, and special), ENGINEERING AND ENVIRONMENTAL DESIGN (engineering technology and industrial administration/management), HEALTH PROFESSIONS (speech pathology/audiology and sports medicine), SOCIAL SCIENCE (anthropology, economics, geography, history, parks and recreation management, philosophy, political science/government, psychology, religion, and sociology). Science and technology, humanities and social and behavioral sciences, and business administration are the largest.

Required: To graduate, students must complete 124 credit hours, including 30 in the major, with a GPA of 2.0. They must fulfill the university's distribution requirements in humanities, natural science, and social science, earn 30 hours in interpretive and area studies, and demonstrate written, oral, and math competency. A course in advanced English composition is required.

Special: CMU offers internships in business administration, study abroad in 11 countries, and dual majors in chemistry/physics and computer science/math. Student-designed majors are available for a B.A. in individual studies, and there is credit for life, military, and work experience. A 3-2 engineering degree is available with Michigan Technological University. Students may take up to 25 hours for pass/fail grades. The Institute for Personal and Career Development offers external degree programs in which students can get degrees without attending classes on campus. There are 30 national honor societies, a freshman honors program, and 21 departmental honors programs.

Faculty/Classroom: 60% of faculty are male; 40%, female. Graduate students teach 1% of introductory courses. The average class size in an introductory lecture is 35; in a laboratory, 29; and in a regular course, 21.

Admissions: 70% of the 2001-2002 applicants were accepted. The SAT I scores for the 2001-2002 freshman class were: Verbal--44% below 500, 40% between 500 and 599, 13% between 600 and 700, and 1% above 700; Math--33% below 500, 44% between 500 and 599, 21% between 600 and 700, and 3% above 700. The ACT scores were 35% below 21, 32% between 21 and 23, 22% between 24 and 26, 7% between 27 and 28, and 4% above 28.

Requirements: The ACT is recommended. In addition, applicants must be high school graduates or hold a GED. The university strongly recommends 4 years each of English and math, 3 each of science and social studies, and 2 of foreign language, as well as 1 course each in computer science and fine arts. AP and CLEP credits are accepted. Students may apply on-line at *http://eweb.cmich.edu/apptype.htm*

Procedure: Freshmen are admitted to all sessions. Entrance exams should be taken during the junior or senior year of high school. There is a deferred admissions plan. Application deadlines are open. The application fee is $25. Notificationis sent on a rolling basis. A waiting list is an active part of the admissions procedure.

Transfer: 1076 transfer students enrolled in 2001-2002. Transfer students must have a GPA of 2.5. 30 credits of 124 must be completed at CMU.

Visiting: There are guides for informal visits and visitors may sit in on classes and stay overnight. To schedule a visit, contact Admissions.

Financial Aid: In 2001-2002, 94% of all freshmen and 76% of continuing students received some form of financial aid. 69% of freshmen and 45% of continuing students received need-based aid. The average freshman award was $7247. Of that total, scholarships or need-based grants averaged $3927 ($17,152 maximum); loans averaged $2856 ($11,957 maximum); and work contracts averaged $464 ($3822 maximum). 22% of undergraduates work part time. Average annual earnings from campus work are $1584. The average financial indebtedness of the 2001 graduate was $14,898. The FAFSA is required. The fall application deadline is February 15.

International Students: There are 229 international students enrolled. The school actively recruits these students. They must score 520 on the written TOEFL.

Computers: The mainframe is an IBM 9672 model R32. There are 273 Mac and IBM PCs available for student use throughout the campus and in the dorms; 21 languages and software packages are available. All students may access the system at any time. There are no time limits and no fees.

Graduates: In 2001, 2922 bachelor's degrees were awarded. The most popular majors were psychology (6%), marketing (4%), and health fitness (4%). In an average class, 1% graduate in 3 years, 15% in 4 years, 42% in 5 years, and 51% in 6 years. 606 companies recruited on campus in 2000-2001.

Admissions Contact: Betty Wagner, Director of Admissions.
E-mail: *cmuadmit@cmuvm.csv.cmich.edu* Web: *www.cmich.edu*

CLEARY COLLEGE — E-5
Ann Arbor, MI 48197 — (517) 548-3670 (Howell)
(800) 589-1979; Fax: (517) 548-2170

Full-time: 150 men, 240 women	**Faculty:** 11; III, --$
Part-time: 65 men, 200 women	**Ph.D.s:** 12%
Graduate: none	**Student/Faculty:** 35 to 1
Year: quarters, summer session	**Tuition:** $10,350
Application Deadline: open	**Room & Board:** n/app
Freshman Class: n/av	**ACT:** recommended
	LESS COMPETITIVE

Cleary College, founded in 1883, is a private college of business offering bachelor's and associate degrees in business. Enrollment figures in the above capsule are approximate. The college serves an entirely commuter student body. A second campus, similar in size and programs, is located in Howell, and there are extension sites throughout southeastern Michigan. The library contains 7877 volumes and 175 audiovisual forms/CDs, and subscribes to 30 periodicals. Computerized library services include the card catalog, interlibrary loans, and database searching. Special learning facilities include a learning resource center. The 27-acre campus is in a suburban area 25 miles east of Lansing and 40 miles west of Detroit. There is one building.

Student Life: 99% of undergraduates are from Michigan. Others are from 2 states, 1 foreign country, and Canada. 90% are from public schools. 91% are white. The average age of all undergraduates is 36.

Housing: There are no residence halls. All students commute. Alcohol is not permitted. All students may keep cars.

Activities: There are no fraternities or sororities. Popular campus events include picnics.

Sports: There is no sports program at Cleary.

Disabled Students: All of the campus is accessible. Wheelchair ramps, special parking, specially equipped rest rooms, lowered drinking fountains, and lowered telephones are available.

Services: Counseling and information services are available, as is tutoring in some subjects, including English, math, computers. There is remedial math and writing.

Campus Safety and Security: Measures include informal discussions, pamphlets/posters/films, and lighted pathways/sidewalks.

Programs of Study: Cleary confers the B.B.A. degree. Associate degrees are also awarded. Bachelor's degrees are awarded in BUSINESS (accounting, banking and finance, business administration and management, human resources, and marketing management), COMPUTER AND PHYSICAL SCIENCE (information sciences and systems), HEALTH PROFESSIONS (health care administration). Accounting is the strongest academically. Business Administration is the largest.

Required: Core requirements include 90 quarter credits of business courses in economics, management, basic accounting, communication, and ethics. To graduate, students must complete a senior project and at least 180 quarter credit hours with a minimum GPA of 2.5

Special: Cleary offers internships, work study, and co-op programs in all majors, accelerated degree programs in accounting, marketing, finance, management information technology, quality management, human resource management, health services management, corporate and public accounting, and business management. Cleary also offers credit for prior learning experiences and opportunities for individualized study. Nondegree study is possible.

Faculty/Classroom: 45% of faculty are male; 55%, female. All teach undergraduates. The average class size in an introductory lecture is 15; in a laboratory, 12; and in a regular course, 12.

Requirements: The ACT is recommended. In addition, applicants must be graduates of an accredited secondary school or have earned a GED and have a minimum GPA of 2.5. A GPA of 2.5 is required. AP and CLEP credits are accepted.

Procedure: Freshmen are admitted to all sessions. There are early decision, early admissions, and deferred admissions plans. Application deadlines are open. The fall 2001 application fee was $25.

Transfer: Applicants must submit official transcripts from all institutions previously attended and have a minimum GPA of 2.5. 45 credits of 180 must be completed at Cleary.

Visiting: There are regularly scheduled orientations for prospective students. There are guides for informal visits and visitors may sit in on classes. To schedule a visit, contact Admissions.

Financial Aid: 1% of undergraduates work part time. Average annual earnings from campus work are $2500. Cleary is a member of CSS. The FAFSA is required. Check with the school for current deadlines.

International Students: There was 1 international student enrolled in a recent year. They must score 600 on the written TOEFL and also take the MELAB.

Computers: The mainframe consists of several Windows NT servers. Each campus has 2 computer labs equipped with IBM PCs for academic use. The Internet is available for distance learning classes. All students may access the system. There are no time limits and no fees. All students are required to have personal computers.

Graduates: In a recent year, 235 bachelor's degrees were awarded.

Admissions Contact: Carrie Bonofiglio, Director of Admissions.
Web: *www.cleary.edu*

COLLEGE FOR CREATIVE STUDIES (Formerly Center For Creative Studies) — E-5
Detroit, MI 48202-4034 — (313) 664-7425
(800) 952-ARTS; Fax: (313) 872-2739

Full-time: 590 men, 383 women	**Faculty:** 44
Part-time: 91 men, 88 women	**Ph.D.s:** 81%
Graduate: none	**Student/Faculty:** 22 to 1
Year: semesters, summer session	**Tuition:** $17,638
Application Deadline: March 1	**Room & Board:** $3300
Freshman Class: 719 applied, 577 accepted, 353 enrolled	
SAT I Verbal/Math: 521/526	**ACT:** 21 — **SPECIAL**

The College for Creative Studies, established in 1926, is a private, independent institution offering comprehensive 4-year B.F.A programs in animation and digital media, crafts, fine arts, communication design, industrial design, interior design, and photography. In addition to regional accreditation, CCS has baccalaureate program accreditation with NASAD. The library contains 21,000 volumes, and subscribes to 100 periodicals. Special learning facilities include a learning resource center and art gallery. The 11-acre campus is in an urban area 3 miles from downtown Detroit in the University Cultural Center, which includes the Detroit Institute of Art. Including residence halls, there are 6 buildings.

Student Life: 83% of undergraduates are from Michigan. Others are from 31 states, 15 foreign countries, and Canada. 64% are white. The average age of freshmen is 18; all undergraduates, 23. 25% do not continue beyond their first year; 50% remain to graduate.

Housing: 265 students can be accommodated in college housing, which includes coed on-campus apartments. On-campus housing is available on a first-come, first-served basis. Priority is given to out-of-town students. 77% of students commute. Alcohol is not permitted. All students may keep cars.

Activities: There are no fraternities or sororities. There are 6 groups on campus, including ethnic, professional, and student government. Popular campus events include an annual student exhibition, Noel Night, and Detroit Festival of the Arts.

Sports: There is no sports program at CCS.

Disabled Students: 75% of the campus is accessible. Wheelchair ramps, elevators, special parking, specially equipped rest rooms, and lowered telephones are available.

Services: Counseling and information services are available, as is tutoring in every subject. There is remedial reading and writing.

Campus Safety and Security: Measures include 24-hour foot and vehicle patrol, escort service, informal discussions, and pamphlets/posters/films. There are lighted pathways/sidewalks.

Programs of Study: CCS confers the B.F.A degree. Bachelor's degrees are awarded in COMMUNICATIONS AND THE ARTS (advertising, animation, ceramic art and design, fine arts, glass, graphic design, illustration, industrial design, metal/jewelry, painting, photography, printmaking, and sculpture), ENGINEERING AND ENVIRONMENTAL DESIGN (interior design), SOCIAL SCIENCE (textiles and clothing). Industrial design and communication design are the strongest academically. Animation and digital media are the largest.

Required: Degree requirements include work in English, behavioral science, art, history, history, speech, philosophy, and art and design. Students must complete 48 credits in liberal arts. A minimum GPA of 2.0 is required, and students must complete 126 credits to graduate.

Special: Internships are available within the student's departmental major. Credit for internships is available. Study abroad is possible.

Faculty/Classroom: 62% of faculty are male; 38%, female. All teach undergraduates. The average class size in an introductory lecture is 20; in a laboratory, 15; and in a regular course, 18.

Admissions: 80% of the 2001-2002 applicants were accepted.

Requirements: The SAT I or ACT is required. In addition, applicants must graduate from an accredited secondary school or earn a GED. A portfolio of representative work and an essay are required. A GPA of 2.5 is required. AP and CLEP credits are accepted. Important factors in the admissions decision are evidence of special talent and advanced placement or honor courses. Applications are accepted on-line at the school's web site or via Apply Yourself.

Procedure: Freshmen are admitted fall and winter. There is a deferred admissions plan. Applications should be filed by March 1 for fall entry and December 1 for spring entry. The fall 2001 application fee was $35. Notification is sent on a rolling basis.

Transfer: 165 transfer students enrolled in 2001-2002. Transfer applicants should submit a portfolio that includes artwork done at the previous college. Transcripts and portfolio review will determine how many credits may transfer. The approval of the chairperson of the department to which the student is applying is required for transfer of studio credit. The minimum GPA is 2.0. 33 credits of 126 must be completed at CCS.

Visiting: There are regularly scheduled orientations for prospective students, including an introduction to the college by an admission professional, a digital presentation of student work, application/financial aid information, and a campus tour. The orientations are scheduled every other week from September through April. There are guides for informal visits and visitors may sit in on classes. To schedule a visit, contact the Admission Office.

Financial Aid: In 2001-2002, 99% of all freshmen and 95% of continuing students received some form of financial aid. 14% of undergraduates work part time. Average annual earnings from campus work are $1200. The average financial indebtedness of the 2001 graduate was $20,850. The FAFSA is required. The fall application deadline is February 21.

International Students: There are 68 international students enrolled. The school actively recruits these students. They must score 500 on the written TOEFL and also take the SAT I or the ACT.

Computers: All students may access the system. There are no time limits and no fees. It is strongly recommended that all students have a personal computer.

Graduates: In 2001, 169 bachelor's degrees were awarded. The most popular majors were graphic communications (33%), industrial design (24%), and fine arts (12%). In an average class, 48% graduate in 6 years. 25 companies recruited on campus in 2000-2001.

Admissions Contact: Admissions Officer.
E-mail: *admissions@ccscad.edu* Web: *www.ccscad.edu*

CONCORDIA UNIVERSITY

Ann Arbor, MI 48105 — E-5

(734) 995-7322
(800) 253-0680; Fax: (734) 995-7455

Full-time: 208 men, 250 women	**Faculty:** 40
Part-time: 27 men, 48 women	**Ph.D.s:** 68%
Graduate: 12 men, 23 women	**Student/Faculty:** 11 to 1
Year: semesters	**Tuition:** $14,700
Application Deadline: September 1	**Room & Board:** $5800

Freshman Class: 298 applied, 256 accepted, 106 enrolled
ACT: 23 — **COMPETITIVE**

Concordia University, (formerly Concordia College), established in 1963, is a private institution affiliated with the Missouri Synod of the Lutheran Church, offering undergraduate and graduate degrees in the arts and sciences, business, education, and human services. There are 4 undergraduate schools and 1 graduate school. In addition to regional accreditation, Concordia has baccalaureate program accreditation with NCATE. The library contains 112,000 volumes, 36,000 microform items, and 6550 audiovisual forms/CDs, and subscribes to 1320 periodicals. Computerized library services include the card catalog, interlibrary loans, and database searching. Special learning facilities include a learning resource center and art gallery. The 234-acre campus is in a suburban area 40 miles west of Detroit. Including residence halls, there are 30 buildings.

Student Life: 80% of undergraduates are from Michigan. Others are from 22 states, 4 foreign countries, and Canada. 62% are from public schools. 85% are white. 79% are Protestant; 13% Catholic. The average age of freshmen is 18; all undergraduates, 21. 35% do not continue beyond their first year.

Housing: 448 students can be accommodated in college housing, which includes single-sex dormitories and married-student housing. On-campus housing is guaranteed for all 4 years. 74% of students live on campus; of those, 60% remain on campus on weekends. Alcohol is not permitted. All students may keep cars.

Activities: There are no fraternities or sororities. There are 21 groups on campus, including band, cheerleading, choir, chorale, chorus, computers, debate, drama, ethnic, jazz band, musical theater, pep band, religious, social, social service, student government, and yearbook. Popular campus events include Boar's Head Festival and Servant Events.

Sports: There are 5 intercollegiate sports for men and 6 for women, and 7 intramural sports for men and 7 for women. Facilities include a soccer field, baseball and softball diamonds, sand volleyball courts, and a phys ed building.

Disabled Students: 90% of the campus is accessible. Wheelchair ramps, elevators, special parking, specially equipped rest rooms, and lowered drinking fountains are available.

Services: Counseling and information services are available, as is tutoring in every subject. There is remedial math, reading, and writing.

Campus Safety and Security: Measures include 24-hour foot and vehicle patrol, escort service, informal discussions, and lighted pathways/sidewalks.

Programs of Study: Concordia confers the B.A. degree. Associate and master's degrees are also awarded. Bachelor's degrees are awarded in BIOLOGICAL SCIENCE (biology/biological science), BUSINESS (business administration and management and sports management), COMMUNICATIONS AND THE ARTS (art, communications, English, and music), COMPUTER AND PHYSICAL SCIENCE (computer management, information sciences and systems, mathematics, and science), EDUCATION (elementary, physical, and secondary), ENGINEERING AND ENVIRONMENTAL DESIGN (aircraft mechanics), HEALTH PROFESSIONS (health care administration), SOCIAL SCIENCE (biblical languages, criminal justice, family/consumer studies, history, psychology, religion, social studies, and sociology). Education is the strongest academically. Business administration, teacher education, and health care administration are the largest.

Required: Degree requirements include completion of 128 credit hours, with 30 to 36 in the major, 33 credit hours of integrated studies, and a minimum GPA of 2.0. The student must also demonstrate proficiency in foreign language, writing, speech, and math. Required courses include upper-level general studies, writing-intensive, physical activities, and computer applications. A senior project is required.

Special: Internships are available in most academic majors. Students may study abroad in 7 countries. Accelerated degree programs are available in business administration, criminal justice administration, and health care administration. The college confers credit for life, military, and work experience through the School of Adult and Continuing Education. Nondegree study, dual majors in many combinations, and a pass/fail grading option are available.

Faculty/Classroom: 55% of faculty are male; 45%, female. All teach undergraduates. The average class size in an introductory lecture is 25; in a laboratory, 10; and in a regular course, 15.

Admissions: 86% of the 2001-2002 applicants were accepted. The ACT scores for the 2001-2002 freshman class were: 37% below 21, 23% between 21 and 23, 20% between 24 and 26, 9% between 27 and 28, and 11% above 28.

Requirements: The SAT I or ACT is required; the ACT is preferred, with a minimum score of 21. Applicants must graduate from an accredited secondary school or have the GED. 20 Carnegie units are required, including 4 units in English, and 3 each in math, science, and social studies. AP and CLEP credits are accepted. Important factors in the admissions decision are evidence of special talent, advanced placement or honor courses, and leadership record. Applications are accepted on-line via Apply Web and the school's web site, *www.cuaa.edu*

Procedure: Freshmen are admitted fall and winter. There is a deferred admissions plan. Applications should be filed by September 1 for fall entry and January 3 for winter entry. The fall 2001 application fee was $25. Notification is sent on a rolling basis.

Transfer: 70 transfer students enrolled in 2001-2002. A GPA of 2.0 is required for transfer students; a GPA of 2.5 is required for admittance to the teacher education program. Transfer students who have earned 12 or more credits are not required to take the ACT. Interviews are recommended. 30 credits of 128 must be completed at Concordia.

Visiting: There are regularly scheduled orientations for prospective students, including 3 Discover Concordia days, Teacher Education Information Day, Senior Day, Junior Day, Art Day, Music Day, and Theatre Day. There are guides for informal visits and visitors may sit in on classes and stay overnight. To schedule a visit, contact the Admissions Office.

Financial Aid: In a recent year, 92% of all freshmen and 87% of continuing students received some form of financial aid. 83% of freshmen and 78% of continuing students received need-based aid. The average freshman award was $13,175. Of that total, scholarships or need-based grants averaged $4509 ($12,000 maximum); loans averaged $2500 ($5650 maximum); work contracts averaged $800 ($1650 maximum); and federal and state grants averaged $3500 ($5150 maximum). 68% of undergraduates work part time. Average annual earnings from campus work are $750. The average financial indebtedness of the 2001 graduate was $20,026. The FAFSA and the college's own financial statement are required. The fall application deadline is May 1.

International Students: There are 4 international students enrolled. They must score 520 on the written TOEFL or 180 on the electronic version or take the MELAB. They must also take the SAT I or the ACT.

Computers: More than 40 PCs are available for student use in the library and in clusters around the campus. All students may access the system 8 A.M. to midnight, with 24-hour access from dorm rooms. There are no time limits and no fees.

Graduates: In 2001, 140 bachelor's degrees were awarded. The most popular majors were business (42%), teacher education (20%), and health care administration (10%).

Admissions Contact: Kathleen Rowe, Director of Admissions. E-mail: *admissions@cuaa.edu*

CORNERSTONE UNIVERSITY AND GRAND RAPIDS BAPTIST SEMINARY D-4
Grand Rapids, MI 49525 (616) 222-1426
(800) 787-9778; Fax: (616) 222-1400

Full-time: 589 men, 943 women
Part-time: 76 men, 108 women
Graduate: 121 men, 44 women
Year: semesters, summer session
Application Deadline: open
Freshman Class: 841 applied, 805 accepted, 325 enrolled
ACT: 23
Faculty: 57; IIB, --$
Ph.D.s: 51%
Student/Faculty: 27 to 1
Tuition: $13,070
Room & Board: $5022
COMPETITIVE

Cornerstone University and Grand Rapids Baptist Seminary, founded in 1941, is a liberal arts college and graduate seminary educating students from a Christian perspective. Major undergraduate programs include business, teacher education, music, and ministry. There are 3 undergraduate and 3 graduate schools. In addition to regional accreditation, Cornerstone has baccalaureate program accreditation with NASM. The library contains 119,041 volumes, 289,150 microform items, and 4792 audiovisual forms/CDs, and subscribes to 996 periodicals. Computerized library services include the card catalog, interlibrary loans, and database searching. Special learning facilities include a learning resource center and radio station. The 132-acre campus is in a suburban area on the northeast side of Grand Rapids. Including residence halls, there are 23 buildings.

Student Life: 80% of undergraduates are from Michigan. Others are from 27 states, 9 foreign countries, and Canada. 62% are from public schools. 92% are white. All are Protestant. The average age of freshmen is 18; all undergraduates, 22. 36% do not continue beyond their first year; 33% remain to graduate.

Housing: 900 students can be accommodated in college housing, which includes single-sex dormitories, on-campus apartments, and married-student housing. In addition, there are honors houses. On-campus housing is guaranteed for all 4 years. 62% of students live on campus; of those, 50% remain on campus on weekends. Alcohol is not permitted. All students may keep cars.

Activities: There are no fraternities or sororities. There are 18 groups on campus, including band, cheerleading, choir, chorale, chorus, drama, ethnic, honors, jazz band, musical theater, pep band, political, religious, social, social service, student government, symphony, and yearbook. Popular campus events include Sibling Weekends, musicals, and Friends Weekend.

Sports: There are 6 intercollegiate sports for men and 7 for women, and 6 intramural sports for men and 6 for women. Facilities include a 2700-seat basketball/volleyball arena, a field house servicing tennis, volleyball, basketball, soccer, and softball, a baseball diamond, 2 soccer fields/intramural fields, a softball field, sand volleyball court, fitness center, human performance labs, 6 locker rooms, and a training room.

Disabled Students: All of the campus is accessible. Wheelchair ramps, elevators, special parking, specially equipped rest rooms, special class scheduling, large computer monitors for the visually impaired, and soundproof rooms for using tape recorders that read books-on-tape are available.

Services: Counseling and information services are available, as is tutoring in every subject. There is a Learning Center that offers a computer lab and special adaptive software, tutoring by appointment in the residence halls, test-taking assistance, and readers and typists as needed. There is a reader service for the blind and remedial math and writing.

Campus Safety and Security: Measures include 24-hour foot and vehicle patrol, escort service, informal discussions, and pamphlets/posters/films. There are emergency telephones and lighted pathways/sidewalks. First Aid/CPR certification is available.

Programs of Study: Cornerstone confers B.A., B.S., and B.Mus. degrees. Associate and master's degrees are also awarded. Bachelor's degrees are awarded in BIOLOGICAL SCIENCE (biology/biological science), BUSINESS (accounting, business administration and management, and marketing/retailing/merchandising), COMMUNICATIONS AND THE ARTS (communications, English, fine arts, music, music performance, music theory and composition, and speech/debate/rhetoric), EDUCATION (elementary, middle school, music, physical, science, and secondary), HEALTH PROFESSIONS (predentistry, premedicine, and preveterinary science), SOCIAL SCIENCE (biblical languages, biblical studies, history, interdisciplinary studies, prelaw, psychology, religion, religious education, social work, and sociology). English, music, and education are the strongest academically. Business and education are the largest.

Required: To graduate, the student must complete 129 credit hours, including 58 in the liberal arts core consisting of the humanities, math, social sciences, science, Bible/religion, foreign language, and phys ed. Specific courses include 2 phys ed courses, freshman rhetoric, biology, math, psychology or sociology, world civilization, fine arts, philosophy, Old Testament, and inductive Bible study. The number of hours in the major varies. The student must have an overall GPA of 2.0, 2.5 in the major, 2.0 in the minor, and pass a comprehensive exam.

Special: All students choose a student-ministries assignment each semester. Cornerstone requires internships in all areas of study. Study abroad in 5 countries, an accelerated degree program in organizational leadership, a Washington semester, and an interdisciplinary major, missionary aviation, are available.

Faculty/Classroom: 73% of faculty are male; 27%, female. 88% teach undergraduates. The average class size in an introductory lecture is 75; in a laboratory, 30; and in a regular course, 21.

Admissions: 96% of the 2001-2002 applicants were accepted. The ACT scores for the 2001-2002 freshman class were: 30% below 21, 27% between 21 and 23, 24% between 24 and 26, 11% between 27 and 28, and 8% above 28.

Requirements: The ACT is required, with a minimum score of 18, or 870 on the SAT I. The college requires a high school transcript or GED certificate, and recommends 15 Carnegie units, including 4 years of English, 3 each of math and social sciences, 2 of science, as well as 10 semesters of electives. The college recommends that the student appear for an interview and requires auditions for music scholarships. A pastoral reference is required. A GPA of 2.25 is required. AP and CLEP credits are accepted. Important factors in the admissions decision are personality/intangible qualities, extracurricular activities record, and leadership record.

Procedure: Freshmen are admitted to all sessions. Entrance exams should be taken during the junior or senior year. There is a deferred admissions plan. Application deadlines are open. The fall 2001 application fee was $25. Notification is sent on a rolling basis.

Transfer: The college requires high school and college transcripts from students, as well as a pastor's reference. The applicant must have taken the ACT if under 25 years of age with fewer than 30 hours of college credit. 32 credits of 129 must be completed at Cornerstone.

Visiting: There are regularly scheduled orientations for prospective students, including admissions and financial aid presentations, class visits, and course preregistration. There are guides for informal visits and visitors may sit in on classes and stay overnight. To schedule a visit, contact the Admissions Office.

Financial Aid: In 2001-2002, 98% of all freshmen and 91% of continuing students received some form of financial aid. 67% of all students received need-based aid. The average freshman award was $10,785. Of that total, scholarships or need-based grants averaged $6533 ($17,800 maximum); loans averaged $4130 ($16,626 maximum); and work contracts averaged $122 ($3736 maximum). 42% of undergraduates work part time. Average annual earnings from campus work are $1600. The average financial indebtedness of the 2001 graduate was $16,882. The FAFSA is required. The fall application deadline is February 20.

International Students: They must score 500 on the written TOEFL.

Computers: The mainframe is a DEC VAX 8300. Terminals are located in several buildings throughout campus for word processing and e-mail. All students may access the system Monday through Thursday from 8 A.M. to 11 P.M., Friday from 8 A.M. to 5 P.M., and Saturday from 1 P.M. to 5 P.M. There are no time limits and no fees.

Graduates: In 2001, 184 bachelor's degrees were awarded. The most popular majors were education (29%), business (18%), and psychology (7%).

Admissions Contact: Brent Rudin, Director of Undergraduate Admissions. E-mail: *admissions@cornerstone.edu*
Web: *www.cornerstone.edu*

DAVENPORT UNIVERSITY D-4
Grand Rapids, MI 49503 (616) 732-1200
(800) 632-9569; Fax: (616) 732-1167

Full-time: 306 men, 545 women
Part-time: 425 men, 758 women
Graduate: 51 men, 31 women
Year: quarters, summer session
Application Deadline: open
Freshman Class: 765 applied, 765 accepted, 457 enrolled
SAT I or ACT: recommended
Faculty: 27
Ph.D.s: 37%
Student/Faculty: 32 to 1
Tuition: $7657
Room & Board: $2400
NONCOMPETITIVE

Davenport University, founded in 1866, is an independent institution specializing in business education. It serves 15,000 students at 24 campuses throughout Michigan and northern Indiana. Davenport offers business-focused degrees. In May 2000, Davenport College, Detroit College of Business, and Great Lakes College began operation as Davenport University. The university also offers online courses. In addition to re-

gional accreditation, Davenport has baccalaureate program accreditation with GAAI ICP. The library contains 28,680 volumes, 802 microform items, and 805 audiovisual forms/CDs, and subscribes to 1000 periodicals. Computerized library services include database searching. Special learning facilities include a learning resource center. The 10-acre campus is in a suburban area 150 miles west of Detroit. Including residence halls, there are 9 buildings.
Student Life: 97% of undergraduates are from Michigan. Others are from 26 foreign countries and Canada. 97% are from public schools. 74% are white. The average age of all undergraduates is 29. 25% do not continue beyond their first year.
Housing: 50 students can be accommodated in college housing, which includes coed dormitories. On-campus housing is guaranteed for all 4 years. Alcohol is not permitted. All students may keep cars.
Activities: There are no fraternities or sororities. There are 5 groups on campus, including ethnic, professional, religious, student government, and yearbook. Popular campus events include Diversity Book Club.
Sports: There is no sports program at Davenport.
Disabled Students: All of the campus is accessible. Wheelchair ramps, elevators, special parking, specially equipped rest rooms, special class scheduling, lowered drinking fountains, and lowered telephones are available.
Services: Counseling and information services are available, as is tutoring in most subjects. There are tutoring labs for math, English, and computers, and there is a learning assistance center. There is remedial math, reading, and writing.
Campus Safety and Security: Measures include shuttle buses, lighted pathways/sidewalks, and 24-hour foot patrols.
Programs of Study: Davenport confers the B.B.A. degree. Associate and master's degrees are also awarded. Bachelor's degrees are awarded in BUSINESS (accounting, business administration and management, hotel/motel and restaurant management, and marketing/retailing/merchandising), COMPUTER AND PHYSICAL SCIENCE (computer programming), HEALTH PROFESSIONS (allied health), SOCIAL SCIENCE (paralegal studies). Business is the strongest academically. Accounting and management are the largest.
Required: Davenport requires all students to complete 184.5 credit hours, 58.5 in the major, with a minimum GPA of 2.0 overall and in career courses. The general education core consists of 72 credits, and the business core of 36 credits. At least 18 credits must be completed on campus in the classroom.
Special: Davenport offers co-op programs in administrative services, sales and marketing, and paralegal studies. There are internships in most disciplines. Study abroad is available through C.I.E.E. and A.I.F.S.
Faculty/Classroom: 49% of faculty are male; 51%, female. All teach undergraduates. The average class size in an introductory lecture is 13 and in a regular course, 13.
Admissions: All the 2001-2002 applicants were accepted. The school has an open admissions policy.
Requirements: The SAT I or ACT is recommended. Graduation from an accredited secondary school is required. A GED is accepted. An interview is recommended. CLEP credit is accepted. Important factors in the admissions decision are ability to finance college education, recommendations by school officials, and personality/intangible qualities. Applications are accepted on-line.
Procedure: Freshmen are admitted to all sessions. Entrance exams should be taken . There is an early decision plan. Application deadlines are open. The application fee is $25. Notification is sent on a rolling basis.
Transfer: 118 transfer students enrolled in 2001-2002. C is the minimum grade accepted for transfer. There is a 75% maximum credit transfer for the bachelor's degree. 59 credits of 185 must be completed at Davenport.
Visiting: There are regularly scheduled orientations for prospective students, consisting of an appointment, set up in advance. There are guides for informal visits and visitors may sit in on classes and stay overnight. To schedule a visit, contact Admissions at *gr_admiss@davenport.edu*.
Financial Aid: In 2001-2002, 70% of all freshmen received some form of financial aid. 91% of undergraduates work part time. Average annual earnings from campus work are $4200. The average financial indebtedness of the 2001 graduate was $8097. The FAFSA is required.
International Students: There are 120 international students enrolled. The school actively recruits these students. They must score 500 on the written TOEFL.
Computers: The mainframe is an HP 3000/Series 58. A complete lab with PCs is available. All students may access the system 8 A.M. to midnight on weekdays, and noon to 6 P.M. on weekends. There are no time limits and no fees.
Graduates: In 2001, 324 bachelor's degrees were awarded. The most popular majors were management (23%), management/business studies (23%), and marketing/CIS-micronetwork (11%). Of the 2000 graduating class, 9% were enrolled in graduate school within 6 months of graduation.
Admissions Contact: Larry Veeneman, Admissions Representative.
E-mail: *kellis@davenport.edu* Web: *www.davenport.edu*

DETROIT COLLEGE OF BUSINESS
(See Davenport University)

EASTERN MICHIGAN UNIVERSITY E-5
Ypsilanti, MI 48197 (734) 487-0193
(800) GO TO EMU; Fax: (734) 487-1484

Full-time: 5063 men, 7940 women	**Faculty:** 762
Part-time: 2208 men, 3291 women	**Ph.D.s:** 80%
Graduate: 1861 men, 3435 women	**Student/Faculty:** 17 to 1
Year: semesters, summer session	**Tuition:** $4603 ($12,230)
Application Deadline: July 31	**Room & Board:** $5252
Freshman Class: 9212 applied, 6868 accepted, 2810 enrolled	
SAT I or ACT: required	**COMPETITIVE**

Eastern Michigan University, founded in 1849, is a public institution offering programs in arts and sciences, business, education, health and human services, and technology. There are 5 undergraduate schools and 1 graduate school. In addition to regional accreditation, EMU has baccalaureate program accreditation with AACN, AACSB, ABET, ACCE, ACS, ADA, AHEA, AOTA, ASLA, ASLHA, CACREP, CAHEA, CCNE, CED, CSWE, FIDER, NAACLS, NASM, NCATE, NLN, and NRPA. The library contains 978,844 volumes, 969,468 microform items, and 8451 audiovisual forms/CDs, and subscribes to 4461 periodicals. Computerized library services include the card catalog, interlibrary loans, and database searching. Special learning facilities include a learning resource center, art gallery, and radio station. The 460-acre campus is in a suburban area 8 miles east of Ann Arbor. Including residence halls, there are 112 buildings.
Student Life: 91% of undergraduates are from Michigan. Others are from 43 states, 67 foreign countries, and Canada. 90% are from public schools. 77% are white; 18% African American. The average age of freshmen is 19; all undergraduates, 22. 29% do not continue beyond their first year; 35% remain to graduate.
Housing: 3760 students can be accommodated in college housing, which includes single-sex and coed dormitories, on-campus apartments, married-student housing, and sorority houses. In addition, there are honors houses, special-interest houses, special housing known as Community of Scholars, upper-class halls, and a first-year center. On-campus housing is available on a first-come, first-served basis and on a lottery system for upperclassmen. 77% of students commute. All students may keep cars.
Activities: 3% of men belong to 2 local and 13 national fraternities; 3% of women belong to 1 local and 14 national sororities. There are 150 groups on campus, including art, band, cheerleading, chess, choir, chorale, chorus, computers, dance, debate, drama, drill team, ethnic, film, forensics, gay, honors, international, jazz band, literary magazine, marching band, musical theater, opera, orchestra, pep band, photography, political, professional, radio and TV, religious, social, social service, student government, symphony, and yearbook. Popular campus events include Martin Luther King Birthday Celebration and Family Weekend.
Sports: There are 8 intercollegiate sports for men and 11 for women, and 25 intramural sports for men and 25 for women. Facilities include a 30,000-seat stadium, outdoor playing fields, a field house, a student recreation and intramural center, and an outdoor park including a lake, amphitheater, lighted basketball courts, volleyball courts, and lake house. There are 2 pools, a whirlpool/sauna, softball and soccer fields, 4 weight rooms, an aerobic studio, and a pro shop.
Disabled Students: 93% of the campus is accessible. Wheelchair ramps, elevators, special parking, specially equipped rest rooms, special class scheduling, lowered drinking fountains, lowered telephones, as well as special housing accommodations are available.
Services: Counseling and information services are available, as is tutoring in every subject. There is a reader service for the blind, and remedial math, reading, and writing. Notetakers and interpreters are provided for the disabled.
Campus Safety and Security: Measures include 24-hour foot and vehicle patrol, self-defense education, escort service, and shuttle buses. There are informal discussions, pamphlets/posters/films, emergency telephones, lighted pathways/sidewalks, and bicycle patrols, a crime prevention officer, area police officers in dorms, an anonymous tip line, Operation Identification, vehicle glass etching, and a bike lock lease program.
Programs of Study: EMU confers B.A., B.S., B.A.E., B.A.in Language and World Business, B.B.A., B.B.E., B.F.A., B.M.E., B.M.P., B.M.T., and B.S.N. degrees. Master's and doctoral degrees are also awarded. Bachelor's degrees are awarded in AGRICULTURE (forestry and related sciences), BIOLOGICAL SCIENCE (biochemistry, biology/biological science, botany, microbiology, and zoology), BUSINESS (accounting, banking and finance, business administration and management, business data processing, business economics, business systems analysis, fashion merchandising, hospitality management services, insurance and risk management, international business management, labor studies, management information systems, management science, marketing/retailing/merchandising, office supervision and management, personnel

management, real estate, recreation and leisure services, secretarial studies/office management, and tourism), COMMUNICATIONS AND THE ARTS (advertising, American literature, applied music, art, arts administration/management, classical languages, communications, communications technology, dance, design, dramatic arts, English, English as a second/foreign language, English literature, film arts, fine arts, French, German, graphic design, historic preservation, Japanese, journalism, linguistics, literature, music, music performance, performing arts, piano/organ, Spanish, speech/debate/rhetoric, and telecommunications), COMPUTER AND PHYSICAL SCIENCE (actuarial science, applied mathematics, astronomy, chemistry, computer programming, computer science, earth science, geology, information sciences and systems, mathematics, physics, polymer science, and statistics), EDUCATION (art, bilingual/bicultural, business, computer, drama, early childhood, education, education of the deaf and hearing impaired, education of the emotionally handicapped, education of the mentally handicapped, education of the multiply handicapped, education of the physically handicapped, education of the visually handicapped, educational media, elementary, English, foreign languages, health, industrial arts, mathematics, middle school, music, physical, psychology, reading, school psychology, science, secondary, social foundations, social science, special, and teaching English as a second/foreign language (TESOL/TEFOL)), ENGINEERING AND ENVIRONMENTAL DESIGN (aviation administration/management, city/community/regional planning, computer graphics, computer technology, construction management, interior design, land use management and reclamation, manufacturing technology, military science, plastics technology, preengineering, and urban planning technology), HEALTH PROFESSIONS (allied health, health care administration, medical laboratory technology, music therapy, nursing, occupational therapy, predentistry, premedicine, preoptometry, prepharmacy, recreation therapy, speech pathology/audiology, and sports medicine), SOCIAL SCIENCE (African American studies, anthropology, area studies, clothing and textiles management/production/services, counseling/psychology, criminal justice, dietetics, economics, family/consumer studies, geography, gerontology, history, interdisciplinary studies, international relations, liberal arts/general studies, paralegal studies, parks and recreation management, philosophy, political science/government, prelaw, psychology, public administration, social science, social work, sociology, and women's studies). Education, business, and health/nursing are the strongest academically. Elementary education, arts/sciences, and business are the largest.

Required: To graduate, students must have a GPA of 2.0, and complete a minimum of 124 semester hours, including usually 30 in the major, and 40 or more of basic studies. Required courses include English composition, political science, computer literacy, and phys ed.

Special: EMU offers internships, work-study programs, a Washington semester in public administration, and co-op programs and cross-registration with the University of Michigan at Ann Arbor, Concordia University, and Washtenaw Community College. Students may study abroad in more than 23 countries. EMU allows dual majors, nondegree study, B.A.-B.S. degrees in all majors and student-designed majors, accelerated degree programs, and confers a general studies degree, as well as a B.A.-B.B.A. degree in language and world business. Students may receive credit for life, military, and work experience, and pass/fail options are open. There are 11 national honor societies, a freshman honors program, and 36 departmental honors programs.

Faculty/Classroom: 56% of faculty are male; 44%, female. 70% teach undergraduates. Graduate students teach 2% of introductory courses. The average class size in a laboratory is 15 and in a regular course, 27.

Admissions: 75% of the 2001-2002 applicants were accepted.

Requirements: The SAT I or ACT is required, with a minimum composite of 17 on the ACT or 789 on the SAT I. Applicants should be high school graduates or hold a GED. The university recommends that students complete 19 academic credits in high school, consisting of 4 in English, 3 each in math, science, and social studies, 2 each in foreign language and history, and 2 to 3 in other traditional college-preparatory courses. A portfolio is required for applicants to the art program, and an audition is required for music students. A GPA of 2.0 is required. AP and CLEP credits are accepted.

Procedure: Freshmen are admitted to all sessions. Entrance exams should be taken by November of the senior year of high school. Applications should be filed by July 31 for fall entry, December 9 for winter entry, April 15 for spring entry, and June 6 for summer entry. The fall 2001 application fee was $25. Notification is sent on a rolling basis.

Transfer: 1786 transfer students enrolled in 2001-2002. Transfer students must have at least 12 semester hours of college credit, with a GPA of 2.0. 30 credits of 124 must be completed at EMU.

Visiting: There are regularly scheduled orientations for prospective students, including tours scheduled every morning and afternoon, as well as Saturday morning, with trained student tour guides. There are guides for informal visits and visitors may sit in on classes and stay overnight. To schedule a visit, contact the admissions On-Campus Programs at (734) 487-1111.

Financial Aid: In 2001-2002, 58% of all freshmen and 73% of continuing students received some form of financial aid. 52% of freshmen and 59% of continuing students received need-based aid. The average freshman award was $11,685. Of that total, scholarships or need-based grants averaged $3519 ($12,069 maximum); loans averaged $2243 ($6625 maximum); and work contracts averaged $2499 ($2600 maximum). 20% of undergraduates work part time. Average annual earnings from campus work are $2499. The average financial indebtedness of the 2001 graduate was $12,018. The FAFSA is required. The fall application deadline is December 21.

International Students: There are 318 international students enrolled. The school actively recruits these students. They must score 500 on the written TOEFL or 173 on the electronic version or take the MELAB.

Computers: The mainframes are 2 DEC ALPHA Servers 1000 A, 2 DEC ALPHA 4000, and 1 IBM 2003-125. Computer labs and stations are available throughout the campus, and residence halls are 75% networked. All workstations have Internet access. All students may access the system at all times. Dial-in access is limited to 1 to 2 hours per session if, using a modem. On campus there is no limit. Fees are included in tuition.

Graduates: In 2001, 2747 bachelor's degrees were awarded. The most popular majors were elementary education (9%), psychology (5%), and special education (5%). In an average class, 8% graduate in 4 years, 24% in 5 years, and 35% in 6 years. 840 companies recruited on campus in 2000-2001. Of the 2000 graduating class, 93% were employed within 6 months of graduation.

Admissions Contact: Judy Benfield-Tatum, Director of Admissions. Web: *www.emich.edu/public/admissions/admissions.html*

FERRIS STATE UNIVERSITY — D-4

Big Rapids, MI 49307 — (231) 591-2100

(800) 433-7747; Fax: (231) 591-3944

Full-time: 4484 men, 3477 women	**Faculty:** 435; IIA, -$
Part-time: 970 men, 1161 women	**Ph.D.s:** 43%
Graduate: 398 men, 440 women	**Student/Faculty:** 18 to 1
Year: semesters, summer session	**Tuition:** $5188 ($10,408)
Application Deadline: open	**Room & Board:** $5628
Freshman Class: 6409 applied, 3263 accepted, 2204 enrolled	
ACT: 19	**COMPETITIVE**

Ferris State University, established in 1884, is a public institution offering day and evening courses through its Schools of Arts and Sciences, Education, Allied Health, Technology, Business, and Pharmacy, College of Optometry, University College, and Kendall College of Art and Design. There are 9 undergraduate and 2 graduate schools. In addition to regional accreditation, Ferris State has baccalaureate program accreditation with ABET, ACPE, ADA, AHEA, CAHEA, CSWE, and NLN. The library contains 341,132 volumes and 2528 microform items, and subscribes to 9300 periodicals. Computerized library services include the card catalog, interlibrary loans, and database searching. Special learning facilities include a learning resource center, art gallery, planetarium, and TV station. The 650-acre campus is in a small town 55 miles north of Grand Rapids. Including residence halls, there are 98 buildings.

Student Life: 95% of undergraduates are from Michigan. Others are from 44 states, 76 foreign countries, and Canada. 78% are white. The average age of freshmen is 19; all undergraduates, 23. 38% do not continue beyond their first year.

Housing: 4333 students can be accommodated in college housing, which includes single-sex and coed dormitories, on-campus apartments, and married-student housing. In addition, there are honors houses. On-campus housing is guaranteed for all 4 years. All students may keep cars.

Activities: 6% of men belong to 21 national fraternities; 4% of women belong to 10 national sororities. There are 130 groups on campus, including art, band, cheerleading, chess, choir, chorale, chorus, computers, dance, drama, drill team, drum and bugle corps, ethnic, film, gay, honors, international, jazz band, marching band, newspaper, orchestra, pep band, photography, political, professional, radio and TV, religious, social, social service, student government, and symphony. Popular campus events include Little Brother/Little Sister Weekend and Mock Rock.

Sports: There are 7 intercollegiate sports for men and 8 for women, and 21 intramural sports for men and 19 for women. Facilities include a golf course, a racquetball and fitness club, an ice arena, a 10,000-seat stadium, a student recreation center with a pool, and tennis courts.

Disabled Students: All of the campus is accessible. Wheelchair ramps, elevators, special parking, specially equipped rest rooms, special class scheduling, lowered drinking fountains, and lowered telephones are available.

Services: Counseling and information services are available, as is tutoring in most subjects. There is a reader service for the blind, and remedial math, reading, and writing.

Campus Safety and Security: Measures include 24-hour foot and vehicle patrol, self-defense education, escort service, and informal discussions. There are pamphlets/posters/films, emergency telephones, and lighted pathways/sidewalks.

Programs of Study: Ferris State confers B.A., B.S., B.F.A, B.S.N, and B.S.W. degrees. Associate, master's, and doctoral degrees are also awarded. Bachelor's degrees are awarded in BIOLOGICAL SCIENCE (biology/biological science), BUSINESS (accounting, banking and finance, business administration and management, hospitality management services, human resources, insurance, international business management, marketing/retailing/merchandising, and small business management), COMMUNICATIONS AND THE ARTS (advertising and public relations), COMPUTER AND PHYSICAL SCIENCE (applied mathematics and computer programming), EDUCATION (business, mathematics, and technical), ENGINEERING AND ENVIRONMENTAL DESIGN (construction management, engineering technology, plastics engineering, and surveying engineering), HEALTH PROFESSIONS (health care administration, nuclear medical technology, nursing, and pharmacy), SOCIAL SCIENCE (criminal justice and social work). Pharmacy is the strongest academically. Business administration and marketing are the largest.

Required: Degree requirements include a minimum 2.0 GPA, 12 semester credit hours in English and speech communications, 9 each in the humanities and social sciences, and 7 to 8 in natural sciences. The number of credits students must earn in the major and the total required for graduation vary by course of study.

Special: Ferris State offers internships, study abroad, work-study programs, accelerated degrees, dual and student-designed majors, credit for life, military, and work experience, and a pass/fail grading option. There are 6 national honor societies, and a freshman honors program.

Faculty/Classroom: 70% of faculty are male; 30%, female. All teach undergraduates. The average class size in an introductory lecture is 40; in a laboratory, 18; and in a regular course, 30.

Admissions: 51% of the 2001-2002 applicants were accepted.

Requirements: The ACT is required. In addition, applicants must graduate from an accredited secondary school or earn a GED. Four years each of English and math, 3 years each of biophysical/physical sciences and history, 2 years each of a foreign language and fine arts, and 1 year of computer literacy are advised. Interviews are recommended. A GPA of 2.0 is required. AP and CLEP credits are accepted. Important factors in the admissions decision are advanced placement or honor courses, evidence of special talent, and recommendations by school officials.

Procedure: Freshmen are admitted to all sessions. Entrance exams should be taken before course registration. Application deadlines are open. Notification is sent on a rolling basis. 1% of all applicants are on a waiting list.

Transfer: 1239 transfer students enrolled in 2001-2002. A GPA of at least 2.0 is required. 30 credits must be completed at Ferris State.

Visiting: There are regularly scheduled orientations for prospective students. There are guides for informal visits and visitors may sit in on classes and stay overnight. To schedule a visit, contact the Admissions Office.

Financial Aid: In 2001-2002, 87% of all freshmen and 76% of continuing students received some form of financial aid. 60% of freshmen and 58% of continuing students received need-based aid. The average freshman award was $6750. Of that total, scholarships or need-based grants averaged $3000 ($6000 maximum); loans averaged $1800 ($5500 maximum); and work contracts averaged $1600 ($2300 maximum). 41% of undergraduates work part time. Average annual earnings from campus work are $2100. The average financial indebtedness of the 2001 graduate was $13,000. Ferris State is a member of CSS. The FAFSA is required. The fall application deadline is March 15.

International Students: There are 201 international students enrolled. The school actively recruits these students. They must score 500 on the written TOEFL and also take a supplemental math exam.

Computers: The mainframe is an IBM 3090 200E. Residence hall rooms and apartments have access to local and worldwide computer networks. Computer labs are available in every residence hall and at various locations on campus. All students may access the system at any time; labs are open 16 hours daily. There are no time limits and no fees.

Graduates: In 2001, 1217 bachelor's degrees were awarded. The most popular majors were pharmacy (8%), criminal justice (8%), and business administration (6%). 210 companies recruited on campus in a recent year.

Admissions Contact: Admissions Officer. A video is available.
Web: *www.ferris.edu/admissions/quesform.htm*

GMI INSTITUTE
(See Kettering University)

GRACE BIBLE COLLEGE
Grand Rapids, MI 49509 — D-4
(616) 538-2330
(800) 968-1887; (616) 538-2330

Full-time: 72 men, 61 women	**Faculty:** 9
Part-time: 6 men, 10 women	**Ph.D.s:** 22%
Graduate: none	**Student/Faculty:** 15 to 1
Year: semesters	**Tuition:** $7950
Application Deadline: open	**Room & Board:** $4650
Freshman Class: 122 applied, 62 accepted, 31 enrolled	
ACT: 21	**COMPETITIVE**

Grace Bible College, founded in 1939, is a private institution affiliated with the Grace Gospel Fellowship. Its mission is to provide a curriculum that integrates general education and biblical studies and prepares students for service in their career, church, and society. In addition to regional accreditation, GBC has baccalaureate program accreditation with AABC. The library contains 38,464 volumes and 1718 audiovisual forms/CDs, and subscribes to 192 periodicals. Computerized library services include the card catalog and database searching. The 16-acre campus is in a suburban area on the southwest side of Grand Rapids. Including residence halls, there are 11 buildings.

Student Life: 68% of undergraduates are from Michigan. Others are from 15 states and 2 foreign countries. 92% are white. Most are Protestant. The average age of freshmen is 18; all undergraduates, 22.

Housing: 80 students can be accommodated in college housing, which includes single-sex dormitories, on-campus apartments, off-campus apartments, and married-student housing. On-campus housing is guaranteed for all 4 years. 64% of students live on campus; of those, 85% remain on campus on weekends. Alcohol is not permitted. All students may keep cars.

Activities: There are no fraternities or sororities. There are some groups and organizations on campus, including drama, musical theater, newspaper, religious, and student government. Popular campus events include Opera Dinner Theater, Winter Formal, and Missions Conference.

Sports: There are 2 intercollegiate sports for men and 2 for women. Facilities include a 1000-seat soccer field and an athletic center with a 500-seat gym for basketball and volleyball, a racquetball court, and an exercise and weight room.

Disabled Students: 85% of the campus is accessible. Wheelchair ramps, elevators, special parking, specially equipped rest rooms, and lowered drinking fountains are available.

Services: Counseling and information services are available, as is tutoring in most subjects.

Campus Safety and Security: Measures include informal discussions, pamphlets/posters/films, lighted pathways/sidewalks, and evening and overnight foot patrol.

Programs of Study: GBC confers B.S., B.Mus., B.R.E., and B.Th. degrees. Associate degrees are also awarded. Bachelor's degrees are awarded in BUSINESS (business administration and management), EDUCATION (elementary and secondary), SOCIAL SCIENCE (early childhood studies, human services, interdisciplinary studies, missions, pastoral studies, religion, religious education, religious music, and youth ministry).

Required: To graduate, students must complete 126 to 158 credits, depending on the major, with a minimum GPA of 2.0 and must be considered worthy in character and conduct by the faculty. Course work is required in arts and sciences, ministry studies, Bible/theology, math/computer science, lab science, and phys ed. Attendance is expected at worship services twice a week.

Special: Cross-registration is available with Cornerstone and Davenport Universities. GBC offers 6-month internships for theology majors.

Faculty/Classroom: 69% of faculty are male; 31%, female. All teach undergraduates. The average class size in a regular course is 25.

Admissions: 51% of the 2001-2002 applicants were accepted. The ACT scores for the 2001-2002 freshman class were: 48% below 21, 32% between 21 and 23, 14% between 24 and 26, and 6% above 28. 19% of the current freshmen were in the top fifth of their class; 48% were in the top two fifths. 2 freshmen graduated first in their class.

Requirements: The ACT is required. In addition, applicants must be graduates of accredited secondary schools or have earned a GED. The application must show involvement in Christian activities and personal salvation through Jesus Christ. GBC requires applicants to be in the upper 50% of their class. A GPA of 2.5 is required. AP and CLEP credits are accepted.

Procedure: Freshmen are admitted fall and spring. Application deadlines are open. Notification is sent on a rolling basis.

Transfer: 19 transfer students enrolled in 2001-2002. Applicants must present a GPA of 2.0 and be in good standing at their previous school. Those with fewer than 24 college credit hours must submit high school records. 24 credits of 126 must be completed at GBC.

Visiting: There are regularly scheduled orientations for prospective students, consisting of 7 Friday programs a year that include workshops, class visits, and campus tours. There are guides for informal visits and visitors may sit in on classes and stay overnight. To schedule a visit, contact Kevin Gilliam, Director of Enrollment at *enrollment@gbcol.edu*.

Financial Aid: In 2001-2002, 99% of all freshmen and 98% of continuing students received some form of financial aid. 65% of freshmen and 86% of continuing students received need-based aid. The average freshman award was $500. Of that total, scholarships or need-based grants averaged $4475 ($3750 maximum); loans averaged $1404 ($2625 maximum); and work contracts averaged $600 ($700 maximum). 37% of undergraduates work part time. Average annual earnings from campus work are $1500. The average financial indebtedness of the 2001 graduate was $9818. The FAFSA is required. The fall application deadline is February 15 for in-state applicants and March 15 for all others.

International Students: There are 2 international students enrolled. They must score 500 on the written TOEFL or 173 on the electronic version.

Computers: GBC operates a LAN system with a Windows NT 4.0 server. Internet and library collection searches are available on 6 PC's in the library. Students who bring a PC to school need a Windows-based system to interface with GBC's network.

Graduates: In 2001, 13 bachelor's degrees were awarded. The most popular majors were liberal arts/biblical (23%), music (15%), and education (15%).

Admissions Contact: Kevin Gilliam, Director of Enrollment.
E-mail: *enrollment@gbcol.edu* Web: *www.gbcol.edu*

GRAND VALLEY STATE UNIVERSITY — D-4

Allendale, MI 49401-9403 — (616) 895-2025
(800) 748-0246; Fax: (616) 895-2000

Full-time: 5423 men, 7948 women	**Faculty:** 693; IIA, av$
Part-time: 1202 men, 1812 women	**Ph.D.s:** 70%
Graduate: 1129 men, 2248 women	**Student/Faculty:** 19 to 1
Year: semesters, summer session	**Tuition:** $4660 ($10,080)
Application Deadline: July 31	**Room & Board:** $5380

Freshman Class: 9593 applied, 7506 accepted, 3097 enrolled
ACT: 23 — **COMPETITIVE**

Grand Valley State University, founded in 1960, is a comprehensive public institution offering graduate and undergraduate liberal arts and professional education. There are 12 undergraduate and 9 graduate schools. In addition to regional accreditation, Grand Valley has baccalaureate program accreditation with ABET, APTA, CSWE, NASAD, NASM, NCATE, and NLN. The 2 libraries contain 672,000 volumes, 577,780 microform items, and 9816 audiovisual forms/CDs, and subscribe to 3422 periodicals. Computerized library services include the card catalog, interlibrary loans, and database searching. Special learning facilities include a learning resource center, art gallery, radio station, TV station, cadaver lab, 2 Great Lakes research vessels, a performance auditorium, and dance studios. The 900-acre campus is in a small town 12 miles west of Grand Rapids. Including residence halls, there are 58 buildings.

Student Life: 96% of undergraduates are from Michigan. Others are from 40 states, 38 foreign countries, and Canada. 75% are from public schools. 89% are white. The average age of freshmen is 18; all undergraduates, 22. 22% do not continue beyond their first year; 48% remain to graduate.

Housing: 4335 students can be accommodated in college housing, which includes coed dormitories, on-campus apartments, off-campus apartments, and married-student housing. In addition, there are honors houses, language houses, and special-interest houses. On-campus housing is guaranteed for the freshman year only, is available on a first-come, first-served basis, and is available on a lottery system for upperclassmen. Priority is given to out-of-town students. 73% of students commute. Alcohol is not permitted. All students may keep cars.

Activities: 3% of men belong to 2 local and 8 national fraternities; 3% of women belong to 2 local and 9 national sororities. There are 130 groups on campus, including art, band, cheerleading, chess, choir, chorale, chorus, computers, dance, drama, ethnic, film, gay, honors, international, jazz band, literary magazine, marching band, newspaper, orchestra, pep band, photography, political, professional, radio and TV, religious, social, social service, student government, and symphony. Popular campus events include Family Day, Hispanic Awareness Week, and Black History Month.

Sports: There are 9 intercollegiate sports for men and 10 for women, and 22 intramural sports for men and 21 for women. Facilities include a football stadium, a baseball field, a basketball arena, swimming and diving pools, an indoor track, a weight room, a fitness building/intramural center, and an outdoor cross-country track.

Disabled Students: 98% of the campus is accessible. Wheelchair ramps, elevators, special parking, specially equipped rest rooms, special class scheduling, lowered drinking fountains, and lowered telephones are available.

Services: Counseling and information services are available, as is tutoring in most subjects. There is a reader service for the blind, and remedial math, reading, and writing.

Campus Safety and Security: Measures include 24-hour foot and vehicle patrol, self-defense education, escort service, and shuttle buses. There are informal discussions, pamphlets/posters/films, emergency telephones, and lighted pathways/sidewalks.

Programs of Study: Grand Valley confers B.A., B.S., B.B.A., B.F.A., B.M., B.M.E., B.S.E., B.S.N., and B.S.W. degrees. Master's degrees are also awarded. Bachelor's degrees are awarded in BIOLOGICAL SCIENCE (biology/biological science), BUSINESS (accounting, banking and finance, business administration and management, business economics, hotel/motel and restaurant management, international business management, management science, marketing/retailing/merchandising, and personnel management), COMMUNICATIONS AND THE ARTS (advertising, broadcasting, communications, design, dramatic arts, English, film arts, fine arts, journalism, languages, music, and photography), COMPUTER AND PHYSICAL SCIENCE (chemistry, computer science, geology, mathematics, and physics), EDUCATION (art, elementary, foreign languages, middle school, music, science, and secondary), ENGINEERING AND ENVIRONMENTAL DESIGN (engineering and industrial engineering technology), HEALTH PROFESSIONS (health science, medical laboratory technology, nursing, physical therapy, physician's assistant, predentistry, and premedicine), SOCIAL SCIENCE (anthropology, criminal justice, economics, geography, history, international relations, philosophy, political science/government, prelaw, psychology, public administration, social science, social work, and sociology). Health sciences, English, and psychology are the largest.

Required: To graduate, students must have earned 30 credits in general education, comprised of 10 courses selected from specific groups, and have completed the university's required courses in English and math, as well as the upper-division writing course. A total of 120 credits, with 36 to 60 in the major, and a GPA of 2.0, are required to graduate.

Special: Many programs offer dual majors and internships, and most majors qualify for B.A.-B.S. degrees. There is an engineering cooperative program, a student-designed major in liberal studies, and many work-study programs. Outside opportunities include study abroad in 10 countries and a Washington semester. There are 14 national honor societies, a freshman honors program, and 12 departmental honors programs.

Faculty/Classroom: 54% of faculty are male; 46%, female. 94% teach undergraduates. No introductory courses are taught by graduate students. The average class size in an introductory lecture is 47; in a laboratory, 18; and in a regular course, 27.

Admissions: 78% of the 2001-2002 applicants were accepted. The ACT scores for the 2001-2002 freshman class were: 26% below 21, 34% between 21 and 23, 25% between 24 and 26, 8% between 27 and 28, and 7% above 28. 33% of the current freshmen were in the top fifth of their class; 67% were in the top two fifths.

Requirements: Michigan residents must submit ACT test scores, nonresidents either ACT or SAT I scores. In addition, high school transcripts should indicate 4 years of English with 1 composition course, and 3 each of history, math (including 2 years of algebra), science, and social studies. Foreign language is recommended. Applicants who graduated from high school more than 3 years ago need not show test results. The GED is accepted. A GPA of 2.9 is required. AP and CLEP credits are accepted. Important factors in the admissions decision are recommendations by school officials, evidence of special talent, and leadership record. The university accepts applications on computer disk and on-line at *www.gvsu.edu*.

Procedure: Freshmen are admitted to all sessions. Entrance exams should be taken during the junior year. Applications should be filed by July 31 for fall entry, November 15 for winter entry, April 10 for spring entry, and May 10 for summer entry. The 2001 fall application fee waas $20. Notification is sent on a rolling basis.

Transfer: 1340 transfer students enrolled in 2001-2002. Transfer students must have a minimum of 30 college credits with a 2.0 GPA. 30 credits of 120 must be completed at Grand Valley.

Visiting: There are regularly scheduled orientations for prospective students, including registration activities. There are guides for informal visits and visitors may sit in on classes and stay overnight. To schedule a visit, contact the Admissions Office.

Financial Aid: In 2001-2002, 74% of all freshmen and 68% of continuing students received some form of financial aid. 55% of freshmen and 51% of continuing students received need-based aid. The average freshman award was $6108. Of that total, scholarships or need-based grants averaged $3485 ($10,000 maximum); loans averaged $1977 ($4425 maximum); and work contracts averaged $1000 ($2400 maximum). 73% of undergraduates work part time. Average annual earnings from campus work are $1800. The average financial indebtedness of the 2001 graduate was $6565. Grand Valley is a member of CSS. The FAFSA is required. The fall application deadline is February 15.

International Students: There are 78 international students enrolled. The school actively recruits these students. They must score 550 on the written TOEFL or take the MELAB or the Comprehensive English Language Test.

Computers: The mainframe is an IBM 9672-R12 system 390 parallel server. There is a 5-to-1 student/computer ratio with computers spread

throughout the campus. LANs and computing labs are open 7 days a week, and PCs are connected to LAN and mainframe networks. All students have e-mail and access to the Internet. All students may access the system. There are no time limits and no fees. It is strongly recommended that all students have a personal computer.
Graduates: In 2001, 2024 bachelor's degrees were awarded. The most popular majors were business (20%), health sciences (18%), and psychology (10%). In an average class, 48% graduate in 6 years. 125 companies recruited on campus in 2000-2001. Of the 2000 graduating class, 87% were employed within 6 months of graduation.
Admissions Contact: Jodi Chycinski, Director of Admissions. A video is available. E-mail: *go2gvsu@gvsu.edu* Web: *www.gvsu.edu*

HILLSDALE COLLEGE D-5
Hillsdale, MI 49242 (517) 607-2327; Fax: (517) 607-2298

Full-time: 554 men, 544 women	**Faculty:** 89
Part-time: 13 men, 27 women	**Ph.D.s:** 90%
Graduate: none	**Student/Faculty:** 12 to 1
Year: semesters, summer session	**Tuition:** $14,700
Application Deadline: July 15	**Room & Board:** $5886
Freshman Class: 950 applied, 808 accepted, 349 enrolled	
SAT I Verbal/Math: 630/600	**ACT:** 26 **VERY COMPETITIVE+**

Hillsdale College, founded in 1844, is a private liberal arts college emphasizing preprofessional, business, and education programs. The 3 libraries contain 175,000 volumes, 42,000 microform items, and 6500 audiovisual forms/CDs, and subscribe to 1500 periodicals. Computerized library services include the card catalog, interlibrary loans, and database searching. Special learning facilities include a learning resource center and a media center, an early childhood education lab, an arboretum, a 3000-book economics library, and a rare books room. The 250-acre campus is in a small town 120 miles southwest of Detroit. Including residence halls, there are 50 buildings.
Student Life: 51% of undergraduates are from Michigan. Others are from 47 states, 14 foreign countries, and Canada. 50% are from public schools. 96% are white. 47% are claim no religious affiliation; 35% Protestant; 17% Catholic. The average age of freshmen is 18; all undergraduates, 20. 10% do not continue beyond their first year.
Housing: 950 students can be accommodated in college housing, which includes single-sex dormitories, on-campus apartments, fraternity houses, and sorority houses. In addition, there are honors houses and special-interest houses. On-campus housing is guaranteed for all 4 years. 80% of students live on campus; of those, 85% remain on campus on weekends. Alcohol is not permitted. All students may keep cars.
Activities: 35% of men belong to 4 national fraternities; 50% of women belong to 4 national sororities. There are 50 groups on campus, including art, bagpipe band, cheerleading, choir, chorale, chorus, computers, dance, debate, drama, drill team, drum and bagpipe corps, ethnic, forensics, honors, international, jazz band, literary magazine, musical theater, newspaper, orchestra, pep band, photography, political, professional, radio and TV, religious, social, student government, and yearbook. Popular campus events include Parents Weekend, President's Ball, and Greek Week.
Sports: There are 9 intercollegiate sports for men and 9 for women, and 7 intramural sports for men and 7 for women. Facilities include an athletic complex with a prescription turf football field, a swimming pool, a 200-meter indoor track, a basketball arena, a weight room, an outdoor Olympic track, an exercise/physiology room, and volleyball, handball, racquetball, wallyball, and indoor tennis courts. The campus stadium seats 8000; the gym, 2600.
Disabled Students: 85% of the campus is accessible. Wheelchair ramps, elevators, special parking, specially equipped rest rooms, and lowered drinking fountains are available.
Services: Counseling and information services are available, as is tutoring in every subject. A writing center on campus and a peer tutoring program are administered by current students.
Campus Safety and Security: Measures include 24-hour foot and vehicle patrol, informal discussions, pamphlets/posters/films, and lighted pathways/sidewalks.
Programs of Study: Hillsdale confers B.A. and B.S. degrees. Bachelor's degrees are awarded in BIOLOGICAL SCIENCE (biology/biological science), BUSINESS (accounting, banking and finance, business administration and management, international business management, and marketing/retailing/merchandising), COMMUNICATIONS AND THE ARTS (classics, comparative literature, dramatic arts, English, fine arts, French, German, music, Spanish, and speech/debate/rhetoric), COMPUTER AND PHYSICAL SCIENCE (chemistry, mathematics, and physics), EDUCATION (art, early childhood, elementary, foreign languages, middle school, music, physical, science, and secondary), HEALTH PROFESSIONS (predentistry, premedicine, and preveterinary science), SOCIAL SCIENCE (American studies, Christian studies, economics, European studies, history, political science/government, prelaw, psychology, religion, social science, and sociology). History, economics, and biology are the strongest academically. Business, history, and English are the largest.
Required: To graduate, the student must complete 124 semester hours with a GPA of 2.0. Required courses include 1 year of English, 1 year of science, 1 semester of Western Heritage and 1 semester of American Heritage, 9 hours of the humanities, 8 of the natural sciences and math, 6 of the social sciences, and 2 of phys ed. Students must also enroll in 2 seminars at the school's Center for Constructive Alternatives. 12 credit hours in a foreign language for a B.A. degree and 36 credit hours in math and science for a B.S. degree are also required.
Special: Special academic programs include the Washington Journalism Internship at the National Journalism Center and the Washington-Hillsdale Intern Program (WHIP), which places students in congressional or government offices. Students may study abroad in France, Germany, or Spain, and qualified students are chosen to attend Oxford University for a year. A business internship is offered in London at Regents College. The college offers an accelerated degree; interdisciplinary majors, including political economy combining economics, history, and political science; 3-2 and 2-2 engineering degrees; and work-study programs at the city radio station WCSR and the city newspaper, the *Hillsdale Daily News*. There are 18 national honor societies, and a freshman honors program.
Faculty/Classroom: 75% of faculty are male; 25%, female. All teach undergraduates and 1% both teach and do research. The average class size in an introductory lecture is 24; in a laboratory, 7; and in a regular course, 21.
Admissions: 85% of the 2001-2002 applicants were accepted. The SAT I scores for the 2001-2002 freshman class were: Verbal--6% below 500, 31% between 500 and 599, 40% between 600 and 700, and 23% above 700; Math--8% below 500, 39% between 500 and 599, 41% between 600 and 700, and 12% above 700. The ACT scores were 6% below 21, 20% between 21 and 23, 35% between 24 and 26, 14% between 27 and 28, and 25% above 28. 65% of the current freshmen were in the top fifth of their class; 90% were in the top two fifths. There were 11 National Merit finalists and 60 semifinalists. 17 freshmen graduated first in their class.
Requirements: The SAT I or ACT is required. In addition, the student must be a high school graduate or have earned a GED, and must have completed 4 years of English, 3 each of math and science, and 2 each of history, social studies, and foreign language. The college requires a letter of recommendation and an essay. An interview is also recommended. For music majors, an audition is required. The school recommends taking SAT II: Subject tests. Hillsdale requires applicants to be in the upper 50% of their class. A GPA of 3.1 is required. AP and CLEP credits are accepted. Important factors in the admissions decision are advanced placement or honor courses, leadership record, and extracurricular activities record. Applications can be obtained on-line at *www.hillsdale.edu*.
Procedure: Freshmen are admitted to all sessions. Entrance exams should be taken in the spring of the junior year and/or the fall of the senior year. Applications should be filed by July 15 for fall entry, December 15 for spring entry, and May 1 for summer entry, along with a $15 fee. Notification is sent on a rolling basis.
Transfer: 41 transfer students enrolled in 2001-2002. Transfer students must have a GPA of 3.0, and have a transfer evaluation form completed by the dean of students of their school. Hillsdale also requires high school and college transcripts. 24 credits of 124 must be completed at Hillsdale.
Visiting: There are regularly scheduled orientations for prospective students, including a spring orientation and a formal junior and senior visitation program. There are guides for informal visits and visitors may sit in on classes and stay overnight. To schedule a visit, contact Shannon Pellecchia at the Admissions Office at *admissions@hillsdale.edu*.
Financial Aid: In 2001-2002, 85% of all freshmen and 89% of continuing students received some form of financial aid. 80% of freshmen received need-based aid. The average freshman award was $10,500. Of that total, scholarships or need-based grants averaged $6500 ($14,400 maximum); loans averaged $3500 ($500 maximum); and work contracts averaged $1000. 65% of undergraduates work part time. Average annual earnings from campus work are $1300. The average financial indebtedness of the 2001 graduate was $11,000. Hillsdale is a member of CSS. The FAFSA and the college's own financial statement are required. The fall application deadline is April 15.
International Students: There are 23 international students enrolled. They must score 520 on the written TOEFL or 190 on the electronic version or take the MELAB, the Comprehensive English Language Test, or the college's own test. Applicants can also complete ESL level 108, with a minimum score of 15 in the motivational and proficiency categories.
Computers: The mainframe is an IBM AS/400. The computer lab, located in the student center, has more than 100 PCs available for student use. Laser printers are also available, along with word-processing and software workshops, e-mail, Internet, and the World Wide Web. All students may access the system at any time. There are no time limits and no fees.
Graduates: In 2001, 235 bachelor's degrees were awarded. The most popular majors were business (27%), biology (15%), and history (11%). In an average class, 1% graduate in 3 years, 68% in 4 years, 71% in 5

years, and 71% in 6 years. 50 companies recruited on campus in 2000-2001. Of the 2000 graduating class, 18% were enrolled in graduate school within 6 months of graduation and 80% were employed.

Admissions Contact: Jeffrey S. Lantis, Director of Admissions. A video is available. E-mail: *jeff.lantis@hillsdale.edu*
Web: *http://www.hillsdale.edu*

HOPE COLLEGE — C-4
Holland, MI 49423 (616) 395-7850
(800) 968-7850; Fax: (616) 395-7130

Full-time: 1127 men, 1744 women	**Faculty:** 208; IIB, av$
Part-time: 63 men, 65 women	**Ph.D.s:** 83%
Graduate: none	**Student/Faculty:** 14 to 1
Year: semesters, summer session	**Tuition:** $17,448
Application Deadline: open	**Room & Board:** $5474
Freshman Class: 2110 applied, 1852 accepted, 736 enrolled	
SAT I Verbal/Math: 595/603	**ACT:** 25 **COMPETITIVE+**

Hope College, founded by Dutch pioneers in 1866, is a liberal arts institution affiliated with the Reformed Church in America. In addition to regional accreditation, Hope has baccalaureate program accreditation with ABET, ACS, CSWE, NASAD, NASD, NASM, NAST, NCATE, and NLN. The 2 libraries contain 336,755 volumes, 340,419 microform items, and 11,173 audiovisual forms/CDs, and subscribe to 1959 periodicals. Computerized library services include the card catalog, interlibrary loans, and database searching. Special learning facilities include a learning resource center, art gallery, planetarium, radio station, TV station, an academic support center, and a modern and classical language lab. The 45-acre campus is in a suburban area 26 miles southwest of Grand Rapids and 5 miles east of Lake Michigan. Including residence halls, there are 105 buildings.

Student Life: 77% of undergraduates are from Michigan. Others are from 38 states, 40 foreign countries, and Canada. 86% are from public schools. 93% are white. 51% are Protestant; 16% unknown 20%, non-Christian 1%; 12% Catholic. The average age of freshmen is 18; all undergraduates, 20.

Housing: 2200 students can be accommodated in college housing, which includes single-sex and coed dormitories, on-campus apartments, married-student housing, fraternity houses, and sorority houses. In addition, there are language houses and student cottages. On-campus housing is guaranteed for all 4 years. 81% of students live on campus; of those, 75% remain on campus on weekends. Alcohol is not permitted. All students may keep cars.

Activities: 6% of men belong to 6 local fraternities; 15% of women belong to 6 local sororities. There are 67 groups on campus, including art, band, cheerleading, choir, chorale, chorus, computers, dance, drama, ethnic, film, honors, international, jazz band, literary magazine, musical theater, newspaper, orchestra, pep band, photography, political, professional, radio and TV, religious, social, social service, student government, and yearbook. Popular campus events include Winter Fantasia, Spring Festival, and Nykerk Cup Competition.

Sports: There are 9 intercollegiate sports for men and 9 for women, and 16 intramural sports for men and 13 for women. Facilities include athletic fields, a field house, a tennis center, and a health and phys ed center that contains gyms, a running track, a swimming and diving pool, exercise rooms, a dance studio, racquetball courts, gymnastics rooms, and health-fitness equipment.

Disabled Students: 95% of the campus is accessible. Wheelchair ramps, elevators, special parking, specially equipped rest rooms, special class scheduling, and lowered drinking fountains are available.

Services: Counseling and information services are available, as is tutoring in every subject. There is a reader service for the blind.

Campus Safety and Security: Measures include 24-hour foot and vehicle patrol, escort service, shuttle buses, and informal discussions. There are pamphlets/posters/films, emergency telephones, lighted pathways/sidewalks, and free taxi services.

Programs of Study: Hope confers B.A., B.S., B.Mus., and B.S.N. degrees. Bachelor's degrees are awarded in BIOLOGICAL SCIENCE (biochemistry and biology/biological science), BUSINESS (accounting and business administration and management), COMMUNICATIONS AND THE ARTS (communications, dance, dramatic arts, English, fine arts, French, German, music, and Spanish), COMPUTER AND PHYSICAL SCIENCE (chemistry, computer science, geology, mathematics, and physics), EDUCATION (art, business, elementary, foreign languages, music, science, secondary, and special), ENGINEERING AND ENVIRONMENTAL DESIGN (engineering), HEALTH PROFESSIONS (nursing, predentistry, and premedicine), SOCIAL SCIENCE (economics, history, international relations, philosophy, physical fitness/movement, political science/government, prelaw, psychology, religion, social work, and sociology). Preprofessional, biological sciences, and psychology are the strongest academically. Business, biology, and English are the largest.

Required: To graduate, students must complete 126 semester hours with a 2.0 GPA. All students must take 51 hours of the general education program, including a first-year seminar, 10 hours of math and natural science, 8 of cultural heritage, 6 each of social science, performing and fine arts, and religion, 4 each of a language and writing, 3 in a senior seminar, 2 of health dynamics, and a cultural diversity course.

Special: The college offers internships in all academic areas as well as on-campus work-study programs, study abroad in more than 40 countries, and Washington, Chicago, New York, and Philadelphia semesters. Students may take dual majors or work toward a 3-2 engineering degree with Michigan, Case Western, and Washington Universities, as well as others. There are 20 national honor societies, including Phi Beta Kappa, and 1 departmental honors program.

Faculty/Classroom: 58% of faculty are male; 42%, female. All teach undergraduates. The average class size in an introductory lecture is 25; in a laboratory, 25; and in a regular course, 25.

Admissions: 88% of the 2001-2002 applicants were accepted. The SAT I scores for the 2001-2002 freshman class were: Verbal--12% below 500, 39% between 500 and 599, 37% between 600 and 700, and 12% above 700; Math--13% below 500, 30% between 500 and 599, 41% between 600 and 700, and 16% above 700. The ACT scores were 2% between 12 and 17, 34% between 18 and 23, 49% between 24 and 29, and 15% between 30 and 36. 52% of the current freshmen were in the top fifth of their class; 87% were in the top two fifths. There were 13 National Merit finalists. 17 freshmen graduated first in their class.

Requirements: The SAT I or ACT is required. In addition, the college requires a high school transcript, which must include 4 years of English, 2 each of math, a foreign language, and social science, and 1 year of a lab science, as well as 5 other academic courses. The college requires submission of an essay and recommends an interview. A portfolio or audition is required for certain majors. The GED is considered. AP and CLEP credits are accepted. Important factors in the admissions decision are advanced placement or honor courses, leadership record, and evidence of special talent. Applications are accepted on-line via CollegeNet.

Procedure: Freshmen are admitted fall, winter, and spring. Entrance exams should be taken during spring of the junior year or fall of the senior year. There are early admissions and deferred admissions plans. Application deadlines are open. The fall 2001 application fee was $25. 2% of all applicants are on a waiting list; 35 were accepted in 2001.

Transfer: 57 transfer students enrolled in 2001-2002. Transfer students must have a GPA of 2.0 in at least 1 year of liberal arts courses. 32 credits of 126 must be completed at Hope.

Visiting: There are regularly scheduled orientations for prospective students, including tours, classes, lunch with a current student, and appointments with professors. There are guides for informal visits and visitors may sit in on classes and stay overnight. To schedule a visit, contact the Admissions Office.

Financial Aid: In 2001-2002, 90% of all students received some form of financial aid. 61% of freshmen and 57% of continuing students received need-based aid. The average freshman award was $15,745. Of that total, scholarships or need-based grants averaged $10,920 ($22,922 maximum); loans averaged $3325 ($5125 maximum); and work contracts averaged $1500 (maximum). 52% of undergraduates work part time. Average annual earnings from campus work are $1056. The average financial indebtedness of the 2001 graduate was $16,675. Hope is a member of CSS. The FAFSA and the college's own financial statement are required. The fall application deadline is February 15.

International Students: There are 47 international students enrolled. The school actively recruits these students. They must score 550 on the written TOEFL and also take the SAT I or the ACT.

Computers: The mainframe is a DEC VAX 4200. Terminals and PCs are located in most dorms and academic buildings and in the library and the student center. All students may access the system 24 hours a day. There are no time limits and no fees.

Graduates: In 2001, 579 bachelor's degrees were awarded. The most popular majors were business administration (12%), biology (9%), and English (8%). In an average class, 47% graduate in 4 years, 66% in 5 years, and 67% in 6 years. 63 companies recruited on campus in 2000-2001. Of the 2000 graduating class, 27% were enrolled in graduate school within 6 months of graduation and 67% were employed.

Admissions Contact: James R. Bekkering, Vice President for Admissions. E-mail: *admissions@hope.edu* Web: *www.hope.edu*

KALAMAZOO COLLEGE

Kalamazoo, MI 49006-3295 D-5

(616) 337-7166

(800) 253-3602; Fax: (616) 337-7390

Full-time: 603 men, 781 women **Faculty:** 97; IIB, av$
Part-time: none **Ph.D.s:** 90%
Graduate: none **Student/Faculty:** 14 to 1
Year: quarters **Tuition:** $20,727
Application Deadline: February 15 **Room & Board:** $6228
Freshman Class: 1328 applied, 1038 accepted, 341 enrolled
SAT I Verbal/Math: 637/624 **ACT:** 28

HIGHLY COMPETITIVE+

Kalamazoo College is a liberal arts and sciences institution founded in 1833. The library contains 346,648 volumes, 54,055 microform items, and 8938 audiovisual forms/CDs, and subscribes to 1250 periodicals. Computerized library services include the card catalog, interlibrary loans, and database searching. Special learning facilities include a learning resource center, art gallery, and radio station. The 60-acre campus is in a suburban area 140 miles from Detroit and Chicago. Including residence halls, there are 30 buildings.

Student Life: 76% of undergraduates are from Michigan. Others are from 42 states, 16 foreign countries, and Canada. 85% are from public schools. 83% are white. 40% are claim no religious affiliation; 34% Protestant; 22% Catholic. The average age of freshmen is 18; all undergraduates, 20. 12% do not continue beyond their first year; 71% remain to graduate.

Housing: 868 students can be accommodated in college housing, which includes coed dormitories. In addition, there are special-interest houses and a wellness house. On-campus housing is guaranteed for all 4 years. 75% of students live on campus; of those, 85% remain on campus on weekends. Upperclassmen may keep cars.

Activities: There are no fraternities or sororities. There are 50 groups on campus, including art, band, cheerleading, choir, chorale, chorus, computers, dance, drama, environmental, ethnic, film, gay, honors, international, jazz band, literary magazine, musical theater, newspaper, orchestra, photography, political, professional, radio and TV, religious, social, social service, student government, symphony, and yearbook. Popular campus events include Monte Carlo Night, Quadstock, and Day of Gracious Living.

Sports: There are 8 intercollegiate sports for men and 8 for women, and 12 intramural sports for men and 11 for women. Facilities include a field house that houses a 2000-seat gym, basketball and volleyball courts, weight-training rooms, and a dance studio; a 1500-seat, 11-court tennis stadium; a racquet center with 4 tennis courts, 3 racquetball courts, and a squash court; a natatorium; a 4000-seat football stadium; and soccer and baseball fields.

Disabled Students: 25% of the campus is accessible. Wheelchair ramps, elevators, special parking, specially equipped rest rooms, and special class scheduling are available.

Services: Counseling and information services are available, as is tutoring in most subjects, a writing center, language labs, and supplemental instruction.

Campus Safety and Security: Measures include 24-hour foot and vehicle patrol, self-defense education, escort service, and informal discussions. There are pamphlets/posters/films, emergency telephones, lighted pathways/sidewalks, and secured residence halls with an electronic entry system.

Programs of Study: Kalamazoo confers the B.A. degree. Bachelor's degrees are awarded in BIOLOGICAL SCIENCE (biology/biological science), BUSINESS (business economics), COMMUNICATIONS AND THE ARTS (art, art history and appreciation, dramatic arts, English, French, German, music, and Spanish), COMPUTER AND PHYSICAL SCIENCE (chemistry, computer science, mathematics, and physics), HEALTH PROFESSIONS (health science), SOCIAL SCIENCE (anthropology, classical/ancient civilization, history, human development, interdisciplinary studies, international relations, international studies, philosophy, political science/government, psychology, religion, and sociology). Foreign languages, international studies and commerce, and health sciences are the strongest academically. Economics, English, and political science are the largest.

Required: To graduate, students must complete 38 academic units, including 8 units in the major, with a minimum 2.0 GPA. Required courses include 4 units in social science, 3 in natural science, computer science, or math, 2 each in literature and philosophy/religion, and 1 in fine arts. The college further requires completion of a senior individualized project, a credit from the liberal arts colloquium, and a passing grade on a comprehensive exam in the major. The student must also take 5 non-credit courses in phys ed and show proficiency in writing as well as in a foreign language.

Special: Students may study abroad in more than 12 countries and choose from among 900 career internships in the United States, Europe, Asia, and Africa. The school offers a Washington semester, allows dual and interdisciplinary majors, and has cross-registration with Western Michigan University. A 3-2 engineering degree is offered with Washington University and the University of Michigan. There are accelerated 3-year programs in predentistry, premedicine, and preveterinary medicine. There are 3 national honor societies, including Phi Beta Kappa.

Faculty/Classroom: 52% of faculty are male; 48%, female. All teach undergraduates. The average class size in an introductory lecture is 18; in a laboratory, 24; and in a regular course, 18.

Admissions: 78% of the 2001-2002 applicants were accepted. The SAT I scores for the 2001-2002 freshman class were: Verbal--1% below 500, 27% between 500 and 599, 52% between 600 and 700, and 20% above 700; Math--1% below 500, 31% between 500 and 599, 52% between 600 and 700, and 16% above 700. The ACT scores were 1% below 21, 5% between 21 and 23, 33% between 24 and 26, 22% between 27 and 28, and 39% above 28. 71% of the current freshmen were in the top fifth of their class; 95% were in the top two fifths. There were 11 National Merit finalists. 21 freshmen graduated first in their class.

Requirements: The SAT I or ACT is required. In addition, the college also requires a high school transcript, an essay, and teacher and counselor recommendations; an interview is recommended. AP credits are accepted. Important factors in the admissions decision are advanced placement or honor courses, evidence of special talent, and leadership record. Applications are accepted on computer disk.

Procedure: Freshmen are admitted fall and winter. Entrance exams should be taken by December of the senior year. There are early decision, early admissions, and deferred admissions plans. Early decision applications should be filed by November 15; regular applications, by February 15 for fall entry. The fee is $25 for on-line, $45 for paper. Notification of early decision is sent December 1; regular decision, April 1. 40 early decision candidates were accepted for the 2001-2002 class; 24 were accepted in 2001.

Transfer: 15 transfer students enrolled in 2001-2002. Applicants must have a 3.0 GPA from previous institution(s). 18 units of 38 must be completed at Kalamazoo.

Visiting: There are regularly scheduled orientations for prospective students, including interviews, tours, and class visits as requested. Special preview events include formal presentation of the unique curriculum and financial aid seminars. There are guides for informal visits and visitors may sit in on classes and stay overnight. To schedule a visit, contact the visit coordinator, Pat Marcinkowski.

Financial Aid: In 2001-2002, 98% of all freshmen and 96% of continuing students received some form of financial aid. 46% of all students received need-based aid. The average freshman award was $17,130. Of that total, scholarships or need-based grants averaged $9180 and tuition remission programs averaged $17,130. 40% of undergraduates work part time. Average annual earnings from campus work are $1045. The average financial indebtedness of the 2001 graduate was $17,400. The CSS/Profile or FAFSA is required. The fall application deadline is February 15.

International Students: There are 31 international students enrolled. The school actively recruits these students. They must score 550 on the written TOEFL or take the MELAB.

Computers: The mainframe is a Sun Ultra 2. There are 130 PCs available for student use, 10 of which are limited to physics students. All PCs and Macs are networked on the Internet. All rooms in the residence halls are wired for network access. All students may access the system. There are no time limits and no fees. It is strongly recommended that all students have personal computers.

Graduates: In 2001, 214 bachelor's degrees were awarded. The most popular majors were economics (14%), English (14%), and biology (12%). In an average class, 65% graduate in 4 years, 71% in 5 years, and 73% in 6 years. 35 companies recruited on campus in 2000-2001. Of the 2000 graduating class, 30% were enrolled in graduate school within 6 months of graduation and 60% were employed.

Admissions Contact: John M. Carroll, Director of Admission. A video is available. E-mail: *admissions@kzoo.edu* Web: *www.kzoo.edu*

KENDALL COLLEGE OF ART AND DESIGN

(See Kendall College of Art and Design of Ferris State University)

KENDALL COLLEGE OF ART AND DESIGN OF FERRIS STATE UNIVERSITY D-4
(Formerly Kendall College of Art and Design)
Grand Rapids, MI 49503-3002

(616) 451-2787
(800) 676-2787; Fax: (616) 831-9689

Full-time: 675 men and women	**Faculty:** 33
Part-time: 181 men and women	**Ph.D.s:** 100%
Graduate: 6 men and women	**Student/Faculty:** 20 to 1
Year: semesters, summer session	**Tuition:** $8820 ($14,000)
Application Deadline: open	**Room & Board:** n/app
Freshman Class: n/av	
SAT I or ACT: required	**SPECIAL**

The Kendall College of Art and Design of Ferris State University, formerly Kendall College of Art and Design, founded in 1928, is a commuter institution specializing in design studies and the fine arts. In addition to regional accreditation, Kendall has baccalaureate program accreditation with FIDER and NASAD. The library contains 23,000 volumes, 1000 microform items, and 3500 audiovisual forms/CDs, and subscribes to 150 periodicals. Computerized library services include the card catalog. Special learning facilities include a learning resource center, art gallery, model/wood shop, photography lab, printmaking lab, fine art studios, and student gallery. The 1-acre campus is in an urban area in downtown Grand Rapids. There are 2 buildings.

Student Life: 91% of undergraduates are from Michigan. 90% are from public schools. 81% are white. The average age of all undergraduates is 24.

Housing: There are no residence halls. All students commute. Alcohol is not permitted.

Activities: There are no fraternities or sororities. There are 9 groups on campus, including art, ethnic, film, gay, international, literary magazine, newspaper, photography, professional, religious, and student government. Popular campus events include Advising Day, pancake supper, and all-campus picnic.

Sports: There is no sports program at Kendall. Upon payment of an annual fee, students may use Grand Rapids Community College's pool, track, and sports facilities.

Disabled Students: All of the campus is accessible. Wheelchair ramps, elevators, special parking, specially equipped rest rooms, lowered drinking fountains, lowered telephones, and special drawing tables are available.

Services: Counseling and information services are available, as is tutoring in every subject. There is a reader service for the blind.

Campus Safety and Security: Measures include escort service, informal discussions, pamphlets/posters/films, and emergency telephones. There are lighted pathways/sidewalks.

Programs of Study: Kendall confers B.S. and B.F.A. degrees. Bachelor's degrees are awarded in COMMUNICATIONS AND THE ARTS (art history and appreciation, fine arts, illustration, industrial design, media arts, and multimedia), ENGINEERING AND ENVIRONMENTAL DESIGN (furniture design and interior design). Illustration and visual communication are the largest.

Required: To graduate, students must complete 120 credit hours, including 30 of liberal arts and sciences, 12 to 18 of a foundation studio core, 12 to 15 of art history, and 12 to 15 of studio electives. All students must complete a graduation portfolio. A minimum GPA of 2.0 is required, with a minimum GPA of 2.25 in the student's major studio core courses.

Special: Cross-registration is offered through a consortium of schools. Internships are available in all majors. Study abroad may be arranged by the student and approved by the college; trips to Peruga, Italy, and London, England, are offered each year. Dual majors are possible.

Faculty/Classroom: 54% of faculty are male; 46%, female. All teach undergraduates. The average class size in an introductory lecture is 35; in a laboratory, 15; and in a regular course, 20.

Requirements: The SAT I or ACT is required. In addition, a high school transcript is required. Scores from either the ACT or the SAT I are not required if the applicant has been out of high school for at least 3 years. The GED certificate is accepted. Students must submit an essay with their application. A portfolio and an interview are also recommended. Prospective students are encouraged to take courses in drawing, painting, and design in high school. Kendall requires applicants to be in the upper 50% of their class. A GPA of 2.25 is required. AP and CLEP credits are accepted. Important factors in the admissions decision are leadership record, personality/intangible qualities, and evidence of special talent.

Procedure: Freshmen are admitted to all sessions. There are early decision and deferred admissions plans. Application deadlines are open. The fall 2001 application fee was $35. Notification is sent on a rolling basis.

Transfer: 95 transfer students enrolled in a recent year. Applicants must have a GPA of 2.25 and pass a portfolio review. An interview is recommended. 60 credits of 120 must be completed at Kendall.

Visiting: There are regularly scheduled orientations for prospective students, including a building tour, faculty introductions, financial aid and housing information, and registration/advising. There are guides for informal visits and visitors may sit in on classes. To schedule a visit, contact the Admissions Office.

Financial Aid: In a recent year, 86% of all freshmen and 81% of continuing students received some form of financial aid. 65% of freshmen and 68% of continuing students received need-based aid. The average freshman award was $7888. Of that total, scholarships or need-based grants averaged $4230; loans averaged $5420 ($15,189 maximum); work contracts averaged $2145 ($3465 maximum); and student-obtained outside awards averaged $1230 ($2500 maximum). 1% of undergraduates work part time. Average annual earnings from campus work are $2475. The average financial indebtedness of a recent graduate was $18,000. The FAFSA is required. The fall application deadline is February 15.

International Students: There were 9 international students enrolled in a recent year. They must score 500 on the written TOEFL and also take the SAT I or the ACT.

Computers: The college provides Mac computers for student use in classroom work and design. Library computers provide Internet access. Students may use the computer labs from 8 A.M. to 12 P.M. There are no time limits. The fee is $25 per semester per student.

Graduates: In a recent year, 87 bachelor's degrees were awarded. The most popular majors were visual communication (36%), illustration (24%), and interior design (15%). In an average class, 20% graduate in 4 years, 33% in 5 years, and 37% in 6 years. 30 companies recruited on campus in a recent year.

Admissions Contact: Amy Packard, Director of Admissions.
E-mail: *packard@kcad.edu* Web: *www.kcad.edu*

KETTERING UNIVERSITY E-4
Flint, MI 48504-4898

(810) 762-7865
(800) 955-4464; Fax: (810) 762-9837

Full-time: 2116 men, 490 women	**Faculty:** 145
Part-time: none	**Ph.D.s:** 87%
Graduate: 504 men, 189 women	**Student/Faculty:** 18 to 1
Year: terms, summer session	**Tuition:** $18,656
Application Deadline: open	**Room & Board:** $4600
Freshman Class: 2413 applied, 1708 accepted, 593 enrolled	
SAT I Verbal/Math: 590/640	**ACT:** 26 **HIGHLY COMPETITIVE**

Kettering University is an independent college founded in 1919. In the 5-year undergraduate program students alternate 11-week terms of full-time classes with 12-week terms of full-time paid professional cooperative education (co-op) work experience in industry. Students typically begin co-op during their freshman year and co-op in 43 states and several countries. In addition to regional accreditation, Kettering has baccalaureate program accreditation with ABET and ACBSP. The library contains 94,738 volumes, 516 microform items, and 276 audiovisual forms/CDs, and subscribes to 540 periodicals. Computerized library services include the card catalog, interlibrary loans, and database searching. Special learning facilities include a learning resource center, art gallery, radio station, and industrial history archives. The 51-acre campus is in a suburban area 60 miles north of Detroit. Including residence halls, there are 7 buildings.

Student Life: 60% of undergraduates are from Michigan. Others are from 48 states, 19 foreign countries, and Canada. 83% are from public schools. 76% are white. The average age of freshmen is 18; all undergraduates, 20. 13% do not continue beyond their first year.

Housing: 552 students can be accommodated in college housing, which includes single-sex and coed dormitories, on-campus apartments, fraternity houses, and sorority houses. On-campus housing is guaranteed for the freshman year only and is available on a lottery system for upperclassmen. Priority is given to out-of-town students. Alcohol is not permitted. All students may keep cars.

Activities: 45% of men belong to 13 national fraternities; 47% of women belong to 8 national sororities. There are 40 groups on campus, including art, chorus, computers, drama, ethnic, honors, international, jazz band, newspaper, pep band, photography, political, professional, radio and TV, religious, social, social service, student government, and yearbook. Popular campus events include Talent Show, Greek Week, and Diversity Week.

Sports: There are 2 intercollegiate sports for men, and 19 intramural sports for men and 19 for women. Facilities include a recreation center with 2 basketball and 2 tennis/basketball courts; 4 racquetball and squash courts; a 1/8-mile track; an Olympic-size pool; free weight, Nautilus, and aerobic rooms; 4 softball and 2 soccer fields; outdoor tennis courts; and a sand volleyball court.

Disabled Students: All of the campus is accessible. Wheelchair ramps, elevators, special parking, specially equipped rest rooms, special class scheduling, lowered drinking fountains, and lowered telephones are available.

Services: Tutoring is routinely available for most subjects in the Academic Support Center, in the residence hall, and with faculty. Supplemental tutoring is coordinated through the Academic Services Department. Math and writing labs are available. A Strategies for Academic Success program is available.

Campus Safety and Security: Measures include 24-hour foot and vehicle patrol, self-defense education, escort service, and informal discussions. There are pamphlets/posters/films, emergency telephones, and lighted pathways/sidewalks. After-hours access (e.g., to the academic building) is secure via the tunnel from the residence hall and campus center.

Programs of Study: Kettering confers B.S.A.M., B.S.A.P., B.S.C.E., B.S.C.S., B.S.E.C., B.S.E.E., B.S.I.E., B.S.M., B.S.M.E., and B.S.M.S.E. degrees. Master's degrees are also awarded. Bachelor's degrees are awarded in BUSINESS (business administration and management), COMPUTER AND PHYSICAL SCIENCE (applied mathematics, applied physics, and computer science), ENGINEERING AND ENVIRONMENTAL DESIGN (computer engineering, electrical/electronics engineering, environmental science, industrial engineering, manufacturing engineering, and mechanical engineering). Mechanical engineering, electrical engineering, and computer engineering are the largest.

Required: Degree requirements include completion of 160 credit hours, with 60 in the major. All students must take specific courses in math, chemistry, physics, written and oral communication, computers, history, humanities, and economics. A minimum grade average of 80 on a scale of 100 is required for graduation. The GPA is determined by a formula combining the numerical grades achieved and the number of credits attempted. Students must complete a fifth-year thesis project.

Special: All Kettering University undergraduate students participate in paid cooperative education work experience. Students may pursue a dual major in electrical and mechanical engineering. Accelerated degree programs in engineering are available in most majors, as is study abroad in 6 countries. There are 7 national honor societies.

Faculty/Classroom: 85% of faculty are male; 15%, female. All teach undergraduates and 55% both teach and do research. No introductory courses are taught by graduate students. The average class size in an introductory lecture is 35; in a laboratory, 18; and in a regular course, 28.

Admissions: 71% of the 2001-2002 applicants were accepted. The SAT I scores for the 2001-2002 freshman class were: Verbal--9% below 500, 48% between 500 and 599, 36% between 600 and 700, and 7% above 700; Math--20% between 500 and 599, 62% between 600 and 700, and 19% above 700. The ACT scores were 3% below 21, 15% between 21 and 23, 44% between 24 and 26, 19% between 27 and 28, and 19% above 28. 59% of the current freshmen were in the top fifth of their class; 91% were in the top two fifths. 20 freshmen graduated first in their class.

Requirements: The SAT I or ACT is required. In addition, applicants must graduate from an accredited secondary school with a minimum of 16 academic credits. Applicants must have completed 3 1/2 years of math, including trigonometry, 3 years of English, and 2 years of lab science, 1 of which must be chemistry or physics (both are strongly recommended). AP credits are accepted. Important factors in the admissions decision are leadership record, advanced placement or honor courses, and extracurricular activities record. Applications can be submitted on-line through the university's web site.

Procedure: Freshmen are admitted fall and summer. Entrance exams should be taken during the spring of junior year and fall of senior year. There is a deferred admissions plan. Application deadlines are open. The fall 2001 application fee was $25. Notification is sent on a rolling basis.

Transfer: 48 transfer students enrolled in 2001-2002. Transfer applicants must present the same minimum preparation as freshmen in math and science and must submit both high school and college transcripts and SAT I or ACT scores. Required courses can be taken in high school or college. A minimum GPA of 3.0 in English, math, and science is expected. Transfers who present fewer than 30 credits of full-time study will be judged on both their college and high school record and test scores. 85 credits of 160 must be completed at Kettering.

Visiting: There are regularly scheduled orientations for prospective students, including meeting/open house programs scheduled 3 Saturdays a year. There are guides for informal visits and visitors may sit in on classes and stay overnight. To schedule a visit, contact the Admissions Office at (800) 955-4464, ext. 7865.

Financial Aid: In 2001-2002, 91% of all freshmen and 71% of continuing students received some form of financial aid. 74% of freshmen and 56% of continuing students received need-based aid. The average freshman award was $13,712. Of that total, scholarships or need-based grants averaged $8059 ($14,760 maximum); loans averaged $2625 ($6625 maximum); work contracts averaged $800 ($1600 maximum); and paid cooperative work experiences averaged $2062 ($3200 maximum). Average annual earnings from campus work are $550. The average financial indebtedness of the 2001 graduate was $29,281. The FAFSA is required. The fall application deadline is February 14.

International Students: There are 128 international students enrolled. The school actively recruits these students. They must score 550 on the written TOEFL or 213 on the electronic version or take the MELAB. They must also take the SAT I.

Computers: The mainframes are a Sun SPARC server and a VAX 11-785. All campus buildings and residence hall rooms are fully networked. Telephone and web access is available from off campus. There are more than 300 workstations, networked PCs, and CAD/CAE workstations for general student use. Standalone and dedicated PCs are available in most labs. All students may access the system 24 hours per day, 7 days per week. There are no time limits and no fees. It is strongly recommended that all students have personal computers.

Graduates: In 2001, 421 bachelor's degrees were awarded. The most popular majors were mechanical engineering (60%), electrical engineering (18%), and industrial and manufacturing (3%). In an average class, 1% graduate in 4 years, 50% in 5 years, and 63% in 6 years. More than 100 companies recruited on campus in 2000-2001. Of the 2000 graduating class, 20% were enrolled in graduate school within 6 months of graduation and 96% were employed.

Admissions Contact: Rawlan Lillard II, Director of Admissions. A video is available. E-mail: *admissions@kettering.edu*
Web: *www.kettering.edu*

LAKE SUPERIOR STATE UNIVERSITY D-2

Sault Sainte Marie, MI 49783-1699 **(906) 635-2231**
(888) 800-5778; Fax: (906) 635-6669

Full-time: 1300 men, 1150 women	**Faculty:** 114; IIA, --$
Part-time: 300 men, 450 women	**Ph.D.s:** 56%
Graduate: 85 men, 65 women	**Student/Faculty:** 22 to 1
Year: semesters, summer session	**Tuition:** $4334 ($8312)
Application Deadline: open	**Room & Board:** $4700
Freshman Class: n/av	
ACT: required	**LESS COMPETITIVE**

Lake Superior State University, founded in 1946, is a business, technical, and liberal arts institution. Figures given in the above capsule, and in this profile, are approximate. There are 3 undergraduate schools and 1 graduate school. In addition to regional accreditation, LSSU has baccalaureate program accreditation with ABET and NLN. The library contains 106,618 volumes and 810 audiovisual forms/CDs, and subscribes to 950 periodicals. Computerized library services include the card catalog, interlibrary loans, and database searching. Special learning facilities include a learning resource center, natural history museum, planetarium, radio station, fish hatchery and aquatics lab, and interactive television for distance education. The 121-acre campus is in a small town 280 miles north of Lansing. Including residence halls, there are 36 buildings.

Student Life: 75% of undergraduates are from Michigan. Others are from 20 states, 7 foreign countries, and Canada. 94% are from public schools. 76% are white; 17% foreign nationals. The average age of all undergraduates is 23. 33% do not continue beyond their first year; 45% remain to graduate.

Housing: 1198 students can be accommodated in college housing, which includes single-sex and coed dormitories, on-campus apartments, married-student housing, fraternity houses, and mobile home lots for student-owned mobile homes. On-campus housing is guaranteed for the freshman year only, is available on a first-come, first-served basis, and is available on a lottery system for upperclassmen. 73% of students commute. All students may keep cars.

Activities: There are 1 local and 4 national fraternities; 10% of women belong to 5 national sororities. There are 44 groups on campus, including band, cheerleading, chess, chorale, computers, drama, ethnic, film, honors, jazz band, literary magazine, musical theater, newspaper, orchestra, pep band, political, professional, radio and TV, religious, social, social service, student government, and symphony. Popular campus events include Winter Carnival, Spring Fling, and Beach Party.

Sports: There are 5 intercollegiate sports for men and 5 for women, and 17 intramural sports for men and 15 for women. Facilities include a 2800-seat gym, 4100-seat ice arena, basketball courts, indoor and outdoor tennis courts, racquetball courts, an indoor pool, weight rooms, a dance studio, and a quarter-mile all-weather track.

Disabled Students: 90% of the campus is accessible. Wheelchair ramps, elevators, special parking, specially equipped rest rooms, special class scheduling, lowered drinking fountains, and lowered telephones are available.

Services: Counseling and information services are available, as is tutoring in most subjects, included on request and free of charge. There is a reader service for the blind, and remedial math, reading, and writing. There are also math, reading, and writing labs.

Campus Safety and Security: Measures include 24-hour foot and vehicle patrol, self-defense education, escort service, and informal discussions. There are pamphlets/posters/films and lighted pathways/sidewalks.

Programs of Study: LSSU confers B.A. and B.S. degrees. Associate and master's degrees are also awarded. Bachelor's degrees are awarded in AGRICULTURE (fish and game management and wildlife management), BIOLOGICAL SCIENCE (biology/biological science), BUSINESS (accounting, business administration and management, and marketing/

retailing/merchandising), COMMUNICATIONS AND THE ARTS (English and fine arts), COMPUTER AND PHYSICAL SCIENCE (computer science, geology, and mathematics), EDUCATION (athletic training, early childhood, elementary, and secondary), ENGINEERING AND ENVIRONMENTAL DESIGN (electrical/electronics engineering, engineering, engineering management, engineering technology, environmental engineering technology, environmental science, manufacturing technology, and mechanical engineering), HEALTH PROFESSIONS (exercise science, medical laboratory technology, nursing, predentistry, premedicine, and recreation therapy), SOCIAL SCIENCE (criminal justice, economics, fire science, history, human services, paralegal studies, parks and recreation management, political science/government, prelaw, psychology, social science, and sociology). Engineering technology, nursing, and biology are the strongest academically. Business and criminal justice are the largest.

Required: To graduate, students must complete 124 semester hours with a GPA of 2.0. The core curriculum includes course work in computer literacy, English, oral communications, aesthetics, critical thinking, humanities, math, science, social science, ethics, and cultural diversity. At least 32 of the final credits, and 50% of all upper-level courses, must be taken in residence at Lake State. Math and English competency must be met.

Special: Lake State offers internships in criminal justice, medical technology, human services, legal assistance studies, natural resources technology, work-study programs, co-op programs in engineering technology, and cross-registration with the Canadian Colleges of Sault and Algoma and Bridge International Consortium. Study abroad, a Washington semester, and student-designed majors are available. Distance learning and weekend college study formats are offered. There is a freshman honors program.

Faculty/Classroom: 71% of faculty are male; 29%, female. All teach undergraduates. No introductory courses are taught by graduate students. The average class size in a laboratory is 14 and in a regular course, 30.

Requirements: The ACT is required. In addition, applicants should be high school graduates with 3 years of English, 2 each of math and social studies, and 1 of history, and should have a GPA of 2.0. The GED is accepted. An interview is recommended. A GPA of 2.0 is required. AP and CLEP credits are accepted. Important factors in the admissions decision are advanced placement or honor courses, recommendations by school officials, and recommendations by alumni.

Procedure: Freshmen are admitted to all sessions. There is a deferred admissions plan. Application deadlines are open.

Transfer: Applicants must be eligible to return to the last institution attended, and must have an overall college GPA of 2.0. An interview is recommended. ACT scores are required if high school graduation was within 26 months of the semester of entry. High school transcripts and GED scores are required if transferring with fewer than 19 semester hours of credit. 32 credits of 124 must be completed at LSSU.

Visiting: There are regularly scheduled orientations for prospective students. There are guides for informal visits and visitors may sit in on classes. To schedule a visit, contact the Admissions Office.

Financial Aid: The FAFSA is required. Check with the school for current deadlines.

International Students: The school actively recruits these students. They must score 550 on the written TOEFL.

Computers: The mainframe is a DEC ALPHA. Students have access to a DEC MicroVAX 3400 through terminals located in the computer lab. There are more than 190 PCs for student use in a number of locations across campus. All students may access the system during lab hours. There are no time limits and no fees.

Admissions Contact: Kevin Pollock, Director of Admissions.
E-mail: *admissions@lakers.lssu.edu* Web: *www.lssu.edu*

LAWRENCE TECHNOLOGICAL UNIVERSITY — E-5
Southfield, MI 48075 (248) 204-3160
(800) CALL-LTU; Fax: (248) 204-3188

Full-time: 1000 men, 375 women	**Faculty:** 112
Part-time: 1200 men, 350 women	**Ph.D.s:** 68%
Graduate: 550 men, 300 women	**Student/Faculty:** 12 to 1
Year: semesters, summer session	**Tuition:** $11,800
Application Deadline: open	**Room & Board:** $3000 (room only)
Freshman Class: n/av	
ACT: required	**COMPETITIVE**

Lawrence Technological University, founded in 1932 as the Lawrence Institute of Technology, is a private institution housing colleges of engineering, management, arts and sciences, and architecture and design. There are 4 undergraduate and 4 graduate schools. Figures in the above capsule, and in this profile, are approximate. In addition to regional accreditation, Lawrence Tech has baccalaureate program accreditation with ABET, ACBSP, FIDER, NAAB, and NASAD. The library contains 70,000 volumes, 93,000 microform items, and 500 audiovisual forms/CDs, and subscribes to 1000 periodicals. Computerized library services include the card catalog, interlibrary loans, and database searching. Special learning facilities include a learning resource center, TV station, a Frank Lloyd Wright-designed home (used as academic resource), and the personal library of the late architect Albert Kahn. The 115-acre campus is in a suburban area 30 minutes north of downtown Detroit. Including residence halls, there are 9 buildings.

Student Life: 90% of undergraduates are from Michigan. Others are from 10 states, 35 foreign countries, and Canada. 83% are white.

Housing: 380 students can be accommodated in college housing, which includes coed on-campus apartments. On-campus housing is available on a first-come, first-served basis. 90% of students commute. All students may keep cars.

Activities: 2% of men belong to 1 local and 3 national fraternities; 1% of women belong to 2 local and 2 national sororities. There are 40 groups on campus, including chess, chorale, computers, drama, ethnic, honors, newspaper, political, professional, radio and TV, religious, social, student government, and yearbook. Popular campus events include Open House, Reunion Weekend, and Greek Week.

Sports: There are 8 intramural sports for men and 8 for women. Facilities include a field house with 4 racquetball courts, a weight room, a track, and a sauna. A gym seats 1500, an arena 350.

Disabled Students: 90% of the campus is accessible. Wheelchair ramps, elevators, special parking, specially equipped rest rooms, special class scheduling, lowered drinking fountains, and lowered telephones are available.

Services: Counseling and information services are available, as is tutoring in some subjects, including math, computers, science, and engineering. There are also writing workshops.

Campus Safety and Security: Measures include 24-hour foot and vehicle patrol, escort service, pamphlets/posters/films, and emergency telephones. There are lighted pathways/sidewalks and closed-circuit camera monitoring.

Programs of Study: Lawrence Tech confers B.S., B.Admin., B. Arch., and B.F.A. degrees. Associate and master's degrees are also awarded. Bachelor's degrees are awarded in BUSINESS (accounting, banking and finance, business administration and management, and small business management), COMPUTER AND PHYSICAL SCIENCE (chemistry, computer science, mathematics, and physics), ENGINEERING AND ENVIRONMENTAL DESIGN (architecture, civil engineering, electrical/electronics engineering, engineering technology, industrial administration/management, and mechanical engineering), SOCIAL SCIENCE (humanities). Math and computer science are the strongest academically. Engineering is the largest.

Required: To graduate, students must have completed (depending on the major) 120 to 131 semester credit hours, with a GPA no lower than 2.0.

Special: The College of Engineering offers a work-study program. Co-op programs are available in engineering and engineering technology as are internships and work-study programs. The A.B. Admin. and any associate degree program may be combined. There are 7 national honor societies and 6 departmental honors programs.

Faculty/Classroom: 93% of faculty are male; 7%, female. 95% teach undergraduates. No introductory courses are taught by graduate students. The average class size in an introductory lecture is 19; in a laboratory, 18; and in a regular course, 19.

Admissions: 35% of the applicants in a recent year were accepted.

Requirements: The ACT is required. In addition, students must have a high school diploma and a GPA of no lower than 2.5, at least 2.0 in each subject area pertaining to their major. Applicants should have taken 4 years each of math, science, and English, and 3 years of social science. The GED is accepted. An interview is recommended. A GPA of 2.5 is required. AP and CLEP credits are accepted. Important factors in the admissions decision are advanced placement or honor courses, personality/intangible qualities, and leadership record. Applications are accepted on-line at *www.ltu.edu*.

Procedure: Freshmen are admitted to all sessions. Entrance exams should be taken in the junior year. There are early admissions and deferred admissions plans. Application deadlines are open.

Transfer: More than 527 transfer students usually enroll every year. They must have earned at least 30 credit hours and a GPA for all college-level work no lower than 2.0, or meet all admission requirements for high school students. 28 credits of 120 must be completed at Lawrence Tech.

Visiting: There are regularly scheduled orientations for prospective students. There are guides for informal visits and visitors may sit in on classes and stay overnight. To schedule a visit, contact the Admissions Office.

Financial Aid: In a recent year, 59% of all freshmen and 63% of continuing students received some form of financial aid. 54% of freshmen and 63% of continuing students received need-based aid. The average freshman award was $10,650. Of that total, scholarships or need-based grants averaged $3675 ($10,100 maximum); loans averaged $2625 ($6625 maximum); work contracts averaged $1225 ($3000 maximum); and state and federal grants $3625 ($6475 maximum). 79% of undergraduates work part time. Average annual earnings from campus work are $1535. The average financial indebtedness of a recent graduate was $13,600. Lawrence Tech is a member of CSS. The FFS is required. Check with the school for current application deadlines.

International Students: There were about 50 international students enrolled in a recent year. The school actively recruits these students. They must score 550 on the written TOEFL or take the MELAB or the Comprehensive English Language Test.

Computers: The mainframe is a DEC VAX Cluster. A computer center is available, as are more than 150 PCs throughout the campus. All students may access the system 24 hours daily. There are no time limits and no fees. It is recommended that freshmen have laptop computers.

Graduates: Nearly 800 bachelor's degrees are awarded annually. The most popular majors are science information systems, (16%), mechanical engineering, and architecture.

Admissions Contact: Lisa Kujawa, Admissions Director. A video is available. E-mail: *admissions@ltu.edu* Web: *http://www.ltu.edu*

MADONNA UNIVERSITY

Livonia, MI 48150-1173 — E-5

(734) 432-5317
(800) 852-4951; Fax: (734) 432-5424

Full-time: 296 men, 1109 women	**Faculty:** 114; IIB, av$
Part-time: 370 men, 1268 women	**Ph.D.s:** 55%
Graduate: 226 men, 552 women	**Student/Faculty:** 12 to 1
Year: terms, summer session	**Tuition:** $6652
Application Deadline: open	**Room & Board:** $4852
Freshman Class: 496 applied, 351 accepted, 230 enrolled	
ACT: 23	**VERY COMPETITIVE**

Madonna University, founded in 1947, is a liberal arts institution affiliated with the Roman Catholic Church. There are 6 undergraduate schools and 1 graduate school. In addition to regional accreditation, MU has baccalaureate program accreditation with ADA, CSWE, NCATE, and NLN. The 2 libraries contain 171,000 volumes, 451,000 microform items, and 6540 audiovisual forms/CDs, and subscribe to 3566 periodicals. Computerized library services include interlibrary loans and database searching. Special learning facilities include a learning resource center, art gallery, radio station, TV station, computerized writing lab, and the Center for Personalized Instruction. The 48-acre campus is in a suburban area 20 miles west of Detroit. Including residence halls, there are 4 buildings.

Student Life: 96% of undergraduates are from Michigan. Others are from 13 states, 6 foreign countries, and Canada. 85% are from public schools. 77% are white; 12% African American. 41% are Catholic; 18% Protestant. The average age of freshmen is 29; all undergraduates, 30. 22% do not continue beyond their first year.

Housing: 180 students can be accommodated in college housing, which includes single-sex dormitories. On-campus housing is guaranteed for all 4 years. 96% of students commute. Alcohol is not permitted. All students may keep cars.

Activities: There are no fraternities or sororities. There are 22 groups on campus, including art, chorale, computers, environmental, ethnic, honors, newspaper, orchestra, peace and justice, photography, political, professional, radio and TV, religious, social, social service, and student government. Popular campus events include Founders Day, Halloween Magic, and Christmas for Kids.

Sports: There are 3 intercollegiate sports for men and 4 for women. Facilities include an activities center, a weight training room, a 700-seat gym, and an outdoor softball arena.

Disabled Students: All of the campus is accessible. Wheelchair ramps, elevators, special parking, specially equipped rest rooms, special class scheduling, lowered drinking fountains, lowered telephones, and telecommunication devices and visible fire alarms for hearing-impaired students are available.

Services: Counseling and information services are available, as is tutoring in most subjects. There is a reader service for the blind, remedial math, reading, and writing, and interpreters and note takers for hearing-impaired and visually impaired students.

Campus Safety and Security: Measures include 24-hour foot and vehicle patrol, escort service, informal discussions, and pamphlets/posters/films. There are emergency telephones, lighted pathways/sidewalks, and an emergency car service.

Programs of Study: MU confers B.A., B.S., B.A.S., B.S.M.T., B.S.N., and B.S.W. degrees. Associate and master's degrees are also awarded. Bachelor's degrees are awarded in BIOLOGICAL SCIENCE (biochemistry, biology/biological science, and nutrition), BUSINESS (accounting, business administration and management, hospitality management services, international business management, management science, and marketing/retailing/merchandising), COMMUNICATIONS AND THE ARTS (art, English, fine arts, graphic design, journalism, music, Spanish, technical and business writing, and video), COMPUTER AND PHYSICAL SCIENCE (chemistry, computer science, information sciences and systems, mathematics, natural sciences, and science), EDUCATION (music and secondary), ENGINEERING AND ENVIRONMENTAL DESIGN (commercial art and occupational safety and health), HEALTH PROFESSIONS (allied health, hospice care, medical laboratory technology, and nursing), SOCIAL SCIENCE (child psychology/development, criminal justice, dietetics, family/consumer studies, fire science, food science, gerontology, history, interpreter for the deaf, liberal arts/general studies, pastoral studies, psychology, religion, religious music, safety and security technology, social science, social work, and sociology). Nursing is the strongest academically. Nursing and business administration are the largest.

Required: To graduate, students must complete at least 120 semester hours with a 2.0 GPA; required hours in the major vary from 30 to 62. A minimum of 52 hours of general education courses are required, including 25 hours in humanities, 15 in social science, and 12 in math and science. All students are required to take English 101 and 102 and a senior seminar, which includes a comprehensive exam.

Special: MU offers cross-registration with Marygrove and St. Mary of Orchard Lake Colleges, Sacred Heart Seminary, and the University of Detroit Mercy. Students may pursue co-op programs in 43 majors, internships, a B.A.-B.S. degree in gerontology, and credit for life, military, or work experience. MU also has affiliations with universities in Argentina, Belgium, Great Britain, Japan, Poland, and Taiwan. There are 7 national honor societies, including Phi Beta Kappa, and 7 departmental honors programs.

Faculty/Classroom: 46% of faculty are male; 54%, female. All both teach and do research. No introductory courses are taught by graduate students. The average class size in an introductory lecture is 22; in a laboratory, 13; and in a regular course, 17.

Admissions: 71% of the 2001-2002 applicants were accepted. The ACT scores for the 2001-2002 freshman class were: 23% below 21, 42% between 21 and 23, 30% between 24 and 26, and 5% between 27 and 28. 47% of the current freshmen were in the top fifth of their class; 86% were in the top two fifths. There were 3 National Merit semifinalists. 6 freshmen graduated first in their class.

Requirements: The ACT is required. In addition, students should have completed 4 years of English, 3 of math, 2 of science, and 1 of history. The school accepts the GED. An essay is required. For some majors, students are asked to submit a portfolio or to appear for an interview or audition. A GPA of 2.75 is required. AP and CLEP credits are accepted. Important factors in the admissions decision are advanced placement or honor courses, recommendations by school officials, and leadership record. Applications are accepted on computer disk or on-line via the school's web site, ApplyYourself, or Catholic Colleges On-line.

Procedure: Freshmen are admitted to all sessions. Entrance exams should be taken during either the junior or senior year. Application deadlines are open. Notification is sent on a rolling basis.

Transfer: 529 transfer students enrolled in 2001-2002. Applicants must be in good academic and personal standing at their previous colleges and must submit official transcripts of college and high school work. Courses completed at an accredited institution with a grade of C or better will be considered for transfer credit. 30 credits of 120 must be completed at MU.

Visiting: There are regularly scheduled orientations for prospective students, including an interview and a tour of the campus. There are guides for informal visits and visitors may sit in on classes and stay overnight. To schedule a visit, contact the Office of Undergraduate Admissions at (734) 432-5339 or *admis@madonna.edu*

Financial Aid: In 2001-2002, 60% of all freshmen and 48% of continuing students received some form of financial aid. 46% of freshmen and 39% of continuing students received need-based aid. The average freshman award was $6067. Of that total, scholarships or need-based grants averaged $4187 ($14,308 maximum); loans averaged $3329 ($6625 maximum); and work contracts averaged $2498 ($4920 maximum). 9% of undergraduates work part time. The average financial indebtedness of the 2001 graduate was $15,126. The FAFSA is required. The fall application deadline is February 21.

International Students: There are 43 international students enrolled. The school actively recruits these students. They must score 540 on the written TOEFL or take the MELAB, or an equivalent English proficiency test and the ACT.

Computers: The mainframe is an IBM AS/400. The mainframe, networked with 20 PCs that can be used for class assignments, uses COBOL and RPG. 80 PCs are networked via a Novell LAN in the computer lab and in the library. Library research is done via CD-ROM files and national databases. Smaller, decentralized labs are found in the Health Instruction Center, the tutoring center, the physics lab, and various faculty and staff offices. All students may access the system 9 A.M. to 10 P.M. daily, 9 A.M. to 5 P.M. Saturday, and 1 P.M. to 5 P.M. Sunday. Students may access the system only 3 hours per day if others are waiting. There are no fees.

Graduates: In 2001, 536 bachelor's degrees were awarded. The most popular majors were nursing (10%), business (5%), and criminal justice (4%). In an average class, 22% graduate in 4 years, 65% in 5 years, and 81% in 6 years. 25 companies recruited on campus in 2000-2001. Of the 2000 graduating class, 8% were enrolled in graduate school within 6 months of graduation.

Admissions Contact: Frank Hribar, Director for Enrollment Management. A video is available. E-mail: *fhribar@madonna.edu* Web: *www.madonna.edu*

MARYGROVE COLLEGE

Detroit, MI 48221-2599 E-5
(313) 927-1240
(866) 313-1927; Fax: (313) 927-1345

Full-time: 88 men, 322 women
Part-time: 88 men, 381 women
Graduate: 1059 men, 4135 women
Year: semesters, summer session
Application Deadline: August 15
Faculty: 49
Ph.D.s: 75%
Student/Faculty: 8 to 1
Tuition: $10,875
Room & Board: $5200
Freshman Class: 395 applied, 217 accepted, 115 enrolled
ACT: 19.5 COMPETITIVE

Founded in 1905 and grounded in the liberal arts, Marygrove College is a private comprehensive institution affiliated with the Catholic Church. In addition to regional accreditation, Marygrove has baccalaureate program accreditation with ADA, CAHEA, CSWE, and NCATE. The library contains 98,817 volumes, 61,183 microform items, and 1559 audiovisual forms/CDs, and subscribes to 500 periodicals. Computerized library services include the card catalog, interlibrary loans, and database searching. Special learning facilities include a learning resource center, art gallery, a writing center, a learning clinic, and a theater. The 50-acre campus is in an urban area 11 miles from downtown Detroit. Including residence halls, there are 3 buildings.

Student Life: 99% of undergraduates are from Michigan. Others are from 3 states, 2 foreign countries, and Canada. 76% are African American. The average age of freshmen is 29; all undergraduates, 34. 33% do not continue beyond their first year.

Housing: 70 students can be accommodated in college housing, which includes coed dormitories. 92% of students commute. Alcohol is not permitted. All students may keep cars.

Activities: There are no fraternities or sororities. There are 17 groups on campus, including art, choir, chorale, computers, honors, religious, social service, and student government. Popular campus events include Honors Day, Martin Luther King Day, and contemporary American authors lecture series.

Sports: There is 1 intercollegiate sport for men and 1 for women. Facilities include a fitness center and a gym.

Disabled Students: 90% of the campus is accessible. Wheelchair ramps, elevators, special parking, specially equipped rest rooms, lowered drinking fountains, and portable wheelchair ramps are available.

Services: Counseling and information services are available, as is tutoring in most subjects. There is remedial math, reading, and writing.

Campus Safety and Security: Measures include 24-hour foot and vehicle patrol, self-defense education, escort service, and informal discussions. There are pamphlets/posters/films, emergency telephones, and lighted pathways/sidewalks.

Programs of Study: Marygrove confers B.A., B.S., B.A.S., B.B.A., B.F.A., B.M., and B.S.W. degrees. Associate and master's degrees are also awarded. Bachelor's degrees are awarded in BIOLOGICAL SCIENCE (biology/biological science and nutrition), BUSINESS (business administration and management), COMMUNICATIONS AND THE ARTS (art, dance, English, language arts, and music), COMPUTER AND PHYSICAL SCIENCE (chemistry, information sciences and systems, mathematics, radiological technology, and science), EDUCATION (early childhood, social studies, and special), ENGINEERING AND ENVIRONMENTAL DESIGN (environmental science), HEALTH PROFESSIONS (allied health and art therapy), SOCIAL SCIENCE (child psychology/development, family/consumer studies, food production/management/services, food science, history, home economics, political science/government, psychology, religion, social science, and social work). Business, computer science, and education are the largest.

Required: To graduate, students must complete 128 semester hours with a minimum GPA of 2.0. The required core program includes a first-year seminar, 18 hours in arts and letters, 12 in social sciences, 8 in math and natural science (including 1 lab science), and courses in communications (composition, oral communication, and computer literacy). The required number of hours in the major varies.

Special: A consortium program is offered with the University of Detroit Mercy, Saint Mary's College, Sacred Heart Seminary, and Madonna University. Also available are nondegree study, student-designed and dual majors, study abroad in 5 countries, internships, pass/fail options, and work-study programs. Students may acquire credit for life experience by documenting their achievements in a portfolio. There are 4 national honor societies, a freshman honors program, and 1 departmental honors program.

Faculty/Classroom: 35% of faculty are male; 65%, female. All both teach and do research. No introductory courses are taught by graduate students. The average class size in an introductory lecture is 17 and in a laboratory, 10.

Admissions: 55% of the 2001-2002 applicants were accepted.

Requirements: The ACT is required. In addition, the applicant must be a graduate of an accredited high school. An interview is recommended. The student's average, class rank, recommendations, and special talents are important factors in admission. Entering students must take the College Placement Examinations. A GPA of 2.0 is required. AP and CLEP credits are accepted. Important factors in the admissions decision are recommendations by school officials, evidence of special talent, and advanced placement or honor courses.

Procedure: Freshmen are admitted to all sessions. There is a deferred admissions plan. Applications should be filed by August 15 for fall entry. The fall 2001 application fee was $25. Notification of early decision and regular decision, is sent on a rolling basis.

Transfer: 104 transfer students enrolled in 2001-2002. Transfer students must have a minimum 2.0 GPA. An associate degree or 24 completed credit hours and an interview are recommended. 30 credits of 128 must be completed at Marygrove.

Visiting: There are regularly scheduled orientations for prospective students, including a tour of the campus followed by college workshops, first-year-student panels, and a college financial planning seminar. There are guides for informal visits and visitors may sit in on classes. To schedule a visit, contact the Admissions Office at *info@marygrove.edu*

Financial Aid: In a recent year, 95% of all students received some form of financial aid, including need-based aid. The average freshman award was $9200. Of that total, scholarships or need-based grants averaged $7200 ($10,950 maximum); loans averaged $2000 ($3625 maximum); and work contracts averaged $2000 ($3000 maximum). 14% of undergraduates work part time. Average annual earnings from campus work are $2700. The average financial indebtedness of the 2001 graduate was $25,000. Marygrove is a member of CSS. The CSS/Profile or FAFSA and the college's own financial statement are required. The fall application deadline is March 15.

International Students: There are 7 international students enrolled. They must score 520 on the written TOEFL.

Computers: The mainframes are a Burroughs Bl000 and a Unisys AY. There is a computer center and lab in the liberal arts building and a computer-aided instruction lab. All students may access the system. There are no time limits and no fees.

Graduates: In 2001, 86 bachelor's degrees were awarded. The most popular majors were business and management (26%), social work (24%), and education (15%). 16 companies recruited on campus in 2000-2001.

Admissions Contact: Fred Schebor, Dean of Admission. A video is available. E-mail: *fschebor@marygrove.edu* Web: *www.marygrove.edu*

MICHIGAN STATE UNIVERSITY

East Lansing, MI 48824-1046 D-4
(517) 355-8332
Fax: (517) 353-1647

Full-time: 14,153 men, 16,436 women
Part-time: 2090 men, 2201 women
Graduate: 4106 men, 5247 women
Year: semesters, summer session
Application Deadline: July 25
Faculty: 2468; I, av$
Ph.D.s: 95%
Student/Faculty: 12 to 1
Tuition: $5708 ($14,056)
Room & Board: $4678
Freshman Class: 24,246 applied, 15,812 accepted, 6767 enrolled
SAT I Verbal/Math: 560/580 **ACT:** 24 VERY COMPETITIVE

Michigan State University, a pioneer land-grant institution, was founded in 1855. Its 14 colleges and more than 100 departments offer undergraduate and graduate degrees in more than 200 fields of study. The university's Honors College offers students an alternative education program. There are 11 undergraduate and 13 graduate schools. In addition to regional accreditation, MSU has baccalaureate program accreditation with AACSB, ABET, ACEJMC, ADA, ASLA, CAHEA, CSWE, FIDER, NASM, NCATE, NLN, and SAF. The 16 libraries contain 4,206,032 volumes, 5,061,423 microform items, and 34,611 audiovisual forms/CDs, and subscribe to 28,007 periodicals. Computerized library services include the card catalog, interlibrary loans, and database searching. Special learning facilities include a learning resource center, art gallery, natural history museum, planetarium, radio station, TV station, the Beal Botanical Garden, a superconducting cyclotron lab, the Center for Environmental Toxicology, the Pesticide Research Center, and the Case Center for Computer-Aided Engineering and Manufacturing. The 5239-acre campus is in a suburban area 80 miles west of Detroit. Including residence halls, there are 564 buildings.

Student Life: 91% of undergraduates are from Michigan. Others are from 49 states, 115 foreign countries, and Canada. 79% are white. The average age of freshmen is 18; all undergraduates, 20. 15% do not continue beyond their first year; 70% remain to graduate.

Housing: 17,000 students can be accommodated in college housing, which includes single-sex and coed dormitories, on-campus apartments, and married-student housing. In addition, there are honors houses and special-interest houses. On-campus housing is guaranteed for all 4 years. 55% of students commute. Upperclassmen may keep cars.

Activities: 8% of men belong to 37 national fraternities; 8% of women belong to 19 national sororities. There are 350 groups on campus, including art, band, cheerleading, chess, choir, chorale, chorus, computers, dance, debate, drama, ethnic, film, gay, honors, international, jazz band, marching band, musical theater, newspaper, orchestra, pep band, photography, political, professional, radio and TV, religious, social, social service, student government, symphony, and yearbook. Popular campus events include MSU vs. University of Michigan football game, Greek Week, and Siblings Weekend.

Sports: There are 12 intercollegiate sports for men and 12 for women, and 25 intramural sports for men and 25 for women. Facilities include a 76,000-seat stadium, a 4000-seat gym and field house, an ice arena, and a multipurpose 15,500-seat student events center. The university also has an indoor football practice facility, 3 intramural facilities, indoor and outdoor tennis courts, ball fields, a running track, 2 golf courses, and 4 swimming pools, including 1 Olympic-size outdoor pool.

Disabled Students: 75% of the campus is accessible. Wheelchair ramps, elevators, special parking, specially equipped rest rooms, special class scheduling, lowered drinking fountains, lowered telephones, tape recorders, videotaped classes, reading machines, readers, and note takers are available.

Services: Counseling and information services are available, as is tutoring in most subjects. There is a reader service for the blind and remedial math and writing.

Campus Safety and Security: Measures include 24-hour foot and vehicle patrol, self-defense education, escort service, and shuttle buses. There are informal discussions, pamphlets/posters/films, emergency telephones, lighted pathways/sidewalks, and campus buses.

Programs of Study: MSU confers B.A., B.S., B.F.A., B.Land.Arch., B.Mus., and B.S. in Nursing degrees. Master's and doctoral degrees are also awarded. Bachelor's degrees are awarded in AGRICULTURE (agriculture, animal science, forestry and related sciences, horticulture, and soil science), BIOLOGICAL SCIENCE (biochemistry, biology/biological science, botany, entomology, microbiology, nutrition, and zoology), BUSINESS (accounting, business administration and management, marketing management, marketing/retailing/merchandising, and personnel management), COMMUNICATIONS AND THE ARTS (advertising, applied music, art history and appreciation, communications, English, French, German, journalism, Latin, linguistics, music, music theory and composition, Russian, Spanish, studio art, and telecommunications), COMPUTER AND PHYSICAL SCIENCE (astrophysics, chemistry, computer science, earth science, geology, mathematics, physical sciences, physics, science, and statistics), EDUCATION (agricultural, art, early childhood, elementary, foreign languages, home economics, music, physical, science, secondary, and special), ENGINEERING AND ENVIRONMENTAL DESIGN (chemical engineering, city/community/regional planning, civil engineering, computer engineering, construction management, electrical/electronics engineering, engineering, interior design, landscape architecture/design, materials engineering, and mechanical engineering), HEALTH PROFESSIONS (clinical science, medical laboratory technology, music therapy, nursing, predentistry, premedicine, and speech pathology/audiology), SOCIAL SCIENCE (American studies, anthropology, classical/ancient civilization, criminal justice, dietetics, economics, family/consumer resource management, food production/management/services, food science, geography, history, humanities, international relations, philosophy, political science/government, prelaw, psychology, public administration, religion, social science, social work, and sociology). Teacher education, audiology and speech sciences are the strongest academically. Psychology, general business administration, and accounting are the largest.

Required: To graduate, students must complete a freshman writing course and a writing course specified by the major and degree program. Students must complete the 26-credit University Integrative Studies requirement consisting of 8 credits of arts and humanitites, 8 of social, behavioral, and economic sciences, 7 of general science, and 3 of a trans-collegiate course. Students must also demonstrate knowledge in math equivalent to 4 years of college preparatory math at the high school level, including 2 years of algebra, 1 year of geometry, and 1 year of either probability, trigonometry, or calculus. A total of 120 semester hours is required, as is a minimum 2.0 GPA.

Special: Special academic programs include an engineering co-op program with business and industry; internships in business, education, political science, agriculture, and communication arts; study abroad in more than 51 countries; on-campus work-study programs; and a sea semester. An accelerated degree program in all majors and student-designed majors are offered at the Honors College. Nondegree study, pass/fail options in some courses, and dual majors are possible. Educationally disadvantaged students may avail themselves of the College Achievement Admissions Program (CAAP). Cross-registration with the Committee on Institutional Cooperation schools is available. There are 48 national honor societies, including Phi Beta Kappa, and a freshman honors program.

Faculty/Classroom: 74% of faculty are male; 26%, female. The average class size in an introductory lecture is 100; in a laboratory, 30; and in a regular course, 30.

Admissions: 65% of the 2001-2002 applicants were accepted. The SAT I scores for the 2001-2002 freshman class were: Verbal--25% below 500, 42% between 500 and 599, 26% between 600 and 700, and 7% above 700; Math--19% below 500, 38% between 500 and 599, 33% between 600 and 700, and 10% above 700. The ACT scores were 17% below 21, 28% between 21 and 23, 30% between 24 and 26, 12% between 27 and 28, and 13% above 28. 52% of the current freshmen were in the top fifth of their class; 87% were in the top two fifths.

Requirements: The SAT I or ACT is required. In addition, applicants must be graduates of an accredited secondary school and have completed 4 years of English, 3 years each of math and social studies, including history, and 2 years of science. The GED is accepted. Music majors must audition. Applications are available on diskette for DOS, Mac, and Windows. AP and CLEP credits are accepted. Important factors in the admissions decision are recommendations by school officials, advanced placement or honor courses, and evidence of special talent.

Procedure: Freshmen are admitted to all sessions. Entrance exams should be taken during the junior year of high school. There is a deferred admissions plan. Applications should be filed by July 25 for fall entry, December 1 for spring entry, and April 15 for summer entry. The fall 2001 application fee was $40. Notification is sent on a rolling basis. A waiting list is an active part of the admissions procedure.

Transfer: A minimum GPA of 2.0 is required. 30 credits of 120 must be completed at MSU.

Visiting: There are regularly scheduled orientations for prospective students, including a presentation and a tour of the campus. There are guides for informal visits and visitors may sit in on classes and stay overnight. To schedule a visit, contact the Student Admissions Committee at (517) 353-1615.

Financial Aid: In 2001-2002, 83% of all freshmen and 64% of continuing students received some form of financial aid. MSU is a member of CSS. The FAFSA is required.

International Students: The school actively recruits these students. They must score 550 on the written TOEFL or 213 on the electronic version or take the MELAB, the Comprehensive English Language Test, or the college's own test.

Computers: The mainframes are an IBM 3090, a CONVEX 220, and a 96 Node GP1000. There are more than 5000 networked PCs from various vendors located in 25 public microlabs and numerous restricted micro-facilities. Seven residence halls have public labs with computers that are on the Internet. All residence halls have modem-compatible phone lines in the living quarters. All students may access the system 16 hours per day; 7 days per week. There are no time limits and no fees.

Admissions Contact: Dr. Gordon E. Stanley, Director of Admissions and Scholarships. A video is available. E-mail: *admis@msu.edu*
Web: *admissions.msu.edu*

MICHIGAN TECHNOLOGICAL UNIVERSITY B-1

Houghton, MI 49931-1295 **(906) 487-2335**
(888) MTU-1885; Fax: (906) 487-2125

Full-time: 3622 men, 1256 women	**Faculty:** 370; I, -$
Part-time: 828 men, 232 women	**Ph.D.s:** 86%
Graduate: 455 men, 217 women	**Student/Faculty:** 13 to 1
Year: semesters, summer session	**Tuition:** $5887 ($13,165)
Application Deadline: open	**Room & Board:** $5201
Freshman Class: 3033 applied, 2785 accepted, 1202 enrolled	
SAT I Verbal/Math: 580/610	**ACT:** 25 **VERY COMPETITIVE**

Michigan Technological University, founded in 1885, is a state-supported institution offering degrees in engineering, liberal arts, sciences, forestry, business, and technology. There are 5 undergraduate schools and 1 graduate school. In addition to regional accreditation, Michigan Tech has baccalaureate program accreditation with ABET and SAF. The library contains 815,630 volumes, 529,170 microform items, and 3808 audiovisual forms/CDs, and subscribes to 10,463 periodicals. Computerized library services include the card catalog, interlibrary loans, and database searching. Special learning facilities include a learning resource center, radio station, mineral museum, observatory, forestry center, and performing arts center. The 240-acre campus is in a small town 380 miles northwest of Milwaukee, Wisconsin. Including residence halls, there are 42 buildings.

Student Life: Most students are from the Midwest. Others are from 43 states, 70 foreign countries, and Canada. 81% are white; 10% foreign nationals. The average age of freshmen is 19; all undergraduates, 21. 24% do not continue beyond their first year.

Housing: 2714 students can be accommodated in college housing, which includes coed dormitories, on-campus apartments, and married-student housing. In addition, a floor in 1 dorm is for seniors and graduate students. Also, each form has chemical-free areas where tobacco and alcohol are not allowed. Plus, there are separate areas for international students and the fisrt year experience program. On-campus housing is guaranteed for the freshman year only and is available on a first-come, first-served basis. 60% of students commute. All students may keep cars.

Activities: 9% of men belong to 4 local and 11 national fraternities; 14% of women belong to 4 local and 4 national sororities. There are 180 groups on campus, including art, band, cheerleading, chess, choir, chorale, chorus, computers, dance, drama, drill team, ethnic, film, gay, honors, international, jazz band, literary magazine, musical theater, newspaper, orchestra, pep band, photography, political, professional, radio and TV, religious, social, social service, student government, and symphony. Popular campus events include Winter Carnival, K-Day, and Spring Fling.

Sports: There are 7 intercollegiate sports for men and 6 for women, and 38 intramural sports for men and 37 for women. Facilities include a complex with a 4200-seat ice arena and a 3200-seat gym, a lakeside golf course, football and softball fields, a tennis center, Mont Ripley Ski Hill and a cross-country ski trail, a multipurpose room, pool, fitness center, racquetball/squash courts, dance room, and gymnastics room.

Disabled Students: 85% of the campus is accessible. Wheelchair ramps, elevators, special parking, specially equipped rest rooms, special class scheduling, and lowered drinking fountains are available.

Services: Counseling and information services are available, as is tutoring in some subjects. There is remedial math, reading, and writing. Learning centers for English, math, chemistry, and physics are available.

Campus Safety and Security: Measures include 24-hour foot and vehicle patrol, self-defense education, escort service, and shuttle buses. There are informal discussions, pamphlets/posters/films, emergency telephones, and lighted pathways/sidewalks.

Programs of Study: Michigan Tech confers B.A. and B.S. degrees. Associate, master's, and doctoral degrees are also awarded. Bachelor's degrees are awarded in AGRICULTURE (forestry and related sciences), BIOLOGICAL SCIENCE (biology/biological science and ecology), BUSINESS (business administration and management and business economics), COMMUNICATIONS AND THE ARTS (technical and business writing), COMPUTER AND PHYSICAL SCIENCE (chemistry, computer science, geology, geophysics and seismology, mathematics, and physics), ENGINEERING AND ENVIRONMENTAL DESIGN (biomedical engineering, chemical engineering, civil engineering, computer engineering, electrical/electronics engineering, engineering, engineering technology, environmental engineering, geological engineering, mechanical engineering, mining and mineral engineering, and surveying engineering), HEALTH PROFESSIONS (medical laboratory technology), SOCIAL SCIENCE (liberal arts/general studies and social science). Engineering, forestry, and physical science are the strongest academically. Mechanical, electrical, and chemical engineering are the largest.

Required: To graduate, students must complete 120 to 146 credit hours, maintain a miminum GPA of 2.0, and fulfill basic general education requirements. The basic general education curriculum consists of 4 core courses to be taken by every baccalaureate student, a 5-course distribution requirement, physed, and a science/math requirement. In general, 30 of the last 36 credit hours and 30 credit hours of advanced level courses must be completed at MTU.

Special: Michigan Tech offers co-op programs in almost all majors, internships in medical technology and secondary teacher education, work-study programs, study abroad in more than 20 countries, dual majors, and a B.A.-B.S. degree in scientific and technical communication. There are interinstitutional programs with Northwestern Michigan College, Gogebic Community College, Lansing Community College, and Delta College. A 3-2 engineering degree is possible in conjunction with the University of Wisconsin/Superior, the College of St. Scholastica, and Adrian, Albion, Augsburg, Northland, and Mount Senario Colleges. There are 17 national honor societies.

Faculty/Classroom: 75% of faculty are male; 25%, female. All teach undergraduates, 73% also do research. Graduate students teach 6% of introductory courses. The average class size in an introductory lecture is 61; in a laboratory, 20; and in a regular course, 29.

Admissions: 92% of the 2001-2002 applicants were accepted. The SAT I scores for the 2001-2002 freshman class were: Verbal--14% below 500, 44% between 500 and 599, 36% between 600 and 700, and 6% above 700; Math--8% below 500, 36% between 500 and 599, 44% between 600 and 700, and 12% above 700. The ACT scores were 10% below 21, 20% between 21 and 23, 32% between 24 and 26, 18% between 27 and 28, and 20% above 28. 52% of the current freshmen were in the top fifth of their class; 81% were in the top two fifths. There were 9 National Merit finalists. 70 freshmen graduated first in their class.

Requirements: The SAT I or ACT is required. Scores are used for admission and placement. Admissions requirements include graduation from an accredited secondary school, with 15 academic credits. These must include 3 credits each in English and in math for engineering and science curricula; 1 credit of chemistry or physics; credits in social studies and foreign language are recommended. The GED is accepted. AP and CLEP credits are accepted. Important factors in the admissions decision are advanced placement or honor courses, leadership record, and recommendations by school officials. Applications are accepted on-line at the school's web site, *www.mtu.edu*

Procedure: Freshmen are admitted to all sessions. Entrance exams should be taken in the junior year. There is a deferred admissions plan. Application deadlines are open. The fall 2001 application fee was $30. Notification is sent on a rolling basis.

Transfer: 234 transfer students enrolled in 2001-2002. Transfer students must have a minimum GPA of 2.5 on a 4.0 scale; grades of B or better are expected in math and science courses. 30 credits of 120 to 146 must be completed at Michigan Tech.

Visiting: There are regularly scheduled orientations for prospective students, including campus tours at 10 A.M. and 2 P.M. Monday through Friday. Separate interviews are available with academic department personnel and admissions representatives. There are guides for informal visits and visitors may sit in on classes and stay overnight. To schedule a visit, contact the Admissions Office at *mtu4u@mtu.edu*

Financial Aid: In 2001-2002, 81% of all freshmen and 74% of continuing students received some form of financial aid. 43% of continuing students received need-based aid. The average freshman award was $7031. Of that total, scholarships or need-based grants averaged $4600 ($19,558 maximum); loans averaged $4945 ($18,162 maximum); and work contracts averaged $1335 ($1545 maximum). 29% of undergraduates work part time. Average annual earnings from campus work are $4500. The average financial indebtedness of the 2001 graduate was $11,665. Michigan Tech is a member of CSS. The FAFSA is required. The fall application deadline is March 1.

International Students: There are 297 international students enrolled. The school actively recruits these students. They must score 500 on the written TOEFL or 173 on the electronic version.

Computers: Almost every department has 1 or more student computing labs. Equipment varies but includes PCs, Macs, Sun workstations, laser printers, electrostatic plotters, and scanners. Software includes general productivity packages, such as word processing and spreadsheets, and specialized applications, such as CAD/CAM, GIS, and publishing. All students may access the system 24 hours a day. There are no time limits. The fee varies with major.

Graduates: In 2001, 1074 bachelor's degrees were awarded. The most popular majors were mechanical engineering (21%), electrical engineering (12%), and civil engineering (10%). In an average class, 29% graduate in 4 years, 59% in 5 years, and 64% in 6 years. 280 companies recruited on campus in 2000-2001. Of the 2000 graduating class, 15% were enrolled in graduate school within 6 months of graduation and 95% were employed.

Admissions Contact: Nancy Rehling, Director of Undergraduate Admissions. E-mail: *mtu4u@mtu.edu* Web: *www.mtu.edu/apply/*

NORTHERN MICHIGAN UNIVERSITY — C-2

Marquette, MI 49855 (906) 227-2650
(800) 682-9797; Fax: (906) 227-1747

Full-time: 3159 men, 3555 women	**Faculty:** 294; IIA, av$
Part-time: 399 men, 560 women	**Ph.D.s:** 80%
Graduate: 235 men, 395 women	**Student/Faculty:** 23 to 1
Year: semesters, summer session	**Tuition:** $4257 ($7041)
Application Deadline: open	**Room & Board:** $5436
Freshman Class: 4467 applied, 3776 accepted, 1703 enrolled	
SAT I or ACT: required	**COMPETITIVE**

Northern Michigan University, founded in 1899, is a public institution offering undergraduate programs in the arts and sciences, business, education, health science, human services, nursing, and technology. There are 4 undergraduate schools and 1 graduate school. Figures in the above capsule are approximate. In addition to regional accreditation, NMU has baccalaureate program accreditation with ADA, CSWE, NASM, NCATE, and NLN. The library contains 1,111,373 volumes, 594,089 microform items, and 22,587 audiovisual forms/CDs, and subscribes to 1862 periodicals. Computerized library services include the card catalog, interlibrary loans, and database searching. Special learning facilities include a learning resource center, art gallery, radio station, TV station, and an observatory. The 320-acre campus is in an urban area on the southern shores of Lake Superior. Including residence halls, there are 55 buildings.

Student Life: 85% of undergraduates are from Michigan. Others are from 49 states, 36 foreign countries, and Canada. 91% are white. The average age of freshmen is 19; all undergraduates, 21. 31% do not continue beyond their first year.

Housing: 2500 students can be accommodated in college housing, which includes coed dormitories, on-campus apartments, and married-student housing. In addition, there are honors houses, special-interest houses, smoke-free, and chemical-free houses. On-campus housing is guaranteed for all 4 years. 62% of students commute. All students may keep cars.

Activities: 1% of men and about 1% of women belong to 4 national fraternities; 1% of women belong to 3 national sororities. There are 200 groups on campus, including art, band, cheerleading, chess, choir, chorale, chorus, computers, dance, drama, drill team, ethnic, film, gay, honors, international, jazz band, literary magazine, marching band, musical theater, newspaper, orchestra, pep band, photography, political, professional, radio and TV, religious, social, social service, student government, and symphony. Popular campus events include Winterfest, Be a Part from the Start, and U.P. 200 Dog Sled Race.

Sports: There are 5 intercollegiate sports for men and 8 for women, and 10 intramural sports for men and 10 for women. Facilities include

indoor and outdoor playing fields, an aerobic and fitness training area, an ice rink, a swimming pool, a diving tank, a field house, an 8000-seat stadium, a 4000-seat basketball and hockey arena, a rock-climbing wall, racquetball courts, the neighboring forests and rivers, and Lake Superior.

Disabled Students: 90% of the campus is accessible. Wheelchair ramps, elevators, special parking, specially equipped rest rooms, lowered drinking fountains, and lowered telephones are available.

Services: Counseling and information services are available, as is tutoring in every subject. There is a reader service for the blind, and remedial math, reading, and writing.

Campus Safety and Security: Measures include 24-hour foot and vehicle patrol, escort service, shuttle buses, and informal discussions. There are pamphlets/posters/films, emergency telephones, lighted pathways/sidewalks, and a crime prevention program with a full-time staff.

Programs of Study: NMU confers B.A., B.S., B.F.A., B.M.Ed., B.S.N., and B.S.W. degrees. Associate and master's degrees are also awarded. Bachelor's degrees are awarded in BIOLOGICAL SCIENCE (biochemistry, biology/biological science, botany, ecology, microbiology, physiology, wildlife biology, and zoology), BUSINESS (accounting, banking and finance, business administration and management, entrepreneurial studies, and marketing/retailing/merchandising), COMMUNICATIONS AND THE ARTS (broadcasting, ceramic art and design, communications, design, dramatic arts, drawing, English, film arts, fine arts, French, graphic design, illustration, metal/jewelry, music, painting, photography, printmaking, public relations, sculpture, Spanish, and speech/debate/rhetoric), COMPUTER AND PHYSICAL SCIENCE (chemistry, computer programming, computer science, earth science, information sciences and systems, mathematics, and physics), EDUCATION (art, business, computer, early childhood, education of the mentally handicapped, elementary, foreign languages, health, industrial arts, music, physical, science, and secondary), ENGINEERING AND ENVIRONMENTAL DESIGN (construction management, electrical/electronics engineering technology, furniture design, industrial engineering technology, land use management and reclamation, and manufacturing technology), HEALTH PROFESSIONS (clinical science, cytotechnology, medical laboratory technology, nursing, predentistry, premedicine, preveterinary science, and speech pathology/audiology), SOCIAL SCIENCE (corrections, criminal justice, dietetics, economics, geography, history, international studies, parks and recreation management, philosophy, physical fitness/movement, political science/government, prelaw, psychology, public administration, social studies, social work, sociology, and water resources). Biology, chemistry, and education are the strongest academically. Business, education, and biology are the largest.

Required: Students must earn 40 semester credits in liberal studies requirements, including courses in humanities, composition, natural sciences/math, social sciences, communications, and visual and performing arts. Graduation requirements vary by degree program; at the minimum, students must earn 124 semester credits, including 32 in a major field, with a GPA of 2.0. Courses in phys ed/health and world culture and a writing proficiency exam are also required.

Special: Cross-registration is available with other Michigan universities and colleges. Students may study abroad in Europe, Latin America, and Japan. NMU also offers internships, a co-op program in business, accelerated degree programs, a combined accounting/computer information systems major, dual and student-designed majors, limited pass/fail options, and nondegree study. There are 9 national honor societies and a freshman honors program.

Faculty/Classroom: 63% of faculty are male; 37%, female. All teach undergraduates. Graduate students teach 1% of introductory courses. The average class size in an introductory lecture is 23; in a laboratory, 16; and in a regular course, 23.

Admissions: 85% of applicants in a recent year were accepted. 16 freshmen graduated first in their class in a recent year.

Requirements: The SAT I or ACT is required, with a minimum composite score of 900 for the SAT I and 19 for the ACT. Applicants must be graduates of accredited secondary schools or have earned a GED. NMU requires 12 to 16 Carnegie units; recommended secondary school preparation includes 4 years of English, 3 each of math, history, social studies, foreign language, and science, 2 of fine arts or performing arts, and 1 of computer instruction. Students seeking art scholarships must submit a portfolio; those seeking music and theater scholarships must audition. Applications are accepted on-line. A GPA of 2.25 is required. AP and CLEP credits are accepted. Important factors in the admissions decision are advanced placement or honor courses, evidence of special talent, and recommendations by school officials.

Procedure: Freshmen are admitted to all sessions. Entrance exams should be taken during the year prior to enrollment. There is a deferred admissions plan. Application deadlines are open. Application fee is $25.

Transfer: 484 transfer students enrolled in a recent year. Applicants must present a minimum GPA of 2.0 in at least 12 semester credits of college-level work. 32 credits of 124 must be completed at NMU.

Visiting: There are regularly scheduled orientations for prospective students, including an admissions interview, a tour, and a faculty visit. Visitors may sit in on classes and stay overnight. To schedule a visit, contact the Campus Visit Office at (906) 227-1709 or (800) 682-9797.

Financial Aid: In a recent year, 83% of all freshmen and 82% of continuing students received some form of financial aid. 65% of undergraduates work part time. Average annual earnings from campus work are $935. The average financial indebtedness of a recent graduate was $13,784. The FAFSA is required. The fall application deadline is February 1.

International Students: There were 107 international students enrolled in a recent year. The school actively recruits these students. They must score 500 on the written TOEFL or 173 on the electronic version, or 19 on the ACT. Canadian students must take the SAT I or ACT.

Computers: The mainframe is an IBM 9672-R11. There are more than 400 terminals and PCs located in 2 computer labs, the library, residence halls, and academic departments. Those students who use the computer for instruction or research may access the mainframe from 7 A.M. to midnight daily. There are no time limits and no fees.

Graduates: In a recent year, 979 bachelor's degrees were awarded. The most popular majors were business (16%), education (13%), and criminal justice (8%). In an average class, 12% graduate in 4 years, 32% in 5 years, and 37% in 6 years. 57 companies recruited on campus in a recent year. Of graduating class in a recent year, 15% were enrolled in graduate school within 6 months of graduation and 88% were employed.

Admissions Contact: Gerri Daniels, Director of Admissions. A video is available. E-mail: *admiss@nmu.edu* Web: *www.nmu.edu*

NORTHWOOD UNIVERSITY — D-4

Midland, MI 48640 — (989) 837-4273
(800) 457-7878; Fax: (989) 837-4104

Full-time: 1117 men, 680 women	**Faculty:** 44
Part-time: 29 men, 20 women	**Ph.D.s:** 75%
Graduate: 168 men, 72 women	**Student/Faculty:** 41 to 1
Year: terms, summer session	**Tuition:** $12,531
Application Deadline: August 1	**Room & Board:** $5829
Freshman Class: 1341 applied, 1186 accepted, 489 enrolled	
SAT I Verbal/Math: 460/490	**ACT:** 20 **LESS COMPETITIVE**

Northwood University, founded in 1959, is a private, nonprofit college offering undergraduate and graduate programs in business management. Campuses are located in Florida, Michigan, and Texas. The library contains 46,695 volumes and 47,000 microform items, and subscribes to 400 periodicals. Computerized library services include the card catalog, interlibrary loans, and database searching. Special learning facilities include an art gallery and and a creativity center. The 270-acre campus is in a suburban area 135 miles north of Detroit. Including residence halls, there are 27 buildings.

Student Life: 82% of undergraduates are from Michigan. Others are from 41 states, 65 foreign countries, and Canada. 70% are from public schools. 70% are white; 15% African American, 13% foreign nationals. The average age of freshmen is 19; all undergraduates, 20. 22% do not continue beyond their first year.

Housing: 864 students can be accommodated in college housing, which includes single-sex dormitories and on-campus apartments. On-campus housing is guaranteed for the freshman year only and is available on a first-come, first-served basis. 52% of students live on campus; of those, 60% remain on campus on weekends. All students may keep cars.

Activities: 45% of men belong to 3 local and 3 national fraternities; 40% of women belong to 1 local and 4 national sororities. There are 27 groups on campus, including cheerleading, chorale, computers, dance, drama, ethnic, forensics, honors, international, investment, newspaper, pep band, political, professional, religious, social, social service, student government, and yearbook. Popular campus events include Auto Show Weekend, Greek Week, and Values Emphasis Week.

Sports: There are 9 intercollegiate sports for men and 7 for women, and 10 intramural sports for men and 9 for women. Facilities include a sports center with a 1500-seat indoor gym, and a 3500-seat stadium.

Disabled Students: 95% of the campus is accessible. Wheelchair ramps, elevators, special parking, specially equipped rest rooms, special class scheduling, and lowered drinking fountains are available.

Services: Counseling and information services are available, as is tutoring in most subjects. There is remedial math, reading, and writing.

Campus Safety and Security: Measures include 24-hour foot and vehicle patrol, informal discussions, pamphlets/posters/films, and lighted pathways/sidewalks. There is a professional security force.

Programs of Study: Northwood confers the B.B.A. degree. Associate and master's degrees are also awarded. Bachelor's degrees are awarded in BUSINESS (accounting, banking and finance, business administration and management, business economics, fashion merchandising, hospitality management services, hotel/motel and restaurant management, international business management, and transportation and travel marketing), COMMUNICATIONS AND THE ARTS (advertising), COMPUTER AND PHYSICAL SCIENCE (computer management). Accounting is the strongest academically. Marketing/management is the largest.

Required: To graduate, all students must complete a minimum of 180 credit hours, with 36 credit hours in the major. A minimum GPA of 2.0 must be maintained, and 6 credits of computer science management and 2 credits of executive fitness must be completed. Internships for 1 to 6 credits are required in some majors.

Special: Northwood offers on- and off-campus work-study and a competitive study-abroad program in Europe, which is based in Paris and includes extensive travel. Dual majors with management are available in all majors. Credit for life and military work experience is possible through a plan of study. Nondegree study, accelerated degree programs, externships in most majors, and pass/fail options are offered. There is a freshman honors program.

Faculty/Classroom: 58% of faculty are male; 42%, female. All teach undergraduates. No introductory courses are taught by graduate students. The average class size in an introductory lecture is 30; in a laboratory, 20; and in a regular course, 25.

Admissions: 88% of the 2001-2002 applicants were accepted. The SAT I scores for the 2001-2002 freshman class were: Verbal--65% below 500, 21% between 500 and 599, and 15% between 600 and 700; Math--53% below 500, 34% between 500 and 599, and 13% between 600 and 700. The ACT scores were 59% below 21, 23% between 21 and 23, 13% between 24 and 26, 3% between 27 and 28, and 2% above 28. 19% of the current freshmen were in the top fifth of their class; 47% were in the top two fifths. 8 freshmen graduated first in their class.

Requirements: The SAT I or ACT is required. In addition, graduation from an accredited secondary school is required. The GED is accepted. A GPA of 2.0 is required. AP and CLEP credits are accepted. Important factors in the admissions decision are advanced placement or honor courses, evidence of special talent, and leadership record. Applications are accepted on-line.

Procedure: Freshmen are admitted to all sessions. Entrance exams should be taken in the spring of the junior year. There is a deferred admissions plan. Applications should be filed by August 1 for fall entry, November 15 for winter entry, February 15 for spring entry, and June 1 for summer entry, along with a $25 fee. Notification is sent on a rolling basis.

Transfer: 256 transfer students enrolled in 2001-2002. Transfer students must have a minimum of 12 credit hours and a minimum GPA of 2.0. An associate degree and an interview are recommended. 45 credits of 180 must be completed at Northwood.

Visiting: There are regularly scheduled orientations for prospective students, including academic and social seminars and presentations. There are guides for informal visits and visitors may sit in on classes and stay overnight. To schedule a visit, contact the Admissions Department at *admissions@northwood.edu*

Financial Aid: In 2001-2002, 75% of all freshmen and 74% of continuing students received some form of financial aid. 89% of freshmen and 92% of continuing students received need-based aid. The average freshman award was $13,721. Of that total, scholarships or need-based grants averaged $6177; loans averaged $2576; and work contracts averaged $2875. All undergraduates work part time. Average annual earnings from campus work are $1400. The average financial indebtedness of the 2001 graduate was $17,125. The FAFSA is required. The fall application deadline is March 15.

International Students: There were 181 international students enrolled in a recent year. The school actively recruits these students. They must score 500 on the written TOEFL or 173 on the electronic version and also take the SAT I or the ACT, scoring 16 on the ACT.

Computers: The mainframe is an IBM RS/6000. All students may access the system at any time. There are no time limits. The fee is $35.

Graduates: In 2001, 426 bachelor's degrees were awarded. 115 companies recruited on campus in 2000-2001. Of the 2000 graduating class, 4% were enrolled in graduate school within 6 months of graduation and 98% were employed.

Admissions Contact: Dan Toland, Director of Admissions. A video is available. E-mail: *admissions@northwood.edu*
Web: *www.northwood.edu*

OAKLAND UNIVERSITY E-4

Rochester, MI 48309-4401 (248) 370-3360; Fax: (800) OAK-UNIV

Full-time: 3129 men, 5458 women	**Faculty:** 448; IIA, +$
Part-time: 1452 men, 2490 women	**Ph.D.s:** 90%
Graduate: 1181 men, 2165 women	**Student/Faculty:** 19 to 1
Year: semesters, summer session	**Tuition:** $4440 ($11,392)
Application Deadline: open	**Room & Board:** $4978

Freshman Class: 5468 applied, 4220 accepted, 1907 enrolled
ACT: 21 **COMPETITIVE**

Oakland University, established in 1957, is a comprehensive state-supported institution serving a primarily commuter student body. There are 6 undergraduate schools and 1 graduate school. In addition to regional accreditation, Oakland has baccalaureate program accreditation with AACSB, ABET, APTA, CSAB, NASM, NCATE, and NLN. The 2 libraries contain 688,000 volumes, 1,131,000 microform items, and 4361 audiovisual forms/CDs, and subscribe to 2600 periodicals. Computerized library services include the card catalog, interlibrary loans, and database searching. Special learning facilities include a learning resource center, art gallery, and radio station. The 1444-acre campus is in a suburban area 25 miles north of Detroit. Including residence halls, there are 46 buildings.

Student Life: 97% of undergraduates are from Michigan. Others are from 42 states, 59 foreign countries, and Canada. 84% are white. The average age of freshmen is 18; all undergraduates, 24. 26% do not continue beyond their first year.

Housing: 1464 students can be accommodated in college housing, which includes single-sex and coed dormitories and married-student housing. In addition, there are honors houses, special-interest houses and a wellness dorm. On-campus housing is guaranteed for all 4 years and is available on a first-come, first-served basis. Priority is given to out-of-town students. 88% of students commute. All students may keep cars.

Activities: 3% of men and about 1% of women belong to 6 national fraternities; 2% of women belong to 7 national sororities. There are 95 groups on campus, including art, band, cheerleading, choir, chorale, chorus, computers, dance, drama, ethnic, forensics, gay, honors, international, jazz band, musical theater, newspaper, orchestra, pep band, political, professional, radio and TV, religious, social, social service, student government, and symphony. Popular campus events include Pig Roast, African-American celebration month, and Midnight Madness Meadowbrook Ball.

Sports: There are 6 intercollegiate sports for men and 8 for women, and 6 intramural sports for men and 6 for women. Facilities include a health enhancement institute, a 250,000-square-foot student recreation and athletic center that includes softball and baseball diamonds, an indoor track, soccer and touch football fields, and facilities for swimming, basketball, weight training, dance, fencing, handball, squash, racquetball, and golf.

Disabled Students: 90% of the campus is accessible. Wheelchair ramps, elevators, special parking, specially equipped rest rooms, special class scheduling, lowered drinking fountains, lowered telephones, and automatic door openers are available.

Services: Counseling and information services are available, as is tutoring in every subject. There is a reader service for the blind, remedial math and writing, and a mentorship program.

Campus Safety and Security: Measures include 24-hour foot and vehicle patrol, self-defense education, escort service, and informal discussions. There are pamphlets/posters/films, emergency telephones, and lighted pathways/sidewalks.

Programs of Study: Oakland confers B.A., B.S., B.G.S., B.Mus., B.S.E., and B.S.N. degrees. Master's and doctoral degrees are also awarded. Bachelor's degrees are awarded in BIOLOGICAL SCIENCE (biochemistry and biology/biological science), BUSINESS (accounting, banking and finance, business administration and management, business economics, human resources, management information systems, marketing/retailing/merchandising, and personnel management), COMMUNICATIONS AND THE ARTS (art history and appreciation, Chinese, communications, English, fine arts, French, German, Japanese, journalism, linguistics, music, performing arts, Russian, and Spanish), COMPUTER AND PHYSICAL SCIENCE (chemistry, computer science, information sciences and systems, mathematics, physics, and statistics), EDUCATION (elementary and music), ENGINEERING AND ENVIRONMENTAL DESIGN (computer engineering, electrical/electronics engineering, engineering and applied science, engineering physics, industrial engineering, mechanical engineering, and systems engineering), HEALTH PROFESSIONS (environmental health science, health science, industrial hygiene, medical laboratory science, medical science, nursing, and physical therapy), SOCIAL SCIENCE (African American studies, anthropology, Asian/Oriental studies, East Asian studies, economics, history, Latin American studies, liberal arts/general studies, philosophy, political science/government, psychology, public administration, Russian and Slavic studies, sociology, South Asian studies, and women's studies). Physical sciences, biological sciences, and engineering are the strongest academically. Psychology, elementary education, and communications are the largest.

Required: To graduate, students must complete 124 credit hours for a B.A. (128 for a B.Mus. or a B.S. in environmental health), including 32 to 36 in the major. A minimum GPA of 2.0 is required. The core curriculum must include 1 course each in humanities, social science, natural science, language, math/logic, international studies, and Western civilization, and completion of 1 course that meets the ethnic diversity requirement; writing proficiency must be demonstrated as well.

Special: Special academic programs include internships, cooperative programs for most disciplines, and many work-study opportunities. There are organized programs for study abroad in 7 countries; independent programs can be arranged. Oakland also offers a B.A.-B.S. degree in biology and economics, a general studies program, dual majors, and preprofessional studies in medicine, dentristry, optometry, and veterinary medicine. There are 6 national honor societies, a freshman honors program, and 39 departmental honors programs.

Faculty/Classroom: 60% of faculty are male; 40%, female. 99% teach undergraduates; all do research. No introductory courses are taught by graduate students.
Admissions: 77% of the 2001-2002 applicants were accepted. The ACT scores for the 2001-2002 freshman class were: 43% below 21, 29% between 21 and 23, 19% between 24 and 26, 5% between 27 and 28, and 4% above 28.
Requirements: The ACT is required. In addition, admissions requirements include graduation from an accredited secondary school and high school level college preparatory work including 4 years of English, and 3 years each of math, science, and social studies. 2 years of foreign language and 1 semester of computer science are recommended as well. Music and dance majors must audition. A GPA of 2.5 is required. AP and CLEP credits are accepted. Important factors in the admissions decision are evidence of special talent, leadership record, and advanced placement or honor courses.
Procedure: Freshmen are admitted to all sessions. Entrance exams should be taken during the spring of the junior year or early fall of the senior year. There is a deferred admissions plan. The fall 2001 application fee was $25. Notification is sent on a rolling basis.
Transfer: 1294 transfer students enrolled in 2001-2002. Applicants must have at least a 2.5 GPA; a higher GPA is required in some majors. 32 credits of 124 to 128 must be completed at Oakland.
Visiting: There are regularly scheduled orientations for prospective students, including a review of services, academic advising, and course registration. There are guides for informal visits and visitors may sit in on classes and stay overnight. To schedule a visit, contact the Admissions Office.
Financial Aid: In 2000-2001, 33% of all freshmen and 40% of continuing students received some form of financial aid. 25% of freshmen and 28% of continuing students received need-based aid. The average freshman award was $5560. Of that total, scholarships or need-based grants averaged $3100; loans averaged $2250. Oakland is a member of CSS. The FAFSA and the college's own financial statement are required. The fall application deadline is April 1.
International Students: There are 124 international students enrolled. They must score 550 on the written TOEFL.
Computers: There are 39 networked labs with 558 stations, and 9 non-networked labs with 55 stations. All students may access the system. There are no time limits and no fees.
Graduates: In 2001, 1794 bachelor's degrees were awarded. The most popular majors were elementary education (17%), human resource development (7%), and communication (7%). In an average class, 10% graduate in 4 years, 29% in 5 years, and 40% in 6 years.
Admissions Contact: Peter Nacy, Director of Admissions. A video is available. E-mail: *ouinfo@oakland.edu*

OLIVET COLLEGE
Olivet, MI 49076 — D-4
(616) 749-7635
(800) 456-7189; Fax: (616) 749-3821

Full-time: 430 men, 390 women	**Faculty:** 51; IIB, --$
Part-time: 40 men, 35 women	**Ph.D.s:** 36%
Graduate: 5 men, 40 women	**Student/Faculty:** 16 to 1
Year: 4-4-1, summer session	**Tuition:** $13,200
Application Deadline: open	**Room & Board:** $4300
Freshman Class: n/av	
ACT: recommended	**COMPETITIVE**

Olivet College, founded in 1844, is a private liberal arts institution affiliated with both the United Church of Christ and the Congregational Christian Churches. There is 1 graduate school. The information in the above capsule, and in this profile, is approximate. The library contains 85,000 volumes and 117 microform items, and subscribes to 450 periodicals. Computerized library services include the card catalog. Special learning facilities include a learning resource center, art gallery, planetarium, radio station, and an observatory, and a nature preserve. The 92-acre campus is in a small town 30 miles south of Lansing and 120 miles west of Detroit. Including residence halls, there are 24 buildings.
Student Life: 82% of undergraduates are from Michigan. Others are from 21 states, 15 foreign countries, and Canada. 77% are white; 14% African American. 21% are Catholic; 18% claim no religious affiliation. The average age of freshmen is 19; all undergraduates, 23. 40% do not continue beyond their first year; 40% remain to graduate.
Housing: About 660 students can be accommodated in college housing, which includes single-sex and coed dormitories, fraternity houses, and sorority houses. In addition, there are honors houses. On-campus housing is guaranteed for the freshman year only and is available on a first-come, first-served basis. 66% of students live on campus; of those, 48% remain on campus on weekends. All students may keep cars.
Activities: 9% of men and about 2% of women belong to 4 local fraternities; 7% of women belong to 2 local sororities. There are 27 groups on campus, including art, cheerleading, choir, chorale, chorus, computers, drama, ethnic, honors, international, literary magazine, musical theater, newspaper, photography, professional, radio and TV, religious, social, student government, and yearbook. Popular campus events include Diversity Week, Community Service Week, Honors Convocation, and Welcome Week.
Sports: There are 9 intercollegiate sports for men and 9 for women, and 4 intramural sports for men and 3 for women. Facilities include an athletic center, football field, gym, fitness center, soccer fields, softball and baseball fields, tennis courts, a student center, and a pool.
Disabled Students: 25% of the campus is accessible. Wheelchair ramps, elevators, special parking, and specially equipped rest rooms are available.
Services: Counseling and information services are available, as is tutoring in most subjects. There is remedial math, reading, and writing.
Campus Safety and Security: Measures include 24-hour foot and vehicle patrol, self-defense education, escort service, and informal discussions. There are lighted pathways/sidewalks.
Programs of Study: Olivet confers the B.A. degree. Master's degrees are also awarded. Bachelor's degrees are awarded in BIOLOGICAL SCIENCE (biochemistry and biology/biological science), BUSINESS (accounting, business administration and management, insurance, international business management, and marketing management), COMMUNICATIONS AND THE ARTS (communications, design, English, fine arts, illustration, and journalism), COMPUTER AND PHYSICAL SCIENCE (chemistry, computer science, and mathematics), EDUCATION (athletic training, elementary, physical, and secondary), ENGINEERING AND ENVIRONMENTAL DESIGN (environmental science), HEALTH PROFESSIONS (health, predentistry, premedicine, and preveterinary science), SOCIAL SCIENCE (anthropology, criminal justice, economics, history, prelaw, psychology, social studies, and sociology). Business administration, teacher education, and psychology are the strongest academically.
Required: To graduate, students must complete 120 semester hours, 36 to 60 in the major. Their minimum GPA must be 2.0; those seeking certification must maintain a minimum 2.5 GPA in all education courses and in all courses in their major and minor fields. Students must demonstrate competency in 16 areas and complete a 33-hour general education program. In addition, a 40-hour service learning course and senior experience class are required.
Special: Olivet offers internships, cooperative education opportunies, and both student-designed and dual majors. There are 2 national honor societies, and 2 departmental honors programs.
Faculty/Classroom: 55% of faculty are male; 45%, female. All teach undergraduates. No introductory courses are taught by graduate students. The average class size in an introductory lecture is 20; in a laboratory, 14; and in a regular course, 16.
Admissions: In a recent year, 25% of the current freshmen were in the top fifth of their class; 50% were in the top two fifths.
Requirements: The SAT I or ACT is recommended; the minimum score considered on the ACT is 13. Students must be graduates of an accredited secondary school, with a scholastic GPA of at least 2.6 and completion of college-preparatory courses. The GED is accepted. Individual consideration is given to applicants not meeting these criteria, but demonstrating other potential. A GPA of 2.7 is required. AP and CLEP credits are accepted. Important factors in the admissions decision are evidence of special talent, leadership record, and extracurricular activities record.
Procedure: Freshmen are admitted fall, spring, and summer. Check with the school for current application deadlines.
Transfer: 65 transfer students enrolled in a recent year. Transcripts of college work completed elsewhere must show a 2.0 GPA. Transfer applicants must be high school graduates or the equivalent. 30 credits of 120 must be completed at Olivet.
Visiting: There are regularly scheduled orientations for prospective students. There are guides for informal visits and visitors may sit in on classes and stay overnight. To schedule a visit, contact the Admissions Office.
Financial Aid: In a recent year, 94% of all freshmen and 95% of continuing students received some form of financial aid. 88% of freshmen and 92% of continuing students received need-based aid. The average freshman award was $7400. Of that total, scholarships or need-based grants averaged $8214 ($13,900 maximum); loans averaged $2266 ($2625 maximum); and work contracts averaged $1177 ($1600 maximum). 59% of undergraduates work part time. Average annual earnings from campus work are $709. The average financial indebtedness of a recent graduate was $18,000. Olivet is a member of CSS. The FAFSA is required. Check with the school for current deadlines.
International Students: There are 40 international students enrolled. The school actively recruits these students. They must score 500 on the written TOEFL.
Computers: The mainframe is a DEC ALPHA 1000. There are 40 PCs available to all students, which are networked and provide access to the Web. All students may access the system. There are no time limits and no fees.
Graduates: In a recent year, 120 bachelor's degrees were awarded. The most popular majors were business adminstration (17%), psychology (11%), and biology (11%).

Admissions Contact: Kevin Leonard, Director. A video is available. E-mail: *kleonard@olivetnet.edu* Web: *olivetnet.edu*

ROCHESTER COLLEGE E-4
Rochester Hills, MI 48307 (248) 218-2031
(800) 521-6010; Fax: (248) 218-2035

Full-time: 276 men, 358 women
Part-time: 126 men, 167 women
Graduate: none
Year: semesters
Application Deadline: open
Freshman Class: n/av
SAT I or ACT: required
Faculty: 32
Ph.D.s: 28%
Student/Faculty: 20 to 1
Tuition: $10,062
Room & Board: $5342
COMPETITIVE+

Rochester College, founded in 1959, is a private institution affiliated with the Churches of Christ. It offers undergraduate programs in business, behavioral sciences, Christian services, English, interdisciplinary studies, history, music, communication, and general science. The library contains 68,922 volumes, 16,725 microform items, and 956 audiovisual forms/CDs, and subscribes to 642 periodicals. Computerized library services include interlibrary loans and database searching. The 83-acre campus is in a suburban area 25 miles north of Detroit. Including residence halls, there are 12 buildings.

Student Life: 82% of undergraduates are from Michigan. Others are from 19 states, 10 foreign countries, and Canada. 83% are white; 11% African American. 84% are Protestant; 15% Catholic. The average age of freshmen is 20; all undergraduates, 21.

Housing: 366 students can be accommodated in college housing, which includes single-sex dormitories and married-student housing. On-campus housing is available on a first-come, first-served basis. 50% of students live on campus. Alcohol is not permitted. All students may keep cars.

Activities: There are no fraternities or sororities. There are 22 groups on campus, including cheerleading, chorale, chorus, drama, jazz band, newspaper, professional, religious, social, social service, student government, and yearbook. Popular campus events include Celebration.

Sports: There are 5 intercollegiate sports for men and 5 for women, and 9 intramural sports for men and 9 for women. Facilities include a gym, plus soccer, baseball, and softball fields.

Disabled Students: 75% of the campus is accessible. Wheelchair ramps, elevators, special parking, specially equipped rest rooms, and special class scheduling are available.

Services: Counseling and information services are available, as is tutoring in some subjects, including Bible. There is remedial math, reading, and writing.

Campus Safety and Security: Measures include lighted pathways/sidewalks and evening security guards.

Programs of Study: The college confers B.S., B.B.A., and B.R.E. degrees. Associate degrees are also awarded. Bachelor's degrees are awarded in BUSINESS (accounting, business administration and management, and marketing management), COMMUNICATIONS AND THE ARTS (communications, English, and music), COMPUTER AND PHYSICAL SCIENCE (computer management and science), SOCIAL SCIENCE (behavioral science, biblical studies, Christian studies, history, interdisciplinary studies, ministries, and psychology). Management, interdisciplinary studies, and psychology are the largest.

Required: All students must follow a core curriculum that includes courses in religion, communication, humanities, phys ed, science, math, and social science. To graduate, students must complete 128 credits with a minimum GPA of 2.0.

Special: A co-op program in education is available. Cross-registration with Oakland University, Madonna University, Oakland Community College, and Macomb Community College is offered. Internships, which are required for many majors, study abroad, and work-study programs are also offered. There are 2 national honor societies and 1 departmental honors program.

Faculty/Classroom: 65% of faculty are male; 35%, female. All teach undergraduates. The average class size in an introductory lecture is 40; in a laboratory, 10; and in a regular course, 23.

Requirements: The SAT I or ACT is required. A GPA of 2.25 is required. AP and CLEP credits are accepted. Applications are accepted on-line at *www.rc.edu*

Procedure: Freshmen are admitted to all sessions. Entrance exams should be taken as early as possible. There are early admissions and deferred admissions plans. Application deadlines are open. The application fee is $25. Notification is sent on a rolling basis.

Transfer: 54 transfer students enrolled in 2001-2002. A 2.0 college GPA is required. 32 credits of 128 must be completed at the college.

Visiting: There are regularly scheduled orientations for prospective students, including several College Life Preview Days in fall and winter and Celebration Saturday in March. There are guides for informal visits and visitors may sit in on classes and stay overnight. To schedule a visit, contact the Enrollment Services Office.

Financial Aid: In 2001-2002, 93% of all freshmen and 91% of continuing students received some form of financial aid. 59% of freshmen and 58% of continuing students received need-based aid. The average freshman award was $7766. Of that total, scholarships or need-based grants averaged $5004; loans averaged $2072; and work contracts averaged $690. 25% of undergraduates work part time. Average annual earnings from campus work are $994. The average financial indebtedness of the 2001 graduate was $10,416. The CSS/Profile, FAFSA, FFS, or SFS and the college's own financial statement are required. The fall application deadline is August 31.

International Students: There are 29 international students enrolled. The school actively recruits these students. They must score 500 on the written TOEFL or 173 on the electronic version.

Computers: Students may use Pentium 200 MXX workstations in the student computer lab, IBM workstations in the learning lab or library, or dial-up access from the residence halls. Internet access is available. All students may access the system. Schedules for computer use vary. There are no time limits and no fees.

Graduates: In 2001, 136 bachelor's degrees were awarded. The most popular majors were management (28%), early childhood education (8%), and business communication (5%). In an average class, 8% graduate in 4 years, 10% in 5 years, and 12% in 6 years.

Admissions Contact: Larry Norman, Vice President for Enrollment Management. E-mail: *admissions@rc.edu* Web: *www.rc.edu*

SAGINAW VALLEY STATE UNIVERSITY D-4
University Center, MI 48710-0001 (517) 790-4200
(800) 968-9500; Fax: (517) 790-0180

Full-time: 1800 men, 2500 women
Part-time: 1000 men, 1600 women
Graduate: 430 men, 1090 women
Year: semesters, summer session
Application Deadline: open
Freshman Class: 2373 applied, 2307 accepted, 1070 enrolled
ACT: 21
Faculty: 212
Ph.D.s: 82%
Student/Faculty: 20 to 1
Tuition: $4265 ($8528)
Room & Board: $5200
COMPETITIVE

Saginaw Valley State University, founded in 1963, is a state-supported institution offering undergraduate and graduate degrees in arts and behavioral sciences, business and management, education, nursing and health sciences, and science, engineering, and technology. There are 5 undergraduate and 6 graduate schools. In addition to regional accreditation, SVSU has baccalaureate program accreditation with ABET, CSWE, NCATE, and NLN. The library contains 222,925 volumes, 359,991 microform items, and 21,953 audiovisual forms/CDs, and subscribes to 3138 periodicals. Computerized library services include the card catalog, interlibrary loans, and database searching. Special learning facilities include a learning resource center, art gallery, and an observatory. The 782-acre campus is in a suburban area 5 miles north of Saginaw. Including residence halls, there are 42 buildings.

Student Life: 96% of undergraduates are from Michigan. Others are from 18 states, 52 foreign countries, and Canada. 97% are from public schools. 85% are white. The average age of all undergraduates is 24. 32% do not continue beyond their first year.

Housing: 1029 students can be accommodated in college housing, which includes coed dormitories, on-campus apartments, and married-student housing. In addition, there are healthy lifestyle floors and buildings, and first-year suites. On-campus housing is guaranteed for all 4 years. 87% of students commute. Alcohol is not permitted. All students may keep cars.

Activities: 5% of men and about 1% of women belong to 10 national fraternities; 5% of women belong to 6 national sororities. There are 75 groups on campus, including art, band, cheerleading, choir, chorus, computers, dance, drama, ethnic, film, gay, honors, international, jazz band, literary magazine, marching band, musical theater, newspaper, orchestra, pep band, photography, political, professional, religious, social, social service, and student government. Popular campus events include Comedy Night, Family Festival Day, and Cards Party.

Sports: There are 9 intercollegiate sports for men and 8 for women, and 20 intramural sports for men and 18 for women. Facilities include a health and phys ed complex with an Olympic-size pool, indoor track, and racquetball courts; tennis courts; intramural, baseball, softball, and soccer fields; archery; a fitness trail; a football stadium; a golf and tee range; and horseshoe pits.

Disabled Students: 99% of the campus is accessible. Wheelchair ramps, elevators, special parking, specially equipped rest rooms, special class scheduling, lowered drinking fountains, lowered telephones, electronically opened doors, and special access to the library are offered. All buildings are interconnected on the second floor, and special provisions have been made in dorms.

Services: Counseling and information services are available, as is tutoring in most subjects, including most 100- and 200-level classes. There is a reader service for the blind, and remedial math, reading, and writing.

Campus Safety and Security: Measures include 24-hour foot and vehicle patrol, self-defense education, escort service, and informal discus-

sions. There are pamphlets/posters/films, emergency telephones, and lighted pathways/sidewalks. The SVSU public safety department has commissioned police officers to provide police services.

Programs of Study: SVSU confers B.A., B.S., B.A.S., B.B.A., B.F.A., B.P.A., B.S.E.E., B.S.M.E., B.S.N., and B.S.W. degrees. Master's degrees are also awarded. Bachelor's degrees are awarded in BIOLOGICAL SCIENCE (biochemistry and biology/biological science), BUSINESS (accounting, banking and finance, business administration and management, business economics, business law, and marketing management), COMMUNICATIONS AND THE ARTS (art, communications, design, dramatic arts, English, fine arts, French, music, and Spanish), COMPUTER AND PHYSICAL SCIENCE (applied physics, chemistry, computer mathematics, computer science, mathematics, optics, and physics), EDUCATION (art, elementary, English, foreign languages, mathematics, music, physical, and special), ENGINEERING AND ENVIRONMENTAL DESIGN (electrical/electronics engineering, environmental science, industrial administration/management, and mechanical engineering), HEALTH PROFESSIONS (allied health, nursing, and occupational therapy), SOCIAL SCIENCE (criminal justice, economics, history, interdisciplinary studies, international studies, political science/government, psychology, public administration, social work, and sociology). Mechanical engineering, criminal justice, and elementary education are the largest.

Required: Students must complete a minimum of 124 credits, satisfy basic skills and general education requirements, maintain a minimum GPA of 2.0, complete at least 31 credits at SVSU, and be enrolled on campus the last semester.

Special: Opportunities are provided for student-designed majors, work-study, internships, co-op education, credit by exam, nondegree study, pass/fail options, and study abroad in Japan, Mexico, Poland, Austria, England, France, and Italy. There are 3 national honor societies.

Faculty/Classroom: 65% of faculty are male; 35%, female. All teach undergraduates. No introductory courses are taught by graduate students. The average class size in an introductory lecture is 27; in a laboratory, 13; and in a regular course, 25.

Admissions: 97% of the 2001-2002 applicants were accepted. The ACT scores for the 2001-2002 freshman class were: 51% below 21, 25% between 21 and 23, 15% between 24 and 26, 6% between 27 and 28, and 3% above 28. 55 freshmen graduated first in their class.

Requirements: The ACT is required. In addition, graduation from an accredited secondary school or a GED is required. Applicants should submit records of successful completion of 4 years each of English and math, 3 each of social science and science, 2 each of a foreign language and fine arts, and 1 course in computer literacy. A GPA of 2.5 is required. AP and CLEP credits are accepted.

Procedure: Freshmen are admitted to all sessions. Application deadlines are open. The fall 2001 application fee was $25. Notification is sent on a rolling basis.

Transfer: 639 transfer students enrolled in 2001-2002. Transfer students with fewer than 45 credits from a previous college must submit high school and college transcripts. A minimum GPA of 2.0 is needed. An interview may be required. 31 credits of 124 must be completed at SVSU.

Visiting: There are regularly scheduled orientations for prospective students, including tours help with schedules, basic information, and counseling. There are guides for informal visits. To schedule a visit, contact the Office of Admissions.

Financial Aid: In a recent year, 54% of all freshmen and 51% of continuing students received some form of financial aid. 75% of freshmen and 74% of continuing students received need-based aid. The average freshman award was $4753. Of that total, scholarships or need-based grants averaged $1000 ($8553 maximum); loans averaged $2625 ($6625 maximum); and work contracts averaged $1128 ($2000 maximum). 12% of undergraduates work part time. Average annual earnings from campus work are $1600. The average financial indebtedness of the 2001 graduate was $9580. The FAFSA is required.

International Students: There were 158 international students enrolled in a recent year. The school actively recruits these students. They must score 500 on the written TOEFL.

Computers: The mainframe is a DEC ALPHA 1000. The mainframe is accessible from any of 300 Macs or PCs available in networked student computer labs or via Internet dial-in. All stations have access to the Internet and the Web. All students may access the system. There are no time limits and no fees.

Graduates: In 2001, 809 bachelor's degrees were awarded. The most popular majors were elementary education (12%), criminal justice (9%), and nursing (8%). 15 companies recruited on campus in 2000-2001.

Admissions Contact: James Dwyer, Director of Admissions.
E-mail: *admissions@svsu.edu* Web: *www.svsu.edu*

SAINT MARY'S COLLEGE — E-4
Orchard Lake, MI 48324 — (248) 683-0528; Fax: (248) 683-0402

Full-time: 120 men, 70 women	**Faculty:** 19
Part-time: 70 men, 85 women	**Ph.D.s:** 80%
Graduate: none	**Student/Faculty:** 10 to 1
Year: semesters, summer session	**Tuition:** $8514
Application Deadline: see profile	**Room & Board:** $4800
Freshman Class: n/av	
ACT: required	**LESS COMPETITIVE**

Saint Mary's College, founded in 1885, is an independent institution affiliated with the Roman Catholic Church. Figures in above capsule are approximate. The library contains 75,000 volumes and 6199 microform items, and subscribes to 450 periodicals. Computerized library services include the card catalog, interlibrary loans, and database searching. Special learning facilities include a learning resource center and art gallery. The 122-acre campus is in a suburban area 17 miles from Detroit. Including residence halls, there are 13 buildings.

Student Life: 95% of undergraduates are from Michigan. Others are from 11 states, 16 foreign countries, and Canada. 70% are from public schools. 91% are white. 60% are Catholic; 34% Protestant. The average age of freshmen is 19; all undergraduates, 29. 31% do not continue beyond their first year; 20% remain to graduate.

Housing: 150 students can be accommodated in college housing, which includes single-sex dormitories. On-campus housing is guaranteed for all 4 years. 74% of students commute. Alcohol is not permitted. All students may keep cars.

Activities: There are no fraternities or sororities. There are 12 groups on campus, including dance, drama, ethnic, honors, international, literary magazine, newspaper, religious, social, social service, student government, and yearbook.

Sports: There are 3 intercollegiate sports for men and 1 for women, and 5 intramural sports for men and 5 for women. Facilities include a stadium, 2 gyms, a weight room, an outdoor track, and baseball, football, and soccer fields.

Disabled Students: 80% of the campus is accessible. Wheelchair ramps, special parking, and specially equipped rest rooms are available.

Services: Counseling and information services are available, as is tutoring in most subjects. There is remedial math, reading, and writing.

Campus Safety and Security: Measures include informal discussions, pamphlets/posters/films, emergency telephones, and lighted pathways/sidewalks. There is evening security in dorms.

Programs of Study: Saint Mary's confers B.A., B.S., B.G.S., and B.H.S. degrees. Bachelor's degrees are awarded in BIOLOGICAL SCIENCE (biology/biological science), BUSINESS (business administration and management), COMMUNICATIONS AND THE ARTS (communications, English, and modern language), COMPUTER AND PHYSICAL SCIENCE (chemistry, computer science, and radiological technology), EDUCATION (education), HEALTH PROFESSIONS (health science and premedicine), SOCIAL SCIENCE (community services, human services, philosophy, prelaw, psychology, religious education, social science, sociology, and theological studies). Premedicine, communication arts, and theology are the strongest academically. Business, communication arts, and psychology are the largest.

Required: To graduate, students must complete 120 credit hours, with 30 to 36 hours in the major and a minimum GPA of 2.0. All students must take 60 hours of core curriculum courses in the following areas: communications, ultimate meaning and value, interpretation and analysis of the arts, historical consciousness, foreign language, social science, natural science, and math. The college requires that students demonstrate writing proficiency.

Special: The college offers co-op programs with colleges in the Detroit Area Consortium of Catholic Colleges. Internships, study abroad, an accelerated degree program in organizational managements, dual majors, a general studies degree, directed study, and nondegree study are available. A program in Polish studies is offered at the school's Center of Polish Studies and Culture.

Faculty/Classroom: 60% of faculty are male; 40%, female. All teach undergraduates.

Requirements: The ACT is required, with a minimum composite score of 19. Applicants must be graduates of an accredited secondary school. The GED is accepted. Students must complete 16 high school academic credits. A GPA of 2.5 is required. CLEP credit is accepted. Important factors in the admissions decision are evidence of special talent, advanced placement or honor courses, and leadership record. Students may submit applications on-line.

Procedure: Freshmen are admitted fall, winter, and spring. There are early decision and early admissions plans. Notification is sent on a rolling basis. Check with the school for current deadlines. The fall 2001 application fee was $25.

Transfer: 35 transfer students enrolled in a recent year. Applicants must have a minimum GPA of 2.0. The ACT is required unless the student is classified as a nontraditional student or has 12 or more semester hours of college credit. 30 credits of 120 must be completed at Saint Mary's.

Visiting: There are regularly scheduled orientations for prospective students, Transfer students may attend a day or evening orientation prior to the fall semester. There are guides for informal visits and visitors may sit in on classes and stay overnight. To schedule a visit, contact the Admissions Office at (248) 683-1757.

Financial Aid: Saint Mary's is a member of CSS. The CSS/Profile and the college's own financial statement are required. Check with the school for current deadlines.

International Students: The school actively recruits these students. They must score 500 on the written TOEFL or take the MELAB.

Computers: The mainframe is an IBM/36. The college makes available a substantial number of PCs for students. . There are no time limits and no fees. It is strongly recommended that all students have a personal computer.

Graduates: In a recent year, 37 bachelor's degrees were awarded.

Admissions Contact: David Sichterman, Assistant Director of Admissions. E-mail: *stmcoll@aol.com* Web: *www.stmarys-orchardlake.edu*

SIENA HEIGHTS UNIVERSITY

Adrian, MI 49221 — E-5

(517) 264-7183
(800) 521-0009; Fax: (517) 264-7745

Full-time: 270 men, 480 women	**Faculty:** 53; IIB, -$
Part-time: 70 men, 160 women	**Ph.D.s:** 64%
Graduate: 50 men, 110 women	**Student/Faculty:** 14 to 1
Year: semesters, summer session	**Tuition:** $12,000
Application Deadline: open	**Room & Board:** $4400
Freshman Class: n/av	
ACT: required	**LESS COMPETITIVE**

Siena Heights University, founded in 1919, is a private liberal arts institution affiliated with the Roman Catholic Church. There is 1 graduate school. Information in the above capsule, and in this profile, is approximate. In addition to regional accreditation, Siena has baccalaureate program accreditation with NASAD. The library contains 112,049 volumes, 24,214 microform items, and 4730 audiovisual forms/CDs, and subscribes to 451 periodicals. Computerized library services include the card catalog, interlibrary loans, and database searching. Special learning facilities include an art gallery. The 140-acre campus is in a small town 75 miles southwest of Detroit. Including residence halls, there are 12 buildings.

Student Life: 80% are from public schools. 84% are white. The average age of freshmen is 18; all undergraduates, 25. 45% do not continue beyond their first year.

Housing: About 450 students can be accommodated in college housing, which includes coed dormitories. On-campus housing is available on a first-come, first-served basis and is available on a lottery system for upperclassmen. Priority is given to out-of-town students. 69% of students commute. All students may keep cars.

Activities: 10% of men belong to 2 national fraternities; 10% of women belong to 2 national sororities. There are 30 groups on campus, including art, cheerleading, choir, chorale, chorus, computers, drama, ethnic, international, jazz band, literary magazine, musical theater, newspaper, professional, religious, social, social service, student government, and symphony. Popular campus events include Alumni/Family Weekend, International Dinner, and athletic banquets.

Sports: There are 6 intercollegiate sports for men and 6 for women, and 6 intramural sports for men and 6 for women. Facilities include a 57000-square-foot student activity center, which houses 5 basketball, 4 volleyball, and 2 tennis courts, a 200-meter, 4-lane track, a baseball batting cage, training and exercise rooms, ballrooms, and the Sage Union. The indoor gym seats 4000. There is also a soccer field and a sand volleyball pit.

Disabled Students: 70% of the campus is accessible. Wheelchair ramps, elevators, special parking, specially equipped rest rooms, and lowered drinking fountains are available.

Services: Counseling and information services are available, as is tutoring in most subjects. There is remedial math, reading, and writing.

Campus Safety and Security: Measures include 24-hour foot and vehicle patrol, self-defense education, escort service, and informal discussions. There are pamphlets/posters/films and lighted pathways/sidewalks.

Programs of Study: Siena confers B.A., B.S., B.A.S., and B.F.A. degrees. Associate and master's degrees are also awarded. Bachelor's degrees are awarded in BIOLOGICAL SCIENCE (biology/biological science), BUSINESS (accounting, business administration and management, hotel/motel and restaurant management, and retailing), COMMUNICATIONS AND THE ARTS (art history and appreciation, communications, English, fine arts, music, and Spanish), COMPUTER AND PHYSICAL SCIENCE (chemistry, information sciences and systems, mathematics, and natural sciences), EDUCATION (business, elementary, and music), HEALTH PROFESSIONS (premedicine), SOCIAL SCIENCE (American studies, child psychology/development, criminal justice, history, human services, humanities, liberal arts/general studies, philosophy, psychology, public administration, religion, social science, and social work). Art, business, and biology are the strongest academically. Business, art, and education are the largest.

Required: To graduate, students must complete 120 semester hours, including 30 hours in the major, and maintain at least a 2.0 GPA. A core curriculum of 33 to 35 semester hours is required, including 2 courses in English composition and 1 each in literature, math, science, fine/performing arts, social science, history, philosophy, and religious studies. A seminar in education is also required.

Special: Special academic programs include 2-2 engineering co-op programs with the University of Detroit and the University of Michigan, a 2-2 business administration program at Lake Michigan College, internships in a student's major, study abroad in Mexico for various majors and in Siena, Italy, for art students, and on-and off-campus work-study. Also offered are dual and inverted majors, B.A.-B.S. degrees, a general studies degree, and student-designed majors. 3-year bachelor's degrees may be earned, and a directed student-teaching program is available for education majors. Flexible learning formats include weekend and evening courses. There is 1 national honor society.

Faculty/Classroom: 52% of faculty are male; 48%, female. 95% teach undergraduates. No introductory courses are taught by graduate students. The average class size in a regular course is 15.

Requirements: The ACT is required with a minimum score of 17. Admissions requirements include graduation from an accredited secondary school. The GED is accepted. A GPA of 2.3 is required. AP and CLEP credits are accepted. Important factors in the admissions decision are recommendations by school officials, parents or siblings attending the school, and recommendations by alumni. Applications are accepted online.

Procedure: Freshmen are admitted to all sessions. SAT I or ACT scores should be available when the application is filed. There is a deferred admissions plan. Application deadlines are open. Check with the school for current application deadlines and fee.

Transfer: 70 transfer students enrolled in in a recent year. Applicants must have a 2.0 GPA. High school and college transcripts must be submitted. 30 credits of 120 must be completed at Siena.

Visiting: There are regularly scheduled orientations for prospective students. There are guides for informal visits and visitors may sit in on classes and stay overnight. To schedule a visit, contact the Admissions Office at (517) 264-7180 or (800) 521-0009, ext. 7180.

Financial Aid: In a recent year, 95% of all freshmen and 92% of continuing students received some form of financial aid. 66% of freshmen and 68% of continuing students received need-based aid. Scholarships or need-based grants averaged $6900 ($10,700 maximum); loans averaged $2400 ($6400 maximum); and work contracts averaged $1600 ($2400 maximum). 75% of undergraduates work part time. Average annual earnings from campus work are $1300. The average financial indebtedness of a recent graduate was $12,500. Siena is a member of CSS. The FAFSA is required. Check with the school for current deadlines.

International Students: The school actively recruits these students. They must score 500 on the written TOEFL and also take the ACT, scoring 17.

Computers: The mainframe is an IBM RS/6000 320H. The PC lab has Mac and IBM computers for student use, with access to the Internet and the Web. All students may access the system from 8 A.M. to 11 P.M., except when classes are in session. There are no time limits and no fees.

Graduates: In a recent year, 171 bachelor's degrees were awarded. The most popular majors were business administration (17%), art (11%), and psychology (8%).

Admissions Contact: Kevin C. Kucera, Dean of Admissions and Enrollment Services. E-mail: *admissions@sienahts.edu*

SPRING ARBOR COLLEGE
(See Spring Arbor University)

SPRING ARBOR UNIVERSITY (Formerly Spring Arbor College)

Spring Arbor, MI 49283-9799 — D-5

(517) 750-6468
(800) 968-0011; Fax: (517) 750-6620

Full-time: 367 men, 619 women	**Faculty:** 84
Part-time: 54 men, 99 women	**Ph.D.s:** 52%
Graduate: 149 men, 294 women	**Student/Faculty:** 12 to 1
Year: 4-1-4, summer session	**Tuition:** $13,136
Application Deadline: open	**Room & Board:** $4840
Freshman Class: 565 applied, 488 accepted, 225 enrolled	
ACT: 22	**COMPETITIVE**

Spring Arbor University (formerly Spring Arbor College), founded in 1873, is a private institution affiliated with the Free Methodist Church. It offers undergraduate programs in fine arts, humanities, philosophy, religion, natural science, social science, and education. Graduate programs in business and education are also offered. In addition to regional accreditation, SAU has baccalaureate program accreditation with CSWE and NCATE. The library contains 93,307 volumes, 315,412 microform items, and 5291 audiovisual forms/CDs, and subscribes to 634 periodicals. Computerized library services include the card catalog, interlibrary loans, and database searching. Special learning facilities include a learning resource center, radio station, and TV production facilities and equipment. The 70-acre campus is in a small town 8 miles west of Jackson. Including residence halls, there are 27 buildings.

Student Life: 87% of undergraduates are from Michigan. Others are from 19 states, 14 foreign countries, and Canada. 83% are white; 19% Asian American, 11% African American. 69% are Protestant; 20% claim no religious affiliation. 17% do not continue beyond their first year; 49% remain to graduate.

Housing: 686 students can be accommodated in college housing, which includes single-sex dormitories, on-campus apartments, and married-student housing. On-campus housing is guaranteed for all 4 years. 70% of students live on campus; of those, 50% remain on campus on weekends. Alcohol is not permitted. All students may keep cars.

Activities: There are no fraternities or sororities. There are 21 groups on campus, including band, cheerleading, choir, chorale, drama, ethnic, honors, international, jazz band, newspaper, radio and TV, religious, social, social service, student government, and yearbook. Popular campus events include Arbor Games, Midnight Breakfast, and Spring Banquet.

Sports: There are 7 intercollegiate sports for men and 7 for women, and 8 intramural sports for men and 4 for women. Facilities include a 500-seat stadium, a 2600-seat gym, all-weather and indoor tracks, tennis courts, a basketball court, an Olympic pool, a weight-training room with cardiovascular equipment, and baseball, softball, and soccer fields.

Disabled Students: 80% of the campus is accessible. Wheelchair ramps, elevators, special parking, specially equipped rest rooms, lowered drinking fountains, and lowered telephones, are available.

Services: Counseling and information services are available, as is tutoring in most subjects. There is a reader service for the blind, remedial math, reading, and writing, religious counseling, and health services.

Campus Safety and Security: Measures include self-defense education, escort service, informal discussions, and lighted pathways/sidewalks. There is a night security guard and a bike patrol.

Programs of Study: SAU confers B.A. and B.S.W. degrees. Associate and master's degrees are also awarded. Bachelor's degrees are awarded in BIOLOGICAL SCIENCE (biochemistry and biology/biological science), BUSINESS (accounting, business administration and management, and management information systems), COMMUNICATIONS AND THE ARTS (art, communications, English, language arts, music, and Spanish), COMPUTER AND PHYSICAL SCIENCE (chemistry, computer science, mathematics, and physics), HEALTH PROFESSIONS (exercise science), SOCIAL SCIENCE (history, ministries, philosophy, physical fitness/movement, psychology, religion, social science, social work, and sociology). Business, teacher education, and social science are the strongest academically. English, business, and communications are the largest.

Required: Students must complete 4 Christian perspective courses, cross-cultural studies, writing skills, speech, and physical fitness. Liberal arts requirements are in fine arts, humanities, natural science/math, philosophy/religion, and social science. To graduate, at least 124 semester hours, 30 to 48 in the major, with a minimum GPA of 2.0 overall and 2.2 in the major, are needed.

Special: Each student participates in a cross-cultural experience, which includes travel to a foreign country or to an urban center in the United States. Additional study-abroad opportunities can be arranged. A Washington semester is available through the American Studies Program. The university also offers cross-registration with Jackson Community College, work-study, a dual major in physics/math, student-designed majors, pass/fail options, and nondegree study. Alternative programs for adult learners provide field-based study and assign credit for life experience. An accelerated B.A. program for such students is also offered. There are 3 national honor societies and a freshman honors program.

Faculty/Classroom: 62% of faculty are male; 38%, female. No introductory courses are taught by graduate students. The average class size in an introductory lecture is 35; in a laboratory, 12; and in a regular course, 15.

Admissions: 86% of the 2001-2002 applicants were accepted. The ACT scores for the 2001-2002 freshman class were: 31% below 21, 30% between 21 and 23, 22% between 24 and 26, 11% between 27 and 28, and 6% above 28. 40% of the current freshmen were in the top fifth of their class; 66% were in the top two fifths. 12 freshmen graduated first in their class.

Requirements: The ACT is required, with a composite score of 20 recommended. Applicants must be graduates of accredited secondary schools or have a GED. An interview is advised for those who do not meet the requirements. Home-schooled applicants must take the ACT or the SAT I, provide transcripts of course work, and submit a 2- to 3-page paper. A GPA of 2.6 is required. AP and CLEP credits are accepted. Important factors in the admissions decision are personality/intangible qualities, parents or siblings attending the school, and leadership record.

Procedure: Freshmen are admitted to all sessions. Entrance exams should be taken in the spring of the junior year or fall of the senior year. There are early admissions and deferred admissions plans. Application deadlines are open. The fall 2001 application fee was $30. Notification is sent on a rolling basis.

Transfer: 100 transfer students enrolled in 2001-2002. Applicants should have a minimum GPA of 2.0 and are encouraged to arrange an interview. A release of information form is required from the previous college attended. 30 credits of 124 must be completed at SAU.

Visiting: There are regularly scheduled orientations for prospective students, including a tour, class and chapel attendance, lunch, and a student panel discussion. There are guides for informal visits and visitors may sit in on classes and stay overnight. To schedule a visit, contact the Admissions Office.

Financial Aid: In 2001-2002, 95% of all freshmen and 90% of continuing students received some form of financial aid. 75% of freshmen received need-based aid. The average freshman award was $12,044. Of that total, scholarships or need-based grants averaged $8399; loans averaged $3613 ($9625 maximum). 26% of undergraduates work part time. Average annual earnings from campus work are $1000. SAU is a member of CSS. The FAFSA is required. The fall application deadline is May 1.

International Students: There are 33 international students enrolled. They must score 525 on the written TOEFL or take the MELAB, and also take the ACT.

Computers: The mainframes are an HP 828 and an HP E35. Computer labs in the science building, art building, student center, and Lowell lounge are open to all students. A lab in the Learning Center is for the special needs population. All students may access the system. There are no time limits and no fees. It is strongly recommended that all students have personal computers.

Graduates: In 2001, 773 bachelor's degrees were awarded. The most popular majors were business (39%), family life (26%), and health service (7%). In an average class, 30% graduate in 4 years, 55% in 5 years, and 57% in 6 years.

Admissions Contact: Shelley Ashley, Director of Admissions. A video is available. E-mail: *admissions@admin.arbor.edu*
Web: *www.arbor.edu*

UNIVERSITY OF DETROIT MERCY — E-5

Detroit, MI 48219-0900 — **(313) 993-1245**
(800) 635-5020; Fax: (313) 993-3317

Full-time: 1000 men, 1000 women	**Faculty:** 217
Part-time: 400 men, 1600 women	**Ph.D.s:** 85%
Graduate: 800 men, 1000 women	**Student/Faculty:** 10 to 1
Year: semesters, summer session	**Tuition:** $16,300
Application Deadline: see profile	**Room & Board:** $5320
Freshman Class: n/av	
SAT I or ACT: required	**LESS COMPETITIVE**

University of Detroit Mercy, founded in 1877, is a private, independent institution affiliated with the Jesuits and Sisters of Mercy. It offers undergraduate programs in liberal arts, education and human services, business administration, engineering and science, architecture, and nursing and health sciences. Figures in the above capsule, and in this profile, are approximate. There are 8 undergraduate and 5 graduate schools. In addition to regional accreditation, U of DM has baccalaureate program accreditation with AACSB, ABET, ADA, CSWE, NAAB, and NLN. The 5 libraries contain 500,000 volumes, 700,000 microform items, and 15,000 audiovisual forms/CDs, and subscribe to 3100 periodicals. Computerized library services include the card catalog, interlibrary loans, and database searching. Special learning facilities include a learning resource center and radio station. The 70-acre campus is in an urban area 7 miles north of downtown Detroit. Including residence halls, there are 43 buildings.

Student Life: 93% of undergraduates are from Michigan. Others are from 24 states, 27 foreign countries, and Canada. 50% are white; 40% African American. 30% are Catholic; 30% a variety of denominations and religions; 24% claim no religious affiliation; 16% Protestant. The average age of freshmen is 18; all undergraduates, 29.

Housing: 1000 students can be accommodated in college housing, which includes coed dormitories, married-student housing, and a freshman residence program. On-campus housing is guaranteed for all 4 years. 85% of students commute. All students may keep cars.

Activities: 12% of men belong to 3 national fraternities; 12% of women belong to 3 national sororities. There are 70 groups on campus, including cheerleading, chorale, computers, drama, ethnic, honors, international, literary magazine, newspaper, pep band, political, professional, radio and TV, religious, social, social service, student government, and yearbook. Popular campus events include Engineering and Architecture Week.

Sports: There are 7 intercollegiate sports for men and 7 for women, and 11 intramural sports for men and 11 for women. Facilities include a fitness center, gym, racquetball/handball courts, an indoor track, a game room in the Student Union, and soccer, softball, and baseball fields.

Disabled Students: 50% of the campus is accessible. Wheelchair ramps, elevators, special parking, and special class scheduling are available.

Services: Counseling and information services are available, as is tutoring in some subjects, including all freshman courses and many other courses. There is remedial math, reading, and writing.

Campus Safety and Security: Measures include 24-hour foot and vehicle patrol, self-defense education, escort service, and informal discussions. There are pamphlets/posters/films, emergency telephones, and lighted pathways/sidewalks.

Programs of Study: U of DM confers B.A., B.S., B.Arch., B.B.A., B.C.E., B.Ch.E., B.E.E., B.En., B.F.A., B.M.E., B.S.Ed., B.S.N., and B.S.W. degrees. Associate, master's, and doctoral degrees are also awarded. Bachelor's degrees are awarded in BIOLOGICAL SCIENCE (biochemistry and biology/biological science), BUSINESS (accounting and business administration and management), COMMUNICATIONS AND THE ARTS (communications, dramatic arts, and English), COMPUTER AND PHYSICAL SCIENCE (chemistry, computer science, information sciences and systems, and mathematics), EDUCATION (early childhood, elementary, health, middle school, secondary, and special), ENGINEERING AND ENVIRONMENTAL DESIGN (architecture, chemical engineering, civil engineering, electrical/electronics engineering, engineering, industrial engineering technology, and mechanical engineering), HEALTH PROFESSIONS (dental hygiene, health care administration, nuclear medical technology, nursing, predentistry, premedicine, and sports medicine), SOCIAL SCIENCE (addiction studies, criminal justice, economics, history, human services, liberal arts/general studies, paralegal studies, philosophy, political science/government, prelaw, psychology, religion, social work, and sociology). Engineering, nursing, and business administration are the strongest academically. Business administration, nursing, and mechanical engineering are the largest.

Required: Students must successfully complete at least 126 credit hours, including a core curriculum, and maintain a minimum GPA of 2.0. Required courses include English composition, religion, philosophy, and speech fundamentals.

Special: Cooperative education is mandatory for engineering and architecture majors and is optional for others. Cross-registration is available with a consortium of Catholic colleges in the Detroit area. There are internships, and a B.A.-B.S. degree is available for math, chemistry, and biology majors. An accelerated 6-year degree program in dentistry is provided. Study abroad is available in England, China, Canada, Mexico, Italy, Poland, Israel, and Greece. Academic exploration courses are provided to help students who are undecided about a future vocation. There are 5 national honor societies, and a freshman honors program.

Faculty/Classroom: 75% both teach and do research.

Requirements: The SAT I or ACT is required. In addition, graduation from an accredited secondary school is required; a GED will be accepted. Students must submit 16 academic credits, which should include, as a minimum, 4 units of English, 3 of math, and 2 each of history or social studies and natural science, including a lab course. Remaining credits should be distributed in a foreign language, speech, music, art, and other college preparatory electives. An interview is recommended. A GPA of 2.5 is required. AP and CLEP credits are accepted. Advanced placement or honor courses is an important factor in the admission decision.

Procedure: Freshmen are admitted to all sessions. Entrance exams should be taken during the junior or senior year. There is an early admissions plan. Notification is sent on a rolling basis. Check with the school for current deadlines. The fall 2001 application fee was $25.

Transfer: Transfer applicants with fewer than 24 semester hours of credit at an accredited institution must submit SAT I or ACT scores and have maintained a minimum GPA of 2.0. If the student is older than 23 years of age, the SAT I/ACT scores need not be submitted. 32 credits of 126 must be completed at U of DM.

Visiting: There are regularly scheduled orientations for prospective students, including a look at student life, testing and advising, and registration. There are guides for informal visits and visitors may sit in on classes and stay overnight. To schedule a visit, contact the Admissions Office.

Financial Aid: U of DM is a member of CSS. The FAFSA is required. Check with the school for current deadlines.

International Students: The school actively recruits these students. They must take the college's own test.

Computers: The mainframe is a Unisys A3K. PCs are available throughout the campus. All students may access the system. There are no time limits.

Admissions Contact: Admissions Counselors.
E-mail: *admissions@udmercy.edu*

UNIVERSITY OF MICHIGAN/ANN ARBOR E-5

Ann Arbor, MI 48109 **(734) 764-7433; Fax: (734) 936-0740**

Full-time: 11,410 men, 11,779 women	**Faculty:** 1795; I, +$
Part-time: 749 men, 609 women	**Ph.D.s:** 92%
Graduate: 7818 men, 5883 women	**Student/Faculty:** 13 to 1
Year: trimesters, summer session	**Tuition:** $6935 ($21,645)
Application Deadline: February 1	**Room & Board:** $6068
Freshman Class: 24,141 applied, 12,594 accepted, 5540 enrolled	
SAT I Verbal/Math: 630/660	**ACT:** 28

HIGHLY COMPETITIVE+

The University of Michigan/Ann Arbor, founded in 1817, is the main campus of the University of Michigan. The public institution offers undergraduate programs in the arts and sciences, architecture, business administration, education, engineering, fine arts, kinesiology, natural resources, nursing, and professional studies, as well as a wide range of graduate and professional programs. There are 12 undergraduate and 19 graduate schools. In addition to regional accreditation, UM has baccalaureate program accreditation with AACSB, ABET, ACEJMC, ACPE, ADA, ASLA, CSWE, NAAB, NASAD, NASM, NCATE, NLN, and SAF. The 24 libraries contain 7,348,460 volumes, 6,037,194 microform items, and 56,512 audiovisual forms/CDs, and subscribe to 68,798 periodicals. Computerized library services include the card catalog, interlibrary loans, and database searching. Special learning facilities include a learning resource center, art gallery, natural history museum, planetarium, radio station, TV station, archeology museum, botanical gardens, and 2 historical museums. The 3114-acre campus is in a suburban area 38 miles west of Detroit. Including residence halls, there are 210 buildings.

Student Life: 65% of undergraduates are from Michigan. Others are from 50 states, 90 foreign countries, and Canada. 71% are white; 12% Asian American. The average age of freshmen is 18; all undergraduates, 20. 5% do not continue beyond their first year.

Housing: 10,936 students can be accommodated in college housing, which includes single-sex and coed dormitories, on-campus apartments, married-student housing, fraternity houses, and sorority houses. In addition, there are honors houses, language houses, special-interest houses, substance-free dorm rooms, women-in-science housing, and cooperative housing. On-campus housing is guaranteed for the freshman year only, is available on a first-come, first-served basis, and on a lottery system for upperclassmen. 63% of students commute. All students may keep cars.

Activities: 17% of men belong to 1 local and 37 national fraternities; 17% of women belong to 24 national sororities. There are 900 groups on campus, including art, band, cheerleading, chess, choir, chorale, chorus, computers, dance, debate, drama, ethnic, film, gay, honors, international, jazz band, literary magazine, marching band, musical theater, newspaper, opera, orchestra, pep band, photography, political, professional, radio and TV, religious, social, social service, student government, symphony, and yearbook. Popular campus events include Martin Luther King Day, Native American Pow Wow, and Holocaust conference.

Sports: There are 12 intercollegiate sports for men and 13 for women, and 25 intramural sports for men and 25 for women. Facilities include a 107,501-seat stadium, a 1000-seat gym, an indoor track and tennis complex, an indoor practice center, 3 recreational buildings, 2 golf courses, a natatorium and separate swimming pools, an ice arena, and several other athletic arenas, the largest of which seats 13,000.

Disabled Students: 97% of the campus is accessible. Wheelchair ramps, elevators, special parking, specially equipped rest rooms, special class scheduling, lowered drinking fountains, lowered telephones, special housing, para-transit service, specially equipped vans, talking calculators, telecommunication devices for the deaf, and an adaptive technology computing site that includes a high-speed scanner, voice input and voice output, braille display and large-print screens, and a braille printer are available.

Services: Counseling and information services are available, as is tutoring in some subjects, including introductory English and math. There is a reader service for the blind.

Campus Safety and Security: Measures include 24-hour foot and vehicle patrol, self-defense education, escort service, and shuttle buses. There are informal discussions, pamphlets/posters/films, emergency telephones, lighted pathways/sidewalks, a nite-owl bus service, officer bicycle patrols, and a taxi service.

Programs of Study: UM confers A.B., B.S., A.B.E.D., B.B.A., B.D.A., B.F.A., B.F.A.D., B.F.A.M.T., B.F.A.(T), B.G.S., B.Mus., B.Mus.A., B.S.A.O.S., B.S.Chem., B.S.D.Hyg., B.S.E.AET., B.S.E.C.E., B.S.E.Ch., B.S.E.Civ., B.S.E.Comp., B.S.Ed., B.S.E.E.E., B.S.E.E.P., B.S.E.E.S., B.S.E.I.O., B.S.E.I.S., B.S.E.M.A., B.S.E.M.E., B.S.E.Met., B.S.E.M.S., B.S.E.Nav., B.S.Eng., B.S.M.C., B.S.MET., B.S.N., B.S.(NRE), B.S.P.O., and B.S.P.S. degrees. Master's and doctoral degrees are also awarded. Bachelor's degrees are awarded in AGRICULTURE (natural resource management), BIOLOGICAL SCIENCE (biochemistry, biology/biological science, biophysics, botany, cell biology, ecology, microbiology, nutrition, wildlife biology, and zoology), BUSINESS (business administration and management, recreation and leisure services, and sports management), COMMUNICATIONS AND THE ARTS (applied music, Arabic, art history and appreciation, ceramic art and design, Chinese, classical languages, communications, comparative literature, creative writing, dance, design, dramatic arts, English, fiber/textiles/weaving, film arts, French, German, graphic design, Greek, Hebrew, industrial design, Italian, Japanese, jazz, journalism, Latin, linguistics, literature, media arts, metal/jewelry, music, music history and appreciation, music performance, music theory and composition, musical theater, painting, percussion, performing arts, photography, piano/organ, printmaking, romance languages and literature, Russian, sculpture, Spanish, speech/debate/rhetoric, strings, voice, and winds), COMPUTER AND PHYSICAL SCIENCE (applied mathematics, astronomy, astrophysics, atmospheric sciences and meteorology, chemistry, computer science, geoscience, mathematics, oceanography, physics, and statistics), EDUCATION (art, elementary, music, physical, and secondary), ENGINEERING AND ENVIRONMENTAL DESIGN (aeronautical engineering, architecture, chemical engineering, civil engineering, computer engineering, electrical/electronics engineering, engineering, engineering and applied science, engineering physics, environmental engineering, environmental science, industrial engineering, interior design, landscape architecture/design, materials engineering, materials science, mechanical engineering, naval architecture and marine engineering, and nuclear engineering), HEALTH PROFESSIONS (biomedical science, dental hygiene, medical technology, nursing, and pharmacy), SOCIAL SCIENCE (African American studies, African studies, American studies, anthropology, archeology, Asian/Oriental studies, biblical languages, biblical studies, biopsychology, classical/ancient civilization, economics, geography, Hispanic American studies, history, humanities, Islamic studies, Judaic studies, Latin American studies, liberal arts/general studies, medieval studies, Middle Eastern studies, Near Eastern studies, philosophy, physical fitness/movement, political science/government, psychology, religion, Russian and Slavic studies, Scandinavian studies, social science, sociology, Western European studies, and women's studies). Classics, English, and political science are the strongest academically. Psychology, engineering, and business administration are the largest.

Required: Academic requirements vary by program. For the College of Literature, Science, and the Arts, most students must complete 9 semester hours each of humanities, social science, and natural science/math, fulfill requirements in English (including composition), race and ethnicity (1 course), and foreign language. Students must also meet the quantitative reasoning requirement, designed to ensure proficiency in using and analyzing quantitative information. To graduate, students must complete 120 to 128 semester hours, including 24 to 30 in a major field, with a minimum GPA of 2.0.

Special: A co-op program in engineering and cross-registration with Big Ten institutions and the University of Chicago are available, as are internships, study abroad in 35 countries, and a Washington semester. B.A.-B.S. degrees, dual and student-designed majors, and a 3-2 engineering degree with several colleges and universities are possible. Interdisciplinary majors are offered in anthropology and zoology, music and technology, natural resources and biometry, materials and metallurgical engineering, materials science and engineering, biopsychology and cognitive science, and social anthropology. Interdisciplinary liberal arts programs offering small group living/learning environments are available in the Residential College and the Lloyd Scholars Program. Also available are Honors College preferred admission to professional programs and a Women in Science Program. There are 21 national honor societies, including Phi Beta Kappa, and a freshman honors program.

Faculty/Classroom: 63% of faculty are male; 37%, female. All both teach and do research. The average class size in a regular course is 29.

Admissions: 52% of the 2001-2002 applicants were accepted. The SAT I scores for the 2001-2002 freshman class were: Verbal--5% below 500, 29% between 500 and 599, 47% between 600 and 700, and 17% above 700; Math--3% below 500, 16% between 500 and 599, 48% between 600 and 700, and 33% above 700. The ACT scores were 3% below 21, 9% between 21 and 23, 22% between 24 and 26, 23% between 27 and 28, and 42% above 28. 88% of the current freshmen were in the top fifth of their class; 98% were in the top two fifths. There were 76 National Merit finalists.

Requirements: The SAT I or ACT is required. In addition, applicants must be graduates of accredited secondary schools or have earned a GED. The university requires 15 academic credits or 20 Carnegie units, including 4 in English, 3 in math (4 for engineering majors), 3 in history and social studies, and 2 each in foreign language and in science. The following are recommended electives: 1 unit of hands-on computer study and 1 unit of fine or performing arts. An essay is required for all applicants. Students applying to the School of Art must submit a portfolio; those applying to the School of Music must present an audition. AP and CLEP credits are accepted. Applications are available on CD-ROM at *www.weapply.com*, or a PDF application can be downloaded from *www.umich.edu/~info/admissions*. Applications may also be submitted on-line at *embark.com*

Procedure: Freshmen are admitted to all sessions. Entrance exams should be taken at the end of the junior year or the beginning of the senior year. There is a deferred admissions plan. Applications should be filed by February 1 for fall entry, November 1 for winter entry, or February 1 for spring or summer entry. The fall 2001 application fee was $40. Notification is sent on a rolling basis. 4% of all applicants are on a waiting list.

Transfer: 900 transfer students enrolled in 2001-2002. A minimum college GPA of 3.0 is required for junior-level transfers. 60 credits of 120 must be completed at UM.

Visiting: There are regularly scheduled orientations for prospective students, including placement testing, academic counseling, course registration, social activities, and informational programs on student life, computing resources, campus safety, and career planning. There are guides for informal visits and visitors may sit in on classes.

Financial Aid: In 2001-2002, 74% of all freshmen and 58% of continuing students received some form of financial aid. 31% of freshmen and 36% of continuing students received need-based aid. The average freshman award was $8826. Of that total, scholarships or need-based grants averaged $5865 ($20,000 maximum); loans averaged $5514 ($10,500 maximum); and work contracts averaged $1333 ($2400 maximum). 42% of undergraduates work part time. Average annual earnings from campus work are $1205. The average financial indebtedness of the 2001 graduate was $16,024. The FAFSA and tax returns are required. The fall application deadline is September 30.

International Students: There are 1051 international students enrolled. They must score 560 on the written TOEFL take the MELAB.

Computers: The mainframes is comprised of an IBM system 390 Multiprise 2000 Series Processor, CMOS, Model 2003-135. 1,400 PCs are available to members of the university community. The 15 campus computing sites provide networked computers, laser printers, and hundreds of software programs. There are also 15 residence hall sites, 10 computer-equipped classrooms, special multimedia labs, and an adaptive technology computing site for users with disabilities. All resident hall rooms are wired with Ethernet for Internet connectivity. Business administration provides an additional 155 workstations for its students' use only. Engineering provides an additional 440 workstations for its students' use only. Students also have access to 550 workstations in the Media Union. All students may access the system at any time. There are no time limits and no fees.

Graduates: In 2001, 5606 bachelor's degrees were awarded. The most popular majors were engineering (18%), psychology (10%), and English (6%). In an average class, 2% graduate in 3 years, 62% in 4 years, 80% in 5 years, and 82% in 6 years. 999 companies recruited on campus in 2000-2001.

Admissions Contact: Theodore L. Spencer, Director of Admissions. A video is available. E-mail: *ugadmiss@umich.edu*
Web: *www.admissions.umich.edu*

UNIVERSITY OF MICHIGAN/DEARBORN — E-5

Dearborn, MI 48128 — **(313) 593-5658/ (313) 593-5550**
Fax: (313) 436-9167

Full-time: 362 men, 366 women	**Faculty:** 247; IIA, av$
Part-time: none	**Ph.D.s:** 63%
Graduate: none	**Student/Faculty:** 3 to 1
Year: semesters, summer session	**Tuition:** $4677 ($11,359)
Application Deadline: open	**Room & Board:** n/app
Freshman Class: 2187 applied, 1534 accepted, 718 enrolled	
ACT: 23	**VERY COMPETITIVE**

The University of Michigan/Dearborn, founded in 1959, is a public, comprehensive commuter institution that is part of the University of Michigan system. The emphasis of its degree programs is on the liberal arts, management, engineering, and education. There are 4 undergraduate and 4 graduate schools. In addition to regional accreditation, University of Michigan/Dearborn has baccalaureate program accreditation with ABET and NCATE. The library contains 300,000 volumes, 385,000 microform items, and 2000 audiovisual forms/CDs, and subscribes to 1600 periodicals. Computerized library services include the card catalog, interlibrary loans, and database searching. Special learning facilities include a learning resource center, art gallery, natural history museum, radio station, TV station, nature preserve, Armenian research center, child development center, engineering education and practice center, and the Henry Ford Estate, a National Historic Landmark. The 196-acre campus is in a suburban area 10 miles from Detroit. There are 20 buildings.

Student Life: 99% of undergraduates are from Michigan. Others are from 16 states, 22 foreign countries, and Canada. 77% are from public schools. 82% are white. The average age of freshmen is 18; all undergraduates, 23. 18% do not continue beyond their first year; 53% remain to graduate.

Housing: There are no residence halls. All students commute. Alcohol is not permitted. All students may keep cars.

Activities: 5% of men and about 1% of women belong to 7 national fraternities; 3% of women belong to 4 national sororities. There are 92 groups on campus, including art, cheerleading, chess, choir, computers, debate, drama, ethnic, film, gay, honors, international, literary magazine, newspaper, pep band, photography, political, professional, radio and TV, religious, social, social service, and student government. Popular campus events include Martin Luther King Diversity Celebration, Native American Pow Wow, and Fallfest.

Sports: There is 1 intercollegiate sport for men and 2 for women, and 21 intramural sports for men and 20 for women. Facilities include a 1200-seat gym, an ice rink, an indoor/outdoor track, a playing field, sand volleyball courts, weight and exercise rooms, and outdoor tennis courts.

Disabled Students: All of the campus is accessible. Wheelchair ramps, elevators, special parking, specially equipped rest rooms, lowered drinking fountains, and lowered telephones are available.

Services: Counseling and information services are available, as is tutoring in most subjects, including science, computer classes, composition, and math. There is a reader service for the blind, and remedial math, reading, and writing.

Campus Safety and Security: Measures include 24-hour foot and vehicle patrol, self-defense education, escort service, and informal discussions. There are pamphlets/posters/films, emergency telephones, lighted pathways/sidewalks, vehicle etching, Crime Prevention Day, CPR training, and a rape awareness seminar.

Programs of Study: University of Michigan/Dearborn confers B.A., B.S., B.B.A., B.G.S., B.S.A., and B.S.E. degrees. Master's degrees are also awarded. Bachelor's degrees are awarded in BIOLOGICAL SCIENCE (biochemistry, biology/biological science, and microbiology), BUSINESS (business administration and management), COMMUNICATIONS AND THE ARTS (art history and appreciation, arts administration/management, English, languages, and music history and appreciation), COMPUTER AND PHYSICAL SCIENCE (chemistry, computer science, mathematics, physics, and science), EDUCATION (early childhood, elementary, science, secondary, and social studies), ENGINEERING AND ENVIRONMENTAL DESIGN (computer engineering, electrical/electronics engineering, environmental science, industrial engineering, manufacturing engineering, and mechanical engineering), SOCIAL SCIENCE (American studies, anthropology, behavioral science, economics, history, humanities, international studies, liberal arts/general studies, philosophy, political science/government, psychology, social science, and sociology). Electrical engineering and business administration are the strongest academically. Mechanical engineering, prebusiness, and business administration are the largest.

Required: Each college within the university has its own unique requirements. To graduate, students must complete 120 to 128 credit hours.

Special: UMD offers internships, study abroad, work-study and accelerated degree programs, a general studies degree, a dual major in engineering mathematics, student-designed majors, and co-op programs in engineering, business administration, and arts and sciences. Nondegree study and pass/fail options are possible. There is a freshman honors program.

Faculty/Classroom: 68% of faculty are male; 32%, female. The average class size in an introductory lecture is 43 and in a regular course, 28.

Admissions: 70% of the 2001-2002 applicants were accepted. 12 freshmen graduated first in their class.

Requirements: The ACT, with a minimum composite score of 22, or the SAT I is required. Other admissions requirements normally include graduation from an accredited secondary school, with 4 years each in math and English, 3 in science, and 2 each in art, foreign language, and history. The GED is accepted with a minimum score of 55. An essay and interview are recommended. A GPA of 3.0 is required. AP credits are accepted. Important factors in the admissions decision are advanced placement or honor courses, recommendations by school officials, and leadership record.

Procedure: Freshmen are admitted to all sessions. Entrance exams should be taken in the spring of the junior year or the fall of the senior year. Application deadlines are open for fall entry. The fall 2001 application fee was $30. Notification is sent on a rolling basis.

Transfer: Applicants are required to have 25 to 30 transferable semester/credit hours; if they have fewer than 25, the SAT I or ACT is mandatory. The required minimum GPA ranges from 2.5 to 3.0, depending on the intended major. 30 credits of 120 to 128 must be completed at University of Michigan/Dearborn.

Visiting: There are regularly scheduled orientations for prospective students, consisting of a tour, a student panel, academic unit introduction, and campus life sessions. There are guides for informal visits and visitors may sit in on classes. To schedule a visit, contact the Admissions Office at (313) 593-5100 or *admissions@umd.umich.edu*

Financial Aid: In 2001-2002, 70% of all students received some form of financial aid, including need-based aid. 85% of undergraduates work part time. Average annual earnings from campus work are $2000. The FAFSA is required. The fall application deadline is February 1.

International Students: There are 100 international students enrolled. They must score 550 on the written TOEFL or 213 on the electronic version and also take the MELAB.

Computers: There is a minicomputer with 400 networked PCs for students, including Macs and Sun models. All students may access the system. There are no time limits and no fees.

Graduates: In 2001, 979 bachelor's degrees were awarded. The most popular majors were mechanical engineering (8%), management (8%), and psychology (8%). In an average class, 1% graduate in 3 years, 8% in 4 years, 37% in 5 years, and 47% in 6 years.

Admissions Contact: Gabrielle Williams, Assistant Director of Admissions and Orientation. E-mail: *gjwillms@umd.umich.edu*

UNIVERSITY OF MICHIGAN/FLINT — E-4

Flint, MI 48502 — **(810) 762-3300; Fax: (810) 762-3272**

Full-time: 1229 men, 2195 women	**Faculty:** 203; IIA, --$
Part-time: 833 men, 1622 women	**Ph.D.s:** 79%
Graduate: 235 men, 283 women	**Student/Faculty:** 17 to 1
Year: semesters, summer session	**Tuition:** $4323 ($8323)
Application Deadline: February 15	**Room & Board:** n/app
Freshman Class: 1540 applied, 1248 accepted, 649 enrolled	
ACT: 22	**COMPETITIVE**

The University of Michigan/Flint, established in 1956, is a public institution offering programs in the liberal arts and sciences. There are 3 undergraduate and 5 graduate schools. In addition to regional accreditation, UM-Flint has baccalaureate program accreditation with AACSB, NASM, NCATE, and NLN. The library contains 200,100 volumes, 632,407 microform items, and 15,395 audiovisual forms/CDs, and subscribes to 1108 periodicals. Computerized library services include the card catalog, interlibrary loans, and database searching. Special learning facilities include a learning resource center, art gallery, radio station, and TV station. The 72-acre campus is in an urban area 60 miles northwest of Detroit, 50 miles east of Lansing, and 55 miles north of Ann Arbor. There are 9 buildings.

Student Life: 99% of undergraduates are from Michigan. Others are from 14 states, 8 foreign countries, and Canada. 95% are from public schools. 78% are white; 11% African American. The average age of freshmen is 18; all undergraduates, 26. 18% do not continue beyond their first year.

Housing: There are no residence halls. College-sponsored living facilities include off-campus apartments. All students commute. Alcohol is not permitted. All students may keep cars.

Activities: 3% of men belong to 5 local and 2 national fraternities; 4% of women belong to 3 local and 2 national sororities. There are 50 groups on campus, including art, band, chess, choir, chorale, chorus, computers, dance, drama, ethnic, gay, honors, jazz band, literary magazine, musical theater, newspaper, orchestra, political, professional, radio and TV, religious, social, social service, student government, and symphony. Popular campus events include Flintstock Music Festival and Flint Comedy Jam.

Sports: There are 15 intramural sports for men and 15 for women. Facilities include a recreation building housing a multipurpose gym, racquetball courts, a weight training area, and a swimming pool.

Disabled Students: 95% of the campus is accessible. Wheelchair ramps, elevators, special parking, specially equipped rest rooms, special class scheduling, lowered drinking fountains, lowered telephones, and a telephone for the hearing impaired are available. Reasonable accommodations may be made for students with documented disabilities.

Services: Counseling and information services are available, as is tutoring in every subject. There is a reader service for the blind, and remedial math, reading, and writing.

Campus Safety and Security: Measures include 24-hour foot and vehicle patrol, self-defense education, escort service, and informal discussions. There are pamphlets/posters/films, emergency telephones, and lighted pathways/sidewalks.

Programs of Study: UM-Flint confers B.A., B.S., B.A.S., B.B.A., B.F.A., B.G.S., B.Mus.Ed., and B.S.N. degrees. Master's degrees are also awarded. Bachelor's degrees are awarded in BIOLOGICAL SCIENCE (biology/biological science and ecology), BUSINESS (accounting, banking and finance, business administration and management, human resources, management engineering, and marketing/retailing/merchandising), COMMUNICATIONS AND THE ARTS (communications, dramatic arts, English, French, German, Germanic languages and literature, music, Spanish, and speech/debate/rhetoric), COMPUTER AND PHYSICAL SCIENCE (chemistry, computer science, earth science, mathematics, physical sciences, and physics), EDUCATION (early childhood, elementary, foreign languages, music, science, and secondary), ENGINEERING AND ENVIRONMENTAL DESIGN (engineering), HEALTH PROFESSIONS (environmental health science, health care administration, health science, medical laboratory technology, nursing, physical therapy, predentistry, premedicine, prepharmacy, preveterinary science, and radiation therapy), SOCIAL SCIENCE (anthropology, community psychology, criminal justice, economics, geography, history, international studies, philosophy, political science/government, prelaw, psychology, public administration, social science, social work, sociology, and urban studies). Business, physical therapy, and nursing are the strongest academically. Business and education are the largest.

Required: To graduate, all students must complete at least 120 credits, including 30 to 70 in the major along with satisfying all major requirements, and maintain a GPA of 2.0. Distribution requirements total 50 credits in English composition, humanities, fine arts, social science, and natural science.

Special: Special arrangements include co-op programs and dual majors, student-designed majors, cross-registration with Mott Community College, internships, study abroad, work-study, a 3-2 engineering program, an accelerated business degree, a general studies degree, nondegree study, and pass/fail options. There is a chapter of Phi Beta Kappa and a freshman honors program.

Faculty/Classroom: 53% of faculty are male; 47%, female. All both teach and do research. No introductory courses are taught by graduate students. The average class size in an introductory lecture is 40; in a laboratory, 20; and in a regular course, 24.

Admissions: 81% of the 2001-2002 applicants were accepted. 47% of the current freshmen were in the top fifth of their class; 78% were in the top two fifths. There were 15 National Merit semifinalists. 3 freshmen graduated first in their class.

Requirements: The SAT I or ACT is required, with the ACT preferred. Graduation from secondary school is required, with 4 years of English, 3 each of math and social studies, and 2 of science. The GED is accepted. SAT II: Subject tests and an interview are recommended. Applied music students must audition. AP and CLEP credits are accepted. Important factors in the admissions decision are advanced placement or honor courses, evidence of special talent, and leadership record. Applications are accepted on-line at *www.umflint.edu*

Procedure: Freshmen are admitted to all sessions. Entrance exams should be taken in the spring of the junior year or fall of the senior year. There is a deferred admissions plan. Applications should be filed by February 15 for fall entry and December 15 for winter entry. The fall 2001 application fee was $30. Notification is sent on a rolling basis.

Transfer: 587 transfer students enrolled in 2001-2002. Applicants must have at least 12 college credits and a minimum GPA of 2.0 in transferable courses. An associate degree and an interview are recommended. 45 credits of a minimum of 120 must be completed at UM-Flint.

Visiting: There are regularly scheduled orientations for prospective students. There are guides for informal visits and visitors may sit in on classes. To schedule a visit, contact the Admissions Office at *admissions@umflint.edu*

Financial Aid: In 2001-2002, 73% of all freshmen and 53% of continuing students received some form of financial aid. 51% of freshmen and 37% of continuing students received need-based aid. The CSS/Profile or FFS is required. The fall application deadline is March 15.

International Students: There are 18 international students enrolled. They must score 550 on the written TOEFL or 213 on the electronic version or take the MELAB.

Computers: PCs are available with e-mail capabilities. All students may access the system. There are no fees.

Graduates: In 2001, 892 bachelor's degrees were awarded. The most popular majors were business (18%), elementary education (11%), and English (5%).

Admissions Contact: Michelle Gurley, Interim Director of Admissions. E-mail: *admissions@list.umich.edu* Web: *www.flint.umich.edu*

WAYNE STATE UNIVERSITY — E-5

Detroit, MI 48202 — **(313) 577-3577; Fax: (313) 577-7536**

Full-time: 3804 men, 5468 women	**Faculty:** 1689; I, -$
Part-time: 3577 men, 5640 women	**Ph.D.s:** 85%
Graduate: 5828 men, 6723 women	**Student/Faculty:** 6 to 1
Year: semesters, summer session	**Tuition:** $4330 ($9352)
Application Deadline: August 1	**Room & Board:** $2390 ($6450)
Freshman Class: 6015 applied, 4322 accepted, 2585 enrolled	
ACT: 20	**COMPETITIVE**

Wayne State University, founded in 1868, is a state-supported, nonprofit institution. Primarily a commuter college, it offers a variety of academic and professional programs. There are 11 undergraduate and 14 graduate schools. In addition to regional accreditation, Wayne State has baccalaureate program accreditation with AACSB, ABET, ABFSE, ACPE, ACS, ADA, AOTA, APTA, ASLHA, CAHEA, CCNE, CSWE, NAACLS, NASM, NCATE, and NLN. The 6 libraries contain 1,813,249 volumes, 3,567,450 microform items, and 57,444 audiovisual forms/CDs, and subscribe to 19,531 periodicals. Computerized library services include the card catalog and database searching. Special learning facilities include a learning resource center, art gallery, natural history museum, planetarium, and TV station. The 203-acre campus is in an urban area 2 miles north of downtown Detroit in the New Center area. There are 95 buildings.

Student Life: 94% of undergraduates are from Michigan. Others are from 31 states, 67 foreign countries, and Canada. 87% are from public schools. 49% are white; 30% African American. The average age of freshmen is 22; all undergraduates, 26.

Housing: There are no residence halls. College-sponsored living facilities include coed on-campus apartments, which are available on a first-come, first-served basis. 65% of students commute. All students may keep cars.

Activities: 2% of men belong to 8 national fraternities; 2% of women belong to 10 national sororities. There are 114 groups on campus, including band, chess, choir, computers, dance, ethnic, film, forensics, gay, honors, international, jazz band, marching band, newspaper, orchestra, pep band, political, professional, radio and TV, religious, social, social service, student government, symphony, and yearbook. Popular campus events include Student Organization Day, the International Fair, and Detroit Festival of the Arts.

Sports: There are 9 intercollegiate sports for men and 8 for women, and 10 intramural sports for men and 10 for women. Facilities include a phys ed building, a recreation and finess center, various swimming pools, courts, and soccer and softball fields.

Disabled Students: All of the campus is accessible. Wheelchair ramps, elevators, special parking, specially equipped rest rooms, lowered drinking fountains, lowered telephones, and educational accessibility services are available.

Services: Counseling and information services are available, as is tutoring in every subject. There is a reader service for the blind, and remedial math, reading, and writing. Tutorial services are available through centralized counseling or academic departments.

Campus Safety and Security: Measures include 24-hour foot and vehicle patrol, self-defense education, escort service, and informal discussions. There are pamphlets/posters/films, emergency telephones, and lighted pathways/sidewalks.

Programs of Study: Wayne State confers B.A., B.S., B.A.S., B.F.A., B.I.S., B.Mus., B.P.A., B.S.A.H.S., B.S.C.T., B.S.E.T., B.S.M.S., B.S.N., B.S.W., and B.T.I.S. degrees. Master's and doctoral degrees are also awarded. Bachelor's degrees are awarded in BIOLOGICAL SCIENCE (biology/biological science), BUSINESS (accounting, banking and finance, business economics, funeral home services, labor studies, management information systems, management science, and marketing/retailing/merchandising), COMMUNICATIONS AND THE ARTS (Arabic, art, art history and appreciation, broadcasting, classics, communications, dance, design, dramatic arts, English, film arts, fine arts, German, Italian, journalism, linguistics, music, public relations, Russian, Slavic languages, and Spanish), COMPUTER AND PHYSICAL SCIENCE (chemistry, computer science, geology, information sciences and systems, mathematics, and physics), EDUCATION (art, business, elementary, mathematics, physical, science, special, and technical), ENGINEERING AND ENVIRONMENTAL DESIGN (chemical engineering, civil engineering, computer technology, electrical/electronics engineering, industrial engineering technology, manufacturing technology, mechanical engineering, and mechanical engineering technology), HEALTH PROFESSIONS (nursing, occupational therapy, pharmacy, radiation therapy, and speech pathology/audiology), SOCIAL SCIENCE (African American studies, African studies, American studies, anthropology, criminal justice, dietetics, economics, food science, geography, history, human development, international studies, liberal arts/general studies, Mexican-American/Chicano studies, Near Eastern studies, parks and recreation management, peace studies, philosophy, political science/government, psychology, public affairs, social work, sociology, urban studies, and women's studies). Chemistry, biology, and pharmacy are the strongest academically. Elementary education, art, and psychology are the largest.

Required: To graduate, students must complete at least 120 credit hours and have a minimum GPA of 2.0. General Education has 2 components. Students must complete competencies in written communication, math, oral communication, and computer literacy. In addition, students must complete group requirements in natural science, social science, American society and institutions, foreign culture, humanities, and the university and its libraries.

Special: Special academic programs include cross-registration with Macomb University Center, the University of Michigan, and the University of Windsor; internships in business, industry, or communications; study abroad in Germany, Japan, or England; on-campus work-study programs; a general studies degree; co-op programs; nondegree study; and limited pass/fail options. The College of Lifelong Learning offers televised, weekend, and evening courses. There is 1 national honor society, Phi Beta Kappa, a freshman honors program, and 23 departmental honors programs.

Faculty/Classroom: 62% of faculty are male; 38%, female. 62% teach undergraduates, 92% do research, and 54% do both. Graduate students teach 13% of introductory courses. The average class size in an introductory lecture is 100; in a laboratory, 20; and in a regular course, 30.

Admissions: 72% of the 2001-2002 applicants were accepted. 40% of the current freshmen were in the top fifth of their class.

Requirements: The SAT I or ACT is required , with the ACT preferred. Admissions requirements include graduation from an accredited secondary school; the GED with an acceptable SAT I or ACT score is also allowable. If the GPA is below 2.75, the applicant must have composite SAT I scores totaling at least 990 or an ACT score of 21. A GPA of 2.75

is required. AP and CLEP credits are accepted. Applications are accepted on-line at *www.apply.wayne.edu*

Procedure: Freshmen are admitted to all sessions. If necessary, the ACT should be taken in the junior year or the SAT I in the senior year. There is a deferred admissions plan. Applications should be filed by August 1 for fall entry, December 1 for winter entry, and April 1 for spring or summer entry, along with a $20 fee. Notification is sent on a rolling basis.

Transfer: 2001 transfer students enrolled in 2001-2002. Applicants must have 30 transferable credit hours with a 3.0 GPA, and an overall minimum GPA of 2.0. 30 credits of 120 must be completed at Wayne State.

Visiting: There are guides for informal visits and visitors may sit in on classes. To schedule a visit, contact the Office of Admissions.

Financial Aid: In a recent year, 41% of all freshmen and 37% of continuing students received some form of financial aid. 29% of freshmen and 25% of continuing students received need-based aid. The average freshman award was $4499. Of that total, scholarships or need-based grants averaged $3000 ($5000 maximum); loans averaged $2600 ($5500 maximum); and work contracts averaged $3696 ($4000 maximum). 11% of undergraduates work part time. Average annual earnings from campus work are $2786. The average financial indebtedness of the 2001 graduate was $15,457. Wayne State is a member of CSS. The FAFSA, federal tax returns, and W-2s are required. The fall priority application deadline is March 1.

International Students: There are 951 international students enrolled. The school actively recruits these students. They must score 550 on the written TOEFL or 213 on the electronic version or take the MELAB.

Computers: The mainframes are a CRAY J-916, an IBM 9672 R24, an RS/6000 Model 595, and an IBM 9121-411. There are 1000 Macs and PCs available in the libraries, the student union, and academic departments. All students may access the system 24 hours a day. There are no time limits and no fees.

Graduates: In 2001, 2235 bachelor's degrees were awarded. The most popular majors were elementary education (9%), psychology (7%), and nursing (6%). In an average class, 12% graduate in 3 years, 27% in 4 years, 37% in 5 years, and 42% in 6 years. 93 companies recruited on campus in 2000-2001. Of the 2000 graduating class, 36% were enrolled in graduate school within 6 months of graduation and 98% were employed.

Admissions Contact: Michael Wood, Director of Admissions.
E-mail: *admissions@wayne.edu* Web: *www.wayne.edu*

WESTERN MICHIGAN UNIVERSITY

Kalamazoo, MI 49008 — D-5

(616) 387-2000
(800) 400-4968; Fax: (616) 387-2096

Full-time: 9626 men, 10,269 women	**Faculty:** 832; I, --$
Part-time: 1519 men, 1742 women	**Ph.D.s:** 93%
Graduate: 2356 men, 3419 women	**Student/Faculty:** 24 to 1
Year: semesters, summer session	**Tuition:** $4499 ($10,255)
Application Deadline: open	**Room & Board:** $5517
Freshman Class: 13,517 applied, 11,362 accepted, 4601 enrolled	
ACT: 22	**COMPETITIVE**

Western Michigan University, founded in 1903, is a public institution offering 225 degree programs in the liberal arts and sciences, aviation, business, education, engineering, fine arts, health and human services, and preprofessional studies. There are 7 undergraduate schools and 1 graduate school. In addition to regional accreditation, WMU has baccalaureate program accreditation with AACSB, ABET, AHEA, ASLA, CSAB, CSWE, NASAD, NASM, NCATE, and NLN. The 5 libraries contain 4,109,238 volumes, 1,820,779 microform items, and 28,557 audiovisual forms/CDs, and subscribe to 7743 periodicals. Computerized library services include the card catalog, interlibrary loans, and database searching. Special learning facilities include a learning resource center, art gallery, radio station, aviation flight simulators, electron microscope, particle accelerator, and a paper manufacturing and fiber recovery pilot plant. The 504-acre campus is in an urban area 140 miles west of Detroit. Including residence halls, there are 130 buildings.

Student Life: 76% of undergraduates are from Michigan. Others are from 49 states, 104 foreign countries, and Canada. 87% are white. The average age of freshmen is 18; all undergraduates, 21. 23% do not continue beyond their first year; 52% remain to graduate.

Housing: 6180 students can be accommodated in college housing, which includes single-sex and coed dormitories, on-campus apartments, off-campus apartments, married-student housing, fraternity houses, and sorority houses. In addition, there are honors houses, special-interest houses, a health and wellness, and an international house. On-campus housing is guaranteed for the freshman year only and is available on a first-come, first-served basis. 73% of students commute. All students may keep cars.

Activities: There are 2 local and 22 national fraternities and 1 local and 16 national sororities. There are 300 groups on campus, including art, band, cheerleading, chess, choir, chorale, chorus, computers, dance, drama, ethnic, film, gay, honors, international, jazz band, literary magazine, marching band, musical theater, orchestra, pep band, photography, political, professional, radio and TV, religious, social, social service, student government, symphony, and yearbook. Popular campus events include Family Weekend, Into the Streets, and Campus Classic Races.

Sports: There are 7 intercollegiate sports for men and 9 for women, and 24 intramural sports for men and 24 for women. Facilities include a recreation center designed as a sports village, which includes a recreational swimming pool, a swirl pool, a weight and fitness room with more than 100 stations, facilities for basketball, floor hockey, and indoor soccer, a climbing wall, baseball/softball infields, a golf driving range, an elevated track for jogging, and facilities for aerobics, archery, badminton, tennis, and volleyball. The field house includes a 5800-seat arena for basketball and volleyball competition and facilities for gymnasts. There is also a 400-meter Olympic model Martin-surface track, a cross-country course, bowling lanes, a video game area, tennis courts, a 30,000-seat stadium, a competition swimming pool, an ice arena, and outdoor baseball, softball, touch football, and soccer fields.

Disabled Students: 85% of the campus is accessible. Wheelchair ramps, elevators, special parking, specially equipped rest rooms, special class scheduling, lowered drinking fountains, and lowered telephones are available. Some campus apartments have been renovated for wheelchair students. A lift-equipped van to take disabled students to classes and adaptive computer equipment are also available.

Services: Counseling and information services are available, as is tutoring in most subjects. There is a reader service for the blind, and remedial math, reading, and writing.

Campus Safety and Security: Measures include 24-hour foot and vehicle patrol, self-defense education, escort service, and shuttle buses. There are informal discussions, pamphlets/posters/films, emergency telephones, and lighted pathways/sidewalks. There is also a Student Watch Program, Operation Identification, an enhanced telephone system, and a residence hall security system.

Programs of Study: WMU confers B.A., B.S., B.B.A., B.F.A., B.Mus., B.S., B.S.E., B.S.N., and B.S.W. degrees. Master's and doctoral degrees are also awarded. Bachelor's degrees are awarded in BIOLOGICAL SCIENCE (biochemistry and biology/biological science), BUSINESS (accounting, banking and finance, business administration and management, business economics, business statistics, insurance, management information systems, management science, marketing/retailing/merchandising, recreation and leisure services, and tourism), COMMUNICATIONS AND THE ARTS (advertising, applied music, art, art history and appreciation, broadcasting, ceramic art and design, communications, creative writing, dance, dramatic arts, English, English literature, French, German, graphic design, industrial design, jazz, journalism, media arts, music, music history and appreciation, music theory and composition, painting, public relations, Spanish, telecommunications, and theater design), COMPUTER AND PHYSICAL SCIENCE (applied mathematics, chemistry, computer science, earth science, geology, geophysics and seismology, hydrology, information sciences and systems, mathematics, physics, and statistics), EDUCATION (art, business, education, elementary, health, home economics, marketing and distribution, music, physical, science, and secondary), ENGINEERING AND ENVIRONMENTAL DESIGN (aeronautical engineering, aeronautical science, aeronautical technology, aircraft mechanics, automotive technology, aviation administration/management, chemical engineering, computer engineering, construction engineering, construction management, electrical/electronics engineering, engineering, engineering management, environmental science, industrial engineering, interior design, manufacturing technology, materials engineering, mechanical engineering, paper and pulp science, paper engineering, and printing technology), HEALTH PROFESSIONS (community health work, exercise science, music therapy, nursing, occupational therapy, predentistry, premedicine, and speech pathology/audiology), SOCIAL SCIENCE (American studies, anthropology, behavioral science, criminal justice, dietetics, economics, European studies, family/consumer studies, fashion design and technology, food production/management/services, geography, history, home economics, interdisciplinary studies, liberal arts/general studies, philosophy, political science/government, prelaw, psychology, public administration, religion, social science, social work, sociology, textiles and clothing, and women's studies). Marketing, finance and commercial law, and education are the largest.

Required: Students must complete 122 semester hours, including 35 of general education courses and a minimum of 24 in the major. A minimum GPA of 2.0 is required. Students must complete 2 phys ed hours, courses in science, social science, humanities, and fine arts, and 1 course in non-Western world study. Comprehensive exams are required in some departments. All students must demonstrate computer literacy.

Special: Cross-registration is available through the Kalamazoo Consortium. Opportunities are provided for internships in occupational and music therapy, teaching, business, history, and engineering. Also available are work-study programs, student-designed majors, pass/fail options, and credit by exam. Students may study abroad in more than 20 countries on 4 continents. There are 25 national honor societies, including

Phi Beta Kappa, a freshman honors program, and 6 departmental honors programs.

Faculty/Classroom: 66% of faculty are male; 34%, female. 87% teach undergraduates, all do research, and 87% do both. Graduate students teach 17% of introductory courses. The average class size in an introductory lecture is 43; in a laboratory, 22; and in a regular course, 24.

Admissions: 84% of the 2001-2002 applicants were accepted. The ACT scores for the 2001-2002 freshman class were: 36% below 21, 31% between 21 and 23, 21% between 24 and 26, 7% between 27 and 28, and 5% above 28. 33% of the current freshmen were in the top fifth of their class; 71% were in the top two fifths.

Requirements: The ACT is required. In addition, applicants must submit an official high school transcript. An audition is required for music majors. An interview may be recommended. The College of Fine Arts requires an audition/portfolio/interview of all applicants. A GPA of 2.0 is required. AP and CLEP credits are accepted. Important factors in the admissions decision are advanced placement or honor courses, extracurricular activities record, and recommendations by school officials. Applications are accepted on-line via the WMU web site.

Procedure: Freshmen are admitted to all sessions. Entrance exams should be taken late in the junior year or early in the senior year. There is a deferred admissions plan. Application deadlines are open. The fall 2001 application fee was $25. Notification is sent on a rolling basis.

Transfer: 1925 transfer students enrolled in 2001-2002. Applicants must have a minimum GPA of 2.0 in transferable college courses. Consideration will also be given to the trend of grades and recent course work. 30 credits of 122 must be completed at WMU.

Visiting: There are regularly scheduled orientations for prospective students, including an admission presentation, departmental advising, lunch, and a campus tour. Visitors may sit in on classes and stay overnight. To schedule a visit, call (616) 387-2289.

Financial Aid: In 2001-2002, 38% of all freshmen and 55% of continuing students received some form of financial aid. 42% of freshmen and 45% of continuing students received need-based aid. The average freshman award was $6078. 21% of undergraduates work part time. Average annual earnings from campus work are $3178. The average financial indebtedness of the 2001 graduate was $12,297. The FAFSA is required. The fall application deadline is April 1.

International Students: There are 834 international students enrolled. The school actively recruits these students. They must score 550 on the written TOEFL or take the MELAB.

Computers: The mainframes are a DEC VAX 7620 and an IBM 3090/300J. The mainframe is used for institutional and research purposes as well as for course work. About 2000 workstations are available in classroom buildings, dorms, and the student center. A Sun operating system is networked in labs for student use. All students may access the system 24 hours a day. Time limits are set individually. There are no fees.

Graduates: In 2001, 3645 bachelor's degrees were awarded. The most popular majors were education (10%), marketing (5%), and finance (4%). In an average class, 17% graduate in 4 years, 44% in 5 years, and 53% in 6 years. 258 companies recruited on campus in 2000-2001. Of the 2000 graduating class, 9% were enrolled in graduate school within 6 months of graduation and 81% were employed.

Admissions Contact: John Fraire, Dean, Admissions and Orientation. E-mail: *ask-wmu@wmich.edu; www.wmich.edu*
Web: *http://www.wmich.edu/*

WILLIAM TYNDALE COLLEGE — E-5

Farmington Hills, MI 48331-3147 — (248) 553-7200
(800) 483-0707; Fax: (248) 553-5963

Full-time: 148 men, 168 women	**Faculty:** 5
Part-time: 132 men, 160 women	**Ph.D.s:** 87%
Graduate: none	**Student/Faculty:** 63 to 1
Year: semesters, summer session	**Tuition:** $7950
Application Deadline: open	**Room & Board:** $3200
Freshman Class: n/av	
ACT: 23	**COMPETITIVE**

William Tyndale College, established in 1945, is a Christian liberal arts college offering undergraduate degrees in Christian studies, humanities and social sciences, math and natural sciences, and professional studies. The library contains 60,000 volumes, 2125 microform items, and 3300 audiovisual forms/CDs, and subscribes to 230 periodicals. Computerized library services include interlibrary loans and database searching. The 28-acre campus is in a suburban area 15 miles west of Detroit. Including residence halls, there are 2 buildings.

Student Life: 96% of undergraduates are from Michigan. Others are from 5 states, 10 foreign countries, and Canada. 73% are from public schools. 63% are white; 31% African American. 76% are Protestant; 22% claim no religious affiliation. The average age of freshmen is 21; all undergraduates, 26. 20% do not continue beyond their first year.

Housing: 54 students can be accommodated in college housing, which includes coed dormitories. On-campus housing is available on a first-come, first-served basis. Priority is given to out-of-town students. 92% of students commute. Alcohol is not permitted. All students may keep cars.

Activities: There are no fraternities or sororities. There are 9 groups on campus, including choir, drama, honors, international, newspaper, religious, social, social service, and student government. Popular campus events include New Student Retreat and Billy T's Coffee House.

Sports: There is 1 intramural sport for men and 1 for women. Facilities include a soccer field and access to local school gyms.

Disabled Students: All of the campus is accessible. Wheelchair ramps, elevators, special parking, specially equipped rest rooms, lowered drinking fountains, and lowered telephones are available.

Services: Counseling and information services are available, as is tutoring in every subject. There is remedial math, reading, and writing.

Campus Safety and Security: Measures include lighted pathways/sidewalks.

Programs of Study: Tyndale confers B.A., B.B.A., B.Mus., and B.R.E. degrees. Associate degrees are also awarded. Bachelor's degrees are awarded in BUSINESS (business administration and management), COMMUNICATIONS AND THE ARTS (English, music, and music performance), COMPUTER AND PHYSICAL SCIENCE (mathematics), SOCIAL SCIENCE (biblical studies, Christian studies, history, Near Eastern studies, pastoral studies, prelaw, psychology, religious music, social science, and theological studies). Business administration, Christian thought, and psychology are the largest.

Required: Students must complete 120 credits, with at least 30 in the major, and maintain a minimum GPA of 2.0. Special curriculum requirements include 28 hours of social and natural sciences, 27 hours of humanities, and 24 of Christian thought.

Special: Internships in youth studies and pastoral studies majors are available. An accelerated degree program in business administration allows students to complete a B.B.A. degree in 19 months, attending class once a week. Dual majors in music/youth are offered. There are 2 national honor societies.

Faculty/Classroom: 67% of faculty are male; 33%, female. All teach undergraduates. The average class size in an introductory lecture is 18.

Admissions: The ACT scores for the 2001-2002 freshman class were: 29% below 21, 25% between 21 and 23, 25% between 24 and 26, 14% between 27 and 28, and 7% above 28. 7% of the current freshmen were in the top fifth of their class; 26% were in the top two fifths.

Requirements: The ACT is required, with a minimum composite score of 18. Graduation from an accredited secondary school is required; the GED is accepted. Music majors must audition. In addition, home-schooled students must provide writing samples, a recommendation, and an interview; business administration students must submit an essay. A GPA of 2.25 is required. AP and CLEP credits are accepted. Important factors in the admissions decision are advanced placement or honor courses, leadership record, and parents or siblings attending the school. Applications are accepted on-line.

Procedure: Freshmen are admitted to all sessions. Entrance exams should be taken in the senior year. There is a deferred admissions plan. Application deadlines are open. The fall 2001 application fee was $50. Notification is sent on a rolling basis.

Transfer: 110 transfer students enrolled in 2001-2002. Transfer students must have a GPA of 2.0 for college work. A high school transcript is required if they have fewer than 30 college credits. 45 credits of 120 must be completed at Tyndale.

Visiting: There are regularly scheduled orientations for prospective students, including an overview of academic programs, student life, campus activities, financial aid, registration, and advising. There are guides for informal visits and visitors may sit in on classes and stay overnight. To schedule a visit, contact the Admissions Counselor, Office of Admissions at *admissions@williamtyndale.edu*

Financial Aid: In 2001-2002, 57% of all freshmen and 62% of continuing students received some form of financial aid. 43% of freshmen and 57% of continuing students received need-based aid. The average freshman award was $2750. Of that total, scholarships or need-based grants averaged $4000 ($2750 maximum); loans averaged $2625 ($10,500 maximum); and grants averaged $2300 (maximum). 6% of undergraduates work part time. Average annual earnings from campus work are $2000. The average financial indebtedness of the 2001 graduate was $4000. Tyndale is a member of CSS. The FAFSA and the college's own financial statement are required. The fall application deadline is May 1.

International Students: There were 20 international students enrolled in a recent year. The school actively recruits these students. They must score 525 on the written TOEFL.

Computers: The mainframes are a Novell server and an NT 4.0 server. There is a computer lab for students and faculty. All students may access the system 7 A.M. to 10 P.M. Monday through Saturday. There are no time limits and no fees. It is recommended that all students have PC's.

Graduates: In a recent year, 190 bachelor's degrees were awarded. The most popular majors were business administration (57%), psychology (12%), and Christian thought (5%). In an average class, 7% graduate in 3 years, 17% in 4 years, 28% in 5 years, and 28% in 6 years. 15 companies recruited on campus in 2000-2001.

Admissions Contact: Fred A. Schebor, Dean of Admissions.
Web: *www.tyndalecollege.edu*

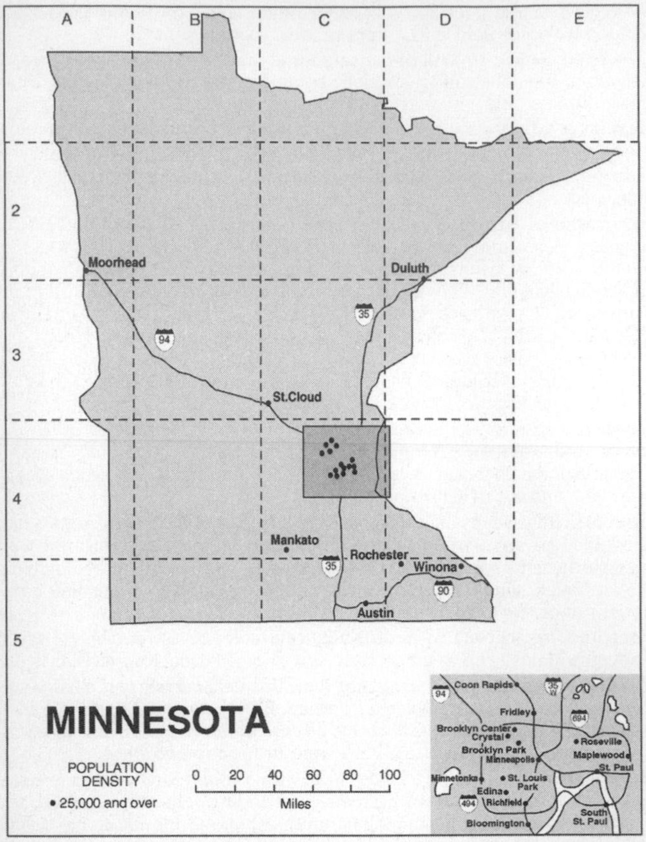

AUGSBURG COLLEGE

Minneapolis, MN 55454 — C-4

(612) 330-1001
(800) 788-5678; Fax: (612) 330-1590

Full-time: 985 men, 1290 women	**Faculty:** 135; IIB, -$
Part-time: 178 men, 327 women	**Ph.D.s:** 64%
Graduate: 17 men, 114 women	**Student/Faculty:** 17 to 1
Year: semesters, summer session	**Tuition:** $17,438
Application Deadline: August 15	**Room & Board:** $5540
Freshman Class: 869 applied, 656 accepted, 337 enrolled	
SAT I Verbal/Math: 541/542	**ACT:** 23 **COMPETITIVE**

Augsburg College, established in 1869, is a private liberal arts institution affiliated with the Evangelical Lutheran Church in America. In addition to regional accreditation, Augsburg has baccalaureate program accreditation with CSWE, NASM, NCATE, and NLN. The library contains 142,739 volumes, 17,640 microform items, and 2355 audiovisual forms/CDs, and subscribes to 800 periodicals. Computerized library services include the card catalog, interlibrary loans, and database searching. Special learning facilities include a learning resource center, art gallery, radio station, and a TV studio. The 23-acre campus is in an urban area in Minneapolis. Including residence halls, there are 25 buildings.

Student Life: 87% of undergraduates are from Minnesota. Others are from 37 states, 39 foreign countries, and Canada. 69% are white. 45% are Protestant; 35% claim no religious affiliation; 17% Catholic. The average age of freshmen is 18; all undergraduates, 26. 24% do not continue beyond their first year.

Housing: 904 students can be accommodated in college housing, which includes coed dormitories, on-campus apartments, and married-student housing. In addition, there are special-interest houses. On-campus housing is available on a first-come, first-served basis and on a lottery system for upperclassmen. Priority is given to out-of-town students. 54% of students live on campus; of those, 60% remain on campus on weekends. All students may keep cars.

Activities: There are no fraternities or sororities. There are 40 groups on campus, including art, band, cheerleading, choir, chorus, dance, drama, ethnic, gay, honors, international, jazz band, literary magazine, newspaper, orchestra, pep band, political, professional, radio and TV, religious, social, social service, student government, and yearbook. Popular campus events include Days in May, Spring Affair, and Advent Vespers.

Sports: There are 10 intercollegiate sports for men and 9 for women, and 4 intramural sports for men and 4 for women. Facilities include a 1500-seat sports field, a 2800-seat gym, tennis courts, a double-rink ice arena, and a domed field facility for winter.

Disabled Students: 92% of the campus is accessible. Wheelchair ramps, elevators, special parking, specially equipped rest rooms, special class scheduling, lowered drinking fountains, and lowered telephones are available.

Services: Counseling and information services are available, as is tutoring in every subject. There is a reader service for the blind, remedial math and writing, taped textbooks, and adaptive computer technology, including a text scanner, speaking software, a touch tablet, and text magnification software.

Campus Safety and Security: Measures include 24-hour foot and vehicle patrol, self-defense education, escort service, and informal discussions. There are pamphlets/posters/films, emergency telephones, and lighted pathways/sidewalks.

Programs of Study: Augsburg confers B.A., B.S., and B.M. degrees. Master's degrees are also awarded. Bachelor's degrees are awarded in BIOLOGICAL SCIENCE (biology/biological science), BUSINESS (accounting, business administration and management, international business management, management information systems, and marketing/retailing/merchandising), COMMUNICATIONS AND THE ARTS (art history and appreciation, communications, dramatic arts, English, French, German, music, Scandinavian languages, Spanish, speech/debate/rhetoric, and studio art), COMPUTER AND PHYSICAL SCIENCE (chemistry, computer science, mathematics, and physics), EDUCATION (elementary, health, music, physical, and secondary), HEALTH PROFESSIONS (music therapy), SOCIAL SCIENCE (East Asian studies, economics, history, international relations, philosophy, political science/government, psychology, religion, Russian and Slavic studies, Scandinavian studies, social work, sociology, urban studies, and women's studies). Physics, chemistry, and English are the strongest academically. Business, communication, and education are the largest.

Required: To graduate, all students must have a minimum GPA of 2.0 and a total of 32 course credits, with 10 to 15 in the major. They must complete 15 courses from 8 Perspective areas, and first-year fall orientation and seminar. Students must also satisfy entry-level and graduation skills requirements in writing, critical thinking, math, quantitative reasoning, and speaking, and demonstrate proficiency in 2 sports.

Special: Special academic programs include internships and co-op programs in business, government, and nonprofit and community-based organizations, a Washington semester, and study abroad in Europe, Latin America, and Africa. There are student-designed majors, cross-registration through the Associated Colleges of the Twin Cities (ACTC), dual and 3-2 engineering degrees with Washington University, Michigan Technological University, and the University of Minnesota, and preprofessional programs in dentistry, law, medicine, physical therapy, pharmacy, theology, and veterinary medicine. Credit for previous learning experience may be granted, and pass/fail options are possible. There is 1 national honor society, and a freshman honors program.

Faculty/Classroom: 49% of faculty are male; 51%, female. 99% teach undergraduates. No introductory courses are taught by graduate students. The average class size in an introductory lecture is 20; in a laboratory, 16; and in a regular course, 16.

Admissions: 75% of the 2001-2002 applicants were accepted. The SAT I scores for the 2001-2002 freshman class were: Verbal--32% below 500, 34% between 500 and 599, 30% between 600 and 700, and 4% above 700; Math--24% below 500, 52% between 500 and 599, 20% between 600 and 700, and 4% above 700. The ACT scores were 29% below 21, 28% between 21 and 23, 26% between 24 and 26, 8% between 27 and 28, and 9% above 28. 38% of the current freshmen were in the top fifth of their class; 63% were in the top two fifths. 11 freshmen graduated first in their class.

Requirements: The SAT I or ACT is required, with minimum scores of 430 (verbal) and 430 (math) on the SAT I or 20 on the ACT. Admissions requirements include graduation from an accredited secondary school, with 4 years of English. The GED is also accepted. An essay is required and an interview is recommended. Augsburg requires applicants to be in the upper 50% of their class. A GPA of 2.5 is required. AP and CLEP credits are accepted. Important factors in the admissions decision are advanced placement or honor courses, leadership record, and recommendations by school officials.

Procedure: Freshmen are admitted fall and spring. Entrance exams should be taken during the fall of the senior year in high school. There is a deferred admissions plan. Early decision applications should be filed by December 15; regular applications, by August 15 for fall entry and December 15 for spring entry. The fall 2001 application fee was $25. Notification is sent on a rolling basis.

Transfer: 330 transfer students enrolled in 2001-2002. Applicants must have a minimum GPA of 2.2 in college course work. 9 credits of 32 must be completed at Augsburg.

Visiting: There are regularly scheduled orientations for prospective students, including admissions interviews and campus tours. Students may also arrange to meet with professors and coaches, and to attend lectures. There are guides for informal visits and visitors may sit in on classes and stay overnight. To schedule a visit, contact the Admissions Office at *admissions@augsburg.edu*

Financial Aid: In 2001-2002, 92% of all freshmen and 81% of continuing students received some form of financial aid. 69% of freshmen and 66% of continuing students received need-based aid. The average freshman award was $18,618. Of that total, scholarships or need-based grants averaged $11,439 ($24,061 maximum); loans averaged $6530 ($23,382 maximum); and work contracts averaged $2179 ($3000 maximum). 96% of undergraduates work part time. Average annual earnings from campus work are $1307. The average financial indebtedness of the 2001 graduate was $21,456. Augsburg is a member of CSS. The FAFSA and the college's own financial statement are required. The fall application deadline is August 1.

International Students: There are 74 international students enrolled. The school actively recruits these students. They must score 520 on the written TOEFL or take the MELAB.

Computers: The mainframe is an IBM AS400. There are 55 PCs located in the main computer center. There are also 2 satellite centers with a total of 35 PCs, and 3 computer classrooms with 20 computers each. There are 4 computer classrooms with a total of 41 PC Windows workstations and 26 Mac workstations. In the library there are 14 PC Windows workstations, 2 Mac workstations, and 43 IBM ThinkPad and 13 Mac G3 laptops available for checkout. In the dorm lab, there are 11 Windows PC workstations and 19 other workstations. Anyone with an Augsburg network account has access to the Internet, Intranet, and printing. All students may access the system. There are no time limits and no fees.

Graduates: In 2001, 475 bachelor's degrees were awarded. The most popular majors were business administration (29%), education (15%), and communication (6%). In an average class, 2% graduate in 3 years, 36% in 4 years, 48% in 5 years, and 52% in 6 years. 91 companies recruited on campus in 2000-2001. Of the 2000 graduating class, 15% were enrolled in graduate school within 6 months of graduation and 95% were employed.

Admissions Contact: Sally Daniels, Director of Admissions.
E-mail: *daniels@augsburg.edu* Web: *http://www.augsburg.edu*

BEMIDJI STATE UNIVERSITY

Bemidji, MN 56601-2699 — **B-2** — **(218) 755-2040**
(800) 475-2001; Fax: (218) 755-2074

Full-time: 1630 men, 1788 women	**Faculty:** 191; IIB, av$
Part-time: 240 men, 656 women	**Ph.D.s:** 82%
Graduate: 61 men, 132 women	**Student/Faculty:** 18 to 1
Year: semesters, summer session	**Tuition:** $3903 ($6984)
Application Deadline: open	**Room & Board:** $4054
Freshman Class: n/av	
ACT: 22	**COMPETITIVE**

Bemidji State University, founded in 1919, is a public liberal arts university. There are 3 undergraduate schools and 1 graduate school. In addition to regional accreditation, Bemidji State University has baccalaureate program accreditation with CSWE, NASM, NCATE, and NLN. The library contains 190,000 volumes, 721,255 microform items, and 2500 audiovisual forms/CDs, and subscribes to 907 periodicals. Computerized library services include the card catalog, interlibrary loans, and database searching. Special learning facilities include a learning resource center, art gallery, radio station, and TV station. The 89-acre campus is in a small town 220 miles northwest of Minneapolis. Including residence halls, there are 21 buildings.

Student Life: 80% of undergraduates are from Minnesota. Others are from 46 states, 34 foreign countries, and Canada. 95% are from public schools. 89% are white. The average age of freshmen is 20; all undergraduates, 25. 30% do not continue beyond their first year; 43% remain to graduate.

Housing: 1700 students can be accommodated in college housing, which includes single-sex and coed dormitories and on-campus apartments. In addition, there are special-interest houses and single parent apartments. On-campus housing is available on a first-come, first-served basis. 68% of students commute. Alcohol is not permitted. All students may keep cars.

Activities: 2% of men belong to 2 national fraternities; 1% of women belong to 1 national sorority. There are 80 groups on campus, including art, band, cheerleading, choir, chorus, computers, dance, drama, ethnic, gay, honors, international, jazz band, literary magazine, musical theater, newspaper, opera, orchestra, pep band, political, professional, radio and TV, religious, social, social service, and student government. Popular campus events include Funtastic Dance Follies, madrigal music, and plays and concerts.

Sports: There are 7 intercollegiate sports for men and 7 for women, and 7 intramural sports for men and 4 for women. Facilities include a basketball gym, an Olympic-size pool, a hockey arena, a football stadium, indoor and outdoor tracks, baseball and softball fields, tennis, racquetball, and handball courts, weight rooms, and a dance studio.

Disabled Students: 90% of the campus is accessible. Wheelchair ramps, elevators, special parking, specially equipped rest rooms, lowered drinking fountains, and lowered telephones are available.

Services: Counseling and information services are available, as is tutoring in every subject. There is a reader service for the blind, and remedial math, reading, and writing.

Campus Safety and Security: Measures include 24-hour foot and vehicle patrol, escort service, informal discussions, and pamphlets/posters/films. There are emergency telephones and lighted pathways/sidewalks.

Programs of Study: Bemidji State University confers B.A., B.S., and B.F.A. degrees. Associate and master's degrees are also awarded. Bachelor's degrees are awarded in BIOLOGICAL SCIENCE (biology/biological science), BUSINESS (accounting and business administration and management), COMMUNICATIONS AND THE ARTS (broadcasting, communications, English, fine arts, German, journalism, languages, music, and Spanish), COMPUTER AND PHYSICAL SCIENCE (chemistry, computer science, earth science, geology, mathematics, and physics), EDUCATION (art, early childhood, elementary, foreign languages, health, industrial arts, middle school, science, and secondary), ENGINEERING AND ENVIRONMENTAL DESIGN (industrial engineering technology), HEALTH PROFESSIONS (medical laboratory technology, nursing, predentistry, and premedicine), SOCIAL SCIENCE (community services, criminal justice, economics, geography, history, parks and recreation management, philosophy, political science/government, prelaw, psychology, social science, social work, and sociology). Nursing and accounting are the strongest academically. Business administration and elementary and secondary education are the largest.

Required: All students must complete at least 128 semester hours, of which 42 are general education, including courses in freshman English, the humanities, social science, physical science, liberal education activities, and phys ed. Students must maintain a minimum GPA of 2.0; a 2.3 GPA is required in the major (2.5 for education majors).

Special: Students may attend other schools within the Minnesota State University system. Students may study abroad in England, China, Japan, and Malaysia. Paid internships and work-study programs are available in many fields. Students may receive credit for life, military, and work experience. Student-designed dual majors, nondegree study, and pass/fail options are offered. There are 2 national honor societies, and a freshman honors program.

Faculty/Classroom: 61% of faculty are male; 39%, female. All teach undergraduates and 15% do research. Graduate students teach less than 1% of introductory courses. The average class size in an introductory lecture is 35; in a laboratory, 20; and in a regular course, 23.

Admissions: The ACT scores for the 2001-2002 freshman class were: 27% below 20, 47% between 21 and 23, 20% between 24 and 26, and 6% between 27 and 28. 31% of a recent freshmen class were in the top fifth of their class; 64% were in the top two fifths. 10 freshmen graduated first in their class in a recent year.

Requirements: The ACT is required. In addition, applicants must have a minimum high school rank of 50% or a composite score of 21 on the ACT. They should have had 4 years of English and 3 years each of math, science, and social studies. AP and CLEP credits are accepted. Important factors in the admissions decision are recommendations by school officials, advanced placement or honor courses, and extracurricular activities record.

Procedure: Freshmen are admitted to all sessions. Entrance exams should be taken during the junior year. There is a deferred admissions plan. Application deadlines are open. The fall 2001 application fee was $20. Notification is sent on a rolling basis.

Transfer: 451 transfer students enrolled in 2001-2002. Applicants must have a minimum GPA of 2.0. 32 credits of 128 must be completed at Bemidji State University.

Visiting: There are regularly scheduled orientations for prospective students, including an interview with an admissions counselor, a tour of the campus, and visits with faculty. There are guides for informal visits and visitors may sit in on classes and stay overnight. To schedule a visit, contact the Admissions Office at (888) 345-1721.

Financial Aid: In 2001-2002, 78% of all freshmen and 79% of continuing students received some form of financial aid. 68% of freshmen and 72% of continuing students received need-based aid. The average freshman award was $5120. Of that total, scholarships or need-based grants averaged $1520 ($2000 maximum); loans averaged $1900 ($4000 maximum); and work contracts averaged $1700. 35% of undergraduates work part time. Average annual earnings from campus work are $1950. The average financial indebtedness of the 2001 graduate was $12,400. The FAFSA and the college's own financial statement are required. The application deadline is 2 months prior to the beginning of the semester.

International Students: There are 210 international students enrolled. The school actively recruits these students. They must score 550 on the written TOEFL.

Computers: The mainframes are a DEC VAX 785 and a Sperry UNIVAC 1180. There are PC labs and 135 terminals in various campus locations. Approximately 35 mainframe access terminals are located in 4 locations. All residence hall rooms are connected to the network. All students may access the system 24 hours a day on campus; 18 hours a day in other locations. There are no time limits. The fee is $1 per credit.

Graduates: In 2001, 741 bachelor's degrees were awarded. The most popular majors were education (18%), business/accounting (8%), and industrial technology (7%). In an average class, 1% graduate in 3 years, 16% in 4 years, 22% in 5 years, and 37% in 6 years. 45 companies recruited on campus in 2000-2001.

Admissions Contact: Paul Muller, Associate Director, Admissions. A video is available. E-mail: *admissions@bemidjistate.edu*

BETHEL COLLEGE

St. Paul, MN 55112 C-4

(651) 638-6242

(800) 255-8706; Fax: (651) 635-1490

Full-time: 971 men, 1464 women	**Faculty:** 146; IIB, av$
Part-time: 82 men, 183 women	**Ph.D.s:** 75%
Graduate: 73 men, 218 women	**Student/Faculty:** 17 to 1
Year: trimesters, summer session	**Tuition:** $16,780
Application Deadline: December 1	**Room & Board:** $5960
Freshman Class: 1580 applied, 1055 accepted, 667 enrolled	
SAT I Verbal/Math: 590/593	**ACT:** 24 **VERY COMPETITIVE**

Bethel College, established in 1871, is a private liberal arts college affiliated with the Baptist General Conference. In addition to regional accreditation, Bethel has baccalaureate program accreditation with CSWE, NCATE, and NLN. The 2 libraries contain 150,203 volumes, 116,405 microform items, and 6270 audiovisual forms/CDs, and subscribe to 842 periodicals. Computerized library services include the card catalog, interlibrary loans, and database searching. Special learning facilities include a learning resource center, art gallery, and radio station. The 231-acre campus is in a suburban area 10 miles north of Minneapolis/St. Paul.

Student Life: 62% of undergraduates are from Minnesota. Others are from 38 states and Canada. 94% are white. Most are Protestant. The average age of freshmen is 18; all undergraduates, 21. 17% do not continue beyond their first year; 72% remain to graduate.

Housing: 1479 students can be accommodated in college housing, which includes single-sex dormitories, on-campus apartments, and off-campus apartments. In addition, there are townhouses. On-campus housing is guaranteed for the freshman year only, is available on a first-come, first-served basis, and on a lottery system for upperclassmen. 70% of students live on campus; of those, 40% remain on campus on weekends. Alcohol is not permitted. Upperclassmen may keep cars.

Activities: There are no fraternities or sororities. There are 37 groups on campus, including art, band, cheerleading, choir, chorale, chorus, debate, drama, ethnic, film, forensics, honors, international, jazz band, literary magazine, musical theater, newspaper, orchestra, pep band, political, professional, radio and TV, religious, social, social service, student government, and yearbook. Popular campus events include Snow Daze and Royal Cup Competition.

Sports: There are 9 intercollegiate sports for men and 8 for women, and 12 intramural sports for men and 12 for women. Facilities include a gym, an indoor recreation center, with 1/8-mile track and 4 multipurpose courts, weight room, racquetball courts, football and baseball fields, and tennis courts.

Disabled Students: 99% of the campus is accessible. Wheelchair ramps, elevators, special parking, specially equipped rest rooms, special class scheduling, lowered drinking fountains, and lowered telephones are available.

Services: Counseling and information services are available, as is tutoring in most subjects. There is a reader service for the blind. An academic enrichment and support center offers tutoring, a writing lab, and time management and study skills workshops.

Campus Safety and Security: Measures include 24-hour foot and vehicle patrol, escort service, shuttle buses, and pamphlets/posters/films. There are emergency telephones and lighted pathways/sidewalks.

Programs of Study: Bethel confers B.A., B.S., B.Mus., and B.Mus.Ed. degrees. Associate and master's degrees are also awarded. Bachelor's degrees are awarded in BIOLOGICAL SCIENCE (biochemistry and biology/biological science), BUSINESS (accounting, banking and finance, business administration and management, and marketing/retailing/merchandising), COMMUNICATIONS AND THE ARTS (communications, dramatic arts, English, fine arts, multimedia, music, Spanish, and speech/debate/rhetoric), COMPUTER AND PHYSICAL SCIENCE (chemistry, computer science, mathematics, and physics), EDUCATION (art, athletic training, business, early childhood, elementary, foreign languages, health, mathematics, music, physical, science, and secondary), ENGINEERING AND ENVIRONMENTAL DESIGN (engineering and applied science and environmental science), HEALTH PROFESSIONS (nursing), SOCIAL SCIENCE (economics, ethnic studies, history, international relations, philosophy, political science/government, psychology, religion, social work, and youth ministry). Physical sciences, life sciences, and computer science are the strongest academically. Education, business, and biology are the largest.

Required: Students must complete a minimum of 122 semester credit hours, with 30 to 60 in the major and 51 in general education. Specific general education courses include introduction to the Bible, Christianity and Western culture, college writing, creativity in fine arts, and physical wellness. An overall GPA of 2.0 and a GPA of 2.25 in the major are needed.

Special: Students may arrange internships, study abroad in various countries, participate in a Washington semester with the Christian College Coalition, and select various work-study programs. Dual majors in cross-cultural studies are available. Students may design their own majors, earn a 3-2 engineering degree, and select limited pass/fail options. An adult degree completion program is offered. There is a freshman honors program.

Faculty/Classroom: 54% of faculty are male; 46%, female. All teach undergraduates. No introductory courses are taught by graduate students. The average class size in a laboratory is 20 and in a regular course, 22.

Admissions: 67% of the 2001-2002 applicants were accepted. The SAT I scores for the 2001-2002 freshman class were: Verbal--19% below 500, 37% between 500 and 599, 38% between 600 and 700, and 6% above 700; Math--21% below 500, 40% between 500 and 599, 31% between 600 and 700, and 8% above 700. 47% of the current freshmen were in the top fifth of their class; 90% were in the top two fifths. There were 6 National Merit finalists and 3 semifinalists.

Requirements: The SAT I or ACT is required. The PSAT is accepted. In addition, applicants must be graduates of an accredited secondary school or have a GED. An interview is recommended. Bethel requires applicants to be in the upper 50% of their class. AP and CLEP credits are accepted. Important factors in the admissions decision are advanced placement or honor courses, extracurricular activities record, and personality/intangible qualities. Applications are accepted on-line at *Applyweb.com*

Procedure: Freshmen are admitted fall, winter, and spring. Entrance exams should be taken during spring of junior year. There is an early admissions plan. Applications should be filed by December 1 for fall entry, November 1 for winter entry, and December 1 for spring entry, along with a $25 fee. Notification is sent January 15. 20% of all applicants are on a waiting list.

Transfer: 96 transfer students enrolled in 2001-2002. Applicants must have a minimum GPA of 2.5 and must submit all college transcripts. 28 credits of 122 must be completed at Bethel.

Visiting: There are regularly scheduled orientations for prospective students, throughout the school year. There are guides for informal visits and visitors may sit in on classes and stay overnight. To schedule a visit, contact the Admissions Office.

Financial Aid: The average financial indebtedness of the 2001 graduate was $17,000. The FAFSA, the college's own financial statement, and students' and parents' most recent federal tax returns are required. The fall application deadline is April 15.

International Students: They must score 525 on the written TOEFL or 195 on the electronic version and also take the SAT I or the ACT.

Computers: The mainframes are a Dell system PC and an 850 workgroup server for Macs. The computer labs have more than 125 Macs and PCs; the on-campus housing options are fully wired, allowing for 2 mainframe connections per room. All students may access the system 24 hours a day. There are no time limits and no fees.

Graduates: In a recent year, 647 bachelor's degrees were awarded. In an average class, 65% graduate in 4 years, 71% in 5 years, and 74% in 6 years.

Admissions Contact: Jay T. Fedje, Director of Admissions. E-mail: *bcoll-admit@bethel.edu* Web: *http://www.bethel.edu*

CARLETON COLLEGE

Northfield, MN 55057 C-4

(507) 646-4190

(800) 995-CARL; Fax: (507) 646-4526

Full-time: 922 men, 1010 women	**Faculty:** 184; IIB, ++$
Part-time: 5 men, 11 women	**Ph.D.s:** 95%
Graduate: none	**Student/Faculty:** 11 to 1
Year: trimesters	**Tuition:** $25,530
Application Deadline: January 15	**Room & Board:** $5250
Freshman Class: 4065 applied, 1511 accepted, 516 enrolled	
SAT I or ACT: required	**MOST COMPETITIVE**

Carleton College, founded in 1866, is a private liberal arts college. The library contains 639,707 volumes, 127,753 microform items, and 778 audiovisual forms/CDs, and subscribes to 1538 periodicals, plus 2300 electronic journals. Computerized library services include the card catalog, interlibrary loans, and database searching. Special learning facilities include a learning resource center, art gallery, radio station, an observatory, and an 850-acre arboretum. The 945-acre campus is in a small town 35 miles south of Minneapolis-St. Paul. Including residence halls, there are 29 buildings.

Student Life: 78% of undergraduates are from out of state, mostly the Midwest. Others are from 50 states, 26 foreign countries, and Canada. 75% are from public schools. 81% are white. The average age of freshmen is 18; all undergraduates, 20. 4% do not continue beyond their first year; 89% remain to graduate.

Housing: 1648 students can be accommodated in college housing, which includes single-sex and coed dormitories, on-campus apartments, and off-campus apartments. In addition, there are language houses and special-interest houses. On-campus housing is guaranteed for all 4 years. 89% of students live on campus; of those, 97% remain on campus on weekends. No one may keep cars.

Activities: There are no fraternities or sororities. There are 134 groups on campus, including art, band, chess, choir, chorale, chorus, computers, dance, debate, drama, ethnic, film, gay, honors, international, jazz band, literary magazine, musical theater, newspaper, orchestra, photography, political, professional, radio and TV, religious, social, social service, student government, symphony, and yearbook. Popular campus events include Mai Fete, spring concert, and Winter Ball.

Sports: There are 12 intercollegiate sports for men and 12 for women, and 11 intramural sports for men and 12 for women. Facilities include a gym with a 1220-seat arena, 6-lane swimming pool, and wrestling room; 2 recreation centers with gym, dance studio, indoor tennis court, sauna, 5-lane swimming pool, 200-meter indoor track, sport courts, weight room, dance studio, and climbing wall. The 7000-seat stadium complex has handball and racquetball courts, 200-meter indoor track, baseball batting cage, and weight room; the 800-acre arboretum has baseball, softball, soccer, ultimate frisbee, lacrosse, rugby, and field hockey fields, 12 outdoor tennis courts, and 16 miles of running, biking, hiking, and cross-country skiing trails.

Disabled Students: 28% of the campus is accessible. Wheelchair ramps, elevators, special parking, specially equipped rest rooms, special class scheduling, and lowered drinking fountains are available.

Services: Counseling and information services are available, as is tutoring in every subject. There are also writing and math skills assistance centers, and a reader service for the blind.

Campus Safety and Security: Measures include 24-hour foot and vehicle patrol, escort service, informal discussions, and pamphlets/posters/films. There are emergency telephones, lighted pathways/sidewalks, and nighttime transport service.

Programs of Study: Carleton confers the B.A degree. Bachelor's degrees are awarded in BIOLOGICAL SCIENCE (biology/biological science), COMMUNICATIONS AND THE ARTS (art history and appreciation, classics, English, French, German, Greek, Latin, music, romance languages and literature, Russian, Spanish, and studio art), COMPUTER AND PHYSICAL SCIENCE (chemistry, computer science, geology, mathematics, and physics), SOCIAL SCIENCE (African American studies, African studies, American studies, anthropology, Asian/Oriental studies, classical/ancient civilization, economics, history, international relations, Latin American studies, philosophy, political science/government, psychology, religion, sociology, and women's studies). Social sciences and history, physical sciences, and biological life sciences are the largest.

Required: Students are required to demonstrate proficiency in English composition and in a foreign language, and to take 1 course centrally concerned with another culture. 4 terms of phys ed are required. Students must complete 210 credits or 117 semester hours, including 18 credits each from the social sciences, math, and science, and 12 credits each from arts, literature, and humanities. Students must maintain a minimum GPA of 2.0. The total number of hours required for the major varies by department (72 is the norm). All seniors must complete a senior integrative exercise in their major, which may consist of a comprehensive exam, an extensive research project or paper, a public lecture, or a combination of these.

Special: Students may cross-register with Saint Olaf College and pursue a variety of internships. The college offers study abroad in 46 countries. Dual majors in all areas and student-designed majors are available. Students may earn a 3-2 engineering degree with Washington or Columbia University, a 3-2 degree in nursing, and a 3-3 degree in law. Pass/fail options are offered. There is a chapter of Phi Beta Kappa.

Faculty/Classroom: 60% of faculty are male; 40%, female. All both teach and do research. The average class size in an introductory lecture is 23; in a laboratory, 15; and in a regular course, 16.

Admissions: 37% of the 2001-2002 applicants were accepted. The SAT I scores for the 2001-2002 freshman class were: Verbal--2% below 500, 8% between 500 and 599, 41% between 600 and 700, and 49% above 700; Math--1% below 500, 11% between 500 and 599, 46% between 600 and 700, and 42% above 700. The ACT scores were 1% below 21, 5% between 21 and 23, 43% between 24 and 28, and 51% above 28. 89% of the current freshmen were in the top fifth of their class; 99% were in the top two fifths. There were 88 National Merit finalists. 59 freshmen graduated first in their class.

Requirements: The SAT I or ACT is required. There are no secondary school requirements, but it is recommended that applicants have completed 4 years of English, 3 years each of math and a foreign language, 2 years each of history and science, and 1 year of social studies. An essay and 2 teacher recommendations are required. Applications are accepted on-line via CollegeLink and Apply. AP credits are accepted. Important factors in the admissions decision are advanced placement or honor courses, personality/intangible qualities, and evidence of special talent.

Procedure: Freshmen are admitted in the fall. Entrance exams should be taken before March 1. There are early decision and deferred admissions plans. Early decision applications should be filed by November 15; regular applications, by January 15 for fall entry. The fall 2001 application fee was $30. Notification of early decision is sent December 15; regular decision, by April 15. 204 early decision candidates were accepted for the 2001-2002 class. 34% of all applicants are on a waiting list.

Transfer: 5 transfer students enrolled in 2001-2002. Transfers are usually accepted for sophomore and junior classes. A 3.0 GPA is recommended. 108 credits of 210 must be completed at Carleton.

Visiting: There are guides for informal visits and visitors may sit in on classes and stay overnight. To schedule a visit, contact the Admissions Office.

Financial Aid: In 2000-2001, 57% of all freshmen and 77% of continuing students received some form of financial aid. The average freshman award was $18,483. Of that total, scholarships or need-based grants averaged $15,885; and loans averaged $1749. 80% of undergraduates work part time. Average annual earnings from campus work are $1900. The average financial indebtedness of the 2001 graduate was $14,882. Carleton is a member of CSS. The CSS/Profile or FAFSA is required. The fall application deadline is February 15.

International Students: There are 55 international students enrolled. The school actively recruits these students. They must take the TOEFL, the SAT I, or the ACT.

Computers: All students may access the system 24 hours a day. There are no time limits and no fees.

Graduates: In 2001, 439 bachelor's degrees were awarded. The most popular majors were social science and history (30%), physical sciences (13%), and biological/life sciences (13%). In an average class, 85% graduate in 4 years, 87% in 5 years, and 89% in 6 years. 49 companies recruited on campus in 2000-2001. Of the 2000 graduating class, 16% were enrolled in graduate school within 6 months of graduation and 52% were employed.

Admissions Contact: Paul Thiboutot, Dean of Admissions. A video is available. E-mail: *admissions@acs.carleton.edu*
Web: *www.carleton.edu*

COLLEGE OF SAINT BENEDICT — C-3

St. Joseph, MN 56374-2099 — **(320) 363-5308**
(800) 544-1489; Fax: (320) 363-5010

Full-time: 2029 women	**Faculty:** 137
Part-time: 71 women	**Ph.D.s:** 70%
Graduate: none	**Student/Faculty:** 15 to 1
Year: semesters	**Tuition:** $18,315
Application Deadline: open	**Room & Board:** $5606
Freshman Class: 1431 applied, 1172 accepted, 556 enrolled	
SAT I Verbal/Math: 600/600	**ACT:** 25 **VERY COMPETITIVE**

The College of Saint Benedict, established in 1887, is a private, Benedictine Catholic institution offering undergraduate liberal arts study for women in conjunction with St. John's University, a Benedictine Catholic institution for men. The coordinate institutions share an academic calendar, academic curriculum, and most cocurriculum programs. In addition to regional accreditation, St. Benedict has baccalaureate program accreditation with ACS, ADA, CSWE, NASM, NCATE, and NLN. The 3 libraries contain 800,685 volumes, 196,063 microform items, and 21,400 audiovisual forms/CDs, and subscribe to 8942 periodicals. Computerized library services include the card catalog, interlibrary loans, and database searching. Special learning facilities include a learning resource center, art gallery, natural history museum, radio station, a pottery studio, an arboretum, an observatory, a greenhouse and Hill Monastic Manuscript library at St. John's University. The 315-acre campus is in a small town 70 miles northwest of Minneapolis and 10 miles west of St. Cloud. Including residence halls, there are 33 buildings.

Student Life: 83% of undergraduates are from Minnesota. Others are from 31 states, 24 foreign countries, and Canada. 78% are from public schools. 92% are white. 69% are Catholic; 25% Protestant. The average age of freshmen is 18; all undergraduates, 20. 12% do not continue beyond their first year; 70% remain to graduate.

Housing: 1543 students can be accommodated in college housing, which includes single-sex dormitories, on-campus apartments, and off-campus apartments. On-campus housing is guaranteed for the freshman year only, is available on a first-come, first-served basis, and on a lottery system for upperclassmen. 80% of students live on campus. All students may keep cars.

Activities: There are no fraternities. There are 80 groups on campus, including academic clubs such as chemistry and biology, art, band, choir, chorale, chorus, computers, dance, drama, ethnic, gay, honors, international, jazz band, literary magazine, musical theater, opera, orchestra, political, professional, radio and TV, religious, social, social service, student government, symphony, and yearbook. Popular campus events include Pinestock, Festival of Cultures, and Insane at the Haehn.

Sports: Facilities include a 1000-seat volleyball and basketball arena, racquetball, indoor, and outdoor tennis courts, a weight room, an indoor pool, a field house with indoor running track, an aerobics studio, a fitness center with exercise and weight-training equipment, a softball diamond, soccer fields, and 30 miles of cross-country ski trails. Students have access to St. John's University facilities as well, including a 4-story climbing wall and a fitness center.

Disabled Students: 90% of the campus is accessible. Wheelchair ramps, elevators, special parking, specially equipped rest rooms, special class scheduling, lowered drinking fountains, and lowered telephones are available.

Services: Counseling and information services are available, as is tutoring in most subjects. There is a reader service for the blind. A writing center, a math skills center study courses, and test-taking skills instruction.

Campus Safety and Security: Measures include 24-hour foot and vehicle patrol, self-defense education, escort service, and shuttle buses. There are informal discussions, pamphlets/posters/films, emergency telephones, and lighted pathways/sidewalks.

Programs of Study: St. Benedict confers B.A. and B.S.N. degrees. Bachelor's degrees are awarded in AGRICULTURE (forestry and related sciences), BIOLOGICAL SCIENCE (biochemistry, biology/biological science, and nutrition), BUSINESS (accounting and management science), COMMUNICATIONS AND THE ARTS (art, classics, communications, dramatic arts, English, fine arts, French, German, music, and Spanish), COMPUTER AND PHYSICAL SCIENCE (chemistry, computer science, mathematics, natural sciences, and physics), EDUCATION (elementary), ENGINEERING AND ENVIRONMENTAL DESIGN (preengineering), HEALTH PROFESSIONS (medical laboratory technology, nursing, occupational therapy, physical therapy, predentistry, premedicine, prepharmacy, and preveterinary science), SOCIAL SCIENCE (dietetics, economics, history, humanities, liberal arts/general studies, ministries, pastoral studies, peace studies, philosophy, political science/government, prelaw, psychology, social science, social work, sociology, and theological studies). The humanities is the strongest academically. Nursing, elementary education, and management are the largest.

Required: To graduate, students must complete the core curriculum of writing, discussion, quantitative reasoning, and gender and global perspectives. Distribution requirements include 6 credits in fine arts, 5 in humanities, 2 each in natural science and social science, and 1 in math. All students must prove math and foreign language proficiency. A total of 124 credits must be earned, with 40 credits in upper-division courses and an overall GPA of 2.0. Students must complete a first-year symposium and a senior seminar.

Special: Students may cross-register with St. John's University and St. Cloud State University. There are study-abroad programs in Ireland, China, South America, South Africa, Central America, Australia, Scandinavia, and various European cities. Internships, dual and student-designed majors in math/computer science and in preprofessional programs, and liberal studies degrees may be pursued. A 3-2 engineering program is offered through University of Minnesota. Nondegree study and a pass/fail grading option are also available. There is 1 national honor society and a freshman honors program.

Faculty/Classroom: 44% of faculty are male; 56%, female. All both teach and do research. The average class size in an introductory lecture is 25; in a laboratory, 18; and in a regular course, 20.

Admissions: 82% of the 2001-2002 applicants were accepted. The SAT I scores for the 2001-2002 freshman class were: Verbal--18% below 500, 26% between 500 and 599, 45% between 600 and 700, and 11% above 700; Math--16% below 500, 31% between 500 and 599, 50% between 600 and 700, and 3% above 700. The ACT scores were 7% below 21, 27% between 21 and 23, 33% between 24 and 26, 13% between 27 and 28, and 20% above 28. 69% of the current freshmen were in the top fifth of their class; 95% were in the top two fifths. There were 4 National Merit finalists. 20 freshmen graduated first in their class.

Requirements: The SAT I or ACT is required. In addition, students should be graduates of an accredited secondary school. Academic preparation should include 17 units, including 4 of English, 3 of math, 2 each of a science and social studies, and 6 electives. A foreign language is recommended. The GED is accepted. An essay is required. Home-schooled applicants are not required to have a high school diploma but are required to provide appropriate documentation of college preparatory curriculum. St. Benedict requires applicants to be in the upper 50% of their class. A GPA of 3.0 is required. AP and CLEP credits are accepted. Important factors in the admissions decision are leadership record, evidence of special talent, and extracurricular activities record. The college accepts electronic applications via CollegeNET and on its web site *www.csbsju.edu/admission/*.

Procedure: Freshmen are admitted fall and spring. Entrance exams should be taken during the spring of the junior year or fall of the senior year. There are early admissions and deferred admissions plans. Application deadlines are open. Notification of regular decision is sent on a rolling basis beginning October 1. The fall 2001 application fee was $25. A waiting list is an active part of the admissions procedure.

Transfer: 57 transfer students enrolled in 2001-2002. Transfer applicants must have a minimum college GPA of 2.75. An essay or personal statement, high school and college transcripts, and a transfer student evaluation form are required. Standardized test scores may be required of some. 45 credits of 124 must be completed at St. Benedict.

Visiting: There are regularly scheduled orientations for prospective students, including programs that vary with student interest. Information can be found at the college's web site. There are guides for informal visits and visitors may sit in on classes and stay overnight. To schedule a visit, contact the Admissions Office.

Financial Aid: In 2001-2002, 94% of all freshmen and 91% of continuing students received some form of financial aid. 68% of freshmen and 64% of continuing students received need-based aid. The average freshman award was $15,389. Of that total, scholarships or need-based grants averaged $11,068; loans averaged $3649; and work contracts averaged $802. 25% of undergraduates work part time. Average annual earnings from campus work are $2100. The average financial indebtedness of the 2001 graduate was $19,480. The FAFSA and the college's own financial statement are required. The fall application deadline is May 1.

International Students: There are 78 international students enrolled. The school actively recruits these students. They must score 500 on the written TOEFL or 173 on the electronic version or take the MELAB. They must also take the SAT I or ACT, scoring 500 on SAT I verbal or 21 on ACT verbal.

Computers: The mainframe is a Windows NT network. Students have free 24-hour access to computers in each college residence, in numerous departments, and in 4 public access areas. Most residence halls and apartments are computer-wired. All students may access the system 24 hours per day. There are no time limits and no fees.

Graduates: In 2001, 479 bachelor's degrees were awarded. The most popular majors were nursing (13%), management (12%), and psychology (9%). In an average class, 2% graduate in 3 years, 75% in 4 years, 80% in 5 years, and 80% in 6 years. 40 companies recruited on campus in 2000-2001. Of the 2000 graduating class, 11% were enrolled in graduate school within 6 months of graduation and 89% were employed.

Admissions Contact: Mary Milbert, Dean of Admission. A video is available. E-mail: *admissions@csbsju.edu* Web: *www.csbsju.edu*

COLLEGE OF SAINT CATHERINE C-4

St. Paul, MN 55105 **(651) 690-6505**

(800) 945-4599 ext. 6505; Fax: (651) 690-8824

Full-time: 20 men, 2283 women	**Faculty:** 184
Part-time: 69 men, 1228 women	**Ph.D.s:** 74%
Graduate: 112 men, 910 women	**Student/Faculty:** 13 to 1
Year: 4-1-4, summer session	**Tuition:** $17,402
Application Deadline: open	**Room & Board:** $4922
Freshman Class: 814 applied, 671 accepted, 359 enrolled	
SAT I or ACT: required	**VERY COMPETITIVE**

The College of Saint Catherine, founded in 1905, is a private, comprehensive, women's college affiliated with the Roman Catholic Church. The 2 libraries contain 390,613 volumes, 169,236 microform items, and 13,627 audiovisual forms/CDs, and subscribe to 2166 periodicals. Computerized library services include the card catalog, interlibrary loans, and database searching. Special learning facilities include a learning resource center, art gallery, and observatory. The 110-acre campus is in an urban area 6 miles southwest of downtown St. Paul. Including residence halls, there are 18 buildings.

Student Life: 86% of undergraduates are from Minnesota. Others are from 29 states, 30 foreign countries, and Canada. 80% are from public schools. 76% are white. 45% are Catholic; 20% Protestant. The average age of freshmen is 19; all undergraduates, 28. 20% do not continue beyond their first year.

Housing: 700 students can be accommodated in college housing, which includes single-sex dormitories and on-campus apartments. On-campus housing is guaranteed for all 4 years. 63% of students commute. All students may keep cars.

Activities: Tthere are 2 local sororities. There are no fraternities. There are 42 groups on campus, including art, band, choir, chorale, chorus, dance, drama, drill team, ethnic, gay, honors, international, jazz band, literary magazine, musical theater, newspaper, orchestra, photography, political, professional, religious, social, social service, and student government. Popular campus events include Suitcase Dance, Student Life Week, and Dew Drop Bop.

Sports: Facilities include a fitness facility, a gym, a weight room, a swimming pool, an outdoor fitness course, tennis courts, a soccer field, and a softball field.

Disabled Students: 85% of the campus is accessible. Wheelchair ramps, elevators, special parking, specially equipped rest rooms, special class scheduling, lowered drinking fountains, and lowered telephones are available.
Services: Counseling and information services are available, as is tutoring in most subjects. There is a reader service for the blind, and remedial math, reading, and writing.
Campus Safety and Security: Measures include 24-hour foot and vehicle patrol, self-defense education, escort service, and informal discussions. There are pamphlets/posters/films, emergency telephones, and lighted pathways/sidewalks.
Programs of Study: CSC confers B.A. and B.S. degrees. Associate and master's degrees are also awarded. Bachelor's degrees are awarded in BIOLOGICAL SCIENCE (biochemistry, biology/biological science, and nutrition), BUSINESS (accounting, business administration and management, fashion merchandising, and international economics), COMMUNICATIONS AND THE ARTS (communications, dramatic arts, English, fine arts, French, music, Spanish, and speech/debate/rhetoric), COMPUTER AND PHYSICAL SCIENCE (chemistry, information sciences and systems, and mathematics), EDUCATION (art, early childhood, elementary, home economics, music, and physical), HEALTH PROFESSIONS (health care administration, nursing, and occupational therapy), SOCIAL SCIENCE (dietetics, economics, family/consumer studies, history, international relations, philosophy, physical fitness/movement, political science/government, psychology, social studies, social work, sociology, and theological studies). Nursing, occupational therapy, and elementary education are the largest.
Required: To graduate, students must complete 130 semester credits, including a liberal arts core with courses in history, foreign language, philosophy, math, fine arts, literature, and theology, and 80 credits outside the major. Required courses are The Reflective Woman and The Global Search for Justice. At least 36 hours are required in the major. Students must have a minimum 2.0 GPA and demonstrate proficiency in composition, math, and computer literacy.
Special: CSC offers co-op programs with Carondolet College, the University of Minnesota, and George Washington University, and cross-registration with the Associated Colleges of the Twin Cities and other colleges sponsored by the Sisters of St. Joseph. Students may arrange internships, a Washington semester, and study abroad. Dual majors are available in the sciences and engineering. Students may receive credit for life, military, or work experience. Student-designed majors, nondegree study, and pass/fail options are available. The Weekend College offers a B.A. degree. There are 24 national honor societies, including Phi Beta Kappa, and a freshman honors program.
Faculty/Classroom: 20% of faculty are male; 80%, female. All teach undergraduates. No introductory courses are taught by graduate students. The average class size in an introductory lecture is 16; in a laboratory, 14; and in a regular course, 13.
Admissions: 82% of the 2001-2002 applicants were accepted. The SAT I scores for the 2001-2002 freshman class were: Verbal--30% below 500, 30% between 500 and 599, 34% between 600 and 700, and 6% above 700; Math--18% below 500, 36% between 500 and 599, 37% between 600 and 700, and 9% above 700. The ACT scores were 27% below 21, 26% between 21 and 23, 28% between 24 and 26, 10% between 27 and 28, and 8% above 28. 47% of the current freshmen were in the top fifth of their class; 80% were in the top two fifths. There were 3 National Merit semifinalists. 12 freshmen graduated first in their class.
Requirements: The SAT I or ACT is required. In addition, applicants must have completed a college preparatory program including 4 courses in English, 3 in math, and 2 each in a foreign language, science, and social studies. Applications are accepted on-line via the Catholic College Admission Application, ExPAN, and Apply. CSC requires applicants to be in the upper 50% of their class. A GPA of 2.5 is required. AP and CLEP credits are accepted. Important factors in the admissions decision are advanced placement or honor courses, recommendations by school officials, and extracurricular activities record.
Procedure: Freshmen are admitted to all sessions. Entrance exams should be taken during the senior year. There is a deferred admissions plan. Application deadlines are open.
Transfer: 772 transfer students enrolled in 2001-2002. Transfer applicants must submit high school and college transcripts. 48 credits of 130 must be completed at CSC.
Visiting: There are regularly scheduled orientations for prospective students, including a tour, an admissions interview, and an appointment with a faculty member. There are guides for informal visits and visitors may sit in on classes and stay overnight. To schedule a visit, contact the Admissions Office.
Financial Aid: In a recent year, 94% of all freshmen and 88% of continuing students received some form of financial aid. 77% of freshmen and 73% of continuing students received need-based aid. The average freshman award was $19,436. 93% of undergraduates work part time. Average annual earnings from campus work are $1800. The average financial indebtedness of a recent year's graduate was $22,642. CSC is a member of CSS. The FAFSA and the college's own financial statement are required. The fall application deadline is April 1.
International Students: The school actively recruits these students. They must score 500 on the written TOEFL or take the MELAB or the college's own test, The SAT I is required only if the student attended a U.S. high school, whether in this country or overseas.
Computers: The mainframe is an HP 9000/826. More than 350 PCs are available throughout campus for students to access the Internet and work on class assignments. All students may access the system 24 hours a day. There are no time limits and no fees.
Graduates: In 2001, 539 bachelor's degrees were awarded. The most popular majors were occupational therapy (18%), nursing (13%), and elementary education (10%). In an average class, 3% graduate in 3 years, 40% in 4 years, 52% in 5 years, and 55% in 6 years. 9 companies recruited on campus in 2000-2001. Of the 2000 graduating class, 15% were enrolled in graduate school within 6 months of graduation and 88% were employed.
Admissions Contact: Marlene Mohs, Associate Dean of Admissions. E-mail: *admissions@stkate.edu* Web: *www.stkate.edu*

COLLEGE OF SAINT SCHOLASTICA — D-3
Duluth, MN 55811 — **(218) 723-6046**
(800) 249-6412; Fax: (218) 723-5991

Full-time: 442 men, 1055 women	**Faculty:** 113; IIB, --$
Part-time: 63 men, 140 women	**Ph.D.s:** 49%
Graduate: 154 men, 377 women	**Student/Faculty:** 13 to 1
Year: semesters, summer session	**Tuition:** $17,180
Application Deadline: open	**Room & Board:** $5198
Freshman Class: 960 applied, 844 accepted, 300 enrolled	
SAT I Verbal/Math: 560/580	**ACT:** 23 **COMPETITIVE+**

The College of St. Scholastica, founded in 1912, is a private liberal arts college affiliated with the Roman Catholic Church. There is 1 graduate school. In addition to regional accreditation, College of Saint Scholastica has baccalaureate program accreditation with ADA, APTA, CAHEA, CSWE, and NLN. The library contains 128,266 volumes, 86 microform items, and 8250 audiovisual forms/CDs, and subscribes to 697 periodicals. Computerized library services include the card catalog, interlibrary loans, and database searching. Special learning facilities include a learning resource center. The 160-acre campus is in a suburban area 150 miles north of Minneapolis and St. Paul. Including residence halls, there are 16 buildings.
Student Life: 89% of undergraduates are from Minnesota. Others are from 21 states, 13 foreign countries, and Canada. 90% are white. 34% are Catholic; 31% claim no religious affiliation; 29% Protestant. The average age of freshmen is 23; all undergraduates, 25. 20% do not continue beyond their first year.
Housing: 681 students can be accommodated in college housing, which includes coed dormitories and on-campus apartments. Single-parent housing space is available. On-campus housing is available on a first-come, first-served basis and on a lottery system for upperclassmen. 61% of students commute. All students may keep cars.
Activities: There are no fraternities or sororities. There are 45 groups on campus, including band, cheerleading, choir, chorale, chorus, computers, dance, drama, ethnic, gay, honors, international, jazz band, literary magazine, newspaper, pep band, photography, political, professional, religious, social, social service, student government, and yearbook. Popular campus events include Mayfest Week, Fall Fest, and Welcome Back Week.
Sports: There are 6 intercollegiate sports for men and 6 for women, and 6 intramural sports for men and 6 for women. Facilities include a recreation center.
Disabled Students: 95% of the campus is accessible. Wheelchair ramps, elevators, special parking, specially equipped rest rooms, special class scheduling, lowered drinking fountains, lowered telephones, and special dorm rooms are available.
Services: Counseling and information services are available, as is tutoring in most subjects. There is a reader service for the blind, sign language interpreters, a note-taking service, tape recorders, voice input computers, and remedial study skills.
Campus Safety and Security: Measures include 24-hour foot and vehicle patrol, self-defense education, escort service, and informal discussions. There are pamphlets/posters/films, emergency telephones, lighted pathways/sidewalks, electronically operated dormitory entrances, and student door monitors in the evening and night.
Programs of Study: College of Saint Scholastica confers the B.A. degree. Master's degrees are also awarded. Bachelor's degrees are awarded in BIOLOGICAL SCIENCE (biochemistry and biology/biological science), BUSINESS (accounting, business administration and management, and international business management), COMMUNICATIONS AND THE ARTS (communications, English, languages, and music), COMPUTER AND PHYSICAL SCIENCE (chemistry, computer science, information sciences and systems, mathematics, and natural sciences), EDUCATION (education, educational media, elementary, and social science), HEALTH PROFESSIONS (exercise science, health care administration, health science, and nursing), SOCIAL SCIENCE (behav-

ioral science, economics, history, humanities, psychology, religion, and social work). English, biology, and chemistry are the strongest academically. Education, nursing, and health sciences are the largest.

Required: To graduate, students must complete 128 semester credits, with a 2.0 GPA. 44 credits of general education courses are required, including 4 credits each of English composition, social science, natural science, oral communication, literature, history, fine arts, philosophy, religious studies, math, and cultural diversity and 2 to 8 credits in a foreign language. The hours required in the major vary. Computer literacy is required of all students. Most majors require an internship for graduation.

Special: Students may cross-register with the University of Minnesota at Duluth and the University of Wisconsin at Superior. Self-designed majors, internships, study abroad in 5 countries, accelerated degrees, nondegree study, pass/fail options, and credit for life, military, or work experience are available. There is a 3-2 engineering degree with the Institute of Technology of the University of Minnesota. There are 2 national honor societies and a freshman honors program.

Faculty/Classroom: 42% of faculty are male; 58%, female. 95% teach undergraduates and 13% both teach and do research. No introductory courses are taught by graduate students. The average class size in an introductory lecture is 24; in a laboratory, 14; and in a regular course, 19.

Admissions: 88% of the 2001-2002 applicants were accepted. The SAT I scores for the 2001-2002 freshman class were: Verbal--14% below 500, 57% between 500 and 599, 22% between 600 and 700, and 7% above 700; Math--14% below 500, 50% between 500 and 599, 29% between 600 and 700, and 7% above 700. The ACT scores were 19% below 21, 32% between 21 and 23, 27% between 24 and 26, and 19% between 27 and 28. 52% of the current freshmen were in the top fifth of their class; 79% were in the top two fifths. 12 freshmen graduated first in their class.

Requirements: The SAT I or ACT is required. In addition, PSAT scores may also be submitted. Students are also required to send official high school transcripts. AP and CLEP credits are accepted. Important factors in the admissions decision are personality/intangible qualities, advanced placement or honor courses, and recommendations by school officials. Applications are accepted on-line via Peterson's, Apply, or ACT College Connector.

Procedure: Freshmen are admitted to all sessions. Entrance exams should be taken by January of the senior year of high school. There are early decision, early admissions, and deferred admissions plans. The fall 2001 application fee was $25. Notification is sent on a rolling basis. Application deadlines are open. 21 early decision candidates were accepted for the 2001-2002 class.

Transfer: 121 transfer students enrolled in 2001-2002. Applicants must have a GPA of 2.0 or a college aptitude rating score of 50 or higher. 32 credits of 128 must be completed at College of Saint Scholastica.

Visiting: There are regularly scheduled orientations for prospective students, including a class placement survey, peer and academic advisement, and registration. There are guides for informal visits and visitors may sit in on classes and stay overnight. To schedule a visit, contact the Admissions Office at *admissions@css.edu*

Financial Aid: In 2001-2002, 98% of all freshmen and 96% of continuing students received some form of financial aid. 79% of freshmen and 84% of continuing students received need-based aid. The average freshman award was $12,129. Of that total, scholarships or need-based grants averaged $10,138 ($23,909 maximum); loans averaged $5496 ($15,284 maximum); work contracts averaged $851 ($2000 maximum); and institutional discounts (employee, multiple siblings) averaged $596 ($20,100 maximum). 33% of undergraduates work part time. Average annual earnings from campus work are $1782. The average financial indebtedness of the 2001 graduate was $23,098. College of Saint Scholastica is a member of CSS. The FAFSA and the college's own financial statement are required. The fall application deadline is March 15.

International Students: There are 12 international students enrolled. They must score 550 on the written TOEFL or 213 on the electronic version or take the MELAB.

Computers: The mainframes are an IBM System 36 and a DEC ALPHA 4100. There are 140 PCs on network in labs throughout the campus. Web access will allow students to see accounts, grades, schedules, financial aid, and transcripts. All students may access the system 7 A.M. to midnight Monday through Thursday, 7 A.M. to 5 P.M. on Fridays, 9 A.M. to 5 P.M. on Saturdays, and 2 P.M. to midnight on Sundays. There are no time limits and no fees.

Graduates: In 2001, 296 bachelor's degrees were awarded. The most popular majors were nursing (21%), health sciences (11%), and biology (10%). In an average class, 6% graduate in 3 years, 50% in 4 years, 55% in 5 years, and 60% in 6 years. 3 companies recruited on campus in 2000-2001. Of the 2000 graduating class, 31% were enrolled in graduate school within 6 months of graduation and 60% were employed.

Admissions Contact: Brian Dalton, Vice President for Enrollment Management. A video is available. E-mail: *bdalton@css.edu*
Web: *www.css.edu*

COLLEGE OF ST. BENEDICT
(See Saint John's University)

COLLEGE OF VISUAL ARTS C-4
St. Paul, MN 55102 (651) 224-3416
(800) 224-1536; Fax: (651) 224-8854

Full-time: 103 men, 136 women	**Faculty:** 11
Part-time: 10 men, 20 women	**Ph.D.s:** 58%
Graduate: none	**Student/Faculty:** 22 to 1
Year: semesters, summer session	**Tuition:** $12,185
Application Deadline: open	**Room & Board:** n/app
Freshman Class: 121 applied, 106 accepted, 81 enrolled	
SAT I or ACT: recommended	**SPECIAL**

Founded in 1924, the College of Visual Arts is a fully accredited, private college of art and design, offering degrees in communication design, photography, illustration, and fine arts (painting, drawing, sculpture, and printmaking). The library contains 5780 volumes and 27,500 audiovisual forms/CDs, and subscribes to 35 periodicals. Computerized library services include the card catalog, interlibrary loans, and database searching. Special learning facilities include a learning resource center and art gallery. The 3-acre campus is in an urban area in a historic residential area near downtown St. Paul. There are 4 buildings.

Student Life: 93% of undergraduates are from Minnesota. Others are from 8 states and 4 foreign countries. 86% are white.

Housing: There are no residence halls. College-sponsored living facilities include off-campus apartments. All of students commute. Housing assistance is offered. Alcohol is not permitted. All students may keep cars.

Activities: There are no fraternities or sororities. There are some groups and organizations on campus, including professional. Popular campus events include an annual lecture series and exhibit openings.

Sports: There is no sports program at CVA.

Disabled Students: 30% of the campus is accessible. Special parking, specially equipped rest rooms, and lowered drinking fountains are available.

Services: Counseling and information services are available, as is tutoring in most subjects. There is remedial math, reading, and writing.

Campus Safety and Security: Measures include escort service and a security guard for evenings and weekends.

Programs of Study: CVA confers the B.F.A. degree. Bachelor's degrees are awarded in COMMUNICATIONS AND THE ARTS (drawing, fine arts, graphic design, illustration, painting, photography, printmaking, and sculpture).

Required: All students must complete 126 semester hours, including an 18-credit first-year foundation program, 48 hours of liberal arts requirements, 33 to 39 hours in the major, 9 to 12 hours of supportive art/design requirements, and 18 hours of studio electives. A minimum GPA of 2.0 is needed, and projects in art and design must be completed.

Special: Juniors and seniors are encouraged to take internships with various area organizations and businesses. CVA also offers study abroad in France, Italy, and England and a German exchange program.

Faculty/Classroom: 51% of faculty are male; 49%, female. All teach undergraduates. The average class size in an introductory lecture is 20 and in a laboratory, 15.

Admissions: 88% of the 2001-2002 applicants were accepted.

Requirements: The SAT I or ACT is recommended. In addition, applicants must submit a personal statement of interest and a portfolio. An interview and a visit to the college are highly recommended. A GPA of 2.6 is required. Important factors in the admissions decision are personality/intangible qualities, evidence of special talent, and recommendations by school officials.

Procedure: Freshmen are admitted fall and spring. Entrance exams should be taken in fall or spring of the junior year or fall of the senior year. There are early admissions and deferred admissions plans. Application deadlines are open. Notification is sent on a rolling basis. The application fee is $40.

Transfer: 35 transfer students enrolled in 2001-2002. Required are a personal statement, an interview, transcripts from all postsecondary institutions attended, and a faculty review of work done in studio art classes at other postsecondary institutions. 66 credits of 126 must be completed at CVA.

Visiting: There are regularly scheduled orientations for prospective students, consisting of annual open house events, including slide presentations of student artwork, financial aid discussion, a tour of facilities, and student panel discussion. There are guides for informal visits and visitors may sit in on classes. To schedule a visit, contact the Admissions Office.

Financial Aid: In 2001-2002, 80% of all freshmen and 82% of continuing students received some form of financial aid. 61% of freshmen and 68% of continuing students received need-based aid. The average freshman award was $8400. Of that total, scholarships or need-based grants averaged $3100 ($11,851 maximum); and loans averaged $5300

($7125 maximum). 19% of undergraduates work part time. Average annual earnings from campus work are $3000. The average financial indebtedness of the 2001 graduate was $17,000. The FAFSA and the college's own financial statement are required.

International Students: There were 6 international students enrolled in a recent year. They must score 500 on the written TOEFL or 173 on the electronic version and also take the ACT scoring 16, or the college's own entrance exam.

Computers: Student computer labs are networked to allow classes to share and transfer graphics files. All students may access the system. There are no time limits. The fee is $75. It is strongly recommended that all students have personal computers.

Graduates: In a recent year, 28 bachelor's degrees were awarded. The most popular majors were communication design (36%), photography (20%), and fine arts (14%). In an average class, 50% graduate in 4 years, 83% in 5 years, and 100% in 6 years. Of the 2000 graduating class, 75% were employed within 6 months of graduation.

Admissions Contact: Lynn E. Tanaka, Director of Admissions. A video is available. E-mail: *info@cva.edu* Web: *www.cva.edu*

CONCORDIA COLLEGE
(See Concordia University)

CONCORDIA COLLEGE/MOORHEAD A-2

Moorhead, MN 56562 (218) 299-3004 (collect)
(800) 699-9897; Fax: (218) 299-3947

Full-time: 1030 men, 1780 women	**Faculty:** 183; IIB, -$
Part-time: 40 men, 70 women	**Ph.D.s:** 72%
Graduate: none	**Student/Faculty:** 15 to 1
Year: semesters, summer session	**Tuition:** $14,725
Application Deadline: open	**Room & Board:** $4110
Freshman Class: n/av	
SAT I or ACT: required	**COMPETITIVE**

Concordia College, founded in 1891, is a private, liberal arts institution affiliated with the Evangelical Lutheran Church in America. Figures in above capsule are approximate. In addition to regional accreditation, Concordia has baccalaureate program accreditation with ADA, CSWE, NASM, NCATE, and NLN. The library contains 300,000 volumes, 43,296 microform items, and 11,048 audiovisual forms/CDs, and subscribes to 1463 periodicals. Computerized library services include the card catalog, interlibrary loans, and database searching. Special learning facilities include a learning resource center, art gallery, radio station, TV station, and an observatory. The 120-acre campus is in an urban area 240 miles northwest of Minneapolis and St. Paul. Including residence halls, there are 36 buildings.

Student Life: 61% of undergraduates are from Minnesota. Others are from 37 states, 34 foreign countries, and Canada. 96% are from public schools. 93% are white. 81% are Protestant; 13% Catholic. The average age of freshmen is 18; all undergraduates, 20. 21% do not continue beyond their first year; 70% remain to graduate.

Housing: 1850 students can be accommodated in college housing, which includes single-sex dormitories and on-campus apartments. In addition, there are language houses. On-campus housing is guaranteed for the freshman year only, is available on a first-come, first-served basis, and is available on a lottery system for upperclassmen. Priority is given to out-of-town students. 56% of students live on campus; of those, 75% remain on campus on weekends. Alcohol is not permitted. All students may keep cars.

Activities: There are no fraternities or sororities. There are 150 groups on campus, including art, band, cheerleading, choir, chorale, chorus, dance, debate, drama, drill team, ethnic, film, forensics, gay, honors, international, jazz band, literary magazine, musical theater, newspaper, orchestra, pep band, photography, political, professional, radio and TV, religious, social, social service, student government, symphony, and yearbook. Popular campus events include Family Weekend, Winter Meltdown, and Black History Week.

Sports: There are 10 intercollegiate sports for men and 10 for women, and 9 intramural sports for men and 10 for women. Facilities include a health club, a 200-meter indoor track with 4 multipurpose basketball/tennis courts, an indoor swimming pool and sauna, a 7000-seat stadium with an all-weather track, a field house with a 4500-seat auditorium, 2 more basketball courts, 2 auxiliary gyms and a weight room, 6 outdoor tennis courts, softball and soccer competition fields, a baseball complex, and soccer practice fields.

Disabled Students: 95% of the campus is accessible. Wheelchair ramps, elevators, special parking, specially equipped rest rooms, special class scheduling, lowered drinking fountains, and automatic doors are available.

Services: Counseling and information services are available, as is tutoring in most subjects. There is a reader service for the blind and an interpreter service for the deaf.

Campus Safety and Security: Measures include 24-hour foot and vehicle patrol, escort service, informal discussions, and pamphlets/posters/films. There are lighted pathways/sidewalks.

Programs of Study: Concordia confers B.A. and B.M. degrees. Bachelor's degrees are awarded in BIOLOGICAL SCIENCE (biology/biological science), BUSINESS (accounting, business administration and management, international business management, and office supervision and management), COMMUNICATIONS AND THE ARTS (advertising, apparel design, art history and appreciation, classical languages, communications, creative writing, dramatic arts, English, French, German, journalism, Latin, literature, music, music performance, public relations, Spanish, speech/debate/rhetoric, and studio art), COMPUTER AND PHYSICAL SCIENCE (chemistry, computer science, mathematics, and physics), EDUCATION (art, business, elementary, foreign languages, health, home economics, middle school, music, physical, science, secondary, and social studies), ENGINEERING AND ENVIRONMENTAL DESIGN (environmental science and preengineering), HEALTH PROFESSIONS (health, health care administration, medical laboratory technology, nursing, predentistry, premedicine, and preveterinary science), SOCIAL SCIENCE (dietetics, economics, family/consumer studies, history, humanities, international relations, ministries, philosophy, political science/government, prelaw, psychology, religion, Russian and Slavic studies, Scandinavian studies, social work, and sociology). Premedicine, prelaw, and math are the strongest academically. Business administration, communications, and biology are the largest.

Required: All students must maintain a minimum GPA of 2.0 while taking 126 semester hours, including at least 32 in the major. Required courses include freshman English, an introduction to liberal arts, an integration course, and 2 courses each in phys ed and religion. Distribution requirements include 7 courses taken from 5 areas: science and math, social science, foreign language, foundation/premises of civilization, and literature/fine arts.

Special: Cross-registration is offered through the Tri-College University Consortium. Co-op programs and internships are available in most majors, and accelerated degree programs and dual majors are available in all majors. There is a Washington semester and an urban studies semester in Chicago. Study abroad in more than 30 countries, on- and off-campus work-study, a B.A.-B.M. degree in music, and 3-2 and 2-2 engineering degrees with Washington and North Dakota State universities and the University of Minnesota are possible. Nondegree study for special students and pass/fail options are also available. There are 10 national honor societies, a freshman honors program, and 11 departmental honors programs.

Faculty/Classroom: 60% of faculty are male; 40%, female. All teach undergraduates. The average class size in an introductory lecture is 25; in a laboratory, 18; and in a regular course, 19.

Admissions: There were 5 National Merit finalists and 5 semifinalists in a recent year.

Requirements: The SAT I or ACT is required. In addition, 2 character references are required, and an interview is recommended. The GED is accepted. Academic performance and preparation, as evidenced in a high school transcript, is the single most important factor in the admissions decision. AP and CLEP credits are accepted. Important factors in the admissions decision are recommendations by school officials, advanced placement or honor courses, and personality/intangible qualities. Applications are accepted on disk or on-line via the college's home page on the World Wide Web or through CollegeLink.

Procedure: Freshmen are admitted to all sessions. Entrance exams should be taken by the first semester of the senior year. There are early admissions and deferred admissions plans. Application deadlines are open. A waiting list is an active part of the admissions procedure. The fall 2001 application fee was $20.

Transfer: 63 transfer students enrolled in a recent year. Transfer applicants must have a minimum 2.0 GPA, and provide official transcripts from previously attended schools. 32 credits of 126 must be completed at Concordia.

Visiting: There are regularly scheduled orientations for prospective students, including an extensive campus tour and meetings with admissions counselors and faculty members. There are guides for informal visits and visitors may sit in on classes and stay overnight. To schedule a visit, contact the Office of Admissions.

Financial Aid: In a recent year, 85% of all freshmen and 87% of continuing students received some form of financial aid. 70% of freshmen received need-based aid. The average freshman award was $11,611. Of that total, scholarships or need-based grants averaged $6835 ($16,860 maximum); loans averaged $4903 ($18,500 maximum); and work contracts averaged $1136 ($3000 maximum). 52% of undergraduates work part time. Average annual earnings from campus work are $1058. The average financial indebtedness of a recent year's graduate was $18,135. Concordia is a member of CSS. The FAFSA and the college's own financial statement are required. The fall application deadline is April 1.

International Students: There were 106 international students enrolled in a recent year. The school actively recruits these students. They must score 500 on the written TOEFL.

Computers: The mainframe is a Unisys A2400 Model 311. IBM and Mac PCs are available in 16 computer labs on campus and in each residence hall. All students are assigned an e-mail account. and have access to about 265 computers, which all have Internet access. All students may access the system 20 to 24 hours per day. There are no time limits and no fees.

Graduates: In a recent year, 624 bachelor's degrees were awarded. The most popular majors were business administration (16%), languages (14%), and English (11%). In an average class, 59% graduate in 4 years, 67% in 5 years, and 68% in 6 years. 86 companies recruited on campus in a recent year.

Admissions Contact: Office of Admissions, Concordia College/ Moorhead. E-mail: *admissions@gloria.cord.edu* Web: *www.cord.edu*

CONCORDIA UNIVERSITY

St. Paul, MN 55104-5494 C-4

(651) 641-8718

(800) 333-4705; Fax: (651) 659-0207

Full-time: 555 men, 817 women	**Faculty:** 96
Part-time: 50 men, 89 women	**Ph.D.s:** 77%
Graduate: 88 men, 174 women	**Student/Faculty:** 16 to 1
Year: semesters, summer session	**Tuition:** $14,752
Application Deadline: August 1	**Room & Board:** $5160
Freshman Class: 937 applied, 503 accepted, 200 enrolled	
ACT: recommended	**COMPETITIVE**

Concordia University, founded in 1893 and a unit of the Concordia University system, is a private institution affiliated with the Lutheran Church – Missouri Synod and offering programs in teacher education, business, church vocations, and the liberal arts. There are 2 undergraduate schools and 1 graduate school. In addition to regional accreditation, CSP has baccalaureate program accreditation with NCATE. The library contains 127,146 volumes, 10,090 microform items, and 6441 audiovisual forms/ CDs, and subscribes to 406 periodicals. Computerized library services include the card catalog, interlibrary loans, and database searching. Special learning facilities include a learning resource center, art gallery, and natural history museum. The 27-acre campus is in an urban area in the Midway area of St. Paul. Including residence halls, there are 28 buildings.

Student Life: 72% of undergraduates are from Minnesota. Others are from 38 states and Canada. 75% are from public schools. 84% are white. 44% are Protestant; 12% Catholic. The average age of freshmen is 18; all undergraduates, 23. 39% do not continue beyond their first year.

Housing: 481 students can be accommodated in college housing, which includes single-sex dormitories, on-campus apartments, and married-student housing. On-campus housing is guaranteed for the freshman year only and is available on a first-come, first-served basis. Priority is given to out-of-town students. 70% of students commute. Alcohol is not permitted. All students may keep cars.

Activities: There are no fraternities or sororities. There are 40 groups on campus, including art, band, cheerleading, choir, drama, ethnic, jazz band, musical theater, newspaper, pep band, religious, social, student government, and yearbook.

Sports: There are 6 intercollegiate sports for men and 7 for women, and 5 intramural sports for men and 5 for women. Facilities include a 4500-seat stadium, a 1200-seat gym, a health and wellness center, a rock climbing wall, a 200-meter track, and several playing fields for various sports.

Disabled Students: 95% of the campus is accessible. Wheelchair ramps, elevators, special parking, specially equipped rest rooms, special class scheduling, lowered drinking fountains, lowered telephones, and touch-pad doors are available.

Services: Counseling and information services are available, as is tutoring in every subject. There is remedial math, reading, and writing.

Campus Safety and Security: Measures include 24-hour foot and vehicle patrol, self-defense education, escort service, and informal discussions. There are pamphlets/posters/films, emergency telephones, and lighted pathways/sidewalks.

Programs of Study: CSP confers B.A., and B.B.A. degrees. Associate and master's degrees are also awarded. Bachelor's degrees are awarded in BIOLOGICAL SCIENCE (biology/biological science), BUSINESS (accounting, banking and finance, business administration and management, management information systems, marketing management, and organizational behavior), COMMUNICATIONS AND THE ARTS (art, art history and appreciation, communications, dramatic arts, English, music, and studio art), COMPUTER AND PHYSICAL SCIENCE (natural sciences), EDUCATION (early childhood, elementary, English, mathematics, middle school, music, physical, science, secondary, and social studies), ENGINEERING AND ENVIRONMENTAL DESIGN (environmental science), SOCIAL SCIENCE (child care/child and family studies, criminal justice, history, psychology, religion, religious education, religious music, sociology, and theological studies). Elementary education is the strongest academically. Elementary education and business are the largest.

Required: To graduate, students must complete 128 credit hours in the form of 1 major or 2 minors. GPA varies from 2.0 to 2.75 and required hours in the major vary from 32 to 44, depending on the program. The core curriculum consists of 42 hours of liberal arts courses.

Special: CSP offers cross-registration with other area colleges and other members of the Concordia University system, internships in most programs, and study abroad in England, India, and Mexico. Accelerated degree programs, B.A. degrees, and interdisciplinary majors are also available. Credit for life experience, nondegree study, and pass/fail options are possible.

Faculty/Classroom: 66% of faculty are male; 34%, female. 95% teach undergraduates. No introductory courses are taught by graduate students.

Admissions: 54% of the 2001-2002 applicants were accepted. 25% of the current freshmen were in the top fifth of their class; 53% were in the top two fifths. 3 freshmen graduated first in their class.

Requirements: The ACT is recommended. In addition, applicants are required to have 4 years of English, 2 each of math, science, fine arts, and history/social studies, and 1 each of health or phys ed. An interview and essay are recommended. 2 letters of recommendation are required. The GED is accepted. CSP requires applicants to be in the upper 50% of their class. A GPA of 2.0 is required. AP and CLEP credits are accepted. Important factors in the admissions decision are recommendations by school officials, leadership record, and extracurricular activities record. Applications are accepted on-line via CollegeNET, CollegeLink, or the school's web site.

Procedure: Freshmen are admitted to all sessions. Entrance exams should be taken during the senior year. There is a deferred admissions plan. Applications should be filed by August 1 for fall entry and December 1 for spring entry. The fall 2001 application fee was $25. Notification is sent on a rolling basis.

Transfer: 92 transfer students enrolled in 2001-2002. Applicants must have a 2.0 GPA and submit 2 letters of recommendation. Students with fewer than 1 year of college credits must also submit ACT scores and an official high school transcript. 32 credits of 128 must be completed at CSP.

Visiting: There are regularly scheduled orientations for prospective students, including a 3-day program before classes begin, with class visits, lunch, and meetings with professors. There are guides for informal visits and visitors may sit in on classes and stay overnight. To schedule a visit, contact the Director of Freshman Admission at *severeid@csp.edu*

Financial Aid: In 2001-2002, 93% of all freshmen and 80% of continuing students received some form of financial aid. 67% of freshmen and 74% of continuing students received need-based aid. The average freshman award was $16,707. Of that total, scholarships or need-based grants averaged $9451 ($21,052 maximum); loans averaged $3475 ($6625 maximum); and work contracts averaged $1679 ($1750 maximum). 33% of undergraduates work part time. Average annual earnings from campus work are $999. The average financial indebtedness of the 2001 graduate was $12,784. The FAFSA, the college's own financial statement, and a federal tax return are required. The fall application deadline is March 1.

International Students: There are 2 international students enrolled. The school actively recruits these students. They must score 500 on the written TOEFL or 173 on the electronic version or take the MELAB or Level 109 of ELS.

Computers: The mainframe is a DEC ALPHA 2100 200. All full-time undergraduates are issued IBM ThinkPad computers. All students may access the system during the hours the media center and science building are open. There are no time limits and no fees.

Graduates: In 2001, 450 bachelor's degrees were awarded. The most popular majors were organizational management (36%), teacher education (16%), and marketing (12%). In an average class, 38% graduate in 6 years. 25 companies recruited on campus in 2000-2001.

Admissions Contact: Rhonda Behm-Severeid, Director of Freshman Admission. E-mail: *admiss@csp.edu* Web: *www.csp.edu*

GUSTAVUS ADOLPHUS COLLEGE

St. Peter, MN 56082-1498 C-4

(507) 933-7676

(800) GUSTAVU; Fax: (507) 933-6270

Full-time: 1087 men, 1481 women	**Faculty:** 174; IIB, av$
Part-time: 6 men, 18 women	**Ph.D.s:** 87%
Graduate: none	**Student/Faculty:** 15 to 1
Year: 4-1-4	**Tuition:** $19,290
Application Deadline: May 1	**Room & Board:** $4900
Freshman Class: 2009 applied, 1637 accepted, 670 enrolled	
SAT I Verbal/Math: 600/620	**ACT:** 26 **VERY COMPETITIVE+**

Gustavus Adolphus College, founded in 1862, is a private liberal arts college affiliated with the Lutheran Church. In addition to regional accreditation, Gustavus has baccalaureate program accreditation with NASM, NCATE, and NLN. The library contains 273,748 volumes, 31,385 microform items, and 15,407 audiovisual forms/CDs, and subscribes to 1072 periodicals. Computerized library services include the card catalog, interlibrary loans, and database searching. Special learning facilities include an art gallery, radio station, and an arboretum. The 330-acre campus is in a small town 65 miles southwest of Minneapolis. Including residence halls, there are 55 buildings.

Student Life: 71% of undergraduates are from Minnesota. Others are from 45 states, 24 foreign countries, and Canada. 93% are from public schools. 93% are white. 79% are Protestant; 19% Catholic. The average age of freshmen is 18; all undergraduates, 20. 9% do not continue beyond their first year; 77% remain to graduate.

Housing: 1960 students can be accommodated in college housing, which includes coed dormitories and on-campus apartments. In addition, there are language houses and special-interest houses. On-campus housing is guaranteed for all 4 years. 85% of students live on campus; of those, 85% remain on campus on weekends. Upperclassmen may keep cars.

Activities: 27% of men and about 1% of women belong to 7 local fraternities; 22% of women belong to 5 local sororities. There are 85 groups on campus, including band, cheerleading, choir, chorus, dance, debate, drama, ethnic, forensics, gay, honors, international, jazz band, literary magazine, newspaper, orchestra, pep band, political, professional, radio and TV, religious, social, social service, student government, and yearbook. Popular campus events include Christmas in Christ Chapel and Frost Week.

Sports: There are 12 intercollegiate sports for men and 13 for women, and 17 intramural sports for men and 10 for women. Facilities include an ice arena, an Olympic-size pool, a gymnastics area, an indoor tennis center, an arena, playing fields, racquetball and tennis courts, a weight room, an indoor running track, and varsity and intramural fields for soccer, softball, baseball, lacrosse, rugby, and ultimate frisbee.

Disabled Students: 90% of the campus is accessible. Wheelchair ramps, elevators, special parking, specially equipped rest rooms, special class scheduling, and lowered drinking fountains are available.

Services: Counseling and information services are available, as is tutoring in most subjects and a writing lab.

Campus Safety and Security: Measures include 24-hour foot and vehicle patrol, escort service, shuttle buses, and informal discussions. There are pamphlets/posters/films, emergency telephones, and lighted pathways/sidewalks.

Programs of Study: Gustavus confers the B.A. degree. Bachelor's degrees are awarded in BIOLOGICAL SCIENCE (biochemistry and biology/biological science), BUSINESS (accounting, business administration and management, business economics, and international business management), COMMUNICATIONS AND THE ARTS (classics, communications, dance, dramatic arts, English, fine arts, French, German, music, Russian, Scandinavian languages, Spanish, and speech/debate/rhetoric), COMPUTER AND PHYSICAL SCIENCE (chemistry, computer science, geology, mathematics, and physics), EDUCATION (art, business, elementary, foreign languages, health, middle school, music, science, and secondary), HEALTH PROFESSIONS (nursing, physical therapy, predentistry, and premedicine), SOCIAL SCIENCE (anthropology, criminal justice, economics, geography, history, philosophy, political science/government, prelaw, psychology, religion, social science, and sociology). Physical science and social science are the strongest academically. Business, biology, and social science are the largest.

Required: All students are required to complete 35 courses totaling 140 semester hours, including 3 January-term courses and 1 course in phys ed. Core and distribution requirements include a first-term seminar and 2 additional writing classes, 4 courses in language and humanities, 2 each in fine arts, math/science, social science, and foreign culture, and 1 in religion. A minimum GPA of 2.0 is necessary for graduation. A total of 7 to 11 courses is required in the major.

Special: Co-op programs in nursing with St. Olaf College and cross-registration with Minnesota State University are available. The college offers internships, a Washington semester, study abroad in 22 countries, student-designed majors, nondegree study, and pass/fail options for some courses. A 3-2 engineering degree program with Washington University and the University of Minnesota is offered. The Curriculum II core offers a 12-course interdisciplinary program. There are 16 national honor societies, including Phi Beta Kappa, and 12 departmental honors programs.

Faculty/Classroom: 60% of faculty are male; 40%, female. 97% both teach and do research. The average class size in an introductory lecture is 25; in a laboratory, 15; and in a regular course, 15.

Admissions: 81% of the 2001-2002 applicants were accepted. The SAT I scores for the 2001-2002 freshman class were: Verbal--14% below 500, 34% between 500 and 599, 34% between 600 and 700, and 18% above 700; Math--10% below 500, 34% between 500 and 599, 41% between 600 and 700, and 15% above 700. The ACT scores were 8% below 21, 22% between 21 and 23, 31% between 24 and 26, 16% between 27 and 28, and 23% above 28. 60% of the current freshmen were in the top fifth of their class; 89% were in the top two fifths. There were 18 National Merit finalists and 6 semifinalists. 58 freshmen graduated first in their class.

Requirements: The SAT I or ACT is required. In addition, in addition, applicants must have completed 4 years of English, 3 each of math and science, and 2 each of a foreign language, history, and social studies. AP credits are accepted. Important factors in the admissions decision are advanced placement or honor courses, evidence of special talent, and parents or siblings attending the school. Applications are accepted on-line via CollegeNET or the school's own web site.

Procedure: Freshmen are admitted fall, winter, and spring. Entrance exams should be taken in the fall of the senior year. There are early decision, early admissions, and deferred admissions plans. Early decision applications should be filed by November 15; regular applications, by May 1 for fall entry, December 15 for winter entry, and January 15 for spring entry. The fall 2001 application fee was $25. Notification of early decision is sent December 1; regular decision, on a rolling basis. 141 early decision candidates were accepted for the 2001-2002 class.

Transfer: 46 transfer students enrolled in 2001-2002. Transfer applicants must have earned a 2.4 GPA at their previous college. 72 credits of 140 must be completed at Gustavus.

Visiting: There are regularly scheduled orientations for prospective students, consisting of an interview, a tour, and meetings with faculty and students. There are guides for informal visits and visitors may sit in on classes and stay overnight. To schedule a visit, contact the Admissions Office at *admission@gustavus.edu*

Financial Aid: In 2001-2002, 93% of all freshmen and 82% of continuing students received some form of financial aid. 63% of all students received need-based aid. The average freshman award was $13,263. Of that total, scholarships or need-based grants averaged $7963; loans averaged $3500 ($4500 maximum); and work contracts averaged $1800 (maximum). 71% of undergraduates work part time. Average annual earnings from campus work are $1600. The average financial indebtedness of the 2001 graduate was $16,900. Gustavus is a member of CSS. The FAFSA and the college's own financial statement are required. The fall application deadline is April 1.

International Students: There were 45 international students enrolled in a recent year. The school actively recruits these students. They must score 550 on the written TOEFL or 213 on the electronic version or take the MELAB.

Computers: The mainframes are a DEC MicroVAX 3600 and a MicroVAX II. Students have access to 6 computer networks, some of which are connected with the Minnesota State University System. These include 55 Mac, 50 IBM, and 27 NeXT PCs located in the library and various academic buildings. There is also an electronic music lab. All students may access the system. There are no time limits and no fees. It is strongly recommended that all students have personal computers.

Graduates: In 2001, 542 bachelor's degrees were awarded. The most popular majors were communications (9%), biology (8%), and management (8%). In an average class, 1% graduate in 3 years, 78% in 4 years, 81% in 5 years, and 81% in 6 years. 40 companies recruited on campus in 2000-2001. Of the 2000 graduating class, 30% were enrolled in graduate school within 6 months of graduation and 65% were employed.

Admissions Contact: Mark H. Anderson, Dean of Admission. A video is available. E-mail: *markande@gustavus.edu* Web: *www.gustavus.edu*

HAMLINE UNIVERSITY — C-4
St. Paul, MN 55104-1284 — (651) 523-2207
(800) 753-9753; Fax: (651) 523-2458

Full-time: 652 men, 1115 women	**Faculty:** 104; IIB, +$
Part-time: 26 men, 80 women	**Ph.D.s:** 100%
Graduate: 660 men, 1590 women	**Student/Faculty:** 11 to 1
Year: trimesters, summer session	**Tuition:** $17,664
Application Deadline: May 1	**Room & Board:** $5675
Freshman Class: 1460 applied, 1159 accepted, 421 enrolled	
SAT I Verbal/Math: recommended	**ACT:** required **COMPETITIVE+**

Hamline University, founded in 1854, is a private liberal arts and sciences university affiliated with the United Methodist Church. There are graduate schools. In addition to regional accreditation, Hamline has baccalaureate program accreditation with NASM and NCATE. The 2 libraries contain 292,178 volumes, 931,602 microform items, and 2642 audiovisual forms/CDs, and subscribe to 3858 periodicals. Computerized library services include the card catalog, interlibrary loans, and database searching. Special learning facilities include a learning resource center, art gallery, centers for environmental education and applied research, the Jewish History Society Archives, and the Center for Excellence in Urban Teaching. The 50-acre campus is in an urban area between the downtowns of Minneapolis and St. Paul. Including residence halls, there are 27 buildings.

Student Life: 66% of undergraduates are from Minnesota. Others are from 35 states, 37 foreign countries, and Canada. 78% are from public schools. 72% are white. 23% are Catholic; 19% Protestant. The average age of freshmen is 18; all undergraduates, 21. 20% do not continue beyond their first year.

Housing: 917 students can be accommodated in college housing, which includes coed dormitories, on-campus apartments, and sorority houses. In addition, there are smoke-free, substance-free, and living/learning floors, language houses and special-interest houses. On-campus housing is guaranteed for all 4 years. 53% of students live on campus; of those, 90% remain on campus on weekends. All students may keep cars.

Activities: 55% of women belong to 1 local sorority. There are no fraternities. There are 80 groups on campus, including art, band, cheerleading, chess, choir, chorale, chorus, computers, dance, drama, ethnic, film, gay, honors, international, jazz band, literary magazine, marching band, musical theater, newspaper, orchestra, pep band, political, professional, religious, social, social service, student government, symphony, and yearbook. Popular campus events include World Fest, Community Service Week, and Fall Fair.

Sports: There are 9 intercollegiate sports for men and 9 for women, and 8 intramural sports for men and 10 for women. Facilities include a stadium, a field house and swimming pool, a playing field, and an athletic center.

Disabled Students: 75% of the campus is accessible. Wheelchair ramps, elevators, special parking, specially equipped rest rooms, special class scheduling, lowered drinking fountains, and lowered telephones are available.

Services: Counseling and information services are available, as is tutoring in every subject . There is a reader service for the blind and remedial math and writing.

Campus Safety and Security: Measures include 24-hour foot and vehicle patrol, self-defense education, escort service, and informal discussions. There are pamphlets/posters/films, emergency telephones, and lighted pathways/sidewalks.

Programs of Study: Hamline confers the B.A. degree. Master's and doctoral degrees are also awarded. Bachelor's degrees are awarded in BIOLOGICAL SCIENCE (biology/biological science), BUSINESS (business administration and management and international business management), COMMUNICATIONS AND THE ARTS (art, art history and appreciation, communications, dramatic arts, English, fine arts, French, German, music, and Spanish), COMPUTER AND PHYSICAL SCIENCE (chemistry, mathematics, and physics), EDUCATION (athletic training, elementary, foreign languages, physical, science, and secondary), ENGINEERING AND ENVIRONMENTAL DESIGN (environmental science), HEALTH PROFESSIONS (predentistry and premedicine), SOCIAL SCIENCE (anthropology, criminal justice, East Asian studies, economics, European studies, history, international relations, Latin American studies, paralegal studies, philosophy, political science/government, prelaw, psychology, religion, social science, sociology, urban studies, and women's studies). Prelaw, premedicine, and international relations are the strongest academically. Psychology, English, and political science are the largest.

Required: To graduate, students must complete 32 course credits (128 semester hours) with a minimum overall GPA of 2.0. In their first year, all students are required to take a freshman seminar and freshman English, and demonstrate computer literacy. All students must also take 3 writing-intensive courses, 1 each year following, and 3 courses on human or cultural diversity; 2 speaking-intensive courses and 2 courses each in fine arts, humanities, natural sciences, and social sciences; and 1 course each in computer utilization and formal reasoning. An independent study project and an internship are also required.

Special: Cross-registration with Augsburg, Macalester, Saint Catherine, and Saint Thomas Colleges is possible. Students may select cooperative programs, study abroad, a Washington semester with American University, dual majors, student-designed majors, and pass/fail options. Students may earn a 3-2 or 4-2 engineering degree at the University of Minnesota or Washington University. On-campus work-study is available, as are extensive internship opportunities on and off campus. There are 18 national honor societies, including Phi Beta Kappa, a freshman honors program, and 10 departmental honors programs.

Faculty/Classroom: 50% of faculty are male; 50%, female. All teach undergraduates. No introductory courses are taught by graduate students. The average class size in an introductory lecture is 27; in a laboratory, 14; and in a regular course, 19.

Admissions: 79% of the 2001-2002 applicants were accepted. 56% of the current freshmen were in the top fifth of their class; 72% were in the top two fifths. There were 6 National Merit finalists and 6 semifinalists. 16 freshmen graduated first in their class.

Requirements: The ACT is required and the SAT I is recommended. In addition, it is recommended that candidates for admission complete 4 years of English with 1 year of college preparatory writing, 3 years each of math, lab science, and social science, and 2 years of a foreign language. AP and CLEP credits are accepted. Important factors in the admissions decision are advanced placement or honor courses, recommendations by school officials, and leadership record. Applications are accepted on-line at *http://lutsen.hamline.edu/cla/admission/applyonline.index.html*

Procedure: Freshmen are admitted in the fall. Entrance exams should be taken by February of the senior year. There are early admissions and deferred admissions plans. Applications should be filed by May 1 for fall entry. Notification of early decision is sent December 15; regular decision, on a rolling basis.

Transfer: 135 transfer students enrolled in 2001-2002. 42 credits of 128 must be completed at Hamline.

Visiting: There are guides for informal visits and visitors may sit in on classes and stay overnight. To schedule a visit, contact the Admissions Office.

Financial Aid: In 2001-2002, 71% of all freshmen and 70% of continuing students received some form of financial aid. 70% of all students received need-bases aid. The average freshman award was $16,837. Of that total, scholarships or need-based grants averaged $13,970 ($17,414 maximum); loans averaged $744; and work contracts averaged $2123 ($2500 maximum). All undergraduates work part time. Average annual earnings from campus work are $2100. The average financial indebtedness of the 2001 graduate was $18,708. The FAFSA and the college's own financial statement are required. The fall application deadline is March 15.

International Students: There are 68 international students enrolled. The school actively recruits these students. They must score 550 on the written TOEFL or take the MELAB.

Computers: The mainframe is a Sequent NUMA-Q 2000 high-end Enterprise Server. There are 360 PCs available for student use in the computer center, the library, and classrooms. All students may access the system 24 hours a day, year-round. There are no time limits and no fees.

Graduates: In 2001, 318 bachelor's degrees were awarded. The most popular majors were psychology (13%), business (8%), and biology (6%). In an average class, 3% graduate in 3 years, 55% in 4 years, 60% in 5 years, and 62% in 6 years. Of the 2000 graduating class, 21% were enrolled in graduate school within 6 months of graduation and 91% were employed.

Admissions Contact: Steven Bjork, Director of Admissions.
E-mail: *cla-admis@gw.hamline.edu* Web: *www.hamline.edu*

MACALESTER COLLEGE — C-4
St. Paul, MN 55105 — (651) 696-6357
(800) 231-7974; Fax: (651) 696-6724

Full-time: 745 men, 1024 women	**Faculty:** 148; IIB, +$
Part-time: 14 men, 39 women	**Ph.D.s:** 93%
Graduate: none	**Student/Faculty:** 12 to 1
Year: semesters	**Tuition:** $22,608
Application Deadline: January 15	**Room & Board:** $6206
Freshman Class: 3480 applied, 1749 accepted, 505 enrolled	
SAT I Verbal/Math: 690/660	**ACT:** 29
	HIGHLY COMPETITIVE+

Macalester College, founded in 1855, is a nonsectarian liberal arts and sciences institution affiliated with the United Presbyterian Church. In addition to regional accreditation, Macalester has baccalaureate program accreditation with NASM. The library contains 417,732 volumes, 73,509 microform items, and 9753 audiovisual forms/CDs, and subscribes to 4558 periodicals. Computerized library services include the card catalog, interlibrary loans, and database searching. Special learning facilities include a learning resource center, art gallery, radio station, and a 280-acre natural history study area 25 miles from campus. The 53-acre campus is in an urban area midway between downtown St. Paul and Minneapolis. Including residence halls, there are 36 buildings.

Student Life: 77% of undergraduates are from out of state, mostly the Midwest. Others are from 50 states, 78 foreign countries, and Canada. 66% are from public schools. 74% are white; 14% foreign nationals. The average age of freshmen is 18; all undergraduates, 20. 9% do not continue beyond their first year; 78% remain to graduate.

Housing: 1225 students can be accommodated in college housing, which includes single-sex and coed dormitories and on-campus apartments. In addition, there are language houses, special-interest houses, a vegetarian co-op, and a Hebrew house. On-campus housing is available on a lottery system for upperclassmen. 70% of students live on campus; of those, 99% remain on campus on weekends. Upperclassmen may keep cars.

Activities: There are no fraternities or sororities. There are 70 groups on campus, including art, bagpipe band, band, chess, choir, chorale, chorus, computers, dance, debate, drama, ethnic, forensics, gay, honors, international, jazz band, literary magazine, musical theater, newspaper, opera, orchestra, pep band, photography, political, professional, radio and TV, religious, social, social service, student government, and symphony. Popular campus events include Scottish Country Fair, Volunteer Service Week, and Fall Festival.

Sports: There are 10 intercollegiate sports for men and 11 for women, and 20 intramural sports for men and 20 for women. Facilities include a field house, a 650-seat gym, a 4000-seat stadium, a swimming pool, 2 racquetball courts, 6 tennis courts, a dance studio, a track, 2 weight rooms, and baseball and softball diamonds.

Disabled Students: 80% of the campus is accessible. Wheelchair ramps, elevators, special parking, specially equipped rest rooms, special class scheduling, lowered drinking fountains, and lowered telephones are available.

Services: Counseling and information services are available, as is tutoring in most subjects. There is a reader service for the blind, and remedial math, reading, and writing.

Campus Safety and Security: Measures include 24-hour foot and vehicle patrol, self-defense education, escort service, and informal discussions. There are pamphlets/posters/films, emergency telephones, lighted pathways/sidewalks, and a security site on the school's web site.

Programs of Study: Macalester confers the B.A. degree. Bachelor's degrees are awarded in BIOLOGICAL SCIENCE (biology/biological science and neurosciences), COMMUNICATIONS AND THE ARTS (art, classics, communications, dramatic arts, English, French, Japanese, linguistics, music, Russian, and Spanish), COMPUTER AND PHYSICAL SCIENCE (chemistry, computer science, geology, mathematics, and physics), ENGINEERING AND ENVIRONMENTAL DESIGN (environmental science), SOCIAL SCIENCE (anthropology, Asian/Oriental studies, economics, geography, German area studies, history, international relations, Latin American studies, philosophy, political science/government, psychology, religion, Russian and Slavic studies, sociology, urban studies, and women's studies). International studies, economics, and biology are the strongest academically. Math/computer science, Spanish, and history are the largest.

Required: All students are required to complete 128 semester hours, with 32 to 44 in the major, and an overall minimum GPA of 2.0. Required courses include 12 hours in humanities and fine arts, 8 hours in natural science and/or math, 8 hours in social science, 4 hours each in domestic diversity and international diversity, and a first-year course. Second language proficiency equivalent to 2 years of college-level language must be shown, and every major requires a capstone experience.

Special: Cross-registration at Minneapolis College of Art and Design is offered; in addition, the college belongs to several consortiums, including the Associated Colleges of the Twin Cities. There also are cooperative programs in liberal arts and architecture with Washington University in St. Louis, engineering with the same school and the University of Minnesota, and nursing with Rush-Presbyterian-St. Luke's Medical Center in Chicago. Internships are available in government, financial services, law, medicine, research, the arts, and other fields. Students may study abroad in more than 40 countries. Credit by exam under supervision of individual instructors, nondegree study, student-designed majors, and pass/fail options for no more than 1 course per semester also are available. There are 15 national honor societies, including Phi Beta Kappa.

Faculty/Classroom: 54% of faculty are male; 46%, female. All teach undergraduates and 90% both teach and do research. The average class size in an introductory lecture is 19; in a laboratory, 11; and in a regular course, 14.

Admissions: 50% of the 2001-2002 applicants were accepted. The SAT I scores for the 2001-2002 freshman class were: Verbal--8% between 500 and 599, 52% between 600 and 700, and 40% above 700; Math--17% between 500 and 599, 58% between 600 and 700, and 25% above 700. The ACT scores were 2% between 21 and 23, 13% between 24 and 26, 23% between 27 and 28, and 62% above 28. 89% of the current freshmen were in the top fifth of their class; 99% were in the top two fifths. There were 51 National Merit finalists and 7 semifinalists. 55 freshmen graduated first in their class.

Requirements: The SAT I or ACT is required. In addition, applicants should have earned at least 16 academic credits, including 4 years of English and 3 each in math, science, foreign language, and social studies/history. The college also expects applicants to have taken honors, AP, or IB courses where available. An essay is required, and an interview is recommended. AP credits are accepted. Important factors in the admissions decision are advanced placement or honor courses, extracurricular activities record, and recommendations by school officials. Applications are accepted on-line via Next Stop College, Common App., and CollegeNET.

Procedure: Freshmen are admitted in the fall. Entrance exams should be taken in the fall of the senior year. There are early decision and deferred admissions plans. Early decision applications should be filed by November 15; regular applications, by January 15 for fall entry, along with a $40 fee. Notification of early decision is sent December 15; regular decision, April 1. 113 early decision candidates were accepted for the 2001-2002 class. 4% of all applicants are on a waiting list; none were accepted in 2001.

Transfer: 21 transfer students enrolled in 2001-2002. Transfer students usually must present a GPA of 3.33 (B+), a secondary school transcript, and recommendations from 2 teachers and from the dean of students. In addition, the SAT I or ACT is required, and an interview is recommended. Transferable grades are evaluated on the basis of the nature and quality of work. Generally, a grade of C or better is accepted. 64 credits of 128 must be completed at Macalester.

Visiting: There are regularly scheduled orientations for prospective students, including interviews, information sessions, a class visit, and a tour of campus. There are guides for informal visits and visitors may sit in on classes and stay overnight. To schedule a visit, contact the Admissions Office.

Financial Aid: In 2001-2002, 74% of all freshmen and 80% of continuing students received some form of financial aid. 68% of freshmen and 78% of continuing students received need-based aid. The average freshman award was $17,975. Of that total, scholarships or need-based grants averaged $15,212 ($29,000 maximum); loans averaged $1343 ($3500 maximum); and work contracts averaged $1420 ($1500 maximum). 66% of undergraduates work part time. Average annual earnings from campus work are $1240. The average financial indebtedness of the 2001 graduate was $14,200. Macalester is a member of CSS. The CSS/Profile or FAFSA, parents' W-2s and tax forms, and student tax forms are required. The fall application deadline is February 8.

International Students: There are 258 international students enrolled. The school actively recruits these students. They must score 573 on the written TOEFL or 230 on the electronic version or take the MELAB.

Computers: The mainframe is a DEC ALPHA 2000 server. The central computer provides access to the Internet and to e-mail. There are approximately 300 PCs and Macs available for general student use. All students may access the system 24 hours a day. There are no time limits and no fees.

Graduates: In 2001, 403 bachelor's degrees were awarded. The most popular majors were biology (11%), economics (11%), and psychology (10%). In an average class, 69% graduate in 4 years, 76% in 5 years, and 79% in 6 years. 97 companies recruited on campus in 2000-2001. Of the 2000 graduating class, 29% were enrolled in graduate school within 6 months of graduation and 67% were employed.

Admissions Contact: Lorne T. Robinson, Dean of Admissions and Financial Aid. E-mail: *admissions@macalester.edu*
Web: *www.macalester.edu*

METROPOLITAN STATE UNIVERSITY — C-4

St. Paul, MN 55106 — **(651) 772-7664; Fax: (651) 772-7519**

Full-time: 673 men, 866 women	**Faculty:** 103; IIA, -$
Part-time: 1561 men, 2562 women	**Ph.D.s:** 68%
Graduate: 184 men, 164 women	**Student/Faculty:** 15 to 1
Year: semesters, summer session	**Tuition:** $2943 ($6462)
Application Deadline: open	**Room & Board:** n/app
Freshman Class: n/av	
SAT I or ACT: required	**SPECIAL**

Metropolitan State University, founded in 1971, is a public institution primarily serving working adults through a variety of majors and individually designed degree programs. There are 4 undergraduate and 2 graduate schools. Figures in the above capsule are approximate. In addition to regional accreditation, Metro State has baccalaureate program accreditation with NLN. Computerized library services include interlibrary loans and database searching. Special learning facilities include a learning resource center. The campus is in an urban area. It is composed of several small dispersed sites throughout the Twin Cities Metro.

Student Life: 99% of undergraduates are from Minnesota. Others are from 12 states, 53 foreign countries, and Canada. 95% are from public schools. 42% are white. The average age of freshmen is 28; all undergraduates, 33.

Housing: There are no residence halls. All students commute. Alcohol is not permitted.

Activities: There are no fraternities or sororities. There are 18 groups on campus, including ethnic, gay, honors, international, newspaper, professional, religious, and student government.

Sports: There is no sports program at Metro State.

Disabled Students: Elevators, special parking, specially equipped rest rooms, lowered drinking fountains, and lowered telephones are available.

Services: Counseling and information services are available, as is tutoring in some subjects, including accounting, finance, economics, writing, math, and ESL.

Campus Safety and Security: Measures include an escort service.

Programs of Study: Metro State confers B.A., B.S., and B.S.N. degrees. Master's degrees are also awarded. Bachelor's degrees are awarded in BIOLOGICAL SCIENCE (biology/biological science), BUSINESS (accounting, banking and finance, business administration and management, hospitality management services, human resources, international business management, management information systems, and marketing management), COMMUNICATIONS AND THE ARTS (advertising, communications, dramatic arts, English, public relations, and technical and business writing), COMPUTER AND PHYSICAL SCIENCE (applied mathematics, computer science, and information sciences and systems), HEALTH PROFESSIONS (nursing), SOCIAL SCIENCE (child psychology/development, counseling/psychology, criminal justice, economics, ethnic studies, history, human services, law enforcement and corrections, liberal arts/general studies, philosophy, psychology, public administration, social science, social work, and women's studies). Nursing is the strongest academically. Accounting and business administration are the largest.

Required: To graduate, all students must complete 120 to 124 semester credits, with a varying number of hours required in the major, 40 credits in a core curriculum, and a 2.0 GPA.

Special: Internships and student-designed programs are offered.

Faculty/Classroom: 51% of faculty are male; 49%, female. All teach undergraduates. No introductory courses are taught by graduate students. The average class size in an introductory lecture is 24; in a laboratory, 24; and in a regular course, 19.

Requirements: The SAT I or ACT is required. In addition, Metro State requires applicants to be in the upper 50% of their class or have ACT, PSAT, or SAT I scores at or above the national median. Applicants not meeting these requirements will be considered in the alternative admissions process. The GED is accepted. Metro State requires applicants to be in the upper 50% of their class. A GPA of 3.0 is required. CLEP credit is accepted.

Procedure: Freshmen are admitted to all sessions. There is a deferred admissions plan. Application deadlines are open. Application fee is $20.

Transfer: Applicants must have at least a C average. 30 credits of 120 to 124 must be completed at Metro State.

Visiting: There are regularly scheduled orientations for prospective students.

Financial Aid: In a recent year, 10% of all students received some form of financial aid, including need-based aid. The average freshman award was $3000. 3% of undergraduates work part time. Average annual earnings from campus work are $3000. The average financial indebtedness of a recent graduate was $10,100. Metro State is a member of CSS. The FAFSA is required. The fall application deadline is August 1.

International Students: There were 112 international students enrolled in a recent year. They must score 500 on the written TOEFL or take the MELAB.

Computers: There are 2 student computer centers with a total of 180 Macintosh and IBM PCs. Software is accessed through servers. All students may access the system numerous hours on weekdays and weekends. There are no time limits. The fee $1 per quarter credit hour. It is strongly recommended that all students have a personal computer.

Graduates: In a recent year, 857 bachelor's degrees were awarded. The most popular majors were individualized (24%), business (9%), and accounting (6%). 187 companies recruited on campus in a recent year.

Admissions Contact: Vang Vang, Admissions Counselor.
E-mail: *vang.vang@metrostate.edu*

MINNEAPOLIS COLLEGE OF ART AND DESIGN — C-4

Minneapolis, MN 55404 — (612) 874-3760
(800) 874-6223; Fax: (612) 874-3701

Full-time: 300 men, 205 women	**Faculty:** 39; IIB, -$
Part-time: 35 men, 40 women	**Ph.D.s:** 67%
Graduate: 10 men, 15 women	**Student/Faculty:** 13 to 1
Year: semesters, summer session	**Tuition:** $19,360
Application Deadline: open	**Room & Board:** $4200
Freshman Class: n/av	
SAT I or ACT: required	**SPECIAL**

The Minneapolis College of Art and Design, founded in 1886, is a private college of art. Figures in the above capsule, and in this profile, are approximate. In addition to regional accreditation, MCAD has baccalaureate program accreditation with NASAD. The library contains 59,067 volumes, 9 microform items, and 2103 audiovisual forms/CDs, and subscribes to 192 periodicals. Computerized library services include interlibrary loans and database searching. Special learning facilities include a learning resource center and art gallery. The 7-acre campus is in an urban area 1 mile south of downtown Minneapolis. Including residence halls, there are 9 buildings.

Student Life: 64% of undergraduates are from Minnesota. Others are from 36 states, 21 foreign countries, and Canada. 90% are from public schools. 80% are white. The average age of freshmen is 19; all undergraduates, 22. 18% do not continue beyond their first year; 33% remain to graduate.

Housing: 195 students can be accommodated in college housing, which includes coed on-campus apartments. On-campus housing is available on a first-come, first-served basis. Priority is given to out-of-town students. 65% of students commute. All students may keep cars.

Activities: There are no fraternities or sororities. There are 9 groups on campus, including art, computers, drama, film, gay, photography, professional, and student government. Popular campus events include Senior Show, Thanksgiving Dinner, and Art Sale.

Sports: There are 2 intramural sports for men and 2 for women. Students have the use of off-campus facilities.

Disabled Students: 95% of the campus is accessible. Wheelchair ramps, elevators, special parking, specially equipped rest rooms, and special class scheduling are available.

Services: Counseling and information services are available, as is tutoring in most subjects.

Campus Safety and Security: Measures include 24-hour foot and vehicle patrol, self-defense education, escort service, and informal discussions. There are pamphlets/posters/films, emergency telephones, lighted pathways/sidewalks, and a taxi service.

Programs of Study: MCAD confers B.F.A. and B.S. degrees. Master's degrees are also awarded. Bachelor's degrees are awarded in COMMUNICATIONS AND THE ARTS (advertising, design, drawing, film arts, fine arts, graphic design, illustration, media arts, painting, photography, printmaking, sculpture, studio art, and video), ENGINEERING AND ENVIRONMENTAL DESIGN (furniture design). Design and illustration are the largest.

Required: All B.F.A. students must satisfactorily complete 120 semester credits, including 12 in foundation studies, 69 in a studio major, and 39 in liberal arts. A 2.0 minimum GPA must be maintained. A senior project is required.

Special: MCAD offers cross-registration with Macalester College, internships, study abroad in Italy, Japan, Canada, Germany, France, England, Mexico, and Denmark, and work-study programs.

Faculty/Classroom: 55% of faculty are male; 45%, female. All teach undergraduates. No introductory courses are taught by graduate students. The average class size in an introductory lecture is 25; in a laboratory, 18; and in a regular course, 18.

Admissions: 1 freshman graduated first in the class in a recent year.

Requirements: The SAT I or ACT is required. In addition, applicants must submit a personal statement of interest, an essay, a letter of recommendation, transcripts, and a portfolio (B.F.A.). An interview is strongly encouraged. The GED is accepted. AP credits are accepted. Important factors in the admissions decision are evidence of special talent, personality/intangible qualities, and recommendations by school officials.

Procedure: Freshmen are admitted fall and spring. Entrance exams should be taken in the spring of the junior year in high school. There is a deferred admissions plan. Application deadlines are open. The fall 2001 application fee was $35.

Transfer: 75 transfer students enrolled in a recent year. B.F.A. applicants must submit a portfolio for the transfer of studio credit and an official transcript from all postsecondary schools. 45 credits of 120 must be completed at MCAD.

Visiting: There are regularly scheduled orientations for prospective students, consisting of tours, a program about putting a portfolio together, career information, and financial aid information. There are guides for informal visits and visitors may sit in on classes and stay overnight. To schedule a visit, contact the Admissions Office.

Financial Aid: In a recent year, 71% of all freshmen and 94% of continuing students received some form of financial aid. 62% of freshmen and 75% of continuing students received need-based aid. The average freshman award was $10,034. Of that total, scholarships or need-based grants averaged $4997 ($6500 maximum); loans averaged $2674 ($5000 maximum); and work contracts averaged $1825. 24% of undergraduates work part time. Average annual earnings from campus work are $1825. The average financial indebtedness of a recent year's graduate was $22,240. MCAD is a member of CSS. The FAFSA and parent and student federal income tax forms are required. The fall priority application deadline is April 20.

International Students: There were 16 international students enrolled in a recent year. They must score 550 on the written TOEFL and also take or take ESL level 9.

Computers: The Computer Center services more than 118 workstations in 7 locations. There is software for word processing, painting, drawing, 2- and 3-dimensional design, programming, electronic imaging (digitizing), scanning, image processing, page layout prepress color separation, 2- and 3-dimensional animation, and modeling on Mac IIcx, computers, a NeXT Dimension, NeXT stations, Apollo 3 AT&T Targa-based PCs, and Amigas. All students may access the system. There are no time limits.

Graduates: In a recent year, 99 bachelor's degrees were awarded. The most popular majors were graphic design (44%), media arts (29%), and fine arts studio (26%). In an average class, 29% graduate in 4 years, 34% in 5 years, and 35% in 6 years.

Admissions Contact: Susan Neppl, Director of Enrollment and Student Financial Services. E-mail: *admissions@mn.mcad.edu*
Web: *www.mcad.edu*

MINNESOTA STATE UNIVERSITY, MANKATO — C-4

Mankato, MN 56001 — (507) 389-1822
(800) 722-0544; Fax: (507) 389-1511

Full-time: 5003 men, 5308 women	**Faculty:** 454; IIA, av$
Part-time: 611 men, 718 women	**Ph.D.s:** 78%
Graduate: 580 men, 1022 women	**Student/Faculty:** 23 to 1
Year: semesters, summer session	**Tuition:** $3619 ($7037)
Application Deadline: open	**Room & Board:** $3677
Freshman Class: 5402 applied, 4423 accepted, 2185 enrolled	
SAT I: n/av	**ACT:** required
	LESS COMPETITIVE

Minnesota State University, Mankato, founded in 1868 and a unit of Minnesota State Colleges and Universities, offers programs in the liberal arts and sciences, as well as business, education, engineering and technology, and nursing. There are 6 undergraduate schools and 1 graduate school. In addition to regional accreditation, Minnesota State or MSU has baccalaureate program accreditation with AACSB, ABET, ADA,

CSWE, NASAD, NASM, NCATE, NLN, and NRPA. The library contains 1,107,354 volumes, 253,560 microform items, and 30,686 audiovisual forms/CDs, and subscribes to 3126 periodicals. Computerized library services include the card catalog, interlibrary loans, and database searching. Special learning facilities include a learning resource center, art gallery, radio station, and 2 observatories. The 354-acre campus is in a rural area 85 miles southwest of Minneapolis-St. Paul. Including residence halls, there are 18 buildings.

Student Life: 87% of undergraduates are from Minnesota. Others are from 39 states, 57 foreign countries, and Canada. 93% are white. The average age of freshmen is 19; all undergraduates, 22. 22% do not continue beyond their first year; 43% remain to graduate.

Housing: 3100 students can be accommodated in college housing, which includes coed dormitories. In addition, there are special-interest floors, including freshmen quiet-study floors, engineering floors, and computer science floors. On-campus housing is guaranteed for the freshman year only, is available on a first-come, first-served basis, and is available on a lottery system for upperclassmen. 75% of students commute. Alcohol is not permitted. All students may keep cars.

Activities: 1% of men belong to 7 national fraternities; 1% of women belong to 4 national sororities. There are 114 groups on campus, including art, band, cheerleading, choir, chorale, chorus, computers, dance, debate, drama, ethnic, film, forensics, gay, honors, international, jazz band, literary magazine, marching band, musical theater, newspaper, opera, orchestra, pep band, photography, political, professional, radio and TV, religious, social, social service, and student government. Popular campus events include Greek Week and multicultural activities and celebrations.

Sports: There are 10 intercollegiate sports for men and 10 for women, and 35 intramural sports for men and 35 for women. Facilities include a 7000-seat stadium, 2 gyms, a field house, indoor tracks, tennis and racquetball courts, an indoor swimming pool, and a 5000-seat ice hockey arena (city-owned).

Disabled Students: 90% of the campus is accessible. Wheelchair ramps, elevators, special parking, specially equipped rest rooms, special class scheduling, lowered drinking fountains, lowered telephones, and assistive technology are available.

Services: Counseling and information services are available, as is tutoring in most subjects. There is a reader service for the blind, and remedial math, reading, and writing. Also available are alternative testing accommodations, note taking, sign language interpreting, and taped texts.

Campus Safety and Security: Measures include 24-hour foot and vehicle patrol, self-defense education, escort service, and shuttle buses. There are informal discussions, pamphlets/posters/films, emergency telephones, lighted pathways/sidewalks, closed-circuit parking lot cameras, and motion-sensitive lights in low-traffic areas.

Programs of Study: Minnesota State or MSU confers B.A., B.S., B.F.A., B.Mus., B.S.E.E., and B.S.M.E. degrees. Associate and master's degrees are also awarded. Bachelor's degrees are awarded in BIOLOGICAL SCIENCE (avian sciences, biochemistry, biology/biological science, and biotechnology), BUSINESS (accounting, banking and finance, business administration and management, international business management, management science, and marketing/retailing/merchandising), COMMUNICATIONS AND THE ARTS (applied art, art, communications, dance, dramatic arts, English, French, German, journalism, music, music business management, Spanish, and speech/debate/rhetoric), COMPUTER AND PHYSICAL SCIENCE (astronomy, chemistry, earth science, information sciences and systems, mathematics, and physics), EDUCATION (art, athletic training, elementary, foreign languages, health, industrial arts, music, physical, science, and secondary), ENGINEERING AND ENVIRONMENTAL DESIGN (automotive technology, aviation administration/management, construction management, electrical/electronics engineering, electrical/electronics engineering technology, engineering technology, environmental science, interior design, manufacturing technology, mechanical engineering, and preengineering), HEALTH PROFESSIONS (dental hygiene, health science, medical laboratory technology, nursing, predentistry, premedicine, preosteopathy, prepharmacy, prepodiatry, preveterinary science, public health, and speech pathology/audiology), SOCIAL SCIENCE (anthropology, corrections, dietetics, economics, ethnic studies, family/consumer studies, food science, geography, history, humanities, law enforcement and corrections, parks and recreation management, philosophy, political science/government, prelaw, psychology, social studies, social work, sociology, urban studies, and women's studies). Engineering, nursing, and sciences are the strongest academically. Business, social work, and psychology are the largest.

Required: To graduate, students must complete 128 semester hours of credit, with a minimum GPA of 2.0. and 45 hours in the major. Most programs require 44 hours of general education, including courses in English, speech, science, math, social/behavioral science, arts and humanities, cultural diversity, global perspective, ethnic/civic responsibility, and people and the environment.

Special: The university offers cross-registration within the Minnesota State University System and with Gustavus Adolphus College. Students may serve internships, study abroad, or participate in an accelerated degree program. B.A.-B.S. degrees, dual and student-designed majors, nondegree study, and pass/fail options also are available. There are 11 national honor societies, a freshman honors program, and 1 departmental honors program.

Faculty/Classroom: 58% of faculty are male; 42%, female. 96% teach undergraduates and 51% do research. Graduate students teach 4% of introductory courses. The average class size in an introductory lecture is 43; in a laboratory, 11; and in a regular course, 21.

Admissions: 82% of the 2001-2002 applicants were accepted. 27% of the current freshmen were in the top fifth of their class; 60% were in the top two fifths. 13 freshmen graduated first in their class in a rent year

Requirements: The ACT is required. In addition applicants must be graduates of an accredited secondary school and rank in the top 50% of their high school class or have an ACT composite score of 21 or higher along with a satisfactory class rank. AP and CLEP credits are accepted.

Procedure: Freshmen are admitted to all sessions. Entrance exams should be taken in the spring of the junior year or the fall of the senior year. There is a deferred admissions plan. Application deadlines are open. The fall 2001 application fee was $20. Notification is sent on a rooling basis.

Transfer: 1009 transfer students enrolled in 2001-2002. Transfer applicants must have a minimum GPA of 2.0 and have completed at least 75% of all college-level courses attempted. 30 credits of 128 must be completed at Minnesota State or MSU.

Visiting: There are regularly scheduled orientations for prospective students, consisting of overview presentations, campus tours, and academic information fairs. Visitors may sit in on classes. To schedule a visit, contact the Admissions Office.

Financial Aid: In 2001-2002, 45% of all freshmen and 46% of continuing students received some form of financial aid. 32% of freshmen and 33% of continuing students received need-based aid. The average freshman award was $4977. Of that total, scholarships or need-based grants averaged $2863; and loans averaged $3036. 35% of undergraduates work part time. The FAFSA is required. The fall application deadline is March 15.

International Students: There are 460 international students enrolled. They must score 500 on the written TOEFL or 173 on the electronic version and also take an English placement test at matriculation.

Computers: The mainframe is a Unisys 2200; Dec 4000/500. Mac and IBM PCs are available at several campus locations, including a centralized lab with 475 computers and 6 computerized classrooms. All students may access the system. There are no time limits. The fee is $3.11 per semester credit. It is recommended that students have personal computers. For the College of Business, a laptop PC is required.

Graduates: In 2001, 1606 bachelor's degrees were awarded. The most popular majors were elementary education (15%), computer science (13%), and nursing (9%). In an average class, 1% graduate in 3 years, 15% in 4 years, 35% in 5 years, and 44% in 6 years. 260 companies recruited on campus in a recent year. Of the 2000 graduating class, 5% were enrolled in graduate school within 6 months of graduation.

Admissions Contact: Walt Wolff, Director of Admissions.
E-mail: *admissions@mankato.msus.edu* Web: *www.mankato.msus.edu*

MOORHEAD STATE UNIVERSITY — A-2

Moorhead, MN 56563 (218) 236-2161
(800) 593-7246; Fax: (218) 236-2168

Full-time: 1800 men, 3000 women	**Faculty:** 255
Part-time: 300 men, 800 women	**Ph.D.s:** 75%
Graduate: 70 men, 230 women	**Student/Faculty:** 19 to 1
Year: semesters, summer session	**Tuition:** $3600 ($6600)
Application Deadline: see profile	**Room & Board:** $3600
Freshman Class: n/av	
SAT I or ACT: n/av	**LESS COMPETITIVE**

Moorhead State University, founded in 1885, is a public liberal arts institution. Figures in the above capsule, and in this profile, are approximate. In addition to regional accreditation, Moorhead State has baccalaureate program accreditation with CSWE, NASAD, NASM, NCATE, and NLN. The library contains 365,000 volumes, 45,000 microform items, and 7000 audiovisual forms/CDs, and subscribes to 1626 periodicals. Computerized library services include the card catalog, interlibrary loans, and database searching. Special learning facilities include an art gallery, planetarium, radio station, TV station, and a science center. The 104-acre campus is in a suburban area 240 miles northwest of Minneapolis-St. Paul and across the river from Fargo, North Dakota. Including residence halls, there are 23 buildings.

Student Life: 96% are white. The average age of freshmen is 18; all undergraduates, 24.

Housing: 2164 students can be accommodated in college housing, which includes single-sex and coed dormitories. On-campus housing is available on a first-come, first-served basis. 67% of students commute. Alcohol is not permitted. All students may keep cars.

Activities: 2% of men belong to 1 local fraternity and 1 national fraternity; 1% of women belong to 3 national sororities. There are 150 groups on campus, including art, band, cheerleading, choir, chorus, computers, dance, drama, drill team, ethnic, film, gay, honors, international, jazz band, literary magazine, musical theater, newspaper, orchestra, pep band, photography, political, professional, radio and TV, religious, social, social service, and student government. Popular campus events include Parents Day, Straw Hat Summer Theatre, and Meltdown Concert.
Sports: There are 5 intercollegiate sports for men and 9 for women, and 18 intramural sports for men and 18 for women. Facilities include 4 gyms, racquetball and volleyball courts, 2 swimming pools, indoor and outdoor tennis courts, weight and wrestling rooms, a running track, and 3 softball diamonds.
Disabled Students: Wheelchair ramps, elevators, special parking, specially equipped rest rooms, lowered drinking fountains, and lowered telephones are available.
Services: Counseling and information services are available, as is tutoring in every subject. There is a reader service for the blind, and remedial math, reading, and writing.
Campus Safety and Security: Measures include 24-hour foot and vehicle patrol, self-defense education, escort service, and informal discussions. There are pamphlets/posters/films, emergency telephones, and lighted pathways/sidewalks.
Programs of Study: Moorhead State confers B.A., B.S., B.F.A., B.M., B.S.N., and B.S.W. degrees. Associate and master's degrees are also awarded. Bachelor's degrees are awarded in BIOLOGICAL SCIENCE (biology/biological science), BUSINESS (accounting, banking and finance, business administration and management, hotel/motel and restaurant management, international business management, marketing/retailing/merchandising, and trade and industrial supervision and management), COMMUNICATIONS AND THE ARTS (advertising, broadcasting, communications, dramatic arts, English, fine arts, French, German, journalism, music, public relations, Spanish, and speech/debate/rhetoric), COMPUTER AND PHYSICAL SCIENCE (chemistry, computer science, mathematics, and physics), EDUCATION (art, early childhood, elementary, foreign languages, health, industrial arts, music, science, secondary, social studies, and special), ENGINEERING AND ENVIRONMENTAL DESIGN (construction engineering), HEALTH PROFESSIONS (medical laboratory technology, nursing, predentistry, premedicine, prepharmacy, preveterinary science, and speech pathology/audiology), SOCIAL SCIENCE (American studies, anthropology, criminal justice, economics, history, paralegal studies, philosophy, political science/government, prelaw, psychology, social science, social work, and sociology). Music and speech/theater are the strongest academically. Business, education, and mass communications are the largest.
Required: To graduate students must have a 2.0 GPA and complete 128 semester hours, including a liberal arts core of 45 credits and 43 semester hours in upper-division courses. Required courses include 6 hours each of natural science, social science, humanities, and communications, language, or symbolic systems, and 5 credits in cultural diversity. All students must complete an upper-level writing requirement.
Special: Internships are available in most disciplines. The university offers cross-registration with North Dakota State University and Concordia College, and is a member of the National Student Exchange. Students may study abroad in more than 60 countries. Student-designed and dual majors, credit for military experience, nondegree study, and pass/fail options are possible. There are 7 national honor societies, a freshman honors program, and 1 departmental honors program.
Requirements: In addition, a high school diploma is required, and the GED is accepted. An SAT I combined score of 900 or ACT of 21 is required for applicants whose high school rank is below the top half. Moorhead State requires applicants to be in the upper 50% of their class. AP and CLEP credits are accepted.
Procedure: Freshmen are admitted to all sessions. Entrance exams should be taken in the junior or senior year of high school. Notification is sent on a rolling basis. Check with the school for current application deadlines and fee.
Transfer: Applicants must submit a high school transcript or GED score and all other transcripts for postsecondary schools attended. A minimum GPA of 2.0 (higher for entry in some departments) is necessary for transfer credit. 30 credits of 128 must be completed at Moorhead State.
Visiting: There are regularly scheduled orientations for prospective students, including a campus tour, lunch, and meetings with faculty and an admissions officer. There are guides for informal visits. To schedule a visit, contact the Admissions Office.
Financial Aid: 80% of undergraduates work part time. Average annual earnings from campus work are $1571. The average financial indebtedness of a recent year's graduate was $10,762. The FAFSA and the college's own financial statement are required. Check with the school for current deadlines.
International Students: There were 99 international students enrolled in a recent year. The school actively recruits these students. They must score 500 on the written TOEFL.
Computers: The mainframe is a DEC 4000/700A. There are 450 PCs available for student use, as well as 7 DEC and Data General minicomputers with more than 200 terminals. All students may access the system 24 hours a day, 7 days a week. There are no time limits.
Admissions Contact: Director of Admissions.

NORTH CENTRAL UNIVERSITY
Minneapolis, MN 55404 — C-4
(612) 343-4480
(800) 289-6222; Fax: (612) 343-4778

Full-time: 495 men, 665 women	**Faculty:** 33
Part-time: none	**Ph.D.s:** 13%
Graduate: none	**Student/Faculty:** 35 to 1
Year: semesters, summer session	**Tuition:** $9034
Application Deadline: June 1	**Room & Board:** $3810
Freshman Class: n/av	
SAT I or ACT: required	**LESS COMPETITIVE**

North Central University, founded in 1930 and affiliated with the Assemblies of God, is a Christian university that emphasizes rigorous academic training and spiritual passion. Figures in the above capsule are approximate. The library contains 70,041 volumes and 29 microform items, and subscribes to 399 periodicals. Computerized library services include the card catalog, interlibrary loans, and database searching. Special learning facilities include a learning resource center, radio station, and TV station. The 9-acre campus is in an urban area in downtown Minneapolis. Including residence halls, there are 15 buildings.
Student Life: 65% of undergraduates are from out of state, mostly the Midwest. Others are from 42 states, 7 foreign countries, and Canada. 94% are white.
Housing: University sponsored housing includes single-sex dormitories and on-campus apartments. In addition, there are honors houses. 64% of students commute. Alcohol is not permitted. Upperclassmen may keep cars.
Activities: There are no fraternities or sororities. There are 34 groups on campus, including art, band, choir, chorale, drama, jazz band, literary magazine, musical theater, newspaper, orchestra, photography, political, radio and TV, social, student government, and yearbook. Popular campus events include All-College Picnic, Community Outreach Day, and Winter Extravaganza Days.
Sports: There are 2 intercollegiate sports for men and 2 for women, and 2 intramural sports for men and 2 for women. Facilities include Elliot Park and the Clark-Danielson College Life Center gym.
Disabled Students: All of the campus is accessible. Wheelchair ramps, elevators, special parking, specially equipped rest rooms, special class scheduling, lowered drinking fountains, and lowered telephones are available.
Services: Counseling and information services are available, as is tutoring in some subjects, including English composition. There is remedial math, reading, and writing.
Campus Safety and Security: Measures include 24-hour foot and vehicle patrol, escort service, and pamphlets/posters/films.
Programs of Study: NCU confers B.A. and B.S. degrees. Associate degrees are also awarded. Bachelor's degrees are awarded in COMMUNICATIONS AND THE ARTS (communications), EDUCATION (elementary), SOCIAL SCIENCE (behavioral science, biblical languages, ministries, pastoral studies, religion, religious education, and religious music). Ministries is the largest.
Required: Students must complete at least 126 credits for the bachelor's degree. Each program has specific requirements, including general education and biblical studies core classes. Internships are required for all programs. Students must take 60 or more total hours in their major, with a minimum overall GPA of 2.0 (2.2 for teacher education).
Special: Students may pursue co-op programs in nursing or secondary education, study in 6 countries, earn a general studies degree, pursue nondegree study, or receive credit for life, military, or work experience.
Faculty/Classroom: 65% of faculty are male; 35%, female. All teach undergraduates.
Requirements: The SAT I or ACT is required. In addition, the college requires a minimum ACT score of 18, high school transcripts, and academic and pastoral references. AP and CLEP credits are accepted.
Procedure: Freshmen are admitted fall and spring. There is an early admissions plan. Applications should be filed by June 1 for fall entry and December 31 for spring entry, along with a $25 fee. Notification is sent on a rolling basis.
Transfer: Transfer applicants must submit a completed application, a pastor's reference, a high school transcript or the GED, and college transcripts. Applicants with less than a year of college credit must also submit ACT or SAT I scores and academic references. 27 credits of 126 must be completed at NCU.
Visiting: There are regularly scheduled orientations for prospective students. There are guides for informal visits and visitors may sit in on classes and stay overnight. To schedule a visit, contact the Admissions Office.
Financial Aid: The FFS and the college's own financial statement are required.
International Students: They must score 500 on the written TOEFL and also take the ACT, scoring 18 on the ACT.

Computers: PCs are available in the library and in the computer lab. All students may access the system. There are no time limits and no fees.
Admissions Contact: Jim Hubert, Admissions Director.
E-mail: *jghubert@northcentral.edu* Web: *www.northcentral.edu*

NORTHWESTERN COLLEGE C-4
St. Paul, MN 55113-1598 **(651) 631-5209**
(800) 827-6827; Fax: (651) 631-5680

Full-time: 583 men, 971 women	**Faculty:** 68; IIB, --$
Part-time: 17 men, 31 women	**Ph.D.s:** 76%
Graduate: none	**Student/Faculty:** 23 to 1
Year: quarters, summer session	**Tuition:** $14,982
Application Deadline: August 1	**Room & Board:** $4834
Freshman Class: 742 applied, 733 accepted, 404 enrolled	
SAT I Verbal/Math: 591/568	**ACT:** 24 **COMPETITIVE+**

Northwestern College, founded in 1902, is a Christian college offering traditional undergraduate programs in Bible, liberal arts, and professional studies and providing nontraditional educational opportunities through its degree completion and distance education divisions. In addition to regional accreditation, Northwestern has baccalaureate program accreditation with NASM. The library contains 92,410 volumes, 281 microform items, and 5785 audiovisual forms/CDs, and subscribes to 1989 periodicals. Computerized library services include the card catalog, interlibrary loans, and database searching. Special learning facilities include a learning resource center, art gallery, radio station, and language labs. The 100-acre campus is in a suburban area 7 miles north of downtown St. Paul. Including residence halls, there are 12 buildings.

Student Life: 62% of undergraduates are from Minnesota. Others are from 32 states, 27 foreign countries, and Canada. 81% are from public schools. 94% are white. Most are Protestant. The average age of freshmen is 18; all undergraduates, 20. 22% do not continue beyond their first year.

Housing: 978 students can be accommodated in college housing, which includes single-sex dormitories and on-campus apartments. On-campus housing is guaranteed for the freshman year only and is available on a first-come, first-served basis. Priority is given to out-of-town students. 61% of students live on campus; of those, 70% remain on campus on weekends. Alcohol is not permitted. All students may keep cars.

Activities: There are no fraternities or sororities. There are 25 groups on campus, including art, band, cheerleading, choir, chorale, chorus, drama, ethnic, forensics, international, jazz band, literary magazine, musical theater, newspaper, opera, orchestra, pep band, photography, political, professional, radio and TV, religious, social, social service, student government, and yearbook. Popular campus events include Spiritual Emphasis Week, Parents Weekend, and residence hall open house.

Sports: There are 8 intercollegiate sports for men and 8 for women, and 15 intramural sports for men and 15 for women. Facilities include softball, baseball, and football/soccer fields, outdoor tennis courts, and a waterfront for aquatic sports in summer and broomball in winter. There is a health and phys ed center, with a full basketball court, 2 racquetball courts, an elevated jogging surface, a fitness center, and an athletic training room. The student center has a small swimming pool.

Disabled Students: 70% of the campus is accessible. Wheelchair ramps, elevators, special parking, specially equipped rest rooms, special class scheduling, lowered drinking fountains, and lowered telephones are available.

Services: Counseling and information services are available, as is tutoring in some subjects, including including math, English, Bible, Greek, biology, and accounting. There is remedial math, reading, and writing.

Campus Safety and Security: Measures include 24-hour foot and vehicle patrol, self-defense education, escort service, and shuttle buses. There are informal discussions, pamphlets/posters/films, emergency telephones, and lighted pathways/sidewalks.

Programs of Study: Northwestern confers B.A., B.S., B.M.E. (music education), and B.Mus. degrees. Associate degrees are also awarded. Bachelor's degrees are awarded in BIOLOGICAL SCIENCE (biology/biological science), BUSINESS (accounting, banking and finance, business administration and management, international business management, management information systems, marketing management, and sports management), COMMUNICATIONS AND THE ARTS (broadcasting, communications, dramatic arts, English, graphic design, journalism, music, music performance, Spanish, and studio art), COMPUTER AND PHYSICAL SCIENCE (mathematics), EDUCATION (art, Christian, early childhood, elementary, English, mathematics, music, physical, social studies, and teaching English as a second/foreign language (TESOL/TEFOL)), HEALTH PROFESSIONS (sports medicine), SOCIAL SCIENCE (biblical studies, criminal justice, history, ministries, missions, pastoral studies, psychology, social science, and youth ministry). Elementary/secondary education, business, and music are the strongest academically. Education, business, and psychology are the largest.

Required: To graduate, students must complete 124 semester credits with a 2.0 GPA. The number of credits required in the major varies from 36 to 102 (average of 58). Core courses include 30 credits of Bible, 10 credits of composition/speech/computer literacy, 7 to 8 credits of Western civilization/social science and foreign language/cross-cultural courses, 6 to 8 credits of math and science, 6 credits each of fine arts/literature/philosophy, and 1 credit of phys ed.

Special: The college offers 5 study-abroad programs and 4 U.S. off-campus programs through the Council for Christian Colleges and Universities. International business majors are placed in 6-month internships in Japan. There are also co-op programs in engineering, environmental studies, law, and ROTC training. A 3-2 engineering degree with the University of Minnesota-Twin Cities is offered. There are 2 national honor societies, and a freshman honors program.

Faculty/Classroom: 56% of faculty are male; 44%, female. All teach undergraduates. The average class size in an introductory lecture is 33; in a laboratory, 14; and in a regular course, 24.

Admissions: 99% of the 2001-2002 applicants were accepted. The SAT I scores for the 2001-2002 freshman class were: Verbal--19% below 500, 28% between 500 and 599, 41% between 600 and 700, and 12% above 700; Math--25% below 500, 40% between 500 and 599, 16% between 600 and 700, and 19% above 700. The ACT scores were 25% below 21, 25% between 21 and 23, 26% between 24 and 26, 14% between 27 and 28, and 10% above 28. 42% of the current freshmen were in the top fifth of their class; 70% were in the top two fifths. There were 5 National Merit semifinalists. 9 freshmen graduated first in their class.

Requirements: The ACT is required and the SAT I is recommended. A high school diploma is required; the GED is accepted. The minimum high school GPA is 2.0, but a 3.0 or higher is recommended. Applicants are expected to have completed the following Carnegie units: 4 in English, 3 each in math, science, and social studies, and 2 in foreign language. A statement of Christian faith and an assent to a lifestyle agreement are required. 2 letters of reference must be submitted, 1 from the applicant's pastor. A personal interview is required for some applicants. AP and CLEP credits are accepted. Important factors in the admissions decision are personality/intangible qualities, recommendations by school officials, and extracurricular activities record.

Procedure: Freshmen are admitted to all sessions. Entrance exams should be taken no later than June of the year of intended fall entry. There are early admissions and deferred admissions plans. Applications should be filed by August 1 for fall entry, December 15 for spring entry, and May 1 for summer entry, along with a $25 fee. Notification is sent on a rolling basis.

Transfer: 97 transfer students enrolled in 2001-2002. Applicants must have an average of C or better from an accredited institution. 30 credits of 124 must be completed at Northwestern.

Visiting: There are regularly scheduled orientations for prospective students. There are guides for informal visits and visitors may sit in on classes and stay overnight. To schedule a visit, contact the Admissions Office at (651) 631-5111 or *admissions@nwc,edu.*

Financial Aid: In 2001-2002, 98% of all students received some form of financial aid. 83% of freshmen and 82% of continuing students received need-based aid. The average freshman award was $11,609. Of that total, scholarships or need-based grants averaged $8437; and loans averaged $3172. 71% of undergraduates work part time. Average annual earnings from campus work are $1750. The average financial indebtedness of the 2001 graduate was $15,500. The FAFSA and the college's own financial statement are required. The fall application deadline is March 1.

International Students: There are 11 international students enrolled. They must score 530 on the written TOEFL or 197 on the electronic version or take the MELAB. They must also take the SAT I or the ACT.

Computers: The mainframe is an IBM RS/6000, for administrative use only. 100 PCs are available for student use in 5 computer labs, including 1 in the student center/residence hall complex. 85 are IBM-compatibles with Internet access; the other 15 are Macs for education majors. All students may access the system. There are no time limits and no fees.

Graduates: In 2001, 259 bachelor's degrees were awarded. The most popular majors were elementary and secondary education (25%), business administration (11%), and psychology (7%). In an average class, 2% graduate in 3 years, 44% in 4 years, 53% in 5 years, and 54% in 6 years. 144 companies recruited on campus in 2000-2001. Of the 2000 graduating class, 4% were enrolled in graduate school within 6 months of graduation and 74% were employed.

Admissions Contact: Kenneth K. Faffler, Director of Recruitment. A video is available. E-mail: *kkf@nwc.edu* Web: *www.nwc.edu*

SAINT CLOUD STATE UNIVERSITY

St. Cloud, MN 56301-4498 C-3
(320) 255-2244
(800) 369-4260; Fax: (320) 255-2243

Full-time: 5506 men, 6379 women	**Faculty:** 605; IIA, -$
Part-time: 1196 men, 1633 women	**Ph.D.s:** 75%
Graduate: 446 men, 801 women	**Student/Faculty:** 20 to 1
Year: semesters, summer session	**Tuition:** $3566 ($7146)
Application Deadline: open	**Room & Board:** $3614

Freshman Class: 5145 applied, 4260 accepted, 2250 enrolled
ACT: 21 **COMPETITIVE**

Saint Cloud State University, founded in 1869, is a comprehensive university with 5 colleges plus 5 graduate schools offering programs that include the liberal arts and career preparation with emphasis on diversity, hands-on learning, and service to the community. In addition to regional accreditation, SCSU has baccalaureate program accreditation with AACSB, ABET, ACEJMC, ASLA, CSWE, NASAD, NASM, and NCATE. The library contains 579,275 volumes, 525,501 microform items, and 20,795 audiovisual forms/CDs, and subscribes to 12,054 periodicals. Computerized library services include the card catalog, interlibrary loans, and database searching. Special learning facilities include a learning resource center, art gallery, natural history museum, planetarium, radio station, TV station, and a National Hockey Center. The 158-acre campus is in a suburban area 60 miles northwest of Minneapolis. Including residence halls, there are 35 buildings.

Student Life: 88% of undergraduates are from Minnesota. Others are from 49 states, 77 foreign countries, and Canada. 99% are from public schools. 71% are white. 56% are Protestant; 38% Catholic. The average age of freshmen is 19; all undergraduates, 22. 27% do not continue beyond their first year.

Housing: 3000 students can be accommodated in college housing, which includes single-sex and coed dormitories. In addition, there are honors houses and a nontraditional student floor.. On-campus housing is guaranteed for all 4 years. 81% of students commute. Alcohol is not permitted. All students may keep cars.

Activities: 2% of men belong to 5 national fraternities; 2% of women belong to 5 local and 2 national sororities. There are 240 groups on campus, including art, band, cheerleading, chess, choir, chorale, chorus, computers, dance, drama, entrepreneurial, ethnic, film, gay, hobby, honors, international, jazz band, literary magazine, marching band, musical theater, opera, orchestra, pep band, photography, political, professional, radio and TV, religious, social, social service, sports, student government, symphony, travel, and yearbook. Popular campus events include Music Festival, Ethnic Awareness Week, and major speakers and workshops.

Sports: There are 14 intercollegiate sports for men and 12 for women, and 37 intramural sports for men and 37 for women. Facilities include a wrestling room, a weight room, a dance studio, a racquetball court, gyms, swimming and diving pools, indoor and outdoor tracks, and baseball and football fields.

Disabled Students: 88% of the campus is accessible. Wheelchair ramps, elevators, special parking, specially equipped rest rooms, special class scheduling, lowered drinking fountains, and lowered telephones are available.

Services: Counseling and information services are available, as is tutoring in every subject. There is a reader service for the blind, and remedial math, reading, and writing.

Campus Safety and Security: Measures include 24-hour foot and vehicle patrol, self-defense education, escort service, and shuttle buses. There are informal discussions, pamphlets/posters/films, emergency telephones, lighted pathways/sidewalks, and a required short safety course.

Programs of Study: SCSU confers B.A., B.S., B.E.S., B.F.A., and B.Mus. degrees. Associate, master's, and doctoral degrees are also awarded. Bachelor's degrees are awarded in BIOLOGICAL SCIENCE (biology/biological science), BUSINESS (accounting, banking and finance, business administration and management, business economics, international business management, marketing/retailing/merchandising, and personnel management), COMMUNICATIONS AND THE ARTS (advertising, broadcasting, communications, dramatic arts, English, fine arts, journalism, languages, music, and speech/debate/rhetoric), COMPUTER AND PHYSICAL SCIENCE (atmospheric sciences and meteorology, chemistry, computer science, earth science, geology, mathematics, physics, and statistics), EDUCATION (art, early childhood, elementary, foreign languages, guidance, health, industrial arts, music, science, and secondary), ENGINEERING AND ENVIRONMENTAL DESIGN (aviation administration/management, electrical/electronics engineering, engineering technology, and manufacturing engineering), HEALTH PROFESSIONS (predentistry, premedicine, public health, and speech pathology/audiology), SOCIAL SCIENCE (anthropology, criminal justice, economics, geography, history, international relations, philosophy, political science/government, prelaw, psychology, public administration, social science, social work, sociology, and urban studies). Business, computer science, and mass communications are the strongest academically. Business, education, and communications are the largest.

Required: Students must complete a minimum of 120 semester credit hours, including 40 hours of general education requirements and 60 to 80 hours in the major, and must maintain at least a 2.0 GPA, higher for many majors. Students must complete English 191, English 192, Speech 192, 2 credits in phys ed, and 24 credits in philosophy/humanities/fine arts, natural science and math, and social and behavioral science.

Special: The university offers cross-registration with St. John's University and the College of St. Benedict, internships in almost all majors, work-study programs, and study abroad in 7 countries. Students may take dual majors, design their own majors for a Bachelor of Elective Studies degree, and earn a general degree or a B.A.-B.S. degree in most majors, including meteorology and photographic technology. The university gives credit for military experience and allows nondegree study and pass/fail options. There are 4 national honor societies, a freshman honors program, and 1 departmental honors program.

Faculty/Classroom: 59% of faculty are male; 41%, female. 93% teach undergraduates, 2% do research, and 5% do both. Graduate students teach 1% of introductory courses. The average class size in an introductory lecture is 36; in a laboratory, 20; and in a regular course, 25.

Admissions: 83% of the 2001-2002 applicants were accepted. The ACT scores for the 2001-2002 freshman class were: 46% below 21, 29% between 21 and 23, 18% between 24 and 26, 4% between 27 and 28, and 2% above 28. 21% of the current freshmen were in the top fifth of their class; 56% were in the top two fifths. There were 3 National Merit finalists.

Requirements: The ACT is required. SCSU requires applicants to be in the upper 50% of their class. A GPA of 2.5 is required. AP and CLEP credits are accepted.

Procedure: Freshmen are admitted to all sessions. Entrance exams should be taken in the junior or senior year. Application deadlines are open. The fall 2001 application fee was $20. Notification is sent in 2 weeks.

Transfer: 1453 transfer students enrolled in 2001-2002. Applicants must have a minimum 2.0 GPA from their previous college if they transfer with 12 or more credits. If transferring with fewer than 12 credits, they are treated as entering freshmen. 30 credits of 120 must be completed at SCSU.

Visiting: There are regularly scheduled orientations for prospective students. There are guides for informal visits and visitors may sit in on classes. To schedule a visit, contact the Admissions Office.

Financial Aid: 20% of undergraduates work part time. Average annual earnings from campus work are $2180. The average financial indebtedness of the 2001 graduate was $14,864. The FAFSA and the college's own financial statement are required. The fall application deadline is open.

International Students: There are 578 international students enrolled. The school actively recruits these students. They must score 500 on the written TOEFL or take the MELAB or the Comprehensive English Language Test, plus the university's own test. They must also take the ACT.

Computers: The mainframe is a Digital Alpha Model 4100. There are 16 computer labs and 650 PCs for student use; 175 are networked to share printers and 60 are networked to the mainframe for disk sharing and file server capabilities. All students may access the system 8 A.M. to midnight. There are no time limits and no fees.

Graduates: In 2001, 2350 bachelor's degrees were awarded. The most popular majors were elementary education (9%), psychology (7%), and mass communication/business CIS/biology (each at 6%). In an average class, 13% graduate in 4 years, 36% in 5 years, and 43% in 6 years. 100 companies recruited on campus in 2000-2001. Of the 2000 graduating class, 6% were enrolled in graduate school within 6 months of graduation and 80% were employed.

Admissions Contact: Pat Krueger, Associate Director of Admissions. A video is available. E-mail: *scsu4u@stcloud.state.edu*
Web: *www.stcloudstate.edu*

SAINT JOHN'S UNIVERSITY

Collegeville, MN 56321-7155 B-3
(320) 363-2196
(800) 245-6467; Fax: (320) 363-3206

Full-time: 1853 men	**Faculty:** 157; IIB, av$
Part-time: 35 men	**Ph.D.s:** 75%
Graduate: 70 men, 81 women	**Student/Faculty:** 12 to 1
Year: trimesters	**Tuition:** $18,325
Application Deadline: open	**Room & Board:** $5315

Freshman Class: 1115 applied, 950 accepted, 502 enrolled
SAT I Verbal/Math: 580/620 **ACT:** 25 **VERY COMPETITIVE**

St. John's University, founded in 1857 by Benedictine monks, is a private institution offering programs in the liberal arts. The university is a college for men but shares an academic calendar, academic curriculum, and most cocurricular programs with the College of St. Benedict, a college for women 4 miles away. There is 1 graduate school. In addition to regional accreditation, St. John's has baccalaureate program accreditation with ACS, ADA, ATS, CSWE, NASM, NCATE, and NLN. The 3 libraries contain 800,685 volumes, 196,063 microform items, and 21,400 audiovisual forms/CDs, and subscribe to 8942 periodicals. Computerized library services include the card catalog, interlibrary loans, and database searching. Special learning facilities include a learning resource center, art gallery, natural history museum, radio station, TV station, an observatory, a greenhouse, an arboretum, an herbarium, a pottery studio, and Hill Monastic Manuscript Library. The 2400-acre campus is in a rural area 15 miles west of St. Cloud and 70 miles northwest of Minneapolis and St. Paul. Including residence halls, there are 35 buildings.

Student Life: 83% of undergraduates are from Minnesota. Others are from 31 states, 21 foreign countries, and Canada. 78% are from public schools. 94% are white. 70% are Catholic; 23% Protestant. The average age of freshmen is 19; all undergraduates, 20. 8% do not continue beyond their first year; 70% remain to graduate.

Housing: 1529 students can be accommodated in college housing, which includes single-sex dormitories and on-campus apartments. In addition, there is a health and wellness floor, a christian living floor, and accommodations for disable students. Students are required to live on campus for the first 2 years. On-campus housing is available on a first-come, first-served basis, and on a lottery system for upperclassmen. 85% of students live on campus. All students may keep cars.

Activities: There are 80 groups on campus, including art, band, biology, chemistry, choir, chorale, chorus, computers, dance, debate, drama, ethnic, gay, honors, international, jazz band, literary magazine, musical theater, opera, orchestra, political, professional, radio and TV, religious, social, social service, student government, symphony, and yearbook. Popular campus events include Pinestock, Spirit Week, and Involvement on the Mall.

Sports: Facilities include basketball and racquetball courts, soccer, baseball, and rugby fields, indoor and outdoor tennis courts, indoor and sand volleyball courts, indoor and outdoor tracks, an aerobics studio, a fitness center, a swimming pool, a 4-story climbing wall, 5 lakes for canoeing, fishing, swimming, rowing, and wind sailing, and access to facilities at College of Saint Benedict.

Disabled Students: 90% of the campus is accessible. Wheelchair ramps, elevators, special parking, specially equipped rest rooms, special class scheduling, lowered drinking fountains, lowered telephones, and specially equipped dorm rooms are available.

Services: Counseling and information services are available, as is tutoring in every subject. There is a reader service for the blind. There is a skills center, math and writing labs, and study and test-taking skills instruction.

Campus Safety and Security: Measures include 24-hour foot and vehicle patrol, self-defense education, escort service, and shuttle buses. There are informal discussions, pamphlets/posters/films, emergency telephones, and lighted pathways/sidewalks.

Programs of Study: St. John's confers the B.A. degree. Master's degrees are also awarded. Bachelor's degrees are awarded in AGRICULTURE (forestry and related sciences), BIOLOGICAL SCIENCE (biochemistry, biology/biological science, and nutrition), BUSINESS (accounting and management science), COMMUNICATIONS AND THE ARTS (art, classics, communications, dramatic arts, English, fine arts, French, German, music, and Spanish), COMPUTER AND PHYSICAL SCIENCE (chemistry, computer science, mathematics, natural sciences, and physics), EDUCATION (elementary), ENGINEERING AND ENVIRONMENTAL DESIGN (preengineering), HEALTH PROFESSIONS (medical laboratory technology, nursing, occupational therapy, physical therapy, predentistry, premedicine, prepharmacy, and preveterinary science), SOCIAL SCIENCE (dietetics, economics, history, humanities, pastoral studies, peace studies, philosophy, political science/government, prelaw, psychology, social science, social work, sociology, and theological studies). The humanities is the strongest academically. Management, biology, and computer science are the largest.

Required: To graduate, students must complete 124 credit hours with a 2.0 GPA. The required core curriculum includes 6 credits in fine arts, 5 courses in humanities, 2 courses each in natural science and social science, and 1 course in math. A first-year symposium and a senior seminar are also required, and students must participate in 1 approved physical activity.

Special: There is cross-registration with the College of St. Benedict and St. Cloud State University. An extensive program of internships and fieldwork, including programs in Latin America, South America, and Scandinavia, is offered. Students may design their own majors and individual learning projects, and may study abroad in 12 countries. There is a 3-2 engineering program with the University of Minnesota. Double majors, including math/computer science and preprofessional programs, nondegree study, and pass/fail options are available. There is 1 national honor society, and a freshman honors program.

Faculty/Classroom: 70% of faculty are male; 30%, female. All both teach and do research. No introductory courses are taught by graduate students. The average class size in an introductory lecture is 25; in a laboratory, 18; and in a regular course, 20.

Admissions: 85% of the 2001-2002 applicants were accepted. The SAT I scores for the 2001-2002 freshman class were: Verbal--14% below 500, 44% between 500 and 599, 33% between 600 and 700, and 9% above 700; Math--8% below 500, 36% between 500 and 599, 47% between 600 and 700, and 9% above 700. The ACT scores were 6% below 21, 26% between 21 and 23, 33% between 24 and 26, 17% between 27 and 28, and 18% above 28. 44% of the current freshmen were in the top fifth of their class; 77% were in the top two fifths. There were 3 National Merit finalists. 20 freshmen graduated first in their class.

Requirements: The SAT I or ACT is required. In addition, students should be graduates of an accredited secondary school. Academic preparation should include 17 units, including 4 of English, 3 of math, 2 each of science and social studies, and 6 electives. A foreign language is recommended. The GED is accepted. An essay is required. Home-schooled applicants are not required to have a high school diploma but are required to provide appropriate documentation of college preparatory curriculum. St. John's requires applicants to be in the upper 50% of their class. A GPA of 3.0 is required. AP and CLEP credits are accepted. Important factors in the admissions decision are advanced placement or honor courses, evidence of special talent, and extracurricular activities record. The college accepts electronic applications via CollegeNET and on its own web site, *http://www.csbsju.edu/admission/index.html*

Procedure: Freshmen are admitted fall and spring. Entrance exams should be taken by the fall of the senior year. There are early admissions and deferred admissions plans. Application deadlines are open. The fall 2001 application fee was $25. Notification is sent on a rolling basis. A waiting list is an active part of the admissions procedure.

Transfer: 31 transfer students enrolled in 2001-2002. Transfer applicants must have a minimum college GPA of 2.75. An essay or personal statement, high school and college transcripts, and a transfer student evaluation form are also required. Standardized test scores may be required of some 45 credits of 124 must be completed at St. John's.

Visiting: There are regularly scheduled orientations for prospective students. Programs vary according to student interest. Information can be found at the St. John's web site. There are guides for informal visits and visitors may sit in on classes and stay overnight. To schedule a visit, contact the Admissions Office.

Financial Aid: In 2001-2002, 92% of all freshmen and 88% of continuing students received some form of financial aid. 62% of freshmen and 59% of continuing students received need-based aid. The average freshman award was $13,719. Of that total, scholarships or need-based grants averaged $11,420; loans averaged $3710; and work contracts averaged $1047. 63% of undergraduates work part time. Average annual earnings from campus work are $2100. The average financial indebtedness of the 2001 graduate was $18,835. The FAFSA, the college's own financial statement, and federal tax returns and W-2s are required. The fall application deadline is May 1.

International Students: There are 49 international students enrolled. The school actively recruits these students. They must score 500 on the written TOEFL or 173 on the electronic version or take the MELAB.

Computers: The mainframe is a Windows NT network. Networked PCs are available in the computer center, library, and academic buildings. Most student residences are connected to PC and Mac networks. All students may access the system 24 hours a day. There are no time limits and no fees.

Graduates: In 2001, 374 bachelor's degrees were awarded. The most popular majors were business and management (25%), biology (8%), and political science (6%). In an average class, 1% graduate in 3 years, 79% in 4 years, 84% in 5 years, and 84% in 6 years. 40 companies recruited on campus in 2000-2001. Of the 2000 graduating class, 15% were enrolled in graduate school within 6 months of graduation and 80% were employed.

Admissions Contact: Mary Milbert, Dean of Admissions. A video is available. E-mail: *admissions@csbsju.edu* Web: *www.csbsju.edu*

SAINT MARY'S UNIVERSITY OF MINNESOTA D-5

Winona, MN 55987-1399 **(507) 457-1700**
(800) 635-5987; Fax: (507) 457-1722

Full-time: 595 men, 707 women	**Faculty:** 101; IIA, --$
Part-time: 25 men, 41 women	**Ph.D.s:** 80%
Graduate: 353 men, 986 women	**Student/Faculty:** 13 to 1
Year: semesters	**Tuition:** $15,195
Application Deadline: May 1	**Room & Board:** $4780

Freshman Class: 1055 applied, 910 accepted, 397 enrolled
ACT: 23 **COMPETITIVE**

Saint Mary's University of Minnesota, founded in 1912, is a private liberal arts college affiliated with the Roman Catholic Church and sponsored by the La Sallian Christian Brothers. There are 4 undergraduate schools and 1 graduate school. The library contains 151,643 volumes, 129,075 microform items, and 7485 audiovisual forms/CDs, and subscribes to 699 periodicals. Computerized library services include the card catalog, interlibrary loans, and database searching. Special learning facilities include a learning resource center, art gallery, radio station, observatory, and natural resource center. The 400-acre campus is in a small town 110 miles southeast of Minneapolis-St. Paul, and 275 miles northwest of Chicago. Including residence halls, there are 48 buildings.

Student Life: 62% of undergraduates are from Minnesota. Others are from 24 states, 18 foreign countries, and Canada. 62% are from public schools. 92% are white. 68% are Catholic; 18% Protestant. The average age of freshmen is 18; all undergraduates, 20. 23% do not continue beyond their first year.

Housing: 1125 students can be accommodated in college housing, which includes single-sex and coed dormitories and on-campus apartments. On-campus housing is guaranteed for all 4 years. In addition, there are student-directed communities and drug/alcohol/tobacco-free dorms. 83% of students live on campus; of those, 75% remain on campus on weekends. All students may keep cars.

Activities: 4% of men belong to 2 national fraternities; 4% of women belong to 2 national sororities. There are 88 groups on campus, including art, band, cheerleading, choir, chorale, chorus, computers, dance, drama, ethnic, film, gay, honors, international, jazz band, literary magazine, musical theater, newspaper, orchestra, pep band, photography, political, professional, radio and TV, religious, social, social service, sports clubs, student government, symphony, and yearbook. Popular campus events include Casino Night, Winter Sports Weekend, and Olympic Day.

Sports: There are 10 intercollegiate sports for men and 11 for women, and 9 intramural sports for men and 9 for women. Facilities include 7 basketball courts, indoor tennis courts, indoor ice arena, 4 racquetball courts, exercise and weight rooms, baseball, softball, and soccer fields, Nordic skiing, running trails, and indoor track.

Disabled Students: 93% of the campus is accessible. Wheelchair ramps, elevators, special parking, specially equipped rest rooms, lowered drinking fountains, lowered telephones, and TDD phones are available.

Services: Counseling and information services are available, as is tutoring in every subject. There is a reader service for the blind, and remedial math, reading, and writing.

Campus Safety and Security: Measures include 24-hour foot and vehicle patrol, self-defense education, escort service, and shuttle buses. There are informal discussions, pamphlets/posters/films, emergency telephones, and lighted pathways/sidewalks.

Programs of Study: SMU confers the B.A. degree. Master's and doctoral degrees are also awarded. Bachelor's degrees are awarded in BIOLOGICAL SCIENCE (biology/biological science, biophysics, and environmental biology), BUSINESS (accounting, business administration and management, international business management, and marketing/retailing/merchandising), COMMUNICATIONS AND THE ARTS (creative writing, dramatic arts, French, graphic design, literature, music business management, music performance, public relations, publishing, Spanish, and studio art), COMPUTER AND PHYSICAL SCIENCE (chemistry, computer science, mathematics, physical chemistry, and physics), EDUCATION (elementary, English, foreign languages, middle school, music, science, and social science), ENGINEERING AND ENVIRONMENTAL DESIGN (preengineering), HEALTH PROFESSIONS (cytotechnology, medical laboratory technology, nuclear medical technology, physical therapy, predentistry, premedicine, and preveterinary science), SOCIAL SCIENCE (criminal justice, history, human services, philosophy, political science/government, prelaw, psychology, public administration, social science, sociology, theological studies, and youth ministry). Biology, accounting, and childhood/early adolescent education are the strongest academically. Management, marketing, and biology are the largest.

Required: Students must have a 2.0 cumulative major GPA and complete a minimum of 122 semester credits, including at least 45 at the upper-division level. Students must complete 32 to 59 credits in the major and the general education program. Students must spend their final year in academic residence.

Special: Students may cross-register with Winona State University. Internships, co-op programs, student teaching, study abroad, work-study programs, and a Washington semester are available. The university also offers dual and student-designed majors, a 3-2 engineering degree, nondegree study, pass/fail options, credit for life, military, and work experience, and an honors program that also serves as an alternative general education program. There are 13 national honor societies and a freshman honors program.

Faculty/Classroom: 57% of faculty are male; 43%, female. All teach undergraduates and 15% both teach and do research. No introductory courses are taught by graduate students. The average class size in an introductory lecture is 22; in a laboratory, 12; and in a regular course, 13.

Admissions: 86% of the 2001-2002 applicants were accepted. The ACT scores for the 2001-2002 freshman class were: 30% below 21, 26% between 21 and 23, 21% between 24 and 26, 13% between 27 and 28, and 9% above 28. 37% of the current freshmen were in the top fifth of their class; 70% were in the top two fifths. There were 2 National Merit finalists and 3 semifinalists. 10 freshmen graduated first in their class.

Requirements: The ACT is required. In addition, candidates for admission should have completed 4 units of English, 3 each of natural science, math, social studies, and academic electives, and 2 of foreign language. SMU requires applicants to be in the upper 50% of their class. A GPA of 2.5 is required. AP and CLEP credits are accepted. Important factors in the admissions decision are advanced placement or honor courses, leadership record, and ability to finance college education. The University accepts applications on-line at *www.smumn.edu*

Procedure: Freshmen are admitted fall and spring. Entrance exams should be taken by the fall of the senior year. There is a deferred admissions plan. Applications should be filed by May 1 for fall entry and December 1 for spring entry, along with a $25 fee. Notification is sent on a rolling basis.

Transfer: 42 transfer students enrolled in 2001-2002. Applicants must have a 2.0 GPA with at least 12 credits. 60 credits of 122 must be completed at SMU.

Visiting: There are regularly scheduled orientations for prospective students, including an interview, a tour, class visits, and lunch. There are guides for informal visits and visitors may sit in on classes and stay overnight. To schedule a visit, contact the Office of Admissions.

Financial Aid: In 2001-2002, 84% of all freshmen and 89% of continuing students received some form of financial aid. 62% of freshmen and 63% of continuing students received need-based aid. The average freshman award was $13,331. Of that total, loans averaged $3992 ($9625 maximum); and work contracts averaged $1300 ($1800 maximum). 52% of undergraduates work part time. Average annual earnings from campus work are $1062. The average financial indebtedness of the 2001 graduate was $16,686. The FAFSA and the college's own financial statement are required. The fall application deadline is open.

International Students: There are 25 international students enrolled. The school actively recruits these students. They must score 520 on the written TOEFL.

Computers: The mainframe is a VAX. 356 Macs, PCs, and silicon graphics workstations are available in computer labs, departmental areas, dorms, and classrooms. All students may access the system 7:15 A.M. to 2 A.M., Monday through Thursday; 7:15 A.M. to 10 P.M., Friday; 10 A.M. to 10 P.M., Saturday; and 10 A.M. to 2 A.M. Sunday. There are no time limits and no fees.

Graduates: In 2001, 322 bachelor's degrees were awarded. The most popular majors were marketing (9%), psychology (7%), and human services (5%). In an average class, 1% graduate in 3 years, 51% in 4 years, 55% in 5 years, and 56% in 6 years. 118 companies recruited on campus in 2000-2001. Of the 2000 graduating class, 23% were enrolled in graduate school within 6 months of graduation and 60% were employed.

Admissions Contact: Anthony M. Piscitiello, Vice President for Admission. A video is available. E-mail: *admissions@smumn.edu*
Web: *http://www.smumn.edu*

SAINT OLAF COLLEGE — C-4

Northfield, MN 55057-1098 — **(507) 646-3025**
(800) 800-3025; Fax: (507) 646-3832

Full-time: 1237 men, 1704 women	**Faculty:** 227; IIB, +$
Part-time: 21 men, 49 women	**Ph.D.s:** 89%
Graduate: none	**Student/Faculty:** 13 to 1
Year: 4-1-4, summer session	**Tuition:** $21,280
Application Deadline: February 1	**Room & Board:** $4600
Freshman Class: 2464 applied, 1883 accepted, 747 enrolled	
SAT I or ACT: required	**HIGHLY COMPETITIVE**

St. Olaf College, founded in 1874, is a private liberal arts institution affiliated with the Evangelical Lutheran Church in America. In addition to regional accreditation, St. Olaf has baccalaureate program accreditation with CSWE, NASAD, NASM, NCATE, and NLN. The 4 libraries contain 623,414 volumes, 59,430 microform items, and 26,471 audiovisual forms/CDs, and subscribe to 2216 periodicals. Computerized library services include the card catalog, interlibrary loans, and database searching. Special learning facilities include a learning resource center, art gallery, radio station, and TV station. The 350-acre campus is in a small town 40 miles south of Minneapolis. Including residence halls, there are 29 buildings.

Student Life: 53% of undergraduates are from Minnesota. Others are from 49 states and 20 foreign countries. 80% are from public schools. 87% are white. 69% are Protestant; 15% Catholic; 12% various denominations. The average age of freshmen is 18; all undergraduates, 20. 8% do not continue beyond their first year.

Housing: 2676 students can be accommodated in college housing, which includes coed dormitories. In addition, there are honors houses, language houses, and special-interest houses. On-campus housing is guaranteed for all 4 years. 96% of students live on campus; of those, 80% remain on campus on weekends. Alcohol is not permitted. No one may keep cars.

Activities: There are no fraternities or sororities. There are 96 groups on campus, including art, band, cheerleading, chess, choir, chorus, dance, debate, drama, ethnic, film, forensics, gay, honors, international, jazz band, literary magazine, musical theater, newspaper, opera, orchestra, pep band, photography, political, professional, radio and TV, religious, social, social service, student government, symphony, and yearbook. Popular campus events include Christmas Festival, Black History Month, and Fine Arts Week.

Sports: There are 14 intercollegiate sports for men and 13 for women, and 11 intramural sports for men and 11 for women. Facilities include 2 athletic complexes, a field house with batting cages, a long jump pit, 5 indoor tennis courts, and a 6-lane indoor track, a soccer pitch, softball and baseball diamonds, 2 weight rooms, a football field, an 8-lane all-weather track and field, a 9-hole frisbee golf course, and practice and recreation space.
Disabled Students: 70% of the campus is accessible. Wheelchair ramps, elevators, special parking, specially equipped rest rooms, special class scheduling, and lowered drinking fountains are available.
Services: Counseling and information services are available, as is tutoring in every subject. There is a reader service for the blind. Study sessions are available.
Campus Safety and Security: Measures include 24-hour foot and vehicle patrol, self-defense education, escort service, and shuttle buses. There are informal discussions, pamphlets/posters/films, emergency telephones, and lighted pathways/sidewalks.
Programs of Study: St. Olaf confers B.A., B.Mus., and B.S.N. degrees. Bachelor's degrees are awarded in BIOLOGICAL SCIENCE (biology/biological science), COMMUNICATIONS AND THE ARTS (art history and appreciation, communications, dance, dramatic arts, English, fine arts, French, German, Greek, Latin, music, music performance, music theory and composition, Russian, Scandinavian languages, Spanish, and studio art), COMPUTER AND PHYSICAL SCIENCE (chemistry, mathematics, and physics), EDUCATION (art, English, foreign languages, music, and social studies), ENGINEERING AND ENVIRONMENTAL DESIGN (environmental science), HEALTH PROFESSIONS (nursing), SOCIAL SCIENCE (American studies, Asian/Oriental studies, classical/ancient civilization, crosscultural studies, economics, family/consumer resource management, Hispanic American studies, history, medieval studies, philosophy, political science/government, psychology, religion, religious music, Russian and Slavic studies, social work, sociology, and women's studies). Biology, English, and psychology are the largest.
Required: To graduate, students must complete 35 courses, including 18 in upper-division work and 8 to 10 in the major, with a 2.0 GPA. Foundation courses include 4 writing-intensive courses, 4 in foreign language, 2 in phys ed, and 1 each in oral communication, math, and first-year writing. Students must also complete core requirements of 2 courses each in history, literature and art, science, human behavior, Bible and theology, and multicultural studies as well as 1 in ethics.
Special: St. Olaf offers cross-registration with Carleton College, study abroad in 48 countries, a Washington semester, preprofessional programs, internships, and a 3-2 B.A.-B.S.E. degree in engineering with Washington University in St. Louis. There are dual majors, nondegree study, and pass/fail options. The Center for Integrative Studies allows students to design individual majors with an emphasis on tutorials and seminars. There are 15 national honor societies, including Phi Beta Kappa.
Faculty/Classroom: 57% of faculty are male; 43%, female. All both teach and do research. The average class size in an introductory lecture is 27; in a laboratory, 17; and in a regular course, 21.
Admissions: 76% of the 2001-2002 applicants were accepted. The SAT I scores for the 2001-2002 freshman class were: Verbal--3% below 500, 29% between 500 and 599, 52% between 600 and 700, and 16% above 700; Math--3% below 500, 31% between 500 and 599, 51% between 600 and 700, and 15% above 700. The ACT scores were 10% between 21 and 23, 28% between 24 and 26, 26% between 27 and 28, and 36% above 28. 76% of the current freshmen were in the top fifth of their class; 97% were in the top two fifths. There were 32 National Merit finalists. 59 freshmen graduated first in their class.
Requirements: The SAT I or ACT is required. In addition, applicants should have completed 4 years of English, 3 to 4 each of math and social studies, and 2 to 3 each of science and a foreign language. AP and CLEP credits are accepted. Important factors in the admissions decision are advanced placement or honor courses, recommendations by school officials, and leadership record. Applications are accepted on-line via CollegeNET.
Procedure: Freshmen are admitted fall, winter, and spring. Entrance exams should be taken in the spring of the junior year or the fall of the senior year. There are early decision and deferred admissions plans. Early decision applications should be filed by November 15; regular applications, by February 1 for fall entry, along with a $35 fee. Notification of early decision is sent December 1; regular decision, on a rolling basis. 128 early decision candidates were accepted for the 2001-2002 class. 4% of all applicants are on a waiting list; 19 were accepted in 2001.
Transfer: 40 transfer students enrolled in 2001-2002. Applicants must have a 3.0 GPA at their previous institution. 17 courses of 35 must be completed at St. Olaf.
Visiting: There are regularly scheduled orientations for prospective students, consisting of information sessions in an open-house format. There are guides for informal visits and visitors may sit in on classes and stay overnight. To schedule a visit, contact Janice Malecha, Visit Coordinator at (800) ASK-OLAF or *visit@stolaf.edu*
Financial Aid: In 2001-2002, 80% of all freshmen and 73% of continuing students received some form of financial aid. 61% of freshmen and 64% of continuing students received need-based aid. The average freshman award was $15,255. Of that total, scholarships or need-based grants averaged $8144 ($16,500 maximum); loans averaged $3559 ($5625 maximum); and work contracts averaged $1600 ($2100 maximum). 82% of undergraduates work part time. Average annual earnings from campus work are $1200. The average financial indebtedness of the 2001 graduate was $15,490. The CSS/Profile or FAFSA and the college's own financial statement are required. The fall application deadline is March 1.
International Students: There are 48 international students enrolled. The school actively recruits these students. They must score 550 on the written TOEFL or 213 on the electronic version.
Computers: The mainframes are 2 DEC VAX 11/780s. More than 180 public-area PCs and Macs are available. Many departments and all residence halls have computer rooms as well. All students may access the system. There are no time limits and no fees.
Graduates: In 2001, 648 bachelor's degrees were awarded. The most popular majors were biology (17%), English (10%), and economics (9%). In an average class, 75% graduate in 4 years, 79% in 5 years, and 80% in 6 years. 155 companies recruited on campus in 2000-2001. Of the 2000 graduating class, 25% were enrolled in graduate school within 6 months of graduation and 68% were employed.
Admissions Contact: Sara Kyle, Director of Admissions.
E-mail: *admissions@stolaf.edu* Web: *http://www.stolaf.edu*

SOUTHWEST STATE UNIVERSITY — B-4

Marshall, MN 56258 — (507) 537-7021
(800) 642-0684; Fax: (507) 537-7154

Full-time: 800 men, 950 women	**Faculty:** 115; IIB, av$
Part-time: 450 men, 650 women	**Ph.D.s:** 77%
Graduate: 70 men, 70 women	**Student/Faculty:** 15 to 1
Year: semesters, summer session	**Tuition:** $3717 ($6130)
Application Deadline: open	**Room & Board:** $3400
Freshman Class: n/av	
SAT I or ACT: required	**LESS COMPETITIVE**

Southwest State University, founded in 1963, is a public institution offering programs in liberal arts, technology, and preprofessional training. Figures given in athe bove capsule, and in this profile, are approximate. The library contains 165,000 volumes, 37,000 microform items, and 12,000 audiovisual forms/CDs, and subscribes to 800 periodicals. Computerized library services include the card catalog, interlibrary loans, and database searching. Special learning facilities include an art gallery, natural history museum, planetarium, radio station, and TV station. The 216-acre campus is in a rural area 150 miles southwest of Minneapolis. Including residence halls, there are 51 buildings.
Student Life: 77% of undergraduates are from Minnesota. Others are from 27 states and 23 foreign countries. 95% are from public schools. 91% are white. The average age of all undergraduates is 22. 20% do not continue beyond their first year; 35% remain to graduate.
Housing: 1250 students can be accommodated in college housing, which includes single-sex and coed dormitories. In addition, there are special-interest houses and a quiet house. On-campus housing is guaranteed for the freshman year only. 61% of students live on campus. Alcohol is not permitted. All students may keep cars.
Activities: There are no fraternities or sororities. There are 60 groups on campus, including art, band, cheerleading, chess, choir, chorus, computers, dance, drama, ethnic, honors, international, jazz band, literary magazine, marching band, newspaper, pep band, political, radio and TV, religious, student government, and symphony. Popular campus events include Prairie Festival and Rural Writer's Conference.
Sports: There are 5 intercollegiate sports for men and 4 for women. Facilities include a gym, baseball and softball facilities, handball and squash courts, a track, a football field, tennis courts, wrestling rooms, a weight room, an Olympic-size pool, and a 5000-seat stadium.
Disabled Students: 95% of the campus is accessible. Wheelchair ramps, elevators, special parking, specially equipped rest rooms, special class scheduling, lowered drinking fountains, and lowered telephones are available.
Services: Counseling and information services are available, as is tutoring in most subjects. There is a reader service for the blind, and remedial math, reading, and writing.
Campus Safety and Security: Measures include 24-hour foot and vehicle patrol, escort service, informal discussions, and pamphlets/posters/films. There are emergency telephones and lighted pathways/sidewalks.
Programs of Study: SSU confers B.A. and B.S. degrees. Associate and master's degrees are also awarded. Bachelor's degrees are awarded in AGRICULTURE (agricultural business management), BIOLOGICAL SCIENCE (biology/biological science), BUSINESS (accounting, business administration and management, marketing/retailing/merchandising, and office supervision and management), COMMUNICATIONS AND THE ARTS (art, communications, creative writing, literature, music, and Spanish), COMPUTER AND PHYSICAL SCIENCE (chemistry, computer science, and mathematics), EDUCATION (art, business, early child-

hood, elementary, health, mathematics, music, and physical), HEALTH PROFESSIONS (medical technology), SOCIAL SCIENCE (history, interdisciplinary studies, political science/government, psychology, social work, and sociology). Education, business administration, and accounting are the largest.

Required: To graduate, students must complete at least 128 semester credit hours, a minimum of 27 of which must be the 300 or 400 level, and a liberal arts core curriculum, with a minimum GPA of 2.0.

Special: SSU has cooperative programs with various local colleges, cross-registration with several state universities, and an accelerated degree in business administration. SSU also offers internships in every discipline, work-study programs, study abroad in Japan, student-designed and interdisciplinary majors including speech communication and theater arts, nondegree study, pass/fail options, and credit for life, military, and work experience. There are 2 national honor societies and a freshman honors program.

Faculty/Classroom: 73% of faculty are male; 27%, female. 95% teach undergraduates.

Requirements: The SAT I or ACT is required, the ACT is preferred, with a composite score of 21, or a combined verbal and math score of 970 on the SAT I. Students should be graduates of an accredited secondary school or have a GED certificate. An interview is recommended. SSU requires applicants to be in the upper 50% of their class. AP and CLEP credits are accepted. Important factors in the admissions decision are recommendations by school officials, leadership record, and personality/intangible qualities.

Procedure: Freshmen are admitted to all sessions. Entrance exams should be taken during the junior or senior year. There are early decision, early admissions, and deferred admissions plans. Application deadlines are open for fall entry. Notification is sent on a rolling basis. The fall 2001 application fee was $20.

Transfer: Applicants need a minimum GPA of 2.0 in previous college-level work at an accredited institution. High school transcripts are required if students are transferring with fewer than 24 semester credits. 48 credits of 128 must be completed at SSU.

Visiting: There are regularly scheduled orientations for prospective students. There are guides for informal visits and visitors may sit in on classes and stay overnight. To schedule a visit, contact the Admissions Office.

Financial Aid: In a recent year, 81% of all freshmen and 80% of continuing students received some form of financial aid. 82% of freshmen and 78% of continuing students received need-based aid. The average freshman award was $3043. Of that total, scholarships or need-based grants averaged $800 ($2500 maximum); loans averaged $3000 ($5500 maximum); and work contracts averaged $700 ($1200 maximum). 70% of undergraduates work part time. Average annual earnings from campus work are $875. The average financial indebtedness of a recent year's graduate was $6100. The FAFSA is required. Check with the school for current deadlines.

International Students: The school actively recruits these students. They must score 500 on the written TOEFL.

Computers: The mainframes are a DEC ALPHA system 2100 VMS and a DEC ALPHA server 1000 UNIX system. There are Mac and IBM PCs available. All students may access the system 24 hours per day. There are no time limits.

Admissions Contact: Richard Shearer, Director of Enrollment. A video is available. E-mail: *shearerr@southwest.msus.edu*
Web: *www.southwest.msus.edu*

UNIVERSITY OF MINNESOTA SYSTEM

The University of Minnesota System, established in 1851, is a public system governed by a board of regents. The chief administrator is the president. The primary goal of the system is teaching, research, and public service. The total enrollment of all four campuses is 51,835, with 3182 faculty members. There are 268 baccalaureate, 220 master's, and 116 doctoral degree programs offered through the system. The U of M four-year campuses are located in Duluth, Morris, and Twin Cities.

UNIVERSITY OF MINNESOTA/CROOKSTON A-2

Crookston, MN 56716-5001 (218) 281-8569
(800) 232-6466; Fax: (218) 281-8050

Full-time: 1050 men and women	**Faculty:** IIB, av$
Part-time: 1120 men and women	**Ph.D.s:** n/av
Graduate: none	**Student/Faculty:** n/av
Year: n/av	**Tuition:** $5626
Application Deadline: open	**Room & Board:** $4100
Freshman Class: n/av	**ACT:** required
	NONCOMPETITIVE

University of Minnesota/Crookston, founded in 1965, is a public institution offering undergraduate degrees in agriculture, business, and hotel, restaurant, and institutional management. Figures given in the above capsule, and in this profile, are approximate. In addition to regional accreditation, UMC has baccalaureate program accreditation with AACSB and ADA. The library contains 30,684 volumes, 264 microform items, and 2280 audiovisual forms/CDs, and subscribes to 770 periodicals. Computerized library services include the card catalog, interlibrary loans, and database searching. Special learning facilities include a learning resource center. The 95-acre campus is in a rural area 25 miles from Grand Forks, North Dakota. Including residence halls, there are 28 buildings.

Student Life: 75% of undergraduates are from Minnesota. Others are from 12 states, 6 foreign countries, and Canada. 98% are from public schools. 94% are white. The average age of freshmen is 18; all undergraduates, 26. 45% do not continue beyond their first year.

Housing: 400 students can be accommodated in college housing, which includes coed dormitories and on-campus apartments. On-campus housing is available on a first-come, first-served basis. Priority is given to out-of-town students. 55% of students commute. Alcohol is not permitted. All students may keep cars.

Activities: There are no fraternities or sororities. There are 9 groups on campus, including cheerleading, choir, computers, drama, ethnic, newspaper, pep band, student government, and yearbook. Popular campus events include Agriculture Activities Day and Business Activities Day.

Sports: There are 4 intercollegiate sports for men and 3 for women, and 6 intramural sports for men and 6 for women. Facilities include a large indoor and outdoor sports complex.

Disabled Students: 95% of the campus is accessible. Wheelchair ramps, elevators, special parking, specially equipped rest rooms, special class scheduling, lowered drinking fountains, and lowered telephones are available.

Services: Counseling and information services are available, as is tutoring in most subjects. There is a reader service for the blind, and remedial math, reading, and writing. An academic assistance center is also available.

Campus Safety and Security: Measures include pamphlets/posters/films and lighted pathways/sidewalks.

Programs of Study: Bachelor's degrees are awarded in AGRICULTURE (agricultural business management, and natural resource management), BUSINESS (accounting, business administration and management, hotel/motel and restaurant management, management science, and sports management), COMPUTER AND PHYSICAL SCIENCE (information sciences and systems), ENGINEERING AND ENVIRONMENTAL DESIGN (environmental engineering technology and technological management), HEALTH PROFESSIONS (health care administration), SOCIAL SCIENCE (food production/management/services).

Requirements: The ACT is required. In addition, students with a high school diploma or equivalent are eligible for admission. AP and CLEP credits are accepted.

Procedure: Freshmen are admitted fall and spring. There are early admissions and deferred admissions plans. Application deadlines are open. Check with the school for current application fee.

Transfer: 30 credits of 120 must be completed at UMC.

Visiting: There are guides for informal visits and visitors may sit in on classes and stay overnight. To schedule a visit, contact the Admissions Office.

Financial Aid: Average annual earnings from campus work are $900. UMC is a member of CSS. The FAFSA is required. Check with the school for current deadlines.

International Students: The school actively recruits these students. They must score 500 on the written TOEFL.

Computers: All full-time students pay an access fee to the local area network and are issued a notebook computer. All students may access the system. There are no time limits.

Admissions Contact: Russell L. Kreager, Director of Enrollment Management. E-mail: *infor@crk.umn.edu*
Web: *www.crk.umn.edu/people/admissions*

UNIVERSITY OF MINNESOTA/DULUTH D-3

Duluth, MN 55812-2496 (218) 726-7171
(800) 232-1339; Fax: (218) 726-6394

Full-time: 3750 men, 3904 women	**Faculty:** 346; IIA, av$
Part-time: 551 men, 575 women	**Ph.D.s:** 81%
Graduate: 227 men, 236 women	**Student/Faculty:** 23 to 1
Year: semesters, summer session	**Tuition:** $5844 ($14,881)
Application Deadline: August 1	**Room & Board:** $4592
Freshman Class: 6339 applied, 5018 accepted, 2153 enrolled	
ACT: 23	**COMPETITIVE**

The University of Minnesota Duluth, founded in 1947, is a liberal arts institution offering undergraduate and graduate programs as a campus of the University of Minnesota. There are 5 undergraduate and 2 graduate schools. In addition to regional accreditation, UMD has baccalaureate program accreditation with ABET, ASLA, CSAB, CSWE, NASM, and NCATE. The library contains 705,000 volumes, 750,000 microform items, and 14,000 audiovisual forms/CDs, and subscribes to 2737 periodicals. Computerized library services include the card catalog, interlibrary loans, and database searching. Special learning facilities include a learning resource center, art gallery, planetarium, radio station, TV station, and and a performing arts center. The 244-acre campus is in a suburban area 150 miles north of Minneapolis and St. Paul. Including residence halls, there are 50 buildings.

Student Life: 87% of undergraduates are from Minnesota. Others are from 27 states, 30 foreign countries, and Canada. 95% are from public schools. 92% are white. The average age of freshmen is 18; all undergraduates, 21. 26% do not continue beyond their first year; 38% remain to graduate.

Housing: 2796 students can be accommodated in college housing, which includes single-sex and coed dormitories and on-campus apartments. On-campus housing is available on a first-come, first-served basis and on a lottery system for upperclassmen. 62% of students commute. Alcohol is not permitted. All students may keep cars.

Activities: 1% of men belong to 2 local and 2 national fraternities; 1% of women belong to 1 national and 2 local sororities. There are 130 groups on campus, including band, chamber orchestra, cheerleading, chess, choir, chorale, chorus, dance, drama, ethnic, gay, honors, international, jazz band, jazz choir, jazz ensemble, musical theater, newspaper, opera, orchestra, pep band, political, professional, radio and TV, religious, social, social service, student government, and wind ensemble. Popular campus events include Winter Festival, Black History Month, and Hispanic Heritage Month.

Sports: There are 7 intercollegiate sports for men and 8 for women, and 16 intramural sports for men and 16 for women. Facilities include a multipurpose ice center, a football and track-and-field stadium, a baseball park, softball and soccer fields, a field house for track and tennis, and a gym for basketball and volleyball, as well as a nearby country club for cross country and golf.

Disabled Students: All of the campus is accessible. Wheelchair ramps, elevators, special parking, specially equipped rest rooms, lowered drinking fountains, lowered telephones, and specially equipped residence hall rooms are available.

Services: Counseling and information services are available, as is tutoring in some subjects, including math, business, economics, sciences, accounting, computer science, and writing. There is a reader service for the blind and remedial math and writing. Workshops and seminars are also offered on study skills, note taking, time management, test-taking strategies, and goal setting.

Campus Safety and Security: Measures include 24-hour foot and vehicle patrol, self-defense education, escort service, and pamphlets/posters/films. There are emergency telephones and lighted pathways/sidewalks.

Programs of Study: UMD confers B.A., B.S., B.A.A., B.Ac., B.A.S., B.B.A., B.Ch.E., B.E.C.E., B.F.A., B.I.E., B.M., B.S.CH.E., B.S.E.C.E, and B.S.I.E. degrees. Master's degrees are also awarded. Bachelor's degrees are awarded in BIOLOGICAL SCIENCE (biology/biological science), BUSINESS (business administration and management), COMMUNICATIONS AND THE ARTS (art, communications, dramatic arts, English, graphic design, jazz, music, music performance, and Spanish), COMPUTER AND PHYSICAL SCIENCE (chemistry, computer science, earth science, geology, mathematics, and physics), EDUCATION (art, athletic training, elementary, English, foreign languages, health, mathematics, music, physical, recreation, science, and social studies), ENGINEERING AND ENVIRONMENTAL DESIGN (chemical engineering, computer engineering, electrical/electronics engineering, environmental science, and industrial engineering), HEALTH PROFESSIONS (speech pathology/audiology), SOCIAL SCIENCE (anthropology, criminology, early childhood studies, economics, geography, history, interdisciplinary studies, international studies, Native American studies, philosophy, political science/government, psychology, sociology, urban studies, and women's studies). Business, sciences, and engineering are the strongest academically. Business administration, communication, and biology are the largest.

Required: To graduate, students must complete 120 to 136 semester credits, including 2 courses in college writing and a liberal education distribution of at least 35 credits in 10 academic areas. At least 4 credits of course work must emphasize cultural diversity, and 4 should emphasize an international perspective.

Special: Students may study abroad in England, Sweden, and Finland. UMD also offers a 3-2 engineering degree with the University of Minnesota Twin Cities, cross-registration with the College of St. Scholastica and the University of Wisconsin/Superior, internships, work-study programs, a B.A.-B.S. degree in several fields, dual degrees such as biochemistry and molecular biology, student-designed majors, and nondegree study. There are 6 national honor societies, including Phi Beta Kappa, a freshman honors program, and 17 departmental honors programs.

Faculty/Classroom: 58% of faculty are male; 42%, female. 95% teach undergraduates. No introductory courses are taught by graduate students. The average class size in an introductory lecture is 65.

Admissions: 79% of the 2001-2002 applicants were accepted. The ACT scores for the 2001-2002 freshman class were: 19% below 21, 28% between 21 and 23, 35% between 24 and 26, 15% between 27 and 28, and 3% above 28. 70 freshmen graduated first in their class.

Requirements: The ACT is required and the SAT I is recommended. In addition, applicants must have completed 4 years in English, 3 each in math and sciences, and 2 each in a single second language and social studies. Course work in the visual and performing arts and computer skills is recommended. Students with a GED certificate will be admitted selectively as space permits. AP and CLEP credits are accepted. Important factors in the admissions decision are advanced placement or honor courses, recommendations by school officials, and evidence of special talent.

Procedure: Freshmen are admitted to all sessions. Entrance exams should be taken at the end of the junior year or the beginning of the senior year. Applications should be filed by August 1 for fall entry and November 15 for spring entry. The fall 2001 application fee was $25. Notification is sent on a rolling basis.

Transfer: 409 transfer students enrolled in 2001-2002. Applicants who have completed 26 or more semester credits must have a minimum 2.0 GPA and a 75% completion ratio; applicants who have attempted fewer than 26 semester credits must have a high school rank at or above the 50th percentile, a 1.8 GPA in their previous college work, and a 75% completion ratio. 30 credits of 120 must be completed at UMD.

Visiting: There are regularly scheduled orientations for prospective students, including a campus tour and an appointment with admissions counselors, faculty, or coaches, if requested. There are guides for informal visits and visitors may sit in on classes. To schedule a visit, contact the Admissions Office.

Financial Aid: 7% of undergraduates work part time. The FAFSA is required. The fall application deadline is March 31.

International Students: There were 87 international students enrolled in a recent year. The school actively recruits these students. They must score 550 on the written TOEFL.

Computers: The mainframe is a UNIX operating system with Novell servers. Mainframe access is available through 6 computer labs across campus. Students may also open an account for personal use on the central UNIX system. All students may access the system 8 A.M. to 12 P.M. weekdays; Saturday and Sunday hours are also available. There are no time limits. The fee is $2 per credit for basic Internet access.

Graduates: In 2001, 1164 bachelor's degrees were awarded. The most popular majors were business administration (18%), communication (18%), and criminology (10%). In an average class, 5% graduate in 3 years, 19% in 4 years, 17% in 5 years, and 5% in 6 years. 51 companies recruited on campus in 2000-2001.

Admissions Contact: Beth Esselstrom, Director of Admissions.
E-mail: *umdadmis@d.umn.edu* Web: *http://www.d.umn.edu*

UNIVERSITY OF MINNESOTA/MORRIS — B-3

Morris, MN 56267-2199 (320) 589-6035
(800) 992-8863; Fax: (320) 589-1673

Full-time: 736 men, 1057 women	**Faculty:** 120; IIB, av$
Part-time: 48 men, 86 women	**Ph.D.s:** 87%
Graduate: none	**Student/Faculty:** 15 to 1
Year: semesters, May inter- and summer session	**Tuition:** $6246 ($10,763)
	Room & Board: $4470
Application Deadline: March 15	
Freshman Class: 1269 applied, 1064 accepted, 480 enrolled	
SAT I Verbal/Math: 584/572	**ACT:** 24 **VERY COMPETITIVE**

The University of Minnesota/Morris, founded in 1959, is a public liberal arts institution within the University of Minnesota system. In addition to regional accreditation, UMM has baccalaureate program accreditation with NCATE. The library contains 191,000 volumes, 218,549 microform items, and 1923 audiovisual forms/CDs, and subscribes to 6911 periodicals. Computerized library services include the card catalog, interlibrary loans, and database searching. Special learning facilities include a learning resource center, art gallery, radio station, TV studios, language lab, observatory, and agricultural experiment station. The 130-acre campus is in a small town 150 miles northwest of Minneapolis. Including residence halls, there are 36 buildings.

Student Life: 79% of undergraduates are from Minnesota. Others are from 32 states, 15 foreign countries, and Canada. 95% are from public schools. 81% are white. The average age of freshmen is 18; all undergraduates, 21. 18% do not continue beyond their first year; 60% remain to graduate.

Housing: 1032 students can be accommodated in college housing, which includes coed dormitories and on-campus apartments. On-campus housing is guaranteed for the freshman year only and is available on a lottery system for upperclassmen. 51% of students commute. All students may keep cars.

Activities: There are no fraternities or sororities. There are 84 groups on campus, including art, band, campus activities, cheerleading, chess, choir, chorus, computers, dance, drama, ethnic, forensics, gay, honors, international, jazz band, literary magazine, mentoring, musical theater, newspaper, orchestra, political, professional, radio and TV, reading instruction, religious, riding, social, social service, student government, swing dancing, and yearbook. Popular campus events include Cultural Heritage Week, Diversity Jam, and Jazz Fest.

Sports: There are 7 intercollegiate sports for men and 9 for women, and 12 intramural sports for men and 12 for women. Facilities include a 4500-seat stadium, a phys ed center, 5 gyms, wrestling, exercise, and weight rooms, an Olympic-size pool, handball and racquetball courts, a track, fields for softball, baseball, soccer, and football, a diving well, a warm-water pool and slide, an indoor track, and a cardiovascular fitness room.

Disabled Students: 70% of the campus is accessible. Wheelchair ramps, elevators, special parking, specially equipped rest rooms, special class scheduling, lowered drinking fountains, and a disability services coordinator are available. Special learning equipment and services are available through the academic assistance center.

Services: Counseling and information services are available, as is tutoring in every subject. There is a reader service for the blind, and remedial math, reading, and writing.

Campus Safety and Security: Measures include 24-hour foot and vehicle patrol, self-defense education, escort service, and shuttle buses. There are informal discussions, pamphlets/posters/films, emergency telephones, and lighted pathways/sidewalks.

Programs of Study: UMM confers the B.A. degree. Bachelor's degrees are awarded in BIOLOGICAL SCIENCE (biology/biological science), BUSINESS (management science), COMMUNICATIONS AND THE ARTS (art history and appreciation, dramatic arts, English, French, German, music, Spanish, speech/debate/rhetoric, and studio art), COMPUTER AND PHYSICAL SCIENCE (chemistry, computer science, geology, mathematics, and physics), EDUCATION (elementary and secondary), HEALTH PROFESSIONS (premedicine), SOCIAL SCIENCE (anthropology, economics, European studies, history, Latin American studies, liberal arts/general studies, philosophy, political science/government, prelaw, psychology, social science, sociology, and women's studies). Psychology and sciences are the strongest academically. Economics, education, and English are the largest.

Required: In addition to 40 semester hours in the major, students are required to complete 60 credits of a general education curriculum, including courses in writing, computing, foreign language or equivalent, and advanced study, as well as courses focusing on the arts, the physical and abstract worlds, and the self and others. In order to graduate, students must complete at least 120 semester credits with a minimum GPA of 2.0.

Special: UMM offers work-study programs, internships, study abroad, dual majors, student-designed majors, nondegree study, pass/fail options, and credit for life, military, and work experience. There is a 2-3 engineering degree with the University of Minnesota at Twin Cities. A competitive, merit-based program that pairs students and professors in order to undertake creative projects is available. There is a freshman honors program.

Faculty/Classroom: 58% of faculty are male; 42%, female. All teach undergraduates and 89% both teach and do research. The average class size in an introductory lecture is 25; in a laboratory, 20; and in a regular course, 18.

Admissions: 84% of the 2001-2002 applicants were accepted. The SAT I scores for the 2001-2002 freshman class were: Verbal--17% below 500, 39% between 500 and 599, 32% between 600 and 700, and 12% above 700; Math--22% below 500, 44% between 500 and 599, 26% between 600 and 700, and 8% above 700. The ACT scores were 15% below 21, 26% between 21 and 23, 30% between 24 and 26, 14% between 27 and 28, and 15% above 28. 74% of the current freshmen were in the top fifth of their class; 92% were in the top two fifths. There were 2 National Merit finalists and 7 semifinalists. 25 freshmen graduated first in their class.

Requirements: The SAT I or ACT is required. In addition, applicants should be graduates of an accredited secondary school or have a GED certificate. They must have completed 4 years of English, 3 each of math and science, 2 of a single foreign language, and 1 eah of social studies and American history. A GPA of 3.0 is required. AP and CLEP credits are accepted. Important factors in the admissions decision are leadership record, extracurricular activities record, and advanced placement or honor courses. Applications are accepted on-line at *http://www.mrs.umn.edu/admissions.*

Procedure: Freshmen are admitted fall and spring. Entrance exams should be taken before December 1 of the senior year. There are early decision and deferred admissions plans. Early decision applications should be filed by December 1; regular applications, by March 15 for fall entry and November 1 for winter entry, along with a $25 fee. Notification of early decision is sent December 20; regular decision, April 1.

Transfer: 82 transfer students enrolled in 2001-2002. Applicants must submit a high school transcript or GED scores, all college transcripts, and have maintained a minimum GPA of 2.5. 30 credits of 120 must be completed at UMM.

Visiting: There are regularly scheduled orientations for prospective students, including a campus tour, lunch with faculty, a session with admissions staff, and a student panel. There are guides for informal visits and visitors may sit in on classes and stay overnight. To schedule a visit, contact the Admissions Office.

Financial Aid: In 2001-2002, 85% of all freshmen and 94% of continuing students received some form of financial aid. 76% of freshmen and 80% of continuing students received need-based aid. The average freshman award was $5000. Of that total, scholarships or need-based grants averaged $3212; loans averaged $2891; and work contracts averaged $376. 90% of undergraduates work part time. Average annual earnings from campus work are $740. The average financial indebtedness of the 2001 graduate was $10,100. The FAFSA is required. The fall application deadline is April 1.

International Students: There are 23 international students enrolled. They must score 550 on the written TOEFL and also take the SAT I or the ACT.

Computers: The mainframes are a cluster of VAX and UNIX computers and shared mainframe resources with University of Minnesota/Twin Cities. There are 7 PC and Mac computer labs on campus, with a student-to-computer ratio of about 13 to 1. All dorm rooms have access to the system. All students may access the system 24 hours per day. There are no time limits and no fees.

Graduates: In 2001, 241 bachelor's degrees were awarded. The most popular majors were elementary education (13%), English (10%), and biology (10%). In an average class, 44% graduate in 4 years, 60% in 5 years, and 67% in 6 years. 37 companies recruited on campus in 2000-2001. Of the 2000 graduating class, 29% were enrolled in graduate school within 6 months of graduation and 71% were employed.

Admissions Contact: Scott Hagg, Director of Admissions. A video is available. E-mail: *admissions@mrs.umn.edu*
Web: *http://www.mrs.umn.edu*

UNIVERSITY OF MINNESOTA/TWIN CITIES C-4
Minneapolis, MN 55455 **(612) 625-2008**
(800) 752-1000; Fax: (612) 625-1693

Full-time: 11,474 men, 10,475 women — **Faculty:** 2463; I, +$
Part-time: 3763 men, 4424 women — **Ph.D.s:** 91%
Graduate: 6889 men, 7572 women — **Student/Faculty:** 8 to 1
Year: semesters, summer session — **Tuition:** $5536 ($15,002)
Application Deadline: December 15 — **Room & Board:** $5587
Freshman Class: 15,436 applied, 11,673 accepted, 5344 enrolled
SAT I Verbal/Math: 590/620 — **ACT:** 25 **VERY COMPETITIVE**

University of Minnesota/Twin Cities, founded in 1851, is a land-grant institution offering programs in liberal and fine arts, physical and biological sciences, health sciences, education, natural resources, human ecology, business, agriculture, engineering, and professional training in law, medicine, dentistry, pharmacy, and veterinary medicine. There are 18 undergraduate schools and 1 graduate school. In addition to regional accreditation, the university has baccalaureate program accreditation with AACSB, ABET, ABFSE, ACEJMC, ADA, APTA, ASLA, CSWE, FIDER, NAAB, NASM, NCATE, NLN, and SAF. The 17 libraries contain 565 million volumes, 5.4 million microform items, and 500,000 audiovisual forms/CDs, and subscribe to 48,105 periodicals. Computerized library services include the card catalog, interlibrary loans, and database searching. Special learning facilities include a learning resource center, art gallery, natural history museum, planetarium, radio station, and TV station. The 2000-acre campus is in an urban area within both Minneapolis and St. Paul. Including residence halls, there are 205 buildings.

Student Life: 72% of undergraduates are from Minnesota. Others are from 49 states, 110 foreign countries, and Canada. 85% are from public schools. 83% are white. The average age of freshmen is 18; all undergraduates, 22. 17% do not continue beyond their first year; 56% remain to graduate.

Housing: 5636 students can be accommodated in college housing, which includes single-sex and coed dormitories, on-campus apartments, off-campus apartments, married-student housing, fraternity houses, and sorority houses. In addition, there are honors houses and special-interest houses. On-campus housing is guaranteed for the freshman year only, is available on a first-come, first-served basis, and is available on a lottery system for upperclassmen. 88% of students commute. Alcohol is not permitted. All students may keep cars.

Activities: There are 33 local fraternities and 18 local sororities. There are 525 groups on campus, including art, band, cheerleading, chess, choir, chorale, chorus, computers, dance, debate, drama, ethnic, film, gay, honors, international, jazz band, literary magazine, marching band, musical theater, newspaper, orchestra, pep band, photography, political, professional, radio and TV, religious, social, social service, student government, symphony, and yearbook. Popular campus events include Campus Carnival.

Sports: There are 12 intercollegiate sports for men and 11 for women, and 16 intramural sports for men and 16 for women. Facilities include a domed stadium, 3 gyms, 2 field houses, a hockey rink, an Olympic-size aquatic center, and a student recreation center.

Disabled Students: 75% of the campus is accessible. Wheelchair ramps, elevators, special parking, specially equipped rest rooms, special class scheduling, lowered drinking fountains, lowered telephones, listening devices, TTY and volume-control phones, print enlargers, and adaptive computers are available. In addition, support groups and counselors provide assistance with all areas of university life and career planning.

Services: Counseling and information services are available, as is tutoring in every subject. There is a reader service for the blind, remedial math, reading, and writing, test proctoring, and sign language interpreters.

Campus Safety and Security: Measures include 24-hour foot and vehicle patrol, self-defense education, escort service, and shuttle buses. There are informal discussions, pamphlets/posters/films, emergency telephones, lighted pathways/sidewalks, a 20-member university police force, and blue light phone centers.

Programs of Study: The university confers B.A., B.S., B.Aerospace Eng., B.Agr.Eng., B.C.E., B.Ch., B.Ch.E., B.Comp.Sci., B.E.E., B.F.A., B.G.E., B.I.S., B.M., B.Materials Sci., B.Mathematics, B.M.E., B.Pcs., B.S.Bus., B.S.G., B.S. in Astrophysics, B.S. in Geophysics, B.S.N., and B.Statistics. degrees. Master's and doctoral degrees are also awarded. Bachelor's degrees are awarded in AGRICULTURE (agricultural business management, agricultural economics, fishing and fisheries, forestry and related sciences, forestry production and processing, and natural resource management), BIOLOGICAL SCIENCE (biochemistry, biology/biological science, botany, cell biology, ecology, evolutionary biology, genetics, microbiology, nutrition, physiology, and wildlife biology), BUSINESS (accounting, business administration and management, management science, marketing/retailing/merchandising, recreation and leisure services, recreational facilities management, and retailing), COMMUNICATIONS AND THE ARTS (art history and appreciation, Chinese, classical languages, dance, English, film arts, French, German, Greek, Hebrew, Italian, Japanese, languages, Latin, linguistics, music, Russian, Scandinavian languages, Spanish, speech/debate/rhetoric, and studio art), COMPUTER AND PHYSICAL SCIENCE (actuarial science, astronomy, astrophysics, chemistry, computer science, geology, geophysics and seismology, mathematics, physics, and statistics), EDUCATION (agricultural, art, bilingual/bicultural, business, early childhood, elementary, English, home economics, industrial arts, mathematics, music, physical, science, social studies, and teaching English as a second/foreign language (TESOL/TEFOL)), ENGINEERING AND ENVIRONMENTAL DESIGN (aeronautical engineering, agricultural engineering, architecture, chemical engineering, civil engineering, electrical/electronics engineering, environmental design, geological engineering, industrial engineering, interior design, landscape architecture/design, materials engineering, materials science, mechanical engineering, and metallurgical engineering), HEALTH PROFESSIONS (dental hygiene, medical laboratory technology, music therapy, nursing, occupational therapy, pharmacy, physical therapy, predentistry, premedicine, prepharmacy, preveterinary science, and speech pathology/audiology), SOCIAL SCIENCE (African American studies, African studies, American Indian studies, American studies, anthropology, child psychology/development, East Asian studies, economics, food science, geography, history, humanities, international relations, Mexican-American/Chicano studies, Middle Eastern studies, philosophy, political science/government, prelaw, psychology, Russian and Slavic studies, sociology, South Asian studies, textiles and clothing, urban studies, and women's studies). Chemical engineering, psychology, and economics are the strongest academically. Mechanical engineering, psychology, and electrical engineering are the largest.

Required: To graduate, students must complete 120 to 130 semester credits, including 45 in the major, with a minimum GPA of 2.0. Distribution requirements include course work in the 4 areas of communication, language, and symbolic systems, physical and biological sciences, the individual and society, and artistic expression. Other requirements vary by program.

Special: The university offers cooperative programs, cross-registration with the Minnesota Community College system, internships, study abroad in 65 countries, work-study programs both on and off campus, a B.A.-B.S. degree in all majors, a general studies degree, and dual and student-designed majors. Pass/fail options and credit for life, military, or work experience are available. There are 21 national honor societies, including Phi Beta Kappa, a freshman honors program, and 8 departmental honors programs.

Faculty/Classroom: 75% of faculty are male; 25%, female. All both teach and do research. The average class size in an introductory lecture is 29.

Admissions: 76% of the 2001-2002 applicants were accepted. The SAT I scores for the 2001-2002 freshman class were: Verbal--14% below 500, 36% between 500 and 599, 38% between 600 and 700, and 12% above 700; Math--11% below 500, 28% between 500 and 599, 42% between 600 and 700, and 20% above 700. The ACT scores were 17% below 21, 22% between 21 and 23, 28% between 24 and 26, 16% between 27 and 28, and 17% above 28. 52% of the current freshmen were in the top fifth of their class; 85% were in the top two fifths. 266 freshmen graduated first in their class in a recent year.

Requirements: The ACT is recommended. In addition, the university uses a formula index in evaluating high school rank and ACT test scores. A portfolio is required for studio arts and architecture, an audition for music, and an interview for architecture and education. AP and CLEP credits are accepted. Important factors in the admissions decision are advanced placement or honor courses, evidence of special talent, and leadership record. Applications are accepted on-line at the university's web site *http://admissions.tc.umn.edu.*

Procedure: Freshmen are admitted to all sessions. Entrance exams should be taken by the end of the junior year or October/November/December of the senior year. There is an early admissions plan. Applications should be filed by December 15 for fall entry and October 15 for spring entry. Notification is sent on a rolling basis.

Transfer: 2136 transfer students enrolled in a recent year. Admission requirements vary by major/program, with a minimum 2.2 GPA needed for consideration. 30 credits of 120 must be completed at the university.

Visiting: There are regularly scheduled orientations for prospective students. There are guides for informal visits and visitors may sit in on classes and stay overnight. To schedule a visit, contact The Visit Line at (612) 625-0000.

Financial Aid: In 2001-2002, 72% of all freshmen and 59% of continuing students received some form of financial aid. The FAFSA is required. The fall application deadline is open.

International Students: There were 666 international students enrolled in a recent year. They must score 550 on the written TOEFL or take the MELAB or the college's own test, the Minnesota Battery, or the Institutional TOEFL, and also take the ACT (residents of Minnesota and neighboring states), or the SAT I (residents of other states).

Computers: The mainframes are an IBM/CMS, CDC CYBER NOSNE, NOS, EP/IX, and DEC VMS. There are about 250 terminals and 1000 PCs for public use. All the PCs are networked. All students may access the system 24 hours a day, 7 days a week. Students may access the system 2 hours per session if there are others waiting or signed on. The fee is $45 per quarter. It is strongly recommended that all students have a personal computer.

Graduates: In a recent year, 5131 bachelor's degrees were awarded. The most popular majors were business administration (6%), psychology (5%), and mechanical engineering (3%). In an average class, 1% graduate in 3 years, 18% in 4 years, 39% in 5 years, and 48% in 6 years. 200 companies recruited on campus in 2000-2001.

Admissions Contact: Dr. Wayne Sigler, Ph.D., Director of Admissions. A video is available. E-mail: *admissions@tc.umn.edu.*
Web: *www.umn.edu*

UNIVERSITY OF SAINT THOMAS — C-4

St. Paul, MN 55105 — (651) 962-6150
(800) 328-6819, ext. 2; Fax: (651) 962-6160

Full-time: 2242 men, 2478 women	**Faculty:** 270; IIA, av$
Part-time: 318 men, 378 women	**Ph.D.s:** 84%
Graduate: 3012 men, 3045 women	**Student/Faculty:** 12 to 1
Year: 4-1-4, summer session	**Tuition:** $18,421
Application Deadline: open	**Room & Board:** $5623
Freshman Class: 3257 applied, 2639 accepted, 1071 enrolled	
SAT I Verbal/Math: 570/600	**ACT:** 25 **VERY COMPETITIVE**

The University of Saint Thomas, founded in 1885, is a private liberal arts institution affiliated with the Roman Catholic Church. There are 4 undergraduate and 9 graduate schools. In addition to regional accreditation, Saint Thomas has baccalaureate program accreditation with ABET, ACS, CSWE, NASM, and NCATE. The 3 libraries contain 408,473 volumes, 878,519 microform items, and 5270 audiovisual forms/CDs, and subscribe to 2621 periodicals. Computerized library services include the card catalog, interlibrary loans, and database searching. Special learning facilities include a learning resource center. The 78-acre campus is in an urban area 5 miles west of St. Paul and 5 miles east of Minneapolis. Including residence halls, there are 74 buildings.

Student Life: 82% of undergraduates are from Minnesota. Others are from 42 states and 48 foreign countries. 73% are from public schools. 88% are white. 54% are Catholic; 26% Protestant; 11% Muslim, Orthodox, Buddhist, Hindu, and other denominations. The average age of freshmen is 18; all undergraduates, 21. 16% do not continue beyond their first year.

Housing: 2000 students can be accommodated in college housing, which includes single-sex dormitories, on-campus apartments, and off-campus apartments. In addition, there are special-interest houses. Chemical-free lifestyle, first-year experience, and women in science housing. On-campus housing is available on a first-come, first-served basis and on a lottery system for upperclassmen. 57% of students commute. All students may keep cars.

Activities: There are no fraternities or sororities. There are 94 groups on campus, including art, band, cheerleading, chess, choir, chorus, computers, dance, debate, drama, drill team, ethnic, gay, honors, international, jazz band, lecture committee, literary magazine, multicultural organizations, musical theater, newspaper, pep band, photography, political, professional, radio and TV, religious, social, social service, student government, student programming board, and yearbook. Popular campus events include Spring Fling, Taste of St. Thomas, and Senior Send-off.

Sports: There are 10 intercollegiate sports for men and 10 for women, and 10 intramural sports for men and 10 for women. Facilities include a field house with a 1/10-mile track, 5 volleyball courts, a 2000-seat gym, 4 basketball courts, 4 tennis courts, 6 racquetball courts, a fitness center, weight training and aerobics rooms, 2 swimming pools, 2 squash courts, a 5000-seat football and track stadium that includes an 8-lane Olympic caliber track, a baseball diamond, soccer, softball, and other playing fields, and 6 outdoor tennis courts.

Disabled Students: 80% of the campus is accessible. Wheelchair ramps, elevators, special parking, specially equipped rest rooms, special class scheduling, lowered drinking fountains, and lowered telephones are available.

Services: Counseling and information services are available, as is tutoring in most subjects. There is a reader service for the blind.

Campus Safety and Security: Measures include 24-hour foot and vehicle patrol, escort service, shuttle buses, and informal discussions. There are pamphlets/posters/films, emergency telephones, and lighted pathways/sidewalks.

Programs of Study: Saint Thomas confers B.A., B.S., B.S.E., and B.S.M.E. degrees. Master's and doctoral degrees are also awarded. Bachelor's degrees are awarded in BIOLOGICAL SCIENCE (biology/biological science and neurosciences), BUSINESS (accounting, banking and finance, business administration and management, entrepreneurial studies, international business management, marketing management, personnel management, and real estate), COMMUNICATIONS AND THE ARTS (art history and appreciation, classical languages, communications, dramatic arts, English, French, German, journalism, Latin, literature, music, music business management, Russian, and Spanish), COMPUTER AND PHYSICAL SCIENCE (actuarial science, chemistry, computer science, geology, mathematics, and physics), EDUCATION (elementary, health, music, physical, science, and secondary), ENGINEERING AND ENVIRONMENTAL DESIGN (electrical/electronics engineering, environmental science, and mechanical engineering), HEALTH PROFESSIONS (community health work), SOCIAL SCIENCE (Christian studies, classical/ancient civilization, criminal justice, East Asian studies, economics, geography, history, international studies, peace studies, philosophy, political science/government, psychology, Russian and Slavic studies, social science, social studies, social work, sociology, theological studies, and women's studies). Business is the largest.

Required: All students must maintain a minimum GPA of 2.0 and complete at least 33 courses, or 132 semester credits, plus 1 in phys ed for no credit. Core curriculum requirements include 3 courses each in language and culture, faith and Catholic tradition, natural science and mathematical and quantitative reasoning, 2 courses each in moral and philosophical reasoning and literature and writing, and 1 course each in fine arts, historical studies, social analysis, and human diversity. Students must complete 84 credits outside their major and demostrate proficiency in operating a computer.

Special: Students may cross-register with Augsburg and Macalester Colleges, the College of Saint Catherine, and Hamline University. Study abroad is available in more than 40 countries, and there are several work-study programs. There are formal 3-2 engineering degree arrangements with Washington and Notre Dame Universities and the University of Minnesota, and 3-2 engineering degrees can also be arranged with many other accredited engineering programs. Nondegree study and pass/fail options also are available. There are 13 national honor societies and a freshman honors program.

Faculty/Classroom: 62% of faculty are male; 38%, female. 80% teach undergraduates. No introductory courses are taught by graduate students. The average class size in an introductory lecture is 24; in a laboratory, 15; and in a regular course, 21.

Admissions: 81% of the 2001-2002 applicants were accepted. The SAT I scores for the 2001-2002 freshman class were: Verbal--20% below 500, 41% between 500 and 599, 33% between 600 and 700, and 6% above 700; Math--16% below 500, 34% between 500 and 599, 46% between 600 and 700, and 4% above 700. The ACT scores were 11% below 21, 25% between 21 and 23, 29% between 24 and 26, 19% between 27 and 28, and 16% above 28. 50% of the current freshmen were in the top fifth of their class; 80% were in the top two fifths. There were 8 National Merit finalists. 43 freshmen graduated first in their class.

Requirements: The SAT I or ACT is required. In addition, Saint Thomas recommends 4 units each of English, foreign language, and math (with 3 units of math required), and 2 each of science and history or social sciences. An essay is required. The GED is accepted. AP and CLEP credits are accepted. Important factors in the admissions decision are recommendations by school officials, geographic diversity, and parents or siblings attending the school. Applications are accepted on computer disk and on-line through the Admissions Office at the school's web site.

Procedure: Freshmen are admitted fall and spring. Entrance exams should be taken by the fall of the senior year. There is a deferred admissions plan. Application deadlines are open. The fall 2001 application fee was $30. Notification is sent on a rolling basis.

Transfer: 273 transfer students enrolled in 2001-2002. Transfer applicants must have a minimum GPA of 2.3 in transferable college credits. 32 credits of 132 must be completed at Saint Thomas.

Visiting: There are regularly scheduled orientations for prospective students, consisting of an open house in fall and spring that includes an admissions counselor presentation, a tour, a faculty fair, lunch, and a financial aid presentation. Other smaller orientations are also available. There are guides for informal visits and visitors may sit in on classes and stay overnight. To schedule a visit, contact the Visit Coordinator at (651) 962-6154 or *admvisit@stthomas.edu*

Financial Aid: In 2001-2002, 93% of all freshmen and 76% of continuing students received some form of financial aid. 43% of freshmen and 46% of continuing students received need-based aid. The average freshman award was $11,767. Of that total, scholarships or need-based grants averaged $7263 ($27,751 maximum); loans averaged $2944 ($25,125 maximum); and work contracts averaged $1560 ($4500 maximum). 45% of undergraduates work part time. Average annual earnings from campus work are $2265. The average financial indebtedness of the 2001 graduate was $19,708. The FAFSA is required. The fall application deadline is April 1.

International Students: There are 63 international students enrolled. They must score 550 on the written TOEFL or take the MELAB.

Computers: The mainframes are a VMS cluster, comprised of a Compaq ES (Enterprise Server) 40 and an AXP4100. Connection to the network is via fastnet, with full access from all resident hall rooms. Students are given access to the Internet via our network, a personal e-mail account, personal web page space, and NT storage space. All computers in all labs have Internet access. There are 7 public labs, 7 resident hall labs, and 58 discipline-specific labs with a total of 570 PCs. All students may access the system at any time. There are no time limits and no fees.

Graduates: In 2001, 1129 bachelor's degrees were awarded. The most popular majors were business administration/marketing (40%), journalism/communications (10%), and social science/history (9%). In an average class, 50% graduate in 4 years, 66% in 5 years, and 68% in 6 years. 70 companies recruited on campus in 2000-2001. Of the 2000 graduating class, 15% were enrolled in graduate school within 6 months of graduation and 96% were employed.

Admissions Contact: Marla Friederichs, Associate Vice President for Enrollment Management. E-mail: *admissions@stthomas.edu*
Web: *http://www.stthomas.edu*

WINONA STATE UNIVERSITY — D-5

Winona, MN 55987-5838 — **(507) 457-5100**
(800) DIAL-WSU; Fax: (507) 457-5620

Full-time: 2283 men, 3947 women	**Faculty:** 300; IIB, ++$
Part-time: 338 men, 546 women	**Ph.D.s:** 80%
Graduate: 185 men, 448 women	**Student/Faculty:** 18 to 1
Year: semesters, summer session	**Tuition:** $4630 ($8360)
Application Deadline: open	**Room & Board:** $3940

Freshman Class: 4032 applied, 3420 accepted, 1634 enrolled
ACT: 23 — **COMPETITIVE**

Winona State University, founded in 1858, is a public liberal arts institution and part of the Minnesota State Colleges and Universities system. There are 5 undergraduate schools and 1 graduate school. In addition to regional accreditation, WSU has baccalaureate program accreditation with ABET, ACCE, CSWE, NCATE, and NLN. The library contains 245,000 volumes and 831,000 microform items, and subscribes to 1400 periodicals. Computerized library services include interlibrary loans and database searching. Special learning facilities include a learning resource center, art gallery, radio station, and TV station. The 47-acre campus is in a small town 100 miles southeast of Minneapolis and St. Paul. Including residence halls, there are 26 buildings.

Student Life: 60% of undergraduates are from Minnesota. Others are from 40 states, 45 foreign countries, and Canada. 85% are from public schools. 94% are white. 40% are Catholic; 40% Protestant. The average age of freshmen is 18; all undergraduates, 23. 25% do not continue beyond their first year; 50% remain to graduate.

Housing: 2100 students can be accommodated in college housing, which includes single-sex and coed dormitories. In addition, there are honors houses. On-campus housing is guaranteed for all 4 years. Alcohol is not permitted. All students may keep cars.

Activities: 3% of men belong to 3 national fraternities; 3% of women belong to 3 national sororities. There are 130 groups on campus, including art, band, cheerleading, chess, choir, chorale, chorus, computers, dance, debate, drama, ethnic, forensics, gay, honors, international, jazz band, literary magazine, musical theater, newspaper, orchestra, pep band, photography, political, professional, radio and TV, religious, social, social service, student government, and symphony.

Sports: There are 5 intercollegiate sports for men and 9 for women, and 15 intramural sports for men and 15 for women. Facilities include a 4000-seat stadium, a bowling alley, 8 outdoor tennis courts, and a field house with 10 gyms, 3 weight rooms, a swimming pool, indoor track and tennis facilities, and handball/racquetball courts.

Disabled Students: Wheelchair ramps, elevators, special parking, specially equipped rest rooms, special class scheduling, lowered drinking fountains, lowered telephones, and special apartments are available.

Services: Counseling and information services are available, as is tutoring in most subjects.

Campus Safety and Security: Measures include 24-hour foot and vehicle patrol, self-defense education, escort service, and shuttle buses. There are informal discussions, pamphlets/posters/films, emergency telephones, and lighted pathways/sidewalks.

Programs of Study: WSU confers B.A., B.S., B.S.E., and B.S.N. degrees. Associate and master's degrees are also awarded. Bachelor's degrees are awarded in BIOLOGICAL SCIENCE (biology/biological science), BUSINESS (accounting, banking and finance, business administration and management, business economics, management information systems, marketing/retailing/merchandising, and personnel management), COMMUNICATIONS AND THE ARTS (advertising, broadcasting, communications, dramatic arts, English, fine arts, French, German, journalism, music, Spanish, and speech/debate/rhetoric), COMPUTER AND PHYSICAL SCIENCE (chemistry, computer science, earth science, geology, mathematics, physics, and statistics), EDUCATION (art, business, early childhood, elementary, foreign languages, health, music, science, secondary, and special), ENGINEERING AND ENVIRONMENTAL DESIGN (materials engineering), HEALTH PROFESSIONS (cytotechnology, medical laboratory technology, nursing, physical therapy, predentistry, premedicine, preveterinary science, and public health), SOCIAL SCIENCE (community services, criminal justice, economics, history, international relations, paralegal studies, parks and recreation management, physical fitness/movement, political science/government, prelaw, psychology, public administration, social science, social work, and sociology). Engineering, nursing, and accounting are the strongest academically. Business administration, mass communication, and education are the largest.

Required: To graduate, students must complete 128 credit hours with a minimum GPA of 2.5 in most majors. General education requirements include 6 credits each in humanities, science/math, social science, and a different culture, 4 in English, 3 each in speech and math, and 2 in phys ed. Majors average 40 credits and some require a capstone experience.

Special: WSU offers cross-registration with St. Mary's University, study abroad in 25 countries, internships, work-study programs, student-designed majors, dual majors, pass/fail options, and credit for life, military, and work experience. Students may earn accelerated degrees in all majors and a general studies degree. There are 12 national honor societies, a freshman honors program, and 8 departmental honors programs.

Faculty/Classroom: 60% of faculty are male; 40%, female. 90% teach undergraduates, 10% do research, and 25% do both. No introductory courses are taught by graduate students. The average class size in an introductory lecture is 35; in a laboratory, 20; and in a regular course, 30.

Admissions: 85% of the 2001-2002 applicants were accepted. 40% of the current freshmen were in the top fifth of their class; 75% were in the top two fifths. In a recent year, there were 3 National Merit finalists and 45 semifinalists. 50 freshmen graduated first in their class.

Requirements: The SAT I or ACT is required. In addition, candidates should have completed 4 units of English, 1 of which may be speech; 3 each of math, social studies, and science; 2 of a world language; and 1 elective, preferably in world culture, the arts, or computer science. WSU requires applicants to be in the upper 50% of their class. AP and CLEP credits are accepted. Important factors in the admissions decision are advanced placement or honor courses, leadership record, and evidence of special talent. Applications are accepted on computer disk and on-line.

Procedure: Freshmen are admitted to all sessions. Entrance exams should be taken in the junior year. There are early admissions and deferred admissions plans. Application deadlines are open. The application fee is $20. Notification is sent on a rolling basis.

Transfer: Applicants must have completed 24 semester hours of credit with a minimum GPA of 2.4. 32 credits of 128 must be completed at WSU.

Visiting: There are regularly scheduled orientations for prospective students, including daily tours and admissions visits from October through February on Saturday mornings. There are guides for informal visits and visitors may sit in on classes and stay overnight. To schedule a visit, contact the Admissions Office.

Financial Aid: In 2001-2002, 73% of all freshmen and 70% of continuing students received some form of financial aid. The average freshman award in a recent year was $3500. Of that total, scholarships or need-based grants averaged $1500 ($2500 maximum); loans averaged $1000 ($4000 maximum); and work contracts averaged $1000 ($2000 maximum). 40% of undergraduates work part time. Average annual earnings from campus work are $1800. The average financial indebtedness of a recent year's graduate was $7000. The FAFSA is required. The fall application deadline is April 1.

International Students: There were 325 international students enrolled in a recent year. The school actively recruits these students. They must score 550 on the written TOEFL or take the MELAB.

Computers: The mainframes are comprised of Unisys, DEC VAX, IBM AS/400, and other models. There are more than 1400 terminals located throughout the campus, and more than 1400 jacks in the library. All students may access the system 8 A.M. to 12 P.M. There are no time limits and no fees. All students are required to have personal computers. An IBM ThinkPad Model 390 is recommended.

Admissions Contact: Douglas R. Schacke, Director of Admissions. A video is available. E-mail: *admissions@winona.edu*
Web: *http://www.winona.edu*

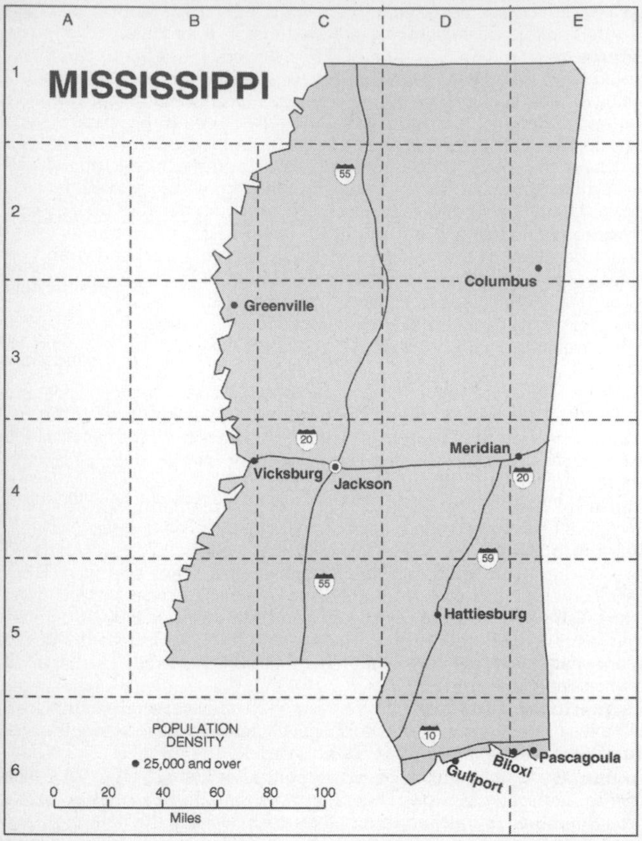

ALCORN STATE UNIVERSITY B-4

Alcorn State, MS 39096-7500 **(601) 877-6147**
(800) 222-6790; Fax: (601) 877-6347

Full-time: 947 men, 1322 women
Part-time: 63 men, 211 women
Graduate: 170 men, 383 women
Year: semesters, summer session
Application Deadline: open
Freshman Class: 1307 accepted, 495 enrolled
SAT I or ACT: required
Faculty: 167; IIB, -$
Ph.D.s: 59%
Student/Faculty: 14 to 1
Tuition: $2785 ($6413)
Room & Board: $2809
LESS COMPETITIVE

Alcorn State University, founded in 1871, is a public institution offering programs in agriculture, the arts and sciences, business, engineering, and nursing. There are 6 undergraduate schools and 1 graduate school. In addition to regional accreditation, Alcorn State University has baccalaureate program accreditation with AAFCS, AHEA, NCATE, and NLN. The library contains 200,907 volumes, 526,492 microform items, and 6276 audiovisual forms/CDs, and subscribes to 1046 periodicals. Computerized library services include the card catalog, interlibrary loans, and database searching. Special learning facilities include a learning resource center and radio station. The 1756-acre campus is in a rural area 45 miles south of Vicksburg. Including residence halls, there are 94 buildings.

Student Life: 83% of undergraduates are from Mississippi. Others are from 31 states, 7 foreign countries, and Canada. 95% are from public schools. 94% are African American. The average age of freshmen is 18; all undergraduates, 23. 28% do not continue beyond their first year.

Housing: 2261 students can be accommodated in college housing, which includes single-sex dormitories. In addition, there are honors houses. On-campus housing is guaranteed for all 4 years. 66% of students live on campus; of those, 45% remain on campus on weekends. Alcohol is not permitted. All students may keep cars.

Activities: 8% of men belong to 5 local and 4 national fraternities; 10% of women belong to 4 local and 4 national sororities. There are 83 groups on campus, including band, cheerleading, choir, chorus, drama, honors, jazz band, marching band, newspaper, photography, religious, student government, and yearbook. Popular campus events include High School Day and Career Development Day.

Sports: There are 7 intercollegiate sports for men and 8 for women, and 8 intramural sports for men and 9 for women. Facilities include a 10,000-seat stadium and a 5000-seat gym.

Disabled Students: 15% of the campus is accessible. Wheelchair ramps, elevators, special parking, specially equipped rest rooms, and lowered drinking fountains are available.

Services: Counseling and information services are available, as is tutoring in most subjects. There is remedial math, reading, writing, and remedial English.

Campus Safety and Security: Measures include 24-hour foot and vehicle patrol, pamphlets/posters/films, and lighted pathways/sidewalks.

Programs of Study: Alcorn State University confers B.A., B.S., B.Mus.Ed., and B.S.N. degrees. Associate and master's degrees are also awarded. Bachelor's degrees are awarded in AGRICULTURE (agricultural economics, agriculture, agronomy, and animal science), BIOLOGICAL SCIENCE (biology/biological science and nutrition), BUSINESS (accounting, business administration and management, and office supervision and management), COMMUNICATIONS AND THE ARTS (communications and English), COMPUTER AND PHYSICAL SCIENCE (chemistry, computer science, and mathematics), EDUCATION (elementary, industrial arts, music, physical, recreation, and special), ENGINEERING AND ENVIRONMENTAL DESIGN (industrial administration/management), HEALTH PROFESSIONS (health science and nursing), SOCIAL SCIENCE (criminal justice, economics, family/consumer studies, history, liberal arts/general studies, political science/government, psychology, and sociology). Elementary education is the largest.

Required: To graduate, students must complete at least 128 semester hours with a minimum GPA of 2.0. Core requirements include 12 hours of social science, 9 each of natural science and creative arts, 6 of English, 4 of phys ed or military science, and 3 each of math and oral communications, as well as 1 of student adjustment.

Special: The university offers cooperative programs in medical technology and physical therapy, internships, and work-study programs. There is 1 national honor society, including Phi Beta Kappa, a freshman honors program, and 5 departmental honors programs.

Faculty/Classroom: 57% of faculty are male; 43%, female. 87% teach undergraduates. The average class size in a laboratory is 19 and in a regular course, 18.

Admissions: The ACT scores for the 2001-2002 freshman class were: 87% between 21 and 23, 12% between 24 and 26, and 1% between 27 and 28. 18% of the current freshmen were in the top fifth of their class.

Requirements: The SAT I or ACT is required, with a minimum composite score of 700 to 710 on the SAT I or 15 on the ACT. In addition, applicants should be graduates of an accredited secondary school or have a GED certificate. They should have completed 4 units of English, 3 each of math and sciences, 2.5 of social sciences, and 1 of a required elective. A GPA of 2.0 is required. AP and CLEP credits are accepted.

Procedure: Freshmen are admitted to all sessions. Entrance exams should be taken so that scores may be submitted at the time application is made. There are early decision, early admissions, and deferred admissions plans. Application deadlines are open. Notification is sent on a rolling basis.

Transfer: 170 transfer students enrolled in 2001-2002. Applicants must have at least 6 hours each of composition and lab sciences, 3 hours of college algebra or above, and 9 other transferable elective hours, and have maintained an overall minimum GPA of 2.0. 104 credits of 128 must be completed at Alcorn State University.

Visiting: There are regularly scheduled orientations for prospective students. There are guides for informal visits and visitors may sit in on classes and stay overnight. To schedule a visit, contact Emanuel F. Barnes, Director of Admissions.

Financial Aid: In 2001-2002, 68% of all freshmen and 73% of continuing students received some form of financial aid. 36% of freshmen received need-based aid. The average freshman award was $6503. Of that total, scholarships or need-based grants averaged $3146 ($6039 maximum); loans averaged $2157 ($2625 maximum); and work contracts averaged $1200 ($1600 maximum). 65% of undergraduates work part time. Average annual earnings from campus work are $2200. The average financial indebtedness of the 2001 graduate was $3700. Alcorn State University is a member of CSS. The CSS/Profile or FAFSA is required.

International Students: There are 30 international students enrolled. The school actively recruits these students. They must score 525 on the written TOEFL, take the college's own test, and also take the ACT, scoring 21, or the SAT I.

Computers: The mainframe is an IBM 4361/PO2. All students may access the system. There are no time limits and no fees.

Graduates: In 2001, 573 bachelor's degrees were awarded.

Admissions Contact: Emanuel F. Barnes, Director of Admissions.
E-mail: *ebarnes@lorman.alcorn.edu* Web: *www.alcorn.edu*

BELHAVEN COLLEGE
Jackson, MS 39202 C-4
(601) 968-5940
(800) 960-5940; Fax: (601) 968-8946

Full-time: 564 men, 946 women
Part-time: 57 men, 99 women
Graduate: 76 men, 141 women
Year: semesters, summer session
Application Deadline: open
Freshman Class: 538 applied, 361 accepted, 206 enrolled
SAT I Verbal/Math: 609/583
Faculty: 51
Ph.D.s: 79%
Student/Faculty: 30 to 1
Tuition: $11,600
Room & Board: $4440
ACT: 24 **COMPETITIVE+**

Belhaven College, founded in 1883, is a private liberal arts institution with a Presbyterian heritage. There is 1 undergraduate school and 1 graduate school. In addition to regional accreditation, Belhaven has baccalaureate program accreditation with NASAD and NASM. The library contains 115,283 volumes, 9032 microform items, and 15,594 audiovisual forms/CDs, and subscribes to 559 periodicals. Computerized library services include the card catalog, interlibrary loans, and database searching. Special learning facilities include an art gallery. The 42-acre campus is in an urban area in Jackson. Including residence halls, there are 13 buildings.

Student Life: 69% of undergraduates are from Mississippi. Others are from 35 states, 11 foreign countries, and Canada. 61% are white; 35% African American. Most are Protestant. The average age of freshmen is 18; all undergraduates, 29. 38% do not continue beyond their first year; 43% remain to graduate.

Housing: 540 students can be accommodated in college housing, which includes single-sex dormitories. On-campus housing is guaranteed for all 4 years. 73% of students commute. Alcohol is not permitted. All students may keep cars.

Activities: There are no fraternities or sororities. There are 22 groups on campus, including art, cheerleading, choir, chorus, dance, drama, ethnic, honors, literary magazine, musical theater, newspaper, political, professional, religious, social service, student government, and yearbook. Popular campus events include Singing Christmas Tree, concert and lecture series, and Lake Day.

Sports: There are 7 intercollegiate sports for men and 7 for women, and 4 intramural sports for men and 4 for women. Facilities include a gym, 5 tennis courts, a lake, an intramural and soccer field, a baseball field, a football/soccer practice field, an athletic training facility, and an exercise, weight, and conditioning complex.

Disabled Students: 25% of the campus is accessible. Wheelchair ramps, elevators, special parking, specially equipped rest rooms, special class scheduling, and lowered drinking fountains are available.

Services: There is remedial math and writing, and study halls for athletes.

Campus Safety and Security: Measures include 24-hour foot and vehicle patrol, escort service, informal discussions, and lighted pathways/sidewalks.

Programs of Study: Belhaven confers B.A., B.S., B.A.A., B.B.A., B.F.A., and B.S.M. degrees. Associate and master's degrees are also awarded. Bachelor's degrees are awarded in BIOLOGICAL SCIENCE (biology/biological science), BUSINESS (accounting and business administration and management), COMMUNICATIONS AND THE ARTS (art, ballet, communications, dance, dramatic arts, English, and music), COMPUTER AND PHYSICAL SCIENCE (chemistry, computer science, information sciences and systems, and mathematics), EDUCATION (athletic training and elementary), HEALTH PROFESSIONS (exercise science), SOCIAL SCIENCE (biblical studies, history, humanities, philosophy, political science/government, psychology, religious music, and social work). Biology and chemistry are the strongest academically. Business administration and education are the largest.

Required: Requirements for graduation vary by degree, but students must complete at least 124 semester hours, including 25 hours of World View Curriculum courses, with a minimum 2.0 GPA.

Special: Students may participate in various internships, including one in Washington, D.C., or in 6 countries through the study-travel program. Belhaven also offers, dual majors, nondegree study, pass/fail options, a 3-2 engineering degree with Mississippi State University, and work-study. 2 1-month summer sessions and 2 2-week minisessions offer additional opportunities for credit. There are 3 national honor societies, a freshman honors program, and 1 departmental honors program.

Faculty/Classroom: 66% of faculty are male; 34%, female. 90% teach undergraduates. No introductory courses are taught by graduate students. The average class size in an introductory lecture is 24; in a laboratory, 16; and in a regular course, 18.

Admissions: 67% of the 2001-2002 applicants were accepted. The SAT I scores for the 2001-2002 freshman class were: Verbal--26% below 500, 29% between 500 and 599, 35% between 600 and 700, and 9% above 700; Math--36% below 500, 40% between 500 and 599, 17% between 600 and 700, and 7% above 700. The ACT scores were 32% below 21, 25% between 21 and 23, 15% between 24 and 26, 15% between 27 and 28, and 13% above 28. 31% of the current freshmen were in the top fifth of their class; 51% were in the top two fifths. There was 1 National Merit finalist and 5 semifinalists. 5 freshmen graduated first in their class.

Requirements: The SAT I or ACT is required; the ACT is preferred. Applicants should be graduates of an accredited secondary school, with 16 academic units, including 4 of English, 2 of math, 1 each of history and natural science, a recommended 2 of a foreign language, and 6 of electives. A personal recommendation is also required. A GPA of 2.0 is required. AP and CLEP credits are accepted. Important factors in the admissions decision are advanced placement or honor courses, evidence of special talent, and extracurricular activities record.

Procedure: Freshmen are admitted to all sessions. Entrance exams should be taken in the junior year. There is an early admissions plan. Application deadlines are open. The fall 2001 application fee was $25. Notification is sent on a rolling basis.

Transfer: 318 transfer students enrolled in 2001-2002. Transfer applicants must have a minimum 2.0 GPA and submit all college transcripts. 31 credits of 124 must be completed at Belhaven.

Visiting: There are guides for informal visits and visitors may sit in on classes and stay overnight. To schedule a visit, contact the Admissions Office.

Financial Aid: In a recent year, 90% of all freshmen and 92% of continuing students received some form of financial aid. 86% of all students received need-based aid. Scholarships or need-based grants averaged $4253; loans averaged $2000; work contracts averaged $1545; and state grants averaged $1055. 12% of undergraduates work part time. Average annual earnings from campus work are $1545. The average financial indebtedness of the 2001 graduate was $17,800. The FAFSA and the college's own financial statement are required. The fall application deadline is March 1.

International Students: There are 24 international students enrolled. The school actively recruits these students. They must score 500 on the written TOEFL or 173 on the electronic version.

Computers: More than 30 PCs are available for academic use in the library and computer lab. All are wired to the campus fiber-optic network, the Internet, and the World Wide Web. All students may access the system. There are no time limits and no fees.

Graduates: In 2001, 299 bachelor's degrees were awarded. The most popular majors were business administration (52%), psychology (8%), and elementary education (7%). In an average class, 34% graduate in 4 years, 43% in 5 years, and 44% in 6 years. 20 companies recruited on campus in 2000-2001.

Admissions Contact: Dr. Stephen D. Livesay, Vice President for Advancement. E-mail: *admissions@belhaven.edu*
Web: *www.belhaven.edu*

BLUE MOUNTAIN COLLEGE
Blue Mountain, MS 38610-0160 D-1
(662) 685-4161
(800) 235-0136; Fax: (662) 685-4776

Full-time: 59 men, 250 women
Part-time: 14 men, 81 women
Graduate: none
Year: semesters, summer session
Application Deadline: open
Freshman Class: 108 applied, 100 accepted, 42 enrolled
SAT I Verbal/Math: 470/435
Faculty: 21
Ph.D.s: 55%
Student/Faculty: 15 to 1
Tuition: $6100
Room & Board: $3000
ACT: 19 **LESS COMPETITIVE**

Blue Mountain College, founded in 1873 and affiliated with the Southern Baptist Church, is a private, liberal arts college for women that also admits men who are preparing for a church-related vocation. The 2 libraries contain 60,500 volumes, 380 microform items, and 4320 audiovisual forms/CDs, and subscribe to 200 periodicals. Computerized library services include the card catalog and database searching. The 44-acre campus is in a rural area 70 miles southwest of Memphis. Including residence halls, there are 14 buildings.

Student Life: 89% of undergraduates are from Mississippi. Others are from 10 states and 1 foreign country. 83% are from public schools. 88% are white; 10% African American. Most are Protestant. The average age of freshmen is 21; all undergraduates, 27. 43% do not continue beyond their first year.

Housing: 234 students can be accommodated in college housing, which includes single-sex dormitories. In addition, there are special-interest houses. On-campus housing is guaranteed for all 4 years. 79% of students commute. Alcohol is not permitted. All students may keep cars.

Activities: There are no fraternities or sororities. There are 30 groups on campus, including art, choir, chorale, chorus, drama, honors, literary magazine, musical theater, professional, religious, social, student government, and yearbook. Popular campus events include High School Weekend, Field Day, and formal dinners and plays.

Sports: There are 2 intercollegiate sports for women, and 3 intramural sports for men and 7 for women. Facilities include a gym, a swimming pool, and a softball field.

Disabled Students: 10% of the campus is accessible. Wheelchair ramps, special parking, and special class scheduling are available.

Services: There is remedial writing.

Campus Safety and Security: Measures include lighted pathways/sidewalks.

Programs of Study: BMC confers B.A., B.S., B.S.Ed., and B.Mus. degrees. Bachelor's degrees are awarded in BIOLOGICAL SCIENCE (biology/biological science), BUSINESS (business administration and management), COMMUNICATIONS AND THE ARTS (dramatic arts, English, music, and piano/organ), COMPUTER AND PHYSICAL SCIENCE (chemistry and mathematics), EDUCATION (business, elementary, English, foreign languages, mathematics, music, physical, science, secondary, and social science), HEALTH PROFESSIONS (medical technology, nursing, and premedicine), SOCIAL SCIENCE (history, prelaw, psychology, and social science). Education is the strongest academically. Elementary education is the largest.

Required: All students must take 120 semester hours, including 6 hours each of English composition, literature, history, and Bible, 3 hours of psychology, and 2 semesters of phys ed. Students must maintain a minimum GPA of 2.5 for the teaching degree and 2.0 for other degrees. Majors require 30 or more hours.

Special: Students may take summer business internships. The college offers pass/fail options and dual majors. There is 1 national honor society, and 14 departmental honors programs.

Faculty/Classroom: 45% of faculty are male; 55%, female. 97% teach undergraduates. The average class size in an introductory lecture is 19; in a laboratory, 13; and in a regular course, 15.

Admissions: 93% of the 2001-2002 applicants were accepted. The SAT I scores for the 2001-2002 freshman class were: Verbal--50% below 500, and 50% between 500 and 599; Math--50% below 500, and 50% between 500 and 599. The ACT scores were 64% below 21, 20% between 21 and 23, 11% between 24 and 26, 4% between 27 and 28, and 1% above 28. 6 freshmen graduated first in their class.

Requirements: The SAT I or ACT is required. In addition, BMC recommends that applicants for admission have completed 4 units of English, 3 each of math, science, and social studies, and 2 of a foreign language. A GPA of 2.0 is required. AP and CLEP credits are accepted. Important factors in the admissions decision are ability to finance college education, extracurricular activities record, and geographic diversity.

Procedure: Freshmen are admitted fall, spring, and summer. Entrance exams should be taken starting in the junior year. There is an early admissions plan. Application deadlines are open. The application fee is $10. Notification is sent on a rolling basis.

Transfer: 106 transfer students enrolled in 2001-2002. 30 credits of 120 must be completed at BMC.

Visiting: There are regularly scheduled orientations for prospective students. There are guides for informal visits and visitors may sit in on classes and stay overnight. To schedule a visit, contact the Office of Admissions.

Financial Aid: In 2001-2002, 80% of all freshmen and 76% of continuing students received some form of financial aid. 58% of freshmen and 64% of continuing students received need-based aid. The average freshman award was $3200. Of that total, scholarships or need-based grants averaged $800 ($5700 maximum); loans averaged $2492 ($2625 maximum); and work contracts averaged $1400 (maximum). 24% of undergraduates work part time. Average annual earnings from campus work are $1400. The average financial indebtedness of the 2001 graduate was $11,000. BMC is a member of CSS. The FAFSA and the college's own financial statement are required. The fall application deadline is March 1.

International Students: There is 1 international student enrolled. They must score 500 on the written TOEFL or 173 on the electronic version and also take the SAT I or the ACT.

Computers: There are no time limits and no fees.

Graduates: In 2001, 97 bachelor's degrees were awarded. The most popular majors were elementary education (38%), biology/chemistry (14%), and English (11%). In an average class, 1% graduate in 3 years, 25% in 4 years, 12% in 5 years, and 2% in 6 years. Of the 2000 graduating class, 8% were enrolled in graduate school within 6 months of graduation and 75% were employed.

Admissions Contact: Tina Barkley, Director of Admissions.
E-mail: *tbarkley@bmc.edu* Web: *www.bmc.edu*

DELTA STATE UNIVERSITY — C-2

Cleveland, MS 38733 — (662) 846-4018
(800) 468-6378; Fax: (662) 846-4683

Full-time: 1152 men, 1670 women	**Faculty:** IIA, --$
Part-time: 150 men, 320 women	**Ph.D.s:** 38%
Graduate: 137 men, 317 women	**Student/Faculty:** 15 to 1
Year: semesters, summer session	**Tuition:** $2696 ($6412)
Application Deadline: August 1	**Room & Board:** $2720
Freshman Class: 430 enrolled	
ACT: 21	**COMPETITIVE**

Delta State University, founded in 1924, is a public liberal arts institution offering degrees in arts and sciences, business, education, health science, and nursing. There are 4 undergraduate and 4 graduate schools. In addition to regional accreditation, DSU has baccalaureate program accreditation with AAFCS, ACBSP, ACEJMC, ACS, AHEA, CAAHEP, CSWE, NASAD, NASM, NCATE, and NLN. The library contains 312,631 volumes, 754,713 microform items, and 15,470 audiovisual forms/CDs, and subscribes to 1365 periodicals. Computerized library services include the card catalog, interlibrary loans, and database searching. Special learning facilities include a learning resource center, art gallery, natural history museum, planetarium, and a performing arts center. The 332-acre campus is in a small town 110 miles south of Memphis, and 130 miles north of Jackson. Including residence halls, there are 46 buildings.

Student Life: 92% of undergraduates are from Mississippi. Others are from 29 states, 7 foreign countries, and Canada. 67% are white; 32% African American. The average age of freshmen is 19; all undergraduates, 26. 24% do not continue beyond their first year; 50% remain to graduate.

Housing: 1807 students can be accommodated in college housing, which includes single-sex dormitories and married-student housing. On-campus housing is guaranteed for all 4 years. 62% of students commute. Alcohol is not permitted. All students may keep cars.

Activities: 17% of men belong to 8 national fraternities; 13% of women belong to 6 national sororities. There are 116 groups on campus, including art, band, cheerleading, choir, chorale, chorus, computers, dance, drama, drill team, ethnic, honors, jazz band, literary magazine, marching band, musical theater, newspaper, opera, orchestra, pep band, photography, political, professional, religious, social, social service, student government, and yearbook. Popular campus events include Springfest and Christmas Madrigal Feast.

Sports: There are 7 intercollegiate sports for men and 6 for women, and 16 intramural sports for men and 16 for women. Facilities include a coliseum, an indoor pool, a gym, a baseball field, a softball field, a football stadium, a 9-hole golf course, outdoor tennis courts, 2 intramural fields, an outdoor walking facility, and a fitness center.

Disabled Students: 90% of the campus is accessible. Wheelchair ramps, elevators, special parking, specially equipped rest rooms, special class scheduling, lowered drinking fountains, and lowered telephones are available.

Services: Counseling and information services are available, as is tutoring in every subject. There is remedial math, reading, and writing.

Campus Safety and Security: Measures include 24-hour foot and vehicle patrol, self-defense education, escort service, and informal discussions. There are pamphlets/posters/films, emergency telephones, and lighted pathways/sidewalks.

Programs of Study: DSU confers B.A., B.S., B.B.A., B.C.A., B.F.A., B.M., B.M.E., B.S.C.J., B.S.E., B.S.G.S. B.S.N., and B.S.W. degrees. Master's and doctoral degrees are also awarded. Bachelor's degrees are awarded in BIOLOGICAL SCIENCE (biology/biological science), BUSINESS (accounting, business administration and management, fashion merchandising, hospitality management services, insurance, management science, marketing/retailing/merchandising, and secretarial studies/office management), COMMUNICATIONS AND THE ARTS (art, English, journalism, music, and music performance), COMPUTER AND PHYSICAL SCIENCE (chemistry, information sciences and systems, and mathematics), EDUCATION (athletic training, business, elementary, English, foreign languages, health, mathematics, music, science, secondary, social science, social studies, and special), ENGINEERING AND ENVIRONMENTAL DESIGN (aviation administration/management and environmental science), HEALTH PROFESSIONS (nursing, predentistry, premedicine, and speech pathology/audiology), SOCIAL SCIENCE (criminal justice, family/consumer studies, history, political science/government, psychology, social science, social work, and sociology). Elementary education, biology, and computer information systems are the largest.

Required: To graduate, students must complete 128 semester hours, including 30 to 54 in the major, with a minimum GPA of 2.0. General education requirements include 6 hours each of English composition, English literature, history, lab science, and social science; 3 hours each of fine arts, math, psychology, and speech; and 2 hours of phys ed.

Special: DSU offers internships in several majors. A general studies degree and nondegree study are also available. There are 16 national honor societies, a freshman honors program, and 7 departmental honors programs.

Faculty/Classroom: 59% of faculty are male; 41%, female. No introductory courses are taught by graduate students.

Admissions: The ACT scores for the 2001-2002 freshman class were: 58% below 21, 22% between 21 and 23, 12% between 24 and 26, 4% between 27 and 28, and 3% above 28. 42% of the current freshmen were in the top fifth of their class; 75% were in the top two fifths.

Requirements: The SAT I or ACT is required. In addition, students may gain admission by completing the college prep curriculum with a minimum of 3.2 GPA; by completing the college prep curriculum with a minimum of 2.5 GPA and scoring at least 16 on the ACT (at least 650 on the SAT I); by ranking in the upper 50% of the class and scoring at least 16 on the ACT (at least 650 on the SAT I); or by completing the college prep curriculum with a minimum 2.0 GPA and scoring 18 or higher on the ACT (at least 740 on the SAT I). The Nelson Denny Reading Test and Math Placement Test must also be taken. Applicants must be graduates of an accredited secondary school or have the GED. They should have completed 4 courses in English; 3 each in math, science, and social studies; 2 in a foreign language, world geography, or additional science/math; and 1/2 in computer applications. Students may apply on-line at the school's web site address. A GPA of 2.0 is required. AP credits are accepted.

Procedure: Freshmen are admitted to all sessions. Entrance exams should be taken as early as possible. Applications should be filed by August 1 for fall entry. Notification is sent on a rolling basis.

Transfer: 578 transfer students enrolled in 2001-2002. A minimum GPA of 2.0 is required, and an associate degree and ACT or SAT I scores are recommended. 30 credits of 128 must be completed at DSU.

Visiting: There are regularly scheduled orientations for prospective students, including campus tours and introduction to faculty and staff. There are guides for informal visits and visitors may sit in on classes and stay overnight. To schedule a visit, contact School Relations and Recruitment at (662) 846-4656.

Financial Aid: In 2001-2002, 93% of all freshmen and 88% of continuing students received some form of financial aid. 10% of undergraduates work part time. The average financial indebtedness of the 2001 graduate was $11,178. The FAFSA is required. The fall application deadline is June 1.

International Students: There are 24 international students enrolled. They must score 525 on the written TOEFL and also take the SAT I or the ACT, scoring 21 on the ACT or 970 on the SAT I.

Computers: The mainframe is an IBM RS/6000 Model 540. There are 257 PCs available in various locations. Students have access to the Internet and Web from computer labs, dorm rooms, and the library. All students may access the system from 8 A.M. to 11 P.M. daily. There are no time limits and no fees. It is recommended that students in the executive MBA program have personal computers.

Graduates: In 2001, 598 bachelor's degrees were awarded. The most popular majors were elementary education (12%), computer information systems (7%), and biology (7%). In an average class, 1% graduate in 3 years, 19% in 4 years, 37% in 5 years, and 42% in 6 years. 130 companies recruited on campus in 2000-2001.

Admissions Contact: Debbie Heslep, Director of Admissions.
E-mail: *dheslep@dsu.deltast.edu* Web: *http://www.deltast.edu*

JACKSON STATE UNIVERSITY — C-4
Jackson, MS 39217 (601) 968-2100
(800) 848-6817; Fax: (601) 973-3445

Full-time: 1815 men, 2455 women	**Faculty:** 360; IIA, --$
Part-time: 360 men, 570 women	**Ph.D.s:** 66%
Graduate: 410 men, 750 women	**Student/Faculty:** 13 to 1
Year: semesters, summer session	**Tuition:** $3206 ($7376)
Application Deadline: open	**Room & Board:** $3570
Freshman Class: n/av	
SAT I or ACT: required	**LESS COMPETITIVE**

Jackson State University, founded in 1877, is a public institution with an emphasis on liberal arts, business, music, and teacher preparation. Figures in the above capsule, and in this profile, are approximate. There are 5 undergraduate schools and 1 graduate school. In addition to regional accreditation, JSU has baccalaureate program accreditation with AACSB, CSWE, NASAD, NASM, and NCATE. The library contains 435,552 volumes, 60,552 microform items, and 16,331 audiovisual forms/CDs, and subscribes to 1589 periodicals. Computerized library services include database searching. Special learning facilities include a learning resource center and radio station. The 150-acre campus is in an urban area 190 miles north of New Orleans. Including residence halls, there are 39 buildings.

Student Life: 73% of undergraduates are from Mississippi. Others are from 40 states and 29 foreign countries. 94% are African American. The average age of freshmen is 21; all undergraduates, 23. 35% do not continue beyond their first year; 37% remain to graduate.

Housing: 2600 students can be accommodated in college housing, which includes single-sex dormitories. In addition, there are honors houses and athletic houses. On-campus housing is available on a first-come, first-served basis. 53% of students commute. Alcohol is not permitted. All students may keep cars.

Activities: 5% of men belong to 4 national fraternities; 5% of women belong to 4 national sororities. There are 20 groups on campus, including art, band, cheerleading, choir, dance, drama, drill team, ethnic, honors, jazz band, marching band, musical theater, newspaper, opera, orchestra, pep band, photography, political, radio and TV, religious, social service, student government, symphony, and yearbook.

Sports: There are 7 intercollegiate sports for men and 4 for women, and 2 intramural sports for men and 2 for women. Facilities include an Olympic-size swimming pool, a gym with 2 basketball courts, indoor and outdoor tennis courts, badminton and volleyball courts, a dance studio, a baseball diamond, soccer and athletic fields, an archery range, and a track.

Disabled Students: All of the campus is accessible. Wheelchair ramps, elevators, special parking, specially equipped rest rooms, lowered drinking fountains, and lowered telephones are available.

Services: Counseling and information services are available, as is tutoring in every subject. There is remedial math, reading, and writing.

Campus Safety and Security: Measures include 24-hour foot and vehicle patrol, self-defense education, informal discussions, and pamphlets/posters/films.

Programs of Study: JSU confers B.A., B.S., B.B.A, B.M., B.M.E., B.S.Ed., and B.S.W. degrees. Master's and doctoral degrees are also awarded. Bachelor's degrees are awarded in BIOLOGICAL SCIENCE (biology/biological science), BUSINESS (accounting, banking and finance, business administration and management, marketing/retailing/merchandising, and office supervision and management), COMMUNICATIONS AND THE ARTS (art, communications, English, languages, piano/organ, and speech/debate/rhetoric), COMPUTER AND PHYSICAL SCIENCE (atmospheric sciences and meteorology, chemistry, computer science, mathematics, and physics), EDUCATION (business, elementary, health, industrial arts, mathematics, music, social science, and special), HEALTH PROFESSIONS (premedicine), SOCIAL SCIENCE (child care/child and family studies, corrections, criminal justice, economics, history, political science/government, psychology, social work, sociology, and urban studies). Computer science, biology, and accounting are the strongest academically. Biology, elementary education, and computer science are the largest.

Required: To graduate, students must complete at least 128 semester hours with a minimum GPA of 2.0. At least 30 upper-division hours must be earned in the major. Distribution requirements include a total of 49 to 59 hours in communications, humanities and fine arts, social and behavioral sciences, natural sciences, health and physical education, and concepts for success in college.

Special: Internships with various corporations, nondegree study, work-study programs, a cooperative education program, accelerated degrees, combined B.A.-B.S. degrees, and a student-exchange program are available. There are 4 national honor societies, a freshman honors program, and 14 departmental honors programs.

Faculty/Classroom: 58% of faculty are male; 42%, female.

Requirements: The SAT I or ACT is required. In addition, applicants must be graduates of an accredited secondary school or have a GED certificate. They must have earned 15½ Carnegie units, including 4 of English, 3 each of math, social studies, and sciences, ½ of computer applications, and 2 of advanced electives. A composite ACT score of 20 or above, or an SAT I score of 800 or above exempts students from the specific high school unit requirements. An interview is recommended. A GPA of 2.0 is required. AP and CLEP credits are accepted. Important factors in the admissions decision are recommendations by school officials, leadership record, and extracurricular activities record. Applications are accepted on computer disk and on-line at *www.jsums.edu*.

Procedure: Freshmen are admitted to all sessions. Entrance exams should be taken during the first semester of the senior year. There are early admissions and deferred admissions plans. Application deadlines are open.

Transfer: Applicants should submit an official transcript from each institution attended, be in good standing at the last college or university attended, and have a minimum cumulative GPA of 2.0. 30 credits of 128 must be completed at JSU.

Visiting: There are regularly scheduled orientations for prospective students. There are guides for informal visits and visitors may sit in on classes and stay overnight. To schedule a visit, contact the Office of Admissions.

Financial Aid: JSU is a member of CSS. The FAFSA is required. Check with the school for current deadlines.

International Students: The school actively recruits these students. They must score 525 on the written TOEFL and also take a placement test and the SAT I or the ACT, scoring 20 on the ACT.

Computers: The mainframe is a 2 DEC VAX 11/780s. There are also PCs available throughout the campus. All students may access the system 7 A.M. to 12 A.M., with access to PCs during business hours. There are no time limits and no fees.

Admissions Contact: Stephanie Chatman, Associate Director of Admissions. E-mail: *schatman@ccaix.jsums.edu* Web: *www.jsums.edu*

MILLSAPS COLLEGE
C-4

Jackson, MS 39210
(601) 974-1050
(800) 352-1050; Fax: (601) 974-1059

Full-time: 531 men, 634 women	**Faculty:** 93; IIB, av$
Part-time: 24 men, 32 women	**Ph.D.s:** 92%
Graduate: 61 men, 48 women	**Student/Faculty:** 13 to 1
Year: semesters, summer session	**Tuition:** $16,546
Application Deadline: February 1	**Room & Board:** $6062
Freshman Class: 952 applied, 815 accepted, 324 enrolled	
SAT I Verbal/Math: 600/590	**ACT:** 26 **VERY COMPETITIVE+**

Millsaps College, founded in 1890, is a private liberal arts institution affiliated with the United Methodist Church. In addition to regional accreditation, Millsaps has baccalaureate program accreditation with AACSB and NCATE. The library contains 209,900 volumes, 78,719 microform items, and 7732 audiovisual forms/CDs, and subscribes to 631 periodicals. Computerized library services include the card catalog, interlibrary loans, and database searching. Special learning facilities include an art gallery and an observatory. The 100-acre campus is in an urban area in the capital city of Jackson. Including residence halls, there are 36 buildings.

Student Life: 57% of undergraduates are from Mississippi. Others are from 25 states, 10 foreign countries, and Canada. 65% are from public schools. 84% are white; 11% African American. 58% are Protestant; 21% claim no religious affiliation; 17% Catholic. The average age of freshmen is 18; all undergraduates, 20. 17% do not continue beyond their first year.

Housing: 857 students can be accommodated in college housing, which includes single-sex and coed dormitories and fraternity houses. In addition, there are special-interest houses and designated housing for freshmen. On-campus housing is guaranteed for the freshman and sophomore years only, is available on a first-come, first-served basis, and is available on a lottery system for upperclassmen. 78% of students live on campus; of those, 75% remain on campus on weekends. All students may keep cars.

Activities: 51% of men belong to 5 national fraternities; 60% of women belong to 6 national sororities. There are 74 groups on campus, including art, cheerleading, choir, chorus, computers, dance, drama, ethnic, honors, international, literary magazine, musical theater, newspaper, photography, political, professional, radio and TV, religious, social, social service, student government, and yearbook. Popular campus events include Major Madness, Multicultural Festival, and Millsaps Forums.

Sports: There are 7 intercollegiate sports for men and 7 for women, and 5 intramural sports for men and 5 for women. Facilities include 6 tennis courts, a swimming pool, a jogging course, 4 playing fields, and a physical activities center with a weight room and basketball, tennis, and volleyball courts.

Disabled Students: 90% of the campus is accessible. Wheelchair ramps, elevators, special parking, specially equipped rest rooms, special class scheduling, lowered drinking fountains, and lowered telephones are available. Other needs can be addressed through the ADA coordinator on an individual basis.

Services: Counseling and information services are available, as is tutoring in most subjects, a writing center, a language lab, and a math lab for assistance.

Campus Safety and Security: Measures include 24-hour foot and vehicle patrol, self-defense education, escort service, and informal discussions. There are pamphlets/posters/films, emergency telephones, lighted pathways/sidewalks, key card access to buildings, and night-time staffed entrances.

Programs of Study: Millsaps confers B.A., B.S., B.B.A., and B.L.S. degrees. Master's degrees are also awarded. Bachelor's degrees are awarded in BIOLOGICAL SCIENCE (biology/biological science), BUSINESS (accounting and business administration and management), COMMUNICATIONS AND THE ARTS (art, classics, dramatic arts, English, French, German, music, and Spanish), COMPUTER AND PHYSICAL SCIENCE (chemistry, computer science, geology, mathematics, and physics), EDUCATION (elementary), SOCIAL SCIENCE (economics, European studies, history, philosophy, political science/government, psychology, religion, and sociology). Business administration, English, and psychology are strongest academically and have the largest enrollments.

Required: To graduate, students must complete 128 credit hours with a minimum GPA of 2.0. The core curriculum includes 4 interdisciplinary courses in the humanities and 4 in the sciences and math. Students must also demonstrate writing proficiency at the sophomore level and pass a comprehensive exam in their main field of study.

Special: Millsaps offers many opportunities for study abroad, a Washington semester, internships, dual majors, a B.A.-B.S. degree in most majors, 3-2 degree programs in engineering with Washington, Auburn, Vanderbilt, and Columbia Universities and Georgia Tech, and a 3-2 degree in business administration. There are 25 national honor societies, including Phi Beta Kappa, and 25 departmental honors programs.

Faculty/Classroom: 62% of faculty are male; 38%, female. All teach undergraduates and 90% both teach and do research. No introductory courses are taught by graduate students. The average class size in an introductory lecture is 21; in a laboratory, 16; and in a regular course, 16.

Admissions: 86% of the 2001-2002 applicants were accepted. The SAT I scores for the 2001-2002 freshman class were: Verbal--8% below 500, 39% between 500 and 599, 41% between 600 and 700, and 12% above 700; Math--12% below 500, 39% between 500 and 599, 39% between 600 and 700, and 10% above 700. The ACT scores were 4% below 21, 23% between 21 and 23, 25% between 24 and 26, 17% between 27 and 28, and 31% above 28. 66% of the current freshmen were in the top fifth of their class; 71% were in the top two fifths. 19 freshmen graduated first in their class.

Requirements: The SAT I or ACT is required. In addition, applicants should be graduates of an accredited secondary school or have a GED certificate, and have completed at least 14 academic units of English, math, social studies, natural sciences, or foreign languages (4 units of English should be included). An essay is required. Millsaps requires applicants to be in the upper 50% of their class. A GPA of 2.5 is required. AP and CLEP credits are accepted. Important factors in the admissions decision are advanced placement or honor courses, extracurricular activities record, and recommendations by school officials. Applications are accepted on computer disk and on-line via the web sites at *www.millsaps.edu* and *www.commonapp.org*

Procedure: Freshmen are admitted fall and spring. Entrance exams should be taken in the spring of the junior year or fall of the senior year. There are early admissions and deferred admissions plans. Early action application should be filed by December 1; regular applications, by February 1 for fall entry and December 1 for spring entry, along with a $25 fee. Notification of early action is sent December 20; regular decision, on a rolling basis, beginning January 15.

Transfer: 48 transfer students enrolled in 2001-2002. Applicants must have a minimum GPA of 2.75 and be in good standing at their previous school. 64 credits of 128 must be completed at Millsaps.

Visiting: There are regularly scheduled orientations for prospective students, including meetings with faculty and student services personnel. There are guides for informal visits and visitors may sit in on classes and stay overnight. To schedule a visit, contact the Admissions Office.

Financial Aid: In 2001-2002, 97% of all freshmen and 93% of continuing students received some form of financial aid. 58% of all students received need-based aid. The average freshman award was $16,647. Of that total, scholarships or need-based grants averaged $12,700 ($24,750 maximum); loans averaged $3117 ($17,900 maximum); and work contracts averaged $1166 ($1500 maximum). 81% of undergraduates work part time. Average annual earnings from campus work are $900. The average financial indebtedness of the 2001 graduate was $18,743. The FAFSA and the college's own financial statement are required. The fall application deadline is March 1.

International Students: There are 13 international students enrolled. The school actively recruits these students. They must score 550 on the written TOEFL.

Computers: The mainframes are a VMS 2 VAX 4000-50 and 2 VAX 4000-500A, ALPHA 4100 (Unix), ALPHA 1000 (NT), plus additional area servers. There are also 55 PCs in 2 academic labs and 50 terminals in 6 student labs. All students may access the system at any time. There are no time limits and no fees. It is strongly recommended that all students have a personal computer.

Graduates: In 2001, 276 bachelor's degrees were awarded. The most popular majors were business administration (23%), psychology (10%), and English (9%). In an average class, 62% graduate in 4 years, 69% in 5 years, and 70% in 6 years. Of the 2000 graduating class, 46% were enrolled in graduate school within 6 months of graduation and 99% were employed.

Admissions Contact: John Gaines, Director of Admissions.
E-mail: *admissions@millsaps.edu* Web: *http://www.millsaps.edu/admiss*

MISSISSIPPI COLLEGE
C-4

Clinton, MS 39058
(601) 925-3800
(800) 738-1236; Fax: (601) 925-3950

Full-time: 842 men, 1175 women	**Faculty:** 143
Part-time: 106 men, 166 women	**Ph.D.s:** 67%
Graduate: 402 men, 532 women	**Student/Faculty:** 14 to 1
Year: semesters, summer session	**Tuition:** $10,150
Application Deadline: open	**Room & Board:** $4424
Freshman Class: 525 applied, 457 accepted, 300 enrolled	
ACT: 23	**COMPETITIVE**

Mississippi College, founded in 1826 and affiliated with the Southern Baptist Church, is a private institution offering degrees in liberal arts, business, education, and health sciences. There are 4 undergraduate and 2 graduate schools. In addition to regional accreditation, MC has baccalaureate program accreditation with ACBSP, CSWE, NASM, NCATE, and NLN. The 2 libraries contain 235,000 volumes, 265,000 microform items, and 13,000 audiovisual forms/CDs, and subscribe to 750 periodicals. Computerized library services include the card catalog, interlibrary loans, and database searching. Special learning facilities include a learning resource center, art gallery, radio station, and TV station. The 320-acre campus is in a suburban area 5 miles west of Jackson. Including residence halls, there are 30 buildings.

Student Life: 82% of undergraduates are from Mississippi. Others are from 31 states and 5 foreign countries. 87% are white; 11% African American. Most are Protestant. The average age of freshmen is 18; all undergraduates, 22. 21% do not continue beyond their first year.

Housing: 1599 students can be accommodated in college housing, which includes single-sex dormitories and married-student housing. On-campus housing is available on a first-come, first-served basis. 61% of students live on campus. Alcohol is not permitted. All students may keep cars.

Activities: There are no fraternities or sororities. There are 55 groups on campus, including art, band, cheerleading, choir, chorale, chorus, computers, debate, drama, ethnic, forensics, honors, international, jazz band, literary magazine, marching band, musical theater, newspaper, opera, pep band, political, professional, radio and TV, religious, social, social service, student government, and yearbook. Popular campus events include I Love America Day, Derby Day, and Spring Fever Week.

Sports: There are 6 intercollegiate sports for men and 6 for women, and 6 intramural sports for men and 6 for women. Facilities include a coliseum, an 8300-seat stadium, tennis courts, soccer and softball fields, a swimming pool, a 4000-seat gym, a fitness facility, and a campus weight-training facility.

Disabled Students: 95% of the campus is accessible. Wheelchair ramps, elevators, special parking, specially equipped rest rooms, special class scheduling, lowered drinking fountains, lowered telephones, wide doors, and special dorm rooms equipped for the physically disabled are available.

Services: Counseling and information services are available, as is tutoring in most subjects. There is remedial math, reading, and writing and study skills classes.

Campus Safety and Security: Measures include 24-hour foot and vehicle patrol, escort service, informal discussions, and emergency telephones. There are lighted pathways/sidewalks.

Programs of Study: MC confers B.A., B.S., B.M., B.M.Ed., B.S.B.A., B.S.Ed., B.S.N., and B.S.W. degrees. Master's degrees are also awarded. Bachelor's degrees are awarded in BIOLOGICAL SCIENCE (biochemistry and biology/biological science), BUSINESS (accounting, business administration and management, and marketing/retailing/merchandising), COMMUNICATIONS AND THE ARTS (applied music, art, communications, English, French, graphic design, languages, modern language, music, music theory and composition, piano/organ, Spanish, voice, and winds), COMPUTER AND PHYSICAL SCIENCE (chemistry, computer science, mathematics, and physics), EDUCATION (art, business, elementary, music, and special), ENGINEERING AND ENVIRONMENTAL DESIGN (engineering physics and interior design), HEALTH PROFESSIONS (nursing), SOCIAL SCIENCE (American studies, Christian studies, criminal justice, family/consumer studies, history, paralegal studies, political science/government, psychology, religious music, social studies, social work, and sociology). Premedicine, nursing, and business are the strongest academically. Business, education, and biology are the largest.

Required: To graduate, students must complete 130 credit hours, with an average of C or better in the major. The core curriculum includes English, history, economics, computer science, religion, math, art, social science, phys ed, and chapel. 30 hours are usually required in the major; some majors require 36 to 45. Students must pass a writing proficiency exam. B.A. candidates and English majors must take 12 hours of a foreign language.

Special: Cooperative programs, including a 3-2 engineering degree and a program in agriculture, are offered with the University of Mississippi, Mississippi State University, and Auburn University. MC also offers study abroad in up to 10 countries, a 3-3 law school program with the School of Law, work-study programs, internships, B.A.-B.S. degrees, and credit for military experience and by exam. There are 18 national honor societies and a freshman honors program.

Faculty/Classroom: 62% of faculty are male; 38%, female. 82% teach undergraduates. Graduate students teach 19% of introductory courses. The average class size in an introductory lecture is 30; in a laboratory, 25; and in a regular course, 25.

Admissions: 87% of the 2001-2002 applicants were accepted. The ACT scores for the 2001-2002 freshman class were: 23% below 21, 30% between 21 and 23, 27% between 24 and 26, 7% between 27 and 28, and 13% above 28. There was 1 National Merit semifinalist.

Requirements: The SAT I or ACT is required (ACT is preferred). A minimum ACT score of 18 or SAT I composite score of 870 is required for regular admission. Students scoring below these levels may be considered for acceptance into the developmental program. In addition to the application for admission, students must submit a 250-word essay, at least 1 letter of recommendation (3 are recommended for scholarship consideration), and a transcript from all schools previously attended. A well-rounded high school program is advisable. An interview is recommended, as is a portfolio or audition for some majors. A GPA of 2.0 is required. AP and CLEP credits are accepted. Important factors in the admissions decision are personality/intangible qualities, extracurricular activities record, and leadership record.

Procedure: Freshmen are admitted fall, spring, and summer. Entrance exams should be taken by December of the senior year. Application deadlines are open. The application fee is $25. Notification is sent as applications are received and reviewed.

Transfer: 324 transfer students enrolled in 2001-2002. Applicants must be junior college graduates or students in good academic standing with the college they last attended. They must have a minimum GPA of 2.0. Transfer students will be considered as freshmen if fewer than 12 semester hours or 16 quarter hours have been completed. Applicants must submit transcripts from all schools previously attended. 33 credits of 130 must be completed at MC.

Visiting: There are regularly scheduled orientations for prospective students, including attending classes, touring the campus, and meeting with administrators and departmental representatives. There are guides for informal visits and visitors may sit in on classes and stay overnight. To schedule a visit, contact Chad Phillips, Director of Admissions.

Financial Aid: In 2001-2002, 83% of all freshmen and 86% of continuing students received some form of financial aid. 41% of freshmen and 52% of continuing students received need-based aid. The average freshman award was $9821. Of that total, scholarships or need-based grants averaged $6994 ($13,100 maximum); loans averaged $1893 ($13,125 maximum); and work contracts averaged $116 ($1050 maximum). 19% of undergraduates work part time. Average annual earnings from campus work are $1052. The average financial indebtedness of the 2001 graduate was $20,570. The FAFSA is required. The fall application deadline is March 1.

International Students: There are 16 international students enrolled. They must score 550 on the written TOEFL or 213 on the electronic version.

Computers: The mainframe is an HP 3000/Series III. Students may access the collegewide network through various points on campus. The academic computer labs consist of some 200 workstations that are attached to Novell servers and connected to the Internet. Students who have been assigned an account may access the system from 8 A.M. to midnight Monday through Thursday, from 8 A.M. to 11 P.M. Friday, from 8 A.M. to 6 P.M. Saturday, and from 1 P.M. to 11 P.M. Sunday. There are no time limits and no fees.

Graduates: In 2001, 442 bachelor's degrees were awarded. The most popular majors were business administration (10%), nursing (9%), and biology (9%). 83 companies recruited on campus in 2000-2001.

Admissions Contact: Chad Phillips, Director of Admissions.
E-mail: *enrollment-services@mc.edu* Web: *www.mc.edu*

MISSISSIPPI STATE UNIVERSITY — E 3
Mississippi State, MS 39762 — (662) 325-2224
Fax: (662) 325-7360

Full-time: 6309 men, 5608 women	**Faculty:** 883; I, --$
Part-time: 912 men, 775 women	**Ph.D.s:** 81%
Graduate: 1614 men, 1660 women	**Student/Faculty:** 13 to 1
Year: semesters, summer session	**Tuition:** $3018 ($6120)
Application Deadline: May 1	**Room & Board:** $4835
Freshman Class: 5447 applied, 3911 accepted, 1777 enrolled	
SAT I or ACT: required	**COMPETITIVE**

Mississippi State University, founded in 1878 as a land-grant institution, offers degree programs in the arts and sciences, agriculture, business and industry, education, engineering, forest resources, architecture, accounting, and professional training in veterinary medicine. There are 9 undergraduate schools and 1 graduate school. In addition to regional accreditation, State has baccalaureate program accreditation with AACSB, ABET, ACS, ADA, AHEA, APA, ASLA, CACREP, CSWE, NAAB, NASAD, NASM, NASPAA, NCATE, and SAF. The 3 libraries contain 1,576,409 volumes, 2,290,785 microform items, and 17,648 audiovisual forms/CDs, and subscribe to 16,202 periodicals. Computerized library services include the card catalog, interlibrary loans, and database searching. Special learning facilities include a learning resource center, art gallery, natural history museum, planetarium, radio station, TV station, music museum, archeology museum, and entomology museum. The campus is in a small town.

Student Life: 79% of undergraduates are from Mississippi. Others are from 49 states, 69 foreign countries, and Canada. 76% are white; 17% African American. The average age of freshmen is 20; all undergraduates, 22. 21% do not continue beyond their first year.

Housing: 3935 students can be accommodated in college housing, which includes single-sex and coed dormitories, on-campus apartments, married-student housing, fraternity houses, and sorority houses. In addition, there are honors houses. 79% of students commute. Alcohol is not permitted. All students may keep cars.

Activities: 17% of men belong to 18 national fraternities; 18% of women belong to 1 local sorority and 11 national sororities. There are 300 groups on campus, including art, band, cheerleading, chess, choir, chorale, chorus, computers, dance, drama, drill team, ethnic, gay, honors, international, jazz band, literary magazine, marching band, musical theater, newspaper, orchestra, pep band, political, professional, radio and TV, religious, social, social service, student government, symphony, and yearbook. Popular campus events include pep rallies, concerts, and dance programs.

Sports: There are 7 intercollegiate sports for men and 9 for women, and 32 intramural sports for men and 32 for women. Facilities include a 41,200-seat football stadium, a 6,700-seat baseball park, a 9,200-seat multipurpose coliseum, a physical fitness complex, an all-weather track, 4 practice football fields, a 6-court tennis complex, an 18-hole golf course, 5 lighted tennis courts, the Sanderson Center, which consists of 7 basketball courts, 6 volleyball courts, 8 racquetball courts, 10000 square feet for strength and aerobic conditioning, 3 full-size dance studios, an indoor rock-climbing wall, a 1/8-mile walking track, and RecPlex, which is a multipurpose field complex with 4 softball, 2 soccer, and 6 flag football fields.

Disabled Students: 90% of the campus is accessible. Wheelchair ramps, elevators, special parking, specially equipped rest rooms, special class scheduling, lowered drinking fountains, lowered telephones, and phones equipped with TTY in the union and library are available.

Services: Counseling and information services are available, as is tutoring in some subjects, including math, English, chemistry, physics, and study skills. There is a reader service for the blind, remedial math, reading, and writing, study assistance, preparation for professional exams, and credit courses in reading and study skills.

Campus Safety and Security: Measures include 24-hour foot and vehicle patrol, self-defense education, escort service, and shuttle buses. There are informal discussions, pamphlets/posters/films, emergency telephones, lighted pathways/sidewalks, and bicycle patrol.

Programs of Study: State confers B.A., B.S., B.Arch., B.B.A., B.F.A., B.Land.Arch., B.Mus.Ed., B.P.A., and B.S.W. degrees. Master's and doctoral degrees are also awarded. Bachelor's degrees are awarded in AGRICULTURE (agricultural business management, agricultural economics, agriculture, agronomy, animal science, fishing and fisheries, forestry production and processing, horticulture, plant protection (pest management), poultry science, and wildlife management), BIOLOGICAL SCIENCE (biochemistry, biology/biological science, and microbiology), BUSINESS (accounting, banking and finance, business administration and management, insurance, marketing/retailing/merchandising, real estate, and trade and industrial supervision and management), COMMUNICATIONS AND THE ARTS (art, communications, English, and languages), COMPUTER AND PHYSICAL SCIENCE (chemistry, computer science, geoscience, information sciences and systems, mathematics, physics, and science), EDUCATION (agricultural, business, education, elementary, music, physical, secondary, special, and technical), ENGINEERING AND ENVIRONMENTAL DESIGN (aerospace studies, agricultural engineering technology, architecture, bioengineering, chemical engineering, civil engineering, computer engineering, electrical/electronics engineering, industrial engineering, industrial engineering technology, landscape architecture/design, and mechanical engineering), HEALTH PROFESSIONS (medical technology), SOCIAL SCIENCE (anthropology, economics, food science, history, interdisciplinary studies, liberal arts/general studies, philosophy, political science/government, psychology, social work, and sociology). Accounting, biochemistry, and physics are the strongest academically. General business administration, elementary education, and biology are the largest.

Required: The core curriculum includes 6 to 9 hours of math and natural science, 6 each of humanities, English composition, and social behavior, and 3 each of public speaking, computer literacy, and fine arts, and junior/senior-level writing. The total number of hours required for graduation and in the major varies. A minimum GPA of 2.0 must be maintained.

Special: Cooperative education, cross-registration with the Academic Common Market, internships, and study abroad in 15 countries are offered. Work-study programs, a Washington semester, accelerated degree programs, a general studies degree, 3-2 engineering degrees, nondegree study, student-designed majors, B.A.-B.S. degrees, and pass/fail options for some courses are available. There are 43 national honor societies, a freshman honors program, and 27 departmental honors programs.

Faculty/Classroom: 65% of faculty are male; 35%, female.

Admissions: 72% of the 2001-2002 applicants were accepted. There were 32 National Merit finalists and 46 semifinalists. 12 freshmen graduated first in their class.

Requirements: The SAT I or ACT is required. In addition, applicants should have completed 15 1/2 high school academic credits, including 4 in English, 3 each in math, science, and social science, 2 advanced electives (foreign language, world geography, 4th year lab-based science, or 4th year math), and 1/2 credit in the computer as a productivity tool (not keyboarding). Full admission is granted with all of the above and 1 of the following: minimum 3.2 GPA on required high school courses; 2.5 GPA on required high school classes or class standing in top 50% with ACT score of 16 or higher/SAT I combined score of 750 or higher; 2.0 GPA on required high school classes with ACT score of 18 or higher/SAT I combined 840 or higher; or satisfy National Collegiate Athletic Association standards for student-athletes who are full qualifiers under Division I guidelines. Students with a GED are accepted with the required ACT/SAT I score. AP and CLEP credits are accepted. Applications may be submitted on-line at the school's web site.

Procedure: Freshmen are admitted fall, spring, and summer. Entrance exams should be taken in the spring semester of the junior year or the fall semester of the senior year. There are early admissions and deferred admissions plans. Applications should be filed by May 1 for fall entry (August 1 for transfer students), November 15 for spring entry, and May 15 for summer entry. The fall 2001 application fee was $25 (out of state and international students only). Notification is sent on a rolling basis.

Transfer: 1692 transfer students enrolled in 2001-2002. Applicants must submit an official college transcript from each college attended, indicating a minimum GPA of 2.0 (some departments require 2.5), and must be in good standing at their previous school. 32 credits of 136 must be completed at State.

Visiting: There are regularly scheduled orientations for prospective students, including 2-day sessions for freshmen and 1-day sessions for transfers. There are guides for informal visits and visitors may sit in on classes and stay overnight. To schedule a visit, contact John Dickerson, Director of Enrollment Services at (662) 325-3076.

Financial Aid: In 2001-2002, 72% of all freshmen and 74% of continuing students received some form of financial aid. 34% of freshmen and 39% of continuing students received need-based aid. The average freshman award was $5122. Of that total, scholarships or need-based grants averaged $2568 ($14,500 maximum); loans averaged $4250 ($19,165 maximum); and work contracts averaged $2981 ($3160 maximum). 34% of undergraduates work part time. Average annual earnings from campus work are $2146. The average financial indebtedness of the 2001 graduate was $13,499. The FAFSA is required. The fall application deadline is April 1.

International Students: There are 150 international students enrolled. They must score 525 on the written TOEFL or 197 on the electronic version. They must also take the SAT I or ACT, scoring 980 on the SAT I or 21 on the ACT.

Computers: The mainframes are a Sun E10000, a Sun Enterprise Server 6000, and a Sun Enterprise Server 2000. Mainframes, servers, and PCs are connected to a campus ATM/Ethernet network. 2 public labs and several departmental labs provide several hundred PCs for student use. All have access to the Internet. All students may access the system 24 hours a day. There are no time limits and no fees. It is recommended that students in preveterinary medicine, architecture, and engineering have personal computers.

Graduates: In 2001, 2345 bachelor's degrees were awarded. The most popular majors were elementary education (8%), marketing (7%), and business administration (6%). In an average class, 21% graduate in 4 years, 41% in 5 years, and 53% in 6 years. 285 companies recruited on campus in 2000-2001.

Admissions Contact: Jerry Inmon, Director of Admissions.
E-mail: *admit@admissions.msstate.edu*
Web: *http://www.msuinfo.ur.msstate.edu/admissions*

MISSISSIPPI UNIVERSITY FOR WOMEN — E-2
Columbus, MS 39701 — **(601) 329-7106**
(877) 462-8439; Fax: (601) 241-7481

Full-time: 300 men, 1600 women	**Faculty:** 116; IIB, --$
Part-time: 300 men, 1000 women	**Ph.D.s:** 68%
Graduate: 20 men, 120 women	**Student/Faculty:** 16 to 1
Year: semesters, summer session	**Tuition:** $2656 ($6412)
Application Deadline: open	**Room & Board:** $2790
Freshman Class: n/av	
SAT I or ACT: recommended	**LESS COMPETITIVE**

Mississippi University for Women, founded in 1884, is a public institution offering degrees in liberal arts, education, business and communications, nursing, human sciences, science and math, health and kinesiology, and culinary arts. Figures given in above capsule are approximate. There are 8 undergraduate and 2 graduate schools. In addition to regional accreditation, MUW has baccalaureate program accreditation with AHEA, NASAD, NASM, NCATE, and NLN. The library contains 232,638 volumes, 569,448 microform items, and 98 audiovisual forms/CDs, and subscribes to 1620 periodicals. Computerized library services include the card catalog, interlibrary loans, and database searching. Special learning facilities include a learning resource center, art gallery, radio station, TV station, and distance learning studio. The 110-acre campus is in a small town 120 miles west of Birmingham, Alabama. Including residence halls, there are 53 buildings.

Student Life: 89% of undergraduates are from Mississippi. Others are from 20 states, 25 foreign countries, and Canada. 84% are from public schools. 70% are white; 27% African American. The average age of freshmen is 19; all undergraduates, 29. 30% do not continue beyond their first year; 43% remain to graduate.

Housing: 1100 students can be accommodated in college housing, which includes single-sex dormitories, on-campus apartments, and married-student housing. On-campus housing is available on a first-come, first-served basis. 77% of students commute. Alcohol is not permitted. All students may keep cars.

Activities: 10% of men belong to 2 local fraternities and 1 national fraternity; 20% of women belong to 12 local and 3 national sororities. There are 84 groups on campus, including art, band, choir, chorale, chorus, computers, dance, drama, ethnic, film, honors, international, jazz band, literary magazine, musical theater, newspaper, orchestra, photography, political, professional, radio and TV, religious, social, social service, student government, and yearbook. Popular campus events include Mardi Gras, Oktoberfest, and Nutcracker.

Sports: There are 4 intercollegiate sports for women, and 5 intramural sports for men and 5 for women. Facilities include 3 gyms, a softball field, tennis and racquetball courts, indoor and outdoor swimming pools, a gymnastics room, a weight room, a dance studio, a 3-hole pitch-and-putt golf course, a soccer and flag football field, and a Vita course.

Disabled Students: 95% of the campus is accessible. Wheelchair ramps, elevators, special parking, specially equipped rest rooms, special class scheduling, lowered drinking fountains, and lowered telephones are available.

Services: Counseling and information services are available, as is tutoring in most subjects. There is remedial math, reading, and writing.

Campus Safety and Security: Measures include 24-hour foot and vehicle patrol, escort service, informal discussions, and pamphlets/posters/films. There are lighted pathways/sidewalks and guard gates, and freshman orientation class.

Programs of Study: MUW confers B.A., B.S., B.F.A., B.M., and B.S.N. degrees. Associate and master's degrees are also awarded. Bachelor's degrees are awarded in BIOLOGICAL SCIENCE (biology/biological science and microbiology), BUSINESS (accounting, business administration and management, fashion merchandising, and sports management), COMMUNICATIONS AND THE ARTS (communications, English, fine arts, music, and Spanish), COMPUTER AND PHYSICAL SCIENCE (chemistry, mathematics, and physical sciences), EDUCATION (art, elementary, and music), HEALTH PROFESSIONS (nursing and speech pathology/audiology), SOCIAL SCIENCE (clothing and textiles management/production/services, food production/management/services, history, human development, paralegal studies, physical fitness/movement, political science/government, psychology, and social science). Biology, chemistry, and English are the strongest academically. Business, nursing, and elementary education are the largest.

Required: To graduate, students must complete 128 credit hours, including 30 to 39 in a major, with a minimum GPA of 2.0. The core curriculum requires 12 hours of English, 8 of lab-based science, 6 each of history and social sciences, 3 each of speech or philosophy, fine arts, and math, 2 of phys ed, and 1 of a freshman seminar. Students must also pass a comprehensive exam.

Special: Cross-registration and a 3-2 engineering degree are available with Mississippi State University. MUW also offers internships in all divisions, co-op and work-study programs, several combinations of dual majors, study abroad in 5 countries, credit for experience, nondegree study, and a pass/fail option. There are 15 national honor societies, a freshman honors program, and 3 departmental honors programs.

Faculty/Classroom: 39% of faculty are male; 61%, female. 94% teach undergraduates. No introductory courses are taught by graduate students. The average class size in an introductory lecture is 35; in a laboratory, 23; and in a regular course, 25.

Requirements: The SAT I or ACT is recommended. In addition, prospective students should have completed 4 units of English; 3 each of math, science, and social studies courses in U.S. history, world history, government, and economics or geography; 2 of advanced electives, including foreign language or geography, and a course in computer applications. A GPA of 2.0 is required. AP and CLEP credits are accepted. Important factors in the admissions decision are recommendations by school officials, leadership record, and advanced placement or honor courses.

Procedure: Freshmen are admitted to all sessions. Entrance exams should be taken as early as possible. There are early decision and early admissions plans. Application deadlines are open. The fall 2001 application fee was $25.

Transfer: Applicants must have a GPA of 2.0 in 6 semester hours of both English composition and a lab science, 3 of college algebra or above, and 9 of transferable electives. High school and college transcripts are required. 32 credits of 128 must be completed at MUW.

Visiting: There are regularly scheduled orientations for prospective students, including talks with various student services officers and preregistering. There are guides for informal visits and visitors may sit in on classes and stay overnight. To schedule a visit, contact the Director of Admissions.

Financial Aid: MUW is a member of CSS. The FAFSA is required. Check with the school for current deadlines.

International Students: The school actively recruits these students. They must score 525 on the written TOEFL and also take the SAT I or the ACT, scoring 16 on the ACT.

Computers: The mainframe is an IBM ES9000. The academic computing center offers access to mainframe terminals and more than 100 networked PCs. Computer labs on campus house additional networked PCs. Internet access is available to all students. All students may access the system 8 A.M. to 12 A.M. Monday through Friday. There are no time limits and no fees. It is strongly recommended that all students have a personal computer.

Admissions Contact: Melanie Freeman, Director of Admissions.
E-mail: *mfreeman@muw.edu* Web: *www.muw.edu*

MISSISSIPPI VALLEY STATE UNIVERSITY C-2

Itta Bena, MS 38941-1400 (662) 254-3347; Fax: (662) 254-7900

Full-time: 748 men, 1398 women	**Faculty:** 121
Part-time: 70 men, 420 women	**Ph.D.s:** 60%
Graduate: 90 men, 355 women	**Student/Faculty:** 18 to 1
Year: semesters, summer session	**Tuition:** $3158 ($7375)
Application Deadline: August 10	**Room & Board:** $3187
Freshman Class: 506 accepted, 232 enrolled	
SAT I Verbal/Math: 480/428	**ACT:** 18 **COMPETITIVE**

Mississippi Valley State University, founded in 1946, offers programs in the arts and sciences, business, and education. There are 5 undergraduate schools and 1 graduate school. In addition to regional accreditation, MVSU has baccalaureate program accreditation with NASAD, NASM, and NCATE. The library contains 150,000 volumes, 295,500 microform items, and 3525 audiovisual forms/CDs, and subscribes to 650 periodicals. Computerized library services include the card catalog, interlibrary loans, and database searching. Special learning facilities include a learning resource center, art gallery, radio station, TV station, and a campus nursery/preschool. The 450-acre campus is in a small town 8 miles from Greenwood and 100 miles north of Jackson. Including residence halls, there are 35 buildings.

Student Life: 94% of undergraduates are from Mississippi. Others are from 24 states, 7 foreign countries, and Canada. 92% are from public schools. 95% are African American. Most are Protestant. The average age of freshmen is 18; all undergraduates, 20. 15% do not continue beyond their first year; 40% remain to graduate.

Housing: 1914 students can be accommodated in college housing, which includes single-sex dormitories. In addition, there are honors houses. On-campus housing is available on a first-come, first-served basis. 66% of students commute. Alcohol is not permitted. All students may keep cars.

Activities: There are 5 local and 4 national fraternities and 5 local and 4 national sororities. There are 44 groups on campus, including art, band, cheerleading, choir, chorale, chorus, computers, dance, drama, drill team, honors, jazz band, literary magazine, marching band, newspaper, performing, political, professional, radio and TV, religious, social, social service, student government, and yearbook. Popular campus events include Founders Day, Pride Day, and Black History Month.

Sports: There are 8 intercollegiate sports for men and 6 for women, and 10 intramural sports for men and 9 for women. Facilities include a stadium for football and track, a gymnastics room, a dance studio, an indoor pool, a 2200-seat gym, basketball arena, a weight-training room, and handball, squash, and paddleball courts.

Disabled Students: 99% of the campus is accessible. Wheelchair ramps, elevators, special parking, specially equipped rest rooms, and lowered drinking fountains are available.

Services: Counseling and information services are available, as is tutoring in most subjects. There is remedial math, reading, and writing.

Campus Safety and Security: Measures include 24-hour foot and vehicle patrol, informal discussions, pamphlets/posters/films, and emergency telephones. There are lighted pathways/sidewalks.

Programs of Study: MVSU confers B.A., B.S., B.M.E., B.S.E, and B.S.W. degrees. Master's degrees are also awarded. Bachelor's degrees are awarded in BIOLOGICAL SCIENCE (biology/biological science), BUSINESS (accounting, business administration and management, and office supervision and management), COMMUNICATIONS AND THE ARTS (art, communications, English, fine arts, and speech/debate/rhetoric), COMPUTER AND PHYSICAL SCIENCE (chemistry, computer science, and mathematics), EDUCATION (early childhood, elementary, English, mathematics, music, physical, science, and social science), ENGINEERING AND ENVIRONMENTAL DESIGN (industrial engineering technology), HEALTH PROFESSIONS (environmental health science), SOCIAL SCIENCE (criminal justice, history, political science/government, public administration, social work, and sociology). Biology, computer science, and business are the strongest academically. Criminal justice, business, and education are the largest.

Required: General education requirements include 12 semester hours in English, 6 each in social studies and lab science, 3 each in college algebra, speech, fine arts, psychology, and health ed, and 2 in phys ed. To graduate, students must complete at least 124 credit hours with a minimum GPA of 2.0 overall and in the major.

Special: MVSU offers a special cooperative education program, B.A.-B.S. degree, internships in social work and environmental health, work-study, and nondegree study. Credit may be granted for military experience. A pass/fail option is possible. There are 4 national honor societies, a freshman honors program, and 2 departmental honors programs.

Faculty/Classroom: 65% of faculty are male; 35%, female. All teach undergraduates and 20% both teach and do research. No introductory courses are taught by graduate students. The average class size in an introductory lecture is 30; in a laboratory, 25; and in a regular course, 30.

Admissions: 16% of the 2001-2002 applicants were accepted. The ACT scores were 91% below 21, 7% between 21 and 23, 1% between 24 and 26, and 1% between 27 and 28. 47% of the current freshmen were in the top fifth of their class; 80% were in the top two fifths.

Requirements: The ACT is required for Mississippi residents. Out-of-state students may submit SAT I scores. Applicants must be graduates of a secondary school or have a GED and have completed 4 credits in English, 3 each in math and natural sciences, 2 1/2 in social sciences, and 1 in a foreign language. Recommendations are considered important. A GPA of 2.0 is required. AP and CLEP credits are accepted. Important factors in the admissions decision are evidence of special talent, leadership record, and advanced placement or honor courses. Applications are accepted on-line at the school's web site.

Procedure: Freshmen are admitted fall, spring, and summer. There is an early admissions plan. Applications should be filed by August 10 for fall entry, January for spring entry, and May for summer entry. Notification is sent on a rolling basis.

Transfer: 223 transfer students enrolled in 2001-2002. Transfers must have a minimum 2.0 GPA in at least 24 specified credit hours. 30 credits of 124 must be completed at MVSU.

Visiting: There are regularly scheduled orientations for prospective students, including campus tours with a student guide. Visitors may sit in on classes. To schedule a visit, contact the Dean of Students at (601) 254-3637.

Financial Aid: In a recent year, scholarships or need-based grants averaged $3175 (maximum); loans averaged $625 ($2625 maximum); work contracts averaged $800 ($1400 maximum); and institutional scholarships (which will award up to cost of education minus other grant aid) averaged $4823. 95% of undergraduates work part time. The CSS/Profile or FAFSA and the college's own financial statement are required. The fall application deadline is June 1.

International Students: There are 11 international students enrolled. The school actively recruits these students. They must score 525 on the written TOEFL.

Computers: The mainframe is an IBM 4331. PCs are available in the physics lab and 5 additional computer labs. Students enrolled in computer science courses may access the system 8 A.M. to midnight. There are no time limits and no fees. It is strongly recommended that all students have a personal computer.

Graduates: In 2001, 279 bachelor's degrees were awarded. The most popular majors were biology (13%), business (11%), and criminal justice (9%). In an average class, 38% graduate in 4 years, and 2% in 5 years. 30 companies recruited on campus in 2000-2001.

Admissions Contact: Tameka Jones, Acting Director.
E-mail: *admsn@mvsu.edu*

RUST COLLEGE D-1

Holly Springs, MS 38635 (662) 252-8000, ext. 4059
(888) 886-8492, ext. 4059; Fax: (662) 252-8895

Full-time: 211 men, 384 women	**Faculty:** 46
Part-time: 71 men, 135 women	**Ph.D.s:** 45%
Graduate: none	**Student/Faculty:** 13 to 1
Year: semesters, summer session	**Tuition:** $5400
Application Deadline: July 15	**Room & Board:** $2400
Freshman Class: 1760 applied, 752 accepted, 174 enrolled	
ACT: 15	**COMPETITIVE+**

Rust College, founded in 1866, is a private liberal arts college affiliated with the United Methodist Church. The academic year consists of semesters, each divided into two 8-week modules, plus a summer term. The library contains 122,097 volumes, 8919 microform items, and 884 audiovisual forms/CDs, and subscribes to 340 periodicals. Computerized library services include the card catalog and interlibrary loans. Special learning facilities include a learning resource center, radio station, TV station, and Dr. Ron Trojak collection of African tribal art. The 126-acre campus is in a small town 35 miles southeast of Memphis, Tennessee. Including residence halls, there are 23 buildings.

Student Life: 63% of undergraduates are from Mississippi. Others are from 21 states and 6 foreign countries. 90% are from public schools. 90% are African American. 66% are Protestant; 31% claim no religious affiliation. The average age of freshmen is 19; all undergraduates, 22. 52% do not continue beyond their first year.

Housing: 856 students can be accommodated in college housing, which includes single-sex dormitories. In addition, there are honors houses. On-campus housing is guaranteed for all 4 years. 56% of students live on campus; of those, 50% remain on campus on weekends. Alcohol is not permitted. All students may keep cars.

Activities: 10% of men belong to 4 national fraternities; 14% of women belong to 4 local and 4 national sororities. There are 32 groups on campus, including band, cheerleading, choir, chorale, computers, drama, ethnic, honors, international, newspaper, photography, political, radio and TV, religious, social, social service, student government, and yearbook. Popular campus events include Career Day, Founders Day, and Religious Emphasis Week.

Sports: There are 7 intercollegiate sports for men and 7 for women. Facilities include a 2500-seat gym, a swimming pool, tennis courts, a track, a 2000-seat stadium, a bowling alley, pool tables, and the Magic Johnson Sports Arena.

Disabled Students: Wheelchair ramps, elevators, special parking, specially equipped rest rooms, and lowered drinking fountains are available.

Services: Counseling and information services are available, as is tutoring in most subjects. There is remedial math, reading, and writing.

Campus Safety and Security: Measures include 24-hour foot and vehicle patrol, escort service, informal discussions, and pamphlets/posters/films. There are lighted pathways/sidewalks.

Programs of Study: Rust confers B.A. and B.S. degrees. Associate degrees are also awarded. Bachelor's degrees are awarded in BIOLOGICAL SCIENCE (biology/biological science), BUSINESS (business administration and management), COMMUNICATIONS AND THE ARTS (communications, English, journalism, and music), COMPUTER AND PHYSICAL SCIENCE (chemistry, computer science, and mathematics), EDUCATION (elementary), HEALTH PROFESSIONS (health), SOCIAL SCIENCE (political science/government, social work, and sociology). Business administration and management is the strongest academically. Biology, computer science, and social work are the largest.

Required: All students must earn a minimum of 124 semester hours while maintaining a cumulative GPA of 2.0. Distribution requirements include 59 1/2 general education credits in the fields of education, humanities, science and math, and a required freshman program. A minimum of 50 credits constitutes a major, and comprehensive exams are given in all programs.

Special: Internships are available in all areas and may be required for some majors. On-campus work-study, study abroad, credit by exam, independent study, B.A.-B.S. degrees, and dual majors in a variety of science programs are available. There are 3-2 degrees in preprofessional programs and medical technology, and a 3-2 engineering degree with the student's school of choice. There are 3 national honor societies, a freshman honors program, and 5 departmental honors programs.

Faculty/Classroom: 64% of faculty are male; 36%, female. All teach undergraduates. The average class size in an introductory lecture is 10; in a laboratory, 10; and in a regular course, 25.

Admissions: 43% of the 2001-2002 applicants were accepted. The ACT scores for the 2001-2002 freshman class were: 81% below 21, 18% between 21 and 23, and 1% between 24 and 26.

Requirements: The ACT is required. In addition, Rust students must submit 19 academic credits, including 4 in English, 3 each in math, science, and social studies, and 6 electives. An audition, an interview, and 2 letters of recommendation are required. The GED is accepted. An essay and portfolio are recommended. A GPA of 2.0 is required. AP and CLEP credits are accepted. Important factors in the admissions decision are evidence of special talent, extracurricular activities record, and recommendations by school officials.

Procedure: Freshmen are admitted fall, spring, and summer. Entrance exams should be taken prior to the first semester of the freshman year. Applications should be filed by July 15 for fall entry and December 15 for spring entry. The fall 2001 application fee was $10. Notification is sent on a rolling basis.

Transfer: 32 transfer students enrolled in 2001-2002. Transfer applicants with at least 15 semester hours of credit need not take the ACT or SAT I. Only C grades or better transfer. 30 credits of 124 must be completed at Rust.

Visiting: There are regularly scheduled orientations for prospective students, including a campus tour, departmental visits, introduction to the application process, financial-aid orientation, and question-and-answer session. There are guides for informal visits and visitors may sit in on classes and stay overnight. To schedule a visit, contact Johnny McDonald, Enrollment Services.

Financial Aid: In 2001-2002, 88% of all freshmen received some form of financial aid. 92% of freshmen received need-based aid. Scholarships or need-based grants averaged $2387 ($8000 maximum); loans averaged $1584 ($2625 maximum); and work contracts averaged $764 ($1000 maximum). 41% of undergraduates work part time. Average annual earnings from campus work are $1300. The average financial indebtedness of the 2001 graduate was $11,668. The FFS and the college's own financial statement are required. The fall application deadline is July 15.

International Students: There are 47 international students enrolled. They must score 540 on the written TOEFL.
Computers: The mainframe is an IBM AS/400. Computer labs are located in 5 of 7 academic divisions. 9 PC labs exist for academic programs. Internet access is available at the library. Computer science majors and work-aid students may access the system at assigned times. There are no time limits and no fees.
Graduates: In 2001, 100 bachelor's degrees were awarded. The most popular majors were business administration and management (32%), mass communication (12%), and biology (12%). In an average class, 24% graduate in 4 years, 10% in 5 years, and 1% in 6 years. 42 companies recruited on campus in 2000-2001. Of the 2000 graduating class, 13% were enrolled in graduate school within 6 months of graduation and 69% were employed.
Admissions Contact: Johnny McDonald, Director of Enrollment Services. E-mail: *jbmcdonald@rustcollege.edu* Web: *rustcollege.edu*

TOUGALOO COLLEGE
Tougaloo, MS 39174 C-4
(601) 977-7764
(888) 424-2566; (601) 977-6185

Full-time: 270 men, 600 women	**Faculty:** 66
Part-time: 20 men, 50 women	**Ph.D.s:** 52%
Graduate: none	**Student/Faculty:** 13 to 1
Year: semesters	**Tuition:** $6200
Application Deadline: open	**Room & Board:** $3000
Freshman Class: n/av	
SAT I or ACT: required	**NONCOMPETITIVE**

Tougaloo College, founded in 1869, is a private liberal arts institution affiliated with the United Church of Christ. Figures given in above capsule are approximate. The library contains 117,000 volumes, 7200 microform items, and 4300 audiovisual forms/CDs, and subscribes to 370 periodicals. Computerized library services include the card catalog, interlibrary loans, and database searching. Special learning facilities include a learning resource center and art gallery. The 500-acre campus is in a suburban area 1 mile north of Jackson. Including residence halls, there are 18 buildings.
Student Life: 87% of undergraduates are from Mississippi. Others are from 23 states and 2 foreign countries. Most are from public schools. Most are African American. Most are Baptist. The average age of freshmen is 18; all undergraduates, 20. 18% do not continue beyond their first year; 42% remain to graduate.
Housing: 632 students can be accommodated in college housing, which includes single-sex dormitories. On-campus housing is available on a first-come, first-served basis. 60% of students live on campus; of those, 80% remain on campus on weekends. Alcohol is not permitted. All students may keep cars.
Activities: 35% of men belong to 4 national fraternities; 40% of women belong to 4 national sororities. There are many groups and organizations on campus, including art, cheerleading, choir, chorus, computers, honors, international, newspaper, photography, political, professional, religious, social, social service, student government, and yearbook. Popular campus events include Founders Day.
Sports: There are 2 intercollegiate sports for men and 1 for women. Facilities include a gym, a tennis court, and access to a bowling alley and a golf course.
Disabled Students: 20% of the campus is accessible. Wheelchair ramps, elevators, and specially equipped rest rooms are available.
Services: Counseling and information services are available, as is tutoring in every subject. There is remedial math, reading, and writing.
Campus Safety and Security: Measures include 24-hour foot and vehicle patrol, self-defense education, informal discussions, and pamphlets/posters/films. There are emergency telephones and lighted pathways/sidewalks.
Programs of Study: Tougaloo confers B.A. and B.S. degrees. Associate degrees are also awarded. Bachelor's degrees are awarded in BIOLOGICAL SCIENCE (biology/biological science), BUSINESS (recreation and leisure services), COMMUNICATIONS AND THE ARTS (art, English, and music), COMPUTER AND PHYSICAL SCIENCE (chemistry, mathematics, and physics), EDUCATION (elementary, health, and physical), SOCIAL SCIENCE (economics, history, political science/government, psychology, and sociology). Physical sciences is the strongest academically. Biology and economics are the largest.
Required: To graduate, students must complete 124 credit hours, including 27 to 48 in the major, with a minimum GPA of 2.0. Students must fulfill about 56 hours of general education requirements, take computer science and phys ed courses, and complete a senior paper.
Special: Tougaloo offers cooperative programs with Brown and Boston universities, study abroad in Africa, a Washington semester in conjunction with American University, internships, work-study programs, credit for military service, pass/fail options, and a 3-2 engineering degree with Georgia Tech, the University of Wisconsin at Madison, and Brown, Mississippi, Tuskegee, and Howard universities. There are 3 national honor societies, and a freshman honors program.
Faculty/Classroom: 55% of faculty are male; 45%, female. All teach undergraduates.
Requirements: The SAT I or ACT is required. In addition, candidates should be graduates of an accredited secondary school or have a GED certificate. They should have completed 3 credits of English, 2 each of math and science, and 1 each of history and social studies. An interview is recommended. A GPA of 2.0 is required. AP and CLEP credits are accepted. Important factors in the admissions decision are advanced placement or honor courses, evidence of special talent, and extracurricular activities record.
Procedure: Freshmen are admitted in the fall. Entrance exams should be taken by March of the senior year. There is an early admissions plan. Application deadlines are open. The fall application fee was $5.
Transfer: Applicants must submit transcripts of all college coursework and have a minimum GPA of 2.0. 30 credits of 124 must be completed at Tougaloo.
Visiting: Visitors may sit in on classes and stay overnight. To schedule a visit, contact the Office of Student Enrollment at (601) 977-7765.
Financial Aid: Tougaloo is a member of CSS. The CSS/Profile, FAFSA, FFS, or SFS is required. Check with the school for current deadlines.
International Students: They must score 500 on the written TOEFL and also take the SAT I or the ACT.
Computers: The mainframe is a DEC. Mac, IBM, and AT&T PCs are available in the Academic Computing Center. There are no time limits and no fees.
Admissions Contact: Carolyn L. Evans, Enrollment Services. A video is available.

UNIVERSITY OF MISSISSIPPI
University, MS 38677 D-2
(662) 915-7226
(800) OLE-MISS; Fax: (662) 915-5869

Full-time: 4529 men, 4743 women	**Faculty:** 495; I, --$
Part-time: 283 men, 326 women	**Ph.D.s:** 83%
Graduate: 1000 men, 982 women	**Student/Faculty:** 17 to 1
Year: semesters, summer session	**Tuition:** $3626 ($8172)
Application Deadline: April 1	**Room & Board:** $4040
Freshman Class: 6601 applied, 5287 accepted, 2091 enrolled	
SAT I or ACT: required	**COMPETITIVE**

The University of Mississippi, founded in 1844, is a public institution offering undergraduate and graduate programs in the liberal arts, business, pharmacy, engineering, accountancy, and education. There are 6 undergraduate and 2 graduate schools. In addition to regional accreditation, Ole Miss has baccalaureate program accreditation with AACSB, ABET, ACEJMC, CSAB, CSWE, NASAD, NASM, and NCATE. The 3 libraries contain 1 million volumes and 42,056 audiovisual forms/CDs, and subscribe to 6427 periodicals. Computerized library services include the card catalog, interlibrary loans, and database searching. Special learning facilities include a learning resource center, art gallery, radio station, TV station, a museum, the Center for the Study of Southern Culture, the National Center for Physical Acoustics, Rowan Oak, the home of William Faulkner, the National Center for Development of Natural Products, National Food Service Management Institute, and the Croft Institute for International Studies. The 2000-acre campus is in a small town 70 miles southeast of Memphis, Tennessee. Including residence halls, there are 193 buildings.
Student Life: 65% of undergraduates are from Mississippi. Others are from 47 states, 70 foreign countries, and Canada. 70% are from public schools. 82% are white; 12% African American. The average age of all undergraduates is 21. 26% do not continue beyond their first year; 54% remain to graduate.
Housing: 4513 students can be accommodated in college housing, which includes single-sex dormitories, on-campus apartments, married-student housing, fraternity houses, and sorority houses. On-campus housing is guaranteed for the freshman year only, is available on a first-come, first-served basis, and is available on a lottery system for upperclassmen. Alcohol is not permitted. All students may keep cars.
Activities: 35% of men belong to 19 national fraternities; 40% of women belong to 13 national sororities. There are 200 groups on campus, including art, band, cheerleading, chess, choir, chorale, chorus, computers, dance, drama, drill team, ethnic, gay, honors, international, jazz band, literary magazine, marching band, musical theater, newspaper, orchestra, pep band, political, professional, radio and TV, religious, social, social service, student government, symphony, and yearbook. Popular campus events include Faulkner and Yoknapatawpha Conference, Red and Blue Week, and Oxford Conference for the Book.
Sports: There are 8 intercollegiate sports for men and 10 for women, and 35 intramural sports for men and 35 for women. Facilities include a 50,577-seat football stadium, an 8800-seat gym, a baseball diamond, an indoor pool, 10 racquetball courts, 23 outdoor tennis courts, 3 playing fields, women's soccer and softball fields, volleyball, an indoor tennis facility, and a fitness center.
Disabled Students: 25% of the campus is accessible. Wheelchair ramps, elevators, special parking, specially equipped rest rooms, special

class scheduling, lowered drinking fountains, and lowered telephones are available.

Services: Counseling and information services are available, as is tutoring in every subject. There is a reader service for the blind and remedial math and reading.

Campus Safety and Security: Measures include 24-hour foot and vehicle patrol, self-defense education, escort service, and informal discussions. There are pamphlets/posters/films, emergency telephones, lighted pathways/sidewalks, and a full-time campus safety officer.

Programs of Study: Ole Miss confers B.A., B.S., B.Ac., B.A.E., B.A.Ed., B.A.L.M., B.B.A, B.C.R., B.E., B.F.A., B.Mus., B.P.A., B.S.C.E., B.S.Ch.E., B.S.C.S., B.S.E.E., B.S.E.S., B.S.F.C.S., B.S.G.E., B.S.J., B.S.M.E., B.S.Pharm., and B.S.W. degrees. Master's and doctoral degrees are also awarded. Bachelor's degrees are awarded in BIOLOGICAL SCIENCE (biology/biological science), BUSINESS (accounting, banking and finance, business administration and management, business economics, court reporting, insurance, international business management, investments and securities, management information systems, management science, marketing/retailing/merchandising, real estate, recreation and leisure services, and recreational facilities management), COMMUNICATIONS AND THE ARTS (advertising, art, art history and appreciation, broadcasting, design, dramatic arts, English, French, German, journalism, linguistics, music, radio/television technology, and Spanish), COMPUTER AND PHYSICAL SCIENCE (chemistry, computer science, geology, and physics), EDUCATION (elementary, English, foreign languages, home economics, mathematics, science, social science, and special), ENGINEERING AND ENVIRONMENTAL DESIGN (chemical engineering, civil engineering, electrical/electronics engineering, engineering, geological engineering, and mechanical engineering), HEALTH PROFESSIONS (biomedical science, exercise science, medical laboratory technology, medical technology, pharmacy, speech pathology/audiology, and speech therapy), SOCIAL SCIENCE (anthropology, area studies, classical/ancient civilization, economics, family/consumer studies, forensic studies, history, international studies, liberal arts/general studies, philosophy, political science/government, psychology, public administration, social work, and sociology). General business, accountancy, and biological sciences are the largest.

Required: Students must maintain a minimum GPA of 2.0 (2.5 in teacher education) while taking 126 to 139 semester hours, including 24 to 42 in the major. Other requirements include 6 hours each of English composition and lab science and 3 each of college algebra and humanities and fine arts.

Special: Internships in journalism, accounting, and engineering, study abroad in numerous countries, and work-study programs within the college are offered. Dual majors, a general studies degree, credit by exam, special testing in music and languages, credit for military experience, and limited pass/fail options also are available. There are 24 national honor societies, and a freshman honors program.

Faculty/Classroom: 69% of faculty are male; 31%, female.

Admissions: 80% of the 2001-2002 applicants were accepted. The ACT scores for the 2001-2002 freshman class were: 27% below 21, 26% between 21 and 23, 21% between 24 and 26, 11% between 27 and 28, and 15% above 28. There were 27 National Merit finalists and 10 semifinalists in a recent year.

Requirements: The SAT I or ACT is required, with a minimum composite score of 840 on the SAT I or 18 on the ACT. Applicants need 15 academic credits, including 4 units in English, 3 each in math, science lab courses, and social studies, 2 in foreign language or world geography, and 1/2 in computer applications. A portfolio for art majors and an audition for theater and music majors are required. The GED is not accepted. Applications are accepted on-line. A GPA of 2.0 is required. AP and CLEP credits are accepted.

Procedure: Freshmen are admitted to all sessions. There are early admissions and deferred admissions plans. Applications should be filed by April 1 for fall entry, December 1 for spring entry, and April 1 for summer entry, along with a $40 (nonresidents) or $25 (residents) fee. Notification is sent on a rolling basis.

Transfer: 783 transfer students enrolled in a recent year. Transfer students must have earned a minimum 2.0 GPA on previous college work. The SAT I or ACT may be required depending on credits earned. 30 credits of 126 must be completed at Ole Miss.

Visiting: There are regularly scheduled orientations for prospective students, including academic information/student life discussions and tours. Class attendance and academic appointments can be arranged. There are guides for informal visits and visitors may sit in on classes and stay overnight. To schedule a visit, contact the Office of Admissions.

Financial Aid: In 2001-2002, 75% of all freshmen and 74% of continuing students received some form of financial aid. The average freshman award in a recent year was $5351. Of that total, scholarships or need-based grants averaged $3136 ($16,510 maximum); loans averaged $2043 ($12,000 maximum); and work contracts averaged $172 ($2400 maximum). The average financial indebtedness of a recent year's graduate was $11,658. Ole Miss is a member of CSS. The FAFSA is required. The fall application deadline is March 15.

International Students: There were 134 international students enrolled in a recent year. The school actively recruits these students. They must score 550 on the written TOEFL or 213 on the electronic version and also take the college's own test, the SAT I (scoring 970) or the ACT (scoring 21).

Computers: The mainframes are an IBM ES 9000, an SGI Challenge L, an SGI Power Challenge L, a CRAY Y-MP83, and a CRAY J916. The computer center runs a 120-unit general-access lab housing Novell networked PCs with mainframe connection via the campus fiber optic network. Various academic departments operate their own PC labs, some of which are networked and connected to the campus backbone fiber. All students may access the system 24 hours daily. There are no time limits and no fees. It is strongly recommended that all students have a personal computer.

Graduates: In a recent year, 1567 bachelor's degrees were awarded. The most popular majors were business/management/accounting (31%), education (9%), and health professions (8%). In an average class, 32% graduate in 4 years, 50% in 5 years, and 54% in 6 years.

Admissions Contact: Beckett Howorth, Director of Admissions and Records. A video is available. E-mail: *admissions@olemiss.edu*
Web: *www.olemiss.edu*

UNIVERSITY OF SOUTHERN MISSISSIPPI — D-5

Hattiesburg, MS 39406-5166 — (601) 266-5000
Fax: (601) 266-5148

Full-time: 3850 men, 5675 women	**Faculty:** 630; I, --$
Part-time: 445 men, 635 women	**Ph.D.s:** 84%
Graduate: 780 men, 1200 women	**Student/Faculty:** 15 to 1
Year: semesters, summer session	**Tuition:** $3416 ($7932)
Application Deadline: see profile	**Room & Board:** $3285
Freshman Class: n/av	
ACT: required	**LESS COMPETITIVE**

The University of Southern Mississippi, founded in 1910, is a public institution offering comprehensive undergraduate and graduate programs. Some information in this profile is approximate. There are 8 undergraduate schools and 1 graduate school. In addition to regional accreditation, Southern Miss has baccalaureate program accreditation with AACSB, ABET, ACEJMC, ADA, AHEA, ASLA, CAHEA, CSAB, CSWE, FIDER, NASAD, NASM, NCATE, NLN, and NRPA. The 2 libraries contain 976,660 volumes, 3,858,617 microform items, and 16,003 audiovisual forms/CDs, and subscribe to 7031 periodicals. Computerized library services include the card catalog and database searching. Special learning facilities include a learning resource center, art gallery, natural history museum, radio station, TV station, TV production studios, the Museum of Natural Science, and a music resource center. The 1090-acre campus is in a suburban area 90 miles southeast of Jackson, and 105 miles north of New Orleans, Louisiana. Including residence halls, there are 168 buildings.

Student Life: 85% of undergraduates are from Mississippi. Others are from 48 states, 61 foreign countries, and Canada. 83% are from public schools. 76% are white; 20% African American. The average age of freshmen is 19; all undergraduates, 25. 27% do not continue beyond their first year; 47% remain to graduate.

Housing: 3225 students can be accommodated in college housing, which includes single-sex dormitories, married-student housing, and fraternity houses. On-campus housing is guaranteed for the freshman year only and is available on a first-come, first-served basis. 70% of students commute. Alcohol is not permitted. All students may keep cars.

Activities: 16% of men belong to 16 local and 16 national fraternities; 15% of women belong to 12 local and 12 national sororities. There are 211 groups on campus, including art, band, cheerleading, choir, chorale, chorus, computers, dance, drama, ethnic, gay, honors, international, jazz band, marching band, musical theater, newspaper, opera, orchestra, pep band, photography, political, professional, radio and TV, religious, social, social service, student government, symphony, and yearbook.

Sports: There are 7 intercollegiate sports for men and 7 for women, and 41 intramural sports for men and 41 for women. Facilities include a recreational lake, a football stadium, a basketball coliseum, a baseball park, tennis courts, a golf course, an equestrian center, a fitness institute, a natatorium, and playing fields for softball, flag football, and soccer.

Disabled Students: 80% of the campus is accessible. Wheelchair ramps, elevators, special parking, specially equipped rest rooms, special class scheduling, lowered drinking fountains, lowered telephones, and an Office of Support Services for students with disabilities are available.

Services: Counseling and information services are available, as is tutoring in most subjects. There is a reader service for the blind, and remedial math, reading, and writing.

Campus Safety and Security: Measures include 24-hour foot and vehicle patrol, self-defense education, escort service, and shuttle buses. There are informal discussions, pamphlets/posters/films, emergency telephones, and lighted pathways/sidewalks.

Programs of Study: Southern Miss confers B.A., B.S., B.F.A., B.M., B.M.E., and B.S.B.A degrees. Master's and doctoral degrees are also awarded. Bachelor's degrees are awarded in BIOLOGICAL SCIENCE (biology/biological science), BUSINESS (accounting, banking and finance, business administration and management, business economics, hotel/motel and restaurant management, international business management, marketing/retailing/merchandising, and personnel management), COMMUNICATIONS AND THE ARTS (advertising, communications, dance, design, dramatic arts, English, fine arts, journalism, languages, music, radio/television technology, and speech/debate/rhetoric), COMPUTER AND PHYSICAL SCIENCE (chemistry, computer science, geology, information sciences and systems, mathematics, physics, polymer science, and statistics), EDUCATION (art, business, early childhood, elementary, foreign languages, guidance, health, home economics, industrial arts, middle school, music, science, and secondary), ENGINEERING AND ENVIRONMENTAL DESIGN (architectural technology, computer technology, construction technology, electrical/electronics engineering technology, engineering technology, and mechanical engineering technology), HEALTH PROFESSIONS (medical laboratory technology, nursing, predentistry, premedicine, and speech pathology/audiology), SOCIAL SCIENCE (anthropology, criminal justice, economics, geography, history, international studies, parks and recreation management, philosophy, political science/government, prelaw, psychology, social science, social work, and sociology). Polymer science and accounting are the strongest academically. Accounting is the largest.

Required: To graduate, students must complete at least 128 semester hours, including 64 at the senior college level, with a minimum GPA of 2.0. Core requirements include courses in reasoning and communication skills, humanities and fine arts, social and behavioral sciences, human wellness, and natural and applied sciences.

Special: USM offers many cooperative programs, internships, dual majors, nondegree study, limited pass/fail options, credit for life experience, and study abroad in England, Germany, Austria, and Italy. The university also participates in the Title IV College Work-Study Program. There are 27 national honor societies, and a freshman honors program.

Faculty/Classroom: 63% of faculty are male; 37%, female. 91% teach undergraduates and 75% do research. The average class size in an introductory lecture is 37; in a laboratory, 32; and in a regular course, 29.

Admissions: There were 10 National Merit finalists in a recent year.

Requirements: The ACT is required, with a minimum score of 15. Applicants must be graduates of an accredited secondary school or have a GED certificate. They should have completed 4 units of English, 3 each of math, science, and social studies, 2 of advanced electives, and 1/2 of computer applications. Applications are accepted on-line at the school's home page. A GPA of 2.0 is required. AP and CLEP credits are accepted.

Procedure: Freshmen are admitted to all sessions. Entrance exams should be taken in the fall of the senior year. There are early decision and early admissions plans. Check with school for current application deadlines.

Transfer: Applicants must be eligible to return to their previous institution. 32 credits of 128 must be completed at Southern Miss.

Visiting: There are regularly scheduled orientations for prospective students, including campus tours and general session orientations. There are guides for informal visits and visitors may sit in on classes. To schedule a visit, contact Homer Wesley.

Financial Aid: In a recent year, 70% of all freshmen and 64% of continuing students received some form of financial aid. 47% of freshmen and 45% of continuing students received need-based aid. The average freshman award was $2828. Of that total, scholarships or need-based grants averaged $3027 ($14,600 maximum); loans averaged $2938 ($9125 maximum); and work contracts averaged $2240. 10% of undergraduates work part time. Average annual earnings from campus work are $2472. The FAFSA is required. The fall application deadline is March 15.

International Students: The school actively recruits these students. They must score 525 on the written TOEFL and also take the ACT, scoring 18.

Computers: The mainframes are a Honeywell DPS90 and a DEC/ALPHA server 8200. There are also 570 IBM, Mac, and Zenith PCs available throughout the campus. All students may access the system at any time. There are no time limits and no fees.

Graduates: In an average class, 20% graduate in 4 years, 38% in 5 years, and 46% in 6 years. 918 companies recruited on campus in a recent year.

Admissions Contact: Wayne Pyle, Admissions Office. A video is available. Web: *http://www.usm.ed/*

WILLIAM CAREY COLLEGE
Hattiesburg, MS 39401-5499

D-5
(601) 582-6103
(800) 962-5991; (601) 582-6454

Full-time: 500 men, 900 women	**Faculty:** 80
Part-time: 150 men, 300 women	**Ph.D.s:** 57%
Graduate: none	**Student/Faculty:** 17 to 1
Year: trimesters, summer session	**Tuition:** $7150
Application Deadline: see profile	**Room & Board:** $3000
Freshman Class: n/av	
ACT: required	**LESS COMPETITIVE**

William Carey College, founded in 1906, is a private liberal arts college affiliated with the Mississippi Baptist Convention. There are 4 undergraduate and 2 graduate schools. Figures in the above capsule are approximate. In addition to regional accreditation, Carey has baccalaureate program accreditation with NASDTEC, NASM, and NLN. The 4 libraries contain 135,000 volumes, 30,000 microform items, and 3000 audiovisual forms/CDs, and subscribe to 600 periodicals. Computerized library services include the card catalog, interlibrary loans, and database searching. Special learning facilities include a learning resource center and art gallery. The 120-acre campus is in a small town 100 miles from New Orleans, Louisiana. Including residence halls, there are 15 buildings.

Student Life: The average age of freshmen is 18.

Housing: 428 students can be accommodated in college housing, which includes single-sex dormitories and on-campus apartments. 50% of students live on campus. Alcohol is not permitted. All students may keep cars.

Activities: There is 1 national fraternity and there are 2 local sororities and 1 national sorority. There are 20 groups on campus, including art, cheerleading, choir, chorale, drama, ethnic, honors, international, literary magazine, newspaper, pep band, professional, religious, social, social service, student government, and yearbook. Popular campus events include Hydromania and Mudbowl, Spring Fling Week, and Crawfish Boil.

Sports: There are 4 intercollegiate sports for men and 4 for women, and 3 intramural sports for men and 3 for women. Facilities include a gym, a baseball field, an intramural field, and tennis courts.

Disabled Students: 80% of the campus is accessible. Wheelchair ramps, special parking, specially equipped rest rooms, and special class scheduling are available.

Services: Counseling and information services are available, as is tutoring in every subject. There is remedial math, reading, and writing.

Campus Safety and Security: Measures include 24-hour foot and vehicle patrol, escort service, informal discussions, and pamphlets/posters/films. There are emergency telephones, and lighted pathways/sidewalks. Campus security personnel are on duty 24 hours a day.

Programs of Study: Carey confers B.A., B.S., B.F.A., B.G.S., B.L.S., B.M., B.S.B., and B.S.N. degrees. Master's degrees are also awarded. Bachelor's degrees are awarded in BIOLOGICAL SCIENCE (biology/biological science), BUSINESS (business administration and management), COMMUNICATIONS AND THE ARTS (art, communications, dramatic arts, English, music, music performance, and Spanish), COMPUTER AND PHYSICAL SCIENCE (chemistry, mathematics, and radiological technology), EDUCATION (elementary, music, and physical), HEALTH PROFESSIONS (medical laboratory technology, music therapy, and nursing), SOCIAL SCIENCE (history, liberal arts/general studies, psychology, religion, religious music, and social science). Education, music, and nursing are the strongest academically. Education and nursing are the largest.

Required: Students must complete a core curriculum, including 6 credits each in religion, English, history, and social and behavioral science; 4 in lab science; 3 each in math, fine arts, communication, and literature; and 2 in phys ed. A total of 128 trimester hours, with a minimum 2.0 GPA overall and in the major, is needed to graduate.

Special: Internships are available in some disciplines, and nondegree study, a 3-2 program in forestry, and a 3-1 program in medical technology are also available. 2-year professional programs are possible in engineering, physical therapy, medical records administration, radiological technology, optometry, and pharmacy. Upperclassmen may choose 1 pass/fail option per trimester. There are 7 national honor societies, and a freshman honors program.

Requirements: The ACT is required. In addition, applicants must have earned 16 Carnegie units, including courses in English, foreign language, social studies, science, and math. The admissions committee also considers special skills or aptitudes and other evidence of academic potential. Recommendations from high school officials and college alumni, extracurricular activities, honors courses, leadership potential, and ability to pay also are considered. Carey requires applicants to be in the upper 50% of their class. A GPA of 2.0 is required. AP and CLEP credits are accepted.

Procedure: Freshmen are admitted to all sessions. There are early admissions and deferred admissions plans. Notification is sent on a rolling basis. Check with the school for current application deadlines and fee.

Transfer: Transfer students must have a minimum GPA of 1.4 for freshmen, 1.7 for sophomores, and 2.0 for juniors. 30 credits of 128 must be completed at Carey.

Visiting: There are regularly scheduled orientations for prospective students, including panel discussions, campus tours, faculty advising, and financial aid seminars. There are guides for informal visits and visitors may sit in on classes and stay overnight. To schedule a visit, contact the Admissions Office.

Financial Aid: The FAFSA is required. Check with the school for current deadlines.

International Students: They must score 525 on the written TOEFL or take the MELAB or the college's own test and the SAT I or the ACT.

Computers: The computer lab is located in the learning resource center. All students may access the system. There are no time limits and no fees.

Admissions Contact: Thomas Huebner, Jr., Director of Admissions. E-mail: *admiss@wmcarey.edu* Web: *www.wmcarey.edu*

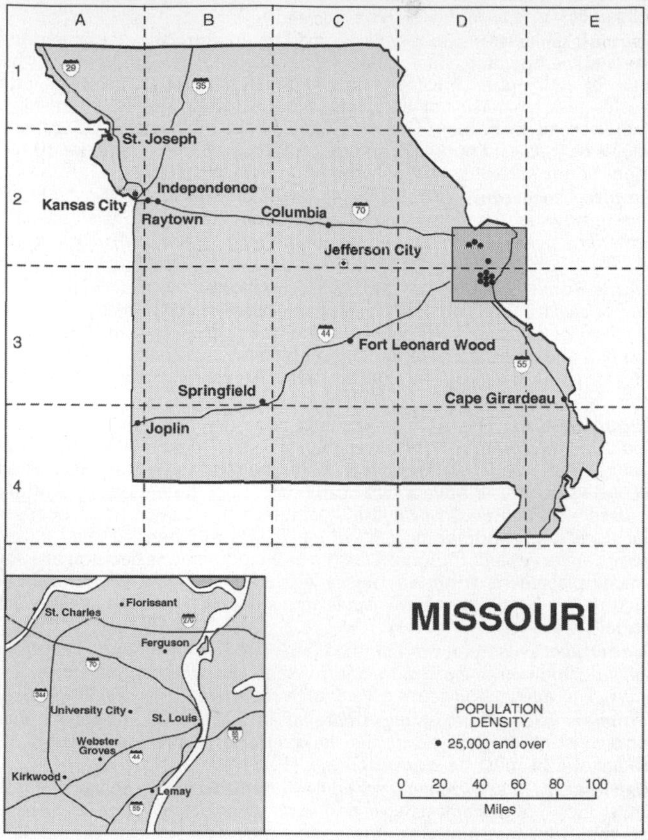

AVILA COLLEGE
Kansas City, MO 64145 — A-2

(816) 501-2400
(800) GO-AVILA; Fax: (816) 501-2453

Full-time: 307 men, 488 women
Part-time: 117 men, 323 women
Graduate: 120 men, 289 women
Year: semesters, summer session
Application Deadline: open
Freshman Class: 435 applied, 402 accepted, 163 enrolled
SAT I Verbal/Math: 475/545
Faculty: 59; IIB, --$
Ph.D.s: 77%
Student/Faculty: 14 to 1
Tuition: $12,720
Room & Board: $5000
ACT: 22
COMPETITIVE

Avila College, founded in 1916, is a comprehensive liberal arts institution sponsored by the Sisters of St. Joseph of Carondelet. In addition to regional accreditation, Avila has baccalaureate program accreditation with CAHEA, CCNE, and CSWE. The library contains 70,935 volumes, 480,000 microform items, and 3094 audiovisual forms/CDs, and subscribes to 551 periodicals. Computerized library services include the card catalog, interlibrary loans, and database searching. Special learning facilities include a learning resource center, art gallery, TV station, 500-seat theater, interactive video library, and video production facilities. The 48-acre campus is in a suburban area in Kansas City, Missouri. Including residence halls, there are 11 buildings.

Student Life: 70% of undergraduates are from Missouri. Others are from 16 states, 20 foreign countries, and Canada. 90% are from public schools. 74% are white; 13% African American. 30% are Catholic. The average age of freshmen is 18; all undergraduates, 27. 30% do not continue beyond their first year.

Housing: 230 students can be accommodated in college housing, which includes coed dormitories. On-campus housing is guaranteed for all 4 years. 82% of students commute. Alcohol is not permitted. All students may keep cars.

Activities: There are no fraternities or sororities. There are 23 groups on campus, including cheerleading, choir, chorus, computers, dance, debate, drama, ethnic, film, forensics, honors, international, literary magazine, musical theater, photography, political, professional, radio and TV, religious, social, social service, student government, and yearbook. Popular campus events include sports and theatrical events, Family Day, and International Festival.

Sports: There are 4 intercollegiate sports for men and 4 for women, and 8 intramural sports for men and 8 for women. Facilities include a field house with basketball and volleyball courts, a training room, and weight and fitness equipment. There is also an athletic complex with baseball, softball, and soccer fields, tennis courts, and practice fields.

Disabled Students: 80% of the campus is accessible. Wheelchair ramps, elevators, special parking, specially equipped rest rooms, special class scheduling, lowered drinking fountains, and lowered telephones are available.

Services: Counseling and information services are available, as is tutoring in most subjects. There is a reader service for the blind, and remedial math, reading, and writing.

Campus Safety and Security: Measures include self-defense education, escort service, informal discussions, and pamphlets/posters/films. There are lighted pathways/sidewalks, evening and night security patrols, and 24-hour closed-circuit television in residence hall entryways.

Programs of Study: Avila confers B.A., B.S., B.F.A., B.S.B.A., B.S.N., and B.S.W. degrees. Master's degrees are also awarded. Bachelor's degrees are awarded in BIOLOGICAL SCIENCE (biology/biological science), BUSINESS (accounting, banking and finance, business administration and management, international business management, management science, and marketing/retailing/merchandising), COMMUNICATIONS AND THE ARTS (art, communications, dramatic arts, English, and music), COMPUTER AND PHYSICAL SCIENCE (chemistry, computer science, information sciences and systems, mathematics, natural sciences, and radiological technology), EDUCATION (business, elementary, middle school, and special), HEALTH PROFESSIONS (medical laboratory technology, nursing, premedicine, and sports medicine), SOCIAL SCIENCE (history, liberal arts/general studies, paralegal studies, political science/government, psychology, social work, sociology, and theological studies). Nursing, education, and communications are the strongest academically. Nursing, education, and radiologic technology are the largest.

Required: To graduate, students must complete at least 128 semester hours with a minimum 2.0 GPA. The 42- to 47-hour core curriculum consists of courses in composition, communication, math, history, literature, theology, philosophy, the arts, the sciences, and social institutions.

Special: Students may cross-register with the Kansas City Area Student Exchange, the Sisters of Saint Joseph College Consortium, and the Council of Independent Colleges Student Exchange. Avila also offers internships, work-study, a Washington center program, dual majors in science, math, and health professions, and accelerated degree programs in business administration and psychology. There are 6 national honor societies.

Faculty/Classroom: 42% of faculty are male; 58%, female. All both teach and do research. No introductory courses are taught by graduate students. The average class size in an introductory lecture is 22; in a laboratory, 16; and in a regular course, 16.

Admissions: 92% of the 2001-2002 applicants were accepted. The ACT scores for the 2001-2002 freshman class were: 30% below 21, 49% between 21 and 23, 12% between 24 and 26, 6% between 27 and 28, and 3% above 28. 25% of the current freshmen were in the top fifth of their class; 49% were in the top two fifths. 1 freshman graduated first in the class.

Requirements: The SAT I or ACT is required. A minimum ACT score of 20 or SAT I composite score of 900 is recommended. Applicants must be graduates of an accredited secondary school or have a GED certificate. They should have completed 16 academic units, including 4 in English, 3 in math, 2 to 4 in foreign language, 2 to 3 in natural and social sciences, and 1 to 2 in fine arts. An interview is advised. A GPA of 2.5 is required. AP and CLEP credits are accepted. Important factors in the admissions decision are recommendations by school officials, extracurricular activities record, and leadership record.

Procedure: Freshmen are admitted to all sessions. Entrance exams should be taken in the spring or summer of the junior year. Application deadlines are open. Notification is sent on a rolling basis.

Transfer: 185 transfer students enrolled in 2001-2002. Applicants must have a minimum GPA of 2.0. 30 credits of 128 must be completed at Avila.

Visiting: There are regularly scheduled orientations for prospective students, including a visit with admissions and a faculty member and a campus tour. There are guides for informal visits and visitors may sit in on classes and stay overnight. To schedule a visit, contact the Director of Admissions.

Financial Aid: In 2001-2002, 97% of all freshmen and 87% of continuing students received some form of financial aid. 76% of freshmen and 74% of continuing students received need-based aid. The average freshman award was $8825. Of that total, scholarships or need-based grants averaged $5000 ($11,150 maximum); loans averaged $2625 ($3625 maximum); and work contracts averaged $1200 (maximum). 92% of undergraduates work part time. Average annual earnings from campus work are $1200. The average financial indebtedness of the 2001 graduate was $11,000. The FAFSA is required.

International Students: There are 73 international students enrolled. The school actively recruits these students. They must score 550 on the written TOEFL.

Computers: The mainframe is a Compaq DEC ALPHA 2100 4/233. There are 60 IBM PCs and 27 Macs located in computer labs, residence halls, and the library. All students may access the system. There are no time limits and no fees.

Graduates: In 2001, 170 bachelor's degrees were awarded. The most popular majors were business (25%), education (14%), and radiologic technology (10%). In an average class, 31% graduate in 4 years, 43% in 5 years, and 44% in 6 years. Of the 2000 graduating class, 18% were enrolled in graduate school within 6 months of graduation and 97% were employed.

Admissions Contact: Paige Illum, Director of Admissions.
E-mail: *admissions@mail.avila.edu* Web: *www.avila.edu*

CENTRAL METHODIST COLLEGE — C-2

Fayette, MO 65248 (660) 248-6247
(888) CMC-1854; Fax: (660) 248-1872

Full-time: 385 men, 400 women	**Faculty:** 64
Part-time: 21 men, 25 women	**Ph.D.s:** 50%
Graduate: 9 men, 46 women	**Student/Faculty:** 12 to 1
Year: semesters, summer session	**Tuition:** $12,130
Application Deadline: open	**Room & Board:** $4330
Freshman Class: 1056 applied, 880 accepted, 247 enrolled	
ACT: 20	**COMPETITIVE**

Central Methodist College, founded in 1854, is a private liberal arts institution affiliated with the Methodist Church. In addition to regional accreditation, CMC has baccalaureate program accreditation with NASM. The library contains 102,695 volumes, 140,812 microform items, and 3736 audiovisual forms/CDs, and subscribes to 447 periodicals. Computerized library services include the card catalog, interlibrary loans, and database searching. Special learning facilities include a learning resource center, art gallery, natural history museum, radio station, TV station, and an observatory. The 52-acre campus is in a small town 30 miles northwest of Columbia. Including residence halls, there are 22 buildings.

Student Life: 90% of undergraduates are from Missouri. Others are from 20 states, 8 foreign countries, and Canada. 96% are from public schools. 87% are white. 77% are Protestant; 20% Catholic. The average age of freshmen is 18; all undergraduates, 21. 39% do not continue beyond their first year.

Housing: 667 students can be accommodated in college housing, which includes single-sex and coed dormitories, off-campus apartments, and married-student housing. On-campus housing is guaranteed for all 4 years. 70% of students live on campus; of those, 60% remain on campus on weekends. Alcohol is not permitted. All students may keep cars.

Activities: 40% of men belong to 6 local fraternities; 40% of women belong to 5 local sororities. There are 30 groups on campus, including band, cheerleading, choir, chorale, chorus, computers, debate, drama, drill team, honors, jazz band, literary magazine, marching band, newspaper, pep band, photography, political, professional, radio and TV, religious, social, social service, student government, and yearbook. Popular campus events include the Music Festival.

Sports: There are 7 intercollegiate sports for men and 7 for women, and 10 intramural sports for men and 10 for women. Facilities include a field house with a 2000-seat gym, playing fields, and a recreation center.

Disabled Students: 65% of the campus is accessible. Wheelchair ramps, elevators, special parking, specially equipped rest rooms, special class scheduling, and lowered drinking fountains are available.

Services: Counseling and information services are available, as is tutoring in some subjects. There is remedial math, reading, and writing.

Campus Safety and Security: Measures include 24-hour foot and vehicle patrol, escort service, informal discussions, and pamphlets/posters/films. There are emergency telephones and lighted pathways/sidewalks.

Programs of Study: CMC confers B.A., B.S., B.M., B.M.E., B.S.E., and B.S.N. degrees. Associate degrees are also awarded. Bachelor's degrees are awarded in BIOLOGICAL SCIENCE (biology/biological science), BUSINESS (accounting, business administration and management, and recreational facilities management), COMMUNICATIONS AND THE ARTS (broadcasting, communications, dramatic arts, English, French, music, and Spanish), COMPUTER AND PHYSICAL SCIENCE (chemistry, computer science, mathematics, and physics), EDUCATION (athletic training, early childhood, elementary, foreign languages, music, physical, science, and social science), ENGINEERING AND ENVIRONMENTAL DESIGN (environmental science), HEALTH PROFESSIONS (nursing), SOCIAL SCIENCE (criminal justice, economics, history, interdisciplinary studies, philosophy, political science/government, psychology, public administration, religion, and sociology). Sciences, music, and preprofessional programs are the strongest academically. Business and education are the largest.

Required: To graduate, students must complete 124 to 131 credit hours, including at least 24 in the major, depending on the degree sought. A minimum GPA of 2.0 is required for all but the athletic training and education programs, which require a 2.5. Students must complete 53 hours of a distribution curriculum, including computer literacy, phys ed or a competency exam, religion, philosophy, freshman orientation to college life, and a senior capstone.

Special: CMC offers cooperative programs in medical technology and physical therapy, and 3-2 engineering degrees with the University of Missouri at Rolla, the University of Evansville, Stanford University, and Washington University at St. Louis. Work-study programs, internships, study abroad in France, Germany, and Spain, dual majors, a general studies degree, and nondegree study are also available. There are 10 national honor societies, and a freshman honors program.

Faculty/Classroom: 60% of faculty are male; 40%, female. All teach undergraduates. No introductory courses are taught by graduate students. The average class size in a laboratory is 9 and in a regular course, 14.

Admissions: 83% of the 2001-2002 applicants were accepted. The ACT scores for the 2001-2002 freshman class were: 51% below 21, 25% between 21 and 23, 13% between 24 and 26, 8% between 27 and 28, and 3% above 28. 27% of the current freshmen were in the top fifth of their class; 51% were in the top two fifths. 4 freshmen graduated first in their class.

Requirements: The ACT is required with a minimum score of 18. Those students with a GPA lower than 2.0 may write a letter of appeal and have an interview. Applicants should be graduates of an accredited secondary school or have a GED certificate. Recommended preparatory courses include 4 units of English, 3 of math, and 2 each of science, social studies, and humanities. A GPA of 2.0 is required. AP and CLEP credits are accepted. Important factors in the admissions decision are advanced placement or honor courses, evidence of special talent, and extracurricular activities record. Applications are accepted on-line on the school's web site.

Procedure: Freshmen are admitted fall, winter, and summer. There are early decision and early admissions plans. Application deadlines are open. The application fee is $20. Notification is sent on a rolling basis.

Transfer: 158 transfer students enrolled in 2001-2002. Transfer applicants must be in good academic standing at their previous college. 30 credits of 124 must be completed at CMC.

Visiting: There are regularly scheduled orientations for prospective students, including a campus tour and visits with faculty members. There are guides for informal visits and visitors may sit in on classes and stay overnight. To schedule a visit, contact Admissions/Student Affairs at (660) 248-2242.

Financial Aid: In 2001-2002, all freshmen and 96% of continuing students received some form of financial aid. 87% of freshmen and 81% of continuing students received need-based aid. The average freshman award was $12,144. Of that total, scholarships or need-based grants averaged $6591; loans averaged $2625 (maximum); and work contracts averaged $500 ($750 maximum). 35% of undergraduates work part time. Average annual earnings from campus work are $700. The average financial indebtedness of the 2001 graduate was $17,617. The FAFSA is required. The fall application deadline is April 1.

International Students: There are 15 international students enrolled. The school actively recruits these students. They must score 500 on the written TOEFL or take the MELAB.

Computers: The mainframes are a DEC VAX 3100 and an IBM 80. There are also 24 terminals and 50 PCs available throughout the campus. All students may access the system during lab hours for up to an hour at a time. There are no time limits. The fee is $100 per year.

Graduates: In 2001, 287 bachelor's degrees were awarded. The most popular majors were elementary education (30%), nursing (11%), and biology (6%).

Admissions Contact: Office of Admissions. A video is available.
E-mail: *admissions@cmu.edu* Web: *www.cmc.edu*

CENTRAL MISSOURI STATE UNIVERSITY — B-2

Warrensburg, MO 64093 (660) 543-4290
(800) 956-0177; Fax: (660) 543-8517

Full-time: 3452 men, 3935 women	**Faculty:** 439; IIA, -$
Part-time: 819 men, 862 women	**Ph.D.s:** 80%
Graduate: 637 men, 1117 women	**Student/Faculty:** 17 to 1
Year: semesters, summer session	**Tuition:** $3510 ($6960)
Application Deadline: see profile	**Room & Board:** $4410
Freshman Class: 3720 applied, 2664 accepted, 1502 enrolled	
ACT: 22	**COMPETITIVE**

Central Missouri State University, founded in 1871, is a public liberal arts institution offering a comprehensive range of degree programs. There are 5 undergraduate schools and 1 graduate school. In addition to regional accreditation, Central has baccalaureate program accreditation with AACSB, ABET, ACCE, ACS, ADA, ADDA, ASLA, CAA, CSWE, NAIT, NASAD, NASM, NASPE, NCATE, NLN, and SOA. The library contains 3,020,197 volumes, 1,576,341 microform items, and 23,690 audiovisual forms/CDs, and subscribes to 3582 periodicals. Computerized library services include the card catalog, interlibrary loans, and database searching. Special learning facilities include a learning resource center, art gallery, natural history museum, radio station, TV station, an instructional airport, a 200-acre farm, a driving/safety range, a speech and hearing clinic, a child development lab, and an English Language Center. The 1300-acre campus is in a small town 50 miles southeast of Kansas City. Including residence halls, there are 50 buildings.

Student Life: 89% of undergraduates are from Missouri. Others are from 41 states, 65 foreign countries, and Canada. 90% are from public schools. 87% are white. 59% are Protestant; 24% Catholic. The average age of freshmen is 19; all undergraduates, 23. 28% do not continue beyond their first year; 40% remain to graduate.

Housing: 3425 students can be accommodated in college housing, which includes single-sex and coed dormitories, on-campus apartments, off-campus apartments, married-student housing, fraternity houses, and sorority houses. In addition, there are honors houses, special-interest houses, and quiet dorms. On-campus housing is available on a first-come, first-served basis. 68% of students commute. All students may keep cars.

Activities: 16% of men belong to 13 national fraternities; 13% of women belong to 10 national sororities. There are 180 groups on campus, including art, band, cheerleading, chess, choir, chorale, chorus, computers, dance, debate, drama, drill team, ethnic, film, forensics, gay, honors, international, jazz band, literary magazine, marching band, musical theater, newspaper, opera, orchestra, pep band, photography, political, professional, radio and TV, religious, social, social service, student government, symphony, and yearbook. Popular campus events include Performing Arts Series, Technology Fair, and Repertory Theater.

Sports: There are 7 intercollegiate sports for men and 7 for women, and 45 intramural sports for men and 45 for women. Facilities include a stadium seating more than 12,000, 3 gyms, baseball, softball, and practice fields, a bowling alley, tennis courts, and a multipurpose building that contains a swimming pool, weight rooms, and courts for basketball, racquetball, and volleyball. A nearby outdoor recreation area has an 18-hole golf course and facilities for swimming and other activities.

Disabled Students: 95% of the campus is accessible. Wheelchair ramps, elevators, special parking, specially equipped rest rooms, special class scheduling, lowered drinking fountains, lowered telephones, and a limited number of handicapped-accessible dorms are available.

Services: Counseling and information services are available, as is tutoring in some subjects, including, for a fee, math, chemistry, physics, biology, accounting, economics, and business. There is a reader service for the blind and remedial math. Writing and learning labs are available for all students. Tutoring is available through TRIO Student Support Services.

Campus Safety and Security: Measures include 24-hour foot and vehicle patrol, self-defense education, escort service, and informal discussions. There are pamphlets/posters/films, emergency telephones, lighted pathways/sidewalks, and a bike patrol.

Programs of Study: Central confers B.A., B.S., B.F.A., B.M., B.M.E., B.S.B.A., B.S.Ed., and B.S.W. degrees. Associate and master's degrees are also awarded. Bachelor's degrees are awarded in AGRICULTURE (agricultural business management, agricultural economics, and conservation and regulation), BIOLOGICAL SCIENCE (biology/biological science), BUSINESS (accounting, banking and finance, business administration and management, hotel/motel and restaurant management, human resources, management science, marketing/retailing/merchandising, organizational behavior, recreation and leisure services, and tourism), COMMUNICATIONS AND THE ARTS (broadcasting, communications, English, French, German, journalism, music, photography, public relations, Spanish, speech/debate/rhetoric, studio art, and theater design), COMPUTER AND PHYSICAL SCIENCE (actuarial science, chemistry, computer science, earth science, geology, information sciences and systems, mathematics, and physics), EDUCATION (agricultural, art, business, early childhood, elementary, English, foreign languages, home economics, industrial arts, mathematics, middle school, music, physical, science, secondary, social studies, and special), ENGINEERING AND ENVIRONMENTAL DESIGN (agricultural engineering technology, automotive technology, aviation computer technology, commercial art, construction management, drafting and design technology, electrical/electronics engineering, electrical/electronics engineering technology, engineering, engineering technology, graphic arts technology, industrial engineering technology, interior design, manufacturing technology, and occupational safety and health), HEALTH PROFESSIONS (medical laboratory technology, nursing, predentistry, premedicine, and speech pathology/audiology), SOCIAL SCIENCE (child care/child and family studies, criminal justice, dietetics, economics, geography, history, political science/government, prelaw, psychology, safety management, social work, sociology, and textiles and clothing). Curriculum and instruction, criminal justice, and business management are the largest.

Required: To graduate, students must complete a minimum of 124 hours, including 35 to 64 in the major, and have a minimum GPA of 2.0; several majors require a higher cumulative GPA. General education requirements include a total of 39 to 45 hours in humanities, social sciences, multicultural studies, technology, English and oral communications, math, science, and individual development.

Special: Central offers cross-registration with the Midwest Student Exchange Program, credit and noncredit internships, study abroad in more than 15 countries, a B.A.-B.S. degree, dual and student-designed majors, credit for military service, pass/fail options, nondegree study, and a 3-2 engineering degree with the University of Missouri at Columbia and at Rolla and with the University of Kansas. There are 25 national honor societies, and a freshman honors program.

Faculty/Classroom: 63% of faculty are male; 37%, female. The average class size in an introductory lecture is 30.

Admissions: 72% of the 2001-2002 applicants were accepted. The ACT scores for the 2001-2002 freshman class were: 39% below 21, 33% between 21 and 23, 16% between 24 and 26, 7% between 27 and 28, and 5% above 28. 31% of the current freshmen were in the top fifth of their class; 61% were in the top two fifths. There was 1 National Merit finalist. 31 freshmen graduated first in their class.

Requirements: The ACT is required. In addition, applicants must have completed 16 academic credits, including 4 in English with a writing emphasis, and 3 each in math (algebra and beyond) and social science, 2 in natural sciences, and 1 in fine or performing arts, as well as 3 in academic electives. A foreign language is recommended. The GED is accepted. Central requires applicants to be in the upper 50% of their class. AP and CLEP credits are accepted. Applications are accepted on-line via the college's web site.

Procedure: Freshmen are admitted to all sessions. Entrance exams should be taken preferably in the junior year. Applications should be filed by the day before classes begin. The 20001 application fee was $25. Notification is sent on a rolling basis.

Transfer: 773 transfer students enrolled in 2001-2002. Applicants must have a minimum GPA of 2.0, as indicated by an official college transcript. 30 credits of 124 must be completed at Central.

Visiting: There are regularly scheduled orientations for prospective students, including orientation sessions on housing, general education requirements, and enrollment for fall classes. There are guides for informal visits and visitors may sit in on classes and stay overnight. To schedule a visit, contact the Office of Admissions.

Financial Aid: In 2001-2002, 83% of all freshmen and 82% of continuing students received some form of financial aid. 76% of freshmen and 75% of continuing students received need-based aid. The average freshman award was $5875. Of that total, scholarships or need-based grants averaged $1875 ($11,750 maximum); loans averaged $2100 ($2625 maximum); and work contracts averaged $1900 ($2400 maximum). 39% of undergraduates work part time. Average annual earnings from campus work are $1800. The average financial indebtedness of the 2001 graduate was $8900. Central is a member of CSS. The FAFSA is required. The fall application deadline is March 1.

International Students: There are 337 international students enrolled. The school actively recruits these students. They must score 500 on the written TOEFL and also take institutional assessment.

Computers: The mainframes are an IBM 4381 and an ES 9000 9121 Model 210. There are 350 terminals in the 2 mainframe labs, as well as 1300 lab/classroom PCs in various buildings, and 8 open labs for student use. All students may access the system from 7:30 A.M. to 1 A.M. There are no time limits and no fees.

Graduates: In 2001, 1535 bachelor's degrees were awarded. The most popular majors were criminal justice (20%), teacher education (18%), and computer information systems and business (9%). In an average class, 1% graduate in 3 years, 20% in 4 years, 39% in 5 years, and 42% in 6 years. 507 companies recruited on campus in 2000-2001. Of the 2000 graduating class, 12% were enrolled in graduate school within 6 months of graduation and 94% were employed.

Admissions Contact: Margaret Herron, Executive Director of Enrollment Management. A video is available.
E-mail: *admit@cmsuvmb.cmsu.edu* Web: *cmsu.edu*

COLLEGE OF THE OZARKS — B-4
Point Lookout, MO 65726 — **(417) 334-6411, ext. 4219**
(800) 222-0525; Fax: (417) 335-2618

Full-time: 577 men, 709 women	**Faculty:** 89; IIB, -$
Part-time: 42 men, 67 women	**Ph.D.s:** 62%
Graduate: none	**Student/Faculty:** 14 to 1
Year: semesters	**Tuition:** $150
Application Deadline: February 1	**Room & Board:** $2500

Freshman Class: 2129 applied, 311 accepted, 283 enrolled
ACT: 21 — **COMPETITIVE+**

College of the Ozarks, founded in 1906, is a private liberal arts college affiliated with the Presbyterian Church (U.S.A.). Instead of paying tuition, students work a total of 560 hours in campus jobs and are responsible only for room and board, books, personal expenses, and an incidental fee of $150. Students may also elect to work in a summer program, which will cover their room and board costs as well. The library contains 118,235 volumes, 30,604 microform items, and 5193 audiovisual forms/CDs, and subscribes to 503 periodicals. Computerized library services include the card catalog, interlibrary loans, and database searching. Special learning facilities include a learning resource center, art gallery, radio station, museum, grist mill, weaving studio, airport, firehouse, print shop, orchid greenhouses, fruitcake/jelly kitchens, day care center, and 3 farm operations. The 1000-acre campus is in a small town 40 miles south of Springfield, adjacent to the resort town of Branson. Including residence halls, there are 82 buildings.

Student Life: 63% of undergraduates are from Missouri. Others are from 26 states, 22 foreign countries, and Canada. 85% are from public schools. 86% are white; 10% foreign nationals. 74% are Protestant; 20% claim no religious affiliation. The average age of freshmen is 19; all undergraduates, 21. 24% do not continue beyond their first year; 70% remain to graduate.

Housing: 1031 students can be accommodated in college housing, which includes single-sex dormitories. Student members of the volunteer fire department have living facilities in the campus fire station. On-campus housing is guaranteed for all 4 years. 68% of students live on campus; of those, 80% remain on campus on weekends. Alcohol is not permitted. All students may keep cars.

Activities: There are no fraternities or sororities. There are 49 groups on campus, including academic, art, band, cheerleading, choir, chorale, computers, dance, departmental, drama, film, international, jazz band, literary magazine, major, musical theater, newspaper, orchestra, pep band, photography, political, professional, radio and TV, religious, social service, student government, and yearbook. Popular campus events include Fourth of July, lectures, and concerts.

Sports: There are 2 intercollegiate sports for men and 2 for women, and 12 intramural sports for men and 12 for women. Facilities include an all-weather track, an indoor walking track, horseshoe pit, softball and baseball fields, tennis courts, handball courts, volleyball and sand volleyball, badminton and table tennis facilities, an aerobics room and rehabilitation training room, and a field house with a 4500-seat gym, 3 basketball courts, an Olympic-size pool, a weight training room, racquetball courts, and a dance studio.

Disabled Students: 95% of the campus is accessible. Wheelchair ramps, elevators, special parking, and specially equipped rest rooms are available.

Services: Counseling and information services are available, as is tutoring in some subjects, including math and foreign language. There is also a center for writing and thinking. There is remedial math.

Campus Safety and Security: Measures include 24-hour foot and vehicle patrol, informal discussions, pamphlets/posters/films, and emergency telephones. There are lighted pathways/sidewalks, a parking lot security system, and a 24-hour paramedic service on campus. The front gate is locked at 1 P.M. daily and women's dorms are locked at closing hours.

Programs of Study: C of O confers B.A. and B.S. degrees. Bachelor's degrees are awarded in AGRICULTURE (agricultural business management, agriculture, agronomy, animal science, horticulture, and poultry science), BIOLOGICAL SCIENCE (biology/biological science), BUSINESS (accounting, business administration and management, hotel/motel and restaurant management, international business management, and marketing management), COMMUNICATIONS AND THE ARTS (art, broadcasting, communications, English, French, German, journalism, media arts, music, musical theater, performing arts, Spanish, studio art, and theater design), COMPUTER AND PHYSICAL SCIENCE (chemistry, computer science, information sciences and systems, and mathematics), EDUCATION (agricultural, art, business, elementary, English, foreign languages, industrial arts, mathematics, middle school, physical, secondary, social studies, technical, and vocational), ENGINEERING AND ENVIRONMENTAL DESIGN (aviation computer technology, graphic arts technology, industrial engineering technology, and preengineering), HEALTH PROFESSIONS (medical technology, nursing, premedicine, prepharmacy, preveterinary science, and speech pathology/audiology), SOCIAL SCIENCE (child psychology/development, clothing and textiles management/production/services, corrections, criminal justice, criminology, dietetics, family/consumer studies, food science, gerontology, history, home economics, interdisciplinary studies, law enforcement and corrections, philosophy, political science/government, psychology, religion, religious music, safety management, social work, and sociology). Business administration, sciences, and history are the strongest academically. Business administration is the largest.

Required: 55 to 58 hours of general education requirements include specific courses in English, speech, religion, history and political science, math, and phys ed. Students must also select courses from an arts and letters, social science, and physical science distribution. B.A. candidates must complete 8 credit hours of foreign language, and B.S. candidates must complete 6 to 8 credit hours of additional physical science, biology, or math. To graduate, all students must complete at least 124 credit hours, including 36 upper level and 30 in a major field, with a minimum GPA of 2.0 in the major as well as overall. A portfolio is required. A comprehensive exam in psychology is required.

Special: The college offers co-op programs, study abroad in the Netherlands, Korea, Bali, Indonesia, and Thailand, internships through numerous departments, preprofessional programs in nursing, medical technology, and engineering, a 3-2 engineering degree program, independent study/practicum courses, student-designed interdisciplinary majors, and credit for military experience. Pass/fail grading is allowed for proficiency exams. There are 4 national honor societies and 4 departmental honors programs.

Faculty/Classroom: 70% of faculty are male; 30%, female. All teach undergraduates. The average class size in an introductory lecture is 40; in a laboratory, 16; and in a regular course, 21.

Admissions: 15% of the 2001-2002 applicants were accepted. The ACT scores for the 2001-2002 freshman class were: 10% below 17, 65% between 18 and 23, 22% between 24 and 29, and 3% between 30 and 36. 7 freshmen graduated first in their class.

Requirements: The SAT I or ACT is required. Applicants must be graduates of accredited secondary schools, have earned a GED, or have an ACT score of 19 or better. A physical exam, financial aid application, 2 recommendations (preferably from school personnel), and an interview are required. C of O requires applicants to be in the upper 50% of their class. A GPA of 2.0 is required. AP and CLEP credits are accepted. Important factors in the admissions decision are leadership record, extracurricular activities record, and advanced placement or honor courses. Applications are accepted on-line at the school's web site, *www.cofo.edu*

Procedure: Freshmen are admitted fall and spring. Entrance exams should be taken in October or December of the senior year. Early decision applications should be filed by February 15; regular applications, by February 1 for fall entry. Notification of early decision is sent in February; regular decision, February 1. 5% of all applicants are on a waiting list.

Transfer: 67 transfer students enrolled in 2001-2002. Transfer applicants must present a minimum GPA of 2.0 and may not have a previous disciplinary or loan default record. The ACT or the SAT I is required if the applicant has completed fewer than 48 credit hours. An interview is required. The dean of students at the transfer college must complete a form attesting to the positive character of the applicant. All transfer students must submit a financial aid transcript. 45 credits of 125 must be completed at C of O.

Visiting: There are regularly scheduled orientations for prospective students, including College Days, an orientation provided for local area high schools. There are guides for informal visits and visitors may sit in on classes. To schedule a visit, contact the Admissions Office at (417) 334-6411.

Financial Aid: In 2001-2002, all students received some form of financial aid. 90% of all students received need-based aid. The average freshman award was $10,888. Of that total, scholarships or need-based grants averaged $6600 ($8102 maximum); and work contracts averaged $2884 (maximum). All undergraduates work part time. Average annual earnings from campus work are $2884. The average financial indebtedness of the 2001 graduate was $2211. The FAFSA and student and parent federal tax returns are required. The fall application deadline is March 15.

International Students: There were 43 international students enrolled in a recent year. They must score 550 on the written TOEFL and it is recommended that they also take the ACT or the SAT I.

Computers: There are 136 PCs. Various other campus departments have computers for classroom instruction and use. All students may access the system from 8 A.M. to 11 P.M. There are no time limits and no fees.

Graduates: In 2001, 292 bachelor's degrees were awarded. The most popular majors were education (22%), business (10%), and psychology (9%). In an average class, 21% graduate in 4 years, 39% in 5 years, and 44% in 6 years. 172 companies recruited on campus in 2000-2001.

Admissions Contact: Marci Linson, Dean of Admissions.
E-mail: *admiss4@cofo.edu* Web: *http://www.cofo.edu*

COLUMBIA COLLEGE
Columbia, MO 65216

C-2
(573) 875-7352
(800) 231-2391; Fax: (573) 875-7506

Full-time: 287 men, 382 women	**Faculty:** 53; IIB, --$
Part-time: 77 men, 109 women	**Ph.D.s:** 85%
Graduate: 47 men, 94 women	**Student/Faculty:** 13 to 1
Year: semesters, summer session	**Tuition:** $10,506
Application Deadline: open	**Room & Board:** $4576
Freshman Class: 657 applied, 392 accepted, 149 enrolled	
ACT: 22	**COMPETITIVE**

Columbia College, founded in 1851, is a private liberal arts institution affiliated with the Disciples of Christ. In addition to regional accreditation, Columbia has baccalaureate program accreditation with CSWE. The library contains 80,000 volumes, 18,000 microform items, and 3000 audiovisual forms/CDs, and subscribes to more than 600 periodicals. Computerized library services include the card catalog, interlibrary loans, and database searching. Special learning facilities include a learning resource center and art gallery. The 39-acre campus is in a small town 120 miles east of Kansas City and 120 miles west of St. Louis. Including residence halls, there are 13 buildings.

Student Life: 88% of undergraduates are from Missouri. Others are from 17 states and 30 foreign countries. 81% are white. 57% claim no religious affiliation; 28% Protestant; 13% Catholic. The average age of freshmen is 19; all undergraduates, 24. 30% do not continue beyond their first year; 37% remain to graduate.

Housing: 326 students can be accommodated in college housing, which includes single-sex and coed dormitories. In addition, there is a wellness floor. On-campus housing is guaranteed for all 4 years. 65% of students commute. Alcohol is not permitted. All students may keep cars.

Activities: There are no fraternities or sororities. There are 28 groups on campus, including art, cheerleading, choir, chorale, computers, ethnic, honors, international, literary magazine, pep band, photography, political, professional, religious, social, social service, student government, and yearbook. Popular campus events include International Student Festival, Black History Convocation, and Women's History Convocation.

Sports: There are 3 intercollegiate sports for men and 2 for women, and 16 intramural sports for men and 16 for women. Facilities include a 650-seat gym, softball and soccer fields, an indoor pool, a dance studio, tennis courts, and an exercise/weight room.

Disabled Students: 97% of the campus is accessible. Wheelchair ramps, elevators, special parking, specially equipped rest rooms, special class scheduling, lowered drinking fountains, and lowered telephones are available.

Services: Counseling and information services are available, as is tutoring in most subjects, including accounting, English composition, geography, math, history, and psychology, as well as in study skills. There is remedial math and writing.

Campus Safety and Security: Measures include 24-hour foot and vehicle patrol, escort service, informal discussions, and pamphlets/posters/films. There are emergency telephones and lighted pathways/sidewalks.

Programs of Study: Columbia confers B.A., B.S., B.A.G.S, B.F.A., and B.S.W. degrees. Associate and master's degrees are also awarded. Bachelor's degrees are awarded in BUSINESS (business administration and management), COMMUNICATIONS AND THE ARTS (art, English, and fine arts), COMPUTER AND PHYSICAL SCIENCE (computer science, information sciences and systems, and natural sciences), EDUCATION (elementary and secondary), SOCIAL SCIENCE (criminal justice, forensic studies, history, interdisciplinary studies, political science/government, psychology, social work, and sociology). Art, history/government, and education are the strongest academically. Business administration is the largest.

Required: To graduate, students must complete 120 semester hours, including 39 to 72 in the major, with a minimum GPA of 2.0. Distribution requirements include 18 hours in humanities, 9 in basic skills such as English composition and computers, 9 in social science, and 8 in math and science.

Special: Columbia offers cross-registration with the University of Missouri/Columbia and Stephens College, internships, study abroad in more than 20 countries, B.A.-B.S. degrees in most disciplines, an individual studies degree, student-designed and dual majors, nondegree study, and pass/fail options. Select students who complete a special 2-semester project earn a bachelor's degree with distinction (B.A.D.). There are 4 national honor societies, a freshman honors program, and 10 departmental honors programs.

Faculty/Classroom: 55% of faculty are male; 45%, female. All teach undergraduates and 50% also do research. No introductory courses are taught by graduate students. The average class size in an introductory lecture is 23; in a laboratory, 22; and in a regular course, 15.

Admissions: 60% of the 2001-2002 applicants were accepted. The SAT I scores for the 2001-2002 freshman class were: Verbal--50% between 500 and 599, and 50% between 600 and 700; Math--50% between 500 and 599, and 50% between 600 and 700. The ACT scores were 42% below 21, 26% between 21 and 23, 22% between 24 and 26, 6% between 27 and 28, and 4% above 28. 11% of the current freshmen were in the top fifth of their class; 46% were in the top two fifths.

Requirements: The ACT is required. In addition, applicants must be graduates of an accredited secondary school or have a GED certificate. Students should have completed 4 units of English, 3 of math including 2 of algebra and 1 of geometry, and 2 each of natural science and social studies. Columbia requires applicants to be in the upper 50% of their class. A GPA of 2.0 is required. AP and CLEP credits are accepted. Important factors in the admissions decision are advanced placement or honor courses, leadership record, and evidence of special talent. Applications are accepted on-line via the school's web site.

Procedure: Freshmen are admitted to all sessions. Entrance exams should be taken in spring of the junior year or fall of the senior year. There is a deferred admissions plan. Application deadlines are open. The fall 2001 application fee was $25. Notification is sent on a rolling basis.

Transfer: 125 transfer students enrolled in 2001-2002. Applicants must have a minimum GPA of 2.0 overall and in the last semester attended and must submit a high school transcript and SAT I or ACT scores. 24 credits of 120 must be completed at Columbia.

Visiting: There are regularly scheduled orientations for prospective students, including a campus tour, a workshop in financial aid, an academic/organization fair, and a luncheon. There are guides for informal visits and visitors may sit in on classes and stay overnight. To schedule a visit, contact the Admissions Office.

Financial Aid: In 2001-2002, 78% of all freshmen and 66% of continuing students received some form of financial aid. 54% of freshmen and 44% of continuing students received need-based aid. The average freshman award was $9878. Of that total, scholarships or need-based grants averaged $2846 ($17,682 maximum); loans averaged $5111 ($11,625 maximum); and work contracts averaged $2100 ($2240 maximum). 64% of undergraduates work part time. Average annual earnings from campus work are $2100. Columbia is a member of CSS. The FAFSA and the college's own financial statement are required. The fall application deadline is April 30.

International Students: There are 51 international students enrolled. The school actively recruits these students. They must score 500 on the written TOEFL or 173 on the electronic version.

Computers: The mainframe is an HP 9000/Model K370. There are terminals located in the computer lab, library, and residence halls. All students may access the system from 8 A.M. to 10 P.M. in the computer lab. There are no time limits. The fee is $35. It is strongly recommended that all students have a personal computer.

Graduates: In 2001, 123 bachelor's degrees were awarded. The most popular majors were business administration (24%), liberal arts (24%), and education (19%). In an average class, 24% graduate in 4 years, 34% in 5 years, and 35% in 6 years.

Admissions Contact: Regina Morin, Director of Admissions.
E-mail: *admissions@email.ccis.edu* Web: *www.ccis.edu*

CULVER-STOCKTON COLLEGE C-1

Canton, MO 63435-1299 (217) 231-6331
(800) 537-1883; Fax: (217) 231-6618

Full-time: 350 men, 395 women	**Faculty:** 56; IIB, --$
Part-time: 21 men, 55 women	**Ph.D.s:** 68%
Graduate: none	**Student/Faculty:** 13 to 1
Year: semesters, summer session	**Tuition:** $10,650
Application Deadline: open	**Room & Board:** $4750
Freshman Class: 697 applied, 656 accepted, 199 enrolled	
SAT I Verbal/Math: 490/490	**ACT:** 21 **LESS COMPETITIVE**

Culver-Stockton College, established in 1853, is a private liberal arts institution affiliated with the Disciples of Christ. In addition to regional accreditation, C-SC has baccalaureate program accreditation with NLN. The library contains 154,181 volumes, 4979 microform items, and 4065 audiovisual forms/CDs, and subscribes to 778 periodicals. Computerized library services include the card catalog, interlibrary loans, and database searching. Special learning facilities include a learning resource center, art gallery, radio station, and a rare books collection, a performing arts center, a publications lab, and a tutorial center. The 143-acre campus is in a rural area 125 miles north of St. Louis. Including residence halls, there are 19 buildings.

Student Life: 55% of undergraduates are from Missouri. Others are from 28 states, 8 foreign countries, and Canada. 89% are from public schools. 88% are white. 62% are Protestant; 23% Catholic; 14% claim no religious affiliation. The average age of freshmen is 18; all undergraduates, 21. 36% do not continue beyond their first year.

Housing: 650 students can be accommodated in college housing, which includes single-sex and coed dormitories, fraternity houses, and sorority houses. On-campus housing is guaranteed for all 4 years. 70% of students live on campus; of those, 50% remain on campus on weekends. Alcohol is not permitted. All students may keep cars.

Activities: 37% of men belong to 4 national fraternities; 39% of women belong to 3 national sororities. There are 37 groups on campus, including art, band, cheerleading, choir, chorus, dance, drama, ethnic, forensics, honors, international, jazz band, literary magazine, musical theater, newspaper, opera, pep band, photography, political, professional, radio and TV, religious, social, social service, and student government. Popular campus events include National Collegiate Alcohol Awareness Week, Spring Fling, and Family Weekend.

Sports: There are 5 intercollegiate sports for men and 5 for women, and 9 intramural sports for men and 9 for women. Facilities include a 2000-seat football stadium, a soccer field, a baseball field, intramural fields, a swimming pool, a dance studio, a weight room, and a field house with basketball, volleyball, tennis, and racquetball courts.

Disabled Students: 40% of the campus is accessible. Wheelchair ramps, elevators, special parking, and specially equipped rest rooms are available.

Services: Counseling and information services are available, as is tutoring in most subjects. There is remedial math and writing.

Campus Safety and Security: Measures include self-defense education, escort service, informal discussions, and pamphlets/posters/films. There are emergency telephones, lighted pathways/sidewalks, and nighttime security patrol.

Programs of Study: C-SC confers B.A., B.S., B.F.A., B.M.E., and B.S.N. degrees. Bachelor's degrees are awarded in BIOLOGICAL SCIENCE (biology/biological science), BUSINESS (accounting, banking and finance, business administration and management, management science, and recreational facilities management), COMMUNICATIONS AND THE ARTS (art, arts administration/management, communications, dramatic arts, English, and music), COMPUTER AND PHYSICAL SCIENCE (chemistry, information sciences and systems, and mathematics), EDUCATION (art, athletic training, drama, education, music, and physical), HEALTH PROFESSIONS (medical technology and nursing), SOCIAL SCIENCE (criminal justice, history, psychology, religion, and sociology). Education and nursing are the strongest academically. Education, business, and nursing are the largest.

Required: To graduate, students must complete 124 credit hours, including 24 to 64 in the major, with a minimum GPA of 2.0. Distribution requirements include 6 hours in a foreign language, 3 hours in the fine arts and 5 to 9 each in social science, 4 to 9 in humanities, 3 to 9 in natural science, 3 to 6 in math, and 2 to 3 in computer science for the B.A. degree. Specific English composition, speech, phys ed, introductory computer, and Christian heritage courses are required.

Special: Culver-Stockton offers joint-degree programs in nursing in conjunction with Blessing-Rieman College of Nursing, a 2-2 degree in engineering with the University of Missouri/Rolla, and 3-2 degree in occupational therapy with Washington University at St. Louis. Study abroad, internships, and dual and individualized majors are also available. A course titled Decades of Destiny is presented in nontraditional 5-week modules. There are 8 national honor societies, a freshman honors program, and 18 departmental honors programs.

Faculty/Classroom: 75% of faculty are male; 25%, female. All teach undergraduates. The average class size in an introductory lecture is 22; in a laboratory, 15; and in a regular course, 16.

Admissions: 94% of the 2001-2002 applicants were accepted. The SAT I scores for the 2001-2002 freshman class were: Verbal--62% below 500, 30% between 500 and 599, 4% between 600 and 700, and 4% above 700; Math--52% below 500, 33% between 500 and 599, and 14% between 600 and 700. The ACT scores were 51% below 21, 25% between 21 and 23, 15% between 24 and 26, 5% between 27 and 28, and 4% above 28. 25% of the current freshmen were in the top fifth of their class; 50% were in the top two fifths. 7 freshmen graduated first in their class.

Requirements: The SAT I or ACT is required. In addition, secondary school preparation should include 4 years of English, 2 to 4 each in math and science, and 1 to 3 each in history and social studies. Applications are accepted on-line at the school's web site. C-SC requires applicants to be in the upper 50% of their class. A GPA of 2.0 is required. AP and CLEP credits are accepted. Important factors in the admissions decision are advanced placement or honor courses, leadership record, and evidence of special talent.

Procedure: Freshmen are admitted fall and spring. Entrance exams should be taken by April of the entering school year. Application deadlines are open. There is a rolling admissions plan. Application fee is $25.

Transfer: 79 transfer students enrolled in 2001-2002. Grades of C or better earned at regionally accredited institutions will be accepted if the work is relevant to the Culver curriculum. No more than 64 semester or 96 quarter hours of credit from a junior college may be transferred. 30 credits of 124 must be completed at C-SC.

Visiting: There are regularly scheduled orientations for prospective students, including meetings with academic professors, students, coaches, extracurricular advisers, plus financial aid information, student life panel, and campus tours. There are guides for informal visits and visitors may sit in on classes and stay overnight. To schedule a visit, contact Enrollment Services.

Financial Aid: In 2001-2002, 99% of all freshmen and 81% of continuing students received some form of financial aid. 73% of freshmen and 64% of continuing students received need-based aid. The average freshman award was $13,531. Of that total, scholarships or need-based grants averaged $6077 ($11,100 maximum); loans averaged $2804 ($6625 maximum); and work contracts averaged $1068 ($3600 maximum). 31% of undergraduates work part time. Average annual earnings from campus work are $1281. The average financial indebtedness of the 2001 graduate was $12,915. C-SC is a member of CSS. The FAFSA is required. The fall application deadline is August 1.

International Students: There are 18 international students enrolled. The school actively recruits these students. They must score 500 on the written TOEFL but International students are not required to take the TOEFL if they have resided in this country for 1 semester. The college prefers that they also take the SAT I or ACT.

Computers: The mainframe is an HP Netserver LC IV. There are 70 IBM PCs available in the library, computer lab, various classroom buildings, and residence halls. Mainframe access is also available from student rooms through student-owned PCs. All students may access the system days, evenings, and weekends. There are no time limits and no fees.

Graduates: In 2001, 175 bachelor's degrees were awarded. The most popular majors were nursing (14%), business administration (11%), and psychology and elementary education (10%). In an average class, 1% graduate in 3 years, 43% in 4 years, and 48% in 5 years. 50 companies recruited on campus in 2000-2001. Of the 2000 graduating class, 10% were enrolled in graduate school within 6 months of graduation and 89% were employed.

Admissions Contact: Ron Cronacher, Director of Enrollment Services. A video is available. E-mail: *enrollment@culver.edu*
Web: *www.culver.edu*

DEACONESS COLLEGE OF NURSING — D-2
St. Louis, MO 63139 — (314) 768-3044
(800) 942-4310; (314) 768-5673

Full-time: 10 men, 166 women	**Faculty:** 16
Part-time: 1 man, 69 women	**Ph.D.s:** 15%
Graduate: none	**Student/Faculty:** 11 to 1
Year: semesters, summer session	**Tuition:** $8500
Application Deadline: open	**Room & Board:** $4200
Freshman Class: n/av	
SAT I or ACT: required	**SPECIAL**

Deaconess College of Nursing, established in 1889 and affiliated with the United Church of Christ, is a private college offering undergraduate programs in nursing. Figures in above capsule are approximate. In addition to regional accreditation, Deaconess has baccalaureate program accreditation with NLN. The library contains 8000 volumes and 130 audiovisual forms/CDs, and subscribes to 230 periodicals. Computerized library services include interlibrary loans and database searching. Special learning facilities include a learning resource center and nursing archives and a nursing arts lab. The 15-acre campus is in an urban area 4 miles west of downtown St. Louis. Including residence halls, there are 10 buildings.

Student Life: 72% of undergraduates are from Missouri. Others are from 4 states and 2 foreign countries. 78% are from public schools. 87% are white; 10% African American. 46% are Catholic; 40% Protestant; 14% claim no religious affiliation. The average age of freshmen is 21; all undergraduates, 23. 13% do not continue beyond their first year; 65% remain to graduate.

Housing: 98 students can be accommodated in college housing, which includes coed dormitories. On-campus housing is available on a first-come, first-served basis. Priority is given to out-of-town students. 72% of students commute. Alcohol is not permitted. Upperclassmen may keep cars.

Activities: There are no fraternities or sororities. There are 7 groups on campus, including newspaper, professional, religious, social, and student government. Popular campus events include Dedication Ceremony, Christmas Tea, and Welcome Week.

Sports: There is no sports program at Deaconess. Facilities include a weight room.

Disabled Students: 90% of the campus is accessible. Wheelchair ramps, elevators, special parking, and specially equipped rest rooms are available.

Services: Counseling and information services are available, as is tutoring in some subjects, including sciences and statistics. There is remedial math, reading, and writing. Each student is assigned an academic adviser.

Campus Safety and Security: Measures include 24-hour foot and vehicle patrol, self-defense education, escort service, and shuttle buses. There are informal discussions, pamphlets/posters/films, emergency telephones, lighted pathways/sidewalks, and a card reader security system.

Programs of Study: Deaconess confers the B.S.N. degree. Associate degrees are also awarded. Bachelor's degrees are awarded in HEALTH PROFESSIONS (nursing).

Required: To graduate, students must complete 128 credit hours, including 62 in nursing courses, with a minimum GPA of 2.0. General education requirements include 30 hours of math and science, 24 of liberal arts and humanities, and 12 of social science.

Special: Students may opt for credit by exam. A work-study program with Deaconess Hospital and cross-registration with Fontbonne College are available.

Faculty/Classroom: All of faculty are female. All teach undergraduates and 2% both teach and do research. The average class size in an introductory lecture is 30; in a laboratory, 20; and in a regular course, 25.

Requirements: The SAT I or ACT is required; the ACT is preferred. Applicants must be graduates of an accredited secondary school or have a GED certificate. They should have completed 3 years each of math and science and 4 years of English. An essay must be submitted. Academic ranking in the upper third of the high school graduating class and a cumulative GPA of 2.5 or above is preferred. AP and CLEP credits are accepted. Important factors in the admissions decision are advanced placement or honor courses, recommendations by school officials, and recommendations by alumni.

Procedure: Freshmen are admitted in the fall. Entrance exams should be taken by December of the senior year. Application deadlines are open. The fall 2001 application fee was $30.

Transfer: Applicants must have a minimum ACT score of 21 and a GPA of 2.5 or above in high school, and academic ranking in the top third of the high school graduating class is preferred. A cumulative GPA of 2.5 in postsecondary work is preferred. 44 credits of 128 must be completed at Deaconess.

Visiting: There are regularly scheduled orientations for prospective students, consisting of an introduction to the school and its program, a review of the curriculum, admissions procedures, and financial aid, and tours. There are guides for informal visits and visitors may sit in on classes and stay overnight. To schedule a visit, contact the Admissions Office.

Financial Aid: The FAFSA is required. Check with the school for current deadlines.

International Students: They must score 500 on the written TOEFL.

Computers: There are 7 stand-alone PCs in the library and 13 networked PCs in the computer lab. All students may access the system. There are no time limits and no fees.

Graduates: The most popular major was nursing (100%) in a recent year. In an average class, 65% graduate in 4 years, and 5% in 5 years.

Admissions Contact: June Marlowe, Admissions Coordinator.

DEVRY UNIVERSITY/KANSAS CITY A-2
Kansas City, MO 64131-3626 **(816) 941-2810**
(800) 821-3766; Fax: (816) 941-0896

Full-time: 1434 men, 410 women	**Faculty:** 77
Part-time: 541 men, 235 women	**Ph.D.s:** n/av
Graduate: none	**Student/Faculty:** 24 to 1
Year: semesters, summer session	**Tuition:** $8805
Application Deadline: open	**Room & Board:** n/app
Freshman Class: 841 applied, 760 accepted, 545 enrolled	
SAT I or ACT: recommended	**LESS COMPETITIVE**

The DeVry University/Kansas City, formerly DeVry Institute of Technology, a private institution founded in 1931, joined the DeVry schools in 1969. One of 23 institutes in the United States and Canada owned by DeVry University, Inc., the school offers undergraduate programs in business administration, electronics, engineering, telecommunications, computer information systems, technical management, information technology, and computer engineering technology. In addition to regional accreditation, DeVry has baccalaureate program accreditation with ABET. The library contains 9724 volumes, 36,138 microform items, and 333 audiovisual forms/CDs, and subscribes to 121 periodicals. Computerized library services include the card catalog, interlibrary loans, and database searching. Special learning facilities include a learning resource center and electronics and other labs. The 11-acre campus is in an urban area. There is 1 building.

Student Life: 58% of undergraduates are from Missouri. Others are from 30 states and 3 foreign countries. 78% are white; 14% African American. The average age of all undergraduates is 28. 54% do not continue beyond their first year; 39% remain to graduate.

Housing: There are no residence halls. All students commute. Housing referrals may be obtained through the Student Housing Office. Alcohol is not permitted. All students may keep cars.

Activities: There are no fraternities or sororities. There are 8 groups on campus, including ethnic, honors, international, newspaper, paintball, professional, religious, social, and student government. Popular campus events include Try-Athalon, Student Picnic, and Casino Night.

Sports: There are 3 intramural sports for men and 3 for women.

Disabled Students: All of the campus is accessible. Wheelchair ramps, elevators, special parking, specially equipped rest rooms, special class scheduling, lowered drinking fountains, and lowered telephones are available.

Services: Counseling and information services are available, as is tutoring in every subject.

Campus Safety and Security: Measures include 24-hour foot and vehicle patrol, lighted pathways/sidewalks, and a security detection system that is deployed when the facility is closed.

Programs of Study: DeVry confers the B.S. degree. Associate degrees are also awarded. Bachelor's degrees are awarded in BUSINESS (business administration and management), COMMUNICATIONS AND THE ARTS (telecommunications), COMPUTER AND PHYSICAL SCIENCE (information sciences and systems), ENGINEERING AND ENVIRONMENTAL DESIGN (computer engineering, computer technology, electrical/electronics engineering technology, and technological management). Telecommunications and computer information systems are the largest.

Required: To graduate, students must achieve a GPA of at least 2.0 and satisfactorily complete all curriculium requirements. Course requirements vary according to program. All first-semester students take courses in business organization, computer applications, algebra, psychology, and student success strategies.

Special: Nondegree study, co-op programs, accelerated degree programs, and evening and weekend classes are possible. There are 2 national honor societies.

Faculty/Classroom: All teach undergraduates. The average class size in an introductory lecture is 30; in a laboratory, 30; and in a regular course, 30.

Admissions: 90% of the 2001-2002 applicants were accepted.

Requirements: The SAT I or ACT is recommended. In addition, admissions requirements include graduation from a secondary school; the GED is also accepted. Applicants must pass the DeVry entrance exam or present satisfactory ACT or SAT I scores. An interview is required. Applications are accepted on-line at *Embark.com*. CLEP credit is accepted.

Procedure: Freshmen are admitted fall, spring, and summer. There is a deferred admissions plan. Application deadlines are open. The application fee is $50. Notification is sent on a rolling basis.

Transfer: 465 transfer students enrolled in 2001-2002. Applicants must present passing grades in all completed college course work, demonstrate language skills proficiency with at least 24 completed semester credits, and evidence math proficiency by appropriate college-level credits. 35 % of 48 to 154 credits must be completed at DeVry.

Visiting: There are regularly scheduled orientations for prospective students. There are guides for informal visits. To schedule a visit, contact Anna Diamond, New Student Coordinator at (816) 941-0430.

Financial Aid: In a recent year, 38% of all freshmen and 87% of continuing students received some form of financial aid. 21% of freshmen and 40% of continuing students received need-based aid. Scholarships or need-based grants averaged $1558; and loans averaged $5339. 5% of undergraduates work part time. Average annual earnings from campus work are $7200. The FAFSA is required.

International Students: There are 19 international students enrolled. They must score 500 on the written TOEFL or 173 on the electronic version.

Computers: The mainframe is an IBM 3081K. Lab facilities include IBM PCs in stand-alone and network configurations, with access to the mainframe. LANs provide access to a wide range of applications software. Hard copy from the mainframe is provided through a local minicomputer and medium- and high-speed printers. Students in the computer information systems program may access the system during published lab hours. There are no fees.

Graduates: In 2001, 427 bachelor's degrees were awarded. The most popular majors were business (54%), computer information systems (34%), and electronics engineering technology (12%). 40 companies recruited on campus in 2000-2001.

Admissions Contact: Trudy Lomonaco, Acting Director of Admissions. Web: *www.kc.devry.edu*

DRURY UNIVERSITY B-3
Springfield, MO 65802 **(417) 873-7205**
(800) 922-2274; Fax: (417) 866-3873

Full-time: 610 men, 805 women	**Faculty:** 104; IIB, -$
Part-time: 22 men, 13 women	**Ph.D.s:** 96%
Graduate: 96 men, 231 women	**Student/Faculty:** 11 to 1
Year: semesters, summer session	**Tuition:** $11,204
Application Deadline: August 1	**Room & Board:** $4046
Freshman Class: 974 applied, 826 accepted, 340 enrolled	
SAT I Verbal/Math: 543/556	**ACT:** 25 **VERY COMPETITIVE**

Drury University, founded in 1873, is a private university with degree programs emphasizing the liberal arts, architecture, business, communications, economics, education, and health sciences. There are 3 undergraduate and 5 graduate schools. In addition to regional accreditation, Drury has baccalaureate program accreditation with ACBSP, NAAB, and NCATE. The 2 libraries contain 254,000 volumes, 119,639 microform items, and 58,641 audiovisual forms/CDs, and subscribe to 721 periodicals. Computerized library services include the card catalog, interlibrary loans, and database searching. Special learning facilities include an art gallery, radio station, a teleconference facility, and an art and architecture slide collection. The 60-acre campus is in an urban area 200 miles southwest of St. Louis and 150 miles southeast of Kansas City. Including residence halls, there are 19 buildings.

Student Life: 75% of undergraduates are from Missouri. Others are from 35 states, 50 foreign countries, and Canada. 83% are from public schools. 90% are white. The average age of freshmen is 18; all undergraduates, 20. 19% do not continue beyond their first year; 63% remain to graduate.

Housing: 795 students can be accommodated in college housing, which includes single-sex and coed dormitories, on-campus apartments, married-student housing, and fraternity houses. On-campus housing is guaranteed for all 4 years. 52% of students commute. All students may keep cars.

Activities: 39% of men belong to 4 national fraternities; 42% of women belong to 4 national sororities. There are 50 groups on campus, including art, band, cheerleading, chess, choir, chorale, chorus, computers, dance, drama, gay, honors, international, jazz band, leadership, literary magazine, musical theater, newspaper, opera, orchestra, pep band, photography, political, professional, radio and TV, religious, social, social service, student government, student life, symphony, and yearbook. Popular campus events include Family Weekend and Fall Festival.

Sports: There are 6 intercollegiate sports for men and 6 for women, and 10 intramural sports for men and 10 for women. Facilities include a gym, lighted tennis and racquetball courts, playing fields, an Olympic-size pool, a fitness center, a running track, a lighted soccer field, and a 2200-seat indoor stadium for basketball and volleyball.

Disabled Students: 90% of the campus is accessible. Wheelchair ramps, elevators, special parking, specially equipped rest rooms, special class scheduling, lowered drinking fountains, and lowered telephones are available.

Services: Counseling and information services are available, as is tutoring in every subject. There is a reader service for the blind, a math and reading learning center, a writing center, and a communications center.

Campus Safety and Security: Measures include 24-hour foot and vehicle patrol, self-defense education, escort service, and shuttle buses. There are informal discussions, pamphlets/posters/films, emergency telephones, lighted pathways/sidewalks, and lighted parking lots with security cameras monitored 24 hours a day.

Programs of Study: Drury confers B.A., B.Arch., B.M., and B.M.Ed. degrees. Master's degrees are also awarded. Bachelor's degrees are awarded in BIOLOGICAL SCIENCE (biology/biological science), BUSINESS (accounting, business administration and management, international business management, and sports management), COMMUNICATIONS AND THE ARTS (advertising, art history and appreciation, arts administration/management, broadcasting, communications, dramatic arts, English, fine arts, French, German, journalism, music, public relations, Spanish, and speech/debate/rhetoric), COMPUTER AND PHYSICAL SCIENCE (chemistry, computer science, information sciences and systems, mathematics, and physics), EDUCATION (elementary, music, physical, secondary, and special), ENGINEERING AND ENVIRONMENTAL DESIGN (architecture and environmental science), HEALTH PROFESSIONS (exercise science, nursing, predentistry, premedicine, and preveterinary science), SOCIAL SCIENCE (criminology, economics, history, international studies, philosophy, physical fitness/movement, political science/government, prelaw, psychology, and sociology). Premedicine, education, and preprofessional programs are the strongest academically. Business administration, biology, and architecture are the largest.

Required: To graduate, students must complete 124 credit hours (150 for accounting and 170 for B.Arch.). They must also maintain a minimum GPA of 2.7 and complete 26 to 32 credit hours in the major (99 for architecture). Students pursue a broad curriculum called Global Perspectives that includes requirements in science, math, humanities, fine arts, fitness, foreign language, and social science, with specific classes in Alpha Seminar, Math and Science Inquiry, Global Awareness, Global Futures, and Value Analysis. All students who complete the curriculum are awarded a minor in global studies.

Special: Drury offers work-study, cross-registration with Regents College in London, co-op programs in international business, computer information systems, and arts administration, study abroad in 6 countries, internships, a Washington semester, credit by exam, nondegree study, dual majors in most majors, satisfactory/unsatisfactory options, and a 3-2 engineering degree in conjunction with the University of Missouri and Washington University in St. Louis, as well as a premedical early admission arrangement with St. Louis University and the University of Missouri-Columbia. There are 17 national honor societies, a freshman honors program, and 19 departmental honors programs.

Faculty/Classroom: 61% of faculty are male; 39%, female. All teach undergraduates and 40% both teach and do research. No introductory courses are taught by graduate students. The average class size in an introductory lecture is 26; in a laboratory, 24; and in a regular course, 13.

Admissions: 85% of the 2001-2002 applicants were accepted. The SAT I scores for the 2001-2002 freshman class were: Verbal--30% below 500, 49% between 500 and 599, 19% between 600 and 700, and 2% above 700; Math--14% below 500, 61% between 500 and 599, 16% between 600 and 700, and 9% above 700. The ACT scores were 10% below 21, 25% between 21 and 23, 27% between 24 and 26, 14% between 27 and 28, and 23% above 28. 59% of the current freshmen were in the top fifth of their class; 83% were in the top two fifths. There was 1 National Merit semifinalist. 25 freshmen graduated first in their class.

Requirements: The SAT I or ACT is required. In addition, applicants must be graduates of an accredited secondary school or have a GED certificate. Recommended high school credits include 4 units of English and at least 3 each of math through algebra II, natural science, and social studies. An essay and a reference from the high school counselor or principal are required. Drury requires applicants to be in the upper 50% of their class. A GPA of 2.7 is required. AP and CLEP credits are accepted. Important factors in the admissions decision are advanced placement or honor courses, extracurricular activities record, and leadership record. Applications are acepted on-line at the school's web site, *www.devry.edu*.

Procedure: Freshmen are admitted to all sessions. Entrance exams should be taken in the spring of the junior year or fall of the senior year. There is a deferred admissions plan. Applications should be filed by August 1 for fall entry and December 1 for spring entry, along with a $20 fee. Notification is sent on a rolling basis.

Transfer: 88 transfer students enrolled in 2001-2002. Applicants must have a minimum GPA of 2.0 in all college work completed, and supply an essay or writing sample and reference from the current student services office. 30 credits of 124 must be completed at Drury.

Visiting: There are regularly scheduled orientations for prospective students, consisting of special visit days for pre-med, architecture, communications, pre-engineering, math, physics, and computer science. There are guides for informal visits and visitors may sit in on classes and stay overnight. To schedule a visit, contact the Admissions Office.

Financial Aid: In 2001-2002, 84% of all freshmen and 83% of continuing students received some form of financial aid. 77% of freshmen and 70% of continuing students received need-based aid. The average freshman award was $7052. Of that total, scholarships or need-based grants averaged $2327 ($11,690 maximum); loans averaged $2625 (maximum); and work contracts averaged $2100 (maximum). 87% of undergraduates work part time. Average annual earnings from campus work are $2000. The average financial indebtedness of the 2001 graduate was $13,950. The FAFSA and the college's own financial statement are required. The fall application deadline is March 15.

International Students: There are 83 international students enrolled. The school actively recruits these students. They must score 550 on the written TOEFL or 200 on the electronic version or take the MELAB or the college's own test.

Computers: The mainframes are an IBM AS/400, available only to office employees. The technology center has more than 100 PCs available to all students for academic use, including teleconferencing and access to the Internet. All students may access the system 24 hours a day, 7 days a week in the technology center. There are no time limits and no fees.

Graduates: In 2001, 231 bachelor's degrees were awarded. The most popular majors were business administration (22%), biology (20%), and chemistry (9%). In an average class, 1% graduate in 3 years, 47% in 4 years, 63% in 5 years, and 63% in 6 years. 23 companies recruited on campus in 2000-2001. Of the 2000 graduating class, 29% were enrolled in graduate school within 6 months of graduation and 69% were employed.

Admissions Contact: Michael G. Thomas, Director of Admission.
E-mail: *druryad@drury.edu* Web: *www.drury.edu*

EVANGEL COLLEGE
(See Evangel University)

EVANGEL UNIVERSITY B-3
(Formerly Evangel College)
Springfield, MO 65802

(417) 865-2811
(800) EVANGEL; Fax: (417) 865-9599

Full-time: 630 men, 820 women	**Faculty:** 84
Part-time: 32 men, 47 women	**Ph.D.s:** 53%
Graduate: 21 men, 20 women	**Student/Faculty:** 17 to 1
Year: semesters, summer session	**Tuition:** $10,150
Application Deadline: n/av	**Room & Board:** $3900
Freshman Class: 813 applied, 720 accepted, 402 enrolled	
ACT: 21	**COMPETITIVE**

Evangel University, formerly Evangel College, established in 1955, is a private facility affiliated with the Assemblies of God. In addition to regional accreditation, Evangel has baccalaureate program accreditation with CSWE, NASM, and NCATE. The library contains 96,487 volumes, 11,386 microform items, and 6801 audiovisual forms/CDs, and subscribes to 748 periodicals. Computerized library services include interlibrary loans. Special learning facilities include a learning resource center, radio station, and TV station. The 80-acre campus is in an urban area 225 miles west of St. Louis. Including residence halls, there are 14 buildings.

Student Life: 61% of undergraduates are from out of state, mostly the Midwest. Others are from 47 states, 11 foreign countries, and Canada. 79% are from public schools. 90% are white and most are Protestant. The average age of freshmen is 18; all undergraduates, 20. 29% do not continue beyond their first year.

Housing: 1460 students can be accommodated in college housing, which includes single-sex and coed dormitories and married-student housing. On-campus housing is guaranteed for all 4 years. 78% of students live on campus; of those, all remain on campus on weekends. Alcohol is not permitted. All students may keep cars.

Activities: There are no fraternities or sororities. There are 16 groups on campus, including band, cheerleading, choir, chorale, chorus, drama, forensics, honors, jazz band, musical theater, newspaper, orchestra, pep band, photography, political, professional, radio and TV, religious, student government, and yearbook. Popular campus events include College Weekend and performances of the Springfield Symphony.

Sports: There are 5 intercollegiate sports for men and 6 for women, and 4 intramural sports for men and 4 for women. Facilities include a student activities center and a 2000-seat gym.
Disabled Students: All of the campus is accessible. Wheelchair ramps, elevators, special parking, specially equipped rest rooms, lowered drinking fountains, and lowered telephones are available.
Services: Counseling and information services are available, as is tutoring in every subject. There is a reader service for the blind, and remedial math, reading, and writing.
Campus Safety and Security: Measures include 24-hour foot and vehicle patrol, escort service, emergency telephones, and lighted pathways/sidewalks.
Programs of Study: Evangel confers B.A., B.S., B.B.A., B.F.A., B.M., and B.S.W. degrees. Associate and master's degrees are also awarded. Bachelor's degrees are awarded in BIOLOGICAL SCIENCE (biology/biological science), BUSINESS (accounting, management science, and marketing/retailing/merchandising), COMMUNICATIONS AND THE ARTS (art, broadcasting, communications, design, dramatic arts, English, journalism, music, music performance, Spanish, and speech/debate/rhetoric), COMPUTER AND PHYSICAL SCIENCE (chemistry, computer science, and mathematics), EDUCATION (business, early childhood, elementary, foreign languages, music, physical, science, secondary, and special), HEALTH PROFESSIONS (medical laboratory technology), SOCIAL SCIENCE (biblical studies, criminal justice, history, international studies, missions, parks and recreation management, political science/government, psychology, public administration, religion, religious music, social science, social work, and sociology). Business, education, and music are the strongest academically. Business and education are the largest.
Required: All students must complete 50 to 53 general education hours, including courses in phys ed, computer literacy, and Bible study. A minimum GPA of 2.0 is required for graduation. Students must complete 124 credit hours, 36 of which are upper division level, with approximately 30 credit hours in the major.
Special: There are 3-2 engineering degrees available in conjunction with Washington University and the University of Missouri at Columbia. Other options include work-study, credit by exam, and a Washington semester. There are 9 national honor societies, and 7 departmental honors program.
Faculty/Classroom: 62% of faculty are male; 38%, female. All teach undergraduates. No introductory courses are taught by graduate students. The average class size in an introductory lecture is 40 and in a regular course, 20.
Admissions: 89% of the 2001-2002 applicants were accepted. The ACT scores for the 2001-2002 freshman class were: 6% below 21, 49% between 21 and 23, 22% between 24 and 26, 18% between 27 and 28, and 5% above 28. 21 freshmen graduated first in their class.
Requirements: The SAT I or ACT is recommended. In addition, the recommended preparatory curriculum includes 3 credits in English, 2 each in math and social studies, and 1 in lab science. The GED is accepted. A GPA of 2.0 is required. AP and CLEP credits are accepted.
Procedure: Freshmen are admitted to all sessions. Entrance exams should be taken before high school graduation. Notification is sent on a rolling basis. The application fee was $25 in 2001.
Transfer: 110 transfer students enrolled in 2001-2002. Transfer applicants must be in good standing with their previous institutions and have a cumulative GPA of 2.0. 30 credits of 124 must be completed at Evangel.
Visiting: There are regularly scheduled orientations for prospective students, consisting of scheduled visits every Friday and by appointment. There are guides for informal visits and visitors may sit in on classes and stay overnight. To schedule a visit, contact Office of Admissions at *dentona@evangel.edu*
Financial Aid: In 2001-2002, 87% of all freshmen and 94% of continuing students received some form of financial aid. 71% of freshmen and 76% of continuing students received need-based aid. The average freshman award was $5682. 26% of undergraduates work part time. Average annual earnings from campus work are $1875. Evangel is a member of CSS. The FAFSA is required. The fall application deadline is August 1.
International Students: There are 21 international students enrolled. They must score 490 on the written TOEFL and also take the SAT I or the ACT.
Computers: The mainframes are a DEC VAX II/750 and a DEC MicroVAX II. There are 3 computer labs with PCs available for student use. Computers are also located in each residence hall. All students may access the system during hours of operation. There are no time limits and no fees. It is strongly recommended that all students have a personal computer.
Graduates: In 2001, 298 bachelor's degrees were awarded. The most popular majors were education (21%), behavioral science (15%), and business (13%). In an average class, 96% graduate in 4 years, and 4% in 5 years. 54 companies recruited on campus in 2000-2001.
Admissions Contact: Andrew Denton, Director of Admissions. A video is available. E-mail: *admissions@evangel.edu*
Web: *http://www.evangel.edu/*

FONTBONNE UNIVERSITY — D-2

Fontbonne University
St. Louis, MO 63105 — **(314) 889-1400; Fax: (314) 889-1451**

Full-time: 310 men, 879 women	**Faculty:** 60
Part-time: 100 men, 227 women	**Ph.D.s:** 66%
Graduate: 196 men, 480 women	**Student/Faculty:** 20 to 1
Year: semesters, summer session	**Tuition:** $12,746
Application Deadline: August 1	**Room & Board:** $5300

Freshman Class: 426 applied, 357 accepted, 177 enrolled
ACT: 22 — **COMPETITIVE**

Fontbonne University, founded in 1917, is a private institution affiliated with the Catholic Church. It offers undergraduate degree programs in education, natural sciences, human environmental sciences, business, and communication and fine arts. In addition to regional accreditation, Fontbonne has baccalaureate program accreditation with ADA and ASLA. The library contains 90,000 volumes and 6000 audiovisual forms/CDs, and subscribes to 510 periodicals. Computerized library services include the card catalog, interlibrary loans, and database searching. Special learning facilities include a learning resource center, art gallery, a biological field station, a broadcast center, and a communications disorder clinic. The 13-acre campus is in a suburban area 1 mile west of St. Louis. Including residence halls, there are 10 buildings.
Student Life: 80% of undergraduates are from Missouri. Others are from 17 states and 19 foreign countries. 48% are from public schools. 80% are white; 17% African American. 55% are Catholic; 23% Protestant; 10% claim no religious affiliation. The average age of freshmen is 18; all undergraduates, 24. 20% do not continue beyond their first year; 65% remain to graduate.
Housing: 270 students can be accommodated in college housing, which includes single-sex and coed dormitories and on-campus apartments. On-campus housing is guaranteed for the freshman year only and is available on a first-come, first-served basis. Priority is given to out-of-town students. 75% of students commute. All students may keep cars.
Activities: There is 1 local fraternity. There are no sororities. There are 24 groups on campus, including cheerleading, choir, chorus, computers, drama, drill team, ethnic, gay, honors, international, literary magazine, musical theater, photography, political, professional, radio and TV, religious, social, social service, student government, and yearbook. Popular campus events include Spring Fest, art shows, and musical performances.
Sports: There are 7 intercollegiate sports for men and 8 for women, and 4 intramural sports for men and 7 for women. Facilities include a student activity center that houses a 2000-seat gym, weight room, track, aerobics room, and cafe.
Disabled Students: 70% of the campus is accessible. Wheelchair ramps, elevators, special parking, specially equipped rest rooms, lowered drinking fountains, lowered telephones, and special class scheduling when possible are available.
Services: Counseling and information services are available, as is tutoring in most subjects. There is remedial math, reading, and writing.
Campus Safety and Security: Measures include self-defense education, informal discussions, pamphlets/posters/films, and emergency telephones. There are lighted pathways/sidewalks and security personnel as needed.
Programs of Study: Fontbonne confers B.A., B.S., and B.F.A. degrees. Master's degrees are also awarded. Bachelor's degrees are awarded in BIOLOGICAL SCIENCE (biology/biological science), BUSINESS (business administration and management and fashion merchandising), COMMUNICATIONS AND THE ARTS (art, broadcasting, communications, English, fine arts, and performing arts), COMPUTER AND PHYSICAL SCIENCE (computer science, information sciences and systems, and mathematics), EDUCATION (art, early childhood, education of the deaf and hearing impaired, elementary, middle school, and special), HEALTH PROFESSIONS (speech pathology/audiology), SOCIAL SCIENCE (dietetics, family/consumer studies, history, human services, liberal arts/general studies, and prelaw). Education, computer science, and math are the strongest academically. Business, communication studies, and education are the largest.
Required: To graduate, students must complete 128 credit hours, including 44 in general education requirements, with a minimum GPA of 2.0. The number of hours required for the major varies.
Special: Fontbonne offers cross-registration with several area colleges and a student exchange program with the Sisters of St. Joseph Consortium. There are also cooperative programs in all majors except education, internships with major companies, study abroad in 2 countries, work-study programs, student-designed and dual majors, credit by exam, nondegree study, pass/fail options, and B.A.-B.S. degrees. In addition, an accelerated degree program in business is available, as are 3-2 degrees in engineering and social work with Washington University. There are 4 national honor societies, and a freshman honors program.
Faculty/Classroom: 46% of faculty are male; 54%, female. 91% teach undergraduates, 2% do research, and 2% do both. The average class

size in an introductory lecture is 21; in a laboratory, 8; and in a regular course, 15.

Admissions: 84% of the 2001-2002 applicants were accepted. The ACT scores for the 2001-2002 freshman class were: 37% below 21, 34% between 21 and 23, 18% between 24 and 26, 7% between 27 and 28, and 4% above 28. 41% of the current freshmen were in the top fifth of their class; 64% were in the top two fifths. 2 freshmen graduated first in their class in a recent year.

Requirements: The SAT I or ACT is required, with a minimum SAT I composite score of 900 or ACT score of 20 recommended. Applicants must be graduates of an accredited secondary school or have a GED certificate. They must have completed 16 academic credits, including 4 in English, 3 in math, 2 each in science and social studies, and 1 in history. An audition or portfolio may be required. Fontbonne requires applicants to be in the upper 50% of their class. A GPA of 2.5 is required. AP and CLEP credits are accepted. Important factors in the admissions decision are advanced placement or honor courses, extracurricular activities record, and leadership record. Applications are accepted on disk and online.

Procedure: Freshmen are admitted to all sessions. Entrance exams should be taken prior to registration. There are early admissions and deferred admissions plans. Applications should be filed by August 1 for fall entry and January 1 for spring entry. The fall 2001 application fee was $25. Notification is sent on a rolling basis.

Transfer: 136 transfer students enrolled in 2001-2002. Applicants must have a minimum GPA of 2.0 and either submit the ACT or the SAT I scores or take a placement test. Students with fewer than 30 credits must submit a high school transcript. An interview is recommended. 32 credits of 128 must be completed at Fontbonne.

Visiting: There are regularly scheduled orientations for prospective students, including a campus tour, a financial aid presentation, and visits with faculty and current students. There are guides for informal visits and visitors may sit in on classes and stay overnight. To schedule a visit, contact the Admissions Office.

Financial Aid: In 2001-2002, 92% of all freshmen and 99% of continuing students received some form of financial aid. 62% of freshmen and 79% of continuing students received need-based aid. The average freshman award was $11,830. Of that total, scholarships or need-based grants averaged $6300 ($12,596 maximum); loans averaged $2625 ($4125 maximum); and work contracts averaged $1500 ($2500 maximum). 22% of undergraduates work part time. Average annual earnings from campus work are $1243. The average financial indebtedness of the 2001 graduate was $22,000. The CSS/Profile, FAFSA, or FFS and the college's own financial statement are required. The fall application deadline is April 1.

International Students: There are 27 international students enrolled. The school actively recruits these students. They must score 500 on the written TOEFL.

Computers: The mainframe is an HP9000 D350. More than 40 IBM and Mac PCs are available, as is Internet access. All students may access the system during regular hours. There are no time limits. The fee is $35.

Graduates: In 2001, 333 bachelor's degrees were awarded. The most popular majors were business (56%), communication disorders (9%), and fine arts (8%). In an average class, 50% graduate in 4 years, and 52% in 5 years. 25 companies recruited on campus in 2000-2001. Of the 2000 graduating class, 97% were employed within 6 months of graduation.

Admissions Contact: Peggy Musen, Associate Dean for Enrollment Management. E-mail: *pmusen@fontbonne.edu*
Web: *www.fontbonne.edu*

HANNIBAL-LAGRANGE COLLEGE — D-2
Hannibal, MO 63401 — (573) 221-3113
(800) HLG-1119; Fax: (573) 221-6594

Full-time: 265 men, 439 women	**Faculty:** 48
Part-time: 146 men, 249 women	**Ph.D.s:** 39%
Graduate: none	**Student/Faculty:** 15 to 1
Year: semesters, summer session	**Tuition:** $9130
Application Deadline: August 29	**Room & Board:** $3400
Freshman Class: 584 applied, 221 accepted, 165 enrolled	
SAT I Verbal/Math: 540/580	**ACT:** 21 — **COMPETITIVE**

Hannibal-LaGrange College, founded in 1858, is a private facility affiliated with the Southern Baptist Church. In addition to regional accreditation, HLG has baccalaureate program accreditation with NLN. The library contains 89,700 volumes, 20,852 microform items, and 7085 audiovisual forms/CDs, and subscribes to 507 periodicals. Computerized library services include the card catalog, interlibrary loans, and database searching. Special learning facilities include and a nature trail. The 110-acre campus is in a small town 100 miles north of St. Louis. Including residence halls, there are 17 buildings.

Student Life: 80% of undergraduates are from Missouri. Others are from 24 states and 8 foreign countries. 98% are from public schools. 97% are white. The average age of freshmen is 19; all undergraduates. 23. 6% do not continue beyond their first year.

Housing: 416 students can be accommodated in college housing, which includes single-sex dormitories and on-campus apartments. On-campus housing is guaranteed for all 4 years. 60% of students live on campus; of those, 71% remain on campus on weekends. Alcohol is not permitted. All students may keep cars.

Activities: There are no fraternities or sororities. There are 27 groups on campus, including band, cheerleading, choir, chorus, drama, honors, jazz band, newspaper, pep band, political, professional, religious, science, social, social service, student government, and yearbook. Popular campus events include Spring Campus Visitation Days and Encounter Visitation Days.

Sports: There are 2 intercollegiate sports for men and 2 for women, and 6 intramural sports for men and 6 for women. Facilities include baseball, softball, and soccer fields and a 41,000-square-foot sports complex that contains a gym, weight and aerobics rooms, and volleyball, tennis, and racquetball courts.

Disabled Students: 65% of the campus is accessible. Wheelchair ramps, elevators, special parking, specially equipped rest rooms, special class scheduling, lowered drinking fountains, and limited dorm space are available.

Services: Counseling and information services are available, as is tutoring in some subjects, including math and business/accounting. There is a reader service for the blind, and remedial math, reading, and writing, and sign language for hearing-impaired students.

Campus Safety and Security: Measures include 24-hour foot and vehicle patrol, escort service, pamphlets/posters/films, and emergency telephones. There are lighted pathways/sidewalks.

Programs of Study: HLG confers B.A., B.S., B.C.E., B.C.M., B.R.S., B.S.Ed., and B.S.N. degrees. Associate degrees are also awarded. Bachelor's degrees are awarded in BIOLOGICAL SCIENCE (biology/biological science), BUSINESS (accounting, business administration and management, personnel management, and recreational facilities management), COMMUNICATIONS AND THE ARTS (art, communications, dramatic arts, English, music, music performance, piano/organ, and speech/debate/rhetoric), COMPUTER AND PHYSICAL SCIENCE (computer programming, information sciences and systems, and mathematics), EDUCATION (Christian, early childhood, elementary, music, and secondary), HEALTH PROFESSIONS (nursing), SOCIAL SCIENCE (biblical studies, criminal justice, history, human services, liberal arts/general studies, psychology, and religious music). Accounting and business administration are the strongest academically. Education, business, and organizational management are the largest.

Required: All students must complete 124 credit hours with a 2.0 GPA to graduate. The major usually requires 36 or more credit hours of study. General education requirements include 8 hours in natural science; 6 hours each in Bible, composition, literature, foreign language, history, fine arts, and social science; 3 hours each in speech and algebra; 2 hours in phys ed; and 1 hour in Success in Education. Different core requirements pertain to education and nursing students.

Special: Internships are available for students taking courses in human services, data processing, criminal justice, and Bible studies. Study abroad in England and a Washington semester are also available. There are accelerated-degree programs in administration of justice and organizational management. Student-designed majors, credit by examination, and nondegree study are possible. There is 1 national honor society, Phi Beta Kappa, and a freshman honors program.

Faculty/Classroom: 56% of faculty are male; 44%, female. All teach undergraduates. The average class size in an introductory lecture is 17; in a laboratory, 18; and in a regular course, 16.

Admissions: 38% of the 2001-2002 applicants were accepted. The ACT scores for the 2001-2002 freshman class were: 25% below 21, 47% between 21 and 23, 21% between 24 and 26, and 7% above 28. 28% of the current freshmen were in the top fifth of their class; 72% were in the top two fifths. There was 1 National Merit finalist. 7 freshmen graduated first in their class.

Requirements: The SAT I or ACT is required. In addition, in addition, applicants must be graduates of an accredited secondary school or have the GED. An interview is required. A GPA of 2.0 is required. AP and CLEP credits are accepted. Applications are accepted on-line at *www.hlg.edu*

Procedure: Freshmen are admitted to all sessions. Entrance exams should be taken before registration. Applications should be filed by August 29 for fall entry and January 8 for spring entry, along with a $25 fee. Notification is sent on a rolling basis.

Transfer: Applicants must submit transcripts from all colleges attended. Students applying with fewer than 30 credit hours must also submit a high school transcript along with ACT or SAT I scores. 32 credits of 124 must be completed at HLG.

Visiting: There are regularly scheduled orientations for prospective students, Encounter Days, which are organized tours of the campus covering financial aid, student affairs, and academic areas, and including lunch in the cafeteria. There are guides for informal visits and visitors may sit in on classes and stay overnight. To schedule a visit, contact the Admissions Office at (800) HLG-1119 or *sdouglas@hlg.edu*

Financial Aid: In 2001-2002, 94% of all freshmen and 84% of continuing students received some form of financial aid. 93% of freshmen received need-based aid. The average freshman award was $7623. 68% of undergraduates work part time. Average annual earnings from campus work are $1100. The average financial indebtedness of the 2001 graduate was $11,300. The FAFSA is required. The fall application deadline is July 1.

International Students: There are 13 international students enrolled. The school actively recruits these students. They must score 520 on the written TOEFL and also take the ACT.

Computers: Mainframes are an EXL 320 and 316, a 325 Sperry 5000/40, and a Data General AV620. PCs are available in the technical center for all students. All students may access the system. There are no time limits and no fees.

Graduates: In 2001, 135 bachelor's degrees were awarded. The most popular majors were education (29%), organizational management (13%), and administration of justice (11%). In an average class, 60% graduate in 4 years, and 64% in 6 years. 24 companies recruited on campus in 2000-2001. Of the 2000 graduating class, 5% were enrolled in graduate school within 6 months of graduation.

Admissions Contact: Ray Carty, Dean of Enrollment Management. E-mail: *rcarty@hlg.edu*

HARRIS-STOWE STATE COLLEGE D-2

St. Louis, MO 63103 (314) 340-3300; Fax: (314) 340-3555

Full-time: 204 men, 349 women	**Faculty:** 52; IIB, -$
Part-time: 187 men, 566 women	**Ph.D.s:** 65%
Graduate: none	**Student/Faculty:** 14 to 1
Year: semesters, summer session	**Tuition:** $2310 ($4522)
Application Deadline: open	**Room & Board:** n/app
Freshman Class: 219 applied, 188 accepted, 170 enrolled	
SAT I or ACT: required	**SPECIAL**

Harris-Stowe State College, founded in 1854, is a state-supported, commuter institution offering undergraduate programs in teacher and urban education. In addition to regional accreditation, Harris-Stowe has baccalaureate program accreditation with NCATE. The library contains 90,000 volumes and 30,000 microform items, and subscribes to 300 periodicals. Computerized library services include the card catalog, interlibrary loans, and database searching. Special learning facilities include a learning resource center. The 8-acre campus is in an urban area in metropolitan St. Louis. There are 2 buildings.

Student Life: The average age of all undergraduates is 28.

Housing: There are no residence halls. All of students commute. Alcohol is not permitted.

Activities: There are some groups and organizations on campus, including cheerleading, chorale, dance, drama, ethnic, literary magazine, newspaper, professional, student government, and yearbook. Popular campus events include Mistletoe Dinner Dance and Awards Breakfast.

Sports: There are 3 intercollegiate sports for men and 4 for women.

Disabled Students: All of the campus is accessible. Wheelchair ramps, elevators, special parking, specially equipped rest rooms, and lowered telephones are available.

Services: There is remedial math, reading, and writing and tutoring.

Campus Safety and Security: Measures include lighted pathways/sidewalks.

Programs of Study: Harris-Stowe confers B.S.T.E. and B.S.U.E. degrees. Bachelor's degrees are awarded in EDUCATION (early childhood, elementary, and middle school).

Required: Students are required to complete 120 to 129 semester hours, including a 40-hour core curriculum of general education courses, and must maintain a minimum GPA of 2.5.

Special: Opportunities are provided for internships as part of the degree in urban education, credit by examination, and pass/fail options in developmental courses. There are 3 national honor societies.

Admissions: 86% of the 2001-2002 applicants were accepted.

Requirements: The SAT I or ACT is required. In addition, applicants should have completed 16 academic units at an accredited secondary school or hold a GED. A GPA of 2.0 is required.

Procedure: Entrance exams should be taken before the close of registration. There is a deferred admissions plan. Application deadlines are open. Notification is sent on a rolling basis.

Transfer: 30 credits of 120 must be completed at Harris-Stowe.

Visiting: There are guides for informal visits and visitors may sit in on classes. To schedule a visit, contact the Director of Admissions/Academic Advisement.

Financial Aid: In 2001-2002, 81% of continuing students received some form of financial aid. The FAFSA is required. Check with school for curremt deadlines.

International Students: They must score 500 on the written TOEFL or 173 on the electronic version and also take the SAT I, ACT, or Harris-Stowe's own examination if ACT/SAT I scores are not high enough.

Computers: PCs are available for student use in the academic support center and the PC lab. All students may access the system. There are no time limits and no fees.

Admissions Contact: Valerie A. Beeson, Director of Admissions/Academic Advisement. E-mail: *beesonv@hssc.edu* Web: *www.hssc.edu*

JEWISH HOSPITAL COLLEGE OF NURSING AND ALLIED HEALTH D-2

St. Louis, MO 63110-1091 (314) 454-7055
(800) 832-9009; (314) 454-5239

Full-time: 175 men and women	**Faculty:** 23
Part-time: 210 men and women	**Ph.D.s:** 33%
Graduate: 90 men and women	**Student/Faculty:** 8 to 1
Year: 8-week terms, summer session	**Tuition:** $8700
Application Deadline: open	**Room & Board:** $2500
Freshman Class: n/av	**ACT:** required **SPECIAL**

Jewish Hospital College of Nursing and Allied Health, founded in 1993, is a small college located within the Washington University Medical Center. Figures in above capsule are approximate. There is 1 graduate school. In addition to regional accreditation, Jewish Hospital College has baccalaureate program accreditation with NLN. The library contains 2400 volumes and 450 audiovisual forms/CDs, and subscribes to 150 periodicals. Computerized library services include the card catalog, interlibrary loans, and database searching. The 4-acre campus is in an urban area in the central west end of the city of St. Louis. Including residence halls, there is 1 building.

Student Life: 60% of undergraduates are from Missouri. Others are from 10 states. 75% are white; 20% African American. The average age of freshmen is 26; all undergraduates, 29. 10% do not continue beyond their first year; 85% remain to graduate.

Housing: 117 students can be accommodated in college housing, which includes coed dormitories. On-campus housing is available on a first-come, first-served basis. 92% of students commute. Alcohol is not permitted. All students may keep cars.

Activities: There are no fraternities or sororities. There are some groups and organizations on campus, including professional and student government. Popular campus events include Holiday Party, Lobby Day, and walkathons.

Sports: There is no sports program at Jewish Hospital College.

Disabled Students: 60% of the campus is accessible. Wheelchair ramps, elevators, specially equipped rest rooms, and lowered drinking fountains are available.

Services: Counseling and information services are available, as is tutoring in most subjects.

Campus Safety and Security: Measures include 24-hour foot and vehicle patrol, escort service, shuttle buses, and informal discussions. There are pamphlets/posters/films and lighted pathways/sidewalks.

Programs of Study: Jewish Hospital College confers B.S. and B.S.N. degrees. Associate and master's degrees are also awarded. Bachelor's degrees are awarded in HEALTH PROFESSIONS (clinical science, cytotechnology, nursing, and radiological science). Nursing is the largest.

Required: To graduate, 121 credit hours are required with a minimum GPA of 2.0.

Special: A postbaccalaureate dietetic internship is available, and study abroad in 1 country is offered.

Faculty/Classroom: 8% of faculty are male; 92%, female. All teach undergraduates. The average class size in a laboratory is 10.

Requirements: The ACT is required. Jewish Hospital College requires applicants to be in the upper 50% of their class. A GPA of 2.5 is required. CLEP credit is accepted. Advanced placement or honor courses is an important factor in the admission decision.

Procedure: Freshmen are admitted fall and spring. There are early decision and deferred admissions plans. Application deadlines are open. 20% of all applicants are on a waiting list. The fall 2001 application fee was $25.

Transfer: Applicants should be high school graduates in the upper half of their class, with a 2.5 GPA in high school and college and with a composite score of 21 on the ACT or 1000 on the SAT I. 30 credits of 121 must be completed at Jewish Hospital College.

Visiting: There are regularly scheduled orientations for prospective students, including an overview of the college and programs offered, tours given by current students, and a question-and-answer period. There are guides for informal visits and visitors may sit in on classes. To schedule a visit, contact the recruiter at (314) 454-7057.

Financial Aid: 88% of undergraduates work part time. Average annual earnings from campus work are $1000. The FAFSA and the college's own financial statement are required. Check with the school for current deadlines.

International Students: They must score 550 on the written TOEFL and also take the SAT I or the ACT, scoring 21 on the ACT.

Computers: All students may access the system. There are no time limits and no fees.

Graduates: In a recent year, 47 bachelor's degrees were awarded. 5 companies recruited on campus in a recent year. Of the 2000 graduating class, 10% were enrolled in graduate school within 6 months of graduation and 96% were employed.

Admissions Contact: Director of Enrollment Management.

KANSAS CITY ART INSTITUTE A-2

Kansas City, MO 64111 (816) 474-5224
(800) 522-5224; Fax: (816) 802-3309

Full-time: 246 men, 279 women	**Faculty:** 42; IIB, -$
Part-time: 8 men, 4 women	**Ph.D.s:** 88%
Graduate: none	**Student/Faculty:** 13 to 1
Year: semesters, summer session	**Tuition:** $19,580
Application Deadline: rolling	**Room & Board:** $6300
Freshman Class: 550 applied, 438 accepted, 179 enrolled	
SAT I Verbal/Math: 552/522	**ACT:** 23 **SPECIAL**

The Kansas City Art Institute, founded in 1885, is an independent professional college of art and design. In addition to regional accreditation, KCAI has baccalaureate program accreditation with NASAD. The library contains 30,000 volumes and subscribes to 125 periodicals. Computerized library services include the card catalog, interlibrary loans, and database searching. Special learning facilities include a learning resource center and art gallery. The 17-acre campus is in an urban area. Including residence halls, there are 14 buildings.

Student Life: 62% of undergraduates are from out of state, mostly the Midwest. Others are from 40 states, 7 foreign countries, and Canada. 60% are from public schools. 82% are white. The average age of freshmen is 19.3; all undergraduates, 21.6. 28% do not continue beyond their first year.

Housing: 180 students can be accommodated in college housing, which includes single-sex and coed dormitories and off-campus apartments. On-campus housing is guaranteed for the freshman year only and is available on a first-come, first-served basis. 75% of students commute. Alcohol is not permitted. All students may keep cars.

Activities: There are no fraternities or sororities. There are some groups and organizations on campus, including literary magazine and newspaper. Popular campus events include dances, film series, and poetry readings.

Sports: There is no sports program at KCAI.

Disabled Students: 50% of the campus is accessible. Wheelchair ramps and specially equipped rest rooms are available.

Services: Counseling and information services are available, as is tutoring in every subject. There is remedial reading and writing.

Campus Safety and Security: Measures include 24-hour foot and vehicle patrol, escort service, informal discussions, and pamphlets/posters/films. There are emergency telephones, lighted pathways/sidewalks, and free taxi service.

Programs of Study: KCAI confers the B.F.A. degree. Bachelor's degrees are awarded in COMMUNICATIONS AND THE ARTS (art history and appreciation, ceramic art and design, creative writing, design, fiber/textiles/weaving, illustration, painting, photography, printmaking, sculpture, and video).

Required: Students must maintain a minimum GPA of 2.0 overall and within their studio major. A total of 129 credit hours is needed, including 81 in studio classes; 45 distributed among courses in history of Western thought, art history, literature, humanities, and other liberal arts; and 3 in electives.

Special: KCAI offers internships with major corporations such as Hallmark and Disney, independent study, work-study programs, study abroad, cross-registration, intermedia majors, an exchange program, and nondegree study.

Faculty/Classroom: 67% of faculty are male; 33%, female. All teach undergraduates. The average class size in an introductory lecture is 24; in a laboratory, 19; and in a regular course, 14.

Admissions: 80% of the 2001-2002 applicants were accepted. The SAT I scores for the 2001-2002 freshman class were: Verbal--26% below 500, 39% between 500 and 599, 29% between 600 and 700, and 6% above 700; Math--39% below 500, 37% between 500 and 599, 20% between 600 and 700, and 4% above 700. The ACT scores were 28% below 21, 33% between 21 and 23, 25% between 24 and 26, 12% between 27 and 28, and 2% above 28.

Requirements: The SAT I or ACT is required, and a GPA of 2.5. In addition, applicants must submit a portfolio consisting of 10 to 20 pieces of artwork, 2 letters of recommendation, and high school transcripts. The GED is accepted. A statement of purpose and an interview are required. AP and CLEP credits are accepted. Important factors in the admissions decision are evidence of special talent, advanced placement or honor courses, and recommendations by school officials.

Procedure: Freshmen are admitted fall and spring. Entrance exams should be taken in spring of the junior year or fall of the senior year. There is a deferred admissions plan. Applications are rolling for fall entry, along with a $25 fee. Notification is sent on a rolling basis.

Transfer: 66 transfer students enrolled in 2001-2002. Transfer applicants must submit official transcripts and a portfolio. A minimum GPA of 2.0 is required. 72 credits of 129 must be completed at KCAI.

Visiting: There are regularly scheduled orientations for prospective students, consisting of information sessions offered every other Friday. There are guides for informal visits and visitors may sit in on classes and stay overnight. To schedule a visit, contact the Admissions Office.

Financial Aid: In 2001-2002, 95% of all freshmen and 80% of continuing students received some form of financial aid. 79% of freshmen and 84% of continuing students received need-based aid. The average freshman award was $12,814. Of that total, scholarships or need-based grants averaged $6638 ($9000 maximum); loans averaged $2625 ($3625 maximum); and work contracts averaged $1000. 60% of undergraduates work part time. Maximum annual earnings from campus work are $1500. The average financial indebtedness of the 2001 graduate was $17,125. The FAFSA, the college's own financial statement, and the student and parent IRS tax forms, if requested. are required. The fall application deadline is March 1.

International Students: There are 7 international students enrolled. They must score 500 on the written TOEFL or 213 on the electronic version.

Computers: There is a computer graphics center with software for computer-generated art and design, including digital painting, image processing and composing, layout and illustration, and 3-D modeling and animation. All students may access the system. There are no time limits and no fees. It is recommended that students in design and illustration majors have personal computers.

Graduates: In 2001, 108 bachelor's degrees were awarded. The most popular majors were painting (21%), sculpture (14%), and illustration and ceramics (12%). In an average class, 53% graduate in 4 years, 57% in 5 years, and 60% in 6 years. Of the 2000 graduating class, 11% were enrolled in graduate school within 6 months of graduation and 50% were employed.

Admissions Contact: Larry Stone, Vice President for Enrollment Management. E-mail: *admiss@kcai.edu* Web: *www.kcai.edu*

LESTER L. COX COLLEGE OF NURSING AND HEALTH SCIENCES B-3

Springfield, MO 65802 (417) 269-3069; Fax: (417) 269-3581

Full-time: 12 men, 164 women	**Faculty:** 19
Part-time: 8 men, 128 women	**Ph.D.s:** 5%
Graduate: none	**Student/Faculty:** 9 to 1
Year: semesters	**Tuition:** $6430
Application Deadline: February 1	**Room & Board:** $1650
Freshman Class: n/av	
ACT: 22	**SPECIAL**

Lester L. Cox College of Nursing and Health Sciences, founded in 1994, is a private institution. The library contains 5685 volumes, and subscribes to 284 periodicals. Computerized library services include interlibrary loans and database searching. Special learning facilities include a learning resource center, nursing skills lab, and an audiovisual learning center. The campus is in an urban area. There is 1 building.

Student Life: 99% of undergraduates are from Missouri. 96% are white. The average age of all undergraduates is 27.

Housing: 60 students can be accommodated in college housing, which includes coed dormitories. On-campus housing is available on a first-come, first-served basis. 90% of students commute. Alcohol is not permitted. All students may keep cars.

Activities: There are no fraternities or sororities. There are some groups and organizations on campus, including professional, religious, and student government. Popular campus events include Fall Fling, Wellness Days, and Diversity Day.

Sports: There is no sports program at Cox College.

Disabled Students: Wheelchair ramps, elevators, and special parking are available.

Services: Counseling and information services are available, as is tutoring in some subjects, including math and writing. There is remedial math and writing. Peer tutoring is available for most science courses.

Campus Safety and Security: Measures include 24-hour foot and vehicle patrol, escort service, pamphlets/posters/films, and lighted pathways/sidewalks.

Programs of Study: Cox College confers the B.S.N. degree. Associate degrees are also awarded. Bachelor's degrees are awarded in HEALTH PROFESSIONS (nursing).

Required: A total of 122 credit hours is required for the B.S.N.

Faculty/Classroom: 26% of faculty are male; 74%, female. All teach undergraduates. The average class size in an introductory lecture is 25; in a laboratory, 33; and in a regular course, 25.

Admissions: The ACT scores for the 2001-2002 freshman class were: 94% between 21 and 23, 5% between 24 and 26, and 1% above 28.

Requirements: The ACT is required. In addition, an ACT score of 22 or better is required. A GPA of 2.5 is required. AP and CLEP credits are accepted.

Procedure: Freshmen are admitted fall and spring. There is an early decision plan. Early decision application should be filed by November 1, regular applications, by February 1 for fall entry and September 1 for spring entry. The college accepts all applicants. Notification of early decision is sent December 1; regular decision, March 1 and October 1. 10 early decision candidates were accepted for the 2001-2002 class. The application fee was $30 in 2001.

Transfer: 59 transfer students enrolled in 2001-2002. A GPA of 2.0 or better is required, with 12 or more hours of credit. Only courses with a grade of C or better will be considered for transfer. Transfer applicants are not required to submit an ACT score. 30 credits of 122 must be completed at Cox College.

Visiting: There are guides for informal visits and visitors may sit in on classes. To schedule a visit, contact Virginia Mace.

Financial Aid: In 2001-2002, 92% of all freshmen and 90% of continuing students received some form of financial aid. 71% of freshmen and 77% of continuing students received need-based aid. The average freshman award was $7254. Of that total, scholarships or need-based grants averaged $2767 ($7750 maximum); and loans averaged $4450 ($8625 maximum). 5% of undergraduates work part time. Average annual earnings from campus work are $858. The average financial indebtedness of the 2001 graduate was $13,480. The FAFSA is required. The fall application deadline is April 1.

International Students: They must score 500 on the written TOEFL and also take the ACT, scoring 22.

Computers: There are computer labs with 26 workstations, 13 of those with Internet access. . There are no time limits and no fees.

Graduates: In 2001, 1 bachelor's degrees were awarded. 20 companies recruited on campus in 2000-2001. Of the 2000 graduating class, all were employed within 6 months of graduation.

Admissions Contact: Virginia Mace, Admissions Counselor. A video is available. E-mail: *vsmace@coxcollege.edu* Web: *coxcollege.edu*

LINCOLN UNIVERSITY C-2
Jefferson City, MO 65102-0029 (573) 681-5599
(800) 521-5052; Fax: (573) 681-5889

Full-time: 925 men, 1100 women	**Faculty:** 141; IIA, --$
Part-time: 350 men, 700 women	**Ph.D.s:** 30%
Graduate: 70 men, 185 women	**Student/Faculty:** 14 to 1
Year: semesters, summer session	**Tuition:** $3368 ($6578)
Application Deadline: July 15	**Room & Board:** $3790
Freshman Class: n/av	**ACT:** required

NONCOMPETITIVE

Lincoln University, established in 1866, is a land-grant institution offering degree programs in agriculture, arts and sciences, business, applied technology, and education. Figures in above capsule are approximate. There are 3 undergraduate schools and 1 graduate school. In addition to regional accreditation, LU has baccalaureate program accreditation with NASM and NCATE. The library contains 340,000 volumes, 100,000 microform items, and 3000 audiovisual forms/CDs, and subscribes to 1000 periodicals. Computerized library services include the card catalog, interlibrary loans, and database searching. Special learning facilities include a learning resource center, radio station, TV station, and ethnic studies center. The 155-acre campus is in a small town 130 miles west of St. Louis. Including residence halls, there are 36 buildings.

Student Life: 89% of undergraduates are from Missouri. Others are from 28 states, 29 foreign countries, and Canada. 63% are white; 30% African American. The average age of freshmen is 18; all undergraduates, 22.

Housing: 630 students can be accommodated in college housing, which includes single-sex dormitories. On-campus housing is available on a first-come, first-served basis. 82% of students commute. Alcohol is not permitted. All students may keep cars.

Activities: 3% of men belong to 4 national fraternities. There are 4 national sororities. There are 28 groups on campus, including art, band, cheerleading, choir, dance, drama, honors, international, jazz band, marching band, newspaper, opera, professional, radio and TV, religious, student government, and yearbook. Popular campus events include Black History Week and Unity Awards in Media.

Sports: There are 6 intercollegiate sports for men and 4 for women, and 2 intramural sports for men. Facilities include a 5600-seat stadium and a 2500-seat gym.

Disabled Students: Wheelchair ramps, elevators, special parking, specially equipped rest rooms, special class scheduling, lowered drinking fountains, and lowered telephones are available.

Services: Counseling and information services are available, as is tutoring in most subjects. There is a reader service for the blind, and remedial math, reading, and writing.

Campus Safety and Security: Measures include 24-hour foot and vehicle patrol, self-defense education, escort service, and informal discussions. There are pamphlets/posters/films, emergency telephones, and lighted pathways/sidewalks.

Programs of Study: LU confers B.A., B.S., B.M.E., and B.S.Ed. degrees. Associate and master's degrees are also awarded. Bachelor's degrees are awarded in AGRICULTURE (agriculture), BIOLOGICAL SCIENCE (biology/biological science), BUSINESS (accounting, business administration and management, marketing/retailing/merchandising, and office supervision and management), COMMUNICATIONS AND THE ARTS (art, English, French, journalism, and Spanish), COMPUTER AND PHYSICAL SCIENCE (chemistry, information sciences and systems, mathematics, and physics), EDUCATION (art, business, elementary, home economics, music, physical, social science, and special), ENGINEERING AND ENVIRONMENTAL DESIGN (civil engineering technology, engineering, and mechanical design technology), HEALTH PROFESSIONS (medical technology and nursing), SOCIAL SCIENCE (criminal justice, economics, history, liberal arts/general studies, philosophy, political science/government, psychology, public administration, and sociology). Business administration, nursing, and education are the largest.

Required: To graduate, students must complete 121 semester hours including at least 30 in the major, with 18 hours in upper-division courses. Students must maintain a minimum GPA of 2.0. Coursework is required in math, English, speech, humanities, history, social science, cultural diversity, and phys ed. Seniors must pass a major field exit exam.

Special: LU offers cross-registration with the University of Missouri/Columbia and William Woods, Westminster, and Columbia colleges; federal, state, local, and private internships; co-op programs, and a 3-2 engineering degree with the University of Missouri Rolla. Credit by exam, student-designed majors, and a continuing education program are available. There is a freshman honors program.

Faculty/Classroom: 61% of faculty are male; 39%, female. All teach undergraduates and 14% do research. No introductory courses are taught by graduate students. The average class size in an introductory lecture is 50; in a laboratory, 13; and in a regular course, 25.

Requirements: The ACT is required. In addition, students must be graduates of an accredited secondary school or have the GED. A GPA of 2.0 is required. CLEP credit is accepted.

Procedure: Freshmen are admitted to all sessions. Entrance exams should be taken prior to registration. There is an early admissions plan. Applications should be filed by July 15 for fall entry and November 20 for spring entry, along with a $17 fee. The college accepts all in-state residents. Notification is sent on a rolling basis.

Transfer: 213 transfer students enrolled in a recent year. All applicants must submit a college transcript from each institution previously attended; those students transferring fewer than 30 hours must also submit the high school transcript and ACT scores. 30 credits of 121 must be completed at LU.

Visiting: There are regularly scheduled orientations for prospective students, consisting of a freshman orientation held each July. There are guides for informal visits and visitors may sit in on classes and stay overnight. To schedule a visit, contact the Enrollment Services Office at (573) 681-5022.

Financial Aid: In a recent year, 72% of all freshmen and 65% of continuing students received some form of financial aid. 62% of freshmen and 52% of continuing students received need-based aid. The average freshman award in a recent year was $5750. Of that total, scholarships or need-based grants averaged $2070 ($3100 maximum); loans averaged $2625; and work contracts averaged $1100 ($1400 maximum). 12% of undergraduates work part time. Average annual earnings from campus work are $1000. The average financial indebtedness of a recent year's graduate was $1600. LU is a member of CSS. The FAFSA is required. The fall application deadline is March 15.

International Students: There were 143 international students enrolled in a recent year. They must score 500 on the written TOEFL or take the MELAB and the ACT and placement tests.

Computers: The mainframes are a Unisys B5935, AL-FS, and A6-KX. The mainframes are networked with the Internet. There are also 5 PC labs with a total of 150 computers for student use. All students may access the system 8 A.M. to 10 P.M. Monday through Friday, 8 A.M. to 7 P.M. Saturday, and 9 A.M. to 2 P.M. Sunday. There are no time limits and no fees.

Admissions Contact: Constance Williams, Vice President, Student Affairs. Web: *www.lincolnu.edu*

LINDENWOOD UNIVERSITY D-2
St. Charles, MO 63301 (636) 949-4949; Fax: (636) 949-4910

Full-time: 1596 men, 2129 women	**Faculty:** 153
Part-time: 73 men, 55 women	**Ph.D.s:** 46%
Graduate: 752 men, 1495 women	**Student/Faculty:** 24 to 1
Year: 4-1-4, summer session	**Tuition:** $11,650
Application Deadline: open	**Room & Board:** $5600
Freshman Class: n/av	
ACT: required	

COMPETITIVE

Lindenwood University, founded in 1827, is a private institution offering undergraduate degree programs in the arts and sciences, business, education, and preprofessional fields. There are 5 undergraduate and 9 graduate schools. The library contains 138,232 volumes, 84,340 microform items, and 2623 audiovisual forms/CDs, and subscribes to 445 periodicals. Computerized library services include the card catalog, interlibrary loans, and database searching. Special learning facilities include a learning resource center, art gallery, radio station, TV station, and a greenhouse. The 200-acre campus is in a suburban area 25 miles west of St. Louis. Including residence halls, there are 19 buildings.

Student Life: 75% of undergraduates are from Missouri. Others are from 34 states, 60 foreign countries, and Canada. 74% are white. 49% are Catholic; 45%, Protestant. The average age of freshmen is 18; all undergraduates, 21.

Housing: 2300 students can be accommodated in college housing, which includes single-sex dormitories, on-campus apartments, and married-student housing. In addition, there are honors houses. On-campus housing is guaranteed for all 4 years. 70% of students live on campus. Alcohol is not permitted. All students may keep cars.

Activities: 20% of men belong to 3 national fraternities; 8% of women belong to 2 national sororities. There are 50 groups on campus, including art, band, cheerleading, chess, choir, chorale, chorus, computers, dance, drama, drill team, film, honors, international, jazz band, literary magazine, marching band, musical theater, newspaper, pep band, photography, political, professional, radio and TV, religious, social, social service, student government, and yearbook. Popular campus events include Spring Fling, Alumni Weekend, and Christmas Walk.

Sports: There are 15 intercollegiate sports for men and 15 for women, and 6 intramural sports for men and 6 for women. Facilities include an indoor pool, a gym, weight rooms, a 5000-seat stadium, a 3000-seat performance arena, a sand volleyball court, tennis courts, and softball, baseball, soccer, and track fields. Students may use the local golf course for a discounted fee.

Disabled Students: 40% of the campus is accessible. Wheelchair ramps, elevators, special parking, specially equipped rest rooms, special class scheduling, lowered drinking fountains, and lowered telephones are available.

Services: Counseling and information services are available, as is tutoring in every subject. There is a reader service for the blind.

Campus Safety and Security: Measures include 24-hour foot and vehicle patrol, escort service, informal discussions, and pamphlets/posters/films. There are emergency telephones and lighted pathways/sidewalks.

Programs of Study: Lindenwood confers B.A., B.S., and B.F.A. degrees. Master's degrees are also awarded. Bachelor's degrees are awarded in AGRICULTURE (agricultural business management), BIOLOGICAL SCIENCE (biology/biological science), BUSINESS (accounting, banking and finance, business administration and management, human resources, management information systems, marketing/retailing/merchandising, and sports management), COMMUNICATIONS AND THE ARTS (art history and appreciation, communications, creative writing, dance, dramatic arts, English, French, music, performing arts, Spanish, studio art, and technical and business writing), COMPUTER AND PHYSICAL SCIENCE (chemistry, computer science, and mathematics), EDUCATION (art, athletic training, business, early childhood, elementary, music, physical, science, and secondary), ENGINEERING AND ENVIRONMENTAL DESIGN (engineering), HEALTH PROFESSIONS (medical technology), SOCIAL SCIENCE (criminal justice, fashion design and technology, history, human services, international studies, liberal arts/general studies, political science/government, prelaw, psychology, public administration, religion, social work, and sociology). Biology, education, and mass communications are the strongest academically. Business, education, and mass communications are the largest.

Required: In order to graduate, students must complete a minimum of 128 credit hours, including at least 36 in the major and 42 in upper-division courses, with a minimum GPA of 2.0. Core curriculum courses include 10 hours of math and science, 9 each of social sciences, humanities, and civilization, 6 of English, and 3 each of fine arts and communications.

Special: The university offers internships in most majors, a co-op program in computer science, study abroad and a Washington semester for juniors, and cross-registration with the Greater St. Louis College Consortium. The B.A.-B.S. degree, dual and student-designed majors, accelerated degree programs, 3-2 degrees in engineering and social work with Washington University in St. Louis, work-study programs, and nondegree study are also available. Lindenwood is also designed to meet the needs of working adults; there are evening and weekend classes and 5-year bachelor's programs. There are 4 national honor societies, and a freshman honors program.

Faculty/Classroom: 59% of faculty are male; 41%, female. All teach undergraduates. No introductory courses are taught by graduate students. The average class size in an introductory lecture is 30; in a laboratory, 25; and in a regular course, 25.

Admissions: 83% of the 2001-2002 applicants were accepted. 20% of the current freshmen were in the top fifth of their class; 50% were in the top two fifths.

Requirements: The SAT I or ACT is required; the minimum required score on the ACT is 18. Applicants must be graduates of an accredited secondary school or have a GED. High school preparation should include at least 16 academic units, based on 4 years of English, 2 to 3 each of math, science, and social studies, 2 of a foreign language, and some study of fine or performing arts. An essay and an interview are recommended. Lindenwood requires applicants to be in the upper 50% of their class. A GPA of 2.0 is required. AP and CLEP credits are accepted. Important factors in the admissions decision are evidence of special talent, advanced placement or honor courses, and leadership record.

Procedure: Freshmen are admitted to all sessions. There are early admissions and deferred admissions plans. Application deadlines are open. The fall 2001 application fee was $25. Notification is sent on a rolling basis.

Transfer: 337 transfer students enrolled in 2001-2002. Applicants must have a minimum GPA of 2.0 and should submit official college transcripts in order to transfer credits. 30 credits of 128 must be completed at Lindenwood.

Visiting: There are regularly scheduled orientations for prospective students, including an admissions interview, a campus tour, and advising. There are guides for informal visits and visitors may sit in on classes and stay overnight. To schedule a visit, contact the Office of Undergraduate Admissions.

Financial Aid: 91% of undergraduates work part time. Average annual earnings from campus work are $1800. Lindenwood is a member of CSS. The FAFSA is required. The fall application deadline for state aid is April 1.

International Students: There are 300 international students enrolled. The school actively recruits these students. They must score 500 on the written TOEFL or 173 on the electronic version or take the MELAB.

Computers: The mainframe is a DEC VAX 11/750. There are also 65 PCs, 10 of which are networked, in the library and the science and business halls. All students may access the system. There are no time limits and no fees.

Graduates: In 2001, 652 bachelor's degrees were awarded. The most popular majors were business administration (27%), education (11%), and communications (11%). In an average class, 5% graduate in 3 years, 25% in 4 years, 39% in 5 years, and 40% in 6 years.

Admissions Contact: John Guffey, Dean of Admissions.
Web: *http://www.lindenwood.edu*

MARYVILLE UNIVERSITY OF SAINT LOUIS — D-2

St. Louis, MO 63141-7299 — (314) 529-9350
(800) 627-9855; Fax: (314) 529-9927

Full-time: 335 men, 1043 women	**Faculty:** 85; IIA, --$
Part-time: 347 men, 907 women	**Ph.D.s:** 90%
Graduate: 148 men, 382 women	**Student/Faculty:** 16 to 1
Year: semesters, summer session	**Tuition:** $13,000
Application Deadline: see profile	**Room & Board:** $5600
Freshman Class: n/av	
SAT I or ACT: required	**COMPETITIVE**

Maryville University of Saint Louis, established in 1872, is an independent institution offering undergraduate programs in arts, sciences, business, education, and health-related fields and graduate programs in business administration, education, health administration, nursing, occupational therapy, physical therapy, and rehabilitation counseling. There are 4 undergraduate and 3 graduate schools. In addition to regional accreditation, Maryville has baccalaureate program accreditation with AACN, APTA, FIDER, NASAD, NCATE, and NLN. The library contains 203,526 volumes, 468,949 microform items, and 10,661 audiovisual forms/CDs, and subscribes to 4658 periodicals. Computerized library services include the card catalog, interlibrary loans, and database searching. Special learning facilities include a learning resource center, art gallery, an observatory, a teaching lab, art and design labs, clinical labs for nursing, occupational therapy, and physical therapy, video conferencing facilities on all campuses, 4 multimedia-ready classrooms, and residence hall computer labs. The 130-acre campus is in a suburban area 20 miles west of downtown St. Louis. Including residence halls, there are 13 buildings.

Student Life: 88% of undergraduates are from Missouri. Others are from 15 states, 33 foreign countries, and Canada. 80% are from public schools. 87% are white. 75% claim no religious affiliation; 17% Catholic. The average age of freshmen is 18; all undergraduates, 28. 20% do not continue beyond their first year; 73% remain to graduate.

Housing: 372 students can be accommodated in college housing, which includes single-sex and coed dormitories. On-campus housing is guaranteed for all 4 years. 76% of students commute. All students may keep cars.

Activities: There are no fraternities or sororities. There are 37 groups on campus, including art, band, cheerleading, chorale, dance, departmental, drama, ethnic, honors, international, jazz band, literary magazine, newspaper, political, professional, religious, social, social service, and student government. Popular campus events include Christmas tree-lighting ceremony, Fall Festival, and Cram Jam.

Sports: There are 6 intercollegiate sports for men and 6 for women, and 10 intramural sports for men and 10 for women. Facilities include a new university center, an outdoor swimming pool, tennis courts, soccer, softball, and baseball fields, a gym, outdoor and indoor basketball hoops, a fitness center, a student center with table tennis and billiards, a sand volleyball court, and outdoor walking/hiking trails.

Disabled Students: 90% of the campus is accessible. Wheelchair ramps, elevators, special parking, specially equipped rest rooms, special class scheduling, lowered drinking fountains, lowered telephones, electronic doors, note takers, and interpreters for hearing-impaired students are available.

Services: Counseling and information services are available, as is tutoring in some subjects, including English, math, accounting, statistics, biology, chemistry, physics, anatomy and physiology, computer science, calculus, French, and algebra. There is a reader service for the blind, remedial writing, peer tutoring, study skills materials, workshops, and individual consultations.

Campus Safety and Security: Measures include 24-hour foot and vehicle patrol, self-defense education, escort service, and pamphlets/posters/films. There are emergency telephones, lighted pathways/sidewalks, video security systems in residence halls, and security key operated dormitory entrances.

Programs of Study: Maryville confers B.A., B.S., B.F.A., B.S.C.L.S., B.S.M.T., and B.S.N. degrees. Master's degrees are also awarded. Bachelor's degrees are awarded in AGRICULTURE (environmental studies), BIOLOGICAL SCIENCE (biology/biological science), BUSINESS (accounting, business administration and management, electronic business, management science, marketing/retailing/merchandising, and organizational behavior), COMMUNICATIONS AND THE ARTS (communications, English, graphic design, music, and studio art), COMPUTER AND PHYSICAL SCIENCE (actuarial science, chemistry, computer science, information sciences and systems, mathematics, and science), EDUCATION (art, early childhood, elementary, middle school, and secondary), ENGINEERING AND ENVIRONMENTAL DESIGN (environmental science and interior design), HEALTH PROFESSIONS (clinical science, health care administration, health science, music therapy, and nursing), SOCIAL SCIENCE (criminology, history, liberal arts/general studies, paralegal studies, psychology, and sociology). Actuarial science, education, and physical therapy are the strongest academically. Information systems, business administration, and nursing are the largest.

Required: To graduate, all students must complete a minimum of 128 credit hours, with a minimum GPA of 2.0. The core curriculum consists of 12 credit hours each of humanities, math and science, and social and behavioral science, and 8 credit hours each of communication skills and fine arts. 48 upper-division credits must be completed.

Special: Opportunities are available for co-op programs in some majors. There is cross-registration with Fontbonne and Missouri Baptist Colleges, and with Webster and Lindenwood Universities. Students may choose internships in various fields, and cooperative programs are available with such employers as Ameritech and ITT. Other options include dual majors, study abroad in England, Japan, Korea, China, and other countries, a Washington semester, nondegree study, and pass-fail grading. A 3-2 engineering degree is available in conjunction with Washington University. There are 8 national honor societies, and a freshman honors program.

Faculty/Classroom: 37% of faculty are male; 63%, female. All teach undergraduates. No introductory courses are taught by graduate students. The average class size in an introductory lecture is 17; in a laboratory, 15; and in a regular course, 16.

Admissions: 47% of the current freshmen were in the top fifth of their class; 74% were in the top two fifths. 10 freshmen graduated first in their class.

Requirements: The SAT I or ACT is required. In addition, students must have graduated from an accredited secondary school with 22 academic credits or have the GED. Expected preparatory courses include 4 units of English, 3 each of math and a foreign language, and 2 each of science and social studies, plus 8 electives. Some majors have additional admission requirements. A GPA of 2.5 is required. AP and CLEP credits are accepted. Important factors in the admissions decision are recommendations by school officials, advanced placement or honor courses, and leadership record. Applications are accepted on-line via the school's web site.

Procedure: Freshmen are admitted to all sessions. Entrance exams should be taken during the junior year. Application deadlines vary with the semester start date. The fall 2001 application fee was $20. Notification is sent on a rolling basis.

Transfer: 370 transfer students enrolled in a recent year. A minimum GPA of 2.0, higher for some majors, is required. Some majors may require ACT or SAT I scores. 30 credits of 128 must be completed at Maryville.

Visiting: There are regularly scheduled orientations for prospective students, including visiting the campus and arranging a personal interview with an admissions counselor. There are guides for informal visits and visitors may sit in on classes and stay overnight. To schedule a visit, contact the Admissions Office.

Financial Aid: In 2001-2002, 91% of all freshmen and 59% of continuing students received some form of financial aid. 84% of freshmen and 56% of continuing students received need-based aid. The average freshman award was $11,570. Of that total, scholarships or need-based grants averaged $8739 ($19,650 maximum); loans averaged $3267 ($8625 maximum); work contracts averaged $1435 ($2000 maximum); and discounts averaged $3107 ($12,160 maximum). 21% of undergraduates work part time. Average annual earnings from campus work are $954. The average financial indebtedness of the 2001 graduate was $12,638. Maryville is a member of CSS. The FAFSA is required. The fall application deadline is April 1.

International Students: There are 88 international students enrolled. The school actively recruits these students. They must score 500 on the written TOEFL or 173 on the electronic version.

Computers: The mainframe is an HP 9000K210. There are more than 300 IBM and Mac PCs available for academic use at several computer centers, residence halls, and the library. All students may access the system in the computer center lab from 8 A.M. to 10 P.M.; 24-hour access from 2 residence hall computer labs. There are no time limits and no fees.

Graduates: In 2001, 505 bachelor's degrees were awarded. The most popular majors were information systems (10%), physical therapy (8%), and management (8%). In an average class, 46% graduate in 4 years, 59% in 5 years, and 61% in 6 years. 70 companies recruited on campus in 2000-2001.

Admissions Contact: Beth Triplett, Vice President for Enrollment. A video is available. E-mail: *admissions@maryville.edu*
Web: *www.maryville.edu*

MISSOURI BAPTIST COLLEGE — D-2
St. Louis, MO 63141-8660 — **(314) 392-2290**
(877) 434-1115; Fax: (314) 434-7596

Full-time: 365 men, 593 women	**Faculty:** 46; IIB, --$
Part-time: 669 men, 1107 women	**Ph.D.s:** 56%
Graduate: 48 men, 323 women	**Student/Faculty:** 21 to 1
Year: semesters, summer session	**Tuition:** $10,682
Application Deadline: open	**Room & Board:** $5080
Freshman Class: 378 applied, 290 accepted, 176 enrolled	
ACT: 21	**LESS COMPETITIVE**

Missouri Baptist College, established in 1964, is a private liberal arts institution affiliated with the Missouri Baptist Convention. There are 6 undergraduate schools and 1 graduate school. The library contains 103,747 volumes, 52,216 microform items, and 4327 audiovisual forms/CDs, and subscribes to 446 periodicals. Computerized library services include the card catalog, interlibrary loans, and database searching. Special learning facilities include an audiovisual production lab. The 63-acre campus is in a suburban area 15 miles west of St. Louis. Including residence halls, there are 6 buildings.

Student Life: 94% of undergraduates are from Missouri. Others are from 19 states, 22 foreign countries, and Canada. 71% are from public schools. 88% are white. 46% are Protestant; 31% claim no religious affiliation; 24% are members of the school's denomination; 16% are Catholic. The average age of freshmen is 19; all undergraduates, 22. 36% do not continue beyond their first year.

Housing: 260 students can be accommodated in college housing, which includes single-sex dormitories and off-campus apartments. In addition, there are honors houses. On-campus housing is available on a first-come, first-served basis. 70% of students commute. Alcohol is not permitted. All students may keep cars.

Activities: There are no fraternities or sororities. There are 31 groups on campus, including band, business, cheerleading, choir, chorale, chorus, computers, drama, film, honors, international, jazz band, literary magazine, musical theater, newspaper, opera, professional, religious, and student government. Popular campus events include Spring Musical, Christmas Concert, and Hanging of the Green.

Sports: There are 7 intercollegiate sports for men and 5 for women, and 4 intramural sports for men and 4 for women. Facilities include a gym, weight training rooms, a game room, and baseball, softball, and soccer fields.

Disabled Students: 64% of the campus is accessible. Wheelchair ramps, elevators, special parking, specially equipped rest rooms, and lowered drinking fountains are available.

Services: Counseling and information services are available, as is tutoring in some subjects, by arrangement. There is a reader service for the blind, remedial math and writing, and a writing lab.

Campus Safety and Security: Measures include 24-hour foot and vehicle patrol, self-defense education, and lighted pathways/sidewalks.

Programs of Study: MBC confers B.A., B.S., B.M., B.P.S., B.S.E., and B.S.N. degrees. Associate and master's degrees are also awarded. Bachelor's degrees are awarded in BIOLOGICAL SCIENCE (biology/biological science), BUSINESS (accounting, business administration and management, management science, and sports management), COMMUNICATIONS AND THE ARTS (communications, English, and music performance), COMPUTER AND PHYSICAL SCIENCE (chemistry, information sciences and systems, mathematics, and science), EDUCATION (athletic training, early childhood, elementary, middle school, and music), HEALTH PROFESSIONS (health science, nursing, and sports medicine), SOCIAL SCIENCE (behavioral science, child psychology/development, criminal justice, history, human services, ministries, physical fitness/movement, psychology, religion, religious education, religious music, and social science). Education, business, and religion are the strongest academically. Education, business, and communications are the largest.

Required: All students must take courses in the humanities/fine arts, social and behavorial sciences, natural sciences, phys ed, computer literacy, and Old and New Testament history. A minimum GPA of 2.0 is required (some majors require a GPA of 2.5 or better). To graduate, students must complete at least 128 credit hours, with a minimum of 30 hours in the major and 45 hours of upper-division courses; pass a general education exam and an exit exam or other assessment in the major; and complete a capstone project.

Special: There is cross-registration with Fontbonne College and Maryville, Lindenwood, and Webster Universities. Students may opt for credit by exam, nondegree study, and student-designed majors. A 3-2 engineering degree with the University of Missouri/Columbia or a 2-2 engineering degree with the University of Missouri/Rolla is available. Study abroad is possible at Harlaxton College in England and at Hong Kong Baptist University. MBC also offers internships in various disciplines and dual majors in some business and education fields. There are 5 national honor societies.

Faculty/Classroom: 60% of faculty are male; 40%, female. 94% teach undergraduates. No introductory courses are taught by graduate students. The average class size in an introductory lecture is 22; in a laboratory, 10; and in a regular course, 13.

Admissions: 77% of the 2001-2002 applicants were accepted. The ACT scores for the 2001-2002 freshman class were: 48% below 21, 25% between 21 and 23, 7% between 24 and 26, 5% between 27 and 28, and 5% above 28. 19% of the current freshmen were in the top fifth of their class; 51% were in the top two fifths. 4 freshmen graduated first in their class.

Requirements: The SAT I or ACT is required, with a minimum score of 800 on the SAT I or 18 on the ACT. Applicants must be graduates of an accredited secondary school. GED and home-schooled students are accepted. MBC requires applicants to be in the upper 50% of their class. A GPA of 2.0 is required. AP and CLEP credits are accepted. Important factors in the admissions decision are advanced placement or honor courses, leadership record, and evidence of special talent. Applications are accepted on-line via the school's website.

Procedure: Freshmen are admitted to all sessions. Entrance exams should be taken in the junior year. Application deadlines are open. The application fee is $25. Notification is sent on a rolling basis.

Transfer: 235 transfer students enrolled in 2001-2002. Applicants must have a 2.0 GPA, with some programs requiring 2.5 or better. Students must submit official transcripts from all previous colleges attended, along with a character reference. 24 of the last 30 credits of the minimum total 128 must be completed at MBC.

Visiting: There are regularly scheduled orientations for prospective students, consisting of Welcome Weekend, open houses, and campus tours. There are guides for informal visits and visitors may sit in on classes and stay overnight. To schedule a visit, contact the Admissions Office.

Financial Aid: In 2001-2002, 90% of all freshmen and 65% of continuing students received some form of financial aid. 51% of freshmen and 42% of continuing students received need-based aid. The average freshman award was $7179. Of that total, scholarships or need-based grants averaged $5731 ($13,495 maximum); loans averaged $2157 ($6063 maximum); work contracts averaged $1741 ($4000 maximum); and outside scholarships averaged $999 ($2500 maximum). 6% of undergraduates work part time. Average annual earnings from campus work are $1133. The FAFSA and the college's own financial statement are required. The fall application deadline is November 15.

International Students: There are 35 international students enrolled. They must score 500 on the written TOEFL or 173 on the electronic version; those with a TOEFL between 430 and 499 (paper) or 117 and 172 (electronic) are eligible for provisional admission and must take the Intensive English sequence. Applicants bust also take the SAT I, scoring 800, or the ACT, scoring 18.

Computers: On the main campus there are 30 PCs available for academic use in the computer lab, 2 labs with 5 PCs each in the residence halls, a music lab with Macs, an education lab with Macs, a math/science lab with 5 PCs, and an additional 14 PCs in the library. All are networked and have access to the Internet and the Web. All residence hall rooms are networked and Internet ready for students who bring their own PCs to campus. All students may access the system. There are no time limits. In a recent year, the fee was $4 per credit hour.

Graduates: In 2001, 170 bachelor's degrees were awarded. The most popular majors were elementary education (21%), business administration (12%), and psychology (8%). In an average class, 42% graduate in 6 years. 63 companies recruited on campus in 2000-2001.

Admissions Contact: Thomas Smith, Director of Admissions.
E-mail: *admissions@mobap.edu* Web: *www.mobap.edu*

MISSOURI SOUTHERN STATE COLLEGE — A-4
Joplin, MO 64801-1595 — (417) 782-6772
(800) 606-6772; Fax: (417) 659-4429

Full-time: 1721 men, 2142 women	**Faculty:** 203; IIB, -$
Part-time: 831 men, 1223 women	**Ph.D.s:** 61%
Graduate: none	**Student/Faculty:** 19 to 1
Year: semesters, summer session	**Tuition:** $2866 ($5566)
Application Deadline: August 21	**Room & Board:** $3800

Freshman Class: 1772 applied, 1399 accepted, 879 enrolled
ACT: 22 — **COMPETITIVE**

Missouri Southern State College, founded in 1937, is a public, primarily commuter institution offering undergraduate degree programs in the arts and sciences, business, education, psychology, and technology. International or global education is a distinctive theme of the college mission. There are 4 undergraduate schools. In addition to regional accreditation, MSSC has baccalaureate program accreditation with ABET, ACBSP, ADA, NCATE, NLN, and NAACLS. The library contains 427,068 volumes, 688,951 microform items, and 13,811 audiovisual forms/CDs, and subscribes to 1200 periodicals. Computerized library services include the card catalog, interlibrary loans, and database searching. Special learning facilities include a learning resource center, art gallery, radio station, TV station, biology pond, and child development center. The 334-acre campus is in a small town in the southwest corner of the state, 138 miles south of Kansas City. Including residence halls, there are 40 buildings.

Student Life: 87% of undergraduates are from Missouri. 91% are white. The average age of freshmen is 23; all undergraduates, 29. 27% of freshmen remain to graduate.

Housing: 750 students can be accommodated in college housing, which includes single-sex dormitories and on-campus apartments. On-campus housing is available on a first-come, first-served basis. 90% of students commute. Alcohol is not permitted. All students may keep cars.

Activities: 1% of men belong to 2 national fraternities; 1% of women belong to 2 national sororities. There are many groups and organizations on campus, including art, band, cheerleading, chess, choir, chorale, chorus, computers, dance, debate, drama, ethnic, film, forensics, gay, honors, international, jazz band, literary magazine, marching band, musical theater, newspaper, orchestra, pep band, photography, political, professional, radio and TV, religious, social, social service, student government, and symphony. Popular campus events include Spring Fling, Natural High, and Welcome Week.

Sports: Facilities include a 10,000-seat astroturf football stadium, a 4000-seat gym, a 4000-seat auditorium, a natatorium, a student life center, a black box theatre, a 3240-seat gym with a basketball court, a 6-lane 200-meter indoor track, a training and weight room, and chair-back seating on both sides of the gym.

Disabled Students: 99% of the campus is accessible. Wheelchair ramps, elevators, special parking, specially equipped rest rooms, special class scheduling, lowered drinking fountains, and lowered telephones are available.

Services: There is a reader service for the blind, and remedial math, reading, and writing. Assistance is also provided for improving time management and test-taking skills.

Campus Safety and Security: Measures include 24-hour foot and vehicle patrol, informal discussions, pamphlets/posters/films, and emergency telephones. There are lighted pathways/sidewalks.

Programs of Study: MSSC confers B.A., B.S., B.G.S., B.S.B.A., and B.S.E. degrees. Associate degrees are also awarded. Bachelor's degrees are awarded in BIOLOGICAL SCIENCE (biology/biological science, biotechnology, ecology, genetics, marine biology, and microbiology), BUSINESS (accounting, banking and finance, business administration and management, business economics, international business management, management information systems, management science, and marketing/retailing/merchandising), COMMUNICATIONS AND THE ARTS (art, communications, dramatic arts, English, fine arts, French, German, graphic design, music, Spanish, and speech/debate/rhetoric), COMPUTER AND PHYSICAL SCIENCE (chemistry, computer mathematics, computer science, information sciences and systems, mathematics, and physics), EDUCATION (art, business, drama, early childhood, elementary, English, foreign languages, health, mathematics, middle school, music, physical, reading, science, secondary, social science, social studies, and special), ENGINEERING AND ENVIRONMENTAL DESIGN (computer technology and manufacturing technology), HEALTH PROFESSIONS (environmental health science, medical laboratory technology, nursing, physical therapy, predentistry, premedicine, preoptometry, prepharmacy, and preveterinary science), SOCIAL SCIENCE (criminal justice, economics, history, international studies, liberal arts/general studies, political science/government, psychology, social science, social studies, and sociology). Preengineering/physical science is the strongest academically. Business, education, and criminal justice are the largest.

Required: General education requirements include a total of 51 credit hours, with 15 in basic studies, 12 each in science and cultural studies, 9 in humanities, and 3 in international studies. Students must also demonstrate proficiency in computer skills and writing. To graduate, students must complete at least 124 credit hours, including a minimum of 40 in the major, and present a minimum GPA of 2.0, 2.75 for the B.S.E.
Special: Students may study abroad at Oxford or Cambridge, England, as well as other countries. MSSC also offers internships in many majors, accelerated degree programs, a 3-2 engineering degree with the University of Missouri/Rolla, a general studies degree, and credit for life experience. Nondegree study is possible. There are 13 national honor societies, a freshman honors program, and 1 departmental honors program.
Faculty/Classroom: 61% of faculty are male; 39%, female. All teach undergraduates. The average class size in an introductory lecture is 24; in a laboratory, 18; and in a regular course, 15.
Admissions: 79% of the 2001-2002 applicants were accepted. The ACT scores for the 2001-2002 freshman class were: 45% below 21, 24% between 21 and 23, 18% between 24 and 26, 8% between 27 and 28, and 5% above 28. 32% of the current freshmen were in the top fifth of their class; 56% were in the top two fifths. 17 freshmen graduated first in their class.
Requirements: The ACT is required, with a minimum composite score of 18. Applicants must be graduates of accredited secondary schools or have earned a GED. The college requires completion of 16 Carnegie units in core courses for high school graduates. AP and CLEP credits are accepted. Advanced placement or honor courses are an important factor in the admission decision. Applications are accepted on computer disk and on-line at the school's web site.
Procedure: Freshmen are admitted to all sessions. Entrance exams should be taken during the junior or senior year of high school. There is a deferred admissions plan. Applications should be filed by August 21 for fall entry, January 15 for spring entry, and June 5 for summer entry. The fall 2001 application fee was $15. Notification is sent on a rolling basis.
Transfer: 425 transfer students enrolled in 2001-2002. Applicants must have a GPA of 2.0. They must be able to return to their previous college. 30 credits of 124 must be completed at MSSC.
Visiting: There are regularly scheduled orientations for prospective students, including a preenrollment tour during the summer. There are guides for informal visits and visitors may sit in on classes and stay overnight. To schedule a visit, contact the Admissions Office.
Financial Aid: In 2001-2002, 84% of all freshmen and 88% of continuing students received some form of financial aid. The FAFSA is required. The fall application deadline is August 1.
International Students: There are 111 international students enrolled. The school actively recruits these students. They must score 535 on the written TOEFL or take the MELAB and also take the ACT, scoring 18.
Computers: The mainframe is an ES/9000 with USE/ESA. There are 391 Windows 95/98/NT based PCs in open student labs equipped with Internet and productivity software. Also available are some 36 Macs equipped with productivity software, some with Internet capability. All students may access the system. There are no time limits. The fee is $20.
Graduates: In 2001, 607 bachelor's degrees were awarded. The most popular majors were education (27%), business (25%), and criminal justice (10%). In an average class, 10% graduate in 4 years, 24% in 5 years, and 29% in 6 years. 210 companies recruited on campus in 2000-2001. Of the 2000 graduating class, 10% were enrolled in graduate school within 6 months of graduation and 84% were employed.
Admissions Contact: Derek S. Skaggs, Director of Enrollment Services. E-mail: *admissions@mail.mssc.edu* Web: *http://www.mssc.edu*

MISSOURI VALLEY COLLEGE B-2

Marshall, MO 65340 **(660) 831-4157; Fax: (660) 831-4039**

Full-time: 790 men, 515 women	**Faculty:** 57
Part-time: 100 men, 160 women	**Ph.D.s:** 58%
Graduate: none	**Student/Faculty:** 23 to 1
Year: 4-1-4, summer session	**Tuition:** $12,400
Application Deadline: open	**Room & Board:** $5000
Freshman Class: n/av	
SAT I or ACT: required	**LESS COMPETITIVE**

Missouri Valley College, founded in 1889, is a private liberal arts college, affiliated with the Presbyterian Church (U.S.A.), offering 25 majors. Figures in the above capsule are approximate. The library contains 71,000 volumes, 1700 microform items, and 1100 audiovisual forms/CDs, and subscribes to 400 periodicals. Computerized library services include interlibrary loans and database searching. Special learning facilities include a learning resource center, radio station, and TV station. The 140-acre campus is in a small town 80 miles from Kansas City and 150 miles from St. Louis. Including residence halls, there are 17 buildings.
Student Life: 66% of undergraduates are from Missouri. Others are from 43 states, 9 foreign countries, and Canada. 75% are from public schools. 79% are white; 13% African American. 73% are Protestant; 20% Catholic. The average age of freshmen is 19; all undergraduates, 21. 25% do not continue beyond their first year; 20% remain to graduate.
Housing: 1100 students can be accommodated in college housing, which includes single-sex dormitories, on-campus apartments, married-student housing, fraternity houses, and sorority houses. In addition, there are honors houses and special-interest houses. On-campus housing is guaranteed for all 4 years. 81% of students live on campus; of those, 50% remain on campus on weekends. Alcohol is not permitted. All students may keep cars.
Activities: 30% of men belong to 4 national fraternities; 20% of women belong to 3 national sororities. There are 40 groups on campus, including art, band, cheerleading, choir, chorale, chorus, computers, dance, drama, drill team, ethnic, film, honors, international, jazz band, literary magazine, musical theater, newspaper, orchestra, pep band, photography, radio and TV, religious, SADD, social, social service, student government, symphony, and yearbook. Popular campus events include Springfest and Parents Weekend.
Sports: There are 8 intercollegiate sports for men and 7 for women, and 7 intramural sports for men and 7 for women. Facilities include a 2000-seat gym, tennis and basketball courts, football and soccer fields, a 1000-seat stadium, and horse stables.
Disabled Students: 20% of the campus is accessible. Wheelchair ramps, elevators, special parking, specially equipped rest rooms, special class scheduling, and lowered drinking fountains are available.
Services: Counseling and information services are available, as is tutoring in most subjects. There is remedial math, reading, and writing.
Campus Safety and Security: Measures include escort service, informal discussions, pamphlets/posters/films, and emergency telephones. There are lighted pathways/sidewalks and 5 P.M. to 3 A.M. foot and vehicle patrol.
Programs of Study: MVC confers B.A. and B.S. degrees. Associate degrees are also awarded. Bachelor's degrees are awarded in AGRICULTURE (agricultural business management), BIOLOGICAL SCIENCE (biology/biological science), BUSINESS (accounting, business administration and management, and recreational facilities management), COMMUNICATIONS AND THE ARTS (art, communications, dramatic arts, English, and speech/debate/rhetoric), COMPUTER AND PHYSICAL SCIENCE (actuarial science, information sciences and systems, and mathematics), EDUCATION (elementary, physical, and social studies), HEALTH PROFESSIONS (exercise science), SOCIAL SCIENCE (addiction studies, criminal justice, economics, history, human services, liberal arts/general studies, philosophy, political science/government, psychology, public administration, religion, and sociology). Education is the strongest academically. Business administration, phys ed, and psychology are the largest.
Required: All students must complete 128 credit hours, including 35 to 40 hours in their major, with a GPA of at least 2.0. Distribution requirements include the 40-hour core curriculum of English, phys ed, math, fine arts, and science. A computer course is strongly recommended. All students must complete a senior assessment.
Special: Accelerated degree programs, internships, work-study, co-op programs, nondegree study, and pass/fail options are available. There are 3 national honor societies and 3 departmental honors programs.
Faculty/Classroom: 73% of faculty are male; 27%, female. All teach undergraduates. The average class size in an introductory lecture is 30; in a laboratory, 25; and in a regular course, 28.
Admissions: There were 5 National Merit semifinalists in a recent year.
Requirements: The SAT I or ACT is required. In addition, students must have graduated from an accredited secondary school or have the GED. Applications are accepted on-line. AP and CLEP credits are accepted. Important factors in the admissions decision are advanced placement or honor courses, evidence of special talent, and extracurricular activities record.
Procedure: Freshmen are admitted to all sessions. Entrance exams should be taken as early as possible. Application deadlines are open. Notification is rolling. The application fee is $10.
Transfer: 158 transfer students enrolled in a recent year. A minimum GPA of 2.0 is recommended; D grades do not transfer. 30 credits of 128 must be completed at MVC.
Visiting: There are regularly scheduled orientations for prospective students, including jump-start days in the summer and registration days during the school year. There are guides for informal visits and visitors may sit in on classes and stay overnight. To schedule a visit, contact the Admission Coordinator at (660) 831-4114.
Financial Aid: In a recent year, most freshmen and all continuing students received some form of financial aid. 70% of freshmen received need-based aid. The average freshman award was $8000. Of that total, scholarships or need-based grants averaged $10,000 ($12,000 maximum); loans averaged $2120 ($5500 maximum); and work contracts averaged $1500. 80% of undergraduates work part time. Average annual earnings from campus work are $1500. The average financial indebtedness of a recent graduate was $10,000. MVC is a member of CSS. The FAFSA is required. Check with the school for current deadlines.
International Students: The school actively recruits these students. They must take the TOEFL and also take the SAT I or the ACT.

Computers: 150 PCs and Macs are available on campus. Free access to the Internet is available to students on 25 computers in the library. All students may access the system. There are no time limits and no fees. It is strongly recommended that all students have a personal computer.

Graduates: In a recent year, 154 bachelor's degrees were awarded. The most popular majors were business (16%), education (13%), and human services (12%). In an average class, 2% graduate in 3 years, 20% in 4 years, and 25% in 5 years. Of a recent graduating class, 15% were enrolled in graduate school within 6 months of graduation and 80% were employed.

Admissions Contact: Jamie L. Gold-Naylor, Director of Admissions. E-mail: *naylorj@moval.edu* Web: *www.moval.edu*

MISSOURI WESTERN STATE COLLEGE — A-2

St. Joseph, MO 64507 — (816) 271-4266
(800) 662-7041; Fax: (816) 271-5833

Full-time: 1563 men, 2351 women	**Faculty:** 190; IIB, -$
Part-time: 439 men, 749 women	**Ph.D.s:** 71%
Graduate: none	**Student/Faculty:** 21 to 1
Year: semesters, summer session	**Tuition:** $3224 ($5690)
Application Deadline: July 25	**Room & Board:** $3638

Freshman Class: 2453 applied, 2453 accepted, 1176 enrolled
ACT: 19 — **NONCOMPETITIVE**

Missouri Western State College, founded in 1915, is a public institution offering undergraduate degrees in the arts and sciences, business administration, education, nursing, technology, and social work. There are 2 undergraduate schools. In addition to regional accreditation, MWSC has baccalaureate program accreditation with ABET, CSWE, NASM, NCATE, and NLN. The library contains 207,383 volumes, 111,544 microform items, and 16,024 audiovisual forms/CDs, and subscribes to 1504 periodicals. Computerized library services include the card catalog, interlibrary loans, and database searching. Special learning facilities include a learning resource center, planetarium, and a biology nature study area. The 740-acre campus is in a suburban area 50 miles north of Kansas City. Including residence halls, there are 15 buildings.

Student Life: 90% of undergraduates are from Missouri. Others are from 35 states, 10 foreign countries, and Canada. 88% are white. The average age of freshmen is 20; all undergraduates, 25. 44% do not continue beyond their first year.

Housing: 1050 students can be accommodated in college housing, which includes single-sex and coed dormitories and on-campus apartments. On-campus housing is available on a first-come, first-served basis. 80% of students commute. Alcohol is not permitted. All students may keep cars.

Activities: 7% of men belong to 5 national fraternities; 3% of women belong to 7 national sororities. There are 51 groups on campus, including art, band, cheerleading, choir, dance, drama, drill team, ethnic, honors, international, jazz band, marching band, musical theater, newspaper, pep band, political, professional, religious, social, social service, student government, symphony, and yearbook. Popular campus events include Spring Fest, Fall Convocation, and Family Day.

Sports: There are 4 intercollegiate sports for men and 4 for women, and 20 intramural sports for men and 20 for women. Facilities include tennis and racquetball courts, a 6000-seat football stadium, a 468-seat auditorium, a swimming pool, a jogging/walking trail, a fitness center, baseball and softball fields, a trapshooting range, a volleyball area, a track, and 2 gyms, the larger seating 4000.

Disabled Students: Nearly all of the campus is accessible. Wheelchair ramps, elevators, special parking, specially equipped rest rooms, lowered drinking fountains, and lowered telephones are available.

Services: Counseling and information services are available, as is tutoring in some subjects. There is a reader service for the blind, and remedial math, reading, and writing.

Campus Safety and Security: Measures include 24-hour foot and vehicle patrol, self-defense education, escort service, and informal discussions. There are pamphlets/posters/films, emergency telephones, and lighted pathways/sidewalks.

Programs of Study: MWSC confers B.A., B.S., B.I.S., B.S.B.A., B.S.E., B.S.N., B.S.T., and B.S.W. degrees. Associate degrees are also awarded. Bachelor's degrees are awarded in BIOLOGICAL SCIENCE (biology/biological science), BUSINESS (accounting, business administration and management, and marketing/retailing/merchandising), COMMUNICATIONS AND THE ARTS (communications, English, fine arts, French, music, Spanish, and speech/debate/rhetoric), COMPUTER AND PHYSICAL SCIENCE (chemistry, computer programming, computer science, information sciences and systems, mathematics, and natural sciences), EDUCATION (art, early childhood, elementary, foreign languages, middle school, music, and secondary), ENGINEERING AND ENVIRONMENTAL DESIGN (commercial art and engineering technology), HEALTH PROFESSIONS (medical laboratory technology and nursing), SOCIAL SCIENCE (criminal justice, economics, history, parks and recreation management, political science/government, psychology, and social work). Physical sciences is the strongest academically. Education, nursing, and criminal justice are the largest.

Required: The core curriculum consists of 12 credit hours of basic skills (English composition, algebra, and speech), 9 to 10 of humanities, 9 of social sciences, 8 to 10 of natural sciences, and 4 of physical health. To graduate, students must complete at least 124 credit hours, including 45 to 71 in the major, with a minimum GPA of 2.0.

Special: MWSC offers internships, work-study programs with local employers, dual majors, a 3-2 engineering degree program with the University of Missouri/Rolla, credit for life experience, pass/fail options, and nondegree study. There are 6 national honor societies, a freshman honors program, and 12 departmental honors program.

Faculty/Classroom: 63% of faculty are male; 37%, female. All teach undergraduates. The average class size in an introductory lecture is 35; in a laboratory, 25; and in a regular course, 25.

Admissions: All of the 2001-2002 applicants were accepted. The ACT scores for the 2001-2002 freshman class were: 63% below 21, 21% between 21 and 23, 11% between 24 and 26, 3% between 27 and 28, and 2% above 28. 20% of the current freshmen were in the top fifth of their class; 46% were in the top two fifths. 11 freshmen graduated first in their class.

Requirements: The ACT is required. In addition, applicants must be graduates of an accredited secondary school or have earned a GED. AP and CLEP credits are accepted.

Procedure: Freshmen are admitted to all sessions. Entrance exams should be taken at least 6 months prior to enrollment. Applications should be filed by July 25 for fall entry, December 20 for spring entry, and May 15 for summer entry, along with a $15 fee. The college accepts all applicants.

Transfer: 303 transfer students enrolled in 2001-2002. The required GPA depends on the number of credit hours completed, but a minimum of 2.0 is standard. 30 credits of 124 must be completed at MWSC.

Visiting: There are regularly scheduled orientations for prospective students. There are guides for informal visits. To schedule a visit, contact the Admissions Office at *admissn@mwsc.edu*

Financial Aid: In a recent year, 75% of all freshmen and 85% of continuing students received some form of financial aid. 70% of freshmen and 80% of continuing students received need-based aid. The average freshman award was $3566. Of that total, scholarships or need-based grants averaged $3000; and loans averaged $2746. 69% of undergraduates work part time. Average annual earnings from campus work are $1900. The FAFSA is required. The fall application deadline is March 1.

International Students: There are 15 international students enrolled. They must score 500 on the written TOEFL and also take the ACT.

Computers: The mainframes are an HP 3000/ Models 58 and 42/ and an IBM RISC/6000 UNIX system. About 250 PCs are available, most in departmental labs and nearly 50 in other areas for general student access. About 30 terminals are also available. Students have access to E-mail and to the Internet system. A computer lab is located in the residence complex. All students may access the system. There are no time limits. All students are charged $2 per credit hour (maximum of $24 per semester) for computer use. This fee is included in the required fees.

Graduates: In 2001, 712 bachelor's degrees were awarded. The most popular majors were management (15%), criminal justice (15%), and elementary education (7%). In an average class, 12% graduate in 4 years, 24% in 5 years, and 29% in 6 years. Of the 2000 graduating class, 20% were enrolled in graduate school within 6 months of graduation and 90% were employed.

Admissions Contact: Howard McCauley, Director of Admissions. A video is available. E-mail: *admissn@mwsc.edu* Web: *www.mwsc.edu*

NORTHWEST MISSOURI STATE UNIVERSITY — A-1

Maryville, MO 64468 — (660) 562-1595
(800) 633-1175; Fax: (660) 562-1121

Full-time: 2184 men, 2772 women	**Faculty:** 244; IIA, --$
Part-time: 290 men, 354 women	**Ph.D.s:** 71%
Graduate: 285 men, 735 women	**Student/Faculty:** 20 to 1
Year: trimesters, summer session	**Tuition:** $3600 ($6068)
Application Deadline: open	**Room & Board:** $4322

Freshman Class: 3573 applied, 2285 accepted, 1197 enrolled
SAT I or ACT: required — **LESS COMPETITIVE**

Northwest Missouri State University, founded in 1905, is a public institution offering undergraduate courses in agriculture, science, arts and humanities, business, government, computer science, and education. There are 3 undergraduate schools and 1 graduate school. In addition to regional accreditation, Northwest has baccalaureate program accreditation with ADA, AHEA, NASM, and NCATE. The library contains 286,302 volumes, 15,864 microform items, and 1937 audiovisual forms/CDs, and subscribes to 3411 periodicals. Computerized library services include the card catalog, interlibrary loans, and database searching. Special learning facilities include a learning resource center, art gallery, radio station, TV station, and a model elementary library collection with curriculum materials for grades K-6. The 240-acre campus is in a rural area

90 miles north of Kansas City. Including residence halls, there are 33 buildings.

Student Life: 66% of undergraduates are from Missouri. Others are from 41 states, 23 foreign countries, and Canada. 95% are from public schools. 93% are white. The average age of freshmen is 19; all undergraduates, 21. 35% do not continue beyond their first year; 40% remain to graduate.

Housing: 2800 students can be accommodated in college housing, which includes single-sex and coed dormitories and sorority houses. On-campus housing is guaranteed for all 4 years. 51% of students live on campus; of those, 65% remain on campus on weekends. Alcohol is not permitted. All students may keep cars.

Activities: 10% of men belong to 9 national fraternities; 10% of women belong to 5 national sororities. There are 162 groups on campus, including band, cheerleading, choir, chorale, chorus, computers, drama, drill team, drum and bugle corps, ethnic, international, jazz band, literary magazine, marching band, newspaper, pep band, photography, political, professional, radio and TV, religious, social, student government, and yearbook. Popular campus events include Tower Dance, Black Awareness Week, and Greek Week.

Sports: There are 6 intercollegiate sports for men and 5 for women, and 35 intramural sports for men and 35 for women. Facilities include a 7000-seat stadium, a 3000-seat basketball arena, 3 gyms, 4 racquetball courts, a weight-lifting area, volleyball and tennis courts, dance areas, and an aquatic center with 2 pools.

Disabled Students: 90% of the campus is accessible. Wheelchair ramps, elevators, special parking, specially equipped rest rooms, special class scheduling, lowered drinking fountains, and lowered telephones are available.

Services: Counseling and information services are available, as is tutoring in most subjects. There is a reader service for the blind, and remedial math, reading, and writing.

Campus Safety and Security: Measures include 24-hour foot and vehicle patrol, escort service, informal discussions, and pamphlets/posters/films. There are lighted pathways/sidewalks.

Programs of Study: Northwest confers B.A., B.S., B.F.A., B.S.Ed., B.S.Med.Tech., and B.Tech. degrees. Master's degrees are also awarded. Bachelor's degrees are awarded in AGRICULTURE (agricultural business management, agricultural mechanics, agriculture, agronomy, animal science, conservation and regulation, forestry and related sciences, horticulture, and wildlife management), BIOLOGICAL SCIENCE (biology/biological science, botany, and zoology), BUSINESS (accounting, banking and finance, business administration and management, business economics, international business management, marketing/retailing/merchandising, personnel management, and recreation and leisure services), COMMUNICATIONS AND THE ARTS (advertising, art, broadcasting, communications, dramatic arts, English, fine arts, French, journalism, music, public relations, Spanish, and speech/debate/rhetoric), COMPUTER AND PHYSICAL SCIENCE (chemistry, computer management, computer science, earth science, geology, information sciences and systems, mathematics, physics, science, and statistics), EDUCATION (agricultural, art, business, early childhood, education of the mentally handicapped, elementary, mathematics, middle school, music, physical, recreation, science, secondary, special, and specific learning disabilities), ENGINEERING AND ENVIRONMENTAL DESIGN (preengineering), HEALTH PROFESSIONS (predentistry, premedicine, prepharmacy, and preveterinary science), SOCIAL SCIENCE (child care/child and family studies, clothing and textiles management/production/services, economics, family/consumer resource management, food science, geography, history, home economics, humanities, industrial and organizational psychology, philosophy, political science/government, prelaw, psychology, public administration, social science, sociology, and textiles and clothing). Education, mass communications, and agriculture are the strongest academically.

Required: All students must maintain a minimum GPA of 2.0 while taking at least 124 credit hours. Distribution requirements include 9 hours each in social science and humanities, 8 in natural science, 6 in composition, 4 each in math and phys ed, 3 each in oral communications and behavioral sciences, and 1 in the freshman seminar.

Special: Co-op programs with the University of Missouri/Rolla, cross-registration with Missouri Western State College, campuswide internships, study abroad in England and Mexico, and a Washington semester are available. Work-study programs, student-designed majors, a 3-2 engineering degree with the University of Missouri/Rolla, credit for military experience, nondegree study, and pass/fail options are possible. There are 3 national honor societies.

Faculty/Classroom: 61% of faculty are male; 39%, female. All teach undergraduates. No introductory courses are taught by graduate students. The average class size in an introductory lecture is 40; in a laboratory, 20; and in a regular course, 24.

Admissions: 64% of the 2001-2002 applicants were accepted. The ACT scores for the 2001-2002 freshman class were: 33% below 21, 32% between 21 and 23, 21% between 24 and 26, 8% between 27 and 28, and 5% above 28. 43% of the current freshmen were in the top fifth of their class; 78% were in the top two fifths.

Requirements: The SAT I or ACT is required, with a minimum composite score of 970 on the SAT I or 21 on the ACT; if scores are below those levels, a combined percentile index obtained from the SAT I or ACT score and high school rank will be used. Northwest requires applicants to be in the upper 50% of their class. A GPA of 2.0 is required. AP and CLEP credits are accepted. Important factors in the admissions decision are evidence of special talent, leadership record, and recommendations by alumni. Applications are accepted on-line via CollegeLink.

Procedure: Freshmen are admitted fall, spring, and summer. Entrance exams should be taken in the fall of the senior year. Application deadlines are open. The fall 2001 application fee was $15. Notification is sent on a rolling basis.

Transfer: 360 transfer students enrolled in 2001-2002. Applicants must present a minimum GPA of 2.0. 30 credits of 124 must be completed at Northwest.

Visiting: There are regularly scheduled orientations for prospective students. There are guides for informal visits and visitors may sit in on classes and stay overnight. To schedule a visit, contact the Mable Cook Admissions and Visitors Center at (660) 562-1562.

Financial Aid: In 2001-2002, 81% of all freshmen and 69% of continuing students received some form of financial aid. 56% of freshmen and 63% of continuing students received need-based aid. The average freshman award was $5234. Of that total, scholarships or need-based grants averaged $1234 ($3000 maximum); loans averaged $3000 ($6000 maximum); and work contracts averaged $1000 ($2000 maximum). 50% of undergraduates work part time. Average annual earnings from campus work are $1138. The average financial indebtedness of the 2001 graduate was $15,144. The FAFSA is required.

International Students: There are 196 international students enrolled. They must score 500 on the written TOEFL.

Computers: The mainframe are 10 clustered DEC VAX computers. Students may access the mainframe from more than 3400 PCs and notebook computers located in residence halls, the library, and labs. Students may also use the networks available to access libraries, campuses, and computers located around the country. All students may access the system 24 hours daily. There are no time limits and no fees. It is strongly recommended that all students have a personal computer.

Graduates: In 2001, 977 bachelor's degrees were awarded. The most popular majors were education (24%), business marketing (21%), and social science history (10%).

Admissions Contact: Shari Morley, Associate Director, Admissions. A video is available. E-mail: *bevs@mail.nwmissour.edu*
Web: *www.nwmissouri.edu*

PARK UNIVERSITY — A-2

Parkville, MO 64152-9974 — (816) 584-6215
(800) 745-7275; Fax: (816) 741-4462

Full-time: 351 men, 598 women	**Faculty:** 54; IIB, --$
Part-time: 4420 men, 3893 women	**Ph.D.s:** 54%
Graduate: 90 men, 130 women	**Student/Faculty:** 18 to 1
Year: semesters, summer session	**Tuition:** $4816
Application Deadline: August 15	**Room & Board:** $5000

Freshman Class: 405 applied, 274 accepted, 141 enrolled
ACT: 19 — **COMPETITIVE**

Park University, formerly Park College, founded in 1875, is a private institution offering degree programs in the humanities, performing arts, natural and life sciences, and social and administrative sciences. There are 2 undergraduate and 3 graduate schools. In addition to regional accreditation, Park has baccalaureate program accreditation with NLN. The library contains 141,870 volumes, 195,530 microform items, and 670 audiovisual forms/CDs, and subscribes to 775 periodicals. Computerized library services include the card catalog, interlibrary loans, and database searching. Special learning facilities include a learning resource center, art gallery, radio station, and TV station. The 800-acre campus is in a suburban area 12 miles north of Kansas City. Including residence halls, there are 17 buildings.

Student Life: 80% of undergraduates are from Missouri. Others are from 37 states, 58 foreign countries, and Canada. 80% are from public schools. 61% are white; 21% African American; 14% Hispanic. Most are claim no religious affiliation. The average age of freshmen is 18; all undergraduates, 33. 27% do not continue beyond their first year; 34% remain to graduate.

Housing: 226 students can be accommodated in college housing, which includes coed dormitories and on-campus apartments. On-campus housing is guaranteed for all 4 years. 98% of students commute. Alcohol is not permitted. All students may keep cars.

Activities: There are no fraternities or sororities. There are 30 groups on campus, including art, cheerleading, choir, computers, drama, ethnic, honors, international, literary magazine, newspaper, outdoor, photography, political, professional, radio and TV, religious, social, social service, student government, symphony, and yearbook. Popular campus events include Fall Harvest Festival, Spring Fling, and International Week.

Sports: There are 6 intercollegiate sports for men and 6 for women, and 3 intramural sports for men and 3 for women. Facilities include an 800-seat indoor gym with basketball and volleyball courts, a 350-seat indoor gym with basketball and volleyball courts, an all-weather outdoor track, soccer and softball fields, a sports medicine room, 4 tennis courts, and an outdoor sand volleyball and basketball court.

Disabled Students: 95% of the campus is accessible. Wheelchair ramps, elevators, special parking, specially equipped rest rooms, special class scheduling, and lowered drinking fountains are available.

Services: Counseling and information services are available, as is tutoring in most subjects. There is a reader service for the blind, and remedial math, reading, and writing.

Campus Safety and Security: Measures include 24-hour foot and vehicle patrol, escort service, informal discussions, and pamphlets/posters/films. There are lighted pathways/sidewalks.

Programs of Study: Park confers B.A., B.S., and B.P.A. degrees. Associate and master's degrees are also awarded. Bachelor's degrees are awarded in BIOLOGICAL SCIENCE (biology/biological science), BUSINESS (accounting, banking and finance, business administration and management, business economics, human resources, management information systems, and marketing management), COMMUNICATIONS AND THE ARTS (communications, English, fine arts, graphic design, public relations, and Spanish), COMPUTER AND PHYSICAL SCIENCE (chemistry, computer science, information sciences and systems, mathematics, and natural sciences), EDUCATION (athletic training, early childhood, and elementary), ENGINEERING AND ENVIRONMENTAL DESIGN (aviation administration/management, engineering management, and interior design), HEALTH PROFESSIONS (health care administration), SOCIAL SCIENCE (child care/child and family studies, criminal justice, economics, fire protection, history, human services, law, liberal arts/general studies, political science/government, psychology, public administration, social psychology, sociology, and systems science). Management information systems, management, and human resources are the largest.

Required: All students must complete core requirements, including 3 semesters of English composition, and 1 of algebra, as well as 1 science course. They must also complete 24 to 27 hours of general education courses and 9 hours of Liberal Learning courses. Of the 120 credit hours needed for the bachelor's degree, 45 must be completed in upper-division work and 30 to 60 in the major, with a minimum GPA of 2.0.

Special: Cross-registration is available through a Kansas City consortium, and study abroad is possible through other schools. The college also offers internships in most majors, work-study programs with local companies, a Washington semester, credit for life and military experience, pass/fail options, and nondegree study. An accelerated degree program is offered in some majors. There are 2 national honor societies, and a freshman honors program.

Faculty/Classroom: 69% of faculty are male; 31%, female. All teach undergraduates and 80% do research. No introductory courses are taught by graduate students. The average class size in an introductory lecture is 20; in a laboratory, 10; and in a regular course, 15.

Admissions: 68% of the 2001-2002 applicants were accepted. The ACT scores for the 2001-2002 freshman class were: 73% below 21, 13% between 21 and 23, 10% between 24 and 26, 2% between 27 and 28, and 1% above 28. 33% of the current freshmen were in the top fifth of their class; 54% were in the top two fifths. 3 freshmen graduated first in their class.

Requirements: The SAT I or ACT is required. In addition, the GED is accepted with a minimum total score of 225 and no area less than 35. Park requires applicants to be in the upper 50% of their class. A GPA of 2.0 is required. AP and CLEP credits are accepted. Important factors in the admissions decision are advanced placement or honor courses, leadership record, and extracurricular activities record. Applications are accepted on-line through the school's web site.

Procedure: Freshmen are admitted fall, spring, and summer. Entrance exams should be taken during the junior year or early in the senior year. There is an early admissions plan. Applications should be filed by August 15 for fall entry and December 15 for spring entry. The fall 2001 application fee was $25. Notification is sent on a rolling basis.

Transfer: 2052 transfer students enrolled in 2001-2002. The college requires a GPA of at least 2.0. A minimum ACT composite score of 20 is recommended, but is waived for students age 25 or older. 24 credits of 120 must be completed at Park.

Visiting: There are regularly scheduled orientations for prospective students, including a campus tour, lunch, an information session with a student panel, sessions on admissions, scholarships, and financial aid, and a chance to attend a class and meet with a faculty member. There are guides for informal visits and visitors may sit in on classes and stay overnight. To schedule a visit, contact Dr. Ron Carruth, Director of Student Recruiting.

Financial Aid: The average freshman award was $5130. Of that total, scholarships or need-based grants averaged $2500 ($10,500 maximum); loans averaged $2625 (maximum); and work contracts averaged $1000 (maximum). 85% of undergraduates work part time. Average annual earnings from campus work are $1000. The average financial indebtedness of the 2001 graduate was $10,000. The FAFSA and the college's own financial statement are required. The fall application deadline is April 1.

International Students: The school actively recruits these students. They must score 500 on the written TOEFL.

Computers: The mainframe is an HP 9000/Series 857. There are also 135 PCs available for student use with access to the Internet mostly in academic buildings, dorms, the library, and computer labs;~ 80 are in a lab environment with access to the Internet. All students may access the system Monday through Thursday, 8 A.M. to 11 P.M.; Friday, 8 A.M. to 5 p.m; Saturday, 10 A.M. to 5 P.M.; Sunday, 12 noon to 5 P.M. There are no time limits and no fees.

Graduates: In 2001, 1983 bachelor's degrees were awarded. The most popular majors were management (19%), human resources (15%), and management information systems (13%). In an average class, 2% graduate in 3 years, 20% in 4 years, and 36% in 5 years. 15 companies recruited on campus in 2000-2001. Of the 2000 graduating class, 9% were enrolled in graduate school within 6 months of graduation and 94% were employed.

Admissions Contact: Dr. Ron Carruth, Director of Student Recruiting. E-mail: *admissions@mail.park.edu* Web: *www.park.edu*

RESEARCH COLLEGE OF NURSING — A-2

Kansas City, MO 64132 — (816) 501-4654
(800) 842-6776; Fax: (816) 501-4241

Full-time: 13 men, 134 women	**Faculty:** 33
Part-time: 1 man, 4 women	**Ph.D.s:** 23%
Graduate: 1 man, 10 women	**Student/Faculty:** 4 to 1
Year: semesters, summer session	**Tuition:** $15,390
Application Deadline: June 30	**Room & Board:** $4920

Freshman Class: 66 applied, 53 accepted, 14 enrolled
ACT: 22 — **SPECIAL**

Research College of Nursing, founded in 1980, is a private college of nursing affiliated with Rockhurst University of Kansas City, a Jesuit-run, 25-acre liberal arts college with an enrollment of about 1500 undergraduates. Located on the campus of the Research Medical Center, the Research College of Nursing offers classes on its home campus, on the Rockhurst campus, and in a variety of health-related settings in the Kansas City area. In addition to regional accreditation, Research College has baccalaureate program accreditation with NLN and and AACN. The library contains 109,000 volumes, 150,000 microform items, and 1100 audiovisual forms/CDs, and subscribes to 700 periodicals. Computerized library services include the card catalog, interlibrary loans, and database searching. Special learning facilities include a learning resource center, art gallery, and radio station. The campus is in an urban area in Kansas City. Including residence halls, there are 3 buildings.

Student Life: 90% of undergraduates are from Missouri. Others are from 6 states and 1 foreign country. 55% are from public schools. 79% are white. 45% are Catholic; 17% Protestant. The average age of freshmen is 18; all undergraduates, 22. 30% do not continue beyond their first year; 63% remain to graduate.

Housing: 815 students can be accommodated in college housing, which includes single-sex and coed dormitories, on-campus apartments, married-student housing, and fraternity houses. In addition, there are special-interest houses. On-campus housing is guaranteed for all 4 years. 65% of students live on campus; of those, 60% remain on campus on weekends. All students may keep cars.

Activities: 27% of men belong to 4 national fraternities; 12% of women belong to 2 national sororities. There are 35 groups on campus, including art, cheerleading, chess, choir, chorus, computers, drama, drill team, ethnic, honors, international, literary magazine, musical theater, newspaper, political, professional, radio and TV, religious, social, social service, student government, and yearbook. Popular campus events include Mass of the Holy Spirit.

Sports: There are 6 intercollegiate sports for men and 5 for women, and 30 intramural sports for men and 30 for women. Facilities include a gym, an exercise facility, a fitness center, and racquetball courts.

Disabled Students: 80% of the campus is accessible. Wheelchair ramps, elevators, special parking, specially equipped rest rooms, lowered drinking fountains, and lowered telephones are available.

Services: Counseling and information services are available, as is tutoring in some subjects, including primarily freshman-and sophomore-level courses. There is remedial writing. The learning center offers assistance with college writing tasks and study strategies.

Campus Safety and Security: Measures include 24-hour foot and vehicle patrol, escort service, informal discussions, and emergency telephones. There are lighted pathways/sidewalks.

Programs of Study: Research College confers the B.S.N. degree. Master's degrees are also awarded. Bachelor's degrees are awarded in HEALTH PROFESSIONS (nursing).

Required: To earn the B.S.N., students must complete a total of 128 semester hours, with 66 in liberal arts and sciences and 62 in the nursing

major. A 2.25 GPA overall and in all nursing course work is required to graduate.
Special: Work-study, co-op, and accelerated degree programs, study abroad in 7 countries, and a Washington semester are available. There is a chapter of Phi Beta Kappa and a freshman honors program.
Faculty/Classroom: 2% of faculty are male; 98%, female. All teach undergraduates. No introductory courses are taught by graduate students. The average class size in an introductory lecture is 55 and in a laboratory, 8.
Admissions: 80% of the 2001-2002 applicants were accepted. The ACT scores for the 2001-2002 freshman class were: 23% below 21, 46% between 21 and 23, and 31% between 24 and 26. 33% of the current freshmen were in the top fifth of their class; 67% were in the top two fifths.
Requirements: The ACT is required, with a minimum composite score of 20 on each area. A minimum score of 960 on the SAT I may be substituted. Applicants should graduate from an accredited secondary school or have the GED. Applicants must be in the upper 50% of their class, and a GPA of 2.0 is required. An interview is recommended. Applicants should have completed 3 years of high school math, including algebra II, 3 years of English, and 2 years of science, including chemistry. AP and CLEP credits are accepted. Important factors in the admissions decision are advanced placement or honor courses, recommendations by school officials, and leadership record.
Procedure: Freshmen are admitted to all sessions. Entrance exams should be taken during the junior or senior year of high school. There is a deferred admissions plan. Applications should be filed by June 30 for fall entry, along with a $20 fee. Notification is sent on a rolling basis.
Transfer: 15 transfer students enrolled in 2001-2002. A minimum GPA of 2.5 is required to interview for the Research/Rockhurst Joint B.S.N. Program. Students must complete the sophomore-level nursing course before entering the junior-level clinical; this course is offered only in the spring. Admission requires an interview along with all official transcripts. Admission for transfers is very limited. 30 credits of 128 must be completed at Research College.
Visiting: There are regularly scheduled orientations for prospective students. There is 1 senior visit weekend in November and 1 in February. There are guides for informal visits and visitors may sit in on classes and stay overnight. To schedule a visit, contact the Admission and Financial Aid Office at (800) 842-6776 or (816) 502-4100 or *marisa.ferrara@rockhurst.edu*
Financial Aid: 29% of undergraduates work part time. Average annual earnings from campus work are $1500. Research College is a member of CSS. The FAFSA is required. The fall application deadline is April 1.
International Students: There is 1 international student enrolled. They must score 550 on the written TOEFL and also score 900 on the SAT I or 20 on the ACT.
Computers: The mainframe is a DEC VAX 8530. Computers are available for student use in all academic buildings and the library. All students may access the system. There are no time limits and no fees.
Admissions Contact: Marisa Ferrara, Admission Counselor.
E-mail: *marisa.ferrara@rockhurst.edu* Web: *www.researchcollege.edu*

ROCKHURST UNIVERSITY — A-2
Kansas City, MO 64110-2561 — **(816) 501-4100**
(800) 842-6776; Fax: (816) 501-4241

Full-time: 567 men, 647 women	**Faculty:** 131; IIB, av$
Part-time: 319 men, 478 women	**Ph.D.s:** 76%
Graduate: 364 men, 355 women	**Student/Faculty:** 9 to 1
Year: semesters, summer session	**Tuition:** $15,140
Application Deadline: June 30	**Room & Board:** $4950
Freshman Class: n/av	
SAT I or ACT: required	**COMPETITIVE**

Rockhurst University, founded in 1910, is a comprehensive, Catholic Jesuit institution that offers undergraduate programs in the arts and sciences, education, nursing, and business. There are 4 undergraduate and 2 graduate schools. In addition to regional accreditation, Rockhurst has baccalaureate program accreditation with APTA, CAHEA, and NLN. The library contains 305,200 volumes, 223,100 microform items, and 3339 audiovisual forms/CDs, and subscribes to 765 periodicals. Computerized library services include the card catalog, interlibrary loans, and database searching. Special learning facilities include a learning resource center, art gallery, radio station, and and multimedia classrooms. The 55-acre campus is in an urban area in Kansas City. Including residence halls, there are 19 buildings.
Student Life: 67% of undergraduates are from Missouri. Others are from 22 states, 24 foreign countries, and Canada. 58% are from public schools. 82% are white. 54% are Catholic; 23% Protestant; 21% claim no religious affiliation. The average age of freshmen is 18; all undergraduates, 21. 18% do not continue beyond their first year; 66% remain to graduate.
Housing: 815 students can be accommodated in college housing, which includes single-sex and coed dormitories and on-campus apartments. On-campus housing is available on a first come, first served basis. Priority is given to out-of-town students. 53% of students live on campus; of those, 45% remain on campus on weekends. All students may keep cars.
Activities: 17% of men belong to 3 national fraternities; 17% of women belong to 2 national sororities. There are 55 groups on campus, including art, cheerleading, choir, chorale, chorus, computers, drama, ethnic, honors, international, literary magazine, musical theater, newspaper, photography, political, professional, radio and TV, religious, social, social service, student government, and yearbook. Popular campus events include fraternity socials, coffee house events, and Rockstock (live bands).
Sports: There are 5 intercollegiate sports for men and 5 for women, and 12 intramural sports for men and 12 for women. Facilities include athletic and soccer fields; tennis, handball, racquetball, badminton, basketball, and volleyball courts; a weight and exercise room, and gymnastics facilities.
Disabled Students: 80% of the campus is accessible. Wheelchair ramps, elevators, special parking, specially equipped rest rooms, and lowered drinking fountains and telephones are available.
Services: Counseling and information services are available, as is tutoring in some subjects, including primarily freshman- and sophomore-level courses. The Learning Center offers tutoring in many subjects, assistance with any college writing task, and study strategies.
Campus Safety and Security: Measures include 24-hour foot and vehicle patrol, self-defense education, escort service, and shuttle buses. There are informal discussions, pamphlets/posters/films, emergency telephones, lighted pathways/sidewalks, and formal presentations, and a full in-house security program geared toward integration of security into the overall campus operation.
Programs of Study: Rockhurst confers B.A., B.S., B.L.S., B.P.S., B.S.B.A., and B.S.N. degrees. Master's degrees are also awarded. Bachelor's degrees are awarded in BIOLOGICAL SCIENCE (biology/biological science), BUSINESS (accounting, banking and finance, business administration and management, business economics, human resources, institutional management, management information systems, management science, marketing/retailing/merchandising, and personnel management), COMMUNICATIONS AND THE ARTS (communications, dramatic arts, English, French, and Spanish), COMPUTER AND PHYSICAL SCIENCE (chemistry, computer science, information sciences and systems, mathematics, and physics), EDUCATION (elementary, foreign languages, and secondary), ENGINEERING AND ENVIRONMENTAL DESIGN (computer technology and industrial administration/management), HEALTH PROFESSIONS (clinical science, nursing, and speech pathology/audiology), SOCIAL SCIENCE (economics, history, international relations, philosophy, political science/government, psychology, sociology, and theological studies). Chemistry, psychology, and philosophy are the strongest academically. Biology, nursing, and psychology are the largest.
Required: Students must complete 120 to 128 credit hours with a minimum of 18 in the major, with at least a 2.0 GPA. 52 prescribed semester hours in philosophy, theology, history, literature, science, social studies, and the arts are required. Students must also demonstrate proficiency in oral and written communication and math.
Special: Students may obtain career-related work experience through the Cooperative Education Program. Internships for credit and salary are available. Students are encouraged to study abroad in 1 of 5 countries for a semester, to take a semester in New York at Fordham University, or to participate in a congressional intern/study program in Washington, D.C., through Marquette University. B.A.-B.S. degrees research programs, work-study, and an accelerated degree in nursing are also available. Students may pursue a 3-2 engineering degree and interdisciplinary majors. There are 3 national honor societies, including Phi Beta Kappa, a freshman honors program, and 11 departmental honors program.
Faculty/Classroom: 58% of faculty are male; 42%, female. 94% teach undergraduates. No introductory courses are taught by graduate students. The average class size in an introductory lecture is 22; in a laboratory, 11; and in a regular course, 20.
Admissions: 34% of the current freshmen were in the top fifth of their class; 60% were in the top two fifths. 4 freshmen graduated first in their class.
Requirements: The SAT I or ACT is required. In addition, minimum composite scores of 960 (480 on each part) on the SAT I, or 20 on the ACT are required. In addition, the applicant must be a graduate of an accredited secondary school or have earned a GED. The university requires completion of 15 academic credits, including 4 years of English, 3 to 4 of history/social science, 3 of math, 2 to 4 of a foreign language, and 1 of visual or performing arts. An interview is recommended, and a recommendation is required. Applications are accepted on disk or online through Embark. Rockhurst requires applicants to be in the upper 50% of their class. A GPA of 2.0 is required. AP and CLEP credits are accepted. Important factors in the admissions decision are advanced placement or honor courses, recommendations by school officials, and leadership record.

Procedure: Freshmen are admitted to all sessions. Entrance exams should be taken in April or June of the junior year or October, December, or February of the senior year. There are early decision and deferred admissions plans. Early decision application should be filed by May 1; regular applications, by June 30 for fall entry. Notification of early decision is sent July 1; regular decision, on a rolling basis. 50 early decision candidates were accepted for the 2001-2002 class.

Transfer: 148 transfer students enrolled in 2001-2002. Transfer applicants must have a GPA of at least 2.25. An interview is recommended. All college transcripts must be submitted; a high school transcript and test scores are required if the applicant has completed fewer than 24 college semester hours. 30 credits of 128 must be completed at Rockhurst.

Visiting: There are regularly scheduled orientations for prospective students, including a campus tour, an interview with an admissions counselor, and a classroom visit or meeting with a faculty member. There are guides for informal visits and visitors may sit in on classes and stay overnight. To schedule a visit, contact Laura Long in Admissions at (816) 501-4172 or (816) 501-2345 or *peg.millard@rockhurst.edu*

Financial Aid: In 2001-2002, 95% of all freshmen and 85% of continuing students received some form of financial aid. 75% of freshmen and 59% of continuing students received need-based aid. The average freshman award was $15,011. Of that total, scholarships or need-based grants averaged $6175 ($14,800 maximum); loans averaged $3813 ($6625 maximum); and work contracts averaged $1500 ($1850 maximum). 28% of undergraduates work part time. Average annual earnings from campus work are $1500. The average financial indebtedness of the 2001 graduate was $16,000. The FAFSA and the college's own financial statement are required. The fall application deadline is February 15.

International Students: There are 32 international students enrolled. The school actively recruits these students. They must score 550 on the written TOEFL and also take the SAT I or the ACT, scoring 20.

Computers: The mainframes are a 1 DEC ALPHA 4100 and 2 ALPHA 2100s. There are approximately 500 PCs and Macs available in computer labs, classrooms, the library, and residence halls. All students can connect to the Internet. All students may access the system 24 hours a day. There are no time limits and no fees.

Graduates: In 2001, 364 bachelor's degrees were awarded. The most popular majors were business/marketing (28%), nursing/health professions (17%), and psychology/social science/history (12%). In an average class, 53% graduate in 4 years, 62% in 5 years, and 66% in 6 years. 120 companies recruited on campus in 2000-2001. Of the 2000 graduating class, 26% were enrolled in graduate school within 6 months of graduation and 52% were employed.

Admissions Contact: Mark Kopenski, Vice President for Enrollment Management. A video is available. E-mail: *admission@rockhurst.edu*
Web: *rockhurst.edu*

SAINT LOUIS UNIVERSITY

St. Louis, MO 63103-2097 — D-2
(314) 977-2500
(800) SLUFORU; Fax: (314) 977-7136

Full-time: 2972 men, 3545 women	**Faculty:** 1205; I, --$
Part-time: 259 men, 381 women	**Ph.D.s:** 96%
Graduate: 1650 men, 2267 women	**Student/Faculty:** 5 to 1
Year: semesters, summer session	**Tuition:** $9830
Application Deadline: August 1	**Room & Board:** $6760
Freshman Class: 5547 applied, 3834 accepted, 1335 enrolled	
SAT I Verbal/Math: 592/601	**ACT:** 26 **VERY COMPETITIVE+**

Saint Louis University, founded in 1818, is a private institution affiliated with the Jesuit Order of the Roman Catholic Church. There are 9 undergraduate schools and 1 graduate school. In addition to regional accreditation, SLU has baccalaureate program accreditation with AACSB, ABET, AHEA, APTA, CSWE, NCATE, and NLN. The 3 libraries contain 1,785,604 volumes, 2,392,846 microform items, and 202,409 audiovisual forms/CDs, and subscribe to 13,408 periodicals. Computerized library services include the card catalog, interlibrary loans, and database searching. Special learning facilities include a learning resource center, art gallery, radio station, and TV station. The 300-acre campus is in an urban area in the Midtown Arts District of St. Louis. Including residence halls, there are 151 buildings.

Student Life: 52% of undergraduates are from Missouri. Others are from 49 states, 80 foreign countries, and Canada. 70% are white. 44% are Catholic; 17%, Protestant; 11% claim no religious affiliation. The average age of freshmen is 18; all undergraduates, 22. 14% do not continue beyond their first year; 69% remain to graduate.

Housing: 3289 students can be accommodated in college housing, which includes single-sex and coed dormitories, on-campus apartments, married-student housing, and fraternity houses. In addition, there are honors houses, language houses, and special-interest houses. 50% of students live on campus; of those, 75% remain on campus on weekends. All students may keep cars.

Activities: 17% of men belong to 12 national fraternities; 20% of women belong to 5 national sororities. There are 100 groups on campus, including band, cheerleading, choir, chorale, chorus, computers, debate, drama, drill team, ethnic, film, gay, honors, international, musical theater, newspaper, pep band, political, professional, radio and TV, religious, social, social service, student government, and yearbook. Popular campus events include Student Activities Fair, Spring Fever, and Billiken World Festival.

Sports: There are 9 intercollegiate sports for men and 10 for women, and 22 intramural sports for men and 22 for women. Facilities include A 2,000-seat gym, a 6.050-seat outdoor sports center, a 19,000-seat off-campus arena, a recreation center with multipurpose courts, a swimming pool and a diving well, track facilities, a weight-training room, and a natural grass soccer facility.

Disabled Students: 90% of the campus is accessible. Wheelchair ramps, elevators, special parking, specially equipped rest rooms, special class scheduling, lowered drinking fountains, and lowered telephones are available. There is also tutoring and assistance in finding student services. A reader/scanner is available.

Services: Counseling and information services are available, as is tutoring in most subjects, including math, English, history, economics, and natural sciences. There is a reader service for the blind, and remedial math, reading, and writing. books on tape, academic success seminars, time management, and test-taking techniques dealing with test anxiety and study skills.

Campus Safety and Security: Measures include 24-hour foot and vehicle patrol, self-defense education, escort service, and shuttle buses. There are informal discussions, pamphlets/posters/films, emergency telephones, and lighted pathways/sidewalks. There are metrolink field trips, residence hall presentations, community building programs, 24-hour emergency telephone/alarm devices, and electronically operated dorm entrances.

Programs of Study: SLU confers B.A. and B.S. degrees. Associate, master's, and doctoral degrees are also awarded. Bachelor's degrees are awarded in BIOLOGICAL SCIENCE (biology/biological science and nutrition), BUSINESS (accounting, banking and finance, business administration and management, human resources, international business management, management science, marketing/retailing/merchandising, organizational behavior, and personnel management), COMMUNICATIONS AND THE ARTS (art history and appreciation, communications, dramatic arts, English, French, German, Greek, Latin, music, Russian, Spanish, and studio art), COMPUTER AND PHYSICAL SCIENCE (applied mathematics, atmospheric sciences and meteorology, chemistry, computer science, earth science, geology, geophysics and seismology, information sciences and systems, mathematics, and physics), EDUCATION (education), ENGINEERING AND ENVIRONMENTAL DESIGN (aeronautical engineering, aircraft mechanics, airline piloting and navigation, aviation administration/management, biomedical engineering, computer technology, electrical/electronics engineering, engineering management, environmental science, and mechanical engineering), HEALTH PROFESSIONS (clinical science, exercise science, health care administration, nuclear medical technology, nursing, occupational therapy, physician's assistant, and speech pathology/audiology), SOCIAL SCIENCE (American studies, classical/ancient civilization, criminal justice, economics, history, humanities, international studies, philosophy, political science/government, psychology, social science, social work, sociology, theological studies, and urban studies). Physical therapy, aerospace engineering, and psychology are the strongest academically. Biology, psychology, and communications are the largest.

Required: Students must complete distribution requirements in international cultures, fine arts, English, literature, science, social/behavioral science, math, and history, as well as specific courses in philosophy, theology, and rhetoric/research. The bachelor's degree requires completion of at least 120 credit hours, including 30 in a major field, with a minimum GPA of 2.0.

Special: Students may study abroad in Spain, France, and Germany. Cross-registration with Washington University and the University of Missouri at St. Louis, internships with local financial institutions, work-study programs on campus, an accelerated degree program in nursing, a 3-2 engineering degree program with Washington University in St. Louis, dual majors, student-designed majors, and pass/fail options are also possible. There are 18 national honor societies, including Phi Beta Kappa, and a freshman honors program.

Faculty/Classroom: 68% of faculty are male; 32%, female. The average class size in an introductory lecture is 27; in a laboratory, 15; and in a regular course, 22.

Admissions: 69% of the 2001-2002 applicants were accepted. The SAT I scores for the 2001-2002 freshman class were: Verbal--12% below 500, 38% between 500 and 599, 42% between 600 and 700, and 8% above 700; Math--12% below 500, 33% between 500 and 599, 43% between 600 and 700, and 12% above 700. The ACT scores were 6% below 21, 16% between 21 and 23, 28% between 24 and 26, 20% between 27 and 28, and 30% above 28. 57% of the current freshmen were in the top fifth of their class; 83% were in the top two fifths. There were 27 National Merit finalists and 18 semifinalists.

Requirements: The ACT is required. In addition, applicants must be graduates of accredited secondary schools or have earned a GED. Students are encouraged to take 4 or more academic courses each semester of high school including 4 years of English, 3 each of math, academic electives, and sciences, 2 of social sciences and foreign language. Other requirements include courses in biology and chemistry for the School of Nursing and the School of Allied Health Professions; physics, an additional year of natural science, and 4 years of math for the physical therapy program; a third year of natural science (preferably physics) for admission to the occupational therapy and nutrition and dietetics programs; and a fourth year of math for the Parks College engineering or aviation programs. AP and CLEP credits are accepted. Important factors in the admissions decision are advanced placement or honor courses, extracurricular activities record, and leadership record. Applications are accepted on computer disk or on-line at *http://www.slu.edu/admissions/*

Procedure: Freshmen are admitted fall, spring, and summer. Entrance exams should be taken in the fall of the senior year. There is a deferred admissions plan. Applications should be filed by August 1 for fall entry. Notification is sent on a rolling basis. A waiting list is an active part of the admissions procedure. The fall 2001 application fee was $25.

Transfer: 437 transfer students enrolled in 2001-2002. The university recommends that transfer applicants present an associate degree or a minimum of 12 credit hours with a GPA of at least 2.0. 30 credits of 120 must be completed at SLU.

Visiting: There are regularly scheduled orientations for prospective students, consisting of a campus tour, individual and group visits to a class or an academic department, and admissions and financial aid counseling. There are guides for informal visits and visitors may sit in on classes and stay overnight. To schedule a visit, contact Admissions.

Financial Aid: In 2001-2002, 97% of all freshmen and 85% of continuing students received some form of financial aid. 77% of all students received need-based aid. The average freshman award was $17,484. Of that total, scholarships or need-based grants averaged $14,503 ($27,420 maximum); loans averaged $3681 ($20,625 maximum); and work contracts averaged $2600 (maximum). 24% of undergraduates work part time. Average annual earnings from campus work are $2600. The average financial indebtedness of the 2001 graduate was $14,231. The FAFSA is required. The fall application deadline is July 1.

International Students: There are 297 international students enrolled. The school actively recruits these students. They must score 500 on the written TOEFL or take the MELAB, and must pass a writing test.

Computers: The mainframe is a DEC ALPHA 2000 Cluster. There are more than 1200 PCs available for student use in various labs, which have Internet and Web access. All students may access the system. There are no time limits and no fees.

Graduates: In 2001, 1498 bachelor's degrees were awarded. The most popular majors were management information systems (7%), psychology (6%), and nursing (6%). In an average class, 2% graduate in 3 years, 52% in 4 years, 68% in 5 years, and 69% in 6 years. 178 companies recruited on campus in 2000-2001. Of the 2000 graduating class, 21% were enrolled in graduate school within 6 months of graduation and 64% were employed.

Admissions Contact: Edwin Harris, Associate Provost. A video is available. E-mail: *admitme@slu.edu* Web: *imagine.slu.edu*

SOUTHEAST MISSOURI STATE UNIVERSITY E-3

Cape Girardeau, MO 63701 (573) 651-2590; Fax: (573) 651-5936

Full-time: 2457 men, 3669 women	**Faculty:** 370; IIA, -$
Part-time: 777 men, 1195 women	**Ph.D.s:** 67%
Graduate: 326 men, 928 women	**Student/Faculty:** 17 to 1
Year: semesters, summer session	**Tuition:** $3525 ($6360)
Application Deadline: open	**Room & Board:** $4842
Freshman Class: 3391 applied, 1859 accepted, 1606 enrolled	
ACT: 22	**COMPETITIVE+**

Southeast Missouri State University, founded in 1873, is a public institution offering undergraduate and graduate programs in arts and sciences, business, agriculture, education, and health. It includes a school of polytechnic studies. There are 6 undergraduate schools and 1 graduate school. In addition to regional accreditation, Southeast has baccalaureate program accreditation with AACSB, ADA, APTA, ASLA, CSWE, NASM, NCATE, NLN, and NRPA. The library contains 411,992 volumes, 1,233,490 microform items, and 9400 audiovisual forms/CDs, and subscribes to 2781 periodicals. Computerized library services include the card catalog, interlibrary loans, and database searching. Special learning facilities include a learning resource center, radio station, and museum of archeological items and artworks. The 693 acre campus is in a small town 120 miles south of St. Louis. Including residence halls, there are 69 buildings.

Student Life: 85% of undergraduates are from Missouri. Others are from 37 states, 41 foreign countries, and Canada. 90% are white. 50% are Protestant; 34% Catholic; 11% claim no religious affiliation. The average age of freshmen is 19; all undergraduates, 22. 30% do not continue beyond their first year; 45% remain to graduate.

Housing: 2384 students can be accommodated in college housing, which includes single-sex and coed dormitories, fraternity houses, and sorority houses. In addition, there are honors houses and special-interest houses. On-campus housing is guaranteed for the freshman year only and is available on a first-come, first-served basis. 72% of students commute. Alcohol is not permitted. All students may keep cars.

Activities: 19% of men belong to 11 national fraternities; 9% of women belong to 9 national sororities. There are 174 groups on campus, including art, band, cheerleading, choir, chorus, dance, drama, drill team, ethnic, honors, international, jazz band, literary magazine, marching band, musical theater, orchestra, pep band, political, professional, radio and TV, religious, social, social service, student government, symphony, and yearbook. Popular campus events include Family Weekends, Spring Fling, and International Week.

Sports: There are 6 intercollegiate sports for men and 8 for women, and 30 intramural sports for men and 30 for women. Facilities include an indoor pool and a student recreation center housing an indoor track, a climbing wall, 6 racquetball courts, 3 indoor basketball courts, a weight room, volleyball courts, and bicycle and rowing machines.

Disabled Students: All of the campus is accessible. Wheelchair ramps, elevators, special parking, specially equipped rest rooms, special class scheduling, lowered drinking fountains, and lowered telephones are available.

Services: Counseling and information services are available, as is tutoring in most subjects. There is a reader service for the blind, and remedial math, reading, and writing.

Campus Safety and Security: Measures include 24-hour foot and vehicle patrol, self-defense education, escort service, and shuttle buses. There are informal discussions, pamphlets/posters/films, emergency telephones, and lighted pathways/sidewalks.

Programs of Study: Southeast confers B.A., B.S., B.G.S., B.S.B.A., B.S.Ed., B.S.M., B.S.Mus.Ed., B.S.N., and B.S.Voc.HomeEcon.Ed. degrees. Associate and master's degrees are also awarded. Bachelor's degrees are awarded in AGRICULTURE (agricultural business management, agriculture, agronomy, animal science, and horticulture), BIOLOGICAL SCIENCE (biology/biological science), BUSINESS (accounting, banking and finance, business economics, fashion merchandising, marketing/retailing/merchandising, and office supervision and management), COMMUNICATIONS AND THE ARTS (advertising, art, communications, dramatic arts, English, French, German, journalism, music, music performance, music theory and composition, public relations, radio/television technology, and Spanish), COMPUTER AND PHYSICAL SCIENCE (chemistry, computer science, earth science, geoscience, mathematics, and physics), EDUCATION (art, athletic training, business, early childhood, elementary, English, foreign languages, industrial arts, mathematics, music, physical, science, secondary, social studies, special, and speech correction), ENGINEERING AND ENVIRONMENTAL DESIGN (engineering technology, environmental science, industrial engineering technology, and interior design), HEALTH PROFESSIONS (nursing, speech pathology/audiology, and sports medicine), SOCIAL SCIENCE (anthropology, corrections, criminal justice, economics, family/consumer studies, food science, geography, history, law enforcement and corrections, liberal arts/general studies, parks and recreation management, philosophy, political science/government, psychology, social work, and sociology). Teacher education is the strongest academically. Health and human service are the largest.

Required: Students must complete 124 credit hours, up to 64 in the major. The core curriculum includes 48 credit hours in the University Studies program, as well as interdisciplinary studies, English, and math. Minimum GPAs (at least 2.0) and other graduation requirements vary by program. A writing exam must also be passed.

Special: Southeast offers co-op programs in education and communication disorders, and cross-registration with Southern Illinois University. Opportunities are provided for individually arranged internships and work-study, study abroad in 48 countries, a general studies degree, dual and student-designed majors (interdisciplinary studies), credit by exam, nondegree study, and pass/fail options. A 3-2 engineering degree is possible in conjunction with the University of Missouri at Rolla or at Columbia. There are 8 national honor societies, a freshman honors program, and 10 departmental honors programs.

Faculty/Classroom: 51% of faculty are male; 49%, female. All teach undergraduates.

Admissions: 55% of the 2001-2002 applicants were accepted. The ACT scores for the 2001-2002 freshman class were: 39% below 21, 28% between 21 and 23, 18% between 24 and 26, 8% between 27 and 28, and 7% above 28. 28% of the current freshmen were in the top fifth of their class; 55% were in the top two fifths. There was 1 National Merit finalist. 47 freshmen graduated first in their class.

Requirements: The ACT is required. In addition, graduation from an accredited secondary school is required; the GED is accepted. Applicants should submit an academic record with 4 credits in English, 3 in social studies, 3 in algebra or higher math, 3 in science, 3 additional credits in English, math, science, social studies, speech, or a foreign language, and 1 unit in visual/performing arts. A GPA of 2.0 is required. AP and CLEP credits are accepted.

Procedure: Freshmen are admitted fall, spring, and summer. Entrance exams should be taken in the spring of the junior year or fall of the senior year. Application deadlines are open. The fall 2001 application fee was $20. Notification is sent on a rolling basis.

Transfer: 471 transfer students enrolled in 2001-2002. Transcripts of the student's previous college must be submitted, listing at least 24 credits earned and a minimum GPA of 2.0. The ACT is not required. 30 credits of 124 must be completed at Southeast.

Visiting: There are regularly scheduled orientations for prospective students, including academic advising and other university information. There are guides for informal visits and visitors may sit in on classes and stay overnight. To schedule a visit, contact the Admissions Office at *admissions@semovm.semo.edu*

Financial Aid: 15% of undergraduates work part time. Average annual earnings from campus work are $1500. The average financial indebtedness of the 2001 graduate was $14,301. The FAFSA is required. The fall application deadline is July 1.

International Students: There are 194 international students enrolled. The school actively recruits these students. They must score 550 on the written TOEFL and also take the ACT, scoring 18.

Computers: The mainframe is an IBM 4381. There are also 650 terminals and PCs in various campus locations, including the dorms. All students may access the system. There are no time limits and no fees.

Graduates: In 2001, 1552 bachelor's degrees were awarded. In an average class, 25% graduate in 4 years, 43% in 5 years, and 48% in 6 years.

Admissions Contact: Deborah Below, Director of Admissions. A video is available. Web: *semo.edu*

SOUTHWEST BAPTIST UNIVERSITY B-3

Bolivar, MO 65613 (417) 328-1810
(800) 526-5859; Fax: (417) 328-1514

Full-time: 732 men, 1137 women	**Faculty:** 87
Part-time: 183 men, 662 women	**Ph.D.s:** 69%
Graduate: 186 men, 664 women	**Student/Faculty:** 21 to 1
Year: 4-1-4, summer session	**Tuition:** $10,326
Application Deadline: open	**Room & Board:** $3100
Freshman Class: 884 applied, 754 accepted, 420 enrolled	
SAT I Verbal/Math: 520/540	**ACT:** 23 **LESS COMPETITIVE**

Southwest Baptist University, founded in 1878, is a private liberal arts institution affiliated with the Southern Baptist Convention. There are 5 undergraduate and 3 graduate schools. In addition to regional accreditation, SBU has baccalaureate program accreditation with ACBSP, ADA, CAPTE, NASM, and NLN. The library contains 165,000 volumes, 429,626 microform items, and 10,576 audiovisual forms/CDs, and subscribes to 1973 periodicals. Computerized library services include the card catalog, interlibrary loans, and database searching. Special learning facilities include a learning resource center and child study center. The 152-acre campus is in a rural area 28 miles north of Springfield. Including residence halls, there are 37 buildings.

Student Life: 76% of undergraduates are from Missouri. Others are from 39 states, 7 foreign countries, and Canada. 94% are white. 23% are Protestant. The average age of freshmen is 20; all undergraduates, 21. 29% do not continue beyond their first year.

Housing: 1110 students can be accommodated in college housing, which includes single-sex dormitories and on-campus apartments. On-campus housing is guaranteed for all 4 years. 63% of students commute. Alcohol is not permitted. All students may keep cars.

Activities: There are no fraternities or sororities. There are many groups and organizations on campus, including art, band, cheerleading, choir, chorale, chorus, computers, debate, drama, forensics, honors, international, jazz band, musical theater, newspaper, opera, orchestra, pep band, photography, political, professional, radio and TV, religious, social service, student government, and yearbook. Popular campus events include fall and spring visitation days and Parents Day.

Sports: There are 7 intercollegiate sports for men and 6 for women, and 12 intramural sports for men and 12 for women. Facilities include a 2500-seat field house and a 1260-seat gym, weight rooms, training facilities, a baseball diamond, a football stadium, an outdoor track, and 5 tennis courts. There are also fields for flag football, soccer, and softball, and a natatorium with a 25-meter swimming pool.

Disabled Students: 75% of the campus is accessible. Wheelchair ramps, elevators, special parking, specially equipped rest rooms, special class scheduling, and lowered drinking fountains are available.

Services: Counseling and information services are available, as is tutoring in every subject. There is remedial math, reading, and writing.

Campus Safety and Security: Measures include 24-hour foot and vehicle patrol, informal discussions, emergency telephones, and lighted pathways/sidewalks.

Programs of Study: SBU confers B.A., B.S., B.A.S., B.M., and B.S.N. degrees. Associate and master's degrees are also awarded. Bachelor's degrees are awarded in BIOLOGICAL SCIENCE (biology/biological science), BUSINESS (accounting, business administration and management, recreation and leisure services, and sports management), COMMUNICATIONS AND THE ARTS (art, communications, dramatic arts, English, music, and Spanish), COMPUTER AND PHYSICAL SCIENCE (chemistry, computer science, information sciences and systems, and mathematics), EDUCATION (art, athletic training, early childhood, elementary, middle school, music, physical, and social science), ENGINEERING AND ENVIRONMENTAL DESIGN (commercial art and occupational safety and health), HEALTH PROFESSIONS (medical technology and nursing), SOCIAL SCIENCE (biblical studies, criminal justice, history, human services, ministries, political science/government, psychology, religion, religious education, religious music, and sociology). Education, nursing, and business administration are the largest.

Required: To graduate, students must complete 128 credit hours, with 40 in upper-division courses, and maintain a 2.0 GPA. Distribution requirements for most bachelor's degrees include 10 to 11 hours in science and math, 9 to 12 in humanities, 9 in communications, 8 in religion, 6 in business and community leadership, 5 in personal and family development, and 3 in computer literacy. B.A. students must demonstrate foreign language proficiency. All students must also fulfill the chapel attendance requirement.

Special: SBU offers internships, study abroad, and Washington, Russian, Latin American, Middle Eastern, and Hollywood semester programs. 3-2 engineering degrees with the University of Missouri-Rolla and Washington University are also offered. On-campus work-study, dual majors, pass-fail options, correspondence courses, and nondegree study are available. There are 2 national honor societies, and 5 departmental honors program.

Faculty/Classroom: 66% of faculty are male; 34%, female. All teach undergraduates. No introductory courses are taught by graduate students. The average class size in an introductory lecture is 35; in a laboratory, 60; and in a regular course, 20.

Admissions: 85% of the 2001-2002 applicants were accepted. The SAT I scores for the 2001-2002 freshman class were: Verbal--33% below 500, 50% between 500 and 599, 14% between 600 and 700, and 3% above 700; Math--40% below 500, 38% between 500 and 599, 17% between 600 and 700, and 5% above 700. The ACT scores were 25% below 21, 29% between 21 and 23, 29% between 24 and 26, 8% between 27 and 28, and 9% above 28. 42% of the current freshmen were in the top fifth of their class; 56% were in the top two fifths.

Requirements: The SAT I or ACT is required with a minimum score of 890 on the SAT I or 19 on the ACT for unconditional admission. Sutdents must be graduates of an accredited secondary school or have earned a GED. Applicants are required to have 13 academic credits, including a recommended 4 credits in English, 3 in math, 2 each in natural science and history or social science, and 2 in English, math, foreign language, computer science, social studies, and natural science electives. An interview and, where applicable, an audition are recommended. AP and CLEP credits are accepted.

Procedure: Freshmen are admitted to all sessions. Entrance exams should be taken at any time prior to admission. There are early decision and deferred admissions plans. Application deadlines are open with a rolling admissions plan.

Transfer: 117 transfer students enrolled in 2001-2002. Applicants must submit official college and high school transcripts and have a minimum GPA of 2.0. An interview is encouraged. Students who have not yet met SBU's English and math requirements must present scores from the ACT, SAT I, or other approved placement test. Only 6 hours of D credit will be accepted. 30 credits of 128 must be completed at SBU.

Visiting: There are regularly scheduled orientations for prospective students, including fall and spring visitation days. There are guides for informal visits and visitors may sit in on classes and stay overnight. To schedule a visit, contact Rob Harris, Director of Admissions at *rharris@sbuniv.edu*

Financial Aid: In 2001-2002, 95% of all freshmen and 76% of continuing students received some form of financial aid. 75% of freshmen and 83% of continuing students received need-based aid. The average freshman award was $6354. Of that total, scholarships or need-based grants averaged $3958 ($14,275 maximum); loans averaged $2395 ($8125 maximum); and work contracts averaged $1061 ($1224 maximum). 28% of undergraduates work part time. Average annual earnings from campus work are $822. The average financial indebtedness of the 2001 graduate was $15,417. The FAFSA and the college's own financial statement are required. The fall application deadline is March 1.

International Students: There are 10 international students enrolled. They must score 550 on the written TOEFL and also take the SAT I or the ACT.

Computers: The mainframe is an HP 9000-D330 midrange system for administrative records systems. There are 220 terminals or PCs located in the computer center, the library, and classrooms and available for student use. 7 dormitories are wired for connection to the campus network and for e-mail and Internet access. There are also 48 dial-up lines for access from off campus or from unwired residence halls. All students may access the system from 8 A.M. to 1:30 A.M. daily. There are no time limits. The fee is $35.

Graduates: In 2001, 377 bachelor's degrees were awarded. The most popular majors were education (31%), nursing (14%), and business

(11%). In an average class, 12% graduate in 3 years, 55% in 4 years, 68% in 5 years, and 70% in 6 years. 74 companies recruited on campus in 2000-2001.

Admissions Contact: Rob Harris, Director of Admissions. A video is available. E-mail: *rharris@sbuniv.edu* Web: *www.sbuniv.edu*

SOUTHWEST MISSOURI STATE UNIVERSITY B-3

Springfield, MO 65804 (417) 836-5521
(800) 492-7900; Fax: (417) 836-6334

Full-time: 5400 men, 6400 women	**Faculty:** 668; IIA, -$
Part-time: 1200 men, 1550 women	**Ph.D.s:** 81%
Graduate: 990 men, 1875 women	**Student/Faculty:** 17 to 1
Year: semesters, summer session	**Tuition:** $3600 ($6800)
Application Deadline: see profile	**Room & Board:** $4000
Freshman Class: n/av	
SAT I or ACT: required	**LESS COMPETITIVE**

Southwest Missouri State University, founded in 1905, is a public institution offering undergraduate programs in arts and letters, business administration, humanities and social sciences, education and psychology, health and applied sciences, and science and math. Figures in above capsule are approximate. There are 7 undergraduate schools and 1 graduate school. In addition to regional accreditation, SMSU has baccalaureate program accreditation with AACSB, ADA, AHEA, ASLA, CSAB, CSWE, NASM, NCATE, NLN, and NRPA. The library contains 675,000 volumes, 900,000 microform items, and 30,000 audiovisual forms/CDs, and subscribes to 5000 periodicals. Computerized library services include the card catalog, interlibrary loans, and database searching. Special learning facilities include a learning resource center, art gallery, and radio station. The 225-acre campus is in a suburban area 220 miles southwest of St. Louis. Including residence halls, there are 60 buildings.

Student Life: 92% of undergraduates are from Missouri. Others are from 47 states, 66 foreign countries, and Canada. 90% are from public schools. 89% are white. The average age of freshmen is 18; all undergraduates, 21. 32% do not continue beyond their first year.

Housing: 4170 students can be accommodated in college housing, which includes single-sex and coed dormitories, on-campus apartments, married-student housing, fraternity houses, and sorority houses. In addition, there are honors houses, wellness houses, and housing for international students and nontraditional students (age 23 and older). On-campus housing is guaranteed for all 4 years. Alcohol is not permitted. All students may keep cars.

Activities: 14% of men and about 9% of women belong to 15 national fraternities; 10% of women belong to 10 national sororities. There are 252 groups on campus, including art, band, cheerleading, chess, choir, chorale, chorus, computers, dance, drama, drill team, ethnic, gay, honors, international, jazz band, literary magazine, marching band, musical theater, newspaper, orchestra, pep band, political, professional, radio and TV, religious, social, social service, student government, symphony, and yearbook. Popular campus events include Tent Theater, New Student Festival, Family Weekend, Spring Fling, and Leadership Conference.

Sports: There are 10 intercollegiate sports for men and 9 for women, and 19 intramural sports for men and 19 for women. Facilities include a 16,600-seat stadium, a 9000-seat arena, a 9000-seat gym, a student center, an athletic center, a swimming pool, softball and practice fields, tennis courts, and bowling lanes.

Disabled Students: 95% of the campus is accessible. Wheelchair ramps, elevators, special parking, specially equipped rest rooms, special class scheduling, lowered drinking fountains, lowered telephones, TDD terminals, automatic door openers, and special housing are available.

Services: Counseling and information services are available, as is tutoring in some subjects. There is a reader service for the blind, and remedial math, reading, and writing. and a math center and writing center for student use. Proctors are available for tests given to those with disabilities.

Campus Safety and Security: Measures include 24-hour foot and vehicle patrol, self-defense education, escort service, and shuttle buses. There are informal discussions, pamphlets/posters/films, emergency telephones, and lighted pathways/sidewalks.

Programs of Study: SMSU confers B.A., B.S., B.F.A., B.M., B.S.E., B.S.N., and B.S.W. degrees. Master's degrees are also awarded. Bachelor's degrees are awarded in AGRICULTURE (agriculture, agronomy, animal science, conservation and regulation, horticulture, and wildlife management), BIOLOGICAL SCIENCE (biology/biological science, cell biology, and nutrition), BUSINESS (accounting, banking and finance, business administration and management, hotel/motel and restaurant management, institutional management, insurance, marketing/retailing/merchandising, and recreation and leisure services), COMMUNICATIONS AND THE ARTS (art, broadcasting, communications, dance, design, dramatic arts, English, film arts, French, German, Latin, music, music performance, Spanish, speech/debate/rhetoric, and technical and business writing), COMPUTER AND PHYSICAL SCIENCE (chemistry, computer science, earth science, geology, information sciences and systems, mathematics, and physics), EDUCATION (agricultural, art, athletic training, business, early childhood, elementary, foreign languages, health, home economics, industrial arts, middle school, music, physical, science, secondary, and special), ENGINEERING AND ENVIRONMENTAL DESIGN (cartography, construction management, drafting and design, electrical/electronics engineering technology, engineering physics, industrial administration/management, interior design, manufacturing technology, mechanical design technology, printing technology, and urban planning technology), HEALTH PROFESSIONS (medical laboratory technology, nursing, predentistry, radiograph medical technology, respiratory therapy, and speech pathology/audiology), SOCIAL SCIENCE (anthropology, child care/child and family studies, clothing and textiles management/production/services, dietetics, economics, geography, gerontology, history, parks and recreation management, philosophy, political science/government, psychology, public administration, religion, social science, social work, and sociology). Education and business are the largest.

Required: A total of 125 to 130 semester hours, including 30 to 60 in the major, and a minimum GPA of 2.0 are required. 45 general education semester hours are required, to include 8 in natural sciences, 6 to 9 each in social sciences and humanities, 6 in American studies, 4 in phys ed, 3 to 6 in English composition, 3 each in math and speech, and 1 in freshman orientation.

Special: Southwest Missouri offers co-op programs, internships, study abroad in 40 countries, and work-study programs. Also available are B.A.-B.S. degrees in 12 majors, preprofessional programs in law and medicine, and student-designed and interdisciplinary majors, including antiquities, agriculture business and agriculture education, chemistry/biochemistry, communication management, and finance/real estate. A 3-2 engineering degree is available through the University of Missouri-Rolla. Credit for military experience and pass/not-pass options are offered. There are 31 national honor societies and a freshman honors program.

Faculty/Classroom: 70% of faculty are male; 30%, female. 97% teach undergraduates. Graduate students teach 4% of introductory courses. The average class size in a regular course is 23.

Requirements: The SAT I or ACT is required; the ACT is preferred. Admission is based on a sliding scale of rank or GPA and test score. Freshmen must also have a 16-unit high school core curriculum, including 4 in English, 3 each in math and social studies, 2 in science, 1 in visual and performing arts, and 3 electives. AP and CLEP credits are accepted.

Procedure: Freshmen are admitted to all sessions. Entrance exams should be taken as early as possible. Notification is sent on a rolling basis. Check with the school for current application deadlines and fee.

Transfer: Applicants must present a minimum GPA of 2.0 on transferable courses. If they have completed less than 24 semester hours, they are also required to meet freshman admission requirements. 30 credits of 125 must be completed at SMSU.

Visiting: There are regularly scheduled orientations for prospective students, including academic advising and enrollment for classes. There are guides for informal visits. To schedule a visit, contact the Admissions Office.

Financial Aid: In a recent year, 49% of all students received some form of financial aid. 44% of all students received need-based aid. The average freshman award was $4425. Of that total, scholarships or need-based grants averaged $1854 ($7000 maximum); loans averaged $2275 ($5000 maximum); and work contracts averaged $84 ($1300 maximum). 51% of undergraduates work part time. Average annual earnings from campus work are $1500. The average financial indebtedness of a recent graduate was $13,455. SMSU is a member of CSS. The FAFSA is required. Check with the school for current deadlines.

International Students: There were 328 international students enrolled in a recent year. The school actively recruits these students. They must score 500 on the written TOEFL.

Computers: The mainframes are a UNIX processors and Novell servers. 3 computer labs contain approximately 300 PCs, most of which are connected to the campus network. Access to the campus network is available through the residence halls and through dial-in services. All students may access the system. There are no time limits and no fees.

Admissions Contact: Donald E. Simpson, Director of Admissions. A video is available. E-mail: *smsuinfo@mail.smsu.edu*
Web: *www.smsu.edu*

STEPHENS COLLEGE
Columbia, MO 65215 C-2
(573) 876-7207
(800) 876-7207; Fax: (573) 876-7237

Full-time: 16 men, 420 women
Part-time: 16 men, 166 women
Graduate: 5 men, 46 women
Year: semesters
Application Deadline: open
Freshman Class: 284 applied, 282 accepted, 129 enrolled
SAT I Verbal/Math: 560/500
Faculty: 51
Ph.D.s: 88%
Student/Faculty: 9 to 1
Tuition: $16,245
Room & Board: $6050
ACT: 23 COMPETITIVE

Stephens College, founded in 1833, is a private college primarily for women, offering undergraduate programs in the arts and sciences, business, education, and fine arts. There are 6 undergraduate and 2 graduate schools. The library contains 122,609 volumes, 11,234 microform items, and 4831 audiovisual forms/CDs, and subscribes to 336 periodicals. Computerized library services include interlibrary loans and database searching. Special learning facilities include a learning resource center, art gallery, radio station, and TV station. The 86-acre campus is in an urban area 126 miles west of St. Louis. Including residence halls, there are 35 buildings.

Student Life: 52% of undergraduates are from out of state, mostly the Midwest. Others are from 41 states and 3 foreign countries. 83% are white. The average age of freshmen is 18; all undergraduates, 24. 37% do not continue beyond their first year; 63% remain to graduate.

Housing: 775 students can be accommodated in college housing, which includes single-sex dormitories and on-campus apartments. In addition, there are honors houses, special-interest houses for intercultural scholars and fine arts majors, and houses with designated academic floors or non-smoking floors. On-campus housing is guaranteed for all 4 years. 75% of students live on campus. All students may keep cars.

Activities: 88% of women belong to 2 national sororities. There are no fraternities. There are 45 groups on campus, including art, choir, chorale, chorus, dance, drama, ethnic, gay, honors, international, literary magazine, musical theater, newspaper, photography, political, professional, radio and TV, religious, social, social service, student government, and yearbook. Popular campus events include the opening convocation, Honors Convocation, and Haunted House.

Sports: Facilities include a 300-seat gym, an Olympic-size pool, and tennis courts.

Disabled Students: 80% of the campus is accessible. Wheelchair ramps, elevators, special parking, specially equipped rest rooms, special class scheduling, lowered drinking fountains, and specially modified residence hall rooms and bathrooms are available.

Services: Counseling and information services are available, as is tutoring in most subjects, including English and courses with written expectations. There is remedial writing.

Campus Safety and Security: Measures include 24-hour foot and vehicle patrol, self-defense education, escort service, and informal discussions. There are pamphlets/posters/films, emergency telephones, and lighted pathways/sidewalks.

Programs of Study: Stephens confers B.A., B.S., and B.F.A. degrees. Associate and master's degrees are also awarded. Bachelor's degrees are awarded in AGRICULTURE (equine science), BIOLOGICAL SCIENCE (biology/biological science), BUSINESS (accounting, business administration and management, and fashion merchandising), COMMUNICATIONS AND THE ARTS (creative writing, dance, dramatic arts, English, graphic design, public relations, and Spanish), COMPUTER AND PHYSICAL SCIENCE (mathematics), EDUCATION (early childhood and elementary), ENGINEERING AND ENVIRONMENTAL DESIGN (environmental science), SOCIAL SCIENCE (fashion design and technology, international studies, liberal arts/general studies, philosophy, political science/government, prelaw, and social science). Theater arts, fashion, and education are the largest.

Required: All students must complete English 101 and 102, a math course, and a distribution of 9 courses in lower-division work. The bachelor's degree requires completion of at least 120 semester hours, including 30 to 72 in a major field, with a minimum GPA of 2.0.

Special: Students may study abroad in England, Canada, Mexico, and Spain. Stephens also offers cross-registration with the Mid-Missouri Association of Colleges and Universities, a Washington semester, dual and student-designed majors, a 3-2 occupational therapy degree program with Washington University, and pass/fail options for electives. There are 8 national honor societies, and a freshman honors program.

Faculty/Classroom: 45% of faculty are male; 55%, female. All both teach and do research.

Admissions: 99% of the 2001-2002 applicants were accepted. The SAT I scores for the 2001-2002 freshman class were: Verbal--11% below 500, 51% between 500 and 599, and 38% between 600 and 700; Math--27% below 500, 62% between 500 and 599, 9% between 600 and 700, and 2% above 700. The ACT scores were 26% below 21, 29% between 21 and 23, 28% between 24 and 26, 10% between 27 and 28, and 7% above 28. 40% of the current freshmen were in the top fifth of their class; 65% were in the top two fifths. 2 freshmen graduated first in their class.

Requirements: The SAT I or ACT is required. In addition, applicants must be graduates of accredited secondary schools or have earned a GED. An essay is also required, and an interview is recommended. A GPA of 2.5 is required. AP and CLEP credits are accepted. Important factors in the admissions decision are advanced placement or honor courses, leadership record, and recommendations by school officials. Applications are accepted on-line at the school's web site.

Procedure: Freshmen are admitted fall and spring. There are early decision, early admissions, and deferred admissions plans. Application deadlines are open. The application fee is $25. Notification is sent on a rolling basis.

Transfer: 27 transfer students enrolled in 2001-2002. Applicants must submit official transcripts from all college work attempted or completed as well as a recommendation from an academic college instructor. Transfers must submit an official high school transcript. 36 credits of 120 must be completed at Stephens.

Visiting: There are regularly scheduled orientations for prospective students, consisting of attendance at classes, a campus tour, an appointment with instructors, and an interview. There are guides for informal visits and visitors may sit in on classes and stay overnight. To schedule a visit, contact the campus visit coordinator at *apply@stephens.edu*

Financial Aid: In 2001-2002, 85% of all students received some form of financial aid, including need-based aid. The average freshman award was $13,400. Of that total, scholarships or need-based grants averaged $10,600 ($12,000 maximum); loans averaged $2000 ($6625 maximum); and work contracts averaged $800 ($1500 maximum). 55% of undergraduates work part time. Average annual earnings from campus work are $800. The average financial indebtedness of the 2001 graduate was $14,080. The FAFSA is required.

International Students: The school actively recruits these students. They must score 550 on the written TOEFL or 213 on the electronic version.

Computers: The mainframe is a DEC ALPHA 2000. There is an academic lab with 25 computers with access to the Internet and the web; the library has 10 computers with access to the Internet and the web. Departmental labs have 3 to 10 computers each. Each residence hall has a lab with 4 to 8 computers, all with Internet access. All students may access the system. There are no time limits and no fees. It is strongly recommended that all students have a personal computer.

Graduates: In 2001, 119 bachelor's degrees were awarded. The most popular majors were performing arts (32%), business (11%), and fashion (10%). In an average class, 20% graduate in 3 years, 43% in 4 years, and 49% in 6 years. 16 companies recruited on campus in 2000-2001.

Admissions Contact: Patricia M. Gibbs, Dean of Enrollment.
E-mail: *pgibbs@stephens.edu* Web: *www.stephens.edu*

TRUMAN STATE UNIVERSITY
Kirksville, MO 63501 C-1
(660) 785-4114
(800) 892-7792; Fax: (660) 785-7456

Full-time: 2313 men, 3203 women
Part-time: 82 men, 87 women
Graduate: 70 men, 164 women
Year: semesters, summer session
Application Deadline: March 1
Freshman Class: 5002 applied, 4107 accepted, 1470 enrolled
SAT I Verbal/Math: 610/590
Faculty: 359; IIA, --$
Ph.D.s: 78%
Student/Faculty: 15 to 1
Tuition: $3832 ($6960)
Room & Board: $4736
ACT: 27 VERY COMPETITIVE+

Truman State University, founded in 1867, and formerly known as Northeast Missouri State University, is a public liberal arts institution offering undergraduate and graduate degree programs in business and accountancy, education, fine arts, human potential and performance, language and literature, mathematics and computer science, science, and social science. There are 7 undergraduate and 9 graduate schools. In addition to regional accreditation, Truman has baccalaureate program accreditation with AACSB, ASLA, NASM, NCATE, and NLN. The library contains 429,873 volumes, 1.5 million microform items, and 35,085 audiovisual forms/CDs, and subscribes to 3498 periodicals. Computerized library services include the card catalog, interlibrary loans, and database searching. Special learning facilities include a learning resource center, art gallery, radio station, and a TV studio, a biofeedback lab, an independent learning center for nursing students, an observatory, a greenhouse chamber, and a speech and hearing clinic. The 140-acre campus is in a small town 170 miles northeast of Kansas City and 200 miles north of St. Louis. Including residence halls, there are 39 buildings.

Student Life: 73% of undergraduates are from Missouri. Others are from 39 states, 50 foreign countries, and Canada. 80% are from public schools. 89% are white. 38% are no affiliation, unknown affiliation, or other religious affiliation; 33% are Catholic and 28% Protestant. The average age of freshmen is 18; all undergraduates, 20. 16% do not continue beyond their first year; 64% remain to graduate.

Housing: 2970 students can be accommodated in college housing, which includes single-sex and coed dormitories, on-campus apartments,

married-student housing, and sorority houses. On-campus housing is guaranteed for the freshman year only and is available on a first-come, first-served basis. 54% of students commute. Alcohol is not permitted. All students may keep cars.

Activities: 30% of men belong to 2 national fraternities; 20% of women belong to 1 local and 9 national sororities. There are 221 groups on campus, including art, band, cheerleading, chess, choir, chorus, computers, dance, debate, drama, drill team, ethnic, gay, honors, international, jazz band, literary magazine, marching band, musical theater, newspaper, orchestra, pep band, photography, political, professional, radio and TV, religious, social, social service, student government, and yearbook. Popular campus events include Dog Days (Spring Carnival), Family Day, and International Week.

Sports: There are 11 intercollegiate sports for men and 10 for women, and 21 intramural sports for men and 21 for women. Facilities include a 5000-seat football stadium, a soccer field, tennis and racquetball courts, a softball diamond, a baseball diamond, a 3000-seat arena with 3 basketball courts, an Olympic-size pool, weight training rooms, indoor and outdoor track facilities, and a 60,000-square-foot student recreation center.

Disabled Students: 90% of the campus is accessible. Wheelchair ramps, elevators, special parking, specially equipped rest rooms, special class scheduling, and lowered drinking fountains and telephones. The swimming pool is equipped with a lift to assist physically disabled swimmers. Adaptive living arrangements are possible are available.

Services: Counseling and information services are available, as is tutoring in most subjects, with services for the hearing impaired that include a braille scanner and printer. There is a reader service for the blind. Services for individuals with disabilities provides recording, note-taking, test-taking, and advising services.

Campus Safety and Security: Measures include 24-hour foot and vehicle patrol, self-defense education, escort service, and informal discussions. There are pamphlets/posters/films, emergency telephones, lighted pathways/sidewalks, and personal body alarms, available on a limited basis.

Programs of Study: Truman confers B.A., B.S., B.F.A., B.M., and B.S.N. degrees. Master's degrees are also awarded. Bachelor's degrees are awarded in AGRICULTURE (agricultural economics, agriculture, agronomy, animal science, and equine science), BIOLOGICAL SCIENCE (biology/biological science), BUSINESS (accounting and business administration and management), COMMUNICATIONS AND THE ARTS (art, art history and appreciation, classics, communications, dramatic arts, English, fine arts, French, German, journalism, music, music performance, Russian, Spanish, and speech/debate/rhetoric), COMPUTER AND PHYSICAL SCIENCE (chemistry, computer science, mathematics, and physics), EDUCATION (physical), ENGINEERING AND ENVIRONMENTAL DESIGN (preengineering), HEALTH PROFESSIONS (health science, medical technology, nursing, physical therapy, predentistry, premedicine, preoptometry, prepharmacy, preveterinary science, and speech pathology/audiology), SOCIAL SCIENCE (criminal justice, economics, history, philosophy, physical fitness/movement, political science/government, prelaw, psychology, religion, and sociology). Chemistry, physics, and math are the strongest academically. Business administration, biology, and English are the largest.

Required: All students must complete 63 hours of course work in the liberal arts, 16 of which must be in written and oral communication, math and statistics, computer literacy, and personal well-being, and 23 of which must be in history, science, social science, philosophy/religion, and aesthetics. The B.A.,B.F.A., and B.M. degree require intermediate proficiency in one foreign language, and the B.S. and B.S.N. require additional course work in science, math, statistics, computer science, social sciences, or logic. Skills such as writing, quantitative analysis, problem solving, and critical thinking are reinforced throughout the curriculum, and all seniors end their studies with a capstone, or culminating experience, in their majors. Students must also complete a nationally normed exam in their subject area as part of Truman's assessment program.

Special: Study abroad in 39 countries is offered through Truman's own programs and those of the College Consortium for International Studies, the Council on International Educational Exchange, and the International Student Exchange Program. The university requires internships in education and agricultural science. Voluntary legislative internships are offered to all students at the state capitol, and internships through the Washington Center. There is a 2-2 engineering program with the University of Missouri-Rolla and Columbia campuses. Work-study programs, B.A.-B.S. degrees, dual majors, student-designed majors in health and exercise science, credit for military experience, pass/fail options for internships, and nondegree study are available. There are 18 national honor societies, including Phi Beta Kappa, a freshman honors program, and 11 departmental honors program.

Faculty/Classroom: 61% of faculty are male; 39%, female. 97% teach undergraduates. Graduate students teach 6% of introductory courses. The average class size in an introductory lecture is 29; in a laboratory, 18; and in a regular course, 23.

Admissions: 82% of the 2001-2002 applicants were accepted. The SAT I scores for the 2001-2002 freshman class were: Verbal--8% below 500, 37% between 500 and 599, 39% between 600 and 700, and 17% above 700; Math--10% below 500, 40% between 500 and 599, 40% between 600 and 700, and 10% above 700. The ACT scores were 2% below 21, 15% between 21 and 23, 30% between 24 and 26, 21% between 27 and 28, and 33% above 28. 73% of the current freshmen were in the top fifth of their class; 96% were in the top two fifths. There were 12 National Merit finalists. 131 freshmen graduated first in their class.

Requirements: The SAT I or ACT is required; the university prefers the ACT, with a recommended minimum score of 22. Recommended minimum composite score on the SAT I is 960, or 480 on each part. Applicants should have completed 4 units of English, 3 each of science and social studies, 2 of foreign language, and 1 of art or music. 4 units of math are strongly recommended. An essay is required and an interview or visit is recommended. Applications are accepted on-line via Apply, Next Stop College, CollegeLink, or the school's web site, *www.truman.edu*. Truman requires applicants to be in the upper 70% of their class. A GPA of 2.75 is required. AP and CLEP credits are accepted. Important factors in the admissions decision are leadership record, advanced placement or honor courses, and extracurricular activities record.

Procedure: Freshmen are admitted to all sessions. Entrance exams should be taken during the spring or summer following the junior year. There is a deferred admissions plan. Early decision application should be filed by November 15; regular applications, by March 1 for fall entry. Notification of early decision is sent December 15; regular decision is rolling.

Transfer: 100 transfer students enrolled in 2001-2002. Transfer applicants must present a minimum 2.75 GPA on transferable hours and must meet minimum criteria for entering freshmen. 45 credits of 124 must be completed at Truman.

Visiting: There are regularly scheduled orientations for prospective students, including an interview with an admission counselor, a student-led campus tour, an appointment with a faculty member in the student's major, appointments in any areas of special interest, and the opportunity to observe a class. There are guides for informal visits and visitors may sit in on classes and stay overnight. To schedule a visit, contact the Admissions Office at (660) 785-4135.

Financial Aid: In 2001-2002, 97% of all freshmen and 94% of continuing students received some form of financial aid. 32% of freshmen and 28% of continuing students received need-based aid. The average freshman award was $6048. Of that total, scholarships or need-based grants averaged $3327 ($11,216 maximum); loans averaged $1572 ($2625 maximum); and work contracts averaged $967 ($1500 maximum). 36% of undergraduates work part time. Average annual earnings from campus work are $1037. The average financial indebtedness of the 2001 graduate was $14,382. Truman is a member of CSS. The FAFSA, FFS, or SFS and the college's own financial statement are required. The fall application deadline is April 1.

International Students: There are 217 international students enrolled. The school actively recruits these students. They must score 550 on the written TOEFL and also take the Comprehensive English Language Test.

Computers: Students have access to the university's PC-based network. All students receive free computer accounts for e-mail, printing, and saving files. Approximately 745 workstations are available for student use; PCs are located in 8 residence halls and most academic buildings. All residence hall rooms are wired with network connections. All students may access the system Labs are open until midnight in the academic buildings, and 2 A.M. in the library. Residence hall labs are always open. An individual time limit of 30 minutes is imposed only when other students are waiting. There are no fees.

Graduates: In 2001, 1229 bachelor's degrees were awarded. The most popular majors were business administration (17%), biology (10%), and English (10%). In an average class, 2% graduate in 3 years, 37% in 4 years, 61% in 5 years, and 64% in 6 years. 294 companies recruited on campus in 2000-2001. Of the 2000 graduating class, 36% were enrolled in graduate school within 6 months of graduation and 60% were employed.

Admissions Contact: Kathy Rieck, Dean of Admissions and Records. E-mail: *admissions@truman.edu* Web: *www.truman.edu*

UNIVERSITY OF MISSOURI SYSTEM

The University of Missouri System, established in 1966, is a public system of higher education. It is governed by a board of curators and the chief administrator is the president. The primary goals of the system are teaching, research, extension, and other public service. The main priorities are to provide the highest quality of instructional and research programs, to provide educational access to qualified students who demonstrate likelihood of academic success, and to operate in an effective and cost-efficient manner. The total enrollment of all 4 campuses usually exceeds 55,000, with approximately 9500 faculty members. Altogether there are 224 baccalaureate (including 19 postbaccalaureate), 202 master's (including 10 education specialist), and 117 doctoral programs, plus professional programs in dentistry, law, medicine, optometry, and veterinary medicine offered. The system consists of 4 4-year institutions located in Columbia, Kansas City, Rolla, and St. Louis. Profiles of these campuses are included in this section.

UNIVERSITY OF MISSOURI/COLUMBIA C-2

Columbia, MO 65211 (573) 882-7786
(800) 225-6075; Fax: (573) 882-7887

Full-time: 8276 men, 9103 women	**Faculty:** 1688; I, -$
Part-time: 527 men, 525 women	**Ph.D.s:** 87%
Graduate: 2506 men, 2730 women	**Student/Faculty:** 10 to 1
Year: semesters, summer session	**Tuition:** $4887 ($13,332)
Application Deadline: May 1	**Room & Board:** $4916

Freshman Class: 9678 applied, 6197 accepted, 4167 enrolled
ACT: 26 HIGHLY COMPETITIVE

The University of Missouri/Columbia, established in 1839, offers a comprehensive array of undergraduate and graduate programs as well as professional training in law, medicine, and veterinary medicine. There are 10 undergraduate and 20 graduate schools. In addition to regional accreditation, MU has baccalaureate program accreditation with AACSB, ABET, ACEJMC, ADA, APTA, CAHEA, CSWE, FIDER, NASAD, NASM, NRPA, and SAF. The 11 libraries contain 3,060,509 volumes and 6,737,867 microform items, and subscribe to 16,684 periodicals. Computerized library services include the card catalog, interlibrary loans, and database searching. Special learning facilities include a learning resource center, art gallery, natural history museum, radio station, TV station, astronomy observatory, freedom of information center, herbarium, and anthropology, fishery, and wildlife collections. The 1377-acre campus is in a small town 120 miles west of St. Louis and 120 miles east of Kansas City. Including residence halls, there are 375 buildings.

Student Life: 86% of undergraduates are from Missouri. Others are from 49 states, 99 foreign countries, and Canada. 85% are white. The average age of freshmen is 18; all undergraduates, 20. 16% do not continue beyond their first year; 60% remain to graduate.

Housing: 5640 students can be accommodated in college housing, which includes single-sex and coed dormitories, married-student housing, fraternity houses, and sorority houses. In addition, there are honors houses, language houses, and special-interest houses, international houses, quiet houses, and graduate/professional houses. On-campus housing is guaranteed for all 4 years. 58% of students commute. Alcohol is not permitted. All students may keep cars.

Activities: 23% of men belong to 28 national fraternities; 27% of women belong to 20 national sororities. There are 420 groups on campus, including art, band, cheerleading, choir, chorale, chorus, computers, dance, debate, drama, drill team, drum and bugle corps, ethnic, gay, honors, international, jazz band, literary magazine, marching band, musical theater, newspaper, orchestra, pep band, photography, political, professional, radio and TV, religious, social, social service, student government, symphony, and yearbook. Popular campus events include Big Twelve athletics, academic weeks, and Meet Mizzou Day.

Sports: There are 7 intercollegiate sports for men and 9 for women, and 35 intramural sports for men and 30 for women. Facilities include a recreation center with more than 10 multicourts, 21 racquetball courts, a natatorium, an indoor running track, and 2 weight rooms. There is a 62,000-seat stadium, a 1300-seat indoor gym, and an 18,000-seat auditorium.

Disabled Students: All of the campus is accessible. Wheelchair ramps, elevators, special parking, specially equipped rest rooms, special class scheduling, lowered drinking fountains, and lowered telephones are available.

Services: Counseling and information services are available, as is tutoring in some subjects. There is a reader service for the blind.

Campus Safety and Security: Measures include 24-hour foot and vehicle patrol, self-defense education, escort service, and shuttle buses. There are informal discussions, pamphlets/posters/films, emergency telephones, lighted pathways/sidewalks, and a 24-hour bicycle patrol.

Programs of Study: MU confers A.B., B.S., B.E.S., B.F.A., B.G.S., B.H.S., B.J., B.M., B.S.Acc., B.S.B.A., B.S.B.E., B.S.ChE., B.S.CiE., B.S.C.E., B.S.E.E., B.S.Ed., B.S.F., B.S.F.W., B.S.H.E.S., B.S.I.E., B.S.M.E., B.S.N., and B.S.W. degrees. Master's and doctoral degrees are also awarded. Bachelor's degrees are awarded in AGRICULTURE (agricultural economics, agriculture, animal science, and soil science), BIOLOGICAL SCIENCE (biochemistry and biology/biological science), BUSINESS (accounting, banking and finance, business administration and management, business economics, hotel/motel and restaurant management, marketing/retailing/merchandising, real estate, and tourism), COMMUNICATIONS AND THE ARTS (advertising, art history and appreciation, broadcasting, classics, communications, design, dramatic arts, English, French, German, journalism, music, Russian, and Spanish), COMPUTER AND PHYSICAL SCIENCE (atmospheric sciences and meteorology, chemistry, computer science, geology, mathematics, physics, and statistics), EDUCATION (art, early childhood, education, elementary, middle school, music, and secondary), ENGINEERING AND ENVIRONMENTAL DESIGN (chemical engineering, civil engineering, computer engineering, electrical/electronics engineering, industrial engineering, and mechanical engineering), HEALTH PROFESSIONS (nursing, occupational therapy, physical therapy, radiological science, and respiratory therapy), SOCIAL SCIENCE (anthropology, archeology, dietetics, economics, food science, geography, history, international studies, parks and recreation management, philosophy, political science/government, psychology, religion, social science, social work, and sociology). Biological sciences, business administration, and psychology are the strongest academically. Business, journalism, and engineering are the largest.

Required: To graduate, students must maintain a minimum 2.0 GPA and complete at least 120 credits, of which at least 30 must be in their major, although credit requirement can vary by degree program. They are required to take courses in English, math, and American history or political science. Additionally, course work leading to computer and math profiency is required, as are 2 writing-intensive courses. A capstone experience is required.

Special: Available academic programs include co-op programs and cross-registration with other schools, internships, study abroad, a Washington semester, and work-study programs. Special degrees or studies include an accelerated degree, dual majors, a general studies degree, and student-designed majors. Nondegree study and pass/fail options are available. For highly motivated students there is an honors college and the possibility of early admission to the schools of law and medicine. The university also has an easy-access program for nondegree-seeking community residents. There are 31 national honor societies, including Phi Beta Kappa, and a freshman honors program.

Faculty/Classroom: 67% of faculty are male; 33%, female.

Admissions: 64% of the 2001-2002 applicants were accepted. The ACT scores for the 2001-2002 freshman class were: 7% below 21, 23% between 21 and 23, 29% between 24 and 26, 17% between 27 and 28, and 24% above 28. 53% of the current freshmen were in the top fifth of their class; 82% were in the top two fifths. There were 19 National Merit finalists. 86 freshmen graduated first in their class.

Requirements: The ACT is required. In addition, students may gain probationary admission with sufficient GED scores. The usual requirements are completion of 17 Carnegie units, including 4 each in English and math, 3 each in social studies and science, 2 in a foreign language, and 1 in fine arts. Admission is determined by these units and a combination of class rank and ACT score. AP and CLEP credits are accepted. Important factors in the admissions decision are advanced placement or honor courses and evidence of special talent. Applications are accepted on-line.

Procedure: Freshmen are admitted to all sessions. Entrance exams should be taken late in the junior year or in the senior year. There is a deferred admissions plan. Applications should be filed by May 1 for fall entry. The fall 2001 application fee was $25. Notification is sent on a rolling basis.

Transfer: 1125 transfer students enrolled in 2001-2002. Transfer students must present 24 hours of completed college-level course work with a minimum 2.0 GPA, and show a C average in all course work attempted. An interview is recommended.

Visiting: There are regularly scheduled orientations for prospective students, consisting of a campus tour, a visit with an admissions representative, and a visit with an academic representative on request. There are guides for informal visits and visitors may sit in on classes. To schedule a visit, contact High School and Transfer Relations at (573) 882-2456.

Financial Aid: In 2001-2002, 80% of all freshmen and 75% of continuing students received some form of financial aid. 41% of freshmen and 40% of continuing students received need-based aid. The average freshman award was $5832. 6% of undergraduates work part time. Average annual earnings from campus work are $1525. The average financial indebtedness of the 2001 graduate was $17,085. The FAFSA is required. The fall application deadline is March 1.

International Students: There are 311 international students enrolled. They must score 500 on the written TOEFL.

Computers: The mainframe is an IBM 7060-HSP. There are 39 general access computing sites with more than 1400 workstations equipped with Macs, Windows, and Silicon Graphics, and laser printers for output from the mainframe or PCs. 30 sites house more than 150 Windows and Mac workstations for students in residence halls. All students may access the system 24 hours daily by modem; lab hours vary, but they are open 7 days a week and 3 are 21 hours. There are no time limits. The fee is $8.90 per credit hour.

Graduates: In 2001, 3716 bachelor's degrees were awarded. The most popular majors were business (15%), journalism (11%), and engineering (8%). In an average class, 1% graduate in 3 years, 32% in 4 years, 60% in 5 years, and 65% in 6 years. More than 1500 companies recruited on campus in 2000-2001.

Admissions Contact: Georgeanne Porter, Director Undergraduate Admissions. E-mail: *MU4U@missouri.edu* Web: *www.missouri.edu*

UNIVERSITY OF MISSOURI/KANSAS CITY A-2

Kansas City, MO 64110 (816) 235-1111; Fax: (816) 235-5544

Full-time: 1775 men, 2593 women | **Faculty:** 520; 1, --$
Part-time: 1671 men, 2260 women | **Ph.D.s:** 91%
Graduate: 1984 men, 2686 women | **Student/Faculty:** 8 to 1
Year: semesters, summer session | **Tuition:** $4585 ($13,997)
Application Deadline: open | **Room & Board:** $5100
Freshman Class: 2523 applied, 1853 accepted, 784 enrolled
ACT: 24 **VERY COMPETITIVE**

The University of Missouri/Kansas City, which opened in 1933, is a public institution offering undergraduate and graduate programs in the arts and sciences, engineering, business, education, health fields, preprofessional, and professional studies. It offers most of the degree programs in the evening to a primarily commuter student body. There are 9 undergraduate and 13 graduate schools. In addition to regional accreditation, UMKC has baccalaureate program accreditation with AACSB, ABET, ACPE, ADA, NASM, NCATE, and NLN. The 4 libraries contain 1,432,792 volumes, 1,972,257 microform items, and 438,821 audiovisual forms/CDs, and subscribe to 6842 periodicals. Computerized library services include the card catalog, interlibrary loans, and database searching. Special learning facilities include a learning resource center, art gallery, natural history museum, planetarium, and radio station. The 262-acre campus is in an urban area in Kansas City. Including residence halls, there are 42 buildings.

Student Life: 82% of undergraduates are from Missouri. Others are from 45 states, 53 foreign countries, and Canada. 66% are white; 13% African American. The average age of freshmen is 19; all undergraduates, 23. 27% do not continue beyond their first year; 39% remain to graduate.

Housing: 325 students can be accommodated in college housing, which includes coed dormitories and on-campus apartments. On-campus housing is available on a first-come, first-served basis. 95% of students commute. Alcohol is not permitted. All students may keep cars.

Activities: 6% of men belong to 4 national fraternities; 4% of women belong to 2 local and 3 national sororities. There are 202 groups on campus, including art, band, cheerleading, chess, choir, chorale, chorus, computers, dance, debate, drama, ethnic, gay, honors, international, jazz band, literary magazine, newspaper, opera, orchestra, photography, political, professional, radio and TV, religious, social, social service, student government, and yearbook. Popular campus events include International Food and Culture Night, Welcome Back Week, and Spring Fling.

Sports: There are 6 intercollegiate sports for men and 7 for women, and 13 intramural sports for men and 13 for women. Facilities include a recreation center with 5 gyms, an indoor/outdoor pool, indoor and outdoor tracks, a fitness center, and handball, racquetball, and squash courts. There are also recreation facilities at the University Center.

Disabled Students: 95% of the campus is accessible. Wheelchair ramps, elevators, special parking, specially equipped rest rooms, special class scheduling, lowered drinking fountains, and lowered telephones are available.

Services: There is a reader service for the blind.

Campus Safety and Security: Measures include 24-hour foot and vehicle patrol, self-defense education, escort service, and shuttle buses. There are informal discussions, pamphlets/posters/films, emergency telephones, and lighted pathways/sidewalks.

Programs of Study: UMKC confers B.A., B.S., B.B.A., B.F.A., B.I.T., B.L.A., B.M., B.M.E., B.S.C.I.E., B.S.D.H., B.S.E.E., B.S.M.E., and B.S.N. degrees. Master's and doctoral degrees are also awarded. Bachelor's degrees are awarded in BIOLOGICAL SCIENCE (biology/biological science), BUSINESS (accounting and business administration and management), COMMUNICATIONS AND THE ARTS (art, art history and appreciation, communications, dance, dramatic arts, English, fine arts, French, German, music, music performance, music theory and composition, performing arts, Spanish, speech/debate/rhetoric, and studio art), COMPUTER AND PHYSICAL SCIENCE (chemistry, computer science, earth science, geology, information sciences and systems, mathematics, and physics), EDUCATION (elementary, health, music, physical, and secondary), ENGINEERING AND ENVIRONMENTAL DESIGN (civil engineering, electrical/electronics engineering, environmental science, and mechanical engineering), HEALTH PROFESSIONS (dental hygiene, medical technology, music therapy, and nursing), SOCIAL SCIENCE (American studies, criminal justice, economics, geography, history, Judaic studies, liberal arts/general studies, philosophy, political science/government, psychology, sociology, and urban studies). Health sciences and performing arts are the strongest academically. Liberal arts is the largest.

Required: Most candidates for the B.A. and B.S. degrees must complete a core curriculum that consists of courses in English, a foreign language, math, philosophy, fine arts, history, literature, natural sciences, and social sciences. They must complete 120 credit hours, including 36 in their major, with a 2.0 GPA.

Special: Special academic programs include co-op programs and internships in several majors, study abroad in 8 countries, an accelerated degree program, and numerous work-study opportunities in the Kansas City area. Special degrees include a B.A.-B.S. degree in the computer science program and a liberal arts degree offered by the adult program. The pass/fail option is available in some courses. Freshmen may enter 6-year medical and dental programs. There are 4 national honor societies, a freshman honors program, and 1 departmental honors program.

Faculty/Classroom: 64% of faculty are male; 36%, female. The average class size in an introductory lecture is 30; in a laboratory, 16; and in a regular course, 24.

Admissions: 73% of the 2001-2002 applicants were accepted. The ACT scores for the 2001-2002 freshman class were: 25% below 21, 23% between 21 and 23, 22% between 24 and 26, 15% between 27 and 28, and 15% above 28. 49% of the current freshmen were in the top fifth of their class; 80% were in the top two fifths. 38 freshmen graduated first in their class in a recent year.

Requirements: The ACT is required. A combination of the student's test score and class rank determines admissibility; if the rank is 47 or below, the ACT score must be 24 or higher. Graduation from an accredited secondary school is a requirement for admission; the GED is also accepted. Required high school subjects include 4 units of English, 3 each of math and social studies, 2 of science, 1 of arts, and 3 more units selected from the above subjects or from a foreign language. A portfolio is required for art majors, an audition for music majors, and an interview for only those students applying for the pharmacy degree or the 6-year medical and dental programs. AP and CLEP credits are accepted.

Procedure: Freshmen are admitted to all sessions. Entrance exams should be taken by March of the senior year. Application deadlines are open. The fall 2001 application fee was $25. Notification is sent on a rolling basis.

Transfer: 1260 transfer students enrolled in 2001-2002. A maximum of 60 semester hours from community colleges or 30 hours earned within the University of Missouri System will be accepted. Transfer students must have maintained a 2.0 GPA. The SAT I or ACT is recommended. 30 credits of 120 must be completed at UMKC.

Visiting: There are regularly scheduled orientations for prospective students, consisting of a 1-day program for new freshmen or a half-day optional program for transfer students. There are guides for informal visits. To schedule a visit, contact the UMKC Welcome Center at (816) 235-8652.

Financial Aid: In 2001-2002, 71% of all freshmen and 58% of continuing students received some form of financial aid. 56% of freshmen and 54% of continuing students received need-based aid. The average freshman award was $11,663. Of that total, scholarships or need-based grants averaged $2227 ($19,704 maximum); loans averaged $2305 ($4000 maximum); work contracts averaged $3096 ($5000 maximum); and VA benefits averaged $4713 ($8648 maximum). 10% of undergraduates work part time. Average annual earnings from campus work are $3096. The FAFSA is required. The fall application deadline is March 1.

International Students: There are 289 international students enrolled. The school actively recruits these students. They must score 500 on the written TOEFL.

Computers: The mainframe consists of 5 Compaq ALPHA 2100 minicomputers. There are more than 400 PCs available at various student computer labs. All students may access the system 24 hours, 7 days a week. Students may access the system dial-up limit of 15 hours; no limit for lab use. The fee is $30 per credit hour.

Graduates: In 2001, 1138 bachelor's degrees were awarded. The most popular majors were liberal arts (19%), business administration (13%), and biology (8%). In an average class, 9% graduate in 4 years, 18% in 5 years, and 39% in 6 years. 475 companies recruited on campus in 2000-2001.

Admissions Contact: Melvin Tyler, Director of Admissions.
E-mail: *admit@umkc.edu* Web: *http://www.umkc.edu*

UNIVERSITY OF MISSOURI/ROLLA C-3

Rolla, MO 65409-0910 (573) 341-4164
(800) 522-0938; Fax: (573) 341-4082

Full-time: 2590 men, 756 women | **Faculty:** 275; I, av$
Part-time: 278 men, 107 women | **Ph.D.s:** 90%
Graduate: 651 men, 193 women | **Student/Faculty:** 12 to 1
Year: semesters, summer session | **Tuition:** $4974 ($13,419)
Application Deadline: July 1 | **Room & Board:** $5060
Freshman Class: 1789 applied, 1716 accepted, 715 enrolled
ACT: 27 **COMPETITIVE**

The University of Missouri/Rolla, founded in 1870, is part of the University of Missouri system. A public institution, it offers comprehensive undergraduate and graduate programs and confers degrees in arts and sciences, engineering, mines and metallurgy, and management and information systems. There are 4 undergraduate and 4 graduate schools. In addition to regional accreditation, UMR has baccalaureate program accreditation with ABET and CSAB. The library contains 435,008 volumes, 51,443 microform items, and 6268 audiovisual forms/CDs, and subscribes to 1508 periodicals. Computerized library services include the card catalog, interlibrary loans, and database searching. Special learning facilities include a learning resource center, radio station, writing center, student design center, nuclear reactor, observatory, explosives testing labs, and underground mine. The 284-acre campus is in a small town 90 miles southwest of St. Louis. Including residence halls, there are 71 buildings.

Student Life: 78% of undergraduates are from Missouri. Others are from 47 states, 38 foreign countries, and Canada. 85% are from public schools. 83% are white. 37% are Protestant; 34% claim no religious affiliation; 22% Catholic. The average age of freshmen is 18; all undergraduates, 21. 17% do not continue beyond their first year; 57% remain to graduate.

Housing: 1365 students can be accommodated in college housing, which includes single-sex and coed dormitories, on-campus apartments, and married-student housing. In addition, there is the Voyager Program and community learning centers. On-campus housing is guaranteed for the freshman year only and is available on a first-come, first-served basis. 53% of students live on campus; of those, 65% remain on campus on weekends. Alcohol is not permitted. All students may keep cars.

Activities: 27% of men belong to 20 national fraternities; 24% of women belong to 1 local sorority and 5 national sororities. There are 197 groups on campus, including bagpipe band, band, cheerleading, chess, choir, chorale, chorus, computers, drama, drill team, ethnic, gay, honors, international, jazz band, literary magazine, marching band, musical theater, newspaper, orchestra, pep band, political, professional, radio and TV, religious, social, social service, student government, and yearbook. Popular campus events include St. Patrick's Day, Black Culture Month, and Hispanic Culture Month.

Sports: There are 9 intercollegiate sports for men and 5 for women, and 16 intramural sports for men and 15 for women. Facilities include a gym, a weight room, a pool, a golf course, a track, racquetball and tennis courts, ball and soccer fields, and a 5000-seat stadium.

Disabled Students: 95% of the campus is accessible. Wheelchair ramps, elevators, special parking, specially equipped rest rooms, special class scheduling, lowered drinking fountains, lowered telephones, assistive listening devices, closed-circuit TV, wheelchairs, signers, aides, and specialized testing accommodations are available.

Services: Counseling and information services are available, as is tutoring in 24 subjects. There is a reader service for the blind.

Campus Safety and Security: Measures include 24-hour foot and vehicle patrol, escort service, informal discussions, and pamphlets/posters/films. There are emergency telephones, lighted pathways/sidewalks, and crime prevention and rape/sexual assault programs.

Programs of Study: UMR confers B.A. and B.S. degrees. Master's and doctoral degrees are also awarded. Bachelor's degrees are awarded in BIOLOGICAL SCIENCE (biology/biological science, environmental biology, and life science), BUSINESS (business administration and management, electronic business, and management information systems), COMMUNICATIONS AND THE ARTS (English and technical and business writing), COMPUTER AND PHYSICAL SCIENCE (applied mathematics, chemistry, computer science, geology, geophysics and seismology, information sciences and systems, mathematics, physics, polymer science, and statistics), EDUCATION (secondary), ENGINEERING AND ENVIRONMENTAL DESIGN (aeronautical engineering, architectural engineering, ceramic engineering, chemical engineering, civil engineering, computer engineering, electrical/electronics engineering, engineering, engineering management, engineering mechanics, geological engineering, industrial engineering, manufacturing engineering, materials engineering, mechanical engineering, metallurgical engineering, mining and mineral engineering, nuclear engineering, petroleum/natural gas engineering, plastics engineering, and systems engineering), HEALTH PROFESSIONS (environmental health science, predentistry, and premedicine), SOCIAL SCIENCE (economics, history, philosophy, prelaw, and psychology). Engineering, science, and technology are the strongest academically. Engineering, arts, sciences and mines, and metallurgy are the largest.

Required: Candidates for graduation must maintain at least a 2.0 GPA. A total of 120 to 132 credits, depending on the degree, is required. An assessment exam is required.

Special: UMR offers internships in business and government, co-op programs in which students work and attend school on alternating schedules, and study abroad in 8 countries. Accelerated degrees in science and engineering, dual majors, B.A.-B.S. degrees, a 3-2 engineering degree, work-study programs, a 5 year master's degree program, credit for life/military/work experience, and pass/fail options in certain courses are also available. There are 23 national honor societies, a freshman honors program, and 24 departmental honors programs.

Faculty/Classroom: 87% of faculty are male; 13%, female. 88% teach undergraduates. Graduate students teach 25% of introductory courses. The average class size in an introductory lecture is 36; in a laboratory, 18; and in a regular course, 25.

Admissions: 96% of the 2001-2002 applicants were accepted. The ACT scores for the 2001-2002 freshman class were: 5% below 21, 15% between 21 and 23, 25% between 24 and 26, 16% between 27 and 28, and 39% above 28. 61% of the current freshmen were in the top fifth of their class; 88% were in the top two fifths. There were 44 National Merit finalists. 26 freshmen graduated first in their class.

Requirements: The SAT I or ACT is required. In addition, the sum of the high school student's class rank percentile and aptitude exam percentile must be 120 or higher. Candidates must be graduates of an accredited secondary school or have the GED. The applicant must have completed 16 academic credit units, including 4 each in English and math, 3 each in science and social studies, and 2 in a foreign language. AP and CLEP credits are accepted. Important factors in the admissions decision are leadership record, extracurricular activities record, and advanced placement or honor courses. Applications are accepted on-line at *http://www.umr.edu/enrol*

Procedure: Freshmen are admitted to all sessions. Entrance exams should be taken late in the junior year or early in the senior year. Applications should be filed by July 1 for fall entry, December 1 for spring entry, and May 1 for summer entry, along with a $25 fee. Notification is sent on a rolling basis. 10% of all applicants are on a waiting list.

Transfer: 231 transfer students enrolled in 2001-2002. Applicants with fewer than 24 semester hours of college-level work must apply as freshmen; those with 24 or more must have attained at least a 2.0 GPA in all college-level courses. 30 credits of 120 to 132 must be completed at UMR.

Visiting: There are regularly scheduled orientations for prospective students, including a tour with a student, admissions and financial aid counseling, special interest contact, and a departmental visit with a faculty member. There are guides for informal visits and visitors may sit in on classes and stay overnight. To schedule a visit, contact UMR Visitor's Center at (573) 341-4165.

Financial Aid: In 2001-2002, 92% of all freshmen and 84% of continuing students received some form of financial aid. 50% of all students received need-based aid. The average freshman award was $8652. Of that total, scholarships or need-based grants averaged $6007 ($19,408 maximum); loans averaged $3012 ($16,000 maximum); and work contracts averaged $1080 ($4600 maximum). 38% of undergraduates work part time. Average annual earnings from campus work are $1080. The average financial indebtedness of the 2001 graduate was $16,850. UMR is a member of CSS. The FAFSA is required. The fall application priority deadline is March 1.

International Students: There are 141 international students enrolled. They must score 550 on the written TOEFL or 213 on the electronic version or take the MELAB, the Comprehensive English Language Test, or the college's own test.

Computers: The mainframe consists of Unix Servers. All students have free access to campus servers and to 700 networked PCs and Macs at 40 locations. Also available are 100 UNIX workstations (HP and Sun). A complete array of software is provided on all platforms, and 24-hour service is offered. All students may access the system. There are no time limits and no fees.

Graduates: In 2001, 685 bachelor's degrees were awarded. The most popular majors were mechanical engineering (15%), electrical engineering (12%), and civil engineering (10%). In an average class, 14% graduate in 4 years, 43% in 5 years, and 57% in 6 years. 561 companies recruited on campus in 2000-2001. Of the 2000 graduating class, 17% were enrolled in graduate school within 6 months of graduation and 79% were employed.

Admissions Contact: Jay Goff, Acting Director, Admissions and Dean of Enrollment Management. A video is available.
E-mail: *umrolla@umr.edu* Web: *http://www.umr.edu/admissions*

UNIVERSITY OF MISSOURI/ST. LOUIS — D-2

St. Louis, MO 63121-4499 — **(314) 516-5451**
888 GO-2-UMSL; Fax: (314) 516-5310

Full-time: 2251 men, 3235 women	**Faculty:** 496; I, --$
Part-time: 2622 men, 4143 women	**Ph.D.s:** 76%
Graduate: 846 men, 1733 women	**Student/Faculty:** 11 to 1
Year: semesters, summer session	**Tuition:** $5116 ($13,561)
Application Deadline: July 1	**Room & Board:** $4850

Freshman Class: 2165 applied, 1136 accepted, 634 enrolled
ACT: required — **COMPETITIVE**

The University of Missouri/St. Louis, founded in 1963, is a public institution offering undergraduate and graduate programs and conferring degrees in arts and sciences, business, nursing, education, and engineering. There are 6 undergraduate and 2 graduate schools. In addition to regional accreditation, UM-St. Louis has baccalaureate program accreditation with AACSB, CSWE, NASM, NCATE, and NLN. The 3 libraries contain 778,867 volumes, 1,255,484 microform items, and 3871 audiovisual forms/CDs, and subscribe to 3596 periodicals. Computerized library services include interlibrary loans and database searching. Special learning facilities include a learning resource center, art gallery, planetarium, and radio station. The Mercantile Library Collection is housed in the Thomas Jefferson Library. The more than 275-acre campus is in an urban area 10 miles north of downtown St. Louis. Including residence halls, there are 42 buildings.

Student Life: 92% of undergraduates are from Missouri. Others are from 40 states, 60 foreign countries, and Canada. 73% are white; 14%, African American. The average age of freshmen is 18; all undergraduates, 22. 38% do not continue beyond their first year; 61% remain to graduate.

Housing: 1100 students can be accommodated in college housing, which includes coed dormitories, on-campus apartments, and married-student housing. In addition, there are honors houses. On-campus housing is available on a first-come, first-served basis. Priority is given to out-of-town students. 92% of students commute. Alcohol is not permitted. All students may keep cars.

Activities: 1% of men belong to 2 national fraternities; 3% of women belong to 3 national sororities. There are more than 200 groups on campus, including art, band, cheerleading, chess, choir, chorale, chorus, computers, dance, debate, drama, ethnic, forensics, gay, honors, international, jazz band, literary magazine, newspaper, pep band, photography, political, professional, radio and TV, religious, social, social service, and student government. Popular campus events include Mirthday, Expo, and Welcome Week.

Sports: There are 5 intercollegiate sports for men and 6 for women, and 10 intramural sports for men and 10 for women. Facilities include indoor handball/racquetball, basketball, volleyball, and badminton courts; wrestling, dance, and conditioning rooms, and a swimming pool; outdoors, there are intramural fields and facilities for baseball, soccer, handball, racquetball, and tennis.

Disabled Students: The entire campus is accessible to physically disabled persons. Wheelchair ramps, elevators, special parking, specially equipped rest rooms, special class scheduling, lowered drinking fountains, and lowered telephones are available.

Services: Counseling and information services are available, as is tutoring in most subjects. There is a reader service for the blind, and remedial math, reading, and writing.

Campus Safety and Security: Measures include 24-hour foot and vehicle patrol, self-defense education, escort service, and shuttle buses. There are informal discussions, pamphlets/posters/films, emergency telephones, and lighted pathways/sidewalks.

Programs of Study: UM-St. Louis confers B.A., B.S., B.F.A., B.G.S., B.H.S., B.M., B.S.Acc., B.S.B.A., B.S.C.E., B.S.Ed., B.S.E.E., B.S.M.E., B.S.MIS., B.ME., B.S.N., B.S.P.A., and B.S.W. degrees. Master's and doctoral degrees are also awarded. Bachelor's degrees are awarded in BIOLOGICAL SCIENCE (biology/biological science), BUSINESS (accounting, business administration and management, and management information systems), COMMUNICATIONS AND THE ARTS (art history and appreciation, communications, English, fine arts, French, German, music, and Spanish), COMPUTER AND PHYSICAL SCIENCE (applied mathematics, chemistry, computer science, mathematics, and physics), EDUCATION (early childhood, elementary, music, physical, secondary, and special), ENGINEERING AND ENVIRONMENTAL DESIGN (civil engineering, electrical/electronics engineering, engineering, industrial engineering, and mechanical engineering), HEALTH PROFESSIONS (health science and nursing), SOCIAL SCIENCE (anthropology, criminal justice, economics, history, philosophy, political science/government, psychology, public administration, social work, and sociology). Business, chemistry, and education are the strongest academically. Business, education, and nursing are the largest.

Required: To graduate, students must complete 120 credit hours, 42 of which must be in the area of general education. They must maintain a 2.0 GPA.

Special: Cross-registration with Washington University, St. Louis University, and St. Louis Community College and cooperative programs in all majors are offered. Study abroad in 30 countries, including England, France, and Germany, and a general studies degree in which credit can be earned for life, military, or work experience are available. Almost all the degree programs are available through the Evening College. Some work-study is available. There is an accelerated nursing degree program and student-designed majors for the B.G.S. There are 18 national honor societies, a freshman honors program, and 16 departmental honors program.

Faculty/Classroom: 49% of faculty are male; 51%, female.

Admissions: 52% of the 2001-2002 applicants were accepted. The SAT I scores for the 2001-2002 freshman class were: Verbal--33% below 500, 36% between 500 and 599, 26% between 600 and 700, and 5% above 700; Math--31% below 500, 40% between 500 and 599, 24% between 600 and 700, and 5% above 700. The ACT scores were 4% below 18, 52% between 18 and 23, 37% between 24 and 29, and 6% above 29. 47% of the current freshmen were in the top fifth of their class; 79% were in the top two fifths.

Requirements: The ACT is required. In addition, applicants are required to have a total of 17 units, including 4 in English, 4 in math, 3 each in social studies and science, 2 in the same foreign language, and 1 in fine arts. Class rank and test scores are used to determine eligibility for admission. AP and CLEP credits are accepted. Applications are accepted on-line through CollegeView and via the university's web site, *www.umsl.edu*

Procedure: Freshmen are admitted to all sessions. Applications should be filed by July 1 for fall entry, December 1 for winter entry, and May 1 for summer entry, along with a $25 fee. Notification is sent on a rolling basis.

Transfer: 1825 transfer students enrolled in 2001-2002. Transfer students must have earned a minimum of 24 credit hours and maintained a minimum 2.0 GPA. 30 credits of 120 must be completed at UM-St. Louis.

Visiting: There are regularly scheduled orientations for prospective students. There are guides for informal visits and visitors may sit in on classes and stay overnight. To schedule a visit, contact Regina Walton at (314) 516-5460 or *walton@umsl.edu*

Financial Aid: In 2001-2002, 66% of all freshmen received some form of financial aid. The average freshman award was $2500. The FAFSA is required. The fall application deadline is March 30.

International Students: The school actively recruits these students. They must score 500 on the written TOEFL or 173 on the electronic version and also take the university's own test.

Computers: The mainframe is a Sun Microsystems Enterprise 4000. Students may access 7 instructional computing labs with 700 computers, and dial-up access is available 24 hours a day, 7 days a week. All students may access the system. There are no time limits. The fee is $8.90 per credit hour. It is strongly recommended that all students have a personal computer.

Graduates: In 2001, 1777 bachelor's degrees were awarded. The most popular majors were business (28%), education (19%), and social science/history (10%). Of the 2000 graduating class, 93% were employed within 6 months of graduation.

Admissions Contact: Melissa Hattman, Acting Director of Undegraduate Admissions. E-mail: *admissionsu@msx.umsl.edu*
Web: *http://www.umsl.edu*

WASHINGTON UNIVERSITY IN ST. LOUIS D-2

St. Louis, MO 63130-4899 (314) 935-6000
(800) 638-0700; Fax: (314) 935-4290

Full-time: 2923 men, 2986 women	**Faculty:** 715; I, +$
Part-time: 366 men, 497 women	**Ph.D.s:** 99%
Graduate: 2884 men, 2531 women	**Student/Faculty:** 8 to 1
Year: semesters, summer session	**Tuition:** $26,377
Application Deadline: January 15	**Room & Board:** $8216

Freshman Class: 20,834 applied, 4888 accepted, 1272 enrolled
SAT I or ACT: required **MOST COMPETITIVE**

Washington University, founded in 1853, is a private, independent institution offering undergraduate and graduate programs in arts and sciences, business, architecture, engineering, art, and professional programs in law, medicine (including physical therapy and occupational therapy), and social work. There are 5 undergraduate and 8 graduate schools. In addition to regional accreditation, Washington U. has baccalaureate program accreditation with AACSB, ABET, and NASAD. The 14 libraries contain 3,486,079 volumes, 3,175,017 microform items, and 43,569 audiovisual forms/CDs, and subscribe to 18,302 periodicals. Computerized library services include the card catalog, interlibrary loans, and database searching. Special learning facilities include a learning resource center, art gallery, planetarium, radio station, TV station, dance studio, professional theater, observatory, and studio theater. The 169-acre campus is in a suburban area 7 miles west of downtown St. Louis. Including residence halls, there are 101 buildings.

Student Life: 89% of undergraduates are from out of state, mostly the Midwest. Others are from 49 states, 82 foreign countries, and Canada. 61% are from public schools. 66% are white; 10%, Asian American. 30% are Catholic; 30%, Jewish; 30%, Protestant. The average age of freshmen is 18; all undergraduates, 20. 4% do not continue beyond their first year; 88% remain to graduate.

Housing: 4400 students can be accommodated in college housing, which includes single-sex and coed dormitories, on-campus apartments, off-campus apartments, married-student housing, and fraternity houses. In addition, there are special-interest houses, language and special-interest suites within residence halls, upper-class housing, single sex floors in coed buildings, and small group housing for students who share common interests and goals. On-campus housing is guaranteed for the freshman year only and is available on a lottery system for upperclassmen. 65% of students live on campus; of those, 97% remain on campus on weekends. Upperclassmen may keep cars.

Activities: 25% of men belong to 11 national fraternities; 18% of women belong to 5 national sororities. There are 200 groups on campus, including art, band, cheerleading, chess, choir, chorale, chorus, computers, dance, debate, drama, ethnic, film, forensics, gay, honors, international, jazz band, literary magazine, musical theater, newspaper, opera, orchestra, pep band, photography, political, professional, radio and TV, religious, social, social service, student government, symphony, and yearbook. Popular campus events include multicultural celebrations, College Bowl, and all-student theater.

Sports: There are 9 intercollegiate sports for men and 9 for women, and 26 intramural sports for men and 26 for women. Facilities include gyms, a swimming pool, tracks, a weight room, saunas, recreational playing fields, a football stadium, a fitness center, and racquetball, tennis, handball, and squash courts.

Disabled Students: 95% of the campus is accessible. Wheelchair ramps, elevators, special parking, specially equipped rest rooms, special class scheduling, lowered drinking fountains, lowered telephones, and magnification devices and hearing-assist devices are available.

Services: Counseling and information services are available, as is tutoring in every subject. There is a reader service for the blind.

Campus Safety and Security: Measures include 24-hour foot and vehicle patrol, self-defense education, escort service, and shuttle buses. There are informal discussions, pamphlets/posters/films, emergency telephones, and lighted pathways/sidewalks.

Programs of Study: Washington U. confers B.A., B.S., B.F.A., B.M., B.S.B.A, B.S.B.M.E., B.S.C.E., B.S.Ch.E., B.S.C.S., B.S.Co.E., B.S.E.E., B.S.I.M., B.S.M.E., and B.S.S.S.E., degrees. Master's and doctoral degrees are also awarded. Bachelor's degrees are awarded in AGRICULTURE (plant science), BIOLOGICAL SCIENCE (biochemistry, biology/biological science, biophysics, and neurosciences), BUSINESS (accounting, banking and finance, business administration and management, business economics, human resources, international business management, international economics, marketing management, marketing/retailing/merchandising, and trade and industrial supervision and management), COMMUNICATIONS AND THE ARTS (advertising, American literature, Arabic, art history and appreciation, ceramic art and design, Chinese, classics, comparative literature, creative writing, dance, design, dramatic arts, drawing, East Asian languages and literature, English, English literature, film arts, fine arts, French, German, graphic design, Greek (classical), Hebrew, Italian, Japanese, languages, Latin, literature, music, music theory and composition, painting, performing arts, photography, printmaking, romance languages and literature, Russian, sculpture, Spanish, studio art, and visual and performing arts), COMPUTER AND PHYSICAL SCIENCE (applied mathematics, chemistry, computer programming, computer science, earth science, information sciences and systems, mathematics, physical sciences, physics, and statistics), EDUCATION (art, education, elementary, foreign languages, mathematics, middle school, science, secondary, social science, and social studies), ENGINEERING AND ENVIRONMENTAL DESIGN (architecture, bioengineering, biomedical engineering, chemical engineering, civil engineering, commercial art, computer engineering, electrical/electronics engineering, engineering, engineering mechanics, engineering physics, environmental science, geological engineering, mechanical engineering, systems engineering, and technology and public affairs), HEALTH PROFESSIONS (pharmacy, predentistry, premedicine, prepharmacy, and preveterinary science), SOCIAL SCIENCE (African American studies, African studies, American studies, anthropology, archeology, area studies, Asian/Oriental studies, biopsychology, East Asian studies, Eastern European studies, economics, ethnic studies, European studies, fashion design and technology, history, humanities, international relations, international studies, Islamic studies, Judaic studies, Latin American studies, medieval studies, Middle Eastern studies, philosophy, political science/government, psychology, religion, Russian and Slavic studies, social science, South Asian studies, systems science, urban studies, Western European studies, and women's studies). Natural sciences and engineering are the strongest academically. Natural sciences, engineering, and business are the largest.

Required: Students must complete 120 credits and maintain a minimum GPA of 2.0. In addition, all students must complete a course in English composition and 3 courses in the major liberal arts disciplines.

Special: Opportunities are provided for cooperative programs with other schools, internships, work-study programs, study abroad, a Washington (D.C.) semester, accelerated degree programs, a B.A.-B.S. engineering degree, credit by examination, nondegree study, pass/fail options, and dual and student-designed majors. There are 18 national honor societies, including Phi Beta Kappa.

Faculty/Classroom: 71% of faculty are male; 29%, female. The average class size in an introductory lecture is 26; in a laboratory, 17; and in a regular course, 21.

Admissions: 23% of the 2001-2002 applicants were accepted. The SAT I scores for the 2001-2002 freshman class were: Verbal--1% below 500, 7% between 500 and 599, 48% between 600 and 700, and 44% above 700; Math--3% between 500 and 599, 38% between 600 and 700, and 59% above 700. The ACT scores were 2% between 21 and 23, 6% between 24 and 26, 16% between 27 and 28, and 76% above 28. 98% of the current freshmen were in the top fifth of their class; 100% were in the top two fifths. There were 174 National Merit finalists. 129 freshmen graduated first in their class.

Requirements: The SAT I or ACT is required. In addition, an essay is required from all applicants. Fine arts students may submit portfolios. 4 years of English, 3 each of math, science, and social science/history, and 2 of a foreign language are recommended. Also required are recommendations from a teacher and a counselor. AP credits are accepted. Important factors in the admissions decision are advanced placement or honor courses, evidence of special talent, and extracurricular activities record. Applications are accepted on-line.

Procedure: Freshmen are admitted in the fall. Entrance exams should be taken by December of the senior year. There are early decision and deferred admissions plans. Early decision applications should be filed by November 15; regular applications, by January 15 for fall entry, along with a $55 fee. Notification of early decision is sent December 15; regular decision, April 1. 314 early decision candidates were accepted for the 2001-2002 class. 185 wait-listed applicants were accepted in 2001.

Transfer: 182 transfer students enrolled in 2001-2002. Students less than 5 years out of high school must submit an offical transcript from secondary schools previously attended. A minimum GPA of 3.0 is required. An interview is recommended. If the student has taken the SAT I or the ACT in the last 5 years, results must be submitted. College transcript(s) and recommendations from a professor and dean/adviser are required. 36 credits of 120 must be completed at Washington U.

Visiting: There are regularly scheduled orientations for prospective students, consisting of group presentations followed by a campus tour, as well as visits to classes and meetings with current students and faculty. There are guides for informal visits and visitors may sit in on classes and stay overnight. To schedule a visit, contact the Office of Undergraduate Admissions at (314) 935-8888 or (800) 676-2114.

Financial Aid: In 2001-2002, 58% of all freshmen and 62% of continuing students received some form of financial aid. 39% of freshmen and 47% of continuing students received need-based aid. 50% of undergraduates work part time. Average annual earnings from campus work are $2000. Washington U. is a member of CSS. The CSS/Profile or FAFSA is required. The fall application deadline is February 15.

International Students: There are 313 international students enrolled. The school actively recruits these students. They must score 550 on the written TOEFL or 213 on the electronic version and also take the SAT I or the ACT.

Computers: The mainframes are an IBM 7060-H55 and IBM 9121-621. Specialized computing resources are available to students. The Center for Engineering Computing provides access to about 100 computing stations accessible from the campus-wide network. The School of Business provides a student lab with more than 65 computers. In addition, Residential Technology Services provides 11 computer clusters throughout the residence halls that are available 24 hours a day. All rooms in residence halls have Internet connections. All students may access the system 24 hours per day, 7 days per week. There are no time limits and no fees.

Graduates: In 2001, 1408 bachelor's degrees were awarded. The most popular majors were biology and psychology (17%), engineering (17%), and business (15%). In an average class, 1% graduate in 3 years, 77% in 4 years, 87% in 5 years, and 88% in 6 years. 250 companies recruited on campus in 2000-2001. Of the 2000 graduating class, 33% were enrolled in graduate school within 6 months of graduation and 58% were employed.

Admissions Contact: Office of Undergraduate Admissions. A video is available. E-mail: *admissions@wustl.edu*
Web: *http://admissions.wustl.edu*

WEBSTER UNIVERSITY — D-2

St. Louis, MO 63119-3194 — (314) 968-6991
(800) 75-ENROL; Fax: (314) 968-7115

Full-time: 1174 men, 1745 women	**Faculty:** 157; IIA, -$
Part-time: 682 men, 1110 women	**Ph.D.s:** 80%
Graduate: 5979 men, 7035 women	**Student/Faculty:** 19 to 1
Year: semesters, summer session	**Tuition:** $13,920
Application Deadline: March 1	**Room & Board:** $5884
Freshman Class: 1029 applied, 613 accepted, 397 enrolled	
SAT I Verbal/Math: 565/542	**ACT:** 24 **VERY COMPETITIVE**

Webster University, founded in 1915, is an independent institution with programs in fine and performing arts, liberal arts and sciences, education, nursing, and business. There are 5 undergraduate and 5 graduate schools. In addition to regional accreditation, Webster has baccalaureate program accreditation with AACSB, ACBSP, NASM, and NLN. The library contains 253,955 volumes, 136,500 microform items, and 10,969 audiovisual forms/CDs, and subscribes to 4918 periodicals. Computerized library services include the card catalog, interlibrary loans, and database searching. Special learning facilities include a learning resource center, art gallery, radio station, and a media center, a writing center, and a theater. The 47-acre campus is in a suburban area 12 miles southwest of St. Louis. Including residence halls, there are 44 buildings.

Student Life: 58% of undergraduates are from Missouri. Others are from 45 states, 100 foreign countries, and Canada. 67% are from public schools. 58% are white; 24% African American; 10% foreign nationals. The average age of freshmen is 19; all undergraduates, 26. 19% do not continue beyond their first year; 55% remain to graduate.

Housing: 500 students can be accommodated in college housing, which includes single-sex and coed dormitories and on-campus apartments. In addition, there are special-interest houses. On-campus housing is guaranteed for the freshman year only, is available on a first-come, first-served basis, and is available on a lottery system for upperclassmen. Priority is given to out-of-town students. 80% of students commute. All students may keep cars.

Activities: There are no fraternities or sororities. There are 48 groups on campus, including amnesty, art, band, cheerleading, chess, choir, chorale, chorus, computers, dance, debate, departmental, drama, ethnic, film, forensics, gay, honors, international, jazz band, literary magazine, musical theater, newspaper, opera, orchestra, outdoor, photography, political, professional, radio and TV, religious, social, social service, student government, symphony, and women. Popular campus events include Spring Fest, Back-to-School Dance, and Annual Semiformal.

Sports: There are 5 intercollegiate sports for men and 7 for women, and 4 intramural sports for men and 4 for women. Facilities include a gym, an athletic training center, a sauna, a fitness center, and a chipping and putting green, along with a 25-yard, 6-lane, indoor swiming pool.

Disabled Students: 75% of the campus is accessible. Wheelchair ramps, elevators, special parking, specially equipped rest rooms, special class scheduling, lowered drinking fountains, lowered telephones, and telephones for the hearing impaired, automatic door openers, a reading machine, computer for paraplegic students, deaf interpreters, note takers, and textbooks on tape. All TV monitors in classrooms have closed-caption capabilities.

Services: Counseling and information services are available, as is tutoring in most subjects. There is a reader service for the blind, peer tutoring, and study skills training.

Campus Safety and Security: Measures include 24-hour foot and vehicle patrol, self-defense education, escort service, and informal discussions. There are pamphlets/posters/films, emergency telephones, and lighted pathways/sidewalks.

Programs of Study: Webster confers B.A., B.S., B.B.A., B.F.A., B.M., B.M.Ed., and B.S.N. degrees. Master's and doctoral degrees are also awarded. Bachelor's degrees are awarded in BIOLOGICAL SCIENCE (biology/biological science), BUSINESS (accounting, business administration and management, and management science), COMMUNICATIONS AND THE ARTS (advertising, art, audio technology, broadcasting, communications, dance, dramatic arts, English, film arts, French, German, journalism, literature, media arts, music, musical theater, photography, public relations, Spanish, theater design, and video), COMPUTER AND PHYSICAL SCIENCE (computer science, information sciences and systems, and mathematics), EDUCATION (education and music), ENGINEERING AND ENVIRONMENTAL DESIGN (environmental science), HEALTH PROFESSIONS (nursing), SOCIAL SCIENCE (anthropology, economics, history, international relations, law, philosophy, political science/government, psychology, religion, social science, and sociology). Liberal arts is the strongest academically. Business and communications are the largest.

Required: To graduate, students must complete at least 128 semester hours with a minimum GPA of 2.0. A freshman seminar is required; otherwise, the curriculum requires specific courses within the major field of study only, as well as successful completion of an approved major, and successful completion of 9 general education goals, usually by taking a 3-credit hour course in each area. At least 30 semester credits of a student's final 36 credits must be earned at Webster.

Special: Students may cross-register with Washington University and the University of Missouri/Columbia, and with Fontbonne, Maryville, Lindenwood, and Missouri Baptist Colleges and Eden Seminary. The university offers co-op programs, work-study programs, internships, dual majors, student-designed majors, B.A.-B.S. degrees, a 3-2 engineering degree with the University of Missouri/Columbia and Washington University, and a 3-4 architecture program with Washington University. Study abroad, nondegree study, pass/fail options, and credit for life, military, and work experience are available. There is 1 national honor society.

Faculty/Classroom: 53% of faculty are male; 47%, female. No introductory courses are taught by graduate students. The average class size in an introductory lecture is 20; in a laboratory, 12; and in a regular course, 15.

Admissions: 60% of the 2001-2002 applicants were accepted. The SAT I scores for the 2001-2002 freshman class were: Verbal--12% below 500, 46% between 500 and 599, 30% between 600 and 700, and 12% above 700; Math--27% below 500, 53% between 500 and 599, 16% between 600 and 700, and 4% above 700. The ACT scores were 22% below 21, 25% between 21 and 23, 26% between 24 and 26, 12% between 27 and 28, and 15% above 28. 44% of the current freshmen were in the top fifth of their class; 76% were in the top two fifths. There was 1 National Merit finalist and 2 semifinalists. 11 freshmen graduated first in their class.

Requirements: The SAT I or ACT is required. In addition, applicants must be graduates of an accredited secondary school. The GED is accepted. Webster recommends that students complete 16 high school academic units, including 4 units of English, 3 each of social studies/history and math, and 2 each of foreign language, science, and electives. An essay is required of all students, and a portfolio or audition is required for art, dance, music, musical theater, theater, and film applicants. Applications are accepted on computer disk and on-line at *www.webster.edu*. Webster requires applicants to be in the upper 50% of their class. A GPA of 2.5 is required. AP and CLEP credits are accepted. Important factors in the admissions decision are advanced placement or honor courses, leadership record, and recommendations by school officials.

Procedure: Freshmen are admitted fall and spring. Entrance exams should be taken in the spring of the junior year. There are early admissions and deferred admissions plans. Applications should be filed by March 1 for fall entry and December 1 for spring entry, along with a $25 fee. Notification is sent on a rolling basis.

Transfer: 467 transfer students enrolled in 2001-2002. Applicants for transfer must have a minimum GPA of 2.5 for college credit completed. If they have fewer than 30 transferable hours, they must submit high school transcripts. 30 credits of 128 must be completed at Webster.

Visiting: There are regularly scheduled orientations for prospective students consisting of an open house, which includes classes, meetings with faculty, a financial aid workshop, a tour of the university, and an athletics department overview. There are guides for informal visits and visitors may sit in on classes and stay overnight. To schedule a visit, contact Bridget Stewart at (800) 753-6765 or *bstewart@webster.edu*.

Financial Aid: In 2001-2002, 95% of all freshmen and 45% of continuing students received some form of financial aid. 68% of freshmen and 34% of continuing students received need-based aid. The average freshman award was $12,220. Of that total, scholarships or need-based grants averaged $6781 ($13,720 maximum); loans averaged $3179 ($6625 maximum); and work contracts averaged $2260 ($2500 maximum). 18% of undergraduates work part time. Average annual earnings from campus work are $2379. The FAFSA and the college's own financial statement are required. The fall application deadline is April 1.

International Students: There are 152 international students enrolled. The school actively recruits these students. They must score 490 on the written TOEFL and also take written and oral/listening tests. If they are graduates of U.S. high schools or international secondary schools that use English as the language of instruction, they must also take the SAT I or ACT.

Computers: The mainframe is an HP 9000. Student dormitories use the mainframe. In addition, there are 300 Pentium PCs and Macs available in the central labs, student lounges, and distributed departments. 10 e-mail stations are located in dormitories and classroom buildings. All computers access the Internet and the Web. There are no time limits. The fee is $200.

Graduates: In 2001, 833 bachelor's degrees were awarded. The most popular majors were management (24%), business administration (12%), and computer science (11%). In an average class, 40% graduate in 4 years, 49% in 5 years, and 55% in 6 years. 51 companies recruited on campus in 2000-2001. Of the 2000 graduating class, 17% were enrolled in graduate school within 6 months of graduation and 95% were employed.

Admissions Contact: Niel DeVasto, Director, Freshman Admissions. A video is available. E-mail: *admit@websteruniv.edu*
Web: *www.webster.edu*

WESTMINSTER COLLEGE

Fulton, MO 65251 — **C-2**
(573) 592-5251
(800) 475-3361; Fax: (573) 592-5255

Full-time: 429 men, 318 women	**Faculty:** 49; IIB, av$
Part-time: 10 men, 11 women	**Ph.D.s:** 80%
Graduate: none	**Student/Faculty:** 14 to 1
Year: semesters, summer session	**Tuition:** $14,870
Application Deadline: open	**Room & Board:** $5120
Freshman Class: 666 applied, 535 accepted, 248 enrolled	
ACT: 24	**COMPETITIVE+**

Westminster College, founded in 1851, is an independent liberal arts and sciences college affiliated with the Presbyterian Church (U.S.A.). The 2 libraries contain 93,705 volumes, 16,282 microform items, and 6914 audiovisual forms/CDs, and subscribe to 409 periodicals. Computerized library services include the card catalog, interlibrary loans, and database searching. Special learning facilities include a learning resource center a photospectrometer lab, a multimedia language and learning lab, and a multimedia classroom. The 65-acre campus is in a small town 20 miles east of Columbia. Including residence halls, there are 26 buildings.

Student Life: 62% of undergraduates are from Missouri. Others are from 23 states and 8 foreign countries. 70% are from public schools. 91% are white. 47% are Protestant; 22% claim no religious affiliation; 20% Catholic. The average age of freshmen is 18; all undergraduates, 20. 30% do not continue beyond their first year; 48% remain to graduate.

Housing: 442 students can be accommodated in college housing, which includes single-sex and coed dormitories, off-campus apartments, and fraternity houses. In addition, there are special-interest houses. On-campus housing is guaranteed for all 4 years. 85% of students live on campus; of those, 95% remain on campus on weekends. All students may keep cars.

Activities: 66% of men belong to 6 national fraternities; 65% of women belong to 3 national sororities. There are 56 groups on campus, including art, cheerleading, choir, chorale, chorus, drama, ethnic, honors, international, literary magazine, musical theater, newspaper, pep band, photography, political, professional, religious, social, social service, student government, and yearbook. Popular campus events include Alumni Weekend, College Bowl, and Fulton Jazz Festival.

Sports: Facilities include an 800-seat gym, a weight room and a training room, baseball, softball, and soccer fields, a field sports area, tennis, racquetball, and sand volleyball courts, a swimming pool, an indoor rifle range, and a 1500-seat auditorium/arena.

Disabled Students: 50% of the campus is accessible. Wheelchair ramps, elevators, special parking, specially equipped rest rooms, and special class scheduling are available.

Services: Counseling and information services are available, as is tutoring in most subjects. There is remedial math and reading.

Campus Safety and Security: Measures include 24-hour foot and vehicle patrol, self-defense education, escort service, and informal discussions. There are pamphlets/posters/films, emergency telephones, and lighted pathways/sidewalks.

Programs of Study: Westminster confers the B.A. degree. Bachelor's degrees are awarded in BIOLOGICAL SCIENCE (biology/biological science), BUSINESS (accounting, business administration and management, international business management, and management information systems), COMMUNICATIONS AND THE ARTS (English, French, and Spanish), COMPUTER AND PHYSICAL SCIENCE (chemistry, computer science, mathematics, and physics), EDUCATION (elementary, middle school, physical, and secondary), ENGINEERING AND ENVIRONMENTAL DESIGN (environmental science), SOCIAL SCIENCE (anthropology, economics, history, international studies, philosophy, political science/government, psychology, religion, and sociology). English, biology, and history are the strongest academically. Business administration, political science, and psychology are the largest.

Required: To graduate, students must complete 122 credit hours, including a maximum of 40 hours in their major, with a minimum GPA of 2.0. Students must take 6 to 10 hours (37–42 total) in scientific inquiry, historical awareness, fundamental questions, artistic expression, human behaviors and institutions, cultural diversity, and global interdependence.

Special: Westminster offers co-op programs with colleges of the Mid-Missouri Associated Colleges and Universities, cross-registration with William Woods University, internships in all areas, study abroad in 15 countries, a Washington semester, a United Nations semester, and an urban studies program in Chicago. Student-designed majors are available as well as a 3-2 engineering degree with Washington University in St. Louis. The pass/fail option and dual majors are available. There are 15 national honor societies, a freshman honors program, and 8 departmental honors programs.

Faculty/Classroom: 71% of faculty are male; 29%, female. All teach undergraduates, 75% do research, and 75% do both. The average class size in an introductory lecture is 19; in a laboratory, 20; and in a regular course, 15.

Admissions: 80% of the 2001-2002 applicants were accepted. 40% of the current freshmen were in the top fifth of their class; 65% were in the top two fifths. In a recent year, there were 2 National Merit finalists and 3 semifinalists; 6 freshmen graduated first in their class.

Requirements: The SAT I or ACT is required. In addition, applicants must be graduates of an accredited secondary school. The GED is also accepted. Students must have completed 4 years each of social studies and English, 3 years each of math and science, and 2 years each of a foreign language and history. An essay is required and an interview is recommended. AP and CLEP credits are accepted. Important factors in the admissions decision are advanced placement or honor courses, leadership record, and extracurricular activities record. Applications are accepted on computer disk and on-line via the school's web site at *www.wcmo.edu*.

Procedure: Freshmen are admitted to all sessions. Entrance exams should be taken in the junior year of high school. There are early decision, early admissions, and deferred admissions plans. Application deadlines are open. The application fee is $25. Notification is sent on a rolling basis.

Transfer: Applicants must have taken either the ACT or the SAT I and must complete at least 4 semesters at Westminster as full-time students. 48 credits of 122 must be completed at Westminster.

Visiting: There are regularly scheduled orientations for prospective students, including 1-day summer programs with a general orientation and class registration. There are guides for informal visits and visitors may sit in on classes and stay overnight. To schedule a visit, contact Barbara Mc Gee, Office of Enrollment Services.

Financial Aid: In a recent year, 98% of all freshmen and 97% of continuing students received some form of financial aid. 57% of freshmen and 54% of continuing students received need-based aid. The average freshman award was $11,100. Of that total, scholarships or need-based grants averaged $8200 ($17,400 maximum); loans averaged $2000 ($6625 maximum); and work contracts averaged $1000 ($2000 maximum). 42% of undergraduates work part time. Average annual earnings from campus work are $825. The average financial indebtedness of a recent year's graduate was $12,600. Westminster is a member of CSS. The FAFSA is required. The fall application deadline is February 28.

International Students: There were 26 international students enrolled in a recent year. The school actively recruits these students. They must score 550 on the written TOEFL or 213 on the electronic version.

Computers: The mainframes are a DEC ALPHA server 21009, a DEC ALPHA server 1000a, a DEC Prioris XL server, a Gateway P5-200 server, and Power Macintosh 9500/150. There are 130 PCs and Macs available for student use. All residential halls, fraternities, and office areas are wired to a campus network and the Internet. All students may access the system. There are no time limits and no fees.

Graduates: In a recent year, 143 bachelor's degrees were awarded. The most popular majors were business administration (26%), psychology (12%), and political science (9%). In an average class, 35% graduate in 4 years, 43% in 5 years, and 41% in 6 years. 56 companies recruited on campus in a recent year. Of the 2000 graduating class, 94% were employed within 6 months of graduation.

Admissions Contact: Patrick Kirby, Dean of Enrollment Services. E-mail: *kirbypt@jaynet.wcmo.edu* Web: *http://www.wcmo.edu*

WILLIAM JEWELL COLLEGE — B-2
Liberty, MO 64068 — (816) 781-7700, ext. 5137
(800) 753-7009; Fax: (816) 415-5027

Full-time: 434 men, 620 women	**Faculty:** 84; IIB, av$
Part-time: 17 men, 18 women	**Ph.D.s:** 85%
Graduate: none	**Student/Faculty:** 13 to 1
Year: semesters, summer session	**Tuition:** $13,100
Application Deadline: March 15	**Room & Board:** $4050
Freshman Class: 635 applied, 508 accepted, 243 enrolled	
SAT I or ACT: required	**VERY COMPETITIVE**

William Jewell College, founded in 1849, is a small liberal arts college affiliated with the Baptist Church and offers undergraduate programs in the arts and sciences, business, education, and health fields. Tuition figures in the above capsule are approximate. In addition to regional accreditation, Jewell has baccalaureate program accreditation with NASM and NLN. The library contains 265,182 volumes, 215,981 microform items, and 29,064 audiovisual forms/CDs, and subscribes to 819 periodicals. Computerized library services include the card catalog, interlibrary loans, and database searching. Special learning facilities include a learning resource center, art gallery, planetarium, and radio station. The 149-acre campus is in a suburban area 15 miles northeast of Kansas City. Including residence halls, there are 23 buildings.

Student Life: 80% of undergraduates are from Missouri. Others are from 28 states, 12 foreign countries, and Canada. 90% are from public schools. 93% are white. The average age of freshmen is 18; all undergraduates, 19. 25% do not continue beyond their first year.

Housing: 872 students can be accommodated in college housing, which includes single-sex and coed dormitories, married-student housing, fraternity houses, and sorority houses. In addition, there are honors houses. On-campus housing is guaranteed for all 4 years. 67% of students live on campus; of those, 50% remain on campus on weekends. Alcohol is not permitted. All students may keep cars.

Activities: 41% of men belong to 4 national fraternities; 34% of women belong to 4 national sororities. There are 71 groups on campus, including art, band, cheerleading, choir, chorale, chorus, computers, dance, debate, drama, drill team, ethnic, honors, international, jazz band, marching band, ministries, musical theater, newspaper, orchestra, pep band, photography, political, professional, radio and TV, religious, social, social service, student government, symphony, and yearbook. Popular campus events include Serve and Celebrate, Parents/Grandparents Day, and CUA Picnic.

Sports: There are 9 intercollegiate sports for men and 9 for women, and 14 intramural sports for men and 5 for women. Facilities include a football stadium, a sports complex for baseball, soccer, and softball, and a phys ed center with an indoor track, a dance room, and facilities for basketball, racquetball, swimming, indoor tennis, volleyball, and weight lifting. The total seating capacity of the stadiums is 7000 and that of the indoor gym is 2000.

Disabled Students: 30% of the campus is accessible. Wheelchair ramps, elevators, special parking, specially equipped rest rooms, special class scheduling, and lowered drinking fountains are available.

Services: Counseling and information services are available, as is tutoring in most subjects.

Campus Safety and Security: Measures include 24-hour foot and vehicle patrol, self-defense education, informal discussions, and pamphlets/posters/films. There are emergency telephones and lighted pathways/sidewalks.

Programs of Study: Jewell confers B.A. and B.S. degrees. Bachelor's degrees are awarded in BIOLOGICAL SCIENCE (biochemistry and biology/biological science), BUSINESS (accounting, business administration and management, business economics, international business management, and management information systems), COMMUNICATIONS AND THE ARTS (art, communications, dramatic arts, English, French, music, and Spanish), COMPUTER AND PHYSICAL SCIENCE (chemistry, computer science, information sciences and systems, mathematics, and physics), EDUCATION (elementary, music, and secondary), HEALTH PROFESSIONS (medical laboratory technology, medical technology, and nursing), SOCIAL SCIENCE (history, international relations, Japanese studies, philosophy, political science/government, psychology, and religion). Business is the largest.

Required: To graduate, students must complete a minimum of 124 credits with a minimum 2.0 GPA, fulfilling the proper core requirements for their major and degree. All students must take The Responsible Self in their first semester and must also take courses in oral and written communication, phys ed, math, and foreign language, interdisciplinary courses in 4 categories, and a general education capstone course. Comprehensive exams in most majors are required.

Special: Internships for juniors or seniors, study abroad in Europe, Japan, and Hong Kong, and a Washington semester are offered. B.A.-B.S. degrees, dual majors of any combination, student-designed majors, and 3-2 engineering degrees with Washington University and the Universities of Missouri and Kansas are available. The pass/fail option is also available. The Oxbridge Honors Program for major study is patterned after the teaching methods of Oxford and Cambridge. Leadership and service learning programs are offered. There are 13 national honor societies, a freshman honors program, and 13 departmental honors programs.

Faculty/Classroom: 55% of faculty are male; 45%, female. All teach undergraduates. The average class size in an introductory lecture is 30; in a laboratory, 20; and in a regular course, 15.

Admissions: 80% of the 2001-2002 applicants were accepted. The SAT I scores for the 2001-2002 freshman class were: Verbal--20% below 500, 46% between 500 and 599, 20% between 600 and 700, and 14% above 700; Math--19% below 500, 33% between 500 and 599, 41% between 600 and 700, and 7% above 700. The ACT scores were 2% below 17, 45% between 18 and 23, 43% between 24 and 29, and 12% above 29.

Requirements: The SAT I or ACT is required. In addition, students must be graduates of an accredited secondary school; the GED is also accepted. The college recommends that applicants have taken 4 English courses, 3 courses each in math, social studies, and science, and 2 in foreign language. An interview is recommended. An audition is advised for music applicants. AP and CLEP credits are accepted. Important factors in the admissions decision are advanced placement or honor courses, extracurricular activities record, and leadership record. Applications are accepted on computer disk via CollegeLink and are accepted on-line at *admission@william.jewell.edu*

Procedure: Freshmen are admitted fall, spring, and summer. Entrance exams should be taken in the junior year. There is a deferred admissions plan. Applications should be filed by March 15 for fall entry, along with a $25 fee. Notification is sent on a rolling basis beginning September 1.

Transfer: 54 transfer students enrolled in 2001-2002. Transfer students must have maintained a 2.0 GPA and be in good academic standing with their former schools. Education majors must take the ACT, achieving a minimum score of 20. An interview is recommended for all students. 30 credits of 124 must be completed at Jewell.

Visiting: There are regularly scheduled orientations for prospective students, and personalized visits can be arranged upon request. There are guides for informal visits and visitors may sit in on classes and stay overnight. To schedule a visit, contact the Admission Office.

Financial Aid: In 2001-2002, 68% of all freshmen and 60% of continuing students received some form of financial aid. Including need-based aid. The average freshman award was $9229. The average financial indebtedness of the 2001 graduate was $17,500. Jewell is a member of CSS. The FAFSA and the college's own financial statement are required. The fall application deadline is March 1.

International Students: The school actively recruits these students. They must score 550 on the written TOEFL or take the MELAB.

Computers: The mainframe is a Data General-UNIX. The college provides approximately 100 PCs for academic use. All students may access the system. There are no time limits and no fees. It is strongly recommended that all students have a personal computer.

Graduates: In 2001, 258 bachelor's degrees were awarded. The most popular majors were business (24%), education (13%), and psychology (12%). In an average class, 46% graduate in 4 years, 59% in 5 years, and 60% in 6 years.

Admissions Contact: Chad Jolly, Dean of Enrollment Development. E-mail: *admission@william.jewell.edu* Web: *www.jewell.edu*

WILLIAM WOODS UNIVERSITY C-2

Fulton, MO 65251 (573) 592-4221
(800) 995-3159; Fax: (573) 592-1146

Full-time: 247 men, 599 women	**Faculty:** 62
Part-time: 40 men, 103 women	**Ph.D.s:** 61%
Graduate: 249 men, 421 women	**Student/Faculty:** 14 to 1
Year: semesters, summer session	**Tuition:** $13,790
Application Deadline: open	**Room & Board:** $5600
Freshman Class: 411 applied, 393 accepted, 181 enrolled	
SAT I Verbal/Math: 523/509	**ACT:** 22 **LESS COMPETITIVE**

William Woods University, founded in 1870, is a professions-oriented liberal arts university. Affiliated with the Christian Church (Disciples of Christ), it offers undergraduate programs in equestrian studies, international studies, education, arts and sciences, and selected preprofessional areas and graduate programs. In addition to regional accreditation, William Woods has baccalaureate program accreditation with ABA, and CSWE. The library contains 130,427 volumes, 10,841 microform items, and 28,204 audiovisual forms/CDs, and subscribes to 419 periodicals. Computerized library services include the card catalog, interlibrary loans, and database searching. Special learning facilities include a learning resource center, art gallery, labs for photography, foreign languages, and art, equestrian studies stables, a model courtroom, an American Sign Language interpreting lab, and an observatory. The 170-acre campus is in a small town 100 miles west of St. Louis. Including residence halls, there are 35 buildings.

Student Life: 75% of undergraduates are from Missouri. Others are from 36 states, 16 foreign countries, and Canada. 86% are from public schools. 88% are white. 37% are Protestant; 23% Catholic. The average age of freshmen is 18; all undergraduates, 21. 19% do not continue beyond their first year; 60% remain to graduate.

Housing: 750 students can be accommodated in college housing, which includes single-sex and coed dormitories, on-campus apartments, fraternity houses, and sorority houses. In addition, there are special-interest houses and nonsmoking and independent housing. On-campus housing is guaranteed for all 4 years. 88% of students live on campus; of those, 75% remain on campus on weekends. All students may keep cars.

Activities: 40% of men belong to 2 national fraternities; 46% of women belong to 4 national sororities. There are 30 groups on campus, including art, drama, honors, international, literary magazine, musical theater, photography, political, professional, religious, social, social service, student government, and yearbook. Popular campus events include Salute to the Arts, Campus Involvement and Activities Fair, and horse shows.

Sports: There are 4 intercollegiate sports for men and 5 for women. Facilities include a gym, a fitness center, a sand volleyball court, tennis courts, soccer, baseball, and softball fields, a weight room, a lake with a sand beach, table tennis and pool tables, and a sauna.

Disabled Students: 66% of the campus is accessible. Wheelchair ramps, elevators, special parking, specially equipped rest rooms, special class scheduling, lowered drinking fountains, lowered telephones, and campus access to TTY phones are available.

Services: Counseling and information services are available, as is tutoring in most subjects. There is a reader service for the blind and remedial math and writing. Interpreting is provided for the deaf upon request and receipt of supporting documentation. Study skills improvement courses are available.

Campus Safety and Security: Measures include 24-hour foot and vehicle patrol, self-defense education, escort service, and informal discussions. There are pamphlets/posters/films and lighted pathways/sidewalks.

Programs of Study: William Woods confers B.A., B.S., B.F.A., and B.S.W. degrees. Master's degrees are also awarded. Bachelor's degrees are awarded in AGRICULTURE (equine science), BIOLOGICAL SCIENCE (biology/biological science), BUSINESS (accounting and business administration and management), COMMUNICATIONS AND THE ARTS (art, communications, dramatic arts, English, graphic design, journalism, and studio art), COMPUTER AND PHYSICAL SCIENCE (computer science, information sciences and systems, mathematics, and science), EDUCATION (athletic training, early childhood, elementary, middle school, physical, and special), SOCIAL SCIENCE (family/juvenile justice, history, interdisciplinary studies, international studies, interpreter for the deaf, paralegal studies, political science/government, psychology, and social work). Business, equestrian studies, and political/legal studies are the strongest academically. Business, equestrian studies, and ASL/English interpreting are the largest.

Required: Students must complete a minimum of 122 credits to graduate, including at least 30 in the major and 52 in Common Studies, with 7 in the natural sciences, 6 each in English, the humanities, and behavioral and social sciences, 3 each in oral communication, math, and fine or performing arts, and 2 in freshman seminar. They must have maintained a minimum GPA of 2.0.

Special: William Woods University offers cross-registration with schools in the Mid-Missouri Association of Colleges and Universities, internships in various fields, including equestrian studies and computer information systems, study abroad, a Washington semester, and work-study. An accelerated degree program in most majors, B.A.-B.S. degrees, and student-designed and dual majors are possible. Credit for life, military, and work experience and pass/fail options are available. There are 11 national honor societies, and a freshman honors program.

Faculty/Classroom: 48% of faculty are male; 52%, female. All teach undergraduates. No introductory courses are taught by graduate students. The average class size in an introductory lecture is 25; in a laboratory, 15; and in a regular course, 25.

Admissions: 96% of the 2001-2002 applicants were accepted. 31% of the current freshmen were in the top fifth of their class; 23% were in the top two fifths.

Requirements: The SAT I or ACT is required with a recommended composite SAT I score of 900 and ACT score of 21. To be admitted to the college, applicants must be graduates of an accredited secondary school; the GED is also accepted. They must have completed 16 course units, 11 of which must be distributed among English, a foreign language, math, natural sciences, and social sciences. 2 references and an interview are recommended. Application are accepted on-line. AP and CLEP credits are accepted. Important factors in the admissions decision are personality/intangible qualities, leadership record, and recommendations by school officials.

Procedure: Freshmen are admitted to all sessions. Entrance exams should be taken in the spring of the junior year or the fall of the senior year. There is an early admissions plan. Application deadlines are open. The application fee is $25. Notification is sent on a rolling basis.

Transfer: 59 transfer students enrolled in 2001-2002. Transfer students must submit high school transcripts or GED and all college transcripts. They must also provide 2 references and be in good standing with their previous institution. 30 credits of 122 must be completed at William Woods.

Visiting: There are regularly scheduled orientations for prospective students, including the opportunity to talk with an academic adviser and an extensive student development-directed orientation to campus life. There are guides for informal visits and visitors may sit in on classes and stay overnight. To schedule a visit, contact the Office of Enrollment Services at (800) 995-3159, ext. 4221.

Financial Aid: In 2001-2002, all freshmen and 95% of continuing students received some form of financial aid. 56% of freshmen and 51% of continuing students received need-based aid. The average freshman award was $10,732. Of that total, scholarships or need-based grants averaged $8237 ($13,200 maximum); loans averaged $2714 ($4625 maximum); and work contracts averaged $830 ($1200 maximum). 52% of undergraduates work part time. Average annual earnings from campus work are $840. The average financial indebtedness of the 2001 graduate was $20,290. The FAFSA is required. The fall application deadline is March 1.

International Students: The school actively recruits these students. They must score 550 on the written TOEFL.

Computers: The mainframe is an AS/400 Model 200. The college provides 175 PCs and Macs for academic use. These can be found in classrooms, dorms, computer labs, and the library. E-mail and connections to the Internet are also available. Students have access to the campus network from all residence hall rooms. All students may access the system 7 days a week. There are no time limits and no fees. It is strongly recommended that all students have a personal computer.

Graduates: In 2001, 146 bachelor's degrees were awarded. The most popular majors were business administration/business management (25%), equestrian studies/equestrian administration (13%), and computer information science/computer information managment (6%).

Admissions Contact: Laura Archuleta, Executive Director of Enrollment Services. E-mail: *admissions@williamwoods.edu*
Web: *www.williamwoods.edu*

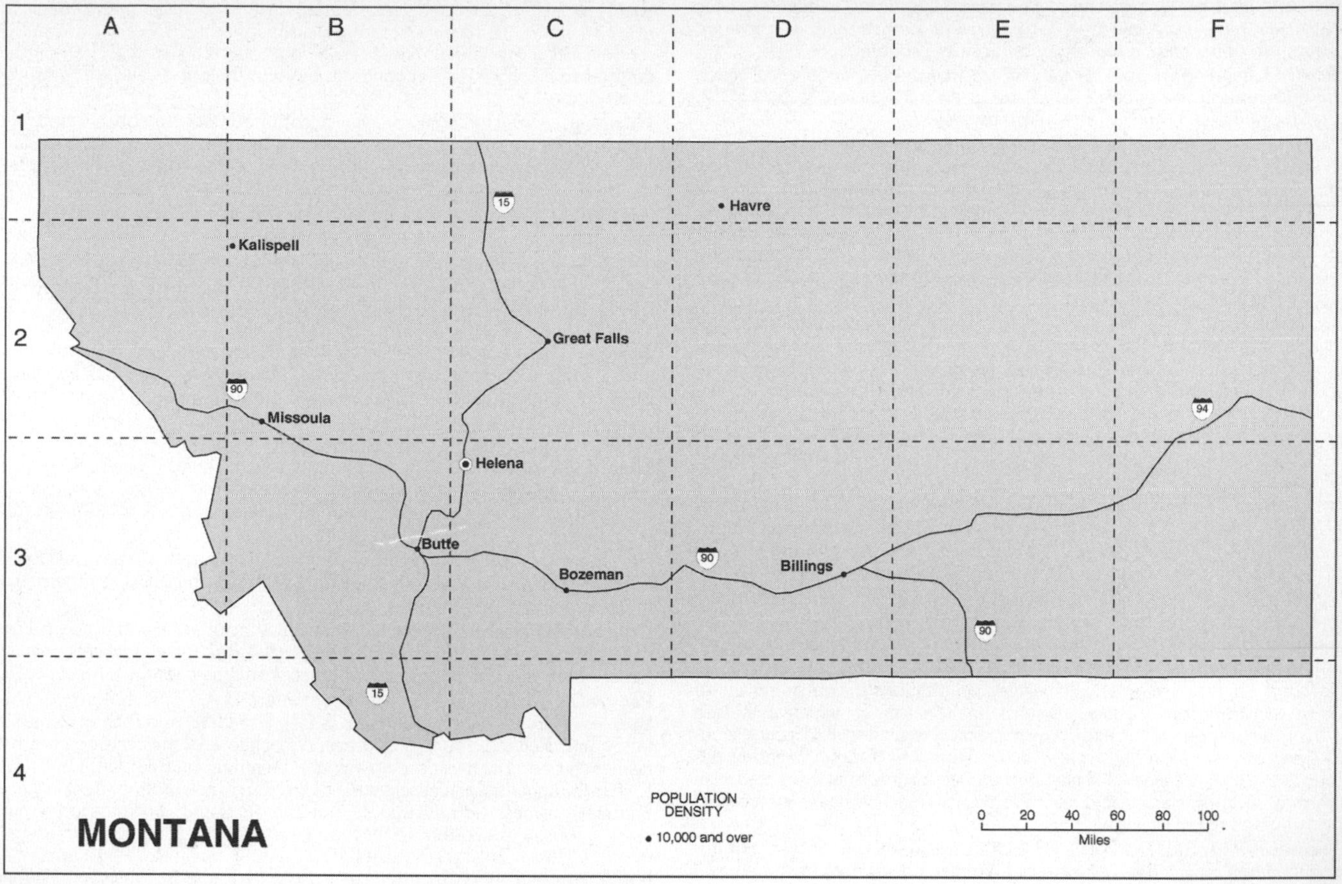

CARROLL COLLEGE
Helena, MT 59625-0002 C-2
(406) 447-4384
(800) 992-3648; (406) 447-4533

Full-time: 458 men, 693 women	**Faculty:** 79; IIB, --$
Part-time: 69 men, 127 women	**Ph.D.s:** 67%
Graduate: none	**Student/Faculty:** 15 to 1
Year: semesters, summer session	**Tuition:** $13,768
Application Deadline: June 1	**Room & Board:** $5372
Freshman Class: 842 applied, 753 accepted, 344 enrolled	
SAT I or ACT: required	**COMPETITIVE**

Carroll College, founded in 1909, is a small liberal arts college affiliated with the Roman Catholic Church. It offers undergraduate programs in arts and sciences, business, engineering, education, religion, and selected preprofessional training. In addition to regional accreditation, Carroll has baccalaureate program accreditation with CAHEA, CSWE, NLN, and NRPA. The library contains 89,003 volumes, 64,500 microform items, and 3890 audiovisual forms/CDs, and subscribes to 504 periodicals. Computerized library services include the card catalog, interlibrary loans, and database searching. Special learning facilities include a learning resource center and radio station. The 64-acre campus is in a small town 110 miles east of Missoula and 100 miles west of Bozeman. Including residence halls, there are 12 buildings.

Student Life: 68% of undergraduates are from Montana. Others are from 21 states, 10 foreign countries, and Canada. 77% are white. The average age of freshmen is 19; all undergraduates, 22. 19% do not continue beyond their first year.

Housing: 800 students can be accommodated in college housing, which includes single-sex and coed dormitories. On-campus housing is guaranteed for all 4 years. 50% of students live on campus. All students may keep cars.

Activities: There are no fraternities or sororities. There are 35 groups on campus, including cheerleading, choir, drama, ethnic, film, honors, international, jazz band, literary magazine, musical theater, newspaper, pep band, political, professional, radio and TV, religious, social, social service, student government, and yearbook. Popular campus events include theme dances, Casino night, and softball tournament.

Sports: There are 3 intercollegiate sports for men and 5 for women, and 10 intramural sports for men and 10 for women. Facilities include basketball, tennis, and racquetball courts, weight-lifting, aerobics, and dance rooms, a swimming pool, and a 4200-seat gym.

Disabled Students: 75% of the campus is accessible. Wheelchair ramps, elevators, special parking, specially equipped rest rooms, special class scheduling, and lowered drinking fountains are available.

Services: Counseling and information services are available, as is tutoring in most subjects, including writing, math, statistics, economics, chemistry, accounting, and anatomy and physiology. There is remedial math, reading, and writing.

Campus Safety and Security: Measures include escort service, informal discussions, and lighted pathways/sidewalks.

Programs of Study: Carroll confers the B.A. degree. Associate degrees are also awarded. Bachelor's degrees are awarded in BIOLOGICAL SCIENCE (biology/biological science), BUSINESS (accounting and business administration and management), COMMUNICATIONS AND THE ARTS (classical languages, communications, creative writing, dramatic arts, English, French, performing arts, public relations, and Spanish), COMPUTER AND PHYSICAL SCIENCE (chemistry, computer science, and mathematics), EDUCATION (elementary, foreign languages, physical, secondary, and teaching English as a second/foreign language (TESOL/TEFOL)), ENGINEERING AND ENVIRONMENTAL DESIGN (civil engineering and environmental science), HEALTH PROFESSIONS (clinical science, health care administration, nursing, predentistry, premedicine, preoptometry, prepharmacy, and preveterinary science), SOCIAL SCIENCE (history, international relations, philosophy, political science/government, prelaw, psychology, public administration, religion, social science, social work, and sociology). Business, nursing, and biology are the largest.

Required: To graduate, students must complete 122 semester hours and maintain the specific GPA and credit concentration required by their major. The college's general liberal arts requirements include courses in writing, communications, history, math, natural and social sciences, philosophy, theology, and fine arts.

Special: Carroll College offers a 3-2 engineering program leading to acceptance at any of 6 cooperating universities. In addition, internships, study abroad in Paris, Japan, Spain, Gemany, Korea and many other countries through a consortium for international studies, and work-study programs in certain fields are available. Students may take a dual major in any 2 fields of study, select an interdisciplinary major such as health information management, earn credit for life, military, and work experience, or pursue nondegree study. The pass/fail option is available. There are 6 national honor societies, including Phi Beta Kappa, a freshman honors program, and 5 departmental honors programs.

Faculty/Classroom: 56% of faculty are male; 44%, female. All teach undergraduates. The average class size in an introductory lecture is 22; in a laboratory, 13; and in a regular course, 17.

Admissions: 89% of the 2001-2002 applicants were accepted. The SAT I scores for the 2001-2002 freshman class were: Verbal--22% below 500, 49% between 500 and 599, 25% between 600 and 700, and 5% above 700; Math--24% below 500, 50% between 500 and 599, 22% between 600 and 700, and 4% above 700. The ACT scores were 2% below 17, 43% between 18 and 23, 46% between 24 and 29, and 9% above 29. 57% of the current freshmen were in the top quarter of their class; 85% were in the top half.

Requirements: The SAT I or ACT is required; composite scores of 1000 on the SAT I or 21 on the ACT are recommended. Students must be graduates of an accredited secondary school or have a GED. An essay is required. A GPA of 2.5 is required. AP and CLEP credits are accepted. Important factors in the admissions decision are advanced placement or honor courses, recommendations by school officials, and leadership record. Applications are accepted on-line at Carroll College's web page, or via CollegeLink.

Procedure: Freshmen are admitted fall and spring. Entrance exams should be taken in the fall of the senior year. There is a deferred admissions plan. Applications should be filed by June 1 for fall entry, along with a $25 fee. Notification is sent on a rolling basis.

Transfer: 64 transfer students enrolled in 2001-2002. Transfer students need a 2.5 GPA and must submit ACT or SAT I scores if fewer than 30 college credits have been completed. Letters of recommendation are required. 30 credits of 122 must be completed at Carroll.

Visiting: There are regularly scheduled orientations for prospective students, consisting of 3 visiting sessions in the summer, which include a tour of the campus, overnight housing, social activities, and preregistration for classes. Orientation takes place Thursday through Monday before the start of fall classes. There are guides for informal visits and visitors may sit in on classes and stay overnight. To schedule a visit, contact the Admissions Office.

Financial Aid: In 2001-2002, 69% of all freshmen and 66% of continuing students received some form of financial aid. 61% of freshmen and 60% of continuing students received need-based aid. The average freshman award was $12,198. The average financial indebtedness of the 2001 graduate was $22,450. Carroll is a member of CSS. The FAFSA is required. The fall application deadline is March 1.

International Students: The school actively recruits these students. They must score 550 on the written TOEFL and also take the college's own test. English-speaking students must submit SAT I or ACT scores.

Computers: The mainframe is an IBM AS/400. All residence hall rooms are wired for access to the network, with access also available in computer labs and the library. Internet access is available. There are 100 computers available for student use in various locations around campus. All students may access the system. There are no time limits and no fees.

Graduates: In 2001, 203 bachelor's degrees were awarded. The most popular majors were business (19%), biology (13%), and education (13%). In an average class, 39% graduate in 4 years, 49% in 5 years, and 50% in 6 years.

Admissions Contact: Candace Cain, Director of Admissions. A video is available. E-mail: *enroll@carroll.edu* Web: *www.carroll.edu*

MONTANA STATE UNIVERSITY-BILLINGS D-3

Billings, MT 59101-0298 **(406) 657-2158**
(800) 656-MSUB; Fax: (406) 657-2302

Full-time: 1094 men, 1924 women	**Faculty:** 148; IIA, --$
Part-time: 293 men, 561 women	**Ph.D.s:** 87%
Graduate: 130 men, 341 women	**Student/Faculty:** 20 to 1
Year: semesters, summer session	**Tuition:** $3153 ($8532)
Application Deadline: open	**Room & Board:** $4500
Freshman Class: n/av	
SAT I Verbal/Math: 477/490	**ACT:** 20 **NONCOMPETITIVE**

Montana State University-Billings, founded in 1927, is a comprehensive, regional, public university offering instructional and learning opportunities in the arts and sciences as well as professional programs in business, technology, human services, rehabilitation, and education. There are 5 undergraduate schools and 1 graduate school. In addition to regional accreditation, MSU-Billings has baccalaureate program accreditation with NASAD, NASM, and NCATE. The library contains 281,258 volumes, 850,000 microform items, and 1713 audiovisual forms/CDs, and subscribes to 794 periodicals. Computerized library services include the card catalog, interlibrary loans, and database searching. Special learning facilities include a learning resource center, art gallery, radio station, and scientific field station, small business institute, urban institute, special education learning center, disabilities center, center for business enterprise, and center for applied economic research. The 92-acre campus is in an urban area in Billings. Including residence halls, there are 21 buildings.

Student Life: 92% of undergraduates are from Montana. Others are from 34 states, 18 foreign countries, and Canada. 97% are from public schools. 83% are white. The average age of freshmen is 21; all undergraduates, 25. 53% do not continue beyond their first year; 27% remain to graduate.

Housing: 558 students can be accommodated in college housing, which includes single-sex and coed dormitories and married-student housing. On-campus housing is available on a first-come, first-served basis. 88% of students commute. All students may keep cars.

Activities: There are no fraternities or sororities. There are 53 groups on campus, including art, band, cheerleading, choir, chorale, chorus, computers, drama, ethnic, honors, jazz band, literary magazine, newspaper, orchestra, pep band, political, professional, radio and TV, religious, social, social service, and student government. Popular campus events include Powwow and Native American Day.

Sports: There are 4 intercollegiate sports for men and 6 for women, and 7 intramural sports for men and 7 for women. Facilities include a phys ed building with an Olympic-sized pool, 2 gyms, a running track, weight-training equipment, 6 racquetball courts, and a soccer/softball field.

Disabled Students: All of the campus is accessible. Wheelchair ramps, elevators, special parking, specially equipped rest rooms, special class scheduling, lowered drinking fountains, and lowered telephones are available.

Services: Counseling and information services are available, as is tutoring in most subjects. There is a reader service for the blind, and remedial math, reading, and writing.

Campus Safety and Security: Measures include 24-hour foot and vehicle patrol, escort service, informal discussions, and pamphlets/posters/films. There are emergency telephones and lighted pathways/sidewalks.

Programs of Study: MSU-Billings confers B.A., B.S., B.A. or B.S. in Business Administration, B.A.S., B.S.Ed., B.S.H.S., and B.S. in Rehabilitation and Related Services degrees. Associate and master's degrees are also awarded. Bachelor's degrees are awarded in BIOLOGICAL SCIENCE (biology/biological science), BUSINESS (accounting, banking and finance, business administration and management, business data processing, business economics, human resources, and marketing management), COMMUNICATIONS AND THE ARTS (art history and appreciation, communications, dramatic arts, English, fine arts, music, and public relations), COMPUTER AND PHYSICAL SCIENCE (chemistry, information sciences and systems, and mathematics), EDUCATION (art, early childhood, education, elementary, health, mathematics, middle school, music, physical, science, secondary, social science, social studies, and special), ENGINEERING AND ENVIRONMENTAL DESIGN (environmental science), HEALTH PROFESSIONS (health, health care administration, and rehabilitation therapy), SOCIAL SCIENCE (history, liberal arts/general studies, psychology, sociology, and Spanish studies). The sciences, business, and education are the strongest academically. Education and business are the largest.

Required: To graduate, students must have earned a minimum of 120 semester credits, including 30 in their major. They must maintain a minimum 2.0 GPA; education and human services majors must maintain a minimum 2.7 GPA. General education requirements must also be fulfilled.

Special: MSU-Billings offers co-op programs in business, human services, and liberal arts, internships, work-study programs, B.A.-B.S. degrees, dual majors, nondegree study, and pass/fail options. There are 10 national honor societies, a freshman honors program, and 1 departmental honors program.

Faculty/Classroom: 65% of faculty are male; 35%, female. All teach undergraduates. Graduate students teach 1% of introductory courses. The average class size in an introductory lecture is 30 and in a laboratory, 20.

Admissions: The SAT I scores for the 2001-2002 freshman class were: Verbal--60% below 500, 32% between 500 and 599, and 7% between 600 and 700; Math--49% below 500, 41% between 500 and 599, 9% between 600 and 700, and 1% above 700. The ACT scores were 56% below 21, 27% between 21 and 23, 11% between 24 and 26, 5% between 27 and 28, and 1% above 28. 17% of the current freshmen were in the top fifth of their class; 41% were in the top two fifths. 10 freshmen graduated first in their class.

Requirements: The SAT I or ACT is required. In addition, applicants must be graduates of an accredited secondary school; the GED is also accepted. The applicant must have taken 4 years of English, 3 each of social science and math, and 2 each of science, foreign languages, or humanities. Students need to meet 1 of 3 criteria: be in the upper 50% of their class; have a GPA of 2.0 or better; or have minimum composite scores of 22 on the ACT or 1030 on the SAT I. Applications are accepted on-line via CollegeNet. MSU-Billings requires applicants to be in the upper 50% of their class. A GPA of 2.5 is required. AP and CLEP credits are accepted. Important factors in the admissions decision are advanced placement or honor courses, geographic diversity, and evidence of special talent.

Procedure: Freshmen are admitted to all sessions. Entrance exams should be taken in the senior year of high school. There is a deferred admissions plan. Application deadlines are open, and notification is on a rolling basis. The fee was $30 in 2001.

Transfer: 365 transfer students enrolled in 2001-2002. Out-of-state transfer students must have earned a 2.0 GPA; in-state transfer students must be in good academic standing. 32 credits of 120 must be completed at MSU-Billings.

Visiting: There are regularly scheduled orientations for prospective students. There are guides for informal visits and visitors may sit in on classes and stay overnight. To schedule a visit, contact Shelly Beatty at *sbeatty@msubillings.edu*.

Financial Aid: In a recent year, 58% of all freshmen and 61% of continuing students received some form of financial aid. 46% of freshmen and 56% of continuing students received need-based aid. The average freshman award was $4325. Of that total, scholarships or need-based grants averaged $1300; loans averaged $2425; and work contracts averaged $600. Average annual earnings from campus work were $1245. The average financial indebtedness of a recent graduate was $13,554. The FAFSA and the college's own financial statement are required. The fall application deadline is March 1.

International Students: There are 31 international students enrolled. The school actively recruits these students. They must score 525 on the written TOEFL and also take the SAT I or the ACT.

Computers: The mainframe is a DEC 8100. There are also 500 PCs available at various campus locations. All have access to e-mail, the Web, and on-line library resources, course registration, and courses. All students may access the system 24 hours a day. There are no time limits. The fee is $2.65/per credit hour. It is strongly recommended that all students have a personal computer.

Graduates: In 2001, 503 bachelor's degrees were awarded. The most popular majors were arts and sciences (39%), business (32%), and education (26%). In an average class, 9% graduate in 4 years, 25% in 5 years, and 31% in 6 years. 100 companies recruited on campus in 2000-2001. Of the 2000 graduating class, 7% were enrolled in graduate school within 6 months of graduation and 89% were employed.

Admissions Contact: Karen Everett, Director of Admissions and Records and Registrar. E-mail: *keverett@msubillings.edu*
Web: *www.msubillings.edu*

MONTANA STATE UNIVERSITY-BOZEMAN C-3

Bozeman, MT 59717 **(406) 994-2452; Fax: (406) 994-1923**

Full-time: 4976 men, 4115 women	**Faculty:** 522; I, --$
Part-time: 757 men, 689 women	**Ph.D.s:** n/av
Graduate: 630 men, 578 women	**Student/Faculty:** 17 to 1
Year: semesters, summer session	**Tuition:** $3381 ($10,147)
Application Deadline: open	**Room & Board:** $5050
Freshman Class: 3641 applied, 3156 accepted, 1894 enrolled	
SAT I Verbal/Math: 540/550	**ACT:** 23 **COMPETITIVE**

Montana State University-Bozeman, founded in 1893, is a public, land-grant institution offering programs in agriculture, business, arts and architecture, education, engineering, health and human development, nursing, and letters and science. There are 7 undergraduate schools and 1 graduate school. In addition to regional accreditation, MSU-Bozeman has baccalaureate program accreditation with AACSB, AAFCS, ABET, ADA, CACREP, CCNE, CSAB, NAAB, NASAD, NASM, NCATE, and NLN. The 2 libraries contain 615,068 volumes, 2,089,818 microform items, and 4336 audiovisual forms/CDs, and subscribe to 4492 periodicals. Computerized library services include the card catalog, interlibrary loans, and database searching. Special learning facilities include a learning resource center, art gallery, natural history museum, planetarium, radio station, TV station, Center for Biofilm Engineering, Burns Telecommunication Center, and a geographic information and analysis center. The 1170-acre campus is in a small town 140 miles west of Billings and 90 miles north of Yellowstone National Park. Including residence halls, there are 83 buildings.

Student Life: 71% of undergraduates are from Montana. Others are from 50 states, 46 foreign countries, and Canada. 86% are white. The average age of freshmen is 19; all undergraduates, 22. 29% do not continue beyond their first year; 43% remain to graduate.

Housing: 5400 students can be accommodated in college housing, which includes coed dormitories and married-student housing. In addition, there are honors houses, international houses, houses for older students, nonsmoking floors, and wellness floors. On-campus housing is guaranteed for the freshman year only and is available on a first-come, first-served basis. 78% of students commute. All students may keep cars.

Activities: 6% of men belong to 9 national fraternities; 6% of women belong to 5 national sororities. There are 150 groups on campus, including art, band, cheerleading, chess, choir, chorale, chorus, computers, dance, drama, drill team, ethnic, film, gay, honors, international, jazz band, marching band, musical theater, newspaper, orchestra, pep band, photography, political, professional, radio and TV, religious, social, social service, student government, and symphony. Popular campus events include International Food Bazaar and Native American Pow-Wow.

Sports: There are 6 intercollegiate sports for men and 8 for women, and 38 intramural sports for men and 40 for women. Facilities include a 10,000-seat stadium, numerous gyms, handball courts, weight rooms, and 2 pools.

Disabled Students: 90% of the campus is accessible. Wheelchair ramps, elevators, special parking, specially equipped rest rooms, special class scheduling, lowered drinking fountains, lowered telephones, services through the resource center, and a taping service for the blind are available.

Services: Counseling and information services are available, as is tutoring in most subjects. There is a reader service for the blind, and remedial math, reading, and writing.

Campus Safety and Security: Measures include 24-hour foot and vehicle patrol, self-defense education, escort service, and informal discussions. There are pamphlets/posters/films, emergency telephones, and lighted pathways/sidewalks.

Programs of Study: MSU-Bozeman confers B.A., B.S., B.F.A., and B.Mus.Ed. degrees. Master's and doctoral degrees are also awarded. Bachelor's degrees are awarded in AGRICULTURE (agricultural business management, animal science, horticulture, natural resource management, plant science, range/farm management, and soil science), BIOLOGICAL SCIENCE (biology/biological science, biotechnology, and microbiology), BUSINESS (business administration and management), COMMUNICATIONS AND THE ARTS (art, dramatic arts, English, fine arts, media arts, modern language, and music), COMPUTER AND PHYSICAL SCIENCE (chemistry, computer science, earth science, mathematics, and physics), EDUCATION (agricultural, elementary, music, secondary, and technical), ENGINEERING AND ENVIRONMENTAL DESIGN (agricultural engineering technology, chemical engineering, civil engineering, computer engineering, construction engineering, electrical/electronics engineering, environmental design, environmental science, industrial engineering, land use management and reclamation, mechanical engineering, and mechanical engineering technology), HEALTH PROFESSIONS (health, health care administration, and nursing), SOCIAL SCIENCE (anthropology, economics, history, human development, philosophy, political science/government, psychology, and sociology). Engineering, physical science, and architecture are the strongest academically. Business, education, and nursing are the largest.

Required: To graduate, students must complete a core curriculum of 8 credits of natural sciences, 6 credits each of multicultural studies, humanities, social science, and communications, and 3 credits each of fine arts and math. The total number of credits required varies by program, with 120 being the minimum; at least one third must be in upper-division courses. A minimum 2.0 GPA is needed. Students must be officially registered in their chosen curriculum for at least 2 semesters before graduation.

Special: MSU-Bozeman offers internships in selected majors, study in 40 countries, cross-registration in selected programs, B.A.-B.S. degrees, dual and interdisciplinary majors, nondegree study, and pass/fail options. There are 23 national honor societies and a university-wide honors program.

Faculty/Classroom: 60% of faculty are male; 40%, female. All both teach and do research. Graduate students teach 21% of introductory courses. The average class size in an introductory lecture is 79; in a laboratory, 24; and in a regular course, 26.

Admissions: 87% of the 2001-2002 applicants were accepted. The SAT I scores for the 2001-2002 freshman class were: Verbal--31% below 500, 45% between 500 and 599, 22% between 600 and 700, and 2% above 700; Math--25% below 500, 44% between 500 and 599, 26% between 600 and 700, and 5% above 700. The ACT scores were 27% below 21, 30% between 21 and 23, 23% between 24 and 26, 11% between 27 and 28, and 9% above 28. 31% of the current freshmen were in the top fifth of their class; 45% were in the top two fifths. 64 freshmen graduated first in their class.

Requirements: The SAT I or ACT is required. In addition, MSU-Bozeman requires applicants to have a minimum GPA of 2.5 and rank in the upper 50% of their graduating class or have minimum composite scores of 22 on the ACT or 1030 on the SAT I. They must be graduates of an accredited secondary school. The GED is accepted. Students should have completed 4 years of English, 3 years each of social studies and math, 2 years of lab science, and 2 years of language, computer science, visual and performing arts, or vocational education. AP and CLEP credits are accepted. Applications are accepted on-line at the school's web site: *www.montana.edu/wwwcat/appopts.html*. Applicants will be billed a $30 nonrefundable processing fee when the on-line application is received.

Procedure: Freshmen are admitted fall, spring, and summer. Entrance exams should be taken in the fall of the senior year. There are early admissions and deferred admissions plans. Application deadlines are open. Notification is on a rolling basis. The fall 2001 application fee was $30.

Transfer: 821 transfer students enrolled in 2001-2002. Applicants must have a minimum GPA of 2.0; grades of D or better transfer for credit. 30 credits of 120 must be completed at MSU-Bozeman.

Visiting: There are regularly scheduled orientations for prospective students, including program overviews, a tour, and meeting with assistant deans. There are guides for informal visits and visitors may sit in on classes and stay overnight. To schedule a visit, contact the Office of New Student Services.

Financial Aid: In a recent year, 74% of all freshmen and 65% of continuing students received some form of financial aid. 50% of all students received need-based aid. The average freshman award was $6677. Of that total, scholarships or need-based grants averaged $1274 ($10,650 maximum); loans averaged $2291 ($11,425 maximum); work contracts averaged $847 ($3925 maximum); and non-need based aid, including institutional and External sholarships and grants,nonparent loans, parent loans, tuition waivers, and athletic aid averaged $2603 ($17,087 maximum). 20% of undergraduates work part time. Average annual earnings from campus work are $1800. The average financial indebtedness of the 2001 graduate was $17,000. The FAFSA is required. The fall application deadline is March 1.

International Students: There are 204 international students enrolled. The school actively recruits these students. They must score 525 on the written TOEFL or 195 on the electronic version. Students must also submit proof of American Cultural Exchange Language Institute Level 5.

Computers: The mainframe is a Digital Alpha Server 8400 clustered with an Alpha Server 4100. Labs, residence halls, the library, and departments have 850 computers available for student use. All students may access the system. There are no time limits. The fee is included in the mandatory fees. It is recommended that students in environmental design have personal computers.

Graduates: In 2001, 1672 bachelor's degrees were awarded. The most popular majors were business (12%), nursing (7%), and biological sciences (6%). In an average class, 12% graduate in 4 years, 46% in 5 years, and 90% in 6 years. 169 companies recruited on campus in 2000-2001. Of the 2000 graduating class, 7% were enrolled in graduate school within 6 months of graduation and 80% were employed.

Admissions Contact: Ronda Russell, Director, Office of New Student Services. A video is available. E-mail: *admissions@montana.edu*
Web: *http://www.montana.edu/wwwnss/*

MONTANA STATE UNIVERSITY-NORTHERN D-1

Havre, MT 59501-7751 (406) 265-3704
(800) 662-6132; Fax: (406) 265-3792

Full-time: 640 men, 540 women	**Faculty:** 71; IIA, --$
Part-time: 100 men, 210 women	**Ph.D.s:** 47%
Graduate: 43 men, 70 women	**Student/Faculty:** 16 to 1
Year: semesters, summer session	**Tuition:** $3200 ($8400)
Application Deadline: open	**Room & Board:** $5400
Freshman Class: n/av	
SAT I or ACT: required	**NONCOMPETITIVE**

Montana State University-Northern, founded in 1929, is part of the Montana University System and offers programs in the liberal arts, teacher education, business, and technology. Figures given in above capsule are approximate. There is 1 graduate school. In addition to regional accreditation, MSU-Northern has baccalaureate program accreditation with NLN. The library contains 100,000 volumes and 600,000 microform items, and subscribes to 650 periodicals. Computerized library services include the card catalog, interlibrary loans, and database searching. Special learning facilities include a learning resource center and radio station. The 105-acre campus is in a small town 115 miles north of Great Falls. Including residence halls, there are 21 buildings.

Student Life: The average age of freshmen is 21; all undergraduates, 28.

Housing: 450 students can be accommodated in college housing, which includes single-sex and coed dormitories, on-campus apartments, and married-student housing. On-campus housing is guaranteed for all 4 years. 60% of students live on campus. All students may keep cars.

Activities: There are no fraternities or sororities. There are 30 groups on campus, including dance, ethnic, musical theater, newspaper, pep band, religious, social service, student government, and yearbook. Popular campus events include concerts, dances, and theatrical productions.

Sports: There are 3 intercollegiate sports for men and 3 for women, and 11 intramural sports for men and 9 for women. Facilities include tennis courts, a swimming pool, weight and wrestling rooms, and 2 gyms, the larger seating 2500. Nearby Glacier National Park offers outdoor facilities.

Disabled Students: Wheelchair ramps, elevators, special parking, and specially equipped rest rooms are available.

Services: Counseling and information services are available, as is tutoring in every subject. There is remedial math, reading, and writing.

Campus Safety and Security: Measures include lighted pathways/sidewalks.

Programs of Study: MSU-Northern confers B.A., B.S., B.S.Ed., and B.T. degrees. Associate and master's degrees are also awarded. Bachelor's degrees are awarded in AGRICULTURE (agricultural mechanics), BIOLOGICAL SCIENCE (biology/biological science and ecology), COMMUNICATIONS AND THE ARTS (communications, dramatic arts, English, fine arts, French, and music), COMPUTER AND PHYSICAL SCIENCE (chemistry), EDUCATION (business, elementary, industrial arts, physical, science, secondary, and social science), ENGINEERING AND ENVIRONMENTAL DESIGN (automotive technology, civil engineering technology, construction technology, drafting and design technology, electrical/electronics engineering technology, engineering technology, environmental science, and manufacturing technology), HEALTH PROFESSIONS (nursing), SOCIAL SCIENCE (history, humanities, interdisciplinary studies, Native American studies, and social science). Business technology, nursing, and education are the largest.

Required: To graduate, students must complete at least 128 credits with a minimum GPA of 2.0 overall and 2.25 in their major and minor. Distribution requirements include 12 credits each of humanities, social science, math/science, and technology/applied arts. Students also must demonstrate proficiency in computing and in written and oral communication.

Special: B.A.-B.S. and other dual-degree programs, pass/fail options, cooperative programs in most disciplines, independent study, dual majors, and work-study programs are available.

Faculty/Classroom: All teach undergraduates. No introductory courses are taught by graduate students.

Requirements: The SAT I or ACT is required, with a minimum composite scores of 20. Applicants must be graduates of an accredited high school or have a GED certificate. They should have completed 4 years of English, 3 each of math, social science, and history, including global studies and U.S. history, and 2 each of lab science and electives. MSU-Northern requires applicants to be in the upper 50% of their class. A GPA of 2.5 is required. CLEP credit is accepted.

Procedure: Freshmen are admitted to all sessions. There is an early admissions plan. Application deadlines are open. Notificacion is rolling. The application fee is $30.

Transfer: Nonresidents must have a minimum GPA of 2.0. Any applicant with fewer than 12 transfer credits must submit a transcript of college work completed and meet standard freshman requirements. 36 credits of 128 must be completed at MSU-Northern.

Visiting: There are regularly scheduled orientations for prospective students. There are guides for informal visits and visitors may sit in on classes and stay overnight. To schedule a visit, contact the Admissions Office.

Financial Aid: The college's own financial statement is required. Check with the school for current deadlines.

International Students: There were 13 international students enrolled in a recent year. The school actively recruits these students. They must score 500 on the written TOEFL.

Computers: There are Apple computers available in various locations. All students may access the system when the buildings are open. There are no time limits.

Admissions Contact: Stacey Gonsalez, Admissions Counselor.
E-mail: *msunadmit@msun.edu* Web: *www.msun.edu*

MONTANA TECH OF THE UNIVERSITY OF MONTANA C-3

Butte, MT 59701-8997 (406) 496-4178
(800) 445-TECH; Fax: (406) 496-4710

Full-time: 968 men, 686 women	**Faculty:** 107; IIA, av$
Part-time: 129 men, 222 women	**Ph.D.s:** 75%
Graduate: 49 men, 32 women	**Student/Faculty:** 15 to 1
Year: semesters, summer session	**Tuition:** $3404 ($9911)
Application Deadline: open	**Room & Board:** $4441
Freshman Class: 1002 applied, 951 accepted, 791 enrolled	
SAT I Verbal/Math: 528/550	**ACT:** 21 **COMPETITIVE**

Founded in 1893 as the Montana School of Mines, Montana Tech still focuses on its original programs in minerals and energy engineering and has expanded its offerings to include new science, engineering, business, computer science, technical communications, health care, and related programs. There are 4 undergraduate schools and 1 graduate school. In addition to regional accreditation, Montana Tech has baccalaureate program accreditation with ABET and ACS. The library contains 167,262 volumes, 259,581 microform items, and 2947 audiovisual forms/CDs, and subscribes to 394 periodicals. Computerized library services include the card catalog, interlibrary loans, and database searching. Special learning facilities include a learning resource center, radio station, a mineral museum, and METNET 2-way interactive communication studio. The 56-acre campus is in a small town in Butte. Including residence halls, there are 19 buildings.

Student Life: 86% of undergraduates are from Montana. Others are from 33 states, 17 foreign countries, and Canada. 90% are from public schools. 92% are white. The average age of freshmen is 19; all undergraduates, 22. 39% do not continue beyond their first year; 58% remain to graduate.

Housing: 426 students can be accommodated in college housing, which includes coed dormitories, off-campus apartments, and married-student housing. On-campus housing is guaranteed for the freshman year only and is available on a first-come, first-served basis. Priority is given to out-of-town students. 87% of students commute. All students may keep cars.

Activities: There are no fraternities or sororities. There are 33 groups on campus, including band, cheerleading, choir, chorale, computers, ethnic, international, newspaper, pep band, photography, professional, radio and TV, religious, social, social service, student government, and symphony. Popular campus events include M-Day, International Dinner, and Comedy Night.

Sports: There are 3 intercollegiate sports for men and 3 for women, and 10 intramural sports for men and 10 for women. Facilities include an athletic/ recreational complex housing 4 basketball courts, a 25-meter swimming pool, volleyball courts, a weight-lifting room, 6 handball/ raquetball courts, tennis courts, a stadium with skybox seating, 3 classrooms and 2 practice fields, and a baseball facility.

Disabled Students: 75% of the campus is accessible. Wheelchair ramps, elevators, special parking, specially equipped rest rooms, special class scheduling, lowered drinking fountains, and lowered telephones are available.

Services: Counseling and information services are available, as is tutoring in most subjects, including mathematics, physics, chemistry, biology, engineering science, and business and computer science. There is a reader service for the blind and remedial math. Tutoring in additional subject areas is available upon request.

Campus Safety and Security: Measures include 24-hour foot and vehicle patrol, self-defense education, informal discussions, and pamphlets/ posters/films. There are emergency telephones, lighted pathways/ sidewalks, and a foot patrol.

Programs of Study: Montana Tech confers B.S. and B.A.S degrees. Associate and master's degrees are also awarded. Bachelor's degrees are awarded in BIOLOGICAL SCIENCE (biology/biological science), BUSINESS (business systems analysis), COMMUNICATIONS AND THE ARTS (communications and communications technology), COMPUTER AND PHYSICAL SCIENCE (chemistry, computer programming, computer science, mathematics, and science), ENGINEERING AND ENVIRONMENTAL DESIGN (computer engineering, engineering, environmental engineering, geological engineering, geophysical engineering, metallurgical engineering, mining and mineral engineering, occupational safety and health, and petroleum/natural gas engineering), SOCIAL SCIENCE (humanities and social science and liberal arts/general studies). Engineering and science are the strongest programs academically and have the largest enrollments.

Required: For graduation, students must complete at least 120 semester credits (more for engineering degrees) and maintain a minimum 2.0 GPA. Requirements include 6 hours each of communications, humanities, mathematical sciences, and social sciences, and 6 to 7 hours of physical and life sciences. Engineering students must satisfy specific requirements within the individual curriculum.

Special: Montana Tech has cooperative programs in all areas with 7 other institutions and cross-registration with Flathead Valley Community College, Montana State University, and the University of Montana. Internships are available, and there is a student-faculty exchange program with the People's Republic of China and a mining exchange program with Peru. Work-study, accelerated degree programs, 3-2 engineering degrees, student-designed majors, nondegree study, and credit for military experience are available. There are 3 national honor societies.

Faculty/Classroom: 81% of faculty are male; 20%, female. All teach undergraduates, 25% do research, and 25% do both. The average class size in an introductory lecture is 34; in a laboratory, 15; and in a regular course, 21.

Admissions: 95% of the 2001-2002 applicants were accepted. The SAT I scores for the 2001-2002 freshman class were: Verbal--35% below 500, 38% between 500 and 599, 24% between 600 and 700, and 3% above 700; Math--26% below 500, 36% between 500 and 599, 31% between 600 and 700, and 7% above 700. The ACT scores were 49% below 21, 20% between 21 and 23, 18% between 24 and 26, 7% between 27 and 28, and 6% above 28. 41% of the current freshmen were in the top fifth of their class; 70% were in the top two fifths. 19 freshmen graduated first in their class.

Requirements: The SAT I or ACT is required. In addition, applicants must be graduates of an accredited secondary school. The GED is accepted. 14 academic credits are required, including English, 4 years; math and social studies, 3 years each; science, 2 years; plus 2 years chosen from foreign language, computer science, visual and performing arts, or vocational education. Applicants must have minimum composite scores of 22 on the ACT or 1030 on the SAT I or a 2.5 GPA, or be in the top half of their graduating class. Other factors regarding admissions are considered only if the preceding standards are not met. Applications are accepted on computer disk and on-line via CollegeNet. AP and CLEP credits are accepted.

Procedure: Freshmen are admitted to all sessions. Entrance exams should be taken in the senior year. There is a deferred admissions plan. Early decision applications should be filed by March 1; regular applications, on an open basis for fall entry, along with a $30 fee. Notification is sent on a rolling basis.

Transfer: 123 transfer students enrolled in 2001-2002. Transfer applicants must have a minimum GPA of 2.0. Grades of C and above transfer for credit. 30 credits of 120 must be completed at Montana Tech.

Visiting: There are regularly scheduled orientations for prospective students, There is an official fall orientation, though visits are welcome anytime. There are guides for informal visits and visitors may sit in on classes and stay overnight. To schedule a visit, contact the Admissions Office.

Financial Aid: In 2001-2002, 75% of all students received some form of financial aid. 60% of freshmen and 70% of continuing students received need-based aid. The average freshman award was $4000. Of that total, scholarships or need-based grants averaged $1047 ($7863 maximum); loans averaged $2539 ($11,493 maximum); work contracts averaged $1500; and grants averaged $1675 ($2300 maximum). 63% of undergraduates work part time. Average annual earnings from campus work are $1800. The average financial indebtedness of the 2001 graduate was $11,500. Montana Tech is a member of CSS. The FAFSA is required. The fall application deadline is March 1.

International Students: There are 56 international students enrolled. The school actively recruits these students. They must score 525 on the written TOEFL or 195 on the electronic version and also take the SAT I or the ACT, scoring 22 on the ACT or 1020 on the SAT I.

Computers: The mainframe is a series of Compaq servers. There are some 1500 PCs connected to the campus LAN. All have access to both the Internet and campus intranet resources. Many PCs on both campuses are designated as "general use" for all students. Additionally, departments provide PCs configured for the requirements of their individual programs. All students may access the system anytime. There are no time limits. The fee is $36 per semester.

Graduates: In 2001, 243 bachelor's degrees were awarded. The most popular majors were general engineering (17%), petroleum engineering (14%), and business and information technology (12%). In an average class, 1% graduate in 3 years, 40% in 4 years, 60% in 5 years, and 67% in 6 years. 153 companies recruited on campus in 2000-2001. Of the 2000 graduating class, 10% were enrolled in graduate school within 6 months of graduation and 95% were employed.

Admissions Contact: Ray Rogers, Director of College Relations and Marketing. A video is available. E-mail: *admissions@mtech.edu*
Web: *www.mtech.edu*

MONTANA UNIVERSITY SYSTEM

The Montana University System, established in 1972, is a public system. It is governed by a board of regents whose chief administrator is the Commissioner of Higher Education. The primary goal of the system is teaching first, then research and public service. The main priorities are funding, system structure, and transfer articulation. The total enrollment of all 6 4-year campuses is approximately 28,000, with about 1100 faculty members. There are 148 baccalaureate, 92 master's, and 33 doctoral programs offered in the system. Profiles of the 4-year campuses are included in this section.

ROCKY MOUNTAIN COLLEGE — D-3

Billings, MT 59102 — **(406) 657-1000 or 657-1026**
(800) 877-6259; Fax: (406) 259-9751

Full-time: 337 men, 375 women	**Faculty:** 45
Part-time: 26 men, 39 women	**Ph.D.s:** 67%
Graduate: none	**Student/Faculty:** 16 to 1
Year: semesters, summer session	**Tuition:** $12,835
Application Deadline: August 1	**Room & Board:** $5278
Freshman Class: 452 applied, 377 accepted, 140 enrolled	
SAT I Verbal/Math: 493/501	**ACT:** 22 — **COMPETITIVE**

Rocky Mountain College, established in 1878, is a private liberal arts institution affiliated with the United Church of Christ, the United Methodist Church, and the Presbyterian Church (U.S.A.). In addition to regional accreditation, Rocky has baccalaureate program accreditation with CAAHEP and IACBE. The library contains 86,689 volumes, 52 microform items, and 709 audiovisual forms/CDs, and subscribes to 364 periodicals. Computerized library services include the card catalog, interlibrary loans, and database searching. Special learning facilities include a learning resource center and art gallery. The 60-acre campus is in a small town 550 miles north of Denver, Colorado, in south-central Montana. Including residence halls, there are 16 buildings.

Student Life: 75% of undergraduates are from Montana. Others are from 32 states, 16 foreign countries, and Canada. 82% are white; 10% Native American/Eskimo. 45% are Protestant; 36% claim no religious affiliation; 18% Catholic. The average age of freshmen is 19; all undergraduates, 24. 33% do not continue beyond their first year; 33% remain to graduate.

Housing: 303 students can be accommodated in college housing, which includes coed dormitories and on-campus apartments. On-campus housing is guaranteed for the freshman year only and is available on a first-come, first-served basis. 63% of students commute. All students may keep cars.

Activities: There are no fraternities or sororities. There are 25 groups on campus, including band, cheerleading, choir, chorale, chorus, computers, drama, forensics, honors, international, jazz band, literary magazine, marching band, musical theater, newspaper, pep band, photography, professional, religious, social, social service, student government, and yearbook. Popular campus events include Convocations, intercollegiate athletics, and Woodrow Wilson Visiting Fellow.

Sports: There are 4 intercollegiate sports for men and 4 for women, and 12 intramural sports for men and 12 for women. Facilities include a bicycle and ski repair shop and an equipment rental shop. Activities include backpacking in Glacier National Park, white-water river rafting in the Tetons, and climbing at Beartooth Mountain.

Disabled Students: 60% of the campus is accessible. Wheelchair ramps, elevators, special parking, specially equipped rest rooms, special class scheduling, and lowered drinking fountains are available.

Services: Counseling and information services are available, as is tutoring in most subjects. There is a reader service for the blind, and remedial math, reading, and writing.

Campus Safety and Security: Measures include self-defense education, escort service, informal discussions, and pamphlets/posters/films. There are lighted pathways/sidewalks and security cameras.

Programs of Study: Rocky confers B.A. and B.S. degrees. Associate degrees are also awarded. Bachelor's degrees are awarded in AGRICULTURE (equine science), BIOLOGICAL SCIENCE (biology/biological science), BUSINESS (accounting, business administration and management, and business economics), COMMUNICATIONS AND THE ARTS (art, communications, dramatic arts, literature, and music performance), COMPUTER AND PHYSICAL SCIENCE (chemistry, computer science, earth science, information sciences and systems, mathematics, and natural sciences), EDUCATION (art, education, elementary, English, mathematics, music, physical, psychology, science, social science, and social studies), ENGINEERING AND ENVIRONMENTAL DESIGN (aeronautical science and aviation administration/management), HEALTH PROFESSIONS (physician's assistant), SOCIAL SCIENCE (anthropology, economics, history, philosophy, political science/government, psychology, religion, and sociology). Education, business and economics, and aviation are the largest.

Required: To graduate, students must complete 124 credit hours, 24 in a major and 18 in a minor, with a minimum overall GPA of 2.0 and 2.25 in the major. There are general education requirements in humanities, the natural and social sciences, fine arts, and religious thought, as well as writing, speech, math, computer, and health requirements.

Special: The college offers co-op programs, internships, study abroad in 32 countries, work-study, dual majors, individualized programs of study, and credit for life, military, and work experience. Juniors and seniors may elect to take 1 course on a pass/fail basis each semester. There is a freshman honors program, and all departments have honors programs.

Faculty/Classroom: 56% of faculty are male; 44%, female. All teach undergraduates and 15% do research. The average class size in an introductory lecture is 19; in a laboratory, 11; and in a regular course, 12.

Admissions: 83% of the 2001-2002 applicants were accepted. The SAT I scores for the 2001-2002 freshman class were: Verbal--50% below 500, 39% between 500 and 599, and 11% between 600 and 700; Math--41% below 500, 48% between 500 and 599, and 11% between 600 and 700. The ACT scores were 42% below 21, 17% between 21 and 23, 28% between 24 and 26, 7% between 27 and 28, and 5% above 28. 21% of the current freshmen were in the top fifth of their class; 50% were in the top two fifths. 3 freshmen graduated first in their class.

Requirements: The SAT I or ACT is required. In addition, applicants must be graduates of an accredited secondary school; the GED is accepted. Students must have completed 4 units of English, 1 unit of history, and 2 units each in 3 of the following: foreign language, math, natural sciences, and social sciences. The school recommends a portfolio for admission to the art program, an audition for admission to the music program, and an interview for academically weak students. A GPA of 2.5 is required. AP and CLEP credits are accepted. Applications may be submitted on-line at *www.rocky.edu/admissions/whichone.shtml*.

Procedure: Freshmen are admitted to all sessions. There are early admissions and deferred admissions plans. Applications should be filed by August 1 for fall entry, along with a $25 fee. Notification is sent on a rolling basis, beginning October 1.

Transfer: 111 transfer students enrolled in 2001-2002. Transfer students must have a minimum GPA of 2.0; grades of 2.0 and higher transfer for credit. Transfers are admitted every term. 24 credits of 124 must be completed at Rocky.

Visiting: There are regularly scheduled orientations for prospective students, in late spring and summer. There are guides for informal visits and visitors may sit in on classes and stay overnight. To schedule a visit, contact the Director of Admissions.

Financial Aid: In a recent year, 95% of all freshmen and 97% of continuing students received some form of financial aid. 73% of freshmen and 80% of continuing students received need-based aid. The average freshman award was $9311. Of that total, scholarships or need-based grants averaged $6063; loans averaged $2803; and work contracts averaged $1000. Average annual earnings from campus work are $1000. The average financial indebtedness of a recent graduate was $16,606. The FAFSA and the college's own financial statement are required. The fall application deadline is April 1.

International Students: There are 26 international students enrolled. The school actively recruits these students. They must score 500 on the written TOEFL or 173 on the electronic version.

Computers: The mainframe is an HP. 7 student computer labs housing 193 PCs are available. All students may access the system. There are no time limits and no fees.

Graduates: In 2001, 159 bachelor's degrees were awarded. The most popular majors were education (16%), physician assistant (14%), and aviation (13%). 75 companies recruited on campus in 2000-2001. Of the 2000 graduating class, 13% were enrolled in graduate school within 6 months of graduation and 99% were employed.

Admissions Contact: LynAnn Henderson, Director of Admissions. E-mail: *admissions@rocky.edu* Web: *www.rocky.edu*

UNIVERSITY OF GREAT FALLS

Great Falls, MT 59405 — C-2

(406) 791-5200
(800) 856-9544; Fax: (406) 791-5209

Full-time: 158 men, 329 women	**Faculty:** 41
Part-time: 78 men, 191 women	**Ph.D.s:** 54%
Graduate: 27 men, 96 women	**Student/Faculty:** 12 to 1
Year: semesters, summer session	**Tuition:** $10,260
Application Deadline: August 1	**Room & Board:** $5100
Freshman Class: 200 applied	
SAT I or ACT: recommended	**COMPETITIVE**

The University of Great Falls, established in 1932, is a private, liberal arts institution affiliated with the Roman Catholic Church. There are 2 undergraduate schools and 1 graduate school. The library contains 106,135 volumes, 124,608 microform items, and 3894 audiovisual forms/CDs, and subscribes to 587 periodicals. Computerized library services include the card catalog, interlibrary loans, and database searching. Special learning facilities include a learning resource center and art gallery. The 40-acre campus is in an urban area. Including residence halls, there are 13 buildings.

Student Life: 93% of undergraduates are from Montana. Others are from 20 states and Canada. 99% are from public schools. 80% are white. 28% are Catholic; 22% claim no religious affiliation; 19%, Protestant. The average age of freshmen is 26; all undergraduates, 33. 46% do not continue beyond their first year; 20% remain to graduate.

Housing: 189 students can be accommodated in college housing, which includes single-sex and coed dormitories, off-campus apartments, and married-student housing. On-campus housing is guaranteed for the freshman year only and is available on a first-come, first-served basis. Priority is given to out-of-town students. 88% of students commute. Alcohol is not permitted. All students may keep cars.

Activities: There are no fraternities or sororities. There are 15 groups on campus, including art, business, cheerleading, chess, choir, chorus, computers, drama, ethnic, forensics, honors, literary magazine, musical theater, newspaper, orchestra, photography, professional, religious, social, social service, student government, and symphony. Popular campus events include Orientation Barbecue, Halloween Dance, and Intramural Festival.

Sports: There is 1 intercollegiate sport for men and 2 for women, and 7 intramural sports for men and 7 for women. Facilities include a gym, Olympic-size pool, game room, and workout room.

Disabled Students: All of the campus is accessible. Wheelchair ramps, elevators, special parking, specially equipped rest rooms, special class scheduling, and lowered drinking fountains are available.

Services: Counseling and information services are available, as is tutoring in some subjects, including 100-level courses, 200-level courses, and selected 300-level courses. There is a reader service for the blind, remedial math, reading, and writing, and tutoring in basic skills.

Campus Safety and Security: Measures include 24-hour foot and vehicle patrol, self-defense education, escort service, and informal discussions. There are pamphlets/posters/films, emergency telephones, and lighted pathways/sidewalks.

Programs of Study: UGF confers B.A. and B.S. degrees. Associate and master's degrees are also awarded. Bachelor's degrees are awarded in BIOLOGICAL SCIENCE (biology/biological science, botany, microbiology, molecular biology, and physiology), BUSINESS (accounting, business administration and management, management science, and marketing/retailing/merchandising), COMMUNICATIONS AND THE ARTS (art, English, and fine arts), COMPUTER AND PHYSICAL SCIENCE (computer management, computer programming, computer science, mathematics, physical sciences, and science), EDUCATION (education of the exceptional child, elementary, health, mathematics, middle school, physical, reading, science, secondary, social studies, and special), ENGI-

NEERING AND ENVIRONMENTAL DESIGN (computer graphics), HEALTH PROFESSIONS (health care administration, predentistry, and premedicine), SOCIAL SCIENCE (counseling/psychology, criminal justice, history, human services, law enforcement and corrections, paralegal studies, political science/government, prelaw, psychology, religion, social science, sociology, and theological studies). Biology, paralegal studies, and computer science are the strongest academically. Education, criminal justice, and business are the largest.

Required: Students must complete 128 credit hours, including 30 to 65 in the major, plus 15 to 21 minor credits, maintaining a minimum GPA of 2.0. The 52-credit-hour core curriculum includes math, computer science, art, behavioral science, history, literature, philosophy, science, writing, theology, and religion. Specific disciplines required include human nature, intellectual inquiry, and religious dimension.

Special: Internships are offered in sociology, criminal justice, paralegal studies, health care administration, and chemical-dependency counseling. Opportunities are provided for work-study programs, B.A.-B.S. degrees in most majors, dual majors, a general studies degree, credit by exam or for military service, and nondegree study. A 3-2 engineering degree for applied computer science and applied math majors is offered with Montana State University-Bozeman. Specialized instruction is available through the use of videotape and telephone discussions in 14 locations throughout Montana and Canada. There is 1 national honor society.

Faculty/Classroom: 59% of faculty are male; 42%, female. All teach undergraduates. No introductory courses are taught by graduate students. The average class size in an introductory lecture is 15; in a laboratory, 10; and in a regular course, 14.

Admissions: 68% of the 2001-2002 applicants were accepted. The SAT I scores for the 2001-2002 freshman class were: Verbal--44% below 500, 25% between 500 and 599, and 31% between 600 and 700; Math--47% below 500, 40% between 500 and 599, and 13% between 600 and 700. The ACT scores were 44% below 21, 28% between 21 and 23, 18% between 24 and 26, 3% between 27 and 28, and 8% above 28.

Requirements: The SAT I or ACT is recommended. In addition, graduation from an accredited secondary school is required; the GED is accepted. Applicants should have 4 years of English, 3 of math, and 2 each of social studies, science, and electives, including foreign language, art, music, and vocational education. An interview is recommended. A GPA of 2.0 is required. AP and CLEP credits are accepted.

Procedure: Freshmen are admitted fall, spring, and summer. Entrance exams should be taken prior to registration. Applications should be filed by August 1 for fall entry. Notification is sent on a rolling basis. The fall application fee was $25.

Transfer: 98 transfer students enrolled in 2001-2002. Transfer applicants must be in good academic standing from another accredited college or university, and must submit official transcripts from all colleges or universities attended. Those without a bachelor's degree must also submit an official high school transcript. 30 credits of 128 must be completed at UGF.

Visiting: There are regularly scheduled orientations for prospective students, including meeting with prospective advisers and staff, financial aid presentation, campus tour, and lunch. There are guides for informal visits and visitors may sit in on classes and stay overnight. To schedule a visit, contact the Office of Admissions.

Financial Aid: In 2001-2002, 81% of all freshmen and 83% of continuing students received some form of financial aid. 82% of freshmen and 61% of continuing students received need-based aid. The average freshman award was $9578. Of that total, scholarships or need-based grants averaged $3507 ($4500 maximum); loans averaged $2720 ($3978 maximum); and work contracts averaged $3075 ($3500 maximum). 39% of undergraduates work part time. Average annual earnings from campus work are $3000. The average financial indebtedness of the 2001 graduate was $20,470. UGF is a member of CSS. The FAFSA is required.

International Students: There are 19 international students enrolled. The school actively recruits these students. They must score 550 on the written TOEFL.

Computers: There are 250 Pentium PCs with full Internet access via a T1 line. All students may access the system 7 days a week. There are no time limits and no fees. It is strongly recommended that all students have a personal computer.

Graduates: In 2001, 180 bachelor's degrees were awarded. The most popular majors were education (29%), criminal justice (13%), and business (11%). In an average class, 6% graduate in 3 years, 6% in 4 years, 14% in 5 years, and 20% in 6 years. 70 companies recruited on campus in 2000-2001. Of the 2000 graduating class, 18% were employed within 6 months of graduation.

Admissions Contact: Cathy Day, Director of Admissions.
E-mail: *adminrec@ugf.edu* Web: *www.ugf.edu*

UNIVERSITY OF MONTANA — B-2
Missoula, MT 59812 (406) 243-6266
(800) 462-8636; Fax: (406) 243-5711

Full-time: 4395 men, 4826 women	**Faculty:** 439; I, --$
Part-time: 577 men, 656 women	**Ph.D.s:** 86%
Graduate: 1024 men, 1135 women	**Student/Faculty:** 21 to 1
Year: semesters, summer session	**Tuition:** $3520 ($9532)
Application Deadline: July 1	**Room & Board:** $4518
Freshman Class: 3562 applied, 3144 accepted, 1874 enrolled	
SAT I Verbal/Math: 546/538	**ACT:** 23 **COMPETITIVE**

The University of Montana, founded in 1893, is a public institution with programs in arts and sciences, business administration, fine arts, education, forestry, journalism, and pharmacy and allied health sciences. It is part of the Montana University System. There are 8 undergraduate and 2 graduate schools. In addition to regional accreditation, U of M has baccalaureate program accreditation with AACSB, ACCE, ACPE, APTA, CAHEA, CSAB, CSWE, NASAD, NASDTEC, NASM, NCATE, and SAF. The 4 libraries contain 913,000 volumes, 1,991,267 microform items, and 27,600 audiovisual forms/CDs, and subscribe to 4700 periodicals. Computerized library services include the card catalog, interlibrary loans, and database searching. Special learning facilities include an art gallery, radio station, TV station, experimental forest, biological station, ranch, Center for People and Forests, geology field camp, international language lab, wilderness institute, observatory, and fresh water research center. The 220-acre campus is in an urban area 200 miles east of Spokane. Including residence halls, there are 57 buildings.

Student Life: 70% of undergraduates are from Montana. Others are from 49 states, 67 foreign countries, and Canada. 80% are from public schools. 93% are white. The average age of freshmen is 19; all undergraduates, 25. 22% do not continue beyond their first year; 39% remain to graduate.

Housing: 2600 students can be accommodated in college housing, which includes single-sex and coed dormitories, off-campus apartments, and married-student housing. In addition, there are honors houses and special-interest houses, an international house, and nontraditional houses. On-campus housing is guaranteed for the freshman year only. 75% of students commute. All students may keep cars.

Activities: 10% of men belong to 9 national fraternities; 8% of women belong to 4 national sororities. There are 130 groups on campus, including academic, art, band, cheerleading, chess, choir, chorale, chorus, computers, creative writing, dance, drill team, ethnic, forestry, gay, honors, international, jazz band, literary magazine, marching band, newspaper, opera, orchestra, pep band, political, professional, radio and TV, religious, social, social service, student government, and symphony. Popular campus events include Foresters Day, Founders Day, and International Week.

Sports: There are 6 intercollegiate sports for men and 8 for women, and 16 intramural sports for men and 12 for women. Facilities include a field house, a 10,000-seat gym, an 18,000-seat stadium, a fitness center, a golf course, soccer and rugby fields, an Olympic-size pool, a game room, a climbing wall, weight rooms, and mountain trails.

Disabled Students: 75% of the campus is accessible. Wheelchair ramps, elevators, special parking, specially equipped rest rooms, special class scheduling, lowered drinking fountains, lowered telephones, specially equipped dorm rooms, and stadium access are available.

Services: Counseling and information services are available, as is tutoring in every subject. There is a reader service for the blind, and remedial math, reading, and writing. Mentors and note takers are available, as are books on tape for LD students.

Campus Safety and Security: Measures include 24-hour foot and vehicle patrol, self-defense education, escort service, and informal discussions. There are pamphlets/posters/films, emergency telephones, and lighted pathways/sidewalks.

Programs of Study: U of M confers B.A., B.S., B.A.E., B.S.H.P.E., and B.S.M. degrees. Associate, master's, and doctoral degrees are also awarded. Bachelor's degrees are awarded in AGRICULTURE (environmental studies forestry and related sciences), BIOLOGICAL SCIENCE (biology/biological science, botany, microbiology, wildlife biology, and zoology), BUSINESS (accounting, banking and finance, business administration and management, marketing/retailing/merchandising, personnel management, and small business management), COMMUNICATIONS AND THE ARTS (classics, communications, dramatic arts, English, fine arts, French, German, Japanese, journalism, music, music performance, radio/television technology, Russian, and Spanish), COMPUTER AND PHYSICAL SCIENCE (chemistry, computer science, geology, mathematics, and physics), EDUCATION (elementary, music, physical, science, and secondary), HEALTH PROFESSIONS (medical technology and pharmacy), SOCIAL SCIENCE (anthropology, economics, geography, history, liberal arts/general studies, Native American studies, philosophy, political science/government, psychology, social work, sociology, and women's studies). Journalism, forestry, and liberal arts are the strongest academically. Business, forestry, and education are the largest.

Required: A total of 120 credits is required for graduation in most majors. The number of hours in the major varies; some majors require a thesis. There are competency requirements in writing, math, and foreign language or symbolic systems. Juniors must pass writing exams. Distribution requirements include courses in expressive arts, literary and artistic studies, historical and cultural studies, social sciences, ethical and human values, and natural sciences. A minimum GPA of 2.0 must be maintained.

Special: Students may cross-register with Montana Tech and Western Montana College. Co-op programs exist in business, communications, economics, management, and liberal studies; internships in most majors, work-study programs with nonprofit organizations, and study abroad in 12 countries are available. The school offers a B.A.-B.S. degree in chemistry, pass/fail options in classes other than major requirements, and dual majors in physics and computer science as well as history and political science. There are 7 national honor societies, including Phi Beta Kappa, a freshman honors program, and 5 departmental honors programs.

Faculty/Classroom: 67% of faculty are male; 33%, female. All both teach and do research. Graduate students teach 2% of introductory courses. The average class size in an introductory lecture is 35; in a laboratory, 25; and in a regular course, 35.

Admissions: 88% of the 2001-2002 applicants were accepted. The SAT I scores for the 2001-2002 freshman class were: Verbal--26% below 500, 46% between 500 and 599, 22% between 600 and 700, and 5% above 700; Math--30% below 500, 45% between 500 and 599, 22% between 600 and 700, and 3% above 700. The ACT scores were 27% below 21, 33% between 21 and 23, 23% between 24 and 26, 10% between 27 and 28, and 7% above 28. 30% of the current freshmen were in the top fifth of their class; 62% were in the top two fifths. There were 11 National Merit finalists and 10 semifinalists in a recent year. 73 freshmen graduated first in their class in a recent year.

Requirements: The SAT I or ACT is required, with a minimum composite ACT score of 22 or a minimum SAT I composite score of 1030. Applicants must be graduates of an accredited secondary school. The GED is accepted. Students should have completed 4 years of English, 3 of math, 3 of social studies, 2 of lab science, and 2 elective credits (foreign language recommended). U of M requires applicants to be in the upper 50% of their class. A GPA of 2.5 is required. AP and CLEP credits are accepted. Important factors in the admissions decision are advanced placement or honor courses, evidence of special talent, and geographic diversity. Applications are accepted on disk or on-line by contacting U of M on the Internet or via CollegeNET, Apply, or Education Connect.

Procedure: Freshmen are admitted to all sessions. There is a deferred admissions plan. Applications should be filed by July 1 for fall entry and November 15 for spring entry. The fall 2001 application fee was $30. Notification is sent on a rolling basis.

Transfer: 946 transfer students enrolled in a recent year. Applicants must have a minimum GPA of 2.0. Grades of 2.0 or better transfer for credit. 30 credits of 120 must be completed at U of M.

Visiting: There are regularly scheduled orientations for prospective students, including placement testing, advising, workshops, and social events. There are guides for informal visits and visitors may sit in on classes. To schedule a visit, contact the Office of Admissions and New Student Services.

Financial Aid: U of M is a member of CSS. The FAFSA is required. The fall application deadline is March 1.

International Students: There were 385 international students enrolled in a recent year. The school actively recruits these students. They must score 500 on the written TOEFL.

Computers: The mainframe consists of 2 DEC ALPHA 8200 servers. Terminal rooms are located campuswide, including in dorms. Several academic departments have their own terminal rooms. Off-campus services have access through Interact. All students may access the system anytime. There are no time limits. The fee is $3 per credit. It is strongly recommended that all students have a personal computer.

Graduates: In a recent year, 1795 bachelor's degrees were awarded. The most popular majors were business (17%), education (11%), and forestry (9%). In an average class, 27% graduate in 4 years, 29% in 5 years, and 57% in 6 years. 76 companies recruited on campus in a recent year. Of a recent year's graduating class, 29% were enrolled in graduate school within 6 months of graduation and 96% were employed.

Admissions Contact: Frank Matule, Director of Admissions and New Student Services. A video is available. E-mail: *admiss@selway.umt.edu* Web: *http://www.umt.edu/nss*

UNIVERSITY OF MONTANA--WESTERN B-3
(Formerly Western Montana College of the University of Montana)

Dillon, MT 59725 **(406) 683-7331**
(866) UMW-MONT; Fax: (406) 683-7493

Full-time: 417 men, 474 women	**Faculty:** 50; IIB, --$
Part-time: 47 men, 225 women	**Ph.D.s:** 80%
Graduate: none	**Student/Faculty:** 18 to 1
Year: semesters, summer session	**Tuition:** $2915 ($8832)
Application Deadline: July 1	**Room & Board:** $4000
Freshman Class: 278 applied, 278 accepted, 183 enrolled	
SAT I or ACT: required	**NONCOMPETITIVE**

The University of Montana--Western College, formerly Western Montana College of the University of Montana and established in 1893, is a public institution, part of the University of Montana system. The college emphasizes teacher education and liberal studies. In addition to regional accreditation, Western has baccalaureate program accreditation with NCATE. The library contains 63,000 volumes and 35 audiovisual forms/CDs, and subscribes to 550 periodicals. Computerized library services include the card catalog, interlibrary loans, and database searching. Special learning facilities include a learning resource center, art gallery, radio station, and a humanities resource center. The 34-acre campus is in a small town 60 miles south of Butte and 150 miles from Yellowstone National Park. Including residence halls, there are 22 buildings.

Student Life: 90% of undergraduates are from Montana. Others are from 24 states, 3 foreign countries, and Canada. 90% are from public schools. 87% are white. The average age of freshmen is 20; all undergraduates, 25. 30% do not continue beyond their first year.

Housing: 616 students can be accommodated in college housing, which includes single-sex and coed dormitories, on-campus apartments, and married-student housing. On-campus housing is guaranteed for all 4 years. All students may keep cars.

Activities: There are no fraternities or sororities. There are 18 groups on campus, including art, band, cheerleading, choir, chorale, drama, ethnic, honors, musical theater, newspaper, pep band, political, radio and TV, religious, social, social service, student government, and yearbook. Popular campus events include Alumni Weekend and International Week.

Sports: There are 4 intercollegiate sports for men and 4 for women, and 7 intramural sports for men and 7 for women. Facilities include a 5000-seat gym, 3 basketball and 4 racquetball courts, a dance floor, tennis courts, 2 weight rooms, an aerobics room, circuit training, an indoor arena, and a 3000-seat stadium.

Disabled Students: 98% of the campus is accessible. Wheelchair ramps, elevators, special parking, specially equipped rest rooms, special class scheduling, lowered drinking fountains, and lowered telephones are available.

Services: Counseling and information services are available, as is tutoring in most subjects, and remedial math.

Campus Safety and Security: Measures include 24-hour foot and vehicle patrol, escort service, informal discussions, and pamphlets/posters/films. There are lighted pathways/sidewalks.

Programs of Study: Western confers B.A., B.S. Business, B.Applied Sc., and B.S.Ed. degrees. Associate degrees are also awarded. Bachelor's degrees are awarded in COMMUNICATIONS AND THE ARTS (art, communications, creative writing, English literature, and technical and business writing), EDUCATION (art, business, elementary, industrial arts, middle school, music, science, and secondary), ENGINEERING AND ENVIRONMENTAL DESIGN (environmental science), SOCIAL SCIENCE (liberal arts/general studies, and social science). Elementary education is the largest.

Required: For graduation, students must complete 120 credit hours (128 for education) and maintain a minimum GPA of 2.0. Other requirements vary by major.

Special: The college offers co-op programs, work-study programs, B.A.-B.S. degrees, dual majors, and pass/fail options. The Rural Education Program is designed to prepare students for teaching in smaller rural school settings. There are 2 national honor societies, and a freshman honors program.

Faculty/Classroom: 60% of faculty are male; 40%, female. All teach undergraduates. The average class size in an introductory lecture is 35; in a laboratory, 20; and in a regular course, 19.

Admissions: All of the 2001-2002 applicants were accepted. 15% of the current freshmen were in the top fifth of their class; 37% were in the top two fifths. 4 freshmen graduated first in their class in a recent year.

Requirements: The SAT I or ACT is required; new students who have not taken one of them must complete one during their first semester of attendance. Applicants must be graduates of an accredited secondary school. The GED is accepted. Students should have completed 4 years of English, 3 each of social studies and math, 2 years of lab science, and 2 years of electives. Western requires applicants to be in the upper 50%

of their class. A GPA of 2.5 is required. AP and CLEP credits are accepted.

Procedure: Freshmen are admitted to all sessions. There is a deferred admissions plan. Applications should be filed by July 1 for fall entry, December 1 for spring entry, and May 1 for summer entry, along with a $30 fee. The college accepts all applicants. Notification is sent on a rolling basis.

Transfer: 91 transfer students enrolled in 2001-2002. Transfers must have attempted a minimum of 12 credit hours and have a cumulative GPA of 2.0. Credits earned at any accredited college can be used to satisfy curriculum or degree requirements only after evaluation. 30 credits of 120 must be completed at Western.

Visiting: There are regularly scheduled orientations for prospective students, including Sunday through Monday overnight stays. There are guides for informal visits and visitors may sit in on classes. To schedule a visit, contact the Admissions Office.

Financial Aid: In 2001-2002, 65% of all freshmen and 75% of continuing students received some form of financial aid. 72% of freshmen and 51% of continuing students received need-based aid. The average freshman award was $5239. Of that total, scholarships or need-based grants averaged $2077 ($5000 maximum); loans averaged $2412 ($2625 maximum); and work contracts averaged $750 ($1500 maximum). 99% of undergraduates work part time. Average annual earnings from campus work are $1500. The average financial indebtedness of the 2001 graduate was $20,433. Western is a member of CSS. The FAFSA is required. The fall application deadline is March 1.

International Students: There are 5 international students enrolled. They must score 500 on the written TOEFL or 173 on the electronic version; the ACT or SAT I is required of Canadian high school students.

Computers: The mainframe is a DEC PDP 11/60. PCs are available in the computer learning center/office simulation center, with access to the Internet. All students may access the system from 8 A.M. to 10 P.M. without time limits. The fee is $36.

Graduates: In 2001, 148 bachelor's degrees were awarded. The most popular majors were elementary education (35%), liberal arts and sciences (35%), and secondary education (20%). In a recent graduating class, 80% were employed within 6 months of graduation.

Admissions Contact: Arlene Williams, Dean of Enrollment Management. E-mail: *admissions@umwestern.edu* Web: *www.umwestern.edu*

WESTERN MONTANA COLLEGE OF THE UNIVERSITY OF MONTANA
(See University of Montana--Western)

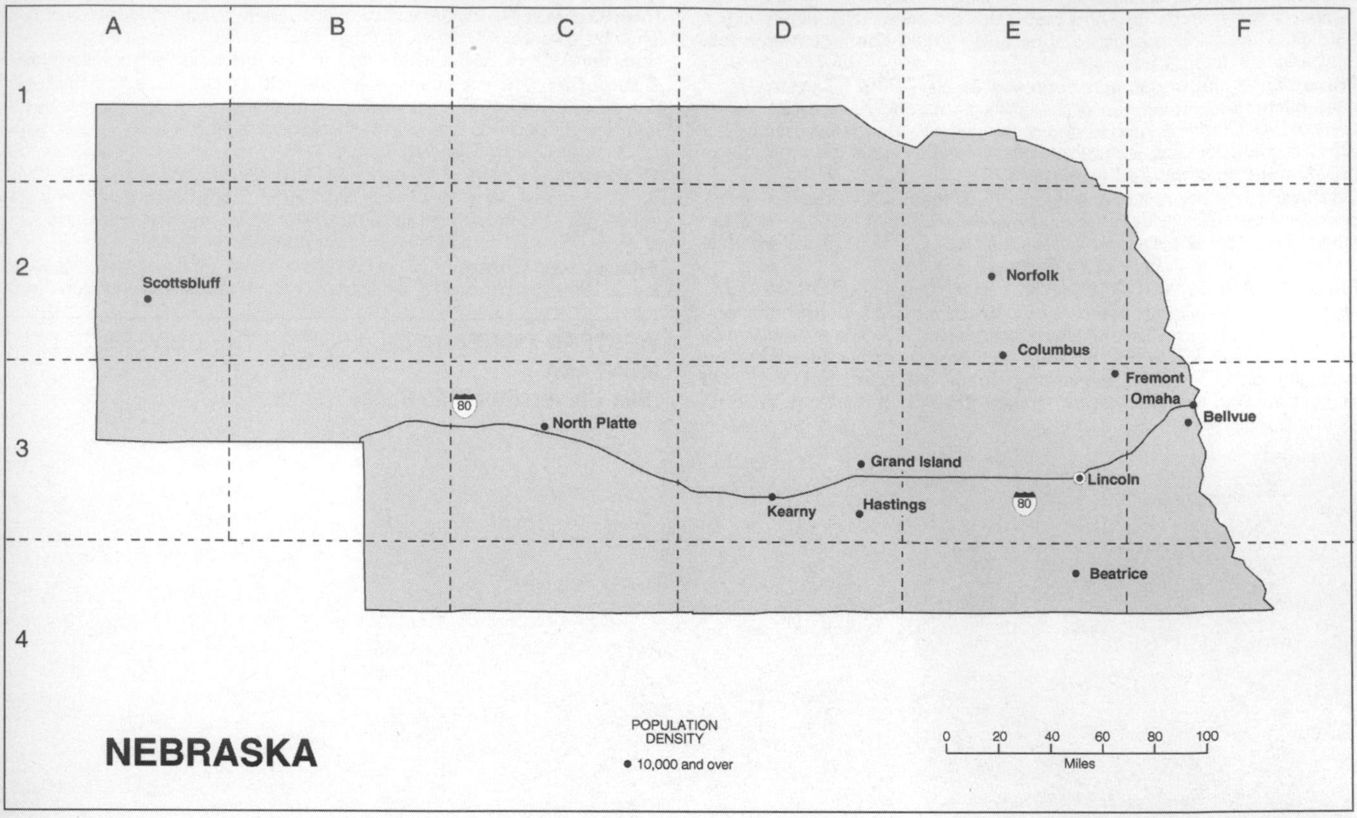

BELLEVUE UNIVERSITY

Bellevue, NE 68005 — F-3

(402) 293-3767

(800) 756-7920; Fax: (402) 293-3730

Full-time: 1127 men, 995 women	**Faculty:** 48
Part-time: 472 men, 611 women	**Ph.D.s:** 56%
Graduate: 386 men, 334 women	**Student/Faculty:** 44 to 1
Year: semesters, summer session	**Tuition:** $4125
Application Deadline: open	**Room & Board:** n/app
Freshman Class: 172 applied, 172 accepted, 103 enrolled	
SAT I: n/av	**ACT:** required

NONCOMPETITIVE

Bellevue University, established in 1966, is a private commuter institution offering undergraduate degrees in arts and sciences, professional studies, and business. There are 3 undergraduate schools and 1 graduate school. The library contains 122,000 volumes and 6700 microform items, and subscribes to 507 periodicals. Computerized library services include the card catalog, interlibrary loans, and database searching. Special learning facilities include a learning resource center and art gallery. The 19-acre campus is in a suburban area 5 miles south of Omaha. There are 6 buildings.

Student Life: 95% of undergraduates are from Nebraska. 90% are from public schools. 86% are white. The average age of all undergraduates is 25. 12% do not continue beyond their first year; 40% remain to graduate.

Housing: There are no residence halls. All students commute. Alcohol is not permitted.

Activities: There are no fraternities or sororities. There are some groups and organizations on campus, including cheerleading, newspaper, and professional. Popular campus events include Halloween and Christmas parties, Black History Month, and Spring Bash.

Sports: There are 2 intercollegiate sports for men and 1 for women. Facilities include racquetball, basketball, and volleyball courts, and weightlifting equipment.

Disabled Students: All of the campus is accessible. Wheelchair ramps, special parking, specially equipped rest rooms, and lowered drinking fountains are available.

Services: Counseling and information services are available, as is tutoring in most subjects.

Campus Safety and Security: Measures include self-defense education, informal discussions, pamphlets/posters/films, and lighted pathways/sidewalks.

Programs of Study: Bellevue University confers B.A., B.S., and B.F.A. degrees. Master's degrees are also awarded. Bachelor's degrees are awarded in BUSINESS (accounting, business administration and management, and personnel management), COMMUNICATIONS AND THE ARTS (communications, English, fine arts, and photography), COMPUTER AND PHYSICAL SCIENCE (information sciences and systems), EDUCATION (physical), SOCIAL SCIENCE (criminal justice, geography, history, philosophy, political science/government, psychology, social science, sociology, and urban studies). Business administration is the strongest academically.

Required: To graduate, students must complete the core curriculum, with course work in communicative arts, a foreign language, art, English literature, foreign language literature, culture, civilization, music, philosophy, biology, chemistry, geology, math, geography, physics, psychology, sociology, economics, history, and political science. The required number of core credits varies by degree program from 63 to 66, and the total number of hours in the major varies by major. Students must earn 127 to 132 credits, depending on the degree. The minimum required GPA is 2.0 overall and 2.5 in the major.

Special: Bellevue University offers co-op programs with Buena Vista Colleges and Grace College of the Bible, internships, and work-study. Students may earn B.A.-B.S. degrees, and an accelerated degree program is possible in professional studies. The university permits dual majors, and composite, interdisciplinary majors are available in the social sciences and urban studies. Credit may be conferred for military experience. Nondegree study is possible. The Lockstep Degree Competition Program offers an alternative to the traditional academic structure. The School of Arts and Sciences operates on a 4-day academic week to provide flexibility. There is 1 national honor society.

Faculty/Classroom: 91% teach undergraduates. No introductory courses are taught by graduate students. The average class size in an introductory lecture is 35; in a laboratory, 25; and in a regular course, 25.

Admissions: All of the 2001-2002 applicants were accepted.

Requirements: The ACT, with a recommended minimum score of 19, or the SAT I is required for those entering college within 2 years after high school graduation; submission of ACT/SAT I scores is recommended for all others. Applicants must be graduates of an accredited secondary school or have a GED. Interviews are recommended. AP and CLEP credits are accepted.

Procedure: Freshmen are admitted to all sessions. Entrance exams should be taken in April. There are early decision and early admissions plans. Application deadlines are open. Notification is on a rolling basis. The fall 2001 application fee was $10.
Transfer: 30 credits of 127 must be completed at Bellevue University.
Visiting: There are regularly scheduled orientations for prospective students. There are guides for informal visits and visitors may sit in on classes. To schedule a visit, contact the Admissions Office.
Financial Aid: In a recent year, 82% of all freshmen and 74% of continuing students received some form of financial aid. 67% of freshmen and 90% of continuing students received need-based aid. The average freshman award was $5884. 3% of undergraduates work part time. Average annual earnings from campus work are $1520. The FAFSA is required. The fall application deadline is July 1.
International Students: The school actively recruits these students. They must score 500 on the written TOEFL or take the MELAB, and also take the ACT.
Computers: The mainframe is an HP. There are 8 terminals and 25 PCs in the computer lab and computer classroom. Use is on a first-come, first-served basis. Students enrolled in classes where a computer fee is charged may access the system. There are no time limits.
Admissions Contact: Sharon Thonen, Director of Admissions.
E-mail: *set@scholars.bellevue.edu* Web: *http://bruins.bellevue.edu*

CHADRON STATE COLLEGE — B-1
Chadron, NE 69337 (308) 432-6263
(800) CHADRON; Fax: (308) 432-6229

Full-time: 767 men, 974 women	**Faculty:** 100; IIA, --$
Part-time: 217 men, 436 women	**Ph.D.s:** 74%
Graduate: 107 men, 303 women	**Student/Faculty:** 17 to 1
Year: semesters, summer session	**Tuition:** $2481 ($4573)
Application Deadline: open	**Room & Board:** $3730
Freshman Class: 754 applied, 754 accepted, 399 enrolled	
ACT: 22	**NONCOMPETITIVE**

Chadron State College, founded in 1911, is a public college offering programs in liberal arts and professional training. There are 4 undergraduate schools and 1 graduate school. In addition to regional accreditation, CSC has baccalaureate program accreditation with CSWE and NCATE. The library contains 129,660 volumes, 325,063 microform items, and 5596 audiovisual forms/CDs, and subscribes to 112,500 periodicals. Computerized library services include the card catalog, interlibrary loans, and database searching. Special learning facilities include a learning resource center, natural history museum, planetarium, and radio station. The 281-acre campus is in a small town 100 miles south of Rapid City, South Dakota. Including residence halls, there are 27 buildings.
Student Life: 74% of undergraduates are from Nebraska. Others are from 32 states, 6 foreign countries, and Canada. 97% are from public schools. 90% are white. 45% are Protestant; 40% Catholic; 13% claim no religious affiliation. The average age of freshmen is 20; all undergraduates, 22. 35% do not continue beyond their first year; 33% remain to graduate.
Housing: 1200 students can be accommodated in college housing, which includes single-sex and coed dormitories and married-student housing. In addition, there are honors houses. On-campus housing is guaranteed for all 4 years. 65% of students commute. Alcohol is not permitted. All students may keep cars.
Activities: There are no fraternities or sororities. There are 71 groups on campus, including art, band, cheerleading, choir, dance, ethnic, gay, honors, international, jazz band, musical theater, newspaper, orchestra, pep band, photography, political, radio and TV, science fiction, student government, symphony and video. Popular campus events include Spring Daze.
Sports: There are 5 intercollegiate sports for men and 5 for women, and 46 intramural sports for men and 46 for women. Facilities include a 3000-seat stadium, a gym, a swimming pool, and an activity center.
Disabled Students: All of the campus is accessible. Wheelchair ramps, elevators, special parking, specially equipped rest rooms, special class scheduling, and lowered drinking fountains are available.
Services: Counseling and information services are available, as is tutoring in most subjects. There is a reader service for the blind, and remedial math, reading, and writing.
Campus Safety and Security: Measures include 24-hour foot and vehicle patrol, self-defense education, informal discussions, and pamphlets/posters/films. There are emergency telephones and lighted pathways/sidewalks.
Programs of Study: CSC confers B.A., B.S., and B.S.E. degrees. Master's degrees are also awarded. Bachelor's degrees are awarded in BIOLOGICAL SCIENCE (biology/biological science), BUSINESS (business administration and management), COMMUNICATIONS AND THE ARTS (art, dramatic arts, English, music, and speech/debate/rhetoric), COMPUTER AND PHYSICAL SCIENCE (chemistry, mathematics, and physics), EDUCATION (early childhood, elementary, health, science, and secondary), ENGINEERING AND ENVIRONMENTAL DESIGN (industrial engineering technology), HEALTH PROFESSIONS (predentistry, and premedicine), SOCIAL SCIENCE (criminal justice, history, political science/government, prelaw, psychology, social science, social work, and sociology). Education, business, and health professions are the strongest academically. Education, business, and justice studies are the largest.
Required: For graduation, students must complete 125 credit hours, including 47 hours of general education courses, and maintain a 2.0 GPA for the B.A. and a 2.5 GPA for the B.S.E. Other requirements vary by major.
Special: The college offers internships, a Washington semester, and work-study programs. Dual majors, co-op programs, and credit for life, military, and work experience are possible. There are 12 national honor societies, and a freshman honors program.
Faculty/Classroom: 72% of faculty are male; 28%, female. All teach undergraduates. Graduate students teach 2% of introductory courses. The average class size in an introductory lecture is 36; in a laboratory, 19; and in a regular course, 25.
Admissions: All of the 2001-2002 applicants were accepted. The SAT I scores for the 2001-2002 freshman class were: Verbal--67% below 500, and 33% between 500 and 599; Math--50% below 500, 33% between 500 and 599, and 17% between 600 and 700. The ACT scores were 45% below 21, 21% between 21 and 23, 19% between 24 and 26, 9% between 27 and 28, and 5% above 28. 32% of the current freshmen were in the top fifth of their class; 56% were in the top two fifths. In a recent year, 2 freshmen graduated first in their class.
Requirements: The SAT I or ACT is recommended unless the applicant has been out of high school for more than 5 years. Applicants need not be graduates of an accredited secondary school. The GED is accepted. High school work should include a minimum of 15 academic units with at least 3 units in English, and others in math, science, social studies, and foreign language. AP and CLEP credits are accepted. Important factors in the admissions decision are advanced placement or honor courses, evidence of special talent, and leadership record.
Procedure: Freshmen are admitted to all sessions. Entrance exams should be taken . Application deadlines are open. The fee was $15 in 2001.
Transfer: A maximum of 66 semester credits earned at an accredited 2-year college may be transferred. The registrar will evaluate credit earned at a 3- or 4-year college to determine the student's classification. All passing credit obtained from an institution is accepted in programs offered by Chadron State. Transfers are admitted every term. 30 credits of 125 must be completed at CSC.
Visiting: There are regularly scheduled orientations for prospective students, including visits with faculty, tours of the campus, meetings with financial aid and housing advisers, and complimentary meals. There are guides for informal visits and visitors may sit in on classes and stay overnight. To schedule a visit, contact the Admissions Office at *inquire@csc.edu*.
Financial Aid: In 2001-2002, 78% of all freshmen and 73% of continuing students received some form of financial aid. 54% of all students received need-based aid. The average freshman award was $2168. Of that total, scholarships or need-based grants averaged $1348; and loans averaged $820. Average annual earnings from campus work are $1000. The FAFSA is are required. The fall application deadline is June 1.
International Students: There are 17 international students enrolled. They must score 550 on the written TOEFL and also take the SAT I or the ACT.
Computers: The mainframe is a DEC ALPHA 3800. There are 3 networked labs with 12 PCs, 10 Macs, and 8 digital terminals. All students may access the system 7:30 A.M. to 10:30 P.M.
Graduates: In 2001, 476 bachelor's degrees were awarded. The most popular majors were education (27%), business (25%), and justice studies (15%). In an average class, 1% graduate in 3 years, 12% in 4 years, 30% in 5 years, and 34% in 6 years. 7 companies recruited on campus in 2000-2001.
Admissions Contact: Tena Cook Gould, Director of Admissions.
E-mail: *tgould@csc.edu* Web: *www.csc.edu*

CLARKSON COLLEGE — F-3
Omaha, NE 68131 (402) 552-3041
(800) 647-5500; Fax: (402) 552-6057

Full-time: 12 men, 192 women	**Faculty:** 43; IIB, --$
Part-time: 16 men, 142 women	**Ph.D.s:** 36%
Graduate: 6 men, 90 women	**Student/Faculty:** 4 to 1
Year: semesters, summer session	**Tuition:** $9378
Application Deadline: open	**Room & Board:** $2800
Freshman Class: 238 applied, 195 accepted, 155 enrolled	
ACT: 22	**COMPETITIVE**

Clarkson College, established in 1888 and affiliated with the Episcopal Church, and offers undergraduate and graduate degrees in the health care professions and business. There are 3 undergraduate and 2 graduate schools. In addition to regional accreditation, Clarkson has baccalaureate program accreditation with NLN. The library contains 8097 volumes, 115 microform items, and 559 audiovisual forms/CDs, and subscribes to 299 periodicals. Computerized library services include the card catalog, interlibrary loans, and database searching. Special learning facilities include a learning resource center, art gallery, and regional medical center. The 29-acre campus is in an urban area in Omaha. Including residence halls, there are 13 buildings.

Student Life: 61% of undergraduates are from Nebraska. Others are from 13 states and 1 foreign country. 90% are from public schools. 90% are white. 50% are Catholic; 45% Protestant. The average age of freshmen is 23; all undergraduates, 27. 10% do not continue beyond their first year; 87% remain to graduate.

Housing: 54 students can be accommodated in college housing, which includes coed on-campus apartments. On-campus housing is available on a first-come, first-served basis. Priority is given to out-of-town students. 90% of students commute. Alcohol is not permitted. All students may keep cars.

Activities: There are no fraternities or sororities. There are 12 groups on campus, including chorus, newspaper, professional, social, social service, and student government. Popular campus events include holiday dances and parties.

Sports: There is no sports program at Clarkson. Facilities are available at the adjacent University of Nebraska Medical Center and include basketball and volleyball courts, exercise equipment, and a weight room.

Disabled Students: 95% of the campus is accessible. Wheelchair ramps, elevators, special parking, specially equipped rest rooms, special class scheduling, lowered drinking fountains, and lowered telephones are available.

Services: Counseling and information services are available, as is tutoring in every subject.

Campus Safety and Security: Measures include 24-hour foot and vehicle patrol, self-defense education, escort service, and informal discussions. There are pamphlets/posters/films, emergency telephones, and lighted pathways/sidewalks.

Programs of Study: Clarkson confers B.S. and B.S.N. degrees. Associate and master's degrees are also awarded. Bachelor's degrees are awarded in BUSINESS (business administration and management), COMPUTER AND PHYSICAL SCIENCE (radiological technology), HEALTH PROFESSIONS (nursing and radiograph medical technology). Radiological technology and nursing are the strongest academically. Nursing is the largest.

Required: To graduate, students must complete 128 credit hours, including 68 in the major, and maintain a minimum GPA of 2.0. General education requirements include courses in the humanities, English, behavioral and social sciences, science and math, and phys ed. A 9-hour core curriculum is also required.

Special: A co-op program in nursing, study abroad in England, work-study programs, and dual majors are available. Credit is given for military experience, and nondegree study is possible. The distance education option allows advanced placement students living a distance from the campus to complete their studies at home. There is 1 national honor society.

Faculty/Classroom: 21% of faculty are male; 79%, female. All teach undergraduates. No introductory courses are taught by graduate students. The average class size in an introductory lecture is 45; in a laboratory, 10; and in a regular course, 35.

Admissions: 82% of the 2001-2002 applicants were accepted. The ACT scores for the 2001-2002 freshman class were: 5% below 21, 90% between 21 and 23, and 5% between 24 and 26. 29% of the current freshmen were in the top fifth of their class; 88% were in the top two fifths. 3 freshmen graduated first in their class in a recent year.

Requirements: The SAT I or ACT is required with a minimum composite score of 20 on the ACT or 850 on the SAT I. The ACT is preferred. Tests are not required for applicants more than 2 years out of high school. Applicants must be graduates of an accredited secondary school, with 3 years of English and 2 each of social science, algebra, and science (including lab science). The GED is accepted. Clarkson requires applicants to be in the upper 50% of their class. A GPA of 2.0 is required. AP and CLEP credits are accepted. Important factors in the admissions decision are advanced placement or honor courses, extracurricular activities record, and evidence of special talent.

Procedure: Freshmen are admitted to all sessions. Entrance exams should be taken during the junior year or first semester of the senior year. There is a deferred admissions plan. Application deadlines are open. The fall 2001 application fee was $15. Notification is sent on a rolling basis. 5% of all applicants are on a waiting list.

Transfer: Transfer students must have a minimum GPA of 2.5. Grades of C or better transfer for credit. Transfers are admitted for fall and spring. An interview is sometimes required. 64 credits of 128 must be completed at Clarkson.

Visiting: There are regularly scheduled orientations for prospective students. There are guides for informal visits and visitors may sit in on classes. To schedule a visit, contact the Admissions Office.

Financial Aid: Clarkson is a member of CSS. The FAFSA and the college's own financial statement are required. The fall application deadline is May 1.

International Students: They must score 600 on the written TOEFL, 85 on the MELAB, or 5 on the TWE and also take the SAT I or the ACT.

Computers: The mainframe is a DEC VAX 4400. There are IBM and Mac systems available for student use. 20 IBM and Mac PCs, with 10 mainframe terminals, are housed in special labs for their instruction and use. In addition, there are 10 terminals in the residence hall computer lab. All students may access the system 7 A.M. to 8:30 P.M. There are no time limits and no fees.

Admissions Contact: Tami Bartunek, Director of Admissions.
E-mail: *bartunek@clarksoncollege.edu* Web: *www.clarksoncollege.edu*

COLLEGE OF SAINT MARY — F-2

Omaha, NE 68124 — (402) 399-2407
(800) 926-5534; Fax: (402) 399-2412

Full-time: 549 women	**Faculty:** 36
Part-time: 19 men, 362 women	**Ph.D.s:** 36%
Graduate: none	**Student/Faculty:** 15 to 1
Year: semesters, summer session	**Tuition:** $13,750
Application Deadline: open	**Room & Board:** $4976
Freshman Class: 192 applied, 130 accepted, 59 enrolled	
ACT: 22	**COMPETITIVE**

College of Saint Mary, founded in 1923, is a Roman Catholic women's college offering a program that combines training for professional careers with a liberal arts component. In addition to regional accreditation, CSM has baccalaureate program accreditation with ACOTE, AHIMA, CAHEA and NLN. The library contains 66,034 volumes and 2052 audiovisual forms/CDs, and subscribes to 1420 periodicals. Computerized library services include the card catalog, interlibrary loans, and database searching. Special learning facilities include a learning resource center and art gallery. The 25-acre campus is in a suburban area 5 miles west of downtown Omaha. Including residence halls, there are 8 buildings.

Student Life: 86% of undergraduates are from Nebraska. Others are from 17 states and 5 foreign countries. 82% are from public schools. 90% are white. 35% are Catholic. The average age of freshmen is 20; all undergraduates, 30. 32% do not continue beyond their first year; 49% remain to graduate.

Housing: 257 students can be accommodated in college housing, which is available on a first-come, first-served basis. 83% of students commute. All students may keep cars.

Activities: There are no sororities. There are 12 groups on campus, including choir, computers, ethnic, honors, international, political, professional, religious, social, social service, and student government. Popular campus events include Fine Arts Festival, Spirit Day, and the Queen of Hearts dance.

Sports: There are 6 intercollegiate sports for women and 3 intramural sports for women. Facilities include a gym, a 6-lane swimming pool, a weight room, an elevated running track, 2 racquetball courts, an exercise room, a training room, 4 outdoor tennis courts, 2 soccer fields, and 2 softball fields.

Disabled Students: 85% of the campus is accessible. Wheelchair ramps, elevators, special parking, specially equipped rest rooms, special class scheduling, lowered drinking fountains, and electric door openers are available.

Services: Counseling and information services are available, as is tutoring in most subjects. There is a reader service for the blind, remedial math, reading, and writing, and study groups.

Campus Safety and Security: Measures include 24-hour foot and vehicle patrol, self-defense education, escort service, and informal discussions. There are pamphlets/posters/films, emergency telephones, lighted pathways/sidewalks, and camera-monitored and coded entrances to residence halls.

Programs of Study: CSM confers B.A., B.S., B.B.C., B.B.L., and B.G.S. degrees. Associate degrees are also awarded. Bachelor's degrees are awarded in BIOLOGICAL SCIENCE (biology/biological science), BUSINESS (business administration and management), COMMUNICATIONS AND THE ARTS (art, and English), COMPUTER AND PHYSICAL SCIENCE (chemistry, computer management, mathematics, and natural sciences), EDUCATION (early childhood, education, elementary, and special), HEALTH PROFESSIONS (medical laboratory technology, nursing, and occupational therapy), SOCIAL SCIENCE (human services, humanities, liberal arts/general studies, paralegal studies, and psychology). Preprofessional studies and occupational therapy are the strongest academically. Nursing, business, and education are the largest.

Required: To graduate, students must complete 128 semester hours, with a minimum of 30 hours in the major and a 2.0 GPA in the major and overall. Required general education courses total 47 hours, with 9 in math and science, 6 in English, 3 each in communications, computer, ethics, fine arts, liberal arts, history, philosophy, social science, and theology, and 1 each in phys ed and a core seminar. Students must demonstrate competency in math and English.

Special: Students may pursue internships in any major, including research courses in the sciences. CSM also offers dual majors, study abroad in 11 countries, nondegree study, pass/fail options, an accelerated degree program in business leadership, and credit for life, military, and work experience. There are 2 national honor societies.
Faculty/Classroom: 21% of faculty are male; 79%, female. All teach undergraduates. The average class size in an introductory lecture is 35; in a laboratory, 25; and in a regular course, 10.
Admissions: 68% of the 2001-2002 applicants were accepted. In a recent year, 2 freshmen graduated first in their class.
Requirements: The SAT I or ACT is required. In addition, students must meet 2 out of 3 criteria: a minimum composite score of 19 on the ACT, a GPA of at least 2.0, and rank in the upper 50% of their class. Applicants must be graduates of an accredited secondary school. The GED is accepted. Students should have completed 16 academic units, including 4 years of English and 2 each of math, social studies and science, with biology and chemistry required for the various health profession majors. An interview is recommended. Applications are accepted on-line via the school's web site. CSM requires applicants to be in the upper 50% of their class. A GPA of 2.0 is required. AP and CLEP credits are accepted.
Procedure: Freshmen are admitted to all sessions. Entrance exams should be taken in the junior or senior year. There is a deferred admissions plan. Application deadlines are open. The fee was $25 in 2001. Notification is sent within 2 weeks of receipt of application.
Transfer: 220 transfer students enrolled in 2001-2002. Applicants should have a minimum GPA of 2.0 and submit official transcripts from previous colleges attended. Students with fewer than 12 credit hours must also submit ACT OR SAT I scores. Grades of C or better transfer for credit. Students are admitted every term. 30 credits of 128 must be completed at CSM.
Visiting: There are regularly scheduled orientations for prospective students, consisting of touring the campus, attending financial aid and student-life presentations, and sitting in on classes of a student's choice. Visitors are CSM's guests for lunch or overnight. There are guides for informal visits and visitors may sit in on classes and stay overnight. To schedule a visit, contact the Office of Enrollment Services at (402) 399-2405 or *enroll@csm.edu*.
Financial Aid: In 2001 2002, 98% of all freshmen and 65% of continuing students received some form of financial aid. 54% of freshmen and 74% of continuing students received need-based aid. The average freshman award was $11,527. Of that total, scholarships or need-based grants averaged $6215; loans averaged $4497; and work contracts averaged $815. 12% of undergraduates work part time. Average annual earnings from campus work are $1200. The average financial indebtedness of the 2001 graduate was $16,000. The FAFSA is required. The fall application deadline is April 1.
International Students: There are 5 international students enrolled. The school actively recruits these students. They must score 550 on the written TOEFL.
Computers: The mainframe is a Compaq client/server network. Students may access the campus network and the Internet via 95 PCs in various locations. All students may access the system 8 A.M. to midnight Monday through Thursday, 8 A.M. to 5 P.M. Friday, 10 A.M. to 5 P.M. Saturday, and 1 P.M. to midnight Sunday. There are no time limits and no fees.
Graduates: In 2001, 120 bachelor's degrees were awarded. The most popular majors were business (23%), occupational therapy (15%), and education (13%). In an average class, 41% graduate in 4 years, 46% in 5 years, and 49% in 6 years. 86 companies recruited on campus in 2000-2001. Of the 2000 graduating class, 12% were enrolled in graduate school within 6 months of graduation and 91% were employed.
Admissions Contact: Christy Hutchison, Vice President for Enrollment Services. E-mail: *enroll@csm.edu* Web: *www.csm.edu*

CONCORDIA UNIVERSITY NEBRASKA E-3
Seward, NE 68434 (402) 643-7233
(800) 535-5494; Fax: (402) 643-4073

Full-time: 521 men, 647 women	**Faculty:** 66; IIB, --$
Part-time: 23 men and women	**Ph.D.s:** 85%
Graduate: 56 men and women	**Student/Faculty:** 18 to 1
Year: semesters, summer session	**Tuition:** $13,468
Application Deadline: August 1	**Room & Board:** $4302
Freshman Class: 856 applied, 776 accepted, 372 enrolled	
ACT: 23	**COMPETITIVE**

Concordia University Nebraska, founded in 1894, is a private university owned and operated by the Lutheran Church-Missouri Synod, with degree programs in professional education and liberal arts. Among Concordia's major programs are those for professional work in the Lutheran Church: teacher education, director of Christian education, preseminary pastoral training, and church music. In addition to regional accreditation, Concordia has baccalaureate program accreditation with NCATE. The 3 libraries contain 177,683 volumes, 10,719 microform items, and 13,214 audiovisual forms/CDs, and subscribe to 545 periodicals. Computerized library services include the card catalog and database searching. Special learning facilities include a learning resource center, art gallery, natural history museum, and observatory. The 120-acre campus is in a small town 25 miles west of Lincoln. Including residence halls, there are 25 buildings.
Student Life: 59% of undergraduates are from out of state, mostly the Midwest. Others are from 37 states and 9 foreign countries. 95% are white. Most are Protestant. The average age of freshmen is 18; all undergraduates, 21. 48% of freshmen remain to graduate.
Housing: 815 students can be accommodated in college housing, which includes single-sex dormitories, off-campus apartments, and married-student housing. On-campus housing is guaranteed for all 4 years. 90% of students live on campus; of those, 90% remain on campus on weekends. Alcohol is not permitted. All students may keep cars.
Activities: There are no fraternities or sororities. There are 35 groups on campus, including band, cheerleading, choir, chorale, chorus, computers, debate, drama, drill team, ethnic, forensics, honors, international, jazz band, literary magazine, newspaper, orchestra, pep band, photography, professional, religious, social, social service, student government, and yearbook. Popular campus events include Fall Fest and Spring Weekend.
Sports: There are 8 intercollegiate sports for men and 8 for women, and 7 intramural sports for men and 7 for women. Facilities include a gym, a weight-training room, an indoor pool, football, baseball, and soccer fields, and a track and field stadium.
Disabled Students: 35% of the campus is accessible. Wheelchair ramps, elevators, special parking, specially equipped rest rooms, lowered drinking fountains, and lowered telephones are available.
Services: Counseling and information services are available, as is tutoring in every subject. There is a reader service for the blind, talking books, and tape recorders.
Campus Safety and Security: Measures include 24-hour foot and vehicle patrol, self-defense education, escort service, and informal discussions. There are pamphlets/posters/films, emergency telephones, lighted pathways/sidewalks, vehicle and bicycle registration, and a possession ID engraving program.
Programs of Study: Concordia confers B.A., B.S., B.F.A., B.S.Med.Tech., B.Mus., and B.Sacred Music degrees. Master's degrees are also awarded. Bachelor's degrees are awarded in BIOLOGICAL SCIENCE (biology/biological science), BUSINESS (accounting, business administration and management, and sports management), COMMUNICATIONS AND THE ARTS (communications, dramatic arts, English, fine arts, music, speech/debate/rhetoric, and studio art), COMPUTER AND PHYSICAL SCIENCE (chemistry, computer science, mathematics, natural sciences, and physical sciences), EDUCATION (business, Christian, early childhood, elementary, home economics, industrial arts, middle school, music, physical, science, secondary, and special), HEALTH PROFESSIONS (exercise science, health, medical laboratory technology, predentistry, and premedicine), SOCIAL SCIENCE (behavioral science, geography, history, physical fitness/movement, prelaw, psychology, and theological studies). Education, business, and art are the strongest academically. Education is the largest.
Required: To graduate, students must complete a minimum of 128 credits with a GPA of at least 2.0. Required general education courses include 12 hours of theology, 9 hours each of English/speech, social science, and science, 6 of fine arts, 3 each of math and health and phys ed, 2 to 3 of electives, and 1 hour minimum of computer literacy.
Special: Concordia offers cross-registration with the University of Nebraska in Lincoln. Internships are available in education, business, and Christian education. B.A.-B.S. degrees, student-designed majors, dual majors, study abroad in England, India, and China, nondegree studies, and pass/fail options are available. There is an accelerated degree program in organizational management. There is a freshman honors program.
Faculty/Classroom: 71% of faculty are male; 29%, female. All teach undergraduates. Graduate students teach 1% of introductory courses. The average class size in an introductory lecture is 20; in a laboratory, 15; and in a regular course, 15.
Admissions: 91% of the 2001-2002 applicants were accepted.
Requirements: The SAT I or ACT is required. In addition, a minimum composite score of 18 is recommended for the ACT. Applicants need not be graduates of an accredited secondary school. The GED is accepted. The school strongly encourages high school courses in art, English, foreign language, history, math, music, phys ed, science, and social studies. An interview is recommended. Concordia requires applicants to be in the upper 50% of their class. A GPA of 2.0 is required. Applications are accepted on-line at *www.applyweb.com*. AP and CLEP credits are accepted. Important factors in the admissions decision are ability to finance college education, leadership record, and recommendations by alumni.
Procedure: Freshmen are admitted to all sessions. Entrance exams should be taken in the junior or senior year. Applications should be filed by August 1 for fall entry and January 1 for spring entry. The fall 2001 application fee was $15. Notification is sent on a rolling basis.

Transfer: 74 transfer students enrolled in 2001-2002. Applicants should have a minimum GPA of 2.0 and a minimum ACT score of 18. An interview is recommended. Passing grades transfer for credit. Transfers are admitted every term. 30 credits of 128 must be completed at Concordia.

Visiting: There are regularly scheduled orientations for prospective students, including a campus tour, visits with professors/coaches, and an admission interview. There are guides for informal visits and visitors may sit in on classes and stay overnight. To schedule a visit, contact the Office of Admission.

Financial Aid: The FAFSA and the college's own financial statement are required. The fall application deadline is August 15.

International Students: There are 15 international students enrolled. The school actively recruits these students. They must score 500 on the written TOEFL and also take the SAT I or the ACT.

Computers: The mainframe is a DEC VAX 4105A. More than 150 PCs are available across campus, with Internet and web access on all. All students may access the system. There are no time limits and no fees.

Graduates: The most popular majors were teacher education (75%), business/marketing (10%), and social science/history (4%). In an average class, 57% graduate in 6 years.

Admissions Contact: Office of Admission.
E-mail: *admiss@seward.cune.edu* Web: *www.cune.edu/*

CREIGHTON UNIVERSITY

F-3

Omaha, NE 68178-0001 **(402) 280-2703**
(800) 282-5835; Fax: (402) 280-2685

Full-time: 1373 men, 1871 women	**Faculty:** 242; IIA, av$
Part-time: 167 men, 244 women	**Ph.D.s:** 92%
Graduate: 1272 men, 1346 women	**Student/Faculty:** 13 to 1
Year: semesters, summer session	**Tuition:** $17,136
Application Deadline: August 1	**Room & Board:** $6340
Freshman Class: 2605 applied, 2348 accepted, 746 enrolled	
SAT I Verbal/Math: 577/576	**ACT:** 25 **VERY COMPETITIVE**

Creighton University, established in 1878, is a private Catholic institution conducted by the Jesuits and offering undergraduate programs in arts and sciences, business, and nursing. Tuition and fees for freshmen total $17,136; room and board is $6,190. Tuition and fees for sophomores, juniors, and seniors total $15,808; room and board is $6340. There are 4 undergraduate and 5 graduate schools. In addition to regional accreditation, Creighton has baccalaureate program accreditation with AACSB, ACPE, NCATE, and NLN. The 3 libraries contain 796,801 volumes, 287,561 microform items, and 17,517 audiovisual forms/CDs, and subscribe to 9859 periodicals. Computerized library services include the card catalog, interlibrary loans, and database searching. Special learning facilities include a learning resource center, art gallery, planetarium, radio station, and TV station. The 78-acre campus is in an urban area near downtown Omaha. Including residence halls, there are 46 buildings.

Student Life: 51% of undergraduates are from out of state, mostly the Midwest. Others are from 42 states, 73 foreign countries, and Canada. 60% are from public schools. 78% are white; 10% Asian American. 61% are Catholic; 20% Protestant; 16% claim no religious affiliation. The average age of freshmen is 18; all undergraduates, 20. 15% do not continue beyond their first year; 72% remain to graduate.

Housing: 1860 students can be accommodated in college housing, which includes single-sex and coed dormitories, on-campus apartments, and married-student housing. In addition, there are special-interest houses. Creighton House combines independent study projects with community living and a special interdisciplinary seminar. On-campus housing is guaranteed for all 4 years. 57% of students commute. Alcohol is not permitted. All students may keep cars.

Activities: 33% of men belong to 7 national fraternities; 30% of women belong to 6 national sororities. There are 100 groups on campus, including art, band, cheerleading, chess, choir, chorale, chorus, computers, dance, debate, drama, drill team, ethnic, film, forensics, honors, international, jazz band, literary magazine, musical theater, newspaper, pep band, photography, political, professional, radio and TV, religious, social, social service, student government, and yearbook. Popular campus events include Comedy Club, Noon Music Series, and lectures.

Sports: There are 6 intercollegiate sports for men and 7 for women, and 20 intramural sports for men and 20 for women. Facilities include a sports complex, an outdoor artificial turf area with baseball, softball, and soccer fields, a natural grass intercollegiate soccer facility, and a physical fitness center with courts for basketball, volleyball, badminton, or gymnastics, a pool, a weight room, and a jogging track; another center offers practice courts and training rooms for all intercollegiate sports.

Disabled Students: 80% of the campus is accessible. Wheelchair ramps, elevators, special parking, specially equipped rest rooms, special class scheduling, lowered drinking fountains, and lowered telephones are available.

Services: Counseling and information services are available, as is tutoring in most subjects. There is a reader service for the blind, and remedial math, reading, and writing.

Campus Safety and Security: Measures include 24-hour foot and vehicle patrol, self-defense education, escort service, and shuttle buses. There are informal discussions, pamphlets/posters/films, emergency telephones, and lighted pathways/sidewalks.

Programs of Study: Creighton confers B.A., B.S., B.F.A., B.S. Atmospheric Science, B.S.B.A., B.S.Chem., B.S. Computer Science, B.S. Environmental Science, B.S. Mathematics, B.S.N., B.S. Physics, B.S.Soc., and B.S.W. degrees. Associate, master's, and doctoral degrees are also awarded. Bachelor's degrees are awarded in BIOLOGICAL SCIENCE (biology/biological science), BUSINESS (accounting, banking and finance, business administration and management, international business management, management information systems, and marketing/retailing/merchandising), COMMUNICATIONS AND THE ARTS (art, communications, dramatic arts, English, fine arts, French, German, Greek, journalism, Latin, music, Spanish, and speech/debate/rhetoric), COMPUTER AND PHYSICAL SCIENCE (atmospheric sciences and meteorology, chemistry, computer science, mathematics, and physics), EDUCATION (elementary, secondary, and special), ENGINEERING AND ENVIRONMENTAL DESIGN (environmental science), HEALTH PROFESSIONS (emergency medical technologies and nursing), SOCIAL SCIENCE (American studies, classical/ancient civilization, economics, history, ministries, philosophy, political science/government, prelaw, psychology, social work, sociology, and theological studies). Nursing, biology, and psychology are the largest.

Required: For graduation, students must complete a minimum of 128 credit hours and maintain a GPA of 2.0. Each school has general education requirements.

Special: The university offers preengineering co-op programs with the University of Detroit and Washington University in St. Louis, study abroad at more than 110 partner institutions in 40 countries, a Washington semester, internships, and work-study programs. Nursing students may take an accelerated degree program, and B.A.-B.S. degrees are possible. Dual majors, nondegree study, pass/fail options, and credit for life, military, and work experience are available. There are 13 national honor societies, a freshman honors program, and 1 departmental honors program.

Faculty/Classroom: 68% of faculty are male; 32%, female. No introductory courses are taught by graduate students. The average class size in an introductory lecture is 29; in a laboratory, 22; and in a regular course, 25.

Admissions: 90% of the 2001-2002 applicants were accepted. The SAT I scores for the 2001-2002 freshman class were: Verbal--16% below 500, 47% between 500 and 599, 32% between 600 and 700, and 7% above 700; Math--17% below 500, 42% between 500 and 599, 32% between 600 and 700, and 9% above 700. The ACT scores were 11% below 21, 21% between 21 and 23, 28% between 24 and 26, 21% between 27 and 28, and 19% above 28. 56% of the current freshmen were in the top fifth of their class; 82% were in the top two fifths. 56 freshmen graduated first in their class.

Requirements: The SAT I or ACT is required. In addition, applicants must be graduates of an accredited secondary school. The GED is accepted. Students should have completed 16 credits, including 4 credits in English, 3 each in math and electives, and 2 each in foreign language, science, and social studies. Home-schooled students are welcome. Creighton requires applicants to be in the upper 50% of their class. A GPA of 2.75 is required. AP and CLEP credits are accepted. Important factors in the admissions decision are recommendations by school officials, advanced placement or honor courses, and leadership record. Online applications may be submitted via Creighton's web site.

Procedure: Freshmen are admitted to all sessions. Entrance exams should be taken prior to May 1 of the senior year. Applications should be filed by August 1 for fall entry and January 1 for spring entry, along with a $40 fee. Notification is sent on a rolling basis.

Transfer: Applicants must have a 2.0 minimum GPA in a regionally accredited school. A minimum score of 21 on the ACT or 990 on the SAT I is recommended. Grades of C or better transfer for credit. Transfers are admitted every semester. 48 credits of 128 must be completed at Creighton.

Visiting: There are regularly scheduled orientations for prospective students, consisting of an open house program with various presentations and campus tours. There are guides for informal visits and visitors may sit in on classes and stay overnight. To schedule a visit, contact the Admissions Office.

Financial Aid: In 2001-2002, 92% of all freshmen and 86% of continuing students received some form of financial aid. 57% of freshmen and 56% of continuing students received need-based aid. The average freshman award was $14,070. Of that total, scholarships or need-based grants averaged $7369 ($17,186 maximum); loans averaged $4820 ($5625 maximum); and work contracts averaged $1830 ($2000 maximum). 42% of undergraduates work part time. Average annual earnings from campus work are $1357. The average financial indebtedness of the 2001 graduate was $20,517. The FAFSA and the college's own financial statement are required. The fall application deadline is April 1.

International Students: There are 125 international students enrolled. The school actively recruits these students. They must score 550 on the written TOEFL or 213 on the electronic version.

Computers: The mainframes are 18 HP 9000s and numerous network servers. There are also 500 personal computers available throughout the campus and in computer labs. All students may access the system any time. There are no time limits and no fees. It is strongly recommended that all students have a personal computer. It is required that first-year pharmacy students have personal computers.

Graduates: In 2001, 750 bachelor's degrees were awarded. The most popular majors were nursing (17%), biology (8%), and psychology (7%). In an average class, 1% graduate in 3 years, 57% in 4 years, 70% in 5 years, and 72% in 6 years. 102 companies recruited on campus in 2000-2001.

Admissions Contact: Dennis O'Driscoll, Director of Admissions. A video is available. E-mail: *admissions@creighton.edu*
Web: *www.creighton.edu*

DANA COLLEGE

Blair, NE 68008-1099 F-2
(402) 426-7222
(800) 444-3262; Fax: (402) 426-7386

Full-time: 300 men, 253 women	**Faculty:** 45
Part-time: 7 men, 5 women	**Ph.D.s:** 53%
Graduate: none	**Student/Faculty:** 12 to 1
Year: 4-1-4, summer session	**Tuition:** $13,950
Application Deadline: August 1	**Room & Board:** $4096
Freshman Class: 757 applied, 533 accepted, 156 enrolled	
SAT I Verbal/Math: 490/505	**ACT:** 22 COMPETITIVE

Dana College, established in 1884, is a private liberal arts institution affiliated with the Evangelical Lutheran Church in America. In addition to regional accreditation, Dana has baccalaureate program accreditation with ACBSP, CSWE, and NCATE. The library contains 198,863 volumes, 13,061 microform items, and 3993 audiovisual forms/CDs, and subscribes to 537 periodicals. Computerized library services include the card catalog, interlibrary loans, and database searching. Special learning facilities include a learning resource center, art gallery, radio station, TV station, and theater. The 150-acre campus is in a small town 20 miles north of Omaha. Including residence halls, there are 17 buildings.

Student Life: 51% of undergraduates are from Nebraska. Others are from 32 states and 8 foreign countries. 87% are white. 54% are Protestant; 21% Catholic. The average age of freshmen is 19; all undergraduates, 21. 34% do not continue beyond their first year; 52% remain to graduate.

Housing: 617 students can be accommodated in college housing, which includes single-sex and coed dormitories, on-campus apartments, and married-student housing. On-campus housing is guaranteed for all 4 years. 73% of students live on campus; of those, 50% remain on campus on weekends. Alcohol is not permitted. All students may keep cars.

Activities: There are no fraternities or sororities. There are 35 groups on campus, including art, band, cheerleading, choir, chorale, chorus, computers, drama, drill team, environmental, ethnic, honors, international, jazz band, literary magazine, musical theater, newspaper, orchestra, pep band, photography, political, professional, radio and TV, religious, social, social service, student government, and yearbook. Popular campus events include Sights and Sounds of Christmas, Spring Fling, and the Staley Foundation Distinguished Scholar Lecture Series.

Sports: There are 8 intercollegiate sports for men and 7 for women, and 14 intramural sports for men and 14 for women. Facilities include fields for socccer, cross-country, football/track, softball, and baseball, and a coliseum for basketball, swimming, tennis, racquetball, volleyball, wrestling, and weight training.

Disabled Students: 70% of the campus is accessible. Wheelchair ramps, elevators, special parking, specially equipped rest rooms, special class scheduling, and lowered drinking fountains are available.

Services: Counseling and information services are available, as is tutoring in some subjects, including most 100- and 200-level general education courses. There is remedial math and writing. a study skills course, and study sessions for individual courses.

Campus Safety and Security: Measures include 24-hour foot and vehicle patrol, self-defense education, escort service, and informal discussions. There are pamphlets/posters/films, emergency telephones, and lighted pathways/sidewalks.

Programs of Study: Dana confers the B.A. degree. Bachelor's degrees are awarded in BIOLOGICAL SCIENCE (biology/biological science), BUSINESS (accounting, and business administration and management), COMMUNICATIONS AND THE ARTS (art, communications, English, German, music, and Spanish), COMPUTER AND PHYSICAL SCIENCE (chemistry, computer science, and mathematics), EDUCATION (art, business, drama, elementary, English, foreign languages, mathematics, music, physical, science, secondary, social science, social studies, and special), ENGINEERING AND ENVIRONMENTAL DESIGN (environmental science), SOCIAL SCIENCE (history, interdisciplinary studies, international relations, liberal arts/general studies, psychology, religion, social science, social work, and sociology). Social work, education, and business are the strongest academically. Elementary education, biology, and business administration are the largest.

Required: To graduate, students must complete 128 credit hours, including at least 30 in the major and 40 at the 300 or 400 level, with a minimum GPA of 2.0. Other requirements include demonstrated competency in verbal and written communication skills, 15 core hours in liberal arts, 2 credits in wellness, and 1 religion course. Also required are 18 distributive hours in 3 of 4 areas of study: human culture, human scientific inquiry, human development and organizations, and human aesthetic expression.

Special: Dana offers cross-registration with Midland Lutheran College, internships in most majors, study abroad, and work-study programs. Integratred studies, credit for life, military, and work experience, nondegree study, and pass/fail options are available. There are preprofessional programs in prechiropractic, preoccupational therapy, prephysician's assistant, preseminary, and prelaw. Students in the medical arts major, leading to a degree or certification in a medical technology field, spend senior year in a hospital-based program. There are 3 national honor societies, a freshman honors program, and a schoolwide honors program.

Faculty/Classroom: 53% of faculty are male; 46%, female. All teach undergraduates and 60% do research. The average class size in an introductory lecture is 35; in a laboratory, 10; and in a regular course, 24.

Admissions: 70% of the 2001-2002 applicants were accepted. The SAT I scores for the 2001-2002 freshman class were: Verbal--60% below 500, 23% between 500 and 599, 10% between 600 and 700, and 7% above 700; Math--57% below 500, 33% between 500 and 599, and 10% between 600 and 700. The ACT scores were 41% below 21, 23% between 21 and 23, 24% between 24 and 26, 6% between 27 and 28, and 6% above 28. 31% of the current freshmen were in the top fifth of their class; 64% were in the top two fifths. 2 freshmen graduated first in their class.

Requirements: The SAT I or ACT is required with a recommended minimum composite score of 890 on the SAT I or 19 on the ACT. Applicants must be graduates of an accredited secondary school. The GED is accepted. Prospective students are encouraged to take college-preparatory courses, including 4 years each of English and social science, 3 each of science and math, and 2 of a foreign language. An interview is recommended. Applications are accepted on computer disk and on line via the school's web site. Dana requires applicants to be in the upper 50% of their class. A GPA of 2.0 is required. AP and CLEP credits are accepted. Important factors in the admissions decision are advanced placement or honor courses, recommendations by school officials, and leadership record.

Procedure: Freshmen are admitted to all sessions. Entrance exams should be taken in the spring of the junior year or fall of the senior year. There are early admissions and deferred admissions plans. The prefered application dates are August 1 for fall entry and January 10 for spring entry, along with a $20 fee. Notification is sent on a rolling basis.

Transfer: 30 transfer students enrolled in 2001-2002. Applicants with an associate degree and a minimum college GPA of 2.0 will be considered, those with less than a 2.0 GPA will be evaluated on the basis of high school performance and an interview with the admissions committee. Grades of C or better transfer for credit. Students are admitted every term. 32 credits of 128 must be completed at Dana.

Visiting: There are regularly scheduled orientations for prospective students, including appointments with faculty, coaches, and activity directors, a campus tour, a financial-aid session, an admissions session, and lunch. Overnight lodging is available at no charge. There are guides for informal visits and visitors may sit in on classes and stay overnight. To schedule a visit, contact the Admissions Office at *jconneal@fs1.dana.edu*.

Financial Aid: In 2001-2002, nearly all freshmen and continuing students received some form of financial aid. 83% of freshmen and 81% of continuing students received need-based aid. The average freshman award was $13,863. Of that total, scholarships or need-based grants averaged $8354 ($13,400 maximum); loans averaged $4531 ($5125 maximum); work contracts averaged $1500 ($2000 maximum); and outside resources, including a church scholarship of $1000. 53% of undergraduates work part time. Average annual earnings from campus work are $641. The average financial indebtedness of the 2001 graduate was $18,890. The FAFSA and the college's own financial statement are required. The fall application deadline is April 1.

International Students: There are 12 international students enrolled. The school actively recruits these students. They must score 500 on the written TOEFL; applicants with TOEFL scores of at least 460 may be accepted into a program supported by ESL courses.

Computers: The campus is fully networked. Approximately 250 PCs are distributed among the 7 computer labs and 5 residence halls. Internet access is available without charge. All students may access the system. There are no time limits and no fees.

Graduates: In 2001, 106 bachelor's degrees were awarded. The most popular majors were education (29%), business (17%), and social work (17%). In an average class, 1% graduate in 3 years, 74% in 4 years, and

99% in 5 years. 19 companies recruited on campus in 2000-2001. Of the 2000 graduating class, 7% were enrolled in graduate school within 6 months of graduation and 96% were employed.
Admissions Contact: James Lynes, Director of Admissions.
E-mail: *admissions@fs1.dana.edu* Web: *www.dana.edu*

DOANE COLLEGE

Crete, NE 68333 — **E-3**

(402) 826-8222
(800) 333-6263; Fax: (402) 826-8600

Full-time: 485 men, 477 women	**Faculty:** 70; IIA, --$
Part-time: 4 men, 5 women	**Ph.D.s:** 56%
Graduate: none	**Student/Faculty:** 14 to 1
Year: 4-1-4, summer session	**Tuition:** $13,470
Application Deadline: August 15	**Room & Board:** $4130
Freshman Class: 1079 applied, 910 accepted, 235 enrolled	
ACT: 23	**LESS COMPETITIVE**

Doane College, founded in 1872 and the oldest liberal arts college in Nebraska, is a private, independent, comprehensive college that maintains historic ties with the United Church of Christ. In addition to regional accreditation, Doane has baccalaureate program accreditation with NCATE. The library contains 256,562 volumes and 2630 audiovisual forms/CDs. Computerized library services include the card catalog, interlibrary loans, and database searching. Special learning facilities include a learning resource center, art gallery, radio station, TV station, and an observatory. The 300-acre campus is in a small town 25 miles southwest of Lincoln. Including residence halls, there are 27 buildings.
Student Life: 82% of undergraduates are from Nebraska. Others are from 23 states and 1 foreign country. 80% are from public schools. 94% are white. 34% are Protestant; 23% Catholic. The average age of freshmen is 18; all undergraduates, 21. 18% do not continue beyond their first year; 62% remain to graduate.
Housing: 875 students can be accommodated in college housing, which includes single-sex and coed dormitories, on-campus apartments, and married-student housing. In addition, there are honors houses and special interest houses. On-campus housing is guaranteed for all 4 years. 74% of students live on campus. All students may keep cars.
Activities: 48% of men belong to 5 local fraternities; 40% of women belong to 4 local sororities. There are 50 groups on campus, including alternative spring beak, art, band, cheerleading, choir, chorale, chorus, computers, dance, drama, ethnic, forensics, gay, Hanson Leadership program, honors, international, investment club, jazz band, literary magazine, marching band, musical theater, newspaper, pep band, photography, political, professional, radio and TV, religious, social, social service, speech team, student government, wildlife/conservation club, and yearbook. Popular campus events include Parents Day, Stop Day, and Christmas festival and concert.
Sports: There are 8 intercollegiate sports for men and 8 for women, and 4 intramural sports for men and 4 for women. Facilities include a phys ed building, field house, sports field, fitness center, gym, pool, nature and cross-country trails, challenge course, and indoor and outdoor tracks.
Disabled Students: 60% of the campus is accessible. Wheelchair ramps, elevators, special parking, specially equipped rest rooms, and special class scheduling are available.
Services: Counseling and information services are available, as is tutoring in every subject. There is remedial math, reading, and writing.
Campus Safety and Security: Measures include escort service, informal discussions, pamphlets/posters/films, and emergency telephones. There are lighted pathways/sidewalks and and evening patrols by trained security personnel.
Programs of Study: Doane confers B.A. and B.S. degrees. Master's degrees are also awarded. Bachelor's degrees are awarded in BIOLOGICAL SCIENCE (biology/biological science), BUSINESS (accounting, and business administration and management), COMMUNICATIONS AND THE ARTS (art, communications, dramatic arts, English, English as a second/foreign language, French, German, language arts, music, Spanish, speech/debate/rhetoric, and technical and business writing), COMPUTER AND PHYSICAL SCIENCE (chemistry, computer science, mathematics, physical sciences, and physics), EDUCATION (business, elementary, physical, science, social science, and special), ENGINEERING AND ENVIRONMENTAL DESIGN (environmental science), HEALTH PROFESSIONS (industrial hygiene), SOCIAL SCIENCE (economics, history, international studies, philosophy, political science/government, psychology, public administration, religion, and sociology). Education is the strongest academically. Education and business administration are the largest.
Required: The Doane Plan requires students to complete 60 to 70 credits in heritage studies, contemporary issues, international/multicultural perspective, natural science, quantitative reasoning, communication, aesthetic perspective, health and well-being, and community and leadership. Students are also required to complete 2 hours of phys ed, demonstrate computer skills in word processing, and in most disciplines, complete a senior seminar. Students must complete 132 credit hours and have a minimum GPA of 2.0 in the major to graduate.

Special: Internships for sophomores through seniors, a Washington semester, and study abroad in numerous countries are possible. A 3-2 engineering program in conjunction with Washington at St. Louis and Columbia universities, work study, student-designed and interdisciplinary majors, dual majors and accelerated degrees in all areas, credit by exam, nondegree study, and pass/fail options are available. Doane also offers the HELPS program, designed for Doane College graduates who wish to return as full-time students to seek further education in preparation for career advancement. Students may pursue a 3-2 environmental studies/forestry degree in conjunction with Duke University. Doane's Lincoln campus, designed for adults, offers intensive 8-week classes in the evening and on weekends in both undergraduate and graduate programs. Doane offers an honors program, leadership development program, and the opportunity to conduct summer research projects with faculty. There are 7 national honor societies, a freshman honors program, and 2 departmental honors program.

Faculty/Classroom: 63% of faculty are male; 37%, female. All teach undergraduates. The average class size in an introductory lecture is 24; in a laboratory, 16; and in a regular course, 18.

Admissions: 38% of the current freshmen were in the top fifth of their class; 68% were in the top two fifths.

Requirements: The SAT I or ACT is required. In addition, the ACT is preferred. Applicants must be graduates of an accredited secondary school. The GED is accepted. It is recommended that 4 units of English and 3 units each of math, science, and the social sciences be completed. An interview is recommended. Art students must submit a portfolio, and music and drama students must audition. Students may submit applications via *www.doane.edu*. AP and CLEP credits are accepted. Important factors in the admissions decision are advanced placement or honor courses, recommendations by school officials, and ability to finance college education.

Procedure: Freshmen are admitted fall, winter, and spring. Entrance exams should be taken by spring of junior year or early senior year. There is a deferred admissions plan. Applications should be filed by August 15 for fall entry. The fee was $15 in 2001. Notification is sent on a rolling basis.

Transfer: Transfer students must submit a transcript from previously attended colleges and have been in good standing. The SAT I or ACT is usually required. Grades of 2.0 or higher generally transfer for credit. 30 credits of 132 must be completed at Doane.

Visiting: There are regularly scheduled orientations for prospective students, including 4 scheduled half-day visits that incorporate a parents program. There are guides for informal visits and visitors may sit in on classes and stay overnight. To schedule a visit, contact the Admissions Office at *dkunzman@doane.edu*.

Financial Aid: In 2001-2002, 80% of all freshmen and 75% of continuing students received some form of financial aid. 81% of freshmen and 70% of continuing students received need-based aid. The average freshman award was $11,913. Of that total, scholarships or need-based grants averaged $8662 ($16,010 maximum); loans averaged $2832 ($4125 maximum); and work contracts averaged $771 ($1800 maximum). 48% of undergraduates work part time. Average annual earnings from campus work are $766. The average financial indebtedness of the 2001 graduate was $14,009. The FAFSA is required. The fall application deadline is March 1.

International Students: There are usually about 5 international students enrolled. The school actively recruits these students. They must score 550 on the written TOEFL.

Computers: The mainframe is a Compaq DS-20. Every residence hall has a PC lab networked to the server and Internet. Several large labs are available 73 hours a week. All students have E-mail, Internet services, and web access. All residence rooms have unlimited access. All students may access the system any time. There are no time limits and no fees.

Graduates: In 2001, 171 bachelor's degrees were awarded. The most popular majors were elementary education (14%), business administration (11%), and biology (10%). In an average class, 1% graduate in 3 years, 85% in 4 years, 99% in 5 years, and 100% in 6 years. 45 companies recruited on campus in 2000-2001. Of the 2000 graduating class, 37% were enrolled in graduate school within 6 months of graduation and 83% were employed.

Admissions Contact: Dan Kunzman, Dean of Admissions. A video is available. E-mail: *admissions@doane.edu* Web: *www.doane.edu*

HASTINGS COLLEGE
Hastings, NE 68901 D-3
(402) 461-7315
(800) 532-7642; Fax: (402) 461-7490

Full-time: 510 men, 527 women | **Faculty:** 74; IIB, --$
Part-time: 15 men, 15 women | **Ph.D.s:** 73%
Graduate: 15 men, 26 women | **Student/Faculty:** 14 to 1
Year: 4-1-4, summer session | **Tuition:** $13,666
Application Deadline: August 1 | **Room & Board:** $4188
Freshman Class: 1065 applied, 955 accepted, 315 enrolled
ACT: 24 **COMPETITIVE+**

Hastings College, founded in 1882 and affiliated with the Presbyterian Church (U.S.A.), offers programs in the liberal arts and sciences, education, business, and prehealth professions. In addition to regional accreditation, Hastings College has baccalaureate program accreditation with NASM and NCATE. The library contains 115,000 volumes, 60,000 microform items, and 2600 audiovisual forms/CDs, and subscribes to 600 periodicals. Computerized library services include the card catalog, interlibrary loans, and database searching. Special learning facilities include a learning resource center, art gallery, radio station, TV station, and an observatory, and a glass blowing studio. The 104-acre campus is in a rural area 150 miles west of Omaha. Including residence halls, there are 31 buildings.

Student Life: 76% of undergraduates are from Nebraska. Others are from 25 states, 10 foreign countries, and Canada. 90% are from public schools. 93% are white. 59% are Protestant; 25% Catholic; 15% claim no religious affiliation. The average age of freshmen is 18; all undergraduates, 21. 25% do not continue beyond their first year; 57% remain to graduate.

Housing: 619 students can be accommodated in college housing, which includes single-sex and coed dormitories. In addition, there are honors houses. On-campus housing is guaranteed for the freshman and sophomore years only and is available on a first-come, first-served basis. Priority is given to out-of-town students. 50% of students live on campus; of those, 60% remain on campus on weekends. Alcohol is not permitted. All students may keep cars.

Activities: 20% of men belong to 4 local fraternities; 30% of women belong to 4 local sororities. There are 84 groups on campus, including art, band, cheerleading, choir, chorus, dance, debate, drama, ethnic, flag team, forensics, gay, health advisory council, honors, jazz band, literary magazine, marching band, musical theater, newspaper, nontraditional students, opera, orchestra, peer educators, pep band, photography, political, professional, public relations, radio and TV, religious, social, social service, student government, symphony, and yearbook. Popular campus events include May Fete, Festival of Lessons and Carols, and Artist Lecture Series.

Sports: There are 9 intercollegiate sports for men and 9 for women, and 9 intramural sports for men and 9 for women. Facilities include a physical fitness center, a pool, a weight room, indoor and outdoor tennis courts, a 2200-seat stadium, a 3500-seat gym, and an all-weather track.

Disabled Students: 90% of the campus is accessible. Wheelchair ramps, elevators, special parking, specially equipped rest rooms, special class scheduling, lowered drinking fountains, and lowered telephones are available.

Services: Counseling and information services are available, as is tutoring in most subjects, including all core subjects and most lower-division courses.

Campus Safety and Security: Measures include escort service, pamphlets/posters/films, emergency telephones, and lighted pathways/sidewalks. There is a night security patrol.

Programs of Study: Hastings College confers B.A. and B.M. degrees. Master's degrees are also awarded. Bachelor's degrees are awarded in BIOLOGICAL SCIENCE (biology/biological science), BUSINESS (accounting, and business administration and management), COMMUNICATIONS AND THE ARTS (broadcasting, communications, dramatic arts, English, fine arts, German, music, Spanish, and speech/debate/rhetoric), COMPUTER AND PHYSICAL SCIENCE (chemistry, computer science, mathematics, and physics), EDUCATION (art, business, elementary, foreign languages, music, science, secondary, and special), HEALTH PROFESSIONS (health care administration), SOCIAL SCIENCE (economics, history, human services, philosophy, political science/government, psychology, religion, social science, and sociology). Physics is the strongest academically. Business administration and education are the largest.

Required: Students are required to take courses in written and oral communication, physical and life science, foreign language, history, social and political science, literature, philosophy, religion, health/wellness, computer science, the fine arts, and phys ed. A minimum 2.0 GPA and 127 credit hours, with 30 to 36 in the major, are required to graduate.

Special: There is a co-op nursing program with Creighton University, a 3-2 engineering program with Columbia and Washington Universities and Georgia Institute of Technology, and a 3-2 degree in occupational therapy with Boston and Washington Universities. Internships, study abroad in England, Spain, Russia, Ireland, Holland, and Germany, work-study, dual majors in all areas, and student-designed majors are possible. Credit by exam, credit for military experience, and pass/fail options are available. There are 14 national honor societies.

Faculty/Classroom: 70% of faculty are male; 30%, female. All teach undergraduates and 25% both teach and do research. No introductory courses are taught by graduate students. The average class size in an introductory lecture is 25; in a laboratory, 25; and in a regular course, 18.

Admissions: 90% of the 2001-2002 applicants were accepted. The ACT scores for the 2001-2002 freshman class were: 15% below 21, 31% between 21 and 23, 24% between 24 and 26, 16% between 27 and 28, and 14% above 28. 49% of the current freshmen were in the top fifth of their class; 81% were in the top two fifths. A recent class included 2 National Merit finalists and 2 semifinalists and 20 freshmen graduated first in that class.

Requirements: The SAT I or ACT is required. In addition, applicants should graduate from an accredited secondary school with a minimum of 4 academic credits in English and 2 each in math, science, social studies, and a foreign language. Generally, placement in the upper half of the graduating class, a minimum GPA of 2.0, or a composite score of 20 on the enhanced ACT is a minimal requirement for consideration for admission. Hastings College requires applicants to be in the upper 50% of their class. A GPA of 2.0 is required. AP and CLEP credits are accepted. Important factors in the admissions decision are advanced placement or honor courses, leadership record, and personality/intangible qualities.

Procedure: Freshmen are admitted to all sessions. Entrance exams should be taken before November. Applications should be filed by August 1 for fall entry, December 1 for winter entry, January 1 for spring entry, and May 15 for summer entry. The fee was $20 in 2001. Notification of both early and regular decision is on a rolling basis.

Transfer: 42 transfer students enrolled in 2001-2002. Transfer students must have completed course work equivalent by description to that of Hastings and have earned grades of C or better. 30 credits of 127 must be completed at Hastings College.

Visiting: There are regularly scheduled orientations for prospective students, including academic department presentations, a financial aid session, a student panel discussion, a student guided tour, and an activities fair. There are guides for informal visits and visitors may sit in on classes and stay overnight. To schedule a visit, contact the Admissions Office at (402) 461-7316.

Financial Aid: In 2001-2002, nearly all students received some form of financial aid. 78% of freshmen and 74% of continuing students received need-based aid. The average freshman award was $12,066. Of that total, scholarships or need-based grants averaged $7844 ($15,900 maximum); loans averaged $4090 ($16,125 maximum); and work contracts averaged $700 ($1000 maximum). 54% of undergraduates work part time. Average annual earnings from campus work are $775. The average financial indebtedness of the 2001 graduate was $15,778. Hastings College is a member of CSS. The FAFSA is required. The fall application deadline is May 1.

International Students: There were 15 international students enrolled in a recent class. The school actively recruits these students. They must score 500 on the written TOEFL. International athletes should take a standardized test for athletic eligibility.

Computers: The mainframes consist of multiple servers, including Compaq-Dell and Hewlett-Packard. 94 Windows-based PCs and 42 Macs are available for academic use in several computer labs across campus. All students can connect their computers to the campus network to access Internet resources. All library resources are available and each student has an e-mail address. All students may access the system. There are no time limits and no fees.

Graduates: In 2001, 224 bachelor's degrees were awarded. The most popular majors were business administration (19%), education (17%), and biology (9%). In an average class, 44% graduate in 4 years, and 58% in 5 years. 23 companies recruited on campus in 2000-2001. Of the 2000 graduating class, 19% were enrolled in graduate school within 6 months of graduation and 66% were employed.

Admissions Contact: Michael Karloff, Director of Admissions. A video is available. E-mail: *admissions@hastings.edu* Web: *www.hastings.edu*

MIDLAND LUTHERAN COLLEGE
Fremont, NE 68025 E-2
(402) 941-6501
(800) 642-8382; Fax: (402)-721-2050

Full-time: 407 men, 534 women | **Faculty:** 69; IIB, --$
Part-time: 17 men, 33 women | **Ph.D.s:** 45%
Graduate: none | **Student/Faculty:** 14 to 1
Year: 4-1-4, summer session | **Tuition:** $14,600
Application Deadline: July 15 | **Room & Board:** $4000
Freshman Class: 865 applied, 735 accepted, 280 enrolled
ACT: 22 **COMPETITIVE**

Midland Lutheran College, established in 1883, is a private liberal arts institution affiliated with the Evangelical Lutheran Church in America. In addition to regional accreditation, Midland has baccalaureate program accreditation with NLN. The library contains 105,000 volumes and 1000 audiovisual forms/CDs, and subscribes to 900 periodicals. Computerized library services include interlibrary loans and database searching. Special learning facilities include a learning resource center and planetarium. The 27-acre campus is in a small town 30 miles northwest of Omaha. Including residence halls, there are 18 buildings.

Student Life: 75% of undergraduates are from Nebraska. Others are from 23 states, 10 foreign countries, and Canada. 94% are from public schools. 91% are white. 57% are Protestant; 32%, Catholic; 10% claim no religious affiliation. The average age of freshmen is 18; all undergraduates, 20. 16% do not continue beyond their first year; 56% remain to graduate.

Housing: 575 students can be accommodated in college housing, which includes single-sex and coed dormitories and off-campus apartments. On-campus housing is guaranteed for all 4 years, is available on a first-come, first-served basis, and is available on a lottery system for upperclassmen. 52% of students live on campus; of those, 50% remain on campus on weekends. Alcohol is not permitted. All students may keep cars.

Activities: 20% of men belong to 4 local fraternities; 20% of women belong to 4 local sororities. There are 36 groups on campus, including art, band, cheerleading, choir, chorale, chorus, computers, drama, drill team, ethnic, film, forensics, honors, jazz band, literary magazine, musical theater, newspaper, pep band, photography, political, professional, radio and TV, religious, social, social service, student government, and yearbook. Popular campus events include Journalism Day, Greek Games, Snow Week, and Martin Luther King Day.

Sports: There are 9 intercollegiate sports for men and 9 for women, and 6 intramural sports for men and 6 for women. Facilities include a phys ed center, an athletic practice field, an indoor pool, an indoor track, and a weight room.

Disabled Students: 90% of the campus is accessible. Wheelchair ramps, elevators, special parking, specially equipped rest rooms, special class scheduling, lowered drinking fountains, and lowered telephones are available.

Services: Counseling and information services are available, as is tutoring in every subject. There is remedial reading and writing.

Campus Safety and Security: Measures include 24-hour foot and vehicle patrol, escort service, informal discussions, and pamphlets/posters/films. There are lighted pathways/sidewalks.

Programs of Study: Midland confers B.A., B.S., B.S.B.A., and B.S.N. degrees. Associate degrees are also awarded. Bachelor's degrees are awarded in BIOLOGICAL SCIENCE (biology/biological science), BUSINESS (accounting, business administration and management, business economics, management information systems, and marketing/retailing/merchandising), COMMUNICATIONS AND THE ARTS (advertising, communications, English, fine arts, journalism, and music), COMPUTER AND PHYSICAL SCIENCE (chemistry, computer programming, computer science, and mathematics), EDUCATION (art, business, early childhood, elementary, middle school, music, science, and secondary), HEALTH PROFESSIONS (nursing, predentistry, and premedicine), SOCIAL SCIENCE (community services, economics, history, parks and recreation management, prelaw, psychology, religion, social science, and sociology). Business, journalism, and education are the strongest academically. Business, education, and nursing are the largest.

Required: To graduate, students need a total of 128 credit hours, with 33 of these in distribution requirements of the student's selection. 1 course each in English, speech, and math is required, as well as 1 year of foreign language on the high school or college level. The total number of hours in the major varies from 34 to 48, and students must maintain a GPA of at least 2.0 overall and 2.25 in the major, with some departments requiring a higher minimum GPA.

Special: There is cross-registration with Dana College in Blair, internships in business, public relations, journalism, and art, study abroad in 3 countries, student-designed majors, work-study programs, and a 3-2 engineering degree with Washington University. Other options include dual majors, independent study, directed study, and the pass/no credit grading system. There are 2 national honor societies.

Faculty/Classroom: 60% of faculty are male; 40%, female. All teach undergraduates. The average class size in a laboratory is 20 and in a regular course, 20.

Admissions: 85% of the 2001-2002 applicants were accepted. The ACT scores for the 2001-2002 freshman class were: 9% below 21, 64% between 21 and 23, 15% between 24 and 26, 10% between 27 and 28, and 2% above 28. 48% of the current freshmen were in the top fifth of their class; 85% were in the top two fifths. 19 freshmen graduated first in their class.

Requirements: The SAT I or ACT is recommended. In addition, applicants should be graduates of an accredited secondary school. The GED is accepted. Recommended preparation includes 3 units of English, 2 each of math, and foreign language, and 10 of electives. An interview is recommended. Midland requires applicants to be in the upper 50% of their class. AP and CLEP credits are accepted. Important factors in the admissions decision are leadership record, extracurricular activities record, and evidence of special talent. Applications are accepted on computer disk and on-line.

Procedure: Freshmen are admitted fall and winter. Entrance exams should be taken during the fall of the senior year. There are early decision, early admissions, and deferred admissions plans. Applications should be filed by July 15 for fall entry and January 10 for spring entry, along with a $20 fee. Notification of early decision is sent December 15; regular decision, on a rolling basis. 25 early decision candidates were accepted for the 2001-2002 class.

Transfer: 60 transfer students enrolled in 2001-2002. Applicants must be in good standing at their previous college and generally have a 2.0 minimum GPA. Grades of C or higher transfer for credit. 30 credits of 128 must be completed at Midland.

Visiting: Campus visits are scheduled on an individual basis and as much as possible include visits with faculty, students, and financial aid counselors. There are guides for informal visits and visitors may sit in on classes and stay overnight. To schedule a visit, contact the Admissions Office at *admissions@admin.mlc.edu*

Financial Aid: In 2001-2002, 93% of all freshmen and 90% of continuing students received some form of financial aid. 75% of freshmen and 80% of continuing students received need-based aid. The average freshman award was $12,400. Of that total, scholarships or need-based grants averaged $6700 ($14,600 maximum); loans averaged $3500 ($4500 maximum); work contracts averaged $1000 ($1200 maximum); and outside scholarships averaged $3000. 80% of undergraduates work part time. Average annual earnings from campus work are $800. The average financial indebtedness of the 2001 graduate was $18,200. Midland is a member of CSS. The FAFSA or FFS is required. The fall application deadline is May 1.

International Students: There are 16 international students enrolled. The school actively recruits these students. They must score 500 on the written TOEFL.

Computers: The mainframes are a DEC Vax VMS 4400 and 4106 models. 65 Mac and IBM computers are available with complete access to the Web and Internet. All students have e-mail accounts. All students may access the system. There are no time limits and no fees. It is recommended that students in business and education have personal computers.

Graduates: In 2001, 170 bachelor's degrees were awarded. The most popular majors were business (30%), education (25%), and nursing (20%). In an average class, 1% graduate in 3 years, 52% in 4 years, 55% in 5 years, and 56% in 6 years. 38 companies recruited on campus in 2000-2001. Of the 2000 graduating class, 11% were enrolled in graduate school within 6 months of graduation and 86% were employed.

Admissions Contact: John Klockentager, Vice President for Enrollment Services. E-mail: *klock@admin.mlc.edu* Web: *www.mlc.edu*

NEBRASKA METHODIST COLLEGE OF NURSING AND ALLIED HEALTH F-3

Omaha, NE 68114 (402) 354-4879
(800) 335-5510; Fax: (402) 354-8875

Full-time: 25 men, 191 women	**Faculty:** 28
Part-time: 11 men, 120 women	**Ph.D.s:** 10%
Graduate: 5 men, 28 women	**Student/Faculty:** 8 to 1
Year: semesters, summer session	**Tuition:** $9600
Application Deadline: April 1	**Room & Board:** $1500
Freshman Class: 30 applied, 28 accepted, 20 enrolled	
ACT: 20	**SPECIAL**

Nebraska Methodist College of Nursing and Allied Health, founded in 1891 as the Methodist School of Nursing and chartered in the state of Nebraska in 1985 with its present name, is part of the Nebraska Methodist Health Systems. The college is a private, primarily commuter institution offering career training in the health sciences. In addition to regional accreditation, Nebraska Methodist College has baccalaureate program accreditation with CAHEA and NLN. The 2 libraries contain 13,059 volumes, 1722 microform items, and 500 audiovisual forms/CDs, and subscribe to 598 periodicals. Computerized library services include the card catalog, interlibrary loans, and database searching. Special learning facilities include a learning resource center, an assessment lab for nursing and respiratory care studies, and a human cadaver lab. The 5-acre campus is in an urban area in the center of Omaha. Including residence halls, there are 3 buildings on 3 campus locations.

Student Life: 95% of undergraduates are from Nebraska. Others are from 10 states and 2 foreign countries. 95% are from public schools. 89% are white. The average age of freshmen is 18; all undergraduates, 24. 2% do not continue beyond their first year; 74% remain to graduate.

Housing: 80 students can be accommodated in college housing, which includes coed dormitories. On-campus housing is available on a first-come, first-served basis. Priority is given to out-of-town students. 80% of students commute. Alcohol is not permitted. All students may keep cars.

Activities: There are no fraternities or sororities. There are 10 groups on campus, including ethnic, professional, social, social service, and student government. Popular campus events include Honors Convocation and pledging ceremonies.

Sports: There is no sports program at Nebraska Methodist College. Facilities include a fitness center.

Disabled Students: 75% of the campus is accessible. Elevators, special parking, and specially equipped rest rooms are available.

Services: Counseling and information services are available, as is tutoring in most subjects. There is remedial math, reading, and writing. A reader service for the blind is available in the metropolitan area.

Campus Safety and Security: Measures include self-defense education, informal discussions, pamphlets/posters/films, and lighted pathways/sidewalks.

Programs of Study: Nebraska Methodist College confers B.S. and B.S.N. degrees. Associate and master's degrees are also awarded. Bachelor's degrees are awarded in HEALTH PROFESSIONS (nursing, respiratory therapy, and ultrasound technology). Nursing is the strongest program academically and has the largest enrollment.

Required: All students must complete 45 credit hours of core curriculum courses in the humanities, social and behavioral sciences, and natural and applied sciences. A total of 127 credit hours is required, 55 of these in the major. Students must maintain a minimum GPA of 2.0.

Special: There is nondegree study and credit by exam. Credit by correspondence may be considered. There is 1 national honor society, and 2 departmental honors programs.

Faculty/Classroom: 15% of faculty are male; 85%, female. All teach undergraduates. No introductory courses are taught by graduate students. The average class size in an introductory lecture is 35; in a laboratory, 10; and in a regular course, 20.

Admissions: 93% of the 2001-2002 applicants were accepted. The ACT scores for the 2001-2002 freshman class were: 60% below 21, 30% between 21 and 23, 5% between 24 and 26, and 5% above 28. 30% of the current freshmen were in the top fifth of their class; 70% were in the top two fifths.

Requirements: The ACT is required with a minimum acceptable score of 18. Students must be graduates of an accredited secondary school with the number of academic credits required under Nebraska state law. The GED is accepted. Students should have completed 4 years of English and 2 years each of math, science, and social studies. An essay and an interview are required. Nebraska Methodist College requires applicants to be in the upper 75% of their class. A GPA of 2.0 is required. Applications are accepted on-line at the school's web site. AP and CLEP credits are accepted. Important factors in the admissions decision are personality/intangible qualities, advanced placement or honor courses, and leadership record.

Procedure: Freshmen are admitted fall and spring. Entrance exams should be taken as early as possible. Applications should be filed by April 1 for fall entry and November 1 for spring entry, along with a $25 fee. Notification is sent on a rolling basis.

Transfer: 60 transfer students enrolled in 2001-2002. Applicants must have a GPA above 2.0. Grades of C and above can be transferred for credit. An interview is required. 30 credits of 127 must be completed at Nebraska Methodist College.

Visiting: There are regularly scheduled orientations for prospective students. There are guides for informal visits and visitors may sit in on classes. To schedule a visit, contact the Admissions Office.

Financial Aid: In a recent year, 65% of all freshmen and 75% of continuing students received some form of financial aid. 60% of freshmen and 75% of continuing students received need-based aid. The average freshman award was $6000. Of that total, scholarships or need-based grants averaged $2500 ($5340 maximum); and loans averaged $4100 ($10,000 maximum). 66% of undergraduates work part time. The average financial indebtedness of a recent year's graduate was $7000. The FAFSA and the college's own financial statement are required. The fall application deadline is May 1.

International Students: There is 1 international student enrolled. They must score 550 on the written TOEFL.

Computers: The mainframe is an IBM. 60 IBM PCs are available in labs on each campus. Students have access to e-mail and the Internet. All students may access the system. There are no time limits and no fees.

Graduates: In 2001, 68 bachelor's degrees were awarded. The most popular majors were nursing (90%) and allied health (10%). In an average class, 74% graduate in 4 years. 4 companies recruited on campus in 2000-2001. Of the 2000 graduating class, 90% were employed within 6 months of graduation.

Admissions Contact: Admissions Officer.
E-mail: *admissions@methodistcollege.edu*
Web: *www.methodistcollege.edu*

NEBRASKA WESLEYAN UNIVERSITY E-3

Lincoln, NE 68504 (402) 465-2218
(800) 541-3818; Fax: (402) 465-2179

Full-time: 655 men, 819 women	**Faculty:** 99; IIB, -$
Part-time: 43 men, 104 women	**Ph.D.s:** 86%
Graduate: 19 men, 79 women	**Student/Faculty:** 15 to 1
Year: semesters, summer session	**Tuition:** $14,641
Application Deadline: May 1	**Room & Board:** $4126
Freshman Class: 1128 applied, 945 accepted, 392 enrolled	
ACT: 24	**VERY COMPETITIVE**

Nebraska Wesleyan University, founded in 1887, is a private liberal arts institution affiliated with the United Methodist Church. In addition to regional accreditation, NWU has baccalaureate program accreditation with ACBSP, CSWE, NASM, NCATE, and NLN. The library contains 198,261 volumes, 4506 microform items, and 5413 audiovisual forms/CDs, and subscribes to 732 periodicals. Computerized library services include the card catalog, interlibrary loans, and database searching. Special learning facilities include a learning resource center, art gallery, and planetarium. The 50-acre campus is in a suburban area 50 miles west of Omaha. Including residence halls, there are 17 buildings.

Student Life: 94% of undergraduates are from Nebraska. Others are from 22 states and 8 foreign countries. 95% are white. 60% are Protestant; 28% Catholic. The average age of freshmen is 18; all undergraduates, 21. 16% do not continue beyond their first year; 63% remain to graduate.

Housing: 981 students can be accommodated in college housing, which includes single-sex and coed dormitories, off-campus apartments, fraternity houses, and sorority houses. In addition, there are speial interest houses. On-campus housing is guaranteed for all 4 years. 52% of students live on campus; of those, 70% remain on campus on weekends. All students may keep cars.

Activities: 29% of men belong to 1 local and 3 national fraternities; 26% of women belong to 2 local and 2 national sororities. There are 80 groups on campus, including art, band, cheerleading, choir, chorus, computers, debate, drama, drill team, ethnic, forensics, gay, honors, international, jazz band, literary magazine, musical theater, newspaper, opera, orchestra, pep band, political, professional, religious, social, social service, student government, and yearbook. Popular campus events include Wesleyan Weekend and annual orientation event.

Sports: There are 8 intercollegiate sports for men and 8 for women, and 10 intramural sports for men and 10 for women. Facilities include a recreation and fitness center, a field house and gym, a stadium, a swimming pool, an outdoor track, football and baseball fields, and tennis courts.

Disabled Students: 85% of the campus is accessible. Wheelchair ramps, elevators, special parking, specially equipped rest rooms, special class scheduling, and lowered drinking fountains, and telephones. All academic programs can be moved or adapted as needed to accommodate students.

Services: Counseling and information services are available, as is tutoring in some subjects, including sciences, social sciences, humanities, and math.

Campus Safety and Security: Measures include escort service, informal discussions, emergency telephones, and lighted pathways/sidewalks. There is a nighttime foot patrol.

Programs of Study: NWU confers B.A., B.S., B.F.A., B.M., and B.S.N. degrees. Master's degrees are also awarded. Bachelor's degrees are awarded in BIOLOGICAL SCIENCE (biochemistry, biology/biological science, and molecular biology), BUSINESS (business administration and management, international business management, and sports management), COMMUNICATIONS AND THE ARTS (applied music, art, communications, design, dramatic arts, English, French, German, music, and Spanish), COMPUTER AND PHYSICAL SCIENCE (chemistry, computer science, information sciences and systems, mathematics, and physics), EDUCATION (athletic training, elementary, middle school, music, physical, and special), HEALTH PROFESSIONS (exercise science, and nursing), SOCIAL SCIENCE (anthropology, biopsychology, economics, history, international studies, paralegal studies, philosophy, political science/government, psychology, religion, social work, sociology, and women's studies). Biological science, psychology, and English are the strongest academically. Business administration, biology, and psychology are the largest.

Required: To graduate, students must complete approximately 42 to 48 hours of general education requirements including 9 hours in First-year Experience, 8 in Developing Foundations courses, 7 in Scientific Inquiry, 6 in U.S. Culture and Society, 3 to 11 in Global Perspectives, 3 in Western Intellectual and Religious Traditions, and 3 in Fine Arts. At least 126 credit hours, including 30 in the major, must be completed with a minimum GPA of 2.0. A senior comprehensive is also needed, consisting of a comprehensive exam in the major discipline, a thesis or independent study, or an internship, presentation, or performance.

Special: NWU offers cross-registration with Union College, the Capitol Hill Internship Program, study abroad in 35 countries, a global studies major, and a department of interdisciplinary studies. Internships are available in most departments and required in many. Other options include nondegree study, pass/fail options, dual majors, credit by examination, and a 3-2 engineering degree in conjunction with Washington and Columbia Universities. There are 20 national honor societies.

Faculty/Classroom: 47% of faculty are male; 53%, female. All teach undergraduates. No introductory courses are taught by graduate students. The average class size in an introductory lecture is 25; in a laboratory, 16; and in a regular course, 20.

Admissions: 84% of the 2001-2002 applicants were accepted. The ACT scores for the 2001-2002 freshman class were: 13% below 21, 30% between 21 and 23, 31% between 24 and 26, 14% between 27 and 28, and 12% above 28. 48% of the current freshmen were in the top fifth of their class; 80% were in the top two fifths. 17 freshmen graduated first in their class.

Requirements: The SAT I or ACT is required. In addition, a minimum composite score of 950 on the SAT I or 20 on the ACT is required. Freshmen must be graduates of an accredited secondary school or submit the GED. An interview is recommended. NWU requires applicants to be in the upper 50% of their class. AP and CLEP credits are accepted. Important factors in the admissions decision are advanced placement or honor courses, leadership record, and recommendations by school officials.

Procedure: Freshmen are admitted fall and spring. Entrance exams should be taken no later than December of the senior year. There are early decision and deferred admissions plans. Early decision application should be filed by November 15; regular applications, by May 1 for fall entry, December 15 for spring entry, and April 15 for summer entry. Notification of early decision is sent December 15; regular decision, January 15. The application fee was $20 in 2001. 139 early decision candidates were accepted for the 2001-2002 class.

Transfer: 42 transfer students enrolled in 2001-2002. Applicants must be in good standing at their previous school and have a 2.0 GPA or higher. A minimum of 950 on the SAT I or 20 on the ACT is recommended. Grades of C- or better transfer for credit. 30 credits of 126 must be completed at NWU.

Visiting: There are regularly scheduled orientations for prospective students, consisting of a tour, classroom visits, and meetings with faculty and financial aid and admissions personnel. There are guides for informal visits and visitors may sit in on classes and stay overnight. To schedule a visit, contact the Admissions Office at *admissions@nebrwesleyan.edu.*

Financial Aid: In 2001-2002, 94% of all freshmen and 92% of continuing students received some form of financial aid. 70% of freshmen and 66% of continuing students received need-based aid. The average freshman award was $10,135. Of that total, scholarships or need-based grants averaged $7067 ($15,400 maximum); loans averaged $2640 ($4025 maximum); and work contracts averaged $400 ($1000 maximum). 91% of undergraduates work part time. Average annual earnings from campus work are $1100. The average financial indebtedness of the 2001 graduate was $16,130. The FAFSA is required. The fall application deadline is August 15.

International Students: There are 13 international students enrolled. The school actively recruits these students. They must score 525 on the written TOEFL or 195 on the electronic version or take the MELAB.

Computers: 30 computer labs--9 general use labs (including one in each of the 5 residence halls) and 21 departmental labs--containing a total of 336 computers are available for student use. All computer labs, classrooms, offices and residence hall rooms are wired and networked for campus and Internet access. All students may access the system 24 hours a day, 7 days a week. There are no time limits and no fees.

Graduates: In 2001, 334 bachelor's degrees were awarded. The most popular majors were business administration (22%), psychology (9%), and elementary education (7%). In an average class, 46% graduate in 4 years, 60% in 5 years, and 62% in 6 years. 147 companies recruited on campus in 2000-2001.

Admissions Contact: Kendal E. Sieg, Director of Admissions. A video is available. E-mail: *admissions@nebrwesleyan.edu*
Web: *http://www.nebrwesleyan.edu*

PERU STATE COLLEGE
Peru, NE 68421-0010 — F-3

(402) 872-2221
(800) 742-4412; Fax: (402) 872-2296

Full-time: 417 men, 457 women	**Faculty:** 39; IIB, --$
Part-time: 242 men, 330 women	**Ph.D.s:** 64%
Graduate: 44 men, 135 women	**Student/Faculty:** 23 to 1
Year: semesters, summer session	**Tuition:** $2546 ($4638)
Application Deadline: open	**Room & Board:** $3796

Freshman Class: 350 applied, 350 accepted, 187 enrolled
ACT: recommended — **NONCOMPETITIVE**

Peru State College, established in 1867 and a part of the Nebraska State College System, is a public institution offering curricula in the arts, business, military studies, teacher preparation, and technical studies. In addition to regional accreditation, Peru State has baccalaureate program accreditation with NCATE. The library contains 102,432 volumes, 494,101 microform items, and 10,403 audiovisual forms/CDs, and subscribes to 313 periodicals. Computerized library services include the card catalog, interlibrary loans, and database searching. Special learning facilities include a learning resource center and art gallery. The 103-acre campus is in a rural area 60 miles south of Omaha. Including residence halls, there are 21 buildings.

Student Life: Students come from 12 states, 8 foreign countries, and Canada. 98% are from public schools. 87% are white. The average age of freshmen is 18; all undergraduates, 22. 28% do not continue beyond their first year; 35% remain to graduate.

Housing: 590 students can be accommodated in college housing, which includes single-sex dormitories, on-campus apartments, and married-student housing. On-campus housing is guaranteed for all 4 years. 65% of students live on campus; of those, 27% remain on campus on weekends. Alcohol is not permitted. All students may keep cars.

Activities: There are no fraternities or sororities. There are 27 groups on campus, including art, band, cheerleading, choir, chorus, computers, drama, ethnic, gay, honors, jazz band, pep band, photography, professional, religious, social, social service, student government, and yearbook. Popular campus events include Spring Break Trip.

Sports: There are 3 intercollegiate sports for men and 3 for women, and 7 intramural sports for men and 7 for women. Facilities include a playing field; an activity trail; a 2500-seat stadium; and a health and recreation complex containing basketball and tennis courts, an indoor track, and an Olympic-sized swimming pool.

Disabled Students: 80% of the campus is accessible. Wheelchair ramps, elevators, special parking, specially equipped rest rooms, special class scheduling, lowered drinking fountains, and lowered telephones are available.

Services: Counseling and information services are available, as is tutoring in most subjects. There is a reader service for the blind, and remedial math, reading, and writing. Tutoring is available in writing and other subjects.

Campus Safety and Security: Measures include 24-hour foot and vehicle patrol, escort service, informal discussions, and pamphlets/posters/films. There are lighted pathways/sidewalks.

Programs of Study: Bobcats confers B.A., B.S., and B.T. degrees. Master's degrees are also awarded. Bachelor's degrees are awarded in AGRICULTURE (wildlife management), BIOLOGICAL SCIENCE (biology/biological science), BUSINESS (accounting, business administration and management, marketing/retailing/merchandising, and sports management), COMMUNICATIONS AND THE ARTS (English, music, and music business management), COMPUTER AND PHYSICAL SCIENCE (computer management, computer programming, computer science, mathematics, nuclear technology, and physical sciences), EDUCATION (art, elementary, music, physical, science, secondary, and special), ENGINEERING AND ENVIRONMENTAL DESIGN (preengineering), HEALTH PROFESSIONS (premedicine, prepharmacy, and preveterinary science), SOCIAL SCIENCE (history, prelaw, psychology, social science, and sociology).

Required: To graduate, students must complete 45 to 53 hours of general education requirements in literature, communications, fine arts, social and behavioral sciences, health and hygiene, computer science, and natural sciences, as well as a phys ed requirement. Teacher education majors must have a GPA of 2.5; all others must have a GPA of 2.0. The college requires 125 credit hours for graduation.

Special: The college offers cooperative programs, internships, B.A.-B.S. degrees, dual majors, work-study programs, and nondegree study. Credit may be granted for military experience. There are 2 national honor societies and a freshman honors program.

Faculty/Classroom: 79% of faculty are male; 21%, female. All teach undergraduates. No introductory courses are taught by graduate students. The average class size in an introductory lecture is 40; in a laboratory, 25; and in a regular course, 25.

Admissions: All of the 2001-2002 applicants were accepted. The ACT scores for the 2001-2002 freshman class were: 49% below 21, 32% between 21 and 23, 14% between 24 and 26, 4% between 27 and 28, and 1% above 28. 14% of the current freshmen were in the top fifth of their class; 43% were in the top two fifths.

Requirements: The ACT is recommended. In addition, applicants who have graduated from an accredited Nebraska secondary school will be admitted; holders of the GED will be considered. Out-of-state applicants should have earned 16 Carnegie units. A GPA of 2.0 is required. AP and CLEP credits are accepted.

Procedure: Freshmen are admitted to all sessions. Entrance exams should be taken. There is a deferred admissions plan. Application deadlines are open; the fee is $10.

Transfer: 149 transfer students enrolled in 2001-2002. Transfer students must be in good standing with the previously attended institution. 30 credits of 125 must be completed at Bobcats.

Visiting: There are regularly scheduled orientations for prospective students. There are guides for informal visits and visitors may sit in on classes and stay overnight. To schedule a visit, contact the Admissions Office at *www.peru.edu*.

Financial Aid: In 2001-2002, 73% of all freshmen received some form of financial aid. 40% of undergraduates work part time. Average annual earnings from campus work are $800. The average financial indebtedness of the 2001 graduate was $14,000. The FAFSA is required. The fall application deadline is May 1.

International Students: There are 12 international students enrolled. They must score 550 on the written TOEFL or 230 on the electronic version.

Computers: Peru State provides 48 Macs in labs for students enrolled in computer courses. . There are no time limits and no fees.

Graduates: In 2001, 229 bachelor's degrees were awarded. The most popular majors were education (38%) and business administration (38%). In an average class, 11% graduate in 4 years, 20% in 5 years, and 30% in 6 years. 10 companies recruited on campus in 2000-2001. Of the 2000 graduating class, 10% were enrolled in graduate school within 6 months of graduation and 93% were employed.

Admissions Contact: Janelle Moran, Director of Admission and Recruitment. E-mail: *jmoran@oakmail.peru.edu*
Web: *http://www.peru.edu*

UNION COLLEGE
Lincoln, NE 68506

E-3
(402) 486-2504
(800) 228-4600; Fax: (402) 486-2895

Full-time: 336 men, 446 women	**Faculty:** 57
Part-time: 68 men, 72 women	**Ph.D.s:** 39%
Graduate: none	**Student/Faculty:** 14 to 1
Year: semesters, summer session	**Tuition:** $11,390
Application Deadline: open	**Room & Board:** $3260
Freshman Class: n/av	**ACT:** required **COMPETITIVE**

Union College, established in 1891, is a nonprofit, private, liberal arts institution affiliated with the Seventh-Day Adventist Church. In addition to regional accreditation, College of the Golden Cords has baccalaureate program accreditation with CSWE, NCATE, and NLN. The library contains 144,199 volumes, 1026 microform items, and 4098 audiovisual forms/CDs, and subscribes to 1558 periodicals. Computerized library services include the card catalog, interlibrary loans, and database searching. Special learning facilities include a learning resource center, art gallery, and and a state-run natural arboretum. The 26-acre campus is in a suburban area 5 miles southeast of Lincoln. Including residence halls, there are 11 buildings.

Student Life: 81% of undergraduates are from out of state, mostly the Midwest. Others are from 44 states, 34 foreign countries, and Canada. 18% are from public schools. 74% are white; 14% foreign nationals. The average age of freshmen is 18; all undergraduates, 21. 23% do not continue beyond their first year; 47% remain to graduate.

Housing: 635 students can be accommodated in college housing, which includes single-sex dormitories, on-campus apartments, and married-student housing. On-campus housing is guaranteed for the freshman year only and is available on a first-come, first-served basis. 64% of students live on campus; of those, 67% remain on campus on weekends. Alcohol is not permitted. All students may keep cars.

Activities: There are no fraternities or sororities. There are 15 groups on campus, including art, band, choir, chorale, computers, drama, ethnic, honors, international, literary magazine, newspaper, orchestra, photography, religious, student government, and yearbook.

Sports: There is 1 intercollegiate sport for men and 1 for women, and 8 intramural sports for men and 8 for women. Facilities include an Olympic-size indoor swimming pool, a weight room, tennis courts, and a sandlot volleyball court.

Disabled Students: 75% of the campus is accessible. Wheelchair ramps, elevators, special parking, specially equipped rest rooms, and lowered telephones are available.

Services: Counseling and information services are available, as is tutoring in most subjects. There is remedial math, reading, and writing. Tutoring is available upon request.

Campus Safety and Security: Measures include escort service and lighted pathways/sidewalks.

Programs of Study: The college confers B.A., B.S., B.A.T., B.Ed., B.M., B.S.W., and B.T. degrees. Associate degrees are also awarded. Bachelor's degrees are awarded in BIOLOGICAL SCIENCE (biology/biological science), BUSINESS (accounting, banking and finance, business administration and management, management science, marketing and distribution, and small business management), COMMUNICATIONS AND THE ARTS (communications, English, journalism, literature, modern language, music, music performance, public relations, and studio art), COMPUTER AND PHYSICAL SCIENCE (chemistry, computer science, mathematics, physics, and science), EDUCATION (art, business, computer, elementary, English, mathematics, music, physical, secondary, and social science), ENGINEERING AND ENVIRONMENTAL DESIGN (commercial art), HEALTH PROFESSIONS (medical laboratory technology, nursing, and physician's assistant), SOCIAL SCIENCE (history, international studies, pastoral studies, physical fitness/movement, psychology, religion, religious education, social science, social work, and theological studies). Physician's assistant and physical science are the strongest academically. Business administration and nursing are the largest.

Required: Students must complete 128 semester hours with fulfillment of a major, and maintain a minimum GPA of 2.0. There are 39 hours of core classes, including those in art/fine arts, computer science, English, history, math, science, and philosophy/religion.

Special: Special academic programs include study abroad in 4 countries, co-op programs with 9 Adventist institutions abroad, and cross-registration with the University of Nebraska, Nebraska Wesleyan University, and Southeast Community College. Student-designed majors are available through the Personalized Bachelor's Degree Program. There are pass/fail options in electives for upperclassmen with a minimum cumulative GPA of 2.0. Some internships are available. There is a freshman honors program.

Faculty/Classroom: 57% of faculty are male; 43%, female. The average class size in an introductory lecture is 21 and in a regular course, 18.

Admissions: 33% of the current freshmen were in the top fifth of their class; 63% were in the top two fifths. There were 3 National Merit finalists in a recent year.

Requirements: The ACT is required. In addition, freshmen with a high school GPA below 2.5 and/or an ACT composite score below the 20th percentile will be enrolled in the freshman development program. Applicants must have graduated from an accredited secondary school with 18 academic credits, including 3 units of English and 1 unit each of math, science, and history. For math and science programs, 2 units of algebra, and 1 unit each of geometry and trigonometry are recommended. For majors in nursing, biology, chemistry, physics, or engineering, applicants should complete physics and chemistry courses. The GED is also accepted. An essay and interview are advised, and music students should audition. A GPA of 2.5 is required. AP and CLEP credits are accepted.

Procedure: Freshmen are admitted fall and spring. Entrance exams should be taken by fall of the senior year. Application deadlines are open and there is no fee.

Transfer: 74 transfer students enrolled in 2001-2002. Transfer students must have a minimum GPA of 2.0. The ACT is required, and high school and college transcripts must be submitted. 30 credits of 128 must be completed at Union College.

Visiting: There are regularly scheduled orientations for prospective students. There are guides for informal visits and visitors may sit in on classes and stay overnight. To schedule a visit, contact the Admissions Office Campus Hostess.

Financial Aid: In 2001-2002, 100% of all freshmen and 95% of continuing students received some form of financial aid. 55% of freshmen and 54% of continuing students received need-based aid. The average freshman award was $7152. Of that total, scholarships or need-based grants averaged $5193 ($13,930 maximum); loans averaged $3320 ($12,443 maximum); and work contracts averaged $1805 ($3800 maximum). 48% of undergraduates work part time. Average annual earnings from campus work are $1960. The average financial indebtedness of the 2001 graduate was $17,913. College of the Golden Cords is a member of CSS. The FAFSA is required. The fall application deadline is May 15.

International Students: There are 144 international students enrolled. The school actively recruits these students. They must score 550 on the written TOEFL.

Computers: The mainframes are an HP 3000 and an HP 9000. There are also 65 computers in labs and ethernet for student-owned PCs. All students may access the system. There are no time limits and no fees. It is strongly recommended that all students have a personal computer.

Graduates: In 2001, 137 bachelor's degrees were awarded. The most popular majors were physician's assistant (14%), nursing (11%), and business administration (11%). In an average class, 29% graduate in 4 years, and 39% in 6 years. 32 companies recruited on campus in 2000-2001. Of the 2000 graduating class, 11% were enrolled in graduate school within 6 months of graduation and 85% were employed.

Admissions Contact: Daryl Cole, Vice President of Enrollment Services. E-mail: *ucenrol@ucollege.edu* Web: *www.ucollege.edu*

UNIVERSITY OF NEBRASKA SYSTEM

The University of Nebraska System, established in 1869, is a public system. It is governed by a board of regents and a central administration, whose chief administrator is the president. The primary mission and priorities of the system are teaching, research, and service. The total enrollment of all campuses is nearly 46,000, with more than 2600 faculty members. Altogether there are 330 baccalaureate, 160 master's, and 45 doctoral programs offered. There are 4-year campus located in Kearney, Lincoln and Omaha. Profiles of these campuses are included in this section.

UNIVERSITY OF NEBRASKA AT KEARNEY D-3

Kearney, NE 68849 (308) 865-8526
(800) KEARNEY; Fax: (308) 865-8987

Full-time: 2300 men, 2800 women	**Faculty:** 314; IIA, --$
Part-time: 300 men, 440 women	**Ph.D.s:** 74%
Graduate: 365 men, 615 women	**Student/Faculty:** 18 to 1
Year: semesters, summer session	**Tuition:** $3148 ($5503)
Application Deadline: open	**Room & Board:** $3900
Freshman Class: n/av	
SAT I or ACT: required	**NONCOMPETITIVE**

The University of Nebraska at Kearney, founded in 1903, is a public facility. Figures in above capsule are approximate. There are 4 undergraduate schools and 1 graduate school. In addition to regional accreditation, UNK has baccalaureate program accreditation with ADA, CSWE, NASM, NCATE, and NLN. The library contains 287,000 volumes, 985,000 microform items, and 1300 audiovisual forms/CDs, and subscribes to 1650 periodicals. Computerized library services include the card catalog, interlibrary loans, and database searching. Special learning facilities include a learning resource center, art gallery, planetarium, radio station, TV station, and writing center. The 235-acre campus is in a small town 180 miles west of Omaha. Including residence halls, there are 36 buildings.

Student Life: 91% of undergraduates are from Nebraska. Others are from 39 states, 46 foreign countries, and Canada. 93% are white. The average age of freshmen is 19; all undergraduates, 21. 22% do not continue beyond their first year; 47% remain to graduate.

Housing: 2600 students can be accommodated in college housing, which includes single-sex and coed dormitories, off-campus apartments, married-student housing, fraternity houses, and sorority houses. In addition, there are honors houses and special-interest houses. On-campus housing is guaranteed for the freshman year only and is available on a first-come, first-served basis. 69% of students commute. Alcohol is not permitted. All students may keep cars.

Activities: 11% of men belong to 7 national fraternities; 10% of women belong to 4 national sororities. There are 160 groups on campus, including art, band, cheerleading, choir, chorale, chorus, computers, dance, debate, drama, drill team, ethnic, forensics, gay, honors, international, jazz band, marching band, musical theater, newspaper, opera, orchestra, pep band, photography, political, professional, radio and TV, religious, social, social service, student government, symphony, and yearbook. Popular campus events include Welcome Week, Bike Bowl, and the Midwest Conference on World Affairs.

Sports: There are 8 intercollegiate sports for men and 8 for women, and 14 intramural sports for men and 14 for women. Facilities include a field, tennis courts, and health and sports facility.

Disabled Students: Wheelchair ramps, elevators, special parking, specially equipped rest rooms, and lowered drinking fountains are available.

Services: Counseling and information services are available, as is tutoring in most subjects. There is a reader service for the blind, and remedial math, reading, and writing.

Campus Safety and Security: Measures include 24-hour foot and vehicle patrol, escort service, informal discussions, and pamphlets/posters/films. There are emergency telephones, and lighted pathways/sidewalks.

Programs of Study: UNK confers B.A., B.S. B.A.Ed., B.F.A., B.G.S., and B.S.Ed. degrees. Master's degrees are also awarded. Bachelor's degrees are awarded in BIOLOGICAL SCIENCE (biology/biological science), BUSINESS (accounting, banking and finance, business administration and management, business economics, marketing/retailing/merchandising, personnel management, and tourism), COMMUNICATIONS AND THE ARTS (advertising, broadcasting, communications, dramatic arts, English, fine arts, French, German, journalism, music, Spanish, speech/debate/rhetoric, and telecommunications), COMPUTER AND PHYSICAL SCIENCE (chemistry, computer programming, computer science, information sciences and systems, mathematics, physics, and statistics), EDUCATION (art, business, early childhood, elementary, foreign languages, health, home economics, middle school, music, physical, science, secondary, special, and teaching English as a second/foreign language (TESOL/TEFOL)), HEALTH PROFESSIONS (nursing, predentistry, and premedicine), SOCIAL SCIENCE (criminal justice, dietetics, economics, family/consumer studies, geography, history, human development, international studies, political science/government, prelaw, psychology, social science, social work, and sociology). Business, communication, and psychology are the strongest academically. Business administration, elementary education, and special education are the largest.

Required: To graduate, all students must complete courses in humanities, communications, civilization, math, natural sciences, and social and behavioral sciences. A minimum of 125 credit hours is required, with approximately 60 in the major. Students must maintain a GPA of 2.0 or higher.

Special: Special arrangements include internships, work-study programs, study at other U.S. colleges and universities under the auspices of the National Student Exchange Program, and study abroad in more than 40 countries through the International Student Exchange Program. Cooperative programs in some health science majors, an international studies degree, and a credit/no credit grading option are available. There is a chapter of Phi Beta Kappa and a freshman honors program.

Faculty/Classroom: 66% of faculty are male; 34%, female. 99% teach undergraduates. The average class size in an introductory lecture is 32; in a laboratory, 25; and in a regular course, 20.

Admissions: In a recent year, 50% of the current freshmen were in the top fifth of their class; 30% were in the top two fifths.

Requirements: Applicants must be graduates of an accredited secondary school. The GED is accepted. They should have completed 4 years of high school English, 3 years each of math, science, and social studies, 2 years of the same foreign language, and 1 year of an academic elective. They should score 20 or above on the ACT or 950 on the SAT I, or be in the top half of their graduating class. UNK requires applicants to be in the upper 50% of their class. AP and CLEP credits are accepted. Important factors in the admissions decision are recommendations by school officials, evidence of special talent, and advanced placement or honor courses. Applications are accepted on-line at *www.unk.edu*

Procedure: Freshmen are admitted fall, spring, and summer. Entrance exams should be taken at the end of the junior year or beginning of the senior year. Application deadlines are open. Notification is rolling. The application fee is $25.

Transfer: 395 transfer students enrolled in a recent year. Transfer students must supply transcripts from previous institutions. If the GPA from the previous school is lower than 2.0, students will be evaluated by the Admissions Director. Transfers must show proof of honorable dismissal from the last institution attended. Grades of C and above transfer for credit. 45 credits of 125 must be completed at UNK.

Visiting: There are regularly scheduled orientations for prospective students, including registration for classes and campus orientation. There are guides for informal visits and visitors may sit in on classes and stay overnight. To schedule a visit, contact the Admissions Office at *admissionsug@unk.edu*

Financial Aid: In a recent year, 81% of all freshmen and 76% of continuing students received some form of financial aid. 55% of freshmen and 51% of continuing students received need-based aid. The average freshman award was $4523. 90% of undergraduates work part time. Average annual earnings from campus work are $1250. The average financial indebtedness of a recent graduate was $13,570. The FAFSA and the college's own financial statement are required. Check with the school for current deadlines.

International Students: There were 178 international students enrolled in a recent year. The school actively recruits these students. They must score 500 on the written TOEFL.

Computers: The mainframe is an ALPHA 1000A. There are 700 Mac and IBM PCs available. All students may access the system. There are no time limits. It is strongly recommended that all students have a personal computer.

Admissions Contact: John Kundel, Director of Admissions.
E-mail: *admissionsug@unk.edu* Web: *www.unk.edu*

UNIVERSITY OF NEBRASKA AT LINCOLN E-3

Lincoln, NE 68588-0417 (402) 472-2023
(800) 742-8800; Fax: (402) 472-0670

Full-time: 8484 men, 7625 women	**Faculty:** I, -$
Part-time: 1034 men, 842 women	**Ph.D.s:** 93%
Graduate: 2315 men, 2464 women	**Student/Faculty:** 15 to 1
Year: semesters, summer session	**Tuition:** $3760 ($9362)
Application Deadline: June 30	**Room & Board:** $4565
Freshman Class: 7266 applied, 6578 accepted, 5532 enrolled	
SAT I Verbal/Math: 567/583	**ACT:** 24 **COMPETITIVE+**

University of Nebraska-Lincoln, part of the University of Nebraska system, was founded in 1869 as a land-grant facility. There are 9 undergraduate schools and 1 graduate school. In addition to regional accreditation, UNL has baccalaureate program accreditation with ABET, ACCE, ACEJMC, ADA, FIDER, and NCATE. The 12 libraries contain 2,612,706 volumes, 4,355,285 microform items, and 31,340 audiovisual forms/CDs, and subscribe to 22,836 periodicals. Computerized library services include the card catalog, interlibrary loans, and database searching. Special learning facilities include a learning resource center, art gallery, natural history museum, planetarium, radio station, TV station, a center for mass spectrometry, an observatory, the Buros Institute of Mental Measurements, an animal sciences complex, and a center for performing arts. The 628-acre campus is in an urban area 55 miles southwest of Omaha. Including residence halls, there are 236 buildings.

Student Life: 86% of undergraduates are from Nebraska. Others are from 49 states, 122 foreign countries, and Canada. 89% are from public schools. 85% are white. The average age of freshmen is 18; all undergraduates, 21. 20% do not continue beyond their first year; 53% remain to graduate.

Housing: 5200 students can be accommodated in college housing, which includes single-sex and coed dormitories, on-campus apartments,

off-campus apartments, married-student housing, fraternity houses, and sorority houses. In addition, there are honors houses, language houses, special-interest houses, floors for modern languages, scholars, engineering, business, and journalism, and an international house. On-campus housing is guaranteed for the freshman year only and is available on a first-come, first-served basis. 74% of students commute. Alcohol is not permitted. All students may keep cars.

Activities: 15% of men belong to 1 local fraternity and 24 national fraternities; 17% of women belong to 15 national sororities. There are 335 groups on campus, including art, band, cheerleading, chess, choir, chorale, chorus, computers, dance, debate, drama, ethnic, film, forensics, gay, honors, international, jazz band, literary magazine, marching band, musical theater, newspaper, opera, orchestra, pep band, photography, political, professional, radio and TV, religious, social, social service, student government, symphony, and yearbook. Popular campus events include Cornstock, Parents Weekend, and Freshmen Friday.

Sports: There are 11 intercollegiate sports for men and 14 for women, and 65 intramural sports for men and 45 for women. Facilities include a recreation center and 34 acres of outdoor recreational space.

Disabled Students: 80% of the campus is accessible. Wheelchair ramps, elevators, special parking, specially equipped rest rooms, special class scheduling, lowered drinking fountains, lowered telephones, and the Office of Handicapped Services are available.

Services: Counseling and information services are available, as is tutoring in most subjects. There is a reader service for the blind.

Campus Safety and Security: Measures include 24-hour foot and vehicle patrol, escort service, shuttle buses, and informal discussions. There are pamphlets/posters/films, emergency telephones, and lighted pathways/sidewalks.

Programs of Study: UNL confers B.A., B.S., B.A.Ed., B.B.A., B.F.A., B.F.A.Ed., B.J., B.M., B.M.Ed., B.S.A.E., B.S.Agr., B.S.Arch., B.S.B.A., B.S.B.S.E., B.S.C., B.S.C.E., B.S.C.M., B.S.C.S., B.S.Ch.E., B.S.E.E., B.S.E.T., B.S.Ed., B.S.H.E., B.S.H.R.E.S., B.S.I.C.E., B.S.I.E., B.S.I.T., B.S.M.E., and B.S.N.R. degrees. Associate, master's, and doctoral degrees are also awarded. Bachelor's degrees are awarded in AGRICULTURE (agricultural business management, agricultural economics, agricultural mechanics, agriculture, agronomy, animal science, environmental studies, fish and game management, horticulture, natural resource management, plant protection (pest management), range/farm management, and soil science), BIOLOGICAL SCIENCE (biochemistry and biology/biological science), BUSINESS (accounting, banking and finance, business administration and management, business economics, international business management, management science, and marketing/retailing/merchandising), COMMUNICATIONS AND THE ARTS (advertising, art, art history and appreciation, broadcasting, classics, communications, dance, design, dramatic arts, English, English as a second/foreign language, film arts, fine arts, French, German, Greek, journalism, languages, Latin, music, Russian, Spanish, and speech/debate/rhetoric), COMPUTER AND PHYSICAL SCIENCE (actuarial science, atmospheric sciences and meteorology, chemistry, computer science, geology, mathematics, and physics), EDUCATION (agricultural, art, athletic training, business, early childhood, education, elementary, foreign languages, guidance, health, home economics, industrial arts, middle school, music, science, secondary, and special), ENGINEERING AND ENVIRONMENTAL DESIGN (agricultural engineering, architectural engineering, architecture, bioengineering, chemical engineering, civil engineering, computer engineering, construction management, construction technology, drafting and design technology, electrical/electronics engineering, electrical/electronics engineering technology, environmental science, fire protection engineering, industrial engineering, industrial engineering technology, manufacturing technology, and mechanical engineering), HEALTH PROFESSIONS (dental hygiene, exercise science, medical laboratory technology, predentistry, premedicine, prepharmacy, public health, speech pathology/audiology, and veterinary science), SOCIAL SCIENCE (anthropology, dietetics, economics, family/consumer studies, food science, geography, history, human development, international relations, Latin American studies, law, medieval studies, parks and recreation management, philosophy, political science/government, psychology, sociology, textiles and clothing, water resources, Western European studies, and women's studies). Biochemistry, engineering, and journalism are the strongest academically. Psychology, business administration, and education are the largest.

Required: Distribution requirements include 9 courses across 8 areas of essential studies and 10 courses from integrative studies area. A minimum GPA of 2.0 is required. Each college and major has its own requirements; there are few graduation requirements that apply to all students.

Special: There is cross-registration with many schools, and co-op programs are available in the Colleges of Engineering and Technology and Agriculture. Through membership in the International Student Exchange Program, the university can place students in more than 90 universities around the world. Internship opportunities abound, as do work-study programs. Accelerated degree programs, a Washington semester, B.A.-B.S. degrees, dual majors, combined pre-professional programs, student-designed majors, credit by exam, nondegree study, and pass/fail options are also available. There are 51 national honor societies, including Phi Beta Kappa, a freshman honors program, and 18 departmental honors program.

Faculty/Classroom: 75% of faculty are male; 25%, female. Graduate students teach 30% of introductory courses. The average class size in an introductory lecture is 43; in a laboratory, 16; and in a regular course, 29.

Admissions: 91% of the 2001-2002 applicants were accepted. The SAT I scores for the 2001-2002 freshman class were: Verbal--23% below 500, 39% between 500 and 599, 28% between 600 and 700, and 10% above 700; Math--19% below 500, 35% between 500 and 599, 33% between 600 and 700, and 13% above 700. The ACT scores were 19% below 21, 44% between 21 and 23, 25% between 24 and 26, and 12% above 28. 41% of the current freshmen were in the top fifth of their class; 70% were in the top two fifths. There were 29 National Merit finalists and 122 semifinalists.

Requirements: The SAT I or ACT is recommended. In addition, applicants must be graduates of an accredited secondary school. The GED is accepted. Students must have completed 3 years of English, 2 years each of math, science, and social studies, and an additional year of language arts. UNL requires applicants to be in the upper 50% of their class. AP and CLEP credits are accepted.

Procedure: Freshmen are admitted to all sessions. Entrance exams should be taken in April of the junior year. Applications should be filed by June 30 for fall entry and December 15 for spring entry, along with a $25 fee. Notification is sent on a rolling basis.

Transfer: 910 transfer students enrolled in 2001-2002. Transfer students must have a 2.0 GPA for both the cumulative average of all postsecondary facilities attended and for the most recent term of attendance. In certain majors, a higher GPA and/or extra course work may be required. 30 credits must be completed at UNL.

Visiting: There are regularly scheduled orientations for prospective students, including an information session, a campus tour, a visit to areas of academic interest, and a meeting with a department representative. There are guides for informal visits and visitors may sit in on classes and stay overnight. To schedule a visit, contact High School and College Relations at (402) 472-4887.

Financial Aid: In 2001-2002, 77% of all freshmen and 67% of continuing students received some form of financial aid. 42% of freshmen and 38% of continuing students received need-based aid. The average freshman award was $5926. Of that total, scholarships or need-based grants averaged $3864; loans averaged $3596; and work contracts averaged $2300. All undergraduates work part time. Average annual earnings from campus work are $1200. The average financial indebtedness of the 2001 graduate was $16,592. The FAFSA is required. The fall application deadline is March 1.

International Students: There are 457 international students enrolled. The school actively recruits these students. They must score 500 on the written TOEFL.

Computers: The mainframes are comprised of several DEC ALPHA server 2100s, a cluster of Sun Systems, and an IBM RS/6000 /F50. There are 500 PCs in public facilities located throughout both city and east campuses. Colleges and departments have additional facilities for their own students. PC facilities are in all residence complexes. All facilities are part of the campus network. All students may access the system 24 hours a day, 7 days per week. There are no time limits and no fees. It is recommended that students in architecture and community and regional planning have personal computers.

Graduates: In 2001, 2997 bachelor's degrees were awarded. The most popular majors were business/marketing (21%), engineering/engineering technologies (12%), and communications/communications technologies (10%). In an average class, 21% graduate in 4 years, 47% in 5 years, and 53% in 6 years. 261 companies recruited on campus in 2000-2001.

Admissions Contact: Pat McBride, Interim Director of Admissions. E-mail: *nuhusker@unl.edu* Web: *http://www.unl.edu*

UNIVERSITY OF NEBRASKA AT OMAHA F-3

Omaha, NE 68182 (402) 554-2393

(800) 858-8648; Fax: (402) 554-3472

Full-time: 3655 men, 4251 women	**Faculty:** 494; IIA, -$
Part-time: 1505 men, 1727 women	**Ph.D.s:** 82%
Graduate: 1153 men, 1852 women	**Student/Faculty:** 16 to 1
Year: semesters, summer session	**Tuition:** $2638 ($6676)
Application Deadline: August 1	**Room & Board:** $4229

Freshman Class: 4121 applied, 3527 accepted, 1892 enrolled

ACT: 22 **COMPETITIVE**

The University of Nebraska at Omaha, established in 1908, is a public institution and part of the University of Nebraska system. There are 10 undergraduate schools and 1 graduate school. In addition to regional accreditation, UNOmaha has baccalaureate program accreditation with AACSB, AHEA, CSWE, and NCATE. The library contains 750,000 volumes, 2 million microform items, and 7000 audiovisual forms/CDs, and subscribes to 3000 periodicals. Computerized library services include the card catalog, interlibrary loans, and database searching. Special learning facilities include a learning resource center, art gallery, planetarium, radio station, and TV station. The 158-acre campus is in a suburban area within the Omaha city limits. Including residence halls, there are 28 buildings.

Student Life: 87% of undergraduates are from Nebraska. Others are from 45 states, 72 foreign countries, and Canada. 84% are from public schools. 82% are white. The average age of freshmen is 20; all undergraduates, 24. 28% do not continue beyond their first year; 37% remain to graduate.

Housing: 576 students can be accommodated in college housing, which includes single-sex and coed dormitories and on-campus apartments. On-campus housing is available on a first-come, first-served basis. 95% of students commute. Alcohol is not permitted. All students may keep cars.

Activities: 7% of men belong to 8 national fraternities; 4% of women belong to 9 national sororities. There are 110 groups on campus, including band, cheerleading, choir, chorale, chorus, dance, drama, drill team, ethnic, gay, honors, international, jazz band, marching band, newspaper, pep band, political, professional, radio and TV, religious, social, social service, and student government. Popular campus events include Celebrate UNO, International Week, and Black History Month.

Sports: There are 5 intercollegiate sports for men and 7 for women, and 16 intramural sports for men and 16 for women. Facilities include a football field, a field house, and a health/phys ed/recreation building housing basketball and volleyball courts, weight rooms, and a swimming pool.

Disabled Students: All of the campus is accessible. Wheelchair ramps, elevators, special parking, specially equipped rest rooms, special class scheduling, lowered drinking fountains, and lowered telephones are available.

Services: Counseling and information services are available, as is tutoring in some subjects, including math and psychology. There is a reader service for the blind and remedial math, reading, and writing.

Campus Safety and Security: Measures include 24-hour foot and vehicle patrol, self-defense education, escort service, and shuttle buses. There are emergency telephones and lighted pathways/sidewalks.

Programs of Study: UNOmaha confers B.A., B.S., B.F.A., B.G.S., B.S.B.A., and B.S.Ed. degrees. Associate, master's, and doctoral degrees are also awarded. Bachelor's degrees are awarded in BIOLOGICAL SCIENCE (biology/biological science), BUSINESS (accounting, banking and finance, business administration and management, management information systems, management science, and marketing/retailing/merchandising), COMMUNICATIONS AND THE ARTS (broadcasting, communications, dramatic arts, English, fine arts, French, German, journalism, music, Spanish, and speech/debate/rhetoric), COMPUTER AND PHYSICAL SCIENCE (chemistry, computer science, geology, mathematics, and physics), EDUCATION (early childhood, elementary, health, physical, secondary, and special), ENGINEERING AND ENVIRONMENTAL DESIGN (engineering physics), HEALTH PROFESSIONS (premedicine), SOCIAL SCIENCE (criminal justice, economics, geography, history, interdisciplinary studies, philosophy, political science/government, prelaw, psychology, public administration, social work, sociology, and urban studies). Prebusiness and elementary education are the largest.

Required: To graduate, students must complete 30 hours of distribution requirements in natural and physical sciences, humanities and fine arts, and social and behavioral sciences; 15 hours in fundamental academic skills in English writing, math, and public speaking; and 6 hours in cultural diversity.

Special: UNOmaha offers internships for business students, cooperative programs, and credit by examination. Students may study abroad in various European countries. There is a freshman honors program.

Faculty/Classroom: 63% of faculty are male; 37%, female. 97% teach undergraduates. Graduate students teach 5% of introductory courses. The average class size in an introductory lecture is 34; in a laboratory, 17; and in a regular course, 30.

Admissions: 86% of the 2001-2002 applicants were accepted. The ACT scores for the 2001-2002 freshman class were: 39% below 21, 31% between 21 and 23, 18% between 24 and 26, 6% between 27 and 28, and 6% above 28. 25% of the current freshmen were in the top fifth of their class; 54% were in the top two fifths.

Requirements: The SAT I or ACT is required. In addition, in addition, students must be graduates of an accredited secondary school. The GED is accepted. Students must have completed 4 units of English and 2 each of math, social sciences, and sciences. UNOmaha requires applicants to be in the upper 50% of their class. A GPA of 2.0 is required. AP and CLEP credits are accepted. Important factors in the admissions decision are recommendations by school officials, evidence of special talent, and personality/intangible qualities.

Procedure: Freshmen are admitted fall, spring, and summer. Entrance exams should be taken by the senior year. Applications should be filed by August 1 for fall entry, December 1 for spring entry, and June 1 for summer entry, along with a $25 fee. Notification is sent on a rolling basis.

Transfer: 1209 transfer students enrolled in 2001-2002. Applicants must present evidence of good standing at the last institution they attended. Grades of C or better transfer for credit. A minimum GPA of 2.0 is required. 30 credits of 125 must be completed at UNOmaha.

Visiting: There are regularly scheduled orientations for prospective students. There are guides for informal visits and visitors may sit in on classes. To schedule a visit, contact the Admissions Office or Office of Orientation at (402) 554-2677.

Financial Aid: In 2001-2002, 43% of all freshmen and 45% of continuing students received some form of financial aid. 41% of freshmen and 43% of continuing students received need-based aid. The average freshman award was $4900. 4% of undergraduates work part time. Average annual earnings from campus work are $3700. The average financial indebtedness of the 2001 graduate was $16,900. The FAFSA is required. The fall application deadline is March 1.

International Students: There are 253 international students enrolled. The school actively recruits these students. They must score 500 on the written TOEFL or 173 on the electronic version and also take the SAT I or the ACT.

Computers: The mainframe is a DEC VAX 8650. There are also PCs available in 16 student user rooms. All students may access the system at any time. There are no time limits and no fees.

Graduates: In 2001, 1414 bachelor's degrees were awarded. The most popular majors were criminal justice (11%), elementary education (10%), and management information systems (5%). In an average class, 5% graduate in 4 years, 19% in 5 years, and 27% in 6 years.

Admissions Contact: Jolene Adams, Associate Director of Admissions. E-mail: *unoadm@unomaha.edu* Web: *www.unomaha.edu*

WAYNE STATE COLLEGE — E-2
Wayne, NE 68787 — (402) 375-7000
(800) 228-9972; Fax: (402) 375-7204

Full-time: 1103 men, 1485 women	**Faculty:** 128; IIA, --$
Part-time: 80 men, 167 women	**Ph.D.s:** 81%
Graduate: 171 men, 305 women	**Student/Faculty:** 20 to 1
Year: semesters, summer session	**Tuition:** $2735 ($4827)
Application Deadline: open	**Room & Board:** $3520
Freshman Class: 1287 applied, 1287 accepted, 597 enrolled	
ACT: 21	**NONCOMPETITIVE**

Wayne State College, founded in 1910, is a public liberal arts facility. There are 4 undergraduate and 2 graduate schools. In addition to regional accreditation, Wayne State has baccalaureate program accreditation with NCATE. The library contains 221,300 volumes, 777,350 microform items, and 6822 audiovisual forms/CDs, and subscribes to 630 periodicals. Computerized library services include the card catalog and database searching. Special learning facilities include a learning resource center, art gallery, planetarium, radio station, TV station, and arboretum. The 128-acre campus is in a rural area 45 miles southwest of Sioux City, Iowa. Including residence halls, there are 25 buildings.

Student Life: 84% of undergraduates are from Nebraska. Others are from 24 states, 19 foreign countries, and Canada. 90% are from public schools. 92% are white. 44% are Protestant; 29% Catholic; 27% claim no religious affiliation. The average age of freshmen is 18; all undergraduates, 22. 32% do not continue beyond their first year; 46% remain to graduate.

Housing: 1584 students can be accommodated in college housing, which includes single-sex and coed dormitories. On-campus housing is guaranteed for the freshman year only, is available on a first-come, first-served basis, and is available on a lottery system for upperclassmen. 58% of students commute. Alcohol is not permitted. All students may keep cars.

Activities: There is 1 national fraternity and 2 local sororities and 1 national sorority. There are 88 groups on campus, including art, band, cheerleading, choir, chorale, chorus, computers, drama, drill team, ethnic, gay, honors, international, jazz band, literary magazine, marching band, newspaper, orchestra, pep band, political, professional, radio and TV, religious, social, student government, and symphony. Popular campus events include International Dinner, Elizabethan Dinners, and Greek Olympics.

Sports: There are 6 intercollegiate sports for men and 6 for women, and 38 intramural sports for men and 38 for women. Facilities include tennis courts, softball, flag football, and soccer fields, a gym, and a 33,000-square-foot recreation center, which has an indoor track, weight room, pool, and handball, volleyball, basketball, and tennis courts.

Disabled Students: 90% of the campus is accessible. Wheelchair ramps, elevators, special parking, specially equipped rest rooms, special class scheduling, lowered drinking fountains, lowered telephones, and a residence hall with accessibility for the disabled are available. In addition, the school's pool is equipped with special steps.

Services: Counseling and information services are available, as is tutoring in most subjects. There is a reader service for the blind.

Campus Safety and Security: Measures include 24-hour foot and vehicle patrol, self-defense education, escort service, and lighted pathways/

sidewalks. In addition, there are articles in the campus newspaper relating to safety and security.

Programs of Study: Wayne State confers B.A. and B.S. degrees. Master's degrees are also awarded. Bachelor's degrees are awarded in BIOLOGICAL SCIENCE (life science), BUSINESS (business administration and management and sports management), COMMUNICATIONS AND THE ARTS (art, communications, dramatic arts, English, graphic design, modern language, music, Spanish, and speech/debate/rhetoric), COMPUTER AND PHYSICAL SCIENCE (chemistry, computer science, and mathematics), EDUCATION (elementary, foreign languages, health, home economics, industrial arts, music, science, and special), ENGINEERING AND ENVIRONMENTAL DESIGN (technological management), SOCIAL SCIENCE (counseling/psychology, criminal justice, early childhood studies, family/consumer studies, food production/management/services, history, interdisciplinary studies, parks and recreation management, political science/government, psychology, social science, and sociology). Business, education, and social sciences are the largest.

Required: Students must complete a specified 46-credit general education curriculum. A minimum of 125 credit hours is required for graduation, with 30 to 62 in the major and 40 in upper-division courses. Students must maintain at least a 2.0 GPA.

Special: There are co-op programs and cross-registration with Northeast Community College. Also offered are pass/fail options, internships, credit by exam, any combination of dual majors, a B.A.-B.S. degree in certain instances, and some student-designed majors. There are 3 national honor societies, a freshman honors program, and 7 departmental honors programs.

Faculty/Classroom: 56% of faculty are male; 44%, female. All teach undergraduates. Graduate students teach 6% of introductory courses.

Admissions: 100% of the 2001-2002 applicants were accepted. The ACT scores for the 2001-2002 freshman class were: 52% below 21, 23% between 21 and 23, 16% between 24 and 26, 5% between 27 and 28, and 4% above 28. 23% of the current freshmen were in the top fifth of their class; 48% were in the top two fifths. 20 freshmen graduated first in their class.

Requirements: The ACT is recommended. In addition, applicants must be graduates of an accredited secondary school. The GED is accepted. Entering freshmen must have completed 16 credits, with a recommended 4 units of English, 3 each of math and social studies, and 2 of science. Additional units in foreign language, fine and performing arts, and computer literacy are recommended. AP and CLEP credits are accepted. Important factors in the admissions decision are advanced placement or honor courses, evidence of special talent, and leadership record.

Procedure: Freshmen are admitted fall, winter, and summer. Entrance exams should be taken in the spring of the junior year or fall of the senior year. There is a deferred admissions plan. Application deadlines are open. Application fee is $20.

Transfer: 182 transfer students enrolled in 2001-2002. Transfer students must have a minimum GPA of 2.0. Grades of C and above transfer for credit. An interview is recommended. 30 credits of 125 must be completed at Wayne State.

Visiting: There are guides for informal visits and visitors may sit in on classes and stay overnight. To schedule a visit, contact the Admissions Office at (402) 375-7234.

Financial Aid: In 2001-2002, 62% of all freshmen and 59% of continuing students received some form of financial aid. Wayne State is a member of CSS. The FAFSA and the college's own financial statement are required. The fall application deadline is open.

International Students: There are 31 international students enrolled. They must score 550 on the written TOEFL.

Computers: The mainframe is a DEC VAX 4000 Model 300. There are networked computer labs in the library and the education, business, applied science, and math/science buildings. Dorms are wired for network access. All students may access the system any time. There are no time limits and no fees.

Graduates: In 2001, 580 bachelor's degrees were awarded. The most popular majors were business (27%), education (25%), and psychology (9%). In an average class, 1% graduate in 3 years, 19% in 4 years, 36% in 5 years, and 40% in 6 years. 35 companies recruited on campus in 2000-2001.

Admissions Contact: Teresa Moore, Director of Admissions.
E-mail: *wscadmit@wscgate.wsc.edu* Web: *www.wsc.edu*

YORK COLLEGE — E-3

York, NE 68467-2699 — (402) 363-5712
(800) 950-YORK (9675); Fax: (402) 363-5623

Full-time: 182 men, 245 women	**Faculty:** 36
Part-time: 12 men, 16 women	**Ph.D.s:** 30%
Graduate: none	**Student/Faculty:** 12 to 1
Year: semesters, summer session	**Tuition:** $10,300
Application Deadline: see profile	**Room & Board:** $3200
Freshman Class: 208 applied, 199 accepted, 117 enrolled	
ACT: recommended	**COMPETITIVE**

York College, founded in 1890, is an independent undergraduate college affiliated with the Churches of Christ. There are 6 undergraduate schools. The library contains 50,280 volumes, 21,011 microform items, and 5923 audiovisual forms/CDs, and subscribes to 329 periodicals. Computerized library services include the card catalog, interlibrary loans, and database searching. The 40-acre campus is in a small town 45 miles west of Lincoln. Including residence halls, there are 17 buildings.

Student Life: 70% of undergraduates are from out of state, mostly the Midwest. Others are from 33 states, 12 foreign countries, and Canada. 90% are from public schools. 91% are white. Most are Protestant. The average age of freshmen is 18; all undergraduates, 22. 10% do not continue beyond their first year; 51% remain to graduate.

Housing: 472 students can be accommodated in college housing, which includes single-sex dormitories and on-campus apartments. On-campus housing is guaranteed for all 4 years. 64% of students live on campus; of those, 85% remain on campus on weekends. Alcohol is not permitted. All students may keep cars.

Activities: 65% of men belong to 4 local fraternities; 56% of women belong to 4 local sororities. There are 25 groups on campus, including art, choir, chorus, computers, drama, honors, international, literary magazine, musical theater, newspaper, photography, political, professional, religious, social, social service, student government, and yearbook. Popular campus events include High School Days, Fall Musical, and All School Banquet.

Sports: There are 6 intercollegiate sports for men and 6 for women, and 6 intramural sports for men and 6 for women. Facilities include basketball and volleyball courts, a gym, soccer, baseball, and intramural fields, and a weight room.

Disabled Students: 50% of the campus is accessible. Wheelchair ramps, elevators, special parking, specially equipped rest rooms, lowered drinking fountains, and lowered telephones are available.

Services: Counseling and information services are available, as is tutoring in every subject. There is remedial math, reading, and writing, and a peer tutoring program.

Campus Safety and Security: Measures include self-defense education, pamphlets/posters/films, emergency telephones, and lighted pathways/sidewalks. There is an evening/night foot patrol.

Programs of Study: York confers B.A., B.S., B.B.A., and B.Mus. Degrees. Associate degrees are also awarded. Bachelor's degrees are awarded in BIOLOGICAL SCIENCE (biology/biological science), BUSINESS (accounting, banking and finance, business administration and management, and human resources), COMMUNICATIONS AND THE ARTS (communications, English, music, and music performance), COMPUTER AND PHYSICAL SCIENCE (natural sciences), EDUCATION (education and music), SOCIAL SCIENCE (biblical studies, history, human services, liberal arts/general studies, and psychology). Education, natural science, and psychology are the strongest academically. Education and business are the largest.

Required: To graduate, students must complete 128 to 130 credits with a 2.0 GPA. Course work includes a general education requirement of 18 hours of humanities, 10 of science, 12 of social science, 16 of Bible, and 3 of math or computer science. The major requirements vary according to concentration; typically, 40 hours or more are required. Some majors and minors require a 2.5 GPA.

Special: Summer internships are required in biblical studies, and work-study is available on campus. Honors and independent study are available as adjuncts to a normal course load. An accelerated degree program is offered in human resource management. A joint B.B.A.-B.S. is offered in finance and accounting. There are 2 national honor societies, a freshman honors program, and 2 departmental honors programs.

Faculty/Classroom: 66% of faculty are male; 34%, female. All teach undergraduates. The average class size in an introductory lecture is 30; in a laboratory, 20; and in a regular course, 25.

Admissions: 96% of the 2001-2002 applicants were accepted. The SAT I scores for the 2001-2002 freshman class were: Verbal--25% below 500, 50% between 500 and 599, and 25% between 600 and 700; Math--25% below 500, 37% between 500 and 599, and 38% between 600 and 700. The ACT scores were 48% below 21, 22% between 21 and 23, 14% between 24 and 26, 11% between 27 and 28, and 5% above 28. 20% of the current freshmen were in the top fifth of their class; 49% were in the top two fifths.

Requirements: The ACT is recommended. In addition, for regular acceptance, students must meet 2 of the following 3 requirements: a 2.0

cumulative GPA; graduate in the top half of their graduating class; score 18 on the ACT or 860 on the SAT I. AP and CLEP credits are accepted. Important factors in the admissions decision are ability to finance college education, personality/intangible qualities, and evidence of special talent.

Procedure: Freshmen are admitted to all sessions. Entrance exams should be taken before April. Check with the school for current application deadlines. Notification is sent on a rolling basis.

Transfer: 26 transfer students enrolled in 2001-2002. Transcripts of previous work must be submitted as well as 2 personal references. Cumulative college GPA should not be lower than 2.0 if student is transferring in more than 60 hours. 30 credits of 128 must be completed at York.

Visiting: There are regularly scheduled orientations for prospective students, including financial aid and admissions consultations and a campus tour. There are guides for informal visits and visitors may sit in on classes and stay overnight. To schedule a visit, contact Keri Mathews at (402) 363-5627 or *kmathews@york.edu*

Financial Aid: In 2001-2002, 98% of all freshmen and 93% of continuing students received some form of financial aid. 57% of freshmen and 64% of continuing students received need-based aid. The average freshman award was $9706. Of that total, scholarships or need-based grants averaged $3721; loans averaged $4567; work contracts averaged $1087. 92% of undergraduates work part time. Average annual earnings from campus work are $825. The average financial indebtedness of the 2001 graduate was $18,107. The FAFSA is required. Check with the school for current application deadlines.

International Students: There are 19 international students enrolled. They must score 500 on the written TOEFL or 173 on the electronic version and also take the SAT I or the ACT, scoring 860 on the SAT I or 18 on the ACT.

Computers: The mainframe is a 586 fileserver in Novell Netware 3.12. 30 PCs are located in a computer lab. An additional 12 PCs are scattered around the library and other academic buildings. All students may access the system 8 A.M. to 10:30 P.M. weekdays, and various times on weekends. There are no time limits and no fees.

Graduates: In 2001, 84 bachelor's degrees were awarded. The most popular majors were education (29%), business (22%), and psychology (15%). In an average class, 88% graduate in 4 years, and 12% in 5 years. Of the 2000 graduating class, 5% were enrolled in graduate school within 6 months of graduation and 95% were employed.

Admissions Contact: Dr. Jim White, Vice President of Enrollment Management. E-mail: *jlwhite@york.edu* Web: *www.york.edu*

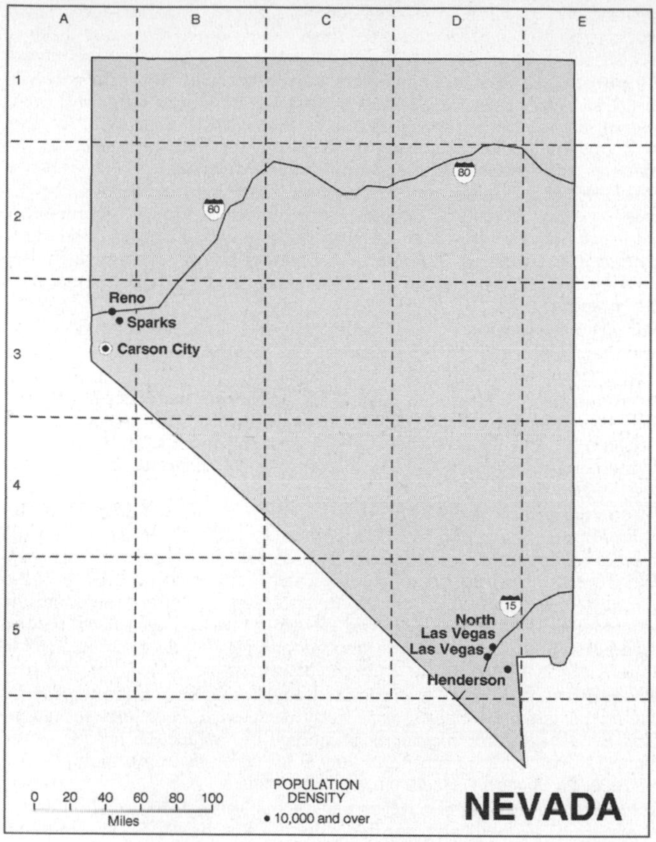

SIERRA NEVADA COLLEGE-LAKE TAHOE

A-3

Incline Village, NV 89450

(775) 831-1314

(800) 332-8666; Fax: (775) 831-1347

Full-time: 170 men, 130 women	**Faculty:** 20
Part-time: 10 men, 10 women	**Ph.D.s:** n/av
Graduate: 40 men, 75 women	**Student/Faculty:** 15 to 1
Year: semesters, summer session	**Tuition:** $15,000
Application Deadline: March 15	**Room & Board:** $6060
Freshman Class: n/av	
SAT I or ACT: required	**LESS COMPETITIVE**

Sierra Nevada College, founded in 1969, is a private institution offering programs in liberal arts, fine arts, business, hotel resort management, ski business management, environmental science, and teacher education. There are 7 undergraduate schools. Figures in the above capsule are approximate. The library contains 20,000 volumes and 10,000 microform items, and subscribes to 100 periodicals. Computerized library services include interlibrary loans. Special learning facilities include an art gallery and observatory, and recording studio. The 35-acre campus is in a rural area 25 miles west of Reno. Including residence halls, there are 7 buildings.

Student Life: 70% of undergraduates are from out of state, mostly the West. Others are from 30 states, 8 foreign countries, and Canada. 60% are from public schools. 95% are white. The average age of freshmen is 19; all undergraduates, 22. 20% do not continue beyond their first year; 50% remain to graduate.

Housing: 120 students can be accommodated in college housing, which includes single-sex dormitories and on-campus apartments. On-campus housing is guaranteed for all 4 years. 50% of students commute. Alcohol is not permitted. All students may keep cars.

Activities: There are no fraternities or sororities. There are many groups and organizations on campus, including art, choir, chorale, chorus, dance, honors, international, musical theater, newspaper, political, student government, and yearbook. Popular campus events include Bohemia Night, Nevada Day, and a faculty-student softball game.

Sports: There is 1 intercollegiate sport for men and 1 for women, and 2 intramural sports for men and 2 for women. Facilities include nearby ski areas, hiking and mountain biking trails, volleyball and softball areas, community tennis courts and golf courses, and sites for water sports and beach volleyball.

Disabled Students: Wheelchair ramps, specially equipped rest rooms, and special class scheduling are available.

Services: Counseling and information services are available, as is tutoring in most subjects. There is remedial math, reading, and writing.

Campus Safety and Security: Measures include informal discussions.

Programs of Study: Sierra Nevada College-Lake Tahoe confers B.A., B.S., and B.F.A. degrees. Bachelor's degrees are awarded in BUSINESS (business administration and management, and recreational facilities management), COMMUNICATIONS AND THE ARTS (fine arts and music), COMPUTER AND PHYSICAL SCIENCE (science), ENGINEERING AND ENVIRONMENTAL DESIGN (environmental science), SOCIAL SCIENCE (humanities). Environmental science/ecology is the strongest academically. Business administration is the largest.

Required: All students must complete at least 120 semester hours, including 40 in upper-division courses with a minimum GPA of 2.0. Students also must pass the writing proficiency exam and meet distribution requirements in 4 interdisciplinary themes: symbols, relationships with nature and humans, memberships in groups and institutions, and ethics, values, and beliefs.

Special: Business administration concentrations are offered in ski business and resort management and in hotel, restaurant, and resort management. Student-designed majors, work-study programs, internships, credit for life experiences and volunteer community work, and nondegree study are available.

Faculty/Classroom: 60% of faculty are male; 40%, female. All teach undergraduates. The average class size in an introductory lecture is 15; in a laboratory, 8; and in a regular course, 15.

Requirements: The SAT I or ACT is required. In addition, all applicants are reviewed individually. An essay and 2 letters of recommendation are required, and an interview is recommended. The GED is accepted. Applications are accepted on-line. A GPA of 2.0 is required. AP and CLEP credits are accepted. Important factors in the admissions decision are ability to finance college education, advanced placement or honor courses, and extracurricular activities record.

Procedure: Freshmen are admitted to all sessions. Entrance exams should be taken in the senior year. There is a deferred admissions plan. Applications should be filed by March 15 for fall entry. Notification is sent on a rolling basis.

Transfer: The college accepts applications from students who have completed any course at an accredited postsecondary institution. If fewer than 15 credits have been earned, the high school transcript and standardized test scores are also needed. 96 credits of 120 must be completed at Sierra Nevada College-Lake Tahoe.

Visiting: There are regularly scheduled orientations for prospective students, consisting of a 2-day campus visit with overnight stay and mandatory class attendance. There are guides for informal visits and visitors may sit in on classes and stay overnight. To schedule a visit, contact the Office of Admissions.

Financial Aid: In a recent year, 70% of all students received some form of financial aid. 50% of all students received need-based aid. The average freshman award was $3500. Of that total, scholarships or need-based grants averaged $2500 ($4000 maximum); loans averaged $6625 ($18,000 maximum); and work contracts averaged $2000. 75% of undergraduates work part time. Average annual earnings from campus work are $1500. The average financial indebtedness of a recent graduate was $10,000. The FAFSA and the college's own financial statement are required. The fall application deadline is April 1.

International Students: The school actively recruits these students. They must score 500 on the written TOEFL or take any other English proficiency test.

Computers: The mainframe is an IBM. There are computer labs with 25 terminals on campus. The freshman dormitory has Internet access. All students may access the system 8 A.M. to 9 P.M. daily. There are no time limits and no fees. It is strongly recommended that all students have a personal computer.

Graduates: In a recent year, the most popular majors were business administration (50%) and humanities (25%).

Admissions Contact: Admissions Office.
E-mail: *admissions@sierranevada.edu* Web: *www.sierranevada.edu*

UNIVERSITY AND COMMUNITY COLLEGE SYSTEM OF NEVADA

The University and Community College System of Nevada, established in 1865, is a public system. It is governed by a board of regents, whose chief executive is the chancellor. The primary goals of the system are teaching, research, and public service. The main priorities are to provide all public programs of postsecondary instruction in Nevada, to sponsor programs of basic and applied research that contribute to the cultural, economic, and social development of Nevada, and to sponsor programs of public service for citizens of the state. The total enrollment in fall 2001 of all 7 campuses exceeds 70,000, with more than 2080 full-time faculty members. There are 172 baccalaureate, 133 master's, and 65 doctoral programs offered within the system. Profiles of the 4-year campuses in Las Vegas and Reno are included in this section. 4-year programs have also been offered at one community college since 1999. A new state college is slated to enroll its first class in fall 2002.

UNIVERSITY OF NEVADA/LAS VEGAS — D-5

Las Vegas, NV 89154-1021 (702) 895-3443; Fax: (702) 895-1118

Full-time: 5492 men, 6742 women	**Faculty:** IIA, +$
Part-time: 2835 men, 3537 women	**Ph.D.s:** 87%
Graduate: 2077 men, 3292 women	**Student/Faculty:** 19 to 1
Year: semesters, summer session	**Tuition:** $2481 ($9696)
Application Deadline: August 15	**Room & Board:** $5800
Freshman Class: 5587 applied, 4463 accepted, 2541 enrolled	
SAT I or ACT: recommended	**VERY COMPETITIVE**

University of Nevada/Las Vegas, established in 1957, is a state-supported institution offering undergraduate and graduate programs in business, education, health science, engineering, science and math, hotel administration, fine arts, liberal arts, urban affairs, and honors. There are 10 undergraduate schools and 1 graduate school. In addition to regional accreditation, UNLV has baccalaureate program accreditation with AACSB, ABET, CSWE, NASM, NCATE, and NLN. The 4 libraries contain 888,198 volumes, 1,705,020 microform items, and 120,128 audiovisual forms/CDs, and subscribe to 6380 periodicals. Computerized library services include the card catalog and interlibrary loans. Special learning facilities include a learning resource center, art gallery, natural history museum, and radio station. The 335-acre campus is in an urban area. Including residence halls, there are 60 buildings.

Student Life: 77% of undergraduates are from Nevada. Others are from 49 states, 77 foreign countries, and Canada. 74% are white; 10% Asian American. The average age of freshmen is 18; all undergraduates, 25. 25% do not continue beyond their first year; 74% remain to graduate.

Housing: 1500 students can be accommodated in college housing, which includes single-sex and coed dormitories. In addition, there are special-interest houses and substance-free, study-intensive recess housing.. On-campus housing is guaranteed for the freshman year only and is available on a first-come, first-served basis. Priority is given to out-of-town students. 94% of students commute. All students may keep cars.

Activities: 5% of men belong to 15 national fraternities; 5% of women belong to 1 local sorority and 7 national sororities. There are 160 groups on campus, including band, cheerleading, choir, chorus, computers, dance, drama, drill team, ethnic, gay, honors, international, jazz band, marching band, musical theater, newspaper, orchestra, pep band, political, professional, radio and TV, religious, social, student government, and symphony. Popular campus events include Unityfest, Majors Exploration Fair, and Career Day.

Sports: There are 7 intercollegiate sports for men and 8 for women, and 8 intramural sports for men and 8 for women. Facilities include an arena, a football stadium, tennis courts, softball and soccer fields, racquetball courts, a weight room, 2 gyms, and separate athletic/training facilities for intercollegiate athletes.

Disabled Students: All of the campus is accessible. Wheelchair ramps, elevators, special parking, specially equipped rest rooms, special class scheduling, lowered drinking fountains, lowered telephones, and priority class registration are available.

Services: Counseling and information services are available, as is tutoring in every subject. There is a reader service for the blind, and remedial math, reading, and writing.

Campus Safety and Security: Measures include 24-hour foot and vehicle patrol, self-defense education, escort service, and shuttle buses. There are emergency telephones and lighted pathways/sidewalks.

Programs of Study: UNLV confers B.A., B.S., and B.F.A. degrees. Master's and doctoral degrees are also awarded. Bachelor's degrees are awarded in BIOLOGICAL SCIENCE (biology/biological science), BUSINESS (accounting, banking and finance, hotel/motel and restaurant management, human resources, international business management, management information systems, management science, marketing/retailing/merchandising, real estate, and recreational facilities management), COMMUNICATIONS AND THE ARTS (art history and appreciation, communications, dance, dramatic arts, English, film arts, fine arts, French, German, music, romance languages and literature, and Spanish), COMPUTER AND PHYSICAL SCIENCE (applied physics, chemistry, computer science, earth science, geology, mathematics, physics, and radiological technology), EDUCATION (elementary, health, physical, recreation, secondary, special, and trade and industrial), ENGINEERING AND ENVIRONMENTAL DESIGN (architectural engineering, civil engineering, computer engineering, construction management, electrical/electronics engineering, environmental science, interior design, landscape architecture/design, mechanical engineering, and urban planning technology), HEALTH PROFESSIONS (clinical science, exercise science, health care administration, nuclear medical technology, nursing, and sports medicine), SOCIAL SCIENCE (anthropology, criminal justice, economics, food production/management/services, history, interdisciplinary studies, philosophy, physical fitness/movement, political science/government, psychology, public administration, social science, social work, sociology, and women's studies). Hotel administration and dance are the strongest academically. Liberal arts and business are the largest.

Required: Students must complete 124 credits, with 45 of these credits in the student's major, and must maintain a minimum GPA of 2.0. All students must meet core requirements that include courses in English, logic and math, the Constitution, social science, fine arts, science, humanities, and international and multicultural diversity.

Special: Opportunities are provided for internships, an accelerated degree program, B.A.-B.S. degrees, dual majors, credit by examination, credit for military service, nondegree study, pass/fail options, and study abroad in 8 countries. There are 16 national honor societies, including Phi Beta Kappa, a freshman honors program, and 11 departmental honors programs.

Faculty/Classroom: 63% of faculty are male; 37%, female. 95% teach undergraduates and 5% do research. The average class size in an introductory lecture is 21 and in a laboratory, 20.

Admissions: 80% of the 2001-2002 applicants were accepted. The ACT scores for the 2001-2002 freshman class were: 15% below 21, 55% between 21 and 23, 27% between 24 and 26, and 2% above 28. 46% of the current freshmen were in the top fifth of their class; 81% were in the top two fifths.

Requirements: The SAT I or ACT is recommended. In addition, graduation from an accredited secondary school is required. Applicants should submit an academic record distributed as follows: 4 credits in English, and 3 each in history, social studies, math, and science. A GPA of 2.5 is required. AP and CLEP credits are accepted. Important factors in the admissions decision are advanced placement or honor courses, recommendations by school officials, and geographic diversity. On-line applications are available at the university's web site.

Procedure: Freshmen are admitted to all sessions. Entrance exams should be taken by February 1. Early decision applications should be filed by January 15; regular applications, by August 15 for fall entry, January 3 for spring entry, and July 9 for summer entry, along with a $40 fee. Notification is sent on a rolling basis.

Transfer: Applicants should present a minimum GPA of 2.0. and a minimum of 12 credits for transfer. The SAT I or the ACT is recommended. Applicants must be in good academic standing and eligible to return to the educational institution last attended. 30 credits of 124 must be completed at UNLV.

Visiting: There are regularly scheduled orientations for prospective students, consisting of a complete introduction to the campus, student services, and parent orientation. There are guides for informal visits and visitors may sit in on classes. To schedule a visit, contact the Admissions Office.

Financial Aid: In a recent year, 68% of all freshmen and 66% of continuing students received some form of financial aid. 76% of freshmen and 71% of continuing students received need-based aid. The average freshman award was $2710. 75% of undergraduates work part time. UNLV is a member of CSS. The CSS/Profile, FAFSA, FFS, or SFS, the college's own financial statement, and the Singlefile Form are required. The fall application deadline is February 1.

International Students: The school actively recruits these students. They must score 500 on the written TOEFL, take the MELAB, or prove English proficiency by other means.

Computers: The mainframe is a CDC CYBER 830. There are also 100 PCs and Macs available in computer labs. All students may access the system 24 hours a day, 7 days a week. There are no time limits. The fee is $25.

Graduates: In an average class, 9% graduate in 3 years, 12% in 4 years, 10% in 5 years, and 8% in 6 years.

Admissions Contact: Kristi Rodriguez, Assistant Director of Admissions. A video is available. E-mail: *gounlv@ccmail.nevada.edu*
Web: *http://www.unlv.edu*

UNIVERSITY OF NEVADA/RENO — A-3

Reno, NV 89557 (775) 784-6865
(800) 622-4867; Fax: (775) 784-4283

Full-time: 3672 men, 4595 women	**Faculty:** 594; I, av$
Part-time: 966 men, 1245 women	**Ph.D.s:** 83%
Graduate: 1262 men, 1771 women	**Student/Faculty:** 12 to 1
Year: semesters, summer session	**Tuition:** $2547 ($9762)
Application Deadline: March 1	**Room & Board:** $6190
Freshman Class: 10,134 applied, 8572 accepted, 4891 enrolled	
SAT I Verbal/Math: 517/524	**ACT:** 22 **COMPETITIVE**

The University of Nevada, Reno, established in 1874, is a land-grant institution and part of the University and Community College System of Nevada. It offers programs in agriculture, arts and science, business administration, education, engineering, human and community sciences, journalism, medicine, and mining, as well as interdisciplinary studies. There are 10 undergraduate schools and 1 graduate school. In addition to regional accreditation, Nevada has baccalaureate program accreditation with AACSB, ABET, ACEJMC, AHEA, CSWE, NASM, NCATE, and NLN. The 6 libraries contain 956,282 volumes, 3,311,040 microform items, and 395,862 audiovisual forms/CDs, and subscribe to 5567 periodicals. Computerized library services include the card catalog, interlibrary loans, and database searching. Special learning facilities include a learning resource center, art gallery, planetarium, radio station, TV station, and the Nevada Historical Society Museum. The 200-acre campus is in an urban area 200 miles east of San Francisco. Including residence halls, there are 86 buildings.

Student Life: 80% of undergraduates are from Nevada. Others are from 42 states, 48 foreign countries, and Canada. 76% are white. The average age of freshmen is 19; all undergraduates, 23. 25% do not continue beyond their first year.

Housing: 1158 students can be accommodated in college housing, which includes single-sex and coed dormitories, on-campus apartments, off-campus apartments, and married-student housing. In addition, there are honors houses. On-campus housing is available on a first-come, first-served basis. 90% of students commute. All students may keep cars.

Activities: 10% of men belong to 2 local and 11 national fraternities; 3% of women belong to 4 national sororities. There are 100 groups on campus, including art, band, cheerleading, chess, choir, chorale, chorus, computers, dance, debate, drama, drill team, ethnic, film, gay, honors, international, jazz band, literary magazine, marching band, musical theater, newspaper, orchestra, pep band, photography, political, professional, radio and TV, religious, social, social service, student government, symphony, and yearbook. Popular campus events include Mackay Week and Winter Carnival.

Sports: There are 7 intercollegiate sports for men and 8 for women, and 14 intramural sports for men and 11 for women. Facilities include a recreation center, a 30,000-seat stadium, a 6000-seat gym, a 12,500-seat auditorium, and an 11,600 seat indoor events center.

Disabled Students: 99% of the campus is accessible. Wheelchair ramps, elevators, special parking, specially equipped rest rooms, special class scheduling, lowered drinking fountains, lowered telephones, and automatic door openers are available.

Services: Counseling and information services are available, as is tutoring in most subjects. There is a reader service for the blind, and remedial math, reading, and writing. Students are mainstreamed with special services for the disabled.

Campus Safety and Security: Measures include 24-hour foot and vehicle patrol, self-defense education, escort service, and shuttle buses. There are pamphlets/posters/films, emergency telephones, and lighted pathways/sidewalks.

Programs of Study: Nevada confers B.A., B.S., B.A.C.J., B.A.Ed., B.F.A., B.G.S., B.M., B.S.Bus.Ad., B.S.C.E., B.S.Chem.E., B.S.Chem., B.S.C.S., B.S.Ed., B.S.E.E., B.S.E.P., B.S.Geog., B.S.Geol., B.S.Geol.E., B.S.Geophys., B.S.M.E., B.S.Met.E., B.S.Min.E., B.S.Nurs., and B.S.Vet.Sc. degrees. Master's and doctoral degrees are also awarded. Bachelor's degrees are awarded in AGRICULTURE (agricultural economics, animal science, and natural resource management), BIOLOGICAL SCIENCE (biochemistry, biology/biological science, and nutrition), BUSINESS (accounting, banking and finance, business economics, management science, and marketing/retailing/merchandising), COMMUNICATIONS AND THE ARTS (applied music, art, dramatic arts, English, French, German, journalism, music, Spanish, and speech/debate/rhetoric), COMPUTER AND PHYSICAL SCIENCE (chemistry, computer science, geology, geophysics and seismology, hydrology, information sciences and systems, mathematics, and physics), EDUCATION (elementary, music, secondary, and special), ENGINEERING AND ENVIRONMENTAL DESIGN (chemical engineering, civil engineering, electrical/electronics engineering, engineering physics, environmental science, geological engineering, interior design, mechanical engineering, metallurgical engineering, and mining and mineral engineering), HEALTH PROFESSIONS (nursing, and speech pathology/audiology), SOCIAL SCIENCE (anthropology, child care/child and family studies, criminal justice, geography, history, human ecology, international relations, liberal arts/general studies, philosophy, political science/government, psychology, social work, and sociology). Psychology, biology, and criminal justice are the largest.

Required: To graduate, all students must complete 124 to 138 semester credits and earn a GPA of 2.0. The core curriculum includes 9 credits of Western Traditions, 6 each of capstone courses and natural science, 3 to 6 of writing, 3 each of math, social science, and fine arts, and fulfillment of the diversity requirement.

Special: Students may study abroad in 6 countries, pursue internships, and complete dual majors in many subject areas. There is a freshman honors program.

Faculty/Classroom: 68% of faculty are male; 32%, female. All both teach and do research. Graduate students teach 13% of introductory courses. The average class size in an introductory lecture is 36; in a laboratory, 16; and in a regular course, 36.

Admissions: 85% of the 2001-2002 applicants were accepted. The SAT I scores for the 2001-2002 freshman class were: Verbal--41% below 500, 41% between 500 and 599, 16% between 600 and 700, and 2% above 700; Math--38% below 500, 40% between 500 and 599, 14% between 600 and 700, and 3% above 700. The ACT scores were 34% below 21, 30% between 21 and 23, 21% between 24 and 26, 8% between 27 and 28, and 7% above 28.

Requirements: The SAT I or ACT is required. However, test scores are used for placement purposes only. Applicants should have completed 13 1/2 academic credits, including 4 in English, 3 each in math, science, and social studies/history, and a half credit in computer literacy. The GED is not accepted. A GPA of 2.5 is required. AP and CLEP credits are accepted. Important factors in the admissions decision are advanced placement or honor courses, recommendations by school officials, and leadership record.

Procedure: Freshmen are admitted fall and spring. Entrance exams should be taken in October of the senior year. There are early admissions and deferred admissions plans. Applications should be filed by March 1 for fall entry and November 1 for spring entry. The fall 2001 application fee was $40. Notification is sent on a rolling basis.

Transfer: Applicants should have a 2.0 GPA and 12 transferable credits. 32 credits of 124 must be completed at Nevada.

Visiting: There are regularly scheduled orientations for prospective students. There are guides for informal visits and visitors may sit in on classes. To schedule a visit, contact the Office of Outreach Services/the Office for Prospective Students.

Financial Aid: In a recent year 14% of freshmen and 19% of continuing students received need-based aid. The average freshman award was $8300. The FAFSA and the college's own financial statement are required.

International Students: There were 279 international students enrolled in a recent year. The school actively recruits these students. They must score 500 on the written TOEFL.

Computers: The mainframe is a multiple UNIX-based platforms. There are various computer labs within each college designed for local area networks, as well as for networking with the mainframe. All students may access the system. There are no time limits. The fee varies per class session.

Graduates: In an average class, 11% graduate in 4 years, 33% in 5 years, and 42% in 6 years.

Admissions Contact: Dr. Melisa N. Choroszy, Assistant Vice President, Records/Enrollment Services. E-mail: *choroszy@admin.unr.edu or unrug@unr.edu* Web: *www.unr.edu*

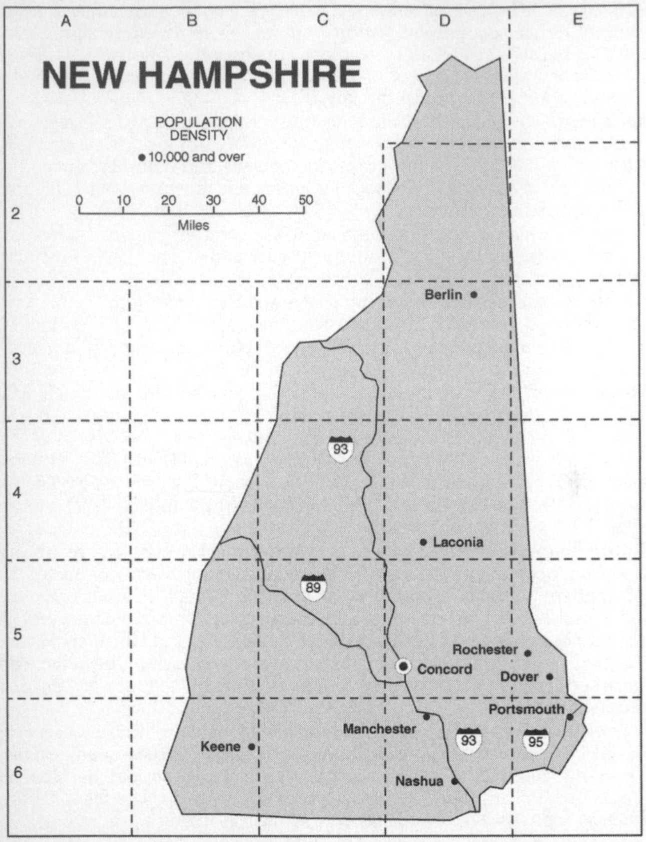

COLBY-SAWYER COLLEGE C-5
New London, NH 03257 (603) 526-3700
(800) 272-1015; Fax: (603) 526-3452

Full-time: 316 men, 555 women	**Faculty:** 49; IIB, -$
Part-time: 11 men, 19 women	**Ph.D.s:** 78%
Graduate: none	**Student/Faculty:** 18 to 1
Year: semesters	**Tuition:** $20,130
Application Deadline: open	**Room & Board:** $7720
Freshman Class: 1246 applied, 1083 accepted, 285 enrolled	
SAT I Verbal/Math: 500/500	**ACT:** 20 **LESS COMPETITIVE**

Colby-Sawyer College, established in 1837, is an independent institution offering a variety of undergraduate majors, including fine arts, nursing, business, and communications, as well as education certification. In addition to regional accreditation, Colby-Sawyer has baccalaureate program accreditation with CAAHEP and NLN. The library contains 92,116 volumes, 197,625 microform items, and 2119 audiovisual forms/CDs, and subscribes to 4148 periodicals. Computerized library services include the card catalog, interlibrary loans, and database searching. Special learning facilities include a learning resource center, art gallery, radio station, academic development center, and laboratory school (K-3). The 200-acre campus is in a small town 100 miles northwest of Boston, MA. Including residence halls, there are 28 buildings.

Student Life: 69% of undergraduates are from out of state, mostly the Northeast. Others are from 27 states and 9 foreign countries. 79% are from public schools. 95% are white. 39% claim no religious affiliation; 35%, Catholic; 18%, Protestant. The average age of freshmen is 18; all undergraduates, 20. 19% do not continue beyond their first year; 58% remain to graduate.

Housing: 835 students can be accommodated in college housing, which includes single-sex, coed dormitories, and a substance-free residence hall. On-campus housing is guaranteed for all 4 years. 88% of students live on campus; of those, 70% remain on campus on weekends. All students may keep cars.

Activities: There are no fraternities or sororities. There are 40 groups on campus, including academic counseling, art, chorus, dance, drama, environmental, film, honors, international, literary magazine, musical theater, newspaper, outing, photography, professional, radio and TV, religious, social, social service, student government, and yearbook. Popular campus events include Fall and Spring Weekends and Mountain Day.

Sports: There are 8 intercollegiate sports for men and 9 for women, and 15 intramural sports for men and 15 for women. Facilities include 6 outdoor and 3 indoor tennis courts, a fitness center, an NCAA-approved swimming pool, a suspended track, squash and racquetball courts, 4 outdoor competitive fields, and nearby golf courses, ski and biking trails, and an indoor riding arena.

Disabled Students: 50% of the campus is accessible. Wheelchair ramps, elevators, special parking, specially equipped rest rooms, special class scheduling, and handicap accessible residence hall suites are available.

Services: Counseling and information services are available, as is tutoring in every subject. There is a reader service for the blind, and remedial math, reading, and writing.

Campus Safety and Security: Measures include 24-hour foot and vehicle patrol, self-defense education, escort service, and shuttle buses. There are informal discussions, pamphlets/posters/films, emergency telephones, lighted pathways/sidewalks, and monthly meetings between students and campus safety personnel.

Programs of Study: Colby-Sawyer confers B.A., B.S., and B.F.A. degrees. Associate degrees are also awarded. Bachelor's degrees are awarded in AGRICULTURE (environmental studies), BIOLOGICAL SCIENCE (biology/biological science), BUSINESS (business administration and management and sports management), COMMUNICATIONS AND THE ARTS (art, communications, design, English, and graphic design), EDUCATION (art, athletic training, early childhood, English, science, and social studies), HEALTH PROFESSIONS (exercise science and nursing), SOCIAL SCIENCE (child psychology/development, history, and psychology). Exercise and sport sciences, business administration, and child development are the largest.

Required: Required courses include writing, math, and computer literacy. Four required interdisciplinary core courses are Creative Expression, Process of Discovery, Social Analysis, and Judgment and Belief. Required electives include 1 each in fine and performing arts and natural sciences, and 2 each in social sciences and humanities. Most majors must also complete an internship or a senior research project. A total of 120 credit hours, with a minimum GPA of 2.0, is needed for graduation.

Special: There is cross-registration through the New Hampshire College and University Council. Students may choose internships (required in some majors) and may study abroad in Australia, Canada, and several European countries. A Washington semester with American University is available. Other options include student-designed majors, education certification, credit by exam, a general studies degree, and interdisciplinary majors such as History, Society, and Culture. There is 1 national honor society, a freshman honors program, and 2 departmental honors programs.

Faculty/Classroom: 45% of faculty are male; 55%, female. All teach undergraduates. The average class size in a regular course is 18.

Admissions: 87% of the 2001-2002 applicants were accepted.

Requirements: The SAT I or ACT is required. In addition, the GED is accepted. A minimum of 15 college preparatory credits is recommended for admission, including 4 years of English, 3 or more of social studies, 3 of math, 2 of the same foreign language, and 2 or more of lab science. An essay is required, as are 2 letters of recommendation. Interviews are strongly recommended. A GPA of 2.0 is required. AP and CLEP credits are accepted. Important factors in the admissions decision are advanced placement or honor courses, recommendations by school officials, and leadership record. Applications are accepted on-line via CollegeLink and Common App.

Procedure: Freshmen are admitted fall and spring. Entrance exams should be taken in the fall of the senior year. There is a deferred admissions plan. Application deadlines are open. Notification is on a rolling basis. The application fee is $40.

Transfer: 24 transfer students enrolled in 2001-2002. College-level work will be emphasized. College transcripts, course descriptions, and a dean's form are required in addition to the standard requirements. 60 credits of 120 must be completed at Colby-Sawyer.

Visiting: There are regularly scheduled orientations for prospective students, including tours and interviews. 2 open house programs offer tours as well as academic, athletic, campus life, career development, and academic development presentations; several visiting-day programs offer tours, interviews, and class visits. There are guides for informal visits and visitors may sit in on classes and stay overnight. To schedule a visit, contact the Admissions Office.

Financial Aid: Colby-Sawyer is a member of CSS. The FAFSA and the college's own financial statement are required. The fall application deadline is March 1.

International Students: There are 26 international students enrolled. The school actively recruits these students. They must score 450 on the written TOEFL.

Computers: There are 3 student computer labs on campus, housing 55 PCs; 2 "smart" classrooms housing 25 PCs; a library with 17 PCs; and a student center with 4 PCs. All students may access the system. There are no time limits and no fees.

Graduates: In 2001, 167 bachelor's degrees were awarded. The most popular majors were exercise and sports science (16%), child development (16%), and business administration (11%). In an average class, 50% graduate in 4 years, 57% in 5 years, and 58% in 6 years. 5 companies recruited on campus in 2000-2001. Of the 2000 graduating class, 12% were enrolled in graduate school within 6 months of graduation and 89% were employed.

Admissions Contact: Office of Admissions and Financial Aid.
E-mail: *csadmiss@colby-sawyer.edu* Web: *http://www.colby-sawyer.edu*

COLLEGE FOR LIFELONG LEARNING D-4
Concord, NH 03301-6430 (603) 228-3000, ext. 313
(800) 582-7248; Fax: (603) 229-0964

Full-time: 30 men, 60 women	**Faculty:** n/av
Part-time: 460 men, 1650 women	**Ph.D.s:** n/av
Graduate: none	**Student/Faculty:** n/av
Year: trimesters, summer session	**Tuition:** $4100 ($4500)
Application Deadline: open	**Room & Board:** n/app
Freshman Class: n/av	
SAT I or ACT: not required	**SPECIAL**

The College for Lifelong Learning, established as part of the University System of New Hampshire in 1972, is a state-supported commuter institution offering undergraduate programs in general and professional studies for adults. Figures in the above capsule are approximate. Computerized library services include interlibrary loans and database searching. Special learning facilities include a learning resource center. The campus is in a small town.

Student Life: 92% of undergraduates are from New Hampshire. Others are from 4 states and 1 foreign country. 77% are white. The average age of all undergraduates is 35.

Housing: There are no residence halls. All of students commute. Alcohol is not permitted.

Activities: There are no fraternities or sororities.

Sports: There is no sports program at CLL.

Disabled Students: All of the campus is accessible. Wheelchair ramps, special parking, and specially equipped rest rooms are available.

Services: There is remedial math, reading, and writing.

Campus Safety and Security: Measures include informal discussions and pamphlets/posters/films.

Programs of Study: CLL confers B.G.S. and B.S. degrees. Associate degrees are also awarded. Bachelor's degrees are awarded in BUSINESS (management science), SOCIAL SCIENCE (behavioral science and liberal arts/general studies). Behavioral science is the largest.

Required: Students must complete 124 credits, 34 to 36 in the major, and must maintain a minimum GPA of 2.0. All students are required to complete courses in computer competency, critical thinking/problem solving, mathematical reasoning, and written and oral communications. General education requirements include courses in humanities/arts, science and technology, and social science.

Special: Opportunities are provided for internships, cross-registration with all USNH schools, student-designed and dual majors, credit by exam, nondegree study, and pass/fail options (for degree students only). CLL offers programs throughout the state through a network of 9 regional centers. There is 1 national honor society.

Faculty/Classroom: 44% of faculty are male; 56%, female. All teach undergraduates. The average class size in a regular course is 10.

Requirements: A GED will be considered if submitted for admission evaluation. An interview is required. AP and CLEP credits are accepted.

Procedure: Freshmen are admitted to all sessions. Application deadlines are open. The fall 2001 application fee was $35.

Transfer: 30 credits of 124 must be completed at CLL.

Visiting: There are regularly scheduled orientations for prospective students, consisting of an overview of college programs, financial aid, services, and transfer policies. Visitors may sit in on classes. To schedule a visit, contact a regional center.

Financial Aid: The FAFSA is required.

International Students: They must score 500 on the written TOEFL.

Computers: The mainframe is a DEC VAX. There are 9 PC labs available for student use. All students may access the system. There are no time limits and no fees.

Graduates: In a recent year, 138 bachelor's degrees were awarded. The most popular majors in a recent year were behavioral science (70%), management (27%), and self-designed studies (3%).

Admissions Contact: Ruth Nawn, Assistant Registrar.
E-mail: *rnawn@unhf.unh.edu*

DANIEL WEBSTER COLLEGE D-6
Nashua, NH 03063-1300 (603) 577-6600
(800) 325-6876; Fax: (603) 577-6001

Full-time: 412 men, 96 women	**Faculty:** 33
Part-time: 62 men, 8 women	**Ph.D.s:** 43%
Graduate: none	**Student/Faculty:** 15 to 1
Year: semesters, summer session	**Tuition:** $17,870
Application Deadline: open	**Room & Board:** $7000
Freshman Class: 936 applied, 658 accepted, 214 enrolled	
SAT I Verbal/Math: 523/536	**COMPETITIVE**

Daniel Webster College, founded in 1965, is a private college offering study in the fields of aviation, business, computer sciences, engineering, sports management, and social sciences. There are 5 undergraduate schools. The library contains 32,000 volumes, 55,294 microform items, and 1457 audiovisual forms/CDs, and subscribes to 390 periodicals. Computerized library services include the card catalog, interlibrary loans, and database searching. Special learning facilities include a learning resource center and a flight center, a flight tower, air traffic control labs, flight simulators, a hangar, and a fleet of airplanes. The 54-acre campus is in a suburban area 35 miles northwest of Boston. Including residence halls, there are 13 buildings.

Student Life: 72% of undergraduates are from out of state, mostly the Middle Atlantic. Others are from 27 states, 18 foreign countries, and Canada. 79% are from public schools. 91% are white. The average age of freshmen is 18; all undergraduates, 20. 35% do not continue beyond their first year; 51% remain to graduate.

Housing: 500 students can be accommodated in college housing, which includes single-sex and coed dormitories and on-campus apartments. In addition, there are suites, quiet-floors in residence halls, smoke-free areas, and a substance-free, 10-month housing option. On-campus housing is guaranteed for all 4 years. 72% of students live on campus; of those, 80% remain on campus on weekends. All students may keep cars.

Activities: There are no fraternities or sororities. There are 16 groups on campus, including computers, drama, film, flight team, honors, jazz band, newspaper, professional, religious, social, social service, student government, and yearbook. Popular campus events include Ski Day, Family Weekend, and a whitewater rafting trip.

Sports: There are 7 intercollegiate sports for men and 5 for women, and 6 intramural sports for men and 5 for women. Facilities include an indoor basketball/volleyball court, a weight room, tennis courts, soccer, lacrosse, and softball fields, and cross-country trails.

Disabled Students: 75% of the campus is accessible. Wheelchair ramps, elevators, special parking, specially equipped rest rooms, special class scheduling, and lowered drinking fountains are available.

Services: Counseling and information services are available, as is tutoring in every subject. There is remedial math and writing, study skills and test skills workshops, study groups, a math/ science center, a writing center, and accommodations for students with learning disabilities.

Campus Safety and Security: Measures include 24-hour foot and vehicle patrol, self-defense education, escort service, and informal discussions. There are pamphlets/posters/films, emergency telephones, and lighted pathways/sidewalks.

Programs of Study: DWC confers the B.S. degree. Associate degrees are also awarded. Bachelor's degrees are awarded in BUSINESS (business administration and management, management information systems, and sports management), COMPUTER AND PHYSICAL SCIENCE (computer science and information sciences and systems), ENGINEERING AND ENVIRONMENTAL DESIGN (air traffic control, airline piloting and navigation, aviation administration/management, and computer technology), SOCIAL SCIENCE (social science). Aviation, computer science, and information systems are the strongest academically. Aviation is the largest.

Required: Students must complete general education courses in communication, computer literacy, math, natural science, the humanities, and the social sciences. At least 120 credits, with 45 to 58 in the major, are required for graduation. Students must maintain a minimum overall GPA of 2.0. and grades of C or better in their major.

Special: There is cross-registration with the New Hampshire College and University Council. All programs offer credit by exam. Interdisciplinary majors, including aviation flight operations and aviation management/air traffic management, are available. Study abroad, internships in aviation, business management, computer sciences, and sport management, a general studies degree, and a 2-2 engineering program with the Universities of New Hampshire and Massachusetts at Lowell, Kettering University, and Clarkson University are additional options. There is 1 national honor society.

Faculty/Classroom: 76% of faculty are male; 24%, female. All both teach and do research. The average class size in an introductory lecture is 17 to 20; in a laboratory, 12; and in a regular course, 20.

Admissions: 70% of the 2001-2002 applicants were accepted. The SAT I scores for the 2001-2002 freshman class were: Verbal--36% below

500, 50% between 500 and 599, 12% between 600 and 700, and 2% above 700. 24% of the current freshmen were in the top fifth of their class; 57% were in the top two fifths.

Requirements: The SAT I is required. In addition, applicants must be graduates of an accredited secondary school or submit the GED. Students should have taken 4 years of English, 3 of math, 2 each of social studies and science, and 1 of history. An essay and an interview are recommended. AP and CLEP credits are accepted. Important factors in the admissions decision are advanced placement or honor courses, recommendations by school officials, and leadership record. Applications are accepted on-line at the school's web site.

Procedure: Freshmen are admitted to all sessions. There are early admissions and deferred admissions plans. Application deadlines are open.The application fee is $35. Notification is sent on a rolling basis.

Transfer: 21 transfer students enrolled in a recent year. Transfer students must have a minimum college GPA of 2.0. The SAT I is required. Grades of C or better transfer for credit. 30 credits of a minimum of 120 must be completed at DWC.

Visiting: There are regularly scheduled orientations for prospective students, including a tour and an admissions interview; also available are meetings with faculty and coaches and an aerial tour of the campus. There are guides for informal visits and visitors may sit in on classes and stay overnight. To schedule a visit, contact the Office of Admissions.

Financial Aid: In 2001-2002, 92% of all freshmen and 90% of continuing students received some form of financial aid. 87% of freshmen and 78% of continuing students received need-based aid. The average freshman award was $13,550. Of that total, scholarships or need-based grants averaged $8405 ($17,300 maximum); loans averaged $3625 ($5500 maximum); and work contracts averaged $2000. 25% of undergraduates work part time. Average annual earnings from campus work are $1500. The average financial indebtedness of the 2001 graduate was $18,500. The FAFSA and the college's own financial statement are required. The fall application deadline is March 1.

International Students: There are 9 international students enrolled. They must score 520 on the written TOEFL.

Computers: There are 14 servers connected to more than 150 PCs for student use. All residence halls are wired for Internet access. All students may access the system when the computer center is open. There are no time limits. There is a one-time technology fee of $120. It is strongly recommended that all students have a personal computer.

Graduates: In 2001, 76 bachelor's degrees were awarded. The most popular majors were aviation management/flight operations (22%), aviation management (21%), and computer science (13%). In an average class, 46% graduate in 4 years, and 49% in 5 years. Of the 2000 graduating class, 10% were enrolled in graduate school within 6 months of graduation and 81% were employed.

Admissions Contact: Jim Thatcher, Enrollment Services.
E-mail: *admissions@dwc.edu* Web: *www.dwc.edu*

DARTMOUTH COLLEGE — B-4

Hanover, NH 03755 — **(603) 646-2875; Fax: (603) 646-1216**

Full-time: 2099 men, 1982 women	**Faculty:** 406; I, +$
Part-time: 16 men, 21 women	**Ph.D.s:** 95%
Graduate: 842 men, 535 women	**Student/Faculty:** 10 to 1
Year: terms	**Tuition:** $26,562
Application Deadline: January 1	**Room & Board:** $7896
Freshman Class: 9720 applied, 2220 accepted, 1135 enrolled	
SAT I Verbal/Math: 710/720	**MOST COMPETITIVE**

Dartmouth College, chartered in 1769, is a private liberal arts institution offering a wide range of graduate and undergraduate programs. There is a year-round academic calendar of 4 10-week terms. There are 1 undergraduate and 4 graduate schools. The 10 libraries contain 2,355,700 volumes, 2,554,823 microform items, and 78,471 audiovisual forms/CDs, and subscribe to 20,679 periodicals. Computerized library services include the card catalog, interlibrary loans, and database searching. Special learning facilities include a learning resource center, art gallery, radio station, and creative and performing arts center, life sciences lab, physical and social sciences centers, and observatory. The 265-acre campus is in a rural area 140 miles northwest of Boston. Including residence halls, there are 100 buildings.

Student Life: 97% of undergraduates are from out of state, mostly the Middle Atlantic. Others are from 50 states, 74 foreign countries, and Canada. 63% are from public schools. 61% are white; 11% Asian American. 27% are Protestant; 25% claim no religious affiliation; 24% Catholic; 11% Jewish. The average age of freshmen is 19; all undergraduates, 20. 4% do not continue beyond their first year; 95% remain to graduate.

Housing: 3500 students can be accommodated in college housing, which includes coed dormitories, on-campus apartments, married-student housing, fraternity houses, and sorority houses. In addition, there are language houses and special-interest houses as well as faculty-in-residence and academic affinity programs. On-campus housing is guaranteed for the freshman year only, is available on a first-come, first-served basis, and is available on a lottery system for upperclassmen. 87% of students live on campus. Alcohol is permitted, and upperclass students may keep cars.

Activities: 23% of men belong to 7 local and 7 national fraternities; 21% of women belong to 3 local and 5 national sororities. There are more than 250 groups on campus, including art, band, cheerleading, chess, choir, chorale, chorus, computers, dance, debate, drama, ethnic, film, forensics, gay, honors, international, jazz band, literary magazine, marching band, musical theater, newspaper, opera, orchestra, outing, pep band, photography, political, professional, radio and TV, religious, social, social service, student government, symphony, and yearbook. Popular campus events include Dartmouth Night/Homecoming, Winter and Summer Carnivals, and Green Key Service Weekend.

Sports: There are 16 intercollegiate sports for men and 16 for women, and 25 intramural sports for men and 25 for women. Facilities include a 2100-seat stadium, a fitness center, squash and racquetball courts, a dance studio, a 5000-seat arena, a gym, a 21,000-seat football stadium, a boat house, a tennis center with indoor and outdoor courts, a golf course, a ski slope with 3 chairlifts, and a riding farm.

Disabled Students: 75% of the campus is accessible. Wheelchair ramps, elevators, special parking, specially equipped rest rooms, special class scheduling, lowered drinking fountains, lowered telephones, and accessible residence halls are available.

Services: Counseling and information services are available, as is tutoring in every subject. There is a reader service for the blind. There is an academic skills center for all students. Readers, note takers, tape recorders, and support for learning-disabled students are available.

Campus Safety and Security: Measures include 24-hour foot and vehicle patrol, self-defense education, escort service, and shuttle buses. There are informal discussions, pamphlets/posters/films, emergency telephones, and lighted pathways/sidewalks.

Programs of Study: Dartmouth confers B.A. and B.Eng. degrees. Master's and doctoral degrees are also awarded. Bachelor's degrees are awarded in BIOLOGICAL SCIENCE (biochemistry, biology/biological science, evolutionary biology, and genetics), COMMUNICATIONS AND THE ARTS (Arabic, art history and appreciation, Chinese, classics, comparative literature, creative writing, dramatic arts, English, English literature, film arts, French, German, Italian, linguistics, music, romance languages and literature, Russian, Spanish, and studio art), COMPUTER AND PHYSICAL SCIENCE (chemistry, computer science, earth science, mathematics, and physics), ENGINEERING AND ENVIRONMENTAL DESIGN (engineering and applied science, engineering physics, and environmental science), SOCIAL SCIENCE (African American studies, African studies, anthropology, Asian/Oriental studies, Caribbean studies, classical/ancient civilization, cognitive science, economics, geography, German area studies, Hispanic American studies, history, Latin American studies, Middle Eastern studies, Native American studies, philosophy, political science/government, psychology, religion, Russian and Slavic studies, social science, sociology, Spanish studies, and women's studies). Economics, psychology, and government are the largest.

Required: All students must take 35 courses, 10 of which must be distributed in the following fields: arts; social analysis; literature; quantitative or deductive science; philosophical, religious, or historical analysis; natural science; technology or applied science; and international or comparative study. 3 world culture courses are required from the U.S., Europe, and at least 1 non-Western society. A multidisciplinary or interdisciplinary course, a freshman seminar, a senior project, and foreign language proficiency are also required.

Special: Students may design programs using the college's unique Dartmouth Plan, which divides the academic calender into 4 10-week terms, based on the seasons. The plan permits greater flexibility for vacations and for the 40 study-abroad programs in 15 countries, including Italy, France, Scotland, Russia, and Brazil. Cross-registration is offered through the Twelve College Exchange Network, which includes Amherst and Mount Holyoke. Exchange programs also exist with the University of California at San Diego, McGill University in Montreal, selected German universities, Keio University in Tokyo, and Beijing Normal University in China. There are special academic programs in Washington, D.C., and Tucson, Arizona. Students may design their own interdisciplinary majors, involving multiple departments if desired, take dual majors in all fields, or satisfy a modified major involving 2 departments, with emphasis in 1. Hands-on computer science education, internships, combined B.A.-B.S. degrees, and work-study programs also are available. A 3-2 engineering degree is offered with Dartmouth's Thayer School of Engineering. There is a freshman honors program and all departments have honor programs.

Faculty/Classroom: 66% of faculty are male; 34%, female. All both teach and do research. No introductory courses are taught by graduate students. The average class size in an introductory lecture is 34; in a laboratory, 16; and in a regular course, 23.

Admissions: 23% of the 2001-2002 applicants were accepted. The SAT I scores for the 2001-2002 freshman class were: Verbal--7% between 500 and 599, 33% between 600 and 700, and 60% above 700; Math--1% below 500, 4% between 500 and 599, 30% between 600 and 700, and 66% above 700. 95% of the current freshmen were in the top fifth of their class and all were in the top two fifths. There were 63 National Merit finalists. 156 freshmen graduated first in their class.

Requirements: The SAT I or ACT is required as are 3 SAT II: Subject tests. Evidence of intellectual capacity, motivation, and personal integrity are prime considerations in the highly competitive admissions process, which also considers talent, accomplishment, and involvement in nonacademic areas. Course requirements are flexible, but students are urged to take English, foreign language, math, lab science, and history. The GED is accepted. AP credits are accepted.

Procedure: Freshmen are admitted in the fall. Entrance exams should be taken no later than January of the senior year. There are early decision and deferred admissions plans. Early decision applications should be filed by November 1; regular applications, by January 1 for fall entry. Notification of early decision is sent December 15; regular decision, April 15. 376 early decision candidates were accepted for the 2001-2002 class. The application fee is $65. A waiting list is an active part of the admissions procedure.

Transfer: 28 transfer students enrolled in 2001-2002. Applicants must demonstrate high achievement and intellectual motivation through college transcripts as well as standardized test scores and high school transcripts.

Visiting: There are regularly scheduled orientations for prospective students, including tours, group information sessions, and interviews. There are guides for informal visits and visitors may sit in on classes and stay overnight. To schedule a visit, contact the Office of Admissions.

Financial Aid: In 2001-2002, 61% of all freshmen received some form of financial aid. 42% of freshmen received need-based aid. The average freshman award was $25,154. Of that total, scholarships or need-based grants averaged $20,959 ($35,653 maximum); loans averaged $2519 ($3350 maximum); and work contracts averaged $1530 ($2075 maximum). The average financial indebtedness of the 2001 graduate was $14,719. Dartmouth is a member of CSS. The CSS/Profile or FAFSA and parents' and student's federal income tax returns. In addition, a Noncustodial Parents' statement, tax returns, and W-2s, and a Business/Farm Supplement may be required. Foreign students must provide a certificate of finances and parents' tax returns or statements. The fall application deadline is February 1.

International Students: There are 187 international students enrolled. The school actively recruits these students. And also take the SAT I or the ACTStudents must take SAT II: Subject tests in any 3 subjects along with the SAT I or ACT.

Computers: The mainframes are an IBM RS/6000 4P-270, an SG 1 ORIGIN 200, and a Sun E450. More than 12,000 network ports are available for student use. The computer network (which includes wireless network station) links dormitory rooms, administrative and academic buildings, and mainframe computers on and off campus. Students can access scholarly databases, a collegewide e-mail system, and the Internet. All students may access the system 24 hours daily. There are no time limits and no fees. All students are required to have personal computers.

Graduates: In 2001, 1056 bachelor's degrees were awarded. The most popular majors were economics (12%), history (10%), and government (10%). In an average class, 86% graduate in 4 years, 93% in 5 years, and 95% in 6 years. 300 companies recruited on campus in 2000-2001. Of the 2000 graduating class, 18% were enrolled in graduate school within 6 months of graduation and 70% were employed.

Admissions Contact: Karl Furstenberg, Dean of Admissions.
E-mail: *undergraduate.admissions@dartmouth.edu*
Web: *www.dartmouth.edu*

FRANKLIN PIERCE COLLEGE — C-8
Rindge, NH 03461-0060 — (603) 899-4054
(800) 437-0048; Fax: (603) 899-4372

Full-time: 716 men, 761 women	**Faculty:** 65
Part-time: 34 men, 37 women	**Ph.D.s:** 72%
Graduate: none	**Student/Faculty:** 23 to 1
Year: semesters, summer session	**Tuition:** $19,875
Application Deadline: open	**Room & Board:** $6250
Freshman Class: 3850 applied, 3109 accepted, 529 enrolled	
SAT I Verbal/Math: 500/483	**LESS COMPETITIVE**

Franklin Pierce College, founded in 1962, is a private liberal arts institution that also has an extensive continuing education program, which offers undergraduate and graduate degrees at locations in Concord, Keene, Lebanon, Salem, Nashua, and Portsmouth in New Hampshire. The library contains 106,045 volumes, 26,061 microform items, and 9957 audiovisual forms/CDs, and subscribes to 1362 periodicals. Computerized library services include the card catalog, interlibrary loans, and database searching. Special learning facilities include a learning resource center, art gallery, radio station, TV station, computer labs, theaters, and studios. The 1000-acre campus is in a rural area 65 miles northwest of Boston. Including residence halls, there are 30 buildings.

Student Life: 86% of undergraduates are from out of state, mostly the Northeast. Others are from 27 states, 18 foreign countries, and Canada. 87% are from public schools. 89% are white. The average age of freshmen is 18; all undergraduates, 20. 32% do not continue beyond their first year; 49% remain to graduate.

Housing: 1345 students can be accommodated in college housing, which includes single-sex and coed dormitories, on-campus apartments, and off-campus apartments. On-campus housing is guaranteed for all 4 years. 86% of students live on campus; of those, 70% remain on campus on weekends. All students may keep cars.

Activities: There are no fraternities or sororities. There are 35 groups on campus, including art, cheerleading, chess, choir, chorale, computers, dance, drama, ethnic, gay, honors, international, jazz band, literary magazine, musical theater, newspaper, outing, photography, political, professional, radio and TV, religious, social, social service, student government, and yearbook. Popular campus events include Winter Carnival, Spring and Fall Weekends, and Up All Night Mardi Gras.

Sports: There are 8 intercollegiate sports for men and 10 for women, and 6 intramural sports for men and 3 for women. Facilities include a 72,000-square-foot airframe activity center, a field house, a fitness center, an 800-seat gym, an athletic trainer, playing fields, a track, a lake with a beach, a fleet of sailboats, cross-country and hiking trails, and courts for tennis, basketball, and volleyball.

Disabled Students: 90% of the campus is accessible. Wheelchair ramps, elevators, special parking, specially equipped rest rooms, special class scheduling, lowered drinking fountains, and lowered telephones are available.

Services: Counseling and information services are available, as is tutoring in every subject. There is a reader service for the blind, remedial math, reading, and writing, note takers, a professional reading specialist, alternative testing, reduced course loads, study skills workshops, and content-area study skills courses.

Campus Safety and Security: Measures include 24-hour foot and vehicle patrol, escort service, shuttle buses, and informal discussions. There are pamphlets/posters/films, emergency telephones, and lighted pathways/sidewalks.

Programs of Study: FPC confers B.A. and B.S. degrees. Master's degrees are also awarded. Bachelor's degrees are awarded in BIOLOGICAL SCIENCE (biology/biological science), BUSINESS (accounting, banking and finance, business administration and management, business economics, international economics, management science, marketing/retailing/merchandising, and sports management), COMMUNICATIONS AND THE ARTS (advertising, arts administration/management, communications, dance, dramatic arts, English, fine arts, graphic design, music, performing arts, and theater design), COMPUTER AND PHYSICAL SCIENCE (computer science, information sciences and systems, and mathematics), EDUCATION (education, elementary, and secondary), ENGINEERING AND ENVIRONMENTAL DESIGN (environmental science), SOCIAL SCIENCE (American studies, anthropology, criminal justice, history, political science/government, psychology, social work, and sociology). Anthropology, biology, and environmental science are the strongest academically. Criminal justice, mass communication, and psychology are the largest.

Required: Students must complete 120 semester hours with a cumulative GPA of at least 2.0 and pass exams for writing and math competency. Individual and Community core requirements total 11 courses, including Individual and Community, College Writing, Integrated Science, American Experience, Twentieth Century, Foundations of Mathematics, Experiencing the Arts, Ancient and Medieval Worlds, Reason and Romanticism, Science of Society, and a senior liberal arts seminar.

Special: Cross-registration is offered in nearly every subject through the New Hampshire College and University Council, a 13-member consortium of area institutions. Study at Richmond College in London, Oxford University, and American College Dublin, internships in most majors on or off campus, a Washington semester, and work-study through the college are possible. In addition, accelerated degree programs in all majors, dual majors in most fields, student-designed majors, credit for life experience, and nondegree study are available. There are 5 national honor societies, and a freshman honors program.

Faculty/Classroom: 60% of faculty are male; 40%, female. All teach undergraduates and 50% both teach and do research. The average class size in an introductory lecture is 60; in a laboratory, 16; and in a regular course, 19.

Admissions: 81% of the 2001-2002 applicants were accepted. The SAT I scores for the 2001-2002 freshman class were: Verbal--57% below 500, 32% between 500 and 599, and 10% between 600 and 700; Math--63% below 500, 30% between 500 and 599, 6% between 600 and 700, and 1% above 700. 17% of the current freshmen were in the top fifth of their class; 40% were in the top two fifths.

Requirements: The SAT I or ACT is required, but with no minimum score. Applicants must have earned 10 academic units or 16 Carnegie units in high school, including 4 years of English, 2 years each in math and science, and 1 year each in history and social studies. An interview is recommended. The GED is accepted. A GPA of 2.0 is required. AP and CLEP credits are accepted. Important factors in the admissions decision are recommendations by school officials, advanced placement or honor courses, and leadership record. Applications are accepted on-line; a hard copy still needs to be submitted with a signature.

Procedure: Freshmen are admitted to all sessions. Entrance exams should be taken in the fall of the senior year. There are early admissions and deferred admissions plans. Application deadlines are open. Notification is sent on a rolling basis.

Transfer: 47 transfer students enrolled in 2001-2002. A minimum 2.0 GPA in college work is required. Students with fewer than 30 credits must submit the SAT I results (no minimum score) and official high school transcripts. A personal recommendation is necessary and an interview recommended. 30 credits of 120 must be completed at FPC.

Visiting: There are regularly scheduled orientations for prospective students, including open houses held each spring and fall and interviews and tours available weekdays and most Saturdays. There are guides for informal visits and visitors may sit in on classes and stay overnight. To schedule a visit, contact the Admissions Office at (603) 899-4055.

Financial Aid: In 2001-2002, 95% of all students received some form of financial aid. 94% of freshmen and 96% of continuing students received need-based aid. The average freshman award was $14,500. Of that total, scholarships or need-based grants averaged $10,878 ($23,630 maximum); loans averaged $3589 ($4800 maximum); work contracts averaged $1500 ($1800 maximum); and private scholarships averaged $300 ($16,135 maximum). 74% of undergraduates work part time. Average annual earnings from campus work are $1800. The average financial indebtedness of the 2001 graduate was $19,308. The FAFSA is required. The fall application deadline is rolling.

International Students: There are 47 international students enrolled. The school actively recruits these students. They must score 500 on the written TOEFL and also take and also take ELS Level 109. The SAT I or ACT may be substituted for the TOEFL.

Computers: There are 3 computer labs (PCs and Macs) available for student use 7 days per week, in addition to Internet access ports in all residence halls for students with PCs. All students may access the system 16 hours daily. There are no time limits and no fees. It is strongly recommended that all students have a personal computer.

Graduates: In 2001, 241 bachelor's degrees were awarded. The most popular majors were criminal justice (14%), psychology (8%), and mass communication (8%). 35 companies recruited on campus in 2000-2001. Of the 2000 graduating class, 13% were enrolled in graduate school within 6 months of graduation and 91% were employed.

Admissions Contact: Lucy C. Shonk, Dean of Admissions. A video is available. E-mail: *admissions@fpc.edu* Web: *www.fpc.edu*

HESSER COLLEGE
Manchester, NH 03101

(603) 668-6660
(800) 526-9231; Fax: (603) 666-4722

Full-time: 190 men, 265 women	**Faculty:** 29
Part-time: 5 men, 6 women	**Ph.D.s:** 1%
Graduate: none	**Student/Faculty:** 16 to 1
Year: semesters, summer session	**Tuition:** $10,210
Application Deadline: open	**Room & Board:** $6000
Freshman Class: n/av	
SAT I or ACT: not required	**LESS COMPETITIVE**

Hesser College, founded in 1900, is a small, private institution offering more than 30 associate and bachelor degree programs. The library contains 30,000 volumes. Computerized library services include the card catalog, interlibrary loans, and database searching. Special learning facilities include a learning resource center, radio station, TV station, and medical labs. The 2-acre campus is in a medium-size city.

Student Life: The average age of freshmen is 18; all undergraduates, 19.

Housing: More than 500 students can be accommodated in college housing, which includes single-sex dormitories. On-campus housing is guaranteed for the freshman year only and is available on a lottery system for upperclassmen. 50% of students live on campus; of those, 50% remain on campus on weekends. Alcohol is not permitted. All students may keep cars.

Activities: There are no fraternities or sororities. There are some groups and organizations on campus, including cheerleading, honors, international, newspaper, professional, radio and TV, social, and student government.

Sports: There are 3 intercollegiate sports for men and 3 for women. Basketball, volleyball, soccer, and softball programs are available.

Services: Counseling and information services are available, as is tutoring in every subject. There is remedial math, reading, and writing. There is a center for teaching, learning, and assessment.

Campus Safety and Security: Measures include 24-hour foot and vehicle patrol and escort service.

Programs of Study: Hesser College confers B.B.A. and B.C.J. degrees. Associate degrees are also awarded. Bachelor's degrees are awarded in BUSINESS (accounting, business administration and management, and marketing/retailing/merchandising), SOCIAL SCIENCE (criminal justice). Criminal justice is the largest.

Required: A minimum 2.0 GPA is required. Contact the school for specific program information.

Special: Internships and work-study programs are available. The college offers a J.D. degree through an articulation agreement with the Massachusetts School of Law, Andover. There is 1 national honor society, and a freshman honors program.

Faculty/Classroom: 54% of faculty are male; 46%, female. The average class size in a regular course is 20.

Admissions: 25% of the current freshmen were in the top fifth of their class; 60% were in the top two fifths.

Requirements: Applicants must be high school graduates. The GED is accepted. An interview is required. A GPA of 2.0 is required. Applications are accepted on-line via the school's web site. Important factors in the admissions decision are personality/intangible qualities, recommendations by school officials, and leadership record.

Procedure: Freshmen are admitted fall and spring. Entrance exams should be taken at orientation. Application deadlines are open. The application fee is $10. Notification is sent on a rolling basis.

Visiting: There are regularly scheduled orientations for prospective students, including campus tours Monday through Friday during the school year and Monday through Thursday during the summer. Open House and Saturday tour days are also available. There are guides for informal visits and visitors may sit in on classes. To schedule a visit, contact Kevin Wilkinson, Director of Admissions at (603) 668-6660, ext. 2110.

Financial Aid: The FAFSA and the college's own financial statement are required. The fall application deadline is rolling.

International Students: There are about 30 international students enrolled. The school actively recruits these students. They must score 450 on the written TOEFL or take the MELAB or Kaplan English Language Proficiency Test.

Computers: There are Dell computer labs and Mac G4 computer labs.

Admissions Contact: Kevin Wilkinson, Director of Admissions. A video is available. E-mail: *kwilkinson@hesser.edu* Web: *www.hesser.edu*

KEENE STATE COLLEGE
Keene, NH 03435

B-6
(603) 358-2276
(800) KSC-1909; Fax: (603) 358-2767

Full-time: 1555 men, 2249 women	**Faculty:** 178; IIB, -$
Part-time: 306 men, 290 women	**Ph.D.s:** 81%
Graduate: 78 men, 155 women	**Student/Faculty:** 21 to 1
Year: semesters, summer session	**Tuition:** $5554 ($11,054)
Application Deadline: March 1	**Room & Board:** $5726
Freshman Class: 3428 applied, 2682 accepted, 956 enrolled	
SAT I Verbal/Math: 490/480	**ACT:** 19 **COMPETITIVE**

Keene State College, founded in 1909, is part of the public University System of New Hampshire and offers a liberal arts program that includes teacher preparation, art, and business emphases. In addition to regional accreditation, KSC has baccalaureate program accreditation with CAAHEP, NASM, and NCATE. The library contains 238,297 volumes, 690,421 microform items, and 4797 audiovisual forms/CDs, and subscribes to 1195 periodicals. Computerized library services include the card catalog, interlibrary loans, and database searching. Special learning facilities include a learning resource center, art gallery, planetarium, radio station, TV station, and and the Holocaust Resource Center. The 150-acre campus is in a suburban area 90 miles northwest of Boston. Including residence halls, there are 70 buildings.

Student Life: 58% of undergraduates are from New Hampshire. Others are from 26 states, 18 foreign countries, and Canada. 80% are from public schools. 92% are white. 48% are Catholic; 21% claim no religious affiliation; 20% Protestant; 10% unspecified. The average age of freshmen is 18; all undergraduates, 21. 23% do not continue beyond their first year; 57% remain to graduate.

Housing: 2076 students can be accommodated in college housing, which includes single-sex and coed dormitories, on-campus apartments, married-student housing, fraternity houses, and sorority houses. In addition, there are special interest houses. On-campus housing is guaranteed for the freshman year only and is available on a lottery system for upperclassmen. 55% of students live on campus. Upperclassmen may keep cars.

Activities: 11% of men belong to 2 local and 3 national fraternities; 8% of women belong to 3 local and 2 national sororities. There are 81 groups on campus, including art, band, cheerleading, choir, chorale, chorus, computers, dance, drama, ethnic, film, gay, honors, international, jazz band, literary magazine, musical theater, newspaper, orchestra, photography, political, professional, radio and TV, religious, social, social service, student government, and yearbook. Popular campus events include Parent and Family Weekend, Winter Carnival, and Diversity Day.

Sports: There are 7 intercollegiate sports for men and 9 for women, and 12 intramural sports for men and 12 for women. Facilities include a 1500-seat gym, a 1000-seat stadium for soccer and field hockey, an indoor pool, a fitness center, racquetball, tennis, and squash courts, and a training room.

Disabled Students: 90% of the campus is accessible. Wheelchair ramps, elevators, special parking, specially equipped rest rooms, lowered drinking fountains, and lowered telephones are available.

Services: Counseling and information services are available, as is tutoring in most subjects. There is a writing process center, a reading center, and a math center. There is also a reader service for the blind and remedial math and reading.

Campus Safety and Security: Measures include 24-hour foot and vehicle patrol, escort service, shuttle buses, and informal discussions. There are pamphlets/posters/films, emergency telephones, and lighted pathways/sidewalks.

Programs of Study: KSC confers B.A., B.S., and B.M. degrees. Associate and master's degrees are also awarded. Bachelor's degrees are awarded in BIOLOGICAL SCIENCE (biology/biological science), BUSINESS (management science), COMMUNICATIONS AND THE ARTS (art, communications, dramatic arts, English, fine arts, French, journalism, music, music performance, and Spanish), COMPUTER AND PHYSICAL SCIENCE (chemistry, computer mathematics, computer science, geology, and mathematics), EDUCATION (early childhood, elementary, foreign languages, home economics, industrial arts, mathematics, music, physical, science, secondary, special, and vocational), ENGINEERING AND ENVIRONMENTAL DESIGN (environmental science, industrial engineering technology, and occupational safety and health), HEALTH PROFESSIONS (health science), SOCIAL SCIENCE (American studies, dietetics, geography, history, political science/government, psychology, safety management, social science, and sociology). Education, safety studies, and health science are the strongest academically. Education, management, and psychology are the largest.

Required: All students must take 120 to 142 credits, with 40 to 50 hours in their major, while maintaining a 2.0 GPA. Distribution requirements include 5 courses in the arts and humanities, 4 each in the social sciences, math, and sciences, and 1 in English composition. Students also must demonstrate proficiency in math.

Special: Cross-registration through New Hampshire College and the University Council, internships and co-op programs in all areas of study, study abroad anywhere in the world, and work-study at the college are available. Students also may pursue dual majors, a general studies degree, individualized majors, accelerated degrees in the psychology honors program, and a 3-2 engineering degree with Clarkson University or the University of New Hampshire. In addition, there are pass/fail options and credit for life experience. There are 18 national honor societies, and 1 departmental honors program.

Faculty/Classroom: 54% of faculty are male; 46%, female. All teach undergraduates. No introductory courses are taught by graduate students. The average class size in an introductory lecture is 20; in a laboratory, 8; and in a regular course, 13.

Admissions: 78% of the 2001-2002 applicants were accepted. The SAT I scores for the 2001-2002 freshman class were: Verbal--52% below 500, 38% between 500 and 599, 9% between 600 and 700, and 1% above 700; Math--58% below 500, 34% between 500 and 599, 9% between 600 and 700, and 1% above 700. The ACT scores were 70% below 21, 20% between 21 and 23, 7% between 24 and 26, and 2% between 27 and 28. 10% of the current freshmen were in the top fifth of their class; 39% were in the top two fifths.

Requirements: The SAT I is required with scores of 450 verbal and 450 math. Applicants need at least 11 academic credits, including 4 years of English, and 2 each of math, science, social studies, and history. An essay, portfolio, and audition are required for certain programs, and an interview is recommended. A GPA of 2.5 is required. AP and CLEP credits are accepted. Important factors in the admissions decision are advanced placement or honor courses, recommendations by school officials, and evidence of special talent.

Procedure: Freshmen are admitted fall and spring. Entrance exams should be taken during the spring of the junior year or fall of the senior year. There is a deferred admissions plan. Applications should be filed by March 1 for fall entry and December 1 for spring entry. The fee was $25 to $35 in 2001. Notification is sent on a rolling basis.

Transfer: 188 transfer students enrolled in 2001-2002. Transfer students must have a 2.0 cumulative GPA and at least 12 college credits. An interview is recommended. 24 credits of 120 to 142 must be completed at KSC.

Visiting: There are regularly scheduled orientations for prospective students, consisting of a personal interview with the professional staff and a tour. There are guides for informal visits and visitors may sit in on classes. To schedule a visit, contact the Admissions Office.

Financial Aid: 59% of freshmen and 53% of continuing students received need-based aid. The average freshman award was $6462. Of that total, scholarships or need-based grants averaged $3556; and loans averaged $2827. The average financial indebtedness of the 2001 graduate was $16,607. The FAFSA and IRS tax returns are required. The fall application deadline is March 1.

International Students: There are 62 international students enrolled. They must score 500 on the written TOEFL.

Computers: The mainframe is a DEC ALPHA 4000. 365 PCs are available in 29 special interest and general purpose labs. All students may access the system 24 hours per day. There are no time limits and no fees.

Graduates: In 2001, 660 bachelor's degrees were awarded. The most popular majors were education (12%), psychology (9%), and safety studies (7%). In an average class, 27% graduate in 4 years, 51% in 5 years, and 57% in 6 years. 20 companies recruited on campus in 2000-2001. Of the 2000 graduating class, 10% were enrolled in graduate school and 46% were employed prior to graduation.

Admissions Contact: Peggy Richmond, Director of Admissions. A video is available. E-mail: *admissions@keene.edu* Web: *www.keene.edu*

NEW ENGLAND COLLEGE

Henniker, NH 03242 — **C-5**

(603) 428-2223

(800) 521-7642; Fax: (608) 428-7230

Full-time: 371 men, 371 women	**Faculty:** 53; IIB, --$
Part-time: 18 men, 36 women	**Ph.D.s:** 75%
Graduate: 25 men, 39 women	**Student/Faculty:** 14 to 1
Year: semesters, summer session	**Tuition:** $19,590
Application Deadline: open	**Room & Board:** $7116
Freshman Class: 1012 applied, 897 accepted, 238 enrolled	
SAT I Verbal/Math: 460/450	**LESS COMPETITIVE**

New England College, founded in 1946, is an independent, liberal arts institution emphasizing small classes and a cocurricular leadership program. The library contains 104,000 volumes, 36,000 microform items, and 2000 audiovisual forms/CDs, and subscribes to 650 periodicals. Computerized library services include the card catalog, interlibrary loans, and database searching. Special learning facilities include a learning resource center, art gallery, radio station, and Center for Educational Innovation, with a high-tech classroom building. The 225-acre campus is in a small town 17 miles west of Concord and 80 miles north of Boston, Massachusetts. Including residence halls, there are 31 buildings.

Student Life: 72% of undergraduates are from out of state, mostly the Northeast. Others are from 27 states, 12 foreign countries, and Canada. 70% are from public schools. 89% are white; 10% Hispanic. The average age of freshmen is 18; all undergraduates, 20. 28% do not continue beyond their first year; 50% remain to graduate.

Housing: 590 students can be accommodated in college housing, which includes coed dormitories, on-campus apartments, fraternity houses, and sorority houses. In addition, there are special-interest houses. Students may choose to live in cooperative substance-free housing. On-campus housing is guaranteed for all 4 years. 70% of students live on campus; of those, 80% remain on campus on weekends. All students may keep cars.

Activities: 12% of men and about 3% of women belong to 3 local fraternities; 8% of women belong to 1 local and 1 national sorority. There are 26 groups on campus, including choir, dance, drama, ethnic, film, honors, international, newspaper, photography, political, professional, radio and TV, social, social service, student government, and yearbook. Popular campus events include International Week and Spring Weekend.

Sports: There are 7 intercollegiate sports for men and 8 for women, and 7 intramural sports for men and 7 for women. Facilities include a gym, field house, Nautilus, 26 acres of playing fields, indoor and outdoor basketball and tennis courts, cross-country ski trails, Alpine skiing at a local ski area, and a fitness center.

Disabled Students: 80% of the campus is accessible. Wheelchair ramps, elevators, special parking, specially equipped rest rooms, and special class scheduling are available.

Services: Counseling and information services are available, as is tutoring in every subject.

Campus Safety and Security: Measures include 24-hour foot and vehicle patrol, escort service, informal discussions, and pamphlets/posters/films. There are emergency telephones and lighted pathways/sidewalks.

Programs of Study: NEC confers B.A. and B.S. degrees. Associate and master's degrees are also awarded. Bachelor's degrees are awarded in BIOLOGICAL SCIENCE (biology/biological science), BUSINESS (business administration and management and sports management), COMMUNICATIONS AND THE ARTS (art history and appreciation, communications, comparative literature, creative writing, dramatic arts, English literature, and fine arts), COMPUTER AND PHYSICAL SCIENCE (mathematics), EDUCATION (elementary, physical, secondary, and special), ENGINEERING AND ENVIRONMENTAL DESIGN (environmental science), HEALTH PROFESSIONS (health science), SOCIAL SCIENCE (criminal justice, philosophy, physical fitness/movement, political science/government, psychology, sociology, and women's studies). Business, education, and psychology are the strongest academically. Business, education, and kinesiology are the largest.

Required: All students must earn a minimum GPA of 2.0 and take 120 credit hours, including an average of 40 in their major. Distribution requirements cover 4 general education areas, including science, humanities, social science, math, and world culture and human rights. Specific requirements include College Writing I and II, a math course (or passing grade on a placement test), computer science, and science courses.

Special: Cross-registration is available with the New Hampshire College and University Council. Also available are internships for juniors and seniors with a GPA of 2.5, study abroad in 6 countries, work-study programs, dual majors, student-designed majors, interdisciplinary majors, nondegree study, pass/fail options, and a 3-2 engineering degree with Clarkson University. There is a freshman honors program.

Faculty/Classroom: 50% of faculty are male; 50%, female. All teach undergraduates and 20% both teach and do research. No introductory courses are taught by graduate students. The average class size in an introductory lecture is 20; in a laboratory, 14; and in a regular course, 16.

Admissions: 89% of the 2001-2002 applicants were accepted. The SAT I scores for the 2001-2002 freshman class were: Verbal--64% below 500, 30% between 500 and 599, 5% between 600 and 700, and 1% above 700; Math--71% below 500, 24% between 500 and 599, and 5% between 600 and 700. 11% of the current freshmen were in the top fifth of their class; 41% were in the top two fifths.

Requirements: In addition, 4 years of English, 3 years each of math and social studies, and 2 years each of science and electives are recommended. An essay is required and an interview is recommended. A GPA of 2.0 is required. AP and CLEP credits are accepted. Important factors in the admissions decision are recommendations by school officials, extracurricular activities record, and parents or siblings attending the school.

Procedure: Freshmen are admitted fall and spring. There are early decision and deferred admissions plans. Early decision applications should be filed by December 9; the deadline for regular applications is open for fall entry. The fall 2001 application fee was $30. Notification of early decision is sent December 20; regular decision, on a rolling basis. 163 early decision candidates were accepted for the 2001-2002 class.

Transfer: 22 transfer students enrolled in a recent year. Transfer students should have a 2.0 minimum GPA from the previous college. A recommendation from the Dean of Students is required. An interview is recommended. 30 credits of 120 must be completed at NEC.

Visiting: There are regularly scheduled orientations for prospective students, including class registration and meeting faculty and other students. There are guides for informal visits and visitors may sit in on classes and stay overnight. To schedule a visit, contact Muriel Schlosser in the Admissions Office.

Financial Aid: In 2001-2002, 85% of all freshmen and 83% of continuing students received some form of financial aid. 61% of freshmen and 63% of continuing students received need-based aid. The average freshman award was $15,323. Of that total, scholarships or need-based grants averaged $1212; loans averaged $2738; and work contracts averaged $1193. 50% of undergraduates work part time. Average annual earnings from campus work are $1500. The average financial indebtedness of the 2001 graduate was $22,519. The FAFSA is required. The fall application deadline is March 1.

International Students: There were 40 international students enrolled in a recent year. The school actively recruits these students. They must score 450 on the written TOEFL.

Computers: The mainframe is a Sun Server Network. 75 PCs are available in the computer labs. All are Internet-connected through a fiber-optic network. There are 16 Macs in the graphic design lab, and 30 in the library. All students may access the system. There are no time limits and no fees. It is strongly recommended that all students have personal computers.

Graduates: In 2001, 141 bachelor's degrees were awarded. The most popular majors were business (25%), psychology (10%), and visual and performing arts (10%). In an average class, 50% graduate in 4 years, and 55% in 5 years. Of the 2000 graduating class, 95% were employed within 6 months of graduation.

Admissions Contact: Office of Admissions.
E-mail: *admis@necl.nec.edu* Web: *www.nec.edu*

NEW HAMPSHIRE COLLEGE
(See Southern New Hampshire University)

PLYMOUTH STATE COLLEGE
Plymouth, NH 03264-1595 D-4

(603) 535-2237
(800) 842-6900; Fax: (603) 535-2714

Full-time: 1604 men, 1707 women	**Faculty:** 168; IIA, av$
Part-time: 56 men, 62 women	**Ph.D.s:** 90%
Graduate: 95 men, 217 women	**Student/Faculty:** 20 to 1
Year: semesters, summer session	**Tuition:** $5550 ($11,050)
Application Deadline: April 1	**Room & Board:** $5474
Freshman Class: n/av	
SAT I or ACT: required	**LESS COMPETITIVE**

Plymouth State College, founded in 1871, is a public institution offering programs in business, education, and liberal arts and sciences. In addition to regional accreditation, PSC has baccalaureate program accreditation with ACBSP, CAAHEP, CSWE, and NCATE. The library contains 296,479 volumes, 731,476 microform items, and 9068 audiovisual forms/CDs, and subscribes to 1071 periodicals. Computerized library services include the card catalog, interlibrary loans, and database searching. Special learning facilities include a learning resource center, art gallery, planetarium, radio station, a major performing arts center, a NAEYC-accredited lab school for children ages 2 to 6, geographic information systems lab, meteorology lab, graphic design, computer lab, MIDI lab, and weather technology evaluation center. The 170-acre campus is in a small town 2 hours north of Boston. Including residence halls, there are 47 buildings.

Student Life: 56% of undergraduates are from New Hampshire. Others are from 32 states and 9 foreign countries. 96% are from public schools. 90% are white. The average age of freshmen is 18; all undergraduates, 21. 27% do not continue beyond their first year; 53% remain to graduate.

Housing: 2062 students can be accommodated in college housing, which includes coed dormitories, on-campus apartments, married-student housing, fraternity houses, and sorority houses. In addition, there are special-interest houses, a wellness residence hall, 2 language apartments, and special-interest areas in the residence halls for skiing, showboarding, biking, hiking, music/theater, fine arts, community service, and fitness. On-campus housing is guaranteed for all 4 years. 57% of students live on campus; of those, 70% remain on campus on weekends. All students may keep cars.

Activities: 4% of men belong to 2 national fraternities; 7% of women belong to 2 local and 2 national sororities. There are 90 groups on campus, including art, band, cheerleading, choir, chorale, computers, dance, debate, drama, ethnic, gay, honors, international, jazz band, leadership effectiveness and development seminar, literary magazine, musical theater, newspaper, OSSIPEE (student wellness organization), professional, radio and TV, religious, social, social service, student government, and yearbook. Popular campus events include Spring Fling and Family Weekend.

Sports: There are 9 intercollegiate sports for men and 9 for women, and 14 intramural sports for men and 14 for women. Facilities include a 2500-seat stadium, a 2000-seat gym, playing fields, and facilities for basketball, racquetball, indoor soccer, swimming, tennis, volleyball, softball, and lacrosse. There is also a 75,000-square-foot recreation student center separate from athletics, as well as a ropes course.

Disabled Students: 75% of the campus is accessible. Wheelchair ramps, elevators, special parking, specially equipped rest rooms, lowered drinking fountains,and lowered telephones are available. The shuttle service is wheelchair-accessible, and there are handicap-accessible student apartment units, ADA compliant alarm systems, and TDD/TTY.

Services: Counseling and information services are available, as is tutoring in some subjects, including 100-and 200-level courses and some upper-level courses. Peer tutoring is available.

Campus Safety and Security: Measures include 24-hour foot and vehicle patrol, self-defense education, escort service, and shuttle buses. There are informal discussions, pamphlets/posters/films, emergency telephones, and lighted pathways/sidewalks. There are also programs in defensive driving, alcohol awareness, drug identification, and personal safety.

Programs of Study: PSC confers B.A., B.S., and B.F.A. degrees. Master's degrees are also awarded. Bachelor's degrees are awarded in BIOLOGICAL SCIENCE (biology/biological science, biotechnology, and environmental biology), BUSINESS (accounting, business administration and management, marketing management, and recreation and leisure services), COMMUNICATIONS AND THE ARTS (art, communications, English, French, graphic design, music, performing arts, and Spanish), COMPUTER AND PHYSICAL SCIENCE (atmospheric sciences and meteorology, chemistry, computer science, information sciences and systems, and mathematics), EDUCATION (art, athletic training, health, mathematics, music, physical, science, and social science), ENGINEERING AND ENVIRONMENTAL DESIGN (city/community/regional planning), SOCIAL SCIENCE (anthropology, child care/child and family studies, early childhood studies, economics, geography, history, humanities, interdisciplinary studies, medieval studies, philosophy, political science/government, psychology, public administration, and social work). Childhood studies, management, and phys ed are the largest.

Required: All students must maintain a minimum GPA of 2.0 while enrolled in 122 semester hours, including 2 credits in phys ed, 1 credit of introduction to the academic community, and 1 course each in composition and math foundations. Distribution requirements are part of the general education program, which requires 7 credits in scientific and science lab, 6 credits in social and psychological, 3 credits in technological, and 3 credits each in the following perspectives: fine and performing arts, global, historical, literary, philosophical, and quantitative reasoning. Some majors have a higher GPA and total credit requirement.

Special: Cross-registration with the New Hampshire College and University Council is available. Internships, study abroad in 3 countries, and college work-study programs are available. Dual majors, an accelerated degree program offering an undergraduate business and M.B.A. degree in 5 years, and student-designed majors are possible. There are 9 national honor societies, a freshman honors program, and 2 departmental honors programs.

Faculty/Classroom: 57% of faculty are male; 43%, female. All teach undergraduates. The average class size in an introductory lecture is 24; in a laboratory, 16; and in a regular course, 20.

Admissions: 3 freshmen graduated first in their class.

Requirements: The SAT I or ACT is required. In addition, PSC requires that applicants have completed 4 units of English, 3 of math, 2 each of social studies and science, 1 of history, and recommends 2 in foreign language. An audition for certain programs is required, and an essay is required. The GED is accepted. AP and CLEP credits are accepted. Important factors in the admissions decision are advanced placement or honor courses, recommendations by school officials, and leadership record. Applications are accepted on-line via the school's web site and CollegeLink.

Procedure: Freshmen are admitted fall and spring. Entrance exams should be taken in November of the senior year. There is a deferred admissions plan. Applications should be filed by April 1 for fall entry and January 1 for spring entry, along with a $30 fee. Notification is sent on a rolling basis.

Transfer: 189 transfer students enrolled in 2001-2002. Transfer students must have a minimum GPA of 2.0 on prior work to be considered. 30 credits of 122 must be completed at PSC.

Visiting: There are regularly scheduled orientations for prospective students, including an admission presentation, a tour of the campus, and a meal in the dining hall. There are guides for informal visits and visitors may sit in on classes. To schedule a visit, contact the Admission Office at (800) 842-6900, ext. 2237.

Financial Aid: In a recent year, 81% of all freshmen and 73% of continuing students received some form of financial aid. 63% of freshmen and 58% of continuing students received need-based aid. The average freshman award was $7561. Of that total, scholarships or need-based grants averaged $3569 ($6200 maximum); loans averaged $3339 ($8025 maximum); work contracts averaged $1816 ($2000 maximum); and local and private scholarships averaged $1158 ($5000 maximum). 34% of undergraduates work part time. Average annual earnings from campus work are $852. The average financial indebtedness of the 2001 graduate was $16,343. The FAFSA is required. The fall application deadline is March 1.

International Students: There are 11 international students enrolled. The school actively recruits these students. They must score 520 on the written TOEFL or 190 on the electronic version, or provide proof of English proficiency during secondary education.

Computers: 349 PCs and 121 Mac workstations are available to students in 29 different computing facilities. In addition, all campus residence halls provide computer ports for students in their rooms. All systems are connected to the campus network, the Internet, and the Web. All students may access the system. There are no time limits. There is a $276 annual technology fee. It is strongly recommended that all students have a personal computer.

Graduates: In 2001, 558 bachelor's degrees were awarded. The most popular majors were childhood studies (19%), management (9%), and physical education (8%). In an average class, 20% graduate in 4 years, 41% in 5 years, and 50% in 6 years. 68 companies recruited on campus in 2000-2001.

Admissions Contact: Eugene D. Fahey, Senior Associate of Admission. E-mail: *pscadmit@mail.psc.plymouth.edu*
Web: *www.plymouth.edu*

RIVIER COLLEGE

Nashua, NH 03060-5086 D-6
(603) 897-8507
(800) 44-RIVIER; Fax: (603) 891-1799

Full-time: 165 men, 605 women	**Faculty:** 63; IIA, --$
Part-time: 121 men, 577 women	**Ph.D.s:** 88%
Graduate: 238 men, 670 women	**Student/Faculty:** 12 to 1
Year: semesters, summer session	**Tuition:** $17,565
Application Deadline: open	**Room & Board:** $6650
Freshman Class: 200 enrolled	
SAT I Verbal/Math: 480/470	**COMPETITIVE**

Rivier College, founded in 1933 by the Sisters of the Presentation of Mary, is a Catholic college offering a liberal arts and professional curriculum. In addition to regional accreditation, Rivier has baccalaureate program accreditation with NLN. The library contains 107,200 volumes, 89,572 microform items, and 29,094 audiovisual forms/CDs, and subscribes to 480 periodicals. Computerized library services include the card catalog, interlibrary loans, and database searching. Special learning facilities include a learning resource center, art gallery, education curriculum resources center, legal reference center, early childhood center/laboratory school, and language lab. The 67-acre campus is in a suburban area 45 miles north of Boston. Including residence halls, there are 37 buildings.

Student Life: 68% of undergraduates are from New Hampshire. Others are from 13 states, 13 foreign countries, and Canada. 80% are from public schools. 93% are white. The average age of freshmen is 18; all undergraduates, 28. 22% do not continue beyond their first year.

Housing: 300 students can be accommodated in college housing, which includes coed dormitories. In addition, there is a substance-free/wellness residence hall. On-campus housing is guaranteed for all 4 years. 56% of students commute. All students may keep cars.

Activities: There are no fraternities or sororities. There are 32 groups on campus, including art, behavioral sciences, chorus, computers, debate, drama, ethnic, history, honors, international, literary magazine, newspaper, nursing, paralegal, political, professional, religious, social, social sciences, social service, student government, and yearbook. Popular campus events include Spirit Week, Black History Month, and Women's History Month.

Sports: There are 5 intercollegiate sports for men and 5 for women, and 7 intramural sports for men and 7 for women. Facilities include a 300-seat gym, a weight room, tennis courts, and soccer and softball fields.

Disabled Students: 75% of the campus is accessible. Wheelchair ramps, elevators, special parking, specially equipped rest rooms, and lowered drinking fountains are available.

Services: Counseling and information services are available, as is tutoring in some subjects, including math, English, business, and languages. Tutoring is available in other subject areas. There is remedial math and writing. There is a full-service writing center.

Campus Safety and Security: Measures include 24-hour foot and vehicle patrol, escort service, informal discussions, and pamphlets/posters/films. There are emergency telephones, lighted pathways/sidewalks, 24-hour access by telephone or walkie-talkie, and electronically operated dorm entrances using security cards.

Programs of Study: Rivier confers B.A., B.S., and B.F.A. degrees. Associate and master's degrees are also awarded. Bachelor's degrees are awarded in BIOLOGICAL SCIENCE (biology/biological science), BUSINESS (accounting, business administration and management, management information systems, and management science), COMMUNICATIONS AND THE ARTS (communications, design, English, French, graphic design, illustration, photography, Spanish, and studio art), COMPUTER AND PHYSICAL SCIENCE (chemistry, computer science, and mathematics), EDUCATION (art, athletic training, early childhood, elementary, English, foreign languages, mathematics, science, secondary, social studies, and special), HEALTH PROFESSIONS (nursing, physical therapy, predentistry, premedicine, preveterinary science, and sports medicine), SOCIAL SCIENCE (history, human development, law, liberal arts/general studies, paralegal studies, political science/government, prelaw, psychology, safety management, and sociology). Art, education, and nursing are the strongest academically. Education, psychology, and business are the largest.

Required: A writing sample is required at entry, and a demonstration of writing proficiency must be shown prior to graduation. Students must complete at least 120 credit hours, ordinarily consisting of 40 3-credit courses with 35 to 60 credits in the student's major, and they must maintain a minimum GPA of 2.0. Distribution requirements include 17 core courses in basic skills of writing and math, the humanities, and the sciences. These courses include religious studies, philosophy, physical and life sciences, fine arts, modern languages, literature, behavioral and social sciences, and Western civilization.

Special: Rivier offers cross-registration through the New Hampshire College and University Council, internships in most majors, a B.A.-B.S. degree in chemistry, an accelerated master's program in English, dual majors, a liberal studies degree, credit by challenge examination, nondegree study, and pass/fail options. There is 1 national honor society and a freshman honors program.

Faculty/Classroom: 38% of faculty are male; 62%, female. 88% teach undergraduates. No introductory courses are taught by graduate students. The average class size in an introductory lecture is 25; in a laboratory, 20; and in a regular course, 17.

Admissions: 24% of the current freshmen were in the top fifth of their class; 70% were in the top two fifths.

Requirements: The SAT I is required. In addition, applicants must be high school graduates or hold the GED. The recommended college preparatory curriculum includes 4 years of English, 3 of math, 2 or more each of foreign language and social studies, 1 of lab science, and 4 academic electives. An essay and 1 or 2 letters of recommendation are required, and an interview is highly recommended. Prospective art majors must submit a portfolio. Rivier requires applicants to be in the upper 50% of their class and have a minimum high school average of 78; 80 for nursing candidates. AP and CLEP credits are accepted. Important factors in the admissions decision are advanced placement or honor courses, recommendations by school officials, and extracurricular activities record. Applications are accepted on-line via the Rivier web site.

Procedure: Freshmen are admitted fall and spring. Entrance exams should be taken in the junior or senior year. There are deferred admissions and rolling admissions plans. Application deadlines are open.

Transfer: 153 transfer students enrolled in a recent year. Transfer applicants should have a minimum GPA of 2.5 and submit SAT I or ACT scores if they have earned fewer than 12 credits at the previous institution. Official college transcripts are required and an interview is recommended. 60 credits of 120 must be completed at Rivier.

Visiting: There are regularly scheduled orientations for prospective students, including an opportunity to interview, a tour, class visits, and opportunities to meet with faculty, coaches, and current students. There are guides for informal visits and visitors may sit in on classes and stay overnight. To schedule a visit, contact the Office of Undergraduate Admissions.

Financial Aid: In a recent year, 88% of all freshmen and 82% of continuing students received some form of financial aid. 92% of freshmen and 71% of continuing students received need-based aid. The average freshman award was $7100. Of that total, scholarships or need-based grants averaged $7841 ($10,000 maximum); loans averaged $2536 ($2625 maximum); and work contracts averaged $2000 ($2000 maximum). 35% of undergraduates work part time. Average annual earnings from campus work are $546. The average financial indebtedness of the 2001 graduate was $16,554. Rivier is a member of CSS. The FAFSA is required. The fall application deadline is February 1.

International Students: The school actively recruits international students. They must score 500 on the written TOEFL and also take the college's own test.

Computers: The mainframes consist of a Sun SPARC 20 with NEC and DEC ALPHA servers. The Academic Computing Center houses high-speed Pentium workstations with a wide range of software and services. All students are provided with private server storage, Internet access, and an e-mail account. Residence halls are wired for access to the college network and the Web. All students may access the system 24 hours a day. There are no time limits. The fee varies.

Graduates: In a recent year, 200 bachelor's degrees were awarded. The most popular majors were education (25%), nursing (21%), and paralegal studies (15%). Of the 2000 graduating class, 21% were enrolled in graduate school within 6 months of graduation and 99% were employed.

Admissions Contact: Heather Hardcastle.
E-mail: *rivadmit@rivier.edu* Web: *www.rivier.edu*

SAINT ANSELM COLLEGE — D-6

Manchester, NH 03102 — (603) 641-7500
(888) 4 ANSELM; Fax: (603) 641-7550

Full-time: 842 men, 1046 women	**Faculty:** 122; IIB, -$
Part-time: 44 men, 32 women	**Ph.D.s:** 94%
Graduate: none	**Student/Faculty:** 15 to 1
Year: semesters, summer session	**Tuition:** $20,055
Application Deadline: March 1	**Room & Board:** $7350
Freshman Class: 2553 applied, 1912 accepted, 546 enrolled	
SAT I Verbal/Math: 560/560	**COMPETITIVE**

Saint Anselm College, founded in 1889, is a private Roman Catholic institution offering a liberal arts education. In addition to regional accreditation, Saint Anselm has baccalaureate program accreditation with NLN. The library contains 219,000 volumes, 65,000 microform items, and 8000 audiovisual forms/CDs, and subscribes to 3900 periodicals. Computerized library services include the card catalog, interlibrary loans, and database searching. Special learning facilities include a learning resource center, art gallery, and planetarium. The 404-acre campus is in a suburban area 50 miles north of Boston. Including residence halls, there are 63 buildings.

Student Life: 74% of undergraduates are from out of state, mostly the Northeast. Others are from 27 states, 16 foreign countries, and Canada. 67% are from public schools. 93% are white. Most are Catholic. The average age of freshmen is 18; all undergraduates, 20. 20% do not continue beyond their first year; 70% remain to graduate.

Housing: 1644 students can be accommodated in college housing, which includes single-sex dormitories and on-campus apartments. On-campus housing is guaranteed for all 4 years. 88% of students live on campus; of those, 85% remain on campus on weekends. All students may keep cars.

Activities: There are no fraternities or sororities. There are 64 groups on campus, including art, cheerleading, chess, choir, chorale, chorus, computers, dance, debate, drama, ethnic, honors, international, jazz band, literary magazine, newspaper, pep band, photography, political, professional, religious, social, social service, student government, and yearbook. Popular campus events include Winter Weekend, Family Weekend, and Road for Hope.

Sports: There are 10 intercollegiate sports for men and 9 for women, and 13 intramural sports for men and 13 for women. Facilities include a 1500-seat gym, an activity center that houses basketball, volleyball, tennis, and racquetball courts, and weight and training rooms, a 2500-seat stadium, a 500-seat baseball stadium, and athletic fields.

Disabled Students: 60% of the campus is accessible. Wheelchair ramps, elevators, special parking, specially equipped rest rooms, special class scheduling, and lowered drinking fountains are available.

Services: Counseling and information services are available, as is tutoring in most subjects. There is a reader service for the blind.

Campus Safety and Security: Measures include 24-hour foot and vehicle patrol, informal discussions, pamphlets/posters/films, and emergency telephones. There are lighted pathways/sidewalks and security escort upon request.

Programs of Study: Saint Anselm confers B.A. and B.S.N. degrees. Bachelor's degrees are awarded in BIOLOGICAL SCIENCE (biochemistry and biology/biological science), BUSINESS (accounting, banking and finance, and business administration and management), COMMUNICATIONS AND THE ARTS (classics, English, fine arts, French, and Spanish), COMPUTER AND PHYSICAL SCIENCE (chemistry, computer science, mathematics, and natural sciences), EDUCATION (secondary), ENGINEERING AND ENVIRONMENTAL DESIGN (engineering and environmental science), HEALTH PROFESSIONS (nursing, predentistry, and premedicine), SOCIAL SCIENCE (criminal justice, economics, history, liberal arts/general studies, philosophy, political science/government, prelaw, psychology, sociology, and theological studies). Business, English, and psychology are the largest.

Required: All students must maintain a GPA of 2.0 in the major while completing at least 40 semester courses, including 4 semesters in the humanities, 2 each in English and lab science, 3 each in philosophy and theology, and 2 to 4 in foreign language; 10 to 13 courses are required in the major area of study.

Special: Saint Anselm offers a 5-year liberal arts and a 3-2 engineering program in cooperation with Manhattan College, Notre Dame University, University of Massachusetts Lowell, and Catholic University of America. Cross-registration is possible. In addition, internships, a Washington semester, study abroad, and nondegree study are available. There are 11 national honor societies, and a freshman honors program.

Faculty/Classroom: 57% of faculty are male; 43%, female. All teach undergraduates. The average class size in an introductory lecture is 20; in a laboratory, 14; and in a regular course, 24.

Admissions: 75% of the 2001-2002 applicants were accepted. The SAT I scores for the 2001-2002 freshman class were: Verbal--18% below 500, 54% between 500 and 599, 26% between 600 and 700, and 2% above 700; Math--17% below 500, 57% between 500 and 599, 24% between 600 and 700, and 2% above 700. 37% of the current freshmen were in the top fifth of their class; 72% were in the top two fifths. 5 freshmen graduated first in their class.

Requirements: The SAT I is required. In addition, applicants must have 16 academic credits and 16 Carnegie units, including 4 years of English, 3 each of math and science, 2 of foreign language, and 1 each of history and social studies. An essay is required and an interview is recommended. The GED is accepted. A GPA of 2.0 is required. AP and CLEP credits are accepted. Important factors in the admissions decision are advanced placement or honor courses, leadership record, and recommendations by school officials. Applications are accepted on disk or on-line via Common App.

Procedure: Freshmen are admitted fall and spring. Entrance exams should be taken during the spring of the junior year or fall of the senior year. There are early decision, early admissions, and deferred admissions plans. Early decision applications should be filed by December 1; regular applications, by March 1 for fall entry and December 1 for spring entry, along with a $50 fee. Notification of early decision is sent December 15; regular decision, on a rolling basis. 46 early decision candidates were accepted for the 2001-2002 class. 2% of all applicants are on a waiting list.

Transfer: 23 transfer students enrolled in 2001-2002. Transfer students must have a minimum GPA of 2.5 after earning at least 30 college credits. The SAT I is required and an interview is recommended. In addition, 2 letters of recommendation are necessary. 20 courses of 40 must be completed at Saint Anselm.

Visiting: There are regularly scheduled orientations for prospective students, consisting of daily individual interviews and/or group information sessions followed by a campus tour. There are guides for informal visits and visitors may sit in on classes and stay overnight. To schedule a visit, contact the Admissions Office.

Financial Aid: In 2001-2002, 82% of all freshmen and 84% of continuing students received some form of financial aid. 85% of freshmen and 84% of continuing students received need-based aid. The average freshman award was $16,189. Of that total, scholarships or need-based grants averaged $8287 ($19,460 maximum); loans averaged $2500 ($5125 maximum); and work contracts averaged $1000 (maximum). 45% of undergraduates work part time. Average annual earnings from campus work are $641. The average financial indebtedness of the 2001 graduate was $17,897. The CSS/Profile or FAFSA is required. The fall application deadline is March 15.

International Students: There are 16 international students enrolled. The school actively recruits these students. They must score 550 on the written TOEFL or 213 on the electronic version and also take the SAT I or the ACT.

Computers: The mainframe is an IBM AS/400. 3 main computer centers on campus contain more than 50 Macs and 125 PCs. All are networked to print- and file-sharing servers and all have high-speed (T3) Internet access. Additional computers are located in psychology, physics, chemistry, biology, and math department labs. All students may access the system 8:30 A.M. to midnight, Monday through Friday; 10 a.m to 6 p.m Saturday; 1 P.M. to 12 A.M., Sunday. Students also have 24-hour, 7 days a week connection to the Internet from all residence halls and classrooms. There are no time limits and no fees.

Graduates: In 2001, 408 bachelor's degrees were awarded. The most popular majors were economics/business (19%), psychology (12%), and nursing (10%). In an average class, 67% graduate in 4 years, 71% in 5 years, and 71% in 6 years. 75 companies recruited on campus in 2000-2001. Of the 2000 graduating class, 13% were enrolled in graduate school within 6 months of graduation and 80% were employed.

Admissions Contact: Admissions Office.
E-mail: *admissions@anselm.edu* Web: *www.anselm.edu*

SOUTHERN NEW HAMPSHIRE UNIVERSITY (Formerly New Hampshire College) D-6

Manchester, NH 03106-1045 (603) 645-9611
(800) 642-4968; Fax: (603) 645-9693

Full-time: 1144 men, 1287 women	**Faculty:** 65; IIA, av$
Part-time: 633 men, 843 women	**Ph.D.s:** 65%
Graduate: 865 men, 812 women	**Student/Faculty:** 37 to 1
Year: semesters, summer session	**Tuition:** $16,786
Application Deadline: March 15	**Room & Board:** $7066

Freshman Class: 1953 applied, 1602 accepted, 491 enrolled
SAT I Verbal/Math: 473/482 **COMPETITIVE**

Southern New Hampshire University, founded in 1932, is a private institution offering business, liberal arts, and hospitality disciplines. In addition to regional accreditation, SNHU has baccalaureate program accreditation with ACBSP. The library contains 79,621 volumes, 320,236 microform items, and 2105 audiovisual forms/CDs, and subscribes to 529 periodicals. Computerized library services include the card catalog, interlibrary loans, and database searching. Special learning facilities include a learning resource center, art gallery, radio station, TV station, and an audiovisual studio. The 280-acre campus is in a suburban area 55 miles north of Boston. Including residence halls, there are 25 buildings.

Student Life: 70% of undergraduates are from out of state, mostly the Northeast. Others are from 23 states, 60 foreign countries, and Canada. 80% are from public schools. 42% are white. 50% are Catholic; 35% Protestant; 10% Jewish. The average age of freshmen is 19; all undergraduates, 21. 30% do not continue beyond their first year; 50% remain to graduate.

Housing: 1138 students can be accommodated in college housing, which includes single-sex and coed dormitories and on-campus apartments. In addition, there are special-interest houses, and a wellness housing area. On-campus housing is guaranteed for the freshman year only and is available on a first-come, first-served basis. 80% of students live on campus; of those, 75% remain on campus on weekends. All students may keep cars.

Activities: 3% of men belong to 4 national fraternities; 3% of women belong to 1 national and 3 local sororities. There are 35 groups on campus, including cheerleading, dance, drama, ethnic, honors, international, literary magazine, musical theater, newspaper, professional, radio and TV, religious, social, social service, student government, and yearbook. Popular campus events include Fall, Winter, and Spring Weekends, Family Weekend, and International Night.

Sports: There are 8 intercollegiate sports for men and 7 for women, and 7 intramural sports for men and 6 for women. Facilities include an Olympic-size swimming pool, racquetball court, 2 gyms, a Nautilus weight room, a mirrored dance/exercise room, 2 training rooms, an equipment room, 4 tennis courts, baseball and softball fields, a lighted varsity game field, and several practice fields.

Disabled Students: 90% of the campus is accessible. Wheelchair ramps, elevators, special parking, specially equipped rest rooms, special class scheduling, lowered drinking fountains, lowered telephones, and automatic door openers are available.

Services: Counseling and information services are available, as is tutoring in every subject. There is a reader service for the blind, and remedial math, reading, and writing.

Campus Safety and Security: Measures include 24-hour foot and vehicle patrol, self-defense education, escort service, and informal discussions. There are pamphlets/posters/films, emergency telephones, lighted pathways/sidewalks, and winter driving seminars for international students.

Programs of Study: SNHU confers B.A. and B.S. degrees. Associate, master's, and doctoral degrees are also awarded. Bachelor's degrees are awarded in BUSINESS (accounting, banking and finance, business administration and management, hospitality management services, hotel/motel and restaurant management, international business management, management science, marketing/retailing/merchandising, retailing, sports management, and tourism), COMMUNICATIONS AND THE ARTS (communications, English, and English literature), COMPUTER AND PHYSICAL SCIENCE (information sciences and systems), EDUCATION (business, English, and marketing and distribution), ENGINEERING AND ENVIRONMENTAL DESIGN (technological management), SOCIAL SCIENCE (American studies, economics, humanities, psychology, and social science). Business and culinary arts are the strongest academically. Business administration, accounting, and hotel/restaurant management are the largest.

Required: To graduate, students must complete 120 credit hours, including a maximum of 33 in their major, with a GPA of 2.0. Distribution requirements total 69 credits from the college core, including 2 to 3 courses in writing, 2 in economics, and 1 in math, computer science, public speaking, statistics, and social science, plus a freshman seminar and electives in fine arts or humanities, literature, and the social and natural sciences.

Special: Co-op programs with the area business community are strongly promoted, as is cross-registration through the New Hampshire College and University Council. Students may study abroad in England, the Netherlands, and Malaysia. A general business studies degree with 10 different concentrations, work-study programs, dual majors, an accelerated degree program in business administration, combined B.A.-B.S. degrees, credit for life experience, and nondegree study are available. There are 4 national honor societies and a freshman honors program.

Faculty/Classroom: 60% of faculty are male; 40%, female. 39% teach undergraduates. No introductory courses are taught by graduate students. The average class size in an introductory lecture is 22 and in a regular course, 25.

Admissions: 82% of the 2001-2002 applicants were accepted. The SAT I scores for the 2001-2002 freshman class were: Verbal--65% below 500, 28% between 500 and 599, and 7% between 600 and 700; Math--58% below 500, 32% between 500 and 599, and 7% between 600 and 700. 15% of the current freshmen were in the top fifth of their class; 30% were in the top two fifths.

Requirements: The SAT I is required. In addition, students must have completed 4 years of English and 3 of math. An essay and a letter of recommendation from a guidance counselor or 2 teachers are required, and an interview is strongly recommended. The GED is accepted. SNHU requires applicants to be in the upper 50% of their class. A GPA of 2.0 is required. AP and CLEP credits are accepted. Important factors in the admissions decision are advanced placement or honor courses, recommendations by school officials, and leadership record. Applications are accepted on-line via any educational service, such as Apply, and at the school's web site.

Procedure: Freshmen are admitted to all sessions. There are early decision, early admissions, and deferred admissions plans. Early decision applications should be filed by November 15; regular applications, by March 15 for fall entry and December 1 for spring entry. The 2001 application fee was $25. If the application is received via the school's web site, the application fee is waived. Notification is sent on a rolling basis.

Transfer: 151 transfer students enrolled in 2001-2002. Applicants must have a minimum GPA of 2.0, submit official high school and college transcripts, an essay, and a letter of recommendation. An interview is recommended. 30 credits of 120 must be completed at SNHU.

Visiting: There are regularly scheduled orientations for prospective students, including a greeting from college administrators, campus tours with students, and informal discussions with faculty. There are guides for informal visits and visitors may sit in on classes. To schedule a visit, contact the Admission Office.

Financial Aid: In 2001-2002, 80% of all students received some form of financial aid, including need-based aid. The FAFSA is required. The fall application deadline is March 15.

International Students: The school actively recruits these students. They must score 500 on the written TOEFL.

Computers: The mainframe is an IBM 4381. There are more than 350 terminals, with access available to the Internet and Web. All students may access the system 16 hours daily. There are no time limits and no fees. It is strongly recommended that all students have a personal computer. Students in 3-year degree programs are required to have personal computers. An IBM is recommended.

Graduates: In 2001, 669 bachelor's degrees were awarded. The most popular majors were business administration (37%), hotel and restaurant management (10%), and marketing (6%). In an average class, 25% graduate in 4 years, 30% in 5 years, and 35% in 6 years. 150 companies recruited on campus in 2000-2001.

Admissions Contact: Brad Poznanski, Director of Admission and Enrollment Planning. A video is available. E-mail: *admission@snhu.edu*
Web: *www.snhu.edu*

THOMAS MORE COLLEGE OF LIBERAL ARTS D-6

Merrimack, NH 03054 (603) 880-8308
(800) 880-8308; Fax: (603) 880-9280

Full-time: 37 men, 32 women
Part-time: none
Graduate: none
Year: semesters
Application Deadline: open
Freshman Class: n/av
SAT I or ACT: required
Faculty: 5
Ph.D.s: 100%
Student/Faculty: 14 to 1
Tuition: $10,000
Room & Board: $7700
COMPETITIVE

Thomas More College of Liberal Arts, founded in 1978 by Roman Catholic educators, is an undergraduate institution. In addition to regional accreditation, TMC has baccalaureate program accreditation with AALE. The library contains 50,000 volumes, and subscribes to 20 periodicals. The 12-acre campus is in a suburban area between Nashua and Manchester, 40 miles north of Boston. Including residence halls, there are 5 buildings.

Student Life: 81% of undergraduates are from out of state, mostly the Northeast. Others are from 20 states, 2 foreign countries, and Canada. 84% are white. The average age of freshmen is 18; all undergraduates, 20. 9% do not continue beyond their first year.

Housing: Housing includes single-sex dormitories. On-campus housing is guaranteed for all 4 years. Alcohol is not permitted. All students may keep cars.

Activities: There are no fraternities or sororities.

Disabled Students: 70% of the campus is accessible. Wheelchair ramps, special parking, and specially equipped rest rooms are available.

Services: Informal tutoring is available by request.

Campus Safety and Security: Measures include escort service, informal discussions, and lighted pathways/sidewalks.

Programs of Study: TMC confers the B.A. degree. Bachelor's degrees are awarded in BIOLOGICAL SCIENCE (biology/biological science), COMMUNICATIONS AND THE ARTS (literature), SOCIAL SCIENCE (philosophy and political science/government).

Required: To graduate, students must complete 120 credit hours, (125 for biology majors), including 48 in humanities, 12 in writing workshop, 12 in classical languages, 12 in math and science, 6 in theology, and 3 in fine arts. At least 24 hours (32 for biology majors) in the major are required. In addition, students must complete a junior project of independent study and a senior thesis.

Special: A semester in Rome for sophomores is required unless waived.

Faculty/Classroom: 80% of faculty are male; 20%, female. All teach undergraduates, 80% do research, and 80% do both.

Admissions: There were 2 National Merit finalists.

Requirements: The SAT I or ACT is required. In addition, applicants should be high school graduates with 4 college preparatory units of English, 3 of math, and 2 each of foreign language, social science, and lab science. The GED is accepted. An essay and 2 letters of recommendation are required. An interview is strongly recommended. Important factors in the admissions decision are personality/intangible qualities, evidence of special talent, and leadership record. Applications are accepted on-line at the school's web site.

Procedure: Freshmen are admitted fall and spring. Application deadlines are open. The fall 2001 application fee was $25. Notification is sent on a rolling basis.

Transfer: 4 transfer students enrolled in 2001-2002. Applicants must submit a transcript from all higher institutions attended.

Visiting: There are guides for informal visits and visitors may sit in on classes and stay overnight. To schedule a visit, contact Kristen S. Kelly, Director of Admissions.

Financial Aid: In a recent year, 80% of all freshmen and 90% of continuing students received some form of financial aid. 65% of freshmen and 77% of continuing students received need-based aid. The average freshman award was $8768. Of that total, scholarships or need-based grants averaged $6117 ($9200 maximum); loans averaged $2625; and work contracts averaged $1960. 59% of undergraduates work part time. Average annual earnings from campus work are $1960. The average financial indebtedness of a recent year's graduate was $13,056. TMC is a member of CSS. The FAFSA is required.

International Students: There are 2 international students enrolled. The school actively recruits these students. It is strongly recommended that students take either the SAT I or the ACT.

Computers: There are 6 computers in the library for e-mail, Internet access, and word processing. All students may access the system durning library hours. There are no time limits and no fees.

Graduates: In 2001, 12 bachelor's degrees were awarded. The most popular majors were philosophy (33%), political science (33%), and literature (25%). In an average class, all graduate in 4 years. Of the 2000 graduating class, 27% were enrolled in graduate school within 6 months of graduation and 73% were employed.

Admissions Contact: Kristen S. Kelly, Director of Admissions.
E-mail: *admissions@thomasmorecollege.edu*
Web: *www.thomasmorecollege.edu*

UNIVERSITY OF NEW HAMPSHIRE E-5

Durham, NH 03824 (603) 862-1360; Fax: (603) 862-0077

Full-time: 4174 men, 5796 women
Part-time: 185 men, 245 women
Graduate: 880 men, 1124 women
Year: semesters, summer session
Application Deadline: February 1
Faculty: 476; I, -$
Ph.D.s: 95%
Student/Faculty: 21 to 1
Tuition: $7693 ($17,113)
Room & Board: $5514
Freshman Class: 10,093 applied, 7708 accepted, 2555 enrolled
SAT I Verbal/Math: 550/550
COMPETITIVE

The University of New Hampshire, founded in 1866, is part of the public university system of New Hampshire and offers degree programs in liberal arts, engineering, physical sciences, business, economics, life sciences, agriculture, and health and human services. There are 7 undergraduate schools and 1 graduate school. In addition to regional accreditation, UNH has baccalaureate program accreditation with AACSB, ABET, ADA, AHEA, CAHEA, CSAB, CSWE, NASM, NLN, and SAF. The 5 libraries contain 1,683,444 volumes, 2,050,726 microform items, and 22,761 audiovisual forms/CDs, and subscribe to 9200 periodicals. Computerized library services include the card catalog, interlibrary loans, and database searching. Special learning facilities include a learning resource center, art gallery, radio station, TV station, observatory, marine labs, experiential learning center, child development center, and various agricultural and equine facilities. The 2600-acre campus is in a rural area 60 miles north of Boston. Including residence halls, there are 135 buildings.

Student Life: 59% of undergraduates are from New Hampshire. Others are from 40 states, 27 foreign countries, and Canada. 79% are from public schools. 89% are white. 35% are Catholic; 31% claim no religious affiliation; 26% Protestant. The average age of freshmen is 18; all undergraduates, 20. 14% do not continue beyond their first year; 71% remain to graduate.

Housing: 5700 students can be accommodated in college housing, which includes single-sex and coed dormitories, on-campus apartments, and married-student housing. In addition, there are honors houses, language houses, special-interest houses, international and independent living residence halls. On-campus housing is guaranteed for the freshman year only, is available on a first-come, first-served basis, and is available on a lottery system for upperclassmen. 50% of students live on campus; of those, 25% remain on campus on weekends. Upperclassmen may keep cars.

Activities: 5% of men belong to 1 local fraternity and 11 national fraternities; 5% of women belong to 5 national sororities. There are 133 groups on campus, including art, band, cheerleading, chess, choir, chorale, chorus, computers, dance, drama, ethnic, film, gay, honors, international, jazz band, literary magazine, marching band, musical theater, newspaper, opera, orchestra, pep band, photography, political, professional, radio and TV, religious, social, social service, student government, symphony, and yearbook. Popular campus events include International Day, Family Weekend, and Spring Fling.

Sports: There are 10 intercollegiate sports for men and 14 for women, and 12 intramural sports for men and 13 for women, and 12 coed intramural sports. Facilities include indoor and outdoor swimming pools, tracks, tennis courts, gyms, wrestling and gymnastics rooms, a dance studio, playing fields, an indoor ice rink, and cross-country ski trails. A 3-story recreation and sports complex, which seats 6000 at hockey and basketball games and special events, includes a fitness center, jogging track, a weight room, racquetball courts, an international squash court, aerobics and martial arts studios, multipurpose courts, and basketball courts.

Disabled Students: 80% of the campus is accessible. Wheelchair ramps, elevators, special parking, specially equipped rest rooms, special class scheduling, lowered drinking fountains, lowered telephones are available. Accommodations made on a case-by-case basis include sign language interpreters, reduced course loads, extended exam time, accessible transportation, academic modifications, note takers, text on tape, and readers.

Services: Counseling and information services are available. Instruction in learning strategies, study skills, time management, and organizational skills is available. The university writing center offers free assistance by trained consultants.

Campus Safety and Security: Measures include 24-hour foot and vehicle patrol, self-defense education, escort service, and shuttle buses. There are informal discussions, pamphlets/posters/films, emergency telephones, and lighted pathways/sidewalks.

Programs of Study: UNH confers B.A., B.S., B.F.A., B.M., and B.S.F. degrees. Associate, master's, and doctoral degrees are also awarded. Bachelor's degrees are awarded in AGRICULTURE (animal science, dairy science, equine science, forestry and related sciences, horticulture, natural resource management, plant science, soil science, and wildlife management), BIOLOGICAL SCIENCE (biochemistry, biology/biological science, biotechnology, ecology, marine biology, microbiology, molecular biology, nutrition, and zoology), BUSINESS (business administration and management, hotel/motel and restaurant management, recreation and leisure services, and tourism), COMMUNICATIONS AND

THE ARTS (art history and appreciation, classics, communications, dramatic arts, English, fine arts, French, German, Greek, journalism, Latin, linguistics, music, music history and appreciation, music performance, music theory and composition, performing arts, Russian, Spanish, studio art, and voice), COMPUTER AND PHYSICAL SCIENCE (chemistry, computer science, earth science, geology, hydrology, mathematics, and physics), EDUCATION (athletic training, English, mathematics, music, physical, and recreation), ENGINEERING AND ENVIRONMENTAL DESIGN (chemical engineering, city/community/regional planning, civil engineering, computer engineering, electrical/electronics engineering, energy management technology, engineering technology, environmental engineering, environmental science, mechanical engineering, and mechanical engineering technology), HEALTH PROFESSIONS (health care administration, medical laboratory science, nursing, occupational therapy, preveterinary science, and speech pathology/audiology), SOCIAL SCIENCE (anthropology, economics, family/consumer studies, French studies, geography, history, humanities, international studies, philosophy, physical fitness/movement, political science/government, psychology, social work, sociology, water resources, and women's studies). Psychology, English, and biological sciences are the strongest academically. Business administration, biology, and psychology are the largest.

Required: To graduate, all students must maintain a GPA of 2.0 and complete at least 128 credits, with a minimum of 36 credits and 10 classes in the major. General education requirements include 4 writing-intensive courses, including freshman composition; 3 courses each in quantitative reasoning and science; and 1 course each in historical perspectives, social science, fine arts, foreign culture, and philosophy/literature. Honors students and most seniors write a thesis or complete a project.

Special: Co-op programs with Cornell University in marine science are available. Extensive cross-registration is possible through the New Hampshire College and University Council Consortium. There also is nationwide study through the National Student Exchange and worldwide study through the Center for International Education. Internships, a Washington semester, work-study, B.A.-B.S. degrees, dual majors, a general studies degree, student-designed majors, extensive 3-2 B.S./M.B.A. programs and other bachelor's/graduate degree plans, nondegree study, and pass/fail options are available. A 3-2 engineering degree is offered with the New Hampshire Technical Institute, Vermont Technical College, Keene State College, and other institutions. There are 21 national honor societies, including Phi Beta Kappa, a freshman honors program, and 53 departmental honors program.

Faculty/Classroom: 62% of faculty are male; 38%, female. 82% teach undergraduates, all do research, and 82% do both. Graduate students teach 8% of introductory courses. The average class size in an introductory lecture is 37; in a laboratory, 23; and in a regular course, 17.

Admissions: 76% of the 2001-2002 applicants were accepted. The SAT I scores for the 2001-2002 freshman class were: Verbal--24% below 500, 50% between 500 and 599, 23% between 600 and 700, and 3% above 700; Math--19% below 500, 48% between 500 and 599, 29% between 600 and 700, and 4% above 700. 45% of the current freshmen were in the top fifth of their class; 86% were in the top two fifths. There were 10 National Merit semifinalists. 29 freshmen graduated first in their class.

Requirements: The SAT I or ACT is required, with a composite SAT I score of 1080 recommended. Applicants should have 18 academic credits, including 4 years each in English, math, and lab science and 3 each in foreign language and 2 social studies. Students with a specific major in mind are encouraged to take SAT II: Subject tests relating to that major. An essay is required for all students and an informational interview recommended. For art students, a portfolio is required, as is an audition for music students. The GED is accepted. AP and CLEP credits are accepted. Important factors in the admissions decision are advanced placement or honor courses, recommendations by school officials, and evidence of special talent. Applications are accepted by mail; on computer disk; or on-line at the school's web site or via College View, Apply, CollegeLink, or Common App.

Procedure: Freshmen are admitted fall and spring. Entrance exams should be taken before February 1 of the senior year. There are early admissions and deferred admissions plans. Applications should be filed by February 1 for fall entry and November 1 for spring entry, along with a $35 fee ($50 out of state). Notification is sent April 15.

Transfer: 472 transfer students enrolled in 2001-2002. Applicants must submit an overall minimum GPA of 2.5 and 3.0 in a general education curriculum. The SAT I or the ACT is required. 32 credits of 128 must be completed at UNH.

Visiting: There are regularly scheduled orientations for prospective students, including campus tours, a student panel, and general information sessions. There are guides for informal visits and visitors may sit in on classes. To schedule a visit, contact the Admissions Office.

Financial Aid: In 2001-2002, 75% of all freshmen and 67% of continuing students received some form of financial aid. 52% of freshmen and 47% of continuing students received need-based aid. The average freshman award was $11,075. Of that total, scholarships or need-based grants averaged $3437 ($22,410 maximum); loans averaged $5793 ($6625 maximum); and work contracts averaged $1845 ($2500 maximum). 25% of undergraduates work part time. Average annual earnings from campus work are $1817. The average financial indebtedness of the 2001 graduate was $19,515. UNH is a member of CSS. The FAFSA is required. The fall application deadline is March 1.

International Students: There are 76 international students enrolled. The school actively recruits these students. They must score 550 on the written TOEFL or 213 on the electronic version and also take the SAT I or the ACT.

Computers: The mainframes are a Compaq Alpha Server 2100 and 4100. Each dorm room is fitted with Ethernet ports for each student to access the campus network mainframe and Internet. In addition, there are nearly 280 computers located in 6 clusters on the campus, more than 100 computers in the library, and 200 active Ethernet ports available in the library for students with laptop computers. All students may access the system. There are no time limits and no fees.

Graduates: In 2001, 2148 bachelor's degrees were awarded. The most popular majors were business administration (13%), English (8%), and psychology (7%). In an average class, 49% graduate in 4 years, 69% in 5 years, and 71% in 6 years. 194 companies recruited on campus in 2000-2001.

Admissions Contact: Cecilia J. Leslie, Executive Director, Admissions. E-mail: *admissions@unh.edu* Web: *www.unh.edu/admissions/*

UNIVERSITY SYSTEM OF NEW HAMPSHIRE

The University System of New Hampshire, established in 1963, consists of the Universities of New Hampshire at Durham and Manchester, the State Colleges at Keene and Plymouth, and the statewide College for Lifelong Learning. A dozen more organizations—such as the NH Agricultural Experiment Station, Cooperative Extension, and NH Public Television—are also affiliated with the university system. The University System is governed by a single Board of Trustees, which is assigned management and control of the property and affairs of the system. Under state law the board is comprised of 27 trustees—11 members appointed by the governor, with the advice and consent of the 5 person Executive Council; 4 members, at least 1 of whom is a resident of New Hampshire, are elected by the alumni of the University of New Hampshire; 1 member is elected by the Keene State College alumni; 1 member is elected by the Plymouth State College alumni; and 2 members are students elected by the student body, on a rotating basis, of each of the residential institutions of the system. In addition, there are 8 ex-officio members of the board, including the presidents of the four member institutions, the chancellor, the Commissioner of the Department of Agriculture, the Commissioner of the Department of Education, and the governor. The total enrollment at all campuses is just under 30,000, with more than 1000 faculty members. There are 181 baccalaureate, 80 master's, and 21 doctoral programs offered in the system. 4-year campuses are located in Durham, Keene, and Plymouth. Profiles of those campuses are included in this section.

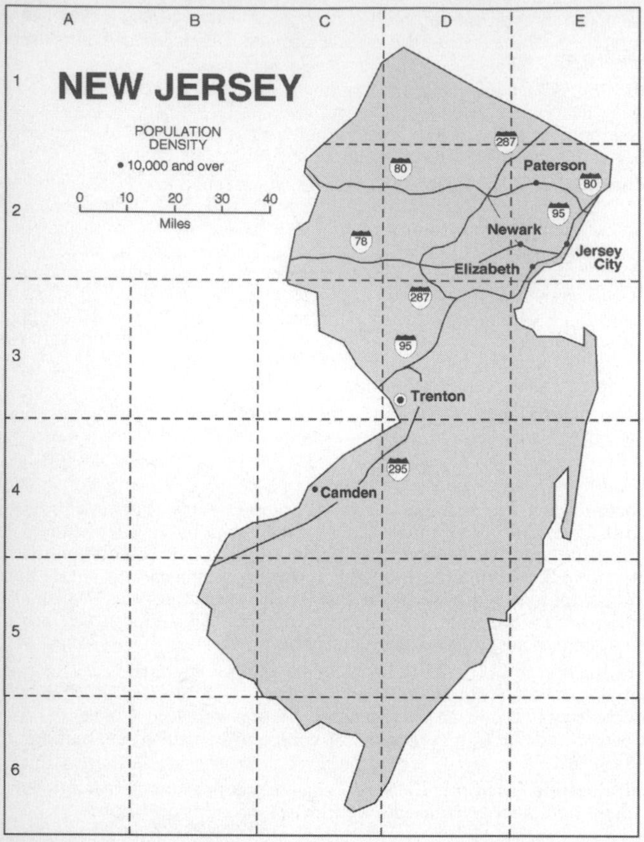

BLOOMFIELD COLLEGE E-2
Bloomfield, NJ 07003 **(973) 748-9000, ext. 392**
(800) 848-4555; Fax: (973) 748-0916

Full-time: 420 men, 833 women
Part-time: 161 men, 348 women
Graduate: none
Year: semesters, summer session
Application Deadline: open
Freshman Class: 1437 applied, 802 accepted, 312 enrolled
SAT I Verbal/Math: 430/430
Faculty: 61; IIB, av$
Ph.D.s: 78%
Student/Faculty: 21 to 1
Tuition: $11,450
Room & Board: $5550
COMPETITIVE

Bloomfield College, founded in 1868 and affiliated with the Presbyterian Church (U.S.A.), is an independent institution offering programs in liberal arts and sciences, creative arts and technology, professional studies, and the clinical and health sciences. In addition to regional accreditation, Bloomfield has baccalaureate program accreditation with NLN. The library contains 64,700 volumes, 59 microform items, and 1148 audiovisual forms/CDs, and subscribes to 456 periodicals. Computerized library services include interlibrary loans and database searching. Special learning facilities include a learning resource center, art gallery, and electronic classrooms. The 12-acre campus is in a suburban area 15 miles from New York City. Including residence halls, there are 35 buildings.

Student Life: 96% of undergraduates are from New Jersey. Others are from 15 states and 2 foreign countries. 70% are from public schools. 50% are African American; 19% white; 17% Hispanic. The average age of freshmen is 21; all undergraduates, 28. 66% do not continue beyond their first year; 33% remain to graduate.

Housing: 259 students can be accommodated in college housing, which includes single-sex and coed dormitories, fraternity houses, and sorority houses. In addition, there are honors houses and special-interest houses. On-campus housing is available on a first-come, first-served basis. Priority is given to out-of-town students. 85% of students commute. All students may keep cars.

Activities: 5% of men belong to 1 local fraternity and 3 national fraternities; 2% of women belong to 1 local sorority and 2 national sororities. There are 37 groups on campus, including art, choir, dance, drama, ethnic, film, gay, honors, international, literary magazine, musical theater, newspaper, photography, professional, radio and TV, religious, social, social service, student government, and yearbook. Popular campus events include Formal Dinners, Multicultural Festivals, and Comedy Shows.

Sports: There are 4 intercollegiate sports for men and 4 for women, and 4 intramural sports for men and 4 for women. Facilities include a 600-seat gym, weightlifting facilities, and volleyball court.

Disabled Students: 65% of the campus is accessible. Wheelchair ramps, elevators, special parking, specially equipped rest rooms, lowered drinking fountains, lowered telephones, ADA signage, and lever handles for classroom access are available.

Services: Counseling and information services are available, as is tutoring in most subjects. There is a reader service for the blind, and remedial math, reading, and writing.

Campus Safety and Security: Measures include 24-hour foot and vehicle patrol, escort service, informal discussions, and pamphlets/posters/films. There are emergency telephones, lighted pathways/sidewalks, and security cameras installed in all high-traffic areas.

Programs of Study: Bloomfield confers B.A. and B.S. degrees. Bachelor's degrees are awarded in BIOLOGICAL SCIENCE (biology/biological science), BUSINESS (accounting and business administration and management), COMMUNICATIONS AND THE ARTS (English, fine arts, French, music technology, Spanish, and video), COMPUTER AND PHYSICAL SCIENCE (applied mathematics, chemistry, and information sciences and systems), ENGINEERING AND ENVIRONMENTAL DESIGN (graphic arts technology), HEALTH PROFESSIONS (clinical science and nursing), SOCIAL SCIENCE (history, humanities, interdisciplinary studies, philosophy, political science/government, psychology, religion, and sociology). Nursing is the strongest academically. Business, sociology, and psychology are the largest.

Required: General education includes common core courses totaling 13.5 course units. To graduate, students must complete 33 course units, with a GPA of 2.0 overall and in the major.

Special: A special B.S./M.S. program in computer information systems is available with the New Jersey Institute of Technology. Internships are avaiable in many programs as well as study abroad in Europe, Asia, Africa, and Latin America. Double and contract majors permitted. There is 1 national honor society, a freshman honors program, and 2 departmental honors programs.

Faculty/Classroom: 55% of faculty are male; 45%, female. All teach undergraduates. The average class size in an introductory lecture is 15; in a laboratory, 12; and in a regular course, 14.

Admissions: 56% of the 2001-2002 applicants were accepted. The SAT I scores for the 2001-2002 freshman class were: Verbal--82% below 500, 15% between 500 and 599, and 2% between 600 and 700; Math--84% below 500, 15% between 500 and 599, and 1% between 600 and 700. 17% of the current freshmen were in the top fifth of their class; 43% were in the top two fifths.

Requirements: The SAT I or ACT is required. In addition, the college requires at least 14 academic units, which should include English, math, history, and lab science. 2 personal recommendations are required. A GPA of 2.4 is required. AP and CLEP credits are accepted. Important factors in the admissions decision are advanced placement or honor courses, recommendations by school officials, and extracurricular activities record. Applications are accepted on-line via the college's web site and Common App.

Procedure: Freshmen are admitted to all sessions. Entrance exams should be taken during the senior year. There are early decision, early admissions, and deferred admissions plans. Application deadlines are open. The fall 2001 application fee was $35. Notification is sent on a rolling basis.

Transfer: 62 transfer students enrolled in 2001-2002. Applicants must present a minimum GPA of 2.0 from an accredited institution and submit official transcripts from all previously attended colleges. 16 credits of 33 must be completed at Bloomfield.

Visiting: There are regularly scheduled orientations for prospective students, consisting of a campus tour, an admissions interview, and other activities by request. There are guides for informal visits and visitors may sit in on classes. To schedule a visit, contact the Office of Admissions at (973) 748-9000, ext. 230.

Financial Aid: In 2001-2002, 95% of all freshmen and 90% of continuing students received some form of financial aid. 91% of freshmen and 89% of continuing students received need-based aid. The average freshman award was $10,900. Of that total, scholarships or need-based grants averaged $7575 ($16,100 maximum); loans averaged $2155 ($6625 maximum); and work contracts averaged $1250 ($3000 maximum). 15% of undergraduates work part time. Average annual earnings from campus work are $1250. The average financial indebtedness of the 2001 graduate was $9900. The FAFSA and the college's own financial statement are required. The fall application deadline is June 1.

International Students: There were 33 international students enrolled in a recent year. They must score 550 on the written TOEFL or 173 on the electronic version.

Computers: The mainframe is an Alpha server DS 20E. Students have access to the Internet and networks through 200 PCs within various computer labs in several buildings. All students may access the system. There are no time limits and no fees.
Graduates: In 2001, 231 bachelor's degrees were awarded. The most popular majors were business administration (24%), sociology (20%), and nursing (12%). In an average class, 14% graduate in 4 years, 27% in 5 years, and 33% in 6 years. 23 companies recruited on campus in 2000-2001. Of the 2000 graduating class, 6% were enrolled in graduate school within 6 months of graduation and 74% were employed.
Admissions Contact: Lourdes Delgado, Dean of Admissions.
E-mail: *admission@bloomfield.edu* Web: *http://www.bloomfield.edu*

CALDWELL COLLEGE E-2
Caldwell, NJ 07006 (973) 618-3224
(800) 831-9178; Fax: (973) 618-3600

Full-time: 372 men, 623 women **Faculty:** 72; IIB, -$
Part-time: 238 men, 690 women **Ph.D.s:** 77%
Graduate: 58 men, 257 women **Student/Faculty:** 13 to 1
Year: semesters, summer session **Tuition:** $14,340
Application Deadline: open **Room & Board:** $6600
Freshman Class: 1150 applied, 887 accepted, 293 enrolled
SAT I Verbal/Math: 460/460 **LESS COMPETITIVE**

Caldwell College, founded in 1939, is a private school offering programs in liberal arts, science, business, fine arts, and education. It is affiliated with the Roman Catholic Church. There is 1 graduate school. The library contains 126,805 volumes, 3921 microform items, and 3994 audiovisual forms/CDs, and subscribes to 890 periodicals. Computerized library services include the card catalog, interlibrary loans, and database searching. Special learning facilities include a learning resource center, art gallery, and TV station. The 80-acre campus is in a suburban area 20 miles west of New York City. Including residence halls, there are 7 buildings.
Student Life: 91% of undergraduates are from New Jersey. Others are from 7 states and 13 foreign countries. 70% are from public schools. 65% are white; 12% African American. The average age of freshmen is 18; all undergraduates, 20. 21% do not continue beyond their first year; 55% remain to graduate.
Housing: 315 students can be accommodated in college housing, which includes coed dormitories. On-campus housing is guaranteed for all 4 years. 63% of students commute. All students may keep cars.
Activities: There are no fraternities or sororities. There are 25 groups on campus, including art, band, cheerleading, choir, ethnic, honors, international, literary magazine, newspaper, orchestra, pep band, professional, radio and TV, religious, social, social service, student government, and yearbook. Popular campus events include Founders Day, Freshman Investiture, and Fall Festival.
Sports: There are 5 intercollegiate sports for men and 5 for women, and 5 intramural sports for men and 5 for women. Facilities include a multipurpose gym, a training room, tennis courts, weight rooms, playing fields, and a pool.
Disabled Students: 85% of the campus is accessible. Wheelchair ramps, elevators, special parking, specially equipped rest rooms, special class scheduling, lowered drinking fountains, and lowered telephones are available.
Services: Counseling and information services are available, as is tutoring in most subjects. There is a reader service for the blind, remedial math, reading, and writing, and a writing lab.
Campus Safety and Security: Measures include 24-hour foot and vehicle patrol, self-defense education, escort service, and informal discussions. There are pamphlets/posters/films, emergency telephones, and lighted pathways/sidewalks.
Programs of Study: Caldwell confers B.A., B.S., and B.F.A. degrees. Master's degrees are also awarded. Bachelor's degrees are awarded in BIOLOGICAL SCIENCE (biology/biological science), BUSINESS (accounting, business administration and management, international business management, management science, and marketing and distribution), COMMUNICATIONS AND THE ARTS (art, communications, English, fine arts, French, music, Spanish, and studio art), COMPUTER AND PHYSICAL SCIENCE (chemistry, computer management, computer science, information sciences and systems, and mathematics), EDUCATION (elementary), HEALTH PROFESSIONS (medical laboratory technology), SOCIAL SCIENCE (criminal justice, history, political science/government, psychology, religion, social studies, and sociology). Liberal arts, education, and sciences are the strongest academically. Business, education, and psychology are the largest.
Required: Students must maintain a minimum GPA of 2.0 while taking 122 credit hours, including a minimum of 30 in the major. The 55-credit core includes 15 credits in religion/philosophy, 6 each in history, English, language, social science, math and computer science, and fine arts, 2 in communication arts, and 1 in phys ed. Students must participate in an outcome assessment that is unique for each department. It is a comprehensive examination for some.
Special: Caldwell offers co-op and internship programs in all majors; study abroad in 3 countries; a Washington semester; 1-semester internships; and work study with Dominican Adult Day Care, Hill Top Day Care, and Family and Child Services of North Essex. B.A.-B.S. degrees in 27 fields, dual majors in all majors, credit for life experience in adult education, nondegree study,student-designed majors, and pass/fail options are possible. The Continuing Education Program offers adults (23 years or older) a chance to complete degree requirements in the evening and Saturdays, and the External Degree Program gives adults an opportunity to earn a degree off campus. There are 13 national honor societies, and a freshman honors program.
Faculty/Classroom: 43% of faculty are male; 57%, female. All teach undergraduates. No introductory courses are taught by graduate students. The average class size in an introductory lecture is 24; in a laboratory, 12; and in a regular course, 16.
Admissions: 77% of the 2001-2002 applicants were accepted. The SAT I scores for the 2001-2002 freshman class were: Verbal--69% below 500, 26% between 500 and 599, and 5% between 600 and 700; Math--67% below 500, 27% between 500 and 599, 5% between 600 and 700, and 1% above 700. 15% of the current freshmen were in the top fifth of their class; 50% were in the top two fifths. 1 freshman graduated first in the class in a recent year.
Requirements: The SAT I is required. In addition, applicants need 16 academic credits or 16 Carnegie units, including 4 years in English, 2 each in foreign language, math, and science, and 1 in history. A written recommendation from a high school counselor is required. A portfolio, audition, and interview are recommended, depending on the field of study. The GED is accepted. A GPA of 2.0 is required. AP and CLEP credits are accepted. Important factors in the admissions decision are advanced placement or honor courses, leadership record, and recommendations by school officials. Applications are accepted on-line at the school's web site and via Apply.
Procedure: Freshmen are admitted to all sessions. Entrance exams should be taken in fall of the senior year. Application deadlines are open. The fall 2001 application fee was $40. Notification is sent on a rolling basis.
Transfer: 62 transfer students enrolled in a recent year. Transfer students must have a minimum GPA of 2.0 (2.5 in teacher education) and 12 transferable credits. 45 credits of 122 must be completed at Caldwell.
Visiting: There are regularly scheduled orientations for prospective students, including a brief presentation by faculty and students, followed by a tour. There are guides for informal visits and visitors may sit in on classes and stay overnight. To schedule a visit, contact the Admissions Office at (973) 618-3500.
Financial Aid: In 2001-2002, 80% of all freshmen and 74% of continuing students received some form of financial aid. Average annual earnings from campus work are $700. The average financial indebtedness of a recent year's graduate was $10,225. Caldwell is a member of CSS. The FAFSA and the college's own financial statement are required. The fall application deadline is June 1.
International Students: The school actively recruits these students. They must score 500 on the written TOEFL.
Computers: The mainframe is an IBM AS/400. Some 75 networked PCs located in labs and computer classrooms are available for word processing, spreadsheet, database, desktop publishing, presentation software, and Internet access. 18 Macs are used for similar purposes, except Internet access. All dorm rooms are wired for Internet access. All students may access the system Monday to Thursday 9 A.M. to 9:30 P.M., Friday 10:30 A.M. to 4 P.M., and weekends 12 P.M. to 5 P.M. There are no time limits and no fees.
Graduates: In a recent year, 232 bachelor's degrees were awarded. The most popular majors were business administration (25%), psychology (13%), and education (12%). In an average class, 1% graduate in 3 years, 41% in 4 years, 53% in 5 years, and 55% in 6 years.
Admissions Contact: Richard Ott, Vice President for Enrollment. A video is available. E-mail: *rott@caldwell.edu* Web: *www.caldwell.edu*

CENTENARY COLLEGE C-2
Hackettstown, NJ 07840 (908) 852-1400
(800) 236-8679; Fax: (908) 852-3454

Full-time: 287 men, 793 women **Faculty:** 47
Part-time: 127 men, 246 women **Ph.D.s:** 60%
Graduate: 44 men, 153 women **Student/Faculty:** 23 to 1
Year: semesters, summer session **Tuition:** $16,030
Application Deadline: open **Room & Board:** $6400
Freshman Class: 514 applied, 425 accepted, 197 enrolled
SAT I Verbal/Math: 496/493 **ACT:** 22 **COMPETITIVE**

Centenary College, founded in 1867, is a private institution affiliated with the United Methodist Church. The college offers undergraduate and graduate programs in liberal arts, business, international studies, education, equine studies, fashion, and fine arts. In addition to regional accreditation, Centenary has baccalaureate program accreditation with NASDTEC. The library contains about 68,000 volumes, 20,000 microform items, and 5000 audiovisual forms/CDs, and subscribes to 375 periodicals. Computerized library services include the card catalog, interlibrary loans, and database searching. Special learning facilities include a learning resource center, art gallery, radio station, TV station, and an equestrian center, a language lab, and a CAD lab. The 42-acre campus is in a suburban area 55 miles west of New York City. Including residence halls, there are 14 buildings.

Student Life: 85% of undergraduates are from New Jersey. Others are from 21 states, 16 foreign countries, and Canada. 76% are from public schools. 55% are white. 72% are claim no religious affiliation; 16% Catholic. The average age of freshmen is 24; all undergraduates, 26. 39% do not continue beyond their first year; 30% remain to graduate.

Housing: 460 students can be accommodated in college housing, which includes single-sex and coed dormitories. On-campus housing is guaranteed for all 4 years. 51% of students commute. All students may keep cars.

Activities: 20% of men belong to 1 local fraternity; 60% of women belong to 3 local sororities. There are 27 groups on campus, including art, cheerleading, chorus, dance, drama, ethnic, honors, international, literary magazine, newspaper, photography, professional, radio and TV, religious, social, social service, student government, and yearbook. Popular campus events include Presidents Ball and Centenary Weekend.

Sports: There are 7 intercollegiate sports for men and 7 for women and a number of intramural sports for both men and women. Facilities include a gym, a fitness center and indoor pool, tennis courts, playing fields, and an equine center and stables.

Disabled Students: 50% of the campus is accessible. Wheelchair ramps, special parking, specially equipped rest rooms, special class scheduling, and lowered telephones are available.

Services: There is remedial math, reading, and writing. Peer tutors are available in most subject areas upon request.

Campus Safety and Security: Measures include self-defense education, escort service, informal discussions, and pamphlets/posters/films. There are lighted pathways/sidewalks.

Programs of Study: Centenary confers B.A., B.S., and B.F.A. degrees. Associate and master's degrees are also awarded. Bachelor's degrees are awarded in AGRICULTURE (equine science), BIOLOGICAL SCIENCE (biology/biological science), BUSINESS (accounting and business administration and management), COMMUNICATIONS AND THE ARTS (applied art, communications, dramatic arts, and English), COMPUTER AND PHYSICAL SCIENCE (mathematics), EDUCATION (elementary and secondary), SOCIAL SCIENCE (criminal justice, fashion design and technology, history, interdisciplinary studies, international studies, political science/government, psychology, and sociology). Equine studies, business, and education certification are the strongest academically. Education certification, equine studies, and business are the largest.

Required: Students must complete a distribution of 40 to 46 semester hours in core courses, including college seminars, and 9 credits in liberal arts studies, as well as the required number of credits, usually 48, for their major. At least 128 semester hours and a minimum GPA of 2.0 are needed to earn the bachelor's degree.

Special: Centenary offers internships in every major. The college offers study abroad in England and other countries, dual and student-designed majors, work-study on-campus, and a pass/fail option. Students aged 25 or older may earn life experience credits. There is 1 national honor society and a freshman honors program.

Faculty/Classroom: 36% of faculty are male; 64%, female. All both teach and do research. No introductory courses are taught by graduate students. The average class size in an introductory lecture is 25; in a laboratory, 20; and in a regular course, 15.

Admissions: 83% of the 2001-2002 applicants were accepted. The SAT I scores for the 2001-2002 freshman class were: Verbal--56% below 500, 33% between 500 and 599, and 11% between 600 and 700; Math--53% below 500, 40% between 500 and 599, 6% between 600 and 700, and 1% above 700. The ACT scores were 29% below 21, 43% between 21 and 23, 14% between 24 and 26, and 14% between 27 and 28. 25% of the current freshmen were in the top fifth of their class; 56% were in the top two fifths. 1 freshman graduated as valedictorian.

Requirements: The SAT I or ACT is required. In addition, minimum scores include an SAT I composite of 800, 400 verbal and 400 math, or an ACT score of 18. Applicants must be graduates of accredited secondary schools or have earned a GED. Centenary requires 16 academic credits or Carnegie units, based on 4 years of English, math, and science, and 2 years each of foreign language and history. An essay is required for freshmen, and an interview is recommended. Applicants to specific fine arts programs must also submit a portfolio. Application may be made on-line at *www.centenarycollege.edu*. Centenary requires applicants to be in the upper 50% of their class. A GPA of 2.0 is required. AP and CLEP credits are accepted. Important factors in the admissions decision are advanced placement or honor courses, leadership record, and ability to finance college education.

Procedure: Freshmen are admitted fall and spring. Entrance exams should be taken as early as possible in the senior year. There is a deferred admissions plan. Application deadlines are open. The fee in 2001 was $30.

Transfer: 129 transfer students enrolled in 2001-2002. Applicants must have a minimum college GPA of 2.0 and submit proof of high school graduation or the equivalent. 32 credits of 128 must be completed at Centenary.

Visiting: There are regularly scheduled orientations for prospective students, including basic skills testing, advising, registration, and social events. Visitors may sit in on classes and stay overnight. To schedule a visit, contact the Admissions Office at *admissions@centenarycollege.edu*

Financial Aid: In 2001-2002, 89% of all freshmen and 86% of continuing students received some form of financial aid. 66% of freshmen and 68% of continuing students received need-based aid. The average freshman award was $12,083. Of that total, scholarships or need-based grants averaged $6903 ($9600 maximum); loans averaged $4677 ($6625 maximum); work contracts averaged $561 ($1200 maximum); and grants in return for institutional service or community project $1396 ($9600 maximum). 75% of undergraduates work part time. Average annual earnings from campus work are $800. The average financial indebtedness of the 2001 graduate was $16,534. The FAFSA and the college's own financial statement are required. The fall application deadline is September 1.

International Students: There are 90 international students enrolled. The school actively recruits these students. They must score 450 on the written TOEFL and also take the SAT I or the ACT.

Computers: The PC and CAD labs are available for instructional and student use. Access to the Internet is available in the library. All resident students are issued a PC, and each residence room is equipped with a color printer, a telephone line, voice mail, and Internet access. The library is fully equipped with an automated, integrated library system. All students may access the system. Computer and CAD lab use depends on lab hours. The fee is $350 annual technology fee.

Graduates: 126 bachelor's degrees were awarded for a recent class. The most popular majors were business administration (21%), psychology (13%), and liberal arts (13%). In an average class, 25% graduate in 4 years, and 60% in 5 years. 35 companies recruited on campus in 2000-2001. Of the 2000 graduating class, 10% were enrolled in graduate school within 6 months of graduation and 70% were employed.

Admissions Contact: Glenna Warren, Dean of Admissions.
E-mail: *admissions@centenarycollege.edu* Web: *centenarycollege.edu*

COLLEGE OF NEW JERSEY, THE — D-3

Ewing, NJ 08628-0718 (609) 771-2131
(800) 624-0967; Fax: (609) 637-5174

Full-time: 2324 men, 3303 women	**Faculty:** 329
Part-time: 124 men, 222 women	**Ph.D.s:** 88%
Graduate: 159 men, 715 women	**Student/Faculty:** 17 to 1
Year: semesters, summer session	**Tuition:** $6661 ($10,409)
Application Deadline: February 15	**Room & Board:** $6764
Freshman Class: 5988 applied, 3069 accepted, 1262 enrolled	
SAT I Verbal/Math: 620/650	**HIGHLY COMPETITIVE**

The College of New Jersey, founded in 1855, is a public institution offering programs in the liberal arts, sciences, business, engineering, nursing, and education. There are 7 undergraduate schools and 1 graduate school. In addition to regional accreditation, TCNJ has baccalaureate program accreditation with AACSB, ABET, CSAB, NASDTEC, NASM, NCATE, and NLN. The library contains 566,460 volumes, 319,021 microform items, and 22,950 audiovisual forms/CDs, and subscribes to 1341 periodicals. Computerized library services include the card catalog, interlibrary loans, and database searching. Special learning facilities include a learning resource center, art gallery, planetarium, radio station, TV station, an electron microscopy lab, and greenhouses. The 289-acre campus is in a suburban area between Princeton and Trenton. Including residence halls, there are 38 buildings.

Student Life: 95% of undergraduates are from New Jersey. Others are from 22 states and 12 foreign countries. 65% are from public schools. 81% are white. 50% are Catholic; 20% Protestant; 14% claim no religious affiliation; 12% Eastern Orthodox, Buddhist, Muslim, Islamic, Quaker. The average age of freshmen is 18; all undergraduates, 20. 4% do not continue beyond their first year; 80% remain to graduate.

Housing: 3624 students can be accommodated in college housing, which includes single-sex and coed dormitories, on-campus apartments, and off-campus apartments. In addition, there are honors houses, special-interest houses, a music house, an engineering house, study floors with extended quiet hours, wellness housing units, and a living-learning center for the First-Year Experience taken by all entering students. On-campus housing is guaranteed for the freshman year only and is available on a lottery system for upperclassmen. 61% of students live on campus; of those, 70% remain on campus on weekends. Upperclassmen may keep cars.

Activities: 6% of men belong to 2 local and 9 national fraternities; 8% of women belong to 13 national sororities. There are 186 groups on campus, including art, band, cheerleading, choir, chorale, chorus, computers, dance, drama, ethnic, film, foreign language, gay, honors, international, jazz band, literary magazine, musical theater, newspaper, opera, orchestra, pep band, photography, political, professional, radio and TV, recreational, religious, social, social service, student government, symphony, and yearbook. Popular campus events include Welcome Week, Ewing Community Day, and Heritage Day.

Sports: There are 11 intercollegiate sports for men and 10 for women, and 7 intramural sports for men and 7 for women. Facilities include a 5000-seat stadium with an Astroturf field, an aquatic center, baseball and softball diamonds, an NCAA-approved all-weather track, lighted tennis courts, a sand volleyball court, a 1200-seat gym, and a student recreation center with a wellness center, tennis, racquetball, and basketball courts, and a weight room.

Disabled Students: 90% of the campus is accessible. Wheelchair ramps, elevators, special parking, specially equipped rest rooms, special class scheduling, lowered drinking fountains, lowered telephones, TDD machines for the deaf, and a library room equipped for students who are hearing-impaired, visually impaired, or motor impaired are available.

Services: Counseling and information services are available, as is tutoring in every subject. There is a reader service for the blind, and remedial math, reading, and writing. The school also offers science lab tutoring and evaluative testing services.

Campus Safety and Security: Measures include 24-hour foot and vehicle patrol, self-defense education, escort service, and informal discussions. There are pamphlets/posters/films, emergency telephones, and lighted pathways/sidewalks.

Programs of Study: TCNJ confers B.A., B.S., B.F.A., B.M., and B.S.N. degrees. Master's degrees are also awarded. Bachelor's degrees are awarded in BIOLOGICAL SCIENCE (biology/biological science), BUSINESS (accounting, business administration and management, international business management, management science, and marketing/retailing/merchandising), COMMUNICATIONS AND THE ARTS (communications, English, fine arts, graphic design, journalism, music, and Spanish), COMPUTER AND PHYSICAL SCIENCE (chemistry, computer science, mathematics, physics, and statistics), EDUCATION (art, early childhood, education of the deaf and hearing impaired, elementary, English, health, music, physical, special, and technical), ENGINEERING AND ENVIRONMENTAL DESIGN (engineering and applied science), HEALTH PROFESSIONS (nursing), SOCIAL SCIENCE (criminal justice, economics, history, international studies, philosophy, political science/government, psychology, sociology, and women's studies). Biology, English, and computer science are the strongest academically. Biology, elementary education, and business are the largest.

Required: To graduate, the student must earn 120 semester hours, with a minimum GPA of 2.0. The student must complete a general education curriculum that includes 26 hours in perspectives on the world, 3 to 21 hours in intellectual skills, and 6 hours in an interdisciplinary core. The credits required in the major vary by program.

Special: TCNJ offers cross-registration with the New Jersey Marine Science Consortium, numerous internships in the public and private sectors, and study abroad in more than a dozen countries through the International Student Exchange program (ISEP). Pass/fail options and some dual majors are possible. Specially designed research courses allow students to participate in collaborative scholarly projects with members of the faculty. Combined advanced-degree professional programs are offered in law and justice, medicine, and optometry with other area schools. There are 9 national honor societies, a freshman honors program, and 17 departmental honors programs.

Faculty/Classroom: 58% of faculty are male; 42%, female. All teach undergraduates and 50% both teach and do research. No introductory courses are taught by graduate students. The average class size in an introductory lecture is 24; in a laboratory, 20; and in a regular course, 21.

Admissions: 51% of the 2001-2002 applicants were accepted. The SAT I scores for the 2001-2002 freshman class were: Verbal--2% below 500, 34% between 500 and 599, 51% between 600 and 700, and 13% above 700; Math--1% below 500, 20% between 500 and 599, 59% between 600 and 700, and 20% above 700. 95% of the current freshmen were in the top fifth of their class; 97% were in the top two fifths. There were 4 National Merit finalists and 14 semifinalists. 14 freshmen graduated first in their class.

Requirements: The SAT I is required. In addition, applicants must have earned 16 academic credits in high school, consisting of 4 in English, 2 each in math, science, and social studies, and 6 others distributed among math, science, social studies, and a foreign language. An essay is required. Art majors must submit a portfolio, and music majors must audition. The GED is accepted. AP and CLEP credits are accepted. Important factors in the admissions decision are advanced placement or honor courses, leadership record, and evidence of special talent. Applications are accepted on-line through an enrollment services system at *www.princetonreview.com*

Procedure: Freshmen are admitted fall and spring. Entrance exams should be taken by the end of the junior year or early in the senior year. There are early decision and early admissions plans. Early decision applications should be filed by November 15; regular applications, by February 15 for fall entry, November 1 for spring entry, and May 1 for summer entry, along with a $50 fee. Notification of early decision is sent December 15; regular decision, on a rolling basis. 200 early decision candidates were accepted for the 2001-2002 class. A waiting list is an active part of the admissions process.

Transfer: 213 transfer students enrolled in 2001-2002. Transfer students must have a minimum GPA of 2.5, and those with fewer than 33 credits must submit the SAT I scores. An associate degree is recommended. All transfer students must submit high school transcripts. 42 credits of 120 must be completed at TCNJ.

Visiting: There are regularly scheduled orientations for prospective students, consisting of an admissions presentation and a tour of campus. Reservations are required. There are guides for informal visits and visitors may sit in on classes and stay overnight. To schedule a visit, contact the Admissions Office.

Financial Aid: In 2001-2002, 73% of all freshmen and 75% of continuing students received some form of financial aid. 50% of all students received need-based aid. The average freshman award was $4600. Of that total, scholarships or need-based grants averaged $2600 ($10,500 maximum); loans averaged $3200 ($10,500 maximum); and work contracts averaged $1200 ($2000 maximum). 95% of undergraduates work part time. Average annual earnings from campus work are $750. The average financial indebtedness of the 2001 graduate was $13,000. The FAFSA and copies of students' and parents' tax returns as applicable are required. The fall application deadline is March 5.

International Students: There are 17 international students enrolled. They must score 550 on the written TOEFL and also take the SAT I or the ACT. The SAT I is required for merit scholarship consideration.

Computers: The mainframe is an IBM ES9000 9121-320. There are 500 networked PCs and workstations available in 22 academic computing labs throughout the campus, including 3 in residence halls. Students have access to the campuswide network from their residence hall rooms. In addition, more than 3000 student PCs are connected through the campus residence network. All students may access the system. There are no time limits. The fee is $180 annually. It is strongly recommended that all students have a personal computer.

Graduates: In 2001, 1308 bachelor's degrees were awarded. The most popular majors were business administration (20%), elementary/early childhood education (14%), and biology (9%). In an average class, 58% graduate in 4 years, 80% in 5 years, and 80% in 6 years. 518 companies recruited on campus in 2000-2001. Of the 2000 graduating class, 21% were enrolled in graduate school within 6 months of graduation and 85% were employed.

Admissions Contact: Lisa Angeloni, Director of Admissions.
E-mail: *admiss@tcnj.edu* Web: *www.tcnj.edu*

COLLEGE OF SAINT ELIZABETH — E-2

Morristown, NJ 07960-6989 (973) 290-4700
(800) 210-7900; Fax: (973) 290-4710

Full-time: 1 man, 596 women	**Faculty:** 54; IIB, av$
Part-time: 87 men, 567 women	**Ph.D.s:** 79%
Graduate: 52 men, 438 women	**Student/Faculty:** 11 to 1
Year: semesters, summer session	**Tuition:** $15,310
Application Deadline: August 15	**Room & Board:** $7200
Freshman Class: 409 applied, 326 accepted, 149 enrolled	
SAT I Verbal/Math: 450/460	**COMPETITIVE**

The College of St. Elizabeth, founded in 1899, is a private Roman Catholic college primarily for women. Undergraduate programs are offered in the arts and sciences, business administration, education, foods and nutrition, and upper-level nursing. There are graduate programs in education, management, health care management, nutrition, psychology, and theology. Adult undergraduate degree programs and graduate programs are coeducational. In addition to regional accreditation, CSE has baccalaureate program accreditation with ADA and NLN. The library contains 110,272 volumes, 104,965 microform items, and 1612 audiovisual forms/CDs, and subscribes to 633 periodicals. Computerized library services include the card catalog, interlibrary loans, and database searching. Special learning facilities include a learning resource center and a television studio. The 188-acre campus is in a suburban area 40 miles west of New York City. Including residence halls, there are 11 buildings.

Student Life: 93% of undergraduates are from New Jersey. Others are from 7 states and 25 foreign countries. 68% are from public schools. 62% are white; 14% Hispanic; 11% African American. 68% are Catholic; 16% claim no religious affiliation; 11% Protestant. The average age of freshmen is 18; all undergraduates, 27. 18% do not continue beyond their first year; 62% remain to graduate.

Housing: 402 students can be accommodated in college housing, which includes single-sex dormitories. On-campus housing is guaranteed for all 4 years, is available on a first-come, first-served basis, and is available on a lottery system for upperclassmen. 73% of students live on campus; of those, 22% remain on campus on weekends. All students may keep cars.

Activities: There are 28 groups on campus, including chorale, drama, ethnic, honors, international, literary magazine, newspaper, professional, religious, social, social service, student government, and yearbook. Popular campus events include Oktoberfest, International Night, and Christmas celebrations.

Sports: There are 8 intercollegiate sports for women. Facilities include a student center that houses a swimming pool, a weight room, an archery range, and a gym. Tennis courts are also available, as is a bike and fitness trail.

Disabled Students: 75% of the campus is accessible. Wheelchair ramps, elevators, special parking, specially equipped rest rooms, special class scheduling, and handrails are available.

Services: Counseling and information services are available, as is tutoring in most subjects. There is remedial math, reading, and writing, books on tape, large monitor computers, and notetakers.

Campus Safety and Security: Measures include 24-hour foot and vehicle patrol, escort service, informal discussions, and pamphlets/posters/films. There are emergency telephones and lighted pathways/sidewalks.

Programs of Study: CSE confers B.A., B.S., and B.S.N. degrees. Master's degrees are also awarded. Bachelor's degrees are awarded in BIOLOGICAL SCIENCE (biochemistry, biology/biological science, nutrition, and toxicology), BUSINESS (accounting, business administration and management, marketing management, and office supervision and management), COMMUNICATIONS AND THE ARTS (art, communications, English, fine arts, music, and Spanish), COMPUTER AND PHYSICAL SCIENCE (chemistry, computer science, and mathematics), EDUCATION (early childhood, elementary, and special), HEALTH PROFESSIONS (cytotechnology, medical technology, nursing, predentistry, and premedicine), SOCIAL SCIENCE (American studies, economics, history, international studies, peace studies, philosophy, prelaw, psychology, sociology, and theological studies). Math, chemistry, and education are the strongest academically. Business administration, education, and psychology are the largest.

Required: To graduate, students must complete 128 semester hours, with a minimum of 32 in the major, while maintaining a GPA of 2.0, or 2.75 for education majors. Core requirements include 27 credits in specific humanities courses focusing on theology, philosophy, literature, history, foreign language, and fine arts, 6 to 8 in math and science, and 6 in social science. In addition, 2 credits in fitness/wellness and an interdisciplinary course are required. Students must also demonstrate proficiency in writing and complete a comprehensive or capstone experience.

Special: There is cross-registration with Drew and Fairleigh Dickinson Universities. CSE also offers internships in business, law, technology, health, government, sports, and television. On-campus work-study, accelerated degree programs, dual majors, student-designed majors, study abroad, credit for life experience, pass/fail options, and nondegree study are also available. Continuing studies programs are geared to the working student. There are 10 national honor societies and a freshman honors program.

Faculty/Classroom: 34% of faculty are male; 66%, female. 84% teach undergraduates. No introductory courses are taught by graduate students. The average class size in an introductory lecture is 19; in a laboratory, 13; and in a regular course, 15.

Admissions: 80% of the 2001-2002 applicants were accepted. The SAT I scores for the 2001-2002 freshman class were: Verbal--56% below 500, 34% between 500 and 599, 8% between 600 and 700, and 2% above 700; Math--56% below 500, 33% between 500 and 599, 7% between 600 and 700, and 4% above 700. 35% of the current freshmen were in the top fifth of their class; 63% were in the top two fifths. 1 freshman graduated as valedictorian.

Requirements: The SAT I is required with a minimum composite score of 1000, 500 on each part, recommended. Applicants must be graduates of accredited secondary schools or have earned a GED. The college requires 16 academic units, including 3 each in English and math/science, 2 each in foreign language, and 1 in history. An essay and 2 letters of recommendaiton are required and an interview is recommended. CSE requires applicants to be in the upper 50% of their class. A GPA of 2.0 is required. AP and CLEP credits are accepted. Important factors in the admissions decision are advanced placement or honor courses, recommendations by school officials, and leadership record.

Procedure: Freshmen are admitted fall and spring. Entrance exams should be taken early in the senior year. There is a deferred admissions plan. Applications should be filed by August 15 for fall entry and December 15 for spring entry, along with a $35 fee. Notification is sent on a rolling basis.

Transfer: 52 transfer students enrolled in 2001-2002. Applicants must present a minimum GPA of 2.0 in course work from an accredited college. SAT I or ACT scores, an associate degree, and an interview are also recommended. 56 credits of 128 must be completed at CSE.

Visiting: There are regularly scheduled orientations for prospective students, including interviews, tours, and class visitation. There are guides for informal visits and visitors may sit in on classes and stay overnight. To schedule a visit, contact Donna Tartarka, Dean of Admission.

Financial Aid: In 2001-2002, 98% of all freshmen and 71% of continuing students received some form of financial aid. 77% of freshmen and 56% of continuing students received need-based aid. The average freshman award was $15,685. Of that total, scholarships or need-based grants averaged $11,947 ($15,310 maximum); loans averaged $2699 ($4425 maximum); and work contracts averaged $1039 ($1500 maximum). 95% of undergraduates work part time. Average annual earnings from campus work are $1000. The average financial indebtedness of the 2001 graduate was $17,168. The FAFSA is required. The fall application deadline is March 1.

International Students: There are 51 international students enrolled. The school actively recruits these students. Applicants from English-speaking countries may submit scores from either the TOEFL or the SAT I and also take other approved assessment tests.

Computers: The mainframe is a Hewlett-Packard Netfinity LHH Server controlling a Microsoft Windows NT network. There are a total of 152 computers (128 PCs and 24 Macs) in general and special purpose labs throughout campus. All systems have access to the Internet, and e-mail services from their dorm room and other locations on campus. All students may access the system. There are no time limits and no fees.

Graduates: In 2001, 218 bachelor's degrees were awarded. The most popular majors were business (30%), education (17%), and psychology (11%). In an average class, 1% graduate in 3 years, 56% in 4 years, 61% in 5 years, and 62% in 6 years. 3 companies recruited on campus in 2000-2001. Of the 2000 graduating class, 21% were enrolled in graduate school within 6 months of graduation and 66% were employed.

Admissions Contact: Donna Tartarka, Dean of Admission. A video is available. E-mail: *apply@liza.st-elizabeth.edu*
Web: *www.st-elizabeth.edu*

DEVRY COLLEGE OF TECHNOLOGY/NORTH BRUNSWICK — D-3

North Brunswick, NJ 08902-3362 — (732) 435-4850
Fax: (732) 435-4856

Full-time: 1877 men, 500 women	**Faculty:** 70
Part-time: 1140 men, 395 women	**Ph.D.s:** n/av
Graduate: none	**Student/Faculty:** 34 to 1
Year: semesters, summer session	**Tuition:** $8805
Application Deadline: open	**Room & Board:** n/app
Freshman Class: 2015 applied, 1650 accepted, 966 enrolled	
SAT I or ACT: recommended	**LESS COMPETITIVE**

DeVry College of Technology/North Brunswick, formerly DeVry Institute of Technology/North Brunswick, founded in 1969, is a private institution offering hands-on programs in electronics, business administration, computer information systems, and information technology. The school is 1 of 15 DeVry campuses throughout the United States and Canada. In addition to regional accreditation, DeVry has baccalaureate program accreditation with ABET. The library contains 32,201 volumes and 1870 audiovisual forms/CDs, and subscribes to 210 periodicals. Computerized library services include the card catalog, interlibrary loans, and database searching. Special learning facilities include a learning resource center. The 15-acre campus is in a small town. There is 1 building.

Student Life: 87% of undergraduates are from New Jersey. Others are from 22 states and 25 foreign countries. 43% are white; 24% African American; 17% Hispanic. The average age of all undergraduates is 26. 48% do not continue beyond their first year.

Housing: There are no residence halls. All students commute. Housing referrals may be obtained through the Student Housing Office. Alcohol is not permitted. All students may keep cars.

Activities: There are no fraternities or sororities. There are 11 groups on campus, including ethnic, honors, and professional. Popular campus events include Student Appreciation Day.

Sports: There is no sports program at DeVry.

Disabled Students: All of the campus is accessible. Wheelchair ramps, elevators, special parking, specially equipped rest rooms, special class scheduling, lowered drinking fountains, and lowered telephones are available.

Services: Counseling and information services are available, as is tutoring in every subject.

Programs of Study: DeVry confers the B.S. degree. Associate degrees are also awarded. Bachelor's degrees are awarded in COMMUNICATIONS AND THE ARTS (telecommunications), ENGINEERING AND ENVIRONMENTAL DESIGN (electrical/electronics engineering technology). Telecommunications is the largest.

Required: To graduate, students must achieve a GPA of at least 2.0, complete 48 to 154 credit hours, and satisfactorily complete all curriculum requirements. Course requirements vary according to program. All first-semester students take courses in business organization, computer application, algebra, psychology, and student success strategies.

Special: Evening and weekend classes, co-op programs, and an accelerated degree program are offered. There are 2 national honor societies, including Phi Beta Kappa.

Faculty/Classroom: All teach undergraduates. The average class size in an introductory lecture is 30; in a laboratory, 30; and in a regular course, 30.

Admissions: 82% of the 2001-2002 applicants were accepted.

Requirements: The SAT I or ACT is recommended. In addition, admissions requirements include graduation from a secondary school; the

GED is also accepted. Applicants must pass the DeVry entrance exam or present satisfactory ACT or SAT I scores. An interview is required. Applications are accepted on-line at *Embark.com*. CLEP credit is accepted.
Procedure: Freshmen are admitted fall, spring, and summer. There is a deferred admissions plan. Application deadlines are open. The application fee is $50. Notification is sent on a rolling basis.
Transfer: 1 transfer student enrolled in a recent year. Applicants must present passing grades in all completed college course work, demonstrate language skills proficiency with at least 24 completed semester hours, and present evidence of math proficiency by appropriate college-level credits. 35% of 48 to 54 credits must be completed at DeVry.
Visiting: There are regularly scheduled orientations for prospective students. There are guides for informal visits and visitors may sit in on classes. To schedule a visit, contact Danielle DiNapoli, Dean of Admissions at (732) 435-4880.
Financial Aid: In 2001-2002, 31% of all freshmen and 82% of continuing students received some form of financial aid. 22% of freshmen and 41% of continuing students received need-based aid. 8% of undergraduates work part time. Average annual earnings from campus work are $3300. The FAFSA is required.
International Students: There are 52 international students enrolled. They must score 500 on the written TOEFL or 173 on the electronic version and also take DeVry's computerized placement test, achieving a minimum score that varies by program.
Computers: Lab facilities include PCs in stand-alone and network configurations with access to the mainframe. LANs provide access to a wide range of applications software. Hard copy from the mainframe is provided through a local microcomputer and medium- and high-speed printers. Computer information students may access the system during published lab hours. Students may access the system. There are no fees. It is recommended that students in the Information Technology program have DeVry-issued laptop computers. There is a $55 per creidt hour technology fee.
Graduates: In 2001, 86 bachelor's degrees were awarded. The most popular majors were business (76%) and electronics engineering technology (24%). 173 companies recruited on campus in 2000-2001.
Admissions Contact: Danielle DeNapoli, Dean of Admissions.
Web: *www.nj.devry.edu*

DREW UNIVERSITY/COLLEGE OF LIBERAL ARTS D-2

Madison, NJ 07940 (973) 408-DREW; Fax: (973) 408-3068

Full-time: 578 men, 905 women	**Faculty:** 120; IIA, +$
Part-time: 14 men, 39 women	**Ph.D.s:** 96%
Graduate: 359 men, 360 women	**Student/Faculty:** 12 to 1
Year: semesters, summer session	**Tuition:** $25,122
Application Deadline: February 15	**Room & Board:** $7030
Freshman Class: 2513 applied, 1804 accepted, 396 enrolled	
SAT I Verbal/Math: 610/600	**VERY COMPETITIVE**

The College of Liberal Arts was added to Drew University in 1928 and is part of an educational complex that includes a theological school and a graduate school. Drew is a private, independent institution affiliated with the United Methodist Church. The library contains 499,417 volumes and 366,323 microform items, and subscribes to 3755 periodicals. Computerized library services include the card catalog, interlibrary loans, and database searching. Special learning facilities include a learning resource center, art gallery, radio station, TV station, observatory, photography gallery, and TV satellite dish. The 186-acre campus is in a small town 30 miles west of New York City. Including residence halls, there are 57 buildings.
Student Life: 57% of undergraduates are from New Jersey. Others are from 37 states and 18 foreign countries. 66% are from public schools. 61% are white. The average age of freshmen is 18; all undergraduates, 20. 15% do not continue beyond their first year; 75% remain to graduate.
Housing: 1306 students can be accommodated in college housing, which includes single-sex and coed dormitories, on-campus apartments, and married-student housing. In addition, there are language houses and special-interest houses. On-campus housing is guaranteed for all 4 years. 89% of students live on campus; of those, 70% remain on campus on weekends. Upperclassmen may keep cars.
Activities: There are no fraternities or sororities. There are 80 groups on campus, including art, choir, chorale, computers, dance, drama, ecology, ethnic, film, gay, honors, international, jazz band, literary magazine, newspaper, orchestra, pep band, photography, political, professional, radio and TV, religious, social, social service, student government, women's, and yearbook. Popular campus events include Holiday Semiformal, Annual Picnic, and Multicultural Awareness Day.
Sports: There are 11 intercollegiate sports for men and 12 for women, and 12 intramural sports for men and 12 for women. Facilities include an artificial turf athletic field with a 1000-seat gym, a 1000-seat auditorium, a swimming pool, a lighted tennis complex, a weight training room, a game room, an indoor track, a forest preserve, and an arboretum.
Disabled Students: Wheelchair ramps, elevators, special parking, specially equipped rest rooms, special class scheduling, lowered drinking fountains, lowered telephones are available. The main dining facility, the student center and commons, and the ground floor of every dorm and classroom building are accessible to students with physical disabilities.
Services: Counseling and information services are available, as is tutoring in most subjects. There is a reader service for the blind.
Campus Safety and Security: Measures include 24-hour foot and vehicle patrol, self-defense education, escort service, and informal discussions. There are pamphlets/posters/films, emergency telephones, and lighted pathways/sidewalks.
Programs of Study: Drew confers the B.A. degree. Master's and doctoral degrees are also awarded. Bachelor's degrees are awarded in BIOLOGICAL SCIENCE (biology/biological science), COMMUNICATIONS AND THE ARTS (art, classics, dramatic arts, English, French, German, music, Russian, and Spanish), COMPUTER AND PHYSICAL SCIENCE (chemistry, computer science, mathematics, and physics), SOCIAL SCIENCE (American studies, anthropology, behavioral science, economics, ethnic studies, history, philosophy, political science/government, psychobiology, psychology, religion, sociology, and women's studies). Psychology, political science, and English are the largest.
Required: To graduate, students must earn at least 128 credits, of which at least 64 must be beyond the lower level and at least 32 must be at the upper level. All students must fulfill the requirements of a major and those of the general education program. For graduation, the cumulative GPA, both overall and in the major, must be at least 2.0. General education requirements include a first-year seminar, demonstration of writing competency, at least 8 credits in foreign language and fulfillment of a language-in-context requirement, and completion of at least 4 credits in each of 2 different departments in the following 4 divisions: natural and mathematical sciences, social sciences, humanities, and arts and literature. Each student must also complete a minor.
Special: Drew offers co-op programs with Duke University, as well as cross-registration with the College of Saint Elizabeth and Fairleigh Dickinson University. There are also dual majors, study abroad, a Wall Street semester, a Washington semester, student-designed majors, internships, 3-2 engineering programs with Washington University in St. Louis, the Stevens Institute of Technology, and Columbia University in New York City, and a 7-year B.A.-M.D. program in medicine with UMDNJ. There are 11 national honor societies, including Phi Beta Kappa, and 12 departmental honors programs.
Faculty/Classroom: 57% of faculty are male; 43%, female. All both teach and do research. Graduate students teach 1% of introductory courses. The average class size in an introductory lecture is 25; in a laboratory, 20; and in a regular course, 18.
Admissions: 72% of the 2001-2002 applicants were accepted. The SAT I scores for the 2001-2002 freshman class were: Verbal--8% below 500, 32% between 500 and 599, 44% between 600 and 700, and 16% above 700; Math--10% below 500, 39% between 500 and 599, 39% between 600 and 700, and 12% above 700. 68% of the current freshmen were in the top fifth of their class; 94% were in the top two fifths. 4 freshmen graduated first in their class.
Requirements: The SAT I or ACT is required. The SAT I is preferred. The university strongly recommends 18 academic credits or Carnegie units, including 4 in English, 3 in math, and 2 each in foreign language, science, social studies, and history, with the remaining 3 in additional academic courses. 3 SAT II: Subject tests are recommended, including 1 in writing. An essay is also required, and an interview is recommended. Drew requires applicants to be in the upper 94% of their class. AP and CLEP credits are accepted. Important factors in the admissions decision are advanced placement or honor courses, extracurricular activities record, and leadership record. Applicatiojna are accepted on-line.
Procedure: Freshmen are admitted fall and spring. Entrance exams should be taken by January of the senior year. There are early decision, early admissions, and deferred admissions plans. Early decision applications should be filed by December 1 or January 15; regular applications, by February 15 for fall entry and December 1 for spring entry, along with a $40 fee. Notification of early decision is sent December 24 or February 15; regular decision, March 15. 55 early decision candidates were accepted for the 2001-2002 class. 5% of all applicants are on a waiting list.
Transfer: 42 transfer students enrolled in 2001-2002. Applicants must submit satisfactory high school and college academic records, SAT I or ACT scores, a personal essay, and a statement of good standing from previous schools attended. An interview also may be required. Students with fewer than 12 credits must apply as entering freshmen. 56 credits of 128 must be completed at Drew.
Visiting: There are regularly scheduled orientations for prospective students. There are guides for informal visits and visitors may sit in on classes and stay overnight. To schedule a visit, contact the Admissions Office.
Financial Aid: In 2001-2002, 81% of all freshmen and 77% of continuing students received some form of financial aid. 46% of freshmen and 49% of continuing students received need-based aid. The average freshman award was $13,492. Of that total, scholarships or need-based grants averaged $11,428 ($20,866 maximum); loans averaged $2096 ($4600 maximum); and work contracts averaged $1594 ($1700 maximum). 47% of undergraduates work part time. Average annual earnings

from campus work are $1080. The average financial indebtedness of the 2001 graduate was $13,106. The CSS/Profile and FAFSA are required. The fall application deadline is February 15.

International Students: There are 24 international students enrolled. The school actively recruits these students. They must score 550 on the written TOEFL or 213 on the electronic version and also take the SAT I or the ACT.

Computers: The mainframe is a Compaq. All full-time students are provided with a free Pentium notebook computer, a printer, and accompanying software. An extensive software library and additional computers are located on campus. Students also have access to the Internet and e-mail, with connections in many of the residence halls. All students may access the system. There are no time limits and no fees.

Graduates: In 2001, 350 bachelor's degrees were awarded. The most popular majors were poliical science (17%), psychology (12%), and English (9%). In an average class, 70% graduate in 4 years. 78 companies recruited on campus in 2000-2001. Of the 2000 graduating class, 11% were enrolled in graduate school within 6 months of graduation and 71% were employed.

Admissions Contact: Roberto Noya, Dean of Admissions and Financial Aid. E-mail: *cadm@drew.edu* Web: *http://www.drew.edu*

FAIRLEIGH DICKINSON UNIVERSITY SYSTEM

Established in 1942, Fairleigh Dickinson University is an independent, nonsectarian institution of higher education offering career-oriented undergraduate and graduate programs. It is governed by a board of trustees whose chief administrator is the president. The 2 northern New Jersey campuses are in Florham-Madison and Teaneck-Hackensack; the Wroxton College campus is in Oxfordshire, England. The University has also established a branch campus in Tel Aviv, Israel, in cooperation with Israel's Biotechnical Institute. Teaching and research are the primary goals of the institution, with a student-faculty ratio of about 14:1. All courses are taught by full- or part-time faculty. The university seeks to provide an academically challenging learning experience to prepare students for employment or enrollment in graduate or professional schools. The university offers 53 undergraduate programs and 50 graduate programs including the Ph.D. in clinical psychology and a Psy.D. in school psychology.

FAIRLEIGH DICKINSON UNIVERSITY/MADISON CAMPUS D-3

Madison, NJ 07940 (201) 692-7304
(800) 338-8803; Fax: (201) 692-7309

Full-time: 949 men, 1040 women	**Faculty:** 111
Part-time: 191 men, 247 women	**Ph.D.s:** 80%
Graduate: 351 men, 682 women	**Student/Faculty:** 18 to 1
Year: semesters, summer session	**Tuition:** $18,000
Application Deadline: March 1	**Room & Board:** $7500
Freshman Class: 2524 applied, 1752 accepted, 500 enrolled	
SAT I or ACT: required	**COMPETITIVE**

Fairleigh Dickinson University, founded in 1942, is an independent university comprised of 2 campuses, Teaneck/Hackensack and Florham/Madison, offering undergraduate and graduate degrees in business, arts and sciences, professional studies, public administration, and hotel, restaurant, and tourism management. Tuition and room and board figures in the above capsule are approximate. There are 3 undergraduate and 3 graduate schools. In addition to regional accreditation, FDU has baccalaureate program accreditation with AACSB, ACS, and APTA. The library contains 176,222 volumes, 13,273 microform items, and 591 audiovisual forms/CDs, and subscribes to 1259 periodicals. Computerized library services include the card catalog, interlibrary loans, and database searching. Special learning facilities include a learning resource center. The 178-acre campus is in a suburban area 27 miles west of New York City, in Morris County. Including residence halls, there are 32 buildings.

Student Life: 86% of undergraduates are from New Jersey. Others are from 22 states, 33 foreign countries, and Canada. 72% are white. The average age of freshmen is 18; all undergraduates, 22. 22% do not continue beyond their first year.

Housing: 1369 students can be accommodated in college housing, which includes single-sex and coed dormitories, off-campus apartments, fraternity houses, and sorority houses. On-campus housing is guaranteed for all 4 years and is available on a first-come, first-served basis. 53% of students live on campus. Upperclassmen may keep cars.

Activities: There are 4 national fraternities; 10% of women belong to 4 national sororities. There are 60 groups on campus, including art, cheerleading, computers, drama, ethnic, film, gay, honors, international, jazz band, literary magazine, musical theater, newspaper, photography, political, professional, radio and TV, religious, social, social service, student government, and yearbook. Popular campus events include dances, Welcome Week Softball Marathon, and Senior Days.

Sports: There are 9 intercollegiate sports for men and 9 for women, and 11 intramural sports for men and 10 for women. Facilities include football, baseball, men's and women's soccer, softball, lacrosse, and field hockey fields, 5 tennis courts, and 2 full outdoor basketball courts. There is an 82,000-square foot recreation center, a 6000-square foot fitness center, 2 racquetball courts, basketball seating for 2500, an 8-lane competition pool, an aerobics room, and a training room.

Disabled Students: Wheelchair ramps, elevators, special parking, specially equipped rest rooms, special class scheduling, lowered drinking fountains, lowered telephones, and oral interpretation for the hearing impaired are available.

Services: Counseling and information services are available, as is tutoring in most subjects. There is a reader service for the blind, and remedial math, reading, and writing. Workshops also offer assistance with study skills and time management, and support services for basic skills students and freshmen are available. There is a regional center for learning disabled students.

Campus Safety and Security: Measures include 24-hour foot and vehicle patrol, self-defense education, escort service, and informal discussions. There are pamphlets/posters/films, emergency telephones, lighted pathways/sidewalks, an active crime prevention program, and bike patrol.

Programs of Study: FDU confers B.A. and B.S. degrees. Associate and master's degrees are also awarded. Bachelor's degrees are awarded in BIOLOGICAL SCIENCE (biology/biological science and marine biology), BUSINESS (accounting, business administration and management, entrepreneurial studies, hotel/motel and restaurant management, and marketing/retailing/merchandising), COMMUNICATIONS AND THE ARTS (communications, dramatic arts, English, fine arts, and video), COMPUTER AND PHYSICAL SCIENCE (chemistry, computer science, mathematics, and radiological technology), HEALTH PROFESSIONS (medical laboratory technology), SOCIAL SCIENCE (economics, French studies, history, humanities, philosophy, political science/government, psychology, sociology, and Spanish studies). Psychology, business management, and marketing are the largest.

Required: To graduate, students must complete a minimum of 128 credits, including 30 to 44 in the major, with an overall minimum 2.0 GPA (2.5 in the major). Distribution requirements include courses in English, communications, math, phys ed, foreign language, humanities, social and behavioral sciences, lab and computer science, an integrated, interdisciplinary university core sequence, and freshman seminar.

Special: FDU offers co-op programs in all majors, internships, and study abroad. A Washington semester, work-study, accelerated degrees, and student-designed majors in the humanities and general studies are possible. A prepharmacy program, as well as joint baccalaureate dental programs are available. There are 14 national honor societies, a freshman honors program, and 19 departmental honors programs.

Faculty/Classroom: 70% of faculty are male; 30%, female. All teach undergraduates. No introductory courses are taught by graduate students.

Admissions: 28% of the current freshmen were in the top quarter of their class; 62% were in the top half. 69% of the 2001-2002 applicants were accepted. The SAT I scores for the 2001-2002 freshman class were: Verbal--48% below 500, 40% between 500 and 599, and 12% between 600 and 700; Math--42% below 500, 45% between 500 and 599, 12% between 600 and 700, and 1% above 700. 3 freshmen graduated first in their class.

Requirements: The SAT I or ACT is required. In addition, applicants should be graduates of an accredited high school or have a GED certificate. They should have completed a minimum of 16 academic units, including 4 in English, 3 in math, 2 each in history, foreign language, and lab science (3 are recommended), and 3 in electives. Those students applying to science and health sciences programs must meet additional requirements. An interview may be requested by the university. FDU requires applicants to be in the upper 50% of their class. AP and CLEP credits are accepted. Important factors in the admissions decision are advanced placement or honor courses, personality/intangible qualities, and recommendations by school officials. Applications are accepted on-line at *www.fdu.edu*

Procedure: Freshmen are admitted to all sessions. There are early admissions and deferred admissions plans. Applications should be filed by March 1 for fall entry. The fall 2001 application fee was $40. Notification is sent on a rolling basis beginning November 1.

Transfer: 140 transfer students enrolled in 2001-2002. All transfer applicants must submit official transcripts for all college work taken. Those students with fewer than 24 credits must also submit a high school transcript or a copy of their state department of education's equivalency score, and SAT I scores. 50 credits of 128 must be completed at FDU.

Visiting: There are regularly scheduled orientations for prospective students, including an overnight stay during the week, standardized placement testing, faculty advisement, class registration, and educational and social activities to prepare students for entrance in the fall. There are guides for informal visits and visitors may sit in on classes and stay overnight. To schedule a visit, contact the Admissions Office.

Financial Aid: The institution's own financial statement is required. The fall application deadline is March 15.

International Students: There are 62 international students enrolled. The school actively recruits these students. They must score 550 on the written TOEFL or 213 on the electronic version or take the MELAB, the Comprehensive English Language Test, or the college's own test.The SAT I or ACT is highly recommended.

Computers: The mainframes are a DEC ALPHA 2100 and 4100, and Sun 250 and 450. There are 7 PC labs, each consisting of more than 20 IBM NetVista Pentium III PCs connected to a central Novell file server and to the network, which is connected to the Internet. Each dormitory room has access to the campus LAN and to the Internet. All students may access the system. There are no time limits. The fee is $420 per year.

Graduates: In 2001, 937 bachelor's degrees were awarded. The most popular majors were business/marketing (27%), liberal arts (14%), and psychology (11%). 92 companies recruited on campus in 2000-2001.

Admissions Contact: Gary Hamme, Vice President for Enrollment Management. E-mail: *globaleducation@fdu.edu* Web: *www.fdu.edu*

FAIRLEIGH DICKINSON UNIVERSITY/TEANECK CAMPUS E-2

Teaneck, NJ 07666 (201) 692-7304
(800) 338-8803; Fax: (201) 692-7309

Full-time: 810 men, 1050 women	**Faculty:** 164
Part-time: 918 men, 1335 women	**Ph.D.s:** 78%
Graduate: 895 men, 1084 women	**Student/Faculty:** 11 to 1
Year: semesters, summer session	**Tuition:** $17,474
Application Deadline: March 1	**Room & Board:** $7172

Freshman Class: 2343 applied, 1630 accepted, 497 enrolled
SAT I or ACT: required **COMPETITIVE**

Fairleigh Dickinson University/Teaneck, founded in 1942, is an independent university offering undergraduate and graduate degrees in business, arts and sciences, professional studies, public administration, and hotel, restaurant, and tourism management. There are 3 undergraduate and 3 graduate schools. In addition to regional accreditation, FDU has baccalaureate program accreditation with ABET, APTA, CSAB, NASDTEC, and NLN. The 3 libraries contain 48,837 microform items and 3779 audiovisual forms/CDs. Computerized library services include the card catalog, interlibrary loans, and database searching. Special learning facilities include a learning resource center, computer labs, ITV multimedia classrooms, a photonics lab, and a regional center for learning disabilities. The 88-acre campus is in a suburban area 13 miles from midtown Manhattan. Including residence halls, there are 52 buildings.

Student Life: 69% of undergraduates are from New Jersey. Others are from 20 states, 53 foreign countries, and Canada. 48% are white; 14% African American; 10% Hispanic. The average age of freshmen is 18; all undergraduates, 25.

Housing: 737 students can be accommodated in college housing. College-sponsored housing is single-sex and coed. There is housing for international students. On-campus housing is available on a first-come, first-served basis and is available on a lottery system for upperclassmen. Priority is given to out-of-town students. 71% of students commute. Alcohol is not permitted in residence halls. All students may keep cars.

Activities: 8% of men belong to 4 national fraternities; 8% of women belong to 7 national sororities. There are 65 groups on campus, including art, cheerleading, choir, computers, dance, drama, ethnic, film, honors, international, literary magazine, musical theater, newspaper, photography, political, professional, radio and TV, religious, social, social service, student government, and yearbook. Popular campus events include dances, dinner parties, and concerts.

Sports: There are 8 intercollegiate sports for men and 9 for women, and 15 intramural sports for men and 15 for women. Facilities include a 5000-seat facility with a 6-lane, 200-meter track, 4 full basketball courts, 2 volleyball courts, 4 racquetball courts, and a fully equipped weight room; 6 tennis courts; a baseball field and soccer field with bleachers; outdoor basketball courts; and a training room and fitness center in the Student Union Building.

Disabled Students: Wheelchair ramps, elevators, special parking, specially equipped rest rooms, special class scheduling, lowered drinking fountains, lowered telephones, and oral interpretation for the hearing impaired are available.

Services: Counseling and information services are available, as is tutoring in most subjects. There is a reader service for the blind, and remedial math, reading, and writing. Workshops offer assistance with academic study skills, time management, and advanced reading and writing. There is also a regional center for learning disabled students.

Campus Safety and Security: Measures include 24-hour foot and vehicle patrol, self-defense education, escort service, and informal discussions. There are pamphlets/posters/films, emergency telephones, lighted pathways/sidewalks, an active crime prevention program, and a bike patrol.

Programs of Study: FDU confers B.A., B.S., B.S.Civ.E.T., B.S.C.L.S., B.S.Con.E.T., B.S.E.E., B.S.E.E.T., B.S.M.E.T., and B.S.N. degrees. Associate, master's, and doctoral degrees are also awarded. Bachelor's degrees are awarded in BIOLOGICAL SCIENCE (biochemistry, biology/biological science, and marine biology), BUSINESS (accounting, business administration and management, entrepreneurial studies, hotel/motel and restaurant management, and marketing/retailing/merchandising), COMMUNICATIONS AND THE ARTS (communications, dramatic arts, English, fine arts, French, and Spanish), COMPUTER AND PHYSICAL SCIENCE (chemistry, computer science, mathematics, radiological technology, and science), ENGINEERING AND ENVIRONMENTAL DESIGN (civil engineering technology, construction engineering, electrical/electronics engineering, electrical/electronics engineering technology, environmental science, and mechanical engineering technology), HEALTH PROFESSIONS (allied health, clinical science, medical laboratory technology, nursing, predentistry, premedicine, and preveterinary science), SOCIAL SCIENCE (criminal justice, economics, history, humanities, international studies, liberal arts/general studies, philosophy, political science/government, psychology, and sociology). Business management and psychology are the largest.

Required: To graduate, students must complete 120 to 128 credits, including 30 to 44 in the major, with an overall minimum 2.0 GPA. Students must complete a 4-semester interdisciplinary sequence and 1 course in freshman seminar.

Special: FDU offers co-op programs in all majors, cross-registration, internships, and study abroad in England. A Washington semester, work-study, accelerated degrees, and student-designed majors in the humanities and general studies are possible. A 7-year medical program is available with Karol Marcinkowski School of Medicine in Poland, as is an accelerated chiropractic program with New York Chiropractic College and Logan Chiropractic College. There are 14 national honor societies, a freshman honors program, and 19 departmental honors programs.

Faculty/Classroom: 62% of faculty are male; 38%, female. All teach undergraduates. No introductory courses are taught by graduate students.

Admissions: 70% of the 2001-2002 applicants were accepted. The SAT I scores for the 2001-2002 freshman class were: Verbal--65% below 500, 29% between 500 and 599, and 6% between 600 and 700; Math--60% below 500, 33% between 500 and 599, 7% between 600 and 700, and 1% above 700. 27% of the current freshmen were in the top quarter of their class; 66% were in the top half. 5 freshmen graduated first in their class.

Requirements: The SAT I or ACT is required. In addition, applicants should be graduates of an accredited high school or have a GED certificate. They should have completed a minimum of 16 academic units, including 4 in English, 3 in math, 2 each in history, foreign language, and lab science (3 are recommended), and 3 in electives. Those students applying to science, engineering, and health sciences programs must meet additional requirements. An interview may be requested by the university. FDU requires applicants to be in the upper 50% of their class. AP and CLEP credits are accepted. Important factors in the admissions decision are advanced placement or honor courses, recommendations by school officials, and leadership record. Applications are available on the school's web site, and through *Embark.com*.

Procedure: Freshmen are admitted to all sessions. There is a deferred admissions plan. Applications should be filed by March 1 for fall entry. The fall 2001 application fee was $40. Notification is sent on a rolling basis.

Transfer: 390 transfer students enrolled in 2001-2002. All applicants must submit official transcripts for all college work taken. Those students with fewer than 24 credits must also submit a high school transcript or a copy of their state department of education's equivalency score, and SAT I scores. 50 credits of 128 must be completed at FDU.

Visiting: There are regularly scheduled orientations for prospective students, including an overnight stay during the summer, standardized placement testing, faculty advisement, class registration, and educational and social activities to prepare students for entrance in the fall. There are guides for informal visits and visitors may sit in on classes and stay overnight. To schedule a visit, contact the Admissions Office.

Financial Aid: In a recent year, 84% of all freshmen and 86% of continuing students received some form of financial aid. 75% of all students received need-based aid. Scholarships or need-based grants averaged $10,607; loans averaged $3302; and work contracts averaged $1178.

International Students: There are 317 international students enrolled. The school actively recruits these students. They must score 550 on the written TOEFL or 213 on the electronic version, or take the MELAB, the Comprehensive English Language Test, or the college's own test.

Computers: The mainframes are DEC ALPHA 4100 and 2100 systems, and Sun Enterprise 250 and 450 systems. Each PC lab has 20 or more IBM NetVista Pentium III PCs with connectivity to LAN-based file servers and the Internet. Each dorm room has access to the campus LAN and to the Internet. All students may access the system. There are no time limits. The fee is $420 per year.

Graduates: In 2001, 937 bachelor's degrees were awarded. The most popular majors were business marketing (27%), liberal arts (14%), and psychology (11%). 300 companies recruited on campus in 2000-2001.

Admissions Contact: Gary Hamme, Vice President for Enrollment Management. E-mail: *globaleducation@fdu.edu* Web: *www.fdu.edu*

FELICIAN COLLEGE E-2

Lodi, NJ 07644 (201) 559-6131; Fax: (201) 559-6188

Full-time: 272 men, 687 women	**Faculty:** 72; IIB, --$
Part-time: 118 men, 541 women	**Ph.D.s:** 55%
Graduate: 18 men, 81 women	**Student/Faculty:** 13 to 1
Year: semesters, summer session	**Tuition:** $13,450
Application Deadline: open	**Room & Board:** $6600
Freshman Class: 1421 applied, 886 accepted, 541 enrolled	
SAT I Verbal/Math: 450/455	**COMPETITIVE**

Felician College, founded in 1942, is a private, Roman Catholic, liberal arts school with concentrations in health science, teacher education, and arts and sciences. There are 3 undergraduate and 3 graduate schools. In addition to regional accreditation, Felician has baccalaureate program accreditation with CAHEA and NLN. The library contains 120,000 volumes, 74,477 microform items, and 4870 audiovisual forms/CDs, and subscribes to 795 periodicals. Computerized library services include interlibrary loans and database searching. Special learning facilities include a learning resource center and a nursing clinical lab. The 32-acre campus is in a suburban area 10 miles east of New York City. Including residence halls, there are 5 buildings.

Student Life: 96% of undergraduates are from New Jersey. Others are from 8 states, 6 foreign countries, and Canada. 65% are from public schools. 57% are white; 15% Hispanic; 13% African American. The average age of freshmen is 18; all undergraduates, 25. 10% do not continue beyond their first year; 35% remain to graduate.

Housing: 700 students can be accommodated in college housing, which includes single-sex dormitories. On-campus housing is guaranteed for all 4 years. 87% of students commute. Alcohol is not permitted. Upperclassmen may keep cars.

Activities: There are no fraternities or sororities. There are 17 groups on campus, including art, cheerleading, chess, choir, computers, drama, education, ethnic, free enterprise, honors, international, karate, literary magazine, professional, religious, science, social service, and student government. Popular campus events include College festival, springfest, and sibling weekend.

Sports: There are 4 intercollegiate sports for men and 4 for women. Facilities include 2 fitness centers and a gym.

Disabled Students: 90% of the campus is accessible. Wheelchair ramps, elevators, special parking, specially equipped rest rooms, lowered drinking fountains, lowered telephones, and wheelchair lifts are available.

Services: Counseling and information services are available, as is tutoring in most subjects. There is remedial math, reading, and writing.

Campus Safety and Security: Measures include 24-hour foot and vehicle patrol, lighted pathways/sidewalks, and guards on duty 24 hours a day.

Programs of Study: Felician confers B.A., B.S., and B.S.N. degrees. Associate and master's degrees are also awarded. Bachelor's degrees are awarded in BIOLOGICAL SCIENCE (biology/biological science), BUSINESS (business administration and management and institutional management), COMMUNICATIONS AND THE ARTS (art and English), COMPUTER AND PHYSICAL SCIENCE (computer science and mathematics), EDUCATION (elementary and special), HEALTH PROFESSIONS (clinical science and nursing), SOCIAL SCIENCE (history, humanities, philosophy, psychology, and religion). Education and nursing are the strongest academically.

Required: All students must earn a minimum GPA of 2.0 (2.5 in medical lab technology, 2.75 in nursing, and 3.0 in education), while taking 120 credit hours (128 to 130 in education), with 39 to 57 hours in their majors. Distribution requirements include 45 to 47 hours from a core curriculum, including courses in English, philosophy, religious studies, humanities, historical tradition, science, and social-cultural studies.

Special: Co-op programs are available in clinical lab sciences with the University of Medicine and Dentistry of New Jersey. In addition, internships for credit, work-study at the college, dual majors in education, an interdisciplinary studies degree, an accelerated degree in organizational management, student-designed majors within humanities and social and behavioral sciences, weekend college, and pass/fail options are possible. There is a freshman honors program.

Faculty/Classroom: 45% of faculty are male; 55%, female. The average class size in an introductory lecture is 25; in a laboratory, 20; and in a regular course, 15.

Admissions: 62% of the 2001-2002 applicants were accepted. The SAT I scores for the 2001-2002 freshman class were: Verbal--78% below 500, 20% between 500 and 599, and 2% between 600 and 700; Math--75% below 500, 23% between 500 and 599, and 2% between 600 and 700. 35% of the current freshmen were in the top fifth of their class; 70% were in the top two fifths.

Requirements: The SAT I is required, with a minimum composite score of 850 recommended. The college also recommends that applicants have 16 academic credits, including 4 in English, 2 to 3 each in math, science, and social studies, and 3 to 6 in academic electives, including foreign language. An interview is recommended. The GED is accepted. A GPA of 2.75 is required. AP and CLEP credits are accepted. Important factors in the admissions decision are recommendations by school officials, advanced placement or honor courses, and extracurricular activities record. Applications are accepted on-line at the school's web site.

Procedure: Freshmen are admitted fall, spring, and summer. Application deadlines are open. The fall 2001 application fee was $30. Notification is sent on a rolling basis.

Transfer: 263 transfer students enrolled in 2001-2002. Applicants must have maintained a minimum GPA of 2.5 (2.75 in nursing and 3.0 in education). An interview is recommended. Nursing majors require previous college-level lab science. 30 credits of 120 must be completed at Felician.

Visiting: There are guides for informal visits and visitors may sit in on classes. To schedule a visit, contact the Admissions Office.

Financial Aid: In 2001-2002, 65% of all students received some form of financial aid. 45% of freshmen and 40% of continuing students received need-based aid. The average freshman award was $7500. Of that total, scholarships or need-based grants averaged $2200 ($3125 maximum); loans averaged $2500; and work contracts averaged $2800 ($3000 maximum). 97% of undergraduates work part time. Average annual earnings from campus work are $3000. The average financial indebtedness of the 2001 graduate was $18,000. The FAFSA and the college's own financial statement are required. The fall application deadline is June 1.

International Students: There are more than 35 international students enrolled. The school actively recruits these students. They must score 500 on the written TOEFL or 200 on the electronic version.

Computers: There are 250 Macs and PCs available for academic use. All students have full access to the Internet. All students may access the system. There are no time limits and no fees.

Graduates: In 2001, 132 bachelor's degrees were awarded. The most popular majors were nursing (25%), education (20%), and English (15%). 40 companies recruited on campus in 2000-2001.

Admissions Contact: Cynthia Sievewright, Director of Admissions. E-mail: *admissions@inet.felician.edu* Web: *www.felician.edu*

GEORGIAN COURT COLLEGE E-4

Lakewood, NJ 08701-2697 (732) 364-2200, ext. 760
(800) 458-8422; (732) 364-4442

Full-time: 50 men, 1000 women	**Faculty:** 82; IIA, --$
Part-time: 100 men, 430 women	**Ph.D.s:** 72%
Graduate: 155 men, 680 women	**Student/Faculty:** 13 to 1
Year: semesters, summer session	**Tuition:** $13,840
Application Deadline: August 1	**Room & Board:** $5200
Freshman Class: n/av	
SAT I or ACT: required	**LESS COMPETITIVE**

Georgian Court College, founded in 1908, is an independent Roman Catholic college. The day division matriculates only women; the evening and graduate divisions are coeducational. Undergraduate programs are offered in the arts and sciences, business administration, religion, social work, and teacher preparation. Figures in the above capsule are approximate. In addition to regional accreditation, The Court has baccalaureate program accreditation with ACBSP and NASDTEC. The library contains 130,000 volumes, 620,000 microform items, and 2000 audiovisual forms/CDs, and subscribes to 1400 periodicals. Computerized library services include the card catalog, interlibrary loans, and database searching. Special learning facilities include a learning resource center, art gallery, and an arboretum. The 150-acre campus is in a suburban area 60 miles south of New York City and 60 miles east of Philadelphia. Including residence halls, there are 17 buildings.

Student Life: 99% of undergraduates are from New Jersey. Others are from 5 states and 3 foreign countries. 83% are from public schools. 78% are white. 48% are Catholic. The average age of freshmen is 18; all undergraduates, 26. 1% do not continue beyond their first year; 84% remain to graduate.

Housing: 356 students can be accommodated in college housing, which includes single-sex dormitories. On-campus housing is guaranteed for all 4 years and is available on a first-come, first-served basis. 74% of students commute. All students may keep cars.

Activities: There are no fraternities or sororities. There are 38 groups on campus, including art, band, choir, chorale, ethnic, honors, international, literary magazine, newspaper, professional, religious, social, social service, student government, and yearbook. Popular campus events include Irish Afternoon, Family Day, and Christmas Reception.

Sports: There are 4 intercollegiate sports for women. Facilities include a porcelain-faced swimming pool, basketball and volleyball courts, a 300-seat gym, a fitness center, athletic fields, and a tennis court.

Disabled Students: 73% of the campus is accessible. Wheelchair ramps, elevators, special parking, specially equipped rest rooms, special

class scheduling, lowered drinking fountains, lowered telephones, and special equipment for the visually and hearing impaired are available.
Services: Counseling and information services are available, as is tutoring in most subjects. There is remedial math, reading, and writing.
Campus Safety and Security: Measures include 24-hour foot and vehicle patrol, escort service, informal discussions, and pamphlets/posters/films. There are lighted pathways/sidewalks.
Programs of Study: The Court confers B.A., B.S., B.F.A., and B.S.W. degrees. Master's degrees are also awarded. Bachelor's degrees are awarded in BIOLOGICAL SCIENCE (biochemistry and biology/biological science), BUSINESS (accounting and business administration and management), COMMUNICATIONS AND THE ARTS (art, art history and appreciation, English, French, music, and Spanish), COMPUTER AND PHYSICAL SCIENCE (chemistry, mathematics, and physics), EDUCATION (elementary and special), SOCIAL SCIENCE (history, humanities, psychology, religion, social work, and sociology). Education, psychology, and business administration are the largest.
Required: General education requirements include 9 semester courses in humanities, 5 in social science, and 3 in natural science/math. Students under 25 also must complete a semester course in phys ed. The bachelor's degree requires completion of at least 132 credit hours, including a minimum of 30 in a major field. Students must maintain a GPA of at least 2.0 overall and 2.5 in all majors but social work, which requires a 3.0.
Special: Business administration majors may participate in cooperative programs and work-study programs with various employers. Georgian Court also offers study abroad through the College Consortium for International Studies, internships in history, social work, and political science, dual majors in education, a general studies degree in humanities, field experience externships in art, psychology, education, and social work, credit for life experience, and pass/fail options. Nondegree study is possible. There are 15 national honor societies and 13 departmental honors programs.
Faculty/Classroom: 47% of faculty are male; 53%, female. 79% teach undergraduates. No introductory courses are taught by graduate students. The average class size in an introductory lecture is 19; in a laboratory, 7; and in a regular course, 13.
Admissions: 27% of the current freshmen were in the top fifth of their class; 54% were in the top two fifths.
Requirements: The SAT I or ACT is required. In addition, applicants must be graduates of accredited secondary schools or have earned a GED. The college requires 16 academic credits or Carnegie units, based on 6 years of academic electives, 4 of English, 2 each of foreign language and math, and 1 each of history and a lab science. An interview is recommended for all students, and an audition is required for applied music majors. The Court requires applicants to be in the upper 50% of their class. AP and CLEP credits are accepted.
Procedure: Freshmen are admitted fall and spring. Entrance exams should be taken by January of the senior year. There is an early admissions plan. Applications should be filed by August 1 for fall entry and January 1 for spring entry. Notification is sent on a rolling basis. The fall 2001 application fee was $30.
Transfer: Applicants with fewer than 24 credits must fulfill freshman requirements. 50 credits of 132 must be completed at The Court.
Visiting: There are regularly scheduled orientations for prospective students, including visits with faculty and students and a tour of facilities. There are guides for informal visits and visitors may sit in on classes and stay overnight. To schedule a visit, contact Director of Admissions.
Financial Aid: In a recent year, 91% of all freshmen and 83% of continuing students received some form of financial aid. 91% of freshmen and 82% of continuing students received need-based aid. The average freshman award was $11,714. Of that total, scholarships or need-based grants averaged $9378 ($18,531 maximum); loans averaged $3971 ($18,783 maximum); and work contracts averaged $993 ($1000 maximum). 30% of undergraduates work part time. Average annual earnings from campus work are $993. The average financial indebtedness of a recent graduate was $14,047. The Court is a member of CSS. The FAFSA, the college's own financial statement, and the parent and student 1040 tax forms are required. Check with the school for current deadlines.
International Students: There were 4 international students enrolled in a recent year. The school actively recruits these students. They must score 550 on the written TOEFL.
Computers: 6 modern computer labs with 131 networked computers are available to all students. All students may access the system from 8 A.M. to 10 P.M. daily. There are no time limits and no fees.
Graduates: In a recent year, 344 bachelor's degrees were awarded. The most popular majors were psychology (18%), special education (17%), and business (14%). In an average class, 47% graduate in 4 years, 60% in 5 years, and 64% in 6 years. 79 companies recruited on campus in a recet year. Of a recent graduating class, 16% were enrolled in graduate school within 6 months of graduation and 89% were employed.
Admissions Contact: Director of Admissions.
E-mail: *admissions-ugrad@georgian.edu* Web: *www.georgian.edu*

JERSEY CITY STATE COLLEGE
(See New Jersey City University)

KEAN UNIVERSITY E-2
Union, NJ 07083-0411 (908) 527-2195; Fax: (908) 351-5187

Full-time: 2531 men, 4182 women	**Faculty:** 376
Part-time: 776 men, 1978 women	**Ph.D.s:** 90%
Graduate: 599 men, 2028 women	**Student/Faculty:** 18 to 1
Year: semesters, summer session	**Tuition:** $5121 ($7041)
Application Deadline: June 15	**Room & Board:** $6038
Freshman Class: 4684 applied, 2382 accepted, 1195 enrolled	
SAT I Verbal/Math: 494/505	**COMPETITIVE**

Kean University, founded in 1855, is a public institution offering undergraduate and graduate programs in the arts and sciences, business, education, government, nursing, and technology. Kean is primarily a metropolitan commuter university. There are 4 undergraduate schools and 1 graduate school. In addition to regional accreditation, Kean has baccalaureate program accreditation with APTA, ASLA, CAHEA, CSWE, NASAD, NASDTEC, NASM, NCATE, and NLN. The library contains 271,000 volumes, 792,000 microform items, and 6000 audiovisual forms/CDs, and subscribes to 14,200 periodicals. Computerized library services include the card catalog, interlibrary loans, and database searching. Special learning facilities include a learning resource center, art gallery, radio station, TV station, and Holocaust Resource Center. The 151-acre campus is in a suburban area 12 miles west of New York City. Including residence halls, there are 35 buildings.
Student Life: 95% of undergraduates are from New Jersey. Others are from 15 states and 89 foreign countries. 52% are white; 20% African American; 17% Hispanic. The average age of freshmen is 21; all undergraduates, 26. 21% do not continue beyond their first year; 39% remain to graduate.
Housing: 1250 students can be accommodated in college housing, which includes coed dormitories and on-campus apartments. On-campus housing is guaranteed for all 4 years. 88% of students commute. Alcohol is not permitted. All students may keep cars.
Activities: There are 12 local and 3 national fraternities and 12 local and 4 national sororities. There are 130 groups on campus, including cheerleading, chorus, computers, dance, drama, ethnic, gay, honors, international, jazz band, literary magazine, musical theater, newspaper, pep band, political, professional, radio and TV, religious, social, social service, student government, and yearbook. Popular campus events include Campus Awareness Festival.
Sports: There are 8 intercollegiate sports for men and 7 for women, and 13 intramural sports for men and 9 for women. Facilities include a 3000-seat stadium, an 8-lane track, 7 playing fields, 4 gyms, basketball courts, 22 tennis courts, swimming pools, a track, a weight training room, pool tables, and pinball and video machines.
Disabled Students: All of the campus is accessible. Wheelchair ramps, elevators, special parking, and specially equipped rest rooms are available.
Services: Counseling and information services are available, as is tutoring in most subjects. There is a reader service for the blind, remedial math, reading, and writing, and a full program for learning-disabled students.
Campus Safety and Security: Measures include 24-hour foot and vehicle patrol, escort service, shuttle buses, and informal discussions. There are pamphlets/posters/films, emergency telephones, and lighted pathways/sidewalks.
Programs of Study: Kean confers B.A., B.S., and B.F.A., B.S.N and B.S.W. degrees. Master's degrees are also awarded. Bachelor's degrees are awarded in BIOLOGICAL SCIENCE (biology/biological science), BUSINESS (accounting, banking and finance, business administration and management, marketing/retailing/merchandising, and recreation and leisure services), COMMUNICATIONS AND THE ARTS (art history and appreciation, communications, dramatic arts, English, fine arts, graphic design, industrial design, multimedia, music, Spanish, studio art, and telecommunications), COMPUTER AND PHYSICAL SCIENCE (chemistry, computer science, earth science, and mathematics), EDUCATION (drama, early childhood, elementary, industrial arts, music, physical, special, and technical), ENGINEERING AND ENVIRONMENTAL DESIGN (graphic arts technology, industrial engineering technology, and interior design), HEALTH PROFESSIONS (health care administration, medical technology, nursing, occupational therapy, rehabilitation therapy, and speech pathology/audiology), SOCIAL SCIENCE (criminal justice, economics, history, philosophy, political science/government, psychology, public administration, social work, and sociology). Allied health and technology are the strongest academically. Business is the largest.
Required: Students must complete a freshman seminar, 18 credits of core requirements, 2 upper-level writing courses, and at least 30 credits in a major field. The bachelor's degree requires completion of 124 to 129 semester hours with a minimum GPA of 2.0.

Special: Students may study abroad in 7 countries, and Kean offers cooperative programs and cross-registration with other members of the Consortium of East New Jersey. There are also dual majors in elementary education, a B.A.- B.S. degree in chemistry, internships in selected majors, a Washington semester, accelerated degrees in chemistry and social work, credit for life experience, and pass/fail options. There are 5 national honor societies, a freshman honors program, and 18 departmental honors programs.

Faculty/Classroom: 53% of faculty are male; 47%, female. All teach undergraduates. No introductory courses are taught by graduate students. The average class size in an introductory lecture is 25; in a laboratory, 15; and in a regular course, 17.

Admissions: 51% of the 2001-2002 applicants were accepted. The SAT I scores for the 2001-2002 freshman class were: Verbal--54% below 500, 42% between 500 and 599, and 4% between 600 and 700; Math--45% below 500, 49% between 500 and 599, and 6% between 600 and 700. 19% of the current freshmen were in the top fifth of their class; 47% were in the top two fifths.

Requirements: The SAT I is required, with a minimum composite score of 1000. Applicants must be graduates of accredited secondary schools or have earned a GED. College preparatory study includes 4 courses in English, 3 in math, 2 each in lab science and social studies, and 5 in academic electives. An essay is also required, and an interview is recommended. Kean requires applicants to be in the upper 50% of their class. A GPA of 2.0 is required. AP and CLEP credits are accepted. Important factors in the admissions decision are leadership record, advanced placement or honor courses, and recommendations by school officials.

Procedure: Freshmen are admitted to all sessions. Applications should be filed by June 15 for fall entry and November 1 for spring entry. The fall application fee was $35. Notification is sent on a rolling basis.

Transfer: 1084 transfer students enrolled in 2001-2002. Applicants must present a minimum GPA of 2.0. Those students tranferring fewer than 15 credits must also submit SAT I scores. 32 credits of 124 must be completed at Kean.

Visiting: There are regularly scheduled orientations for prospective students. There are guides for informal visits. To schedule a visit, contact the Admissions Office.

Financial Aid: In 2001-2002, 61% of all freshmen and 40% of continuing students received some form of financial aid. 50% of freshmen and 32% of continuing students received need-based aid. The average freshman award was $6024. Of that total, scholarships or need-based grants averaged $3928 ($9751 maximum); loans averaged $4374 ($6625 maximum); work contracts averaged $1521 ($2000 maximum); and institutional scholarships averaged $1121 ($2000 maximum). 10% of undergraduates work part time. Average annual earnings from campus work are $1925. The average financial indebtedness of the 2001 graduate was $24,106. The FAFSA is required. The fall application deadline is March 15.

International Students: There are 240 international students enrolled. The school actively recruits these students.

Computers: The Computer Services Department operates a Prime 6550 for academic use and a Prime 5340 for CAD/CAM use by the Technology Department. Major buildings are connected by a campus-wide fiber-optic backbone to the university's central system. More than 30 discipline-based PC labs with software packages are located throughout the campus. All students may access the system. There are no time limits and no fees.

Graduates: The most popular majors were management science (13%), elementary education (9%), and psychology (6%). In an average class, 15% graduate in 4 years, 35% in 5 years, and 43% in 6 years.

Admissions Contact: Audley Bridges, Director of Admissions. A video is available. E-mail: *admitme@turbo.kean.edu* Web: *www.kean.edu*

MONMOUTH UNIVERSITY — E-3

West Long Branch, NJ 07764-1898 — (732) 571-3456
(800) 543-9671; Fax: (732) 263-5166

Full-time: 1594 men, 2041 women	**Faculty:** 211; IIA, av$
Part-time: 176 men, 368 women	**Ph.D.s:** 73%
Graduate: 525 men, 1049 women	**Student/Faculty:** 17 to 1
Year: semesters, summer session	**Tuition:** $17,076
Application Deadline: March 1	**Room & Board:** $6966
Freshman Class: 4964 applied, 4050 accepted, 882 enrolled	
SAT I or ACT: required	**COMPETITIVE**

Monmouth University, founded in 1933, is a private comprehensive institution offering both undergraduate and graduate programs in the arts and sciences, business, education, upper-level nursing, technology, and professional training. There are 5 undergraduate schools and 1 graduate school. In addition to regional accreditation, Monmouth has baccalaureate program accreditation with AACSB, ABET, ACS, CCNE, CSWE, and NLN. The library contains 252,497 volumes and 331,970 microform items, and subscribes to 1250 periodicals. Computerized library services include the card catalog, interlibrary loans, and database searching. Special learning facilities include a learning resource center, art gallery, radio station, and TV station. The 147-acre campus is in a suburban area 60 miles south of New York City. Including residence halls, there are 53 buildings.

Student Life: 92% of undergraduates are from New Jersey. Others are from 23 states, 12 foreign countries, and Canada. 79% are white. The average age of freshmen is 18; all undergraduates, 23. 29% do not continue beyond their first year; 52% remain to graduate.

Housing: 1400 students can be accommodated in college housing, which includes single-sex and coed dormitories and on-campus apartments. On-campus housing is available on a first-come, first-served basis. Priority is given to out-of-town students. 61% of students commute. Alcohol is not permitted. All students may keep cars.

Activities: 8% of men belong to 7 national fraternities; 9% of women belong to 6 national sororities. There are 67 groups on campus, including cheerleading, choir, computers, drama, ethnic, gay, honors, international, jazz band, literary magazine, musical theater, newspaper, pep band, political, professional, radio and TV, religious, social service, student government, symphony, and yearbook. Popular campus events include Springfest, Ebony Night, and Winter Ball.

Sports: There are 8 intercollegiate sports for men and 7 for women, and 7 intramural sports for men and 7 for women. Facilities include a 2800-seat gym, outdoor tennis courts, 3 basketball courts, an 8-lane all-weather track, an indoor Olympic-size pool, exercise, wrestling, and weight rooms, and baseball, softball, and soccer fields.

Disabled Students: 90% of the campus is accessible. Wheelchair ramps, elevators, special parking, specially equipped rest rooms, special class scheduling, lowered drinking fountains, and academic assistance provided within the classroom are available.

Services: There is a reader service for the blind, and remedial math, reading, and writing. Tutoring is offered in every subject for learning disabled and physically challenged students. It is available upon request for others.

Campus Safety and Security: Measures include 24-hour foot and vehicle patrol, self-defense education, escort service, and informal discussions. There are pamphlets/posters/films, emergency telephones, lighted pathways/sidewalks, an official Monmouth University police force, and a student watch organization.

Programs of Study: Monmouth confers B.A., B.S., B.S.N., and B.S.W. degrees. Associate and master's degrees are also awarded. Bachelor's degrees are awarded in BIOLOGICAL SCIENCE (biology/biological science), BUSINESS (accounting, banking and finance, business administration and management, business economics, and marketing/retailing/merchandising), COMMUNICATIONS AND THE ARTS (art, art history and appreciation, communications, English, modern language, music, and music business management), COMPUTER AND PHYSICAL SCIENCE (chemistry, computer programming, computer science, and mathematics), EDUCATION (art, English, foreign languages, mathematics, music, science, secondary, and special), ENGINEERING AND ENVIRONMENTAL DESIGN (computer graphics), HEALTH PROFESSIONS (clinical science, medical laboratory technology, nursing, and premedicine), SOCIAL SCIENCE (anthropology, criminal justice, history, interdisciplinary studies, political science/government, prelaw, psychology, and social work). Business, education, and communication are the largest.

Required: General education requirements include 6 credits each of English composition, literature, history, natural science, social sciences, and cross-cultural studies; 3 each of math, computer science, critical discourse, and global issues; and 1 of phys ed. Students must also pass a writing proficiency exam. To graduate, students must earn at least 128 credits, including 30 or more in a major, with a minimum GPA of 2.0 overall and 2.1 in the major.

Special: Students may study abroad. There are cooperative and internship programs and a Washington semester. Monmouth also offers work-study programs, dual majors, flexible studies programs, and credit for life experience. Nondegree study is possible. There are 7 national honor societies and a freshman honors program.

Faculty/Classroom: 52% of faculty are male; 48%, female. No introductory courses are taught by graduate students.

Admissions: 82% of the 2001-2002 applicants were accepted. The SAT I scores for the 2001-2002 freshman class were: Verbal--34% below 500, 52% between 500 and 599, 13% between 600 and 700, and 1% above 700; Math--28% below 500, 54% between 500 and 599, 17% between 600 and 700, and 1% above 700. 26% of the current freshmen were in the top fifth of their class; 61% were in the top two fifths.

Requirements: The SAT I or ACT is required, with a combined minimum score of 950 on the SAT I. Applicants must be graduates of accredited secondary schools or have earned a GED. The college requires 16 Carnegie units, based on 4 years of English, 3 of math, and 2 each of history and science, with the remaining 5 units in academic electives. An essay and an interview are also recommended. A GPA of 2.25 is required. AP and CLEP credits are accepted. Important factors in the admissions decision are advanced placement or honor courses, recommendations by school officials, and personality/intangible qualities. Applications are accepted on-line.

Procedure: Freshmen are admitted fall, spring, and summer. Entrance exams should be taken by December of the senior year. There are early decision, early admissions, and deferred admissions plans. Early decision applications should be filed by December 1; regular applications, by March 1 for fall entry and January 1 for spring entry. The fall 2001 application fee was $35. Notification of early decision is sent January 1; regular decision, April 1. 147 early decision candidates were accepted for the 2001-2002 class.

Transfer: 420 transfer students enrolled in 2001-2002. Transfers with fewer than 24 transferable college credits must provide a high school transcript and SAT I scores. All transfer applicants must submit college transcripts and a statement of good standing. A minimum college GPA of 2.0 is required. 32 credits of 128 must be completed at Monmouth.

Visiting: There are regularly scheduled orientations for prospective students, including campus tours and interviews. There are guides for informal visits and visitors may sit in on classes. To schedule a visit, contact the Admissions Office.

Financial Aid: In 2001-2002, 66% of all freshmen and 63% of continuing students received some form of financial aid. 31% of freshmen and 33% of continuing students received need-based aid. Scholarships or need-based grants averaged $7182 and loans averaged $4804. The average financial indebtedness of the 2001 graduate was $18,500. Monmouth is a member of CSS. The FAFSA is required.

International Students: There are 12 international students enrolled. The school actively recruits these students. They must score 525 on the written TOEFL. The SAT I or ACT may be substituted for the TOEFL, with a minimum 1050 composite score on the SAT I.

Computers: Classrooms, offices, residence hall rooms, and computer labs are connected via a 10MB Ethernet network encompassing more than 1,000 workstations. More than 500 workstations (Pentium, Mac, Sun, and Silicon Graphics) are dedicated for student use in more than 30 computing labs. There are also areas on campus that are enhanced for laptop connectivity. All students may access the system. There are no time limits and no fees.

Graduates: In 2001, 819 bachelor's degrees were awarded. The most popular majors were business (24%), education (20%), and communication (14%). In an average class, 35% graduate in 4 years, 47% in 5 years, and 52% in 6 years.

Admissions Contact: Kelly McCrum, Director of Undergraduate Admissions. E-mail: *cbenol@mondec.monmouth.edu*
Web: *www.monmouth.edu*

MONTCLAIR STATE UNIVERSITY

Upper Montclair, NJ 07043-1624 E-2
(973) 655-4444
(800) 331-9205; (973) 655-7700

Full-time: 2800 men, 4200 women	**Faculty:** 444; IIA, +$
Part-time: 920 men, 1800 women	**Ph.D.s:** 90%
Graduate: 910 men, 2175 women	**Student/Faculty:** 16 to 1
Year: semesters, summer session	**Tuition:** $4387 ($6302)
Application Deadline: March 1	**Room & Board:** $5900 ($6475)
Freshman Class: n/av	
SAT I or ACT: required	**LESS COMPETITIVE**

Montclair State University, established in 1908, is a public institution offering programs in liberal arts and sciences, business administration, fine and performing arts, and professional studies. Figures given in above capsule are approximate. There are 5 undergraduate schools and 1 graduate school. In addition to regional accreditation, Montclair has baccalaureate program accreditation with ADA, CSAB, NASAD, NASM, NCATE, and NRPA. The library contains 420,000 volumes, 1,100,000 microform items, and 15,000 audiovisual forms/CDs, and subscribes to 3400 periodicals. Computerized library services include the card catalog, interlibrary loans, and database searching. Special learning facilities include a learning resource center, art gallery, radio station, a psychoeducational center, and Academic Success Center. The 200-acre campus is in a suburban area 15 miles west of New York City. Including residence halls, there are 39 buildings.

Student Life: 96% of undergraduates are from New Jersey. Others are from 31 states and 56 foreign countries. 80% are from public schools. 64% are white; 15% Hispanic; 11% African American. The average age of freshmen is 18; all undergraduates, 28. 20% do not continue beyond their first year; 59% remain to graduate.

Housing: 2079 students can be accommodated in college housing, which includes single-sex and coed dormitories and on-campus apartments. On-campus housing is guaranteed for the freshman year only and is available on a lottery system for upperclassmen. Priority is given to out-of-town students. 79% of students commute. Alcohol is not permitted. All students may keep cars.

Activities: There are 13 local and 12 national fraternities and 10 local and 7 national sororities. There are 121 groups on campus, including band, cheerleading, choir, chorus, drama, ethnic, gay, honors, international, jazz band, literary magazine, marching band, newspaper, orchestra, professional, radio and TV, religious, social, social service, student government, and yearbook. Popular campus events include Carnival, Spring Week, and Greek Week.

Sports: There are 11 intercollegiate sports for men and 11 for women, and 10 intramural sports for men and 9 for women. Facilities include a gym complex with a pool, wrestling and weight rooms, a basketball court, an auxiliary gym, a 6000-seat field, a baseball diamond, tennis and platform tennis courts, 2 softball fields, a multipurpose field, an all-weather track, a field house, and a fitness center.

Disabled Students: 85% of the campus is accessible. Wheelchair ramps, elevators, special parking, specially equipped rest rooms, lowered drinking fountains, lowered telephones, and curb cuts, speaker phones, special building signs, TDDs, and priority registration. An office for students with disabilities has been established are available.

Services: Counseling and information services are available, as is tutoring in most subjects. There is remedial math, reading, and writing. Textbooks on tape are available.

Campus Safety and Security: Measures include 24-hour foot and vehicle patrol, self-defense education, escort service, and shuttle buses. There are informal discussions, pamphlets/posters/films, emergency telephones, lighted pathways/sidewalks, a full-time campus police force, a crime prevention officer, and crime prevention programs.

Programs of Study: Montclair confers B.A., B.S., B.F.A., and B.Mus. degrees. Master's degrees are also awarded. Bachelor's degrees are awarded in BIOLOGICAL SCIENCE (biochemistry, biology/biological science, and molecular biology), BUSINESS (business administration and management and recreation and leisure services), COMMUNICATIONS AND THE ARTS (broadcasting, classics, dance, dramatic arts, English, fine arts, French, German, Italian, Latin, linguistics, music, music performance, Spanish, and speech/debate/rhetoric), COMPUTER AND PHYSICAL SCIENCE (chemistry, computer science, geoscience, mathematics, and physics), EDUCATION (art, business, health, music, physical, and technical), HEALTH PROFESSIONS (allied health and music therapy), SOCIAL SCIENCE (anthropology, economics, geography, history, home economics, human ecology, humanities, parks and recreation management, philosophy, political science/government, psychology, religion, and sociology). Business administration, psychology, and biology are the largest.

Required: Students must successfully complete a minimum of 128 semester hours, with 33 to 82 in the major, while maintaining a minimum GPA of 2.0. General education requirements include courses in communications, contemporary issues, art appreciation, a foreign language, humanities, math, natural/physical science, social sciences, and multicultural awareness, as well as 1 semester hour in phys ed and 2 semester hours in computer science.

Special: Internships, co-op programs in all majors, credit by exam, pass/fail options, work-study, credit for life experience, independent study, weekend study, and study abroad in 50 countries are offered. Joint-degree programs are offered in practical anthropology and applied economics, and a 5-year B.A.-B.Mus. program in music is available, as is a 7-year articulated medical program with the University of Medicine and Dentistry of New Jersey. There are 23 national honor societies, a freshman honors program, and 6 departmental honors programs.

Faculty/Classroom: 63% of faculty are male; 37%, female.

Requirements: The SAT I or ACT is required. In addition, applicants must submit 16 Carnegie units, including 4 in English, 3 to 4 in math (including algebra I and II and geometry), 2 each in lab science, social studies, and a foreign language, and the remainder in additional courses in these fields. The GED is accepted. A portfolio, audition, or interview is required for students planning to major in fine arts, music, speech, or theater. Admission to computer science requires 4 years of math, including trigonometry. AP and CLEP credits are accepted. Important factors in the admissions decision are advanced placement or honor courses, recommendations by school officials, and ability to finance college education.

Procedure: Freshmen are admitted fall and spring. Entrance exams should be taken in October, November, or December of the senior year. Applications should be filed by March 1 for fall entry and October 15 for spring entry. Notification is sent on a rolling basis. 5% of all applicants are on a waiting list. The fall 2001 application fee was $40.

Transfer: Applicants must have completed a minimum of 15 credits from an accredited college. A cumulative GPA of 2.5 is required; a GPA of 3.0 is required for business and computer science majors. Applicants must have completed English composition. High school and college transcripts are required. 32 credits of 128 must be completed at Montclair.

Visiting: There are regularly scheduled orientations for prospective students. There are guides for informal visits. To schedule a visit, contact the Admissions Office.

Financial Aid: The FAFSA is required. Check with the school for current deadlines.

International Students: The school actively recruits these students. They must score 500 on the written TOEFL.

Computers: The mainframes are a DEC VAX cluster and a DEC ALPHA cluster. PC and Mac labs are located throughout the campus, with about 400 computers and PC printers. A network of Sun workstations is also available. A wide variety of general and discipline-specific software is offered. Residence hall rooms are wired for network connections, and Internet access is available. All students may access the system. There are no time limits and no fees.

Admissions Contact: Director of Admissions.
E-mail: *msuadm@mail.montclair.edu* Web: *www.montclair.edu*

NEW JERSEY CITY UNIVERSITY (Formerly Jersey City State College)
E-2

Jersey City, NJ 07305
(201) 200-3234
(888) 441-NJCU; (201) 200-2044

Full-time: 1550 men, 2300 women	**Faculty:** 240
Part-time: 700 men, 1250 women	**Ph.D.s:** 79%
Graduate: 380 men, 1150 women	**Student/Faculty:** 16 to 1
Year: semesters, summer session	**Tuition:** $4100 ($7600)
Application Deadline: April 1	**Room & Board:** $5000
Freshman Class: n/av	
SAT I: required	**LESS COMPETITIVE**

New Jersey City University, formerly known as Jersey City State College, founded in 1927, is a public institution offering undergraduate and graduate programs in the arts and sciences, business administration, education, health science, upper-level nursing, and other professional fields. Figures in the above capsule are approximate. There are 3 undergraduate schools and 1 graduate school. In addition to regional accreditation, NJCU has baccalaureate program accreditation with NASAD, NASM, NCATE, and NLN. The library contains 250,000 volumes, 600,000 microform items, and 850 audiovisual forms/CDs, and subscribes to 1500 periodicals. Computerized library services include the card catalog, interlibrary loans, and database searching. Special learning facilities include a learning resource center, art gallery, radio station, media arts center, and laboratory school for special-education instruction. The 17-acre campus is in an urban area 10 miles west of New York City, New York. Including residence halls, there are 14 buildings.

Student Life: 99% of undergraduates are from New Jersey. Others are from 12 states, 50 foreign countries, and Canada. 43% are white; 26% Hispanic; 18% African American. The average age of freshmen is 18; all undergraduates, 22.

Housing: 276 students can be accommodated in college housing, which includes coed dormitories and an academic/scholastic floor in Vodra Hall. On-campus housing is guaranteed for all 4 years and is available on a first-come, first-served basis. Priority is given to out-of-town students. 95% of students commute. Alcohol is not permitted. All students may keep cars.

Activities: 4% of men belong to 4 local and 4 national fraternities; 3% of women belong to 7 local sororities and 1 national sorority. There are 42 groups on campus, including art, band, cheerleading, choir, chorale, chorus, computers, dance, drama, ethnic, film, gay, honors, international, jazz band, literary magazine, musical theater, newspaper, opera, orchestra, photography, political, professional, radio and TV, religious, social, social service, student government, symphony, and yearbook. Popular campus events include President's Picnic, Town and Gown Concert, and lecture series.

Sports: There are 6 intercollegiate sports for men and 6 for women, and 14 intramural sports for men and 14 for women. Facilities include an athletic and fitness center with a 2000-seat arena, jogging track, fitness facilities, 6-lane pool, sauna, racquetball courts, and outdoor football, soccer, and tennis facilities.

Disabled Students: All of the campus is accessible. Wheelchair ramps, elevators, special parking, specially equipped rest rooms, special class scheduling, lowered drinking fountains, and lowered telephones are available.

Services: Counseling and information services are available, as is tutoring in most subjects. There is remedial math, reading, and writing.

Campus Safety and Security: Measures include 24-hour foot and vehicle patrol, escort service, shuttle buses, and informal discussions. There are pamphlets/posters/films, emergency telephones, and lighted pathways/sidewalks.

Programs of Study: NJCU confers B.A., B.S., B.F.A., and B.S.N. degrees. Master's degrees are also awarded. Bachelor's degrees are awarded in BIOLOGICAL SCIENCE (biology/biological science), BUSINESS (accounting, banking and finance, business administration and management, marketing/retailing/merchandising, and retailing), COMMUNICATIONS AND THE ARTS (design, English, fine arts, media arts, music, photography, and Spanish), COMPUTER AND PHYSICAL SCIENCE (chemistry, computer science, earth science, geology, mathematics, and physics), EDUCATION (art, early childhood, elementary, health, music, secondary, and special), HEALTH PROFESSIONS (medical laboratory technology, nuclear medical technology, nursing, predentistry, premedicine, and public health), SOCIAL SCIENCE (criminal justice, economics, geography, history, philosophy, political science/government, prelaw, psychology, and sociology). Business, nursing, criminal justice are the largest.

Required: Students must complete 66 semester hours in general education courses, satisfy college requirements in English, communication, and math, and complete the introductory career exploration and computer usage courses. The bachelor's degree requires completion of at least 128 semester hours, including 36 to 54 in a major field, with a minimum GPA of 2.0. Distribution requirements include 9 credits each in natural science, social science, humanities, and fine and performing arts, and 6 credits in communications and contemporary world.

Special: Co-op programs and internships in all majors are available. NJCU also offers study abroad, work-study programs, numerous health science programs, and some programs affiliated with New Jersey College of Medicine and Dentistry in Newark. Nondegree study is possible. There are 4 national honor societies, a freshman honors program, and 1 departmental honors program.

Faculty/Classroom: 57% of faculty are male; 43%, female. All teach undergraduates. No introductory courses are taught by graduate students. The average class size in an introductory lecture is 25; in a laboratory, 15; and in a regular course, 16.

Requirements: The SAT I is required. In addition, applicants must be graduates of accredited secondary schools or have earned a GED. The college requires 16 Carnegie units, including 4 in English, 3 in math, and 2 each in social studies and a lab science, with the remaining 5 units in a foreign language and additional academic courses. An essay is also required and an interview is recommended. Applications are accepted on-line at the school's web site. NJCU requires applicants to be in the upper 50% of their class. A GPA of 2.5 is required. AP and CLEP credits are accepted. Important factors in the admissions decision are advanced placement or honor courses, evidence of special talent, and recommendations by school officials.

Procedure: Freshmen are admitted fall and spring. Entrance exams should be taken in the spring of the junior year or fall of the senior year. There are early admissions and deferred admissions plans. Applications should be filed by April 1 for fall entry. Notification is sent on a rolling basis. A waiting list is an active part of the admissions procedure. The fall 2001 application fee was $35.

Transfer: 793 transfer students enrolled in a recent year. Applicants must present a minimum GPA of 2.0 in at least 12 credit hours completed at the college level. Students transferring fewer than 12 credits must also submit SAT I scores of at least 480 verbal and 440 math. An interview is recommended for all transfers. A basic skills test is required for transfers who have fewer than 30 credits or have not taken English or math at their previous school. 36 credits of 128 must be completed at NJCU.

Visiting: There are regularly scheduled orientations for prospective students, including a financial aid workshop, guided tours, and open house. There is a summer orientation. There are guides for informal visits and visitors may sit in on classes. To schedule a visit, contact the Admissions Office.

Financial Aid: NJCU is a member of CSS. The FAFSA is required. Check with the school for current deadlines.

International Students: They must score 500 on the written TOEFL and also take the SAT I, scoring 920.

Computers: The mainframes are a DEC VAX 6510, a VAX 8530, 3 MicroVAX 3100s, and a MicroVAX 3800. Students are able to use the Internet as well as other network systems, and a toll-free dial-up system whereby they may use home computers and the mainframe. There are 3 computer labs with 75 terminals. All students may access the system 24 hours a day. There are no time limits and no fees.

Graduates: In a recent year, 896 bachelor's degrees were awarded. The most popular majors were business administration (23%), criminal justice (11%), and nursing (8%). In an average class, 4% graduate in 4 years, 17% in 5 years, and 31% in 6 years. 350 companies recruited on campus in a recent year.

Admissions Contact: Drusilla Blackman, Director of Admissions.
E-mail: *admissions@njcu.edu* Web: *www.njcu.edu*

NEW JERSEY INSTITUTE OF TECHNOLOGY
E-2

Newark, NJ 07102-1982
(973) 596-3300
(800) 222-NJIT; Fax: (973) 596-6085

Full-time: 3224 men, 899 women	**Faculty:** 311
Part-time: 1213 men, 362 women	**Ph.D.s:** 98%
Graduate: 2268 men, 896 women	**Student/Faculty:** 13 to 1
Year: semesters, summer session	**Tuition:** $7200 ($11,852)
Application Deadline: April 1	**Room & Board:** $7490
Freshman Class: 2227 applied, 1456 accepted, 713 enrolled	
SAT I Verbal/Math: 536/593	**VERY COMPETITIVE**

New Jersey Institute of Technology is a public research university providing instruction, research, and public service in engineering, computer science, management, architecture, engineering technology, applied sciences, and related fields. There are 6 undergraduate schools and 1 graduate school. In addition to regional accreditation, NJIT has baccalaureate program accreditation with AACSB, ABET, CSAB, and NAAB. The 2 libraries contain 170,000 volumes, 1000 microform items, and

1000 audiovisual forms/CDs, and subscribe to 10,000 periodicals. Computerized library services include the card catalog, interlibrary loans, and database searching. Special learning facilities include a learning resource center, art gallery, radio station, and 3 TV studios. NJIT is home to many government- and industry-sponsored labs and research centers, including the EPA Northeast Hazardous Substance Research Center, the National Center for Transportation and Industrial Productivity, the Center for Manufacturing Systems, the Emission Reduction Research Center, the Microelectronics Research Center, the Center for Microwave and Lightwave Engineering, and the Multi-Lifecycle Engineering Center. The 45-acre campus is in an urban area 10 miles west of New York City. Including residence halls, there are 25 buildings.

Student Life: 95% of undergraduates are from New Jersey. Others are from 36 states, 100 foreign countries, and Canada. 80% are from public schools. 34% are white; 23% Asian American; 11% African American; 10% Hispanic. 38% are Catholic; 36% Islamic, Buddhist, Eastern Orthodox; 25% Protestant; 19% claim no religious affiliation. The average age of freshmen is 18; all undergraduates, 24. 15% do not continue beyond their first year; 80% remain to graduate.

Housing: 1155 students can be accommodated in college housing, which includes coed dormitories. On-campus housing is available on a first-come, first-served basis and is available on a lottery system for upperclassmen. Priority is given to out-of-town students. 82% of students commute. All students may keep cars.

Activities: 12% of men belong to 4 local and 10 national fraternities; 8% of women belong to 4 local and 5 national sororities. There are 65 groups on campus, including art, chess, computers, drama, drum and bugle corps, ethnic, gay, honors, international, musical theater, newspaper, photography, professional, radio and TV, religious, social, social service, student government, and yearbook. Popular campus events include Miniversity, International Students Food Festival, and Leadership Training Weekend.

Sports: There are 9 intercollegiate sports for men and 6 for women, and 13 intramural sports for men and 7 for women. Facilities include a 1000-seat stadium, a fitness center with an indoor track, a 6-lane swimming pool, 4 tennis courts, 4 racquet sport courts, playing fields, bowling lanes, a table tennis and billiards area, and 3 gyms, the largest of which seats 1200.

Disabled Students: 95% of the campus is accessible. Wheelchair ramps, elevators, special parking, specially equipped rest rooms, special class scheduling, lowered drinking fountains, and lowered telephones are available.

Services: Counseling and information services are available, as is tutoring in most subjects. There is a reader service for the blind, and remedial math, reading, and writing.

Campus Safety and Security: Measures include 24-hour foot and vehicle patrol, self-defense education, escort service, and shuttle buses. There are informal discussions, pamphlets/posters/films, emergency telephones, and lighted pathways/sidewalks.

Programs of Study: NJIT confers B.A., B.S., and B.Arch. degrees. Master's and doctoral degrees are also awarded. Bachelor's degrees are awarded in BIOLOGICAL SCIENCE (biology/biological science), BUSINESS (management science), COMMUNICATIONS AND THE ARTS (technical and business writing), COMPUTER AND PHYSICAL SCIENCE (applied mathematics, applied physics, chemistry, computer management, computer science, information sciences and systems, science technology, and statistics), ENGINEERING AND ENVIRONMENTAL DESIGN (architecture, chemical engineering, civil engineering, computer engineering, electrical/electronics engineering, engineering and applied science, engineering technology, environmental science, geophysical engineering, industrial engineering, manufacturing engineering, and mechanical engineering), HEALTH PROFESSIONS (nursing), SOCIAL SCIENCE (history). Engineering, computer science, and architecture are the strongest academically. Engineering is the largest.

Required: General university requirements include 9 credits of humanities and social science electives, 7 of natural sciences, 6 each of math, cultural history, basic social sciences, and engineering technology, 3 each of English and management, and 2 of computer science. Students must also complete 2 courses in phys ed. To graduate, students must earn between 124 and 164 credits, depending on the program, including 50 in the major, with a minimum GPA of 2.0 in upper-level major courses.

Special: Cross-registration is offered in conjunction with Essex County College, Rutgers University's Newark campus, and the University of Medicine and Dentistry of New Jersey. Cooperative programs, available in all majors, include two 6-month internships. There are 3-2 engineering degree programs with Stockton State College and Lincoln and Seton Hall Universities. NJIT also offers work-study programs, study abroad in 18 countries, dual and interdisciplinary majors, accelerated degree programs, distance learning, and nondegree study. There is 1 national honor society, and a freshman honors program.

Faculty/Classroom: 83% of faculty are male; 17%, female. 74% teach undergraduates, all do research, and 74% do both. The average class size in an introductory lecture is 30; in a laboratory, 27; and in a regular course, 25.

Admissions: 65% of the 2001-2002 applicants were accepted. The SAT I scores for the 2001-2002 freshman class were: Verbal--29% below 500, 49% between 500 and 599, 20% between 600 and 700, and 2% above 700; Math--8% below 500, 44% between 500 and 599, 42% between 600 and 700, and 7% above 700. 1% of the current freshmen were in the top fifth of their class; 8% were in the top two fifths.

Requirements: The SAT I is required. In addition, the SAT II: Subject test in math I or II is also required. Applicants should have completed 16 secondary school units, including 4 each in English and math, 2 in a lab science, and 6 in a distribution of social studies, foreign language, math, and science courses. AP and CLEP credits are accepted. Important factors in the admissions decision are advanced placement or honor courses, recommendations by school officials, and geographic diversity. Applications are accepted on-line at the school's web site.

Procedure: Freshmen are admitted fall and spring. Entrance exams should be taken in May of the junior year or November of the senior year. Applications should be filed by April 1 for fall entry and November 15 for spring entry, along with a $50 fee. Notification is sent on a rolling basis. 15% of all applicants are on a waiting list.

Transfer: 560 transfer students enrolled in 2001-2002. A minimum college GPA of 2.0 is required, but 2.5 or higher is recommended. Students must submit transcripts of all attempted postsecondary academic work. Applicants with fewer than 30 credits may be asked to provide scores on the SAT I and the SAT II: Subject test in math, as well as high school transcripts. Engineering technology students must present an associate degree. Admission to the School of Architecture is very competitive for transfer students. 33 credits of 124 to 164 must be completed at NJIT.

Visiting: There are regularly scheduled orientations for prospective students, including tours and meetings with admissions personnel, students, and faculty. There are guides for informal visits and visitors may sit in on classes and stay overnight. To schedule a visit, contact Kathy Kelly, Director of Admissions.

Financial Aid: In 2001-2002, 70% of all students received some form of financial aid. 50% of all students received need-based aid. 70% of undergraduates work part time. Average annual earnings from campus work are $2150. The average financial indebtedness of the 2001 graduate was $7000. The FAFSA and the college's own financial statement are required.

International Students: There are 295 international students enrolled. The school actively recruits these students. They must score 550 on the written TOEFL or 213 on the electronic version and also take the SAT I. Students must take SAT II: Subject tests in math I or II.

Computers: The mainframes are comprised of a DEC VAX 6430, which serves as the main VMS computer, and a DEC 5900, which serves as the UNIX engine for academic work. All computing facilities are connected to a campuswide network, which has a fiber-optic spine between buildings; all dorm rooms are wired for access. 150 computer nodes can be accessed from 2500 on-campus locations. All students may access the system. There are no time limits and no fees. All students are required to have personal computers.

Graduates: In 2001, 803 bachelor's degrees were awarded. The most popular majors were computer science (22%), engineering technology (11%), and computer engineering (9%). In an average class, 47% graduate in 6 years. 200 companies recruited on campus in 2000-2001. Of the 2000 graduating class, 20% were enrolled in graduate school within 6 months of graduation and 70% were employed.

Admissions Contact: Kathy Kelly, Director of Admissions.
E-mail: *admissions@admin.njit.edu*

PRINCETON UNIVERSITY D-3

Princeton, NJ 08544-0430 **(609) 258-3060; Fax: (609) 258-6743**

Full-time: 2380 men, 2231 women	**Faculty:** 704; I, ++$
Part-time: none	**Ph.D.s:** 83%
Graduate: 1178 men, 675 women	**Student/Faculty:** 7 to 1
Year: semesters	**Tuition:** $27,230
Application Deadline: January 2	**Room & Board:** $7842
Freshman Class: 14,289 applied, 1677 accepted, 1185 enrolled	
SAT I Verbal/Math: 720/740	**ACT:** 33 **MOST COMPETITIVE**

Princeton University, established in 1746, is a private institution offering degrees in the liberal arts and sciences, engineering, applied science, architecture, public and international affairs, interdisciplinary and regional studies, and the creative arts. There are 4 graduate schools. In addition to regional accreditation, Princeton has baccalaureate program accreditation with ABET and NAAB. The 20 libraries contain 5 million volumes, 3 million microform items, and 52,000 audiovisual forms/CDs, and subscribe to 30,000 periodicals. Computerized library services include the card catalog. Special learning facilities include an art gallery, natural history museum, radio station, a music center, a visual and performing arts center, several theaters, an observatory, a plasma physics lab, and a center for environmental and energy studies. The 600-acre campus is in a small town 50 miles south of New York City. Including residence halls, there are 140 buildings.

Student Life: 86% of undergraduates are from out of state, mostly the Middle Atlantic. Others are from 49 states, 70 foreign countries, and

Canada. 71% are white; 10% Asian American. The average age of freshmen is 18; all undergraduates, 20. 2% do not continue beyond their first year; 96% remain to graduate.

Housing: 4400 students can be accommodated in college housing, which includes coed dormitories, on-campus apartments, and married-student housing. On-campus housing is guaranteed for all 4 years. 98% of students live on campus. Alcohol is not permitted. All students may keep cars.

Activities: There are no fraternities or sororities. There are 200 groups on campus, including art, band, cheerleading, chess, choir, chorale, chorus, dance, drama, ethnic, film, gay, international, jazz band, literary magazine, musical theater, newspaper, opera, orchestra, pep band, photography, political, professional, radio and TV, religious, social, social service, student government, symphony, and yearbook. Popular campus events include recitals and theater productions.

Sports: There are 17 intercollegiate sports for men and 16 for women, and 53 intramural sports for men and 53 for women. Facilities include a 45,000-seat football and track stadium, an 18-hole golf course, 2 gyms, an Olympic swimming and diving complex, playing fields, a boathouse and Olympic-level racing course for crew and sailing, a health fitness center, an ice rink, dance studios, and tennis, squash, and volleyball courts.

Disabled Students: Wheelchair ramps, elevators, special parking, specially equipped rest rooms, special class scheduling, and lowered telephones are available.

Services: Counseling and information services are available, as is tutoring in every subject. There is a reader service for the blind.

Campus Safety and Security: Measures include 24-hour foot and vehicle patrol, self-defense education, escort service, and shuttle buses. There are informal discussions, pamphlets/posters/films, emergency telephones, and lighted pathways/sidewalks.

Programs of Study: Princeton confers A.B. and B.S.E. degrees. Master's and doctoral degrees are also awarded. Bachelor's degrees are awarded in BIOLOGICAL SCIENCE (biology/biological science), COMMUNICATIONS AND THE ARTS (classics, comparative literature, English, Germanic languages and literature, music, romance languages and literature, and Slavic languages), COMPUTER AND PHYSICAL SCIENCE (astrophysics, chemistry, computer science, geology, mathematics, and physics), ENGINEERING AND ENVIRONMENTAL DESIGN (aeronautical engineering, architectural engineering, architecture, chemical engineering, civil engineering, electrical/electronics engineering, and mechanical engineering), SOCIAL SCIENCE (anthropology, archeology, East Asian studies, economics, history, international relations, Near Eastern studies, philosophy, political science/government, psychology, religion, and sociology). History, political science, and English are the largest.

Required: To graduate, students must complete 8 semesters, or academic units. Candidates for the A.B. degree must demonstrate proficiency in English composition and a foreign language and complete distribution requirements in the areas of arts and letters, natural science, social science, and history, philosophy, and religion. Candidates for the B.S.E. must satisfy the English composition requirement and, by the end of the sophomore year, complete 4 terms of math, 2 of physics, and 1 each of chemistry and computing. A junior project and senior thesis are required of virtually all students.

Special: Princeton offers independent study, preceptorials, accelerated degree programs, a program in teacher preparation, student-proposed courses and majors, field study, study abroad, seminars, and internships in public affairs. The university operates on an honor code whereby exams are not proctored by faculty members. There are 2 national honor societies, including Phi Beta Kappa.

Faculty/Classroom: 76% of faculty are male; 24%, female. All teach undergraduates and 90% do research. Graduate students teach 1% of introductory courses.

Admissions: 12% of the 2001-2002 applicants were accepted. The SAT I scores for the 2001-2002 freshman class were: Verbal--2% between 500 and 599, 27% between 600 and 700, and 71% above 700; Math--1% between 500 and 599, 24% between 600 and 700, and 75% above 700. 95% of the current freshmen were in the top fifth of their class; 100% were in the top two fifths.

Requirements: The SAT I is required. In addition, the ACT is accepted. SAT II: Subject tests are also required. Applicants must be graduates of an accredited secondary school. Recommended college preparatory courses include 4 years each of English, math, and a foreign language; 2 years each of lab science and history; and some study of art, music, and, if possible, a second foreign language. An essay is required and an interview is recommended. Fine arts majors should submit an audition tape or portfolio. AP credits are accepted.

Procedure: Freshmen are admitted in the fall. Entrance exams should be taken by January of the senior year. There are early decision, early admissions, and deferred admissions plans. Early decision applications should be filed by November 1; regular applications, by January 2 for fall entry, along with a $60 fee. 3% of all applicants are on a waiting list.

Transfer: No transfer students have been admitted in recent years. Since space is limited, only those students with excellent academic records and compelling academic reasons for transferring should apply.

Visiting: There are regularly scheduled orientations for prospective students, including daily tours conducted by student guides, general information sessions, and student sessions with admissions staff. There are guides for informal visits and visitors may sit in on classes and stay overnight. To schedule a visit, contact Orange Key Guide Service at (609) 258-3603.

Financial Aid: In 2001-2002, 80% of all students received some form of financial aid. 67% of undergraduates work part time. Princeton is a member of CSS. The CSS/Profile and the college's own financial statement are required.

International Students: The school actively recruits these students. They must take the TOEFL and also take the SAT I.

Computers: The mainframe is an IBM 9672-RC4 system. There are also 450 PCs, including Macs and IBMs, connected to a central TigerNet system. NeXT, Silicon Graphics, Bitnet, and the Internet are available through Sun workstations. All residence hall rooms are wired through Dormnet, and specialized clusters on campus provide access to very high bandwidth resources. All students may access the system. There are no fees. It is strongly recommended that all students have a personal computer.

Admissions Contact: Fred A. Hargadon, Dean of Admissions.
Web: *www.princeton.edu*

RAMAPO COLLEGE OF NEW JERSEY — D-2

Mahwah, NJ 07430 — **(201) 684-7300**
(800) 9-RAMAPO; Fax: (201) 684-7964

Full-time: 1454 men, 2060 women	**Faculty:** 159; IIB, +$
Part-time: 526 men, 850 women	**Ph.D.s:** 93%
Graduate: 124 men, 185 women	**Student/Faculty:** 22 to 1
Year: semesters, summer session	**Tuition:** $6178 ($9564)
Application Deadline: March 1	**Room & Board:** $7372
Freshman Class: 3549 applied, 1496 accepted, 633 enrolled	
SAT I Verbal/Math: 550/550	**VERY COMPETITIVE**

Ramapo College, founded in 1971, is a public institution offering undergraduate programs in the arts and sciences, American and international studies, business administration, and human services. Personal interaction is incorporated throughout the curriculum as is an international, multicultural component including telecommunications and computer technology. There are 5 undergraduate and 3 graduate schools. In addition to regional accreditation, Ramapo has baccalaureate program accreditation with NLN. The library contains 110,646 volumes, 802 microform items, and 1726 audiovisual forms/CDs, and subscribes to 910 periodicals. Computerized library services include the card catalog, interlibrary loans, and database searching. Special learning facilities include a learning resource center, art gallery, radio station, TV station, and an international telecommunications satellite center. The 314-acre campus is in a suburban area 25 miles northwest of New York City. Including residence halls, there are 48 buildings.

Student Life: 84% of undergraduates are from New Jersey. Others are from 22 states and 64 foreign countries. 77% are white. The average age of freshmen is 18; all undergraduates, 24. 15% do not continue beyond their first year; 48% remain to graduate.

Housing: 1903 students can be accommodated in college housing, which includes coed dormitories and on-campus apartments. In addition, there are special-interest houses and an international house. On-campus housing is available on a first-come, first-served basis. 54% of students live on campus. All students may keep cars.

Activities: 6% of men belong to 6 national fraternities; 6% of women belong to 6 national sororities. There are 60 groups on campus, including cheerleading, choir, chorale, chorus, computers, debate, drama, ethnic, film, gay, honors, international, jazz band, literary magazine, musical theater, newspaper, photography, political, professional, radio and TV, religious, social, social service, student government, and yearbook. Popular campus events include Welcome Week, Springfest, and Earth Day.

Sports: There are 8 intercollegiate sports for men and 8 for women, and 4 intramural sports for men and 2 for women. Facilities include a 1000-seat stadium, 12 lighted tennis courts, playing fields, a 300-seat arena, a track, a 1000-seat gym with a basketball court, an Olympic-size pool, and a fitness and weight training center.

Disabled Students: All of the campus is accessible. Wheelchair ramps, elevators, special parking, specially equipped rest rooms, special class scheduling, lowered drinking fountains, lowered telephones, and specially equipped residence hall facilities are available.

Services: Counseling and information services are available, as is tutoring in every subject. There is a reader service for the blind, and remedial math, reading, and writing.

Campus Safety and Security: Measures include 24-hour foot and vehicle patrol, escort service, shuttle buses, and informal discussions. There are pamphlets/posters/films, emergency telephones, lighted pathways/

sidewalks, surveillance cameras, and emergency telephones in main parking lots and in residence life buildings.

Programs of Study: Ramapo confers B.A., B.S., B.S.N., and B.S.W. degrees. Master's degrees are also awarded. Bachelor's degrees are awarded in BIOLOGICAL SCIENCE (biochemistry and biology/biological science), BUSINESS (accounting, business administration and management, and international business management), COMMUNICATIONS AND THE ARTS (art, communications, fine arts, and literature), COMPUTER AND PHYSICAL SCIENCE (chemistry, computer science, information sciences and systems, mathematics, and physics), ENGINEERING AND ENVIRONMENTAL DESIGN (environmental science), HEALTH PROFESSIONS (clinical science and nursing), SOCIAL SCIENCE (American studies, economics, history, human ecology, international studies, law, political science/government, psychology, social science, social work, and sociology). Physics, biochemistry, and nursing are the strongest academically. Business administration, communication arts, and psychology are the largest.

Required: Students must complete general education requirements of approximately 50 credits in science, social science, humanities, and English composition, as well as core requirements in their school of study and their particular major. A senior seminar is also required. To graduate, students must earn at least 128 credits with a minimum GPA of 2.0.

Special: Ramapo's curriculum emphasizes the interdependence of global society and includes an international dimension in all academic programs. Students may study abroad in 6 countries. Cooperative programs are available with various corporations and in 12 foreign countries. Cross-registration is possible with local state colleges. Ramapo also offers a winter session, accelerated degree programs, dual, student-designed, and interdisciplinary majors, including law and society, credit for life experience, pass/fail options, internships, work-study programs, and nondegree study. There are 6 national honor societies, a freshman honors program, and 10 departmental honors programs.

Faculty/Classroom: 60% of faculty are male; 40%, female. All teach undergraduates. No introductory courses are taught by graduate students. The average class size in an introductory lecture is 31; in a laboratory, 13; and in a regular course, 21.

Admissions: 42% of the 2001-2002 applicants were accepted. The SAT I scores for the 2001-2002 freshman class were: Verbal--18% below 500, 58% between 500 and 599, 22% between 600 and 700, and 2% above 700; Math--16% below 500, 57% between 500 and 599, 25% between 600 and 700, and 2% above 700. 41% of the current freshmen were in the top fifth of their class; 76% were in the top two fifths.

Requirements: The SAT I is required. In addition, applicants must be graduates of accredited secondary schools or have earned a GED. The college requires 16 academic credits, including 4 in English, 3 in math, 2 each in science and social studies, and the remaining 5 in academic electives. Students are encouraged to take 2 years of a foreign language. Students must also submit an essay. An interview is recommended. A GPA of 3.0 is required. AP and CLEP credits are accepted. Important factors in the admissions decision are advanced placement or honor courses, recommendations by school officials, and evidence of special talent. Applications are accepted on computer disk and on-line.

Procedure: Freshmen are admitted fall and spring. Entrance exams should be taken during the senior year. There are early decision and deferred admissions plans. Applications should be filed by March 1 for fall entry and December 1 for spring entry. The fall application fee was $45. Notification is sent on a rolling basis.

Transfer: 505 transfer students enrolled in 2001-2002. Applicants must present a minimum GPA of 2.0; however, students applying to the School of Business with at least 45 credits must submit a GPA of 2.5. There are special requirements for social work, nursing, and communications majors. Any applicant transferring fewer than 30 credits must provide a high school transcript. SAT I scores are recommended. Associate degree recipients are encouraged to apply. 45 credits of 128 must be completed at Ramapo.

Visiting: There are regularly scheduled orientations for prospective students, including orientation, advisement, and registration. There are guides for informal visits and visitors may sit in on classes. To schedule a visit, contact the Admissions Office.

Financial Aid: In 2001-2002, 71% of all freshmen and 55% of continuing students received some form of financial aid. 61% of freshmen and 55% of continuing students received need-based aid. The average freshman award was $8339. Of that total, scholarships or need-based grants averaged $7126 ($16,119 maximum); loans averaged $5190 ($16,842 maximum); and work contracts averaged $956 ($3148 maximum). 4% of undergraduates work part time. Average annual earnings from campus work are $1134. The average financial indebtedness of the 2001 graduate was $13,832. The FAFSA is required. The fall application deadline is March 15.

International Students: There are 240 international students enrolled. The school actively recruits these students. They must score 550 on the written TOEFL.

Computers: The mainframe is a DEC 5500 running UNIX. In addition, 300 PCs are located in the residence halls, the computing lab, and the library. All students may access the system according to posted schedules for lab times.

Graduates: In 2001, 770 bachelor's degrees were awarded. The most popular majors were business administration (21%), communications (13%), and psychology (11%). In an average class, 21% graduate in 4 years, 42% in 5 years, and 47% in 6 years. 81 companies recruited on campus in 2000-2001.

Admissions Contact: Nancy E. Jaeger, Director of Admissions. A video is available. E-mail: *admissions@ramapo.edu*
Web: *www.ramapo.edu*

RICHARD STOCKTON COLLEGE OF NEW JERSEY D-5

Pomona, NJ 08240 **(609) 652-4261; Fax: (609) 748-5541**

Full-time: 2107 men, 2905 women	**Faculty:** 195; IIB, +$
Part-time: 446 men, 680 women	**Ph.D.s:** 97%
Graduate: 106 men, 213 women	**Student/Faculty:** 26 to 1
Year: semesters, summer session	**Tuition:** $6320 ($8768)
Application Deadline: May 1	**Room & Board:** $5845
Freshman Class: 3384 applied, 1533 accepted, 784 enrolled	
SAT I Verbal/Math: 550/570	**VERY COMPETITIVE**

Richard Stockton College of New Jersey, founded in 1969, is a public liberal arts college with 27 undergraduate programs and 6 graduate specialty areas. There are 5 undergraduate schools. In addition to regional accreditation, Stockton has baccalaureate program accreditation with APTA, CSWE, NASDTEC, NCATE, and NLN. The library contains 246,834 volumes, 354,795 microform items, and 14,227 audiovisual forms/CDs, and subscribes to 1360 periodicals. Computerized library services include the card catalog, interlibrary loans, and database searching. Special learning facilities include a learning resource center, art gallery, radio station, TV station, an astronomical observatory, a marine science field lab, a marina with a fleet of small boats, a Holocaust resource center, and an educational technology training center. The 1600-acre campus is in a suburban area 12 miles northwest of Atlantic City. Including residence halls, there are 55 buildings.

Student Life: 98% of undergraduates are from New Jersey. Others are from 23 states, 24 foreign countries, and Canada. 74% are from public schools. 82% are white. The average age of freshmen is 18; all undergraduates, 22. 15% do not continue beyond their first year; 60% remain to graduate.

Housing: 2081 students can be accommodated in college housing, which includes dormitories and on-campus apartments. In addition, there are honors houses, special-interest houses, and wellness, substance-free, and smoke-free housing. On-campus housing is guaranteed for the freshman year only, is available on a first-come, first-served basis, and on a lottery system for upperclassmen. Priority is given to out-of-town students. 58% of students commute. All students may keep cars.

Activities: 5% of men belong to 9 national fraternities; 59% of women belong to 10 national sororities. There are 75 groups on campus, including art, band, cheerleading, chess, choir, chorale, chorus, computers, dance, drama, ethnic, honors, international, jazz band, literary magazine, newspaper, orchestra, pep band, photography, political, professional, radio and TV, religious, social, social service, student government, and yearbook. Popular campus events include Spring Concert, Spring Fling, and Black History Month.

Sports: There are 6 intercollegiate sports for men and 8 for women, and 13 intramural sports for men and 11 for women. Facilities include an indoor 6-lane swimming pool, an indoor track, a weight-lifting gym, 2 multipurpose gyms, a sauna, steam baths, dance studios, playing fields, a 60-acre lake for fishing and canoeing, cross-country courses, bike trails, an all-weather track, and tennis, racquetball, and basketball courts. There are 9 club sports in addition to intramurals.

Disabled Students: 99% of the campus is accessible. Wheelchair ramps, elevators, special parking, specially equipped rest rooms, special class scheduling, lowered drinking fountains, lowered telephones, and electric doors are available.

Services: Counseling and information services are available, as is tutoring in most subjects. There is a reader service for the blind, and remedial math, reading, and writing. In addition, there is a skills center and a learning access program for learning-disabled students.

Campus Safety and Security: Measures include 24-hour foot and vehicle patrol, self-defense education, escort service, and shuttle buses. There are informal discussions, pamphlets/posters/films, emergency telephones, and lighted pathways/sidewalks.

Programs of Study: Stockton confers B.A., B.S., and B.S.N. degrees. Master's degrees are also awarded. Bachelor's degrees are awarded in BIOLOGICAL SCIENCE (biochemistry, biology/biological science, and marine science), BUSINESS (accounting, banking and finance, business administration and management, and management science), COMMUNICATIONS AND THE ARTS (dance, dramatic arts, fine arts, and music), COMPUTER AND PHYSICAL SCIENCE (chemistry, computer science, information sciences and systems, mathematics, and physics), ENGINEERING AND ENVIRONMENTAL DESIGN (environmental science and preengineering), HEALTH PROFESSIONS (nursing, physical therapy, public health, and speech pathology/audiology), SOCIAL SCIENCE (anthropology, criminal justice, economics, history, liberal arts/general studies, philosophy, political science/government, psychology, religion, and social work). Sciences is the strongest academically. Business, psychology, and criminal justice are the largest.

Required: To graduate, students must earn 128 credit hours, with 32 in the general studies curriculum, and maintain a minimum GPA of 2.0. 3 quantitative reasoning and 4 writing courses as well as a freshman seminar are required.

Special: Stockton offers internships in all fields with a wide variety of companies, work-study with various government agencies and corporations, a Washington semester, independent study, and study abroad in 10 countries. Dual majors in all programs, student-designed majors, an accelerated degree in medicine, 3-2 engineering degrees with the New Jersey Institute of Technology and Rutgers University, and general studies degrees are also offered. Nondegree study, pass/fail options, and credit for life, military, and work experience are possible. There are 5 national honor societies.

Faculty/Classroom: 60% of faculty are male; 40%, female. 95% both teach and do research. The average class size in an introductory lecture is 30; in a laboratory, 12; and in a regular course, 17.

Admissions: 45% of the 2001-2002 applicants were accepted. The SAT I scores for the 2001-2002 freshman class were: Verbal--32% below 500, 50% between 500 and 599, 16% between 600 and 700, and 2% above 700; Math--30% below 500, 50% between 500 and 599, 18% between 600 and 700, and 2% above 700. 50% of the current freshmen were in the top fifth of their class; 80% were in the top two fifths. There was 1 National Merit finalist.

Requirements: The SAT I or ACT is required. In addition, applicants must be high school graduates; the GED is accepted. 16 academic credits are required, including 4 years in English, 3 each in math and social studies, 2 in science, and 4 additional years of any of the above or a foreign language, or both. An essay and an interview are recommended, and a portfolio or audition is necessary where appropriate. Stockton requires applicants to be in the upper 50% of their class. A GPA of 2.5 is required. AP and CLEP credits are accepted. Important factors in the admissions decision are advanced placement or honor courses, leadership record, and evidence of special talent.

Procedure: Freshmen are admitted fall and spring. Entrance exams should be taken once in the junior year and again before January in the senior year. There is an early admissions plan. Applications should be filed by May 1 for fall entry and December 1 for spring entry. The fall 2001 application fee was $35. Notification is sent on a rolling basis. 15% of all applicants are on a waiting list.

Transfer: 858 transfer students enrolled in 2001-2002. Transfer students must have earned at least 16 credits at other colleges and must submit college and high school transcripts as well as SAT I scores. 32 credits of 128 must be completed at Stockton.

Visiting: There are regularly scheduled orientations for prospective students, including academic advising and orientation. There are guides for informal visits and visitors may sit in on classes. To schedule a visit, contact Enrollment Management at (609) 652-4251.

Financial Aid: In 2001-2002, 78% of all freshmen and 70% of continuing students received some form of financial aid. 51% of all students received need-based aid. The average freshman award was $8565. Of that total, scholarships or need-based grants averaged $5251 ($10,190 maximum); loans averaged $1811 ($6625 maximum); and work contracts averaged $1556 ($1800 maximum). 27% of undergraduates work part time. Average annual earnings from campus work are $1671. The average financial indebtedness of the 2001 graduate was $14,388. The FAFSA is required. The fall application deadline is March 1.

International Students: There were 35 international students enrolled in a recent year. The school actively recruits these students. They must score 525 on the written TOEFL.

Computers: The mainframes are a DEC VAX 8600 and 6300 and an IBM 3090. There are also 2 Alpha 2104/275 servers, 1 Alpha 2000/233 server, and a DEC 5500 processor. Students may access the Caucus network for conferencing and linkage to the mainframe and the Internet. There are also more than 750 PCs dispersed in 20 computer labs, 34 electronic classrooms, the library, faculty offices, and academic support facilities. All students may access the system 24 hours a day. There are no time limits and no fees.

Graduates: In 2001, 1340 bachelor's degrees were awarded. The most popular majors were social science (27%), natural sciences (21%), and business and management (20%). In an average class, 2% graduate in 3 years, 30% in 4 years, 56% in 5 years, and 60% in 6 years. Of the 2000 graduating class, 34% were enrolled in graduate school within 6 months of graduation and 83% were employed.

Admissions Contact: Sal Catalfamo, Dean, Enrollment Management. E-mail: *admissions@stockton.edu* Web: *www.stockton.edu*

RIDER UNIVERSITY — D-3

Lawrenceville, NJ 08648-3099 — (609) 896-5042
(800) 257-9026; Fax: (609) 895-6645

Full-time: 1514 men, 2004 women	**Faculty:** 207; IIA, ++$
Part-time: 311 men, 547 women	**Ph.D.s:** 94%
Graduate: 361 men, 789 women	**Student/Faculty:** 17 to 1
Year: semesters, summer session	**Tuition:** $19,700
Application Deadline: open	**Room & Board:** $7700

Freshman Class: 4348 applied, 3199 accepted, 916 enrolled
SAT I Verbal/Math: 510/520 — **COMPETITIVE**

Rider University, founded in 1865, is a private institution offering undergraduate programs in the areas of business administration, liberal arts, education, sciences, and continuing studies. Westminster Choir College, located in nearby Princeton, is Rider's fourth college. There are 4 undergraduate and 2 graduate schools. In addition to regional accreditation, Rider has baccalaureate program accreditation with AACSB and NCATE. The library contains 376,495 volumes, 576,545 microform items, and 23,095 audiovisual forms/CDs, and subscribes to 2715 periodicals. Computerized library services include the card catalog, interlibrary loans, and database searching. Special learning facilities include a learning resource center, art gallery, radio station, TV station, journalism and sociology labs, and a holocaust/genocide center. The 340-acre campus is in a suburban area 3 miles north of Trenton and 7 miles south of Princeton. Including residence halls, there are 37 buildings.

Student Life: 76% of undergraduates are from New Jersey. Others are from 30 states, 8 foreign countries, and Canada. 76% are white. 39% are Catholic; 30% claim no religious affiliation; 11% Protestant. The average age of freshmen is 19; all undergraduates, 24. 23% do not continue beyond their first year; 54% remain to graduate.

Housing: 2163 students can be accommodated in college housing, which includes single-sex and coed dormitories, on-campus apartments, fraternity houses, and sorority houses. In addition, there are special-interest houses. On-campus housing is guaranteed for all 4 years. 60% of students live on campus. All students may keep cars.

Activities: 9% of men belong to 2 minority and 5 national fraternities; 9% of women belong to 1 regional sorority and 7 national sororities. There are 104 groups on campus, including art, band, cheerleading, choir, chorus, computers, dance, drama, ethnic, film, gay, honors, international, jazz band, literary magazine, musical theater, newspaper, opera, orchestra, photography, political, professional, radio and TV, religious, social, social service, student government, and yearbook. Popular campus events include Cranberry Fest, Family Day, and Unity Day.

Sports: There are 10 intercollegiate sports for men and 10 for women, and 10 intramural sports for men and 6 for women. Facilities include a gym, a swimming pool, a fitness center and spa, lighted outdoor multipurpose courts, outdoor varsity and intramural fields, and an outdoor track.

Disabled Students: 63% of the campus is accessible. Wheelchair ramps, elevators, special parking, specially equipped rest rooms, special class scheduling, lowered drinking fountains, and lowered telephones are available.

Services: Counseling and information services are available, as is tutoring in most subjects. There is remedial math, reading, and writing.

Campus Safety and Security: Measures include 24-hour foot and vehicle patrol, self-defense education, escort service, and informal discussions. There are pamphlets/posters/films, emergency telephones, lighted pathways/sidewalks, a shuttle car, a staffed kiosk at the entrance, and a security system in residence halls.

Programs of Study: Rider confers B.A., B.S., and B.S.B.A. degrees. Associate and master's degrees are also awarded. Bachelor's degrees are awarded in BIOLOGICAL SCIENCE (biochemistry, biology/biological science, and marine science), BUSINESS (accounting, banking and finance, business administration and management, business economics, human resources, international business management, marketing/retailing/merchandising, and organizational behavior), COMMUNICATIONS AND THE ARTS (advertising, communications, English, fine arts, French, German, journalism, Russian, Spanish, and speech/debate/rhetoric), COMPUTER AND PHYSICAL SCIENCE (actuarial science, chemistry, geology, information sciences and systems, mathematics, and physics), EDUCATION (business, early childhood, elementary, foreign languages, marketing and distribution, science, secondary, social studies, and teaching English as a second/foreign language (TESOL/TEFOL)), ENGINEERING AND ENVIRONMENTAL DESIGN (environmental science), HEALTH PROFESSIONS (predentistry and premedicine), SOCIAL SCIENCE (American studies, biopsychology, economics, history, liberal arts/general studies, philosophy, political science/government, prelaw, psychology, and sociology). Business, actuarial science, and education are the strongest academically. Accounting, elementary education, and finance are the largest.

Required: To graduate, all students must maintain a minimum GPA of 2.0 while taking 120 semester hours. Students also must fulfill core curriculum requirements, including 9 hours in humanities, 7 to 8 in science, 6 each in English writing and foreign language (may be waived if proficiency is demonstrated), social sciences/communications, and history, and 3 in math.

Special: Internships in many programs, a co-op program in marketing, work-study, study abroad in 7 countries, a B.A.-B.S. degree in all liberal arts and sciences, dual majors in education, a liberal studies degree, and nondegree study are possible. There are 28 national honor societies, a freshman honors program, and 19 departmental honors programs.

Faculty/Classroom: 64% of faculty are male; 36%, female. 93% teach undergraduates. No introductory courses are taught by graduate students. The average class size in an introductory lecture is 27; in a laboratory, 11; and in a regular course, 20.

Admissions: 74% of the 2001-2002 applicants were accepted. The SAT I scores for the 2001-2002 freshman class were: Verbal--41% below 500, 46% between 500 and 599, 12% between 600 and 700, and 1% above 700; Math--37% below 500, 48% between 500 and 599, 13% between 600 and 700, and 2% above 700. 19% of the current freshmen were in the top fifth of their class; 32% were in the top two fifths.

Requirements: The SAT I or ACT is required. In addition, applicants need 16 Carnegie units, including 4 years of English. 3 units of math are required for prospective math, science, and business majors. An essay is recommended. An audition is required for theater scholarships. The GED is accepted. Rider requires applicants to be in the upper 50% of their class. A GPA of 2.0 is required. AP and CLEP credits are accepted. Important factors in the admissions decision are advanced placement or honor courses, extracurricular activities record, and leadership record. Applications are accepted on-line via Common Application.

Procedure: Freshmen are admitted fall and spring. Entrance exams should be taken by January of the senior year. There are early admissions and deferred admissions plans. Application deadlines are open. The early application deadline is November 15. Regular application deadlines are open. The fall 2001 application fee was $40. Notification of early action is sent December 15; regular decision, on a rolling basis, generally within 4 weeks after the application is complete.

Transfer: 179 transfer students enrolled in 2001-2002. A GPA of 2.5 or better is required for applicants. If students have fewer than 30 credits, they also must submit high school transcripts and SAT I scores. An essay or personal statement is required, and an interview is recommended. 30 credits of 120 must be completed at Rider.

Visiting: There are regularly scheduled orientations for prospective students, including 4 open houses, with programs that consist of a welcome, a campus tour, and a variety of formal and informal activities to meet faculty, staff, current students, and alumni. There are guides for informal visits and visitors may sit in on classes. To schedule a visit, contact the Office of Admissions.

Financial Aid: In 2001-2002, 70% of all freshmen and 76% of continuing students received some form of financial aid. 58% of freshmen and 66% of continuing students received need-based aid. The average freshman award was $16,541. Of that total, scholarships or need-based grants averaged $8015; loans averaged $3323; and work contracts averaged $4577. 15% of undergraduates work part time. The average financial indebtedness of the 2001 graduate was $16,000. The FAFSA is required. The fall application deadline is March 1.

International Students: There are 5 international students enrolled. The school actively recruits these students. They must score 563 on the written TOEFL or 202 on the electronic version and also take the SAT I or the ACT.

Computers: The mainframes are 2 DEC VAX 4000s and a MicroVAX 3400. The microcomputer labs have IBM PCs available for general use and departmental labs have more than 200 PCs, many of which are networked. In addition, students have assigned voice mail and e-mail accounts. The campus has a comprehensive light guide voice, data, and video network linking residence halls, classrooms, and faculty/administrative offices. All students may access the system during regular lab hours and at any time in residence halls. There are no time limits.

Graduates: In 2001, 759 bachelor's degrees were awarded. The most popular majors were elementary education (11%), finance (9%), and communication (9%). In an average class, 37% graduate in 4 years, 50% in 5 years, and 56% in 6 years. 128 companies recruited on campus in 2000-2001. Of the 2000 graduating class, 13% were enrolled in graduate school within 6 months of graduation and 81% were employed.

Admissions Contact: Susan C. Christian, Director of Admissions. A video is available. E-mail: *admissions@rider.edu* Web: *www.rider.edu*

ROWAN UNIVERSITY

C-4

Glassboro, NJ 08028

(856) 256-4200
(800) 447-1165; Fax: (856) 256-4430

Full-time: 2885 men, 3669 women	**Faculty:** 364
Part-time: 600 men, 1171 women	**Ph.D.s:** 80%
Graduate: 374 men, 1089 women	**Student/Faculty:** 18 to 1
Year: semesters, summer session	**Tuition:** $5779 ($10,279)
Application Deadline: March 15	**Room & Board:** $6586
Freshman Class: 6143 applied, 2818 accepted, 1282 enrolled	
SAT I Verbal/Math: 559/574	**VERY COMPETITIVE**

Rowan University was founded in 1923 as a public institution offering undergraduate programs in the arts and sciences, business administration, education, fine and performing arts, and engineering. There are 6 undergraduate schools and 1 graduate school. In addition to regional accreditation, Rowan has baccalaureate program accreditation with NASM and NCATE. The library contains 316,500 volumes, 478,692 microform items, and 52,834 audiovisual forms/CDs, and subscribes to 1858 periodicals. Computerized library services include database searching. Special learning facilities include an art gallery, planetarium, and radio station. The 200-acre campus is in a small town 20 miles southeast of Philadelphia. Including residence halls, there are 40 buildings.

Student Life: 98% of undergraduates are from New Jersey. Others are from 11 states, 13 foreign countries, and Canada. 65% are from public schools. 81% are white. The average age of freshmen is 20; all undergraduates, 25. 16% do not continue beyond their first year; 57% remain to graduate.

Housing: 2300 students can be accommodated in college housing, which includes single-sex and coed dormitories, on-campus apartments, off-campus apartments, married-student housing, fraternity houses, and sorority houses. In addition, there are honors houses. On-campus housing is guaranteed for the freshman year only and is available on a lottery system for upperclassmen. Priority is given to out-of-town students. Alcohol is not permitted. Upperclassmen may keep cars.

Activities: 9% of men belong to 1 local and 11 national fraternities; 9% of women belong to 5 local and 8 national sororities. There are 150 groups on campus, including art, band, cheerleading, chess, choir, chorale, chorus, computers, concert band, dance, drama, ethnic, film, honors, international, jazz band, literary magazine, marching band, music ensembles, musical theater, newspaper, opera, orchestra, pep band, political, professional, radio and TV, religious, social, social service, student government, symphony, and yearbook. Popular campus events include Spring Fling and Community Day.

Sports: There are 7 intercollegiate sports for men and 9 for women, and 7 intramural sports for men and 6 for women. Facilities include a 3000-seat stadium, an 1800-seat gym, a 1000-seat auditorium, a swimming pool, tennis courts, and playing fields.

Disabled Students: 95% of the campus is accessible. Wheelchair ramps, elevators, special parking, specially equipped rest rooms, special class scheduling, lowered drinking fountains, and lowered telephones are available.

Services: Counseling and information services are available, as is tutoring in most subjects. There is remedial math, reading, and writing.

Campus Safety and Security: Measures include 24-hour foot and vehicle patrol, self-defense education, escort service, and informal discussions. There are pamphlets/posters/films, emergency telephones, and lighted pathways/sidewalks.

Programs of Study: Rowan confers B.A., B.S., B.F.A., and B.M. degrees. Master's and doctoral degrees are also awarded. Bachelor's degrees are awarded in BIOLOGICAL SCIENCE (biology/biological science), BUSINESS (accounting, business administration and management, marketing/retailing/merchandising, personnel management, and small business management), COMMUNICATIONS AND THE ARTS (broadcasting, communications, dramatic arts, English, fine arts, journalism, music, Spanish, and speech/debate/rhetoric), COMPUTER AND PHYSICAL SCIENCE (chemistry, and physics), EDUCATION (early childhood, elementary, foreign languages, music, and science), ENGINEERING AND ENVIRONMENTAL DESIGN (engineering), SOCIAL SCIENCE (criminal justice, economics, history, liberal arts/general studies, political science/government, psychology, and sociology). Communications, business administration, and elementary education are the strongest academically and the largest.

Required: General education requirements include 12 to 18 semester hours of social and behavioral sciences, 12 to 16 of science and math, 6 to 9 of communications, 6 of fine and performing arts, and 3 to 6 of history/humanities/languages/arts. Students must also complete 6 semester hours of writing and 3 of phys ed, lab science, and computer literacy. The bachelor's degree requires completion of at least 120 semester hours, including 30 to 39 in a major field, with a minimum GPA of 2.0.

Special: Students may study abroad in 8 countries. Internships are available both with and without pay. Rowan also offers accelerated degree programs and 3-2 degrees in optometry, podiatry, and pharmacy. There are dual majors, pass/fail options, and credit for military experience. There is a freshman honors program.

Faculty/Classroom: 71% of faculty are male; 29%, female. All teach undergraduates. No introductory courses are taught by graduate students. The average class size in an introductory lecture is 25; in a laboratory, 20; and in a regular course, 25.

Admissions: 46% of the 2001-2002 applicants were accepted. The SAT I scores for the 2001-2002 freshman class were: Verbal--13% below 500, 60% between 500 and 599, 25% between 600 and 700, and 2% above 700; Math--10% below 500, 55% between 500 and 599, 32% between 600 and 700, and 3% above 700. 48% of the current freshmen were in the top fifth of their class; 83% were in the top two fifths.

Requirements: The SAT I is required, with a recommended minimum composite score of 950, or no less than 450 on either part. Students submitting ACT scores should have a minimum composite score of 19. Applicants must be graduates of accredited secondary schools or have earned a GED. Rowan requires 16 academic credits or Carnegie units, including 4 in English, 3 each in math and college preparatory electives, and 2 each in foreign language, history, and a lab science. An essay is required of all students, and a portfolio or audition is required for specific majors. Rowan requires applicants to be in the upper 75% of their class. A GPA of 3.0 is required. AP and CLEP credits are accepted. Important factors in the admissions decision are advanced placement or honor courses, evidence of special talent, and leadership record.

Procedure: Freshmen are admitted fall and spring. Entrance exams should be taken in November or December of the senior year. There is a deferred admissions plan. Applications should be filed by March 15 for fall entry and November 15 for spring entry, along with a $50 fee. Notification is sent on a rolling basis. A waiting list is an active part of the admissions procedure.

Transfer: 742 transfer students enrolled in 2001-2002. Applicants must have a minimum GPA of 2.0, but should present a GPA of 2.5 to be competitive. An associate degree is recommended. Students who have earned fewer than 24 semester hours must also submit a high school transcript and SAT I results. 30 credits of 120 must be completed at Rowan.

Visiting: There are regularly scheduled orientations for prospective students, consisting of a 2-day summer program providing schedule confirmation/adjustment, student activities updates, and workshops for students and parents. There are guides for informal visits and visitors may sit in on classes. To schedule a visit, contact the Admissions Office.

Financial Aid: In 2001-2002, 70% of all students received some form of financial aid. The average freshman award was $7250. Of that total, scholarships or need-based grants averaged $3190; loans averaged $2185 ($2500 maximum); work contracts averaged $900 ($1500 maximum); and grants averaged $900 ($1900 maximum). 10% of undergraduates work part time. Average annual earnings from campus work are $1200. The CSS/Profile or FAFSA, the college's own financial statement and financial aid transcripts are required. The fall application deadline is March 15.

International Students: International students must score 550 on the written TOEFL or take the MELAB. Applicants from English-speaking countries must also submit an SAT I score.

Computers: The mainframes are 2 DEC VAX 8650, series 6000-410. PCs are available in academic and student labs. All students may access the system 7:30 A.M. to midnight. There are no time limits and no fees.

Graduates: In 2001, 1441 bachelor's degrees were awarded. The most popular majors were business administration (18%), communications (13%), and elementary education (11%). In an average class, 20% graduate in 4 years, 48% in 5 years, and 55% in 6 years. 106 companies recruited on campus in 2000-2001.

Admissions Contact: Marvin G. Sills, Director of Admissions.
E-mail: *admissions@rowan.edu* Web: *rowan.edu/admiss/admiss.htm*

RUTGERS, THE STATE UNIVERSITY OF NEW JERSEY

Rutgers, the State University of New Jersey, established in 1766, is a public system governed by a board of governors. Its chief administrator is the president. The primary goals of the system are instruction, research, and service. The main priorities are to continue development as a distinguished comprehensive public university, to enhance undergraduate education, to strengthen graduate education and research, and to develop and improve programs to better serve New Jersey's and society's needs. 4-year campuses are located in New Brunswick, Newark, and Camden. There are more than 100 baccalaureate, 100 master's, and 80 doctoral programs offered through the Rutgers system.

RUTGERS, THE STATE UNIVERSITY OF NEW JERSEY/CAMDEN CAMPUS — C-4

Camden, NJ 08102 — **(856) 225-6104; Fax: (856) 225-6498**

Full-time: 1135 men, 1584 women	**Faculty:** 223; IIA, +$
Part-time: 324 men, 582 women	**Ph.D.s:** 98%
Graduate: 296 men, 283 women	**Student/Faculty:** 12 to 1
Year: semesters, summer session	**Tuition:** $6484 ($11,922)
Application Deadline: open	**Room & Board:** n/app

Freshman Class: 6205 applied, 3662 accepted, 426 enrolled
SAT I or ACT: required — **COMPETITIVE**

Rutgers, The State University of New Jersey/Camden Campus, founded in 1934, is comprised of 2 undergraduate, degree-granting schools: College of the Arts and Sciences and University College--Camden. Each school has individual requirements, policies, and fees. Applicants should contact the particular school for the most current information. There are 2 undergraduate schools. In addition to regional accreditation, Camden has baccalaureate program accreditation with AACSB, CSWE, NASDTEC, and NLN. The 2 libraries contain 714,447 volumes, 259,982 microform items, and 326 audiovisual forms/CDs, and subscribe to 5189 periodicals. Computerized library services include the card catalog, interlibrary loans, and database searching. Special learning facilities include a learning resource center, art gallery, and radio station. The campus is in an urban area 1 mile east of Philadelphia.

Student Life: 97% of undergraduates are from New Jersey. Others are from 5 states. 67% are white; 15% African American. The average age of freshmen is 19; all undergraduates, 25.

Housing: Housing includes coed dormitories and on-campus apartments. In addition, there is special housing for disabled students. 88% of students commute. Alcohol is not permitted.

Activities: There are no fraternities or sororities. There are 70 groups on campus, including choir, computers, drama, ethnic, gay, honors, international, literary magazine, newspaper, orchestra, political, professional, radio and TV, religious, social, social service, student government, and yearbook. Popular campus events include Raptor Day, Springfest, and Bill Maher Lecture.

Sports: There is no sports program at Camden.

Disabled Students: 95% of the campus is accessible. Wheelchair ramps, elevators, special parking, specially equipped rest rooms, special class scheduling, lowered drinking fountains, and lowered telephones are available. Facilities vary from building to building. However, all classes are scheduled in accessible locations for disabled students.

Services: Counseling and information services are available, as is tutoring in some subjects, including introductory classes. There is a reader service for the blind, and remedial math, reading, and writing.

Campus Safety and Security: Measures include 24-hour foot and vehicle patrol, self-defense education, escort service, and shuttle buses. There are informal discussions, pamphlets/posters/films, emergency telephones, and lighted pathways/sidewalks. The police department is supplemented by security guards.

Programs of Study: Camden confers B.A. and B.S. degrees. Master's degrees are also awarded. Bachelor's degrees are awarded in BIOLOGICAL SCIENCE (biochemistry and biology/biological science), BUSINESS (accounting, banking and finance, management science, and marketing/retailing/merchandising), COMMUNICATIONS AND THE ARTS (art, art history and appreciation, dramatic arts, English, French, German, music, and Spanish), COMPUTER AND PHYSICAL SCIENCE (chemistry, computer science, mathematics, physics, and science), EDUCATION (elementary and secondary), HEALTH PROFESSIONS (medical laboratory technology, nursing, predentistry, and premedicine), SOCIAL SCIENCE (African American studies, American studies, economics, history, liberal arts/general studies, philosophy, political science/government, prelaw, psychology, social work, sociology, and urban studies). Psychology, computer science, and economics are the largest.

Required: To graduate, students must complete 120 credits, with 30 to 48 in the major, and maintain a minimum GPA of 2.0. A core curriculum of 60 credits is required, including 3 credits each in literary masterpieces, art, music or theater arts, and a foreign language, with an additional 3 credits in English or a foreign language; and 3 credits in math, with an additional 3 credits in math, computer science, or statistics. 1 interdisciplinary course is required, as are 9 credits from social science disciplines, 6 credits in English composition, 6 credits in history, 6 credits in the natural science disciplines, and an additional 9 credits in courses offered outside the major department.

Special: The university offers co-op programs, cross-registration, internships, accelerated degrees, student-designed majors, dual majors, nondegree study, and pass/fail options. Students may study abroad in numerous countries. In addition, there is an 8-year B.A./M.D. program with U.M.D.N.J., and many combined bachelor's and master's programs. There is a freshman honors program.

Faculty/Classroom: 64% of faculty are male; 36%, female.

Admissions: 59% of the 2001-2002 applicants were accepted. 70% of the current freshmen were in the top quarter of their class; 98% were in the top half.

Requirements: The SAT I or ACT is required, but not for students who have been out of high school for 2 years or more. SATII tests may be required of some students. The GED is accepted. Students must have completed 16 academic credits or Carnegie units, including 4 years of English, 3 years of math, and 2 years each of a foreign language and science, plus 7 additional academic units. AP and CLEP credits are accepted. Important factors in the admissions decision are advanced placement or honor courses, evidence of special talent, and leadership record. Applications are accepted on-line at the Rutgers web site.

Procedure: Freshmen are admitted fall and spring. It is recommended that entrance exams be taken December of senior year. There are deferred admissions and rolling admissions plans. Application deadlines are open; deadline for priority decision is December 1. The application fee is $50. 2% of all applicants are on a waiting list; 79 were accepted in 2001.

Transfer: 386 transfer students enrolled in 2001-2002. Applicants must have a minimum of 12 credit hours. Grades of C or better in courses that correspond in content and credit to those offered by the college transfer for credit. Transfer students are admitted in the fall and spring semesters. All high school and previous college transcripts are required. 30 credits of 120 must be completed at Camden.

Visiting: There are regularly scheduled orientations for prospective students, including an information session with an admissions officer and a campus tour. Visitors may sit in on classes. To schedule a visit, contact the Admissions Office (Camden).

Financial Aid: In 2001-2002, 61% of all freshmen and 62% of continuing students received some form of financial aid. 96% of freshmen and 98% of continuing students received need-based aid. The average freshman award was $7793. The average financial indebtedness of the 2001 graduate was $15,158. The FAFSA is required. The fall application deadline is March 15.

International Students: International students must score 550 on the written TOEFL and also take the SAT I or the ACT.

Computers: The mainframes are a consists of a Sun Ultra 2 SPARC Server, Sun 10/51 SPARC Server, and Sun Enterprise 3500. Workstations and networked PCs and Mac (a total of 187 systems) are located in public labs in 2 major academic buildings, the library, the Campus Center, and the dormitories. All provide access to the central systems, the Web, and the local Camden campus computers. On-campus computer network services include on-line admission, registration, transcripts, e-mail, library searches, library catalog, and full access to the Internet. A complete intranet web service is available for all aspects of student services. All students may access the system. Public labs are open whenever the building housing the lab is open. The main lab is available Monday through Thursday, 8 A.M. to 11 P.M.; Friday and Saturday, 9 A.M. to 5 P.M.; Sunday 2 P.M. to 10 P.M. (24 hours a day, 7 days a week through modem access). There are no time limits. The fee is $200.

Graduates: In 2001, 736 bachelor's degrees were awarded.

Admissions Contact: Dr. Deborah Bowles, Director of Admissions--Camden. E-mail: *admissions@asb-ugadm.rutgers.edu*
Web: *www.rutgers.edu*

RUTGERS, THE STATE UNIVERSITY OF NEW JERSEY/NEW BRUNSWICK CAMPUS D-3

New Brunswick, NJ 08903 (732) 932-4636; Fax: (732) 445-0237

Full-time: 11,942 men, 13,649 women	**Faculty:** 1506; I, av$
Part-time: 1070 men, 1266 women	**Ph.D.s:** 98%
Graduate: 444 men, 751 women	**Student/Faculty:** 17 to 1
Year: semesters, summer session	**Tuition:** $6133 ($11,311)
Application Deadline: open	**Room & Board:** $6576
Freshman Class: 27,074 applied, 16,174 accepted, 5436 enrolled	
SAT I or ACT: required	**COMPETITIVE**

Rutgers, The State University of New Jersey/New Brunswick Campus, founded in 1934, is comprised of 11 undergraduate degree-granting colleges. Students in New Brunswick enroll in 1 of 4 liberal arts colleges: Douglass College, Livingston College, Rutgers College, or University College-New Brunswick, or in 1 of 7 professional schools: Cook College, Mason Gross School of the Arts, College of Pharmacy, School of Business-New Brunswick, School of Communication, Information and Library Studies, School of Engineering, or the Edward J. Bloustein School of Planning and Public Policy. Each school within the New Brunswick campus has individual requirements, policies, and fees. Applicants should contact the particular school for the most current information. There are 11 undergraduate schools. In addition to regional accreditation, New Brunswick has baccalaureate program accreditation with AACSB, NASDTEC, and NASM. The 26 libraries contain 4,737,147 volumes, 3,280,875 microform items, and 91,657 audiovisual forms/CDs, and subscribe to 17,182 periodicals. Computerized library services include the card catalog, interlibrary loans, and database searching. Special learning facilities include a learning resource center, art gallery, radio station, TV station, geology museum, and various research centers. The campus is in a small town 33 miles south of New York City.

Student Life: 92% of undergraduates are from New Jersey. Others are from 19 states. 56% are white; 19% Asian American. The average age of freshmen is 18; all undergraduates, 20.

Housing: Campus housing includes single-sex and coed dormitories, married-student housing, fraternity houses, and sorority houses. In addition, there are language houses, special-interest houses, first-year residence, substance-free, and transfer housing, and a residence for single mothers with children. 54% of students commute. Alcohol is not permitted.

Activities: There are 27 fraternities and 15 sororities. There are more than 400 groups on campus, including art, band, cheerleading, chess, choir, chorale, chorus, computers, dance, drama, drill team, ethnic, film, gay, honors, international, jazz band, literary magazine, marching band, musical theater, newspaper, opera, orchestra, pep band, photography, political, professional, radio and TV, religious, social, social service, student government, symphony, and yearbook. Popular campus events include UC Festival, theater trips, and annual picnic.

Sports: There are 15 intercollegiate sports for men and 15 for women.

Disabled Students: Wheelchair ramps, elevators, special parking, specially equipped rest rooms, special class scheduling, lowered drinking fountains,and lowered telephones are available. Facilities vary from building to building. However, all classes are scheduled in accessible locations for disabled students. Special housing is available.

Services: Counseling and information services are available, as is tutoring in most subjects, with specific assistance in difficult first- and second-level courses, as well as learning assistance. There is remedial math, reading, and writing, computer software with aids, library technology, and assistance.

Campus Safety and Security: Measures include 24-hour foot and vehicle patrol, self-defense education, escort service, and shuttle buses. There are informal discussions, pamphlets/posters/films, emergency telephones, and lighted pathways/sidewalks. The police department is supplemented by security guards and student safety officers.

Programs of Study: New Brunswick confers B.A. and B.S. degrees. Master's and doctoral degrees are also awarded. Bachelor's degrees are awarded in AGRICULTURE (agriculture, animal science, natural resource management, and plant science), BIOLOGICAL SCIENCE (biochemistry, biology/biological science, biotechnology, botany, cell biology, ecology, evolutionary biology, genetics, marine science, microbiology, molecular biology, nutrition, and physiology), BUSINESS (accounting, banking and finance, business administration and management, labor studies, management information systems, management science, and marketing/retailing/merchandising), COMMUNICATIONS AND THE ARTS (art, art history and appreciation, Chinese, classics, communications, comparative literature, dance, dramatic arts, East Asian languages and literature, English, French, German, Italian, journalism, Latin, linguistics, music, Russian, Spanish, and visual and performing arts), COMPUTER AND PHYSICAL SCIENCE (chemistry, computer science, geology, mathematics, physics, and statistics), EDUCATION (vocational), ENGINEERING AND ENVIRONMENTAL DESIGN (ceramic engineering, chemical engineering, civil engineering, electrical/electronics engineering, environmental science, industrial engineering, and mechanical engineering), HEALTH PROFESSIONS (biomedical science, exercise science, medical technology, pharmacy, and public health), SOCIAL SCIENCE (African American studies, American studies, anthropology, Asian/Oriental studies, criminal justice, economics, food science, geography, Hispanic American studies, history, humanities, Judaic studies, Latin American studies, medieval studies, Middle Eastern studies, philosophy, political science/government, psychology, religion, Russian and Slavic studies, social work, sociology, urban studies, and women's studies). Biological sciences, psychology, and English are the largest.

Required: To graduate, students must complete 120 credits, with a minimum GPA of 2.0. A liberal arts core requirement includes 12 credits each of humanities, social sciences, math, and science, and 6 credits of English composition . Check with the individual college for specific program requirements.

Special: The college offers co-op programs, cross registration, and study abroad in numerous countries. A Washington semester, work-study, accelerated degree programs, B.A.-B.S. degrees, student-designed majors, nondegree study, and pass/fail options are available. There is an 8-year B.A.-M.D. program with UMDNJ and several dual degree (5 year and 6 year) programs. There are 2 national honor societies, including Phi Beta Kappa, and a freshman honors program.

Faculty/Classroom: 63% of faculty are male; 37%, female.

Admissions: 60% of the 2001-2002 applicants were accepted. 72% of the current freshmen were in the top quarter of their class; 98% were in the top half.

Requirements: The SAT I or ACT is required, as is a high school diploma. The GED is accepted. Students must have completed 16 academic credits or Carnegie units, including 4 years of English, 3 years of math (algebra I and II, and geometry), 2 years each of a foreign language and science, and 5 additional academic units. AP and CLEP credits are accepted. Important factors in the admissions decision are evidence of special talent, extracurricular activities record, and ability to finance college education. Students may apply on-line by accessing the Rutgers web site.

Procedure: Freshmen are admitted fall and spring. It is recommended, but not required, that entrance exams should be taken December of senior year. There is an early admissions plan. Application deadlines are open. Priority deadline is Debember 1. The application fee is $50. Notificacion is sent on a rolling basis beginning February 28. 8% of all applicants are on a waiting list; 32 were accepted in 2001.

Transfer: 1277 transfer students enrolled in 2001-2002. Applicants must have a minimum of 12 credit hours earned. High school and college transcripts are required. Transfers are admitted in the fall or spring. 30 credits of the last 42 must be completed at New Brunswick.

Visiting: There are regularly scheduled orientations for prospective students, including a preadmission orientation. To schedule a visit, contact University Undergraduate Admissions at (732) 932-7470.

Financial Aid: In 2001-2002, 48% of all freshmen and 46% of continuing students received some form of financial aid. 71% of all students received need-based aid. The average freshman award was $8994. The average financial indebtedness of the 2001 graduate was $15,311. The FAFSA is required. The fall priority application deadline is March 15.

International Students: They must score 550 on the written TOEFL and also take the college's own test.

Computers: The mainframe is a central system that includes 11 Sun UNIX servers dedicated to student use. Individual departments have a variety of PCs. The central system may be accessed from Macs, Windows-based PCs, and X-terminals located in several large public labs. Services include e-mail, newsgroups, software applications, a campus-wide information system, and access to the Internet. All students may access the system 24 hours per day. There are no time limits. The fee is $200.

Graduates: In 2001, 5493 bachelor's degrees were awarded. The most popular majors were social sciences and history (21%), psychology (9%), and biological life science (9%).

Admissions Contact: Raul Barriera, Director of Admissions.
E-mail: *admissions.rutgers.edu* Web: *www.rutgers.edu*

RUTGERS, THE STATE UNIVERSITY OF NEW JERSEY/NEWARK CAMPUS E-2

Newark, NJ 07102 **(973) 353-5205; Fax: (973) 353-1440**

Full-time: 1828 men, 2583 women	**Faculty:** 447; I
Part-time: 522 men, 749 women	**Ph.D.s:** 98%
Graduate: 413 men, 299 women	**Student/Faculty:** 10 to 1
Year: semesters, summer session	**Tuition:** $6394 ($11,832)
Application Deadline: December 1	**Room & Board:** n/av
Freshman Class: 8873 applied, 4618 accepted, 895 enrolled	
SAT I or ACT: required	**COMPETITIVE**

Rutgers, The State University of New Jersey/Newark Campus, founded in 1934, is comprised of 4 undergraduate, degree-granting schools: Newark College of Arts and Sciences, University College-Newark, School of Management, and College of Nursing. Each school has individual requirements, policies, and fees. Applicants should contact the particular school for the most current information. In addition to regional accreditation, Newark has baccalaureate program accreditation with AACSB, CSWE, and NASDTEC. The 4 libraries contain 941,103 volumes, 1,464,368 microform items, and 34,994 audiovisual forms/CDs, and subscribe to 29,005 periodicals. Computerized library services include the card catalog, interlibrary loans, and database searching. Special learning facilities include a learning resource center, art gallery, radio station, molecular and behavioral neuroscience center, and institutes of jazz and animal behavior. The 34-acre campus is in an urban area 7 miles west of New York City.

Student Life: 95% of undergraduates are from New Jersey. Others are from 9 states and 6 foreign countries. 34% are African American; 25% white, 19% Hispanic. The average age of freshmen is 18; all undergraduates, 22.

Housing: Campus housing includes coed apartments, fraternity houses, and sorority houses. In addition, there is special housing for disabled students. 88% of students commute. Alcohol is not permitted.

Activities: There are no fraternities or sororities. There are 85 groups on campus, including chess, chorale, chorus, drama, literary magazine, newspaper, outreach, radio, and yearbook. Popular campus events include Black History Month, Honors Convocation, and Alpha Sigma Lambda.

Disabled Students: 80% of the campus is accessible. Wheelchair ramps, elevators, special parking, specially equipped rest rooms, special class scheduling, lowered drinking fountains, and lowered telephones are available. Facilities vary from building to building. However, all classes are scheduled in accessible locations for disabled students.

Services: Counseling and information services are available, as is tutoring in most subjects. There is a reader service for the blind, and remedial math, reading, and writing.

Campus Safety and Security: Measures include 24-hour foot and vehicle patrol, self-defense education, escort service, and shuttle buses. There are informal discussions, pamphlets/posters/films, emergency telephones, and lighted pathways/sidewalks. Security guards assist Rutgers police in providing public safety services. There is also a student marshal program.

Programs of Study: Newark confers B.A. and B.S. degrees. Master's and doctoral degrees are also awarded. Bachelor's degrees are awarded in BUSINESS (accounting, banking and finance, business administration and management, management science, and marketing/retailing/merchandising), COMMUNICATIONS AND THE ARTS (English), COMPUTER AND PHYSICAL SCIENCE (computer science and information sciences and systems), HEALTH PROFESSIONS (predentistry and premedicine), SOCIAL SCIENCE (criminal justice, economics, history, philosophy, political science/government, prelaw, psychology, social work, and sociology). Accounting, management, and psychology are the largest.

Required: To graduate, students must complete 124 credits with a minimum GPA of 2.0. Distribution requirements include 8 credits in natural science/math or 3 courses in nonlab science, math, or computer science; 6 credits each in history, literature, social sciences, humanities, and fine arts; 1 course in critical thinking; and 15 credits of electives. All students must take English composition and demonstrate math proficiency either by exam or by successfully completing a college algebra course or any other advanced course in math, a college calculus course, (with a grade of C or better) or a precalculus course (with a grade of B or better).

Special: Students may cross-register with the New Jersey Institute of Technology and the University of Medicine and Dentistry of New Jersey. Internships are available. The school offers study abroad, accelerated degree programs in business administration and criminal justice, dual majors, student-designed majors, nondegree study, and pass/fail options. Contact the school for information on the Honors College. There are 12 national honor societies, including Phi Beta Kappa, and a freshman honors program.

Faculty/Classroom: 62% of faculty are male; 38%, female. All both teach and do research. The average class size in an introductory lecture is 30; in a laboratory, 20; and in a regular course, 30.

Admissions: 52% of the 2001-2002 applicants were accepted. 63% of the current freshmen were in the top quarter of their class; 98% were in the top half.

Requirements: The SAT I or ACT is required. The GED is accepted. SAT II: Subject tests may be required of some applicants. Students should have completed 16 high school academic credits or Carnegie units, including 4 years of English, 3 years of math, 2 years of a foreign language, and 7 other academic units. AP and CLEP credits are accepted. Important factors in the admissions decision are advanced placement or honor courses, evidence of special talent, and leadership record. Students may apply on-line by accessing the Rutgers web site.

Procedure: Freshmen are admitted fall and spring. December of senior year is recommended as the date for taking entrance exams. There is an early admissions plan. Priority applications should be filed by December 1 for fall entry and November 1 for spring entry, along with a $50 fee. Notification is sent on a rolling basis. 2% of all applicants are on a waiting list; 108 were accepted in 2001.

Transfer: 469 transfer students enrolled in 2001-2002. Students who have completed at least 12 credit hours at another college with a cumulative GPA of 2.0 are considered for admission as transfer students. Transfers are admitted in the fall and spring. High school and college transcripts are required. 30 of the last 42 credits must be completed at Newark.

Visiting: There are regularly scheduled orientations for prospective students, including an information session with an admissions counselor and a tour of the campus. There are guides for informal visits and visitors may sit in on classes. To schedule a visit, contact the Admissions Office (Newark) at (973) 353-5205.

Financial Aid: Average annual earnings from campus work are $1365. The average financial indebtedness of the 2001 graduate was $15,855. The FAFSA is required. The fall application deadline is March 15.

International Students: There are 32 international students enrolled. They must score 550 on the written TOEFL and also take the college's own test.

Computers: The mainframe is a central system that includes 11 Sun UNIX servers dedicated to student use. Individual departments also have a variety of PCs. All students can generate their own accounts on this system. Access to the central campus system, and other university systems is provided through more than 450 networked PCs in 9 campus labs. 1 dorm has a PC lab, and all dorm rooms are wired for direct connection to the network. All students may access the system. Access to accounts, e-mail, and the Internet is available from the campus labs from 8:30 A.M. to midnight, and 24 hours a day from the dial-up lines. There are no time limits. The fee is $200.

Graduates: In 2001, 953 bachelor's degrees were awarded. The most popular majors were business/marketing (26%), health sciences (13%), and public administration (12%).

Admissions Contact: Bruce Neimeyer, Director of Admissions-Newark. E-mail: *admissions@asb-ugadm.rutgers.edu*
Web: *www.rutgers.edu*

SAINT PETER'S COLLEGE E-2
Jersey City, NJ 07306-5997 **(201) 915-9213**
(888) SPC-9933; (201) 432-5860

Full-time: 1100 men, 1150 women
Part-time: 160 men, 400 women
Graduate: 225 men, 300 women
Year: semesters, summer session
Application Deadline: open
Freshman Class: n/av
SAT I: required
Faculty: 112; IIA, -$
Ph.D.s: 78%
Student/Faculty: 20 to 1
Tuition: $15,696
Room & Board: $6596
LESS COMPETITIVE

Saint Peter's College, founded in 1872, is a private liberal arts and business college affiliated with the Roman Catholic Church and known as New Jersey's Jesuit College. Figures in the above capsule are approximate. There are 2 undergraduate and 3 graduate schools. In addition to regional accreditation, SPC has baccalaureate program accreditation with NLN. The 2 libraries contain 285,000 volumes, 70,000 microform items, and 3800 audiovisual forms/CDs, and subscribe to 1800 periodicals. Computerized library services include the card catalog, interlibrary loans, and database searching. Special learning facilities include a learning resource center, art gallery, radio station, and TV station. The 15-acre campus is in an urban area 2 miles west of New York City. Including residence halls, there are 29 buildings.

Student Life: 87% of undergraduates are from New Jersey. Others are from 26 states and 10 foreign countries. 56% are from public schools. 48% are white; 27% Hispanic; 16% African American. Most are Catholic. The average age of freshmen is 18; all undergraduates, 24. 23% do not continue beyond their first year; 51% remain to graduate.

Housing: 863 students can be accommodated in college housing, which includes single-sex and coed dormitories and on-campus apartments. In addition, there are community service houses. On-campus housing is guaranteed for all 4 years. 70% of students commute. Upperclassmen may keep cars.

Activities: There are no fraternities or sororities. There are 50 groups on campus, including cheerleading, chess, chorus, computers, debate, drama, ethnic, forensics, honors, international, literary magazine, newspaper, pep band, political, professional, radio and TV, religious, social, social service, student government, and yearbook. Popular campus events include International Day, career fairs, and SpringFest.

Sports: There are 10 intercollegiate sports for men and 8 for women, and 20 intramural sports for men and 18 for women. Facilities include a recreational center, a 2000-seat gym, and an athletic field.

Disabled Students: 80% of the campus is accessible. Wheelchair ramps, elevators, special parking, specially equipped rest rooms, special class scheduling, lowered drinking fountains, lowered telephones, and specially equipped rooms in residence halls are available.

Services: Counseling and information services are available, as is tutoring in every subject. There is a reader service for the blind, and remedial math, reading, and writing.

Campus Safety and Security: Measures include 24-hour foot and vehicle patrol, self-defense education, escort service, and shuttle buses. There are informal discussions, pamphlets/posters/films, emergency telephones, and security desk monitoring of access to residence halls.

Programs of Study: SPC confers B.A., B.S., and B.S.N. degrees. Associate and master's degrees are also awarded. Bachelor's degrees are awarded in BIOLOGICAL SCIENCE (biochemistry and biology/biological science), BUSINESS (accounting, business administration and management, international business management, and marketing/retailing/merchandising), COMMUNICATIONS AND THE ARTS (art history and appreciation, classical languages, classics, English, fine arts, and Spanish), COMPUTER AND PHYSICAL SCIENCE (chemistry, computer science, mathematics, natural sciences, and physics), EDUCATION (elementary and secondary), HEALTH PROFESSIONS (health care administration, medical laboratory technology, nursing, predentistry, and premedicine), SOCIAL SCIENCE (American studies, classical/ancient civilization, criminal justice, economics, history, humanities, philosophy, political science/government, prelaw, psychology, social science, sociology, theological studies, and urban studies). Natural sciences and accounting are the strongest academically. Business management, accounting, and computer sciences are the largest.

Required: To graduate, students must complete 129 credit hours, including 57 in the core curriculum, 12 in core electives, between 30 and 45 in the major, and the rest in subjects related to the major. The core curriculum requires 9 credits of natural sciences, 6 to 8 of math, 3 each of social science, philosophy, history, literature, and a modern language, and 3 each of fine arts and composition. Students must earn a GPA of 2.0.

Special: There are co-op programs with local companies, as well as departmental programs, and many internships available in Jersey City and nearby New York City. A Washington semester and study abroad in any of 60 countries are offered. The college also offers dual majors and student-designed majors, credit for life, military, and work experience, nondegree study, and pass/fail options. There are 9 national honor societies, a freshman honors program, and 1 departmental honors program.

Faculty/Classroom: 65% of faculty are male; 35%, female. All teach undergraduates. No introductory courses are taught by graduate students. The average class size in an introductory lecture is 23; in a laboratory, 14; and in a regular course, 16.

Requirements: The SAT I is required. In addition, applicants must be high school graduates or submit the GED certificate. Students should have completed 16 Carnegie units of high school study, including 4 years of English, 3 of math, 2 each of science, history, and a foreign language, and another 3 of additional work in any of these subjects. An essay and 2 letters of recommendation are required, and an interview is recommended. AP and CLEP credits are accepted. Important factors in the admissions decision are advanced placement or honor courses, extracurricular activities record, and recommendations by school officials.

Procedure: Freshmen are admitted fall and spring. Entrance exams should be taken by the fall of the senior year. There are early admissions and deferred admissions plans. Application deadlines are open. The fall 2001 application fee was $30.

Transfer: 93 transfer students enrolled in a recent year. The school requires a 2.0 college GPA of transfer students, as well as a high school transcript and an 800 composite SAT I score for students less than 2 years out of high school. An interview is recommended. 30 credits of 129 must be completed at SPC.

Visiting: There are regularly scheduled orientations for prospective students, including open houses, weekend and weekday visit days with a tour and class and information sessions, as well as tours and interviews by appointment. There are guides for informal visits and visitors may sit in on classes and stay overnight. To schedule a visit, contact the Admissions Office.

Financial Aid: SPC is a member of CSS. The FAFSA is required. The fall application deadline is March 1.

International Students: The school actively recruits these students. They must score 500 on the written TOEFL.

Computers: The mainframes are an IBM 9370, a DEC VAX 780, 2 DEC PDP 11/44s, and a DEC PDP 11/24. There are also a number of PCs available in computer labs throughout the campus, and the VAX can be accessed from outside computers by modem. All students may access the system. The system may be used for remote access 24 hours a day; for local access, about 94 hours a week. There are no time limits and no fees.

Graduates: In a recent year, 392 bachelor's degrees were awarded. The most popular majors were business management (15%), accountancy (15%), and elementary education (10%). In an average class, 1% graduate in 3 years, 30% in 4 years, 47% in 5 years, and 51% in 6 years. 140 companies recruited on campus in a recent year. Of a recent graduating class, 23% were enrolled in graduate school within 6 months of graduation and 88% were employed.

Admissions Contact: Frederick Chesky, Director of Admissions.
E-mail: *admissions@spcvxa.spc.edu* Web: *www.spc.edu*

SETON HALL UNIVERSITY E-2
South Orange, NJ 07079-2691 **(973) 761-9332**
(800) THE-HALL; (973) 275-2040

Full-time: 2000 men, 2350 women
Part-time: 690 men, 450 women
Graduate: 2250 men, 2450 women
Year: semesters, summer session
Application Deadline: March 1
Freshman Class: n/av
SAT I or ACT: required
Faculty: 272
Ph.D.s: 89%
Student/Faculty: 16 to 1
Tuition: $18,410
Room & Board: $8500
LESS COMPETITIVE

Seton Hall University, founded in 1856 by the first bishop of Newark and affiliated with the Roman Catholic Church, has undergraduate programs in the colleges of arts and sciences, business, education and human services, nursing, and diplomacy and international relations. Figures in the above capsule are approximate. There are 5 undergraduate and 8 graduate schools. In addition to regional accreditation, Seton Hall has baccalaureate program accreditation with AACSB, CSWE, and NLN. The 2 libraries contain 500,000 volumes, 600,000 microform items, and 3600 audiovisual forms/CDs, and subscribe to 2500 periodicals. Computerized library services include the card catalog, interlibrary loans, and database searching. Special learning facilities include a learning resource center, art gallery, natural history museum, radio station, and TV station. The 58-acre campus is in a suburban area 14 miles west of New York City. Including residence halls, there are 31 buildings.

Student Life: 81% of undergraduates are from New Jersey. Others are from 42 states, 44 foreign countries, and Canada. 69% are from public schools. 55% are white; 12% African American. 67% are Catholic; 14% Protestant. The average age of freshmen is 18; all undergraduates, 22. 19% do not continue beyond their first year; 65% remain to graduate.

Housing: 2015 students can be accommodated in college housing, which includes single-sex and coed dormitories and off-campus apartments. In addition, there are special-interest houses, an all-quiet residence hall, all female floors, modern language floors, academic teaming floors, smoke-free floors and areas, and substance-free floors and areas. On-campus housing is guaranteed for the freshman year only, is available on a first-come, first-served basis, and is available on a lottery system for upperclassmen. Priority is given to out-of-town students. 61% of students commute. Alcohol is not permitted. Upperclassmen may keep cars.

Activities: 15% of men belong to 1 local and 10 national fraternities; 12% of women belong to 4 local and 8 national sororities. There are 100 groups on campus, including art, cheerleading, choir, chorus, commuter council, computers, drama, drill team, ethnic, forensics, honors, international, literary magazine, musical theater, newspaper, pep band, photography, political, professional, radio and TV, recreation, religious, social, social service, student ambassador society, student government, volunteer, and yearbook. Popular campus events include University Day, Theatre-in-the-Round, and Welcome Weekend.

Sports: There are 9 intercollegiate sports for men and 8 for women, and 25 intramural sports for men and 25 for women. Facilities include a 3400-seat gym, an indoor track, an indoor pool, a dance studio, a weight room, a soccer and baseball field, a softball field, and tennis and racquetball courts. School teams also use the Meadowlands Arena, which seats 19,759.

Disabled Students: 75% of the campus is accessible. Wheelchair ramps, elevators, special parking, specially equipped rest rooms, special class scheduling, lowered drinking fountains, and lowered telephones are available.

Services: Counseling and information services are available, as is tutoring in most subjects. There is a reader service for the blind, and remedial math, reading, and writing. Tutorial assistance for disabled students is available.

Campus Safety and Security: Measures include 24-hour foot and vehicle patrol, escort service, shuttle buses, and informal discussions. There are pamphlets/posters/films, emergency telephones, and lighted pathways/sidewalks. Paid student security attendants are posted at residence hall entrances.

Programs of Study: Seton Hall confers B.A., B.S., B.A.B.A., B.S.B.A., B.S.Ed., and B.S.N. degrees. Master's and doctoral degrees are also awarded. Bachelor's degrees are awarded in BIOLOGICAL SCIENCE (biology/biological science), BUSINESS (accounting, banking and finance, business administration and management, business economics, management information systems, marketing/retailing/merchandising, and sports management), COMMUNICATIONS AND THE ARTS (art, communications, English, French, Italian, modern language, music, and Spanish), COMPUTER AND PHYSICAL SCIENCE (chemistry, computer science, mathematics, and physics), EDUCATION (elementary, secondary, and special), HEALTH PROFESSIONS (nursing), SOCIAL SCIENCE (African American studies, anthropology, Asian/Oriental studies, classical/ancient civilization, criminal justice, economics, history, international relations, liberal arts/general studies, philosophy, political science/government, psychology, religion, social science, social work, and sociology). Business (accounting, finance), biology, and chemistry are the strongest academically. Biology, criminal justice, and communication are the largest.

Required: To graduate, students must complete at least 128 hours, including a minimum of 36 hours in the major, both varying by major. Students must take freshman composition as well as courses in English, math, social science, natural sciences, religious studies, and philosophy, earning a minimum GPA of 2.0 (2.5 in the College of Education and Human Services).

Special: Co-op and work-study are possible through the College of Arts and Sciences and the School of Business; internships are available in many arts and sciences majors. Education majors go into the field during their sophomore year. Cross-registration in engineering and 3-2 engineering degrees are offered with the New Jersey Institute of Technology. Students may take a Washington semester (political science majors) or study abroad in more than 100 countries. An accelerated B.S.N. degree, a 5-year B.A.-M.B.A., a 5-year B.A.-M.P.A., a 5-year B.A.-B.S. degree in engineering, and a 6-year B.S.-M.S. in physical therapy, physician assistant, and occupational therapy are offered. Nondegree study is permitted, as are pass/fail options in electives. There are 20 national honor societies, a freshman honors program, and 3 departmental honors programs.

Faculty/Classroom: 61% of faculty are male; 39%, female. 70% teach undergraduates. No introductory courses are taught by graduate students. The average class size in an introductory lecture is 30; in a laboratory, 10; and in a regular course, 20.

Admissions: 3 freshmen graduated first in their class.

Requirements: The SAT I or ACT is required. In addition, seton Hall recommends a composite score higher than 1050 on the SAT I, with at least 500 on each part, or a minimum composite score of 24 on the ACT. Applicants must supply high school transcripts or a GED certificate. Students should have completed 16 Carnegie units of high school study, including 4 years of English, 3 of math, 2 each of a foreign language and either history or social studies, 1 of science, and 4 academic electives. An essay is optional, and an interview is recommended. A GPA of 2.5 is required. AP and CLEP credits are accepted. Important factors in the admissions decision are advanced placement or honor courses, leadership record, and parents or siblings attending the school. Students have access to an on-line application via Seton Hall's web site at *www.shu.edu/admit*. The application service used is Applyweb.

Procedure: Freshmen are admitted fall and spring. Entrance exams should be taken by January of the senior year. There is a deferred admissions plan. Applications should be filed by March 1 for fall entry and December 1 for spring entry. Notification is sent on a rolling basis. 8% of all applicants are on a waiting list; 340 were accepted in 2001. The fall 2001 application fee was $45.

Transfer: 247 transfer students enrolled in a recent year. Applicants should have earned 30 hours of college credit, with a minimum GPA of 2.5, or 2.8 for the business and science schools. The SAT I is required for students with fewer than 30 credits of college-level work at the time of application, and an interview is recommended. 30 credits of 128 must be completed at Seton Hall.

Visiting: There are regularly scheduled orientations for prospective students, including campus tours weekdays and Saturdays during the academic year and on weekdays during the summer. Open houses for prospective applicants are available each fall. Visitors may sit in on classes. To schedule a visit, contact the Enrollment Services Office.

Financial Aid: In a recent year, 85% of all freshmen and 59% of continuing students received some form of financial aid. 63% of freshmen and 48% of continuing students received need-based aid. The average freshman award was $11,686. Of that total, scholarships or need-based grants averaged $7136 ($26,000 maximum); loans averaged $4327 ($4800 maximum); and work contracts averaged $223 ($5000 maximum). 20% of undergraduates work part time. Average annual earnings from campus work are $1958. The average financial indebtedness of a recent graduate was $15,823. Seton Hall is a member of CSS. The FAFSA is required. Check with the school for current deadlines.

International Students: There were 113 international students enrolled in a recent year. The school actively recruits these students. They must score 550 on the written TOEFL and also take the SAT I or the ACT.

Computers: The mainframe is an IBM 9121. All entering students are required to lease an IBM lap top; in addition, there are more than 300 PCs in public labs. Students have access to the mainframe, networked file servers, the campuswide information system, the library catalog, personal e-mail accounts, and the Internet. Students can connect almost anywhere on campus. All students may access the system. Public labs are available until 11 P.M.; there is 24-hour remote connection availability. There are no time limits and no fees. All students are required to have personal computers. All entering freshmen are required to participate in the Mobile Computing Program. It is recommended that students have personal computers. Pentium-based IBM laptops are recommended.

Graduates: In a recent year, 884 bachelor's degrees were awarded. The most popular majors were communications (11%), nursing (10%), and criminal justice (9%). In an average class, 1% graduate in 3 years, 40% in 4 years, 58% in 5 years, and 61% in 6 years. 100 companies recruited on campus in a recent year. Of a recent graduating class, 20% were enrolled in graduate school within 6 months of graduation and 60% were employed.

Admissions Contact: Arthur W. Blanck, Director of Enrollment Services. A video is available. E-mail: *thehall@shu.edu*
Web: *www.shu.edu*

STEVENS INSTITUTE OF TECHNOLOGY — E-2
Hoboken, NJ 07030 — (201) 216-5194
(800) 458-5323; Fax: (201) 216-8348

Full-time: 1242 men, 405 women	**Faculty:** 110
Part-time: 1 man, 1 woman	**Ph.D.s:** 84%
Graduate: 1907 men, 744 women	**Student/Faculty:** 14 to 1
Year: semesters, summer session	**Tuition:** $23,780
Application Deadline: February 15	**Room & Board:** $7730
Freshman Class: 2622 applied, 1280 accepted, 445 enrolled	
SAT I Verbal/Math: 630/710	**HIGHLY COMPETITIVE+**

Stevens Institute of Technology, founded in 1870, is a private institution offering programs of study in science, computer science, engineering, and humanities. There are 3 undergraduate schools and 1 graduate school. In addition to regional accreditation, Stevens has baccalaureate program accreditation with ABET and CSAB. The library contains 110,575 volumes, 2141 microform items, and 1754 audiovisual forms/CDs, and subscribes to 137 periodicals. Computerized library services include the card catalog, interlibrary loans, and database searching. Special learning facilities include an art gallery, radio station, TV station, lab for ocean and coastal engineering, environmental lab, design and manufacturing institute, technology center, and telecommunications institute. The 55-acre campus is in an urban area 1 mile west of New York City. Including residence halls, there are 50 buildings.

Student Life: 61% of undergraduates are from New Jersey. Others are from 33 states, 46 foreign countries, and Canada. 51% are white; 22% Asian American; 12% Hispanic. The average age of freshmen is 18; all undergraduates, 20. 12% do not continue beyond their first year; 67% remain to graduate.

Housing: 1018 students can be accommodated in college housing, which includes single-sex and coed dormitories, on-campus apartments, off-campus apartments, married-student housing, fraternity houses, and sorority houses. On-campus housing is guaranteed for all 4 years. 66% of students live on campus; of those, 70% remain on campus on weekends. Upperclassmen may keep cars.

Activities: 35% of men belong to 9 national fraternities; 35% of women belong to 3 national sororities. There are 50 groups on campus, including art, band, chess, chorus, computers, drama, ethnic, international, jazz band, literary magazine, musical theater, newspaper, pep band, photography, political, professional, radio and TV, religious, social, social service, student government, and yearbook. Popular campus events include Fall Tech Fest and Spring Boken Festival.

Sports: There are 9 intercollegiate sports for men and 9 for women, and 18 intramural sports for men and 18 for women. Facilities include a 60,000-square-foot complex with an NCAA regulation swimming pool convertible to international size, squash courts, a 1000-seat basketball arena, fitness rooms, racquetball courts, a playing field, a student union, and several outdoor courts.

Disabled Students: 25% of the campus is accessible. Wheelchair ramps, elevators, special parking, specially equipped rest rooms, and lowered drinking fountains are available.

Services: Counseling and information services are available, as is tutoring in every subject.

Campus Safety and Security: Measures include 24-hour foot and vehicle patrol, self-defense education, escort service, and informal discussions. There are pamphlets/posters/films, emergency telephones, and lighted pathways/sidewalks.

Programs of Study: Stevens confers B.A., B.S., and B.E. degrees. Master's and doctoral degrees are also awarded. Bachelor's degrees are awarded in BIOLOGICAL SCIENCE (biochemistry), COMMUNICATIONS AND THE ARTS (literature), COMPUTER AND PHYSICAL SCIENCE (applied mathematics, applied physics, chemistry, computer science, mathematics, physics, and polymer science), ENGINEERING AND ENVIRONMENTAL DESIGN (chemical engineering, civil engineering, computer engineering, electrical/electronics engineering, engineering management, engineering physics, environmental engineering, materials engineering, and mechanical engineering), HEALTH PROFESSIONS (predentistry and premedicine), SOCIAL SCIENCE (history, philosophy, and prelaw). Engineering is the strongest academically, and has the largest enrollments.

Required: To graduate, the student must have earned at least 145 credit hours with a minimum 2.0 GPA; the total hours in the major vary by program. The core curriculum includes courses in engineering, science, computer science, math, liberal arts, and phys ed.

Special: Stevens offers a 3-2 engineering degree with New York University, a work-study program within the school, co-op programs, corporate and research internships through the Undergraduate Projects in Technology and Medicine, study abroad in Scotland, Australia, and Lebanon, and pass/fail options for extra courses. Students may undertake dual majors as well as accelerated degree programs in medicine, dentistry, and law, and can receive a B.A.-B.E. degree or a B.A.-B.S. degree in all majors. Undergraduates may take graduate courses. There are 3 national honor societies, and a freshman honors program.

Faculty/Classroom: 86% of faculty are male; 14%, female. 83% teach undergraduates, 80% do research, and 80% do both. No introductory courses are taught by graduate students. The average class size in an introductory lecture is 100; in a laboratory, 50; and in a regular course, 20.

Admissions: 49% of the 2001-2002 applicants were accepted. The SAT I scores for the 2001-2002 freshman class were: Verbal--8% below 500, 36% between 500 and 599, 44% between 600 and 700, and 12% above 700; Math--2% below 500, 11% between 500 and 599, 55% between 600 and 700, and 34% above 700. 11 freshmen graduated first in their class in a recent year.

Requirements: The SAT I or ACT is required. The SAT I is preferred. Stevens recommends a minimum of 2 SAT II: Subject tests, depending on the intended major. In addition, applicants must provide official high school transcripts. Students should have taken 4 years of English, math, and science. An interview is required. A GPA of 3.0 is required. AP credits are accepted. Important factors in the admissions decision are advanced placement or honor courses and extracurricular activities record. Applications are accepted on computer disk and on-line via the school's web site.

Procedure: Freshmen are admitted in the fall. Entrance exams should be taken by February of the senior year. There are early decision, early admissions, and deferred admissions plans. Early decision applications should be filed by November 15; regular applications, by February 15 for fall entry and December 1 for spring entry. The fall 2001 application fee was $45. Notification of early decision is sent December 15; regular decision, March 15.

Transfer: 60 transfer students enrolled in a recent year. Applicants should have a minimum GPA of 3.0. They must submit all college transcripts, including course descriptions; SAT I or ACT scores are required of those students with fewer than 30 hours of college credit. 50 credits of 126 must be completed at Stevens.

Visiting: There are regularly scheduled orientations for prospective students, including interviews and campus tours. There are guides for informal visits and visitors may sit in on classes and stay overnight. To schedule a visit, contact the Admissions Office.

Financial Aid: In 2001-2002, 90% of all freshmen and 92% of continuing students received some form of financial aid. 55% of undergraduates work part time. Average annual earnings from campus work are $1000. The average financial indebtedness of a recent graduate was $12,400. Stevens is a member of CSS. The FAFSA is required.

International Students: There were 129 international students enrolled in a recent year. The school actively recruits these students. They must score 550 on the written TOEFL and also take the SAT I or the ACT.

Computers: The mainframes are a SGI Challenge and Challenge L servers, Sun SPARE servers, and Intel-based servers. All students may access campus servers, the Internet, the Web, and specialized facilities via the campuswide network that connects every academic, administrative, and residential building. Labs of systems and connections for notebooks are available throughout the campus, including all residence hall rooms, 1 per person. All students may access the system. There are no time limits and no fees. All students are required to have personal computers. It is recommended that all students have Pentium III 500 Notebooks, 64 MB, 5 GB, with a 10/100 network card.

Graduates: In a recent year, 291 bachelor's degrees were awarded. The most popular majors were mechanical engineering (20%), electrical engineering (15%), and computer engineering (13%). In an average class, 45% graduate in 4 years, 55% in 5 years, and 67% in 6 years.

Admissions Contact: Daniel Gallagher, Dean of Undergraduate Admissions. E-mail: *admissions@stevens-tech.edu*
Web: *http://www.stevens-tech.edu*

THOMAS EDISON STATE COLLEGE D-3

Trenton, NJ 08608-1176 **(609) 984-1150; Fax: (609) 984-8447**

Full-time: none	**Faculty:** n/av
Part-time: 4338 men, 3814 women	**Ph.D.s:** n/av
Graduate: 103 men, 80 women	**Student/Faculty:** n/av
Year: see profile	**Tuition:** see profile
Application Deadline: open	**Room & Board:** n/app
Freshman Class: n/av	
SAT I or ACT: not required	**SPECIAL**

Thomas Edison State College, founded in 1972, is a public institution of higher education. The college provides many ways to complete a degree in more than 100 areas of study, including credit by exam, assessment of experiential learning, guided independent study, and credit for corporate and military training, which enables adults to pursue educational goals while attending to the challenges of career and family. Students may pay a flat fee of $2,750 a year ($3,950 out of state) for an unlimited number of credit-earning methods, or $830 a year ($1,480 out of state), plus the fees, for services and credits as they use/earn them. In addition to regional accreditation, Thomas Edison has baccalaureate program accreditation with NLN. Special learning facilities include the New Jersey State Library, an affiliate of the college. The 2-acre campus is in an urban area 40 miles north of Philadelphia. There are 3 buildings.

Student Life: 56% of undergraduates are from New Jersey. Others are from 49 states, 80 foreign countries, and Canada. 75% are white; 10% African American. The average age of all undergraduates is 38.

Housing: There are no residence halls. Alcohol is not permitted.

Activities: There are no fraternities or sororities.

Sports: There is no sports program at Thomas Edison.

Disabled Students: 95% of the campus is accessible. Wheelchair ramps, elevators, special parking, specially equipped rest rooms, and lowered drinking fountains are available. Visually impaired students may make use of a "Talking Browser," pwWebSpeak.

Services: Alumni peer counseling and study groups for the nursing degree are among the counseling and tutorial services available.

Campus Safety and Security: Measures include lighted pathways/sidewalks. There is a guard on the premises 7 A.M. to 11 P.M.; the outside is patrolled by the New Jersey State Police.

Programs of Study: Thomas Edison confers B.A., B.S., B.S.A.S.T., B.S.B.A., B.S.H.S., and B.S.N. degrees. Associate and master's degrees are also awarded. Bachelor's degrees are awarded in AGRICULTURE (environmental studies, forestry and related sciences, and horticulture), BIOLOGICAL SCIENCE (biology/biological science), BUSINESS (accounting, banking and finance, business administration and management, hotel/motel and restaurant management, human resources, insurance, international business management, labor studies, management information systems, management science, marketing and distribution, office supervision and management, purchasing/inventory management, real estate, recreation and leisure services, retailing, small business management, and transportation management), COMMUNICATIONS AND THE ARTS (advertising, art, communications, dramatic arts, journalism, literature, music, and photography), COMPUTER AND PHYSICAL SCIENCE (chemistry, computer science, information sciences and systems, mathematics, natural sciences, nuclear technology, and physics), EDUCATION (foreign languages, health, and nutrition), ENGINEERING AND ENVIRONMENTAL DESIGN (air traffic control, architecture, aviation computer technology, biomedical equipment technology, civil engineering technology, computer technology, construction engineering, drafting and design, electrical/electronics engineering technology, emergency/disaster science, environmental science, manufacturing technology, marine engineering, materials science, mechanical engineering technology, nuclear engineering technology, and survey and mapping technology), HEALTH PROFESSIONS (clinical science, cytotechnology, dental hygiene, health, health care administration, hospital administration, mental health/human services, nuclear medical technology, nursing, radiation therapy, and respiratory therapy), SOCIAL SCIENCE (anthropology, child psychology/development, community services, criminal justice, economics, fire protection, gerontology, history, human services, humanities, liberal arts/general studies, philosophy, political science/government, psychology, public administration, religion, social science, and sociology). Liberal studies is the strongest academically. Liberal studies, general management, and psychology are the largest.

Required: The baccalaureate student must complete a liberal arts requirement that includes courses in written expression, humanities, social science, math, and natural sciences for a total of at least 50% liberal arts credits. To graduate, 120 semester hours are required, with a minimum GPA of 2.0.

Special: Students may design their own majors and take dual majors in all degree programs except nursing. A B.S. in health sciences is available as a joint degree with the University of Medicine and Dentistry of New Jersey (UMDNJ). Credit for college-level knowledge gained through life, military, and work experience is readily granted. Students may receive pass/fail grades. Students work on their own, proceeding at their own pace, depending on the option selected for earning credit. Thomas Edison has no semesters, though the Guided Study program follows a 6-semester calendar. There is 1 national honor society.

Faculty/Classroom: 65% of faculty are male; 35%, female.

Requirements: Applicants must have a high school diploma or the equivalent and be at least 21 years old or have an associate degree from an accredited 2-year college. AP and CLEP credits are accepted. Applications are accepted on-line at the school's website.

Procedure: Application deadlines are open. The fall 2001 application fee was $75. Notification is sent on a rolling basis.

Transfer: Transfers, like other students, must be at least 21 and be high school graduates or the equivalent, or hold an associate degree. The granting of credit for course work successfully completed elsewhere is an intrinsic part of the school's system. Transfer credits are awarded with the grades earned.

Visiting: There are regularly scheduled orientations for prospective students, including group information sessions and seminars. To schedule a visit, contact the Director of Admissions at (888) 442-8372.

Financial Aid: In 2001-2002, 8% of all enrolled students received some form of financial aid. 5% of all enrolled students received need-based aid. The FAFSA and the college's own financial statement are required. Applications are processed on a rolling basis. The priority fall application deadline is June 1.

International Students: There are 207 international students enrolled. They must score 500 on the written TOEFL or 173 on the electronic version.

Computers: The mainframe is an HP 9000. The college web site allows students to apply, register for courses, take on-line courses, contact offices via e-mail, and submit course-related forms. Visitors to the college web site may participate in open on-line discussions and chat areas. All students may access the system at their convenience. There are no time limits and no fees.

Graduates: In 2001, 1002 bachelor's degrees were awarded. The most popular majors were liberal studies (20%), nuclear engineering technology (11%), and psychology (9%).

Admissions Contact: Gordon Holly, Director of Admissions. A video is available. E-mail: *admissions@tesc.edu* Web: *http://www.tesc.edu*

WESTMINSTER CHOIR COLLEGE OF RIDER UNIVERSITY — D-3

Princeton, NJ 08540-3899 — **(609) 921-7144**
(800) 96-CHOIR; (609) 921-2538

Full-time: 120 men, 200 women	**Faculty:** 37
Part-time: none	**Ph.D.s:** 80%
Graduate: 55 men, 105 women	**Student/Faculty:** 7 to 1
Year: semesters, summer session	**Tuition:** $18,000
Application Deadline: open	**Room & Board:** $7400
Freshman Class: n/av	
SAT I or ACT: required	**SPECIAL**

Westminster Choir College, founded in 1926, is a private school of music within Rider University, that focuses on undergraduate and graduate students seeking positions of music leadership in churches, schools, and communities. Figures in the above capsule are approximate. In addition to regional accreditation, Westminster Choir College has baccalaureate program accreditation with NASM. The library contains 60,000 volumes, 425 microform items, and 9000 audiovisual forms/CDs, and subscribes to 170 periodicals. Computerized library services include the card catalog, interlibrary loans, and database searching. Special learning facilities include a learning resource center, a music computer lab, and a vocal lab. The 23-acre campus is in a suburban area 50 miles south of New York City. Including residence halls, there are 12 buildings.

Student Life: 66% of undergraduates are from out of state, mostly the Northeast. Others are from 36 states, 24 foreign countries, and Canada. 75% are white; 19% foreign nationals. The average age of freshmen is 18; all undergraduates, 21. 18% do not continue beyond their first year; 50% remain to graduate.

Housing: 206 students can be accommodated in college housing, which includes single-sex and coed dormitories. On-campus housing is guaranteed for all 4 years. 70% of students live on campus; of those, 85% remain on campus on weekends. All students may keep cars.

Activities: There are no fraternities or sororities. There are 12 groups on campus, including choir, chorus, drama, ethnic, gay, honors, musical theater, newspaper, opera, orchestra, professional, radio and TV, religious, social, student government, and yearbook. Popular campus events include Spring Fling, Christmas at Westminster, and concerts.

Sports: There are 2 intramural sports for men and 2 for women.

Disabled Students: 42% of the campus is accessible. Wheelchair ramps, elevators, special parking, specially equipped rest rooms, and lowered telephones are available.

Services: Counseling and information services are available, as is tutoring in every subject. There is remedial math, reading, and writing.

Campus Safety and Security: Measures include escort service, shuttle buses, pamphlets/posters/films, and emergency telephones. There are lighted pathways/sidewalks and increased campus security from 6 P.M. to 6 A.M.

Programs of Study: Westminster Choir College confers B.A. and B.M. degrees. Master's degrees are also awarded. Bachelor's degrees are awarded in COMMUNICATIONS AND THE ARTS (music, music performance, music theory and composition, piano/organ, and voice), EDUCATION (music), SOCIAL SCIENCE (religious music). Music education is the largest.

Required: All students must maintain a minimum GPA of 2.0 (2.5 for music education majors) while completing 124 semester hours, including 92 to 100 in their majors. All students also must meet English reading and writing proficiency requirements. Distribution requirements include 33 semester hours in arts and sciences with at least 1 course from each of the divisions of the department. Satisfactory performance in recital also is needed.

Special: Cross-registration with Drew University, Princeton University, Rider University, and Princeton Theological Seminary, internships in the arts, church, box office management, and arts administration, work-study programs, dual majors in any combination of 7 majors in music, and pass/fail options are all available. In addition, individualized programs of study in Europe may be pursued. There is 1 national honor society.

Faculty/Classroom: All teach undergraduates. No introductory courses are taught by graduate students. The average class size in an introductory lecture is 18; in a laboratory, 8; and in a regular course, 12.

Requirements: The SAT I or ACT is required; SAT I minimum scores should be 800 composite, 400 verbal and 400 math. Applicants must present 4 years of credits in English, 3 in history, 2 in math, and 1 in science. An essay and music audition are required, whereas an interview is recommended. The GED is accepted. A GPA of 2.0 is required. AP credits are accepted. Important factors in the admissions decision are evidence of special talent, recommendations by alumni, and recommendations by school officials.

Procedure: Freshmen are admitted fall and spring. Entrance exams should be taken at the time of the audition. There are early decision, early admissions, and deferred admissions plans. Application deadlines are open. Notification is sent on a rolling basis. The fall 2001 application fee was $40.

Transfer: Applicants must submit high school and college transcripts and 2 letters of recommendation. An audition is required. 65 credits of 124 must be completed at Westminster Choir College.

Visiting: There are regularly scheduled orientations for prospective students. There are guides for informal visits and visitors may sit in on classes. To schedule a visit, contact the Admissions Office.

Financial Aid: In 2001-2002, 80% of all students received some form of financial aid. The average recent freshman award was $14,724. The average financial indebtedness of a recent graduate was $12,500. Westminster Choir College is a member of CSS. The FAFSA is required. Check with the school for current deadlines.

International Students: They must score 550 on the written TOEFL.

Computers: PCs are available for academic use in the Music, Arts and Sciences, and Learning Center computer labs. All students may access the system. There are no time limits and no fees.

Admissions Contact: Monica A. Tritto, Director of Admissions. E-mail: *wccadmission@rider.edu* Web: *westminster.rider.edu*

WILLIAM PATERSON UNIVERSITY OF NEW JERSEY E-2

Wayne, NJ 07470 (973) 720-2125; (973) 720-2910

Full-time: 2720 men, 3600 women	**Faculty:** 309; IIA, +$
Part-time: 750 men, 1225 women	**Ph.D.s:** 79%
Graduate: 310 men, 1165 women	**Student/Faculty:** 20 to 1
Year: semesters, summer session	**Tuition:** $5000 ($8000)
Application Deadline: see profile	**Room & Board:** $6000
Freshman Class: n/av	
SAT I or ACT: required	**LESS COMPETITIVE**

William Paterson University of New Jersey, founded in 1855 as a college, is a public institution comprised of the Colleges of Arts and Communication; Education; Humanities, and Social Sciences; Science and Health; and Business. Figures in the above capsule are approximate. There are 5 undergraduate and 5 graduate schools. In addition to regional accreditation, WPUNJ has baccalaureate program accreditation with ASLA, NASM, NCATE, and NLN. The library contains 320,000 volumes, 1 million microform items, and 15,000 audiovisual forms/CDs, and subscribes to 1500 periodicals. Computerized library services include the card catalog, interlibrary loans, and database searching. Special learning facilities include an art gallery, radio station, TV station, and a speech and hearing clinic, an academic support center, a computerized writing center, and a teleconference center. The 320-acre campus is in a suburban area 25 miles west of New York City. Including residence halls, there are 35 buildings.

Student Life: 98% of undergraduates are from New Jersey. Others are from 22 states, 58 foreign countries, and Canada. 75% are from public schools. 61% are white; 20% Hispanic; 16% African American. The average age of freshmen is 18; all undergraduates, 24. 22% do not continue beyond their first year; 78% remain to graduate.

Housing: 1800 students can be accommodated in college housing, which includes coed dormitories and on-campus apartments. In addition, there are honors houses. On-campus housing is guaranteed for all 4 years. 69% of students commute. Upperclassmen may keep cars.

Activities: 10% of men belong to 3 local and 8 national fraternities; 12% of women belong to 3 local and 11 national sororities. There are 50 groups on campus, including art, cheerleading, chorus, computers, dance, drama, ethnic, film, gay, honors, international, jazz band, literary magazine, musical theater, newspaper, opera, orchestra, photography, political, professional, radio and TV, religious, student government, and yearbook. Popular campus events include Midday Artist Series, Puerto Rican Heritage Month, and Latin American Week.

Sports: There are 7 intercollegiate sports for men and 7 for women, and 24 intramural sports for men and 24 for women. Facilities include a recreation center with courts for basketball, tennis, racquetball, volleyball, and badminton, weight and exercise rooms, saunas and whirlpools, and a 4000-seat auditorium. The university also offers an Olympic-size pool, 8 additional tennis courts, and an athletic complex with fields for baseball, field hockey, football, soccer, softball, and track.

Disabled Students: Wheelchair ramps, elevators, special parking, specially equipped rest rooms, special class scheduling, lowered drinking fountains, and lowered telephones are available.

Services: Counseling and information services are available, as is tutoring in most subjects. There is remedial math, reading, and writing. There is a science enrichment center, a writing center, and a business tutorial lab.

Campus Safety and Security: Measures include 24-hour foot and vehicle patrol, escort service, shuttle buses, and informal discussions. There are pamphlets/posters/films, emergency telephones, and lighted pathways/sidewalks.

Programs of Study: WPUNJ confers B.A., B.S., B.F.A., and B.M. degrees. Master's degrees are also awarded. Bachelor's degrees are awarded in BIOLOGICAL SCIENCE (biology/biological science and biotechnology), BUSINESS (accounting, banking and finance, and business administration and management), COMMUNICATIONS AND THE ARTS (art history and appreciation, communications, dramatic arts, English, fine arts, music, Spanish, and studio art), COMPUTER AND PHYSICAL SCIENCE (chemistry, computer science, and mathematics), EDUCATION (health, music, physical, and special), ENGINEERING AND ENVIRONMENTAL DESIGN (environmental science), HEALTH PROFESSIONS (community health work, health science, and nursing), SOCIAL SCIENCE (African American studies, anthropology, economics, geography, history, philosophy, political science/government, psychology, and sociology). Biology/biotechnology, computer science, and English are the strongest academically. Management, communications, and education are the largest.

Required: All students must maintain a cumulative GPA of at least 2.0 and take 128 credit hours, typically including 30 to 40 in their major. General education requirements include 21 credits in the humanities, 11 or 12 in science, 9 in the social sciences, and 6 in art and communication. Also required are 1 course in health or movement science, 1 course dealing with racism or sexism, and 1 course in non-Western culture. Students also complete 6 credits of general education electives and a minimum of 9 credits of upper-level elective courses.

Special: Study abroad in 33 countries, cross-registration, internships, work-study programs on campus, accelerated degree programs, dual majors, individual curriculum design, and credit for military experience are available. Nondegree study and some pass/fail options are also possible. In the Learning Clusters Project, students experience how 3 general education courses, taken together, reinforce and better integrate each other. There is a professional program in teacher education leading to certification in early childhood, elementary, middle, and secondary education. There are 6 national honor societies, and 4 departmental honors programs.

Faculty/Classroom: 62% of faculty are male; 38%, female. All teach undergraduates and 40% do research. No introductory courses are taught by graduate students. The average class size in an introductory lecture is 32; in a laboratory, 24; and in a regular course, 19.

Requirements: The SAT I or ACT is required. In addition, applicants must have 16 academic credits or Carnegie units, including 4 in English, 3 in math, 2 each in science lab and social studies, and 5 electives such as foreign language and history. An essay and interview are recommended for some applicants, as are a portfolio and audition. The GED is accepted. WPUNJ requires applicants to be in the upper 50% of their class. A GPA of 2.5 is required. AP and CLEP credits are accepted. Important factors in the admissions decision are advanced placement or honor courses, recommendations by school officials, and evidence of special talent.

Procedure: Freshmen are admitted fall and spring. Entrance exams should be taken by January 31. There are early decision, early admissions, and deferred admissions plans. Notification is sent on a rolling basis. A waiting list is an active part of the admissions procedure. Check with the school for current application deadlines and fee.

Transfer: 886 transfer students enrolled in a recent year. Transfer students need a minimum GPA of 2.0 (business, nursing, computer science, and education students need a 2.5 GPA) and at least 12 credit hours earned. 38 credits of 128 must be completed at WPUNJ.

Visiting: There are regularly scheduled orientations for prospective students, including a campus tour, guest speakers, and dissemination of printed information. There are guides for informal visits and visitors may sit in on classes. To schedule a visit, contact the Admissions Office.

Financial Aid: WPUNJ is a member of CSS. The FAFSA and parent and student federal income tax forms are required. The fall application deadline is open.

International Students: They must score 550 on the written TOEFL.

Computers: The mainframe is an IBM 3099. There are also PCs available for student use. All students may access the system at all times. There are no time limits. The fee is $30.

Admissions Contact: Director of Admissions. Web: *www.wpunj.edu*

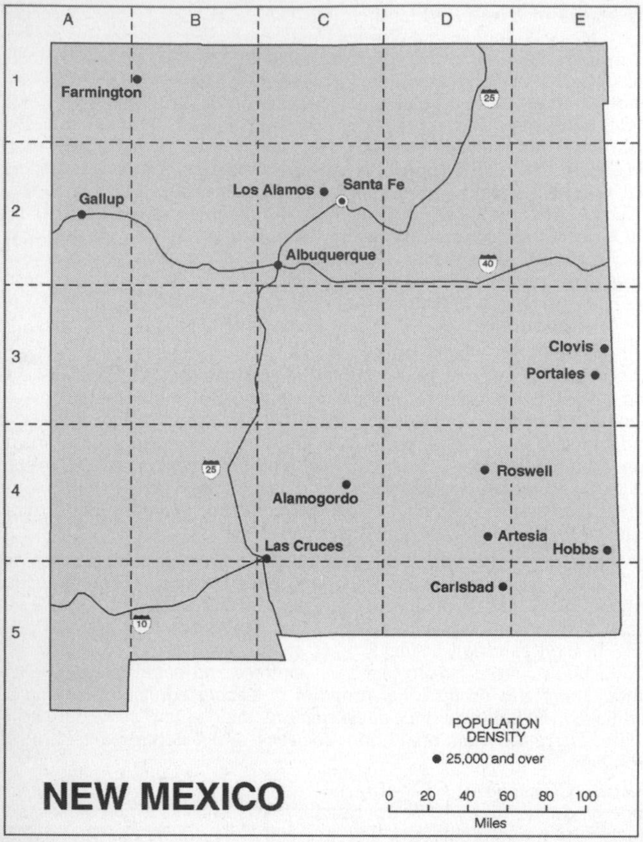

COLLEGE OF SANTA FE
Santa Fe, NM 87505-5634

C-2
(505) 473-6133
(800) 456-2673; (505) 473-6129

Full-time: 300 men, 370 women
Part-time: 220 men, 450 women
Graduate: 55 men, 170 women
Year: semesters, summer session
Application Deadline: open
Freshman Class: n/av
SAT I or ACT: required

Faculty: 57; IIB, -$
Ph.D.s: 25%
Student/Faculty: 13 to 1
Tuition: $15,250
Room & Board: $5000

LESS COMPETITIVE

The College of Santa Fe, founded in 1947 by the Christian Brothers, is a private liberal arts institution offering undergraduate programs in social sciences, humanities, education, science and math, business, visual arts, moving image arts, and performing arts. Figures in the above capsule are approximate. The library contains 165,000 volumes and 7300 audiovisual forms/CDs, and subscribes to 320 periodicals. Computerized library services include the card catalog, interlibrary loans, and database searching. Special learning facilities include a learning resource center, art gallery, and a professional sound stage for film and video, and a professional graphics workshop. The 98-acre campus is in a suburban area 60 miles north of Albuquerque.

Student Life: 70% of undergraduates are from New Mexico. Others are from 41 states, 5 foreign countries, and Canada. 64% are white; 27% Hispanic. 18% are Catholic. The average age of freshmen is 19; all undergraduates, 27. 38% do not continue beyond their first year; 53% remain to graduate.

Housing: 392 students can be accommodated in college housing, which includes single-sex and coed dormitories. In addition, there are honors houses, an alcohol-free dorm, and nontraditional-age student housing. On-campus housing is guaranteed for the freshman year only. 58% of students commute. All students may keep cars.

Activities: There are no fraternities or sororities. There are 15 groups on campus, including art, computers, dance, drama, ethnic, film, gay, honors, international, literary magazine, musical theater, newspaper, photography, political, religious, social, social service, and student government. Popular campus events include Christmas Ball, Music Fest, and President's Pancake Flip.

Sports: There are 5 intramural sports for men and 5 for women. Facilities include a fitness center housing a gym, racquetball/squash courts, a weight room, and a multipurpose exercise room.

Disabled Students: Wheelchair ramps, elevators, special parking, specially equipped rest rooms, lowered drinking fountains, lowered telephones, and lowered light switches and controls in dorms are available.

Services: Counseling and information services are available, as is tutoring in most subjects. There is remedial math, reading, and writing.

Campus Safety and Security: Measures include 24-hour foot and vehicle patrol, self-defense education, informal discussions, and pamphlets/posters/films. There are emergency telephones and lighted pathways/sidewalks.

Programs of Study: CSF confers B.A., B.S., and B.F.A. degrees. Master's degrees are also awarded. Bachelor's degrees are awarded in BIOLOGICAL SCIENCE (biology/biological science), BUSINESS (accounting, and business administration and management), COMMUNICATIONS AND THE ARTS (art history and appreciation, creative writing, design, dramatic arts, English, film arts, music, and visual and performing arts), COMPUTER AND PHYSICAL SCIENCE (chemistry, computer science, information sciences and systems, and mathematics), EDUCATION (education, English, and mathematics), ENGINEERING AND ENVIRONMENTAL DESIGN (environmental science), SOCIAL SCIENCE (human services, humanities, psychology, public administration, religion, and Southwest American studies). The arts, business, and education are the strongest academically. Performing arts, moving image arts, and visual arts are the largest.

Required: Students must successfully complete 128 credit hours, with 64 to 69 hours in the major and a minimum GPA of 2.0. The 45-credit liberal arts core curriculum requires courses in science, humanities, philosophy, religious studies, English, speech, social science, phys ed, and health awareness.

Special: CSF offers co-op programs in art therapy and arts and entertainment management, internships in moving image arts, performing arts, business, psychology, science, and education, and cross-registration with the Institute of American Indian Arts. Work-study, study abroad in London, student-designed majors, pass/fail options, credit by examination, art studies in New York City, and credit for work experience are possible.

Faculty/Classroom: 82% of faculty are male; 18%, female. 10% do research. The average class size in an introductory lecture is 25; in a laboratory, 25; and in a regular course, 20.

Requirements: The SAT I or ACT is required of students who graduated from high school within 2 years of applying to CSF. Graduation from an accredited secondary school is required. The GED is accepted. Applicants must have 16 academic credits, including 3 years of English, 2 each of math, science, and social studies, 1 of foreign language, and the remainder in college-preparatory courses. Letters of recommendation are suggested. A portfolio or an audition is required for specific majors. An essay and an interview are recommended. AP and CLEP credits are accepted. Important factors in the admissions decision are evidence of special talent, leadership record, and advanced placement or honor courses. Applications are accepted on-line via CollegeLink and College Scope.

Procedure: Freshmen are admitted to all sessions. Entrance exams should be taken in the junior year of high school. There are early admissions and deferred admissions plans. Application deadlines are open. The fall 2001 application fee was $25.

Transfer: 97 transfer students enrolled in a recent year. Applicants must submit an official high school transcript and official transcripts from all previous colleges. SAT I or ACT scores and an interview are recommended. 30 credits of 128 must be completed at CSF.

Visiting: There are regularly scheduled orientations for prospective students, including 3 Weekend Fiestas each year during which students attend campus tours, classes, departmental receptions, a meeting with an admissions counselor, a campus event, and an outdoor activity. Students are housed with current students and eat in the campus dining hall. There are guides for informal visits and visitors may sit in on classes and stay overnight. To schedule a visit, contact the Office of Admissions.

Financial Aid: In a recent year, 61% of all freshmen and 95% of continuing students received some form of financial aid. 52% of freshmen and 81% of continuing students received need-based aid. The average freshman award was $14,000. Of that total, scholarships or need-based grants averaged $1500 ($4366 maximum); loans averaged $1750 ($4352 maximum); and work contracts averaged $2000. 25% of undergraduates work part time. Average annual earnings from campus work are $925. The average financial indebtedness of a recent graduate was $17,125. CSF is a member of CSS. The FAFSA and the college's own financial statement are required. Check with the school for current deadlines.

International Students: There were 6 international students enrolled in a recent year. They must score 500 on the written TOEFL and also take the Comprehensive English Language Test, or the SAT I or ACT.
Computers: The mainframe is a Data General MV5600. There are 36 computers available to students through the library or the computer lab. All students may access the system. There are no time limits and no fees.
Admissions Contact: Dale H. Reinhart, Director of Admissions and Enrollment Management. E-mail: *admissions@csf.edu*

COLLEGE OF THE SOUTHWEST E-4
Hobbs, NM 88240-9987 (505) 392-6561
(800) 530-4400; Fax: (505) 392-6006

Full-time: 146 men, 254 women	**Faculty:** 19
Part-time: 63 men, 150 women	**Ph.D.s:** 33%
Graduate: 42 men, 192 women	**Student/Faculty:** 21 to 1
Year: semesters, summer session	**Tuition:** $4690
Application Deadline: open	**Room & Board:** $3766
Freshman Class: 44 applied, 44 accepted, 42 enrolled	
SAT I Verbal/Math: 450/450	**ACT:** 20 NONCOMPETITIVE

College of the Southwest, founded in 1962, is a private institution offering undergraduate programs in arts and sciences, business, education, psychology, and criminal justice. Graduate programs are offered in education. The library contains 67,073 volumes, 17,956 microform items, and 1136 audiovisual forms/CDs, and subscribes to 304 periodicals. Computerized library services include the card catalog, interlibrary loans, and database searching. Special learning facilities include a learning resource center. The 162-acre campus is in a small town 110 miles southwest of Lubbock, Texas. Including residence halls, there are 9 buildings.
Student Life: 79% of undergraduates are from New Mexico. Others are from 7 states, 5 foreign countries, and Canada. 75% are white; 20% Hispanic. The average age of freshmen is 19; all undergraduates, 29. 50% do not continue beyond their first year; 24% remain to graduate.
Housing: 64 students can be accommodated in college housing, which includes single-sex dormitories and on-campus apartments. On-campus housing is available on a first-come, first-served basis. Priority is given to out-of-town students. 84% of students commute. Alcohol is not permitted. All students may keep cars.
Activities: There are no fraternities or sororities. There are 7 groups on campus, including chorus, drama, honors, newspaper, professional, student government, and yearbook. Popular campus events include Annual Students in Free Enterprise Dinner and Award Presentation, Family Week, and speakers' presentations.
Sports: There is 1 intercollegiate sport for men and 2 for women, and 5 intramural sports for men and 5 for women. Facilities include soccer and baseball fields, a game room, and a physical fitness center with a multipurpose gym, racquetball courts, and a physiology lab.
Disabled Students: All of the campus is accessible. Wheelchair ramps, special parking, and specially equipped rest rooms are available.
Services: Counseling and information services are available, as is tutoring in most subjects. There is remedial math and writing.
Campus Safety and Security: Measures include 24-hour foot and vehicle patrol, informal discussions, and pamphlets/posters/films.
Programs of Study: CSW confers B.S., B.A.S., and B.B.A. degrees. Master's degrees are also awarded. Bachelor's degrees are awarded in BIOLOGICAL SCIENCE (biology/biological science), BUSINESS (accounting, business administration and management, and marketing/retailing/merchandising), COMMUNICATIONS AND THE ARTS (English), COMPUTER AND PHYSICAL SCIENCE (mathematics and natural sciences), EDUCATION (athletic training, elementary, physical, secondary, and special), SOCIAL SCIENCE (criminal justice, history, prelaw, psychology, and sociology). Education and business are the strongest academically.
Required: To graduate, students must complete 128 semester hours with a minimum GPA of 2.0 (2.5 for education majors). General education requirements include 12 semester hours each of social science and math/science, 9 each of humanities/fine arts and communications, 6 of religion, and 3 of economics, as well as a course in free enterprise and a senior seminar in leadership and ethics.
Special: Internships are available for students majoring in business, psychology, and education. CSW also offers nondegree study and credit for military experience. There are 2 national honor societies.
Faculty/Classroom: 51% of faculty are male; 49%, female. All teach undergraduates. No introductory courses are taught by graduate students. The average class size in an introductory lecture is 25; in a laboratory, 15; and in a regular course, 18.
Admissions: All 2001-2002 applicants were accepted. The SAT I scores for the 2001-2002 freshman class were: Verbal--64% below 500, 22% between 500 and 599, and 14% between 600 and 700; Math--64% below 500, 22% between 500 and 599, and 14% between 600 and 700. The ACT scores were 56% below 21, 22% between 21 and 23, 9% between 24 and 26, 9% between 27 and 28, and 4% above 28. 27% of the current freshmen were in the top fifth of their class; 84% were in the top two fifths.
Requirements: The SAT I or ACT is required, with a minimum composite score of 910 on the SAT I or 19 on the ACT. Applicants must be graduates of an accredited secondary school or have a GED certificate. CSW requires applicants to be in the upper 50% of their class. A GPA of 2.0 is required. AP and CLEP credits are accepted. Important factors in the admissions decision are advanced placement or honor courses, extracurricular activities record, and ability to finance college education.
Procedure: Freshmen are admitted to all sessions. Application deadlines are open. The fall 2001 application fee was $25. Notification is sent on a rolling basis.
Transfer: 130 transfer students enrolled in 2001-2002. Applicants must present a minimum GPA of 2.0 and official transcripts from all colleges attended. 30 credits of 128 must be completed at CSW.
Visiting: There are guides for informal visits and visitors may sit in on classes and stay overnight. To schedule a visit, contact Charlotte Smith, Director of Admissions.
Financial Aid: In 2001-2002, 93% of all freshmen received some form of financial aid. 43% of freshmen and 84% of continuing students received need-based aid. The average freshman award was $5581. Of that total, scholarships or need-based grants averaged $4457 ($10,792 maximum); loans averaged $2799 ($6625 maximum); and work contracts averaged $220 ($3000 maximum). 17% of undergraduates work part time. Average annual earnings from campus work are $2000. The average financial indebtedness of the 2001 graduate was $10,500. The FAFSA and the college's own financial statement are required. The fall application deadline is June 15.
International Students: There are 10 international students enrolled. They must score 550 on the written TOEFL and also take the SAT I or the ACT.
Computers: Macs and PCs are located in the computer lab and science building. There are no time limits and no fees.
Graduates: In 2001, 142 bachelor's degrees were awarded. The most popular majors were education (56%), psychology (11%), and management (7%). In an average class, 19% graduate in 5 years. 10 companies recruited on campus in 2000-2001. Of the 2000 graduating class, 13% were enrolled in graduate school within 6 months of graduation and 80% were employed.
Admissions Contact: Charlotte Smith, Director of Admissions.
E-mail: *csmith@csw.edu* Web: *www.csw.edu*

EASTERN NEW MEXICO UNIVERSITY E-3
Portales, NM 88130 (505) 562-2178
(800) 367-3668; Fax: (505) 562-2118

Full-time: 1087 men, 1420 women	**Faculty:** 134; IIA, --$
Part-time: 133 men, 340 women	**Ph.D.s:** 96%
Graduate: 162 men, 441 women	**Student/Faculty:** 19 to 1
Year: semesters, summer session	**Tuition:** $2088 ($7644)
Application Deadline: open	**Room & Board:** $2025
Freshman Class: 541 enrolled	
SAT I or ACT: required	LESS COMPETITIVE

Eastern New Mexico University, founded in 1934, is a public institution offering programs in the liberal arts and sciences, as well as education, business, fine arts, and vocational and technical fields. There are 4 undergraduate schools and 1 graduate school. In addition to regional accreditation, Eastern has baccalaureate program accreditation with ACBSP, ASLA, NASM, NCATE, and NLN. The library contains 280,000 volumes and 2000 microform items, and subscribes to 1800 periodicals. Computerized library services include the card catalog, interlibrary loans, and database searching. Special learning facilities include a learning resource center, art gallery, natural history museum, radio station, TV station, and nearby important archeological sites. The 400-acre campus is in a small town 120 miles northeast of Lubbock, Texas. Including residence halls, there are 50 buildings.
Student Life: 83% of undergraduates are from New Mexico. Others are from 47 states, 8 foreign countries, and Canada. 95% are from public schools. 61% are white; 27% Hispanic. 41% are Protestant; 22% Catholic; 16% claim no religious affiliation. The average age of freshmen is 20; all undergraduates, 25.
Housing: 1400 students can be accommodated in college housing, which includes single-sex and coed dormitories, on-campus apartments, married-student housing, and freshmen only living areas. On-campus housing is guaranteed for all 4 years. 71% of students commute. Alcohol is not permitted. All students may keep cars.
Activities: Tthere are 6 national fraternities and 2 national sororities. There are 83 groups on campus, including art, band, cheerleading, choir, chorus, computers, dance, debate, drama, drill team, ethnic, forensics, gay, honors, international, jazz band, literary magazine, marching band, musical theater, newspaper, orchestra, pep band, photography, political, professional, radio and TV, religious, social, social service, steel drum band, student government, and yearbook. Popular campus events include Green and Silver Breakthrough, Peanut Valley Festival, and Fiesta International.

Sports: There are 4 intercollegiate sports for men and 5 for women, and 18 intramural sports for men and 18 for women. Facilities include a 5200-seat arena, tennis courts, an indoor pool, a 5300-seat stadium, and handball and racquetball courts.
Disabled Students: 95% of the campus is accessible. Wheelchair ramps, elevators, special parking, specially equipped rest rooms, special class scheduling, lowered drinking fountains, automatic door openers, and curb cuts are available.
Services: Counseling and information services are available, as is tutoring in every subject. There is a reader service for the blind, and remedial math, reading, and writing.
Campus Safety and Security: Measures include 24-hour foot and vehicle patrol, self-defense education, escort service, and pamphlets/posters/films. There are lighted pathways/sidewalks.
Programs of Study: Eastern confers B.A., B.S., B.A.E., B.B.A., B.F.A., B.M., B.M.E., B.S.E., and B.U.S. degrees. Associate and master's degrees are also awarded. Bachelor's degrees are awarded in AGRICULTURE (agricultural business management, agriculture, and wildlife management), BIOLOGICAL SCIENCE (biology/biological science), BUSINESS (accounting, banking and finance, business administration and management, business economics, marketing/retailing/merchandising, and personnel management), COMMUNICATIONS AND THE ARTS (art, communications, dramatic arts, English, fine arts, journalism, music, music performance, Spanish, and speech/debate/rhetoric), COMPUTER AND PHYSICAL SCIENCE (chemistry, computer science, geology, information sciences and systems, mathematics, physics, and statistics), EDUCATION (agricultural, business, elementary, home economics, music, physical, and special), ENGINEERING AND ENVIRONMENTAL DESIGN (electrical/electronics engineering technology), HEALTH PROFESSIONS (medical laboratory technology, nursing, and speech pathology/audiology), SOCIAL SCIENCE (anthropology, criminal justice, economics, history, human services, political science/government, psychology, religion, social studies, and sociology). Sciences are the strongest academically. Education, biology, and communications are the largest.
Required: To graduate, students must earn 128 credit hours, 36 in the major, with a minimum GPA of 2.0. Required courses include those in English, science, math, social studies, humanities, fine arts, and phys ed.
Special: The school offers co-op programs in wildlife and fisheries and communication, internships, study abroad in 3 countries work-study programs, student-designed majors, a general studies degree, credit for life, military, and work experience, nondegree study, and pass/fail options. There are 10 national honor societies and a freshman honors program.
Faculty/Classroom: 53% of faculty are male; 47%, female. 97% teach undergraduates.
Admissions: 19% of the current freshmen were in the top fifth of their class; 41% were in the top two fifths. 6 freshmen graduated first in their class.
Requirements: The SAT I or ACT is required, with a minimum required composite score of 17 on the ACT or 720 on the SAT I. Applicants must be high school graduates or have the GED, having earned 20 units, including 4 in English, 3 in math, 2 in science, and 1 each in history, music, and social studies. Provisional and special admissions are available. A GPA of 2.25 is required. AP and CLEP credits are accepted. Applications are accepted on-line.
Procedure: Freshmen are admitted to all sessions. Entrance exams should be taken in the junior or senior year. Application deadlines are open. Notification is sent on a rolling basis.
Transfer: 291 transfer students enrolled in 2001-2002. Transfer students must have a minimum GPA of 2.0. 32 credits of 128 must be completed at Eastern.
Visiting: There are regularly scheduled orientations for prospective students, including meetings with admissions, financial aid, and faculty in major, a tour of campus, and a meal in the dining hall. There are guides for informal visits and visitors may sit in on classes and stay overnight. To schedule a visit, contact the Admissions Office.
Financial Aid: In 2001-2002, 61% of all freshmen and 72% of continuing students received some form of financial aid. 59% of freshmen and 62% of continuing students received need-based aid. The average freshman award was $5775. Of that total, scholarships or need-based grants averaged $3290 ($4000 maximum); loans averaged $2521 ($2625 maximum); and work contracts averaged $1400 ($1978 maximum). Average annual earnings from campus work are $2470. The FAFSA, the college's own financial statement, and the institutional scholarship are required. The fall application deadline is March 1.
International Students: There are 10 international students enrolled. The school actively recruits these students. They must score 500 on the written TOEFL or 175 on the electronic version.
Computers: The mainframe is an IBM AS/400. Computer accounts are available to all students on campus. Access includes the Internet and e-mail. Students have access to the College of Business's 30 PCs, the campuswide computer center that houses 75 PCs, and the 30-station library computer center. Network access is also available from all residence halls. All students may access the system. There are no time limits and no fees.
Graduates: In 2001, 503 bachelor's degrees were awarded. The most popular majors were elementary education (20%), sociology (8%), and university studies (6%). In an average class, 9% graduate in 4 years, 20% in 5 years, and 27% in 6 years. 75 companies recruited on campus in 2000-2001.
Admissions Contact: Dr. Karyl Lyne, Admissions.
E-mail: *karyl.lyne@enmu.edu* Web: *www.enmu.edu*

NEW MEXICO HIGHLANDS UNIVERSITY D-2

Las Vegas, NM 87701 (505) 454-3434
(800) 338-6648; Fax: (505) 454-3552

Full-time: 584 men, 690 women	**Faculty:** 123
Part-time: 154 men, 458 women	**Ph.D.s:** 70%
Graduate: 401 men, 958 women	**Student/Faculty:** 10 to 1
Year: semesters, summer session	**Tuition:** $2258 ($9386)
Application Deadline: open	**Room & Board:** $3998
Freshman Class: 895 applied, 760 accepted, 258 enrolled	
SAT I Verbal/Math: 360/415	**ACT:** 18 **NONCOMPETITIVE**

New Mexico Highlands University, founded in 1893, is a state-supported institution offering undergraduate programs in liberal and fine arts, science and engineering, and professional studies. There are 3 undergraduate schools. In addition to regional accreditation, Highlands University has baccalaureate program accreditation with ABET and CSWE. The library contains 522,500 volumes, and subscribes to 1300 periodicals. Computerized library services include the card catalog, interlibrary loans, and database searching. Special learning facilities include a learning resource center, art gallery, radio station, TV station, and a video production studio. The 175-acre campus is in a small town 65 miles northeast of Santa Fe. Including residence halls, there are 38 buildings.
Student Life: 89% of undergraduates are from New Mexico. Others are from 40 states, 10 foreign countries, and Canada. 95% are from public schools. 52% are Hispanic; 35% white. The average age of freshmen is 18; all undergraduates, 26. 46% do not continue beyond their first year; 25% remain to graduate.
Housing: 480 students can be accommodated in college housing, which includes single-sex and coed dormitories, on-campus apartments, and married-student housing. On-campus housing is guaranteed for the freshman year only and is available on a first-come, first-served basis. Alcohol is not permitted. All students may keep cars.
Activities: There are no sororities. There are many groups and organizations on campus, including art, band, cheerleading, choir, chorale, chorus, departmental, drama, ethnic, film, honors, international, jazz band, marching band, newspaper, photography, political, radio and TV, religious, social service, student government, and yearbook. Popular campus events include Multicultural Week and Career Day.
Sports: There are 4 intercollegiate sports for men and 3 for women, and 8 intramural sports for men and 8 for women. Facilities include a 5000-seat football stadium, a 3600-seat arena, an indoor swimming pool, a weight room, athletic fields, a 9-hole golf course, and tennis, racquetball, and basketball courts. Hiking and skiing are nearby.
Disabled Students: 90% of the campus is accessible. Wheelchair ramps, elevators, special parking, specially equipped rest rooms, lowered drinking fountains, and lowered telephones are available.
Services: Counseling and information services are available, as is tutoring in most subjects. There is a reader service for the blind, and remedial math, reading, and writing.
Campus Safety and Security: Measures include 24-hour foot and vehicle patrol, self-defense education, escort service, and informal discussions. There are pamphlets/posters/films, emergency telephones, and lighted pathways/sidewalks.
Programs of Study: Highlands University confers B.A., B.S., B.B.A., B.F.A., B.S.E., and B.S.W. degrees. Associate and master's degrees are also awarded. Bachelor's degrees are awarded in AGRICULTURE (natural resource management), BIOLOGICAL SCIENCE (biology/biological science), BUSINESS (accounting, banking and finance, business administration and management, management information systems, marketing/retailing/merchandising, and recreation and leisure services), COMMUNICATIONS AND THE ARTS (art, communications, English, graphic design, music, and Spanish), COMPUTER AND PHYSICAL SCIENCE (chemistry, computer science, mathematics, and physics), EDUCATION (early childhood, elementary, science, special, and technical), ENGINEERING AND ENVIRONMENTAL DESIGN (engineering and environmental science), HEALTH PROFESSIONS (health, predentistry, premedicine, and preveterinary science), SOCIAL SCIENCE (anthropology, history, physical fitness/movement, political science/government, prelaw, psychology, social work, and sociology). Engineering and physical sciences are the strongest academically. Education, business administration, and social work are the largest.
Required: Students must complete 40 to 51 credits of core curriculum requirements, including courses in English, history, science, social environment, thought and critical analysis, fine arts, literature, communicating skills, and phys ed. Proficiency in language and math must be demonstrated. A minimum of 128 credits, including at least 30 in the major, with a GPA of at least 2.0 is required to graduate.

Special: Highlands offers practicum, internship, and field-study courses; cooperative programs in most majors; internships in education; minors in geology, physics, secondary education, philosophy, and theater; and credit for military training. There are 2 national honor societies, including Phi Beta Kappa, and a freshman honors program.

Faculty/Classroom: 60% of faculty are male; 39%, female. All teach undergraduates.

Admissions: 85% of the 2001-2002 applicants were accepted. The SAT I scores for the 2001-2002 freshman class were: Verbal--77% below 500, and 23% between 500 and 599; Math--65% below 500, 34% between 500 and 599, and 1% between 600 and 700. The ACT scores were 81% below 21, 17% between 21 and 23, 1% between 24 and 26, and 1% above 28. 20% of the current freshmen were in the top fifth of their class; 55% were in the top two fifths. 10 freshmen graduated first in their class in a recent year.

Requirements: The ACT is required; SAT I scores may be substituted. Scores are used for placement purposes. Applicants should be graduates of an accredited secondary school; the GED is accepted. A GPA of 2.0 is required. AP and CLEP credits are accepted. Important factors in the admissions decision are advanced placement or honor courses, evidence of special talent, and recommendations by school officials. Applications are accepted on computer disk and on-line at the school's web site.

Procedure: Freshmen are admitted to all sessions. There are early decision and deferred admissions plans. Application deadlines are open. The fall 2001 application fee was $15. Notification is sent on a rolling basis.

Transfer: Transfer applicants with 16 or more semester credit hours must have at least a 2.0 GPA. 32 credits of 128 must be completed at Highlands University.

Visiting: There are regularly scheduled orientations for prospective students, available on a call-in basis. There are guides for informal visits and visitors may sit in on classes and stay overnight. To schedule a visit, contact the Admissions Office at (505) 454-3593 or (800) 338-6648.

Financial Aid: 25% of undergraduates worked part time in a recent year. Average annual earnings from campus work were $2000. The FAFSA is required.

International Students: There were 30 international students enrolled in a recent year. They must score 500 on the written TOEFL.

Computers: The mainframes are Compaq Alpha servers. There are computer labs located in various buildings, including several dorms. All students may access the system 24 hours daily. There are no time limits and no fees. It is strongly recommended that all students have a personal computer.

Admissions Contact: John Coca, Director of Admissions. A video is available. E-mail: *admissions@nmhu.edu* Web: *www.nmhu.edu*

NEW MEXICO INSTITUTE OF MINING AND TECHNOLOGY C-3

Socorro, NM 87801 **(505) 835-5424**
(800) 428-TECH; Fax: (505) 835-5989

Full-time: 658 men, 290 women	**Faculty:** 92
Part-time: 123 men, 185 women	**Ph.D.s:** 98%
Graduate: 219 men, 113 women	**Student/Faculty:** 10 to 1
Year: semesters, summer session	**Tuition:** $2722 ($8419)
Application Deadline: August 1	**Room & Board:** $4430
Freshman Class: 343 applied, 289 accepted, 218 enrolled	
ACT: 26	**VERY COMPETITIVE+**

New Mexico Institute of Mining and Technology, founded in 1889 as the New Mexico School of Mines, is a science and engineering university. It has 4 research-associated divisions: the New Mexico Bureau of Geology and Mineral Resources, the Energetic Materials Research and Testing Center, the Petroleum Recovery Research Center, and the Langmuir Laboratory for Atmospheric Research. In addition to regional accreditation, New Mexico Tech has baccalaureate program accreditation with ABET. The library contains 242,500 volumes, 180,000 microform items, and 1400 audiovisual forms/CDs, and subscribes to 900 periodicals. Computerized library services include the card catalog, interlibrary loans, and database searching. Special learning facilities include a radio station, mineral museum, seismic research mine, and campus astronomical observatory. The 320-acre campus is in a small town 75 miles south of Albuquerque. Including residence halls, there are 28 buildings.

Student Life: 81% of undergraduates are from New Mexico. Others are from 49 states, 38 foreign countries, and Canada. 87% are from public schools. 66% are white; 16% Hispanic; 10% foreign nationals. The average age of freshmen is 18; all undergraduates, 22. 26% do not continue beyond their first year; 40% remain to graduate.

Housing: 644 students can be accommodated in college housing, which includes single-sex and coed dormitories, on-campus apartments, and married-student housing. On-campus housing is available on a first-come, first-served basis. 56% of students commute. Alcohol is not permitted. All students may keep cars.

Activities: There are no fraternities or sororities. There are 55 groups on campus, including art, band, chess, chorus, computers, drama, ethnic, gay, honors, international, jazz band, musical theater, orchestra, political, professional, radio and TV, religious, social, social service, student government, and yearbook. Popular campus events include 49ers, Spring Fling, and International Student Exhibit.

Sports: There are 9 intramural sports for men and 9 for women. Facilities include 2 gyms, tennis courts, a swimming pool, an 18-hole golf course, an athletic field, sand volleyball courts, a climbing wall, a weight/fitness room, racquetball/squash courts, a Ping-Pong area, and a martial arts/combatives room.

Disabled Students: Most of the campus is wheelchair accessible. Wheelchair ramps, elevators, special parking, specially equipped rest rooms, lowered drinking fountains, and lowered telephones are available.

Services: Counseling and information services are available, as is tutoring in most subjects. There is a reader service for the blind.

Campus Safety and Security: Measures include 24-hour foot and vehicle patrol, self-defense education, escort service, and informal discussions. There are pamphlets/posters/films, emergency telephones, and lighted pathways/sidewalks.

Programs of Study: New Mexico Tech confers B.S. and B.G.S. degrees. Associate, master's, and doctoral degrees are also awarded. Bachelor's degrees are awarded in BIOLOGICAL SCIENCE (biology/biological science), BUSINESS (business administration and management), COMMUNICATIONS AND THE ARTS (technical and business writing), COMPUTER AND PHYSICAL SCIENCE (chemistry, computer science, geology, geophysics and seismology, mathematics, and physics), ENGINEERING AND ENVIRONMENTAL DESIGN (chemical engineering, electrical/electronics engineering, engineering, engineering mechanics, environmental engineering, environmental science, materials engineering, metallurgical engineering, mining and mineral engineering, and petroleum/natural gas engineering), SOCIAL SCIENCE (liberal arts/general studies and psychology). Physics and electrical engineering are the strongest academically. Electrical engineering, computer science, and physics are the largest.

Required: Students must earn at least 130 credit hours to graduate, including 42 hours of basic science, consisting in part of 10 hours of physics and 8 each of chemistry, calculus, and biology/geology/engineering. Further distribution requirements include 18 hours of literature, philosophy, the arts, and social science, 9 hours each of written and spoken English, and a senior seminar or senior design project. The credit hours required in the major vary by program. The student must also maintain a cumulative GPA of 2.0.

Special: New Mexico Tech offers co-op programs in computer science and all engineering majors, internships in technical communications, and cross-registration with New Mexico State, University of New Mexico, and Los Alamos National Laboratories in the WERC consortium. Dual majors are offered in engineering, computer science, physics, and math. Work programs, student-designed majors in environmental science, general studies, and basic science, nondegree study, and pass/fail options are also available. There are 3-2 accelerated degree programs in geology and in science or engineering and hydrology. There are 4 national honor societies and 4 departmental honors programs.

Faculty/Classroom: 87% of faculty are male; 13%, female. All teach undergraduates and 95% also do research. Graduate students teach 12% of introductory courses. The average class size in an introductory lecture is 18; in a laboratory, 12; and in a regular course, 18.

Admissions: 84% of the 2001-2002 applicants were accepted. The SAT I scores for the 2001-2002 freshman class were: Verbal--12% below 500, 36% between 500 and 599, 40% between 600 and 700, and 12% above 700; Math--14% below 500, 26% between 500 and 599, 43% between 600 and 700, and 17% above 700. The ACT scores were 6% below 21, 22% between 21 and 23, 27% between 24 and 26, 15% between 27 and 28, and 30% above 28. 60% of the current freshmen were in the top fifth of their class; 87% were in the top two fifths.

Requirements: The ACT is required, with a minimum score of 21. Applicants must be high school graduates or present a GED certificate. Students should have earned 15 academic credits, consisting of 4 units of English, 3 each of social science and math (2 beyond general math), and 2 of science (including 1 of lab science), and electives. A GPA of 2.5 is required. AP credits are accepted. Important factors in the admissions decision are advanced placement or honor courses, evidence of special talent, and extracurricular activities record. On-line applications are available at *http://www.nmt.edu/mainpage/uginfo/application.html*, but the printout must be sent to the school.

Procedure: Freshmen are admitted to all sessions. Entrance exams should be taken by December of the senior year. There are early decision, early admissions, and deferred admissions plans. Applications should be filed by August 1 for fall entry and December 1 for spring entry. The fall 2001 application fee was $15. Notification is sent on a rolling basis.

Transfer: 40 transfer students enrolled in 2001-2002. Transfer students must have a GPA of 2.0 and have completed 30 semester hours of transferable credit. Those who have fewer than 30 credit hours, or who have not completed freshman English, must present a minimum ACT score of

21, as well as high school transcripts. 30 credits of 130 must be completed at New Mexico Tech.

Visiting: There are regularly scheduled orientations for prospective students, including 2 days of get-aquainted social activities, information sessions for parents and students, and transition sessions for parents. There are guides for informal visits and visitors may sit in on classes and stay overnight. To schedule a visit, contact the Admission Office.

Financial Aid: 47% of undergraduates work part time. The FAFSA is required. The fall application deadline is March 1.

International Students: There are 30 international students enrolled. They must score 540 on the written TOEFL or 207 on the electronic version.

Computers: The mainframes are a dual SPARC 20, DEC ALPHA 500 and DEC ALPHA 400. Students may access the mainframe from PCs located in the computer center and in most departments as well as from their rooms via Ethernet connection or modem. All students may access the system 16.5 hours a day on site; 24 hours a day via network. There are no time limits. The fee is $2 per semester. It is strongly recommended that all students have a personal computer.

Graduates: In 2001, 182 bachelor's degrees were awarded. The most popular majors were engineering (42%), physical sciences (21%), and computer and information sciences (9%). In an average class, 33% graduate in 5 years, and 40% in 6 years.

Admissions Contact: Melissa Jaramillo-Fleming, Director Admission. E-mail: *admission@admin.nmt.edu* Web: *http://www.nmt.edu*

NEW MEXICO STATE UNIVERSITY — C-4

Las Cruces, NM 88003-8001 — **(505) 646-3121**
(800) 662-6678; Fax: (505) 646-6330

Full-time: 4620 men, 5224 women	**Faculty:** 660; I, --$
Part-time: 1190 men, 1550 women	**Ph.D.s:** 83%
Graduate: 1214 men, 1426 women	**Student/Faculty:** 15 to 1
Year: semesters, summer session	**Tuition:** $3006 ($10,014)
Application Deadline: open	**Room & Board:** $4296
Freshman Class: 5489 applied, 4386 accepted, 2235 enrolled	
SAT I: accepted	**ACT:** required **COMPETITIVE**

New Mexico State University, founded in 1888, is a public institution offering undergraduate and graduate programs that include study in liberal arts, agriculture, business, engineering, health science, education, and visual and performing arts. There are 6 undergraduate schools and 1 graduate school. In addition to regional accreditation, NMSU has baccalaureate program accreditation with AACSB, ABET, ADA, AHEA, APA, CACREP, CCNE, CSWE, NASM, NCATE, and NLN. The 2 libraries contain 1,541,887 volumes, 1,181,153 microform items, and 1066 audiovisual forms/CDs, and subscribe to 6747 periodicals. Computerized library services include the card catalog, interlibrary loans, and database searching. Special learning facilities include a learning resource center, art gallery, natural history museum, radio station, TV station, a 289-acre experimental farm and orchard, a 61,760-acre cattle and experimental ranch, and a 2160-acre recreational area in the Organ Mountains. The 900-acre campus is in an urban area 40 miles north of El Paso. Including residence halls, there are 284 buildings.

Student Life: 77% of undergraduates are from New Mexico. Others are from 49 states, 79 foreign countries, and Canada. 48% are white; 40%, Hispanic. The average age of freshmen is 18; all undergraduates, 23. 28% do not continue beyond their first year; 72% remain to graduate.

Housing: 3800 students can be accommodated in college housing, which includes single-sex and coed dormitories, on-campus apartments, married-student housing, fraternity houses, and sorority houses. In addition, there are honors houses. On-campus housing is guaranteed for all 4 years. 80% of students commute. All students may keep cars.

Activities: 4% of men belong to 14 national fraternities; 3% of women belong to 7 national sororities. There are 255 groups on campus, including art, band, cheerleading, chess, choir, chorale, chorus, computers, dance, drama, drill team, drum and bugle corps, ethnic, gay, honors, international, jazz band, literary magazine, marching band, musical theater, newspaper, opera, orchestra, pep band, photography, political, professional, radio and TV, religious, social, social service, student government, and symphony. Popular campus events include Chicano Week, American Indian Week, and Black Week.

Sports: There are 6 intercollegiate sports for men and 8 for women, and 29 intramural sports for men and 29 for women. Facilities include a game room, natatorium, tennis courts, playing fields, a gym, and rodeo grounds. One campus stadium seats 30,342 while the other seats more than 13,000.

Disabled Students: 95% of the campus is accessible. Wheelchair ramps, elevators, special parking, specially equipped rest rooms, lowered drinking fountains, lowered telephones, and priority registration are available.

Services: Counseling and information services are available, as is tutoring in most subjects. There is a reader service for the blind. Remedial classes are offered at the Dona Ana Branch Community College. There is also an interpreter for the hearing impaired.

Campus Safety and Security: Measures include 24-hour foot and vehicle patrol, self-defense education, escort service, and shuttle buses. There are informal discussions, pamphlets/posters/films, emergency telephones, and lighted pathways/sidewalks.

Programs of Study: NMSU confers B.A., B.S., B.Ac., B.A.Ec., B.B.A., B.C.J., B.F.A., B.I.S., B.M., B.M.Ed., B.S.Ag., B.S.A.T.Ed., B.S.C.H., B.S.Ed., B.S.in Environmental Science, B.S.E.T., B.S. in Family and Consumer Sciences, B.S.G.E., B.S.H.R.T.S., B.S.N., and B.S.W. degrees. Associate, master's, and doctoral degrees are also awarded. Bachelor's degrees are awarded in AGRICULTURE (agricultural business management, agriculture, agronomy, animal science, horticulture, range/farm management, and soil science), BIOLOGICAL SCIENCE (biochemistry and biology/biological science, microbiology, nutrition, and wildlife biology), BUSINESS (accounting, banking and finance, business administration and management, business economics, fashion merchandising, hotel/motel and restaurant management, international business management, management information systems, marketing/retailing/merchandising, recreational facilities management, and tourism), COMMUNICATIONS AND THE ARTS (art, communications, dance, dramatic arts, English, fine arts, journalism, languages, and music), COMPUTER AND PHYSICAL SCIENCE (chemistry, computer science, geology, mathematics, and physics), EDUCATION (agricultural, athletic training, early childhood, elementary, home economics, music, physical, secondary, and special), ENGINEERING AND ENVIRONMENTAL DESIGN (chemical engineering, city/community/regional planning, civil engineering, electrical/electronics engineering, engineering technology, environmental engineering, environmental science, geological engineering, industrial engineering, mechanical engineering, and surveying engineering), HEALTH PROFESSIONS (community health work, nursing, and speech pathology/audiology), SOCIAL SCIENCE (anthropology, child psychology/development, criminal justice, economics, family/consumer studies, geography, history, philosophy, political science/government, psychology, social work, and sociology). Elementary education, electrical engineering, and criminal justice are the largest.

Required: All students must complete a minimum of 128 credits including at least 50 upper-division credits. A minimum GPA of 2.0 is needed. Distribution requirements include communications, humanities, math, natural sciences, and social sciences.

Special: Internships, cooperative programs in engineering, math, science, teacher education, business and other majors, dual majors, study abroad in 33 countries, work-study, nondegree study, and B.A.-B.S. degrees in biology, chemistry, and physics are available. There is cross-registration with the Dona Ana Branch Community College. There are 24 national honor societies, and a freshman honors program.

Faculty/Classroom: 66% of faculty are male; 34%, female. All both teach and do research. Graduate students teach 10% of introductory courses. The average class size in an introductory lecture is 37; in a laboratory, 16; and in a regular course, 30.

Admissions: 80% of the 2001-2002 applicants were accepted. The ACT scores for the 2001-2002 freshman class were: 49% below 21, 27% between 21 and 23, 15% between 24 and 26, 6% between 27 and 28, and 3% above 28. 9% of the current freshmen were in the top quarter of their class; 33% were in the top half. 27 freshmen graduated first in their class.

Requirements: The ACT is required. Applicants must score 20 on the ACT or may take the SAT I (accepted, but not recommended), and submit a composite score of 780. The GED is accepted. Minimum high school preparation of 4 units of English, 3 of math, 2 beyond general science, and 1 foreign language/fine arts is required. A GPA of 2.0 is required. AP and CLEP credits are accepted. Applications are accepted on-line at *http://www.nmsu.edu/~admision/admit-form.html*

Procedure: Freshmen are admitted to all sessions. Entrance exams should be taken during the high school junior or senior year. There is an early admissions plan. Application deadlines are open. Notification is sent on a rolling basis. The application fee is $15.

Transfer: 573 transfer students enrolled in 2001-2002. Applicants must have a minimum GPA of 2.0. They need 30 credits to avoid freshman admission requirements. If the applicant has earned 30 academic credit hours or more, the ACT score will be waived. If the applicant has earned 48 academic credit hours or more, the high school transcript will be waived. 30 credits of 128 must be completed at NMSU.

Visiting: There are regularly scheduled orientations for prospective students, including meetings with admissions counselors, faculty members, financial aid advisors, and a tour of campus. There are guides for informal visits and visitors may sit in on classes and stay overnight. To schedule a visit, contact the Office of Admissions.

Financial Aid: In 2000-2001, 64% of all freshmen received some form of financial aid. 65% of freshmen received need-based aid. The average freshman award was $2370. 16% of undergraduates work part time. Average annual earnings from campus work are $3033. NMSU is a member of CSS. The FAFSA is required. The fall application deadline is March 1.

International Students: There are 152 international students enrolled. They must score 500 on the written TOEFL or take the MELAB.

Computers: The mainframe is an IBM 9672-R24. A number of PCs are available in academic areas, the library, and the student union. All students may access the system at any time. There are no time limits and no fees.
Graduates: In 2001, 1827 bachelor's degrees were awarded. The most popular majors were elementary education (7%), criminal justice (5%), and acounting (4%). In an average class, 10% graduate in 4 years, 34% in 5 years, and 43% in 6 years. 663 companies recruited on campus in 2000-2001.
Admissions Contact: Angela Mora-Riley, Director of Admissions. A video is available. E-mail: *admissions@nmsu.edu*
Web: *http://www.nmsu.edu/admissions.html*

SAINT JOHN'S COLLEGE C-2
Santa Fe, NM 87505 (505) 984-6060
(800) 331-5232; Fax: (505) 984-6003

Full-time: 240 men, 200 women **Faculty:** 58
Part-time: 3 men, 2 women **Ph.D.s:** 76%
Graduate: 43 men, 40 women **Student/Faculty:** 8 to 1
Year: semesters, summer session **Tuition:** $26,065
Application Deadline: open **Room & Board:** $6770
Freshman Class: 360 applied, 308 accepted, 136 enrolled
SAT I Verbal/Math: 680/620 **ACT:** 30 **VERY COMPETITIVE+**

St. John's College, founded in 1696, offers a curriculum based on the Great Books Program in which students and faculty work together in small discussion classes without lecture courses, written finals, or emphasis on grades. The program is a rigorous interdisciplinary curriculum based on great books — literature, math, philosophy, theology, sciences, political theory, music, history, economics — from Homer to Freud, Euclid to Einstein. There is 1 graduate school. The library contains 65,000 volumes and 8205 audiovisual forms/CDs, and subscribes to 135 periodicals. Computerized library services include the card catalog, interlibrary loans, and database searching. Special learning facilities include an art gallery, a music library, a search and rescue headquarters, and music practice rooms. The 250-acre campus is in a suburban area in Santa Fe. Including residence halls, there are 31 buildings.
Student Life: 86% of undergraduates are from out of state, mostly the Southwest. Students are from 43 states, 7 foreign countries, and Canada. 85% are from public schools. 90% are white. The average age of freshmen is 18; all undergraduates, 21. 10% do not continue beyond their first year; 60% remain to graduate.
Housing: 329 students can be accommodated in college housing, which includes single-sex and coed dormitories and on-campus apartments. In addition, there are smoke-free and alcohol-free residences. On-campus housing is guaranteed for the freshman year only and is available on a lottery system for upperclassmen. 68% of students live on campus; of those, all remain on campus on weekends. All students may keep cars.
Activities: There are no fraternities or sororities. There are 32 groups on campus, including art, chess, choir, chorale, chorus, computers, dance, drama, fencing, film, gay, jazz band, literary magazine, newspaper, orchestra, photography, search and rescue, social service, student government, and yearbook. Popular campus events include Oktoberfest, Halloween and Christmas parties, and Reality weekend.
Sports: There are 5 intramural sports for men and 5 for women. Facilities include a soccer field, a track, tennis courts, an outdoor basketball court, a gymnasium with weight room, racquetball, squash, and basketball courts, nearby mountains, and a ski mountain 30 minutes from campus.
Disabled Students: 75% of the campus is accessible. Wheelchair ramps, elevators, special parking, specially equipped rest rooms, and special class scheduling are available.
Services: Counseling and information services are available, as is tutoring in every subject.
Campus Safety and Security: Measures include 24-hour foot and vehicle patrol, self-defense education, escort service, and shuttle buses. There are informal discussions, pamphlets/posters/films, emergency telephones, and lighted pathways/sidewalks.
Programs of Study: St. John's confers the B.A. degree. Master's degrees are also awarded. Bachelor's degrees are awarded in SOCIAL SCIENCE (liberal arts/general studies).
Required: The college has one curriculum, based on the Great Books of the Western World, which the student must complete to graduate. It includes 4 years of math, seminar, and a language, 3 years of science, and 1 year of music. There are 2 electives in the 4 years. A total of 135 semester hours is required, and the student must have no grade below C in the senior year. An oral exam on the senior thesis is required.
Special: Internships with alumni in a wide range of fields are available and students may transfer between the Santa Fe and Annapolis campuses. Premedical studies at universities around the country and 4-1 teaching certification through the University of New Mexico are possible.
Faculty/Classroom: 75% of faculty are male; 25%, female. All teach undergraduates. No introductory courses are taught by graduate students. The average class size in an introductory lecture is 15; in a laboratory, 15; and in a regular course, 15.
Admissions: 86% of the 2001-2002 applicants were accepted. The SAT I scores for the 2001-2002 freshman class were: Verbal--2% below 500, 15% between 500 and 599, 38% between 600 and 700, and 46% above 700; Math--6% below 500, 36% between 500 and 599, 41% between 600 and 700, and 18% above 700. 43% of the current freshmen were in the top fifth of their class; 75% were in the top two fifths. There were 4 National Merit finalists and 11 semifinalists. 6 freshmen graduated first in their class.
Requirements: Applicants must write 3 personal essays and submit 2 teacher references, a secondary school report including a reference from a school official, and transcripts of all academic work in high school and college. A campus visit and interview are recommended. 3 years of math and 2 years of foreign language are required; 4 years each of math, foreign language, English, and science are recommended. The GED is accepted for early admission candidates. The SAT I or ACT is required of early admission candidates. Important factors in the admissions decision are advanced placement or honor courses, evidence of special talent, and recommendations by school officials.
Procedure: Freshmen are admitted fall and spring. There are early admissions and deferred admissions plans. Application deadlines are open. Notification is sent on a rolling basis.
Transfer: 17 transfer students enrolled in a recent year. St. John's accepts transfers only for its freshman class; no previous college credit is recognized. Admission requirements are the same as for freshmen. 135 credits of 135 must be completed at St. John's.
Visiting: There are regularly scheduled orientations for prospective students, including a tour of the campus and housing, class visits, and an interview. There are guides for informal visits and visitors may sit in on classes and stay overnight. To schedule a visit, contact the Admissions Office.
Financial Aid: In 2001-2002, 64% of all freshmen and 66% of continuing students received some form of financial aid. 71% of freshmen and 66% of continuing students received need-based aid. The average freshman award was $18,272. Of that total, scholarships or need-based grants averaged $13,450 ($23,000 maximum); loans averaged $3125 ($5500 maximum); and work contracts averaged $2200 (maximum). 61% of undergraduates work part time. Average annual earnings from campus work are $2400. The average financial indebtedness of the 2001 graduate was $18,025. St. John's is a member of CSS. The CSS/Profile or FAFSA, the Business/FARM Supplement, and the noncustodial parent statement are required. The fall application deadline is February 15.
International Students: There are 7 international students enrolled. The school actively recruits these students. They must score 550 on the written TOEFL or 213 on the electronic version.
Computers: A computer lab with Macs, PCs, and printers is available to students. All students may access the system. There are no time limits. The fee is $20.
Graduates: In 2001, 88 bachelor's degrees were awarded. The most popular major was liberal arts (100%). In an average class, 50% graduate in 4 years, 52% in 5 years, and 60% in 6 years. 20 companies recruited on campus in 2000-2001.
Admissions Contact: Larry Clendenin, Director of Admissions.
E-mail: *admissions@mail.sjcsf.edu* Web: *http://www.sjcsf.edu*

UNIVERSITY OF NEW MEXICO C-2
Albuquerque, NM 87131 (505) 277-2446
(800) 225-5866; Fax: (505) 277-6686

Full-time: 5549 men, 7141 women **Faculty:** 1660; I, --$
Part-time: 1544 men, 2207 women **Ph.D.s:** 87%
Graduate: 2618 men, 3668 women **Student/Faculty:** 8 to 1
Year: semesters, summer session **Tuition:** $3026 ($11,424)
Application Deadline: June 23 **Room & Board:** $5000
Freshman Class: 5678 applied, 4306 accepted, 2406 enrolled
SAT I Verbal/Math: 540/520 **ACT:** 21 **COMPETITIVE**

The University of New Mexico, founded in 1889, is a public university offering instruction in liberal and fine arts, business, engineering, health science, teacher preparation, law, and technology. In addition to the main campuses, it has 4 campuses for 2-year study and 2 for graduate study. There are 11 undergraduate and 5 graduate schools. In addition to regional accreditation, UNM has baccalaureate program accreditation with AACSB, ABET, ACPE, CAHEA, NAAB, NASM, NCATE, NLN, and NRPA. The 10 libraries contain 2,372,378 volumes, 4,563,569 microform items, and 52,426 audiovisual forms/CDs, and subscribe to 21,287 periodicals. Computerized library services include the card catalog, interlibrary loans, and database searching. Special learning facilities include a learning resource center, art gallery, planetarium, radio station, TV station, robotics lab, photo-history collection, lithography and meteoritic institutes, observatory, and museums of geology, anthropology, biology, and art. The 769-acre campus is in an urban area within the city of Albuquerque. Including residence halls, there are 269 buildings.

Student Life: 90% of undergraduates are from New Mexico. Others are from 49 states, 90 foreign countries, and Canada. 56% are white; 27% Hispanic. The average age of freshmen is 18; all undergraduates, 24. 27% do not continue beyond their first year; 40% remain to graduate.

Housing: 2292 students can be accommodated in college housing, which includes single-sex and coed dormitories, on-campus apartments, married-student housing, fraternity houses, and sorority houses. In addition, there are honors houses and special-interest houses. On-campus housing is guaranteed for all 4 years. 92% of students commute. Alcohol is not permitted. All students may keep cars.

Activities: 3% of men belong to 9 national fraternities; 2% of women belong to 4 national sororities. There are 250 groups on campus, including art, band, cheerleading, chess, choir, chorale, chorus, computers, dance, drama, drill team, ethnic, film, forensics, gay, honors, international, jazz band, literary magazine, marching band, musical theater, newspaper, opera, orchestra, pep band, photography, political, professional, radio and TV, religious, social, social service, student government, symphony, and yearbook. Popular campus events include Spring Fiesta, Welcome Back Days, and Hanging of the Greens.

Sports: There are 10 intercollegiate sports for men and 11 for women, and 32 intramural sports for men and 26 for women. Facilities include 2 gyms, a football field, basketball courts, 2 pools, weights, and racquetball and tennis courts. The stadium seats 30,000, the gym 7000, and the largest arena 20,000.

Disabled Students: 95% of the campus is accessible. Wheelchair ramps, elevators, special parking, specially equipped rest rooms, special class scheduling, lowered drinking fountains, and lowered telephones are available.

Services: Counseling and information services are available, as is tutoring in most subjects. There is a reader service for the blind, and remedial math, reading, and writing.

Campus Safety and Security: Measures include 24-hour foot and vehicle patrol, self-defense education, escort service, and shuttle buses. There are informal discussions, pamphlets/posters/films, emergency telephones, and lighted pathways/sidewalks.

Programs of Study: UNM confers B.A., B.S., B.A.Ed., B.B.A., B.F.A., and B.S.Ed. degrees. Associate, master's, and doctoral degrees are also awarded. Bachelor's degrees are awarded in BIOLOGICAL SCIENCE (biochemistry, biology/biological science, life science, and nutrition), BUSINESS (accounting, banking and finance, business administration and management, entrepreneurial studies, international business management, management science, marketing/retailing/merchandising, personnel management, and tourism), COMMUNICATIONS AND THE ARTS (art history and appreciation, classics, communications, comparative literature, creative writing, dance, dramatic arts, English, fine arts, French, German, journalism, languages, linguistics, media arts, music, Portuguese, Spanish, studio art, and technical and business writing), COMPUTER AND PHYSICAL SCIENCE (astrophysics, chemistry, computer science, earth science, mathematics, physics, and planetary and space science), EDUCATION (art, athletic training, bilingual/bicultural, business, early childhood, elementary, health, music, physical, science, special, and teaching English as a second/foreign language (TESOL/TEFOL)), ENGINEERING AND ENVIRONMENTAL DESIGN (architecture, chemical engineering, civil engineering, computer engineering, construction engineering, electrical/electronics engineering, environmental design, manufacturing engineering, mechanical engineering, and nuclear engineering), HEALTH PROFESSIONS (dental hygiene, emergency medical technologies, exercise science, medical laboratory technology, nursing, occupational therapy, pharmacy, physical therapy, physician's assistant, predentistry, premedicine, radiological science, and speech pathology/audiology), SOCIAL SCIENCE (African American studies, American studies, anthropology, Asian/Oriental studies, child care/child and family studies, criminal justice, dietetics, economics, European studies, family/consumer studies, geography, history, interpreter for the deaf, Latin American studies, parks and recreation management, philosophy, physical fitness/movement, political science/government, prelaw, psychology, and sociology). Biology, elementary education, and psychology are the largest.

Required: All students must take 2 English courses, including English composition. A minimum of 128 credit hours is required, along with a GPA of 2.0.

Special: There is a 3-2 engineering program with the Anderson School of Management. Study abroad is available in 11 countries. The university offers cooperative programs, a Washington semester, work-study, dual and student-designed majors, a general studies degree, credit by exam, credit for military experience, nondegree study, and pass/fail options. There are 10 national honor societies, including Phi Beta Kappa, and a freshman honors program.

Faculty/Classroom: 60% of faculty are male; 40%, female.

Admissions: 76% of the 2001-2002 applicants were accepted. The SAT I scores for the 2001-2002 freshman class were: Verbal--34% below 500, 38% between 500 and 599, 24% between 600 and 700, and 4% above 700; Math--39% below 500, 39% between 500 and 599, 20% between 600 and 700, and 3% above 700. The ACT scores were 41% below 21, 27% between 21 and 23, 20% between 24 and 26, 7% between 27 and 28, and 6% above 28. 37% of the current freshmen were in the top fifth of their class; 69% were in the top two fifths.

Requirements: The SAT I or ACT is required. In addition, a total of 13 academic credits is required, including 4 years of English, 3 years of math, and 2 years each of foreign language, natural science (1 lab), and social science (1 U.S. history). A GED is accepted. A GPA of 2.25 is required. AP and CLEP credits are accepted. Important factors in the admissions decision are leadership record, evidence of special talent, and advanced placement or honor courses. Applications are accepted on-line via the university's web site.

Procedure: Freshmen are admitted fall, spring, and summer. Entrance exams should be taken late in the junior or early in the senior year. There is an early admissions plan. Deadlines are rolling for early decision applications; regular applications should be filed by June 23 for fall entry, November 15 for spring entry, and May 1 for summer entry. The fall 2001 application fee was $20. Notification of early decision and regular decision is sent on a rolling basis.

Transfer: 1744 transfer students enrolled in a recent year. Applicants must have at least a 2.0 GPA in all transferable courses. 30 credits of 128 must be completed at UNM.

Visiting: There are regularly scheduled orientations for prospective students, including academic advisement, admissions and financial aid counseling, and a tour of the campus and housing. There are guides for informal visits and visitors may stay overnight. To schedule a visit, contact Recruitment Services at (505) 277-2260 or *www.unmlobos.edu*.

Financial Aid: The FAFSA is required. The fall application deadline is March 1.

International Students: There were 146 international students enrolled in a recent year. They must score 550 on the written TOEFL or 213 on the electronic version or take the MELAB or have the University of Cambridge English Examination Certificate.

Computers: The mainframes are an IBM 9672-RA15, IBM RS 6000/370, 2 IBM RS 6000/390s, operating system: AIX 4.1, and 3 IBM RS 6000/370s. 345 terminals and PCs are available in 7 computing pods and 4 classrooms in various locations. All students may access the system. There are no time limits and no fees.

Graduates: In 2001, 2548 bachelor's degrees were awarded. The most popular majors were university studies (9%), elementary education (8%), and biology (7%). In an average class, 40% graduate in 6 years. 252 companies recruited on campus in 2000-2001.

Admissions Contact: Cynthia Stuart, Director of Admissions.
E-mail: *apply@unm.edu* Web: *http://www.unm.edu*

WESTERN NEW MEXICO UNIVERSITY — B-4

Silver City, NM 88061 — (505) 538-6106; (800) 222-9668; (505) 538-6155

Full-time: 200 men, 300 women	**Faculty:** IIA, --$
Part-time: 40 men, 80 women	**Ph.D.s:** n/av
Graduate: 70 men, 130 women	**Student/Faculty:** 7 to 1
Year: semesters, summer session	**Tuition:** $2142 ($7806)
Application Deadline: see profile	**Room & Board:** $3808
Freshman Class: n/av	
SAT I or ACT: required	**LESS COMPETITIVE**

Western New Mexico University, founded in 1893, is a public institution offering vocational, liberal arts, science, and professional programs. Figures given in above capsule are approximate. There are 2 undergraduate and 3 graduate schools. The library contains 120,000 volumes, 500,000 microform items, and 500 audiovisual forms/CDs, and subscribes to 950 periodicals. Computerized library services include the card catalog, interlibrary loans, and database searching. Special learning facilities include a learning resource center, art gallery, natural history museum, and instrumental-vocal music center with individual practice rooms. The 80-acre campus is in a small town 113 miles northwest of Las Cruces and a few minutes from the Gila National Forest. Including residence halls, there are 40 buildings.

Housing: 285 students can be accommodated in college housing, which includes dormitories and married-student housing.

Activities: There are some groups and organizations on campus, including academic, religious, social, and social service.

Programs of Study: WNMU confers B.A., B.S., B.B.A., B.S.V.T., and B.S.W. degrees. Associate and master's degrees are also awarded. Bachelor's degrees are awarded in AGRICULTURE (forestry and related sciences), BIOLOGICAL SCIENCE (biology/biological science, botany, and zoology), BUSINESS (accounting, business administration and management, international business management, management information systems, and marketing/retailing/merchandising), COMMUNICATIONS AND THE ARTS (English, fine arts, music, and Spanish), COMPUTER AND PHYSICAL SCIENCE (chemistry, computer science, mathematics, and science), EDUCATION (art, business, elementary, physical, science, secondary, special, and vocational), HEALTH PROFESSIONS (medical laboratory technology, predentistry, premedicine, prepharmacy, and public health), SOCIAL SCIENCE (Hispanic American studies, history, human services, humanities, law enforcement and corrections, psychology, public administration, social science, social work, and sociology).

Required: To graduate, students must earn at least 128 credit hours, including 30 to 54 in the major, with a minimum GPA of 2.0, and complete 51 hours of general education requirements.

Special: VNMU offers internships, dual and student-designed majors, and work-study programs.

Requirements: The SAT I or ACT is required. In addition, applicants should be graduates of an accredited secondary school or present a GED. Students should have completed at least 3 units of English, and 2 of social studies, including U.S. history, as well as 2 each of science and math. Intermediate algebra and plane geometry are advised for students planning to enter certain fields. WNMU recommends a 2.0 GPA, but lower averages will be considered if applicants' test scores and personal recommendations are strong. CLEP credit is accepted.

Procedure: Freshmen are admitted to all sessions. Entrance exams should be taken before registration, preferably in the senior year. There is an early admissions plan. Notification is sent on a rolling basis. Check with the school for current application deadlines and fee.

Transfer: Transfer students must have a GPA of 2.0. Those with fewer than 32 hours of college credit must supply ACT or SAT I scores and a high school transcript. 30 credits of 128 must be completed at WNMU.

Visiting: There are regularly scheduled orientations for prospective students. There are guides for informal visits and visitors may sit in on classes and stay overnight. To schedule a visit, contact the Admissions Office.

Financial Aid: The FAFSA is required. Check with the school for current deadlines.

International Students: The school actively recruits these students. They must score 550 on the written TOEFL and also take the SAT I or the ACT.

Computers: The mainframe is a comprised of 2 DEX VAX computers. More than 250 Macs and PCs are available to the university community. All are networked for access to e-mail and the Internet. Several campus locations house special-purpose computers. There are no time limits and no fees.

Admissions Contact: Michael Alecksen, Director of Admissions/Recruitment.

NEW YORK

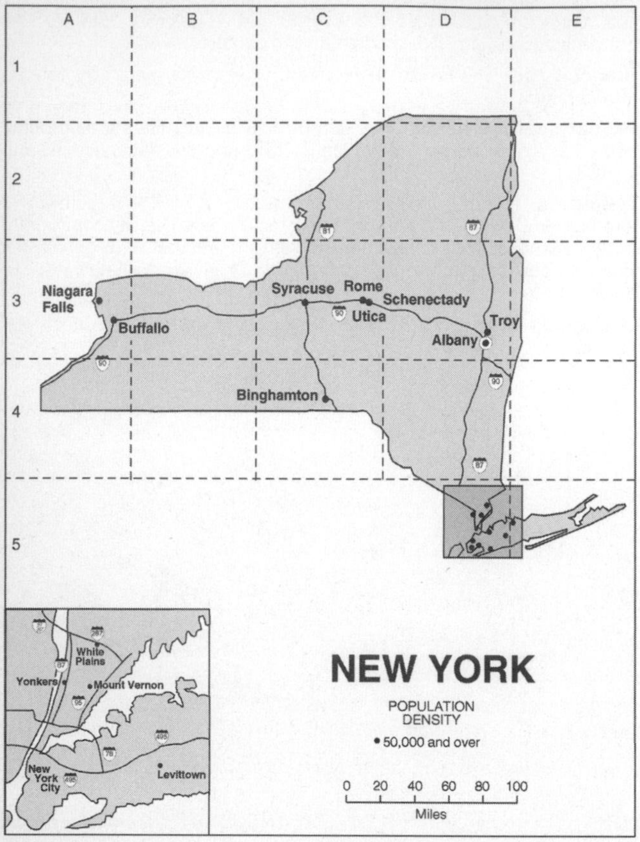

ADELPHI UNIVERSITY

Garden City, NY 11530 D-5
(516) 877-3050
(800) ADELPHI; Fax: (516) 877-3039

Full-time: 819 men, 1897 women
Part-time: 163 men, 512 women
Graduate: 600 men, 2442 women
Year: semesters, summer session
Application Deadline: open
Faculty: 186; I, -$
Ph.D.s: 80%
Student/Faculty: 15 to 1
Tuition: $16,270
Room & Board: $7050
Freshman Class: 3703 applied, 2530 accepted, 690 enrolled
SAT I Verbal/Math: 530/530 **VERY COMPETITIVE**

Adelphi University, founded in 1896, is a private liberal arts institution. There are 7 undergraduate and 6 graduate schools. In addition to regional accreditation, Adelphi has baccalaureate program accreditation with CCNE, CSWE, and NLN. The 2 libraries contain 632,515 volumes, 813,380 microform items, and 43,336 audiovisual forms/CDs, and subscribe to 1785 periodicals. Computerized library services include the card catalog, interlibrary loans, and database searching. Special learning facilities include a learning resource center, art gallery, radio station, observatory, theater, sculpture and ceramics studios, bronze casting foundry, and language labs. The 75-acre campus is in a suburban area 20 miles east of New York City. Including residence halls, there are 22 buildings.

Student Life: 89% of undergraduates are from New York. Others are from 40 states, 53 foreign countries, and Canada. 75% are from public schools. 67% are white; 15% African American. 57% are Catholic; 21% Protestant. The average age of freshmen is 19; all undergraduates, 25. 24% do not continue beyond their first year; 50% remain to graduate.

Housing: 950 students can be accommodated in college housing, which includes coed dormitories. On-campus housing is available on a first-come, first-served basis and is available on a lottery system for upperclassmen. Priority is given to out-of-town students. 75% of students commute. Alcohol is not permitted. All students may keep cars.

Activities: 6% of men belong to 3 national fraternities; 6% of women belong to 1 local sorority and 6 national sororities. There are 76 groups on campus, including band, cheerleading, chorale, computers, dance, drama, ethnic, film, honors, international, jazz band, literary magazine, musical theater, newspaper, orchestra, political, professional, radio and TV, religious, social, social service, student government, and yearbook. Popular campus events include Senior Week, Halloween Party, and Fall Fest.

Sports: There are 9 intercollegiate sports for men and 9 for women, and 25 intramural sports for men and 25 for women. Facilities include a 3000-seat stadium, a 600-seat gym, a swimming pool, racquetball, squash, tennis, and handball courts, exercise rooms, a dance studio, a track, and playing fields for baseball, softball, and soccer.

Disabled Students: 95% of the campus is accessible. Wheelchair ramps, elevators, special parking, specially equipped rest rooms, special class scheduling, lowered drinking fountains, and lowered telephones are available.

Services: Counseling and information services are available, as is tutoring in most subjects. A learning center offers tutoring in writing, quantitative skills, and with class assignments. There is a reader service for the blind.

Campus Safety and Security: Measures include 24-hour foot and vehicle patrol, self-defense education, escort service, and shuttle buses. There are informal discussions, pamphlets/posters/films, emergency telephones, and lighted pathways/sidewalks. Dorm main entrances are videotaped and dorm doors are locked 24 hours a day.

Programs of Study: Adelphi confers B.A., B.S., B.B.A., B.F.A., B.S.Ed., and B.S.S.W. degrees. Associate, master's, and doctoral degrees are also awarded. Bachelor's degrees are awarded in AGRICULTURE (environmental studies), BIOLOGICAL SCIENCE (biochemistry and biology/biological science), BUSINESS (accounting, banking and finance, business administration and management, and management information systems), COMMUNICATIONS AND THE ARTS (art history and appreciation, communications, dance, design, dramatic arts, English, fine arts, French, languages, music, performing arts, Spanish, theater design, and visual and performing arts), COMPUTER AND PHYSICAL SCIENCE (chemistry, computer science, earth science, mathematics, natural sciences, and physics), EDUCATION (art, education of the deaf and hearing impaired, elementary, English, foreign languages, mathematics, music, physical, science, secondary, and social studies), HEALTH PROFESSIONS (nursing and speech pathology/audiology), SOCIAL SCIENCE (anthropology, economics, history, Latin American studies, liberal arts/general studies, philosophy, physical fitness/movement, political science/government, psychology, social science, social work, and sociology). Business management, psychology, and social studies are the largest.

Required: To graduate, students need at least a 2.0 cumulative GPA (higher in some programs) and 120 credit hours with a minimum of 27 in the major. 6 credits each are required in the arts, humanities and languages, natural sciences and math, and social sciences. Other course requirements include English composition, freshman seminar (3 credits each), and a 1-credit freshman orientation experience.

Special: Internships are available in accounting, banking and money management, and communications, among others. Study abroad is available in more than 20 countries, including Spain, France, Denmark, and England. A 5-year bachelor's/master's degree in a number of fields, including biology, social work, and education is offered. In addition, work-study programs, double majors, the B.A.-B.S. degree, an accelerated degree program, a Washington semester, cross-registration with Tufts, credit for life experience for adult students, nondegree study in special cases, and pass/fail options are possible. A 3-2 engineering degree is offered with Rensselaer Polytechnic Institute, Columbia University, Polytechnic University, and Stevens Institute of Technology, and joint degree programs are offered in computer science, dentistry, engineering, environmental studies, law, optometry, and physical therapy with other universities and technical institutes. There are 13 national honor societies and a freshman honors program. There is also an Honors College.

Faculty/Classroom: 48% of faculty are male; 52%, female. All teach undergraduates. No introductory courses are taught by graduate students. The average class size in a regular course is 22.

Admissions: 68% of the 2001-2002 applicants were accepted. The SAT I scores for the 2001-2002 freshman class were: Verbal--32% below 500, 47% between 500 and 599, 20% between 600 and 700, and 1% above 700; Math--31% below 500, 45% between 500 and 599, 22% between 600 and 700, and 2% above 700. 38% of the current freshmen were in the top fifth of their class; 78% were in the top two fifths.

Requirements: The SAT I or ACT is required; composite scores should be 900 on the SAT I or 19 on the ACT. Applicants should have 16 academic credits, including a recommended 4 units of English, history, and social studies, 3 each of math and science, and 2 or 3 of foreign language. An essay is required and an interview recommended for all applicants. A portfolio for art and technical theater candidates, an audition for music, dance, and theater candidates, and an interview for nursing, social work, and honors candidates are required. The SAT I is recommended for the general studies and learning disabilities programs. A GPA of 2.5 is required. AP credits are accepted. Important factors in the admissions decision are advanced placement or honor courses, leadership record, and personality/intangible qualities. Applications are accepted on-line at the school's web site and via Common App.

Procedure: Freshmen are admitted fall and spring. Entrance exams should be taken in October of the senior year or May of the junior year. There is a deferred admissions plan. Application deadlines are open. The fall 2001 application fee was $25. Notification is sent on a rolling basis.

Transfer: 511 transfer students enrolled in 2001-2002. A GPA of 2.5 is recommended in addition to an essay, an official high school transcript, and official records of all work completed or in progress from previous colleges and universities. An interview is required for students in social work and nursing, while an audition is needed for music, dance, and theater students, and a portfolio for art and technical theater students. 30 credits of 120 must be completed at Adelphi.

Visiting: There are guides for informal visits and visitors may sit in on classes. To schedule a visit, contact Undergraduate Admissions.

Financial Aid: In 2001-2002, 92% of all freshmen and 86% of continuing students received some form of financial aid. 69% of freshmen and 64% of continuing students received need-based aid. The average freshman award was $12,500. Of that total, scholarships or need-based grants averaged $8467 ($17,000 maximum); loans averaged $3384; work contracts averaged $1265; and funding from private sources outside the university averaged $280. The average financial indebtedness of the 2001 graduate was $20,385. Adelphi is a member of CSS. The FAFSA is required. The fall application deadline is February 15.

International Students: There are 124 international students enrolled. The school actively recruits these students. They must score 550 on the written TOEFL or 213 on the electronic version and also take the SAT I or the ACT.

Computers: The mainframe is an AV 3700 Data General. There are 525 PC, Mac, and UNIX workstations located throughout the campus and in special-purpose labs. There are 6 general-access computer labs. All workstations have the ability to access e-mail and the Internet and can also utilize the software and services provided on several UNIX servers via the campuswide data network. All students may access the system. There are no time limits and no fees.

Graduates: In 2001, 666 bachelor's degrees were awarded. The most popular majors were business (28%), social science (21%), and education (11%). In an average class, 2% graduate in 3 years, 44% in 4 years, 48% in 5 years, and 50% in 6 years. 247 companies recruited on campus in 2000-2001. Of the 1999 graduating class, 58% were enrolled in graduate school within 6 months of graduation and 98% were employed.

Admissions Contact: Rory Shaffer Walsh, Director, Office of University Admissions. E-mail: *admissions@adelphi.edu*
Web: *www.adelphi.edu*

ALBANY COLLEGE OF PHARMACY — D-3

Albany, NY 12208 (518) 445-7221
(888) 203-8010; Fax: (518) 445-7202

Full-time: 211 men, 371 women	**Faculty:** 44; IIB, +$
Part-time: 3 men, 3 women	**Ph.D.s:** 75%
Graduate: 48 men, 76 women	**Student/Faculty:** 13 to 1
Year: semesters	**Tuition:** $14,370
Application Deadline: February 1	**Room & Board:** $5100
Freshman Class: 403 applied, 271 accepted, 147 enrolled	
SAT I or ACT: required	**SPECIAL**

Albany College of Pharmacy, founded in 1881, is a private, 6-year institution and a division of Union University. In addition to regional accreditation, Albany College of Pharmacy has baccalaureate program accreditation with ACPE. The library contains 12,314 volumes, 28,388 microform items, and 2676 audiovisual forms/CDs, and subscribes to 1399 periodicals. Computerized library services include the card catalog, interlibrary loans, and database searching. Special learning facilities include a learning resource center and the Throop Pharmacy Museum. The 1-acre campus is in an urban area in the University Heights area of Albany. Including residence halls, there are 4 buildings.

Student Life: 90% of undergraduates are from New York. Others are from 11 states, 6 foreign countries, and Canada. 75% are from public schools. 85% are white; 10% Asian American. The average age of freshmen is 18; all undergraduates, 21. 15% do not continue beyond their first year; 81% remain to graduate.

Housing: 300 students can be accommodated in college housing, which includes coed dormitories and off-campus apartments. Priority for on-campus housing is given to out-of-town students. Alcohol is not permitted. All students may keep cars.

Activities: 45% of men and about 43% of women belong to 6 national fraternities. There are 16 groups on campus, including bowling, chorus, ethnic, honors, international, literary magazine, multicultural, newspaper, outdoors, photography, professional, skiing, social service, student government, and yearbook. Popular campus events include Parents Weekend, Open House, and Interview Day.

Sports: There are 4 intercollegiate sports for men and 4 for women, and 3 intramural sports for men and 3 for women. Facilities include a gym, a fitness center, an outdoor track, and a soccer field.

Disabled Students: 98% of the campus is accessible. Wheelchair ramps, elevators, special parking, and specially equipped rest rooms are available.

Services: Counseling and information services are available, as is tutoring in most subjects.

Campus Safety and Security: Measures include 24-hour foot and vehicle patrol, self-defense education, informal discussions, and pamphlets/posters/films. There are emergency telephones and lighted pathways/sidewalks.

Programs of Study: Albany College of Pharmacy confers the B.S.Pharm. Sciences degree. Master's and doctoral degrees are also awarded. Bachelor's degrees are awarded in HEALTH PROFESSIONS (pharmacy).

Required: To graduate, students must complete 162 credits, including core curriculum courses, with a minimum GPA of 2.0.

Special: The college offers cross-registration with other area colleges, dual majors leading to master's and doctoral degrees, an accelerated degree, and work-study programs. There is 1 national honor society.

Faculty/Classroom: 50% of faculty are male; 50%, female. No introductory courses are taught by graduate students. The average class size in an introductory lecture is 140; in a laboratory, 30; and in a regular course, 125.

Admissions: 3 freshmen graduated first in their class.

Requirements: The SAT I or ACT is required. In addition, applicants must be graduates of an accredited high school with at least 17 credits, including 4 each of English and math through precalculus, and 3 of science, including chemistry. The GED is accepted. Albany College of Pharmacy requires applicants to be in the upper 50% of their class. A GPA of 3.0 is required. AP and CLEP credits are accepted. Important factors in the admissions decision are advanced placement or honor courses, extracurricular activities record, and recommendations by alumni. Applications are accepted on-line through CollegeNet.

Procedure: Freshmen are admitted in the fall. Entrance exams should be taken in the junior year. Applications should be filed by February 1 for fall entry. The fall 2001 application fee was $50. Notification is sent on a rolling basis.

Transfer: Applicants must have a GPA of 3.2. 83 credits of 162 must be completed at Albany College of Pharmacy.

Visiting: There are regularly scheduled orientations for prospective students, including a tour of the school and residence halls and a discussion of admissions requirements, financial aid, and student activities. There are guides for informal visits and visitors may sit in on classes and stay overnight. To schedule a visit, contact the Admissions Office.

Financial Aid: The FAFSA is required.

International Students: There are 10 international students enrolled. They must score 600 on the written TOEFL or 250 on the electronic version or take the TSE. They must also take the SAT I or the ACT.

Computers: The mainframe is a DEC VAX 11/750. Entering students receive laptop computers through a lease program. A number of PCs are also available. All students may access the system 24 hours a day. There are no time limits and no fees.

Admissions Contact: Craig Tynan, Admissions Counselor. A video is available. E-mail: *admissions@acp.edu* Web: *www.acp.edu*

ALBERT A. LIST COLLEGE OF JEWISH STUDIES — D-5

New York, NY 10027-4649 (212) 678-8832; Fax: (212) 678-8947

Full-time: 80 men, 81 women	**Faculty:** 40
Part-time: 8 men, 8 women	**Ph.D.s:** 98%
Graduate: none	**Student/Faculty:** 4 to 1
Year: semesters, summer session	**Tuition:** $10,000
Application Deadline: February 15	**Room & Board:** $8500
Freshman Class: 138 applied, 87 accepted, 48 enrolled	
SAT I Verbal/Math: required	**HIGHLY COMPETITIVE+**

Albert A. List College of Jewish Studies, the undergraduate division of the Jewish Theological Seminary, founded in 1886, is a private institution affiliated with the Conservative branch of the Jewish faith. List College offers programs in all aspects of Judaism, including Bible, rabbinics, literature, history, philosophy, education, and communal service. There is also a combined liberal arts program with Columbia University and Barnard College. The library contains 320,000 volumes and 3500 microform items, and subscribes to 750 periodicals. Computerized library services include the card catalog, interlibrary loans, and database searching. Special learning facilities include a learning resource center, art gallery, music center, Jewish education, research center, and the Jewish Museum Archives Center. The 1-acre campus is in an urban area on the upper west side of Manhattan. Including residence halls, there are 6 buildings.

Student Life: 75% of undergraduates are from out of state, mostly the Middle Atlantic. Others are from 12 states, 3 foreign countries, and Canada. 70% are from public schools. All are white and Jewish. The average age of freshmen is 18; all undergraduates, 20. 96% of freshmen remain to graduate.

Housing: 212 students can be accommodated in college housing, which includes coed dormitories, on- and off-campus apartments, Kosher housing, and married-student housing. On-campus housing is guaranteed for all 4 years. 93% of students live on campus; of those, 95% remain on campus on weekends. Alcohol is not permitted. All students may keep cars.

Activities: Through Columbia University, 12% of men belong to fraternities; 4% of women belong to sororities. There are many groups and organizations on campus, including art, band, choir, chorus, computers, dance, drama, ethnic, film, gay, honors, international, literary magazine, musical theater, newspaper, orchestra, photography, political, professional, radio and TV, religious, social, social service, student government, and yearbook. List College students have access to all clubs and organizations at Columbia and Barnard. Popular campus events include Purim, Simchat Torah, and Orientation.

Sports: There are 3 intramural sports for men and 3 for women. List College students may use the facilities at Columbia University.

Disabled Students: All of the campus is accessible. Wheelchair ramps, elevators, special parking, specially equipped rest rooms, lowered drinking fountains, lowered telephones, and elevators with braille panels are available.

Services: Counseling and information services are available, as is tutoring in most subjects.

Campus Safety and Security: Measures include 24-hour foot and vehicle patrol, escort service, informal discussions, and pamphlets/posters/films. There are emergency telephones and lighted pathways/sidewalks.

Programs of Study: List College confers the B.A. degree in SOCIAL SCIENCE (biblical studies and Judaic studies).

Required: Students must take a Hebrew language requirement, 24 credits in Jewish history, 9 in literature, and 6 each in Bible, Jewish philosophy, and Talmud. In addition, there are 60 required credits in liberal arts, including 6 credits each in English, history/philosophy/social science, and math or lab science to be completed at another college or university. A total of 156 credits (96 taken at List College) is required for graduation, with 21 in a major field.

Special: There is a joint program with Columbia University and a double-degree program with Barnard College, which enable students to earn 2 B.A. degrees in 4 to 4 1/2 years. Study abroad is available in Israel, England, France, and Spain. Student-designed majors, credit by exam, and nondegree study are also offered. There is a chapter of Phi Beta Kappa and a freshman honors program.

Faculty/Classroom: 68% of faculty are male; 32%, female. All both teach and do research. The average class size in an introductory lecture is 30 and in a regular course, 10.

Admissions: 63% of the 2001-2002 applicants were accepted. The SAT I scores for the 2001-2002 freshman class were: Verbal--2% below 500, 20% between 500 and 599, 52% between 600 and 700, and 26% above 700; Math--4% below 500, 22% between 500 and 599, 70% between 600 and 700, and 4% above 700. The ACT scores were 10% between 21 and 23, 20% between 24 and 26, 40% between 27 and 28, and 30% above 28.

Requirements: The SAT I is required as is the SAT II: Subject tests. Applicants must be graduates of an accredited secondary school or have the GED. An essay and 2 recommendations are required; an interview is strongly recommended. AP credits are accepted. Important factors in the admissions decision are advanced placement or honor courses, extracurricular activities record, and personality/intangible qualities. Students can print on-line applications and submit them by mail.

Procedure: Freshmen are admitted fall and spring. Entrance exams should be taken in the spring of the junior year. There are early decision, early admissions, and deferred admissions plans. Early decision application should be filed by November 15; regular applications, by February 15 for fall entry and November 1 for spring entry. Notification of early decision is sent December 15; regular decision, April 15. 14 early decision candidates were accepted for the 2001-2002 class. The fall 2001 application fee was $60.

Transfer: In a recent year, 7 transfer students enrolled. Applicants must submit SAT I or ACT scores, an essay, high school and college transcripts, and 2 academic recommendations. A minimum college GPA of 2.5 is required. An interview is recommended. 48 credits of 156 must be completed at List College.

Visiting: There are regularly scheduled orientations for prospective students, including a tour of the campus and of Columbia University, an interview with the dean, and an overnight dormitory stay. There are guides for informal visits and visitors may sit in on classes and stay overnight. To schedule a visit, contact Reena Kamins, Admissions Director at (212) 678-8832.

Financial Aid: In 2001-2002, 75% of all freshmen and 65% of continuing students received some form of financial aid. The average freshman award was $17,800. 15% of undergraduates work part time. List College is a member of CSS. The CSS/Profile, the college's own financial statement, and 1040 tax forms are required. The fall application deadline is March 1.

International Students: In a recent year, there were 10 international students enrolled. These students must score 500 on the written TOEFL and also take the college's own test or the American Language English Placement Test and the SAT I or the ACT.

Computers: All dormitories have Internet connections. All students may access the system. There are no time limits and no fees.

Graduates: In 2001, 39 bachelor's degrees were awarded. In an average class, 60% graduate in 4 years, and 100% in 5 years.

Admissions Contact: Reena Kamins, Director of Admissions.
E-mail: *lcadmissions@jtsa.edu* Web: *www.jtsa.edu*

ALFRED UNIVERSITY — B-4

Alfred, NY 14802-1205 — (607) 871-2115
(800) 541-9229; Fax: (607) 871-2198

Full-time: 952 men, 1060 women	**Faculty:** 173; IIA, -$
Part-time: 42 men, 60 women	**Ph.D.s:** 93%
Graduate: 133 men, 195 women	**Student/Faculty:** 12 to 1
Year: semesters, summer session	**Tuition:** $19,196
Application Deadline: February 1	**Room & Board:** $8016
Freshman Class: 2048 applied, 1538 accepted, 508 enrolled	
SAT I Verbal/Math: 556/561	**ACT:** 24 **COMPETITIVE+**

Alfred University, founded in 1836, is a private institution offering programs in business administration, liberal arts and sciences, engineering, and professional studies, and in art and design and ceramic engineering through the New York State College of Ceramics. The above tuition figures are for incoming freshmen. Contact the school for tuition rates at other academic levels. There are 5 undergraduate and 7 graduate schools. In addition to regional accreditation, AU has baccalaureate program accreditation with AACSB, ABET, and NASAD. The 2 libraries contain 323,944 volumes and 94,298 microform items, and subscribe to 6467 periodicals. Computerized library services include the card catalog, interlibrary loans, and database searching. Special learning facilities include a learning resource center, art gallery, radio station, TV station, and observatory. The 232-acre campus is in a rural area 70 miles south of Rochester. Including residence halls, there are 54 buildings.

Student Life: 69% of undergraduates are from New York. Others are from 38 states, 12 foreign countries, and Canada. 90% are from public schools. 88% are white. The average age of freshmen is 18; all undergraduates, 20. 20% do not continue beyond their first year; 65% remain to graduate.

Housing: 1330 students can be accommodated in college housing, which includes coed dormitories, on-campus apartments, fraternity houses, and sorority houses. In addition, there are honors houses, language houses, and special-interest houses. On-campus housing is available on a first-come, first-served basis and is available on a lottery system for upperclassmen. 65% of students live on campus; of those, 90% remain on campus on weekends. All students may keep cars.

Activities: 20% of men belong to 2 local and 6 national fraternities; 15% of women belong to 3 local sororities and 1 national sorority. There are 91 groups on campus, including art, band, cheerleading, chess, chorale, chorus, computers, dance, drama, ethnic, film, gay, honors, international, jazz band, literary magazine, newspaper, orchestra, pep band, photography, political, professional, radio and TV, religious, social, social service, student activities board, student government, and yearbook. Popular campus events include Alumni Weekend, Hot Dog Day, and Family Weekend.

Sports: There are 11 intercollegiate sports for men and 12 for women, and 14 intramural sports for men and 13 for women. Facilities include an omniturf football surface, a soccer and lacrosse field, an Olympic-size pool, tennis courts, racquetball and squash courts, a weight room, and a dance and exercise studio. The campus stadium seats 4200, the indoor gym, 3000. There is also a fitness center and facilities for horseback riding nearby.

Disabled Students: 50% of the campus is accessible. Wheelchair ramps, elevators, special parking, specially equipped rest rooms, special class scheduling, and lowered drinking fountains are available.

Services: Counseling and information services are available, as is tutoring in most subjects. There is a reader service for the blind, and remedial math, reading, and writing. Time management and study skills workshops and advocacy and support for students with learning and physical disabilities are available.

Campus Safety and Security: Measures include escort service, informal discussions, pamphlets/posters/films, and emergency telephones. There are lighted pathways/sidewalks and vehicle and foot patrol.

Programs of Study: AU confers B.A., B.S., and B.F.A. degrees. Master's and doctoral degrees are also awarded. Bachelor's degrees are awarded in BIOLOGICAL SCIENCE (biology/biological science), BUSINESS (accounting, banking and finance, business administration and management, business economics, management science, and marketing/retailing/merchandising), COMMUNICATIONS AND THE ARTS (ceramic art and design, communications, dramatic arts, English, fine arts,

French, German, glass, performing arts, and Spanish), COMPUTER AND PHYSICAL SCIENCE (chemistry, computer science, geology, mathematics, physics, and science), EDUCATION (art, athletic training, business, elementary, English, foreign languages, mathematics, science, secondary, and social studies), ENGINEERING AND ENVIRONMENTAL DESIGN (ceramic engineering, electrical/electronics engineering, environmental science, materials engineering, and mechanical engineering), HEALTH PROFESSIONS (health care administration), SOCIAL SCIENCE (criminal justice, crosscultural studies, economics, gerontology, history, interdisciplinary studies, philosophy, political science/government, psychology, public administration, and sociology). Ceramic engineering, electrical engineering, and business are the strongest academically. Art and design, business administration, and ceramic engineering are the largest.

Required: To graduate, students must complete 120 to 137 credits, depending on the major, with 36 to 48 credits in the major. Students must demonstrate basic competencies in writing, oral communication, math, and computers. Freshmen must attend 10 freshman forums. Distribution requirements include 8 credits each of social studies and natural science and 4 credits each of philosophy or religion, literature, art, and history. A minimum GPA of 2.0 is required.

Special: There are cooperative programs in engineering and business with Duke, Clarkson, and Columbia Universities and SUNY/Brockport. There is cross-registration with the SUNY College of Technology and a 5-year program in environmental management/forestry with Duke. Alfred offers internships in all programs, extensive study abroad, Washington and Albany semesters, work-study, accelerated-degree programs, a general studies degree, student-designed majors, dual majors, credit by exam, and pass/fail options. A special feature is the New York State College of Ceramics, which offers programs and facilities in ceramic engineering and science as well as art and design. There are 12 national honor societies, a freshman honors program, and 42 departmental honors programs.

Faculty/Classroom: 64% of faculty are male; 36%, female. 90% both teach and do research. No introductory courses are taught by graduate students. The average class size in an introductory lecture is 25; in a laboratory, 15; and in a regular course, 18.

Admissions: 75% of the 2001-2002 applicants were accepted. The SAT I scores for the 2001-2002 freshman class were: Verbal--24% below 500, 44% between 500 and 599, 27% between 600 and 700, and 5% above 700; Math--18% below 500, 48% between 500 and 599, 30% between 600 and 700, and 4% above 700. The ACT scores were 4% below 19, 19 % between 19 and 21, 30% between 22 and 24, 27% between 25 and 27, and 20% above 27. 43% of the current freshmen were in the top fifth of their class; 74% were in the top two fifths. There were 8 National Merit finalists. 7 freshmen graduated first in their class.

Requirements: The SAT I or ACT is required. A GED is accepted. A minimum of 16 Carnegie units is required, including 4 years of English and 2 to 3 years each of math, history/social studies, and science. The remaining units may be either in a foreign language or any of the previously mentioned fields. An essay is required, and applicants to B.F.A. programs must submit a portfolio. Interviews are encouraged. AP credits are accepted. Important factors in the admissions decision are advanced placement or honor courses, personality/intangible qualities, and extracurricular activities record. Applications are accepted on-line at the school's web site.

Procedure: Freshmen are admitted fall and spring. Entrance exams should be taken in the junior year. There are early decision, early admissions, and deferred admissions plans. Early decision applications should be filed by December 1; regular applications, by February 1 for fall entry and December 1 for spring entry, along with a $40 fee. Notification of early decision is sent December 15; regular decision, March 15. 55 early decision candidates were accepted for the 2001-2002 class.

Transfer: 85 transfer students enrolled in 2001-2002. Transfer applicants must have a GPA of at least 2.5. They must submit at least 1 letter of recommendation and official high school and college transcripts. Art students must submit a portfolio. 30 credits of 120 must be completed at AU.

Visiting: There are regularly scheduled orientations for prospective students, including a campus tour, a social activities panel, a financial aid presentation, faculty discussions, and on-campus interviews. There are guides for informal visits and visitors may sit in on classes and stay overnight. To schedule a visit, contact Scott Hooker, Director of Admissions.

Financial Aid: In 2001-2002, 85% of all students received some form of financial aid. The average freshman award was $18,444 to $20,694. 50% of undergraduates work part time. Average annual earnings from campus work are $1000. The average financial indebtedness of the 2001 graduate was $17,500. The FAFSA, the college's own financial statement, the state aid form, the Business/Farm Supplement, and the noncustodial parent statement are required. The fall application deadline is May 1.

International Students: There are 38 international students enrolled. The school actively recruits these students. They must score 550 on the written TOEFL.

Computers: The mainframe is a Compaq Alpha ES 40. All buildings are connected to the campus network. There are numerous high-speed, laser, and color printers. More than 400 terminals are located across campus for student use. All students may access the system 24 hours a day, 7 days a week. There are no time limits and no fees.

Graduates: In 2001, 379 bachelor's degrees were awarded. The most popular majors were art and design (25%), business administration (13%), and psychology (7%). In an average class, 1% graduate in 3 years, 50% in 4 years, 65% in 5 years, and 66% in 6 years. 78 companies recruited on campus in 2000-2001. Of the 2000 graduating class, 24% were enrolled in graduate school within 6 months of graduation and 70% were employed.

Admissions Contact: Scott Hooker, Director of Admissions. A video is available. E-mail: *hooker@alfred.edu* or *admwww@alfred.edu*
Web: *http://www.alfred.edu*

AUDREY COHEN COLLEGE

New York, NY 10013 — **D-5**

(212) 343-1234, ext. 5001
(800) 33-THINK; Fax: (212) 343-8470

Full-time: 234 men, 1062 women	**Faculty:** 23
Part-time: none	**Ph.D.s:** 90%
Graduate: 40 men, 183 women	**Student/Faculty:** 56 to 1
Year: trimesters, summer session	**Tuition:** $14,715
Application Deadline: August 1	**Room & Board:** n/app
Freshman Class: 405 applied, 266 accepted, 153 enrolled	
SAT I or ACT: not required	**COMPETITIVE**

Audrey Cohen College, founded in 1964, is a private institution offering programs in human services and business management. The college operates on a 3 semester calendar, including a complete summer semester. All bachelor degree programs involve a combination of class work and field work and may be completed in 2 years and 8 months. There are 2 undergraduate and 2 graduate schools. The library contains 32,000 volumes and 1800 microform items, and subscribes to 3300 periodicals. Computerized library services include the card catalog, interlibrary loans, and database searching. Special learning facilities include a learning resource center. The campus is in an urban area. There is 1 building.

Student Life: 95% of undergraduates are from New York. Others are from 4 states, 9 foreign countries, and Canada. 68% are from public schools. 60% are African American; 18% Hispanic. The average age of freshmen is 32; all undergraduates, 32. 28% do not continue beyond their first year; 59% remain to graduate.

Housing: There are no residence halls. All students commute. Alcohol is not permitted.

Activities: There are no fraternities or sororities. There are several groups on campus, including computers, ethnic, gay, honors, professional, social, social service, student government, and yearbook. Popular campus events include career fairs, admissions open house, and dean's list ceremonies.

Sports: There is no sports program at the college.

Disabled Students: All of the campus is accessible. Wheelchair ramps, elevators, specially equipped rest rooms, special class scheduling, lowered drinking fountains, and lowered telephones are available.

Services: Counseling and information services are available, as is tutoring in every subject. There is remedial math, reading, and writing.

Campus Safety and Security: Measures include 24-hour foot and vehicle patrol, lighted pathways/sidewalks, fire drills, and a fire escape stairwell.

Programs of Study: The college confers B.B.A. and B.P.S. degrees. Associate and master's degrees are also awarded. Bachelor's degrees are awarded in BUSINESS (business administration and management), EDUCATION (early childhood), HEALTH PROFESSIONS (mental health/human services), SOCIAL SCIENCE (child care/child and family studies, community services, gerontology, human services, prelaw, psychology, and social work). Business management is the strongest academically. Human services is the largest.

Required: To graduate, students must complete 128 credit hours with a minimum GPA of 2.0. The curriculum is prescribed and no electives are featured. A constructive action document based on performance in the field and mastery of course work is required each semester.

Special: Internships, study abroad in 3 countries, work-study programs, accelerated degree programs, credit by exam, and credit for life experience are offered.

Faculty/Classroom: 63% of faculty are male; 37%, female. 95% teach undergraduates. No introductory courses are taught by graduate students. The average class size in an introductory lecture is 25; in a laboratory, 18; and in a regular course, 20.

Admissions: 66% of the 2001-2002 applicants were accepted.

Requirements: Students must take the Test of Adult Basic Education (TABE) in English, reading, and math; recent high school graduates who have a minimum composite SAT I score of 1050 may present the SAT I instead. Applicants must have graduated from an accredited secondary school. The GED is accepted. An essay and an interview are required. CLEP credit is accepted. Important factors in the admissions decision are evidence of special talent, leadership record, and personality/intangible qualities. Applications are accepted on-line.

Procedure: Freshmen are admitted to all sessions. Entrance exams should be taken in the senior year. Applications should be filed by August 1 for fall entry, December 1 for spring entry, and April 1 for summer entry, along with a $30 fee. Notification is sent on a rolling basis.

Transfer: Admission is based on current skills and abilities as measured on the entrance exam and essay. 64 credits of 128 must be completed at the college.

Visiting: There are regularly scheduled orientations for prospective students. There are guides for informal visits and visitors may sit in on classes. To schedule a visit, contact the Admissions Office.

Financial Aid: The CSS/Profile or FAFSA and the New York State Higher Education Financial statement are required. The fall application deadline is August 15.

International Students: They must score 550 on the written TOEFL and also take TABE.

Computers: The mainframe is a Unisys Clearpath. There are also 120 Unisys PW300 PCs available in the computer labs and the library. All students may access the system whenever the college is open. There are no time limits. The fee is $75. It is strongly recommended that all students have a personal computer.

Graduates: In 2001, 252 bachelor's degrees were awarded. In an average class, 40% graduate in 4 years. 35 companies recruited on campus in a recent year. Of a recent graduating class, 50% were enrolled in graduate school within 6 months of graduation and 93% were employed.

Admissions Contact: Steven K. Lenhart, Director of Admissions.
E-mail: *slenhart@audreycohen.edu* Web: *www.audreycohen.edu*

BARD COLLEGE
D-4

Annandale-on-Hudson, NY 12504

(845) 758-7472
Fax: (845) 758-5208

Full-time: 564 men, 720 women	**Faculty:** 113; IIB, ++$
Part-time: 28 men, 31 women	**Ph.D.s:** 97%
Graduate: 54 men, 118 women	**Student/Faculty:** 11 to 1
Year: 4-1-4	**Tuition:** $26,170
Application Deadline: January 15	**Room & Board:** $7742
Freshman Class: 2970 applied, 1320 accepted, 358 enrolled	
SAT I Verbal/Math: 660/620	**HIGHLY COMPETITIVE**

Bard College, founded in 1860, is an independent liberal arts and sciences institution affiliated historically with the Association of Episcopal Colleges. Discussion-oriented seminars and independent study are encouraged, tutorials are on a one-to-one basis, and most classes are kept small, with fewer than 20 students. The library contains 260,000 volumes, 5670 microform items, and 5600 audiovisual forms/CDs, and subscribes to 850 periodicals. Computerized library services include the card catalog, interlibrary loans, and database searching. Special learning facilities include a learning resource center, art gallery, radio station, ecology field station, the Jerome Levy International Economics Institute, the Institute for Writing and Thinking, the International Academy for Scholarship and the Arts, the Center for Curatorial Studies and Art in Contemporary Culture, and an archeological field school. The 600-acre campus is in a rural area 100 miles north of New York City. Including residence halls, there are 70 buildings.

Student Life: 74% of undergraduates are from out of state, mostly the Northeast. Students are from 50 states, 47 foreign countries, and Canada. 70% are from public schools. 82% are white. The average age of freshmen is 18; all undergraduates, 20. 13% do not continue beyond their first year; 70% remain to graduate.

Housing: 1200 students can be accommodated in college housing, which includes single-sex and coed dormitories. In addition, there are special-interest houses and quiet dorms. On-campus housing is guaranteed for the freshman year only and is available on a lottery system for upperclassmen. 85% of students live on campus; of those, 75% remain on campus on weekends. All students may keep cars.

Activities: There are no fraternities or sororities. There are 60 groups on campus, including art, band, chamber groups, chess, choir, chorus, computers, dance, drama, ethnic, film, gay, international, jazz band, literary magazine, newspaper, opera, orchestra, photography, political, radio and TV, religious, social, social service, student government, and yearbook. Popular campus events include Winter Carnival, Spring Festival, and comedy night.

Sports: There are 7 intercollegiate sports for men and 7 for women, and 13 intramural sports for men and 13 for women. Facilities include a gym and pool, soccer and softball fields, squash and tennis courts, cross-country trails, bike paths, a 300-seat auditorium, and a film center.

Disabled Students: 70% of the campus is accessible. Wheelchair ramps, elevators, special parking, specially equipped rest rooms, lowered drinking fountains, and lowered telephones are available.

Services: Counseling and information services are available, as is tutoring in every subject. There is a reader service for the blind.

Campus Safety and Security: Measures include 24-hour foot and vehicle patrol, self-defense education, escort service, and shuttle buses. There are informal discussions, pamphlets/posters/films, emergency telephones, lighted pathways/sidewalks, volunteer emergency medical technicians on call 24 hours a day, and Bard Response to Rape and Associated Violence Education (BRAVE) volunteers.

Programs of Study: Bard confers B.A. and B.S. degrees. Master's and doctoral degrees are also awarded. Bachelor's degrees are awarded in BIOLOGICAL SCIENCE (biochemistry, biology/biological science, cell biology, ecology, microbiology, and molecular biology), COMMUNICATIONS AND THE ARTS (American literature, art history and appreciation, Chinese, classical languages, classics, creative writing, dance, dramatic arts, drawing, English, English literature, film arts, French, German, Germanic languages and literature, Italian, music history and appreciation, music performance, music theory and composition, painting, photography, Russian, sculpture, and Spanish), COMPUTER AND PHYSICAL SCIENCE (chemistry, mathematics, natural sciences, and physics), ENGINEERING AND ENVIRONMENTAL DESIGN (environmental science), HEALTH PROFESSIONS (predentistry and premedicine), SOCIAL SCIENCE (African studies, American studies, anthropology, archeology, area studies, Asian/Oriental studies, British studies, Celtic studies, clinical psychology, developmental psychology, Eastern European studies, economics, European studies, French studies, history, history of philosophy, history of science, human development, interdisciplinary studies, Italian studies, Judaic studies, Latin American studies, medieval studies, philosophy, political science/government, prelaw, religion, Russian and Slavic studies, social psychology, social science, sociology, and Spanish studies). Languages and literature, the arts, and social studies are the largest.

Required: All students must complete a 3-week workshop in language and thinking, a year-long freshman seminar, and a senior project. A conference in the junior year is required, and through a moderation process in the sophomore year, the student chooses a concentration in an academic department. A distribution of at least 1 course in each of the 7 academic areas, including a quantitative analysis course, is required, with a maximum of 84 hours in the student's major and a total of 124 credit hours needed to graduate.

Special: Bard offers opportunities for study abroad, internships (no academic credit), Washington and New York semesters, dual majors, student-designed majors, accelerated degree programs, and pass/fail options. Cross-registration is available with Vassar College and SUNY/New Paltz. A 3-2 engineering degree is available with the Columbia Univesity School of Engineering. Other 3-2 degrees are available in forestry and environmental studies, social work, architecture, city and regional planning, public health, and business administration. There are also opportunities for independent study, multicultural and ethnic studies, community, regional, and environmental studies, area studies, and the International Honors Program.

Faculty/Classroom: 57% of faculty are male; 43%, female. All teach undergraduates and do research. No introductory courses are taught by graduate students. The average class size in an introductory lecture is 20; in a laboratory, 15; and in a regular course, 15.

Admissions: 44% of the 2001-2002 applicants were accepted. The SAT I scores for the 2001-2002 freshman class were: Verbal--13% between 500 and 599, 53% between 600 and 700, and 34% above 700; Math--26% between 500 and 599, 54% between 600 and 700, and 20% above 700. 80% of the current freshmen were in the top fifth of their class; 98% were in the top two fifths. There were 2 National Merit finalists and 16 semifinalists. 20 freshmen graduated first in their class in a recent year.

Requirements: Bard places strong emphasis on the academic background and intellectual curiosity of applicants, as well as indications of the student's commitment to social and environmental concerns, independent research, volunteer work, and other important extracurricular activities. Students applying for admission are expected to have graduated from an accredited secondary school (the GED is accepted) and must submit written essays with the application. The high school record should include a full complement of college-preparatory courses. Honors and advanced placement courses are also considered. An interview is recommended. Bard requires applicants to be in the upper 50% of their class. A GPA of 3.0 is required. AP credits are accepted. Important factors in the admissions decision are advanced placement or honor courses, evidence of special talent, and extracurricular activities record. Students may apply on-line with Common Application or Peterson's.

Procedure: Freshmen are admitted fall and spring. There are early admissions and deferred admissions plans. Early action applications should be filed by November 1; regular applications, by January 15 for fall entry and November 1 for spring entry, along with a $50 fee. Notification of early action is sent January 1; regular decision, April 1. 9% of all applicants are on a waiting list; 10 were accepted in 2001.

Transfer: 33 transfer students enrolled in 2001-2002. Admission requirements are the same as for regular applicants. A minimum GPA of 3.0 and an interview are recommended. 60 credits of 124 must be completed at Bard.

Visiting: There are regularly scheduled orientations for prospective students, consisting of regularly scheduled daily tours and interviews (each 1/2 to 1 hour), which are strongly recommended. There are guides for informal visits and visitors may sit in on classes. To schedule a visit, contact the Admissions Office.

Financial Aid: In 2001-2002, 61% of all freshmen and 66% of continuing students received some form of financial aid. 57% of freshmen and 61% of continuing students received need-based aid. The average freshman award was $19,099. Of that total, scholarships or need-based grants averaged $15,900 ($20,000 maximum); loans averaged $2625 ($4125 maximum); and work contracts averaged $1500. 50% of undergraduates work part time. Average annual earnings from campus work are $1200. The average financial indebtedness of the 2001 graduate was $16,000. The CSS/Profile or FAFSA is required. The fall application deadline is February 15.

International Students: There are 75 international students enrolled. They must score 600 on the written TOEFL or 250 on the electronic version.

Computers: The computer center houses more than 90 networked Macs and PCs. There are more than 400 additional terminals and PCs located in the library, academic departments, and throughout the campus. All students may access the system. There are no time limits and no fees.

Graduates: In 2001, 250 bachelor's degrees were awarded. The most popular majors were social studies (37%), visual and performing arts (30%), and language and literature (25%). In an average class, 3% graduate in 3 years, 50% in 4 years, 70% in 5 years, and 72% in 6 years. 100 companies recruited on campus in 2000-2001. Of the 2000 graduating class, 45% were enrolled in graduate school within 6 months of graduation and 50% were employed.

Admissions Contact: Mary Backlund, Director of Admissions. A video is available. E-mail: *admissions@bard.edu* Web: *www.bard.edu*

BERKELEY COLLEGE D-5
White Plains, NY 10601

(914) 694-1122
(800) 446-5400; (914) 328-9469

Full-time: 150 men, 420 women	**Faculty:** 15
Part-time: 20 men, 100 women	**Ph.D.s:** 54%
Graduate: none	**Student/Faculty:** 38 to 1
Year: quarters,summer session	**Tuition:** $13,545
Application Deadline: open	**Room & Board:** $8000
Freshman Class: n/av	
SAT I or ACT: n/av	**LESS COMPETITIVE**

Berkeley College, established in 1945, is a private institution with 5 campuses in New York and New Jersey. Its programs are designed to prepare students for careers in business by providing an education that balances academic studies, professional training, and hands-on experience. Figures in the above capsule are approximate. The library contains 9500 volumes and 800 audiovisual forms/CDs, and subscribes to 80 periodicals. Computerized library services include the card catalog, interlibrary loans, and database searching. Special learning facilities include a learning resource center. The 10-acre campus is in a suburban area. Including residence halls, there are 3 buildings.

Student Life: 80% of undergraduates are from New York. Others are from 8 states and 14 foreign countries. 66% are white; 16% African American; 11% Hispanic. The average age of freshmen is 19; all undergraduates, 20.

Housing: 96 students can be accommodated in college housing, which includes coed dormitories. Priority for on-campus housing is given to out-of-town students. 86% of students commute. Alcohol is not permitted. All students may keep cars.

Activities: There are no fraternities or sororities. There are 6 groups on campus, including international, newspaper, professional, social, social service, and student government. Popular campus events include Multicultural Month and Commuter Appreciation Day.

Sports: There is no sports program at Berkeley College. Students have access to the sports and exercise facilities at nearby Manhattanville College.

Disabled Students: Wheelchair ramps, elevators, and special parking are available.

Services: Counseling and information services are available, as is tutoring in every subject. There is remedial math, reading, and writing.

Campus Safety and Security: Measures include lighted pathways/sidewalks and and night patrols by trained security personnel.

Programs of Study: Berkeley College confers the B.B.A. degree. Associate degrees are also awarded. Bachelor's degrees are awarded in BUSINESS (accounting, business administration and management, international business management, and marketing/retailing/merchandising).

Requirements: In addition, graduation from an accredited high school or the equivalent (GED) and an entrance exam or the SAT I or ACT scores are basic requirements for admission. A personal interview is strongly recommended. Applications are accepted on-line at the school's web site. AP and CLEP credits are accepted.

Procedure: Freshmen are admitted to all sessions. Entrance exams should be taken as soon as the application is submitted, if possible. There is a deferred admissions plan. Application deadlines are open. Notification is sent on a rolling basis. The fall 2001 application fee was $35.

Transfer: 49 transfer students enrolled in a recent year. Applicants must submit a transcript from each college attended and a high school transcript or equivalent (GED). 60 credits of 180 must be completed at Berkeley College.

Visiting: There are guides for informal visits.

Financial Aid: In a recent year, 90% of all students received some form of financial aid. The FAFSA, the college's own financial statement and the state income tax return are required. Check with the school for current aplication deadlines and fee.

International Students: There were 20 international students enrolled in a recent year. The school actively recruits these students. .

Computers: More than 150 PCs are available to students, all with access to the Internet and the Web. All students may access the system. There are no time limits and no fees.

Admissions Contact: Admissions Officer.
E-mail: *wpcampus@berkeleycollege.edu*
Web: *www.berkeleycollege.edu*

BERKELEY COLLEGE OF NEW YORK CITY D-5
New York, NY 10017

(212) 986-4343
(800)446-5400; (212) 697-3371

Full-time: 400 men, 1120 women	**Faculty:** 30
Part-time: 50 men, 150 women	**Ph.D.s:** 33%
Graduate: none	**Student/Faculty:** 50 to 1
Year: quarters, summer session	**Tuition:** $12,500
Application Deadline: open	**Room & Board:** n/app
Freshman Class: n/av	
SAT I or ACT: n/av	**LESS COMPETITIVE**

Berkeley College of New York City, founded in 1936, is a private institution offering undergraduate programs in business. Figures in the above capsule are approximate. The library contains 11,005 volumes, and subscribes to 130 periodicals. Computerized library services include the card catalog, interlibrary loans, and database searching. Special learning facilities include a learning resource center. The campus is in an urban area in midtown Manhattan, a short walk from Grand Central Station. There are 2 buildings.

Housing: There are no residence halls.

Programs of Study: Berkeley College of New York City confers the B.B.A. degree. Associate degrees are also awarded. Bachelor's degrees are awarded in BUSINESS (accounting, business administration and management, international business management, and marketing/retailing/merchandising).

Faculty/Classroom: All teach undergraduates.

Requirements: In addition, graduation from an accredited high school or the GED, and an entrance exam, or the SAT I or ACT scores are basic requirements for admission. A personal interview is strongly recommended. Applications are accepted on-line at the school's web site. AP and CLEP credits are accepted.

Procedure: Freshmen are admitted to all sessions. Entrance exams should be taken any time. There is a deferred admissions plan. Application deadlines are open. Notification is on a rolling basis. The fall 2001 application fee was $35.

Transfer: 60 transfer students enrolled in a recent year. A transcript from each college or university attended must be submitted to receive credit. 60 credits of 180 must be completed at Berkeley College of New York City.

Visiting: There are guides for informal visits.

Financial Aid: In a recent year, 90% of all freshmen received some form of financial aid. The FAFSA, the college's own financial statement and the state income tax form are required. Check with the school for current deadlines.

International Students: There were 130 international students enrolled in a recent year. The school actively recruits these students. .

Computers: More than 200 PCs are available to students with access to the Internet and Web. All students may access the system. There are no time limits and no fees.

Admissions Contact: Admissions Officer.
E-mail: *nycampus@berkeleycollege.edu*
Web: *www.berkeleycollege.edu*

BORICUA COLLEGE
New York, NY 10032 D-5

(212) 694-1000 or (718) 782-2200
Fax: (212) 694-1015 or (718) 782-2050

Full-time: 250 men, 900 women
Part-time: none
Graduate: none
Year: trimesters, summer session
Application Deadline: open
Freshman Class: 672 applied, 438 accepted, 391 enrolled
SAT I or ACT: not required
Faculty: n/av
Ph.D.s: n/av
Student/Faculty: n/av
Tuition: $7375
Room & Board: n/app
COMPETITIVE

Boricua College, founded in 1974, is a private college for bilingual students, designed to meet the needs of a Spanish-speaking population. Figures in the above capsule are approximate. There are 2 graduate schools. The library contains 128,727 volumes and 3000 audiovisual forms/CDs, and subscribes to 227 periodicals. Computerized library services include the card catalog and database searching. Special learning facilities include a learning resource center and art gallery. The campus is in an urban area in Manhattan and Brooklyn. There are 4 buildings.

Student Life: 70% are from public schools. 85% are Hispanic; 10% African American. The average age of freshmen is 29; all undergraduates, 32. 12% do not continue beyond their first year; 80% remain to graduate.

Housing: There are no residence halls. Alcohol is not permitted. No one may keep cars.

Activities: There are no fraternities or sororities. There are 5 groups on campus, including art, chorus, drama, newspaper, and student government. Popular campus events include cultural programs, Puerto Rican Discovery Day, and Christmas and Spring concerts with chorus and orchestra.

Sports: Facilities include a gym.

Disabled Students: Elevators and specially equipped rest rooms are available.

Services: Counseling and information services are available, as is tutoring in most subjects.

Campus Safety and Security: Measures include shuttle buses, informal discussions, pamphlets/posters/films, and emergency telephones. There are lighted pathways/sidewalks.

Programs of Study: Bachelor's degrees are awarded in BUSINESS (business administration and management), EDUCATION (elementary), SOCIAL SCIENCE (human services and liberal arts/general studies).

Required: Check with the school for current information.

Admissions: 65% of the 2001-2002 applicants were accepted.

Requirements: Boricua administers its own tests to prospective students, although either the SAT I or ACT is accepted. Applicants must be graduates of an accredited secondary school or have a GED. 2 letters of recommendation and an admissions interview are required. Applicants must demonstrate a working knowledge of English and Spanish to a faculty panel. CLEP credit is accepted. Important factors in the admissions decision are leadership record, personality/intangible qualities, and recommendations by school officials.

Procedure: Freshmen are admitted fall, spring, and summer. There is an early decision plan. Application deadlines are open. The application fee is $30. Notification is sent on a rolling basis.

Transfer: 176 transfer students enrolled in a recent year. Applicants with associate degrees may transfer up to 60 credits. All college credits passed with grade C and above are accepted. 80 credits of 124 must be completed at Boricua.

Visiting: There are regularly scheduled orientations for prospective students. Letters are sent to prospective students advising them of scheduled orientations. To schedule a visit, contact Abraham Cruzat or Miriam Prefferat at (212) 694-1000 or (718) 782-2200.

Financial Aid: In 2001-2002, 95% of all freshmen and 70% of continuing students received some form of financial aid. Boricua is a member of CSS. The FAFSA and income tax forms are required. The fall application deadline is March 31.

Computers: The mainframe is an IBM 486 SX. There are computers available for student use in the computer lab. All students may access the system. There are no time limits and no fees.

Graduates: In a recent year, 160 bachelor's degrees were awarded. The most popular majors were elementary education (53%), human services (35%), and administration (12%). In an average class, 80% graduate in 3 years, and 20% in 4 years. Of a recent graduating class, 28% were enrolled in graduate school within 6 months of graduation and 70% were employed.

Admissions Contact: Abraham Cruz (Manhattan) or Miriam Pfeffer, Director of Student Services. E-mail: *acruz@boricuacollege.edu* or *mpfeffer@boricuacolleg*

BROOKLYN CAMPUS OF LONG ISLAND UNIVERSITY
(See Long Island University/Brooklyn Campus)

C. W. POST CAMPUS OF LONG ISLAND UNIVERSITY
(See Long Island University/C.W. Post Campus)

CANISIUS COLLEGE
Buffalo, NY 14208 A-3

(716) 888-2200
(800) 843-1517; Fax: (716) 888-3230

Full-time: 1430 men, 1553 women
Part-time: 165 men, 228 women
Graduate: 604 men, 888 women
Year: semesters, summer session
Application Deadline: open
Freshman Class: 3276 applied, 2650 accepted, 719 enrolled
SAT I Verbal/Math: 540/550
Faculty: 203; IIA, av$
Ph.D.s: 92%
Student/Faculty: 15 to 1
Tuition: $17,536
Room & Board: $7160
ACT: 24
COMPETITIVE+

Canisius College, founded in 1870, is a private Roman Catholic college in the Jesuit tradition. It offers undergraduate programs in the liberal arts and sciences, business, education, and human services. There are 3 undergraduate and 3 graduate schools. In addition to regional accreditation, Canisius has baccalaureate program accreditation with AACSB, ACS, and CED. The library contains 321,012 volumes, 562,156 microform items, and 7509 audiovisual forms/CDs, and subscribes to 9238 periodicals. Computerized library services include the card catalog, interlibrary loans, and database searching. Special learning facilities include a learning resource center, planetarium, radio station, television studio, foreign language lab, and 78 media-assisted classrooms. The 32-acre campus is in an urban area. Including residence halls, there are 50 buildings.

Student Life: 91% of undergraduates are from New York. Others are from 33 states, 26 foreign countries, and Canada. 69% are from public schools. 72% are white. 67% are Catholic; 18% Protestant; 10% claim no religious affiliation. The average age of freshmen is 18; all undergraduates, 22. 16% do not continue beyond their first year; 65% remain to graduate.

Housing: 1304 students can be accommodated in college housing, which includes single-sex and coed dormitories, on-campus apartments, and off-campus apartments. In addition, there are honors houses, special-interest houses, and an international students house. On-campus housing is guaranteed for all 4 years. 63% of students commute. Alcohol is not permitted. All students may keep cars.

Activities: 3% of men belong to 1 national fraternity; 2% of women belong to 1 national sorority. There are 90 groups on campus, including art, band, cheerleading, chess, choir, chorale, computers, dance, drama, drill team, ethnic, gay, honors, international, jazz band, literary magazine, newspaper, pep band, political, professional, radio and TV, religious, social, social service, student government, and yearbook. Popular campus events include Fall Semiformal, Senior Week, and Parents Weekend.

Sports: There are 12 intercollegiate sports for men and 12 for women, and 10 intramural sports for men and 10 for women. Facilities include an 1800-seat athletic center with a 25-yard pool, racquetball courts, and training rooms, a 1000-seat sports complex with Astroturf playing fields and perimeter track, a rifle range, a mirrored dance studio, and outdoor tennis courts.

Disabled Students: 90% of the campus is accessible. Wheelchair ramps, elevators, special parking, specially equipped rest rooms, special class scheduling, lowered drinking fountains, lowered telephones, automatic doors, TDD, a shuttle service for students with disabilities, distraction-free testing spaces, and adjustable classroom desks are available.

Services: Counseling and information services are available, as is tutoring in every subject. There is a reader service for the blind, and remedial math, reading, and writing.

Campus Safety and Security: Measures include 24-hour foot and vehicle patrol, self-defense education, escort service, and shuttle buses. There are informal discussions, pamphlets/posters/films, emergency telephones, lighted pathways/sidewalks, a crime prevention officer, and crime prevention programs.

Programs of Study: Canisius confers B.A. and B.S. degrees. Associate and master's degrees are also awarded. Bachelor's degrees are awarded in BIOLOGICAL SCIENCE (biochemistry, biology/biological science, and genetics), BUSINESS (accounting, banking and finance, business administration and management, management information systems, and marketing/retailing/merchandising), COMMUNICATIONS AND THE ARTS (art history and appreciation, communications, English, French, German, languages, and Spanish), COMPUTER AND PHYSICAL SCIENCE (chemistry, computer science, digital arts/technology, mathematics, and physics), EDUCATION (athletic training, business, elementary, English, foreign languages, mathematics, physical, science, secondary, social studies, and special), ENGINEERING AND ENVIRONMENTAL DESIGN (environmental science), HEALTH PROFESSIONS (clinical science and medical laboratory technology), SOCIAL SCIENCE (anthropology, criminal justice, economics, European studies, history, humanities, international relations, philosophy, political science/government, psychology, religion, social science, sociology, and urban studies). Accounting, chemistry, and computer science are the strongest academically. Accounting, psychology, and management are the largest.

Required: All students must complete a core curriculum consisting of 4 courses in general studies (literature, philosophy, and religion) and 14 courses in area studies (natural sciences, social studies, art and literature, history, philosophy, religious studies, math, and languages). In addition, students must take 10 3-credit courses in the major. A minimum of 120 credit hours and a minimum GPA of 2.0 are required for graduation.

Special: Canisius offers internships, credit by exam, pass/fail options, nondegree studies, dual majors, including anthropology/sociology, a Washington semester, work-study programs, and study abroad in 10 countries. Cooperative programs are available with the Fashion Institute of Technology in New York City and the SUNY College of Environmental Science and Forestry in Syracuse. Cross-registration is permitted with 14 schools in the Western New York Consortium of Higher Education. Canisius also offers early assurance and joint degree programs with SUNY health professions schools in Buffalo and Syracuse. There are 9 national honor societies, a freshman honors program, and 2 departmental honors programs.

Faculty/Classroom: 64% of faculty are male; 36%, female. 97% teach undergraduates, 75% do research, and 65% do both. No introductory courses are taught by graduate students. The average class size in an introductory lecture is 24; in a laboratory, 21; and in a regular course, 26.

Admissions: 81% of the 2001-2002 applicants were accepted. The SAT I scores for the 2001-2002 freshman class were: Verbal--31% below 500, 47% between 500 and 599, 20% between 600 and 700, and 2% above 700; Math--26% below 500, 46% between 500 and 599, 25% between 600 and 700, and 3% above 700. The ACT scores were 30% below 21, 25% between 21 and 23, 22% between 24 and 26, 12% between 27 and 28, and 11% above 28. 39% of the current freshmen were in the top fifth of their class; 70% were in the top two fifths. There were 3 National Merit semifinalists. 12 freshmen graduated first in their class.

Requirements: The SAT I or ACT is required. Minimum scores recommended are SAT I composite 800 and 21 ACT. Applicants must have graduated from an accredited secondary school (a GED will be accepted) and have acquired 4 credits in English, 3 to 3 1/2 in math, 2 each in social studies and a foreign language, 1 to 2 in science, and 2 1/2 to 4 in other electives. An essay and an interview are recommended. A GPA of 2.0 is required. AP and CLEP credits are accepted. Important factors in the admissions decision are advanced placement or honor courses, recommendations by school officials, and leadership record. Applications are accepted on computer disk and on-line at the school's web site and via ExPAN, CollegeLink, CollegeView, Apply, and others.

Procedure: Freshmen are admitted fall and spring. Entrance exams should be taken during the junior or senior year. There are early admissions and deferred admissions plans. Application deadlines are open. The fall 2001 application fee was $25. Notification is sent on a rolling basis.

Transfer: 174 transfer students enrolled in 2001-2002. Applicants must present a minimum GPA of 2.0. 30 credits of 120 must be completed at Canisius.

Visiting: There are regularly scheduled orientations for prospective students, including campus weekends, single-day visits, and overnights. Also available are summer visitations for families, an open house in the fall and in the spring, and a financial aid workshop in January. There are guides for informal visits and visitors may sit in on classes and stay overnight. To schedule a visit, contact the Admissions Office.

Financial Aid: In 2001-2002, 96% of all freshmen and 89% of continuing students received some form of financial aid. 85% of freshmen and 86% of continuing students received need-based aid. The average freshman award was $15,870. Of that total, scholarships or need-based grants averaged $11,521 ($16,990 maximum); loans averaged $3446; and work contracts averaged $904 ($2000 maximum). 20% of undergraduates work part time. Average annual earnings from campus work are $1244. The average financial indebtedness of the 2001 graduate was $19,782. Canisius is a member of CSS. The FAFSA and the college's own financial statement are required. The fall application deadline is February 2.

International Students: There are 127 international students enrolled. The school actively recruits these students. They must score 500 on the written TOEFL or 173 on the electronic version if English is not the first language and also take the SAT I or the ACT.

Computers: The mainframe is a Sun SPARC. 14 student-accessible locations contain 131 networked Macs and 150 networked Windows PCs. Student labs are open to all currently registered students; 3 are reserved for residence hall students. Personal network accounts with e-mail and web access are available to all current students. All students may access the system. The Web can be accessed at any time. There are no time limits and no fees. It is strongly recommended that all students have a personal computer.

Graduates: In 2001, 582 bachelor's degrees were awarded. The most popular majors were education (20%), psychology (10%), and communication studies (8%). In an average class, 34% graduate in 4 years, 48% in 5 years, and 52% in 6 years. 55 companies recruited on campus in 2000-2001. Of the 2000 graduating class, 25% were enrolled in graduate school within 6 months of graduation and 60% were employed.

Admissions Contact: Penelope H. Lips, Director of Admissions.
E-mail: *admissions@canisius.edu* Web: *http://www.canisius.edu*

CAZENOVIA COLLEGE

Cazenovia, NY 13035 — C-3

(315) 655-7208
(800) 654-3210; Fax: (315) 655-2190

Full-time: 215 men, 535 women	**Faculty:** 46; IIB, --$
Part-time: 50 men, 110 women	**Ph.D.s:** 63%
Graduate: none	**Student/Faculty:** 16 to 1
Year: semesters, summer session	**Tuition:** $13,385
Application Deadline: open	**Room & Board:** $6500
Freshman Class: 978 applied, 840 accepted, 748 enrolled	
SAT I Verbal/Math: 455/446	**ACT:** 19 **LESS COMPETITIVE**

Cazenovia College, founded in 1824, is a private institution offering degree programs in applied arts and sciences and preprofessional studies. The library contains more than 64,000 volumes, nearly 13,000 microform items, and more than 3000 audiovisual forms/CDs, and subscribes to 456 periodicals. Computerized library services include interlibrary loans and database searching. Special learning facilities include a learning resource center, art gallery, radio station, and and nearby campus farm with equine center. The 40-acre campus is in a small town 18 miles southeast of Syracuse. Including residence halls, there are 24 buildings.

Student Life: 88% of undergraduates are from New York. Others are from 20 states and 2 foreign countries. 91% are from public schools. 84% are white. The average age of freshmen is 18. 33% do not continue beyond their first year; 32% remain to graduate.

Housing: 600 students can be accommodated in college housing, which includes single-sex and coed dormitories and on-campus apartments. In addition, there is a quiet building, a wellness center, a global awareness cluster, an all-female residence hall, and an upperclass-only section. On-campus housing is guaranteed for all 4 years. 76% of students live on campus; of those, 60% remain on campus on weekends. Alcohol is not permitted. All students may keep cars.

Activities: There are no fraternities or sororities. There are many groups and organizations on campus, including cheerleading, chorale, computers, drama, ethnic, gay, honors, literary magazine, musical theater, newspaper, political, social service, student government, and yearbook. Popular campus events include Spring Day, Parents Weekend, and athletic events.

Sports: There are 5 intercollegiate sports for men and 6 for women, and 8 intramural sports for men and 9 for women. Facilities include an athletic center that houses an Olympic-size pool, 2 gyms, a weight room, 2 racquetball courts, outdoor tennis courts, and athletic fields.

Disabled Students: 86% of the campus is accessible. Wheelchair ramps, elevators, special parking, specially equipped rest rooms, special class scheduling, lowered telephones, and special dormitory facilities are available.

Services: Counseling and information services are available, as is tutoring in every subject. There is a reader service for the blind, and remedial math, reading, and writing.

Campus Safety and Security: Measures include escort service, informal discussions, pamphlets/posters/films, and emergency telephones. There are lighted pathways/sidewalks and a night foot patrol.

Programs of Study: Cazenovia confers B.A., B.S., B.F.A., and B.P.S. degrees. Associate degrees are also awarded. Bachelor's degrees are awarded in BUSINESS (management science), COMMUNICATIONS AND THE ARTS (English and studio art), EDUCATION (early childhood and elementary), ENGINEERING AND ENVIRONMENTAL DESIGN (commercial art and interior design), SOCIAL SCIENCE (human services, liberal arts/general studies, psychology, and social science). Interior design, liberal arts, and human services are the strongest academically. Graphic design is the largest.

Required: A total of 120 semester credits and a GPA of 2.0 are required for the bachelor's degree. Students must take courses in speech, academic writing, diversity and social consciousness, science or math, visual literacy, communications, ethics, cultural literacy, and research methods. They must also demonstrate math proficiency and complete a senior capstone course.

Special: Cazenovia offers internships, a Washington semester, work-study, B.A.-B.S. degrees in liberal studies and liberal and professional studies, and study abroad. There is cross-registration with the American International University in London and the Institute for Experimental Learning. There is 1 national honor society, a freshman honors program, and 2 departmental honors programs.

Faculty/Classroom: 39% of faculty are male; 61%, female. All teach undergraduates and 1% also do research. The average class size in an introductory lecture is 28; in a laboratory, 15; and in a regular course, 22.

Admissions: 86% of the 2001-2002 applicants were accepted. The SAT I scores for the 2001-2002 freshman class were: Verbal--72% below 500, 21% between 500 and 599, and 7% between 600 and 700; Math--

74% below 500, 24% between 500 and 599, and 2% between 600 and 700. The ACT scores were 75% below 21, 18% between 21 and 23, 4% between 24 and 26, and 3% between 27 and 28.
Requirements: The SAT I or ACT is recommended. In addition, applicants should be graduates of an accredited secondary school or the equivalent. A recommendation from a guidance counselor or teacher is required. A GPA of 2.0 is required. AP and CLEP credits are accepted. Important factors in the admissions decision are evidence of special talent, personality/intangible qualities, and recommendations by school officials.
Procedure: Freshmen are admitted fall and spring. Entrance exams should be taken by the fall of the senior year. There are early admissions and deferred admissions plans. Application deadlines are open, but priority is given to applications filed before March 1. The application fee is $25. Notification is on a rolling basis. 5% of all applicants are on a waiting list.
Transfer: 58 transfer students enrolled in 2001-2002. Applicants must present at least 12 college credits, with a minimum GPA of 2.0, and official transcripts from previous colleges attended. Students with fewer than 24 credits must also submit a high school transcript. 30 credits of 120 must be completed at Cazenovia.
Visiting: There are regularly scheduled orientations for prospective students, consisting of a welcome by the president and deans, financial aid sessions, placement testing, academic advising, and registration. There are guides for informal visits and visitors may sit in on classes and stay overnight. To schedule a visit, contact the Admissions and Financial Aid Office.
Financial Aid: In 2001-2002, 85% of all freshmen and 97% of continuing students received some form of financial aid. 82% of freshmen and 93% of continuing students received need-based aid. The average freshman award was $11,664. Of that total, scholarships or need-based grants averaged $9943 ($19,650 maximum); loans averaged $2625 (maximum); and work contracts averaged $1000 (maximum). 22% of undergraduates work part time. Average annual earnings from campus work are $1000. The average financial indebtedness of the 2001 graduate was $14,808. The FAFSA and Express TAP are required. The fall application deadline is March 15.
International Students: There are 2 international students enrolled. They must score 550 on the written TOEFL and also take the SAT I or the ACT.
Computers: The mainframe is a networked IBM-type LAN. Students access a network designed for the computer lab that houses approximately 70 PCs. Network access is also available in residence halls and is linked to the Internet. All students may access the system daily from 8 A.M. to midnight. There are no time limits. The fee is $100.
Graduates: In 2001, 106 bachelor's degrees were awarded. 23 companies recruited on campus in 2000-2001.
Admissions Contact: Robert A. Croot, Dean for Admissions and Financial Aid. E-mail: *admission@cazcollege.edu*
Web: *www.cazcollege.edu*

CITY UNIVERSITY OF NEW YORK

The City University of New York (CUNY), established in 1847, is a public system in New York City. It is governed by a board of trustees whose chief administrator is the chancellor. The primary goal of the system is to maintain and expand its commitment to academic excellence and to the provision of equal access and opportunity. The main priorities are providing access for all students who seek to enroll, ensuring student success, and enhancing instructional and research excellence. The total enrollment of all 21 campuses is 200,000, with nearly 6000 faculty members. There are some 600 baccalaureate, 350 master's, and 50 doctoral programs offered. Profiles of the 4-year campuses (located in New York's 5 boroughs of Manhattan, Brooklyn, Queens, Staten Island and the Bronx) appear in this section.

CITY UNIVERSITY OF NEW YORK/BARUCH COLLEGE D-5

New York, NY 10010-5585 **(646) 312-1400**

Full-time: 3935 men, 5019 women	**Faculty:** 405
Part-time: 1725 men, 2509 women	**Ph.D.s:** 87%
Graduate: 1388 men, 1390 women	**Student/Faculty:** 22 to 1
Year: semesters, summer session	**Tuition:** $3275 ($6875)
Application Deadline: May 1	**Room & Board:** n/app
Freshman Class: 15,337 applied, 5045 accepted, 1725 enrolled	
SAT I Verbal/Math: 500/540	**VERY COMPETITIVE+**

Baruch College was founded in 1919 and became a separate unit of the City University of New York in 1968. It offers undergraduate programs in business and public administration, liberal arts and sciences, and public administration. There are 3 undergraduate and 3 graduate schools. In addition to regional accreditation, Baruch has baccalaureate program accreditation with AACSB. The library contains 427,268 volumes, 2,064,811 microform items, and 1017 audiovisual forms/CDs, and subscribes to 4154 periodicals. Computerized library services include the card catalog, interlibrary loans, and database searching. Special learning facilities include a learning resource center, art gallery, and radio station. The campus is in Manhattan. There are 6 buildings.
Student Life: 90% of undergraduates are from New York. Others are from 15 states, 144 foreign countries, and Canada. 70% are from public schools. 26% are Asian American; 26% white; 20% Hispanic; 17% African American; 11% foreign nationals. The average age of freshmen is 18; all undergraduates, 23. 16% do not continue beyond their first year.
Housing: There are no residence halls. All students commute. Alcohol is not permitted. No one may keep cars.
Activities: 1% of men belong to 1 local fraternity and 2 national fraternities; 1% of women belong to 1 local sorority and 2 national sororities. There are 98 groups on campus, including cheerleading, chess, chorus, computers, drama, ethnic, gay, honors, international, literary magazine, newspaper, photography, political, professional, radio and TV, religious, social, social service, student government, and yearbook. Popular campus events include club fairs, street fairs, and Caribbean Week.
Sports: There are 5 intercollegiate sports for men and 5 for women, and 4 intramural sports for men and 2 for women. Facilities include a gym, a swimming pool, a weight room, an exercise room, and racquetball courts.
Disabled Students: All of the campus is accessible. Wheelchair ramps, elevators, specially equipped rest rooms, and special class scheduling are available.
Services: Counseling and information services are available, as is tutoring in most subjects. There is a reader service for the blind, and remedial math, reading, and writing. Note takers, large-print computer screens, and interpreters for the deaf are available.
Campus Safety and Security: Measures include 24-hour foot and vehicle patrol, self-defense education, escort service, and informal discussions. There are pamphlets/posters/films, lighted pathways/sidewalks, emergency phones, fire safety directors, and an ID system that uses card swipe in turnstiles for entry.
Programs of Study: Baruch confers B.A., B.S., and B.B.A. degrees. Master's and doctoral degrees are also awarded. Bachelor's degrees are awarded in BUSINESS (accounting, investments and securities, management science, marketing management, marketing/retailing/merchandising, operations research, personnel management, and real estate), COMMUNICATIONS AND THE ARTS (advertising, communications, English, journalism, music, and Spanish), COMPUTER AND PHYSICAL SCIENCE (actuarial science, information sciences and systems, mathematics, and statistics), SOCIAL SCIENCE (economics, history, industrial and organizational psychology, philosophy, political science/government, psychology, public affairs, and sociology). Economics, English, and math are the strongest academically. Accounting, finance, and computer information systems are the largest.
Required: Students must complete a minimum of 120 credits for the B.A. or B.S., and 124 for the B.B.A., with at least 24 hours in the major, and maintain a GPA of 2.0 overall in the major. Students' core curriculum should include courses in English, literature, communications, history, philosophy, and fine and performing arts.
Special: Students may take courses at all CUNY schools. The college offers internships and study abroad in Great Britain, France, Germany, Mexico, and Israel. Students may design their own liberal arts major. A federal work-study program is available, and pass/fail options are permitted for liberal arts majors. Students may combine any undergraduate major with a masters in accountancy. There are 7 national honor societies, and a freshman honors program. Most departments have honors programs.
Faculty/Classroom: 65% of faculty are male; 35%, female. 93% teach undergraduates. Graduate students teach 4% of introductory courses. The average class size in an introductory lecture is 250; in a laboratory, 20; and in a regular course, 35.
Admissions: 33% of the 2001-2002 applicants were accepted. The SAT I scores for the 2001-2002 freshman class were: Verbal--48% below 500, 40% between 500 and 599, 11% between 600 and 700, and 1% above 700; Math--22% below 500, 47% between 500 and 599, 27% between 600 and 700, and 4% above 700. 36% of the current freshmen were in the top fifth of their class; 89% were in the top two fifths. 45 freshmen graduated first in their class.
Requirements: The SAT I is required. In addition, applicants must present an official high school transcript (a GED will be accepted) indicating a minimum average grade of 81% in academic subjects (minimum of 14 credits). A grade average of 82 is required. AP and CLEP credits are accepted.
Procedure: Freshmen are admitted fall and spring. Entrance exams should be taken March 1. There is an early decision plan. Applications should be filed by May 1 for fall entry and November 5 for spring entry. The fall 2001 application fee was $40. Notification of early decision is sent January 4; regular decision, February 1.
Transfer: 1102 transfer students enrolled in 2001-2002. All other applicants must have a minimum GPA of 2.5 for 12 to 34.9 credits submitted, a minimum GPA of 2.25 for 35 to 59.9 credits, and a minimum GPA of

2.0 for 60 or more credits. Business applicants must have a 2.75 GPA. Students applying for transfer with fewer than 12 credits earned must have a minimum GPA of 2.5 and a minimum high school average of 80%. 32 credits of 128 must be completed at Baruch.
Visiting: There are regularly scheduled orientations for prospective students, including a meeting with an admissions counselor. There are guides for informal visits. To schedule a visit, contact the Admissions Office.
Financial Aid: In 2001-2002, 92% of all freshmen and 68% of continuing students received some form of financial aid. 67% of freshmen and 59% of continuing students received need-based aid. The average freshman award was $2060. Of that total, scholarships or need-based grants averaged $5400; loans averaged $1500; and work contracts averaged $900. 75% of undergraduates work part time. Average annual earnings from campus work are $2500. The average financial indebtedness of the 2001 graduate was $9660. Baruch is a member of CSS. The FAFSA is required. The fall application deadline is May 1.
International Students: There are 1185 international students enrolled. They must score 620 on the written TOEFL or 260 on the electronic version and also take the college's own test.
Computers: There are 1,200 PCs available in the computer center, media center, resource center, library, computer labs, and classrooms throughout the entire campus for student use. All students may access the system. There are no time limits and no fees.
Graduates: In 2001, 2356 bachelor's degrees were awarded. The most popular majors were accounting (29%), finance and investments (15%), and human resource management (9%). In an average class, 5% graduate in 4 years, 23% in 5 years, and 35% in 6 years. 350 companies recruited on campus in 2000-2001.
Admissions Contact: James Murphy, Director of Undergraduate Admissions and Financial Aid. A video is available.
E-mail: *jmurphy@baruch.cuny.edu*

CITY UNIVERSITY OF NEW YORK/BROOKLYN COLLEGE D-5

Brooklyn, NY 11210-2889 (718) 951-5001; Fax: (718) 951-4506

Full-time: 2668 men, 4049 women	**Faculty:** 516
Part-time: 1204 men, 2191 women	**Ph.D.s:** 100%
Graduate: 1514 men, 3511 women	**Student/Faculty:** 13 to 1
Year: semesters, summer session	**Tuition:** $3403 ($7003)
Application Deadline: open	**Room & Board:** n/app
Freshman Class: n/av	
SAT I or ACT: required	**LESS COMPETITIVE**

Brooklyn College, established in 1930, is a publicly supported college of liberal arts, sciences, preprofessional, and professional studies. It is part of the City University of New York and serves the commuter student. There are 2 undergraduate schools and 1 graduate school. In addition to regional accreditation, Brooklyn College has baccalaureate program accreditation with ADA. The library contains 1,305,602 volumes, 1,624,712 microform items, and 21,731 audiovisual forms/CDs, and subscribes to 9374 (electronic) and 4167 (print) periodicals. Computerized library services include the card catalog, interlibrary loans, and database searching. Special learning facilities include a learning resource center, art gallery, radio station, TV station, 3 color studios, and a speech and hearing clinic. The 26-acre campus is in an urban area in Brooklyn, New York. There are 8 buildings.
Student Life: 95% of undergraduates are from New York. Others are from 20 states, 65 foreign countries, and Canada. 74% are from public schools. 47% are white; 28% African American; 11% Hispanic. The average age of freshmen is 19; all undergraduates, 25. 19% do not continue beyond their first year; 81% remain to graduate.
Housing: There are no residence halls. All students commute. Alcohol is not permitted. No one may keep cars.
Activities: 2% of men belong to 1 local fraternity and 6 national fraternities; 2% of women belong to 4 local and 3 national sororities. There are 150 groups on campus, including academic, art, choir, chorus, computers, dance, drama, ethnic, film, gay, honors, literary magazine, musical theater, newspaper, orchestra, photography, political, professional, radio and TV, religious, social, social service, student government, symphony, and yearbook. Popular campus events include Country Fair, Fall Festival, and Black Solidarity Day.
Sports: There are 8 intercollegiate sports for men and 8 for women, and 8 intramural sports for men and 8 for women. Facilities include swimming pools, a soccer field, volleyball, racquetball, squash, tennis, and basketball courts, a weight-training room, and a jogging track.
Disabled Students: All of the campus is accessible. Wheelchair ramps, elevators, special parking, specially equipped rest rooms, special class scheduling, lowered drinking fountains, and lowered telephones are available.
Services: Counseling and information services are available, as is tutoring in every subject. There is a reader service for the blind.
Campus Safety and Security: Measures include 24-hour foot and vehicle patrol, escort service, shuttle buses, and informal discussions. There are pamphlets/posters/films, emergency telephones, and lighted pathways/sidewalks.
Programs of Study: Brooklyn College confers B.A., B.S., B.F.A., and B.M. degrees. Master's degrees are also awarded. Bachelor's degrees are awarded in BIOLOGICAL SCIENCE (biology/biological science), BUSINESS (accounting, banking and finance, and business administration and management), COMMUNICATIONS AND THE ARTS (art, art history and appreciation, broadcasting, classics, comparative literature, creative writing, dance, dramatic arts, English, film arts, French, German, Greek, Hebrew, Italian, journalism, languages, Latin, linguistics, music, music performance, music theory and composition, radio/television technology, Russian, Spanish, speech/debate/rhetoric, theater management, and visual and performing arts), COMPUTER AND PHYSICAL SCIENCE (applied mathematics, chemistry, computer science, geology, information sciences and systems, mathematics, and physics), EDUCATION (art, bilingual/bicultural, early childhood, education of the deaf and hearing impaired, elementary, English, foreign languages, health, mathematics, music, physical, science, secondary, social studies, and special), ENGINEERING AND ENVIRONMENTAL DESIGN (preengineering), HEALTH PROFESSIONS (health science, predentistry, premedicine, and speech pathology/audiology), SOCIAL SCIENCE (African studies, American studies, anthropology, archeology, Caribbean studies, economics, Hispanic American studies, history, Judaic studies, Latin American studies, philosophy, political science/government, prelaw, psychology, religion, sociology, urban studies, and women's studies). Education, business, and computer science are the strongest academically and have the largest enrollments.
Required: 10 required, interrelated courses cover the following core curriculum areas: classics, art, music, political science, sociology, history, literature, math, computer science, chemistry, physics, biology, geology, philosophy, and comparative cultures. There are basic skills requirements in reading, composition, speech, and math, as well as a foreign language requirement. A 2.0 GPA and a minimum of 120 credit hours, with 31 to 36 in the major, are required to graduate.
Special: There are numerous cooperative and cross-registration programs with colleges and universities in the area. Many internships and work-study programs are available. Study abroad is possible in Israel, Paris, Puerto Rico, and Africa. Summer programs are available in London, Florence, Madrid, Tokyo, and Ireland. A B.A.-M.D., B.S.-M.P.S., and accelerated B.A.-M.A. programs are available. A number of B.A.-B.S. degrees, dual majors, a 3-2 engineering degree, and student-designed majors are possible. Credit by exam, credit for life experience, nondegree study, and pass/fail options are offered. There are 13 national honor societies, including Phi Beta Kappa, a freshman honors program, and 26 departmental honors programs.
Faculty/Classroom: 58% of faculty are male; 42%, female. 80% teach undergraduates and 80% do research. The average class size in a laboratory is 15 and in a regular course, 35.
Requirements: The SAT is required with a composite score of 960 (480 verbal and 480 math). Alternatively, the ACT is accepted with 20-20 verbal and math scores. The GED, with a score of 300 or higher, is accepted. Requirements are higher for B.A.-M.D. entrants and for the scholars program. Applicants not meeting the standard requirements are eligible for admission to the City University's community colleges. AP and CLEP credits are accepted.
Procedure: Freshmen are admitted fall and spring. Entrance exams should be taken prior to admission. There is an early admissions plan. Application deadlines are open. The application fee is $40. Notification is sent on a rolling basis.
Transfer: 1090 transfer students enrolled in 2001-2002. Transfer students must have a minimum 2.0 GPA with 24 or more credits; 2.25 with 15 to 23 credits; and 2.5 with 7 to 14 credits. Students with less than 7 credits must have an acceptable high school average and a 2.0 college GPA. 48 credits of 120 must be completed at Brooklyn College.
Visiting: There are regularly scheduled orientations for prospective students. There are guides for informal visits. To schedule a visit, contact the Office of Admissions.
Financial Aid: In 2001-2002, 67% of all freshmen and 63% of continuing students received some form of financial aid. 65% of freshmen and 64% of continuing students received need-based aid. The average freshman award was $4674. Of that total, scholarships or need-based grants averaged $3600 ($7150 maximum); loans averaged $1000 ($6625 maximum); and work contracts averaged $800 ($2000 maximum). 71% of undergraduates work part time. Average annual earnings from campus work are $1100. The average financial indebtedness of the 2001 graduate was $9500. The FAFSA is required. The fall application deadline is March 1.
International Students: There are 366 international students enrolled. The school actively recruits these students. They must score 500 on the written TOEFL and also take the college's own test and the SAT I or the ACT, scoring 960 on the SAT I or 20 on the ACT.
Computers: The Office of Information Technology Services (ITS) has labs containing 300 networked PCs, all of which provide Internet access, and provide a full complement of adaptive equipment for students with special needs. Wired and wireless connectivity is available for students

who wish to use their own laptops. A variety of software applications is available, along with assistance by expert lab technicians, free laser printing, and videoconferencing. Additionally, the Student Union Building Learning Center has 40 Internet-equipped computers and several color printers and has 12 workstations. Additional computers are available in the library and individual academic departments. All students may access the system. Students may access the system 1 hour, when other students are waiting. There are no fees.

Graduates: In 2001, 1421 bachelor's degrees were awarded. The most popular majors were education (15%), psychology (13%), and business (13%). 68 companies recruited on campus in 2000-2001.

Admissions Contact: Marianne Booufall Tynan, Director of Admissions. E-mail: *adminqry@brooklyn.cuny.edu*
Web: *www.brooklyn.cuny.edu*

CITY UNIVERSITY OF NEW YORK/CITY COLLEGE D-5

New York, NY 10031 (212) 650-6977; Fax: (212) 650-6417

Full-time: 2622 men, 2432 women	**Faculty:** 473
Part-time: 1336 men, 1677 women	**Ph.D.s:** 85%
Graduate: 971 men, 1445 women	**Student/Faculty:** 11 to 1
Year: semesters, summer session	**Tuition:** $3309 ($6909)
Application Deadline: December 1	**Room & Board:** n/app
Freshman Class: 735 enrolled	
SAT I: required	**LESS COMPETITIVE**

City College, founded in 1847, is a public liberal arts college that is part of the City University of New York. The college offers programs through 4 undergraduate and 4 graduate schools and 2 professional centers. In addition to regional accreditation, CCNY has baccalaureate program accreditation with ABET, ABFSE, NAAB, and NCATE. The 4 libraries contain 1,397,720 volumes, 838,027 microform items, and 19,586 audiovisual forms/CDs, and subscribe to 2207 periodicals. Computerized library services include the card catalog, interlibrary loans, and database searching. Special learning facilities include an art gallery, planetarium, radio station, TV station, weather station, laser labs, and microwave labs. The 34-acre campus is in an urban area in New York City. There are 14 buildings.

Student Life: 87% of undergraduates are from New York. Others are from 49 states, 60 foreign countries, and Canada. 90% are from public schools. 30% are African American; 26%, Hispanic; 13%, Asian American. The average age of freshmen is 18; all undergraduates, 27. 10% do not continue beyond their first year.

Housing: There are no residence halls. Alcohol is not permitted.

Activities: There are no fraternities or sororities. There are 100 groups on campus, including art, band, cheerleading, chess, chorus, computers, drama, ethnic, gay, honors, international, jazz band, literary magazine, newspaper, orchestra, political, professional, radio and TV, religious, social, social service, student government, and yearbook. Popular campus events include Langston Hughes Poetry Contest and Dance Theater of Harlem performances at Davis Center.

Sports: There are 6 intercollegiate sports for men and 4 for women. Facilities include swimming pools, 2 gyms, and a weight room.

Disabled Students: 90% of the campus is accessible. Wheelchair ramps, elevators, special parking, specially equipped rest rooms, special class scheduling, lowered drinking fountains, and lowered telephones are available.

Services: Counseling and information services are available, as is tutoring in most subjects, including science, economics, engineering, and math. There is a reader service for the blind.

Campus Safety and Security: Measures include 24-hour foot and vehicle patrol, escort service, shuttle buses, and informal discussions. There are pamphlets/posters/films and emergency telephones.

Programs of Study: CCNY confers B.A., B.S., B.Arch., B.E., B.F.A., and B.S.Ed. degrees. Master's degrees are also awarded. Bachelor's degrees are awarded in BIOLOGICAL SCIENCE (biology/biological science), BUSINESS (business administration and management), COMMUNICATIONS AND THE ARTS (communications, comparative literature, dramatic arts, English, film arts, fine arts, French, music, and Spanish), COMPUTER AND PHYSICAL SCIENCE (chemistry, computer science, earth science, geology, mathematics, and physics), EDUCATION (art, early childhood, elementary, foreign languages, secondary, and special), ENGINEERING AND ENVIRONMENTAL DESIGN (chemical engineering, civil engineering, electrical/electronics engineering, and mechanical engineering), HEALTH PROFESSIONS (predentistry and premedicine), SOCIAL SCIENCE (anthropology, Asian/Oriental studies, economics, ethnic studies, history, international studies, Latin American studies, philosophy, political science/government, prelaw, psychology, and sociology). Engineering, architecture, and sciences are the strongest academically. Engineering, architecture, and psychology are the largest.

Required: Students must successfully complete 120 credits, with 32 to 48 in the major, and maintain a minimum GPA of 2.0. A core curriculum must be met, and students must complete courses in basic writing, world humanities, world civilizations, computer literacy, world arts, and U.S. society.

Special: Cross-registration is permitted with other City University colleges. A 6-year urban legal studies degree and a 7-year biomedical education degree are available. Opportunities are provided for internships, a Washington semester, work-study programs, a wide variety of accelerated degree programs, credit by exam, credit for life experience, and study abroad in Europe, China, Africa, the Dominican Republic, and Japan. There is a chapter of Phi Beta Kappa and a freshman honors program.

Faculty/Classroom: 62% of faculty are male; 38%, female. No introductory courses are taught by graduate students. The average class size in an introductory lecture is 135 and in a regular course, 25.

Admissions: The SAT I scores for the 2001-2002 freshman class were: Verbal--62% below 500, 25% between 500 and 599, 11% between 600 and 700, and 2% above 700; Math--48% below 500, 31% between 500 and 599, 15% between 600 and 700, and 5% above 700. 26% of the current freshmen were in the top fifth of their class; 51% were in the top two fifths.

Requirements: A minimum composite SAT I score of 1100 or an ACT score of 22 is recommended. Graduation from an accredited secondary school is generally required, but a GED will be accepted. 14 academic credits should be presented, with a minimum grade average of 80%. A GPA of 80.0 is required. AP credits are accepted. Applications are accepted on-line at *www.applyto.uapc.cuny.edu*

Procedure: Freshmen are admitted fall and spring. Entrance exams should be taken prior to registration. There is an early admissions plan. Applications should be filed by December 1 for fall entry and October 15 for spring entry. Notification is sent on a rolling basis. The fall application fee was $40.

Transfer: 839 transfer students enrolled in 2001-2002. Transfer applicants must have earned a minimum of 24 credit hours and maintained a GPA of 2.0. Selected programs have more competitive requirements. 32 credits of 120 must be completed at CCNY.

Visiting: There are regularly scheduled orientations for prospective students. There are guides for informal visits and visitors may sit in on classes. To schedule a visit, contact the Admissions Office at (212) 650-6476.

Financial Aid: In a recent year, 65% of all freshmen and 75% of continuing students received some form of financial aid. The average freshman award was $6005. The college's own financial statement is required.

International Students: There are 516 international students enrolled. They must score 500 on the written TOEFL.

Computers: The mainframe is an IBM 3090 located at the City University central computer facility. A campuswide fiber-optic network is the backbone; more than 4000 PCs are networked throughout campus; 50 computer languages are available. All students may access the system. There are no time limits.

Graduates: In 2001, 1109 bachelor's degrees were awarded. 100 companies recruited on campus in 2000-2001. Of the 2000 graduating class, 14% were enrolled in graduate school within 6 months of graduation.

Admissions Contact: Director of Admissions. A video is available.
E-mail: *admissions@admin.ccny.cuny.edu* Web: *www.ccny.cuny.edu*

CITY UNIVERSITY OF NEW YORK/COLLEGE OF STATEN ISLAND D-5

Staten Island, NY 10314 (718) 982-2010; Fax: (718) 982-2500

Full-time: 2828 men, 3435 women	**Faculty:** 313
Part-time: 1191 men, 2422 women	**Ph.D.s:** 97%
Graduate: 287 men, 1121 women	**Student/Faculty:** 19 to 1
Year: semesters, summer session	**Tuition:** $3358 ($6958)
Application Deadline: open	**Room & Board:** n/app
Freshman Class: n/av	
SAT I Verbal/Math: 430/440	**NONCOMPETITIVE**

The College of Staten Island, a public institution founded in 1955, is committed to excellence. It offers associate, baccalaureate, and master degrees and Ph.D.s in conjunction with CUNY Graduate Center. In addition to regional accreditation, CSI has baccalaureate program accreditation with ABET, APTA, CAHEA, NAACLS, and NLNAC. The library contains 212,554 volumes, 877,357 microform items, and 14,500 audiovisual forms/CDs, and subscribes to 994 periodicals. Computerized library services include the card catalog, interlibrary loans, and database searching. Special learning facilities include an art gallery, planetarium, and radio station. The 204-acre campus is in an urban area in New York City's borough of Staten Island. There are 19 buildings.

Student Life: 99% of undergraduates are from New York. Others are from 12 states, 116 foreign countries, and Canada. 48% are white. Most are Catholic. The average age of freshmen is 23; all undergraduates, 25. 18% do not continue beyond their first year; 44% remain to graduate.

Housing: There are no residence halls. All students commute. Alcohol is not permitted. All students may keep cars.

Activities: There are no fraternities or sororities. There are 41 groups on campus, including art, chorus, computers, dance, drama, ethnic, film, gay, honors, international, jazz band, literary magazine, newspaper, photography, political, professional, radio and TV, religious, social, social service, student government, and yearbook. Popular campus events include Kwanzaa, Spring Festival, and cultural dances.

Sports: There are 5 intercollegiate sports for men and 5 for women, and 16 intramural sports for men and 16 for women. Facilities include a 1200-seat gym, an indoor pool, baseball, soccer, and football fields, tennis courts, outdoor recreational basketball courts, shuffleboard and bocce courts, outdoor track and field facilities, 4 volleyball fields, a softball field, an ancillary gym, and a softball field.

Disabled Students: 95% of the campus is accessible. Wheelchair ramps, elevators, special parking, specially equipped rest rooms, special class scheduling, lowered drinking fountains, lowered telephones, and wheelchair accessible campus bus, assistance with registration, and special accommodations in computer labs are available.

Services: Counseling and information services are available, as is tutoring in most subjects. There is a reader service for the blind, and remedial math, reading, and writing.

Campus Safety and Security: Measures include 24-hour foot and vehicle patrol, escort service, shuttle buses, and informal discussions. There are pamphlets/posters/films, emergency telephones, lighted pathways/sidewalks, and an emergency "blue light" system, radar-controlled traffic monitoring, and bicycle patrol.

Programs of Study: CSI confers B.A., B.S. degrees. Associate, master's, and doctoral degrees are also awarded. Bachelor's degrees are awarded in BIOLOGICAL SCIENCE (biochemistry and biology/biological science), BUSINESS (accounting and business administration and management), COMMUNICATIONS AND THE ARTS (art, communications, dramatic arts, English, film arts, music, and Spanish), COMPUTER AND PHYSICAL SCIENCE (chemistry, computer science, information sciences and systems, mathematics, and physics), EDUCATION (education), ENGINEERING AND ENVIRONMENTAL DESIGN (engineering and applied science), HEALTH PROFESSIONS (medical technology, nursing, physical therapy, and physician's assistant), SOCIAL SCIENCE (African American studies, American studies, economics, history, international studies, liberal arts/general studies, philosophy, political science/government, psychology, social work, sociology, and women's studies). Business, education, and psychology are the largest.

Required: The curriculum varies for each degree, but phys ed and English are required for all majors as well as courses from each of three areas: science/technology/math, social sciences/history/philosophy, and humanities. A minimum 2.0 GPA and 120 credit hours are required to graduate.

Special: Internships are available in most fields. Study abroad is possible in Italy, Ecuador, China, and Greece. There are student-designed majors and interdisciplinary majors, including computer science-math, sociology-anthropology, and science, letters, and society. Credit by exam, credit for life experience, and nondegree study are available. There are 8 national honor societies, a freshman honors program, and 18 departmental honors programs.

Faculty/Classroom: 60% of faculty are male; 40%, female. 94% teach undergraduates, 80% do research, and 78% do both. No introductory courses are taught by graduate students. The average class size in an introductory lecture is 32; in a laboratory, 15; and in a regular course, 26.

Admissions: The SAT I scores for the 2001-2002 freshman class were: Verbal--79% below 500, 18% between 500 and 599, and 3% between 600 and 700; Math--75% below 500, 22% between 500 and 599, and 3% between 600 and 700.

Requirements: All graduates of an accredited secondary school, or students holding a GED equivalent, are accepted for admission. Applicants must have an 80 grade average or graduate in the upper two-thirds of their class to be eligible for admission to the 4-year programs. AP and CLEP credits are accepted.

Procedure: Freshmen are admitted fall and spring. Application deadlines are open. The application fee is $40. Notification is sent on a rolling basis.

Transfer: 505 transfer students enrolled in 2001-2002. Applicants must have a minimum 2.0 GPA. 30 credits of 120 must be completed at CSI.

Visiting: There are regularly scheduled orientations for prospective students, including campus tours, presentations, and lunch. There are guides for informal visits and visitors may sit in on classes. To schedule a visit, contact the Office of Student Recruitment at (718) 982-2259.

Financial Aid: In 2001-2002, 35% of all students received some form of financial aid. 60% of freshmen and 52% of continuing students received need-based aid. The average freshman award was $3863. Of that total, scholarships or need-based grants averaged $2201 ($5580 maximum); loans averaged $1462 ($3475 maximum); and work contracts averaged $200 ($1000 maximum). The FAFSA is required. The fall application deadline is May 31.

International Students: There are 316 international students enrolled. The school actively recruits these students. They must score 550 on the written TOEFL or 213 on the electronic version.

Computers: A total of 1086 Macs and PCs are located in 16 computer labs and 15 academic labs. All are connected to the campuswide system and the Internet. Most students have e-mail accounts. All students may access the system 8 A.M. to midnight Monday through Thursday, 8.a.m to 10 P.M. Friday, 9 A.M. to 5 P.M. Saturday, and noon to 5 P.M. Sunday.

Graduates: In 2001, 911 bachelor's degrees were awarded. The most popular majors were business (17%), education (11%), and psychology (10%). In an average class, 2% graduate in 3 years, 13% in 4 years, 31% in 5 years, and 38% in 6 years. 150 companies recruited on campus in 2000-2001.

Admissions Contact: Mary Beth Riley, Director of Admissions and Recruitment. E-mail: *reilly@postbox.csi.cuny.edu*
Web: *www.csi.cuny.edu/index.htm/*

CITY UNIVERSITY OF NEW YORK/HERBERT H. LEHMAN COLLEGE — D-5

Bronx, NY 10468 — **(718) 960-8700; (718) 960-8712**

Full-time: 4200 men and women	**Faculty:** 296
Part-time: 3000 men and women	**Ph.D.s:** 89%
Graduate: 1860 men and women	**Student/Faculty:** 14 to 1
Year: semesters, summer session	**Tuition:** $3320 ($6920)
Application Deadline: rolling	**Room & Board:** n/app
Freshman Class: n/av	
SAT I or ACT: recommended	**LESS COMPETITIVE**

Lehman College, established in 1968 as an independent unit of the City University of New York, is a commuter institution offering programs in the arts and humanities, natural and social sciences, nursing, and professional studies. There are 5 undergraduate and 4 graduate schools. Figures in the above capsule are approximate. In addition to regional accreditation, Lehman has baccalaureate program accreditation with ADA, CSWE, NCATE, and NLN. The library contains 556,275 volumes, 620,660 microform items, and 1832 audiovisual forms/CDs, and subscribes to 1513 periodicals. Computerized library services include the card catalog and database searching. Special learning facilities include a learning resource center, art gallery, radio station, TV station, and center for performing arts. The 37-acre campus is in an urban area in the Bronx, New York City. There are 15 buildings.

Student Life: Others are from 90 foreign countries. 74% are from public schools. 44% are Hispanic; 33% African American; 16% white. 54% are Catholic; 14% claim no religious affiliation. The average age of freshmen is 20; all undergraduates, 29.

Housing: There are no residence halls. All students commute. Alcohol is not permitted. All students may keep cars.

Activities: There are no fraternities. There are 54 groups on campus, including art, band, chess, choir, chorus, computers, dance, drama, ethnic, film, honors, international, literary magazine, musical theater, newspaper, professional, radio and TV, religious, social, social service, student government, and yearbook.

Sports: There are 9 intercollegiate sports for men and 7 for women, and 9 intramural sports for men and 9 for women. Facilities include 3 gyms, an exercise room, a swimming pool, outdoor tennis courts, soccer and baseball fields, and a dance studio.

Disabled Students: 90% of the campus is accessible. Wheelchair ramps, elevators, special parking, specially equipped rest rooms, and special class scheduling are available.

Services: Counseling and information services are available, as is tutoring in every subject. There is a reader service for the blind, and remedial math, reading, and writing. A writing center offers individual and small group tutorials and workshops.

Campus Safety and Security: Measures include 24-hour foot and vehicle patrol, pamphlets/posters/films, emergency telephones, and lighted pathways/sidewalks.

Programs of Study: Lehman confers B.A., B.S., and B.F.A. degrees. Master's degrees are also awarded. Bachelor's degrees are awarded in BIOLOGICAL SCIENCE (biology/biological science), BUSINESS (accounting, business administration and management, and management science), COMMUNICATIONS AND THE ARTS (communications, comparative literature, dance, English, fine arts, French, German, Greek, Hebrew, Italian, languages, Latin, linguistics, music, Russian, Spanish, and speech/debate/rhetoric), COMPUTER AND PHYSICAL SCIENCE (chemistry, computer science, geology, mathematics, and physics), EDUCATION (art, business, early childhood, elementary, foreign languages, health, science, and secondary), HEALTH PROFESSIONS (health care administration, nursing, predentistry, premedicine, and speech pathology/audiology), SOCIAL SCIENCE (African American studies, American studies, anthropology, dietetics, economics, geography, history, international relations, philosophy, political science/government, prelaw, psychology, social work, and sociology). Economics and accounting, education, and nursing are the largest.

Required: To graduate, students must successfully complete 120 credits, including 64 in the major, with a minimum GPA of 2.0. Requirements include 17 credits of core courses, 8 of English composition, 3 to 10 of a foreign language, and 3 of oral communication, as well as 22 credits distributed among courses in comparative culture, historical studies, social science, natural science, literature, art, and knowledge, self, and values. Students must demonstrate proficiency in basic reading, writing, and math skills before entering the upper division.

Special: Lehman offers internships, study abroad, work-study programs, dual and student-designed majors, nondegree study, pass/fail options, and credit for life experience. A 3-2 social work degree is offered in conjunction with the senior college of CUNY, Bard, and Sarah Lawrence. Transfer programs in preengineering, prepharmacy, and preenvironmental science and forestry allow students to complete their degrees at specialized colleges of other New York universities. There are 21 national honor societies, including Phi Beta Kappa, a freshman honors program, and 60 departmental honors programs.

Faculty/Classroom: 53% of faculty are male; 47%, female. No introductory courses are taught by graduate students. The average class size in an introductory lecture is 25 and in a laboratory, 12.

Requirements: The SAT I or ACT is recommended. This requirement may also be satisfied by an SAT I composite score of 1100. Graduation from an accredited secondary school is required; a GED will be accepted. A grade average of 80 is required. AP and CLEP credits are accepted.

Procedure: Freshmen are admitted fall and spring. Entrance exams should be taken before registration. There are early decision, early admissions, and deferred admissions plans. Notification is sent on a rolling basis. Check with the school for current application deadlines and fee.

Transfer: Applicants must submit all educational records and show a minimum GPA of 2.0 in previous college work. Applicants with fewer than 13 college credits must also have a high school average of 80 in academic subjects. 38 credits of 120 must be completed at Lehman.

Visiting: There are regularly scheduled orientations for prospective students. There are guides for informal visits and visitors may sit in on classes. To schedule a visit, contact the Office of Student Recruitment at (718) 960-8713.

Financial Aid: The college's own financial statement is required. Merit awards are available. Check with the school for current deadlines.

International Students: They must score 500 on the written TOEFL and also take the college's own test.

Computers: The mainframe is a DEC VAX 11/750. There are Mac and PCs located in the Academic Computer Center and specific classrooms. A UNIX-based network includes an IBM PC/RT file server and 8 IBM 6152 RISC workstations. All students may access the system. There are no time limits and no fees.

Graduates: In a recent year, 1156 bachelor's degrees were awarded. The most popular majors were psychology (12%), nursing (10%), and sociology (8%). Of a recent graduating class, 24% were enrolled in graduate school within 6 months of graduation and 73% were employed.

Admissions Contact: Clarence A. Wilkes, Director of Admissions. A video is available. E-mail: *enroll@alpha.lehman.cuny.edu*
Web: *www.lehman.cuny.edu*

CITY UNIVERSITY OF NEW YORK/HUNTER COLLEGE D-5
New York, NY 10021 (212) 772-4490; (800) 772-4000

Full-time: 3091 men, 6996 women	**Faculty:** 584
Part-time: 1650 men, 3966 women	**Ph.D.s:** 85%
Graduate: 1003 men, 3692 women	**Student/Faculty:** 17 to 1
Year: semesters, summer session	**Tuition:** $3350 ($6950)
Application Deadline: see profile	**Room & Board:** $1800
Freshman Class: 8147 applied, 3852 accepted, 1946 enrolled	
SAT I Verbal/Math: 500/500	**COMPETITIVE+**

Hunter College, a comprehensive, nonprofit institution established in 1870, is part of the City University of New York and is both city- and state-supported. Some information in this profile is approximate. Primarily a commuter college, it emphasizes liberal arts in its undergraduate and graduate programs. There are 3 undergraduate and 4 graduate schools. In addition to regional accreditation, Hunter has baccalaureate program accreditation with ADA, APTA, ASLA, CSWE, NCATE, and NLN. The library contains 753,465 volumes, 1,111,737 microform items, and 12,515 audiovisual forms/CDs, and subscribes to 2287 periodicals. Computerized library services include the card catalog and database searching. Special learning facilities include a learning resource center, an art gallery, a radio station, a geography/geology lab, on-campus elementary and secondary schools, and a theater. The 3-acre campus is in an urban area in New York City. Including residence halls, there are 6 buildings.

Student Life: 91% of undergraduates are from New York. Others are from 35 states, 136 foreign countries, and Canada. 36% are white; 24%, Hispanic; 20%, African American; 14%, Asian American. The average age of freshmen is 18; all undergraduates, 25. 23% do not continue beyond their first year; 49% remain to graduate.

Housing: 500 students can be accommodated in college housing, which includes coed dormitories. On-campus housing is available on a first-come, first-served basis and is available on a lottery system for upperclassmen. 99% of students commute. No one may keep cars.

Activities: 2% of men belong to 1 local and 1 national fraternity; 1% of women belong to sororities. There are 130 groups on campus, including art, band, cheerleading, choir, chorale, chorus, drama, ethnic, film, gay, honors, international, jazz band, literary magazine, musical theater, newspaper, orchestra, political, professional, radio and TV, religious, social, social service, student government, symphony, and yearbook. Popular campus events include Major Day Fair.

Sports: There are 9 intercollegiate sports for men and 11 for women. Facilities include fencing, dance, and weight rooms, racquetball courts, a pool, outdoor tennis courts, and a gym.

Disabled Students: All of the campus is accessible. Wheelchair ramps, elevators, special parking, specially equipped rest rooms, special class scheduling, lowered drinking fountains, lowered telephones, special advisement office, and a student organization are available.

Services: Counseling and information services are available, as is tutoring in every subject. There is a reader service for the blind, and remedial math, reading, and writing. Review of graduate-level papers through the writing center and a math tutoring center are available.

Campus Safety and Security: Measures include self-defense education, shuttle buses, pamphlets/posters/films, and emergency telephones. There is a 24-hour foot patrol.

Programs of Study: Hunter confers B.A., B.S., B.F.A., B.Mus., and B.S.Ed degrees. Master's degrees are also awarded. Bachelor's degrees are awarded in BIOLOGICAL SCIENCE (biology/biological science and nutrition), BUSINESS (accounting), COMMUNICATIONS AND THE ARTS (Chinese, classics, comparative literature, creative writing, dance, dramatic arts, English, English literature, film arts, fine arts, French, German, Greek, Hebrew, Italian, languages, Latin, media arts, music, Russian, and Spanish), COMPUTER AND PHYSICAL SCIENCE (chemistry, computer science, mathematics, physics, and statistics), EDUCATION (art, early childhood, elementary, foreign languages, health, middle school, music, science, and secondary), ENGINEERING AND ENVIRONMENTAL DESIGN (energy management technology, environmental science, and preengineering), HEALTH PROFESSIONS (medical laboratory technology, nursing, physical therapy, predentistry, premedicine, and public health), SOCIAL SCIENCE (African American studies, anthropology, archeology, economics, geography, Hispanic American studies, history, international relations, Judaic studies, Latin American studies, philosophy, political science/government, prelaw, psychology, religion, social science, sociology, urban studies, and women's studies). Physical therapy is the strongest academically. Psychology is the largest.

Required: To graduate, students must complete 120 credits (up to 131 for the B.S. degree). The total number of hours in a major varies from 24 credits for a liberal arts major to 63 credits for a professional concentration; a minimum GPA of 2.0 is needed overall and in the major. Distribution requirements include 12 credits of social sciences, up to 12 credits of a foreign language, 10 or more of math and science, 9 of humanities and the arts, 6 of literature, and 3 of English composition.

Special: Special academic programs include internships, student-designed majors, work-study, study abroad in 8 countries, and dual majors. There is cross-registration with the Brooklyn School of Law, Marymount Manhattan College, and the YIVO Institute. Through the National Student Exchange Program, Hunter students can study for 1 or 2 semesters at any of 150 U.S. campuses. Accelerated degree programs are offered in anthropology, biopharmacology, economics, English, history, math, physics, sociology, and social research. Exchange programs in Paris or Puerto Rico are possible. There are 2 national honor societies, including Phi Beta Kappa, a freshman honors program, and 19 departmental honors programs.

Faculty/Classroom: The average class size in a laboratory is 19 and in a regular course, 30.

Admissions: 47% of the 2001-2002 applicants were accepted. The SAT I scores for the 2001-2002 freshman class were: Verbal--52% below 500, 38% between 500 and 599, 9% between 600 and 700, and 1% above 700; Math--48% below 500, 41% between 500 and 599, 10% between 600 and 700, and 1% above 700.

Requirements: The SAT I is required. Admission is based on a combination of high school grade average, high school academic credits, including English and math, and SAT I scores. AP and CLEP credits are accepted.

Procedure: Freshmen are admitted fall and spring. There is an early admissions plan. For priority consideration, applications should be filed by January 15. The fall 2001 application fee was $40.

Transfer: 1531 transfer students enrolled in a recent year. Applicants must have at least a 2.0 GPA. All students must complete 30 of the 120 to 131 credits required for a bachelor's degree at the college, including half of those needed for both the major and the minor.

Visiting: There are regularly scheduled orientations for prospective students, including presentations and tours every Friday. Please call (212) 772-4490 for details. There are guides for informal visits and visitors may sit in on classes. To schedule a visit, contact the Office of Admissions.

Financial Aid: 25% of undergraduates work part time. The college's own financial statement is required. Check with the school for current deadlines.

International Students: International students must score 500 on the written TOEFL and also take the college's own test.

Computers: The mainframes are an IBM 3090 and a Sun. There are 600 PCs networked in 10 computer labs. All students may access the system 24 hours a day. Students may access the system 1 hour when students are waiting. The fee is $25.

Graduates: In a recent year, 1799 bachelor's degrees were awarded. The most popular majors were psychology (15%), English (11%), and sociology (10%).

Admissions Contact: Office of Admissions.
E-mail: *admissions@hunter.cuny.edu* Web: *www.hunter.cuny.edu*

CITY UNIVERSITY OF NEW YORK/JOHN JAY COLLEGE OF CRIMINAL JUSTICE D-5

New York, NY 10019 (212) 237-8878; Fax: (212) 237-8777

Full-time: 2669 men, 4420 women | **Faculty:** 275
Part-time: 1533 men, 1806 women | **Ph.D.s:** 85%
Graduate: 391 men, 650 women | **Student/Faculty:** 26 to 1
Year: semesters, summer session | **Tuition:** $3300 ($6900)
Application Deadline: open | **Room & Board:** n/app
Freshman Class: 3339 applied, 2733 accepted, 1357 enrolled
SAT I Verbal/Math: 459/442 **COMPETITIVE**

John Jay College of Criminal Justice, established in 1964, is a liberal arts college and part of the City University of New York, with special emphasis in the fields of criminology, forensic science, correction administration, and other areas of the criminal justice system. Some information in this profile is approximate. There are 5 graduate schools. The library contains 215,609 volumes, 198,832 microform items, and 3000 audiovisual forms/CDs, and subscribes to 10,335 periodicals. Computerized library services include the card catalog, interlibrary loans, and database searching. Special learning facilities include a learning resource center, art gallery, radio station, TV station, fire science lab, security technology lab, and explosion-proof forensic science/toxicology lab. The 1-acre campus is in an urban area in midtown Manhattan. There are 3 buildings.

Student Life: 95% of undergraduates are from New York. 80% are from public schools. 37% are Hispanic; 29%, African American; 24%, white. The average age of freshmen is 19; all undergraduates, 24. 20% do not continue beyond their first year; 40% remain to graduate.

Housing: There are no residence halls. All students commute. All students may keep cars.

Activities: There are no fraternities or sororities. There are 26 groups on campus, including art, cheerleading, chess, choir, chorale, chorus, computers, dance, drama, ethnic, film, gay, honors, international, literary magazine, musical theater, newspaper, photography, political, professional, radio and TV, religious, social, social service, student government, and yearbook.

Sports: There are 5 intercollegiate sports for men and 5 for women, and 15 intramural sports for men and 15 for women. Facilities include 2 gyms, 2 racquetball courts, a fitness center, a swimming pool, a strength training center, and a rooftop outdoor tennis court and jogging track.

Disabled Students: 99% of the campus is accessible. Wheelchair ramps, elevators, special parking, specially equipped rest rooms, special class scheduling, lowered drinking fountains, and lowered telephones are available.

Services: Counseling and information services are available, as is tutoring in most subjects, including English, math and reading. There is a reader service for the blind, and remedial math, reading, and writing.

Campus Safety and Security: Measures include 24-hour foot and vehicle patrol, self-defense education, informal discussions, and pamphlets/posters/films. There are emergency telephones and lighted pathways/sidewalks.

Programs of Study: John Jay confers B.A. and B.S. degrees. Associate and master's degrees are also awarded. Bachelor's degrees are awarded in BIOLOGICAL SCIENCE (toxicology), COMPUTER AND PHYSICAL SCIENCE (information sciences and systems), SOCIAL SCIENCE (corrections, criminal justice, criminology, fire science, forensic studies, law enforcement and corrections, political science/government, public administration, and safety management). Forensic science is the strongest academically. Criminal justice, police science, and legal studies are the largest.

Required: Students are required to complete 128 credit hours, with 36 to 42 of these hours in the student's major, and must maintain a minimum GPA of 2.0. 1 credit in phys ed is required of all students.

Special: The school offers cross-registration with other schools in the City University of New York. Internships are available with the Manhattan District Attorney, the Queens Supreme Court, the New York City Police Department, the United States Marshal's Service, and the New York City Corrections Department. Opportunities are provided for work-study programs, a Washington semester, interdisciplinary and student-designed majors, including forensic psychology, pass/fail options, nondegree study, credit for life experience, B.A.-M.A. programs in forensic psychology, criminal justice, and public administration, and study abroad in England, Barbados, and Israel. There is 1 national honor society and a freshman honors program.

Faculty/Classroom: 56% of faculty are male; 44%, female. 94% teach undergraduates and 80% both teach and do research. Graduate students teach 5% of introductory courses. The average class size in an introductory lecture is 25; in a laboratory, 15; and in a regular course, 20.

Admissions: 82% of the 2001-2002 applicants were accepted. The SAT I scores for the 2001-2002 freshman class were: Verbal--64% below 500, 31% between 500 and 599, 4% between 600 and 700, and 1% above 700; Math--70% below 500, 25% between 500 and 599, 4% between 600 and 700, and 1% above 700.

Requirements: The SAT I is recommended. In addition, applicants must have graduated from an accredited secondary school, or a GED certificate will be accepted. Admission to associate degree programs requires a minimum SAT I score of 900, a high school average of 72, or a GED score of 300. Admission to baccalaureate degree programs requires a minimum SAT I score of 1020 or a high school average of 80 and 12 academic units with 4 units in English and math and 1 unit in each discipline. John Jay requires applicants to be in the upper 50% of their class. AP and CLEP credits are accepted.

Procedure: Freshmen are admitted fall and spring. There is an early admissions plan. Application deadlines are open. The fall 2001 application fee was $40.

Transfer: Applicants must have completed 24 credits with a cumulative GPA of 2.0. If fewer than 24 credits are presented, a high school transcript should be presented. Half of the credits required for the major must be completed at John Jay.

Visiting: There are regularly scheduled orientations for prospective students, consisting of a freshman/transfer workshop. There are guides for informal visits and visitors may sit in on classes. To schedule a visit, contact Christopher Williams at (212) 237-8868.

Financial Aid: In 2001-2002, 70% of all students received some form of financial aid. 5% of undergraduates work part time. Average annual earnings from campus work are $1000. The average financial indebtedness of a recent graduate was $10,000. The FAFSA is required.

International Students: There were 52 international students enrolled in a recent year. They must score 500 on the written TOEFL.

Computers: The mainframe is an IBM 3090/400. Some 540 PCs are available to students. There are open access facilities in the academic computing center and hands-on classes in departmental labs and the library. All students may access the system. There are no time limits and no fees.

Graduates: In a recent year, 1186 bachelor's degrees were awarded. The most popular majors were criminal justice (36%), forensic psychology (21%), and legal studies (11%). In an average class, 2% graduate in 3 years, 8% in 4 years, 21% in 5 years, and 39% in 6 years. 75 companies recruited on campus in a recent year. Of a recent graduating class, 19% were enrolled in graduate school within 6 months of graduation and 82% were employed.

Admissions Contact: Richard Saulnier, Dean of Admissions and Registration. E-mail: *rsaulnier@jjay.cuny.edu* Web: *www.jjay.cuny.edu*

CITY UNIVERSITY OF NEW YORK/MEDGAR EVERS COLLEGE D-5

Brooklyn, NY 11225-2201 (718) 270-6021; Fax: (718) 270-6198

Full-time: 636 men, 1938 women | **Faculty:** 113
Part-time: 381 men, 1761 women | **Ph.D.s:** 72%
Graduate: none | **Student/Faculty:** 23 to 1
Year: semesters, summer session | **Tuition:** $3282 ($6882)
Application Deadline: open | **Room & Board:** n/app
Freshman Class: 651 enrolled
SAT I: recommended **NONCOMPETITIVE**

Medgar Evers College, established in 1969 as part of the City University of New York, is an undergraduate commuter institution offering programs in business, education, natural sciences and math, nursing, and social sciences. There are 6 undergraduate schools. The library contains 74,000 volumes, 40,000 microform items, and 13,000 audiovisual forms/CDs, and subscribes to 700 periodicals. Computerized library services include the card catalog and interlibrary loans. Special learning facilities include a learning resource center and radio station. The campus is in an urban area located in the Crown Heights section of Brooklyn.

Student Life: The average age of freshmen is 22; all undergraduates, 27. 25% do not continue beyond their first year.

Housing: There are no residence halls. Alcohol is not permitted. No one may keep cars.

Activities: 2% of men belong to 2 national fraternities. There is 1 national sorority. There are 10 groups on campus, including choir, dance, ethnic, newspaper, political, radio and TV, religious, social service, student government, and yearbook. Popular campus events include Kwaanza and Black Solidarity Day.

Sports: There are 4 intercollegiate sports for men and 3 for women, and 5 intramural sports for men and 3 for women. Facilities include a swimming pool, a gym, and an exercise room.

Disabled Students: Wheelchair ramps, elevators, special parking, specially equipped rest rooms, lowered drinking fountains, and lowered telephones are available.
Services: Counseling and information services are available, as is tutoring in every subject. There is a reader service for the blind, and remedial math, reading, and writing.
Campus Safety and Security: Measures include 24-hour foot and vehicle patrol.
Programs of Study: MEC confers B.A. and B.S. degrees. Associate degrees are also awarded. Bachelor's degrees are awarded in BIOLOGICAL SCIENCE (biology/biological science), BUSINESS (accounting and business administration and management), EDUCATION (elementary and special), ENGINEERING AND ENVIRONMENTAL DESIGN (environmental science), HEALTH PROFESSIONS (nursing), SOCIAL SCIENCE (liberal arts/general studies, psychology, and public administration).
Required: To graduate, students must complete 128 credits with a minimum GPA of 2.0. The core curriculum requires a total of 42 credits in English, philosophy, speech, math, liberal arts, career planning, and phys ed. Students must demonstrate proficiency in basic reading, writing, and math skills prior to entering their junior year.
Special: MEC offers exchange programs with other CUNY institutions, evening and weekend classes, credit for military and prior learning experience, pass/fail options, and nondegree study. Study abroad in 3 countries is also possible. There is 1 national honor society, a freshman honors program, and 11 departmental honors programs.
Requirements: The SAT I is recommended. In addition, MEC accepts all applicants who either are graduates of an accredited secondary school or have earned a GED with a score of 225 or higher. Students must meet the university's health standards. CLEP credit is accepted.
Procedure: Freshmen are admitted fall and spring. Application deadlines are open. The fall 2001 application fee was $40. Notification is sent on a rolling basis.
Transfer: 442 transfer students enrolled in 2001-2002. Applicants must have a minimum GPA of 2.0. Those students with fewer than 24 college credits must also submit a high school transcript. 32 credits of 120 must be completed at MEC.
Financial Aid: The FAFSA and CUNY Student Aid Form (CSAF) are required. The fall application deadline is August 15.
International Students: The school actively recruits these students. They must score 475 on the written TOEFL and also take the ACT or the college's own entrance exam.
Computers: The mainframe is an IBM 3033. There are also PCs and Macs available in the data processing center. All students may access the system. There are no time limits and no fees.
Graduates: In 2001, 207 bachelor's degrees were awarded. The most popular majors were business (22%), elementary education (18%), and nursing (16%). 15 companies recruited on campus in 2000-2001.
Admissions Contact: Greg Thomas, Enrollment Management.
Web: *www.mec.cuny.edu*

CITY UNIVERSITY OF NEW YORK/NEW YORK CITY TECHNICAL COLLEGE D-5

Brooklyn, NY 11201-2983 **(718) 260-5500; (718) 260-5504**

Full-time: 3758 men, 3649 women	**Faculty:** 281
Part-time: 1788 men, 1834 women	**Ph.D.s:** n/av
Graduate: none	**Student/Faculty:** 26 to 1
Year: semesters, summer session	**Tuition:** $3319 ($6919)
Application Deadline: open	**Room & Board:** n/app
Freshman Class: n/av	
SAT I or ACT: recommended	**NONCOMPETITIVE**

New York City Technical College, founded in 1946 and made part of the City University of New York system in 1964, is an undergraduate commuter college offering day and evening programs in technology. The library contains 175,000 volumes, 87 microform items, and 6000 audiovisual forms/CDs, and subscribes to 700 periodicals. Computerized library services include the card catalog, interlibrary loans, and database searching. Special learning facilities include a learning resource center and art gallery. The campus is in an urban area. There are 9 buildings.
Student Life: 96% of undergraduates are from New York. 36% are African American; 23% Hispanic; 11% Asian American. The average age of freshmen is 23; all undergraduates, 25.
Housing: There are no residence halls.
Activities: There are 2 local fraternities and 1 local sorority. There are many groups and organizations on campus, including computers, drama, ethnic, gay, honors, international, musical theater, professional, religious, social, and student government.
Services: Counseling and information services are available, as is tutoring in most subjects.
Campus Safety and Security: Measures include 24-hour foot and vehicle patrol, informal discussions, pamphlets/posters/films, and emergency telephones. There are lighted pathways/sidewalks.
Programs of Study: City Tech confers B.S. and B.T. degrees. Associate degrees are also awarded. Bachelor's degrees are awarded in BUSINESS (hotel/motel and restaurant management), COMMUNICATIONS AND THE ARTS (telecommunications), EDUCATION (technical and vocational), ENGINEERING AND ENVIRONMENTAL DESIGN (electromechanical technology and graphic and printing production), SOCIAL SCIENCE (human services).
Required: Students must receive CUNY certification in reading, writing, and math and complete associate degree requirements. General education requirements include selections from African American, Puerto Rican, and Latin American studies, sciences, humanities, social sciences, and education. A total of 120 credits is required for the B.S. or B.T. degree.
Special: B.A. and B.S. degrees are offered through CUNY's university-wide bachelor's exchange credits program. An alternative format program for adults offers credit for life/work experience. Nondegree study and work-study are possible.
Requirements: The SAT I or ACT is recommended. In addition, applicants should be graduates of an accredited secondary school or have the GED equivalent and meet the university's health standards. Students must first apply to the associate degree program and later to the specific bachelor degree program. AP and CLEP credits are accepted.
Procedure: Application deadlines are open. The fall 2001 application fee was $40.
Transfer: 600 transfer students enrolled in a recent year. Candidates must have a 2.0 GPA. They must meet CUNY requirements in reading, writing, and math. 34 credits of 120 must be completed at City Tech.
Visiting: To schedule a visit, contact Admission Office.
Financial Aid: The CUNY Student Aid Form (CSAF) financial statement is required.
Computers: All students may access the system. There are no time limits and no fees.
Graduates: In a recent year, 325 bachelor's degrees were awarded. The most popular majors were hospitality management (23%), human service (20%), and telecommunication (16%).
Admissions Contact: Joseph Lento, Director of Admissions.
E-mail: *jglny@cunyvm.cuny.edu* Web: *www.nyctc.cuny.edu*

CITY UNIVERSITY OF NEW YORK/QUEENS COLLEGE D-5

Flushing, NY 11367-1597 **(718) 997-5608; Fax: (718) 997-5617**

Full-time: 2797 men, 4386 women	**Faculty:** 464
Part-time: 1324 men, 2706 women	**Ph.D.s:** 95%
Graduate: 1160 men, 3018 women	**Student/Faculty:** 16 to 1
Year: semesters, summer session	**Tuition:** $3403 ($7003)
Application Deadline: see profile	**Room & Board:** n/app
Freshman Class: 5086 applied, 2350 accepted, 913 enrolled	
SAT I Verbal/Math: 504/537 (mean)	**VERY COMPETITIVE**

Queens College, founded in 1937, is a public commuter institution within the City University of New York system. In addition to regional accreditation, Queens has baccalaureate program accreditation with ADA, ACS, APA, and ASLHA. The 2 libraries contain 711,737 volumes, 767,153 microform items, and 27,300 audiovisual forms/CDs, and subscribe to 3156 periodicals. Computerized library services include the card catalog, interlibrary loans, and database searching. Special learning facilities include a learning resource center, art gallery, radio station, a center for the performing arts, and a center for environmental teaching and research located on Long Island. The 76-acre campus is in an urban area 10 miles from Manhattan. There are 20 buildings.
Student Life: 99% of undergraduates are from New York. Others are from 15 states, 118 foreign countries, and Canada. 55% are from public schools. 51% are white; 19% Asian American; 15% Hispanic; 10% African American. 44% are Catholic; 23% Jewish; 11% Protestant; 11% Muslim, Hindu, Buddhist, Taoist. The average age of freshmen is 19; all undergraduates, 26. 15% do not continue beyond their first year; 40% remain to graduate.
Housing: There are no residence halls. All of students commute. Alcohol is not permitted. All students may keep cars.
Activities: 1% of men and about 1% of women belong to 3 national fraternities and 3 national sororities. There are 100 groups on campus, including band, choir, chorus, drama, ethnic, honors, international, jazz band, literary magazine, musical theater, newspaper, orchestra, political, radio and TV, religious, social, social service, student government, symphony, and yearbook. Popular campus events include fall and spring campus fests and a spring job fair.
Sports: There are 10 intercollegiate sports for men and 12 for women, and 10 intramural sports for men and 7 for women. Facilities include a gym complex, a swimming pool, dance studios, weight rooms, an outdoor quarter-mile track, soccer, lacrosse, and baseball fields, and 18 tennis courts.
Disabled Students: 90% of the campus is accessible. Wheelchair ramps, elevators, special parking, specially equipped rest rooms, and special class scheduling are available.

Services: Counseling and information services are available, as is tutoring in most subjects. There is a reader service for the blind.

Campus Safety and Security: Measures include 24-hour foot and vehicle patrol, pamphlets/posters/films, emergency telephones, and lighted pathways/sidewalks.

Programs of Study: Queens confers B.A., B.S., B.F.A., and B.Mus. degrees. Master's degrees are also awarded. Bachelor's degrees are awarded in AGRICULTURE (environmental studies), BIOLOGICAL SCIENCE (biochemistry and biology/biological science), BUSINESS (accounting and labor studies), COMMUNICATIONS AND THE ARTS (art, art history and appreciation, communications, comparative literature, dance, dramatic arts, English, film arts, French, German, Greek, Hebrew, Italian, Latin, linguistics, media arts, music, Russian, Spanish, and studio art), COMPUTER AND PHYSICAL SCIENCE (chemistry, computer science, geology, mathematics, and physics), EDUCATION (art, early childhood, elementary, home economics, music, physical, and secondary), ENGINEERING AND ENVIRONMENTAL DESIGN (environmental science), HEALTH PROFESSIONS (health science, predentistry, and premedicine), SOCIAL SCIENCE (African studies, American studies, anthropology, classical/ancient civilization, East Asian studies, economics, family/consumer studies, history, home economics, interdisciplinary studies, Judaic studies, Latin American studies, philosophy, political science/government, psychology, religion, social work, sociology, urban studies, and women's studies). Music, English, and linguistics are the strongest academically. Accounting, computer science, and psychology are the largest.

Required: To graduate, students must complete 120 credits with a minimum GPA of 2.0. They must fulfill requirements in the major and 35 to 40 credits of a liberal arts core curriculum.

Special: Queens offers co-op programs, cross-registration with other CUNY campuses, internships in business, liberal arts, journalsim, and social sciences, study abroad, work-study, accelerated degrees, dual and student-designed majors, pass/fail options, and nondegree study. There are preprofessional programs in engineering, law, medicine, and dentistry. The SEEK program provides financial and educational resources for underprepared freshmen. There are 15 national honor societies, including Phi Beta Kappa, and a freshman honors program.

Faculty/Classroom: 55% of faculty are male; 45%, female. Graduate students teach 1% of introductory courses. The average class size in an introductory lecture is 35; in a laboratory, 20; and in a regular course, 27.

Admissions: 46% of the 2001-2002 applicants were accepted. The SAT I scores for the 2001-2002 freshman class were: Verbal--47% below 500, 38% between 500 and 599, 13% between 600 and 700, and 2% above 700; Math--31% below 500, 45% between 500 and 599, 21% between 600 and 700, and 3% above 700.

Requirements: The SAT I is required. In addition, high school preparation should include 4 years each of English and social studies, 3 each of math and foreign language, and 2 of lab science. A GPA of 3.0 is required. AP and CLEP credits are accepted.

Procedure: Freshmen are admitted fall and spring. Entrance exams should be taken in the spring of the junior year or the fall of the senior year. There is an early admissions plan. For priority consideration, applications should be filed by January 1 for fall entry and October 15 for spring entry. The fall 2001 application fee was $40. Notification is sent on a rolling basis.

Transfer: 1318 transfer students enrolled in 2001-2002. First-year transfers should have a minimum GPA of 2.5 and must meet freshman criteria; most others need a 2.25 for consideration. 45 credits of 120 must be completed at Queens.

Visiting: There are regularly scheduled orientations for prospective students, including information sessions and a campus tour. To schedule a visit, contact the Admissions Office at (718) 997-5614.

Financial Aid: In 2001-2002, 80% of all freshmen and 55% of continuing students received some form of financial aid. 76% of freshmen and 44% of continuing students received need-based aid. The average freshman award was $7500. Of that total, scholarships, need-based grants, work contracts, and loans averaged $2500. Average annual earnings from campus work are $2500. The average financial indebtedness of the 2001 graduate was $12,000. The FAFSA is required. The fall application deadline is May 1.

International Students: There are 540 international students enrolled. They must score 500 on the written TOEFL and also take the SAT I or the CUNY Skills Assessment Test. Honors students should take SAT II: Subject tests.

Computers: The mainframe is an IBM. 450 Dell Pentiums and Apple Power Mac computers are available to students in computer labs. All students may access the system during day and evening hours, 7 days a week. There are no time limits. The fee is $38 per year for part-time students or $150 per year for full-time students.

Graduates: In 2001, the most popular majors were sociology (14%), accounting (11%), and political science (10%). In an average class, 3% graduate in 3 years, 21% in 4 years, 33% in 5 years, and 39% in 6 years. 100 companies recruited on campus in a recent year. Of the 2000 graduating class, 21% were enrolled in graduate school within 6 months of graduation and 70% were employed.

Admissions Contact: Dr. Vincent J. Angrisani, Executive Director of Admissions, Marketing, and Sholarship. A video is available.
Web: *www.qc.edu*

CITY UNIVERSITY OF NEW YORK/YORK COLLEGE D-5

Jamaica, NY 11451 **(718) 262-2165; (718) 262-2601**

Full-time: 885 men, 1965 women	**Faculty:** 168
Part-time: 638 men, 1765 women	**Ph.D.s:** 71%
Graduate: none	**Student/Faculty:** 17 to 1
Year: semesters, summer session	**Tuition:** $3292 ($6892)
Application Deadline: open	**Room & Board:** n/app
Freshman Class: n/av	
SAT I or ACT: required	**NONCOMPETITIVE**

York College, established in 1966, is a public liberal arts commuter college and part of the City University of New York. In addition to regional accreditation, York has baccalaureate program accreditation with CAHEA, CSWE, NLN, and ACOTE. The library contains 180,000 volumes, 154,000 microform items, and 4613 audiovisual forms/CDs, and subscribes to 1100 periodicals. Computerized library services include the card catalog, interlibrary loans, and database searching. Special learning facilities include a learning resource center, art gallery, TV station, a cardio-pneumo simulator, and a theater. The 50-acre campus is in an urban area in New York City. There are 5 buildings.

Student Life: 96% of undergraduates are from New York. Others are from 4 states, 82 foreign countries, and Canada. 44% are African American; 14% Hispanic. The average age of freshmen is 21; all undergraduates, 29. 19% do not continue beyond their first year; 24% remain to graduate.

Housing: There are no residence halls. All students commute. Alcohol is not permitted. All students may keep cars.

Activities: There are no fraternities or sororities. There are 50 groups on campus, including art, cheerleading, choir, chorus, computers, drama, ethnic, honors, international, jazz band, literary magazine, musical theater, newspaper, political, professional, radio and TV, religious, social, social service, student government, and yearbook. Popular campus events include club fairs, talent shows, and ethnic fairs.

Sports: There are 9 intercollegiate sports for men and 10 for women, and 9 intramural sports for men and 10 for women. Facilities include a 1200-seat gym, a 25-meter, 6-lane swimming pool with diving boards, a health risk appraisal center, an exercise therapy room, outdoor track; tennis courts; soccer field; indoor walking/jogging track; weight room; aerobics room; handball courts; and multipurpose room.

Disabled Students: All of the campus is accessible. Wheelchair ramps, elevators, special parking, specially equipped rest rooms, special class scheduling, lowered drinking fountains, and lowered telephones are available.

Services: Counseling and information services are available, as is tutoring in every subject. There is a reader service for the blind, and remedial math, reading, and writing.

Campus Safety and Security: Measures include 24-hour foot and vehicle patrol, escort service, informal discussions, and pamphlets/posters/films. There are emergency telephones and lighted pathways/sidewalks.

Programs of Study: York confers B.A. and B.S. degrees. Bachelor's degrees are awarded in BIOLOGICAL SCIENCE (biology/biological science and biotechnology), BUSINESS (accounting, business administration and management, and marketing/retailing/merchandising), COMMUNICATIONS AND THE ARTS (art history and appreciation, dramatic arts, English, French, music, Spanish, speech/debate/rhetoric, and studio art), COMPUTER AND PHYSICAL SCIENCE (chemistry, geology, information sciences and systems, mathematics, and physics), EDUCATION (physical), HEALTH PROFESSIONS (community health work, environmental health science, exercise science, medical laboratory technology, nursing, and occupational therapy), SOCIAL SCIENCE (African American studies, anthropology, economics, gerontology, history, liberal arts/general studies, philosophy, political science/government, psychology, social work, and sociology). Business, psychology, and social work are the largest.

Required: All students are required to complete 120 credits and maintain a minimum GPA of 2.0. The core curriculum of 61 credits includes courses in humanities, behavioral science, cultural diversity, math, natural science, and junior level writing. Students must also take a 2-credit phys ed course and complete 2 semesters of English.

Special: Cross-registration with all schools in the City University of New York is permitted. Also provided are work-study programs, credit by exam, dual majors in physics and math, nondegree study, pass/fail options, credit for life experience, internships, cooperative programs with other schools, and student-designed majors. There are 6 national honor societies, and 4 departmental honors programs.

Faculty/Classroom: 56% of faculty are male; 44%, female. 93% teach undergraduates and 7% both teach and do research.

Requirements: The SAT I or ACT is required; students should achieve a minimum composite score of 1100 on the SAT I. Applicants must have graduated from an accredited secondary school or present a GED certificate. An audition is recommended for music majors. AP and CLEP credits are accepted.

Procedure: Freshmen are admitted fall and spring. There are early admissions and deferred admissions plans. Application deadlines are open. Notification is sent monthly. The fall 2001 application fee was $40.

Transfer: 304 transfer students enrolled in a recent year. Students must present a minimum GPA of 2.0. 40 credits of 120 must be completed at York.

Visiting: There are regularly scheduled orientations for prospective students, including workshops and group meetings with faculty and staff on matriculation; registration; financial aid, degree requirements; and advisement for classes. Visitors may sit in on classes. To schedule a visit, contact the Director of Admissions or Admissions counselor.

Financial Aid: The FAFSA and the college's own financial statement are required.

International Students: There were 283 international students enrolled in a recent year. They must score 470 on the written TOEFL and also take the SAT I, ACT, or Math placement test if student comes from non-English-speaking country, scoring 1100 on SAT I.

Computers: The mainframes are an IBM 3090, 3081KX, and 4361-5. There are also 353 Macs and IBM PCs available throughout the school. All students may access the system during hours of operation of college facilities. There are no time limits and no fees.

Graduates: In a recent year, 768 bachelor's degrees were awarded. In an average class, 1% graduate in 3 years, 4% in 4 years, 15% in 5 years, and 24% in 6 years. 100 companies recruited on campus in a recent year.

Admissions Contact: Sally Nelson, Director of Admissions and Enrollment. A video is available. E-mail: *admissions@york.cuny.edu*
Web: *http://www.york.cuny.edu*

CLARKSON UNIVERSITY D-2
Potsdam, NY 13699

(315) 268-6479
(800) 527-6577; Fax: (315) 268-7647

Full-time: 1932 men, 647 women	**Faculty:** 141; I, -$
Part-time: 13 men, 18 women	**Ph.D.s:** 92%
Graduate: 225 men, 114 women	**Student/Faculty:** 18 to 1
Year: semesters, summer session	**Tuition:** $21,800
Application Deadline: March 1	**Room & Board:** $8084

Freshman Class: 2584 applied, 2082 accepted, 724 enrolled
SAT I Verbal/Math: 570/610 **VERY COMPETITIVE**

Clarkson University, founded in 1896, is a private institution offering undergraduate programs in engineering, business, science, and the liberal arts, and graduate programs in engineering, business, science, and health sciences. There are 4 undergraduate and 4 graduate schools. In addition to regional accreditation, Clarkson has baccalaureate program accreditation with AACSB, ABET, and U.S. Civil Service Commission. The library contains 237,128 volumes, 272,797 microform items, and 3857 audiovisual forms/CDs, and subscribes to 1453 periodicals. Computerized library services include the card catalog, interlibrary loans, and database searching. Special learning facilities include a learning resource center, natural history museum, radio station, and TV station. The 640-acre campus is in a rural area 70 miles north of Watertown and 75 miles south of Ottawa, Canada. Including residence halls, there are 43 buildings.

Student Life: 76% of undergraduates are from New York. Others are from 41 states, 35 foreign countries, and Canada. 87% are from public schools. 85% are white. 36% are Catholic; 34% Buddhist, Hindu, Muslim, Mormon, Orthodox, and others.; 26% claim no religious affiliation. The average age of freshmen is 18; all undergraduates, 20. 12% do not continue beyond their first year; 69% remain to graduate.

Housing: 2072 students can be accommodated in college housing, which includes single-sex and coed dormitories, on-campus apartments, married-student housing, fraternity houses, and sorority houses. In addition, there are special-interest houses. On-campus housing is guaranteed for all 4 years. 83% of students live on campus; of those, 90% remain on campus on weekends. Alcohol is not permitted. All students may keep cars.

Activities: 14% of men belong to 4 local and 5 national fraternities; 14% of women belong to 2 national sororities. There are 56 groups on campus, including cheerleading, chess, computers, drama, ethnic, honors, international, jazz band, literary magazine, musical theater, newspaper, orchestra, pep band, photography, professional, radio and TV, religious, social, social service, student government, and yearbook. Popular campus events include Ice Carnival, Culture Night, and Greek Week.

Sports: There are 10 intercollegiate sports for men and 8 for women, and 12 intramural sports for men and 17 for women. Facilities include a 3000-seat multipurpose ice arena, a fitness center, a gym, a swimming pool, a weight room, a field house, and racquetball, paddleball, and tennis courts.

Disabled Students: 85% of the campus is accessible. Wheelchair ramps, elevators, special parking, specially equipped rest rooms, special class scheduling, lowered drinking fountains, lowered telephones, and special residence hall rooms are available.

Services: Counseling and information services are available, as is tutoring in most subjects, including all freshman- and sophomore-level courses and some junior-level courses.

Campus Safety and Security: Measures include 24-hour foot and vehicle patrol, escort service, shuttle buses, and informal discussions. There are pamphlets/posters/films, emergency telephones, and lighted pathways/sidewalks.

Programs of Study: Clarkson confers B.S. and B.P.S. degrees. Master's and doctoral degrees are also awarded. Bachelor's degrees are awarded in BIOLOGICAL SCIENCE (biology/biological science and molecular biology), BUSINESS (accounting, banking and finance, business administration and management, management information systems, and marketing/retailing/merchandising), COMMUNICATIONS AND THE ARTS (technical and business writing), COMPUTER AND PHYSICAL SCIENCE (applied mathematics, chemistry, computer science, mathematics, physics, and science), ENGINEERING AND ENVIRONMENTAL DESIGN (aeronautical engineering, chemical engineering, civil engineering, computer engineering, electrical/electronics engineering, engineering management, environmental science, industrial administration/management, and mechanical engineering), HEALTH PROFESSIONS (industrial hygiene), SOCIAL SCIENCE (economics, history, humanities, political science/government, psychology, social science, and sociology). Engineering, business, and sciences are the strongest academically. Mechanical and computer engineering, and management are the largest.

Required: Students must complete at least 120 credit hours, with 30 in the major and a minimum GPA of 2.0 to graduate. Students must meet a foundation curriculum requirement and take the Personal Wellness unit.

Special: Clarkson offers cross-registration with the Associate Colleges of the St. Lawrence Valley: St. Lawrence University and Potsdam and Canton colleges. Co-op programs in all academic areas, dual majors in business and liberal arts, interdisciplinary majors, internships, accelerated degree programs, student-designed majors in the B.P.S. degree program, and study abroad in England, Sweden, Germany, Australia, France, and Canada are possible. There are 3-2 engineering programs with many institutions in the Northeast; students who participate take the first 3 years of the prescribed program at a 4-year liberal arts institution and then transfer with junior standing into one of Clarkson's 4-year engineering curricula. There are interdisciplinary programs in biomolecular science, environmental science and policy, environmental and occupational health, and software engineering. There are 9 national honor societies, including Phi Beta Kappa, a freshman honors program, and 1 departmental honors program.

Faculty/Classroom: 77% of faculty are male; 23%, female. 92% teach undergraduates, 56% do research, and 38% do both. No introductory courses are taught by graduate students. The average class size in an introductory lecture is 73; in a laboratory, 25; and in a regular course, 30.

Admissions: 81% of the 2001-2002 applicants were accepted. The SAT I scores for the 2001-2002 freshman class were: Verbal--16% below 500, 46% between 500 and 599, 31% between 600 and 700, and 7% above 700; Math--5% below 500, 34% between 500 and 599, 48% between 600 and 700, and 13% above 700. 65% of the current freshmen were in the top fifth of their class; 89% were in the top two fifths. There were 2 National Merit finalists. 23 freshmen graduated first in their class.

Requirements: The SAT I or ACT is required. In addition, SAT II: Subject tests are also recommended. Applicants must have graduated from an accredited secondary school or have the GED. A campus visit and interview are also recommended. Applications are accepted on computer disk and on-line via the Internet. AP and CLEP credits are accepted. Important factors in the admissions decision are advanced placement or honor courses, recommendations by school officials, and extracurricular activities record.

Procedure: Freshmen are admitted fall and spring. There are early decision, early admissions, and deferred admissions plans. Early decision application should be filed by December 1 or January 15; regular applications, by March 1 for fall entry and December 1 for spring entry, along with a $30 fee. Notification of early decision is sent January 1 or February 1; regular decision, beginning in February. 179 early decision candidates were accepted for the 2001-2002 class. A waiting list is an active part of the admissions process; 2 wait-list applicants were accepted in 2001.

Transfer: 91 transfer students enrolled in 2001-2002. Transfer students should submit transcripts from all colleges attended and 2 letters of recommendation, including 1 from an academic professsor or instructor. An associate degree will be considered, and an interview is recommended. 30 credits of 120 must be completed at Clarkson.

Visiting: There are regularly scheduled orientations for prospective students, including meetings with administration and faculty. There are guides for informal visits and visitors may sit in on classes and stay overnight. To schedule a visit, contact the Admissions Office.

Financial Aid: In 2001-2002, 97% of all freshmen and 91% of continuing students received some form of financial aid. 85% of freshmen and

82% of continuing students received need-based aid. The average freshman award was $18,873. Of that total, scholarships or need-based grants averaged $12,421 ($30,484 maximum); loans averaged $5356 ($8625 maximum); work contracts averaged $1100 ($1200 maximum); and externally sponsored scholarships/awards averaged $650. 50% of undergraduates work part time. Average annual earnings from campus work are $930. The average financial indebtedness of the 2001 graduate was $17,809. The FAFSA is required. The fall application deadline is February 15.

International Students: There are 90 international students enrolled. They must score 550 on the written TOEFL or 213 on the electronic version and also take the SAT I if first-year students.

Computers: The mainframes are an IBM 4381 and an RS 6000. About 100 terminals are available in clusters throughout the campus. All students may access the system. There are no time limits and no fees. All students are required to have personal computers.

Graduates: In 2001, 536 bachelor's degrees were awarded. The most popular majors were engineering and management (15%), mechanical engineering (14%), and civil engineering (13%). In an average class, 56% graduate in 4 years, 70% in 5 years, and 71% in 6 years. 170 companies recruited on campus in 2000-2001. Of the 2000 graduating class, 14% were enrolled in graduate school within 6 months of graduation and 83% were employed.

Admissions Contact: Brian T. Grant, Director of Enrollment Operations. E-mail: *grantbt@clarkson.edu* Web: *http://www.clarkson.edu*

COLGATE UNIVERSITY C-3

Hamilton, NY 13346 (315) 228-7401; Fax: (315) 228-7544

Full-time: 1364 men, 1410 women	**Faculty:** 217; IIB, ++$
Part-time: 5 men, 2 women	**Ph.D.s:** 99%
Graduate: 2 men, 2 women	**Student/Faculty:** 13 to 1
Year: semesters	**Tuition:** $27,025
Application Deadline: January 15	**Room & Board:** $6455
Freshman Class: 6059 applied, 2238 accepted, 741 enrolled	
SAT I Verbal/Math: 680/685	**ACT:** 31 **MOST COMPETITIVE**

Colgate University, founded in 1819, is a private liberal arts institution. Some information in this profile is approximate. There is 1 graduate school. The 2 libraries contain 615,940 volumes, 474,987 microform items, and 7877 audiovisual forms/CDs, and subscribe to 2299 periodicals. Computerized library services include the card catalog, interlibrary loans, and database searching. Special learning facilities include an art gallery, radio station, TV station, anthropology museum, and observatory. The 550-acre campus is in a rural area 45 miles southeast of Syracuse and 35 miles southwest of Utica. Including residence halls, there are 86 buildings.

Student Life: 68% of undergraduates are from out of state, mostly the Northeast. Others are from 44 states, 29 foreign countries, and Canada. 71% are from public schools. 82% are white. 20% are Jewish. The average age of freshmen is 18; all undergraduates, 20. 2% do not continue beyond their first year; 89% remain to graduate.

Housing: 2400 students can be accommodated in college housing, which includes coed dormitories, on-campus apartments, fraternity houses, and sorority houses. In addition, there are language houses and special-interest houses. On-campus housing is guaranteed for all 4 years. 90% of students live on campus; of those, 95% remain on campus on weekends. All students may keep cars.

Activities: 33% of men belong to 1 local and 8 national fraternities; 31% of women belong to 4 national sororities. There are 100 groups on campus, including art, band, cheerleading, chess, choir, chorale, chorus, computers, dance, debate, drama, ethnic, film, forensics, gay, honors, international, jazz band, literary magazine, marching band, musical theater, newspaper, orchestra, pep band, photography, political, professional, radio and TV, religious, social, social service, student government, symphony, and yearbook. Popular campus events include Family Weekend, Peace Jam, and Winter Carnival.

Sports: There are 11 intercollegiate sports for men and 12 for women, and 20 intramural sports for men and 20 for women. Facilities include numerous athletic fields, a softball diamond, an outdoor artificial surface field, a football stadium, an athletic center, a 3000-seat gym, a golf course, a field house, a ski center, a 50-meter pool, a bowling center, a hockey rink, a 9000-square-foot fitness center, running trails, a trap range, and courts for basketball, tennis, squash, handball, and racquetball.

Disabled Students: 20% of the campus is accessible. Wheelchair ramps, elevators, special parking, specially equipped rest rooms, special class scheduling, and lowered drinking fountains are available.

Services: Counseling and information services are available, as is tutoring in every subject. There is a reader service for the blind, remedial writing, a note taker service for students with learning and sensory disabilities, and a writing center.

Campus Safety and Security: Measures include 24-hour foot and vehicle patrol, self-defense education, escort service, and informal discussions. There are pamphlets/posters/films, emergency telephones, and lighted pathways/sidewalks.

Programs of Study: Colgate confers the B.A. degree. Master's degrees are also awarded. Bachelor's degrees are awarded in BIOLOGICAL SCIENCE (biochemistry, biology/biological science, molecular biology, and neurosciences), COMMUNICATIONS AND THE ARTS (art history and appreciation, classics, dramatic arts, English, French, German, Greek, Latin, music, Russian, Spanish, and studio art), COMPUTER AND PHYSICAL SCIENCE (astronomy, chemistry, computer science, geology, geophysics and seismology, mathematics, natural sciences, physical sciences, and physics), EDUCATION (education), ENGINEERING AND ENVIRONMENTAL DESIGN (environmental science), SOCIAL SCIENCE (African studies, anthropology, Asian/Oriental studies, economics, geography, history, humanities, international relations, Latin American studies, Native American studies, peace studies, philosophy, political science/government, psychology, religion, Russian and Slavic studies, social science, sociology, and women's studies). English, economics, and history are the largest.

Required: To graduate, students must complete a first-year seminar course and the core curriculum, including 4 general education courses and 2 courses each in the natural sciences, social sciences, and humanities. A total of 32 courses is required, with 8 to 12 courses in the major. Study in a foreign language, phys ed, and a swimming test are also required. Students need a 2.0 GPA overall and in the major.

Special: Colgate offers various internships, semester and summer research opportunities with faculty, work-study, study abroad in 16 countries, accelerated degree programs, dual majors, and student-designed majors. A 3-2 engineering degree with Columbia and Washington Universities and Rensselaer Polytechnic Institute, a 3-4 architecture degree with Washington University, credit by exam, and pass/fail options are available. There are 8 national honor societies, including Phi Beta Kappa and a freshman honors program.

Faculty/Classroom: 58% of faculty are male; 42%, female. All both teach and do research. No introductory courses are taught by graduate students. The average class size in an introductory lecture is 21; in a laboratory, 17; and in a regular course, 20.

Admissions: 37% of the 2001-2002 applicants were accepted. The SAT I scores for the 2001-2002 freshman class were: Verbal--3% below 500, 16% between 500 and 599, 53% between 600 and 700, and 28% above 700; Math--2% below 500, 11% between 500 and 599, 55% between 600 and 700, and 32% above 700. The ACT scores were 2% between 21 and 23, 11% between 24 and 26, 20% between 27 and 28, and 67% above 28. 85% of recent freshmen were in the top fifth of their class; 97% were in the top two fifths. 31 freshmen graduated first in their class in a recent year.

Requirements: Students may submit the SAT I and SAT II: Subject tests in writing and 2 other disciplines, or the ACT. 2 teacher recommendations and a counselor's report are required. An interview, though not evaluated, is recommended. Students should present 16 or more Carnegie credits, based on 4 years each of English and math and at least 3 of lab science, social science, and a foreign language, with electives in the arts. AP and CLEP credits are accepted. Important factors in the admissions decision are advanced placement or honor courses, recommendations by school officials, and leadership record. Colgate accepts applications on computer disk or on-line, via Mac Apply, CollegeLink, ExPAN, and the Common Application.

Procedure: Freshmen are admitted in the fall. Entrance exams should be taken in time for score reports to reach the University by January 15. There are early decision, early admissions, and deferred admissions plans. Early decision application should be filed by November 15; regular applications, by January 15 for fall entry, along with a $55 fee. Notification of early decision is sent December 15; regular decision, April 1. 233 early decision candidates were accepted for a recent class. 7% of all applicants are on a waiting list.

Transfer: 17 transfer students enrolled in a recent year. Either the SAT I or the ACT is required, as well as college and high school transcripts, a dean's report, and faculty recommendations. 16 courses of 32 must be completed at Colgate.

Visiting: There are regularly scheduled orientations for prospective students, including fall open house programs, nonevaluative interviews, group information sessions, and student-led tours. There are guides for informal visits and visitors may sit in on classes and stay overnight. To schedule a visit, contact the Office of Admission.

Financial Aid: In 2001-2002, 40% of all freshmen and 42% of continuing students received some form of financial aid. 50% of undergraduates work part time. Average annual earnings from campus work are $890. The average financial indebtedness of a recent graduate was $12,750. Colgate is a member of CSS. The CSS/Profile or FAFSA is required. Check with the school for current deadlines.

International Students: There were 69 international students enrolled in a recent year. The school actively recruits these students. They must score 600 on the written TOEFL or 250 on the electronic version and also take the SAT I or the ACT.

Computers: The mainframe is a DEC VAX 11/780. There are 400 terminals on campus offering a wide variety of applications software. In addition, all residence halls are wired for networked computers. All students

may access the system. There are no time limits and no fees. It is strongly recommended that all students have a personal computer.
Graduates: In a recent year, 677 bachelor's degrees were awarded. The most popular majors were economics (12%), English (10%), and history (10%). In an average class, 1% graduate in 3 years, 84% in 4 years, 88% in 5 years, and 89% in 6 years. 70 companies recruited on campus in a recent year. Of a recent graduating class, 14% were enrolled in graduate school within 6 months of graduation and 84% were employed.
Admissions Contact: Gary L. Ross, Dean of Admission.
E-mail: *admission@mail.colgate.edu* Web: *www.colgate.edu*

COLLEGE OF AERONAUTICS

Flushing, NY 11369 — D-5
(718) 429-6600
(800) 776-2376; Fax: (718) 779-2231

Full-time: 804 men, 76 women	**Faculty:** 109; III, +$
Part-time: 397 men, 24 women	**Ph.D.s:** 10%
Graduate: none	**Student/Faculty:** 8 to 1
Year: semesters, summer session	**Tuition:** $10,730
Application Deadline: open	**Room & Board:** n/app
Freshman Class: 637 applied, 454 accepted, 284 enrolled	
SAT I Verbal/Math: 450/450	**SPECIAL**

The College of Aeronautics, founded in 1932, is a private aviation school offering undergraduate degrees in aeronautical engineering technology, computerized design/animated graphics, airport management, avionics, aviation maintenance, and aircraft operations. In addition to regional accreditation, COA has baccalaureate program accreditation with ABET. The library contains 62,000 volumes and 10,000 microform items. Computerized library services include the card catalog and database searching. Special learning facilities include a learning resource center and a flight simulator, nondestructive testing labs, and a 5000-square-foot hangar facility. The 6-acre campus is in an urban area at LaGuardia Airport, 4 miles east of Manhattan. There are 2 buildings.
Student Life: 95% of undergraduates are from New York. Others are from 9 states, 19 foreign countries, and Canada. 96% are from public schools. 39% are Hispanic; 24% African American; 17% white; 13% Asian American. The average age of freshmen is 21; all undergraduates, 23. 27% do not continue beyond their first year; 68% remain to graduate.
Housing: There are no residence halls. College-sponsored housing is coed. Alcohol is not permitted. All students may keep cars.
Activities: There are no fraternities or sororities. There are 4 groups on campus, including ethnic, professional, social, student government, and yearbook. Popular campus events include Open House-Techno Expo, Winter Fest, and Spring Fest.
Sports: There are 3 intramural sports for men and 3 for women. Facilities include nearby areas for softball, flag football, weight lifting, and basketball.
Disabled Students: 95% of the campus is accessible. Wheelchair ramps, elevators, special parking, specially equipped rest rooms, special class scheduling, lowered drinking fountains, and lowered telephones are available.
Services: Counseling and information services are available, as is tutoring in most subjects. There is remedial math, reading, and writing.
Campus Safety and Security: Measures include 24-hour foot and vehicle patrol, informal discussions, and pamphlets/posters/films.
Programs of Study: COA confers B.S. and B.Tech. degrees. Associate degrees are also awarded. Bachelor's degrees are awarded in ENGINEERING AND ENVIRONMENTAL DESIGN (aircraft mechanics, airline piloting and navigation, and aviation administration/management). Maintenance technology, flight operations, and airport management are the strongest academically. Maintenance technology is the largest.
Required: All students must satisfy English, math, and science requirements and fulfill appropriate licensing requirements while maintaining a GPA of at least 2.0. Students with advanced credit must complete 30 credits in residency. A total of 134 credits is required to graduate.
Special: Work-study programs are available with the College of Aeronautics, and internships may be arranged through the career development office. B.A.-B.S. degrees are offered.
Faculty/Classroom: 90% of faculty are male; 10%, female. All teach undergraduates. The average class size in an introductory lecture is 25; in a laboratory, 20; and in a regular course, 20.
Admissions: 71% of the 2001-2002 applicants were accepted.
Requirements: The SAT I is recommended, with scores of 400 verbal and 400 math. Applicants are required to have 3 years of math and 2 years each of English and science. An interview is also recommended. A GPA of 2.0 is required. AP credits are accepted. Important factors in the admissions decision are evidence of special talent, advanced placement or honor courses, and personality/intangible qualities.
Procedure: Freshmen are admitted fall and spring. There are early decision and early admissions plans. Application deadlines are open. The fall 2001 application fee was $30. Notification is sent on a rolling basis. 60 early decision candidates were accepted for the 2001-2002 class.
Transfer: A minimum 2.0 GPA is required. 30 credits of 134 must be completed at COA.
Visiting: There are regularly scheduled orientations for prospective students, scheduled prior to registration, which include a tour and academic advisement. There are guides for informal visits and visitors may sit in on classes. To schedule a visit, contact the Admissions Office at (718) 429-6600 ext. 118 or *admissions@aero.edu*.
Financial Aid: In a recent year, 88% of all freshmen and 82% of continuing students received some form of financial aid. 74% of freshmen and 78% of continuing students received need-based aid. The average freshman award was $4300. Of that total, scholarships or need-based grants averaged $2100 ($7249 maximum); loans averaged $1200 ($2625 maximum); and work contracts averaged $1000 ($2628 maximum). 86% of undergraduates work part time. Average annual earnings from campus work are $2550. The average financial indebtedness of a recent year's graduate was $18,000. The CSS/Profile or FAFSA and the college's own financial statement are required. The fall application deadline is April 15.
International Students: The school actively recruits these students. They must score 500 on the written TOEFL or have an English Proficiency Certificate.
Computers: The mainframe is an AS400/IBM, networked for both PC and Mac use. All students may access the system. There are no time limits and no fees.
Graduates: In 2001, 134 bachelor's degrees were awarded. In an average class, 30% graduate in 3 years, 60% in 4 years, 80% in 5 years, and 100% in 6 years. 25 companies recruited on campus in 2000-2001.
Admissions Contact: Suzanne Phillips, Interim Dean of Admissions.
E-mail: *admissions@aero.edu* Web: *www.aero.edu*

COLLEGE OF INSURANCE
(See Saint John's University)

COLLEGE OF MOUNT SAINT VINCENT

Riverdale, NY 10471 — D-5
(718) 405-3267
(800) 665-CMSV; Fax: (718) 549-7945

Full-time: 230 men, 703 women	**Faculty:** 65
Part-time: 27 men, 201 women	**Ph.D.s:** 76%
Graduate: 40 men, 178 women	**Student/Faculty:** 14 to 1
Year: semesters, summer session	**Tuition:** $17,330
Application Deadline: March 1	**Room & Board:** $7020
Freshman Class: 1181 applied, 825 accepted, 300 enrolled	
SAT I Verbal/Math: 490/480	**COMPETITIVE**

The College of Mount Saint Vincent, founded as an academy in 1847 and chartered as a college in 1911, is a private liberal arts institution in the Catholic tradition. In addition to regional accreditation, CMSV has baccalaureate program accreditation with ACBSP and NLN. The library contains 159,284 volumes, 6006 microform items, and 6224 audiovisual forms/CDs, and subscribes to 576 periodicals. Computerized library services include the card catalog, interlibrary loans, and database searching. Special learning facilities include a learning resource center, radio station, and TV station. The 70-acre campus is in an urban area 11 miles north of midtown Manhattan. Including residence halls, there are 11 buildings.
Student Life: 93% of undergraduates are from New York. Others are from 10 states, 10 foreign countries, and Canada. 39% are from public schools. 40% are white; 35% Hispanic; 10% African American; 10% Asian American. Most are Catholic. The average age of freshmen is 18; all undergraduates, 25. 20% do not continue beyond their first year; 66% remain to graduate.
Housing: 556 students can be accommodated in college housing, which includes single-sex and coed dormitories. On-campus housing is guaranteed for all 4 years. 56% of students commute. All students may keep cars.
Activities: There are no fraternities or sororities. There are 30 groups on campus, including art, choir, chorus, computers, dance, drama, environmental, ethnic, film, gay, honors, international, literary magazine, musical theater, newspaper, photography, professional, radio and TV, religious, social, social service, student government, and yearbook. Popular campus events include Annual Block Party, Bachelor Auction, and Renaissance Faire.
Sports: There are 5 intercollegiate sports for men and 8 for women, and 6 intramural sports for men and 6 for women. Facilities include a gym, a swimming pool, a weight room, a dance studio, a recreation room, a fitness center with aerobic and Nautilus facilities, and basketball, squash, and tennis courts.
Disabled Students: 90% of the campus is accessible. Wheelchair ramps, elevators, special parking, specially equipped rest rooms, lowered drinking fountains, and lowered telephones are available.
Services: Counseling and information services are available, as is tutoring in most subjects, including computer science, math, chemistry, biology, languages, psychology, sociology, writing, and economics. There is a reader service for the blind, and remedial math, reading, and writing.

Campus Safety and Security: Measures include 24-hour foot and vehicle patrol, escort service, shuttle buses, and informal discussions. There are pamphlets/posters/films, emergency telephones, lighted pathways/sidewalks, and a college committee on safety and security on campus.

Programs of Study: CMSV confers B.A. and B.S. degrees. Associate and master's degrees are also awarded. Bachelor's degrees are awarded in BIOLOGICAL SCIENCE (biochemistry and biology/biological science), BUSINESS (business administration and management), COMMUNICATIONS AND THE ARTS (communications, English, French, modern language, and Spanish), COMPUTER AND PHYSICAL SCIENCE (chemistry, computer science, mathematics, and physics), EDUCATION (health, physical, and special), HEALTH PROFESSIONS (allied health and nursing), SOCIAL SCIENCE (economics, history, liberal arts/general studies, philosophy, psychology, religion, sociology, and urban studies). Nursing, biology, and communications are the strongest academically. Nursing, psychology, and business are the largest.

Required: All students must complete a 56-credit core curriculum with courses in humanities, social sciences, math and computers, and natural sciences. A total of 121 credits for a B.A. or 126 credits for a B.S., with a minimum of 30 credits in the major, and a minimum GPA of 2.0 are required.

Special: Cross-registration with Manhattan College offers cooperative B.A. programs in international studies, philosophy, phys ed, physics, religious studies, and urban affairs. Internships, work-study, study abroad in 6 countries, a 3-2 engineering degree with Manhattan College, dual majors, and student-designed majors in liberal arts are available. B.A.-B.S. degrees in computer science, health education, math, and psychology, and teacher dual certification programs with special education and elementary, middle school, and secondary education are possible. There are 15 national honor societies, a freshman honors program, and 5 departmental honors programs.

Faculty/Classroom: 36% of faculty are male; 64%, female. 92% teach undergraduates and 50% both teach and do research. No introductory courses are taught by graduate students. The average class size in an introductory lecture is 25; in a laboratory, 15; and in a regular course, 15.

Admissions: 70% of the 2001-2002 applicants were accepted. The SAT I scores for the 2001-2002 freshman class were: Verbal--54% below 500, 36% between 500 and 599, 9% between 600 and 700, and 1% above 700; Math--53% below 500, 41% between 500 and 599, and 6% between 600 and 700. 38% of the current freshmen were in the top fifth of their class; 65% were in the top two fifths.

Requirements: The SAT I or ACT is required. In addition, applicants should have completed 4 high school academic units of English, 3 of science, and 2 each of math, foreign language, and social sciences, as well as electives. An essay is required, and an interview is recommended. One letter of recommendation is required, and additional letters are encouraged. CMSV requires applicants to be in the upper 70% of their class. A grade average of 80 is required. AP and CLEP credits are accepted. Important factors in the admissions decision are advanced placement or honor courses, recommendations by school officials, and extracurricular activities record.

Procedure: Freshmen are admitted fall and spring. Entrance exams should be taken during the junior year and/or fall of the senior year. There are early decision and early admissions plans. Early decision applications should be filed by November 15; regular applications, by March 1 for fall entry. The 2001 application fee was $35. Notification of early decision is sent December 15; regular decision, on a rolling basis.

Transfer: 149 transfer students enrolled in a recent year. Transfer applicants should have a minimum GPA of 2.0. Those majoring in nursing, the sciences, math, or computer science need at least a 2.5 GPA. An interview is recommended. 45 (for B.A.) to 51 (for B.S.) credits of 121 (B.A.) to 126 (B.S.)must be completed at CMSV.

Visiting: There are regularly scheduled orientations for prospective students. Upon request, students may have an interview with an admissions counselor, sit in on classes, and tour the campus. All students are invited to an open house. Accepted students may have a one-on-one meeting with a student on campus. There are guides for informal visits and visitors may sit in on classes and stay overnight. To schedule a visit, contact the Admissions Office at (800) 665-2678, ext. 3267.

Financial Aid: In a recent year, 90% of all freshmen and 75% of continuing students received some form of financial aid. 80% of freshmen and 75% of continuing students received need-based aid. The average freshman award was $9600. Of that total, scholarships or need-based grants averaged $6000 ($21,930 maximum); loans averaged $2625 ($6625 maximum); and work contracts averaged $700 ($1000 maximum). 65% of undergraduates work part time. Average annual earnings from campus work are $500. The average financial indebtedness of a recent year's graduate was $10,000. CMSV is a member of CSS. The FAFSA, the college's own financial statement, and the TAP application for New York state residents are required. The fall application deadline is March 15.

International Students: There were 40 international students enrolled in a recent year. The school actively recruits these students. They must score 550 on the written TOEFL or complete ELS Level 109, available on campus, and also take the SAT I or the ACT, scoring 900 on the SAT I.

Computers: The mainframe is a client-server environment running Novell. 150 PCs are available. All students may access the system 9 A.M. to 10 P.M. Monday through Thursday and 9 A.M. to 4 P.M. Friday, Saturday, and Sunday. There are no time limits. The fee is $150.

Admissions Contact: Timothy P. Nash, Dean of Admission and Financial Aid. A video is available. E-mail: *admissns@cmsv.edu*
Web: *www.cmsv.edu*

COLLEGE OF NEW ROCHELLE

D-5

New Rochelle, NY 10805-2339 **(914) 654-5452**
(800) 933-5923; Fax: (914) 654-5464

Full-time: 6 men, 579 women	**Faculty:** 68
Part-time: 28 men, 295 women	**Ph.D.s:** 75%
Graduate: 144 men, 1454 women	**Student/Faculty:** 9 to 1
Year: semesters, summer session	**Tuition:** $13,150
Application Deadline: August 15	**Room & Board:** $6850
Freshman Class: 804 applied, 478 accepted, 118 enrolled	
SAT I Verbal/Math: 480/460	**ACT:** 18 **COMPETITIVE**

The College of New Rochelle was founded in 1904 by the Ursuline order as the first Catholic college for women in New York State and is now independent. There are 3 undergraduate schools. The School of Arts and Sciences offers liberal arts baccalaureate education for women only; the School of Nursing is coeducational. The School of New Resources is described in a separate profile. There is also 1 graduate school. In addition to regional accreditation, CNR has baccalaureate program accreditation with CSWE and NLN. The library contains 224,000 volumes, 277 microform items, and 5700 audiovisual forms/CDs, and subscribes to 1432 periodicals. Computerized library services include the card catalog, interlibrary loans, and database searching. Special learning facilities include a learning resource center, art gallery, and the Learning Center for Nursing. The 20-acre campus is in a suburban area 12 miles north of New York City. Including residence halls, there are 20 buildings.

Student Life: 79% of undergraduates are from New York. Others are from 13 states and 4 foreign countries. 73% are from public schools. 44% are African American; 29%, white; 20%, Hispanic. 77% are Catholic; 18%, Protestant. The average age of freshmen is 18; all undergraduates, 21. 24% do not continue beyond their first year; 55% remain to graduate.

Housing: 500 students can be accommodated in college housing, which includes dormitories. On-campus housing is guaranteed for all 4 years. 55% of students commute. No one may keep cars.

Activities: There are 18 groups on campus, including art, choir, chorus, drama, ethnic, film, honors, international, literary magazine, musical theater, newspaper, photography, political, professional, radio and TV, religious, social, social service, student government, and yearbook. Popular campus events include Junior Ring Dance, 100 and 200 days dances, and Parents Weekend.

Sports: There is an intercollegiate sports program. Facilities include a gym, a dance studio, a swimming pool, a tennis court, and a Nautilus room.

Disabled Students: 50% of the campus is accessible. Wheelchair ramps, elevators, special parking, specially equipped rest rooms, and special class scheduling are available.

Services: Counseling and information services are available, as is tutoring in some subjects, including science and languages. There is remedial math, reading, and writing. Individual counseling and educational workshops about self-development and personal concerns are available, as are self-help materials.

Campus Safety and Security: Measures include 24-hour foot and vehicle patrol, self-defense education, escort service, and shuttle buses. There are informal discussions, pamphlets/posters/films, emergency telephones, lighted pathways/sidewalks, card access to dorms, and surveillance cameras.

Programs of Study: CNR confers B.A., B.S., B.F.A., and B.S.N. degrees. Master's degrees are also awarded. Bachelor's degrees are awarded in BIOLOGICAL SCIENCE (biology/biological science), BUSINESS (business administration and management), COMMUNICATIONS AND THE ARTS (art history and appreciation, classics, communications, English, fine arts, French, and Spanish), COMPUTER AND PHYSICAL SCIENCE (chemistry, mathematics, and physics), EDUCATION (art, early childhood, elementary, foreign languages, middle school, and secondary), HEALTH PROFESSIONS (art therapy, nursing, predentistry, and premedicine), SOCIAL SCIENCE (economics, history, international studies, philosophy, political science/government, prelaw, psychology, religion, social work, and sociology). Nursing, art, and psychology are the largest.

Required: Students must complete 120 credit hours, 60 to 90 in liberal arts courses, depending on the major, meet specific course distribution requirements, and maintain a minimum GPA of 2.0 to graduate. 4 phys ed courses are also required.

Special: CNR provides cooperative programs in all disciplines, cross-registration with Iona College, work-study programs, dual majors in all majors, interdisciplinary studies, an accelerated degree program in nursing, a Washington semester, internships, study abroad in 9 countries, pass/fail options, student-designed majors, a general studies degree, and nondegree study. There is 1 national honor society, and a freshman honors program.

Faculty/Classroom: 26% of faculty are male; 74%, female. All both teach and do research. No introductory courses are taught by graduate students. The average class size in an introductory lecture is 15; in a laboratory, 10; and in a regular course, 15.

Admissions: 59% of the 2001-2002 applicants were accepted. The SAT I scores for the 2001-2002 freshman class were: Verbal--60% below 500, 30% between 500 and 599, 9% between 600 and 700, and 1% above 700; Math--68% below 500, 25% between 500 and 599, 6% between 600 and 700, and 1% above 700. 28% of the current freshmen were in the top fifth of their class; 59% were in the top two fifths.

Requirements: The SAT I is required. In addition, graduation from an accredited secondary school is required; the GED is accepted. Applicants must have completed 15 academic credits, with 4 in English, 3 each in math, science, and social studies, and 2 in a foreign language. A portfolio is required for art majors. An essay and interview are recommended. AP credits are accepted. Important factors in the admissions decision are advanced placement or honor courses, recommendations by school officials, and leadership record.

Procedure: Freshmen are admitted to all sessions. Entrance exams should be taken in the junior year or the fall of the senior year. There are early decision, early admissions, and deferred admissions plans. Early decision application should be filed by November 1; regular applications, by August 15 for fall entry and January 10 for spring entry. The fall 2001 application fee was $20. Notification of early decision is sent December 15; regular decision, on a rolling basis.

Transfer: 60 transfer students enrolled in 2001-2002. Applicants must submit a transcript from their previous college showing courses completed and a minimum GPA of 2.0. High school records and the SAT I scores are required. An interview is recommended. 30 credits of 120 must be completed at CNR.

Visiting: There are guides for informal visits and visitors may sit in on classes and stay overnight. To schedule a visit, contact the Office of Admissions.

Financial Aid: In 2001-2002, 80% of all students received some form of financial aid, including need-based aid. The average freshman award was $13,800. Of that total, scholarships or need-based grants averaged $8879; loans averaged $1921; work contracts averaged $1000; and institutional waivers and external aid averaged $200. 60% of undergraduates work part time. Average annual earnings from campus work are $1200. The average financial indebtedness of the 2001 graduate was $25,000. The CSS/Profile, FAFSA, FFS, or SFS, the college's own financial statement, and income documentation are required. The fall application deadline is open.

International Students: The school actively recruits these students. They must score 550 on the written TOEFL and also take the SAT I or ACT; the SAT I is preferred.

Computers: The mainframe is an IBM PS 80. The computer center contains 120 PCs for student use. All students may access the system from 8:30 A.M. to 11 P.M. daily. There is a time limit of 2 hours during peak usage. There are no fees.

Graduates: In 2001, 206 bachelor's degrees were awarded. In an average class, 41% graduate in 4 years, 53% in 5 years, and 57% in 6 years. 27 companies recruited on campus in 2000-2001. Of the 2000 graduating class, 20% were enrolled in graduate school within 6 months of graduation and 60% were employed.

Admissions Contact: Stephanie Decker, Director of Admission. A video is available. E-mail: *sdecker@cnr.edu* Web: *www.cnr.edu*

COLLEGE OF NEW ROCHELLE - SCHOOL OF NEW RESOURCES — D-5

New Rochelle, NY 10805-2339 — (914) 654-5522

(800) 288-4767; Fax: (914) 654-5664

Full-time: 540 men, 3236 women	**Faculty:** 22
Part-time: 67 men, 372 women	**Ph.D.s:** 27%
Graduate: none	**Student/Faculty:** 191 to 1
Year: semesters, summer session	**Tuition:** $4970
Application Deadline: August 15	**Room & Board:** n/app
Freshman Class: 825 enrolled	
SAT I or ACT: not required	**SPECIAL**

The College of New Rochelle's School of New Resources is a liberal arts institution serving adult baccalaureate students. The library contains 224,000 volumes, 277 microform items, and 5700 audiovisual forms/CDs, and subscribes to 1432 periodicals. Computerized library services include the card catalog, interlibrary loans, and database searching. Special learning facilities include a learning resource center, art gallery, TV station, and the Learning Center for Nursing. The campus is in an urban area 12 miles north of New York City. Six additional campuses are located within city. There are 20 buildings.

Student Life: 98% of undergraduates are from New York. Others are from 3 states and 3 foreign countries. 79% are African American; 14% Hispanic. The average age of freshmen is 33; all undergraduates, 37. 35% do not continue beyond their first year; 68% remain to graduate.

Housing: There are no residence halls. All students commute. Alcohol is not permitted. All students may keep cars.

Activities: There are no fraternities or sororities. There are some groups and organizations on campus, including student government.

Sports: There is no sports program at SNR.

Services: There is remedial math, reading, and writing. Individual counseling and educational workshops about self-development and personal concerns are available, as are self-help materials.

Campus Safety and Security: Measures include 24-hour foot and vehicle patrol, self-defense education, escort service, and shuttle buses. There are informal discussions, pamphlets/posters/films, emergency telephones, lighted pathways/sidewalks, and surveillance cameras.

Programs of Study: SNR confers the B.A. degree. Bachelor's degrees are awarded in SOCIAL SCIENCE (liberal arts/general studies).

Required: Students must complete 120 credit hours, meet specific course distribution requirements, and maintain a minimum GPA of 2.0 to graduate. Entrance, core, and exit seminars are required, as are degree-planning courses.

Special: SNR provides a voluntary work-study program.

Faculty/Classroom: 50% of faculty are male; 50%, female. All teach undergraduates. The average class size in an introductory lecture is 15; in a laboratory, 10; and in a regular course, 15.

Requirements: AP credits are accepted.

Procedure: Freshmen are admitted to all sessions. Entrance exams should be taken in the junior year or fall of the senior year. Early decision applications should be filed by November 1; regular applications, by August 15 for fall entry and January 10 for spring entry. Notification of early decision is sent December 15; regular decision, on a rolling basis.

Transfer: 520 transfer students enrolled in 2001-2002. Transfer students must submit a transcript from their previous college, showing courses completed and a minimum GPA of 2.0. An interview is required. 30 credits of 120 must be completed at SNR.

Financial Aid: In 2001-2002, 90% of all students received some form of financial aid, including need-based aid. The average freshman award was $8600. Of that total, scholarships or need-based grants averaged $6836; loans averaged $3614; work contracts averaged $100; and external aid averaged $200. 5% of undergraduates work part time. Average annual earnings from campus work are $2000. The average financial indebtedness of the 2001 graduate was $10,000. The FAFSA, the college's own financial statement, and income documentation are required. The fall application deadline is open.

Computers: The main campus computer center contains 120 PCs for student use. All students may access the system from 8:30 A.M. to 11 P.M. daily. Students may access the system 2 hours during peak usage. There are no fees.

Graduates: In 2001, 843 bachelor's degrees were awarded. In an average class, 12% graduate in 4 years, 23% in 5 years, and 28% in 6 years. Of the 2000 graduating class, 18% were enrolled in graduate school within 6 months of graduation.

Admissions Contact: Donna Tyler, Associate Dean. A video is available.

COLLEGE OF SAINT ROSE — D-3

Albany, NY 12203 — (518) 454-5150

(800) 637-8556; Fax: (518) 454-2013

Full-time: 568 men, 1673 women	**Faculty:** 139; IIA, --$
Part-time: 171 men, 397 women	**Ph.D.s:** 75%
Graduate: 404 men, 1151 women	**Student/Faculty:** 16 to 1
Year: semesters, summer session	**Tuition:** $13,918
Application Deadline: February 1	**Room & Board:** $6746
Freshman Class: 1619 applied, 1252 accepted, 491 enrolled	
SAT I Verbal/Math: 580/520	**ACT:** 22 — **COMPETITIVE**

The College of Saint Rose, established in 1920, is an independent liberal arts institution sponsored by the Sisters of St. Joseph of Carondelet. Some information in this profile is approximate. There are 4 undergraduate schools and 1 graduate school. In addition to regional accreditation, CSR has baccalaureate program accreditation with ACBSP, ASLA, and NASAD. The library contains 199,151 volumes, 252,117 microform items, and 1135 audiovisual forms/CDs, and subscribes to 975 periodicals. Computerized library services include the card catalog, interlibrary loans, and database searching. Special learning facilities include a learning resource center, art gallery, and TV station. The 22-acre campus is in a suburban area in a residential section, 1 1/2 miles from downtown Albany. Including residence halls, there are 63 buildings.

Student Life: 97% of undergraduates are from New York. Others are from 16 states, 30 foreign countries, and Canada. 60% are from public

schools. 85% are white. 60% are Catholic; 32%, Protestant. The average age of freshmen is 18; all undergraduates, 22. 18% do not continue beyond their first year; 65% remain to graduate.

Housing: 921 students can be accommodated in college housing, which includes single-sex and coed dormitories, on-campus apartments, and married-student housing. On-campus housing is available on a first-come, first-served basis and is available on a lottery system for upperclassmen. 60% of students commute. Upperclassmen may keep cars.

Activities: There are no fraternities or sororities. There are 34 groups on campus, including art, cheerleading, chess, chorale, computers, drama, ethnic, gay, international, jazz band, literary magazine, newspaper, orchestra, political, professional, religious, social, social service, student government, and yearbook. Popular campus events include Harvest Fest, Rose Rock, and Land and Water Olympics.

Sports: There are 5 intercollegiate sports for men and 6 for women, and 3 intramural sports for men and 3 for women. Facilities include a gym with basketball and volleyball courts, a weight room, an indoor swimming pool, and access to city soccer, baseball, and softball fields.

Disabled Students: 98% of the campus is accessible. Wheelchair ramps, elevators, special parking, specially equipped rest rooms, lowered drinking fountains, lowered telephones, and some automatic-open doors are available.

Services: Counseling and information services are available, as is tutoring in most subjects, including writing, math, accounting, computer science, and others as needed. There is a reader service for the blind, and remedial math, reading, and writing. There is also a full-time director of disabled student services.

Campus Safety and Security: Measures include 24-hour foot and vehicle patrol, shuttle buses, informal discussions, and pamphlets/posters/films. There are emergency telephones, lighted pathways/sidewalks, a student volunteer escort service, and fire drills.

Programs of Study: CSR confers B.A., B.S., and B.F.A. degrees. Master's degrees are also awarded. Bachelor's degrees are awarded in BIOLOGICAL SCIENCE (biochemistry and biology/biological science), BUSINESS (accounting and business administration and management), COMMUNICATIONS AND THE ARTS (communications, English, graphic design, music, public relations, Spanish, and studio art), COMPUTER AND PHYSICAL SCIENCE (chemistry, information sciences and systems, and mathematics), EDUCATION (art, elementary, English, foreign languages, mathematics, music, science, social studies, and special), ENGINEERING AND ENVIRONMENTAL DESIGN (environmental science), HEALTH PROFESSIONS (cytotechnology, medical laboratory technology, and speech pathology/audiology), SOCIAL SCIENCE (American studies, history, interdisciplinary studies, psychology, religion, social work, and sociology). Education, art, and music are the strongest academically. Business, special education, and elememntary education are the largest.

Required: To graduate, students must complete 122 credits with a minimum GPA of 2.0 overall and in the major; these requirements are higher for certain majors. Liberal education requirements consist of 6 credits in college writing and speech and 30 credits in the humanities, science and math, social science and business, and the arts. Students must also complete 2 credits in phys ed.

Special: CSR offers cross-registration with the Hudson-Mohawk Association and the CSI Consortium, internships, work-study programs, study abroad in 29 countries, dual and student-designed majors, nondegree study, and pass/fail options. There are 3-2 engineering degree programs with Alfred and Clarkson Universities and Union College, as well as a 6-year law program with Albany Law School. There are 6 national honor societies and 5 departmental honors programs.

Faculty/Classroom: 47% of faculty are male; 53%, female. 96% teach undergraduates. No introductory courses are taught by graduate students. The average class size in a laboratory is 14 and in a regular course, 25.

Admissions: 77% of the 2001-2002 applicants were accepted. The SAT I scores for the 2001-2002 freshman class were: Verbal--31% below 500, 52% between 500 and 599, 16% between 600 and 700, and 1% above 700; Math--35% below 500, 51% between 500 and 599, 13% between 600 and 700, and 1% above 700. The ACT scores were 30% below 21, 36% between 21 and 23, 24% between 24 and 26, 6% between 27 and 28, and 4% above 28. 36% of the current freshmen were in the top fifth of their class; 74% were in the top two fifths. 4 freshmen graduated first in their class in a recent year.

Requirements: The SAT I or ACT is required. In addition, applicants must be graduates of an accredited secondary school or have a GED certificate. They should have completed college preparatory programs. All students must submit a letter of recommendation. Art students must submit portfolios, and music students must audition. CSR requires applicants to be in the upper 50% of their class. A grade average of 80 is required. AP and CLEP credits are accepted. Important factors in the admissions decision are advanced placement or honor courses, leadership record, and recommendations by school officials. Applications are accepted on-line through ExPAN.

Procedure: Freshmen are admitted fall and spring. Entrance exams should be taken no later than November. There are early admissions and deferred admissions plans. Applications should be filed by February 1 for fall entry and November 1 for spring entry. The fall 2001 application fee was $30. Notification is sent on a rolling basis.

Transfer: 341 transfer students enrolled in a recent year. Applicants must submit official transcripts, a letter of recommendation, and a personal statement of the reasons for seeking transfer. Art majors must submit a portfolio, and music majors must audition. 60 credits of 122 must be completed at CSR.

Visiting: There are regularly scheduled orientations for prospective students, including visits with admissions and financial aid representatives, an overnight program hosted by students, Saturday information sessions in November, an open house, and Accepted Student Day in April. There are guides for informal visits and visitors may sit in on classes and stay overnight. To schedule a visit, contact the Admissions Office.

Financial Aid: In 2001-2002, 95% of all freshmen and 93% of continuing students received some form of financial aid. 16% of undergraduates work part time. Average annual earnings from campus work are $770. The average financial indebtedness of a recent graduate was $16,379. CSR is a member of CSS. The FAFSA is required. Check with the school for current deadlines.

International Students: The school actively recruits these students. They must score 500 on the written TOEFL or take the MELAB.

Computers: The mainframe is an IBM RS/6000/990. The college network provides connectivity to various application services located throughout the campus. More than 300 PCs are available for student use in computer labs, classrooms, and the library. All dorms are networked with 1 connection per bed. Dial-up access is also available via a modem pool. All PCs have access to the Internet, e-mail, and the Web. All students may access the system 24 hours a day Monday through Saturday, and additional hours on Sunday. There are no time limits.

Graduates: In a recent year, 466 bachelor's degrees were awarded. The most popular majors were elementary education (22%), business (10%), and special education (10%). In an average class, 60% graduate in 4 years, 61% in 5 years, and 65% in 6 years. 125 companies recruited on campus in a recent year. Of a recent graduating class, 47% were enrolled in graduate school within 6 months of graduation and 74% were employed.

Admissions Contact: Mary Grondahl, Associate Vice President for Undergraduate Admissions. A video is available.
E-mail: *admit@rosnet.strose.edu* Web: *www.strose.edu*

COLUMBIA UNIVERSITY SYSTEM

Columbia University System, established in 1754, is a private system in New York. It is governed by a board of trustees whose chief administrator is the president. The primary goals of the system are teaching and research. The main priorities are providing outstanding undergraduate instruction; conducting research to develop new knowledge and methods; and training of professionals in law, business, social work, and medicine. Graduate and professional programs include architecture, fine arts, public health, international affairs, public affairs, dentistry, education, and engineering. The total undergraduate enrollment of the four campuses is about 9,000. There are approximately 110 baccalaureate, 160 master's, and 80 doctoral programs offered at Columbia University. Profiles of the 4-year campuses are included in this section.

COLUMBIA UNIVERSITY/BARNARD COLLEGE
(See Columbia University/Barnard College)

COLUMBIA UNIVERSITY/BARNARD COLLEGE D-5

New York, NY 10027-6598	**(212) 854-2014; Fax: (212) 854-6220**
Full-time: 2213 women	**Faculty:** 183; IIB, +$
Part-time: 48 women	**Ph.D.s:** 93%
Graduate: none	**Student/Faculty:** 12 to 1
Year: semesters	**Tuition:** $24,036
Application Deadline: January 1	**Room & Board:** $9658
Freshman Class: 4074 applied, 1355 accepted, 541 enrolled	
SAT I Verbal/Math: 670/660	**ACT:** 28 **MOST COMPETITIVE**

Barnard College, founded in 1889, is an independent affiliate of Columbia University. It is an undergraduate women's liberal arts college. The library contains 195,354 volumes, 17,419 microform items, and 15,395 audiovisual forms/CDs, and subscribes to 548 periodicals. Computerized library services include the card catalog, interlibrary loans, and database searching. Special learning facilities include a learning resource center, art gallery, radio station, TV station, greenhouse, history of physics lab, child development research and study center, dance studio, modern theater, women's research archives within a women's center, and multimedia labs and classrooms. The 4-acre campus is in an urban area occupying 4 city blocks of Manhattan's Upper West Side. Including residence halls, there are 15 buildings.

Student Life: 65% of undergraduates are from out of state, mostly the Middle Atlantic. Students are from 50 states, 27 foreign countries, and

Canada. 58% are from public schools. 65% are white; 21% Asian American. The average age of freshmen is 19; all undergraduates, 20. 7% do not continue beyond their first year; 87% remain to graduate.

Housing: 2021 students can be accommodated in college housing, which includes single-sex and coed dormitories, on-campus apartments, and off-campus apartments. In addition, there are special-interest houses and special housing for disabled students. On-campus housing is guaranteed for all 4 years. 88% of students live on campus; of those, 75% remain on campus on weekends. Alcohol is not permitted. All students may keep cars.

Activities: There are no sororities. There are 100 groups on campus, including art, band, cheerleading, choir, chorale, chorus, dance, debate, drama, ethnic, film, gay, international, jazz band, literary magazine, marching band, musical theater, newspaper, opera, orchestra, photography, political, professional, radio and TV, religious, social, social service, student government, symphony, and yearbook. Popular campus events include Spring and Winter Festivals, Founders Day, and Take Back the Night.

Sports: Facilities include pools, weight rooms, gyms, tennis courts, an indoor track, a boat slip, and a bowling alley.

Disabled Students: 90% of the campus is accessible. Wheelchair ramps, elevators, special parking, specially equipped rest rooms, special class scheduling, lowered drinking fountains, and lowered telephones are available. The Office of Disability Services provides a variety of support services to students with permanent and temporary disabilities.

Services: Counseling and information services are available, as is tutoring in every subject. There is a reader service for the blind. A student-staffed writing room is available for students of all levels of writing ability, and a math help room is also available to students in all math courses.

Campus Safety and Security: Measures include 24-hour foot and vehicle patrol, escort service, shuttle buses, and informal discussions. There are pamphlets/posters/films, emergency telephones, lighted pathways/sidewalks, and safety and security education programs.

Programs of Study: Barnard confers the B.A. degree. Bachelor's degrees are awarded in BIOLOGICAL SCIENCE (biochemistry and biology/biological science), COMMUNICATIONS AND THE ARTS (art history and appreciation, classics, comparative literature, dance, dramatic arts, English, French, German, Greek, Italian, Latin, linguistics, music, Russian, and Spanish), COMPUTER AND PHYSICAL SCIENCE (astronomy, chemistry, computer science, mathematics, physics, and statistics), ENGINEERING AND ENVIRONMENTAL DESIGN (architecture and environmental science), SOCIAL SCIENCE (American studies, anthropology, biopsychology, classical/ancient civilization, East Asian studies, economics, European studies, history, international studies, medieval studies, Middle Eastern studies, philosophy, political science/government, psychology, religion, sociology, urban studies, and women's studies). English, biology, and psychology are the strongest academically. Psychology, English, and economics are the largest.

Required: A total of 120 credits is required, with a minimum GPA of 2.0. All students must take 4 semesters each of a foreign language, humanities, or social sciences outside the major, and geographic and cultural diversity courses that may satisfy the major or other requirements, 2 semesters each of lab science and phys ed, and 1 semester each in first-year seminar, first-year English, and quantitative reasoning.

Special: Barnard offers cross-registration with Columbia University, more than 2500 internships with New York City firms and institutions, and study abroad worldwide. A 3-2 engineering program with the Columbia School of Engineering and double-degree programs with the Columbia University Schools of International and Public Affairs, Law, and Dentistry, the Juilliard School, and the Jewish Theological Seminary are possible. The college offers dual and student-designed majors and multidisciplinary majors, including economic history. There is 1 national honor society, Phi Beta Kappa.

Faculty/Classroom: 38% of faculty are male; 62%, female. All both teach and do research. The average class size in an introductory lecture is 41; in a laboratory, 11; and in a regular course, 16.

Admissions: 33% of the 2001-2002 applicants were accepted. The SAT I scores for the 2001-2002 freshman class were: Verbal--1% below 500, 10% between 500 and 599, 52% between 600 and 700, and 37% above 700; Math--2% below 500, 12% between 500 and 599, 57% between 600 and 700, and 29% above 700. The ACT scores were 8% between 21 and 23, 21% between 24 and 26, 19% between 27 and 28, and 52% above 28. 94% of the current freshmen were in the top fifth of their class; 97% were in the top two fifths. There were 4 National Merit finalists.

Requirements: The SAT I or ACT is required. In addition, if taking the SAT I, an applicant must also take 3 SAT II: Subject tests, one of which must be in writing or literature. A GED is accepted. Applicants should prepare with 4 years of English, 3 of math, 3 or 4 of a foreign language, 2 of a lab science, and 1 of history. An interview is recommended. AP credits are accepted. Important factors in the admissions decision are advanced placement or honor courses, evidence of special talent, and extracurricular activities record. Applications are accepted on-line via Apply or the school's web site.

Procedure: Freshmen are admitted fall and spring. Entrance exams should be taken by January of the senior year. There are early decision and deferred admissions plans. Early decision applications should be filed by November 15; regular applications, by January 1 for fall entry. The fall 2001 application fee was $45. Notification of early decision is sent December 15; regular decision, April 1. 135 early decision candidates were accepted for the 2001-2002 class. 21% of all applicants are on a waiting list; 55 were accepted in 2001.

Transfer: 67 transfer students enrolled in 2001-2002. Applicants must complete at least 1 college course. The SAT I or ACT is required. Deadlines for transfer applicants are April 1 (fall term) and November 1 (spring term). 60 credits of 120 must be completed at the college.

Visiting: There are regularly scheduled orientations for prospective students, consisting of open house programs regularly scheduled throughout the fall. There are guides for informal visits and visitors may sit in on classes and stay overnight. To schedule a visit, contact the Office of Admissions.

Financial Aid: In 2001-2002, 50% of all freshmen and 55% of continuing students received some form of financial aid. 37% of freshmen and 41% of continuing students received need-based aid. The average freshman award was $24,306. Of that total, scholarships or need-based grants averaged $21,000 ($36,480 maximum); loans averaged $2600 (maximum); and work contracts averaged $1700 (maximum). 37% of undergraduates work part time. The average financial indebtedness of the 2001 graduate was $13,430. Barnard is a member of CSS. The CSS/Profile or FAFSA, the college's own financial statement, the parents' and student's federal tax returns, and the business and/or noncustodial parent statement, if applicable, are required. The fall application deadline is February 1.

International Students: There are 78 international students enrolled. The school actively recruits these students. They must score 600 on the written TOEFL and also take the SAT I or ACT. Applicants who take the SAT I must also take SAT II: Subject tests in writing or literature and 2 others.

Computers: The mainframe is an IBM RS/6000. All students have access to 3 academic computer labs that provide networked access to software, bibliographic searching, and Columbia University mainframe links. Several academic departments maintain computer labs for student use. All dorms are also wired for full Internet access. All students may access the system. There are no time limits and no fees. It is strongly recommended that all students have a personal computer.

Graduates: In 2001, 583 bachelor's degrees were awarded. The most popular majors were psychology (13%), English (12%), and economics (12%). In an average class, 3% graduate in 3 years, 72% in 4 years, 82% in 5 years, and 85% in 6 years. 130 companies recruited on campus in 2000-2001. Of the 2000 graduating class, 26% were enrolled in graduate school within 6 months of graduation and 55% were employed.

Admissions Contact: Jennifer Fondiller, Dean of Admissions.
E-mail: *admissions@barnard.edu* Web: *http://www.barnard.edu*

COLUMBIA UNIVERSITY/COLUMBIA COLLEGE — D-5

New York, NY 10027 — **(212) 854-2522; Fax: (212) 854-1209**

Full-time: 2018 men, 2079 women	**Faculty:** 656; I, ++$
Part-time: none	**Ph.D.s:** 100%
Graduate: none	**Student/Faculty:** 6 to 1
Year: semesters, summer session	**Tuition:** $26,908
Application Deadline: January 2	**Room & Board:** $8282
Freshman Class: 14,094 applied, 1729 accepted, 1005 enrolled	
SAT I Verbal/Math: 720/710	**ACT:** 30 **MOST COMPETITIVE**

Columbia College of Columbia University, founded in 1754, is a private college offering programs in the liberal arts and sciences. There is 1 undergraduate school. The 20 libraries contain 7.2 million volumes. Computerized library services include the card catalog, interlibrary loans, and database searching. Special learning facilities include an art gallery, planetarium, radio station, TV station, and an observatory. The 36-acre campus is in an urban area of New York City. Including residence halls, there are 50 buildings.

Student Life: 74% of undergraduates are from out of state, mostly the Middle Atlantic. Others are from 49 states, 59 foreign countries, and Canada. 60% are from public schools. 52% are white; 13% Asian American. The average age of freshmen is 18; all undergraduates, 20. 2% do not continue beyond their first year; 91% remain to graduate.

Housing: All students can be accommodated in college housing, which includes single-sex and coed dormitories, on-campus apartments, fraternity houses, and sorority houses. In addition, there are language houses and special-interest houses. On-campus housing is guaranteed for all 4 years. 95% of students live on campus. All students may keep cars.

Activities: 15% of men belong to 19 national fraternities; 9% of women belong to 9 national sororities. There are 300 groups on campus, including art, band, cheerleading, chess, choir, chorale, chorus, computers, dance, debate, drama, ethnic, film, gay, honors, international, jazz band, literary magazine, marching band, musical theater, newspaper, opera, orchestra, outdoor, pep band, photography, political, professional, radio and TV, religious, social, social service, student government, symphony, and yearbook. Popular campus events include Columbia Fest, United Minorities Board Ethnic Festival, and Holiday Lighting Ceremony/Yule Log.

Sports: There are 14 intercollegiate sports for men and 14 for women, and 10 intramural sports for men and 10 for women. Facilities include a football stadium, indoor and outdoor track and field facilities, a baseball field, a soccer stadium, a recreational gym with a swimming pool, basketball/volleyball courts, aerobic, fencing, wrestling, martial arts, weight rooms, a boat house, and tennis, squash, handball, and racquetball courts.

Disabled Students: All of the campus is accessible. Wheelchair ramps, elevators, special parking, specially equipped rest rooms, special class scheduling, lowered drinking fountains, lowered telephones, and chair lifts are available.

Services: Counseling and information services are available, as is tutoring in every subject. There is a reader service for the blind.

Campus Safety and Security: Measures include 24-hour foot and vehicle patrol, self-defense education, escort service, and shuttle buses. There are informal discussions, pamphlets/posters/films, emergency telephones, and lighted pathways/sidewalks.

Programs of Study: Columbia confers the A.B. degree. Bachelor's degrees are awarded in BIOLOGICAL SCIENCE (biochemistry, biology/biological science, biophysics, environmental biology, and neurosciences), COMMUNICATIONS AND THE ARTS (art history and appreciation, classics, comparative literature, dance, dramatic arts, English, film arts, French, German, Germanic languages and literature, Greek, Latin, linguistics, music, Russian, Spanish, and visual and performing arts), COMPUTER AND PHYSICAL SCIENCE (astronomy, astrophysics, chemistry, computer science, earth science, geochemistry, geology, geophysics and seismology, mathematics, physics, and statistics), EDUCATION (education), ENGINEERING AND ENVIRONMENTAL DESIGN (architecture and environmental science), SOCIAL SCIENCE (African American studies, American studies, anthropology, archeology, area studies, Asian/American studies, Asian/Oriental studies, classical/ancient civilization, East Asian studies, economics, Hispanic American studies, history, Italian studies, Latin American studies, medieval studies, Middle Eastern studies, philosophy, political science/government, psychology, religion, Russian and Slavic studies, sociology, urban studies, and women's studies). Economics, English, and history are the largest.

Required: All students complete a core curriculum consisting of classes in literature and philosophy, history, social science, art, sculpture and architecture, and music of the Western tradition; 2 courses in non-Western areas are also required. Distribution requirements include 2 years of foreign language (unless competency can be demonstrated), 3 semesters of science, 1 year of phys ed, and 1 semester of writing. A total of 124 credit hours is required; usually 30 to 40 of these are in the major. The minimum required GPA is 2.0.

Special: There is a study abroad program with Oxford and Cambridge Universities in England and the Kyoto Center for Japanese Studies in Japan, and cross-registration with the Juilliard School and Barnard College. Combined B.A.-B.S. degrees are offered via 3-2 or 4-1 engineering programs. There is also a 5-year B.A./M.I.A. with Columbia's School of International and Public Affairs. The college offers study abroad in France, work-study, internships, credit by exam, pass/fail options, and dual, student-designed, and interdisciplinary majors including regional studies and ancient studies. There is a chapter of Phi Beta Kappa.

Faculty/Classroom: 70% of faculty are male; 30%, female. All both teach and do research. The average class size in an introductory lecture is 70; in a laboratory, 15; and in a regular course, 25.

Admissions: 12% of the 2001-2002 applicants were accepted. The SAT I scores for the 2001-2002 freshman class were: Verbal--7% between 500 and 599, 29% between 600 and 700, and 64% above 700; Math--6% between 500 and 599, 34% between 600 and 700, and 60% above 700. The ACT scores were 4% between 21 and 23, 38% between 24 and 26, and 58% above 28. 94% of the current freshmen were in the top fifth of their class; 99% were in the top two fifths.

Requirements: The SAT I or ACT is required. In addition, 3 SAT II: Subject tests, one of which must be writing, are also required. A GED is accepted. Students should prepare with 4 years of English and 3 or 4 years each of foreign language, and social studies, history, math, and laboratory science. An essay is required; interviews are not required. 2 academic faculty recommendations and a written evaluation or recommendation from a school official are also required. AP credits are accepted. Important factors in the admissions decision are advanced placement or honor courses, recommendations by school officials, and leadership record. Applications are accepted on-line at the school's web site.

Procedure: Freshmen are admitted in the fall. Entrance exams should be taken. The College prefers that these exams be taken no later than October or November of the senior year. There are early decision, early admissions, and deferred admissions plans. Early decision applications should be filed by November 1; regular applications, by January 2 for fall entry, along with a $65 fee. Notification of early decision is sent December 15; regular decision, April 1. 475 early decision candidates were accepted for the 2001-2002 class. 4% of all applicants are on a waiting list; 7 were accepted.

Transfer: 74 transfer students enrolled in 2001-2002. Applicants must have completed 1 full year of college (24 credits) with a GPA of at least 3.0. They must submit high school and college transcripts. 60 credits of 124 must be completed at Columbia.

Visiting: There are regularly scheduled orientations for prospective students, consisting of group information sessions and student-led tours. There are guides for informal visits and visitors may sit in on classes and stay overnight. To schedule a visit, contact Visitors Center at (212) 854-4900.

Financial Aid: In 2001-2002, 49% of all freshmen and 41% of continuing students received some form of financial aid. 42% of freshmen and 35% of continuing students received need-based aid. The average freshman award was $23,112. The average financial indebtedness of the 2001 graduate was $16,358. Columbia is a member of CSS. The CSS/Profile or FAFSA, the college's own financial statement, and the federal tax returns, and the business/farm supplement, and/or the divorced/separated parents statement if applicable, are required. The fall application deadline is February 10.

International Students: There are 193 international students enrolled. The school actively recruits these students. They must score 600 on the written TOEFL or 250 on the electronic version and also take the SAT I, or ACT and 3 SATII subject tests, one of them in writing.

Computers: The mainframes are comprised of 3 Sun 4/280s, a DEC VAX 8700, and an IBM 4341. There are computer labs and stand-alone terminals throughout the campus and computer clusters in residence halls. Every dorm room has an ethernet connection. All students may access the system 24 hours a day, 7 days a week. There are no time limits.

Graduates: In 2001, 967 bachelor's degrees were awarded. The most popular majors were economics (13%), political science (12%), and history (11%). 370 companies recruited on campus in 2000-2001.

Admissions Contact: Admissions Officer, Office of Undergraduate Admissions. A video is available.
Web: *http://www.studentaffairs.columbia.edu/admissions*

COLUMBIA UNIVERSITY/FU FOUNDATION SCHOOL OF ENGINEERING AND APPLIED SCIENCE D-5

New York, NY 10027 (212) 854-2521; Fax: (212) 854-1209

Full-time: 917 men, 347 women	**Faculty:** 113; I, ++$
Part-time: none	**Ph.D.s:** 100%
Graduate: none	**Student/Faculty:** 11 to 1
Year: semesters, summer session	**Tuition:** $26,908
Application Deadline: January 2	**Room & Board:** $8282
Freshman Class: 2466 applied, 649 accepted, 312 enrolled	
SAT I Verbal/Math: 690/760	**ACT:** 29 **MOST COMPETITIVE**

The Fu Foundation School of Engineering and Applied Science of Columbia University, founded in 1754, offers undergraduate and graduate degree programs in engineering and applied science. There is 1 undergraduate and 1 graduate school. In addition to regional accreditation, Columbia Engineering has baccalaureate program accreditation with ABET. The 20 libraries contain 7.2 million volumes and 48,000 microform items. Computerized library services include the card catalog, interlibrary loans, and database searching. Special learning facilities include an art gallery, radio station, TV station, and an observatory. The 36-acre campus is in an urban area in New York City. Including residence halls, there are 50 buildings.

Student Life: 60% of undergraduates are from out of state, mostly the Middle Atlantic. Others are from 41 states, 59 foreign countries, and Canada. 75% are from public schools. 34% are Asian American; 32% white; 12% foreign nationals. The average age of freshmen is 18; all undergraduates, 20. 3% do not continue beyond their first year; 89% remain to graduate.

Housing: All students can be accommodated in college housing, which includes single-sex and coed dormitories, on-campus apartments, off-campus apartments, married-student housing, fraternity houses, and sorority houses. In addition, there are language houses and special interest houses. 95% of students live on campus. All students may keep cars.

Activities: 15% of men belong to 19 national fraternities; 9% of women belong to 9 national sororities. There are 300 groups on campus, including art, band, cheerleading, chess, choir, chorus, computers, dance, debate, drama, ethnic, film, gay, honors, international, jazz band, literary magazine, marching band, musical theater, newspaper, opera, orchestra, pep band, photography, political, professional, radio and TV, religious, social, social service, student government, symphony, and yearbook. Popular campus events include Columbia Fest, Holiday Lighting Ceremony/Yule Log, and Ethnic Festival.

Sports: There are 14 intercollegiate sports for men and 14 for women, and 10 intramural sports for men and 10 for women. Facilities include a football stadium, indoor and outdoor track-and-field facilities, a baseball field, a soccer stadium, recreational gym with swimming pool, basketball/volleyball courts, aerobic exercise, fencing, wrestling, martial arts, weight rooms, a boat house, and tennis, squash, handball, and racquetball courts.

Disabled Students: All of the campus is accessible. Wheelchair ramps, elevators, special parking, specially equipped rest rooms, and chair lifts are available.

Services: Counseling and information services are available, as is tutoring in every subject. There is a reader service for the blind.

Campus Safety and Security: Measures include 24-hour foot and vehicle patrol, self-defense education, escort service, and shuttle buses. There are pamphlets/posters/films, emergency telephones, and lighted pathways/sidewalks.

Programs of Study: Columbia Engineering confers the B.S. degree. Master's and doctoral degrees are also awarded. Bachelor's degrees are awarded in BUSINESS (operations research), COMPUTER AND PHYSICAL SCIENCE (applied mathematics, applied physics, and computer science), ENGINEERING AND ENVIRONMENTAL DESIGN (biomedical engineering, chemical engineering, civil engineering, computer engineering, electrical/electronics engineering, engineering management, engineering mechanics, geological engineering, industrial engineering technology, materials science, mechanical engineering, metallurgical engineering, and mining and mineral engineering). Computer science, computer engineering, and biomedical engineering are the largest.

Required: All students must complete 128 semester hours, including 38 hours of technical coursework in math, physics, chemistry, and computer science, and 27 hours in nontechnical courses covering the humanities and economics. Courses in logic and rhetoric, and economics, and 1 year of phys ed are required. Students must take 66 hours in the major and maintain a 2.5 GPA.

Special: Students may study at Columbia College or any of more than 90 other liberal arts colleges throughout the country in a 5-year program leading to the combined B.A.-B.S. degree or a 3-2 engineering degree. There is cross-registration with Barnard College, Teacher's College, and The Juilliard School. The school offers study abroad in more than 100 locations, internships, work-study, and pass/fail options. There is a chapter of Phi Beta Kappa.

Faculty/Classroom: 95% of faculty are male; 5%, female. All both teach undergraduates, and do research. The average class size in an introductory lecture is 50; in a laboratory, 15; and in a regular course, 25.

Admissions: 26% of the 2001-2002 applicants were accepted. The SAT I scores for the 2001-2002 freshman class were: Verbal--1% below 500, 5% between 500 and 599, 49% between 600 and 700, and 44% above 700; Math--14% between 600 and 700, and 86% above 700. The ACT scores were 53% between 27 and 28, and 47% above 28. 92% of the current freshmen were in the top fifth of their class; 99% were in the top two fifths.

Requirements: The SAT I or ACT is required as are 3 SAT II: Subject tests in mathematics I or II, chemistry or physics, and writing. Applicants must be graduates of an accredited secondary school with a recommended 4 years of English, 3 or 4 of history and social studies, 2 or 3 of a foreign language, 1 each of physics and chemistry, and math courses through calculus. Also required are a written evaluation or recommendation from a college adviser or guidance counselor and 2 recommendations from teachers of academic classroom subjects (1 from a teacher of math). An essay is required, and an interview is recommended. AP credits are accepted. Important factors in the admissions decision are advanced placement or honor courses, evidence of special talent, and recommendations by alumni. Applications are accepted on-line via the college web site.

Procedure: Freshmen are admitted in the fall. All testing must be completed by November of the senior year of high school (October for early decision applicants). There are early decision, early admissions, and deferred admissions plans. Early decision applications should be filed by November 1; regular applications, by January 2 for fall entry, along with a $65 fee. Notification of early decision is sent December 15; regular decision, April 1. 108 early decision candidates were accepted for the 2001-2002 class. 5% of all applicants are on a waiting list.

Transfer: 20 transfer students enrolled in 2001-2002. Applicants should have completed 1 year each of calculus, physics, and chemistry with lab, in addition to appropriate liberal arts courses. 60 credits of 128 must be completed at Columbia Engineering.

Visiting: There are regularly scheduled orientations for prospective students, consisting of group information sessions and student-led tours. There are guides for informal visits and visitors may sit in on classes and stay overnight. To schedule a visit, contact the Visitor Center at (212) 854-4900.

Financial Aid: In 2001-2002, 50% of all freshmen and 52% of continuing students received some form of financial aid. 43% of continuing students received need-based aid. The average freshman award was $23,174. The average financial indebtedness of the 2001 graduate was $17,384. Columbia Engineering is a member of CSS. The CSS/Profile or FAFSA and the college's own financial statement are required. The fall application deadline is February 10.

International Students: There are 146 international students enrolled. The school actively recruits these students. They must take the TOEFL or the college's own test. Students must take SAT II: Subject tests in writing, mathematics I or II, and physics or chemistry.

Computers: The mainframes are comprised of a Prime, 13 DEC VAX 11/750s, 3 AT&T 3B20s, 75 AT&T 3B2 supermicros, an HP 9050, a system of HP 9900s, 2 IRIS computers, and an IBM Interactive Graphics Lab. There are PCs available in labs and classrooms. Academic buildings and residence halls are wired to the campus network. There is a high-speed modem pool for off-campus access. Every residence hall room has an ethernet connection. All students may access the system 24 hours a day, 7 days a week. There are no time limits. The cost is included in the student fee.

Graduates: In 2001, 308 bachelor's degrees were awarded. The most popular majors were computer science (15%), electrical engineering (14%), and operations research (13%). 370 companies recruited on campus in 2000-2001.

Admissions Contact: Admissions Officer.
Web: *http://www.studentaffairs.columbia.edu/admissions*

COLUMBIA UNIVERSITY/SCHOOL OF GENERAL STUDIES — D-5

New York, NY 10027 — **(212) 854-2772; (212) 854-6316**

Full-time: 260 men, 290 women	**Faculty:** n/av
Part-time: 250 men, 340 women	**Ph.D.s:** n/av
Graduate: none	**Student/Faculty:** n/av
Year: semesters, summer session	**Tuition:** $25,000
Application Deadline: see profile	**Room & Board:** $10,000
Freshman Class: n/av	
SAT I or ACT: recommended	**COMPETITIVE**

The School of General Studies of Columbia University, founded in 1947, offers liberal arts degree programs and postgraduate studies for adult men and women whose post-high school education has been interrupted or postponed by at least 1 year. Figures in the above capsule are approximate. Computerized library services include the card catalog, interlibrary loans, and database searching. Special learning facilities include a learning resource center, art gallery, and radio station. The campus is in an urban area on the upper west side of Manhattan in New York City.

Student Life: Others are from Canada. 65% are white; 10% foreign nationals. The average age of all undergraduates is 28.

Housing: Available housing includes off-campus apartments, married-student housing, and fraternity houses. On-campus housing is available on a first-come, first-served basis. Alcohol is not permitted. No one may keep cars.

Activities: There are many groups and organizations on campus, including band, cheerleading, chess, choir, computers, drama, ethnic, film, gay, international, jazz band, literary magazine, marching band, musical theater, newspaper, orchestra, photography, political, professional, radio and TV, religious, social, social service, student government, symphony, writer's women's, and yearbook.

Sports: Facilities include 2 gyms, a swimming pool, tennis, squash, and racquetball courts, a training center, 2 dance/martial arts studios, a fencing room, a wrestling room, and an indoor track.

Disabled Students: Wheelchair ramps, elevators, specially equipped rest rooms, lowered drinking fountains, and lowered telephones are available.

Services: Counseling and information services are available, as is tutoring in some subjects, including English composition, math, languages, and sciences.

Campus Safety and Security: Measures include 24-hour foot and vehicle patrol, escort service, pamphlets/posters/films, and emergency telephones. There are lighted pathways/sidewalks.

Programs of Study: GS confers B.A. and B.S. degrees. Master's and doctoral degrees are also awarded. Bachelor's degrees are awarded in BIOLOGICAL SCIENCE (biology/biological science), COMMUNICATIONS AND THE ARTS (art history and appreciation, classics, comparative literature, dance, dramatic arts, English literature, film arts, French, German, Italian, literature, music, Slavic languages, Spanish, and visual and performing arts), COMPUTER AND PHYSICAL SCIENCE (applied mathematics, astronomy, chemistry, computer science, geoscience, mathematics, physics, and statistics), ENGINEERING AND ENVIRONMENTAL DESIGN (architecture and environmental science), SOCIAL SCIENCE (African American studies, anthropology, archeology, classical/ancient civilization, East Asian studies, economics, French studies, German area studies, Hispanic American studies, history, Italian studies, Latin American studies, Middle Eastern studies, philosophy, political science/government, psychology, religion, sociology, urban studies, and women's studies).

Required: All students must complete 124 credit hours, including 56 distribution requirement credits in literature, humanities, foreign language or literature, social science, science, and cultural diversity. Proficiency in English composition and math is required. A GPA of 2.0 is necessary to graduate.

Special: Preprofessional studies in allied health and medical fields and interdisciplinary majors, minors, and concentrations are offered. Internships in New York City, work-study programs on campus, study abroad, a 3-2 engineering degree at Columbia University School of Engineering and Applied Science, B.A.-B.S. degrees, and dual majors are available. There is a chapter of Phi Beta Kappa.
Requirements: The SAT I or ACT is recommended. SAT I, ACT, or Columbia's General Studies Admissions Exam scores should be submitted along with high school and all college transcripts. An autobiographical statement is required. An interview is encouraged. A GPA of 2.5 is required. AP credits are accepted. Important factors in the admissions decision are advanced placement or honor courses, personality/intangible qualities, and evidence of special talent. Applications are accepted on-line at the school's web site.
Procedure: Freshmen are admitted to all sessions. Entrance exams should be taken as early as possible. Notification is sent on a rolling basis. Check with the school for current application deadlines and fee.
Transfer: 64 credits of 124 must be completed at GS.
Visiting: There are regularly scheduled orientations for prospective students, consisting of an admissions information session every other Wednesday, preceeded by a campus tour. For information call (212) 854-5109. There are guides for informal visits.
Financial Aid: In a recent year, 75% of all freshmen received some form of financial aid. 25% of freshmen and 30% of continuing students received need-based aid. The average freshman award was $2100. Of that total, scholarships or need-based grants averaged $4000 ($8500 maximum); and work contracts averaged $2500 ($5000 maximum). 75% of undergraduates work part time. Average annual earnings from campus work are $2500. The average financial indebtedness of a recent graduate was $30,000. GS is a member of CSS. The FAFSA and the college's own financial statement are required. Check with the school for current deadlines.
International Students: There were 250 international students enrolled in a recent year. The school actively recruits these students. They must score 600 on the written TOEFL and also take the college's own test. Submission of recent SAT I scores is encouraged.
Computers: The mainframe is an IBM. Computer accounts allow access to the Internet, e-mail, commercial news wires, labs, and on-line services. All students may access the system. Students may access the system 1 hour. There are no fees. It is strongly recommended that all students have a personal computer.
Admissions Contact: Carlos Alberto Porro, Director of Admissions.
E-mail: *gs-admit@columbia.edu* Web: *www.gs.columbia.edu*

CONCORDIA COLLEGE D-5
Bronxville, NY 10708 (914) 337-9300
(800) 937-2655; Fax: (914) 395-4636

Full-time: 223 men, 319 women | **Faculty:** 35
Part-time: 37 men, 83 women | **Ph.D.s:** 79%
Graduate: none | **Student/Faculty:** 16 to 1
Year: semesters | **Tuition:** $16,700
Application Deadline: March 15 | **Room & Board:** $7500
Freshman Class: 502 applied, 361 accepted, 132 enrolled
SAT I Verbal/Math: 465/457 | **ACT:** 23 **VERY COMPETITIVE**

Concordia College, founded in 1881, is a Christian liberal arts college offering undergraduate majors, including business, education, music, social work, and professional training in ministry. Some information in this profile is approximate. In addition to regional accreditation, Concordia has baccalaureate program accreditation with CSWE. The library contains 85,000 volumes and 25,000 microform items, and subscribes to 450 periodicals. Computerized library services include the card catalog, interlibrary loans, and database searching. Special learning facilities include a learning resource center, art gallery, education center, family center, and Lutheran education service. The 33-acre campus is in a suburban area 15 miles north of New York City. Including residence halls, there are 21 buildings.
Student Life: 69% of undergraduates are from New York. Others are from 21 states, 31 foreign countries, and Canada. 64% are white; 16%, African American; 12%, Hispanic. 40% are Protestant; 38%, Catholic; 18%, unknown. The average age of freshmen is 18; all undergraduates, 22. 26% do not continue beyond their first year; 60% remain to graduate.
Housing: 420 students can be accommodated in college housing, which includes single-sex dormitories. In addition, there are special-interest houses. On-campus housing is guaranteed for all 4 years. 66% of students live on campus; of those, 75% remain on campus on weekends. All students may keep cars.
Activities: There are no fraternities or sororities. There are 25 groups on campus, including art, choir, chorus, drama, ethnic, honors, international, jazz band, literary magazine, musical theater, newspaper, orchestra, photography, professional, religious, social, social service, student government, symphony, and yearbook. Popular campus events include guest lectures, dramatic presentations, and spring and fall festivals.
Sports: There are 5 intercollegiate sports for men and 5 for women, and 10 intramural sports for men and 10 for women. Facilities include an athletic center, a field house, indoor and outdoor tennis courts, squash and racquetball courts, a weight room, a fitness center, and 3 athletic fields.
Disabled Students: 50% of the campus is accessible. Elevators, special parking, specially equipped rest rooms, lowered drinking fountains, and lowered telephones are available.
Services: Counseling and information services are available, as is tutoring in most subjects, including reading, writing, and math. There is remedial math, reading, and writing.
Campus Safety and Security: Measures include 24-hour foot and vehicle patrol, escort service, informal discussions, and emergency telephones. There are lighted pathways/sidewalks.
Programs of Study: Concordia confers B.A., B.S., and B.M. degrees. Associate degrees are also awarded. Bachelor's degrees are awarded in BIOLOGICAL SCIENCE (biology/biological science), BUSINESS (business administration and management), COMMUNICATIONS AND THE ARTS (applied music, arts administration/management, English, and music), COMPUTER AND PHYSICAL SCIENCE (mathematics), EDUCATION (business, early childhood, education, elementary, music, and secondary), ENGINEERING AND ENVIRONMENTAL DESIGN (environmental science), HEALTH PROFESSIONS (physical therapy), SOCIAL SCIENCE (behavioral science, history, interdisciplinary studies, international studies, ministries, religion, religious music, and social work). Education, music, and behavioral science are the strongest academically. Education, business administration, and music are the largest.
Required: To graduate, students must complete 122 semester hours with a minimum GPA of 2.0. General education requirements include 39 semester hours of liberal arts, 18 of foundation courses in basic skills and values, 12 of integrated studies, and 9 of religion. Students are required to take 3 credits each of phys ed and computers. A thesis is required in some majors.
Special: A registered professional nurse program is offered in cooperation with Mount Vernon Hospital School of Nursing. Concordia also offers co-op programs in social work and education, a dual degree program in physical therapy, cross-registration with a consortium of nearby colleges, internships, study abroad in England, B.A.- B.S. degrees, an interdisciplinary studies degree including a major in educational services, and credit for life experience. Accelerated degree programs are available in business administration and behavioral studies. There is 1 national honor society, a freshman honors program, and 10 departmental honors programs.
Faculty/Classroom: 69% of faculty are male; 31%, female. All teach undergraduates. The average class size in an introductory lecture is 19; in a laboratory, 12; and in a regular course, 12.
Admissions: 72% of the 2001-2002 applicants were accepted. The SAT I scores for the 2001-2002 freshman class were: Verbal--41% below 500, 41% between 500 and 599, 16% between 600 and 700, and 2% above 700; Math--44% below 500, 45% between 500 and 599, and 10% between 600 and 700. The ACT scores were 19% below 21, 30% between 21 and 23, 20% between 24 and 26, 15% between 27 and 28, and 20% above 28. 30% of the current freshmen were in the top fifth of their class; 62% were in the top two fifths. 4 freshmen graduated first in their class in a recent.
Requirements: The SAT I or ACT is required. In addition, applicants should be graduates of an accredited secondary school or have a GED certificate. Concordia prefers completion of 16 academic units, including 4 of English, and 2 each of math, history or social studies, science (at least 1 with lab), and a foreign language. An interview is recommended, and those students applying to the music program must audition. A GPA of 2.5 is required. AP and CLEP credits are accepted. Important factors in the admissions decision are advanced placement or honor courses, evidence of special talent, and extracurricular activities record. Applications are available on disk through CollegeLink, and on-line at *concordia-ny.edu*.
Procedure: Freshmen are admitted fall and spring. Entrance exams should be taken in the fall of the senior year. There are early decision, early admissions, and deferred admissions plans. Early decision application should be filed by November 15; regular applications, by March 15 for fall entry and December 30 for spring entry, along with a $30 fee. Notification of early decision is sent December 1; regular decision, on a rolling basis. 12 early decision candidates were accepted for a recent class.
Transfer: 44 transfer students enrolled in a recent year. A 2.0 GPA is recommended. Applicants must submit official transcripts from previous colleges attended. The last 30 credits of 122 must be completed at Concordia.
Visiting: There are regularly scheduled orientations for prospective students. There are guides for informal visits and visitors may sit in on classes and stay overnight. To schedule a visit, contact the Admissions Office.
Financial Aid: In 2001-2002, 94% of all freshmen and 95% of continuing students received some form of financial aid. 36% of undergraduates work part time. Average annual earnings from campus work are

$1275. The average financial indebtedness of a recent graduate was $12,530. The FAFSA is required. Check with the school for current deadlines.

International Students: There were 58 international students enrolled in a recent year. The school actively recruits these students. They must score 550 on the written TOEFL or 213 on the electronic version and also take the SAT I.

Computers: The mainframe is a Condurrent CPU 3212. There are 2 labs with 50 PCs available to students. All students may access the system any time. There are no time limits and no fees.

Graduates: In a recent year, 122 bachelor's degrees were awarded. The most popular majors were business administration (32%), elementary education (18%), and social work (6%). In an average class, 2% graduate in 3 years, 41% in 4 years, 45% in 5 years, and 51% in 6 years. Of a recent graduating class, 18% were enrolled in graduate school within 6 months of graduation and 79% were employed.

Admissions Contact: Becky Hendricks, Director of Admission. A video is available. E-mail: *ec@concordia-ny.edu*
Web: *www.concordia-ny.edu*

COOPER UNION FOR THE ADVANCEMENT OF SCIENCE AND ART D-5

New York, NY 10003 (212) 353-4120; (212) 353-4342

Full-time: 560 men, 300 women	**Faculty:** 53
Part-time: 10 men, 10 women	**Ph.D.s:** 82%
Graduate: 20 men, 8 women	**Student/Faculty:** 16 to 1
Year: semesters, summer session	**Tuition:** 0
Application Deadline: April 1	**Room & Board:** $6000
Freshman Class: n/av	
SAT I: required	**ACT:** n/av **MOST COMPETITIVE**

The Cooper Union for the Advancement of Science and Art, founded in 1859, is a privately endowed institution. Students who are U.S. residents are admitted under full scholarship, which covers the tuition of about $25000. There is an additional fee of about $600. Figures in the above capsule are approximate. Cooper Union offers undergraduate degrees in architecture, art, and engineering, and graduate degrees in engineering. Figures in the above capsule are approximate. There are 3 undergraduate schools and 1 graduate school. In addition to regional accreditation, Cooper Union has baccalaureate program accreditation with ABET, NAAB, and NASAD. The library contains 100,000 volumes, 50,000 microform items, and 300 audiovisual forms/CDs, and subscribes to 350 periodicals. Computerized library services include the card catalog, interlibrary loans, and database searching. Special learning facilities include a learning resource center, art gallery, a center for speaking and writing, an electronic resources center, and a visual resources center. The campus is in an urban area located in the heart of lower Manhattan. Including residence halls, there are 5 buildings.

Student Life: 61% of undergraduates are from New York. Others are from 40 states, 10 foreign countries, and Canada. 70% are from public schools. 56% are white; 27% Asian American. The average age of freshmen is 18; all undergraduates, 20. 8% do not continue beyond their first year; 77% remain to graduate.

Housing: 183 students can be accommodated in college housing, which includes coed on-campus apartments. 78% of students commute. All students may keep cars.

Activities: 20% of men belong to 2 national fraternities; 10% of women belong to 1 local sorority. There are 60 groups on campus, including chorale, computers, debate, drama, environmental, ethnic, gay, honors, international, literary magazine, newspaper, political, professional, religious, social, social service, student government, and yearbook. Popular campus events include an end-of-the-year student art and architecture exhibit.

Sports: There are 5 intercollegiate sports for men and 2 for women, and 12 intramural sports for men and 12 for women. Facilities include weight, martial arts, and fencing rooms, a nearby swimming pool, and basketball courts.

Disabled Students: 60% of the campus is accessible. Wheelchair ramps, elevators, and specially equipped rest rooms are available.

Services: Counseling and information services are available, as is tutoring in some subjects, including math, physics, speech, and writing.

Campus Safety and Security: Measures include pamphlets/posters/films, emergency telephones, lighted pathways/sidewalks, and community security and police.

Programs of Study: Cooper Union confers B.S., B.Arch., B.E., and B.F.A. degrees. Master's degrees are also awarded. Bachelor's degrees are awarded in COMMUNICATIONS AND THE ARTS (fine arts and graphic design), ENGINEERING AND ENVIRONMENTAL DESIGN (architecture, chemical engineering, civil engineering, electrical/electronics engineering, engineering, and mechanical engineering). Engineering is the largest.

Required: The 5-year architecture program requires 160 credits, including 30 in liberal arts and electives, for graduation. Art students must complete 128 credits, including 38 in liberal arts and electives, with a minimum overall GPA of 2.0 to graduate. A 2.5 GPA is expected in studio work. Engineering students are required to complete a minimum of 135 credits, including a computer literacy course and 24 credits in humanities and social sciences, with a minimum GPA of 2.0.

Special: Cross-registration with New School University, internships, study abroad for art students in 8 countries, and for engineering students in 6 countries, and some pass/fail options are available. Nondegree study is possible. An accelerated degree in engineering is also available. There are 4 national honor societies, and 1 departmental honors program.

Faculty/Classroom: 74% of faculty are male; 26%, female. All both teach and do research. No introductory courses are taught by graduate students. The average class size in an introductory lecture is 28; in a laboratory, 20; and in a regular course, 20.

Requirements: The SAT I is required. In addition, engineering applicants must take SAT II: Subject tests in mathematics I or II and physics or chemistry. Graduation from an approved secondary school is required. Applicants should have completed 16 to 18 high school academic credits, depending on their major. An essay is part of the application process. Art students must submit a portfolio. Art and architecture applicants must complete a project called the hometest. AP credits are accepted. Important factors in the admissions decision are evidence of special talent, advanced placement or honor courses, and personality/intangible qualities. Applications are accepted on-line at *www.cooper.edu*.

Procedure: Freshmen are admitted in the fall. Entrance exams should be taken before February 1. There are early decision, early admissions, and deferred admissions plans. A waiting list is an active part of the admissions procedure. Check with the school for current application deadlines and fee.

Transfer: 33 transfer students enrolled in a recent year. Art and architecture transfer applicants must present a portfolio and a minimum of 24 credits in studio classes. Engineering transfer applicants must submit a transcript with grades of B or better in at least 24 credits of appropriate courses.

Visiting: There are regularly scheduled orientations for prospective students, consisting of open house and portfolio review days for art and open house for engineering; architecture tours by appointment. To schedule a visit, contact the Office of Admissions and Records.

Financial Aid: In a recent year, 43% of all freshmen and 34% of continuing students received some form of financial aid. The average freshman award was $3600. Of that total, scholarships or need-based grants averaged $2700 ($4000 maximum); loans averaged $2470 ($2625 maximum); and work contracts averaged $1000 ($2000 maximum). 27% of undergraduates work part time. Average annual earnings from campus work are $1545. The average financial indebtedness of a recent graduate was $10,080. Cooper Union is a member of CSS. The FAFSA is required. The fall application deadline is April 15.

International Students: There were 50 international students enrolled in a recent year. They must score 600 on the written TOEFL. All freshman applicants must take the SAT I; art and architecture students must also take the hometest. SAT II: Subject tests in math and physics or chemistry are required for engineering applicants only.

Computers: The mainframe is a DEC VAX 11/780. The computer center, located in the Engineering Building, contains more than 100 workstations and PCs, all available for student use. All students have access to e-mail and the Internet. All students may access the system whenever the Engineering Building is open. There are no time limits and no fees.

Graduates: In a recent year, 205 bachelor's degrees were awarded. The most popular majors were fine arts (26%), electrical engineering (20%), and civil engineering (15%). In an average class, 55% graduate in 4 years, 70% in 5 years, and 75% in 6 years. 80 companies recruited on campus in a recent year. Of a recent graduating class, 54% were enrolled in graduate school within 6 months of graduation and 42% were employed.

Admissions Contact: Admissions Representative.
E-mail: *admissions@cooper.edu* Web: *www.cooper.edu*

CORNELL UNIVERSITY C-3

Ithaca, NY 14850 (607) 255-5241

Full-time: 7153 men, 6648 women	**Faculty:** 1469; I, +$
Part-time: none	**Ph.D.s:** 97%
Graduate: 3273 men, 2346 women	**Student/Faculty:** 9 to 1
Year: semesters, summer session	**Tuition:** $26,062
Application Deadline: January 1	**Room & Board:** $8552
Freshman Class: 21,519 applied, 5861 accepted, 2988 enrolled	
SAT I Verbal/Math: 660/700	**MOST COMPETITIVE**

Cornell University was founded in 1865 as a land-grant institution. Privately supported undergraduate divisions include the College of Architecture, Art, and Planning; the College of Arts and Sciences; the College of Engineering; and the School of Hotel Administration. State-assisted undergraduate divisions include the College of Agriculture and Life Sciences, the College of Human Ecology, and the School of Industrial and

Labor Relations. There are 7 undergraduate and 4 graduate schools. In addition to regional accreditation, Cornell has baccalaureate program accreditation with AACSB, ABET, ASLA, CSWE, and FIDER. The 17 libraries contain 6,797,144 volumes, 7,787,351 microform items, and 388,894 audiovisual forms/CDs, and subscribe to 62,731 periodicals. Computerized library services include the card catalog, interlibrary loans, and database searching. Special learning facilities include a learning resource center, art gallery, planetarium, radio station, a bird sanctuary, 4 designated national resource centers, and 2 local optical observatories. The 745-acre campus is in a rural area 60 miles south of Syracuse. Including residence halls, there are 770 buildings.

Student Life: 52% of undergraduates are from out of state, mostly the Middle Atlantic. Others are from 49 states, 82 foreign countries, and Canada. 61% are white; 16% Asian American; 12% foreign nationals. The average age of freshmen is 18; all undergraduates, 19. 4% do not continue beyond their first year; 90% remain to graduate.

Housing: 7330 students can be accommodated in college housing, which includes single-sex and coed dormitories, on-campus apartments, married-student housing, fraternity houses, and sorority houses. In addition, there are language houses and special-interest houses. On-campus housing is guaranteed for the freshman year only and is available on a lottery system for upperclassmen. 54% of students live on campus; of those, 90% remain on campus on weekends. All students may keep cars.

Activities: 21% of men belong to 3 local and 39 national fraternities; 19% of women belong to 5 local and 18 national sororities. There are 400 groups on campus, including art, band, cheerleading, choir, chorale, chorus, computers, dance, debate, drama, drill team, drum and bugle corps, ethnic, film, forensics, gay, honors, international, literary magazine, marching band, musical theater, newspaper, orchestra, pep band, photography, political, professional, radio and TV, religious, social, social service, student government, symphony, and yearbook. Popular campus events include Third World Festival of the Arts, Student Leadership Conference, and College Bowl.

Sports: There are 17 intercollegiate sports for men and 17 for women, and 36 intramural sports for men and 36 for women. Facilities include indoor and outdoor tracks, a 5000-seat indoor gym, 3 swimming pools, a 25000-seat stadium, 16 intercollegiate fields, a bowling alley, intramural fields, a boat house, and indoor and outdoor tennis courts.

Disabled Students: 90% of the campus is accessible. Wheelchair ramps, elevators, special parking, specially equipped rest rooms, special class scheduling, lowered drinking fountains, lowered telephones, alternative test arrangements, and bus passes or van transportation are available.

Services: Counseling and information services are available, as is tutoring in most subjects. There is a reader service for the blind, note takers, biology and math student support centers, and writing workshops.

Campus Safety and Security: Measures include 24-hour foot and vehicle patrol, self-defense education, escort service, and shuttle buses. There are informal discussions, pamphlets/posters/films, emergency telephones, and lighted pathways/sidewalks.

Programs of Study: Cornell confers B.A., B.S., B.Arch., and B.F.A. degrees. Master's and doctoral degrees are also awarded. Bachelor's degrees are awarded in AGRICULTURE (agricultural business management, agricultural economics, agriculture, agronomy, animal science, horticulture, international agriculture, natural resource management, plant science, and soil science), BIOLOGICAL SCIENCE (biology/biological science, biometrics and biostatistics, botany, entomology, evolutionary biology, genetics, and nutrition), BUSINESS (hotel/motel and restaurant management, labor studies, and operations research), COMMUNICATIONS AND THE ARTS (art history and appreciation, classics, communications, comparative literature, dance, design, dramatic arts, English, film arts, fine arts, French, German, Greek, Italian, languages, Latin, linguistics, music, Russian, and Spanish), COMPUTER AND PHYSICAL SCIENCE (astronomy, atmospheric sciences and meteorology, chemistry, computer science, earth science, geology, mathematics, physics, science technology, and statistics), EDUCATION (education), ENGINEERING AND ENVIRONMENTAL DESIGN (aerospace studies, agricultural engineering, architecture, chemical engineering, city/community/regional planning, civil engineering, computer engineering, electrical/electronics engineering, engineering physics, environmental engineering technology, landscape architecture/design, materials science, and mechanical engineering), SOCIAL SCIENCE (African studies, American studies, anthropology, archeology, Asian/Oriental studies, classical/ancient civilization, economics, family/consumer studies, food production/management/services, food science, German area studies, history, human development, Near Eastern studies, philosophy, political science/government, psychology, public affairs, religion, rural sociology, Russian and Slavic studies, sociology, textiles and clothing, urban studies, and women's studies). Hotel administration, industrial and labor relations, and engineering are the largest.

Required: Entering freshmen must meet basic swimming and water safety competency requirements. All undergraduates must take 2 semesters each of freshman writing seminar and phys ed. Graduation requirements vary by program, including a minimum of 120 credits.

Special: Co-op programs are offered in the College of Engineering and the School of Industrial and Labor Relations. Cross-registration is available with Ithaca College. Public-policy internships are available in Washington, D.C., Albany, and New York City. Cornell also offers study abroad in more than 50 countries, B.A.-B.S. and B.A.-B.F.A. degrees, interdisciplinary/intercollegiate options, student-designed and dual majors, work-study programs, accelerated degree programs, pass/fail options, and limited nondegree study. There are 3 national honor societies, including Phi Beta Kappa.

Faculty/Classroom: 77% of faculty are male; 23%, female. All both teach undergraduates and do research. Graduate students teach 1% of introductory courses. The average class size in an introductory lecture is 58; in a laboratory, 13; and in a regular course, 31.

Admissions: 27% of the 2001-2002 applicants were accepted. The SAT I scores for the 2001-2002 freshman class were: Verbal--2% below 500, 13% between 500 and 599, 48% between 600 and 700, and 37% above 700; Math--8% between 500 and 599, 36% between 600 and 700, and 56% above 700. 93% of the current freshmen were in the top fifth of their class; 99% were in the top two fifths. There were 63 National Merit finalists.

Requirements: The SAT I or ACT is required. In addition, an essay is required as part of the application process. Other requirements vary by division or program, including specific SAT II: Subject tests and selection of courses within the minimum 16 secondary-school academic units needed. An interview and/or portfolio is required for specific majors. AP credits are accepted. Important factors in the admissions decision are advanced placement or honor courses, evidence of special talent, and leadership record. Applications are accepted on-line via ExPAN and Apply.

Procedure: Freshmen are admitted fall and spring. Entrance exams should be taken by December of the senior year. There are early decision and deferred admissions plans. Early decision applications should be filed by November 10; regular applications, by January 1 for fall entry and November 10 for spring entry. The fall 2001 application fee was $65. Notification of early decision is sent mid-December; regular decision, mid-April. 976 early decision candidates were accepted for the 2001-2002 class. 10% of all applicants are on a waiting list; 283 were accepted in 2001.

Transfer: 542 transfer students enrolled in 2001-2002. All applicants must submit high school and college transcripts, as well as scores from the SAT I or ACT if taken previously. Other admission requirements vary by program, including the number of credits that must be completed at Cornell.

Visiting: There are regularly scheduled orientations for prospective students, including campus tours and information sessions. There are guides for informal visits and visitors may sit in on classes and stay overnight. To schedule a visit, contact the Red Carpet Society at (607) 255-3447.

Financial Aid: In 2001-2002, 63% of all freshmen and 61% of continuing students received some form of financial aid. 45% of freshmen and 49% of continuing students received need-based aid. The average freshman award was $21,270. Of that total, scholarships or need-based grants averaged $15,616 ($36,000 maximum); loans averaged $5792 ($6640 maximum); and work contracts averaged $1800 ($2200 maximum). The average financial indebtedness of the 2001 graduate was $20,213. The CSS/Profile or FAFSA is required and the IRS form is required after enrollment. The fall application deadline is February 11.

International Students: There are 1038 international students enrolled. The school actively recruits these students. They must score 600 on the written TOEFL and also take the SAT I or the ACT. Some divisions require SAT II: Subject tests.

Computers: The mainframe is 2 IBM 3090/600s. Students have access to 7 campuswide computer centers and more than 20 departmental facilities with more than 700 PCs/terminals, as well as networks in the residence halls. All students may access the system. There are no time limits and no fees. It is recommended that students in engineering have personal computers.

Graduates: In 2001, 3585 bachelor's degrees were awarded. The most popular majors were engineering (15%), social sciences and history (12%), and biological sciences/life sciences (9%). In an average class, 5% graduate in 3 years, 86% in 4 years, 89% in 5 years, and 90% in 6 years. 830 companies recruited on campus in 2000-2001. Of the 2000 graduating class, 30% were enrolled in graduate school within 6 months of graduation and 54% were employed.

Admissions Contact: Wendy Schaerer, Director of Undergraduate Admissions. A video is available. E-mail: *admissions@cornell.edu*
Web: *http://www.cornell.edu*

DAEMEN COLLEGE
Amherst, NY 14226-3592 — A-3
(716) 839-8225
(800) 462-7652; Fax: (716) 839-8370

Full-time: 335 men, 1088 women	**Faculty:** 70; IIB, -$
Part-time: 98 men, 354 women	**Ph.D.s:** 77%
Graduate: 31 men, 84 women	**Student/Faculty:** 20 to 1
Year: semesters, summer session	**Tuition:** $13,620
Application Deadline: see profile	**Room & Board:** $7000
Freshman Class: 1792 applied, 1375 accepted, 342 enrolled	
SAT I Verbal/Math: 490/480	**ACT:** 21 **COMPETITIVE**

Daemen College, founded in 1947, is a private institution offering undergraduate and graduate programs in the liberal and fine arts, business, education, allied health professions, and natural sciences. There is 1 graduate school. In addition to regional accreditation, Daemen has baccalaureate program accreditation with APTA, CAAHEP, CSWE, and NLN. The library contains 140,176 volumes, 23,778 microform items, and 5045 audiovisual forms/CDs, and subscribes to 945 periodicals. Computerized library services include the card catalog, interlibrary loans, and database searching. Special learning facilities include a learning resource center, art gallery, and a video conference center. The 35-acre campus is in a suburban area 5 miles northeast of downtown Buffalo. Including residence halls, there are 22 buildings.

Student Life: 81% of undergraduates are from New York. Others are from 24 states, 9 foreign countries, and Canada. 70% are white; 14%, foreign nationals; 11%, African American. 45% are Catholic; 26%, Protestant. The average age of freshmen is 18; all undergraduates, 26. 32% do not continue beyond their first year; 35% remain to graduate.

Housing: 524 students can be accommodated in college housing, which includes coed dormitories, a quiet dorm, and on-campus apartments. On-campus housing is guaranteed for all 4 years. 72% of students commute. All students may keep cars.

Activities: 3% of men belong to 1 local fraternity; 4% of women belong to 4 local sororities. There are 35 groups on campus, including art, cheerleading, chorale, drama, honors, literary magazine, multicultural, musical theater, newspaper, professional, religious, social, social service, student government, and yearbook. Popular campus events include Welcome Back Week, Springfest, and Fallfest.

Sports: There are 4 intercollegiate sports for men and 4 for women, and 5 intramural sports for men and 4 for women. Facilities include a gym, weight and exercise rooms, and saunas.

Disabled Students: 90% of the campus is accessible. Wheelchair ramps, elevators, special parking, specially equipped rest rooms, lowered drinking fountains, and lowered telephones are available.

Services: Counseling and information services are available, as is tutoring in every subject. There is remedial math, reading, and writing.

Campus Safety and Security: Measures include 24-hour foot and vehicle patrol, escort service, informal discussions, and pamphlets/posters/films. There are emergency telephones, lighted pathways/sidewalks, and video monitors.

Programs of Study: Daemen confers B.A., B.S., and B.F.A. degrees. Master's degrees are also awarded. Bachelor's degrees are awarded in BIOLOGICAL SCIENCE (biology/biological science), BUSINESS (accounting and business administration and management), COMMUNICATIONS AND THE ARTS (applied art, art, English, fine arts, French, graphic design, and Spanish), COMPUTER AND PHYSICAL SCIENCE (chemistry, mathematics, and natural sciences), EDUCATION (art, business, elementary, English, foreign languages, mathematics, science, social studies, and special), HEALTH PROFESSIONS (health care administration, nursing, physical therapy, and physician's assistant), SOCIAL SCIENCE (history, humanities, political science/government, psychology, religion, and social work). Physical therapy, physician assistant, and natural science are the strongest academically. Physical therapy, nursing, and physician assistant are the largest.

Required: To graduate, students must complete 120 to 155 hours with a minimum GPA of 2.0. The core curriculum includes 6 credit hours each in literature, philosophy/religion, and history/government; 3 each in composition, fine or performing arts, math, science, economics/sociology, psychology, and liberal arts colloquium; and 6 additional hours outside the major for most programs.

Special: Daemen offers cooperative programs in all majors, internships, cross-registration within the Western New York Consortium of Colleges and Universities, student-designed majors, work-study programs, an accelerated degree program in nursing, dual majors, a Washington semester, and study abroad in Spain, France, Canada, and Mexico. There are 6 national honor societies.

Faculty/Classroom: 45% of faculty are male; 55%, female. 99% teach undergraduates. No introductory courses are taught by graduate students. The average class size in an introductory lecture is 24; in a laboratory, 11; and in a regular course, 14.

Admissions: 77% of the 2001-2002 applicants were accepted. The SAT I scores for the 2001-2002 freshman class were: Verbal--54% below 500, 38% between 500 and 599, and 8% between 600 and 700; Math--56% below 500, 35% between 500 and 599, and 9% between 600 and 700. The ACT scores were 47% below 21, 28% between 21 and 23, 18% between 24 and 26, 5% between 27 and 28, and 2% above 28. 27% of the current freshmen were in the top fifth of their class; 55% were in the top two fifths. 1 freshman graduated first in their class.

Requirements: The SAT I or ACT is required. In addition, applicants must be graduates of an accredited secondary school or have the GED equivalent. Some departments have further admissions requirements, including a portfolio review for art majors, 3-year sequences of math and science for all natural science programs, and 2 essays, 3 letters of recommendation, and a supplemental application for the physician assistant program. A GPA of 2.0 is required. AP and CLEP credits are accepted. Important factors in the admissions decision are advanced placement or honor courses, leadership record, and evidence of special talent. Applications are available at the college's web site.

Procedure: Freshmen are admitted to all sessions. Entrance exams should be taken by the summer following the senior year. There are early admissions and deferred admissions plans. The application deadline for the physician assistant and physical therapy programs is January 15. All other application deadlines are open. Notification is sent on a rolling basis. The fall 2001 application fee was $25.

Transfer: 186 transfer students enrolled in 2001-2002. Applicants must present college transcripts and an indication of good standing from the last institution attended and a minimum GPA of 2.0. to 2.8. Physician assistant applicants should submit essays, 3 letters of recommendation, and supplemental applications. 30 credits of 120 must be completed at Daemen.

Visiting: There are regularly scheduled orientations for prospective students, consisting of a 5-day orientation that includes a campus tour, interview, and placement testing in math and English during July and August. There are guides for informal visits and visitors may sit in on classes and stay overnight. To schedule a visit, contact the Admissions Office.

Financial Aid: In 2000-2001, 47% of all freshmen and 72% of continuing students received some form of financial aid. 45% of freshmen and 65% of continuing students received need-based aid. The average freshman award was $11,689. Of that total, scholarships or need-based grants averaged $5641 ($10,000 maximum); loans averaged $1986 ($2625 maximum); work contracts averaged $704 ($2000 maximum); and parent loan for student averaged $978 ($1500 maximum). 21% of undergraduates work part time. Average annual earnings from campus work are $704. The average financial indebtedness of the 2001 graduate was $11,527. The FAFSA is required. The fall application deadline is February 15.

International Students: There are 129 international students enrolled. The school actively recruits these students. They must score 500 on the written TOEFL.

Computers: 146 PCs are available on campus in the Academic Resource Center, the library, and departmental computer labs. Internet access is available at all terminals. All students may access the system. There are no time limits and no fees.

Graduates: In 2001, 327 bachelor's degrees were awarded. The most popular majors were physical therapy (30%), nursing (22%), and physician assistant (10%). In an average class, 19% graduate in 4 years, 31% in 5 years, and 34% in 6 years. 80 companies recruited on campus in 2000-2001. Of the 2000 graduating class, 18% were enrolled in graduate school within 6 months of graduation and 89% were employed.

Admissions Contact: Patricia Brown, Dean of Enrollment Management. A video is available. E-mail: *admissions@daeman.edu*
Web: *http://www.daemen.edu*

DEVRY INSTITUTE OF TECHNOLOGY/NEW YORK
Long Island City, NY 11101 — D-5
(718) 361-0004
(888) 71-DeVry; Fax: (718) 269-4288

Full-time: 1199 men, 319 women	**Faculty:** 55
Part-time: 413 men, 105 women	**Ph.D.s:** n/av
Graduate: none	**Student/Faculty:** 28 to 1
Year: semesters, summer session	**Tuition:** $9865
Application Deadline: open	**Room & Board:** n/app
Freshman Class: 1506 accepted, 655 enrolled	
SAT I or ACT: recommended	**LESS COMPETITIVE**

DeVry Institute of Technology/New York, founded in 1998, is a private institution offering hands-on programs in electronics, business administration, computer information systems, telecommunications, and computer technology. The school is 1 of 23 Devry Institutes throughout the United States and Canada. The library contains 9752 volumes and 708 audiovisual forms/CDs, and subscribes to 120 periodicals. Computerized library services include the card catalog, interlibrary loans, and database searching. Special learning facilities include a learning resource center and electronics and other labs. The 2-acre campus is in an urban area. There is 1 building.

Student Life: 96% of undergraduates are from New York. Others are from 16 states and 29 foreign countries. 22% are African American; 16% Hispanic. The average age of all undergraduates is 26. 41% do not continue beyond their first year.

Housing: There are no residence halls. All students commute. Alcohol is not permitted. All students may keep cars.
Activities: There are no fraternities or sororities. There are 7 groups on campus, including chess, international, professional, social, and yearbook. Popular campus events include DSA Time Out, End of Semester Bashment, and Post Ramadan Celebration.
Sports: There is no sports program at DeVry.
Disabled Students: All of the campus is accessible. Elevators, special parking, specially equipped rest rooms, special class scheduling, lowered drinking fountains, and lowered telephones are available.
Services: Counseling and information services are available, as is tutoring in every subject.
Campus Safety and Security: Measures include 24-hour foot and vehicle patrol, escort service, informal discussions, and pamphlets/posters/films. There are emergency telephones and lighted pathways/sidewalks.
Programs of Study: DeVry confers the B.S. degree. Associate degrees are also awarded. Bachelor's degrees are awarded in BUSINESS (business administration and management), COMMUNICATIONS AND THE ARTS (telecommunications), COMPUTER AND PHYSICAL SCIENCE (information sciences and systems), ENGINEERING AND ENVIRONMENTAL DESIGN (computer technology and electrical/electronics engineering technology). Electronics, computer information systems, and business administration are the largest.
Required: To graduate, students must complete 48 to 154 credit hours with a 2.0 minimum GPA. Course requirements vary according to program. All first-semester students take courses in algebra, psychology, and student success strategies.
Special: Evening and weekend classes, co-op programs, and an accelerated degree program are offered.
Faculty/Classroom: All teach undergraduates. The average class size in an introductory lecture is 30; in a laboratory, 30; and in a regular course, 30.
Requirements: The SAT I or ACT is recommended. Admissions requirements include graduation from a secondary school; the GED is also accepted. Applicants must pass the DeVry entrance exam or present satisfactory ACT or SAT I scores. An interview is required. CLEP credit is accepted. Applications are accepted on-line at *www.ny.devry.edu*
Procedure: Freshmen are admitted fall, spring, and summer. There is a deferred admissions plan. Application deadlines are open. The application fee is $50. Notification is sent on a rolling basis.
Transfer: 22 transfer students enrolled in 2001-2002. Applicants must present passing grades in all completed college course work, demonstrate language skills proficiency with at least 24 completed semester hours, and present evidence of math proficiency by appropriate college-level credits. 35 credits of 48 to 154 must be completed at DeVry.
Visiting: There are regularly scheduled orientations for prospective students. There are guides for informal visits and visitors may sit in on classes. To schedule a visit, contact Edith Bolancos, Director of Admissions at (718) 472-2728.
Financial Aid: In a recent year, 70% of all freshmen and 86% of continuing students received some form of financial aid. 57% of freshmen and 55% of continuing students received need-based aid. 3% of undergraduates work part time. Average annual earnings from campus work are $5000. The average financial indebtedness of the 2001 graduate was $7680. The FAFSA is required.
International Students: There are 101 international students enrolled. They must score 500 on the written TOEFL or 173 on the electronic version and also take DeVry computerized placement test, achieving a minimum score that varies by program.
Computers: Lab facilities include PCs in stand-alone and network configurations, with access to the mainframe. LANs provide access to a wide range of applications software. Hard copy from the mainframe is provided through a local minicomputer and medium- and high-speed printers. Computer information systems students may access the system during lab hours. There are no fees.
Graduates: In 2001, 5 bachelor's degrees were awarded. The most popular majors were electronics technology (80%) and business (20%). 21 companies recruited on campus in 2000-2001.
Admissions Contact: Newton Myrett, Director of Admissions.
Web: *www.ny.devry.edu*

DOMINICAN COLLEGE D-5
Orangeburg, NY 10962 (845) 359-7800, ext. 208; (845) 365-3150

Full-time: 220 men, 540 women	**Faculty:** 56; IIB, -$
Part-time: 200 men, 700 women	**Ph.D.s:** 46%
Graduate: 10 men, 30 women	**Student/Faculty:** 14 to 1
Year: semesters, summer session	**Tuition:** $13,400
Application Deadline: open	**Room & Board:** $7000
Freshman Class: n/av	
SAT I: required	**LESS COMPETITIVE**

Dominican College, founded in 1952, is an independent Catholic institution offering undergraduate programs in business, biology, education, liberal arts, nursing, premedicine, occupational therapy, and social sciences. Figures in the above capsule are approximate. In addition to regional accreditation, Dominican has baccalaureate program accreditation with CSWE and NLN. The library contains 103,000 volumes, 15,000 microform items, and 1000 audiovisual forms/CDs, and subscribes to 650 periodicals. Computerized library services include interlibrary loans. Special learning facilities include a learning resource center. The 24-acre campus is in a suburban area 17 miles north of New York City. Including residence halls, there are 9 buildings.
Student Life: 74% of undergraduates are from New York. Others are from 11 states and 5 foreign countries. 70% are from public schools. 69% are white; 12% African American; 10% Hispanic. 75% are Catholic; 10% Jewish; 10% Protestant. The average age of freshmen is 19; all undergraduates, 23. 23% do not continue beyond their first year; 45% remain to graduate.
Housing: 250 students can be accommodated in college housing, which includes coed dormitories. On-campus housing is guaranteed for all 4 years. 85% of students commute. Alcohol is not permitted. All students may keep cars.
Activities: There are no fraternities or sororities. There are 17 groups on campus, including cheerleading, chorus, computers, drama, honors, international, literary magazine, musical theater, newspaper, professional, religious, social service, student government, and yearbook. Popular campus events include Family Day, craft fair, and Springfest.
Sports: There are 3 intercollegiate sports for men and 4 for women. Facilities include a baseball field and a basketball court.
Disabled Students: All of the campus is accessible. Wheelchair ramps, special parking, specially equipped rest rooms, lowered drinking fountains, and lowered telephones are available.
Services: Counseling and information services are available, as is tutoring in some subjects, including English and math. There is remedial math, reading, and writing. There is a writing center.
Campus Safety and Security: Measures include shuttle buses, informal discussions, emergency telephones, and lighted pathways/sidewalks. There are night security guards in dorms.
Programs of Study: Dominican confers B.A., B.S., B.S.Ed., and B.S.N. degrees. Associate and master's degrees are also awarded. Bachelor's degrees are awarded in BIOLOGICAL SCIENCE (biology/biological science), BUSINESS (accounting, business administration and management, business economics, international business management, and marketing/retailing/merchandising), COMMUNICATIONS AND THE ARTS (English, languages, and Spanish), COMPUTER AND PHYSICAL SCIENCE (actuarial science and mathematics), EDUCATION (athletic training, elementary, science, secondary, and special), ENGINEERING AND ENVIRONMENTAL DESIGN (preengineering), HEALTH PROFESSIONS (nursing, occupational therapy, physical therapy, and premedicine), SOCIAL SCIENCE (American studies, history, humanities, prelaw, psychology, public administration, social science, and social work). Occupational therapy and nursing are the strongest academically. Business, nursing, and occupational therapy are the largest.
Required: Computer courses are required for business majors. In order to graduate, all students must complete 120 semester hours, including a general education curriculum of 36 to 39 credits. Nursing and occupational therapy majors must maintain a minimum GPA of 2.5, while all other majors require at least a 2.0.
Special: Accelerated degree programs are available in business majors, as well as co-op programs in business administration, arts and sciences, nursing, social sciences, education, and social work. Individualized internships in all fields, work-study programs, B.A.-B.S. degrees, dual majors, and a 3-2 engineering degree with Manhattan College are also offered. Dual teacher certification in elementary and special education is available. Credit for life experience is granted through submission of a portfolio. Weekend College, offered on a trimester basis, is designed to meet the needs of working adults. There are 3 national honor societies, a freshman honors program, and 3 departmental honors programs.
Faculty/Classroom: 38% of faculty are male; 62%, female. 96% teach undergraduates. The average class size in a regular course is 16.
Requirements: The SAT I is required. In addition, applicants should be graduates of an accredited secondary school or possess a GED equivalent. An interview and an essay are recommended. Applications are accepted on-line via CollegeLink and Princeton Review. A grade average of 70.0 is required. AP and CLEP credits are accepted. Important factors in the admissions decision are advanced placement or honor courses, leadership record, and extracurricular activities record.
Procedure: Freshmen are admitted to all sessions. Entrance exams should be taken by November of the senior year. There are early decision, early admissions, and deferred admissions plans. Application deadlines are open. The application fee is $35.
Transfer: 104 transfer students enrolled in a recent year. Applicants must submit a transcript from their previous school. A minimum GPA of 2.0 is required. An interview should be scheduled. Departmental approval is required for acceptance into all major areas of study. 30 credits of 120 must be completed at Dominican.
Visiting: There are regularly scheduled orientations for prospective students. There are guides for informal visits and visitors may sit in on classes. To schedule a visit, contact Joyce Elbe, Director of Admissions.

Financial Aid: In a recent year, 98% of all freshmen and 79% of continuing students received some form of financial aid. 76% of freshmen and 68% of continuing students received need-based aid. The average freshman award was $10,215. Of that total, scholarships or need-based grants averaged $4750 ($12,000 maximum); loans averaged $3965 ($8750 maximum); and work contracts averaged $1500. 37% of undergraduates work part time. Average annual earnings from campus work are $1485. The average financial indebtedness of a recent graduate was $15,000. Dominican is a member of CSS. The FAFSA and the college's own financial statement are required. The fall application deadline is May 1.

International Students: The school actively recruits these students. They must score 500 on the written TOEFL and also take the SAT I or the ACT.

Computers: The mainframe is a DEC MicroVAX 3100-40. There are 4 PC computer labs on campus. One lab is located in the residence hall. All students may access the system. There are no time limits and no fees.

Graduates: In a recent, 308 bachelor's degrees were awarded. The most popular majors were business (28%), nursing (28%), and occupational therapy (16%). In an average class, 40% graduate in 4 years, 42% in 5 years, and 44% in 6 years. Of a recent graduating class, 8% were enrolled in graduate school within 6 months of graduation and 99% were employed.

Admissions Contact: Joyce Elbe, Director of Admissions. A video is available. E-mail: *admissions@dc.edu* Web: *www.dc.edu*

DOWLING COLLEGE

Oakdale, NY 11769-1999 — E-5

(631) 244-3436
(800) DOWLING; Fax: (631) 563-3827

Full-time: 732 men, 1104 women	**Faculty:** 91
Part-time: 368 men, 659 women	**Ph.D.s:** 90%
Graduate: 856 men, 1836 women	**Student/Faculty:** 17 to 1
Year: 4-1-4, summer session	**Tuition:** $12,735
Application Deadline: open	**Room & Board:** $7546
Freshman Class: 1386 applied, 1370 accepted, 398 enrolled	
SAT I or ACT: recommended	**LESS COMPETITIVE**

Dowling College, founded in 1955, is a small, independent institution offering programs in the arts and sciences, aviation and transportation, business, and education. There are 4 undergraduate and 3 graduate schools. The library contains 174,947 volumes, 558,811 microform items, and 108 audiovisual forms/CDs, and subscribes to 1259 periodicals. Computerized library services include the card catalog, interlibrary loans, and database searching. Special learning facilities include a learning resource center, art gallery, radio station, government documents, and the Federal Aviation Administration (FAA) Aviation Education Resource Center. The 156-acre campus is in a suburban area 50 miles east of New York City. Including residence halls, there are 10 buildings.

Student Life: 95% of undergraduates are from New York. Others are from 25 states, 61 foreign countries, and Canada. 89% are from public schools. 65% are white. The average age of freshmen is 20; all undergraduates, 28. 20% do not continue beyond their first year; 36% remain to graduate.

Housing: 481 students can be accommodated in college housing, which includes coed on-campus apartments. On-campus housing is available on a first-come, first-served basis. Priority is given to out-of-town students. 86% of students commute. Alcohol is not permitted. All students may keep cars.

Activities: There are no fraternities or sororities. There are 39 groups on campus, including aeronautics, art, cheerleading, chorus, computers, drama, ethnic, gay, gospel choir, honors, international, literary magazine, martial arts, newspaper, orchestra, photography, professional, psychology, radio and TV, religious, social, student government, and yearbook. Popular campus events include Freshman Mixer, Holiday Party, and Spring Cotillion.

Sports: There are 7 intercollegiate sports for men and 6 for women. Facilities include a basketball court, a weight room, tennis courts, and a fitness center.

Disabled Students: 90% of the campus is accessible. Wheelchair ramps, elevators, special parking, specially equipped rest rooms, special class scheduling, lowered drinking fountains, and lowered telephones are available.

Services: Counseling and information services are available, as is tutoring in most subjects. There is remedial math, reading, and writing.

Campus Safety and Security: Measures include 24-hour foot and vehicle patrol, escort service, shuttle buses, and informal discussions. There are pamphlets/posters/films, emergency telephones, and lighted pathways/sidewalks.

Programs of Study: Dowling confers B.A., B.S., and B.B.A. degrees. Master's and doctoral degrees are also awarded. Bachelor's degrees are awarded in BIOLOGICAL SCIENCE (biology/biological science and marine biology), BUSINESS (accounting, banking and finance, business administration and management, international business management, marketing/retailing/merchandising, tourism, and transportation management), COMMUNICATIONS AND THE ARTS (communications, English, fine arts, languages, music, romance languages and literature, speech/debate/rhetoric, and visual and performing arts), COMPUTER AND PHYSICAL SCIENCE (applied mathematics, computer programming, computer science, information sciences and systems, mathematics, and natural sciences), EDUCATION (elementary, music, secondary, and special), ENGINEERING AND ENVIRONMENTAL DESIGN (aeronautical science and aeronautical technology), SOCIAL SCIENCE (anthropology, economics, history, humanities, liberal arts/general studies, philosophy, political science/government, psychology, social science, and sociology). Business, education, and computer sciences are the largest.

Required: To graduate, students must complete 122 credits with a minimum GPA of 2.0. The required 36-credit general education core includes a senior seminar.

Special: Dowling offers a B.S. in professional and liberal studies, internships, independent study, work-study, and nondegree study. There are cooperative programs in several majors, including aeronautics and airway science majors with the FAA. There are 10 national honor societies, a freshman honors program, and 3 departmental honors programs.

Faculty/Classroom: 65% of faculty are male; 35%, female. 66% teach undergraduates. No introductory courses are taught by graduate students. The average class size in an introductory lecture is 20; in a laboratory, 15; and in a regular course, 17.

Admissions: 99% of the 2001-2002 applicants were accepted.

Requirements: The SAT I or ACT is recommended. In addition, applicants should be graduates of an accredited secondary school and have completed at least 16 Carnegie units, including 4 in English. An interview is strongly recommended. AP and CLEP credits are accepted. Important factors in the admissions decision are advanced placement or honor courses, evidence of special talent, and recommendations by school officials. Applicants can apply on-line at *http://www.dowling.edu.*

Procedure: Freshmen are admitted to all sessions. Entrance exams should be taken by January of the senior year. There is a deferred admissions plan. Application deadlines are open. The application fee is $25. Notification is sent on a rolling basis.

Transfer: 342 transfer students enrolled in 2001-2002. Applicants must submit official transcripts from all colleges attended. Courses completed with a grade of C or better may transfer. 30 credits of 122 must be completed at Dowling.

Visiting: There are regularly scheduled orientations for prospective students, including a campus tour and meetings with enrollment services members, staff, and faculty. There are guides for informal visits and visitors may sit in on classes and stay overnight. To schedule a visit, contact the Enrollment Services Office.

Financial Aid: In a recent year, 73% of all freshmen and 68% of continuing students received some form of financial aid. 71% of freshmen and 70% of continuing students received need-based aid. The average freshman award was $6473. Of that total, scholarships or need-based grants averaged $1618 ($12,015 maximum); loans averaged $2500 ($6625 maximum); and work contracts averaged $1510 ($3000 maximum). All undergraduates work part time. Average annual earnings from campus work are $1510. The average financial indebtedness of a recent year's graduate was $6810. The FAFSA and the college's own financial statement are required. The fall application deadline is May 1.

International Students: There are 100 international students enrolled. The school actively recruits these students. They must score 500 on the written TOEFL.

Computers: The mainframe is an IBM RS6000 Model 7017-570. There are Compaq and IBM PCs in the academic computing center and library. All students may access the system 7 A.M. to 10:45 P.M., Monday through Thursday and 7 A.M. to 5 P.M., Friday through Sunday. There are no time limits and no fees.

Graduates: In 2001, 602 bachelor's degrees were awarded. The most popular majors were elementary education (13%), management (12%), and accounting (11%). In an average class, 21% graduate in 4 years, 27% in 5 years, and 33% in 6 years. 115 companies recruited on campus in 2000-2001.

Admissions Contact: Bridget Masturzo, Assistant Director of Communication. A video is available. E-mail: *masturzb@dowling.edu*
Web: *www.dowling.edu*

D'YOUVILLE COLLEGE
Buffalo, NY 14201

A-3
(716) 881-7600
(800) 777-3921; Fax: (716) 881-7790

Full-time: 192 men, 545 women	**Faculty:** 106
Part-time: 50 men, 174 women	**Ph.D.s:** 60%
Graduate: 343 men, 1182 women	**Student/Faculty:** 7 to 1
Year: semesters, summer session	**Tuition:** $12,550
Application Deadline: open	**Room & Board:** $6154
Freshman Class: 652 applied, 464 accepted, 95 enrolled	
SAT I Verbal/Math: 460/480	**ACT:** 23 **COMPETITIVE**

D'Youville College, founded in 1908, is a private, nonsectarian liberal arts institution. In addition to regional accreditation, D'Youville has baccalaureate program accreditation with ADA, APTA, CAHEA, CSWE, and NLN. The library contains 95,995 volumes, 181,884 microform items, and 3342 audiovisual forms/CDs, and subscribes to 690 periodicals. Computerized library services include the card catalog and database searching. Special learning facilities include a learning resource center and radio station. The 7-acre campus is in an urban area 1 mile north of Buffalo. Including residence halls, there are 8 buildings.

Student Life: 94% of undergraduates are from New York. Others are from 23 states, 26 foreign countries, and Canada. 80% are from public schools. 61% are white; 17% foreign nationals; 11% African American. The average age of freshmen is 19; all undergraduates, 25. 30% do not continue beyond their first year; 47% remain to graduate.

Housing: 308 students can be accommodated in college housing, which includes single-sex and coed dormitories. In addition, there are honors floors. On-campus housing is guaranteed for all 4 years. 80% of students commute. All students may keep cars.

Activities: There are no fraternities or sororities. There are 35 groups on campus, including chorus, computers, ethnic, honors, international, literary magazine, newspaper, professional, radio and TV, religious, social, social service, student government, and yearbook. Popular campus events include Moving Up Days, Family and Friends, and Honors Convocation.

Sports: There are 6 intercollegiate sports for men and 6 for women, and 9 intramural sports for men and 9 for women. Facilities include a 200-seat indoor gym, a basketball court, a swimming pool, a fitness room, and a dance studio.

Disabled Students: 95% of the campus is accessible. Wheelchair ramps, elevators, special parking, specially equipped rest rooms, lowered drinking fountains, and lowered telephones are available.

Services: Counseling and information services are available, as is tutoring in some subjects, based on tutor accessibility. There is a reader service for the blind, and remedial math, reading, and writing.

Campus Safety and Security: Measures include 24-hour foot and vehicle patrol, self-defense education, escort service, and informal discussions. There are pamphlets/posters/films, emergency telephones, lighted pathways/sidewalks, a special focus program, and a security committee.

Programs of Study: D'Youville confers B.A., B.S., and B.S.N. degrees. Master's degrees are also awarded. Bachelor's degrees are awarded in BIOLOGICAL SCIENCE (biology/biological science), BUSINESS (accounting, business administration and management, and international business management), COMMUNICATIONS AND THE ARTS (English), COMPUTER AND PHYSICAL SCIENCE (information sciences and systems), EDUCATION (business, elementary, and special), HEALTH PROFESSIONS (nursing, occupational therapy, physical therapy, and physician's assistant), SOCIAL SCIENCE (dietetics, history, philosophy, psychology, and sociology). Education and health professions are the strongest academically. Health professions, business, and nursing are the largest.

Required: All students must complete general program and core curriculum requirements, including 5 courses in humanities, 2 each in English and natural sciences, and 1 each in ethics, philosophy or religion, history, sociology, psychology, economics or political science, math, and computer science. A minimum of 120 to 144 credit hours, varying by major, with a minimum GPA of 2.0, is required to graduate.

Special: D'Youville has cross-registration with member colleges of the Western New York Consortium. Internships, work-study programs, dual majors, and pass/fail options are available. Accelerated 5-year B.S.-M.S. programs in physical therapy, occupational therapy, international business, nursing, and dietetics are offered. For freshmen with undecided majors, the Career Discovery Program offers special courses, internships, and faculty advisers. There is 1 national honor society, and 6 departmental honors programs.

Faculty/Classroom: 40% of faculty are male; 60%, female. All both teach and do research. No introductory courses are taught by graduate students. The average class size in an introductory lecture is 30; in a laboratory, 12; and in a regular course, 23.

Admissions: 71% of the 2001-2002 applicants were accepted. The SAT I scores for the 2001-2002 freshman class were: Verbal--61% below 500, 34% between 500 and 599, and 5% between 600 and 700; Math--64% below 500, 30% between 500 and 599, 4% between 600 and 700, and 2% above 700. The ACT scores were 16% below 21, 50% between 21 and 23, 25% between 24 and 26, and 8% above 28. 29% of the current freshmen were in the top fifth of their class; 65% were in the top two fifths.

Requirements: The SAT I or ACT is required. In addition, applicants should have completed 16 Carnegie units, including 4 years of high school English, 3 of social studies, and 1 each of math and science; some majors require additional years of math and science. The GED is accepted. An interview is recommended. A GPA of 2.0 is required. AP and CLEP credits are accepted. Important factors in the admissions decision are advanced placement or honor courses, evidence of special talent, and leadership record. Applications are accepted on-line.

Procedure: Freshmen are admitted fall and spring. Entrance exams should be taken by the end of the junior year. There is a deferred admissions plan. Application deadlines are open. The fall 2001 application fee was $25. Notification is sent on a rolling basis.

Transfer: 153 transfer students enrolled in 2001-2002. Applicants need a minimum GPA of 2.0, or 2.5 for some programs. An interview is recommended. There are very few openings for transfers seeking part-time studies. 30 credits of 120 must be completed at D'Youville.

Visiting: There are regularly scheduled orientations for prospective students. There are guides for informal visits and visitors may sit in on classes and stay overnight. To schedule a visit, contact the Admissions Office.

Financial Aid: In a recent year, 98% of all freshmen and 82% of continuing students received some form of financial aid. 85% of freshmen and 80% of continuing students received need-based aid. The average freshman award was $5844. Of that total, scholarships or need-based grants averaged $5000 ($10,000 maximum); loans averaged $3400 ($5125 maximum); and work contracts averaged $800. 26% of undergraduates work part time. Average annual earnings from campus work are $800. The average financial indebtedness of a recent year's graduate was $14,000. D'Youville is a member of CSS. The FAFSA and New York State TAP are required. The fall application deadline is March 15.

International Students: There are 97 international students enrolled. The school actively recruits these students. They must score 500 on the written TOEFL and also take the SAT I or the ACT.

Computers: The mainframe is a Sun. There are 3 computer labs as well as computers located in the residence hall. Mac and Windows computers are networked. There is a fiber optic computer network with ports throughout the college, including the dorms. All students may access the system. There are no time limits and no fees.

Graduates: In 2001, 206 bachelor's degrees were awarded. The most popular majors were physical/occupational therapy (43%), physician assistant (17%), and nursing (13%). 92 companies recruited on campus in a recent year. Of a recent year's graduating class, 10% were enrolled in graduate school within 6 months of graduation and 96% were employed.

Admissions Contact: Ron H. Dannecker, Director of Admissions and Financial Aid. E-mail: *admiss@dyc.edu* Web: *www.dyc.edu*

EASTMAN SCHOOL OF MUSIC
Rochester, NY 14604

B-3
(585) 274-1060
(800) 388-9695; Fax: (585) 232-8601

Full-time: 494 men and women	**Faculty:** 89
Part-time: none	**Ph.D.s:** 55%
Graduate: 326 men and women	**Student/Faculty:** 6 to 1
Year: semesters	**Tuition:** $22,499
Application Deadline: December 1	**Room & Board:** $8185
Freshman Class: 899 applied, 234 accepted, 111 enrolled	
SAT I: recommended	**SPECIAL**

Eastman School of Music, founded in 1921, is a private professional school of music within the University of Rochester. In addition to regional accreditation, Eastman has baccalaureate program accreditation with NASM. The library contains 350,000 volumes, 16,000 microform items, and 100,000 audiovisual forms/CDs, and subscribes to 650 periodicals. Computerized library services include the card catalog, interlibrary loans, and database searching. Special learning facilities include a learning resource center, art gallery, recording studios, a music library, a theater, and 3 recital halls. The 3-acre campus is in an urban area in downtown Rochester. Including residence halls, there are 4 buildings.

Student Life: 73% of undergraduates are from out of state, mostly the Middle Atlantic. Others are from 40 states, 23 foreign countries, and Canada. 90% are from public schools. 70% are white; 15% foreign nationals. The average age of freshmen is 18; all undergraduates, 20. 11% do not continue beyond their first year; 80% remain to graduate.

Housing: 360 students can be accommodated in college housing, which includes single-sex and coed dormitories, fraternity houses, and sorority houses. The Student Living Center is divided into separate "houses" that can be organized by special interest. On-campus housing is guaranteed for all 4 years. 90% of students live on campus; of those, all remain on campus on weekends. Alcohol is not permitted. All students may keep cars.

Activities: 5% of men and about 2% of women belong to 2 national fraternities; 4% of women belong to 1 national sorority. There are more than 15 groups on campus, including Association for Injury Prevention, band, chorale, chorus, computers, gay, international, jazz band, literary magazine, newspaper, opera, orchestra, professional, religious, social, student government, symphony, and yearbook. Popular campus events include Holiday Sing and Boo Blast.

Sports: There is no sports program at Eastman. All athletic facilities of the University of Rochester, as well as a nearby YMCA, are available to students.

Disabled Students: 95% of the campus is accessible. Wheelchair ramps, elevators, special parking, specially equipped rest rooms, lowered drinking fountains, and lowered telephones are available.

Services: Counseling and information services are available, as is tutoring in every subject. There is a reader service for the blind, remedial writing, and English tutoring for nonnative English speakers.

Campus Safety and Security: Measures include 24-hour foot and vehicle patrol, self-defense education, escort service, and shuttle buses. There are informal discussions, pamphlets/posters/films, emergency telephones, lighted pathways/sidewalks, and security cameras.

Programs of Study: Eastman confers the B.M. degree. Master's and doctoral degrees are also awarded. Bachelor's degrees are awarded in COMMUNICATIONS AND THE ARTS (jazz, music, music performance, and music theory and composition), EDUCATION (music). Performance is the largest.

Required: All students must complete core requirements in a major instrument or voice, music theory, music history, and Western cultural tradition, as well as English and humanities electives. A total of 120 to 148 credit hours, varying by program, with a minimum GPA of 2.0, is required to graduate.

Special: The school and the University of Rochester cooperatively offer the B.A. degree with a music concentration. All the facilities of the university are open to Eastman students. Cross-registration is also available with colleges in the Rochester Consortium. Dual majors are available in all areas of study. Internships and study abroad are also possible. There is 1 national honor society.

Faculty/Classroom: 60% of faculty are male; 40%, female. All both teach and do research. Graduate students teach 10% of introductory courses. The average class size in an introductory lecture is 30 and in a regular course, 15.

Admissions: 26% of the 2001-2002 applicants were accepted.

Requirements: The SAT I is recommended. The SAT I or ACT is required only of home-schooled applicants. Applicants should be graduates of an accredited secondary school with 16 academic credits, including 4 years of English. The GED is accepted. An audition and an interview are required, as are 3 letters of recommendation. Some majors have other specific requirements. AP credits are accepted. Important factors in the admissions decision are evidence of special talent, recommendations by alumni, and personality/intangible qualities.

Procedure: Freshmen are admitted fall and spring. There is a deferred admissions plan. Applications should be filed by December 1 for fall entry and November 1 for spring entry, along with a $80 fee. Notification is sent on a rolling basis. 10% of all applicants are on a waiting list; 10 were accepted in 2001.

Transfer: 15 transfer students enrolled in 2001-2002. Requirements include satisfactory academic standing at the previous institution, a successful audition, and an interview. The number of credits that must be completed at Eastman varies.

Visiting: There are regularly scheduled orientations for prospective students, including group information sessions and a tour of the facilities. To schedule a visit, contact the Admissions Office.

Financial Aid: In a recent year, 99% of all freshmen and 98% of continuing students received some form of financial aid. 73% of freshmen and 71% of continuing students received need-based aid. 70% of undergraduates work part time. Average annual earnings from campus work are $800. The average financial indebtedness of a recent year's graduate was $10,000. Eastman is a member of CSS. The CSS/Profile or FAFSA and the college's own financial statement are required. The fall application deadline is February 1.

International Students: There are 64 international students enrolled. The school actively recruits these students. They must score 500 on the written TOEFL or 173 on the electronic version.

Computers: The mainframe is an SGI origin 200 (UNIX). IBM PCs and Macs are located in residence halls, the library, and the main building. There is also a computer music center with Musical Instrument Digital Interface. Residence hall rooms are wired for Internet access. An Internet Cafe is located in the main building. All students may access the system. There are no time limits. The fee is $50.

Graduates: In 2001, 83 bachelor's degrees were awarded. The most popular majors were music performance (76%), music education (11%), and composition (6%). In an average class, 74% graduate in 6 years. 35 companies recruited on campus in 2000-2001. Of the 2000 graduating class, 70% were enrolled in graduate school within 6 months of graduation and 16% were employed.

Admissions Contact: Kathleen Tesar, Director of Admissions.
E-mail: *esmadmit@mail.rochester.edu*
Web: *www.rochester.edu/Eastman*

ELMIRA COLLEGE — C-4

Elmira, NY 14901 — (607) 735-1724
(800) 935-6472; Fax: (607) 735-1718

Full-time: 391 men, 838 women	**Faculty:** 80; IIB, -$
Part-time: 98 men, 257 women	**Ph.D.s:** 98%
Graduate: 85 men, 272 women	**Student/Faculty:** 15 to 1
Year: terms, summer session	**Tuition:** $23,540
Application Deadline: June 15	**Room & Board:** $7530
Freshman Class: 1833 applied, 1345 accepted, 372 enrolled	
SAT I Verbal/Math: 550/540	**ACT:** 25 **VERY COMPETITIVE+**

Elmira College, founded in 1855, is a private liberal arts institution offering general and preprofessional programs. In addition to regional accreditation, Elmira has baccalaureate program accreditation with NLN. The library contains 389,000 volumes, 1,320,000 microform items, and 2200 audiovisual forms/CDs, and subscribes to 1755 periodicals. Computerized library services include the card catalog, interlibrary loans, and database searching. Special learning facilities include a learning resource center, art gallery, radio station, speech and hearing clinic, and Mark Twain's study. The 42-acre campus is in a suburban area 90 miles southwest of Syracuse. Including residence halls, there are 25 buildings.

Student Life: 55% of undergraduates are from New York. Others are from 35 states, 23 foreign countries, and Canada. 65% are from public schools. 87% are white. The average age of freshmen is 18; all undergraduates, 21. 12% do not continue beyond their first year; 65% remain to graduate.

Housing: 1068 students can be accommodated in college housing, which includes single-sex and coed dormitories, honors floors, and on-campus apartments. On-campus housing is guaranteed for all 4 years. 92% of students live on campus; of those, 90% remain on campus on weekends. All students may keep cars.

Activities: There are no fraternities or sororities. There are 70 groups on campus, including art, band, cheerleading, chorale, chorus, dance, drama, honors, international, literary magazine, musical theater, newspaper, orchestra, pep band, political, professional, radio, religious, social, social service, student government, and yearbook. Popular campus events include Mountain Day, Midnight Breakfast, and Spring Weekend.

Sports: There are 6 intercollegiate sports for men and 10 for women, and 21 intramural sports for men and 21 for women. Facilities include 2500-seat and 950-seat gyms, indoor tennis facilities, a 3500-seat hockey arena, racquetball courts, a fitness center, a dance studio, and a swimming pool.

Disabled Students: 25% of the campus is accessible. Wheelchair ramps, elevators, special parking, specially equipped rest rooms, and special class scheduling are available.

Services: Counseling and information services are available, as is tutoring in most subjects. Tutoring in math and freshman English is available in each freshman dorm.

Campus Safety and Security: Measures include 24-hour foot and vehicle patrol, escort service, informal discussions, and pamphlets/posters/films. There are lighted pathways/sidewalks.

Programs of Study: Elmira confers B.A. and B.S. degrees. Bachelor's degrees are awarded in BIOLOGICAL SCIENCE (biochemistry and biology/biological science), BUSINESS (accounting, business administration and management, business economics, international business management, and marketing/retailing/merchandising), COMMUNICATIONS AND THE ARTS (art, classics, dramatic arts, English literature, fine arts, French, languages, music, and Spanish), COMPUTER AND PHYSICAL SCIENCE (chemistry and mathematics), EDUCATION (art, elementary, foreign languages, science, and secondary), ENGINEERING AND ENVIRONMENTAL DESIGN (environmental science), HEALTH PROFESSIONS (medical laboratory technology, nursing, predentistry, premedicine, and speech pathology/audiology), SOCIAL SCIENCE (American studies, anthropology, criminal justice, history, human services, international studies, philosophy, political science/government, prelaw, psychology, and sociology). History, theater, and premedicine are the strongest academically. Psychology, management, and education are the largest.

Required: All students must complete general degree requirements, including communication skills, writing courses, math competency, and computer literacy; a core curriculum; distribution requirements in culture and civilization, contemporary social institutions, the scientific method, the creative process, and phys ed; and a field experience program. A total of 120 credit hours with a minimum GPA of 2.0 overall and in the major is required to graduate.

Special: The required field experience program provides a career-related internship as well as community service. A junior year abroad program, a Washington semester, an accelerated degree program, a general studies degree, student-designed majors, and pass/fail options are available. A 3-2 chemical engineering degree is offered with Clarkson University. B.A.-B.S. degrees are offered in biochemistry, biology, chemistry, economics, education, environmental studies, history, math, political science, and psychology. Elmira is a member of the Spring Term Consortium, enabling students to take 6-week courses at participating institutions. There are 10 national honor societies, including Phi Beta Kappa.

Faculty/Classroom: 52% of faculty are male; 48%, female. All both teach and do research. The average class size in an introductory lecture is 20; in a laboratory, 10; and in a regular course, 16.

Admissions: 73% of the 2001-2002 applicants were accepted. The SAT I scores for the 2001-2002 freshman class were: Verbal--31% below 500, 43% between 500 and 599, 23% between 600 and 700, and 3% above 700; Math--32% below 500, 48% between 500 and 599, 18% between 600 and 700, and 2% above 700. The ACT scores were 20% below 21, 26% between 21 and 23, 32% between 24 and 26, 16% between 27 and 28, and 6% above 28. 50% of the current freshmen were in the top fifth of their class; 77% were in the top two fifths. There were 2 National Merit finalists and 7 semifinalists. 39 freshmen graduated first in their class.

Requirements: The SAT I or ACT is required. In addition, applicants should have completed 4 years of high school English, 3 of math, and 2 of science, or GED equivalent. An essay is part of the application process. An interview is strongly recommended. A GPA of 2.0 is required. AP and CLEP credits are accepted. Important factors in the admissions decision are advanced placement or honor courses, extracurricular activities record, and recommendations by school officials. Applications are accepted on-line via CollegeNet and Common App.

Procedure: Freshmen are admitted fall and winter. Entrance exams should be taken by January of the entry year. There are early decision, early admissions, and deferred admissions plans. Early decision applications should be filed by January 15; regular applications, by June 15 for fall entry and December 1 for winter entry. Notification of early decision is sent January 31; regular decision, on a rolling basis. 58 early decision candidates were accepted for the 2001-2002 class. 3% of all applicants are on a waiting list; 3 were accepted in 2001. The fall 2001 application fee was $40.

Transfer: 61 transfer students enrolled in 2001-2002. Applicants should have a minimum GPA of 2.0. An interview is strongly recommended. 30 credits of 120 must be completed at Elmira.

Visiting: There are regularly scheduled orientations for prospective students, consisting of an open house format and overview, a tour, lunch, a student panel, a faculty panel, general admissions and scholarship information, and an optional interview. Individual visits for interviews and tours are available year-round, including Saturday mornings. There are guides for informal visits and visitors may sit in on classes and stay overnight. To schedule a visit, contact the Office of Admissions at *admissions@elmira.edu*

Financial Aid: 90% of all students received some form of aid. 75% of all students received need-based aid. The average freshman award was $20,700. Of that total, scholarships or need-based grants averaged $13,200 ($22,960 maximum); loans averaged $5000 ($8125 maximum); work contracts averaged $1300 ($1800 maximum); and federal and state grants averaged $1200 ($8750 maximum). 50% of undergraduates work part time. Average annual earnings from campus work are $1000. The average financial indebtedness of the 2001 graduate was $17,137. Elmira is a member of CSS. The FAFSA and state application if applicable are required. The fall application deadline is February 1.

International Students: 75 international students were enrolled in a recent year. The school actively recruits these students. They must score 500 on the written TOEFL or 173 on the electronic version.

Computers: More than 90 PCs connected to the Internet and Windows NT file servers are available to students in the computer center and the library. All students may access the system weekdays 15 hours per day and weekends 8 to 10 hours per day. There are no time limits and no fees.

Graduates: In 2001, 231 bachelor's degrees were awarded. The most popular majors were education (19%), business (15%), and psychology (13%). In an average class, 1% graduate in 3 years, 60% in 4 years, 65% in 5 years, and 65% in 6 years. 40 companies recruited on campus in 2000-2001. Of the 2000 graduating class, 43% were enrolled in graduate school within 6 months of graduation and 55% were employed.

Admissions Contact: William S. Neal, Dean of Admissions.
E-mail: *admissions@elmira.edu* Web: *elmira.edu*

EUGENE LANG COLLEGE OF NEW SCHOOL UNIVERSITY D-3

New York, NY 10011 (212) 229-5665; (212) 229-5355

Full-time: 150 men, 300 women	**Faculty:** 14
Part-time: 15 men, 50 women	**Ph.D.s:** 100%
Graduate: none	**Student/Faculty:** 33 to 1
Year: semesters	**Tuition:** $20,300
Application Deadline: February 1	**Room & Board:** $10,000
Freshman Class: n/av	
SAT I or ACT: required	**COMPETITIVE**

Eugene Lang College, established in 1978, is the liberal arts undergraduate division of New School University (formerly the New School for Social Research). Figures in the above capsule are approximate. There are 4 undergraduate and 6 graduate schools. The 4 libraries contain 142,000 volumes and 65,000 microform items, and subscribe to 750 periodicals. Computerized library services include the card catalog, interlibrary loans, and database searching. Special learning facilities include an art gallery and and writing center. The 5-acre campus is in an urban area in the heart of Greenwich Village. Including residence halls, there are 14 buildings.

Student Life: 59% of undergraduates are from out of state, mostly the Northeast. Others are from 34 states, 12 foreign countries, and Canada. 60% are from public schools. 50% are white; 11% Hispanic. The average age of freshmen is 18; all undergraduates, 20. 15% do not continue beyond their first year; 85% remain to graduate.

Housing: 500 students can be accommodated in college housing, which includes coed dormitories and off-campus apartments. On-campus housing is available on a first-come, first-served basis and is available on a lottery system for upperclassmen. Priority is given to out-of-town students. 57% of students commute. Alcohol is not permitted. All students may keep cars.

Activities: There are no fraternities or sororities. There are 15 groups on campus, including chorus, drama, ethnic, gay, international, jazz band, literary magazine, newspaper, photography, political, social, social service, and student government. Popular campus events include Lang in the City, a program that makes cultural events available to students.

Sports: Students receive discounted rates at area gyms and city recreation facilities.

Disabled Students: Wheelchair ramps, elevators, specially equipped rest rooms, and lowered telephones are available.

Services: Counseling and information services are available, as is tutoring in some subjects, including writing and remedial writing at the writing center.

Campus Safety and Security: Measures include informal discussions, pamphlets/posters/films, and 24-hour dormitory security.

Programs of Study: Eugene Lang College confers the B.A. degree. Master's and doctoral degrees are also awarded. Bachelor's degrees are awarded in COMMUNICATIONS AND THE ARTS (creative writing, dramatic arts, and English), EDUCATION (education), SOCIAL SCIENCE (crosscultural studies, economics, history, political science/government, prelaw, psychology, social science, sociology, urban studies, and women's studies). Creative writing, history, urban studies, and education are the strongest academically. Writing and cultural studies are the largest.

Required: To graduate, students must complete 120 credit hours with a GPA of 2.0 and a minimum of 36 hours in 1 of 5 areas of concentration: writing, literature, and the arts; urban studies; social and historical inquiry; cultural studies; or mind, nature, and value. Also required are 88 credit hours in Lang College courses and 4 credits of senior work. Required courses include a first-year writing seminar and a freshman workshop program. A senior project must be completed.

Special: Lang College offers a concentration rather than a traditional major; there is no core curriculum and students are instructed in small seminars. Students may cross-register with other New School divisions. A large variety of internships for credit, study abroad, B.A/M.A. and B.A./M.S.T. options, a B.A./B.F.A. degree with Parsons School of Design and the New School's Jazz and Contemporary Music Program, student-designed majors, and nondegree study are available.

Faculty/Classroom: 38% of faculty are male; 62%, female. All have postgraduate degrees and all teach undergraduates. The average class size in a laboratory is 15 and in a regular course, 15.

Requirements: The SAT I or ACT is required. In addition, 4 SAT II: Subject tests may be substituted for either test. Applicants must be enrolled in a strong college preparatory program. The GED is accepted. An essay and an interview are required. Art students must present a portfolio and complete a home exam. Jazz students are required to audition. AP credits are accepted. Important factors in the admissions decision are personality/intangible qualities, advanced placement or honor courses, and recommendations by school officials.

Procedure: Freshmen are admitted fall and spring. Entrance exams should be taken in May of the junior year or October of the senior year. There are early decision, early admissions, and deferred admissions plans. A waiting list is an active part of the admissions procedure. Contact the school for current application deadlines and fee.

Transfer: 84 transfer students enrolled in a recent year. Applicants must have a minimum college GPA of 2.5 and must submit high school transcripts, ACT or SAT I scores (if taken in the last 5 years), and 2 recommendations. An interview is required. Grades of C or better transfer for credit. 60 credits of 120 must be completed at Eugene Lang College.

Visiting: There are regularly scheduled orientations for prospective students, including a campus tour, visits to classes, and panel discussions. There are guides for informal visits and visitors may sit in on classes. To schedule a visit, contact the Admissions Office.

Financial Aid: In a recent year, 78% of all freshmen and 80% of continuing students received some form of financial aid. 75% of freshmen and 79% of continuing students received need-based aid. The average freshman award was $14,566. Of that total, scholarships or need-based grants averaged $10,906; and loans averaged $3125. 40% of undergraduates work part time. The average financial indebtedness of a recent graduate was $17,125. The FAFSA is required. Check with the school for current application deadlines.

International Students: There are usually about 25 international students enrolled. The school actively recruits these students. They must score 600 on the written TOEFL and also take the SAT I or the ACT.

Computers: The mainframe is an HP. Macs and PCs are available for student use in an academic computing center. Students can arrange for access for statistical course work and dissertation research. There are no time limits and no fees. It is strongly recommended that all students have a personal computer.

Graduates: Some 90 to 100 bachelor's degrees are awarded annually.

Admissions Contact: Jennifer Gill Fondiller, Director of Admissions. E-mail: *lang@newschool.edu* Web: *www.lang.edu*

EUGENE LANG COLLEGE OF THE NEW SCHOOL FOR SOCIAL RESEARCH
(See Eugene Lang College of New School University)

EXCELSIOR COLLEGE D-3
(Formerly Regents College)

Albany, NY 12203-5159 (518) 464-8500
(888) 674-2388; Fax: (518) 464-8777

Full-time: none	**Faculty:** 442
Part-time: 7255 men, 11,605 women	**Ph.D.s:** n/av
Graduate: 57 men, 214 women	**Student/Faculty:** n/app
Year: see profile	**Tuition:** $915
Application Deadline: open	**Room & Board:** n/app
Freshman Class: n/av	
SAT I or ACT: not required	**SPECIAL**

Excelsior College, founded in 1971, is an external degree, noninstructional institution that is a member of the University of the State of New York. Students earn degrees without attending classes at Excelsior College. Credit is earned through proficiency exams, course credit from other accredited colleges, military training, and on-the-job training. There are 4 undergraduate and 2 graduate schools. In addition to regional accreditation, Excelsior has baccalaureate program accreditation with ABET and NLN. Computerized library services include the card catalog, interlibrary loans, and database searching. Special learning facilities include an electronic peer network available on the Internet. The campus is in a suburban area in Albany. There is 1 building.

Student Life: 87% of undergraduates are from out of state. Others are from 49 states, 52 foreign countries, and Canada. 72% are white; 13% African American. The average age of all undergraduates is 40.

Housing: There are no residence halls. Alcohol is not permitted.

Activities: There are no fraternities or sororities. Popular campus events include commencement.

Disabled Students: Wheelchair ramps, elevators, special parking, specially equipped rest rooms, and lowered drinking fountains are available.

Services: Counseling and information services are available, as is tutoring in some subjects, including statistics and writing.

Programs of Study: Excelsior confers B.A., B.S., B.S.Comp.Tech, B.S.Elect.Tech, B.S.N., B.S.Nuc.T, and B.S.T. degrees. Associate and master's degrees are also awarded. Bachelor's degrees are awarded in BUSINESS (accounting, banking and finance, business administration and management, human resources, insurance and risk management, international business management, management information systems, and marketing/retailing/merchandising), COMPUTER AND PHYSICAL SCIENCE (information sciences and systems and nuclear technology), ENGINEERING AND ENVIRONMENTAL DESIGN (computer technology, electrical/electronics engineering technology, and technological management), HEALTH PROFESSIONS (nursing), SOCIAL SCIENCE (liberal arts/general studies). Nursing and liberal studies are the largest.

Required: To graduate, students must complete 120 credits with 30 in the major and a minimum 2.0 GPA. At least 50% of course work must be in the arts and sciences. The required core courses must include 6 to 12 credits each in humanities, math/science, and social science/history. The nursing program requires a different set of core courses as well as the nursing performance exams. All students must fulfill a written English requirement.

Special: B.A. or B.S. candidates may major in liberal studies or in most traditional academic disciplines. Faculty consultants design curricula, approve sources of credit, create exams, and assess student learning. They do not offer instruction. Students receive academic advising by telephone, letter, computer, or in person. The flexibility of this alternate program enables adults to pursue an undergraduate degree independently. Exams are available. Pass/fail options are possible.

Faculty/Classroom: 30% of faculty are male; 70%, female.

Requirements: There are no admissions requirements except for nursing students. Applicants need not be residents of New York State. Students without a high school diploma or equivalent are admitted as special students. Nursing enrollment is available only to students with certain health care backgrounds. AP and CLEP credits are accepted.

Procedure: Freshmen are admitted to all sessions. Application deadlines are open. The fall 2001 application fee was $40. Notification is sent on a rolling basis.

Transfer: 9930 transfer students enrolled in 2001-2002.

Financial Aid: The college's own financial statement is required. The fall application deadline is July 1.

International Students: There are 410 international students enrolled part-time. The school actively recruits these students.

Computers: The mainframe is a DEC ALPHA. Students are encouraged to access a database of more than 20,000 exams and courses available through distance learning. They also have access to Excelsior College study groups and administrative offices via the Web. All students may access the system 24 hours a day, 7 days a week, via the Internet. There are no time limits and no fees.

Graduates: In 2001, 2705 bachelor's degrees were awarded. The most popular majors were liberal arts (83%), business (10%), and technology (4%). In an average class, 54% graduate in 3 years, 55% in 4 years, 57% in 5 years, and 57% in 6 years.

Admissions Contact: Prospective Student Adviser.
E-mail: *info@excelsior.edu* Web: *www.excelsior.edu*

FASHION INSTITUTE OF TECHNOLOGY/STATE UNIVERSITY OF NEW YORK D-5

New York, NY 10001-5992 (212) 217-7675
(800) Go-To-FIT; Fax: (212) 217-7481

Full-time: 1004 men, 5363 women	**Faculty:** 211
Part-time: 915 men, 3398 women	**Ph.D.s:** n/av
Graduate: 10 men, 96 women	**Student/Faculty:** 30 to 1
Year: 4-1-4, summer session	**Tuition:** $3366 ($7894)
Application Deadline: January 1	**Room & Board:** $6138
Freshman Class: 4339 applied, 1743 accepted, 1021 enrolled	
SAT I or ACT: not required	**COMPETITIVE+**

The Fashion Institute of Technology, founded in 1944 as part of the State University of New York, is an art and design, business, and technology college that prepares students for careers in fashion and related design professions and industries. In addition to regional accreditation, FIT has baccalaureate program accreditation with FIDER and NASAD. The library contains 154,015 volumes, 7907 microform items, and 12,040 audiovisual forms/CDs, and subscribes to 850 periodicals. Computerized library services include the card catalog, interlibrary loans, and database searching. Special learning facilities include an art gallery, radio station, design lab, lighting lab, quick response center, computer-aided design and communications facility, and the Annette Green Fragrance Foundation Studio Collections of the Museum at FIT. The 5-acre campus is in an urban area in Manhattan. Including residence halls, there are 8 buildings.

Student Life: 69% of undergraduates are from New York. Others are from 49 states, 80 foreign countries, and Canada. 41% are white; 15% foreign nationals, 11% Asian American, 10% Hispanic. The average age of freshmen is 19; all undergraduates, 25.

Housing: 1250 students can be accommodated in college housing, which includes single-sex and coed dormitories and on-campus apartments. On-campus housing is available on a lottery system for upperclassmen. Priority is given to out-of-town students. 84% of students commute. Alcohol is not permitted. No one may keep cars.

Activities: There are no fraternities or sororities. There are 70 groups on campus, including art, cheerleading, chess, dance, drama, ethnic, gay, honors, literary magazine, musical theater, newspaper, photography, political, professional, radio and TV, religious, social, social service, student government, and yearbook. Popular campus events include fashion shows, a lecture series, and craft center events.

Sports: There are 4 intercollegiate sports for men and 4 for women, and 4 intramural sports for men and 4 for women. Facilities include 2 gyms, a dance studio, and a weight room.

Disabled Students: 95% of the campus is accessible. Wheelchair ramps, elevators, special parking, specially equipped rest rooms, lowered drinking fountains, lowered telephones, services/facilities for the hearing impaired, and library tapes are available.

Services: Counseling and information services are available, as is tutoring in every subject. There is remedial math, reading, and writing. The school has a special program for the learning disabled.

Campus Safety and Security: Measures include 24-hour foot and vehicle patrol, self-defense education, informal discussions, and pamphlets/posters/films. There are emergency telephones, lighted pathways/sidewalks, and lectures by the New York City Police Department.

Programs of Study: FIT confers B.F.A. and B.S. degrees. Associate and master's degrees are also awarded. Bachelor's degrees are awarded in BUSINESS (apparel and accessories marketing, fashion merchandising, and marketing/retailing/merchandising), COMMUNICATIONS AND THE ARTS (advertising, design, fiber/textiles/weaving, graphic design, illustration, and toy design), ENGINEERING AND ENVIRONMENTAL DESIGN (computer graphics, interior design, and textile technology), SOCIAL SCIENCE (fashion design and technology, home furnishings and equipment management/production/services, and textiles and clothing). Fashion merchandising management is the strongest academically. Advertising and marketing communications are the largest.

Required: To graduate, students must complete the credit and course requirements for their majors with a 2.0 GPA. Students may qualify for a degree in 2 ways: by earning 60 credits, with half in the major while in residence at the upper-division level, or by earning 30 credits at the upper-division level in addition to an FIT associate degree. There is a 2-credit phys ed requirement.

Special: Internships are offered, and students may study abroad in 8 countries. Nondegree study is available. There is 1 departmental honors program.

Faculty/Classroom: 48% of faculty are male; 52%, female. All teach undergraduates. No introductory courses are taught by graduate students. The average class size in an introductory lecture is 25; in a laboratory, 18; and in a regular course, 25.

Admissions: 40% of the 2001-2002 applicants were accepted. 42% of the current freshmen were in the top fifth of their class; 58% were in the top two fifths.

Requirements: Applicants must be high school graduates or have a GED certificate. An essay and, when appropriate, a portfolio are required. FIT requires applicants to be in the upper 50% of their class. A GPA of 2.0 is required. AP and CLEP credits are accepted. Important factors in the admissions decision are personality/intangible qualities, leadership record, and evidence of special talent. Applications are accepted on-line at the school's web site.

Procedure: Freshmen are admitted fall and spring. There is an early decision plan. Applications should be filed by January 1 for fall entry and October 1 for spring entry, along with a $40 fee. Notification is sent on a rolling basis. 5% of all applicants are on a waiting list; 582 were accepted in 2001.

Transfer: 966 transfer students enrolled in 2001-2002. Applicants must have a GPA of 2.0 and at least 30 college credits. An interview is required for art and design applicants, as well as a portfolio when appropriate. 30 credits of 60 must be completed at FIT.

Visiting: There are regularly scheduled orientations for prospective students, including a presentation and group information session with a counselor. To schedule a visit, contact the Admissions Office at *fitinfo@fitsuny.edu*

Financial Aid: In 2001-2002, 53% of all freshmen received some form of financial aid. 55% of freshmen and 47% of continuing students received need-based aid. The average freshman award was $5234. FIT is a member of CSS. The CSS/Profile is required. The fall application deadline is March 15.

International Students: There are 1086 international students enrolled. They must score 550 on the written TOEFL.

Computers: The mainframe is an Alpha ES40. There are 240 PCs available in various academic computer labs and college areas. All students may access the system. There are no fees.

Graduates: In 2001, 767 bachelor's degrees were awarded. The most popular majors were fashion merchandising management (32%), advertising, marketing, and communications (15%), and fashion design (11%). In an average class, 51% graduate in 3 years. 90 companies recruited on campus in 2000-2001. Of the 2000 graduating class, 18% were enrolled in graduate school within 6 months of graduation and 73% were employed.

Admissions Contact: Dolores Lombardi, Director of Admissions.
E-mail: *lombardd@fitsuny.edu* Web: *www.fitnyc.suny.edu*

FIVE TOWNS COLLEGE

Dix Hills, NY 11746 — E-5
(631) 424-7000, ext. 2110
Fax: (631) 424-7008

Full-time: 669 men, 327 women	**Faculty:** 35
Part-time: 22 men, 11 women	**Ph.D.s:** 42%
Graduate: 37 men, 17 women	**Student/Faculty:** 28 to 1
Year: semesters, summer session	**Tuition:** $11,050
Application Deadline: open	**Room & Board:** $7800
Freshman Class: 834 applied, 440 accepted, 397 enrolled	
SAT I Verbal/Math: 482/467	**ACT:** 18 SPECIAL

Five Towns College, founded in 1972, is a private institution offering undergraduate programs in music, music business, business, liberal arts, theater, and elementary education. The library contains 28,000 volumes, 50 microform items, and 9575 audiovisual forms/CDs, and subscribes to 550 periodicals. Computerized library services include interlibrary loans and database searching. Special learning facilities include a learning resource center, 48- and 24-track recording studios, a MIDI studio, and a video/TV studio. The 40-acre campus is in a suburban area 48 miles east of New York City. Including residence halls, there is 1 building.

Student Life: 95% of undergraduates are from New York. Others are from 11 states and 9 foreign countries. 91% are from public schools. 62% are white; 22%, African American; 15%, Hispanic. The average age of freshmen is 19; all undergraduates, 21. 28% do not continue beyond their first year; 60% remain to graduate.

Housing: 180 students can be accommodated in college housing, which includes coed dormitories and off-campus apartments. Priority for on-campus housing is given to out-of-town students. 90% of students commute. Alcohol is not permitted. All students may keep cars.

Activities: There are no fraternities or sororities. There are 12 groups on campus, including art, audio, band, barbershop quartet, booster, choir, chorale, chorus, drama, honors, international, jazz band, musical theater, newspaper, orchestra, photography, professional, radio and TV, readers theater, social, student government, symphony, theatrical concert, and yearbook. Popular campus events include the Cultural Hour, the Annual Picnic, and spring and fall festivals.

Sports: There are 2 intercollegiate sports for men and 2 for women. Facilities include a gym with basketball and volleyball courts and an outdoor baseball/football field.

Disabled Students: 50% of the campus is accessible. Wheelchair ramps, special parking, specially equipped rest rooms, special class scheduling, lowered drinking fountains, and lowered telephones are available.

Services: Counseling and information services are available, as is tutoring in most subjects. There is remedial math, reading, and writing.

Campus Safety and Security: Measures include 24-hour foot and vehicle patrol, shuttle buses, informal discussions, and pamphlets/posters/films. There are lighted pathways/sidewalks.

Programs of Study: FTC confers B.S., B.F.A., B.P.S., and Mus.B. degrees. Associate degrees are also awarded. Bachelor's degrees are awarded in COMMUNICATIONS AND THE ARTS (audio technology, dramatic arts, jazz, music business management, music performance, music theory and composition, and video), EDUCATION (elementary and music). Music education is the strongest academically. Audio recording technology is the largest.

Required: To graduate, all students must complete a total of 128 credits for a Mus.B. or B.F.A. degree, 120 for a B.P.S. degree, or 130 for a B.S. degree. Students must maintain at least a C average in their major concentration and have a minimum GPA of 2.0 to graduate. Distribution requirements include 45 credits in core courses in liberal arts. The core curriculum consists of English Composition 101 and 102, Speech 101, 3 credits each of either psychology or sociology, and various upper-division liberal arts and social science courses. All music students must pass a jury examination. Music majors and elementary education majors must take a comprehensive exam.

Special: Cross-registration is available with schools in the Long Island Regional Advisory Council on Higher Education. Co-op programs in audio recording technology, music business, video arts, and broadcasting are available, and internships are possible. Work-study programs are offered on campus. Students can have dual majors in music, audio recording technology, business, music business, and video production. There is 1 national honor society and 3 departmental honors programs.

Faculty/Classroom: 65% of faculty are male; 35%, female. All both teach and do research. The average class size in an introductory lecture is 30; in a laboratory, 20; and in a regular course, 30.

Admissions: 53% of the 2001-2002 applicants were accepted. The SAT I scores for the 2001-2002 freshman class were: Verbal--75% below 500, 24% between 500 and 599, and 1% between 600 and 700; Math--60% below 500, 39% between 500 and 599, and 1% between 600 and 700. The ACT scores were 98% below 21, and 2% between 21 and 23.

Requirements: The SAT I or ACT is required. In addition, a minimum high school average of 75 is required. A GED with a minimum score of

250 is accepted. An interview is required for all students, and music students are required to audition. AP and CLEP credits are accepted. Important factors in the admissions decision are advanced placement or honor courses, evidence of special talent, and personality/intangible qualities.

Procedure: Freshmen are admitted to all sessions. Entrance exams should be taken prior to admission. There is a deferred admissions plan. Application deadlines are open. A waiting list is an active part of the admissions procedure. Notification is sent on a rolling basis. The fall 2001 application fee was $25.

Transfer: 110 transfer students enrolled in 2001-2002. Students must be in good academic standing at their former school. 45 credits of 120 to 130 must be completed at FTC.

Visiting: There are regularly scheduled orientations for prospective students, including a campus tour, academic counseling, and financial aid counseling. There are guides for informal visits and visitors may sit in on classes. To schedule a visit, contact the Admissions Office at *www.ftc.edu*

Financial Aid: In 2001-2002, 72% of all freshmen and 68% of continuing students received some form of financial aid. 70% of freshmen and 68% of continuing students received need-based aid. The average freshman award was $4000. Of that total, scholarships or need-based grants averaged $2000 ($10,500 maximum); loans averaged $2467 ($5500 maximum); and work contracts averaged $600 ($3000 maximum). 53% of undergraduates work part time. Average annual earnings from campus work are $1000. The average financial indebtedness of the 2001 graduate was $10,000. The FAFSA and the college's own financial statement are required.

International Students: There are 10 international students enrolled. The school actively recruits these students. They must score 520 on the written TOEFL and also take the SAT I or the college's own entrance exam.

Computers: The mainframe is an IBM AS/400. There are 100 terminals available in a computer labs and the library. All students may access the system during school hours. There are no time limits and no fees.

Graduates: The most popular majors were business (54%), music education (24%), and music performance (22%). 45 companies recruited on campus in 2000-2001. Of the 2000 graduating class, 5% were enrolled in graduate school within 6 months of graduation and 80% were employed.

Admissions Contact: Jerry Cohen, Director of Admissions.
E-mail: *admissions@ftc.edu*

FORDHAM UNIVERSITY SYSTEM

The Fordham University System, established in 1841, is a private system in the Jesuit tradition. It is governed by a board of trustees whose chief administrator is the president. The primary goal of the system is to educate talented men and women in the liberal arts and basic sciences. The main priorities are excellence in undergraduate and selected graduate/professional programs, and commitment to teaching, research, and service. The total enrollment of all 3 campuses is about 4600, with more than 500 faculty members. There are 69 baccalaureate, 71 master's, and 25 doctoral programs through Fordham University. Profiles of the 4-year campuses are included in this section.

FORDHAM UNIVERSITY

Bronx, NY 10458 — **D-5**
(718) 817-4000
(800) FORDHAM; Fax: (718) 367-3426

Full-time: 2566 men, 3717 women	**Faculty:** 447; I, av$
Part-time: 274 men, 505 women	**Ph.D.s:** 95%
Graduate: 2507 men, 4274 women	**Student/Faculty:** 14 to 1
Year: semesters, summer session	**Tuition:** $22,170
Application Deadline: February 1	**Room & Board:** $8540
Freshman Class: 10,663 applied, 5901 accepted, 1663 enrolled	
SAT I Verbal/Math: 580/580	**ACT:** 25 **VERY COMPETITIVE**

Fordham University, founded in 1841, is an independent institution offering an education based on the Jesuit tradition, with 2 campuses in New York City, 1 in the Bronx and the other in Manhattan near Lincoln Center. There are 4 undergraduate and 6 graduate schools. In addition to regional accreditation, Fordham University has baccalaureate program accreditation with AACSB and NCATE. The 2 libraries contain 1,749,713 volumes, 2,586,483 microform items, and 7784 audiovisual forms/CDs, and subscribe to 12,022 periodicals. Computerized library services include the card catalog, interlibrary loans, and database searching. Special learning facilities include a radio station, a seismic station, and an archeological site on campus. The 85-acre campus is in an urban area adjacent to the Bronx Zoo and New York Botanical Garden. Including residence halls, there are 32 buildings.

Student Life: 63% of undergraduates are from New York. Others are from 46 states, 38 foreign countries, and Canada. 40% are from public schools. 56% are white; 10%, Hispanic. 68% are Catholic; 15% claim no religious affiliation. The average age of freshmen is 19; all undergraduates, 20. 11% do not continue beyond their first year; 74% remain to graduate.

Housing: 3468 students can be accommodated in college housing, which includes coed dormitories, on-campus apartments, and off-campus apartments. In addition, there is a residental college. On-campus housing is guaranteed for all 4 years. 58% of students live on campus; of those, 90% remain on campus on weekends. All students may keep cars.

Activities: There are no fraternities or sororities. There are 85 groups on campus, including art, band, cheerleading, choir, chorale, chorus, computers, dance, drama, ethnic, film, honors, international, literary magazine, marching band, musical theater, newspaper, pep band, photography, political, professional, radio and TV, religious, social, social service, student government, and yearbook. Popular campus events include Spring Weekend, Spring Semiformal, and Senior Week.

Sports: There are 18 intercollegiate sports for men and 16 for women, and 22 intramural sports for men and 22 for women. Facilities include a 6000-seat football stadium, an Olympic-size pool with a separate diving area, an indoor track, a 3200-seat gym, and tennis, squash, and racquetball courts.

Disabled Students: 80% of the campus is accessible. Wheelchair ramps, elevators, special parking, specially equipped rest rooms, special class scheduling, and lowered drinking fountains are available.

Services: Counseling and information services are available, as is tutoring in most subjects.

Campus Safety and Security: Measures include 24-hour foot and vehicle patrol, escort service, shuttle buses, and informal discussions. There are pamphlets/posters/films, emergency telephones, and lighted pathways/sidewalks.

Programs of Study: Fordham University confers B.A., B.S., and B.F.A. degrees. Master's and doctoral degrees are also awarded. Bachelor's degrees are awarded in BIOLOGICAL SCIENCE (biology/biological science), BUSINESS (accounting, business administration and management, business economics, international business management, and marketing management), COMMUNICATIONS AND THE ARTS (art history and appreciation, broadcasting, classical languages, communications, comparative literature, creative writing, dance, dramatic arts, English, film arts, fine arts, French, German, Italian, journalism, music, performing arts, photography, Russian, Spanish, and visual and performing arts), COMPUTER AND PHYSICAL SCIENCE (chemistry, computer science, information sciences and systems, mathematics, physics, and science), EDUCATION (education and mathematics), ENGINEERING AND ENVIRONMENTAL DESIGN (preengineering), HEALTH PROFESSIONS (predentistry, premedicine, and preveterinary science), SOCIAL SCIENCE (African American studies, African studies, American studies, anthropology, classical/ancient civilization, criminal justice, economics, French studies, German area studies, history, international studies, Italian studies, Latin American studies, medieval studies, Middle Eastern studies, peace studies, philosophy, political science/government, prelaw, psychology, religion, Russian and Slavic studies, social science, social work, sociology, Spanish studies, theological studies, urban studies, and women's studies). Communications, social sciences, and English are the strongest academically. Business, psychology, and history are the largest.

Required: All students must complete a core curriculum, including 2 courses each in English literature, history, philosophy, theology, natural sciences, social sciences, and foreign language and 1 each in math, English composition, and fine arts. A total of 124 credits with 30 in the major and a 2.0 minimum GPA are required. A thesis is required for the honors program.

Special: Fordham University offers career-oriented internships in communications and other majors during the junior or senior year with New York City companies and institutions. A combined 3-2 engineering program is available with Columbia and Case Western Reserve Universities. Study abroad, a Washington semester, dual and student-designed majors, and pass/fail options are available. There are 6 national honor societies, including Phi Beta Kappa, and a freshman honors program.

Faculty/Classroom: 64% of faculty are male; 36%, female. 74% both teach and do research. No introductory courses are taught by graduate students. The average class size in an introductory lecture is 21; in a laboratory, 11; and in a regular course, 17.

Admissions: 55% of the 2001-2002 applicants were accepted. 56% of the current freshmen were in the top fifth of their class; 85% were in the top two fifths. In a recent year, there were 9 National Merit semifinalists. 20 freshmen graduated first in their class.

Requirements: The SAT I or ACT is required. In addition, applicants should have completed 4 years of high school English and 3 each of math, science, social studies, history, and foreign language. An essay is part of the application process. An interview is recommended. Auditions are required for theater and dance majors. Fordham University requires applicants to be in the upper 40% of their class. A GPA of 3.0 is required. AP and CLEP credits are accepted. Important factors in the admissions decision are leadership record, parents or siblings attending the school, and recommendations by school officials. Applications care accepted on-line via *Embark.com*.

Procedure: Freshmen are admitted fall and spring. Entrance exams should be taken by December of the senior year. There are early decision and deferred admissions plans. Early decision applications should be filed by November 1; regular applications, by February 1 for fall entry and November 1 for spring entry, along with a $50 fee. Notification of early decision is sent December 15; regular decision, April 1. 91 early decision candidates were accepted for the 2001-2002 class. 9% of all applicants are on a waiting list; 29 were accepted in 2001.

Transfer: 280 transfer students enrolled in 2001-2002. A 3.0 minimum GPA is recommended. Applicants under age 21 should submit SAT I or ACT scores. An interview is recommended. 64 credits of 124 must be completed at Fordham University.

Visiting: There are regularly scheduled orientations for prospective students. There are guides for informal visits and visitors may sit in on classes and stay overnight. To schedule a visit, contact the Admissions Office.

Financial Aid: In a recent year, 73% of all freshmen and 69% of continuing students received some form of financial aid. 69% of freshmen and 59% of continuing students received need-based aid. The average freshman award was $16,570. Of that total, scholarships or need-based grants averaged $11,689; loans averaged $2820; and work contracts averaged $3471. 95% of undergraduates work part time. Average annual earnings from campus work are $1600. The average financial indebtedness of a recent graduate was $15,379. Fordham University is a member of CSS. The CSS/Profile or FAFSA is required. The fall application deadline is February 1.

International Students: There are 97 international students enrolled. The school actively recruits these students. They must score 550 on the written TOEFL or 231 on the electronic version and also take the university's own test and the SAT I or the ACT.

Computers: The mainframe is a DEC VAX system. More than 900 PCs are available to students in labs throughout both campuses. Labs can be found in the libraries, academic buildings, and residence halls. Most are connected to the mainframe and have access to the World Wide Web. All residence halls are also wired for hookup to the university network and the Internet. All students may access the system. There are no time limits and no fees.

Graduates: In 2001, 1392 bachelor's degrees were awarded. The most popular majors were business administration (17%), communications (12%), and psychology (9%). In an average class, 1% graduate in 3 years, 64% in 4 years, 73% in 5 years, and 74% in 6 years. 500 companies recruited on campus in a recent year. Of a recent graduating class, 25% were enrolled in graduate school within 6 months of graduation and 90% were employed.

Admissions Contact: John W. Buckley, Dean of Admission.
E-mail: *enroll@fordham.edu* Web: *www.fordham.edu*

FRIENDS WORLD PROGRAM

Southampton, NY 11968 — E-5 — (631) 287-8474
(800)LIU-PLAN; Fax: (631) 287-8463

Full-time: 49 men, 124 women	**Faculty:** 24
Part-time: 4 men, 15 women	**Ph.D.s:** 70%
Graduate: none	**Student/Faculty:** 10 to 1
Year: semesters	**Tuition:** $17,960
Application Deadline: open	**Room & Board:** $8280
Freshman Class: 86 applied, 40 accepted, 27 enrolled	
SAT I or ACT: not required	**COMPETITIVE**

Friends World Program, founded in 1965, offers student-designed majors in the liberal arts and is located on the campus of Southampton College. Some information in this profile is approximate. Friends World has campuses in Costa Rica, England, Israel, Kenya, India, China, and Japan, and during the 4-year program, students study at 2 or 3 of them. Much of the learning is through individually designed off-campus field experience and internships in 2 or more cultures. Students attend the Southampton campus only during their first semester. The library contains 1 million volumes, 1000 microform items, and 500 audiovisual forms/CDs, and subscribes to 690 periodicals. Computerized library services include the card catalog, interlibrary loans, and database searching. Special learning facilities include a learning resource center, art gallery, radio station, and marine lab. The 110-acre campus is in a rural area 90 miles east of New York City. Including residence halls, there are 33 buildings.

Student Life: 80% of undergraduates are from out of state, mostly the Northwest. Others are from 29 states, 10 foreign countries, and Canada. 75% are from public schools. 83% are white; 10%, foreign nationals. Most claim no religious affiliation. The average age of freshmen is 19; all undergraduates, 22. 20% do not continue beyond their first year; 60% remain to graduate.

Housing: 700 students can be accommodated in college housing, which includes single-sex and coed dormitories and off-campus apartments. On-campus housing is guaranteed for the freshman year only. Priority is given to out-of-town students. 95% of students live on campus; of those, 80% remain on campus on weekends. All students may keep cars.

Activities: There are no fraternities or sororities. There are 50 groups on campus, including art, drama, ethnic, film, gay, honors, international, literary magazine, newspaper, photography, political, radio and TV, religious, social service, student government, and yearbook. Popular campus events include Ingatherings--weekend events where students on field internships return to campus for sharing and community meetings on college governance. There are also multicultural awareness activities.

Sports: There is no sports program at Friends World.

Disabled Students: 15% of the campus is accessible. Wheelchair ramps and special parking are available.

Services: Counseling and information services are available. The Study Center offers faculty tutoring in every subject. There is remedial math, reading, and writing.

Campus Safety and Security: Measures include 24-hour foot and vehicle patrol, self-defense education, informal discussions, and pamphlets/posters/films. There are emergency telephones and lighted pathways/sidewalks.

Programs of Study: Friends World confers the B.A. in Interdisciplinary Studies degree. Bachelor's degrees are awarded in SOCIAL SCIENCE (interdisciplinary studies).

Required: All students must complete 1 writing course and the Friends World Education Seminar. Distribution requirements include 12 credits each in area studies, human issues, and foreign language and 24 credits in liberal arts. Students are required to study 2 cultures other than their own. All students demonstrate learning by keeping portfolios. Submission of a completed portfolio is required to advance to the next year of study. There are no grades. A senior thesis and a total of 120 credit hours are required, with at least 24 hours in a major subject area.

Special: There is cross-registration with Long Island University, including a 4-1 education program with the C.W. Post campus. All students carry out fieldwork and internships and live abroad. Friends World offers a general studies degree, and the wide range of subjects includes women's studies, anthropology, politics, archaeology, comparative religions, music, education, holistic medicine and healing, alternative agriculture, ecology, the arts, and peace studies.

Faculty/Classroom: 40% of faculty are male; 60%, female. All teach undergraduates and 60% do research. The average class size in an introductory lecture is 22 and in a regular course, 10.

Admissions: 47% of the 2001-2002 applicants were accepted.

Requirements: The SAT I or ACT is not required for regular admission, but is considered if submitted. The GED is accepted, as is evidence of equivalent life experience. An essay and interview are required. A grade average of 80 is required. AP and CLEP credits are accepted. Important factors in the admissions decision are personality/intangible qualities, extracurricular activities record, and evidence of special talent. Applications are accepted on-line.

Procedure: Freshmen are admitted in the fall. There are early admissions and deferred admissions plans. Application deadlines are open. The application fee is $30. A waiting list is an active part of the admissions procedure.

Transfer: Transfer applicants with a 2.0 GPA in 30 academic credits and other candidates showing interest are considered. Applicants with fewer than 30 credits must submit high school as well as college transcripts. All must have an interview. 60 credits of 120 must be completed at Friends World.

Visiting: There are guides for informal visits and visitors may sit in on classes and stay overnight. To schedule a visit, contact the Admissions Office.

Financial Aid: In 2001-2002, 96% of all freshmen and 87% of continuing students received some form of financial aid. 10% of undergraduates work part time. Average annual earnings from campus work are $500. Friends World is a member of CSS. The FAFSA and the college's own financial statement are required.

International Students: They must score 550 on the written TOEFL or 213 on the electronic version.

Computers: The mainframe is an IBM. In Southhampton, the students use the LIU network, which is a node on the Internet connecting Friends World students to computers worldwide. There are 125 PCs in 6 campus locations, a 12-to-1 student/computer ratio, and computer hookups in all dormitory rooms. Overseas, students have access to Friends World administrative computers, and some centers have PCs for student use. All students may access the system. There are no time limits and no fees.

Admissions Contact: Joyce Tuttle, Admissions Counselor.
E-mail: *fw@southampton.liunet.edu* Web: *www.liu.edu/friendsworld*

HAMILTON COLLEGE
Clinton, NY 13323 — C-3
(315) 859-4421
(800) 843-2655; Fax: (315) 859-4457

Full-time: 842 men, 864 women	**Faculty:** 197; IIB, +$
Part-time: 1 woman	**Ph.D.s:** 83%
Graduate: none	**Student/Faculty:** 9 to 1
Year: semesters	**Tuition:** $27,350
Application Deadline: see profile	**Room & Board:** $6800
Freshman Class: 4601 applied, 1615 accepted, 465 enrolled	
SAT I Verbal/Math: 640/640	**HIGHLY COMPETITIVE**

Hamilton College, founded in 1793, is a private, nonsectarian, liberal arts school offering undergraduate programs in the arts and sciences. The 3 libraries contain 558,808 volumes, 435,977 microform items, and 55,327 audiovisual forms/CDs, and subscribe to 2560 periodicals. Computerized library services include the card catalog and database searching. Special learning facilities include an art gallery, radio station, and an observatory. The 1200-acre campus is in a rural area 9 miles southwest of Utica. Including residence halls, there are 51 buildings.

Student Life: 59% of undergraduates are from out of state, mostly the Northeast. Others are from 43 states, 29 foreign countries, and Canada. 60% are from public schools. 85% are white. 31% are Catholic; 30% Protestant; 25% claim no religious affiliation. The average age of freshmen is 18; all undergraduates, 20. 8% do not continue beyond their first year; 92% remain to graduate.

Housing: 1449 students can be accommodated in college housing, which includes coed dormitories, on-campus apartments, and married-student housing. In addition, there are language houses, special-interest houses, quiet floors, substance-free areas, and a cooperative. On-campus housing is guaranteed for all 4 years. 96% of students live on campus; of those, 95% remain on campus on weekends. Upperclassmen may keep cars.

Activities: 29% of men belong to 8 national fraternities; 12% of women belong to 3 local sororities. There are 60 groups on campus, including art, chess, choir, chorale, chorus, computers, dance, drama, ethnic, film, gay, honors, international, jazz band, literary magazine, musical theater, newspaper, pep band, photography, political, professional, radio, religious, social, social service, student government, and yearbook. Popular campus events include Class and Charter Day, Winterfest, and Springfest.

Sports: There are 13 intercollegiate sports for men and 13 for women, and 26 intramural sports for men and 29 for women. Facilities include a gym, a field house, squash and racquetball courts, indoor and outdoor tennis courts, a football stadium, a 9-hole golf course, a swimming pool, indoor and outdoor tracks, numerous grass fields, an artificial turf field, paddle tennis courts, and an ice rink.

Disabled Students: Wheelchair ramps, elevators, special parking, specially equipped rest rooms, and special class scheduling are available.

Services: Counseling and information services are available, as is tutoring in some subjects through the New York State Higher Education Opportunity Program (HEOP).

Campus Safety and Security: Measures include 24-hour foot and vehicle patrol, self-defense education, escort service, and shuttle buses. There are informal discussions, pamphlets/posters/films, emergency telephones, and lighted pathways/sidewalks.

Programs of Study: Hamilton confers the B.A. degree. Bachelor's degrees are awarded in BIOLOGICAL SCIENCE (biochemistry, biology/biological science, and neurosciences), COMMUNICATIONS AND THE ARTS (art, art history and appreciation, classics, communications, comparative literature, creative writing, dance, dramatic arts, English, French, German, languages, music, Spanish, and studio art), COMPUTER AND PHYSICAL SCIENCE (chemistry, computer science, geology, mathematics, and physics), SOCIAL SCIENCE (African studies, American studies, anthropology, archeology, Asian/Oriental studies, classical/ancient civilization, economics, history, international relations, philosophy, political science/government, psychobiology, psychology, public affairs, religion, Russian and Slavic studies, sociology, and women's studies). English, government, and history are the largest.

Required: Students must successfully complete 128 credits, with 32 to 40 of these in the student's major, and must maintain at least a 72 average in half the courses taken. Students are required to take 2 courses in each academic division, 3 courses designated as writing intensive, and at least 2 courses covering human diversity and ethical issues, as well as 2 semesters of physical education. A senior project in the student's major is also required.

Special: Cross-registration is permitted with Colgate University and Utica College of Syracuse University. Opportunities are provided for internships, a cooperative program through the Williams College Mystic Seaport Program in Connecticut, and a Washington semester. Accelerated degree programs, dual majors, nondegree study, pass/fail options, student-designed majors, a program for early assurance of acceptance to medical school, and study abroad in many countries are available. 3-2 engineering degrees are offered with Washington University, Rensselaer Polytechnic Institute, and Columbia University. There are 4 national honor societies, including Phi Beta Kappa.

Faculty/Classroom: 59% of faculty are male; 41%, female. All teach undergraduates. The average class size in an introductory lecture and in a regular course is 18.

Admissions: 35% of the 2001-2002 applicants were accepted. The SAT I scores for the 2001-2002 freshman class were: Verbal--4% below 500, 21% between 500 and 599, 51% between 600 and 700, and 24% above 700; Math--3% below 500, 21% between 500 and 599, 58% between 600 and 700, and 18% above 700. 87% of the current freshmen were in the top fifth of their class; 93% were in the top two fifths.

Requirements: The SAT I or ACT is required. In addition, although graduation from an accredited secondary school or a GED is desirable, and a full complement of college-preparatory courses is recommended, Hamilton will consider all highly recommended candidates who demonstrate an ability and desire to perform at intellectually demanding levels. An essay is required, and an interview is recommended. AP credits are accepted. Important factors in the admissions decision are advanced placement or honor courses, recommendations by school officials, and parents or siblings attending the school. Applications may be submitted on-line at *www.hamilton.edu/admission/application/download.html*.

Procedure: Freshmen are admitted in the fall. Entrance exams should be taken prior to February of the senior year. There are early decision, early admissions, and deferred admissions plans. 191 early decision candidates were accepted for the 2001-2002 class. 5% of all applicants are on a waiting list; 15 were accepted in 2001. The fall 2001 application fee was $50. Check with the school for current application deadlines.

Transfer: In a recent year, 17 transfer students enrolled. Transfer applicants must submit high school and college transcripts, an essay or personal statement, and standardized test scores, and must present a minimum GPA of 3.0 in all college-level work. 64 credits of 128 must be completed at Hamilton.

Visiting: There are regularly scheduled orientations for prospective students, consisting of an interview, tour, class visit, and open house program. There are guides for informal visits and visitors may sit in on classes and stay overnight. To schedule a visit, contact the Admissions Office.

Financial Aid: In 2001-2002, 55% of all freshmen and 59% of continuing students received some form of financial aid. 52% of freshmen and 56% of continuing students received need-based aid. The average freshman award was $21,520. Of that total, scholarships or need-based grants averaged $19,364; loans averaged $2531; and work contracts averaged $3495. 48% of undergraduates work part time. Average annual earnings from campus work are $1400. The average financial indebtedness of the 2001 graduate was $16,776. Hamilton is a member of CSS. The CSS/Profile or FAFSA is required. The fall application deadline is February 1.

International Students: There are 59 international students enrolled. The school actively recruits these students. They must take the SAT I or the ACT.

Computers: The mainframes are comprised of a DEC 5100, DEC 5000/25, and DEC 5500. There are 100 Macs and 50 PCs in public computer labs. Students have full access to the Internet, including in residence halls. All students may access the system more than 100 hours per week. There are no time limits and no fees.

Graduates: In 2001, 439 bachelor's degrees were awarded. The most popular majors were social sciences and history (36%), English (9%), and visual and performing arts (8%). In an average class, 80% graduate in 4 years, 84% in 5 years, and 85% in 6 years.

Admissions Contact: Richard M. Fuller, Dean of Admissions.
E-mail: *admission@hamilton.edu* Web: *www.hamilton.edu*

HARTWICK COLLEGE
Oneonta, NY 13820-4020 — D-3
(607) 431-4150
(888) HARTWICK; Fax: (607) 431-4154

Full-time: 576 men, 734 women	**Faculty:** 106; IIB, av$
Part-time: 65 men, 71 women	**Ph.D.s:** n/av
Graduate: none	**Student/Faculty:** 12 to 1
Year: 4-1-4	**Tuition:** $26,040
Application Deadline: February 15	**Room & Board:** $7050
Freshman Class: 1970 applied, 1746 accepted, 433 enrolled	
SAT I Verbal/Math: 555/556	**ACT:** 24 **COMPETITIVE+**

Hartwick College, founded in 1797, is a private undergraduate liberal arts and sciences college. In addition to regional accreditation, Hartwick has baccalaureate program accreditation with NASAD, NASM, and NLN. The library contains 348,699 volumes, 56,817 microform items, and 1400 audiovisual forms/CDs. Computerized library services include the card catalog, interlibrary loans, and database searching. Special learning facilities include an art gallery, radio station, TV station, museum, 914-acre environmental study center, observatory, and an environmental field station. The 425-acre campus is in a small town 75 miles southwest of Albany. Including residence halls, there are 28 buildings.

Student Life: 64% of undergraduates are from New York. Others are from 30 states, 35 foreign countries, and Canada. 84% are from public

schools. 65% are white. The average age of freshmen is 18; all undergraduates, 20. 24% do not continue beyond their first year; 57% remain to graduate.

Housing: 1200 students can be accommodated in college housing, which includes single-sex and coed dormitories, on-campus apartments, fraternity houses, and sorority houses. In addition, there are special-interest houses, substance-free houses, and an environmental campus. On-campus housing is guaranteed for all 4 years. 86% of students live on campus; of those, 90% remain on campus on weekends. All students may keep cars.

Activities: 15% of men belong to 1 local fraternity and 4 national fraternities; 17% of women belong to 3 local sororities and 1 national sorority. There are 60 groups on campus, including art, band, cheerleading, choir, chorale, chorus, computers, dance, drama, ethnic, film, gay, honors, international, jazz band, literary magazine, musical theater, newspaper, orchestra, pep band, photography, political, professional, radio and TV, religious, social, social service, student government, and yearbook. Popular campus events include Holiday Ball, Earth Day, and Multicultural Month.

Sports: There are 11 intercollegiate sports for men and 13 for women, and 9 intramural sports for men and 9 for women. Facilities include 2 gyms, an indoor pool, a dance room, athletic and training facilities, a track, a Nautilus exercise gym, a fitness center, a lighted all-weather playing field, a lighted soccer field, a minor league field for baseball, an equestrian complex, and courts for handball, racquetball, squash, and tennis.

Disabled Students: 50% of the campus is accessible. Wheelchair ramps, elevators, special parking, specially equipped rest rooms, special class scheduling, lowered drinking fountains, and lowered telephones are available.

Services: Counseling and information services are available, as is tutoring in every subject. There is a reader service for the blind. There are writing and math centers and an academic center for excellence.

Campus Safety and Security: Measures include 24-hour foot and vehicle patrol, self-defense education, escort service, and shuttle buses. There are informal discussions, pamphlets/posters/films, emergency telephones, and lighted pathways/sidewalks.

Programs of Study: Hartwick confers B.A. and B.S. degrees. Bachelor's degrees are awarded in BIOLOGICAL SCIENCE (biochemistry and biology/biological science), BUSINESS (accounting and business administration and management), COMMUNICATIONS AND THE ARTS (art, art history and appreciation, dramatic arts, English, French, German, languages, music, and Spanish), COMPUTER AND PHYSICAL SCIENCE (chemistry, computer science, geology, information sciences and systems, mathematics, and physics), EDUCATION (music), HEALTH PROFESSIONS (medical technology and nursing), SOCIAL SCIENCE (anthropology, economics, history, philosophy, political science/government, psychology, religion, and sociology). Anthropology, chemistry, and nursing are the strongest academically. Psychology, management, and nursing are the largest.

Required: Students must complete 36 course units with at least a 2.0 GPA. Core requirements are in the study areas of continuity, interdependence, science and technology, critical thinking, effective communication, and electives. Courses are chosen from offerings in humanities, science and math, social and behavioral sciences, foreign language, and phys ed. A first-year seminar and a contemporary issues seminar for juniors and seniors are required. Students are strongly urged to include an off-campus learning experience.

Special: Students may design their own majors and choose independent study. Cross-registration with SUNY College at Oneonta is possible and local and international internships are available. There is a January thematic term, a Washington semester, and study abroad in 30 countries. First-year students may participate in specially designated off-campus programs. Experiential programs include Outward Bound and the National Outdoor Leadership School. All departments offer dual majors and accelerated degree options. There is a 3-2 engineering program with Clarkson University or Columbia University, a 3-3 program with Albany Law School, and a 4-1 business program with Clarkson University. There are 10 national honor societies and a freshman honors program.

Faculty/Classroom: All teach undergraduates. The average class size in an introductory lecture is 20; in a laboratory, 20; and in a regular course, 30.

Admissions: 89% of the 2001-2002 applicants were accepted. The SAT I scores for the 2001-2002 freshman class were: Verbal--23% below 500, 48% between 500 and 599, 26% between 600 and 700, and 4% above 700; Math--19% below 500, 52% between 500 and 599, 26% between 600 and 700, and 2% above 700. 37% of the current freshmen were in the top fifth of their class; 71% were in the top two fifths. 5 freshmen graduated first in their class in a recent year.

Requirements: Reporting of SAT I and ACT scores is optional. The recommended secondary course of study includes 4 years of English, and 3 years each of math, a foreign language, history, and lab science. Hartwick strongly recommends that applicants plan a campus visit and interview. Prospective art majors should submit a portfolio, and music majors must audition. Computer disks are offered to all prospective students, providing information about the college as well as an application. Students may also use various application services and apply on-line via Hartwick's web site. AP and CLEP credits are accepted. Important factors in the admissions decision are advanced placement or honor courses, recommendations by school officials, and ability to finance college education.

Procedure: Freshmen are admitted to all sessions. Entrance exams should be taken in the spring of the junior year and/or the fall of the senior year. There are early decision and deferred admissions plans. Early decision applications should be filed by January 15; regular applications, by February 15 for fall entry, December 1 for winter entry, and January 1 for spring entry. The fall 2001 application fee was $35. Notification of early decision is sent on a rolling basis; regular decision, March 15. 75 early decision candidates were accepted for the 2001-2002 class. A waiting list is an active part of the admissions procedure.

Transfer: 45 transfer students enrolled in 2001-2002. Applicants should present a minimum GPA of 2.0. 18 units of 36 must be completed at Hartwick.

Visiting: There are regularly scheduled orientations for prospective students, consisting of an interview and tour, lunch, departmental open houses, presentations on student life, off-campus programs, and a career planning process. There are guides for informal visits and visitors may sit in on classes and stay overnight. To schedule a visit, contact the Admissions Office.

Financial Aid: In 2001-2002, 79% of all freshmen and 78% of continuing students received some form of financial aid. The average freshman award was $22,000. 66% of undergraduates work part time. Average annual earnings from campus work are $1400. The average financial indebtedness of the 2001 graduate was $19,364. Hartwick is a member of CSS. The FAFSA and the college's own financial statement are required. The fall application deadline is February 15.

International Students: There are 56 international students enrolled. The school actively recruits these students. They must score 500 on the written TOEFL or take the MELAB.

Computers: The mainframe is comprised of 3 IBM Netfinity 5500 MZ0 servers. All students are provided with a printer and a notebook computer, which they can connect to the network from anywhere on campus. All students may access the system 24 hours per day, 7 days per week. There are no time limits and no fees.

Graduates: In 2001, 312 bachelor's degrees were awarded. The most popular majors were management (19%), psychology (10%), and English (7%). In an average class, 51% graduate in 4 years, 57% in 5 years, and 57% in 6 years. 20 companies recruited on campus in 2000-2001.

Admissions Contact: Susan DiLeno, Dean of Admission.
E-mail: *admissions@hartwick.edu* Web: *www.hartwick.edu*

HILBERT COLLEGE

Hamburg, NY 14075-1597 — **A-3**
(716) 649-7900, ext. 211
(800) 649-8003; Fax: (716) 649-0702

Full-time: 271 men, 380 women	**Faculty:** 36; IIB, --$
Part-time: 84 men, 229 women	**Ph.D.s:** 60%
Graduate: none	**Student/Faculty:** 18 to 1
Year: semesters, summer session	**Tuition:** $12,100
Application Deadline: open	**Room & Board:** $4730
Freshman Class: 317 applied, 285 accepted, 152 enrolled	
SAT I Verbal/Math: 447/451	**ACT:** 19 **LESS COMPETITIVE**

Hilbert College, founded in 1957, is a private institution offering degree programs in business, criminal justice, and social sciences. The library contains 33,000 volumes, 18,103 microform items, and 650 audiovisual forms/CDs, and subscribes to 3337 periodicals. Computerized library services include the card catalog, interlibrary loans, and database searching. Special learning facilities include a learning resource center. The 44-acre campus is in an urban area about 15 miles south of Buffalo. Including residence halls, there are 6 buildings.

Student Life: 99% of undergraduates are from New York. Others are from 4 states, 3 foreign countries, and Canada. 89% are from public schools. 89% are white. The average age of freshmen is 19; all undergraduates, 27. 26% do not continue beyond their first year; 74% remain to graduate.

Housing: 93 students can be accommodated in college housing, which includes 1 coed dorms. On-campus housing is available on a first-come, first-served basis and is available on a lottery system for upperclassmen. 90% of students commute. All students may keep cars.

Activities: There are no fraternities or sororities. There are 20 groups on campus, including academic, chorus, ethnic, honors, literary magazine, professional, religious, social, student government, and yearbook. Popular campus events include Quad Party, Welcome Back Picnic, and Fall Family Weekend.

Sports: There are 5 intercollegiate sports for men and 6 for women, and 2 intramural sports for men and 2 for women. Facilities include a soccer/lacrosse field, baseball and softball diamonds, a practice field, a weight room, and a 900-seat NCAA regulation indoor athletic facility.

Disabled Students: 95% of the campus is accessible. Wheelchair ramps, elevators, special parking, specially equipped rest rooms, special class scheduling, lowered drinking fountains, and lowered telephones are available.

Services: Counseling and information services are available, as is tutoring in some subjects, including writing, accounting, and math. There is remedial math and writing.

Campus Safety and Security: Measures include 24-hour foot and vehicle patrol, self-defense education, escort service, and informal discussions. There are pamphlets/posters/films, emergency telephones, and lighted pathways/sidewalks.

Programs of Study: Hilbert confers B.A. and B.S. degrees. Associate degrees are also awarded. Bachelor's degrees are awarded in BUSINESS (accounting and business administration and management), COMMUNICATIONS AND THE ARTS (English), SOCIAL SCIENCE (criminal justice, criminology, human services, liberal arts/general studies, paralegal studies, and psychology). Economic crime investigation, paralegal studies, and accounting are the strongest academically. Criminal justice, human services, and business administration are the largest.

Required: To graduate, students must complete 120 credit hours, including at least 36 in the major and 60 in liberal arts, with a minimum 2.0 GPA. Students must fulfill requirements in English, math, philosophy, social sciences, and senior seminar.

Special: Hilbert offers cross-registration with other members of the Western New York College Consortium, internships in most majors, and work-study programs. The college maintains articulation agreements with New York State community colleges. There are 3 national honor societies, a freshman honors program, and 3 departmental honors programs.

Faculty/Classroom: 65% of faculty are male; 35%, female. All teach undergraduates and 10% do research. The average class size in an introductory lecture is 20; in a laboratory, 4; and in a regular course, 15.

Admissions: 90% of the 2001-2002 applicants were accepted. The SAT I scores for the 2001-2002 freshman class were: Verbal--77% below 500, 17% between 500 and 599, and 6% between 600 and 700; Math--70% below 500, 25% between 500 and 599, and 5% between 600 and 700. The ACT scores were 60% below 21, 28% between 21 and 23, 6% between 24 and 26, and 6% between 27 and 28. 12% of the current freshmen were in the top fifth of their class; 34% were in the top two fifths. 1 freshman graduated first in their class.

Requirements: The SAT I or ACT is recommended. A grade average of 70 is required. AP and CLEP credits are accepted. Important factors in the admissions decision are leadership record, recommendations by school officials, and advanced placement or honor courses. Applications are accepted on-line.

Procedure: Freshmen are admitted to all sessions. There is a deferred admissions plan. Application deadlines are open. The fall 2001 application fee was $20. Notification is sent on a rolling basis.

Transfer: 146 transfer students enrolled in 2001-2002. Applicants must submit official transcripts from all colleges attended and, in somes cases, the high school transcript. 30 credits of 120 must be completed at Hilbert.

Visiting: There are regularly scheduled orientations for prospective students, consisting of a campus tour, a student panel, and admissions, financial aid, and academic information sessions. There are guides for informal visits and visitors may sit in on classes and stay overnight. To schedule a visit, contact the Office of Admissions.

Financial Aid: In 2001-2002, 98% of all freshmen and 75% of continuing students received some form of financial aid. 92% of freshmen and 55% of continuing students received need-based aid. The average freshman award was $10,828. Of that total, scholarships or need-based grants averaged $6481 ($13,750 maximum); loans averaged $2638 ($6625 maximum); and work contracts averaged $1589 ($1800 maximum). 7% of undergraduates work part time. Average annual earnings from campus work are $1589. The average financial indebtedness of the 2001 graduate was $10,450. Hilbert is a member of CSS. The FAFSA is required. The fall application deadline is December 1.

International Students: They must score 500 on the written TOEFL.

Computers: The mainframe is a Sun Micro system. There are several other servers available for student use. All students may access the system. There are no time limits and no fees.

Graduates: In 2001, 139 bachelor's degrees were awarded. The most popular majors were criminal justice (31%), business administration (20%), and paralegal studies (17%). In an average class, 23% graduate in 3 years, 39% in 4 years, and 44% in 5 years. 10 companies recruited on campus in 2000-2001. Of the 2000 graduating class, 8% were enrolled in graduate school within 6 months of graduation and 68% were employed.

Admissions Contact: Director of Admissions. A video is available.
E-mail: *admissions@hilbert.edu* Web: *www.hilbert.edu*

HOBART AND WILLIAM SMITH COLLEGES C-3

Geneva, NY 14456-3397 H: (315) 781-3622; WS: (315) 781-3472
H: (800) 852-2256; WS: (800) 245-0100; Fax: (315) 781-3471

Full-time: 831 men, 1050 women	**Faculty:** 148; IIB, +$
Part-time: 5 men, 6 women	**Ph.D.s:** 93%
Graduate: none	**Student/Faculty:** 13 to 1
Year: semesters	**Tuition:** $26,177
Application Deadline: February 1	**Room & Board:** $7018
Freshman Class: 2928 applied, 2003 accepted, 548 enrolled	
SAT I or ACT: required	**VERY COMPETITIVE**

Hobart College, a men's college founded in 1822, shares campus, classes, and faculty with William Smith College, a women's college founded in 1908. Together, these coordinate colleges offer degree programs in the liberal arts. The library contains 367,222 volumes, 77,092 microform items, and 8178 audiovisual forms/CDs, and subscribes to 3266 periodicals. Computerized library services include the card catalog, interlibrary loans, and database searching. Special learning facilities include a learning resource center, art gallery, radio station, 100-acre natural preserve, and 70-foot research vessel. The 170-acre campus is in a small town 50 miles west of Syracuse and 50 miles east of Rochester, on the north shore of Seneca Lake. Including residence halls, there are 92 buildings.

Student Life: 51% of undergraduates are from out of state, mostly the Northeast. Others are from 40 states, 19 foreign countries, and Canada. 65% are from public schools. 86% are white. 30% are Catholic; 30% Protestant; 20% claim no religious affiliation; 15% Jewish. The average age of freshmen is 18; all undergraduates, 20. 15% do not continue beyond their first year; 75% remain to graduate.

Housing: 1500 students can be accommodated in college housing, which includes single-sex and coed dormitories, on-campus apartments, and fraternity houses. In addition, there are honors houses, language houses, special-interest houses, cooperative houses in which students plan and prepare their own meals, and townhouses for upperclassmen. On-campus housing is guaranteed for all 4 years. 92% of students live on campus; of those, 93% remain on campus on weekends. All students may keep cars.

Activities: 15% of men belong to 5 national fraternities. There are no sororities. There are 70 groups on campus, including art, chess, choir, chorale, chorus, computers, dance, debate, drama, ethnic, film, forensics, gay, honors, international, jazz band, literary magazine, musical theater, newspaper, orchestra, photography, political, professional, radio and TV, religious, social, social service, student government, symphony, and yearbook. Popular campus events include Folk Festival, Charter Day, and Moving Up Day.

Sports: There are 11 intercollegiate sports for men and 10 for women, and 23 intramural sports for men and 23 for women. Facilities include a sport and recreation center, 2 gyms, numerous athletic fields, a swimming pool, 5 indoor tennis courts, 2 weight rooms, basketball and racquetball courts, an indoor track, international squash courts, and a boathouse.

Disabled Students: Wheelchair ramps, elevators, special parking, specially equipped rest rooms, special class scheduling, and lowered drinking fountains are available.

Services: Counseling and information services are available, as is tutoring in every subject. There is a reader service for the blind, and remedial math, reading, and writing. There is a counseling center staffed by 5 therapists/counselors as well as various support groups and educational workshops.

Campus Safety and Security: Measures include 24-hour foot and vehicle patrol, self-defense education, escort service, and shuttle buses. There are informal discussions, pamphlets/posters/films, emergency telephones, and lighted pathways/sidewalks.

Programs of Study: HWS confers B.A. and B.S. degrees. Bachelor's degrees are awarded in BIOLOGICAL SCIENCE (biology/biological science), COMMUNICATIONS AND THE ARTS (Chinese, classics, comparative literature, dance, English, fine arts, French, Japanese, music, and Spanish), COMPUTER AND PHYSICAL SCIENCE (chemistry, computer science, geoscience, mathematics, and physics), ENGINEERING AND ENVIRONMENTAL DESIGN (architecture, and environmental science), SOCIAL SCIENCE (American studies, anthropology, Asian/Oriental studies, economics, history, international relations, philosophy, political science/government, psychology, religion, Russian and Slavic studies, sociology, urban studies, and women's studies). Natural sciences, environmental studies, and creative writing are the strongest academically. English, economics, and political science are the largest.

Required: All first-year students must take a seminar. Students should complete a major of 14 to 18 courses and a minor of 6 to 8 courses, or a second major. Of the major or the minor (or second major), one must be disciplinary and the other interdisciplinary. Minimum grade and GPA standards apply. In addition, all students must meet the 8 goals established by the faculty to ensure breadth across the disciplines as well as depth in the major.

Special: Students are encouraged to spend at least 1 term in a study-abroad program, offered in more than 29 countries and locales within the United States. Options include a United Nations term, a Washington semester, an urban semester, and prearchitecture semesters in New York, Paris, Florence, or Copenhagen. HWS offers dual and student-designed majors, credit for life/military/work experience, nondegree study, and pass/fail options. There are also advanced business degree programs with Clarkson University and Rochester Institute of Technology and 3-2 engineering degrees with Columbia University, Rensselaer Polytechnic Institute, and Dartmouth College. There are 9 national honor societies, including Phi Beta Kappa. All departments have honor programs.

Faculty/Classroom: 60% of faculty are male; 40%, female. All both teach and do research. The average class size in an introductory lecture is 41; in a laboratory, 18; and in a regular course, 18.

Admissions: 68% of the 2001-2002 applicants were accepted. The SAT I scores for the 2001-2002 freshman class were: Verbal--13% below 500, 50% between 500 and 599, 33% between 600 and 700, and 4% above 700; Math--12% below 500, 52% between 500 and 599, 33% between 600 and 700, and 3% above 700. 49% of the current freshmen were in the top fifth of their class; 81% were in the top two fifths. 2 freshmen graduated first in their class.

Requirements: The SAT I or ACT is required. SAT II: Subject tests are not required but will be considered if taken. A GED is accepted. A total of 18 academic credits is required, including 4 years of English, 3 of math, and at least 2 each of lab science, foreign language, and history. An essay is required; an interview is recommended. AP credits are accepted. Important factors in the admissions decision are advanced placement or honor courses, evidence of special talent, and leadership record. Applications are accepted on computer disk and on-line at the college's web site or via Common App or Embark.

Procedure: Freshmen are admitted in the fall. Entrance exams should be taken in the junior or senior year. There are early decision, early admissions, and deferred admissions plans. Early decision applications should be filed by January 1; regular applications, by February 1 for fall entry, along with a $45 fee. Notification of early decision is sent February 1; regular decision, April 1. 117 early decision candidates were accepted for the 2001-2002 class. 10% of all applicants are on a waiting list; 10 were accepted in 2001.

Transfer: 33 transfer students enrolled in 2001-2002. Applicants must have a 2.5 GPA and have completed 1 year of college study. They are required to take the SAT I or ACT. An interview is recommended. 16 credits of 32 must be completed at HWS.

Visiting: There are regularly scheduled orientations for prospective students, including 7 open houses in the spring, summer, and fall and daily tours and personal interviews year round. There are guides for informal visits and visitors may sit in on classes and stay overnight. To schedule a visit, contact the Offices of Admissions at (800) 852-2256 or *admissions@hws.edu*

Financial Aid: In 2001-2002, 70% of all students received some form of financial aid. 59% of freshmen and 66% of continuing students received need-based aid. The average freshman award was $24,119. Of that total, scholarships or need-based grants averaged $17,599 ($30,750 maximum); loans averaged $2625 ($6625 maximum); and work contracts averaged $1200 ($1800 maximum). 53% of undergraduates work part time. Average annual earnings from campus work are $687. The average financial indebtedness of the 2001 graduate was $17,294. HWS is a member of CSS. The CSS/Profile or FAFSA is required. The fall application deadline is February 15.

International Students: There are 29 international students enrolled. The school actively recruits these students. They must score 550 on the written TOEFL or 220 on the electronic version and also take the SAT I or the ACT.

Computers: The mainframes are a DEC ALPHA 2100 and a DEC VAX 6520. There are 122 PCs and 60 terminals directly connected to the mainframe, with 114 PCs networked. The 4 PC labs provide access to the on-line library catalog system, e-mail, and the Internet. All students have e-mail accounts, and computers in student rooms are directly connected to the mainframe. All students may access the system from 8 A.M. to 1 A.M., 7 days a week. There are no time limits and no fees.

Graduates: In 2001, 399 bachelor's degrees were awarded. The most popular majors were English (19%), economics (14%), and history (9%). In an average class, 70% graduate in 4 years, 82% in 5 years, and 83% in 6 years. Of the 2000 graduating class, 27% were enrolled in graduate school within 6 months of graduation and 82% were employed.

Admissions Contact: Mara O'Laughlin, Director of Admissions.
E-mail: *olaughlin@hws.edu* Web: *http://www.hws.edu*

HOFSTRA UNIVERSITY — D-5

Hempstead, NY 11549 (516) 463-6700
(800) HOFSTRA; Fax: (516) 560-7660

Full-time: 3909 men, 4497 women — **Faculty:** 367; I, av$
Part-time: 584 men, 655 women — **Ph.D.s:** 90%
Graduate: 1346 men, 2437 women — **Student/Faculty:** 23 to 1
Year: 4-1-4, summer session — **Tuition:** $15,722
Application Deadline: see profile — **Room & Board:** $7530
Freshman Class: 11,613 applied, 8949 accepted, 1978 enrolled
SAT I Verbal/Math: 540/550 — **ACT:** 22 — **COMPETITIVE**

Hofstra University, founded in 1935, is an independent institution offering programs in liberal arts and sciences, business, communications, and education. There are 7 undergraduate and 5 graduate schools. In addition to regional accreditation, Hofstra has baccalaureate program accreditation with AACSB, ABET, ACS, ASHA, CAAHEP, and NCATE. The 4 libraries contain 1.6 million volumes, 3.4 million microform items, and 7000 audiovisual forms/CDs, and subscribe to 7017 periodicals. Computerized library services include the card catalog, interlibrary loans, and database searching. Special learning facilities include a learning resource center, art gallery, radio station, TV station, museum, arboretum, bird sanctuary, writing center, career center, cultural center, language lab, technology lab, and child care institute. The 240-acre campus is in a suburban area 25 miles east of New York City. Including residence halls, there are 130 buildings.

Student Life: 79% of undergraduates are from New York. Others are from 44 states, 67 foreign countries, and Canada. 74% are white; 11% African American. The average age of freshmen is 18; all undergraduates, 22. 23% do not continue beyond their first year; 61% remain to graduate.

Housing: 4000 students can be accommodated in college housing, which includes single-sex and coed dormitories, off-campus apartments, and married-student housing. In addition, there are special-interest houses, international student housing, special housing for disabled students, a freshman center, and nonsmoking and quiet-hour floors. On-campus housing is available on a first-come, first-served basis and is available on a lottery system for upperclassmen. 61% of students commute. All students may keep cars.

Activities: 6% of men belong to 2 local and 17 national fraternities; 7% of women belong to 6 local and 8 national sororities. There are 120 groups on campus, including art, band, cheerleading, chess, choir, chorale, chorus, commuter, computers, dance, debate, drama, drum and bugle corps, ethnic, film, forensics, gay, honors, international, jazz, commuter, band, literary magazine, musical theater, newspaper, opera, orchestra, pep band, photography, political, professional, radio and TV, religious, resident student, social, social service, student government, symphony, and yearbook. Popular campus events include Spring Shakespeare Festival, Italian American Festival, and Spring Irish Festival.

Sports: There are 9 intercollegiate sports for men and 9 for women, and 8 intramural sports for men and 8 for women. Facilities include a 15,000-seat stadium, a 5,000-seat arena, a physical fitness center, a swim center with an Olympic-size swimming pool and high-dive area, a softball stadium, a recreation center, a gym, an indoor jogging track, a wrestling room, and courts for badminton, basketball, tennis, and volleyball.

Disabled Students: All of the campus is accessible. Wheelchair ramps, elevators, special parking, specially equipped rest rooms, special class scheduling, lowered drinking fountains, lowered telephones, automated door openings, and TTY visual telephones are available.

Services: Counseling and information services are available, as is tutoring in every subject. There is a reader service for the blind, and remedial math, reading, and writing.

Campus Safety and Security: Measures include 24-hour foot and vehicle patrol, self-defense education, escort service, and shuttle buses. There are informal discussions, pamphlets/posters/films, emergency telephones, lighted pathways/sidewalks, security cameras in residence halls, and a motorist assistance program.

Programs of Study: Hofstra confers B.A., B.S., B.B.A., B.E., B.F.A., and B.S.Ed. degrees. Master's and doctoral degrees are also awarded. Bachelor's degrees are awarded in AGRICULTURE (natural resource management), BIOLOGICAL SCIENCE (biochemistry, biology/biological science, and marine biology), BUSINESS (accounting, banking and finance, business administration and management, international business management, management information systems, and marketing/retailing/merchandising), COMMUNICATIONS AND THE ARTS (art history and appreciation, audio technology, broadcasting, classics, communications, communications technology, comparative literature, dance, dramatic arts, English, film arts, fine arts, French, German, Hebrew, Italian, journalism, languages, media arts, music, public relations, Russian, Spanish, and speech/debate/rhetoric), COMPUTER AND PHYSICAL SCIENCE (chemistry, computer science, geology, mathematics, natural sciences, and physics), EDUCATION (art, athletic training, bilingual/bicultural, business, early childhood, elementary, foreign languages, health, music, physical, science, and secondary), ENGINEERING AND

ENVIRONMENTAL DESIGN (electrical/electronics engineering, engineering, engineering and applied science, industrial engineering, and mechanical engineering), HEALTH PROFESSIONS (community health work and speech pathology/audiology), SOCIAL SCIENCE (African studies, American studies, anthropology, area studies, Asian/Oriental studies, crosscultural studies, economics, geography, history, humanities, interdisciplinary studies, Judaic studies, liberal arts/general studies, philosophy, physical fitness/movement, political science/government, psychology, social science, and sociology). Accounting, marketing, and English are the strongest academically. Marketing and business computer information systems are the largest.

Required: A total of 124 to 135 credit hours is required for graduation, with 30 to 36 in the major and a minimum GPA of 2.0. Students must take 2 semesters of English and pass a writing proficiency test. A minimum of 9 semester hours each are required in humanities, natural sciences/math/computer science, and social science, and 3 in cross-cultural. Foreign language study is required for the B.A. and B.B.A. in international business, and students in New College must submit a thesis.

Special: Internships, a Washington semester, study abroad in 19 countries, and dual and student-designed majors are offered. Credit for military and work experience and credit by exam are given. Hofstra offers nondegree study and pass/fail options. There are 30 national honor societies, including Phi Beta Kappa, a freshman honors program, and 13 departmental honors programs.

Faculty/Classroom: 55% of faculty are male; 45%, female. 74% both teach and do research. The average class size in an introductory lecture is 27; in a laboratory, 15; and in a regular course, 24.

Admissions: 77% of the 2001-2002 applicants were accepted. The SAT I scores for the 2001-2002 freshman class were: Verbal--21% below 500, 58% between 500 and 599, 19% between 600 and 700, and 2% above 700; Math--18% below 500, 57% between 500 and 599, 23% between 600 and 700, and 2% above 700. The ACT scores were 26% below 21, 38% between 21 and 23, 22% between 24 and 26, 10% between 27 and 28, and 4% above 28. 34% of the current freshmen were in the top fifth of their class; 75% were in the top two fifths. 8 freshmen graduated first in their class.

Requirements: The SAT I or ACT is required. In addition, applicants should graduate from an accredited secondary school or have a GED. Preparatory work should include 4 years of English, 3 of history and social studies, 2 each of math and foreign language, and 1 of science, plus 4 academic electives. Engineering students require 4 years of math and 1 each of chemistry and physics. An essay and interview are recommended. AP and CLEP credits are accepted. Important factors in the admissions decision are advanced placement or honor courses, recommendations by school officials, and leadership record. Applications are accepted on-line.

Procedure: Freshmen are admitted fall and spring. Entrance exams should be taken in the junior or senior year. There are early decision, early admissions, and deferred admissions plans. Early decision applications should be filed by December 1. The fall 2001 application fee was $40. Notification of early decision is sent December 15; regular decision, on a rolling basis. 86 early decision candidates were accepted for the 2001-2002 class.

Transfer: 777 transfer students enrolled in 2001-2002. Admission is based primarily on prior college work. A maximum of 64 credits from a 2-year school and 94 credits from a 4-year school are accepted. The minimum GPA is 2.0. 30 credits of 124 must be completed at Hofstra.

Visiting: There are regularly scheduled orientations for prospective students, including an open house, a campus tour, and a program in which a prospective student spends the day with a current student in a similar major. There are guides for informal visits and visitors may sit in on classes and stay overnight. To schedule a visit, contact the Ambassador Program at (516) 463-6798.

Financial Aid: In 2001-2002, 76% of all freshmen and 74% of continuing students received some form of financial aid. 73% of freshmen and 71% of continuing students received need-based aid. The average freshman award was $10,258. Of that total, scholarships or need-based grants averaged $4786 ($24,888 maximum); loans averaged $4296 ($31,536 maximum); and work contracts averaged $2467 ($2500 maximum). The average financial indebtedness of the 2001 graduate was $10,018. Hofstra is a member of CSS. The FAFSA is required. The fall application deadline is February 15.

International Students: There are 222 international students enrolled. The school actively recruits these students. They must score 550 on the written TOEFL or 213 on the electronic version and also take the college's own test.

Computers: The mainframes are an IBM 9121, a DEC VAX 8530, and a DEC VAX 6410. The university's computer network provides individual accounts for all students for Internet, e-mail, and more than 250 networked software programs. More than 750 PC, Mac, and UNIX workstations are available to students in the various labs and classrooms on campus. The labs are staffed, and 1 computer lab is open 24 hours a day, 7 days per week. All campus workstations have high-speed (OC3) Internet access. All resident students are provided with Internet and e-mail access from their dorm rooms. All students may access the system. There are no time limits and no fees.

Graduates: In 2001, 1703 bachelor's degrees were awarded. The most popular majors were psychology (13%), banking and finance (8%), and marketing (7%). In an average class, 1% graduate in 3 years, 41% in 4 years, 56% in 5 years, and 60% in 6 years. 261 companies recruited on campus in 2000-2001.

Admissions Contact: Mary Beth Carey, Vice President for Enrollment Services. E-mail: *hofstra@hofstra.edu* Web: *www.hofstra.edu*

HOUGHTON COLLEGE — B-3

Houghton, NY 14744 — (585) 567-9353
(800) 777-2556; Fax: (585) 567-9522

Full-time: 496 men, 864 women	**Faculty:** 81; IIB, -$
Part-time: 22 men, 45 women	**Ph.D.s:** 80%
Graduate: none	**Student/Faculty:** 17 to 1
Year: 4-4-1	**Tuition:** $16,290
Application Deadline: open	**Room & Board:** $5520
Freshman Class: 1025 applied, 935 accepted, 355 enrolled	
SAT I Verbal/Math: 592/576	**ACT:** 26 **VERY COMPETITIVE+**

Houghton College, founded in 1883, is a Christian liberal arts college with more than 40 majors and programs. In addition to regional accreditation, Houghton has baccalaureate program accreditation with NASM. The library contains 226,092 volumes, 30,281 microform items, and 7441 audiovisual forms/CDs, and subscribes to 3651 periodicals. Computerized library services include the card catalog, interlibrary loans, and database searching. Special learning facilities include an art gallery, radio station, and equestrian center. The 1300-acre campus is in a rural area 65 miles southeast of Buffalo and 70 miles southwest of Rochester. Including residence halls, there are 17 buildings.

Student Life: 57% of undergraduates are from New York. Others are from 39 states, 24 foreign countries, and Canada. 78% are from public schools. 90% are white. 73% are Protestant; 19%, nondenominational. The average age of freshmen is 18; all undergraduates, 21. 15% do not continue beyond their first year; 73% remain to graduate.

Housing: 990 students can be accommodated in college housing, which includes single-sex dormitories and on-campus apartments. In addition, there are language houses and special-interest houses. On-campus housing is guaranteed for the freshman year only and is available on a lottery system for upperclassmen. Priority is given to out-of-town students. 77% of students live on campus; of those, 65% remain on campus on weekends. Alcohol is not permitted. All students may keep cars.

Activities: There are no fraternities or sororities. There are 40 groups on campus, including art, bagpipe band, band, cheerleading, choir, chorale, chorus, drama, ethnic, honors, international, jazz band, literary magazine, mission, musical theater, newspaper, opera, orchestra, outreach, political, professional, radio and TV, religious, social service, student government, and yearbook. Popular campus events include Christian Life Emphasis Week, Winter Weekend, and Madrigal Dinners.

Sports: There are 4 intercollegiate sports for men and 6 for women, and 8 intramural sports for men and 6 for women. Facilities include 3 basketball and 4 racquetball courts, a swimming pool, an indoor track, a downhill ski slope, cross-country ski trails, 6 tennis courts, a climbing wall, an 8-lane all weather track, and a 386-acre equestrian center with an indoor riding ring. The gym seats 1800; the auditorium, 1300.

Disabled Students: 80% of the campus is accessible. Wheelchair ramps, elevators, special parking, specially equipped rest rooms, special class scheduling, lowered drinking fountains, and lowered telephones are available.

Services: Counseling and information services are available, as is tutoring in some subjects, including general education courses. There is a reader service for the blind and support for learning-disabled students.

Campus Safety and Security: Measures include 24-hour foot and vehicle patrol, escort service, shuttle buses, and informal discussions. There are pamphlets/posters/films, emergency telephones, and lighted pathways/sidewalks.

Programs of Study: Houghton confers B.A., B.S., and B.M. degrees. Associate degrees are also awarded. Bachelor's degrees are awarded in BIOLOGICAL SCIENCE (biology/biological science), BUSINESS (accounting, business administration and management, and recreation and leisure services), COMMUNICATIONS AND THE ARTS (art, communications, creative writing, English, French, music performance, music theory and composition, and Spanish), COMPUTER AND PHYSICAL SCIENCE (chemistry, computer science, mathematics, physics, and science), EDUCATION (elementary, music, physical, science, and secondary), ENGINEERING AND ENVIRONMENTAL DESIGN (environmental science), HEALTH PROFESSIONS (medical technology), SOCIAL SCIENCE (biblical studies, crosscultural studies, history, humanities, international relations, ministries, philosophy, political science/government, psychology, religion, and sociology). Biology, religion, and music are the strongest academically. Education, biology, and psychology are the largest.

Required: Required courses include 10 hours of math and science, 9 of religion, 8 of language, 6 to 9 of English, 6 of social science, 4 each of philosophy and Western civilization, 3 of fine arts, 2 to 6 of communication, 2 of phys ed, and a research component. A total of between 124 and 129 credits, with at least 24 in the major, and a minimum GPA of 2.0 are required to graduate.

Special: Students may cross-register with members of the Western New York Consortium. Internships are available in psychology, social work, business, graphic design, communication, athletic training, recreation, English, and Christian education. Study abroad in 25 countries, a Washington semester, dual majors, and a 3-2 engineering degree with Clarkson and Washington Universities are available. Credit for military experience and nondegree study are possible. There are 2 national honor societies and a freshman honors program.

Faculty/Classroom: 75% of faculty are male; 25%, female. All teach undergraduates and 15% do research. The average class size in an introductory lecture is 29; in a laboratory, 14; and in a regular course, 17.

Admissions: 91% of the 2001-2002 applicants were accepted. The SAT I scores for the 2001-2002 freshman class were: Verbal--15% below 500, 39% between 500 and 599, 31% between 600 and 700, and 15% above 700; Math--18% below 500, 42% between 500 and 599, 32% between 600 and 700, and 8% above 700. The ACT scores were 16% below 21, 21% between 21 and 23, 25% between 24 and 26, 15% between 27 and 28, and 23% above 28. 54% of the current freshmen were in the top fifth of their class; 83% were in the top two fifths. There were 2 National Merit finalists and 3 semifinalists. 29 freshmen graduated first in their class.

Requirements: The SAT I or ACT is required, with a minimum composite score of 900 on the SAT I or 20 on the ACT recommended. Applicants must graduate from an accredited secondary school or have a GED. A total of 16 academic credits is recommended, including 4 of English, 3 of social studies, and 2 each of foreign language, math, and science. An essay is required. Music students must audition. An interview is recommended. Houghton requires applicants to be in the upper 50% of their class. A GPA of 2.5 is required. AP and CLEP credits are accepted. Important factors in the admissions decision are personality/intangible qualities, recommendations by school officials, and advanced placement or honor courses. Applications are accepted on-line.

Procedure: Freshmen are admitted fall and spring. Entrance exams should be taken in the spring of the junior year or fall of the senior year. There are early admissions and deferred admissions plans. Application deadlines are open. Notification is sent on a rolling basis beginning January 1. The fall 2001 application fee was $25.

Transfer: 50 transfer students enrolled in 2001-2002. Applicants should have a 2.5 or better GPA. A pastor's recommendation and high school transcripts must be submitted. The SAT I or ACT and an interview are recommended. 30 credits of 125 must be completed at Houghton.

Visiting: There are regularly scheduled orientations for prospective students, including a tour, an admissions interview, a financial aid session, a class visit, and academic program sessions. There are guides for informal visits and visitors may sit in on classes and stay overnight. To schedule a visit, contact Andy Cahill, Campus Visit Coordinator.

Financial Aid: In 2001-2002, 91% of all freshmen and 93% of continuing students received some form of financial aid. 80% of freshmen and 78% of continuing students received need-based aid. The average freshman award was $10,720. Of that total, scholarships or need-based grants averaged $6885 ($21,500 maximum); loans averaged $6408 ($15,000 maximum); and work contracts averaged $1500 (maximum). 50% of undergraduates work part time. Average annual earnings from campus work are $658. The average financial indebtedness of the 2001 graduate was $9898. Houghton is a member of CSS. The FAFSA and the college's own financial statement are required. The fall application deadline is March 1.

International Students: There are 57 international students enrolled. The school actively recruits these students. They must score 550 on the written TOEFL.

Computers: The mainframe is a DEC VAX 8200. All students receive a laptop when they enroll full time at Houghton. The laptop is included in tuition. There are data jacks in all residence rooms, 1 per student. The college has several fully wired classrooms as well as access in study areas, the library, and the snack shop. There is a general-use lab that is open 24 hours a day, 7 days a week and various labs for specialized departmental use. All students may access the system. There are no time limits and no fees.

Graduates: In 2001, 343 bachelor's degrees were awarded. The most popular majors were elementary education (14%), biology (9%), and music (8%). In an average class, 2% graduate in 3 years, 61% in 4 years, 71% in 5 years, and 73% in 6 years. 30 companies recruited on campus in 2000-2001. Of the 2000 graduating class, 17% were enrolled in graduate school within 6 months of graduation and 85% were employed.

Admissions Contact: Bruce Campbell, Director of Admission.
E-mail: *admission@houghton.edu* Web: *www.houghton.edu*

IONA COLLEGE D-5
New Rochelle, NY 10801-1890 **(914) 633-2503**
(800) 231-IONA; Fax: (914) 633-2096

Full-time: 1477 men, 1444 women	**Faculty:** 171; IIA, av$
Part-time: 201 men, 295 women	**Ph.D.s:** 83%
Graduate: 386 men, 585 women	**Student/Faculty:** 17 to 1
Year: semesters, summer session	**Tuition:** $17,140
Application Deadline: March 15	**Room & Board:** $9416
Freshman Class: 3384 applied, 2704 accepted, 842 enrolled	
SAT I Verbal/Math: 500/500	**ACT:** 19 **COMPETITIVE**

Iona College, founded in 1940, is a private, largely commuter college offering programs through schools of general studies, arts and science, and business. It has campuses in Rockland County and Manhattan in addition to the main campus in New Rochelle. There are 2 undergraduate and 2 graduate schools. In addition to regional accreditation, Iona has baccalaureate program accreditation with AACSB, CSWE, and NLN. The library contains 264,917 volumes, 458,551 microform items, and 2852 audiovisual forms/CDs, and subscribes to 803 periodicals. Computerized library services include the card catalog, interlibrary loans, and database searching. Special learning facilities include a learning resource center, art gallery, radio station, TV station, an electron microscope, and a speech and hearing clinic. The 35-acre campus is in a suburban area 20 miles northeast of New York City. Including residence halls, there are 44 buildings.

Student Life: 84% of undergraduates are from New York. Others are from 31 states, 13 foreign countries, and Canada. 73% are white; 13%, Hispanic; 11%, African American. The average age of freshmen is 18; all undergraduates, 20. 23% do not continue beyond their first year; 56% remain to graduate.

Housing: 540 students can be accommodated in college housing, which includes single-sex and coed dormitories and off-campus apartments. On-campus housing is available on a first-come, first-served basis and is available on a lottery system for upperclassmen. Priority is given to out-of-town students. 84% of students commute. Alcohol is not permitted. All students may keep cars.

Activities: There are 8 local and 2 national fraternities and 7 local and 2 national sororities. There are 74 groups on campus, including academic, bagpipe band, cheerleading, choir, chorale, computers, dance, drama, ethnic, honors, international, literary magazine, musical theater, newspaper, pep band, photography, political, professional, radio and TV, religious, social, social service, student government, and yearbook. Popular campus events include Founders Day, Day of the Peacemaker, and Columbus Day Carnival.

Sports: There are 23 intercollegiate sports for men and 23 for women, and 2 intramural sports for men and 2 for women. Facilities include an all-weather football-soccer field, a gym, a Nautilus fitness center, a baseball field, saunas, a track, and a swimming pool. The campus stadium seats 1200 and the indoor gym, 3,000.

Disabled Students: 80% of the campus is accessible. Wheelchair ramps, elevators, special parking, specially equipped rest rooms, special class scheduling, lowered drinking fountains, and lowered telephones are available. All classes are on the first floor.

Services: Counseling and information services are available, as is tutoring in some subjects, including math, statistics, computer science, English composition, history, Spanish, scientific and technological literacy, accounting, business, and management science. There is a reader service for the blind.

Campus Safety and Security: Measures include 24-hour foot and vehicle patrol, shuttle buses, informal discussions, and pamphlets/posters/films. There are emergency telephones and lighted pathways/sidewalks.

Programs of Study: Iona confers B.A., B.S., and B.B.A. degrees. Master's degrees are also awarded. Bachelor's degrees are awarded in BIOLOGICAL SCIENCE (biology/biological science and ecology), BUSINESS (accounting, banking and finance, business administration and management, business economics, business law, management information systems, management science, and marketing/retailing/merchandising), COMMUNICATIONS AND THE ARTS (advertising, communications, dramatic arts, English, film arts, French, Italian, journalism, and Spanish), COMPUTER AND PHYSICAL SCIENCE (computer science, information sciences and systems, mathematics, and physics), EDUCATION (elementary, foreign languages, middle school, science, and secondary), HEALTH PROFESSIONS (health care administration, medical laboratory technology, predentistry, premedicine, prepharmacy, preveterinary science, and speech pathology/audiology), SOCIAL SCIENCE (criminal justice, economics, history, international relations, philosophy, political science/government, prelaw, psychology, religion, social science, social work, sociology, and urban studies). Accounting, computer science, and management information systems are the strongest academically. Communication arts, accounting, and management are the largest.

Required: The core curriculum includes 24 credits of humanities, 12 credits of natural and symbolic languages, and 6 credits each of communications, social science, and science and technology. Computer literacy is required. The total number of credits required in liberal arts is 120, with 39 to 46 in the major; the business program requires 126 credits, with 30 in the major. The minimum GPA is 2.0.

Special: There is cross-registration and co-op programs with Concordia College, Marymount College Tarrytown, and the College of New Rochelle. There are internships for upperclassmen. Study abroad is available in Ireland, Belgium, France, Spain, Italy, and Morocco. There is work-study in Iona offices and academic departments. Students may earn a combined B.A.-B.S. degree in economics, psychology, elementary education, early secondary education, and math education. The college offers dual and student-designed majors, a general studies degree, and credit by examination and for life/military/work experience. There are 20 national honor societies, and a freshman honors program.

Faculty/Classroom: 63% of faculty are male; 37%, female. 95% teach undergraduates. No introductory courses are taught by graduate students. The average class size in an introductory lecture is 22; in a laboratory, 16; and in a regular course, 21.

Admissions: 80% of the 2001-2002 applicants were accepted. The SAT I scores for the 2001-2002 freshman class were: Verbal--47% below 500, 41% between 500 and 599, 11% between 600 and 700, and 1% above 700; Math--47% below 500, 40% between 500 and 599, 12% between 600 and 700, and 1% above 700.

Requirements: The SAT I is required and the ACT is recommended. In addition, applicants must complete 16 academic credits including 4 units of English, 3 of math, 2 of foreign language, and 1 each of history, science, and social studies. A GED is accepted. An essay and an interview are recommended. Iona requires applicants to be in the upper 60% of their class. A GPA of 2.5 is required. AP and CLEP credits are accepted. Important factors in the admissions decision are recommendations by school officials, extracurricular activities record, and leadership record.

Procedure: Freshmen are admitted fall and spring. Entrance exams should be taken in the spring of the senior year. There is a deferred admissions plan. Applications should be filed by March 15 for fall entry and January 1 for spring entry. Notification is sent on a rolling basis. The fall 2001 application fee was $25.

Transfer: 194 transfer students enrolled in 2001-2002. Transfer applicants must have a GPA of at least 2.5 and must submit high school transcripts if they have earned less than 30 college credits. An interview is recommended. 30 credits of 120 must be completed at Iona.

Visiting: There are regularly scheduled orientations for prospective students, including a meeting with an admissions counselor, a campus tour, and a variety of on-campus programs during the spring and summer. There are guides for informal visits and visitors may sit in on classes. To schedule a visit, contact the Admissions Office at (914) 633-2502 or *icad@iona.edu*

Financial Aid: In 2001-2002, 96% of all freshmen and 80% of continuing students received some form of financial aid. 15% of all students received need-based aid. The average freshman award was $5827. Of that total, scholarships or need-based grants averaged $3659 ($8570 maximum); loans averaged $1716 ($5250 maximum); work contracts averaged $733 ($1500 maximum); and state and federal entitlements averaged $1963 ($4975 maximum). The average financial indebtedness of the 2001 graduate was $17,096. The FAFSA, the college's own financial statement, and the and the TAP (Tuition Assistance Program) are required.

International Students: There are 18 international students enrolled. They must score 550 on the written TOEFL and also take the SAT I scoring 700, or the ACT.

Computers: The mainframe is an IBM ES 9000 Model 320. The campus WAN consists of 30 file servers (10 Novell, 17 NT, and 3 UNIX) and 1100 workstations. 500 Pentium workstations are available on campus for student use. All students may access the system. There is unlimited access to PC software (24 hours) and mainframe facilities. There are no time limits. The fee is $25 per semester.

Graduates: In 2001, 608 bachelor's degrees were awarded. The most popular majors were mass communication (15%), education (10%), and business (9%). In an average class, 1% graduate in 3 years, 40% in 4 years, 54% in 5 years, and 58% in 6 years. 62 companies recruited on campus in 2000-2001.

Admissions Contact: Thomas Weede, Director of Admissions.
E-mail: *icad@iona.edu* Web: *http://www.iona.edu*

ITHACA COLLEGE — C-3

Ithaca, NY 14850-7020 — (607) 274-3124
(800) 429-4274; Fax: (607) 274-1900

Full-time: 2714 men and 3364 women — **Faculty:** 419; IIA, -$
Part-time: 63 men and 68 women — **Ph.D.s:** 88%
Graduate: 66 men and 208 women — **Student/Faculty:** 14 to 1
Year: semesters, summer session — **Tuition:** $20,104
Application Deadline: March 1 — **Room & Board:** $8615
Freshman Class: 10,505 applied, 6192 accepted, 1755 enrolled
SAT I Verbal/Math: 580/580 — **HIGHLY COMPETITIVE**

Ithaca College, founded in 1892, is a private college offering undergraduate and graduate programs in business, communications, health science and human performance, humanities and sciences, and music. There are 5 undergraduate schools and 1 graduate school. In addition to regional accreditation, Ithaca or IC has baccalaureate program accreditation with AOTA, APTA, NASM, and NRPA. The library contains 599,755 volumes, 305,164 microform items, and 25,547 audiovisual forms/CDs, and subscribes to 2305 periodicals. Computerized library services include the card catalog, interlibrary loans, and database searching. Special learning facilities include an art gallery, radio station, TV station, and digital audio and video labs; speech, hearing, wellness, and physical therapy clinics; greenhouse; financial "trading room"; observatory; and electroacoustic music studios. The 757-acre campus is in a small town 250 miles northwest of New York City. Including residence halls, there are 60 buildings.

Student Life: 52% of undergraduates are from out of state, mostly the Middle Atlantic. Others are from 45 states, 77 foreign countries, and Canada. 75% are from public schools. The average age of freshmen is 18; all undergraduates, 20. 15% do not continue beyond their first year; 72% remain to graduate.

Housing: 3607 students can be accommodated in college housing, which includes single-sex and coed dormitories and on-campus apartments. In addition, there are first-year students only housing, a quiet study residence hall, music honor fraternities, smoke-free buildings and floors, coed by door buildings, honors floors, a substance-free building, multicultural housing, and several freshman seminar groups housed together. On-campus housing is guaranteed for all 4 years. 70% of students live on campus; of those, 95% remain on campus on weekends. All students may keep cars.

Activities: 2% of men and about 1% of women belong to 3 national fraternities; 2% of women belong to 1 local sorority. There are 140 groups on campus, including art, band, chess, choir, chorale, chorus, College Bowl, computers, dance, debate, drama, ethnic, film, gay, honors, international, jazz band, literary magazine, musical theater, newspaper, opera, orchestra, pep band, photography, political, professional, radio and TV, religious, social, social service, sports clubs, student government, symphony, and yearbook. Popular campus events include Winter Fest, Fall Madness, and Day of Service.

Sports: There are 12 intercollegiate sports for men and 13 for women, and 15 intramural sports for men and 15 for women. Facilities include 5 gyms, 2 dance studios, a student union, indoor and outdoor pools, a fitness center and wellness clinic, tennis courts, and baseball, football, lacrosse, field hockey, and soccer fields.

Disabled Students: Wheelchair ramps, elevators, special parking, specially equipped rest rooms, special class scheduling, lowered drinking fountains, and lowered telephones are available.

Services: Nonremedial tutoring is available.

Campus Safety and Security: Measures include 24-hour foot and vehicle patrol, escort service, pamphlets/posters/films, and emergency telephones. There are lighted pathways/sidewalks and crime prevention programs.

Programs of Study: Ithaca or IC confers B.A., B.S., B.F.A., and Mus.B. degrees. Master's degrees are also awarded. Bachelor's degrees are awarded in BIOLOGICAL SCIENCE (biochemistry and biology/biological science), BUSINESS (accounting, banking and finance, business administration and management, business economics, electronic business, human resources, international business management, management science, marketing management, marketing/retailing/merchandising, organizational behavior, personnel management, recreation and leisure services, and sports management), COMMUNICATIONS AND THE ARTS (art, art history and appreciation, broadcasting, communications, creative writing, dramatic arts, English, film arts, fine arts, French, German, jazz, journalism, languages, media arts, modern language, music, music performance, music theory and composition, musical theater, performing arts, photography, public relations, Spanish, speech/debate/rhetoric, studio art, telecommunications, theater design, theater management, video, and visual and performing arts), COMPUTER AND PHYSICAL SCIENCE (chemistry, computer mathematics, computer science, information sciences and systems, mathematics, and physics), EDUCATION (athletic training, education, education of the deaf and hearing impaired, educational media, English, foreign languages, health, mathematics, middle school, music, physical, secondary, social studies, and speech correction), ENGINEERING AND ENVIRONMEN-

TAL DESIGN (environmental science), HEALTH PROFESSIONS (allied health, clinical science, community health work, exercise science, health, health care administration, health science, hospital administration, occupational therapy, physical therapy, predentistry, premedicine, public health, recreation therapy, rehabilitation therapy, speech pathology/audiology, speech therapy, and sports medicine), SOCIAL SCIENCE (anthropology, economics, history, industrial and organizational psychology, interdisciplinary studies, liberal arts/general studies, philosophy, physical fitness/movement, political science/government, prelaw, psychology, social studies, and sociology). Physical therapy, theater, and music are the strongest academically. Music, television-radio, and business administration are the largest.

Required: Students must successfully complete a minimum of 120 credit hours. In addition, each student must meet the requirements of a core curriculum, which varies with each school within the college and includes courses in the liberal arts and professional courses outside the student's major.

Special: Cross-registration is available with Cornell University and Wells College. Opportunities are also provided for internships, work-study programs, dual majors, accelerated degree programs, nondegree study, pass/fail options, student-designed majors, a 3-2 engineering degree with Cornell University, Clarkson University, Rensselaer Polytechnic Institute, and SUNY Binghamton, and study abroad in London, Valencia, and other foreign cities. A 4-1 advanced business degree program and a 3-1 optometry program are also available. There are 24 national honor societies, a freshman honors program, and 16 departmental honors programs.

Faculty/Classroom: All teach undergraduates. No introductory courses are taught by graduate students. The average class size in an introductory lecture is 21 and in a regular course, 19.

Admissions: 59% of the 2001-2002 applicants were accepted. The SAT I scores for the 2001-2002 freshman class were: Verbal--10% below 500, 48% between 500 and 599, 37% between 600 and 699, and 5% above 700; Math--8% below 500, 49% between 500 and 599, 40% between 600 and 700, and 4% above 700. 56% of the current freshmen were in the top fifth of their class; 86% were in the top two fifths. There were 6 National Merit finalists. 26 freshmen graduated first in their class.

Requirements: The SAT I or ACT is required. In addition, applicants should be graduates of an accredited secondary school with a minimum of 16 Carnegie units, including 4 years of English, 3 each of math, science, and social studies, 2 of foreign language, and other college-preparatory electives. The GED is accepted. An essay is required, as is an audition for music and theater students. In some majors, a portfolio and an interview are recommended. Applications are accepted on-line at the school's web site. Ithaca requires applicants to be in the upper 25% of their class. AP and CLEP credits are accepted.

Procedure: Freshmen are admitted fall and spring. Entrance exams should be taken in spring of the junior year or fall of the senior year. There are early decision and deferred admissions plans. Early decision applications should be filed by November 1; regular applications, by March 1 for fall entry and December 1 for spring entry. The fall 2001 application fee was $55. Notification of early decision is sent December 15; regular decision, on a rolling basis.

Transfer: Transfer applicants must submit SAT I or ACT scores, a high school transcript, transcripts from previously attended colleges, and a personal recommendation from their adviser or Dean of Students. A minimum college GPA of 2.75 is recommended. 30 credits of 120 must be completed at Ithaca.

Visiting: There are regularly scheduled orientations for prospective students, including a campus tour and an interview with an admissions counselor. Fall open house programs offering personal meetings with faculty are available by appointment. There are guides for informal visits and visitors may sit in on classes and stay overnight. To schedule a visit, contact the Director of Admission.

Financial Aid: In 2001-2002, 84% of all freshmen and 79% of continuing students received some form of financial aid. 64% of all students received need-based aid. The average freshman award was $15,164. Of that total, scholarships or need-based grants averaged $10,713 ($31,207 maximum); loans averaged $2576 ($8625 maximum); and work contracts averaged $1875 ($2900 maximum). 42% of undergraduates work part time. Average annual earnings from campus work are $2200. Ithaca is a member of CSS. The FAFSA is required; the CSS/Profile is required for early decision applicants only. The fall application deadline is February 1.

International Students: There are 165 international students enrolled. The school actively recruits these students. They must score 550 on the written TOEFL or 213 on the electronic version and also take the ACT or the SAT I.

Computers: The mainframes are a DEC VAX 11/750 and a DEC VAX 11/785. Students may access the VAX mainframes from approximately 685 PCs/terminals in the library, computer labs, and classrooms. All residence halls are fully networked and have access to the Internet and Web. All students may access the system 24 hours a day. There are no time limits and no fees.

Graduates: In 2001, 1258 bachelor's degrees were awarded. The most popular majors were television-radio (11%), music (8%), and physical therapy (7%). In an average class, 1% graduate in 3 years, 64% in 4 years, 72% in 5 years, and 72% in 6 years. 421 companies recruited on campus in 2000-2001. Of the 2000 graduating class, 33% were enrolled in graduate school within 6 months of graduation and 83% were employed.

Admissions Contact: Paula Mitchell, Director of Admission. A video is available. E-mail: *admission@ithaca.edu* Web: *www.ithaca.edu*

JEWISH THEOLOGICAL SEMINARY/LIST COLLEGE OF JEWISH STUDIES

(See Albert A. List College of Jewish Studies)

JUILLIARD SCHOOL

New York, NY 10023-6588 — **D-5**

(212) 799-5000, ext. 223
Fax: (212) 724-6420

Full-time: 246 men, 259 women	**Faculty:** 100
Part-time: 1 man	**Ph.D.s:** n/av
Graduate: 162 men, 145 women	**Student/Faculty:** 5 to 1
Year: semesters	**Tuition:** $19,000
Application Deadline: December 1	**Room & Board:** $7395
Freshman Class: 1643 applied, 145 accepted, 114 enrolled	
SAT I or ACT: not required	**SPECIAL**

The Juilliard School, founded in 1905, is a private college of dance, music, and drama. The library contains 73,000 volumes, 1399 microform items, and 20,500 audiovisual forms/CDs, and subscribes to 205 periodicals. Computerized library services include the card catalog, interlibrary loans, and database searching. Special learning facilities include 200 practice rooms, 5 theaters, scenery and costume shops, and dance studios. The campus is in an urban area at Lincoln Center in New York City. Including residence halls, there are 2 buildings.

Student Life: 84% of undergraduates are from out of state, mostly the Northeast. Others are from 42 states, 29 foreign countries, and Canada. 38% are white; 27% foreign nationals, 18% Asian American, 11% African American. The average age of freshmen is 18; all undergraduates, 20. 6% do not continue beyond their first year; 75% remain to graduate.

Housing: 350 students can be accommodated in college housing, which includes single-sex and coed dormitories and off-campus apartments. All floors are smoke-free. There are quiet, alcohol-free, and singel-sex (all female) floors. On-campus housing is guaranteed for the freshman year only, is available on a first-come, first-served basis, and on a lottery system for upperclassmen. 52% of students commute. All students may keep cars.

Activities: There are no fraternities or sororities. There are 20 groups on campus, including band, choir, chorale, chorus, dance, drama, environmental consciousness, ethnic, gay, international, jazz band, marching band, opera, orchestra, professional, religious, social, social service, student government, and symphony. Popular campus events include performances by the Juilliard orchestras at Lincoln Center, dance concerts, and drama and opera productions.

Sports: There is no sports program at Juilliard. Facilities include a health recreational facility in the residence hall.

Disabled Students: All of the campus is accessible. Wheelchair ramps, elevators, specially equipped rest rooms, lowered drinking fountains, and lowered telephones are available.

Services: Counseling and information services are available, as is tutoring in some subjects, including ear training and literature and materials of music.

Campus Safety and Security: Measures include 24-hour foot and vehicle patrol, self-defense education, informal discussions, and pamphlets/posters/films. There are emergency telephones, lighted pathways/sidewalks, 24-hour guards in residence halls and the main building, video cameras, and turnstiles with ID card access.

Programs of Study: Juilliard confers B.F.A. and B.Mus. degrees. Master's and doctoral degrees are also awarded. Bachelor's degrees are awarded in COMMUNICATIONS AND THE ARTS (dance, dramatic arts, music theory and composition, percussion, piano/organ, strings, voice, and winds). Piano, voice, and violin are the largest.

Required: Each division has its own requirements for graduation.

Special: A joint program with Columbia University and Barnard College allows students to obtain a 5-year B.A.-B.Mus. degree. Internships are available with cultural organizations in New York City. There is study abroad in music academies in England, Israel, and Russia. Work-study programs, accelerated degrees and dual majors in music, a combined B.Mus.-M.Mus. degree, nondegree study, and pass/fail options are available.

Faculty/Classroom: 65% of faculty are male; 35%, female. All teach undergraduates. The average class size in a regular course is 12.

Admissions: 9% of the 2001-2002 applicants were accepted.

Requirements: A high school diploma or GED is required. Students are accepted primarily on the basis of personal auditions rather than tests. Important factors in the admissions decision are evidence of special talent and personality/intangible qualities.

Procedure: Freshmen are admitted in the fall. Personal auditions should be completed in December for opera, February for drama and regionals in dance and music, and March for dance and music. There is an early admissions plan. Applications should be filed by December 1 for fall entry, along with a $100 fee. Notification is sent April 1. 1% of all applicants are on a waiting list; 20 were accepted in 2001.

Transfer: 26 transfer students enrolled in 2001-2002. Transfer applicants must audition in person.

Visiting: There are regularly scheduled orientations for prospective students, including guided tours and question-and-answer sessions, Monday to Friday at 2:30 P.M. Visitors may sit in on classes and stay overnight. To schedule a visit, contact Sarah J. Adriance, Admissions Assistant at *sadriance@juilliard.edu*

Financial Aid: In 2001-2002, 94% of all freshmen and 92% of continuing students received some form of financial aid, including need-based aid. The average freshman award was $18,169. Of that total, scholarships or need-based grants averaged $13,267 ($25,775 maximum); loans averaged $3417 ($6625 maximum); and work contracts averaged $1500 (maximum). 83% of undergraduates work part time. Average annual earnings from campus work are $1225. The average financial indebtedness of the 2001 graduate was $21,588. The FAFSA and the college's own financial statement are required. The fall application deadline is March 1.

International Students: There are 232 international students enrolled. They must take the TOEFL, the college's own test, and TWE. All students must audition in person.

Computers: All students may access the system during lab hours. There are no fees.

Graduates: In a recent year, 105 bachelor's degrees were awarded. The most popular majors were music (76%), dance (17%), and drama (7%). In an average class, 70% graduate in 4 years, 73% in 5 years, and 75% in 6 years.

Admissions Contact: Office of Admissions.
E-mail: *mgray@juilliard.edu* Web: *www.juilliard.edu*

KEUKA COLLEGE

B-3

Keuka Park, NY 14478

(315) 536-5254, ext. 254
(800) 33-KEUKA; Fax: (315) 536-5386

Full-time: 279 men, 753 women	**Faculty:** 50; IIB, --$
Part-time: 7 men, 24 women	**Ph.D.s:** 60%
Graduate: none	**Student/Faculty:** 21 to 1
Year: 4-1-4, summer session	**Tuition:** $14,290
Application Deadline: open	**Room & Board:** $6880
Freshman Class: n/av	
SAT I Verbal/Math: required	**ACT:** 21 **COMPETITIVE**

Keuka College, founded in 1890, is an independent college affiliated with American Baptist Churches and offers instruction in the liberal arts. In addition to regional accreditation, Keuka has baccalaureate program accreditation with AHEA, CSWE, and NLN. The library contains 83,108 volumes, 3991 microform items, and 2764 audiovisual forms/CDs, and subscribes to 17,287 periodicals. Computerized library services include the card catalog, interlibrary loans, and database searching. Special learning facilities include a learning resource center, art gallery, and radio station. The 203-acre campus is in a rural area 60 miles south of Rochester. Including residence halls, there are 19 buildings.

Student Life: 92% of undergraduates are from New York. Others are from 23 states, 3 foreign countries, and Canada. 80% are from public schools. 92% are white. 30% are Protestant. The average age of freshmen is 18; all undergraduates, 22. 19% do not continue beyond their first year; 52% remain to graduate.

Housing: 719 students can be accommodated in college housing, which includes single-sex and coed dormitories. In addition, there are honors houses and special-interest houses. On-campus housing is guaranteed for all 4 years. 68% of students live on campus; of those, 60% remain on campus on weekends. Alcohol is not permitted. Upperclassmen may keep cars.

Activities: There are no fraternities or sororities. There are 42 groups on campus, including art, cheerleading, choir, chorale, community service, dance, drama, ethnic, honors, international, leadership, literary magazine, newspaper, political, professional, religious, social, social service, student government, and yearbook. Popular campus events include Spring Weekend, May Day, and Family Weekend.

Sports: There are 5 intercollegiate sports for men and 6 for women, and 8 intramural sports for men and 8 for women. Facilities include an Olympic-size pool, a gym, a fitness center, a weight room, and an outdoor athletic facility.

Disabled Students: 60% of the campus is accessible. Wheelchair ramps, elevators, special parking, specially equipped rest rooms, special class scheduling, lowered drinking fountains, and specially equipped residence rooms are available.

Services: Counseling and information services are available, as is tutoring in every subject. There is a reader service for the blind, and remedial math, reading, and writing. Individual and group tutoring is available free through the college's academic support services.

Campus Safety and Security: Measures include 24-hour foot and vehicle patrol, self-defense education, shuttle buses, and informal discussions. There are pamphlets/posters/films, emergency telephones, and lighted pathways/sidewalks.

Programs of Study: Keuka confers B.A. and B.S. degrees. Master's degrees are also awarded. Bachelor's degrees are awarded in BIOLOGICAL SCIENCE (biochemistry and biology/biological science), BUSINESS (accounting, business administration and management, hotel/motel and restaurant management, and marketing/retailing/merchandising), COMMUNICATIONS AND THE ARTS (American Sign Language, communications, and English), EDUCATION (elementary and secondary), ENGINEERING AND ENVIRONMENTAL DESIGN (environmental science), HEALTH PROFESSIONS (medical laboratory technology, nursing, occupational therapy, predentistry, premedicine, and preveterinary science), SOCIAL SCIENCE (criminal justice, political science/government, prelaw, psychology, social work, and sociology). Occupational therapy, biology, and education are the strongest academically. Occupational therapy, education, and management are the largest.

Required: Students must complete 1 field period combining academic study and professional experience for each year of enrollment. The core curriculum consists of 43 to 46 credits, including but not limited to required courses in phys ed, computer science, and integrative studies. A total of 120 credit hours is required for graduation with a minimum of 30 credits in the major and a major/cumulative GPA of 2.0.

Special: There are co-op programs with other members of the Rochester Area Colleges Consortium. The college offers internships, study abroad, a Washington semester, dual majors, and student-designed majors. Credit is also given by exam and for work experience. There are 16 national honor societies.

Faculty/Classroom: 45% of faculty are male; 55%, female. All teach undergraduates. The average class size in an introductory lecture is 22; in a laboratory, 12; and in a regular course, 22.

Admissions: 96% of the 2001-2002 applicants were accepted.

Requirements: The SAT I or ACT is required. In addition, students should graduate from an accredited secondary school with a minimum GPA of 2.8. The GED is accepted. A minimum of 15 Carnegie units is required, including 4 years of English, 3 of history, 2 to 3 of math and science, 2 of foreign language, and 1 of social studies. An essay is required, and an interview is recommended. Keuka requires applicants to be in the upper 50% of their class. A GPA of 2.8 is required. AP and CLEP credits are accepted. Important factors in the admissions decision are recommendations by school officials, extracurricular activities record, and leadership record. Applications are accepted on-line at the school's web site.

Procedure: Freshmen are admitted fall and spring. Entrance exams should be taken in the spring of the junior year or the fall of the senior year. There are early decision, early admissions, and deferred admissions plans. Early decision applications should be filed by December 1 for fall entry; the deadline for regular applications is open. The fall 2001 application fee was $30. Notification of early decision is sent December 1; regular decision, on a rolling basis.

Transfer: 69 transfer students enrolled in 2001-2002. Applicants must take the SAT I or ACT and submit transcripts. An interview is recommended. A minimum GPA of 2.5 is required in college work. 30 credits of 120 must be completed at Keuka.

Visiting: There are regularly scheduled orientations for prospective students, including open houses held in October and April, when students can speak with faculty, student affairs and financial aid representatives, and current students. There are guides for informal visits and visitors may sit in on classes and stay overnight. To schedule a visit, contact the Admissions Office at (315) 279-4411.

Financial Aid: In 2001-2002, 96% of all freshmen and 92% of continuing students received some form of financial aid, including need-based aid. The average freshman award was $12,045. Of that total, scholarships or need-based grants averaged $5500 ($12,730 maximum); loans averaged $2625 (maximum); and work contracts averaged $1700 ($1800 maximum). 61% of undergraduates work part time. Average annual earnings from campus work are $880. The average financial indebtedness of the 2001 graduate was $18,645. Keuka is a member of CSS. The FAFSA and the college's own financial statement are required. The fall application deadline is March 15.

International Students: There are 8 international students enrolled. They must score 588 on the written TOEFL or 238 on the electronic version and also take the SAT I or the ACT.

Computers: The mainframe is a DEC ALPHA 4000. There are 2 fully equipped PC labs that provide students with word processing, graphics, spreadsheet, other academic support functions, Internet, and e-mail access. All students may access the system. There are no time limits and no fees. It is strongly recommended that all students have a personal computer.

Graduates: In 2001, 144 bachelor's degrees were awarded. The most popular majors were occupational therapy (34%), unified elementary/special education (23%), and nursing (7%). In an average class, 35% graduate in 4 years, 52% in 5 years, and 52% in 6 years.

Admissions Contact: Robert Callahan, Dean of Enrollment Management. A video is available. E-mail: *admissions@mail.keuka.edu* Web: *www.keuka.edu*

LABORATORY INSTITUTE OF MERCHANDISING D-5
New York, NY 10022-5268 (212) 752-1530
(800) 677-1323; Fax: (212) 421-4341

Full-time: 17 men, 321 women
Part-time: 2 women
Graduate: none
Year: semesters, summer session
Application Deadline: open
Freshman Class: 261 applied, 194 accepted, 81 enrolled
SAT I Verbal/Math: 484/459
Faculty: 9
Ph.D.s: n/av
Student/Faculty: 38 to 1
Tuition: $13,550
Room & Board: n/app
SPECIAL

The Laboratory Institute of Merchandising, founded in 1939, is a private college offering programs in fashion merchandising, marketing, and visual merchandising. The library contains 11,352 volumes and 452 audiovisual forms/CDs, and subscribes to 100 periodicals. Computerized library services include database searching. Special learning facilities include a learning resource center. The campus is in an urban area. There is one building.

Student Life: 56% of undergraduates are from New York. Others are from 18 states, 8 foreign countries, and Canada. 58% are from public schools. 65% are white; 17%, Hispanic. The average age of freshmen is 18; all undergraduates, 20. 85% of freshmen remain to graduate.

Housing: There are no residence halls. Alcohol is not permitted.

Activities: There are no fraternities or sororities. There are 8 groups on campus, including ethnic, fashion, film, honors, professional, religious, student government, and yearbook. Popular campus events include an annual fashion show, a ski trip, and a Halloween costume party.

Sports: There is no sports program at LIM.

Disabled Students: Elevators are available.

Services: Counseling and information services are available, as is tutoring in most subjects. There is remedial math, reading, and writing.

Campus Safety and Security: Measures include informal discussions and pamphlets/posters/films.

Programs of Study: LIM confers B.B.A. and B.P.S. degrees. Associate degrees are also awarded. Bachelor's degrees are awarded in BUSINESS (fashion merchandising and marketing/retailing/merchandising).

Required: Students must complete 34 credits in the liberal arts and a minimum of 72 in fashion/business courses. Freshmen and sophomores must successfully complete a 3-credit work project each year. Seniors must complete a 13-credit, semester-long co-op program. A total of 126 credits and a GPA of 2.0 are required to graduate.

Special: Internships are required in the first, second, and fourth years. Study abroad is available in China, Italy, Spain, France, and England. There are co-op programs as well as work-study programs with major department stores and specialty shops, manufacturers, showrooms, magazine publishers, and cosmetics companies. There is 1 national honor society.

Faculty/Classroom: 39% of faculty are male; 61%, female. The average class size in an introductory lecture is 20 and in a regular course, 23.

Admissions: 74% of the 2001-2002 applicants were accepted. The SAT I scores for the 2001-2002 freshman class were: Verbal--61% below 500, 36% between 500 and 599, and 3% between 600 and 700; Math--68% below 500, 31% between 500 and 599, and 1% between 600 and 700. 11% of the current freshmen were in the top fifth of their class; 28% were in the top two fifths.

Requirements: The SAT I or ACT is required. In addition, an essay and interview are required. Applicants should be high school graduates or hold the GED. AP and CLEP credits are accepted. Important factors in the admissions decision are personality/intangible qualities, leadership record, and extracurricular activities record.

Procedure: Freshmen are admitted fall and spring. Application deadlines are open. Notification is on a rolling basis. The fall 2001 application fee was $35.

Transfer: 51 transfer students enrolled in 2001-2002. Applicants must submit their official high school and college transcripts. Students with fewer than 30 college credits must submit the SAT I or ACT scores. Interviews are required of all applicants, and recommendation letters are encouraged but not required. 46 credits of 126 must be completed at LIM.

Visiting: There are regularly scheduled orientations for prospective students, consisting of the Student for a Day program, which includes a tour, 2 presentations, a financial aid overview, lunch, interviews, and a scholarship exam. There are guides for informal visits and visitors may sit in on classes. To schedule a visit, contact the Admissions Office.

Financial Aid: In 2001-2002, 78% of all freshmen and 85% of continuing students received some form of financial aid. 82% of freshmen and 76% of continuing students received need-based aid. The average freshman award was $9000. Of that total, scholarships or need-based grants averaged $737 ($3125 maximum); loans averaged $2625; and work contracts averaged $2800 (maximum). 5% of undergraduates work part time. The average financial indebtedness of the 2001 graduate was $15,000. The FAFSA and the college's own financial statement are required. The fall application deadline is April 1.

International Students: There are 4 international students enrolled. They must score 550 on the written TOEFL.

Computers: All students may access the system. There are no time limits and no fees.

Graduates: In 2001, 39 bachelor's degrees were awarded. In an average class, 89% graduate in 4 years. Of the 2000 graduating class, All were employed within 6 months of graduation.

Admissions Contact: Karen Hamill Iglio, Director of Admissions. E-mail: *admissions@limcollege.edu* Web: *http://www.limcollege.edu*

LE MOYNE COLLEGE C-3
Syracuse, NY 13214-1399 (315) 445-4300
(800) 333-4733; Fax: (315) 445-4711

Full-time: 877 men, 1273 women
Part-time: 130 men, 165 women
Graduate: 305 men, 416 women
Year: semesters, summer session
Application Deadline: March 1
Freshman Class: 2443 applied, 1881 accepted, 502 enrolled
SAT I Verbal/Math: 550/555
Faculty: 139; IIB, +$
Ph.D.s: 90%
Student/Faculty: 15 to 1
Tuition: $16,850
Room & Board: $6990
ACT: 23
COMPETITIVE

Le Moyne College, founded in 1946, is a private institution in the Catholic and Jesuit tradition offering programs in the liberal arts and sciences. The library contains 242,233 volumes, 557,198 microform items, and 7694 audiovisual forms/CDs, and subscribes to 1308 periodicals. Computerized library services include the card catalog, interlibrary loans, and database searching. Special learning facilities include a learning resource center, art gallery, and radio station. The 151-acre campus is in a suburban area on the eastern edge of Syracuse. Including residence halls, there are 34 buildings.

Student Life: 95% of undergraduates are from New York. Others are from 22 states and 7 foreign countries. 76% are from public schools. 88% are white. 40% are Catholic; 40% Buddhist, Muslim, Baptist, or unknown; 13% claim no religious affiliation. The average age of freshmen is 18; all undergraduates, 22. 16% do not continue beyond their first year; 72% remain to graduate.

Housing: 1450 students can be accommodated in college housing, which includes single-sex and coed dormitories, on-campus apartments, and off-campus apartments. In addition, there are special-interest houses. On-campus housing is guaranteed for all 4 years. 67% of students live on campus; of those, 85% remain on campus on weekends. All students may keep cars.

Activities: There are no fraternities or sororities. There are 70 groups on campus, including art, band, cheerleading, chess, choir, chorale, chorus, computers, dance, drama, ethnic, honors, international, jazz band, literary magazine, musical theater, newspaper, pep band, political, professional, radio and TV, religious, social, social service, student government, and yearbook. Popular campus events include Winter/Spring Olympics, Model UN, and Senior Week Activities.

Sports: There are 8 intercollegiate sports for men and 8 for women, and 8 intramural sports for men and 7 for women. Facilities include a 2500-seat gym, indoor batting cages, team rooms, a 25-yard lap pool with diving capabilities, a whirlpool, a fitness center, an athletic training room, a jogging track, racquetball courts, a recreational gym, and locker rooms. Outdoor facilities include fields for intercollegiate baseball, softball, soccer, and lacrosse, tennis courts, a cross-country trail, and several intramural fields.

Disabled Students: 95% of the campus is accessible. Wheelchair ramps, elevators, special parking, specially equipped rest rooms, lowered drinking fountains, lowered telephones, automatic door openers, and a hydraulic lift for the swimming pool are available.

Services: Counseling and information services are available, as is tutoring in most subjects. There is a reader service for the blind and remedial math and writing. Study groups are available for selected courses.

Campus Safety and Security: Measures include 24-hour foot and vehicle patrol, self-defense education, escort service, and shuttle buses. There are informal discussions, pamphlets/posters/films, emergency telephones, lighted pathways/sidewalks, a campus watch program, 5 Blue Light Security Phones, 18 stationary closed-circuit security cameras, AT&T campuswide card access, and 6 Pan Tilt Zoom closed-circuit security cameras.

Programs of Study: Le Moyne confers B.A. and B.S. degrees. Master's degrees are also awarded. Bachelor's degrees are awarded in BIOLOGICAL SCIENCE (biochemistry and biology/biological science), BUSINESS (accounting, business administration and management, human resources, and labor studies), COMMUNICATIONS AND THE ARTS (communications, creative writing, dramatic arts, English, French, and

Spanish), COMPUTER AND PHYSICAL SCIENCE (applied mathematics, chemistry, information sciences and systems, mathematics, physics, and science), EDUCATION (elementary, English, foreign languages, mathematics, science, secondary, and social studies), HEALTH PROFESSIONS (physician's assistant, predentistry, premedicine, preoptometry, prepharmacy, prepodiatry, and preveterinary science), SOCIAL SCIENCE (criminology, economics, history, international studies, philosophy, political science/government, prelaw, psychology, religion, and sociology). Business, English, and psychology are the largest.

Required: A core curriculum of 14 courses in the humanities, natural sciences, and social sciences is required. Students must earn a GPA of 2.0, 30 hours in the major, and 120 total credit hours to graduate.

Special: Internships are available to students in all majors. A campus work-study program, study abroad in 8 countries, dual majors, and a Washington semester are offered. A 3-2 engineering degree is available with Manhattan College, Clarkson University, and University of Detroit Mercy, and there are early assurance medical and dental programs and a physician assistant program. Some pass/fail options are offered. There are 14 national honor societies, a freshman honors program, and 10 departmental honors programs.

Faculty/Classroom: 61% of faculty are male; 39%, female. All both teach and do research. No introductory courses are taught by graduate students. The average class size in an introductory lecture is 25; in a laboratory, 16; and in a regular course, 22.

Admissions: 77% of the 2001-2002 applicants were accepted. The SAT I scores for the 2001-2002 freshman class were: Verbal--24% below 500, 53% between 500 and 599, 20% between 600 and 700, and 3% above 700; Math--18% below 500, 57% between 500 and 599, 23% between 600 and 700, and 2% above 700. The ACT scores were 24% below 21, 37% between 21 and 23, 24% between 24 and 26, 8% between 27 and 28, and 6% above 28. 43% of the current freshmen were in the top fifth of their class; 77% were in the top two fifths. 4 freshmen graduated first in their class.

Requirements: The SAT I or ACT is required. In addition, students should graduate from an accredited high school, having completed 16 academic units that include 4 in English, 3 to 4 each in math, science, and social studies, and 3 in foreign language. A personal statement and letters of recommendation from a teacher and a counselor are required. AP and CLEP credits are accepted. Important factors in the admissions decision are recommendations by school officials and advanced placement or honor courses. Applications are accepted on-line via Common App, Embark, and NYMentor.

Procedure: Freshmen are admitted fall and spring. Entrance exams should be taken in the spring of the junior year or fall of the senior year. There are early decision, early admissions, and deferred admissions plans. Early decision applications should be filed by December 1; regular applications, by March 1 for fall entry (priority deadline) and December 1 for spring entry, along with a $35 fee. Notification of early decision is sent December 15; regular decision, on a rolling basis beginning in January. 49 early decision candidates were accepted for the 2001-2002 class. 3% of all applicants are on a waiting list; 27 were accepted in 2001.

Transfer: 167 transfer students enrolled in 2001-2002. A 2.6 GPA is usually required. High school and college transcripts, a letter of recommendation from an academic official at the last college attended, and a personal statement must be submitted. SAT I or ACT scores are needed for students out of high school for less than 3 years or with fewer than 30 completed college credits. 30 credits of a minimum of 120 must be completed at Le Moyne.

Visiting: There are regularly scheduled orientations for prospective students, including a campus tour and an interview with admissions counselors. Accepted students are invited to attend class and stay overnight in a residence hall. There are guides for informal visits and visitors may sit in on classes and stay overnight. To schedule a visit, contact the Admission Office.

Financial Aid: In 2001-2002, 94% of all freshmen and 92% of continuing students received some form of financial aid. 81% of freshmen and 80% of continuing students received need-based aid. The average freshman award was $14,780. Of that total, scholarships or need-based grants averaged $9155 ($22,875 maximum); loans averaged $4126 ($4625 maximum); and work contracts averaged $1500 (maximum). 90% of undergraduates work part time. Average annual earnings from campus work are $1300. The average financial indebtedness of the 2001 graduate was $17,125. Le Moyne is a member of CSS. The FAFSA and the college's own financial statement are required. The fall application deadline is February 1.

International Students: There are 18 international students enrolled. The school actively recruits these students. They must score 550 on the written TOEFL or 213 on the electronic version and also take the SAT I or the ACT.

Computers: All academic computing for students and faculty is run from Novell and NT servers. Connected to the campus network are about 300 PCs and Macs in public and departmental labs across campus, providing access to the library system, the Internet, and Novell servers with a multitude of applications. There is access to personal space on these servers. Access from residence hall rooms includes the library system, personal space, and the Internet. All students may access the system 24 hours a day. There are no time limits and no fees.

Graduates: In 2001, 473 bachelor's degrees were awarded. The most popular majors were business (23%), psychology (20%), and biology (12%). In an average class, 68% graduate in 4 years, 72% in 5 years, and 73% in 6 years. 52 companies recruited on campus in 2000-2001. Of the 2000 graduating class, 27% were enrolled in graduate school within 1 year of graduation and 69% were employed.

Admissions Contact: Dennis J. Nicholson, Director of Admission. A video is available. E-mail: *admission@lemoyne.edu*
Web: *www.lemoyne.edu*

LONG ISLAND UNIVERSITY SYSTEM

Long Island University, established in 1886, is a private system in New York. It is governed by a board of trustees, whose chief administrator is the president. The primary goal of the system is to provide Long Island's communities with high-quality higher education. The main priorities are teaching in the liberal arts and professions, extending higher education to underrepresented populations, and providing every student with opportunities for cooperative education placements in a field related to his or her major. The total enrollment of the 3 4-year campuses is about 13,500 with some 1000 faculty members. Altogether there are 142 baccalaureate, 148 master's, and 4 doctoral programs offered at Long Island University. The 4-year campuses are located in Brooklyn, Brookville, and Southampton. Profiles are included in this section.

LONG ISLAND UNIVERSITY/BROOKLYN CAMPUS D-5

Brooklyn, NY 11201 **(718) 488-1292**
(800) LIU-PLAN; Fax: (718) 797-2399

Full-time: 1326 men, 3098 women	**Faculty:** 211; IIA, +$
Part-time: 259 men, 826 women	**Ph.D.s:** 76%
Graduate: 913 men, 1192 women	**Student/Faculty:** 21 to 1
Year: semesters, summer session	**Tuition:** $16,680
Application Deadline: open	**Room & Board:** $5610
Freshman Class: 2375 applied, 2343 accepted, 941 enrolled	
SAT I: recommended	**ACT:** n/av **COMPETITIVE**

Long Island University/Brooklyn Campus, founded in 1926, is part of the Long Island University system. It is a private institution offering programs in liberal arts and sciences, pharmacy, health professions, education, business, nursing, and special programs. It is largely a commuter school. There are 6 undergraduate and 5 graduate schools. In addition to regional accreditation, LIU has baccalaureate program accreditation with ACPE and NLN. The library contains 2.1 million volumes, 813,544 microform items, and 7902 audiovisual forms/CDs, and subscribes to 8042 periodicals. Computerized library services include the card catalog and interlibrary loans. Special learning facilities include a learning resource center, art gallery, radio station, and TV station. The 10-acre campus is in an urban area. Including residence halls, there are 11 buildings.

Student Life: 86% of undergraduates are from New York. Others are from 35 states, 21 foreign countries, and Canada. 75% are from public schools. 43% are African American; 27% white, 19% Hispanic, 11% Asian American. The average age of freshmen is 21; all undergraduates, 25. 36% do not continue beyond their first year; 61% remain to graduate.

Housing: 525 students can be accommodated in college housing, which includes single-sex and coed dormitories and married-student housing. On-campus housing is available on a first-come, first-served basis. 89% of students commute. Alcohol is not permitted. No one may keep cars.

Activities: There are 75 groups on campus, including band, cheerleading, chess, chorale, computers, dance, ethnic, honors, international, jazz band, literary magazine, newspaper, pep band, photography, political, radio and TV, religious, student government, and yearbook.

Sports: There are 7 intercollegiate sports for men and 6 for women, and 6 intramural sports for men and 6 for women. Facilities include a baseball/soccer field and a basketball gym.

Disabled Students: All of the campus is accessible. Wheelchair ramps, elevators, specially equipped rest rooms, special class scheduling, lowered drinking fountains, and lowered telephones are available.

Services: Counseling and information services are available, as is tutoring in most subjects. There is remedial math, reading, and writing.

Campus Safety and Security: Measures include 24-hour foot and vehicle patrol, pamphlets/posters/films, emergency telephones, and lighted pathways/sidewalks.

Programs of Study: LIU confers B.A., B.S., and B.F.A. degrees. Associate, master's, and doctoral degrees are also awarded. Bachelor's degrees are awarded in BIOLOGICAL SCIENCE (biology/biological science), BUSINESS (accounting, banking and finance, business administration and management, and marketing/retailing/merchandising), COMMUNICATIONS AND THE ARTS (broadcasting, communications, English, fine arts, journalism, languages, music, and speech/debate/rhetoric), COMPUTER AND PHYSICAL SCIENCE (chemistry, computer science, information sciences and systems, and mathematics), EDUCATION (art, business, early childhood, elementary, music, science, secondary, special, and teaching English as a second/foreign language (TESOL/TEFOL)), HEALTH PROFESSIONS (nursing, occupational therapy, pharmacy, physical therapy, physician's assistant, predentistry, and premedicine), SOCIAL SCIENCE (anthropology, economics, history, philosophy, political science/government, prelaw, psychology, social science, social work, and sociology). Health professions, pharmacy, and liberal arts are the strongest academically. Health professions, liberal arts, and business are the largest.

Required: Proficiency courses include basic English and math, English composition, and speech. Distribution requirements are 6 credits each in foreign language, math, and science. Students must complete a core curriculum of 18 credits in the humanities, 12 in social sciences, 8 in natural sciences, and 6 in math. A total of 128 credits (197 for pharmacy) is required for graduation, with 36 credits in the major, and a GPA of 2.0.

Special: Accelerated degree programs are available in all majors. Students may cross-register with other LIU campuses. Internships in career-related jobs provide cooperative education credits. Study abroad, dual majors, credit for life, military, and work experience, and pass/fail options are also offered. There is a chapter of Phi Beta Kappa and a freshman honors program.

Faculty/Classroom: All teach undergraduates. The average class size in a regular course is 22.

Admissions: 99% of the 2001-2002 applicants were accepted.

Requirements: The SAT I is recommended. LIU requires applicants to be in the upper 75% of their class. A GPA of 2.0 is required. AP and CLEP credits are accepted. Important factors in the admissions decision are recommendations by school officials, advanced placement or honor courses, and evidence of special talent. Applications are accepted on-line at *www.liu.edu*

Procedure: Freshmen are admitted to all sessions. Entrance exams should be taken by January of the senior year. There is a deferred admissions plan. Application deadlines are open. The application fee is $30. Notification is sent on a rolling basis.

Transfer: 724 transfer students enrolled in 2001-2002. A GPA of 2.5 is required. 32 credits of 128 must be completed at LIU.

Visiting: There are regularly scheduled orientations for prospective students. Visitors may sit in on classes. To schedule a visit, contact the Admissions Office at (718) 488-1011.

Financial Aid: The CSS/Profile and the college's own financial statement are required. The fall application deadline is November 15.

International Students: There are 101 international students enrolled. The school actively recruits these students. They must score 500 on the written TOEFL and also take the SAT I or the ACT.

Computers: The mainframe is a DEC VAX 8600. PCs are available in the library for academic use. All students may access the system during library hours. There are no time limits and no fees.

Graduates: In 2001, 900 bachelor's degrees were awarded. In an average class, 30% graduate in 4 years, 60% in 5 years, and 70% in 6 years. 150 companies recruited on campus in 2000-2001.

Admissions Contact: Alan B. Chaves, Dean of Admissions.
E-mail: *attend@liu.edu* Web: *www.liu.edu*

LONG ISLAND UNIVERSITY/C.W. POST CAMPUS D-5
Brookville, NY 11548-1300 (516) 299-2900
(800) LIU-PLAN; Fax: (516) 299-2137

Full-time: 1550 men, 2318 women	**Faculty:** 311
Part-time: 1155 men, 1473 women	**Ph.D.s:** 91%
Graduate: 997 men, 2640 women	**Student/Faculty:** 12 to 1
Year: semesters, summer session	**Tuition:** $18,090
Application Deadline: February 1	**Room & Board:** $7290
Freshman Class: 4499 applied, 3484 accepted, 876 enrolled	
SAT I Verbal/Math: 489/492	**COMPETITIVE**

Long Island University/C.W. Post Campus, founded in 1954 as part of the private Long Island University system, offers 100 undergraduate and 63 graduate majors in education, liberal arts and sciences, accountancy, business, public service, health professions and nursing, and information and computer science. There are 6 undergraduate and 6 graduate schools. In addition to regional accreditation, C.W. Post has baccalaureate program accreditation with AACSB, ADA, ASLA, CAHEA, CSWE, and NLN. The library contains 893,513 volumes, 790,513 microform items, and 33,469 audiovisual forms/CDs, and subscribes to 11,044 periodicals. Computerized library services include the card catalog, interlibrary loans, and database searching. Special learning facilities include a learning resource center, art gallery, radio station, TV station, art museum, a tax institute, a speech and hearing center, a center for business research, a federal depository, and a multimedia computer center. The 307-acre campus is in a suburban area 25 miles east of New York City, on the former estate of Marjorie Merriweather Post. Including residence halls, there are 53 buildings.

Student Life: 91% of undergraduates are from New York. Others are from 32 states, 46 foreign countries, and Canada. 71% are from public schools. 13% are white. The average age of freshmen is 18; all undergraduates, 21. 31% do not continue beyond their first year; 37% remain to graduate.

Housing: 1619 students can be accommodated in college housing, which includes single-sex, coed, and quiet dormitories. On-campus housing is guaranteed for all 4 years. 60% of students commute. All students may keep cars.

Activities: There are 6 national fraternities and 9 national sororities. There are 80 groups on campus, including art, band, chamber singing, cheerleading, chess, choir, chorale, chorus, computers, dance, drama, equestrian, ethnic, film, gay, honors, international, jazz band, literary magazine, madrigal, musical theater, newspaper, orchestra, pep band, photography, political, professional, radio and TV, religious, Renaissance music, social, social service, student government, vocal music, and yearbook. Popular campus events include Theater Festival, Spring Fling, and Cereal Bowl: The Inter-Residential Hall Competition.

Sports: There are 7 intercollegiate sports for men and 10 for women, and 4 intramural sports for men and 2 for women. Facilities include a 5,000-seat football stadium, an equestrian center, tennis courts, 70 acres of baseball, soccer, lacrosse, softball, and practice fields, a recreational center with an 8-lane swimming pool, 3 basketball courts with spectator seating for 3,000, racquetball courts, indoor track, and weight and aerobic rooms.

Disabled Students: 75% of the campus is accessible. Wheelchair ramps, elevators, special parking, specially equipped rest rooms, lowered drinking fountains, and electric doors are available.

Services: Counseling and information services are available, as is tutoring in most subjects. There is a reader service for the blind, remedial math, reading, and writing, and an academic resource center for learning-disabled students.

Campus Safety and Security: Measures include 24-hour foot and vehicle patrol, self-defense education, escort service, and shuttle buses. There are informal discussions, pamphlets/posters/films, emergency telephones, lighted pathways/sidewalks, restricted night access to campus, card-access residence entrances, and electronic keyless locking system for dorm rooms.

Programs of Study: C.W. Post confers B.A., B.S., B.F.A., and B.S.Ed. degrees. Associate, master's, and doctoral degrees are also awarded. Bachelor's degrees are awarded in AGRICULTURE (conservation and regulation), BIOLOGICAL SCIENCE (biology/biological science, molecular biology, and nutrition), BUSINESS (accounting, banking and finance, business administration and management, and marketing/retailing/merchandising), COMMUNICATIONS AND THE ARTS (arts administration/management, broadcasting, communications, dance, dramatic arts, English, film arts, fine arts, French, German, Italian, journalism, music, photography, public relations, and Spanish), COMPUTER AND PHYSICAL SCIENCE (chemistry, computer science, geology, information sciences and systems, mathematics, physics, and radiological technology), EDUCATION (art, early childhood, elementary, English, foreign languages, health, music, science, and secondary), ENGINEERING AND ENVIRONMENTAL DESIGN (preengineering), HEALTH PROFESSIONS (art therapy, biomedical science, health care administration, medical laboratory technology, medical records administration/services, nursing, predentistry, premedicine, prepharmacy, and speech pathology/audiology), SOCIAL SCIENCE (criminal justice, economics, geography, history, international studies, philosophy, political science/government, prelaw, psychology, public administration, and social work). Accounting, radiologic technology, and biology are the strongest academically. Business, education, and media arts are the largest.

Required: Core requirements include 8 credits of lab science, 9 each of history and philosophy, 6 each of language and literature, arts, political science and economics, sociology, psychology, and geography or anthropology, and 3 of math. A minimum of 128 credits is required to graduate. GPA requirements range from 2.0 to 2.5 in most departments, 3.0 in interdisciplinary studies. Students must demonstrate competency in writing, quantitative skills, computer skills, oral communications, and library use.

Special: There is cross-registration with several other Long Island colleges. C.W. Post offers co-op programs in all majors, internships, study abroad in 11 countries, work-study in most departments, accelerated degree programs, and a Washington semester for outstanding criminal justice students. Dual majors and student-designed majors are available. There is a 3-2 engineering degree with Polytechnic University, Pratt Institute, and Arizona State University, and credit is available for life, military, and work experience. Nondegree study is available, as are pass/fail options. There are 14 national honor societies, a freshman honors program, and 16 departmental honors programs.

Faculty/Classroom: 38% of faculty are male; 62%, female. 95% teach undergraduates, 72% do research, and 72% do both. No introductory courses are taught by graduate students. The average class size in an introductory lecture is 26; in a laboratory, 20; and in a regular course, 19.

Admissions: 77% of the 2001-2002 applicants were accepted. The SAT I scores for the 2001-2002 freshman class were: Verbal--54% below

500, 35% between 500 and 599, 10% between 600 and 700, and 1% above 700; Math--55% below 500, 35% between 500 and 599, and 10% between 600 and 700. 30% of the current freshmen were in the top fifth of their class; 61% were in the top two fifths. There were 4 National Merit finalists.

Requirements: The SAT I or ACT is required, with a minimum composite SAT I score of 900 or a minimum ACT score of 20. Applicants should be graduates of an accredited secondary school with a B average or have a GED. Preparatory work should include 4 years of English, 4 of social science, 2 of foreign language, 2 of college preparatory math, and 2 of lab science. A grade average of 75 is required. AP and CLEP credits are accepted. Important factors in the admissions decision are advanced placement or honor courses, recommendations by school officials, and evidence of special talent. Applications are accepted on-line at the school's web site.

Procedure: Freshmen are admitted to all sessions. Entrance exams should be taken from May of the junior year through December of the senior year. There are early admissions and deferred admissions plans. Applications should be filed by February 1 for fall entry, along with a $30 fee. Notification is sent on a rolling basis.

Transfer: 900 transfer students enrolled in 2001-2002. Applicants should have appropriate high school credentials and a minimum college GPA of 2.25. 32 credits of 128 must be completed at C.W. Post.

Visiting: There are regularly scheduled orientations for prospective students, consisting of Post Preview Days, which include meeting the faculty, an admissions and financial aid overview, and a campus tour. There are guides for informal visits and visitors may sit in on classes. To schedule a visit, contact the Office of Admissions.

Financial Aid: In 2001-2002, 85% of all students received some form of financial aid; 65% received need-based aid. Scholarships or need-based grants averaged $9600 ($25,100 maximum); loans averaged $2000 ($4625 maximum); and work contracts averaged $1500 ($2000 maximum). 31% of undergraduates work part time. Average annual earnings from campus work are $1200. The average financial indebtedness of the 2001 graduate was $15,000. C.W. Post is a member of CSS. The CSS/Profile or FAFSA is required. The fall application deadline is May 15.

International Students: There are 96 international students enrolled. The school actively recruits these students. They must score 500 on the written TOEFL or 173 on the electronic version. SAT I or ACT scores are recommended to help evaluate students' admissions eligibility.

Computers: The mainframes are UNIX, NT/2000 servers in the Information Technology Department and a fiber-based network throughout campus. The Office of Information Technology supports 25 campus-wide labs for student use with more than 500 computers (PCs and Macs), free LaserJet printing services, and a wide range of software from graphic to statistical packages; 25 smart classrooms are connected to the Internet; e-mail accounts are provided to every member of the campus community; all dorm rooms are connected to the campus network, and a web-based student information system providing student information about grades, bills, degree requirements, and many other services is available. Dial-up capability is available 24 hours a day. There are no time limits and no fees.

Graduates: In 2001, 904 bachelor's degrees were awarded. The most popular majors were elementary education (14%), psychology (7%), and criminal justice (6%). 500 companies recruited on campus in 2000-2001. Of the 2001 graduating class, 29% were enrolled in graduate school within 6 months of graduation and 84% were employed.

Admissions Contact: Susan Reantillo, Executive Director of Admissions and Recruitment. E-mail: *enroll@cwpost.liu.edu*
Web: *www.liu.edu*

LONG ISLAND UNIVERSITY/SOUTHAMPTON COLLEGE — E-5

Southampton, NY 11968 — **(631) 287-8200**
(800) LIU-PLAN, ext. 2; Fax: (631) 287-8130

Full-time: 356 men, 808 women	**Faculty:** 74; IIA, +$
Part-time: 940 men, 1101 women	**Ph.D.s:** 86%
Graduate: 44 men, 189 women	**Student/Faculty:** 16 to 1
Year: semesters, summer session	**Tuition:** $18,120
Application Deadline: open	**Room & Board:** $8150
Freshman Class: 1298 applied, 865 accepted, 243 enrolled	
SAT I Verbal/Math: 522/503	**ACT:** 23 — **COMPETITIVE**

Long Island University/Southampton College, established in 1963, is a private liberal arts institution offering undergraduate and graduate programs in the arts and sciences, business, and education. There are 6 undergraduate and 3 graduate schools. The library contains 150,000 volumes, 1000 microform items, and 500 audiovisual forms/CDs, and subscribes to 700 periodicals. Computerized library services include the card catalog, interlibrary loans, and database searching. Special learning facilities include a learning resource center, art gallery, radio station, on-campus marine station, seawater laboratories, and research vessels. The 110-acre campus is in a rural area 90 miles east of New York City. Including residence halls, there are 43 buildings.

Student Life: 60% of undergraduates are from New York. Others are from 46 states, 15 foreign countries, and Canada. 85% are from public schools. 82% are white. 65% are Catholic; 20% Protestant. The average age of freshmen is 18; all undergraduates, 21. 10% do not continue beyond their first year; 78% remain to graduate.

Housing: 710 students can be accommodated in college housing, which includes single-sex and coed dormitories. In addition, there are honors houses, special-interest houses, a nonsmoking house, and honors, quiet-study, all-women, smoke-free, and substance-free dorms. On-campus housing is guaranteed for all 4 years. 80% of students live on campus; of those, 55% remain on campus on weekends. All students may keep cars.

Activities: There are no fraternities or sororities. There are 50 groups on campus, including art, cheerleading, choir, chorus, computers, dance, drama, environmental, ethnic, film, gay, honors, jazz band, literary magazine, marine sciences, musical theater, newspaper, photography, political, professional, radio and TV, religious, social, social service, student government, submersibles-scuba diving, and yearbook. Popular campus events include Spring Fest, Fall Fest, and Friday Night Phenomenon.

Sports: There are 5 intercollegiate sports for men and 5 for women, and 6 intramural sports for men and 5 for women. Facilities include a gym, an outdoor swimming pool, basketball and volleyball courts, a weight room, a fitness trail, and soccer, softball, and lacrosse fields.

Disabled Students: 15% of the campus is accessible. Wheelchair ramps, elevators, special parking, specially equipped rest rooms, lowered drinking fountains, and lowered telephones are available.

Services: Counseling and information services are available, as is tutoring in every subject. There is remedial math, reading, and writing.

Campus Safety and Security: Measures include 24-hour foot and vehicle patrol, self-defense education, shuttle buses, and informal discussions. There are pamphlets/posters/films, emergency telephones, and lighted pathways/sidewalks. The college also conducts an alcohol awareness week and date-rape seminars.

Programs of Study: Southampton College confers B.A., B.S., and B.F.A. degrees. Master's degrees are also awarded. Bachelor's degrees are awarded in BIOLOGICAL SCIENCE (biology/biological science and marine science), COMMUNICATIONS AND THE ARTS (communications, English, fine arts, and graphic design), COMPUTER AND PHYSICAL SCIENCE (chemistry), EDUCATION (art and elementary), SOCIAL SCIENCE (history, liberal arts/general studies, political science/government, prelaw, psychology, social science, and sociology). Marine science and fine arts are the strongest academically. Marine science, fine arts, and social science are the largest.

Required: To graduate, students must complete 128 credits with an overall 2.0 GPA and a 2.25 GPA in the major. Core courses consist of 3 required courses in English, (including Introduction to Composition), and 2 each in humanities, social science, science/math, and fine arts. 45 to 88 hours must be completed in the major. All students must pass a writing proficiency exam.

Special: Cross-registration is permitted with the C.W. Post and Brooklyn campuses of Long Island University and the Friends World Program. Opportunities are provided for internships in science research, legislative offices, and the Smithsonian Institution. Study abroad, work-study programs, an accelerated degree program in accounting, dual majors in psychology and biology, credit by examination, credit for life experience, nondegree study, and pass/fail options are also available. In the Friends World Program, students design their own majors and receive credit based on experiential education, fieldwork, and overseas travel. There are 2 national honor societies, a freshman honors program, and 2 departmental honors programs.

Faculty/Classroom: 79% of faculty are male; 21%, female. All teach undergraduates and 86% both teach and do research. No introductory courses are taught by graduate students. The average class size in an introductory lecture is 20; in a laboratory, 15; and in a regular course, 15.

Admissions: 67% of the 2001-2002 applicants were accepted. The SAT I scores for the 2001-2002 freshman class were: Verbal--29% below 500, 42% between 500 and 599, 25% between 600 and 700, and 4% above 700; Math--29% below 500, 47% between 500 and 599, 21% between 600 and 700, and 3% above 700. The ACT scores were 15% below 21, 45% between 21 and 23, and 40% between 24 and 26. 25% of the current freshmen were in the top fifth of their class; 40% were in the top two fifths. 5 freshmen graduated first in their class.

Requirements: The SAT I or ACT is required, with a minimum composite score of 1000 (500 verbal and 500 math) on the SAT I or 21 on the ACT. Graduation from an accredited secondary school is required; the GED will be accepted. The academic record should include 4 credits in English, 3 each in history and social studies, 2 each in math and science, and 1 in art. An essay, portfolio, audition, or interview may be recommended. A grade average of 80 is required. AP and CLEP credits are accepted. Important factors in the admissions decision are advanced placement or honor courses, personality/intangible qualities, and evidence of special talent. Applications are accepted on disk and on-line via

CollegeLink, Peterson's, Common App, and College Board, and via the college own on-line application, *www.southampton.liu.edu*

Procedure: Freshmen are admitted fall and spring. Entrance exams should be taken during the junior year. There are early decision, early admissions, and deferred admissions plans. Early decision applications should be filed by December 1; regular applications have open deadlines for fall entry. The fall 2001 application fee was $30. Notification of early decision is sent December 23; regular decision, on a rolling basis. 161 early decision candidates were accepted for the 2001-2002 class.

Transfer: Applicants must have a 2.0 GPA in previous college work. An interview is recommended. High school grades and SAT I scores are required if the student has fewer than 30 college credits. 32 credits of 128 must be completed at Southampton College.

Visiting: There are regularly scheduled orientations for prospective students, including an interview, a tour, and lunch or dinner. Students may also attend a class, meet with a coach, and attend a cooperative education meeting. There are guides for informal visits and visitors may sit in on classes and stay overnight. To schedule a visit, contact the Admissions Office at *admissions@southampton.liu.edu*

Financial Aid: In a recent year, 54% of all freshmen and 70% of continuing students received some form of financial aid. 49% of freshmen received need-based aid. Work contracts averaged $1200. Average annual earnings from campus work are $1200. The average financial indebtedness of a recent graduate was $15,235. The FAFSA and the college's own financial statement are required. The fall application deadline is June 1.

International Students: There weare 30 international students enrolled in a recent year. They must score 500 on the written TOEFL or 197 on the electronic version and also take the SAT I or the ACT.

Computers: The mainframes are a DEC VAX 750, 8600, and 6210 and an IBM 520. The Long Island University Network is connected to the Internet. There are 120 PCs located at 6 campus locations and there are in-room PC hookups. The student-to-computer ratio is 12 to 1. A Silicon Graphics Lab is also available for student use. All students may access the system 24 hours a day. There are no time limits and no fees.

Admissions Contact: Bernetta C. McCall, Director of Admissions. A video is available. E-mail: *info@southampton.liu.edu*
Web: *http://www.southampton.liu.edu*

MANHATTAN COLLEGE

Riverdale, NY 10471 D-5
(718) 862-7200
(800) 622-9235; Fax: (718) 862-8019

Full-time: 1259 men, 1188 women	**Faculty:** 155; IIA, +$
Part-time: 94 men, 67 women	**Ph.D.s:** 94%
Graduate: 176 men, 162 women	**Student/Faculty:** 16 to 1
Year: semesters, summer session	**Tuition:** $17,800
Application Deadline: March 1	**Room & Board:** $7700
Freshman Class: 3947 applied, 2491 accepted, 593 enrolled	
SAT I Verbal/Math: 530/540	**VERY COMPETITIVE**

Manhattan College, founded in 1853, is a private institution affiliated with the Christian Brothers of the Catholic Church. It offers degree programs in the arts and sciences, education and human services, business, and engineering. There are 5 undergraduate and 3 graduate schools. In addition to regional accreditation, Manhattan has baccalaureate program accreditation with ABET, AHEA, and CAHEA. The 4 libraries contain 193,100 volumes, 383,480 microform items, and 3244 audiovisual forms/CDs, and subscribe to 1527 periodicals. Computerized library services include the card catalog, interlibrary loans, and database searching. Special learning facilities include a learning resource center, radio station, nuclear reactor lab, and media center. The 26-acre campus is in an urban area 10 miles north of midtown Manhattan. Including residence halls, there are 28 buildings.

Student Life: 75% of undergraduates are from New York. Others are from 33 states and 10 foreign countries. 60% are from public schools. 67% are white; 14% Hispanic. The average age of freshmen is 18; all undergraduates, 20. 15% do not continue beyond their first year; 68% remain to graduate.

Housing: 1440 students can be accommodated in college housing, which includes coed dormitories and off-campus apartments. On-campus housing is guaranteed for all 4 years. 54% of students live on campus; of those, 80% remain on campus on weekends. All students may keep cars.

Activities: 2% of men belong to 1 international and 3 local fraternities; 1% of women belong to 4 local sororities. There are 70 groups on campus, including bagpipe band, cheerleading, choir, chorus, computers, dance, debate, drama, ethnic, honors, international, jazz band, literary magazine, musical theater, newspaper, orchestra, pep band, political, professional, radio and TV, religious, social, social service, student government, and yearbook. Popular campus events include Annual Springfest, Special Olympics, and Jasper Jingle.

Sports: There are 8 intercollegiate sports for men and 8 for women, and 7 intramural sports for men and 7 for women. Facilities include 5 full basketball courts, which can also be used for volleyball and tennis, an indoor track, a weight room, a swimming pool, and a Nautilus center.

Disabled Students: All of the campus is accessible. Wheelchair ramps, elevators, special parking, and specially equipped rest rooms are available.

Services: Counseling and information services are available, as is tutoring in every subject.

Campus Safety and Security: Measures include 24-hour foot and vehicle patrol, escort service, informal discussions, and pamphlets/posters/films. There are emergency telephones and lighted pathways/sidewalks.

Programs of Study: Manhattan confers B.A., B.S., and B.S.E. degrees. Master's degrees are also awarded. Bachelor's degrees are awarded in BIOLOGICAL SCIENCE (biochemistry and biology/biological science), BUSINESS (accounting, banking and finance, business economics, international business management, and marketing/retailing/merchandising), COMMUNICATIONS AND THE ARTS (communications, English, French, and Spanish), COMPUTER AND PHYSICAL SCIENCE (chemistry, computer science, information sciences and systems, mathematics, and physics), EDUCATION (early childhood, elementary, foreign languages, health, middle school, physical, science, secondary, and special), ENGINEERING AND ENVIRONMENTAL DESIGN (chemical engineering, civil engineering, electrical/electronics engineering, environmental engineering, and mechanical engineering), HEALTH PROFESSIONS (predentistry, premedicine, and radiological science), SOCIAL SCIENCE (economics, history, peace studies, philosophy, political science/government, prelaw, psychology, religion, sociology, and urban studies). Engineering and business are the strongest academically. Arts, business, and education are the largest.

Required: All students must take courses in English composition and literature, religious studies, philosophy, humanities, social science, science, math, and a modern foreign language. About 130 credit hours are required for graduation, with about 36 in the major. The minimum GPA is 2.0.

Special: Manhattan offers co-op programs in 11 majors, cross-registration with the College of Mount St. Vincent, and off-campus internships in business, industry, government, and social or cultural organizations. Students may study abroad in 10 countries and enter work-study programs with major U.S. corporations, health services, or in the arts. A general studies degree, a 3-2 engineering degree, a dual major in international business, credit by exam, and nondegree study are also available. There are 22 national honor societies, including Phi Beta Kappa, a freshman honors program, and 28 departmental honors programs.

Faculty/Classroom: 70% of faculty are male; 30%, female. All teach undergraduates and 80% both teach and do research. No introductory courses are taught by graduate students. The average class size in an introductory lecture is 15 and in a regular course, 22.

Admissions: 63% of the 2001-2002 applicants were accepted. The SAT I scores for the 2001-2002 freshman class were: Verbal--27% below 500, 55% between 500 and 599, 16% between 600 and 700, and 2% above 700; Math--23% below 500, 50% between 500 and 599, 24% between 600 and 700, and 3% above 700. 16 freshmen graduated first in their class.

Requirements: The SAT I is required. Applicants must graduate from an accredited secondary school or have earned a GED. 16 academic units are required, including 4 of English, 3 each of math and social studies, and 2 of foreign language, lab sciences, and electives. An essay is required and an interview is recommended. AP and CLEP credits are accepted. Important factors in the admissions decision are advanced placement or honor courses, leadership record, and recommendations by school officials. The college accepts applications on-line via Common App, ExPAN, CollegeView, CollegeLink, and the college's web site *www.manhattan.edu*

Procedure: Freshmen are admitted fall and spring. Entrance exams should be taken in the spring of the junior year or the fall of the senior year. There are early decision and deferred admissions plans. Early decision applications should be filed by November 15; regular applications, by March 1 for fall entry and December 1 for spring entry. The 2001 fall application fee was $40. Notification of early decision is sent December 1; regular decision, on a rolling basis, beginning December 15. 20 early decision candidates were accepted for the 2001-2002 class. 4% of all applicants are on a waiting list.

Transfer: 125 transfer students enrolled in 2001-2002. Applicants must have a GPA of 2.5 and meet subject course requirements according to their course of study. They must submit transcripts from colleges and high schools attended. An interview is recommended. 66 credits of 130 must be completed at Manhattan.

Visiting: There are regularly scheduled orientations for prospective students during 2 days in the summer, which include scheduling, parent workshops, loan seminars, and English and math testing. There are guides for informal visits and visitors may sit in on classes and stay overnight. To schedule a visit, contact the Admission Center.

Financial Aid: In 2001-2002, 82% of all freshmen and 71% of continuing students received some form of financial aid. 73% of freshmen and 63% of continuing students received need-based aid. The average fresh-

man award was $11,454. Of that total, scholarships or need-based grants averaged $6520 ($24,910 maximum); loans averaged $3321 ($4625 maximum); and work contracts averaged $1500. 15% of undergraduates work part time. Average annual earnings from campus work are $600. The average financial indebtedness of the 2001 graduate was $12,100. The FAFSA and the college's own financial statement are required. The fall application deadline is February 1.

International Students: There are 39 international students enrolled. The school actively recruits these students. They must score 550 on the written TOEFL and also take the SAT I or the ACT.

Computers: The mainframe is a DEC VAX 8350. Terminals and PCs are located in the computer center and in engineering labs. In addition, all residence halls are capable of providing Internet access to students who have their own computers. All students may access the system 13 hours a day in the labs and 24 hours a day in residence halls or by modem. There are no time limits and no fees.

Graduates: In 2001, 552 bachelor's degrees were awarded. The most popular majors were arts and science (33%), business (22%), and engineering (18%). In an average class, 53% graduate in 4 years, 64% in 5 years, and 68% in 6 years. 200 companies recruited on campus in 2000-2001. Of the 2000 graduating class, 16% were enrolled in graduate school within 6 months of graduation and 61% were employed.

Admissions Contact: William J. Bisset, Jr., Assistant Vice President for Enrollment Management. A video is available.

E-mail: *admit@manhattan.edu* Web: *www.manhattan.edu*

MANHATTAN SCHOOL OF MUSIC D-5

New York, NY 10027-4678 (212) 749-2802, ext. 4501
Fax: (212) 749-5471

Full-time: 184 men, 188 women	**Faculty:** 35
Part-time: 7 men, 16 women	**Ph.D.s:** 40%
Graduate: 173 men, 263 women	**Student/Faculty:** 11 to 1
Year: semesters	**Tuition:** $21,500
Application Deadline: December 3	**Room & Board:** $10,000
Freshman Class: 588 applied, 281 accepted, 86 enrolled	
SAT I or ACT: recommended	**SPECIAL**

The Manhattan School of Music, founded in 1917, is a private college offering undergraduate and graduate degrees in music performance and composition. The library contains 73,405 volumes and 21,074 audiovisual forms/CDs, and subscribes to 128 periodicals. Computerized library services include the card catalog, interlibrary loans, and database searching. Special learning facilities include 2 electronic music studios and a recording studio. The 1-acre campus is in an urban area in New York City. Including residence halls, there are 2 buildings.

Student Life: 77% of undergraduates are from out of state, mostly the Northeast. Others are from 41 states, 46 foreign countries, and Canada. 81% are from public schools. 36% are foreign nationals; 36%, white. The average age of freshmen is 18; all undergraduates, 21. 17% do not continue beyond their first year; 54% remain to graduate.

Housing: 380 students can be accommodated in college housing, which includes single-sex and coed dormitories. On-campus housing is guaranteed for the freshman year only and is available on a lottery system for upperclassmen. Priority is given to out-of-town students. 50% of students live on campus; of those, 95% remain on campus on weekends. All students may keep cars.

Activities: 10% of men belong to 2 local fraternities; 20% of women belong to 2 local sororities. There are 13 groups on campus, including choir, chorale, chorus, ethnic, gay, international, jazz band, musical theater, opera, orchestra, student government, and symphony. Popular campus events include a Halloween party, a Christmas/Chanukah party, and post-opera party.

Sports: There is no sports program at MSM.

Disabled Students: 70% of the campus is accessible. Wheelchair ramps, elevators, specially equipped rest rooms, special class scheduling, and lowered telephones are available.

Services: Counseling and information services are available, as is tutoring in most subjects. There is a reader service for the blind.

Campus Safety and Security: Measures include 24-hour foot and vehicle patrol, informal discussions, pamphlets/posters/films, and lighted pathways/sidewalks.

Programs of Study: MSM confers the B.Mus. degree. Master's and doctoral degrees are also awarded. Bachelor's degrees are awarded in COMMUNICATIONS AND THE ARTS (jazz, music, music performance, music theory and composition, piano/organ, strings, and voice). Classical piano, classical voice, and jazz are the largest.

Required: All students must take 4 music theory courses, a 4-course core curriculum in the humanities, and 4 elective humanities courses, and perform a final, senior-year recital. Composition majors must complete an original symphonic work. To graduate, students must earn 120 to 130 credit hours, including 90 to 100 in the major, with a minimum GPA of 2.0.

Special: There is cross-registration with Barnard College. Credit by exam in theory and music history is available.

Faculty/Classroom: 69% of faculty are male; 31%, female. All teach undergraduates. Graduate students teach 1% of introductory courses. The average class size in an introductory lecture is 20 and in a regular course, 15.

Admissions: 48% of the 2001-2002 applicants were accepted.

Requirements: The SAT I or ACT is recommended. In addition, applicants should graduate from an accredited high school with a minimum GPA of 2.5. The GED is accepted. Admission is based on a performance audition, evaluation of scholastic achievements, and available openings in the major field. A GPA of 2.9 is required. AP and CLEP credits are accepted. Important factors in the admissions decision are evidence of special talent, personality/intangible qualities, and extracurricular activities record.

Procedure: Freshmen are admitted in the fall. Applications should be filed by December 3 for fall entry, along with a $100 fee. Notification is sent April 1. 2% of all applicants are on a waiting list; 10 were accepted in 2001.

Transfer: 67 transfer students enrolled in 2001-2002. Applicants must audition and submit college transcripts. 60 credits of 120 must be completed at MSM.

Visiting: There are regularly scheduled orientations for prospective students, consisting of a tour of the facility and a discussion with a counselor. There are guides for informal visits and visitors may sit in on classes. To schedule a visit, contact the Office of Admission and Financial Aid at (212) 749-2802, ext. 2.

Financial Aid: The CSS/Profile or FAFSA and the college's own financial statement are required. The fall application deadline is April 15.

International Students: There are 111 international students enrolled. The school actively recruits these students. They must score 500 on the written TOEFL or 173 on the electronic version and also take the International English Language Testing System (IELTS).

Computers: Stand alone PCs are available in the computer lab. All students may access the system. There are no time limits and no fees.

Graduates: In 2001, 79 bachelor's degrees were awarded. The most popular majors were piano (26%), voice (21%), and strings (14%). In an average class, 4% graduate in 3 years, 47% in 4 years, 52% in 5 years, and 54% in 6 years.

Admissions Contact: Lee Cioppa, Director of Admission.

E-mail: *admission@msmnyc.edu* Web: *www.msmnyc.edu*

MANHATTANVILLE COLLEGE D-5

Purchase, NY 10577 (914) 323-5464
(800) 32 VILLE; Fax: (914) 694-1732

Full-time: 444 men, 964 women	**Faculty:** 74
Part-time: 53 men, 117 women	**Ph.D.s:** 99%
Graduate: 137 men, 753 women	**Student/Faculty:** 19 to 1
Year: semesters, summer session	**Tuition:** $20,410
Application Deadline: open	**Room & Board:** $8320
Freshman Class: 2328 applied, 1342 accepted, 402 enrolled	
SAT I Verbal/Math: 530/530	**ACT:** 24 **VERY COMPETITIVE**

Manhattanville College, founded in 1841, is an independent institution offering programs in liberal and fine arts, business, health science, and teacher preparation. In addition to regional accreditation, M'ville has baccalaureate program accreditation with NASM. The library contains 184,412 volumes, 529,595 microform items, and 2710 audiovisual forms/CDs, and subscribes to 12,435 periodicals. Computerized library services include the card catalog, interlibrary loans, and database searching. Special learning facilities include a learning resource center, art gallery, and radio station. The 100-acre campus is in a suburban area 25 miles north of New York City. Including residence halls, there are 21 buildings.

Student Life: 63% of undergraduates are from New York. Others are from 33 states, 48 foreign countries, and Canada. 59% are white; 13%, Hispanic. 79% are claim no religious affiliation; 18%, Catholic. The average age of freshmen is 18; all undergraduates, 21. 28% do not continue beyond their first year; 60% remain to graduate.

Housing: 980 students can be accommodated in college housing, which includes single-sex and coed dormitories. In addition, there are special-interest houses, an intercultural residence hall, and a substance-free living area. On-campus housing is guaranteed for all 4 years. 69% of students live on campus; of those, 75% remain on campus on weekends. All students may keep cars.

Activities: There are no fraternities or sororities. There are 60 groups on campus, including art, band, cheerleading, chess, choir, chorale, chorus, computers, dance, debate, drama, ethnic, film, gay, honors, international, jazz band, literary magazine, musical theater, newspaper, orchestra, photography, political, professional, radio and TV, religious, social, social service, student government, and yearbook. Popular campus events include Black History Month, Quad Jam, and Fall Jam.

Sports: There are 8 intercollegiate sports for men and 10 for women, and 3 intramural sports for men and 3 for women. Facilities include a 1000-seat gym, a 25-yard indoor pool, 6 deco-turf tennis courts, a

healthworks-wellness center, and baseball, lacrosse, field hockey, softball fields, and batting cages.
Disabled Students: All of the campus is accessible. Wheelchair ramps, elevators, special parking, specially equipped rest rooms, and special class scheduling are available.
Services: Counseling and information services are available, as is tutoring in every subject and a program for students with documented learning disabilities.
Campus Safety and Security: Measures include 24-hour foot and vehicle patrol, escort service, shuttle buses, and informal discussions. There are pamphlets/posters/films, emergency telephones, and lighted pathways/sidewalks.
Programs of Study: M'ville confers B.A., B.F.A., and B.Mus. degrees. Master's degrees are also awarded. Bachelor's degrees are awarded in BIOLOGICAL SCIENCE (biochemistry and biology/biological science), BUSINESS (banking and finance, management science, and organizational behavior), COMMUNICATIONS AND THE ARTS (art, art history and appreciation, classics, dance, dramatic arts, English, fine arts, French, German, music, romance languages and literature, and Spanish), COMPUTER AND PHYSICAL SCIENCE (chemistry, computer science, mathematics, and physics), EDUCATION (art and music), SOCIAL SCIENCE (American studies, Asian/Oriental studies, behavioral science, economics, history, international studies, liberal arts/general studies, philosophy, political science/government, psychology, religion, and sociology). Management, art, and psychology are the strongest academically. Psychology, management, and sociology are the largest.
Required: Distribution requirements include 18 credits in social sciences and humanities and either a major or minor in foreign language or 18 credits in Western and non-Western courses, 8 credits in math and natural sciences, and 6 in the arts. A year-long freshman humanities course, courses in library skills, writing, and global perspective, and a preceptorial are required. A total of 120 credit hours and a minimum GPA of 2.0 are needed to graduate.
Special: Manhattanville offers cross-registration with SUNY Purchase, internships in all majors for credit, and study abroad in 10 countries. Dual, student-designed, and interdisciplinary majors, and pass/fail options are also available. Under the portfolio degree plan, students develop an individualized program combining both academic and nonacademic training. There are 3 national honor societies, a freshman honors program, and 16 departmental honors programs.
Faculty/Classroom: 47% of faculty are male; 53%, female. All teach undergraduates. No introductory courses are taught by graduate students. The average class size in an introductory lecture is 15; in a laboratory, 12; and in a regular course, 10.
Admissions: 58% of the 2001-2002 applicants were accepted.
Requirements: The SAT I or ACT is required. In addition, applicants should graduate in the upper 50% of their class with 4 years of English, 3 each of history, math, and science, including 2 of lab science, and one half year each of art and music. The GED is accepted. Interviews are strongly encouraged. Art applicants must submit a portfolio; music applicants must audition. A GPA of 2.0 is required. AP and CLEP credits are accepted. Important factors in the admissions decision are leadership record, recommendations by alumni, and recommendations by school officials. Applications are accepted on-line at *www.mville.edu*
Procedure: Freshmen are admitted fall and spring. Entrance exams should be taken in the spring of the junior or fall of the senior year. There are early decision, early admissions, and deferred admissions plans. Application deadlines are open. Notification is on a rolling basis. The application fee is $50. 80% of all applicants are on a waiting list; 2 were accepted in 2001.
Transfer: 74 transfer students enrolled in 2001-2002. Applicants must submit college transcripts. A minimum GPA of 2.5 and a statement of good standing are required. Applicants with fewer than 40 credits must submit all high school records and SAT I scores. 60 credits of 120 must be completed at M'ville.
Visiting: There are regularly scheduled orientations for prospective students. There are guides for informal visits and visitors may sit in on classes and stay overnight. To schedule a visit, contact the Office of Admissions and Financial Aid at *admissions@mville.edu*
Financial Aid: In 2001-2002, 88% of all freshmen and 70% of continuing students received some form of financial aid. 79% of freshmen and 55% of continuing students received need-based aid. The average freshman award was $17,284. 31% of undergraduates work part time. Average annual earnings from campus work are $1700. The FAFSA, the college's own financial statement, and the state aid form are required. The fall application deadline is April 15.
International Students: There are 110 international students enrolled. The school actively recruits these students. They must score 550 on the written TOEFL or 220 on the electronic version and also take the SAT I or the ACT.
Computers: The mainframe is an HPK 380. Students may access the campus network and the Internet via 120 PCs on campus and in labs in the library. All dorm rooms and public spaces are wired for Internet access. All students may access the system. Internet and intranet are usable 24 hours per day, 7 days a week. Computer labs are open about 64 to 70 hours throughout the week. There are no time limits and no fees.
Graduates: In 2001, 295 bachelor's degrees were awarded. The most popular majors were management (16%), psychology (13%), and art (11%). In an average class, 55% graduate in 4 years, 60% in 5 years, and 60% in 6 years. 51 companies recruited on campus in 2000-2001. Of the 2000 graduating class, 69% were enrolled in graduate school within 6 months of graduation and 28% were employed.
Admissions Contact: Jose Flores, Director of Admissions. A video is available. E-mail: *floresj@mville.edu*
Web: *http://www.manhattanville.edu*

MANNES COLLEGE OF MUSIC — D-5
New York, NY 10024 — (212) 580-0210, ext. 247
(800) 292-3040; Fax: (212) 580-1738

Full-time: 46 men, 78 women	**Faculty:** 23
Part-time: none	**Ph.D.s:** n/av
Graduate: 72 men, 86 women	**Student/Faculty:** 5 to 1
Year: semesters	**Tuition:** $21,330
Application Deadline: December 15	**Room & Board:** $7570
Freshman Class: n/av	
SAT I or ACT: not required	**SPECIAL**

Mannes College of Music, founded in 1916 and today part of the New School University, is a private institution offering instruction in music. The library contains 36,500 volumes, 3 microform items, and 8800 audiovisual forms/CDs, and subscribes to 77 periodicals. Computerized library services include the card catalog, interlibrary loans, and database searching. Special learning facilities include 2 concert/recital halls, a recording studio, and an electronic music studio. The campus is in an urban area in Manhattan. Including residence halls, there are 3 buildings.
Student Life: 71% of undergraduates are from out of state, mostly the Northeast. Others are from 18 states, 18 foreign countries, and Canada. The average age of freshmen is 19; all undergraduates, 21. 17% do not continue beyond their first year; 47% remain to graduate.
Housing: 30 students can be accommodated in college housing, which includes coed dormitories. On-campus housing is guaranteed for the freshman and sophomore years only and is available on a first-come, first-served basis. Priority is given to out-of-town students. Alcohol is not permitted.
Activities: There are no fraternities or sororities. There are 6 groups on campus, including choir, chorus, jazz band, opera, orchestra, and symphony. Popular campus events include orchestra/chorus concerts, Christmas parties, and recitals.
Sports: There is no sports program at Mannes.
Disabled Students: All of the campus is accessible. Elevators are available.
Services: Counseling and information services are available, as is tutoring in most subjects.
Campus Safety and Security: There is a security guard 24 hours a day at the front entrance of the dormitory and from 8 A.M. to 11 P.M. at the front desk of the college lobby.
Programs of Study: Mannes confers B.S. and B.Mus. degrees. Master's degrees are also awarded. Bachelor's degrees are awarded in COMMUNICATIONS AND THE ARTS (music, music performance, music theory and composition, and voice). Voice, piano, and violin are the largest.
Required: The required core curriculum includes courses in English, Western civilization, art history, and literature. Students majoring in instruments and voice must participate in various ensemble classes. Courses are also required in techniques and history of music. To graduate, performance majors must perform before a faculty jury, and composition majors must submit 5 original pieces for juried consideration.
Special: Mannes offers cross-registration with New School University. There are some dual majors by permission.
Faculty/Classroom: No introductory courses are taught by graduate students. The average class size in an introductory lecture is 10 to 12.
Requirements: Applicants must be graduates of an accredited secondary school or have a GED certificate. An audition, an interview, a letter of recommendation, and a written test in music theory and musicianship are required. Important factors in the admissions decision are evidence of special talent, personality/intangible qualities, and recommendations by school officials.
Procedure: Freshmen are admitted fall and spring. Entrance exams should be taken at the time of the audition. There is a deferred admissions plan. Applications should be filed by December 15 for fall entry, along with a $100 fee. Notification is sent on a rolling basis.
Transfer: 27 transfer students enrolled in 2001-2002. Transfer applicants must complete the same procedures as entering freshmen and submit transcripts from all secondary schools and colleges attended.
Visiting: There are guides for informal visits and visitors may sit in on classes. To schedule a visit, contact the Admissions Office.
Financial Aid: In a recent year, 70% of all freshmen and 60% of continuing students received some form of financial aid. 45% of freshmen

and 35% of continuing students received need-based aid. The average freshman award was $6625. Of that total, scholarships or need-based grants averaged $3000 ($19,800 maximum); and loans averaged $2625. 18% of undergraduates work part time. Average annual earnings from campus work are $1200. The average financial indebtedness of a recent year's graduate was $36,000. Mannes is a member of CSS. The FAFSA and the college's own financial statement are required. The fall application deadline is March 1.

International Students: There are 108 international students enrolled. They must score 550 on the written TOEFL and also take the college's own entrance exam.

Computers: All students may access the system. There are no time limits and no fees.

Graduates: In 2001, 30 bachelor's degrees were awarded. The most popular majors were voice (32%), piano (16%), and composition (16%). In an average class, 38% graduate in 4 years, 38% in 5 years, and 38% in 6 years.

Admissions Contact: Allison Scola, Associate Director of Admissions. E-mail: *mannesadmissions@mannes.edu* Web: *www.mannes.edu*

MARIST COLLEGE

Poughkeepsie, NY 12601 — D-4
(845) 575-3226
(800) 436-5483; Fax: (845) 575-3215

Full-time: 1755 men, 2324 women	**Faculty:** 178; IIA, --$
Part-time: 271 men, 363 women	**Ph.D.s:** 83%
Graduate: 395 men, 445 women	**Student/Faculty:** 23 to 1
Year: semesters, summer session	**Tuition:** $16,972
Application Deadline: February 15	**Room & Board:** $7964
Freshman Class: 6254 applied, 3236 accepted, 910 enrolled	
SAT I Verbal/Math: 567/580	**ACT:** 25 **VERY COMPETITIVE**

Marist College, founded in 1946, is an independent liberal arts college with a Catholic tradition. In addition to regional accreditation, Marist has baccalaureate program accreditation with CSWE. The library contains 169,643 volumes, 224,092 microform items, and 4638 audiovisual forms/CDs, and subscribes to 5950 periodicals. Computerized library services include interlibrary loans and database searching. Special learning facilities include a learning resource center, art gallery, radio station, TV station, gallery of Lowell Thomas memorabilia, estuarine and environmental studies laboratory, public opinion institute, and economic research center. The 150-acre campus is in a suburban area 75 miles north of New York City on the Hudson River. Including residence halls, there are 46 buildings.

Student Life: 64% of undergraduates are from New York. Others are from 36 states, 19 foreign countries, and Canada. 70% are from public schools. 90% are white. 60% are Catholic; 20% Protestant. The average age of freshmen is 18; all undergraduates, 20. 10% do not continue beyond their first year; 68% remain to graduate.

Housing: 2668 students can be accommodated in college housing, which includes coed dormitories, on-campus apartments, and off-campus apartments. In addition, there are freshman dorms with mentors and housing for upperclassmen. 71% of students live on campus; of those, 80% remain on campus on weekends. Alcohol is not permitted. Upperclassmen may keep cars.

Activities: 6% of men belong to 3 national fraternities; 9% of women belong to 1 local sorority and 4 national sororities. There are 75 groups on campus, including art, bagpipe band, band, cheerleading, chess, choir, chorale, chorus, computers, dance, debate, drama, ethnic, film, gay, honors, international, jazz band, literary magazine, marching band, musical theater, newspaper, pep band, photography, political, professional, radio and TV, religious, social, social service, student government, and yearbook. Popular campus events include President's Cup Regatta, Community Unity, and Foxfest.

Sports: There are 11 intercollegiate sports for men and 12 for women, and 5 coed intramural sports. Facilities include 2 boathouses, a 4000-seat basketball arena, a 3000-seat stadium, 30 acres of playing fields, a field house, a swimming pool, a diving tank, racquetball courts, a dance and aerobics studio, a weight room, rowing tanks, 9 intramural basketball courts, an all-purpose playing space, and a state-of-the-art fitness center.

Disabled Students: All of the campus is accessible. Wheelchair ramps, elevators, special parking, specially equipped rest rooms, special class scheduling, lowered drinking fountains, and lowered telephones are available.

Services: Counseling and information services are available, as is tutoring in every subject. There is a reader service for the blind, and remedial math, reading, and writing.

Campus Safety and Security: Measures include 24-hour foot and vehicle patrol, escort service, informal discussions, and pamphlets/posters/films. There are emergency telephones, lighted pathways/sidewalks, and security personnel in residence halls.

Programs of Study: Marist confers B.A., B.S., and B.P.S. degrees. Master's degrees are also awarded. Bachelor's degrees are awarded in BIOLOGICAL SCIENCE (biology/biological science), BUSINESS (accounting, business administration and management, and fashion merchandising), COMMUNICATIONS AND THE ARTS (communications, English, fine arts, French, and Spanish), COMPUTER AND PHYSICAL SCIENCE (chemistry, computer mathematics, computer science, information sciences and systems, and mathematics), EDUCATION (athletic training and special), ENGINEERING AND ENVIRONMENTAL DESIGN (environmental science), HEALTH PROFESSIONS (medical technology), SOCIAL SCIENCE (American studies, child psychology/development, criminal justice, economics, fashion design and technology, history, interdisciplinary studies, political science/government, psychology, and social work). Computer science, computer information systems, and natural sciences are the strongest academically. Business administration, communications, and psychology are the largest.

Required: To graduate, students must maintain a GPA of 2.0 in the major while taking 120 credits. A 30-credit core curriculum and 30 to 36 credits in a major are required. Distribution requirements include 6 credits each in natural sciences, social sciences, history, literature, and math and 3 credits each in fine arts and philosophy/religious studies. Specific course requirements include English writing skills and foundation courses in those areas defined by major programs.

Special: Marist offers cross-registration with schools in the mid-Hudson area and study abroad in Europe, Africa, Latin America, Central America, and the Far East. The school also offers a 3-year degree in social work, co-op programs in computer science and computer information systems, work-study programs, a B.A.-B.S. degree, and dual and student-designed majors. There are internships available with more than 250 organizations in the United States and abroad, including New York State Legislature and White House programs. There are 4 national honor societies and a freshman honors program.

Faculty/Classroom: 62% of faculty are male; 38%, female. All teach undergraduates. No introductory courses are taught by graduate students. The average class size in an introductory lecture is 18; in a laboratory, 7; and in a regular course, 19.

Admissions: 52% of the 2001-2002 applicants were accepted. The SAT I scores for the 2001-2002 freshman class were: Verbal--9% below 500, 59% between 500 and 599, 29% between 600 and 700, and 3% above 700; Math--8% below 500, 54% between 500 and 599, 36% between 600 and 700, and 2% above 700. 43% of the current freshmen were in the top fifth of their class; 85% were in the top two fifths. In a recent year, there were 3 National Merit finalists and 16 semifinalists; 7 freshmen graduated first in their class.

Requirements: The SAT I or ACT is required. In addition, applicants should have 16 high school units, including a recommended 4 in English, 3 in math, 2 each in science, language, and social studies, and 1 in U.S. history, art, and music. The GED is accepted. An essay and campus visit are recommended. Marist requires applicants to be in the upper 50% of their class. A grade average of 83 is required. AP and CLEP credits are accepted. Important factors in the admissions decision are leadership record, advanced placement or honor courses, and recommendations by school officials. Applications are accepted on-line via the Marist web page.

Procedure: Freshmen are admitted fall and spring. Entrance exams should be taken during the fall of the senior year. There are early decision, early admissions, and deferred admissions plans. Early decision applications should be filed by December 1; regular applications, by February 15 for fall entry and December 1 for spring entry. The fall 2001 application fee was $40. Notification of early decision is sent January 15; regular decision, March 15. 926 early decision candidates were accepted for the 2001-2002 class. 8% of all applicants are on a waiting list.

Transfer: 168 transfer students enrolled in 2001-2002. Applicants must have at least a 2.8 GPA (depending on the college and major program) in at least 30 college credits. Students with fewer than 25 credits will be treated as freshmen. Grades of C or better transfer. 30 credits of 120 must be completed at Marist.

Visiting: There are regularly scheduled orientations for prospective students, including 1-day June visits for freshmen plus a 3-day orientation before fall classes begin. There are guides for informal visits and visitors may sit in on classes and stay overnight. To schedule a visit, contact the Admissions Office receptionist.

Financial Aid: In 2001-2002, 81% of all freshmen and 72% of continuing students received some form of financial aid. 66% of freshmen and 64% of continuing students received need-based aid. The average freshman award was $10,880. Of that total, scholarships or need-based grants averaged $6000 ($12,000 maximum); loans averaged $2500 ($5125 maximum); and work contracts averaged $600 ($1200 maximum). 34% of undergraduates work part time. Average annual earnings from campus work are $1200. The FAFSA is required. The fall application deadline is February 15.

International Students: There are 27 international students enrolled. The school actively recruits these students. They must score 550 on the written TOEFL.

Computers: The mainframe is an IBM 9672-RC4. The campus center has a drop-in lab available to all students from 8 A.M. to midnight during the week and longer on weekends. All dorm rooms are equipped with data jacks allowing students to hook up PCs with the mainframe and to access library files. Overall, there are 12 areas on campus providing more than 300 terminals for student use, as well as 185 PCs and numerous printers. All students may access the system. There are no time limits and no fees.

Graduates: In 2001, 948 bachelor's degrees were awarded. The most popular majors were communications (22%), business (18%), and criminal justice (12%). In an average class, 56% graduate in 4 years, 66% in 5 years, and 67% in 6 years. 270 companies recruited on campus in 2000-2001. Of the 2000 graduating class, 12% were enrolled in graduate school within 6 months of graduation and 70% were employed.

Admissions Contact: Sean Kaylor, Vice President of Admissions and Enrollment. E-mail: *admissions@marist.edu* Web: *www.marist.edu*

MARYMOUNT COLLEGE/TARRYTOWN D-5

Tarrytown, NY 10591 (914) 332-8295
(800) 724-4312; Fax: (914) 332-4956

Full-time: 17 men, 810 women	**Faculty:** 57; IIB, -$
Part-time: 31 men, 143 women	**Ph.D.s:** 93%
Graduate: none	**Student/Faculty:** 15 to 1
Year: semesters, summer session	**Tuition:** $15,750
Application Deadline: August 1	**Room & Board:** $8100
Freshman Class: 678 applied, 548 accepted, 217 enrolled	
SAT I Verbal/Math: 485/465	**COMPETITIVE**

Marymount College/Tarrytown, founded in 1907, is an independent women's undergraduate institution in the Catholic tradition. The Weekend College is for both men and women. The college offers programs in liberal arts and career preparation. In addition to regional accreditation, the college has baccalaureate program accreditation with ADA and CSWE. The library contains 119,461 volumes, 14,143 microform items, and 422 audiovisual forms/CDs, and subscribes to 363 periodicals. Computerized library services include the card catalog, interlibrary loans, and database searching. Special learning facilities include a learning resource center and a multimedia teaching and learning center. The 25-acre campus is in a suburban area 30 miles north of New York City. Including residence halls, there are 12 buildings.

Student Life: 67% of undergraduates are from New York. Others are from 32 states and 20 foreign countries. 77% are from public schools. 39% are white; 16%, Hispanic; 14%, African American. 45% are Catholic; 24% other religions, no preference, and unknown; 20%, Protestant; 10% claim no religious affiliation. The average age of freshmen is 18; all undergraduates, 21. 35% do not continue beyond their first year; 60% remain to graduate.

Housing: 638 students can be accommodated in college housing, which includes dormitories. In addition, there are honors, special-interest, intercultural, and quiet floors. On-campus housing is guaranteed for all 4 years. 62% of students live on campus. Alcohol is not permitted. All students may keep cars.

Activities: There are no fraternities or sororities. There are 25 groups on campus, including art, chorale, commuter, computers, dance, drama, ethnic, honors, international, literary magazine, newspaper, photography, political, professional, radio and TV, religious, social, social service, student government, and yearbook. Popular campus events include Talent Show, Fashion Show and Competition, and Women's Day.

Sports: There are 5 intercollegiate sports for women and 2 intramural sports for women. Facilities include a swimming pool, dance studio, fitness center, tennis court, and an athletic field. The campus stadium seats 350, the indoor gym 250.

Disabled Students: 85% of the campus is accessible. Wheelchair ramps, elevators, special parking, specially equipped rest rooms, special class scheduling, automatic door openers, paid note takers, and an ASL interpreter are available.

Services: Counseling and information services are available, as is tutoring in every subject. There is remedial math, reading, and writing. There are writing and math labs.

Campus Safety and Security: Measures include 24-hour foot and vehicle patrol, self-defense education, shuttle buses, and informal discussions. There are pamphlets/posters/films, emergency telephones, and lighted pathways/sidewalks.

Programs of Study: The college confers B.A. and B.S. degrees. Associate degrees are also awarded. Bachelor's degrees are awarded in BIOLOGICAL SCIENCE (biology/biological science), BUSINESS (business administration and management, fashion merchandising, and international business management), COMMUNICATIONS AND THE ARTS (art history and appreciation, communications, dramatic arts, English, fine arts, French, and Spanish), COMPUTER AND PHYSICAL SCIENCE (chemistry, computer science, information sciences and systems, and mathematics), EDUCATION (art, elementary, foreign languages, home economics, mathematics, science, secondary, and special), ENGINEERING AND ENVIRONMENTAL DESIGN (interior design), SOCIAL SCIENCE (American studies, economics, fashion design and technology, food science, history, home economics, interdisciplinary studies, international studies, liberal arts/general studies, political science/government, psychology, public affairs, social work, and sociology). Business, education, and psychology are the largest.

Required: All students must take 19 courses in 10 disciplines. A total of 120 credits is required for graduation, as is a minimum GPA of 2.0. Students must complete 5 courses on college mission themes, and 2 sets of learning community courses.

Special: Juniors and seniors in all disciplines may receive up to 12 credits for on-site internships. The college offers study abroad in 7 countries, a Washington semester, work-study programs, dual and student-designed majors, credit by exam, nondegree study, and pass/fail options. There are 3-2 business and education programs with Fordham University and a 6-year joint program in physical therapy and occupational therapy with Touro College. A Weekend College is available to working men and women. There are 3 national honor societies and a freshman honors program.

Faculty/Classroom: 39% of faculty are male; 61%, female. All teach undergraduates and 60% do research. The average class size in an introductory lecture is 20; in a laboratory, 16; and in a regular course, 15.

Admissions: 81% of the 2001-2002 applicants were accepted. The SAT I scores for the 2001-2002 freshman class were: Verbal--57% below 500, 32% between 500 and 599, 10% between 600 and 700, and 1% above 700; Math--64% below 500, 31% between 500 and 599, and 5% between 600 and 700.

Requirements: The SAT I is required, but ACT scores may be submitted instead. Applicants must complete 16 academic credits, including 4 years of English, and 3 years each of foreign language, math, science, and history or social studies. The GED is accepted. An interview is recommended. A GPA of 2.5 is required. AP and CLEP credits are accepted. Important factors in the admissions decision are recommendations by school officials, extracurricular activities record, and leadership record. Applications are accepted on-line via Common App and NY Mentor.

Procedure: Freshmen are admitted fall and spring. Entrance exams should be taken in the fall of the year preceding enrollment. There are early admissions and deferred admissions plans. Early decision applications should be filed by October 31; regular applications, by August 1 for fall entry and January 10 for spring entry. Notification of early decision is sent December 1; regular decision, on a rolling basis. The fall 2001 application fee was $30.

Transfer: 96 transfer students enrolled in 2001-2002. Applicants with fewer than 24 college credits must submit SAT I scores and a high school transcript. A GPA of at least 2.0 is required. 45 credits of 120 must be completed at the college.

Visiting: There are regularly scheduled orientations for prospective students, including meeting with a counselor and touring the campus. There are guides for informal visits and visitors may sit in on classes. To schedule a visit, contact Daniela Esposito, Director of Admissions at *admiss@mmc.marymt.edu*

Financial Aid: In 2001-2002, 81% of all freshmen and 90% of continuing students received some form of financial aid. 80% of freshmen and 65% of continuing students received need-based aid. The average freshman award was $15,085. Of that total, scholarships or need-based grants averaged $6525 ($15,300 maximum); loans averaged $3748 ($10,500 maximum); and work contracts averaged $1289 ($1900 maximum). 34% of undergraduates work part time. Average annual earnings from campus work are $1289. The average financial indebtedness of the 2001 graduate was $11,793. The FAFSA is required. The fall application deadline is May 1.

International Students: There are 73 international students enrolled. The school actively recruits these students. They must score 500 on the written TOEFL.

Computers: The mainframe is a DEC ALPHA. There are about 135 workstations available to students in 5 main labs, a small lab in each dorm, the library, and various other locations. Nearly all are linked with a campuswide LAN. Available software and services include Microsoft Office, graphics, desktop and web publishing, CAD, statistical, e-mail, Internet, and library database access. All dorm rooms provide connectivity, and dial-up service is available off campus. All students may access the system 7 days a week. There are no time limits and no fees.

Graduates: In 2001, 171 bachelor's degrees were awarded. The most popular majors were education (19%), business (14%), and nutrition (8%). In an average class, 52% graduate in 4 years, 57% in 5 years, and 60% in 6 years. 64 companies recruited on campus in 2000-2001. Of the 2000 graduating class, 25% were enrolled in graduate school within 6 months of graduation and 81% were employed.

Admissions Contact: Daniela Esposito, Director of Admissions.
E-mail: *admiss@mmc.marymt.edu* Web: *www.marymt.edu*

MARYMOUNT MANHATTAN COLLEGE

D-5

New York, NY 10021

(212) 517-0555

(800) MARYMOUNT; Fax: (212) 517-0448

Full-time: 443 men, 1385 women	**Faculty:** 70; IIB, --$
Part-time: 127 men, 752 women	**Ph.D.s:** 49%
Graduate: none	**Student/Faculty:** 26 to 1
Year: semesters, summer session	**Tuition:** $14,695
Application Deadline: open	**Room & Board:** $8500
Freshman Class: 1804 applied, 1028 accepted, 508 enrolled	
SAT I Verbal/Math: 534/500	**ACT:** 25 **VERY COMPETITIVE**

Marymount Manhattan College is an urban, independent liberal arts college, offering programs in the arts and sciences for all ages, as well as substantial preprofessional preparation. The library contains 75,000 volumes, 70 microform items, and 1643 audiovisual forms/CDs, and subscribes to 600 periodicals. Computerized library services include the card catalog, interlibrary loans, and database searching. Special learning facilities include a learning resource center, art gallery, radio station, TV station, and a communications arts multimedia suite featuring digital editing technology. The 1-acre campus is in an urban area in Manhattan. Including residence halls, there are 3 buildings.

Student Life: 65% of undergraduates are from New York. Others are from 48 states, 62 foreign countries, and Canada. 50% are from public schools. 53% are white; 20%, African American; 16%, Hispanic. The average age of freshmen is 19; all undergraduates, 26. 19% do not continue beyond their first year; 74% remain to graduate.

Housing: 500 students can be accommodated in college housing, which includes single-sex and coed dormitories and off-campus apartments. On-campus housing is available on a first-come, first-served basis and is available on a lottery system for upperclassmen. Priority is given to out-of-town students. 77% of students commute. Alcohol is not permitted. All students may keep cars.

Activities: 33% of women belong to 1 national sorority. There are no fraternities. There are 30 groups on campus, including art, choir, computers, dance, drama, ethnic, film, gay, honors, international, literary magazine, musical theater, newspaper, photography, political, professional, radio and TV, religious, social, social service, student government, and yearbook. Popular campus events include Strawberry Festival, International Day, and Holiday Soiree.

Sports: There are 3 intramural sports for men and 3 for women. Facilities include an Olympic-size pool and a 300-seat auditorium.

Disabled Students: All of the campus is accessible. Wheelchair ramps, elevators, specially equipped rest rooms, special class scheduling, and lowered drinking fountains are available.

Services: Counseling and information services are available, as is tutoring in every subject. There is remedial math, reading, and writing.

Campus Safety and Security: Measures include 24-hour foot and vehicle patrol, self-defense education, shuttle buses, and informal discussions. There are pamphlets/posters/films, lighted pathways/sidewalks, security cameras, and photo ID check-in.

Programs of Study: MMC confers B.A., B.S., and B.F.A. degrees. Bachelor's degrees are awarded in BIOLOGICAL SCIENCE (biology/biological science), BUSINESS (accounting and business administration and management), COMMUNICATIONS AND THE ARTS (communications, dance, dramatic arts, English, and fine arts), EDUCATION (elementary, secondary, and special), HEALTH PROFESSIONS (premedicine and speech pathology/audiology), SOCIAL SCIENCE (history, international studies, liberal arts/general studies, political science/government, psychology, and sociology). Bio/premedicine, English, and liberal arts are the strongest academically. Theater, business, and communication arts are the largest.

Required: To graduate, students must complete 120 credit hours, including 37 to 70 in the major, with a minimum GPA of 2.5. The core curriculum totals 43 credits in the areas of critical thinking, psychology and philosophy, quantitative reasoning and science, the modern world, communications/language, and the arts.

Special: MMC offers study abroad, interdisciplinary courses, pass/fail options, nondegree study, credit for life experience, and some 250 internships in all majors. Cooperative programs in business and finance, dance, music, languages, nursing, and urban education are offered in conjunction with local colleges and institutes. There is a January minisession, cross-registration with Hunter College, and a 5-year masters in publishing with Pace University. There are 6 national honor societies and a freshman honors program.

Faculty/Classroom: 65% teach undergraduates and 35% both teach and do research. The average class size in an introductory lecture is 30; in a laboratory, 6; and in a regular course, 16.

Admissions: 57% of the 2001-2002 applicants were accepted. In a recent year, 11 freshmen graduated first in their class.

Requirements: The SAT I or ACT is required. In addition, applicants should be graduates of an accredited secondary school or have a GED certificate. MMC recommends completion of 16 academic units, including 4 each in English and electives, and 3 each in language, math, social science, and science. Recommendations are required, and an interview is strongly advised. Applicants to the dance and acting programs must audition. A GPA of 2.5 is required. AP and CLEP credits are accepted. Important factors in the admissions decision are personality/intangible qualities, evidence of special talent, and leadership record. Applications are accepted via MMC's web site at *marymount.mmm.edu* or via *Embark.com*

Procedure: Freshmen are admitted to all sessions. Entrance exams should be taken as early as possible. There are early decision and deferred admissions plans. Early decision applications should be filed by November 1; regular applications are open. Notification of early decision is sent December 15; regular decision, on a rolling basis. 12 early decision candidates were accepted for the 2001-2002 class. The fall 2001 application fee was $50.

Transfer: 121 transfer students enrolled in 2001-2002. Applicants who have graduated from high school since 1989 must meet standard freshman requirements and must submit official transcripts from all colleges attended. 30 credits of 120 must be completed at MMC.

Visiting: There are regularly scheduled orientations for prospective students, including an interview with an admissions counselor, a tour of the school and dormitories, and a meeting with a financial aid adviser. There are guides for informal visits and visitors may sit in on classes. To schedule a visit, contact the Admissions Office at *admissions@mmm.edu*

Financial Aid: In a recent year, 85% of all students received some form of aid. 75% of all students received need-based aid. The average freshman award was $18,500. Of that total, scholarships or need-based grants averaged $6765 ($13,050 maximum); loans averaged $2625 (maximum); work contracts averaged $1500 ($3000 maximum); and PLUS loans averaged $9650 ($22,000 maximum). 65% of undergraduates work part time. Average annual earnings from campus work are $2000. The average financial indebtedness of the 2001 graduate was $12,000. The FAFSA and TAP for (New York state residents) are required. The fall application deadline is February 15.

International Students: There are 138 international students enrolled. The school actively recruits these students. They must score 500 on the written TOEFL or 173 on the electronic version.

Computers: The mainframe is a Colleague, version 16. There are IBM PCs in the computer lab, as well as Macs in the multimedia suite for graphics work. Wireless Internet connections are available in the library. All students may access the system. There are no time limits and no fees.

Graduates: In 2001, 305 bachelor's degrees were awarded. The most popular majors were theater/acting (19%), business/accounting (17%), and communication arts (14%). In an average class, 60% graduate in 4 years, 70% in 5 years, and 72% in 6 years. 18 companies recruited on campus in 2000-2001. Of the 2000 graduating class, 29% were enrolled in graduate school within 6 months of graduation and 61% were employed.

Admissions Contact: Thomas Friebel, Associate Vice President for Enrollment Services. E-mail: *admissions@mmm.edu*
Web: *www.marymount.mmm.edu*

MEDAILLE COLLEGE

C-1

Buffalo, NY 14214

(716) 884-3281

(800) 292-1582; Fax: (716) 884-0291

Full-time: 366 men, 940 women	**Faculty:** 58; IIB, -$
Part-time: 70 men, 136 women	**Ph.D.s:** 66%
Graduate: 111 men, 165 women	**Student/Faculty:** 23 to 1
Year: semesters, summer session	**Tuition:** $12,520
Application Deadline: August 15	**Room & Board:** $5800
Freshman Class: 553 applied, 348 accepted, 215 enrolled	
SAT I Verbal/Math: 470/450	**COMPETITIVE**

Medaille College, founded in 1875, is a private, nonsectarian institution offering undergraduate programs in liberal arts, education, business, and sciences, and graduate programs in business and education, to a primarily commuter student body. The library contains 56,478 volumes, 1495 microform items, and 2279 audiovisual forms/CDs, and subscribes to 295 periodicals. Computerized library services include the card catalog, interlibrary loans, and database searching. Special learning facilities include a learning resource center, radio station, TV station, and a media institute. The 13-acre campus is in an urban area 3 miles from downtown Buffalo. Including residence halls, there are 16 buildings.

Student Life: 90% of undergraduates are from New York. Others are from 4 states, 2 foreign countries, and Canada. 70% are white; 14%, African American. The average age of freshmen is 20; all undergraduates, 26. 30% do not continue beyond their first year; 39% remain to graduate.

Housing: 200 students can be accommodated in college housing, which includes single-sex and coed on-campus apartments and off-campus apartments. On-campus housing is guaranteed for all 4 years. 90% of students commute. All students may keep cars.

Activities: There are no fraternities or sororities. There are 16 groups on campus, including academic, art, cheerleading, ethnic, honors, literary magazine, newspaper, photography, professional, radio and TV, social, student government, and yearbook. Popular campus events include Founders Day, Silent Auction, and Honors Convocation.

Sports: There are 6 intercollegiate sports for men and 6 for women, and 3 intramural sports for men and 3 for women. Facilities include an NCAA regulation gym located in the student center, and a softball and soccer field.

Disabled Students: 99% of the campus is accessible. Wheelchair ramps, elevators, special parking, specially equipped rest rooms, lowered drinking fountains, and lowered telephones are available.

Services: Counseling and information services are available, as is tutoring in most subjects. There is a reader service for the blind, and remedial math, reading, and writing.

Campus Safety and Security: Measures include escort service, shuttle buses, informal discussions, and pamphlets/posters/films. There are emergency telephones and lighted pathways/sidewalks.

Programs of Study: Medaille confers B.A., B.S., B.B.A., and B.S.Ed. degrees. Associate and master's degrees are also awarded. Bachelor's degrees are awarded in BIOLOGICAL SCIENCE (biology/biological science), BUSINESS (banking and finance, business administration and management, human resources, and sports management), COMMUNICATIONS AND THE ARTS (communications), COMPUTER AND PHYSICAL SCIENCE (information sciences and systems), EDUCATION (elementary), SOCIAL SCIENCE (child care/child and family studies, criminal justice, human services, humanities, liberal arts/general studies, political science/government, psychology, and social science). Psychology and humanities are the strongest academically. Education, business administration, and veterinary technology are the largest.

Required: The bachelor's degree requires successful completion of 120 credit hours or 128 for elementary education and biology majors. In addition to specific course requirements for each major, students must maintain a minimum GPA of 2.0. Five theme areas must be satisfied: Theme I - Self and others; Theme II - Global Perspectives; Theme III - Creative Expression; Theme IV - Science, Technology, and Environment; and Theme V - Communication. Students must also complete 6 credits in baccalaureate capstone courses.

Special: Cross-registration is available with colleges in the Western New York Consortium. Most degree programs require internships. Opportunities are provided for student-designed majors, credit by examination, pass/fail options, and credit for work experience. The 2-year veterinary technology program combined with additional liberal arts and sciences courses leads to the B.S. in liberal studies degree. A modular program of evening courses, as well as Weekend College classes, enable students to maintain full-time status by attending classes either 2 nights a week or on weekends. There are 2 national honor societies and a freshman honors program.

Faculty/Classroom: 60% of faculty are male; 40%, female. All teach undergraduates and 15% both teach and do research. No introductory courses are taught by graduate students. The average class size in an introductory lecture is 20; in a laboratory, 10; and in a regular course, 14.

Admissions: 63% of the 2001-2002 applicants were accepted. The SAT I scores for the 2001-2002 freshman class were: Verbal--70% below 500, 25% between 500 and 599, and 5% between 600 and 700; Math--80% below 500, 18% between 500 and 599, and 2% between 600 and 700. 19% of the current freshmen were in the top fifth of their class; 62% were in the top two fifths.

Requirements: The SAT I is required. In addition, applicants must be graduates of an accredited secondary school or hold the GED. An essay and an interview are required. A GPA of 70.0 is required. AP and CLEP credits are accepted. Important factors in the admissions decision are advanced placement or honor courses, personality/intangible qualities, and leadership record. Applications are accepted on-line at *www.medaille.edu*

Procedure: Freshmen are admitted to all sessions. Entrance exams should be taken in May. There is a deferred admissions plan. Applications should be filed by August 15 for fall entry, January 15 for spring entry, and June 15 for summer entry, along with a $25 fee. Notification is sent on a rolling basis.

Transfer: 354 transfer students enrolled in 2001-2002. Transfer applicants must have a minimum GPA of 2.0 in their previous college work. An interview and recommendations are required. 30 credits of 120 must be completed at Medaille.

Visiting: There are regularly scheduled orientations for prospective students, including campus tours, academic program meetings, icebreakers, and a review of policies and procedures. There are guides for informal visits and visitors may sit in on classes and stay overnight. To schedule a visit, contact Jacqueline S. Matheny at *jmatheny@medaille.edu*

Financial Aid: In 2001-2002, 95% of all freshmen and 93% of continuing students received some form of financial aid. 85% of all students received need-based aid. The average freshman award was $11,432. Of that total, scholarships or need-based grants averaged $5000 ($12,375 maximum); loans averaged $2625 ($6625 maximum); and work contracts averaged $1500 ($3000 maximum). 15% of undergraduates work part time. Average annual earnings from campus work are $1500. The average financial indebtedness of the 2001 graduate was $18,350. Medaille is a member of CSS. The FAFSA and the college's own financial statement are required. The fall application deadline is April 1.

International Students: There are 153 international students enrolled. They must score 550 on the written TOEFL or 213 on the electronic version and also take the SAT I.

Computers: There are 100 IBM and 25 Mac PCs available for academic use. All students may access the system. There are no time limits and no fees.

Graduates: In 2001, 313 bachelor's degrees were awarded. The most popular majors were elementary teacher education (35%), business administration (31%), and liberal studies (8%). In an average class, 30% graduate in 4 years, 38% in 5 years, and 39% in 6 years. 63 companies recruited on campus in 2000-2001. Of the 2000 graduating class, 18% were enrolled in graduate school within 6 months of graduation and 96% were employed.

Admissions Contact: Jacqueline S. Matheny, Director Enrollment Management. E-mail: *jmatheny@medaille.edu* Web: *www.medaille.edu*

MERCY COLLEGE D-5

Dobbs Ferry, NY 10522-1189 **(914) 693-7600**
(800)MERCY NY; (914) 674-7382

Full-time: 1505 men, 34,230 women	**Faculty:** 125; IIA, av$
Part-time: 700 men, 2130 women	**Ph.D.s:** 63%
Graduate: 230 men, 1020 women	**Student/Faculty:** 39 to 1
Year: semesters, summer session	**Tuition:** $7875
Application Deadline: open	**Room & Board:** $8000
Freshman Class: 884 enrolled	
SAT I or ACT: recommended	**LESS COMPETITIVE**

Mercy College, founded in 1950, is an independent institution offering programs in liberal arts, fine arts, business, and health science. Figures in above capsule are approximate. There are 8 graduate schools. In addition to regional accreditation, Mercy has baccalaureate program accreditation with CSWE, ACOTE, and CCNE. The 5 libraries contain 7 million volumes, and subscribe to 1170 periodicals. Computerized library services include the card catalog, interlibrary loans, and database searching. Special learning facilities include a learning resource center, art gallery, radio station, TV station, computer lab, and reference library. The 40-acre campus is in a suburban area 12 miles north of New York City. Including residence halls, there are 12 buildings.

Student Life: 97% of undergraduates are from New York. Others are from 14 states and 10 foreign countries. 95% are from public schools. 60% are white; 20% African American; 19% Hispanic. The average age of freshmen is 19; all undergraduates, 28. 25% do not continue beyond their first year; 60% remain to graduate.

Housing: 200 students can be accommodated in college housing, which includes coed dormitories. On-campus housing is available on a first-come, first-served basis. Priority is given to out-of-town students. 99% of students commute. Alcohol is not permitted. All students may keep cars.

Activities: There are no fraternities or sororities. There are 28 groups on campus, including art, chess, computers, drama, ethnic, film, honors, international, literary magazine, newspaper, political, professional, radio and TV, religious, social, social service, student government, and yearbook. Popular campus events include plays and special honors programs.

Sports: There are 6 intercollegiate sports for men and 5 for women. Facilities include a 200-seat gym, a soccer/baseball field, a swimming pool, tennis courts, and a track.

Disabled Students: 75% of the campus is accessible. Wheelchair ramps, elevators, special parking, specially equipped rest rooms, special class scheduling, and lowered drinking fountains are available.

Services: Counseling and information services are available, as is tutoring in every subject. There is a reader service for the blind, and remedial math, reading, and writing.

Campus Safety and Security: Measures include shuttle buses, informal discussions, and lighted pathways/sidewalks.

Programs of Study: Mercy confers B.A. and B.S. degrees. Associate and master's degrees are also awarded. Bachelor's degrees are awarded in BIOLOGICAL SCIENCE (biology/biological science), BUSINESS (accounting and business administration and management), COMMUNICATIONS AND THE ARTS (English, journalism, music, and speech/debate/rhetoric), COMPUTER AND PHYSICAL SCIENCE (computer science, information sciences and systems, and mathematics), EDUCATION (education of the deaf and hearing impaired, elementary, special, and teaching English as a second/foreign language (TESOL/TEFOL)), HEALTH PROFESSIONS (medical laboratory technology, nursing, recreation therapy, and veterinary science), SOCIAL SCIENCE (behavioral science, criminal justice, history, interdisciplinary studies, paralegal studies, political science/government, psychology, social work, and sociology). The health professions programs is the strongest academically. Business and education are the largest.

Required: To graduate, students must complete 120 semester hours with a minimum GPA of 2.0 overall and in the major. Distribution requirements include 12 credits each of math/natural science and philosophy/language/fine arts, 9 of social science, 6 each of English and history, and 3 of speech.

Special: Mercy offers internships in each major, co-op programs in education, work-study programs through the Westchester Employee Association, study abroad, dual majors and degrees, credit for life experience, nondegree study, and pass/fail options. There are 14 national honor societies, including Phi Beta Kappa, a freshman honors program, and 14 departmental honors programs.

Faculty/Classroom: 98% teach undergraduates and 5% do research. No introductory courses are taught by graduate students. The average class size in an introductory lecture is 15; in a laboratory, 12; and in a regular course, 14.

Requirements: The SAT I or ACT is recommended. In addition, applicants must be graduates of an accredited secondary school or have a GED certificate. They should have completed at least 16 academic units. An interview is required and a letter of recommendation from the high school counselor or principal is required. Art students must submit a portfolio; music students must audition. Applications are accepted on-line at *www.merlin.mercynet.edu*. AP and CLEP credits are accepted.

Procedure: Freshmen are admitted to all sessions. Entrance exams should be taken between October and January of the senior year. There are early admissions and deferred admissions plans. Application deadlines are open. Notification is on a rolling basis. The fall 2001 application fee was $35.

Transfer: 1537 transfer students enrolled in a recent year. Applicants must submit official transcripts from all colleges attended. Students with fewer than 15 college credits must also submit their high school transcript. An interview is required. 30 credits of 120 must be completed at Mercy.

Visiting: There are regularly scheduled orientations for prospective students. There are guides for informal visits and visitors may sit in on classes. To schedule a visit, contact the Admissions Office.

Financial Aid: Mercy is a member of CSS. The FAFSA is required. The fall application deadline is May 1.

International Students: There were 225 international students enrolled in a recent year. The school actively recruits these students. They must take the college's own test.

Computers: The mainframe is an IBM 4381. There are also 250 IBM PCs and Macs, as well as graphics workstations with IBM XTs and Vectrix graphics boards. All students may access the system. There are no time limits. The fee is $35.

Admissions Contact: Joy Colelli, Vice President for Enrollment Management. Web: *www.mercynet.edu*

MOLLOY COLLEGE

D-5

Rockville Centre, NY 11570 — **(516) 678-5000, ext. 6240**
(888) 4MOLLOY; Fax: (516) 256-2247

Full-time: 354 men, 1055 women	**Faculty:** 120; IIB, av$
Part-time: 106 men, 497 women	**Ph.D.s:** 54%
Graduate: 65 men, 463 women	**Student/Faculty:** 12 to 1
Year: semesters, summer session	**Tuition:** $13,940
Application Deadline: open	**Room & Board:** n/app
Freshman Class: 594 applied, 515 accepted	
SAT I Verbal/Math: 501/509	**COMPETITIVE**

Molloy College, founded in 1955 in the Catholic and Dominican tradition, is an independent commuter college. It offers programs in liberal arts and sciences, business, nursing and health professions, social work, teacher certification, and preprofessional studies. In addition to regional accreditation, Molloy has baccalaureate program accreditation with CSWE and NLN. The library contains 135,000 volumes, 13,850 microform items, and 2700 audiovisual forms/CDs, and subscribes to 700 periodicals. Computerized library services include the card catalog, interlibrary loans, and database searching. Special learning facilities include a learning resource center, art gallery, and TV station. The 30-acre campus is in a suburban area 20 miles east of New York City. There are 4 buildings.

Student Life: 98% of undergraduates are from New York. Others are from 1 state and 9 foreign countries. 66% are from public schools. 68% are white; 16% African American. Most are Catholic. The average age of freshmen is 18; all undergraduates, 22. 18% do not continue beyond their first year; 57% remain to graduate.

Housing: There are no residence halls. Alcohol is not permitted. All students may keep cars.

Activities: There are no fraternities or sororities. There are 23 groups on campus, including band, cheerleading, choir, chorus, dance, drama, ethnic, honors, international, jazz band, literary magazine, musical theater, newspaper, professional, radio, religious, social, social service, student government, and yearbook. Popular campus events include Tree-Trimming Party, Senior 55 Nights Party, and Junior Ring Night.

Sports: There are 6 intercollegiate sports for men and 7 for women. Facilities include a gym, a dance studio, a weight room, sports fields, and basketball and tennis courts.

Disabled Students: All of the campus is accessible. Wheelchair ramps, elevators, special parking, specially equipped rest rooms, special class scheduling, lowered drinking fountains, and lowered telephones are available.

Services: Counseling and information services are available, as is tutoring in every subject. There is a reader service for the blind, and remedial math, reading, and writing.

Campus Safety and Security: Measures include 24-hour foot and vehicle patrol, escort service, pamphlets/posters/films, and emergency telephones. There are lighted pathways/sidewalks and a Campus Concerns Committee.

Programs of Study: Molloy confers B.A. and B.S. degrees. Associate and master's degrees are also awarded. Bachelor's degrees are awarded in BIOLOGICAL SCIENCE (biology/biological science), BUSINESS (accounting and business administration and management), COMMUNICATIONS AND THE ARTS (art, communications, English, music, and Spanish), COMPUTER AND PHYSICAL SCIENCE (computer science, information sciences and systems, and mathematics), EDUCATION (elementary, secondary, and special), ENGINEERING AND ENVIRONMENTAL DESIGN (environmental science), HEALTH PROFESSIONS (music therapy, nursing, and speech pathology/audiology), SOCIAL SCIENCE (criminal justice, gerontology, history, interdisciplinary studies, peace studies, philosophy, political science/government, psychology, social work, sociology, and theological studies). Nursing, education, and social work are the strongest academically. Nursing, business, and psychology are the largest.

Required: Core requirements consist of 9 credits of philosophy and theology, 6 each of English and modern language, 1 of phys ed, and courses in art, music history, speech, history, political science, psychology, sociology, math, and science. A total of 128 to 137 credit hours is required for graduation.

Special: Students may cross-register with 16 area colleges. The college offers internships, a Washington semester, study abroad, and dual and student-designed majors. Credit by examination and for life, military, and work experience, nondegree study, and pass/fail options are available. There are 15 national honor societies and a freshman honors program.

Faculty/Classroom: 19% of faculty are male; 81%, female. 91% teach undergraduates and 25% do research. No introductory courses are taught by graduate students. The average class size in an introductory lecture is 27; in a laboratory, 15; and in a regular course, 18.

Admissions: 87% of the 2001-2002 applicants were accepted. The SAT I scores for the 2001-2002 freshman class were: Verbal--49% below 500, 40% between 500 and 599, and 11% between 600 and 700; Math--47% below 500, 39% between 500 and 599, 12% between 600 and 700, and 2% above 700. 34% of the current freshmen were in the top fifth of their class; 53% were in the top two fifths.

Requirements: The SAT I or ACT is required; the SAT I is preferred. Applicants should be graduates of a secondary school or have a GED. Preparation should include 4 years of English, 3 each of math and history, and 2 each of foreign language and science. An essay is required, and an interview is recommended. Music students must audition and take a theory exam. A high school grade average of 80 is required. AP and CLEP credits are accepted. Important factors in the admissions decision are advanced placement or honor courses, recommendations by school officials, and extracurricular activities record.

Procedure: Freshmen are admitted fall and spring. Entrance exams should be taken in the fall of the senior year. There are early decision and deferred admissions plans. Application deadlines are open. The fall 2001 application fee was $30. Notification is sent on a rolling basis.

Transfer: 375 transfer students enrolled in 2001-2002. A minimum college GPA of 2.0 is required, with some majors requiring a higher GPA. An interview is recommended. 30 credits of 128 to 137 must be completed at Molloy.

Visiting: There are regularly scheduled orientations for prospective students, including an address by the president of Molloy, department presentations, campus tours, and admissions, financial aid, and scholarship information. There are guides for informal visits and visitors may sit in on classes. To schedule a visit, contact the Admissions Office.

Financial Aid: In 2001-2002, 93% of all freshmen and 91% of continuing students received some form of financial aid. 77% of freshmen and 84% of continuing students received need-based aid. The average freshman award was $4125. Of that total, scholarships or need-based grants averaged $4000 ($6700 maximum); loans averaged $1000 ($2600 maximum); and work contracts averaged $1440. 23% of undergraduates work part time. Average annual earnings from campus work are $2000. The average financial indebtedness of the 2001 graduate was $15,000. Molloy is a member of CSS. The FAFSA is required. The fall application deadline is May 1.

International Students: There were 10 international students enrolled in a recent year. They must score 500 on the written TOEFL or take the MELAB.

Computers: Molloy College is a wireless campus. Students can use their own laptop computers or borrow from the lab. There are 244 PCs available to students in 4 campus computer labs. In addition, numerous PCs are available for student use within individual departments. Internet and e-mail access is available to students in the library, computer labs, and many departments. All students may access the system. There are no time limits and no fees.

Graduates: In 2001, 448 bachelor's degrees were awarded. The most popular majors were nursing (39%), psychology (14%), and business (9%). In an average class, 42% graduate in 4 years, 55% in 5 years, and 57% in 6 years. 70 companies recruited on campus in 2000-2001.

Admissions Contact: Marguerite Lane, Director of Admissions. E-mail: *mlane@molloy.edu* Web: *www.molloy.edu*

MONROE COLLEGE D-5

Bronx, NY 10468 (718) 933-6700 ext. 250
(800) 55 MONROE; Fax: (718) 364-3552

Full-time: 2300 men, 2700 women
Part-time: none
Graduate: none
Year: semesters, summer session
Application Deadline: August 15
Freshman Class: n/av
SAT I: recommended
Faculty: n/av
Ph.D.s: n/av
Student/Faculty: n/av
Tuition: $8460
Room & Board: $6200
LESS COMPETITIVE

Monroe College, founded in 1933 as the Monroe School of Business, offers undergraduate programs in business.

Housing: College-sponsored living facilities include off-campus apartments.

Programs of Study: Monroe confers B.B.A. degrees. Associate degrees are also awarded. Bachelor's degrees are awarded in accounting, business administration and management, and management information systems.

Required: To receive a bachelor's degree, students must earn a minimum of 120 total credits, with a minimum of 60 in the major. General education requirements include 9 credits in English and 6 each in math and electives. 2 computer courses are also required.

Special: Internships are available through a cooperative education program, and there are accelerated degree programs.

Admissions: 10% of the current freshmen were in the top fifth of their class; 25% were in the top two fifths.

Requirements: The SAT I is recommended. In addition, an application, an essay, and an interview are required. Monroe College requires applicants to be in the upper 50% of their class. An average of 70.0 is required. Applications are available on-line.

Procedure: Early decision applications should be filed by December 15; regular applications, by August 15 for fall entry, January 5 for spring entry, and April 15 for summer entry, along with a $25 fee.

Financial Aid: In 2001-2002, 80% of all students received some form of financial aid. The FAFSA, the college's own form, and federal and state tax returns are required.

Admissions Contact: Luke D. Schultheis, Director of Admissions. A video is available. E-mail: *admissions@monroecollege.edu*
Web: *www.monroecollege.edu*

MOUNT SAINT MARY COLLEGE D-4

Newburgh, NY 12550 (845) 569-3248
(888) YES-MSMC; Fax: (845) 562-6762

Full-time: 414 men, 1028 women
Part-time: 113 men, 251 women
Graduate: 57 men, 308 women
Year: semesters, summer session
Application Deadline: open
Freshman Class: 1347 applied, 1109 accepted, 333 enrolled
SAT I Verbal/Math: 516/502
Faculty: 59; IIB, av$
Ph.D.s: 78%
Student/Faculty: 24 to 1
Tuition: $12,675
Room & Board: $6150
COMPETITIVE

MSMC is a liberal arts college offering undergraduate programs leading to bachelor of arts and bachelor of science degrees, and graduate programs leading to a master's in education, nursing, and business administration. An accelerated evening program is offered for non-traditional and adult students. There is 1 undergraduate school and 3 graduate divisions. In addition to regional accreditation, the Mount has baccalaureate program accreditation with NLN. The 2 libraries contain 101,696 volumes, 690,442 microform items, and 27,879 audiovisual forms/CDs, and subscribe to 876 periodicals. Computerized library services include the card catalog, interlibrary loans, and database searching. Special learning facilities include a learning resource center, an elementary school, and an herbarium field station. The 70-acre campus is in a suburban area 58 miles north of New York City. Including residence halls, there are 41 buildings.

Student Life: 85% of undergraduates are from New York. Others are from 16 states, 6 foreign countries, and Canada. 60% are from public schools. 80% are white; 11% African American. 59% are Catholic; 38% Christian, Unknown, Baptist, Methodist, other. The average age of freshmen is 19; all undergraduates, 26. 20% do not continue beyond their first year; 70% remain to graduate.

Housing: 745 students can be accommodated in college housing, which includes single-sex dormitories. In addition, there are on-campus townhouses. On-campus housing is guaranteed for all 4 years. 61% of students commute. All students may keep cars.

Activities: There are no fraternities or sororities. There are 29 groups on campus, including art, cheerleading, choir, computers, drama, ethnic, honors, literary magazine, musical theater, newspaper, photography, political, professional, radio and TV, religious, social, student government, and yearbook. Popular campus events include Octoberfest, Siblings Weekend, and Holiday Formal.

Sports: There are 5 intercollegiate sports for men and 6 for women, and 15 intramural sports for men and 15 for women. Facilities include a gym, a weight room, tennis and handball courts, an indoor running track, a swimming pool, a Nautilus room, a game room, and an aerobics/dance studio.

Disabled Students: All of the campus is accessible. Wheelchair ramps, elevators, special parking, specially equipped rest rooms, lowered telephones, and special equipment in the library and computer centers to accommodate students with low vision are available.

Services: Counseling and information services are available, as is tutoring in every subject. There is remedial math, reading, and writing.

Campus Safety and Security: Measures include 24-hour foot and vehicle patrol, self-defense education, escort service, and shuttle buses. There are informal discussions, pamphlets/posters/films, emergency telephones, and lighted pathways/sidewalks.

Programs of Study: The Mount confers B.A., B.S., B.S.Ed., and B.S.N. degrees. Master's degrees are also awarded. Bachelor's degrees are awarded in BIOLOGICAL SCIENCE (biology/biological science), BUSINESS (accounting and business administration and management), COMMUNICATIONS AND THE ARTS (communications, English, media arts, and public relations), COMPUTER AND PHYSICAL SCIENCE (chemistry, computer science, information sciences and systems, and mathematics), EDUCATION (elementary, secondary, and special), HEALTH PROFESSIONS (medical laboratory technology, nursing, premedicine, and preveterinary science), SOCIAL SCIENCE (criminal justice, Hispanic American studies, history, human services, interdisciplinary studies, international studies, political science/government, prelaw, psychology, social science, and sociology). Education, nursing, and business are the strongest academically. Education, business, and social sciences are the largest.

Required: The required core curriculum includes 39 credits in natural sciences, math, computer science, philosophy and religion, arts and letters, and social sciences. A total of 120 credit hours is required for the B.A. or B.S., with 24 to 40 in the major and a minimum GPA of 2.0. Overall requirements are higher for nursing, medical technology, and education students. All students must achieve computer literacy before graduation.

Special: Co-op programs and internships are available in all majors. There is cross-registration with other mid-Hudson area colleges, as well as accelerated degree programs in business, accounting, nursing, computer science, and public relations. There is a 3-2 degree in physical therapy with New York Medical College and a 3-2 engineering degree with Catholic University. The college also offers study abroad in more than 22 countries, a Washington semester, work-study, and dual and student-designed majors. Credit by exam and for life, military, and work experience, nondegree study, and pass/fail options are available. There are 8 national honor societies, including Phi Beta Kappa, a freshman honors program, and 6 departmental honors programs.

Faculty/Classroom: 43% of faculty are male; 57%, female. 88% teach undergraduates, 40% do research, and 40% do both. No introductory courses are taught by graduate students. The average class size in an introductory lecture is 33; in a laboratory, 8; and in a regular course, 22.

Admissions: 82% of the 2001-2002 applicants were accepted. The SAT I scores for the 2001-2002 freshman class were: Verbal--41% below 500, 46% between 500 and 599, 9% between 600 and 700, and 1% above 700; Math--47% below 500, 42% between 500 and 599, 9% between 600 and 700, and 1% above 700.

Requirements: The SAT I or ACT is required. In addition, students should be graduates of an accredited secondary school. The GED is accepted. Applicants should prepare with 4 years each of English and history and at least 3 each of math and science and 2 of foreign language. An essay and an interview are recommended. Students must be in the top 35% of their class. A grade average of 85 is required. AP and CLEP credits are accepted. Important factors in the admissions decision are advanced placement or honor courses, personality/intangible qualities, evidence of special talent, and recommendations by school officials. Applications are accepted on-line.

Procedure: Freshmen are admitted to all sessions. Entrance exams should be taken as early as possible. There is a deferred admissions plan. Application deadlines are open. The fall 2001 application fee was $30. Notification is sent on a rolling basis.

Transfer: 194 transfer students enrolled in 2001-2002. Applicants must have a GPA of at least 2.0 in all college work. The SAT I or ACT, an associate degree, and an interview are recommended. 30 credits of 120 must be completed at the Mount.

Visiting: There are regularly scheduled orientations for prospective students, including 6 open houses per year, a 4-day fall orientation program, and a Spend a Day with a Current Student program in the spring. There are guides for informal visits and visitors may sit in on classes and stay overnight. To schedule a visit, contact Admissions.

Financial Aid: In 2001-2002, 83% of all freshmen and 80% of continuing students received some form of financial aid. 20% of undergraduates work part time. Average annual earnings from campus work are $1000. The average financial indebtedness of the 2001 graduate was $15,000. The Mount is a member of CSS. The FAFSA and the college's own financial statement are required. The fall application deadline is March 15.

International Students: There is 1 international student enrolled. They must score 500 on the written TOEFL and also take the SAT I, ACT, or the college's own entrance exam.

Computers: The student-computer ratio is 14 to 1. PCs are located in the main computer center, labs, classrooms, and the library. All students may access the system weekdays from 10 A.M. to 11 P.M., and weekends from 10 A.M. to 5 P.M. There are no time limits and no fees. It is strongly recommended that all students have a personal computer.

Graduates: In 2001, 332 bachelor's degrees were awarded. The most popular majors were business (25%), education (18%), and nursing (11%). In an average class, 44% graduate in 4 years, 54% in 5 years, and 55% in 6 years. 10 companies recruited on campus in 2000-2001. Of the 2000 graduating class, 25% were enrolled in graduate school within 6 months of graduation and 89% were employed.

Admissions Contact: J. Randall Ognibene, Director of Admissions. A video is available. E-mail: *mtstmary@msmc.edu* Web: *www.msmc.edu*

NAZARETH COLLEGE OF ROCHESTER — B-3

Rochester, NY 14618-3790 — (585) 389-2860

(800) 462-3944; Fax: (585) 389-2826

Full-time: 409 men, 1229 women	**Faculty:** 135; IIA, -$
Part-time: 53 men, 207 women	**Ph.D.s:** 94%
Graduate: 199 men, 1010 women	**Student/Faculty:** 12 to 1
Year: semesters, summer session	**Tuition:** $15,376
Application Deadline: February 15	**Room & Board:** $6660
Freshman Class: 1750 applied, 1328 accepted, 360 enrolled	
SAT I Verbal/Math: 570/570	**ACT:** 25 **VERY COMPETITIVE**

Nazareth College of Rochester, founded in 1924, is an independent institution offering programs in the liberal arts and sciences and preprofessional areas. In addition to regional accreditation, Nazareth has baccalaureate program accreditation with CSWE, NASM, and NLN. The library contains 261,686 volumes, 424,883 microform items, and 17,928 audiovisual forms/CDs, and subscribes to 1896 periodicals. Computerized library services include the card catalog, interlibrary loans, and database searching. Special learning facilities include a learning resource center, art gallery, and radio station. The 95-acre campus is in a suburban area 7 miles east of Rochester. Including residence halls, there are 21 buildings.

Student Life: 96% of undergraduates are from New York. Others are from 20 states, 9 foreign countries, and Canada. 90% are from public schools. 91% are white. The average age of freshmen is 18; all undergraduates, 21. 16% do not continue beyond their first year; 68% remain to graduate.

Housing: 1044 students can be accommodated in college housing, which includes single-sex and coed dormitories and on-campus apartments. In addition, there are language houses, special-interest houses, and substance-free, freshman experience, and honors floors. On-campus housing is guaranteed for all 4 years. 62% of students live on campus; of those, 88% remain on campus on weekends. All students may keep cars.

Activities: There are no fraternities or sororities. There are 33 groups on campus, including art, band, cheerleading, choir, chorale, chorus, computers, dance, drama, ethnic, gay, honors, jazz band, literary magazine, musical theater, newspaper, opera, orchestra, political, religious, student government, and yearbook. Popular campus events include Springfest, Parents Weekend, and Siblings Weekend.

Sports: There are 7 intercollegiate sports for men and 9 for women, and 20 intramural sports for men and 20 for women. Facilities include a gym, a 25-meter swimming pool, soccer and lacrosse fields, including an outdoor turf field, tennis and racquetball courts, a fitness center, and a sauna.

Disabled Students: 80% of the campus is accessible. Wheelchair ramps, elevators, special parking, specially equipped rest rooms, and special class scheduling are available.

Services: Counseling and information services are available, as is tutoring in every subject.

Campus Safety and Security: Measures include 24-hour foot and vehicle patrol, escort service, informal discussions, and pamphlets/posters/films. There are emergency telephones, lighted pathways/sidewalks, an alarm system, and security beepers free to all students.

Programs of Study: Nazareth confers B.A., B.S., and B.Mus. degrees. Master's degrees are also awarded. Bachelor's degrees are awarded in BIOLOGICAL SCIENCE (biochemistry and biology/biological science), BUSINESS (accounting and business administration and management), COMMUNICATIONS AND THE ARTS (art, art history and appreciation, dramatic arts, English, fine arts, French, German, Italian, music, music history and appreciation, music performance, and Spanish), COMPUTER AND PHYSICAL SCIENCE (chemistry, information sciences and systems, and mathematics), EDUCATION (art, business, elementary, English, foreign languages, mathematics, middle school, music, science, social studies, and special), ENGINEERING AND ENVIRONMENTAL DESIGN (environmental science), HEALTH PROFESSIONS (music therapy, nursing, physical therapy, and speech pathology/audiology), SOCIAL SCIENCE (American studies, anthropology, economics, history, international studies, philosophy, political science/government, psychology, religion, social science, social work, and sociology). Physical therapy, math, and English are the strongest academically. Business, psychology, and art are the largest.

Required: All students must take courses in English, math, lab science, philosophy, social science, history, and religious studies. 2 semesters of phys ed, a course in computer literacy, and a writing competency exam in the junior year are required. Other requirements vary according to the major, with a total of 30 to 75 upper-division credits needed. A total of 120 credit hours is required to graduate. The minimum GPA is 2.0.

Special: There is cross-registration with members of the Rochester Area Colleges Consortium. Internships and a Washington semester are offered. There is study abroad in France, Spain, Italy, and Germany, and there are exchange programs in Australia, Japan, Italy, and Wales. There are 20 national honor societies and 13 departmental honors programs.

Faculty/Classroom: 42% of faculty are male; 58%, female. All teach undergraduates. No introductory courses are taught by graduate students. The average class size in an introductory lecture is 25; in a laboratory, 15; and in a regular course, 24.

Admissions: 76% of the 2001-2002 applicants were accepted. The SAT I scores for the 2001-2002 freshman class were: Verbal--13% below 500, 53% between 500 and 599, 31% between 600 and 700, and 3% above 700; Math--14% below 500, 54% between 500 and 599, 28% between 600 and 700, and 5% above 700. The ACT scores were 13% below 21, 26% between 21 and 23, 35% between 24 and 26, 14% between 27 and 28, and 12% above 28. 67% of the current freshmen were in the top fifth of their class; 91% were in the top two fifths. There were 3 National Merit semifinalists. 5 freshmen graduated first in their class.

Requirements: The SAT I or ACT is required, with minimum scores of 500 verbal and 500 math on the SAT I and 21 on the ACT. Applicants should graduate from an accredited secondary school or have a GED. A minimum of 16 academic credits is required, including 4 years of English and 3 each of social studies, foreign language, math, and science. An essay is required, as are an audition for music and theater students and a portfolio for art students. An interview is recommended. Nazareth requires applicants to be in the upper 50% of their class. A GPA of 2.75 is required. AP and CLEP credits are accepted. Important factors in the admissions decision are geographic diversity, advanced placement or honor courses, and evidence of special talent.

Procedure: Freshmen are admitted fall and spring. Entrance exams should be taken by December of the senior year. There are early decision and deferred admissions plans. Early decision applications should be filed by December 1; regular applications, by February 15 for fall entry and November 15 for spring entry, along with a $40 fee. Notification of early decision is sent January 1; regular decision, February 1. 47 early decision candidates were accepted for the 2001-2002 class. 6% of all applicants are on a waiting list; 24 were accepted in 2001.

Transfer: 127 transfer students enrolled in 2001-2002. Applicants must have a college GPA of 2.5 (2.75 for education and physical therapy students). Those with fewer than 30 credits must submit high school transcripts. 30 credits of 120 must be completed at Nazareth.

Visiting: There are regularly scheduled orientations for prospective students, including individual appointments, group sessions, open houses, and summer academic orientation. There are guides for informal visits and visitors may sit in on classes and stay overnight. To schedule a visit, contact the Admissions Office.

Financial Aid: In 2001-2002, 95% of all freshmen and 90% of continuing students received some form of financial aid. 91% of freshmen and 90% of continuing students received need-based aid. The average freshman award was $14,271. Of that total, scholarships or need-based grants averaged $10,016 ($14,940 maximum); loans averaged $2953 ($4125 maximum); and work contracts averaged $967 ($1900 maximum). 69% of undergraduates work part time. Average annual earnings from campus work are $1421. The average financial indebtedness of the 2001 graduate was $21,118. Nazareth is a member of CSS. The FAFSA is required. The CSS Profile is required for early decision applicants only. The fall application deadline is February 15.

International Students: There are 9 international students enrolled. The school actively recruits these students. They must score 550 on the written TOEFL or 213 on the electronic version and also take the SAT I or the ACT.

Computers: The mainframe is a Compact Alpha System. There are 150 PCs available for academic use in 6 labs. 2 labs are open 24 hours a day. All students may access the system. There are no time limits and no fees.

Graduates: In 2001, 439 bachelor's degrees were awarded. The most popular majors were business (15%), English (11%), and psychology (10%). In an average class, 61% graduate in 4 years, 65% in 5 years, and 68% in 6 years. 35 companies recruited on campus in 2000-2001. Of the 2000 graduating class, 39% were enrolled in graduate school within 6 months of graduation and 82% were employed.

Admissions Contact: Thomas DaRin, Vice President of Enrollment Management. E-mail: *admissions@naz.edu* Web: *ww.naz.edu*

NEW YORK INSTITUTE OF TECHNOLOGY D-5

Old Westbury, NY 11568-8000 (516) 686-7925
(800) 345-NYIT; (516) 686-7613

Full-time: 2395 men, 1523 women	**Faculty:** 230; IIA, ++$
Part-time: 1029 men, 602 women	**Ph.D.s:** 87%
Graduate: 1758 men, 1627 women	**Student/Faculty:** 15 to 1
Year: semesters, summer session	**Tuition:** $14,876
Application Deadline: February 1	**Room & Board:** $6880
Freshman Class: 3251 applied, 2568 accepted, 815 enrolled	
SAT I Verbal/Math: 530/570	**ACT:** 23 **COMPETITIVE**

The New York Institute of Technology, founded in 1955, is a nonsectarian, nonprofit institution of higher learning that provides undergraduate, graduate, and professional programs in allied health, architecture, art, business, culinary arts, communication, arts, education, engineering, hospitality management, and medicine and technology. Traditional, and accelerated formats in day, evening, and weekend sessions are available, in addition to noncredit and personal enrichment programs and off campus independent study. NYIT maintains additional campuses on Long Island, and in Manhattan. NUIT'S on-line campus is an innovative virtual campus. Students can take courses or acquire a 4 year degree entirely through web-based computer conferencing with no campus classes required. There are 7 undergraduate and 8 graduate schools. In addition to regional accreditation, NYIT has baccalaureate program accreditation with ABET, ACOTE, ADA, ARC-PA, CADE, FIDER, and NAAB. The 5 libraries contain 215,375 volumes, 743,882 microform items, and 45,423 audiovisual forms/CDs, and subscribe to 2929 periodicals. Computerized library services include the card catalog, interlibrary loans, and database searching. Special learning facilities include a learning resource center, art gallery, radio station, TV station, and and TV studios. The 525-acre campus is in a suburban area. The Old Westbury campus is 25 miles east of New York City, 10 miles from Queens.

Student Life: 91% of undergraduates are from New York. Others are from 33 states, 92 foreign countries, and Canada. 33% are white; 13% foreign nationals; 10% African American; 10% Asian American. The average age of freshmen is 18; all undergraduates, 24. 33% do not continue beyond their first year; 67% remain to graduate.

Housing: 1000 students can be accommodated in college housing, which includes single-sex and coed dormitories and on-campus apartments. In addition, there are special-interest houses, facilities for international, graduate, architecture, and first-year students, for student leaders, and for the student government executive board members, and Greek life organization. On-campus housing is guaranteed for all 4 years. 91% of students commute. Alcohol is not permitted. All students may keep cars.

Activities: 2% of men belong to 1 local fraternity and 4 national fraternities; 1% of women belong to 2 local sororities and 1 national sorority. There are 100 groups on campus, including academic, art, cheerleading, chorale, computers, dance, drama, ethnic, film, honors, international, literary magazine, musical theater, newspaper, political, professional, radio and TV, religious, social, social service, special interest, student government, student media, and yearbook. Popular campus events include May Fest, Club Fair Day, and Earth Day.

Sports: There are 7 intercollegiate sports for men and 7 for women, and 9 intramural sports for men and 9 for women. Facilities include a gym, soccer, softball and baseball fields, a track, courts for tennis, handball, and basketball, a fitness center, aquatic facilities, and a weight room.

Disabled Students: All of the campus is accessible. Wheelchair ramps, elevators, special parking, specially equipped rest rooms, and lowered drinking fountains are available.

Services: Counseling and information services are available, as is tutoring in every subject. There is remedial math, reading, and writing.

Campus Safety and Security: Measures include 24-hour foot and vehicle patrol, escort service, shuttle buses, and informal discussions. There are pamphlets/posters/films, emergency telephones, and lighted pathways/sidewalks.

Programs of Study: NYIT confers B.A., B.S., B.Arch., B.F.A., B.P.S., and B.Tech. degrees. Associate and master's degrees are also awarded. Bachelor's degrees are awarded in BIOLOGICAL SCIENCE (biology/biological science, life science, and nutrition), BUSINESS (accounting, banking and finance, business administration and management, hospitality management services, marketing and distribution, and marketing/retailing/merchandising), COMMUNICATIONS AND THE ARTS (advertising, communications, English, fine arts, graphic design, technical and business writing, and telecommunications), COMPUTER AND PHYSICAL SCIENCE (chemistry, computer science, mathematics, and physics), EDUCATION (art, business, education, elementary, health, middle school, science, secondary, technical, and trade and industrial), ENGINEERING AND ENVIRONMENTAL DESIGN (aeronautical engineering, architecture, biomedical engineering, computer engineering, computer graphics, electrical/electronics engineering, electrical/electronics engineering technology, engineering technology, environmental design, environmental engineering technology, industrial engineering, interior design, manufacturing engineering, mechanical engineering, and technological management), HEALTH PROFESSIONS (clinical science, nursing, occupational therapy, physical therapy, physician's assistant, and preosteopathy), SOCIAL SCIENCE (behavioral science, interdisciplinary studies, political science/government, prelaw, social studies, and sociology). Architecture, allied health programs, and engineering are the strongest academically. Computer science, business administration, and architectural technology are the largest.

Required: All students take a core curriculum, sequenced over 8 semesters, that includes 42 credits in English, speech, behavioral and natural science, social science, philosophy, economics, and a capstone course in the major field. A total of 120 to 169 credits and a minimum GPA of 2.0, both overall and in the major, are required for graduation.

Special: NYIT offers cooperative programs, summer study abroad, internships, student-designed majors, a B.A.-B.S. degree in interdisciplinary studies, accelerated degree programs in osteopathic medicine, mechanical engineering, physical therapy, occupational therapy, and criminal justice, and nondegree study. There are 7 national honor societies, a freshman honors program, and 2 departmental honors programs.

Faculty/Classroom: 67% of faculty are male; 33%, female. 88% teach undergraduates, 28% do research, and 28% do both. No introductory courses are taught by graduate students. The average class size in an introductory lecture is 20; in a laboratory, 15; and in a regular course, 17.

Admissions: 79% of the 2001-2002 applicants were accepted. The SAT I scores for the 2001-2002 freshman class were: Verbal--35% below 500, 47% between 500 and 599, 18% between 600 and 700, and 2% above 700; Math--13% below 500, 47% between 500 and 599, 35% between 600 and 700, and 5% above 700. The ACT scores were 50% below 21, 12% between 21 and 23, 10% between 24 and 26, 10% between 27 and 28, and 18% above 28.

Requirements: The SAT I or ACT is required. In addition, all students must present evidence of completion of high school degree or an equivalence. Architecture, engineering, combined baccalaureate/doctor of osteopathic medicine, nursing, occupational therapy, physical therapy, and physician assistant programs requirements include interviews, essays, letters of recommendation, volunteer hours, and Regents units. Recommendations are required for education program applicants. Portfolios are required for fine arts applicants. AP and CLEP credits are accepted. Important factors in the admissions decision are leadership record, evidence of special talent, and geographic diversity. Applications are accepted on-line, through the school's web site.

Procedure: Freshmen are admitted fall and spring. There is a deferred admissions plan. Applications should be filed by February 1 for fall entry. The fall 2001 application fee was $50. Notification is sent on a rolling basis.

Transfer: 608 transfer students enrolled in 2001-2002. Applicants must submit official transcripts from all colleges attended. Engineering applicants must have a 2.3 GPA in math, physics, and engineering courses. 30 credits of 120 must be completed at NYIT.

Visiting: There are regularly scheduled orientations for prospective students, including open houses in fall and spring, with campus tours, a president's address, financial aid seminars, honors receptions, sessions with faculty advisers, and major-specific receptions. There are guides for informal visits and visitors may sit in on classes. To schedule a visit, contact the Admissions Office at (516) 686-7520.

Financial Aid: In 2001-2002, 86% of all freshmen and 76% of continuing students received some form of financial aid. 80% of freshmen and 72% of continuing students received need-based aid. Scholarships or need-based grants averaged $5218 ($20,800 maximum); loans averaged $2964 ($8355 maximum); and work contracts averaged $1749 ($4000 maximum). 77% of undergraduates work part time. Average annual earnings from campus work are $2000. The average financial indebtedness of the 2001 graduate was $15,000. The FAFSA is required.

International Students: There are 361 international students enrolled. The school actively recruits these students. They must score 550 on the written TOEFL or 213 on the electronic version and also take the college's own test and the SAT I or the ACT.

Computers: The mainframe is a Sun Ultra Enterprise 4500. There are 3 open access labs with Internet access, 26 classroom labs with 25 computers each, 4 distance learning labs on each campus with full computer capacity, and 703 PC, Mac, and Silicon Graphics workstations available for student use. Open access and reserve computers in 4 libraries are Internet connected. All students may access the system. There are no time limits and no fees. All students are required to have personal computers.

Graduates: In 2001, 735 bachelor's degrees were awarded. The most popular majors were business administration (14%), life sciences (12%), and interdisciplinary studies (8%). In an average class, 2% graduate in 3 years, 14% in 4 years, 38% in 5 years, and 46% in 6 years. 185 companies recruited on campus in 2000-2001. Of the 2000 graduating class, 43% were enrolled in graduate school within 6 months of graduation and 90% were employed.

Admissions Contact: Jacquelyn Nealon, Dean of Admissions and Financial Aid. A video is available. E-mail: *admissions@nyit.edu*
Web: *www.nyit.edu*

NEW YORK UNIVERSITY D-5

New York, NY 10011 (212) 998-4500; Fax: (212) 995-4902

Full-time: 6785 men, 10,177 women	**Faculty:** 1705; I, +$
Part-time: 831 men, 1235 women	**Ph.D.s:** 94%
Graduate: 7723 men, 10,383 women	**Student/Faculty:** 10 to 1
Year: semesters, summer session	**Tuition:** $25,380
Application Deadline: January 15	**Room & Board:** $9820
Freshman Class: 30,533 applied, 8701 accepted, 3753 enrolled	
SAT I Verbal/Math: 670/670	**ACT:** 29 **MOST COMPETITIVE**

New York University, founded in 1831, is a private research university offering undergraduate, graduate, and professional degrees in arts and sciences, business, education, health professions, nursing, social work, and individualized study. NYU consists of 14 colleges and schools located in New York City. There are 7 undergraduate and 11 graduate schools. In addition to regional accreditation, NYU has baccalaureate program accreditation with AACSB, ACEJMC, ACOTE, ADA, AMA-LCME, APA, APTA, ASLHA, CAAHEP, CSWE, NASPAA, and NLN. The 8 libraries contain 4,495,381 volumes, 4,459,879 microform items, and 73,216 audiovisual forms/CDs, and subscribe to 34,047 periodicals. Computerized library services include the card catalog, interlibrary loans, and database searching. Special learning facilities include a learning resource center, art gallery, radio station, TV station, and a speech/language/hearing clinic. The campus is in an urban area in New York City's Greenwich Village. Including residence halls, there are 150 buildings.

Student Life: 54% of undergraduates are from out of state, mostly the Northeast. Others are from 49 states, 137 foreign countries, and Canada. 70% are from public schools. 40% are white; 14%, Asian American. The average age of freshmen is 19; all undergraduates, 22. 9% do not continue beyond their first year; 75% remain to graduate.

Housing: 10,391 students can be accommodated in college housing, which includes coed dormitories, on-campus apartments, and fraternity houses. In addition, there are special-interest houses and SAFE (Substance and Alcohol Free Environment) housing. On-campus housing is guaranteed for all 4 years. 55% of students live on campus. All students may keep cars.

Activities: 5% of men belong to 13 national fraternities; 2% of women belong to 9 local and 4 national sororities. There are 250 groups on campus, including art, bagpipe band, band, cheerleading, chess, choir, chorale, chorus, computers, dance, debate, drama, ethnic, film, forensics, gay, honors, international, jazz band, literary magazine, musical theater, newspaper, orchestra, pep band, photography, political, professional, radio and TV, religious, social, social service, student government, symphony, and yearbook. Popular campus events include Spring Strawberry Festival, Grad Alley, and Career Services Fair.

Sports: There are 11 intercollegiate sports for men and 9 for women, and 11 intramural sports for men and 11 for women. Facilities include a sports and recreation center that includes a pool, tennis courts, a track, a dance studio, an exercise prescription facility, a weight room, handball, racquetball, and squash courts, a fencing area, a rock-climbing wall, and multipurpose courts.

Disabled Students: 95% of the campus is accessible. Wheelchair ramps, elevators, special parking, specially equipped rest rooms, lowered drinking fountains, and lowered telephones are available.

Services: Counseling and information services are available, as is tutoring in every subject. There is a reader service for the blind.

Campus Safety and Security: Measures include self-defense education, escort service, shuttle buses, and informal discussions. There are pamphlets/posters/films, emergency telephones, lighted pathways/sidewalks, vehicle patrol, 24-hour security in residence halls, and a neighborhood-merchant emergency help service.

Programs of Study: NYU confers B.A., B.S., B.F.A., B.S./B.E., and Mus.B. degrees. Associate, master's, and doctoral degrees are also awarded. Bachelor's degrees are awarded in BIOLOGICAL SCIENCE (biochemistry, biology/biological science, neurosciences, and nutrition), BUSINESS (accounting, banking and finance, business administration and management, business economics, hotel/motel and restaurant management, international business management, marketing/retailing/merchandising, operations research, recreation and leisure services, and sports management), COMMUNICATIONS AND THE ARTS (American literature, art history and appreciation, classics, communications, comparative literature, dance, dramatic arts, English, English literature, film arts, fine arts, French, German, Germanic languages and literature, Greek, Greek (classical), Hebrew, Italian, journalism, Latin, linguistics, music, music business management, music performance, music theory and composition, photography, Portuguese, radio/television technology, romance languages and literature, Russian, Spanish, speech/debate/rhetoric, studio art, and voice), COMPUTER AND PHYSICAL SCIENCE (actuarial science, chemistry, computer science, information sciences and systems, mathematics, physics, and statistics), EDUCATION (early childhood, English, foreign languages, mathematics, music, science, secondary, social studies, and special), ENGINEERING AND ENVIRONMENTAL DESIGN (chemical engineering, civil engineering, computer engineering, electrical/electronics engineering, engineering physics, environmental engineering, graphic arts technology, materials engineering, mechanical engineering, and urban design), HEALTH PROFESSIONS (nursing, predentistry, premedicine, preoptometry, prepodiatry, and speech pathology/audiology), SOCIAL SCIENCE (African studies, anthropology, classical/ancient civilization, East Asian studies, economics, European studies, history, Judaic studies, Latin American studies, Luso-Brazilian studies, medieval studies, Middle Eastern studies, philosophy, political science/government, prelaw, psychology, religion, social work, sociology, urban studies, Western European studies, and women's studies). Finance, theater, and film and television are the largest.

Required: All students must complete a minimum of 128 credit hours and maintain a minimum GPA of 2.0. A course in expository writing is required. Students must complete a core liberal arts curriculum in addition to major and elective credit.

Special: A 3-2 engineering degree (B.S./B.E.) is available with the Stevens Institute of Technology in New Jersey. A vast array of internships is available, as well as study worldwide at 6 sites: Florence, Paris, Madrid, Prague, London, and Buenos Aires. B.A.-B.S. degree options, accelerated degrees in more than 140 majors, dual and student-designed majors, credit by exam, and pass/fail options are also available. A Washington semester is available to political science majors. There are exchange programs with several historically black colleges. There is a chapter of Phi Beta Kappa and a freshman honors program.

Faculty/Classroom: 63% of faculty are male; 37%, female. No introductory courses are taught by graduate students.

Admissions: 28% of the 2001-2002 applicants were accepted. The SAT I scores for the 2001-2002 freshman class were: Verbal--12% between 500 and 599, 53% between 600 and 700, and 35% above 700; Math--1% below 500, 12% between 500 and 599, 50% between 600 and 700, and 37% above 700. The ACT scores were 4% between 21 and 23, 9% between 24 and 26, 28% between 27 and 28, and 59% above 28. 89% of the current freshmen were in the top fifth of their class; 99% were in the top two fifths. There were 132 National Merit finalists.

Requirements: The SAT I or ACT is required. In addition, applicants must graduate from an accredited secondary school. The GED is accepted. Students must present at least 16 Carnegie units, including 4 in English. Some majors require an audition or submission of a creative portfolio. AP and CLEP credits are accepted. Important factors in the admissions decision are advanced placement or honor courses and evidence of special talent. All applicants must submit an essay and 2 letters of recommendation. Students may apply on-line at the school's web site, at *Embark.com*, or via NY State Mentor.

Procedure: Freshmen are admitted fall, spring, and summer. Entrance exams should be taken by November of the senior year. There is an early decision plan. Early decision applications should be filed by November 15; regular applications, by January 15 for fall entry, December 1 for spring entry, and May 1 for summer entry, along with a $55 fee. Notification of early decision is sent December 15; regular decision, April 1. 992 early decision candidates were accepted for the 2001-2002 class. 3% of all applicants are on a waiting list; 65 were accepted in 2001.

Transfer: 748 transfer students enrolled in 2001-2002. Students must submit official college transcripts from all postsecondary institutions attended, a final high school transcript, and SAT I scores. 32 credits of 128 must be completed at NYU.

Visiting: There are regularly scheduled orientations for prospective students, including campus tours and weekday information sessions by appointment. There are also 2 fall open houses. Visitors may sit in on classes. To schedule a visit, contact the Admissions Office at (212) 998-4524 or via the school's web site.

Financial Aid: In 2001-2002, 76% of all freshmen and 72% of continuing students received some form of financial aid. 56% of freshmen and 54% of continuing students received need-based aid. The average freshman award was $17,567. 16% of undergraduates work part time. Average annual earnings from campus work are $1917. The average financial indebtedness of the 2001 graduate was $20,079. The FAFSA is required. The fall application deadline is February 15.

International Students: There are 837 international students enrolled. The school actively recruits these students. They must take the college's own test or have ESL testing, and also take the SAT I or the ACT. Students must take SAT II: Subject tests; 3 total are recommended, English and 2 other tests.

Computers: The mainframes are a 1 Sun E 10000, 6 Sun E 3500s, 2 IBM Sp2s, an IBM ES 9000 Mainframe Computer(9672-RB6) running both the Var/ESA and the OS/390 operating systems, and IBM 12S/6000, SP2(9076-206) running the AIX operating system; and a number of Novell servers and AIX servers. Students in degree/diploma programs are eligible for an NYUHome account. This account provides e-mail, a personal web page, software, and easy access to the World Wide Web, network news, and other Internet services. Facilities include Macs and PCs at 4 computer labs; more than 100 public terminals for walk-up access to e-mail and Internet; laptop plug-in ports and circulating laptops at the library; DIAL service for fast PPP phone and modem connectors from home or while traveling; ResNet for in-room Ethernet access in virtually all residence halls. There are no time limits and no fees.

Graduates: In 2001, 4139 bachelor's degrees were awarded. The most popular majors were business (15%), drama/theater arts (10%), and film/cinema studies (8%). In an average class, 65% graduate in 4 years, 72% in 5 years, and 74% in 6 years. 700 companies recruited on campus in 2000-2001. Of the 2000 graduating class, 23% were enrolled in graduate school within 6 months of graduation and 88% were employed.

Admissions Contact: Office of Undergraduate Admissions. A video is available. Web: *www.nyu.edu/ugadmissions/*

NIAGARA UNIVERSITY A-3

Niagara University, NY 14109 (716) 286-8700
(800) 462-2111; Fax: (716) 286-8710

Full-time: 908 men, 1360 women	**Faculty:** 129; IIA, -$
Part-time: 67 men, 125 women	**Ph.D.s:** 93%
Graduate: 255 men, 563 women	**Student/Faculty:** 18 to 1
Year: semesters, summer session	**Tuition:** $15,300
Application Deadline: August 15	**Room & Board:** $6950
Freshman Class: 2481 applied, 2065 accepted, 598 enrolled	
SAT I Verbal/Math: 521/523	**ACT:** 21 **COMPETITIVE+**

Niagara University, founded in 1856 by the Vincentian fathers and brothers, is today a private, institution rooted in a Roman Catholic tradition. Programs offered include those in liberal arts, business, education, nursing, and travel, hotel, and restaurant administration. There are 4 undergraduate and 3 graduate schools. In addition to regional accreditation, Niagara has baccalaureate program accreditation with AACSB, ACCE, CSWE, NCATE, and NLN. The library contains 271,101 volumes, 78,311 microform items, and 772 audiovisual forms/CDs, and subscribes to 4700 periodicals. Computerized library services include the card catalog, interlibrary loans, and database searching. Special learning facilities include a learning resource center, art gallery, radio station, TV station, and 2 theaters, and a greenhouse. The 160-acre campus is in a suburban area 4 miles north of Niagara Falls, overlooking the Niagara River gorge, 20 miles north of Buffalo. Including residence halls, there are 25 buildings.

Student Life: 87% of undergraduates are from New York. Others are from 31 states, 10 foreign countries, and Canada. 75% are from public schools. 81% are white. 65% are Catholic; 18%, Protestant. The average age of freshmen is 18; all undergraduates, 21. 19% do not continue beyond their first year; 60% remain to graduate.

Housing: 1315 students can be accommodated in college housing, which includes single-sex and coed dormitories. In addition, there are honors houses, international, and special-interest houses. On-campus housing is guaranteed for all 4 years. 51% of students live on campus; of those, 75% remain on campus on weekends. All students may keep cars.

Activities: 2% of men belong to 2 national fraternities. There are no sororities. There are 78 groups on campus, including art, aviation, cheerleading, choir, chorale, computers, drama, drill team, ethnic, film, honors, international, musical theater, newspaper, pep band, political, professional, radio and TV, religious, social, social service, student government, and yearbook. Popular campus events include Orientation, CARE, and University Ball.

Sports: There are 7 intercollegiate sports for men and 6 for women, and 25 intramural sports for men and 25 for women. Facilities include a 3400-seat gym, a 6-lane swimming and diving pool, exercise and weight rooms, saunas and dance areas, outdoor tennis courts, baseball and soccer fields, basketball and racquetball courts, and multipurpose courts with an indoor track. Hiking and biking trails are nearby.

Disabled Students: 75% of the campus is accessible. Wheelchair ramps, elevators, special parking, specially equipped rest rooms, special class scheduling, lowered drinking fountains, and campus accommodation for the vision-impaired are available.

Services: Counseling and information services are available, as is tutoring in most subjects. There is a reader service for the blind, and remedial math, reading, and writing. Study skills development, note taking, and escort-assistance services are available, as are educational assistant services for the vision-impaired, educational/classroom assistance and machines for the hearing-impaired, and services for the learning disabled.

Campus Safety and Security: Measures include 24-hour foot and vehicle patrol, self-defense education, escort service, and informal discussions. There are pamphlets/posters/films, emergency telephones, lighted pathways/sidewalks, and a campus security advisory board.

Programs of Study: Niagara confers B.A., B.S., B.B.A., and B.F.A. degrees. Associate and master's degrees are also awarded. Bachelor's degrees are awarded in BIOLOGICAL SCIENCE (biochemistry, biology/biological science, and life science), BUSINESS (accounting, business administration and management, business economics, hotel/motel and restaurant management, human resources, marketing/retailing/merchandising, tourism, and transportation management), COMMUNICATIONS AND THE ARTS (communications, dramatic arts, English, French, and Spanish), COMPUTER AND PHYSICAL SCIENCE (chemistry, computer science, information sciences and systems, and mathematics), EDUCATION (elementary, English, foreign languages, mathematics, science, secondary, and social studies), ENGINEERING AND ENVIRONMENTAL DESIGN (preengineering), HEALTH PROFESSIONS (nursing, predentistry, and premedicine), SOCIAL SCIENCE (criminal justice, history, international studies, philosophy, political science/government, prelaw, psychology, religion, social science, social work, and sociology). Business, social sciences, and education are the strongest academically. Business administration, travel and tourism, and social services are the largest.

Required: To graduate, students must earn 120 to 126 credit hours and a GPA of at least 2.0; 60 to 66 such hours are required in the major, 20 in specific disciplines, and 20 in liberal arts classes. A comprehensive exam is required in some majors; a thesis is required of honor students and some majors.

Special: Niagara offers a Washington semester, a semester at the state capitol in Albany, on-campus work-study, internships in most majors with such companies as the Big 6 accounting firms and Walt Disney World, and co-op programs in all areas except nursing, education, and social work. Students may study abroad in 4 countries and cross-register through the Western New York Consortium. Accelerated degree programs in business and nursing, B.A.-B.S. degrees, dual majors, a 2-3 engineering program with the University of Detroit, nondegree study, credit for life, military, and work experience, pass/fail options, and research are also available. There is also an academic exploration program for undeclared majors. There are 14 national honor societies and a freshman honors program.

Faculty/Classroom: 63% of faculty are male; 37%, female. All teach undergraduates. No introductory courses are taught by graduate students. The average class size in an introductory lecture is 25 and in a regular course, 20.

Admissions: 83% of the 2001-2002 applicants were accepted. The SAT I scores for the 2001-2002 freshman class were: Verbal--40% below 500, 45% between 500 and 599, 14% between 600 and 700, and 1% above 700; Math--37% below 500, 46% between 500 and 599, 16% between 600 and 700, and 1% above 700. 32% of the current freshmen were in the top fifth of their class; 61% were in the top two fifths.

Requirements: The SAT I or ACT is required. In addition, applicants should be graduates of an accredited high school. The GED is accepted. The high school program should include 16 academic credits, with 4 in English and 2 each in foreign language, history, math, science, social studies, as well as academic electives. Science, math, and computer majors should have 3 credits each in math and science. A grade average of 80 is required. AP and CLEP credits are accepted. Important factors in the admissions decision are advanced placement or honor courses, parents or siblings attending the school, and recommendations by school officials. The university accepts applications on-line via ExPAN.

Procedure: Freshmen are admitted to all sessions. Entrance exams should be taken in the junior year or fall of the senior year. There are early decision and deferred admissions plans. Early decision applications should be filed by August 15; regular applications, by August 15 for fall entry and January 10 for spring entry. Notification is sent on a rolling basis. The fall 2001 application fee was $30.

Transfer: 137 transfer students enrolled in 2001-2002. Applicants must have a minimum GPA of 2.0 in travel, hotel, and restaurant administration, arts and sciences, and academic exploration (except for 2.25 in business and 2.5 for nursing and education majors) and submit all high school and college transcripts. The SAT I or ACT is recommended. 30 credits of 120 to 126 must be completed at Niagara.

Visiting: There are regularly scheduled orientations for prospective students, including individual interviews and campus tours. Other arrangements can be made individually, such as to attend a class, eat in the student cafeteria, and/or speak with a faculty member. There are guides for informal visits and visitors may sit in on classes and stay overnight. To schedule a visit, contact the Admissions Office appointment desk.

Financial Aid: In 2001-2002, 99% of all freshmen and 95% of continuing students received some form of financial aid. 82% of freshmen and 83% of continuing students received need-based aid. The average fresh-

man award was $13,689. Of that total, scholarships or need-based grants averaged $11,267 ($22,350 maximum); loans averaged $1974 ($4625 maximum); and work contracts averaged $448 ($2300 maximum). 21% of undergraduates work part time. Average annual earnings from campus work are $1592. The average financial indebtedness of the 2001 graduate was $17,606. Niagara is a member of CSS. The FAFSA is required. The fall application deadline is February 15.

International Students: There are 129 international students enrolled. The school actively recruits these students. They must score 500 on the written TOEFL.

Computers: The mainframe is a DEC MicroVAX 3800. There are 150 terminals/PCs available to students in several academic computing labs and in the academic computing center. All dorms are networked, and some rooms are tied in so students can access the system. All students may access the system 9 A.M. to 11 P.M. Monday to Thursday, 9 A.M. to 5 P.M. Friday, noon to 5 P.M. Saturday, and 3 P.M. to 10 P.M. Sunday. There are no time limits and no fees.

Graduates: In 2001, 528 bachelor's degrees were awarded. The most popular majors were commerce and accounting (23%), education (20%), and hospitality/tourism (9%). In an average class, 46% graduate in 4 years, 54% in 5 years, and 54% in 6 years. 139 companies recruited on campus in 2000-2001. Of the 2000 graduating class, 22% were enrolled in graduate school within 6 months of graduation and 76% were employed.

Admissions Contact: Mike Koropski, Director of Admissions. E-mail: *admissions@niagara.edu* Web: *niagara.edu*

NYACK COLLEGE

Nyack, NY 10960 — D-5

(845) 358-1710
(800) 336-9225; Fax: (845) 358-3047

Full-time: 685 men, 1032 women	**Faculty:** 71
Part-time: 68 men, 112 women	**Ph.D.s:** 62%
Graduate: 290 men, 267 women	**Student/Faculty:** 16 to 1
Year: semesters, summer session	**Tuition:** $12,740
Application Deadline: open	**Room & Board:** $5800
Freshman Class: 1023 applied, 688 accepted, 338 enrolled	
SAT I or ACT: required	**COMPETITIVE**

Nyack College, founded in 1882, is a private liberal arts institution affiliated with the Christian and Missionary Alliance.The enrollment figures in the above capsule include the Manhattan Center and Adult Degree Completion Program students. There is 1 graduate school. In addition to regional accreditation, Nyack has baccalaureate program accreditation with NASM. The 3 libraries contain 99,000 volumes and 208,000 microform items, and subscribe to 871 periodicals. Computerized library services include the card catalog, interlibrary loans, and database searching. Special learning facilities include a learning resource center and radio station. The 102-acre campus is in a suburban area 20 miles north of New York City. Including residence halls, there are 22 buildings.

Student Life: 67% of undergraduates are from New York. Others are from 42 states, 58 foreign countries, and Canada. 36% are white; 27% African American, 23% Hispanic. Most are Protestant. The average age of freshmen is 21; all undergraduates, 27. 35% do not continue beyond their first year; 46% remain to graduate.

Housing: 715 students can be accommodated in college housing, which includes single-sex dormitories and on-campus apartments. In addition, there are honors houses. On-campus housing is guaranteed for all 4 years. 81% of students live on campus. Alcohol is not permitted. All students may keep cars.

Activities: There are no fraternities or sororities. There are 19 groups on campus, including band, cheerleading, choir, chorale, drama, ethnic, handbell choir, honors, ladies' glee club, literary magazine, musical theater, newspaper, orchestra, professional, radio and TV, religious, social service, student government, and yearbook. Popular campus events include music festivals and the Cultural Events Series.

Sports: There are 5 intercollegiate sports for men and 5 for women. Facilities include a gym, soccer field, fitness center, training room, softball field, tennis courts, outdoor basketball courts, and a baseball field.

Disabled Students: 70% of the campus is accessible. Elevators, special parking, specially equipped rest rooms, and lowered drinking fountains are available.

Services: Counseling and information services are available, as is tutoring in every subject. There is a reader service for the blind.

Campus Safety and Security: Measures include 24-hour foot and vehicle patrol, escort service, pamphlets/posters/films, and lighted pathways/sidewalks.

Programs of Study: Nyack confers B.A., B.S., B.Mus., and S.M.B. degrees. Associate and master's degrees are also awarded. Bachelor's degrees are awarded in BUSINESS (accounting and business administration and management), COMMUNICATIONS AND THE ARTS (communications, English, music, music performance, music theory and composition, piano/organ, and voice), COMPUTER AND PHYSICAL SCIENCE (computer science and mathematics), EDUCATION (elementary, music, secondary, and teaching English as a second/foreign language (TESOL/TEFOL)), SOCIAL SCIENCE (biblical studies, crosscultural studies, history, interdisciplinary studies, missions, pastoral studies, philosophy, psychology, religion, religious education, religious music, social science, social work, and youth ministry). Psychology, education, and ministry-related programs are the largest.

Required: To graduate, students must complete 126 to 130 credits with a minimum GPA of 2.0 or 2.5 for education majors. General education and major requirements vary by degree program. Students must adhere to the college's standards of Christian living and behavior and complete Bible courses.

Special: Nyack offers internships, cooperative programs with other schools, study abroad in 6 countries, a semester in Hollywood for communications majors, dual and student-designed majors, independent study, nondegree study, a Washington semester, and pass/fail options. The business program provides advanced standing for the M.B.A. program at St. Thomas Aquinas College in Sparkill, NY. There is a freshman honors program.

Faculty/Classroom: 60% of faculty are male; 40%, female. 70% teach undergraduates. No introductory courses are taught by graduate students. The average class size in a laboratory is 15 and in a regular course, 20.

Admissions: 67% of the 2001-2002 applicants were accepted. The ACT scores for the 2001-2002 freshman class were: 42% below 21, 21% between 21 and 23, 19% between 24 and 26, 7% between 27 and 28, and 12% above 28. 23% of the current freshmen were in the top fifth of their class; 51% were in the top two fifths. 1 freshman graduated first in the class.

Requirements: The SAT I or ACT is required. High school graduation or its equivalent is essential. Completion of 16 academic credits is required; the college recommends 4 units of English, 3 of history or social science, 3 of any combination of math and science, 2 of a foreign language, and 4 of electives. Students must demonstrate sound Christian character through personal testimony and recommendations. An interview may be required. AP and CLEP credits are accepted.

Procedure: Freshmen are admitted fall and spring. Application deadlines are open. The fall 2001 application fee was $15. Notification is sent on a rolling basis.

Transfer: 101 transfer students enrolled in 2001-2002. Applicants must provide all transcripts from previous schools attended. 30 credits of 126 to 130 must be completed at Nyack.

Visiting: There are regularly scheduled orientations for prospective students. There are guides for informal visits and visitors may sit in on classes and stay overnight. To schedule a visit, contact the Office of Admissions.

Financial Aid: The FAFSA and parent and student tax returns, if selected for verification, are required.

International Students: There are 287 international students enrolled. The school actively recruits these students. They must score 550 on the written TOEFL and also take the SAT I or the ACT.

Computers: Some 125 PCs are available in computer labs, the libraries, and the resource center. Students may access e-mail to on- and off-campus addresses, as well as the Internet and Web. All students may access the system. There are no time limits and no fees.

Graduates: In 2001, 319 bachelor's degrees were awarded. The most popular majors were business (55%), philosophy/religion/theology (10%), and interdisciplinary studies (8%). In an average class, 35% graduate in 4 years, 45% in 5 years, and 46% in 6 years. 50 companies recruited on campus in 2000-2001.

Admissions Contact: Miguel Sanchez, Director of Admissions. A video is available. E-mail: *enroll@nyack.edu* Web: *www.nyackcollege.edu*

PACE UNIVERSITY

New York, NY 10038-1508 — D-5

(212) 346-1225 or (914) 773-3321
(800) 874-PACE; Fax: (212) 346-1040 or (914) 773-3851

Full-time: 2736 men, 4095 women	**Faculty:** 428; I, +$
Part-time: 849 men, 1233 women	**Ph.D.s:** 82%
Graduate: 2166 men, 2419 women	**Student/Faculty:** 16 to 1
Year: semesters, summer session	**Tuition:** $17,030
Application Deadline: open	**Room & Board:** $7170
Freshman Class: 7072 applied, 5362 accepted, 1644 enrolled	
SAT I Verbal: 514	**ACT:** 22 **COMPETITIVE**

Pace University, founded in 1906, is a private institution offering programs in arts and sciences, business, nursing, education, and computer and information science on 3 campuses, with undergraduate studies in New York City and Pleasantville and graduate studies in White Plains. There are 5 undergraduate and 5 graduate schools. In addition to regional accreditation, Pace has baccalaureate program accreditation with AACSB, CCNE, and CSAB. The 3 libraries contain 786,132 volumes, 71,030 microform items, and 976 audiovisual forms/CDs, and subscribe to 2637 periodicals. Computerized library services include the card catalog, interlibrary loans, and database searching. Special learning facilities include a learning resource center, radio station, TV station, 2 art galleries, a performing arts center, biological research labs, an environmental center, a language lab, and computer labs. There is an urban campus in downtown New York City and a 200-acre suburban campus in Pleasantville/Briarcliff Manor. Including residence halls, there are 41 buildings.

Student Life: 75% of undergraduates are from New York. Others are from 46 states, 58 foreign countries, and Canada. 70% are from public schools. 42% are white; 11%, African American; 11%, Asian American; 11%, Hispanic. 39% are Catholic; 21% claim no religious affiliation; 16%, Protestant; 13%, Jewish. The average age of freshmen is 20; all undergraduates, 24. 24% do not continue beyond their first year; 54% remain to graduate.

Housing: 2350 students can be accommodated in college housing, which includes coed dormitories, on-campus apartments, and off-campus apartments. In addition, there are honors houses, special-interest houses, and a wellness floor. 77% of students commute. All students may keep cars.

Activities: 10% of men belong to 2 local and 6 national fraternities; 10% of women belong to 10 local and 2 national sororities. There are 100 groups on campus, including art, cheerleading, chorus, computers, dance, debate, drama, ethnic, film, gay, honors, international, literary magazine, musical theater, newspaper, photography, political, professional, radio and TV, religious, social, social service, student government, and yearbook. Popular campus events include Carribbean Festival, Spirit Night, and Chill Out Day.

Sports: There are 9 intercollegiate sports for men and 9 for women, and 4 intramural sports for men and 4 for women. Facilities include the Civic Center Gym in New York City and gyms, tennis courts, and playing fields at the Pleasantville/Briarcliff Manor campus.

Disabled Students: 70% of the campus is accessible. Wheelchair ramps, elevators, special parking, special class scheduling, lowered drinking fountains, lowered telephones, and other facilities that vary by campus are available.

Services: Counseling and information services are available, as is tutoring in every subject. There is remedial math, reading, and writing. All services are provided in the University's center for academic excellence.

Campus Safety and Security: Measures include 24-hour foot and vehicle patrol, escort service, shuttle buses, and informal discussions. There are pamphlets/posters/films, emergency telephones, and lighted pathways/sidewalks.

Programs of Study: Pace confers B.A., B.S., B.B.A., B.F.A., and B.S.N. degrees. Associate, master's, and doctoral degrees are also awarded. Bachelor's degrees are awarded in BIOLOGICAL SCIENCE (biology/biological science), BUSINESS (accounting, banking and finance, business administration and management, business economics, international business management, and marketing/retailing/merchandising), COMMUNICATIONS AND THE ARTS (communications, dramatic arts, English, fine arts, French, journalism, Spanish, and theater design), COMPUTER AND PHYSICAL SCIENCE (chemistry, computer science, information sciences and systems, mathematics, and physics), EDUCATION (business, early childhood, elementary, and secondary), ENGINEERING AND ENVIRONMENTAL DESIGN (industrial administration/management), HEALTH PROFESSIONS (medical laboratory technology, nursing, physician's assistant, predentistry, premedicine, and speech pathology/audiology), SOCIAL SCIENCE (anthropology, criminal justice, economics, history, political science/government, psychology, social science, and sociology). Accounting is the strongest academically. Business and finance are the largest.

Required: To graduate, students must complete 128 to 133 credit hours, including 32 to 50 in the major, with a minimum GPA of 2.0. A core curriculum of 60 credits and an introductory computer science course are required.

Special: Internships, study abroad, a Washington semester, and a cooperative education program in all majors are available. Pace also offers accelerated degree programs, B.A.-B.S. degrees, dual majors, general studies degrees, and 3-2 engineering degrees with Manhattan College and Rensselaer Polytechnic Institute. Credit for life, military, and work experience, nondegree study, and pass/fail options are available. There are 15 national honor societies and a freshman honors program.

Faculty/Classroom: 60% of faculty are male; 40%, female. 84% teach undergraduates and 24% do research. No introductory courses are taught by graduate students. The average class size in an introductory lecture is 35; in a laboratory, 11; and in a regular course, 23.

Admissions: 76% of the 2001-2002 applicants were accepted. The SAT I scores for the 2001-2002 freshman class were: Verbal--38% below 500, 49% between 500 and 599, 12% between 600 and 700, and 1% above 700; Math--29% below 500, 48% between 500 and 599, 22% between 600 and 700, and 1% above 700. The ACT scores were 35% below 21, 41% between 21 and 23, 12% between 24 and 26, and 12% between 27 and 28. 43% of the current freshmen were in the top fifth of their class; 74% were in the top two fifths.

Requirements: The SAT I or ACT is required. In addition, applicants should be graduates of an accredited secondary school, with at least 16 academic credits, including 4 in English, 3 to 4 each in math, science, and history, and 2 to 3 in foreign language. The GED is accepted. An essay and an interview are recommended. A GPA of 3.0 is required. AP and CLEP credits are accepted. Important factors in the admissions decision are advanced placement or honor courses, recommendations by school officials, and leadership record. Applications are accepted on computer disk via College Board exam or CollegeView and on-line through Pace's web site.

Procedure: Freshmen are admitted fall and spring. Entrance exams should be taken by December of the student's senior year. There are early admissions and deferred admissions plans. Application deadlines are open. Notification is sent on a rolling basis. The fall 2001 application fee was $45.

Transfer: 685 transfer students enrolled in 2001-2002. Applicants are admitted in the fall or spring. A college GPA of 2.5 is required. Grades of C or better transfer for credit. A maximum of 68 credits will be accepted from a 2-year school. 32 credits of 128 must be completed at Pace.

Visiting: There are regularly scheduled orientations for prospective students, consisting of student-for-a-day programs and overnight visits by appointment. There are guides for informal visits and visitors may sit in on classes and stay overnight. To schedule a visit, contact the Office of Undergraduate Admission at *ugnyc@pace.edu* or *infoctr@pace.edu*

Financial Aid: In 2001-2002, 78% of all freshmen and 67% of continuing students received some form of financial aid. 94% of freshmen received need-based aid. The average freshman award was $9747. Average annual earnings from campus work are $3600. The average financial indebtedness of the 2001 graduate was $13,520. The FAFSA is required. The fall application deadline is February 15.

International Students: There are 482 international students enrolled. The school actively recruits these students. They must score 550 on the written TOEFL and also take the university's own test.

Computers: The mainframe is an IBM S/390 Model MP 3000H30. There are about 850 terminals on both campuses and at the midtown center. All students may access the system 24 hours a day. There are no time limits and no fees.

Graduates: In 2001, 1699 bachelor's degrees were awarded. The most popular majors were computer science information systems (17%), finance (13%), and accounting (10%). In an average class, 1% graduate in 3 years, 35% in 4 years, 52% in 5 years, and 56% in 6 years. 412 companies recruited on campus in 2000-2001. Of the 2000 graduating class, 81% were employed within 6 months of graduation.

Admissions Contact: Richard P. Alvarez (NYC) and Joanna Broda, Directors of Undergraduate Admissions. E-mail: *infoctr@pace.edu*
Web: *www.pace.edu*

PARSONS SCHOOL OF DESIGN — D-5
New York, NY 10011 — (877) 528-3321; (877) 528-3324; (212) 229-5166

Full-time: 551 men, 1573 women	**Faculty:** 56
Part-time: 36 men, 151 women	**Ph.D.s:** n/av
Graduate: 142 men, 280 women	**Student/Faculty:** n/av
Year: semesters, summer session	**Tuition:** $22,630
Application Deadline: open	**Room & Board:** $9612
Freshman Class: 1690 applied, 738 accepted, 356 enrolled	
SAT I or ACT: required	**SPECIAL**

Parsons School of Design, founded in 1896, is a private professional art school and is part of the New School for Social Research. In addition to regional accreditation, Parsons has baccalaureate program accreditation with NASAD. The 2 libraries contain 177,000 volumes and 5000 audiovisual forms/CDs, and subscribe to 230 periodicals. Computerized library services include the card catalog and database searching. Special learning facilities include an art gallery. The 2-acre campus is in an urban area in Manhattan's Greenwich Village. Including residence halls, there are 8 buildings.

Student Life: 52% of undergraduates are from New York. Others are from 49 states, 39 foreign countries, and Canada. 80% are from public schools. 32% are white; 29% foreign nationals; 20% Asian American. The average age of freshmen is 19; all undergraduates, 23.

Housing: 700 students can be accommodated in college housing, which includes coed dormitories and off-campus apartments. On-campus housing is available on a first-come, first-served basis and is available on a lottery system for upperclassmen. Priority is given to out-of-town students. Alcohol is not permitted. All students may keep cars.

Activities: There are no fraternities or sororities. There are some groups and organizations on campus, including ethnic, gay, international, literary magazine, political, religious, social, and student government. Popular campus events include the Fashion Critics Award Show and annual senior shows.

Sports: There is no sports program at Parsons.

Disabled Students: 95% of the campus is accessible. Wheelchair ramps, elevators, and specially equipped rest rooms are available.

Services: Counseling and information services are available, as is tutoring in some subjects, including English and art history. There is remedial reading and writing.

Campus Safety and Security: Measures include informal discussions and pamphlets/posters/films.
Programs of Study: Parsons confers B.A.-B.F.A., B.B.A., and B.F.A. degrees. Associate and master's degrees are also awarded. Bachelor's degrees are awarded in BUSINESS (marketing/retailing/merchandising), COMMUNICATIONS AND THE ARTS (advertising, design, fine arts, graphic design, illustration, photography, and studio art), ENGINEERING AND ENVIRONMENTAL DESIGN (architectural engineering and interior design), SOCIAL SCIENCE (fashion design and technology). Communication design, illustration, and fashion design are the largest.
Required: To graduate, students must complete 134 credit hours, including 97 in the major, with a minimum GPA of 2.0. Parsons requires a minimum of 30 credits in liberal arts and 12 in art history.
Special: Students may cross-register at the New School for Social Research, Cooper Union, and Pratt Institute. Internships are required for some majors. Students may study abroad at the Parsons campus in Paris or in 4 other countries. The 5-year combined B.A.-B.F.A. degree requires 180 credits for graduation. A mobility semester or year at any AICAD school is available, and interdisciplinary majors, including architecture and environmental design and design marketing, are possible.
Faculty/Classroom: 89% of faculty teach undergraduates. No introductory courses are taught by graduate students. The average class size in an introductory lecture is 30 and in a regular course, 17.
Admissions: 44% of the 2001-2002 applicants were accepted. The SAT I scores for the 2001-2002 freshman class were: Verbal--43% below 500, 32% between 500 and 599, 19% between 600 and 700, and 6% above 700; Math--32% below 500, 40% between 500 and 599, 22% between 600 and 700, and 6% above 700.
Requirements: The SAT I or ACT is required. In addition, applicants must be graduates of an accredited secondary school. The GED is accepted. Applicants should have completed 4 years each of art, English, history, and social studies. A portfolio and home exam are required, and an interview is recommended. AP credits are accepted. Important factors in the admissions decision are evidence of special talent, advanced placement or honor courses, and personality/intangible qualities.
Procedure: Freshmen are admitted fall and spring. Entrance exams should be taken by the spring of the junior year. There is an early admissions plan. Application deadlines are open. Application fee is $40. Notification is sent on a rolling basis. A waiting list is an active part of the admissions procedure.
Transfer: 420 transfer students enrolled in 2001-2002. Applicants will receive credit for grade C work or better in college courses that are similar in content, purpose, and standards to the courses offered at Parsons. A high school transcript is required for undergraduates, and the SAT I or ACT is recommended. All students must present a portfolio and home exam. Transfers are admitted in the fall or spring. 67 credits of 134 must be completed at Parsons.
Visiting: There are guides for informal visits. To schedule a visit, contact the Office of Admissions.
Financial Aid: In 2001-2002, 70% of all freshmen and 59% of continuing students received some form of financial aid. 64% of freshmen and 58% of continuing students received need-based aid. The average freshman award was $12,684. The average financial indebtedness of the 2001 graduate was $23,450. Parsons is a member of CSS. The FAFSA is required. International students must file an institutional application. The fall application deadline is March 1.
International Students: The school actively recruits these students. They must score 550 on the written TOEFL.
Computers: 800 Macs/PCs are available, as well as graphical software, e-mail and Internet access, and AutoCAD and fashion-design labs. All students may access the system. There are no time limits and no fees. It is strongly recommended that all students have a personal computer.
Graduates: In 2001, 198 bachelor's degrees were awarded. The most popular majors were visual and performing arts (94%) and architecture (6%). In an average class, 46% graduate in 4 years, 56% in 5 years, and 61% in 6 years.
Admissions Contact: Nadine M. Bourgeois, Assistant Dean and Director of Admissions. E-mail: *parsadm@newschool.edu*
Web: *www.parsons.edu*

POLYTECHNIC UNIVERSITY/BROOKLYN D-5
Brooklyn, NY 11201-2999 (718) 260-3100
POLYTEC; Fax: (718) 260-3136

Full-time: 1062 men, 286 women	**Faculty:** 105; I, -$
Part-time: 96 men, 21 women	**Ph.D.s:** 93%
Graduate: 815 men, 221 women	**Student/Faculty:** 8 to 1
Year: semesters, summer session	**Tuition:** $22,940
Application Deadline: open	**Room & Board:** $10,150

Freshman Class: 1573 applied, 1079 accepted, 454 enrolled
SAT I Verbal/Math: 590/660 **HIGHLY COMPETITIVE**

Polytechnic University, founded in 1854, is a private, multicampus university offering undergraduate and graduate programs through the divisions of arts and sciences, engineering, and management. In addition to regional accreditation, Brooklyn Poly has baccalaureate program accreditation with ABET and CSAB. The library contains 197,302 volumes and 56,628 microform items, and subscribes to 821 periodicals. Computerized library services include the card catalog, interlibrary loans, and database searching. Special learning facilities include a learning resource center and radio station. The 3-acre campus is in an urban area 5 minutes from downtown Manhattan. Including residence halls, there are 6 buildings.
Student Life: 92% of undergraduates are from New York. Others are from 10 states, 19 foreign countries, and Canada. 83% are from public schools. 41% are Asian American; 27% white, 10% African American. The average age of freshmen is 19; all undergraduates, 21. 19% do not continue beyond their first year; 52% remain to graduate.
Housing: 400 students can be accommodated in college housing, which includes coed dormitories and fraternity houses. On-campus housing is available on a first-come, first-served basis. Priority is given to out-of-town students. 97% of students commute. Alcohol is not permitted. No one may keep cars.
Activities: 12% of men and about 3% of women belong to 2 local and 3 national fraternities; 3% of women belong to 1 national sorority. There are 60 groups on campus, including arts and music, chess, computers, ethnic, film, honors, international, literary magazine, newspaper, photography, professional, radio and TV, religious, social, social service, student government, and yearbook. Popular campus events include Chinese New Year, film festivals, and International Food Fair.
Sports: There are 7 intercollegiate sports for men and 7 for women, and 7 intramural sports for men and 7 for women. Facilities include soccer, lacrosse, and baseball fields, and 2 student centers.
Disabled Students: 70% of the campus is accessible. Wheelchair ramps, elevators, special parking, specially equipped rest rooms, lowered drinking fountains, and lowered telephones are available.
Services: Counseling and information services are available, as is tutoring in every subject. There is remedial writing.
Campus Safety and Security: Measures include 24-hour foot and vehicle patrol, informal discussions, pamphlets/posters/films, and emergency telephones. There are lighted pathways/sidewalks.
Programs of Study: Brooklyn Poly confers the B.S. degree. Master's and doctoral degrees are also awarded. Bachelor's degrees are awarded in COMMUNICATIONS AND THE ARTS (technical and business writing), COMPUTER AND PHYSICAL SCIENCE (chemistry, computer science, information sciences and systems, mathematics, and physics), ENGINEERING AND ENVIRONMENTAL DESIGN (chemical engineering, civil engineering, computer engineering, electrical/electronics engineering, and mechanical engineering), SOCIAL SCIENCE (humanities, liberal arts/general studies, and social science). Engineering, management, and physical sciences are the strongest academically. Electrical engineering, computer engineering, and computer science are the largest.
Required: Students must complete all university and departmental course requirements, including 24 credits in humanities/social science, 16 in math, 12 in chemistry/physics, 4 in computers with Pascal, and 4 in engineering design. A total of 124 to 128 credits must be earned, with 32 in the major, and a minimum GPA of 2.0 is required to graduate. A senior design project is also required.
Special: Cooperative programs are available in all majors. Opportunities are provided for internships, work-study programs, study abroad, accelerated degree programs in engineering and computer science, dual majors, student-designed majors, and nondegree study. There are 9 national honor societies, a freshman honors program, and 3 departmental honors programs.
Faculty/Classroom: 79% of faculty are male; 21%, female. 49% teach undergraduates. No introductory courses are taught by graduate students. The average class size in an introductory lecture is 24; in a laboratory, 19; and in a regular course, 30.
Admissions: 69% of the 2001-2002 applicants were accepted. The SAT I scores for the 2001-2002 freshman class were: Verbal--4% below 500, 57% between 500 and 599, 35% between 600 and 700, and 3% above 700; Math--13% between 500 and 599, 62% between 600 and 700, and 25% above 700.
Requirements: The SAT I is required. Graduation from an accredited secondary school is required; a GED will be accepted. Applicants must submit a minimum of 16 credit hours, including 4 each in English, math and science, and 1 each in foreign language, art, music, and social studies. SAT II: Subject tests in writing, math I or II, and chemistry or physics are recommended. An essay and an interview are recommended. AP credits are accepted. Important factors in the admissions decision are advanced placement or honor courses, leadership record, and evidence of special talent. Applications are accepted on computer disk in a readable format such as Word, WordPerfect, or ASCII and on-line at the school's web site.
Procedure: Freshmen are admitted fall, spring, and summer. Entrance exams should be taken by November of the senior year. There is a deferred admissions plan. Application deadlines are open. The fall 2001 application fee was $40. Notification is sent on a rolling basis.
Transfer: 56 transfer students enrolled in 2001-2002. Transfer applicants must have a 2.75 cumulative GPA. Students with fewer than 30

credits must submit SAT I scores and secondary school transcripts in addition to official college-level transcripts. 36 credits of 124 to 128 must be completed at Brooklyn Poly.

Visiting: There are regularly scheduled orientations for prospective students, including a keynote speaker, major presentations, financial aid and scholarship sessions, and student life and career services sessions. There are guides for informal visits and visitors may stay overnight. To schedule a visit, contact the Dean of Admissions.

Financial Aid: In 2001-2002, 96% of all freshmen and 90% of continuing students received some form of financial aid. 76% of freshmen and 73% of continuing students received need-based aid. The average freshman award was $18,460. Of that total, scholarships or need-based grants averaged $10,029 ($22,050 maximum); loans averaged $4586 ($6550 maximum); and work contracts averaged $1689 ($2000 maximum). 14% of undergraduates work part time. Average annual earnings from campus work are $1500. The average financial indebtedness of the 2001 graduate was $13,490. The FAFSA and the college's own financial statement are required. The fall application deadline is March 1.

International Students: There are 54 international students enrolled. The school actively recruits these students. They must score 500 on the written TOEFL and also take the SAT I or the ACT.

Computers: There are also 100 Pentium Win NT4 microcomputers and 22 Pentium/Pentium Pro workstations available for student use, located primarily in 4 main computer labs. All students may access the system. 24-hour dial-up service is available. Computer labs are open 13 hours a day. There are no time limits and no fees. All students are required to have personal computers. An IBM Think Pad purchased through the university is recommended.

Graduates: In 2001, 310 bachelor's degrees were awarded. The most popular majors were computer science (41%), computer engineering (18%), and electrical engineering (16%). In an average class, 1% graduate in 3 years, 33% in 4 years, 48% in 5 years, and 52% in 6 years. 150 companies recruited on campus in 2000-2001. Of the 2000 graduating class, 5% were enrolled in graduate school within 6 months of graduation and 84% were employed.

Admissions Contact: Steven Kerge, Dean of Admissions.
E-mail: *admitme@poly.edu* Web: *www.poly.edu*

PRATT INSTITUTE
Brooklyn, NY 11205 — D-5
(718) 636-3669
(800) 331-0834; (718) 636-3670

Full-time: 1250 men, 1200 women	**Faculty:** 67; IIA, --$
Part-time: 200 men, 200 women	**Ph.D.s:** 64%
Graduate: 500 men, 855 women	**Student/Faculty:** 37 to 1
Year: 4-1-4, summer session	**Tuition:** $19,550
Application Deadline: February 1	**Room & Board:** $8000
Freshman Class: n/av	
SAT I or ACT: required	**SPECIAL**

Pratt Institute, founded in 1887, is a private institution offering undergraduate and graduate programs in architecture, art and design education, art history, industrial/interior/communication design, fine arts, design management, arts and cultural management, writing for publication, performance and media, and professional studies. Figures in the above capsule are approximate. There are 2 undergraduate and 3 graduate schools. In addition to regional accreditation, Pratt has baccalaureate program accreditation with FIDER, NAAB, and NASAD. The library contains 208,000 volumes, 50,000 microform items, and 3500 audiovisual forms/CDs, and subscribes to 500 periodicals. Computerized library services include the card catalog and database searching. Special learning facilities include a learning resource center, art gallery, radio station, and bronze foundry and metal forge. The 25-acre campus is in an urban area 25 miles east of downtown Manhattan. Including residence halls, there are 23 buildings.

Student Life: 50% of undergraduates are from New York. Others are from 48 states, 65 foreign countries, and Canada. 81% are from public schools. 55% are white; 13% Asian American; 10% African American. The average age of freshmen is 19; all undergraduates, 23. 8% do not continue beyond their first year; 65% remain to graduate.

Housing: 1180 students can be accommodated in college housing, which includes single-sex and coed dormitories, on-campus apartments, and married-student housing. In addition, there are honors houses. On-campus housing is guaranteed for the freshman year only, is available on a first-come, first-served basis, and is available on a lottery system for upperclassmen. Priority is given to out-of-town students. 55% of students live on campus; of those, 80% remain on campus on weekends. All students may keep cars.

Activities: 3% of men belong to 1 local and 1 national fraternity; 1% of women belong to 1 local sorority. There are 60 groups on campus, including art, cheerleading, chess, drama, ethnic, film, gay, honors, international, literary magazine, musical theater, newspaper, professional, radio and TV, religious, social, student government, and yearbook. Popular campus events include Springfest, International Food Fair, and Holiday Ball.

Sports: There are 6 intercollegiate sports for men and 4 for women, and 3 intramural sports for men and 1 for women. Facilities include an activities resource center containing 5 indoor tennis courts, a 200-meter indoor track, volleyball and basketball courts, a weight room, and 2 dance studios.

Disabled Students: 75% of the campus is accessible. Wheelchair ramps, elevators, special parking, specially equipped rest rooms, lowered drinking fountains, and specially equipped residence hall spaces are available.

Services: Counseling and information services are available, as is tutoring in some subjects, including math, English, science, social science, and art history. There is a reader service for the blind and individual tutoring and testing services are also available.

Campus Safety and Security: Measures include 24-hour foot and vehicle patrol, escort service, shuttle buses, and informal discussions. There are pamphlets/posters/films, emergency telephones, lighted pathways/sidewalks, and trained security officers.

Programs of Study: Pratt confers B.Arch., B.F.A., B.I.D., and B.P.S. degrees. Associate and master's degrees are also awarded. Bachelor's degrees are awarded in COMMUNICATIONS AND THE ARTS (art history and appreciation, communications, creative writing, film arts, fine arts, industrial design, and photography), EDUCATION (art), ENGINEERING AND ENVIRONMENTAL DESIGN (architecture, computer graphics, construction management, and interior design), SOCIAL SCIENCE (fashion design and technology). Fine arts, industrial design, and communications design are the strongest academically. Architecture and communications design are the largest.

Required: The number of credits needed for graduation varies with the major, but a minimum of 132 is required, one quarter of which must be in liberal arts. Undergraduates must maintain a GPA of 2.0. All students must take 13 credits (15 for architecture majors) of liberal arts electives, 6 credits each of social sciences or philosophy, English, and cultural history, and 3 credits of science.

Special: Pratt offers co-op programs with the East Coast Consortium (art and design schools) and cross-registration with St. John's College and Queen's College. Internships, study abroad in 4 countries, accelerated degree programs, work-study programs, dual majors, credit for work experience, nondegree study, and pass/fail options are available. There are 4 national honor societies.

Faculty/Classroom: 65% of faculty are male; 35%, female. 92% teach undergraduates and 1% do research. No introductory courses are taught by graduate students. The average class size in an introductory lecture is 22; in a laboratory, 20; and in a regular course, 15.

Requirements: The SAT I or ACT is required. In addition, SAT II: Subject tests in writing and mathematics level I or II are recommended for architecture applicants. Applicants must be graduates of an accredited secondary school. The GED is accepted. Students should have completed 4 years of English, 3 of math, and 2 each of science, social studies, and history. A portfolio is required, as is an interview for all applicants who live within 100 miles of Pratt. Applications are accepted on-line at the school's web site. A GPA of 3.0 is required. AP and CLEP credits are accepted. Important factors in the admissions decision are evidence of special talent, advanced placement or honor courses, and recommendations by school officials.

Procedure: Freshmen are admitted fall and spring. Entrance exams should be taken by November of the senior year. There is an early decision plan. A waiting list is an active part of the admissions procedure. Check with the school for current application deadlines.

Transfer: 302 transfer students enrolled in a recent year. Applicants should present college transcripts and recommendations. Students with fewer than 30 college credits must submit the SAT I or ACT scores. All transfer applicants without an associate degree must submit high school transcripts as well. A portfolio is required for architecture and art and design students. An interview is recommended. 48 credits of 132 must be completed at Pratt.

Visiting: There are regularly scheduled orientations for prospective students, including a campus tour, schoolwide presentations, departmental presentations, and financial aid workshops. There are guides for informal visits and visitors may sit in on classes and stay overnight. To schedule a visit, contact the Office of Admissions.

Financial Aid: In a recent year, 75% of continuing students received some form of financial aid and 70% of continuing students received need-based aid. Pratt is a member of CSS. The CSS/Profile or FAFSA, the college's own financial statement, and the parents' and student's tax returns are required.

International Students: There are usually about 750 international students enrolled. The school actively recruits these students. They must score 500 on the written TOEFL and also take the college's own test.

Computers: The mainframe is a DEC VAX 6210, it may be reached via 12 VT340 terminals in the engineering lab or by dial-up modem. All students may access the system 24-hours a day, 7 days a week. There are no time limits and no fees. It is strongly recommended that all students have a personal computer.

Admissions Contact: Judith Aaron, Vice President for Enrollment. A video is available. E-mail: *jaaron@pratt.edu* Web: *www.pratt.edu*

PURCHASE COLLEGE, SUNY
(See State University of New York/College at Purchase)

REGENTS COLLEGE
(See Excelsior College)

RENSSELAER POLYTECHNIC INSTITUTE D-3

Troy, NY 12180-3590 (518) 276-6216
(800) 448-6562; Fax: (518) 276-4072

Full-time: 3942 men, 1244 women	**Faculty:** 356; I, av$
Part-time: 41 men, 45 women	**Ph.D.s:** 98%
Graduate: 2046 men, 788 women	**Student/Faculty:** 15 to 1
Year: semesters, summer session	**Tuition:** $25,555
Application Deadline: January 1	**Room & Board:** $8308
Freshman Class: 5542 applied, 3748 accepted, 1112 enrolled	
SAT I Verbal/Math: 625/683	**ACT:** 26

HIGHLY COMPETITIVE+

Rensselaer Polytechnic Institute, founded in 1824, is a private institution that emphasizes technology in its Schools of Engineering, Architecture, Management, Humanities, Social Sciences, and Science. There are 5 undergraduate and 5 graduate schools. In addition to regional accreditation, Rensselaer has baccalaureate program accreditation with AACSB, ABET, and NAAB. The 2 libraries contain 309,171 volumes and 91,435 audiovisual forms/CDs, and subscribe to 3112 periodicals. Computerized library services include the card catalog, interlibrary loans, and database searching. Special learning facilities include a learning resource center, art gallery, radio station, and observatory. The 262-acre campus is in a suburban area 10 miles north of Albany. Including residence halls, there are 185 buildings.

Student Life: 51% of undergraduates are from New York. Others are from 49 states, 81 foreign countries, and Canada. 78% are from public schools. 70% are white; 12%, Asian American. The average age of freshmen is 18; all undergraduates, 21. 9% do not continue beyond their first year; 77% remain to graduate.

Housing: 2933 students can be accommodated in college housing, which includes single-sex and coed dormitories, on-campus apartments, married-student housing, fraternity houses, and sorority houses. In addition, there are special-interest houses and a Black cultural center. On-campus housing is guaranteed for the freshman year only, is available on a first-come, first-served basis, and is available on a lottery system for upperclassmen. 55% of students live on campus. Upperclassmen may keep cars.

Activities: 30% of men and about 1% of women belong to 1 local fraternity and 28 national fraternities; 17% of women belong to 1 local sorority and 4 national sororities. There are 170 groups on campus, including art, band, cheerleading, chess, chorale, chorus, computers, dance, drama, drill team, ethnic, gay, honors, international, jazz band, literary magazine, musical theater, newspaper, orchestra, pep band, photography, political, professional, radio and TV, religious, social, social service, student government, symphony, and yearbook. Popular campus events include Grand Marshal Week, International Festival, and Activities Fair.

Sports: There are 12 intercollegiate sports for men and 11 for women, and 22 intramural sports for men and 21 for women. Facilities include a 5300-seat field house, 2 pools, a stadium, 2 gyms, a sports and recreation center, several playing fields, 2 weight rooms, 6 tennis courts, 7 handball/squash courts, an artificial turf field, an indoor track, an ice hockey rink, and a fitness center.

Disabled Students: 55% of the campus is accessible. Wheelchair ramps, elevators, special parking, specially equipped rest rooms, special class scheduling, lowered drinking fountains, and lowered telephones are available.

Services: Counseling and information services are available, as is tutoring in every subject. There is a reader service for the blind and a writing center.

Campus Safety and Security: Measures include 24-hour foot and vehicle patrol, self-defense education, escort service, and shuttle buses. There are informal discussions, pamphlets/posters/films, emergency telephones, lighted pathways/sidewalks, card-access residence halls, on-campus bicycle patrol, and a student volunteer program.

Programs of Study: Rensselaer confers B.S. and B.Arch. degrees. Master's and doctoral degrees are also awarded. Bachelor's degrees are awarded in BIOLOGICAL SCIENCE (biochemistry, biology/biological science, and biophysics), BUSINESS (management information systems, and management science), COMMUNICATIONS AND THE ARTS (communications and media arts), COMPUTER AND PHYSICAL SCIENCE (chemistry, computer science, geology, mathematics, physics, and science technology), ENGINEERING AND ENVIRONMENTAL DESIGN (aeronautical engineering, architecture, biomedical engineering, chemical engineering, civil engineering, computer engineering, construction engineering, electrical/electronics engineering, engineering, engineering physics, environmental engineering, industrial engineering, materials engineering, mechanical engineering, and nuclear engineering), HEALTH PROFESSIONS (predentistry and premedicine), SOCIAL SCIENCE (economics, interdisciplinary studies, philosophy, prelaw, and psychology). Mechanical engineering, electrical engineering, and computer and systems engineering are the strongest academically. General engineering, management, and computer science are the largest.

Required: For graduation, students must earn at least 124 credits in all majors except engineering and B.S. architecture (128 needed) and the B.Arch. program (168 needed). The core curriculum includes 24 credits in physical, life, and engineering sciences and 24 credits in humanities and social sciences. Students must maintain a minimum GPA of 1.8 and must fulfill a writing requirement.

Special: Rensselaer offers an exchange program with Williams and Harvey Mudd Colleges and cross-registration with 14 regional colleges and universities. Co-op programs, internships, study abroad in several countries, and pass/fail options are available. Students may pursue dual and student-designed majors, a 3-2 engineering degree, and accelerated 4-year B.S.-M.S. degrees in engineering, computer science, geophysics, and math. Continuing education programs are broadcast via TV satellite to various industrial locations. There are 14 national honor societies, and 3 departmental honors programs.

Faculty/Classroom: 85% of faculty are male; 15%, female. No introductory courses are taught by graduate students. The average class size in an introductory lecture is 250; in a laboratory, 25; and in a regular course, 24.

Admissions: 68% of the 2001-2002 applicants were accepted. The SAT I scores for the 2001-2002 freshman class were: Verbal--4% below 500, 29% between 500 and 599, 50% between 600 and 700, and 17% above 700; Math--7% between 500 and 599, 50% between 600 and 700, and 43% above 700. The ACT scores were 4% below 21, 20% between 21 and 23, 32% between 24 and 26, 24% between 27 and 28, and 20% above 28. 84% of the current freshmen were in the top fifth of their class; 97% were in the top two fifths. 53 freshmen graduated first in their class.

Requirements: The SAT I or ACT is required. In addition, SAT II: Subject tests in writing, math, and science are recommended (required for accelerated-program applicants). Applicants must be graduates of an accredited secondary school and have completed 4 years each of English, math (through precalculus), and science (including chemistry and physics), and 3 years of social studies. An essay is required. Architecture and electronic arts applicants must submit a portfolio. AP credits are accepted. Important factors in the admissions decision are advanced placement or honor courses, recommendations by school officials, and leadership record. Rensselaer offers its application for use on PC systems; an application can be accessed on-line from the school's web site.

Procedure: Freshmen are admitted fall and spring. Entrance exams should be taken in the junior or senior year. There are early decision and deferred admissions plans. Early decision applications should be filed by November 15; regular applications, by January 1 for fall entry and November 1 for spring entry, along with a $50 fee. Notification of early decision is sent December 19; regular decision, March 15. 183 early decision candidates were accepted for the 2001-2002 class.

Transfer: 145 transfer students enrolled in 2001-2002. The SAT I or ACT is required for applicants with fewer than 30 credits. All students are encouraged to have an interview and must present faculty recommendations; B.Arch. applicants must present a portfolio. Grades of C or better transfer for credit. 48 credits of 124 must be completed at Rensselaer.

Visiting: There are regularly scheduled orientations for prospective students. There are guides for informal visits and visitors may sit in on classes and stay overnight. To schedule a visit, contact the Admissions Office at *admissions@rpi.edu*

Financial Aid: In a recent year, 86% of all students received some form of aid. 60% of freshmen and 62% of continuing students received need-based aid. The average freshman award was $19,375. Of that total, scholarships or need-based grants averaged $14,961; loans averaged $3432; and work contracts averaged $981. 24% of undergraduates work part time. Average annual earnings from campus work are $810. The average financial indebtedness of the 2001 graduate was $25,000. The FAFSA and The New York State form is only required if the student chooses to apply for New York State TAP and not for financial assistance from the federal government. The fall application deadline is February 15.

International Students: There are 218 international students enrolled. The school actively recruits these students. They must score 570 on the written TOEFL or 230 on the electronic version and also take the SAT I or the ACT.

Computers: The mainframe is an IBM ES/9000. There are several PC labs on campus as well as sites in the dormitories. Students use more than 500 networked workstations. There are no time limits and no fees. All students may access the system. All students are required to have personal computers.

Graduates: In 2001, 1041 bachelor's degrees were awarded. The most popular majors were mechanical engineering (16%), management (9%), and computer and systems engineering (9%). In an average class, 53%

graduate in 4 years, 76% in 5 years, and 77% in 6 years. 370 companies recruited on campus in 2000-2001. Of the 2000 graduating class, 13% were enrolled in graduate school within 6 months of graduation and 85% were employed.

Admissions Contact: Teresa C. Duffy, Dean, Enrollment Management. E-mail: *admissions@rpi.edu* Web: *admissions.rpi.edu*

ROBERTS WESLEYAN COLLEGE B-3

Rochester, NY 14624-1997 (585) 594-6400
(800) 777-4792; Fax: (585) 594-6371

Full-time: 380 men, 742 women	**Faculty:** 67
Part-time: 40 men, 73 women	**Ph.D.s:** 58%
Graduate: 68 men, 146 women	**Student/Faculty:** 17 to 1
Year: semesters, summer session	**Tuition:** $14,916
Application Deadline: February 1	**Room & Board:** $5244
Freshman Class: 586 applied, 549 accepted, 247 enrolled	
SAT I Verbal/Math: 562/547	**ACT:** 24 **COMPETITIVE+**

Roberts Wesleyan College, founded in 1866, is a private institution affiliated with the Free Methodist Church. The curriculum offers a liberal arts education in the Christian tradition. In addition to regional accreditation, Roberts has baccalaureate program accreditation with ACBSP, CSWE, NASAD, NASM, and NLN. The library contains 115,921 volumes, 170,978 microform items, and 3662 audiovisual forms/CDs, and subscribes to 864 periodicals. Computerized library services include the card catalog, interlibrary loans, and database searching. Special learning facilities include a learning resource center, art gallery, and radio station. The 75-acre campus is in a suburban area 8 miles southwest of Rochester. Including residence halls, there are 32 buildings.

Student Life: 86% of undergraduates are from New York. Others are from 29 states, 15 foreign countries, and Canada. 76% are white. 70% are Protestant; 16% claim no religious affiliation; 14% Catholic. The average age of freshmen is 19; all undergraduates, 22. 19% do not continue beyond their first year; 54% remain to graduate.

Housing: 784 students can be accommodated in college housing, which includes single-sex dormitories, on-campus apartments, and off-campus apartments. On-campus housing is guaranteed for all 4 years. 69% of students live on campus; of those, 60% remain on campus on weekends. Alcohol is not permitted. All students may keep cars.

Activities: There are no fraternities or sororities. There are many groups and organizations on campus, including band, choir, chorale, drama, ethnic, honors, international, jazz band, musical theater, newspaper, orchestra, pep band, radio and TV, religious, social, social service, student government, and yearbook. Popular campus events include Winter Weekend and Spring Formal.

Sports: There are 6 intercollegiate sports for men and 7 for women, and 20 intramural sports for men and 21 for women. Facilities include an athletic center with facilities for basketball, volleyball, tennis, badminton, track, soccer, weightlifting, walleyball, racquetball, swimming, and diving.

Disabled Students: 60% of the campus is accessible. Wheelchair ramps, elevators, special parking, specially equipped rest rooms, special class scheduling, lowered drinking fountains, and lowered telephones are available.

Services: Counseling and information services are available, as is tutoring in every subject. There is a reader service for the blind, and remedial math, reading, and writing.

Campus Safety and Security: Measures include 24-hour foot and vehicle patrol, self-defense education, escort service, and informal discussions. There are pamphlets/posters/films, emergency telephones, lighted pathways/sidewalks, and personal-safety education programs.

Programs of Study: Roberts confers B.A. and B.S. degrees. Associate and master's degrees are also awarded. Bachelor's degrees are awarded in BIOLOGICAL SCIENCE (biochemistry and biology/biological science), BUSINESS (accounting, business administration and management, and personnel management), COMMUNICATIONS AND THE ARTS (communications, English, fine arts, and music), COMPUTER AND PHYSICAL SCIENCE (chemistry, computer science, mathematics, and physics), EDUCATION (art, elementary, and music), HEALTH PROFESSIONS (nursing, premedicine, prepharmacy, and preveterinary science), SOCIAL SCIENCE (criminal justice, history, prelaw, psychology, social work, and sociology). Nursing and engineering are the strongest academically. Elementary education and organizational management are the largest.

Required: To graduate, students must complete a minimum of 124 credit hours, with a minimum of 30 hours in the major and a GPA of 2.0. Required courses include first year experience, phys ed, modern technology, world issues, speech, writing, history, Bible, and philosophy.

Special: Students may cross-register with members of the Rochester Area Colleges consortium. Internships, study abroad in 8 countries, a Washington semester, co-op programs, a B.A.-B.S. degree in natural science and math, dual majors, and 3-2 engineering degrees with Clarkson University, Rensselaer Polytechnic Institute, and Rochester Institute of Technology are available. Nondegree study, pass/fail options, and credit for life, military, and work experience are also offered. The organizational management program, geared to adults, consists of 4-hour weekly sessions, with reliance on out-of-class work. There is a freshman honors program.

Faculty/Classroom: 63% of faculty are male; 37%, female. 85% teach undergraduates. No introductory courses are taught by graduate students. The average class size in an introductory lecture is 38; in a laboratory, 15; and in a regular course, 23.

Admissions: 94% of the 2001-2002 applicants were accepted. The SAT I scores for the 2001-2002 freshman class were: Verbal--25% below 500, 50% between 500 and 599, 21% between 600 and 700, and 4% above 700; Math--30% below 500, 40% between 500 and 599, 17% between 600 and 700, and 1% above 700. The ACT scores were 32% below 21, 32% between 21 and 23, 20% between 24 and 26, 8% between 27 and 28, and 7% above 28. 40% of the current freshmen were in the top fifth of their class; 68% were in the top two fifths. There were 2 National Merit semifinalists. 8 freshmen graduated first in their class.

Requirements: The SAT I or ACT is required. In addition, applicants must be graduates of an accredited secondary school. The GED is accepted. At least 12 academic credits are required, including 4 years of English and 2 years each of math and science. A foreign language and 3 years of social studies are recommended. The chosen major may modify requirements. An essay is required and an interview is recommended. Applications are accepted on-line at the school's web site. Roberts requires applicants to be in the upper 50% of their class. A GPA of 2.3 is required. AP and CLEP credits are accepted. Important factors in the admissions decision are advanced placement or honor courses, personality/intangible qualities, and extracurricular activities record.

Procedure: Freshmen are admitted to all sessions. There are early admissions and deferred admissions plans. Applications should be filed by February 1 for fall entry and December 1 for spring entry. The fall 2001 application fee was $55. Notification is sent on a rolling basis.

Transfer: 265 transfer students enrolled in 2001-2002. Applicants must submit transcripts from all previous institutions attended. Credit is usually accepted for courses with grade C or better. 30 credits of 124 must be completed at Roberts.

Visiting: There are regularly scheduled orientations for prospective students, including a campus tour, class visits, admissions and departmental interviews, and a financial-aid presentation. There are guides for informal visits and visitors may sit in on classes and stay overnight. To schedule a visit, contact the Admissions Office.

Financial Aid: In a recent year, 88% of all freshmen and 91% of continuing students received some form of financial aid. 87% of all students received need-based aid. The average freshman award was $9680. Of that total, scholarships or need-based grants averaged $5112 ($13,100 maximum); loans averaged $3496 ($10,500 maximum); and work contracts averaged $1073 ($1500 maximum). 35% of undergraduates work part time. Average annual earnings from campus work are $974. The CSS/Profile, FAFSA, FFS or SFS, the college's own financial statement, and the TAP (New York residents only) are required. The fall application deadline is March 15.

International Students: They must score 550 on the written TOEFL or 213 on the electronic version.

Computers: Macs, Apple IIe's, and PCs are available to students for academic or personal use in the science center, for about 90 hours per week, and in the library learning center, for about 48 hours per week. All students may access the system. There are no time limits and no fees.

Graduates: In 2001, 307 bachelor's degrees were awarded. The most popular majors were organizational management (25%), nursing (10%), and elementary education (8%). In an average class, 46% graduate in 4 years, 50% in 5 years, and 52% in 6 years. 103 companies recruited on campus in a recent year. Of a recent graduating class, 19% were enrolled in graduate school within 6 months of graduation and 89% were employed.

Admissions Contact: Linda Kurtz, Dean of Admissions. A video is available. E-mail: *admissions@roberts.edu* Web: *www.roberts.edu*

ROCHESTER INSTITUTE OF TECHNOLOGY B-3

Rochester, NY 14623 (585) 475-6631; Fax: (585) 475-7424

Full-time: 6887 men, 3080 women	**Faculty:** 655; IIA, +$
Part-time: 1317 men, 745 women	**Ph.D.s:** 80%
Graduate: 1512 men, 889 women	**Student/Faculty:** 15 to 1
Year: quarters, summer session	**Tuition:** $18,966
Application Deadline: open	**Room & Board:** $7266
Freshman Class: 8493 applied, 5950 accepted, 2272 enrolled	
SAT I or ACT: required	**VERY COMPETITIVE+**

Rochester Institute of Technology, a private institution founded in 1829, offers programs in science, computer science, allied health, engineering, fine arts, business, hotel management, graphic arts, and photography, as well as liberal arts, and includes the National Technical Institute for the Deaf. Most programs include a cooperative education component, which provides full-time work experience to complement classroom studies. There are 13 undergraduate and 13 graduate schools. In addition to regional accreditation, RIT has baccalaureate program accreditation with AACSB, ABET, ADA, CAHEA, CSAB, CSWE, and NASAD. The library contains 350,000 volumes, 438,000 microform items, and 9940 audio-visual forms/CDs, and subscribes to 15,000 periodicals. Computerized library services include the card catalog, interlibrary loans, and database searching. Special learning facilities include a learning resource center, art gallery, radio station, TV station, a computer chip manufacturing facility, a student-operated restaurant, an electronic prepress lab, an imaging science facility, and an observatory. The 1300-acre campus is in a suburban area 5 miles south of Rochester. Including residence halls, there are 185 buildings.

Student Life: 57% of undergraduates are from New York. Others are from 49 states, 85 foreign countries, and Canada. 85% are from public schools. 78% are white. The average age of freshmen is 18; all undergraduates, 21. 13% do not continue beyond their first year; 62% remain to graduate.

Housing: 6500 students can be accommodated in college housing, which includes single-sex and coed dormitories, on-campus apartments, married-student housing, fraternity houses, and sorority houses. In addition, there are honors houses and special-interest houses. On-campus housing is guaranteed for the freshman year only, is available on a first-come, first-served basis, and is available on a lottery system for upperclassmen. 65% of students live on campus; of those, 90% remain on campus on weekends. All students may keep cars.

Activities: 7% of men belong to 17 national fraternities; 5% of women belong to 7 national sororities. There are 150 groups on campus, including art, band, cheerleading, chess, choir, chorale, chorus, computers, dance, drama, ethnic, film, gay, gospel choir, honors, international, jazz band, literary magazine, newspaper, orchestra, pep band, photography, political, professional, radio and TV, religious, social, social service, student government, and yearbook. Popular campus events include Fall, Spring, and Winter Weekends and Martin Luther King Celebration.

Sports: There are 12 intercollegiate sports for men and 12 for women, and 29 intramural sports for men and 25 for women. Facilities include 3 gyms, an ice rink, a swimming pool, 12 tennis courts, a fitness trail, athletic fields, and a student life center with 8 racquetball courts, dance facilities, weight training facilities, and an indoor track.

Disabled Students: 90% of the campus is accessible. Wheelchair ramps, elevators, special parking, specially equipped rest rooms, special class scheduling, lowered drinking fountains, lowered telephones, and special fire alarm systems for hearing-impaired students are available.

Services: Counseling and information services are available, as is tutoring in most subjects. There is a reader service for the blind. and comprehensive support services for students with physical or learning disabilities and for first-generation college students.

Campus Safety and Security: Measures include 24-hour foot and vehicle patrol, self-defense education, escort service, and shuttle buses. There are informal discussions, pamphlets/posters/films, emergency telephones, and lighted pathways/sidewalks.

Programs of Study: RIT confers B.S. and B.F.A. degrees. Associate, master's, and doctoral degrees are also awarded. Bachelor's degrees are awarded in BIOLOGICAL SCIENCE (biochemistry, biology/biological science, biotechnology, and nutrition), BUSINESS (accounting, banking and finance, business administration and management, business systems analysis, hotel/motel and restaurant management, international business management, management information systems, management science, marketing management, and tourism), COMMUNICATIONS AND THE ARTS (applied art, ceramic art and design, communications, crafts, design, film arts, fine arts, glass, graphic design, illustration, industrial design, metal/jewelry, painting, photography, publishing, sculpture, studio art, telecommunications, and video), COMPUTER AND PHYSICAL SCIENCE (applied mathematics, chemistry, computer mathematics, computer science, information sciences and systems, mathematics, physics, polymer science, statistics, and systems analysis), EDUCATION (education of the deaf and hearing impaired), ENGINEERING AND ENVIRONMENTAL DESIGN (aerospace studies, automotive technology, civil engineering technology, computer engineering, computer graphics, computer technology, electrical/electronics engineering, electrical/electronics engineering technology, engineering, engineering technology, environmental engineering technology, environmental science, furniture design, graphic and printing production, graphic arts technology, industrial engineering, interior design, manufacturing engineering, manufacturing technology, materials science, mechanical engineering, mechanical engineering technology, military science, printing technology, and woodworking), HEALTH PROFESSIONS (allied health, medical laboratory technology, medical technology, nuclear medical technology, physician's assistant, predentistry, premedicine, preveterinary science, and ultrasound technology), SOCIAL SCIENCE (criminal justice, dietetics, economics, experimental psychology, food production/management/services, interpreter for the deaf, prelaw, psychology, public affairs, and social work). Engineering, computer science, and photography are the strongest academically. Engineering, information technology, and photography are the largest.

Required: Students must have a GPA of 2.0 and have completed 180 quarter credit hours to graduate. Distribution requirements include English, social sciences, and humanities; specific courses include writing and literature, senior seminar, and phys ed. B.S. programs also require a minimum of 20 quarter credit hours in science and math. There are no general science or math requirements for the B.F.A. programs in art, design, photography, or film/video.

Special: RIT offers internships in social science and allied health majors, and cooperative education programs with 1300 co-op employers. Cooperative education is required or recommended in most programs and provides full-time paid work experience. Cross-registration with Rochester-area colleges is available. There are accelerated degree programs in science, engineering, public policy, math, computer science, and business. Students may study abroad in 15 countries, and student-designed majors are permitted in applied arts and sciences. There are 6 national honor societies, a freshman honors program, and 7 colleges have honors programs.

Faculty/Classroom: 68% of faculty are male; 32%, female. 95% teach undergraduates and 50% both teach and do research. No introductory courses are taught by graduate students. The average class size in an introductory lecture is 30; in a laboratory, 16; and in a regular course, 20.

Admissions: 70% of the 2001-2002 applicants were accepted. The SAT I scores for the 2001-2002 freshman class were: Verbal--12% below 500, 43% between 500 and 599, 37% between 600 and 700, and 8% above 700; Math--4% below 500, 33% between 500 and 599, 48% between 600 and 700, and 15% above 700. The ACT scores were 7% below 21, 19% between 21 and 23, 27% between 24 and 26, 24% between 27 and 28, and 23% above 28. 55% of the current freshmen were in the top fifth of their class; 85% were in the top two fifths. There were 16 National Merit finalists and 2 semifinalists. 40 freshmen graduated first in their class.

Requirements: The SAT I or ACT is required. In addition, applicants must be high school graduates or have a GED certificate. Applicants are required to submit an essay, and an interview is recommended. The School of Art and the School of Design emphasize a required portfolio of artwork. Required high school math and science credits vary by program, with 3 years in each area generally acceptable. RIT requires applicants to be in the upper 50% of their class. A grade average of 85 is required. AP and CLEP credits are accepted. Important factors in the admissions decision are advanced placement or honor courses, recommendations by school officials, and extracurricular activities record. Applications are accepted on-line via RIT's web site and through EXPAN and Common Application.

Procedure: Freshmen are admitted to all sessions. Entrance exams should be taken during the junior or senior year. There are early decision and deferred admissions plans. Early decision application should be filed by December 15; the regular application deadline is open. The application fee is $50. Notification of early decision is sent January 15; regular decision, on a rolling basis beginning March 15. 583 early decision candidates were accepted for the 2001-2002 class. 2% of all applicants are on a waiting list; 25 were accepted in 2001.

Transfer: 905 transfer students enrolled in 2001-2002. Transfer students must have a GPA of 2.5 for admission to most programs; those with fewer than 30 college credits must supply a high school transcript. Other requirements vary by program. 45 credits of 180 must be completed at RIT.

Visiting: There are regularly scheduled orientations for prospective students, including academic advising and information on housing and student services. There are guides for informal visits and visitors may sit in on classes and stay overnight. To schedule a visit, contact Mary Menard at (585) 475-6736.

Financial Aid: In 2001-2002, 85% of all freshmen and 75% of continuing students received some form of financial aid. 75% of freshmen and 65% of continuing students received need-based aid. The average freshman award was $15,000. Of that total, scholarships or need-based grants averaged $8000 ($18,633 maximum); loans averaged $3800 ($6625 maximum); work contracts averaged $1500 ($2300 maximum); and federal and state grants averaged $1700 ($8300 maximum). 60% of undergraduates work part time. Average annual earnings from campus work are $1700. The FAFSA is required. The fall application deadline is March 1.

International Students: There are 501 international students enrolled. The school actively recruits these students. They must score 525 on the written TOEFL or 197 on the electronic version and also take the SAT I or the ACT.

Computers: The mainframes are a VMS cluster of networked Digital VAX and Alpha computers. RIT has 17 computer centers and computer labs on campus for student use. There are more than 300 mainframe terminals available, as well as hundreds of PCs. Students may link their terminals or PCs to the mainframe system from individual dorm rooms or campus apartments linked to the campus network. All students may access the system 7 days per week, 24-hour access. There are no time limits and no fees.

Graduates: In 2001, 1811 bachelor's degrees were awarded. The most popular majors were engineering (13%), engineering technology (11%), and photography (10%). In an average class, 62% graduate in 6 years. 600 companies recruited on campus in 2000-2001. Of the 2000 graduating class, 8% were enrolled in graduate school within 6 months of graduation and 90% were employed.

Admissions Contact: Daniel Shelley, Director of Admissions. A video is available. E-mail: *admissions@rit.edu* Web: *www.rit.edu*

RUSSELL SAGE COLLEGE

Troy, NY 12180	**D-3**
	(518) 244-2217
	(888) Very-Sage; Fax: (518) 244-6880
Full-time: 742 women	**Faculty:** 65
Part-time: 55 women	**Ph.D.s:** 72%
Graduate: none	**Student/Faculty:** 11 to 1
Year: semesters, summer session	**Tuition:** $17,510
Application Deadline: August 1	**Room & Board:** $6164
Freshman Class: 579 applied, 496 accepted, 258 enrolled	
SAT I Verbal/Math: 516/510	**ACT:** 24 **COMPETITIVE+**

Russell Sage, a private, comprehensive college, was founded in 1916 to prepare women for successful professional careers. Baccalaureate degrees in the traditional arts and sciences are offered, along with professional programs in nutrition, athletic training, nursing, physical and occupational therapy, theater, musical theater, creative arts in therapy, business, forensic science, communications, and education. There is 1 undergraduate and 1 graduate school. In addition to regional accreditation, Russell Sage has baccalaureate program accreditation with ADA, AOTA, APTA, NASAD, NCATE, and NLN. The library contains 373,106 volumes, 3937 microform items, and 34,260 audiovisual forms/CDs, and subscribes to 1057 periodicals. Computerized library services include the card catalog, interlibrary loans, and database searching. Special learning facilities include a learning resource center, the New York State Theatre Institute, Robinson Athletic Center, and Helen Upton Center for Women's Studies. The 14-acre campus is in an urban area 10 miles from Albany and Schenectady. Including residence halls, there are 38 buildings.

Student Life: 89% of undergraduates are from New York. Others are from 15 states and 2 foreign countries. 75% are white. The average age of freshmen is 18; all undergraduates, 22. 15% do not continue beyond their first year; 68% remain to graduate.

Housing: 738 students can be accommodated in college housing, which includes single-sex dormitories and on-campus apartments. In addition, there are language houses, special-interest houses, and substance-free/wellness housing. On-campus housing is guaranteed for all 4 years. 51% of students commute. Upperclassmen may keep cars.

Activities: There are no fraternities or sororities. There are 26 groups on campus, including academic, choir, chorus, dance, drama, equestrian, ethnic, gay, honors, leadership, literary magazine, musical theater, newspaper, orchestra, political, religious, social, social service, student government, and yearbook. Popular campus events include Rally Day, Sage Fest, and Family Weekend.

Sports: Facilities include a weight and fitness center, a sports medicine facility, swimming pool, 4 tennis courts, a practice field, 2 gyms, and a large multipurpose room for indoor recreation.

Disabled Students: 70% of the campus is accessible. Wheelchair ramps, elevators, special parking, specially equipped rest rooms, special class scheduling, computer center access, electronic access via blackboard for a variety of information and courses, specially equipped science labs and equipment, and visits to administrative offices by arrangement are available.

Services: Counseling and information services are available, as is tutoring in most subjects. There is remedial math, reading, and writing.

Campus Safety and Security: Measures include 24-hour foot and vehicle patrol, self-defense education, escort service, and shuttle buses. There are informal discussions, pamphlets/posters/films, emergency telephones, lighted pathways/sidewalks, an evening escort service, and monitored video cameras.

Programs of Study: Russell Sage confers B.A. and B.S. degrees. Master's degrees are also awarded. Bachelor's degrees are awarded in BIOLOGICAL SCIENCE (biochemistry, biology/biological science, and nutrition), BUSINESS (business administration and management), COMMUNICATIONS AND THE ARTS (communications, dramatic arts, English, and Spanish), COMPUTER AND PHYSICAL SCIENCE (chemistry, computer science, information sciences and systems, and mathematics), EDUCATION (athletic training and elementary), HEALTH PROFESSIONS (art therapy, nursing, occupational therapy, and physical therapy), SOCIAL SCIENCE (biopsychology, criminal justice, history, interdisciplinary studies, international studies, political science/government, psychology, and sociology). Physical therapy, psychology, and English are the strongest academically. Physical therapy, psychology, and nursing are the largest.

Required: To graduate, students must complete 120 credits with a 2.0 GPA overall and at least 30 credits and a 2.2 GPA in the major. B.A. candidates must earn a minimum of 90 credits in the liberal arts and sciences and B.S. candidates must earn a minimum of 60. A general education requirement of 36 credits focuses on the experiences of women in a multicultural society, understanding technology, writing skills, and a broad exposure to the various arts and sciences. Students must also complete 6 credits in a single language or show proficiency.

Special: Students may cross-register with the 14 area schools of the Hudson-Mohawk Association of Colleges. A theater major is offered in conjunction with NYSTI. Study abroad, internships, and work-study programs are available. There are several accelerated 5-year programs, a 3-3 program with Albany Law School, and a 3-2 engineering degree with nearby Rensselaer Polytechnic Institute. 9 centers for interdisciplinary inquiry draw students from across majors. The college confers credit for life, military, or work experience. Nondegree study, student-designed majors, and pass/fail options are also available. There are 14 national honor societies and a freshman honors program.

Faculty/Classroom: 34% of faculty are male; 66%, female. All both teach and do research. The average class size in an introductory lecture is 19; in a laboratory, 9; and in a regular course, 16.

Admissions: 86% of the 2001-2002 applicants were accepted. The SAT I scores for the 2001-2002 freshman class were: Verbal--31% below 500, 53% between 500 and 599, 15% between 600 and 700, and 1% above 700; Math--39% below 500, 42% between 500 and 599, and 18% between 600 and 700. The ACT scores were 15% below 21, 31% between 21 and 23, 31% between 24 and 26, 8% between 27 and 28, and 15% above 28. 32% of the current freshmen were in the top fifth of their class; 60% were in the top two fifths.

Requirements: The SAT I or ACT is required. In addition, applicants must be graduates of an accredited secondary school or have a GED. A minimum of 16 academic units are required, including courses in English, social sciences, natural sciences, math, and foreign language. An essay, for applicants still in high school, is required, and an interview is recommended. A GPA of 2.0 is required. AP and CLEP credits are accepted. Important factors in the admissions decision are advanced placement or honor courses, leadership record, and evidence of special talent. Applications are available on-line at *www.sage.edu*.

Procedure: Freshmen are admitted fall and spring. Entrance exams should be taken during spring of the junior year or fall of the senior year. There are early decision, early admissions, and deferred admissions plans. Early decision applications should be filed by December 1; regular applications, by August 1 for fall entry and December 15 for spring entry. The fall 2001 application fee was $30. Notification of early decision is sent December 15; regular decision, on a rolling basis. 19 early decision candidates were accepted for the 2001-2002 class.

Transfer: 119 transfer students enrolled in 2001-2002. Applicants must have a minimum GPA of 2.5. Interviews are strongly encouraged and may be required in some instances. 45 credits of 120 must be completed at Russell Sage.

Visiting: There are regularly scheduled orientations for prospective students including meetings with faculty, a campus tour, a financial aid session, and an admissions interview. There are guides for informal visits and visitors may sit in on classes and stay overnight. To schedule a visit, contact the Office of Admission at (518) 244-2218.

Financial Aid: In 2001-2002, 97% of all freshmen and 95% of continuing students received some form of financial aid. 80% of freshmen and 78% of continuing students received need-based aid. The average freshman award was $17,165. Of that total, scholarships or need-based grants averaged $9300 ($15,300 maximum); loans averaged $3900 ($13,500 maximum); and work contracts averaged $1400 ($1500 maximum). 58% of undergraduates work part time. Average annual earnings from campus work are $1000. The average financial indebtedness of the 2001 graduate was $18,200. The FAFSA is required. The fall application deadline is March 1.

International Students: There is 1 international student enrolled. The school actively recruits these students. They must score 550 on the written TOEFL and also take the SAT I or the ACT if English is their native language.

Computers: The mainframes are an HP and Sun. A campuswide network (SageNet) provides hard-wired and dial-up access to e-mail and the Internet for all students. Labs for student use are equipped with PCs. Word processing, spreadsheet, statistical analysis, graphics, and course-specific software are available. All students may access the system. The public computer labs are open 14 hours per day, 7 days a week; dial-in access is available 24 hours a day. There are no time limits and no fees. It is strongly recommended that all students have a personal computer.

Graduates: In 2001, 251 bachelor's degrees were awarded. The most popular majors were nursing (17%), physical therapy (15%), and elementary education (12%). In an average class, 29% graduate in 4 years, 55% in 5 years, and 59% in 6 years. 61 companies recruited on campus in 2000-2001. Of the 2000 graduating class, 61% were enrolled in graduate school within 6 months of graduation and 34% were employed.

Admissions Contact: Elizabeth Robertson, Senior Associate Director of Admissions. E-mail: *rscadm@sage.edu* Web: *www.sage.edu*

SAINT BONAVENTURE UNIVERSITY A-3

St. Bonaventure, NY 14778-2284 (716) 375-2400
(800) 462-5050; Fax: (716) 375-2005

Full-time: 971 men, 1105 women | **Faculty:** 120; IIA, --$
Part-time: 39 men, 49 women | **Ph.D.s:** 85%
Graduate: 178 men, 368 women | **Student/Faculty:** 17 to 1
Year: semesters, summer session | **Tuition:** $16,156
Application Deadline: April 1 | **Room & Board:** $5800
Freshman Class: 1579 applied, 1487 accepted, 520 enrolled
SAT I Verbal/Math: 535/530 | **ACT:** 21 | **COMPETITIVE**

Saint Bonaventure University, founded in 1858, is a private Roman Catholic institution in the Franciscan tradition, offering programs in the arts and sciences, education, business, and journalism and mass communication. There are 4 undergraduate schools and 1 graduate school. The library contains 241,000 volumes, 97,000 microform items, and 7000 audiovisual forms/CDs, and subscribes to 1500 periodicals. Computerized library services include the card catalog, interlibrary loans, and database searching. Special learning facilities include a learning resource center, art gallery, radio station, TV station, and observatory. The 900-acre campus is in a small town 70 miles southeast of Buffalo. Including residence halls, there are 29 buildings.

Student Life: 76% of undergraduates are from New York. Others are from 39 states, 10 foreign countries, and Canada. 58% are from public schools. 93% are white. The average age of freshmen is 18; all undergraduates, 21. 15% do not continue beyond their first year; 72% remain to graduate.

Housing: 1450 students can be accommodated in college housing, which includes single-sex and coed dormitories and on-campus apartments. On-campus housing is guaranteed for all 4 years. 76% of students live on campus; of those, 90% remain on campus on weekends. All students may keep cars.

Activities: There are no fraternities or sororities. There are 73 groups on campus, including academic, art, band, cheerleading, chess, choir, chorale, chorus, computers, drama, ethnic, honors, international, jazz band, literary magazine, newspaper, orchestra, pep band, photography, political, professional, radio and TV, religious, social, social service, student government, and yearbook. Popular campus events include Family Weekend, Spring and Winter Weekends, and varsity basketball games.

Sports: There are 7 intercollegiate sports for men and 7 for women, and 10 intramural sports for men and 9 for women. Facilities include a 6000-seat gym with basketball and volleyball courts, an indoor swimming pool, a 9-hole golf course, weight facilities and free weights, and a fitness center with racquetball courts, Nautilus equipment, and an aerobics room. There is also a 77-acre area on campus with soccer, baseball, softball, rugby, and intramural fields.

Disabled Students: 90% of the campus is accessible. Wheelchair ramps, elevators, special parking, specially equipped rest rooms, a counseling center staffed by 2 professionals, and a teaching and learning center with a coordinator for disabled services are available.

Services: Counseling and information services are available, as is tutoring in some subjects. There is remedial math, reading, and writing.

Campus Safety and Security: Measures include 24-hour foot and vehicle patrol, self-defense education, escort service, and shuttle buses. There are informal discussions, pamphlets/posters/films, emergency telephones, and lighted pathways/sidewalks.

Programs of Study: SBU confers B.A., B.S., B.B.A., and B.S.Ed. degrees. Master's degrees are also awarded. Bachelor's degrees are awarded in BIOLOGICAL SCIENCE (biochemistry, biology/biological science, and biophysics), BUSINESS (accounting, banking and finance, management science, and marketing/retailing/merchandising), COMMUNICATIONS AND THE ARTS (classical languages, English, French, journalism, Spanish, and visual and performing arts), COMPUTER AND PHYSICAL SCIENCE (chemistry, computer science, mathematics, and physics), EDUCATION (elementary and physical), ENGINEERING AND ENVIRONMENTAL DESIGN (engineering physics and environmental science), HEALTH PROFESSIONS (medical laboratory technology and premedicine), SOCIAL SCIENCE (history, philosophy, political science/government, prelaw, psychology, social science, and sociology). Psychology, accounting, and biology are the strongest academically. Mass communication, biology, and elementary education are the largest.

Required: To graduate, students must complete 120 credit hours, 30 of them in the major, with a minimum GPA of 2.0. Students must also demonstrate writing competency through testing or course work.

Special: Cross-registration can be arranged almost anywhere in the United States through the Visiting Student Program. Internships are available in business, mass communication, political science, psychology, and social science. Study abroad in 18 countries, B.A.-B.S. degrees, accelerated degree programs, dual and student-designed majors, a Washington semester with American University, and pass/fail options are offered. Students may complete a 2-2 or 2-3 engineering degree with the University of Detroit or a 2-3 engineering degree with Clarkson University. There are 10 national honor societies and a freshman honors program.

Faculty/Classroom: 80% of faculty are male; 20%, female. 92% teach undergraduates and 1% both teach and do research. Graduate students teach 1% of introductory courses. The average class size in an introductory lecture is 25; in a laboratory, 12; and in a regular course, 18.

Admissions: 94% of the 2001-2002 applicants were accepted. The SAT I scores for the 2001-2002 freshman class were: Verbal--38% below 500, 44% between 500 and 599, 17% between 600 and 700, and 1% above 700. The ACT scores were 62% below 21, 22% between 21 and 23, 9% between 24 and 26, 5% between 27 and 28, and 1% above 28. 28% of the current freshmen were in the top fifth of their class; 63% were in the top two fifths. 1 freshman graduated first in the class.

Requirements: The SAT I or ACT is required, with a minimum composite score of 1000 on the SAT I (500 verbal, 500 math) or 24 on the ACT. Applicants must be graduates of an accredited secondary school or have a GED. 16 academic credits are required, including 4 years each of English and social studies, 3 each of math and science, and 2 of a foreign language. An essay and an interview are recommended. SBU requires applicants to be in the upper 60% of their class. A grade average of 83 is required. AP and CLEP credits are accepted. Important factors in the admissions decision are recommendations by school officials, advanced placement or honor courses, and extracurricular activities record. Applications may be submitted on-line via NYMentor, CollegeLink, and the Princeton Review (*www.review.com*).

Procedure: Freshmen are admitted to all sessions. Entrance exams should be taken during the spring of the junior year or the fall of the senior year. There are early admissions and deferred admissions plans. Applications should be filed by April 1 for fall entry and December 1 for spring entry. The fall 2001 application fee was $30. Notification is sent on a rolling basis.

Transfer: 92 transfer students enrolled in 2001-2002. Applicants must have a minimum 2.5 GPA. Grades of D or better transfer for credit except in the major. 60 credits of 120 must be completed at SBU.

Visiting: There are regularly scheduled orientations for prospective students, including interviews, tours, class visits, and meetings with professors. There are guides for informal visits and visitors may sit in on classes. To schedule a visit, contact the Admissions Office.

Financial Aid: In a recent year, 93% of all freshmen and 75% of continuing students received some form of financial aid. 90% of freshmen and 86% of continuing students received need-based aid. The average freshman award was $12,416. Of that total, scholarships or need-based grants averaged $7278 ($8000 maximum); loans averaged $2182 ($4825 maximum); work contracts averaged $432 ($1200 maximum); and outside private aid averaged $421. 38% of undergraduates work part time. Average annual earnings from campus work are $700. The average financial indebtedness of a recent graduate was $9500. The FAFSA is required. The fall application deadline is February 1.

International Students: There were 38 international students enrolled in a recent year. They must score 550 on the written TOEFL.

Computers: SBU has 5 PC and 2 Mac labs, housing more than 100 computers connected to a campuswide network. The computer science lab is equipped with 5 Sun workstations and provides a UNIX environment used to support upper-division courses in computer science. Students have full Internet access. All students may access the system 24 hours per day via residence hall rooms or at designated laboratory hours. There are no time limits and no fees.

Graduates: In a recent year, 422 bachelor's degrees were awarded. The most popular majors were elementary education (12%), accounting (11%), and marketing (9%). In an average class, 59% graduate in 4 years, 68% in 5 years, and 71% in 6 years. 40 companies recruited on campus in a recent year. Of the 2000 graduating class, 23% were enrolled in graduate school within 6 months of graduation.

Admissions Contact: James Di Risio, Director of Admissions.
E-mail: *admissions@sbu.edu* Web: *www.sbu.edu*

SAINT FRANCIS COLLEGE D-5

Brooklyn, NY 11201 (718) 489-5200, ext. 200; Fax: (718) 522-1274

Full-time: 871 men, 1125 women | **Faculty:** 66; IIB, av$
Part-time: 135 men, 269 women | **Ph.D.s:** 79%
Graduate: none | **Student/Faculty:** 30 to 1
Year: semesters, summer session | **Tuition:** $9610
Application Deadline: open | **Room & Board:** n/app
Freshman Class: 1558 applied, 1263 accepted, 471 enrolled
SAT I Verbal/Math: 480/490 | **COMPETITIVE**

Saint Francis College, chartered in 1884 by the Franciscan Brothers, is an independent Catholic institution conferring degrees in the arts, sciences, business, and health sciences. The library contains 135,000 volumes, 240 microform items, and 2100 audiovisual forms/CDs, and subscribes to 570 periodicals. Computerized library services include interlibrary loans and database searching. Special learning facilities include a learning resource center, a greenhouse, and a television studio. The 1-acre campus is in an urban area in Brooklyn, New York. There are 5 buildings.

Student Life: 99% of undergraduates are from New York. Others are from 3 states, 42 foreign countries, and Canada. 40% are from public

schools. 53% are white; 21% African American, 14% Hispanic, 10% foreign nationals. The average age of freshmen is 18; all undergraduates, 21. 24% do not continue beyond their first year; 47% remain to graduate.

Housing: There are no residence halls. Alcohol is not permitted. No one may keep cars.

Activities: There is 1 national fraternity; 5% of women belong to 1 local sorority. There are 25 groups on campus, including art, cheerleading, choir, computers, departmental, drama, ethnic, international, literary magazine, newspaper, political, professional, radio and TV, religious, social, social service, student government, and yearbook. Popular campus events include Charter Day, Brooklyn Accents, and personal issues and public interest lecture series.

Sports: There are 9 intercollegiate sports for men and 8 for women, and 6 intramural sports for men and 6 for women. Facilities include a 1100-seat gym, an Olympic-size swimming pool, a weight-training room, and a roof recreation area.

Disabled Students: All of the campus is accessible. Wheelchair ramps, elevators, specially equipped rest rooms, lowered drinking fountains, and lowered telephones are available.

Services: There is a reader service for the blind, and remedial math, reading, and writing. In addition, there are workshops in academic skills such as note- and test-taking techniques and study skills.

Campus Safety and Security: Measures include self-defense education, informal discussions, and pamphlets/posters/films.

Programs of Study: St. Francis confers B.A. and B.S. degrees. Associate degrees are also awarded. Bachelor's degrees are awarded in BIOLOGICAL SCIENCE (biology/biological science), BUSINESS (accounting), COMMUNICATIONS AND THE ARTS (communications and English), COMPUTER AND PHYSICAL SCIENCE (mathematics), EDUCATION (elementary, middle school, physical, and secondary), ENGINEERING AND ENVIRONMENTAL DESIGN (aviation administration/management), HEALTH PROFESSIONS (biomedical science, health care administration, health science, medical laboratory technology, physician's assistant, premedicine, and radiological science), SOCIAL SCIENCE (criminal justice, economics, history, philosophy, political science/government, psychology, social studies, and sociology). Biology, accounting, and psychology are the strongest academically. Management, accounting, and psychology are the largest.

Required: The core curriculum varies according to the major, but all baccalaureate degree programs require courses in communications, English, fine arts, phys ed, history, philosophy, sociology, and science or math. A minimum 2.0 GPA and 128 credit hours are required to graduate.

Special: There are co-op programs in aviation, physical therapy, nursing, and computer science. A variety of internships are available in such areas as industrial and public accounting, and with the NYC Transit Authority, Public Interest Research, the NYS Assembly, and the Urban Fellow Program. Work-study with Methodist Hospital or the borough president's office is possible, and there are pre-professional health programs with the State University of New York Health Science Center at Brooklyn. Study abroad in England, dual majors, pass/fail options, and credit for life experience are possible. There are 15 national honor societies and a freshman honors program.

Faculty/Classroom: 61% of faculty are male; 39%, female. All teach undergraduates and 25% both teach and do research. The average class size in an introductory lecture is 30; in a laboratory, 19; and in a regular course, 23.

Admissions: 81% of the 2001-2002 applicants were accepted. The SAT I scores for the 2001-2002 freshman class were: Verbal--56% below 500, 32% between 500 and 599, 11% between 600 and 700, and 1% above 700; Math--51% below 500, 34% between 500 and 599, 14% between 600 and 700, and 1% above 700. 7 freshmen graduated first in their class.

Requirements: The SAT I is required. In addition, applicants should graduate from an accredited secondary school or have a GED. An entrance essay is required. A grade average of 80 is required. AP and CLEP credits are accepted. Important factors in the admissions decision are recommendations by school officials, leadership record, and advanced placement or honor courses. Applications are accepted on-line at *www.stfranciscollege.edu*

Procedure: Freshmen are admitted to all sessions. Application deadlines are open. The fall 2001 application fee was $200. Notification is sent on a rolling basis.

Transfer: 147 transfer students enrolled in a recent year. A minimum 2.0 GPA is required for transfer students. 30 credits of 128 must be completed at St. Francis.

Visiting: There are regularly scheduled orientations for prospective students, including meetings with faculty, if desired. There are guides for informal visits and visitors may sit in on classes. To schedule a visit, contact the Office of Admissions.

Financial Aid: In a recent year, 82% of all freshmen and 91% of continuing students received some form of financial aid. 57% of freshmen and 60% of continuing students received need-based aid. The average freshman award was $6750. Of that total, scholarships or need-based grants averaged $5250 ($8410 maximum); loans averaged $1250 ($2625 maximum); and college work-study averaged $875 ($1500 maximum). 5% of undergraduates work part time. Average annual earnings from campus work are $1350. The average financial indebtedness of a recent graduate was $2381. The FAFSA, the college's own financial statement, and the NY State TAP application are required. The fall application deadline is February 15.

International Students: There are 53 international students enrolled. The school actively recruits these students. They must score 500 on the written TOEFL.

Computers: A computer center is available to students. It has 40 PCs that are connected to a Local Area Network (LAN). All students may access the system. There are no time limits. The fee is $35 per course.

Graduates: In a recent year, 310 bachelor's degrees were awarded. The most popular majors were management (20%), special studies (17%), and psychology (11%). In an average class, 1% graduate in 3 years, 18% in 4 years, 33% in 5 years, and 47% in 6 years. 51 companies recruited on campus in a recent year.

Admissions Contact: Brother George Larkin, O.S.F., Admissions Dean. A video is available. E-mail: *glarkin@stfranciscollege.edu*
Web: *www.stfranciscollege.edu*

SAINT JOHN FISHER COLLEGE — B-3

Rochester, NY 14618 — (585) 385-8064
(800) 444-4640; Fax: (585) 385-8386

Full-time: 800 men, 1124 women	**Faculty:** 120; IIB, av$
Part-time: 147 men, 279 women	**Ph.D.s:** 87%
Graduate: 202 men, 416 women	**Student/Faculty:** 16 to 1
Year: semesters, summer session	**Tuition:** $15,200
Application Deadline: open	**Room & Board:** $6600
Freshman Class: 1939 applied, 1392 accepted, 540 enrolled	
SAT I Verbal/Math: 530/540	**ACT:** 23 **COMPETITIVE**

St. John Fisher College is an independent, liberal arts institution in the Catholic tradition of American higher education. Guided since its inception in 1948 by the educational philosophy of the Congregation of St. Basil, the college emphasizes liberal learning for students in traditional academic disciplines, as well as for those in more directly career-oriented fields. The college welcomes qualified students, faculty, and staff regardless of religious or cultural background. In addition to regional accreditation, Fisher has baccalaureate program accreditation with ACS and NLN. The library contains 207,343 volumes, 193,805 microform items, and 29,052 audiovisual forms/CDs, and subscribes to 1214 periodicals. Computerized library services include the card catalog, interlibrary loans, and database searching. Special learning facilities include a learning resource center, radio station, TV station, multimedia center, "wet" and "dry" multidisciplinary science labs, animal labs, growth chambers, and a dance and fitness facility. The 136-acre campus is in a suburban area 12 miles southeast of Rochester. Including residence halls, there are 14 buildings.

Student Life: 98% of undergraduates are from New York. Others are from 17 states, 11 foreign countries, and Canada. 65% are from public schools. 88% are white. The average age of freshmen is 19; all undergraduates, 20. 18% do not continue beyond their first year.

Housing: 1100 students can be accommodated in college housing, which includes single-sex and coed dormitories and off-campus apartments. Living facilities include residence halls providing a year-lomg wellness program. On-campus housing is guaranteed for all 4 years. 54% of students live on campus; of those, 85% remain on campus on weekends. All students may keep cars.

Activities: There are no fraternities or sororities. There are 40 groups on campus, including cheerleading, choir, chorale, chorus, College Bowl, computers, drama, ethnic, gay, honors, international, literary magazine, musical theater, newspaper, photography, political, professional, radio and TV, religious, social, social service, Student Activities Board, student government, and yearbook. Popular campus events include Senior Week, Winter Olympics, and TEDDI, a 24-hour dance marathon for charity.

Sports: There are 8 intercollegiate sports for men and 7 for women, and 5 intramural sports for men and 4 for women. Facilities include racquetball, squash, and tennis courts, baseball and softball fields, an all-weather playing field for football, soccer, lacrosse, and intramural athletics, a 9-hole golf course, weight/exercise facilities, varsity gym for intercollegiate basketball, and a multipurpose student life center for indoor tennis, volleyball, and basketball.

Disabled Students: 90% of the campus is accessible. Wheelchair ramps, elevators, special parking, specially equipped rest rooms, special class scheduling, lowered drinking fountains, and lowered telephones are available.

Services: Counseling and information services are available, as is tutoring in most subjects. There is a reader service for the blind. Math and writing centers provide help to students at all levels. Peer tutoring is available to all students in most undergraduate subject areas.

Campus Safety and Security: Measures include 24-hour foot and vehicle patrol, escort service, shuttle buses, and informal discussions. There are pamphlets/posters/films, emergency telephones, and lighted pathways/sidewalks.

Programs of Study: Fisher confers B.A. and B.S. degrees. Master's degrees are also awarded. Bachelor's degrees are awarded in BIOLOGICAL SCIENCE (biology/biological science), BUSINESS (accounting, management science, and sports management), COMMUNICATIONS AND THE ARTS (communications, English, French, German, Italian, and Spanish), COMPUTER AND PHYSICAL SCIENCE (chemistry, computer science, mathematics, physics, and science technology), EDUCATION (early childhood and special), HEALTH PROFESSIONS (nursing), SOCIAL SCIENCE (American studies, anthropology, economics, history, interdisciplinary studies, international studies, philosophy, political science/government, psychology, religion, and sociology). Education, management, and communication/journalism are the largest.

Required: To graduate, students must complete at least 120 credit hours, including at least 30 in the major, and maintain a 2.0 minimum GPA. Core curriculum requirements include 3 to 4 courses each in literature/foreign languages, social sciences, and religious studies/philosophy, 3 in math/natural science,and up to 3 in arts. Freshmen must participate in one of the integrative learning communities.

Special: The college has cooperative programs with the Pennsylvania College of Optometry, and cross-registration with Rochester area colleges. The college offers internships in most majors, independent research in 16 majors, study abroad, work-study programs, accelerated degree programs in many areas, Washington semesters, dual and student-designed majors, and degrees in interdisciplinary studies or liberal studies. A 3-2 engineering degree is offered with Columbia and Clarkson Universities, University of Detroit-Mercy, SUNY at Buffalo, University of Rochester, Rensselaer Polytechnic Institute, and Manhattan College. There are 10 national honor societies, a freshman honors program, and 7 departmental honors programs.

Faculty/Classroom: 57% of faculty are male; 43%, female. All teach undergraduates and 65% both teach and do research. No introductory courses are taught by graduate students. The average class size in an introductory lecture is 27; in a laboratory, 11; and in a regular course, 23.

Admissions: 72% of the 2001-2002 applicants were accepted. The SAT I scores for the 2001-2002 freshman class were: Verbal--29% below 500, 53% between 500 and 599, 18% between 600 and 700, and 1% above 700; Math--26% below 500, 51% between 500 and 599, 22% between 600 and 700, and 1% above 700. The ACT scores were 25% below 21, 34% between 21 and 23, 31% between 24 and 26, 7% between 27 and 28, and 4% above 28. 40% of the current freshmen were in the top fifth of their class; 73% were in the top two fifths. 2 freshmen graduated first in their class.

Requirements: The SAT I or ACT is required. In addition, applicants must be graduates of an accredited secondary school. 16 academic credits are required, including 4 years each in English, history, and social studies, 3 years each in math and science, and 2 years in a foreign language. Interviews are recommended. AP and CLEP credits are accepted. Important factors in the admissions decision are advanced placement or honor courses, extracurricular activities record, and evidence of special talent. Applications are accepted on-line via the college's web site, *www.sjfc.edu*

Procedure: Freshmen are admitted to all sessions. There are early decision and deferred admissions plans. Early decision applications should be filed by December 1; regular applications have open deadlines for fall entry. The fall 2001 application fee was $25. Notification of early decision is sent November 1; regular decision, on a rolling basis. 24 early decision candidates were accepted for the 2001-2002 class.

Transfer: 175 transfer students enrolled in 2001-2002. Applicants must have a minimum GPA of 2.0 to be considered (mean GPA is 2.8). A high school transcript is required for students with fewer than 24 college credits. Interviews are recommended. 30 credits of 120 must be completed at Fisher.

Visiting: There are regularly scheduled orientations for prospective students, including a tour, an interview with a member of the admissions staff, meetings with faculty and coaches, and lunch on campus. There are guides for informal visits and visitors may sit in on classes and stay overnight. To schedule a visit, contact the Admissions Office.

Financial Aid: In 2001-2002, 94% of all freshmen and 82% of continuing students received some form of financial aid. 74% of freshmen and 65% of continuing students received need-based aid. The average freshman award was $12,672. Of that total, scholarships or need-based grants averaged $8815; loans averaged $2264; and work contracts averaged $1600. 25% of undergraduates work part time. Average annual earnings from campus work are $1000. The average financial indebtedness of the 2001 graduate was $18,400. The FAFSA is required. The fall application deadline is February 15.

International Students: There are 11 international students enrolled. The school actively recruits these students. They must score 550 on the written TOEFL and also take the SAT I or the ACT.

Computers: The mainframes are dual SUN 420Rs and numerous NT and WIN 2000 servers. A variety of programming languages is available on the DEC system, including COBOL and FORTRAN. Facilities include Mac and SUN computers, 5 PC labs in the academic computing center, and 3 remote labs on campus. There is also a 50-station PC lab in Kearney Hall. All students may access the system 24 hours daily. There are no time limits and no fees. It is strongly recommended that all students have personal computers.

Graduates: In 2001, 441 bachelor's degrees were awarded. The most popular majors were business and management (20%), psychology (10%), and communication/journalism (9%). In an average class, 56% graduate in 4 years, 58% in 5 years, and 58% in 6 years. 50 companies recruited on campus in 2000-2001. Of the 2000 graduating class, 12% were enrolled in graduate school within 6 months of graduation and 89% were employed.

Admissions Contact: Stacy A. Ledermann, Director of Freshman Admissions. E-mail: *admissions@sjfc.edu* Web: *http://www.sjfc.edu*

SAINT JOHN'S UNIVERSITY

Jamaica, NY 11439 — D-5

(718) 990-2000

(888) 9 STJOHNS; Fax: (718) 990-5827

Full-time: 5027 men, 6575 women	**Faculty:** 491; I, av$
Part-time: 1138 men, 1745 women	**Ph.D.s:** 90%
Graduate: 1621 men, 2517 women	**Student/Faculty:** 24 to 1
Year: semesters, summer session	**Tuition:** $17,330
Application Deadline: open	**Room & Board:** $9330

Freshman Class: 10,254 applied, 8186 accepted, 2689 enrolled

SAT I Verbal/Math: 510/530 — **COMPETITIVE**

Saint John's University, founded in 1870 by the Vincentian Fathers, is a private Roman Catholic institution offering programs in the arts and sciences, education, business, pharmacy and allied health professions, theology, and professional studies. There are 5 undergraduate and 6 graduate schools. In addition to regional accreditation, St. John's has baccalaureate program accreditation with AACSB and ACPE. The 4 libraries contain 1,129,832 volumes, 2,612,445 microform items, and 15,525 audiovisual forms/CDs, and subscribe to 6108 periodicals. Computerized library services include the card catalog, interlibrary loans, and database searching. Special learning facilities include a learning resource center, art gallery, radio station, TV station, health education resource center, model pharmacy, speech and hearing clinic, instructional materials center, instructional Media Center, and Institute of Asian Studies. The 95-acre campus is in a suburban area in the Jamaica section of Queens. There is also a 16 acre branch campus in Staten Island and a 10-story building located in Manhattan's financial district. Including residence halls, there are 33 buildings.

Student Life: 92% of undergraduates are from New York. Others are from 44 states, 134 foreign countries, and Canada. 59% are from public schools. 49% are white; 13% Hispanic, 12% African American, 11% Asian American. 53% are Catholic; 19% claim no religious affiliation; 15% are Muslim, Hindu, Buddhist, Greek Orthodox, Mormon, or Russian Orthodox. The average age of freshmen is 18; all undergraduates, 21. 20% do not continue beyond their first year; 68% remain to graduate.

Housing: 1704 students can be accommodated in college housing, which includes coed dormitories. On-campus housing is available on a first-come, first-served basis and on a lottery system for upperclassmen. Priority is given to out-of-town students. 88% of students commute. All students may keep cars.

Activities: 7% of men belong to 20 local and 14 national fraternities; 7% of women belong to 11 local and 8 national sororities. There are 187 groups on campus, including art, cheerleading, choir, chorus, computers, dance, debate, drama, environmental, ethnic, film, forensics, honors, human rights, international, jazz band, literary magazine, musical theater, newspaper, pep band, photography, political, professional, radio and TV, religious, social, social service, student government, and yearbook. Popular campus events include International Night, Spring Fling, and Student Activities Fair.

Sports: There are 10 intercollegiate sports for men and 9 for women, and 13 intramural sports for men and 12 for women. Facilities include gyms, a swimming pool, squash and tennis courts, weight and exercise rooms, baseball and softball diamonds, fields for football, lacrosse, and soccer, and basketball and racquetball courts.

Disabled Students: 90% of the campus is accessible. Wheelchair ramps, elevators, special parking, specially equipped rest rooms, special class scheduling, lowered drinking fountains, and lowered telephones are available.

Services: Counseling and information services are available, as is tutoring in most subjects. There is a reader service for the blind, remedial math, reading, and writing, note-taking services, tape recorders, assistance in study skills, and a program for at-risk freshmen.

Campus Safety and Security: Measures include 24-hour foot and vehicle patrol, escort service, informal discussions, and pamphlets/posters/films. There are emergency telephones, lighted pathways/sidewalks, and a crime prevention awareness program.

Programs of Study: St. John's confers B.A., B.S., B.F.A., B.S.Ed., and B.S.Med.Tech. degrees. Associate, master's, and doctoral degrees are also awarded. Bachelor's degrees are awarded in BIOLOGICAL SCIENCE (biology/biological science, ecology, and toxicology), BUSINESS (accounting, banking and finance, business administration and management, business economics, funeral home services, hospitality management services, insurance and risk management, management science, marketing and distribution, office supervision and management, real estate, sports management, and transportation management), COMMUNICATIONS AND THE ARTS (art, communications, English, film arts, fine arts, French, German, graphic design, illustration, Italian, journalism, languages, literature, multimedia, photography, Spanish, and speech/debate/rhetoric), COMPUTER AND PHYSICAL SCIENCE (chemistry, computer science, data processing, mathematics, physical sciences, and physics), EDUCATION (art, bilingual/bicultural, early childhood, education of the deaf and hearing impaired, elementary, English, foreign languages, mathematics, middle school, science, secondary, social science, social studies, and special), ENGINEERING AND ENVIRONMENTAL DESIGN (aircraft mechanics, computer technology, environmental science, and preengineering), HEALTH PROFESSIONS (cytotechnology, health care administration, medical technology, nursing, pharmacy, physician's assistant, predentistry, premedicine, and speech pathology/audiology), SOCIAL SCIENCE (American studies, anthropology, Asian/Oriental studies, criminal justice, economics, history, human services, liberal arts/general studies, paralegal studies, philosophy, political science/government, prelaw, psychology, public administration, safety and security technology, social science, sociology, and theological studies). Pharmacy, biology, and psychology are the strongest academically. Pharmacy, finance, and computer science are the largest.

Required: To graduate, students must complete at least 126 credit hours, including core courses and distribution requirements, with a minimum GPA of 2.0 overall and in the major. Other requirements vary by program.

Special: St. John's offers internships, study abroad in Europe, Central and South America, and Asia, an accelerated degree program in many majors, B.A.-B.S. degrees, dual majors and combined degree programs, pass/fail options, and some credit for life, military, and work experience. There are cooperative programs in dentistry with Columbia University, in engineering with Manhattan College, in photography with the International Center of Photography, in funeral service administration with the McAllister Institute, and in optometry with SUNY College of Optometry. There is a 6-year doctor of pharmacy program for incoming freshmen. There are 13 national honor societies and a freshman honors program.

Faculty/Classroom: 64% of faculty are male; 36%, female. 87% teach undergraduates, 91% do research, and 78% do both. No introductory courses are taught by graduate students. The average class size in an introductory lecture is 29; in a laboratory, 23; and in a regular course, 27.

Admissions: 80% of the 2001-2002 applicants were accepted. The SAT I scores for the 2001-2002 freshman class were: Verbal--39% below 500, 46% between 500 and 599, 14% between 600 and 700, and 1% above 700; Math--30% below 500, 46% between 500 and 599, 22% between 600 and 700, and 2% above 700. 33% of the current freshmen were in the top fifth of their class; 63% were in the top two fifths. 10 freshmen graduated first in their class.

Requirements: The SAT I or ACT is required. Admissions decisions are made by committee and are based on several criteria, including standardized test scores, academic curriculum, and high school average. A GPA of 3.0 is required. AP and CLEP credits are accepted. Important factors in the admissions decision are advanced placement or honor courses, recommendations by school officials, and extracurricular activities record. Applications are accepted on-line through the Saint John's web site at (CollegEdge) or through the New York Mentor program (*ny.xap.com*).

Procedure: Freshmen are admitted fall, spring, and summer. Entrance exams should be taken late in the junior year or early in the senior year. There are early admissions and deferred admissions plans. Application deadlines are open. The fall 2001 application fee was $30. Notification is sent on a rolling basis.

Transfer: 647 transfer students enrolled in 2001-2002. Applicants must present official transcripts of high school and college work, as well as a list of courses in progress. If the student has been out of school a semester or more, a letter of explanation is also required. Admissions requirements for transfer students to the 6-year pharmacy program are stricter and placement is limited. 30 credits of 126 must be completed at St. John's.

Visiting: There are regularly scheduled orientations for prospective students, including small group presentations and a tour of the campus. There are guides for informal visits and visitors may sit in on classes by appointment only. To schedule a visit, contact Robert Pennacchio, Associate Director.

Financial Aid: In 2001-2002, 93% of all freshmen and 87% of continuing students received some form of financial aid. 85% of freshmen and 74% of continuing students received need-based aid. The average freshman award was $14,655. Of that total, scholarships or need-based grants averaged $4527 ($16,900 maximum); loans averaged $3749 ($8625 maximum); work contracts averaged $1717 ($4000 maximum); and tuition remission and external grants averaged $5092 ($16,900 maximum). 84% of undergraduates work part time. Average annual earnings from campus work are $4000. The average financial indebtedness of the 2001 graduate was $16,947. The FAFSA is required. The fall application deadline is March 1.

International Students: There are 438 international students enrolled. The school actively recruits these students. They must score 500 on the written TOEFL or 173 on the electronic version and also take the college's own test, and the SAT I, scoring 1000, or the ACT. This requirement may be waived for international students educated outside of the United States.

Computers: There are more than 1000 workstations available with full access to the Internet and the Web. They are located in the library, computer lab, classrooms, student center, and residence halls. All students may access the system. There are no time limits and no fees.

Graduates: In 2001, 2194 bachelor's degrees were awarded. The most popular majors were pharmacy (9%), finance (9%), and criminal justice (8%). In an average class, 2% graduate in 3 years, 43% in 4 years, 63% in 5 years, and 68% in 6 years. 280 companies recruited on campus in 2000-2001. Of the 2000 graduating class, 18% were enrolled in graduate school within 6 months of graduation and 77% were employed.

Admissions Contact: Patricia Armstrong, Director.
E-mail: *admissions@stjohns.edu* Web: *www.stjohns.edu*

SAINT JOSEPH'S COLLEGE, NEW YORK D-5
Brooklyn, NY 11205 (718) 636-6868
(866) AT ST JOE; Fax: (718) 636-8303

Full-time: 88 men, 427 women	**Faculty:** 39
Part-time: 156 men, 452 women	**Ph.D.s:** 52%
Graduate: 18 men, 48 women	**Student/Faculty:** 15 to 1
Year: semesters, summer session	**Tuition:** $9802
Application Deadline: August 1	**Room & Board:** n/app
Freshman Class: 425 applied, 217 accepted, 67 enrolled	
SAT I Verbal/Math: 517/511	**COMPETITIVE**

Saint Joseph's College, established in 1916, is a private, independent, multicampus commuter institution offering undergraduate degrees in arts and sciences, child study, business, accounting, health professions, and nursing. Some information in this profile is approximate. There is a branch campus in Patchogue, Long Island. There is 1 graduate school. In addition to regional accreditation, Saint Joseph's has baccalaureate program accreditation with NLN. The library contains 75,000 volumes, 4341 microform items, and 4504 audiovisual forms/CDs, and subscribes to 434 periodicals. Computerized library services include interlibrary loans and database searching. Special learning facilities include an on-campus lab preschool. The 3-acre campus is in an urban area 1 mile east of Manhattan. There are 5 buildings.

Student Life: 99% of undergraduates are from New York. Others are from 2 states and 2 foreign countries. 20% are from public schools. 50% are white; 36%, African American. The average age of freshmen is 18; all undergraduates, 33. 12% do not continue beyond their first year; 73% remain to graduate.

Housing: There are no residence halls. All students commute. Alcohol is not permitted. All students may keep cars.

Activities: 15% of men belong to 1 local fraternity; 6% of women belong to 1 local sorority. There are 22 groups on campus, including art, cheerleading, chorus, computers, dance, drama, ethnic, honors, literary magazine, newspaper, political, professional, religious, social, social service, student government, and yearbook. Popular campus events include an annual dinner dance, Junior Class Night, and a holiday party.

Sports: There are 3 intercollegiate sports for men and 4 for women, and 4 intramural sports for men and 4 for women. Facilities include a gym, a handball court, an outdoor mall, recreation rooms, and an exercise/weight room.

Disabled Students: 10% of the campus is accessible. Wheelchair ramps, elevators, and specially equipped rest rooms are available.

Services: Counseling and information services are available, as is tutoring in most subjects. There is remedial writing.

Campus Safety and Security: Measures include self-defense education, escort service, informal discussions, and pamphlets/posters/films. There are lighted pathways/sidewalks.

Programs of Study: Saint Joseph's confers B.A. and B.S. degrees. Master's degrees are also awarded. Bachelor's degrees are awarded in BIOLOGICAL SCIENCE (biology/biological science), BUSINESS (accounting and business administration and management), COMMUNICATIONS AND THE ARTS (English, Spanish, and speech/debate/rhetoric), COMPUTER AND PHYSICAL SCIENCE (chemistry and mathematics), EDUCATION (early childhood, elementary, secondary, and special), HEALTH PROFESSIONS (community health work, health care administration, and nursing), SOCIAL SCIENCE (history, psychology, and social science). Child study, psychology, and biology are the largest.

Required: To graduate, students must complete a 51-credit core curriculum requirement consisting of 8 courses in humanities, 3 in social science and math/science, and 1 English composition course. The minimum GPA is 2.0. Students must earn 128 credits, with 30 to 36 credits in the major. Most majors require a thesis.

Special: The college offers internship programs in English, history, political science, psychology, sociology, speech, and business/accounting, and an interdisciplinary major in human relations. Adult students may pursue a general studies degree in which the college allows credit for life, military, and work experience. There are 5 national honor societies and a freshman honors program.

Faculty/Classroom: 39% of faculty are male; 62%, female. All teach undergraduates and 10% do research. The average class size in an introductory lecture is 15; in a laboratory, 15; and in a regular course, 12.

Admissions: 51% of the 2001-2002 applicants were accepted. The SAT I scores for the 2001-2002 freshman class were: Verbal--40% below 500, 49% between 500 and 599, and 11% between 600 and 700; Math--54% below 500, 39% between 500 and 599, and 7% between 600 and 700. 32% of the current freshmen were in the top fifth of their class; 45% were in the top two fifths. 3 freshmen graduated first in their class in a recent year.

Requirements: The SAT I is required, with a minimum required composite score of 900. Applicants must graduate from an accredited secondary school or earn a GED. 16 Carnegie units are required, including 4 units of English and social studies, 3 of math, 2 of languages and science, and 3 elective units. Interviews are recommended. A GPA of 3.0 is required. AP and CLEP credits are accepted. Important factors in the admissions decision are advanced placement or honor courses, recommendations by school officials, and leadership record.

Procedure: Freshmen are admitted fall and spring. There are early decision, early admissions, and deferred admissions plans. Applications should be filed by August 1 for fall entry and January 1 for spring entry, along with a $25 fee. Notification is sent on a rolling basis.

Transfer: 152 transfer students enrolled in a recent year. Transfer applicants must have a minimum GPA of 2.0. If fewer than 40 credits have been earned, the SAT I is required with a minimum composite score of 900. 48 credits of 128 must be completed at Saint Joseph's.

Visiting: There are regularly scheduled orientations for prospective students, including meetings with faculty advisers and student-to-student sessions. There are guides for informal visits and visitors may sit in on classes. To schedule a visit, contact the Admissions Office.

Financial Aid: In 2001-2002, 95% of all freshmen and 87% of continuing students received some form of financial aid. 4% of undergraduates work part time. Average annual earnings from campus work are $1000. Saint Joseph's is a member of CSS. The FAFSA and the college's own financial statement are required. Check with the school for current deadlines.

International Students: They must score 550 on the written TOEFL and also take the SAT I.

Computers: The mainframe is an IBM AS/400/System 36. PCs are available to students in the 3 computer labs, in department offices, and in the library. Students also have access to the Internet, and on-line databases at 20 additional workstations. All students may access the system. There are no time limits and no fees.

Graduates: In an average class, 71% graduate in 4 years, 73% in 5 years, and 73% in 6 years. 32 companies recruited on campus in a recent year. Of a recent graduating class, 42% were enrolled in graduate school within 6 months of graduation and 75% were employed.

Admissions Contact: Theresa LaRocca Meyer, Director of Admissions. Web: *www.sjcny.edu*

SAINT LAWRENCE UNIVERSITY — C-2
Canton, NY 13617 — (315) 229-5261
(800) 285-1856; Fax: (315) 229-5818

Full-time: 918 men, 1040 women	**Faculty:** 156; IIB, +$
Part-time: 16 men, 14 women	**Ph.D.s:** 98%
Graduate: 42 men, 87 women	**Student/Faculty:** 13 to 1
Year: semesters, summer session	**Tuition:** $24,850
Application Deadline: February 15	**Room & Board:** $7755
Freshman Class: 2745 applied, 1674 accepted, 511 enrolled	
SAT I Verbal/Math: 570/570	**VERY COMPETITIVE**

St. Lawrence University, established in 1856, is a private liberal arts institution. In addition to regional accreditation, St. Lawrence has baccalaureate program accreditation with ACS. The 2 libraries contain 522,722 volumes, 580,532 microform items, and 3958 audiovisual forms/CDs, and subscribe to 2035 periodicals. Computerized library services include the card catalog, interlibrary loans, and database searching. Special learning facilities include a learning resource center, art gallery, radio station, and TV station. The 1000-acre campus is in a rural area 80 miles south of Ottawa, Canada. Including residence halls, there are 30 buildings.

Student Life: 51% of undergraduates are from New York. Others are from 37 states, 19 foreign countries, and Canada. 73% are from public schools. 73% are white. The average age of freshmen is 18; all undergraduates, 20. 16% do not continue beyond their first year; 71% remain to graduate.

Housing: 1478 students can be accommodated in college housing, which includes coed dormitories, fraternity houses, and sorority houses. In addition, there are language houses, special-interest houses,and theme cottages, such as Habitat for Humanity. On-campus housing is guaranteed for all 4 years. 96% of students live on campus; of those, 90% remain on campus on weekends. All students may keep cars.

Activities: 14% of men belong to 4 national fraternities; 25% of women belong to 1 local sorority and 3 national sororities. There are 127 groups on campus, including art, chess, choir, chorus, dance, drama, ethnic, forensics, gay, honors, international, literary magazine, newspaper, outdoor, photography, political, professional, radio and TV, religious, social, social service, student government, and yearbook. Popular campus events include St. Lawrence Festival of the Arts, Black History Week, and Holiday Candlelight Service.

Sports: There are 15 intercollegiate sports for men and 16 for women, and 12 intramural sports for men and 9 for women. 45% of men and women participate. Facilities include basketball, squash, and tennis courts, a swimming pool, and weight, Nautilus, and exercise rooms. There are also 2 field houses, an arena, an artificial ice rink, an 18-hole golf course, riding stables, jogging and cross-country ski trails, a fitness center, a 9-line track, and soccer, baseball, and softball fields.

Disabled Students: 75% of the campus is accessible. Wheelchair ramps, elevators, special parking, specially equipped rest rooms, special class scheduling, and visual fire alarms are available.

Services: Counseling and information services are available, as is tutoring in every subject. There is a reader service for the blind, a writing center, and science and technology counseling.

Campus Safety and Security: Measures include 24-hour foot and vehicle patrol, self-defense education, escort service, and shuttle buses. There are informal discussions, pamphlets/posters/films, emergency telephones, lighted pathways/sidewalks, and student patrols.

Programs of Study: St. Lawrence confers B.A. and B.S. degrees. Master's degrees are also awarded. Bachelor's degrees are awarded in BIOLOGICAL SCIENCE (biochemistry, biology/biological science, and neurosciences), COMMUNICATIONS AND THE ARTS (dramatic arts, English, fine arts, French, German, music, and Spanish), COMPUTER AND PHYSICAL SCIENCE (chemistry, computer science, geology, mathematics, and physics), ENGINEERING AND ENVIRONMENTAL DESIGN (environmental science), SOCIAL SCIENCE (African studies, anthropology, Asian/Oriental studies, Canadian studies, economics, history, interdisciplinary studies, international studies, philosophy, political science/government, psychology, religion, and sociology). Psychology, English, and economics are the strongest academically and have the largest enrollments.

Required: To graduate, students must maintain a minimum GPA of 2.0 and complete 120 course hours, with 29 to 43 in the major. Freshmen must take a first-year program, a 2-semester team-taught course. Requirements also include 1 course in arts/expression, 1 in humanities, 1 in social science, 1 in math or foreign language, 2 in natural science/science studies, and 2 in diversity.

Special: Students may cross-register with the Associated Colleges of the St. Lawrence Valley. Internships are available through the sociology, psychology, and English departments and through a service learning program. Study-abroad in 13 countries and a Washington semester are offered. Dual majors and student-designed majors can be arranged. Students may earn 3-2 engineering degrees in conjunction with 7 engineering schools. Nondegree study and pass/fail options are available. An Adirondack semester and a leadership academy are also offered. There are 20 national honor societies, including Phi Beta Kappa, and 17 departmental honors programs.

Faculty/Classroom: 58% of faculty are male; 42%, female. 98% teach undergraduates and all do research. No introductory courses are taught by graduate students. The average class size in a regular course is 16.

Admissions: 61% of the 2001-2002 applicants were accepted. The SAT I scores for the 2001-2002 freshman class were: Verbal--17% below 500, 46% between 500 and 599, 31% between 600 and 700, and 6% above 700; Math--15% below 500, 46% between 500 and 599, 34% between 600 and 700, and 4% above 700. 60% of the current freshmen were in the top fifth of their class; 87% were in the top two fifths. 15 freshmen graduated first in their class in a recent year.

Requirements: The SAT I is required. In addition, applicants must be graduates of an accredited high school. 16 or more academic credits are required, including 4 years of English and 3 years each of foreign languages, math, science, and social studies. Essays are required and interviews are recommended for all applicants. AP and CLEP credits are accepted. Important factors in the admissions decision are advanced placement or honor courses, extracurricular activities record, and recommendations by school officials. Applications are accepted on-line at the university's web site.

Procedure: Freshmen are admitted fall and spring. Entrance exams should be taken during the spring of the junior year or the fall of the senior year. There are early decision and deferred admissions plans. Early decision applications should be filed by November 15; regular applications, by February 15 for fall entry and December 1 for spring entry, along with a $50 fee. Notification is sent within 4 weeks for early decision; by March 15 for regular decision. 114 early decision candidates were accepted for the 2001-2002 class. 13% of all applicants are on a waiting list; 84 were accepted in 2001.

Transfer: 28 transfer students enrolled in 2001-2002. Applicants must have a 3.0 GPA and a minimum of 4 courses must have been completed. The high school transcript and SAT I scores will be evaluated, but college work is more important. Interviews and high school and college recommendations are required. 58 credits of 120 must be completed at St. Lawrence.

Visiting: There are regularly scheduled orientations for prospective students, including interviews and tours. There are guides for informal visits and visitors may sit in on classes and stay overnight. To schedule a visit, contact the Admissions Office.

Financial Aid: In 2001-2002, 86% of all students received some form of financial aid. 70% of all students received need-based aid. The average freshman award was $14,830. Of that total, scholarships or need-based grants averaged $14,830; loans averaged $3910; work contracts averaged $1113; and HEOP, TAP, PELL, SEOG, and outside grants averaged $1980. 43% of undergraduates work part time. Average annual earnings from campus work are $1113. St. Lawrence is a member of CSS. Either the CSS Profile or the college's own application is required. The fall application deadline is February 15.

International Students: There are 70 international students enrolled. The school actively recruits these students. They must score 600 on the written TOEFL or 250 on the electronic version or take the SAT I or ACT.

Computers: 600 PCs are linked to multiple servers and a card catalog. Word processing, spreadsheet, database, and course-specific software, e-mail, calendars, bulletin boards, and Internet and World Wide Web access are available. Computer labs are located throughout campus in academic and resident buildings. All students may access the system 24 hours per day. There are no time limits and no fees.

Graduates: In 2001, 399 bachelor's degrees were awarded. The most popular majors were psychology (12%), government (11%), and English (10%). In an average class, 1% graduate in 3 years, 65% in 4 years, 72% in 5 years, and 72% in 6 years. 20 companies recruited on campus in 2000-2001. Of the 2000 graduating class, 15% were enrolled in graduate school within 6 months of graduation and 80% were employed.

Admissions Contact: Teresa Cowdrey, Dean of Admissions and Financial Aid. E-mail: *admissions@stlawu.edu* Web: *www.stlawu.ed*

SAINT THOMAS AQUINAS COLLEGE

Sparkill, NY 10976 D-5

(914) 398-4100

(800) 999-STAC; Fax: (914) 398-4224

Full-time: 1310 men and women	**Faculty:** 76; IIB, +$
Part-time: 700 men and women	**Ph.D.s:** 75%
Graduate: 65 men, 115 women	**Student/Faculty:** 17 to 1
Year: 4-1-4, summer session	**Tuition:** $13,440
Application Deadline: rolling	**Room & Board:** $7150
Freshman Class: n/av	
SAT I or ACT: required	**LESS COMPETITIVE**

Saint Thomas Aquinas College, founded in 1952, is an independent liberal arts institution. Figures in above capsule are approximate. The library contains 102,943 volumes and 45,900 microform items, and subscribes to 108 periodicals. Computerized library services include the card catalog, interlibrary loans, and database searching. Special learning facilities include a learning resource center, radio station, and TV station. The 43-acre campus is in a suburban area 15 miles north of New York City. Including residence halls, there are 12 buildings.

Student Life: 75% of undergraduates are from New York. Others are from 6 states, 8 foreign countries, and Canada. 80% are from public schools. 84% are white. 62% are Catholic; 23% Protestant. The average age of freshmen is 18; all undergraduates, 23. 16% do not continue beyond their first year; 62% remain to graduate.

Housing: 450 students can be accommodated in college housing, which includes single-sex dormitories and on-campus apartments. On-campus housing is guaranteed for all 4 years. 65% of students commute. Alcohol is not permitted. All students may keep cars.

Activities: There are no fraternities or sororities. There are 15 groups on campus, including cheerleading, chorus, computers, drama, honors, international, literary magazine, musical theater, newspaper, professional, radio and TV, religious, social service, student government, and yearbook. Popular campus events include trips to Broadway shows and Halloween and Christmas mixers.

Sports: There are 5 intercollegiate sports for men and 4 for women, and 6 intramural sports for men and 5 for women. Facilities include an auditorium, a 750-seat gym, a weight room, and basketball and tennis courts.

Disabled Students: 90% of the campus is accessible. Wheelchair ramps, elevators, special parking, specially equipped rest rooms, special class scheduling, and lowered telephones are available.

Services: Counseling and information services are available, as is tutoring in most subjects. There is remedial math and writing.

Campus Safety and Security: Measures include 24-hour foot and vehicle patrol, escort service, pamphlets/posters/films, and emergency telephones. There are lighted pathways/sidewalks.

Programs of Study: STAC confers B.A., B.S., and B.S.E. degrees. Associate and master's degrees are also awarded. Bachelor's degrees are awarded in BUSINESS (accounting, banking and finance, business administration and management, marketing/retailing/merchandising, and recreation and leisure services), COMMUNICATIONS AND THE ARTS (communications, English, fine arts, romance languages and literature, and Spanish), EDUCATION (art, bilingual/bicultural, elementary, foreign languages, science, secondary, and special), ENGINEERING AND ENVIRONMENTAL DESIGN (commercial art), HEALTH PROFESSIONS (medical laboratory technology and premedicine), SOCIAL SCIENCE (criminal justice, history, philosophy, prelaw, psychology, religion, and social science). Education, business administration, and natural sciences are the strongest academically. Business administration is the largest.

Required: To graduate, all students must complete a total of 120 credit hours, with 36 to 54 in the major and a minimum GPA of 2.0. A core curriculum of 51 credits in liberal arts courses is required.

Special: The college offers cross-registration with Barry University and Aquinas College and internships in business, criminal justice, commercial design, recreation and leisure, and communications. Study abroad in Europe and Asia, a 3-2 engineering degree with George Washington University and Manhattan College, and in physical therapy with New York Medical College, and work-study programs are available. Nondegree study and pass/fail options are possible. There are 7 national honor societies, including Phi Beta Kappa, and a freshman honors program.

Faculty/Classroom: 55% of faculty are male; 45%, female. 99% teach undergraduates, 50% do research, and 50% do both. No introductory courses are taught by graduate students. The average class size in an introductory lecture is 35; in a laboratory, 15; and in a regular course, 20.

Requirements: The SAT I or ACT is required. In addition, applicants must be graduates of an accredited secondary school or have a GED certificate. 16 Carnegie units are recommended, including 4 years of English, 3 years of social science, 2 years each of math and science, and 1 year each of foreign language and history. An interview is recommended. Applications are accepted on computer disk and on-line via ExPAN or at the college's web site. A GPA of 2.2 is required. AP and CLEP credits are accepted. Important factors in the admissions decision are leadership record, extracurricular activities record, and advanced placement or honor courses.

Procedure: Freshmen are admitted in fall and spring. Entrance exams should be taken by the spring of the junior year. There are early decision, early admissions, and deferred admissions plans. Notification is sent on a rolling basis. Check with the school for current deadlines. The fall 2001 application fee was $30.

Transfer: 200 transfer students enrolled in a recent year. Applicants must have a 2.0 GPA from the previous school. 30 credits of 120 must be completed at STAC.

Visiting: There are guides for informal visits and visitors may sit in on classes and stay overnight. To schedule a visit, contact the Admissions Office.

Financial Aid: The average freshman award was $7047. STAC is a member of CSS. The FAFSA is required. Check with the school for current deadlines.

International Students: The school actively recruits these students. They must score 500 on the written TOEFL.

Computers: The mainframe is an HP 3000. There are also 50 IBM, Zenith, Mac, and HP PCs available throughout campus. The campus is served by an intranet system with access to the Internet and e-mail. All students may access the system. There are no time limits. The fee is $100.

Admissions Contact: Tracey A. Howard-Ubelhoer, Director of Admissions. A video is available. E-mail: *thoward@stac.edu*
Web: *www.stac.edu*

SARAH LAWRENCE COLLEGE

Bronxville, NY 10708 D-5

(914) 395-2510

(800) 888-2858; Fax: (914) 395-2515

Full-time: 317 men, 826 women	**Faculty:** 176; IIB, +$
Part-time: 9 men, 62 women	**Ph.D.s:** 90%
Graduate: 55 men, 284 women	**Student/Faculty:** 6 to 1
Year: semesters	**Tuition:** $27,982
Application Deadline: January 15	**Room & Board:** $9534
Freshman Class: 2782 applied, 1027 accepted, 323 enrolled	
SAT I Verbal/Math: 670/590	**ACT:** 27 **HIGHLY COMPETITIVE**

Sarah Lawrence College, established in 1926, is an independent institution conferring liberal arts degrees. The academic structure is based on the British don system. Students meet biweekly with professors in tutorials and are enrolled in small seminars. While there are no formal majors, students develop individual concentrations that are usually interdisciplinary. The 3 libraries contain 202,265 volumes, 21,247 microform items, and 8422 audiovisual forms/CDs, and subscribe to 880 periodicals. Computerized library services include the card catalog, interlibrary loans, and database searching. Special learning facilities include an art gallery, radio station, a slide library with 75,000 slides of art and architecture, early childhood center, electronic music studio, music library, student-run theater and student-run art gallery. The 41-acre campus is in a suburban area 15 miles north of midtown Manhattan. Including residence halls, there are 50 buildings.

Student Life: 78% of undergraduates are from out of state, mostly the Northeast. Others are from 48 states, 27 foreign countries, and Canada. 65% are from public schools. 69% are white. The average age of freshmen is 18; all undergraduates, 20. 6% do not continue beyond their first year; 74% remain to graduate.

Housing: 880 students can be accommodated in college housing, which includes single-sex and coed dormitories, on-campus apartments, and off-campus apartments. On-campus housing is guaranteed for all 4 years. 87% of students live on campus; of those, 85% remain on campus on weekends. Upperclassmen may keep cars.

Activities: There are no fraternities or sororities. There are 30 groups on campus, including art, band, choir, chorale, chorus, computers, cultural, dance, drama, ethnic, film, gay, international, jazz band, literary magazine, musical theater, newspaper, orchestra, photography, poetry, political, prose, radio and TV, religious, social, social service, student government, and yearbook. Popular campus events include Mayfair, "Deb Ball," and a student scholarship fundraising auction.

Sports: There are 5 intercollegiate sports for men and 6 for women, and 5 intramural sports for men and 5 for women. Facilities include a sports center with a gym, a jogging track, a 6-lane swimming pool, a rowing tank, a multipurpose studio, and 3 squash courts; a fitness center and weight room; tennis courts; and a number of open fields and lawns. Off-campus, the college has the use of a boat house and stables.

Disabled Students: 50% of the campus is accessible. Wheelchair ramps, elevators, special parking, specially equipped rest rooms, special class scheduling, lowered drinking fountains, and lowered telephones are available.

Services: Counseling and information services are available, as is tutoring in some subjects, including writing. There is a reader service for the blind.

Campus Safety and Security: Measures include 24-hour foot and vehicle patrol, self-defense education, escort service, and shuttle buses. There are informal discussions, pamphlets/posters/films, emergency telephones, and lighted pathways/sidewalks.

Programs of Study: Sarah Lawrence confers the B.A. degree. Master's degrees are also awarded. Bachelor's degrees are awarded in the liberal arts. Students may concentrate in BIOLOGICAL SCIENCE (biology/biological science), COMMUNICATIONS AND THE ARTS (art history and appreciation, classics, creative writing, dance, dramatic arts, English, film arts, fine arts, French, German, Greek, Italian, Latin, literature, music, Russian, Spanish, and visual and performing arts), COMPUTER AND PHYSICAL SCIENCE (chemistry and mathematics), HEALTH PROFESSIONS (premedicine), SOCIAL SCIENCE (anthropology, Asian/Oriental studies, economics, history, liberal arts/general studies, philosophy, political science/government, psychology, religion, Russian and Slavic studies, sociology, and women's studies).

Required: To graduate, students must complete 120 credit hours and meet distribution requirements in 3 of 4 academic areas, including history and social sciences, creative and performing arts, natural science and math, and humanities. Students must fulfill a first-year studies requirement in one of 18 areas and meet a phys ed requirement. Students must also take 2 lecture courses, where the average class size is 40.

Special: Internships are available in a variety of fields, with the school offering proximity to New York City art galleries and agencies. Study abroad in many countries, work-study programs, dual concentrations, and a general degree may be pursued. All concentrations are self-designed and can be combined.

Faculty/Classroom: 51% of faculty are male; 49%, female. All teach undergraduates. No introductory courses are taught by graduate students. The average class size in a regular course is 11.

Admissions: 37% of the 2001-2002 applicants were accepted. The SAT I scores for the 2001-2002 freshman class were: Verbal--3% below 500, 18% between 500 and 599, 48% between 600 and 700, and 31% above 700; Math--8% below 500, 43% between 500 and 599, 43% between 600 and 700, and 7% above 700. The ACT scores were 3% below 21, 14% between 21 and 23, 31% between 24 and 26, 20% between 27 and 28, and 32% above 28. 66% of the current freshmen were in the top fifth of their class; 95% were in the top two fifths. There were 6 National Merit finalists. 5 freshmen graduated first in their class.

Requirements: The SAT I or ACT or 3 SAT II: Subject tests are required. Applicants must graduate from an accredited secondary school or have a GED. The number of academic credits required depends on the high school attended. The college recommends completion of 4 years of English, 3 each of math, science, social studies, and a foreign language, 2 to 3 of history, and 1 each of art and music. 3 essays are required. An interview is recommended. AP credits are accepted. Important factors in the admissions decision are advanced placement or honor courses, academic writing ability, and personality/intangible qualities. Applications are accepted on-line via the Common Application and the college web site *www.sarahlawrence.edu*.

Procedure: Freshmen are admitted fall and spring. There are early decision, early admissions, and deferred admissions plans. Early decision applications should be filed by November 15; regular applications, by January 15 for fall entry and December 1 for spring entry. The fall 2001 application fee was $50. Notification of early decision is sent December 15; regular decision, April 1. 92 early decision candidates were accepted for the 2001-2002 class. 14% of all applicants are on a waiting list; 5 were accepted in 2001.

Transfer: 30 transfer students enrolled in 2001-2002. Applicants must submit the Application for Admission (Form A). Applicants must also submit the College Dean's Report form, high school and college transcripts, and 2 teacher evaluations. A GPA of 3.0 is recommended. Students must have completed 1 full year of college. Sarah Lawrence has a 2-year residency requirement. An interview is strongly recommended. 60 credits of 120 must be completed at Sarah Lawrence.

Visiting: There are regularly scheduled orientations for prospective students, consisting of a full day of faculty and student panels, lectures, tours, and discussion with admissions officers, offered twice each fall. There are guides for informal visits and visitors may sit in on classes and stay overnight. To schedule a visit, contact Linda Bloom, Receptionist, Admissions Office.

Financial Aid: In 2001-2002, 65% of all freshmen and 57% of continuing students received some form of financial aid. 47% of freshmen and 45% of continuing students received need-based aid. The average freshman award was $23,531. Of that total, scholarships or need-based grants averaged $17,803 ($37,665 maximum); loans averaged $2315 ($2625 maximum); and work contracts averaged $1800 (maximum). 43% of undergraduates work part time. Average annual earnings from campus work are $1769. The average financial indebtedness of the 2001 graduate was $13,042. Sarah Lawrence is a member of CSS. The CSS/Profile or FAFSA and non-custodial parent statement are required. The fall application deadline is February 1.

International Students: The school actively recruits these students. They must score 600 on the written TOEFL or take SAT II: English as a second language test and also take the SAT I, ACT, or 3 SAT II: Subject tests.

Computers: There are 60 Macs and PCs with laser printers located in the student computer center, 19 located in the library, and 31 divided between 2 computer classrooms. All PCs are networked with full access to the Internet. All students may access the system 24 hours a day. There are no time limits and no fees.

Graduates: In 2001, 245 bachelor's degrees were awarded. In an average class, 51% graduate in 4 years, 62% in 5 years, and 66% in 6 years. Of the 2000 graduating class, 30% were enrolled in graduate school within 6 months of graduation and 70% were employed.

Admissions Contact: Thyra L. Briggs, Dean of Admission.
E-mail: *slcadmit@alc.edu* Web: *www.slc.edu*

SCHOOL OF VISUAL ARTS — D-5
New York, NY 10010-3994 — (212) 592-2100
(800) 436-4204; Fax: (212) 592-2116

Full-time: 1530 men, 1470 women	**Faculty:** 94
Part-time: 780 men, 1060 women	**Ph.D.s:** 36%
Graduate: 145 men, 182 women	**Student/Faculty:** 32 to 1
Year: semesters, summer session	**Tuition:** $17,000
Application Deadline: March 15	**Room & Board:** $9000

Freshman Class: 1822 applied, 1127 accepted, 419 enrolled
SAT I or ACT: required — **SPECIAL**

The School of Visual Arts, established in 1947, is a private institution conferring undergraduate and graduate degrees in fine arts. There are 8 undergraduate and 5 graduate schools. In addition to regional accreditation, SVA has baccalaureate program accreditation with FIDER and NASAD. The library contains 68,800 volumes, 1070 microform items, and 2990 audiovisual forms/CDs, and subscribes to 278 periodicals. Computerized library services include the card catalog and database searching. Special learning facilities include a learning resource center, art gallery, radio station, 5 student galleries, 3 media arts workshops, 3 film and 2 video studios, numerous editing facilities, animation studio with 3 pencil test facilities, digital audio room, tape transfer room, and multimedia facility with digital printing and editing systems. The campus is in an urban area in the middle of Manhattan. Including residence halls, there are 8 buildings.

Student Life: 60% of undergraduates are from New York. Others are from 45 states, 19 foreign countries, and Canada. 60% are from public schools. 57% are white. The average age of freshmen is 18; all undergraduates, 21. 14% do not continue beyond their first year; 41% remain to graduate.

Housing: 1000 students can be accommodated in college housing, which includes single-sex and coed dormitories and off-campus apartments. On-campus housing is available on a first-come, first-served basis. 75% of students commute. Alcohol is not permitted. All students may keep cars.

Activities: There are no fraternities or sororities. There are many groups and organizations on campus, including art, computers, drama, ethnic, film, gay, honors, international, literary magazine, newspaper, photography, political, professional, radio and TV, religious, social, social service, student government, and yearbook. Popular campus events include an annual ski trip, a Halloween party, and 2 annual paintball trips.

Disabled Students: All of the campus is accessible. Wheelchair ramps, elevators, specially equipped rest rooms, special class scheduling, and lowered telephones are available.

Services: There is remedial reading and writing.

Campus Safety and Security: Measures include 24-hour foot and vehicle patrol, shuttle buses, informal discussions, and pamphlets/posters/films. There are emergency telephones and lighted pathways/sidewalks.

Programs of Study: SVA confers the B.F.A. degree. Master's degrees are also awarded. Bachelor's degrees are awarded in COMMUNICATIONS AND THE ARTS (advertising, animation, film arts, fine arts, graphic design, illustration, photography, and video), ENGINEERING AND ENVIRONMENTAL DESIGN (computer graphics and interior design). Graphic design and advertising, illustration and cartooning, and fine arts are the largest.

Required: To graduate, students must complete 120 credits, including at least 72 in the major, with a minimum GPA of 2.0. These credits must include 30 in humanities and sciences, 12 in art history, and 6 in electives. Students must complete 2 introductory courses in literature and writing and must pass a proficiency exam in the first semester.

Special: SVA offers study abroad in 8 countries, accelerated degree programs, and for-credit internships with more than 200 media-related, design, and advertising firms, including DC Comics, MTV, and Pentagram Design. A summer internship with Walt Disney Studios is possible for illustration/cartooning majors.

Faculty/Classroom: 63% of faculty are male; 37%, female. 86% teach undergraduates. No introductory courses are taught by graduate students. The average class size in an introductory lecture is 45 and in a regular course, 20.

Admissions: 62% of the 2001-2002 applicants were accepted. The SAT I scores for the 2001-2002 freshman class were: Verbal--35% below 500, 44% between 500 and 599, 16% between 600 and 700, and 4% above 700; Math--42% below 500, 41% between 500 and 599, 15% between 600 and 700, and 1% above 700.

Requirements: The SAT I or ACT is required. In addition, applicants must graduate from an accredited secondary school or have a GED. A statement of intent is required of all students. A portfolio is also required, except for film and video applicants, who must submit a 2-part essay. A personal interview and letters of recommendation are considered helpful. A GPA of 2.3 is required. AP and CLEP credits are accepted. Important factors in the admissions decision are evidence of special talent, personality/intangible qualities, and leadership record.

Procedure: Freshmen are admitted fall and spring. There are early decision and deferred admissions plans. Early decision applications should be filed by December 1; regular applications, by March 15 for fall entry and December 1 for spring entry. The fall 2001 application fee was $45. Notification of early decision is sent by January 14; regular decision, within 1 to 2 months after receipt of applications through April 1 or as space permits thereafter. 48 early decision candidates were accepted for a recent class.

Transfer: 503 transfer students enrolled in a recent year. 60 credits of 120 must be completed at SVA.

Visiting: There are regularly scheduled orientations for prospective students, including 6 Saturday Open House receptions and weekly tours. There are guides for informal visits. To schedule a visit, contact the Office of Admissions.

Financial Aid: In 2001-2002, 80% of all freshmen and 61% of continuing students received some form of financial aid. 55% of freshmen and 47% of continuing students received need-based aid. The average freshman award was $9400. Of that total, scholarships or need-based grants averaged $4490 ($17,400 maximum); loans averaged $3600 ($8625 maximum); and work contracts averaged $4900 ($5000 maximum). 5% of undergraduates work part time. Average annual earnings from campus work are $5000. The average financial indebtedness of the 2001 graduate was $14,000. The FAFSA is required. The fall application deadline is February 1.

International Students: There were 434 international students enrolled in a recent year. The school actively recruits these students. They must score 550 on the written TOEFL or 213 on the electronic version or earn a minimum score of 6 in all categories of the NYU English proficiency exam.

Computers: The mainframe is a Sun Enterprise 3500. There are 555 PCs available in the computer art department, digital imaging center, writing resource center, and library. All students may access the system during normal operating hours of the library and the writing resource center; use in other buildings varies by major. There are no time limits and no fees. It is strongly recommended that all students have a personal computer.

Graduates: In 2001, 544 bachelor's degrees were awarded. The most popular majors were graphic design/advertising (27%), illustration/cartooning (19%), and fine arts (15%). In an average class, 35% graduate in 4 years, 41% in 5 years, and 54% in 6 years. 50 companies recruited on campus in 2000-2001.

Admissions Contact: Rick Longo, Executive Director of Admissions.
E-mail: *admissions@adm.schoolofvisualarts.edu*
Web: *www.schoolofvisualarts.edu*

SIENA COLLEGE — D-3

Loudonville, NY 12211-1462 — (518) 783-2423
(888) AT SIENA; Fax: (518) 783-2436

Full-time: 1367 men, 1549 women	**Faculty:** 163; IIB, +$
Part-time: 195 men, 266 women	**Ph.D.s:** 85%
Graduate: 2 men, 3 women	**Student/Faculty:** 18 to 1
Year: semesters, summer session	**Tuition:** $15,870
Application Deadline: March 1	**Room & Board:** $6815
Freshman Class: 3346 applied, 2308 accepted, 712 enrolled	
SAT I Verbal/Math: 545/561	**ACT:** 24 **VERY COMPETITIVE**

Siena College, established in 1937, is a small Franciscan college providing degree programs in the liberal arts, business, and science. There are 3 undergraduate schools and 1 graduate school. In addition to regional accreditation, Siena has baccalaureate program accreditation with ACS and CSWE. The library contains 307,270 volumes, 27,335 microform items, and 4681 audiovisual forms/CDs, and subscribes to 1428 periodicals. Computerized library services include the card catalog, interlibrary loans, and database searching. Special learning facilities include a radio station. The 155-acre campus is in a suburban area 2 miles north of Albany. Including residence halls, there are 26 buildings.

Student Life: 85% of undergraduates are from New York. Others are from 24 states, 7 foreign countries, and Canada. 70% are from public schools. 90% are white. The average age of freshmen is 18; all undergraduates, 21. 12% do not continue beyond their first year; 80% remain to graduate.

Housing: 2219 students can be accommodated in college housing, which includes coed dormitories and townhouses. On-campus housing is guaranteed for the freshman year only and is available on a lottery system for upperclassmen. 74% of students live on campus; of those, 90% remain on campus on weekends. Upperclassmen may keep cars.

Activities: There are no fraternities or sororities. There are 75 groups on campus, including cheerleading, choir, chorus, community service, computers, dance, drama, ethnic, film, honors, international, literary magazine, model U.N., musical theater, newspaper, opera, orchestra, outing, pep band, political, professional, radio and TV, religious, social, social service, student government, symphony, and yearbook. Popular campus events include Family Weekend, Winter Weekend, and Junior/Senior Formal.

Sports: There are 8 intercollegiate sports for men and 11 for women, and 20 intramural sports for men and 20 for women. Facilities include an athletic complex with free weights, a training facility, an indoor track, an 8-lane 25-meter pool, fitness equipment, life cycles, 4 multipurpose courts, 6 outdoor tennis courts, 5 outdoor fields, 2 squash courts, and racquetball courts.

Disabled Students: 90% of the campus is accessible. Wheelchair ramps, elevators, special parking, specially equipped rest rooms, special class scheduling, and an office for students with disabilities that provides various resources are available.

Services: Counseling and information services are available, as is tutoring in most subjects. There is a reader service for the blind, remedial math and writing, and a writing center that offers free one-to-one assistance.

Campus Safety and Security: Measures include 24-hour foot and vehicle patrol, escort service, informal discussions, and pamphlets/posters/films. There are emergency telephones, lighted pathways/sidewalks, and a card access system for dorms, radio dispatch, and a 911 on-campus telephone system.

Programs of Study: Siena confers B.A., B.S., and B.B.A. degrees. Bachelor's degrees are awarded in BIOLOGICAL SCIENCE (biochemistry and biology/biological science), BUSINESS (accounting, banking and finance, business economics, and marketing management), COMMUNICATIONS AND THE ARTS (classical languages, English, French, and Spanish), COMPUTER AND PHYSICAL SCIENCE (chemistry, computer science, mathematics, and physics), ENGINEERING AND ENVIRONMENTAL DESIGN (environmental science), SOCIAL SCIENCE (American studies, economics, history, philosophy, political science/government, psychology, religion, social work, and sociology). Biology, political science, and accounting are the strongest academically. Accounting, marketing/management, and biology are the largest.

Required: To graduate, students must earn 120 credits, including 30 to 39 in the major, with at least a 2.0 GPA. The required core curriculum of 42 credits must include 3 math/science courses, 2 foundation courses, 2 social science courses, 1 to 2 courses in English, history, philosophy, and religious studies, and 1 creative arts course.

Special: The college offers a cooperative 4-1 business program with Clarkson University and a cooperative 2-2 program in environmental science and forestry with Syracuse University. Cross-registration with the Hudson-Mohawk Association and a Washington semester with American University are possible. Domestic and international internships, dual majors, B.A.-B.S. degrees, study abroad in 15 countries, and pass/fail options are available. Students may earn 3-2 engineering degrees with Clarkson and Catholic Universities, Manhattan College, Western New England College, SUNY at Binghamton, and Rensselaer Polytechnic Institute. Siena also offers a 4-4 early assurance program with the Columbia University School of Dental and Oral Surgery and SUNY College of Optometry, a 3-4 program with Boston University School of Graduate Dentistry, and a 4-4 medical program with Albany Medical College. There are 7 national honor societies, and 2 departmental honors program.

Faculty/Classroom: 67% of faculty are male; 33%, female. All teach undergraduates. No introductory courses are taught by graduate students. The average class size in an introductory lecture is 25; in a laboratory, 20; and in a regular course, 22.

Admissions: 69% of the 2001-2002 applicants were accepted. The SAT I scores for the 2001-2002 freshman class were: Verbal--21% below 500, 57% between 500 and 599, 21% between 600 and 700, and 1% above 700; Math--17% below 500, 54% between 500 and 599, 27% between 600 and 700, and 2% above 700. 50% of the current freshmen were in the top fifth of their class; 70% were in the top two fifths.

Requirements: The SAT I is required. In addition, applicants must be graduates of an accredited secondary school or have a GED. Sixteen academic credits are required, including 4 years each of English and history, 3 to 4 years each of math and science, and a recommended 3 years of foreign language study. All applicants must submit an essay; an interview is recommended. AP and CLEP credits are accepted. Important factors in the admissions decision are advanced placement or honor courses, personality/intangible qualities, and extracurricular activities record. An on-line application is available in the Admissions section of Siena's web site, *www.siena.edu/admissions*.

Procedure: Freshmen are admitted fall and spring. Entrance exams should be taken during May of the junior year or November of the senior year. There are early decision, early admissions, and deferred admissions plans. Early decision applications should be filed by December 1; regular applications, by March 1 for fall entry, December 1 for spring entry, and January 1 for summer entry, along with a $40 fee. Notification of early decision is sent January 15; regular decision, March 15. 38 early decision candidates were accepted for the 2001-2002 class. 5% of all applicants are on a waiting list; 30 were accepted in 2001.

Transfer: 137 transfer students enrolled in 2001-2002. Applicants must have a minimum 2.5 GPA. An interview is recommended. 30 credits of 120 must be completed at Siena.

Visiting: There are regularly scheduled orientations for prospective students, Students may interview with an admissions counselor, tour campus, or attend a group information session. There are guides for informal visits and visitors may sit in on classes and stay overnight. To schedule a visit, contact the Admissions Office.

Financial Aid: In 2001-2002, 88% of all freshmen and 82% of continuing students received some form of financial aid. 65% of freshmen and 63% of continuing students received need-based aid. The average freshman award was $10,095. Of that total, scholarships or need-based grants averaged $8117 ($20,995 maximum); loans averaged $2390 ($6625 maximum); and work contracts averaged $987 ($1000 maximum). 65% of undergraduates work part time. Average annual earnings from campus work are $776. The average financial indebtedness of the 2001 graduate was $14,000. The FAFSA and New York State Express TAP application are required. The fall application deadline is April 1.

International Students: There are 10 international students enrolled. The school actively recruits these students. They must score 500 on the written TOEFL and also take the SAT I or the ACT.

Computers: The mainframe is a network of more than 25 servers. All students have accounts established for them prior to arrival. Students may access more than 350 PCs, Macs, and terminals in more than a dozen locations, some of which are open 24 hours a day, 7 days a week. Every residence space includes a network connection for student use. All students may access the system 24 hours per day. There are no time limits and no fees.

Graduates: In 2001, 613 bachelor's degrees were awarded. The most popular majors were marketing/management (23%), psychology (11%), and English (10%). In an average class, 70% graduate in 4 years, 77% in 5 years, and 79% in 6 years. 144 companies recruited on campus in 2000-2001. Of the 2000 graduating class, 19% were enrolled in graduate school within 6 months of graduation and 78% were employed.

Admissions Contact: Edward Jones, Director of Admissions.
E-mail: *admit@siena.edu* Web: *www.siena.edu*

SKIDMORE COLLEGE — D-3

Saratoga Springs, NY 12866-1632 — (518) 580-5570; (800) 867-6007; (518) 580-5584

Full-time: 924 men, 1325 women	**Faculty:** 196; IIB, +$
Part-time: 75 men, 164 women	**Ph.D.s:** 84%
Graduate: 18 men, 38 women	**Student/Faculty:** 11 to 1
Year: semesters, summer session	**Tuition:** $26,676
Application Deadline: January 15	**Room & Board:** $7525
Freshman Class: 5633 applied, 2383 accepted, 599 enrolled	
SAT I Verbal/Math: 620/610	**ACT:** 27 **VERY COMPETITIVE+**

Skidmore College, established in 1903, is an independent institution offering undergraduate programs in liberal arts and sciences, as well as business, social work, education, studio art, dance, and theater. In addition to regional accreditation, Skidmore has baccalaureate program accreditation with CSWE and NASAD. The library contains 323,706 volumes, 234,179 microform items, and 133,484 audiovisual forms/CDs, and subscribes to 3696 periodicals. Computerized library services include the card catalog and database searching. Special learning facilities include a learning resource center, art gallery, radio station, TV station, electronic music studio, music and art studios, theater teaching facility, anthropology lab, and special biological habitats on campus. The 888-acre campus is in a small town 30 miles north of Albany. Including residence halls, there are 42 buildings.

Student Life: 71% of undergraduates are from out of state, mostly the Northeast. Students are from 46 states, 19 foreign countries, and Canada. 61% are from public schools. 75% are white. The average age of freshmen is 18; all undergraduates, 20. 7% do not continue beyond their first year.

Housing: 1700 students can be accommodated in college housing, which includes single-sex and coed dormitories and on-campus apartments. In addition, there are language houses, special-interest houses, and special housing for disabled students. On-campus housing is guaranteed for all 4 years. 77% of students live on campus. All students may keep cars.

Activities: There are no fraternities or sororities. There are 80 groups on campus, including art, chorale, chorus, computers, dance, drama, ethnic, film, gay, honors, international, jazz band, literary magazine, musical theater, newspaper, orchestra, photography, political, professional, radio and TV, religious, social, social service, student government, and yearbook. Popular campus events include Martin Luther King Week, Oktoberfest, and Spring Fling.

Sports: There are 10 intercollegiate sports for men and 10 for women, and 15 intramural sports for men and 13 for women. Facilities include a fitness center, an indoor swimming and diving pool, 2 gyms with 4 basketball courts, an indoor jogging track, a weight room, fields for baseball and other sports, dance studios, cross-country ski trails, a riding center, courts for tennis, handball, racquetball, and squash, and an outdoor facility with a synthetic surface soccer/lacrosse field, an all-weather 400-meter track, lights, and permanent stands.

Disabled Students: 75% of the campus is accessible. Wheelchair ramps, elevators, special parking, specially equipped rest rooms, and lowered drinking fountains are available.

Services: Counseling and information services are available, as is tutoring in most subjects. There is a reader service for the blind. Diagnostic services, note takers, and books on tape are also offered.

Campus Safety and Security: Measures include 24-hour foot and vehicle patrol, escort service, shuttle buses, and informal discussions. There are pamphlets/posters/films, emergency telephones, lighted pathways/sidewalks, a special security alert system, rigorous fire response procedures, and a lock system on dormitory entrances after 8 P.M.

Programs of Study: Skidmore confers B.A. and B.S. degrees. Master's degrees are also awarded. Bachelor's degrees are awarded in BIOLOGICAL SCIENCE (biochemistry and biology/biological science), BUSINESS (business administration and management and business economics), COMMUNICATIONS AND THE ARTS (art, art history and appreciation, classics, dance, dramatic arts, English, fine arts, French, German, music, and Spanish), COMPUTER AND PHYSICAL SCIENCE (chemistry, computer science, geology, mathematics, and physics), EDUCATION (elementary), HEALTH PROFESSIONS (exercise science), SOCIAL SCIENCE (American studies, anthropology, Asian/Oriental studies, economics, French studies, history, liberal arts/general studies, philosophy, political science/government, psychology, religion, social science, social work, sociology, and women's studies). Business, psychology and English are the largest.

Required: To graduate, students must complete 120 credits, including at least 24 at the 300 level, with a minimum GPA of 2.0 overall and in the major. B.A. candidates require 90 credits in the liberal arts to graduate; B.S. candidates require 60 credits. Students must fulfill a 2-course liberal studies sequence and complete distribution requirements of 1 course each in writing, quantitative reasoning, foreign language, lab science, the arts, humanities, and social science and 1 course in either non-Western cultures or cultural diversity.

Special: Skidmore offers cross-registration with the Hudson-Mohawk Consortium, individually designed internships, various study-abroad programs, a Washington semester in conjunction with American University, dual and student-designed majors, credit for life and experience, and pass/fail options, as well as a nondegree study program for senior citizens. There are cooperative programs in engineering with Dartmouth College and Clarkson University, in business with Clarkson and Rensselaer Polytechnic Institute, in education with Union College, and in law with the Benjamin Cardozo Law School. There is a 6-week internship period available at the end of the spring term. There are 9 national honor societies, including Phi Beta Kappa, and a freshman honors program.

Faculty/Classroom: 56% of faculty are male; 44%, female. 90% both teach and do research. No introductory courses are taught by graduate students. The average class size in a regular course is 16.

Admissions: 42% of the 2001-2002 applicants were accepted. The SAT I scores for the 2001-2002 freshman class were: Verbal--5% below 500, 33% between 500 and 599, 50% between 600 and 700, and 13% above 700; Math--4% below 500, 33% between 500 and 599, 54% between 600 and 700, and 9% above 700. The ACT scores were 16% between 18 and 23, 70% between 24 and 29, and 11% above 29. 95% of the current freshmen were in the top half of their class.

Requirements: The SAT I or ACT is required. AP and CLEP credits are accepted. Important factors in the admissions decision are advanced placement or honor courses, recommendations by school officials, and evidence of special talent.

Procedure: Freshmen are admitted fall and spring. Entrance exams should be taken by December of the senior year. There are early decision, early admissions, and deferred admissions plans. Applications should be filed by January 15 for fall entry, along with a $50 fee. Notification is sent April 1. 211 early decision candidates were accepted for the 2001-2002 class. A waiting list is an active part of the admissions procedure.

Transfer: 26 transfer students enrolled in 2001-2002. 60 credits of 120 must be completed at Skidmore.

Visiting: There are regularly scheduled orientations for prospective students, including full open-house day programs. There are guides for informal visits and visitors may sit in on classes and stay overnight. To schedule a visit, contact the Admissions Office at (518) 580-5000.

Financial Aid: In 2001-2002, 42% of all freshmen and 41% of continuing students received some form of financial aid. 41% of freshmen and 39% of continuing students received need-based aid. The average freshman award was $22,555. The average financial indebtedness of the 2001 graduate was $15,400. The CSS/Profile or FAFSA is required. The fall application deadline is January 15.

International Students: The school actively recruits these students. They must score 570 on the written TOEFL and also take the SAT I or the ACT.

Computers: All students may access the system 24 hours per day. There are no time limits and no fees. It is strongly recommended that all students have a personal computer.

Graduates: In 2001, 506 bachelor's degrees were awarded. The most popular majors were business (17%), psychology (11%), and English (10%). In an average class, 72% graduate in 4 years, 77% in 5 years, and 77% in 6 years. Of the 2000 graduating class, 13% were enrolled in graduate school within 6 months of graduation and 96% were employed.

Admissions Contact: Mary Lou Bates, Director of Admissions. A video is available. E-mail: *admissions@skidmore.edu*
Web: *www.skidmore.edu*

SOUTHAMPTON COLLEGE OF LONG ISLAND UNIVERSITY (See Long Island University/Southampton College)

STATE UNIVERSITY OF NEW YORK

The State University of New York (informally known as SUNY), established in 1948, is 1 of 2 public university systems in New York State. Governed by a board of trustees, whose chief administrator is the chancellor, the university's broad mission focuses on improving the lives of New York citizens and on bolstering the state's economy through teaching, research, and public service. Its 64 campuses, located in urban, suburban, and rural communities throughout the state, offer prospective students degrees at every level of higher education, up to and including doctoral and professional degrees. SUNY's comprehensive academic programs and its other academic enhancements have resulted in greater selectivity and continued growth in enrollment. Because of its large community college enrollment (more than 185,000 students annually), the university has enacted numerous programs to facilitate the transfer of students from the 2-year campuses to its senior institutions. Total enrollment is currently more than 380,000 students, taught by a full-time faculty of approximately 12,000 members. Degrees are offered in 1837 associate, 1730 baccalaureate, 1073 master's, 312 doctoral, and 17 first professional degree programs. Profiles of the 4-year institutions follow.

STATE UNIVERSITY OF NEW YORK AT BINGHAMTON (See State University of New York/University at Binghamton)

STATE UNIVERSITY OF NEW YORK/COLLEGE AT BROCKPORT B-3

Brockport, NY 14420 **(585) 395-2751**
(800) 382-8447; Fax: (585) 395-5452

Full-time: 2486 men, 3291 women	**Faculty:** 259; IIA, av$
Part-time: 385 men, 602 women	**Ph.D.s:** 90%
Graduate: 673 men, 1197 women	**Student/Faculty:** 22 to 1
Year: semesters, summer session	**Tuition:** $4127 ($9027)
Application Deadline: open	**Room & Board:** $6140
Freshman Class: 6947 applied, 3782 accepted, 1023 enrolled	
SAT I Verbal/Math: 527/535	**ACT:** 23 **COMPETITIVE**

The State University of New York/College at Brockport, established in 1867, is a public institution offering undergraduate programs in liberal arts, sciences, business, and teacher preparation. There are 3 undergraduate and 3 graduate schools. In addition to regional accreditation, SUNY Brockport has baccalaureate program accreditation with AACSB, CSAB, CSWE, NLN, and NRPA. The library contains 584,687 volumes, 2,044,866 microform items, and 8228 audiovisual forms/CDs, and subscribes to 1340 periodicals. Computerized library services include the card catalog, interlibrary loans, and database searching. Special learning facilities include a learning resource center, art gallery, planetarium, radio station, aquaculture ponds, weather information system, nuclear lab, high-resolution germanium detector, research vessel on Lake Ontario, electron microscope, 2 supercomputers, Doppler Radar system, ultramodern dance facilities including green room, and hydrotherapy room. The 435-acre campus is in a small town 16 miles west of Rochester. Including residence halls, there are 41 buildings.

Student Life: 98% of undergraduates are from New York. Others are from 33 states. 89% are white. The average age of freshmen is 18; all undergraduates, 22. 24% do not continue beyond their first year; 49% remain to graduate.

Housing: 2461 students can be accommodated in college housing, which includes coed dormitories. In addition, there are special-interest houses, special living facilities for transfer and first-year students, and adult/international, 24-hour quiet, and substance-free floors. On-campus housing is guaranteed for the freshman year only and is available on a first-come, first-served basis. 63% of students commute. All students may keep cars.

Activities: 2% of men belong to 6 national fraternities; 2% of women belong to 4 national sororities. There are 60 groups on campus, including art, business, cheerleading, chess, choir, chorus, computers, criminal justice, dance, drama, ethnic, film, gay, honors, international, jazz band, literary magazine, musical theater, newspaper, ouotdoors, photography, political, professional, radio and TV, religious, social, social service, and student government. Popular campus events include Health Week, Honors Convocation, and Scholars Day.

Sports: There are 10 intercollegiate sports for men and 12 for women, and 20 intramural sports for men and 20 for women. Facilities include field hockey, baseball, and softball fields; a soccer pitch; a swimming pool, 6 gyms, a gymnastics area, and wrestling and weight rooms; handball, squash, tennis, and racquetball courts; an ice arena; and a Special Olympics stadium.

Disabled Students: 95% of the campus is accessible. Wheelchair ramps, elevators, special parking, specially equipped rest rooms, special class scheduling, lowered drinking fountains, lowered telephones, and special classroom accommodations are available.

Services: Counseling and information services are available, as is tutoring in some subjects, which vary from semester to semester. There is remedial math and writing. Study skills support is available to all students.

Campus Safety and Security: Measures include 24-hour foot and vehicle patrol, escort service, shuttle buses, and informal discussions. There are pamphlets/posters/films, emergency telephones, lighted pathways/sidewalks, a community policing program, bicycle patrols, and 24-hour locked residence halls.

Programs of Study: SUNY Brockport confers B.A., B.S., B.F.A., and B.S.N. degrees. Master's degrees are also awarded. Bachelor's degrees are awarded in AGRICULTURE (environmental studies), BIOLOGICAL SCIENCE (biology/biological science), BUSINESS (accounting, business administration and management, international business management, and recreation and leisure services), COMMUNICATIONS AND THE ARTS (communications, dance, dramatic arts, English, French, journalism, Spanish, and studio art), COMPUTER AND PHYSICAL SCIENCE (actuarial science, atmospheric sciences and meteorology, chemistry, computer science, earth science, geology, information sciences and systems, mathematics, and physics), EDUCATION (physical), HEALTH

PROFESSIONS (health science, medical technology, and nursing), SOCIAL SCIENCE (African American studies, African studies, anthropology, criminal justice, history, interdisciplinary studies, international studies, philosophy, political science/government, psychology, social work, sociology, and water resources). Biological sciences, meteorology, and computer science are the strongest academically. Physical education, business administration, and psychology are the largest.

Required: To graduate, students must complete a minimum of 120 credits, including 30 to 56.5 credits in the major, with a 2.0 GPA. The core curriculum includes 6 credits each in fine arts, humanities, social science, and natural science and math. All students must take courses in computer literacy, contemporary issues, perspectives on women, comparative culture, quantitative skills, and composition. An academic planning seminar is also required of entering freshmen.

Special: Co-op programs, internships in most majors, and work-study programs in education are available. Brockport offers cross-registration with Rochester area colleges, a Washington semester, study abroad in 23 countries, accelerated degree programs, and an interdisciplinary major in arts for children, emphasizing art, dance, music, and theater. A 3-2 engineering degree is offered with SUNY Binghamton, SUNY Buffalo, and Clarkson, Case Western Reserve, and Syracuse Universities. Credit for life, military, and work experience, nondegree study, and pass/fail grading options are available. An alternative learning approach, Delta College, is an interdisciplinary program that emphasizes global issues and provides opportunities for work or study in other countries, as well as locally, regionally, and nationally. There are 20 national honor societies, a freshman honors program, and 3 departmental honors programs.

Faculty/Classroom: 54% of faculty are male; 46%, female. 87% teach undergraduates. The average class size in a regular course is 22.

Admissions: 54% of the 2001-2002 applicants were accepted. The SAT I scores for the 2001-2002 freshman class were: Verbal--33% below 500, 55% between 500 and 599, 12% between 600 and 700, and 1% above 700; Math--29% below 500, 54% between 500 and 599, 17% between 600 and 700, and 1% above 700. The ACT scores were 28% below 21, 33% between 21 and 23, 22% between 24 and 26, 10% between 27 and 28, and 7% above 28. 22% of the current freshmen were in the top fifth of their class; 54% were in the top two fifths. 11 freshmen graduated first in their class.

Requirements: The SAT I or ACT is required. In addition, SUNY Brockport seeks students who have demonstrated academic success and who show persistence. Applicants must have a high school diploma (preferably from the New York State Regents Program) or have completed a minimum of 18 academic units: 4 each in English and social studies, 3 each in math and science (1 with lab), and 4 in academic electives. An essay and letters of recommendation are encouraged. An audition is required for dance and theater applicants. SUNY Brockport requires applicants to be in the upper 50% of their class. A grade average of 80 to 85 is required. AP and CLEP credits are accepted. Important factors in the admissions decision are advanced placement or honor courses, leadership record, and extracurricular activities record. Applications are accepted on-line via SUNY Online Direct, ExPAN, and other services.

Procedure: Freshmen are admitted fall and spring. Entrance exams should be taken during the spring of the junior year and the fall of the senior year. There are early admissions and deferred admissions plans. Application deadlines are open. The application fee is $40. Notification is sent on a rolling basis.

Transfer: 931 transfer students enrolled in 2001-2002. The applicant must have a minimum GPA of 2.25. Many departments specify prerequisite courses and a higher GPA. SUNY Brockport recommends that transfer applicants have an associate degree or 54 credit hours, with preference given to degree holders. 24 credits of 120 must be completed at SUNY Brockport.

Visiting: There are regularly scheduled orientations for prospective students, including daily admissions information presentations and campus tours. Visits may be arranged on selected Saturdays and holidays. There are guides for informal visits and visitors may sit in on classes and stay overnight. To schedule a visit, contact the Office of Undergraduate Admissions.

Financial Aid: In 2001-2002, 60% of all freshmen and 64% of continuing students received some form of financial aid. 55% of freshmen and 58% of continuing students received need-based aid. The average freshman award was $6471. Of that total, scholarships or need-based grants averaged $2695 ($12,500 maximum); loans averaged $2715 ($12,500 maximum); and work contracts averaged $2000 (maximum). 80% of undergraduates work part time. Average annual earnings from campus work are $840. The average financial indebtedness of the 2001 graduate was $16,451. The FAFSA is required. The fall application deadline is February 15.

International Students: There are 44 international students enrolled. The school actively recruits these students. They must score 530 on the written TOEFL or take the MELAB.

Computers: The mainframes are a Sun E4500 and an IBM 2003. More than 500 networked PCs, Macs, and Suns are available for student use in 23 labs distributed throughout the campus. All are connected to the Internet and World Wide Web and include wiring in residence halls. All students may access the system 24 hours per day. There are no time limits and no fees.

Graduates: In 2001, 1454 bachelor's degrees were awarded. The most popular majors were physical education (10%), business administration (10%), and criminal justice (10%). In an average class, 1% graduate in 3 years, 26% in 4 years, 45% in 5 years, and 49% in 6 years. 300 companies recruited on campus in 2000-2001. Of the 2000 graduating class, 20% were enrolled in graduate school within 6 months of graduation and 74% were employed.

Admissions Contact: J. Scott Atkinson, Assistant Vice President for Enrollment Management. E-mail: *admit@brockport.edu*
Web: *www.brockport.edu*

STATE UNIVERSITY OF NEW YORK/COLLEGE AT BUFFALO — A-3

Buffalo, NY 14222 — (716) 878-4017; Fax: (716) 878-6100

Full-time: 3023 men, 4825 women	**Faculty:** 410; IIA, -$
Part-time: 843 men, 899 women	**Ph.D.s:** 89%
Graduate: 636 men, 1517 women	**Student/Faculty:** 19 to 1
Year: semesters, summer session	**Tuition:** $4029 ($8929)
Application Deadline: open	**Room & Board:** $3996
Freshman Class: 7167 applied, 4090 accepted, 1413 enrolled	
SAT I Verbal/Math: 490/490	**ACT:** 21 **COMPETITIVE**

The State University of New York/College at Buffalo, established in 1867, is a public institution conferring undergraduate liberal arts degrees. In addition to regional accreditation, Buffalo State College has baccalaureate program accreditation with ABET, ADA, ASLA, CSWE, and NCATE. The library contains 470,176 volumes, 910,297 microform items, and 10,863 audiovisual forms/CDs, and subscribes to 2948 periodicals. Computerized library services include the card catalog, interlibrary loans, and database searching. Special learning facilities include a learning resource center, art gallery, planetarium, radio station, a speech, language, and hearing clinic, and a center for performing arts. The 115-acre campus is in an urban area in Buffalo. Including residence halls, there are 36 buildings.

Student Life: 99% of undergraduates are from New York. Others are from 25 states, 28 foreign countries, and Canada. 85% are from public schools. 82% are white; 11% African American. The average age of freshmen is 18; all undergraduates, 24. 23% do not continue beyond their first year; 40% remain to graduate.

Housing: 2086 students can be accommodated in college housing, which includes coed dormitories and on-campus apartments. On-campus housing is available on a first-come, first-served basis. There is also an international student dorm. 84% of students commute. Alcohol is not permitted. All students may keep cars.

Activities: There are 1 local and 9 national fraternities and 3 local and 7 national sororities. There are 75 groups on campus, including art, cheerleading, chess, choir, chorus, computers, dance, drama, ethnic, gay, honors, international, jazz band, literary magazine, musical theater, newspaper, orchestra, political, professional, radio and TV, religious, social, social service, student government, and yearbook. Popular campus events include Commuter Daze, The Gathering, and Welcome Back Week.

Sports: There are 8 intercollegiate sports for men and 10 for women, and 5 intramural sports for men and 3 for women. Facilities include a gym, a natatorium, a basketball/volleyball arena, an ice rink, a game field for football, soccer, and lacrosse, a six-lane track, and a softball diamond.

Disabled Students: 93% of the campus is accessible. Wheelchair ramps, elevators, special parking, specially equipped rest rooms, special class scheduling, lowered drinking fountains, lowered telephones, and special dormitory accommodations are available.

Services: Counseling and information services are available, as is tutoring in every subject. There is a reader service for the blind, and remedial math, reading, and writing. Tutors for visually impaired and hearing-impaired students are also available.

Campus Safety and Security: Measures include 24-hour foot and vehicle patrol, self-defense education, escort service, and shuttle buses. There are informal discussions, pamphlets/posters/films, emergency telephones, lighted pathways/sidewalks, and community policing.

Programs of Study: Buffalo State College confers B.A., B.S., B.F.A., B.S.Ed., and B.T. degrees. Master's degrees are also awarded. Bachelor's degrees are awarded in BIOLOGICAL SCIENCE (biology/biological science), BUSINESS (business administration and management and hospitality management services), COMMUNICATIONS AND THE ARTS (art, art history and appreciation, broadcasting, communications, design, dramatic arts, English, fine arts, French, Italian, journalism, music, painting, photography, printmaking, sculpture, and Spanish), COMPUTER AND PHYSICAL SCIENCE (chemistry, earth science, geology, information sciences and systems, mathematics, and physics), EDUCATION (art, business, elementary, foreign languages, industrial arts, science, secondary, and special), ENGINEERING AND ENVIRONMEN-

TAL DESIGN (electrical/electronics engineering technology, industrial engineering technology, and mechanical engineering technology), HEALTH PROFESSIONS (health and speech pathology/audiology), SOCIAL SCIENCE (anthropology, criminal justice, dietetics, economics, geography, history, humanities, philosophy, political science/government, psychology, social work, sociology, and urban studies). Elementary education and exceptional education are the strongest academically. Elementary education, psychology, and business studies are the largest.

Required: To graduate, students must complete a 60-hour general education requirement consisting of 42 core credits in applied science and education, arts, humanities, math and science, and social science, and 18 hours of electives. Students must earn 123 credits with a minimum GPA of 2.0. The number of hours in the major varies.

Special: Students may cross-register with the Western New York Consortium and exchange with 160 campus members of the National Student Exchange. Internships, Washington and Albany semesters, study abroad in 5 countries, dual majors, and a general studies degree are offered. Students may earn 3-2 engineeing degrees in association with the State University of New York centers at Buffalo and Binghamton, and Clarkson University. There is a cooperative program with the Fashion Institute of Technology. Credit for life, military, and work experience, nondegree study, and pass/fail grading options are available. There is a chapter of Phi Beta Kappa and a freshman honors program.

Faculty/Classroom: 59% of faculty are male; 41%, female. All teach undergraduates. The average class size in an introductory lecture is 34; in a laboratory, 12; and in a regular course, 18.

Admissions: 57% of the 2001-2002 applicants were accepted. The SAT I scores for the 2001-2002 freshman class were: Verbal--54% below 500, 37% between 500 and 599, 8% between 600 and 700, and 1% above 700; Math--52% below 500, 41% between 500 and 599, 6% between 600 and 700, and 1% above 700. The ACT scores were 63% below 21, 23% between 21 and 23, 11% between 24 and 26, 1% between 27 and 28, and 3% above 28. 17% of the current freshmen were in the top fifth of their class; 49% were in the top two fifths.

Requirements: The SAT I is required. In addition, students must graduate from an accredited secondary school or have a GED. They must complete 4 years of English, 3 years each of math, science, and social studies, and 2 years of a foreign language. A portfolio is required for fine arts applicants. A grade average of 85 is required. AP and CLEP credits are accepted. Important factors in the admissions decision are advanced placement or honor courses, evidence of special talent, and recommendations by school officials.

Procedure: Freshmen are admitted to all sessions. Entrance exams should be taken during the junior or senior years. There are early decision, early admissions, and deferred admissions plans. Early decision applications should be filed by November 15; deadline for regular applications is open for fall entry. The fall 2001 application fee was $30. Notification of early decision is sent December 15; regular decision, on a rolling basis. A waiting list is an active part of the admissions procedure.

Transfer: 1047 transfer students enrolled in 2001-2002. Transfer applicants must have a minimum GPA of 2.0. An associate degree is recommended, and a minimum of 15 credit hours must have been earned. 32 credits of 123 must be completed at Buffalo State College.

Visiting: There are regularly scheduled orientations for prospective students. There are guides for informal visits and visitors may sit in on classes. To schedule a visit, contact the Admissions Office.

Financial Aid: The FAFSA and TAP are required. The fall application deadline is March 15.

International Students: There are 61 international students enrolled. The school actively recruits these students. They must score 500 on the written TOEFL.

Computers: The mainframes are an AXP-7600, OPEN VMS AXP Version 6.1. Students have access to the mainframe and the Internet through the campus local area network. Approximately 750 computers are available at various campus sites including the library, classrooms, Computing Services' general access computing facilities, and departmental computer labs. All students may access the system during site hours. Dial-in access is available 24 hours per day. There are no time limits and no fees.

Graduates: In 2001, 1640 bachelor's degrees were awarded. The most popular majors were elementary education (11%), business studies (10%), and social work (6%). In an average class, 1% graduate in 3 years, 14% in 4 years, 34% in 5 years, and 40% in 6 years. 100 companies recruited on campus in 2000-2001. Of the 2000 graduating class, 26% were enrolled in graduate school within 6 months of graduation and 85% were employed.

Admissions Contact: Lesa Loritts, Admissions Director.
E-mail: *admissio@buffalostate.edu* Web: *www.buffalostate.edu*

STATE UNIVERSITY OF NEW YORK/COLLEGE AT CORTLAND C-3

Cortland, NY 13045 **(607) 753-4712; (607) 753-5998**

Full-time: 2296 men, 3271 women	**Faculty:** 247; IIA, --$
Part-time: 123 men, 160 women	**Ph.D.s:** 88%
Graduate: 561 men, 1294 women	**Student/Faculty:** 23 to 1
Year: semesters, summer session	**Tuition:** $4174 ($9074)
Application Deadline: open	**Room & Board:** $6390
Freshman Class: 8341 applied, 4613 accepted, 1303 enrolled	
SAT I or ACT: required	**COMPETITIVE**

The State University of New York College at Cortland, founded in 1868, is a public institution offering academic programs leading to baccalaureate and master's degrees in liberal arts and professional studies. There are 2 undergraduate and 2 graduate schools. In addition to regional accreditation, SUNY Cortland has baccalaureate program accreditation with CAHEA and NRPA. The library contains 400,000 volumes, 750,000 microform items, and 5000 audiovisual forms/CDs, and subscribes to 3000 periodicals. Computerized library services include the card catalog, interlibrary loans, and database searching. Special learning facilities include a learning resource center, art gallery, natural history museum, planetarium, radio station, TV station, natural science museum, greenhouse, center for speech and hearing disorders, classrooms equipped with integrated technologies (multimedia enhanced instruction), and many specialized labs to support various program offerings. The 191-acre campus is in a small town 18 miles north of Ithaca and 29 miles south of Syracuse. Including residence halls, there are 37 buildings.

Student Life: 98% of undergraduates are from New York. Others are from 8 states and 2 foreign countries. 91% are from public schools. 89% are white. The average age of freshmen is 18; all undergraduates, 21. 26% do not continue beyond their first year; 53% remain to graduate.

Housing: 2775 students can be accommodated in college housing, which includes coed dormitories, off-campus apartments, fraternity houses, and sorority houses. In addition, there are special-interest houses, a wellness floor in a residence hall, a computer residence hall, quiet residence halls, a residence for Americans majoring in international studies and/or studying abroad, and a hall for students 21 years or older. 55% of students live on campus. All students may keep cars.

Activities: 4% of men belong to 1 national fraternity; 9% of women belong to 1 local sorority and 4 national sororities. There are 100 groups on campus, including art, band, cheerleading, chess, choir, chorale, chorus, computers, dance, drama, ethnic, film, gay, honors, international, jazz band, literary magazine, musical theater, newspaper, orchestra, political, professional, radio and TV, religious, social, social service, student government, symphony, and yearbook. Popular campus events include the annual Cortland-Ithaca College football game, Winterfest, and Multicultural Festival.

Sports: There are 11 intercollegiate sports for men and 13 for women, and 52 intramural sports for men and 52 for women. Facilities include an Olympic-size pool, a 3600-seat gym, an ice arena, a gymnastics arena, wrestling and weight rooms, dance studio, handball/racquetball courts, squash courts, an athletic training facility, fitness centers, a free-swimming pool, a track, a baseball field, a football/lacrosse/track field seating 4000, a lighted soccer field, a field house, and 50 acres of athletic fields.

Disabled Students: 75% of the campus is accessible. Wheelchair ramps, elevators, special parking, specially equipped rest rooms, special class scheduling, lowered drinking fountains, and lowered telephones are available.

Services: Counseling and information services are available, as is tutoring in some subjects. There is a fully staffed Academic Support and Achievement Program for writing, math, study skills, and learning strategies. Specific course tutoring is available with peer tutors. There is a reader service for the blind.

Campus Safety and Security: Measures include 24-hour foot and vehicle patrol, self-defense education, escort service, and shuttle buses. There are informal discussions, pamphlets/posters/films, emergency telephones, and lighted pathways/sidewalks. State University police maintain a web site with safety information and links. University police also have a Silent Witness Program for reporting crimes anonymously.

Programs of Study: SUNY Cortland confers B.A., B.S., and B.S.E. degrees. Master's degrees are also awarded. Bachelor's degrees are awarded in BIOLOGICAL SCIENCE (biology/biological science), BUSINESS (management science), COMMUNICATIONS AND THE ARTS (art, communications, English, and film arts), COMPUTER AND PHYSICAL SCIENCE (chemistry, geochemistry, geology, geophysics and seismology, mathematics, and physics), EDUCATION (athletic training, foreign languages, health, middle school, physical, recreation, and secondary), ENGINEERING AND ENVIRONMENTAL DESIGN (environmental science), HEALTH PROFESSIONS (health science and speech pathology/audiology), SOCIAL SCIENCE (African American studies, anthropology, economics, geography, history, human services, international studies, philosophy, political science/government, psychology, and sociology).

Biology, political science, and speech pathology/audiology are the strongest academically. Elementary education, phys ed, and communication studies are the largest.

Required: To graduate, undergraduates must complete 6 hours in English composition and at least 6 hours of a writing-intensive course, with 3 of those in the major. 1 course meeting the quantitative skills criteria must also be passed. 28 to 29 hours of courses in the general education program must also be completed, with no more than 2 courses taken in any 1 of the 8 disciplines in the program. A major of 30 to 36 hours, with no more than 45 credits in discipline-specific courses, must be completed. Completion of 90 credits of liberal arts and science courses toward a B.A., 60 credits toward a B.S.E., or 75 credits toward a B.S. is required. A 2.0 GPA, both overall and in all minors and concentrations, must be maintained. Special requirements may be designated by each school of the college.

Special: Cortland offers cross-registration with Tompkins Cortland Community College and has cooperative programs with the State University of New York College of Environmental Science and Forestry, and Centers at Binghamton and Buffalo, and Cornell and Case Western Reserve Universities. Students may study abroad in 11 countries, and they may enroll in a Washington semester. Work-study programs are available. The college confers an individualized studies degree and allows dual majors. Students may pursue a 3-2 engineering degree in conjunction with Alfred, Case Western Reserve, and Clarkson Universities, and the State University of New York Centers at Binghamton, Buffalo, and Stony Brook. Cortland offers nondegree study opportunities. There are 15 national honor societies, including Phi Beta Kappa, a freshman honors program, and 3 departmental honors programs.

Faculty/Classroom: 54% of faculty are male; 46%, female. All teach undergraduates, and 15% also do research. No introductory courses are taught by graduate students. The average class size in an introductory lecture is 38; in a laboratory, 26; and in a regular course, 22.

Admissions: 55% of the 2001-2002 applicants were accepted. The SAT I scores for the 2001-2002 freshman class were: Verbal--39% below 500, 52% between 500 and 599, and 8% between 600 and 700; Math--28% below 500, 60% between 500 and 599, and 12% between 600 and 700. The ACT scores were 2% below 18, 58% between 18 and 23, 39% between 24 and 29, and 1% above 28. 18% of the current freshmen were in the top fifth of their class; 60% were in the top two fifths.

Requirements: The SAT I or ACT is required. In addition, applicants must graduate from an accredited secondary school or have a GED. They must have earned 16 Carnegie units and 16 to 20 academic credits, including 4 units each in English and history or social studies and 2 (3 units preferred) each in math and science; the other 4 units must be taken in areas listed above or in a foreign language. Essays and recommendations are required, and in some cases auditions as well. Interviews are strongly recommended. AP and CLEP credits are accepted. Important factors in the admissions decision are advanced placement or honor courses, extracurricular activities record, and recommendations by school officials. On-line application is possible through the State University of New York Common Application Processing Center.

Procedure: Freshmen are admitted fall and spring. Entrance exams should be taken during the spring of the junior year or fall of the senior year. There are early decision, early admissions, and deferred admissions plans. Early decision applications should be filed by November 15; the deadline for regular applications is open for fall entry. There is a $30 fee. Notification is sent on a rolling basis. 64 early decision candidates were accepted for the 2001-2002 class.

Transfer: 650 transfer students enrolled in 2001-2002. Applicants must have a minimum GPA of 2.5. Some programs are more competitive. Interviews are encouraged. 45 credits of 124 must be completed at SUNY Cortland.

Visiting: There are regularly scheduled orientations for prospective students, consisting of Autumn Preview Days for prospective students as well as Spring Open House for accepted students. There are guides for informal visits and visitors may sit in on classes. To schedule a visit, contact the Admissions Appointment Secretary.

Financial Aid: In 2001-2002, 61% of all freshmen and 60% of continuing students received some form of financial aid. 56% of freshmen and 54% of continuing students received need-based aid. The average freshman award was $6977. The FAFSA and New York State TAP application are required. The fall application deadline is April 1.

International Students: There are 18 international students enrolled. The school actively recruits these students. They must score 550 on the written TOEFL.

Computers: The mainframes are an ALPHA AXT 2100 and multiple servers. There are also 745 IBM and Mac PCs available throughout the campus in 33 student-use labs. There are network connections in all residence hall rooms. All students may access the system 24 hours per day in some labs connected to the campus network. There are no time limits and no fees.

Graduates: In 2001, 1174 bachelor's degrees were awarded. The most popular majors were health science (31%), education (26%), and social science (16%). In an average class, 30% graduate in 4 years, 50% in 5 years, and 53% in 6 years.

Admissions Contact: Gradin Avery, Director of Admissions. A video is available. E-mail: *admssn_info@snycorva.cortland.edu*
Web: *www.cortland.edu*

STATE UNIVERSITY OF NEW YORK/COLLEGE AT FREDONIA — A-4

Fredonia, NY 14063 (716) 673-3251
(800) 252-1212; Fax: (716) 673-3249

Full-time: 1920 men, 2716 women	**Faculty:** 239
Part-time: 105 men, 168 women	**Ph.D.s:** 95%
Graduate: 103 men, 296 women	**Student/Faculty:** 19 to 1
Year: semesters, summer session	**Tuition:** $4175 ($9075)
Application Deadline: open	**Room & Board:** $5950
Freshman Class: n/av	
SAT I or ACT: required	**COMPETITIVE**

The State University of New York at Fredonia, established in 1826, is a public institution offering undergraduate programs in the arts and sciences, business and professional curricula, teacher preparation, and the fine and performing arts. In addition to regional accreditation, Fredonia has baccalaureate program accreditation with NASAD and NASM. The library contains 391,121 volumes, 1,060,631 microform items, and 26,574 audiovisual forms/CDs, and subscribes to 1983 periodicals. Computerized library services include the card catalog, interlibrary loans, and database searching. Special learning facilities include a learning resource center, art gallery, radio station, TV station, a greenhouse, a day-care center, a speech clinic, and an arts center. The 266-acre campus is in a small town 50 miles south of Buffalo and 45 miles north of Erie, Pennsylvania. Including residence halls, there are 25 buildings.

Student Life: 98% of undergraduates are from New York. Others are from 22 states, 6 foreign countries, and Canada. 65% are from public schools. 95% are white. The average age of freshmen is 19; all undergraduates, 21. 20% do not continue beyond their first year; 61% remain to graduate.

Housing: 2621 students can be accommodated in college housing, which includes single-sex and coed dormitories and on-campus apartments. In addition, there are special-interest houses. Living space for fraternities and sororities is available in residence halls. In addition, there are houses for computer students, athletes, and there are quiet-hour centers. On-campus housing is guaranteed for all 4 years. 50% of students live on campus; of those, 80% remain on campus on weekends. All students may keep cars.

Activities: 7% of men belong to 4 national fraternities; 4% of women belong to 3 national sororities. There are 120 groups on campus, including art, band, cheerleading, choir, chorale, chorus, computers, dance, drama, drill team, ethnic, gay, honors, international, jazz band, literary magazine, musical theater, newspaper, opera, orchestra, pep band, photography, political, professional, radio and TV, religious, ski, social, social service, student government, symphony, and yearbook. Popular campus events include various Art Center presentations, Spring Fest, and Little Siblings Weekend.

Sports: There are 8 intercollegiate sports for men and 9 for women, and 8 intramural sports for men and 8 for women. Facilities include a basketball arena, an ice rink, a swimming pool, a gym, a weight room, dance studios, soccer fields, indoor and outdoor tracks, and racquetball, tennis, and volleyball courts.

Disabled Students: 85% of the campus is accessible. Wheelchair ramps, elevators, special parking, specially equipped rest rooms, special class scheduling, lowered drinking fountains, and lowered telephones are available.

Services: Counseling and information services are available, as is tutoring in most subjects. There is a reader service for the blind.

Campus Safety and Security: Measures include 24-hour foot and vehicle patrol, escort service, shuttle buses, and informal discussions. There are pamphlets/posters/films, emergency telephones, lighted pathways/sidewalks, and card swipe access to residence halls.

Programs of Study: Fredonia confers B.A., B.S., B.F.A., B.S.Ed., and Mus.B. degrees. Master's degrees are also awarded. Bachelor's degrees are awarded in BIOLOGICAL SCIENCE (biochemistry and biology/biological science), BUSINESS (accounting, business administration and management, and business economics), COMMUNICATIONS AND THE ARTS (audio technology, communications, dramatic arts, English, fine arts, French, graphic design, media arts, music, and Spanish), COMPUTER AND PHYSICAL SCIENCE (chemistry, computer science, earth science, geology, mathematics, and physics), EDUCATION (early childhood, elementary, foreign languages, middle school, music, science, and secondary), HEALTH PROFESSIONS (health care administration, medical laboratory technology, predentistry, premedicine, and speech pathology/audiology), SOCIAL SCIENCE (history, interdisciplinary studies, philosophy, political science/government, psychology, social work, and sociology). Business, education, music, and psychology are the largest.

Required: To graduate, students must complete 120 hours, including 33 to 45 or more in the major, with a 2.0 GPA. Students must take specific courses in English and math and complete 36 hours of general education courses, including writing, statistical/quantitative abilities, oral communication, natural and social sciences, humanities, and arts.

Special: Cooperative programs are available with many other institutions. Students may cross-register with colleges in the Western New York Consortium. Fredonia offers a variety of internships, study-abroad programs in more than 90 countries, and a Washington semester. Accelerated degrees, a general studies degree, dual and student-designed majors, a 3-2 engineering degree program, nondegree study, and pass/fail grading options are available. There are 19 national honor societies, a freshman honors program, and 19 departmental honors programs.

Faculty/Classroom: 63% of faculty are male; 37%, female. All both teach and do research. No introductory courses are taught by graduate students. The average class size in an introductory lecture is 26; in a laboratory, 16; and in a regular course, 20.

Admissions: 10 freshmen graduated first in their class in a recent year.

Requirements: The SAT I or ACT is required with a minimum composite score of 950 on the SAT I or 20 on the ACT. Applicants must possess a high school diploma or have a GED. 16 academic credits are recommended, including 4 credits each in English and social studies and 3 each in math, science, and a foreign language. 4 years of math and science are encouraged. Essays and interviews are recommended, and, where applicable, an audition or portfolio is required. Fredonia requires applicants to be in the upper 50% of their class. A GPA of 2.7 is required. AP and CLEP credits are accepted. Important factors in the admissions decision are advanced placement or honor courses, evidence of special talent, and recommendations by school officials. Applications are accepted on-line at *http://www.fredonia.edu/admissions/applying.html*.

Procedure: Freshmen are admitted fall and spring. Entrance exams should be taken during the spring of the junior year or fall of the senior year. There are early decision, early admissions, and deferred admissions plans. Early decision applications should be filed by November 1 for fall entry; regular applications have an open deadline. The fee is $40. Notification of early decision is sent December 15; regular decision, on a rolling basis. 55 early decision candidates were accepted for the 2001-2002 class.

Transfer: 525 transfer students enrolled in 2001-2002. Applicants should have a minimum GPA of 2.0. and appropriate academic course work to be considered. An interview is recommended. 45 credits of 120 must be completed at Fredonia.

Visiting: There are regularly scheduled orientations for prospective students, including various open house programs and information sessions and tours Monday through Friday, morning and afternoon. Visitors may sit in on classes and stay overnight. To schedule a visit, contact the Office of Admissions.

Financial Aid: In 2001-2002, 83% of all freshmen and 72% of continuing students received some form of financial aid. 62% of freshmen and 65% of continuing students received need-based aid. The average freshman award was $5299. Of that total, scholarships or need-based grants averaged $1964 ($10,000 maximum); loans averaged $3646 ($11,500 maximum); and work contracts averaged $1320. 20% of undergraduates work part time. Average annual earnings from campus work are $1100. The average financial indebtedness of the 2001 graduate was $12,752. The FAFSA and Express TAP Application (ETA) are required.

International Students: There are 22 international students enrolled. The school actively recruits these students. They must score 500 on the written TOEFL or 175 on the electronic version.

Computers: The mainframe is a DEC Alpha 4100. PCs for student use are located in the computer center, all academic buildings, and various residence halls. There is ethernet access in all student residence hall rooms. All students may access the system. There are no time limits and no fees. It is strongly recommended that all students have a personal computer.

Graduates: In 2001, 935 bachelor's degrees were awarded. The most popular majors were elementary education (20%), business administration (8%), and psychology (6%). In an average class, 43% graduate in 4 years, 55% in 5 years, and 57% in 6 years. 55 companies recruited on campus in 2000-2001. Of the 2000 graduating class, 26% were enrolled in graduate school within 6 months of graduation and 87% were employed.

Admissions Contact: J. Denis Bolton, Director of Admissions.
E-mail: *admissions.office@fredonia.edu* Web: *fredonia.edu*

STATE UNIVERSITY OF NEW YORK/COLLEGE AT GENESEO — B-3

Geneseo, NY 14454 (585) 245-5571; Fax: (585) 245-5550

Full-time: 1840 men, 3405 women	**Faculty:** 258; IIA, --$
Part-time: 44 men, 82 women	**Ph.D.s:** 86%
Graduate: 39 men, 239 women	**Student/Faculty:** 20 to 1
Year: semesters, summer session	**Tuition:** $4310 ($9210)
Application Deadline: January 15	**Room & Board:** $5660
Freshman Class: 7794 applied, 4044 accepted, 1087 enrolled	
SAT I Verbal/Math: 602/610	**ACT:** 26 **HIGHLY COMPETITIVE**

The State University of New York/College at Geneseo, founded in 1871, is a public institution offering liberal arts, business, and accounting programs, teaching certification, and training in communicative disorders and sciences. In addition to regional accreditation, Geneseo has baccalaureate program accreditation with ASLA. The library contains 502,537 volumes, 910,054 microform items, and 4748 audiovisual forms/CDs, and subscribes to 2526 periodicals. Computerized library services include the card catalog, interlibrary loans, and database searching. Special learning facilities include a learning resource center, art gallery, planetarium, radio station, TV station, and and 3 theaters. The 220-acre campus is in a small town 30 miles south of Rochester. Including residence halls, there are 40 buildings.

Student Life: 98% of undergraduates are from New York. Others are from 19 states, 19 foreign countries, and Canada. 83% are from public schools. 89% are white. 47% are Catholic; 29% Protestant; 18% claim no religious affiliation. The average age of freshmen is 18; all undergraduates, 20. 10% do not continue beyond their first year; 80% remain to graduate.

Housing: 3100 students can be accommodated in college housing, which includes coed dormitories. In addition, there are special-interest houses, including science and math houses. On-campus housing is guaranteed for the freshman year only and is available on a first-come, first-served basis. 54% of students live on campus. All students may keep cars.

Activities: 12% of men belong to 10 local and 2 national fraternities; 9% of women belong to 10 local and 3 national sororities. There are 164 groups on campus, including art, band, cheerleading, choir, chorale, chorus, computers, dance, drama, ethnic, gay, honors, international, jazz band, literary magazine, musical theater, newspaper, orchestra, political, professional, radio and TV, religious, social, social service, student government, symphony, and yearbook. Popular campus events include Siblings Weekend, Parents Weekend, and Spring Weekend.

Sports: There are 8 intercollegiate sports for men and 11 for women, and 24 intramural sports for men and 24 for women. Facilities include an ice arena, 2 swimming pools, 3 gyms, 8 squash and 8 tennis courts, an indoor jogging area, Nautilus and weight rooms, a sauna, an outdoor track, and several playing fields. The largest auditorium/arena seats 3000.

Disabled Students: 90% of the campus is accessible. Wheelchair ramps, elevators, special parking, specially equipped rest rooms, special class scheduling, lowered drinking fountains, lowered telephones, and fire alarms for hearing-impaired students are available.

Services: Counseling and information services are available, as is tutoring in every subject. There is a reader service for the blind and remedial math and writing.

Campus Safety and Security: Measures include 24-hour foot and vehicle patrol, self-defense education, escort service, and informal discussions. There are pamphlets/posters/films, emergency telephones, and lighted pathways/sidewalks.

Programs of Study: Geneseo confers B.A., B.S., and B.S.Ed. degrees. Master's degrees are also awarded. Bachelor's degrees are awarded in BIOLOGICAL SCIENCE (biochemistry, biology/biological science, and biophysics), BUSINESS (accounting, business administration and management, and management science), COMMUNICATIONS AND THE ARTS (art history and appreciation, communications, comparative literature, dramatic arts, English, French, music, Spanish, and studio art), COMPUTER AND PHYSICAL SCIENCE (applied physics, chemistry, computer science, geochemistry, geology, geophysics and seismology, mathematics, natural sciences, and physics), EDUCATION (elementary and special), HEALTH PROFESSIONS (speech pathology/audiology), SOCIAL SCIENCE (African American studies, American studies, anthropology, economics, geography, history, international relations, philosophy, political science/government, psychology, and sociology). Biology, special education, and psychology are the largest.

Required: To graduate, students must complete 120 credit hours with a minimum 2.0 GPA. The total number of hours in the major varies. The required core curriculum includes 2 courses each in humanities, fine arts, social sciences, and natural sciences and 1 course each in non-Western tradition, writing, and analytical and numerical analysis.

Special: The college offers a cooperative 3-2 engineering degree with Alfred, Case Western Reserve, Clarkson, Columbia, Penn State, and Syracuse Universities, SUNY at Binghamton and Buffalo, and the University of Rochester, as well as a 3-3 degree with Rochester Institute of Technology. There is also a 3-2 M.B.A. degree offered with Pace, SUNY/Buffalo, or Syracuse; a 4-1 M.B.A. with Alfred, Clarkson, RIT, or Union; and 3-4 degrees with SUNY/Buffalo for Dentistry, SUNY College of Optometry, and NYS College of Osteopathic Medicine. Cross-registration is available with the Rochester Area Colleges Consortium. Geneseo offers internships in all majors, study abroad through more than 95 programs, a Washington semester, dual majors, including theater/English, credit for military experience, and pass/fail options. There are 13 national honor societies, a freshman honors program, and 5 departmental honors programs.

Faculty/Classroom: 60% of faculty are male; 40%, female. All teach undergraduates. No introductory courses are taught by graduate students. The average class size in an introductory lecture is 40; in a laboratory, 24; and in a regular course, 24.

Admissions: 52% of the 2001-2002 applicants were accepted. The SAT I scores for the 2001-2002 freshman class were: Verbal--4% below 500, 41% between 500 and 599, 48% between 600 and 700, and 7% above 700; Math--3% below 500, 37% between 500 and 599, 53% between 600 and 700, and 7% above 700. The ACT scores were 2% below 21, 20% between 21 and 23, 31% between 24 and 26, 22% between 27 and 28, and 25% above 28. 79% of the current freshmen were in the top fifth of their class; 98% were in the top two fifths. 53 freshmen graduated first in their class.

Requirements: The SAT I or ACT is required. In addition, applicants must be graduates of an accredited secondary school or have a GED certificate. The academic program must have included 4 years each of English, math, science, and social studies and 3 years of a foreign language. An essay is required. A portfolio or audition for certain programs and an interview are recommended. Geneseo requires applicants to be in the upper 50% of their class. AP and CLEP credits are accepted. Important factors in the admissions decision are advanced placement or honor courses, recommendations by school officials, and evidence of special talent. Applications are available on-line.

Procedure: Freshmen are admitted fall and spring. Entrance exams should be taken during the spring of the junior year. There are early decision and deferred admissions plans. Early decision applications should be filed by November 15; regular applications, by January 15 for fall entry and September 15 for spring entry. The fall 2001 application fee was $30. Notification of early decision is sent December 15; regular decision, on a rolling basis. 97 early decision candidates were accepted for the 2001-2002 class. A waiting list is an active part of the admissions procedure.

Transfer: 340 transfer students enrolled in 2001-2002. Applicants must provide transcripts from all previously attended colleges. A minimum 2.0 GPA is required. Students with fewer than 24 credit hours must submit SAT I or ACT scores. An essay is required, and an interview is recommended. 30 credits of 120 must be completed at Geneseo.

Visiting: There are regularly scheduled orientations for prospective students, including a day-and-a-half summer program consisting of academic advisement, registration, and adjustment to college life activities. There are guides for informal visits and visitors may sit in on classes and stay overnight. To schedule a visit, contact the Office of Admissions.

Financial Aid: In 2001-2002, 65% of all freshmen and 70% of continuing students received some form of financial aid. 60% of freshmen and 65% of continuing students received need-based aid. The average freshman award was $6565. Of that total, scholarships or need-based grants averaged $1585 ($8000 maximum); loans averaged $3720 ($4625 maximum); and work contracts averaged $1000 ($2000 maximum). 68% of undergraduates work part time. The average financial indebtedness of the 2001 graduate was $15,000. The FAFSA is required. The fall application deadline is February 15.

International Students: There are 42 international students enrolled. The school actively recruits these students. They must score 525 on the written TOEFL.

Computers: The mainframe is a DEC ALPHA 4100. Mac, DOS/Windows, and Sun workstations are located in more than 30 computer labs, supported by fiber-optic network connectivity and full Internet access. All students may access the system 24 hours a day. There are no time limits. The fee is $100. It is strongly recommended that all students have a personal computer.

Graduates: In 2001, 1156 bachelor's degrees were awarded. The most popular majors were education (22%), psychology (9%), and biology (9%). In an average class, 1% graduate in 3 years, 67% in 4 years, and 80% in 5 years. 62 companies recruited on campus in 2000-2001. Of the 2000 graduating class, 27% were enrolled in graduate school within 6 months of graduation and 60% were employed.

Admissions Contact: Kris Shay, Associate Director of Admissions. A video is available. E-mail: *admissions@geneseo.edu*
Web: *www.geneseo.edu*

STATE UNIVERSITY OF NEW YORK/COLLEGE AT OLD WESTBURY D-5

Old Westbury, NY 11568-0210 **(516) 876-3073**
Fax: (516) 876-3307

Full-time: 943 men, 1388 women
Part-time: 296 men, 449 women
Graduate: none
Year: semesters, summer session
Application Deadline: open
Freshman Class: n/av
SAT I: required
Faculty: 122; IIB, +$
Ph.D.s: 83%
Student/Faculty: 19 to 1
Tuition: $3981 ($8881)
Room & Board: $5837
LESS COMPETITIVE

The State University of New York/College at Old Westbury, founded in 1965, is a public institution offering degree programs in the arts and sciences, business, education, fine arts, and health science. The library contains 216,289 volumes, 187,833 microform items, and 4119 audiovisual forms/CDs, and subscribes to 862 periodicals. Computerized library services include the card catalog, interlibrary loans, and database searching. Special learning facilities include a learning resource center, art gallery, and radio station. The 605-acre campus is in a suburban area 20 miles east of New York City. Including residence halls, there are 14 buildings.

Student Life: 99% of undergraduates are from New York. Others are from 7 states, 20 foreign countries, and Canada. 34% are white; 15% Hispanic. The average age of freshmen is 19; all undergraduates, 26. 34% do not continue beyond their first year; 31% remain to graduate.

Housing: 792 students can be accommodated in college housing, which includes coed dormitories. In addition, there are honors houses. On-campus housing is available on a first-come, first-served basis. Priority is given to out-of-town students. 75% of students commute. Alcohol is not permitted. All students may keep cars.

Activities: 6% of men belong to 7 local and 6 national fraternities; 7% of women belong to 6 local and 4 national sororities. There are 55 groups on campus, including art, choir, computers, ethnic, gay, honors, international, newspaper, political, professional, radio and TV, religious, social, social service, student government, and yearbook. Popular campus events include Welcome Back Festival, Wellness at Old Westbury, and Mayfest.

Sports: There are 5 intercollegiate sports for men and 5 for women, and 7 intramural sports for men and 7 for women. Facilities include a 3000-seat gym, an auxiliary gym, a cross-country course, playing fields, a swimming pool, a fitness center, a weight room, jogging trails, and courts for tennis, paddleball, handball, racquetball, and squash.

Disabled Students: 90% of the campus is accessible. Wheelchair ramps, elevators, special parking, specially equipped rest rooms, special class scheduling, lowered drinking fountains, lowered telephones, and limited volunteer transportation are available.

Services: Counseling and information services are available, as is tutoring in most subjects. There is a reader service for the blind, and remedial math, reading, and writing.

Campus Safety and Security: Measures include 24-hour foot and vehicle patrol, escort service, shuttle buses, and informal discussions. There are pamphlets/posters/films, emergency telephones, lighted pathways/sidewalks, an officer dormitory patrol from 6 P.M. to 2 A.M., and student safety aides for escort service and night patrol.

Programs of Study: SUNY Old Westbury confers B.A., B.S., and B.P.S. degrees. Bachelor's degrees are awarded in BIOLOGICAL SCIENCE (biology/biological science), BUSINESS (accounting, banking and finance, business administration and management, management information systems, and marketing/retailing/merchandising), COMMUNICATIONS AND THE ARTS (media arts, Spanish, and visual and performing arts), COMPUTER AND PHYSICAL SCIENCE (chemistry, computer science, and mathematics), EDUCATION (bilingual/bicultural, elementary, foreign languages, mathematics, science, secondary, and special), HEALTH PROFESSIONS (community health work), SOCIAL SCIENCE (American studies, criminology, humanities, international studies, philosophy, political science/government, psychology, and sociology). Teacher education, business, and psychology are the strongest academically and have the largest enrollments.

Required: To graduate, students must maintain a GPA of 2.0 in 120 or 128 semester credits; accounting and special education majors require 128 credits. General education requirements include courses in writing and reasoning skills, creative arts, ideas and ideology, cross-cultural perspectives, U.S. society and history, physical or life science, and foreign language.

Special: SUNY Old Westbury offers cross-registration with SUNY Empire State, Lirache, and colleges in Nassau and Suffolk counties, internships in teacher education, study abroad, a B.A.-B.S. in biological science, dual majors, and a 3-2 engineering degree with SUNY at Stony Brook and SUNY Maritime College. Credit for military and life experience, nondegree study, and pass/fail options are available.

Faculty/Classroom: 51% of faculty are male; 49%, female. All teach undergraduates. The average class size in an introductory lecture is 31; in a laboratory, 10; and in a regular course, 25.

Requirements: The SAT I is required. In addition, applicants must be graduates of an accredited secondary school or have the GED. An essay, portfolio, and interview also are recommended. Students are evaluated according to qualifying categories of academic achievement (80 high school average or 1000 SAT I score), special knowledge and creative ability, paid work experience, and social or personal experience. Applications are accepted on-line at the school's web site. AP and CLEP credits are accepted. Important factors in the admissions decision are leadership record, recommendations by school officials, and evidence of special talent.

Procedure: Freshmen are admitted fall and spring. There are early decision and deferred admissions plans. Application deadlines are open. Notification is sent on a rolling basis. 14 early decision candidates were accepted for a recent class. The fall 2001 application fee was $30.

Transfer: 592 transfer students enrolled in a recent year. Applicants must submit official transcripts from all colleges attended. Those students with fewer than 24 college credits must also submit a high school transcript. The college requires a minimum overall GPA of 2.0. Specific academic majors may require a higher GPA. 48 credits of 120 must be completed at SUNY Old Westbury.

Visiting: There are regularly scheduled orientations for prospective students. There are guides for informal visits. To schedule a visit, contact Enrollment Services.

Financial Aid: In a recent year, 23% of all freshmen received some form of financial aid, including need-based aid. The average freshman award was $5342. 15% of undergraduates work part time. Average annual earnings from campus work are $952. The FAFSA, the college's own financial statement, the IFAA (Institutional application), and previous years' household income are required. The fall application deadline is April 19.

International Students: There were 32 international students enrolled in a recent year. The school actively recruits these students. They must score 500 on the written TOEFL and also take the college's own test.

Computers: The mainframes are a DEC VAX 6620 and a DEC ALPHA 4100. The student computing center houses labs that include 50 Pentium-class PCs and 35 Macs supporting a wide variety of business, academic, and graphics application programs. Other discipline-specific, academic computing labs on the campus include more than 45 Pentium-class PCs running specialized academic programs, and the library provides more than 20 PCs for student use. All students may access the system daily. There are no time limits and no fees.

Graduates: In a recent year, 619 bachelor's degrees were awarded. The most popular majors were school of business (32%), teacher education (16%), and psychology (11%).

Admissions Contact: Mary Marquez Bell, Director. A video is available. Web: *www.oldwestbury.edu*

STATE UNIVERSITY OF NEW YORK/COLLEGE AT ONEONTA D-3

Oneonta, NY 13820-4015 (607) 436-2524
(800) 786-9123; Fax: (607) 436-3074

Full-time: 2095 men, 3146 women	**Faculty:** 252; IIA, -$
Part-time: 77 men, 140 women	**Ph.D.s:** 76%
Graduate: 69 men, 213 women	**Student/Faculty:** 21 to 1
Year: semesters, summer session	**Tuition:** $4231 ($9131)
Application Deadline: May 1	**Room & Board:** $5750
Freshman Class: 9286 applied, 4826 accepted, 1144 enrolled	
SAT I Verbal/Math: 527/532	**ACT:** 22 **COMPETITIVE**

The State University of New York/College at Oneonta, founded in 1889, offers undergraduate and graduate programs in the arts and sciences with a campuswide emphasis on educational technology and community service. There is 1 graduate school. In addition to regional accreditation, Oneonta has baccalaureate program accreditation with AAFCS, ACS, ADA, and NCATE. The library contains 549,243 volumes, 990,831 microform items, and 11,705 audiovisual forms/CDs, and subscribes to 9237 periodicals. Computerized library services include the card catalog, interlibrary loans, and database searching. Special learning facilities include a learning resource center, art gallery, planetarium, radio station, TV station, observatory, science discovery center, community service center, college camp, children's center, and off-campus biological field station. The 250-acre campus is in a rural area 75 miles southwest of Albany and 55 miles northeast of Binghamton. Including residence halls, there are 37 buildings.

Student Life: 97% of undergraduates are from New York. Others are from 27 states, 23 foreign countries, and Canada. 82% are white. The average age of freshmen is 18; all undergraduates, 20. 28% do not continue beyond their first year; 53% remain to graduate.

Housing: 2900 students can be accommodated in college housing, which includes single-sex and coed dormitories. There is a math and science wing, an international wing, all-freshmen housing, and other special-interest groupings within residence halls. On-campus housing is available on a first-come, first-served basis and is available on a lottery system for upperclassmen. 54% of students live on campus; of those, 54% remain on campus on weekends. Alcohol is not permitted. Upperclassmen may keep cars.

Activities: 66% of women belong to 3 local and 5 national sororities. There are no fraternities. There are 70 groups on campus, including academic, art, band, cheerleading, choir, chorale, chorus, computers, culture enrichment, dance, drama, ethnic, film, gay, honors, international, jazz band, musical theater, newspaper, orchestra, pep band, photography, political, professional, radio and TV, religious, social, social service, special interest, student government, and yearbook. Popular campus events include Exploration (campus orientation), Into the Streets (community service day), and Reunion Weekend.

Sports: There are 9 intercollegiate sports for men and 10 for women, and 17 intramural sports for men and 17 for women. Facilities include a gym, a field house, dance studios, weight rooms, a pool, indoor racquetball courts, tennis courts, indoor and outdoor tracks, and athletic fields.

Disabled Students: 75% of the campus is accessible. Wheelchair ramps, elevators, special parking, specially equipped rest rooms, special class scheduling, and lowered drinking fountains are available. All academic buildings and some residence halls are accessible.

Services: Counseling and information services are available, as is tutoring in most subjects. There is a reader service for the blind, and remedial math, reading, and writing.

Campus Safety and Security: Measures include 24-hour foot and vehicle patrol, self-defense education, escort service, and shuttle buses. There are informal discussions, pamphlets/posters/films, emergency telephones, lighted pathways/sidewalks, and residence hall workshops.

Programs of Study: Oneonta confers B.A. and B.S. degrees. Master's degrees are also awarded. Bachelor's degrees are awarded in BIOLOGICAL SCIENCE (biology/biological science), BUSINESS (accounting, business economics, and fashion merchandising), COMMUNICATIONS AND THE ARTS (art, communications, dramatic arts, English, fine arts, French, music, music business management, Spanish, and speech/debate/rhetoric), COMPUTER AND PHYSICAL SCIENCE (atmospheric sciences and meteorology, chemistry, computer science, earth science, geology, mathematics, physics, and statistics), EDUCATION (business, elementary, English, foreign languages, home economics, mathematics, science, secondary, and social science), ENGINEERING AND ENVIRONMENTAL DESIGN (environmental science), HEALTH PROFESSIONS (predentistry and premedicine), SOCIAL SCIENCE (African studies, anthropology, child care/child and family studies, dietetics, economics, geography, gerontology, Hispanic American studies, history, home economics, interdisciplinary studies, international studies, philosophy, political science/government, prelaw, psychology, sociology, and water resources). Physical and natural sciences, business economics, and education are the strongest academically. Education, business economics, and music industry are the largest.

Required: Students must complete 122 semester hours, with at least 48 hours in upper-division courses and 30 to 36 hours in the major. A minimum GPA of 2.0 (2.5 for education majors) must be maintained. In addition, students must complete a 36-hour general education requirement including courses in math, natural sciences, social sciences, American history, Western civilization, other world civilizations, humanities, the arts, foreign language, basic communications, writing skills, and oral communication skills. Students must also pass writing and speech proficiency exams.

Special: Oneonta offers limited cross-registration with Hartwick College, internships in most fields, study abroad through SUNY in 50 countries, a Washington semester, work-study programs, interdisciplinary studies, and dual majors. A 3-2 engineering degree and other cooperative programs are offered. Credit for life experience, nondegree study, and pass/fail options are available. There are 14 national honor societies and a freshman honors program.

Faculty/Classroom: 61% of faculty are male; 39%, female. 99% teach undergraduates. No introductory courses are taught by graduate students. The average class size in an introductory lecture is 25; in a laboratory, 24; and in a regular course, 20.

Admissions: 52% of the 2001-2002 applicants were accepted. The SAT I scores for the 2001-2002 freshman class were: Verbal--31% below 500, 56% between 500 and 599, 12% between 600 and 700, and 1% above 700; Math--26% below 500, 60% between 500 and 599, 13% between 600 and 700, and 1% above 700. The ACT scores were 10% below 21, 60% between 21 and 23, 27% between 24 and 26, and 3% between 27 and 28. 40% of the current freshmen were in the top fifth of their class; 80% were in the top two fifths.

Requirements: The SAT I or ACT is required. In addition, applicants should be graduates of an accredited secondary school and have 16 academic credits, including 4 years each of English and history and 8 years combined of foreign language, math, and science, with at least 2 years in each of these 3 broad areas. The GED is accepted. A GPA of 2.0 is required. AP and CLEP credits are accepted. Important factors in the admissions decision are advanced placement or honor courses, evidence of special talent, and leadership record. Applications are accepted online from the common SUNY application as well as from a number of services linked to Oneonta's web site, including CollegeNET, CollegeLink, and Embark.

Procedure: Freshmen are admitted fall and spring. Entrance exams should be taken in the spring of the junior year or the fall of the senior year. There are early decision and deferred admissions plans. Early decision applications should be filed by November 15; regular applications, by May 1 for fall entry and December 15 for spring entry, along with a $30 fee. Notification of early decision is sent November 15; regular decision, on a rolling basis. 71 early decision candidates were accepted for the 2001-2002 class. 5% of all applicants are on a waiting list; 122 were accepted in 2001.

Transfer: 625 transfer students enrolled in 2001-2002. Official transcripts of all previous college work must be submitted. A minimum of 15 semester hours of transferable credit and a GPA of 2.0 are required. 45 credits of 122 must be completed at Oneonta.

Visiting: There are regularly scheduled orientations for prospective students, including 2 fall open houses, a summer open house, individual appointments, and group information sessions. There are guides for informal visits and visitors may sit in on classes and stay overnight. To schedule a visit, contact the Admissions Office.

Financial Aid: In 2001-2002, 57% of all freshmen and 60% of continuing students received some form of financial aid, including need-based aid. The average freshman award was $6311. Of that total, scholarships or need-based grants averaged $3001 ($8125 maximum); loans averaged $3033 ($5125 maximum); and work contracts averaged $1150 ($1200 maximum). 27% of undergraduates work part time. Average annual earnings from campus work are $700. The average financial indebtedness of the 2001 graduate was $7902. The FAFSA is required. The fall application deadline is April 15.

International Students: There are 71 international students enrolled. The school actively recruits these students. They must score 500 on the written TOEFL or 173 on the electronic version. The SAT I or ACT is recommended.

Computers: The mainframes are a Compaq ES40 and 2 Compaq 2100s. More than 500 PCs and Macs are available in labs on campus. Students have access to e-mail, the Web and the Internet, on-line registration, and other services. All residence halls are wired for high-speed connections. All students may access the system. There are no time limits and no fees. It is strongly recommended that all students have a personal computer.

Graduates: In 2001, 1081 bachelor's degrees were awarded. The most popular majors were elementary education (26%), business economics (12%), and psychology (4%). In an average class, 1% graduate in 3 years, 39% in 4 years, 50% in 5 years, and 52% in 6 years. 45 companies recruited on campus in 2000-2001. Of the 2000 graduating class, 36% were enrolled in graduate school within 6 months of graduation and 81% were employed.

Admissions Contact: Karen Brown, Director of Admissions.
E-mail: *admissions@oneonta.edu* Web: *http://www.oneonta.edu*

STATE UNIVERSITY OF NEW YORK/COLLEGE AT OSWEGO C-3

Oswego, NY 13126 **(315) 312-2250; Fax: (315) 312-3260**

Full-time: 2926 men, 3450 women	**Faculty:** 305; IIA, -$
Part-time: 297 men, 389 women	**Ph.D.s:** 79%
Graduate: 468 men, 877 women	**Student/Faculty:** 21 to 1
Year: semesters, summer session	**Tuition:** $4160 ($9060)
Application Deadline: January 15	**Room & Board:** $6696
Freshman Class: 7832 applied, 4958 accepted, 1270 enrolled	
SAT I or ACT: required	**COMPETITIVE**

State University of New York/College at Oswego, founded in 1861, is a comprehensive institution offering more than 100 cooperative, preprofessional, and graduate programs in the arts and sciences, business, and education. There are 3 undergraduate and 3 graduate schools. In addition to regional accreditation, Oswego has baccalaureate program accreditation with NASM and NCATE. The library contains 450,875 volumes, 1.8 million microform items, and 51,000 audiovisual forms/CDs, and subscribes to 1439 periodicals. Computerized library services include the card catalog, interlibrary loans, and database searching. Special learning facilities include a learning resource center, art gallery, planetarium, radio station, TV station, and biological field station. The 696-acre campus is in a small town on the southeast shore of Lake Ontario, 35 miles northwest of Syracuse. Including residence halls, there are 40 buildings.

Student Life: 98% of undergraduates are from New York. Others are from 27 states, 27 foreign countries, and Canada. 90% are from public schools. 90% are white. 42% are Catholic; 41% Protestant; 14% Jewish. The average age of freshmen is 18; all undergraduates, 21. 28% do not continue beyond their first year; 59% remain to graduate.

Housing: 3300 students can be accommodated in college housing, which includes coed dormitories. In addition, there are honors houses. On-campus housing is guaranteed for all 4 years. 50% of students live on campus; of those, 90% remain on campus on weekends. All students may keep cars.

Activities: 6% of men belong to 5 local and 11 national fraternities; 6% of women belong to 6 local and 8 national sororities. There are 101 groups on campus, including art, band, cheerleading, choir, chorale, chorus, computers, dance, drama, ethnic, gay, honors, international, jazz band, literary magazine, musical theater, newspaper, opera, orchestra, photography, political, professional, radio and TV, religious, social, social service, student government, and yearbook. Popular campus events include Honors Convocations and Quest, Parents Weekend, and College Open House.

Sports: There are 12 intercollegiate sports for men and 11 for women, and 12 intramural sports for men and 12 for women. Facilities include an ice hockey rink, a field house with an artificial-grass practice area, 23 tennis courts, an outdoor track, 3 soccer and 3 lacrosse fields, baseball and softball fields, numerous basketball courts, racquetball and squash courts, 2 indoor pools, and a diving well. The gym seats 3500. There are also 2 fitness centers and weight rooms, a cross-country ski lodge, and a martial arts studio.

Disabled Students: 50% of the campus is accessible. Wheelchair ramps, elevators, special parking, specially equipped rest rooms, special class scheduling, lowered drinking fountains, lowered telephones, and a student support group are available.

Services: Counseling and information services are available, as is tutoring in every subject. There is a reader service for the blind, and remedial math, reading, and writing. In addition, the Office of Learning Support Services provides general foundation support.

Campus Safety and Security: Measures include 24-hour foot and vehicle patrol, shuttle buses, informal discussions, and pamphlets/posters/films. There are emergency telephones, lighted pathways/sidewalks, and a campus police force, programs on safety issues and alcohol education, and a security escort—an electronic device that locates student and alerts police office when triggered.

Programs of Study: Oswego confers B.A., B.S., and B.F.A. degrees. Master's degrees are also awarded. Bachelor's degrees are awarded in BIOLOGICAL SCIENCE (biology/biological science and zoology), BUSINESS (accounting, banking and finance, business administration and management, human resources, international economics, management science, and marketing/retailing/merchandising), COMMUNICATIONS AND THE ARTS (art, broadcasting, communications, dramatic arts, English, French, German, graphic design, journalism, linguistics, music, public relations, and Spanish), COMPUTER AND PHYSICAL SCIENCE (applied mathematics, atmospheric sciences and meteorology, chemistry, computer science, geochemistry, geology, information sciences and systems, mathematics, and physics), EDUCATION (business, elementary, foreign languages, secondary, and vocational), ENGINEERING AND ENVIRONMENTAL DESIGN (technological management), SOCIAL SCIENCE (American studies, anthropology, cognitive science, criminal justice, economics, history, human development, international studies, philosophy, political science/government, psychology, sociology, and women's studies). Chemistry, computer science, and accounting are the strongest academically. Elementary/secondary education, business administration, and accounting are the largest.

Required: To graduate, all students must complete 42 to 48 general education credits including 6 in human diversity, and 3 to 6 each in expository writing and math. Students must have a minimum 2.0 GPA and complete 122 total credit hours (127 hours for technology and vocational education students). The total number of hours in the major varies from 30 to 78.

Special: Oswego offers cross-registration with ACUSNY-Visiting Student Program. More than 900 internships are available with business, social, cultural, and government agencies. The university also offers a Washington semester, study abroad in more than 80 programs, accelerated degree programs, dual majors, B.A.-B.S. degrees in several sciences and B.A.-B.F.A. in art, credit for military experience, nondegree study, and pass/fail options. A 3-2 engineering degree is offered with Clarkson University, SUNY at Binghamton, and Case Western Reserve University. A 3-4 degree in optometry with SUNY College of Optometry, a 2-3 degree in zoo technology with Santa Fe Community College, and 2-2 and 2-3 degrees in health sciences with SUNY Health Sciences Center are also possible. There are 21 national honor societies, including Phi Beta Kappa, a freshman honors program, and 9 departmental honors programs.

Faculty/Classroom: 61% of faculty are male; 39%, female. 93% teach undergraduates. No introductory courses are taught by graduate students. The average class size in an introductory lecture is 100–200; in a laboratory, 13; and in a regular course, 24.

Admissions: 63% of the 2001-2002 applicants were accepted. The SAT I scores for the 2001-2002 freshman class were: Verbal--25% below 500, 57% between 500 and 599, 17% between 600 and 700, and 1% above 700; Math--24% below 500, 56% between 500 and 599, 19% between 600 and 700, and 1% above 700.

Requirements: The SAT I or ACT is required. In addition, applicants must be graduates of an accredited secondary school or have a GED certificate. 18 academic credits are required, including 4 years each of

English and social studies, 3 each of math and science, and 2 of a foreign language. An essay and interview are recommended. Applications are accepted on-line. AP and CLEP credits are accepted. Important factors in the admissions decision are advanced placement or honor courses, extracurricular activities record, and evidence of special talent.

Procedure: Freshmen are admitted fall and spring. Entrance exams should be taken during the spring of the junior year or fall of the senior year. There are early decision, early admissions, and deferred admissions plans. Early decision application should be filed by November 15; regular applications, by January 15 for fall entry and November 1 for spring entry, along with a $30 fee. Notification of early decision is sent December 15; regular decision, on a rolling basis. 55 early decision candidates were accepted for the 2001-2002 class.

Transfer: 728 transfer students enrolled in 2001-2002. Applicants must submit official transcripts from previously attended colleges. Students with a minimum GPA of 2.4 are encouraged to apply. SUNY associate degree holders are given preference. Secondary school records may be required for 1-year transfers. 30 credits of 122 must be completed at Oswego.

Visiting: There are regularly scheduled orientations for prospective students, usually including a campus tour and a meeting with a counselor. There are guides for informal visits and visitors may sit in on classes and stay overnight. To schedule a visit, contact the Office of Admissions.

Financial Aid: In 2001-2002, 66% of all freshmen and 63% of continuing students received some form of financial aid. 61% of freshmen and 57% of continuing students received need-based aid. The average freshman award was $6109. Of that total, scholarships or need-based grants averaged $3207; and loans averaged $2948. 33% of undergraduates work part time. Average annual earnings from campus work are $1200. The average financial indebtedness of the 2001 graduate was $16,468. The FAFSA is required. The fall application deadline is April 1.

International Students: The school actively recruits these students. They must score 550 on the written TOEFL or 213 on the electronic version.

Computers: The mainframes are a DEC VAX 6000-520 and 6000-320, a Sun 4/280, 2 Sun SPARC servers, and 15 Sun or 4 VAX Station 4000 Pathworks file servers. There are more than 600 PCs available for student access, with labs located throughout the campus for general access and in support of departmental programs. There is an instructional computing center that provides a 24-hour help line. All students may access the system. There are no time limits and no fees.

Graduates: In 2001, 1406 bachelor's degrees were awarded. The most popular majors were education (25%), business (22%), and communications (9%). In an average class, 1% graduate in 3 years, 44% in 4 years, 58% in 5 years, and 62% in 6 years. 100 companies recruited on campus in 2000-2001. Of the 2000 graduating class, 12% were enrolled in graduate school within 6 months of graduation and 79% were employed.

Admissions Contact: Joseph F. Grant, Jr., Dean of Admissions. A video is available. E-mail: *admiss@oswego.edu*
Web: *www.oswego.edu*

STATE UNIVERSITY OF NEW YORK/COLLEGE AT PLATTSBURGH D-2

Plattsburgh, NY 12901-2681 (518) 564-2040
(888) 673-0012; Fax: (518) 564-2045

Full-time: 2157 men, 2842 women	**Faculty:** 266; IIA, -$
Part-time: 136 men, 247 women	**Ph.D.s:** 83%
Graduate: 241 men, 613 women	**Student/Faculty:** 19 to 1
Year: trimesters, summer session	**Tuition:** $4149 ($9049)
Application Deadline: February 15	**Room & Board:** $5580
Freshman Class: 5211 applied, 3266 accepted, 1073 enrolled	
SAT I Verbal/Math: 530/520	**ACT:** 21 **COMPETITIVE**

The State University of New York/College at Plattsburgh, founded in 1889, is a public institution offering degree programs in the liberal arts and professional programs. In addition to regional accreditation, Plattsburgh State has baccalaureate program accreditation with ADA and NLN. The library contains 781,518 volumes, 925,213 microform items, and 23,474 audiovisual forms/CDs, and subscribes to 1393 periodicals. Computerized library services include the card catalog, interlibrary loans, and database searching. Special learning facilities include a learning resource center, art gallery, planetarium, radio station, TV station, an environmental science institute, a child care center, a research institute, a teacher resource center, a speech and hearing clinic, the Alzheimer's Disease Assistance Center, auditory research labs, a virtual reality simulator, and distance learning facilities. The 300-acre campus is in a suburban area 150 miles north of Albany, 25 miles west of Burlington, Vermont, and 65 miles south of Montreal. Including residence halls, there are 35 buildings.

Student Life: 97% of undergraduates are from New York. Others are from 25 states, 61 foreign countries, and Canada. 98% are from public schools. 79% are white. The average age of freshmen is 18; all undergraduates, 22. 21% do not continue beyond their first year; 62% remain to graduate.

Housing: 2900 students can be accommodated in college housing, which includes single-sex and coed dormitories. In addition, there are special-interest houses, adult student halls/floors, wellness floors, a substance-free building, and vacation housing. On-campus housing is available on a first-come, first-served basis and on a lottery system for upperclassmen. 59% of students live on campus; of those, 90% remain on campus on weekends. All students may keep cars.

Activities: 6% of men belong to 3 local and 4 national fraternities; 5% of women belong to 3 local and 4 national sororities. There are 90 groups on campus, including art, band, cheerleading, choir, chorale, chorus, computers, drama, ethnic, film, gay, honors, international, jazz band, literary magazine, musical theater, newspaper, orchestra, photography, political, professional, radio and TV, religious, social, social service, student government, symphony, and yearbook. Popular campus events include Canada Day, Family Weekend, and Arts and Crafts Fair.

Sports: There are 9 intercollegiate sports for men and 10 for women, and 12 intramural sports for men and 9 for women. Facilities include a 3500-seat ice arena, a 1500-seat gym, an indoor track, soccer and volleyball areas, an indoor swimming pool, exercise and weight rooms, an aerobics studio, racquetball courts, lighted tennis courts, softball, lacrosse, and rugby fields, and a fitness center.

Disabled Students: 80% of the campus is accessible. Wheelchair ramps, elevators, special parking, specially equipped rest rooms, special class scheduling, lowered drinking fountains, lowered telephones, curb cuts, and electronic doors are available.

Services: Counseling and information services are available, as is tutoring in every subject. There is a reader service for the blind, and remedial math, reading, and writing.

Campus Safety and Security: Measures include 24-hour foot and vehicle patrol, escort service, shuttle buses, and informal discussions. There are pamphlets/posters/films, emergency telephones, lighted pathways/sidewalks, bicycle patrols, combination locks on student rooms, a computerized keyless entry system for residence hall access, door viewers, and basement and ground-level security windows in residence halls.

Programs of Study: Plattsburgh State confers B.A., B.S., B.F.A., and B.S.Ed. degrees. Master's degrees are also awarded. Bachelor's degrees are awarded in BIOLOGICAL SCIENCE (biochemistry, biology/biological science, and cell biology), BUSINESS (accounting, business administration and management, business economics, and hotel/motel and restaurant management), COMMUNICATIONS AND THE ARTS (communications, dramatic arts, English, French, journalism, and Spanish), COMPUTER AND PHYSICAL SCIENCE (chemistry, computer science, geology, mathematics, and physics), EDUCATION (education of the deaf and hearing impaired, elementary, English, mathematics, science, secondary, social studies, and special), ENGINEERING AND ENVIRONMENTAL DESIGN (environmental science), HEALTH PROFESSIONS (medical laboratory technology and nursing), SOCIAL SCIENCE (anthropology, Canadian studies, child care/child and family studies, community services, criminal justice, dietetics, economics, geography, history, home economics, interdisciplinary studies, Latin American studies, philosophy, political science/government, social work, and sociology). Business, accounting, and art are the strongest academically. Psychology, education, and business are the largest.

Required: To graduate, students must have a 2.0 GPA and complete at least 120 semester hours. General education courses total 41 to 46 credits. In addition, all students must demonstrate proficiency in writing by completion of an advanced writing requirement.

Special: The college offers cross-registration with Clinton Community College and Empire State College, internships, study abroad in 6 countries, cooperative programs with a variety of employers, B.A.-B.S. degrees, dual and student-designed majors, and an accelerated degree program in any major except nursing. A 3-2 engineering degree is offered with SUNY Stony Brook and Binghamton, Clarkson, Syracuse, and McGill Universities, and the University of Vermont. Credit for military experience, nondegree study if space permits, and limited pass/fail options are possible. There are 18 national honor societies and a freshman honors program.

Faculty/Classroom: 66% of faculty are male; 34%, female. All both teach and do research. No introductory courses are taught by graduate students. The average class size in an introductory lecture is 27; in a laboratory, 19; and in a regular course, 24.

Admissions: 63% of the 2001-2002 applicants were accepted. The SAT I scores for the 2001-2002 freshman class were: Verbal--33% below 500, 50% between 500 and 599, 15% between 600 and 700, and 2% above 700; Math--31% below 500, 52% between 500 and 599, 16% between 600 and 700, and 1% above 700. The ACT scores were 40% below 21, 36% between 21 and 23, 16% between 24 and 26, 6% between 27 and 28, and 3% above 28. 24% of the current freshmen were in the top fifth of their class; 61% were in the top two fifths. 3 freshmen graduated first in their class.

Requirements: The SAT I or ACT is required. In addition, applicants must have at least 12 academic credits, including 5 combined years of math and science, 4 years of English, and 3 years of social studies. An essay, portfolio, audition, and interview may be recommended in some programs. The GED is accepted. Plattsburgh State requires applicants to be in the upper 50% of their class. A grade average of 78 is required. AP and CLEP credits are accepted. Important factors in the admissions decision are advanced placement or honor courses, recommendations by school officials, and leadership record. Applications are accepted on computer disk and on-line via Apply, Apply Yourself, CollegeLink, CollegeSearch, and ExPAN.

Procedure: Freshmen are admitted fall and spring. Entrance exams should be taken during the second half of the junior year or the beginning of the senior year. There are early decision, early admissions, and deferred admissions plans. Early decision applications should be filed by November 1; regular applications, by February 15 for fall entry and November 1 for spring entry. The fall 2001 application fee was $30. Notification of early decision is sent December 15; regular decision, on a rolling basis. 36 early decision candidates were accepted for the 2001-2002 class.

Transfer: 600 transfer students enrolled in 2001-2002. Applicants must have a minimum 2.0 GPA. Most academic programs require a 2.5 GPA or better. 36 credits of 120 must be completed at Plattsburgh State.

Visiting: There are regularly scheduled orientations for prospective students, including a student-led group tour and either a group or individual interview. Special overnight events for accepted freshmen include meals with students and faculty, classroom visits, discussions with faculty, and special workshops. There are guides for informal visits and visitors may sit in on classes and stay overnight. To schedule a visit, contact the Admissions Office at *admissions@plattsburgh.edu*

Financial Aid: In 2001-2002, 70% of all freshmen and 74% of continuing students received some form of financial aid. 69% of freshmen and 65% of continuing students received need-based aid. The average freshman award was $4725. Of that total, scholarships or need-based grants averaged $2748 ($6000 maximum); loans averaged $2370 ($2625 maximum); and work contracts averaged $1100. 37% of undergraduates work part time. Average annual earnings from campus work are $1100. The average financial indebtedness of the 2001 graduate was $15,274. The FAFSA is required and in-state students must also file the TAP application. The fall application deadline is May 1.

International Students: There are 323 international students enrolled. The school actively recruits these students. They must score 450 on the written TOEFL.

Computers: The mainframes are a DEC VAX 6610 and a DEC VAX 6430. There are 278 student access Macs or PCs located on campus. All students may access the system. There are no time limits. The technology fee is $50 per semester. It is strongly recommended that all students have personal computers.

Graduates: In 2001, 1203 bachelor's degrees were awarded. The most popular majors were education (22%), business (18%), and communication arts (10%). In an average class, 1% graduate in 3 years, 29% in 4 years, 53% in 5 years, and 57% in 6 years. 120 companies recruited on campus in a recent year. Of the 2000 graduating class, 87% were employed within 6 months of graduation.

Admissions Contact: Richard Higgins, Director of Admissions.
E-mail: *higginrj@splavb.cc.plattsburgh.edu* Web: *www.plattsburgh.edu*

STATE UNIVERSITY OF NEW YORK/COLLEGE AT POTSDAM C-2

Potsdam, NY 13676 (315) 267-2180
(800) 433-3154; Fax: (315) 267-2163

Full-time: 1351 men, 1956 women	**Faculty:** 238; IIA, --$
Part-time: 57 men, 111 women	**Ph.D.s:** 73%
Graduate: 227 men, 623 women	**Student/Faculty:** 14 to 1
Year: semesters, summer session	**Tuition:** $4129 ($9029)
Application Deadline: open	**Room & Board:** $6390
Freshman Class: 3397 applied, 2291 accepted, 648 enrolled	
SAT I Verbal/Math: 530/530	**ACT:** 23 **COMPETITIVE**

The State University of New York/College at Potsdam, founded in 1816 by early settlers of New York State's North Country, joined the state university system in 1948. The public institution offers liberal arts and teachers programs, and includes the Crane School of Music. There are 3 undergraduate schools and 1 graduate school. In addition to regional accreditation, SUNY Potsdam has baccalaureate program accreditation with NASM. The 2 libraries contain 404,989 volumes, 743,042 microform items, and 17,120 audiovisual forms/CDs, and subscribe to 1253 periodicals. Computerized library services include the card catalog, interlibrary loans, and database searching. Special learning facilities include an art gallery, natural history museum, planetarium, radio station, electronic music and recording studios, and a seismographic lab. The 240-acre campus is in a rural area 140 miles northeast of Syracuse. Including residence halls, there are 36 buildings.

Student Life: 96% of undergraduates are from New York. Others are from 18 states, 10 foreign countries, and Canada. 83% are white. The average age of freshmen is 18; all undergraduates, 24. 25% do not continue beyond their first year; 49% remain to graduate.

Housing: 2400 students can be accommodated in college housing, which includes single-sex and coed dormitories and on-campus apartments. In addition, there are honors houses, special-interest houses, substance-free housing, an international house, and first-year experience housing. On-campus housing is guaranteed for all 4 years. 52% of students live on campus; of those, 85% remain on campus on weekends. All students may keep cars.

Activities: 5% of men belong to 1 national and 2 local fraternities; 7% of women belong to 1 national and 7 local sororities. There are 100 groups on campus, including art, band, cheerleading, choir, chorale, chorus, computers, dance, drama, environmental awareness, ethnic, gay, honors, international, jazz band, literary magazine, musical theater, newspaper, opera, orchestra, pep band, photography, political, professional, radio and TV, social, social service, student government, symphony, and yearbook. Popular campus events include Harvest Ball, Family Weekend, and Spring Fest.

Sports: There are 7 intercollegiate sports for men and 11 for women, and 12 intramural sports for men and 10 for women. Facilities include a 2400-seat ice arena, an Olympic-size pool, a 3000-seat gym, a field house, indoor and outdoor tracks, tennis, squash, handball, and basketball courts, a weight room, and a dance studio. Potsdam's Star Lake Campus provides a recreational setting amidst the Adirondack Mountains wilderness.

Disabled Students: 95% of the campus is accessible. Wheelchair ramps, elevators, special parking, specially equipped rest rooms, special class scheduling, lowered drinking fountains, lowered telephones, and electric doors are available.

Services: Counseling and information services are available, as is tutoring in most subjects. There is a reader service for the blind, language and math labs, a writing center, and a reading clinic.

Campus Safety and Security: Measures include 24-hour foot and vehicle patrol, self-defense education, escort service, and informal discussions. There are pamphlets/posters/films, emergency telephones, and lighted pathways/sidewalks.

Programs of Study: SUNY Potsdam confers B.A., B.S., and B.A. Mus. degrees. Master's degrees are also awarded. Bachelor's degrees are awarded in BIOLOGICAL SCIENCE (biology/biological science), BUSINESS (business administration and management, business economics, and human resources), COMMUNICATIONS AND THE ARTS (art history and appreciation, dance, dramatic arts, English, fine arts, French, music, music business management, music performance, music theory and composition, Spanish, speech/debate/rhetoric, and studio art), COMPUTER AND PHYSICAL SCIENCE (chemistry, computer science, geology, mathematics, and physics), EDUCATION (art, early childhood, elementary, foreign languages, middle school, music, science, and secondary), HEALTH PROFESSIONS (community health work), SOCIAL SCIENCE (anthropology, archeology, criminal justice, economics, history, interdisciplinary studies, philosophy, political science/government, psychology, and sociology). Math, education, and music education are the strongest academically. Music education, elementary education, and psychology are the largest.

Required: To graduate, students must earn 120 to 124 credit hours, with 30 to 33 in the major, and a minimum GPA of 2.0. General education requirements include 10 to 11 semester hours of freshman course work in verbal and quantitative skills, 21 of Modes of Inquiry in liberal arts, and 4 of phys ed, as well as 1 course each in written and oral communication above the freshman level and demonstrated foreign language proficiency.

Special: Cross-registration is offered with Clarkson University, St. Lawrence University, and Canton College of Technology. Political science internships in Albany and many other internships are possible. SUNY Potsdam also offers work-study opportunities, co-op programs in premedicine, prelaw, and optometry, a 3-2 engineering degree with Clarkson University, study abroad in more than 40 countries, accelerated degree programs in math, English, and education, 3-2 management and accounting degrees, student-designed majors, dual majors in interdisciplinary natural science, nondegree study, and pass/fail options. There are 25 national honor societies, a freshman honors program, and 20 departmental honors programs.

Faculty/Classroom: 58% of faculty are male; 42%, female. All teach undergraduates. No introductory courses are taught by graduate students.

Admissions: 67% of the 2001-2002 applicants were accepted. The SAT I scores for the 2001-2002 freshman class were: Verbal--34% below 500, 43% between 500 and 599, 20% between 600 and 700, and 3% above 700; Math--33% below 500, 48% between 500 and 599, 17% between 600 and 700, and 2% above 700. The ACT scores were 29% below 21, 30% between 21 and 23, 19% between 24 and 26, 13% between 27 and 28, and 9% above 28. 27% of the current freshmen were in the top fifth of their class; 63% were in the top two fifths.

Requirements: The SAT I or ACT is required. Applicants must be high school graduates in a college preparatory program or hold a GED. Students should have earned 17 academic credits: 4 years each of English and social studies, 3 each of math and foreign language, 2 of science, and 1 of art or music. An interview is recommended; an audition, when appropriate, is required. SUNY Potsdam requires applicants to be in the upper 50% of their class. A grade average of 80 is required. AP and CLEP credits are accepted. Important factors in the admissions decision are advanced placement or honor courses, evidence of special talent, and leadership record. Applications are accepted on-line at *www.potsdam.edu/admissions*

Procedure: Freshmen are admitted fall, spring, and summer. Entrance exams should be taken in the junior year or early senior year. There are early admissions and deferred admissions plans. Application deadlines are open. The application fee is $30. Notification is sent on a rolling basis. A waiting list is an active part of the admissions procedure.

Transfer: 349 transfer students enrolled in 2001-2002. Applicants must have earned 12 hours of college credit. Transfers with fewer than 24 credit hours must submit a high school transcript showing a minimum 2.0 GPA. An interview is recommended, as are supplemental recommendations. 45 credits of 120 to 124 must be completed at SUNY Potsdam.

Visiting: There are regularly scheduled orientations for prospective students, including open houses, off-campus interviews by faculty, and alumni receptions. There are guides for informal visits and visitors may sit in on classes and stay overnight. To schedule a visit, contact the Admissions Office at (877) POTSDAM.

Financial Aid: In 2001-2002, 91% of all freshmen and 89% of continuing students received some form of financial aid. 68% of freshmen and 79% of continuing students received need-based aid. The average freshman award was $8696. Of that total, scholarships or need-based grants averaged $4042 ($4700 maximum); loans averaged $6290 ($15,625 maximum); work contracts averaged $1000 (maximum); and state and federal grants averaged $2080 ($4700 maximum). Average annual earnings from campus work are $1000. The average financial indebtedness of the 2001 graduate was $19,084. The FAFSA is required. The fall application deadline is rolling.

International Students: There are 54 international students enrolled. The school actively recruits these students. They must score 520 on the written TOEFL or 190 on the electronic version and also take the SAT I or the ACT.

Computers: The mainframes are 2 DEC Alpha boxes (models 4100 and 2100). About 350 Macs and PCs are networked and connected to all campus buildings and residence hall computer labs. Each has complete access to all networked services, including the Internet. All students may access the system 7 days a week, 24 hours per day. There are no time limits. It is strongly recommended that all students have personal computers. Mac and Windows 9.x and higher are recommended.

Graduates: In 2001, 652 bachelor's degrees were awarded. The most popular majors were psychology (15%), music and music education (15%), and sociology (14%). In an average class, 1% graduate in 3 years, 30% in 4 years, 45% in 5 years, and 48% in 6 years. 66 companies recruited on campus in 2000-2001. Of the 2000 graduating class, 32% were enrolled in graduate school within 6 months of graduation and 65% were employed.

Admissions Contact: Thomas Neshitt, Director of Admissions. E-mail: *admissions@potsdam.edu*

STATE UNIVERSITY OF NEW YORK/COLLEGE AT PURCHASE D-5

Purchase, NY 10577-1400 **(914) 251-6300; Fax: (914) 251-6314**

Full-time: 1349 men, 1690 women	**Faculty:** 136
Part-time: 305 men, 522 women	**Ph.D.s:** 100%
Graduate: 69 men, 83 women	**Student/Faculty:** 22 to 1
Year: semesters, summer session	**Tuition:** $4127 ($9027)
Application Deadline: August 15	**Room & Board:** $6460
Freshman Class: 6122 applied, 2199 accepted, 700 enrolled	
SAT I Verbal/Math: 559/528	**VERY COMPETITIVE**

State University of New York/College at Purchase, founded in 1967, is a public institution that offers programs in visual arts, music, acting, dance, film, theater/stage design technology, natural science, social science, and humanities. In addition to regional accreditation, Purchase College SUNY has baccalaureate program accreditation with NASAD and NASM. The library contains 270,090 volumes, 246,975 microform items, and 15,175 audiovisual forms/CDs, and subscribes to 1400 periodicals. Computerized library services include the card catalog, interlibrary loans, and database searching. Special learning facilities include a learning resource center, art gallery, radio station, TV station, listening and viewing center, science and photography labs, music practice rooms and instruments, multitrack synthesizers, experimental stage, typesetting and computer graphics labs, a performing arts complex, an electron microscope, and the Children's Center at Purchase College. The 500-acre campus is in a suburban area 35 miles north of midtown Manhattan. Including residence halls, there are 40 buildings.

Student Life: 81% of undergraduates are from New York. Others are from 46 states, 30 foreign countries, and Canada. 69% are white. The average age of freshmen is 18; all undergraduates, 22. 23% do not continue beyond their first year; 35% remain to graduate.

Housing: 1850 students can be accommodated in college housing, which includes single-sex and coed dormitories, on-campus apartments, and off-campus apartments. In addition, there are special-interest houses, transfer student units, nontraditional-age student units, wellness halls, presidential scholars halls, and learning community halls. On-campus housing is available on a first-come, first-served basis and is available on a lottery system for upperclassmen. Priority is given to out-of-town students. 58% of students live on campus. All students may keep cars.

Activities: There are 40 groups on campus, including art, band, choir, chorale, computers, dance, drama, environmental awareness, ethnic, film, gay, jazz band, literary magazine, newspaper, opera, orchestra, photography, political, professional, radio and TV, religious, social, social service, student government, symphony, and visual arts. Popular campus events include Spring Concert, Alcohol Awareness Week, and film programs.

Sports: There are 4 intercollegiate sports for men and 5 for women, and 38 intramural sports for men and 38 for women. Facilities include 3 basketball courts, a fitness center, a 6-lane pool, an aerobics studio, 4 racquetball courts, 2 squash courts, 6 lighted tennis courts, and a 4-lane bowling alley.

Disabled Students: All of the campus is accessible. Wheelchair ramps, elevators, special parking, specially equipped rest rooms, note takers, extended test times, quiet rooms for tests, interpreters for the hearing impaired, readers for the visually impaired, a reading machine in the library, and special note-taking paper are available.

Services: Counseling and information services are available, as is tutoring in every subject. There is a reader service for the blind, remedial math, reading, and writing, math and writing drop-in sessions, "The P.J. Project," offering tutoring in residence halls in evenings, assistive technology, supplemental instructors, and computer lab study groups.

Campus Safety and Security: Measures include 24-hour foot and vehicle patrol, escort service, informal discussions, and pamphlets/posters/films. There are emergency telephones and lighted pathways/sidewalks.

Programs of Study: Purchase College SUNY confers B.A., B.S., B.A.L.A., B.F.A., and Mus.B. degrees. Master's degrees are also awarded. Bachelor's degrees are awarded in BIOLOGICAL SCIENCE (biology/biological science), COMMUNICATIONS AND THE ARTS (art history and appreciation, creative writing, dance, dramatic arts, film arts, journalism, literature, music, theater design, and visual and performing arts), COMPUTER AND PHYSICAL SCIENCE (chemistry and mathematics), ENGINEERING AND ENVIRONMENTAL DESIGN (environmental science), SOCIAL SCIENCE (anthropology, economics, ethnic studies, history, liberal arts/general studies, philosophy, political science/government, psychology, sociology, and women's studies). Dance, drama, and film are the strongest academically. Visual arts, music, and liberal studies are the largest.

Required: A minimum 2.0 GPA is required with a minimum of 120 credits. Students majoring in the arts complete a minimum of 90 professional credits and the SUNY general education curriculum. Students majoring in the liberal arts and sciences complete the general education curriculum and major requirements and must complete a senior thesis.

Special: Purchase College offers cross-registration with Empire State colleges, internships with corporations, newspapers, and local agencies, student-designed majors, dual majors, study abroad, work-study, nondegree study, and pass/fail options. There is also an arts conservatory program.

Faculty/Classroom: 58% of faculty are male; 43%, female. All teach undergraduates. The average class size in an introductory lecture is 29; in a laboratory, 17; and in a regular course, 21.

Admissions: 36% of the 2001-2002 applicants were accepted. The SAT I scores for the 2001-2002 freshman class were: Verbal--22% below 500, 45% between 500 and 599, 28% between 600 and 700, and 5% above 700; Math--32% below 500, 48% between 500 and 599, 17% between 600 and 700, and 2% above 700.

Requirements: The SAT I is required and the ACT is recommended, with minimum required composite scores of 1100 on the SAT I or 23 on the ACT. Applicants must be graduates of an accredited secondary school and have completed 16 academic credits and 16 Carnegie units. The GED is accepted. Visual arts students must submit an essay and portfolio and have an interview. Film students need an essay and an interview. Design technology students need a portfolio and an interview. Performing arts students must audition. A GPA of 2.0 is required. AP and CLEP credits are accepted. Important factors in the admissions decision are evidence of special talent, recommendations by school officials, and personality/intangible qualities. Applications are accepted on-line at the school's web site.

Procedure: Freshmen are admitted fall and spring. Entrance exams should be taken by the fall of the senior year. There are early decision and deferred admissions plans. Early decision applications should be filed by November 15; regular applications, by August 15 for fall entry and December 1 for spring entry, along with a $30 fee. Notification of early decision is sent December 15; regular decision, on a rolling basis after December 15. 5% of all applicants are on a waiting list.

Transfer: 426 transfer students enrolled in 2001-2002. Students transferring to the School of Arts (visual or performing arts) must pass an audition or portfolio review. Transfer credit is limited; students can contact the Office of Admission to get a preliminary credit evaluation. Students transferring to programs in liberal arts and sciences must have a minimum 2.0 GPA if they have completed 30 or more semester hours; if they have fewer than 30 semester hours, the high school transcript is also reviewed. Liberal arts and science transfers can transfer a maximum of 90 semester hours from 4 year colleges and 75 semester hours from 2 year colleges. 30 credits of 120 must be completed at Purchase College.

Visiting: There are regularly scheduled orientations for prospective students, including group question and answer sessions followed by a tour of the campus. To schedule a visit, contact the Admissions Office.

Financial Aid: In 2001-2002, 74% of all freshmen and 62% of continuing students received some form of financial aid. 52% of freshmen and 50% of continuing students received need-based aid. The average freshman award was $6160. Of that total, scholarships or need-based grants averaged $1500 ($6000 maximum); loans averaged $3076 ($7625 maximum); and work contracts averaged $1150 ($1400 maximum). 12% of undergraduates work part time. Average annual earnings from campus work are $1073. The average financial indebtedness of the 2001 graduate was $13,510. The FAFSA is required. The fall application deadline is February 15.

International Students: There are 92 international students enrolled. The school actively recruits these students. They must score 550 on the written TOEFL or score 1100 on the SAT I.

Computers: The mainframes are PCs and servers. PCs are available in the computer center in the social sciences building. The humanities building, music building, art and design building, dance hall, natural sciences building, library, and dormitories house PCs as well. There are approximately 350 PCs in total. All students may access the system when the computer center is open. There are no time limits. The fee is $150 per semester. It is strongly recommended that all students have a personal computer.

Graduates: In 2000-2001, 594 bachelor's degrees were awarded. The most popular majors were visual arts (20%), liberal arts (18%), and music (12%). In an average class, 22% graduate in 4 years, 33% in 5 years, and 35% in 6 years. 50 companies recruited on campus in 2000-2001.

Admissions Contact: Betsy Immergut, Director of Admissions.
E-mail: *betsy.immergut@purchase.edu* Web: *admissn@purchase.edu*

STATE UNIVERSITY OF NEW YORK/COLLEGE OF AGRICULTURE AND TECHNOLOGY AT COBLESKILL — D-3

Cobleskill, NY 12043 — (518) 255-5525
(800) 295-8988; Fax: (518) 234-5333

Full-time: 1300 men, 974 women	**Faculty:** 118; III, -$
Part-time: 75 men, 101 women	**Ph.D.s:** 32%
Graduate: none	**Student/Faculty:** 19 to 1
Year: semesters, summer session	**Tuition:** $4740 ($6540)
Application Deadline: open	**Room & Board:** $6460
Freshman Class: 3476 applied, 1329 accepted, 1034 enrolled	
SAT I Verbal/Math: 460/460	**ACT:** 19 **COMPETITIVE+**

The State University of New York/College of Agriculture and Technology at Cobleskill, established in 1916, is a public institution conferring the Bachelor of Technology in Agriculture degree. Some information in this profile is approximate. The library contains 86,000 volumes and 55,000 audiovisual forms/CDs, and subscribes to 1000 periodicals. Computerized library services include the card catalog, interlibrary loans, and database searching. Special learning facilities include a learning resource center, art gallery, arboretum, greenhouses, and plant nursery. The 750-acre campus is in a rural area 35 miles south of Albany. Including residence halls, there are 53 buildings.

Student Life: 93% of undergraduates are from New York. Others are from 11 states. 98% are from public schools. 91% are white. The average age of freshmen is 18; all undergraduates, 20. 20% do not continue beyond their first year; 50% remain to graduate.

Housing: College housing includes single-sex and coed dormitories. On-campus housing is guaranteed for the freshman year only and is available on a lottery system for upperclassmen. 80% of students live on campus; of those, 90% remain on campus on weekends. Alcohol is not permitted. All students may keep cars.

Activities: There are no fraternities or sororities. There are 50 groups on campus, including cheerleading, choir, chorus, computers, ethnic, honors, jazz band, musical theater, newspaper, professional, religious, social service, student government, and yearbook. Popular campus events include Parents Weekend and Alumni Weekend.

Sports: There are 10 intercollegiate sports for men and 9 for women, and 11 intramural sports for men and 10 for women. Facilities include indoor and outdoor basketball and tennis courts, playing fields, a gym, an exercise room, a swimming pool, bowling lanes, a field house, badminton, volleyball, and handball courts, archery and golf driving areas, a quarter-mile track, a ski center, and a fitness trail.

Disabled Students: 35% of the campus is accessible. Wheelchair ramps, elevators, special parking, specially equipped rest rooms, lowered drinking fountains, and lowered telephones are available.

Services: Counseling and information services are available, as is tutoring in some subjects, including biology, intermediate algebra, and chemistry. There is a reader service for the blind, and remedial math, reading, and writing. There is also an academic skills center.

Campus Safety and Security: Measures include 24-hour foot and vehicle patrol, informal discussions, pamphlets/posters/films, and emergency telephones. There are lighted pathways/sidewalks.

Programs of Study: SUNY Cobleskill confers the B.T. in Agriculture degree. Associate degrees are also awarded. Bachelor's degrees are awarded in AGRICULTURE (agricultural business management, agricultural mechanics, animal science, and plant science).

Required: Degree requirements include completion of 126 credit hours, with 30 to 32 upper-division credits in the major, 11 credits of technical electives, 7 to 15 credits in other electives, and a 15-credit internship. Students must maintain a minimum 2.0 GPA.

Special: The college sponsors internship programs, and cross-registration is possible with the Hudson-Mohawk Area Consortium. Students may study abroad at Thomas Danby and South Fields Colleges in England. There is 1 national honor society, a freshman honors program, and 1 departmental honors program.

Faculty/Classroom: 70% of faculty are male; 30%, female. 40% do research. The average class size in an introductory lecture is 33; in a laboratory, 15; and in a regular course, 30.

Admissions: 38% of the 2001-2002 applicants were accepted. The SAT I scores for the 2001-2002 freshman class were: Verbal--45% below 500, 13% between 500 and 599, and 2% between 600 and 700; Math--43% below 500, 16% between 500 and 599, and 2% between 600 and 700. The ACT scores were 66% below 21, 19% between 21 and 23, 9% between 24 and 26, 4% between 27 and 28, and 2% above 28. 9% of the current freshmen were in the top fifth of their class; 28% were in the top two fifths.

Requirements: The SAT I or ACT is recommended. In addition, applicants must have graduated from an accredited secondary school or earned a GED, and are encouraged to have completed college-preparatory courses. Students planning to enter the agricultural program should also take vocational agricultural courses. Applicants are required to visit the campus. An average of 75 is required. AP and CLEP credits are accepted. Important factors in the admissions decision are evidence of special talent, advanced placement or honor courses, and leadership record.

Procedure: Freshmen are admitted fall and spring. There are early admissions and deferred admissions plans. Application deadlines are open. The application fee is $30.

Transfer: Applicants must have a minimum GPA of 2.0. 30 credits of 126 must be completed at SUNY Cobleskill.

Visiting: There are regularly scheduled orientations for prospective students. To schedule a visit, contact the Office of Admissions.

Financial Aid: In 2001-2002, 64% of all freshmen and 55% of continuing students received some form of financial aid. 15% of undergraduates work part time. Average annual earnings from campus work are $675. SUNY Cobleskill is a member of CSS. The FAFSA and the college's own financial statement are required. Check with the shool for current deadlines.

International Students: The school actively recruits these students. They must score 500 on the written TOEFL.

Computers: The mainframe is a DEC. There are 3 computer labs, as well as network access in all residence halls. All students may access the system during computer center hours. There are no time limits and no fees.

Graduates: In an average class, 54% graduate in 3 years and 60% in 4 years.

Admissions Contact: Dr. Clayton Smith, Director of Admissions.
E-mail: *smithc@cobleskill.edu* Web: *www.cobleskill.edu*

STATE UNIVERSITY OF NEW YORK/COLLEGE OF ENVIRONMENTAL SCIENCE AND FORESTRY — C-3

Syracuse, NY 13210-2779 — (315) 470-6600
(800) 7777-ESF; Fax: (315) 470-6933

Full-time: 683 men, 431 women	**Faculty:** 122; IIA, +$
Part-time: 87 men, 62 women	**Ph.D.s:** 80%
Graduate: 383 men, 325 women	**Student/Faculty:** 9 to 1
Year: semesters	**Tuition:** $3776 ($8676)
Application Deadline: March 1	**Room & Board:** $8670
Freshman Class: 707 applied, 410 accepted, 201 enrolled	
SAT I Verbal/Math: required	**VERY COMPETITIVE**

The College of Environmental Science and Forestry, founded in 1911 and located adjacent to the campus of Syracuse University, is one of the colleges of the State University of New York. The public institution specializes in undergraduate and graduate degrees in agricultural, biological, environmental, health, and physical sciences, landscape architecture, and engineering. Students have access to the academic, cultural, and social life at Syracuse University. There is 1 graduate school. In addition to regional accreditation, ESF has baccalaureate program accreditation with ABET, ASLA, and SAF. The library contains 130,305 volumes, 200,090 microform items, and 1118 audiovisual forms/CDs, and subscribes to 2001 periodicals. Computerized library services include the card catalog, interlibrary loans, and database searching. Special learning facilities include a learning resource center, art gallery, radio station, and TV station. The 12-acre campus is in an urban area in Syracuse. Including residence halls, there are 7 buildings.

Student Life: 91% of undergraduates are from New York. Others are from 23 states and 2 foreign countries. 85% are from public schools. 90% are white. The average age of freshmen is 18; all undergraduates, 21. 3% do not continue beyond their first year; 75% remain to graduate.

Housing: 450 students can be accommodated in college housing, which includes single-sex and coed dormitories, on-campus apartments, and married-student housing. In addition, there are honors houses, special-interest houses, substance-free floors, quiet floors, and a global living center. On-campus housing is guaranteed for all 4 years. 50% of students live on campus; of those, 90% remain on campus on weekends. Alcohol is not permitted. Upperclassmen may keep cars.

Activities: 3% of men belong to 20 national fraternities; 3% of women belong to 20 national sororities. There are 220 groups on campus, including art, band, cheerleading, choir, chorale, chorus, computers, dance, debate, drama, drum and bugle corps, ethnic, film, gay, honors, international, jazz band, marching band, musical theater, newspaper, orchestra, pep band, photography, political, professional, radio and TV, religious, social, social service, student government, symphony, and yearbook. Popular campus events include Activities Fair, Earth Day, and Awards Banquet.

Sports: There are 21 intercollegiate sports for men and 21 for women, and 30 intramural sports for men and 30 for women. Athletic and recreational facilities are contracted through Syracuse University.

Disabled Students: 90% of the campus is accessible. Wheelchair ramps, elevators, special parking, specially equipped rest rooms, lowered drinking fountains, and lowered telephones are available.

Services: There is a reader service for the blind and remedial math.

Campus Safety and Security: Measures include 24-hour foot and vehicle patrol, escort service, shuttle buses, and informal discussions. There are pamphlets/posters/films, emergency telephones, and lighted pathways/sidewalks.

Programs of Study: ESF confers B.S. and B.L.A. degrees. Associate, master's, and doctoral degrees are also awarded. Bachelor's degrees are awarded in AGRICULTURE (animal science, environmental studies, forest engineering, forestry and related sciences, natural resource management, plant science, soil science, and wood science), BIOLOGICAL SCIENCE (biology/biological science, botany, ecology, entomology, environmental biology, microbiology, molecular biology, plant genetics, and plant physiology), COMPUTER AND PHYSICAL SCIENCE (chemistry and polymer science), EDUCATION (environmental and science), ENGINEERING AND ENVIRONMENTAL DESIGN (chemical engineering, construction management, environmental design, environmental engineering, landscape architecture/design, paper and pulp science, paper engineering, and survey and mapping technology), HEALTH PROFESSIONS (predentistry, premedicine, and prepharmacy), SOCIAL SCIENCE (prelaw). Engineering, chemistry, and biology are the strongest academically. Environmental and forest biology and environmental studies are the largest.

Required: Students must complete 125 to 130 credit hours for the B.S. (160 for the B.L.A.), including 60 in the major, with a minimum 2.0 GPA. Courses in chemistry, English, math, and botany are required.

Special: Cross-registration is offered with Syracuse University. Co-op programs, accelerated degrees in biology and landscape architecture, and dual options in biology and forestry are available. Study abroad is available in landscape architecture and through Syracuse University. There is 1 national honor society, and a freshman honors program. All departments have honors programs.

Faculty/Classroom: 82% of faculty are male; 18%, female. All both teach undergraduates and do research. No introductory courses are taught by graduate students. The average class size in a regular course is 25.

Admissions: 58% of the 2001-2002 applicants were accepted. There was 1 National Merit finalist. 2 freshmen graduated first in their class.

Requirements: The SAT I or ACT is required. In addition, applicants are required to have a minimum of 4 years of math and science, including chemistry, in a college preparatory curriculum. An essay is required, and an interview, letters of recommendation, and a personal portfolio or resume are recommended. A high school average of 85 is required. AP and CLEP credits are accepted. Important factors in the admissions decision are advanced placement or honor courses, leadership record, and recommendations by school officials. Applications are accepted on-line via SUNY and ESF web sites.

Procedure: Freshmen are admitted fall and spring. Entrance exams should be taken by October of the senior year. There are early decision, early admissions, and deferred admissions plans. Early decision applications should be filed by November 15; regular applications, by March 1 for fall entry, along with a $30 fee. Notification of early decision is sent December 15; regular decision, on a rolling basis. 36 early decision candidates were accepted for the 2001-2002 class.

Transfer: 226 transfer students enrolled in 2001-2002. Transfer requirements vary by major. Students must successfully complete prerequisite course work and must have a 2.0 or higher GPA to be considered. 24 credits of 125 to 130 must be completed at ESF.

Visiting: There are regularly scheduled orientations for prospective students, including a fall open house, which provides campus tours, faculty sessions, an activities fair, and student affairs presentations. There are guides for informal visits and visitors may sit in on classes. To schedule a visit, contact the Admissions Office.

Financial Aid: In a recent year, 80% of all freshmen and 85% of continuing students received some form of financial aid. 80% of all students received need-based aid. The average freshman award was $6425. Of that total, scholarships or need-based grants averaged $600; loans averaged $2600 ($4625 maximum); and work contracts averaged $800 ($1200 maximum). 75% of undergraduates work part time. Average annual earnings from campus work are $1200. The average financial indebtedness of the 2001 graduate was $16,500. ESF is a member of CSS. The FAFSA is required. The fall application deadline is March 1.

International Students: There are 7 international students enrolled. They must score 550 on the written TOEFL or 213 on the electronic version and also take the SAT I or the ACT.

Computers: The college has a web-based computer system. Public PC clusters offer current technology and software. All are connected to the World Wide Web. All students may access the system any time. There are no time limits and no fees.

Graduates: In 2001, 257 bachelor's degrees were awarded. The most popular majors were environmental and forest biology (42%), landscape architecture (14%), and resource management (13%). In an average class, 4% graduate in 3 years, 51% in 4 years, 70% in 5 years, and 72% in 6 years. 32 companies recruited on campus in 2000-2001. Of the 2000 graduating class, 24% were enrolled in graduate school within 6 months of graduation and 60% were employed.

Admissions Contact: Susan H. Sanford, Director of Admissions and Inter-Institutional Relations. A video is available.
E-mail: *esfinfo@esf.edu* Web: *www.esf.edu/admissions/htm*

STATE UNIVERSITY OF NEW YORK/COLLEGE OF TECHNOLOGY AT ALFRED — B-4

Alfred, NY 14802 — **(607) 587-4215**
(800) 4-ALFRED; Fax: (607) 587-4299

Full-time: 1932 men, 800 women	**Faculty:** 132; III, -$
Part-time: 109 men, 200 women	**Ph.D.s:** 8%
Graduate: none	**Student/Faculty:** 21 to 1
Year: semesters, summer session	**Tuition:** $3830 ($5630)
Application Deadline: open	**Room & Board:** $5358
Freshman Class: 3979 applied, 2843 accepted, 1391 enrolled	
SAT I Verbal/Math: 464/488	**ACT:** 20 **COMPETITIVE**

The State University of New York College of Technology at Alfred, founded in 1908, is a public institution conferring associate and bachelor's degrees. There are 3 undergraduate schools. In addition to regional accreditation, Alfred State College has baccalaureate program accreditation with ABET. The 2 libraries contain 60,755 volumes, 501 microform items, and 2115 audiovisual forms/CDs, and subscribe to 448 periodicals. Computerized library services include the card catalog, interlibrary loans, database searching, and an integrated library management system. Special learning facilities include a learning resource center and radio station. The 150-acre campus is in a rural area 15 miles north of Pennsylvania, 75 miles south of Rochester, and 90 miles southeast of Buffalo. Including residence halls, there are 48 buildings.

Student Life: 99% of undergraduates are from New York. Others are from 7 states, 5 foreign countries, and Canada. 89% are white. 50% are claim no religious affiliation; 23% Protestant; 21% Catholic. The average age of freshmen is 18; all undergraduates, 19. 52% of freshmen remain to graduate.

Housing: 1237 students can be accommodated in college housing, which includes coed dormitories. In addition, there are baccalaureate houses, special-interest houses, and wellness, computerized, and adult housing. On-campus housing is guaranteed for all 4 years. 70% of students live on campus; of those, 50% remain on campus on weekends. Alcohol is not permitted. All students may keep cars.

Activities: There are 3 local fraternities and 4 local sororities. There are 62 groups on campus, including band, cheerleading, choir, chorale, computers, drama, ethnic, gay, honors, international, karate, jazz band, literary magazine, musical theater, newspaper, peer education network, pep band, professional, radio and TV, rescue and response team, social,

social service, student government, and yearbook. Popular campus events include Family Weekend and Hot Dog Day.

Sports: There are 10 intercollegiate sports for men and 8 for women, and 26 intramural sports for men and 23 for women. Facilities include a fitness center/weight room, an indoor swimming pool, a wrestling room, a full gym, tennis courts, an outdoor track, baseball and softball fields, and practice fields.

Disabled Students: All of the campus is accessible. Wheelchair ramps, elevators, special parking, specially equipped rest rooms, special class scheduling, lowered drinking fountains, lowered telephones, and specially equipped rooms in residence halls are available.

Services: Counseling and information services are available, as is tutoring in most subjects. There is a reader service for the blind, and remedial math, reading, and writing.

Campus Safety and Security: Measures include 24-hour foot and vehicle patrol, self-defense education, escort service, and shuttle buses. There are informal discussions, pamphlets/posters/films, emergency telephones, and lighted pathways/sidewalks.

Programs of Study: Alfred State College confers B.S., B.B.A., and B.T. degrees. Associate degrees are also awarded. Bachelor's degrees are awarded in COMPUTER AND PHYSICAL SCIENCE (information sciences and systems and web services), ENGINEERING AND ENVIRONMENTAL DESIGN (architectural technology, computer technology, construction management, electrical/electronics engineering technology, electromechanical technology, mechanical engineering technology, and survey and mapping technology). Engineering programs are the strongest academically and have the largest enrollments.

Required: To graduate, candidates for a bachelor's degree must complete a total of 120 credits. A core sequence, including courses in math, physical sciences, and liberal studies, and a year-long senior technical project, are required. A phys ed course is also required.

Special: Cross-registration is offered with Alfred University, Houghton College, Rochester area colleges, and the Western New York Consortium. On-campus work-study programs are available, as are summer internships. There are 2 national honor societies, a freshman honors program, and 52 departmental honors programs.

Faculty/Classroom: 68% of faculty are male; 32%, female. All teach undergraduates. The average class size in an introductory lecture is 40; in a laboratory, 20; and in a regular course, 20.

Admissions: 71% of the 2001-2002 applicants were accepted. 10 freshmen graduated first in their class.

Requirements: The SAT I or ACT is required. In addition, applicants must have graduated from an accredited secondary school or earned a GED. Specific course requirements vary by curriculum. A portfolio is required for applicants interested in computer art and design. A GPA of 3.0 is required. AP and CLEP credits are accepted. Important factors in the admissions decision are recommendations by school officials, advanced placement or honor courses, and leadership record. Applications are accepted on-line via the school's web site or CollegeNET.

Procedure: Freshmen are admitted fall and spring. Application deadlines are open. The application fee is $30. Notification is sent on a rolling basis.

Transfer: 192 transfer students enrolled in 2001-2002. Transfer applicants must have a minimum 2.4 GPA. 30 credits of 120 must be completed at Alfred State College.

Visiting: There are regularly scheduled orientations for prospective students, including open houses during the fall and spring semesters. All aspects of campus are open for visitation. There are guides for informal visits and visitors may sit in on classes and stay overnight. To schedule a visit, contact the Admissions Office.

Financial Aid: In 2001-2002, 80% of all freshmen received some form of financial aid, including need-based aid. The average freshman award was $8000. Of that total, scholarships or need-based grants averaged $750 ($1500 maximum); loans averaged $2625 ($8125 maximum); and work contracts averaged $1000. 40% of undergraduates work part time. Average annual earnings from campus work are $1000. The average financial indebtedness of the 2001 graduate was $6000. The FAFSA is required.

International Students: There are 30 international students enrolled. They must score 500 on the written TOEFL.

Computers: The mainframe is a DEC ALPHA 1200. There are 1600 PCs available in residence halls, academic buildings, the library, and the Student Development Center. Full Internet access is available via 9 T-1 lines. All students may access the system 24 hours a day. There are no time limits and no fees. It is recommended that students in Construction Engineering Technology, Surveying Engineering Technology, and Construction have personal computers. Compaq is recommended.

Graduates: In 2001, 50 bachelor's degrees were awarded. The most popular majors were auto trades (7%), liberal arts and social sciences (6%), and human services (5%). Of the 2000 graduating class, 98% were employed within 6 months of graduation.

Admissions Contact: Deborah Goodrich, Director of Admissions and Enrollment Management. E-mail: *alfredstate.edu*
Web: *www.alfredstate.edu*

STATE UNIVERSITY OF NEW YORK/COLLEGE OF TECHNOLOGY AT FARMINGDALE E-5

Farmingdale, NY 11735 **(631) 420-2200; Fax: (631) 420-2633**

Full-time: 2027 men, 1323 women	**Faculty:** 184; IIB, +$
Part-time: 1022 men, 1077 women	**Ph.D.s:** 42%
Graduate: none	**Student/Faculty:** 18 to 1
Year: semesters, summer session	**Tuition:** $4139 ($9039)
Application Deadline: open	**Room & Board:** $7130

Freshman Class: 2949 applied, 2057 accepted, 1125 enrolled
SAT I: required **COMPETITIVE**

The State University of New York/College of Technology at Farmingdale, founded in 1912, is a public institution offering bachelor's degrees in the applied sciences and technology. Some information in this profile is approximate. There are 4 undergraduate schools. In addition to regional accreditation, State University of New York/College of Technology at Farmingdale has baccalaureate program accreditation with ABET and CAHEA. The library contains 150,000 volumes, 63,000 microform items, and 3100 audiovisual forms/CDs, and subscribes to 900 periodicals. Computerized library services include the card catalog, interlibrary loans, and database searching. Special learning facilities include a learning resource center, art gallery, radio station, dental hygiene clinic, CAD/CAM and CIM labs, fleet of single-engine airplanes, and greenhouse complex. The 380-acre campus is in a suburban area on Long Island, about 35 miles east of New York City. Including residence halls, there are 40 buildings.

Student Life: 99% of undergraduates are from New York. Others are from 5 states. 92% are from public schools. 68% are white; 13%, African American. The average age of freshmen is 22; all undergraduates, 26. 19% do not continue beyond their first year; 36% remain to graduate.

Housing: 616 students can be accommodated in college housing, which includes coed dormitories. On-campus housing is available on a first-come, first-served basis and is available on a lottery system for upperclassmen. Priority is given to out-of-town students. 90% of students commute. Alcohol is not permitted. All students may keep cars.

Activities: There are no fraternities or sororities. There are 32 groups on campus, including art, cheerleading, computers, drama, ethnic, honors, literary magazine, musical theater, newspaper, professional, radio and TV, religious, social, student government, and yearbook. Popular campus events include Comedy Nights, Spring Fling, and black, Hispanic, and women's history months.

Sports: There are 9 intercollegiate sports for men and 7 for women, and 11 intramural sports for men and 11 for women. Facilities include basketball, badminton, volleyball, racquetball, handball, squash, and tennis courts, a swimming pool, a wrestling room, bowling alleys, weight training rooms, indoor and outdoor tracks, a golf driving range and 3-hole golf layout, and baseball, softball, soccer/lacrosse, and multipurpose fields.

Disabled Students: 90% of the campus is accessible. Wheelchair ramps, elevators, special parking, specially equipped rest rooms, lowered drinking fountains, and lowered telephones are available.

Services: Counseling and information services are available, as is tutoring in most subjects. There is a reader service for the blind, remedial math, reading, and writing, and a learning disabilities specialist counselor.

Campus Safety and Security: Measures include 24-hour foot and vehicle patrol, escort service, informal discussions, and pamphlets/posters/films. There are emergency telephones and lighted pathways/sidewalks.

Programs of Study: State University of New York/College of Technology at Farmingdale confers B.S. and B.Tech. degrees. Associate degrees are also awarded. Bachelor's degrees are awarded in ENGINEERING AND ENVIRONMENTAL DESIGN (aeronautical science, automotive technology, aviation administration/management, computer technology, construction management, electrical/electronics engineering technology, graphic arts technology, industrial administration/management, industrial engineering technology, and manufacturing technology), SOCIAL SCIENCE (safety and security technology). Electrical engineering technology is the strongest academically. Industrial technology and electrical engineering technology are the largest.

Required: To graduate, students must complete 124 to 141 credits, including 60 to 70 in the major, with a minimum GPA of 2.0. The core curriculum includes 4 courses each in social science, math/science, and English/humanities, including English composition.

Special: Study abroad in 3 countries is available. There is a B.A.-B.S. degree in applied math (joint admissions program with SUNY Stony Brook). There are 3 national honor societies and 1 departmental honors program.

Faculty/Classroom: 62% of faculty are male; 38%, female. All teach undergraduates. The average class size in an introductory lecture is 28; in a laboratory, 15; and in a regular course, 21.

Admissions: 70% of the 2001-2002 applicants were accepted. 7% of the current freshmen were in the top fifth of their class; 21% were in the top two fifths.

Requirements: The SAT I is required. In addition, applicants must be graduates of an accredited secondary school or have earned a GED. Specific entrance requirements vary by program, but recommended preparation includes 4 units of English and 3 each of math, science, and social science. Art programs require a portfolio and an interview. A GPA of 2.0 is required. AP and CLEP credits are accepted. Applications are accepted on-line at the SUNY Application Processing Center at *http://www.infostu.suny.edu/*

Procedure: Freshmen are admitted fall and spring. There are early admissions and deferred admissions plans. Application deadlines are open. The application fee is $30.

Transfer: Applicants must have a minimum GPA of 2.0 and be eligible to return to their previous college. 30 credits of 124 to 141 must be completed at State University of New York/College of Technology at Farmingdale.

Visiting: There are regularly scheduled orientations for prospective students, including a tour of the campus and general information about the college, admissions, financial aid, and residence life. There are guides for informal visits. To schedule a visit, contact the Admissions Office at (631) 420-2200 or (877) 4FARMINGDALE.

Financial Aid: The FAFSA, the college's own financial statement, and a state aid form are required. Check with the school for current deadlines.

International Students: They must score 500 on the written TOEFL.

Computers: The mainframe is a DEC ALPHA cluster. More than 250 PCs, both networked and stand-alone, are located in student labs in several classroom buildings and residence halls. All students may access the system during lab hours of Monday through Friday, 8 A.M. to 10:30 P.M., and Saturday, 9 A.M. to 4 P.M., or through dial-in access. There are no time limits and no fees.

Admissions Contact: Kathleen Fitzwilliam, Assistant Dean for Enrollment Services. E-mail: *fitzwik@farmingdale.edu*
Web: *www.farmingdale.edu*

STATE UNIVERSITY OF NEW YORK/EMPIRE STATE COLLEGE D-3

Saratoga Springs, NY 12866-4390 **(518) 587-2100, ext. 223**
(800) 847-3000, ext. 223; Fax: (518) 580-0105

Full-time: 796 men, 1489 women	**Faculty:** 123; IIB, av$
Part-time: 2825 men, 2950 women	**Ph.D.s:** 80%
Graduate: 124 men, 211 women	**Student/Faculty:** 19 to 1
Year: see profile	**Tuition:** $3545 ($8445)
Application Deadline: open	**Room & Board:** n/app
Freshman Class: n/av	
SAT I or ACT: not required	**SPECIAL**

Empire State College, founded in 1971 as part of the State University of New York, offers degree programs in the arts and sciences through its statewide network of more than 45 regional centers and units. Students study on their own, with guidance from faculty advisers, or mentors, with whom they develop learning contracts. The college maintains year-round operation, and students study on flexible schedules. The college's headquarters, as well as a regional center, is in Saratoga Springs; other regional centers are in Buffalo, Rochester, Albany, Syracuse, Hartsdale in Westchester County, Old Westbury on Long Island, and in New York City along with the college's School of Labor Studies. Computerized library services include the card catalog, interlibrary loans, and database searching. Special learning facilities include a learning resource center and a technology building.

Student Life: 94% of undergraduates are from New York. Others are from 15 states, 14 foreign countries, and Canada. 73% are white; 13% African American. The average age of all undergraduates is 36. 33% do not continue beyond their first year.

Housing: There are no residence halls. All students commute. Alcohol is not permitted.

Activities: There are 17 groups on campus, including literary magazine and student government. Popular campus events include Regional centers sponsor events and outside speakers throughout the year.

Disabled Students: 85% of the campus is accessible.

Programs of Study: Empire State College confers B.A., B.S., and B.P.S. degrees. Associate and master's degrees are also awarded. Bachelor's degrees are awarded in BUSINESS (business administration and management, labor studies, and management science), COMPUTER AND PHYSICAL SCIENCE (mathematics and science), EDUCATION (education), SOCIAL SCIENCE (community services, economics, history, human development, humanities and social science, interdisciplinary studies, liberal arts/general studies, and sociology). Community and human services and business, management, and economics are the largest.

Required: Students must earn 128 credits, including 30 credits that meet SUNY general education requirements, to graduate. Degree programs are customized and will vary in content.

Special: Empire State College uses a range of teaching methods, including independent study, learning contracts, study groups, and residencies, as well as distance learning, in which students confer with faculty by mail and telephone. Students can cross-register with any SUNY or CUNY school, and some private institutions, and may study abroad in England, Denmark, Cyprus, and Israel. Accelerated degree programs, internships through the Albany semester program, dual majors, student-designed majors, nondegree study, and credit for life, military, and work experience are possible.

Faculty/Classroom: 57% of faculty are male; 43%, female. 99% teach undergraduates and 1% both teach and do research. No introductory courses are taught by graduate students.

Requirements: Applicants must be high school graduates, have a GED, or show ability to succeed at the college level. Empire State College also considers the ability of a learning location to meet individual needs. AP and CLEP credits are accepted. Important factors in the admissions decision are recommendations by school officials and personality/intangible qualities. Applications are accepted on-line at the school's web site.

Procedure: Freshmen are admitted to all sessions. There are application deadlines for some programs.

Transfer: 2196 transfer students enrolled in 2001-2002. Empire State College offers maximum flexibility to transfer applicants, who must provide official transcripts from previous colleges attended. 32 credits of 128 must be completed at Empire State College.

Visiting: There are regularly scheduled orientations for prospective students, by invitation, after students attend an information session. There are guides for informal visits. To schedule a visit, contact Melanie Kaiser at (518) 587-2100, ext. 447 or *melaniekaiser@esc.edu*, or contact the dean of the individual regional center.

Financial Aid: In 2001-2002, 50% of all students received some form of financial aid. 45% of all students received need-based aid. Scholarships or need-based grants averaged $1881 ($4500 maximum); and loans averaged $3702 ($6625 maximum). 1% of undergraduates work part time. Average annual earnings from campus work are $3000. The average financial indebtedness of the 2001 graduate was $4328. The FAFSA is required.

International Students: There are 85 international students enrolled.

Computers: The mainframe is a Compaq Alpha 4100. There are also 150 PCs, primarily IBM, distributed among the college's branches. All students may access the system 24 hours a day. There are no time limits and no fees. It is strongly recommended that all students have a personal computer.

Graduates: In 2001, 1489 bachelor's degrees were awarded. The most popular majors were business, management, and economics (38%), community and human services (24%), and human development (9%).

Admissions Contact: Jennifer Riley, Assistant Director of Admissions. A video is available. E-mail: *admissions@esc.edu* Web: *www.esc.edu*

STATE UNIVERSITY OF NEW YORK/FASHION INSTITUTE OF TECHNOLOGY

(See Fashion Institute of Technology/State University of New York)

STATE UNIVERSITY OF NEW YORK/MARITIME COLLEGE D-5

Throgs Neck, NY 10465 **(718) 409-7220**
(800) 642-1874 (Northeast only); Fax: (718) 409-7465

Full-time: 560 men, 80 women	**Faculty:** 56; IIA, -$
Part-time: 10 men, 5 women	**Ph.D.s:** 41%
Graduate: 160 men, 20 women	**Student/Faculty:** 11 to 1
Year: semesters, summer session	**Tuition:** $3525 ($8425)
Application Deadline: open	**Room & Board:** $6500
Freshman Class: n/av	
SAT I: required	**LESS COMPETITIVE**

The Maritime College of the State University of New York, founded in 1874, is a public institution that prepares students for the U.S. Merchant Marine officer's license and for bachelor's degrees in engineering, naval architecture, marine environmental science, and marine transportation/business administration. The college curriculum includes 3 summer semesters at sea aboard the training ship *Empire State VI*. Tuition and fees total approximately $3525 for students from New York, Connecticut, New Jersey, Pennsylavania, Delaware, Maryland, and Virginia. All others pay approximately $8425. Figures in the above capsule are approximate. In addition to regional accreditation, New York Maritime has baccalaureate program accreditation with ABET. The library contains 81,386 volumes, 12,923 microform items, and 3025 audiovisual forms/CDs, and subscribes to 333 periodicals. Computerized library services include interlibrary loans and database searching. Special learning facilities include a learning resource center, planetarium, a 17,000-ton training ship, a tug, a barge, and a center for simulated marine operations, which contains bridge, radar, tanker, and oil spill response simulators. The 55-acre campus is in a suburban area on the Throgs Neck peninsula where Long Island Sound meets the East River. Including residence halls, there are 27 buildings.

Student Life: 72% of undergraduates are from New York. Others are from 23 states and 15 foreign countries. 57% are from public schools. 78% are white. The average age of freshmen is 18; all undergraduates, 20. 12% do not continue beyond their first year; 62% remain to graduate.

Housing: 800 students can be accommodated in college housing, which includes single-sex and coed dormitories. On-campus housing is guaranteed for all 4 years. 97% of students live on campus; of those, 65% remain on campus on weekends. Alcohol is not permitted. Upperclassmen may keep cars.

Activities: There are no fraternities or sororities. There are 38 groups on campus, including art, bagpipe band, band, cheerleading, chess, chorus, computers, drill team, ethnic, honors, international, jazz band, marching band, newspaper, photography, political, professional, religious, social, social service, student government, and yearbook. Popular campus events include spring formal, Friday night mixers, and Admiral's Ball.

Sports: There are 12 intercollegiate sports for men and 8 for women, and 6 intramural sports for men and 4 for women. Facilities include an athletic center containing a 2000-seat gym, a swimming pool, exercise and weight rooms, a rifle and pistol range, and 4 handball/racquetball and squash courts, a sailing center, and baseball, lacrosse, and soccer fields.

Disabled Students: 90% of the campus is accessible. Wheelchair ramps, elevators, special parking, and specially equipped rest rooms are available.

Services: Counseling and information services are available, as is tutoring in every subject.

Campus Safety and Security: Measures include 24-hour foot and vehicle patrol, informal discussions, emergency telephones, and lighted pathways/sidewalks.

Programs of Study: New York Maritime confers B.S. and B.E. degrees. Associate and master's degrees are also awarded. Bachelor's degrees are awarded in BIOLOGICAL SCIENCE (marine science), BUSINESS (business administration and management and transportation management), COMPUTER AND PHYSICAL SCIENCE (atmospheric sciences and meteorology), ENGINEERING AND ENVIRONMENTAL DESIGN (electrical/electronics engineering, engineering, environmental science, marine engineering, maritime science, and naval architecture and marine engineering), SOCIAL SCIENCE (humanities). Engineering, naval architecture, and marine transportation/business administration are the strongest academically. Marine transportation/business administration is the largest.

Required: To graduate, students must complete the U.S. Merchant Marine officer's license program. Bachelor's degree candidates must earn 160 credit hours, with a GPA of 2.0. Distribution requirements and the number of hours required in the major varies. All students must spend 3 summer semesters at sea acquiring hands-on experience aboard the college's training vessel.

Special: The college offers co-op programs in engineering, an accelerated degree program in marine transportation/transportation management, and internships as cadet observers aboard commercial ships. There are 2 national honor societies and 2 departmental honors programs.

Faculty/Classroom: 94% teach undergraduates, 12% do research, and 12% do both. No introductory courses are taught by graduate students. The average class size in an introductory lecture is 25; in a laboratory, 15; and in a regular course, 20.

Requirements: The SAT I is required. In addition, applicants must be high school graduates or hold a GED. Sixteen Carnegie units are required, including 4 years of English, 3 of math (4 are preferred), and 1 of physics or chemistry. An essay is required and an interview is recommended. Students may apply on-line or on blank preformatted disks available from the Admissions Office. AP and CLEP credits are accepted. Important factors in the admissions decision are advanced placement or honor courses, extracurricular activities record, and leadership record.

Procedure: Freshmen are admitted in the fall. Entrance exams should be taken during the junior or senior year. There are early decision, early admissions, and deferred admissions plans. Application deadlines are open. Check with the school for current application deadlines and fees.

Transfer: Transfer students must have a 2.5 GPA. All applicants must complete the Indoctrination Program and fulfill degree and license requirements at New York Maritime. 160 credits of 160 must be completed at New York Maritime.

Visiting: There are regularly scheduled orientations for prospective students, including a tour of the campus and facilities and meetings with faculty and students. There are guides for informal visits and visitors may sit in on classes and stay overnight. To schedule a visit, contact the Admissions Office.

Financial Aid: The FAFSA and student and parent federal income tax returns are required.

International Students: The school actively recruits these students. They must score 500 on the written TOEFL and also take the SAT I or the ACT.

Computers: The mainframe is a Prime 4050. There are 27 terminals, 8 CAD stations, and 58 PCs. All students may access the system from 8:30 A.M. to 11 P.M. The computer center stays open after 11 P.M. when there is sufficient demand. There are no time limits and no fees.

Admissions Contact: Peter Cooney, Director of Admissions and Enrollment Management. A video is available. E-mail: *sunymaritime.edu*
Web: *www.sunymaritime.edu*

STATE UNIVERSITY OF NEW YORK/UNIVERSITY AT ALBANY D-3

Albany, NY 12222 (518) 442-5435
(800) 293-7869; Fax: (518) 442-5383

Full-time: 5410 men, 5342 women	**Faculty:** 401; I, av$
Part-time: 533 men, 599 women	**Ph.D.s:** 94%
Graduate: 2002 men, 3318 women	**Student/Faculty:** 27 to 1
Year: semesters, summer session	**Tuition:** $4720 ($9620)
Application Deadline: March 1	**Room & Board:** $6277

Freshman Class: 17,019 applied, 9853 accepted, 2205 enrolled
SAT I: required **VERY COMPETITIVE**

State University of New York/University at Albany, established in 1844, is a public institution conferring undergraduate degrees in humanities and fine arts, science and math, social and behavioral sciences, business, public policy, education, and social welfare. There are 7 undergraduate and 8 graduate schools. In addition to regional accreditation, University at Albany has baccalaureate program accreditation with AACSB, ACS, ALA, APA, and CSWE. The 3 libraries contain 2,013,526 volumes, 2,782,393 microform items, and 9735 audiovisual forms/CDs, and subscribe to 16,312 periodicals. Computerized library services include the card catalog, interlibrary loans, and database searching. Special learning facilities include a learning resource center, art gallery, radio station, linear accelerator, sophisticated weather data system, national lightning detection system, interactive media center, extensive art studios, and state-of-the-art electronic library. The 560-acre campus is in a suburban area about 5 miles west of downtown Albany. Including residence halls, there are 90 buildings.

Student Life: 96% of undergraduates are from New York. Others are from 37 states, 42 foreign countries, and Canada. 64% are white. The average age of freshmen is 18; all undergraduates, 21. 15% do not continue beyond their first year; 63% remain to graduate.

Housing: 6900 students can be accommodated in college housing, which includes single-sex and coed dormitories, on-campus apartments, and married-student housing. In addition, there are honors houses and special-interest houses. On-campus housing is available on a first-come, first-served basis and is available on a lottery system for upperclassmen. Priority is given to out-of-town students. 54% of students live on campus. Alcohol is not permitted. Upperclassmen may keep cars.

Activities: 15% of men belong to 8 local and 20 national fraternities; 15% of women belong to 7 local and 19 national sororities. There are 160 groups on campus, including band, cheerleading, chess, chorale, computers, dance, debate, drama, ethnic, gay, honors, international, jazz band, literary magazine, newspaper, orchestra, photography, political, professional, radio and TV, religious, social, social service, student government, and yearbook. Popular campus events include the weeklong Rites of Spring, outdoor concerts, and summer training camp of the New York Giants football team.

Sports: There are 8 intercollegiate sports for men and 11 for women, and 13 intramural sports for men and 9 for women. Facilities include a gym with an Olympic-size pool; an ancillary gym with a quarter-mile track; football, softball, soccer, and practice fields; and a 5000-seat recreation and convocation center.

Disabled Students: 99% of the campus is accessible. Wheelchair ramps, elevators, special parking, specially equipped rest rooms, lowered drinking fountains, and lowered telephones are available. Disabled Student Services provides a broad range of personalized services, including preadmission information, to people with disabilities.

Services: Counseling and information services are available, as is tutoring in most subjects. There is a reader service for the blind, and remedial math, reading, and writing.

Campus Safety and Security: Measures include 24-hour foot and vehicle patrol, self-defense education, escort service, and shuttle buses. There are pamphlets/posters/films, emergency telephones, and lighted pathways/sidewalks.

Programs of Study: University at Albany confers B.A. and B.S. degrees. Master's and doctoral degrees are also awarded. Bachelor's degrees are awarded in BIOLOGICAL SCIENCE (biochemistry, biology/biological science, and molecular biology), BUSINESS (accounting and business administration and management), COMMUNICATIONS AND THE ARTS (art history and appreciation, Chinese, communications, dramatic arts, English, fine arts, French, Hebrew, Italian, Latin, linguistics, music, Russian, and Spanish), COMPUTER AND PHYSICAL SCIENCE (actuarial science, applied mathematics, atmospheric sciences and meteorology, chemistry, computer science, earth science, geology, information sciences and systems, mathematics, and physics), EDUCATION

(English, foreign languages, mathematics, science, secondary, and social studies), ENGINEERING AND ENVIRONMENTAL DESIGN (urban design), HEALTH PROFESSIONS (medical laboratory technology, predentistry, and premedicine), SOCIAL SCIENCE (African American studies, anthropology, Asian/Oriental studies, Caribbean studies, classical/ancient civilization, criminal justice, Eastern European studies, economics, geography, Hispanic American studies, history, Latin American studies, medieval studies, philosophy, political science/government, prelaw, psychology, religion, Russian and Slavic studies, social work, sociology, and women's studies). Criminal justice, information technology, and public administration and policy are the strongest academically. Psychology, English, and business are the largest.

Required: To graduate, students must complete a total of 120 credits with a 2.0 GPA in their major and minor, including 30 to 36 credits required in the major for a B.A. degree and 30 to 42 credits for a B.S. degree. B.A. degree candidates must complete 90 credits in liberal arts courses and B.S. candidates must complete 60. All students must complete a writing requirement and a general education core consisting of a minimum of 24 credits in natural sciences, social sciences, humanities, and the arts, 3 credits in an approved course in cultural and historical perspectives, and 3 credits of an approved course in human diversity. Students must also demonstrate a basic proficiency in a language other than English.

Special: Cross-registration is available with Rensselaer Polytechnic Institute, Albany Law School, and Union, Siena, and Russell Sage Colleges. Internships may be arranged with state government agencies and private organizations. Study abroad in many countries, a Washington semester, B.A.-B.S. degrees, and work-study programs are offered. Dual and student-designed majors, nondegree study, and pass/fail grading options are available. A 3-2 engineering degree with one of 4 institutions is also possible. There are 15 national honor societies, including Phi Beta Kappa, a freshman honors program, and 29 departmental honors programs.

Faculty/Classroom: 63% of faculty are male; 37%, female. 90% teach undergraduates and 75% do research. Graduate students teach 21% of introductory courses. The average class size in an introductory lecture is 37; in a laboratory, 18; and in a regular course, 27.

Admissions: 58% of the 2001-2002 applicants were accepted. The SAT I scores for the 2001-2002 freshman class were: Verbal--11% below 500, 55% between 500 and 599, 30% between 600 and 700, and 4% above 700; Math--6% below 500, 52% between 500 and 599, 37% between 600 and 700, and 5% above 700. 39% of the current freshmen were in the top fifth of their class; 80% were in the top two fifths. In a recent year, there were 2 National Merit finalists and 8 semifinalists. 8 freshmen graduated first in their class.

Requirements: The SAT I is required, but the ACT is accepted. Applicants must be graduates of an accredited secondary school or have a GED. 18 academic credits are required, including 2 to 3 units of math and 2 units of lab sciences. Foreign language study is also recommended. AP and CLEP credits are accepted. Important factors in the admissions decision are advanced placement or honor courses, personality/intangible qualities, and leadership record. Applications are accepted online at the school's web site.

Procedure: Freshmen are admitted to all sessions. Entrance exams should be taken by November of the senior year. There are early action, early admissions, and deferred admissions plans. Early action applications should be filed by November 15; regular applications, by March 1 for fall entry, December 1 for spring entry, and May 1 for summer entry, along with a $40 fee. Notification of early action is sent December 1; regular decision, on a rolling basis. 1400 early decision candidates were accepted for the 2001-2002 class. 3% of all applicants are on a waiting list; 170 were accepted in 2001.

Transfer: 1082 transfer students enrolled in 2001-2002. Applicants must have a minimum GPA of 2.5; accounting, business administration, criminal justice, and social welfare programs require a higher GPA. Students will be admitted to programs according to availability of space and degree of competitiveness. 30 credits of 120 must be completed at University at Albany.

Visiting: There are regularly scheduled orientations for prospective students, including a 2-day summer orientation session. There are guides for informal visits and visitors may sit in on classes. To schedule a visit, contact the Undergraduate Admissions Office by phone or at *campusvisit@albany.edu*

Financial Aid: In 2001-2002, 61% of all freshmen and 55% of continuing students received some form of financial aid. 54% of freshmen and 52% of continuing students received need-based aid. The average freshman award was $7685. Of that total, scholarships or need-based grants averaged $4115 and loans averaged $3120. 25% of undergraduates work part time. The average financial indebtedness of the 2001 graduate was $15,439. University at Albany is a member of CSS. The FAFSA is required. The fall application deadline is March 15.

International Students: There are 176 international students enrolled. The school actively recruits these students. They must score 550 on the written TOEFL or 213 on the electronic version or submit their SAT I results.

Computers: The mainframes are an IBM 9672-R21 and VAX and UNIX clusters. The computing services center networks provide e-mail facilities and Internet access. Computer access rooms, terminals in residence halls, and phone hookups provide 24-hour access to mainframe computing facilities. All students may access the system. There are no time limits and no fees.

Graduates: In 2001, 2475 bachelor's degrees were awarded. The most popular majors were psychology (13%), business (12%), and English (10%). In an average class, 52% graduate in 4 years, 60% in 5 years, and 63% in 6 years. 180 companies recruited on campus in 2000-2001. Of the 2000 graduating class, 33% were enrolled in graduate school within 6 months of graduation and 59% were employed.

Admissions Contact: Harry Wood, Director, Undergraduate Admissions. E-mail: *ugadmissions@albany.edu* Web: *www.albany.edu*

STATE UNIVERSITY OF NEW YORK/UNIVERSITY AT BINGHAMTON C-4
(Formerly State University of New York at Binghamton)

Binghamton, NY 13902-6000 (607) 777-2171
Fax: (607) 777-4445

Full-time: 4578 men, 5259 women	**Faculty:** 498; I, -$
Part-time: 125 men, 205 women	**Ph.D.s:** 94%
Graduate: 1351 men, 1302 women	**Student/Faculty:** 20 to 1
Year: semesters, summer session	**Tuition:** $4551 ($9451)
Application Deadline: February 15	**Room & Board:** $6102
Freshman Class: 17,381 applied, 7791 accepted, 2227 enrolled	
SAT I Verbal/Math: 591/624	**ACT:** 26 **HIGHLY COMPETITIVE**

State University of New York/University at Binghamton, founded in 1946, is part of the State University of New York System. The public institution offers programs through the Harpur College of Arts and Sciences and the Schools of Education and Human Development, Nursing, Management, and Engineering and Applied Science. There are 5 undergraduate schools and 1 graduate school. In addition to regional accreditation, Binghamton University has baccalaureate program accreditation with AACSB, ABET, APA, CCNE, CSAB, and NASM. The 2 libraries contain 1,742,907 volumes, 1,781,236 microform items, and 120,734 audiovisual forms/CDs, and subscribe to 7076 periodicals. Computerized library services include the card catalog, interlibrary loans, and database searching. Special learning facilities include a learning resource center, art gallery, radio station, TV station, nature preserve, and 4-climate greenhouse. The 828-acre campus is in a suburban area 1 mile west of Binghamton. Including residence halls, there are 86 buildings.

Student Life: 94% of undergraduates are from New York. Others are from 32 states, 45 foreign countries, and Canada. 87% are from public schools. 63% are white; 21%, Asian American. 31% are Catholic; 21% claim no religious affiliation; 21%, Jewish; 20%, Protestant. The average age of freshmen is 18; all undergraduates, 20. 9% do not continue beyond their first year; 80% remain to graduate.

Housing: 5710 students can be accommodated in college housing, which includes coed dormitories, on-campus apartments, and married-student housing. In addition, there are special-interest houses and chemical- and smoke-free housing. 57% of students live on campus; of those, 95% remain on campus on weekends. Upperclassmen may keep cars.

Activities: 12% of men belong to 5 local and 14 national fraternities; 15% of women belong to 6 local and 9 national sororities. There are 164 groups on campus, including art, band, cheerleading, chess, choir, chorale, chorus, computers, cultural, dance, debate, drama, ethnic, film, gay, honors, international, jazz band, literary magazine, musical theater, newspaper, opera, orchestra, pep band, photography, political, professional, radio and TV, religious, social, social service, student government, symphony, and yearbook. Popular campus events include Caribbean Carnival, Spring Fling, and University Fest.

Sports: There are 11 intercollegiate sports for men and 10 for women, and 20 intramural sports for men and 18 for women. Facilities include 2 gyms with swimming pools, an indoor track, dance and karate studios, basketball, volleyball, squash, racquetball, and tennis courts, a weight room, batting and driving cages, a cross-country course, a fitness center, a 400-meter track and soccer complex, plus many playing fields. The larger gym seats 2600.

Disabled Students: 90% of the campus is accessible. Wheelchair ramps, elevators, special parking, specially equipped rest rooms, special class scheduling, lowered drinking fountains, lowered telephones, a wheelchair van service, adapted computer stations, and a comprehensive array of services for university students with physical or learning disabilities are available.

Services: Counseling and information services are available, as is tutoring in most subjects and some computer-assisted instruction, particularly in languages. Peer walk-in tutoring is available 6 days per week. There is a reader service for the blind.

Campus Safety and Security: Measures include 24-hour foot and vehicle patrol, self-defense education, escort service, and shuttle buses. There are informal discussions, pamphlets/posters/films, emergency telephones, lighted pathways/sidewalks, police officers, monitored entrance to campus with proper identification between midnight and 5 A.M., keycard entry to residence halls, and formal personal safety programs.

Programs of Study: Binghamton University confers B.A., B.S., B.F.A., and B.Mus. degrees. Master's and doctoral degrees are also awarded. Bachelor's degrees are awarded in BIOLOGICAL SCIENCE (biochemistry and biology/biological science), BUSINESS (accounting and business administration and management), COMMUNICATIONS AND THE ARTS (Arabic, art, art history and appreciation, classics, comparative literature, dramatic arts, English, film arts, fine arts, French, German, Hebrew, Italian, Latin, linguistics, music, music performance, Spanish, speech/debate/rhetoric, and studio art), COMPUTER AND PHYSICAL SCIENCE (chemistry, computer science, geology, mathematics, and physics), ENGINEERING AND ENVIRONMENTAL DESIGN (computer engineering, electrical/electronics engineering, environmental science, industrial engineering, and mechanical engineering), HEALTH PROFESSIONS (nursing), SOCIAL SCIENCE (African American studies, anthropology, Caribbean studies, classical/ancient civilization, economics, geography, history, human development, interdisciplinary studies, Judaic studies, Latin American studies, medieval studies, philosophy, political science/government, psychobiology, psychology, and sociology). Accounting and anthropology are the strongest academically. Management, psychology, and economics are the largest.

Required: To graduate, all students must complete 120 to 133 credit hours, including 36 to 72 in the major, with a minimum GPA of 2.0. General education requirements over the first 2 years include courses in language and communication, global vision, science and math, aesthetic perspective, physical activity/wellness, and identity. Other requirements vary by school.

Special: The university offers innovative study through the Innovational Projects Board, internships, study abroad in more than 100 countries, a Washington semester through American University, on- and off-campus work-study programs, and B.A.-B.S. degrees in 28 departments in arts and sciences and in the professional schools. There are also dual and interdisciplinary majors such as philosophy, politics, and law, student-designed majors, pass/fail options, and independent study. The 3-2 engineering degree is possible with SUNY at Buffalo, SUNY at Stony Brook, Columbia University, Rochester Institute of Technology, University of Rochester, and Clarkson University. Binghamton is also a member of the National Student Exchange and International Student Exchange. Other 3-2 degrees are offered through Harpur College. There are 20 national honor societies, including Phi Beta Kappa, a freshman honors program, and 32 departmental honors programs.

Faculty/Classroom: 63% of faculty are male; 37%, female. All both teach and do research. Graduate students teach 15% of introductory courses. The average class size in an introductory lecture is 39; in a laboratory, 14; and in a regular course, 28.

Admissions: 45% of the 2001-2002 applicants were accepted. The SAT I scores for the 2001-2002 freshman class were: Verbal--9% below 500, 43% between 500 and 599, 41% between 600 and 700, and 7% above 700; Math--3% below 500, 31% between 500 and 599, 50% between 600 and 700, and 16% above 700. The ACT scores were 7% below 21, 18% between 21 and 23, 33% between 24 and 26, 21% between 27 and 28, and 21% above 28. 90% of the current freshmen were in the top fifth of their class; 99% were in the top two fifths. 17 freshmen graduated first in their class.

Requirements: The SAT I or ACT is required. In addition, applicants must be graduates of an accredited secondary school, or have a GED certificate, and complete 16 academic credits. These include 4 units of English, 3 units of 1 foreign language or 2 units each of 2 foreign languages, 2.5 units of math, and 2 units each of science and social studies. Students may submit slides of artwork, request an audition for music, prepare a videotape for dance or theater, or share athletic achievements. An essay is required. AP and CLEP credits are accepted. Important factors in the admissions decision are advanced placement or honor courses, extracurricular activities record, and evidence of special talent. The SUNY application is available through the school's web site. Applications are also accepted on computer disk.

Procedure: Freshmen are admitted to all sessions. Entrance exams should be taken in the spring of the junior year or the fall of the senior year. There are early action and deferred admissions plans. Early action applications should be filed by November 1; regular applications, by February 15 for fall entry and November 15 for spring entry. The fall 2001 application fee was $30. Notification of early action is sent December 20; regular decision, on a rolling basis. 6% of all applicants are on a waiting list; 4 were accepted in 2001.

Transfer: 728 transfer students enrolled in 2001-2002. Applicants must submit college transcripts; students who wish to transfer after their first year of college must also submit their high school transcripts. The SAT I and an essay are recommended but not required. 30 credits of 120 to 133 must be completed at Binghamton University.

Visiting: There are regularly scheduled orientations for prospective students, including an information session and a tour of campus, to be scheduled a week in advance of a visit. Visitors may sit in on classes and stay overnight. To schedule a visit, contact the Office of Undergraduate Admissions.

Financial Aid: In 2001-2002, 83% of all freshmen and 70% of continuing students received some form of financial aid. 81% of freshmen and 67% of continuing students received need-based aid. The average freshman award was $12,537. Of that total, scholarships or need-based grants averaged $3872 ($17,630 maximum); loans averaged $6089 ($17,630 maximum); and work contracts averaged $1415 ($1500 maximum). 13% of undergraduates work part time. Average annual earnings from campus work are $1000. The average financial indebtedness of the 2001 graduate was $13,957. Binghamton University is a member of CSS. The FAFSA is required. The fall application deadline is March 1.

International Students: There are 210 international students enrolled. The school actively recruits these students. They must score 550 on the written TOEFL, which replaces the SAT I or ACT for nonnative speakers of English.

Computers: The mainframes are comprised of 2 IBM 9000 series and a cluster of 5 Sun servers. Each student is given a computer account, e-mail account, and personal web space. Terminals and PCs are available in libraries, some academic areas, and some residence halls. All residence hall rooms have Ethernet and Internet connections. More than 90% of residents bring a computer to campus and connect to the network. Public computer labs are available in the library, in 5 academic buildings, and in 3 residence hall complexes. All students may access the system 24 hours per day. There are no time limits and no fees.

Graduates: In 2001, 2334 bachelor's degrees were awarded. The most popular majors were management (12%), psychology (11%), and English/biology (9%). In an average class, 3% graduate in 3 years, 69% in 4 years, 78% in 5 years, and 80% in 6 years. 147 companies recruited on campus in 2000-2001. Of the 2000 graduating class, 38% were enrolled in graduate school within 6 months of graduation and 82% were employed.

Admissions Contact: Cheryl Brown, Director, Undergraduate Admissions. E-mail: *admit@binghamton.edu* Web: *www.binghamton.edu*

STATE UNIVERSITY OF NEW YORK/UNIVERSITY AT BUFFALO A-3

Buffalo, NY 14260 (716) 645-6900
(888) ub-admit; Fax: (716) 645-6498

Full-time: 8398 men, 6923 women	**Faculty:** 1020; I, av$
Part-time: 973 men, 996 women	**Ph.D.s:** 98%
Graduate: 4172 men, 4376 women	**Student/Faculty:** 15 to 1
Year: semesters, summer session	**Tuition:** $4790 ($9690)
Application Deadline: see profile	**Room & Board:** $6318
Freshman Class: 16,027 applied, 10,062 accepted, 3075 enrolled	
SAT I Verbal/Math: 566/589	**ACT:** 25 **VERY COMPETITIVE**

The State University of New York at Buffalo, established in 1846, is a public institution offering undergraduate degrees in liberal arts and sciences, architecture and planning, engineering, health-related professions, medicine, and management. There are 9 undergraduate and 12 graduate schools. In addition to regional accreditation, UB has baccalaureate program accreditation with AACSB, ABET, APTA, CCNE, CSAB, NASAD, and NASM. The 7 libraries contain 3,256,131 volumes, 5,297,079 microform items, and 160,790 audiovisual forms/CDs, and subscribe to 26,832 periodicals. Computerized library services include the card catalog, interlibrary loans, and database searching. Special learning facilities include a learning resource center, art gallery, radio station, anthropology research museum, observatory, concert hall, theater, nature preserve, and nuclear reactor. The 1350-acre campus is in a suburban area 3 miles north of Buffalo. Including residence halls, there are 177 buildings.

Student Life: 93% of undergraduates are from New York. Others are from 44 states, 71 foreign countries, and Canada. 71% are white; 10% Asian American. The average age of freshmen is 18; all undergraduates, 22. 15% do not continue beyond their first year; 63% remain to graduate.

Housing: 7000 students can be accommodated in college housing, which includes coed dormitories and on-campus apartments. In addition, there are honors houses, special-interest houses, and freshmen-only and transfer-only residence halls. On-campus housing is guaranteed for all 4 years. 65% of students commute. All students may keep cars.

Activities: 5% of men belong to 6 local and 6 national fraternities; 5% of women belong to 7 local and 8 national sororities. There are 200 groups on campus, including art, band, cheerleading, chess, choir, chorale, chorus, computers, dance, drama, ethnic, film, gay, honors, international, jazz band, literary magazine, marching band, musical theater, newspaper, orchestra, pep band, photography, political, professional, radio and TV, religious, social, social service, student government, symphony, and yearbook. Popular campus events include Fall Fest, Spring Fest, and International Fiesta.

Sports: There are 10 intercollegiate sports for men and 10 for women, and 10 intramural sports for men and 9 for women. Facilities include racquetball, squash, tennis, basketball, volleyball, badminton, and handball courts; baseball, soccer, hockey, and multipurpose fields; a football and track and field stadium; an indoor jogging track; an Olympic-size pool and diving well; a triple gym; weight training and wrestling rooms; dance studios; and a spinning room.

Disabled Students: 90% of the campus is accessible. Wheelchair ramps, elevators, special parking, specially equipped rest rooms, special class scheduling, lowered drinking fountains, lowered telephones, pool accessibility, wheelchair vans for transport, and specially equipped rooms in residence halls are available.

Services: Counseling and information services are available, as is tutoring in most subjects. There is a reader service for the blind, remedial math, reading, and writing, peer tutoring, and some computer-assisted instruction.

Campus Safety and Security: Measures include 24-hour foot and vehicle patrol, self-defense education, escort service, and shuttle buses. There are informal discussions, pamphlets/posters/films, emergency telephones, lighted pathways/sidewalks, an alarm system, after-hours card access to academic facilities, community patrols, and a university-wide safety committee.

Programs of Study: UB confers B.A., B.S., B.F.A., B.P.S., and Mus.B. degrees. Master's and doctoral degrees are also awarded. Bachelor's degrees are awarded in BIOLOGICAL SCIENCE (biochemistry, biology/biological science, biophysics, and biotechnology), BUSINESS (business administration and management), COMMUNICATIONS AND THE ARTS (art history and appreciation, classics, communications, dance, dramatic arts, English, fine arts, French, German, Italian, linguistics, media arts, music, music performance, musical theater, Spanish, and studio art), COMPUTER AND PHYSICAL SCIENCE (chemistry, computer science, geology, mathematics, and physics), ENGINEERING AND ENVIRONMENTAL DESIGN (aeronautical engineering, architecture, chemical engineering, civil engineering, computer engineering, electrical/electronics engineering, engineering physics, environmental design, environmental engineering, industrial engineering, and mechanical engineering), HEALTH PROFESSIONS (exercise science, medical laboratory technology, nuclear medical technology, nursing, occupational therapy, pharmacy, and speech pathology/audiology), SOCIAL SCIENCE (African American studies, American studies, anthropology, economics, geography, history, philosophy, political science/government, psychology, social science, sociology, and women's studies). Business administration, computer science and engineering, and psychology are the largest.

Required: To graduate, students must complete 120 semester hours with a minimum GPA of 2.0. General education requirements include writing, math, and library skills, intermediate language proficiency, and courses in math or computer science, world civilization, American pluralism, scientific literacy, literature and arts, and social and behavioral sciences.

Special: Students may cross-register with the Western New York Consortium. Internships are available, and students may study abroad in 28 countries. UB offers a Washington semester, work-study programs, accelerated degree programs, B.A.-B.S. degrees, dual, student-designed, and interdisciplinary majors, including biochemical pharmacology and medicinal chemistry, nondegree study, and credit for military experience. A 3-2 engineering degree can be pursued. Students may choose a successful/unsuccessful (S/U) grading option for selected courses. There is an early assurance of admission program to medical school for students who have completed 3 semesters with a GPA of 3.5. There are 29 national honor societies, including Phi Beta Kappa and a freshman honors program.

Faculty/Classroom: 67% of faculty are male; 33%, female. 79% teach undergraduates, and all do research. Graduate students teach 23% of introductory courses. The average class size in an introductory lecture is 43; in a laboratory, 24; and in a regular course, 33.

Admissions: 63% of the 2001-2002 applicants were accepted. The SAT I scores for the 2001-2002 freshman class were: Verbal--16% below 500, 51% between 500 and 599, 28% between 600 and 700, and 5% above 700; Math--8% below 500, 48% between 500 and 599, 37% between 600 and 700, and 7% above 700. The ACT scores were 7% below 21, 23% between 21 and 23, 31% between 24 and 26, 18% between 27 and 28, and 21% above 28. 48% of the current freshmen were in the top fifth of their class; 88% were in the top two fifths. There were 7 National Merit finalists and 10 semifinalists. 15 freshmen graduated first in their class.

Requirements: The SAT I is required. In addition, applicants must be graduates of an accredited secondary school or have a GED. Art applicants must submit a portfolio; music applicants must audition. AP and CLEP credits are accepted. Important factors in the admissions decision are extracurricular activities record, evidence of special talent, and leadership record. For on-line applications, consult the SUNY web site at *http://infostu.suny.edu*.

Procedure: Freshmen are admitted fall and spring. Entrance exams should be taken during the spring of the junior year or the fall of the senior year. There is an early decision plan. Early decision applications should be filed by November 1; regular applications, on arolling basis, with early November recommended. The fall 2001 application fee was $30. Notification of early decision is sent December 10; regular decision, on a rolling basis. 258 early decision candidates were accepted for the 2001-2002 class.

Transfer: 1779 transfer students enrolled in 2001-2002. Applicants must have a minimum GPA of 2.0 with 24 semester hours completed at the time of application. Students with fewer than 24 semester hours will be evaluated according to both college and high school work and SAT I or ACT scores. 30 credits of 120 must be completed at UB.

Visiting: There are regularly scheduled orientations for prospective students, consisting of information sessions and tours 6 days per week. Visitors may sit in on classes. To schedule a visit, contact the Office of Admissions.

Financial Aid: In 2001-2002, 70% of all freshmen and 60% of continuing students received some form of financial aid. 65% of freshmen and 63% of continuing students received need-based aid. The average freshman award was $5960. Of that total, scholarships or need-based grants averaged $3143 ($12,169 maximum); and loans averaged $2625. 7% of undergraduates work part time. Average annual earnings from campus work are $1200. The average financial indebtedness of the 2001 graduate was $17,125. The FAFSA is required. The fall application deadline is March 1.

International Students: There are 812 international students enrolled. The school actively recruits these students. They must score 523 on the written TOEFL or 193 on the electronic version.

Computers: The mainframes are an IBM 2300/35 and a Sun Enterprise 3000. Students have access through 2200 workstations. Dial-up access is also available. Individual libraries offer numerous CD-ROMs and student access to the Web. All students may access the system any time. There are no time limits. The fee is $500. It is strongly recommended that all students have a personal computer.

Graduates: In 2001, 3037 bachelor's degrees were awarded. The most popular majors were business administration (17%), social science (12%), and engineering (11%). In an average class, 32% graduate in 4 years, 51% in 5 years, and 56% in 6 years. 454 companies recruited on campus in 2000-2001. Of the 2000 graduating class, 30% were enrolled in graduate school within 6 months of graduation and 63% were employed.

Admissions Contact: Regina Toomey, Director of Admissions.
E-mail: *ub-admissions@admissions.buffalo.edu* Web: *www.buffalo.edu*

STATE UNIVERSITY OF NEW YORK/UNIVERSITY AT NEW PALTZ D-4

New Paltz, NY 12561-2443 (914) 257-3200
(888) 639-7589; Fax: (914) 257-3209

Full-time: 1900 men, 3272 women	**Faculty:** 278; IIA, -$
Part-time: 324 men, 586 women	**Ph.D.s:** 87%
Graduate: 497 men, 1289 women	**Student/Faculty:** 19 to 1
Year: semesters, summer session	**Tuition:** $4085 ($8985)
Application Deadline: May 1	**Room & Board:** $5600

Freshman Class: 9624 applied, 3974 accepted, 923 enrolled
SAT I Verbal/Math: 560/560 **VERY COMPETITIVE**

State University of New York/University at New Paltz, founded in 1828, is a public institution offering undergraduate and graduate programs in the liberal arts and sciences, business, education, engineering, fine and performing arts, and the health professions. There are 5 undergraduate schools and 1 graduate school. In addition to regional accreditation, SUNY New Paltz has baccalaureate program accreditation with ABET, ASLA, CSAB, NASAD, NASM, and NLN. The library contains 524,000 volumes, 1,061,003 microform items, and 764 audiovisual forms/CDs, and subscribes to 4950 periodicals. Computerized library services include the card catalog, interlibrary loans, and database searching. Special learning facilities include a learning resource center, planetarium, radio station, TV station, greenhouse, robotics lab, electron microscope facility, speech and hearing clinic, art museum, music therapy training facility, observatory, Fournier transform mass spectrometer, honors center, electronic media center, electronic classroom, and an IBM e-business virtual lab. The 216-acre campus is in a small town 100 miles north of New York City and 65 miles south of Albany. Including residence halls, there are 57 buildings.

Student Life: 91% of undergraduates are from New York. Others are from 32 states, 51 foreign countries, and Canada. 90% are from public schools. 74% are white; 10% Hispanic. The average age of freshmen is 18; all undergraduates, 20. 17% do not continue beyond their first year; 52% remain to graduate.

Housing: 2550 students can be accommodated in college housing, which includes coed dormitories. In addition, there are special-interest houses. On-campus housing is guaranteed for the freshman year only and is available on a first-come, first-served basis. Priority is given to out-of-town students. 51% of students live on campus; of those, 90% remain on campus on weekends. Upperclassmen may keep cars.

Activities: 1% of men belong to 5 local and 5 national fraternities; 3% of women belong to 5 local and 9 national sororities. There are 135 groups on campus, including art, band, cheerleading, chess, choir, chorale, chorus, computers, dance, drama, ethnic, gay, honors, international, jazz band, literary magazine, musical theater, newspaper, orchestra, photography, political, professional, radio and TV, religious, social, social service, student government, and yearbook. Popular campus events include Spirit Weekend, New Paltz Summer Repertory Theater, and Rainbow Month.

Sports: There are 9 intercollegiate sports for men and 11 for women, and 20 intramural sports for men and 15 for women. Facilities include a gym with a swimming pool; numerous playing fields; a 35,000-square-foot air-supported structure for tennis, jogging, volleyball, and basketball; and 24 outdoor tennis courts.

Disabled Students: 90% of the campus is accessible. Wheelchair ramps, elevators, special parking, specially equipped rest rooms, special class scheduling, lowered drinking fountains, lowered telephones, and 4 residence halls accessible to the disabled are available.

Services: Counseling and information services are available, as is tutoring in most subjects. There is a reader service for the blind, and remedial math, reading, and writing.

Campus Safety and Security: Measures include 24-hour foot and vehicle patrol, self-defense education, escort service, and informal discussions. There are pamphlets/posters/films, emergency telephones, lighted pathways/sidewalks, a bicycle patrol, locked residence halls, and a campus 911 system.

Programs of Study: SUNY New Paltz confers B.A., B.S., B.F.A., B.S.E.E., and B.S.N. degrees. Master's degrees are also awarded. Bachelor's degrees are awarded in BIOLOGICAL SCIENCE (biology/biological science), BUSINESS (accounting, banking and finance, business administration and management, and marketing/retailing/merchandising), COMMUNICATIONS AND THE ARTS (art history and appreciation, broadcasting, communications, design, dramatic arts, English, fine arts, French, German, journalism, music, photography, Spanish, and speech/debate/rhetoric), COMPUTER AND PHYSICAL SCIENCE (chemistry, computer science, geology, mathematics, and physics), EDUCATION (art, early childhood, elementary, foreign languages, middle school, science, and secondary), ENGINEERING AND ENVIRONMENTAL DESIGN (computer engineering and electrical/electronics engineering), HEALTH PROFESSIONS (premedicine and speech pathology/audiology), SOCIAL SCIENCE (anthropology, economics, geography, history, international relations, Latin American studies, philosophy, political science/government, psychology, social science, and sociology). Business, computer science, and math are the strongest academically. Business, visual arts, and communication are the largest.

Required: To graduate, students must complete a minimum of 120 credits with a 2.0 GPA. The number of credits required in the major varies. Other requirements include 42 to 52 credits in general education, 1 writing-intensive course in the major, and 60 credits in upper-division courses.

Special: There is cross-registration with the Mid-Hudson Consortium of Colleges. The university offers co-op programs and internships in most majors, work-study programs on campus and at the Children's Center of New Paltz, and opportunities for student-designed or dual majors. Students may study abroad in 18 countries. A 3-2 advanced degree in environmental biology is offered with SUNY Environmental Science and Forestry. There are 7-year medical and optometry accelerated degree programs. There are 4 national honor societies, a freshman honors program, and 6 departmental honors programs.

Faculty/Classroom: 57% of faculty are male; 43%, female. 97% both teach and do research. Graduate students teach 1% of introductory courses. The average class size in an introductory lecture is 25; in a laboratory, 10; and in a regular course, 25.

Admissions: 41% of the 2001-2002 applicants were accepted. The SAT I scores for the 2001-2002 freshman class were: Verbal--16% below 500, 56% between 500 and 599, 25% between 600 and 700, and 3% above 700; Math--13% below 500, 59% between 500 and 599, 26% between 600 and 700, and 2% above 700. 38% of the current freshmen were in the top fifth of their class; 80% were in the top two fifths. There were 5 National Merit semifinalists. 5 freshmen graduated first in their class.

Requirements: The SAT I is required and the ACT is recommended. A minimum composite score of 1100 on the SAT I is recommended. Graduation from an accredited secondary school is required; a GED will be accepted. The applicant's academic record must include a college preparatory program of 4 years of English and 3 to 4 years each of social studies, a foreign language, math, and lab science. Where required, a portfolio and an audition are used for placement purposes only. SUNY New Paltz requires applicants to be in the upper 50% of their class. A GPA of 3.0 is required. AP and CLEP credits are accepted. Important factors in the admissions decision are advanced placement or honor courses, extracurricular activities record, and evidence of special talent. Applications are accepted on-line.

Procedure: Freshmen are admitted in the fall. Entrance exams should be taken on or before December 31. There are early admissions and deferred admissions plans. Early action applications should be filed by November 15; regular applications, by May 1 for fall entry, along with a $30 fee. Notification of early action is sent December 15; regular decision, on a rolling basis. 2% of all applicants are on a waiting list.

Transfer: 632 transfer students enrolled in 2001-2002. To be considered, applicants must have maintained a minimum GPA of 2.5 in all previous college work at accredited institutions. Some programs require a higher GPA for consideration. 30 credits of 120 must be completed at SUNY New Paltz.

Visiting: There are regularly scheduled orientations for prospective students, including information sessions with a tour scheduled by appointment Monday through Friday during the academic year. Saturday sessions/tours are available on selected dates. Visitors may sit in on classes. To schedule a visit, contact the Admissions Office.

Financial Aid: In 2001-2002, 75% of all students received some form of financial aid. 60% of freshmen and 75% of continuing students received need-based aid. The average freshman award was $5500. Of that total, scholarships or need-based grants averaged $1100 ($6200 maximum); loans averaged $2700 ($3500 maximum); and work contracts averaged $900 ($1000 maximum). 40% of undergraduates work part time. Average annual earnings from campus work are $800. The average financial indebtedness of the 2001 graduate was $11,000. The FAFSA is required. The fall application deadline is March 15.

International Students: There are 271 international students enrolled. The school actively recruits these students. They must score 550 on the written TOEFL or 213 on the electronic version. Conditional acceptance is available, but the applicant must take ESL courses until required proficiency is achieved. The SAT I is required if the TOEFL has not been taken.

Computers: The mainframe is an IBM ES/9000 9121-210. Computer facilities include 6 large public PC labs, PC classrooms, department-based PC labs and clusters, and PC labs in residence halls. Access is provided in all residence hall rooms to local UNIX and mainframe hosts as well as the Internet. All students may access the system during those hours that the buildings are open; residence hall terminals and personal PCs, 24 hours a day. There are no time limits and no fees. It is strongly recommended that all students have a personal computer.

Graduates: In 2001, 1347 bachelor's degrees were awarded. The most popular majors were elementary and secondary education (26%), communication and media (12%), and business (11%). In an average class, 22% graduate in 4 years, 44% in 5 years, and 52% in 6 years. 457 companies recruited on campus in 2000-2001.

Admissions Contact: Kimberly Lavoie, Coordinator of Freshman/International Admissions. E-mail: *admissions@newpaltz.edu*
Web: *http://www.newpaltz.edu*

STATE UNIVERSITY OF NEW YORK/UNIVERSITY AT STONY BROOK E-5

Stony Brook, NY 11794 **(516) 632-6868; Fax: (516) 632-9027**

Full-time: 6460 men, 5879 women	**Faculty:** 843; I, av$
Part-time: 612 men, 695 women	**Ph.D.s:** 95%
Graduate: 3251 men, 3958 women	**Student/Faculty:** 15 to 1
Year: semesters, summer session	**Tuition:** $4268 ($9168)
Application Deadline: July 10	**Room & Board:** $6730
Freshman Class: 17,065 applied, 8580 accepted, 2190 enrolled	
SAT I Verbal/Math: 550/590	**VERY COMPETITIVE**

The State University of New York/University at Stony Brook, founded in 1957, is a public institution offering degree programs in arts and sciences, engineering and applied sciences, nursing, health technology and management, and social welfare. There are 5 undergraduate and 8 graduate schools. In addition to regional accreditation, Stony Brook has baccalaureate program accreditation with ABET, AOTA, APA, APTA, CAAHEP, CAHEA, CSWE, NLN, and NAACLS. The 7 libraries contain 1,896,697 volumes, 3,770,432 microform items, and 38,926 audiovisual forms/CDs, and subscribe to 11,214 periodicals. Computerized library services include the card catalog, interlibrary loans, and database searching. Special learning facilities include a learning resource center, art gallery, radio station, and the Museum of Long Island Natural Sciences, and the Fine Arts Center, which includes a 1100-seat main theater, a 400-seat recital hall, and 3 experimental theaters. The 1100-acre campus is in a suburban area on Long Island, 60 miles from New York City. Including residence halls, there are 113 buildings.

Student Life: 94% of undergraduates are from New York. Others are from 38 states, 74 foreign countries, and Canada. 85% are from public schools. 34% are white; 23% Asian American. 34% are Catholic; 23% claim no religious affiliation; 21% Buddhist, Islamic, Mormon, and Eastern Orthodox; 15% Protestant. The average age of freshmen is 18; all undergraduates, 22. 15% do not continue beyond their first year; 54% remain to graduate.

Housing: College housing includes coed dormitories, on-campus apartments, and married-student housing. In addition, there are honors houses, special-interest houses, and 7 living/learning centers that integrate academic experience with living environment. On-campus housing is guaranteed for all 4 years. 52% of students commute. Alcohol is not permitted. Upperclassmen may keep cars.

Activities: There are 4 local and 9 national fraternities and 3 local and 8 national sororities. There are 140 groups on campus, including band, cheerleading, choir, chorale, dance, drama, ethnic, film, gay, honors, international, literary magazine, musical theater, newspaper, orchestra, pep band, photography, political, professional, radio and TV, religious, social, student government, and yearbook. Popular campus events include Fall Fest, Opening Week Activities, and Caribbean Weekend.

Sports: There are 11 intercollegiate sports for men and 9 for women, and 25 intramural sports for men and 25 for women. Facilities include a sports complex housing a 5000-seat arena, a 1900-seat gym, an indoor track, a swimming pool, 6 squash and 8 racquetball courts, 3 multipurpose courts, a dance studio, and exercise and Universal gym rooms. Outdoor facilities include 20 tennis courts, a 3000-seat stadium, a 400-meter track, 2 sand volleyball courts, 2 basketball and 4 handball courts, and separate fields for baseball, soccer, football, lacrosse, and intramural football.

Disabled Students: 75% of the campus is accessible. Wheelchair ramps, elevators, special parking, specially equipped rest rooms, special class scheduling, lowered drinking fountains, lowered telephones, automatic door openers, and specially equipped living accommodations are available.

Services: There is a reader service for the blind and remedial math and writing.

Campus Safety and Security: Measures include 24-hour foot and vehicle patrol, self-defense education, escort service, and shuttle buses. There are informal discussions, pamphlets/posters/films, emergency telephones, lighted pathways/sidewalks, and a campus Crime Stoppers program.

Programs of Study: Stony Brook confers B.A., B.S., and B.E. degrees. Master's and doctoral degrees are also awarded. Bachelor's degrees are awarded in AGRICULTURE (environmental studies), BIOLOGICAL SCIENCE (biochemistry and biology/biological science), BUSINESS (business administration and management), COMMUNICATIONS AND THE ARTS (art history and appreciation, comparative literature, dramatic arts, English, film arts, French, Germanic languages and literature, linguistics, music, Russian languages and literature, and studio art), COMPUTER AND PHYSICAL SCIENCE (applied mathematics, astronomy, atmospheric sciences and meteorology, chemistry, computer science, earth science, geology, information sciences and systems, mathematics, oceanography, physics, planetary and space science, and statistics), ENGINEERING AND ENVIRONMENTAL DESIGN (chemical engineering, computer engineering, electrical/electronics engineering, engineering and applied science, and mechanical engineering), HEALTH PROFESSIONS (clinical science, cytotechnology, health science, nursing, pharmacology, physician's assistant, and respiratory therapy), SOCIAL SCIENCE (African studies, American studies, anthropology, economics, ethnic studies, French studies, history, humanities, interdisciplinary studies, Italian studies, philosophy, political science/government, psychology, religion, social science, social work, sociology, Spanish studies, and women's studies). Applied mathematics and statistics, biochemistry, and biology are the strongest academically. Psychology, business, and computer science are the largest.

Required: To graduate, students must have a minimum 2.0 GPA in 120 credit hours (B.A. and B.S.) or 128 (B.E.). The required number of hours in the major varies. At least 39 credits must be earned in upper-division courses. Students must take 14 to 16 courses to satisfy general education requirements in writing and quantitative reasoning skills, literary and philosophic analysis, exposure to the arts, disciplinary diversity, the interrelationship of science and society, and 3 culminating multicultural requirements. Arts and sciences majors must fulfill a foreign language requirement, unless completed through advanced high-school study. Other requirements vary by school.

Special: Cross-registration may be arranged through the Long Island Regional Advisory Council for Higher Education. The university offers a Washington semester and internships with a variety of government, legal, and social agencies, with hospitals and clinics, and in business and industry. The Federated Learning Communities enables students to concentrate on a major issue each year, and the URECA Program allows undergraduates to work with faculty on research and creative projects. An accelerated degree program in nursing, dual majors, student-designed majors, a national student exchange program, study abroad in 7 countries, pass/fail options, and B.A.-B.S. degrees in chemistry, earth and space science, and psychology are available. There are 4 national honor societies, including Phi Beta Kappa, a freshman honors program, and 22 departmental honors programs.

Faculty/Classroom: 67% of faculty are male; 33%, female. 80% teach undergraduates, 90% do research, and 70% do both. Graduate students teach 37% of introductory courses. The average class size in an introductory lecture is 84; in a laboratory, 25; and in a regular course, 38.

Admissions: 50% of the 2001-2002 applicants were accepted. The SAT I scores for the 2001-2002 freshman class were: Verbal--22% below 500, 50% between 500 and 599, 24% between 600 and 700, and 4% above 700; Math--7% below 500, 46% between 500 and 599, 36% between 600 and 700, and 11% above 700. 52% of the current freshmen were in the top fifth of their class; 86% were in the top two fifths.

Requirements: The SAT I is required. In addition, applicants must be graduates of an accredited secondary school or have a GED certificate. 16 or 17 academic credits are required, including 4 years each of English and social studies, 3 or 4 of math, 3 of science (4 for engineering majors), and 2 or 3 of a foreign language. 3 SAT II: Subject tests, an essay, and an interview are recommended. AP and CLEP credits are accepted. Important factors in the admissions decision are advanced placement or honor courses, extracurricular activities record, and evidence of special talent. Stony Brook participates in the SUNY system common application form, available on disk and through ExPAN. Applications are accepted on-line at the school's web site and via Apply!

Procedure: Freshmen are admitted fall, spring, and summer. Entrance exams should be taken during the junior year or in the fall of the senior year. There are early action, early admissions, and deferred admissions plans. Early action applications should be filed by November 1; regular applications, by July 10 for fall entry and December 20 for spring entry. Notification of early action is sent December 15; regular decision, on a rolling basis. The fall 2001 application fee was $30.

Transfer: 1792 transfer students enrolled in 2001-2002. Applicants must have a minimum 2.5 GPA. An associate degree and an interview are recommended. Other requirements vary by program. Applicants who have earned fewer than 24 college credits must submit a high school transcript. 36 credits of 120 must be completed at Stony Brook.

Visiting: There are regularly scheduled orientations for prospective students, consisting of 1-, 2-, or 3-day programs during which students may confer with faculty, register for classes, and take placement exams for English and math. There are guides for informal visits and visitors may sit in on classes and stay overnight. To schedule a visit, contact the Admissions Office.

Financial Aid: 10% of undergraduates work part time. Stony Brook is a member of CSS. The FAFSA and state aid form are required. The fall application deadline is March 1.

International Students: There are 507 international students enrolled. They must score 550 on the written TOEFL.

Computers: The mainframe is an IBM 3090/180E. There are IBM and Mac PCs throughout the campus. There are also large SUNSPARC workstation networks for student use. All students may access the system 24 hours a day. There are no time limits and no fees.

Graduates: In 2001, 2509 bachelor's degrees were awarded. The most popular majors were psychology (14%), business (6%), and biology (6%). About 500 companies recruited on campus in 2000-2001. Of the 2000 graduating class, 47% were enrolled in graduate school within 6 months of graduation and 22% were employed.

Admissions Contact: Gigi Lamens, Dean of Admissions and Enrollment Services. E-mail: *admiss@mail.upsa.sunysb.edu*
Web: *www.infostu.suny.edu*

SYRACUSE UNIVERSITY — C-3

Syracuse, NY 13244 — **(315) 443-3611; Fax: (315) 443-4226**

Full-time: 4799 men, 5794 women	**Faculty:** 790; I, -$
Part-time: 51 men, 58 women	**Ph.D.s:** 86%
Graduate: 1732 men, 1987 women	**Student/Faculty:** 13 to 1
Year: semesters, summer session	**Tuition:** $21,960
Application Deadline: January 1	**Room & Board:** $8750
Freshman Class: 14,514 applied, 9221 accepted, 2627 enrolled	
SAT I or ACT: required	**HIGHLY COMPETITIVE**

Syracuse University, founded in 1870, is a private institution offering more than 200 undergraduate programs in liberal arts and sciences, architecture, public communications, education, management, human services and health professions, information studies, visual and performing arts, engineering, and computer science. There are 9 undergraduate and 11 graduate schools. In addition to regional accreditation, Syracuse has baccalaureate program accreditation with AACSB, ABET, ACEJMC, ACS, APA, ASHA, CACREP, CSWE, FIDER, NAAB, NASAD, NASM, NASPAS, NCATE, and NLN. The 6 libraries contain 3,080,000 volumes, 4,650,000 microform items, and 858,900 audiovisual forms/CDs, and subscribe to 17,600 periodicals. Computerized library services include the card catalog, interlibrary loans, and database searching. Special learning facilities include a learning resource center, art gallery, radio station, TV station, institute for sensory research, center for public and community service, child care and child development laboratory school, English language institute, center for undergraduate research and innovative learning, audio archives, global collaboratory multimedia classroom, center for science and technology, and community darkrooms (photography). The 200-acre campus is in an urban area 250 miles northwest of New York City.

Student Life: 55% of undergraduates are from out of state, mostly the Northeast. Others are from 49 states, 61 foreign countries, and Canada. 78% are from public schools. 72% are white. 35% are claim no religious affiliation; 30% Catholic; 13% Jewish. Students represent more than 20 different religions on campus.; The average age of freshmen is 18; all undergraduates, 20. 10% do not continue beyond their first year; 74% remain to graduate.

Housing: 7461 students can be accommodated in college housing, which includes coed dormitories, on-campus apartments, married-student housing, fraternity houses, and sorority houses. In addition, there are language houses, special-interest houses, single-sex floors and wings of residence halls, learning communities, and theme/interest housing. On-campus housing is guaranteed for all 4 years and is available on a lottery system for upperclassmen. 73% of students live on campus; of those, 85% remain on campus on weekends. Alcohol is not permitted. Upperclassmen may keep cars.

Activities: 8% of men belong to 1 local fraternity and 25 national fraternities; 13% of women belong to 21 national sororities. There are 300 groups on campus, including art, band, cheerleading, chess, choir, chorale, chorus, computers, dance, debate, drama, ethnic, film, gay, honors, international, jazz band, literary magazine, marching band, musical theater, newspaper, orchestra, pep band, photography, political, professional, radio and TV, religious, social, social service, special interest, student government, symphony, and yearbook. Popular campus events include Parents Weekend, Opening Weekend Activities, and Senior Celebration.

Sports: There are 9 intercollegiate sports for men and 12 for women, and 25 intramural sports for men and 25 for women. Facilities include 4 gyms, 2 swimming pools, weight rooms, tennis courts, exercise rooms, a dance studio, courts for racquet sports, an indoor track, grass playing fields, 2 outdoor artificial turf fields, an outdoor track, a soccer stadium, and a softball stadium. The multipurpose domed stadium seats 50,000 for football and 30,000 for basketball.

Disabled Students: 90% of the campus is accessible. Wheelchair ramps, elevators, special parking, specially equipped rest rooms, special class scheduling, lowered drinking fountains, and lowered telephones are available. There are also special supportive services for the learning disabled: note taking services, oral tests, readers, talking books, a reading machine, tape recorders, and learning center, extended-time tests, support group, study circle, and proofreaders.

Services: Counseling and information services are available, as is tutoring in most subjects. There is a reader service for the blind. In addition to tutoring and study-group support, the academic support resource center provides workshops on generic study skills such as time management and test anxiety reduction as well as information on departmental academic support resources.

Campus Safety and Security: Measures include 24-hour foot and vehicle patrol, escort service, shuttle buses, and informal discussions. There are pamphlets/posters/films, emergency telephones, lighted pathways/sidewalks, bicycle registration, a blue light security system placed throughout campus with a direct link to the Department of Public Safety Communications Center in case of an emergency, and a card key access system in all university residence halls.

Programs of Study: Syracuse confers B.A., B.S., B.Arch., B.F.A, B.I.D., and B.Mus. degrees. Master's and doctoral degrees are also awarded. Bachelor's degrees are awarded in BIOLOGICAL SCIENCE (biology/biological science and nutrition), BUSINESS (accounting, banking and finance, business administration and management, entrepreneurial studies, management information systems, marketing management, marketing/retailing/merchandising, and retailing), COMMUNICATIONS AND THE ARTS (advertising, art, art history and appreciation, broadcasting, ceramic art and design, classics, communications, comparative literature, design, dramatic arts, English, English literature, fiber/textiles/weaving, film arts, fine arts, French, Germanic languages and literature, graphic design, illustration, industrial design, journalism, languages, linguistics, media arts, metal/jewelry, modern language, music, music business management, music performance, music theory and composition, musical theater, painting, photography, printmaking, public relations, publishing, Russian, sculpture, Spanish, speech/debate/rhetoric, telecommunications, theater design, theater management, and video), COMPUTER AND PHYSICAL SCIENCE (chemistry, computer science, geology, information sciences and systems, mathematics, physics, and statistics), EDUCATION (art, early childhood, elementary, English, mathematics, middle school, music, physical, science, secondary, social studies, and special), ENGINEERING AND ENVIRONMENTAL DESIGN (aerospace studies, architecture, bioengineering, chemical engineering, civil engineering, computer engineering, computer graphics, electrical/electronics engineering, engineering physics, environmental design, environmental engineering, environmental science, interior design, and mechanical engineering), HEALTH PROFESSIONS (exercise science, health science, nursing, predentistry, premedicine, preveterinary science, and speech pathology/audiology), SOCIAL SCIENCE (African American studies, American studies, anthropology, child care/child and family studies, classical/ancient civilization, consumer services, dietetics, economics, ethics, politics, and social policy, European studies, family/consumer studies, fashion design and technology, food production/management/services, geography, history, international relations, Italian studies, Latin American studies, medieval studies, peace studies, philosophy, political science/government, prelaw, psychology, public affairs, religion, Russian and Slavic studies, social science, social work, sociology, textiles and clothing, and women's studies). Aerospace engineering, art, and computer engineering are the strongest academically. Liberal arts and sciences, radio and television, broadcasting, and graphic design are the largest.

Required: A minimum of 120 credits with a minimum GPA of 2.0 is required to graduate. All students must take a freshman writing seminar and fulfill core requirements in writing and literature, sciences and math, social sciences, and humanities. Additional requirements vary by college and major.

Special: The Syracuse University Internship Program (SUIP) places students in off-campus local or national field positions related to their major. Cooperative education programs are available in engineering, retailing, and information studies. Cross-registration is offered with SUNY College of Environmental Science and Forestry. Study abroad is available in 6 university-operated centers and through other special programs, and a Washington semester is offered through the International Relations Program. Syracuse also offers B.A.-B.S. degrees, dual and student-designed majors, accelerated degree programs, work-study programs, a general studies degree, pass/fail options, and nondegree study. There are 36 national honor societies, including Phi Beta Kappa, and a freshman honors program.

Faculty/Classroom: 61% of faculty are male; 39%, female. 98% teach undergraduates, 2% do research, and 98% do both. Graduate students teach 6% of introductory courses. The average class size in a laboratory is 18 and in a regular course, 27.

Admissions: 64% of the 2001-2002 applicants were accepted. The SAT I scores for the 2001-2002 freshman class were: Verbal--9% below 500, 41% between 500 and 599, 41% between 600 and 700, and 9% above 700; Math--5% below 500, 34% between 500 and 599, 48% between 600 and 700, and 13% above 700. 68% of the current freshmen were in the top fifth of their class; 94% were in the top two fifths. 41 freshmen graduated first in their class.

Requirements: The SAT I or ACT is required. In addition, applicants should have a strong college preparatory record from an accredited secondary school or have a GED equivalent. An essay is required. A portfolio is required for art and architecture majors, and an audition is required for music and drama majors. A secondary school counselor evaluation, or 2 academic recommendations, and a high school transcript, are also required. AP and CLEP credits are accepted. Important factors in the admissions decision are advanced placement or honor courses, evidence of special talent, and recommendations by school officials.

Procedure: Freshmen are admitted fall and spring. Entrance exams should be taken before January of the senior year for regular decision, and before November of the senior year for early decision. There are early decision, early admissions, and deferred admissions plans. Early decision applications should be filed by November 15; regular applications, by January 1 for fall entry and November 15 for spring entry, along with a $50 fee. Notification of early decision is sent late December; regular decision, mid-March. 379 early decision candidates were accepted for the 2001-2002 class.

Transfer: 318 transfer students enrolled in a recent year. Requirements vary by college. The SAT I or ACT scores and secondary school transcripts are required for applicants with fewer than 30 credit hours. A portfolio is required for art and architecture majors, and an audition for music and drama majors. College transcripts of all post secondary work are required. 30 credits of 120 must be completed at Syracuse.

Visiting: There are regularly scheduled orientations for prospective students, including information programs, a campus tour, and personal interviews. There are guides for informal visits and visitors may sit in on classes and stay overnight. To schedule a visit, contact the Admissions Office.

Financial Aid: In 2001-2002, 78% of all freshmen and 80% of continuing students received some form of financial aid. 51% of freshmen and 52% of continuing students received need-based aid. The average freshman award was $17,445. Of that total, scholarships or need-based grants averaged $11,500 ($21,500 maximum); loans averaged $3680 ($4625 maximum); and work contracts averaged $2265 ($2400 maximum). 45% of undergraduates work part time. Average annual earnings from campus work are $1500. The average financial indebtedness of the 2001 graduate was $18,925. Syracuse is a member of CSS. The CSS/Profile or FAFSA is required. The fall application deadline is February 1.

International Students: There are 367 international students enrolled. The school actively recruits these students. They must score 550 on the written TOEFL or 213 on the electronic version or take ELPT or APIEL.

Computers: Syracuse has a networked client/server computing environment that gives students access to almost 1000 Macs, and UNIX workstations located throughout the campus. High-speed connections are available in all campus housing. All students may access the system 24 hours per day. There are no time limits and no fees. It is strongly recommended that all students have a personal computer.

Graduates: In 2001, 2757 bachelor's degrees were awarded. The most popular majors were communications (16%), management (14%), and social sciences (12%). In an average class, 61% graduate in 4 years, 72% in 5 years, and 74% in 6 years. 288 companies recruited on campus in 2000-2001. Of the 2000 graduating class, 14% were enrolled in graduate school within 6 months of graduation and 80% were employed.

Admissions Contact: Susan E. Donovan, Dean of Admissions. A video is available. E-mail: *orange@syr.edu* Web: *http://www.syracuse.edu*

TOURO COLLEGE D-5
New York, NY 10010 (718) 252-7800, ext. 399 Fax: (718) 253-9455

Full-time: 1716 men, 3648 women	**Faculty:** 225
Part-time: 252 men, 503 women	**Ph.D.s:** 65%
Graduate: 211 men, 451 women	**Student/Faculty:** 24 to 1
Year: semesters, summer session	**Tuition:** $10,250
Application Deadline: open	**Room & Board:** $4700
Freshman Class: 1430 applied, 1046 accepted, 856 enrolled	
SAT I Verbal/Math: 570/550	**ACT:** 23 VERY COMPETITIVE

Touro College, founded in 1971, is a private institution offering undergraduate programs primarily through the Lander College of Liberal Arts and Sciences, the School of General Studies, and the School of Health Sciences. Campuses are in midtown Manhattan, Brooklyn, and Queens. There are 6 undergraduate and 6 graduate schools. In addition to regional accreditation, Touro College has baccalaureate program accreditation with AOTA, APTA, and CAHEA. The 11 libraries contain 271,509 volumes, 14,100 microform items, and 4054 audiovisual forms/CDs, and subscribe to 3163 periodicals. Computerized library services include the card catalog, interlibrary loans, and database searching. Special learning facilities include a learning resource center. The campus is in an urban area. Including residence halls, there are 12 buildings.

Student Life: 95% of undergraduates are from New York. Others are from 25 states, 30 foreign countries, and Canada. 27% do not continue beyond their first year; 47% remain to graduate.

Housing: 200 students can be accommodated in college housing, which includes single-sex dormitories, on-campus apartments, and off-campus apartments. On-campus housing is available on a first-come, first-served basis. Priority is given to out-of town students. Alcohol is not permitted. No one may keep cars.

Activities: There are no fraternities or sororities. There are 10 groups on campus, including computers, debate, literary magazine, newspaper, political, professional, religious, social, student government, and yearbook. Popular campus events include a student-sponsored lecture series and student-faculty social events.

Sports: There is no sports program at Touro College. Facilities include 1 baseball field, 2 tennis courts, and 2 basketball courts.

Disabled Students: All of the campus is accessible. Wheelchair ramps, elevators, specially equipped rest rooms, lowered drinking fountains, and lowered telephones are available.

Services: Counseling and information services are available, as is tutoring in some subjects, including accounting, math, English, and natural sciences. There is remedial math, reading, and writing.

Campus Safety and Security: Measures include 24-hour foot and vehicle patrol and pamphlets/posters/films.

Programs of Study: Touro College confers B.A., B.S., and B.P.S. degrees. Associate, master's, and doctoral degrees are also awarded. Bachelor's degrees are awarded in BIOLOGICAL SCIENCE (biology/biological science), BUSINESS (accounting, banking and finance, business administration and management, management science, and marketing/retailing/merchandising), COMMUNICATIONS AND THE ARTS (English, Hebrew, literature, and speech/debate/rhetoric), COMPUTER AND PHYSICAL SCIENCE (chemistry, computer science, mathematics, and physics), EDUCATION (elementary and special), HEALTH PROFESSIONS (occupational therapy, physical therapy, predentistry, and premedicine), SOCIAL SCIENCE (economics, history, human services, interdisciplinary studies, Judaic studies, liberal arts/general studies, philosophy, political science/government, prelaw, psychology, social science, and sociology). Business/accounting, education, and health sciences are the strongest academically. Psychology, education, and business are the largest.

Required: To graduate, all students must complete at least 120 credit hours (varies by major), with 30 to 70 in the major. A minimum 2.0 GPA is required, with 2.3 in the major. Specific disciplines include Judaic studies or ethnic studies. Required courses include English composition, history, literature, math, and social and natural sciences.

Special: The college offers cross-registration with the Fashion Institute of Technology, internships for juniors and seniors, study abroad in Israel, work-study programs, interdisciplinary majors, an accelerated degree program, credit for life, military, and work experience, pass/fail options, and dual majors. Early and/or preferential admission to professional programs is also possible. There are 2 national honor societies.

Faculty/Classroom: 60% of faculty are male; 40%, female. No introductory courses are taught by graduate students. The average class size in an introductory lecture is 16; in a laboratory, 12; and in a regular course, 15.

Admissions: 73% of the 2001-2002 applicants were accepted. The SAT I scores for the 2001-2002 freshman class were: Verbal--22% below 500, 38% between 500 and 599, 32% between 600 and 700, and 8% above 700; Math--27% below 500, 40% between 500 and 599, 27% between 600 and 700, and 6% above 700. The ACT scores were 8% below 21, 50% between 21 and 23, 8% between 24 and 26, 17% between 27 and 28, and 17% above 28. There were 2 National Merit finalists and 15 semifinalists.

Requirements: The SAT I or ACT is recommended for baccalaureate programs, with scores of 550 verbal and 550 math on the SAT I. Applicants must be graduates of an accredited secondary school. A grade average of 80 is required. AP and CLEP credits are accepted. Important factors in the admissions decision are advanced placement or honor courses, recommendations by school officials, and extracurricular activities record.

Procedure: Freshmen are admitted fall, spring, and summer. Entrance exams should be taken in May of the junior year or fall of the senior year. There are early admissions and deferred admissions plans. Application deadlines are open. Application fee is $50. Notification is sent on a rolling basis.

Transfer: 726 transfer students enrolled in 2001-2002. A 2.5 GPA is required. If the student has less than 60 credits, high school documentation is also required. 45 credits of 120 must be completed at Touro College.

Visiting: There are regularly scheduled orientations for prospective students. There are guides for informal visits and visitors may sit in on classes and stay overnight. To schedule a visit, contact Steven Toplan.

Financial Aid: In a recent year, 90% of all freshmen and 75% of continuing students received some form of financial aid. 75% of freshmen and 65% of continuing students received need-based aid. The average freshman award was $7375. 30% of undergraduates work part time. Average annual earnings from campus work are $3000. The average financial indebtedness of a recent year's graduate was $11,000. The CSS/Profile is required. The fall application deadline is October 15.

International Students: There are 67 international students enrolled. They must score 550 on the written TOEFL or 175 on the electronic version and also take the college's own test.

Computers: The mainframe is an AS/400. Students have access to a LAN (local area network) within Touro's WAN connected to the Internet using a T1 line. More than 500 computers are available for student use. All students may access the system. There are no time limits and no fees.

Graduates: In 2001, 900 bachelor's degrees were awarded. The most popular majors were business/accounting (22%), liberal arts (22%), and psychology (12%). In an average class, 47% graduate in 6 years. 50 companies recruited on campus in 2000-2001. Of the 2000 graduating class, 40% were enrolled in graduate school within 6 months of graduation.

Admissions Contact: Steven Toplan, Director of Admissions. E-mail: *lasadmit@admin.touro.edu* Web: *www.touro.edu*

UNION COLLEGE D-3
Schenectady, NY 12308-2311 (518) 388-6112 (888) 843-6688; Fax: (518) 388-6986

Full-time: 1078 men, 1004 women	**Faculty:** 195; IIA, ++$
Part-time: 22 men, 14 women	**Ph.D.s:** 95%
Graduate: 184 men, 125 women	**Student/Faculty:** 11 to 1
Year: trimesters, summer session	**Tuition:** $26,007
Application Deadline: January 15	**Room & Board:** $6639
Freshman Class: 3910 applied, 1616 accepted, 522 enrolled	
SAT I Verbal/Math: 600/630	**ACT:** 26 HIGHLY COMPETITIVE

Union College, founded in 1795, is an independent liberal arts and engineering college. In addition to regional accreditation, Union has baccalaureate program accreditation with ABET. The library contains 294,416 volumes, 794,671 microform items, and 7960 audiovisual forms/CDs, and subscribes to 1972 print periodicals. Computerized library services include the card catalog, interlibrary loans, and database searching. Special learning facilities include a radio station and theater, high-technology classroom, and lab center. The 100-acre campus is in an urban area 15 miles west of Albany. Including residence halls, there are 100 buildings.

Student Life: 53% of undergraduates are from out of state, mostly the Northeast. Others are from 32 states, 22 foreign countries, and Canada. 65% are from public schools. 84% are white. The average age of freshmen is 18; all undergraduates, 20. 6% do not continue beyond their first year; 84% remain to graduate.

Housing: 1704 students can be accommodated in college housing, which includes single-sex and coed dormitories, on-campus apartments, fraternity houses, and sorority houses. In addition, there are language houses, special-interest houses, and 10 theme houses that emphasize various community atmospeheres, substance-free lifestyle living areas, and a 24-hour quiet option for upperclassmen. On-campus housing is available on a lottery system for upperclassmen. 81% of students live on campus; of those, 80% remain on campus on weekends. Upperclassmen may keep cars.

Activities: 22% of men belong to 1 local and 12 national fraternities; 19% of women belong to 4 national sororities. There are 100 groups on campus, including art, band, cheerleading, chess, choir, computers, dance, debate, drama, ethnic, gay, international, jazz band, literary magazine, newspaper, orchestra, photography, political, professional, radio and TV, religious, social, social service, student government, and yearbook. Popular campus events include Women's Week, Black History Month, and Party in the Garden.

Sports: There are 18 intercollegiate sports for men and 11 for women, and 18 intramural sports for men and 11 for women. Facilities include a field house for volleyball, basketball, and track, fields for soccer, football, lacrosse, and field hockey, an ice rink, a gym, a swimming pool, weight rooms, and tennis and racquetball/squash courts.

Disabled Students: 60% of the campus is accessible. Wheelchair ramps, elevators, special parking, specially equipped rest rooms, lowered drinking fountains, and lowered telephones are available.

Services: Counseling and information services are available, as is tutoring in most subjects, including science and math. A writing center is available.

Campus Safety and Security: Measures include 24-hour foot and vehicle patrol, self-defense education, escort service, and informal discussions. There are pamphlets/posters/films, emergency telephones, lighted pathways/sidewalks, and 24-hour locked residence halls, emergency medical assistance, awareness programs, bicycle patrol, and trolley escort service.

Programs of Study: Union confers B.A., B.S., B.S.C.E., B.S.C.S.E., B.S.E.E., and B.S.M.E. degrees. Master's degrees are also awarded. Bachelor's degrees are awarded in BIOLOGICAL SCIENCE (biochemistry and biology/biological science), BUSINESS (business economics and management science), COMMUNICATIONS AND THE ARTS (art history and appreciation, classics, dramatic arts, English, fine arts, French, German, modern language, music, Spanish, and studio art), COMPUTER AND PHYSICAL SCIENCE (chemistry, computer science, geology, information sciences and systems, mathematics, and physics), ENGINEERING AND ENVIRONMENTAL DESIGN (civil engineering, computer engineering, electrical/electronics engineering, environmental science, and mechanical engineering), SOCIAL SCIENCE (American studies, anthropology, Caribbean studies, East Asian studies, economics, history, humanities, interdisciplinary studies, Latin American studies, law, philosophy, political science/government, psychology, Russian and Slavic studies, sociology, and women's studies). Math, chemistry, and classics are the strongest academically. Biology, political science, and psychology are the largest.

Required: Students must complete a minimum of 36 courses and must maintain a minimum GPA of 1.8 overall and 2.0 in the major. Students must also meet the requirements of the freshman preceptorial and the general education program, which includes courses distributed in 4 areas: history, literature, and civilization; social or behavioral science; math and natural science; and foreign languages and non-Western studies.

Special: Cross-registration is permitted with the Hudson Mohawk Consortium. Opportunities are provided for legislative internships in Albany and Washington, D.C. Union also offers pass/fail options, B.A.-B.S. degrees, dual and student-designed majors, a Washington semester, accelerated degree programs in law and medicine, and study abroad in 25 countries. There are 12 national honor societies, including Phi Beta Kappa, a freshman honors program, and 11 departmental honors programs.

Faculty/Classroom: 64% of faculty are male; 36%, female. All teach undergraduates and 97% both teach and do research. No introductory courses are taught by graduate students. The average class size in an introductory lecture is 23; in a laboratory, 13; and in a regular course, 19.

Admissions: 41% of the 2001-2002 applicants were accepted. The SAT I scores for the 2001-2002 freshman class were: Verbal--5% below 500, 43% between 500 and 599, 45% between 600 and 700, and 7% above 700; Math--2% below 500, 30% between 500 and 599, 53% between 600 and 700, and 15% above 700. 79% of the current freshmen were in the top quarter of their class; 96% were in the top half. There was 1 National Merit finalist.

Requirements: The SAT I or ACT is required, or in place of these, 3 SAT II: Subject tests may be submitted, including 1 in writing. Graduation from an accredited secondary school is required. Applicants must submit a minimum of 16 full-year credits, distributed as follows: 4 years of English, 2 of a foreign language, 2 1/2 to 3 1/2 years of math, 2 years each of science and social studies, and the remainder in college-preparatory courses. Engineering and math majors are expected to have completed additional math and science courses beyond the minimum requirements. An essay is also required, and an interview is recommended. AP credits are accepted. Important factors in the admissions decision are advanced placement or honor courses, recommendations by school officials, and extracurricular activities record. Applications are accepted on-line at *apply.embark.com*. They can be accessed through the Union web site (*http://www.union.edu/admissions/applying/applications.html*) by clicking on Online Application Site. A copy of Union's supplement page and a graded, written essay from 11th or 12th grade are required to complete the application.

Procedure: Freshmen are admitted in the fall. Entrance exams should be taken by January of the senior year. There are early decision and deferred admissions plans. Early decision applications should be filed by November 15; regular applications, by January 15 for fall entry. Notification of early decision is sent December 15; regular decision, April 1. 189 early decision candidates were accepted for the 2001-2002 class. 29% of all applicants are on a waiting list; 31 were accepted in 2001. The fall 2001 application fee was $50.

Transfer: 24 transfer students enrolled in 2001-2002. A 3.0 GPA and 1 full year of college academic work are required. Transfer students must study at Union for at least 2 years. 18 courses of 36 must be completed at Union.

Visiting: There are regularly scheduled orientations for prospective students, including interviews and a tour of the campus. There are guides for informal visits and visitors may sit in on classes and stay overnight. To schedule a visit, contact the Admissions Office, Grant Hall.

Financial Aid: In 2001-2002, 50% of all freshmen and 53% of continuing students received some form of financial aid. 48% of freshmen and 53% of continuing students received need-based aid. The average freshman award was $21,900. Of that total, scholarships or need-based grants averaged $18,475 ($28,325 maximum); loans averaged $2225 ($4625 maximum); and work contracts averaged $1200 (maximum). 33% of undergraduates work part time. Average annual earnings from campus work are $900. The average financial indebtedness of the 2001 graduate was $15,100. Union is a member of CSS. The CSS/Profile or FAFSA is required. The fall application deadline is February 1.

International Students: There are 52 international students enrolled. The school actively recruits these students. They must score 600 on the written TOEFL or 250 on the electronic version and also take SAT I or 3 SAT II: Subject tests, including writing, or the ACT.

Computers: The mainframes are 5 Compaq ALPHA servers and 11 Windows NT servers. There are more than 1000 PCs and workstations on campus linking classrooms, labs, offices, and residence hall rooms. There are also 19 electronic classrooms. Departmental computer labs offer Windows and Mac-based systems. 3 computer labs are available 24 hours/day, 7 days/week. Other departmental labs are available, some 24/7. All students may access the system 24 hours per day, 7 days a week. There are no time limits and no fees.

Graduates: In 2001, 470 bachelor's degrees were awarded. The most popular majors were political science (13%), economics (10%), and psychology (9%). In an average class, 78% graduate in 4 years, 83% in 5 years, and 84% in 6 years. 124 companies recruited on campus in 2000-2001. Of the 2000 graduating class, 31% were enrolled in graduate school within 1 year of graduation and 66% were employed.

Admissions Contact: Daniel Lundquist, Vice President, Admissions and Financial Aid. A video is available. E-mail: *admissions@union.edu* Web: *www.union.edu*

UNITED STATES MERCHANT MARINE ACADEMY D-5
Kings Point, NY 11024-1699 (516) 773-5391
(800) 732-6267; Fax: (516) 773-5390

Full-time: 850 men, 100 women	**Faculty:** 74
Part-time: none	**Ph.D.s:** 85%
Graduate: none	**Student/Faculty:** 13 to 1
Year: semesters	**Tuition:** see profile
Application Deadline: March 1	**Room & Board:** n/app
Freshman Class: n/av	
SAT I or ACT: required	**VERY COMPETITIVE**

The United States Merchant Marine Academy, founded in 1943, is a publicly supported institution offering maritime, military, and engineering programs for the purpose of training officers for the U.S. merchant marine and the maritime industry. Students make no conventional tuition and board payments. Required fees for freshmen are approximately $5700; costs in subsequent years are less. Figures in above capsule are approximate. In addition to regional accreditation, Kings Point has baccalaureate program accreditation with ABET. The library contains 225,000 volumes, 110,000 microform items, and 2000 audiovisual forms/CDs, and subscribes to 1000 periodicals. Computerized library services include database searching. Special learning facilities include a maritime museum. The 80-acre campus is in a suburban area 19 miles east of New York City. There are 28 buildings.

Programs of Study: Kings Point confers the B.S. degree. Bachelor's degrees are awarded in BUSINESS (transportation management), ENGINEERING AND ENVIRONMENTAL DESIGN (engineering, marine engineering, and maritime science). Marine engineering systems is the strongest academically. Marine engineering is the largest.

Required: To graduate, students must complete 160 credit hours with a 2.0 minimum GPA. The required core curriculum includes courses in math, science, English, humanities and history, naval science, phys ed, ship's medicine, and computer science. Students must spend 5 months during their junior and senior years at sea on U.S. flagships. All students must pass resident and sea project courses, the U.S. Coast Guard licensing exam and all required certificates, and the academy physical fitness test. Students must apply for and accept, if offered, a commission in the U.S. Naval Reserve.

Special: The college offers internships in the maritime industry and work-study programs with U.S. shipping companies.

Faculty/Classroom: 91% of faculty are male; 9%, female. All teach undergraduates. The average class size in an introductory lecture is 25 and in a laboratory, 15.
Requirements: The SAT I or ACT is required. In addition, SAT II: Subject tests are recommended. Candidates for admission to the academy must be nominated by a member of the U.S. Congress. They must be between the ages of 17 and 25, U.S. citizens (except by special arrangement), and in excellent physical condition. Applicants should be graduates of an accredited secondary school or have a GED equivalent. 16 academic credits are required, including 4 in English, 3 in math, 1 credit in physics or chemistry with a lab, and 8 in electives. An essay is required. Kings Point requires applicants to be in the upper 40% of their class. Important factors in the admissions decision are advanced placement or honor courses, leadership record, and extracurricular activities record.
Procedure: Freshmen are admitted in the fall. Entrance exams should be taken by the first test date of the year of requested admission. 50% of all applicants are on a waiting list. Check with the school for current application deadlines and fees.
Transfer: All students must spend 4 years at the academy.
Visiting: There are guides for informal visits and visitors may sit in on classes and stay overnight. To schedule a visit, contact the Admissions Office.
Financial Aid: Kings Point is a member of CSS. The FAFSA is required. Check with the school for current deadlines.
International Students: There were 12 international students enrolled in a recent year. They must score 500 on the written TOEFL and also take the SAT I or the ACT.
Computers: The mainframes are a DEC VAX 8600, an IBM 4381, and a Honeywell GPS. There are also 1200 PCs and Macs available in dorm and labs. All students may access the system 24 hours per day. There are no time limits and no fees. All students are required to have personal computers.
Admissions Contact: Capt. James Skinner, Director of Admissions. A video is available. E-mail: *admissions@usmma.edu*
Web: *www.usmma.edu*

UNITED STATES MILITARY ACADEMY D-4

West Point, NY 10996- (845) 938-4041; Fax: (845) 938-8121

Full-time: 3530 men, 635 women	**Faculty:** 577
Part-time: none	**Ph.D.s:** 39%
Graduate: none	**Student/Faculty:** 7 to 1
Year: semesters, summer session	**Tuition:** see profile
Application Deadline: n/av	**Room & Board:** see profile
Freshman Class: n/av	
SAT I or ACT: required	**MOST COMPETITIVE**

The United States Military Academy, founded in 1802, offers military, engineering, and comprehensive arts and sciences programs leading to a bachelor's degree and a commission as a second lieutenant in the U.S. Army, with a 5-year active duty service obligation. Some information in this profile is approximate. All students receive free tuition and room and board as well as an annual salary of $7200. An initial deposit of $2400 is required. Figures in above capsule are approximate. In addition to regional accreditation, West Point has baccalaureate program accreditation with ABET. The library contains 442,169 volumes, 748,443 microform items, and 12,378 audiovisual forms/CDs, and subscribes to 1963 periodicals. Computerized library services include the card catalog, interlibrary loans, and database searching. Special learning facilities include a learning resource center, art gallery, radio station, TV station, and military museum. Cadets may conduct research in conjunction with the academic departments through the Operations Research Center, the Photonics Research Center, the Mechanical Engineering Research Center, and the Office of Artificial Intelligence, Analysis, and Evaluation. There is also a visiting artist program featuring painting, sculpture, and photography. The 16,080-acre campus is in a small town 56 miles north of New York City. Including residence halls, there are 902 buildings.
Student Life: 92% of undergraduates are from out of state, mostly the Northeast. Others are from 50 states and 19 foreign countries. 81% are from public schools. 81% are white. 49% are Protestant; 33%, Catholic; 15% claim no religious affiliation. The average age of freshmen is 18; all undergraduates, 20. 8% do not continue beyond their first year; 82% remain to graduate.
Housing: 4500 students can be accommodated in college housing. College-sponsored housing is coed. On-campus housing is guaranteed for all 4 years. All students live on campus. Upperclassmen may keep cars.
Activities: There are no fraternities or sororities. There are 105 groups on campus, including art, bagpipe band, band, cheerleading, chess, choir, chorale, chorus, computers, dance, debate, drama, drill team, drum and bugle corps, ethnic, film, forensics, honors, international, literary magazine, marching band, musical theater, newspaper, pep band, photography, professional, radio and TV, religious, social, social service, student government, and yearbook. Popular campus events include Ring Weekend and 100th Night for Seniors, 500th Night for Juniors, Yearling Winter Weekend for Sophomores, Plebe-Parent Weekend for Freshmen, and graduation week activities.
Sports: There are 15 intercollegiate sports for men and 9 for women, and 18 intramural sports for men and 14 for women. Facilities include a 40,000-seat football stadium; baseball fields, a 2500-seat hockey rink, a 5000-seat basketball arena, a gymnasium with squash, handball, tennis, and racquetball courts, 3 swimming pools, and workout areas; a field house; indoor/outdoor tracks, a golf course, a ski slope; and hunting, fishing, and boating facilities.
Disabled Students: Wheelchair ramps, elevators, special parking, specially equipped rest rooms, lowered drinking fountains, and lowered telephones are available.
Services: Counseling and information services are available, as is tutoring in every subject. The Center for Enhanced Performance offers 2 courses that provide cadets an opportunity to learn and enhance reading, study, and mental skills.
Campus Safety and Security: Measures include 24-hour foot and vehicle patrol, self-defense education, shuttle buses, and lighted pathways/sidewalks.
Programs of Study: West Point confers the B.S. degree. Bachelor's degrees are awarded in BIOLOGICAL SCIENCE (life science), BUSINESS (management science and operations research), COMMUNICATIONS AND THE ARTS (languages and literature), COMPUTER AND PHYSICAL SCIENCE (chemistry, computer science, mathematics, and physics), ENGINEERING AND ENVIRONMENTAL DESIGN (civil engineering, electrical/electronics engineering, engineering management, engineering physics, environmental engineering, mechanical engineering, military science, nuclear engineering, and systems engineering), SOCIAL SCIENCE (behavioral science, economics, geography, history, international studies, law, philosophy, and political science/government). Engineering, behavioral sciences, and history are the largest.
Required: All cadets must complete a core of 31 courses and 9 academic electives pertinent to their field of study. The major requires an additional 1 to 3 electives in the field. In addition, all cadets must complete 4 courses each in phys ed and military science and a senior thesis or design project in the major. A total of 140 credits, including 127 academic, 6 military, and 7 physical, with at least a C average, is required to graduate.
Special: Junior and senior cadets may participate in 3-week summer educational experiences, including Operation Crossroads Africa, research work in technical areas throughout the country, medical internships at Walter Reed Medical Center, work-fellow positions with federal and Department of Defense agencies, language training in foreign countries, and study at other military and civilian institutions. There are 7 national honor societies, including Phi Beta Kappa, a freshman honors program, and 5 departmental honors programs.
Faculty/Classroom: 88% of faculty are male; 12%, female. 40% both teach and do research. The average class size in an introductory lecture is 15; in a laboratory, 15; and in a regular course, 15.
Admissions: 18% of the 2001-2002 applicants were accepted. The SAT I scores for the 2001-2002 freshman class were: Verbal--2% below 500, 33% between 500 and 599, 47% between 600 and 700, and 18% above 700; Math--1% below 500, 23% between 500 and 599, 54% between 600 and 700, and 23% above 700. The ACT scores were 4% between 18 and 23, 62% between 24 and 29, and 34% above 29.
Requirements: The SAT I or ACT is required. In addition, applicants must be qualified academically, physically, and medically. Candidates must be nominated for admission by members of the U.S. Congress or executive sources. West Point recommends that applicants have 4 years each of English and math, 2 years each of foreign language and lab science, such as chemistry and physics, and 1 year of U.S. history. Courses in geography, government, and economics are also suggested. An essay is required, and an interview is recommended. The GED is accepted. Applicants must be 17 to 22 years old, a U.S. citizen at the time of enrollment (except by agreement with another country), unmarried, and not pregnant or legally obligated to support children. AP credits are accepted. Important factors in the admissions decision are leadership record, extracurricular activities record, and recommendations by school officials.
Procedure: Freshmen are admitted in the summer. Entrance exams should be taken in the spring of the junior year and not later than the fall of the senior year. There are early decision and early admissions plans. Check with the school for current appllication deadlines.
Transfer: All applicants must enter as freshmen. 140 credits of 140 must be completed at West Point.
Visiting: There are regularly scheduled orientations for prospective students. Candidates will be escorted by a cadet, will attend class, have lunch with the Corps of Cadets, and talk with cadets about all phases of West Point life. There are guides for informal visits and visitors may sit in on classes and stay overnight. To schedule a visit, contact the Admissions Office.
International Students: They must take the TOEFL and also take the SAT I or the ACT.
Computers: The mainframe is a Unisys 2200/425. Virually every course requires a computer. There is a PC at each desk, which is con-

nected to academic computing services, word processing, worldwide e-mail, spreadsheets, and database access. All students may access the system 24 hours daily. There are no time limits and no fees. All students are required to have personal computers.

Admissions Contact: Colonel Michael L. Jones, Director of Admissions. A video is available. E-mail: *admissions@usma.edu*
Web: *www.usma.edu*

UNIVERSITY OF ROCHESTER — B-3
Rochester, NY 14627-0251 — **(585) 275-3221**
(888) 822-2256; Fax: (585) 461-4595

Full-time: 2456 men, 1984 women	**Faculty:** 499; 1, +$
Part-time: 60 men, 165 women	**Ph.D.s:** 90%
Graduate: 1782 men, 1486 women	**Student/Faculty:** 9 to 1
Year: semesters, summer session	**Tuition:** $24,794
Application Deadline: January 20	**Room & Board:** $8185
Freshman Class: 7262 applied, 5041 accepted, 1003 enrolled	
SAT I or ACT: required	**HIGHLY COMPETITIVE**

The University of Rochester, founded in 1850, is a private institution offering programs in the arts and sciences, engineering and applied science, nursing, medicine and dentistry, business administration, music, and education. There are 4 undergraduate and 7 graduate schools. In addition to regional accreditation, UR has baccalaureate program accreditation with AACSB, ABET, ACPE, NASM, and NLN. The 7 libraries contain 2,922,335 volumes, 4,145,264 microform items, and 71,100 audiovisual forms/CDs, and subscribe to 9829 periodicals. Computerized library services include the card catalog, interlibrary loans, and database searching. Special learning facilities include a learning resource center, art gallery, radio station, labs for nuclear structure research and laser energetics, a center for visual science, Strong Memorial Hospital, art center, observatory, institute of optics, center for electronic imaging systems, and the National Science Foundation Center for Photoinduced Charge Transfer. The 90-acre campus is in a suburban area 2 miles south of downtown Rochester. Including residence halls, there are 143 buildings.

Student Life: 50% of undergraduates are from out of state, mostly the Middle Atlantic. Students are from 50 states, 95 foreign countries, and Canada. 76% are white; 12% Asian American.

Housing: 3022 students can be accommodated in college housing, which includes single-sex and coed dormitories, on-campus apartments, married-student housing, and fraternity houses. In addition, there are language houses, special-interest houses, drama and medieval houses, and faculty-in-residence housing. On-campus housing is guaranteed for the freshman year only and is available on a lottery system for upperclassmen. 75% of students live on campus; of those, 90% remain on campus on weekends. Upperclassmen may keep cars.

Activities: 25% of men belong to 17 national fraternities; 14% of women belong to 11 national sororities. There are 170 groups on campus, including art, band, campus programming, cheerleading, chess, choir, chorale, chorus, computers, dance, debate, drama, drill team, ethnic, film, gay, honors, international, jazz band, literary magazine, musical theater, newspaper, opera, orchestra, pep band, photography, political, professional, radio and TV, religious, social, social service, student government, symphony, and yearbook. Popular campus events include Dandelion Day, Yellowjacket Day, and Boar's Head Dinner.

Sports: There are 11 intercollegiate sports for men and 11 for women, and 17 intramural sports for men and 17 for women. Facilities include a renovated athletic center, a 5000-seat stadium, a 2500-seat gym, a field house, an ice rink, courts for handball, racquetball, squash, and tennis, an indoor track, a fitness center and weight room, a jogging path, and an aquatic center.

Disabled Students: 75% of the campus is accessible. Wheelchair ramps, elevators, special parking, specially equipped rest rooms, special class scheduling, lowered drinking fountains, and lowered telephones are available. There is access to screened reading and adaptive software.

Services: Counseling and information services are available, as is tutoring in every subject. There is a reader service for the blind.

Campus Safety and Security: Measures include 24-hour foot and vehicle patrol, self-defense education, escort service, and shuttle buses. There are informal discussions, pamphlets/posters/films, emergency telephones, and lighted pathways/sidewalks.

Programs of Study: UR confers B.A., B.S., and B.M. degrees. Master's and doctoral degrees are also awarded. Bachelor's degrees are awarded in AGRICULTURE (environmental studies), BIOLOGICAL SCIENCE (biochemistry, biology/biological science, cell biology, ecology, genetics, microbiology, and neurosciences), COMMUNICATIONS AND THE ARTS (American Sign Language, art history and appreciation, classics, comparative literature, English, film arts, fine arts, French, German, Japanese, jazz, linguistics, music, music theory and composition, Russian, Spanish, and studio art), COMPUTER AND PHYSICAL SCIENCE (applied mathematics, chemistry, computer science, geology, mathematics, optics, physics, and statistics), EDUCATION (music), ENGINEERING AND ENVIRONMENTAL DESIGN (biomedical engineering, chemical engineering, electrical/electronics engineering, engineering and applied science, environmental science, geological engineering, and mechanical engineering), HEALTH PROFESSIONS (health, nursing, and public health), SOCIAL SCIENCE (anthropology, cognitive science, economics, history, interpreter for the deaf, philosophy, political science/government, psychology, religion, and women's studies). Psychology, biology, and political science are the largest.

Required: Students focus on the humanities, social sciences, and natural sciences; 1 of the 3 areas will be their major, and they select a 3-course cluster in each of the other 2. A total of 128 credit hours with a minimum GPA of 2.0 is required to graduate. Additionally, all students satisfy a freshman writing requirement and take 2 upper-level courses in their major that are writing intensive.

Special: Cross-registration is offered with other Rochester area colleges. Internships, a Washington semester, B.A.-B.S. degrees, dual and student-designed majors, nondegree study, and pass/fail options are available. Study abroad is possible in 46 university-sponsored programs, including Australia, China, Japan, Egypt, Israel, and the former Soviet Union, and in several European countries. Other options include a fifth year of courses tuition free, courses designed to teach first-year students how to learn and how to make learning a lifetime habit, a management studies certificate, and music lessons for credit at the Eastman School of Music. Qualified freshmen may obtain early assurance of admission to the university's medical school through the Rochester Early Medical Scholars program. Internships are available in the United States and abroad. There are 6 national honor societies, including Phi Beta Kappa, and 13 departmental honors programs.

Faculty/Classroom: 76% of faculty are male; 24%, female. Graduate students teach 5% of introductory courses. The average class size in an introductory lecture is 75; in a laboratory, 20; and in a regular course, 20.

Admissions: 69% of the 2001-2002 applicants were accepted. The SAT I scores for the 2001-2002 freshman class were: Verbal--2% below 500, 17% between 500 and 599, 54% between 600 and 700, and 27% above 700; Math--1% below 500, 9% between 500 and 599, 50% between 600 and 700, and 39% above 700. The ACT scores were 1% below 21, 7% between 21 and 23, 16% between 24 and 26, 22% between 27 and 28, and 53% above 28. 82% of the current freshmen were in the top fifth of their class; 97% were in the top two fifths.

Requirements: The SAT I or ACT is required. In addition, SAT II: Subject tests are recommended. Applicants should be graduates of an accredited secondary school or have a GED equivalent. An audition is required for music majors. AP credits are accepted. Important factors in the admissions decision are advanced placement or honor courses, recommendations by school officials, and leadership record. The school accepts the institutional application through Embark linked to the UR admissions home page.

Procedure: Freshmen are admitted fall and spring. Entrance exams should be taken by December of the senior year. There are early decision and deferred admissions plans. Early decision applications should be filed by November 15; regular applications, by January 20 for fall entry and October 1 for spring entry, along with a $50 fee. Notification of early decision is sent December 15; regular decision, April 1. 168 early decision candidates were accepted for the 2001-2002 class. 3% of all applicants are on a waiting list; 1 was accepted in 2001.

Transfer: 90 transfer students enrolled in 2001-2002. The most important criterion is an applicant's college record. Transfers are accepted on a rolling admissions basis. 32 credits of 128 must be completed at UR.

Visiting: There are regularly scheduled orientations for prospective students, including campus tours and group information sessions. There are guides for informal visits and visitors may sit in on classes and stay overnight. To schedule a visit, contact the Admissions Office.

Financial Aid: In 2001-2002, 88% of all students received some form of financial aid. 65% of all students received need-based aid. The average freshman award was $19,400. Of that total, scholarships or need-based grants averaged $13,000 ($24,150 maximum); loans averaged $4400 ($4875 maximum); and work contracts averaged $2000 ($2250 maximum). 50% of undergraduates work part time. Average annual earnings from campus work are $1100. The average financial indebtedness of the 2001 graduate was $20,998. UR is a member of CSS. The CSS/Profile or FAFSA is required. The fall application deadline is February 1.

International Students: There are 191 international students enrolled. The school actively recruits these students. They must score 550 on the written TOEFL or 213 on the electronic version and also take the SAT I or the ACT.

Computers: The mainframes are an IBM 4381, DEC VAX systems, Sun systems, and a Solbourne computer. Students have access to hundreds of PCs, workstations, printers, and terminals in the libraries, classrooms, labs, and resource centers on campus. All residence hall rooms have lines accessing the mainframe computers and the Internet. All students may access the system 24 hours daily. There are no time limits and no fees.

Graduates: In 2001, 993 bachelor's degrees were awarded. The most popular majors were psychology (16%), biology (16%), and economics

(12%). In an average class, 62% graduate in 4 years, and 75% in 6 years. 229 companies recruited on campus in 2000-2001.

Admissions Contact: W. Jamie Hobba, Director of Admissions. A video is available. E-mail: *admit@admissions.rochester.edu*
Web: *http://www.rochester.edu*

UTICA COLLEGE OF SYRACUSE UNIVERSITY C-3
Utica, NY 13502-4892 (315) 792-3006
(800) 782-8884; Fax: (315) 792-3003

Full-time: 770 men, 1045 women	**Faculty:** 104
Part-time: 86 men, 242 women	**Ph.D.s:** 91%
Graduate: 62 men, 81 women	**Student/Faculty:** 17 to 1
Year: semesters, summer session	**Tuition:** $18,050
Application Deadline: open	**Room & Board:** $6350
Freshman Class: 2109 applied, 1622 accepted, 475 enrolled	
SAT I Verbal/Math: 500/578	**LESS COMPETITIVE**

Utica College of Syracuse University, a private liberal arts institution founded in 1946, is one of the academic divisions of Syracuse University, and confers the Syracuse University undergraduate degree and Utica College masters degrees. In addition to regional accreditation, UC has baccalaureate program accreditation with NLN and AOTA. The library contains 181,558 volumes, 61,198 microform items, and 8823 audiovisual forms/CDs, and subscribes to 2148 periodicals. Computerized library services include the card catalog, interlibrary loans, and database searching. Special learning facilities include a learning resource center, art gallery, radio station, and an early childhood education lab. The 128-acre campus is in a suburban area 50 miles east of Syracuse. Including residence halls, there are 16 buildings.

Student Life: 89% of undergraduates are from New York. Others are from 33 states, 20 foreign countries, and Canada. 80% are from public schools. 62% are white. The average age of freshmen is 18; all undergraduates, 22. 32% do not continue beyond their first year; 57% remain to graduate.

Housing: 866 students can be accommodated in college housing, which includes single-sex and coed dormitories. On-campus housing is guaranteed for all 4 years. All students may keep cars.

Activities: 2% of men and about 1% of women belong to 1 local and 6 national fraternities; 3% of women belong to 3 local and 3 national sororities. There are 68 groups on campus, including art, band, cheerleading, choir, chorus, computers, drama, ethnic, film, gay, honors, international, jazz band, literary magazine, musical theater, newspaper, pep band, photography, political, professional, radio and TV, religious, social, social service, student government, and yearbook. Popular campus events include outdoor concerts, mock elections, and Winter Weekend.

Sports: There are 9 intercollegiate sports for men and 10 for women, and 20 intramural sports for men and 20 for women. Facilities include a 2200-seat gym, a competition-size swimming pool, tennis, racquetball, handball, and squash courts, a sauna, Nautilus and weight rooms, dance and aerobic rooms, playing fields, a stadium, and hockey facilities.

Disabled Students: 80% of the campus is accessible. Wheelchair ramps, elevators, special parking, specially equipped rest rooms, lowered drinking fountains, and automatic doors are available.

Services: Counseling and information services are available, as is tutoring in most subjects. There is a reader service for the blind, remedial math, reading, and writing, a writing center, and a math center.

Campus Safety and Security: Measures include 24-hour foot and vehicle patrol, escort service, shuttle buses, and informal discussions. There are pamphlets/posters/films, emergency telephones, and lighted pathways/sidewalks.

Programs of Study: UC confers B.A. and B.S. degrees. Master's degrees are also awarded. Bachelor's degrees are awarded in BIOLOGICAL SCIENCE (biology/biological science), BUSINESS (accounting, business administration and management, and business economics), COMMUNICATIONS AND THE ARTS (communications, English, fine arts, journalism, and public relations), COMPUTER AND PHYSICAL SCIENCE (actuarial science, chemistry, computer science, mathematics, and physics), ENGINEERING AND ENVIRONMENTAL DESIGN (construction management), HEALTH PROFESSIONS (nursing, occupational therapy, physical therapy, and recreation therapy), SOCIAL SCIENCE (child psychology/development, criminal justice, economics, history, international studies, philosophy, political science/government, psychology, social studies, and sociology). Occupational therapy, psychology, and biology are the strongest academically. Management is the largest.

Required: To graduate, students must complete a total of 120 to 128 hours with a minimum 2.0 GPA. They must complete a general education requirement, including basic skills and distribution requirements.

Special: UC offers co-op programs, internships, work-study programs in all majors, accelerated degrees, dual majors, and cross-registration with Hamilton College. Study abroad may be arranged in 9 countries. There is a 2-2 engineering degree with Syracuse University. There are 5 national honor societies and a freshman honors program.

Faculty/Classroom: 53% of faculty are male; 47%, female. All both teach and do research. The average class size in an introductory lecture is 23; in a laboratory, 10; and in a regular course, 17.

Admissions: 77% of the 2001-2002 applicants were accepted.

Requirements: The SAT I or ACT is recommended. In addition, graduation from an accredited secondary school or satisfactory scores on the GED are required. Recommended high school courses include 4 years of English, 3 years each of math and social studies, and 2 years each of foreign language and science. An essay and an interview are also recommended. AP and CLEP credits are accepted. Important factors in the admissions decision are advanced placement or honor courses, extracurricular activities record, and leadership record.

Procedure: Freshmen are admitted fall and spring. Entrance exams should be taken during the junior year. There are early admissions and deferred admissions plans. Application deadlines are open. The fall 2001 application fee was $35.

Transfer: 222 transfer students enrolled in 2001-2002. Applicants must have a minimum GPA of 2.3. 30 credits of 120 must be completed at UC.

Visiting: There are regularly scheduled orientations for prospective students, including an interview, financial aid information, and a tour of the campus. There are guides for informal visits and visitors may sit in on classes and stay overnight. To schedule a visit, contact the Admissions Office at *admiss@utica.ucsu.edu*.

Financial Aid: In 2001-2002, 90% of all students received some form of financial aid. 89% of all students received need-based aid. Scholarships or need-based grants averaged $13,167; and loans averaged $2770. The FAFSA is required. The fall application deadline is February 15.

International Students: There are 56 international students enrolled. The school actively recruits these students. They must score 529 on the written TOEFL or 195 on the electronic version or take the MELAB, the Comprehensive English Language Test, or the IELTS.

Computers: The mainframe is a Prime 5370. There are also 201 IBM and Mac PCs available in 8 labs. All students may access the system during posted hours. Time limits are imposed only during peak hours. The fee is $150.

Graduates: In 2001, 443 bachelor's degrees were awarded. The most popular majors were occupational therapy (12%), criminal justice (12%), and management (10%). In an average class, 39% graduate in 3 years, 53% in 4 years, 56% in 5 years, and 57% in 6 years. 500 companies recruited on campus in 2000-2001. Of the 2000 graduating class, 10% were enrolled in graduate school within 6 months of graduation and 88% were employed.

Admissions Contact: Patrick Quinn, Vice President for Enrollment Management. E-mail: *admiss@utica.ucsu.edu* Web: *www.utica.edu*

VASSAR COLLEGE D-4
Poughkeepsie, NY 12604 (914) 437-7300
(800) 827-7270; Fax: (914) 437-7063

Full-time: 924 men, 1453 women	**Faculty:** 243; IIB, ++$
Part-time: 21 men, 41 women	**Ph.D.s:** 94%
Graduate: none	**Student/Faculty:** 10 to 1
Year: semesters	**Tuition:** $26,290
Application Deadline: January 1	**Room & Board:** $7160
Freshman Class: 5690 applied, 1921 accepted, 696 enrolled	
SAT I Verbal/Math: 685/660	**ACT:** 30 **MOST COMPETITIVE**

Vassar College, founded in 1861, is a private, independent college of the liberal arts and sciences. The 3 libraries contain 814,614 volumes, 462,660 microform items, and 17,551 audiovisual forms/CDs, and subscribe to 3268 periodicals. Computerized library services include the card catalog, interlibrary loans, and database searching. Special learning facilities include a learning resource center, art gallery, radio station, studio art building, geological museum, observatory, 3 theaters, concert hall, environmental field station, intercultural center, and research-oriented lab facilities for natural sciences. The 1000-acre campus is in a suburban area 75 miles north of New York City. Including residence halls, there are 100 buildings.

Student Life: 72% of undergraduates are from out of state, mostly the Middle Atlantic. Students are from 50 states, 43 foreign countries, and Canada. 60% are from public schools. 74% are white. The average age of freshmen is 18; all undergraduates, 20. 4% do not continue beyond their first year; 87% remain to graduate.

Housing: 2305 students can be accommodated in college housing, which includes single-sex and coed dormitories, on-campus apartments, off-campus apartments, and married-student housing. There is 1 all-women residence hall and 1 cooperative living unit. On-campus housing is guaranteed for all 4 years. 98% of students live on campus; of those, 90% remain on campus on weekends. All students may keep cars.

Activities: There are no fraternities or sororities. There are 85 groups on campus, including art, band, chess, choir, chorale, chorus, computers, dance, debate, drama, ethnic, film, gay, international, jazz band, literary magazine, newspaper, opera, orchestra, photography, political, radio and TV, religious, social service, student government, and yearbook. Popular campus events include Founders Day, spring and fall formals, and All Parents Weekend.

Sports: There are 11 intercollegiate sports for men and 11 for women, and 11 intramural sports for men and 10 for women. Facilities include a field house with a swimming pool, 5 indoor tennis courts, a weight and conditioning room, a gym with squash and racquetball courts and basketball facilities, a 9-hole golf course, 13 outdoor tennis courts, an all-weather track, 2 soccer fields, a baseball diamond, a rugby field, and various club and intramural fields. An addition to the athletic facilities provides a competition basketball gym, a banked running track, and a 5000-square-foot exercise and fitness center.

Disabled Students: 40% of the campus is accessible. Wheelchair ramps, elevators, special parking, specially equipped rest rooms, lowered drinking fountains, signage in braille, and assisted listening devices are available. There is an Office of Disability and Support Services.

Services: Counseling and information services are available, as is tutoring in most subjects. There is a reader service for the blind and remedial math and writing.

Campus Safety and Security: Measures include 24-hour foot and vehicle patrol, escort service, informal discussions, and emergency telephones. There are lighted pathways/sidewalks.

Programs of Study: Vassar confers the A.B. degree. Master's degrees are also awarded. Bachelor's degrees are awarded in BIOLOGICAL SCIENCE (biochemistry and biology/biological science), COMMUNICATIONS AND THE ARTS (art, dramatic arts, English, film arts, fine arts, languages, and music), COMPUTER AND PHYSICAL SCIENCE (astronomy, chemistry, computer science, geology, mathematics, and physics), EDUCATION (foreign languages), ENGINEERING AND ENVIRONMENTAL DESIGN (environmental science and technology and public affairs), HEALTH PROFESSIONS (premedicine), SOCIAL SCIENCE (African studies, American studies, anthropology, Asian/Oriental studies, biopsychology, British studies, cognitive science, economics, geography, history, international studies, Judaic studies, Latin American studies, medieval studies, philosophy, political science/government, prelaw, psychology, religion, social studies, sociology, Spanish studies, urban studies, and women's studies). English, psychology, and political science are the largest.

Required: To graduate, students must have a total of 34 units equivalent to 120 credit hours, with a minimum GPA of 2.0. Of this total, no more than 17 units may be in a single field of concentration and 8 1/2 units must be outside the major field. Entering freshmen must take the freshman course. All students must meet the foreign language proficiency requirement and must take a quantitative skills course before their third year.

Special: The school offers fieldwork in social agencies and schools, a Washington semester, dual majors, independent majors, a 4-year advanced degree program in chemistry, cross-registration with the 12 College Consortium, and nonrecorded grade options. Study-abroad programs may be arranged in 7 countries. A 3-2 engineering degree with Dartmouth College is offered. There is a chapter of Phi Beta Kappa.

Faculty/Classroom: 54% of faculty are male; 46%, female. All both teach and do research. The average class size in an introductory lecture is 21; in a laboratory, 7; and in a regular course, 17.

Admissions: 34% of the 2001-2002 applicants were accepted. The SAT I scores for the 2001-2002 freshman class were: Verbal--7% between 500 and 599, 50% between 600 and 700, and 44% above 700; Math--13% between 500 and 599, 60% between 600 and 700, and 27% above 700. 88% of the current freshmen were in the top fifth of their class; 98% were in the top two fifths. 31 freshmen graduated first in their class.

Requirements: The SAT I and 3 SAT II: Subject tests, preferably 1 in writing, or the ACT, is required. In addition, graduation from an accredited secondary school or satisfactory scores on the GED are required for admission. The high school program should typically include 4 years of English, 3 or more years of a foreign language, 3 or 4 years of social studies, 3 or 4 years of math, and 2 or 3 years of science. An essay and a writing sample are required. AP credits are accepted. Important factors in the admissions decision are advanced placement or honor courses, recommendations by school officials, and leadership record. Applications are accepted on-line at the school's web site or via Common Application.

Procedure: Freshmen are admitted in the fall. Entrance exams should be taken as early as possible, but no later than December of the senior year. There are early decision and deferred admissions plans. Early decision applications should be filed by November 15; regular applications, by January 1 for fall entry, along with a $60 fee. Notification of early decision is sent December 15; regular decision, April 1. 251 early decision candidates were accepted for the 2001-2002 class. 10% of all applicants are on a waiting list; 2 were accepted in 2001.

Transfer: 30 transfer students enrolled in 2001-2002. Applicants must have at least 1 year of liberal arts course work with a minimum GPA of 3.2. 17 credits of 34 must be completed at Vassar.

Visiting: There are regularly scheduled orientations for prospective students, including a campus tour, an information session, and a class visit when possible. There are guides for informal visits and visitors may sit in on classes and stay overnight. To schedule a visit, contact the Admissions Office.

Financial Aid: In 2001-2002, 62% of all freshmen and 61% of continuing students received some form of financial aid. 53% of freshmen and 55% of continuing students received need-based aid. The average freshman award was $22,114. Of that total, scholarships or need-based grants averaged $18,786 ($30,414 maximum); loans averaged $1788 ($4125 maximum); and work contracts averaged $1540 (maximum). 61% of undergraduates work part time. Average annual earnings from campus work are $956. The average financial indebtedness of the 2001 graduate was $15,673. Vassar is a member of CSS. The CSS/Profile, FAFSA, or FFS and the college's own financial statement are required. The fall application deadline is February 10.

International Students: There are 104 international students enrolled. The school actively recruits these students. They must score 600 on the written TOEFL or 250 on the electronic version and also take the SAT I or the ACT. Students must take any 3 SAT II: Subject tests.

Computers: The mainframes are a DEC VAX 6200, an 11/780, an 11/750, and a MicroVAX II. There are also 350 Mac and IBM PCs available throughout the campus. All students may access the system 24 hours per day. There are no time limits and no fees.

Graduates: In 2001, 600 bachelor's degrees were awarded. The most popular majors were English (13%), psychology (11%), and political science (11%). In an average class, 1% graduate in 3 years, 78% in 4 years, 86% in 5 years, and 87% in 6 years. 14 companies recruited on campus in 2000-2001. Of the 2000 graduating class, 17% were enrolled in graduate school within 6 months of graduation and 71% were employed.

Admissions Contact: David Borus, Dean of Admission and Financial Aid. E-mail: *admissions@vassar.edu* Web: *www.vassar.edu*

WAGNER COLLEGE
Staten Island, NY 10301 — D-5
(718) 390-3411
(800) 221-1010; Fax: (718) 390-3105

Full-time: 625 men, 915 women	**Faculty:** 83; IIA, -$
Part-time: 25 men, 55 women	**Ph.D.s:** 85%
Graduate: 120 men, 265 women	**Student/Faculty:** 17 to 1
Year: semesters, summer session	**Tuition:** $20,500
Application Deadline: February 15	**Room & Board:** $6500
Freshman Class: n/av	
SAT I or ACT: required	**COMPETITIVE**

Wagner College, founded in 1883, is a private liberal arts institution. Figures in above capsule are approximate. In addition to regional accreditation, Wagner has baccalaureate program accreditation with NLN. The library contains 300,000 volumes and 225,000 microform items, and subscribes to 1000 periodicals. Computerized library services include interlibrary loans and database searching. Special learning facilities include an art gallery and planetarium. The 105-acre campus is in a suburban area 10 miles from Manhattan. Including residence halls, there are 18 buildings.

Student Life: 69% of undergraduates are from New York. Others are from 36 states and Canada. 63% are from public schools. 85% are white. 44% are Catholic; 36% claim no religious affiliation; 13% Protestant. The average age of freshmen is 18; all undergraduates, 20. 17% do not continue beyond their first year; 68% remain to graduate.

Housing: 1315 students can be accommodated in college housing, which includes coed dormitories, fraternity/sorority floors, and quiet floors in dorms. On-campus housing is guaranteed for all 4 years. 65% of students live on campus; of those, 75% remain on campus on weekends. Alcohol is not permitted. Upperclassmen may keep cars.

Activities: 20% of men belong to 4 local and 4 national fraternities; 20% of women belong to 1 local and 2 national sororities. There are 65 groups on campus, including art, band, cheerleading, chess, choir, chorale, computers, dance, drama, ethnic, gay, honors, international, jazz band, literary magazine, musical theater, newspaper, opera, pep band, political, professional, religious, social service, student government, symphony, and yearbook. Popular campus events include Songfest and Spring Fling Week.

Sports: There are 7 intercollegiate sports for men and 9 for women, and 4 intramural sports for men and 3 for women. Facilities include a football stadium, a gym, a fitness center, a track, and a basketball arena.

Disabled Students: 25% of the campus is accessible. Wheelchair ramps, elevators, special parking, specially equipped rest rooms, and special class scheduling are available.

Services: Counseling and information services are available, as is tutoring in every subject. There is a reader service for the blind, and remedial math, reading, and writing.

Campus Safety and Security: Measures include 24-hour foot and vehicle patrol, escort service, shuttle buses, and informal discussions. There are emergency telephones, lighted pathways/sidewalks, and ID card access into residence halls.

Programs of Study: Wagner confers B.A. and B.S. degrees. Master's degrees are also awarded. Bachelor's degrees are awarded in BIOLOGICAL SCIENCE (biology/biological science and microbiology), BUSINESS (accounting and business administration and management), COMMUNICATIONS AND THE ARTS (arts administration/management, dramatic arts, English, fine arts, and music), COMPUTER AND PHYSICAL SCIENCE (chemistry, computer science, mathematics, and physics), EDUCATION (elementary, middle school, and secondary), HEALTH PROFESSIONS (medical laboratory technology, nursing, and physician's assistant), SOCIAL SCIENCE (anthropology, gerontology, history, political science/government, psychology, public administration, social work, and sociology). Natural sciences is the strongest academically. Business is the largest.

Required: To graduate, students must complete 128 credit hours with 60 hours in the major and a minimum GPA of 2.0. All students must take courses in English, math, and multidisciplinary studies. In addition, students must fulfill distribution requirements in physical science, life science, math and computers, history, literature, philosophy and religion, foreign culture, aesthetics, and human behavior.

Special: Internships are required for business and English majors and are recommended for all majors. Students may earn B.A.-B.S. degrees in math, physics, and psychology. Student-designed and dual majors, credit for life experience, a Washington semester, nondegree study, and pass/fail options are available. Study abroad in 14 countries is possible. There are 9 national honor societies and a freshman honors program.

Faculty/Classroom: 42% of faculty are male; 58%, female. All teach undergraduates. No introductory courses are taught by graduate students. The average class size in an introductory lecture is 23; in a laboratory, 13; and in a regular course, 20.

Requirements: The SAT I or ACT is required. For SAT I, the recommended minimum scores are 510 verbal and 500 math. A composite score of 21 is recommended on the ACT. Graduation from an accredited secondary school is required, with 18 academic credits or Carnegie units, including 4 years of English, 3 years each of history and math, 2 years each of foreign language, science, and social studies, and 1 year each of art and music. An essay is required, and an interview is recommended. Auditions are required for music and theater applicants. Applications are accepted on computer disk. A GPA of 2.5 is required. AP and CLEP credits are accepted. Important factors in the admissions decision are advanced placement or honor courses, recommendations by school officials, and extracurricular activities record.

Procedure: Freshmen are admitted fall and spring. Entrance exams should be taken by December of the senior year. There are early decision, early admissions, and deferred admissions plans. Check with the school for current application deadlines and fees.

Transfer: Transfer students should have a minimum of 30 credit hours earned with a GPA of 2.5. Applicants must submit all college and high school transcripts, a letter of recommendation, and a personal statement. An interview is recommended. SAT I or ACT scores taken within the last 5 years may be submitted. 30 credits of 128 must be completed at Wagner.

Visiting: There are regularly scheduled orientations for prospective students, including a presentation by the Admissions Office, a tour of the campus, and meetings with faculty and staff. There are guides for informal visits and visitors may sit in on classes and stay overnight. To schedule a visit, contact the Admissions Office.

Financial Aid: In a recent year, 78% of all freshmen and 80% of continuing students received some form of financial aid. The average freshman award was $6200. Of that total, scholarships or need-based grants averaged $5500 ($11,000 maximum); loans averaged $3200 ($5000 maximum); and work contracts averaged $1000 ($1200 maximum). 25% of undergraduates work part time. Average annual earnings from campus work are $800. Wagner is a member of CSS. The FAFSA and the college's own financial statement are required. Check with the school for current deadlines.

International Students: The school actively recruits these students. They must score 550 on the written TOEFL and also take the college's own test.

Computers: The mainframe is a DEC VAX. 75 IBM PCs in the computer center are connected to the mainframe. An additional 52 IBM PCs are available for student use. Printers include 4 HP LaserJet, 2 Epson LQ dot-matrix, and 1 HP PaintJet. All students may access the system Monday through Thursday, 9 A.M. to 10 P.M.; Friday, 9 A.M. to 6 P.M.; and Saturday and Sunday, 11 A.M. to 5 P.M. There are no time limits and no fees. It is strongly recommended that all students have a personal computer.

Graduates: In an average class, 62% graduate in 4 years, and 7% in 5 years.

Admissions Contact: Angelo Araimo, Dean of Admissions. A video is available. E-mail: *admissions@wagner.edu* Web: *www.wagner.edu*

WEBB INSTITUTE D-5

Glen Cove, NY 11542 **(516) 671-2213; Fax: (516) 674-9838**

Full-time: 57 men, 16 women	**Faculty:** 8
Part-time: none	**Ph.D.s:** 50%
Graduate: none	**Student/Faculty:** 9 to 1
Year: semesters	**Tuition:** 0
Application Deadline: February 15	**Room & Board:** $6250
Freshman Class: 62 applied, 29 accepted, 22 enrolled	
SAT I Verbal/Math: 640/700	**MOST COMPETITIVE**

Webb Institute, founded in 1889, is a private engineering school devoted to professional knowledge of ship construction, design, and motive power. All students receive 4-year, full-tuition scholarships. In addition to regional accreditation, Webb has baccalaureate program accreditation with ABET. The library contains 50,598 volumes, 1633 microform items, and 1851 audiovisual forms/CDs, and subscribes to 267 periodicals. Computerized library services include the card catalog, interlibrary loans, and database searching. Special learning facilities include a marine engineering lab and a ship model testing/towing tank. The 26-acre campus is in a suburban area 24 miles east of New York City. Including residence halls, there are 11 buildings.

Student Life: 70% of undergraduates are from out of state, mostly the Northeast. Students are from 23 states and 2 foreign countries. 70% are from public schools. 98% are white. The average age of freshmen is 18; all undergraduates, 20. 4% do not continue beyond their first year; 73% remain to graduate.

Housing: 110 students can be accommodated in college housing, which includes single-sex dormitories. On-campus housing is guaranteed for all 4 years. All students live on campus; of those, 80% remain on campus on weekends. All students may keep cars.

Activities: There are no fraternities or sororities. There are some groups and organizations on campus, including chorale, orchestra, professional, social, student government, yachting, and yearbook. Popular campus events include Parents Day and Webbstock.

Sports: There are 6 intercollegiate sports for men and 6 for women, and 2 intramural sports for men and 2 for women. Facilities include a 60-seat gym, tennis courts, an athletic field, a boat house, and a beachfront dock.

Disabled Students: 90% of the campus is accessible. Elevators and special parking are available.

Services: Counseling and information services are available, as is tutoring in most subjects.

Campus Safety and Security: Measures include 24-hour foot and vehicle patrol, informal discussions, pamphlets/posters/films, and emergency telephones. There are lighted pathways/sidewalks and student and professional security services.

Programs of Study: Webb confers the B.S. degree. Bachelor's degrees are awarded in ENGINEERING AND ENVIRONMENTAL DESIGN (naval architecture and marine engineering).

Required: The curriculum is prescribed, with all students taking the same courses in each of the 4 years. The Webb program has 4 practical 8-week paid work periods: freshman year, a helper mechanic in a shipyard; sophomore year, a cadet in the engine room of a ship; and junior and senior years, a draftsman or junior engineer in a design office. All students must complete a senior seminar, thesis, and technical reports, as well as make engineering inspection visits. A total of 146 credits with a minimum passing grade of 70% is required to graduate.

Special: All students are employed 2 months each year through co-op programs.

Faculty/Classroom: All faculty are male. All teach undergraduates, and 40% also do research. The average class size in an introductory lecture is 25; in a laboratory, 9; and in a regular course, 25.

Admissions: 47% of the 2001-2002 applicants were accepted. The SAT I scores for the 2001-2002 freshman class were: Verbal--20% between 500 and 599, 45% between 600 and 700, and 35% above 700; Math--45% between 600 and 700, and 55% above 700. 94% of the current freshmen were in the top fifth of their class; all were in the top two fifths.

Requirements: The SAT I is required, with minimum SAT I scores of 500 verbal and 660 math. Applicants should be graduates of an accredited secondary school with 16 academic credits completed, including 4 each in English and math, 2 each in history and science, 1 in foreign language, and 3 in electives. 3 SAT II: Subject tests in writing, mathematics level I or II, and physics or chemistry are required, as is an interview. Candidates must be U.S. citizens. Webb requires applicants to be in the upper 20% of their class. A GPA of 3.2 is required. Important factors in the admissions decision are advanced placement or honor courses, evidence of special talent, and personality/intangible qualities.

Procedure: Freshmen are admitted in the fall. Entrance exams should be taken by January of the senior year. There is an early decision plan. Early decision applications should be filed by October 15; regular applications, by February 15 for fall entry, along with a $25 fee. Notification of early decision is sent December 10; regular decision, April 15. 4 early decision candidates were accepted for the 2001-2002 class.

Transfer: Transfers must enter as freshmen. A 3.2 GPA is required. SAT I scores and an interview are required. All 146 credits must be completed at Webb.

Visiting: There are regularly scheduled orientations for prospective students, including an open house one weekend each October. There are guides for informal visits and visitors may sit in on classes and stay overnight. To schedule a visit, contact the Director of Admissions.

Financial Aid: The aid reported here is to assist with room and board. In 2001-2002, 10% of all freshmen and 19% of continuing students received some form of financial aid. 5% of freshmen and 8% of continuing students received need-based aid. The average freshman award was $5125. Of that total, scholarships or need-based grants averaged $2100 ($3250 maximum). The average financial indebtedness of the 2001 graduate was $900. The CSS/Profile and the college's own financial statement are required. The fall application deadline is July 1.

Computers: There are 9 PCs available on campus. Access to the Internet and Web is available from labs and dorm rooms. All students are issued a laptop, which connects to the network for access to e-mail and the Internet. Students can connect to the network from dorm rooms, classrooms, labs, the library, and other public areas. All students may access the system 24 hours per day. There are no time limits and no fees.

Graduates: In 2001, 18 bachelor's degrees were awarded. In an average class, 88% graduate in 4 years. 9 companies recruited on campus in 2000-2001. Of the 2000 graduating class, 15% were enrolled in graduate school within 6 months of graduation and 85% were employed.

Admissions Contact: William G. Murray, Director of Admissions.
E-mail: *admissions@webb-institute.edu*
Web: *http://www.webb-institute.edu*

WELLS COLLEGE
Aurora, NY 13026

C-3
(315) 364-3264
(800) 952-9355; Fax: (315) 364-3227

Full-time: 7 men, 427 women	**Faculty:** 50; IIB, av$
Part-time: 21 women	**Ph.D.s:** 100%
Graduate: none	**Student/Faculty:** 9 to 1
Year: semesters	**Tuition:** $13,050
Application Deadline: March 1	**Room & Board:** $6300
Freshman Class: 417 applied, 369 accepted, 102 enrolled	
SAT I Verbal/Math: 580/540	**ACT:** 25 **VERY COMPETITIVE**

Wells College, founded in 1868, is a private liberal arts institution for women. The library contains 252,097 volumes, 13,925 microform items, and 924 audiovisual forms/CDs, and subscribes to 391 periodicals. Computerized library services include the card catalog, interlibrary loans, and database searching. Special learning facilities include an art gallery and the Book Arts Center. The 365-acre campus is in a small town on Cayuga Lake, 30 miles north of Ithaca. Including residence halls, there are 22 buildings.

Student Life: 73% of undergraduates are from New York. Others are from 30 states and 8 foreign countries. 90% are from public schools. 77% are white. The average age of freshmen is 18; all undergraduates, 20. 24% do not continue beyond their first year; 64% remain to graduate.

Housing: 500 students can be accommodated in college housing, which includes single-sex dormitories and off-campus apartments. There is housing for nontraditional-age students. On-campus housing is guaranteed for all 4 years. 84% of students live on campus; of those, 75% remain on campus on weekends. All students may keep cars.

Activities: There are no sororities. There are 39 groups on campus, including choir, chorale, dance, drama, ethnic, gay, international, literary magazine, newspaper, photography, political, professional, religious, social, social service, student government, and yearbook. Popular campus events include the Odd-Even Basketball Game, Spring Weekend, and 100 Days for Seniors.

Sports: Facilities include a competition-size swimming pool, a gym, a fully equipped fitness center, an athletic training room, 2 indoor tennis courts/practice space, a 9-hole golf course, 4 all-weather tennis courts, a platform tennis court, a boat house and dock with canoes and sailboats, and hiking trails.

Disabled Students: 51% of the campus is accessible. Wheelchair ramps, elevators, special parking, specially equipped rest rooms, special class scheduling, lowered drinking fountains, lowered telephones, and a fully compliant residence hall are available.

Services: Counseling and information services are available, as is tutoring in every subject. Assistance is provided on an individual, as-needed basis. Untimed and extended-time testing options are available.

Campus Safety and Security: Measures include 24-hour foot and vehicle patrol, self-defense education, escort service, and shuttle buses. There are informal discussions, pamphlets/posters/films, emergency telephones, and lighted pathways/sidewalks. All students must escort their guests on campus at all times.

Programs of Study: Wells confers the B.A. degree. Bachelor's degrees are awarded in BIOLOGICAL SCIENCE (biochemistry, biology/biological science, and molecular biology), BUSINESS (business administration and management), COMMUNICATIONS AND THE ARTS (dance, dramatic arts, English, fine arts, French, German, language arts, music, Spanish, and visual and performing arts), COMPUTER AND PHYSICAL SCIENCE (chemistry, computer science, mathematics, and physics), EDUCATION (elementary), ENGINEERING AND ENVIRONMENTAL DESIGN (environmental science), SOCIAL SCIENCE (American studies, anthropology, economics, ethics, politics, and social policy, history, international studies, philosophy, political science/government, psychology, public affairs, religion, sociology, and women's studies). Psychology, English, and mathematical and physical sciences are the largest.

Required: To graduate, students must complete a total of 120 credit hours, including 33 to 63 in the major, with a minimum GPA of 2.0 overall and in the major. All students must complete 2 First-Year Experience courses, a comprehensive exam, and a senior project/thesis. Distribution requirements include 4 courses in phys ed and wellness, 3 in natural and social sciences, 3 in arts and humanities, 2 in a foreign language, and 1 in formal reasoning.

Special: Wells offers cross-registration with Cornell University, Cayuga Community College, and Ithaca College, a Washington semester with American University, internships, and accelerated degree programs in all majors. Study abroad in 13 countries is permitted. A 3-2 engineering degree is available with Washington University in St. Louis and Columbia, Clarkson, Case Western Reserve, and Cornell Universities. Students may also earn 3-2 degrees in business and community health with the University of Rochester and a 3-4 degree in veterinary medicine with Cornell University. Student-designed majors and pass-fail options are available. Work-study, B.A.-B.S. degrees, and dual majors are also possible. There are 2 national honor societies, including Phi Beta Kappa.

Faculty/Classroom: 39% of faculty are male; 61%, female. All teach undergraduates. The average class size in an introductory lecture is 22; in a laboratory, 15; and in a regular course, 13.

Admissions: 88% of the 2001-2002 applicants were accepted. The SAT I scores for the 2001-2002 freshman class were: Verbal--15% below 500, 49% between 500 and 599, 31% between 600 and 700, and 5% above 700; Math--27% below 500, 50% between 500 and 599, and 23% between 600 and 700. The ACT scores were 17% below 21, 23% between 21 and 23, 23% between 24 and 26, 27% between 27 and 28, and 10% above 28. 53% of the current freshmen were in the top fifth of their class; 83% were in the top two fifths. 1 freshman graduated first in the class.

Requirements: The SAT I or ACT is required. In addition, graduation from an accredited secondary school should include 20 academic credits or Carnegie units. High school courses must include 4 years of English, 3 each of a foreign language and math, and 2 each of history and lab science. 2 teacher recommendations and an essay/personal statement are required, and an interview is strongly recommended. AP and CLEP credits are accepted. Important factors in the admissions decision are advanced placement or honor courses, recommendations by school officials, and extracurricular activities record. Applications are accepted on-line via Common App, *embark.com*, and the college's web site.

Procedure: Freshmen are admitted in the fall. Entrance exams should be taken prior to application. There are early decision, early admissions, and deferred admissions plans. Early decision applications should be filed by December 15; regular applications, by March 1 for fall entry, along with a $40 fee. Notification of early decision is sent January 15; regular decision, April 1. 22 early decision candidates were accepted for the 2001-2002 class.

Transfer: 46 transfer students enrolled in 2001-2002. Applicants must be in good standing at the institution last attended. A minimum GPA of 2.0 is required. Wells requires official college and high school transcripts, a personal statement, standardized test scores, and a recommendation from a professor. An interview is strongly recommended. 60 credits of 120 must be completed at Wells.

Visiting: There are regularly scheduled orientations for prospective students, including tours, interviews, class attendance, presentations, open houses, and an overnight hostess program. There are guides for informal visits and visitors may sit in on classes and stay overnight. To schedule a visit, contact the Admissions Office.

Financial Aid: In 2001-2002, 87% of all freshmen and 89% of continuing students received some form of financial aid. 80% of freshmen and 76% of continuing students received need-based aid. The average freshman award was $13,682. Of that total, scholarships or need-based grants averaged $10,297 ($13,500 maximum); loans averaged $3075 ($4125 maximum); and work contracts averaged $1200 (maximum). 90% of undergraduates work part time. Average annual earnings from campus work are $1200. The average financial indebtedness of the 2001 graduate was $17,125. Wells is a member of CSS. The FAFSA is required; early decision applicants must submit the CSS/Profile. The fall application deadline is May 1.

International Students: There are 11 international students enrolled. The school actively recruits these students. They must score 550 on the written TOEFL or 213 on the electronic version.

Computers: The mainframe is an IBM AS/400 Model 720. There are 31 Macs (Power Macs and G3s) and 61 Pentium-level PCs available in academic buildings and residence halls. The computer-to-student ratio is 4 to 1. Students have access to the Internet and the World Wide Web. Access to the Internet is available in every dorm room. All students may access the system. There are no time limits and no fees.

Graduates: In 2001, 94 bachelor's degrees were awarded. The most popular majors were psychology (25%), sociology/anthropology (11%), and visual arts (9%). In an average class, 2% graduate in 3 years, 60% in 4 years, 62% in 5 years, and 64% in 6 years. Of the 2000 graduating class, 15% were enrolled in graduate school within 6 months of graduation and 26% were employed.

Admissions Contact: Susan Sloan, Director of Admissions.
E-mail: *admissions@wells.edu* Web: *www.wells.edu*

YESHIVA UNIVERSITY D-5

New York, NY 10033-3201 (212) 960-5277; Fax: (212) 960-0086

Full-time: 1280 men, 970 women	**Faculty:** 120
Part-time: 40 men, 20 women	**Ph.D.s:** 79%
Graduate: 1330 men, 1690 women	**Student/Faculty:** 19 to 1
Year: semesters, summer session	**Tuition:** $14,600
Application Deadline: see profile	**Room & Board:** $6800
Freshman Class: n/av	
SAT I or ACT: required	**COMPETITIVE**

Yeshiva University, founded in 1886, is an independent liberal arts institution offering undergraduate programs through Yeshiva College, its undergraduate college for men; Stern College for Women; and Sy Syms School of Business. Information in the above capsule, and in this profile, is approximate. There are 7 graduate schools. In addition to regional accreditation, YU has baccalaureate program accreditation with CSWE. The 7 libraries contain 900,000 volumes, 759,000 microform items, and 980 audiovisual forms/CDs, and subscribe to 7790 periodicals. Computerized library services include the card catalog, interlibrary loans, and database searching. Special learning facilities include an art gallery, radio station, and museum. The 26-acre campus is in an urban area.

Student Life: 48% of undergraduates are from New York. Others are from 31 states, 16 foreign countries, and Canada. 14% are from public schools. The average age of freshmen is 17; all undergraduates, 19. 8% do not continue beyond their first year; 90% remain to graduate.

Housing: Approximately 1600 students can be accommodated in college housing, which includes single-sex dormitories and off-campus apartments. On-campus housing is guaranteed for all 4 years. 85% of students live on campus. Alcohol is not permitted. All students may keep cars.

Activities: There are no fraternities or sororities. There are 70 groups on campus, including art, choir, computers, drama, honors, international, jazz band, literary magazine, musical theater, newspaper, political, professional, religious, social service, student government, and yearbook. Popular campus events include holiday and dramatic presentations and Parents Day.

Sports: There are 8 intercollegiate sports for men and 2 for women, and 5 intramural sports for men and 4 for women. The athletic center at Yeshiva College houses a variety of facilities, including a 1000-seat gym.

Disabled Students: 95% of the campus is accessible. Wheelchair ramps and elevators are available.

Services: There is remedial reading and writing. There is also a writing center, which helps students with composition and verbal skills.

Campus Safety and Security: Measures include 24-hour foot and vehicle patrol, escort service, shuttle buses, and informal discussions. There are pamphlets/posters/films, lighted pathways/sidewalks, ID cards, vulnerability surveys, fire drills, alarm systems, emergency telephone numbers, and transportation for routine and special events.

Programs of Study: YU confers B.A. and B.S. degrees. Associate degrees are also awarded. Bachelor's degrees are awarded in BIOLOGICAL SCIENCE (biology/biological science), BUSINESS (accounting, business administration and management, and marketing/retailing/merchandising), COMMUNICATIONS AND THE ARTS (classical languages, communications, English, French, Hebrew, music, and speech/debate/rhetoric), COMPUTER AND PHYSICAL SCIENCE (chemistry, computer science, and mathematics), ENGINEERING AND ENVIRONMENTAL DESIGN (preengineering), HEALTH PROFESSIONS (health science), SOCIAL SCIENCE (economics, history, philosophy, political science/government, psychology, religion, and sociology). The dual program of liberal arts and Jewish studies are the strongest academically. Accounting, psychology, and economics are the largest.

Required: To graduate, students must complete a total of 128 credit hours. Under the dual program, students pursue a liberal arts or business curriculum together with courses in Hebrew language, literature, and culture. Courses in Jewish learning are geared to the student's level of preparation.

Special: YU offers a 3-2 degree in occupational therapy with Columbia and New York Universities; a 3-4 degree in podiatry with the New York College of Podiatric Medicine; and a 3-2 or 4-2 degree in engineering with Columbia University. Stern College students may take courses in advertising, photography, and design at the Fashion Institute of Technology. Study abroad programs may be arranged in Israel. The school offers independent study options and an optional pass/no credit system. There are 9 national honor societies, and 20 departmental honors programs.

Faculty/Classroom: 73% of faculty are male; 27%, female. 58% teach undergraduates, 60% do research, and 28% do both. No introductory courses are taught by graduate students. The average class size in an introductory lecture is 38; in a laboratory, 15; and in a regular course, 18.

Requirements: The SAT I or ACT is required. In addition, graduation from an accredited secondary school with 16 academic credits is required for admission. The GED is accepted under limited and specific circumstances. The SAT II: Subject test in Hebrew is recommended for placement purposes. An interview and an essay are required. A GPA of 3.3 is required. AP and CLEP credits are accepted. Important factors in the admissions decision are extracurricular activities record, personality/intangible qualities, and evidence of special talent.

Procedure: Freshmen are admitted to all sessions. There are early admissions and deferred admissions plans. Notification is sent on a rolling basis. A waiting list is an active part of the admissions procedure. Check with the school for current deadlines and fee.

Transfer: 95 credits of 128 must be completed at YU.

Visiting: There are regularly scheduled orientations for prospective students and YU holds open houses for high school students. There are guides for informal visits and visitors may sit in on classes and stay overnight. To schedule a visit, contact the Office of Admissions.

Financial Aid: YU is a member of CSS. The CSS/Profile and the college's own financial statement are required. Check with the school for current deadlines.

International Students: The school actively recruits these students. They must score 500 on the written TOEFL and also take the SAT I or the ACT. Contact the school for further information.

Computers: The mainframe is an IBM RS/6000. There are more than 200 networked and stand-alone PCs and workstations at 4 academic centers, with additional facilities at university libraries. All students may access the system 24 hours per day via modem or when buildings are open. There are no time limits and no fees.

Admissions Contact: Michael Kranzler, Director of Undergraduate Admissions. A video is available. E-mail: *yuadmit@ymail.yu.edu*
Web: *www.yu.edu*

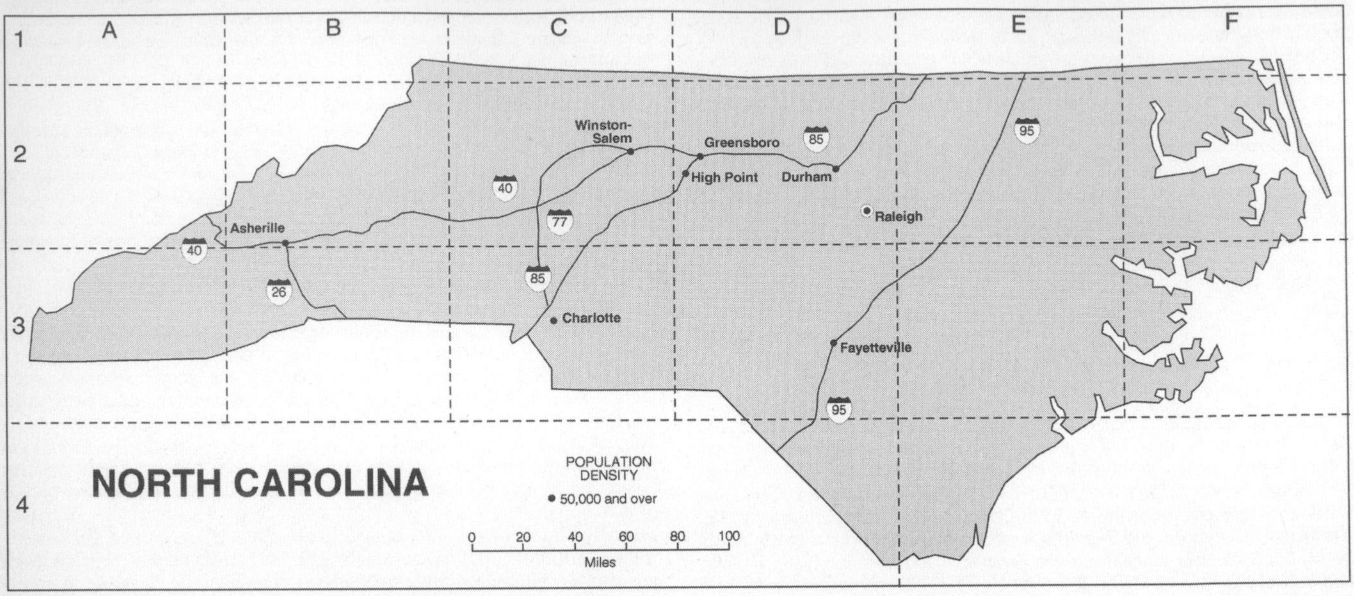

APPALACHIAN STATE UNIVERSITY B-2

Boone, NC 28608 **(828) 262-2120; Fax: (828) 262-3296**

Full-time: 5641 men, 5702 women	**Faculty:** IIA, av$
Part-time: 478 men, 739 women	**Ph.D.s:** n/av
Graduate: 343 men, 859 women	**Student/Faculty:** n/av
Year: semesters, summer session	**Tuition:** $2308 ($10,230)
Application Deadline: open	**Room & Board:** $4045
Freshman Class: 8853 applied, 5770 accepted, 2312 enrolled	
SAT I Math: 548/553	**COMPETITIVE**

Appalachian State University, founded in 1899 and a member of the University of North Carolina system, is a comprehensive university offering undergraduate programs in the arts and sciences, business, teacher education, fine and applied arts, and music. There are 5 undergraduate schools and 1 graduate school. In addition to regional accreditation, App State has baccalaureate program accreditation with AACSB, AAFCS, ADA, ASLA, ASLHA, CAAHEP, CSAB, CSWE, NASAD, NASM, NCATE, NRPA, and SACS-CC. The 2 libraries contain 799,798 volumes, 1,447,300 microform items, and 36,228 audiovisual forms/CDs, and subscribe to 4998 periodicals. Computerized library services include the card catalog, interlibrary loans, and database searching. Special learning facilities include a learning resource center, art gallery, radio station, TV station, an Appalachian cultural center, and a dark sky observatory. The 1100-acre campus is in a rural area in northwest North Carolina. Including residence halls, there are 59 buildings.

Student Life: 88% of undergraduates are from North Carolina. Others are from 38 states, 62 foreign countries, and Canada. 97% are from public schools. 94% are white. The average age of freshmen is 19; all undergraduates, 21. 17% do not continue beyond their first year; 65% remain to graduate.

Housing: 4876 students can be accommodated in college housing, which includes single-sex and coed dormitories, on-campus apartments, and married-student housing. In addition, there is international student housing. On-campus housing is guaranteed for the freshman year only and is available on a lottery system for upperclassmen. 62% of students commute. Alcohol is not permitted. All students may keep cars.

Activities: 5% of men belong to 15 national fraternities; 5% of women belong to 9 national sororities. There are 213 groups on campus, including art, band, cheerleading, chess, choir, chorale, chorus, computers, dance, debate, drama, drill team, ethnic, film, forensics, gay, honors, international, jazz band, literary magazine, marching band, musical theater, opera, orchestra, pep band, photography, political, professional, radio and TV, religious, social, social service, student government, symphony, and yearbook. Popular campus events include Appalachian Summer, fall and spring open houses, and multicultural student weekend.

Sports: There are 11 intercollegiate sports for men and 11 for women, and 43 intramural sports for men and 43 for women. Facilities include a 9000-seat convocation center, a 7000-seat varsity gym, an 18,000-seat stadium, an athletic center, facilities for football, soccer, field hockey, basketball, volleyball, wrestling, indoor and outdoor track, golf, baseball, and tennis, a 2000-seat auditorium, and a fitness center.

Disabled Students: 98% of the campus is accessible. Wheelchair ramps, elevators, special parking, specially equipped rest rooms, special class scheduling, lowered drinking fountains, and lowered telephones are available.

Services: Counseling and information services are available, as is tutoring in most subjects. There is a reader service for the blind, and remedial math, reading, and writing.

Campus Safety and Security: Measures include 24-hour foot and vehicle patrol, self-defense education, escort service, and shuttle buses. There are informal discussions, pamphlets/posters/films, emergency telephones, lighted pathways/sidewalks, and bicycle patrol.

Programs of Study: App State confers B.A., B.S., B.F.A., B.M., B.S.B.A., B.S.C.J., and B.S.W. degrees. Master's and doctoral degrees are also awarded. Bachelor's degrees are awarded in BIOLOGICAL SCIENCE (biology/biological science, ecology, and nutrition), BUSINESS (accounting, banking and finance, hospitality management services, insurance and risk management, marketing/retailing/merchandising, and recreational facilities management), COMMUNICATIONS AND THE ARTS (advertising, art, arts administration/management, communications, dramatic arts, English, French, graphic design, journalism, multimedia, music business management, music performance, public relations, Spanish, and studio art), COMPUTER AND PHYSICAL SCIENCE (chemistry, computer science, geology, information sciences and systems, mathematics, physics, and statistics), EDUCATION (art, business, drama, early childhood, elementary, foreign languages, health, industrial arts, middle school, music, physical, science, secondary, social science, and special), ENGINEERING AND ENVIRONMENTAL DESIGN (construction technology, drafting and design, electrical/electronics engineering technology, environmental science, graphic arts technology, industrial engineering technology, and interior design), HEALTH PROFESSIONS (clinical science, exercise science, health care administration, health science, and music therapy), SOCIAL SCIENCE (anthropology, child psychology/development, clothing and textiles management/production/services, criminal justice, economics, family/consumer studies, geography, history, interdisciplinary studies, philosophy, political science/government, psychology, religion, social work, and sociology). Elementary education, management, and information systems are the largest.

Required: To graduate, students must complete 122 credit hours for most programs, including 60 in the major, with a minimum 2.0 GPA. General education requirements include courses in math, science, history, phys ed, English, social sciences, and humanities.

Special: App State offers co-op programs in clinical lab sciences; cross-registration with Auburn University, Wake Forest University, and the University of North Carolina-Greensboro; internships, work-study programs; B.A.-B.S. degrees; and dual majors. Student-designed majors are possible in some programs, and a 3-2 enfineering degree is possible with Clemson and Auburn Universities. There are 30 national honor societies, a freshman honors program, and 15 departmental honors programs.

Faculty/Classroom: All both teach and do research. Graduate students teach 1% of introductory courses. The average class size in an introductory lecture is 26; in a laboratory, 19; and in a regular course, 20.
Admissions: 65% of the 2001-2002 applicants were accepted. The SAT I scores for the 2001-2002 freshman class were: Verbal--25% below 500, 51% between 500 and 599, 22% between 600 and 700, and 3% above 700; Math--20% below 500, 53% between 500 and 599, 24% between 600 and 700, and 2% above 700. 35% of the current freshmen were in the top fifth of their class; 74% were in the top two fifths. 1 freshman graduated first in their class.
Requirements: The SAT I or ACT is required. In addition, applicants must be graduates of an accredited secondary school; the GED is also accepted. They must have completed 4 course units in high school English, 3 in math and science, and 2 in social studies. AP and CLEP credits are accepted. Important factors in the admissions decision are advanced placement or honor courses, extracurricular activities record, and evidence of special talent.
Procedure: Freshmen are admitted to all sessions. Entrance exams should be taken by November, if possible. Application deadlines are open. The fall 2001 application fee was $45. Notification is sent on a monthly basis, beginning October 15. 8% of all applicants are on a waiting list.
Transfer: 854 transfer students enrolled in 2001-2002. Transfer students must have earned a minimum 2.0 GPA on collegiate work. Those students who have accumulated less than 30 semester credits, or 45 quarter hours, must also meet freshman requirements. 30 credits of 122 must be completed at App State.
Visiting: There are regularly scheduled orientations for prospective students, beginning in July for all new students. There are guides for informal visits and visitors may sit in on classes. To schedule a visit, contact the Visitors Center at (704) 262-2179.
Financial Aid: In 2001-2002, 26% of all freshmen received some form of financial aid. 16% of freshmen received need-based aid. The average freshman award was $4378. The FAFSA is required. The fall application deadline is March 15.
International Students: There are 192 international students enrolled. The school actively recruits these students. They must score 500 on the written TOEFL. The SAT I may be accepted in lieu of the TOEFL.
Computers: The mainframes are clustered VAX machines, a DEC VAX 8550, 8650, Alpha, and a 6310, and an IBM 9370. There are more than 500 PCs in classroom buildings and residence halls. All students may access the system. There are no time limits and no fees.
Graduates: In 2001, 2071 bachelor's degrees were awarded. The most popular majors were business (20%), elementary education (18%), and communications (8%). In an average class, 1% graduate in 3 years, 34% in 4 years, 59% in 5 years, and 62% in 6 years. 300 companies recruited on campus in 2000-2001.
Admissions Contact: Paul Hiatt, Director of Admissions.
E-mail: *admissions@appstate.edu* Web: *appstate.edu*

BARBER-SCOTIA COLLEGE
Concord, NC 28025 — C-3
(704) 789-2903
(800) 610-0778; Fax: (704) 789-2958

Full-time: 281 men, 273 women	**Faculty:** 23; IIB, --$
Part-time: 8 men, 4 women	**Ph.D.s:** 57%
Graduate: none	**Student/Faculty:** 24 to 1
Year: semesters	**Tuition:** $9148
Application Deadline: open	**Room & Board:** $3952
Freshman Class: 1003 applied, 690 accepted, 143 enrolled	
SAT I Verbal/Math: recommended	**COMPETITIVE**

Barber-Scotia College, founded in 1867, is a liberal arts institution affiliated with the Presbyterian Church (U.S.A.) In addition to regional accreditation, Barber-Scotia has baccalaureate program accreditation with NCATE. The library contains 37,000 volumes and 60,000 microform items, and subscribes to 170 periodicals. Computerized library services include interlibrary loans and database searching. Special learning facilities include a learning resource center. The 40-acre campus is in a suburban area 20 miles from Charlotte. Including residence halls, there are 24 buildings.
Student Life: 68% of undergraduates are from North Carolina. Others are from 18 states and Canada. 98% are from public schools. 97% are African American. Most are Protestant. The average age of freshmen is 19; all undergraduates, 22. 30% do not continue beyond their first year; 48% remain to graduate.
Housing: 650 students can be accommodated in college housing, which includes single-sex dormitories and off-campus apartments. On-campus housing is guaranteed for the freshman year only and is available on a first-come, first-served basis. 65% of students live on campus; of those, 85% remain on campus on weekends. Alcohol is not permitted. Upperclassmen may keep cars.
Activities: 25% of men belong to 4 national fraternities; 35% of women belong to 4 national sororities. There are many groups and organizations on campus, including cheerleading, chess, choir, computers, debate, honors, international, newspaper, pep band, political, professional, radio and TV, religious, science, social, social service, student government, and yearbook. Popular campus events include Candlelighting Service, Spring Formal, and Fall Convocation.
Sports: There are 3 intercollegiate sports for men and 5 for women, and 9 intramural sports for men and 8 for women. Facilities include a gym, a tennis court, and an athletic field.
Disabled Students: 50% of the campus is accessible. Wheelchair ramps are available.
Services: Counseling and information services are available, as is tutoring in most subjects. There is remedial math, reading, and writing.
Campus Safety and Security: Measures include 24-hour foot and vehicle patrol, informal discussions, pamphlets/posters/films, and lighted pathways/sidewalks.
Programs of Study: Barber-Scotia confers B.A. and B.S. degrees. Bachelor's degrees are awarded in BIOLOGICAL SCIENCE (biology/biological science), BUSINESS (business administration and management and recreational facilities management), COMMUNICATIONS AND THE ARTS (communications and English), COMPUTER AND PHYSICAL SCIENCE (mathematics), EDUCATION (early childhood), SOCIAL SCIENCE (criminology, political science/government, and sociology). Education and biology are the strongest academically. Sociology, political science, and business are the largest.
Required: To graduate, students must complete 125 credit hours, 36 in the major, with a 55-hour general education requirement that includes religion, English, phys ed, computer science, and 6 other areas. A 2.0 minimum GPA, 2 years of foreign language, a senior seminar, and comprehensive exams are required.
Special: The college offers cross-registration with the Charlotte Area Consortium. There are 2 national honor societies.
Faculty/Classroom: 76% of faculty are male; 24%, female. All teach undergraduates. The average class size in an introductory lecture is 20; in a laboratory, 20; and in a regular course, 15.
Admissions: 69% of the 2001-2002 applicants were accepted. 36% of the current freshmen were in the top fifth of their class; 66% were in the top two fifths.
Requirements: The SAT I or ACT is recommended. AP and CLEP credits are accepted.
Procedure: Freshmen are admitted fall and spring. There is a deferred admissions plan. Application deadlines are open. The fall 2001 application fee was $15. Notification is sent on a rolling basis.
Transfer: Applicants for transfer should have a 2.0 GPA. 30 credits of 125 must be completed at Barber-Scotia.
Visiting: There are guides for informal visits and visitors may sit in on classes and stay overnight. To schedule a visit, contact the Admissions Office at (704) 789-2902.
Financial Aid: The CSS/Profile, FAFSA, FFS, or SFS is required. The fall application deadline is June 30.
Computers: The mainframe is an IBM AS400. Students may use networked labs. All students may access the system 8:30 A.M. to 5 P.M. There are no time limits and no fees.
Admissions Contact: Director of Admissions.

BARTON COLLEGE
Wilson, NC 27893 — E-2
(252) 399-6317
(800) 345-4973; Fax: (252) 399-6572

Full-time: 320 men, 640 women	**Faculty:** 77; IIB, --$
Part-time: 57 men, 212 women	**Ph.D.s:** 73%
Graduate: none	**Student/Faculty:** 13 to 1
Year: 4-1-4, summer session	**Tuition:** $12,264
Application Deadline: open	**Room & Board:** $4570
Freshman Class: 919 applied, 799 accepted, 187 enrolled	
SAT I Verbal/Math: 460/460	**LESS COMPETITIVE**

Barton College, founded in 1902, is a private nonprofit liberal arts college affiliated with the Christian Church (Disciples of Christ). There are 5 undergraduate schools. In addition to regional accreditation, Barton has baccalaureate program accreditation with CED, CSWE, NCATE, and NLN. The library contains 170,282 volumes, 285,772 microform items, and 2813 audiovisual forms/CDs, and subscribes to 453 periodicals. Computerized library services include the card catalog, interlibrary loans, and database searching. Special learning facilities include a learning resource center, TV station, TV studio, writing center, and academic enrichment center. The 62-acre campus is in a suburban area 40 miles east of Raleigh. Including residence halls, there are 23 buildings.
Student Life: 81% of undergraduates are from North Carolina. Others are from 29 states, 16 foreign countries, and Canada. 80% are from public schools. 78% are white; 19% African American. 54% are Protestant; 21% Greek Orthodox, Hindu, Islam, Muslim, and Ukranian Orthodox; 13% claim no religious affiliation; 11% Catholic. The average age of freshmen is 18; all undergraduates, 19. 41% do not continue beyond their first year; 42% remain to graduate.
Housing: 610 students can be accommodated in college housing, which includes single-sex and coed dormitories. On-campus housing is

guaranteed for the freshman year only and is available on a first-come, first-served basis. 60% of students commute. Alcohol is not permitted. All students may keep cars.

Activities: 6% of men belong to 4 national fraternities; 9% of women belong to 3 national sororities. There are 40 groups on campus, including art, band, cheerleading, choir, chorus, computers, drama, ethnic, film, honors, international, jazz band, literary magazine, orchestra, pep band, photography, political, professional, radio and TV, religious, social, social service, student government, symphony, and yearbook. Popular campus events include Pre-exam Jam, Lighting of the Luminaries Christmas Celebration, and Global Focus.

Sports: There are 6 intercollegiate sports for men and 6 for women, and 7 intramural sports for men and 7 for women. Facilities include a gym, a tennis complex, baseball, softball, and soccer fields, community parks for intramural activities, and an indoor pool and track.

Disabled Students: 90% of the campus is accessible. Wheelchair ramps, elevators, special parking, specially equipped rest rooms, special class scheduling, and lowered drinking fountains are available.

Services: Counseling and information services are available, as is tutoring in most subjects. There is a reader service for the blind, interpreting in class for hearing-impaired students upon request, and note takers in class for certain circumstances.

Campus Safety and Security: Measures include 24-hour foot and vehicle patrol, escort service, informal discussions, and pamphlets/posters/films. There are emergency telephones, lighted pathways/sidewalks, campuswide surveillance cameras, and peephole doors to residence rooms.

Programs of Study: Barton confers B.A., B.S., B.F.A., B.S.N., and B.S.W. degrees. Master's degrees are also awarded. Bachelor's degrees are awarded in AGRICULTURE (environmental studies), BIOLOGICAL SCIENCE (biology/biological science), BUSINESS (accounting, business administration and management, human resources, and sports management), COMMUNICATIONS AND THE ARTS (ceramic art and design, communications, dramatic arts, English, graphic design, musical theater, painting, photography, studio art, and theater management), COMPUTER AND PHYSICAL SCIENCE (chemistry, information sciences and systems, and mathematics), EDUCATION (art, athletic training, education of the deaf and hearing impaired, elementary, middle school, music, physical, science, and specific learning disabilities), ENGINEERING AND ENVIRONMENTAL DESIGN (environmental science), HEALTH PROFESSIONS (medical laboratory technology, nursing, and sports medicine), SOCIAL SCIENCE (criminal justice, history, political science/government, psychology, religion, social studies, social work, and Spanish studies). Nursing and education of the deaf and hearing impaired are the strongest academically. Business, nursing, and education are the largest.

Required: All students must complete a minimum of 126 credit hours, including 36 in the major, with a minimum GPA of 2.0. Core requirements include 12 semester hours in humanities and fine arts, 6 to 9 in global and cross-cultural perspective, 7 in natural sciences and math, 6 each in social sciences, and writing proficiency, 3 each in computational and computer proficiency, 2 in sports science, and 2 in freshman and junior seminars.

Special: Barton offers internships, a Washington semester, a general studies degree, dual majors, and credit by exam in entry-level courses. Preprofessional programs are offered in engineering and a variety of health-related fields, as are 3-2 engineering degrees with North Carolina State and North Carolina Agricultural and Technical State Universities and the University of North Carolina at Charlotte. There are 5 national honor societies and a freshman honors program.

Faculty/Classroom: 46% of faculty are male; 54%, female. All teach undergraduates. The average class size in an introductory lecture is 30; in a laboratory, 20; and in a regular course, 20.

Admissions: 87% of the 2001-2002 applicants were accepted. The SAT I scores for the 2001-2002 freshman class were: Verbal--73% below 500, 26% between 500 and 599, and 2% between 600 and 700; Math--69% below 500, 28% between 500 and 599, and 3% between 600 and 700. 19% of the current freshmen were in the top fifth of their class; 40% were in the top two fifths. 2 freshmen graduated first in their class in a recent year.

Requirements: The SAT I or ACT is required. In addition, applicants must be high school graduates with at least 12 college preparatory credits. Barton recommends 4 unities of English, 3 of social science, 2 of math (including algebra), and 2 of natural science (including lab science). A foreign language is encouraged. Barton requires applicants to be in the upper 50% of their class. A GPA of 2.0 is required. AP and CLEP credits are accepted. Important factors in the admissions decision are advanced placement or honor courses, evidence of special talent, and leadership record. Applications are accepted on-line at the school's web site and at *www.xap.com*

Procedure: Freshmen are admitted to all sessions. Entrance exams should be taken in the spring of the junior year and fall of the senior year. Application deadlines are open. The application fee is $25. Notification is sent on a rolling basis.

Transfer: 78 transfer students enrolled in 2001-2002. Applicants must have a college GPA of 2.0 and be eligible to return to the school they last attended. 45 credits of 126 must be completed at Barton.

Visiting: There are regularly scheduled orientations for prospective students, including visiting classes, financial aid and freshman advising workshops, tours of the campus, and meetings with administrators, faculty, and students. There are guides for informal visits and visitors may sit in on classes and stay overnight. To schedule a visit, contact the Admissions Office.

Financial Aid: In 2001-2002, 98% of all freshmen and 94% of continuing students received some form of financial aid. 53% of freshmen and 40% of continuing students received need-based aid. The average freshman award was $10,524. Of that total, scholarships or need-based grants averaged $2452 ($11,914 maximum); loans averaged $4125 ($16,625 maximum); work contracts averaged $510 ($1200 maximum); and merit grant/nonneed and athletic scholarships averaged $3436 ($16,592 maximum). 58% of undergraduates work part time. Average annual earnings from campus work are $1000. The average financial indebtedness of the 2001 graduate was $11,500. The FAFSA is required. The fall application deadline is June 1.

International Students: There are 26 international students enrolled. The school actively recruits these students. They must score 525 on the written TOEFL or 195 on the electronic version.

Computers: The mainframe is an IBM AS/400. PCs are available in computer labs in major buildings for student use. All residence hall rooms are wired for connection to the campus network. All students may access the system 24 hours a day, 7 days a week. There are no time limits and no fees.

Graduates: In 2001, 237 bachelor's degrees were awarded. The most popular majors were nursing (18%), business management (14%), and accounting (9%). In an average class, 29% graduate in 4 years, 40% in 5 years, and 42% in 6 years. 121 companies recruited on campus in a recent year. Of the 2000 graduating class, 4% were enrolled in graduate school within 6 months of graduation.

Admissions Contact: Amy Denton or Amanda Humphrey, Directors of In-State and Out-of-State Admissions. E-mail: *enroll@barton.edu*
Web: *www/barton/edu*

BELMONT ABBEY COLLEGE — C-3
Belmont, NC 28012 — **(704) 825-6665**
(888) BAC-0110; Fax: (704) 825-6670

Full-time: 500 men, 420 women	**Faculty:** 40; IIB, --$
Part-time: 35 men, 100 women	**Ph.D.s:** 83%
Graduate: none	**Student/Faculty:** 23 to 1
Year: semesters, summer session	**Tuition:** $13,350
Application Deadline: open	**Room & Board:** $6280
Freshman Class: n/av	
SAT I or ACT: required	**LESS COMPETITIVE**

Belmont Abbey College, founded in 1876, is a private, nonprofit liberal arts college affiliated with the Roman Catholic Church. Figures in above capsule are approximate. In addition to regional accreditation, Belmont Abbey has baccalaureate program accreditation with NCATE. The library contains 110,050 volumes, 59,000 microform items, and 2042 audiovisual forms/CDs, and subscribes to 609 periodicals. Computerized library services include the card catalog, interlibrary loans, and database searching. Special learning facilities include a learning resource center and radio station. The 650-acre campus is in a suburban area 12 miles southwest of Charlotte. Including residence halls, there are 20 buildings.

Student Life: 73% of undergraduates are from North Carolina. Others are from 35 states, 12 foreign countries, and Canada. 87% are white. 36% are Catholic. The average age of freshmen is 18; all undergraduates, 23. 30% do not continue beyond their first year; 39% remain to graduate.

Housing: 600 students can be accommodated in college housing, which includes single-sex and coed dormitories and on-campus apartments. In addition, there are special-interest houses and a quiet residence hall. Single-occupancy housing is available for all students. On-campus housing is guaranteed for all 4 years. 51% of students live on campus; of those, 50% remain on campus on weekends. All students may keep cars.

Activities: 30% of men belong to 3 local fraternities and 1 national fraternity; 30% of women belong to 3 local sororities. There are 34 groups on campus, including chorus, drama, honors, international, literary magazine, newspaper, political, professional, radio and TV, religious, social, social service, student government, and yearbook. Popular campus events include Spring Weekend, Special Olympics, and Greek Week.

Sports: There are 6 intercollegiate sports for men and 5 for women, and 13 intramural sports for men and 13 for women. Facilities include a phys ed center with a 1200-seat gym, and a college union with a 225-seat auditorium.

Disabled Students: 60% of the campus is accessible. Wheelchair ramps, elevators, special parking, specially equipped rest rooms, special class scheduling, and lowered drinking fountains are available.

Services: Counseling and information services are available, as is tutoring in some subjects, including math, and English.

Campus Safety and Security: Measures include 24-hour foot and vehicle patrol, informal discussions, and lighted pathways/sidewalks.

Programs of Study: Belmont Abbey confers B.A. and B.S. degrees. Bachelor's degrees are awarded in BIOLOGICAL SCIENCE (biology/biological science), BUSINESS (accounting, business administration and management, and recreation and leisure services), COMMUNICATIONS AND THE ARTS (English), COMPUTER AND PHYSICAL SCIENCE (information sciences and systems), EDUCATION (education, elementary, and secondary), ENGINEERING AND ENVIRONMENTAL DESIGN (preengineering), HEALTH PROFESSIONS (medical laboratory technology, predentistry, premedicine, and prepharmacy), SOCIAL SCIENCE (economics, history, liberal arts/general studies, philosophy, political science/government, prelaw, psychology, sociology, and theological studies). Natural and physical sciences, and English are the strongest academically. Business administration, education, and biology are the largest.

Required: To graduate, all students must complete a minimum of 120 credits, including 60 credits of core curriculum and 30 upper-level credits in the major. Among the core requirements are history, math, natural sciences, theology, philosophy, English, fine arts, and Great Books Seminar. A minimum 2.0 GPA must be maintained.

Special: Cross-registration is offered through the Charlotte Area Educational Consortium. There are internships in many majors, including required internships in recreational studies and therapeutic recreation, as well as on-campus work-study, nondegree study, and study abroad. There are 5 national honor societies and a freshman honors program.

Faculty/Classroom: 73% of faculty are male; 27%, female. All teach undergraduates and 60% do research. The average class size in an introductory lecture is 25; in a laboratory, 18; and in a regular course, 17.

Requirements: The SAT I or ACT is required, with a minimum total score of 850 on the SAT I. Candidates must be graduates of an accredited secondary school. A minimum of 16 academic credits must be completed, including 4 in English, 3 each in math and electives, and 2 each in foreign language, history, and science. An interview is recommended. A GPA of 2.3 is required. AP and CLEP credits are accepted. Important factors in the admissions decision are advanced placement or honor courses, extracurricular activities record, and leadership record.

Procedure: Freshmen are admitted fall and spring. Entrance exams should be taken by October of the senior year. There is a deferred admissions plan. Notification is sent on a rolling basis. Check with the school for current application deadlines. The fall 2001 application fee was $25.

Transfer: 56 transfer students enrolled in a recent year. Students with 24 or more credit hours must submit all college transcripts, and those with fewer than 24 credit hours must also submit a high school transcript and the SAT I scores. All candidates must have a minimum 2.0 GPA and must be eligible to return to the last college attended. An interview is recommended. 30 credits of 120 must be completed at Belmont Abbey.

Visiting: There are regularly scheduled orientations for prospective students and a campus tour including meetings with a financial aid adviser, faculty, and students. There are guides for informal visits and visitors may sit in on classes and stay overnight. To schedule a visit, contact the Admissions Office.

Financial Aid: The average freshman award in a recent year was $8700. Of that total, scholarships or need-based grants averaged $4600; loans averaged $2500 ($2625 maximum); and work contracts averaged $1600 ($1800 maximum). 19% of undergraduates work part time. Average annual earnings from campus work are $1600. The average financial indebtedness of a recent year's graduate was $9500. Belmont Abbey is a member of CSS. The FAFSA is required. Check with the school for current deadlines.

International Students: There are 17 international students enrolled. They must score 550 on the written TOEFL.

Computers: Students have access to 65 Pentium PCs, 50 connected to the Internet. All students may access the system at any time. There are no time limits and no fees.

Graduates: In a recent year, 174 bachelor's degrees were awarded. The most popular majors were business management (36%), education (11%), and accounting (6%). In an average class, 31% graduate in 4 years, 40% in 5 years, and 41% in 6 years. 22 companies recruited on campus in a recent year. Of the 2000 graduating class, 22% were enrolled in graduate school within 6 months of graduation and 75% were employed.

Admissions Contact: Denis M. Stokes, Vice President for Enrollment Management. E-mail: *admissions@crusader.bac.edu*
Web: *www.belmontabbeycollege.edu*

BENNETT COLLEGE

Greensboro, NC 27401-3239 — D-2 — (336) 370-8624

Full-time: 513 women	**Faculty:** 57
Part-time: 7 women	**Ph.D.s:** 68%
Graduate: none	**Student/Faculty:** 11 to 1
Year: semesters, summer session	**Tuition:** $10,006
Application Deadline: open	**Room & Board:** $4291
Freshman Class: 1050 applied, 655 accepted, 157 enrolled	
SAT I: required	**COMPETITIVE**

Bennett College, founded in 1873, is a private liberal arts women's institution affiliated with the United Methodist Church. Some information in this profile is approximate. In addition to regional accreditation, Bennett has baccalaureate program accreditation with ADA, CSWE, and NCATE. The library contains 98,000 volumes, 300 microform items, and 1600 audiovisual forms/CDs, and subscribes to 259 periodicals. Computerized library services include the card catalog, interlibrary loans, and database searching. Special learning facilities include a learning resource center and the Women's Leadership Institute. The 55-acre campus is in an urban area 1 mile from downtown Greensboro. Including residence halls, there are 31 buildings.

Student Life: 76% of undergraduates are from out of state, mostly the Northeast. Others are from 34 states and 6 foreign countries. 86% are from public schools. 99% are African American. 77% are Protestant; 11%, Muslim. The average age of freshmen is 18; all undergraduates, 21. 21% do not continue beyond their first year; 35% remain to graduate.

Housing: 608 students can be accommodated in college housing, which includes dormitories. In addition, there are honors houses. On-campus housing is guaranteed for all 4 years. 80% of students live on campus; of those, 50% remain on campus on weekends. Alcohol is not permitted. All students may keep cars.

Activities: 22% of women belong to 4 national sororities. There are 34 groups on campus, including cheerleading, choir, computers, dance, drama, film, honors, international, literary magazine, newspaper, orchestra, professional, religious, student government, and yearbook. Popular campus events include Christmas Concert, President's Ball, and Alumnae Weekend.

Sports: Facilities include a gym, a pool, exercise and gymnastic facilities, an athletic field, and basketball and tennis courts.

Disabled Students: 25% of the campus is accessible. Wheelchair ramps, elevators, special parking, specially equipped rest rooms, and special class scheduling are available.

Services: Counseling and information services are available, as is tutoring in every subject. There is remedial math, reading, and writing.

Campus Safety and Security: Measures include 24-hour foot and vehicle patrol, self-defense education, escort service, and informal discussions. There are pamphlets/posters/films and lighted pathways/sidewalks.

Programs of Study: Bennett confers B.A., B.S., B.A.S.I.S., and B.S.W. degrees. Associate degrees are also awarded. Bachelor's degrees are awarded in BIOLOGICAL SCIENCE (biology/biological science), BUSINESS (accounting, business administration and management, fashion merchandising, and secretarial studies/office management), COMMUNICATIONS AND THE ARTS (arts administration/management, communications, English, music, and visual and performing arts), COMPUTER AND PHYSICAL SCIENCE (chemistry, computer science, and mathematics), EDUCATION (early childhood, elementary, English, mathematics, middle school, music, science, secondary, and special), SOCIAL SCIENCE (dietetics, interdisciplinary studies, political science/government, psychology, social work, and sociology). Biology, math, and education are the strongest academically. Business administration/accounting and biology are the largest.

Required: All students must take 54 to 64 semester hours of general education courses in communication, humanities, math, natural science, reading, history, foreign language, philosophy, phys ed, religion, and women's studies. A total of 124 semester hours, with 60 to 64 in the major, and at least a 2.0 GPA are required for graduation. Comprehensive exams in math and English are required.

Special: Students may cross-register at member colleges of the Greensboro Regional Consortium, study off campus through exchange programs, take a Washington semester, and study abroad. Bennett offers student-designed majors, dual majors in engineering and nursing, nondegree study, a 3-1 nursing program, a B.A.-B.S. degree in interdisciplinary studies, and a 3-2 engineering degree with North Carolina Agricultural and Technical State University. There are 6 national honor societies and 6 departmental honors programs.

Faculty/Classroom: 38% of faculty are male; 62%, female. All teach undergraduates. The average class size in an introductory lecture is 25; in a laboratory, 30; and in a regular course, 20.

Admissions: 62% of the 2001-2002 applicants were accepted.

Requirements: The SAT I is required. In addition, applicants must be graduates of accredited high schools or have earned the GED. Secondary preparation should include 4 years of English, 2 of math, 1 each of science and social studies, and 4 of other academic courses. A personal essay is required, and an interview is recommended. A GPA of 2.5 is required. CLEP credit is accepted. Important factors in the admissions decision are recommendations by school officials, parents or siblings attending the school, and evidence of special talent.

Procedure: Freshmen are admitted fall and spring. Entrance exams should be taken preferably during the senior year. There is a deferred admissions plan. Application deadlines are open. The application fee is $20.

Transfer: An official transcript and a catalog from each college previously attended, 2 letters of recommendation, a statement of honorable dismissal from previous colleges, and a personal essay are required. 64 credits of 124 must be completed at Bennett.

Visiting: There are regularly scheduled orientations for prospective students, including a campus tour and meetings with a financial aid officer and an academic program director. There are guides for informal visits and visitors may sit in on classes and stay overnight. To schedule a visit, contact Linda Torrence, Associate Dean for Enrollment Management.

Financial Aid: In 2001-2002, 84% of all freshmen and 91% of continuing students received some form of financial aid. 24% of undergraduates work part time. Average annual earnings from campus work are $1000. Bennett is a member of CSS. The FAFSA or FFS is required.

International Students: The school actively recruits these students. They must score 500 on the written TOEFL and also take the SAT I or the ACT.

Computers: The college provides 108 PCs for student use and for computer-assisted instruction. All students may access the system 8 A.M. to 11 P.M. There are no time limits.

Admissions Contact: Linda Torrrence, Associate Dean for Enrollment Management. A video is available.
E-mail: *bcinfo@bennett1.bennett.edu* Web: *www.bennett.edu*

CABARRUS COLLEGE OF HEALTH SCIENCES — C-3

Concord, NC 28025-2405 — **(704) 783-1555; Fax: (704) 783-2077**

Full-time: 12 men, 150 women	**Faculty:** n/av
Part-time: 5 men, 113 women	**Ph.D.s:** n/av
Graduate: none	**Student/Faculty:** n/av
Year: semesters	**Tuition:** $6535
Application Deadline: open	**Room & Board:** n/app
Freshman Class: 169 applied, 103 accepted, 63 enrolled	
SAT I or ACT: required	**COMPETITIVE**

Cabarrus College of Health Sciences offers undergraduate completion programs in health services management and nursing.

Programs of Study: Cabarrus confers B.S.H.S.M. and B.S.N. degrees. Associate degrees are also awarded. Bachelor's degrees are awarded in health care administration and nursing.

Required: 120 total credits are required.

Admissions: 61% of the 2001-2002 applicants were accepted.

Requirements: The SAT I or ACT is required. Cabarrus College of Health Sciences requires applicants to be in the upper 50% of their class. A GPA of 2.5 is required.

Procedure: Application deadlines are open. The application fee is $35.

Financial Aid: In 2001-2002, 98% of all freshmen received some form of financial aid.

Admissions Contact: Deborah Deadman Bowman, Director of Admissions. E-mail: *dbowman@northeastmedical.org*
Web: *www.cabarruscollege.edu*

CAMPBELL UNIVERSITY — D-3

Buies Creek, NC 27506 — **(800) 334-4111, ext. 1320**
Fax: (910) 893-1288

Full-time: 1104 men, 1287 women	**Faculty:** 132
Part-time: 25 men, 37 women	**Ph.D.s:** 91%
Graduate: 473 men, 744 women	**Student/Faculty:** 18 to 1
Year: semesters, summer session	**Tuition:** $12,269
Application Deadline: open	**Room & Board:** $4330
Freshman Class: 1848 applied, 1109 accepted, 688 enrolled	
SAT I Verbal/Math: 530/528	**COMPETITIVE**

Campbell University, founded in 1887, is a private, nonsectarian institution affiliated with the North Carolina Baptist Convention and offering degree programs in liberal arts and sciences, business, and education. There are 5 undergraduate and 5 graduate schools. In addition to regional accreditation, Campbell has baccalaureate program accreditation with ACPE, CAAHEP, CSWE, and NCATE. The 5 libraries contain 202,667 volumes, 832,589 microform items, and 3842 audiovisual forms/CDs, and subscribe to 748 periodicals. Computerized library services include the card catalog, interlibrary loans, and database searching. Special learning facilities include a learning resource center, art gallery, radio station, desktop publishing lab, computerized music lab, family and consumer sciences lab, athletic learning resources center, drug information center for the School of Pharmacy, and pharmacy research facility. The 850-acre campus is in a rural area 28 miles south of Raleigh and 30 miles north of Fayetteville. Including residence halls, there are 47 buildings.

Student Life: 63% of undergraduates are from North Carolina. Others are from 49 states, 56 foreign countries, and Canada. 90% are from public schools. 80% are white; 11% African American. 72% are Protestant; 11% Islamic/Muslim, Hindu, Greek Orthodox, Pentecostal. The average age of freshmen is 18; all undergraduates, 20.

Housing: 1500 students can be accommodated in college housing, which includes single-sex dormitories, on-campus apartments, off-campus apartments, and married-student housing. On-campus housing is guaranteed for all 4 years. Alcohol is not permitted. All students may keep cars.

Activities: There are no fraternities or sororities. There are 44 groups on campus, including art, band, cheerleading, choir, chorale, chorus, computers, drama, ethnic, honors, international, jazz band, literary magazine, musical theater, newspaper, orchestra, pep band, photography, political, professional, radio and TV, religious, social, social service, student government, and yearbook. Popular campus events include the Staley Lecture Series, Parents Day, and spring and Christmas formals.

Sports: There are 8 intercollegiate sports for men and 9 for women, and 27 intramural sports for men and 18 for women. Facilities include a 2000-seat gym, an athletic complex, a lake, a coffeehouse, a concert hall, a theater, 2 golf courses, and a nature trail.

Disabled Students: 75% of the campus is accessible. Wheelchair ramps, elevators, special parking, specially equipped rest rooms, special class scheduling, lowered drinking fountains, and lowered telephones are available.

Services: Counseling and information services are available, as is tutoring in most subjects. There is remedial math and writing.

Campus Safety and Security: Measures include 24-hour foot and vehicle patrol, self-defense education, escort service, and informal discussions. There are pamphlets/posters/films, emergency telephones, and lighted pathways/sidewalks.

Programs of Study: Campbell confers B.A., B.S., B.Applied Sci., B.B.A., B.H.S., and B.S.W. degrees. Associate, master's, and doctoral degrees are also awarded. Bachelor's degrees are awarded in BIOLOGICAL SCIENCE (biochemistry and biology/biological science), BUSINESS (accounting, business administration and management, business economics, international business management, investments and securities, and sports management), COMMUNICATIONS AND THE ARTS (advertising, art, broadcasting, communications, dramatic arts, English, French, journalism, music, and Spanish), COMPUTER AND PHYSICAL SCIENCE (chemistry, computer science, information sciences and systems, and mathematics), EDUCATION (athletic training, elementary, and middle school), ENGINEERING AND ENVIRONMENTAL DESIGN (military science and preengineering), HEALTH PROFESSIONS (clinical science and prepharmacy), SOCIAL SCIENCE (criminal justice, economics, family/consumer studies, history, physical fitness/movement, political science/government, prelaw, psychology, religion, and social work). Prelaw, prepharmacy, and trust management are the strongest academically. Prepharmacy, mass communication, and business administration are the largest.

Required: To graduate, students must complete 128 credit hours with a minimum GPA of 2.0 overall and in the major. All students must take English, math, science, religion, fine arts, phys ed, and the Cultural Enrichment Program.

Special: Campbell offers co-op programs, internships, study abroad in 3 countries, a Washington semester, numerous apprenticeships, accelerated degrees, dual majors, and a general studies degree. There is credit for military and work experience. Cross-registration with the North Carolina Model Teacher Education Consortium and B.A.-B.S. degrees are also possible. There are 5 national honor societies, and a freshman honors program.

Faculty/Classroom: 75% of faculty are male; 25%, female. All teach undergraduates and 40% do research. No introductory courses are taught by graduate students. The average class size in an introductory lecture is 30; in a laboratory, 25; and in a regular course, 25.

Admissions: 60% of the 2001-2002 applicants were accepted. The SAT I scores for the 2001-2002 freshman class were: Verbal--43% below 500, 41% between 500 and 599, 13% between 600 and 700, and 4% above 700; Math--41% below 500, 38% between 500 and 599, 17% between 600 and 700, and 3% above 700. 37% of the current freshmen were in the top fifth of their class; 69% were in the top two fifths. 37 freshmen graduated first in their class.

Requirements: The SAT I or ACT is required, with a minimum recommended composite score of 950 on the SAT I. Applicants should have completed 12 high school academic credits, including 4 credits of English, 3 of math, and 2 each of history or social studies, science, and foreign language. An essay, an interview, and a portfolio are recommended. An audition is required for some majors. Campbell requires applicants to be in the upper 50% of their class. A GPA of 2.5 is required. AP and CLEP credits are accepted. Important factors in the admissions decision are advanced placement or honor courses, leadership record, and personality/intangible qualities. Applications may be submitted on-line via the university's web site.

Procedure: Freshmen are admitted to all sessions. Entrance exams should be taken during the junior year or the fall of senior year. There is a deferred admissions plan. Application deadlines are open. The application fee is $25. Notification is sent on a rolling basis.

Transfer: 214 transfer students enrolled in 2001-2002. Applicants should have a minimum GPA of 2.0 and supply transcripts from previously attended colleges. 36 credits of 128 must be completed at Campbell.

Visiting: There are regularly scheduled orientations for prospective students. There are guides for informal visits and visitors may sit in on classes. To schedule a visit, contact the Admissions Office.

Financial Aid: In a recent year, 91% of all freshmen and 81% of continuing students received some form of financial aid. 80% of freshmen and 78% of continuing students received need-based aid. The average freshman award was $17,161. Of that total, scholarships or need-based grants averaged $3000 ($6000 maximum); loans averaged $2625; and work contracts averaged $1000 ($2000 maximum). 30% of undergraduates work part time. Average annual earnings from campus work are $531. The average financial indebtedness of a recent year's graduate was $17,125. The FAFSA is required. The fall priority application deadline is March 15.

International Students: There are 149 international students enrolled. The school actively recruits these students. They must score 500 on the written TOEFL or 173 on the electronic version and also take the SAT I or the ACT, scoring 850 on the SAT I.

Computers: The mainframe is an HP 9000. There are 76 computer terminals in a centralized academic computer center. All students have e-mail accounts, and all dorm rooms have Internet and web access. There are also 21 departmental computer labs ranging from 4 to 25 computers per lab. All students may access the system during posted student hours; generally, Monday through Thursday, 8 A.M. to 11 p.m, with extended hours Friday through Sunday. There are no time limits. There is a $50 Internet fee. It is strongly recommended that all students have a personal computer.

Graduates: In 2001, 794 bachelor's degrees were awarded. The most popular majors were business administration (36%), prepharmacy (17%), and government (10%). In an average class, 1% graduate in 3 years, 58% in 4 years, and 65% in 6 years. 23 companies recruited on campus in 2000-2001. Of the 2000 graduating class, 15% were enrolled in graduate school within 6 months of graduation and 85% were employed.

Admissions Contact: Herbert V. Kerner, Jr., Dean of Admissions. A video is available. E-mail: *adm@mailcenter.campbell.edu*
Web: *www.campbell.edu*

CATAWBA COLLEGE
Salisbury, NC 28144 C-2
(704) 637-4402
(800) 228-2922; Fax: (704) 637-4444

Full-time: 679 men, 705 women	**Faculty:** 73; IIB, --$
Part-time: 19 men, 32 women	**Ph.D.s:** 71%
Graduate: 1 man, 17 women	**Student/Faculty:** 19 to 1
Year: semesters, summer session	**Tuition:** $14,540
Application Deadline: open	**Room & Board:** $5080
Freshman Class: 1107 applied, 910 accepted, 353 enrolled	
SAT I Verbal/Math: 490/490	**COMPETITIVE**

Catawba College, founded in 1851, is an independent institution affiliated with the United Church of Christ and offers undergraduate programs in the arts and sciences, business, education, performing arts, forestry and environmental science, social and behavioral sciences, physical education, and preprofessional fields. There are 8 undergraduate schools and 1 graduate school. In addition to regional accreditation, Catawba has baccalaureate program accreditation with NCATE. The 2 libraries contain 158,959 volumes, 593,783 microform items, and 25,985 audiovisual forms/CDs, and subscribe to 1209 periodicals. Computerized library services include the card catalog, interlibrary loans, and database searching. Special learning facilities include a curriculum materials center, an observatory, and a nature preserve. The 210-acre campus is in a small town 40 miles northeast of Charlotte. Including residence halls, there are 30 buildings.

Student Life: 67% of undergraduates are from North Carolina. Others are from 35 states, 8 foreign countries, and Canada. 87% are from public schools. 79% are white; 16% African American. 76% are Protestant; 11% claim no religious affiliation; 10% Catholic. The average age of freshmen is 18; all undergraduates, 22. 35% do not continue beyond their first year; 45% remain to graduate.

Housing: 770 students can be accommodated in college housing, which includes single-sex and coed dormitories. There are nonsmoking and alcohol-free dormitories. On-campus housing is guaranteed for the freshman year only. 51% of students commute. All students may keep cars.

Activities: There are no fraternities or sororities. There are 25 groups on campus, including art, band, cheerleading, chess, choir, chorale, chorus, computers, dance, drama, ethnic, honors, jazz band, literary magazine, musical theater, newspaper, orchestra, pep band, political, professional, religious, social, social service, student government, symphony, and yearbook. Popular campus events include Winterfest, Inaugural Ball, and Parents Weekend.

Sports: There are 8 intercollegiate sports for men and 8 for women, and 4 intramural sports for men and 4 for women. Facilities include a 5000-seat stadium and a 3500-seat gym, football, baseball, softball, soccer, and field hockey fields, tennis, volleyball, and racquetball courts, weight lifting, a swimming pool, a challenge course, and table tennis and billiards.

Disabled Students: 90% of the campus is accessible. Wheelchair ramps, elevators, special parking, specially equipped rest rooms, lowered drinking fountains, and lowered telephones are available.

Services: Counseling and information services are available, as is tutoring in most subjects.

Campus Safety and Security: Measures include 24-hour foot and vehicle patrol, self-defense education, escort service, and informal discussions. There are pamphlets/posters/films, emergency telephones, and lighted pathways/sidewalks.

Programs of Study: Catawba confers B.A., B.S., B.B.A, and B.F.A. degrees. Master's degrees are also awarded. Bachelor's degrees are awarded in AGRICULTURE (environmental studies and forestry and related sciences), BIOLOGICAL SCIENCE (biology/biological science), BUSINESS (business administration and management, international business management, and recreation and leisure services), COMMUNICATIONS AND THE ARTS (communications, dramatic arts, English, French, music, musical theater, Spanish, speech/debate/rhetoric, and theater management), COMPUTER AND PHYSICAL SCIENCE (chemistry, computer science, information sciences and systems, and mathematics), EDUCATION (athletic training, education, elementary, middle school, music, physical, science, and special), ENGINEERING AND ENVIRONMENTAL DESIGN (environmental science), HEALTH PROFESSIONS (medical technology, physician's assistant, predentistry, premedicine, recreation therapy, and sports medicine), SOCIAL SCIENCE (history, philosophy, political science/government, prelaw, psychology, public administration, religion, and sociology). Premedicine, predentistry, and prelaw are the strongest academically. Business, education, and theater arts are the largest.

Required: To graduate, students must complete at least 120 credit hours, including up to 54 in their major, with a minimum GPA of 2.0. General education requirements include 9 semester hours in humanities, 7 in natural sciences, 6 each in social sciences, English composition, and fine arts, 4 to 9 in math, and 1 in physical fitness, information and technology, college orientation, and foreign language through the elementary level. Students must demonstrate proficiency in math, writing, oral communication, and computer technology.

Special: There are cooperative programs in deaf education with Appalachian State University, forestry and environmental science with Duke University, and physician assistant and medical technician training with Wake Forest University. Cross-registration is possible through the Charlotte Area Educational Consortium. Catawba also offers internships, study abroad in London, a Washington semester, work-study programs, accelerated degree programs, dual majors, a general studies degree, pass/fail options, and student-designed majors. There are 4 national honor societies and a freshman honors program.

Faculty/Classroom: 59% of faculty are male; 41%, female. All teach undergraduates, and 40% also do research. No introductory courses are taught by graduate students. The average class size in an introductory lecture is 25; in a laboratory, 24; and in a regular course, 22.

Admissions: 82% of the 2001-2002 applicants were accepted. The SAT I scores for the 2001-2002 freshman class were: Verbal--51% below 500, 39% between 500 and 599, and 10% between 600 and 700; Math--52% below 500, 39% between 500 and 599, 8% between 600 and 700, and 1% above 700. 22% of the current freshmen were in the top fifth of their class; 49% were in the top two fifths.

Requirements: The SAT I is required; the ACT may be substituted. A minimum SAT I composite score of 800 or ACT score of 21 is required. Applicants must be graduates of an accredited secondary school or have a GED. They must have completed 16 academic credits, of which 12 must be Carnegie units. An essay is required, and an interview is encouraged for all students. An audition is required for music and drama scholarships. A GPA of 2.0 is required. AP and CLEP credits are accepted. Important factors in the admissions decision are advanced placement or honor courses, evidence of special talent, and extracurricular activities record. Applications are accepted on disk and on-line via ExPAN, FishNet, and ReZun, and at the college's web site.

Procedure: Freshmen are admitted to all sessions. Entrance exams should be taken by December of the senior year. There are early decision and deferred admissions plans. Application deadlines are open. The fall 2001 application fee was $25. Notification is sent on a rolling basis.

Transfer: 189 transfer students enrolled in 2001-2002. Applicants must present at least 12 semester hours, a GPA of 2.0 or better, and a minimum SAT I score of 800 or ACT score of 21. Students out of high school for 5 or more years are exempt from the SAT I or ACT requirement. 30 credits of 120 must be completed at Catawba.

Visiting: There are regularly scheduled orientations for prospective students, including campus tours, lunches, meetings with faculty, and financial aid and athletic workshops. There are guides for informal visits and visitors may sit in on classes. To schedule a visit, contact the Office of Admissions at (800) CATAWBA or (704) 637-4222 or *admission@catawaba.edu*

Financial Aid: In 2001-2002, 98% of all freshmen and 94% of continuing students received some form of financial aid. 66% of freshmen and 60% of continuing students received need-based aid. The average freshman award was $12,550. Of that total, scholarships or need-based grants averaged $7381 ($15,120 maximum); loans averaged $6441 ($16,995 maximum); and work contracts averaged $1897 ($2000 maximum). 49% of undergraduates work part time. Average annual earnings from campus work are $1055. The average financial indebtedness of the 2001 graduate was $21,500. Catawba is a member of CSS. The FAFSA and the college's own financial statement are required. The fall application deadline is March 15.

International Students: There are 21 international students enrolled. They must score 525 on the written TOEFL.

Computers: The mainframe is an HP300. All students have access to a PC LAN from their dorm rooms, as well as to 100 PCs in 4 labs on campus. There is full access to the Internet. All students may access the system. There are no time limits and no fees.

Graduates: In 2001, 245 bachelor's degrees were awarded. The most popular majors were communication arts (9%), computer information systems (9%), and business administration (8%). In an average class, 32% graduate in 4 years, 43% in 5 years, and 45% in 6 years. 15 companies recruited on campus in 2000-2001. Of the 2000 graduating class, 7% were enrolled in graduate school within 6 months of graduation.

Admissions Contact: Brian D. Best, Chief Enrollment Officer. A video is available. E-mail: *bdbest@catawba.edu*
Web: *http://www.catawba.edu*

DAVIDSON COLLEGE

Davidson, NC 28035 — C-3

(704) 894-2230
(800) 768-0380; Fax: (704) 894-2016

Full-time: 823 men, 850 women	**Faculty:** 154; IIB, +$
Part-time: 1 woman	**Ph.D.s:** 100%
Graduate: none	**Student/Faculty:** 11 to 1
Year: semesters	**Tuition:** $23,995
Application Deadline: January 2	**Room & Board:** $6828
Freshman Class: 3363 applied, 1164 accepted, 969 enrolled	
SAT I Verbal/Math: 660/660	**ACT:** 29 **MOST COMPETITIVE**

Davidson College, founded in 1837, is a private liberal arts institution affiliated with the Presbyterian Church (U.S.A.). In addition to regional accreditation, Davidson has baccalaureate program accreditation with ACS and NCATE. The library contains 422,035 volumes, 475,788 microform items, and 9494 audiovisual forms/CDs, and subscribes to 2767 periodicals. Computerized library services include the card catalog, interlibrary loans, and database searching. Special learning facilities include a learning resource center, art gallery, radio station, and and arboretum. The 450-acre campus is in a small town 19 miles north of Charlotte. Including residence halls, there are 98 buildings.

Student Life: 81% of undergraduates are from out of state, mostly the South. Others are from 44 states, 32 foreign countries, and Canada. 51% are from public schools. 84% are white. The average age of freshmen is 18; all undergraduates, 20. 4% do not continue beyond their first year; 90% remain to graduate.

Housing: 1551 students can be accommodated in college housing, which includes single-sex and coed dormitories and on-campus apartments. On-campus housing is guaranteed for the freshman year only and is available on a lottery system for upperclassmen. 91% of students live on campus. All students may keep cars.

Activities: There are 7 national fraternities. There are no sororities. There are 106 groups on campus, including art, cheerleading, choir, chorale, chorus, computers, dance, drama, ethnic, gay, honors, international, jazz band, literary magazine, musical theater, newspaper, opera, orchestra, outing, pep band, political, professional, radio and TV, religious, social, social service, student government, symphony, and yearbook. Popular campus events include Solidarity Week, Lunar Luau, and convocations.

Sports: There are 11 intercollegiate sports for men and 10 for women, and 14 intramural sports for men and 11 for women. Facilities include indoor and outdoor tennis courts, 3 racquetball courts, a squash court, a natatorium with a diving well, 2 Nautilus rooms, a gym, a wrestling room, a dance studio, a golf course, a cross-country course and trail, a football and soccer stadium, various other playing fields, and facilities for sailing, swimming, water skiing, and canoeing at the Lake campus.

Disabled Students: 90% of the campus is accessible. Wheelchair ramps, elevators, special parking, specially equipped rest rooms, special class scheduling, lowered drinking fountains, and lowered telephones are available.

Services: Counseling and information services are available. Tutoring is available as needed through the Student Affairs Office. There is a reader service for the blind.

Campus Safety and Security: Measures include 24-hour foot and vehicle patrol, self-defense education, escort service, and informal discussions. There are pamphlets/posters/films, emergency telephones, and lighted pathways/sidewalks.

Programs of Study: Davidson confers A.B. and B.S. degrees. Bachelor's degrees are awarded in BIOLOGICAL SCIENCE (biology/biological science), COMMUNICATIONS AND THE ARTS (art, classics, dramatic arts, English, French, German, music, and Spanish), COMPUTER AND PHYSICAL SCIENCE (chemistry, mathematics, and physics), SOCIAL SCIENCE (anthropology, economics, history, interdisciplinary studies, philosophy, political science/government, psychology, religion, and sociology). Biology, English, and political science are the largest.

Required: Students must complete 32 courses, including 10 to 12 in the major, with a 2.0 GPA in order to graduate. Core curriculum requirements include courses in literature, fine arts, history, religion and philosophy, natural science, math, and social sciences. In addition, students must meet foreign language, composition, cultural diversity, and phys ed requirements. Comprehensive exams and a thesis are required in some majors.

Special: Davidson offers interdisciplinary international and South Asian studies programs and study abroad in several countries as well as through other schools' study-abroad programs. A 3-2 engineering program may be arranged with Georgia Institute of Technology and Columbia, Duke, North Carolina State, and Washington Universities. Students may design their own majors, cross-register with any college in the Charlotte Area Educational Consortium, enroll in a Washington or Philadelphia semester or a semester or month-long environmental program at the School for Field Studies, or undertake independent study. There are 15 national honor societies, including Phi Beta Kappa, and 20 departmental honors programs.

Faculty/Classroom: 69% of faculty are male; 31%, female. All both teach and do research. The average class size in an introductory lecture is 14; in a laboratory, 13; and in a regular course, 14.

Admissions: 35% of the 2001-2002 applicants were accepted. The SAT I scores for the 2001-2002 freshman class were: Verbal--1% below 500, 16% between 500 and 599, 52% between 600 and 700, and 31% above 700; Math--2% below 500, 14% between 500 and 599, 55% between 600 and 700, and 30% above 700. The ACT scores were 2% below 21, 8% between 21 and 23, 17% between 24 and 26, 18% between 27 and 28, and 54% above 28. 90% of the current freshmen were in the top fifth of their class; 99% were in the top two fifths. 18 freshmen graduated first in their class.

Requirements: The SAT I or ACT is required. In addition, SAT II: Subject tests in writing, mathematics level I or II, and 1 other subject are strongly recommended. At least 16 high school units are required, although 20 units are recommended. These should include 4 units of English, 3 units of math, 2 units of the same foreign language, 2 units of science, and 2 units of history/social studies. It is strongly recommended that high school students continue for the third and fourth years in science and in the same foreign language, continue math through calculus, and take additional courses in history. AP credits are accepted. Important factors in the admissions decision are advanced placement or honor courses, recommendations by school officials, and leadership record. Applications are accepted on computer disk via Apply.

Procedure: Freshmen are admitted in the fall. Entrance exams should be taken by the end of the junior year. There are early decision and deferred admissions plans. Early decision applications should be filed by November 15; regular applications, by January 2 for fall entry. The fall 2001 application fee was $50. Notification of early decision is sent December 15; regular decision, April 1. 219 early decision candidates were accepted for the 2001-2002 class. 29% of all applicants are on a waiting list; 14 were accepted in 2001.

Transfer: 10 transfer students enrolled in 2001-2002. Applicants must have at least 1 full year of college work, generally with a 3.0 GPA. They must submit official college and high school transcripts, as well as required letters of recommendation, and be in good standing at their previous college. 16 credits of 32 must be completed at Davidson.

Visiting: There are guides for informal visits and visitors may sit in on classes and stay overnight. To schedule a visit, contact the Admissions Office.

Financial Aid: In 2001-2002, 60% of all freshmen and 61% of continuing students received some form of financial aid. 33% of freshmen and 32% of continuing students received need-based aid. The average freshman award was $15,143. Of that total, scholarships or need-based grants averaged $13,292 ($27,200 maximum); loans averaged $2330 ($5500 maximum); and work contracts averaged $3918. 30% of undergraduates work part time. Average annual earnings from campus work are $2000. The average financial indebtedness of the 2001 graduate was $14,557. The CSS/Profile or FAFSA and the college's own financial statement are required. The fall application deadline is February 15.

International Students: There were 51 international students enrolled in a recent year. The school actively recruits these students. They must score 600 on the written TOEFL or 250 on the electronic version.

Computers: The mainframes are 32 servers, including an HP 9000 K360, Digital Alpha Server 1200, and several Dell PowerEdge 2300s and 6350s. Students may use the host computer and PC network for word processing, computation and graphics (Mathematica, Quattro), statistics (SAS, SPSS, Minitab), and e-mail and the Internet. Access is available from 124 networked PCs in academic buildings, with more than 500 PCs and Macs on the campus. All students may access the system 24 hours per day. There are no time limits and no fees.

Graduates: In 2001, 471 bachelor's degrees were awarded. The most popular majors were English (15%), biology (14%), and history (12%). In an average class, 86% graduate in 4 years, and 90% in 5 years. 229 companies recruited on campus in 2000-2001. Of the 2000 graduating class, 25% were enrolled in graduate school within 6 months of graduation and 65% were employed.

Admissions Contact: Dr. Nancy J. Cable, Dean of Admission and Financial Aid. E-mail: *admission@davidson.edu*
Web: *www.davidson.edu*

DUKE UNIVERSITY D-2

Durham, NC 27706 (919) 684-3214; Fax: (919) 681-8941

Full-time: 3112 men, 2931 women	**Faculty:** 737; I, +$
Part-time: 17 men, 11 women	**Ph.D.s:** 97%
Graduate: 3147 men, 2576 women	**Student/Faculty:** 8 to 1
Year: semesters, summer session	**Tuition:** $26,768
Application Deadline: January 2	**Room & Board:** $7628

Freshman Class: 13,976 applied, 3673 accepted, 1615 enrolled
SAT I Verbal/Math: 700/720 **MOST COMPETITIVE**

Duke University, founded in 1838, is a private institution affiliated with the United Methodist Church and offering undergraduate programs in arts and sciences and engineering. There are 2 undergraduate and 8 graduate schools. In addition to regional accreditation, Duke has baccalaureate program accreditation with AACSB, ABET, ACPE, AHEA, APTA, NCATE, NLN, and SAF. The 9 libraries contain 4,960,746 volumes, 3,855,538 microform items, and 442,106 audiovisual forms/CDs, and subscribe to 31,941 periodicals. Computerized library services include the card catalog, interlibrary loans, and database searching. Special learning facilities include a learning resource center, art gallery, radio station, TV station, marine lab at Beaufort, primate center, center for international studies, nuclear lab, free electron laser, science research center, and institutes of the arts, statistics and decision sciences, policy sciences and public affairs, centers for teaching and learning, community service, geometric computing, culture, and women. The 9350-acre campus is in a suburban area 285 miles southwest of Washington, D.C. Including residence halls, there are 230 buildings.

Student Life: 85% of undergraduates are from out of state, mostly the Northeast. Students are from 49 states, 55 foreign countries, and Canada. 63% are from public schools. 61% are white; 12% Asian American; 10% African American. 49% claim no religious affiliation; 24% are Protestant; 17% Catholic. The average age of freshmen is 18; all undergraduates, 20. 4% do not continue beyond their first year; 93% remain to graduate.

Housing: 5227 students can be accommodated in college housing, which includes single-sex and coed dormitories, on-campus apartments, and married-student housing. In addition, there are language houses, special-interest houses, and theme houses in women's studies, the arts, and community service (APO). On-campus housing is guaranteed for all 4 years. 87% of students live on campus. All students may keep cars.

Activities: 29% of men belong to 17 national fraternities; 42% of women belong to 10 national sororities. There are 350 groups on campus, including art, band, cheerleading, chess, choir, chorale, chorus, computers, dance, debate, drama, drill team, ethnic, film, gay, honors, international, jazz band, literary magazine, marching band, musical theater, newspaper, opera, orchestra, pep band, photography, political, professional, radio and TV, religious, social, social service, student government, symphony, and yearbook. Popular campus events include College Bowl, Oktoberfest, and Springfest.

Sports: There are 11 intercollegiate sports for men and 12 for women, and 15 intramural sports for men and 13 for women. Facilities include stadiums for baseball, basketball/volleyball, football, and soccer/lacrosse; squash, racquetball, and tennis courts; an aquatic center; training and weight rooms; a golf course; cross-country and jogging trails; and practice and intramural sport club fields. The largest stadium seats 33,941; the largest arena, 8564.

Disabled Students: Wheelchair ramps, elevators, special parking, specially equipped rest rooms, special class scheduling, lowered drinking fountains, lowered telephones, and accessible housing arrangements are available. In addition, activities such as concerts can be moved to accessible facilities upon request.

Services: Counseling and information services are available, as is tutoring in every subject. There is a reader service for the blind.

Campus Safety and Security: Measures include 24-hour foot and vehicle patrol, self-defense education, escort service, and shuttle buses. There are informal discussions, pamphlets/posters/films, emergency telephones, lighted pathways/sidewalks, and a crime prevention program.

Programs of Study: Duke confers A.B., B.S., and B.S.E. degrees. Master's and doctoral degrees are also awarded. Bachelor's degrees are awarded in BIOLOGICAL SCIENCE (anatomy and biology/biological science), COMMUNICATIONS AND THE ARTS (African languages, art history and appreciation, classical languages, dramatic arts, English, Germanic languages and literature, linguistics, literature, music, Slavic languages, Spanish, and visual and performing arts), COMPUTER AND PHYSICAL SCIENCE (chemistry, computer science, geology, mathematics, and physics), ENGINEERING AND ENVIRONMENTAL DESIGN (biomedical engineering, civil engineering, electrical/electronics engineering, environmental science, materials science, and mechanical engineering), SOCIAL SCIENCE (African American studies, African studies, anthropology, area studies, Asian/Oriental studies, Canadian studies, classical/ancient civilization, economics, French studies, history, Italian studies, medieval studies, philosophy, political science/government, psychology, public affairs, religion, sociology, and women's studies). The sciences, public policy studies, and political science are the strongest academically. Biology, psychology, and history are the largest.

Required: A minimum of 34 course credits is required for graduation. Students pursue a general course of study, including a writing course and courses in arts and literature, civilizations, foreign languages, natural sciences, quantitative reasoning, and social sciences. No more than 17 course credits are allowed in a major for the B.A. and no more than 19 for the B.S. At least 12 courses must be at or above the 100 level. At least 3 courses designated as seminars, tutorials, independent study, or thesis completion are required. Computer proficiency must be demonstrated by engineering students.

Special: Duke offers cross-registration with the University of North Carolina/Chapel Hill and North Carolina State and North Carolina Central Universities. Also available are internships through the Career Development Center, study abroad in 22 countries, and a Washington semester. An accelerated degree program is possible, achieving graduation in 3 years or combining the senior year with the first graduate year of the law, business, or environment schools. Several 3-2 and 4-1 medical technology programs (degree completed at Duke) are available. Project Calc, an innovative program in calculus, is also offered. Dual majors of any com bination, student-designed majors, nondegree study, and pass/fail options are possible. There are 3 national honor societies, including Phi Beta Kappa.

Faculty/Classroom: 83% of faculty are male; 17%, female. All both teach and do research. Graduate students teach 12% of introductory courses. The average class size in an introductory lecture is 39; in a laboratory, 246; and in a regular course, 21.

Admissions: 26% of the 2001-2002 applicants were accepted. The SAT I scores for the 2001-2002 freshman class were: Verbal--1% below 500, 8% between 500 and 599, 41% between 600 and 700, and 50% above 700; Math--6% between 500 and 599, 31% between 600 and 700, and 63% above 700. The ACT scores were 2% between 18 and 23, 40% between 24 and 29, and 58% above 29. 95% of the current freshmen were in the top fifth of their class; 99% were in the top two fifths.

Requirements: The SAT I or ACT is required. In addition, 3 SAT II: Subject tests, including writing, are required. Applicants must be graduates of an accredited secondary school and have completed 15 academic credits, with 4 in English and 3 each in math, science, and foreign language; an additional 2 in social studies or history are recommended. Engineering students must have 4 credit units in math and 1 in physics or chemistry. An essay is required, and an interview is recommended. A portfolio or audition is advised in appropriate instances. AP credits are accepted. Important factors in the admissions decision are advanced placement or honor courses, recommendations by school officials, and extracurricular activities record.

Procedure: Freshmen are admitted fall and spring. Entrance exams should be taken in October of the junior year for early decision applicants and by January of the senior year for regular decision. There are early decision, early admissions, and deferred admissions plans. Early decision applications should be filed by November 1; regular applications, by January 2 for fall entry and October 15 for spring entry, along with a $65 fee. Notification of early decision is sent December 15; regular decision, April 15. 536 early decision candidates were accepted for the 2001-2002 class. A waiting list is an active part of the admissions procedure.

Transfer: 23 transfer students enrolled in 2001-2002. A minimum 3.6 GPA is recommended. The SAT I, plus 3 SAT II: Subject tests, or the ACT is required. 17 courses of 34 must be completed at Duke.

Visiting: There are regularly scheduled orientations for prospective students, including student-led tours, counselor-led group information sessions, class visits, and lunch with students. There are guides for informal visits and visitors may sit in on classes and stay overnight. To schedule a visit, contact Undergraduate Admissions.

Financial Aid: In 2001-2002, 39% of all freshmen and 36% of continuing students received some form of financial aid. 37% of freshmen and 34% of continuing students received need-based aid. The average freshman award was $19,779. Of that total, scholarships or need-based grants averaged $16,824 ($33,017 maximum); and loans averaged $3617. 30% of undergraduates work part time. Average annual earnings from campus work are $1781. The average financial indebtedness of the 2001 graduate was $16,502. The CSS/Profile or FAFSA is required. The fall application deadline is February 1.

International Students: There are 257 international students enrolled. The school actively recruits these students.

Computers: The mainframe is an IBM 9672. Students may access a number of computer clusters located throughout the campus, providing access to networked and nonnetworked PCs and to workstations. About 600 terminals/PCs are available for general student use. All students have access to e-mail and the Internet. All students may access the system 24 hours a day. There are no time limits and no fees. It is strongly recommended that all students have a personal computer.

Graduates: In 2001, 1589 bachelor's degrees were awarded. The most popular majors were economics (15%), biology (13%), and public policy (10%). In an average class, 1% graduate in 3 years, 87% in 4 years, and 92% in 5 years. 200 companies recruited on campus in 2000-2001. Of the 2000 graduating class, 24% were enrolled in graduate school within 6 months of graduation and 38% were employed.

Admissions Contact: Christoph Guttentag, Director, Undergraduate Admissions. A video is available. E-mail: *askduke@admiss.duke.edu* Web: *http://www.duke.edu/*

EAST CAROLINA UNIVERSITY — E-2

Greenville, NC 27858-4353 (252) 328-6640; Fax: (252) 328-6945

Full-time: 6034 men, 8245 women	**Faculty:** 755; IIA, -$
Part-time: 494 men, 687 women	**Ph.D.s:** 73%
Graduate: 1402 men, 2550 women	**Student/Faculty:** 18 to 1
Year: semesters, summer session	**Tuition:** $2566 ($11,135)
Application Deadline: March 15	**Room & Board:** $5200
Freshman Class: 10,433 applied, 8155 accepted, 3197 enrolled	
SAT I Verbal/Math: 511/519	**ACT:** 20 **COMPETITIVE**

East Carolina University, founded in 1907, is a state-supported institution offering degree programs in the arts and sciences, art, music, business, education, health and human performance, industry and technology, computer science and communication, human environmental sciences, social work and criminal justice studies, medicine, allied health sciences, and nursing. There are 12 undergraduate and 2 graduate schools. In addition to regional accreditation, ECU has baccalaureate program accreditation with AACSB, ACCE, ADA, APTA, CSWE, FIDER, NASAD, NASM, NCATE, NLN, and NRPA. The 2 libraries contain 2,121,239 volumes, 1,841,092 microform items, and 27,830 audiovisual forms/CDs, and subscribe to 4202 periodicals. Computerized library services include the card catalog, interlibrary loans, and database searching. Special learning facilities include a learning resource center, art gallery, and radio station. The 497-acre campus is in an urban area 90 miles east of Raleigh. Including residence halls, there are 166 buildings.

Student Life: 85% of undergraduates are from North Carolina. Others are from 43 states, 53 foreign countries, and Canada. 80% are white; 14% African American. The average age of freshmen is 18; all undergraduates, 22.

Housing: 5045 students can be accommodated in college housing, which includes single-sex and coed dormitories. In addition, there are honors houses, a first-year student's floor, a leadership hall, an extended-quiet-hours floor, a substance-free hall, a nonsmoking floor, and an academic-yerar hall. On-campus housing is guaranteed for the freshman year only and is available on a first-come, first-served basis. 68% of students commute. Alcohol is not permitted. All students may keep cars.

Activities: 10% of men belong to 16 national fraternities; 7% of women belong to 13 national sororities. There are 215 groups on campus, including academic, art, band, cheerleading, choir, chorale, chorus, computers, dance, drama, drill team, ethnic, gay, honors, international, jazz band, literary magazine, marching band, military, musical theater, opera, orchestra, pep band, photography, political, professional, radio and TV, recreation, religious, social, social service, student government, symphony, and yearbook. Popular campus events include Barefoot on the Mall, Mardis Gras, and Midnight Madness.

Sports: There are 9 intercollegiate sports for men and 9 for women, and 21 intramural sports for men and 21 for women. Facilities include a 43,000-seat stadium, an 8,000-seat basketball coliseum, a baseball and softball field, a track, and a natatorium. The Student Recreation Center includes 6 multipurpose courts, a cardiovascular and training area, 3 exercise studios, indoor and outdoor pools, an indoor track, a climbing wall, 7 racquetball courts, a squash court, and a fitness assessment center. The Recreational Sports Complex includes 10 football/soccer fields, 5 softball fields, and a ropes challenge course.

Disabled Students: 94% of the campus is accessible. Wheelchair ramps, elevators, special parking, specially equipped rest rooms, special class scheduling, lowered drinking fountains, lowered telephones, automatic doors, and state-of-the-art adaptive equipment are available.

Services: Counseling and information services are available, as is tutoring in some subjects, including physics, anthropology, biology, chemistry, English, psychology, math, sociology, and philosophy. There is a reader service for the blind and remedial math and reading.

Campus Safety and Security: Measures include 24-hour foot and vehicle patrol, self-defense education, escort service, and shuttle buses. There are informal discussions, pamphlets/posters/films, emergency telephones, lighted pathways/sidewalks, bicycle patrols, bicycle registration, motorist assistance, lost and found, operation ID, the Residence Hall Liaison Officer Program, on-and off-campus crime prevention safety tips, Staff and Faculty Eyes (SAFE) Campus Community Watch Program, and Alcohol Awareness.

Programs of Study: ECU confers B.A., B.S., B.F.A., B.M., B.S.A., B.S.A.P., B.S.B.A., B.S.B.E., B.S.N., B.S.O.T., and B.S.W. degrees. Master's and doctoral degrees are also awarded. Bachelor's degrees are awarded in BIOLOGICAL SCIENCE (biochemistry, biology/biological science, and nutrition), BUSINESS (accounting, banking and finance, business administration and management, hospitality management services, management information systems, marketing management, and recreational facilities management), COMMUNICATIONS AND THE ARTS (art, art history and appreciation, communications, dance, design, dramatic arts, English, French, German, music performance, music theory and composition, and studio art), COMPUTER AND PHYSICAL SCIENCE (applied physics, chemistry, computer science, data processing, geology, mathematics, and physics), EDUCATION (art, athletic training, business, dance, drama, early childhood, education of the emotionally handicapped, education of the mentally handicapped, elementary, English, foreign languages, health, mathematics, middle school, music, physical, science, and special), ENGINEERING AND ENVIRONMENTAL DESIGN (city/community/regional planning, construction management, electrical/electronics engineering technology, environmental engineering technology, industrial engineering technology, interior design, and manufacturing technology), HEALTH PROFESSIONS (environmental health science, exercise science, medical records administration/services, medical technology, music therapy, nursing, occupational therapy, physician's assistant, recreation therapy, rehabilitation therapy, and speech pathology/audiology), SOCIAL SCIENCE (anthropology, child care/child and family studies, clothing and textiles management/production/services, criminal justice, dietetics, economics, family and community services, geography, Hispanic American studies, history, liberal arts/general studies, parks and recreation management, philosophy, physical fitness/movement, political science/government, psychology, social work, sociology, and women's studies). Allied health, art, and music are the strongest academically. Education, health professions and related sciences, and business/marketing are the largest.

Required: To graduate, students must complete 120 to 128 semester hours with a minimum GPA of 2.0 overall and in the major. General education requirements include 12 hours of social science, 10 of humanities and fine arts, 8 of science, 6 of English, 3 of math, and 3 of health and exercise and sport science. The total must include 12 hours of writing-intensive courses and a course in cultural diversity.

Special: ECU offers cooperative programs in most majors, internships, study abroad in 38 countries, dual majors, work-study, and a student-designed major in multidisciplinary studies. There are 19 national honor societies, a freshman honors program, and 39 departmental honors programs.

Faculty/Classroom: 61% of faculty are male; 39%, female. No introductory courses are taught by graduate students. The average class size in an introductory lecture is 56; in a laboratory, 21; and in a regular course, 33.

Admissions: 78% of the 2001-2002 applicants were accepted. The SAT I scores for the 2001-2002 freshman class were: Verbal--43% below 500, 46% between 500 and 599, 10% between 600 and 700, and 1% above 700; Math--38% below 500, 50% between 500 and 599, 11% between 600 and 700, and 1% above 700. The ACT scores were 59% below 21, 29% between 21 and 23, 8% between 24 and 26, 2% between 27 and 28, and 2% above 28. 30% of the current freshmen were in the top fifth of their class; 67% were in the top two fifths. 34 freshmen graduated first in their class.

Requirements: The SAT I or ACT is required. In addition, applicants must be graduates of an accredited secondary school. All degree-seeking students are required to complete 20 academic units, including 4 in English, 3 in math, 3 in science with 1 lab course, and 2 in social studies with 1 in U.S. history. Also recommended are 2 units in a foreign language and 1 unit in fine arts. 1 unit each in foreign language, natural science, and math should be taken in the senior year. Special circumstances exist for applicants with a GED. A GPA of 2.0 is required. AP and CLEP credits are accepted. Applications are accepted on-line at *http://onestop4.ecu.edu/onestop/*

Procedure: Freshmen are admitted to all sessions. Entrance exams should be taken in the spring of the junior year or the fall of the senior year. There is a deferred admissions plan. Applications should be filed by March 15 for fall entry, November 1 for spring entry, and March 15 for summer entry. The fall 2001 application fee was $45. Notification is sent on a rolling basis after April 15.

Transfer: 1135 transfer students enrolled in 2001-2002. Applicants must submit official transcripts from high school and all colleges attended and have a satisfactory GPA in courses attempted. They must meet minimum academic requirements for admission of freshmen. 30 credits of 120 must be completed at ECU.

Visiting: There are regularly scheduled orientations for prospective students, including information sessions and campus tours. There are guides for informal visits. To schedule a visit, contact the Admissions Office.

Financial Aid: In 2001-2002, 60% of all freshmen and 57% of continuing students received some form of financial aid. 40% of freshmen and 41% of continuing students received need-based aid. The average freshman award was $6655. Of that total, scholarships or need-based grants averaged $3868 ($20,421 maximum); loans averaged $4771 ($24,250 maximum); and work contracts averaged $1510 ($5200 maximum). The average financial indebtedness of the 2001 graduate was $16,895. ECU is a member of CSS. The FAFSA is required. The fall application deadline is April 15.

International Students: There are 71 international students enrolled. The school actively recruits these students. They must score 550 on the written TOEFL or 213 on the electronic version.

Computers: The mainframe is an IBM S390/7000 series. There are 6100 PCs and Macs currently on the network. E-mail is provided for each enrolled student. Free Web access is provided to those students living in the residence halls. Students may register for classes, change their local mailing address, and check housing information, financial aid status, parking fines, hold tags, and so forth, using the ECU web site. Students may also register for classes using the automated voice response system. All students may access the system at all times. There are no time limits and no fees. It is strongly recommended that all students have a personal computer.

Graduates: In 2001, 2773 bachelor's degrees were awarded. The most popular majors were nursing (7%), elementary education (5%), and biology (5%). In an average class, 24% graduate in 4 years, 47% in 5 years, and 53% in 6 years. 70 companies recruited on campus in 2000-2001.

Admissions Contact: Thomas E. Powell, Jr., Director of Admissions. E-mail: *admis@mail.ecu.edu* Web: *www.ecu.edu/admissions*

ELIZABETH CITY STATE UNIVERSITY F-2

Elizabeth City, NC 27909 (252) 335-3305
(800) 347-ECSU; Fax: (252) 335-3537

Full-time: 680 men, 1085 women	**Faculty:** 113; IIB, av$
Part-time: 50 men, 150 women	**Ph.D.s:** 68%
Graduate: none	**Student/Faculty:** 16 to 1
Year: semesters, summer session	**Tuition:** $1650 ($8050)
Application Deadline: open	**Room & Board:** $3900
Freshman Class: n/av	
SAT I or ACT: required	**LESS COMPETITIVE**

Elizabeth City State University, founded in 1891 as part of the University of North Carolina System, is a public institution offering undergraduate programs in liberal arts and sciences, education, and business. Figures in above capsule are approximate. The library contains 174,566 volumes, 486,884 microform items, and 1220 audiovisual forms/CDs, and subscribes to 1698 periodicals. Computerized library services include the card catalog and interlibrary loans. Special learning facilities include a learning resource center, art gallery, planetarium, radio station, TV station, farm, and 639-acre educational research tract. The 829-acre campus is in a small town 55 miles from Norfolk, Virginia.

Student Life: 90% of undergraduates are from North Carolina. Others are from 20 states and 5 foreign countries. 75% are African American; 23% white. 25% do not continue beyond their first year; 50% remain to graduate.

Housing: 1019 students can be accommodated in college housing, which includes single-sex dormitories and on-campus apartments. In addition, there are honors houses. On-campus housing is guaranteed for all 4 years. 52% of students commute. Alcohol is not permitted. All students may keep cars.

Activities: There are 4 national fraternities and 4 national sororities. There are many groups and organizations on campus, including band, cheerleading, choir, chorus, dance, drama, honors, international, jazz band, literary magazine, marching band, newspaper, pep band, radio and TV, religious, social, student government, and yearbook.

Sports: Facilities include a 4500-seat gym, a 3500-seat stadium, an all-weather track, a golf range, an Olympic pool, a weight room, 8 tennis courts, dance and exercise studios, handball and racquetball courts, and playing fields.

Disabled Students: Wheelchair ramps, elevators, special parking, specially equipped rest rooms, and lowered drinking fountains are available.

Services: In addition to vocational counseling services, tutoring is available.

Campus Safety and Security: Measures include emergency telephones; ECSU has its own police department on campus.

Programs of Study: ECSU confers B.A., B.S., and B.S.Ed. degrees. Bachelor's degrees are awarded in BIOLOGICAL SCIENCE (biology/biological science), BUSINESS (accounting and business administration and management), COMMUNICATIONS AND THE ARTS (art, English, and music), COMPUTER AND PHYSICAL SCIENCE (chemistry, computer science, geology, mathematics, and physics), EDUCATION (business, elementary, industrial arts, middle school, physical, special, and technical), ENGINEERING AND ENVIRONMENTAL DESIGN (industrial engineering technology), SOCIAL SCIENCE (criminal justice, history, political science/government, psychology, social science, social work, and sociology).

Required: Students must have maintained a minimum GPA of 2.0, fulfilled a major, and completed the requirements of general education courses in the fields of grammar, composition, and literature.

Special: Opportunities are provided for internships, dual majors, weekend/evening degree completion programs, work-study, and credit by exam and for military service. There are 5 national honor societies and a freshman honors program.

Faculty/Classroom: All teach undergraduates.

Requirements: The SAT I or ACT is required. In addition, graduation from an accredited secondary school is required; the GED is accepted. Applicants should submit an academic record with 4 courses in English, 3 each in math and science, and 2 in social studies; it is recommended that applicants have at least 2 course units in foreign languages. Students must also pass the NC Competency Examination or its equivalent. A GPA of 2.0 is required. AP and CLEP credits are accepted.

Procedure: Freshmen are admitted fall, spring, and summer. Entrance exams should be taken as early as possible. There are early admissions and deferred admissions plans. Application deadlines are open. The fall 2001 application fee was $30.

Transfer: 102 transfer students enrolled in a recent year. Applicants must have a minimum college GPA of 2.0 and submit high school and college transcripts. Those with fewer than 30 credit hours must meet both freshman and transfer admission requirements. 30 credits must be completed at ECSU.

Visiting: There are regularly scheduled orientations for prospective students. There are guides for informal visits. To schedule a visit, contact the Admissions Office.

Financial Aid: The FAFSA, the college's own financial statement and income tax forms are required. Check with the school for current deadlines.

International Students: There were 6 international students enrolled in a recent year. They must take the MELAB and also take the SAT I or the ACT.

Computers: The mainframe is a DEC VAX 11/780 with an IBM PC network. The Academic Computing Center houses a computer lab that provides access to the state's major computer network and other systems through LINCNET and BITNET. Students in computer-related courses may access the system. There are no time limits and no fees. It is strongly recommended that all students have a personal computer.

Graduates: In a recent year, 375 bachelor's degrees were awarded. The most popular majors were criminal justice (20%), sociology and social work (16%), and business administration (11%). In an average class, 33% graduate in 4 years, 46% in 5 years, and 49% in 6 years.

Admissions Contact: Bridgett Golham, Director of Admissions and Recruitment. A video is available. E-mail: *admissions@alpha.ecsu.edu* Web: *www.ecsu.edu*

ELON COLLEGE
(See Elon University)

ELON UNIVERSITY D-2
(Formerly Elon College)

Elon, NC 27244-2010 (336) 278-3566
(800) 334-8448; Fax: (336) 278-7699

Full-time: 1580 men, 2484 women	**Faculty:** 210; IIB, av$
Part-time: 44 men, 52 women	**Ph.D.s:** 84%
Graduate: 75 men, 106 women	**Student/Faculty:** 19 to 1
Year: trimesters, summer session	**Tuition:** $14,560
Application Deadline: February 1	**Room & Board:** $4870
Freshman Class: 5328 applied, 3468 accepted, 1214 enrolled	
SAT I Verbal/Math: 560/560	**VERY COMPETITIVE**

Elon University, formerly Elon College, founded in 1889 by the United Church of Christ, is a private comprehensive institution that offers programs in the liberal arts and sciences career-oriented fields of study. There are 4 undergraduate and 3 graduate schools. In addition to regional accreditation, Elon has baccalaureate program accreditation with CAHEA and NCATE. The library contains 156,991 volumes, 825,964 microform items, and 11,061 audiovisual forms/CDs, and subscribes to 16,152 periodicals. Computerized library services include the card catalog, interlibrary loans, and database searching. Special learning facilities include a learning resource center, art gallery, radio station, TV station, a writing center, a botanical preserve, and an observatory. The 502-acre campus is in a suburban area adjacent to Burlington and 17 miles east of Greensboro. Including residence halls, there are 106 buildings.

Student Life: 72% of undergraduates are from out of state, mostly the Middle Atlantic. Others are from 46 states and 30 foreign countries. 84% are from public schools. 89% are white. 43% are Protestant; 25% Catholic. The average age of freshmen is 18; all undergraduates, 20. 17% do not continue beyond their first year; 69% remain to graduate.

Housing: Housing includes single-sex and coed dormitories, on-campus apartments, off-campus apartments, fraternity houses, and sorority houses. In addition, there are honors houses and special-interest houses, theme suites, and academic living-learning communities. On-campus housing is guaranteed for the freshman year only and is available on a lottery system for upperclassmen. 63% of students live on campus; of those, 65% remain on campus on weekends. All students may keep cars.

Activities: 31% of men belong to 9 national fraternities; 40% of women belong to 9 national sororities. There are 125 groups on campus, including art, band, cheerleading, choir, chorale, chorus, computers, dance, drama, drill team, ethnic, film, gay, honors, international, jazz band, literary magazine, marching band, musical theater, newspaper, orchestra, pep band, photography, political, professional, radio and TV, religious, social, social service, student government, symphony, and yearbook. Popular campus events include Family Weekend, Greek Week, and College Coffee.

Sports: There are 7 intercollegiate sports for men and 9 for women, and 21 intramural sports for men and 21 for women. Facilities include an 8250-seat stadium, lighted tennis courts, a baseball stadium, a field house, and 15 athletic fields. The athletic center has racquetball courts, aerobic rooms, a human performance lab, a weight room, a fitness center, 2 gyms, and an indoor swimming pool.

Disabled Students: 75% of the campus is accessible. Wheelchair ramps, elevators, special parking, specially equipped rest rooms, special class scheduling, lowered drinking fountains, lowered telephones, special housing assignments, special class locations, and special headphones for hearing-impaired students in auditoriums are available.

Services: Counseling and information services are available, as is tutoring in most subjects, including many lower-level courses. Preparatory courses are offered, which count as elective credit toward graduation.

Campus Safety and Security: Measures include 24-hour foot and vehicle patrol, self-defense education, escort service, and shuttle buses. There are informal discussions, pamphlets/posters/films, emergency telephones, and lighted pathways/sidewalks.

Programs of Study: Elon confers B.A., B.S., and B.F.A. degrees. Master's degrees are also awarded. Bachelor's degrees are awarded in BIOLOGICAL SCIENCE (biology/biological science), BUSINESS (accounting, business administration and management, and sports management), COMMUNICATIONS AND THE ARTS (art, broadcasting, communications, dramatic arts, English, film arts, French, journalism, music, music performance, musical theater, and Spanish), COMPUTER AND PHYSICAL SCIENCE (chemistry, computer science, mathematics, and physics), EDUCATION (elementary, foreign languages, health, mathematics, middle school, music, physical, science, secondary, social science, and special), ENGINEERING AND ENVIRONMENTAL DESIGN (environmental science, military science, and preengineering), HEALTH PROFESSIONS (medical technology and sports medicine), SOCIAL SCIENCE (economics, history, human services, international studies, philosophy, political science/government, psychology, public administration, religion, and sociology). Business, education, and music theater are the strongest academically. Business, education, and journalism and communication are the largest.

Required: To graduate, students must complete 132 semester hours, including 32 to 68 in the major, with a minimum GPA of 2.0. All students must fulfill the requirements of the General Studies program, which includes a first-year core, experiential learning, liberal studies, and advanced studies, for a total of 59 semester hours, and must satisfactorily complete a comprehensive exam in the major.

Special: Elon offers co-op programs in most majors, dual majors, student-designed majors, cross-registration with 7 other colleges and universities in North Carolina, paid and unpaid internships, study abroad in 25 countries, a Washington semester, work-study programs, pass/fail options, and a 3-2 dual engineering degree program with North Carolina State University. The 3-week January term includes extensive international study opportunites and courses with domestic travel components. There are 22 national honor societies, a freshman honors program, and 7 departmental honors programs.

Faculty/Classroom: 58% of faculty are male; 42%, female. All teach undergraduates, 62% do research, and 62% do both. No introductory courses are taught by graduate students. The average class size in an introductory lecture is 27; in a laboratory, 21; and in a regular course, 22.

Admissions: 65% of the 2001-2002 applicants were accepted. The SAT I scores for the 2001-2002 freshman class were: Verbal--15% below 500, 57% between 500 and 599, 26% between 600 and 700, and 2% above 700; Math--13% below 500, 57% between 500 and 599, 27% between 600 and 700, and 3% above 700. 41% of the current freshmen were in the top fifth of their class; 77% were in the top two fifths. There was 1 National Merit finalist. 7 freshmen graduated first in their class.

Requirements: The SAT I or ACT is required. In addition, students must be graduates of an accredited secondary school or have a GED certificate. They should have completed 4 credits in English, 3 or more in math, 2 or more in a foreign language, 2 or more in science, including at least one lab science, and 2 or more in social studies, including U.S. history. A GPA of 2.6 is required. AP and CLEP credits are accepted. Important factors in the admissions decision are advanced placement or honor courses, evidence of special talent, and leadership record. Applications are accepted on-line.

Procedure: Freshmen are admitted to all sessions. Entrance exams should be taken in the spring of the junior year and the fall of the senior year. There are early decision and deferred admissions plans. Early decision applications should be filed by November 15; regular applications, by February 1 for fall entry and December 1 for spring entry. The fall 2001 application fee was $35. Notification is sent on a rolling basis. 262 early decision candidates were accepted for the 2001-2002 class. 16% of all applicants are on a waiting list; 9 were accepted in 2001.

Transfer: 66 transfer students enrolled in 2001-2002. Applicants must present a high school transcript and a minimum GPA of 2.3 in college course work from a 4-year college. An interview is recommended. A dean's evaluation form is required from the last college or university attended, and the applicant must be eligible to return to that institution. 33 credits of 132 must be completed at Elon.

Visiting: There are regularly scheduled orientations for prospective students, consisting of 2 weekends in spring for deposited freshmen and a spring open house for nondeposited students. There are guides for informal visits and visitors may sit in on classes. To schedule a visit, contact the Admissions Office.

Financial Aid: In 2001-2002, 65% of all freshmen and 62% of continuing students received some form of financial aid. 38% of freshmen and 41% of continuing students received need-based aid. The average freshman award was $8348. Of that total, scholarships or need-based grants averaged $4417 ($19,430 maximum); loans averaged $4128 ($9625 maximum); and work contracts averaged $2357 ($2500 maximum). 26% of undergraduates work part time. Average annual earnings from campus work are $1100. The average financial indebtedness of the 2001 graduate was $11,684. The CSS/Profile or FAFSA and the college's own financial statement are required. The fall application deadline is March 15.

International Students: There are 58 international students enrolled. The school actively recruits these students. They must score 500 on the written TOEFL.

Computers: The mainframe is an HP 9000/series 887. The computer labs have 500 PC workstations connected to the HP mainframe, to 3 Novell servers, to the library, and to the Internet. Macs and PCs are both available. All students may access the system 24 hours a day via modem. There are no time limits and no fees. It is strongly recommended that all students have a personal computer.

Graduates: In 2001, 755 bachelor's degrees were awarded. The most popular majors were business (22%), journalism and communications (18%), and education (12%). In an average class, 62% graduate in 4 years, 65% in 5 years, and 69% in 6 years. 205 companies recruited on campus in 2000-2001. Of the 2000 graduating class, 12% were enrolled in graduate school within 6 months of graduation and 88% were employed.

Admissions Contact: Susan Klopman, Dean of Admissions. A video is available. E-mail: *admissions@elon.edu* Web: *http://www.elon.edu*

FAYETTEVILLE STATE UNIVERSITY D-3

Fayetteville, NC 28301-4298 **(910) 672-1371**
(800) 222-2594; Fax: (910) 437-2512

Full-time: 1199 men, 1927 women	**Faculty:** 202; IIA, -$
Part-time: 199 men, 482 women	**Ph.D.s:** n/av
Graduate: 171 men, 552 women	**Student/Faculty:** 15 to 1
Year: semesters, summer session	**Tuition:** $1770 ($9692)
Application Deadline: see profile	**Room & Board:** $3820
Freshman Class: 1570 applied, 1333 accepted, 776 enrolled	
SAT I or ACT: required	**LESS COMPETITIVE**

Fayetteville State University, founded in 1867 and today part of the University of North Carolina system, is a public institution offering degree programs in the arts and sciences, business, and teacher preparation. There are 3 undergraduate schools and 1 graduate school. In addition to regional accreditation, FSU has baccalaureate program accreditation with NCATE. The library contains 241,022 volumes, 936,006 microform items, and 6656 audiovisual forms/CDs. Computerized library services include the card catalog, interlibrary loans, and database searching. Special learning facilities include a planetarium and radio station. The 156-acre campus is in an urban area 60 miles south of Raleigh. Including residence halls, there are 40 buildings.

Student Life: 90% of undergraduates are from North Carolina. 75% are African American; 19% white. The average age of freshmen is 18; all undergraduates, 24. 29% do not continue beyond their first year; 32% remain to graduate.
Housing: 1200 students can be accommodated in college housing, which includes single-sex and coed dormitories and on-campus apartments. In addition, there is an honors dorm. On-campus housing is available on a first-come, first-served basis. 67% of students commute. Alcohol is not permitted. All students may keep cars.
Activities: 5% of men belong to 5 local and 4 national fraternities; 5% of women belong to 4 national sororities. There are 20 groups on campus, including band, cheerleading, choir, chorus, dance, drama, film, honors, international, jazz band, literary magazine, marching band, newspaper, pep band, political, radio and TV, religious, social service, student government, and yearbook. Popular campus events include The Lyceum, Martin Luther King Day, and Black History Month.
Sports: There are 6 intercollegiate sports for men and 7 for women, and 4 intramural sports for men and 2 for women. Facilities include 2 gyms, a stadium, tennis courts, a bowling alley, a dance studio, a swimming pool, and playing fields.
Disabled Students: 75% of the campus is accessible. Wheelchair ramps, elevators, special parking, specially equipped rest rooms, and lowered drinking fountains are available.
Services: Counseling and information services are available, as is tutoring in some subjects. There is remedial math, reading, and writing.
Campus Safety and Security: Measures include 24-hour foot and vehicle patrol, escort service, and lighted pathways/sidewalks.
Programs of Study: FSU confers B.A. and B.S. degrees. Master's degrees are also awarded. Bachelor's degrees are awarded in BIOLOGICAL SCIENCE (biology/biological science), BUSINESS (accounting, banking and finance, business administration and management, business economics, and office supervision and management), COMMUNICATIONS AND THE ARTS (dramatic arts, English, Spanish, speech/debate/rhetoric, and visual and performing arts), COMPUTER AND PHYSICAL SCIENCE (chemistry, computer science, and mathematics), EDUCATION (business, early childhood, elementary, health, marketing and distribution, middle school, music, secondary, and social science), HEALTH PROFESSIONS (medical laboratory technology, and nursing), SOCIAL SCIENCE (criminal justice, economics, geography, history, political science/government, psychology, public administration, social science, and sociology).
Required: To graduate, students must complete 120 credit hours with a minimum GPA of 2.0 overall and in the major. The core curriculum includes 8 to 11 credits in natural science, 6 to 15 in humanities, 6 to 7 in math, 3 to 9 in social science, 3 each in critical thinking and speech, and 2 each in phys ed/health and university seminar.
Special: FSU offers cooperative programs in business, math, and biological and physical sciences with North Carolina State University, internships, B.A.-B.S. degrees, dual majors, 3-2 engineering degree programs, credit for military experience, and nondegree study. There are 10 national honor societies, a freshman honors program, and 7 departmental honors programs.
Faculty/Classroom: 60% of faculty are male; 40%, female. All both teach and do research. No introductory courses are taught by graduate students. The average class size in an introductory lecture is 30; in a laboratory, 20; and in a regular course, 30.
Admissions: 85% of the 2001-2002 applicants were accepted. The SAT I scores for the 2001-2002 freshman class were: Verbal--82% below 500, 17% between 500 and 599, and 1% between 600 and 700; Math--83% below 500, 16% between 500 and 599, and 1% between 600 and 700.
Requirements: The SAT I or ACT is required. In addition, successful scores are also required on the North Carolina Competency Exam. Applicants must be graduates of an accredited secondary school or have the GED. They should have completed 4 academic units of English, 3 each of math and science with 1 lab course, and 2 of social studies; also recommended are 2 units of a foreign language and completion of 1 unit each of foreign language and math in the senior year. A GPA of 2.0 is required. AP and CLEP credits are accepted. Important factors in the admissions decision are advanced placement or honor courses, recommendations by school officials, and leadership record.
Procedure: Freshmen are admitted to all sessions. Entrance exams should be taken in November. There are early decision, early admissions, and deferred admissions plans. Check with the school for current application deadlines. The fall 2001 application fee was $25. Notification is sent on a rolling basis.
Transfer: 380 transfer students enrolled in 2001-2002. Applicants must submit official transcripts from all colleges attended, have a minimum GPA of 2.0, and be eligible to return to their previous institution. 30 credits of 120 must be completed at FSU.
Visiting: There are regularly scheduled orientations for prospective students, including a campus tour, recreational activity, placement tests, preregistration, and orientation to FSU services. There are guides for informal visits and visitors may sit in on classes and stay overnight. To schedule a visit, contact the Director of Enrollment Management.
Financial Aid: FSU is a member of CSS. The FAFSA is required.
International Students: They must score 550 on the written TOEFL or take some other English proficiency exam administered in their country, and also take the SAT I or the ACT, scoring 700 on the SAT I.
Computers: The mainframes are a DEC VAX 8530 and 6000-320 and a Sequent Balance. There are PC labs as well as teaching labs available to students. Other PCs are available in academic and administrative units. All students may access the system 24 hours a day. There are no time limits and no fees.
Graduates: In 2001, 598 bachelor's degrees were awarded. The most popular majors were business administration (19%), criminal justice (15%), and psychology (12%).
Admissions Contact: Charles Darlington, Director of Enrollment Management. A video is available. E-mail: *cdarlington@uncfsu.edu*
Web: *www.uncfsu.edu/admissions/index.htm*

GARDNER-WEBB UNIVERSITY — C-3
Boiling Springs, NC 28017-9980 — (704) 406-4491, (800) 253-6472

Full-time: 766 men, 1359 women	**Faculty:** 83; IIA, --$
Part-time: 135 men, 318 women	**Ph.D.s:** 70%
Graduate: 434 men, 552 women	**Student/Faculty:** 26 to 1
Year: semesters, summer session	**Tuition:** $12,520
Application Deadline: open	**Room & Board:** $4880
Freshman Class: 1754 applied, 1331 accepted, 378 enrolled	
SAT I Verbal/Math: 510/510	**COMPETITIVE**

Gardner-Webb University, founded in 1905, is an independent institution affiliated with the Southern Baptist Church and offering undergraduate programs in the arts and sciences, business, education, nursing, and preprofessional studies. In addition to regional accreditation, Webb has baccalaureate program accreditation with NASM, NCATE, and NLN. The library contains 220,726 volumes, 593,070 microform items, and 9434 audiovisual forms/CDs, and subscribes to 542 periodicals. Computerized library services include interlibrary loans and database searching. Special learning facilities include a learning resource center, radio station, and observatory. The 200-acre campus is in a small town 50 miles west of Charlotte. Including residence halls, there are 30 buildings.
Student Life: 76% of undergraduates are from North Carolina. Others are from 25 states, 30 foreign countries, and Canada. 88% are white; 11% African American. 78% are Protestant; 15% Catholic. The average age of freshmen is 19; all undergraduates, 24. 30% do not continue beyond their first year; 50% remain to graduate.
Housing: 1085 students can be accommodated in college housing, which includes single-sex dormitories, off-campus apartments, and married-student housing. In addition, there are honors houses. On-campus housing is guaranteed for all 4 years. 65% of students live on campus; of those, 65% remain on campus on weekends. Alcohol is not permitted. All students may keep cars.
Activities: There are no fraternities or sororities. There are 43 groups on campus, including band, cheerleading, choir, chorale, chorus, dance, drama, honors, international, jazz band, literary magazine, musical theater, newspaper, opera, orchestra, pep band, photography, radio and TV, religious, student government, symphony, and yearbook. Popular campus events include Parents Weekend, Spring Jubilee, and Alumni Day.
Sports: There are 7 intercollegiate sports for men and 4 for women, and 12 intramural sports for men and 12 for women. Facilities include a 5000-seat stadium, a gym, tennis and racquetball courts, a weight room, a swimming pool, and playing fields for softball, soccer, football, and baseball.
Disabled Students: All of the campus is accessible. Wheelchair ramps, elevators, special parking, specially equipped rest rooms, special class scheduling, and lowered drinking fountains are available.
Services: Counseling and information services are available, as is tutoring in every subject. There is a reader service for the blind, and remedial math, reading, and writing.
Campus Safety and Security: Measures include 24-hour foot and vehicle patrol, escort service, informal discussions, and pamphlets/posters/films. There are emergency telephones and a foot patrol inside the dorm.
Programs of Study: Webb confers B.A., B.S., and B.S.N. degrees. Associate and master's degrees are also awarded. Bachelor's degrees are awarded in BIOLOGICAL SCIENCE (biology/biological science), BUSINESS (accounting, business administration and management, international business management, and sports management), COMMUNICATIONS AND THE ARTS (American Sign Language, communications, English, French, music, and Spanish), COMPUTER AND PHYSICAL SCIENCE (chemistry, computer science, information sciences and systems, and mathematics), EDUCATION (athletic training, elementary, foreign languages, health, middle school, music, physical, and secondary), ENGINEERING AND ENVIRONMENTAL DESIGN (industrial administration/management), HEALTH PROFESSIONS (medical technology, nursing, and physician's assistant), SOCIAL SCIENCE (history, interpreter for the deaf, psychology, religion, religious music, social science, and

sociology). Preengineering, computer science, and premedicine are the strongest academically. Business is the largest.

Required: To graduate, students must complete 128 credit hours, including 24 to 32 in the major, with a minimum GPA of 2.0. The required core curriculum includes courses in English, history, religion, fine arts, foreign language, natural science, and math.

Special: The university offers work-study programs, internships, study abroad in 18 countries, 3-2 engineering degrees with Auburn University and the University of North Carolina at Charlotte, a 3-1 medical technology degree with the Bowman Gray School of Medicine of Wake Forest University, and a 3-2 physician's assistant program with the Wake Forest University School of Medicine. Independent study is encouraged. There are 2 national honor societies, a freshman honors program, and 3 departmental honors programs.

Faculty/Classroom: 58% of faculty are male; 43%, female. All teach undergraduates. No introductory courses are taught by graduate students. The average class size in an introductory lecture is 30; in a laboratory, 9; and in a regular course, 18.

Admissions: 76% of the 2001-2002 applicants were accepted. The SAT I scores for the 2001-2002 freshman class were: Verbal--49% below 500, 36% between 500 and 599, 13% between 600 and 700, and 1% above 700; Math--49% below 500, 38% between 500 and 599, 12% between 600 and 700, and 1% above 700. 34% of the current freshmen were in the top fifth of their class; 54% were in the top two fifths.

Requirements: The SAT I or ACT is required. In addition, candidates should be graduates of an accredited secondary school or have a GED certificate. The recommended preparatory curriculum includes 4 units of English, 3 of math, and 2 each of social science, natural science, a foreign language, and electives. An interview is encouraged. Webb requires applicants to be in the upper 50% of their class. A GPA of 2.4 is required. AP and CLEP credits are accepted. Important factors in the admissions decision are leadership record, advanced placement or honor courses, and evidence of special talent.

Procedure: Freshmen are admitted to all sessions. Entrance exams should be taken in the senior year. There is a deferred admissions plan. Application deadlines are open. The fall 2001 application fee was $25. Notification is sent on a rolling basis.

Transfer: Applicants must submit the standard application and fee, official high school and college transcripts, and SAT I or ACT scores. High school transcripts and test scores are waived for applicants with 30 or more semester credits and a GPA of 2.0. 32 credits of 128 must be completed at Webb.

Visiting: There are regularly scheduled orientations for prospective students. There are guides for informal visits and visitors may sit in on classes and stay overnight. To schedule a visit, contact the Admissions Office.

Financial Aid: Webb is a member of CSS. The FAFSA and federal tax returns are required.

International Students: The school actively recruits these students. They must score 500 on the written TOEFL.

Computers: The mainframe is an IBM/34. There are PCs available in 5 computer labs, located in the library and 4 other buildings. All students may access the system 7 A.M. to 11 P.M. except when a class is in progress. There are no time limits and no fees.

Admissions Contact: Nathan Alexander, Director of Admissions and Enrollment Management. Web: *www.gardner-webb.edu*

GREENSBORO COLLEGE — D-2
Greensboro, NC 27401-1875 — **(336) 272-7102, ext. 211**
(800) 346-8226; Fax: (336) 378-0154

Full-time: 446 men, 443 women	**Faculty:** 54; IIB, -$
Part-time: 80 men, 170 women	**Ph.D.s:** 78%
Graduate: none	**Student/Faculty:** 17 to 1
Year: semesters, summer session	**Tuition:** $13,700
Application Deadline: open	**Room & Board:** $5380
Freshman Class: 735 applied, 570 accepted, 246 enrolled	
SAT I Verbal/Math: 470/470	**ACT:** 18 **LESS COMPETITIVE**

Greensboro College, founded in 1838, is a private institution affiliated with the United Methodist Church and offering undergraduate programs in the arts and sciences, business, education, health sciences, and preprofessional studies. In addition to regional accreditation, Greensboro College has baccalaureate program accreditation with NCATE. The library contains 104,803 volumes, 2959 microform items, and 2509 audiovisual forms/CDs, and subscribes to 322 periodicals. Computerized library services include the card catalog, interlibrary loans, and database searching. Special learning facilities include a learning resource center, art gallery, and natural history museum. The 40-acre campus is in an urban area bordering downtown Greensboro. Including residence halls, there are 18 buildings.

Student Life: 66% of undergraduates are from North Carolina. Others are from 34 states, 18 foreign countries, and Canada. 79% are white; 16% African American. 62% are Protestant; 14% Catholic; 10% claim no religious affiliation. The average age of freshmen is 18; all undergraduates, 24. 34% do not continue beyond their first year; 46% remain to graduate.

Housing: 557 students can be accommodated in college housing, which includes single-sex and coed dormitories. In addition, there is an on-campus community service house. On-campus housing is guaranteed for all 4 years. 52% of students commute. All students may keep cars.

Activities: There are no fraternities or sororities. There are 52 groups on campus, including art, band, cheerleading, choir, chorale, computers, dance, debate, drama, ethnic, honors, jazz band, literary magazine, marching band, musical theater, newspaper, pep band, photography, professional, religious, social, social service, student government, and yearbook. Popular campus events include Winter Rose Formal, Festival of Lessons and Carols, and Spring Fling.

Sports: There are 8 intercollegiate sports for men and 8 for women, and 5 intramural sports for men and 5 for women. Facilities include an athletic field for soccer and lacrosse, tennis and basketball courts, and a gym with an indoor swimming pool and a weight room.

Disabled Students: 80% of the campus is accessible. Wheelchair ramps, elevators, special parking, specially equipped rest rooms, and special class scheduling are available.

Services: Counseling and information services are available, as is tutoring in most subjects. There is remedial math and writing, a computerized writing center, and a Writing Across the Curriculum program to strengthen communication skills. Professional math tutors are available.

Campus Safety and Security: Measures include 24-hour foot and vehicle patrol, self-defense education, escort service, and shuttle buses. There are informal discussions, pamphlets/posters/films, lighted pathways/sidewalks, and security entrances to residence halls.

Programs of Study: Greensboro College confers B.A. and B.S. degrees. Bachelor's degrees are awarded in BIOLOGICAL SCIENCE (biology/biological science), BUSINESS (accounting and business administration and management), COMMUNICATIONS AND THE ARTS (art, dramatic arts, English, French, music, and Spanish), COMPUTER AND PHYSICAL SCIENCE (chemistry and mathematics), EDUCATION (art, athletic training, drama, early childhood, elementary, English, foreign languages, mathematics, middle school, music, physical, science, secondary, social studies, and special), HEALTH PROFESSIONS (exercise science), SOCIAL SCIENCE (history, political science/government, psychology, religion, and sociology). Business and education are the largest.

Required: To graduate, students must complete 124 credit hours, including 30 to 48 in the major. They must take courses in social science, fine arts, lab science, English and literature, religion, history, phys ed, math, and foreign language. They must also take at least 1 course designated as global awareness and must demonstrate competency in writing, oral communication, and computing.

Special: The college offers cross-registration with members of the Greater Greensboro Consortium and the Piedmont Independent College Association, accelerated degree programs and internships in all majors, B.A.-B.S. degrees, work-study programs, study abroad, dual and student-designed majors, pass/fail options, and credit for life, military, and work experience. Greensboro's Ethics Across the Curriculum program exposes students to ethical issues in a range of disciplines to promote the study and living of ethical principles at the college. There are 11 national honor societies, a freshman honors program, and 10 departmental honors programs.

Faculty/Classroom: 46% of faculty are male; 54%, female. All teach undergraduates and 50% do research. The average class size in an introductory lecture is 21; in a laboratory, 16; and in a regular course, 14.

Admissions: 78% of the 2001-2002 applicants were accepted. The SAT I scores for the 2001-2002 freshman class were: Verbal--64% below 500, 27% between 500 and 599, 7% between 600 and 700, and 2% above 700; Math--60% below 500, 30% between 500 and 599, 8% between 600 and 700, and 2% above 700. The ACT scores were 69% below 21, 11% between 21 and 23, 15% between 24 and 26, 2% between 27 and 28, and 3% above 28. 10% of the current freshmen were in the top fifth of their class; 38% were in the top two fifths.

Requirements: The SAT I or ACT is required. In addition, applicants must be graduates of an accredited secondary school or have a GED certificate. An essay is required, and an interview is recommended. Selected majors must audition or present a portfolio. AP and CLEP credits are accepted. Important factors in the admissions decision are advanced placement or honor courses, leadership record, and evidence of special talent. Applications are accepted on-line at the school's web site.

Procedure: Freshmen are admitted to all sessions. Entrance exams should be taken in the spring of the junior year. There are early action, early admissions, and deferred admissions plans. Early action applications should be filed by December 15; for regular applications, deadlines are open. The fall 2001 application fee was $35. Notification of early action is sent January 31; regular decision, within 2 weeks of receipt of a complete application.

Transfer: 82 transfer students enrolled in 2001-2002. Official transcripts from any college attended are required. Standardized test scores and high school records are required of applicants with fewer than 30 semester hours. An essay is required, and an interview is recommended. 31 credits of 124 must be completed at Greensboro College.

Visiting: There are regularly scheduled orientations for prospective students, including an interview, a campus tour, and meetings with faculty and students. There are guides for informal visits and visitors may sit in on classes and stay overnight. To schedule a visit, contact the Admissions Office.

Financial Aid: In 2001-2002, the average freshman award was $9443. 34% of undergraduates work part time. Average annual earnings from campus work are $700. The average financial indebtedness of a recent year's graduate was $12,229. Greensboro College is a member of CSS. The CSS/Profile or FAFSA is required. The fall application deadline is March 1.

International Students: There are 29 international students enrolled. They must score 550 on the written TOEFL or 213 on the electronic version.

Computers: There are 95 PCs located in classrooms, computer labs, residence halls, the library, and the student center. Students have access to e-mail, the Internet and World Wide Web, and on-line course support; the campuswide network may be accessed from residence halls and off campus. Students have file sharing space on the server and can have a home page. All students may access the system 24 hours a day. There are no time limits and no fees. It is strongly recommended that all students have a personal computer, preferably one that is networkable.

Graduates: In 2001, 134 bachelor's degrees were awarded. The most popular majors were business (26%), education (13%), and sports and exercise studies (11%). In an average class, 1% graduate in 3 years, 30% in 4 years, 44% in 5 years, and 46% in 6 years. 50 companies recruited on campus in 2000-2001. Of a recent graduating class, 9% were enrolled in graduate school within 6 months of graduation and 85% were employed.

Admissions Contact: Tim Jackson, Vice President of Admissions. A video is available. E-mail: *admissions@gborocollege.edu*
Web: *http://www.gborocollege.edu*

GUILFORD COLLEGE D-2

Greensboro, NC 27410 (336) 316-2100
(800) 992-7759; Fax: (336) 316-2954

Full-time: 613 men, 694 women	**Faculty:** 69; IIB, -$
Part-time: 81 men, 102 women	**Ph.D.s:** 70%
Graduate: none	**Student/Faculty:** 19 to 1
Year: semesters, summer session	**Tuition:** $17,645
Application Deadline: February 15	**Room & Board:** $5610
Freshman Class: 1246 applied, 1063 accepted, 327 enrolled	
SAT I or ACT: required	**COMPETITIVE**

Guilford College, founded in 1837 by the Religious Society of Friends (Quakers), is a private liberal arts and sciences institution. In addition to regional accreditation, Guilford College has baccalaureate program accreditation with NCATE. The library contains 215,153 volumes, 19,948 microform items, and 16,116 audiovisual forms/CDs, and subscribes to 916 periodicals. Computerized library services include the card catalog, interlibrary loans, and database searching. Special learning facilities include a learning resource center, art gallery, radio station, observatory, and multimedia learning center for cultures and languages. The 340-acre campus is in a suburban area in northwest Greensboro. Including residence halls, there are 31 buildings.

Student Life: 52% of undergraduates are from out of state, mostly the South. Others are from 43 states, 24 foreign countries, and Canada. 63% are from public schools. 84% are white. 45% are claim no religious affiliation; 43% Protestant. The average age of freshmen is 19; all undergraduates, 22. 23% do not continue beyond their first year; 72% remain to graduate.

Housing: 826 students can be accommodated in college housing, which includes single-sex and coed dormitories, on-campus apartments, and married-student housing. In addition, there are special-interest houses and co-op housing. On-campus housing is guaranteed for the freshman year only and is available on a lottery system for upperclassmen. 73% of students live on campus; of those, 80% remain on campus on weekends. All students may keep cars.

Activities: There are no fraternities or sororities. There are 43 groups on campus, including art, chess, choir, chorale, chorus, dance, drama, ethnic, film, gay, honors, international, jazz band, literary magazine, musical theater, newspaper, pep band, photography, political, professional, radio and TV, religious, social, social service, student government, and yearbook. Popular campus events include Serendipity Spring Festival, Christmas Choir Concert, and International Dinner.

Sports: There are 7 intercollegiate sports for men and 6 for women, and 3 intramural sports for men and 3 for women. Facilities include a 3500-seat football/track stadium, a 2500-seat gym, a field house, a baseball field, basketball courts, a swimming pool and diving tank, playing fields, courts for tennis, badminton, and volleyball, and a weight room.

Disabled Students: 95% of the campus is accessible. Wheelchair ramps, elevators, special parking, specially equipped rest rooms, special class scheduling, lowered drinking fountains, lowered telephones, and an ATM machine are available.

Services: Counseling and information services are available, as is tutoring in every subject. There is a reader service for the blind, and remedial math, reading, and writing. There is faculty tutoring for skills development and student tutoring for course-specific help. Also available are nonremedial writing help, assistance with organizational/time-management skills, and services for students with learning disabilities. Remedial assistance is individually targeted and developmental with a focus on regular assignments.

Campus Safety and Security: Measures include 24-hour foot and vehicle patrol, escort service, informal discussions, and pamphlets/posters/films. There are emergency telephones, lighted pathways/sidewalks, and a whistle program.

Programs of Study: Guilford College confers A.B., B.S., and B.F.A. degrees. Bachelor's degrees are awarded in BIOLOGICAL SCIENCE (biology/biological science), BUSINESS (accounting, business administration and management, and sports management), COMMUNICATIONS AND THE ARTS (dramatic arts, English, fine arts, French, German, music, and Spanish), COMPUTER AND PHYSICAL SCIENCE (chemistry, geology, mathematics, and physics), EDUCATION (elementary, physical, and secondary), ENGINEERING AND ENVIRONMENTAL DESIGN (environmental science), HEALTH PROFESSIONS (health science and sports medicine), SOCIAL SCIENCE (African American studies, criminal justice, economics, history, humanities, international studies, parks and recreation management, peace studies, philosophy, political science/government, psychology, religion, sociology, and women's studies). Psychology, natural sciences, and English are the strongest academically. Management, psychology, and English are the largest.

Required: Students must fulfill requirements in fine arts, English, humanities, sciences, social sciences, and foreign language. They must take a first-year experience and an interdisciplinary capstone course, and courses in historical perspectives, intercultural studies, social justice and environmental responsibility, diversity, and business and policy studies.

Special: There are 3-2 degree programs available in forestry and environmental studies with Duke University, and in physician assistant training with Bowman Gray School of Medicine at Wake Forest University. Guilford also offers many internships, a Washington semester, work-study programs, accelerated degree programs in business management, computer information systems, psychology, and biology, dual majors, student-designed majors, study abroad in 9 countries, and cross-registration with members of the Greater Greensboro Consortium (8 colleges/universities). There are 2 national honor societies and a freshman honors program.

Faculty/Classroom: 54% of faculty are male; 46%, female. All both teach and do research. The average class size in an introductory lecture is 20; in a laboratory, 15; and in a regular course, 17.

Admissions: 85% of the 2001-2002 applicants were accepted. The SAT I scores for the 2001-2002 freshman class were: Verbal--17% below 500, 38% between 500 and 599, 37% between 600 and 700, and 8% above 700; Math--23% below 500, 47% between 500 and 599, 26% between 600 and 700, and 4% above 700. The ACT scores were 19% below 21, 22% between 21 and 23, 23% between 24 and 26, 9% between 27 and 28, and 27% above 28. 33% of the current freshmen were in the top fifth of their class; 66% were in the top two fifths. 8 freshmen graduated first in their class.

Requirements: The SAT I or ACT is required. A minimum SAT I composite score of 1000 or ACT score of 22 is recommended. Applicants should have completed 20 Carnegie units, including 4 in English, 2 each in foreign language and science, and 1 each in history and social studies. The GED is accepted. An essay is required and an interview is recommended. A GPA of 2.0 is required. AP and CLEP credits are accepted. Important factors in the admissions decision are advanced placement or honor courses, extracurricular activities record, and evidence of special talent. Applications are accepted on-line at the Guilford web site.

Procedure: Freshmen are admitted fall and spring. Entrance exams should be taken in spring of the junior year or fall of the senior year. There are early decision, early admissions, and deferred admissions plans. Early decision applications should be filed by November 15; regular applications, by February 15 for fall entry and December 1 for spring entry, along with a $25 fee. Notification of early decision is sent December 15; regular decision, April 1. 38 early decision candidates were accepted for the 2001-2002 class. A waiting list is an active part of the admissions procedure.

Transfer: 42 transfer students enrolled in 2001-2002. Applicants must have a minimum GPA of 2.5 in at least 12 credit hours, submit either SAT I or ACT scores, and provide a letter from the academic adviser or dean of the previous school. An interview is recommended. 64 credits of 128 must be completed at Guilford College.

Visiting: There are regularly scheduled orientations for prospective students, including forums, a campus tour, and presentations by faculty, administrators, and students. There are guides for informal visits and visitors may sit in on classes and stay overnight. To schedule a visit, contact the Admission Office.

Financial Aid: In 2001-2002, 99% of all freshmen received some form of financial aid. The average freshman award was $11,712. Guilford

College is a member of CSS. The CSS/Profile or FAFSA is required. The fall application deadline is March 1.

International Students: There are 37 international students enrolled. The school actively recruits these students. They must score 550 on the written TOEFL or 213 on the electronic version.

Computers: The mainframe consists of Compaq Proliant Windows 2000 servers. There are 250 terminals and PCs in the central lab and classroom building, with access from other buildings through the campus network. All students have e-mail and Internet access, and all residence hall rooms have network connections. All students may access the system 24 hours a day. There are no time limits and no fees.

Graduates: In 2001, 272 bachelor's degrees were awarded. The most popular majors were English (11%), psychology (10%), and business management (10%). In an average class, 51% graduate in 4 years, 65% in 5 years, and 72% in 6 years. 85 companies recruited on campus in 2000-2001. Of the 2000 graduating class, 21% were enrolled in graduate school within 1 year of graduation and 87% were employed.

Admissions Contact: Randy Doss, Vice President of Enrollment and Marketing. E-mail: *admission@guilford.edu* Web: *www.guilford.edu*

HIGH POINT UNIVERSITY — D-2

High Point, NC 27262-3598 — **(336) 841-9216**
(800) 345-6993; Fax: (336) 888-6382

Full-time: 851 men, 1464 women	**Faculty:** 118; IIB, av$
Part-time: 113 men, 162 women	**Ph.D.s:** 83%
Graduate: 63 men, 99 women	**Student/Faculty:** 20 to 1
Year: semesters, summer session	**Tuition:** $13,150
Application Deadline: open	**Room & Board:** $6030
Freshman Class: 1571 applied, 1384 accepted, 489 enrolled	
SAT I Verbal/Math: 503/504	**LESS COMPETITIVE**

High Point University, founded in 1924, is a private institution affiliated with the United Methodist Church. The university offers undergraduate and graduate programs in the arts, science, business, and education, both on its main campus and on its Winston-Salem campus, which accommodates evening students. In addition to regional accreditation, High Point has baccalaureate program accreditation with CAAHEP and NCATE. The library contains 195,658 volumes, 82,000 microform items, and 11,000 audiovisual forms/CDs, and subscribes to 1045 periodicals. Computerized library services include the card catalog, interlibrary loans, and database searching. Special learning facilities include a learning resource center, art gallery, radio station, and TV studio. The 80-acre campus is in a suburban area 15 miles southeast of Winston-Salem and 12 miles southwest of Greensboro. Including residence halls, there are 26 buildings.

Student Life: 55% of undergraduates are from out of state, mostly the Middle Atlantic. Students are from 36 states, 52 foreign countries, and Canada. 88% are from public schools. 78% are white; 17% African American. 76% are Protestant; 15% Catholic. The average age of freshmen is 18; all undergraduates, 20. 24% do not continue beyond their first year; 53% remain to graduate.

Housing: 1044 students can be accommodated in college housing, which includes single-sex and coed dormitories, on-campus apartments, fraternity houses, and sorority houses. In addition, there are special-interest houses and wellness halls. On-campus housing is guaranteed for all 4 years. 60% of students live on campus; of those, 80% remain on campus on weekends. All students may keep cars.

Activities: 38% of men belong to 4 national fraternities; 37% of women belong to 1 local sorority and 4 national sororities. There are 65 groups on campus, including art, band, cheerleading, choir, chorale, chorus, computers, dance, debate, drama, environmental, ethnic, film, honors, international, literary magazine, musical theater, newspaper, outdoor, pep band, political, professional, radio and TV, religious, social, social service, student government, and yearbook. Popular campus events include Greek Week, Family Weekend, and Winter Festival.

Sports: There are 7 intercollegiate sports for men and 7 for women, and 8 intramural sports for men and 8 for women. Facilities include intramural fields, tennis courts, an intramural gym, and a recreation center featuring a swimming pool, racquetball courts, an aerobics center, a weight room, and a 2500-seat arena.

Disabled Students: 90% of the campus is accessible. Wheelchair ramps, elevators, special parking, specially equipped rest rooms, special class scheduling, and lowered drinking fountains are available.

Services: Counseling and information services are available, as is tutoring in every subject. There is remedial math, reading, and writing.

Campus Safety and Security: Measures include 24-hour foot and vehicle patrol, self-defense education, escort service, and informal discussions. There are pamphlets/posters/films, emergency telephones, lighted pathways/sidewalks, 24-hour secured residence halls, and student bike patrols.

Programs of Study: High Point confers B.A. and B.S. degrees. Master's degrees are also awarded. Bachelor's degrees are awarded in AGRICULTURE (forestry and related sciences), BIOLOGICAL SCIENCE (biology/biological science), BUSINESS (accounting, business administration and management, international business management, marketing/retailing/merchandising, recreation and leisure services, and sports management), COMMUNICATIONS AND THE ARTS (art, dramatic arts, English, fine arts, French, modern language, and Spanish), COMPUTER AND PHYSICAL SCIENCE (chemistry, computer science, information sciences and systems, and mathematics), EDUCATION (art, athletic training, elementary, middle school, physical, secondary, and special), ENGINEERING AND ENVIRONMENTAL DESIGN (interior design), HEALTH PROFESSIONS (exercise science, medical laboratory technology, and sports medicine), SOCIAL SCIENCE (American studies, criminal justice, history, home furnishings and equipment management/production/services, human services, industrial and organizational psychology, international studies, philosophy, physical fitness/movement, political science/government, psychology, religion, and sociology). Business administration, exercise science, and education are the largest.

Required: To graduate, students must complete 124 credit hours, including up to 60 in the major, with a minimum GPA of 2.0. The core curriculum consists of 2 courses each in English, history, social science, phys ed, and a modern foreign language, as well as 1 course each in math, lab science, religion, fine arts, ethics, global studies, and senior seminar.

Special: There is cross-registration with the University of North Carolina at Greensboro, North Carolina Agricultural and Technical State University, and Greensboro, Elon, Guilford, and Bennett Colleges. High Point also offers study abroad in 7 countries, the Student Career Internship Program, a dual major in chemistry and business, accelerated degree programs, unique programs in home furnishings marketing/management studies, work-study programs, student-designed majors, and 3-2 forestry and environmental management programs with Duke University. There are 2 national honor societies, a freshman honors program, and 2 departmental honors programs.

Faculty/Classroom: 56% of faculty are male; 44%, female. All teach undergraduates. No introductory courses are taught by graduate students. The average class size in an introductory lecture is 25; in a laboratory, 20; and in a regular course, 16.

Admissions: 88% of the 2001-2002 applicants were accepted. The SAT I scores for the 2001-2002 freshman class were: Verbal--48% below 500, 39% between 500 and 599, 11% between 600 and 700, and 2% above 700; Math--46% below 500, 38% between 500 and 599, 14% between 600 and 700, and 2% above 700. 32% of the current freshmen were in the top fifth of their class; 60% were in the top two fifths. In a recent year, there was 1 National Merit finalist and 4 semifinalists. 7 freshmen graduated first in their class.

Requirements: The SAT I or ACT is required. In addition, applicants should be graduates of an accredited secondary school or have a GED certificate. They should have completed 16 academic units, including 4 in English, 2 each in math and language, 1 each in science and history, and 6 electives. A GPA of 2.0 is required. AP and CLEP credits are accepted. Important factors in the admissions decision are advanced placement or honor courses, evidence of special talent, and extracurricular activities record. Applications are accepted on computer disk and on-line at the school's web site.

Procedure: Freshmen are admitted to all sessions. Entrance exams should be taken prior to high school graduation. There are early admissions and deferred admissions plans. Application deadlines are open. The application fee is $25. Notification is sent on a rolling basis.

Transfer: 245 transfer students enrolled in 2001-2002. Applicants must submit official transcripts from colleges and high schools previously attended, as well as SAT I or ACT scores, if available. Generally, a minimum GPA of 2.0 is required. 31 credits of 124 must be completed at High Point.

Visiting: There are regularly scheduled orientations for prospective students, which are held at the beginning of each term. There are guides for informal visits and visitors may sit in on classes. To schedule a visit, contact the Admissions Office.

Financial Aid: In 2001-2002, 92% of all freshmen and 93% of continuing students received some form of financial aid. 67% of freshmen and 95% of continuing students received need-based aid. The average freshman award was $9200. Of that total, scholarships or need-based grants averaged $5075 ($11,000 maximum); loans averaged $2625 ($6625 maximum); and work contracts averaged $1500 ($2000 maximum). 52% of undergraduates work part time. Average annual earnings from campus work are $1500. The average financial indebtedness of the 2001 graduate was $14,000. High Point is a member of CSS. The FAFSA is required.

International Students: There are 123 international students enrolled. They must score 500 on the written TOEFL or take the MELAB, the Comprehensive English Language Test, or the college's own test.

Computers: The mainframe is an Enterprise 450 minicomputer with13 Intel-based servers. There are 7 computer labs on campus with more than 150 PCs. Student rooms are linked to the Internet. All students may access the system up to 80 hours per week. There are no time limits. The fee is $100. It is strongly recommended that all students have a personal computer.

Graduates: In 2001, 584 bachelor's degrees were awarded. The most popular majors were business administration (38%), computer and information sciences (20%), and education (7%). In an average class, 48% graduate in 4 years, 51% in 5 years, and 53% in 6 years. 115 companies recruited on campus in 2000-2001. Of the 2000 graduating class, 10% were enrolled in graduate school within 6 months of graduation and 87% were employed.
Admissions Contact: James L. Schlimmer, Dean of Enrollment Management. E-mail: *admiss@highpoint.edu* Web: *www.highpoint.edu*

JOHNSON C. SMITH UNIVERSITY C-3
Charlotte, NC 28216 (704) 378-1010
(800) 782-7303; Fax: (704) 378-1242

Full-time: 620 men, 873 women **Faculty:** 92
Part-time: 50 men, 52 women **Ph.D.s:** 77%
Graduate: none **Student/Faculty:** 16 to 1
Year: semesters, summer session **Tuition:** $11,971
Application Deadline: August 1 **Room & Board:** $4589
Freshman Class: 4542 applied, 2019 accepted, 462 enrolled
SAT I Verbal/Math: 483/486 **ACT:** 17 **COMPETITIVE+**

Johnson C. Smith University, founded in 1867, is a progressive historically black private institution offering a liberal arts education and affiliated with the Presbyterian Church (U.S.A.). There are 2 undergraduate schools. In addition to regional accreditation, JCSU has baccalaureate program accreditation with CSWE and NCATE. The library contains 118,000 volumes, 43,000 microform items, and 3000 audiovisual forms/CDs, and subscribes to 700 periodicals. Computerized library services include the card catalog, interlibrary loans, and database searching. Special learning facilities include a learning resource center and radio station. The 105-acre campus is in an urban area in Charlotte. Including residence halls, there are 46 buildings.
Student Life: 73% of undergraduates are from out of state, mostly the Northeast. Students are from 33 states and 5 foreign countries. 97% are from public schools. All are African American. Most are Protestant. The average age of freshmen is 18; all undergraduates, 22. 30% do not continue beyond their first year; 42% remain to graduate.
Housing: 1151 students can be accommodated in college housing, which includes single-sex and coed dormitories. In addition, there are honors houses. On-campus housing is available on a first-come, first-served basis. 80% of students live on campus; of those, 76% remain on campus on weekends. Alcohol is not permitted. Upperclassmen may keep cars.
Activities: 9% of men belong to 4 local and 4 national fraternities; 11% of women belong to 4 local and 4 national sororities. There are 39 groups on campus, including art, band, cheerleading, chess, choir, chorale, chorus, computers, dance, debate, drama, ethnic, film, honors, international, jazz band, literary magazine, marching band, newspaper, orchestra, pep band, photography, political, radio and TV, religious, social service, student government, symphony, and yearbook. Popular campus events include Founders Day, West Fest, and Family Day.
Sports: There are 6 intercollegiate sports for men and 5 for women, and 5 intramural sports for men and 5 for women. Facilities include a 3200-seat gym, a pool, tennis and basketball courts, a weight room, a training room, an Olympic-size track, a football field, and an off-campus, city-owned stadium seating 25,000.
Disabled Students: 5% of the campus is accessible. Wheelchair ramps, special parking, and special class scheduling are available.
Services: Counseling and information services are available, as is tutoring in every subject.
Campus Safety and Security: Measures include 24-hour foot and vehicle patrol, self-defense education, escort service, and informal discussions. There are pamphlets/posters/films, emergency telephones, lighted pathways/sidewalks, and push-button emergency stations.
Programs of Study: JCSU confers B.A., B.S., and B.S.W degrees. Bachelor's degrees are awarded in BIOLOGICAL SCIENCE (biology/biological science), BUSINESS (business administration and management and business economics), COMMUNICATIONS AND THE ARTS (communications, English, music, and music business management), COMPUTER AND PHYSICAL SCIENCE (applied mathematics, chemistry, computer science, mathematics, and physics), EDUCATION (elementary, health, middle school, physical, secondary, and social studies), ENGINEERING AND ENVIRONMENTAL DESIGN (computer engineering and preengineering), HEALTH PROFESSIONS (predentistry and premedicine), SOCIAL SCIENCE (economics, history, liberal arts/general studies, political science/government, prelaw, psychology, social science, social work, and sociology). Business administration is the strongest academically. Business and communication arts are the largest.
Required: To graduate, students must complete 122 credit hours, including 30 to 59 in the major, with a minimum GPA of 2.0. Distribution requirements include 47 hours of courses in English, composition, the humanities, social science, health and phys ed, math, computer science, activities, and natural science. Students must take a competency exam in the sophomore year, write a senior paper, and participate in community service activities.
Special: JCSU offers cooperative programs in business administration, student-designed majors, 3-2 engineering degrees with UNCC and Florida A & M University, cross-registration with the Charlotte Area Educational Consortium, dual majors in engineering and nursing, internships with local businesses, work-study programs, study abroad in 9 countries, and a B.A.-B.S. degree in all majors. Nondegree study in continuing education and pass/fail options are available. There are 9 national honor societies and a freshman honors program.
Faculty/Classroom: 64% of faculty are male; 36%, female. All teach undergraduates, and 2% also do research. The average class size in an introductory lecture is 30; in a laboratory, 15; and in a regular course, 25.
Admissions: 44% of the 2001-2002 applicants were accepted. The SAT I scores for the 2001-2002 freshman class were: Verbal--88% below 500, 11% between 500 and 599, and 1% between 600 and 700; Math--88% below 500, 11% between 500 and 599, and 1% between 600 and 700. 35% of the current freshmen were in the top fifth of their class; 60% were in the top two fifths. 28 freshmen graduated first in their class.
Requirements: The SAT I or ACT is required; a minimum SAT I composite score of 830 or ACT score of 17 is recommended. Applicants should have completed 16 Carnegie units, including 4 in English, 3 in math, 2 each in social science and science, and 5 in electives. The GED is accepted. An essay and an interview are suggested. JCSU requires applicants to be in the upper 60% of their class. A GPA of 2.2 is required. AP credits are accepted. Important factors in the admissions decision are advanced placement or honor courses, recommendations by school officials, and extracurricular activities record. Applications are accepted on-line via CollegeLink and the school's web site.
Procedure: Freshmen are admitted fall and spring. Entrance exams should be taken prior to application. There are early decision and deferred admissions plans. Applications should be filed by August 1 for fall entry. The fall 2001 application fee was $25. Notification is sent on a rolling basis. 100 early decision candidates were accepted for the 2001-2002 class.
Transfer: 40 transfer students enrolled in 2001-2002. Applicants need a minimum GPA of 2.0 in 12 semester hours of transferable course work. 32 credits of 122 must be completed at JCSU.
Visiting: There are regularly scheduled orientations for prospective students. There are guides for informal visits and visitors may sit in on classes and stay overnight. To schedule a visit, contact the Director of Admissions at (704) 378-1000.
Financial Aid: In 2001-2002, 87% of all freshmen and 85% of continuing students received some form of financial aid. The average freshman award was $7500. Of that total, scholarships or need-based grants averaged $2500 ($13,849 maximum); loans averaged $2229 ($2625 maximum); and work contracts averaged $2000. 60% of undergraduates work part time. Average annual earnings from campus work are $1500. The average financial indebtedness of the 2001 graduate was $18,000. JCSU is a member of CSS. The FAFSA is required. The fall application deadline is April 15.
International Students: There were 9 international students enrolled in a recent year. The school actively recruits these students. They must score 500 on the written TOEFL and also take the SAT I or the ACT, scoring 830 on the SAT I.
Computers: The mainframe is an IBM AS/400. More than 400 PCs and printers are located throughout the campus, including some residence halls. Internet access, campus file servers, and e-mail are available. All students may access the system 8:30 A.M. to midnight. There is a 2-hour limit per sitting. There are no fees. All students are required to have personal computers.
Graduates: In a recent year, 237 bachelor's degrees were awarded. The most popular majors were business administration (21%), communication arts (16%), and psychology (10%). In an average class, 30% graduate in 4 years, 37% in 5 years, and 40% in 6 years. 87 companies recruited on campus in a recent year. Of a recent graduating class, 20% were enrolled in graduate school within 6 months of graduation and 45% were employed.
Admissions Contact: Jeffrey A. Smith, Associate Director of Admissions. A video is available. E-mail: *jsmith@jscu.edu*
Web: *http://www.jcsu.edu/*

LEES-MCRAE COLLEGE B-2
Banner Elk, NC 28604 (828) 898-8829
(800) 280-4562; Fax: (828) 898-8707

Full-time: 338 men, 424 women **Faculty:** 54; III, --$
Part-time: 3 men, 27 women **Ph.D.s:** 74%
Graduate: none **Student/Faculty:** 14 to 1
Year: semesters, summer session **Tuition:** $12,442
Application Deadline: open **Room & Board:** $4664
Freshman Class: 524 applied, 488 accepted, 195 enrolled
SAT I Verbal/Math: 490/470 **ACT:** 20 **LESS COMPETITIVE**

Lees-McRae College, founded in 1900, is an independent nonprofit liberal arts institution affiliated with the Presbyterian Church (U.S.A). In addition to regional accreditation, Lees-McRae has baccalaureate program accreditation with NCATE. The library contains 96,628 volumes, 256,447 microform items, and 2326 audiovisual forms/CDs, and subscribes to 343 periodicals. Computerized library services include the card catalog, interlibrary loans, and database searching. Special learning facilities include a learning resource center, art gallery, and an academic advancement center. The 400-acre campus is in a rural area 17 miles south of Boone and 100 miles northwest of Charlotte. Including residence halls, there are 33 buildings.

Student Life: 61% of undergraduates are from North Carolina. Others are from 30 states, 16 foreign countries, and Canada. 86% are white. 65% are Protestant; 21% claim no religious affiliation; 10% Catholic. The average age of freshmen is 18; all undergraduates, 23. 35% do not continue beyond their first year; 37% remain to graduate.

Housing: 488 students can be accommodated in college housing, which includes single-sex and coed dormitories. In addition, there is substance-free housing. On-campus housing is guaranteed for all 4 years. 53% of students live on campus; of those, 30% remain on campus on weekends. Alcohol is not permitted. All students may keep cars.

Activities: There are no fraternities or sororities. There are 20 groups on campus, including cheerleading, choir, chorus, dance, drama, honors, international, musical theater, newspaper, pep band, professional, religious, social, social service, student government, and yearbook. Popular campus events include Staley Distinguished Lectureship, Spring Fling, and Mountain Day.

Sports: There are 8 intercollegiate sports for men and 7 for women, and 11 intramural sports for men and 11 for women. Facilities include a main gym that seats 2000 with basketball/volleyball courts, a match field for soccer/lacrosse, 4 practice fields, a softball field with batting cages, 2 indoor tennis courts, 6 outdoor tennis courts, a secondary gym for intramurals, an indoor Olympic size pool, a fitness center, a weight room facility, outdoor basketball court, and a beach volleyball court.

Disabled Students: 50% of the campus is accessible. Wheelchair ramps, special parking, and specially equipped rest rooms are available.

Services: Counseling and information services are available, as is tutoring in every subject. There is remedial math, reading, and writing.

Campus Safety and Security: Measures include 24-hour foot and vehicle patrol, escort service, informal discussions, and pamphlets/posters/films. There are emergency telephones and lighted pathways/sidewalks.

Programs of Study: Lees-McRae confers B.A. and B.S. degrees. Bachelor's degrees are awarded in BIOLOGICAL SCIENCE (biology/biological science), BUSINESS (business administration and management), COMMUNICATIONS AND THE ARTS (arts administration/management, communications, dramatic arts, English, and musical theater), COMPUTER AND PHYSICAL SCIENCE (mathematics), EDUCATION (elementary and physical), HEALTH PROFESSIONS (sports medicine), SOCIAL SCIENCE (criminal justice, history, humanities, interdisciplinary studies, international studies, psychology, religion, and sociology). Biology, performing arts, and elementary education are the strongest academically. Business, biology, and performing arts are the largest.

Required: To graduate, students must complete at least 124 credit hours, including 57 in the major, with a GPA of 2.0 overall. Core requirements include courses in English, religion, history, natural sciences, social and behavioral sciences, math, computer science, phys ed, and senior seminar.

Special: The college has work-study programs, student-designed majors in the interdisciplinary studies program, and study-abroad opportunities in Ireland and Great Britain. Cross-registration is available with the Marine Science Education Consortium. There is 1 national honor society, a freshman honors program, and 1 departmental honors program.

Faculty/Classroom: 57% of faculty are male; 43%, female. All teach undergraduates. The average class size in an introductory lecture is 21; in a laboratory, 10; and in a regular course, 11.

Admissions: 93% of the 2001-2002 applicants were accepted. The SAT I scores for the 2001-2002 freshman class were: Verbal--56% below 500, 38% between 500 and 599, and 6% between 600 and 700; Math--65% below 500, 25% between 500 and 599, and 10% between 600 and 700. The ACT scores were 64% below 21, 19% between 21 and 23, 13% between 24 and 26, 3% between 27 and 28, and 1% above 28. 14% of the current freshmen were in the top fifth of their class; 40% were in the top two fifths. 1 freshman graduated first in the class.

Requirements: The SAT I or ACT is required. In addition, applicants must have completed 18 units of secondary-school academic courses, including 6 of academic electives, 4 of English, 3 of math, 2 of science (1 with lab work), and 1 each of social studies and history. AP and CLEP credits are accepted. Important factors in the admissions decision are recommendations by school officials, advanced placement or honor courses, and leadership record. Applications are accepted on-line at the school's web site.

Procedure: Freshmen are admitted to all sessions. Entrance exams should be taken in the fall of the senior year. There is a deferred admissions plan. Application deadlines are open. The fall 2001 application fee was $15. Notification is sent on a rolling basis.

Transfer: 124 transfer students enrolled in 2001-2002. Applicants must submit a college GPA of 2.0 and be in good standing at the previous or current institution. Students who have completed 24 semester hours or more must submit a dean's evaluation form; those with fewer than 24 must also submit high school transcripts and SAT I or ACT scores. 32 credits of 124 must be completed at Lees-McRae.

Visiting: There are regularly scheduled orientations for prospective students, consisting of 3 yearly open houses. There are guides for informal visits and visitors may sit in on classes and stay overnight. To schedule a visit, contact the Office of Admissions.

Financial Aid: In 2001-2002, 99% of all freshmen and 98% of continuing students received some form of financial aid. 72% of freshmen and 62% of continuing students received need-based aid. The average freshman award was $12,920. Of that total, scholarships or need-based grants averaged $7143 ($12,292 maximum); loans averaged $3795 ($15,000 maximum); work contracts averaged $1071 ($1545 maximum); and non need-based grants and vocational rehabilitation averaged $913 ($2412 maximum). 62% of undergraduates work part time. Average annual earnings from campus work are $1040. The average financial indebtedness of the 2001 graduate was $6414. Lees-McRae is a member of CSS. The FAFSA is required. The fall application deadline is March 1.

International Students: There are 35 international students enrolled. The school actively recruits these students. They must score 500 on the written TOEFL and also take the SAT I or the ACT.

Computers: The mainframes are a Microsoft Windows NT server and an IBM/AS400. Students have access to 125 PCs on campus offering Internet, e-mail, word processing, spreadsheet, graphics, and programming languages applications. All students may access the system 24 hours a day. There are no time limits and no fees.

Graduates: In 2001, 112 bachelor's degrees were awarded. The most popular majors were elementary education (23%), business administration (19%), and criminal justice (13%). In an average class, 24% graduate in 4 years, 31% in 5 years, and 37% in 6 years.

Admissions Contact: Bart Walker, Director of Admissions. A video is available. E-mail: *admissions@lmc.edu* Web: *www.lmc.edu*

LENOIR-RHYNE COLLEGE — C-2

Hickory, NC 28603 (828) 328-7300
(828) 328-7378; Fax: (828) 328-7378

Full-time: 415 men, 745 women	**Faculty:** 107; IIA, --$
Part-time: 54 men, 102 women	**Ph.D.s:** 73%
Graduate: 46 men, 94 women	**Student/Faculty:** 11 to 1
Year: semesters, summer session	**Tuition:** $14,086
Application Deadline: open	**Room & Board:** $5100
Freshman Class: 1119 applied, 946 accepted, 273 enrolled	
SAT I Verbal/Math: 511/517	**ACT:** 21 **COMPETITIVE**

Lenoir-Rhyne College, founded in 1891, is a private institution affiliated with the Lutheran Church, offering liberal arts programs that focus on business, education, and allied health sciences. In addition to regional accreditation, Lenoir-Rhyne has baccalaureate program accreditation with NCATE and NLN. The library contains 145,960 volumes, 462,878 microform items, and 40,379 audiovisual forms/CDs, and subscribes to 5376 periodicals. Computerized library services include the card catalog, interlibrary loans, and database searching. Special learning facilities include a learning resource center, radio station, TV station, and observatory. The 100-acre campus is in a suburban area 45 miles northwest of Charlotte. Including residence halls, there are 30 buildings.

Student Life: 70% of undergraduates are from North Carolina. Others are from 29 states, 9 foreign countries, and Canada. 89% are from public schools. 87% are white. 68% are Protestant; 23% claim no religious affiliation. The average age of freshmen is 18; all undergraduates, 22. 23% do not continue beyond their first year; 63% remain to graduate.

Housing: 900 students can be accommodated in college housing, which includes single-sex and coed dormitories, on-campus apartments, and fraternity houses. In addition, there is honor housing and hearing-impaired housing. On-campus housing is guaranteed for the first three years and is available on a lottery system for the fourth year. 65% of students live on campus; of those, 70% remain on campus on weekends. All students may keep cars.

Activities: 23% of men belong to 3 national fraternities; 27% of women belong to 4 national sororities. There are 50 groups on campus, including art, band, cheerleading, choir, chorus, computers, dance, debate, drama, ethnic, honors, international, jazz band, literary magazine, marching band, musical theater, newspaper, pep band, photography, political, professional, radio and TV, religious, social, social service, student government, and yearbook. Popular campus events include Spring Fling, Advent Candlelight Service, and Parents Weekend.

Sports: There are 6 intercollegiate sports for men and 6 for women, and 14 intramural sports for men and 14 for women. Facilities include an 8500-seat football stadium, 3600-seat gym, practice fields, racquetball courts, weight rooms, sauna, 25-meter swimming pool, 2 intramural fields, and baseball, softball, and soccer fields.

Disabled Students: All of the campus is accessible. Wheelchair ramps, elevators, special parking, specially equipped rest rooms, lowered drinking fountains, and specially equipped residence halls are available.

Services: Counseling and information services are available, as is tutoring in every subject. There is remedial math and writing. and interpreters and note takers for hearing-impaired students.

Campus Safety and Security: Measures include 24-hour foot and vehicle patrol, self-defense education, escort service, and informal discussions. There are pamphlets/posters/films, emergency telephones, and lighted pathways/sidewalks.

Programs of Study: Lenoir-Rhyne confers B.A., B.S., and B.Mus.Ed. degrees. Master's degrees are also awarded. Bachelor's degrees are awarded in BIOLOGICAL SCIENCE (biology/biological science), BUSINESS (accounting, business administration and management, and international business management), COMMUNICATIONS AND THE ARTS (applied music, classics, communications, dramatic arts, English, French, German, music, and Spanish), COMPUTER AND PHYSICAL SCIENCE (chemistry, computer science, mathematics, and physics), EDUCATION (art, business, early childhood, education of the deaf and hearing impaired, elementary, foreign languages, health, middle school, music, science, and secondary), HEALTH PROFESSIONS (medical laboratory technology, nursing, occupational therapy, physician's assistant, and premedicine), SOCIAL SCIENCE (American studies, economics, history, human services, philosophy, political science/government, prelaw, psychology, religious education, religious music, sociology, and theological studies). Business, education, and nursing are the largest.

Required: To graduate, students must complete 128 credit hours, including 56 to 57 in liberal arts courses, with a minimum GPA of 2.0. The total number of hours in a major varies by program.

Special: Lenoir-Rhyne offers cross-registration in design courses at area schools, study abroad in more than 25 countries, a Washington semester at American University and through the Lutheran College Washington Consortium, internships in most majors, dual majors, a general studies degree, work-study programs, 3-2 enginering degrees with North Carolina State, North Carolina Agricultural and Technical, and Clemson Universities and the University of North Carolina at Charlotte, pass/fail options, and auditing for most courses. In addition, the Broyhill institute for Business Leadership offers programs to promote undestanding of the business community, The college uses the Dartmount method in foreign language and offers an honors program for outstanding students. There are 11 national honor societies, a freshman honors program, and 18 departmental honors programs.

Faculty/Classroom: 55% of faculty are male; 45%, female. All teach undergraduates. No introductory courses are taught by graduate students. The average class size in an introductory lecture is 28; in a laboratory, 20; and in a regular course, 20.

Admissions: 85% of the 2001-2002 applicants were accepted. The SAT I scores for the 2001-2002 freshman class were: Verbal--50% below 500, 34% between 500 and 599, 14% between 600 and 700, and 2% above 700; Math--42% below 500, 46% between 500 and 599, 11% between 600 and 700, and 1% above 700. The ACT scores were 54% below 21, 24% between 21 and 23, 17% between 24 and 26, 2% between 27 and 28, and 3% above 28. 38% of the current freshmen were in the top fifth of their class; 67% were in the top two fifths. 4 freshmen graduated first in their class.

Requirements: The SAT I or ACT is required. In addition, applicants need 16 academic credits and should have 4 units in English, 3 in math, 2 in foreign language, and 1 each in American history and a lab science. An interview is recommended for all students. Music majors must also audition. A GPA of 2.5 is required. Applications are accepted on-line at the school's web site. AP and CLEP credits are accepted. Important factors in the admissions decision are advanced placement or honor courses, personality/intangible qualities, and leadership record.

Procedure: Freshmen are admitted to all sessions. Entrance exams should be taken in the spring of the junior year and thereafter. There are early admissions and deferred admissions plans. Application deadlines are open. The application fee is $25. Notification is sent on a rolling basis.

Transfer: 108 transfer students enrolled in 2001-2002. Applicants with more than 30 semester hours need a 2.0 minimum GPA in general studies programs or a 2.5 minimum GPA in nursing or education programs. Those with fewer than 30 semester hours must meet freshman entrance criteria. 32 credits of 128 must be completed at Lenoir-Rhyne.

Visiting: There are regularly scheduled orientations for prospective students, including a meeting with an admissions counselor and a student-guided tour of the campus. There are guides for informal visits and visitors may sit in on classes and stay overnight. To schedule a visit, contact the Admissions Office.

Financial Aid: In 2001-2002, all freshmen and 92% of continuing students received some form of financial aid. 40% of freshmen and 55% of continuing students received need-based aid. The average freshman award was $18,663. Of that total, scholarships or need-based grants averaged $7594 ($19,186 maximum); loans averaged $8954 ($19,186 maximum); work contracts averaged $1000 ($1500 maximum); and North Carolina Legislative Tutition Grants averaged $1115 ($1800 maximum). 35% of undergraduates work part time. Average annual earnings from campus work are $1000. The average financial indebtedness of the 2001 graduate was $30,000. The FAFSA and the college's own financial statement are required. The fall application deadline is March 15.

International Students: There are 12 international students enrolled. The school actively recruits these students. They must score 500 on the written TOEFL.

Computers: There are 4 computer labs with 77 PCs and 17 Macs. All can be used to access e-mail, the Internet, and the World Wide Web. All students may access the system 24 hours per day via modem; computer lab hours are 8 A.M. to 11:30 P.M. There are no time limits and no fees.

Graduates: In 2001, 275 bachelor's degrees were awarded. The most popular majors were elementary education (12%), psychology (9%), and business (9%). In an average class, 1% graduate in 3 years, 53% in 4 years, 57% in 5 years, and 63% in 6 years. More than 100 companies recruited on campus in 2000-2001. Of the 2000 graduating class, 11% were enrolled in graduate school within 6 months of graduation and 96% were employed.

Admissions Contact: Chad A. Spencer, Assistant Director of Admissions. E-mail: *admission@lrc.edu* Web: *http://www.lrc.edu*

LIVINGSTONE COLLEGE C-2
Salisbury, NC 28144

(704) 638-5502
(800) 835-3435; Fax: (704) 638-5426

Full-time: 690 men and women	**Faculty:** 50
Part-time: 10 men and women	**Ph.D.s:** 55%
Graduate: 50 men and women	**Student/Faculty:** 13 to 1
Year: semesters, summer session	**Tuition:** $9860
Application Deadline: see profile	**Room & Board:** $3500
Freshman Class: n/av	
SAT I or ACT: required	**LESS COMPETITIVE**

Livingstone College, founded in 1879 and affiliated with the African Methodist Episcopal Zion Church, is a private institution offering programs in business, engineering, liberal arts, music, and professional and religious training. Figures given in the above capsule are approximate. In addition to regional accreditation, LC has baccalaureate program accreditation with CSWE. The library contains 80,000 volumes and 1000 microform items, and subscribes to 423 periodicals. Special learning facilities include a learning resource center and natural history museum. The 272-acre campus is in a small town between Greensboro and Charlotte. Including residence halls, there are 22 buildings.

Student Life: 54% of undergraduates are from North Carolina. Others are from 22 states and 7 foreign countries. 90% are from public schools. 96% are African American. The average age of freshmen is 18; all undergraduates, 19.

Housing: 650 students can be accommodated in college housing, which includes single-sex dormitories. In addition, there are honors houses. On-campus housing is guaranteed for all 4 years. 88% of students live on campus; of those, 50% remain on campus on weekends. Alcohol is not permitted. All students may keep cars.

Activities: 20% of men belong to 4 national fraternities; 30% of women belong to 3 national sororities. There are many groups and organizations on campus, including band, cheerleading, choir, chorus, computers, drama, honors, jazz band, marching band, newspaper, pep band, religious, student government, and yearbook.

Sports: There are 4 intercollegiate sports for men and 4 for women, and 5 intramural sports for men and 4 for women. Facilities include a gym and a 4000-seat stadium.

Disabled Students: Special parking and special class scheduling are available.

Services: Counseling and information services are available, as is tutoring in every subject. There is remedial reading and writing.

Campus Safety and Security: Measures include 24-hour foot and vehicle patrol.

Programs of Study: LC confers B.A., B.S., and B.S.W. degrees. Bachelor's degrees are awarded in BIOLOGICAL SCIENCE (biology/biological science), BUSINESS (accounting and business administration and management), COMMUNICATIONS AND THE ARTS (English and music), COMPUTER AND PHYSICAL SCIENCE (chemistry, computer science, and mathematics), EDUCATION (early childhood, elementary, music, science, and secondary), HEALTH PROFESSIONS (predentistry and premedicine), SOCIAL SCIENCE (history, political science/government, prelaw, psychology, social work, and sociology).

Required: At least 126 semester hours with a minimum GPA of 2.0 are required for graduation. Required courses include Freshman English and Religion, 2 semesters each of foreign language and phys ed, 8 hours each of natural science, math, and social science, and 9 hours chosen from offerings in art, literature, music, and philosophy.

Special: Upperclassmen are eligible for a cooperative education program. The college offers internships and 3-2 engineering programs with Georgia Institute of Technology and Clemson University, and a 3-3 law program with Saint John's University. There are 2 national honor societies.

Faculty/Classroom: 40% of faculty are male; 60%, female.

Requirements: The SAT I or ACT is required. In addition, applicants should be high school graduates or have earned the GED. Secondary preparation should include 4 academic credits in English, 2 each in history, math, and music, and 1 each in social studies, science, and art. A GPA of 2.0 is required. AP and CLEP credits are accepted. Important factors in the admissions decision are evidence of special talent, leadership record, and extracurricular activities record.

Procedure: Freshmen are admitted fall and spring. Entrance exams should be taken as early as possible. There is an early decision plan. Notification is sent on a rolling basis. A waiting list is an active part of the admissions procedure. Check with the school for current application deadlines and fees.

Transfer: Transfers should have at least a 2.0 GPA in 30 hours of previous college work. Those with fewer hours must meet freshman requirements. 45 credits of 126 must be completed at LC.

Visiting: There are regularly scheduled orientations for prospective students. There are guides for informal visits and visitors may sit in on classes and stay overnight. To schedule a visit, contact Grady Deese, Director of Admissions, at (704) 638-5530 or (800) 422-5430.

Financial Aid: 50% of undergraduates worked part time in a recent year. Average annual earnings from campus work are $1200. LC is a member of CSS. The FFS is required.

International Students: The school actively recruits these students. They must score 500 on the written TOEFL and also take the SAT I or the ACT.

Computers: The mainframe is an IBM 34. There are also PCs available. All students may access the system. There are no time limits and no fees.

Admissions Contact: Charles M. Alexander, Enrollment Management Specialist.

MARS HILL COLLEGE — B-2
Mars Hill, NC 28754 — (828) 689-1201
(800) 543-1514; Fax: (828) 689-1473

Full-time: 496 men, 605 women	**Faculty:** 80; IIB, --$
Part-time: 39 men, 102 women	**Ph.D.s:** 70%
Graduate: none	**Student/Faculty:** 14 to 1
Year: semesters, summer session	**Tuition:** $13,800
Application Deadline: open	**Room & Board:** $4800
Freshman Class: 1006 applied, 956 accepted, 267 enrolled	
ACT: 19	**LESS COMPETITIVE**

Mars Hill College, founded in 1856, is a private institution affiliated with the Baptist Church and offers undergraduate programs in the arts and sciences, business, education, and preprofessional studies. Some information in this profile is approximate. In addition to regional accreditation, Mars Hill has baccalaureate program accreditation with CSWE, NASM, and NCATE. The library contains 98,150 volumes, 1050 microform items, and 6180 audiovisual forms/CDs, and subscribes to 650 periodicals. Computerized library services include the card catalog, interlibrary loans, and database searching. Special learning facilities include an art gallery, radio station, the Southern Appalachian Center of Regional History and Culture, and the Rural Life Museum. The 180-acre campus is in a rural area 18 miles north of Asheville. Including residence halls, there are 47 buildings.

Student Life: 60% of undergraduates are from North Carolina. Others are from 19 states, 20 foreign countries, and Canada. 14% are African American. 81% are Protestant; 13% claim no religious affiliation. The average age of freshmen is 18; all undergraduates, 21. 20% do not continue beyond their first year; 49% remain to graduate.

Housing: Living facilities include single-sex dormitories, on-campus apartments, and married-student housing. In addition, there are honors houses. On-campus housing is guaranteed for all 4 years. 80% of students live on campus; of those, 33% remain on campus on weekends. Alcohol is not permitted. All students may keep cars.

Activities: 30% of men belong to 4 local and 2 national fraternities; 12% of women belong to 4 local and 1 national sororities. There are 80 groups on campus, including art, band, cheerleading, choir, chorale, chorus, dance, drama, ethnic, honors, international, jazz band, literary magazine, marching band, musical theater, newspaper, orchestra, photography, political, professional, radio and TV, religious, social, social service, student government, and yearbook. Popular campus events include Culturefest, Spring Fling, and the Bascom Lamar Lunsford Festival.

Sports: There are 7 intercollegiate sports for men and 6 for women, and 5 intramural sports for men and 5 for women. Facilities include a 5000-seat stadium, a 3500-seat gym, an indoor Olympic-size swimming pool, and a 10-acre complex that has a track, baseball diamond, soccer field, all-purpose playing field, and 6 tennis courts.

Disabled Students: 41% of the campus is accessible. Wheelchair ramps, elevators, special parking, and specially equipped rest rooms are available.

Services: Counseling and information services are available, as is tutoring in every subject. There is remedial math, reading, and writing.

Campus Safety and Security: Measures include 24-hour foot and vehicle patrol, self-defense education, escort service, and informal discussions. There are pamphlets/posters/films, emergency telephones, and lighted pathways/sidewalks.

Programs of Study: Mars Hill confers B.A., B.S., B.F.A., B.M., and B.S.W. degrees. Bachelor's degrees are awarded in BIOLOGICAL SCIENCE (biology/biological science, botany, and zoology), BUSINESS (accounting, business administration and management, fashion merchandising, and recreation and leisure services), COMMUNICATIONS AND THE ARTS (art history and appreciation, communications, dramatic arts, English, music, music performance, musical theater, performing arts, and Spanish), COMPUTER AND PHYSICAL SCIENCE (chemistry, computer science, and mathematics), EDUCATION (art, athletic training, drama, elementary, mathematics, middle school, music, physical, science, and social studies), HEALTH PROFESSIONS (allied health, physician's assistant, predentistry, premedicine, prepharmacy, and preveterinary science), SOCIAL SCIENCE (history, international studies, political science/government, prelaw, psychology, religion, social work, and sociology). Music, education, and science are the strongest academically. Education is the largest.

Required: To graduate, students must complete at least 128 semester hours with a minimum GPA of 2.0. Distribution requirements include courses in fine arts, literature, American culture, foreign culture, math, natural science, social/behavioral science, ethics, and phys ed.

Special: Mars Hill offers cooperative programs with the Bowman Gray School of Medicine at Wake Forest, internships, study abroad, B.A.-B.S. degrees, dual majors, student-designed majors, and credit for life experience. The Community Life program promotes student involvement in culture and community activities. There are 4 national honor societies and a freshman honors program.

Faculty/Classroom: 58% of faculty are male; 42%, female. All teach undergraduates. The average class size in an introductory lecture is 20; in a laboratory, 15; and in a regular course, 15.

Admissions: 95% of the 2001-2002 applicants were accepted. 27% of the current freshmen were in the top fifth of their class; 48% were in the top two fifths.

Requirements: The SAT I or ACT is required. In addition, applicants need at least 18 academic credits, including 4 in English, 3 in math, and 2 each in history, science, and foreign language. The GED is accepted. A GPA of 2.0 is required. AP and CLEP credits are accepted. Important factors in the admissions decision are advanced placement or honor courses, leadership record, and extracurricular activities record.

Procedure: Freshmen are admitted to all sessions. There are early decision and early admissions plans. Application deadlines are open. The application fee is $25. 3 early decision candidates were accepted for a recent class.

Transfer: 66 transfer students enrolled in a recent year. Transfer applicants must be eligible to return to their previous college or have been out of school for at least 1 semester. They must have a minimum GPA of 2.0 for at least 30 semester credit hours. Remedial and developmental hours do not apply. 32 credits of 128 must be completed at Mars Hill.

Visiting: There are regularly scheduled orientations for prospective students, consisting of 2 days, during which a variety of special programs are offered. Individual students and their families may visit any time throughout the year. There are guides for informal visits and visitors may sit in on classes and stay overnight. To schedule a visit, contact the Admissions Office.

Financial Aid: In 2001-2002, 96% of all freshmen received some form of financial aid. 35% of undergraduates work part time. Average annual earnings from campus work are $1000. Mars Hill is a member of CSS. The FAFSA is required. Check with the school for current deadlines.

International Students: The school actively recruits these students. They must score 500 on the written TOEFL.

Computers: The mainframe is a Wang V565. There are also 90 PCs available, and 10 computer labs fully on-line with the Internet and e-mail. All students may access the system during library hours. Students may access the system for up to 2 hours at a time. There are no fees.

Admissions Contact: Office of Admissions.
E-mail: *admissions@mhc.edu* Web: *www.mhc.edu*

MEREDITH COLLEGE
Raleigh, NC 27607-5298 D-2
(919) 760-8581
(800) MEREDITH; (919) 760-2348

Full-time: 1792 women	**Faculty:** 141; IIB, av$
Part-time: 21 men, 494 women	**Ph.D.s:** 79%
Graduate: 14 men, 80 women	**Student/Faculty:** 13 to 1
Year: semesters, summer session	**Tuition:** $13,100
Application Deadline: February 15	**Room & Board:** $4400

Freshman Class: 1154 applied, 958 accepted, 389 enrolled
SAT I or ACT: required **COMPETITIVE**

Meredith College, founded in 1891, is an independent college for women offering undergraduate and graduate programs in the arts and sciences, business, and professional training. In addition to regional accreditation, Meredith has baccalaureate program accreditation with ADA, CSWE, FIDER, NASM, and NCATE. The library contains 133,963 volumes, 60,580 microform items, and 10,817 audiovisual forms/CDs, and subscribes to 2059 periodicals. Computerized library services include the card catalog, interlibrary loans, and database searching. Special learning facilities include a learning resource center, art gallery, child-care lab, greenhouse, experimental and clinical psychology labs including 1 on autism, astronomy observation deck, and language lab. The 225-acre campus is in a suburban area in the city of Raleigh. Including residence halls, there are 29 buildings.

Student Life: 91% of undergraduates are from North Carolina. Others are from 25 states, 27 foreign countries, and Canada. 87% are from public schools. 88% are white. 63% are Protestant; 29% claim no religious affiliation. The average age of freshmen is 18; all undergraduates, 23. 21% do not continue beyond their first year; 69% remain to graduate.

Housing: 1178 students can be accommodated in college housing, which includes single-sex dormitories with nonsmoking halls. On-campus housing is guaranteed for all 4 years. 52% of students commute. Alcohol is not permitted. All students may keep cars.

Activities: There are no fraternities. There are 89 groups on campus, including art, band, Big Sister/Little Sister, chorale, chorus, commuter, dance, drama, environmental, ethnic, honors, international, literary magazine, marching band, musical theater, newspaper, orchestra, photography, political, professional, religious, social service, student government, symphony, video, and yearbook. Popular campus events include Leadership Awards Day, White Iris Ball, and Fletcher School of Performing Arts performances.

Sports: Facilities include an indoor swimming pool, a dance studio, a fitness center, an archery range, a putting green and driving range, a softball diamond, tennis courts, a soccer field, and a gym with basketball, volleyball, and badminton courts.

Disabled Students: 90% of the campus is accessible. Wheelchair ramps, elevators, special parking, specially equipped rest rooms, special class scheduling, lowered drinking fountains, some specially equipped residence hall rooms, a handicap lift in the swimming pool, and lowered fire alarms are available.

Services: Counseling and information services are available, as is tutoring in some subjects, including math, writing, computer lab, French, Spanish, biology, and chemistry. There is a reader service for the blind.

Campus Safety and Security: Measures include 24-hour foot and vehicle patrol, self-defense education, escort service, and informal discussions. There are pamphlets/posters/films, emergency telephones, lighted pathways/sidewalks, controlled campus access at night, and 24- hour locked residence halls.

Programs of Study: Meredith confers B.A., B.S., and B.M. degrees. Master's degrees are also awarded. Bachelor's degrees are awarded in BIOLOGICAL SCIENCE (biology/biological science and nutrition), BUSINESS (accounting, business administration and management, fashion merchandising, and international business management), COMMUNICATIONS AND THE ARTS (applied music, art, communications, dance, dramatic arts, English, fine arts, French, music, music performance, musical theater, Spanish, and speech/debate/rhetoric), COMPUTER AND PHYSICAL SCIENCE (chemistry, computer science, information sciences and systems, and mathematics), EDUCATION (athletic training and music), ENGINEERING AND ENVIRONMENTAL DESIGN (interior design), HEALTH PROFESSIONS (exercise science), SOCIAL SCIENCE (American studies, child psychology/development, economics, family/consumer studies, food science, history, international studies, political science/government, psychology, public affairs, religion, social work, and sociology). Business, child development, and psychology are the largest.

Required: To graduate, students must complete a total of 124 credit hours, including an average of 36 hours in the major, with a minimum GPA of 2.0. Distribution requirements include 27 to 30 credit hours in the humanities and fine arts, 13 in math and science, 12 in social and behavioral sciences, 6 in foreign language, and 4 to 6 in phys ed. Specific course requirements include English Composition, British Authors, Introduction to Biblical History and Literature, and Western Civilization.

Special: Meredith offers cooperative programs, cross-registration with Cooperating Raleigh Colleges, internships, study abroad in Europe and Asia, a Washington semester at American University, a U.N. semester at Drew University, and work-study programs on campus. Dual majors, interdisciplinary and student-designed majors, preprofessional programs, and pass/fail options are available. Second-degree programs in engineering with North Carolina State University and certification in social work and licensure for teaching are possible. Business administration, management, and social work majors can be completed through evening classes. There are 12 national honor societies, and a freshman honors program.

Faculty/Classroom: 31% of faculty are male; 69%, female. All teach undergraduates. No introductory courses are taught by graduate students. The average class size in an introductory lecture is 17; in a laboratory, 13; and in a regular course, 14.

Admissions: 83% of the 2001-2002 applicants were accepted.

Requirements: The SAT I or ACT is required; the SAT I is preferred. Applicants must have a minimum of 16 units of credit, including 4 in English, 3 each in math, history/social studies, and science, 1 in foreign language (2 recommended), and 2 electives. Grades in academic subjects are very important. An interview may be requested as part of the evaluation process. Applications are available on-line at the Meredith web site. Meredith requires applicants to be in the upper 50% of their class. A GPA of 2.0 is required. AP and CLEP credits are accepted. Important factors in the admissions decision are recommendations by school officials, advanced placement or honor courses, and evidence of special talent.

Procedure: Freshmen are admitted fall and spring. Entrance exams should be taken by January of the senior year. There are early decision and deferred admissions plans. Early decision application should be filed by October 15; regular applications, by February 15 for fall entry and December 1 for spring entry. The fall 2001 application fee was $35. Notification of early decision is sent November 1; regular decision, on a rolling basis. 75 early decision candidates were accepted for the 2001-2002 class.

Transfer: 90 transfer students enrolled in 2001-2002. Applicants must have a minimum GPA of 2.0, be eligible to return to the last college attended, and be recommended by college officials. Those students with fewer than 30 hours of credit must also meet freshman admission requirements. An interview is recommended for all applicants. 31 credits of 124 must be completed at Meredith.

Visiting: There are regularly scheduled orientations for prospective students, including Open Days information sessions for senior students and parents, class visitation, informal conversations with students and faculty/staff, and campus tours. Experience Meredith! for accepted students and their parents includes various off-to-college information sessions, an academic fair, a student activities fair, and campus tours. Individual visitors typically have a conference with an admissions counselor and a campus tour. There are also visitation days for juniors and transfers, and a Legacy Day when alumnae bring prospective students for a visit. There are guides for informal visits and visitors may sit in on classes. To schedule a visit, contact the Admissions Office.

Financial Aid: In a recent year, 86% of all freshmen and 78% of continuing students received some form of financial aid. 51% of freshmen and 60% of continuing students received need-based aid. The average freshman award was $8133. Of that total, scholarships or need-based grants averaged $6213; and self-help averaged $1920. 26% of undergraduates work part time. Average annual earnings from campus work are $900. The average financial indebtedness of a recent graduate was $12,000. Meredith is a member of CSS. The FAFSA and the college's own financial statement are required. The fall application deadline is February 15.

International Students: There were 28 international students enrolled in a recent year. The school actively recruits these students. They must score 500 on the written TOEFL; If English is the student's native language or primary language of instruction, the SAT I should be taken instead of the TOEFL.

Computers: More than 200 PCs are available for student use. All are networked for e-mail, the Internet, and the World Wide Web. Residence halls are wired for network access, and more than 350 residence hall rooms have student-owned computers connected to the campus network. All full-time freshmen are provided with IBM laptop computers. All students may access the system 24 hours per day in residence halls and 1 lab; 7 A.M. to midnight in other labs. There are no time limits and no fees. It is strongly recommended that all students have a personal computer.

Graduates: In 2001, 464 bachelor's degrees were awarded. The most popular majors were business administration (26%), child development (15%), and psychology (10%). In an average class, 1% graduate in 3 years, 58% in 4 years, 65% in 5 years, and 67% in 6 years. 95 companies recruited on campus in 2000-2001. Of the 2000 graduating class, 17% were enrolled in graduate school within 6 months of graduation and 88% were employed.

Admissions Contact: Carol Kercheval, Director of Admissions. A video is available. E-mail: *admissions@meredith.edu*
Web: *www.meredith.edu*

METHODIST COLLEGE D-3
Fayetteville, NC 28311-1420 (910) 630-7027
(800) 488-7110; Fax: (910) 630-7285

Full-time: 1550 men and women	**Faculty:** 90; IIB, --$
Part-time: 295 men and women	**Ph.D.s:** 54%
Graduate: none	**Student/Faculty:** 19 to 1
Year: semesters, summer session	**Tuition:** $14,196
Application Deadline: open	**Room & Board:** $5330
Freshman Class: 1470 applied, 1085 accepted, 366 enrolled	
SAT I Verbal/Math: 490/500	**ACT:** 20 **COMPETITIVE**

Methodist College, founded in 1956, is a private institution affiliated with the United Methodist Church. The college offers programs in the arts and sciences, education, business, and professional training. Enrollment figures in the above capsule are approximate. There are 2 undergraduate schools and 1 graduate school. In addition to regional accreditation, Methodist has baccalaureate program accreditation with ACBSP, CSWE, NCATE, and CAAHEP. The library contains 181,833 volumes, 57,759 microform items, and 13,412 audiovisual forms/CDs, and subscribes to 587 periodicals. Computerized library services include the card catalog, interlibrary loans, and database searching. Special learning facilities include a learning resource center, art gallery, and professional golf and tennis management facilities. The 600-acre campus is in a suburban area 5 miles north of Fayetteville. Including residence halls, there are 30 buildings.

Student Life: 60% of undergraduates are from North Carolina. Others are from 48 states, 37 foreign countries, and Canada. 88% are from public schools. 75% are white; 17% African American. 41% are Protestant; 16% Catholic. The average age of freshmen is 18; all undergraduates, 21. 35% do not continue beyond their first year; 36% remain to graduate.

Housing: 823 students can be accommodated in college housing, which includes single-sex and coed dormitories and on-campus apartments. In addition, there are honors houses and a health and wellness hall. On-campus housing is guaranteed for all 4 years. 52% of students live on campus; of those, 70% remain on campus on weekends. Alcohol is not permitted. All students may keep cars.

Activities: 1% of men belong to 2 local fraternities; 1% of women belong to 2 local sororities and 1 national sorority. There are 72 groups on campus, including art, band, cheerleading, chess, choir, chorale, chorus, computers, dance, debate, drama, ethnic, honors, international, jazz band, literary magazine, musical theater, newspaper, orchestra, pep band, photography, political, professional, religious, social, social service, student government, and yearbook. Popular campus events include Show You Care Day, Annual Woodcutting, and Spring Fest.

Sports: There are 9 intercollegiate sports for men and 10 for women, and 7 intramural sports for men and 4 for women. Facilities include a 1200-seat stadium, a 1500-seat gym, a golf course, a track and field area, tennis courts, and fields for baseball, softball, and soccer.

Disabled Students: 90% of the campus is accessible. Wheelchair ramps, special parking, specially equipped rest rooms, and lowered drinking fountains are available.

Services: Counseling and information services are available, as is tutoring in most subjects. There is a reader service for the blind, and remedial math, reading, and writing.

Campus Safety and Security: Measures include 24-hour foot and vehicle patrol, self-defense education, escort service, and shuttle buses. There are informal discussions, pamphlets/posters/films, emergency telephones, and lighted pathways/sidewalks.

Programs of Study: Methodist confers B.A., B.S., B.H.S, B.M., and B.S.W. degrees. Associate and master's degrees are also awarded. Bachelor's degrees are awarded in BIOLOGICAL SCIENCE (biology/biological science), BUSINESS (accounting, business administration and management, marketing/retailing/merchandising, organizational behavior, and sports management), COMMUNICATIONS AND THE ARTS (art, communications, creative writing, dramatic arts, English, French, music, music performance, and Spanish), COMPUTER AND PHYSICAL SCIENCE (chemistry, computer science, and mathematics), EDUCATION (art, athletic training, elementary, middle school, music, physical, secondary, and special), ENGINEERING AND ENVIRONMENTAL DESIGN (computer technology), HEALTH PROFESSIONS (physician's assistant and predentistry), SOCIAL SCIENCE (criminal justice, economics, history, international studies, political science/government, prelaw, psychology, religion, social studies, social work, and sociology). Business administration, biology, and music are the strongest academically. Business administration, education, and biology are the largest.

Required: To graduate, students must complete at least 124 semester hours, including core requirements, with a minimum GPA of 2.0. A liberal arts core, ranging from 36 to 62 hours, is required in all majors.

Special: Methodist offers internships in political science and social work, study abroad in 2 countries, a Washington semester, a general studies degree, a 3-2 engineering degree with North Carolina State University, pass/fail options, dual majors, and nondegree study. The business administration major offers concentrations in professional golf, tennis, and resort management with specialized facilities and co-op programs. There are 7 national honor societies, a freshman honors program, and 3 departmental honors programs.

Faculty/Classroom: 67% of faculty are male; 33%, female. All teach undergraduates. The average class size in an introductory lecture is 25; in a laboratory, 20; and in a regular course, 20.

Admissions: 74% of the 2001-2002 applicants were accepted. The SAT I scores for the 2001-2002 freshman class were: Verbal--56% below 500, 35% between 500 and 599, 8% between 600 and 700, and 1% above 700; Math--50% below 500, 35% between 500 and 599, 14% between 600 and 700, and 1% above 700. The ACT scores were 55% below 21, 25% between 21 and 23, 15% between 24 and 26, 2% between 27 and 28, and 3% above 28. 27% of the current freshmen were in the top fifth of their class; 52% were in the top two fifths.

Requirements: The SAT I or ACT is required. In addition, applicants should be graduates of an accredited secondary school or have a GED certificate. They must have 16 academic credits, including 4 in English and 3 each in history, math, and science. 2 years of foreign language are recommended. An essay and interview are also recommended. AP and CLEP credits are accepted. Important factors in the admissions decision are advanced placement or honor courses, evidence of special talent, and recommendations by school officials. Applicants can apply on-line at the school's web site.

Procedure: Freshmen are admitted fall, spring, and summer. There is a deferred admissions plan. Application deadlines are open. The application fee is $25. Notification is sent on a rolling basis.

Transfer: 153 transfer students enrolled in 2001-2002. Applicants must have a minimum GPA of 2.0. They must also submit a high school transcript, college transcripts, and the SAT I or ACT scores. 30 credits of 124 must be completed at Methodist.

Visiting: There are regularly scheduled orientations for prospective students, consisting of a 2-day summer orientation in July. There are guides for informal visits and visitors may sit in on classes and stay overnight. To schedule a visit, contact the Admissions Office.

Financial Aid: In 2001-2002, 84% of all freshmen and 87% of continuing students received some form of financial aid. 78% of freshmen and 83% of continuing students received need-based aid. The average freshman award was $9410. Of that total, scholarships or need-based grants averaged $5385 ($9500 maximum); loans averaged $2625 (maximum); and work contracts averaged $1400 ($1600 maximum). 60% of undergraduates work part time. Average annual earnings from campus work are $1000. The average financial indebtedness of the 2001 graduate was $15,400. The FAFSA is required. The fall application deadline is March 15.

International Students: There are 60 international students enrolled. The school actively recruits these students. The TOEFL is required with a minimum score of 500 on the written version or 173 on the electronic version. The student may take the SAT I or ACT in place of the TOEFL if English proficiency is demonstrated.

Computers: The mainframe is an IBM. There are also 150 IBM, AT&T, and leading edge PCs available in various labs. All students may access the system during specified hours. There are no time limits and no fees.

Graduates: In 2001, 254 bachelor's degrees were awarded. The most popular majors were business (46%), social sciences (11%), and education (7%). In an average class, 1% graduate in 3 years, 33% in 4 years, 38% in 5 years, and 40% in 6 years. 180 companies recruited on campus in 2000-2001.

Admissions Contact: Jamie Legg, Director of Admissions.
E-mail: *jlegg@methodist.edu* Web: *www.methodist.edu*

MONTREAT COLLEGE B-2
Montreat, NC 28757-1267 (828) 669-8011, ext. 3784
(800) 622-6968; Fax: (828) 669-0120

Full-time: 393 men, 589 women	**Faculty:** 33; IIB, --$
Part-time: 9 men, 6 women	**Ph.D.s:** 55%
Graduate: 37 men, 78 women	**Student/Faculty:** 32 to 1
Year: semesters	**Tuition:** $12,318
Application Deadline: open	**Room & Board:** $4846
Freshman Class: 394 applied, 330 accepted, 169 enrolled	
SAT I Verbal/Math: 500/500	**COMPETITIVE**

Montreat College, founded in 1916, is a private liberal arts institution affiliated with the Presbyterian Church (U.S.A.) and committed to the integration of faith and learning. The library contains 67,500 volumes, 38,335 microform items, and 230 audiovisual forms/CDs, and subscribes to 438 periodicals. Computerized library services include the card catalog. Special learning facilities include a learning resource center, art gallery, and and the Presbyterian Church (U.S.A.) Historical Foundation. The 100-acre campus is in a rural area 15 miles east of Asheville. Including residence halls, there are 12 buildings.

Student Life: 60% of undergraduates are from North Carolina. Others are from 21 states and 12 foreign countries. 55% are from public schools. 95% are white.

Housing: 392 students can be accommodated in college housing, which includes single-sex dormitories. On-campus housing is guaranteed for all 4 years. 72% of students live on campus; of those, 50% remain on campus on weekends. Alcohol is not permitted. All students may keep cars.

Activities: There are no fraternities or sororities. There are 25 groups on campus, including art, choir, chorus, drama, honors, musical theater, newspaper, photography, political, professional, religious, social, social service, student government, and yearbook.

Sports: There are 5 intercollegiate sports for men and 5 for women, and 4 intramural sports for men and 4 for women. Facilities include standard athletic facilities complemented by opportunities for outdoor recreation activities such as skiing, whitewater sports, mountain climbing, and camping.

Disabled Students: 75% of the campus is accessible. Wheelchair ramps, elevators, special parking, specially equipped rest rooms, special class scheduling, and lowered telephones are available.

Services: Counseling and information services are available, as is tutoring in all academic areas. There is remedial math, reading, and writing.

Campus Safety and Security: Measures include 24-hour foot and vehicle patrol, lighted pathways/sidewalks, and a closed campus.

Programs of Study: Montreat confers B.A., B.S., and B.M. degrees. Associate degrees are also awarded. Bachelor's degrees are awarded in BUSINESS (business administration and management), COMMUNICATIONS AND THE ARTS (English, music business management, and music performance), COMPUTER AND PHYSICAL SCIENCE (mathematics), EDUCATION (elementary, English, environmental, mathematics, secondary, and social studies), ENGINEERING AND ENVIRONMENTAL DESIGN (environmental science), SOCIAL SCIENCE (American studies, biblical studies, crosscultural studies, history, human services, liberal arts/general studies, and religion). English is the strongest academically. Business is the largest.

Required: To graduate, students must complete 126 credit hours with a minimum GPA of 2.0. They must pass a comprehensive exam covering math, computation, oral expression, reading, and writing. A thesis is required for some majors.

Special: Montreat offers internships in all majors, study abroad, a Washington semester, work-study programs, and dual majors. There are 2 national honor societies, a freshman honors program, and 3 departmental honors programs.

Faculty/Classroom: 61% of faculty are male; 39%, female. All teach undergraduates. No introductory courses are taught by graduate students. The average class size in an introductory lecture is 30; in a laboratory, 15; and in a regular course, 10.

Admissions: 84% of the 2001-2002 applicants were accepted. The SAT I scores for the 2001-2002 freshman class were: Verbal--52% below 500, 39% between 500 and 599, and 9% between 600 and 700; Math--53% below 500, 38% between 500 and 599, 8% between 600 and 700, and 1% above 700. 23% of the current freshmen were in the top fifth of their class; 56% were in the top two fifths.

Requirements: The SAT I or ACT is required, and is rated on a sliding scale with the GPA, with a minimum 860 SAT I score or 18 ACT score needed. Applicants must be graduates of an accredited secondary school and have completed 4 years of English, 3 each of math, science, and social studies, and 1 of foreign language. The GED is accepted. A counselor or teacher recommendation is required, and a short autobiographical essay is required unless the student has been interviewed. Montreat requires applicants to be in the upper 50% of their class. A GPA of 2.25 is required. CLEP credit is accepted. Important factors in the admissions decision are advanced placement or honor courses, extracurricular activities record, and evidence of special talent.

Procedure: Freshmen are admitted to all sessions. Application deadlines are open. The fall 2001 application fee was $15. Notification is sent on a rolling basis.

Transfer: 36 transfer students enrolled in a recent year. Applicants must submit official college transcripts, be in good standing at their previous institution, and have completed at least 24 semester hours of college credit with a minimum GPA of 2.0. Students with fewer credits must also submit high school transcripts and SAT I or ACT scores. 18 credits of 126 must be completed at Montreat.

Visiting: There are regularly scheduled orientations for prospective students, including a campus tour, faculty introduction, and student program. There are guides for informal visits and visitors may sit in on classes and stay overnight. To schedule a visit, contact the Admissions Office.

Financial Aid: In a recent year, 91% of all freshmen and 93% of continuing students received some form of financial aid. 72% of freshmen and 73% of continuing students received need-based aid. The average freshman award was $9341. Of that total, scholarships or need-based grants averaged $5316; loans averaged $2625; and work contracts averaged $1400 ($1850 maximum). 67% of undergraduates work part time. Average annual earnings from campus work are $1400. The average financial indebtedness of a recent year's graduate was $16,274. Montreat is a member of CSS. The CSS/Profile and the college's own financial statement are required. The fall application deadline is April 15.

International Students: There were 11 international students enrolled in a recent year. The school actively recruits these students. They must score 500 on the written TOEFL.

Computers: The student-to-computer ratio is 11:1. PCs in dorm rooms can access the Internet and be linked to the campus network. All students may access the system during computer lab hours or at any time by PC. There are no time limits. The fee is $100 as a one-time hook-up fee for student PCs. It is strongly recommended that all students have a personal computer.

Graduates: In a recent year, 57 bachelor's degrees were awarded.

Admissions Contact: Anita F. Darby, Director of Admissions. A video is available. E-mail: *admissions@montreat.edu*
Web: *www.montreat.edu*

MOUNT OLIVE COLLEGE — E-3
Mount Olive, NC 28365 — (919) 658-2502
(800) 653-0854; Fax: (919) 658-7180

Full-time: 650 men, 782 women	**Faculty:** 44
Part-time: 151 men, 192 women	**Ph.D.s:** 79%
Graduate: none	**Student/Faculty:** 33 to 1
Year: semesters, summer session	**Tuition:** $10,010
Application Deadline: open	**Room & Board:** $4400
Freshman Class: 461 applied, 367 accepted, 185 enrolled	
SAT I Verbal/Math: 450/460	**LESS COMPETITIVE**

Mount Olive College, founded in 1951, is a private liberal arts institution affiliated with the Original Free Will Baptist Church. The 2 libraries contain 77,545 volumes, 48,735 microform items, and 2005 audiovisual forms/CDs, and subscribe to 5979 periodicals. Computerized library services include the card catalog, interlibrary loans, and database searching. Special learning facilities include a learning resource center, art gallery, and a church archives collection. The 123-acre campus is in a small town 65 miles southeast of Raleigh. Including residence halls, there are 16 buildings.

Student Life: 92% of undergraduates are from North Carolina. Others are from 21 states, 7 foreign countries, and Canada. 93% are from public schools. 68% are white; 25% African American. The average age of freshmen is 18; all undergraduates, 29. 40% do not continue beyond their first year; 20% remain to graduate.

Housing: 306 students can be accommodated in college housing, which includes single-sex dormitories and on-campus apartments. On-campus housing is guaranteed for the freshman year only. 77% of students commute. Alcohol is not permitted. All students may keep cars.

Activities: There are no fraternities or sororities. There are 20 groups on campus, including art, cheerleading, choir, chorale, chorus, drama, honors, international, literary magazine, newspaper, orchestra, pep band, photography, political, professional, religious, student government, and yearbook. Popular campus events include Founders Day, Pickle Classic Weekend, and the North Carolina Pickle Festival.

Sports: There are 6 intercollegiate sports for men and 6 for women, and 10 intramural sports for men and 8 for women. Facilities include a 2000-seat gym, racquetball and tennis courts, a track, wrestling/gymnastics and weight rooms, an athletic field, outdoor basketball areas, a student center, and baseball, softball, and soccer fields.

Disabled Students: 90% of the campus is accessible. Wheelchair ramps, elevators, special parking, specially equipped rest rooms, and special class scheduling are available.

Services: Counseling and information services are available, as is tutoring in most subjects, including math, English, and science. There is remedial math and reading.

Campus Safety and Security: Measures include informal discussions, pamphlets/posters/films, lighted pathways/sidewalks, and evening and weekend patrols.

Programs of Study: Mount Olive confers B.A., B.S., and B.Applied Sc. degrees. Associate degrees are also awarded. Bachelor's degrees are awarded in BIOLOGICAL SCIENCE (biology/biological science), BUSINESS (accounting, business administration and management, human resources, and recreation and leisure services), COMMUNICATIONS AND THE ARTS (art, communications, English, fine arts, and music), COMPUTER AND PHYSICAL SCIENCE (computer management, information sciences and systems, and mathematics), EDUCATION (middle school and secondary), ENGINEERING AND ENVIRONMENTAL DESIGN (environmental science), SOCIAL SCIENCE (criminal justice, history, human services, liberal arts/general studies, ministries, psychology, and religion). Business, accounting, and psychology are the strongest academically. Business, psychology, and recreation are the largest.

Required: To graduate, students must have completed a total of 126 credit hours, with a minimum 2.0 overall GPA in 63 credit hours for the B.A. or B.S. or in 53 hours for the B. Applied Sc. Distribution requirements include 30 to 36 hours in humanities, 18 in science/math and 12 in social science. Specific course work includes 6 hours of religion, 4 of phys ed, and 3 hours of computer competency.

Special: Mount Olive offers co-op programs and internships in all majors, work-study, B.A.-B.S. degrees, dual majors, and accelerated degree programs in business, accounting, and criminal justice administration. Cross-registration with James Sprunt Community College and Wayne Community College, study abroad, and credit for life, military, and work experience are also possible. Professional degree completion programs run continuously for 55 to 57 weeks. There is 1 national honor society, and a freshman honors program.

Faculty/Classroom: 58% of faculty are male; 42%, female. All teach undergraduates, 14% do research, and 86% do both.

Admissions: 80% of the 2001-2002 applicants were accepted. The SAT I scores for the 2001-2002 freshman class were: Verbal--71% below 500, 25% between 500 and 599, 3% between 600 and 700, and 1% above 700. The ACT scores were 81% below 21, 16% between 21 and 23, 2% between 24 and 26, and 1% between 27 and 28. 24% of the current freshmen were in the top fifth of their class; 56% were in the top two fifths. 4 freshmen graduated first in their class.

Requirements: The SAT I or ACT is required. A minimum SAT I composite score of 700 or ACT score of 16 is recommended. Applicants must be graduates of an accredited secondary school or have a GED certificate. They must have completed 4 units of English, 3 each of math and science, and 2 of history. An essay and interview are suggested. A GPA of 2.0 is required. AP and CLEP credits are accepted.

Procedure: Freshmen are admitted to all sessions. Entrance exams should be taken in the junior or senior year. There are early admissions and deferred admissions plans. Application deadlines are open. The application fee is $20. Notification is sent on a rolling basis.

Transfer: 131 transfer students enrolled in 2001-2002. Applicants must have a minimum GPA of 2.0 and submit an official transcript from the previous institution. An interview may be required. 32 credits of 126 must be completed at Mount Olive.

Visiting: There are regularly scheduled orientations for prospective students, consisting of 2 days of advising, sports, and entertainment. There are guides for informal visits and visitors may sit in on classes. To schedule a visit, contact the Admissions Office at *twoodward@moc.edu*.

Financial Aid: In a recent year, 96% of all students received some form of financial aid. 90% of freshmen and 89% of continuing students received need-based aid. The average freshman award was $6730. 28% of undergraduates work part time. Average annual earnings from campus work are $512. The average financial indebtedness of a recent graduate was $6730. The FAFSA and the college's own financial statement are required. The fall application deadline is March 1.

International Students: There are 8 international students enrolled. The school actively recruits these students. They must score 500 on the written TOEFL and also take the SAT I or the ACT.

Computers: The Internet may be accessed via 45 PCs and Macs located in 2 computer labs, with software and assistance also available. All students may access the system 8 A.M. to 10 P.M. Monday through Friday and during scheduled hours on weekends. Students may access the system for a reasonable length of time. There are no fees. It is strongly recommended that all students have a personal computer.

Graduates: In 2001, 471 bachelor's degrees were awarded. The most popular majors were business (69%), criminal justice administration (16%), and recreation (4%). In an average class, 1% graduate in 3 years, 18% in 4 years, and 22% in 5 years. 91 companies recruited on campus in 2000-2001. Of the 2000 graduating class, 15% were enrolled in graduate school within 6 months of graduation and 8% were employed.

Admissions Contact: Tim Woodard, Director of Admissions. A video is available. E-mail: *admissions@exchanbge.moc.edu*
Web: *www.moc.edu*

NORTH CAROLINA AGRICULTURAL AND TECHNICAL STATE UNIVERSITY D-2

Greensboro, NC 27411 (336) 334-7946
(800) 443-8964; Fax: (336) 334-7136

Full-time: 2800 men, 3100 women	**Faculty:** 442; IIA, av$
Part-time: 350 men, 360 women	**Ph.D.s:** 96%
Graduate: 370 men, 500 women	**Student/Faculty:** 13 to 1
Year: semesters, summer session	**Tuition:** $2189 ($9459)
Application Deadline: June 1	**Room & Board:** $4470
Freshman Class: n/av	
SAT I or ACT: required	**LESS COMPETITIVE**

North Carolina Agricultural and Technical State University, founded in 1891, is a public institution within the University of North Carolina System. A & T offers programs in arts and sciences, education, business and economics, agriculture, nursing, engineering, and technology. Enrollment figures in the above capsule are approximate. There are 7 undergraduate schools and 1 graduate school. In addition to regional accreditation, A & T has baccalaureate program accreditation with AACSB, ABET, ACCE, CSWE, NCATE, and NLN. The library contains 507,036 volumes, 1,038,474 microform items, and 34,025 audiovisual forms/CDs, and subscribes to 5446 periodicals. Computerized library services include the card catalog, interlibrary loans, and database searching. Special learning facilities include an art gallery, planetarium, radio station, TV station, and African Heritage Center. The 191-acre campus is in an urban area 90 miles northeast of Charlotte. Including residence halls, there are 107 buildings.

Student Life: 82% of undergraduates are from North Carolina. Others are from 39 states and 25 foreign countries. 89% are African American. The average age of freshmen is 18; all undergraduates, 22. 25% do not continue beyond their first year; 49% remain to graduate.

Housing: 2959 students can be accommodated in college housing, which includes single-sex and coed dormitories. In addition, there are honors houses. On-campus housing is available on a first-come, first-served basis and is available on a lottery system for upperclassmen. 53% of students commute. Alcohol is not permitted. All students may keep cars.

Activities: 1% of men belong to 5 national fraternities; 1% of women belong to 4 national sororities. There are 150 groups on campus, including art, band, cheerleading, choir, chorus, computers, dance, drama, drill team, ethnic, film, honors, international, jazz band, marching band, newspaper, orchestra, pep band, photography, political, professional, radio and TV, religious, social, social service, student government, symphony, and yearbook. Popular campus events include Graduation, Martin Luther King's Birthday, and Ron McNair Commemoration.

Sports: There are 7 intercollegiate sports for men and 9 for women, and 12 intramural sports for men and 12 for women. Facilities include a gym, a sports center, a stadium, tennis courts, a student union, a field house, and softball/baseball facilities.

Disabled Students: 85% of the campus is accessible. Wheelchair ramps, elevators, special parking, specially equipped rest rooms, special class scheduling, lowered drinking fountains, and lowered telephones are available.

Services: Counseling and information services are available, as is tutoring in every subject. There is a reader service for the blind, and remedial math, reading, and writing.

Campus Safety and Security: Measures include 24-hour foot and vehicle patrol, self-defense education, escort service, and shuttle buses. There are informal discussions, pamphlets/posters/films, emergency telephones, and lighted pathways/sidewalks.

Programs of Study: A & T confers B.A., B.S., B.F.A., B.S.I.E., B.S.M.E., B.S.N., and B.S.W. degrees. Master's and doctoral degrees are also awarded. Bachelor's degrees are awarded in AGRICULTURE (agricultural business management, agricultural economics, and animal science), BIOLOGICAL SCIENCE (biology/biological science), BUSINESS (accounting and business administration and management), COMMUNICATIONS AND THE ARTS (communications, dramatic arts, English, French, music, and speech/debate/rhetoric), COMPUTER AND PHYSICAL SCIENCE (chemistry, computer science, mathematics, and physics), EDUCATION (agricultural, art, business, early childhood, English, home economics, industrial arts, mathematics, music, physical, social science, and special), ENGINEERING AND ENVIRONMENTAL DESIGN (architectural engineering, chemical engineering, civil engineering, electrical/electronics engineering, engineering physics, industrial engineering, landscape architecture/design, mechanical engineering, and occupational safety and health), HEALTH PROFESSIONS (nursing), SOCIAL SCIENCE (child psychology/development, clothing and textiles management/production/services, economics, history, political science/government, psychology, social work, and sociology). Business, accounting, and electronics and computer technology are the strongest academically. Accounting and electronics and computer technology are the largest.

Required: To graduate, students must complete a minimum of 124 credit hours, including at least 80 in the major, with an overall GPA of 2.0 or better. Specific course work is required in English, math, natural science, social science, humanities, and health or phys ed.

Special: A & T offers cross-registration with the Greensboro Regional Consortium, internships, B.A.-B.S. degrees, cooperative programs in most majors, study abroad in 5 countries, work-study programs, and dual majors. There are 3 national honor societies, a freshman honors program, and 13 departmental honors programs.

Faculty/Classroom: 65% of faculty are male; 35%, female. All teach undergraduates. The average class size in an introductory lecture is 26; in a laboratory, 17; and in a regular course, 24.

Requirements: The SAT I or ACT is required with a minimum composite score of 750 on the SAT I or 17 on the ACT. Applicants must be graduates of an accredited secondary school or have a GED certificate. They must have completed at least 16 academic credits, including 4 in English, 3 each in math and science, 2 each in music and social sciences, and a foreign language. An audition is required of fine arts majors, and a portfolio is recommended. An interview is suggested for all applicants. A GPA of 2.0 is required. AP and CLEP credits are accepted. Important factors in the admissions decision are geographic diversity, advanced placement or honor courses, and personality/intangible qualities.

Procedure: Freshmen are admitted to all sessions. Entrance exams should be taken before April 1. There is a deferred admissions plan. Applications should be filed by June 1 for fall entry and December 1 for spring entry. Notification is sent on a rolling basis.

Transfer: 338 transfer students enrolled in a recent year. Applicants must have a minimum GPA of 2.0 in at least 24 semester hours and must be in good standing at their previous school. Specifically, 6 hours of English, history, college algebra, and science are required. 62 credits of 124 must be completed at A & T.

Visiting: There are regularly scheduled orientations for prospective students. There are guides for informal visits and visitors may sit in on classes. To schedule a visit, contact the Admissions Office.

Financial Aid: The average financial indebtedness of the 2001 graduate was $15,008. A & T is a member of CSS. The FAFSA is required. The fall application deadline is March 15.

International Students: There were 53 international students enrolled in a recent year. They must score 550 on the written TOEFL.

Computers: The mainframes are a DEC VAX 6320 and a DEC VAX 11/785. Mac PCs, IBMs, DEC stations, and X terminals are available. All students may access the system. There are no time limits and no fees.

Graduates: In a recent year, 895 bachelor's degrees were awarded. The most popular majors were mechanical engineering (8%), nursing (6%), and accounting (5%). In an average class, 24% graduate in 4 years, 40% in 5 years, and 42% in 6 years. 995 companies recruited on campus in a recent year.

Admissions Contact: John Smith, Admissions Director. A video is available. E-mail: *uadmit@ncat.edu* Web: *www.ncat.edu*

NORTH CAROLINA CENTRAL UNIVERSITY D-2

Durham, NC 27707 (919) 560-6298
Fax: (919) 530-7625 or (919) 560-5462

Full-time: 1259 men, 2134 women	**Faculty:** 257; IIA, +$
Part-time: 272 men, 567 women	**Ph.D.s:** 75%
Graduate: 440 men, 1081 women	**Student/Faculty:** 13 to 1
Year: semesters, summer session	**Tuition:** $2350 ($10,272)
Application Deadline: July 1	**Room & Board:** $4068
Freshman Class: 2167 applied, 1674 accepted, 798 enrolled	
SAT I Verbal/Math: 431/430	**ACT:** 17 **LESS COMPETITIVE**

North Carolina Central University, founded in 1909, is a publicly funded liberal arts institution in the University of North Carolina system. There are 3 undergraduate and 2 graduate schools. In addition to regional accreditation, NCCU has baccalaureate program accreditation with NCATE and NLN. The 6 libraries contain 663,913 volumes, 1,217,019 microform items, and 10,991 audiovisual forms/CDs, and subscribe to 6688 periodicals. Computerized library services include the card catalog and database searching. Special learning facilities include a learning resource center and art gallery. The 103-acre campus is in an urban area 2 miles from the center of Durham. Including residence halls, there are 57 buildings.

Student Life: 90% of undergraduates are from North Carolina. Others are from 34 states and 17 foreign countries. 82% are African American; 14% white. The average age of freshmen is 19; all undergraduates, 24.

Housing: 2377 students can be accommodated in college housing, which includes single-sex and coed dormitories and on-campus apartments. In addition, there are honors houses. On-campus housing is available on a first-come, first-served basis. 63% of students commute. Alcohol is not permitted. All students may keep cars.

Activities: There are 4 national fraternities and 4 national sororities. There are 45 groups on campus, including art, band, cheerleading, chess, choir, computers, dance, drama, drill team, ethnic, honors, international, jazz band, literary magazine, marching band, newspaper, political, professional, radio and TV, religious, social, social service, student government, symphony, and yearbook.

Sports: There are 6 intercollegiate sports for men and 5 for women. Facilities include a 12,000-seat stadium, a 4500-seat gym, a swimming pool, handball and tennis courts, a track, a bowling alley, dance studios, and a weight room.

Disabled Students: 90% of the campus is accessible. Wheelchair ramps, elevators, special parking, specially equipped rest rooms, special class scheduling, lowered drinking fountains, lowered telephones, lowered dormitory intercoms, interpreters, automatic door openers, and adaptive technology are available.

Services: Counseling and information services are available. There is a reader service for the blind, remedial math, reading, and writing, and assistance for students in obtaining needed documentations and with registration. Appropriate individual accomodations and assistance are provided as needed.

Campus Safety and Security: Measures include 24-hour foot and vehicle patrol, escort service, informal discussions, and pamphlets/posters/films. There are emergency telephones and lighted pathways/sidewalks.

Programs of Study: NCCU confers B.A., B.S., B.B.A., B.M., B.S.N., and B.S.W. degrees. Master's degrees are also awarded. Bachelor's degrees are awarded in BIOLOGICAL SCIENCE (biology/biological science and nutrition), BUSINESS (accounting and business administration and management), COMMUNICATIONS AND THE ARTS (art, dramatic arts, English, French, jazz, music, and Spanish), COMPUTER AND PHYSICAL SCIENCE (chemistry, computer science, mathematics, and physics), EDUCATION (elementary, health, middle school, and physical), ENGINEERING AND ENVIRONMENTAL DESIGN (environmental science), HEALTH PROFESSIONS (nursing), SOCIAL SCIENCE (child care/child and family studies, child psychology/development, criminal justice, geography, history, human services, political science/government, psychology, social work, and sociology). Criminal justice is the strongest academically. Business, biology, and political science are the largest.

Required: To graduate, students must complete 124 semester hours, including 30 in the major, with a minimum GPA of 2.0. Core requirements include courses in communications, math and natural science, social science, humanities, and health and phys ed.

Special: NCCU offers internships, work-study programs, dual majors, and nondegree study. There are 10 national honor societies, a freshman honors program, and 10 departmental honors programs.

Faculty/Classroom: 53% of faculty are male; 47%, female. All teach undergraduates.

Admissions: 77% of the 2001-2002 applicants were accepted. The SAT I scores for the 2001-2002 freshman class were: Verbal--83% below 500, 15% between 500 and 599, and 2% between 600 and 700; Math--85% below 500, 14% between 500 and 599, and 1% between 600 and 700. The ACT scores were 94% below 21, 3% between 21 and 23, and 2% between 24 and 26. 11% of the current freshmen were in the top fifth of their class; 31% were in the top two fifths.

Requirements: The SAT I or ACT is required. In addition, applicants must be graduates of an accredited secondary school or have a GED certificate. They must have completed 11 academic credits based on 4 years of English, 3 each of math and science, and 2 each of a foreign language and social studies. Music applicants must audition. A GPA of 2.0 is required. AP and CLEP credits are accepted. Important factors in the admissions decision are advanced placement or honor courses, leadership record, and evidence of special talent.

Procedure: Entrance exams should be taken in the spring of the junior year. Applications should be filed by July 1 for fall entry and November 1 for spring entry. The fall 2001 application fee was $30. Notification is sent on a rolling basis.

Transfer: 339 transfer students enrolled in 2001-2002. Applicants must have a minimum GPA of 2.0 in all college-level courses. 30 credits of 124 must be completed at NCCU.

Visiting: There are regularly scheduled orientations for prospective students. There are guides for informal visits and visitors may sit in on classes and stay overnight. To schedule a visit, contact LuAnn Harris at (919) 530-7349.

Financial Aid: In 2001-2002, 85% of all students received some form of financial aid. 70% of all students received need-based aid. Scholarships or need-based grants averaged $4000 ($7000 maximum); loans averaged $3000 ($6625 maximum); and work contracts averaged $1000 (maximum). The average financial indebtedness of the 2001 graduate was $10,000. 20% of undergraduates work part time on campus. Average annual earnings are $1000. The FAFSA is required. The fall application deadline is August 1.

International Students: They must score 500 on the written TOEFL.

Computers: The mainframe is a Data General MV/15000. All students may access the system 9 A.M. to 5 P.M. Monday through Friday. The computing center also has dial-in service. There are no time limits and no fees.

Graduates: In 2001, 696 bachelor's degrees were awarded. The most popular majors were business administration (18%), education (10%), and biology (10%). 297 companies recruited on campus in 2000-2001.

Admissions Contact: Ms. Jocelyn L. Foy, Director of Admissions. A video is available.

NORTH CAROLINA SCHOOL OF THE ARTS C-2

Winston-Salem, NC 27127-2188 (336) 770-3290
Fax: (336) 770-3370

Full-time: 387 men, 300 women	**Faculty:** 126
Part-time: 15 men, 6 women	**Ph.D.s:** 70%
Graduate: 31 men, 50 women	**Student/Faculty:** 5 to 1
Year: trimesters	**Tuition:** $2877 ($12,282)
Application Deadline: March 1	**Room & Board:** $4920
Freshman Class: 698 applied, 316 accepted, 187 enrolled	
SAT I Verbal/Math: 570/540	**ACT:** 24 **SPECIAL**

North Carolina School of the Arts, founded in 1963 and now part of the University of North Carolina system, is a public institution offering professional training in the performing arts. There are 5 undergraduate and 2 graduate schools. The library contains 114,050 volumes, 25,053 microform items, and 73,025 audiovisual forms/CDs, and subscribes to 490 periodicals. Computerized library services include the card catalog, interlibrary loans, and database searching. Special learning facilities include a learning resource center, art gallery, and numerous performance theaters, screening rooms, and CAD studios. The 45-acre campus is in an urban area 75 miles north of Charlotte. Including residence halls, there are 33 buildings.

Student Life: 52% of undergraduates are from out of state, mostly the Middle Atlantic. Others are from 44 states, 28 foreign countries, and Canada. 80% are from public schools. 84% are white; 10% African American. The average age of freshmen is 19; all undergraduates, 25. 50% do not continue beyond their first year.

Housing: 300 students can be accommodated in college housing, which includes coed dormitories and on-campus apartments. On-campus housing is available on a first-come, first-served basis. Priority is given to out-of-town students. 58% of students live on campus; of those, 90% remain on campus on weekends. Alcohol is not permitted. All students may keep cars.

Activities: There are no fraternities or sororities. There are many groups and organizations on campus, including art, band, choir, chorale, chorus, dance, drama, ethnic, film, gay, international, jazz band, musical theater, newspaper, opera, orchestra, radio and TV, student government, and symphony.

Sports: There is no sports program at NCSA. Facilities include a gym, fitness and weight rooms, a swimming pool, a soccer/touch football field, a golf course, and courts for tennis, basketball, and volleyball.

Disabled Students: 50% of the campus is accessible. Wheelchair ramps, special parking, and elevators in 2 buildings are available.

Services: Counseling and information services are available, as is tutoring in every subject. There is remedial math, reading, and writing. Private tutoring is also offered on a fee basis.

Campus Safety and Security: Measures include 24-hour foot and vehicle patrol, emergency telephones, and lighted pathways/sidewalks.

Programs of Study: NCSA confers B.F.A. and B.M. degrees. Master's degrees are also awarded. Bachelor's degrees are awarded in COMMUNICATIONS AND THE ARTS (ballet, dance, dramatic arts, film arts, music, performing arts, and theater design).

Required: To earn a bachelor's degree, students must demonstrate satisfactory skills in reading, writing, oral communication, and math, take courses in foundations of Western thought, complete studies in fine arts/humanities, social/behavioral sciences, and math/natural science, and meet all requirements in their arts major.

Special: NCSA offers work-study programs, a general studies major, independent study, and design and production apprenticeships. An accelerated degree program is available to high school students in dance, drama, music, and visual arts.

Faculty/Classroom: 67% of faculty are male; 33%, female. All teach undergraduates. No introductory courses are taught by graduate students. The average class size in a regular course is 10.

Admissions: 45% of the 2001-2002 applicants were accepted. The SAT I scores for the 2001-2002 freshman class were: Verbal--17% below 500, 44% between 500 and 599, 30% between 600 and 700, and 8% above 700; Math--25% below 500, 47% between 500 and 599, 24% between 600 and 700, and 3% above 700. 33% of the current freshmen were in the top fifth of their class; 68% were in the top two fifths.

Requirements: The SAT I or ACT is required. In addition, applicants must be graduates of an accredited secondary school or have a GED certificate. They should have completed 4 units in English, 3 in math, 3 in science with 1 in a lab course, and 2 in social studies with 1 in U.S. history. Also recommended are 2 units in a foreign language and 1 unit each in foreign language and math in the senior year. An audition/interview demonstrating evidence of special talent is the primary admissions criterion. Applicants to the School of Design and Production must submit a portfolio. Filmmaking applicants must submit a creative writing sample. CLEP credit is accepted. Important factors in the admissions decision are recommendations by school officials, evidence of special talent, and recommendations by alumni.

Procedure: Freshmen are admitted fall and winter. Applications should be filed by March 1 for fall entry, along with a $45 fee for permanent residents or a $90 fee for international students. Notification is sent on a rolling basis.

Transfer: 62 transfer students enrolled in 2001-2002. Evidence of special talent and good academic standing are required. Placement is based on ability and experience, prior courses, and interviews and auditions.

Visiting: There are regularly scheduled orientations for prospective students, including tours on audition days and question-and-answer sessions with administration and faculty. Visitors may sit in on classes. To schedule a visit, contact the Admissions Office.

Financial Aid: In 2001-2002, 67% of all freshmen and 70% of continuing students received some form of financial aid. 51% of freshmen and 48% of continuing students received need-based aid. The average freshman award was $7158. Of that total, scholarships or need-based grants averaged $4768; loans averaged $2726; and non-need based aid averaged $3197. The average financial indebtedness of the 2001 graduate was $15,566. The FAFSA is required. The fall application deadline is March 1.

International Students: There are 19 international students enrolled. The school actively recruits these students. They must score 550 on the written TOEFL.

Computers: PCs are available in the student computer lab and the library. All students may access the system. There are no time limits and no fees.

Graduates: In 2001, 126 bachelor's degrees were awarded. The most popular majors were filmmaking (38%), design and production (23%), and music (21%). In an average class, 3% graduate in 3 years, 40% in 4 years, 45% in 5 years, and 45% in 6 years.

Admissions Contact: Sheeler Lawson, Director of Admissions. E-mail: *admissions@ncarts.edu* Web: *www.ncarts.edu*

NORTH CAROLINA STATE UNIVERSITY — D-2

Raleigh, NC 27695-7103 — **(919) 515-2434; Fax: (919) 515-5039**

Full-time: 10,350 men, 7506 women	**Faculty:** 1489; I, av$
Part-time: 2257 men, 1660 women	**Ph.D.s:** 90%
Graduate: 3753 men, 3115 women	**Student/Faculty:** 12 to 1
Year: semesters, summer session	**Tuition:** $3206 ($12,372)
Application Deadline: February 1	**Room & Board:** $5474
Freshman Class: 11,835 applied, 7789 accepted, 3831 enrolled	
SAT I Verbal/Math: 520–620/550–660	**ACT:** 22–27

HIGHLY COMPETITIVE

North Carolina State University, founded in 1887, is a member of the University of North Carolina System. Its degree programs emphasize the arts and sciences, agriculture, business, education, engineering, and preprofessional training. There are 10 undergraduate and 10 graduate schools. In addition to regional accreditation, NC State has baccalaureate program accreditation with ABET, CSAB, CSWE, NAAB, NCATE, NRPA, and SAF. The 5 libraries contain 2.9 million volumes, 4,852,892 microform items, and 142,831 audiovisual forms/CDs, and subscribe to 37,000 periodicals. Computerized library services include the card catalog, interlibrary loans, and database searching. Special learning facilities include a learning resource center, art gallery, radio station, TV station, nuclear reactor, phytotron, electron microscope facilities, Materials Research Center, Integrated Manufacturing Systems Engineering Institute, Japan Center, and Precision Engineering Center. The 1,700-acre campus is in an urban area in Raleigh. Including residence halls, there are 150 buildings.

Student Life: 86% of undergraduates are from North Carolina. Others are from 49 states, 66 foreign countries, and Canada. 91% are from public schools. 77% are white; 10% African American. 60% are Protestant; 18% claim no religious affiliation; 14% Catholic. The average age of freshmen is 18; all undergraduates, 21. 12% do not continue beyond their first year; 65% remain to graduate.

Housing: 7300 students can be accommodated in college housing, which includes single-sex and coed dormitories, married-student housing, fraternity houses, and sorority houses. In addition, there are honors houses, and special-interest houses, and international, arts and creative living, computer theme, and fist-year experience halls. On-campus housing is available on a first-come, first-served basis and is available on a lottery system for upperclassmen. 66% of students commute. Alcohol is not permitted. Upperclassmen may keep cars.

Activities: 10% of men belong to 27 national fraternities; 9% of women belong to 10 national sororities. There are 300 groups on campus, including art, bagpipe band, band, cheerleading, chess, choir, chorale, chorus, computers, dance, drama, drill team, drum and bugle corps, ethnic, film, gay, honors, international, jazz band, literary magazine, marching band, musical theater, newspaper, orchestra, pep band, photography, political, professional, radio and TV, religious, social, social service, student government, symphony, and yearbook. Popular campus events include Pan African Festival, Wolfstock, and Greek Week.

Sports: There are 20 intercollegiate sports for men and 16 for women, and 28 intramural sports for men and 26 for women. Facilities include a 55,000-seat football stadium, a 20,000-seat sports arena, a 5000-seat soccer stadium, a baseball stadium, a 12,500-seat gym, a tennis complex, areas for track, 2 indoor pools, and an indoor rock climbing wall.

Disabled Students: 78% of the campus is accessible. Wheelchair ramps, elevators, special parking, specially equipped rest rooms, special class scheduling, lowered drinking fountains, lowered telephones, and van transportation are available.

Services: Counseling and information services are available, as is tutoring in most subjects. There is a reader service for the blind and remedial math and writing.

Campus Safety and Security: Measures include 24-hour foot and vehicle patrol, self-defense education, escort service, and shuttle buses. There are informal discussions, pamphlets/posters/films, emergency telephones, lighted pathways/sidewalks, and bicycle patrol.

Programs of Study: NC State confers B.A., B.S., B.Arch., B.E.D.A., B.L.A., and B.S.W. degrees. Associate, master's, and doctoral degrees are also awarded. Bachelor's degrees are awarded in AGRICULTURE (agricultural business management, agricultural economics, agriculture, agronomy, animal science, conservation and regulation, fishing and fisheries, forestry and related sciences, horticulture, natural resource management, poultry science, soil science, and wood science), BIOLOGICAL SCIENCE (biochemistry, biology/biological science, botany, microbiology, and zoology), BUSINESS (accounting, business administration and management, business economics, and recreation and leisure services), COMMUNICATIONS AND THE ARTS (communications, design, English, French, graphic design, industrial design, and Spanish), COMPUTER AND PHYSICAL SCIENCE (atmospheric sciences and meteorology, chemistry, computer science, earth science, geology, mathematics, physics, and statistics), EDUCATION (agricultural, education, foreign languages, industrial arts, marketing and distribution, mathematics, middle school, science, secondary, social studies, technical, and vocational), ENGINEERING AND ENVIRONMENTAL DESIGN (aeronautical engineering, agricultural engineering, architecture, chemical engineering, civil engineering, computer engineering, construction management, electrical/electronics engineering, engineering, environmental design, environmental engineering, environmental science, furniture design, industrial engineering, landscape architecture/design, materials science, mechanical engineering, nuclear engineering, paper and pulp science, and textile engineering), HEALTH PROFESSIONS (medical laboratory technology, predentistry, premedicine, preveterinary science, and speech pathology/audiology), SOCIAL SCIENCE (clothing and textiles management/production/services, criminal justice, economics, food science, history, interdisciplinary studies, parks and recreation management, philosophy, political science/government, prelaw, psychology, religion, social science, social work, sociology, and textiles and clothing). Electrical engineering, chemical engineering, and architecture are the strongest academically. Business management, mechanical engineering, and electrical engineering are the largest.

Required: To graduate, students must complete 120 to 142 semester hours, including 60 to 70 in the major, with a minimum GPA of 2.0. Distribution requirements include 12 to 18 hours in humanities and social sciences, 6 to 8 each in math and science, 6 in English composition, and 4 in phys ed.

Special: NC State offers cross-registration within the Cooperating Raleigh Colleges network, study abroad in more than 90 countries, internships, work-study programs, an accelerated degree plan, dual majors within any program, a general studies degree in education, a 3-2 engineering degree with the University of North Carolina at Asheville, student-designed multidisciplinary studies majors, credit by examination, nondegree study, and pass/fail options. There are 15 national honor societies, including Phi Beta Kappa, a freshman honors program, and 44 departmental honors programs.

Faculty/Classroom: 75% of faculty are male; 25%, female. All both teach and do research. Graduate students teach 8% of introductory courses. The average class size in an introductory lecture is 35; in a laboratory, 20; and in a regular course, 30.

Admissions: 66% of the 2001-2002 applicants were accepted. The SAT I scores for the 2001-2002 freshman class were: Verbal--12% below 500, 50% between 500 and 599, 35% between 600 and 700, and 3% above 700; Math--2% below 500, 35% between 500 and 599, 50% between 600 and 700, and 13% above 700. The ACT scores were 4% below 21, 7% between 21 and 23, 65% between 24 and 26, 10% between 27 and 28, and 14% above 28. 90% of the current freshmen were in the top fifth of their class; All were in the top two fifths. There were 41 National Merit finalists in a recent year.

Requirements: The SAT I or ACT is required. In addition, the SAT II: Math test is recommended. Applicants must be graduates of an accredited secondary school or have a GED certificate. They must have completed 20 academic credits, including 4 units of English, 3 each of science and math (4 of math is advised), 2 each of social studies and foreign language, and 1 of history. An essay is recommended for all applicants. A portfolio and interview are required for the School of Design. AP and CLEP credits are accepted. Important factors in the admissions decision are advanced placement or honor courses, leadership record, and evidence of special talent. Applications are accepted on-line at the school's web site.

Procedure: Freshmen are admitted to all sessions. Entrance exams should be taken in the spring of the junior year and the fall of the senior year. There are early decision and deferred admissions plans. Early decision applications should be filed by November 15; regular applications, by February 1 for fall entry, November 1 for spring entry, and February 1 for summer entry. The fall 2001 application fee was $55. Notification of early decision is sent December 15; regular decision, on a rolling basis. 3% of all applicants are on a waiting list.

Transfer: 1222 transfer students enrolled in 2001-2002. Applicants must have completed 30 semester hours of college-level work with a minimum GPA of 2.0. Priority is given to students who have completed 60 hours of relevant course work. An associate degree and an interview are recommended. Applicants must have math, English, and foreign language proficiency. 30 credits of 120 must be completed at NC State.

Visiting: There are regularly scheduled orientations for prospective students, consisting of admissions information sessions. There are guides for informal visits and visitors may sit in on classes. To schedule a visit, contact the Admissions Office.

Financial Aid: The FAFSA is required. The fall application deadline is March 1.

International Students: There were 172 international students enrolled in a recent year. The school actively recruits these students. They must score 550 on the written TOEFL and also take the SAT I, ACTif it is available to students in their country.

Computers: The mainframes are an IBM 3081, an IBM 4381/P12, and a DEC VAX 8700. There are also 2300 computer stations located campuswide. Several departments have additional stations available for their majors only. All students may access the system. Students may access the system. Time limits vary by class. The fee is $100.

Graduates: In a recent year, 3688 bachelor's degrees were awarded. The most popular majors were engineering (25%) and business management (16%). In an average class, 1% graduate in 3 years, 27% in 4 years, 58% in 5 years, and 65% in 6 years. 750 companies recruited on campus in 2000-2001.

Admissions Contact: George R. Dixon, Vice Provost and Dir of Admissions. E-mail: *undergrad_admissions@ncsu.edu*
Web: *http://www2.ncsu.edu*

NORTH CAROLINA WESLEYAN COLLEGE — E-2

Rocky Mount, NC 27804 — (252) 985-5200
(800) 488-NCWC; (252) 985-5295

Full-time: 330 men, 410 women	**Faculty:** 46; IIB, --$
Part-time: 20 men, 35 women	**Ph.D.s:** 71%
Graduate: none	**Student/Faculty:** 16 to 1
Year: 4-1-4, summer session	**Tuition:** $9768
Application Deadline: July 15	**Room & Board:** $5882
Freshman Class: n/av	
SAT I or ACT: required	**LESS COMPETITIVE**

North Carolina Wesleyan College, founded in 1956, is a private liberal arts institution affiliated with the United Methodist Church. Figures in above capsule are approximate. In addition to regional accreditation, NCWC has baccalaureate program accreditation with NCATE. The library contains 80,000 volumes, 20,000 microform items, and 4200 audiovisual forms/CDs, and subscribes to 550 periodicals. Computerized library services include the card catalog, interlibrary loans, and database searching. Special learning facilities include a learning resource center, art gallery, and a performing arts center. The 200-acre campus is in a suburban area 57 miles east of Raleigh. Including residence halls, there are 18 buildings.

Student Life: 51% of undergraduates are from out of state, mostly the Middle Atlantic. Others are from 24 states and 9 foreign countries. 70% are from public schools. 56% are white; 39% African American. 70% are Protestant; 16% Catholic; 14% claim no religious affiliation. The average age of freshmen is 18; all undergraduates, 21. 40% do not continue beyond their first year; 28% remain to graduate.

Housing: 504 students can be accommodated in college housing, which includes single-sex and coed dormitories and off-campus apartments. There are single-occupancy residence halls with kitchens on each floor. On-campus housing is guaranteed for all 4 years. 57% of students live on campus; of those, 60% remain on campus on weekends. All students may keep cars.

Activities: 8% of men belong to 3 national fraternities; 4% of women belong to 3 national sororities. There are 23 groups on campus, including cheerleading, chess, choir, chorus, computers, drama, ethnic, gay, honors, international, jazz band, musical theater, newspaper, political, professional, religious, social, social service, student government, and yearbook. Popular campus events include Spring Fling, Parents Weekend, and Alumni Homecoming.

Sports: There are 5 intercollegiate sports for men and 5 for women, and 13 intramural sports for men and 13 for women. Facilities include a 1,200-seat gym with areas for basketball, volleyball, and indoor soccer matches; tennis courts; a skeet range; and fields for intramurals and for varsity baseball, softball, and soccer.

Disabled Students: 90% of the campus is accessible. Wheelchair ramps, elevators, special parking, specially equipped rest rooms, special class scheduling, lowered drinking fountains, and lowered telephones are available.

Services: Counseling and information services are available, as is tutoring in most subjects. There is remedial math, reading, and writing.

Campus Safety and Security: Measures include 24-hour foot and vehicle patrol, escort service, informal discussions, and pamphlets/posters/films. There are emergency telephones and lighted pathways/sidewalks.

Programs of Study: NCWC confers B.A. and B.S. degrees. Bachelor's degrees are awarded in BIOLOGICAL SCIENCE (biology/biological science), BUSINESS (accounting, business administration and management, and hotel/motel and restaurant management), COMMUNICATIONS AND THE ARTS (dramatic arts, English, and music), COMPUTER AND PHYSICAL SCIENCE (chemistry, information sciences and systems, and mathematics), EDUCATION (athletic training, elementary, and middle school), ENGINEERING AND ENVIRONMENTAL DESIGN (environmental science), HEALTH PROFESSIONS (exercise science and premedicine), SOCIAL SCIENCE (criminal justice, history, political science/government, psychology, religion, and sociology). Business administration, justice studies, and computer information systems are the largest.

Required: To graduate, students must complete 124 semester hours, including 30 to 54 in the major, with a minimum GPA of 2.0. Distribution requirements consist of 6 semester hours of English composition or demonstrated proficiency; 4 each of biological and physical science; 3 each of ethics, non-Western culture, math, history, social science, psychology or sociology, religion, literature, and fine arts; 2 of phys ed; and 2 of introduction to college life. Some majors require a thesis.

Special: NCWC offers cooperative programs in all majors, internships, work-study programs through the college offices, credit for military experience, nondegree study, and pass/fail options. The B.A. - B.S. degree may be earned in all majors. There are 2 national honor societies, and a freshman honors program.

Faculty/Classroom: 60% of faculty are male; 40%, female. All teach undergraduates. The average class size in an introductory lecture is 23; in a laboratory, 15; and in a regular course, 18.

Requirements: The SAT I or ACT is required, with a minimum SAT I composite score of 800 or ACT score of 19 recommended. Applicants should be graduates of an accredited secondary school or have a GED. They should have completed at least 13 academic courses, including 4 in English, 3 in math, and 2 each in foreign language, social studies, and lab sciences. NCWC also recommends that students have 2 hours in math and 2 to 3 in science. An essay and interview are advised. Applications are accepted on-line through the school's web site. AP and CLEP credits are accepted. Important factors in the admissions decision are advanced placement or honor courses, extracurricular activities record, and leadership record.

Procedure: Freshmen are admitted fall and spring. Entrance exams should be taken in spring of the junior year or fall or winter of the senior year. There are early admissions and deferred admissions plans. Applications should be filed by July 15 for fall entry, December 1 for spring entry, and June 1 for summer entry, along with a $25 fee. Notification is sent on a rolling basis.

Transfer: 65 transfer students enrolled in a recet year. Applicants must have a minimum GPA of 2.0 in their college courses. They must submit transcripts of all high school and college work, along with proof of high school graduation. 30 credits of 124 must be completed at NCWC.

Visiting: There are regularly scheduled orientations for prospective students, including an individual campus tour, interview, financial aid session, and meetings with faculty and coaches. There are guides for informal visits and visitors may sit in on classes and stay overnight. To schedule a visit, contact the Admissions Office.

Financial Aid: In a recent year, 95% of all freshmen and 80% of continuing students received some form of financial aid. 69% of freshmen and 57% of continuing students received need-based aid. The average freshman award was $8597. Of that total, scholarships or need-based grants averaged $3972 ($7100 maximum); loans averaged $3625; and work contracts averaged $1000. 90% of undergraduates work part time. Average annual earnings from campus work are $1000. The average financial indebtedness of a recent year's graduate was $14,250. NCWC is a member of CSS. The FAFSA is required. The fall application deadline is March 31.

International Students: They must score 500 on the written TOEFL and also take the SAT I.

Computers: The mainframe is an IBM/36. There are also 70 PCs located in the computer lab, residence halls, tutoring center, and library. All students may access the system on a sign-up basis in the computer lab or as available at other locations. There are no time limits and no fees.

Admissions Contact: Alan P. Felton, Director of Admission.
E-mail: *adm@ncwc.edu* Web: *www.ncwc.edu*

PFEIFFER UNIVERSITY

Misenheimer, NC 28109	**C-2**
	(704) 463-1360, ext. 2079
	(800) 338-2060; Fax: (704) 463-1363
Full-time: 396 men, 502 women	**Faculty:** 54; IIA, --$
Part-time: 53 men, 125 women	**Ph.D.s:** 73%
Graduate: 244 men, 351 women	**Student/Faculty:** 15 to 1
Year: semesters, summer session	**Tuition:** $12,780
Application Deadline: August 25	**Room & Board:** $5800
Freshman Class: 599 applied, 441 accepted, 146 enrolled	
SAT I Verbal/Math: 500/510	**ACT:** 21 **COMPETITIVE**

Pfeiffer University, founded in 1885, is a private institution of liberal arts and sciences affiliated with the United Methodist Church. There is 1 graduate school. In addition to regional accreditation, Pfeiffer has baccalaureate program accreditation with NASM and NCATE. The library contains 114,555 volumes, 27,551 microform items, and 2861 audiovisual forms/CDs, and subscribes to 415 periodicals. Computerized library services include the card catalog, interlibrary loans, and database searching. Special learning facilities include a learning resource center and art gallery. The 350-acre campus is in a rural area 35 miles east of Charlotte. Including residence halls, there are 28 buildings.

Student Life: 62% of undergraduates are from North Carolina. Others are from 27 states, 21 foreign countries, and Canada. 67% are white; 23% African American. 51% are Protestant; 30% Catholic. The average age of freshmen is 18; all undergraduates, 22. 28% do not continue beyond their first year; 44% remain to graduate.

Housing: 650 students can be accommodated in college housing, which includes single-sex and coed dormitories and married-student housing. In addition, there are honors houses. On-campus housing is guaranteed for all 4 years. 65% of students live on campus; of those, 60% remain on campus on weekends. All students may keep cars.

Activities: There are no fraternities or sororities. There are 34 groups on campus, including band, cheerleading, chess, choir, chorale, chorus, drama, ethnic, honors, international, jazz band, literary magazine, newspaper, pep band, political, professional, religious, social, social service, and student government. Popular campus events include Winterfest, Aprilfest, and coffee houses.

Sports: There are 7 intercollegiate sports for men and 8 for women, and 21 intramural sports for men and 21 for women. Facilities include an 1800-seat main gym, an indoor pool, exercise rooms, training facilities, and weight rooms. The campus also has 6 tennis courts, fields for baseball, softball, lacrosse, and soccer, areas for golf practice and volleyball, and an indoor batting cage.

Disabled Students: 50% of the campus is accessible. Wheelchair ramps, elevators, special parking, specially equipped rest rooms, and special class scheduling are available.

Services: Counseling and information services are available, as is tutoring in most subjects. There is remedial math, reading, and writing.

Campus Safety and Security: Measures include 24-hour foot and vehicle patrol, self-defense education, escort service, and informal discussions. There are pamphlets/posters/films and lighted pathways/sidewalks.

Programs of Study: Pfeiffer confers A.B. and B.S. degrees. Master's degrees are also awarded. Bachelor's degrees are awarded in BIOLOGICAL SCIENCE (biology/biological science), BUSINESS (accounting, business administration and management, and sports management), COMMUNICATIONS AND THE ARTS (arts administration/management, communications, dramatic arts, English literature, and music), COMPUTER AND PHYSICAL SCIENCE (chemistry, information sciences and systems, and mathematics), EDUCATION (athletic training, Christian, elementary, music, physical, science, secondary, and special), ENGINEERING AND ENVIRONMENTAL DESIGN (environmental science, and preengineering), HEALTH PROFESSIONS (premedicine and sports medicine), SOCIAL SCIENCE (American studies, criminal justice, economics, history, human services, political science/government, prelaw, psychology, religion, religious education, religious music, social studies, and sociology). Chemistry, music, and sports medicine and management are the strongest academically. Business administration, criminal justice, and elementary education are the largest.

Required: All students must complete 120 to 124 semester hours, including 60 credits in writing, language and literature, history/political science, music/art/theater, natural science, math, economics/psychology/sociology, religion, and phys ed. Students must maintain an overall minimum GPA of 2.0 and complete 42 to 72 hours in the major.

Special: A 3-2 program in engineering with Auburn University, work-study programs, many internships in business, education, public service, and phys ed, study abroad in 5 countries, and interdisciplinary majors are offered. There are 4 national honor societies, a freshman honors program, and 10 departmental honors programs.

Faculty/Classroom: 63% of faculty are male; 37%, female. 82% teach undergraduates, 25% do research, and 20% do both. No introductory courses are taught by graduate students. The average class size in an introductory lecture is 20; in a laboratory, 19; and in a regular course, 12.

Admissions: 74% of the 2001-2002 applicants were accepted. The SAT I scores for the 2001-2002 freshman class were: Verbal--48% below 500, 33% between 500 and 599, 10% between 600 and 700, and 1% above 700; Math--42% below 500, 37% between 500 and 599, 13% between 600 and 700, and 1% above 700. The ACT scores were 66% below 21, 22% between 21 and 23, and 11% between 24 and 26. 36% of the current freshmen were in the top fifth of their class; 55% were in the top two fifths.

Requirements: The SAT I is required and the ACT is recommended. In addition, all applicants are required to have completed 4 years of English and 3 years of math, including algebra I. The GED is accepted. A GPA of 2.0 is required. AP and CLEP credits are accepted. Important factors in the admissions decision are advanced placement or honor courses, leadership record, and extracurricular activities record. Applications are accepted on-line.

Procedure: Freshmen are admitted to all sessions. Entrance exams should be taken by January of the senior year. There are early admissions and deferred admissions plans. Applications should be filed by August 25 for fall entry and January 7 for spring entry, along with a $25 fee. Notification is sent on a rolling basis.

Transfer: 74 transfer students enrolled in a recent year. Applicants should be eligible for readmission to the last college attended and have a minimum GPA of 2.0. 45 credits of 120 must be completed at Pfeiffer.

Visiting: There are regularly scheduled orientations for prospective students, including meetings with faculty/staff, a question-and-answer session, a tour, and a lunch. There are guides for informal visits and visitors may sit in on classes and stay overnight. To schedule a visit, contact the Admissions Office.
Financial Aid: In 2001-2002, 77% of all freshmen and 80% of continuing students received some form of financial aid. 40% of undergraduates work part time. Average annual earnings from campus work are $1126. The average financial indebtedness of a recent graduate was $6602. Pfeiffer is a member of CSS. The FAFSA is required. The fall application deadline is open.
International Students: There were 53 international students enrolled in a recent year. They must score 500 on the written TOEFL and also take the SAT I, scoring 900, or proven success at another American School.
Computers: There are 2 main labs and several smaller ones on campus, each with 24 Pentium II computers, which have Internet access, and are available 24 hours per day. Dorms are wired for Internet access. All students may access the system. There are no time limits and no fees.
Graduates: In a recent year, 192 bachelor's degrees were awarded. The most popular majors were business administration (29%), criminal justice (16%), and health care management (9%). In an average class, 30% graduate in 4 years, 39% in 5 years, and 42% in 6 years. 100 companies recruited on campus in a recent year.
Admissions Contact: Steve Cumming, Director of Admissions.
E-mail: *admissions@pfeiffer.edu* Web: *www.pfeiffer.edu*

QUEENS COLLEGE
Charlotte, NC 28274 — C-3
(704) 337-2212
(800) 849-0202; Fax: (704) 337-2403

Full-time: 184 men, 559 women
Part-time: 85 men, 371 women
Graduate: 196 men, 309 women
Year: semesters, summer session
Application Deadline: open
Freshman Class: 677 applied, 538 accepted, 211 enrolled
SAT I or ACT: required
Faculty: 59; IIB, -$
Ph.D.s: 80%
Student/Faculty: 13 to 1
Tuition: $11,360
Room & Board: $5890
COMPETITIVE

Queens College, founded in 1857, is a private liberal arts institution affiliated with the Presbyterian Church (U.S.A.). Undergraduate programs are offered through the College of Arts and Sciences and the Pauline Lewis Hayworth College, a division offering courses in the evening and on Saturday. There are 2 undergraduate schools and 1 graduate school. In addition to regional accreditation, Queens has baccalaureate program accreditation with ACBSP, NASM, NCATE, and NLN. The library contains 107,424 volumes, 368 microform items, and 1344 audiovisual forms/CDs, and subscribes to 1040 periodicals. Computerized library services include the card catalog, interlibrary loans, and database searching. Special learning facilities include a learning resource center, art gallery, rare books and archival collection, photographic lab, ceramics studio, and recital hall. The 25-acre campus is in a suburban area 2 miles south of downtown Charlotte. Including residence halls, there are 29 buildings.
Student Life: 68% of undergraduates are from North Carolina. Others are from 33 states, 22 foreign countries, and Canada. 80% are from public schools. 78% are white; 15% African American. 54% are Protestant; 31% claim no religious affiliation; 12% Catholic. The average age of freshmen is 18; all undergraduates, 20. 23% do not continue beyond their first year; 56% remain to graduate.
Housing: 600 students can be accommodated in college housing, which includes single-sex and coed dormitories. On-campus housing is guaranteed for all 4 years. 72% of students live on campus; of those, 60% remain on campus on weekends. All students may keep cars.
Activities: 20% of men belong to 1 national fraternity; 35% of women belong to 5 national sororities. There are 40 groups on campus, including art, cheerleading, choir, chorale, chorus, computers, dance, drama, ethnic, gay, honors, international, literary magazine, musical theater, newspaper, political, professional, religious, social, social service, student government, and yearbook. Popular campus events include Casino Party, Mardi Gras Festival, and International Symposium.
Sports: There are 5 intercollegiate sports for men and 7 for women, and 8 intramural sports for men and 8 for women. Facilities include an athletic center with a gym, classrooms, dance studios, weight room, training room, and swimming pool. There are also 6 tennis courts (4 lighted) and a soccer/softball complex. In addition, the college center offers various recreational opportunities, and one residence hall has an 8,000 square-foot state-of-the-art fitness center.
Disabled Students: 30% of the campus is accessible. Wheelchair ramps, special parking, specially equipped rest rooms, special class scheduling, and elevators in newer buildings are available.
Services: There is tutoring in English as well as remedial math, reading, and writing.
Campus Safety and Security: Measures include 24-hour foot and vehicle patrol, self-defense education, escort service, and informal discussions. There are pamphlets/posters/films, emergency telephones, and lighted pathways/sidewalks.
Programs of Study: Queens confers B.A., B.S., B.Mus., and B.S.N. degrees. Master's degrees are also awarded. Bachelor's degrees are awarded in BIOLOGICAL SCIENCE (biochemistry and biology/biological science), BUSINESS (accounting and business administration and management), COMMUNICATIONS AND THE ARTS (communications, dramatic arts, English, fine arts, French, music, and Spanish), COMPUTER AND PHYSICAL SCIENCE (mathematics), EDUCATION (elementary), HEALTH PROFESSIONS (music therapy and nursing), SOCIAL SCIENCE (American studies, history, international studies, philosophy, political science/government, psychology, and religion). Liberal arts and sciences are the strongest academically. Business and communications are the largest.
Required: To graduate, students must complete a total of 122 credit hours with a minimum GPA of 2.0. For the B.A., between 30 and 40 hours are required in the student's major. For the B.S., 32 are required. All students must take a sequence of 5 courses in the Core Program in the Liberal Arts. In addition, 2 courses in English composition, 2 in phys ed, and 1 in lab science are required. If entering freshmen do not pass the placement exams giving in math and a foreign language, additional courses will be required. Some majors require a thesis or research project.
Special: Internships in all majors, cross-registration with colleges of the Charlotte Area Educational Consortium, dual majors, nondegree study, and pass/fail options are available. The school offers a Washington semester. A study tour in Europe and Asia (included in the cost of tuition) may be arranged through the school's International Experience Program. There are 5 national honor societies, and a freshman honors program.
Faculty/Classroom: 43% of faculty are male; 57%, female. All teach undergraduates. No introductory courses are taught by graduate students. The average class size in an introductory lecture is 22; in a laboratory, 18; and in a regular course, 16.
Admissions: 79% of the 2001-2002 applicants were accepted. The SAT I scores for the 2001-2002 freshman class were: Verbal--34% below 500, 48% between 500 and 599, 16% between 600 and 700, and 2% above 700; Math--35% below 500, 51% between 500 and 599, and 14% between 600 and 700. The ACT scores were 30% below 21, 34% between 21 and 23, 23% between 24 and 26, 11% between 27 and 28, and 2% above 28. 41% of the current freshmen were in the top fifth of their class; 70% were in the top two fifths. 3 freshmen graduated first in their class.
Requirements: The SAT I or ACT is required. In addition, applicants should have a college preparatory background in an accredited secondary school. The GED is accepted. High school courses should include 4 years of English, 3 of math, 2 each of history or social studies and a foreign language, and 2 years of science, including 1 of lab science. An interview is recommended. An essay is required. An audition or portfolio is recommended for art and music students. Queens' application is available to download and print from the school's web sie and submit as a paper application. AP and CLEP credits are accepted. Important factors in the admissions decision are recommendations by school officials, advanced placement or honor courses, and leadership record.
Procedure: Freshmen are admitted fall and spring. Entrance exams should be taken in the junior year or as early as possible in the senior year. Application deadlines are open. Application fee is $35. Notification is sent on a rolling basis.
Transfer: 77 transfer students enrolled in 2001-2002. Transfer students are accepted in all but the senior class. A GPA of 2.0 is required for all previous college-level work. 45 credits of 122 must be completed at Queens.
Visiting: There are regularly scheduled orientations for prospective students, including a sampling of classes, campus tours, a college overview, a question/answer segment, a meet-the-faculty session, and a scholarship/financial aid session. There are guides for informal visits and visitors may sit in on classes and stay overnight. To schedule a visit, contact the Admissions Office.
Financial Aid: In 2001-2002, 82% of all freshmen and 73% of continuing students received some form of financial aid. 66% of freshmen and 57% of continuing students received need-based aid. The average freshman award was $9259. Of that total, scholarships or need-based grants averaged $5159; loans averaged $2600; and work contracts averaged $1500. Average annual earnings from campus work are $1500. The average financial indebtedness of the 2001 graduate was $14,069. Queens is a member of CSS. The FAFSA is required.
International Students: There are 35 international students enrolled. The school actively recruits these students. They must score 550 on the written TOEFL or 213 on the electronic version and also take the SAT I.
Computers: The mainframe is an IBM AS/400. PCs are available for student use in the computer centers, the library, and the residence halls. All students may access the system. There are no time limits and no fees.
Graduates: In 2001, 220 bachelor's degrees were awarded. The most popular majors were business (32%), nursing (18%), and communica-

tions (12%). In an average class, 49% graduate in 4 years, 55% in 5 years, and 56% in 6 years. 325 companies recruited on campus in 2000-2001.

Admissions Contact: Eileen Dills, Dean for Admissions and Financial Aid. E-mail: *cas@queens.edu* Web: *www.queens.edu*

SAINT ANDREWS PRESBYTERIAN COLLEGE D-3

Laurinburg, NC 28352 (910) 277-5555

(800) 763-0198; Fax: (910) 277-5087

Full-time: 265 men, 328 women | **Faculty:** 35; IIB, --$
Part-time: 7 men, 39 women | **Ph.D.s:** 80%
Graduate: none | **Student/Faculty:** 17 to 1
Year: semesters, summer session | **Tuition:** $14,310
Application Deadline: open | **Room & Board:** $5410
Freshman Class: 588 applied, 505 accepted, 229 enrolled
SAT I or ACT: required **LESS COMPETITIVE**

St. Andrews Presbyterian College is a private liberal arts institution affiliated with the Presbyterian Church (U.S.A.). The library contains 110,105 volumes, 14,204 microform items, and 1676 audiovisual forms/CDs, and subscribes to 416 periodicals. Computerized library services include the card catalog, interlibrary loans, and database searching. Special learning facilities include an art gallery, a 20,000-square-foot science lab, an artronics lab, and a writing lab. The 600-acre campus is in a small town about 100 miles from Charlotte. Including residence halls, there are 17 buildings.

Student Life: 56% of undergraduates are from out of state, mostly the South. Others are from 42 states, 15 foreign countries, and Canada. 80% are white; 10% African American. 53% are claim no religious affiliation; 28% Protestant; 15% Catholic. The average age of freshmen is 18; all undergraduates, 20. 36% do not continue beyond their first year; 34% remain to graduate.

Housing: 770 students can be accommodated in college housing, which includes single-sex and coed dormitories. On-campus housing is guaranteed for all 4 years. 82% of students live on campus; of those, 90% remain on campus on weekends. All students may keep cars.

Activities: There are no fraternities or sororities. There are 32 groups on campus, including art, bagpipe band, cheerleading, chess, chorale, computers, debate, drama, ethnic, film, gay, honors, international, literary magazine, musical theater, newspaper, political, professional, religious, social, social service, and student government. Popular campus events include Writers' Forum, Extravaganza Weekend, and Springfest.

Sports: There are 7 intercollegiate sports for men and 7 for women, and 6 intramural sports for men and 6 for women. Facilities include a basketball and volleyball arena, equestrian facilities, a pool, and soccer, baseball, and softball fields.

Disabled Students: 90% of the campus is accessible. Wheelchair ramps, elevators, special parking, specially equipped rest rooms, lowered drinking fountains, lowered telephones, and personal aides are available.

Services: Counseling and information services are available, as is tutoring in most subjects.

Campus Safety and Security: Measures include 24-hour foot and vehicle patrol, escort service, informal discussions, and pamphlets/posters/films. There are emergency telephones and lighted pathways/sidewalks.

Programs of Study: St. Andrews confers B.A, B.S., and B.F.A. degrees. Bachelor's degrees are awarded in BIOLOGICAL SCIENCE (biology/biological science), BUSINESS (business administration and management and international business management), COMMUNICATIONS AND THE ARTS (communications, creative writing, English, and visual and performing arts), COMPUTER AND PHYSICAL SCIENCE (chemistry and mathematics), EDUCATION (elementary and physical), SOCIAL SCIENCE (Asian/Oriental studies, history, liberal arts/general studies, philosophy, political science/government, psychology, and religion). Business and economics, equine studies, and biology are the strongest academically. Business and economics, elementary education, and phys ed are the largest.

Required: To graduate, students must complete a total of 120 hours with a minimum GPA of 2.0. Between 10 and 15 courses are required in the student's major. All students must complete 15 hours in the interdisciplinary St. Andrews General Education (SAGE) program. In addition, students must satisfy breadth requirements in the arts, humanities, lab sciences, social and behavioral sciences, and phys ed.

Special: St. Andrew's offers student-designed majors for contract and thematic majors, nondegree study, on-campus work-study, and pass/fail options. Students may study abroad in 11 countries. A 3-2 engineering degree with North Carolina State University and 3-2 and 4-2 accounting programs with the University of Georgia are available. There are year-long, semester-long, and summer- and winter-term internships in all majors. There are 3 national honor societies, a freshman honors program, and 8 departmental honors programs.

Faculty/Classroom: 60% of faculty are male; 40%, female. All teach undergraduates and 50% do research. The average class size in an introductory lecture is 15; in a laboratory, 15; and in a regular course, 15.

Admissions: 86% of the 2001-2002 applicants were accepted. The SAT I scores for the 2001-2002 freshman class were: Verbal--50% below 500, 35% between 500 and 599, 11% between 600 and 700, and 4% above 700; Math--56% below 500, 32% between 500 and 599, and 12% between 600 and 700.

Requirements: The SAT I or ACT is required with a minimum score of 950 on the SAT I or 20 on the ACT. Graduation from an accredited secondary school or the GED is required for admission. High school courses should include 4 units of English, 3 each of science and math, and 2 each of a foreign language, social studies, and electives. An essay is required. A GPA of 2.5 is required. AP and CLEP credits are accepted. Important factors in the admissions decision are personality/intangible qualities, recommendations by school officials, and evidence of special talent. Applications are accepted on-line at the school's web site.

Procedure: Freshmen are admitted to all sessions. Entrance exams should be taken as early as possible. There is a deferred admissions plan. Application deadlines are open. Notification is sent on a rolling basis.

Transfer: 51 transfer students enrolled in 2001-2002. Transfer students must have a minimum GPA of 2.0. Up to 65 semester or 97 quarter hours may be transferred from a 2-year college and 90 semester or 135 quarter hours from a 4-year college. 30 credits of 120 must be completed at St. Andrews.

Visiting: There are regularly scheduled orientations for prospective students, including activities, fairs, information sessions, summer orientation sessions with activities, and preregistration. There are guides for informal visits and visitors may sit in on classes and stay overnight. To schedule a visit, contact the Admissions Office.

Financial Aid: In 2001-2002, 90% of all freshmen and 95% of continuing students received some form of financial aid. 80% of freshmen and 72% of continuing students received need-based aid. The average freshman award was $6600. Of that total, scholarships or need-based grants averaged $9500; loans averaged $2625 (maximum); and work contracts averaged $1400 ($2000 maximum). 41% of undergraduates work part time. Average annual earnings from campus work are $1100. The average financial indebtedness of the 2001 graduate was $20,000. The FAFSA is required. The fall application deadline is May 1.

International Students: The school actively recruits these students. They must score 550 on the written TOEFL.

Computers: There is an IBM PC local network, with computer labs. All students may access the system every day, 24 hours a day. There are no time limits and no fees.

Graduates: In an average class, 1% graduate in 3 years, 31% in 4 years, and 33% in 5 years. Of the 2000 graduating class, 24% were enrolled in graduate school within 6 months of graduation and 70% were employed.

Admissions Contact: Glenn Batten, Vice President for Enrollment and Student Services. A video is available. E-mail: *admissions@sapc.edu* Web: *www.sapc.edu*

SAINT AUGUSTINE'S COLLEGE D-2

Raleigh, NC 27610-2298 (919) 516-4000

(800) 948-1126; Fax: (919) 516-5805

Full-time: 513 men, 722 women | **Faculty:** 87
Part-time: 46 men, 79 women | **Ph.D.s:** 59%
Graduate: none | **Student/Faculty:** 16 to 1
Year: semesters, summer session | **Tuition:** $8030
Application Deadline: see profile | **Room & Board:** $4960
Freshman Class: 2181 applied, 893 accepted, 324 enrolled
SAT I or ACT: required **COMPETITIVE+**

Saint Augustine's College, founded in 1867, is a historically black liberal arts institution affiliated with the Episcopal Church. The library contains 70,200 volumes and 500 microform items, and subscribes to 300 periodicals. Computerized library services include database searching. Special learning facilities include a learning resource center, radio station, and TV station. The 110-acre campus is in an urban area 1 mile northeast of downtown Raleigh. Including residence halls, there are 37 buildings.

Student Life: 51% of undergraduates are from North Carolina. Others are from 34 states, 16 foreign countries, and Canada. 99% are from public schools. 90% are African American. 58% are Protestant; 39% claim no religious affiliation. The average age of freshmen is 18; all undergraduates, 22. 38% do not continue beyond their first year; 27% remain to graduate.

Housing: 1143 students can be accommodated in college housing, which includes single-sex dormitories. In addition, there are honors houses. On-campus housing is guaranteed for all 4 years. 62% of students live on campus; of those, 75% remain on campus on weekends. Alcohol is not permitted. All students may keep cars.

Activities: 6% of men belong to 5 national fraternities; 12% of women belong to 4 national sororities. There are 20 groups on campus, including band, cheerleading, chorale, dance, drama, ethnic, honors, international, newspaper, photography, professional, radio and TV, religious, social service, student government, and yearbook. Popular campus events include opening convocation each semester, CIAA tournament, and career/job fairs.

Sports: There are 5 intercollegiate sports for men and 4 for women, and 4 intramural sports for men and 3 for women. Facilities include a 1700-seat gym, a track, baseball fields, and tennis and basketball courts.

Disabled Students: 64% of the campus is accessible. Wheelchair ramps, elevators, special parking, and specially equipped rest rooms are available.

Services: There is remedial math, reading, and writing. Help with writing and test-taking skills is available.

Campus Safety and Security: Measures include 24-hour foot and vehicle patrol, informal discussions, pamphlets/posters/films, and emergency telephones. There are lighted pathways/sidewalks.

Programs of Study: Saint Augustine's College confers B.A. and B.S. degrees. Bachelor's degrees are awarded in BIOLOGICAL SCIENCE (biology/biological science), BUSINESS (accounting, business administration and management, and international business management), COMMUNICATIONS AND THE ARTS (communications, English, fine arts, French, music, music business management, Spanish, and visual and performing arts), COMPUTER AND PHYSICAL SCIENCE (applied mathematics, chemistry, computer science, information sciences and systems, and mathematics), EDUCATION (business, education of the exceptional child, elementary, English, mathematics, music, physical, science, and social studies), ENGINEERING AND ENVIRONMENTAL DESIGN (industrial administration/management and industrial engineering), HEALTH PROFESSIONS (industrial hygiene, medical laboratory technology, and premedicine), SOCIAL SCIENCE (African American studies, criminal justice, history, physical fitness/movement, political science/government, prelaw, psychology, sociology, and urban studies). Engineering, math, and premedicine are the strongest academically. Computer science, business administration, and communications are the largest.

Required: Students must complete at least 120 hours with a minimum 2.0 GPA for graduation. All students must complete a 50 to 55 credit core curriculum that includes courses in reading and communication, foreign language, science, math, philosophy, ethics, humanities, world civilization, psychology, and phys ed. Seniors must pass written and oral examinations in their major fields. Total credit hours required for a degree in offered majors range from 124 to 154.

Special: Students may cross-register at any of 5 area colleges, study abroad, or pursue a 3-2 engineering program with North Carolina State University. There is an accelerated degree program in organizational management for adult learners. Field experience programs, nondegree study, internships, work-study, cooperative programs, and credit for military service are offered. There is 1 national honor society and a freshman honors program.

Faculty/Classroom: 60% of faculty are male; 40%, female. All teach undergraduates. The average class size in an introductory lecture is 22; in a laboratory, 13; and in a regular course, 14.

Admissions: 41% of the 2001-2002 applicants were accepted. 8% of the current freshmen were in the top fifth of their class; 32% were in the top two fifths.

Requirements: The SAT I or ACT is required. In addition, applicants must be graduates of an accredited secondary school with a C+ average in at least 18 academic units, including 4 in English, 3 in math, and 2 each in social studies and science. A GPA of 2.0 is required. AP credits are accepted. Important factors in the admissions decision are geographic diversity, evidence of special talent, and leadership record.

Procedure: Freshmen are admitted to all sessions. There is a deferred admissions plan. Check with school for current application deadlines. The fall 2001 application fee was $25. Notification is sent on a rolling basis.

Transfer: 43 transfer students enrolled in a recent year. Transfers must submit high school and college transcripts and must be eligible to reenter the last institution attended. 30 credits of 124 must be completed at Saint Augustine's College.

Visiting: There are guides for informal visits and visitors may sit in on classes. To schedule a visit, contact the Admissions Office at (919) 516-4016.

Financial Aid: In 2001-2002, 95% of all freshmen and 90% of continuing students received some form of financial aid. 69% of undergraduates work part time. Average annual earnings from campus work are $1572. The average financial indebtedness of a recent year's graduate was $12,850. Saint Augustine's College is a member of CSS. The FAFSA is required. Check with school for current deadlines.

International Students: There were 133 international students enrolled in a recent year. The school actively recruits these students. They must score 500 on the written TOEFL and also take the SAT I or the ACT.

Computers: The mainframe is an IBM RS/6000 Model 590. Students have access to approximately 12 Macs and 150 IBM PCs campuswide that have Microsoft software and are connected to the Internet. All students may access the system. The system may be used during the operating hours of the library, the science building, and the business building. There are no time limits and no fees.

Graduates: In a recent year, 242 bachelor's degrees were awarded. The most popular majors were business (28%), psychology (12%), and criminal justice (8%). In an average class, 1% graduate in 3 years, 12% in 4 years, 25% in 5 years, and 27% in 6 years.

Admissions Contact: Tim Chapman, Interim Director of Admissions. E-mail: *admissions@es.st.aug.edu* Web: *www.st-aug.edu*

SALEM COLLEGE

Winston-Salem, NC 27101 — C-2

(336) 721-2621
(800) 327-2536; Fax: (336) 917-5572

Full-time: 11 men, 651 women	**Faculty:** 52; IIB, --$
Part-time: 19 men, 245 women	**Ph.D.s:** 87%
Graduate: 18 men, 130 women	**Student/Faculty:** 13 to 1
Year: 4-1-4, summer session	**Tuition:** $14,495
Application Deadline: open	**Room & Board:** $8570
Freshman Class: 480 applied, 363 accepted, 181 enrolled	
SAT I Verbal/Math: 584/536	**ACT:** 25 **VERY COMPETITIVE**

Salem College, founded in 1890, traces its roots back to 1772, when it was begun as a school for girls by the Moravians, an early Protestant denomination. Today the private college, which retains a historical relationship with the church, offers a liberal arts education primarily for women. In addition to regional accreditation, Salem has baccalaureate program accreditation with NASM and NCATE. The 2 libraries contain 119,000 volumes, 210,632 microform items, and 8800 audiovisual forms/CDs, and subscribe to 560 periodicals. Computerized library services include the card catalog, interlibrary loans, and database searching. Special learning facilities include a learning resource center, art gallery, radio station, and a learning lab (computer lab with multimedia capability). The 57-acre campus is in an urban area in the center of Old Salem, a restored 18th-century village. Including residence halls, there are 17 buildings.

Student Life: 52% of undergraduates are from North Carolina. Others are from 24 states and 16 foreign countries. 80% are from public schools. 73% are white; 18% African American. The average age of freshmen is 18; all undergraduates, 27. 20% do not continue beyond their first year; 57% remain to graduate.

Housing: 505 students can be accommodated in college housing, which includes single-sex dormitories and off-campus apartments. On-campus housing is guaranteed for all 4 years. 89% of students live on campus; of those, 55% remain on campus on weekends. All students may keep cars.

Activities: There are no fraternities or sororities. There are 41 groups on campus, including chorale, chorus, dance, drama, ethnic, gay, honors, international, literary magazine, marching band, musical theater, newspaper, political, professional, radio and TV, religious, social, social service, student government, and yearbook. Students may also participate in band, marching band, and orchestra at Wake Forest University. Popular campus events include Fall Fest, April Arts, and dance weekends.

Sports: There are 7 intercollegiate sports for women and 7 intramural sports for women. Facilities include 2 athletic fields, an archery range, a swimming pool, 2 basketball/volleyball and tennis courts, 2 dance studios, and a universal weight room.

Disabled Students: 75% of the campus is accessible. Special parking, specially equipped rest rooms, special class scheduling, and lowered drinking fountains are available. Many buildings are historic, so disability access is limited to individual areas that have had recent renovations or were already accessible are available.

Services: Counseling and information services are available, as is tutoring in every subject and a writing center.

Campus Safety and Security: Measures include 24-hour foot and vehicle patrol, escort service, informal discussions, and pamphlets/posters/films. There are emergency telephones and lighted pathways/sidewalks.

Programs of Study: Salem confers B.A., B.S., B.M., and B.S.B.A. degrees. Master's degrees are also awarded. Bachelor's degrees are awarded in BIOLOGICAL SCIENCE (biology/biological science), BUSINESS (accounting, business administration and management, and international business management), COMMUNICATIONS AND THE ARTS (art history and appreciation, arts administration/management, communications, English, French, German, languages, music, Spanish, and studio art), COMPUTER AND PHYSICAL SCIENCE (chemistry and mathematics), ENGINEERING AND ENVIRONMENTAL DESIGN (interior design), HEALTH PROFESSIONS (medical laboratory technology and physician's assistant), SOCIAL SCIENCE (American studies, economics, history, international relations, philosophy, psychology, religion, and sociology). Sociology, business, and communication are the largest.

Required: To graduate, students must complete a total of 36 courses, or 144 semester hours, with a minimum GPA of 2.0. A minimum of 7 courses, or 28 semester hours, is required in the student's major. All students must complete 4 January-term courses, 3 in a modern foreign language, 2 each in English, social science, history, and phys ed, and 1 each in lab science, math, fine arts, and philosophy/religion.

Special: Salem offers an extensive internship program in all majors, cross-registration with Wake Forest University, and study abroad at various locations, including a summer program in Oxford, England. A Washington semester, student-designed and interdisciplinary majors, B.A.-B.S. degrees, nondegree study, and pass/fail options during the January term are available. A 3-2 engineering degree is available with Duke and Vanderbilt Universities. Students may participate in a model U.N. program directed by Drew University in Madison, New Jersey. Interdisciplinary majors are offered in American studies, arts management, international relations, and international business. There are 9 national honor societies and a freshman honors program.

Faculty/Classroom: 42% of faculty are male; 58%, female. All both teach and do research. No introductory courses are taught by graduate students. The average class size in an introductory lecture is 18; in a laboratory, 15; and in a regular course, 15.

Admissions: 76% of the 2001-2002 applicants were accepted. The SAT I scores for the 2001-2002 freshman class were: Verbal--13% below 500, 41% between 500 and 599, 40% between 600 and 700, and 6% above 700; Math--29% below 500, 50% between 500 and 599, 20% between 600 and 700, and 1% above 700. The ACT scores were 19% below 21, 13% between 21 and 23, 29% between 24 and 26, 23% between 27 and 28, and 16% above 28. 44% of the current freshmen were in the top fifth of their class; 70% were in the top two fifths. 3 freshmen graduated first in their class.

Requirements: The SAT I or ACT is required. In addition, graduation from an accredited secondary school or the GED is needed. Students must have 12 academic credits plus electives, including 4 years of high school English, 3 each of math and science, and 2 each of a foreign language and history. An essay is required for all students. Music students must audition. A GPA of 2.5 is required. AP and CLEP credits are accepted. Important factors in the admissions decision are advanced placement or honor courses, leadership record, and evidence of special talent. The college accepts applications on computer disk through CollegeLink and on-line at the school's web site.

Procedure: Freshmen are admitted fall and spring. Entrance exams should be taken by January of the senior year. There are early admissions and deferred admissions plans. Application deadlines are open. The fall 2001 application fee was $25. Notification is sent on a rolling basis.

Transfer: 13 transfer students enrolled in 2001-2002. Applicants must have a minimum GPA of 2.0 in all previous college work and must submit a statement of good standing from the Dean of Students of the college previously attended, 2 letters of recommendation from teachers, a high school transcript, and a transcript and catalog from each college attended. SAT I or ACT scores may be required on an individual basis. An interview is recommended. 36 credits of 144 must be completed at Salem.

Visiting: There are regularly scheduled orientations for prospective students. There are guides for informal visits and visitors may sit in on classes and stay overnight. To schedule a visit, contact the Admissions Office.

Financial Aid: In 2001-2002, 73% of all freshmen and 64% of continuing students received some form of financial aid. 71% of freshmen and 62% of continuing students received need-based aid. The average freshman award was $12,491. Of that total, scholarships or need-based grants averaged $9401 ($14,280 maximum); loans averaged $2625; and work contracts averaged $1600 ($3000 maximum). 66% of undergraduates work part time. Average annual earnings from campus work are $1600. The average financial indebtedness of the 2001 graduate was $14,881. The FAFSA and the college's own financial statement are required. The fall application deadline is March 15.

International Students: There are 27 international students enrolled. The school actively recruits these students. They must score 550 on the written TOEFL.

Computers: The mainframe is a Hewlett-Packard 9000. There are also computers available in the science building, library, and main hall. Salem maintains Mac and Windows labs. All students may access the system when school is in session 24 hours a day. There are no time limits and no fees.

Graduates: In 2001, 163 bachelor's degrees were awarded. The most popular majors were English (14%), communication (11%), and business (10%). In an average class, 1% graduate in 3 years, 63% in 4 years, 64% in 5 years, and 64% in 6 years. Of the 2000 graduating class, 18% were enrolled in graduate school within 6 months of graduation and 77% were employed.

Admissions Contact: Dama E. Evans, Dean of Admissions and Financial Aid. E-mail: *admissions@salem.edu* Web: *www.salem.edu*

SHAW UNIVERSITY — D-2

Raleigh, NC 27601 (919) 546-8275

(800) 214-6683; Fax: (919) 546-8271

Full-time: 671 men, 1284 women	**Faculty:** 90; IIB, --$
Part-time: 117 men, 30 women	**Ph.D.s:** 70%
Graduate: 74 men, 77 women	**Student/Faculty:** 22 to 1
Year: semesters, summer session	**Tuition:** $7930
Application Deadline: July 30	**Room & Board:** $4880
Freshman Class: 2908 applied, 1855 accepted, 475 enrolled	
SAT I or ACT: required	**COMPETITIVE**

Shaw University, founded in 1865, is a private liberal arts university affiliated with the Baptist Church. In addition to regional accreditation, Shaw has baccalaureate program accreditation with NCATE and CAAHEP. The library contains 152,132 volumes, 138,950 microform items, and 875 audiovisual forms/CDs, and subscribes to 9636 periodicals. Computerized library services include the card catalog, interlibrary loans, and database searching. Special learning facilities include a learning resource center, radio station, Praxis lab, Academic Assessment and Achievement Center (AAA), and kinesiotherapy clinic. The 30-acre campus is in an urban area in downtown Raleigh. Including residence halls, there are 23 buildings.

Student Life: 77% of undergraduates are from North Carolina. Others are from 34 states and 10 foreign countries. 93% are African American. The average age of freshmen is 23; all undergraduates, 29.

Housing: 1300 students can be accommodated in college housing, which includes single-sex dormitories. On-campus housing is available on a first-come, first-served basis. 59% of students commute. Alcohol is not permitted. Upperclassmen may keep cars.

Activities: 4% of men belong to 4 national fraternities; 5% of women belong to 4 national sororities. There are 30 groups on campus, including band, business, cheerleading, choir, chorus, criminal justice, dance, drama, ethnic, honors, international, jazz band, musical theater, newspaper, pep band, professional, radio and TV, religious, social, social service, student government, and yearbook. Popular campus events include Career Day, Awards Day, and Religious Emphasis Week.

Sports: There are 6 intercollegiate sports for men and 8 for women, and 5 intramural sports for men and 4 for women.

Disabled Students: Wheelchair ramps, elevators, special parking, specially equipped rest rooms, lowered drinking fountains, and labels in braille are available.

Services: Counseling and information services are available, as is tutoring in some subjects, including English, math, biology, chemistry, physical science, statistics, and social science. There is remedial math, reading, and writing. There is peer tutoring in accounting.

Campus Safety and Security: Measures include 24-hour foot and vehicle patrol, self-defense education, escort service, and informal discussions. There are pamphlets/posters/films, lighted pathways/sidewalks, and and 24-hour electronic surveillance.

Programs of Study: Shaw confers B.A. and B.S. degrees. Associate and master's degrees are also awarded. Bachelor's degrees are awarded in BIOLOGICAL SCIENCE (biology/biological science), BUSINESS (accounting, business administration and management, and recreation and leisure services), COMMUNICATIONS AND THE ARTS (broadcasting, English, and visual and performing arts), COMPUTER AND PHYSICAL SCIENCE (chemistry, computer science, mathematics, and physics), EDUCATION (athletic training, elementary, English, mathematics, physical, science, secondary, social studies, and special), ENGINEERING AND ENVIRONMENTAL DESIGN (environmental science and preengineering), HEALTH PROFESSIONS (recreation therapy, rehabilitation therapy, and speech pathology/audiology), SOCIAL SCIENCE (African studies, criminal justice, gerontology, international relations, international studies, liberal arts/general studies, political science/government, psychology, public administration, religion, social work, and sociology). Business administration/management, criminal justice, and sociology/psychology are the largest.

Required: To graduate (in most majors), students must earn 120 credits, maintain a minimum GPA of 2.0, and successfully complete competency exams in math and English. The general core curriculum includes a total of 54 credits in college orientation, English, math, ethics, humanities, natural sciences, and social sciences.

Special: Shaw offers cross-registration with 4 other North Carolina colleges, internships, a work-study program, a 3-2 engineering degree with North Carolina State University and North Carolina Agricultural and Technical State University, dual and student-designed majors, independent study, and an external degree program for working adults. There are 4 national honor societies and a freshman honors program.

Faculty/Classroom: 65% of faculty are male; 35%, female. 95% teach undergraduates. The average class size in a laboratory is 8 and in a regular course, 13.

Admissions: 64% of the 2001-2002 applicants were accepted.

Requirements: The SAT I or ACT is required. In addition, applicants must be graduates of an accredited secondary school or have a GED certificate. They should have completed 3 units of English, 2 each of math, natural science (with 1 in a lab course), and social science, and 4 of academic electives. Admission to the Teacher Education Program follows separate guidelines. A GPA of 2.0 is required. AP and CLEP credits are accepted. Important factors in the admissions decision are advanced placement or honor courses, personality/intangible qualities, and recommendations by school officials. Applications are accepted on-line or on disk through Apply software.

Procedure: Freshmen are admitted to all sessions. Entrance exams should be taken prior to enrollment. There is a deferred admissions plan. Applications should be filed by July 30 for fall entry and November 30 for spring entry. The fall 2001 application fee was $25. Notification is sent on a rolling basis.

Transfer: 275 transfer students enrolled in 2001-2002. Applicants must submit official transcripts from all colleges attended. Transfer credit is given only for course work of grade C or better completed at an accredited degree-granting institution. 30 credits of 120 must be completed at Shaw.

Visiting: There are regularly scheduled orientations for prospective students, consisting of parent visitation, tours, general administration, and registration. There are guides for informal visits and visitors may sit in on classes. To schedule a visit, contact the Admissions Office.

Financial Aid: 2% of undergraduates work part time. Average annual earnings from campus work are $12,000. The average financial indebtedness of the 2001 graduate was $8781. The FAFSA is required. The fall application deadline is open.

International Students: There are 75 international students enrolled. The school actively recruits these students. The SAT I or the ACT is required.

Computers: The mainframes are an IBM AS/400 and Sun SPARC Station. PCs for student use are located in the library and the science and technology lab. 25 are connected to the Internet. All students may access the system. There are no time limits. The fee is $115 per semester. It is strongly recommended that all students have a personal computer.

Graduates: In 2001, 439 bachelor's degrees were awarded. The most popular majors were business (26%), criminal justice (20%), and sociology (14%). In an average class, 24% graduate in 4 years, 32% in 5 years, and 32% in 6 years.

Admissions Contact: Paul Vandergrift, Director of Admissions and Recruitment. E-mail: *paulv@shawu.edu* Web: *www.shawuniversity.edu*

UNIVERSITY OF NORTH CAROLINA SYSTEM

The University of North Carolina System, established in 1931, is a public system. It is governed by UNC Board of Governors whose chief administrator is the president. The primary goal of the system is to discover, create, transmit, and apply knowledge to address the needs of North Carolina and its people. The main priorities are teaching/instruction, research/scholarship/creative activities, and public service (solving societal problems and enriching quality of life). The total enrollment of all 16 campuses is about 170,000, with approximately 8500 faculty members. There are 983 baccalaureate, 676 master's, and 169 doctoral programs offered through the University of North Carolina System. Profiles of the 4-year campuses are included in this section.

UNIVERSITY OF NORTH CAROLINA AT ASHEVILLE B-2

Asheville, NC 28804-8510 **(828) 251-6481**
(800) 531-9842; Fax: (828) 251-6482

Full-time: 1054 men, 1431 women	**Faculty:** 172; IIB, av$
Part-time: 291 men, 435 women	**Ph.D.s:** 85%
Graduate: 16 men, 20 women	**Student/Faculty:** 14 to 1
Year: semesters, summer session	**Tuition:** $2496 ($9958)
Application Deadline: March 15	**Room & Board:** $4400
Freshman Class: 2020 applied, 1189 accepted, 455 enrolled	
SAT I Verbal/Math: 570/570	**ACT:** 24 **VERY COMPETITIVE**

The University of North Carolina at Asheville, founded in 1927, is a publicly assisted liberal arts institution in the University of North Carolina system. In addition to regional accreditation, UNCA has baccalaureate program accreditation with NCATE. The library contains 378,031 volumes, 813,220 microform items, and 9303 audiovisual forms/CDs, and subscribes to 2034 periodicals. Computerized library services include the card catalog, interlibrary loans, and database searching. Special learning facilities include a learning resource center, art gallery, distance learning facility, center for creative retirement, undergraduate research center, botanical gardens, music recording center, and the Environmental Quality Institute. The 265-acre campus is in a suburban area 130 miles west of Charlotte. Including residence halls, there are 25 buildings.

Student Life: 89% of undergraduates are from North Carolina. Others are from 37 states, 20 foreign countries, and Canada. 85% are from public schools. 91% are white. The average age of freshmen is 18; all undergraduates, 24. 20% do not continue beyond their first year; 53% remain to graduate.

Housing: 1017 students can be accommodated in college housing, which includes single-sex and coed dormitories and off-campus apartments. In addition, there are honors houses and substance-free housing. On-campus housing is guaranteed for all 4 years. 65% of students commute. All students may keep cars.

Activities: 6% of men belong to 4 national fraternities; 3% of women belong to 2 national sororities. There are 80 groups on campus, including art, band, cheerleading, choir, chorus, computers, dance, departmental, drama, ethnic, gay, honors, international, jazz band, literary magazine, pep band, political, professional, religious, social, social service, student government, and yearbook. Popular campus events include International Holiday Fest, Spring Fling, and Fall Fling.

Sports: There are 7 intercollegiate sports for men and 7 for women, and 13 intramural sports for men and 11 for women. Facilities include a sports and health center with a state-of-the-art weight room, 4 basketball courts, volleyball and racquetball courts, a dance studio, an Olympic-size swimming pool, indoor and outdoor tracks, steeplechase and pole vault pits and straight-away chute, outdoor tennis courts, and soccer and baseball fields.

Disabled Students: 94% of the campus is accessible. Wheelchair ramps, elevators, special parking, specially equipped rest rooms, special class scheduling, lowered drinking fountains, and lowered telephones are available.

Services: Counseling and information services are available, as is tutoring in most subjects. There is a reader service for the blind, and remedial math, reading, and writing.

Campus Safety and Security: Measures include 24-hour foot and vehicle patrol, self-defense education, escort service, and informal discussions. There are pamphlets/posters/films and lighted pathways/sidewalks.

Programs of Study: UNCA confers B.A., B.S., and B.F.A. degrees. Master's degrees are also awarded. Bachelor's degrees are awarded in BIOLOGICAL SCIENCE (biology/biological science), BUSINESS (accounting and business administration and management), COMMUNICATIONS AND THE ARTS (art, classics, communications, dramatic arts, French, German, literature, multimedia, music, music technology, and Spanish), COMPUTER AND PHYSICAL SCIENCE (atmospheric sciences and meteorology, chemistry, computer science, mathematics, and physics), ENGINEERING AND ENVIRONMENTAL DESIGN (environmental science and industrial administration/management), SOCIAL SCIENCE (economics, history, philosophy, political science/government, psychology, and sociology). Management, psychology, and environmental science are the largest.

Required: To graduate, students must complete a minimum of 120 credit hours, including 27 to 40 in the major, with a senior capstone experience consisting of undergraduate research, an exam, or a seminar. The core curriculum requires 16 semester hours of humanities, 8 of natural science including lab, 6 of social science, up to 6 of foreign language, 4 each of math and arts, 3 to 7 of English, 2 to 4 of health and fitness, and 1 of library research.

Special: Students may participate in cooperative programs in nursing, forestry, and textile chemistry. UNCA participates in a consortium with Warren Wilson and Mars Hill Colleges, and there is cross-registration with a number of North Carolina universities and colleges. Study-abroad programs are available in more than 7 countries. The school offers internships, dual majors, student-designed interdisciplinary majors, a 2-2 engineering degree with North Carolina State University, and a Washington semester. Nondegree study is available. There are 12 national honor societies, a freshman honors program, and 10 departmental honors programs.

Faculty/Classroom: 60% of faculty are male; 40%, female. All teach undergraduates. No introductory courses are taught by graduate students. The average class size in an introductory lecture is 22; in a laboratory, 17; and in a regular course, 18.

Admissions: 59% of the 2001-2002 applicants were accepted. The SAT I scores for the 2001-2002 freshman class were: Verbal--11% below 500, 48% between 500 and 599, 33% between 600 and 700, and 8% above 700; Math--12% below 500, 49% between 500 and 599, 34% between 600 and 700, and 5% above 700. The ACT scores were 15% below 21, 34% between 21 and 23, 24% between 24 and 26, 12% between 27 and 28, and 15% above 28. 54% of the current freshmen were in the top fifth of their class; 95% were in the top two fifths. There was 1 National Merit finalist. 7 freshmen graduated first in their class.

Requirements: The SAT I or ACT is required. In addition, graduation from an accredited secondary school or the GED is required. UNCA requires a minimum of 16 high school academic units, including 4 of English, 3 each of math (algebra I, geometry, algebra II) and science (biology, physical science, and a lab course), and 2 of social studies/history, with 2 of a foreign language strongly recommended. Applicants are evaluated primarily on their academic achievement record, extracurricular activities that support academic achievement, and SAT I or ACT scores. AP and CLEP credits are accepted. Important factors in the admissions decision are advanced placement or honor courses, leadership record, and evidence of special talent. Applications are accepted on-line at the school's web site or at Embark.com.

Procedure: Freshmen are admitted to all sessions. Entrance exams should be taken at the end of the junior year or the beginning of the senior year. There are early decision and deferred admissions plans. Early decision applications should be filed by October 15; regular applications, by March 15 for fall entry and December 1 for spring entry. The fall 2001 application fee was $50. Notification is sent monthly.

Transfer: 333 transfer students enrolled in 2001-2002. A 2.5 GPA on transfer credit is required; applicants with fewer than 24 semester or 36 quarter credit hours must submit high school transcripts and SAT I or ACT scores. 30 credits of 120 must be completed at UNCA.

Visiting: There are regularly scheduled orientations for prospective students, including meetings with faculty and with student organizations, an information session for students and families, and a campus tour. Preregistration is prior to fall enrollment during the summer months. There are guides for informal visits and visitors may sit in on classes. To schedule a visit, contact Office of Admissions.

Financial Aid: In 2001-2002, 68% of all freshmen and 53% of continuing students received some form of financial aid. 33% of freshmen and 30% of continuing students received need-based aid. The average freshman award was $4706. Of that total, scholarships or need-based grants averaged $2568 ($9864 maximum); loans averaged $3944 ($17,702 maximum); work contracts averaged $1200 ($2279 maximum); and non-need-based grants from outside agencies averaged $2631 ($13,627 maximum). 22% of undergraduates work part time. Average annual earnings from campus work are $1315. The average financial indebtedness of the 2001 graduate was $14,305. The FAFSA is required. The fall application deadline is March 1.

International Students: There are 41 international students enrolled. The school actively recruits these students. They must score 550 on the written TOEFL or 213 on the electronic version and also take the SAT I or the ACT.

Computers: The mainframes are a Compaq VAX 4000, a Compaq Alpha Server 2100, and a Compaq Alpha Server 4100. Students can access the central computing resources and the Internet from one of more than 300 PCs and Macs in campus labs, department labs, residence hall labs, and the library. Additionally, all dorms have a network port for every resident with a PC. There are modems available for access to e-mail and Internet services. All students may access the system 24 hours a day. There are no time limits and no fees.

Graduates: In 2001, 498 bachelor's degrees were awarded. The most popular majors were psychology (16%), management (12%), and environmental science (8%). In an average class, 30% graduate in 4 years, 46% in 5 years, and 53% in 6 years. 170 companies recruited on campus in 2000-2001. Of the 2000 graduating class, 18% were enrolled in graduate school within 6 months of graduation and 92% were employed.

Admissions Contact: Fran Barrett, Director of Admissions. A video is available. E-mail: *admissions@unca.edu* Web: *www.unca.edu*

UNIVERSITY OF NORTH CAROLINA AT CHAPEL HILL D-2

Chapel Hill, NC 27599-2200 **(919) 966-3623**
Fax: (919) 962-3045

Full-time: 5969 men, 9091 women	**Faculty:** 2328; I, +$
Part-time: 325 men, 459 women	**Ph.D.s:** 94%
Graduate: 4052 men, 5598 women	**Student/Faculty:** 6 to 1
Year: semesters, summer session	**Tuition:** $3219 ($13,211)
Application Deadline: see profile	**Room & Board:** $5570
Freshman Class: 15,947 applied, 6339 accepted, 3687 enrolled	
SAT I Verbal/Math: 620/640	**ACT:** 26 **HIGHLY COMPETITIVE**

The University of North Carolina at Chapel Hill, chartered in 1789 and the nation's first public university, offers academic programs leading to 95 bachelor's, 169 master's, and 109 doctoral degrees, as well as professional degrees. There are 9 undergraduate and 12 graduate schools. The 15 libraries contain 4,263,684 volumes, 3,897,013 microform items, and 662,203 audiovisual forms/CDs, and subscribe to 39,044 periodicals. Computerized library services include the card catalog, interlibrary loans, and database searching. Special learning facilities include an art gallery, planetarium, radio station, TV station, and botanical garden. The 720-acre campus is in a suburban area 25 miles west of Raleigh.

Student Life: 82% of undergraduates are from North Carolina. Others are from 49 states, 90 foreign countries, and Canada. 86% are from public schools. 82% are white. The average age of freshmen is 18; all undergraduates, 21. 7% do not continue beyond their first year; 85% remain to graduate.

Housing: 7070 students can be accommodated in college housing, which includes single-sex and coed dormitories and married-student housing. In addition, there are language houses and special-interest houses. On-campus housing is guaranteed for all 4 years. 82% of students commute. Upperclassmen may keep cars.

Activities: 17% of men belong to 30 national fraternities; 17% of women belong to 1 local sorority and 15 national sororities. There are 350 groups on campus, including art, band, cheerleading, chess, choir, chorus, dance, drama, drill team, ethnic, gay, honors, international, jazz band, literary magazine, marching band, musical theater, newspaper, orchestra, pep band, photography, political, professional, radio and TV, religious, social, social service, student government, symphony, and yearbook. Popular campus events include Black Greek Council Stepshow, Apple Chill Festifall, and Jazzfest.

Sports: There are 13 intercollegiate sports for men and 13 for women. Facilities include a 50,000-seat football stadium, 3 swimming pools, a 21,000-seat sports and student activities center, tennis courts, gym facilities, softball fields, and a student recreation center with aerobics, weights, and wellness programs.

Disabled Students: 80% of the campus is accessible. Wheelchair ramps, elevators, special parking, specially equipped rest rooms, special class scheduling, lowered drinking fountains, lowered telephones, and some residence halls are available.

Services: Counseling and information services are available, as is tutoring in every subject. There is a reader service for the blind.

Campus Safety and Security: Measures include 24-hour foot and vehicle patrol, self-defense education, escort service, and shuttle buses. There are informal discussions, pamphlets/posters/films, emergency telephones, lighted pathways/sidewalks, and building security surveys.

Programs of Study: UNC-Chapel Hill confers B.A., B.S., B.A.Ed., B.F.A., B.M., B.Med., B.S.B.A., B.S.N., and B.S.S.T. degrees. Master's and doctoral degrees are also awarded. Bachelor's degrees are awarded in BIOLOGICAL SCIENCE (biology/biological science and zoology), BUSINESS (business administration and management and recreation and leisure services), COMMUNICATIONS AND THE ARTS (art history and appreciation, classical languages, classics, comparative literature, dramatic arts, English, French, German, Greek, Italian, journalism, Latin, linguistics, music, Portuguese, Russian, Slavic languages, Spanish, speech/debate/rhetoric, and studio art), COMPUTER AND PHYSICAL SCIENCE (astronomy, chemistry, geology, mathematics, physics, and statistics), EDUCATION (art, early childhood, education, elementary, foreign languages, middle school, music, physical, science, and secondary), ENGINEERING AND ENVIRONMENTAL DESIGN (industrial administration/management), HEALTH PROFESSIONS (dental hygiene, medical laboratory technology, nursing, pharmacy, public health, and radiological science), SOCIAL SCIENCE (African American studies, African studies, American studies, anthropology, East Asian studies, economics, geography, history, international studies, Latin American studies, liberal arts/general studies, peace studies, philosophy, political science/government, psychology, public affairs, religion, Russian and Slavic studies, sociology, and women's studies). Sociology is the strongest academically. Biology, psychology, and English are the largest.

Required: To graduate, students must complete 120 credits with a 2.0 GPA. All students must take liberal arts courses in their first 2 years, including English, social sciences, history, philosophy, fine arts, foreign language, math, and phys ed. Students must fulfill a cultural diversity requirement by taking 1 course from a list of approved courses.

Special: Students may participate in joint programs with Duke University and North Carolina State University. Internships, study abroad, work-study programs, B.A.-B.S. degrees, and student-designed majors are available. The university offers a 2-2 engineering operations program with North Carolina State University. There are pass/fail options and nondegree study. There are 2 national honor societies, including Phi Beta Kappa, and a freshman honors program.

Faculty/Classroom: 71% of faculty are male; 29%, female. All both teach and do research.

Admissions: 40% of the 2001-2002 applicants were accepted. The SAT I scores for the 2001-2002 freshman class were: Verbal--5% below 500, 30% between 500 and 599, 47% between 600 and 700, and 18% above 700; Math--4% below 500, 25% between 500 and 599, 49% between 600 and 700, and 22% above 700. The ACT scores were 10% below 21, 13% between 21 and 23, 28% between 24 and 26, 17% between 27 and 28, and 32% above 28. 86% of the current freshmen were in the top fifth of their class; 96% were in the top two fifths.

Requirements: The SAT I or ACT is required. In addition, applicants must be graduates of an accredited secondary school. They should complete 16 high school academic credits, including 4 in English, 3 each in math (2 in algebra and 1 in geometry) and science (including at least 1 physical science and 1 lab course), and 2 each in a single foreign language, history, and social studies. A portfolio and an audition are recommended for art and music majors. AP and CLEP credits are accepted. Important factors in the admissions decision are advanced placement or honor courses, leadership record, and recommendations by school officials.

Procedure: Freshmen are admitted in the fall. Entrance exams should be taken in the junior and senior years. There is an early admissions plan. Check with school for current application deadlines. The application fee is $55. Notification is sent on a rolling basis.

Transfer: Most transfers are admitted for the junior year; 50 sophomore transfers are enrolled each fall. Applicants for transfer should have a minimum GPA of 2.0 before seeking admission. 30 credits of 120 must be completed at UNC-Chapel Hill.

Visiting: There are regularly scheduled orientations for prospective students, including campus tours and information sessions, offered twice each day. There are guides for informal visits and visitors may sit in on classes. To schedule a visit, contact the Office of Undergraduate Admissions.

Financial Aid: In 2001-2002, 58% of all freshmen and 51% of continuing students received some form of financial aid. The average financial indebtedness of a recent year's graduate was $12,800. UNC-Chapel Hill is a member of CSS. The CSS/Profile or FAFSA is required. Check with school for current deadlines.

International Students: It is recommended these students take the TOEFL, scoring 600 on the written version or 250 on the electronic version, and also take the SAT I or the ACT.

Computers: The mainframes are a CONVEX supercomputer and a variety of UNIX workstations. More than 300 microcomputers are available for student use throughout the campus. Accounts are available for e-mail and instructional computing. All students may access the system for e-mail; others for course work or independent research may access the system 24 hours a day. There are no time limits and no fees.

Admissions Contact: Jerome A. Lucido, Vice Provost and Director of Undergraduate Admissions. E-mail: *jlucido@email.unc.edu*
Web: *www.unc.edu*

UNIVERSITY OF NORTH CAROLINA AT CHARLOTTE C-3

Charlotte, NC 28223-0001 (704) 687-2213; Fax: (704) 687-6483

Full-time: 5223 men, 6117 women	**Faculty:** 589; IIA, av$
Part-time: 1696 men, 2099 women	**Ph.D.s:** 86%
Graduate: 1286 men, 1887 women	**Student/Faculty:** 19 to 1
Year: semesters, summer session	**Tuition:** $2456 ($10,676)
Application Deadline: July 1	**Room & Board:** $4798
Freshman Class: 7731 applied, 5656 accepted, 2351 enrolled	
SAT I Verbal/Math: 520/530	**ACT:** 21 **COMPETITIVE**

The University of North Carolina at Charlotte, founded in 1946, is a publicly funded institution in the University of North Carolina System. There are 7 undergraduate schools and 1 graduate school. In addition to regional accreditation, UNC-Charlotte has baccalaureate program accreditation with AACSB, ABET, CSWE, NAAB, NCATE, and NLN. The library contains 694,897 volumes, 96,928 microform items, and 8839 audiovisual forms/CDs, and subscribes to 4996 periodicals. Computerized library services include the card catalog, interlibrary loans, and database searching. Special learning facilities include a learning resource center, art gallery, and on-line teleconferencing facility, high-tech research center in engineering, and botanical garden and greenhouse complex that includes a tropical rain forest. The 1000-acre campus is in a suburban area 8 miles northeast of the center of Charlotte. Including residence halls, there are 80 buildings.

Student Life: 88% of undergraduates are from North Carolina. Others are from 48 states, 74 foreign countries, and Canada. 73% are white; 16% African American. 64% claim no religious affiliation; 25% Protestant. The average age of freshmen is 18; all undergraduates, 25. 27% do not continue beyond their first year; 50% remain to graduate.

Housing: 3994 students can be accommodated in college housing, which includes single-sex and coed dormitories and on-campus apartments. In addition, there are honors houses, special-interest houses, an international floor, and 5 sorority floors. On-campus housing is available on a first-come, first-served basis. 78% of students commute. All students may keep cars.

Activities: 7% of men belong to 15 national fraternities; 5% of women belong to 9 national sororities. There are 130 groups on campus, including art, cheerleading, chess, choir, chorale, chorus, computers, dance, debate, drama, ethnic, gay, honors, international, jazz band, literary magazine, newspaper, opera, pep band, photography, political, professional, radio and TV, religious, social, social service, student government, and yearbook. Popular campus events include Greek Week, Miss 49er Pageant, and International Festival.

Sports: There are 7 intercollegiate sports for men and 7 for women, and 35 intramural sports for men and 35 for women. Facilities include a gym, an Olympic-size pool, basketball, tennis, and racquetball courts, a fitness trail, a track, and a training room. There is also a 9100-seat arena, 2 weight rooms, an aerobics studio, an indoor track, indoor basketball/volleyball courts, an indoor climbing wall, and a 7000-square-foot game room.

Disabled Students: 90% of the campus is accessible. Wheelchair ramps, elevators, special parking, specially equipped rest rooms, special class scheduling, lowered drinking fountains, and lowered telephones are available. The Disability Services Office assists students with all academic and physical accommodations.

Services: Counseling and information services are available, as is tutoring in some subjects, including math, science, foreign language, and introductory courses. There is a reader service for the blind.

Campus Safety and Security: Measures include 24-hour foot and vehicle patrol, self-defense education, escort service, and shuttle buses. There are informal discussions, pamphlets/posters/films, emergency telephones, and lighted pathways/sidewalks.

Programs of Study: UNC-Charlotte confers B.A., B.S., B.Arch., B.F.A., B.M., B.S.B.A, B.S.C.E., B.S.E.E., B.S.E.T., B.S.M.E., B.S.N., and B.S.W. degrees. Master's and doctoral degrees are also awarded. Bachelor's degrees are awarded in BIOLOGICAL SCIENCE (biology/biological science), BUSINESS (accounting, banking and finance, business administration and management, business economics, international business management, management information systems, marketing management, and marketing/retailing/merchandising), COMMUNICATIONS AND THE ARTS (communications, dance, dramatic arts, English, fine arts, French, German, music, and Spanish), COMPUTER AND PHYSICAL SCIENCE (chemistry, computer science, earth science, geology, information sciences and systems, mathematics, and physics), EDUCATION (art, dance, drama, elementary, English, foreign languages, mathematics, middle school, music, science, and social studies), ENGINEERING AND ENVIRONMENTAL DESIGN (architecture, civil engineering, civil engineering technology, computer engineering, electrical/electronics engineering, electrical/electronics engineering technology, industrial administration/management, manufacturing engineering, mechanical engineering, and mechanical engineering technology), HEALTH PROFESSIONS (medical technology, and nursing), SOCIAL SCIENCE (African American studies, anthropology, child care/child and family studies, criminal justice, economics, fire control and safety technology, geography, history, international studies, philosophy, physical fitness/movement, political science/government, psychology, religion, social work, and sociology). Architecture, business administration, and geography and earth science are the strongest academically. Business administration, biology, and psychology are the largest.

Required: To graduate, students must complete a minimum of 120 credit hours with an overall minimum GPA of 2.0. Between 30 and 42 hours are required in the major, with a minimum GPA of 2.0 in major and minor courses. All students must complete core requirements in the 6 interrelated areas of communication, problem solving, values, science and technology, arts, literature and ideas, and the individual, society, and culture. A thesis is required.

Special: Cross-registration is available through the Charlotte Area Educational Consortium. Also available are cooperative programs in numerous majors and internships of 1 semester arranged with public and private community organizations. Study abroad, B.A.-B.S. degrees, dual majors, and nondegree study are available. Pass/fail options are limited to 1 course per academic year. There are 39 national honor societies, a freshman honors program, and 12 departmental honors programs.

Faculty/Classroom: 63% of faculty are male; 37%, female. 87% teach undergraduates. Graduate students teach 3% of introductory courses. The average class size in a laboratory is 18 and in a regular course, 30.

Admissions: 73% of the 2001-2002 applicants were accepted. The SAT I scores for the 2001-2002 freshman class were: Verbal--39% below 500, 46% between 500 and 599, 14% between 600 and 700, and 1% above 700; Math--33% below 500, 47% between 500 and 599, 19% between 600 and 700, and 1% above 700. The ACT scores were 45% below 21, 31% between 21 and 23, 15% between 24 and 26, 5% between 27 and 28, and 3% above 28. 41% of the current freshmen were in the top fifth of their class; 79% were in the top two fifths. 17 freshmen graduated first in their class.

Requirements: The SAT I or ACT is required. In addition, graduation from an accredited secondary school or the GED is required. The school requires 14 academic credits, including 4 years of English, 3 each of math and science (including 1 physical science and 1 biological science, 2 of a foreign language, and 2 of social studies, including 1 of U.S. history. Priority is given to students whose senior-year courses include a foreign language, math, world history, and health education. A portfolio and interview are required for art and architecture students only. Admission of students is based on overall performance in a select group of academic courses (80%) and SAT scores (20%). UNC-Charlotte requires applicants to be in the upper 50% of their class. A GPA of 2.0 is required. AP and CLEP credits are accepted. Important factors in the admissions decision are advanced placement or honor courses, leadership record, and recommendations by school officials. Applications are accepted on computer disk and on-line via the school's web site.

Procedure: Freshmen are admitted to all sessions. Entrance exams should be taken at the end of the junior year or by December of the senior year. There are early admissions and deferred admissions plans. Applications should be filed by July 1 for fall entry, November 15 for spring entry, and May 1 for summer entry. Notification is sent on a rolling basis.

Transfer: 1720 transfer students enrolled in 2001-2002. Transfer students must have a minimum GPA of 2.0 on all college courses attempted. Certain majors have limited space and require a higher GPA and/or prerequisites. Applicants with fewer than 24 hours of transferable credit must meet both transfer and freshman admissions requirements. An interview is required only for architecture students. 30 credits of 120 must be completed at UNC-Charlotte.

Visiting: There are regularly scheduled orientations for prospective students, including scheduled tours. There are guides for informal visits and visitors may sit in on classes and stay overnight. To schedule a visit, contact the Admissions Office.

Financial Aid: In 2001-2002, 48% of all freshmen and 46% of continuing students received some form of financial aid. 43% of freshmen and 42% of continuing students received need-based aid. The average freshman award was $4580. Of that total, scholarships or need-based grants averaged $1335 ($6000 maximum); loans averaged $2000 ($6625 maximum); and work contracts averaged $1160 ($1600 maximum). 86% of undergraduates work part time. Average annual earnings from campus work are $1700. The average financial indebtedness of the 2001 graduate was $9458. UNC-Charlotte is a member of CSS. The FAFSA is required. The fall application deadline is April 1.

International Students: There are 383 international students enrolled. They must score 500 on the written TOEFL or 180 on the electronic version or take the MELAB.

Computers: The mainframe is an IBM 9672-R24. About 1,100 PCs are located at various labs on campus. Students can access the Internet and Bitnet. All students may access the system 24 hours per day. There are no time limits. The fee is $25 per semester.

Graduates: In 2001, 2366 bachelor's degrees were awarded. The most popular majors were business administration (26%), engineering (9%), and education (8%). In an average class, 21% graduate in 4 years, 45% in 5 years, and 50% in 6 years. 97 companies recruited on campus in 2000-2001. Of the 2000 graduating class, 9% were enrolled in graduate school within 6 months of graduation and 96% were employed.

Admissions Contact: Craig Fulton, Director of Admissions. A video is available. E-mail: *unccadm@email.uncc.edu* Web: *www.uncc.edu*

UNIVERSITY OF NORTH CAROLINA AT GREENSBORO D-2

Greensboro, NC 27412 (336) 334-5243; Fax: (336) 334-3009

Full-time: 2721 men, 5950 women	**Faculty:** 678; I, --$
Part-time: 609 men, 1096 women	**Ph.D.s:** 86%
Graduate: 917 men, 2050 women	**Student/Faculty:** 13 to 1
Year: semesters, summer session	**Tuition:** $2545 ($10,995)
Application Deadline: August 1	**Room & Board:** $4313

Freshman Class: 6619 applied, 4964 accepted, 1915 enrolled

SAT I Verbal/Math: 520/510 **COMPETITIVE**

The University of North Carolina at Greensboro, founded in 1891, is a publicly funded liberal arts institution in the University of North Carolina system. There are 7 undergraduate and 7 graduate schools. In addition to regional accreditation, UNCG has baccalaureate program accreditation with AACSB, ADA, AHEA, CSWE, FIDER, NASM, NCATE, and NLN. The library contains 844,448 volumes, 1,400,761 microform items, and 59,027 audiovisual forms/CDs, and subscribes to 8714 periodicals. Computerized library services include the card catalog, interlibrary loans, and database searching. Special learning facilities include a learning resource center, art gallery, radio station, and a cooperative observatory/planetarium (off-campus). The 200-acre campus is in an urban area in central Greensboro. Including residence halls, there are 75 buildings.

Student Life: 87% of undergraduates are from North Carolina. Others are from 40 states, 20 foreign countries, and Canada. 95% are from public schools. 73% are white; 20% African American. The average age of freshmen is 18; all undergraduates, 23. 25% do not continue beyond their first year; 46% remain to graduate.

Housing: 3900 students can be accommodated in college housing, which includes single-sex and coed dormitories and on-campus apartments. In addition, there are special-interest houses, an international house, and a Residential College Program. On-campus housing is guaranteed for all 4 years. 64% of students commute. Alcohol is not permitted. All students may keep cars.

Activities: 8% of men belong to 8 national fraternities; 6% of women belong to 8 national sororities. There are 151 groups on campus, including art, band, choir, chorale, chorus, dance, drama, ethnic, film, gay, honors, international, jazz band, literary magazine, musical theater, newspaper, opera, orchestra, pep band, photography, political, professional, radio and TV, religious, social, social service, student government, symphony, and yearbook. Popular campus events include Spring Fling, Fall Kickoff, and Founders Day.

Sports: There are 7 intercollegiate sports for men and 7 for women, and 25 intramural sports for men and 25 for women. Facilities include a physical activities complex and the 44-acre Piney Lake Field Campus, which includes 2 lakes for swimming, boating, and fishing.

Disabled Students: 80% of the campus is accessible. Wheelchair ramps, elevators, special parking, specially equipped rest rooms, special class scheduling, lowered drinking fountains, lowered telephones, and lifts are available.

Services: Counseling and information services are available, as is tutoring in every subject. There is a reader service for the blind and remedial math.

Campus Safety and Security: Measures include 24-hour foot and vehicle patrol, self-defense education, escort service, and shuttle buses. There are informal discussions, pamphlets/posters/films, emergency telephones, and lighted pathways/sidewalks.

Programs of Study: UNCG confers B.A., B.S., B.F.A., B.M., B.S.M.T., B.S.N., and B.S.W. degrees. Master's and doctoral degrees are also awarded. Bachelor's degrees are awarded in BIOLOGICAL SCIENCE (biology/biological science), BUSINESS (accounting, banking and finance, business administration and management, business economics, hotel/motel and restaurant management, marketing/retailing/merchandising, and personnel management), COMMUNICATIONS AND THE ARTS (broadcasting, communications, dance, design, dramatic arts, English, film arts, fine arts, French, German, Greek, Latin, music, Spanish, and speech/debate/rhetoric), COMPUTER AND PHYSICAL SCIENCE (chemistry, earth science, information sciences and systems, mathematics, physics, and statistics), EDUCATION (art, business, early childhood, elementary, foreign languages, health, home economics, middle school, music, and science), HEALTH PROFESSIONS (medical laboratory technology, nursing, predentistry, premedicine, public health, and speech pathology/audiology), SOCIAL SCIENCE (anthropology, child care/child and family studies, dietetics, economics, geography, history, parks and recreation management, philosophy, political science/government, prelaw, psychology, public administration, religion, social science, social work, and sociology). Nursing, education, and business administration are the largest.

Required: In order to graduate, students must complete a minimum of 122 credit hours with a GPA of at least 2.0. Major requirements vary from a minimum of 30 credit hours. The liberal education curriculum for all students requires 45 credit hours chosen from specified courses in the humanities, math and physical sciences, social and behavioral sciences, and a foreign language. Students must take 36 hours at the upper-division level and earn 31 hours of resident credit.

Special: Cooperative programs, internships, accelerated degree programs, and a B.A.-B.S. degree can be arranged in all majors. Cross-registration is offered with the Greater Greensboro Consortium. Students may study abroad in more than 30 countries, including Spain, where UNCG sponsors a semester of study in Madrid. A Washington semester and student-designed majors are also available. The Residential College, a 2-year program for freshmen and sophomores, offers an interdisciplinary curriculum, with faculty and students living in the same residence. Students in this program participate in independent study, community work, and workshops. There are 18 national honor societies, including Phi Beta Kappa, a freshman honors program, and 14 departmental honors programs.

Faculty/Classroom: 50% of faculty are male; 50%, female. 95% teach undergraduates. Graduate students teach 18% of introductory courses. The average class size in an introductory lecture is 30; in a laboratory, 19; and in a regular course, 21.

Admissions: 75% of the 2001-2002 applicants were accepted. The SAT I scores for the 2001-2002 freshman class were: Verbal--41% below 500, 41% between 500 and 599, 15% between 600 and 700, and 3% above 700; Math--44% below 500, 40% between 500 and 599, 14% between 600 and 700, and 1% above 700. 32% of the current freshmen were in the top fifth of their class; 95% were in the top two fifths.

Requirements: The SAT I is required. In addition, graduation from an accredited secondary school or the GED is required. High school courses must include 4 credits of English, 3 each of math and science, 2 of a foreign language, 1 of U.S. history, and 1 of social studies and an elective. A portfolio or audition is required of art and music students. AP and CLEP credits are accepted. Important factors in the admissions decision are advanced placement or honor courses, leadership record, and evidence of special talent.

Procedure: Freshmen are admitted to all sessions. Entrance exams should be taken in June of the junior year or in the fall of the senior year. Applications should be filed by August 1 for fall entry and December 1 for spring entry. The fall 2001 application fee was $35. Notification is sent on a rolling basis.

Transfer: 1022 transfer students enrolled in 2001-2002. Transfer students must have a minimum GPA of 2.0. Students having fewer than 24 semester hours must meet the freshman entrance requirements, including satisfactory scores on the SAT I. 31 credits of 122 must be completed at UNCG.

Visiting: There are regularly scheduled orientations for prospective students. There are guides for informal visits and visitors may sit in on classes and stay overnight. To schedule a visit, contact the Office of Undergraduate Admissions.

Financial Aid: In 2001-2002, 46% of all freshmen and 43% of continuing students received some form of financial aid. 46% of freshmen and 35% of continuing students received need-based aid. The average freshman award was $6784. Of that total, scholarships or need-based grants averaged $2169; loans averaged $3688; and work contracts averaged $1677. 10% of undergraduates work part time. The FAFSA is required. The fall application deadline is March 1.

International Students: There are 120 international students enrolled. They must score 550 on the written TOEFL and also take the SAT I.

Computers: The mainframe is a DEC VAX 8200. PCs and terminals to the mainframe are in labs in most classroom buildings, the student center, and most residence halls. All students may access the system until late-night hours in labs and 24 hours a day via personal modem. There are no time limits and no fees.

Graduates: In 2001, 1794 bachelor's degrees were awarded. The most popular majors were nursing (6%), business administration (6%), and psychology (5%). In an average class, 21% graduate in 4 years, 41% in 5 years, and 46% in 6 years.

Admissions Contact: Jerry Herrelson, Associate Director, Undergraduate Admissions. E-mail: *undergrad_admissions@uncg.edu*
Web: *www.uncg.edu/adm/*

UNIVERSITY OF NORTH CAROLINA AT PEMBROKE D-3

Pembroke, NC 28372-1510 (910) 521-6262
(800) 949-UNCP; Fax: (910) 521-6497

Full-time: 1100 men, 1592 women
Part-time: 223 men, 591 women
Graduate: 141 men, 286 women
Year: semesters, summer session
Application Deadline: July 15
Freshman Class: 1384 applied, 1198 accepted, 700 enrolled
SAT I Verbal/Math: 461/463
Faculty: 162; IIA, -$
Ph.D.s: 71%
Student/Faculty: 17 to 1
Tuition: $2069 ($9991)
Room & Board: $3845
LESS COMPETITIVE

UNC Pembroke, founded in 1887, is part of the University of North Carolina state-supported system. It provides a liberal arts education that includes art, business, health sciences, music, teacher preparation, and preprofessional studies. There are 3 undergraduate schools and 1 graduate school. In addition to regional accreditation, UNCP has baccalaureate program accreditation with CSWE, NASM, and NCATE. The 2 libraries contain 304,079 volumes, 640,834 microform items, and 2081 audiovisual forms/CDs, and subscribe to 1561 periodicals. Computerized library services include the card catalog, interlibrary loans, and database searching. Special learning facilities include a learning resource center, art gallery, TV station, and a Native American resource center. The 126-acre campus is in a small town 30 miles south of Fayetteville, 100 miles south of Raleigh, and 120 miles east of Charlotte. Including residence halls, there are 38 buildings.

Student Life: 98% of undergraduates are from North Carolina. Others are from 32 states, 13 foreign countries, and Canada. 90% are from public schools. 55% are white; 22% Native American/Eskimo; 20% African American. The average age of freshmen is 19; all undergraduates, 26. 31% do not continue beyond their first year; 69% remain to graduate.

Housing: 973 students can be accommodated in college housing, which includes single-sex dormitories. On-campus housing is guaranteed for all 4 years. 64% of students commute. All students may keep cars.

Activities: 4% of men and about 1% of women belong to 2 local and 8 national fraternities; 3% of women belong to 1 local sorority and 7 national sororities. There are 70 groups on campus, including art, band, cheerleading, choir, chorale, chorus, dance, drama, ethnic, gay, honors, international, jazz band, literary magazine, musical theater, newspaper, pep band, political, professional, radio and TV, religious, social, social service, student government, and yearbook. Popular campus events include the Performing Arts Cultural Series, Miss UNCP Scholarship Pageant, and Pembroke Day.

Sports: There are 7 intercollegiate sports for men and 6 for women, and 13 intramural sports for men and 13 for women. Facilities include a 3200-seat gym, an auxiliary gym, a track, tennis courts, a natatorium, weight rooms, a bowling alley, a 1700-seat auditorium, fields for soccer, baseball, and softball, 2 swimming pools, and a wellness center.

Disabled Students: 98% of the campus is accessible. Wheelchair ramps, elevators, special parking, specially equipped rest rooms, special class scheduling, lowered drinking fountains, and lowered telephones are available.

Services: Counseling and information services are available, as is tutoring in every subject. There is a reader service for the blind, and remedial math, reading, and writing as well as Americans with Disabilities services.

Campus Safety and Security: Measures include 24-hour foot and vehicle patrol, self-defense education, escort service, and informal discussions. There are pamphlets/posters/films, emergency telephones, and lighted pathways/sidewalks.

Programs of Study: UNCP confers B.A., B.S., B.M., B.S.A.S., B.S.N., and B.S.W. degrees. Master's degrees are also awarded. Bachelor's degrees are awarded in BIOLOGICAL SCIENCE (biology/biological science), BUSINESS (accounting, business administration and management, and business economics), COMMUNICATIONS AND THE ARTS (art, broadcasting, communications, English, journalism, and music), COMPUTER AND PHYSICAL SCIENCE (chemistry, computer science, and mathematics), EDUCATION (art, elementary, English, mathematics, middle school, music, physical, science, secondary, social studies, and special), HEALTH PROFESSIONS (community health work and premedicine), SOCIAL SCIENCE (American Indian studies, criminal justice, history, parks and recreation management, philosophy, political science/government, prelaw, psychology, public administration, religion, social work, and sociology). Education, business administration, and physical sciences are the strongest academically. Education, business, and social science are the largest.

Required: All students are required to complete 120 to 128 total credits, which include 44 semester hours of general education courses, 39 to 69 hours in a major, and a university orientation class before entrance. A minimum GPA of 2.0 must be maintained.

Special: Co-op programs, cross-registration, internships, study abroad in Sweden, a Washington semester, and work-study programs are available. A 3-1 degree program is offered in medical technology. The B.A.-B.S. degree is available in American Indian studies, broadcasting, or with the B.S.A.S. degree. In addition, dual majors, credit for military experience, and nondegree study are offered. There are 6 national honor societies, including Phi Beta Kappa, a freshman honors program, and 5 departmental honors programs.

Faculty/Classroom: 60% of faculty are male; 40%, female. 98% teach undergraduates, 50% do research, and 80% do both. No introductory courses are taught by graduate students. The average class size in an introductory lecture is 27; in a laboratory, 13; and in a regular course, 20.

Admissions: 87% of the 2001-2002 applicants were accepted. The SAT I scores for the 2001-2002 freshman class were: Verbal--71% below 500, 24% between 500 and 599, 4% between 600 and 700, and 1% above 700; Math--69% below 500, 27% between 500 and 599, and 4% between 600 and 700. The ACT scores were 53% between 12 and 17; 35% between 18 and 23; and 7% between 24 and 29. 21% of the current freshmen were in the top fifth of their class; 48% were in the top two fifths.

Requirements: The SAT I or ACT is required. In addition, applicants must be graduates of an accredited secondary school with 20 academic credits, including 4 courses in English, 3 each in math and science, and 2 in history. An essay and an interview are recommended. Students also must submit an official high school transcript that shows their class rank and GPA. The College Opportunity Program is designed to admit a limited number of students who meet most, but not all, of the regular admissions standards. Students who receive the GED should consult an admissions counselor. UNCP requires applicants to be in the upper 50% of their class. A GPA of 2.0 is required. AP and CLEP credits are accepted. Important factors in the admissions decision are advanced placement or honor courses, recommendations by school officials, and evidence of special talent.

Procedure: Freshmen are admitted to all sessions. Entrance exams should be taken during the junior and senior years. There is a deferred admissions plan. Applications should be filed by July 15 for fall entry, December 1 for spring entry, and May 15 for summer entry. The fall 2001 application fee was $40. Notification is sent on a rolling basis.

Transfer: 375 transfer students enrolled in 2001-2002. Applicants must have a minimum GPA of 2.0, submit transcripts from high school and from all previous colleges, and be eligible to return to the last institution attended. The SAT I and an interview are recommended. 30 credits of 128 must be completed at UNCP.

Visiting: There are regularly scheduled orientations for prospective students, including open houses in the fall, spring, and winter. There are guides for informal visits and visitors may sit in on classes and stay overnight. To schedule a visit, contact the Office of Admissions.

Financial Aid: In a recent year, 71% of all freshmen and 58% of continuing students received some form of financial aid. 49% of freshmen and 46% of continuing students received need-based aid. The average freshman award was $4326. Of that total, scholarships or need-based grants averaged $2952 ($13,259 maximum); loans averaged $2987 ($11,625 maximum); work contracts averaged $1322 ($1546 maximum); and non need-based scholarships averaged $960 ($1500 maximum). 7% of undergraduates work part time. Average annual earnings from campus work are $1299. The FAFSA is required. The fall application deadline is April 15.

International Students: There are 24 international students enrolled. They must score 520 on the written TOEFL or take the MELAB. The SAT I or the ACT is also required.

Computers: The mainframes are an Alpha server 2100 5/250, an Alpha server 2000 4/1233, 2 Compaq DS 20s, a SUN E450, and a SUN E250. There are also PCs available in the computer center classrooms and computer lab. All students may access the system. Students may access the system 1 hour at a time. There are no fees.

Graduates: In 2001, 498 bachelor's degrees were awarded. The most popular majors were protective services (18%), business (18%), and social services (14%). In an average class, 22% graduate in 4 years, 33% in 5 years, and 37% in 6 years. 123 companies recruited on campus in 2000-2001. Of the 2000 graduating class, 11% were enrolled in graduate school within 6 months of graduation and 85% were employed.

Admissions Contact: Jacqueline Clark, VC for Enrollment Management. A video is available. E-mail: *admissions@papa.uncp.edu*
Web: *www.uncp.edu*

UNIVERSITY OF NORTH CAROLINA AT WILMINGTON E-4

Wilmington, NC 28403-3297 (910) 962-3243
Fax: (910) 962-3038

Full-time: 3494 men, 5172 women	**Faculty:** 433; IIA, av$
Part-time: 404 men, 722 women	**Ph.D.s:** 87%
Graduate: 288 men, 519 women	**Student/Faculty:** 20 to 1
Year: semesters, summer session	**Tuition:** $2627 ($10,722)
Application Deadline: February 7	**Room & Board:** $5142

Freshman Class: 5373 applied, 4301 accepted, 1996 enrolled
SAT I Verbal/Math: 543/548 **COMPETITIVE**

The University of North Carolina at Wilmington, founded in 1947, is a publicly funded institution offering programs in the liberal arts and sciences, education, and business. It is a part of the University of North Carolina System. There are 4 undergraduate schools and 1 graduate school. In addition to regional accreditation, UNC at Wilmington has baccalaureate program accreditation with NCATE and NLN. The library contains 493,784 volumes, 758,293 microform items, and 55,744 audiovisual forms/CDs, and subscribes to 4280 periodicals. Computerized library services include the card catalog, interlibrary loans, and database searching. Special learning facilities include a radio station, TV station, a wildflower preserve, a nature preserve, a museum of world cultures, and the research vessel Seahawk, used for a marine biology lab and for research. The 661-acre campus is in a suburban area 125 miles southeast of Raleigh. Including residence halls, there are 71 buildings.

Student Life: 85% of undergraduates are from North Carolina. Others are from 40 states, 37 foreign countries, and Canada. 91% are white. The average age of freshmen is 18; all undergraduates, 22. 21% do not continue beyond their first year; 40% remain to graduate.

Housing: 2106 students can be accommodated in college housing, which includes single-sex and coed dormitories and on-campus apartments. In addition, there are honors houses and an international students dorm. On-campus housing is available on a first-come, first-served basis. 77% of students commute. All students who live at least 1 mile from campus may keep cars.

Activities: 4% of men belong to 13 national fraternities; 5% of women belong to 12 national sororities. There are 114 groups on campus, including academic, art, cheerleading, chorale, computers, dance, drama, ethnic, film, gay, honors, international, jazz band, literary magazine, musical theater, pep band, political, radio and TV, readers theater, religious, social, social service, student government, symphony, team, and yearbook. Popular campus events include Business Week, Greek Week, and Spring Week.

Sports: There are 10 intercollegiate sports for men and 11 for women, and 9 intramural sports for men and 9 for women. Facilities include a 6000-seat coliseum, an Olympic-size swimming pool and separate diving tank, a track and field complex, and basketball, tennis, and racquetball courts.

Disabled Students: 98% of the campus is accessible. Wheelchair ramps, elevators, special parking, specially equipped rest rooms, special class scheduling, lowered drinking fountains, and lowered telephones are available.

Services: Counseling and information services are available, as is tutoring in most subjects. There is a reader service for the blind, and remedial math, reading, and writing.

Campus Safety and Security: Measures include 24-hour foot and vehicle patrol, self-defense education, escort service, and shuttle buses. There are informal discussions, pamphlets/posters/films, emergency telephones, and lighted pathways/sidewalks.

Programs of Study: UNC at Wilmington confers B.A., B.S., B.F.A., and B.S.W. degrees. Master's degrees are also awarded. Bachelor's degrees are awarded in BIOLOGICAL SCIENCE (biology/biological science, marine biology, and marine science), BUSINESS (accounting, banking and finance, business administration and management, business economics, business systems analysis, and marketing/retailing/merchandising), COMMUNICATIONS AND THE ARTS (art history and appreciation, creative writing, dramatic arts, English, film arts, French, music, music performance, Spanish, speech/debate/rhetoric, and studio art), COMPUTER AND PHYSICAL SCIENCE (chemistry, computer science, geology, mathematics, and physics), EDUCATION (athletic training, early childhood, elementary, middle school, music, physical, secondary, and special), ENGINEERING AND ENVIRONMENTAL DESIGN (environmental science), HEALTH PROFESSIONS (medical laboratory technology, nursing, and recreation therapy), SOCIAL SCIENCE (anthropology, criminal justice, geography, history, parks and recreation management, philosophy, political science/government, psychology, religion, social work, and sociology). Psychology is the largest.

Required: Students may qualify for the bachelor's degree by successfully completing the basic studies requirements, an approved course of study in an academic major, a minimum of 124 semester hours of credit, and a minimum quality point average of 2.0. The final 30 semester hours of course credit, including the final 15 semester hours in the major, must be completed at UNC at Wilmington.

Special: UNC at Wilmington offers short-term internships and work-study programs. Dual majors may be pursued if requirements are met, and credit is given for military experience. There are 13 national honor societies, a freshman honors program, and 31 departmental honors programs.

Faculty/Classroom: 59% of faculty are male; 41%, female. 8% do research. The average class size in a regular course is 35.

Admissions: 80% of the 2001-2002 applicants were accepted. The SAT I scores for the 2001-2002 freshman class were: Verbal--30% below 500, 53% between 500 and 599, 16% between 600 and 700, and 1% above 700; Math--24% below 500, 58% between 500 and 599, 17% between 600 and 700, and 1% above 700. The ACT scores were 6% below 21, 31% between 21 and 23, 32% between 24 and 26, 29% between 27 and 28, and 2% above 28. 41% of the current freshmen were in the top fifth of their class; 78% were in the top two fifths.

Requirements: The SAT I or ACT is required; the SAT I is preferred. Graduation from an accredited secondary school or the GED is required for admission. High school courses must include 4 years of English, 3 years of math (algebra I, II, and geometry), 3 units of science (1 year each of biology, physical science, and a lab course), 2 years of social studies including 1 year of U.S. history and 2 years of a foreign language. Students meeting all requirements except that for foreign language will be accepted with a deficiency and will be required to complete a foreign language sequence before receiving a degree. A GPA of 2.0 is required. AP and CLEP credits are accepted.

Procedure: Freshmen are admitted to all sessions. Entrance exams should be taken during the junior or senior year. Applications should be filed by February 7 for fall entry and May 1 for summer entry. The fall 2001 application fee was $45. Notification is sent on a rolling basis. A waiting list is an active part of the admissions procedure.

Transfer: 964 transfer students enrolled in 2001-2002. Transfer students must have a minimum GPA of 2.0 and be eligible to return to the institution last attended. Applicants with fewer than 24 semester hours or 36 quarter hours of transferable credit must also meet the freshman entrance requirements. Prior to admission, transfer applicants must have successfully completed 1 year of freshman-level English and 1 unit of college-level math. One unit of life sciences is also recommended. 30 credits of 124 must be completed at UNC at Wilmington.

Visiting: There are regularly scheduled orientations for prospective students. There are guides for informal visits. To schedule a visit, contact the Admissions Office.

Financial Aid: In 2001-2002, 54% of all freshmen and 48% of continuing students received some form of financial aid. 43% of freshmen and 39% of continuing students received need-based aid. The average freshman award was $7758. Of that total, scholarships or need-based grants averaged $3014 ($20,354 maximum); loans averaged $2786 ($7582 maximum); and work contracts averaged $2718 ($3000 maximum). 80% of undergraduates work part time. Average annual earnings from campus work are $1579. The average financial indebtedness of the 2001 graduate was $12,726. The FAFSA is required, and the college's own financial statement is required for summer session only. The deadline for financial aid applications is the last day of classes.

International Students: There are 69 international students enrolled. The school actively recruits these students. They must score 550 on the written TOEFL. The SAT I (with acceptable scores) will be accepted if TOEFL is not available.

Computers: The mainframes are a DEC VAX 11/785 and a DEC VAX 6000/420. PCs are available in academic and administrative departments. All students may access the system from 8 A.M. to 11 P.M. at on-campus clusters and 24-hours daily via modems. There are no time limits and no fees. It is strongly recommended that all students have a personal computer.

Graduates: In 2001, 1891 bachelor's degrees were awarded. The most popular majors were speech communication (5%), biology (5%), and psychology (4%). In an average class, 34% graduate in 4 years, 51% in 5 years, and 52% in 6 years. 153 companies recruited on campus in 2000-2001. Of the 2000 graduating class, 16% were enrolled in graduate school within 6 months of graduation.

Admissions Contact: Roxie M. Shabazz, Asistant VC for Admissions. A video is available. Web: *www.uncwil.edu*

WAKE FOREST UNIVERSITY C-2

Winston-Salem, NC 27109-7305 (336) 758-5201

Full-time: 1915 men, 2016 women	**Faculty:** 357; IIA, ++$
Part-time: 33 men, 23 women	**Ph.D.s:** 89%
Graduate: 1299 men, 930 women	**Student/Faculty:** 11 to 1
Year: semesters, summer session	**Tuition:** $23,530
Application Deadline: January 15	**Room & Board:** $6760

Freshman Class: 5271 applied, 2421 accepted, 989 enrolled
SAT I: required **ACT:** n/av **MOST COMPETITIVE**

Wake Forest University, established in 1834, is a private institution offering undergraduate programs in the liberal arts and sciences, education, and preprofessional fields. There are 2 undergraduate and 5 graduate schools. In addition to regional accreditation, Wake Forest has baccalaureate program accreditation with AACSB and NCATE. The 3 libraries contain 1,687,457 volumes, 2,085,862 microform items, and 22,997 audiovisual forms/CDs, and subscribe to 16,411 periodicals. Computerized library services include the card catalog, interlibrary loans, and database searching. Special learning facilities include a learning resource center, art gallery, radio station, TV station, fine arts center, anthropology museum, and laser research facility. The 340-acre campus is in a suburban area 4 miles northwest of Winston-Salem. Including residence halls, there are 41 buildings.

Student Life: 74% of undergraduates are from out of state, mostly the South. Others are from 50 states, 20 foreign countries, and Canada. 88% are white. 62% are Protestant; 22% Catholic; 15% Muslim, Hindu, Buddhist, Mormon, not reported. The average age of freshmen is 18; all undergraduates, 20. 7% do not continue beyond their first year; 86% remain to graduate.

Housing: 3063 students can be accommodated in college housing, which includes coed dormitories and on-campus apartments. In addition, there are honors houses, language houses, and special-interest houses. On-campus housing is guaranteed for all 4 years. 75% of students live on campus; of those, 75% remain on campus on weekends. All students may keep cars.

Activities: 37% of men belong to 14 national fraternities; 50% of women belong to 9 national sororities. There are 125 groups on campus, including art, band, cheerleading, choir, chorale, chorus, computers, dance, debate, drama, drill team, environmental, ethnic, film, gay, honors, international, jazz band, literary magazine, marching band, musical theater, newspaper, orchestra, pep band, photography, political, professional, radio and TV, religious, social, social service, student government, symphony, women's, and yearbook. Popular campus events include Convocation, Moravian Christmas Love Feast, and Family Weekend.

Sports: There are 8 intercollegiate sports for men and 8 for women, and 20 intramural sports for men and 16 for women. Facilities include 7 playing fields, 4 indoor basketball courts, a swimming pool, a track, racquetball and tennis courts, an exercise room and weight room, an indoor tennis center, a fitness center, a soccer complex, a golf practice complex, and a cross-country course.

Disabled Students: 80% of the campus is accessible. Wheelchair ramps, elevators, special parking, specially equipped rest rooms, special class scheduling, lowered drinking fountains, and lowered telephones are available.

Services: Counseling and information services are available, as is tutoring in some subjects, primarily in the sciences, math, and foreign languages. There is a reader service for the blind. The Learning Assistance Center offers instructional support and skill development in writing, reading, and study strategies.

Campus Safety and Security: Measures include 24-hour foot and vehicle patrol, self-defense education, escort service, and shuttle buses. There are informal discussions, pamphlets/posters/films, emergency telephones, and lighted pathways/sidewalks. There are gatehouses at 2 of the university's 3 entrances that operate from 10 P.M. to 6 A.M. During those hours, the third entrance is closed.

Programs of Study: Wake Forest confers B.A. and B.S. degrees. Master's and doctoral degrees are also awarded. Bachelor's degrees are awarded in BIOLOGICAL SCIENCE (biology/biological science), BUSINESS (accounting and business administration and management), COMMUNICATIONS AND THE ARTS (art, classics, communications, dramatic arts, English, French, German, Greek, Latin, music, and Spanish), COMPUTER AND PHYSICAL SCIENCE (chemistry, computer science, mathematics, and physics), EDUCATION (education), HEALTH PROFESSIONS (exercise science), SOCIAL SCIENCE (anthropology, economics, history, philosophy, political science/government, psychology, religion, and sociology). Business, biology, and psychology are the largest.

Required: To graduate, students must complete a total of 112 credits with a minimum GPA of 2.0. The number of hours required in the major varies. All students must take 1 semester of a writing seminar, a first year seminar, and 1 course in foreign language literature. In addition, students must complete 3 courses each in natural sciences and math, social and behavioral sciences, and history, religion, and philosophy; 2 courses in literature; and 1 course in fine arts.

Special: The school offers cooperative programs in forestry with Duke University. Cross-registration with Salem College is available. The school sponsors study-abroad programs in more than 10 countries. A Washington semester, internships, work-study programs, dual majors, a 3-2 engineering degree with North Carolina State University, a B.A.-B.S. degree in chemistry/physics, and pass/fail options are available. Accelerated degree programs may be arranged in dentistry and medical technology. Interdisciplinary honors courses and the Open Curriculum program are available for selected students. Wake Forest owns residences in London, Venice, and Vienna where students and professors may attend semester-long courses in a variety of disciplines. There are 11 national honor societies, including Phi Beta Kappa, a freshman honors program, and 21 departmental honors programs.

Faculty/Classroom: 64% of faculty are male; 36%, female. All teach undergraduates. No introductory courses are taught by graduate students. The average class size in a regular course is 20.

Admissions: 46% of the 2001-2002 applicants were accepted. 92% of the current freshmen were in the top quarter of their class; 98% were in the top half. There were 4 National Merit finalists. 93 freshmen graduated first in their class.

Requirements: The SAT I is required. In addition, 3 SAT II: Subject tests, including writing and mathematics, are recommended. Graduation from an accredited secondary school or the GED is required. The school requires 16 academic credits, including 4 credits of English, 2 each of a foreign language, history, and social studies, 3 of math, and 1 of science. 1 credit each of art and music is recommended. All students must submit an essay. Applications can be downloaded and are accepted at the university's web site. AP and CLEP credits are accepted. Important factors in the admissions decision are recommendations by school officials, leadership record, and advanced placement or honor courses.

Procedure: Freshmen are admitted fall and spring. Entrance exams should be taken during the junior year, and at least 1 SAT I should be taken during the senior year. There are early decision and early admissions plans. Early decision application should be filed by November 15; regular applications, by January 15 for fall entry and November 1 for spring entry. Notification of early decision is sent December 15; regular decision, April 1. 488 early decision candidates were accepted for the 2001-2002 class. A waiting list is an active part of the admissions procedure. The fall 2001 application fee was $40.

Transfer: 40 transfer students enrolled in 2001-2002. Transfer students must have a minimum GPA of 2.0 on all college work attempted. The SAT I is required. 56 credits of 112 must be completed at Wake Forest.

Visiting: There are regularly scheduled orientations for prospective students, including group information sessions and tours by appointment. There are guides for informal visits and visitors may sit in on classes and stay overnight. To schedule a visit, contact the Admissions Office.

Financial Aid: In 2001-2002, 64% of all freshmen and 56% of continuing students received some form of financial aid. 31% of freshmen and 28% of continuing students received need-based aid. The average freshman award was $18,817. Of that total, scholarships or need-based grants averaged $14,447; and loans averaged $4883. 25% of undergraduates work part time. Average annual earnings from campus work are $2000. The average financial indebtedness of the 2001 graduate was $20,339. Wake Forest is a member of CSS. The CSS/Profile or FAFSA and the college's own financial statement are required. The fall application deadline is March 1.

International Students: There are 37 international students enrolled. They must take the TOEFL and also take the SAT I.

Computers: The mainframes are an IBM SP2 and HP 3000. Each incoming student receives an IBM ThinkPad laptop computer with mainframe capability. Internet access is available directly from each residence hall room, faculty office, classroom, and the campus library. All have the option of purchasing wireless Ethernet cards. All students may access the system 24 hours per day. There are no time limits and no fees. All students are required to have personal computers.

Graduates: In 2001, 901 bachelor's degrees were awarded. The most popular majors were business (19%), communications (11%), and psychology (8%). In an average class, 77% graduate in 4 years, 86% in 5 years, and 87% in 6 years. 160 companies recruited on campus in 2000-2001. Of the 2000 graduating class, 33% were enrolled in graduate school within 6 months of graduation and 62% were employed.

Admissions Contact: Martha B. Allman, Director of Admissions. A video is available. E-mail: *admissions@wfu.edu* Web: *www.wfu.edu*

WARREN WILSON COLLEGE
B-2

Asheville, NC 28815-9000

(828) 298-3325
(800) 934-3536; Fax: (828) 298-1440

Full-time: 303 men, 470 women	**Faculty:** 57; IIB, --$
Part-time: 1 man, 7 women	**Ph.D.s:** 81%
Graduate: 22 men, 48 women	**Student/Faculty:** 14 to 1
Year: semesters	**Tuition:** $15,094
Application Deadline: March 15	**Room & Board:** $4874
Freshman Class: 628 applied, 545 accepted, 213 enrolled	
SAT I or ACT: required	**COMPETITIVE**

Warren Wilson College, founded in 1894, is a liberal arts institution affiliated with the Presbyterian Church (U.S.A.). All students work 15 hours per week in jobs related to the operation and maintenance of the college. In exchange, room and board is provided at a low rate. In addition to regional accreditation, Warren Wilson College has baccalaureate program accreditation with CSWE and NCATE. The library contains 100,000 volumes, 25,000 microform items, and 5500 audiovisual forms/CDs, and subscribes to 7400 periodicals. Computerized library services include the card catalog, interlibrary loans, and database searching. Special learning facilities include a learning resource center, art gallery, and radio station. The 1175-acre campus is in a small town 5 miles east of Asheville.

Student Life: 79% of undergraduates are from out of state, mostly the South. Others are from 42 states and 21 foreign countries. 74% are from public schools. 90% are white. The average age of freshmen is 18; all undergraduates, 20. 22% do not continue beyond their first year; 60% remain to graduate.

Housing: 684 students can be accommodated in college housing, which includes single-sex and coed dormitories. A wellness house and eco-dorm are also available. On-campus housing is guaranteed for all 4 years. 90% of students live on campus; of those, 95% remain on campus on weekends. Upperclassmen may keep cars.

Activities: There are no fraternities or sororities. There are many groups and organizations on campus, including art, chess, choir, chorus, computers, dance, drama, ethnic, film, gay, honors, international, jazz band, literary magazine, musical theater, newspaper, outdoor activities, photography, political, professional, radio and TV, religious, social, social service, student government, women's, and yearbook. Popular campus events include International Fair, Work Day, and Service Day.

Sports: There are 6 intercollegiate sports for men and 6 for women, and 3 intramural sports for men and 3 for women. Facilities include 2 gyms, an aquatic center, weight and fitness rooms, tennis courts, playing fields, 25 miles of hiking/biking trails, kayak slalom gates, indoor climbing wall, and alpine tower.

Disabled Students: 25% of the campus is accessible. Wheelchair ramps, elevators, special parking, specially equipped rest rooms, special class scheduling, lowered drinking fountains, and lowered telephones are available.

Services: Counseling and information services are available, as is tutoring in most subjects. Tutoring is available through the Peer Assistance Center.

Campus Safety and Security: Measures include 24-hour foot and vehicle patrol, escort service, informal discussions, and lighted pathways/sidewalks.

Programs of Study: Warren Wilson College confers B.A. and B.S. degrees. Master's degrees are also awarded. Bachelor's degrees are awarded in AGRICULTURE (environmental studies), BIOLOGICAL SCIENCE (biology/biological science), BUSINESS (business economics), COMMUNICATIONS AND THE ARTS (art, and English), COMPUTER AND PHYSICAL SCIENCE (chemistry, and mathematics), EDUCATION (elementary, English, middle school, and recreation), SOCIAL SCIENCE (behavioral science, history, humanities, psychology, and social work). Biology is the strongest academically. Environmental studies, biology, and English are the largest.

Required: To graduate, students must complete a total of 128 semester hours with a minimum GPA of 2.0. Between 32 and 40 hours are required in the student's major. All students must complete 36 hours in the core curriculum. All students must also complete 25 hours of community service each year. A first-year seminar and college composition are required.

Special: Cross registration is offered with Mars Hill College and the University of North Carolina at Asheville. Internships related to the major may be arranged. Study-abroad programs in South America, Europe, Japan, and India are available. The college offers an accelerated degree program in education, student-designed majors, nondegree study, and pass/fail options. There are dual majors in history/political science and English/theater arts. Cooperative programs are available in engineering with Washington University in St. Louis. On campus work-study is required.

Faculty/Classroom: 68% of faculty are male; 32%, female. All both teach and do research. No introductory courses are taught by graduate students. The average class size in an introductory lecture is 16; in a laboratory, 15; and in a regular course, 11.

Admissions: 87% of the 2001-2002 applicants were accepted. In a recent year, there were 3 National Merit finalists and 6 semifinalists; 2 freshmen graduated first in the class.

Requirements: The SAT I or ACT is required, with a score of 500 on each section of the SAT I or a composite score of 21 on the ACT. Graduation from an accredited secondary school or the GED is required. Applicants should have a total of 12 academic credits. An essay and an interview are recommended. A GPA of 2.5 is required. AP credits are accepted. Important factors in the admissions decision are advanced placement or honor courses, evidence of special talent, and recommendations by school officials. Applications are accepted on computer disk through CollegeLink.

Procedure: Freshmen are admitted fall and winter. Entrance exams should be taken by January 20 of the senior year. There are early decision, early admissions, and deferred admissions plans. Early decision applications should be filed by November 15; regular applications, by March 15 for fall entry and November 1 for winter entry. Notification of early decision is sent December 1; regular decision, April 1. 48 early decision candidates were accepted for the 2001-2002 class. 10% of all applicants are on a waiting list.

Transfer: 67 transfer students enrolled in 2001-2002. Applicants must have a minimum GPA of 2.75. A year of residence at Warren Wilson is required for graduation. Applicants must be eligible to return to their previous institutions. 32 credits of 128 must be completed at Warren Wilson College.

Visiting: There are guides for informal visits and visitors may sit in on classes and stay overnight. To schedule a visit, contact the campus visit coordinator.

Financial Aid: In 2001-2002, 80% of all freshmen and 77% of continuing students received some form of financial aid. 47% of freshmen and 58% of continuing students received need-based aid. The average freshman award was $9644. Of that total, scholarships or need-based grants averaged $4547; loans averaged $2825; and work contracts averaged $2472. 84% of undergraduates work part time. Average annual earnings from campus work are $2472. The FAFSA and the college's own financial statement are required. The fall application deadline is April 1.

International Students: There are 38 international students enrolled. The school actively recruits these students. They must score 550 on the written TOEFL.

Computers: The mainframe is a McDonnel-Douglas Spirit 6000. PCs and Macs are available for student use in academic buildings and the library. All students may access the system. It is strongly recommended that all students have a personal computer. There are no time limits and no fees.

Graduates: In a recent year, 96 bachelor's degrees were awarded. The most popular majors were behavoral science (21%), environmental studies (17%), and elementary education (7%). In an average class, 1% graduate in 3 years, 32% in 4 years, 5% in 5 years, and 2% in 6 years. 6 companies recruited on campus in 2000-2001. Of the 2000 graduating class, 30% were enrolled in graduate school within 6 months of graduation and 60% were employed.

Admissions Contact: Richard Blomgren, Dean of Admission. A video is available. E-mail: *rickb@warren-wilson.edu*
Web: *www.warren-wilson.edu*

WESTERN CAROLINA UNIVERSITY B-3
Cullowhee, NC 28723 (828) 227-7317
1-877-WCU4YOU; Fax: (828) 227-7319

Full-time: 2450 men, 2422 women	**Faculty:** 326; IIA, -$
Part-time: 281 men, 512 women	**Ph.D.s:** 83%
Graduate: 429 men, 769 women	**Student/Faculty:** 15 to 1
Year: semesters, summer session	**Tuition:** $2243 ($9875)
Application Deadline: July 15	**Room & Board:** $3424
Freshman Class: 3979 applied, 2903 accepted, 1180 enrolled	
SAT I Verbal/Math: 490/500	**COMPETITIVE**

Western Carolina University, founded in 1889, is a publicly funded institution in the University of North Carolina system. There are 5 undergraduate schools and 1 graduate school. In addition to regional accreditation, WCU has baccalaureate program accreditation with AACSB, ABET, ADA, CSWE, FIDER, NASM, NCATE, and NLN. The library contains 583,694 volumes, 1,352,489 microform items, and 6300 audiovisual forms/CDs, and subscribes to 2928 periodicals. Computerized library services include the card catalog, interlibrary loans, and database searching. Special learning facilities include a learning resource center, art gallery, natural history museum, and radio station. The 265-acre campus is in a rural area 160 miles northeast of Atlanta, Georgia, and 50 miles west of Asheville. Including residence halls, there are 88 buildings.

Student Life: 89% of undergraduates are from North Carolina. Others are from 42 states, 34 foreign countries, and Canada. 95% are from public schools. 89% are white. The average age of freshmen is 18; all undergraduates, 20. 30% do not continue beyond their first year; 47% remain to graduate.

Housing: 3000 students can be accommodated in college housing, which includes single-sex and coed dormitories, on-campus apartments, and married-student housing. In addition, there are honors houses. On-campus housing is guaranteed for all 4 years. 55% of students commute. All students may keep cars.

Activities: 15% of men belong to 13 national fraternities; 11% of women belong to 9 national sororities. There are 120 groups on campus, including art, band, cheerleading, choir, chorale, chorus, computers, dance, drama, drill team, ethnic, film, gay, honors, international, literary magazine, marching band, musical theater, newspaper, pep band, photography, political, professional, radio and TV, religious, social, social service, student government, and yearbook. Popular campus events include Mountain Heritage Day, Greek Week, and Madrigal Christmas Dinners.

Sports: There are 6 intercollegiate sports for men and 7 for women, and 37 intramural sports for men and 35 for women. Facilities include a football stadium, a baseball diamond, 6 intramural softball and football fields, a soccer field, 5 gyms, a field house, jogging trails, picnic areas, game rooms, an archery range, a golf driving range, and a golf putting green.

Disabled Students: 90% of the campus is accessible. Wheelchair ramps, elevators, special parking, specially equipped rest rooms, special

class scheduling, lowered drinking fountains, and lowered telephones are available.

Services: Counseling and information services are available, as is tutoring in most subjects. There is a reader service for the blind, and remedial math, reading, and writing.

Campus Safety and Security: Measures include 24-hour foot and vehicle patrol, informal discussions, pamphlets/posters/films, and emergency telephones. There are lighted pathways/sidewalks and crime-prevention education programs.

Programs of Study: WCU confers B.A., B.S., B.F.A., B.S.B.A., B.S.Ed., and B.S.N. degrees. Master's and doctoral degrees are also awarded. Bachelor's degrees are awarded in AGRICULTURE (natural resource management), BIOLOGICAL SCIENCE (biology/biological science, environmental biology, and nutrition), BUSINESS (accounting, banking and finance, business law, hospitality management services, international business management, management science, marketing and distribution, marketing management, and sports management), COMMUNICATIONS AND THE ARTS (art, communications, dramatic arts, English, French, German, music, Spanish, speech/debate/rhetoric, and studio art), COMPUTER AND PHYSICAL SCIENCE (chemistry, computer science, geology, information sciences and systems, mathematics, and physics), EDUCATION (art, early childhood, elementary, English, foreign languages, mathematics, middle school, music, physical, science, secondary, social science, special, and speech correction), ENGINEERING AND ENVIRONMENTAL DESIGN (electrical/electronics engineering technology, engineering technology, industrial engineering technology, interior design, manufacturing technology, and preengineering), HEALTH PROFESSIONS (clinical science, emergency medical technologies, environmental health science, health care administration, medical records administration/services, nursing, predentistry, premedicine, preoptometry, prepharmacy, preveterinary science, and recreation therapy), SOCIAL SCIENCE (anthropology, child care/child and family studies, criminal justice, dietetics, economics, geography, history, parks and recreation management, philosophy, political science/government, prelaw, psychology, social science, social work, and sociology). Elementary education, computer information systems, and nursing are the largest.

Required: In order to graduate, students must complete a total of 120 to 128 credit hours with a minimum GPA of 2.0. Between 30 and 64 hours are required in the major. All students must fulfill liberal studies requirements in writing, oral communication, wellness, social sciences, physical and biological sciences, math, humanities, history, fine and performing arts, world cultures, the Freshman Seminar, and 1 course in upper-level perspectives outside the major.

Special: WCU offers cooperative education programs in most majors, extensive internship opportunities, work-study programs, accelerated degree programs, B.A.-B.S. degrees, dual majors, a special studies degree, nondegree study, pass/fail options in designated courses, and credit for life experience. Study-abroad programs may be arranged in 35 countries. There are 15 national honor societies and a freshman honors program.

Faculty/Classroom: 59% of faculty are male; 41%, female. 93% teach undergraduates. Graduate students teach 5% of introductory courses. The average class size in an introductory lecture is 29; in a laboratory, 20; and in a regular course, 24.

Admissions: 73% of the 2001-2002 applicants were accepted. The SAT I scores for the 2001-2002 freshman class were: Verbal--50% below 500, 38% between 500 and 599, 10% between 600 and 700, and 2% above 700; Math--48% below 500, 40% between 500 and 599, 11% between 600 and 700, and 1% above 700. 20% of the current freshmen were in the top fifth of their class; 45% were in the top two fifths. There were 4 National Merit finalists and 1 semifinalist. 3 freshmen graduated first in their class.

Requirements: The SAT I or ACT is required; the SAT I is preferred. Graduation from an accredited secondary school or the GED is required. High school courses must include 4 units of English, 3 each of math and science, and 2 of social studies, including 1 of U.S. history. 2 units of a foreign language are recommended. WCU requires applicants to be in the upper 25% of their class. A GPA of 2.5 is required. AP and CLEP credits are accepted. Important factors in the admissions decision are advanced placement or honor courses, recommendations by school officials, and evidence of special talent. Applications may be submitted on-line.

Procedure: Freshmen are admitted to all sessions. Entrance exams should be taken during the spring of the junior year or the fall of the senior year. There is an early admissions plan. Applications should be filed by July 15 for fall entry, December 10 for spring entry, and May 1 for summer entry. The fall 2001 application fee was $25. Notification is sent on a rolling basis.

Transfer: 558 transfer students enrolled in 2001-2002. Tranfer students must have a minimum GPA of 2.0 and meet freshman admissions requirements. 30 to 32 credits of 120 to 128 must be completed at WCU.

Visiting: There are regularly scheduled orientations for prospective students, consisting of open houses, 1 in fall, 1 in spring, which include registration, a visit to the department of choice, a campus tour, and an athletic event. There are guides for informal visits and visitors may sit in on classes and stay overnight. To schedule a visit, contact the Admissions Office.

Financial Aid: In 2001-2002, 64% of all freshmen and 69% of continuing students received some form of financial aid. 38% of freshmen and 43% of continuing students received need-based aid. The average freshman award was $6604. Of that total, scholarships or need-based grants averaged $3828 ($14,107 maximum); loans averaged $3085 ($6625 maximum); and work contracts averaged $1332 ($1400 maximum). 30% of undergraduates work part time. Average annual earnings from campus work are $1013. The average financial indebtedness of the 2001 graduate was $15,183. The FAFSA is required. The fall application deadline is April 1.

International Students: There are 44 international students enrolled. The school actively recruits these students. They must score 550 on the written TOEFL or 213 on the electronic version and also take the SAT I.

Computers: The mainframes are 2 DEC VAX 4000/700As, 1 DEC ALPHA 4100, and 1 DEC ALPHA 1000. 10 electronic classrooms are located in 5 classroom buildings. A number of classrooms also contain computer teaching stations. There are also more than 4800 PCs in computer labs, the library, the learning centers, dorm rooms, and faculty and staff offices. All buildings and dorms are wired for network access. All students are required to have a networkable computer with at least a 500-MHz processor. All students may access the system 24 hours a day. There are no time limits and no fees.

Graduates: In 2001, 1042 bachelor's degrees were awarded. The most popular majors were elementary education (7%), nursing (7%), and marketing (7%). In an average class, 1% graduate in 3 years, 22% in 4 years, 40% in 5 years, and 45% in 6 years. 307 companies recruited on campus in 2000-2001.

Admissions Contact: Phil Couley, Admissions Officer.
E-mail: *admiss@email.wcu.edu* Web: *www.admissions.wcu.edu*

WINGATE UNIVERSITY
Wingate, NC 28174

C-3
(704) 233-8200
(800) 755-5550; Fax: (704) 233-8110

Full-time: 573 men, 640 women	**Faculty:** 80; IIB, --$
Part-time: 13 men, 29 women	**Ph.D.s:** 100%
Graduate: 44 men, 58 women	**Student/Faculty:** 15 to 1
Year: semesters, summer session	**Tuition:** $13,680
Application Deadline: open	**Room & Board:** $5460
Freshman Class: 1245 applied, 991 accepted, 396 enrolled	
SAT I Verbal/Math: 510/520	**ACT:** 20 **COMPETITIVE**

Wingate University, founded in 1896, is a private liberal arts institution affiliated with the Baptist State Convention of North Carolina. There are 3 undergraduate and 2 graduate schools. In addition to regional accreditation, Wingate has baccalaureate program accreditation with ACBSP, NASM, and NCATE. The library contains 110,000 volumes, 14,000 microform items, and 5750 audiovisual forms/CDs, and subscribes to 560 periodicals. Computerized library services include the card catalog, interlibrary loans, and database searching. Special learning facilities include a learning resource center, art gallery, and TV station. The 330-acre campus is in a small town 25 miles east of Charlotte. Including residence halls, there are 35 buildings.

Student Life: 59% of undergraduates are from North Carolina. Others are from 35 states, 18 foreign countries, and Canada. 90% are from public schools. 81% are white; 11%, African American. 67% are Protestant; 15%, Catholic; 12% claim no religious affiliation. The average age of freshmen is 18; all undergraduates, 20. 28% do not continue beyond their first year; 43% remain to graduate.

Housing: 1015 students can be accommodated in college housing, which includes single-sex dormitories, on-campus apartments, off-campus apartments, married-student housing, and fraternity houses. In addition, there are honors houses. On-campus housing is guaranteed for all 4 years. 81% of students live on campus; of those, 60% remain on campus on weekends. Alcohol is not permitted. All students may keep cars.

Activities: 9% of men belong to 4 national fraternities; 10% of women belong to 2 national sororities. There are 35 groups on campus, including art, band, cheerleading, choir, chorale, chorus, computers, dance, drama, ethnic, honors, international, jazz band, literary magazine, marching band, musical theater, newspaper, orchestra, pep band, photography, political, professional, radio and TV, religious, running, social, social service, student government, swimming, and yearbook. Popular campus events include Spring Fling and Fall Festival at Campus Lake, and name-band concerts.

Sports: There are 8 intercollegiate sports for men and 8 for women, and 17 intramural sports for men and 17 for women. Facilities include an athletic complex with a gym, a swimming pool, racquetball courts, a weight room, and tennis courts, and a student center with bowling, table tennis, a pool, and a game room.

Disabled Students: 95% of the campus is accessible. Wheelchair ramps, elevators, special parking, specially equipped rest rooms, special class scheduling, and lowered drinking fountains are available.

Services: Counseling and information services are available, as is tutoring in every subject, and additional academic support is available for students with learning disabilities.

Campus Safety and Security: Measures include 24-hour foot and vehicle patrol, self-defense education, escort service, and informal discussions. There are pamphlets/posters/films, emergency telephones, and lighted pathways/sidewalks.

Programs of Study: Wingate confers B.A., B.S., B.F.A., B.L.S., and B.M.Ed. degrees. Master's degrees are also awarded. Bachelor's degrees are awarded in BIOLOGICAL SCIENCE (biology/biological science), BUSINESS (accounting, banking and finance, business administration and management, business economics, management information systems, marketing/retailing/merchandising, and sports management), COMMUNICATIONS AND THE ARTS (art, communications, English, fine arts, music, music business management, and Spanish), COMPUTER AND PHYSICAL SCIENCE (applied mathematics, chemistry, computer mathematics, and mathematics), EDUCATION (art, athletic training, elementary, English, mathematics, middle school, music, physical, reading, and science), ENGINEERING AND ENVIRONMENTAL DESIGN (preengineering), HEALTH PROFESSIONS (predentistry, premedicine, prepharmacy, preveterinary science, and sports medicine), SOCIAL SCIENCE (American studies, economics, history, human services, law, liberal arts/general studies, parks and recreation management, philosophy, prelaw, psychology, religion, and sociology). Biological sciences, history, and English are the strongest academically. Business, athletic training, and communications are the largest.

Required: To graduate, students must complete a minimum of 125 credit hours with a GPA of 2.0. At least 30 hours must be completed in the student's major. All students must take core courses in English composition, literature, religion, fine arts, history, social sciences, foreign language, math, lab science, fitness and wellness, phys ed, and freshman experience.

Special: Cross-registration through the Charlotte Area Education Consortium, internships, a liberal studies degree, B.A.-B.S. degrees, and nondegree study are available. A 3-2 engineering degree is offered with North Carolina State University, Clemson University, and Virginia Polytechnic Institute. Wingate conducts foreign study semesters in London, Denmark, and China. The school also sponsors Winternational, a semester seminar with a 10-day trip to a foreign country for which students earn academic credit at little personal cost. Dual majors are offered in biology and education, history and education, art and education, English and education, math and education, and chemistry and business. There are 9 national honor societies and a freshman honors program.

Faculty/Classroom: 57% of faculty are male; 43%, female. All teach undergraduates. No introductory courses are taught by graduate students. The average class size in an introductory lecture is 26; in a laboratory, 15; and in a regular course, 13.

Admissions: 80% of the 2001-2002 applicants were accepted. The SAT I scores for the 2001-2002 freshman class were: Verbal--42% below 500, 45% between 500 and 599, 11% between 600 and 700, and 2% above 700; Math--39% below 500, 43% between 500 and 599, 16% between 600 and 700, and 2% above 700. The ACT scores were 54% below 21, 13% between 21 and 23, 23% between 24 and 26, and 7% above 28. 32% of the current freshmen were in the top fifth of their class; 60% were in the top two fifths. 3 freshmen graduated first in their class.

Requirements: The SAT I or ACT is required. In addition, graduation from an accredited secondary school or the GED is required. High school curriculum must include 4 courses in English, 3 in math, 2 each in history and science, and 1 in social studies. 2 courses in a foreign language are recommended. An essay is required of all applicants, and an interview is recommended in some cases. A GPA of 2.7 is required. AP and CLEP credits are accepted. Important factors in the admissions decision are advanced placement or honor courses, leadership record, and recommendations by school officials. Applications are accepted on-line.

Procedure: Freshmen are admitted fall, spring, and summer. Entrance exams should be taken in spring of the junior year or fall of the senior year. There is an early decision plan. The application fee is $25. Notification is sent on a rolling basis. 35 early decision candidates were accepted for the 2001-2002 class.

Transfer: 54 transfer students enrolled in 2001-2002. Applicants must have a minimum GPA of 2.0 and must be eligible to return to the institution last attended. The SAT I or ACT is required if a student has been out of high school for less than 5 years or has fewer than 24 transferable hours. An interview may be recommended in some cases. 30 credits of 125 must be completed at Wingate.

Visiting: There are regularly scheduled orientations for prospective students, including Saturday Preview Day 4 times a year, campus tours and presentations of travel programs, academic life, athletics, and student life. New student orientation occurs 4 days prior to opening of school each fall. There are guides for informal visits and visitors may sit in on classes and stay overnight. To schedule a visit, contact the Admissions Office at (704) 233-8201.

Financial Aid: In 2001-2002, 95% of all freshmen and 88% of continuing students received some form of financial aid. 22% of freshmen and 33% of continuing students received need-based aid. The average freshman award was $7800. Of that total, scholarships or need-based grants averaged $6150; and loans averaged $3500. 44% of undergraduates work part time. Average annual earnings from campus work are $1200. The average financial indebtedness of the 2001 graduate was $24,000. The FAFSA is required. The fall application deadline is May 1.

International Students: There are 31 international students enrolled. They must score 550 on the written TOEFL and also take the SAT I or the ACT.

Computers: The mainframe is an HP 3000. PCs are available in labs and offices. All students may access the system 8 A.M. to 11 p.m Sunday to Thursday. There are no time limits and no fees.

Graduates: In 2001, 210 bachelor's degrees were awarded. The most popular majors were business administration (22%), sport management (8%), and athletic training (6%). In an average class, 29% graduate in 4 years, 41% in 5 years, and 42% in 6 years. 45 companies recruited on campus in 2000-2001. Of the 2000 graduating class, 20% were enrolled in graduate school within 6 months of graduation and 80% were employed.

Admissions Contact: Walter Crutchfield, Dean of Admissions.
E-mail: *admit@wingate.edu* Web: *www.wingate.edu*

WINSTON-SALEM STATE UNIVERSITY C-2

Winston-Salem, NC 27110 (336) 750-2070
(800) 257-4052; Fax: (336) 750-2079

Full-time: 773 men, 1653 women	**Faculty:** 176; IIB, +$
Part-time: 161 men, 375 women	**Ph.D.s:** 67%
Graduate: 5 men, 25 women	**Student/Faculty:** 14 to 1
Year: semesters, summer session	**Tuition:** $2063 ($8491)
Application Deadline: open	**Room & Board:** $1932
Freshman Class: 1914 applied, 1451 accepted, 624 enrolled	
SAT I Verbal/Math: 420/420	**LESS COMPETITIVE**

Winston-Salem State University, founded in 1892, is a state-supported liberal arts institution offering undergraduate programs through divisions of arts and sciences, business and economics, education, and nursing and allied health. In addition to regional accreditation, WSSU has baccalaureate program accreditation with NASM, NCATE, and NLN. The library contains 196,168 volumes, 195,003 microform items, and 20,000 audiovisual forms/CDs, and subscribes to 1010 periodicals. Computerized library services include the card catalog, interlibrary loans, and database searching. Special learning facilities include a learning resource center, art gallery, radio station, TV station, Plato laboratory, and an enrichment center. The 94-acre campus is in a suburban area in Winston-Salem. Including residence halls, there are 36 buildings.

Student Life: 93% of undergraduates are from North Carolina. Others are from 30 states. 82% are African American; 15% white. The average age of all undergraduates is 24. 23% do not continue beyond their first year; 10% remain to graduate.

Housing: 1228 students can be accommodated in college housing, which includes single-sex and coed dormitories. On-campus housing is guaranteed for the freshman year only and is available on a first-come, first-served basis. 59% of students commute. Alcohol is not permitted. All students may keep cars.

Activities: There are 70 groups on campus, including art, band, cheerleading, choir, computers, dance, drama, drill team, ethnic, honors, international, jazz band, marching band, newspaper, photography, political, radio and TV, social, student government, and yearbook.

Sports: There are 4 intercollegiate sports for men and 5 for women. Facilities include 2 gyms, tennis courts, an indoor swimming pool, and a track.

Disabled Students: 90% of the campus is accessible. Wheelchair ramps, elevators, special parking, specially equipped rest rooms, lowered drinking fountains, and lowered telephones are available.

Services: Counseling and information services are available, as is tutoring in most subjects. There is remedial math, reading, and writing.

Campus Safety and Security: Measures include 24-hour foot and vehicle patrol, informal discussions, pamphlets/posters/films, and emergency telephones. There are lighted pathways/sidewalks.

Programs of Study: WSSU confers B.A., B.S., B.S.App.Sci., B.S.Med.Tech., B.S.N., and B.S.P.T. degrees. Master's degrees are also awarded. Bachelor's degrees are awarded in BIOLOGICAL SCIENCE (biology/biological science), BUSINESS (accounting, business administration and management, management information systems, and sports management), COMMUNICATIONS AND THE ARTS (art, communications, English, music business management, and Spanish), COMPUTER AND PHYSICAL SCIENCE (chemistry, computer science, and mathematics), EDUCATION (elementary, music, physical, and special), HEALTH PROFESSIONS (medical technology, nursing, physical therapy, and recreation therapy), SOCIAL SCIENCE (economics, history, political science/government, psychology, public administration, and sociology). Phys ed, computer science, and math are the strongest academically. Nursing, business administration, and education are the largest.

Required: Students must complete a minimum of 120 semester hours, with 40 of these hours in upper-level courses, and must maintain an overall minimum GPA of 2.0. All students must also complete the general education core requirement, which includes courses in English composition, social sciences, math and natural sciences, humanities, and phys ed or military science.

Special: Opportunities are provided for cooperative programs, internships, work-study programs, a B.A.-B.S. degree, a general studies degree, and credit for military experience. The nursing division offers flexible scheduling for employed RNs. There is a freshman honors program.

Faculty/Classroom: 46% of faculty are male; 54%, female. All teach undergraduates. The average class size in a laboratory is 25 and in a regular course, 42.

Admissions: 76% of the 2001-2002 applicants were accepted.

Requirements: The SAT I or ACT is required, a minimum composite score of 700 on the SAT I is recommended. Graduation from an accredited secondary school is required; a GED will be accepted. Applicants should submit an academic record including 4 credits in English, 3 each in math and science, 2 in a foreign language, and 1 each in U.S. history, social studies, and phys ed and health. A GPA of 2.0 is required. AP and CLEP credits are accepted. Important factors in the admissions decision are advanced placement or honor courses, leadership record, and recommendations by school officials.

Procedure: Freshmen are admitted to all sessions. Entrance exams should be taken in the summer or early fall of the senior year in high school. There are early admissions and deferred admissions plans. Application deadlines are open.

Transfer: 245 transfer students enrolled in 2001-2002. Transfer applicants must submit official transcripts from all colleges previously attended, showing no grade lower than C. No more than 64 semester hours (96 quarter hours) will be accepted for transfer. Those applicants transferring fewer than 29 credits will be admitted as freshmen and must meet all freshmen admission requirements. 30 credits of 120 must be completed at WSSU.

Visiting: There are regularly scheduled orientations for prospective students, including summer and fall orientation. There are guides for informal visits and visitors may sit in on classes. To schedule a visit, contact Gilbert Wright in the Admissions Office at *wrightg@wssu.edu*.

Financial Aid: In a recent year, 76% of all freshmen and 70% of continuing students received some form of financial aid. 51% of continuing students received need-based aid. The average freshman award was $3125. Of that total, scholarships or need-based grants averaged $2300 ($3300 maximum); loans averaged $1100 ($2700 maximum). All undergraduates work part-time. Average annual earnings from campus work are $1125. The CSS/Profile or FFS and the college's own financial statement are required.

International Students: They must score 540 on the written TOEFL.

Computers: The academic computer center maintains a DEC VAX 11/750 with 20 terminals and 2 on-line printers. All students may access the system. There are no time limits. The $20 fee is included in tuition.

Graduates: In 2001, 518 bachelor's degrees were awarded. The most popular majors were nursing (26%), business administration (11%), and psychology (8%). In an average class, 16% graduate in 4 years, 32% in 5 years, and 37% in 6 years.

Admissions Contact: Ms. Patrice Mitchell, Associate Director of Enrollment Management. A video is available.
E-mail: *mitchellp@wssu.edu* Web: *www.wssu.edu*

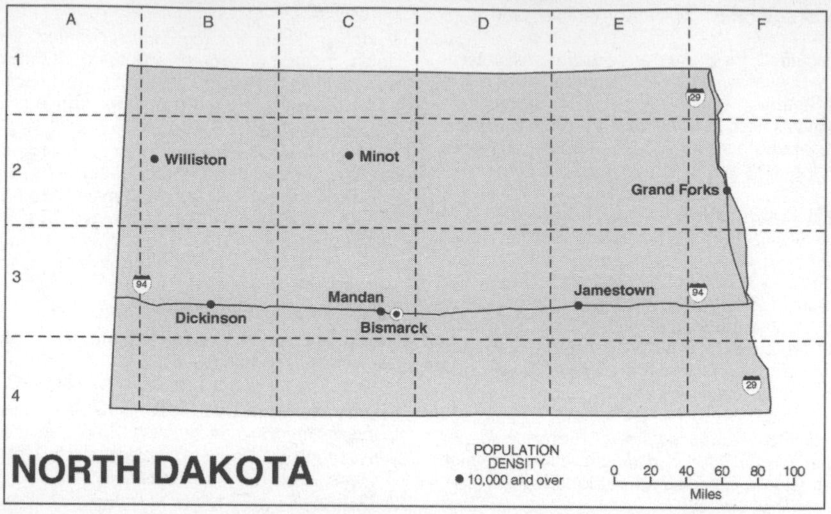

DICKINSON STATE UNIVERSITY

B-3

Dickinson, ND 58601-4896

(701) 483-2175

(800) 279-4295; Fax: (701) 483-2006

Full-time: 690 men, 822 women
Part-time: 213 men, 376 women
Graduate: none
Year: semesters, summer session
Application Deadline: August 15
Faculty: 72; IIB, --$
Ph.D.s: 75%
Student/Faculty: 21 to 1
Tuition: $2463 ($5915)
Room & Board: $3032
Freshman Class: 585 applied, 585 accepted, 417 enrolled
SAT I or ACT: required

NONCOMPETITIVE

Dickinson State University is a public, regional institution offering undergraduate programs in teacher education, the liberal arts, business, health sciences, agriculture, and computer science. There is opportunity for preprofessional study and vocational training in selected areas. There are 2 undergraduate schools. In addition to regional accreditation, DSU has baccalaureate program accreditation with NCATE and NLN. The library contains 81,945 volumes, 37,200 microform items, and 2760 audiovisual forms/CDs, and subscribes to 700 periodicals. Computerized library services include the card catalog, interlibrary loans, and database searching. Special learning facilities include a learning resource center and art gallery. The 100-acre campus is in a rural area 100 miles west of Bismarck. Including residence halls, there are 15 buildings.

Student Life: 75% of undergraduates are from North Dakota. Others are from 26 states, 13 foreign countries, and Canada. 95% are from public schools. 95% are white. 50% are Catholic; 50%, Protestant. The average age of freshmen is 19; all undergraduates, 22. 2% do not continue beyond their first year; 28% remain to graduate.

Housing: 478 students can be accommodated in college housing, which includes single-sex and coed dormitories and married-student housing. In addition, there are honors houses. On-campus housing is guaranteed for the freshman year only and is available on a first-come, first-served basis. 70% of students commute. Alcohol is not permitted. All students may keep cars.

Activities: There are no fraternities or sororities. There are 38 groups on campus, including art, band, cheerleading, choir, chorale, chorus, computers, dance, drama, forensics, honors, international, jazz band, literary magazine, marching band, musical theater, newspaper, pep band, political, professional, religious, social, student government, and yearbook. Popular campus events include Winter, Spring, and Back to School Weeks, and Family Weekend.

Sports: There are 9 intercollegiate sports for men and 8 for women, and 5 intramural sports for men and 3 for women. Facilities include a gym, an outdoor stadium, an indoor/outdoor rodeo arena, and an indoor track.

Disabled Students: 90% of the campus is accessible. Wheelchair ramps, elevators, special parking, specially equipped rest rooms, and special class scheduling are available.

Services: Counseling and information services are available, as is tutoring in every subject. There is a reader service for the blind, and remedial math, reading, and writing.

Campus Safety and Security: Measures include pamphlets/posters/films, lighted pathways/sidewalks, and 10-hour-a-day security.

Programs of Study: DSU confers B.A., B.S., B.S.E., B.S.N., and B.U.S. degrees. Associate degrees are also awarded. Bachelor's degrees are awarded in AGRICULTURE (agricultural business management), BIOLOGICAL SCIENCE (biology/biological science), BUSINESS (accounting, business administration and management, and personnel management), COMMUNICATIONS AND THE ARTS (communications, English, fine arts, journalism, music, Spanish, and speech/debate/rhetoric), COMPUTER AND PHYSICAL SCIENCE (chemistry, computer programming, computer science, earth science, and mathematics), EDUCATION (art, business, early childhood, elementary, middle school, music, science, and secondary), HEALTH PROFESSIONS (nursing), SOCIAL SCIENCE (geography, history, political science/government, social work, and sociology). Elementary education, math, and business are the strongest academically. Education, business, and nursing are the largest.

Required: To graduate, students must complete 128 semester hours, 36 in the major, with a minimum GPA of 2.0. General education requirements include 10 hours in scientific inquiry, including 1 computer science course, 9 hours each in expressions of human civilizations, understanding human civilization, and communication, and 2 hours in phys ed.

Special: DSU offers a co-op program in social work with the University of North Dakota and in agriculture with North Dakota State University. An additional co-op program exists with Bismarck State College. Cross-registration is available within the North Dakota University System. Internships in business and social work, credit for life experience, and pass/fail options are available. Student-designed majors are possible through the Bachelor of University Studies program. There are 5 national honor societies, including Phi Beta Kappa, and a freshman honors program.

Faculty/Classroom: 75% of faculty are male; 25%, female. All teach undergraduates. The average class size in an introductory lecture is 40; in a laboratory, 25; and in a regular course, 20.

Admissions: All of the 2001-2002 applicants were accepted.

Requirements: The SAT I or ACT is required; the ACT is preferred. Graduation from an accredited secondary school is recommended. The GED is accepted. Students must have 20 academic credits. An essay is not required. AP and CLEP credits are accepted. Applications are accepted on-line.

Procedure: Freshmen are admitted to all sessions. Entrance exams should be taken in the spring before fall entrance. Applications should be filed by August 15 for fall entry, January 1 for spring entry, and May 15 for summer entry, along with a $35 fee. The college accepts all applicants. Notification is sent on a rolling basis.

Transfer: 157 transfer students enrolled in a recent year. Transfer students must have a minimum GPA of 2.0. The ACT is preferred, but applicants may submit SAT I scores. 32 credits of 128 must be completed at DSU.

Visiting: There are regularly scheduled orientations for prospective students, consisting of 2 2-day orientations and 2 1-day sessions in July and August. There are guides for informal visits and visitors may sit in on classes and stay overnight. To schedule a visit, contact the Office of Admissions and Academic Records.

Financial Aid: In 2001-2002, 77% of all students received some form of financial aid. 78% of all students received need-based aid. The average freshman award was $3710. Of that total, scholarships or need-based grants averaged $3001 ($8795 maximum); loans averaged $3032 ($6625 maximum); and work contracts averaged $1565 ($4154 maximum). 55% of undergraduates work part time. Average annual earnings from campus work are $1229. The average financial indebtedness of the 2001 graduate was $10,000. The FAFSA is required. The fall application deadline is March 15.

International Students: There are 50 international students enrolled. The school actively recruits these students. They must score 525 on the written TOEFL or 195 on the electronic version and also take the ACT.

Computers: The mainframe is an IBM AS/400. There are 125 PCs available in May Hall and in the residence halls. All students may access the system. There are no time limits and no fees.

Graduates: In 2001, 273 bachelor's degrees were awarded. The most popular majors were teacher education (46%), business administration (18%), and nursing (7%).

Admissions Contact: Marshall Melbye, Director of Admissions and Academic Records. E-mail: *dsu.hawk@dsu.nodak.edu*
Web: *www.dickinsonstate.com*

JAMESTOWN COLLEGE — E-3

Jamestown, ND 58405 — (701) 252-3467, ext. 2548
(800) 336-2554; Fax: (701) 253-4318

Full-time: 464 men, 595 women	**Faculty:** 55; IIB, --$
Part-time: 32 men, 47 women	**Ph.D.s:** 51%
Graduate: none	**Student/Faculty:** 19 to 1
Year: semesters, summer session	**Tuition:** $7925
Application Deadline: open	**Room & Board:** $3385
Freshman Class: 1099 applied, 1090 accepted, 293 enrolled	
ACT: 22	**NONCOMPETITIVE**

Jamestown College, founded in 1883, is a private, nonprofit institution affiliated with the Presbyterian Church (U.S.A.). Its emphases are on the liberal arts, business, arts, health science, music, religious studies, and teacher preparation. In addition to regional accreditation, Jamestown College has baccalaureate program accreditation with NLN. The library contains 120,360 volumes, 9365 microform items, and 2722 audiovisual forms/CDs, and subscribes to 446 periodicals. Computerized library services include the card catalog, interlibrary loans, and database searching. Special learning facilities include a learning resource center and art gallery. The 107-acre campus is in a small town 100 miles west of Fargo. Including residence halls, there are 22 buildings.

Student Life: 65% of undergraduates are from North Dakota. Others are from 29 states, 16 foreign countries, and Canada. 98% are from public schools. 94% are white. 31% are Protestant; 23% claim no religious affiliation; 22% are Catholic. The average age of freshmen is 18; all undergraduates, 22. 27% do not continue beyond their first year; 46% remain to graduate.

Housing: 750 students can be accommodated in college housing, which includes coed dormitories and on-campus apartments. In addition, there are honors houses. On-campus housing is guaranteed for the freshman year only, is available on a first-come, first-served basis, and is available on a lottery system for upperclassmen. 60% of students live on campus; of those, 65% remain on campus on weekends. Alcohol is not permitted. All students may keep cars.

Activities: There are no fraternities or sororities. There are 34 groups on campus, including art, band, cheerleading, choir, chorale, chorus, computers, drama, drill team, honors, international, jazz band, literary magazine, musical theater, newspaper, pep band, political, professional, religious, social, social service, student government, and yearbook. Popular campus events include Foreign Language Week, Family Weekend, and Winter Carnival.

Sports: There are 8 intercollegiate sports for men and 8 for women, and 6 intramural sports for men and 6 for women. Facilities include an athletics center with a basketball court and wrestling practice area; a football stadium with an all-weather track; a soccer field; and a sports center with a swimming pool, weight room, running track, YMCA, and basketball, handball, and racquetball courts. Nearby facilities include a civic arena, softball field, baseball stadium, swimming pool, tennis courts, municipal golf course, and winter sports complex.

Disabled Students: 30% of the campus is accessible. Wheelchair ramps, elevators, special parking, specially equipped rest rooms, special class scheduling, lowered drinking fountains, and lowered telephones are available.

Services: Counseling and information services are available, as is tutoring in most subjects. There is remedial math, reading, and writing.

Campus Safety and Security: Measures include escort service, informal discussions, pamphlets/posters/films, and lighted pathways/sidewalks.

Programs of Study: Jamestown College confers B.A., B.S., and B.S.N. degrees. Bachelor's degrees are awarded in BIOLOGICAL SCIENCE (biochemistry and biology/biological science), BUSINESS (accounting and business administration and management), COMMUNICATIONS AND THE ARTS (communications, English, fine arts, and music), COMPUTER AND PHYSICAL SCIENCE (chemistry, computer science, information sciences and systems, mathematics, and radiological technology), EDUCATION (elementary and physical), HEALTH PROFESSIONS (clinical science and nursing), SOCIAL SCIENCE (criminal justice, history, philosophy, political science/government, psychology, and religion). Business, nursing, and physical sciences are the strongest academically. Business and nursing are the largest.

Required: To graduate, students must have a minimum of 128 semester credits, at least 48 of which must be at the upper-division level, with an average of 48 semester credits in the major. They must maintain at least a 2.0 GPA. General education requirements include 47 to 56 credits, based on degree sought, in the areas of moral and civic education, communication skills, cultural and social heritage, natural science and quantitative reasoning, and phys ed.

Special: Special academic options include co-op programs in business, nursing, computer science, and criminal justice, on-campus work-study, internships, study abroad, dual majors within any of the concentrations, student-designed majors, nondegree study, pass/fail options, and credit for life, military, and work experience. Directed study is also possible. There are preprofessional programs in law, health-related fields, and engineering, including a 3-2 engineering program with North Dakota and South Dakota State Universities and the University of North Dakota. Teacher certification may be earned in secondary education. There are 2 national honor societies, and 10 departmental honors programs.

Faculty/Classroom: 56% of faculty are male; 44%, female. All teach undergraduates. The average class size in an introductory lecture is 35; in a laboratory, 20; and in a regular course, 24.

Admissions: 99% of the 2001-2002 applicants were accepted. The ACT scores for the 2001-2002 freshman class were 39% below 21, 24% between 21 and 23, 20% between 24 and 26, 9% between 27 and 28, and 8% above 28. 34% of the current freshmen were in the top fifth of their class; 59% were in the top two fifths.

Requirements: The ACT is recommended. Admissions requirements include graduation from an accredited secondary school; the GED is also accepted. An interview is highly recommended. Jamestown College requires applicants to be in the upper 50% of their class. A GPA of 2.5 is required. AP and CLEP credits are accepted. Important factors in the admissions decision are evidence of special talent, extracurricular activities record, and leadership record. Applications are accepted on computer disk or on-line via the school's web site or *anycollege.net*.

Procedure: Freshmen are admitted to all sessions. Entrance exams should be taken before or during the fall of the senior year. There is a deferred admissions plan. Application deadlines are open. The application fee is $20. Notification is sent on a rolling basis, within a week of receipt of an application.

Transfer: 51 transfer students enrolled in 2001-2002. Applicants must have at least a 2.5 GPA and be in good standing with their previous college; if suspended, the student must allow 1 semester to elapse before applying for probationary admission. 35 credits of 128 must be completed at Jamestown College.

Visiting: There are guides for informal visits and visitors may sit in on classes and stay overnight. To schedule a visit, contact the Admissions Office at *admissions@jc.edu*.

Financial Aid: In 2001-2002, of all freshmen and 98% of continuing students received some form of financial aid. 71% of freshmen and 74% of continuing students received need-based aid. The average freshman award was $8409. Of that total, scholarships or need-based grants averaged $5311 ($7925 maximum); loans averaged $2273 ($6000 maximum); and work contracts averaged $825 ($3500 maximum). 36% of undergraduates work part time. Average annual earnings from campus work are $825. The average financial indebtedness of the 2001 graduate was $17,675. Jamestown College is a member of CSS. The FAFSA is required. The fall application deadline is August 1.

International Students: There are 40 international students enrolled. The school actively recruits these students. They must score 525 on the written TOEFL or 197 on the electronic version.

Computers: The mainframes are 7 Compaq Proliant 1600s and 1 Compaq Proliant 6000. There are PCs available in the computer center, labs, college library, faculty offices, and residence halls. All 575 computers are networked and have Internet access. Every residence hall room has a Compaq 154 and printer. All students may access the system 24 hours a day. There are no time limits and no fees.

Graduates: In 2001, 193 bachelor's degrees were awarded. The most popular majors were business (25%), elementary education (16%), and nursing (13%). In an average class, 24% graduate in 4 years, 36% in 5 years, and 39% in 6 years. 22 companies recruited on campus in 2000-2001. Of the 2000 graduating class, 5% were enrolled in graduate school within 6 months of graduation and 79% were employed.

Admissions Contact: Judy Erickson, Director of Admissions.
E-mail: *admissions@jc.edu* Web: *www.jc.edu*

MAYVILLE STATE UNIVERSITY

Mayville, ND 58257-1299 E-3
(701) 786-4768
(800) 437-4104; Fax: (701) 786-4748

Full-time: 294 men, 285 women
Part-time: 52 men, 124 women
Graduate: none
Year: semesters, summer session
Application Deadline: open
Freshman Class: 202 applied, 201 accepted, 144 enrolled
ACT: 20
Faculty: 32; IIB, --$
Ph.D.s: 47%
Student/Faculty: 18 to 1
Tuition: $3314 ($6766)
Room & Board: $3126
NONCOMPETITIVE

Mayville State University, founded in 1889, is a public institution that emphasizes teacher education, business, and information technology. There are 5 undergraduate schools. In addition to regional accreditation, Mayville State has baccalaureate program accreditation with NCATE. The library contains 71,595 volumes and 12,530 microform items, and subscribes to 599 periodicals. Computerized library services include the card catalog, interlibrary loans, and database searching. Special learning facilities include a learning resource center, art gallery, and a learning services center. The 55-acre campus is in a rural area 58 miles north of Fargo and 42 miles south of Grand Forks. Including residence halls, there are 19 buildings.

Student Life: 63% of undergraduates are from North Dakota. Others are from 15 states, 2 foreign countries, and Canada. 94% are from public schools. 93% are white. 70% are Protestant; 29% Catholic. The average age of freshmen is 18. 40% do not continue beyond their first year; 35% remain to graduate.

Housing: 410 students can be accommodated in college housing, which includes single-sex and coed dormitories, on-campus apartments, and married-student housing. On-campus housing is guaranteed for the freshman year only and is available on a first-come, first-served basis. 70% of students commute. Alcohol is not permitted. All students may keep cars.

Activities: There are no fraternities or sororities. There are 17 groups on campus, including choir, chorus, computers, debate, drama, ethnic, forensics, musical theater, political, professional, religious, student government, and yearbook. Popular campus events include Spring Fling.

Sports: There are 3 intercollegiate sports for men and 3 for women, and 10 intramural sports for men and 9 for women. Facilities include a 4500-seat football stadium, a track and practice field, a baseball diamond, tennis courts, a swimming pool, and handball and racquetball courts.

Disabled Students: 75% of the campus is accessible. Elevators, special parking, special class scheduling, lowered drinking fountains, and lowered telephones are available.

Services: Counseling and information services are available, as is tutoring in some subjects, including writing, math, reading, and study skills. There is remedial math and writing.

Campus Safety and Security: Measures include informal discussions, pamphlets/posters/films, lighted pathways/sidewalks, and a nighttime foot patrol.

Programs of Study: Mayville State confers B.A., B.S., B.G.S., and B.S.Ed. degrees. Associate degrees are also awarded. Bachelor's degrees are awarded in BIOLOGICAL SCIENCE (biology/biological science), BUSINESS (business administration and management, and office supervision and management), COMMUNICATIONS AND THE ARTS (English), COMPUTER AND PHYSICAL SCIENCE (chemistry, computer programming, mathematics, physical sciences, and science), EDUCATION (business, elementary, health, physical, science, and secondary), SOCIAL SCIENCE (liberal arts/general studies, and social science). Business administration, computer information science, and elementary education are the strongest academically. Business administration and elementary education are the largest.

Required: To graduate, students must complete 128 semester hours with a minimum overall GPA of 2.0 in most programs and 2.5 in education. General requirements include 8 to 10 quarter hours of science, 9 each of humanities and social science, 6 of English, up to 3 of math, and 3 each of computer information systems, psychology, speech, and phys ed.

Special: Through a reciprocity program, residents of all contiguous states and Canadian provinces pay a considerably reduced out-of-state fee. Mayville State also offers preprofessional programs, internships, work-study programs, B.A.-B.S. degrees, dual majors, a general studies degree, credit for life experience, nondegree study, and pass/fail options. Co-op programs are available, including a certified education program for all subject areas. There is also a K-8 math specialist program. There is 1 national honor society.

Faculty/Classroom: 64% of faculty are male; 36%, female. All teach undergraduates. The average class size in an introductory lecture is 20; in a laboratory, 20; and in a regular course, 20.

Admissions: 100% of the 2001-2002 applicants were accepted. The ACT scores for the 2001-2002 freshman class were: 63% below 21, 18% between 21 and 23, 13% between 24 and 26, 2% between 27 and 28, and 2% above 28. 25% of the current freshmen were in the top fifth of their class; 70% were in the top two fifths.

Requirements: The ACT is required. In addition, applicants must be graduates of an accredited secondary school or have a GED certificate. Required core courses include 4 in English, and 3 each in math (algebra I of higher), sciences, and social sciences. A GPA of 2.0 is required. AP and CLEP credits are accepted. Applications are accepted on-line at the school's web site.

Procedure: Freshmen are admitted to all sessions. Entrance exams should be taken during the senior year. There are early decision and early admissions plans. Application deadlines are open. The application fee is $35.

Transfer: 112 transfer students enrolled in 2001-2002. Applicants must submit official transcripts from all colleges attended and should have a minimum GPA of 2.0, with scores on the SAT I or ACT also recommended. 30 credits of 128 must be completed at Mayville State.

Visiting: There are regularly scheduled orientations for prospective students, including a campus tour, meetings with faculty in fields of interest, and meetings with the financial aid director if needed. There are guides for informal visits and visitors may sit in on classes and stay overnight. To schedule a visit, contact the Office of Enrollment Services at (701) 786-4842.

Financial Aid: In 2001-2002, 69% of all freshmen and 81% of continuing students received some form of financial aid. The average freshman award was $5634. Of that total, scholarships or need-based grants averaged $2865; and loans averaged $2766. 31% of undergraduates work part time. The average financial indebtedness of the 2001 graduate was $17,679. Mayville State is a member of CSS. The FAFSA is required. The fall application deadline is March 15.

International Students: There are 4 international students enrolled. The school actively recruits these students. They must score 525 on the written TOEFL or 197 on the electronic version.

Computers: All students have access to the LAN and Internet in classrooms, residence halls, and labs. All students may access the system. There are no time limits and no fees. All students are required to have personal computers. IBM ThinkPad is recommended.

Graduates: In 2001, 106 bachelor's degrees were awarded. The most popular majors were elementary education (41%), business administration (22%), and computer information systems (10%). In an average class, 18% graduate in 4 years, 31% in 5 years, and 36% in 6 years. 6 companies recruited on campus in 2000-2001. Of the 2000 graduating class, 8% were enrolled in graduate school within 6 months of graduation and all were employed.

Admissions Contact: Brian Larson, Director of Enrollment Services. A video is available. E-mail: *admit@mail.masu.nodak.edu*
Web: *www.mayvillestate.edu*

MINOT STATE UNIVERSITY

Minot, ND 58707 C-2
(701) 858-4347
(800) 777-0750; Fax: (701) 839-6933

Full-time: 932 men, 1564 women
Part-time: 323 men, 507 women
Graduate: 50 men, 139 women
Year: semesters, summer session
Application Deadline: open
Freshman Class: 757 applied, 732 accepted, 506 enrolled
ACT: 21
Faculty: 159; IIA, --$
Ph.D.s: 60%
Student/Faculty: 16 to 1
Tuition: $2554 ($6301)
Room & Board: $2912
LESS COMPETITIVE

Minot State University, founded in 1913, is a public institution offering undergraduate and graduate programs in arts and sciences, education, business, nursing, and human services. There are 3 undergraduate schools and 1 graduate school. In addition to regional accreditation, MSU has baccalaureate program accreditation with CSWE, NASM, NCATE, and NLN. The library contains 398,760 volumes, 670,000 microform items, and 8827 audiovisual forms/CDs, and subscribes to 843 periodicals. Computerized library services include the card catalog, interlibrary loans, and database searching. Special learning facilities include a learning resource center, art gallery, natural history museum, radio station, and TV station. The 103-acre campus is in a small town. Including residence halls, there are 21 buildings.

Student Life: 85% of undergraduates are from North Dakota. Others are from 45 states, 15 foreign countries, and Canada. 95% are from public schools. 85% are white. The average age of freshmen is 19; all undergraduates, 21. 40% do not continue beyond their first year; 32% remain to graduate.

Housing: 643 students can be accommodated in college housing, which includes single-sex and coed dormitories, on-campus apartments, and married-student housing. In addition, there are special-interest houses. On-campus housing is guaranteed for the freshman year only, is available on a first-come, first-served basis, and is available on a lottery system for upperclassmen. 85% of students commute. Alcohol is not permitted. All students may keep cars.

Activities: There are no fraternities or sororities. There are 60 groups on campus, including band, cheerleading, choir, chorale, chorus, drama, ethnic, honors, international, jazz band, literary magazine, musical theater, newspaper, orchestra, pep band, political, professional, radio and TV, religious, social service, student government, symphony, and yearbook. Popular campus events include Welcome Week, Final Frenzy, and Native American Awareness Week.

Sports: There are 6 intercollegiate sports for men and 6 for women, and 4 intramural sports for men and 4 for women. Facilities include a 10,000-seat field house, a 2800-seat football stadium, and a 3000-seat gym.

Disabled Students: 99% of the campus is accessible. Wheelchair ramps, elevators, special parking, specially equipped rest rooms, special class scheduling, lowered drinking fountains, and lowered telephones are available, and some dormitory rooms are specially designed for disabled students.

Services: Counseling and information services are available, as is tutoring in most subjects. Special services are offered for disabled students on request.

Campus Safety and Security: Measures include self-defense education, informal discussions, pamphlets/posters/films, and emergency telephones. There are lighted pathways/sidewalks.

Programs of Study: MSU confers B.A., B.S., B.S.Ed., B.S.N., and B.S.W. degrees. Associate and master's degrees are also awarded. Bachelor's degrees are awarded in BIOLOGICAL SCIENCE (biology/biological science), BUSINESS (accounting, banking and finance, international business management, management information systems, management science, and marketing/retailing/merchandising), COMMUNICATIONS AND THE ARTS (art, broadcasting, communications, English, French, German, multimedia, music, and Spanish), COMPUTER AND PHYSICAL SCIENCE (chemistry, computer science, earth science, geology, mathematics, physical sciences, physics, and radiological technology), EDUCATION (business, drama, education of the deaf and hearing impaired, education of the exceptional child, education of the mentally handicapped, elementary, English, foreign languages, mathematics, music, physical, and science), HEALTH PROFESSIONS (dental laboratory technology, nursing, and speech pathology/audiology), SOCIAL SCIENCE (addiction studies, criminal justice, economics, history, liberal arts/general studies, physical fitness/movement, psychology, social science, social work, and sociology). Communication disorders, special education, and elementary education are the strongest academically. Business, criminal justice, and education are the largest.

Required: Students must take a number of general education courses in humanities, communication, math, natural sciences, social and behavorial sciences, and leisure-time education. They must complete at least 128 semester hours, with 30 to 37 in the major and a minimum GPA of 2.0.

Special: A general studies degree, independent research, internships, work-study, and unique programs of study are available. Cross-registration through the North Dakota University System, co-op programs in all majors, and study abroad in 3 countries also are offered. Preliminary programs are available in dental hygiene, dentistry, engineering, law, medicine, and many other areas. There is a freshman honors program.

Faculty/Classroom: 53% of faculty are male, 47%, female. All teach undergraduates and 20% do research. No introductory courses are taught by graduate students. The average class size in an introductory lecture is 60; in a laboratory, 20; and in a regular course, 25.

Admissions: 97% of the 2001-2002 applicants were accepted.

Requirements: The SAT I or ACT is required. In addition, applicants must submit a high school diploma or GED certificate. Core course requirements include 4 years of English and 3 each of math, social studies, and science. Applications are accepted on-line, but a printed copy must also be submitted. AP and CLEP credits are accepted.

Procedure: Freshmen are admitted to all sessions. Entrance exams should be taken any time. There is a deferred admissions plan. Application deadlines are open. The fall 2001 application fee was $25.

Transfer: 419 transfer students enrolled in 2001-2002. Transfers must submit transcripts from each college attended. 30 credits of 128 must be completed at MSU.

Visiting: There are regularly scheduled orientations for prospective students, prior to the beginning of the fall term. There are guides for informal visits and visitors may sit in on classes. To schedule a visit, contact Enrollment Services at (701) 858-3350 or *askmsu@minotstateu.edu*.

Financial Aid: In 2001-2002, 67% of all freshmen and 76% of continuing students received some form of financial aid. 67% of freshmen and 76% of continuing students received need-based aid. The average freshman award was $5268. Of that total, scholarships or need-based grants averaged $2626 ($4850 maximum); loans averaged $2275 ($2625 maximum); work contracts averaged $127 ($2400 maximum); and external aid $524 ($5000 maximum). 1% of undergraduates work part time. Average annual earnings from campus work are $1000. The FAFSA is required. The fall application deadline is October 15.

International Students: There are 26 international students enrolled. The school actively recruits these students. They must score 530 on the written TOEFL or 195 on the electronic version.

Computers: The mainframe consists of 2 Intranet/Novell servers. PCs and Macs are available throughout the campus. Network access to Bitnet, NWNWT, and the Internet is available through a campus Ethernet backbone. All students may access the system 24 hours daily. There are no time limits and no fees.

Graduates: In 2001, 488 bachelor's degrees were awarded. The most popular majors were elementary education (15%), criminal justice (11%), and management (9%). In an average class, 32% graduate in 6 years. 100 companies recruited on campus in 2000-2001. Of the 2000 graduating class, 9% were enrolled in graduate school within 6 months of graduation and 97% were employed.

Admissions Contact: Alexis Hildebrandt, Enrollment Services Representative. E-mail: *hilde@misu.nodak.edu* Web: *www.misu.nodak.edu*

NORTH DAKOTA STATE UNIVERSITY — F-3

Fargo, ND 58105-5454 — (701) 231-8643
(800) 488-NDSU; Fax: (701) 231-8802

Full-time: 4980 men, 3498 women	**Faculty:** 495; IIA, -$
Part-time: 449 men, 502 women	**Ph.D.s:** 82%
Graduate: 617 men, 492 women	**Student/Faculty:** 17 to 1
Year: semesters, summer session	**Tuition:** $3272 ($7871)
Application Deadline: August 15	**Room & Board:** $3732
Freshman Class: 3353 applied, 2221 accepted, 1964 enrolled	
ACT: 23	**VERY COMPETITIVE**

North Dakota State University, founded in 1890, is a comprehensive, public, land-grant institution. Its undergraduate and graduate programs emphasize the liberal arts and sciences, agricultural and technical studies, architecture, business, engineering, teacher preparation, and pharmaceutical studies. There are 8 undergraduate schools and 1 graduate school. In addition to regional accreditation, NDSU has baccalaureate program accreditation with ABET, ACCE, ACPE, ACS, ADA, AHEA, CSAB, FIDER, NAAB, NASM, NCATE, and NLN. The 4 libraries contain 839,000 volumes, 370,000 microform items, and 30,000 audiovisual forms/CDs, and subscribe to 5000 periodicals. Computerized library services include the card catalog, interlibrary loans, and database searching. Special learning facilities include a learning resource center, art gallery, and radio station. The 258-acre campus is in an urban area 229 miles northwest of Minneapolis-St. Paul. Including residence halls, there are 97 buildings.

Student Life: 61% of undergraduates are from North Dakota. Others are from 39 states, 54 foreign countries, and Canada. 93% are from public schools. 95% are white. The average age of freshmen is 19; all undergraduates, 22. 24% do not continue beyond their first year; 46% remain to graduate.

Housing: 3383 students can be accommodated in college housing, which includes single-sex and coed dormitories, on-campus apartments, and married-student housing. On-campus housing is guaranteed for all 4 years. 64% of students commute. Alcohol is not permitted. All students may keep cars.

Activities: 10% of men belong to 10 national fraternities; 5% of women belong to 5 national sororities. There are 200 groups on campus, including academic, art, band, cheerleading, choir, chorus, computers, dance, debate, drama, drill team, ethnic, forensics, gay, honors, international, jazz band, marching band, musical theater, newspaper, pep band, political, professional, radio and TV, recreational, religious, social, social service, and student government. Popular campus events include International Students' Week, Spring Blast, and multicultural activities.

Sports: There are 8 intercollegiate sports for men and 8 for women, and 5 intramural sports for men and 6 for women. Facilities include a sports arena, indoor and outdoor tracks, baseball and softball fields, a pool, wrestling and weight rooms, a multipurpose fitness room, and volleyball, tennis, basketball, and racquetball courts.

Disabled Students: 50% of the campus is accessible. Wheelchair ramps, elevators, special parking, specially equipped rest rooms, special class scheduling, lowered drinking fountains, lowered telephones, and special transportation are available.

Services: Counseling and information services are available, as is tutoring in most subjects. There are note takers, a reader service for the blind, and remedial math, reading, and writing.

Campus Safety and Security: Measures include 24-hour foot and vehicle patrol, self-defense education, escort service, and shuttle buses. There are informal discussions, pamphlets/posters/films, emergency telephones, and lighted pathways/sidewalks.

Programs of Study: NDSU confers B.A., B.S., B.Arch., B.F.A. in Theater Arts, B.L.A., and B.Univ.Studies degrees. Master's and doctoral degrees are also awarded. Bachelor's degrees are awarded in AGRICULTURE (agricultural business management, agricultural economics, agricultural mechanics, agriculture, animal science, equine science, horticulture, natural resource management, plant protection (pest management), plant science, range/farm management, and soil science), BIOLOGICAL SCIENCE (biology/biological science, biotechnology, botany, microbiology, nutrition, and zoology), BUSINESS (accounting, business administration and management, hotel/motel and restaurant management, institutional management, management information systems, and recreation and leisure services), COMMUNICATIONS AND THE ARTS (art, communications, dramatic arts, English, French, music, and Spanish), COMPUTER AND PHYSICAL SCIENCE (actuarial science, chemistry, computer science, earth science, mathematics, physics, radiological technology, and statistics), EDUCATION (agricultural, athletic training, elementary, home economics, music, physical, and secondary), ENGINEERING AND ENVIRONMENTAL DESIGN (agricultural engineering, architecture, civil engineering, computer engineering, construction engineering, construction management, electrical/electronics engineering, environmental design, industrial engineering, interior design, landscape architecture/design, manufacturing engineering, and mechanical engineering), HEALTH PROFESSIONS (clinical science, nursing, pharmacy, preveterinary science, respiratory therapy, and veterinary science), SOCIAL SCIENCE (anthropology, child care/child and family studies, criminal justice, economics, food science, history, humanities, international studies, physical fitness/movement, political science/government, psychology, social science, sociology, and textiles and clothing). Biotechnology and polymers and coatings science are the strongest academically. Sciences, engineering, and human development and education are the largest.

Required: Students must complete at least 122 semester credits, with at least 24 in the major, and maintain at least a 2.0 GPA. General education requirements include 10 credits in science and technology, including a 1 credit lab course, 9 credits in communication, which includes freshman English and public speaking, 6 credits each in humanities and fine arts and in social and behavioral science, 3 credits in quantitative reasoning, at least 2 credits in a wellness course, and a first-year experience course. Included in these courses must be 1 course designated as a cultural diversity course and 1 designated as a global perspectives course.

Special: Special academic programs include cooperative work programs and internships. There is cross-registration with Concordia College and Minnesota State University, both in Moorhead, Minnesota. Student-designed and dual majors, study abroad, a B.A.-B.S. degree, credit for life, military, and work experience, nondegree study, and pass/fail options are possible. There are 22 national honor societies, a freshman honors program, and a university-wide honors program.

Faculty/Classroom: 72% of faculty are male; 28%, female. All teach undergraduates. Graduate students teach 7% of introductory courses. The average class size in an introductory lecture is 88; in a laboratory, 26; and in a regular course, 42.

Admissions: 66% of the 2001-2002 applicants were accepted. The ACT scores for the 2001-2002 freshman class were 28% below 21, 29% between 21 and 23, 24% between 24 and 26, 10% between 27 and 28, and 9% above 28. There were 5 National Merit finalists. 97 freshmen graduated first in their class.

Requirements: The SAT I or ACT is required. In addition, applicants must have completed 4 units of English, and 3 each of math (algebra I or above), laboratory science, and social science. The GED is accepted, with a minimum score of 45 and no subject score lower than 40. A GPA of 2.5 is required. AP and CLEP credits are accepted. Applications are accepted on-line at *www.ndsu.edu*.

Procedure: Freshmen are admitted to all sessions. Entrance exams should be taken in the spring of the junior year or in the fall of the senior year. There is a deferred admissions plan. Applications should be filed by August 15 for fall entry, December 16 for spring entry, and May 20 for summer entry. The fall 2001 application fee was $25. Notification is sent on a rolling basis.

Transfer: 782 transfer students enrolled in 2001-2002. Transfer students must have a minimum GPA of 2.0; ACT or SAT I scores are required if the applicant has less than 24 semester credits. 36 credits of 122 must be completed at NDSU.

Visiting: There are regularly scheduled orientations for prospective students, including tours of the campus, academic appointments, and meetings with admissions counselors and financial aid counselors. There are guides for informal visits and visitors may sit in on classes. To schedule a visit, contact the Office of Admission.

Financial Aid: In 2001-2002, 66% of all freshmen and 76% of continuing students received some form of financial aid. 70% of freshmen and 67% of continuing students received need-based aid. The average freshman award was $4191. 60% of undergraduates work part time. Average annual earnings from campus work are $885. The average financial indebtedness of the 2001 graduate was $20,107. The FAFSA is required. The fall application deadline is April 15.

International Students: There are 360 international students enrolled. The school actively recruits these students. They must score 525 on the written TOEFL.

Computers: The mainframes are an RS 6000 and a SUN 3500. Students access the system from various terminal clusters across campus as well as from their living areas via modem. PCs are also available throughout the campus. All students may access the system 24 hours a day or as posted. There are no time limits and no fees. It is recommended that students in architecture and landscape architecture (sophomore level) have personal computers.

Graduates: In 2001, 1361 bachelor's degrees were awarded. The most popular majors were engineering (17%), business (13%), and health and related sciences (9%). In an average class, 13% graduate in 4 years, 38% in 5 years, and 46% in 6 years. 185 companies recruited on campus in 2000-2001. Of the 2000 graduating class, 16% were enrolled in graduate school within 6 months of graduation and 95% were employed.

Admissions Contact: Dr. Kate Haugen, Associate Dean/Enrollment Management. E-mail: *ndsu.admission@ndsu.nodak.edu*
Web: *www.ndsu.edu*

UNIVERSITY OF MARY — C-3
Bismarck, ND 58504-9652 — (701) 255-7500
(800) 288-6279; Fax: (701) 255-7687

Full-time: 650 men, 1080 women	**Faculty:** 75
Part-time: 60 men, 150 women	**Ph.D.s:** 38%
Graduate: 80 men, 130 women	**Student/Faculty:** 23 to 1
Year: 4-1-4, summer session	**Tuition:** $9000
Application Deadline: open	**Room & Board:** $3900
Freshman Class: n/av	
ACT: 23	**LESS COMPETITIVE**

The University of Mary, founded in 1959, is a private institution affiliated with the Roman Catholic Church. Undergraduate and graduate programs emphasize liberal arts, humanities, social sciences, business, health science, music, professional training, philosophy and religious studies, and teacher preparation. There are 8 undergraduate and 4 graduate schools. In addition to regional accreditation, Mary has baccalaureate program accreditation with CSWE and NLN. The library contains 55,000 volumes and 2500 audiovisual forms/CDs, and subscribes to 550 periodicals. Computerized library services include the card catalog, interlibrary loans, and database searching. Special learning facilities include a learning resource center, art gallery, radio station, and TV station. The 107-acre campus is in a suburban area 7 miles south of Bismarck. Including residence halls, there are 12 buildings.

Student Life: 70% of undergraduates are from North Dakota. Others are from 26 states, 3 foreign countries, and Canada. 95% are from public schools. 96% are white. 60% are Catholic; 30%, Protestant. The average age of freshmen is 18; all undergraduates, 23. 29% do not continue beyond their first year; 40% remain to graduate.

Housing: 755 students can be accommodated in college housing, which includes single-sex and coed dormitories and on-campus apartments. On-campus housing is guaranteed for all 4 years. 50% of students commute. Alcohol is not permitted. All students may keep cars.

Activities: There are no fraternities or sororities. There are 22 groups on campus, including band, cheerleading, choir, chorale, chorus, computers, drama, ethnic, forensics, jazz band, musical theater, newspaper, orchestra, pep band, photography, political, professional, radio and TV, religious, social, social service, student government, symphony, and yearbook. Popular campus events include Parents Day, Cultural Day, and Prayer Day.

Sports: There are 8 intercollegiate sports for men and 7 for women, and 10 intramural sports for men and 10 for women. Facilities include an activity center housing a 1200-seat gym, basketball and racquetball courts, wrestling and weight rooms, and a swimming pool. There are also track/football, intramural, and softball fields, tennis courts, a fitness center, and a 1200-seat stadium.

Disabled Students: All of the campus is accessible. Wheelchair ramps, elevators, special parking, specially equipped rest rooms, special class scheduling, and lowered telephones are available.

Services: Counseling and information services are available, as is tutoring in every subject. There is a reader service for the blind, and remedial math, reading, and writing.

Campus Safety and Security: Measures include escort service, shuttle buses, informal discussions, and pamphlets/posters/films. There are emergency telephones and lighted pathways/sidewalks.

Programs of Study: Mary confers B.A., B.S., and B.Univ.Studies degrees. Master's degrees are also awarded. Bachelor's degrees are awarded in BIOLOGICAL SCIENCE (biology/biological science), BUSINESS (accounting, business administration and management, and management information systems), COMMUNICATIONS AND THE ARTS (communications, English, and music), COMPUTER AND PHYSICAL SCIENCE (mathematics and radiological technology), EDUCATION (athletic training, early childhood, elementary, English, mathematics, music, physical, science, social science, and special), HEALTH PROFESSIONS (medical laboratory science, nursing, occupational therapy, physical therapy, premedicine, and respiratory therapy), SOCIAL SCIENCE (addiction studies, behavioral science, ministries, prelaw, psychology, social science, and social work). Business administration, accounting, and nursing are the strongest academically. Business, nursing, and elementary education are the largest.

Required: To graduate, students must complete 128 semester hours, with 32 to 56 in the major and 44 at the 300-400 level, and have a minimum GPA of 2.0. At least 60 semester hours must be in liberal arts

courses. In addition, a B.A. degree requires 16 semester hours of a foreign language or 20 semester hours of philosophy/theology, with 12 such hours at the 300-400 level. All students must take 3 courses each in humanities, math/science, philosophy/theology, and social sciences.
Special: A co-op program in engineering is available, as is cross-registration with the University of Minnesota. Special academic programs include internships, study abroad in France, Germany, and Spain, on-campus work-study, and a general studies degree. Dual majors include elementary education/early childhood education, elementary education/special education, athletic training/biology, athletic training/phys ed, business/accounting, and business/computer information systems. There are accelerated degree programs in several majors, and a 3-2 engineering program with the University of Minnesota. There are 3 national honor societies, a freshman honors program, and 2 departmental honors programs.
Faculty/Classroom: 49% of faculty are male; 51%, female. All teach undergraduates and 15% both teach and do research. No introductory courses are taught by graduate students. The average class size in an introductory lecture is 30; in a laboratory, 20; and in a regular course, 20.
Requirements: The SAT I or ACT is recommended. In addition, applicants should be graduates of an accredited secondary school; the GED is accepted. For automatic acceptance, 3 requirements must be met: a minimum 2.5 GPA; an 18 or higher on the ACT; and rank in the upper half of the graduating class. The school's own testing can also be used to determine acceptance. A recommendation from a school counselor, teacher, or employer is requested. An interview is advised. AP and CLEP credits are accepted. Applications are accepted on disk and on-line at the school's web site.
Procedure: Freshmen are admitted fall and spring. Entrance exams should be taken in the fall of the senior year. There are early admissions and deferred admissions plans. Application deadlines are open. Notification is sent on a rolling basis.
Transfer: 223 transfer students enrolled in 2001-2002. Transfer students should have a 2.0 minimum GPA and should present a recommendation from a school counselor, instructor, or employer. 32 credits of 128 must be completed at Mary.
Visiting: There are regularly scheduled orientations for prospective students, including a campus tour and meetings with individual professors, coaches, students, and music instructors. There are guides for informal visits and visitors may sit in on classes and stay overnight. To schedule a visit, contact the Admissions Office at *marauder@umary.edu*.
Financial Aid: 70% of undergraduates work part time. Average annual earnings from campus work are $1000. The FAFSA is required.
International Students: They must score 500 on the written TOEFL.
Computers: The mainframe is an IBM 5360 System/36. Students have access to the Internet and World Wide Web and general-purpose and course-specific software through PCs in general-use labs and workstations in faculty offices. All students may access the system 24 hours a day. There are no time limits and no fees. It is recommended that students in computer information systems have personal computers.
Graduates: In 2001, 470 bachelor's degrees were awarded. The most popular majors were management (16%), nursing (12%), and education (11%). In an average class, 2% graduate in 3 years, 35% in 4 years, 42% in 5 years, and 43% in 6 years. 80 companies recruited on campus in 2000-2001. Of the 2000 graduating class, 13% were enrolled in graduate school within 6 months of graduation and 97% were employed.
Admissions Contact: Steph Storey, Director of Admissions. A CD-ROM is available. E-mail: *steph@umary.edu* Web: *www.umary.edu*

UNIVERSITY OF NORTH DAKOTA
Grand Forks, ND 58202 — E-2
(701) 777-4463
(800) CALL UND; Fax: (701) 777-2696

Full-time: 4715 men, 4121 women	**Faculty:** 621; I, --$
Part-time: 468 men, 481 women	**Ph.D.s:** 85%
Graduate: 906 men, 1073 women	**Student/Faculty:** 14 to 1
Year: semesters, summer session	**Tuition:** $3262 ($7862)
Application Deadline: July 1	**Room & Board:** $3805

Freshman Class: 3471 applied, 2346 accepted, 1947 enrolled
SAT I or ACT: required — **VERY COMPETITIVE**

The University of North Dakota, established in 1883, is a state-supported comprehensive institution. Its undergraduate and graduate programs emphasize the liberal arts, fine arts, engineering, medicine, aerospace sciences, nursing, professional training, business and public administration, health science, teacher preparation, law, and computer science. There are 8 undergraduate and 3 graduate schools. In addition to regional accreditation, UND has baccalaureate program accreditation with AACSB, ABET, ACEJMC, ADA, APTA, CSAB, CSWE, NASAD, NASM, NCATE, and NLN. The 3 libraries contain 1,288,003 volumes, 822,557 microform items, and 53,530 audiovisual forms/CDs, and subscribe to 5000 periodicals. Computerized library services include the card catalog, interlibrary loans, and database searching. Special learning facilities include a learning resource center, art gallery, natural history museum, radio station, TV station, an atmospherium, and an art museum and gallery. The 570-acre campus is in an urban area 4 hours from Minneapolis/St. Paul and 2 hours from Winnipeg, Manitoba. Including residence halls, there are 240 buildings.
Student Life: 58% of undergraduates are from North Dakota. Others are from 49 states, 53 foreign countries, and Canada. 95% are from public schools. 88% are white. The average age of freshmen is 19; all undergraduates, 22. 23% do not continue beyond their first year; 77% remain to graduate.
Housing: 4299 students can be accommodated in college housing, which includes single-sex and coed dormitories, on-campus apartments, married-student housing, fraternity houses, and sorority houses. On-campus housing is guaranteed for all 4 years. 64% of students commute. Alcohol is not permitted. All students may keep cars.
Activities: 15% of men belong to 13 national fraternities; 10% of women belong to 7 national sororities. There are 250 groups on campus, including art, band, cheerleading, chess, choir, chorale, chorus, computers, dance, debate, departmental, drama, drill team, ethnic, gay, honors, international, jazz band, literary magazine, marching band, musical theater, orchestra, pep band, photography, political, professional, radio and TV, religious, social, social service, special interest, student government, symphony, and yearbook. Popular campus events include Honors Day, Time Out/Wacipi, and Potato Bowl.
Sports: There are 9 intercollegiate sports for men and 10 for women, and 17 intramural sports for men and 17 for women. Facilities include an ice arena, a golf course, a 15000-seat stadium, a 11400-seat hockey arena, a 6100-seat basketball center, and a sports center/field house with racquetball and basketball courts, pools and weight rooms.
Disabled Students: 98% of the campus is accessible. Wheelchair ramps, elevators, special parking, specially equipped rest rooms, special class scheduling, lowered drinking fountains, lowered telephones, accessible transportation, housing, and academic and personal support services are available.
Services: Counseling and information services are available, as is tutoring in every subject. There is a reader service for the blind.
Campus Safety and Security: Measures include 24-hour foot and vehicle patrol, self-defense education, escort service, and shuttle buses. There are informal discussions, pamphlets/posters/films, emergency telephones, lighted pathways/sidewalks, and emergency phones throughout the campus.
Programs of Study: UND confers B.A., B.S., B.Acc., B.B.A., B.F.A., B.G.S., B.Mus., B.S.A., B.S.A.T., B.S.At Sc., B.S.C.E., B.S.Ch.E., B. S. Chem., B. S. C. J.S., B. S.C.L.S., B.S.C.N., B.S.Cyto., B.S.D., B.S.Ed., B.S.E.E., B.S.E.G., B.S.E.G., B.S.F.W.B., B.S.G., B.S.G.E., B.S.I.T., B.S.M.E., B.S.N., B.S.O.S.E.H., B.S.O.T., B.S.P.A., B.S.P.E., B.S.R.L.S., and B.S.S.W. degrees. Master's and doctoral degrees are also awarded. Bachelor's degrees are awarded in AGRICULTURE (fish and game management), BIOLOGICAL SCIENCE (avian sciences, biology/biological science, and nutrition), BUSINESS (accounting, banking and finance, business economics, entrepreneurial studies, management information systems, management science, marketing/retailing/merchandising, recreation and leisure services, and transportation management), COMMUNICATIONS AND THE ARTS (classical languages, communications, English, fine arts, French, German, music, music performance, Scandinavian languages, Spanish, and visual and performing arts), COMPUTER AND PHYSICAL SCIENCE (applied physics, atmospheric sciences and meteorology, chemistry, computer science, geology, mathematics, and physics), EDUCATION (athletic training, business, early childhood, elementary, middle school, music, physical, science, social studies, and vocational), ENGINEERING AND ENVIRONMENTAL DESIGN (aerospace studies, air traffic control, aviation administration/management, chemical engineering, civil engineering, electrical/electronics engineering, environmental engineering technology, geological engineering, industrial engineering technology, mechanical engineering, and occupational safety and health), HEALTH PROFESSIONS (clinical science, cytotechnology, nursing, occupational therapy, physical therapy, rehabilitation therapy, and speech pathology/audiology), SOCIAL SCIENCE (anthropology, classical/ancient civilization, criminal justice, dietetics, economics, forensic studies, geography, history, humanities and social science, interdisciplinary studies, international studies, liberal arts/general studies, Native American studies, philosophy, political science/government, psychology, public administration, religion, social science, social work, and sociology). Physical therapy is the strongest academically. Health, liberal arts, and business are the largest.
Required: To graduate, students must complete at least 125 credit hours, 30 in the major, with a minimum GPA of 2.0. At least 36 credits must be numbered 300 or above, and at least 60 credits must be from a 4-year institution. Distribution reequirements include 12 credits of math, scienc, and technology, 9 each of social sciences and arts, and humanities, and 6 of English composition. One course in social science or arts and humanities must meet the world cultures designation.
Special: Special academic programs include cooperative programs, accelerated degree programs in most majors, internships in many majors, study abroad in at least 40 countries, work-study, and dual majors in all areas. Also offered are a general studies degree, honors programs, student-designed majors, B.A-B.S. degees, nondegree study, and pass/fail

options. Alternative academic programs include the Division of Continuing Education's correspondence study, the Integrated Studies Program, which offers a means of fulfilling general education requirements by a semester of related course work, and study via telecommunications. Cross-registration with all North Dakota 2- and 4-year public institutions is possible. There are 28 national honor societies, including Phi Beta Kappa, a freshman honors program, and 1 departmental honors program.

Faculty/Classroom: 63% of faculty are male; 37%, female. 85% teach undergraduates, 75% do research, and 75% do both. The average class size in an introductory lecture is 35; in a laboratory, 21; and in a regular course, 27.

Admissions: 68% of the 2001-2002 applicants were accepted. The ACT scores for the 2001-2002 freshman class were: 28% below 21, 28% between 21 and 23, 25% between 24 and 26, 11% between 27 and 28, and 9% above 28. 40% of the current freshmen were in the top fifth of their class; 65% were in the top two fifths. There were 3 National Merit finalists. 88 freshmen graduated first in their class.

Requirements: The SAT I or ACT is required. The ACT is preferred, but SAT I will be accepted. Applicants must be graduates of an accredited secondary school or have passed to GED with an average of 50. A GPA of 2.25 is required. AP and CLEP credits are accepted.

Procedure: Freshmen are admitted to all sessions. Entrance exams should be taken in spring of the junior year or fall of the senior year. There are early decision and early admissions plans. Applications should be filed by July 1 for fall entry, rolling for spring entry, and rolling for summer entry. Notification is sent on a rolling basis.

Transfer: 839 transfer students enrolled in 2001-2002. Transfer students must have a minimum GPA of 2.0 and be in good academic standing. A higher GPA may be required in specific programs. 30 credits of 125 must be completed at UND.

Visiting: There are regularly scheduled orientations for prospective students, including a visit with an admissions counselor, a campus tour, an academic appointment, and an athletic appointment (if applicable). There are guides for informal visits and visitors may sit in on classes and stay overnight. To schedule a visit, contact Enrollment Services at *enrolser@sage.und.hodak.edu.*

Financial Aid: In 2001-2002, 73% of all freshmen and 72% of continuing students received some form of financial aid. 42% of freshmen and 46% of continuing students received need-based aid. The average freshman award was $6393. Of that total, scholarships or need-based grants averaged $2905 ($5000 maximum); loans averaged $3846 ($8625 maximum); and work contracts averaged $1998 ($5000 maximum). 68% of undergraduates work part time. Average annual earnings from campus work are $1997. The average financial indebtedness of the 2001 graduate was $21,199. UND is a member of CSS. The FAFSA is required. The fail application deadline is April 15.

International Students: There are 256 international students enrolled. They must score 525 on the written TOEFL.

Computers: The mainframes are an IBM 7060#50 and Unisys Clear Path 6600. Students may use IBM PCs and Macs at various centrally located campus and departmental labs and residence halls. Network access to mainframe computers and the Internet is available through a dial-in facility (184 lines) and direct access in the PC labs and the residence halls. All students may access the system 24 hours a day. There are no time limits and no fees. It is recommended that students in aviation and medical have personal computers. Dell Latitudes, Pentium II, 366 MHZ, and Gateway 5300 are recommended.

Graduates: In 2001, 1602 bachelor's degrees were awarded. The most popular majors were commercial aviation (8%), elementary education (6%), and communication (5%). In an average class, 16% graduate in 4 years, 20% in 5 years, and 10% in 6 years. 126 companies recruited on campus in 2000-2001. Of the 2000 graduating class, 20% were enrolled in graduate school within 6 months of graduation and 85% were employed.

Admissions Contact: Kenton Pauls, Director, Enrollment Services. A video is available.
E-mail: *kenton_pauls@mail.und.nodak.edu;enrolser@sage.und.*
Web: *http://www.und.edu*

VALLEY CITY STATE UNIVERSITY
E-3

Valley City, ND 58072
(701) 845-7101
(800) 532-8641; (701) 845-7245

Full-time: 349 men, 392 women	**Faculty:** 58; IIB, --$
Part-time: 81 men, 183 women	**Ph.D.s:** 43%
Graduate: none	**Student/Faculty:** 13 to 1
Year: semesters, summer session	**Tuition:** see profile
Application Deadline: open	**Room & Board:** n/app
Freshman Class: 275 applied, 262 accepted, 160 enrolled	
ACT: 21	**LESS COMPETITIVE**

Valley City State University, founded in 1890, is a state-supported institution offering degree programs in the arts and sciences, business, and teacher education. Tuition for North Dakota residents is $2067 per year; for Minnesota residents, $2316; for South Dakota, Montana, and Saskatchewan and Manitoba, Canada, residents, $2584; and for students from the western states, a $3101; and for all other out-of-state students, $5519. In addition to regional accreditation, VCSU has baccalaureate program accreditation with NASM and NCATE. The library contains 103,174 volumes and 15,069 audiovisual forms/CDs, and subscribes to 2982 periodicals. Computerized library services include the card catalog, interlibrary loans, and database searching. Special learning facilities include a learning resource center, art gallery, and planetarium. The 64-acre campus is in a small town 58 miles west of Fargo. Including residence halls, there are 29 buildings.

Student Life: 79% of undergraduates are from North Dakota. Others are from 21 states, 8 foreign countries, and Canada. 99% are from public schools. 90% are white. 62% are Protestant; 31% Catholic. The average age of freshmen is 19; all undergraduates, 23. 36% do not continue beyond their first year; 64% remain to graduate.

Housing: 514 students can be accommodated in college housing, which includes single-sex and coed dormitories and married-student housing. On-campus housing is guaranteed for all 4 years. 68% of students commute. Alcohol is not permitted. All students may keep cars.

Activities: 1% of men belong to 1 local fraternity; 1% of women belong to 1 local sorority. There are 16 groups on campus, including art, band, cheerleading, choir, chorus, computers, drama, honors, international, jazz band, musical theater, newspaper, pep band, photography, political, professional, religious, social, student government, and yearbook. Popular campus events include Sno-Daze, EBC-Hit Parade, and Medicine Wheel Seasonal Celebrations.

Sports: There are 5 intercollegiate sports for men and 5 for women, and 9 intramural sports for men and 9 for women. Facilities include a 2500-seat football stadium with an all-weather track, a 2500-seat arena, an indoor pool, a field house, tennis and racquetball courts, a cross-country course, softball and baseball fields, a golf course, weight rooms, and a fitness room.

Disabled Students: 85% of the campus is accessible. Wheelchair ramps, elevators, special parking, specially equipped rest rooms, special class scheduling, lowered drinking fountains, and lowered telephones are available.

Services: Counseling and information services are available, as is tutoring in most subjects. There is remedial writing.

Campus Safety and Security: Measures include 24-hour foot and vehicle patrol, self-defense education, informal discussions, and pamphlets/posters/films. There are lighted pathways/sidewalks and a night patrol.

Programs of Study: VCSU confers B.A., B.S., B.S.Ed., and B.University Studies degrees. Bachelor's degrees are awarded in BIOLOGICAL SCIENCE (biology/biological science), BUSINESS (business administration and management, human resources, management information systems, and office supervision and management), COMMUNICATIONS AND THE ARTS (art, English, music, and Spanish), COMPUTER AND PHYSICAL SCIENCE (chemistry and mathematics), EDUCATION (art, business, elementary, English, health, mathematics, music, physical, science, secondary, social science, and technical), ENGINEERING AND ENVIRONMENTAL DESIGN (preengineering), HEALTH PROFESSIONS (chiropractic, premedicine, preoptometry, prepharmacy, and preveterinary science), SOCIAL SCIENCE (history, liberal arts/general studies, and social science). Education, business, and computer information systems are the strongest academically. Elementary education and business are the largest.

Required: To graduate, students must complete at least 128 semester hours with a minimum GPA of 2.0, or 2.5 for a B.S.Ed. degree. Except for those pursuing the Bachelor of University Studies degree, all students must complete the foundation studies curriculum, which includes 9 hours in communication, 8 in science, 6 each in humanities and social science, and 3 each in phys ed, computer science, math, and psychology. Students must complete 48 hours in their major if they do not have a minor, or 36 hours in their major if they have a minor.

Special: VCSU offers internships, on-campus work-study, study abroad in 2 countries, pass/fail options for some courses, and credit for life, military, and work experience. There are 6 national honor societies and 4 departmental honors programs.

Faculty/Classroom: 56% of faculty are male; 44%, female. All teach undergraduates, 25% both teach and do research. The average class size in an introductory lecture is 40; in a laboratory, 20; and in a regular course, 25.

Admissions: 95% of the 2001-2002 applicants were accepted. The ACT scores for the 2001-2002 freshman class were: 49% below 21, 27% between 21 and 23, 17% between 24 and 26, 5% between 27 and 28, and 3% above 28. 21% of the current freshmen were in the top fifth of their class; 44% were in the top two fifths. 7 freshmen graduated first in their class.

Requirements: The ACT is required. In addition, applicants must be graduates of an accredited secondary school or have a GED certificate. Core curriculum requirements include 4 units of English and 3 units each of math, lab science, and social science. Applications are accepted on-line. AP and CLEP credits are accepted.

Procedure: Freshmen are admitted to all sessions. There is an early admissions plan. Application deadlines are open. Application fee is $25.

Transfer: 104 transfer students enrolled in 2001-2002. Applicants must be in good academic standing and be eligible to return to their previous institution. Official transcripts from all colleges attended are required. 24 credits of 128 must be completed at VCSU.

Visiting: There are regularly scheduled orientations for prospective students. There are guides for informal visits and visitors may sit in on classes and stay overnight. To schedule a visit, contact the Office of Enrollment Services.

Financial Aid: In 2001-2002, 86% of all freshmen and 74% of continuing students received some form of financial aid. 50% of all students received need-based aid. The average freshman award was $6808. Of that total, scholarships or need-based grants averaged $3157 ($5950 maximum); loans averaged $2736 ($4125 maximum); work contracts averaged $1634 ($2318 maximum); and vocational rehabilitation, housing cost waivers, and tuition waivers for international students averaged $1361 ($1962 maximum). 22% of undergraduates work part time. Average annual earnings from campus work are $1568. The average financial indebtedness of the 2001 graduate was $16,636. VCSU is a member of CSS. The FAFSA is required. The fall application deadline is April 15.

International Students: There are 46 international students enrolled. They must score 500 on the written TOEFL and also take the SAT I or the ACT.

Computers: Each student is issued an IBM Thinkpad 380ED for use during the school year. Every student has network access 24 hours a day to the Internet, the World Wide Web, and the Groupwise e-mail communication system. All students may access the system 24 hours a day. There are no time limits and no fees.

Graduates: In 2001, 163 bachelor's degrees were awarded. The most popular majors were elementary education (50%), business administration (14%), and human resources (6%). In an average class, 18% graduate in 4 years, 37% in 5 years, and 39% in 6 years. 7 companies recruited on campus in 2000-2001. Of the 2000 graduating class, 5% were enrolled in graduate school within 6 months of graduation and 95% were employed.

Admissions Contact: Dan Klein, Director of Enrollment Management. E-mail: *enrollment_services@mail.vcsu.nodak.edu* Web: *www.vcsu.edu*

ANTIOCH COLLEGE

B-4

Yellow Springs, OH 45387

(937) 754-5100

(800) 543-9436; (937) 754-5377

Full-time: 200 men, 380 women
Part-time: 10 men, 10 women
Graduate: none
Year: trimesters, summer session
Application Deadline: February 1
Freshman Class: n/av
SAT I or ACT: recommended

Faculty: 54; IIB, --$
Ph.D.s: 75%
Student/Faculty: 11 to 1
Tuition: $19,940
Room & Board: $5132

LESS COMPETITIVE

Antioch College, established in 1852, is an independent liberal arts institution where students alternate full-time study on campus with full-time related work experience off campus. Figures given in the above capsule are approximate. The library contains 268,000 volumes, 45,123 microform items, and 4666 audiovisual forms/CDs, and subscribes to 1060 periodicals. Computerized library services include the card catalog, interlibrary loans, and database searching. Special learning facilities include a learning resource center, art gallery, radio station, and archives. The 100-acre campus is in a small town 18 miles east of Dayton. Including residence halls, there are 34 buildings.

Student Life: 80% of undergraduates are from out of state, mostly the Northeast. Others are from 45 states, 8 foreign countries, and Canada. 85% are from public schools. 84% are white. The average age of freshmen is 19; all undergraduates, 21. 20% do not continue beyond their first year; 52% remain to graduate.

Housing: 592 students can be accommodated in college housing, which includes single-sex and coed dormitories and on-campus apartments. In addition, there are language houses, special-interest houses, and food cooperatives in the dorms. On-campus housing is guaranteed for all 4 years. 95% of students live on campus; of those, 95% remain on campus on weekends. Alcohol is not permitted. All students may keep cars.

Activities: There are no fraternities or sororities. There are 27 groups on campus, including art, choir, dance, drama, ethnic, film, gay, international, literary magazine, newspaper, photography, political, radio and TV, social, social service, and student government.

Sports: There are 16 intramural sports for men and 16 for women.

Disabled Students: 10% of the campus is accessible. Wheelchair ramps, elevators, special parking, and specially equipped rest rooms are available.

Services: Counseling and information services are available, as is tutoring in most subjects. There is a reader service for the blind and remedial math and writing.

Campus Safety and Security: Measures include 24-hour foot and vehicle patrol, escort service, informal discussions, and pamphlets/posters/films. There are lighted pathways/sidewalks.

Programs of Study: Antioch confers B.A. and B.S. degrees. Bachelor's degrees are awarded in BUSINESS (entrepreneurial studies), COMMUNICATIONS AND THE ARTS (communications, languages, and visual and performing arts), COMPUTER AND PHYSICAL SCIENCE (physical sciences), ENGINEERING AND ENVIRONMENTAL DESIGN (environmental science), SOCIAL SCIENCE (crosscultural studies, humanities and social science, and interdisciplinary studies). Social sciences and environmental studies are the largest.

Required: To graduate, students must complete at least 107 academic credits, with 40 to 56 in the major, and 5 co-op experiences. The general education program consists of 8 4-credit courses. The core curriculum includes writing, math, and foreign language. Distribution requirements include 32 credits in arts, humanities, social sciences, natural sciences, and physical sciences. In addition, students must demonstrate proficiency in a foreign language and must successfully complete a work-study experience of at least 1 term in an international or cross-cultural setting.

Special: An alternating work-study program is required of all students; co-op jobs, normally 16 weeks long and resulting in 1 block of co-op credit, are individually arranged according to the needs, interests, and qualifications of each student. There is cross-registration with 17 higher education institutions in southwestern Ohio, and Antioch's membership in the Great Lakes Colleges Association allows for opportunities for special off-campus programs. An extensive study-abroad program in 15 countries is based on student-designed majors and accelerated degree programs in all majors. A 3-2 engineering degree is offered with Washington University in St. Louis. Within the 8 interdisciplinary majors offered at Antioch, there are dual majors and 25 concentrations available. Nondegree study is possible. All courses are graded on a credit/no credit basis with faculty giving narrative evaluations of each student's work.

Faculty/Classroom: 65% of faculty are male; 35%, female. 89% teach undergraduates. The average class size in a regular course is 13.

Requirements: The SAT I or ACT is recommended. A GPA of 2.5 is required. AP and CLEP credits are accepted. Important factors in the admissions decision are personality/intangible qualities, recommendations by school officials, and evidence of special talent.

Procedure: Freshmen are admitted fall, spring, and summer. There are early admissions and deferred admissions plans. Early action applications should be filed by November 15; regular applications, by February 1 for fall entry, November 1 for spring entry, and April 1 for summer entry. Notification of early action is sent rolling ; regular decision, on a rolling basis.

Transfer: Official college transcripts from previous institutions and a dean's recommendation form are required. 54 credits of 107 must be completed at Antioch.

Visiting: There are regularly scheduled orientations for prospective students, including admissions interviews, co-op presentations, tours, and special events. There are guides for informal visits and visitors may sit in on classes and stay overnight. To schedule a visit, contact the Admissions Office.

Financial Aid: 72% of undergraduates work part time. Average annual earnings from campus work in a recent year were $1700. The FAFSA and the college's own financial statement are required. The fall application deadline is March 1.

International Students: They must score 525 on the written TOEFL.

Computers: The mainframe is a DEC MicroVAX II. There are also 20 Apple IIe and Mac PCs and an IBM XT available in the academic computer center. All students may access the system. There are no time limits. The fee is $75.

Graduates: In an average class, 25% graduate in 4 years, 41% in 5 years, and 46% in 6 years.

Admissions Contact: Director of Admissions. A video is available.
E-mail: *admissions@antioch-college.edu* Web: *antioch-college.edu*

ART ACADEMY OF CINCINNATI
Cincinnati, OH 45202 A-5
(513) 562-8744
(800) 323-5692; Fax: (513) 562-8778

Full-time: 97 men, 117 women
Part-time: 3 men, 1 woman
Graduate: 1 man, 18 women
Year: semesters, summer session
Application Deadline: June 30
Freshman Class: 118 applied, 117 accepted, 64 enrolled
SAT I Verbal/Math: 580/582
Faculty: 18
Ph.D.s: 99%
Student/Faculty: 12 to 1
Tuition: $16,550
Room & Board: n/app
ACT: 22
SPECIAL

The Art Academy of Cincinnati, founded in 1887, is a private professional college offering degrees in fine art, communication arts, and art history. In addition to regional accreditation, the academy has baccalaureate program accreditation with NASAD. The library contains 50,000 volumes, and subscribes to 79 periodicals. Computerized library services include interlibrary loans. Special learning facilities include a learning resource center, art gallery, and an art museum. The 184-acre campus is in an urban area 2 miles northeast of downtown Cincinnati. There are 3 buildings.

Student Life: 53% of undergraduates are from Ohio. Others are from 13 states and 6 foreign countries. 94% are white. The average age of freshmen is 19; all undergraduates, 21. 15% do not continue beyond their first year; 60% remain to graduate.

Housing: There are no residence halls.

Activities: There are no fraternities or sororities.

Services: Counseling and information services are available, as is tutoring in drawing.

Programs of Study: The Academy confers the B.F.A. degree. Associate and master's degrees are also awarded. Bachelor's degrees are awarded in COMMUNICATIONS AND THE ARTS (art history and appreciation, fine arts, graphic design, and illustration). Art history is the strongest academically. Graphic design is the largest.

Required: To graduate, students must complete 132 semester hours, including 30 to 45 in the major, with a GPA of 2.0. The 21-credit foundation curriculum is required of all students, as are a senior thesis and a senior exhibition. Distribution requirements include 15 credits in art history and 6 each in English, social science, natural science, and humanities, as well as 3 each in a cross-disciplinary aesthetics, and electives.

Special: Students may cross-register with member institutions of the Greater Cincinnati Consortium. Co-op programs are available in graphic design, illustration, and art history. Art history majors may intern at the Cincinnati Art Museum.

Faculty/Classroom: 60% of faculty are male; 40%, female. All teach undergraduates. The average class size in an introductory lecture is 25 and in a regular course, 18.

Admissions: 99% of the 2001-2002 applicants were accepted.

Requirements: The SAT I or ACT is required. In addition, applicants should be graduates of an accredited secondary school with a minimum GPA of 2.5. The GED is accepted. A portfolio review or interview is necessary. A GPA of 2.5 is required. AP and CLEP credits are accepted. Important factors in the admissions decision are evidence of special talent, personality/intangible qualities, and recommendations by school officials.

Procedure: Freshmen are admitted in the fall. There is a deferred admissions plan. Early decision applications should be filed by March 1; regular applications, by June 30 for fall entry and December 15 for spring entry, along with a $25 fee. Notification is sent on a rolling basis.

Transfer: 30 transfer students enrolled in 2001-2002. Applicants must present academic transcripts and a portfolio. 65 credits of 132 must be completed at the academy.

Visiting: There are guides for informal visits and visitors may sit in on classes. To schedule a visit, contact Mary Jane Zumwalde in Admissions at (513) 721-5205.

Financial Aid: In 2001-2002, 88% of all freshmen and 68% of continuing students received some form of financial aid. 50% of freshmen and 52% of continuing students received need-based aid. The average freshman award was $6290. 94% of undergraduates work part time. Average annual earnings from campus work are $1500. The average financial indebtedness of the 2001 graduate was $17,135. The FAFSA is required. The fall application deadline is rolling.

International Students: There are 7 international students enrolled. They must score 525 on the written TOEFL and also take the SAT I or the ACT.

Computers: Macs are available to students for art and design functions and word processing. All students may access the system. There are no time limits and no fees.

Graduates: In 2001, 44 bachelor's degrees were awarded. The most popular majors were fine art (20%), communications design (12%), and art history (2%). In an average class, 72% graduate in 4 years, 22% in 5 years, and 16% in 6 years. Of the 2000 graduating class, 2% were enrolled in graduate school within 6 months of graduation and 91% were employed.

Admissions Contact: Mary Jane Zumwalde, Director of Admissions. E-mail: *admissions@artacademy.edu* Web: *artacademy.edu*

ASHLAND UNIVERSITY
Ashland, OH 44805 C-2
(419) 289-5052
(800) 882-1548; Fax: (419) 289-5333

Full-time: 801 men, 1174 women
Part-time: 24 men, 41 women
Graduate: 1166 men, 2661 women
Year: semesters, summer session
Application Deadline: open
Freshman Class: n/av
SAT I Verbal/Math: 510/512
Faculty: 215
Ph.D.s: 79%
Student/Faculty: 16 to 1
Tuition: $16,320
Room & Board: $5862
LESS COMPETITIVE

Ashland University, founded in 1878, is a private liberal arts institution affiliated with the Brethren Church, offering undergraduate and graduate programs in the arts and sciences, business, education, and health services. There are 3 undergraduate and 3 graduate schools. In addition to regional accreditation, Ashland has baccalaureate program accreditation with AACSB, AHEA, CSWE, NASM, NCATE, and NLN. The 2 libraries contain 270,000 volumes, 250,000 microform items, and 8800 audiovisual forms/CDs, and subscribe to 700 periodicals. Computerized library services include the card catalog, interlibrary loans, and database searching. Special learning facilities include a learning resource center, art gallery, radio station, TV station, and writing center, media center, and theater. The 100-acre campus is in a small town midway between Cleveland and Columbus. Including residence halls, there are 36 buildings.

Student Life: 93% of undergraduates are from Ohio. Others are from 27 states, 10 foreign countries, and Canada. 83% are white. 39% are Protestant; 37% claim no religious affiliation; 21% Catholic. The average age of freshmen is 19; all undergraduates, 24. 28% do not continue beyond their first year; 50% remain to graduate.

Housing: 1620 students can be accommodated in college housing, which includes single-sex and coed dormitories and fraternity houses. In addition, there are honors houses, sorority suites, and a resource management residence. On-campus housing is available on a first-come, first-served basis and is available on a lottery system for upperclassmen. 72% of students live on campus. Alcohol is not permitted. All students may keep cars.

Activities: 14% of men belong to 4 national fraternities; 22% of women belong to 5 national sororities. There are 100 groups on campus, including art, band, cheerleading, choir, chorus, dance, drama, drill team, ethnic, honors, international, jazz band, literary magazine, marching band, musical theater, newspaper, orchestra, pep band, photography, political, professional, radio and TV, religious, social, social service, student government, symphony, and yearbook. Popular campus events include Spectrum Series, plays, and Little Sibs Weekend.

Sports: There are 10 intercollegiate sports for men and 8 for women, and 27 intramural sports for men and 27 for women. Facilities include a 5800-seat stadium, a 3000-seat gym, an all-weather track, a field house, a weight-training center, an 8-lane swimming pool with diving board, saunas, exercise rooms, 3 basketball courts, 2 handball/racquetball courts, playing fields, a fitness center, and a soccer complex with 2 full-size fields.

Disabled Students: 5% of the campus is accessible. Wheelchair ramps, elevators, special parking, specially equipped rest rooms, special class scheduling, lowered drinking fountains, and lowered telephones are available.

Services: Counseling and information services are available, as is tutoring in every subject. There is a reader service for the blind.

Campus Safety and Security: Measures include 24-hour foot and vehicle patrol, self-defense education, escort service, and informal discussions. There are pamphlets/posters/films, emergency telephones, lighted pathways/sidewalks, and encoded student identification cards, and an electronic-access system in residence halls.

Programs of Study: Ashland confers B.A., B.S., B.M., B.S.B.A., B.S.Ed., B.S.N., and B.S.W. degrees. Associate, master's, and doctoral degrees are also awarded. Bachelor's degrees are awarded in BIOLOGICAL SCIENCE (biology/biological science, and toxicology), BUSINESS (accounting, banking and finance, business administration and management, business economics, fashion merchandising, hotel/motel and restaurant management, management information systems, marketing/retailing/merchandising, and recreational facilities management), COMMUNICATIONS AND THE ARTS (art, broadcasting, communications, creative writing, dramatic arts, English, fine arts, French, journalism, media arts, music, musical theater, Spanish, and speech/debate/rhetoric), COMPUTER AND PHYSICAL SCIENCE (chemistry, computer science, geology, mathematics, and physics), EDUCATION (art, athletic training, early childhood, education administration, education of the exceptional child, elementary, English, foreign languages, health, home economics, music, physical, science, and secondary), ENGINEERING AND ENVIRONMENTAL DESIGN (commercial art, and environmental science), HEALTH PROFESSIONS (predentistry, premedicine, preoptometry, preveterinary science, and recreation therapy), SOCIAL SCIENCE (American studies, child care/child and family studies, criminal justice, economics, food science, history, international studies, philosophy, physical fitness/movement, political science/government, prelaw, psychology, religion, social science, social work, and sociology). Preprofessional science is the strongest academically. Business and teacher education are the largest.

Required: To graduate, students must complete at least 128 semester hours with a minimum GPA of 2.0 overall and 2.25 in the major. All students must complete 3 semester hours of freshman studies and 44 semester hours of interdisciplinary studies, including courses in English, phys ed, religion, speech, business or economics, fine arts, humanities, science, and social science.

Special: Opportunities are provided for internships, co-op programs in all business majors, work-study programs, dual majors, a 3-2 engineering degree with the University of Akron or the University of Toledo, credit by exam, study abroad in 27 countries, a Washington semester, and pass/fail options. There are 17 national honor societies, a freshman honors program, and 10 departmental honors programs.

Faculty/Classroom: 61% of faculty are male; 39%, female. 81% teach undergraduates. No introductory courses are taught by graduate students. The average class size in an introductory lecture is 20; in a laboratory, 11; and in a regular course, 18.

Admissions: 7 freshmen graduated first in their class.

Requirements: The SAT I or ACT is required. In addition, applicants must be graduates of an accredited secondary school. The GED is accepted. The recommended preparatory program includes 4 units of English, 3 each of science, social studies, and math, and 2 of foreign language. An interview is recommended. AP and CLEP credits are accepted. Important factors in the admissions decision are advanced placement or honor courses, evidence of special talent, and leadership record. Applications may be submitted on-line at the university's web site.

Procedure: Freshmen are admitted to all sessions. Entrance exams should be taken in the spring of the junior year. There is a deferred admissions plan. Application deadlines are open.

Transfer: 112 transfer students enrolled in a recent year. Official transcripts from all previous colleges, showing course credits and a minimum GPA of 2.25, must be submitted when applying for transfer. Generally, if the student has successfully completed a minimum of 1 year of college, the SAT I or ACT will not be required. 32 credits of 128 must be completed at Ashland.

Visiting: There are regularly scheduled orientations for prospective students. There are guides for informal visits and visitors may sit in on classes and stay overnight. To schedule a visit, contact the Office of Admissions at (800) 882-1548, ext. 5052.

Financial Aid: In a recent year, 97% of all students received some form of financial aid. 77% of freshmen and 74% of continuing students received need-based aid. The average freshman award was $15,275. Of that total, scholarships or need-based grants averaged $9965 ($3613 maximum); loans averaged $3613; and work contracts averaged $1000 ($2000 maximum). 30% of undergraduates work part time. Average annual earnings from campus work are $600. The average financial indebtedness of a recent graduate was $17,000. The FAFSA, the college's own financial statement and federal tax returns are required. The fall application deadline is November 15.

International Students: There were 52 international students enrolled in a recent year. The school actively recruits these students. They must score 500 on the written TOEFL.

Computers: The mainframes are a Sun, NT, and Netware servers. There are 10 Windows-based computerized classrooms with more than 200 Pentium PCs, 1 Mac-based classroom with 28 Macs, and 2 staffed multi-platform open labs with 60 Pentium PCs and several more Macs. More than 200 additional computers exist throughout campus for student use. All students may access the system. There are no time limits. The fee is $1.50 per credit hour.

Graduates: In a recent year, 516 bachelor's degrees were awarded. The most popular majors were elementary education (24%), business management (9%), and criminal justice (6%). In an average class, 2% graduate in 3 years, 39% in 4 years, 46% in 5 years, and 52% in 6 years. 33 companies recruited on campus in a recent year. Of the 2000 graduating class, 8% were enrolled in graduate school within 6 months of graduation and 34% were employed.

Admissions Contact: Office of Admissions.
E-mail: *auadmsn@ashland.edu* Web: *http://www.ashland.edu*

BALDWIN-WALLACE COLLEGE D-1

Berea, OH 44017-2088 **(440) 826-2222; Fax: (440) 826-3830**

Full-time: 1232 men, 1810 women	**Faculty:** 160; IIA, -$
Part-time: 296 men, 655 women	**Ph.D.s:** 78%
Graduate: 290 men, 601 women	**Student/Faculty:** 19 to 1
Year: semesters, summer session	**Tuition:** $16,330
Application Deadline: May 1	**Room & Board:** $5680
Freshman Class: 2090 applied, 1695 accepted, 701 enrolled	
SAT I Verbal/Math: 565/570	**ACT:** 24 **VERY COMPETITIVE+**

Baldwin-Wallace College, established in 1845, is a private liberal arts institution affiliated with the United Methodist Church. In addition to regional accreditation, B-W has baccalaureate program accreditation with NASM and NCATE. The 3 libraries contain 250,000 volumes, 103,000 microform items, and 18,500 audiovisual forms/CDs, and subscribe to 1000 periodicals. Computerized library services include the card catalog, interlibrary loans, and database searching. Special learning facilities include a learning resource center, art gallery, and radio station. The 100-acre campus is in a suburban area 14 miles southwest of Cleveland. Including residence halls, there are 59 buildings.

Student Life: 92% of undergraduates are from Ohio. Others are from 29 states, 22 foreign countries, and Canada. 85% are from public schools. 80% are white. 49% are Catholic; 40%, Protestant; 10%, Buddhist, Hindu, Muslim, Orthodox, and Unitarian. The average age of freshmen is 18; all undergraduates, 24. 19% do not continue beyond their first year; 65% remain to graduate.

Housing: 1928 students can be accommodated in college housing, which includes single-sex and coed dormitories and on-campus apartments. In addition, there are honors houses and special-interest houses. On-campus housing is guaranteed for all 4 years. 62% of students live on campus; of those, 40% remain on campus on weekends. All students may keep cars.

Activities: 20% of men belong to 6 national fraternities; 22% of women belong to 6 national sororities. There are 40 groups on campus, including art, band, cheerleading, chess, choir, chorale, chorus, computers, dance, drama, drill team, ethnic, gay, honors, international, jazz band, literary magazine, musical theater, newspaper, opera, orchestra, pep band, political, professional, radio and TV, religious, social, social service, student government, symphony, and yearbook. Popular campus events include May Day Games, Greek Week, and Black History Month.

Sports: There are 11 intercollegiate sports for men and 10 for women, and 12 intramural sports for men and 11 for women. Facilities include an 8000-seat stadium with polyturf and an all-weather track, a 3000-seat gym, baseball fields, and a 6-court tennis complex. The recreation center houses a 200-meter track, a swimming pool, a dance studio, wrestling, gymnastics, and weight rooms, and facilities for basketball, racquetball, volleyball, bowling, and billiards.

Disabled Students: 75% of the campus is accessible. Wheelchair ramps, elevators, special parking, specially equipped rest rooms, special class scheduling, and lowered telephones are available.

Services: Counseling and information services are available, as is tutoring in every subject. There is a reader service for the blind, and remedial math, reading, and writing.

Campus Safety and Security: Measures include 24-hour foot and vehicle patrol, escort service, shuttle buses, and informal discussions. There are pamphlets/posters/films, emergency telephones, and lighted pathways/sidewalks.

Programs of Study: B-W confers B.A., B.S., B.M., B.M.E, and B.S.Ed. degrees. Master's degrees are also awarded. Bachelor's degrees are awarded in BIOLOGICAL SCIENCE (biology/biological science), BUSINESS (accounting, banking and finance, business administration and management, marketing/retailing/merchandising, personnel management, and sports management), COMMUNICATIONS AND THE ARTS (broadcasting, communications, dance, dramatic arts, English, fine arts, French, German, music business management, music performance, Spanish, and speech/debate/rhetoric), COMPUTER AND PHYSICAL SCIENCE (chemistry, computer science, earth science, geology, mathematics, and physics), EDUCATION (art, elementary, foreign languages, health, home economics, music, science, secondary, social studies, and special), ENGINEERING AND ENVIRONMENTAL DESIGN (engineering), HEALTH PROFESSIONS (medical laboratory technology, music therapy, predentistry, premedicine, speech pathology/audiology, and sports medicine), SOCIAL SCIENCE (community services, criminal justice, economics, history, international relations, philosophy, physical fitness/movement, political science/government, prelaw, psychology, religion, and sociology). Business, music, and education are the largest.

Required: All students must complete 124 semester hours and have at least a 2.0 GPA. A total of 45 semester hours must be taken in the liberal arts core, including 20 in humanities, 10 each in natural science and social science, 3 in math/computer science/statistics, and 2 in health and phys ed. Comprehensive exams are required in some majors.

Special: Special academic programs include internships that can qualify for credit, work-study programs, student teaching in England, and study abroad in Europe, India, Japan, Central America, and the Middle East.

There is cross-registration within the Cleveland Commission on Higher Education, as well as 3-2 programs in social work and biology with Case Western Reserve University, in forestry with Duke University, and in engineering with Columbia, Washington, and Case Western Reserve Universities; a 2-2 co-op allied health program is offered with local community colleges. B-W also offers the Consortium for Music Therapy, accelerated degree programs, a general studies degree, a B.A-B.S. degree, dual and student-designed majors, credit for life, military, and work experience, and pass/fail options. The Continuing Education Program offers degrees through evening and weekend colleges. There are 5 national honor societies, a freshman honors program, and 11 departmental honors programs.

Faculty/Classroom: 67% of faculty are male; 33%, female. 99% teach undergraduates. No introductory courses are taught by graduate students. The average class size in an introductory lecture is 20; in a laboratory, 22; and in a regular course, 18.

Admissions: 81% of the 2001-2002 applicants were accepted. The SAT I scores for the 2001-2002 freshman class were: Verbal--16% below 500, 45% between 500 and 599, 33% between 600 and 700, and 6% above 700; Math--17% below 500, 40% between 500 and 599, 35% between 600 and 700, and 8% above 700. The ACT scores were 20% below 21, 30% between 21 and 23, 30% between 24 and 26, 11% between 27 and 28, and 9% above 28. 52% of the current freshmen were in the top fifth of their class; 83% were in the top two fifths. 26 freshmen graduated first in their class.

Requirements: The SAT I or ACT is required. The recommended minimum score for the ACT is 20; for the SAT I, a composite score of 900 (450 each in verbal and math). The scores are used to support data from the high school record; alternative scores are considered. Applicants must be graduates of an accredited secondary school or have earned a GED. 16 academic credits are required, including 4 in English, 3 each in math, natural science, and social science, and 2 in a foreign language; alternative distributions are considered. A teacher's recommendation is required. B-W requires applicants to be in the upper 50% of their class. A GPA of 2.5 is required. AP and CLEP credits are accepted. Important factors in the admissions decision are leadership record, extracurricular activities record, and recommendations by school officials. Applications are accepted on-line.

Procedure: Freshmen are admitted to all sessions. Entrance exams should be taken late in the junior year or early in the senior year. There is a deferred admissions plan. Applications should be filed by May 1 for fall entry, March 15 for spring entry, and June 15 for summer entry, along with a $15 fee. Notification is sent on a rolling basis.

Transfer: 447 transfer students enrolled in 2001-2002. Applicants must have a minimum 2.0 GPA from an accredited institution, be in good standing, and submit a letter of recommendation. High school graduation is required. 32 credits of 124 must be completed at B-W.

Visiting: There are regularly scheduled orientations for prospective students, including an interview, a tour, and classroom visits. There are guides for informal visits and visitors may sit in on classes and stay overnight. To schedule a visit, contact the Admission Office.

Financial Aid: In 2001-2002, 98% of all freshmen and 92% of continuing students received some form of financial aid. 92% of freshmen and 88% of continuing students received need-based aid. The average freshman award was $14,304. Of that total, scholarships or need-based grants averaged $10,629 ($22,010 maximum); loans averaged $3326 ($4425 maximum); and work contracts averaged $1539 ($2000 maximum). 80% of undergraduates work part time. Average annual earnings from campus work are $1800. The average financial indebtedness of the 2001 graduate was $16,185. The FAFSA and the college's own financial statement are required. The fall application deadline is May 1.

International Students: The school actively recruits these students. They must score 500 on the written TOEFL and also take the SAT I or the ACT.

Computers: There are 450 PCs available for student access throughout the campus. There are roughly 550 lab systems with Internet access and many multimedia carts. All students may access the system 24 hours a day. There are no time limits and no lab fees.

Graduates: In 2001, 908 bachelor's degrees were awarded. The most popular majors were business (32%), education (13%), and sport and fitness administration/management (6%). In an average class, 1% graduate in 3 years, 60% in 4 years, 64% in 5 years, and 69% in 6 years. 59 companies recruited on campus in 2000-2001. Of the 2000 graduating class, 25% were enrolled in graduate school within 6 months of graduation and 81% were employed.

Admissions Contact: Juliann K. Baker, Director of Undergraduate Admission. A video is available. E-mail: *jbaker@rs6000baldwinw.edu* Web: *www.baldwinw.edu*

BLUFFTON COLLEGE

B-2

Bluffton, OH 45817

(419) 358-3257
(800) 488-3257; Fax: (419) 358-3232

Full-time: 384 men, 526 women	**Faculty:** 64; IIB, --$
Part-time: 24 men, 42 women	**Ph.D.s:** 78%
Graduate: 30 men, 44 women	**Student/Faculty:** 14 to 1
Year: semesters, summer session	**Tuition:** $15,376
Application Deadline: May 31	**Room & Board:** $5268
Freshman Class: 774 applied, 592 accepted, 239 enrolled	
SAT I Verbal/Math: 541/530	**ACT:** 23 **COMPETITIVE**

Bluffton College, founded in 1899, is a private, Christian, liberal arts institution affiliated with the General Conference Mennonite Church, U.S.A. In addition to regional accreditation, Bluffton College has baccalaureate program accreditation with ADA, CSWE, and NASM. The library contains 147,000 volumes, 95,000 microform items, and 1000 audiovisual forms/CDs, and subscribes to 650 periodicals. Computerized library services include the card catalog, interlibrary loans, and database searching. Special learning facilities include a learning resource center, art gallery, radio station, and the Lion and the Lamb Peace Arts Center. The 65-acre campus is in a small town 60 miles south of Toledo and 70 miles north of Dayton. Including residence halls, there are 25 buildings.

Student Life: 89% of undergraduates are from Ohio. Others are from 15 states, 15 foreign countries, and Canada. 95% are from public schools. 88% are white. 80% are Protestant; 13% Catholic. The average age of freshmen is 18; all undergraduates, 22. 21% do not continue beyond their first year; 57% remain to graduate.

Housing: 736 students can be accommodated in college housing, which includes single-sex dormitories. In addition, there are special-interest houses. On-campus housing is guaranteed for all 4 years. Full time students must live in residence halls unless commuting from home. 75% of students live on campus; of those, 50% remain on campus on weekends. Alcohol is not permitted. All students may keep cars.

Activities: There are no fraternities or sororities. There are 40 groups on campus, including art, band, cheerleading, choir, chorale, chorus, dance, drama, ethnic, honors, international, jazz band, literary magazine, musical theater, newspaper, opera, pep band, photography, political, professional, radio and TV, religious, social, social service, student government, and yearbook. Popular campus events include International Week, Spiritual Emphasis Weeks, and Artist Series.

Sports: There are 8 intercollegiate sports for men and 8 for women, and 10 intramural sports for men and 10 for women. Facilities include 2 gyms, an athletic complex, baseball/softball and football fields, an all-weather track, and a 2600-seat stadium.

Disabled Students: 33% of the campus is accessible. Elevators, special parking, specially equipped rest rooms, special class scheduling, lowered drinking fountains, and special computers for visually impaired students are available.

Services: Counseling and information services are available, as is tutoring in most subjects. There is a reader service for the blind. Tutoring is available for most students, as are classes at the student's request and/or faculty designation.

Campus Safety and Security: Measures include informal discussions, pamphlets/posters/films, emergency telephones, and lighted pathways/sidewalks. There are In a town of only 3,500, village police cruisers regularly patrol the campus during night hours. There are also two night watchwomen who communicate directly with village police.

Programs of Study: Bluffton College confers B.A. and B.S. degrees. Master's degrees are also awarded. Bachelor's degrees are awarded in BIOLOGICAL SCIENCE (biology/biological science, and nutrition), BUSINESS (accounting, apparel and accessories marketing, business administration and management, management science, marketing/retailing/merchandising, recreational facilities management, and sports management), COMMUNICATIONS AND THE ARTS (art, communications, English, music, and Spanish), COMPUTER AND PHYSICAL SCIENCE (chemistry, computer science, and mathematics), EDUCATION (early childhood, elementary, health, home economics, music, physical, and secondary), SOCIAL SCIENCE (child psychology/development, criminal justice, dietetics, economics, family and community services, food science, history, psychology, religion, social work, and sociology). Premedical and English are the strongest academically. Business and elementary education are the largest.

Required: To graduate, students must complete 122 semester hours with 40 to 60 in the major, and have a minimum GPA of 2.0. The general education requirements must be met, and satisfactory achievement in departmental senior comprehensives demonstrated. Distribution requirements are approximately one third for general education requirements, including 6 hours of religion, and one third to one half for the major.

Special: Special arrangements include internships in business, recreation, social work, and education, a Washington semester through the Coalition of Christian Colleges and Universites, and study abroad, including Latin-American exchange programs, student-designed majors and independent study are possible, as is credit for prior learning and for learning in voluntary service. There is an accelerated degree program in organizational management. Nondegree study and pass/fail options are offered. There are 2 national honor societies, and a freshman honors program.

Faculty/Classroom: 62% of faculty are male; 38%, female. All teach undergraduates. No introductory courses are taught by graduate students. The average class size in an introductory lecture is 23; in a laboratory, 12; and in a regular course, 17.

Admissions: 76% of the 2001-2002 applicants were accepted. The SAT I scores for the 2001-2002 freshman class were: Verbal--37% below 500, 41% between 500 and 599, 16% between 600 and 700, and 6% above 700; Math--29% below 500, 51% between 500 and 599, 18% between 600 and 700, and 2% above 700. The ACT scores were 29% below 21, 30% between 21 and 23, 25% between 24 and 26, 9% between 27 and 28, and 7% above 28. 37% of the current freshmen were in the top fifth of their class; 69% were in the top two fifths. 9 freshmen graduated first in their class.

Requirements: The SAT I or ACT is required with a required minimum of 920 composite on the SAT I or 19 on the ACT. The ACT is preferred. Other admissions requirements include graduation from an accredited secondary school, with a 2.3 GPA or clas rank above 50%. Recommended courses include 4 units of English and 3 units each of math, science, social studies, and a foreign language. The GED is accepted. A personal campus visit and an interview are strongly recommended. Music students must audition. Bluffton College requires applicants to be in the upper 50% of their class. A GPA of 2.3 is required. AP and CLEP credits are accepted. Important factors in the admissions decision are recommendations by school officials and extracurricular activities record. Applications are accepted on-line at the school's web site.

Procedure: Freshmen are admitted to all sessions. Entrance exams should be taken in the spring of the junior year or fall of the senior year. There is a deferred admissions plan. Applications should be filed by May 31 for fall entry, along with a $20 fee. Notification is sent on a rolling basis.

Transfer: 47 transfer students enrolled in 2001-2002. Transfer students must have a minimum college GPA of 2.0, meet eligibility criteria from previous institutions, and have met their financial obligations at the former institution. A signed transfer recommendation must be submitted from each college attended. 30 credits of 122 must be completed at Bluffton College.

Visiting: There are regularly scheduled orientations for prospective students, including high school preview days on Saturdays and overnight visit programs; personal visits are arranged on a daily basis and are strongly encouraged. There are guides for informal visits and visitors may sit in on classes and stay overnight. To schedule a visit, contact the Office of Admission.

Financial Aid: In 2001-2002 all students received some form of financial aid. 83% of freshmen and 69% of continuing students received need-based aid. The average freshman award was $13,844. Of that total, scholarships or need-based grants averaged $10,528 ($22,716 maximum); loans averaged $2229 ($3625 maximum); and work contracts averaged $1357 ($2350 maximum). 65% of undergraduates work part time. Average annual earnings from campus work are $1074. The average financial indebtedness of the 2001 graduate was $20,214. The FAFSA is required. The fall application deadline is October 1.

International Students: There are 20 international students enrolled. The school actively recruits these students. They must score 500 on the written TOEFL or 180 on the electronic version.

Computers: The mainframe is an IBM AS/400. PCs are available to all students in a central lab and other various locations, including many academic departments. Several PCs in the computer lab are on the Internet; all students have e-mail addresses. There are no time limits and no fees.

Graduates: In 2001, 225 bachelor's degrees were awarded. The most popular majors were business/marketing (31%), education (21%), and protective services/public administration (7%). In an average class, 1% graduate in 3 years, 50% in 4 years, 57% in 5 years, and 57% in 6 years. 200 companies recruited on campus in 2000-2001. Of the 2000 graduating class, 9% were enrolled in graduate school within 6 months of graduation and 74% were employed.

Admissions Contact: Eric Fulcomer, Director of Admissions. A video is available. E-mail: *admissions@bluffton.edu* Web: *www.bluffton.edu*

BOWLING GREEN STATE UNIVERSITY — B-1

Bowling Green, OH 43403 — **(419) 372-2086; Fax: (419) 372-6955**

Full-time: 6379 men, 8346 women	**Faculty:** 652; I, --$
Part-time: 554 men, 589 women	**Ph.D.s:** 82%
Graduate: 1110 men, 1761 women	**Student/Faculty:** 23 to 1
Year: semesters, summer session	**Tuition:** $5604 ($11,856)
Application Deadline: July 15	**Room & Board:** $5190

Freshman Class: 9941 applied, 9105 accepted, 3624 enrolled

ACT: 22 — **COMPETITIVE**

Bowling Green State University, founded in 1910, is a public liberal arts institution offering more than 165 undergraduate and 75 graduate programs. There are 6 undergraduate schools and 1 graduate school. In addition to regional accreditation, BGSU has baccalaureate program accreditation with AACSB, ACCE, ACEJMC, ADA, APTA, ASLA, CAHEA, CSWE, NASAD, NASM, NCATE, and NLN. The 2 libraries contain 2,285,856 volumes, 2,256,892 microform items, and 672,745 audiovisual forms/CDs. Computerized library services include the card catalog, interlibrary loans, and database searching. Special learning facilities include a learning resource center, art gallery, planetarium, radio station, and TV station. The 1230-acre campus is in a small town 25 miles south of Toledo. Including residence halls, there are 118 buildings.

Student Life: 94% of undergraduates are from Ohio. Others are from 49 states, 85 foreign countries, and Canada. 88% are white. The average age of freshmen is 19; all undergraduates, 21. 22% do not continue beyond their first year; 58% remain to graduate.

Housing: 7000 students can be accommodated in college housing, which includes single-sex and coed dormitories, on-campus apartments, fraternity houses, and sorority houses. In addition, there are honors houses, language houses, special-interest houses, a living learning center, and accommodations for international students. 52% of students commute. All students may keep cars.

Activities: 11% of men belong to 19 national fraternities; 14% of women belong to 18 national sororities. There are 285 groups on campus, including art, band, cheerleading, chess, choir, chorale, chorus, computers, dance, debate, drama, drill team, ethnic, film, gay, honors, international, jazz band, literary magazine, marching band, musical theater, newspaper, opera, orchestra, pep band, photography, political, professional, radio and TV, religious, social, social service, student government, symphony, and yearbook. Popular campus events include Greek Week, International Festival, and all-campus picnic.

Sports: There are 11 intercollegiate sports for men and 11 for women, and 16 intramural sports for men and 16 for women. Facilities include 4 buildings, including a student recreation center and an intramural field house facility, a 30000-seat football stadium, a 5000-seat gym, tennis courts, a golf course, basketball and ice arenas, and softball and intramural fields.

Disabled Students: 80% of the campus is accessible. Wheelchair ramps, elevators, special parking, specially equipped rest rooms, special class scheduling, lowered drinking fountains, lowered telephones, and a shuttle van with lift capabilities are available.

Services: Counseling and information services are available, as is tutoring in some subjects, including writing, math, and 100-level content area classes such as biology, chemistry, and sociology. There is a reader service for the blind, and remedial math, reading, and writing.

Campus Safety and Security: Measures include 24-hour foot and vehicle patrol, escort service, shuttle buses, and informal discussions. There are pamphlets/posters/films, emergency telephones, lighted pathways/sidewalks, and a campus 911 number.

Programs of Study: BGSU confers B.A., B.S., B.A.C., B.F.A., B.A.H.S., B.L.S., B.Mus., B.S.A.M.P.D., B.S.C.F.R.M., B.S.B.A., B.S. in Econ., B.S.Ed., B.S.F.S.N., B.S.J., B.S.Tech., B.S. Applied Microbiology, B.S.A.Therapy, B.S. Child and Family Community Services, B.S. Criminal Justice, B.S. Dietetics, B.S. Environmental Health, B.S. Gerontology, B.S. Interior Design, B.S. Medical Technology, B.S.N., B.S.P.T., B.S.S.W., B.S. Communication Disorders degrees. Master's and doctoral degrees are also awarded. Bachelor's degrees are awarded in BIOLOGICAL SCIENCE (avian sciences, biochemistry, biology/biological science, life science, microbiology, neurosciences, and nutrition), BUSINESS (accounting, apparel and accessories marketing, banking and finance, business administration and management, business economics, business law, fashion merchandising, hospitality management services, hotel/motel and restaurant management, institutional management, international business management, labor studies, management information systems, marketing/retailing/merchandising, personnel management, purchasing/inventory management, recreation and leisure services, sports management, and tourism), COMMUNICATIONS AND THE ARTS (art, art history and appreciation, broadcasting, communications, creative writing, dance, design, dramatic arts, English, film arts, fine arts, French, German, jazz, journalism, Latin, music performance, music theory and composition, Russian, Spanish, technical and business writing, and telecommunications), COMPUTER AND PHYSICAL SCIENCE (chemistry, computer science, geology, information sciences and systems, mathematics, physical sciences, physics, and statistics), EDUCATION (art, business, early childhood, elementary, foreign languages, health, home economics, marketing and distribution, music, physical, secondary, special, and technical), ENGINEERING AND ENVIRONMENTAL DESIGN (computer technology, construction technology, environmental design, environmental science, industrial engineering technology, interior design, manufacturing technology, and mechanical design technology), HEALTH PROFESSIONS (art therapy, environmental health science, exercise science, health care administration, health science, medical laboratory technology, nursing, physical therapy, premedicine, and speech pathology/audiology), SOCIAL SCIENCE (African studies, American studies, Asian/Oriental studies, child care/child and family studies, classical/ancient civilization, criminal justice, dietetics, economics, ethnic studies, family/consumer resource management, food science, geography, gerontology, history, international studies, liberal arts/general studies, parks and recreation management, philosophy, physical fitness/movement, political science/government, psychology, public administration, social science, social work, sociology, and women's studies). Pre-early childhood education, biology, and psychology are the largest.

Required: To graduate, students must complete a minimum of 122 semester hours, including at least 30 in the major, depending on the major, and maintain a minimum 2.0 GPA. The 8-course mandatory general education core includes 2 courses each from natural sciences, social sciences, and humanities and the arts, 1 course from cultural diversity in the United States, and 1 additional course from among natural sciences, social sciences, humanities and the arts, and foreign languages and cultures. At least 1 of the courses in the social sciences or humanities and arts must be designated as foreign cultures or foreign language at the 200 level or above.

Special: Special academic programs include co-op programs in all majors with the National Student Exchange, internships, a Washington semester, work-study, and study abroad. Dual majors are available in all programs, and a B.A.-B.S. degree is offered in computer science, geology, math, psychology, statistics, scientific and technical communication, and individualized planned program. Student-designed majors, independent study, credit for experience, nondegree study, and pass/fail options are possible. There are 20 national honor societies, including Phi Beta Kappa, a freshman honors program, and 40 departmental honors programs.

Faculty/Classroom: 56% of faculty are male; 44%, female. 77% teach undergraduates. Graduate students teach 21% of introductory courses. The average class size in an introductory lecture is 30; in a laboratory, 19; and in a regular course, 29.

Admissions: 92% of the 2001-2002 applicants were accepted. The ACT scores for the 2001-2002 freshman class were: 39% below 21, 30% between 21 and 23, 20% between 24 and 26, 6% between 27 and 28, and 4% above 28. 26% of the current freshmen were in the top fifth of their class; 56% were in the top two fifths. There were 12 National Merit finalists.

Requirements: The SAT I is required and the ACT is recommended. In addition, for all freshmen except those out of high school for 3 or more years, the minimum composite SAT I score is 920 and the minimum ACT score is 20. Performance and test scores must be at minimum and above to be considered. There is no automatic admission. Special circumstances are reviewed as applicable. Other admissions requirements include graduation from an accredited secondary school with a recommended 4 years of English, 3 years each of math, science, and social studies/history, 2 years of a foreign language,and 1 year of art or music. The GED is accepted. Music students must audition. A GPA of 2.5 is required. AP and CLEP credits are accepted. Important factors in the admissions decision are advanced placement or honor courses, recommendations by school officials, and evidence of special talent. Applications are accepted on-line at the schools's web site.

Procedure: Freshmen are admitted to all sessions. Entrance exams should be taken in the junior year. There is a deferred admissions plan. Applications should be filed by July 15 for fall entry, December 15 for spring entry, and May 15 for summer entry. Notification is sent on a rolling basis.

Transfer: 667 transfer students enrolled in 2001-2002. Transfer students who have attempted 12 or more hours at a college are eligible. Applicants with 60 or more semester hours or an associate's degree must have at least a 2.0 GPA; those with fewer hours need a minimum GPA of 2.5 but may petition for admission if it is lower. 30 credits of 122 must be completed at BGSU.

Visiting: There are regularly scheduled orientations for prospective students. There are guides for informal visits and visitors may sit in on classes and stay overnight. To schedule a visit, contact the Office of Admissions at *admissions@bgnet.bgsu.edu*.

Financial Aid: In 2001-2002, 69% of all freshmen and 68% of continuing students received some form of financial aid. 47% of continuing students received need-based aid. The average freshman award was $5500. Of that total, scholarships or need-based grants averaged $3110 ($12,100 maximum); loans averaged $4100 ($18,000 maximum); work contracts averaged $1875 ($2100 maximum); and $3500 ($5300 maximum). 27% of undergraduates work part time. Average annual earnings from campus work are $1900. The average financial indebtedness of the 2001 graduate was $17,000. BGSU is a member of CSS. The FAFSA is required. The application deadline is open.

International Students: There are 153 international students enrolled. The school actively recruits these students. They must score 500 on the written TOEFL or take the MELAB.

Computers: The mainframes are an IBM 9121, an IBM 9221, the Sun SPARCserver cluster, and SGI PowerChallenge L, a BGUNIX, a VAX 6620, and Sun workstations. There are about 1800 computers available in computer labs and in residence halls. Students are able to get accounts on university mainframes through specified classes. All students can receive a BGNet account that provides access to the World Wide Web. All students may access the system during operating hours. There are no time limits and no lab fees.

Graduates: In 2001, 2768 bachelor's degrees were awarded. The most popular majors were elementary education (9%), biology (4%), and nursing (3%). In an average class, 24% graduate in 4 years, 52% in 5 years, and 58% in 6 years.

Admissions Contact: Gary Swegan, Director of Admissions. A video is available. E-mail: *admissions@bgnet.bgsu.edu*
Web: *www.bgsu.edu/offices/admissions/choose/welcome.html*

CAPITAL UNIVERSITY C-3
Columbus, OH 43209-2394 (614) 236-6101
(800) 289-6289; (614) 236-6926

Full-time: 753 men, 1233 women	**Faculty:** 165; IIA, -$
Part-time: 238 men, 484 women	**Ph.D.s:** 80%
Graduate: 633 men, 547 women	**Student/Faculty:** 10 to 1
Year: semesters, summer session	**Tuition:** $17,990
Application Deadline: April 15	**Room & Board:** $5640
Freshman Class: 2223 applied, 1792 accepted, 519 enrolled	
SAT I Verbal/Math: 541/526	**ACT:** 23 **COMPETITIVE**

Capital University, established in 1830, is a private institution affiliated with the Evangelical Lutheran Church in America. Its undergraduate and graduate programs emphasize the liberal arts and sciences, music, and nursing. There are 4 undergraduate and 3 graduate schools. In addition to regional accreditation, Capital has baccalaureate program accreditation with CSWE, NASM, NCATE, and NLN. The 2 libraries contain 177,143 volumes, 112,906 microform items, and 13,558 audiovisual forms/CDs, and subscribe to 750 periodicals. Computerized library services include the card catalog, interlibrary loans, and database searching. Special learning facilities include an art gallery and a TV studio. The 48-acre campus is in a suburban area 3 miles east of downtown Columbus. Including residence halls, there are 24 buildings.

Student Life: 92% of undergraduates are from Ohio. Others are from 23 states, 10 foreign countries, and Canada. 97% are from public schools. 87% are white. 48% are Protestant; 18% Catholic; 12% claim no religious affiliation. The average age of freshmen is 18; all undergraduates, 20. 21% do not continue beyond their first year; 68% remain to graduate.

Housing: 1226 students can be accommodated in college housing, which includes coed dormitories, on-campus apartments, and off-campus apartments. In addition, there are special-interest floors, substance-free floors, Greek organization floors, and a self-governing unit. On-campus housing is guaranteed for all 4 years. 65% of students live on campus; of those, 75% remain on campus on weekends. Upperclassmen may keep cars.

Activities: 25% of men belong to 3 local and 2 national fraternities; 25% of women belong to 4 local and 3 national sororities. There are 60 groups on campus, including art, band, cheerleading, choir, chorale, chorus, dance, debate, drama, drill team, ethnic, gay, honors, international, jazz band, literary magazine, musical theater, newspaper, opera, orchestra, pep band, political, professional, radio and TV, religious, social, social service, student government, symphony, and yearbook. Popular campus events include Kids and Sibs Weekend, Greek Week, and men's and women's basketball games.

Sports: There are 8 intercollegiate sports for men and 6 for women, and 4 intramural sports for men and 4 for women. Facilities include a 2500-seat football stadium, a 2400-seat gym, tennis courts, and weight and game rooms. The recreation center offers bowling, billiards, and other game facilities.

Disabled Students: Elevators, special parking, specially equipped rest rooms, and special class scheduling are available.

Services: Counseling and information services are available, as is tutoring in most subjects. There is remedial math and writing.

Campus Safety and Security: Measures include 24-hour foot and vehicle patrol, self-defense education, escort service, and pamphlets/posters/films. There are lighted pathways/sidewalks.

Programs of Study: Capital confers B.A., B.F.A., B.G.S., B.M., B.S.N., and B.S.W. degrees. Master's degrees are also awarded. Bachelor's degrees are awarded in BIOLOGICAL SCIENCE (biochemistry and biology/biological science), BUSINESS (accounting and business administration and management), COMMUNICATIONS AND THE ARTS (communications, dramatic arts, English, fine arts, French, music, public relations, Spanish, and speech/debate/rhetoric), COMPUTER AND PHYSICAL SCIENCE (chemistry, computer science, and mathematics), EDUCATION (elementary, middle school, physical, and secondary), ENGINEERING AND ENVIRONMENTAL DESIGN (environmental science), HEALTH PROFESSIONS (art therapy, nursing, predentistry, premedicine, and sports medicine), SOCIAL SCIENCE (behavioral science, criminal justice, economics, history, international relations, philosophy, physical fitness/movement, political science/government, prelaw, psychology, religion, social work, and sociology). Business, education, and history are the largest.

Required: To graduate, all students must complete at least 124 semester hours, with a varying number of hours in the major, and maintain a minimum 2.0 GPA. The university core, 36 semester hours, must be followed in an ordered sequence throughout the 4 years; considered an assessment program, it includes specific courses in reading and writing, communication, health, art, science, social science, the humanities, ethics, and religion.

Special: Special academic programs include cross-registration with the Higher Education Council of Columbus, semester internships in most majors, and a Washington semester. Study abroad in 21 countries on 5 continents includes opportunities in Jamaica and at the Kodaly Institute of Music in Hungary. Also possible are a general studies degree and student-designed majors. A dual degree in engineering is offered with Case Western Reserve University and Washington University in St. Louis. Credit for life, military, and work experience may be granted, and nondegree study and pass/fail options are offered. There are 9 national honor societies, and a freshman honors program.

Faculty/Classroom: 57% of faculty are male; 43%, female. 80% teach undergraduates. No introductory courses are taught by graduate students. The average class size in an introductory lecture is 30; in a laboratory, 15; and in a regular course, 20.

Admissions: 81% of the 2001-2002 applicants were accepted. The SAT I scores for the 2001-2002 freshman class were: Math--34% below 500, 41% between 500 and 599, 22% between 600 and 700, and 2% above 700. The ACT scores for the 2001-2002 freshman class were: 26% below 21, 31% between 21 and 23, 24% between 24 and 26, 10% between 27 and 28, and 9% above 28. 42% of the current freshmen were in the top fifth of their class; 74% were in the top two fifths. 7 freshmen graduated first in their class.

Requirements: The SAT I or ACT is required. In addition, other admissions requirements include graduation from an accredited secondary school with 16 academic credits, including 4 units of English, 3 each of math, science, and social science, 2 units of a foreign language, and 1 of electives; nursing applicants need chemistry. The GED is accepted. High school students must submit recommendations from their guidance counselor. An interview is recommended. Students must audition for entry to the Conservatory of Music. A GPA of 2.6 is required. AP and CLEP credits are accepted. Important factors in the admissions decision are advanced placement or honor courses, recommendations by school officials, and evidence of special talent. Applications are available on-line at the school's web site.

Procedure: Freshmen are admitted to all sessions. Entrance exams should be taken by December of the senior year. There is a deferred admissions plan. Applications should be filed by April 15 for fall entry, December 1 for winter entry, and April 1 for summer entry, along with a $25 fee. Notification is sent on a rolling basis.

Transfer: 85 transfer students enrolled in 2001-2002. Transfer students must have a minimum college GPA of 2.25. The SAT I or ACT is recommended, as is an interview. 30 credits of 124 must be completed at Capital.

Visiting: There are regularly scheduled orientations for prospective students, including an interview with a counselor and a campus tour. There are guides for informal visits and visitors may sit in on classes and stay overnight. To schedule a visit, contact the Admissions Office.

Financial Aid: In 2001-2002, 99% of all students received some form of financial aid. 60% of freshmen and 58% of continuing students received need-based aid. The average freshman award was $15,250. Of that total, scholarships or need-based grants averaged $9802 ($17,000 maximum); loans averaged $3690 ($8625 maximum); and work contracts averaged $1630 ($1700 maximum). 40% of undergraduates work part time. Average annual earnings from campus work are $839. The average financial indebtedness of the 2001 graduate was $16,425. Capital is a member of CSS. The FAFSA is required. The fall application deadline is April 1.

International Students: There are 21 international students enrolled. The school actively recruits these students. They must score 500 on the written TOEFL.

Computers: The mainframe is a Sun UltraSPARC II. There are 6 general labs and 90 PCs. The campus is fully networked, including residence hall rooms, a 25-station technology classroom, and an advanced computational lab. All students may access the system 24 hours per day. There are no time limits and no fees.

Graduates: In 2001, 360 bachelor's degrees were awarded. The most popular majors were multidisciplinary (13%), business (11%), and social work (10%). In an average class, 50% graduate in 4 years, 58% in 5 years, and 60% in 6 years. 27 companies recruited on campus in 2000-2001. Of the 2000 graduating class, 21% were enrolled in graduate school within 6 months of graduation and 97% were employed.

Admissions Contact: Kimberly V. Ebbrecht, Director of Admission. A video is available. E-mail: *admissions@capital.edu*
Web: *www.capital.edu*

CASE WESTERN RESERVE UNIVERSITY D-1

Cleveland, OH 44106 **(216) 368-4450; Fax: (216) 368-5111**

Full-time: 1916 men, 1201 women	**Faculty:** 428; I, av$
Part-time: 133 men, 131 women	**Ph.D.s:** 95%
Graduate: 3090 men, 2745 women	**Student/Faculty:** 7 to 1
Year: semesters, summer session	**Tuition:** $21,168
Application Deadline: February 1	**Room & Board:** $6250
Freshman Class: 4663 applied, 3429 accepted, 738 enrolled	
SAT I or ACT: required	**MOST COMPETITIVE**

Case Western Reserve University, founded in 1826, is a private institution offering undergraduate, graduate, and professional programs in arts and sciences, dentistry, engineering, law, management, medicine, nursing, and social work. There are 4 undergraduate and 7 graduate schools. In addition to regional accreditation, CWRU has baccalaureate program accreditation with AACSB, ABET, CAHEA, NASM, and NLN. The 7 libraries contain 2,205,774 volumes, 2,444,697 microform items, and 47,388 audiovisual forms/CDs, and subscribe to 16,773 periodicals. Computerized library services include the card catalog, interlibrary loans, and database searching. Special learning facilities include a learning resource center, art gallery, natural history museum, and radio station. The 152-acre campus is in an urban area 4 miles east of downtown Cleveland. Including residence halls, there are 87 buildings.

Student Life: 58% of undergraduates are from Ohio. Others are from 48 states, 29 foreign countries, and Canada. 70% are from public schools. 73% are white; 13% Asian American. The average age of freshmen is 18; all undergraduates, 20. 10% do not continue beyond their first year; 75% remain to graduate.

Housing: 2285 students can be accommodated in college housing, which includes single-sex and coed dormitories, fraternity houses, and sorority houses. Special housing for students in the College Scholars Program is also available. On-campus housing is guaranteed for all 4 years. 78% of students live on campus; of those, 85% remain on campus on weekends. All students may keep cars.

Activities: 36% of men belong to 18 national fraternities; 17% of women belong to 1 local sorority and 4 national sororities. There are 100 groups on campus, including art, cheerleading, chess, choir, chorale, computers, dance, debate, drama, ethnic, film, gay, honors, international, jazz band, literary magazine, marching band, musical theater, newspaper, orchestra, photography, political, professional, radio, religious, social, social service, student government, symphonic winds ensemble, and yearbook. Popular campus events include Hudson Relays, Greek Week, and African American Heritage Celebration.

Sports: There are 12 intercollegiate sports for men and 10 for women, and 25 intramural sports for men and 25 for women. Facilities include a gym with multipurpose rooms, football, baseball, and soccer fields, indoor and all-weather tracks, softball diamonds, a swimming pool, weight, fencing, and wrestling rooms, basketball, badminton, volleyball, squash, tennis, and racquetball courts, and an archery range.

Disabled Students: Wheelchair ramps, elevators, special parking, specially equipped rest rooms, special class scheduling, lowered drinking fountains, lowered telephones, and TDD, special testing arrangements, note-taking assistance, and individualized academic counseling and planning are available.

Services: Counseling and information services are available, as is tutoring in every subject. There is a reader service for the blind, seminars to improve computing skills and study strategies and supplemental instruction in designated courses in biology, chemistry, math, and physics.

Campus Safety and Security: Measures include 24-hour foot and vehicle patrol, self-defense education, escort service, and shuttle buses. There are informal discussions, pamphlets/posters/films, emergency telephones, lighted pathways/sidewalks, and property crime prevention programs, including bicycle lock rental, vehicle ID etching, and equipment bolting.

Programs of Study: CWRU confers B.A., B.S., B.S.E., and B.S.N. degrees. Master's and doctoral degrees are also awarded. Bachelor's degrees are awarded in BIOLOGICAL SCIENCE (biochemistry, biology/biological science, evolutionary biology, and nutrition), BUSINESS (accounting, and business administration and management), COMMUNICATIONS AND THE ARTS (art history and appreciation, classics, communications, comparative literature, dramatic arts, English, French, German, music, and Spanish), COMPUTER AND PHYSICAL SCIENCE (applied mathematics, astronomy, chemistry, computer science, fluid and thermal science, geology, mathematics, natural sciences, physics, polymer science, and statistics), EDUCATION (art, and music), ENGINEERING AND ENVIRONMENTAL DESIGN (aeronautical engineering, biomedical engineering, chemical engineering, civil engineering, computer engineering, electrical/electronics engineering, engineering, engineering physics, environmental science, materials science, mechanical engineering, and systems engineering), HEALTH PROFESSIONS (nursing), SOCIAL SCIENCE (American studies, anthropology, Asian/Oriental studies, economics, French studies, German area studies, gerontology, history, history of science, international studies, Japanese studies, philosophy, political science/government, psychology, religion, sociology, and women's studies). Engineering, accounting, and biology are the strongest academically. Engineering, biology, and psychology are the largest.

Required: To graduate, students must complete a minimum of 120 semester hours, with at least 30 hours in the major, and maintain a minimum GPA of 2.0. Students must complete a core curriculum as well as courses in English composition and phys ed.

Special: CWRU offers co-op programs with more than 160 employers; students may alternate classroom study with full-time employment. Cross-registration with 13 institutions in the Cleveland area is available, as well as internships in government, corporations, and nonprofit agencies. Students may participate in study abroad, a Washington semester, work-study programs, and accelerated-degree programs. B.A.-B.S. degrees, dual and student-designed majors, 3-2 engineering degrees, nondegree study, independent study, and pass/fail options are possible. There are extensive opportunities for undergraduates to work with faculty on research projects. Preprofessional Scholars Programs in medicine, dentistry, and law are availble. Interdisciplinary majors, such as environmental geology and a double major in pre-architecture, and interdisciplinary majors, such as nutritional biochemistry and metabolism, are available. There are 3 national honor societies, including Phi Beta Kappa.

Faculty/Classroom: 72% of faculty are male; 28%, female. 75% teach undergraduates, 95% do research, and 75% do both. Graduate students teach 5% of introductory courses. The average class size in an introductory lecture is 35 and in a regular course, 30.

Admissions: 74% of the 2001-2002 applicants were accepted. The SAT I scores for the 2001-2002 freshman class were: Verbal--2% below 500, 20% between 500 and 599, 46% between 600 and 700, and 32% above 700; Math--1% below 500, 11% between 500 and 599, 41% between 600 and 700, and 47% above 700. The ACT scores were 2% below 21, 5% between 21 and 23, 14% between 24 and 26, 19% between 27 and 28, and 60% above 28. 88% of the current freshmen were in the top fifth of their class; 98% were in the top two fifths. There were 56 National Merit finalists.

Requirements: The SAT I or ACT is required. In addition, SAT II: Subject tests in writing plus 2 others of the student's choice are strongly recommended for students who take the SAT I. Applicants must be graduates of an accredited secondary school. The GED is accepted. 16 high school academic credits are required, including 4 years of English, 3 of math, (4 for science, math, and engineering majors), and 1 of lab science (2 for science and math majors and premedical students). 2 to 4 years of foreign language are strongly recommended. Engineering, math, and science students should take the SAT II: Subject tests in math I/IC of IIC and physics and/or chemistry. A writing sample of the student's choice is required, and an interview is recommended. AP credits are accepted. Important factors in the admissions decision are advanced placement or honor courses, leadership record, and recommendations by school officials. CWRU accepts applications via its own web site or through the Apply! and Common App web sites.

Procedure: Freshmen are admitted fall, spring, and summer. Entrance exams should be taken by the fall of the senior year; CWRU recommends also taking the test during the spring of the junior year. There are early decision and deferred admissions plans. Early decision applications should be filed by January 1; regular applications, by February 1 for fall entry. Notification is sent April 1. 129 early decision candidates were accepted for the 2001-2002 class. 7% of all applicants are on a waiting list; 80 were accepted in 2001.

Transfer: 75 transfer students enrolled in 2001-2002. Transfer students should have a minimum GPA of 3.0 and meet all high school requirements. Grades of C or better transfer for credit. 60 credits of 120 must be completed at CWRU.

Visiting: There are regularly scheduled orientations for prospective students. There are guides for informal visits and visitors may sit in on classes and stay overnight. To schedule a visit, contact the Office of Undergraduate Admission.

Financial Aid: In 2001-2002, 91% of all freshmen and 90% of continuing students received some form of financial aid. 57% of freshmen and 49% of continuing students received need-based aid. The average freshman award was $20,063. 70% of undergraduates work part time. Average annual earnings from campus work are $2900. The average financial indebtedness of the 2001 graduate was $21,418. CWRU is a member of CSS. The CSS/Profile or FAFSA and parent and student income tax returns and W-2 forms are required. The fall application deadline is February 1.

International Students: There are 116 international students enrolled. The school actively recruits these students. They must score 550 on the written TOEFL or 213 on the electronic version or complete 30 hours of instruction at CWRU's English Language Center.

Computers: The mainframe is an IBM 9672 Model RB5. CWRUnet, the university's high-speed fiber-optic network, connects every residence-hall room with academic departments, libraries, and labs on campus, giving students desktop access to the Internet, a software library, CD-ROM databases, and other electronic resources. All students may access the system 24 hours a day. There are no time limits and no fees. It is strongly recommended that all students have a personal computer.

Graduates: In 2001, 729 bachelor's degrees were awarded. The most popular majors were biology (10%), psychology (7%), and management (7%). In an average class, 1% graduate in 3 years, 51% in 4 years, 73% in 5 years, and 75% in 6 years. 175 companies recruited on campus in 2000-2001. Of the 2000 graduating class, 39% were enrolled in graduate school within 6 months of graduation and 58% were employed.

Admissions Contact: Dean of Undergraduate Admission. A video is available. E-mail: *admission@po.cwru.edu* Web: *http://www.cwru.edu*

CEDARVILLE COLLEGE
(See Cedarville University)

CEDARVILLE UNIVERSITY — B-4
(Formerly Cedarville College)

Cedarville, OH 45314-0601 — **(937) 766-3200**
(800) CEDARVILLE; Fax: (937) 766-2760

Full-time: 1290 men, 1541 women	**Faculty:** 184; IIB, -$
Part-time: 64 men, 48 women	**Ph.D.s:** 61%
Graduate: 2 men, 6 women	**Student/Faculty:** 15 to 1
Year: quarters, summer session	**Tuition:** $12,624
Application Deadline: open	**Room & Board:** $4929
Freshman Class: 2083 applied, 1527 accepted, 735 enrolled	
SAT I Verbal/Math: 590/580	**ACT:** 25 **VERY COMPETITIVE**

Cedarville University, (formerly Cedarville College), founded in 1887, is a private Baptist college of arts and sciences offering programs in engineering, nursing, accounting, computer information systems, and education. The school is known for its religious commitment, conservative values, and community outreach programs. In addition to regional accreditation, the 'Ville has baccalaureate program accreditation with ABET and NLN. The library contains 165,997 volumes, 21,954 microform items, and 5949 audiovisual forms/CDs, and subscribes to 926 periodicals. Computerized library services include the card catalog, interlibrary loans, and database searching. Special learning facilities include a radio station, media resource center, and observatory. The 400-acre campus is in a small town 12 miles south of Springfield. Including residence halls, there are 39 buildings.

Student Life: 67% of undergraduates are from out of state, mostly the Midwest. Others are from 45 states, 10 foreign countries, and Canada. 53% are from public schools. 97% are white. All are Protestant. The average age of freshmen is 18; all undergraduates, 20. 14% do not continue beyond their first year; 58% remain to graduate.

Housing: 2218 students can be accommodated in college housing, which includes single-sex dormitories and married-student housing. On-campus housing is guaranteed for all 4 years. 77% of students live on campus; of those, 80% remain on campus on weekends. Alcohol is not permitted. All students may keep cars.

Activities: There are no fraternities or sororities. There are 49 groups on campus, including band, cheerleading, choir, chorale, chorus, debate, drama, ethnic, forensics, honors, international, jazz band, newspaper, orchestra, pep band, photography, political, professional, radio and TV, religious, social, social service, student government, and yearbook. Popular campus events include Cedar Day and Lil' Sibs Weekend.

Sports: There are 7 intercollegiate sports for men and 7 for women, and 23 intramural sports for men and 23 for women. Facilities include a 3500-seat gym, 5 basketball courts, an indoor track, 3 volleyball courts, 3 racquetball courts, badminton courts, a batting cage, a weight room, a training room, 9 outdoor tennis courts, a 400-meter 9-lane track, soccer, baseball, softball, and intramural playing fields, and an indoor jogging track.

Disabled Students: 60% of the campus is accessible. Wheelchair ramps, elevators, special parking, specially equipped rest rooms, special class scheduling, lowered drinking fountains, and lowered telephones are available.

Services: Counseling and information services are available, as is tutoring in some subjects, including specific science and social science courses and calculus. There is a reader service for the blind, and remedial math, reading, and writing.

Campus Safety and Security: Measures include 24-hour foot and vehicle patrol, escort service, informal discussions, and pamphlets/posters/films. There are emergency telephones and lighted pathways/sidewalks.

Programs of Study: the 'Ville confers B.A., B.S., B.M.E., B.S.E.E., B.S.M.E., and B.S.N. degrees. Associate and master's degrees are also awarded. Bachelor's degrees are awarded in BIOLOGICAL SCIENCE (biology/biological science), BUSINESS (accounting, banking and finance, business administration and management, management information systems, and marketing/retailing/merchandising), COMMUNICATIONS AND THE ARTS (broadcasting, communications, dramatic arts, English, multimedia, music, Spanish, and technical and business writing), COMPUTER AND PHYSICAL SCIENCE (chemistry, computer science, information sciences and systems, mathematics, and physics), ED-

UCATION (athletic training, Christian, early childhood, elementary, foreign languages, mathematics, middle school, music, physical, science, social studies, and special), ENGINEERING AND ENVIRONMENTAL DESIGN (electrical/electronics engineering and mechanical engineering), HEALTH PROFESSIONS (nursing), SOCIAL SCIENCE (American studies, biblical studies, criminal justice, history, international studies, missions, pastoral studies, philosophy, political science/government, pre-law, psychology, public administration, religious music, social science, social work, and sociology). Business, education, and science are the largest.

Required: To graduate, all students must maintain a minimum GPA of 2.0 while taking 192 quarter hours. General education requirements include 24 quarter hours of biblical education, 15 of science and math, 14 to 16 of humanities, 14 of social sciences and history, 10 to 15 of communication, and 3 of phys ed. Students must demonstrate proficiency in English and math and must fulfill the global awareness requirement through foreign language study or intercultural experience.

Special: Internships, study abroad in 9 countries, a Washington semester, dual majors, B.A.-B.S. degrees in biology, chemistry, and math, work-study programs with the college, and pass/fail options are available. Cross-registration with the Southwest Ohio Consortium for Higher Education and the Ohio Learning Network is possible. There are 3 national honor societies, a freshman honors program, and 1 departmental honors program.

Faculty/Classroom: 73% of faculty are male; 27%, female. All teach undergraduates. The average class size in an introductory lecture is 29; in a laboratory, 18; and in a regular course, 24.

Admissions: 73% of the 2001-2002 applicants were accepted. The SAT I scores for the 2001-2002 freshman class were: Verbal--8% below 500, 44% between 500 and 599, 34% between 600 and 700, and 10% above 700; Math--11% below 500, 44% between 500 and 599, 36% between 600 and 700, and 9% above 700. The ACT scores were 3% below 21, 24% between 21 and 23, 36% between 24 and 26, 18% between 27 and 28, and 19% above 28. 55% of the current freshmen were in the top fifth of their class; 87% were in the top two fifths. There were 18 National Merit finalists and 1 semifinalist. 58 freshmen graduated first in their class.

Requirements: The SAT I or ACT is required. In addition, the SAT I or ACT (preferred) is required, with scores above the national average preferred. The college recommends that applicants have 4 years of English and 3 each of social studies, math, science, and a foreign language. The GED is accepted. Recommendations from a local pastor and a high school counselor are required. An interview is recommended. the 'Ville requires applicants to be in the upper 50% of their class. A GPA of 3.0 is required. AP and CLEP credits are accepted. Important factors in the admissions decision are personality/intangible qualities, recommendations by school officials, and advanced placement or honor courses. Applications are accepted on-line at *www.cedarville.edu/admissions*.

Procedure: Freshmen are admitted to all sessions. Entrance exams should be taken by December of the senior year. There are early admissions and deferred admissions plans. Application deadlines are open. The fall 2001 application fee was $30. Notification is sent on a rolling basis. A waiting list is an active part of the admissions procedure.

Transfer: 133 transfer students enrolled in 2001-2002. Applicants must have a minimum college GPA of 3.0. The SAT I or ACT (preferred) is required. 48 quarter credits of 192 must be completed at the 'Ville.

Visiting: There are regularly scheduled orientations for prospective students, including campus tours, chapel services, class visits, and meetings with faculty, coaches, and admissions counselors. There are guides for informal visits and visitors may sit in on classes and stay overnight. To schedule a visit, contact the Admissions Office.

Financial Aid: In 2001-2002, 92% of all freshmen and 75% of continuing students received some form of financial aid. 71% of freshmen and 60% of continuing students received need-based aid. The average freshman award was $9413. Of that total, scholarships or need-based grants averaged $4116 ($16,725 maximum); loans averaged $2904 ($8125 maximum); and work contracts averaged $737 ($2600 maximum). 40% of undergraduates work part time. Average annual earnings from campus work are $1300. The average financial indebtedness of the 2001 graduate was $15,887. The FAFSA and the college's own financial statement are required. The fall application deadline is March 1.

International Students: There are 12 international students enrolled. They must score 550 on the written TOEFL or 213 on the electronic version and also take the SAT I or the ACT.

Computers: The mainframe is an HP 9000/800, model L2000. A network connects 5 public computer labs with more than 125 PCs and about 1100 residence hall rooms, which are equipped with PCs and printers. The network provides access to more than 150 software packages, library resources, e-mail, and the Internet. All students may access the system 24 hours a day for dorm rooms or up to 93 hours a week in the labs. There are no time limits and no fees.

Graduates: In 2001, 579 bachelor's degrees were awarded. The most popular majors were elementary education (17%), nursing (10%), and communication arts (7%). In an average class, 3% graduate in 3 years, 59% in 4 years, 65% in 5 years, and 66% in 6 years. 320 companies recruited on campus in 2000-2001. Of the 2000 graduating class, 9% were enrolled in graduate school within 6 months of graduation and 99% were employed.

Admissions Contact: David Ormsbee, Vice President for Enrollment Management. A video is available. E-mail: *admissions@cedarville.edu* Web: *http://www.cedarville.edu*

CENTRAL STATE UNIVERSITY — B-4
Wilberforce, OH 45384 (937) 376-6348
(800) 388-CSU1; Fax: (937) 376-6648

Full-time: 560 men, 642 women	**Faculty:** 77; IIB, -$
Part-time: 51 men, 67 women	**Ph.D.s:** 62%
Graduate: 28 men, 52 women	**Student/Faculty:** 16 to 1
Year: quarters, summer session	**Tuition:** $3714 ($8118)
Application Deadline: March 31	**Room & Board:** $5208
Freshman Class: 2567 applied, 1270 accepted, 391 enrolled	
ACT: 15	**COMPETITIVE+**

Central State University, founded in 1887, is a public institution offering programs in liberal arts, business, engineering, teacher preparation, and professional training. There are 3 undergraduate schools and 1 graduate school. In addition to regional accreditation, Central State has baccalaureate program accreditation with ABET and NASM. The library contains 179,241 volumes, 622,727 microform items, and 500 audiovisual forms/CDs, and subscribes to 26,316 periodicals. Computerized library services include the card catalog, interlibrary loans, and database searching. Special learning facilities include a learning resource center, art gallery, radio station, and the National Afro-American Museum and Cultural Center. The 60-acre campus is in a rural area 18 miles east of Dayton. Including residence halls, there are 34 buildings.

Student Life: 77% of undergraduates are from Ohio. Others are from 24 states and 2 foreign countries. 96% are African American. The average age of freshmen is 18; all undergraduates, 22. 42% do not continue beyond their first year; 23% remain to graduate.

Housing: 745 students can be accommodated in college housing, which includes single-sex dormitories. On-campus housing is guaranteed for the freshman year only and is available on a first-come, first-served basis. 57% of students live on campus. Alcohol is not permitted. All students may keep cars.

Activities: 1% of men belong to 2 national fraternities; 1% of women belong to 2 national sororities. There are 30 groups on campus, including art, band, cheerleading, choir, chorale, chorus, drama, drill team, ethnic, honors, jazz band, marching band, pep band, political, professional, radio and TV, religious, social, and student government. Popular campus events include Career Day and May Week.

Sports: There are 3 intercollegiate sports for men and 4 for women, and 8 intramural sports for men and 7 for women. Facilities include 2 gyms, a stadium, a swimming pool, a pool room, a baseball diamond, tennis courts, and a weight room.

Disabled Students: All of the campus is accessible. Wheelchair ramps, elevators, special parking, specially equipped rest rooms, lowered drinking fountains, and lowered telephones are available.

Services: Counseling and information services are available, as is tutoring in most subjects.

Campus Safety and Security: Measures include 24-hour foot and vehicle patrol and lighted pathways/sidewalks.

Programs of Study: Central State confers B.A., B.S., B.M., B.S.Ed., and B.S.M.E. degrees. Master's degrees are also awarded. Bachelor's degrees are awarded in BIOLOGICAL SCIENCE (biology/biological science), BUSINESS (accounting, banking and finance, business administration and management, and marketing/retailing/merchandising), COMMUNICATIONS AND THE ARTS (advertising, broadcasting, English, journalism, and music), COMPUTER AND PHYSICAL SCIENCE (chemistry, computer science, and mathematics), EDUCATION (art, elementary, health, music, physical, secondary, and special), ENGINEERING AND ENVIRONMENTAL DESIGN (graphic arts technology and manufacturing engineering), SOCIAL SCIENCE (economics, history, political science/government, psychology, public administration, social work, sociology, and water resources). Communication, music, and education are the strongest academically. Business administration is the largest.

Required: To graduate, students must complete 186 quarter credits, with a minimum GPA of 2.0 (2.5 in education). Required university core courses include 64 credits in English composition, math, computer skills, humanities, natural sciences, social sciences, health and phys ed, and African American history.

Special: Central State offers co-op programs in all majors, cross-registration with 15 area colleges, study abroad in 3 countries, internships, on-campus work-study programs, and B.A.-B.S. degrees. There is a freshman honors program.

Faculty/Classroom: 77% of faculty are male; 23%, female. All teach undergraduates and 75% both teach and do research. No introductory

courses are taught by graduate students. The average class size in an introductory lecture is 25; in a laboratory, 20; and in a regular course, 15.
Admissions: 49% of the 2001-2002 applicants were accepted. The ACT scores for the 2001-2002 freshman class were 89% below 21, 10% between 21 and 23, and 1% between 24 and 26.
Requirements: The ACT is required; the SAT I is accepted. Applicants must be graduates of an accredited secondary school. The GED is accepted. Students should have completed 4 years of high school English, 3 years each of math, science, and social studies, and 2 years of the same foreign language. Ohio applicants should have a GPA of 2.0 and a minimum ACT composite score of 15 or SAT I score of 720. Criteria are higher for out-of-state applicants, including a minimum GPA of 2.5. AP and CLEP credits are accepted. Applications are accepted on-line at *www.centralstate.edu/admissions/apply2.html*.
Procedure: Freshmen are admitted to all sessions. There are early admissions and deferred admissions plans. Applications should be filed by March 31 for fall entry, October 15 for winter entry, February 15 for spring entry, and April 15 for summer entry, along with a $15 fee. Notification is sent on a rolling basis.
Transfer: 127 transfer students enrolled in 2001-2002. Applicants should have a minimum college GPA of 2.0. Grades of C or better transfer for credit. Transfer students with fewer than 47 quarter hours must submit high school transcripts and test scores. Transfers are admitted every term. 45 quarter credits of 186 must be completed at Central State.
Visiting: There are regularly scheduled orientations for prospective students. There are guides for informal visits and visitors may sit in on classes. To schedule a visit, contact the Admissions Office.
Financial Aid: The average freshman award was $10,765. Of that total, scholarships or need-based grants averaged $5958 ($8890 maximum); loans averaged $6040 ($15,975 maximum); and work contracts averaged $1918 ($2000 maximum). 48% of undergraduates work part time. Average annual earnings from campus work are $1920. The FAFSA and the college's own financial statement are required. The fall application deadline is March 31.
International Students: There are 8 international students enrolled. They must score 500 on the written TOEFL and also take the SAT I or the ACT, scoring 19.
Computers: The mainframe is a Microsoft NT server. There are 350 individual PCs available to students in 9 computer labs with access to the Internet and Web. All students may access the system.
Graduates: In 2001, 81 bachelor's degrees were awarded. The most popular majors were education (25%), business (21%), and social sciences and history (17%). In an average class, 1% graduate in 3 years, 9% in 4 years, 20% in 5 years, and 22% in 6 years. 135 companies recruited on campus in 2000-2001. Of the 2000 graduating class, 37% were enrolled in graduate school within 6 months of graduation and 96% were employed.
Admissions Contact: Thandabantu Maceo, Director of Admissions. A video is available. E-mail: *admissions@csu.ces.edu*
Web: *www.centralstate.edu*

CINCINNATI COLLEGE OF MORTUARY SCIENCE A-4
Cincinnati, OH 45224-1462 (513) 761-2020
(888) 377-8433; Fax: (513) 761-3333

Full-time: 78 men, 43 women	**Faculty:** 7
Part-time: 2 men, 3 women	**Ph.D.s:** 33%
Graduate: none	**Student/Faculty:** 17 to 1
Year: quarters, summer session	**Tuition:** $10,850
Application Deadline: October 1	**Room & Board:** n/app
Freshman Class: 75 applied, 73 accepted, 70 enrolled	
SAT I or ACT: required	**SPECIAL**

The Cincinnati College of Mortuary Science, founded in 1882, is the only private mortuary college in the country that is regionally accredited at the bachelor's level. The curriculum encompasses the embalming sciences, funeral directing, and the liberal arts. In addition to regional accreditation, CCMS has baccalaureate program accreditation with ABFSE. The 2 libraries contain 6000 volumes. Computerized library services include the card catalog. Special learning facilities include a clinical embalming lab. The 16-acre campus is in an urban area 8 miles from downtown Cincinnati. There is 1 building.
Student Life: 50% of undergraduates are from out of state, mostly the Midwest. Others are from 15 states. 93% are white. The average age of all undergraduates is 24. 15% do not continue beyond their first year; 85% remain to graduate.
Housing: There are no residence halls. Alcohol is not permitted.
Activities: There are no fraternities or sororities. There are some groups and organizations on campus, including student government and yearbook. Popular campus events include field trips, guest lectures, and welcoming and farewell parties.
Sports: There is no sports program at CCMS.
Disabled Students: All of the campus is accessible. Wheelchair ramps, elevators, special parking, and specially equipped rest rooms are available.
Campus Safety and Security: Measures include informal discussions, pamphlets/posters/films, emergency telephones, and lighted pathways/sidewalks.
Programs of Study: CCMS confers the Bachelor of Mortuary Science degree. Associate degrees are also awarded. Bachelor's degrees are awarded in BUSINESS (funeral home services).
Required: To graduate, students must complete 180 quarter credit hours, including 90 in the major, with a minimum GPA of 2.0. General education requirements consist of 18 quarter hours each in natural science/math, social science, and humanities/arts, and 12 each in English composition and literature, business management, and free electives.
Special: Limited credit may be given for life, military, and work experience.
Faculty/Classroom: 87% of faculty are male; 13%, female. All teach undergraduates. The average class size in an introductory lecture is 50 and in a laboratory, 20.
Admissions: 97% of the 2001-2002 applicants were accepted.
Requirements: The SAT I or ACT is required, with a minimum SAT I composite score of 750 or ACT score of 14. Applicants must be graduates of an accredited secondary school. The GED is accepted. Students must complete 16 high school units, including 8 of electives, 3 of English, 2 each of science and history, and 1 of math. An interview is recommended. A GPA of 2.0 is required. AP and CLEP credits are accepted. Important factors in the admissions decision are leadership record, recommendations by alumni, and parents or siblings attending the school. Applications are accepted on-line.
Procedure: Freshmen are admitted fall and spring. Applications should be filed by October 1 for fall entry and April 1 for spring entry. Notification is sent on a rolling basis.
Transfer: Applicants must submit transcripts from all colleges attended. Grades of D+ or better transfer for credit if students have a GPA of 2.0. Transfers are admitted for the fall and spring terms. 90 credits of 180 must be completed at CCMS.
Visiting: There are regularly scheduled orientations for prospective students, including open house programs in August and February. There are guides for informal visits. To schedule a visit, contact Patsy Leon.
Financial Aid: In a recent year, 80% of all students received some form of financial aid. CCMS is a member of CSS. The CSS/Profile is required. The fall application deadline is September 15.
Computers: There are 16 PCs networked in a lab for instruction at a beginning level. All students may access the system during supervised lab hours. There are no fees.
Graduates: In a recent year, 51 bachelor's degrees were awarded. In an average class, all graduate in 4 years. 4 companies recruited on campus in 2000-2001.
Admissions Contact: Patsy Leon, Admissions/Financial Aid.
E-mail: *ccms@eos.net* Web: *www.ccms.edu*

CLEVELAND INSTITUTE OF ART D-1
Cleveland, OH 44106 (216) 421-7427
(800) 223-4700; Fax: (216) 421-7438

Full-time: 281 men, 292 women	**Faculty:** 48
Part-time: 13 men, 28 women	**Ph.D.s:** 90%
Graduate: 1 woman	**Student/Faculty:** 12 to 1
Year: semesters	**Tuition:** $17,558
Application Deadline: July 1	**Room & Board:** $5122
Freshman Class: 444 applied, 410 accepted, 165 enrolled	
SAT I Verbal/Math: 551/525	**ACT:** 21 **SPECIAL**

Cleveland Institute of Art, founded in 1882, is an independent professional school of art offering a 5-year B.F.A. degree. In addition to regional accreditation, CIA has baccalaureate program accreditation with NASAD. The 3 libraries contain 42,000 volumes and 2800 audiovisual forms/CDs, and subscribe to 260 periodicals. Computerized library services include the card catalog, interlibrary loans, and database searching. Special learning facilities include an art gallery and natural history museum. The 500-acre campus is in an urban area 4 miles east of downtown Cleveland, sharing a campus with Case Western Reserve University. Including residence halls, there are 3 buildings.
Student Life: 66% of undergraduates are from Ohio. Others are from 29 states, 12 foreign countries, and Canada. 97% are from public schools. 87% are white. 50% are Protestant; 41% Catholic. The average age of freshmen is 20; all undergraduates, 22. 10% do not continue beyond their first year; 50% remain to graduate.
Housing: 100 students can be accommodated in college housing, which includes single-sex and coed dormitories. On-campus housing is guaranteed for the freshman year only, is available on a first-come, first-served basis, and is available on a lottery system for upperclassmen. Priority is given to out-of-town students. 80% of students commute. Alcohol is not permitted. All students may keep cars.
Activities: 1% of men belong to 6 national fraternities and 6 national sororities. There are 6 groups on campus, including art, ethnic, gay, international, literary magazine, professional, student government, and

yearbook. The institute shares many social, cultural, and extracurricular activities with Case Western Reserve University. Popular campus events include museum trips, a spring cookout, and student art exhibits.

Sports: There are 8 intramural sports for men and 8 for women. For a fee, students may use the recreation facilities of Case Western Reserve.

Disabled Students: 90% of the campus is accessible. Wheelchair ramps, elevators, special parking, and specially equipped rest rooms are available.

Services: Counseling and information services are available, as is tutoring in most subjects.

Campus Safety and Security: Measures include 24-hour foot and vehicle patrol, escort service, shuttle buses, and informal discussions. There are pamphlets/posters/films, emergency telephones, and lighted pathways/sidewalks.

Programs of Study: CIA confers the B.F.A. degree. Master's degrees are also awarded. Bachelor's degrees are awarded in COMMUNICATIONS AND THE ARTS (advertising, applied art, design, graphic design, industrial design, painting, photography, and studio art). Industrial design, painting, and metals are the strongest academically. Industrial design, graphic design, and painting are the largest.

Required: To graduate, students must complete 150 to 153 credit hours, with 42 to 51 in the major, and must maintain a minimum GPA of 2.0. Distribution requirements call for 105 studio credits and 48 academic credits. A thesis is required, which is encompassed in the B.F.A. show that each student mounts in the spring of the fifth year.

Special: Cross-registration through the Cleveland Commission on Higher Education, internships for third-, fourth-, and fifth-year students with business and industry, and study abroad in 6 countries are available. There are joint programs with Case Western Reserve University in art education and medical illustration.

Faculty/Classroom: 70% of faculty are male; 30%, female. All teach undergraduates. The average class size in an introductory lecture is 40 and in a regular course, 20.

Admissions: 92% of the 2001-2002 applicants were accepted. The SAT I scores for the 2001-2002 freshman class were: Verbal--19% below 500, 48% between 500 and 599, and 33% between 600 and 700; Math--36% below 500, 43% between 500 and 599, and 21% between 600 and 700. The ACT scores were 39% below 21, 22% between 21 and 23, 26% between 24 and 26, 8% between 27 and 28, and 5% above 28. 30% of the current freshmen were in the top fifth of their class; 61% were in the top two fifths.

Requirements: The SAT I or ACT is required with SAT I minimum scores of 350 verbal and 350 math or an ACT minimum composite score of 15. Applicants must be graduates of an accredited secondary school. The GED is accepted. Students should have completed 4 units each of art, English, and math, 2 each of history, science, and social studies, and 1 of a foreign language. An essay and a portfolio are required. An interview is strongly recommended. A GPA of 2.0 is required. AP and CLEP credits are accepted. Important factors in the admissions decision are evidence of special talent, personality/intangible qualities, and leadership record.

Procedure: Freshmen are admitted in the fall. Entrance exams should be taken during the junior year. There are early decision and deferred admissions plans. Applications should be filed by July 1 for fall entry. Notification is sent on a rolling basis. 1% of all applicants are on a waiting list.

Transfer: 51 transfer students enrolled in 2001-2002. Applicants must have a 2.0 GPA and must submit a portfolio. Those who have 30 to 36 credits in comparable studio courses or a strong portfolio will be reviewed by department faculty. Grades of C or better transfer for credit. 72 credits of 150 to 153 must be completed at CIA.

Visiting: There are guides for informal visits and visitors may sit in on classes and stay overnight. To schedule a visit, contact Catherine Redhead, Director of Admissions.

Financial Aid: In 2001-2002, 70% of all freshmen and 80% of continuing students received some form of financial aid. 56% of freshmen and 68% of continuing students received need-based aid. The average freshman award was $10,820. Of that total, scholarships or need-based grants averaged $7033; loans averaged $8813; and work contracts averaged $1949. 33% of undergraduates work part time. Average annual earnings from campus work are $926. The average financial indebtedness of the 2001 graduate was $16,723. The FAFSA, the college's own financial statement and the federal tax forms are required. The fall application deadline is March 15.

International Students: There are 31 international students enrolled. The school actively recruits these students. They must score 525 on the written TOEFL and or complete Level 109 at an ELS center.

Computers: 115 Macs, 65 Wondows NT workstations, and 22 Silicon Graphics PCs are available for student use in 8 separate computer labs. Students may access the system for up to 2 hours. There are no fees.

Graduates: In 2001, 54 bachelor's degrees were awarded. The most popular majors were industrial design (30%), illustration (15%), and interior design and painting (9%). In an average class, 55% graduate in 5 years, and 65% in 6 years. 82 companies recruited on campus in 2000-2001. Of the 2000 graduating class, 24% were enrolled in graduate school within 6 months of graduation and 74% were employed.

Admissions Contact: Catherine Redhead, Director of Admissions. E-mail: *credhead@gate.cia.edu* Web: *www.cia.edu*

CLEVELAND INSTITUTE OF MUSIC — D-1

Cleveland, OH 44106 — **(216) 795-3107; (216) 791-1530**

Full-time: 105 men, 120 women	**Faculty:** 31
Part-time: none	**Ph.D.s:** 9%
Graduate: 60 men, 90 women	**Student/Faculty:** 7 to 1
Year: semesters, summer session	**Tuition:** $20,290
Application Deadline: December 1	**Room & Board:** $5590
Freshman Class: n/av	
SAT I or ACT: required	**SPECIAL**

Cleveland Institute of Music, founded in 1920, is a private music conservatory offering education and training in the arts of performance, composition, and related musical disciplines. Figures in above capsule are approximate. In addition to regional accreditation, CIM has baccalaureate program accreditation with NASM. The library contains 47,878 volumes and 20,500 audiovisual forms/CDs, and subscribes to 115 periodicals. Computerized library services include the card catalog, interlibrary loans, and database searching. Special learning facilities include concert and recital halls, teaching studios, practice rooms, a technology learning center, a specially designed eurhythmics studio, an orchestra library, an opera theater workshop and studio, and music store. The 480-acre campus is in an urban area.

Student Life: 68% of undergraduates are from out of state, mostly the Midwest. Others are from 40 states, 21 foreign countries, and Canada. 95% are from public schools. 71% are white; 20% foreign nationals. The average age of freshmen is 18; all undergraduates, 21. 2% do not continue beyond their first year; 85% remain to graduate.

Housing: 23% of undergraduates live on campus; 99% remain on campus on weekends. College-sponsored housing is coed. On-campus housing is guaranteed for the freshman year only. Alcohol is not permitted. All students may keep cars.

Activities: There are no fraternities or sororities. There are 8 groups on campus, including chorale, chorus, jazz band, opera, orchestra, religious, student government, and symphony. Popular campus events include weekly concerts by the Cleveland Orchestra.

Sports: There is no sports program at CIM. Athletic facilities and a fitness center are available.

Disabled Students: Wheelchair ramps, elevators, special parking, specially equipped rest rooms, and lowered drinking fountains are available.

Services: Counseling and information services are available, as is tutoring in some subjects.

Campus Safety and Security: Measures include 24-hour foot and vehicle patrol, escort service, shuttle buses, and informal discussions. There are pamphlets/posters/films, emergency telephones, and lighted pathways/sidewalks.

Programs of Study: CIM confers B.M.; B.A.Mus.Ed. and B.S.Mus.Ed. degrees. Master's and doctoral degrees are also awarded. Bachelor's degrees are awarded in COMMUNICATIONS AND THE ARTS (music), EDUCATION (music).

Required: CIM requires a minimum of 126 credits with a GPA of 2.0 or higher for graduation. A core curriculum of general education courses, music history, theory, and literature is required. Performance evaluation is based on jury exams and recitals.

Special: Students may take a 5-year double major in performance and audio recording. Cross-registration with schools in the Cleveland Commission on Higher Education Consortium is possible. Music education degrees are offered in conjunction with Case Western Reserve University. There are 2 national honor societies.

Faculty/Classroom: 68% of faculty are male; 32%, female. All teach undergraduates.

Requirements: The SAT I or ACT is required. In addition, an audition and interview are required, at which time freshman applicants must also complete a questionnaire pertaining to general knowledge of music and diagnostic evaluations of rhythmic comprehension as well as sight singing and ear training. Applicants majoring in composition must submit scores and tapes. Other factors in the admissions decision are GPA, class rank, test scores, and recommendations. Applicants should complete a 16 unit college preparatory program. The GED is accepted. On-line application is available at *www.cim.edu/conserv/admissions*. AP credits are accepted.

Procedure: Freshmen are admitted fall and spring. Entrance exams should be taken at the time of the entrance audition. A waiting list is an active part of the admissions procedure. Check with the school for current application deadlines. The fall 2001 application fee was $70.

Transfer: 23 transfer students enrolled in a recent year. Applicants must meet the same criteria as entering freshmen and submit transcripts and letters of recommendation. 48 credits of 126 must be completed at CIM.

Visiting: Visitors may sit in on classes. To schedule a visit, contact the Admission Office.

Financial Aid: In a recent year, 98% of all freshmen and 95% of continuing students received some form of financial aid. 79% of freshmen and 83% of continuing students received need-based aid. The average freshman award was $12,747. Of that total, scholarships or need-based grants averaged $9037 ($17,000 maximum); loans averaged $2982 ($6625 maximum); and work contracts averaged $727 ($2000 maximum). Average annual earnings from campus work are $831. The average financial indebtedness of the 2001 graduate was $19,700. CIM is a member of CSS. The CSS/Profile or FAFSA is required. Check with the school for current deadlines.

International Students: There were 34 international students enrolled in a recent year. They must score 550 on the written TOEFL or take the MELAB.

Computers: Each dorm room is connected to CWRUnet, Case Western Reserve University's fiber-optic computer network. Students are encouraged to bring their own PCs for easy access to this extensive system. Computer facilities are available both at CIM and on the CWRU campus. All students may access the system. There are no time limits and no fees. It is strongly recommended that all students have a personal computer.

Graduates: In a recent year, 54 bachelor's degrees were awarded. In an average class, 80% graduate in 4 years, and 81% in 5 years.

Admissions Contact: Admission Office.
E-mail: *cimadmission@po.cwru.edu* Web: *www.cim.edu*

CLEVELAND STATE UNIVERSITY D-1

Cleveland, OH 44115-2403 (216) 687-2100; Fax: (216) 687-9210

Full-time: 3159 men, 3635 women	**Faculty:** 493; I, --$
Part-time: 1576 men, 2063 women	**Ph.D.s:** 96%
Graduate: 2188 men, 3125 women	**Student/Faculty:** 14 to 1
Year: semesters, summer session	**Tuition:** $4596 ($9054)
Application Deadline: July 15	**Room & Board:** $5550
Freshman Class: 2531 applied, 2165 accepted, 1121 enrolled	
SAT I Verbal/Math: required	**ACT:** required

NONCOMPETITIVE

Cleveland State University, founded in 1964, is a primarily commuter public institution offering undergraduate and graduate programs through the colleges of arts and sciences, business administration, education, engineering, and urban affairs. There are 7 undergraduate and 7 graduate schools. In addition to regional accreditation, CSU has baccalaureate program accreditation with AACSB, ABET, CSWE, NCATE, and NLN. The 2 libraries contain 960,735 volumes, 690,023 microform items and 42,972 audiovisual forms/CDs, and subscribe to 6486 periodicals. Computerized library services include the card catalog, interlibrary loans, and database searching. Special learning facilities include a learning resource center, art gallery, and radio station. The 70-acre campus is in an urban area in downtown Cleveland. Including residence halls, there are 38 buildings.

Student Life: 96% of undergraduates are from Ohio. Others are from 20 states, 79 foreign countries, and Canada. 62% are white; 19% African American. The average age of freshmen is 19; all undergraduates, 27. 40% do not continue beyond their first year; 60% remain to graduate.

Housing: 475 students can be accommodated in college housing, which includes coed dormitories and off-campus apartments. In addition, there are law, quiet study, and first-year experience floors. 96% of students commute. All students may keep cars.

Activities: 1% of men belong to 2 local and 6 national fraternities; 1% of women belong to 8 national sororities. There are 150 groups on campus, including art, cheerleading, chess, choir, chorale, chorus, computers, dance, drama, ethnic, gay, honors, international, jazz band, literary magazine, musical theater, newspaper, opera, orchestra, pep band, photography, political, professional, radio and TV, religious, social, social service, student government, and symphony. Popular campus events include Black Aspiration Week and Springfest.

Sports: There are 8 intercollegiate sports for men and 7 for women, and 5 intramural sports for men and 5 for women. Facilities include a gym, gymnastics and weight rooms, a dance studio, a swimming pool, a fitness trail, an indoor track, handball and squash courts, a 2500-seat soccer stadium, and a convocation center.

Disabled Students: 99% of the campus is accessible. Wheelchair ramps, elevators, special parking, specially equipped rest rooms, and lowered drinking fountains are available.

Services: There is a reader service for the blind, and remedial math, reading, and writing.

Campus Safety and Security: Measures include 24-hour foot and vehicle patrol, escort service, informal discussions, and pamphlets/posters/films. There are emergency telephones, lighted pathways/sidewalks, and a campus watch organization for faculty and staff.

Programs of Study: CSU confers B.A., B.S., B.B.A., B.C.E., B.Ch.E., B.E.E., B.M., B.M.E., B.S.C.I.S., B.S.Ed., B.S.I.E., B.S.N., and B.S.T. degrees. Master's and doctoral degrees are also awarded. Bachelor's degrees are awarded in BIOLOGICAL SCIENCE (biology/biological science), BUSINESS (accounting, banking and finance, business economics, labor studies, management information systems, management science, and marketing/retailing/merchandising), COMMUNICATIONS AND THE ARTS (art, communications, dramatic arts, English, French, German, linguistics, music, and Spanish), COMPUTER AND PHYSICAL SCIENCE (chemistry, computer science, geology, information sciences and systems, mathematics, and physics), EDUCATION (early childhood, elementary, physical, secondary, and special), ENGINEERING AND ENVIRONMENTAL DESIGN (chemical engineering, civil engineering, electrical/electronics engineering, electromechanical technology, environmental science, industrial engineering, mechanical engineering, and mechanical engineering technology), HEALTH PROFESSIONS (medical technology, nursing, occupational therapy, physical therapy, premedicine, and speech therapy), SOCIAL SCIENCE (anthropology, classical/ancient civilization, economics, history, international relations, liberal arts/general studies, philosophy, political science/government, psychology, religion, social science, social studies, social work, sociology, and urban studies). Communications, psychology, and social work are the largest.

Required: Students must complete at least 120 semester hours with a minimum 2.0 GPA for graduation. Requirements include a core curriculum containing courses in English composition, arts and humanities, social science, natural sciences, math and logic, non-Western culture and civilization, Western culture and civilization, and human diversity and the African American experience.

Special: CSU offers a developmental program for Ohio students not qualified for regular freshman admission. There are also cooperative education programs, nondegree study, work-study programs, internships, pass/fail options, and cross-registration at other Cleveland area colleges. Student-designed and dual majors, study abroad in 10 countries, and volunteer opportunities are available, as well as a combined liberal arts and engineering degree and a 3-2 engineering degree. There are 6 national honor societies, and 5 departmental honors programs.

Faculty/Classroom: 62% of faculty are male; 38%, female.

Admissions: 86% of the 2001-2002 applicants were accepted. 15% of the current freshmen were in the top fifth of their class; 31% were in the top two fifths.

Requirements: The SAT I or ACT is required. In addition, the scores should meet the standards of the specific program for which the student is applying. Advanced placement and honors courses are considered in the admissions decision. Applications are accepted on-line via the Apply Yourself Application Network. AP and CLEP credits are accepted.

Procedure: Freshmen are admitted to all sessions. Entrance exams should be taken prior to application. Applications should be filed by July 15 for fall entry, December 1 for spring entry, and April 1 for summer entry. The college accepts all in-state residents. The fall 2001 application fee was $30. Notification is sent on a rolling basis.

Transfer: 1060 transfer students enrolled in 2001-2002. Applicants must have a minimum GPA of 2.0. 30 credits of 120 must be completed at CSU.

Visiting: There are regularly scheduled orientations for prospective students, including general visitation days for the university (in the fall) and each of the colleges (in the spring). There are guides for informal visits and visitors may sit in on classes and stay overnight. To schedule a visit, contact the Office of Undergraduate Admissions at (216) 687-3755.

Financial Aid: In 2001-2002, 23% of all freshmen and 61% of continuing students received some form of financial aid. 19% of freshmen and 41% of continuing students received need-based aid. The average freshman award was $5095. The FAFSA is required. The fall application deadline is April 15.

International Students: There are 220 international students enrolled. They must score 525 on the written TOEFL.

Computers: The mainframes are a Sun 10,000, 3 DEC VAX 750s, and a VAX 8600. The mainframes are accessible by modem or at the university's 10 stations on campus. PC services are available at several networked PC labs on campus. All students may access the system. Hours vary by input center. Modem access is available 24 hours per day. There are no time limits and no fees.

Graduates: In 2001, 1427 bachelor's degrees were awarded. The most popular majors were communications (10%), psychology (8%), and elementary education (6%). In an average class, 9% graduate in 3 years, 24% in 4 years, 31% in 5 years, and 34% in 6 years.

Admissions Contact: Gerald Kiel, Vice Provost of Enrollment Management Services. A video is available. Web: *http://www.csuohio.edu*

COLLEGE OF MOUNT ST. JOSEPH

A-5

Cincinnati, OH 45233-1672

(513) 244-4606
(800) 654-9314; Fax: (513) 244-4851

Full-time: 446 men, 848 women
Faculty: 122; IIB, --$
Part-time: 149 men, 628 women
Ph.D.s: 55%
Graduate: 54 men, 148 women
Student/Faculty: 11 to 1
Year: semesters, summer session
Tuition: $15,040
Application Deadline: August 15
Room & Board: $5250
Freshman Class: 675 applied, 544 accepted, 269 enrolled
SAT I Verbal/Math: 490/490
ACT: 22
COMPETITIVE

The College of Mount St. Joseph, founded in 1920, is a private, liberal arts Catholic institution that fosters a liberal education with career orientation. There is 1 undergraduate school and 4 graduate schools. In addition to regional accreditation, the Mount has baccalaureate program accreditation with ADA, NASM, NCATE, and NLN. The library contains 97,743 volumes, 393,931 microform items, and 1385 audiovisual forms/CDs, and subscribes to 6230 periodicals. Computerized library services include the card catalog, interlibrary loans, and database searching. Special learning facilities include a learning resource center, art gallery, and radio station. The 75-acre campus is in a suburban area 7 miles west of downtown Cincinnati. Including residence halls, there are 7 buildings.

Student Life: 86% of undergraduates are from Ohio. Others are from 12 states and 18 foreign countries. 65% are from public schools. 87% are white. 53% are Catholic; 28% Protestant; 18% not reported. The average age of freshmen is 18; all undergraduates, 26. 12% do not continue beyond their first year; 68% remain to graduate.

Housing: 400 students can be accommodated in college housing, which includes coed dormitories. On-campus housing is guaranteed for all 4 years. 69% of students commute. All students may keep cars.

Activities: There are no fraternities or sororities. There are 41 groups on campus, including art, band, cheerleading, choir, chorale, chorus, computers, dance, departmental, drama, drill team, ethnic, honors, international, jazz band, literary magazine, marching band, musical theater, newspaper, orchestra, pep band, photography, religious, social, social service, and student government. Popular campus events include the Christmas gala, campus fair, and Mission Exploration Day.

Sports: There are 5 intercollegiate sports for men and 6 for women, and 6 intramural sports for men and 6 for women. Facilities include a gym, a track, a wellness center, a weight room, a hockey field, an aerobics center, racquetball courts, 6 lighted tennis courts, a softball field, and a "home" football and baseball stadium located off campus.

Disabled Students: All of the campus is accessible. Wheelchair ramps, elevators, special parking, specially equipped rest rooms, special class scheduling, lowered drinking fountains, lowered telephones, special door openings for wheelchair access, and a chairlift between levels where the science building and classroom building meet are available.

Services: Counseling and information services are available, as is tutoring in most subjects. There is remedial math, reading, and writing, peer tutoring, a skills lab, and a special program for students with learning disabilities.

Campus Safety and Security: Measures include 24-hour foot and vehicle patrol, self-defense education, escort service, and informal discussions. There are pamphlets/posters/films, emergency telephones, and lighted pathways/sidewalks.

Programs of Study: The Mount confers B.A., B.S., B.F.A., and B.S.N. degrees. Associate and master's degrees are also awarded. Bachelor's degrees are awarded in BIOLOGICAL SCIENCE (biology/biological science), BUSINESS (accounting, business administration and management, and purchasing/inventory management), COMMUNICATIONS AND THE ARTS (art, communications, English, fine arts, graphic design, and music), COMPUTER AND PHYSICAL SCIENCE (chemistry, computer mathematics, computer science, mathematics, and natural sciences), EDUCATION (art, athletic training, early childhood, elementary, middle school, music, physical, science, and special), ENGINEERING AND ENVIRONMENTAL DESIGN (interior design), HEALTH PROFESSIONS (health, health care administration, medical laboratory technology, nursing, premedicine, and recreation therapy), SOCIAL SCIENCE (gerontology, history, human services, humanities, liberal arts/general studies, paralegal studies, pastoral studies, psychology, religion, religious education, social work, sociology, theological studies, and women's studies). Physical therapy, nursing, and biology are the strongest academically. Business, education, and nursing are the largest.

Required: To graduate, students must complete 128 credits with an overall minimum GPA of 2.0. and 2.5 in the major. 48 semester hours of liberal arts and sciences and 36 to 40 hours in the major are required. All students must take 3 credits of computer science, 2 credits of phys ed, and written and oral English courses.

Special: The college offers co-op programs in all majors, cross-registration with the Greater Consortium of Colleges and Universities of Ohio, internships, and study abroad in England, Germany, Spain, and Korea. Work-study programs, accelerated degree programs, dual majors, a general studies degree, nondegree study, and pass/fail options are available. The Weekend College offers students an opportunity to earn a degree by enrolling in specially designed classes that meet only on weekends. There is 1 national honor society, a freshman honors program, and 6 departmental honors programs.

Faculty/Classroom: 38% of faculty are male; 62%, female. All teach undergraduates and 25% both teach and do research. The average class size in an introductory lecture is 25; in a laboratory, 20; and in a regular course, 20.

Admissions: 81% of the 2001-2002 applicants were accepted. The SAT I scores for the 2001-2002 freshman class were: Verbal--55% below 500, 34% between 500 and 599, 10% between 600 and 700, and 1% above 700; Math--51% below 500, 39% between 500 and 599, 8% between 600 and 700, and 2% above 700. The ACT scores were 18% below 21, 40% between 21 and 23, 27% between 24 and 26, 12% between 27 and 28, and 3% above 28. 32% of the current freshmen were in the top fifth of their class; 63% were in the top two fifths. There was 1 National Merit finalist. 4 freshmen graduated first in their class.

Requirements: The SAT I or ACT is required. In addition, applicants must be graduates of an accredited secondary school. The GED (with scores in the 50th percentile) is accepted. Students should have completed the following high school academic credits: 4 years of English, 2 of math (including algebra and geometry), 2 of social studies, 2 of foreign language or 2 additional years of previously listed courses, 2 of science, and 1of fine arts. Letters of recommendation and a personal essay are required for those students not meeting at least 3 of the 4 following criteria: completion of above-listed high school core subject courses, class rank in upper three fifths, a minimum GPA of 2.25, or minimum testing scores of 19 on the ACT or 480 verbal and 480 math on the SAT I. An audition is required for music students, and a portfolio is recommended for all art students. The Mount requires applicants to be in the upper 60% of their class. A GPA of 2.25 is required. Applications are accepted on-line at the school's web site.AP and CLEP credits are accepted. Important factors in the admissions decision are recommendations by school officials, advanced placement or honors courses, evidence of special talent, and extracurricular activities record.

Procedure: Freshmen are admitted to all sessions. There is an early admissions plan. Applications should be filed by August 15 for fall entry. The fall 2001 application fee was $25 ($50 for physical therapy). Notification is sent on a rolling basis.

Transfer: 149 transfer students enrolled in 2001-2002. Transfer students must meet 3 of 4 freshman criteria or have a college GPA of 2.0 better in a minimum of 12 semester or 18 quarter hours. All college hours must be presented. 27 credits of 128 must be completed at the Mount.

Visiting: There are regularly scheduled orientations for prospective students, including a meeting with an admissions counselor, a student-guided tour, a visit to financial aid, and a meeting with a faculty member, if requested. There are guides for informal visits and visitors may sit in on classes and stay overnight. To schedule a visit, contact the Admissions Office at (513) 244-4531.

Financial Aid: In 2001-2002, 99% of all freshmen and 90% of continuing students received some form of financial aid. 90% of all students received need-based aid. The average freshman award was $11,223. Of that total, scholarships or need-based grants averaged $7906 ($14,200 maximum); loans averaged $3212 ($5000 maximum); and work contracts averaged $1350 ($2000 maximum). All undergraduates work part time. Average annual earnings from campus work are $2000. The average financial indebtedness of the 2001 graduate was $8900. The FAFSA is required. The fall application deadline is March 1.

International Students: There are 38 international students enrolled. The school actively recruits these students. They must take the MELAB.

Computers: Students have access to 175 network-based workstations and 5 servers. PCs are in 4 large public labs and some smaller department labs, as well as on each floor of the residence hall. All first time, full-time freshmen are required to lease a computer through the college. The Mount is a wireless college. All students may access the system 24 hours a day. There are no time limits and no fees. It is strongly recommended that all students have a personal computer.

Graduates: In 2001, 359 bachelor's degrees were awarded. The most popular majors were business administration (14%), nursing (13%), and education (11%). In an average class, 1% graduate in 3 years, 66% in 4 years, and 68% in 6 years. 56 companies recruited on campus in 2000-2001. Of the 2000 graduating class, 12% were enrolled in graduate school within 6 months of graduation and 90% were employed.

Admissions Contact: Peggy Minnich, Director of Admission. A video is available. E-mail: *peggy-minnich@mail.msj.edu* Web: *www.msj.edu*

COLLEGE OF WOOSTER D-2

Wooster, OH 44691 (330) 263-2270
(800) 877-9905; Fax: (330) 263-2621

Full-time: 847 men, 943 women	**Faculty:** 135; IIB, av$
Part-time: 14 men, 19 women	**Ph.D.s:** 97%
Graduate: none	**Student/Faculty:** 13 to 1
Year: semesters, summer session	**Tuition:** $22,430
Application Deadline: February 15	**Room & Board:** $5920
Freshman Class: 2357 applied, 1704 accepted, 532 enrolled	
SAT I Verbal/Math: 600/590	**ACT:** 25 **VERY COMPETITIVE**

The College of Wooster, founded in 1866, is a liberal arts college. In addition to regional accreditation, Wooster has baccalaureate program accreditation with NASM. The 3 libraries contain 617,864 volumes, 208,268 microform items, and 11,263 audiovisual forms/CDs, and subscribe to 5761 periodicals. Computerized library services include the card catalog, interlibrary loans, and database searching. Special learning facilities include a learning resource center, art gallery, and radio station. The 240-acre campus is in a suburban area 55 miles southwest of Cleveland. Including residence halls, there are 37 buildings.

Student Life: 50% of undergraduates are from out of state, mostly the Midwest. Others are from 44 states, 35 foreign countries, and Canada. 74% are from public schools. 84% are white. The average age of freshmen is 18; all undergraduates, 21. 14% do not continue beyond their first year; 70% remain to graduate.

Housing: 1859 students can be accommodated in college housing, which includes single-sex and coed dormitories. In addition, there are language houses, special-interest houses, and almost 3 dozen small house residential options, most of which are associated with community service/volunteer programs. On-campus housing is guaranteed for all 4 years. 95% of students live on campus; of those, 80% remain on campus on weekends. All students may keep cars.

Activities: 9% of men belong to 3 local fraternities; 9% of women belong to 6 local sororities. There are 11 groups on campus, including art, bagpipe band, band, cheerleading, chess, choir, chorale, chorus, dance, debate, drama, ethnic, forensics, gay, honors, international, jazz band, literary magazine, marching band, musical theater, newspaper, orchestra, photography, political, radio and TV, religious, social service, student government, symphony, and yearbook. Popular campus events include Party on the Green, Winter Gala, and Scot Spirit Day.

Sports: There are 11 intercollegiate sports for men and 11 for women, and 11 intramural sports for men and 11 for women. Facilities include a phys ed center, a stadium, a golf course, tennis courts, a track, baseball and softball fields, a soccer field, a hockey and lacrosse field, a natatorium, and a fitness center.

Disabled Students: 95% of the campus is accessible. Wheelchair ramps, elevators, special parking, specially equipped rest rooms, special class scheduling, and lowered drinking fountains are available.

Services: Counseling and information services are available, as is tutoring in every subject. There is a reader service for the blind, and remedial math, reading, and writing.

Campus Safety and Security: Measures include 24-hour foot and vehicle patrol, escort service, informal discussions, and pamphlets/posters/films. There are emergency telephones and lighted pathways/sidewalks.

Programs of Study: Wooster confers B.A., B.Mus., and B.Mus.Ed. degrees. Bachelor's degrees are awarded in BIOLOGICAL SCIENCE (biochemistry, and biology/biological science), BUSINESS (business economics), COMMUNICATIONS AND THE ARTS (communications, comparative literature, dramatic arts, English, fine arts, French, German, Greek (classical), Latin, music, and Spanish), COMPUTER AND PHYSICAL SCIENCE (chemistry, computer science, geology, mathematics, and physics), SOCIAL SCIENCE (African American studies, anthropology, archeology, area studies, economics, history, interdisciplinary studies, international relations, philosophy, political science/government, psychology, religion, Russian and Slavic studies, sociology, urban studies, and women's studies). Chemistry, history, and English are the strongest academically. History, English, and sociology are the largest.

Required: To graduate students must complete 32 course credits, with 9 to 13 in the major and a minimum GPA of 2.0. All students must take 1 course each in critical inquiry, studies in cultural differences, religious perspectives, and quantitative reasoning, and demonstrate basic writing and foreign language proficiency. Two courses each in social science/history, natural science/math, and arts/humanities are required.

Special: A 3-2 engineering degree is offered in conjunction with Case Western Reserve and Washington universities. A B.A.-B.S. degree is offered in music/music education. Cross-registration is possible with off-campus programs of the Great Lakes Colleges Association. Internships are available in American politics in Washington, D.C., the Ohio State Legislature, and the U.S. State Department, as well as in professional theater and economics. Student-designed majors, dual majors, study abroad in 50 countries, a Washington semester, accelerated degree programs, nondegree study, and pass/fail options for a limited number of courses are available. All seniors participate in a 2-term independent-study project in the major. The student chooses the topic and works on a one-to-one basis with a faculty mentor. A sophomore research program is available by application. There are 12 national honor societies, including Phi Beta Kappa.

Faculty/Classroom: 64% of faculty are male; 36%, female. All both teach and do research. The average class size in an introductory lecture is 15 and in a regular course, 20.

Admissions: 72% of the 2001-2002 applicants were accepted. The SAT I scores for the 2001-2002 freshman class were: Verbal--10% below 500, 37% between 500 and 599, 39% between 600 and 700, and 13% above 700; Math--12% below 500, 39% between 500 and 599, 40% between 600 and 700, and 7% above 700. The ACT scores were 10% below 21, 23% between 21 and 23, 29% between 24 and 26, 17% between 27 and 28, and 21% above 28. 57% of the current freshmen were in the top fifth of their class; 85% were in the top two fifths. There was 1 National Merit finalist and 9 semifinalists. 18 freshmen graduated first in their class.

Requirements: The SAT I or ACT is required with an SAT I composite score of 990 or an ACT minimum composite score of 20. In addition, applicants should be graduates of an accredited secondary school. The GED is accepted. Students should have completed a minimum of 16 high school academic credits. The school also requires an essay and recommends an interview. AP credits are accepted. Important factors in the admissions decision are advanced placement or honor courses, recommendations by school officials, and leadership record. Applications are accepted on computer disk through Common Application and ColleGeLink.

Procedure: Freshmen are admitted fall and winter. Entrance exams should be taken in the fall of the senior year. There are early decision, early admissions, and deferred admissions plans. Early decision applications should be filed by December 1; regular applications, by February 15 for fall entry. Notification of early decision is sent December 15; regular decision, April 1. 77 early decision candidates were accepted for the 2001-2002 class. 4% of all applicants are on a waiting list; 1 was accepted in 2001.

Transfer: 12 transfer students enrolled in 2001-2002. Applicants for transfer must have a minimum GPA of 2.5 and must submit either the SAT I or ACT scores as well as a dean's reference and a high school transcript. An interview is recommended. Grades of C or better transfer for credit. Transfers are admitted every semester. 17 credits of 32 must be completed at Wooster.

Visiting: There are regularly scheduled orientations for prospective students, including an interview, tour, class visits, and meetings with faculty and coaches. There are guides for informal visits and visitors may sit in on classes and stay overnight. To schedule a visit, contact the Admissions Office at *admissions@wooster.edu*.

Financial Aid: In 2001-2002, 99% of all freshmen and 69% of continuing students received some form of financial aid. 61% of freshmen and 44% of continuing students received need-based aid. The average freshman award was $16,186. Of that total, scholarships or need-based grants averaged $14,394 ($29,916 maximum); loans averaged $3210 ($6625 maximum); and work contracts averaged $1394 ($2000 maximum). 50% of undergraduates work part time. Average annual earnings from campus work are $472. The average financial indebtedness of the 2001 graduate was $15,800. Wooster is a member of CSS. The CSS/Profile or FAFSA and the college's own financial statement are required. The fall application deadline is February 15.

International Students: There are 139 international students enrolled. The school actively recruits these students. They must score 550 on the written TOEFL or the MELAB and take the American Language Institute test and the SAT I or the ACT, scoring 900 on the SAT1.

Computers: The mainframe is a Compaq Alpha server 800 5/500. File servers, laser printers, and other minicomputers are available on campus for student use. More than 500 PCs have been linked to WoosterNet, the campuswide local area network that provides computing capabilities 24 hours a day. All students may access the system any time. There are no time limits and no fees.

Graduates: In 2001, 385 bachelor's degrees were awarded. The most popular majors were English (10%), biology (9%), and sociology/anthropology (9%). In an average class, 63% graduate in 4 years, 66% in 5 years, and 67% in 6 years. 28 companies recruited on campus in 2000-2001. Of the 2000 graduating class, 28% were enrolled in graduate school within 6 months of graduation and 70% were employed.

Admissions Contact: Carol Wheatley, Director of Admissions. A video is available. E-mail: *admissions@acs.wooster.edu*
Web: *http://www.wooster.edu*

COLUMBUS COLLEGE OF ART AND DESIGN C-3
Columbus, OH 43215 (614) 224-9101; (614) 222-4040

Full-time: 700 men, 570 women	**Faculty:** 75
Part-time: 165 men, 265 women	**Ph.D.s:** 47%
Graduate: none	**Student/Faculty:** 17 to 1
Year: semesters, summer session	**Tuition:** $16,210
Application Deadline: open	**Room & Board:** $6000
Freshman Class: n/av	
SAT I or ACT: recommended	**SPECIAL**

Columbus College of Art and Design, founded in 1879, is a private institution offering undergraduate programs in art and fine arts. Figures in above capsule are approximate. In addition to regional accreditation, CCAD has baccalaureate program accreditation with NASAD. The library contains 41,396 volumes and 13,475 microform items, and subscribes to 254 periodicals. Computerized library services include the card catalog and database searching. Special learning facilities include a learning resource center, art gallery, and an art museum. The 17-acre campus is in an urban area in Columbus. Including residence halls, there are 15 buildings.

Student Life: 77% of undergraduates are from Ohio. Others are from 49 states, 36 foreign countries, and Canada. 87% are white. The average age of freshmen is 19; all undergraduates, 21. 22% do not continue beyond their first year; 36% remain to graduate.

Housing: 300 students can be accommodated in college housing, which includes single-sex and coed dormitories and off-campus apartments. On-campus housing is guaranteed for the freshman year only and is available on a first-come, first-served basis. Priority is given to out-of-town students. 82% of students commute. Alcohol is not permitted. Upperclassmen may keep cars.

Activities: There are no fraternities or sororities. There are 6 groups on campus, including ethnic, international, literary magazine, newspaper, professional, religious, and student government. Popular campus events include biannual student art sales, International Reception, and International Students Holiday Brunch.

Sports: There are 4 intramural sports for men and 2 for women. Facilities include a game room in the student center.

Disabled Students: 50% of the campus is accessible. Wheelchair ramps, elevators, special parking, specially equipped rest rooms, special class scheduling, and lowered telephones are available.

Services: There is remedial reading and writing.

Campus Safety and Security: Measures include 24-hour foot and vehicle patrol, escort service, informal discussions, and pamphlets/posters/films. There are emergency telephones and lighted pathways/sidewalks.

Programs of Study: CCAD confers the B.F.A. degree. Bachelor's degrees are awarded in COMMUNICATIONS AND THE ARTS (advertising, fine arts, graphic design, illustration, industrial design, and media arts), ENGINEERING AND ENVIRONMENTAL DESIGN (interior design), SOCIAL SCIENCE (fashion design and technology). Illustration and advertising design are the largest.

Required: All students must complete foundation studies, including 4 years of drawing and 3 years of design/color, and courses in English, sociology, psychology, business, art history, science, literature, and painting. A total of 130 credit hours, with 75 to 90 in the major depending on the major, and a minimum GPA of 2.0 are required to graduate. A sophomore English exam must be passed. Students must complete a portfolio of professional caliber, and students in fine arts must have an individual showing of recent works.

Special: Cross-registration is offered with Franklin, Ohio State, and Capital universities; Ohio Dominican, Otterbein, and Pontifical colleges, Columbus State Community College, Mount Carmel College of Nursing, and DeVry Institute of Technology. Internships are available, as are on-campus work-study, dual majors, and nondegree study.

Faculty/Classroom: 71% of faculty are male; 29%, female. All teach undergraduates. The average class size in an introductory lecture is 23; in a laboratory, 18; and in a regular course, 20.

Requirements: The SAT I or ACT is recommended. In addition, applicants should be graduates of an accredited secondary school or have the GED. A portfolio of artwork indicative of abilities must be submitted. An interview is advised. A GPA of 2.0 is required. AP credits are accepted. Important factors in the admissions decision are evidence of special talent, recommendations by school officials, and recommendations by alumni.

Procedure: Freshmen are admitted fall and winter. Application deadlines are open. The fall 2001 application fee was $25.

Transfer: 75 transfer students enrolled in a recent year. Applicants must submit an acceptable portfolio of artwork as well as all high school and college transcripts. A minimum GPA of 2.0 is required. An interview is recommended. 60 credits of 130 must be completed at CCAD.

Visiting: There are regularly scheduled orientations for prospective students, including a personal interview, a portfolio review, and a tour. There are guides for informal visits. To schedule a visit, contact the Admissions Office.

Financial Aid: In a recent year, 72% of all freshmen and 85% of continuing students received some form of financial aid. 60% of freshmen and 80% of continuing students received need-based aid. The average freshman award was $6105. Of that total, scholarships or need-based grants averaged $3000; loans averaged $2625; and work contracts averaged $1563. 53% of undergraduates work part time. Average annual earnings from campus work are $3126. The average financial indebtedness of a recent graduate was $21,730. CCAD is a member of CSS. The FAFSA and the college's own financial statement are required.

International Students: There were 91 international students enrolled in a recent year. The school actively recruits these students. They must score 500 on the written TOEFL or take the MELAB.

Computers: There are 115 computers available for student use. The 3 computer systems include Mac Desktop Publishing, CADD, and SGIs. All students may access the system during scheduled lab hours and class time. There are no time limits. Fees vary.

Graduates: In a recent year, 229 bachelor's degrees were awarded. The most popular majors were illustration (42%), fine arts (21%), and advertising and design (16%). In an average class, 6% graduate in 3 years, and 70% in 4 years. 101 companies recruited on campus in a recent year.

Admissions Contact: Thomas Green, Director of Admissions.

DAVID N. MYERS COLLEGE D-1
Cleveland, OH 44115 (216) 523-3800
(877) DNMYERS; (216) 696-6430

Full-time: 130 men, 443 women	**Faculty:** 17
Part-time: 192 men, 331 women	**Ph.D.s:** 23%
Graduate: 47 men, 34 women	**Student/Faculty:** 12 to 1
Year: semesters, summer session	**Tuition:** $9475
Application Deadline: open	**Room & Board:** n/app
Freshman Class: 130 applied, 76 accepted, 58 enrolled	
SAT I or ACT: required	**COMPETITIVE**

David N. Myers College, founded in 1848, is a private institution offering undergraduate programs in business to commuting students. The library contains 13,250 volumes, 616 microform items, and 471 audiovisual forms/CDs, and subscribes to 140 periodicals. Computerized library services include the card catalog, interlibrary loans, and database searching. Special learning facilities include a learning resource center. The 2-acre campus is in an urban area in Cleveland. There is 1 building.

Student Life: 45% of undergraduates are African American; 42% white. The average age of all undergraduates is 26.

Housing: There are no residence halls. All students commute. Alcohol is not permitted.

Activities: There are no fraternities or sororities. There are a number of groups and organizations on campus, including chorale, student government, and yearbook.

Disabled Students: All of the campus is accessible. Wheelchair ramps, elevators, specially equipped rest rooms, special class scheduling, lowered drinking fountains, and lowered telephones are available.

Services: Counseling and information services are available, as is tutoring in most subjects. There is a reader service for the blind, and remedial math, reading, and writing.

Programs of Study: Myers College confers the B.S. degree. Associate and master's degrees are also awarded. Bachelor's degrees are awarded in BUSINESS (accounting, business administration and management, marketing/retailing/merchandising, office supervision and management, real estate, retailing, and secretarial studies/office management), COMPUTER AND PHYSICAL SCIENCE (information sciences and systems), ENGINEERING AND ENVIRONMENTAL DESIGN (industrial administration/management), HEALTH PROFESSIONS (health care administration), SOCIAL SCIENCE (economics, paralegal studies, public administration, and social science).

Required: All students must complete 51 hours of general education requirements and 27 hours in the business core, plus major requirements and electives. A minimum of 120 semester hours with a minimum GPA of 2.0 is required to graduate.

Special: The external degree program enables working adults to earn a bachelor's degree in a nontraditional manner, including credit by exam and credit for life/work experience. Work-study programs, co-op programs in 7 majors, internships, dual majors, pass/fail options, and cross-registration with other area colleges are offered. Evening and Saturday classes are also available.

Faculty/Classroom: 72% of faculty are male; 28%, female. All teach undergraduates. The average class size in an introductory lecture is 11; in a laboratory, 16; and in a regular course, 11.

Admissions: 58% of the 2001-2002 applicants were accepted.

Requirements: The SAT I or ACT is required for recent high school graduates. Applicants should have completed 19 Carnegie units, including 4 years of high school English, 3 each of math and science, and 2 each of social studies and history. The GED is accepted. An interview is recommended. AP and CLEP credits are accepted. Important factors in the admissions decision are ability to finance college education, advanced placement or honor courses, and recommendations by school officials.

Procedure: Freshmen are admitted to all sessions. Entrance exams should be taken by March of the senior year. There is a deferred admissions plan. Application deadlines are open. Application fee is $25. Notification is sent on a rolling basis.

Transfer: 143 transfer students enrolled in 2001-2002. Applicants should have a minimum GPA of 2.0 in at least 24 semester hours. An associate degree and an interview are recommended. 30 credits of 126 must be completed at Myers College.

Visiting: There are guides for informal visits and visitors may sit in on classes. To schedule a visit, contact Admissions Services.

Financial Aid: In a recent year, 80% of all students received some form of financial aid. 80% of freshmen and 50% of continuing students received need-based aid. The average freshman award was $4025. Myers College is a member of CSS. The FAFSA is required.

International Students: International students must score 500 on the written TOEFL.

Computers: The mainframe is a DEC VAX 4000/300. There are 70 IBM and HP PCs available in the computer lab. All students may access the system on or off campus. There are no time limits and no fees.

Graduates: In 2001, 196 bachelor's degrees were awarded. The most popular majors were business/marketing (50%), information science (8%), and public administration (6%).

Admissions Contact: Tiffiney Payton, Interim Director of Admissions. E-mail: *tpayton@dnmyers.edu* Web: *www.dnmyers.edu*

DEFIANCE COLLEGE — A-2
Defiance, OH 43512 (419) 783-2359
(800) 520-GODC (4632); (419) 783-2468

Full-time: 315 men, 310 women	**Faculty:** 41; IIB, --$
Part-time: 75 men, 130 women	**Ph.D.s:** 70%
Graduate: 205 men and women	**Student/Faculty:** 15 to 1
Year: semesters, summer session	**Tuition:** $15,100
Application Deadline: open	**Room & Board:** $4480
Freshman Class: n/av	
SAT I or ACT: required	**LESS COMPETITIVE**

Defiance College, chartered in 1850, is a small liberal arts institution affiliated with the United Church of Christ. Figures in above capsule are approximate. In addition to regional accreditation, Defiance has baccalaureate program accreditation with CSWE. The library contains 100,000 volumes and 5000 microform items, and subscribes to 500 periodicals. Computerized library services include the card catalog, interlibrary loans, and database searching. Special learning facilities include an art gallery, a nature sanctuary, and a greenhouse. The 150-acre campus is in a small town 55 miles southwest of Toledo. Including residence halls, there are 23 buildings.

Student Life: 89% of undergraduates are from Ohio. Others are from 15 states and 2 foreign countries. 90% are from public schools. 91% are white. 40% are Protestant; 29% Catholic. The average age of freshmen is 18. 37% do not continue beyond their first year; 44% remain to graduate.

Housing: 490 students can be accommodated in college housing, which includes single-sex dormitories, fraternity houses, and sorority houses. On-campus housing is guaranteed for all 4 years. 67% of students commute. Alcohol is not permitted. All students may keep cars.

Activities: 8% of men belong to 1 local and 2 national fraternities; 8% of women belong to 2 local sororities and 1 national sorority. There are 33 groups on campus, including academic clubs, art, band, cheerleading, chess, choir, chorale, drama, ethnic, honors, international, literary magazine, musical theater, newspaper, pep band, photography, professional, religious, social, social service, student government, and yearbook. Popular campus events include Artsfest, Professor Appreciation Week, and Student Senate Service Day.

Sports: There are 9 intercollegiate sports for men and 9 for women, and 12 intramural sports for men and 12 for women. Facilities include a 4000-seat football stadium, baseball, softball, and soccer fields, a cross-country course, a recreation fitness center with a 5000-seat gym, a racquetball court, an indoor track, a weight-lifting room, basketball courts, tennis courts, and an 8-lane all-weather outdoor track.

Disabled Students: 60% of the campus is accessible. Wheelchair ramps, elevators, special parking, specially equipped rest rooms, special class scheduling, lowered drinking fountains, and lowered telephones are available.

Services: Counseling and information services are available, as is tutoring in every subject. There is a reader service for the blind, and remedial math, reading, and writing.

Campus Safety and Security: Measures include escort service, informal discussions, pamphlets/posters/films, and lighted pathways/sidewalks. There are nighttime security guards in residence halls, security cameras in residence hall entrances, and a security guard on the grounds from dusk to dawn.

Programs of Study: Defiance confers B.A. and B.S. degrees. Associate and master's degrees are also awarded. Bachelor's degrees are awarded in BIOLOGICAL SCIENCE (biology/biological science and ecology), BUSINESS (accounting, banking and finance, business administration and management, human resources, management science, marketing/retailing/merchandising, and sports management), COMMUNICATIONS AND THE ARTS (art, communications, and graphic design), COMPUTER AND PHYSICAL SCIENCE (mathematics), EDUCATION (art, Christian, early childhood, elementary, health, mathematics, physical, reading, science, secondary, and social studies), ENGINEERING AND ENVIRONMENTAL DESIGN (environmental science), HEALTH PROFESSIONS (medical laboratory technology), SOCIAL SCIENCE (criminal justice, forensic studies, history, humanities, physical fitness/movement, psychology, religion, and social work). Education is the strongest academically. Business is the largest.

Required: All students must fulfill general education requirements, including written and oral communications and foreign language, and distribution studies in sciences, social sciences, humanities, and fine arts. A freshman seminar, a phys ed course, interdisciplinary studies in Western civilization and the contemporary world, and 2 religion classes, as well as a senior assessment in the major, are also required. A total of 120 semester credits, with at least 30 in the major, and a minimum GPA of 2.0 are required to graduate. Volunteer community service is required in all majors; computer profiency must be demonstrated.

Special: The college offers a strong interdisciplinary emphasis--as, for example, in the wellness and corporate fitness major--and student-designed majors and courses as well as independent study are available. Work-study programs and dual and student-designed majors are available. Numerous cooperative education programs and internships are also offered. B.A.-B.S. degrees, credit for community service not in the student's major, limited pass/fail options, and some credit for life experience are available. There are 8 national honor societies, a freshman honors program, and 1 departmental honors program.

Faculty/Classroom: 65% of faculty are male; 35%, female. All teach undergraduates and 20% do research. No introductory courses are taught by graduate students. The average class size in an introductory lecture is 25; in a laboratory, 18; and in a regular course, 16.

Admissions: 3 freshmen graduated first in their class in a recent year.

Requirements: The SAT I or ACT is required. In addition, applicants should be graduates of an accredited secondary school or have a GED, with 15 Carnegie units completed, including 4 in English, 3 each in math, science, and social studies, and 2 in foreign language. An essay and an interview are recommended. Applications are available at the college's web site at *www.defiance.edu*. Defiance requires applicants to be in the upper 60% of their class. A GPA of 2.0 is required. AP and CLEP credits are accepted. Important factors in the admissions decision are advanced placement or honor courses, personality/intangible qualities, and leadership record.

Procedure: Freshmen are admitted to all sessions. Entrance exams should be taken in the spring of the junior year or the fall of the senior year. There are early admissions and deferred admissions plans. Application deadlines are open. Application fee is $25.

Transfer: 69 transfer students enrolled in a recent year. A minimum college GPA of 2.0 is required; an interview is recommended. 35 credits of 120 must be completed at Defiance.

Visiting: There are regularly scheduled orientations for prospective students, including admissions and financial aid sessions, a campus tour, a complimentary lunch, meetings with faculty, and observing a class in session. Interested applicants can meet with a coach. There are guides for informal visits and visitors may sit in on classes and stay overnight. To schedule a visit, contact the Office of Admission.

Financial Aid: In a recent year, all freshmen and 66% of continuing students received some form of financial aid. 77% of freshmen and 75% of continuing students received need-based aid. The average freshman award was $5608. Of that total, scholarships or need-based grants averaged $5770 ($14,350 maximum); loans averaged $2880 ($5625 maximum); and work contracts averaged $1600 ($2000 maximum). 31% of undergraduates work part time. Average annual earnings from campus work are $800. The average financial indebtedness of a recent year's graduate was $14,323. The FAFSA and the college's own financial statement are required. The fall application deadline is March 1.

International Students: There were 2 international students enrolled in a recent year. They must score 500 on the written TOEFL or take the MELAB.

Computers: The mainframe is a Compaq DS20. PCs and Macs are available in computer labs and faculty offices. All students may access the system 24 hours a day, every day. There are no time limits. The fee is $25.

Graduates: In a recent year, 149 bachelor's degrees were awarded. The most popular majors were management (23%), elementary education (13%), and communications (10%). In an average class, 42% graduate in 4 years, 60% in 5 years, and 69% in 6 years. 390 companies recruited on campus in a recent year. Of the 2000 graduating class, 8% were enrolled in graduate school within 6 months of graduation and 86% were employed.

Admissions Contact: Sarah Ann Bates, Director of Admissions.
E-mail: *admissions@defiance.edu* Web: *www.defiance.edu*

DENISON UNIVERSITY

Granville, OH 43023 — C-3 — (740) 587-6276; (800) DENISON; Fax: (740) 587-6306

Full-time: 902 men, 1187 women	**Faculty:** 179; IIB, +$
Part-time: 2 men, 16 women	**Ph.D.s:** 97%
Graduate: none	**Student/Faculty:** 12 to 1
Year: semesters	**Tuition:** $23,090
Application Deadline: February 1	**Room & Board:** $6550
Freshman Class: 3336 applied, 1947 accepted, 553 enrolled	
SAT I Verbal/Math: 600/610	**ACT:** 27 **HIGHLY COMPETITIVE**

Denison University, founded in 1831, is a private independent institution of liberal arts and sciences. The library contains 371,580 volumes, 100,127 microform items, and 23,377 audiovisual forms/CDs, and subscribes to 4400 periodicals. Computerized library services include the card catalog, interlibrary loans, and database searching. Special learning facilities include a learning resource center, art gallery, planetarium, radio station, TV station, and an observatory, a field research station in a 350-acre biological reserve, high resolution spectometer, economics computer labs, and modern languages laboratory. The 1200-acre campus is in a suburban area 30 miles east of Columbus. Including residence halls, there are 60 buildings.

Student Life: 57% of undergraduates are from out of state, mostly the Midwest. Others are from 48 states, 29 foreign countries, and Canada. 71% are from public schools. 84% are white. 40% are Protestant; 34% Catholic; 16% other (non-Christian) 3%; other (Christian) 10%; other (not identified) 3%. The average age of freshmen is 18; all undergraduates, 20. 13% do not continue beyond their first year; 77% remain to graduate.

Housing: 2194 students can be accommodated in college housing, which includes single-sex and coed dormitories and on-campus apartments. In addition, there are honors houses and special-interest houses. A first year center, substance-free dorms, quiet dorms, all-women dorms, suite-style dorms, and apartments for juniors and seniors with high GPA/leadership is also available. On-campus housing is guaranteed for all 4 years. 98% of students live on campus; of those, 90% remain on campus on weekends. All students may keep cars.

Activities: 32% of men belong to 8 national fraternities; 44% of women belong to 7 national sororities. There are 146 groups on campus, including art, cheerleading, choir, chorale, chorus, computers, dance, drama, ethnic, film, gay, honors, international, jazz band, literary magazine, musical theater, newspaper, orchestra, pep band, photography, political, professional, radio and TV, religious, social, social service, student government, symphony, and yearbook. Popular campus events include an all-campus community picnic and fair, All-Campus Gala, and Academic Awards Convocation.

Sports: There are 11 intercollegiate sports for men and 11 for women, and 13 intramural sports for men and 13 for women. Facilities include a 6000-seat stadium, a 1500-seat gym, 12 outdoor tennis courts, squash courts, an 8-lane quarter-mile track, a field house with a 200-meter track and 4 tennis courts, baseball/softball fields, a recreation gym with 3 volleyball/basketball courts, weight, aerobic, fitness rooms, soccer and men's lacrosse stadium, women's field hockey and lacrosse field, and multiple practice fields.

Disabled Students: 56% of the campus is accessible. Wheelchair ramps, elevators, special parking, specially equipped rest rooms, special class scheduling, lowered drinking fountains, and lowered telephones are available.

Services: Counseling and information services are available, as is tutoring in most subjects. There is a reader service for the blind. A reading and writing center is available, as are study sessions for math, chemistry, and some languages, reduced courseloads, special counselor services, note taking services, oral tests, extended time for tests, untimed tests, talking books, tape recorders, and readers.

Campus Safety and Security: Measures include 24-hour foot and vehicle patrol, self-defense education, escort service, and informal discussions. There are pamphlets/posters/films, emergency telephones, lighted pathways/sidewalks. Residence halls are locked 24 hours a day with entry through a card access system.

Programs of Study: Denison confers B.A., B.S., and B.F.A. degrees. Bachelor's degrees are awarded in BIOLOGICAL SCIENCE (biochemistry, and biology/biological science), COMMUNICATIONS AND THE ARTS (art history and appreciation, communications, dance, dramatic arts, English, film arts, fine arts, French, German, languages, Latin, media arts, music, Spanish, speech/debate/rhetoric, and studio art), COMPUTER AND PHYSICAL SCIENCE (chemistry, computer science, geology, mathematics, and physics), EDUCATION (education, and physical), ENGINEERING AND ENVIRONMENTAL DESIGN (environmental science), SOCIAL SCIENCE (African American studies, classical/ancient civilization, East Asian studies, economics, history, international studies, Latin American studies, philosophy, political science/government, psychology, religion, and women's studies). Psychology, philosophy, and physics are the strongest academically. English, economics, and psychology are the largest.

Required: All students must fulfill aproximately 13 courses of the general education program, including freshman studies in textual, critical, social, scientific, and artistic inquiries, along with oral communication, minority/women's studies, and 2 choices from Western Studies, non-Western studies and American social institutions. A total of 127 semester hours, with 36 in the major and a minimum GPA of 2.0, is required in order to graduate.

Special: Work-study programs, a Washington semester, study-abroad programs in 35 countries, student-designed majors, a math/economics dual major, a dual major in education and various other majors, a philosophy, political science, and economics interdisciplinary major, and pass/fail options are available. A 3-2 engineering program is offered with Rensselaer Polytechnic Institute, Case Western Reserve, and Washington Universities. A May-term internship is available at 200 U.S. locations. A B.A.-B.S. degree, accelerated degree programs, a media technology and arts interdisciplinary major, and nondegree study are possible. There are 15 national honor societies, including Phi Beta Kappa and a freshman honors program. All departments offer honors programs.

Faculty/Classroom: 62% of faculty are male; 38%, female. All teach undergraduates, 100% do research, and 100% do both. The average class size in an introductory lecture is 19; in a laboratory, 21; and in a regular course, 20.

Admissions: 58% of the 2001-2002 applicants were accepted. The SAT I scores for the 2001-2002 freshman class were: Verbal--5% below 500, 44% between 500 and 599, 39% between 600 and 700, and 12% above 700; Math--4% below 500, 41% between 500 and 599, 45% between 600 and 700, and 10% above 700. The ACT scores were 5% below 21, 13% between 21 and 23, 27% between 24 and 26, 23% between 27 and 28, and 32% above 28. 77% of the current freshmen were in the top fifth of their class; 96% were in the top two fifths. There were 8 National Merit finalists and 7 semifinalists. 26 freshmen graduated first in their class.

Requirements: The SAT I or ACT is required. In addition, applicants should have completed 19 Carnegie units, including 4 each in English, math and science, 3 in foreign language, 2 in social studies, and 1 each in history and academic electives. An essay is part of the application process. An interview is advised, and a portfolio or an audition is recommended for art or music majors, respectively. AP credits are accepted. Important factors in the admissions decision are personality/intangible qualities, evidence of special talent, and advanced placement or honor courses. Applications can be downloaded from the admissions web page at *www.denison.edu/admissions*.

Procedure: Freshmen are admitted in the fall. Entrance exams should be taken by December of the senior year. There are early decision and deferred admissions plans. Early decision I applications should be filed by November 15; for scholarship consideration, regular applications, by February 1 for fall entry, along with a $40 fee. Notification of early decision is sent January 1; regular decision, April 1. 117 early decision candidates were accepted for the 2001-2002 class. 1% of all applicants are on a waiting list; 25 were accepted in 2001.

Transfer: 26 transfer students enrolled in 2001-2002. A minimum GPA of 2.75 is required. The SAT I or ACT scores should be submitted. An interview is recommended. 64 credits of 127 must be completed at Denison.

Visiting: There are regularly scheduled orientations for prospective students, including orientation, programs, class visits, tours, and interviews. There are guides for informal visits and visitors may sit in on classes and stay overnight. To schedule a visit, contact the Admissions Office.

Financial Aid: In 2001-2002, 94% of all freshmen and 95% of continuing students received some form of financial aid. 41% of freshmen and 43% of continuing students received need-based aid. The average freshman award was $24,228. Of that total, scholarships or need-based grants averaged $15,475 ($22,250 maximum); loans averaged $3048 ($4625 maximum); and work contracts averaged $2025 (maximum). 53% of undergraduates work part time. Average annual earnings from campus work are $1748. The average financial indebtedness of the 2001 graduate was $13,250. Denison is a member of CSS. The FAFSA and the college's own financial statement are required. The fall application deadline is March 1; priority deadline, February 15; and scolarship deadline, January 1.

International Students: There are 102 international students enrolled. The school actively recruits these students. They must score 550 on the written TOEFL or 213 on the electronic version or take the SAT I or ACT.

Computers: The mainframe is a client/server with 20 servers. More than 1000 PCs are connected to the campus network. 450 of those are available to students in public computer clusters and department labs. All residence halls have network services including e-mail, World Wide Web and the Internet, libraries, directory services, local events calendar, and personal web pages. All students may access the system 24 hours a day. There are no time limits and no fees.

Graduates: In 2001, 476 bachelor's degrees were awarded. The most popular majors were economics (14%), communications (12%), and history (11%). In an average class, 73% graduate in 4 years, 76% in 5 years, and 77% in 6 years. 86 companies recruited on campus in 2000-2001. Of the 2000 graduating class, 22% were enrolled in graduate school within 6 months of graduation and 75% were employed.

Admissions Contact: Perry Robinson, Director of Admissions.
E-mail: *admissions@denison.edu* Web: *http://denison.edu/admissions/*

DEVRY UNIVERSITY/COLUMBUS C-3
Columbus, OH 43209-2705 (614) 253-7291
(800) 426-2206; Fax: (614) 252-4108

Full-time: 2262 men, 630 women	**Faculty:** 83
Part-time: 614 men, 287 women	**Ph.D.s:** n/av
Graduate: none	**Student/Faculty:** 35 to 1
Year: semesters, summer session	**Tuition:** $8805
Application Deadline: open	**Room & Board:** n/app
Freshman Class: 1712 applied, 1503 accepted, 963 enrolled	
SAT I or ACT: recommended	**LESS COMPETITIVE**

DeVry University/Columbus, formerly DeVry Institute of Technology, 1 of 23 DeVry schools in the United States and Canada, opened in 1952. The institute offers undergraduate degrees in business administration, electronics, computer information systems, technical management, information technology, and computer engineering technology. In addition to regional accreditation, DeVry has baccalaureate program accreditation with ABET. The library contains 21,066 volumes, 64,400 microform items, and 1603 audiovisual forms/CDs, and subscribes to 73 periodicals. Computerized library services include the card catalog, interlibrary loans, and database searching. Special learning facilities include a learning resource center and electronics and other labs. The 13-acre campus is in an urban area. There is one building.

Student Life: 83% of undergraduates are from Ohio. Others are from 32 states and 4 foreign countries. 73% are white; 19% African American. The average age of all undergraduates is 25. 55% do not continue beyond their first year.

Housing: There are no residence halls. Housing referrals may be obtained through the Student Housing office. All students commute. Alcohol is not permitted. All students may keep cars.

Activities: There are no fraternities or sororities. There are 9 groups on campus, including ethnic, honors, newspaper, professional, religious, and student government. Popular campus events include Parents Weekend, Student Appreciation Week, and New Student Days.

Sports: There are 3 intramural sports for men and 1 for women.

Disabled Students: 90% of the campus is accessible. Wheelchair ramps, elevators, special parking, specially equipped rest rooms, and special class scheduling are available.

Services: Counseling and information services are available, as is tutoring in every subject.

Campus Safety and Security: Measures include informal discussions, pamphlets/posters/films, emergency telephones, and lighted pathways/sidewalks. Daytime and evening security is provided until the building is closed. Security systems and motion detectors are utilized after business hours.

Programs of Study: DeVry confers the B.S. degree. Associate degrees are also awarded. Bachelor's degrees are awarded in BUSINESS (business administration and management), COMPUTER AND PHYSICAL SCIENCE (information sciences and systems), ENGINEERING AND ENVIRONMENTAL DESIGN (computer technology, electrical/electronics engineering technology, and technological management). Computer information systems and computer engineering technology are the largest.

Required: To graduate, students must achieve a GPA of at least 2.0 and satisfactorily complete all curriculum requirements. Course requirements vary according to program. All first-semester students take courses in business organization, computer applications, algebra, psychology, and student success strategies.

Special: Accelerated degrees, co-op programs, nondegree study, and evening classes are possible. There is 1 national honor society.

Faculty/Classroom: All teach undergraduates. The average class size is 30; in a laboratory, 30.

Admissions: 88% of the 2001-2002 applicants were accepted.

Requirements: The SAT I or ACT is recommended. In addition, admissions requirements include graduation from a secondary school; the GED is also accepted. Applicants must pass the DeVry entrance exam or present satisfactory ACT or SAT I scores. An interview is required. Applications are accepted on-line at *Embark.com*. CLEP credit is accepted.

Procedure: Freshmen are admitted fall, spring, and summer. There is a deferred admissions plan. Application deadlines are open. Notification is sent on a rolling basis. The application fee is $50.

Transfer: 465 transfer students enrolled in 2001-2002. Applicants must present passing grades in all completed college course work, demonstrate language skills proficiency with at least 24 completed semester hours, and evidence math proficiency by appropriate college-level credits. 35% of 48 to 158 credits must be completed at DeVry.

Visiting: There are regularly scheduled orientations for prospective students. There are guides for informal visits and visitors may sit in on classes. To schedule a visit, contact Sheila Brown, New Student Coordinator at (614) 253-0851 or (800) 426-3916.

Financial Aid: In a recent year, 71% of all freshmen and 88% of continuing students received some form of financial aid. 65% of freshmen and 48% of continuing students received need-based aid. The average freshman award was $6215. Of that total, scholarships or need-based grants averaged $2006 and loans averaged $4208. 4% of undergraduates work part time. Average annual earnings from campus work are $7500. DeVry is a member of CSS. The FAFSA is required.

International Students: There are 31 international students enrolled. They must score 500 on the written TOEFL or 173 on the electronic version and also take the college's own entrance exam or DeVry's computerized placement test, achieving a minimum score that varies by program.

Computers: The mainframes are an IBM 3033 and an IBM System 36. Lab facilities include IBM PCs in stand-alone and network configurations, with access to the mainframe. LANs provide access to a wide range of applications software. Hard copy from the mainframe is provided through a local minicomputer and medium- and high-speed printers. Students in the computer information systems program may access the system during lab hours. There are no fees. Students in the Information Technology program must have DeVry-issued laptops. There is a $55 per hour technology fee.

Graduates: In 2001, 486 bachelor's degrees were awarded. The most popular majors were computer information systems (50%), business (29%), and electronics engineering technology (21%). 175 companies recruited on campus in 2000-2001.

Admissions Contact: Bill Holtry, Dean of Admissions.
Web: *www.devry.cols.edu*

FRANCISCAN UNIVERSITY OF STEUBENVILLE E-3
Steubenville, OH 43952-1763 (740) 283-6226
(800) 783-6220; Fax: (740) 284-5456

Full-time: 653 men, 933 women	**Faculty:** 94; IIA, --$
Part-time: 51 men, 96 women	**Ph.D.s:** 69%
Graduate: 212 men, 263 women	**Student/Faculty:** 16 to 1
Year: semesters, summer session	**Tuition:** $13,900
Application Deadline: June 30	**Room & Board:** $5200
Freshman Class: 777 applied, 697 accepted, 325 enrolled	
SAT I Verbal/Math: 570/550	**ACT:** 23.6 **COMPETITIVE+**

Franciscan University of Steubenville, founded in 1946 by the Franciscan Friars, is a Catholic Franciscan, private, liberal arts professional and preprofessional institution committed to the Catholic Church and its renewal. In addition to regional accreditation, Franciscan University has baccalaureate program accreditation with NLN. The library contains 227,109 volumes, 216,268 microform items and 892 audiovisual forms/CDs, and subscribes to 4233 periodicals. Computerized library services include the card catalog, interlibrary loans, and database searching. Special learning facilities include a radio station. The 124-acre campus is in a small town 40 miles west of Pittsburgh. Including residence halls, there are 21 buildings.

Student Life: 78% of undergraduates are from out of state, mostly the Midwest. Others are from 49 states, 26 foreign countries, and Canada. 44% are from public schools. 81% are white. Most are Catholic. The average age of freshmen is 19; all undergraduates, 22. 18% do not continue beyond their first year; 69% remain to graduate.

Housing: 1155 students can be accommodated in college housing, which includes single-sex dormitories and Christian faith households in residence halls. On-campus housing is available on a first-come, first-served basis. 62% of students live on campus; of those, 95% remain on campus on weekends. Upperclassmen may keep cars.

Activities: There is 1 local and 1 national fraternity; 1% of women belong to 1 national sorority. There are 25 groups on campus, including choir, chorale, chorus, computers, drama, ethnic, honors, international, literary magazine, newspaper, orchestra, political, professional, radio and TV, religious, social, social service, student government, and yearbook. Popular campus events include the Feast of St. Francis, Pro-Life Rally, and all school evangelism events.

Sports: There are 4 intramural sports for men and 4 for women. Facilities include a campus athletic center, which houses 2 full-size basketball courts, racquetball courts, saunas, whirlpools, and locker rooms, and provides indoor seating for 2,000. Outdoor athletic facilities include a basketball court, 4 tennis courts, and baseball, softball, flag football, and soccer fields.

Disabled Students: 75% of the campus is accessible. Wheelchair ramps, elevators, special parking, specially equipped rest rooms, special class scheduling, lowered drinking fountains, lowered telephones, fire alarm devices, wider doorways, and curb cuts are available.

Services: Counseling and information services are available, as is tutoring in most subjects. There is a reader service for the blind and remedial reading. Tutoring and counseling are available for learning-disabled students. Tutoring is also available for students on academic probation.

Campus Safety and Security: Measures include 24-hour foot and vehicle patrol, self-defense education, escort service, and shuttle buses. There are informal discussions, pamphlets/posters/films, emergency telephones, and lighted pathways/sidewalks.

Programs of Study: Franciscan University confers B.A., B.S., and B.S.N. degrees. Associate and master's degrees are also awarded. Bachelor's degrees are awarded in BIOLOGICAL SCIENCE (biology/biological science), BUSINESS (accounting and business administration and management), COMMUNICATIONS AND THE ARTS (classics, communications, English, French, and Spanish), COMPUTER AND PHYSICAL SCIENCE (chemistry, computer science, and mathematics), EDUCATION (elementary), ENGINEERING AND ENVIRONMENTAL DESIGN (engineering), HEALTH PROFESSIONS (mental health/human services and nursing), SOCIAL SCIENCE (anthropology, economics, history, humanities and social science, philosophy, political science/government, psychology, religion, sociology, and theological studies). Theology, psychology and education are the strongest academically. Theology, education, and business, are the largest.

Required: All students must complete core liberal arts courses, including 15 credits each in humanities and communications, and 6 credits each in theology, social science, and natural science. A 1-credit thesis seminar is required in all majors. A total of 124 credit hours, with at least 24 in the major, and a minimum GPA of 2.0 are required to graduate.

Special: Dual majors and internships for up to 6 credit hours are available in most majors. A humanities and Catholic culture major in Western tradition and minors in human life issues and music are offered. Study abroad is offered through the university's campus in Gaming, Austria where students spend a semester studying humanities as well as traveling through Europe. There are 5 national honor societies, a freshman honors program, and 25 departmental honors programs.

Faculty/Classroom: 65% of faculty are male; 35%, female. 92% teach undergraduates. No introductory courses are taught by graduate students. The average class size in an introductory lecture is 28; in a laboratory, 15; and in a regular course, 21.

Admissions: 90% of the 2001-2002 applicants were accepted. The SAT I scores for the 2001-2002 freshman class were: Verbal--16% below 500, 44% between 500 and 599, 33% between 600 and 700, and 3% above 700; Math--22% below 500, 51% between 500 and 599, 24% between 600 and 700, and 3% above 700. The ACT scores were 23% below 21, 27% between 21 and 23, 24% between 24 and 26, 14% between 27 and 28, and 12% above 28. 44% of the current freshmen were in the top fifth of their class; 69% were in the top two fifths. 10 freshmen graduated first in their class.

Requirements: The SAT I or ACT is required. In addition, applicants should have completed 15 academic high school units, including 10 in 4 of the 5 following areas: English, foreign language, social science, math, and natural sciences. The GED is accepted. An essay and an interview are recommended. A GPA of 2.4 is required. AP and CLEP credits are accepted. Important factors in the admissions decision are advanced placement or honor courses, evidence of special talent, and leadership record.

Procedure: Freshmen are admitted fall and spring. Entrance exams should be taken in the spring of the junior year or the fall of the senior year. Applications should be filed by June 30 for fall entry and December 15 for spring entry. The application fee for fall 2001 was $20. Notification is sent on a rolling basis.

Transfer: 174 transfer students enrolled in 2001-2002. A minimum 2.0 college GPA is required. High school and college transcripts must be submitted. An interview is recommended. 30 credits of 124 must be completed at Franciscan University.

Visiting: There are regularly scheduled orientations for prospective students, including tours, interviews with professors, admissions, and financial aid officers, and class visits. There are guides for informal visits and visitors may sit in on classes and stay overnight. To schedule a visit, contact the Admissions Office at *visit@franuniv.edu*.

Financial Aid: In 2001-2002, 83% of all freshmen and 84% of continuing students received some form of financial aid. 62% of freshmen and 65% of continuing students received need-based aid. The average freshman award was $8367. Of that total, scholarships or need-based grants averaged $5050 ($11,990 maximum); loans averaged $2818 ($16,650 maximum); and work contracts averaged $1000. 50% of undergraduates work part time. Average annual earnings from campus work are $1000. The average financial indebtedness of the 2001 graduate was $22,940. The FAFSA is required. The fall application deadline is March 15.

International Students: There are 92 international students enrolled. The school actively recruits these students. They must score 550 on the written TOEFL.

Computers: The mainframe is an IBM AS/400. There are also 40 PCs and 30 Macs available in student labs. All students may access the system from 9 A.M. to 11 P.M. Monday through Friday, 10 A.M. to 6 P.M. Saturday, and 1 P.M. to 11 P.M. Sunday. There are no time limits and no fees.

Graduates: In 2001, 400 bachelor's degrees were awarded. The most popular majors were theology (21%), education (10%), and nursing (7%). In an average class, 3% graduate in 3 years, 54% in 4 years, 65% in 5 years, and 69% in 6 years. 35 companies recruited on campus in 2000-2001.

Admissions Contact: Margaret Weber, Director of Admissions. A video is available. E-mail: *admissions@franuniv.edu*
Web: *www.gabriel.franuniv.edu*

FRANKLIN UNIVERSITY
Columbus, OH 43215-5399

C-3
(614) 797-4700
(877) 341-6300; (614) 224-8027

Full-time: 636 men, 808 women	**Faculty:** 33
Part-time: 1353 men, 1853 women	**Ph.D.s:** 43%
Graduate: 456 men, 431 women	**Student/Faculty:** 44 to 1
Year: trimesters, summer session	**Tuition:** $6324
Application Deadline: open	**Room & Board:** n/app
Freshman Class: n/av	
SAT I or ACT: not required	**SPECIAL**

Franklin University is a student-centered, independent, regional institution of lifelong higher education (undergraduate and graduate) working in partnership with Central Ohio's business and professional community in a global context. There are 2 undergraduate schools and 1 graduate school. The library contains 81,730 volumes, 176,468 microform items, and 265 audiovisual forms/CDs, and subscribes to 511 periodicals. Computerized library services include the card catalog, interlibrary loans, and database searching. Special learning facilities include a learning resource center and art gallery. The 14-acre campus is in an urban area located in downtown Columbus. There are 7 buildings.

Student Life: 92% of undergraduates are from Ohio. Others are from 26 states, 66 foreign countries, and Canada. 67% are white; 14% African American; 10% foreign nationals. The average age of all undergraduates is 31.

Housing: There are no residence halls. Alcohol is not permitted. All students may keep cars.

Activities: There are no fraternities or sororities. There are 6 groups on campus, including computers, international, and professional. Popular campus events include New student orientation, awards/scholarship reception, and opening week activities.

Sports: There is no sports program at Franklin.

Disabled Students: All of the campus is accessible. Wheelchair ramps, elevators, special parking, specially equipped rest rooms, special class scheduling, lowered drinking fountains, and lowered telephones are available.

Services: Counseling and information services are available, as is tutoring in most subjects. There is a reader service for the blind, and remedial math, reading, and writing.

Campus Safety and Security: Measures include an escort service. There is a parking guard on duty in each lot and a city police officer on duty during class hours. All such personnel are connected by an emergency radio system.

Programs of Study: Franklin confers the B.S. degree. Associate and master's degrees are also awarded. Bachelor's degrees are awarded in BUSINESS (accounting, banking and finance, business administration and management, human resources, management science, marketing and distribution, and organizational behavior), COMPUTER AND PHYSICAL SCIENCE (computer science), ENGINEERING AND ENVIRONMENTAL DESIGN (technological management), HEALTH PROFESSIONS (health care administration), SOCIAL SCIENCE (safety management). Business administration and computer science are the largest.

Required: Students must complete general education core requirements in communication, math, humanities, socal and behavioral sciences, and science. A total of 122 to 132 semester hours with a minimum GPA of 2.0 (2.25 for some majors) is required to graduate.

Special: Cross-registration is possible with other area colleges and universities through the Higher Education Council of Columbus. Internships are available for accounting, finance, marketing, business administration, computer science, human resources management, and management information sciences. Student-designed majors, ESL, and some pass/fail courses are offered. Bachelor of Science degree completion programs are available through alliances with community colleges in the United States and Canada.

Faculty/Classroom: 58% of faculty are male; 42%, female. 89% teach undergraduates. No introductory courses are taught by graduate students. The average class size in a regular course is 17.

Requirements: Applicants should be graduates of an accredited secondary school or have a GED. AP and CLEP credits are accepted.

Procedure: Freshmen are admitted fall, winter, and summer. There are early admissions and deferred admissions plans. Application deadlines are open.

Transfer: 1113 transfer students enrolled in 2001-2002. The open admission policy applies to transfer students as well as freshmen. 30 credits of 124 must be completed at Franklin.
Visiting: There are guides for informal visits and visitors may sit in on classes. To schedule a visit, contact the Admission Office at *info@franklin.edu*.
Financial Aid: In 2001-2002, 3% of all freshmen and 2% of continuing students received some form of financial aid including need-based aid. The FAFSA and the college's own financial statement are required. The fall application deadline is June 15.
International Students: There are 295 international students enrolled. The school actively recruits these students. They must score 430 on the written TOEFL or 117 on the electronic version or take the MELAB.
Computers: The mainframe is an HP 9000. Several computer labs and classrooms are equipped with 325 networked computers. Students have access to Microsoft Office software and the Internet. All students may access the system. There are no time limits and no fees.
Graduates: In 2001, 814 bachelor's degrees were awarded. The most popular majors were business administration (34%), computer science (14%), and accounting (13%).
Admissions Contact: Student Services Office.
E-mail: *info@franklin.edu* Web: *www.franklin.edu*

HEIDELBERG COLLEGE
Tiffin, OH 44883-2434 — C-2
(419) 448-2330
(800) HEIDELBERG; Fax: (419) 448-2334

Full-time: 489 men, 482 women	**Faculty:** 75; IIB, -$
Part-time: 111 men, 238 women	**Ph.D.s:** 74%
Graduate: 56 men, 153 women	**Student/Faculty:** 13 to 1
Year: semesters, summer session	**Tuition:** $18,132
Application Deadline: May 1	**Room & Board:** $5747
Freshman Class: 1395 applied, 1210 accepted, 281 enrolled	
SAT I Verbal/Math: 515/520	**ACT:** 22 **COMPETITIVE**

Heidelberg College, founded in 1850, is a private liberal arts institution affiliated with the United Church of Christ/Congregational. In addition to regional accreditation, Heidelberg has baccalaureate program accreditation with NASM. The library contains 260,055 volumes, 108,640 microform items, and 8300 audiovisual forms/CDs, and subscribes to 829 periodicals. Computerized library services include the card catalog, interlibrary loans, and database searching. Special learning facilities include a learning resource center, radio station, TV station, a media center, an anthropology museum, a human cadaver lab, an archaeology lab, a physiology lab, and a computer-assisted writing classroom. The 110-acre campus is in a small town 50 miles south of Toledo. Including residence halls, there are 26 buildings.
Student Life: 88% of undergraduates are from Ohio. Others are from 22 states, 8 foreign countries, and Canada. 61% are from public schools. 92% are white. 59% are Protestant; 41% Catholic. The average age of freshmen is 18; all undergraduates, 24. 27% do not continue beyond their first year; 56% remain to graduate.
Housing: 854 students can be accommodated in college housing, which includes single-sex and coed dormitories. On-campus housing is guaranteed for all 4 years. 86% of students live on campus; of those, 85% remain on campus on weekends. All students may keep cars.
Activities: 30% of men belong to 4 local fraternities; 36% of women belong to 4 local sororities. There are 65 groups on campus, including band, cheerleading, choir, chorale, chorus, computers, dance, drama, drill team, ethnic, honors, international, jazz band, literary magazine, musical theater, newspaper, opera, orchestra, pep band, political, professional, radio and TV, religious, social, social service, student government, symphony, and yearbook. Popular campus events include Parents Weekend, Greek Sing, and Tuba Christmas.
Sports: There are 9 intercollegiate sports for men and 8 for women, and 9 intramural sports for men and 8 for women. Facilities include a wrestling arena, an all-weather track, indoor courts for volleyball, basketball, racquetball, and tennis, a weight room and fitness area, a sports medicine clinic, and outdoor tennis, soccer, lacrosse, and football facilities. A YMCA adjacent to the college provides additional recreation options.
Disabled Students: 20% of the campus is accessible. Wheelchair ramps, elevators, special parking, specially equipped rest rooms, and special class scheduling are available.
Services: Counseling and information services are available, as is tutoring in every subject. There is remedial math.
Campus Safety and Security: Measures include 24-hour foot and vehicle patrol, self-defense education, escort service, and informal discussions. There are pamphlets/posters/films, emergency telephones, and lighted pathways/sidewalks.
Programs of Study: Heidelberg confers B.A., B.S., and B.Mus. degrees. Master's degrees are also awarded. Bachelor's degrees are awarded in BIOLOGICAL SCIENCE (biology/biological science and environmental biology), BUSINESS (accounting, business administration and management, business economics, and management science), COMMUNICATIONS AND THE ARTS (communications, dramatic arts, English, German, music, public relations, and Spanish), COMPUTER AND PHYSICAL SCIENCE (chemistry, computer science, information sciences and systems, mathematics, and physics), EDUCATION (elementary, foreign languages, middle school, music, physical, science, and secondary), ENGINEERING AND ENVIRONMENTAL DESIGN (preengineering), HEALTH PROFESSIONS (predentistry, premedicine, and sports medicine), SOCIAL SCIENCE (anthropology, economics, history, international studies, philosophy, political science/government, prelaw, psychology, public administration, religion, social science, and water resources). Business administration, communications, and sciences are the strongest academically. Business administration, sciences, and psychology are the largest.
Required: Students must fulfill 40 semester hours of general education requirements, including English composition and public speaking, arts, languages and literature, civilization, religion and philosophy, social sciences, natural sciences, and math, and 40 semester hours each in the major and electives. 4 units of health and phys ed are needed. A total of 120 semester hours with a minimum GPA of 2.0 overall and 2.5 in the major is required in order to graduate.
Special: There are co-op programs in preengineering and prenursing. A 3-2 engineering degree and a 3-3 nursing degree are offered in cooperation with Case Western Reserve University. Study abroad is possible at the University of Heidelberg, Germany, Seville, Spain, and in Mexico. A Washington semester is available at American University. Dual majors in any combination, an honors program, credit for life experience, internships, and pass/fail options are possible. There are 10 national honor societies, a freshman honors program, and 15 departmental honors programs.
Faculty/Classroom: 71% of faculty are male; 29%, female. 60% both teach and do research. No introductory courses are taught by graduate students. The average class size in an introductory lecture is 25; in a laboratory, 15; and in a regular course, 15.
Admissions: 87% of the 2001-2002 applicants were accepted. 40% of the current freshmen were in the top fifth of their class; 70% were in the top two fifths. There were 6 National Merit semifinalists. 9 freshmen graduated first in their class.
Requirements: The SAT I or ACT is required. In addition, applicants should have completed 22 high school academic credits, including 4 years each of English and social studies, 3 each of math and science, and 2 of a foreign language. An audition is required for music majors. Recommendations and an interview are recommended. The college accepts applications on computer disk through CollegeLink or CollegeView and on-line via Heidelberg's home page, *http://www.heidelberg.edu*. Heidelberg requires applicants to be in the upper 50% of their class. A GPA of 2.4 is required. AP and CLEP credits are accepted. Important factors in the admissions decision are advanced placement or honor courses, leadership record, and extracurricular activities record.
Procedure: Freshmen are admitted to all sessions. Entrance exams should be taken by the end of the junior year or the beginning of the senior year. There is a deferred admissions plan. Applications should be filed by May 1 for fall entry, December 1 for spring entry, and June 1 for summer entry. The fall 2001 application fee was $20. Notification is sent on a rolling basis.
Transfer: 85 transfer students enrolled in a recent year. A minimum GPA of 2.0 and a character reference from the institution most recently attended are required. 30 credits of 120 must be completed at Heidelberg.
Visiting: There are regularly scheduled orientations for prospective students, including coach and faculty sessions, academic overview, student panel, admissions and financial aid presentations, a tour of the college, and lunch. There are guides for informal visits and visitors may sit in on classes and stay overnight. To schedule a visit, contact the Office of Admission.
Financial Aid: In a recent year, 97% of all students received some form of financial aid. 88% of all students received need-based aid. The average freshman award was $8800. Of that total, scholarships or need-based grants averaged $8700 ($18,000 maximum); loans averaged $3500 ($4125 maximum); and work contracts averaged $1000 ($1500 maximum). 65% of undergraduates work part time. Average annual earnings from campus work are $800. The average financial indebtedness of a graduate in a recent year was $18,800. The FAFSA is required. The fall application deadline is May 1.
International Students: There were 15 international students enrolled in a recent year. The school actively recruits these students. They must score 500 on the written TOEFL.
Computers: Terminals are located in all residence halls. All Macs and PCs and special use systems are networked through UNIX hosts for use throughout the campus. Almost every department requires some knowledge of computers. Separate computer centers are located in the sciences complex, the library, the business department, the Honors Center, and the administration building. All students may access the system. There are no time limits and no fees.
Graduates: In a recent year~, 190 bachelor's degrees were awarded. The most popular majors were business administration and management

(27%), biology (11%), and education (6%). In an average class, 50% graduate in 4 years, 52% in 5 years, and 54% in 6 years. 50 companies recruited on campus in 2000-2001. Of the 2000 graduating class, 17% were enrolled in graduate school within 6 months of graduation and 94% were employed.

Admissions Contact: David J. Rhodes, Vice President for Enrollment. E-mail: *adminfo@mail.heidelberg.edu* Web: *http://www.heidelberg.edu*

HIRAM COLLEGE — E-1
Hiram, OH 44234 (330) 569-5169
(800) 362-5280; Fax: (330) 569-5944

Full-time: 427 men, 537 women	**Faculty:** 68; IIB, +$
Part-time: 83 men, 143 women	**Ph.D.s:** 97%
Graduate: none	**Student/Faculty:** 13 to 1
Year: split semesters, summer session	**Tuition:** $20,214
Application Deadline: February 1	**Room & Board:** $6820
Freshman Class: 1024 applied, 894 accepted, 269 enrolled	
SAT I Verbal/Math: 580/570	**ACT:** 24 VERY COMPETITIVE

Hiram College, founded in 1850, is a private, residential liberal arts and sciences institution. In addition to regional accreditation, Hiram has baccalaureate program accreditation with NASM. The library contains 178,776 volumes, 96,049 microform items, and 8795 audiovisual forms/CDs, and subscribes to 885 periodicals. Computerized library services include the card catalog, interlibrary loans, and database searching. Special learning facilities include a learning resource center, art gallery, planetarium, radio station, a 260-acre biological field station and a field station, in the Upper Peninsula of Michigan. The 110-acre campus is in a rural area 35 miles southeast of Cleveland. Including residence halls, there are 28 buildings.

Student Life: 79% of undergraduates are from Ohio. Others are from 23 states and 13 foreign countries. 89% are from public schools. 84% are white. 52% claim no religious affiliation; 22% Protestant; 20% Catholic. The average age of freshmen is 18; all undergraduates, 20. 18% do not continue beyond their first year; 64% remain to graduate.

Housing: 1000 students can be accommodated in college housing, which includes single-sex and coed dormitories. On-campus housing is guaranteed for all 4 years. 93% of students live on campus; of those, 70% remain on campus on weekends. All students may keep cars.

Activities: There are no fraternities or sororities. There are 90 groups on campus, including art, band, cheerleading, choir, chorale, chorus, computers, dance, drama, ethnic, gay, honors, international, jazz band, literary magazine, musical theater, newspaper, opera, orchestra, photography, political, professional, radio and TV, religious, social, social service, student government, and yearbook. Popular campus events include Campus Days, Springfest, and Madrigal Revels.

Sports: There are 9 intercollegiate sports for men and 8 for women, and 10 intramural sports for men and 10 for women. Facilities include a 4000-seat stadium, a gym, sports fields, an all-weather track, a fitness room, a sauna, racquetball and tennis courts, an indoor swimming pool with diving area, an outdoor exercise and fitness trail, a cross-country ski trail, and a fully equipped athletic training facility.

Disabled Students: 40% of the campus is accessible. Wheelchair ramps, elevators, special parking, and specially equipped rest rooms are available.

Services: Counseling and information services are available, as is tutoring in every subject. There is a reader service for the blind. Note takers are available for most classes.

Campus Safety and Security: Measures include 24-hour foot and vehicle patrol, self-defense education, escort service, and informal discussions. There are pamphlets/posters/films, emergency telephones, and lighted pathways/sidewalks.

Programs of Study: Hiram confers the B.A. degree. Bachelor's degrees are awarded in BIOLOGICAL SCIENCE (biology/biological science), BUSINESS (international economics and management science), COMMUNICATIONS AND THE ARTS (art, art history and appreciation, classics, communications, dramatic arts, English, French, German, language arts, music, and Spanish), COMPUTER AND PHYSICAL SCIENCE (applied physics, chemistry, computer science, and mathematics), EDUCATION (elementary), ENGINEERING AND ENVIRONMENTAL DESIGN (environmental science), SOCIAL SCIENCE (economics, history, philosophy, political science/government, psychobiology, psychology, religion, social studies, and sociology). Biology, computer science, and education are the strongest academically. Biology, education, and management are the largest.

Required: All students must complete distribution requirement courses in the fine arts, humanities, natural sciences, and social sciences; the Freshman Institute and Colloquium; a first-year seminar in writing and speaking skills; and 1 upper-division interdisciplinary requirement. A total of 120 academic semester hours and a minimum GPA of 2.0 are required to graduate.

Special: There is cross-registration through the Cleveland Commission on Higher Education and a 3-2 engineering program with Case Western Reserve and Washington Universities. There is a Washington semester and study abroad in many countries with courses taught by Hiram faculty. Double majors and individually arranged internships in all fields, student-designed majors, and pass/no credit options are possible. There are 8 national honor societies, including Phi Beta Kappa.

Faculty/Classroom: 54% of faculty are male; 46%, female. All teach undergraduates. The average class size in an introductory lecture is 21; in a laboratory, 13; and in a regular course, 15.

Admissions: 87% of the 2001-2002 applicants were accepted. The SAT I scores for the 2001-2002 freshman class were: Verbal--22% below 500, 37% between 500 and 599, 31% between 600 and 700, and 10% above 700; Math--24% below 500, 43% between 500 and 599, 29% between 600 and 700, and 4% above 700. The ACT scores were 28% below 21, 23% between 21 and 23, 22% between 24 and 26, 15% between 27 and 28, and 12% above 28. 53% of the current freshmen were in the top fifth of their class; 78% were in the top two fifths. 13 freshmen graduated first in their class in a recent year.

Requirements: The SAT I or ACT is required. In addition, applicants should have completed 16 academic units or the GED equivalent. An essay is required. A portfolio, audition, and interview are recommended. AP and CLEP credits are accepted. Important factors in the admissions decision are advanced placement or honor courses, leadership record, and extracurricular activities record. Applications are accepted on disk or on-line through CollegeLink, Common App, and Apply.

Procedure: Freshmen are admitted fall and spring. Entrance exams should be taken no later than the fall of the senior year. There are early admissions and deferred admissions plans. Early decision applications should be filed by December 1; regular applications, by February 1 for fall entry and December 1 for spring entry, along with a $35 fee. Notification is sent on a rolling basis.

Transfer: 22 transfer students enrolled in a recent year. Applicants should have at least a 2.5 GPA and be in good academic and social standing with the previous institution. An interview is recommended. 60 credits of 120 must be completed at Hiram.

Visiting: There are regularly scheduled orientations for prospective students, 1 week before the semester begins, and campus visits are encouraged while school is in session. There are guides for informal visits and visitors may sit in on classes and stay overnight. To schedule a visit, contact the Admissions Office.

Financial Aid: In 2001-2002, 94% of all freshmen and 93% of continuing students received some form of financial aid. 71% of undergraduates work part time. Average annual earnings from campus work are $1202. The average financial indebtedness of a recent year's graduate was $18,925. Hiram is a member of CSS. The FAFSA is required. Check with the school for current deadlines.

International Students: There were 38 international students enrolled in a recent year. The school actively recruits these students. They must score 550 on the written TOEFL and also take the SAT I or the ACT.

Computers: The mainframe is a DEC ALPHA Server 2100 5/250. The college network may be accessed from student-owned PCs in residence halls and from PC labs throughout the campus. The network allows access to the Internet and the Web. Each residence hall has a lab with 5 to 8 PCs. More than 60 additional PCs are available in classrooms and other locations. All students may access the system 24 hours a day, 7 days per week. There are no time limits and no fees.

Graduates: In a recent year, 222 bachelor's degrees were awarded. The most popular majors were biology (13%), communication (9%), and history (9%). In an average class, 1% graduate in 3 years, 60% in 4 years, 66% in 5 years, and 68% in 6 years.

Admissions Contact: Ed Frato-Sweeney, Director of Admission. A video is available. E-mail: *admission@hiram.edu*
Web: *http://www.hiram.edu*

JOHN CARROLL UNIVERSITY — D-1
University Heights, OH 44118 (216) 397-4294
Fax: (216) 397-4981

Full-time: 1521 men, 1810 women	**Faculty:** 236; IIA, av$
Part-time: 69 men, 108 women	**Ph.D.s:** 89%
Graduate: 297 men, 496 women	**Student/Faculty:** 14 to 1
Year: semesters, summer session	**Tuition:** $17,828
Application Deadline: February 1	**Room & Board:** $6312
Freshman Class: 2764 applied, 2387 accepted, 792 enrolled	
SAT I Verbal/Math: 570/580	**ACT:** 24 VERY COMPETITIVE

John Carroll University, founded in 1886, is a private Catholic institution operated by the Jesuits. It offers undergraduate degree programs in the arts, sciences, and business. There are 2 undergraduate schools and 1 graduate school. In addition to regional accreditation, John Carroll has baccalaureate program accreditation with AACSB and NCATE. The library contains 631,576 volumes, 710,403 microform items, and 4880 audiovisual forms/CDs, and subscribes to 1975 periodicals. Computerized library services include the card catalog, interlibrary loans, and database searching. Special learning facilities include a learning resource center, radio station, and TV station. The 62-acre campus is in a suburban area 10 miles east of Cleveland. Including residence halls, there are 26 buildings.

Student Life: 75% of undergraduates are from Ohio. Others are from 35 states, 21 foreign countries, and Canada. 53% are from public schools. 87% are white. 71% are Catholic; 15% Protestant. The average age of freshmen is 18; all undergraduates, 21. 14% do not continue beyond their first year; 81% remain to graduate.

Housing: 2016 students can be accommodated in college housing, which includes single-sex and coed dormitories. 58% of students live on campus. Upperclassmen may keep cars.

Activities: 13% of men belong to 4 national fraternities; 18% of women belong to 5 national sororities. There are 87 groups on campus, including band, cheerleading, chess, choir, chorale, chorus, computers, dance, debate, drama, drill team, ethnic, honors, international, jazz band, literary magazine, musical theater, newspaper, pep band, photography, political, professional, radio and TV, religious, social, social service, student government, symphony, and yearbook. Popular campus events include Welcome Back Week, Little Siblings Weekend, and Dance Marathon.

Sports: There are 11 intercollegiate sports for men and 10 for women, and 8 intramural sports for men and 8 for women. Facilities include a swimming pool and diving well, a 3800-seat football stadium and track, a baseball stadium, soccer and softball fields, an indoor track, tennis, volleyball, racquetball, and basketball courts, a weight room, a fitness center, and a 33-acre off-campus student villa. Club sports include hockey, rugby, lacrosse, skiing, and sailing.

Disabled Students: 96% of the campus is accessible. Wheelchair ramps, elevators, special parking, specially equipped rest rooms, special class scheduling, lowered drinking fountains, and lowered telephones are available.

Services: Counseling and information services are available, as is tutoring in every subject. There is a reader service for the blind.

Campus Safety and Security: Measures include 24-hour foot and vehicle patrol, self-defense education, escort service, and shuttle buses. There are informal discussions, pamphlets/posters/films, emergency telephones, and lighted pathways/sidewalks.

Programs of Study: John Carroll confers B.A., B.S., B.A.Classics, B.S.B.A., and B.S.Econ. degrees. Master's degrees are also awarded. Bachelor's degrees are awarded in BIOLOGICAL SCIENCE (biology/biological science), BUSINESS (accounting, banking and finance, business administration and management, and marketing/retailing/merchandising), COMMUNICATIONS AND THE ARTS (art history and appreciation, communications, English, French, German, Greek, Latin, literature, and Spanish), COMPUTER AND PHYSICAL SCIENCE (chemistry, computer science, mathematics, and physics), EDUCATION (early childhood, elementary, mathematics, physical, and secondary), ENGINEERING AND ENVIRONMENTAL DESIGN (engineering physics), SOCIAL SCIENCE (economics, history, humanities, philosophy, political science/government, psychology, public administration, religion, and sociology). Accounting, biology, and English are the strongest academically. Communications, biology, and marketing are the largest.

Required: All students must complete a liberal arts core curriculum, which includes 6 credits each in English composition and foreign language, 3 in first-year seminar, and 2 in speech communication. Also, students must take 4 courses each in science/math and the humanities, 3 each in social sciences and philosophy, and 2 in religious studies. Additional requirements include 1 writing-intensive course beyond English composition, 2 international courses, and 1 course in issues of diversity. A total of 128 credit hours with a minimum GPA of 2.0 is required for graduation.

Special: Co-op programs are available, and cross-registration is offered with 16 area colleges through the Northeast Ohio Commission on Higher Education. Study abroad is possible in many countries. Joint engineering degrees are offered with Case Western Reserve University, the University of Detroit Mercy, and Washington University. Work-study programs with local corporations, internships, a Washington semester, student-designed majors, dual majors, and some pass/fail options are available. There are 13 national honor societies, and a freshman honors program.

Faculty/Classroom: 59% of faculty are male; 41%, female. All teach undergraduates, 95% do research, and 95% do both. Graduate students teach 4% of introductory courses. The average class size in an introductory lecture is 21; in a laboratory, 20; and in a regular course, 21.

Admissions: 86% of the 2001-2002 applicants were accepted. The SAT I scores for the 2001-2002 freshman class were: Verbal--16% below 500, 52% between 500 and 599, 26% between 600 and 700, and 6% above 700; Math--12% below 500, 45% between 500 and 599, 39% between 600 and 700, and 4% above 700. The ACT scores were 22% below 21, 29% between 21 and 23, 25% between 24 and 26, 14% between 27 and 28, and 10% above 28. 50% of the current freshmen were in the top fifth of their class; 79% were in the top two fifths. There were 5 National Merit finalists. 12 freshmen graduated first in their class.

Requirements: The SAT I or ACT is required. In addition, applicants should be graduates of an accredited secondary school with 16 academic credits, including 4 in English, 3 in math, 2 each in foreign language, lab science, and social studies, and 3 in electives. An essay is part of the application process, and an interview is recommended. Applications are accepted on computer disk via CollegeLink and Apply Disk, or may be downloaded directly from the University's web site or *embark.com*. AP credits are accepted. Important factors in the admissions decision are advanced placement or honor courses, extracurricular activities record, and recommendations by school officials.

Procedure: Freshmen are admitted fall and spring. Entrance exams should be taken in the spring of the junior year or the fall of the senior year. There is a deferred admissions plan. Applications should be filed by February 1 for fall entry, along with a $25 fee. Notification is sent on a rolling basis.

Transfer: 160 transfer students enrolled in 2001-2002. Students must be in good standing at the time of application. The most recent term average and the cumulative average at the home school must be 2.0 or better to be considered for admission, and the cumulative average for all schools attended must be 2.0 or better. A GPA of at least 2.5 is recommended. 30 credits of 128 must be completed at John Carroll.

Visiting: There are regularly scheduled orientations for prospective students, consisting of open houses, admission and financial aid presentations, campus and Cleveland tours and opportunities to meet faculty and students. There are guides for informal visits and visitors may sit in on classes and stay overnight. To schedule a visit, contact Office of Admission.

Financial Aid: In 2001-2002, 97% of all freshmen and 94% of continuing students received some form of financial aid. 82% of freshmen and 79% of continuing students received need-based aid. The average freshman award was $14,460. Of that total, scholarships or need-based grants averaged $10,425 ($17,478 maximum); loans averaged $3118 ($4625 maximum); and work contracts averaged $917 ($1700 maximum). 34% of undergraduates work part time. The FAFSA is required. The fall application deadline is March 1.

International Students: There are 2 international students enrolled. The school actively recruits these students. They must score 550 on the written TOEFL or 213 on the electronic version and also take the SAT I or the ACT.

Computers: The mainframes are a LAN, Intel-based servers, Alpha server, RISC-based Sun servers, IBM RS6000 servers, and Clustered Network Appliance. Any registered student may obtain a user code for the campus network. There are more than 1000 PCs in various locations on campus. PCs are available in the science and math labs. All residence hall rooms are wired, and students may hook directly into the university system as well as the Internet and World Wide Web. All students may access the system 24 hours a day in some locations. There are no time limits. The technology fee is $300.

Graduates: In 2001, 728 bachelor's degrees were awarded. The most popular majors were communications (14%), biology (10%), and marketing (9%). In an average class, 1% graduate in 3 years, 70% in 4 years, 79% in 5 years, and 81% in 6 years. 163 companies recruited on campus in 2000-2001. Of the 2000 graduating class, 22% were enrolled in graduate school within 6 months of graduation.

Admissions Contact: Thomas P. Fanning, Director of Admission. A video is available. E-mail: *admission@jcu.edu*
Web: *http://www.jcu.edu/*

KENT STATE UNIVERSITY — D-2

Kent, OH 44242-0001 — **(330) 672-2444**
(800) 988-KENT; Fax: (330) 672-2499

Full-time: 6202 men, 9248 women	**Faculty:** 646; I, -$
Part-time: 1203 men, 1729 women	**Ph.D.s:** 85%
Graduate: 1514 men, 2932 women	**Student/Faculty:** 24 to 1
Year: semesters, summer session	**Tuition:** $5954 ($11,441)
Application Deadline: open	**Room & Board:** $5150
Freshman Class: 9694 applied, 8745 accepted, 3653 enrolled	
SAT I Verbal/Math: 500/500	**ACT:** 21 **COMPETITIVE**

Kent State University, founded in 1910, is a public university offering degree programs in liberal and fine arts, business, health science, teacher and professional training, and aviation. There are 7 undergraduate and 7 graduate schools. In addition to regional accreditation, KSU has baccalaureate program accreditation with AACSB, ABET, ACEJMC, FIDER, NAAB, NASAD, NASM, NCATE, and NLN. The 6 libraries contain 1,591,284 volumes, 1,245,139 microform items, and 19,593 audiovisual forms/CDs, and subscribe to 12,400 periodicals. Computerized library services include the card catalog, interlibrary loans, and database searching. Special learning facilities include an art gallery, planetarium, radio station, TV station, fashion museum, and liquid crystal institute. The 1200-acre campus is in a suburban area 45 miles southeast of Cleveland. Including residence halls, there are 110 buildings.

Student Life: 91% of undergraduates are from Ohio. Others are from 49 states, 81 foreign countries, and Canada. 85% are white. The average age of freshmen is 18; all undergraduates, 22. 28% do not continue beyond their first year; 42% remain to graduate.

Housing: 7558 students can be accommodated in college housing, which includes single-sex and coed dormitories and married-student housing. In addition, there are honors houses and special-interest houses. On-campus housing is guaranteed for all 4 years. 67% of students commute. Alcohol is not permitted. All students may keep cars.

Activities: 5% of men belong to 1 local fraternity and 16 national fraternities; 5% of women belong to 3 local and 9 national sororities. There are 230 groups on campus, including art, band, cheerleading, chess, choir, chorale, chorus, computers, dance, drama, drill team, ethnic, film, gay, honors, international, jazz band, literary magazine, marching band, musical theater, newspaper, opera, orchestra, pep band, photography, political, professional, radio and TV, religious, social, social service, student government, and symphony. Popular campus events include Black Squirrel Festival, Community Day, and Spirit Day.

Sports: There are 7 intercollegiate sports for men and 9 for women, and 23 intramural sports for men and 20 for women. Facilities include a gym, a recreation and wellness center, a stadium, a field house, 2 fitness circuits, a golf course, a bowling alley, tennis courts, lighted basketball courts, an ice arena, a pool, a weight room, and soccer, lacrosse, rugby, baseball, and softball fields.

Disabled Students: 90% of the campus is accessible. Wheelchair ramps, elevators, special parking, specially equipped rest rooms, special class scheduling, lowered drinking fountains, lowered telephones, and transportation services are available.

Services: Counseling and information services are available, as is tutoring in most subjects. There is a reader service for the blind, remedial math, reading, and writing, and a writing clinic.

Campus Safety and Security: Measures include 24-hour foot and vehicle patrol, escort service, shuttle buses, and pamphlets/posters/films. There are emergency telephones, lighted pathways/sidewalks, a 24-hour campus police department, overnight security guards, and a 2-key system for residence halls.

Programs of Study: KSU confers B.A., B.S., B.Arch., B.B.A., B.F.A., B.G.S., B.M., B.S.E., and B.S.W. degrees. Associate, master's, and doctoral degrees are also awarded. Bachelor's degrees are awarded in AGRICULTURE (conservation and regulation), BIOLOGICAL SCIENCE (biology/biological science, botany, life science, nutrition, and zoology), BUSINESS (accounting, banking and finance, business administration and management, business economics, fashion merchandising, international economics, management science, marketing/retailing/merchandising, personnel management, real estate, and recreation and leisure services), COMMUNICATIONS AND THE ARTS (advertising, art history and appreciation, broadcasting, classics, communications, crafts, dance, design, dramatic arts, English, film arts, fine arts, French, German, graphic design, industrial design, journalism, Latin, music, photography, public relations, radio/television technology, Russian, Spanish, speech/debate/rhetoric, telecommunications, and visual and performing arts), COMPUTER AND PHYSICAL SCIENCE (applied mathematics, chemistry, computer science, earth science, geology, information sciences and systems, mathematics, physical sciences, and physics), EDUCATION (art, athletic training, business, early childhood, education, elementary, English, foreign languages, health, mathematics, middle school, music, physical, science, secondary, social studies, special, technical, trade and industrial, and vocational), ENGINEERING AND ENVIRONMENTAL DESIGN (aeronautical technology, aircraft mechanics, architecture, aviation administration/management, aviation computer technology, engineering technology, food services technology, industrial administration/management, industrial engineering technology, and interior design), HEALTH PROFESSIONS (community health work, cytotechnology, health science, medical technology, nursing, predentistry, premedicine, preveterinary science, and speech pathology/audiology), SOCIAL SCIENCE (African studies, American studies, anthropology, criminal justice, Eastern European studies, economics, ethnic studies, fashion design and technology, geography, gerontology, history, human development, international relations, Latin American studies, liberal arts/general studies, peace studies, philosophy, political science/government, psychology, Russian and Slavic studies, and sociology). Architecture, education, and fashion design and merchandising are the strongest academically.

Required: Students are required to complete 121 credit hours, of which 42 must be upper division. Distribution requirements include 12 hours in humanities and fine arts, 9 hours in social sciences, and 6 hours each in basic sciences, composition, math, logic, and foreign languages. Students must maintain an overall GPA of 2.0.

Special: A co-op program is available with the School of Technology, and cross-registration is available with the University of Akron and Cleveland State University. Work-study programs and internships are offered. Study abroad in 8 countries, a Washington semester, an accelerated medical degree program, B.A.-B.S. degrees, dual majors, a general studies degree, student-designed majors, credit for military education, nondegree study, and pass/fail options are also possible. The Honors College provides honors course work in all majors. Dual admission with Cuyahoga Community, Lakeland Community, and Lorain County Community Colleges is available. Kent is a member of the National Student Exchange Program. There are 13 national honor societies, including Phi Beta Kappa, and a freshman honors program.

Faculty/Classroom: 53% of faculty are male; 47%, female. Graduate students teach 18% of introductory courses. The average class size in a regular course is 26.

Admissions: 90% of the 2001-2002 applicants were accepted. The SAT I scores for the 2001-2002 freshman class were: Verbal--45% below 500, 41% between 500 and 599, 13% between 600 and 700, and 1% above 700; Math--43% below 500, 41% between 500 and 599, 15% between 600 and 700, and 1% above 700. The ACT scores were 43% below 21, 31% between 21 and 23, 18% between 24 and 26, 5% between 27 and 28, and 3% above 28. 36 freshmen graduated first in their class.

Requirements: The SAT I or ACT is recommended. In addition, applicants must be graduates of an accredited secondary school. KSU strongly recommends a college preparatory program of 4 years of English, 3 each of math, science, and social studies, 2 of foreign language, and 1 in the arts. A GPA of 2.2 is required. AP and CLEP credits are accepted. Applications may be submitted on-line through the school's web site or CollegeNET.

Procedure: Freshmen are admitted fall, spring, and summer. Entrance exams should be taken in the spring of the junior year or the fall of the senior year. Application deadlines are open. The fall 2001 application fee was $30. Notification is sent on a rolling basis. 3% of all applicants are on a waiting list; 406 were accepted in 2001.

Transfer: 1025 transfer students enrolled in 2001-2002. Applicants must present a minimum GPA of 2.0 on completed college course work. For students with fewer than 24 semester hours or 36 quarter hours, a high school transcript and ACT or SAT I scores are also required. 30 credits of 121 must be completed at KSU.

Visiting: There are regularly scheduled orientations for prospective students, including information sessions (financial aid, residence halls, student panel), a campus tour, and meetings with academic representatives. There are guides for informal visits. To schedule a visit, contact the Admissions receptionist.

Financial Aid: In 2001-2002, 66% of all freshmen and 52% of continuing students received some form of financial aid. 55% of freshmen and 48% of continuing students received need-based aid. The average freshman award was $5715. The average financial indebtedness of the 2001 graduate was $14,222. The FAFSA, the college's own financial statement, and the OIG for Ohio residents are required. The fall application priority deadline is March 1.

International Students: There are 202 international students enrolled. They must score 525 on the written TOEFL.

Computers: The mainframes are an IBM RS/6000, an IBM ES/9121/732, and a DEC VAX 4000. Terminals and PC facilities are available for student use in academic buildings and residence halls. 100 dial-up links provide remote access. Students with departmental authorization may access the system 24 hours a day, 7 days a week. There are no time limits and no fees.

Graduates: In 2001, 3076 bachelor's degrees were awarded. The most popular majors were nursing (7%), psychology (5%), and English (4%). In an average class, 13% graduate in 4 years, 34% in 5 years, and 42% in 6 years. 350 companies recruited on campus in 2000-2001. Of the 2000 graduating class, 20% were enrolled in graduate school within 6 months of graduation and 86% were employed.

Admissions Contact: Paul Deutsch, Director of Admissions. A video is available. Web: *www.kent.edu*

KENYON COLLEGE — C-3
Gambier, OH 43022-9623 — (740) 427-5776
(800) 848-2468; Fax: (740) 427-5770

Full-time: 705 men, 853 women	**Faculty:** 142; IIB,
Part-time: 9 men, 20 women	**Ph.D.s:** 97%
Graduate: none	**Student/Faculty:** 11 to 1
Year: semesters	**Tuition:** $27,550
Application Deadline: January 15	**Room & Board:** $4580
Freshman Class: 2002 applied, 1329 accepted, 430 enrolled	
SAT I Verbal/Math: 650/630	**ACT:** 29

HIGHLY COMPETITIVE+

Kenyon College is a private liberal arts and sciences undergraduate college founded in 1824 by Philander Chase, the first Episcopal Bishop of Ohio. The library contains 376,530 volumes, 134,240 microform items, and 170,875 audiovisual forms/CDs, and subscribes to 5621 periodicals. Computerized library services include the card catalog, interlibrary loans, and database searching. Special learning facilities include a learning resource center, art gallery, radio station, TV station, obsesrvatory, and an environmental center. The 800-acre campus is in a rural area 50 miles northeast of Columbus. Including residence halls, there are 65 buildings.

Student Life: 77% of undergraduates are from out of state, mostly the Midwest. Others are from 49 states, 28 foreign countries, and Canada. 51% are from public schools. 84% are white. 27% are claim no religious affiliation; 26% Protestant; 19% a variety of religious practices from Quaker to Zen Buddhists; 17% Catholic; 12% Jewish. The average age of freshmen is 18; all undergraduates, 20. 8% do not continue beyond their first year; 84% remain to graduate.

Housing: 1580 students can be accommodated in college housing, which includes single-sex and coed dormitories and on-campus apartments. In addition, there are special-interest floors, including community service or social group halls, a substance-free hall, a wellness hall, an international wing, and Kosher living section. On-campus housing is guaranteed for all 4 years. 100% of students live on campus; of those, 95% remain on campus on weekends. All students may keep cars.

Activities: 25% of men belong to 1 local and 7 national fraternities; 10% of women belong to 1 local and 3 national sororities. There are 129 groups on campus, including art, band, chess, choir, chorale, chorus, dance, debate, drama, drill team, environmental/conservation, ethnic, film, gay, international, jazz band, literary magazine, martial arts, musical theater, newspaper, orchestra, pep band, photography, political, professional, radio and TV, religious, social, social service, student government, student lectureships, symphony, and yearbook. Popular campus events include Gambier Folk Festival, dance, drama, music, and athletic events, and foreign and domestic film festivals.

Sports: There are 11 intercollegiate sports for men and 11 for women, and 11 intramural sports for men and 11 for women. Facilities include 70 acres of playing, football, softball, and soccer fields, a 50-yard pool, a field house, a Nautilus center and weight rooms, and basketball, tennis, squash, and raquetball courts.

Disabled Students: 13% of the campus is accessible. Wheelchair ramps, elevators, special parking, specially equipped rest rooms, special class scheduling, lowered drinking fountains, lowered telephones, and audio and visual equipment are available.

Services: Counseling and information services are available, as is tutoring in some subjects upon request. There is a reader service for the blind and remedial writing.

Campus Safety and Security: Measures include 24-hour foot and vehicle patrol, self-defense education, escort service, and informal discussions. There are pamphlets/posters/films, emergency telephones, lighted pathways/sidewalks, and and formal saftey awareness events.

Programs of Study: Kenyon confers the B.A. degree. Bachelor's degrees are awarded in BIOLOGICAL SCIENCE (biochemistry, biology/biological science, molecular biology, and neurosciences), COMMUNICATIONS AND THE ARTS (art history and appreciation, classics, dance, dramatic arts, English, French, German, Greek (classical), Latin, modern language, music, Spanish, and studio art), COMPUTER AND PHYSICAL SCIENCE (chemistry, mathematics, and physics), SOCIAL SCIENCE (anthropology, economics, history, international studies, philosophy, political science/government, psychology, religion, and sociology). English, history, and political science are the largest.

Required: Students are required to complete a total of 16 units, including 4 to 7 units in the major and 1 unit in each of 4 divisions representing the arts, humanities, natural sciences, and social sciences. Students must maintain a minimum GPA of 2.0 and complete the senior exercise in their major.

Special: Students may study abroad in many countries. The college also offers dual and student-designed majors, pass/fail options, internships, winter and/or spring break externship programs, a Washington semester consisting of apprenticeships in any of several U.S. programs, and a 3-2 engineering degree with Case Western Reserve, Washington University in St. Louis, and Rensselaer Polytechnic Institute, as well as a 3-2 nursing degree with Case Western Reserve and a 3-2 environmental studies program with Duke University. 3-2 or 4-1 master's (certification) programs with The Bank Street College of Education are also possible. Kenyon's Interdisciplinary Program in Humane Studies offers a tutorial-based concentration on the human predicament. There are 3 national honor societies, including Phi Beta Kappa.

Faculty/Classroom: 61% of faculty are male; 39%, female. All both teach and do research. The average class size in an introductory lecture is 18; in a laboratory, 15; and in a regular course, 11.

Admissions: 66% of the 2001-2002 applicants were accepted. The SAT I scores for the 2001-2002 freshman class were: Verbal--1% below 500, 20% between 500 and 599, 50% between 600 and 700, and 30% above 700; Math--2% below 500, 27% between 500 and 599, 54% between 600 and 700, and 17% above 700. The ACT scores were 5% between 21 and 23, 53% between 24 and 28, and 42% above 29. 75% of the current freshmen were in the top fifth of their class; 95% were in the top two fifths. There were 24 National Merit finalists and 29 semifinalists. 20 freshmen graduated first in their class.

Requirements: The SAT I or ACT is required. In addition, applicants should be graduates of an accredited secondary school. Kenyon recommends 4 units each of English, foreign language, and math and 3 units each of science and social studies. Candidates are encouraged to exceed the minimum requirements, especially in math and science, and to take advance placement or honors work in at least 2 subjects. An essay and interview are important criteria in the admissions decision. Talent in music, theater, art, writing, and athletics is given extra consideration. Students may apply using a computer disk provided a printout is sent with the disk. AP credits are accepted. Important factors in the admissions decision are advanced placement or honor courses, evidence of special talent, and leadership record. Applications are accepted on-line via Common App and *embark.com*.

Procedure: Freshmen are admitted in the fall. Entrance exams should be taken in the fall of the senior year. There are early decision, early admissions, and deferred admissions plans. Early decision applications should be filed by December 1; regular applications, by January 15 for fall entry, along with a $45 fee. Notification of early decision is sent December 15; regular decision, April 1. 95 early decision candidates were accepted for the 2001-2002 class. 9% of all applicants are on a waiting list; 22 were accepted in 2001.

Transfer: 10 transfer students enrolled in 2001-2002. Transfer applicants must have a minimum college GPA of 3.0 and a high school record suggesting ability and potential. 8 units of 16 must be completed at Kenyon.

Visiting: There are regularly scheduled orientations for prospective students, consisting of interviews with staff, a campus tour, and a class visit. Students may also request to meet with faculty and coaches. Kenyon students are also available to host a prospective student overnight in the dorm weekly Sunday–Thursday. There are guides for informal visits and visitors may sit in on classes and stay overnight. To schedule a visit, contact the Admissions Office.

Financial Aid: In 2001-2002, 50% of all freshmen and 45% of continuing students received some form of financial aid. 46% of freshmen and 41% of continuing students received need-based aid. The average freshman award was $22,008. Of that total, scholarships or need-based grants averaged $15,959 ($25,000 maximum); loans averaged $3430 ($4625 maximum); work contracts averaged $968 ($1000 maximum); and federal and state grants and outside awards averaged $1651. 66% of undergraduates work part time. Average annual earnings from campus work are $968. The average financial indebtedness of the 2001 graduate was $20,800. Kenyon is a member of CSS. The CSS/Profile or FAFSA is required. The fall application deadline is February 15.

International Students: There are 42 international students enrolled. The school actively recruits these students. They must score 550 on the written TOEFL or 300 on the electronic version.

Computers: The mainframes are a client/servers-Pentium class PCs running Windows NT and Linux opperative systems. The Student NetworkAccess Plan (SNAP+), Kenyon's residential network program, provides a 10-Base-T ethernet jack in the residence halls for each student, allowing a direct connection to the campus network. There are 289 college-owned computers accessible to students throughout campus. Olin Chalmers labs contain NT and Mac workstations fully configured with application software, as well as stand-up systems for quick e-mail and library resources sessions. 6 additional labs are available for student use when not in use for class sessions, including one 24-hour lab. There are no time limits and no fees. All students may access the system 24 hours a day. It is strongly recommended that all students have a personal computer.

Graduates: In 2001, 379 bachelor's degrees were awarded. The most popular majors were English (22%), political science (12%), and history (11%). In an average class, 79% graduate in 4 years, 82% in 5 years, and 86% in 6 years. 65 companies recruited on campus in 2000-2001. Of the 2000 graduating class, 18% were enrolled in graduate school within 6 months of graduation and 93% were employed.

Admissions Contact: John Anderson, Dean of Admision. A video is available. E-mail: *admissions@kenyon.edu* Web: *www.kenyon.edu*

LAKE ERIE COLLEGE

Painesville, OH 44077 — E-1

(440) 639-7879
(800) 916-0904; Fax: (440) 352-3533

Full-time: 501 men and women	**Faculty:** 27
Part-time: 106 men and women	**Ph.D.s:** 72%
Graduate: 126 men and women	**Student/Faculty:** 16 to 1
Year: semesters, summer session	**Tuition:** $15,750
Application Deadline: open	**Room & Board:** $5600
Freshman Class: n/av	
SAT I Verbal/Math: required	**ACT:** required

LESS COMPETITIVE

Lake Erie College, founded in 1856, is an independent, liberal arts institution. The 2 libraries contain 89,232 volumes, 8091 microform items, and 4469 audiovisual forms/CDs, and subscribe to 767 periodicals. Computerized library services include the card catalog, interlibrary loans, and database searching. Special learning facilities include a learning resource center, art gallery, radio station, an American Indian Museum, and an equestrian center. The 150-acre campus is in a small town 30 miles east of Cleveland. Including residence halls, there are 15 buildings.

Student Life: 85% of undergraduates are from Ohio. Others are from 22 states, 5 foreign countries, and Canada. 90% are from public schools. 96% are white. The average age of freshmen is 18; all undergraduates, 25. 16% do not continue beyond their first year; 65% remain to graduate.

Housing: 256 students can be accommodated in college housing, which includes single-sex and coed dormitories. On-campus housing is guaranteed for all 4 years. 52% of students commute. All students may keep cars.

Activities: There are no fraternities or sororities. There are 20 groups on campus, including art, cheerleading, choir, chorus, dance, drama, equestrian, ethnic, honors, international, musical theater, newspaper, pep band, photography, political, professional, religious, social, social service, student government, and yearbook. Popular campus events include Prix de Ville of North America, international dinners, and class dinners.

Sports: There are 4 intercollegiate sports for men and 5 for women, and 5 intramural sports for men and 5 for women. Facilities include a gym, a 150-acre equestrian center, and playing fields.

Disabled Students: 20% of the campus is accessible. Wheelchair ramps, elevators, special parking, specially equipped rest rooms, special class scheduling, lowered drinking fountains, and lowered telephones are available.

Services: Counseling and information services are available, as is tutoring in most subjects. There is remedial math, reading, and writing.

Campus Safety and Security: Measures include 24-hour foot and vehicle patrol, self-defense education, escort service, and informal discussions. There are pamphlets/posters/films, emergency telephones, and lighted pathways/sidewalks.

Programs of Study: Lake Erie confers B.A., B.S., and B.F.A. degrees. Master's degrees are also awarded. Bachelor's degrees are awarded in AGRICULTURE (equine science), BIOLOGICAL SCIENCE (biology/biological science), BUSINESS (accounting, business administration and management, and international business management), COMMUNICATIONS AND THE ARTS (communications, dance, English, fine arts, French, German, Italian, music, and Spanish), COMPUTER AND PHYSICAL SCIENCE (chemistry and mathematics), EDUCATION (elementary and middle school), ENGINEERING AND ENVIRONMENTAL DESIGN (environmental science), SOCIAL SCIENCE (paralegal studies, psychology, and social science). Languages, education, and business are the strongest academically. Equestrian science, elementary education, and business are the largest.

Required: General education requirements include 6 hours of computers, 4 hours each of math, English, and either a foreign language or math with application, and 2 hours of public speaking. There are specific core requirements for 25 additional semester hours. Students must complete 128 credits, including an average of 64 in the major, with a minimum GPA of 2.0.

Special: Students may choose either national or international internships or study abroad in the Netherlands, France, Germany, Spain, England, and Italy. B.A.-B.S. degrees, student-designed majors, and potential credit for life, military, or work experience are offered. Cross-registration is available with the Northeast Ohio Commission on Higher Education. There is 1 national honor society.

Faculty/Classroom: 63% of faculty are male; 37%, female. All teach undergraduates. No introductory courses are taught by graduate students. The average class size in an introductory lecture is 15; in a laboratory, 16; and in a regular course, 11.

Admissions: 3 freshmen graduated first in their class in a recent year.

Requirements: The SAT I or ACT is required. In addition, applicants should be graduates of an accredited secondary school with a minimum GPA of 2.75. The high school program should include 4 years each of English, math, and science (including 2 years of lab science), and 2 years each of history and social studies, with 2 years of a foreign language recommended. A GPA of 2.5 is required. AP and CLEP credits are accepted. Important factors in the admissions decision are advanced placement or honor courses, recommendations by school officials, and extracurricular activities record. Applications are accepted on-line via NextStopCollege.

Procedure: Freshmen are admitted fall and spring. Entrance exams should be taken by November of the senior year. There is a deferred admissions plan. Application deadlines are open. The fall 2001 application fee was $25. Notification is sent on a rolling basis.

Transfer: 81 transfer students enrolled in 2001-2002. Applicants should submit transcripts from all schools attended and show a GPA of 2.0 in all college work. 32 credits of 128 must be completed at Lake Erie.

Visiting: There are regularly scheduled orientations for prospective students, including a campus tour, a financial aid information session, classroom observation, and faculty or department head interviews. There are guides for informal visits and visitors may sit in on classes and stay overnight. To schedule a visit, contact the Admissions Office.

Financial Aid: In a recent year, 98% of all freshmen and 80% of continuing students received some form of financial aid. 90% of freshmen and 80% of continuing students received need-based aid. The average freshman award was $13,206. Of that total, scholarships or need-based grants averaged $5808 ($10,000 maximum); loans averaged $2625 ($8625 maximum); and work contracts averaged $2100. 25% of undergraduates work part time. Average annual earnings from campus work are $2000. The average financial indebtedness of a recent graduate was $17,125. The FAFSA and the college's own financial statement are required. The fall application deadline is rolling.

International Students: There were 7 international students enrolled in a recent year. They must score 550 on the written TOEFL or take the MELAB and also take the SAT I or the ACT.

Computers: The mainframe is an HP G-30. PCs are available in residence halls, the computer center, and the library. There are no time limits and no fees.

Graduates: In a recent year, 105 bachelor's degrees were awarded. The most popular majors were business (24%), accounting (15%), and education (12%). In an average class, 7% graduate in 3 years, 35% in 4 years, 40% in 5 years, and 41% in 6 years.

Admissions Contact: Danielle Boone, Admissions Counselor.
E-mail: *lecadmit@lec.edu* Web: *www.lec.edu*

LOURDES COLLEGE — B-1

Sylvania, OH 43560 — (419) 885-5291, ext. 299
(800) 878-3210, ext. 1299; Fax: (419) 882-3987

Full-time: 93 men, 358 women	**Faculty:** 57
Part-time: 136 men, 632 women	**Ph.D.s:** 25%
Graduate: none	**Student/Faculty:** 8 to 1
Year: semesters, summer session	**Tuition:** $13,100
Application Deadline: open	**Room & Board:** n/app
Freshman Class: n/av	
ACT: 19	**LESS COMPETITIVE**

Lourdes College, founded in 1958, is a private liberal arts college affiliated with the Roman Catholic Church and sponsored by the Sisters of St. Francis. In addition to regional accreditation, Lourdes has baccalaureate program accreditation with CSWE and NLN. The library contains 71,575 volumes, 10,807 microform items, and 1834 audiovisual forms/CDs, and subscribes to 479 periodicals. Computerized library services include the card catalog, interlibrary loans, and database searching. Special learning facilities include a learning resource center, art gallery, planetarium, and an environmental science lab. The 89-acre campus is in a suburban area 10 miles west of Toledo. There are 8 buildings.

Student Life: 93% of undergraduates are from Ohio. Others are from 2 states, 2 foreign countries, and Canada. 77% are from public schools. 71% are white. 60% are Catholic; 38% Protestant. The average age of freshmen is 29; all undergraduates, 32. 20% do not continue beyond their first year; 45% remain to graduate.

Housing: There are no residence halls. All students commute. Alcohol is not permitted. All students may keep cars.

Activities: There are no fraternities or sororities. There are 15 groups on campus, including art, choir, chorus, honors, humanities, international, literary magazine, newspaper, political, professional, religious, social service, and student government. Popular campus events include End-of-the-Year Picnic, Convocation, and Christmas dinner.

Sports: There are 9 intramural sports for men and 8 for women. Facilities include a gym and exercise room.

Disabled Students: 80% of the campus is accessible. Wheelchair ramps, elevators, special parking, specially equipped rest rooms, special class scheduling, lowered drinking fountains, lowered telephones, and an accessible computer station are available.

Services: Counseling and information services are available, as is tutoring in most subjects. There is remedial math, reading, and writing. Windows for Intellectual Networking Center offers computer-assisted instruction for self-paced learning/tutoring in remedial math, reading, writing, study skills, APA style documentation, Spanish tutorials, advanced math programs, as well as offering professional tutoring services in writing. The center also works with instructors to offer in-class tutorial workshops on specific topics as requested.

Campus Safety and Security: Measures include escort service, pamphlets/posters/films, and lighted pathways/sidewalks.

Programs of Study: Lourdes confers B.A., B.S., B.I.S., B.S.N. degrees. Associate degrees are also awarded. Bachelor's degrees are awarded in BIOLOGICAL SCIENCE (biology/biological science), BUSINESS (business administration and management, entrepreneurial studies, human resources, and international business management), COMMUNICATIONS AND THE ARTS (art, art history and appreciation, English, and fine arts), COMPUTER AND PHYSICAL SCIENCE (chemistry), EDUCATION (education), ENGINEERING AND ENVIRONMENTAL DESIGN (environmental science), HEALTH PROFESSIONS (health and nursing), SOCIAL SCIENCE (criminal justice, gerontology, history, psychology, religion, social work, and sociology). Nursing, chemistry, and education are the strongest academically. Business, nursing and criminal justice are the largest.

Required: Students are required to maintain at least a 2.0 overall GPA, although most disciplines require 2.5. The total number of hours in the major varies from 36 to 59 semester hours depending on the major. Students must complete 128 credit hours, the requirements varying according to the degree sought. Most students will need courses in art/music, religious studies, composition, literature, phys ed, social science, and philosophy.

Special: The college offers internships in social work, criminal justice, occupational therapy, and business, co-op programs in business, work-

study programs, and an accelerated degree program in business and criminal justice. Students may pursue dual majors, nondegree study, or select pass/fail options. The college gives credit for life, military, or work experience. There are 6 national honor societies.
Faculty/Classroom: 25% of faculty are male; 75%, female. All teach undergraduates. The average class size in an introductory lecture is 14; in a laboratory, 10; and in a regular course, 13.
Admissions: The SAT I scores for the 2001-2002 freshman class were: Verbal--50% below 500, and 50% between 500 and 599; Math--50% below 500, and 50% between 500 and 599. 42% of the current freshmen were in the top fifth of their class; 62% were in the top two fifths.
Requirements: The SAT I or ACT is required with an ACT composite of 19 or higher. Candidates for admission should have completed 4 units of English and 3 each of math, science, and social studies. If a GED recipent, a passing score on the GED and satisfactory placement test scores are required. A GPA of 2.0 is required. AP and CLEP credits are accepted.
Procedure: Freshmen are admitted to all sessions. Entrance exams should be taken at least 30 days prior to the beginning of the freshman year of college. There is a deferred admissions plan. Application deadlines are open. The fall 2001 application fee was $25. Notification is sent on a rolling basis.
Transfer: 169 transfer students enrolled in 2001-2002. Transfer students need to submit official transcripts from previously attended colleges/universitites, a completed application and fee, and placement tests when necessary. Regular admission is granted to transfer students with a GPA of 2.0 or better and satisfactory placement test scores, if required. 32 credits of 128 must be completed at Lourdes.
Visiting: There are guides for informal visits and visitors may sit in on classes. To schedule a visit, contact the Office of Admissions at (419) 885-3211.
Financial Aid: In 2001-2002, 82% of all freshmen and 89% of continuing students received some form of financial aid. 68% of freshmen and 77% of continuing students received need-based aid. The average freshman award was $8197. Of that total, scholarships or need-based grants averaged $6252 ($15,972 maximum); loans averaged $4744 ($14,876 maximum); and work contracts averaged $1869 ($4000 maximum). 81% of undergraduates work part time. Average annual earnings from campus work are $1612. The FAFSA is required.
International Students: There are 2 international students enrolled. They must score 500 on the written TOEFL.The college recommends the SAT I or ACT and a placement test depending on the student's academic background.
Computers: The mainframe is a Dell Power Edge server. There are 86 computers available for student use. Students have web and e-mail access. All students may access the system. PCs may be used anytime during open lab hours. There are no time limits and no fees.
Graduates: In 2001, 170 bachelor's degrees were awarded. The most popular majors were business (25%), nursing (20%), and protective services (15%). In an average class, 35% graduate in 6 years. 10 companies recruited on campus in 2000-2001.
Admissions Contact: Director of Admissions.
E-mail: *lcadmits@lourdes.edu* Web: *www.lourdes.edu*

MALONE COLLEGE

Canton, OH 44709 — D-2
(330) 471-8100
(800) 521-1146; Fax: (330) 471-8149

Full-time: 689 men, 1001 women	**Faculty:** 101; IIA, --$
Part-time: 71 men, 139 women	**Ph.D.s:** 58%
Graduate: 97 men, 142 women	**Student/Faculty:** 17 to 1
Year: semesters, summer session	**Tuition:** $13,550
Application Deadline: July 1	**Room & Board:** $5640
Freshman Class: 902 applied, 773 accepted, 357 enrolled	
SAT I Verbal/Math: 550/550	**ACT:** 23 **COMPETITIVE**

Malone College, founded in 1892, is a Christian college for the arts, sciences, and professions in the liberal arts tradition. There are 6 undergraduate schools and 1 graduate school. In addition to regional accreditation, Malone has baccalaureate program accreditation with CSWE and NLN. The library contains 156,898 volumes, 578,838 microform items, and 10,284 audiovisual forms/CDs, and subscribes to 1484 periodicals. Computerized library services include the card catalog, interlibrary loans, and database searching. Special learning facilities include a learning resource center, radio station, and a writing lab. The 78-acre campus is in a suburban area 56 miles southeast of Cleveland. Including residence halls, there are 21 buildings.
Student Life: 91% of undergraduates are from Ohio. Others are from 24 states, 11 foreign countries, and Canada. 90% are from public schools. 92% are white. Most are Protestant. The average age of freshmen is 18; all undergraduates, 24. 26% do not continue beyond their first year; 49% remain to graduate.
Housing: 977 students can be accommodated in college housing, which includes single-sex dormitories and special topic/discipleship floors for upperclassmen. On-campus housing is guaranteed for the freshman year only, is available on a first-come, first-served basis, and is available on a lottery system for upperclassmen. 51% of students commute. Alcohol is not permitted. All students may keep cars.
Activities: There are no fraternities or sororities. There are 41 groups on campus, including art, band, cheerleading, choir, chorale, chorus, computers, debate, drama, drill team, ethnic, forensics, honors, international, jazz band, literary magazine, marching band, musical theater, newspaper, pep band, photography, political, professional, radio and TV, religious, social, social service, student government, and yearbook. Popular campus events include Little Sibs Weekend, Staley Lecture, and Spring Fest.
Sports: There are 9 intercollegiate sports for men and 9 for women, and 14 intramural sports for men and 13 for women. Facilities include a gym and a Nautilus center.
Disabled Students: 90% of the campus is accessible. Wheelchair ramps, elevators, special parking, specially equipped rest rooms, special class scheduling, lowered drinking fountains, and lowered telephones are available.
Services: Counseling and information services are available, as is tutoring in most subjects. There is a reader service for the blind and remedial math and writing.
Campus Safety and Security: Measures include 24-hour foot and vehicle patrol, self-defense education, escort service, and shuttle buses. There are informal discussions, emergency telephones, and lighted pathways/sidewalks.
Programs of Study: Malone confers B.A., B.S.Ed., and B.S.N. degrees. Master's degrees are also awarded. Bachelor's degrees are awarded in BIOLOGICAL SCIENCE (biology/biological science and life science), BUSINESS (accounting, business administration and management, recreational facilities management, and sports management), COMMUNICATIONS AND THE ARTS (art, communications, English, language arts, music, music technology, and Spanish), COMPUTER AND PHYSICAL SCIENCE (chemistry, computer science, mathematics, physical sciences, and science), EDUCATION (art, Christian, early childhood, elementary, foreign languages, health, middle school, music, physical, science, secondary, social studies, and special), HEALTH PROFESSIONS (community health work, exercise science, medical laboratory technology, and nursing), SOCIAL SCIENCE (biblical studies, history, liberal arts/general studies, ministries, physical fitness/movement, political science/government, psychology, religious music, social work, theological studies, and youth ministry). Biology, chemistry, and education are the strongest academically. Business administration, education, and communication arts are the largest.
Required: Students must maintain a GPA of 2.0 overall and 2.25 to 2.75 in the major, depending upon the major. At least 30 hours in the major and 39 hours at the 300 or 400 level are required. To graduate, all students must complete at least 124 credit hours, including a general education curriculum of Stewardship Under God (14 hours), Stewardship and Skills (15 to 16 hours), Stewardship and the Sciences (12 to 13 hours), and Stewardship and Society (15 to 18 hours).
Special: Students may participate in co-op programs and internships in all majors and may cross-register within the Christian College Consortium. Malone offers study abroad in Guatemala, Costa Rica, and Kenya; Hollywood, Martha's Vineyard, Washington, Egypt, China, or Russia semesters through the Council for Christian Colleges and Universities; work-study programs; and degree completion programs in management and nursing. A liberal arts degree, dual and student-designed majors, and credit for life, military, or work experience are also available. The Malone College Management Program offers degree completion for students age 25 or older who have the equivalent of 2 years of college. The BSNDC program offers degree completion for RNs. There are 6 national honor societies, and a freshman honors program.
Faculty/Classroom: 60% of faculty are male; 40%, female. 92% teach undergraduates and 20% both teach and do research. No introductory courses are taught by graduate students. The average class size in an introductory lecture is 26; in a laboratory, 11; and in a regular course, 20.
Admissions: 86% of the 2001-2002 applicants were accepted. The SAT I scores for the 2001-2002 freshman class were: Verbal--21% below 500, 55% between 500 and 599, 21% between 600 and 700, and 3% above 700; Math--29% below 500, 40% between 500 and 599, 26% between 600 and 700, and 5% above 700. The ACT scores were 28% below 21, 29% between 21 and 23, 23% between 24 and 26, 9% between 27 and 28, and 11% above 28. There was 1 National Merit finalist. 11 freshmen graduated first in their class.
Requirements: The ACT or SAT I is required, for traditional students. The ACT is preferred; the SAT I is accepted. Applicants should be graduates of an accredited secondary school with a minimum GPA of 2.5. The GED is accepted. Applications are accepted on-line at the school's web site. AP and CLEP credits are accepted.
Procedure: Freshmen are admitted to all sessions. Entrance exams should be taken in the junior year. There is a deferred admissions plan. Applications should be filed by July 1 for fall entry. The fall 2001 application fee was $20. Notification is sent on a rolling basis.
Transfer: 69 transfer students enrolled in 2001-2002. Applicants must submit an official transcript and a financial aid transcript from each col-

lege attended and a transfer reference form from the most recent school. 30 credits of 124 must be completed at Malone.

Visiting: There are regularly scheduled orientations for prospective students. There are guides for informal visits and visitors may sit in on classes and stay overnight. To schedule a visit, contact the Admissions Office at (330) 471-8145.

Financial Aid: In 2001-2002, 99% of all freshmen and 87% of continuing students received some form of financial aid. 68% of freshmen and 62% of continuing students received need-based aid. The average freshman award was $12,370. Of that total, scholarships or need-based grants averaged $5053 ($17,530 maximum); loans averaged $3961 ($18,625 maximum); work contracts averaged $611 ($2000 maximum); and non-need based grants, tuition waivers, and athletic awards averaged $2743 ($16,062 maximum). 25% of undergraduates work part time. Average annual earnings from campus work are $1677. The average financial indebtedness of the 2001 graduate was $16,072. Malone is a member of CSS. The FAFSA is required. The college's own form is only required for returning students. The fall application deadline is March 1.

International Students: There are 16 international students enrolled. They must score 550 on the written TOEFL or 213 on the electronic version.

Computers: The mainframe is a DEC ALPHA. Malone has 181 PCs available to students, 89 of which are in 5 different labs, 64 in residence halls, and 28 in the library. Students use them for information retrieval from the World Wide Web, for looking up library research materials, for e-mail, for class assignments involving word processing, spreadsheets, databases, and presentations, for on-line courses, for accessing faculty web sites, and for specialized software in accounting, music, and graphic arts. All students may access the system when the library is open, Monday through Thursday 8 A.M. to 11:30 P.M., Friday 8 A.M. to 10 P.M., Saturday 10 A.M. to 5 P.M., Sunday 2 P.M. to 10 P.M. There are no time limits and no fees.

Graduates: In 2001, 492 bachelor's degrees were awarded. The most popular majors were elementary education (11%), business administration (6%), and communication arts (5%). In an average class, 32% graduate in 4 years, 45% in 5 years, and 47% in 6 years. 37 companies recruited on campus in 2000-2001. Of the 2000 graduating class, 22% were enrolled in graduate school within 6 months of graduation and 78% were employed.

Admissions Contact: John Chopka, Vice President for Enrollment Management. A video is available. E-mail: *admissions@malone.edu* Web: *http://www.malone.edu*

MARIETTA COLLEGE

Marietta, OH 45750-4005 — E-5

(740) 376-4600
(800)331-7896; Fax: (740) 376-8888

Full-time: 516 men, 524 women	**Faculty:** 75; IIB, -$
Part-time: 48 men, 60 women	**Ph.D.s:** 92%
Graduate: 11 men, 50 women	**Student/Faculty:** 14 to 1
Year: semesters, summer session	**Tuition:** $19,076
Application Deadline: April 15	**Room & Board:** $5504
Freshman Class: 1152 applied, 1079 accepted, 367 enrolled	
SAT I Verbal/Math: 550/550	**ACT:** 23 **COMPETITIVE**

Marietta College, founded in 1835, is a private liberal arts college. In addition to regional accreditation, Marietta has baccalaureate program accreditation with ABET and CAAHEP. The library contains 250,085 volumes, 128,020 microform items, and 6004 audiovisual forms/CDs, and subscribes to 559 periodicals. Computerized library services include the card catalog, interlibrary loans, and database searching. Special learning facilities include a learning resource center, art gallery, radio station, TV station, an observatory, and a greenhouse. The 120-acre campus is in a small town 115 miles southeast of Columbus. Including residence halls, there are 40 buildings.

Student Life: 57% of undergraduates are from Ohio. Others are from 42 states, 12 foreign countries, and Canada. 89% are from public schools. 92% are white. 60% are Protestant; 30% Catholic; 10% Jewish. The average age of freshmen is 18; all undergraduates, 20. 24% do not continue beyond their first year; 60% remain to graduate.

Housing: 1045 students can be accommodated in college housing, which includes single-sex and coed dormitories, on-campus apartments, fraternity houses, and sorority houses. In addition, there are honors houses and special-interest houses. On-campus housing is guaranteed for all 4 years. 83% of students live on campus; of those, 80% remain on campus on weekends. All students may keep cars.

Activities: 20% of men belong to 3 national fraternities; 25% of women belong to 3 national sororities. There are 75 groups on campus, including Amnesty International, art, Arts and Humanities Council, band, cheerleading, choir, chorale, chorus, computers, dance, debate, drama, drill team, ethnic, film, forensics, Great Outdoors, honors, international, jazz band, literary magazine, musical theater, newspaper, orchestra, pep band, photography, political, professional, radio and TV, religious, ski club circle K, social, social service, student government, and yearbook. Popular campus events include DooDah Day, Winter Weekend, and Little Sibs Weekend.

Sports: There are 11 intercollegiate sports for men and 10 for women, and 4 intramural sports for men and 4 for women. Facilities include a field house, a field park, a Nautilus/Universal room, and an aerobic fitness center.

Disabled Students: 65% of the campus is accessible. Wheelchair ramps, elevators, special parking, specially equipped rest rooms, and special class scheduling are available.

Services: Counseling and information services are available, as is tutoring in most subjects. There is a reader service for the blind and remedial math and writing. and a peer tutoring program.

Campus Safety and Security: Measures include 24-hour foot and vehicle patrol, self-defense education, escort service, and informal discussions. There are pamphlets/posters/films, emergency telephones, and lighted pathways/sidewalks.

Programs of Study: Marietta confers B.A., B.S., and Bach. of Petrol. Engin. degrees. Associate and master's degrees are also awarded. Bachelor's degrees are awarded in BIOLOGICAL SCIENCE (biochemistry and biology/biological science), BUSINESS (accounting, human resources, international business management, management information systems, management science, and marketing/retailing/merchandising), COMMUNICATIONS AND THE ARTS (advertising, broadcasting, communications, dramatic arts, English, fine arts, French, graphic design, journalism, music, public relations, Spanish, speech/debate/rhetoric, and studio art), COMPUTER AND PHYSICAL SCIENCE (chemistry, computer science, geology, information sciences and systems, mathematics, and physics), EDUCATION (elementary and music), ENGINEERING AND ENVIRONMENTAL DESIGN (environmental engineering, environmental science, and petroleum/natural gas engineering), HEALTH PROFESSIONS (sports medicine), SOCIAL SCIENCE (economics, history, philosophy, and psychology). Petroleum engineering is the strongest academically. Economics, management and accounting, and elementary education are the largest.

Required: To graduate, students must complete at least 120 total credit hours, with general education requirements of 4 hours in the humanities and 2 each in fine arts, lab, and social sciences. All students must also take a freshman seminar, English, and speech, and successfully complete at least 1 math course. The minimum number of hours required for a major is 36. A minimum GPA of 2.0 must be maintained. Seniors must complete a capstone project.

Special: There are binary programs with Case Western Reserve and Duke universities and the Universities of Pennsylvania and Michigan. Internships are available in many majors, and students may study abroad in numerous countries and participate in a Washington semester through American University. Preprofessional programs, work-study programs, B.A.-B.S. degrees in all majors, student-designed majors, a 3-2 engineering degree with several universities, pass/fail options, and credit for life, military, and work experience are also available. The freshman year program is designed to assist with the student's academic and social transition to college life. There are 20 national honor societies, including Phi Beta Kappa, a freshman honors program, and 20 departmental honors programs.

Faculty/Classroom: 69% of faculty are male; 31%, female. All teach undergraduates and 30% both teach and do research. No introductory courses are taught by graduate students. The average class size in an introductory lecture is 25; in a laboratory, 12; and in a regular course, 22.

Admissions: 94% of the 2001-2002 applicants were accepted. The SAT I scores for the 2001-2002 freshman class were: Verbal--31% below 500, 41% between 500 and 599, 26% between 600 and 700, and 2% above 700; Math--28% below 500, 41% between 500 and 599, 28% between 600 and 700, and 3% above 700. The ACT scores were 31% below 21, 26% between 21 and 23, 25% between 24 and 26, 11% between 27 and 28, and 7% above 28. 39% of the current freshmen were in the top fifth of their class; 69% were in the top two fifths. There were 6 National Merit semifinalists. 26 freshmen graduated first in their class.

Requirements: The SAT I or ACT is required. In addition, students seeking admission should have completed 4 years of English and 3 of history, math, and science; 2 years of a foreign language is also recommended. An interview is strongly recommended. A GPA of 2.0 is required. AP and CLEP credits are accepted. Important factors in the admissions decision are advanced placement or honor courses, evidence of special talent, and leadership record. Applications are accepted online via the Marietta web site, Common Application, Peterson's, College View, EXPAN, and Apply.

Procedure: Freshmen are admitted fall and spring. Entrance exams should be taken no later than February of the senior year. Applications should be filed by April 15 for fall entry. Notification is sent on a rolling basis. The fall 2001 application fee was $25.

Transfer: 54 transfer students enrolled in 2001-2002. A minimum GPA of 2.5, a recommendation, and an essay are required. 36 credits of 120 must be completed at Marietta.

Visiting: There are regularly scheduled orientations for prospective students, including fall and spring open houses, tours, and meetings with faculty, coaches, and financial aid representatives. There are guides for informal visits and visitors may sit in on classes and stay overnight. To schedule a visit, contact the Office of Admissions.

Financial Aid: In 2001-2002, 96% of all freshmen and 93% of continuing students received some form of financial aid. 77% of freshmen and 70% of continuing students received need-based aid. The average freshman award was $16,520. Of that total, scholarships or need-based grants averaged $10,139 ($26,921 maximum); loans averaged $3612 ($3625 maximum); and work contracts averaged $1819 ($1900 maximum). 72% of undergraduates work part time. Average annual earnings from campus work are $955. The average financial indebtedness of the 2001 graduate was $16,451. Marietta is a member of CSS. The FAFSA is required. The fall application deadline is March 1.

International Students: There are 78 international students enrolled. The school actively recruits these students. They must score 550 on the written TOEFL.

Computers: The mainframes are a DEC ALPHA 2100 RISC system, a DEC APLHA RISC, an IBM RS/6000, and a Multimax 510. The campus-wide network includes 120 PCs and some 80 terminals in 10 academic labs, and offers e-mail, Internet, and World Wide Web access. There are also 150 Macs available for student use. All students may access the system. There are no time limits and no fees. It is strongly recommended that all students have a personal computer.

Graduates: The most popular majors were management (11%), elementary education (9%), and psychology (8%). 41 companies recruited on campus in 2000-2001. Of the 2000 graduating class, 21% were enrolled in graduate school within 6 months of graduation and 60% were employed.

Admissions Contact: Marke M. Vickers, Director of Admission. A video is available. E-mail: *admit@mcnet.marietta.edu*
Web: *www.marietta.edu*

MIAMI UNIVERSITY — A-4
Oxford, OH 45056 — **(513) 529-2531; (513) 529-1550**

Full-time: 6620 men, 8100 women	**Faculty:** 814; I, --$
Part-time: 233 men, 200 women	**Ph.D.s:** 86%
Graduate: 617 men, 1176 women	**Student/Faculty:** 18 to 1
Year: semesters, summer session	**Tuition:** $6915 ($14,589)
Application Deadline: January 31	**Room & Board:** $5970

Freshman Class: 12,500 applied, 9293 accepted, 3439 enrolled
SAT I or ACT: required — **VERY COMPETITIVE+**

Miami University, founded in 1809, is a public institution offering a variety of programs in the liberal arts and pre-professional-vocational training. There are 6 undergraduate schools and 1 graduate school. In addition to regional accreditation, Miami University has baccalaureate program accreditation with AACSB, ABET, ADA, AHEA, ASLA, NAAB, NASAD, NASM, NCATE, and NLN. The 4 libraries contain 2,663,166 volumes, 2,920,326 microform items, and 134,404 audiovisual forms/CDs, and subscribe to 12,234 periodicals. Computerized library services include the card catalog, interlibrary loans, and database searching. Special learning facilities include a learning resource center, art gallery, natural history museum, radio station, and TV station. The 1921-acre campus is in a small town 35 miles northwest of Cincinnati. Including residence halls, there are 162 buildings.

Student Life: 73% of undergraduates are from Ohio. Others are from 48 states, 76 foreign countries, and Canada. 75% are from public schools. 92% are white. The average age of freshmen is 18; all undergraduates, 20. 10% do not continue beyond their first year; 80% remain to graduate.

Housing: 7080 students can be accommodated in college housing, which includes single-sex and coed dormitories, married-student housing, and sorority houses. In addition, there are honors houses, language houses, international houses, and special-interest houses. On-campus housing is guaranteed for the freshman year only and is available on a lottery system for upperclassmen. 55% of students commute. Alcohol is not permitted. Upperclassmen may keep cars.

Activities: 24% of men belong to 28 national fraternities; 27% of women belong to 22 national sororities. There are 325 groups on campus, including art, band, cheerleading, choir, chorale, chorus, dance, debate, drama, drill team, ethnic, forensics, gay, honors, international, jazz band, literary magazine, marching band, musical theater, newspaper, opera, orchestra, pep band, political, professional, radio and TV, religious, social, social service, student government, symphony, and yearbook. Popular campus events include Parents Weekend, Kidsfest Weekend, and Unity Fest.

Sports: There are 8 intercollegiate sports for men and 11 for women, and 25 intramural sports for men and 25 for women. Facilities include a 25,000-seat football stadium, 70 acres of playing fields, 33 outdoor tennis courts, a recreational sports center, 10 indoor basketball/volleyball courts, racquetball, handball, and squash courts, a floor hockey/indoor soccer court, a climbing wall, equestrian stables and dressage course, a world-class aquatic center containing 3 indoor swimming pools, jogging paths, a par course, sand volleyball courts, aerobics and weight rooms, a Frisbee golf course, and an outdoor in-line skating court.

Disabled Students: All of the campus is accessible. Wheelchair ramps, elevators, special parking, specially equipped rest rooms, special class scheduling, lowered drinking fountains, and lowered telephones are available.

Services: Counseling and information services are available, as is tutoring in most subjects. There is a reader service for the blind. Assistance in study skills is available.

Campus Safety and Security: Measures include 24-hour foot and vehicle patrol, self-defense education, escort service, and shuttle buses. There are informal discussions, pamphlets/posters/films, emergency telephones, lighted pathways/sidewalks, and formal crime prevention programs, a community relations officer, a bicycle patrol, and card access into dorms.

Programs of Study: Miami University confers B.A., B.S., B.E.D., B.F.A., B.Mus., and B.Phil. degrees. Master's and doctoral degrees are also awarded. Bachelor's degrees are awarded in BIOLOGICAL SCIENCE (biochemistry, biology/biological science, botany, microbiology, and zoology), BUSINESS (accounting, banking and finance, business administration and management, business economics, management information systems, marketing/retailing/merchandising, operations research, organizational behavior, personnel management, purchasing/inventory management, and sports management), COMMUNICATIONS AND THE ARTS (art, broadcasting, communications, dramatic arts, English, fine arts, French, German, Greek, Latin, linguistics, music, music performance, Russian, Spanish, speech/debate/rhetoric, and telecommunications), COMPUTER AND PHYSICAL SCIENCE (chemistry, computer science, geology, mathematics, physics, and statistics), EDUCATION (art, athletic training, early childhood, elementary, foreign languages, health, middle school, music, physical, science, secondary, and special), ENGINEERING AND ENVIRONMENTAL DESIGN (architecture, engineering, engineering management, engineering physics, engineering technology, environmental design, environmental science, interior design, manufacturing engineering, and paper and pulp science), HEALTH PROFESSIONS (exercise science, health, medical technology, nursing, premedicine, and speech pathology/audiology), SOCIAL SCIENCE (African American studies, American studies, anthropology, classical/ancient civilization, dietetics, economics, family/consumer studies, geography, history, interdisciplinary studies, international relations, international studies, philosophy, physical fitness/movement, political science/government, prelaw, psychology, public administration, religion, social science, social work, sociology, and urban studies). Zoology, chemistry, and accountancy are the strongest academically. Accountancy, elementary education, and marketing are the largest.

Required: To graduate students must complete 128 semester hours, with a minimum 2.0 GPA. Distribution requirements include a total of 36 hours in English composition, fine arts, humanities, social science, world cultures, natural science, math, formal reasoning, and technology. A minimum of 9 hours in a Thematic Sequence outside the major department, and a 3-hour Senior Capstone Experience, which integrates liberal learning and specialized knowledge, are also required.

Special: The university offers cross-registration with Cincinnati area colleges, study abroad in 15 countries, co-op programs in the School of Applied Science, internships in health and sport studies and applied science, a 3-2 engineering degree with Case Western Reserve and Columbia Universities, and a 3-2 forestry degree with Duke University. Students may pursue student-designed majors through the School of Interdisciplinary Studies or interdisciplinary majors, including decision sciences and history of art and architecture. There are 30 national honor societies, including Phi Beta Kappa, and a freshman honors program.

Faculty/Classroom: 60% of faculty are male; 40%, female. All teach undergraduates. Graduate students teach 25% of introductory courses. The average class size in a regular course is 28.

Admissions: 74% of the 2001-2002 applicants were accepted. 77% of the current freshmen were in the top quarter of their class; 97% were in the top half.

Requirements: The SAT I or ACT is required. In addition, candidates for admission must ordinarily be graduates of accredited secondary schools or hold the GED and should have completed 4 units of English, 3 each of math, science, and social studies/history, 2 of a foreign language, and 1 of fine arts. An audition, a portfolio, or an interview is required for direct admission to majors in the School of Fine Arts. Applications are accepted on-line via the university's web site. AP and CLEP credits are accepted. Important factors in the admissions decision are advanced placement or honor courses, evidence of special talent, and extracurricular activities record.

Procedure: Freshmen are admitted to all sessions. Entrance exams should be taken no later than December of the senior year. There is an early decision plan. Early decision application should be filed by November 1; regular applications, by January 31 for fall entry and November 15 for spring entry, along with a $45 fee. Notification of early decision is sent December 15; regular decision, March 15. 616 early decision candidates were accepted for the 2001-2002 class. 4% of all applicants are on a waiting list; 205 were accepted in 2001.

Transfer: 307 transfer students enrolled in 2001-2002. A limited number of transfer students can be accepted. Usually a GPA of 2.75 or

higher is necessary. 32 credits of 128 must be completed at Miami University.
Visiting: There are regularly scheduled orientations for prospective students, consisting of open houses in February and April. There are guides for informal visits and visitors may sit in on classes and stay overnight. To schedule a visit, contact the Office of Admissions, Visit Coordinator at (513) 529-4632 or *visitcoor@muohio.edu*.
Financial Aid: In 2001-2002, 67% of all freshmen and 46% of continuing students received some form of financial aid. 34% of freshmen and 31% of continuing students received need-based aid. The average freshman award was $6636. 30% of undergraduates work part time. Average annual earnings from campus work are $1084. The average financial indebtedness of the 2001 graduate was $16,379. The FAFSA is required. The fall application deadline is February 15.
International Students: There are 105 international students enrolled. They must score 530 on the written TOEFL or take the MELAB. The SAT I or ACT is required only for Canadian applicants, athletes, and those students who have followed a U.S. high school curriculum at a secondary school in the United States or abroad.
Computers: Computer facilities include statistical analysis, database programming, and e-mail, via student computing facilities in academic departments, residence halls, or dial-up. More than 1000 PCs and terminals are available. All residence halls have direct connections to the university network. All students may access the system. There are no time limits. The fee is $90 per semester for full-time on campus and $15 per semester for part-time and off campus. It is strongly recommended that all students have a personal computer.
Graduates: In 2001, 3652 bachelor's degrees were awarded. The most popular majors were marketing (10%), elementary education (9%), and accounting (6%). In an average class, 3% graduate in 3 years, 64% in 4 years, 78% in 5 years, and 80% in 6 years. 336 companies recruited on campus in 2000-2001.
Admissions Contact: Michael Mills, Asst VP/Director of Admissions. A video is available. E-mail: *millsme@muohio.edu*
Web: *www.muohio.edu*

MOUNT UNION COLLEGE
Alliance, OH 44601 — E-2
(330) 821-5320
(800) 992-6682; Fax: (330) 823-3457

Full-time: 903 men, 1157 women	**Faculty:** 118; IIB, -$
Part-time: 93 men, 215 women	**Ph.D.s:** 97%
Graduate: none	**Student/Faculty:** 17 to 1
Year: semesters, summer session	**Tuition:** $16,310
Application Deadline: open	**Room & Board:** $4810

Freshman Class: 2026 applied, 1639 accepted, 608 enrolled
ACT: 22 — **COMPETITIVE**

Mount Union College, founded in 1846, is a private, liberal arts college affiliated with the United Methodist Church. In addition to regional accreditation, Mount Union has baccalaureate program accreditation with NASM. The 3 libraries contain 230,000 volumes and 43,000 microform items, and subscribe to 950 periodicals. Special learning facilities include a learning resource center, art gallery, radio station, two astronomical observatories, a university theater, a playhouse, and a nature center. The 115-acre campus is in a suburban area 20 miles east of Canton. Including residence halls, there are 26 buildings.
Student Life: 88% of undergraduates are from Ohio. Others are from 20 states, 15 foreign countries, and Canada. 89% are from public schools. 94% are white. 39% are Protestant; 31% Catholic; 30% claim no religious affiliation. The average age of freshmen is 19; all undergraduates, 22. 12% do not continue beyond their first year; 61% remain to graduate.
Housing: 1385 students can be accommodated in college housing, which includes single-sex and coed dormitories. In addition, there are honors houses, special-interest houses, and substance-free (tobacco/alcohol) houses. On-campus housing is guaranteed for the freshman year only, is available on a first-come, first-served basis, and is available on a lottery system for upperclassmen. 68% of students live on campus; of those, 70% remain on campus on weekends. All students may keep cars on campus.
Activities: 28% of men belong to 4 national fraternities; 30% of women belong to 1 local and 4 national sororities. There are 74 groups on campus, including art, band, cheerleading, chess, choir, chorale, chorus, computers, dance, debate, drama, drill team, ethnic, forensics, gay, honors, international, jazz band, literary magazine, marching band, musical theater, newspaper, orchestra, pep band, political, professional, radio and TV, religious, social, social service, student government, and yearbook. Popular campus events include Spring Fest, Greek Week, and Schooler Lecture series.
Sports: There are 12 intercollegiate sports for men and 11 for women, and 16 intramural sports for men and 16 for women. Facilities include a gym, field house, stadium, tennis courts, wellness center, exercise and aerobics rooms, and the Hoover-Price Campus Center.
Disabled Students: 90% of the campus is accessible. Wheelchair ramps, elevators, special parking, specially equipped rest rooms, special class scheduling, lowered drinking fountains, and specially equipped residence hall rooms are available.
Services: Counseling and information services are available, as is tutoring in most subjects, including general education courses and most introductory courses. There is a reader service for the blind, remedial writing, and facilitated study groups for most general education courses that meet once a week.
Campus Safety and Security: Measures include 24-hour foot and vehicle patrol, self-defense education, informal discussions, and pamphlets/posters/films. There are emergency telephones and lighted pathways/sidewalks.
Programs of Study: Mount Union confers B.A., B.S., B.Mus., and B.Mus.Ed. degrees. Bachelor's degrees are awarded in BIOLOGICAL SCIENCE (biology/biological science and environmental biology), BUSINESS (accounting, business administration and management, international business management, and sports management), COMMUNICATIONS AND THE ARTS (art, communications, creative writing, dramatic arts, English, French, German, Japanese, media arts, music, music performance, and Spanish), COMPUTER AND PHYSICAL SCIENCE (astronomy, chemistry, computer science, geology, information sciences and systems, mathematics, and physics), EDUCATION (athletic training, early childhood, elementary, middle school, music, and physical), SOCIAL SCIENCE (American studies, economics, history, international studies, Near Eastern studies, philosophy, physical fitness/movement, political science/government, psychology, religion, social science, and sociology). Biology, athletic training, and exercise science are the strongest academically. Business, education, and psychology are the largest.
Required: To graduate, students must complete a minimum of 120 semester hours, including 30 in upper division courses and up to 48 in the major, with a minimum GPA of 2.0. General requirements include 49 hours in a core curriculum encompassing communication skills, analytical skills, religion/philosophy, international studies, Western history, literature, fine arts, phys ed, and the freshman liberal arts experience. Students must also complete a minor requirement and the senior year culminating experience.
Special: Mount Union offers internships for credit in many majors, study abroad in 12 countries, co-op programs in business, work-study programs with various employers, student-designed majors, and pass/fail options. Adults in the nontraditional study program may receive credit for life, military, or work experience. There are 18 national honor societies, a freshman honors program, and 18 departmental honors programs.
Faculty/Classroom: 63% of faculty are male; 37%, female. All teach undergraduates. The average class size in an introductory lecture is 21; in a laboratory, 14; and in a regular course, 16.
Admissions: 81% of the 2001-2002 applicants were accepted. The ACT scores for the 2001-2002 freshman class were: 38% below 21, 29% between 21 and 23, 20% between 24 and 26, 11% between 27 and 28, and 3% above 28. 41% of the current freshmen were in the top fifth of their class; 69% were in the top two fifths. 14 freshmen graduated first in their class.
Requirements: The SAT I or ACT is required. In addition, preference is given to high school graduates who have completed a minimum of 15 academic units, including 4 in English, 3 each in math, social science, and lab science, and 2 in foreign language. Applications are accepted on-line with the form available at the school's web site. A GPA of 2.0 is required. AP and CLEP credits are accepted. Important factors in the admissions decision are advanced placement or honor courses, recommendations by school officials, and personality/intangible qualities.
Procedure: Freshmen are admitted fall and spring. Entrance exams should be taken for the first time in the spring of the junior year. There is a deferred admissions plan. Application deadlines are open. Notification is sent on a rolling basis.
Transfer: 47 transfer students enrolled in a recent year. Applicants must have a college GPA of 2.0 for consideration and must submit a statement of honorable dismissal and an official transcript from the last college attended. A personal statement must accompany the transfer application. 45 credits of 120 must be completed at Mount Union.
Visiting: There are regularly scheduled orientations for prospective students, including interviews, a campus tour, meetings with faculty, and classroom visits. There are guides for informal visits and visitors may sit in on classes and stay overnight. To schedule a visit, contact the Admissions Office at (330) 823-2590 or at: *admission@muc.edu*.
Financial Aid: In a recent year, 96% of all freshmen and 98% of continuing students received some form of financial aid. 79% of freshmen and 74% of continuing students received need-based aid. The average freshman award was $13,669. Of that total, scholarships or need-based grants averaged $9146 ($15,440 maximum); loans averaged $3404 ($3625 maximum); and work contracts averaged $1119 ($1800 maximum). 42% of undergraduates work part time. Average annual earnings from campus work are $1185. The average financial indebtedness of a recent graduate was $14,762. Mount Union is a member of CSS. The FAFSA is required. The fall application deadline is September 1.

International Students: There were 43 international students enrolled in a recent year. The school actively recruits these students. They must score 500 on the written TOEFL.

Computers: Students have network hook-ups in each residence hall-room that provide access to the campus network, including e-mail and the Internet. Students can also use various computer labs located on campus. Students, faculty, and staff share a common e-mail system. All students may access the system. There are no time limits and no fees. It is strongly recommended that all students have a personal computer.

Graduates: In 2001, 420 bachelor's degrees were awarded. The most popular majors were business administration (17%), education (16%), and biology (8%). In an average class, 57% graduate in 4 years, 63% in 5 years, and 65% in 6 years. Of the 2000 graduating class, 25% were enrolled in graduate school within 6 months of graduation and 85% were employed.

Admissions Contact: Amy Tomko, Vice President, Enrollment Services. A video is available. E-mail: *kinggl@muc.edu*
Web: *www.muc.edu*

MOUNT VERNON NAZARENE COLLEGE C-3

Mt. Vernon, OH 43050 **(740) 397-6862, ext. 4510**
(800) 782-2435; Fax: (740) 393-0511

Full-time: 823 men, 1084 women	**Faculty:** 71
Part-time: 102 men, 97 women	**Ph.D.s:** 63%
Graduate: 53 men, 75 women	**Student/Faculty:** 27 to 1
Year: 4-1-4, summer session	**Tuition:** $12,590
Application Deadline: May 31	**Room & Board:** $4437
Freshman Class: 813 applied, 671 accepted, 360 enrolled	
SAT I Verbal/Math: 530/540	**ACT:** 22 **COMPETITIVE**

Mount Vernon Nazarene College, founded in 1964, is a private liberal arts college affiliated with the Church of the Nazarene. The library contains 97,895 volumes, 3382 microform items, and 6782 audiovisual forms/CDs, and subscribes to 586 periodicals. Computerized library services include the card catalog, interlibrary loans, and database searching. Special learning facilities include a learning resource center, art gallery, radio station, and a nature center. The 401-acre campus is in a small town 45 miles northeast of Columbus. Including residence halls, there are 30 buildings.

Student Life: 89% of undergraduates are from Ohio. Others are from 23 states and 6 foreign countries. 84% are from public schools. 97% are white. Most are Protestant. The average age of freshmen is 20; all undergraduates, 24. 23% do not continue beyond their first year; 49% remain to graduate.

Housing: 1108 students can be accommodated in college housing, which includes single-sex dormitories and on-campus apartments. On-campus housing is available on a first-come, first-served basis. 75% of students live on campus; of those, 55% remain on campus on weekends. Alcohol is not permitted. All students may keep cars.

Activities: There are no fraternities or sororities. There are 36 groups on campus, including art, band, cheerleading, choir, chorale, chorus, computers, drama, ethnic, honors, international, jazz band, musical theater, newspaper, orchestra, pep band, photography, political, professional, radio and TV, religious, social, social service, student government, symphony, and yearbook. Popular campus events include community service week, concerts, and Lecture Artists Series.

Sports: There are 4 intercollegiate sports for men and 4 for women, and 9 intramural sports for men and 9 for women. Facilities include a main gym, an intramural/practice gym, a weight room, tennis courts, intramural, baseball, softball, and soccer fields, and a baseball/softball batting facility.

Disabled Students: 90% of the campus is accessible. Wheelchair ramps, elevators, special parking, specially equipped rest rooms, special class scheduling, lowered drinking fountains, and lowered telephones are available.

Services: Counseling and information services are available, as is tutoring in most subjects. There is a reader service for the blind, and remedial math, reading, and writing. Students in the at-risk program are required to take College Survival Skills, Critical Thinking, to meet weekly with academic peer mentors, and take supplemental and peer instruction.

Campus Safety and Security: Measures include 24-hour foot and vehicle patrol, self-defense education, informal discussions, and pamphlets/posters/films. There are emergency telephones, lighted pathways/sidewalks, and fire safety training with Student Leadership, blood-borne pathogen seminars, and Campus Safety and Security Review Committee.

Programs of Study: MVNC confers B.A., B.S., and B.B.A. degrees. Associate and master's degrees are also awarded. Bachelor's degrees are awarded in BIOLOGICAL SCIENCE (biology/biological science), BUSINESS (accounting, business administration and management, office supervision and management, and sports management), COMMUNICATIONS AND THE ARTS (art, communications, English, music, music performance, and Spanish), COMPUTER AND PHYSICAL SCIENCE (chemistry, computer science, and mathematics), EDUCATION (art, business, Christian, early childhood, elementary, English, foreign languages, home economics, mathematics, middle school, music, physical, science, secondary, social studies, and special), HEALTH PROFESSIONS (exercise science and medical technology), SOCIAL SCIENCE (family/consumer studies, history, philosophy, psychology, religion, religious education, social work, sociology, and youth ministry). Premedicine, teacher education, and religion are the strongest academically. Business, teacher education, and biology are the largest.

Required: Students must complete 124 semester hours, at least 40 to 60 hours in the major and 40 in upper-division courses, and maintain a minimum GPA of 2.0. The 43- to 48-hour B.A. general education core includes 12 to 15 hours of general requirements, 18 to 19 in the humanities, 7 to 8 in natural sciences, and 6 in social sciences. Students must also complete 1 semester of a foreign language (or 2 years of one language in high school), intermediate algebra (or complete 2 years of algebra and/or geometry in high school), and the Junior-Senior Testing Program.

Special: MVNC offers internships with local businesses/organizations, on-campus work-study programs, travel abroad during the January interim, dual majors, a general studies degree, and nondegree study. A 2-2 nursing degree in cooperation with Capital University is also available, as is a 2-2 engineering degree with Olivet Nazarene University. There are 3 national honor societies, a freshman honors program, and 18 departmental honors programs.

Faculty/Classroom: 59% of faculty are male; 41%, female. 99% teach undergraduates and 5% both teach and do research. No introductory courses are taught by graduate students. The average class size in an introductory lecture is 28; in a laboratory, 17; and in a regular course, 16.

Admissions: 83% of the 2001-2002 applicants were accepted. The SAT I scores for the 2001-2002 freshman class were: Verbal--38% below 500, 33% between 500 and 599, 25% between 600 and 700, and 5% above 700; Math--21% below 500, 54% between 500 and 599, 18% between 600 and 700, and 7% above 700. The ACT scores were 38% below 21, 27% between 21 and 23, 20% between 24 and 26, 8% between 27 and 28, and 8% above 28. 33% of the current freshmen were in the top fifth of their class; 63% were in the top two fifths. 15 freshmen graduated first in their class.

Requirements: The ACT is required, and a minimum score of 18 is recommended. Applicants should be graduates of an accredited high school and be in the upper two thirds of their class. Required preparatory courses include 3 units in English, 2 units each in math (algebra I and II and geometry) and social studies, and 1 unit in science. 2 units of 1 foreign language and a second science course are recommended. A GPA of 2.5 is required. AP and CLEP credits are accepted. Important factors in the admissions decision are recommendations by school officials, personality/intangible qualities, and leadership record. Applications are accepted on-line.

Procedure: Freshmen are admitted fall, winter, and spring. Entrance exams should be taken in early fall. Applications should be filed by May 31 for fall entry, January 1 for winter entry, January 1 for spring entry, and April 1 for summer entry, along with a $25 fee. Notification is sent on a rolling basis.

Transfer: 91 transfer students enrolled in 2001-2002. Transfer students must be in good standing academically and financially. Official transcripts from all colleges attended must be submitted. 30 credits of 124 must be completed at MVNC.

Visiting: There are regularly scheduled orientations for prospective students. There are guides for informal visits and visitors may sit in on classes and stay overnight. To schedule a visit, contact the Admissions Office at (800) 782-2435 or *admissions@mvnc.edu*.

Financial Aid: In 2001-2002, 98% of all freshmen and 93% of continuing students received some form of financial aid. The average freshman award was $10,700. 35% of undergraduates work part time. Average annual earnings from campus work are $767. The average financial indebtedness of the 2001 graduate was $19,954. The FAFSA and the college's own financial statement are required. The fall application deadline is April 30.

International Students: There are 7 international students enrolled. They must score 500 on the written TOEFL and also take the SAT I or the ACT, scoring 18 on the ACT or 860 on the SAT I.

Computers: The mainframe is an HP 9000/800 G30. 6 labs house HPs, Macs, and PCs. All students may access the system 6 A.M. to midnight everyday. There are no time limits and no fees.

Graduates: In 2001, 359 bachelor's degrees were awarded. The most popular majors were business (47%), social sciences (14%), and education (13%). In an average class, 37% graduate in 4 years, 47% in 5 years, and 50% in 6 years. 52 companies recruited on campus in 2000-2001. Of the 2000 graduating class, 20% were enrolled in graduate school within 6 months of graduation and 90% were employed.

Admissions Contact: Doris Webb, Director of Admissions and Recruitment. E-mail: *admissions@mvnc.edu* Web: *www.mvnc.edu*

MUSKINGUM COLLEGE
D-3

New Concord, OH 43762
(740) 826-8137
(800) 752-6082; Fax: (740) 826-8100

Full-time: 794 men, 798 women	**Faculty:** 87; IIB, -$
Part-time: 19 men, 51 women	**Ph.D.s:** 92%
Graduate: 83 men, 299 women	**Student/Faculty:** 17 to 1
Year: semesters, summer session	**Tuition:** $13,400
Application Deadline: see profile	**Room & Board:** $5360
Freshman Class: 1636 applied, 1403 accepted, 441 enrolled	
SAT I Verbal/Math: 530/530	**ACT:** 22 **COMPETITIVE**

Muskingum College, founded in 1837, is a private liberal arts and sciences institution affiliated with the Presbyterian Church (U.S.A.). There is 1 graduate school. In addition to regional accreditation, Muskingum has baccalaureate program accreditation with NASM and NCATE. The library contains 228,000 volumes, 190,000 microform items, and 9600 audiovisual forms/CDs, and subscribes to 840 periodicals. Computerized library services include the card catalog, interlibrary loans, and database searching. Special learning facilities include a learning resource center, art gallery, radio station, TV station, and greenhouse. The 215-acre campus is in a small town 9 miles west of Cambridge and 50 miles east of Columbus. Including residence halls, there are 33 buildings.

Student Life: 85% of undergraduates are from Ohio. Others are from 26 states, 19 foreign countries, and Canada. 85% are from public schools. 94% are white. 48% are Protestant; 25% Catholic; 25% claim no religious affiliation. The average age of freshmen is 18; all undergraduates, 21. 23% do not continue beyond their first year; 62% remain to graduate.

Housing: 1030 students can be accommodated in college housing, which includes single-sex and coed dormitories, on-campus apartments, fraternity houses, and sorority houses. In addition, there are language houses and special-interest houses. On-campus housing is guaranteed for all 4 years. 85% of students live on campus; of those, 75% remain on campus on weekends. All students may keep cars.

Activities: 45% of men belong to 3 local and 2 national fraternities; 45% of women belong to 3 local and 2 national sororities. There are 60 groups on campus, including art, band, cheerleading, choir, chorus, computers, dance, debate, drama, forensics, gay, honors, international, jazz band, literary magazine, musical theater, newspaper, orchestra, pep band, political, professional, radio and TV, religious, social, social service, student government, symphony, and yearbook. Popular campus events include Parents Weekend, Li'l Sibs Weekend, and Migration Day.

Sports: There are 9 intercollegiate sports for men and 8 for women, and 5 intramural sports for men and 5 for women. Facilities include gyms, weightlifting/training rooms, an aerobics room, a baseball batting cage, a swimming pool, a walking/jogging trail, an all-weather track, football, baseball, and soccer fields, and tennis, basketball, and racquetball courts.

Disabled Students: 30% of the campus is accessible. Wheelchair ramps, elevators, special parking, and lowered drinking fountains are available.

Services: Counseling and information services are available, as is tutoring in every subject. There is a reader service for the blind. The PLUS program is available for learning-disabled and disabled students. The Center for the Advancement of Learning assists all students with study strategies.

Campus Safety and Security: Measures include 24-hour foot and vehicle patrol, escort service, informal discussions, and pamphlets/posters/films. There are emergency telephones and lighted pathways/sidewalks.

Programs of Study: Muskingum confers B.A. and B.S. degrees. Master's degrees are also awarded. Bachelor's degrees are awarded in AGRICULTURE (conservation and regulation), BIOLOGICAL SCIENCE (biology/biological science, molecular biology, and neurosciences), BUSINESS (accounting, business administration and management, and international business management), COMMUNICATIONS AND THE ARTS (art, communications, dramatic arts, English, French, German, journalism, music, Spanish, and speech/debate/rhetoric), COMPUTER AND PHYSICAL SCIENCE (chemistry, computer science, earth science, geology, mathematics, and physics), EDUCATION (Christian, early childhood, elementary, foreign languages, music, physical, reading, science, secondary, and special), ENGINEERING AND ENVIRONMENTAL DESIGN (environmental science), SOCIAL SCIENCE (American studies, economics, history, international relations, philosophy, political science/government, psychology, public affairs, religion, religious education, social science, and sociology). Conservation science, environmental science, and international business are the strongest academically. Education, business, and speech communication are the largest.

Required: To graduate, students must complete a minimum of 124 credit hours, including at least 30 in a major and 40 in upper-level courses. Students must maintain a GPA of at least 2.0, and must also complete the 50 to 55 credit hours of Liberal Arts Essentials, with courses in writing, speech, math, arts and humanities, religion and ethics, science, social science, American studies, and phys ed. Senior capstone experience is required in all areas.

Special: Internships, work-study programs, study abroad in 12 countries, and a Washington semester are possible. Students may earn a 3-2 engineering degree, a B.A.-B.S. degree, or a general studies degree; nearly a third of students pursue dual and student-designed majors. Nondegree study, pass/fail options, and credit for life, military, or work experience are also available. There are 13 national honor societies.

Faculty/Classroom: 60% of faculty are male; 40%, female. All teach undergraduates, 90% do research, and 90% do both. No introductory courses are taught by graduate students. The average class size in an introductory lecture is 30; in a laboratory, 16; and in a regular course, 25.

Admissions: 86% of the 2001-2002 applicants were accepted. The SAT I scores for the 2001-2002 freshman class were: Verbal--37% below 500, 40% between 500 and 599, 20% between 600 and 700, and 3% above 700; Math--33% below 500, 41% between 500 and 599, 22% between 600 and 700, and 4% above 700. The ACT scores were 39% below 21, 28% between 21 and 23, 20% between 24 and 26, 8% between 27 and 28, and 5% above 28. 42% of the current freshmen were in the top fifth of their class; 67% were in the top two fifths. 12 freshmen graduated first in their class in a recent year.

Requirements: The SAT I or ACT is required. In addition, candidates for admission must have a high school diploma or its equivalent, and should have 4 years of English, 3 years of college preparatory math, and 2 years each of science, social science, and foreign language. A GPA of 2.3 is required. AP and CLEP credits are accepted. Important factors in the admissions decision are advanced placement or honor courses, extracurricular activities record, and leadership record. Muskingum accepts applications on computer disk via CollegeLink and Apply.

Procedure: Freshmen are admitted to all sessions. Entrance exams should be taken in the junior year or the fall of the senior year. There are early admissions and deferred admissions plans. Check with school for current deadlines. Notification is sent on a rolling basis.

Transfer: 58 transfer students enrolled in a recent year. Applicants must submit an official college transcript and be in good academic standing from their previous institution. 48 credits of 124 must be completed at Muskingum.

Visiting: There are regularly scheduled orientations for prospective students, consisting of an admission presentation, faculty panel, student panel, and class attendance. There are guides for informal visits and visitors may sit in on classes and stay overnight. To schedule a visit, contact the Admission Office.

Financial Aid: In 2001-2002, 93% of all freshmen and 92% of continuing students received some form of financial aid. 48% of undergraduates work part time. Average annual earnings from campus work are $800. The average financial indebtedness of a recent year's graduate was $14,900. Muskingum is a member of CSS. The FAFSA and student and parents tax returns are required. Check with school for current deadlines.

International Students: There were 43 international students enrolled in a recent year. The school actively recruits these students. They must score 550 on the written TOEFL or 213 on the electronic version.

Computers: There are 6 primary computing labs, and residence hall rooms can access the network. All students may access the system 24 hours a day. There are no time limits and no fees.

Graduates: In a recent year, 228 bachelor's degrees were awarded. The most popular majors were business (24%), elementary education (17%), and history (12%). In an average class, 51% graduate in 4 years, and 61% in 5 years. 23 companies recruited on campus in a recent year.

Admissions Contact: Beth DaLonzo, Director of Admission.
E-mail: *adminfo@muskingum.edu* Web: *www.muskingum.edu*

NOTRE DAME COLLEGE
D-1

South Euclid, OH 44121
(216) 373-5383
(800) NDC-1680, ext. 355; Fax: (216) 381-3802

Full-time: 59 men, 246 women	**Faculty:** 26; IIB, --$
Part-time: 495 men and women	**Ph.D.s:** 65%
Graduate: 123 men and women	**Student/Faculty:** 12 to 1
Year: semesters, summer session	**Tuition:** $14,800
Application Deadline: open	**Room & Board:** $5625
Freshman Class: 284 applied, 211 accepted, 142 enrolled	
SAT I Verbal/Math: 495/470	**ACT:** 21 **COMPETITIVE**

Notre Dame College, formerly Notre Dame College of Ohio, founded in 1922, is a private liberal arts and sciences college affiliated with the Roman Catholic Church. In addition to regional accreditation, NDC has baccalaureate program accreditation with ADA. The library contains 89,292 volumes, 14,200 microform items, and 1768 audiovisual forms/CDs, and subscribes to 300 periodicals. Computerized library services include the card catalog, interlibrary loans, and database searching. Special learning facilities include a learning resource center and tolerance resource center. The 53-acre campus is in a suburban area 13 miles east of Cleveland. Including residence halls, there are 6 buildings.

Student Life: 95% of undergraduates are from Ohio. Others are from 8 states, 7 foreign countries, and Canada. 65% are from public schools. 65% are white; 23% African American. 55% are Catholic; 20% Baptist,

Muslim, and other Christian; 15% Protestant. The average age of freshmen is 18; all undergraduates, 26. 34% do not continue beyond their first year; 52% remain to graduate.

Housing: 222 students can be accommodated in college housing, which includes dormitories. There are nonsmoking floors and quiet floors. Housing is available for weekend college students on WECO weekends. On-campus housing is guaranteed for all 4 years. 78% of students commute. Alcohol is not permitted. All students may keep cars.

Activities: There are no fraternities or sororities. There are 32 groups on campus, including art, choir, computers, dance, drama, ethnic, honors, international, literary magazine, newspaper, political, professional, religious, social, social service, and student government. Popular campus events include Parents Day, Founders Weekend, and Christmas Happening.

Sports: There are 5 intercollegiate sports for men and 7 for women, and 4 intramural sports for men and 4 for women. Facilities include a 500-seat gym, a pool, and a fitness center.

Disabled Students: 75% of the campus is accessible. Wheelchair ramps, elevators, special parking, specially equipped rest rooms, lowered drinking fountains, and lowered telephones are available.

Services: Counseling and information services are available, as is tutoring in most subjects. There is remedial math, reading, and writing.

Campus Safety and Security: Measures include 24-hour foot and vehicle patrol, escort service, informal discussions, and pamphlets/posters/films. There are emergency telephones and lighted pathways/sidewalks.

Programs of Study: NDC confers B.A. and B.S. degrees. Associate and master's degrees are also awarded. Bachelor's degrees are awarded in BIOLOGICAL SCIENCE (biology/biological science), BUSINESS (accounting, business economics, human resources, management science, and marketing/retailing/merchandising), COMMUNICATIONS AND THE ARTS (art, communications, English, graphic design, studio art, and visual and performing arts), COMPUTER AND PHYSICAL SCIENCE (chemistry, information sciences and systems, and mathematics), EDUCATION (early childhood, elementary, middle school, and secondary), ENGINEERING AND ENVIRONMENTAL DESIGN (environmental science), SOCIAL SCIENCE (economics, history, ministries, political science/government, psychology, and theological studies). Business, education, and science are the strongest academically. Business administration, education, and sciences are the largest.

Required: To graduate, students must complete 128 semester hours with a minimum GPA of 2.0. Core requirements include English, speech, literature, fine arts, foreign language, health and phys ed, math, science, social or behavioral science, philosophy/theology, world civilization, and senior seminar.

Special: Students may cross-register with the Cleveland Institutes of Music and Art and through the Northeast Ohio Council on Higher Education. The college offers co-op programs in most majors, internships with local businesses, special degrees, including a B.A. with a diploma in theology, interdisciplinary majors, including visual arts management, credit by exam, nondegree study, and pass/fail options. NDC also offers Weekend College. There are 5 national honor societies.

Faculty/Classroom: 30% of faculty are male; 70%, female. All teach undergraduates. No introductory courses are taught by graduate students. The average class size in an introductory lecture is 20; in a laboratory, 11; and in a regular course, 11.

Admissions: 74% of the 2001-2002 applicants were accepted. The SAT I scores for the 2001-2002 freshman class were: Verbal--50% below 500, 25% between 500 and 599, and 25% between 600 and 700; Math--65% below 500, 15% between 500 and 599, and 20% between 600 and 700. The ACT scores were 30% below 21, 50% between 21 and 23, 19% between 24 and 26, and 1% between 27 and 28. 40% of the current freshmen were in the top fifth of their class; 70% were in the top two fifths.

Requirements: The SAT I or ACT is required, with a minimum composite score of 900 on the SAT I or 19 on the ACT. Applicants should be graduates of an accredited secondary school with 15 academic credits, including 4 of English, 2 of foreign language, 1 each of math, social studies, and science, plus 5 electives. The GED is accepted. An interview is recommended. A GPA of 2.5 is required. AP and CLEP credits are accepted. Important factors in the admissions decision are advanced placement or honor courses, evidence of special talent, and extracurricular activities record.

Procedure: Freshmen are admitted fall and spring. Entrance exams should be taken in the spring of the junior year or the fall of the senior year. There is a deferred admissions plan. Application deadlines are open. The fall 2001 application fee was $30. Notification is sent on a rolling basis.

Transfer: 37 transfer students enrolled in 2001-2002. Applicants must have a college GPA of at least 2.5. An interview is required. 32 credits of 128 must be completed at NDC.

Visiting: There are regularly scheduled orientations for prospective students, including placement testing, academic advising, scheduling, an overview of student services, and a tour of Cleveland. There are guides for informal visits and visitors may sit in on classes and stay overnight. To schedule a visit, contact the Admissions Office.

Financial Aid: In 2001-2002, all freshmen and 90% of continuing students received some form of financial aid. 92% of freshmen and 90% of continuing students received need-based aid. The average freshman award was $13,200. Of that total, scholarships or need-based grants averaged $9075 ($10,000 maximum); loans averaged $2625; and work contracts averaged $1500. 20% of undergraduates work part time. Average annual earnings from campus work are $1500. The average financial indebtedness of the 2001 graduate was $14,825. The FAFSA is required.

International Students: There are 7 international students enrolled. The school actively recruits these students. They must score 550 on the written TOEFL or take the ELS Proficiency Test 109.

Computers: NDC has a Unisys system, and students use individual PCs in the computer lab networked for classroom and homework. There are also PCs located in education and writing labs in dorms. The learning center computer classroom has 31 Pentium MMX computers, and its lab has 16 Pentium computers, all with full Internet access. There is also a 5-seat lab in the residence halls and a Mac lab with 14 Power Mac 5400s. All students may access the system. There are no time limits. The fee is 200.

Graduates: In 2001, 92 bachelor's degrees were awarded. The most popular majors were accounting (19%), human resources (16%), and management (14%). In an average class, 35% graduate in 4 years, and 48% in 5 years. 85 companies recruited on campus in 2000-2001. Of the 2000 graduating class, 10% were enrolled in graduate school within 6 months of graduation and 85% were employed.

Admissions Contact: Meredith Young, Director of Admissions.
E-mail: *myoung@ndc.edu* Web: *http://www.ndc.edu*

OBERLIN COLLEGE — D-2

Oberlin, OH 44074 (440) 775-8411
(800) 622-6243; Fax: (440) 775-6905

Full-time: 1177 men, 1576 women	**Faculty:** 263; IIB, ++$
Part-time: 35 men, 52 women	**Ph.D.s:** 94%
Graduate: 23 men and women	**Student/Faculty:** 11 to 1
Year: 4-1-4	**Tuition:** $26,580
Application Deadline: January 15	**Room & Board:** $6560
Freshman Class: 4570 applied, 1798 accepted, 624 enrolled	
SAT I Verbal/Math: 680/660	**ACT:** 29

HIGHLY COMPETITIVE+

Oberlin College, founded in 1833, is an independent institution offering degree programs in the liberal arts and sciences and music. There are 2 undergraduate schools. In addition to regional accreditation, Oberlin has baccalaureate program accreditation with NASAD and NASM. The 4 libraries contain 1,254,218 volumes, 334,237 microform items, and 71,436 audiovisual forms/CDs, and subscribe to 11,417 periodicals. Computerized library services include the card catalog, interlibrary loans, and database searching. Special learning facilities include a learning resource center, art gallery, radio station, and an observatory, an art museum, and an art library. The 440-acre campus is in a small town 35 miles southwest of Cleveland. Including residence halls, there are 65 buildings.

Student Life: 89% of undergraduates are from out of state, mostly the Midwest. Others are from 49 states, 55 foreign countries, and Canada. 63% are from public schools. 75% are white. The average age of freshmen is 18; all undergraduates, 20. 10% do not continue beyond their first year; 79% remain to graduate.

Housing: 2060 students can be accommodated in college housing, which includes single-sex and coed dormitories. In addition, there are language houses, special-interest houses, and co-ops. On-campus housing is guaranteed for all 4 years. 75% of students live on campus; of those, 99% remain on campus on weekends. Upperclassmen may keep cars.

Activities: There are no fraternities or sororities. There are 120 groups on campus, including art, band, cheerleading, chess, choir, chorale, chorus, computers, dance, drama, ethnic, film, gay, honors, international, jazz band, literary magazine, marching band, musical theater, newspaper, opera, orchestra, photography, political, professional, radio and TV, religious, social, social service, student government, symphony, and yearbook. Popular campus events include Mayfair, Octoberfest, and Mardi Gras.

Sports: There are 11 intercollegiate sports for men and 12 for women, and 10 intramural sports for men and 10 for women. Facilities include a gym, a skating rink, an enclosed and a semi-enclosed field house, a stadium, an indoor 6-lane, 200-meter track, an 8-lane outdoor track, 12 outdoor and 4 indoor tennis courts, a cross-country course, a fitness trail, 2 swimming pools, a Nautilus center, a free-weight room, 22 practice/play fields, and indoor space for football, soccer, and lacrosse practice.

Disabled Students: 90% of the campus is accessible. Wheelchair ramps, elevators, special parking, specially equipped rest rooms, special class scheduling, lowered drinking fountains, lowered telephones, and an indoor/outdoor lift are available.

Services: Counseling and information services are available, as is tutoring in every subject. There is a reader service for the blind, and remedial math, reading, and writing. Computer-assisted services for hearing and visually impaired students and special tutoring and peer-counseling services for learning-disabled students are available.

Campus Safety and Security: Measures include 24-hour foot and vehicle patrol, self-defense education, escort service, and informal discussions. There are pamphlets/posters/films, emergency telephones, lighted pathways/sidewalks, a full-time crime prevention officer, a 24-hour headquarters facility staffed by professional dispatchers, and an electronic card-access system in all dormitories. All security officers are state-certified academy graduates.

Programs of Study: Oberlin confers B.A. and B.Mus. degrees. Master's degrees are also awarded. Bachelor's degrees are awarded in BIOLOGICAL SCIENCE (biochemistry, biology/biological science, and neurosciences), COMMUNICATIONS AND THE ARTS (art, classics, comparative literature, creative writing, dance, dramatic arts, English, fine arts, French, German, music, music history and appreciation, music performance, music theory and composition, romance languages and literature, Russian, and Spanish), COMPUTER AND PHYSICAL SCIENCE (astronomy, chemistry, computer science, geology, mathematics, and physics), EDUCATION (music), ENGINEERING AND ENVIRONMENTAL DESIGN (environmental science), SOCIAL SCIENCE (African American studies, anthropology, archeology, East Asian studies, economics, history, humanities, Judaic studies, Latin American studies, law, Near Eastern studies, philosophy, political science/government, psychology, religion, sociology, and women's studies). Sciences, art and humanities, and music are the strongest academically. English, government, and history are the largest.

Required: Students are required to complete 112 to 124 total credit hours, including 9 hours each in arts/humanities, social/behavioral sciences, natural science/math, and courses dealing with cultural diversity, and 3 winter term projects. In addition, they must earn writing and quantitative proficiency certification. A minimum of 24 credits is required for the major.

Special: Internships are available through the Business Initiatives Program. Students may study abroad in more than 25 countries. The college offers independent and dual majors, 3-2 engineering programs with 4 other institutions, nondegree study for special and visiting students, and a 5-year B.A.-B.Mus. double degree. Pass/no credit options are available to all students. There are 4 national honor societies, including Phi Beta Kappa, and 25 departmental honors programs.

Faculty/Classroom: 66% of faculty are male; 34%, female. All both teach and do research. No introductory courses are taught by graduate students. The average class size in a laboratory is 25 and in a regular course, 21.

Admissions: 39% of the 2001-2002 applicants were accepted. The SAT I scores for the 2001-2002 freshman class were: Verbal--3% below 500, 12% between 500 and 599, 40% between 600 and 700, and 45% above 700; Math--2% below 500, 19% between 500 and 599, 52% between 600 and 700, and 27% above 700. The ACT scores were 3% below 21, 5% between 21 and 23, 16% between 24 and 26, 21% between 27 and 28, and 55% above 28. 71% of the current freshmen were in the top fifth of their class; 94% were in the top two fifths. There were 33 National Merit finalists. 26 freshmen graduated first in their class.

Requirements: The SAT I or ACT is required. In addition, candidates for admission should have completed 4 years each of English and math and 3 each of science, social studies, and a foreign language. AP credits are accepted. Important factors in the admissions decision are advanced placement or honor courses, personality/intangible qualities, and leadership record. Applications are accepted on-line.

Procedure: Freshmen are admitted in the fall. Entrance exams should be taken in the junior year or early in the senior year. There are early decision and deferred admissions plans. Early decision applications should be filed by November 15; regular applications, by January 15 for fall entry and November 15 for spring entry. Notification of early decision is sent December 15; regular decision, April 1. 204 early decision candidates were accepted for the 2001-2002 class. 17% of all applicants are on a waiting list; 35 were accepted in 2001. The fall 2001 application fee was $30.

Transfer: 71 transfer students enrolled in 2001-2002. Applicants should submit official transcripts of all college work completed, plus a list of current courses and midterm grades. An average of B or better should be presented. A high school transcript, recommendations, and standardized test scores are also required. 56 credits of 112 to 124 must be completed at Oberlin.

Visiting: There are regularly scheduled orientations for prospective students, including campus tours, class visits, an interview with an admissions officer, and an overnight stay in the dormitory. There are guides for informal visits and visitors may sit in on classes and stay overnight. To schedule a visit, contact the Admissions Office.

Financial Aid: In 2001-2002, 58% of all freshmen and 55% of continuing students received some form of financial aid. 58% of freshmen and 55% of continuing students received need-based aid. The average freshman award was $24,023. Of that total, scholarships or need-based grants averaged $16,961 ($25,000 maximum); loans averaged $3766 ($4000 maximum); and work contracts averaged $1192 ($1550 maximum). 57% of undergraduates work part time. Average annual earnings from campus work are $1450. The average financial indebtedness of the 2001 graduate was $13,926. Oberlin is a member of CSS. The CSS/Profile or FAFSA and the college's own financial statement are required. The fall application deadline is February 15.

International Students: There are 181 international students enrolled. The school actively recruits these students. They must score 600 on the written TOEFL.

Computers: The mainframe is a DEC VAX 6410. There are 209 Mac, Zenith, and HP PCs and 54 terminals available for student use in the computing center, the music conservatory, residence halls, and classrooms. All students may access the system. There are no time limits and no fees.

Graduates: In 2001, 684 bachelor's degrees were awarded. The most popular majors were English (13%), biology (11%), and history (8%). In an average class, 2% graduate in 3 years, 61% in 4 years, 76% in 5 years, and 77% in 6 years. 49 companies recruited on campus in 2000-2001.

Admissions Contact: Debra Chermonte, Dean of Admissions and Financial Aid. E-mail: *college.admissions@oberlin.edu*
Web: *www.oberlin.edu*

OHIO DOMINICAN COLLEGE

Columbus, OH 43219 — **C-3**
(614) 251-4500
(800) 955-OHIO; Fax: (614) 252-0776

Full-time: 473 men, 1063 women	**Faculty:** 60; IIB, -$
Part-time: 214 men, 447 women	**Ph.D.s:** 80%
Graduate: none	**Student/Faculty:** 26 to 1
Year: semesters, summer session	**Tuition:** $12,730
Application Deadline: open	**Room & Board:** $5370
Freshman Class: 893 applied, 535 accepted, 199 enrolled	
SAT I or ACT: required	**LESS COMPETITIVE**

Ohio Dominican College, founded in 1911 by the Dominican Sisters of St. Mary of the Springs, is a private liberal arts college affiliated with the Roman Catholic Church. The library contains 113,453 volumes, 6994 microform items, and 2848 audiovisual forms/CDs, and subscribes to 518 periodicals. Computerized library services include the card catalog, interlibrary loans, and database searching. Special learning facilities include a learning resource center, art gallery, and radio station. The 62-acre campus is in an urban area 5 miles from downtown Columbus. Including residence halls, there are 9 buildings.

Student Life: 96% of undergraduates are from Ohio. Others are from 12 states and 29 foreign countries. 75% are from public schools. 67% are white; 23% African American. 39% are Protestant; 29% Catholic. The average age of freshmen is 20; all undergraduates, 28. 38% do not continue beyond their first year; 44% remain to graduate.

Housing: 343 students can be accommodated in college housing, which includes single-sex and coed dormitories. On-campus housing is available on a first-come, first-served basis. 88% of students commute. Alcohol is not permitted. All students may keep cars.

Activities: There are no fraternities or sororities. There are 22 groups on campus, including academic, art, association of commuters, association of resident students, board games, cheerleading, choir, dance, drama, drill team, English Circle, ethnic, honors, international, literary magazine, Palette Club, political, professional, radio and TV, religious, social, social service, and student government. Popular campus events include Black History Week, International Student Week, and ODC Day in the Spring.

Sports: There are 4 intercollegiate sports for men and 5 for women, and 6 intramural sports for men and 6 for women. Facilities include an athletic center, a gym, a baseball and softball field, a soccer field, and tennis courts.

Disabled Students: 90% of the campus is accessible. Wheelchair ramps, elevators, special parking, specially equipped rest rooms, and special class scheduling are available.

Services: Counseling and information services are available, as is tutoring in most subjects. There is remedial math, reading, and writing. The Academic Center is a support unit designed to help all students meet their academic commitment and improve their learning skills. The staff offers workshops in study-related topics, provides professional and peer tutoring in a variety of subjects, and counsels students and faculty on learning and study problems.

Campus Safety and Security: Measures include 24-hour foot and vehicle patrol, self-defense education, escort service, and shuttle buses. There are informal discussions, pamphlets/posters/films, emergency telephones, and lighted pathways/sidewalks.

Programs of Study: ODC confers B.A., B.S., and B.S.Ed. degrees. Associate degrees are also awarded. Bachelor's degrees are awarded in BIOLOGICAL SCIENCE (biology/biological science), BUSINESS (business administration and management, international business management, and management information systems), COMMUNICATIONS AND THE ARTS (art, communications, English, graphic design, public relations, and technical and business writing), COMPUTER AND PHYSI-

CAL SCIENCE (chemistry, computer science, information sciences and systems, and mathematics), EDUCATION (early childhood, middle school, special, and teaching English as a second/foreign language (TESOL/TEFOL)), SOCIAL SCIENCE (criminal justice, economics, history, interdisciplinary studies, philosophy, political science/government, psychology, social work, and sociology). Business, education, and computer science and information systems are the largest.

Required: Core curriculum requirements include 12 semester credits in philosophy or theology, 8 each in humanities, English, and behavioral science, 4 each in literature, math, and science, 4 or 8 in language, and 1 in phys ed. All students beyond the freshman year must maintain a GPA of 2.0. Students must complete 124 semester credits. The total hours in the major is set by individual departments.

Special: Students may cross-register with members of the Higher Education Council of Columbus Consortium, study abroad in various countries, and participate in a Washington semester. Internships are required in some majors. ODC offers dual majors and pass/fail options in some courses. Nondegree study and credit for life, military, and work experience are available. The Weekend College Program allows students to attend classes scheduled every other weekend. There are 3 national honor societies and a freshman honors program. All departments have honors programs.

Faculty/Classroom: 44% of faculty are male; 56%, female. All teach undergraduates. The average class size in an introductory lecture is 20 and in a regular course, 20.

Admissions: 60% of the 2001-2002 applicants were accepted. The ACT scores for the 2001-2002 freshman class were: 56% below 21, 26% between 21 and 23, 15% between 24 and 26, 3% between 27 and 28, and 1% above 28.

Requirements: The SAT I or ACT is required. In addition, candidates for admission should have completed 4 units of English and 3 units each of a foreign language, math, science, and social studies. The freshman applicant is required to submit a completed application, transcripts of secondary courses and grades, and official scores from standardized testing (ACT or SAT I). An essay and an interview (in-state applicants) are required. A GPA of 2.0 is required. AP and CLEP credits are accepted.

Procedure: Freshmen are admitted to all sessions. There is a deferred admissions plan. Application deadlines are open. Notification is sent on a rolling basis.

Transfer: 213 transfer students enrolled in 2001-2002. A completed application, an interview, and transcripts of all college work are required of transfer applicants. 32 credits of 124 must be completed at ODC.

Visiting: There are regularly scheduled orientations for prospective students, including an August orientation for fall entry and a January orientation for the second semester. Individual appointments can be arranged. There are guides for informal visits and visitors may sit in on classes and stay overnight. To schedule a visit, contact Victoria Thompson-Campbell, Director of Admissions at *thompson@odc.edu*.

Financial Aid: In a recent year, 94% of all freshmen and 64% of continuing students received some form of financial aid. 75% of freshmen and 73% of continuing students received need-based aid. The average freshman award was $8000. 15% of undergraduates work part time. Average annual earnings from campus work are $1500. The FAFSA is required. The fall application deadline is June 1.

International Students: There are 58 international students enrolled. The school actively recruits these students. They must take the MELAB, TOEFL, or the college's own test .

Computers: ODC has a Windows NT network, with 500 PCs available to students in the library, the science and art buildings, and residence halls. Software for the World Wide Web, word processing, spreadsheet, and database functions is provided, as well as languages for computer science courses. All students may access the system. There are no time limits. The fee is $100 per semester. All students are required to have personal computers.

Graduates: In 2001, 255 bachelor's degrees were awarded. The most popular majors were business administration (41%), elementary education (25%), and criminal justice (6%). In an average class, 6% graduate in 3 years, 28% in 4 years, 42% in 5 years, and 44% in 6 years. 15 companies recruited on campus in 2000-2001.

Admissions Contact: Victoria Thompson-Campbell, Director of Admissions. E-mail: *admissions@odc.edu* Web: *www.odc.edu*

OHIO NORTHERN UNIVERSITY

B-2

Ada, OH 45810 **(419) 772-2260**
(888) 408-4668; Fax: (419) 772-2313

Full-time: 1185 men, 1049 women	**Faculty:** 169; IIB, +$
Part-time: 31 men, 31 women	**Ph.D.s:** 82%
Graduate: 409 men, 570 women	**Student/Faculty:** 13 to 1
Year: quarters, summer session	**Tuition:** $22,275
Application Deadline: August 1	**Room & Board:** $5490
Freshman Class: 2358 applied, 2140 accepted, 732 enrolled	
SAT I Verbal/Math: 560/590	**ACT:** 25 **VERY COMPETITIVE**

Ohio Northern University, founded in 1871, is a private institution affiliated with the United Methodist Church. Undergraduate programs are offered in arts and sciences, business administration, engineering, and pharmacy. There are 4 undergraduate schools and 1 graduate school. In addition to regional accreditation, ONU has baccalaureate program accreditation with ABET, ACPE, ACS, CAAHEP, NASM, and NCATE. The 2 libraries contain 250,518 volumes, 72,067 microform items, and 10,815 audiovisual forms/CDs, and subscribe to 1038 periodicals. Computerized library services include the card catalog, interlibrary loans, and database searching. Special learning facilities include a learning resource center, art gallery, radio station, TV station, and pharmacy museum. The 285-acre campus is in a small town about 75 miles south of Toledo. Including residence halls, there are 39 buildings.

Student Life: 86% of undergraduates are from Ohio. Others are from 42 states, 17 foreign countries, and Canada. 82% are from public schools. 95% are white. 43% are Baptist, Muslim, Lutheran, Presbyterian, United Church of Christ, and others; 26% are Catholic; 19% are members of the shool's denomination; 12% claim no religious affiliation. The average age of freshmen is 18; all undergraduates, 20. 18% do not continue beyond their first year; 66% remain to graduate.

Housing: 1915 students can be accommodated in college housing, which includes single-sex and coed dormitories, on-campus apartments, off-campus apartments, fraternity houses, and sorority houses. In addition, there are honors houses and special-interest houses. On-campus housing is guaranteed for all 4 years. 64% of students live on campus; of those, 70% remain on campus on weekends. All students may keep cars.

Activities: 25% of men belong to 8 national fraternities; 22% of women belong to 4 national sororities. There are more than 170 groups on campus, including art, band, cheerleading, chess, choir, chorale, chorus, computers, dance, debate, drama, drill team, ethnic, honors, international, jazz band, literary magazine, marching band, musical theater, newspaper, orchestra, pep band, political, professional, radio and TV, religious, social, social service, student government, symphony, and yearbook. Popular campus events include Tunes on the Tundra, International Week, and Little Sibs Weekend.

Sports: There are 11 intercollegiate sports for men and 10 for women, and 12 intramural sports for men and 11 for women. Facilities include a 6-lane pool, a wrestling room, weight rooms, indoor/outdoor tennis courts, 3 basketball courts, a football stadium, a training room, bowling lanes, a billiards room, a dance room, a fitness lab, a 200-meter indoor track, an 8-lane, 400-meter outdoor track, 3 racquetball courts, a Nautilus room, and a 2.5-mile jogging/walking path.

Disabled Students: 95% of the campus is accessible. Wheelchair ramps, elevators, special parking, specially equipped rest rooms, special class scheduling, lowered drinking fountains, and lowered telephones are available.

Services: Counseling and information services are available, as is tutoring in most subjects. There is a reader service for the blind and remedial math and writing.

Campus Safety and Security: Measures include 24-hour foot and vehicle patrol, self-defense education, escort service, and informal discussions. There are pamphlets/posters/films, emergency telephones, and lighted pathways/sidewalks.

Programs of Study: ONU confers B.A., B.S., B.F.A., B.M., B.S.B.A., B.S.C.E., B.S.C.P.E., B.S.E.E., B.S.M.E., B.S.M.T., and B.S.Ph. degrees. Doctoral degrees are also awarded. Bachelor's degrees are awarded in AGRICULTURE (environmental studies), BIOLOGICAL SCIENCE (biochemistry, biology/biological science, and molecular biology), BUSINESS (accounting, business administration and management, business economics, international business management, management science, and sports management), COMMUNICATIONS AND THE ARTS (broadcasting, ceramic art and design, communications, creative writing, dramatic arts, English, fine arts, French, graphic design, journalism, language arts, literature, music, music business management, music performance, music theory and composition, public relations, and Spanish), COMPUTER AND PHYSICAL SCIENCE (chemistry, computer science, mathematics, physics, and statistics), EDUCATION (athletic training, early childhood, health, middle school, music, and physical), ENGINEERING AND ENVIRONMENTAL DESIGN (civil engineering, computer engineering, electrical/electronics engineering, mechanical engineering, and technological management), HEALTH PROFESSIONS (health, medical technology, and pharmacy), SOCIAL SCIENCE (criminal justice, history, international studies, philosophy, political science/government, psychology, religion, social studies, sociology, and youth ministry). Chemistry, engineering, and pharmacy are the strongest academically. Pharmacy, engineering, and biology are the largest.

Required: To graduate, students must complete a minimum of 182 quarter hours, maintain a cumulative GPA of 2.0, and fulfill all departmental/college core requirements. Students also must submit a formal application for graduation.

Special: Co-op programs are available in civil, electrical, computer, and mechanical engineering and technology, computer science, and math. Students may take internships in pharmacy, engineering, and business and may study abroad in 15 countries. B.A.-B.S. degrees and dual majors are available in arts/engineering, arts/pharmacy, and arts/business. The university also offers pass/fail options and work-study programs. There are 38 national honor societies, a freshman honors program, and 21 departmental honors programs.

Faculty/Classroom: 67% of faculty are male; 33%, female. 90% both teach and do research. No introductory courses are taught by graduate students. The average class size in an introductory lecture is 29; in a laboratory, 14; and in a regular course, 25.

Admissions: 91% of the 2001-2002 applicants were accepted. The SAT I scores for the 2001-2002 freshman class were: Verbal--20% below 500, 44% between 500 and 599, 33% between 600 and 700, and 3% above 700; Math--18% below 500, 39% between 500 and 599, 38% between 600 and 700, and 5% above 700. The ACT scores were 16% below 21, 22% between 21 and 23, 30% between 24 and 26, 16% between 27 and 28, and 16% above 28. 65% of the current freshmen were in the top quarter of their class; 87% were in the upper half. There were 11 National Merit finalists. 85 graduated first or second in their class.

Requirements: The SAT I or ACT is required. In addition, the preparatory program should include 4 years of English, 3 of math, and 2 each of science, social studies, art, history, and music; 2 years of foreign language are recommended. ONU requires applicants to be in the upper 50% of their class. A GPA of 2.5 is required. AP and CLEP credits are accepted. Important factors in the admissions decision are advanced placement or honor courses, leadership record, and extracurricular activities record. Applications are accepted on-line via ExPAN and at *embark.com*

Procedure: Freshmen are admitted to all sessions. Entrance exams should be taken in the spring of the junior year or the fall of the senior year. There is a deferred admissions plan. Applications should be filed by August 1 for fall entry, November 1 for winter entry, and February 1 for spring entry, along with a $30 fee. Notification is sent on a rolling basis.

Transfer: 88 transfer students enrolled in 2001-2002. Applicants should have a minimum college GPA of 2.0 and submit official transcripts from all schools attended. 45 quarter credits of 182 must be completed at ONU.

Visiting: There are regularly scheduled orientations for prospective students, including a tour, lunch, and appointments in academics, admissions, and financial aid. A meeting with a coach can also be arranged. There are guides for informal visits and visitors may sit in on classes and stay overnight. To schedule a visit, contact the Admissions Office.

Financial Aid: In a recent year, 88% of all freshmen and 89% of continuing students received some form of financial aid. 77% of freshmen and 80% of continuing students received need-based aid. The average freshman award was $19,200. Of that total, scholarships or need-based grants averaged $11,930 ($22,170 maximum); loans averaged $4800 ($10,500 maximum); and work contracts averaged $1200 ($2000 maximum). 65% of undergraduates work part time. Average annual earnings from campus work are $1320. The average financial indebtedness of a recent graduate was $16,000. ONU is a member of CSS. The FAFSA and the college's own financial statement are required. The fall application deadline is April 15.

International Students: There are 23 international students enrolled. The school actively recruits these students. They must score 550 on the written TOEFL or 213 on the electronic version, or score a minimum of 75% on the MELAB.

Computers: The mainframe is an IBM RISC System/6000. PCs for general use are located in all academic buildings and in 9 residence halls. PCs access the other computer hosts around campus via a network. Modem ports may be accessed through telephones on and off campus. The network is connected to OARnet, which provides contact to other research, academic, and commercial institutions connected to the global Internet. All students may access the system during building hours and 24 hours a day via modem. There are no time limits and no fees.

Graduates: In 2001, 475 bachelor's degrees were awarded. The most popular majors were pharmacy (24%), mechanical engineering (7%), and education (6%). In an average class, 66% graduate in 6 years. 342 companies recruited on campus in 2000-2001. Of the 2001 graduating class, 16% were enrolled in graduate school within 6 months of graduation and 84% were employed.

Admissions Contact: Karen P. Condeni, Vice President, Admissions. A video is available. E-mail: *admissions-ug@onu.edu*
Web: *www.onu.edu*

OHIO STATE UNIVERSITY SYSTEM

The Ohio State University System, established in 1870, is a land-grant university. It is governed by a board of trustees, publicly funded through the Ohio Board of Regents. The chief administrator is the president. As a comprehensive flagship institution, its mission includes teaching, research, and public service. The main campus is in Columbus, and regional campuses are located in Lima, Mansfield, Marion, and Newark, while the 2-year Agricultural Technical Institute is in Wooster. The undergraduate enrollment of the 5 4-year campuses is about 52,000, with some 4500 faculty members. There are more than 170 baccalaureate, 113 master's, and 88 doctoral programs offered through The Ohio State University. Profiles of the 4-year campuses are included in this section.

OHIO STATE UNIVERSITY AT LIMA

B-2

Lima, OH 45804 — **(419) 995-8396; Fax: (419) 995-8483**

Full-time: 405 men, 563 women	**Faculty:** 66; IIB, av$
Part-time: 96 men, 149 women	**Ph.D.s:** 91%
Graduate: 23 men, 120 women	**Student/Faculty:** 15 to 1
Year: quarters, summer session	**Tuition:** $3603 ($12,372)
Application Deadline: July 1	**Room & Board:** n/app
Freshman Class: n/av	**ACT:** required

NONCOMPETITIVE

Ohio State University at Lima, founded in 1960, is a regional commuter campus in the Ohio State University system. At Lima, students may earn a bachelor's degree in education, English, and psychology as well as 1 to 3 years of credit toward any degree conferred by OSU. The student may finish the degree at the Columbus campus or transfer to another institution. There are 19 undergraduate and 2 graduate schools. In addition to regional accreditation, Ohio State Lima has baccalaureate program accreditation with NCATE. The library contains 77,984 volumes, 9040 microform items, and 7715 audiovisual forms/CDs, and subscribes to 517 periodicals. Computerized library services include the card catalog, interlibrary loans, and database searching. Special learning facilities include a learning resource center and greenhouse and a geology museum. The 565-acre campus is in a suburban area 3 miles east of Lima. There are 7 buildings.

Student Life: All undergraduates are from Ohio. 95% are from public schools. 94% are white. 27% are Protestant; 25% Catholic; 10% claim no religious affiliation. The average age of freshmen is 19; all undergraduates, 24. 35% do not continue beyond their first year; 50% remain to graduate.

Housing: There are no residence halls. Alcohol is not permitted. All students may keep cars.

Activities: There are no fraternities or sororities. There are 12 groups on campus, including cheerleading, chess, chorus, computers, drama, ethnic, gay, honors, musical theater, religious, and student government. Popular campus events include May Week, Back to School Weiner Roast, and movies.

Sports: There are 3 intramural sports for men and 3 for women. Facilities include a gym and a weight room.

Disabled Students: All of the campus is accessible. Wheelchair ramps, elevators, special parking, specially equipped rest rooms, special class scheduling, and lowered drinking fountains are available.

Services: Counseling and information services are available, as is tutoring in most subjects. There is a reader service for the blind, and remedial math, reading, and writing. Developmental education, taped textbooks, oral testing, test readers and scribes, tape recorders, note takers, and a learning disabilities coordinator/counselor are also available.

Campus Safety and Security: Measures include 24-hour foot and vehicle patrol, self-defense education, escort service, and informal discussions. There are pamphlets/posters/films, emergency telephones, and lighted pathways/sidewalks.

Programs of Study: Ohio State Lima confers B.A., B.S., and B.S.Ed. degrees. Associate and master's degrees are also awarded. Bachelor's degrees are awarded in BUSINESS (business administration and management and hospitality management services), COMMUNICATIONS AND THE ARTS (English), EDUCATION (education), SOCIAL SCIENCE (family/consumer resource management, history, and psychology). Education is the strongest academically.

Required: To graduate, all students must complete 181 to 220 quarter hours, with a minimum GPA of 2.0, and fulfill the general education curriculum requirements.

Special: Students may cross-register with Lima Technical College. Work-study programs, nondegree study, pass/fail options, and credit for life, military, or work experience are available. There is 1 national honor society, a freshman honors program, and 4 departmental honors programs.

Faculty/Classroom: 70% of faculty are male; 30%, female. All teach undergraduates and 50% do research. No introductory courses are taught by graduate students. The average class size in an introductory lecture is 35; in a laboratory, 25; and in a regular course, 20.

Requirements: The ACT is required. In addition, candidates should be high school graduates with 4 years of English, 3 of math, 2 each of foreign language, science, and social studies, 1 of visual or performing arts, and 2 additional years of any of the above subjects. AP and CLEP credits are accepted.

Procedure: Freshmen are admitted to all sessions. Entrance exams should be taken in the spring of the junior year or early fall of the senior year. Applications should be filed by July 1 for fall entry, December 1 for winter entry, March 1 for spring entry, and June 1 for summer entry. The college accepts all in-state residents. Notification is sent on a rolling basis. The fall application fee was $30.

Transfer: 79 transfer students enrolled in a recent year. An overall GPA of 2.0 on all previous college work is required of applicants. 45 credits of 181 must be completed at Ohio State Lima.

Visiting: There are regularly scheduled orientations for prospective students. There are guides for informal visits and visitors may sit in on classes. To schedule a visit, contact the Admissions Office.

Financial Aid: In a recent year, 56% of all freshmen and 58% of continuing students received some form of financial aid. 45% of freshmen and 50% of continuing students received need-based aid. The average freshman award was $3160. Of that total, scholarships or need-based grants averaged $750 ($1800 maximum); loans averaged $1000 ($2625 maximum); and work contracts averaged $2000 ($4000 maximum). 95% of undergraduates work part time. Average annual earnings from campus work are $2000. The average financial indebtedness of a recent graduate was $10,000. The FAFSA is required. The fall application deadline is February 1.

International Students: They must score 500 on the written TOEFL and also take the ACT.

Computers: There are 77 PCs available for student use in labs, the library, and the career center. All students may access the system. There are no time limits and no fees.

Graduates: In a recent year, 31 bachelor's degrees were awarded. In an average class, 15% graduate in 4 years, 49% in 5 years, and 65% in 6 years.

Admissions Contact: Dr. Garlene Smithson, Director of Enrollment Services. E-mail: *penn.40@magnus.ohiostate.edu*
Web: *www.lima.ohio-state.edu*

OHIO STATE UNIVERSITY AT MANSFIELD C-2

Mansfield, OH 44906 (614) 292-9108

Full-time: 330 men, 450 women	**Faculty:** 42; IIB, av$
Part-time: 150 men, 300 women	**Ph.D.s:** 95%
Graduate: 20 men, 95 women	**Student/Faculty:** 19 to 1
Year: quarters, summer session	**Tuition:** $3606 ($12,372)
Application Deadline: open	**Room & Board:** n/app
Freshman Class: n/av	
SAT I or ACT: required	**NONCOMPETITIVE**

Ohio State University at Mansfield, founded in 1958, is a regional commuter campus of the Ohio State University system. At Mansfield, students may earn an undergraduate degree in elementary education. Figures given in the above capsule are approximate. There are 19 undergraduate schools and 1 graduate school. In addition to regional accreditation, OSU Mansfield has baccalaureate program accreditation with NCATE. The library contains 38,874 volumes, 17,559 microform items, and 2155 audiovisual forms/CDs, and subscribes to 410 periodicals. Special learning facilities include a learning resource center, art gallery, radio station, and TV station. The 600-acre campus is in a suburban area 2 miles from Mansfield. There are 7 buildings.

Student Life: 91% are white. The average age of freshmen is 19; all undergraduates, 24.

Housing: There are no residence halls. All students commute. Alcohol is not permitted.

Activities: There are no fraternities or sororities. There are 50 groups on campus, including chorale, drama, ethnic, film, musical theater, newspaper, radio and TV, religious, social, social service, student ambassadors, and student government. Popular campus events include May Day and Buckeye Week.

Sports: There are 12 intramural sports for men and 12 for women. Facilities include a gym and a weight room.

Disabled Students: All of the campus is accessible. Wheelchair ramps, elevators, special parking, specially equipped rest rooms, special class scheduling, lowered drinking fountains, and lowered telephones are available.

Services: Counseling and information services are available, as is tutoring in most subjects. There is a reader service for the blind, and remedial math, reading, and writing. Writing and math labs are provided. Books on tape, test readers and scribes, and priority scheduling are available.

Campus Safety and Security: Measures include 24-hour foot and vehicle patrol, self-defense education, escort service, and informal discussions. There are pamphlets/posters/films, emergency telephones, and lighted pathways/sidewalks.

Programs of Study: OSU Mansfield confers the B.S. in Elem.Ed. degree. Associate degrees are also awarded. Bachelor's degrees are awarded in EDUCATION (elementary).

Required: To graduate, all students must complete 181 to 220 quarter hours, with a minimum GPA of 2.0. General education curriculum requirements must be met.

Special: OSU Mansfield offers co-op programs, study abroad, internships, a general studies degree (no major), nondegree study, pass/fail options, and work-study programs. There are 3 national honor societies and a freshman honors program.

Faculty/Classroom: 92% teach undergraduates.

Requirements: The SAT I or ACT is required. In addition, the GED is accepted. OSU Mansfield follows an open admissions policy. AP and CLEP credits are accepted.

Procedure: Freshmen are admitted to all sessions. There are early admissions and deferred admissions plans. Check with the school for current application deadlines and fees.

Transfer: Applicants must present a minimum 2.0 GPA on previous university course work. 45 credits of 181 must be completed at OSU Mansfield.

Visiting: There are regularly scheduled orientations for prospective students. There are guides for informal visits and visitors may sit in on classes. To schedule a visit, contact Henry Thomas, Coordinator of Admissions.

Financial Aid: OSU Mansfield is a member of CSS. The FAFSA is required. Check with the school for current deadlines.

International Students: They must score 500 on the written TOEFL.

Computers: The mainframe is an Amdahl V8. There are 47 PCs in labs and the library. All students may access the system. There are no time limits and no fees.

Admissions Contact: Henry Thomas, Coordinator of Admissions.

OHIO STATE UNIVERSITY AT MARION C-3

Marion, OH 43302 (614) 389-6786, ext. 6337; Fax: (614) 292-5817

Full-time: none	**Faculty:** 26; IIB, av$
Part-time: none	**Ph.D.s:** 94%
Graduate: none	**Student/Faculty:** 18 to 1
Year: quarters, summer session	**Tuition:** $3606 ($10,818)
Application Deadline: open	**Room & Board:** n/app
Freshman Class: n/av	
SAT I or ACT: recommended	**NONCOMPETITIVE**

Ohio State University at Marion, founded in 1957, is a commuter campus of the Ohio State University system. At Marion, students may earn a bachelor's degree in elementary education English, accounting, business management, and psychology as well as 1 to 3 years of credit applicable to any other degree, including more than 170 academic programs, conferred by OSU, provided the program is completed at the main campus in Columbus. There are 3 graduate schools. In addition to regional accreditation, OSU Marion has baccalaureate program accreditation with NCATE. The library contains 44,000 volumes, 2906 microform items, and 8000 audiovisual forms/CDs, and subscribes to 322 periodicals. Computerized library services include the card catalog, interlibrary loans, and database searching. Special learning facilities include a learning resource center, art gallery, a natural reconstructed prairie site, a greenhouse, a psychology lab, and an early childhood education center. The 180-acre campus is in a rural area 45 miles north of Columbus. There are 6 buildings.

Student Life: 99% of undergraduates are from Ohio. Others are from 3 states. 98% are from public schools. 87% are white. The average age of freshmen is 20; all undergraduates, 24.

Housing: There are no residence halls. All of students commute. Alcohol is not permitted. All students may keep cars.

Activities: There are no fraternities or sororities. There are 8 groups on campus, including art, choir, chorale, chorus, dance, drama, ethnic, honors, jazz band, literary magazine, musical theater, newspaper, political, religious, social, social service, and student government. Popular campus events include Buckeye Week, May Day, and cultural arts events.

Sports: There are 4 intercollegiate sports for men and 3 for women, and 5 intramural sports for men and 5 for women. Facilities include a 740-seat gym, an outdoor fitness court, a weight room, a game room, a rock climbing wall, volleyball courts, and an exercise room.

Disabled Students: All of the campus is accessible. Wheelchair ramps, elevators, special parking, specially equipped rest rooms, lowered drinking fountains, and lowered telephones are available.

Services: Counseling and information services are available, as is tutoring in most subjects. There is remedial math, reading, and writing.

Campus Safety and Security: Measures include self-defense education, informal discussions, pamphlets/posters/films, and emergency telephones. There are lighted pathways/sidewalks.

Programs of Study: OSU Marion confers B.A., B.S., and B.S.Ed. Degrees. Associate and master's degrees are also awarded. Bachelor's degrees are awarded in BUSINESS (accounting), COMMUNICATIONS

AND THE ARTS (English), EDUCATION (elementary), SOCIAL SCIENCE (psychology). Elementary education and psychology are the strongest academically and have the largest enrollments.

Required: Between 181 and 220 credit hours are needed for graduation. Students must complete general education curriculum requirements and maintain a 2.0 GPA.

Special: OSU Marion offers cross-registration with Ohio State University Columbus, various co-op and work-study programs, nondegree study in continuing education, and pass/fail options. There is a freshman honors program.

Faculty/Classroom: 70% of faculty are male; 30%, female. All both teach and do research. The average class size in an introductory lecture is 18; in a laboratory, 24; and in a regular course, 25.

Admissions: 14 freshmen graduated first in their class in a recent year.

Requirements: The SAT I or ACT is recommended. In addition, OSU Marion follows an open admissions policy for in-state students. Applicants should be high school graduates with 4 units of English, 3 of math, 2 each of foreign language, history or social studies, and science, and 1 of art or music. Applications are accepted on-line at *www.marion.ohio-state.edu*. AP and CLEP credits are accepted.

Procedure: Freshmen are admitted to all sessions. Entrance exams should be taken before fall of the senior year in high school. Application deadlines are open.

Transfer: A GPA of 2.0 is required. 45 credits of 181 must be completed at OSU Marion.

Visiting: There are regularly scheduled orientations for prospective students. There are guides for informal visits and visitors may sit in on classes. To schedule a visit, contact the Admissions Office.

Financial Aid: In a recent year, 67% of all freshmen and 48% of continuing students received some form of financial aid. 9% of undergraduates work part time. Average annual earnings from campus work are $1500. The FAFSA is required. The fall application deadline is March 1.

International Students: There were 2 international students enrolled in a recent year. They must score 500 on the written TOEFL.

Computers: 174 PCs are available for student use in a computer center and in labs. All students may access the system. There are no time limits and no fees. It is strongly recommended that all students have a personal computer.

Admissions Contact: Mathieu Moreau, Director of Admissions. E-mail: *moreau.1@osu.edu* Web: *www.marion.ohio-state.edu*

OHIO STATE UNIVERSITY AT NEWARK C-3

Newark, OH 43055 (740) 292-4095
(800) 9NEWARK; Fax: (740) 366-9460

Full-time: 622 men, 902 women	**Faculty:** 59; IIB, av$
Part-time: 197 men, 358 women	**Ph.D.s:** 88%
Graduate: 7 men, 95 women	**Student/Faculty:** 26 to 1
Year: quarters, summer session	**Tuition:** $3603 ($12,372)
Application Deadline: July 1	**Room & Board:** $4500
Freshman Class: n/av	
SAT I Verbal/Math: 490/485	**ACT:** 19 **NONCOMPETITIVE**

The Ohio State University at Newark, founded in 1957, is a regional commuter campus of the Ohio State University system. At Newark, students may earn a bachelor's degree in elementary education, psychology, history, or English, as well as 1 to 3 years of credit applicable to any other degree, including 219 academic programs, conferred by OSU, provided the program is completed at the main campus in Columbus. The library contains 50,008 volumes, 17,465 microform items, and 3649 audiovisual forms/CDs, and subscribes to 427 periodicals. Computerized library services include the card catalog, interlibrary loans, and database searching. Special learning facilities include a learning resource center and art gallery. The 150-acre campus is in a suburban area 40 miles east of Columbus. Including residence halls, there are 5 buildings.

Student Life: 99% of undergraduates are from Ohio. Others are from 3 states and 1 foreign country. 92% are white. The average age of freshmen is 19; all undergraduates, 24. 65% do not continue beyond their first year.

Housing: 140 students can be accommodated in college housing, which includes coed on-campus apartments. On-campus housing is available on a first-come, first-served basis. 95% of students commute. Alcohol is not permitted. All students may keep cars.

Activities: There are no fraternities or sororities. There are 16 groups on campus, including cheerleading, choir, chorale, chorus, drama, ethnic, honors, professional, religious, social, social service, and student government. Popular campus events include Welcome Week, Spring Fling, and Community Service Programs.

Sports: There are 3 intercollegiate sports for men and 3 for women, and 7 intramural sports for men and 7 for women. Facilities include 2 weight rooms, a double gym, and a vita course.

Disabled Students: All of the campus is accessible. Wheelchair ramps, elevators, special parking, specially equipped rest rooms, special class scheduling, lowered drinking fountains, and lowered telephones are available.

Services: Counseling and information services are available, as is tutoring in every subject. There is a reader service for the blind and remedial math and writing. Books on tape, extended test time, readers, scribes, word processing assistance, and loans of specialized equipment are available.

Campus Safety and Security: Measures include 24-hour foot and vehicle patrol, self-defense education, escort service, and informal discussions. There are pamphlets/posters/films and emergency telephones.

Programs of Study: OSU Newark confers B.A., and B.S.Ed. degrees. Associate and master's degrees are also awarded. Bachelor's degrees are awarded in BUSINESS (business administration and management), COMMUNICATIONS AND THE ARTS (English), EDUCATION (elementary), SOCIAL SCIENCE (history and psychology). Elementary education, English, and psychology are the strongest academically. Elementary education is the largest.

Required: Between 181 and 220 credit hours are necessary for graduation, as is a GPA of 2.0. General education requirements include courses in English, math, natural sciences, social sciences, humanities, and foreign language.

Special: Co-op programs and internships are available in some majors, and study abroad in some departments. Cross-registration is possible with Central Ohio Technical College and HECC member schools, and there is work-study with Ohio State. B.A.-B.S. degrees are offered in elementary education, general business, English, history, and psychology. Dual and student-designed majors and nondegree study are possible, and pass/fail options are available. There is a freshman honors program.

Faculty/Classroom: 60% of faculty are male; 40%, female. All teach undergraduates. Graduate students teach 10% of introductory courses. The average class size in an introductory lecture is 35; in a laboratory, 24; and in a regular course, 24.

Admissions: The ACT scores for the 2001-2002 freshman class were: 77% below 21, 15% between 21 and 23, 4% between 24 and 26, 3% between 27 and 28, and 1% above 28. 3 freshmen graduated first in their class.

Requirements: The SAT I or ACT is recommended, for applicants who graduated from high school within the previous 3 years. Candidates should be high school graduates with 4 units of English, 3 of math, 2 each of science, foreign language, and history or social studies, and 1 of visual or performing arts. OSU Newark follows an open admissions policy for Ohio resident applicants. AP and CLEP credits are accepted. Applications are accepted on-line.

Procedure: Freshmen are admitted to all sessions. Entrance exams should be taken in the junior year of high school. Applications should be filed by July 1 for fall entry, December 1 for winter entry, March 1 for spring entry, and June 1 for summer entry, along with a $30 fee. The college accepts all in-state residents. Notification for regular decision is sent 6 weeks after the application is received.

Transfer: A GPA of 2.0 is required. 45 quarter credits of 181 to 220 must be completed at OSU Newark.

Visiting: There are regularly scheduled orientations for prospective students, including a campus tour, meeting with faculty, financial aid, and student services, placement test, class scheduling. There are guides for informal visits and visitors may sit in on classes and stay overnight. To schedule a visit, contact Admissions at (740) 366-9333 or *bruner.4@osu.edu*.

Financial Aid: In 2001-2002, 75% of all freshmen and 62% of continuing students received some form of financial aid. 67% of freshmen and 60% of continuing students received need-based aid. The average freshman award was $10,486. Of that total, scholarships or need-based grants averaged $2881 ($8766 maximum); loans averaged $4174 ($19,315 maximum); and work contracts averaged $2401 ($2500 maximum). 7% of undergraduates work part time. Average annual earnings from campus work are $1111. The average financial indebtedness of the 2001 graduate was $12,125. The FAFSA is required. The fall application deadline is April 1.

International Students: They must score 527 on the written TOEFL or take the MELAB.

Computers: The mainframe is an IBM. Some 400 PCs are available for academic use in computer labs. All students may access the system. There are no time limits and no fees.

Graduates: In 2001, 125 bachelor's degrees were awarded. The most popular majors were elementary education (50%), arts and sciences (40%), and business (10%). Of the 2000 graduating class, 22% were enrolled in graduate school within 6 months of graduation and 97% were employed.

Admissions Contact: Ann Donahue, Director of Enrollment. A video is available. E-mail: *donahue.5@osu.edu*

OHIO UNIVERSITY D-4

Athens, OH 45701-2979 **(740) 593-4100; Fax: (740) 593-0560**

Full-time: 7281 men, 8696 women	**Faculty:** 899; I, --$
Part-time: 474 men, 727 women	**Ph.D.s:** 83%
Graduate: 1522 men, 1463 women	**Student/Faculty:** 18 to 1
Year: quarters, summer session	**Tuition:** $5493 ($11,562)
Application Deadline: February 1	**Room & Board:** $6276
Freshman Class: 12,433 applied, 9747 accepted, 3778 enrolled	
SAT I Verbal/Math: 540/550	**ACT:** 23 **COMPETITIVE**

Ohio University, founded in 1804, is a public university offering programs in liberal and fine arts, aviation, business, communication, engineering, health science, osteopathic medicine, professional training, sciences, and teacher preparation. There are 9 undergraduate and 8 graduate schools. In addition to regional accreditation, Ohio has baccalaureate program accreditation with AACSB, ABET, ACEJMC, ADA, AHEA, CSWE, FIDER, NASAD, NASM, NCATE, and NLN. The 9 libraries contain 2,345,056 volumes, 3,095,313 microform items, and 373,567 audiovisual forms/CDs, and subscribe to 21,374 periodicals. Computerized library services include the card catalog, interlibrary loans, and database searching. Special learning facilities include a learning resource center, art gallery, radio station, TV station, quarterly magazine, accelerator lab, and hearing and speech clinic. The 1700-acre campus is in a small town 75 miles southeast of Columbus. Including residence halls, there are 201 buildings.

Student Life: 91% of undergraduates are from Ohio. Others are from 49 states, 100 foreign countries, and Canada. 82% are from public schools. 93% are white. 43% are Protestant; 30% Catholic. The average age of freshmen is 18; all undergraduates, 20. 15% do not continue beyond their first year; 69% remain to graduate.

Housing: 7528 students can be accommodated in college housing, which includes single-sex and coed dormitories, on-campus apartments, married-student housing, fraternity houses, and sorority houses. In addition, there are honors houses, language houses, and special-interest houses, international houses, quiet halls, and engineering, business, and communication halls. On-campus housing is guaranteed for all 4 years. 59% of students commute. Alcohol is not permitted. Upperclassmen may keep cars.

Activities: 12% of men belong to 20 national fraternities; 16% of women belong to 12 national sororities. There are 288 groups on campus, including art, band, cheerleading, chess, choir, chorale, chorus, computers, dance, drama, ethnic, film, forensics, gay, honors, international, jazz band, literary magazine, marching band, musical theater, newspaper, opera, orchestra, pep band, photography, political, professional, radio and TV, religious, social, social service, student government, symphony, and yearbook. Popular campus events include Parents Weekend, International Street Fair, and Communication Week.

Sports: There are 9 intercollegiate sports for men and 12 for women, and 38 intramural sports for men and 37 for women. Facilities include a recreation center, a football stadium, a basketball and convocation center, an aquatic center, an ice rink, tennis courts, a golf course, an intramural gym, a running track, a fitness and aerobics center, and a baseball field.

Disabled Students: 75% of the campus is accessible. Wheelchair ramps, elevators, special parking, specially equipped rest rooms, special class scheduling, lowered drinking fountains, and lowered telephones are available.

Services: Counseling and information services are available, as is tutoring in most subjects. There is a reader service for the blind, and remedial math, reading, and writing.

Campus Safety and Security: Measures include 24-hour foot and vehicle patrol, self-defense education, escort service, and pamphlets/posters/films. There are emergency telephones and lighted pathways/sidewalks.

Programs of Study: Ohio confers B.A., B.S., B.B.A., B.C.J., B.F.A., B.G.S., B.Mus., B.S.A., B.S.A.S., B.S.A.T., B.S.C., B.S.C.E., B.S.C.S., B.S.Ch.E., B.S.Ed., B.S.E.E., B.S.E.H., B.S.H., B.S.H.C.S., B.S.H.L.S., B.S.I.H., B.S.I.S.E., B.S.I.T., B.S.J., B.S.M.E., B.S.N., B.S.P.E., B.S.R.S., B.S.S., B.S.S.P.S., and B.S.V.C. degrees. Associate, master's, and doctoral degrees are also awarded. Bachelor's degrees are awarded in AGRICULTURE (plant science), BIOLOGICAL SCIENCE (biochemistry, biology/biological science, cell biology, environmental biology, marine biology, microbiology, molecular biology, nutrition, and wildlife biology), BUSINESS (accounting, banking and finance, business administration and management, business economics, business law, fashion merchandising, human resources, international business management, management information systems, management science, marketing management, marketing/retailing/merchandising, personnel management, recreation and leisure services, and sports management), COMMUNICATIONS AND THE ARTS (advertising, art, art history and appreciation, arts administration/management, broadcasting, ceramic art and design, classical languages, communications, creative writing, dance, dramatic arts, English, fiber/textiles/weaving, fine arts, French, German, graphic design, Greek (classical), journalism, Latin, linguistics, music, music history and appreciation, music performance, music theory and composition, painting, photography, piano/organ, printmaking, public relations, romance languages and literature, Russian, Spanish, speech/debate/rhetoric, telecommunications, video, visual and performing arts, and voice), COMPUTER AND PHYSICAL SCIENCE (actuarial science, applied mathematics, chemistry, computer science, earth science, geology, mathematics, physics, and quantitative methods), EDUCATION (art, athletic training, business, early childhood, education of the mentally handicapped, education of the multiple handicapped, education of the physically handicapped, elementary, health, home economics, industrial arts, middle school, music, science, and secondary), ENGINEERING AND ENVIRONMENTAL DESIGN (airline piloting and navigation, aviation administration/management, cartography, chemical engineering, civil engineering, computer engineering, electrical/electronics engineering, environmental science, industrial engineering, interior design, and mechanical engineering), HEALTH PROFESSIONS (clinical science, health care administration, hospital administration, nursing, predentistry, premedicine, preoptometry, prepharmacy, recreation therapy, speech pathology/audiology, and sports medicine), SOCIAL SCIENCE (African American studies, African studies, anthropology, child care/child and family studies, community services, criminal justice, dietetics, early childhood studies, economics, European studies, family and community services, family/consumer resource management, family/consumer studies, food production/management/services, food science, geography, history, international relations, international studies, Latin American studies, liberal arts/general studies, parks and recreation management, philosophy, political science/government, prelaw, psychology, public administration, social studies, social work, sociology, urban studies, and water resources). Communications, business, and engineering are the strongest academically. Journalism, biological sciences, human and consumer services are the largest.

Required: To graduate, students must complete 192 quarter hours, including 45 to 55 in the major, with a minimum GPA of 2.0 in most departments. General education requirements include 2 courses in English composition plus 30 quarter hours in social sciences, natural sciences, humanities, and third world cultures, a minimum of 1 course in math or quantitative skills, and a senior year interdisciplinary course.

Special: The university offers co-op programs in engineering and computer science, internships, study abroad, work-study programs, and an accelerated degree program for students in the Honors Tutorial College. Students may earn a B.A.-B.S. degree in most arts and sciences majors, or a general studies degree. Dual and student-designed majors, nondegree study, limited pass/fail options, and credit for life, military, or work experience are also available. There are 10 national honor societies, including Phi Beta Kappa and a freshman honors program.

Faculty/Classroom: 65% of faculty are male; 35%, female. All both teach and do research. Graduate students teach 15% of introductory courses. The average class size in an introductory lecture is 38; in a laboratory, 16; and in a regular course, 24.

Admissions: 78% of the 2001-2002 applicants were accepted. The SAT I scores for the 2001-2002 freshman class were: Verbal--24% below 500, 51% between 500 and 599, 22% between 600 and 700, and 3% above 700; Math--34% below 500, 49% between 500 and 599, 25% between 600 and 700, and 2% above 700. The ACT scores were 17% below 21, 34% between 21 and 23, 29% between 24 and 26, 10% between 27 and 28, and 10% above 28. 39% of the current freshmen were in the top fifth of their class; 77% were in the top two fifths. There were 8 National Merit finalists. 94 freshmen graduated first in their class.

Requirements: The SAT I or ACT is required. In addition, applicants should graduate with 4 units of English, 3 each of math, science, and social studies, 2 of foreign language, and 1 each of history and visual or performing arts. Ohio requires applicants to be in the upper 50% of their class. A GPA of 2.0 is required. AP and CLEP credits are accepted. Important factors in the admissions decision are advanced placement or honor courses, recommendations by school officials, and evidence of special talent.

Procedure: Freshmen are admitted to all sessions. Entrance exams should be taken in spring of the junior year or fall of the senior year. Applications should be filed by February 1 for fall entry, December 1 for winter entry, March 1 for spring entry, and May 1 for summer entry. Notification is sent on a rolling basis. The fall 2001 application fee was $40.

Transfer: 491 transfer students enrolled in 2001-2002. Transfer students are evaluated individually but must have a GPA of at least 2.5 and 30 quarter hours of transferable college credit. Business and journalism majors usually require a GPA of 3.0 or higher. 48 credits of 192 must be completed at Ohio.

Visiting: There are regularly scheduled orientations for prospective students, including information sessions and campus tours conducted daily Monday to Saturday. There are guides for informal visits and visitors may sit in on classes. To schedule a visit, contact the Admissions Office.

Financial Aid: In 2001-2002, 87% of all freshmen and 68% of continuing students received some form of financial aid. 37% of freshmen and 38% of continuing students received need-based aid. The average freshman award was $9568. Of that total, scholarships or need-based grants averaged $2696 ($18,238 maximum); loans averaged $7024 ($17,907 maximum); and work contracts averaged $1545 ($2060 maximum). 27% of undergraduates work part time. Average annual earnings from campus work are $1886. The average financial indebtedness of the 2001 graduate was $14,832. The FAFSA is required. The fall application deadline is October.

International Students: There are 248 international students enrolled. They must take the TOEFL or the MELAB.

Computers: The mainframes are an IBM Multiprise 3000, 3006 integrated Server, and a DEC ALPHA 3000. More than 6000 PCs are available to students in various campus locations. All students may access the system. There are no time limits and no fees.

Graduates: In 2001, 3754 bachelor's degrees were awarded. The most popular majors were interpersonal communication (9%), elementary education (8%), and journalism (5%). In an average class, 45% graduate in 4 years, 67% in 5 years, and 70% in 6 years. 574 companies recruited on campus in 2000-2001. Of the 2000 graduating class, 25% were enrolled in graduate school within 6 months of graduation and 81% were employed.

Admissions Contact: N. Kip Howard, Director of Admissions.
E-mail: *admissions@ohio.edu*

OHIO WESLEYAN UNIVERSITY

C-3

Delaware, OH 43015

(740) 368-3020
(800) 922-8953; Fax: (740) 368-3314

Full-time: 880 men, 965 women	**Faculty:** 126; IIB, av$
Part-time: 24 men, 17 women	**Ph.D.s:** 99%
Graduate: none	**Student/Faculty:** 15 to 1
Year: semesters, summer session	**Tuition:** $22,860
Application Deadline: March 1	**Room & Board:** $6810
Freshman Class: 2227 applied, 1763 accepted, 584 enrolled	
SAT I Verbal/Math: 605/615	**ACT:** 27 **VERY COMPETITIVE+**

Ohio Wesleyan University, founded in 1842, is an independent liberal arts institution affiliated with the United Methodist Church. In addition to regional accreditation, Ohio Wesleyan has baccalaureate program accreditation with NASM. The 5 libraries contain 367,386 volumes, 93,593 microform items, and 2021 audiovisual forms/CDs, and subscribe to 1127 periodicals. Computerized library services include the card catalog, interlibrary loans, and database searching. Special learning facilities include a learning resource center, art gallery, radio station, TV station, and astronomical observatory. The 200-acre campus is in a small town 20 miles north of Columbus. Including residence halls, there are 55 buildings.

Student Life: 51% of undergraduates are from out of state, mostly the Northeast. Others are from 44 states and 52 foreign countries. 75% are from public schools. 81% are white; 11%, foreign nationals. The average age of freshmen is 18; all undergraduates, 20. 33% do not continue beyond their first year; 74% remain to graduate.

Housing: 1720 students can be accommodated in college housing, which includes single-sex and coed dormitories and fraternity houses. In addition, there are honors houses, language houses, and a wide variety of special-interest houses. Students are invited to submit theme proposals to run a residential house for 8 to 20 students. On-campus housing is guaranteed for all 4 years. 82% of students live on campus; of those, 93% remain on campus on weekends. Upperclassmen may keep cars.

Activities: 44% of men belong to 11 national fraternities; 37% of women belong to 7 national sororities. There are 100 groups on campus, including art, cheerleading, choir, chorale, chorus, computers, dance, debate, drama, ethnic, gay, honors, international, jazz band, literary magazine, musical theater, newspaper, orchestra, pep band, photography, political, professional, radio and TV, religious, social, social service, student government, symphony, and yearbook. Popular campus events include National Colloquium, Fallfest, and Monett Weekend.

Sports: There are 11 intercollegiate sports for men and 11 for women, and 17 intramural sports for men and 17 for women. Facilities include a gym, a football and lacrosse stadium, field hockey and soccer fields, practice fields, a weight room, indoor and outdoor tracks, handball and squash courts, and an indoor pool.

Disabled Students: 60% of the campus is accessible. Wheelchair ramps, special parking, specially equipped rest rooms, and special class scheduling are available.

Services: Counseling and information services are available, as is tutoring in most subjects. Students with learning disabilities may receive special help in writing and organizational skills.

Campus Safety and Security: Measures include 24-hour foot and vehicle patrol, self-defense education, escort service, and informal discussions. There are pamphlets/posters/films, emergency telephones, and lighted pathways/sidewalks.

Programs of Study: Ohio Wesleyan confers B.A., B.F.A., and B.M. degrees. Bachelor's degrees are awarded in BIOLOGICAL SCIENCE (biochemistry, biology/biological science, botany, genetics, microbiology, and zoology), BUSINESS (accounting, business administration and management, business economics, and international business management), COMMUNICATIONS AND THE ARTS (broadcasting, dramatic arts, English, fine arts, French, German, journalism, music, and Spanish), COMPUTER AND PHYSICAL SCIENCE (chemistry, computer science, earth science, geology, mathematics, and physics), EDUCATION (art, early childhood, elementary, foreign languages, middle school, music, physical, science, and secondary), ENGINEERING AND ENVIRONMENTAL DESIGN (environmental science), HEALTH PROFESSIONS (predentistry, premedicine, and preveterinary science), SOCIAL SCIENCE (African American studies, anthropology, economics, geography, history, international relations, philosophy, political science/government, prelaw, psychology, religion, social science, sociology, and women's studies). Psychology, political science and prelaw, and biological sciences are the strongest academically. Economics and business, biological sciences, and political science and government are the largest.

Required: To graduate, most students are required to complete at least 34 units, including 3 units each of humanities/English, social sciences, and science/math and 1 unit of fine or performing arts. Each unit equals a full course and 3.75 semester hours. All students must also take 8 to 12 units in the major, maintain a minimum GPA of 2.0, and satisfy the university writing skills requirements.

Special: Cross-registration is available with members of the Great Lakes College Association. Students may study abroad in 20 countries or participate in a Washington semester, a departmental internship, or a work-study program. Students may also take dual majors in any combination, design their own majors, or pursue a 3-2 engineering degree in conjunction with 4 major universities. Nondegree study and pass/fail options are available. There are 23 national honor societies, including Phi Beta Kappa, and a freshman honors program.

Faculty/Classroom: 66% of faculty are male; 34%, female. All teach undergraduates and 90% also do research. The average class size in an introductory lecture is 22; in a laboratory, 15; and in a regular course, 12.

Admissions: 79% of the 2001-2002 applicants were accepted. The SAT I scores for the 2001-2002 freshman class were: Verbal--10% below 500, 33% between 500 and 599, 45% between 600 and 700, and 12% above 700; Math--9% below 500, 32% between 500 and 599, 45% between 600 and 700, and 14% above 700. The ACT scores were 27% between 21 and 23, 23% between 24 and 26, 27% between 27 and 28, and 23% above 28. 57% of the current freshmen were in the top fifth of their class; 79% were in the top two fifths.

Requirements: The SAT I or ACT is required. In addition, candidates for admission should complete a recommended 4 units of English and 3 each of math, foreign language, social studies, and science. A GPA of 2.5 is required. AP credits are accepted. Important factors in the admissions decision are advanced placement or honor courses, recommendations by school officials, and extracurricular activities record. Applications are accepted on-line and on computer disk using Common App, CollegeLink, CollegeView, and Apply.

Procedure: Freshmen are admitted fall and spring. Entrance exams should be taken in the spring of the junior year or the fall of the senior year. There are early decision and deferred admissions plans. Early decision applications should be filed by December 1; regular applications, by March 1 for fall entry and December 1 for spring entry. The fall 2001 application fee was $35. Notification of early decision is sent December 30; regular decision, on a rolling basis. A waiting list is an active part of the admissions procedure.

Transfer: 23 transfer students enrolled in a recent year. Applicants should have better than a 2.5 college GPA and at least 8 course units of credit. College transcripts and an essay are required, along with a statement of good standing from the previous institution. 18 units of 34 must be completed at Ohio Wesleyan.

Visiting: There are regularly scheduled orientations for prospective students. There are guides for informal visits and visitors may sit in on classes and stay overnight. To schedule a visit, contact the Office of Admission.

Financial Aid: In 2001-2002, 95% of all students received some form of financial aid. The average freshman award was $21,608. Ohio Wesleyan is a member of CSS. The FAFSA and the college's own financial statement are required. The fall application deadline is March 15.

International Students: In a recent year, there were 191 international students enrolled. The school actively recruits these students. They must score 550 on the written TOEFL and also take the SAT I or the ACT.

Computers: The mainframes consist of a DEC ALPHA 2100 and a DEC ALPHA 3000. More than 120 PCs are available for student use in 5 computer labs and in academic departments. Students with their own PCs may network the campus computer. All students may access the system 24 hours a day. There are no time limits and no fees.

Graduates: In a recent class, 316 bachelor's degrees were awarded. The most popular majors were social science and history (22%), business/marketing (21%), and psychology (10%). In an average class, 72% graduate in 4 years, 73% in 5 years, and 74% in 6 years. 20 companies recruited on campus in a recent year. Of a recent graduating class, 30% were enrolled in graduate school within 6 months of graduation.

Admissions Contact: Margaret Drugovich, Vice President of Admission and Financial Aid. E-mail: *owuadmit@cc.owu.edu*
Web: *www.owu.edu*

OTTERBEIN COLLEGE
Westerville, OH 43081 C-3
(614) 823-1500
(800) 488-8144; Fax: (614) 823-1200

Full-time: 724 men, 1194 women	**Faculty:** 143; IIB, av$
Part-time: 167 men, 466 women	**Ph.D.s:** 91%
Graduate: 170 men, 264 women	**Student/Faculty:** 13 to 1
Year: quarters, summer session	**Tuition:** $17,928
Application Deadline: March 1	**Room & Board:** $5511
Freshman Class: 2231 applied, 1891 accepted, 547 enrolled	
SAT I Verbal/Math: 540/534	**ACT:** 23 **COMPETITIVE**

Otterbein College, founded in 1847, is an independent institution affiliated with the United Methodist Church. The college provides a solid liberal arts education combined with professional/career preparation. In addition to regional accreditation, Otterbein College has baccalaureate program accreditation with NASM, NCATE, NLN, and CAAHEP. The library contains more than 300,000 books, microforms, periodicals, audio/video tapes/records/CDs. Computerized library services include the card catalog, interlibrary loans, and database searching. Special learning facilities include a learning resource center, art gallery, planetarium, radio station, TV station, an equine facility, and a theater. The 137-acre campus is in a suburban area 12 miles northeast of Columbus. Including residence halls, there are 28 buildings.

Student Life: 86% of undergraduates are from Ohio. Others are from 29 states and 28 foreign countries. 88% are white. 76% are Protestant; 22% Catholic; 12% claim no religious affiliation. The average age of freshmen is 18; all undergraduates, 22. 7% do not continue beyond their first year; 74% remain to graduate.

Housing: 1029 students can be accommodated in college housing, which includes single-sex dormitories, on-campus apartments, fraternity houses, and sorority houses. In addition, there are honors houses and special-interest houses. On-campus housing is guaranteed for the freshman year only and is available on a first-come, first-served basis. Priority is given to out-of-town students. 52% of students live on campus; of those, 55% remain on campus on weekends. Alcohol is not permitted. All students may keep cars.

Activities: 35% of men belong to 6 local fraternities and 1 national fraternity; 35% of women belong to 6 local sororities. There are 90 groups on campus, including art, band, cheerleading, choir, chorale, chorus, dance, debate, drama, drill team, equestrian, ethnic, forensics, gay, honors, international, intramurals, jazz band, literary magazine, marching band, musical theater, newspaper, opera, orchestra, pep band, photography, political, professional, radio and TV, religious, social, social service, student government, symphony, and yearbook. Popular campus events include Renaissance Festival, Winterfest, and Spring Unity Week.

Sports: There are 8 intercollegiate sports for men and 8 for women, and 15 intramural sports for men and 15 for women. Facilities include a basketball and volleyball center, a football stadium, a soccer field, a weight room, tennis courts, and a cross-country course.

Disabled Students: 81% of the campus is accessible. Wheelchair ramps, elevators, special parking, specially equipped rest rooms, special class scheduling, lowered drinking fountains, and lowered telephones are available.

Services: Counseling and information services are available, as is tutoring in every subject. There is a reader service for the blind, and remedial math, reading, and writing.

Campus Safety and Security: Measures include 24-hour foot and vehicle patrol, self-defense education, escort service, and informal discussions. There are pamphlets/posters/films, emergency telephones, lighted pathways/sidewalks, and 24-hour locked dormitory facilities.

Programs of Study: Otterbein College confers B.A., B.S., B.F.A., B.M., B.Mus.Ed., B.S.E., and B.S.N. degrees. Master's degrees are also awarded. Bachelor's degrees are awarded in AGRICULTURE (equine science), BIOLOGICAL SCIENCE (biochemistry, life science, and molecular biology), BUSINESS (accounting and business administration and management), COMMUNICATIONS AND THE ARTS (art, broadcasting, communications, dramatic arts, English, French, journalism, music, musical theater, public relations, Spanish, speech/debate/rhetoric, and visual and performing arts), COMPUTER AND PHYSICAL SCIENCE (chemistry, computer science, mathematics, and physics), EDUCATION (athletic training, elementary, health, music, and physical), HEALTH PROFESSIONS (nursing), SOCIAL SCIENCE (economics, history, international studies, liberal arts/general studies, philosophy, political science/government, psychology, religion, and sociology). Life science, chemistry, and athletic training are the strongest academically. Business, education, and communications are the largest.

Required: All students must complete 180 quarter hours, including 50 to 100 in the major, with a minimum GPA of 2.0. The liberal arts core includes 15 hours in English composition and literature, 10 hours each in natural and social sciences, 5 hours each in religion/philosophy, fine arts, and non-Western cultures, and 3 in phys ed.

Special: Students may cross-register with members of the Higher Education Council of Columbus, study abroad in 9 countries, have an internship in most majors, or participate in a Washington semester. B.A.-B.S. degrees, 3-2 engineering degrees with Case Western Reserve and Washington universities, credit for military experience, student-designed majors, nondegree study, and limited pass/fail options are also available. There are 9 national honor societies and a freshman honors program.

Faculty/Classroom: 52% of faculty are male; 48%, female. All teach undergraduates. No introductory courses are taught by graduate students. The average class size in an introductory lecture is 20; in a laboratory, 10; and in a regular course, 20.

Admissions: 85% of the 2001-2002 applicants were accepted. The SAT I scores for the 2001-2002 freshman class were: Verbal--27% below 500, 45% between 500 and 599, 25% between 600 and 700, and 3% above 700; Math--32% below 500, 41% between 500 and 599, 26% between 600 and 700, and 1% above 700. The ACT scores were 34% below 21, 25% between 21 and 23, 25% between 24 and 26, 10% between 27 and 28, and 6% above 28. 41% of the current freshmen were in the top fifth of their class.

Requirements: The SAT I or ACT is required. In addition, applicants should be graduates of an accredited secondary school. The recommended preparatory program includes 4 units of English, 3 to 4 units each of math, science, and social studies, 2 to 3 units of foreign language, and 1 to 2 units of performing arts. A high school GPA of 2.5 or better is recommended. Otterbein College requires applicants to be in the upper 50% of their class. A GPA of 2.5 is required. AP and CLEP credits are accepted. Important factors in the admissions decision are advanced placement or honor courses, evidence of special talent, and leadership record. Applications are accepted on-line at the school's web site.

Procedure: Freshmen are admitted to all sessions. Entrance exams should be taken in the spring of the junior year. There is a deferred admissions plan. Applications should be filed by March 1 for fall entry, along with a $25 fee. Notification is sent on a rolling basis.

Transfer: 84 transfer students enrolled in 2001-2002. Applicants should present a college GPA of 2.5. 60 credits of 180 must be completed at Otterbein College.

Visiting: There are regularly scheduled orientations for prospective students, including a conference with an admissions counselor, and a campus tour. There are guides for informal visits and visitors may sit in on classes and stay overnight. To schedule a visit, contact Debbie Jamieson at *uotterb@otterbein.edu*.

Financial Aid: In 2001-2002, 76% of all freshmen and 78% of continuing students received some form of financial aid. 76% of freshmen and 78% of continuing students received need-based aid. The average freshman award was $13,739. 28% of undergraduates work part time. Average annual earnings from campus work are $1500. The FAFSA is required. The fall application deadline is April 1.

International Students: There are 56 international students enrolled. The school actively recruits these students. They must score 500 on the written TOEFL and also take the SAT I or the ACT.

Computers: The mainframe is a DEC VAX/VMS. Terminals and PCs are available in several campus locations. All students may access the system. There are no time limits and no fees.

Graduates: In an average class, 4% graduate in 3 years, 80% in 4 years, and 88% in 5 years. Of the 2000 graduating class, 95% were employed within 6 months of graduation.

Admissions Contact: Dr. Cass Johnson, Director of Admissions.
E-mail: *uotterb@otterbein.edu* Web: *www.otterbein.edu*

SHAWNEE STATE UNIVERSITY
Portsmouth, OH 45662 C-5
(740) 351-4778
(800) 959-2778; Fax: (740) 351-3111

Full-time: 1067 men, 1611 women	**Faculty:** 113; IIB, -$
Part-time: 204 men, 482 women	**Ph.D.s:** 48%
Graduate: none	**Student/Faculty:** 24 to 1
Year: quarters, summer session	**Tuition:** $3402 ($5994)
Application Deadline: open	**Room & Board:** $5232
Freshman Class: 2184 applied, 2184 accepted, 683 enrolled	
ACT: 19	**NONCOMPETITIVE**

Shawnee State University, founded in 1975, is a public institution offering programs in arts and sciences, business, engineering, health sciences, and education. There are 2 undergraduate schools. In addition to regional accreditation, Shawnee State has baccalaureate program accreditation with ACBSP and ADA. The library contains 136,212 volumes, 39,964 microform items, and 19,546 audiovisual forms/CDs, and subscribes to 4792 periodicals. Computerized library services include interlibrary loans and database searching. Special learning facilities include a learning resource center and planetarium. The 50-acre campus is in a small town 90 miles south of Columbus. Including residence halls, there are 27 buildings.

Student Life: 91% of undergraduates are from Ohio. Others are from 9 states, 5 foreign countries, and Canada. 88% are white. The average age of freshmen is 23; all undergraduates, 27. 46% do not continue beyond their first year; 54% remain to graduate.

Housing: 283 students can be accommodated in college housing, which includes single-sex on-campus apartments. On-campus housing is available on a first-come, first-served basis. 90% of students commute. Alcohol is not permitted. All students may keep cars.

Activities: 5% of men belong to 3 national fraternities; 3% of women belong to 2 local sororities. There are 5 groups on campus, including art, cheerleading, choir, chorus, computers, ethnic, honors, international, literary magazine, newspaper, pep band, photography, professional, social, and student government. Popular campus events include Founders Day.

Sports: There are 5 intercollegiate sports for men and 5 for women, and 19 intramural sports for men and 19 for women. Facilities include an activities center with basketball and volleyball courts; a sports center with racquetball courts, Nautilus and weight rooms, a pool, a sauna, and a whirlpool; and a soccer field.

Disabled Students: All of the campus is accessible. Wheelchair ramps, elevators, special parking, specially equipped rest rooms, lowered drinking fountains, and lowered telephones are available.

Services: Counseling and information services are available, as is tutoring in most subjects. There is a reader service for the blind, and remedial math, reading, and writing.

Campus Safety and Security: Measures include 24-hour foot and vehicle patrol, pamphlets/posters/films, emergency telephones, and lighted pathways/sidewalks.

Programs of Study: Shawnee State confers B.A., B.S., B.F.A., B.I.S., and B.S.N. degrees. Associate degrees are also awarded. Bachelor's degrees are awarded in BIOLOGICAL SCIENCE (biology/biological science), BUSINESS (business administration and management), COMMUNICATIONS AND THE ARTS (English and fine arts), COMPUTER AND PHYSICAL SCIENCE (chemistry, mathematics, natural sciences, and physical sciences), EDUCATION (education and elementary), ENGINEERING AND ENVIRONMENTAL DESIGN (computer technology, environmental engineering technology, and plastics technology), HEALTH PROFESSIONS (medical laboratory science, nursing, occupational therapy, premedicine, and sports medicine), SOCIAL SCIENCE (history, humanities, interdisciplinary studies, international relations, prelaw, psychology, social science, and sociology). Engineering technologies is the strongest academically. Early childhood education is the largest.

Required: To graduate, students must complete a general education program and a senior seminar. A total of 180 to 190 quarter credit hours, with a 2.0 GPA in all course work and in the major, is required.

Special: Study abroad in China, Germany, and Spain, and internships and student-designed programs are available. There is 1 national honor society and a freshman honors program.

Faculty/Classroom: 56% of faculty are male; 44%, female. All teach undergraduates. The average class size in an introductory lecture is 38; in a laboratory, 10; and in a regular course, 25.

Admissions: All of the 2001-2002 applicants were accepted. The school has an open admissions policy. The ACT scores for the 2001-2002 freshman class were: 62% below 21, 23% between 21 and 23, 12% between 24 and 26, and 2% between 27 and 28.

Requirements: Applicants must graduate from an accredited high school or have a GED. Applications are accepted on-line and are available at *www.shawnee.edu*. AP and CLEP credits are accepted.

Procedure: Freshmen are admitted to all sessions. Entrance exams should be taken in late spring or early summer. Application deadlines are open.

Transfer: 159 transfer students enrolled in 2001-2002. A completed application and college and high school transcripts sent directly to SSU from previous institutions are required. 45 credits of 180 must be completed at Shawnee State.

Visiting: There are regularly scheduled orientations for prospective students, including fall and spring visitation days, which consist of small sessions with deans and faculty, orientation by student affairs offices, and tours with current college students. There are guides for informal visits and visitors may sit in on classes. To schedule a visit, contact the Office of Admissions.

Financial Aid: The FAFSA is required. The fall application deadline is March 1.

International Students: There are 14 international students enrolled. The school actively recruits these students. They must score 500 on the written TOEFL and also take the college's own test.

Computers: The mainframe is a Compaq ALPHA 4/275. PCs are available in the College of Business and College of Engineering Technologies, Internet Café, and library. All students may access the system. There are no time limits and no fees.

Graduates: In 2001, 278 bachelor's degrees were awarded. The most popular majors were social sciences (12%), business administration (9%), and general studies (7%). In an average class, 9% graduate in 3 years, 19% in 4 years, 30% in 5 years, and 35% in 6 years. 200 companies recruited on campus in 2000-2001.

Admissions Contact: Bob Trusz, Director of Admissions and Retention. A video is available. E-mail: *To_SSU@shawnee.edu*
Web: *www.shawnee.edu*

THE OHIO STATE UNIVERSITY — C-3

Columbus, OH 43210-1200 **(614) 292-3980; Fax: (614) 292-4818**

Full-time: 16,115 men, 15,125 women	**Faculty:** 2713; I, av$
Part-time: 2515 men, 2294 women	**Ph.D.s:** 99%
Graduate: 4271 men, 5181 women	**Student/Faculty:** 12 to 1
Year: quarters, summer session	**Tuition:** $4788 ($13,554)
Application Deadline: February 15	**Room & Board:** $6031
Freshman Class: 19,968 applied, 14,501 accepted, 5996 enrolled	
SAT I Verbal/Math: 575/594	**ACT:** 25 **VERY COMPETITIVE**

Ohio State University, founded in 1870, is a public land-grant institution offering programs in agriculture/natural resources, arts and sciences, business, education, architecture/engineering, nursing, pharmacy, social work, dental hygiene, and human ecology. There are 5 other campuses. There are 14 undergraduate schools and 1 graduate school. In addition to regional accreditation, Ohio State has baccalaureate program accreditation with AACSB, ABET, ACEJMC, ACPE, ADA, APTA, ASLA, CSAB, FIDER, NAAB, NASAD, NASM, NCATE, and NLN. The 18 libraries contain 5,491,498 volumes, 5,316,219 microform items, and 35,969 audiovisual forms/CDs, and subscribe to 42,915 periodicals. Computerized library services include the card catalog, interlibrary loans, and database searching. Special learning facilities include a learning resource center, art gallery, planetarium, radio station, TV station, Museum of Biological Diversity, The John Glenn Institute for Public Service and Public Policy, and the Cartoon Research Library. The 3411-acre campus is in an urban area 2 miles north of downtown Columbus. Including residence halls, there are 421 buildings.

Student Life: 86% of undergraduates are from Ohio. Others are from 49 states, 89 foreign countries, and Canada. 87% are from public schools. 79% are white. 44% are Protestant; 31% Catholic; 22% Buddhist, Islamic; 17% claim no religious affiliation. The average age of freshmen is 18; all undergraduates, 21. 14% do not continue beyond their first year; 56% remain to graduate.

Housing: 9000 students can be accommodated in college housing, which includes single-sex and coed dormitories, on-campus apartments, off-campus apartments, married-student housing, and international houses. In addition, there are honors houses and special-interest houses. On-campus housing is guaranteed for the freshman year only and is available on a first-come, first-served basis. 76% of students commute. All students may keep cars.

Activities: 5% of men belong to 34 national fraternities; 6% of women belong to 21 national sororities. There are 600 groups on campus, including art, band, cheerleading, chess, choir, chorale, chorus, computers, dance, debate, drama, drill team, ethnic, film, forensics, gay, honors, international, jazz band, literary magazine, marching band, musical theater, newspaper, orchestra, pep band, photography, political, professional, radio and TV, religious, social, social service, student government, symphony, and yearbook. Popular campus events include United Black World Month, Medieval and Renaissance Festival, and Greek Week.

Sports: There are 18 intercollegiate sports for men and 19 for women, and 55 intramural sports for men and 55 for women. Facilities include a 100,000-seat football stadium, a 17,500-21,000-seat multipurpose event center, a 13,000-seat arena, archery, running track, sand volleyball courts, a cricket field, an inline hockey rink, weight rooms, swimming pools, basketball, volleyball, and racquetball courts, field houses for tennis, volleyball, basketball, soccer, baseball, and softball fields.

Disabled Students: 99% of the campus is accessible. Wheelchair ramps, elevators, special parking, specially equipped rest rooms, special class scheduling, lowered drinking fountains, lowered telephones, accessible housing, and adaptive transportation are available.

Services: Counseling and information services are available, as is tutoring in most subjects. There is a reader service for the blind, and remedial math, reading, and writing.

Campus Safety and Security: Measures include 24-hour foot and vehicle patrol, self-defense education, escort service, and shuttle buses. There are informal discussions, pamphlets/posters/films, emergency telephones, and lighted pathways/sidewalks.

Programs of Study: Ohio State confers B.A., B.S., B.F.A., B.Mus., and B.Mus.Ed. degrees. Master's and doctoral degrees are also awarded. Bachelor's degrees are awarded in AGRICULTURE (agricultural economics, animal science, fishing and fisheries, forestry and related sciences, natural resource management, and plant science), BIOLOGICAL SCIENCE (biochemistry, biology/biological science, entomology, plant physiology, and zoology), BUSINESS (accounting, business economics, hospitality management services, human resources, international business management, management information systems, marketing and distribution, real estate, and transportation management), COMMUNICATIONS AND THE ARTS (Arabic, art, Chinese, classics, communications, dance, English, German, Hebrew, industrial design, Italian, Japanese, jazz, journalism, linguistics, music, music history and appreciation, music performance, music theory and composition, Portuguese, Russian, and Spanish), COMPUTER AND PHYSICAL SCIENCE (actuarial science, astronomy, chemistry, computer science, geology, information sciences and systems, mathematics, and physics), EDUCATION (agricultural, art, environmental, and music), ENGINEERING AND ENVIRONMENTAL DESIGN (aeronautical engineering, architecture, ceramic engineering, chemical engineering, civil engineering, computer engineering, electrical/electronics engineering, engineering physics, environmental science, industrial engineering, landscape architecture/design, materials engineering, materials science, mechanical engineering, and metallurgical engineering), HEALTH PROFESSIONS (dental hygiene, medical technology, nursing, occupational therapy, physical therapy, radiograph medical technology, and respiratory therapy), SOCIAL SCIENCE (African American studies, anthropology, clothing and textiles management/production/services, criminology, economics, geography, history, human development, human ecology, industrial and organizational psychology, international studies, Islamic studies, Judaic studies, medieval studies, philosophy, political science/government, psychology, social work, sociology, and women's studies). Engineering, business, and social and behavioral sciences are the largest.

Required: To graduate, students must complete 181 to 220 quarter hours, including 40 to 60 in the major, with a minimum GPA of 2.0. The core curriculum consists of courses in writing skills, quantitative and logical skills, foreign language, the sciences, math, and the arts. Distribution requirements include 4 to 5 courses in natural science, 3 in social science, and 5 in arts and humanities.

Special: Students may cross-register with all central Ohio colleges. OSU offers internships, co-op programs, extensive study abroad, work-study programs, dual and student-designed majors, a general degree, a B.A.-B.S. degree, credit by examination, nondegree study, and pass/fail options. There are 22 national honor societies, including Phi Beta Kappa, a freshman honors program, and 20 departmental honors programs.

Faculty/Classroom: 68% of faculty are male; 32%, female. Graduate students teach 40% of introductory courses. The average class size in an introductory lecture is 37; in a laboratory, 16; and in a regular course, 29.

Admissions: 73% of the applicants in a recent year were accepted. The SAT I scores for a recent freshman class were: Verbal--17% below 500, 41% between 500 and 599, 35% between 600 and 700, and 7% above 700; Math--13% below 500, 36% between 500 and 599, 41% between 600 and 700, and 10% above 700. The ACT scores were 10% below 21, 21% between 21 and 23, 23% between 24 and 26, 17% between 27 and 28, and 19% above 28. 57% of the current freshmen were in the top fifth of their class; 84% were in the top two fifths. 245 freshmen graduated first in their class.

Requirements: The SAT I or ACT is required. In addition, applicants must complete high school with at least 18 academic credits, including 4 in English, 3 in math, 2 each in foreign language, science, and history/social studies, and 1 in art or music. The GED is accepted. Students may apply on-line at the school's web site. AP and CLEP credits are accepted. Important factors in the admissions decision are advanced placement or honor courses, evidence of special talent, and geographic diversity.

Procedure: Freshmen are admitted to all sessions. Entrance exams should be taken by October of the senior year. Applications should be filed by February 15 for fall entry, November 1 for winter entry, February 1 for spring entry, and February 15 for summer entry, along with a $30 fee. Notification is sent on a rolling basis from October 15 to March 15. 3% of all applicants are on a waiting list; 32 were accepted in a recent year.

Transfer: 2324 transfer students enrolled in a recent year. High school graduates with 45 hours of college credit and a minimum GPA of 2.0 are admitted for transfer. Those with fewer than 45 hours apply on a competitive basis. 45 credits of 181 must be completed at Ohio State.

Visiting: There are regularly scheduled orientations for prospective students, including campus tours, placement tests, course scheduling, and special sessions designed for parents. There are guides for informal visits and visitors may sit in on classes and stay overnight. To schedule a visit, contact the Student Visitor Center.

Financial Aid: In a recent year, 91% of all freshmen and 67% of continuing students received some form of financial aid. 42% of freshmen and 41% of continuing students received need-based aid. The average freshman award was $5677. Of that total, scholarships or need-based grants averaged $3711 ($13,542 maximum); loans averaged $2759 ($10,345 maximum); and work contracts averaged $2356 ($4000 maximum). 28% of undergraduates work part time. Average annual earnings from campus work are $1557. The average financial indebtedness of a recent graduate was $15,482. The FAFSA is required. The fall application deadline is February 15.

International Students: There were 1537 international students enrolled in a recent year. They must score 527 on the written TOEFL or 197 on the electronic version or take the MELAB.

Computers: The mainframes are an IBM 3081 and 4381, an HP 9000, HP3000, and a DEC VAX 20. More than 1000 PCs are available to students in the main computer center and in libraries, residence halls, labs, and student centers. Students may also connect through university-supplied software from their homes. All students may access the system 24 hours a day. There are no time limits and no fees. It is strongly recommended that all students have a personal computer.

Graduates: In a recent year, 7306 bachelor's degrees were awarded. In an average class, 49% graduate in 5 years, and 56% in 6 years. More than 100 companies recruited on campus in a recent year.

Admissions Contact: Admissions Information Center Representative. A video is available. E-mail: *askabuckeye@osu.edu*
Web: *www.osu.edu*

TIFFIN UNIVERSITY

Tiffin, OH 44883 — C-2
(419) 447-6443
(800) 968-6446; Fax: (419) 443-5006

Full-time: 482 men, 462 women	**Faculty:** 44; IIB, av$
Part-time: 130 men, 305 women	**Ph.D.s:** 65%
Graduate: 111 men, 88 women	**Student/Faculty:** 21 to 1
Year: semesters, summer session	**Tuition:** $11,850
Application Deadline: open	**Room & Board:** $5400
Freshman Class: 1354 applied, 1052 accepted, 267 enrolled	
SAT I Verbal/Math: 520/480	**ACT:** 19 **COMPETITIVE**

Tiffin University, established in 1888, is a private institution emphasizing degree programs in business, liberal studies, and criminal justice. There are 3 undergraduate and 2 graduate schools. In addition to regional accreditation, TU has baccalaureate program accreditation with ACBSP. The library contains 28,700 volumes, 32,500 microform items, and 817 audiovisual forms/CDs, and subscribes to 255 periodicals. Computerized library services include the card catalog, interlibrary loans, and database searching. Special learning facilities include a learning resource center, art gallery, and the Ohio Council on Holocaust Education Information Center. The 103-acre campus is in a small town 90 miles north of Columbus and 60 miles south of Toledo. Including residence halls, there are 27 buildings.

Student Life: 85% of undergraduates are from Ohio. Others are from 24 states, 20 foreign countries, and Canada. 78% are from public schools. 85% are white. The average age of freshmen is 18; all undergraduates, 24. 45% do not continue beyond their first year; 38% remain to graduate.

Housing: 450 students can be accommodated in college housing, which includes single-sex and coed dormitories, on-campus apartments, off-campus apartments, fraternity houses, and sorority houses. In addition, there are honors houses. There is also student development housing, bringing together students who are involved in a number of activities and maintain a 3.2 GPA. On-campus housing is guaranteed for all 4 years. 50% of students live on campus; of those, 60% remain on campus on weekends. All students may keep cars.

Activities: 3% of men belong to 1 local and 1 national fraternity; 2% of women belong to 1 local and 1 national sorority. There are 16 groups on campus, including band, cheerleading, choir, chorale, chorus, computers, drama, drill team, ethnic, gay, honors, international, jazz band, marching band, newspaper, pep band, political, professional, religious, social, social service, student government, and vocal jazz. Popular campus events include Spring Fest, International Students Fair, and Little Siblings Weekend.

Sports: There are 8 intercollegiate sports for men and 8 for women, and 7 intramural sports for men and 7 for women. Facilities include a student center gym, indoor batting cages, a weight room, tennis courts, and soccer, baseball, and softball fields.

Disabled Students: 90% of the campus is accessible. Wheelchair ramps, elevators, special parking, specially equipped rest rooms, special class scheduling, lowered drinking fountains, and lowered telephones are available.

Services: Counseling and information services are available, as is tutoring in most subjects. There is a reader service for the blind, and remedial math, reading, and writing.

Campus Safety and Security: Measures include self-defense education, escort service, informal discussions, and pamphlets/posters/films. There are lighted pathways/sidewalks.

Programs of Study: TU confers B.A., B.B.A., and B.C.J. degrees. Associate and master's degrees are also awarded. Bachelor's degrees are awarded in BUSINESS (accounting, banking and finance, business administration and management, hotel/motel and restaurant management, marketing/retailing/merchandising, and personnel management), COMPUTER AND PHYSICAL SCIENCE (information sciences and systems), SOCIAL SCIENCE (corrections, criminology, international studies, law enforcement and corrections, and liberal arts/general studies). Accounting and forensic psychology are the strongest academically. Accounting and management are the largest.

Required: To graduate, all students must complete 130 to 133 semester hours, including 51 to 54 in the major, with a GPA of 2.0 cumulatively and 2.5 in the major. The 61-semester-hour integrated core curriculum includes courses in computer systems, speech and writing, math and statistics, economics, psychology, sociology, history, literature, philosophy, and cultural heritage.

Special: Internships are recommended for all students. An accelerated degree program in finance, work-study programs, a junior semester in

England, nondegree study, and pass/fail options are also available. There is 1 national honor society on campus.

Faculty/Classroom: 63% of faculty are male; 36%, female. All teach undergraduates and 37% do research. No introductory courses are taught by graduate students. The average class size in an introductory lecture is 28 and in a regular course, 19.

Admissions: 78% of the 2001-2002 applicants were accepted. The SAT I scores for the 2001-2002 freshman class were: Verbal--82% below 500, 17% between 500 and 599, and 5% between 600 and 700; Math--82% below 500, 17% between 500 and 599, and 5% between 600 and 700. The ACT scores were 59% below 21, 18% between 21 and 23, 8% between 24 and 26, and 3% between 27 and 28. 18% of the current freshmen were in the top fifth of their class; 43% were in the top two fifths.

Requirements: The SAT I or ACT is required. In addition, candidates should be graduates of an accredited secondary school, with 4 units of English, 3 of math, 2 each of science and social studies, and 5 of electives. The GED is accepted. An interview is recommended. A GPA of 2.5 is required. AP credits are accepted. Important factors in the admissions decision are leadership record, recommendations by school officials, and extracurricular activities record. Applications are accepted on-line.

Procedure: Freshmen are admitted to all sessions. Application deadlines are open. The fall application fee was $20.

Transfer: 24 transfer students enrolled in 2001-2002. Applicants with 15 or more hours of credit must have a minimum college GPA of 2.0; applicants with fewer hours of credit need a minimum GPA of 1.8 to enter in good standing. The SAT I or ACT and an interview are recommended. 30 credits of 130 must be completed at TU.

Visiting: There are regularly scheduled orientations for prospective students, consisting of placement testing, tours of the campus, lunch with advisers, and an appointment with an individual adviser to schedule fall classes. There are guides for informal visits and visitors may sit in on classes and stay overnight. To schedule a visit, contact the Admissions Office at (419) 448-3423 or (800) 968-6446.

Financial Aid: The average freshman award was $10,000. Average annual earnings from campus work are $1000. The FAFSA is required. The fall application deadline is August 1.

International Students: There are 32 international students enrolled. The school actively recruits these students. They must score 500 on the written TOEFL.

Computers: The computer system operates on a Novell Network, with 60 PCs distributed among 3 computer labs in classroom buildings. All students may access the system. There are no time limits. The fee is $35.

Graduates: In 2001, 231 bachelor's degrees were awarded. The most popular majors were management (45%), accounting (13%), and forensic psychology (11%). In an average class, 27% graduate in 4 years, 32% in 5 years, and 35% in 6 years. 8 companies recruited on campus in 2000-2001. Of a recent graduating class, 14% were enrolled in graduate school within 6 months of graduation and 94% were employed.

Admissions Contact: Darby M. Roggow, Director of Admissions. A video is available. E-mail: *droogow@tiffin.edu* Web: *www.tiffin.edu*

UNION INSTITUTE AND UNIVERSITY

Cincinnati, OH 45206-1925 — A-5

(513) 861-6400

(800)486-3116; Fax: (513) 861-0779

Full-time: 150 men, 255 women	**Faculty:** 28
Part-time: 105 men, 170 women	**Ph.D.s:** 95%
Graduate: 485 men, 695 women	**Student/Faculty:** 14 to 1
Year: semesters, summer session	**Tuition:** $6912
Application Deadline: October 1	**Room & Board:** n/app
Freshman Class: n/av	
SAT I or ACT: not required	**SPECIAL**

The Union Institute, established in 1964, serves the academic needs of mature working adults seeking to earn the B.A. or B.S. degree. In addition to the main Cincinnati campus, there are learning centers in Miami, Los Angeles, San Diego, and Sacramento. The Institute's Center for Distance Learning enables individuals to earn their degrees through a computer-based educational delivery system. Figures in above capsule are approximate. The library contains 3910 volumes and 10 audiovisual forms/CDs, and subscribes to 34 periodicals. Computerized library services include database searching. The campus is in an urban area 2 miles from downtown Cincinnati. There are 3 buildings.

Student Life: 92% of undergraduates are from Ohio. Others are from 22 states, 3 foreign countries, and Canada. 44% are white; 40% African American; 12% Hispanic. The average age of freshmen is 37; all undergraduates, 38. 33% do not continue beyond their first year.

Housing: There are no residence halls. Alcohol is not permitted. All students may keep cars.

Activities: There are no fraternities or sororities. Popular campus events include Commencement.

Sports: There is no sports program at Union.

Disabled Students: All of the campus is accessible. Wheelchair ramps, elevators, special parking, specially equipped rest rooms, lowered drinking fountains, lowered telephones, and audio/visual fire alarms are available.

Campus Safety and Security: Measures include lighted pathways/sidewalks and a security guard during operating hours.

Programs of Study: Union confers B.A. and B.S. degrees. Doctoral degrees are also awarded. Criminal justice studies, business, and education are the largest.

Required: To graduate, students must complete a total of 128 semester credit hours. Distribution requirements include a minimum of 16 semester credits each in humanities and arts, social sciences, language and communications, and natural sciences and math, plus 64 credits in electives and the area of concentration. A senior project, including an oral presentation, is required.

Special: Programs are designed to meet individual learning needs, with tutorial-based courses, often one-on-one. Scheduling is flexible, and there are part-time enrollment options.

Faculty/Classroom: 58% of faculty are male; 42%, female. 30% teach undergraduates. No introductory courses are taught by graduate students. The average class size in an introductory lecture is 8 and in a regular course, 3.

Requirements: The SAT I or ACT are not required. Applicants must show evidence of ability to do college-level work, to be highly motivated, and to have the capacity for self-directed learning. All applicants should present 2 letters of recommendation, a structured personal essay, and transcripts of any previous college work. An interview is required. Applications are accepted on-line at the school's web site. AP and CLEP credits are accepted. Important factors in the admissions decision are evidence of special talent, personality/intangible qualities, and leadership record.

Procedure: Freshmen are admitted to all sessions. There is a deferred admissions plan. Applications should be filed by October 1 for fall entry, February 1 for spring entry, and June 1 for summer entry. Notification is sent on a rolling basis.

Transfer: Grades of C or better from a regionally accredited institution may be transferable. 32 credits of 128 must be completed at Union.

Visiting: There are guides for informal visits and visitors may sit in on classes.

Financial Aid: In a recent year, 69% of all freshmen and 85% of continuing students received some form of financial aid. 69% of freshmen and 74% of continuing students received need-based aid. 94% of undergraduates work part time. The average financial indebtedness of a recent year's graduate was $26,300. The FAFSA and the college's own financial statement are required. Check with the school for current deadlines.

International Students: There were 4 international students enrolled in a recent year.

Computers: The mainframes are an AS400, S30. Learners may access the Internet from privately owned personal computers for a very low fee. All students may access the system. There are no time limits and no fees. It is strongly recommended that all students have a personal computer. It is recommended that students in distance-learning programs have personal computers.

Admissions Contact: Lisa Schrenger, Director, Admissions.
E-mail: *lschrenger@tui.edu* Web: *www.tui.edu*

UNIVERSITY OF AKRON

Akron, OH 44325 — D-2

(330) 972-7077

(800) 655-4884; Fax: (330) 972-7676

Full-time: 6408 men, 6976 women	**Faculty:** 779; I, --$
Part-time: 3287 men, 3509 women	**Ph.D.s:** 87%
Graduate: 1862 men, 2316 women	**Student/Faculty:** 17 to 1
Year: semesters, summer session	**Tuition:** $4930 ($11,132)
Application Deadline: August 15	**Room & Board:** $5600
Freshman Class: 7057 applied, 5986 accepted, 3575 enrolled	
SAT I Verbal/Math: 503/511	**ACT:** 20 **NONCOMPETITIVE**

The University of Akron, founded in 1870, is the public research university for northern Ohio. Primarily a commuter institution, the University offers more than 350 undergraduate and graduate degee programs and approximately 100 certificate programs at its main campus in Akron, its Wayne College branch campus in Orrville, and sites throughout Medina and Summit Counties. There are 8 undergraduate and 8 graduate schools. In addition to regional accreditation, UA has baccalaureate program accreditation with AACSB, ABET, ADA, ASLA, CAHEA, CSWE, NASAD, NASM, NCATE, and NLN. The 4 libraries contain 1,163,501 volumes, 1,940,630 microform items, and 43,448 audiovisual forms/CDs, and subscribe to 12,849 periodicals. Computerized library services include the card catalog, interlibrary loans, and database searching. Special learning facilities include a learning resource center, art gallery, radio station, TV station, nursing center, speech and hearing center, dance institute, educational media lab, and synchronous learning classrooms. The 170-acre campus is in an urban area in downtown Akron, 35 miles south of Cleveland. Including residence halls, there are 79 buildings.

Student Life: 98% of undergraduates are from Ohio. Others are from 33 states, 68 foreign countries, and Canada. 78% are white; 14%, African American. The average age of freshmen is 19; all undergraduates, 22. 30% do not continue beyond their first year; 40% remain to graduate.

Housing: 1800 students can be accommodated in college housing, which includes single-sex and coed dormitories and on-campus apartments. In addition, there are honors houses, special-interest houses, fraternity and sorority houses, private apartment-type halls, and private residence halls. On-campus housing is available on a first-come, first-served basis. Priority is given to out-of-town students. 90% of students commute. Alcohol is not permitted. All students may keep cars.

Activities: 5% of men belong to 1 local and 17 national fraternities; 3% of women belong to 8 national sororities. There are 200 groups on campus, including art, cheerleading, chess, choir, chorale, chorus, computers, dance, drama, ethnic, gay, honors, international, jazz band, marching band, musical theater, newspaper, orchestra, pep band, photography, political, professional, radio and TV, religious, social, social service, student government, symphony, and yearbook. Popular campus events include May Day, Parents/Family Day, and All Campus Leadership Conference.

Sports: There are 9 intercollegiate sports for men and 9 for women, and 12 intramural sports for men and 12 for women. Facilities include a 5500-seat gym, a 35,000-seat stadium, an indoor pool, a student center, indoor and outdoor tracks, 9 racquetball courts, gymnastics and combatives areas, and weight-training and fitness rooms.

Disabled Students: 90% of the campus is accessible. Wheelchair ramps, elevators, special parking, specially equipped rest rooms, special class scheduling, lowered drinking fountains, lowered telephones, and bus service are available.

Services: Counseling and information services are available, as is tutoring in most subjects. There is a reader service for the blind, remedial math, reading, and writing, and TDDs.

Campus Safety and Security: Measures include 24-hour foot and vehicle patrol, self-defense education, escort service, and shuttle buses. There are informal discussions, emergency telephones, and lighted pathways/sidewalks.

Programs of Study: UA confers B.A., B.S., and B.F.A. degrees. Associate, master's, and doctoral degrees are also awarded. Bachelor's degrees are awarded in BIOLOGICAL SCIENCE (biology/biological science, botany, microbiology, and zoology), BUSINESS (accounting, banking and finance, business administration and management, business economics, hospitality management services, international business management, marketing/retailing/merchandising, and personnel management), COMMUNICATIONS AND THE ARTS (advertising, art, broadcasting, classics, communications, dance, design, dramatic arts, English, fine arts, French, German, Latin, music, photography, Russian, Spanish, and speech/debate/rhetoric), COMPUTER AND PHYSICAL SCIENCE (chemistry, computer science, earth science, geology, mathematics, natural sciences, physics, and statistics), EDUCATION (art, athletic training, business, early childhood, elementary, foreign languages, guidance, health, home economics, music, physical, science, secondary, special, and technical), ENGINEERING AND ENVIRONMENTAL DESIGN (biomedical engineering, chemical engineering, civil engineering, computer engineering, construction technology, electrical/electronics engineering, emergency/disaster science, manufacturing technology, mechanical engineering, mechanical engineering technology, and survey and mapping technology), HEALTH PROFESSIONS (medical laboratory technology, nursing, predentistry, premedicine, prepharmacy, preveterinary science, and speech pathology/audiology), SOCIAL SCIENCE (anthropology, criminal justice, dietetics, economics, family/consumer studies, geography, history, home economics, humanities, philosophy, political science/government, prelaw, psychology, public administration, social science, social work, and sociology). Engineering, nursing, and business are the strongest academically. Arts and sciences, business, and engineering are the largest.

Required: To graduate, all students must complete at least 128 credits, with a varying number of hours in the major, and maintain a GPA of 2.0. Specific course requirements include English, Western cultural traditions, math, natural science, social science, humanities, speech, cultural diversity, and phys ed.

Special: UA offers co-op programs with local and out-of-state employers, study abroad in 15 countries, internships and work-study opportunities with community employers, a 6-year accelerated B.S.-M.D. program, a 3-2 engineering degree with Ashland University, B.A.-B.S. degrees in 10 majors, credit for military experience, nondegree study, and pass/fail options. There are 25 national honor societies and a freshman honors program.

Faculty/Classroom: 59% of faculty are male; 41%, female. The average class size in a laboratory is 21 and in a regular course, 26.

Admissions: 85% of the 2001-2002 applicants were accepted. The SAT I scores for the 2001-2002 freshman class were: Verbal--50% below 500, 35% between 500 and 599, 11% between 600 and 700, and 4% above 700; Math--48% below 500, 33% between 500 and 599, 18% between 600 and 700, and 1% above 700. 23% of the current freshmen were in the top fifth of their class; 45% were in the top two fifths. There were 6 National Merit finalists.

Requirements: The SAT I or ACT is required. Applicants must have a diploma from an accredited secondary school or hold the GED. Applicants for unconditional admission must have the following secondary school credits: 4 of English, 3 each of math, science, and social studies, and 2 of foreign language. A portfolio is recommended for art and graphic design students, an audition is required for music and dance students, and an interview is advised for nursing and engineering students. Applications are accepted on-line at the school's web site. AP and CLEP credits are accepted.

Procedure: Freshmen are admitted to all sessions. Entrance exams should be taken by December 1 for scholarship consideration. There are priority decision, early admissions, and deferred admissions plans. Priority decision applications should be filed by February 1; regular applications, by August 15 for fall entry, December 31 for spring entry, and May 27 for summer entry, along with a $30 fee. The college accepts all in-state residents. Notification of priority decision is sent March 15; regular decision, on a rolling basis.

Transfer: 985 transfer students enrolled in 2001-2002. In-state applicants should present a minimum college GPA of 2.0; out-of-state applicants, a GPA of 2.5. There are other requirements for specific academic programs. 32 credits of 128 must be completed at UA.

Visiting: There are regularly scheduled orientations for prospective students, including small groups for information on financial aid, student organizations, campus tours, and meetings with college faculty. There are guides for informal visits and visitors may sit in on classes. To schedule a visit, contact the Office of Undergraduate Admissions at (330) 972-7100.

Financial Aid: In 2001-2002, 74% of all freshmen and 79% of continuing students received some form of financial aid. 61% of freshmen and 53% of continuing students received need-based aid. The average freshman award was $3493. Of that total, scholarships or need-based grants averaged $4331 ($10,000 maximum); loans averaged $3848 ($4050 maximum); work contracts averaged $1228 ($3800 maximum); and non-need-based gift awards averaged $1187 ($10,000 maximum). 95% of undergraduates work part time. Average annual earnings from campus work are $1600. The FAFSA is required. The fall application deadline is March 1.

International Students: There are 218 international students enrolled. The school actively recruits these students. They must score 500 on the written TOEFL.

Computers: The mainframe is an IBM System/390 Enterprise Server. There are 8 public computer labs with 177 workstations and 90 departmental labs with 1725 workstations. All students may access the system from 7 A.M. to 1 A.M. at the computer center. There are no time limits and no fees. Law and honors students are given an IBM laptop for use while enrolled in course.

Graduates: In 2001, 1814 bachelor's degrees were awarded. The most popular majors were business (17%), education (16%), and engineering (13%). In an average class, 10% graduate in 4 years, 30% in 5 years, and 40% in 6 years. 200 companies recruited on campus in 2000-2001.

Admissions Contact: Kim Gentile, Interim Director of Admissions. A video is available. E-mail: *admissions@uakron.edu*
Web: *www.uakron.edu/admissions*

UNIVERSITY OF CINCINNATI — A-5
Cincinnati, OH 45221-0127 (513) 556-1100; Fax: (513) 556-1105

Full-time: 8282 men, 7471 women	**Faculty:** 1229; I, --$
Part-time: 1907 men, 2216 women	**Ph.D.s:** 82%
Graduate: 2739 men, 3294 women	**Student/Faculty:** 13 to 1
Year: quarters, summer session	**Tuition:** $5993 ($15,202)
Application Deadline: July 31	**Room & Board:** $6498
Freshman Class: 10,753 applied, 9713 accepted, 3883 enrolled	
SAT I Verbal/Math: 518/533	**ACT:** 22 **LESS COMPETITIVE**

The University of Cincinnati, founded in 1819, is a state-supported institution offering undergraduate programs in art and architecture, business, engineering, health science, liberal arts and sciences, music, and technical training. Figures in above capsule are approximate. There are 17 undergraduate and 10 graduate schools. In addition to regional accreditation, UC has baccalaureate program accreditation with AACSB and NCATE. The 18 libraries contain 1,948,000 volumes, 2,691,000 microform items, and 21,000 audiovisual forms/CDs, and subscribe to 19,600 periodicals. Computerized library services include the card catalog. Special learning facilities include a learning resource center, art gallery, and radio station. The 270-acre campus is in an urban area downtown Cincinnati. Including residence halls, there are 90 buildings.

Student Life: 93% of undergraduates are from Ohio. Others are from 45 states and 78 foreign countries. 83% are white. The average age of freshmen is 19; all undergraduates, 22. 24% do not continue beyond their first year; 45% remain to graduate.

Housing: 3200 students can be accommodated in college housing, which includes dormitories and on-campus apartments. On-campus housing is guaranteed for the freshman year only. Priority is given to out-of-town students. Alcohol is not permitted. All students may keep cars.

Activities: 11% of men belong to 24 local fraternities; 10% of women belong to 11 local sororities. There are many groups and organizations on campus, including art, band, cheerleading, chess, choir, chorale, chorus, computers, dance, drama, ethnic, gay, honors, international, jazz band, literary magazine, marching band, musical theater, newspaper, opera, orchestra, pep band, photography, political, professional, radio and TV, religious, social, social service, student government, symphony, and yearbook. Popular campus events include Homecoming and College Conservatory of Music productions.

Sports: There are 32 intramural sports for men and 32 for women. Athletic and recreation facilities include a 30000-seat stadium, a field house, a 13000-seat gym, indoor and outdoor tracks, a swimming pool, tennis courts, and athletic fields.

Disabled Students: 95% of the campus is accessible. Wheelchair ramps, elevators, special parking, specially equipped rest rooms, special class scheduling, lowered drinking fountains, and lowered telephones are available.

Services: Counseling and information services are available, as is tutoring in most subjects. There is remedial math, reading, and writing, note taking and reading services for the blind, and interpreting services for the hearing-impaired.

Campus Safety and Security: Measures include escort service, shuttle buses, emergency telephones, and lighted pathways/sidewalks.

Programs of Study: UC confers B.A., B.S., B.Arch., B.B.A., B.F.A., B.G.S., B.M., B.S.Des., B.S.E., B.S.N., B.S.Pharm., B.S.W, B.S.I.M, and B.U.P. degrees. Associate, master's, and doctoral degrees are also awarded. Bachelor's degrees are awarded in BIOLOGICAL SCIENCE (biochemistry and biology/biological science), BUSINESS (accounting, banking and finance, business administration and management, management science, marketing/retailing/merchandising, and real estate), COMMUNICATIONS AND THE ARTS (broadcasting, communications, comparative literature, dance, design, dramatic arts, English, fine arts, French, German, jazz, linguistics, music, music history and appreciation, music theory and composition, piano/organ, Spanish, theater design, and voice), COMPUTER AND PHYSICAL SCIENCE (chemical technology, chemistry, computer science, geology, information sciences and systems, mathematics, physics, and quantitative methods), EDUCATION (art, business, early childhood, elementary, foreign languages, guidance, health, industrial arts, middle school, music, nutrition, science, secondary, and special), ENGINEERING AND ENVIRONMENTAL DESIGN (aeronautical engineering, architectural engineering, architectural technology, chemical engineering, city/community/regional planning, civil engineering, computer engineering, construction management, electrical/electronics engineering, electrical/electronics engineering technology, engineering, engineering mechanics, engineering technology, industrial administration/management, industrial engineering technology, materials engineering, mechanical engineering, mechanical engineering technology, metallurgical engineering, and nuclear engineering), HEALTH PROFESSIONS (medical laboratory technology, nuclear medical technology, nursing, pharmacy, predentistry, premedicine, and speech pathology/audiology), SOCIAL SCIENCE (African American studies, anthropology, Asian/Oriental studies, classical/ancient civilization, criminal justice, economics, geography, history, international studies, Judaic studies, Latin American studies, philosophy, political science/government, prelaw, psychology, social science, social work, sociology, and urban studies). Engineering is the strongest academically. Arts and sciences are the largest.

Required: All students must complete English and humanities requirements. A minimum of 185 quarter credits is required for the baccalaureate degree.

Special: The Professional Practice Program, a 5-year cooperative plan offering alternate work in academic subjects and industry, is available for students in engineering, business, arts and sciences, and design, architecture, and art. Study abroad opportunities include a winter quarter in Spain, an academic program in Paris, and a language/area studies work program in Germany. A general studies degree and nondegree study are available. There is a chapter of Phi Beta Kappa and a freshman honors program.

Faculty/Classroom: 68% of faculty are male; 32%, female.

Admissions: 90% of the 2001-2002 applicants were accepted. The SAT I scores for the 2001-2002 freshman class were: Verbal--38% below 500, 39% between 500 and 599, 20% between 600 and 700, and 4% above 700; Math--35% below 500, 35% between 500 and 599, 25% between 600 and 700, and 5% above 700. The ACT scores were 37% below 21, 23% between 21 and 23, 19% between 24 and 26, 10% between 27 and 28, and 9% above 28. 29% of the current freshmen were in the top fifth of their class; 54% were in the top two fifths.

Requirements: The SAT I or ACT is required. In addition, applicants should be graduates of an accredited secondary school with 4 units of high school English, 3 of math, 2 each of science, social science, foreign language, and electives, and 1 of fine arts. A GPA of 2.0 is required.

Procedure: Freshmen are admitted to all sessions. Entrance exams should be taken in May of the junior year or January or March of the senior year. Applications should be filed by July 31 for fall entry, along with a $35 fee. Notification of early decision and regular decision is sent on a rolling basis.

Transfer: A GPA of 2.0 is required to apply from a 4-year college, a GPA of 2.5 or associate degree from a 2-year college.

Visiting: There are regularly scheduled orientations for prospective students. There are guides for informal visits and visitors may sit in on classes and stay overnight. To schedule a visit, contact the Admissions Office.

Financial Aid: The CSS/Profile or FAFSA is required. The financial aid application must be submitted as soon as possible after January 1.

International Students: There were 203 international students enrolled in a recent year. The school actively recruits these students. They must score 515 on the written TOEFL.

Computers: The mainframes are an Amdahl 5880 and 470, and a DEC VAX. There are also 350 Apple, IBM, and Zenith PCs available in all colleges and in the library. All students may access the system. There are no time limits and no fees.

Graduates: In an average class, 11% graduate in 4 years, 36% in 5 years, and 48% in 6 years.

Admissions Contact: Director of Admissions.
E-mail: *admissions@uc.edu* Web: *www.uc.edu*

UNIVERSITY OF DAYTON

Dayton, OH 45469 — B-4

(937) 229-4411
(800) 837-7433; Fax: (937) 229-4729

Full-time: 3080 men, 3400 women	**Faculty:** 340
Part-time: 335 men, 230 women	**Ph.D.s:** 93%
Graduate: 1425 men, 1790 women	**Student/Faculty:** 19 to 1
Year: semesters, summer session	**Tuition:** $16,000
Application Deadline: open	**Room & Board:** $4900
Freshman Class: n/av	
SAT I Verbal/Math: required	**VERY COMPETITIVE**

The University of Dayton, founded in 1850, is a nonprofit, private, comprehensive institution affiliated with the Roman Catholic Church. Part of the Southwestern Ohio Council for Higher Education, it has undergraduate and graduate programs emphasizing the arts and sciences, business administration, engineering, education, and allied professions and law. There are 4 undergraduate schools and 1 graduate school. Figures in the above capsule are approximate. In addition to regional accreditation, UD has baccalaureate program accreditation with AACSB, ABET, ADA, NASM, and NCATE. The 2 libraries contain 991,020 volumes, 800,531 microform items, and 1858 audiovisual forms/CDs, and subscribe to 5153 periodicals. Computerized library services include the card catalog, interlibrary loans, and database searching. Special learning facilities include a learning resource center, art gallery, radio station, TV station, and an engineering and science research institute, an information sciences center, and a day-care facility that provides a learning environment for education majors. The 110-acre campus is in a suburban area 2 miles south of downtown Dayton. Including residence halls, there are 44 buildings.

Student Life: 61% of undergraduates are from Ohio. Others are from 43 states and Canada. 52% are from public schools. 90% are white. 70% are Catholic; 18% other, no preference, unidentified and Muslim; 12% Protestant. The average age of freshmen is 18; all undergraduates, 19. 14% do not continue beyond their first year; 73% remain to graduate.

Housing: 5500 students can be accommodated in college housing, which includes single-sex and coed dormitories, on-campus apartments, off-campus apartments, fraternity houses, and sorority houses. In addition, there are honors houses and special-interest houses. On-campus housing is available on a first-come, first-served basis and is available on a lottery system for upperclassmen. 95% of students live on campus; of those, 95% remain on campus on weekends. Upperclassmen may keep cars.

Activities: 16% of men and about 20% of women belong to 3 local and 11 national fraternities; 20% of women belong to 1 local and 9 national sororities. There are 160 groups on campus, including art, band, cheerleading, chess, choir, chorale, chorus, computers, dance, debate, drama, drill team, ethnic, gay, honors, international, jazz band, literary magazine, marching band, musical theater, newspaper, orchestra, pep band, photography, political, professional, radio and TV, religious, social, social service, student government, symphony, and yearbook. Popular campus events include Christmas on Campus, Week in Solidarity with Homeless (WISH), and Distinguished Speakers Series.

Sports: There are 7 intercollegiate sports for men and 10 for women. Facilities include a physical activities center, a field house, a 13500-seat arena, a 12000-seat football stadium, soccer and baseball fields, indoor and outdoor tennis courts, racquetball and squash courts, a swimming pool, a basketball court, weight rooms, a fully equipped aerobic conditioning center, a strength and conditioning facility, a weight room, and a sports medicine complex.

Disabled Students: Wheelchair ramps, elevators, special parking, specially equipped rest rooms, special class scheduling, lowered drinking fountains, and lowered telephones are available.

Services: Counseling and information services are available, as is tutoring in every subject. There is a reader service for the blind and developmental math, reading, and writing.

Campus Safety and Security: Measures include 24-hour foot and vehicle patrol, self-defense education, escort service, and shuttle buses. There are informal discussions, pamphlets/posters/films, emergency telephones, lighted pathways/sidewalks, and bike patrol.

Programs of Study: UD confers B.A., B.S., B.C.E., B.Ch.E., B.E.E., B.F.A., B.G.S., B.M., and B.M.E. degrees. Master's and doctoral degrees are also awarded. Bachelor's degrees are awarded in BIOLOGICAL SCIENCE (biochemistry, biology/biological science, environmental biology, and nutrition), BUSINESS (accounting, banking and finance, business economics, management information systems, management science, marketing/retailing/merchandising, and sports management), COMMUNICATIONS AND THE ARTS (broadcasting, communications, design, dramatic arts, English, fine arts, French, German, journalism, music, photography, public relations, and Spanish), COMPUTER AND PHYSICAL SCIENCE (chemistry, computer science, geology, information sciences and systems, mathematics, physical sciences, and physics), EDUCATION (art, business, early childhood, elementary, health, music, secondary, and special), ENGINEERING AND ENVIRONMENTAL DESIGN (chemical engineering, civil engineering, computer engineering, electrical/electronics engineering, electrical/electronics engineering technology, engineering, engineering technology, industrial engineering technology, manufacturing technology, mechanical engineering, and mechanical engineering technology), HEALTH PROFESSIONS (music therapy, predentistry, and premedicine), SOCIAL SCIENCE (American studies, criminal justice, dietetics, economics, history, international studies, philosophy, physical fitness/movement, political science/government, psychology, religion, and sociology). Engineering, business, and exercise science are the strongest academically. Communication, and psychology are the largest.

Required: To graduate, all students must complete a minimum of 120 semester hours with at least 30 in the major, and maintain a minimum GPA of 2.0. The curricula must include general education requirements, including 4 classes in religious studies and philosophy as well as basic skills requirements. Departmental requirements vary.

Special: Special academic programs include co-op and work-study programs, internships, summer study abroad at 5 European sites chosen each year, a summer program in Germany or semester exchange in France for business students, a Washington semester, one-month immersion language programs, and cross-registration with the Southwestern Ohio Council for Higher Education (SOCHE) consortium. Dual major programs are available, as is a B.A.-B.S. degree in economics, chemistry, math, and psychology. A 3-2 engineering degree is offered with Wilberforce University and Thomas More College. A general studies degree, credit for life, military, or work experience, and pass/fail options are also available. There are 23 national honor societies, and a freshman honors program.

Faculty/Classroom: 76% of faculty are male; 24%, female. The average class size in an introductory lecture is 29; in a laboratory, 16; and in a regular course, 27.

Admissions: There were 13 National Merit finalists in a recent year. 39 freshmen graduated first in their class.

Requirements: The SAT I or ACT is required. In addition, applicants should be graduates of an accredited secondary school with 15 to 18 units in English, social sciences, math, foreign language, and lab science. Additional math and science courses may be neessary for certain programs. The GED is accepted. High school transcripts and official scores from the ACT or SAT I must be submitted. An essay or personal statement, recommendation from the high school guidance counselor, and an interview are recommended. Music students must audition. AP and CLEP credits are accepted. Important factors in the admissions decision are advanced placement or honor courses, leadership record, and extracurricular activities record. Applications are accepted on-line at *admission.udayton.edu/application.asp*.

Procedure: Freshmen are admitted fall, winter, and summer. Entrance exams should be taken by December of the senior year. There is a deferred admissions plan. Application deadlines are open. 10% of all applicants are on a waiting list; 183 were accepted in a recent year. Check with the school for current fee.

Transfer: 141 transfer students enrolled in a recent year. Applicants must submit transcripts from all colleges attended and must have a minimum GPA of 2.0; 2.5 is needed for selected programs. An interview is advised. 30 credits of 120 must be completed at UD.

Visiting: There are regularly scheduled orientations for prospective students, including an admission interview, a campus and residence hall tour, meetings with faculty members, and a financial aid discussion. There are guides for informal visits and visitors may sit in on classes and stay overnight. To schedule a visit, contact the campus visit coordinator, Office of Admissions.

Financial Aid: In a recent year, 93% of all freshmen and 96% of continuing students received some form of financial aid. 52% of freshmen and 50% of continuing students received need-based aid. The average freshman award was $12,847. Of that total, scholarships or need-based grants averaged $7219 ($15,020 maximum); loans averaged $4851 ($5625 maximum); and work contracts averaged $1790 ($2100 maximum). 77% of undergraduates work part time. Average annual earnings from campus work are $1460. The average financial indebtedness of a recent graduate was $16,252. UD is a member of CSS. The FAFSA is required. Check with the school for current deadlines.

International Students: There were 37 international students enrolled in a recent year. The school actively recruits these students. They must score 523 on the written TOEFL.

Computers: The mainframe is an NCR 3600. All student housing is connected to the campus voice, video, and data networks. In addition, more than 550 PC, Mac, and Sun computers are available in more than 21 labs around the campus. The university also operates a computer store. All students may access the system 24 hours a day, 7 day a week. There are no time limits and no fees. All students are required to have personal computers.

Graduates: In a recent year, 1441 bachelor's degrees were awarded. The most popular majors were engineering (18%), teacher education (11%), and communication (10%). In an average class, 52% graduate in 4 years, 71% in 5 years, and 73% in 6 years. 195 companies recruited on campus in a recent year. Of a recent graduating class, 96% were enrolled in graduate school within 6 months of graduation.

Admissions Contact: Myron Achbach, Director of Admission. A video is available. E-mail: *admission@udayton.edu*
Web: *http://admission@udayton.edu*

UNIVERSITY OF FINDLAY

Findlay, OH 45840 — **B-2**
(419) 424-4732
(800) 548-0932; Fax: (419) 424-4822

Full-time: 1130 men, 1485 women	**Faculty:** 160; IIA, --$
Part-time: 334 men, 432 women	**Ph.D.s:** 51%
Graduate: 490 men, 714 women	**Student/Faculty:** 16 to 1
Year: semesters, summer session	**Tuition:** $17,528
Application Deadline: June 1	**Room & Board:** $6434
Freshman Class: 2067 applied, 2025 accepted, 613 enrolled	
SAT I Verbal/Math: 504/522	**ACT:** 21 **NONCOMPETITIVE**

The University of Findlay, founded in 1882, is a private, independent institution affiliated with the Churches of God, General Conference, offering liberal arts and sciences and career preparation programs. There are 4 undergraduate and 7 graduate schools. In addition to regional accreditation, Findlay has baccalaureate program accreditation with NCATE. The library contains 135,000 volumes, 90,400 microform items, and 1200 audiovisual forms/CDs, and subscribes to 2511 periodicals. Computerized library services include interlibrary loans and database searching. Special learning facilities include a learning resource center, art gallery, planetarium, radio station, university-owned farm, equine facility, and emergency response training center. The 135-acre campus is in a small town 45 miles south of Toledo and 100 miles north of Columbus. Including residence halls, there are 55 buildings.

Student Life: 80% of undergraduates are from Ohio. Others are from 45 states, 41 foreign countries, and Canada. 80% are from public schools. 85% are white. 60% are Protestant; 35% Catholic. The average age of freshmen is 18; all undergraduates, 22. 25% do not continue beyond their first year; 55% remain to graduate.

Housing: 1000 students can be accommodated in college housing, which includes single-sex dormitories, on-campus apartments, fraternity houses, and sorority houses. In addition, there are honors houses, language houses, and special-interest houses. On-campus housing is guaranteed for all 4 years. 65% of students commute. Alcohol is not permitted. All students may keep cars.

Activities: 4% of men belong to 3 national fraternities; 1% of women belong to 2 national sororities. There are 40 groups on campus, including art, band, cheerleading, choir, chorale, chorus, computers, drama, drum and bugle corps, equestrian, ethnic, honors, international, jazz band, literary magazine, marching band, musical theater, newspaper, pep band, political, preveterinary, professional, radio and TV, religious, social, social service, student government, and yearbook. Popular campus events include Family Weekend, International Night, and Spring Bash.

Sports: There are 14 intercollegiate sports for men and 12 for women, and 15 intramural sports for men and 15 for women. Facilities include a fitness center, a 7200-seat stadium, a 25-meter pool, racquetball courts, and a phys ed center with a 3200-seat gym, an ice arena, indoor track, and four-court athletic building.

Disabled Students: 90% of the campus is accessible. Wheelchair ramps, elevators, special parking, specially equipped rest rooms, special class scheduling, lowered drinking fountains, and specially equipped residence hall rooms are available.

Services: Counseling and information services are available, as is tutoring in most subjects. There is a reader service for the blind, and remedial math, reading, and writing. Other services include assistance with note taking, test taking, research papers, and study skills, and support for the hearing impaired, including interpreters.

Campus Safety and Security: Measures include 24-hour foot and vehicle patrol, self-defense education, escort service, and informal discussions. There are pamphlets/posters/films, emergency telephones, and lighted pathways/sidewalks.

Programs of Study: Findlay confers B.A. and B.S. degrees. Associate and master's degrees are also awarded. Bachelor's degrees are awarded in AGRICULTURE (equine science), BIOLOGICAL SCIENCE (biology/biological science), BUSINESS (accounting, banking and finance, business administration and management, business economics, business systems analysis, hospitality management services, human resources, international business management, and marketing/retailing/merchandising), COMMUNICATIONS AND THE ARTS (arts administration/management, broadcasting, communications, dramatic arts, English, English as a second/foreign language, illustration, Japanese, Spanish, studio art, and technical and business writing), COMPUTER AND PHYSICAL SCIENCE (computer science, mathematics, and science), EDUCATION (art, athletic training, bilingual/bicultural, business, elementary, foreign languages, middle school, physical, and secondary), ENGINEERING AND ENVIRONMENTAL DESIGN (environmental science, occupational safety and health, preengineering, and technological management), HEALTH PROFESSIONS (health science, nuclear medical technology, nursing, occupational therapy, physician's assistant, premedicine, and preveterinary science), SOCIAL SCIENCE (criminal justice, economics, history, international studies, philosophy, political science/government, prelaw, psychology, religion, social work, and sociology). Business administration, preveterinary medicine, and education are the strongest academically. Business administration, equestrian studies, and education are the largest.

Required: All students must complete 33 semester hours of general education requirements, including fine arts, humanities, natural science, math, social science, and religion or philosophy, and most take courses in wellness, computer science, and statistics. There are competency requirements in library use, English and reading, and a wellness course. A total of 124 semester hours with a minimum GPA of 2.0 is required in order to graduate.

Special: Co-op programs are available in accounting and occupational health and safety. There is cross-registration with Mount Carmel College of Nursing and a 3-2 engineering program with the University of Toledo, Ohio Northern University, and Washington University. The field experience program provides up to 20 semester hours in field placement. Internships are available for business, business education, communication, hazardous materials management, and theater majors. Through the College Consortium for International Studies, study abroad is possible in 16 countries. Work-study, a Washington semester, dual and student-designed majors, a general studies degree, pass/fail options, and credit for life experience are offered. Nondegree study is possible. There is a freshman honors program.

Faculty/Classroom: 60% of faculty are male; 40%, female. All teach undergraduates. No introductory courses are taught by graduate students. The average class size in an introductory lecture is 23; in a laboratory, 15; and in a regular course, 22.

Admissions: 98% of the 2001-2002 applicants were accepted. The SAT I scores for the 2001-2002 freshman class were: Verbal--45% below 500, 32% between 500 and 599, 22% between 600 and 700, and 1% above 700; Math--42% below 500, 47% between 500 and 599, 10% between 600 and 700, and 1% above 700. The ACT scores were 30% below 21, 37% between 21 and 23, 22% between 24 and 26, 8% between 27 and 28, and 3% above 28. 30% of the current freshmen were in the top fifth of their class; 60% were in the top two fifths. 21 freshmen graduated first in their class.

Requirements: The SAT I or ACT is required. In addition, applicants should have completed 16 high school credits or GED equivalents, including 4 years of English, 2 years of social studies/history, 3 to 4 math courses, and 2 to 3 science courses. A GPA of 2.3 is required. AP and CLEP credits are accepted. Important factors in the admissions decision are advanced placement or honor courses, evidence of special talent, and extracurricular activities record. Applications are accepted on-line via the university's web site, CollegeView, *Review.com*, CollegeNET, and CollegeLink

Procedure: Freshmen are admitted to all sessions. Entrance exams should be taken during fall of the senior year or the spring of the junior year. There is a deferred admissions plan. Applications should be filed by June 1 for fall entry and December 1 for winter entry. Notification is sent on a rolling basis.

Transfer: 100 transfer students enrolled in 2001-2002. A minimum 2.0 GPA and eligibility to return to the current institution are required. An interview is recommended. 30 credits of 124 must be completed at Findlay.

Visiting: There are regularly scheduled orientations for prospective students, including a tour, interview, coach/faculty visits, and lunch. There are guides for informal visits and visitors may sit in on classes and stay overnight. To schedule a visit, contact the Admissions Office at (800) 548-0932, ext. 4732.

Financial Aid: In 2001-2002, 90% of all students received some form of financial aid. 75% of freshmen and 80% of continuing students received need-based aid. The average freshman award was $11,700. Of that total, scholarships or need-based grants averaged $6200 ($8300 maximum); loans averaged $2500 ($2625 maximum); work contracts averaged $1000 ($1200 maximum); and state and federal aid averaged $2000 ($2769 maximum). 80% of undergraduates work part time. Average annual earnings from campus work are $800. The average financial indebtedness of the 2001 graduate was $14,000. The FAFSA is required. The fall application deadline is April 1.

International Students: There are 426 international students enrolled. The school actively recruits these students. They must score 500 on the written TOEFL.

Computers: The mainframe is an HP G-30. There are 7 student computer labs with networked Pentium-based PCs and Mac G-3s. More than 200 student workstations are available. All residence hall rooms are networked, and off-campus students have free modem access. All students may access the system. There are no time limits and no fees.

Graduates: In 2001, 690 bachelor's degrees were awarded. The most popular majors were business management (15%), business administration (9%), and education (5%). In an average class, 2% graduate in 3 years, 55% in 4 years, 57% in 5 years, and 58% in 6 years. 200 companies recruited on campus in 2000-2001. Of the 2000 graduating class, 10% were enrolled in graduate school within 6 months of graduation and 85% were employed.

Admissions Contact: Michael Momany, Executive Director of Enrollment Services. E-mail: *admissions@findlay.edu* Web: *www.findlay.edu*

UNIVERSITY OF RIO GRANDE — D-5

Rio Grande, OH 45674 — (740) 245-5353

(800) 282-7201; Fax: (740) 245-7260

Full-time: 620 men, 900 women	**Faculty:** 84; IIB, -$
Part-time: 115 men, 220 women	**Ph.D.s:** 52%
Graduate: 25 men, 75 women	**Student/Faculty:** 20 to 1
Year: quarters, summer session	**Tuition:** $4492 ($4948)
Application Deadline: see profile	**Room & Board:** $4236
Freshman Class: n/av	**ACT:** required

NONCOMPETITIVE

The University of Rio Grande, founded in 1876, is a private institution offering degree programs in the liberal arts and sciences, business, and education. Check with the school for specific tuition rates that vary by program. Figures in above capsule are approximate. There are 9 undergraduate schools and 1 graduate school. In addition to regional accreditation, Rio has baccalaureate program accreditation with CSWE, NASDTEC, and NLN. The library contains 96,731 volumes, 274,400 microform items, and 1835 audiovisual forms/CDs, and subscribes to 850 periodicals. Computerized library services include the card catalog, interlibrary loans, and database searching. Special learning facilities include a learning resource center, art gallery, radio station, and TV station. The 194-acre campus is in a rural area 100 miles southeast of Columbus. Including residence halls, there are 27 buildings.

Student Life: 94% of undergraduates are from Ohio. Others are from 12 states, 15 foreign countries, and Canada. 98% are from public schools. 97% are white. The average age of freshmen is 23; all undergraduates, 24.

Housing: 640 students can be accommodated in college housing, which includes single-sex and coed dormitories. In addition, there are special-interest houses. On-campus housing is guaranteed for all 4 years. 76% of students commute. All students may keep cars.

Activities: 6% of men belong to 2 local and 2 national fraternities; 4% of women belong to 5 local sororities. There are 39 groups on campus, including band, cheerleading, choir, chorale, chorus, drama, ecology, ethnic, gay, honors, international, jazz band, musical theater, newspaper, orchestra, pep band, photography, political, professional, radio and TV, religious, social, social service, and student government. Popular campus events include Ethnofest, Bob Evans Farm Festival, and Community Service Day.

Sports: There are 5 intercollegiate sports for men and 5 for women, and 10 intramural sports for men and 10 for women. Facilities include 2 gyms, tennis courts, an indoor Olympic-size pool, an outdoor track, handball, racquetball, and sand volleyball courts, a fitness center, a cross-country track, and soccer, baseball, and softball fields.

Disabled Students: 70% of the campus is accessible. Wheelchair ramps, elevators, special parking, specially equipped rest rooms, special class scheduling, lowered drinking fountains, lowered telephones, note takers, tape recorders, and closed-caption TV are available.

Services: Counseling and information services are available, as is tutoring in every subject. There is a reader service for the blind, and remedial math, reading, and writing. There is also an Accessibility Office.

Campus Safety and Security: Measures include 24-hour foot and vehicle patrol, escort service, informal discussions, and pamphlets/posters/films. There are emergency telephones and lighted pathways/sidewalks.

Programs of Study: Rio confers B.A., B.S., B.S.I.T., B.S.N., and B.S.W. degrees. Associate and master's degrees are also awarded. Bachelor's degrees are awarded in BIOLOGICAL SCIENCE (biology/

biological science), BUSINESS (accounting, business administration and management, business economics, international business management, and marketing management), COMMUNICATIONS AND THE ARTS (art, communications, English, fine arts, music, and public relations), COMPUTER AND PHYSICAL SCIENCE (chemistry, computer science, mathematics, and physical sciences), EDUCATION (art, business, early childhood, education of the mentally handicapped, elementary, English, health, mathematics, music, physical, psychology, reading, science, secondary, social science, and social studies), ENGINEERING AND ENVIRONMENTAL DESIGN (computer technology, drafting and design technology, electrical/electronics engineering technology, environmental science, industrial engineering technology, manufacturing technology, preengineering, and woodworking), HEALTH PROFESSIONS (medical technology, nursing, predentistry, premedicine, and preveterinary science), SOCIAL SCIENCE (American studies, behavioral science, economics, history, humanities, physical fitness/movement, political science/government, prelaw, psychology, social work, and sociology). Education, business, and nursing are the strongest academically. Education, general studies, and business are the largest.

Required: Students must complete 190 to 198 quarter hours, including 47 to 53 in the major, with a minimum GPA of 2.0. The required general studies program, for all but teacher certification and industrial technology majors, includes 13 credit hours in communication skills, 12 hours each in the humanities, math, natural sciences, and social sciences, 3 hours in health and phys ed, and 1 hour in liberal arts.

Special: Rio offers internships in social work, communications, and business, a Washington semester, student-designed majors, limited pass/fail options, and credit for life, military, or work experience. Nondegree study for 1-year certificates in secretarial science and personal computer applications is also available. A community college on the same campus offers technical degree programs that are built into 4-year degrees. There are 3 national honor societies, a freshman honors program, and 1 departmental honors program.

Faculty/Classroom: 67% of faculty are male; 33%, female. All teach undergraduates. The average class size in an introductory lecture is 30; in a laboratory, 20; and in a regular course, 20.

Requirements: The ACT is required. Rio follows an open admissions policy for all applicants. A high school diploma or GED is required. For on-line applications, consult the Rio web site. A GPA of 2.0 is required. AP and CLEP credits are accepted.

Procedure: Freshmen are admitted to all sessions. Entrance exams should be taken no later than December of the senior year for those entering college the following fall. There is an early admissions plan. The college accepts all applicants. Notification is sent on a rolling basis. Check with the school for current application deadlines. The fee is $15.

Transfer: Candidates must submit a final transcript and a dean's evaluation form from the last school attended. 45 credits of 190 must be completed at Rio.

Visiting: There are regularly scheduled orientations for prospective students, with parents and students participating in 1- or 2-day sessions. The program includes half-day placement testing and presentations from various offices, campus e-mail, advising, and registration. Residential students stay in the dorms and have dinner with the president. There are guides for informal visits and visitors may sit in on classes and stay overnight. To schedule a visit, contact the Admissions Office.

Financial Aid: In a recent year, 87% of all freshmen and 85% of continuing students received some form of financial aid. 75% of freshmen and 69% of continuing students received need-based aid. The average freshman award was $4650. Rio is a member of CSS. The FAFSA and the college's own financial statement are required. The fall application deadline is April 15.

International Students: The school actively recruits these students. They must score 400 on the written TOEFL.

Computers: The mainframe is an IBM AS/400 Series 3 for administrative use only. Rio maintains more than 200 PCs on a switched Ethernet local area network. Students have full access to the Web, e-mail, and other Internet services. All students may access the system. The fee is $7 per quarter. It is strongly recommended that all students have a personal computer. Rio recommends a Windows-based PC with Ethernet or modem-based networking and multimedia capabilities.

Admissions Contact: Mark F. Abell, Executive Director, Admissions. E-mail: *mabell@rio.edu* Web: *www.rio.edu*

UNIVERSITY OF TOLEDO

Toledo, OH 43606-3398 — B-1

(419) 530-2696
(800) 5TOLEDO; Fax: (419) 530-5835

Full-time: 6265 men, 6361 women	**Faculty:** 688
Part-time: 1829 men, 2299 women	**Ph.D.s:** 79%
Graduate: 1638 men, 1921 women	**Student/Faculty:** 18 to 1
Year: semesters, summer session	**Tuition:** $5102 ($12,462)
Application Deadline: open	**Room & Board:** $6104
Freshman Class: n/av	
SAT I or ACT: required	**NONCOMPETITIVE**

The University of Toledo, founded in 1872, is a public comprehensive institution emphasizing undergraduate degree programs in the liberal arts and sciences, business, engineering, teacher preparation, and health professions. There are 8 undergraduate and 7 graduate schools. In addition to regional accreditation, UT has baccalaureate program accreditation with AACSB, ABET, ACPE, APTA, NASM, and NCATE. The 3 libraries contain 1,678,250 volumes, 1,597,728 microform items, and 7224 audiovisual forms/CDs, and subscribe to 4527 periodicals. Computerized library services include the card catalog, interlibrary loans, and database searching. Special learning facilities include a learning resource center, art gallery, planetarium, and radio station. The 450-acre campus is in a suburban area 6 miles northwest of downtown Toledo. Including residence halls, there are 85 buildings.

Student Life: 89% of undergraduates are from Ohio. Others are from 47 states, 105 foreign countries, and Canada. 73% are white; 11%, African American. The average age of freshmen is 20; all undergraduates, 23. 29% do not continue beyond their first year; 40% remain to graduate.

Housing: 2889 students can be accommodated in college housing, which includes single-sex and coed dormitories, fraternity houses, and sorority houses. In addition, there are honors houses and special-interest houses. On-campus housing is available on a first-come, first-served basis. 86% of students commute. All students may keep cars.

Activities: 10% of men belong to 1 local and 13 national fraternities; 9% of women belong to 13 national sororities. There are 200 groups on campus, including art, band, cheerleading, chess, choir, chorale, chorus, computers, dance, drama, drill team, ethnic, film, gay, honors, international, jazz band, literary magazine, marching band, musical theater, newspaper, orchestra, pep band, photography, political, professional, radio and TV, religious, social, social service, student government, and symphony. Popular campus events include Songfest, Spring Release, and International Student Dinner.

Sports: There are 9 intercollegiate sports for men and 10 for women, and 48 intramural sports for men and 48 for women. Facilities include a recreation center, a 27,000-seat stadium, a 9000-seat arena, a field house, 3 pools, 12 tennis courts, an indoor/outdoor track, a 4-field recreational softball complex, and recreational/sport club fields.

Disabled Students: 96% of the campus is accessible. Wheelchair ramps, elevators, special parking, specially equipped rest rooms, special class scheduling, lowered drinking fountains, and lowered telephones are available.

Services: Counseling and information services are available, as is tutoring in every subject. There is a reader service for the blind, and remedial math, reading, and writing.

Campus Safety and Security: Measures include 24-hour foot and vehicle patrol, self-defense education, escort service, and shuttle buses. There are informal discussions, pamphlets/posters/films, emergency telephones, lighted pathways/sidewalks, and student patrols. All security officers are state-certified with full arrest authority.

Programs of Study: UT confers B.A., B.S., B.B.A., B.Ed., B. in Eng., B.Eng.Tech., B.F.A., B.Mus., B.S.Admin.Serv., B.S.Criminal Justice, B.S.Exercise Science, B.S.Institutional Health Care, B.S.Med.Tech., B.S.N., B.S.Pharm., B.S. in Physical Therapy, and B.Voc.Ed. degrees. Associate, master's, and doctoral degrees are also awarded. Bachelor's degrees are awarded in BIOLOGICAL SCIENCE (biology/biological science), BUSINESS (accounting, banking and finance, business administration and management, marketing/retailing/merchandising, and recreation and leisure services), COMMUNICATIONS AND THE ARTS (art history and appreciation, communications, dramatic arts, English, film arts, fine arts, French, German, linguistics, music, and Spanish), COMPUTER AND PHYSICAL SCIENCE (chemistry, computer science, geology, information sciences and systems, mathematics, and physics), EDUCATION (art, business, early childhood, elementary, foreign languages, health, music, physical, science, secondary, special, and vocational), ENGINEERING AND ENVIRONMENTAL DESIGN (bioengineering, chemical engineering, civil engineering, computer engineering, electrical/electronics engineering, electromechanical technology, engineering, engineering technology, environmental science, industrial engineering, and mechanical engineering), HEALTH PROFESSIONS (nursing, pharmacy, physical therapy, and speech pathology/audiology), SOCIAL SCIENCE (anthropology, community services, criminal justice, economics, geography, history, humanities, international relations, philosophy, physical fitness/movement, political science/government, psychology, social work, sociology, and women's studies). Engineering, pharmacy, and business are the strongest academically.

Required: To graduate, all students must complete 124 to 169 hours of credit, with 60 in the major, and maintain a minimum GPA of 2.0. A core curriculum is required of all students.

Special: Special academic programs include internships in most majors, study abroad in 14 countries, and on-campus employment through the Financial Aid Office. There is a co-op program with the College of Engineering and cross-registration with Bowling Green State University. The B.A.-B.S. degree and dual majors are available in many areas of study. A general studies degree, student-designed majors, credit for life, military, and work experience, nondegree study, and pass/fail options are also offered. There are 56 national honor societies and a freshman honors program.

Faculty/Classroom: 58% of faculty are male; 41%, female. The average class size in an introductory lecture is 33; in a laboratory, 19; and in a regular course, 28.

Admissions: The SAT I scores for the 2001-2002 freshman class were: Verbal--45% below 500, 39% between 500 and 599, 14% between 600 and 700, and 2% above 700; Math--39% below 500, 37% between 500 and 599, 21% between 600 and 700, and 4% above 700. The ACT scores were 17% between 12 and 17, 49% between 18 and 23, 30% between 24 and 29, and 3% above 29. 35% of the current freshmen were in the top quarter of their class; 64% were in the upper half.

Requirements: The SAT I or ACT is required. In addition, students should be graduates of an accredited secondary school or hold the GED. The preparatory program should include 4 years of English, 3 each of math, natural science, and social studies, and 2 of a foreign language. An interview is advised. AP and CLEP credits are accepted. Important factors in the admissions decision are evidence of special talent, recommendations by school officials, and leadership record. Toledo accepts applications on-line through the ACT College Connector Program.

Procedure: Freshmen are admitted to all sessions. Entrance exams should be taken late in the junior year or early in the senior year. There is a deferred admissions plan. Application deadlines are open. The fall 2001 application fee was $30. The university accepts all in-state applicants. Notification is sent on a rolling basis.

Transfer: 1344 transfer students enrolled in 2001-2002. Applicants must have a minimum of 12 quarter or 8 semester college credits and a GPA of 2.0. An interview is recommended.

Visiting: There are regularly scheduled orientations for prospective students, including an interview with an admissions counselor and a student-guided campus tour. There are guides for informal visits and visitors may sit in on classes and stay overnight. To schedule a visit, contact the Office of Admissions at (419) 530-8888.

Financial Aid: UT is a member of CSS. The FAFSA is required. Check with the school for current deadlines.

International Students: The school actively recruits these students. They must score 500 on the written TOEFL.

Computers: The mainframes are an IBM/9121-511, a DEC 2100 ALPHA Server 4/200, and a DEC 2100 ALPHA Server 4/275. Networked PCs are available at many campus locations. Dorm rooms have Internet access. All students may access the system 24 hours per day, except from Saturday at 5 P.M. to Sunday at noon. There are no time limits and no fees.

Graduates: In 2001, 2031 bachelor's degrees were awarded. The most popular majors were business (18%), education (15%), and engineering (14%).

Admissions Contact: Carolyn Baumgartner, Director of Undergraduate Admissions. A video is available. E-mail: *enroll@utnet.utoledo.edu* Web: *http://www.utoledo.edu*

URBANA UNIVERSITY

Urbana, OH 43078-2091 — B-3

(937) 484-1356

(800) 7-URBANA; Fax: (937) 484-1322

Full-time: 446 men, 414 women	**Faculty:** 49; IIB, --$
Part-time: 164 men, 334 women	**Ph.D.s:** 74%
Graduate: 15 men, 59 women	**Student/Faculty:** 18 to 1
Year: semesters, summer session	**Tuition:** $12,004
Application Deadline: open	**Room & Board:** $5000
Freshman Class: 543 applied, 320 accepted, 213 enrolled	
SAT I or ACT: required	**COMPETITIVE**

Urbana University, founded in 1850 and affiliated with the Swedenborgian Church, is a nonprofit, independent institution emphasizing programs in liberal arts, business, preprofessional training, and teacher preparation. There is 1 graduate school. The library contains 70,000 volumes, 8176 microform items, and 2099 audiovisual forms/CDs, and subscribes to 328 periodicals. Computerized library services include interlibrary loans and database searching. Special learning facilities include a learning resource center, radio station, TV station, rare books room, and history museum. The 128-acre campus is in a small town 40 miles west of Columbus and 50 miles north of Dayton. Including residence halls, there are 29 buildings.

Student Life: 90% of undergraduates are from Ohio. Others are from 5 states and 5 foreign countries. 95% are from public schools. 79% are white; 17% African American. The average age of freshmen is 20; all undergraduates, 24. 23% do not continue beyond their first year; 35% remain to graduate.

Housing: 350 students can be accommodated in college housing, which includes single-sex and coed dormitories. In addition, there are honors houses. On-campus housing is available on a lottery system for upperclassmen. 58% of students commute. All students may keep cars.

Activities: There are no fraternities or sororities. There are 20 groups on campus, including band, cheerleading, choir, chorus, drama, ethnic, honors, international, literary magazine, musical theater, newspaper, pep band, political, professional, radio and TV, religious, social service, student government, and yearbook. Popular campus events include Spring Week, Founders Day, and Activities Fair.

Sports: There are 5 intercollegiate sports for men and 4 for women, and 6 intramural sports for men and 6 for women. Facilities include a community center with a 3500-seat gym, a pool, handball and racquetball courts, a weight room, and outdoor tennis courts.

Disabled Students: 30% of the campus is accessible. Wheelchair ramps, elevators, special parking, and special class scheduling are available.

Services: Counseling and information services are available, as is tutoring in most subjects. There is remedial math, reading, and writing, taped textbooks, reading and writing labs, and study skills seminars.

Campus Safety and Security: Measures include 24-hour foot and vehicle patrol, self-defense education, escort service, and informal discussions. There are pamphlets/posters/films, emergency telephones, and lighted pathways/sidewalks.

Programs of Study: Urbana confers B.A., B.S., and B.S.Ed. degrees. Associate and master's degrees are also awarded. Bachelor's degrees are awarded in BUSINESS (business administration and management and sports management), COMMUNICATIONS AND THE ARTS (communications and English), COMPUTER AND PHYSICAL SCIENCE (science), EDUCATION (elementary, middle school, and secondary), HEALTH PROFESSIONS (premedicine and sports medicine), SOCIAL SCIENCE (criminal justice, liberal arts/general studies, philosophy, physical fitness/movement, prelaw, psychology, and sociology). Business and education are the strongest academically and the largest.

Required: To graduate, all students must complete 126 semester hours, with a minimum overall GPA of 2.0 and 2.5 in the major. Distribution requirements include 12 to 13 credit hours in math and science, 12 each in humanities and social sciences, 9 in communications, and 2 to 3 in health, phys ed, and recreation.

Special: Special academic programs include internships, cross-registration with the Southwestern Ohio Council for Higher Education, study abroad, and accelerated degree programs in teacher certification. B.A.-B.S. degrees, dual and student-designed majors, credit for life, military, and work experience, and nondegree study are also available. There is 1 national honor society and 4 departmental honors programs.

Faculty/Classroom: 60% of faculty are male; 40%, female. All teach undergraduates. No introductory courses are taught by graduate students. The average class size in an introductory lecture is 18; in a laboratory, 7; and in a regular course, 19.

Admissions: 59% of the 2001-2002 applicants were accepted.

Requirements: The SAT I or ACT is required of applicants under 23 years of age, with the ACT preferred. The minimum SAT I score should be 700, and the minimum ACT score, 18. Applicants must be graduates of an accredited secondary school. The GED is accepted. An essay is required of all applicants, and an interview is recommended. A GPA of 2.0 is required. CLEP credit is accepted. Important factors in the admissions decision are advanced placement or honor courses, evidence of special talent, and extracurricular activities record. Applications are accepted on disk or on-line at the Urbana web site.

Procedure: Freshmen are admitted to all sessions. Entrance exams should be taken during the junior or senior year. There is a deferred admissions plan. Application deadlines are open. The fall 2001 application fee was $25. Notification is sent on a rolling basis.

Transfer: 50 transfer students enrolled in a recent year. Applicants must have at least 30 college credits with a GPA of 2.25 and must be in good standing at their previous institution. 30 credits of 126 must be completed at Urbana.

Visiting: There are regularly scheduled orientations for prospective students, consisting of a campus tour and sessions on academics, athletics, performing arts, financial aid, and student life. There are guides for informal visits and visitors may sit in on classes and stay overnight. To schedule a visit, contact the Admissions Office.

Financial Aid: 60% of undergraduates work part time. Average annual earnings from campus work are $1000. Urbana is a member of CSS. The FAFSA, the college's own financial statement, and the state aid form for residents are required. The fall application deadline is May 1.

International Students: There are 4 international students enrolled. The school actively recruits these students. They must score 500 on the written TOEFL.

Computers: The mainframe is a DEC PDP 11/84. Macs and PCs are available for student use in 4 computer labs, the education department, and the library. All students have e-mail accounts. All students may access the system. There are no time limits and no fees.
Graduates: In a recent class, 153 bachelor's degrees were awarded. The most popular majors were business/marketing (48%), education (36%), and protective services/public administration (7%).
Admissions Contact: Admissions Officer.
E-mail: *admiss@urbana.edu* Web: *www.urbana.edu*

URSULINE COLLEGE D-1
Pepper Pike, OH 44124 (440) 442-4203
(888) URSULINE; Fax: (440) 684-6138

Full-time: 34 men, 498 women	**Faculty:** 48; IIB, --$
Part-time: 44 men, 443 women	**Ph.D.s:** 62%
Graduate: 46 men, 216 women	**Student/Faculty:** 11 to 1
Year: semesters, summer session	**Tuition:** $14,730
Application Deadline: open	**Room & Board:** $4700
Freshman Class: 308 applied, 200 accepted, 100 enrolled	
SAT I Verbal/Math: 507/481	**ACT:** 21 **LESS COMPETITIVE**

Ursuline College, established in 1871, is a private, liberal arts, primarily women's college affiliated with the Roman Catholic Church. There are 4 undergraduate schools and 1 graduate school. In addition to regional accreditation, Ursuline has baccalaureate program accreditation with CSWE and NLN. The library contains 125,000 volumes and 7900 audiovisual forms/CDs, and subscribes to 1189 periodicals. Computerized library services include the card catalog, interlibrary loans, and database searching. Special learning facilities include a learning resource center, art gallery, media center, and curriculum library. The 112-acre campus is in a suburban area 13 miles east of Cleveland. Including residence halls, there are 13 buildings.
Student Life: 98% of undergraduates are from Ohio. Others are from 8 states, 7 foreign countries, and Canada. 60% are from public schools. 71% are white; 21%, African American. 42% claim no religious affiliation; 36% are Catholic; 11%, Protestant. The average age of freshmen is 19; all undergraduates, 31. 38% do not continue beyond their first year; 38% remain to graduate.
Housing: 159 students can be accommodated in college housing, which includes single-sex and coed dormitories. On-campus housing is guaranteed for all 4 years and is available on a first-come, first-served basis. 89% of students commute. Alcohol is not permitted. All students may keep cars.
Activities: There are no fraternities or sororities. There are 27 groups on campus, including drama, ethnic, international, literary magazine, professional, religious, social, social service, and student government. Popular campus events include All College Day, a formal dance, and charity benefits.
Sports: There are 4 intercollegiate sports for women and 4 intramural sports for women. Facilities include a fitness center, a swimming pool, a gym, and a campus center.
Disabled Students: 80% of the campus is accessible. Wheelchair ramps, elevators, special parking, and specially equipped rest rooms are available.
Services: Counseling and information services are available, as is tutoring in most subjects. There is a reader service for the blind, and remedial math, reading, and writing.
Campus Safety and Security: Measures include 24-hour foot and vehicle patrol, escort service, informal discussions, and pamphlets/posters/films. There are emergency telephones and lighted pathways/sidewalks.
Programs of Study: Ursuline confers B.A. and B.S.N. degrees. Master's degrees are also awarded. Bachelor's degrees are awarded in BIOLOGICAL SCIENCE (biology/biological science), BUSINESS (accounting, business administration and management, fashion merchandising, human resources, marketing management, and transportation and travel marketing), COMMUNICATIONS AND THE ARTS (art, English, graphic design, historic preservation, and public relations), COMPUTER AND PHYSICAL SCIENCE (mathematics), EDUCATION (early childhood, elementary, and secondary), ENGINEERING AND ENVIRONMENTAL DESIGN (interior design), HEALTH PROFESSIONS (allied health, health care administration, nursing, and premedicine), SOCIAL SCIENCE (American studies, child care/child and family studies, fashion design and technology, history, humanities, philosophy, prelaw, psychology, religion, social work, and sociology). Nursing is the strongest academically. Nursing and business are the largest.
Required: To graduate, students must complete 128 semester hours for the B.A. and 129 for the B.S.N., with a minimum GPA of 2.0 (2.5 in education courses). All students must take 49 credits of general education courses, structured to develop progressive stages of learning.
Special: Ursuline offers co-op programs with the Cleveland College of Jewish Studies and cross-registration with the 8 area colleges in the Cleveland Commission of Higher Education. Internships, a general studies degree, dual and student-designed majors, nondegree study, and accelerated degree programs in business management and health care administration are available. Students may receive credit for life, military, or work experience. There are pass/fail options and a continuing studies program for nontraditional students. There are 2 national honor societies.
Faculty/Classroom: 24% of faculty are male; 76%, female. 88% teach undergraduates. No introductory courses are taught by graduate students. The average class size in an introductory lecture is 18; in a laboratory, 11; and in a regular course, 13.
Admissions: 65% of the 2001-2002 applicants were accepted. The SAT I scores for the 2001-2002 freshman class were: Verbal--53% below 500, 34% between 500 and 599, and 13% between 600 and 700; Math--56% below 500, 41% between 500 and 599, and 3% between 600 and 700. The ACT scores were 44% below 21, 30% between 21 and 23, 18% between 24 and 26, 2% between 27 and 28, and 6% above 28.
Requirements: The SAT I or ACT is required. In addition, students should be graduates of an accredited secondary school. Recommended college-preparatory courses include 4 units of English, 3 each of social studies, math, and science, 2 of a foreign language, and 1 each of fine/performing arts and phys ed/health. A recommendation from a teacher or counselor is required and an interview is encouraged. A GPA of 2.5 is required. AP and CLEP credits are accepted. Important factors in the admissions decision are advanced placement or honor courses, recommendations by school officials, and leadership record. Applications are available on-line at the school's web site.
Procedure: Freshmen are admitted to all sessions. Entrance exams should be taken in the junior year. Application deadlines are open. The application fee is $25. Notification is sent on a rolling basis.
Transfer: 170 transfer students enrolled in 2001-2002. Official copies of all transcripts and a 2.5 GPA are required. Students with less than 24 semester hours of credit must provide high school transcripts. 43 credits of 128 to 129 must be completed at Ursuline.
Visiting: There are regularly scheduled orientations for prospective students, including an open house and overnight visit. There are guides for informal visits and visitors may sit in on classes and stay overnight. To schedule a visit, contact the Admissions Office.
Financial Aid: In 2001-2002, 90% of all freshmen and 86% of continuing students received some form of financial aid. 77% of freshmen and 46% of continuing students received need-based aid. The average freshman award was $1376. Of that total, scholarships or need-based grants averaged $8167 ($10,500 maximum); loans averaged $4275 ($4625 maximum); and work contracts averaged $1318 ($2000 maximum). 97% of undergraduates work part time. Average annual earnings from campus work are $1000. The average financial indebtedness of the 2001 graduate was $19,250. Ursuline is a member of CSS. The FAFSA and the college's own financial statement are required. The priority fall application deadline is March 1.
International Students: There are 6 international students enrolled. The school actively recruits these students. They must score 500 on the written TOEFL or 173 on the electronic version, or take the SAT I, scoring 850, or the ACT, scoring 17.
Computers: The mainframe is a Unisys. There are 8 computer labs on campus for student use. 2 are located in the residence halls. 7 of the labs have PCs and one is a Mac lab. Residence hall rooms are wired so students with their own computers can access the college's network. All students may access the system daily at designated hours. There are no time limits and no fees.
Graduates: In 2001, 290 bachelor's degrees were awarded. The most popular majors were nursing (21%), business (15%), and psychology (5%). In an average class, 23% graduate in 4 years, 36% in 5 years, and 38% in 6 years.
Admissions Contact: Jill Oakley-Jeppe, Director of Admission.
E-mail: *admission@ursuline.edu* Web: *www.ursuline.edu*

WALSH UNIVERSITY D-2
North Canton, OH 44720-3396 (330) 490-7172
(800) 362-9846; Fax: (330) 490-7165

Full-time: 450 men, 605 women	**Faculty:** 60; IIB, -$
Part-time: 126 men, 220 women	**Ph.D.s:** 63%
Graduate: 36 men, 85 women	**Student/Faculty:** 16 to 1
Year: semesters, summer session	**Tuition:** $13,160
Application Deadline: open	**Room & Board:** $5960
Freshman Class: 772 accepted, 266 enrolled	
ACT: 21	**COMPETITIVE**

Walsh University was established in 1958 by the Brothers of Christian Instruction, a religious order of the Roman Catholic Church. The private institution offers undergraduate programs in liberal arts, business, communication, education, professional training, and nursing. There are 4 graduate schools. In addition to regional accreditation, Walsh has baccalaureate program accreditation with NLN. The library contains 129,000 volumes, 8400 microform items, and 1545 audiovisual forms/CDs, and subscribes to 687 periodicals. Computerized library services include the card catalog, interlibrary loans, and database searching. Special learning facilities include a learning resource center, radio station, and a child development center. The 107-acre campus is in a small town 20 miles south of Akron. Including residence halls, there are 11 buildings.

Student Life: 90% of undergraduates are from Ohio. Others are from 5 states and 20 foreign countries. 70% are from public schools. 91% are white. 50% are Catholic; 50% Protestant. The average age of freshmen is 19; all undergraduates, 27. 26% do not continue beyond their first year; 55% remain to graduate.

Housing: 550 students can be accommodated in college housing, which includes single-sex and coed dormitories, on-campus apartments, and married-student housing. In addition, there are special-interest houses. On-campus housing is guaranteed for all 4 years. 65% of students commute. All students may keep cars.

Activities: There are no fraternities or sororities. There are 25 groups on campus, including cheerleading, choir, chorale, computers, dance, drama, ethnic, forensics, honors, international, literary magazine, newspaper, pep band, political, professional, radio and TV, religious, social, social service, student government, and yearbook. Popular campus events include Welcome Week, Candlelight Vigil, and Spring Formal.

Sports: There are 8 intercollegiate sports for men and 8 for women, and 9 intramural sports for men and 9 for women. Facilities include an 1800-seat gym, basketball and tennis courts, a track, an indoor swimming pool, a weight room, and fields for soccer, softball, football, and baseball.

Disabled Students: All of the campus is accessible. Wheelchair ramps, elevators, special parking, specially equipped rest rooms, lowered drinking fountains, and lowered telephones are available.

Services: Counseling and information services are available, as is tutoring in every subject. There is remedial math, reading, and writing.

Campus Safety and Security: Measures include 24-hour foot and vehicle patrol, self-defense education, escort service, and informal discussions. There are pamphlets/posters/films, emergency telephones, and lighted pathways/sidewalks.

Programs of Study: Walsh confers B.A., B.S., and B.S.N. degrees. Associate and master's degrees are also awarded. Bachelor's degrees are awarded in BIOLOGICAL SCIENCE (biology/biological science), BUSINESS (accounting, banking and finance, business administration and management, and marketing/retailing/merchandising), COMMUNICATIONS AND THE ARTS (communications, English, French, and Spanish), COMPUTER AND PHYSICAL SCIENCE (chemistry, computer science, mathematics, and science), EDUCATION (early childhood, elementary, middle school, physical, secondary, and special), HEALTH PROFESSIONS (clinical science, nursing, physical therapy, predentistry, premedicine, and preveterinary science), SOCIAL SCIENCE (history, international studies, pastoral studies, philosophy, political science/government, prelaw, psychology, religion, sociology, and theological studies). Business, psychology, and nursing are the strongest academically. Education, business, and biology are the largest.

Required: To graduate, students must complete 130 semester hours with a minimum 2.0 GPA. The number of hours required in the major varies. A core curriculum of 68 to 71 hours is required, including courses in English, art and music appreciation, economics, social science, math, science, humanities, phys ed, theology, philosophy, and possibly a foreign language.

Special: Work-study programs are available to students having substantial financial need. A 3-2 program in natural resources, including forestry, conservation teaching, fisheries, and wildlife management, is offered with the University of Michigan. Walsh offers co-op programs in business, internships in several majors, accelerated degree programs in business and management and in behavioral science/counseling and human development, evening and continuing education programs, and credit for life experience. There is a chapter of Phi Beta Kappa and a freshman honors program.

Faculty/Classroom: 52% of faculty are male; 48%, female. 96% teach undergraduates, 10% do research, and 10% do both. No introductory courses are taught by graduate students. The average class size in an introductory lecture is 20; in a laboratory, 20; and in a regular course, 19.

Admissions: The ACT scores for the 2001-2002 freshman class were: 44% below 21, 28% between 21 and 23, 20% between 24 and 26, 5% between 27 and 28, and 3% above 28. 35% of the current freshmen were in the top fifth of their class; 62% were in the top two fifths. 8 freshmen graduated first in their class in a recent year.

Requirements: The SAT I or ACT is required. In addition, the applicant must be a graduate of an accredited secondary school; the GED is accepted. Walsh recommends completion of 4 units of English, 3 each of math, science, and social studies, 2 of foreign language, and 1 of fine or performing arts. An essay and an interview are recommended. A GPA of 2.1 is required. AP and CLEP credits are accepted. Important factors in the admissions decision are recommendations by school officials, leadership record, and personality/intangible qualities. Applications are accepted on-line at the school's web site.

Procedure: Freshmen are admitted to all sessions. Entrance exams should be taken during the junior year. There is a deferred admissions plan. Application deadlines are open. The application fee is $25. Notification is sent on a rolling basis.

Transfer: 151 transfer students enrolled in a recent year. Applicants must have a minimum GPA of 2.0 from previous colleges attended. 32 credits of 130 must be completed at Walsh.

Visiting: There are regularly scheduled orientations for prospective students, consisting of a campus tour, a session with financial aid and admissions staff, and an opportunity to meet with faculty, coaches, and other personnel. There are guides for informal visits and visitors may sit in on classes and stay overnight. To schedule a visit, contact the Admissions Office.

Financial Aid: In 2001-2002, 95% of all freshmen and 90% of continuing students received some form of financial aid. 22% of undergraduates work part time. Average annual earnings from campus work are $1360. The average financial indebtedness of a recent year's graduate was $17,000. Walsh is a member of CSS. The FAFSA and the college's own financial statement are required. Check with school for current deadlines.

International Students: There were 20 international students enrolled in a recent year. The school actively recruits these students. They must score 550 on the written TOEFL.

Computers: The mainframe is a DEC VAX. There are 410 networked PCs located in 12 computer labs, one of which is located in a residence hall. Student access to the Internet is available in the labs. All students may access the system. There are no time limits and no fees.

Graduates: In a recent year, 171 bachelor's degrees were awarded. The most popular majors were nursing (20%), management (13%), and biology (11%). In an average class, 24% graduate in 4 years, 39% in 5 years, and 49% in 6 years. 21 companies recruited on campus in a recent year.

Admissions Contact: Brett Freshcer, Dean of Enrollment Management. E-mail: *admissions@walsh.edu* Web: *www.walsh.edu*

WILBERFORCE UNIVERSITY

Wilberforce, OH 45384-1091 — **B-4**
(937) 376-2911, ext. 721
(800) 367-8568; Fax: (937) 376-4751

Full-time: 300 men, 480 women	**Faculty:** 46
Part-time: 10 men, 10 women	**Ph.D.s:** 53%
Graduate: none	**Student/Faculty:** 17 to 1
Year: semesters	**Tuition:** $10,637
Application Deadline: open	**Room & Board:** $4300
Freshman Class: n/av	
SAT I or ACT: recommended	**LESS COMPETITIVE**

Wilberforce University, founded in 1856, is a nonprofit, private institution operated under the auspices of the African Methodist Episcopal Church; it was the first black college in America. Its programs emphasize the liberal arts, business, art and fine arts, engineering, and music. Figures given in the above capsule are approximate. The library contains 60,000 volumes, 12,000 microform items, and 200 audiovisual forms/CDs, and subscribes to 350 periodicals. Special learning facilities include a learning resource center, radio station, and the nearby National Afro-American Museum. The 125-acre campus is in a rural area 20 miles east of Dayton. Including residence halls, there are 21 buildings.

Student Life: 64% of undergraduates are from out of state, mostly the Midwest. Others are from 32 states and 2 foreign countries. All are African American. The average age of freshmen is 18; all undergraduates, 20.

Housing: 775 students can be accommodated in college housing, which includes dormitories and married-student housing. In addition, there are honors houses. On-campus housing is guaranteed for all 4 years. 85% of students live on campus; of those, 70% remain on campus on weekends. Alcohol is not permitted. All students may keep cars.

Activities: 10% of men belong to 3 national fraternities; 10% of women belong to 3 national sororities. There are 30 groups on campus, including choir, computers, dance, ethnic, honors, international, literary magazine, newspaper, political, religious, social, student government, and yearbook. Popular campus events include Fall Festival and Dawn Dance.

Sports: There are 5 intercollegiate sports for men and 4 for women, and 4 intramural sports for men and 4 for women. Facilities include a 1500-seat gym, outdoor and cross-country track, a softball field, and basketball, volleyball, and tennis courts.

Disabled Students: 50% of the campus is accessible. Wheelchair ramps, special parking, specially equipped rest rooms, and limited elevator service in classroom buildings only are available.

Services: Counseling and information services are available, as is tutoring in most subjects. There is a reader service for the blind, and remedial math, reading, and writing.

Programs of Study: Wilberforce confers B.A. and B.S. degrees. Bachelor's degrees are awarded in BIOLOGICAL SCIENCE (biology/biological science), BUSINESS (accounting, banking and finance, business administration and management, business economics, management science, and marketing/retailing/merchandising), COMMUNICATIONS AND THE ARTS (communications, fine arts, literature, and music), COMPUTER AND PHYSICAL SCIENCE (chemistry, computer science, information sciences and systems, mathematics, and science), ENGINEERING AND ENVIRONMENTAL DESIGN (preengineering), HEALTH PROFESSIONS (health care administration and rehabilitation therapy), SOCIAL SCIENCE (economics, liberal arts/general studies, political science/government, prelaw, psychology, social science, social work, and sociology). Business administration, accounting, and banking and finance are the strongest academically.

Required: To graduate, students must complete 126 credit hours with a minimum GPA of 2.0 and no grade in the major below a C. To fulfill the general studies requirements, all students must complete a first-year program, which includes composition and computer literacy courses, and they must also take at least 1 course from each of the following areas: humanistic traditions, music, art, religion, communication arts, literature and language, non-Western studies, behavioral sciences, economics and political science, physical sciences, and life science. 2 credits in health and phys ed and completion of 2 cooperative education experiences are also required.

Special: Wilberforce offers a co-op arrangement with St. John's University School of Law and cross-registration through the Southwestern Ohio Council for Higher Education. B.A.-B.S. degrees are available in all majors, and there are dual majors in engineering along with a 3-2 engineering degree with the University of Dayton. Credit is given for the mandatory co-op education program, in which students participate in paid work experience in their chosen field. Nondegree study is possible in military science. There is 1 national honor society, including Phi Beta Kappa, a freshman honors program, and 4 departmental honors programs.

Faculty/Classroom: 50% of faculty are male; 50%, female. The average class size in an introductory lecture is 12 and in a regular course, 18.

Requirements: The SAT I or ACT is recommended. In addition, students should be graduates of an accredited secondary school and have 15 Carnegie units, including 4 units of English, 2 to 3 of math, including algebra, 2 to 3 of science, including a lab course, and 2 of social studies, including U.S. history. The GED is accepted with a score of 45 or better. SAT II: Subject tests are recommended. A GPA of 2.0 is required. AP and CLEP credits are accepted. Important factors in the admissions decision are recommendations by school officials, advanced placement or honor courses, and evidence of special talent.

Procedure: Freshmen are admitted fall and spring. Entrance exams should be taken by the fall of the senior year. There are early decision and early admissions plans. Application deadlines are open. A waiting list is an active part of the admissions procedure.

Transfer: A minimum college GPA of 2.0 is required. 30 credits of 126 must be completed at Wilberforce.

Visiting: There are regularly scheduled orientations for prospective students. There are guides for informal visits. To schedule a visit, contact the Office of Admissions.

Financial Aid: Wilberforce is a member of CSS. The FAFSA, the college's own financial statement and the parent and student federal income tax returns are required. Check with the school for current deadlines.

International Students: They must score 500 on the written TOEFL and also take the SAT I or the ACT.

Computers: The mainframe is an NCR Tower Series 32/650. There are also 85 NCR 710 PCs available in the computer center. Students enrolled in computer and engineering programs may access the system. There are no time limits and no fees.

Admissions Contact: Kenneth C. Christmon, Director of Admissions. E-mail: *admissions@payne.wilberforce.edu* Web: *www.wilberforce.edu*

WILMINGTON COLLEGE
Wilmington, OH 45177 **B-4**

(937) 382-6661
(800) 341-9318; Fax: (937) 382-7077

Full-time: 532 men, 650 women	**Faculty:** 70; IIB, --$
Part-time: 23 men, 22 women	**Ph.D.s:** 69%
Graduate: none	**Student/Faculty:** 17 to 1
Year: semesters, summer session	**Tuition:** $15,746
Application Deadline: open	**Room & Board:** $6080

Freshman Class: 1260 applied, 1012 accepted, 365 enrolled
ACT: 21 **COMPETITIVE**

Wilmington College, established in 1870, is a private institution sponsored by the Society of Friends. The college offers programs in the liberal arts, business, health science, teacher preparation, agricultural studies, religious studies, and athletic training. In addition to regional accreditation, Wilmington has baccalaureate program accreditation with CAAHEP and NCATE. The library contains 110,000 volumes, 42,000 microform items, and 1400 audiovisual forms/CDs, and subscribes to 400 periodicals. Computerized library services include the card catalog, interlibrary loans, and database searching. Special learning facilities include a learning resource center, art gallery, Peace Resource Center, Quaker museum, observatory, and greenhouse. The 65-acre campus is in a small town 50 miles from Cincinnati and from Columbus. Including residence halls, there are 17 buildings.

Student Life: 96% of undergraduates are from Ohio. Others are from 15 states and 5 foreign countries. 90% are white; 10%, African American. 40% claim no religious affiliation; 17% are Catholic. The average age of freshmen is 19. 29% do not continue beyond their first year; 56% remain to graduate.

Housing: 833 students can be accommodated in college housing, which includes single-sex and coed dormitories, on-campus apartments, fraternity houses, and sorority houses. On-campus housing is guaranteed for all 4 years. 70% of students live on campus. All students may keep cars.

Activities: 17% of men belong to 4 local fraternities and 1 national fraternity; 16% of women belong to 4 local sororities. There are 63 groups on campus, including cheerleading, choir, chorale, drama, ethnic, gay, honors, international, jazz band, literary magazine, musical theater, newspaper, orchestra, photography, political, professional, religious, social, social service, student government, and yearbook. Popular campus events include Community Day, Westheimer Peace Symposium, and Fall Fest.

Sports: There are 11 intercollegiate sports for men and 10 for women, and 8 intramural sports for men and 8 for women. Facilities include an Olympic-size pool, a Nautilus weight-training room, an exercise room, racquetball courts, a 4500-seat gym, and a 3000-seat stadium.

Disabled Students: 20% of the campus is accessible. Wheelchair ramps, elevators, special parking, specially equipped rest rooms, and special class scheduling are available.

Services: Counseling and information services are available, as is tutoring in every subject. There is remedial math, reading, and writing.

Campus Safety and Security: Measures include 24-hour foot and vehicle patrol, escort service, informal discussions, and pamphlets/posters/films. There are emergency telephones and lighted pathways/sidewalks.

Programs of Study: Wilmington confers B.A. and B.S. degrees. Master's degrees are also awarded. Bachelor's degrees are awarded in AGRICULTURE (agriculture), BIOLOGICAL SCIENCE (biology/biological science), BUSINESS (accounting, business administration and management, organizational behavior, and sports management), COMMUNICATIONS AND THE ARTS (art, communications, dramatic arts, English, and Spanish), COMPUTER AND PHYSICAL SCIENCE (chemistry, computer science, and mathematics), EDUCATION (athletic training, early childhood, elementary, physical, and secondary), HEALTH PROFESSIONS (predentistry, premedicine, and preveterinary science), SOCIAL SCIENCE (criminal justice, history, liberal arts/general studies, prelaw, psychology, religion, social science, social work, and sociology). Chemistry, biology, and athletic training are the strongest academically. Business, agriculture, and athletic training are the largest.

Required: To graduate, students must complete 124 semester hours, including no more than 60 hours in the major, with a minimum GPA of 2.0. At least 40 hours must be in upper-division work. General education requirements include courses in English and math competence, international knowledge, basic areas of thought and expression, and personal fitness.

Special: Special academic programs include work-study, internships, a Washington semester, and cross-registration with the Southwest Ohio Consortium. Study abroad may be arranged in Mexico, Austria, France, and other countries. Dual majors in any subject and student-designed majors are offered. Credit for experience, nondegree study, and pass/fail options are possible. There are 2 national honor societies, a freshman honors program, and 3 departmental honors programs.

Faculty/Classroom: 57% of faculty are male; 43%, female. All teach undergraduates. The average class size in an introductory lecture is 25 and in a regular course, 19.

Admissions: 80% of the 2001-2002 applicants were accepted. 17% of the current freshmen were in the top fifth of their class; 32% were in the top two fifths. 8 freshmen graduated first in their class.

Requirements: The SAT I or ACT is required. In addition, applicants must be graduates of an accredited secondary school, with 4 units of English, 2 units each of math, science, and social studies, and a recommended 2 units of a foreign language. An additional 6 units is required in other areas. The GED is accepted. An interview is recommended. An essay may be required. Wilmington requires applicants to be in the upper 50% of their class. A GPA of 2.5 is required. AP and CLEP credits are accepted. Important factors in the admissions decision are recommendations by school officials, parents or siblings attending the school, and recommendations by alumni.

Procedure: Freshmen are admitted fall and spring. Entrance exams should be taken as early as possible. There is a deferred admissions plan. Application deadlines are open. The application fee is $25. Notification is sent on a rolling basis.

Transfer: 70 transfer students enrolled in 2001-2002. Applicants' college and high school transcripts are evaluated on an individual basis. Students must have a 2.0 GPA and a completed transfer recommendation form. 30 credits of 124 must be completed at Wilmington.

Visiting: There are regularly scheduled orientations for prospective students, including meetings with faculty and a tour of the campus. There are guides for informal visits and visitors may sit in on classes and stay overnight. To schedule a visit, contact the Admissions Office.

Financial Aid: In 2001-2002, 95% of all freshmen and 89% of continuing students received some form of financial aid. 85% of all students received need-based aid. The average freshman award was $14,000. Of that total, scholarships or need-based grants averaged $5000 ($9000 maximum); loans averaged $2625 ($5125 maximum); work contracts averaged $1275 ($1550 maximum); and Choice awards averaged $960 (maximum). 35% of undergraduates work part time. Average annual earnings from campus work are $1400. The average financial indebtedness of the 2001 graduate was $17,300. The FAFSA is required. The fall application deadline is March 15.

International Students: There are 8 international students enrolled. The school actively recruits these students. They must score 500 on the written TOEFL if the SAT I is not taken. Students who have been previously enrolled in a U.S. high school must also take the SAT I scoring 410 verbal, or the ACT.

Computers: The mainframes are 2 HP 9000s. There are 150 networked PCs available in public areas. There is full access to the Internet and the Web. All students may access the system at any time. There are no time limits and no fees.

Graduates: In 2001, 145 bachelor's degrees were awarded. The most popular majors were business (38%), education (14%), and agriculture (11%). 52 companies recruited on campus in 2000-2001. Of the 2000 graduating class, 5% were enrolled in graduate school within 6 months of graduation and 21% were employed.

Admissions Contact: Larry Lesick, Vice President for Enrollment Management. E-mail: *admission@wilmington.edu*
Web: *www.wilmington.edu*

WITTENBERG UNIVERSITY — B-3
Springfield, OH 45501 — (937) 327-6314
(800) 677-7558; Fax: (937) 327-6379

Full-time: 970 men, 1075 women	**Faculty:** 141; IIB, av$
Part-time: 50 men, 68 women	**Ph.D.s:** 97%
Graduate: none	**Student/Faculty:** 15 to 1
Year: semesters, summer session	**Tuition:** $22,990
Application Deadline: March 15	**Room & Board:** $5776

Freshman Class: 2405 applied, 2044 accepted, 628 enrolled
SAT I Verbal/Math: required — **VERY COMPETITIVE**

Wittenberg University, founded in 1845, is a private liberal arts and sciences institution affiliated with the Evangelical Lutheran Church in America. The 2 libraries contain 370,000 volumes, 90,000 microform items, and 26,000 audiovisual forms/CDs, and subscribe to 1200 periodicals. Computerized library services include the card catalog, interlibrary loans, and database searching. Special learning facilities include a learning resource center, art gallery, radio station, geology museum, and observatory. The 100-acre campus is in a suburban area 25 miles east of Dayton and 40 miles west of Columbus. Including residence halls, there are 35 buildings.

Student Life: 58% of undergraduates are from Ohio. Others are from 40 states, 23 foreign countries, and Canada. 80% are from public schools. 85% are white. 59% are Protestant; 23% Catholic; 15% claim no religious affiliation. The average age of freshmen is 18; all undergraduates, 20. 16% do not continue beyond their first year; 72% remain to graduate.

Housing: 1200 students can be accommodated in college housing, which includes single-sex and coed dormitories, on-campus apartments, off-campus apartments, married-student housing, fraternity houses, and sorority houses. In addition, there are honors houses, language houses, special-interest houses, and a substance-free residence hall. On-campus housing is guaranteed for all 4 years. 96% of students live on campus; of those, 85% remain on campus on weekends. All students may keep cars.

Activities: 20% of men belong to 5 national fraternities; 35% of women belong to 7 national sororities. There are 110 groups on campus, including art, band, caving, cheerleading, chess, choir, chorale, chorus, computers, dance, drama, ethnic, forensics, gay, honors, international, jazz band, literary magazine, musical theater, newspaper, orchestra, pep band, photography, political, professional, radio and TV, religious, social, social service, student government, symphony, and yearbook. Popular campus events include Wittenberg Series, International Festival, and Professional Alumni Days.

Sports: There are 11 intercollegiate sports for men and 11 for women, and 15 intramural sports for men and 12 for women. Facilities include a multipurpose field house, a swimming pool, 6 racquetball/handball courts, a fitness center, and sports medicine rooms. There is also a 3200-seat gym, a 3200-seat arena, 12 acres of playing fields, and a 500-seat stadium with an artificially lit playing field, a track, and 12 tennis courts.

Disabled Students: 75% of the campus is accessible. Wheelchair ramps, elevators, special parking, specially equipped rest rooms, special class scheduling, lowered drinking fountains, and lowered telephones are available.

Services: Counseling and information services are available, as is tutoring in most subjects. There are also math and writers' workshops.

Campus Safety and Security: Measures include 24-hour foot and vehicle patrol, self-defense education, escort service, and informal discussions. There are pamphlets/posters/films, emergency telephones, and lighted pathways/sidewalks. City police support campus police during the evening. There is also a student Eyes and Ears Program and a campus security committee made up of students and faculty.

Programs of Study: Wittenberg confers B.A., B.F.A., B.M., and B.M.E. degrees. Master's degrees are also awarded. Bachelor's degrees are awarded in BIOLOGICAL SCIENCE (biology/biological science), BUSINESS (business administration and management), COMMUNICATIONS AND THE ARTS (communications, dramatic arts, English, fine arts, French, German, music, Russian, and Spanish), COMPUTER AND PHYSICAL SCIENCE (chemistry, computer science, earth science, geology, mathematics, and physics), EDUCATION (art, business, elementary, foreign languages, middle school, music, science, secondary, and special), HEALTH PROFESSIONS (predentistry and premedicine), SOCIAL SCIENCE (American studies, East Asian studies, economics, geography, history, international relations, philosophy, political science/government, prelaw, psychology, religion, and sociology). Biology, education, and English are the strongest academically. Business, education, and biology are the largest.

Required: To graduate, students must complete at least 130 credits. The required minimum GPA and number of hours in the major varies by department. The liberal arts core includes courses distributed in various areas. All students must take a Common Learning course, and courses in writing proficiency, services, phys ed, and math/computer science. Comprehensive exams are required in some departments. Sophomores must spend 30 hours in volunteer service.

Special: Internships, cross-registration through the Southwest Ohio Consortium, a Washington semester, work-study programs, study-abroad opportunities in many countries, accelerated degree programs, dual and student-designed majors, nondegree study, and pass/fail options are available. A 3-2 engineering degree is offered through Washington, Columbia, and Case Western Reserve Universities and Georgia Institute of Technology. There is also a 3-2 nursing program with Johns Hopkins University and an occupational therapy program with Washington University. There are 6 national honor societies, including Phi Beta Kappa, a freshman honors program, and 10 departmental honors programs.

Faculty/Classroom: 58% of faculty are male; 42%, female. All teach undergraduates and 25% also do research. The average class size in an introductory lecture is 25; in a laboratory, 20; and in a regular course, 18.

Admissions: 85% of the 2001-2002 applicants were accepted. 68% of the current freshmen were in the top fifth of their class; 95% were in the top two fifths. In a recent year, there were 4 National Merit finalists, and 29 freshmen graduated first in their class.

Requirements: The SAT I or ACT is required. The SAT II: Writing test is recommended. In addition, students should have graduated from an accredited secondary school with 16 academic credits, including 4 units of English and 3 each of a foreign language, math, science, and social studies, which includes history. An essay is required and an interview advised. Art students must present a portfolio, and music students must audition. AP credits are accepted. Important factors in the admissions decision are advanced placement or honor courses, evidence of special talent, and extracurricular activities record. Wittenberg will accept applications on-line via CollegeLink, Apply, or similar services; the school has its own free application web site.

Procedure: Freshmen are admitted to all sessions. Entrance exams should be taken by the fall of the senior year, but as early as possible. There are early decision, early admissions, and deferred admissions plans. Early decision applications should be filed by November 15; regular applications, by March 15 for fall entry, December 1 for winter entry, and May 1 for summer entry, along with a $40 fee. Notification of early decision is sent January 1; regular decision, on a rolling basis, within 3 weeks of receipt of the completed application. 27 early decision candidates were accepted for the 2001-2002 class. 2% of all applicants are on a waiting list; 1 was accepted in 2001.

Transfer: 31 transfer students enrolled in 2001-2002. Applicants should have a minimum GPA of 2.25 at an accredited college and be in good academic and social standing. High school transcripts are required in some cases. An interview is recommended. 75 credits of 130 must be completed at Wittenberg.

Visiting: There are regularly scheduled orientations for prospective students, including fall, winter, and summer programs. There are guides for informal visits and visitors may sit in on classes and stay overnight. To schedule a visit, contact the Admissions Office.

Financial Aid: In 2001-2002, 76% of all freshmen and 72% of continuing students received some form of financial aid, including need-based aid. The average freshman award was $19,000. Of that total, scholarships or need-based grants averaged $14,000 ($22,000 maximum); loans averaged $3500 ($4500 maximum); work contracts averaged $1700; and Choice Awards for Ohio residents attending Ohio private colleges, $1060 per year. 55% of undergraduates work part time. Average annual earnings from campus work are $1500. The FAFSA is required. The fall application deadline is March 15.

International Students: There are 90 international students enrolled. The school actively recruits these students. They must score 550 on the written TOEFL or 230 on the electronic version or take the SAT I, if available. In some cases, the SAT I is required.

Computers: The mainframe is a DEC VAX 11/750. There are 500 terminals and PCs located in residence halls and all academic buildings and libraries. All students may access the system 24 hours a day. There are no time limits. The fee is $150. It is strongly recommended that all students have a personal computer, preferably a Pentium.

Graduates: In 2001, 465 bachelor's degrees were awarded. The most popular majors were business (15%), biology (10%), and education (8%). In an average class, 1% graduate in 3 years, 68% in 4 years, 71% in 5 years, and 72% in 6 years. 75 companies recruited on campus in 2000-2001. Of the 2000 graduating class, 16% were enrolled in graduate school within 6 months of graduation and 96% were employed.

Admissions Contact: Kenneth G. Benne, Dean of Admissions. A video is available. E-mail: *admission@wittenberg.edu*
Web: *www.wittenberg.edu*

WRIGHT STATE UNIVERSITY

Dayton, OH 45435 — B-4
(937) 775-5700
(800) 247-1770; Fax: (937) 775-5795

Full-time: 4281 men, 5500 women	**Faculty:** 487; I, --$
Part-time: 1041 men, 1398 women	**Ph.D.s:** 87%
Graduate: 1478 men, 2112 women	**Student/Faculty:** 20 to 1
Year: quarters, summer session	**Tuition:** $4596 ($9192)
Application Deadline: open	**Room & Board:** $4545
Freshman Class: n/av	
SAT I or ACT: required	**LESS COMPETITIVE**

Wright State University, founded in 1964, is a state-supported institution offering undergraduate programs in business and administration, education and human services, engineering and computer science, liberal arts, math and science, and nursing and health. There are 6 undergraduate and 5 graduate schools. In addition to regional accreditation, Wright State has baccalaureate program accreditation with AACSB, ABET, CSWE, NASM, NCATE, and NLN. The 2 libraries contain 695,805 volumes and 1,278,767 microform items, and subscribe to 5523 periodicals. Computerized library services include the card catalog, interlibrary loans, and database searching. Special learning facilities include a learning resource center, art gallery, radio station, TV station, and a TV production studio. The Department of Archives and Special Collections houses one of the most complete depositories of information on the Wright Brothers in the world. The 645-acre campus is in a suburban area 8 miles northeast of Dayton. Including residence halls, there are 53 buildings.

Student Life: 98% of undergraduates are from Ohio. Others are from 49 states, 71 foreign countries, and Canada. 82% are white. The average age of freshmen is 19; all undergraduates, 24. 28% do not continue beyond their first year; 42% remain to graduate.

Housing: 2300 students can be accommodated in college housing, which includes coed dormitories, on-campus apartments, and married-student housing. In addition, there are honors houses and special-interest houses. On-campus housing is available on a first-come, first-served basis and is available on a lottery system for upperclassmen. 80% of students commute. All students may keep cars.

Activities: 5% of men belong to 2 local and 8 national fraternities; 3% of women belong to 5 national sororities. There are 140 groups on campus, including band, cheerleading, chess, choir, chorale, chorus, computers, drill team, ethnic, film, gay, honors, international, jazz band, literary magazine, newspaper, orchestra, pep band, political, professional, radio and TV, religious, social, social service, and student government. Popular campus events include October Daze, May Daze, and Madrigal Dinner.

Sports: There are 7 intercollegiate sports for men and 7 for women, and 12 intramural sports for men and 12 for women. Facilities include an athletic and entertainment center with an arena seating 13,000 spectators, break-off rooms, auxiliary gym, and baseball and practice fields. The student union houses a natatorium, weight rooms, game rooms, and playing courts.

Disabled Students: All of the campus is accessible. Wheelchair ramps, elevators, special parking, specially equipped rest rooms, lowered drinking fountains, lowered telephones, and specially equipped on-campus housing. An underground tunnel system connects all academic buildings. Adaptive technology is available are available.

Services: Counseling and information services are available, as is tutoring in most subjects. There is a reader service for the blind, and remedial math, reading, and writing.

Campus Safety and Security: Measures include 24-hour foot and vehicle patrol, self-defense education, escort service, and shuttle buses. There are informal discussions, pamphlets/posters/films, emergency telephones, and lighted pathways/sidewalks.

Programs of Study: Wright State confers B.A., B.S., B.F.A., B.Mus., B.S.B., B.S.Comp.Eng., B.S.E., B.S.Ed., B.S.M.T., and B.S.N. degrees. Master's and doctoral degrees are also awarded. Bachelor's degrees are awarded in BIOLOGICAL SCIENCE (biology/biological science), BUSINESS (accounting, banking and finance, business economics, management information systems, management science, and marketing/retailing/merchandising), COMMUNICATIONS AND THE ARTS (art history and appreciation, arts administration/management, classical languages, communications, dance, dramatic arts, English, film arts, fine arts, French, German, modern language, music, music history and appreciation, music theory and composition, Spanish, and theater design), COMPUTER AND PHYSICAL SCIENCE (chemistry, computer science, geology, geophysics and seismology, mathematics, and physics), EDUCATION (art, business, elementary, foreign languages, music, physical, science, secondary, and special), ENGINEERING AND ENVIRONMENTAL DESIGN (biomedical engineering, computer engineering, electrical/electronics engineering, engineering physics, materials engineering, mechanical engineering, systems engineering, and water and wastewater technology), HEALTH PROFESSIONS (environmental health science, medical laboratory technology, nursing, predentistry, premedicine, and rehabilitation therapy), SOCIAL SCIENCE (anthropology, economics, geography, history, humanities, international relations, philosophy, political science/government, prelaw, psychology, religion, social work, sociology, and urban studies). Business education, theater arts, and engineering are the strongest academically. Elementary education, accounting, and nursing are the largest.

Required: To graduate, students must complete 183 quarter hours, with a minimum GPA of 2.0. All students are required to take 57 credit hours of general education courses in 4 areas: communication and math skills, the Western experience, the non-Western world, and understanding the contemporary world.

Special: B.A.-B.S. degrees are offered in computer science, geography, urban affairs, biological sciences, chemistry, geological sciences, math, and psychology. Cross-registration with other area colleges is available through the Southwestern Ohio Council for Higher Education. Dual majors, co-op programs, internships, study abroad, work-study programs, student-designed majors, nondegree study, and credit for military experience are available. There are 13 national honor societies, a freshman honors program, and 62 departmental honors programs.

Faculty/Classroom: 64% of faculty are male; 36%, female. The average class size in an introductory lecture is 41; in a laboratory, 27; and in a regular course, 32.

Requirements: The SAT I or ACT is required. In addition, applicants should be graduates of an accredited secondary school and have 4 units in English, 3 units each in math, science, and social studies, 2 units in a foreign language, and 1 units in the arts. A portfolio is required for art majors, an audition for theater and music majors. The GED is accepted. Applications are accepted on computer disk and on-line. AP and CLEP credits are accepted.

Procedure: Freshmen are admitted to all sessions. Entrance exams should be taken in the spring of the junior year. There is a deferred admissions plan. Application deadlines are open. Notification is sent on a rolling basis. The fall 2001 application fee was $30.

Transfer: Applicants must have a 2.0 GPA. 45 credits of 183 must be completed at Wright State.

Visiting: There are regularly scheduled orientations for prospective students, including a campus tour and information on academic and student services. There are guides for informal visits and visitors may sit in on classes. To schedule a visit, contact the Office of Admissions.

Financial Aid: Wright State is a member of CSS. The CSS/Profile, FAFSA, FFS, or SFS, or the college's own financial statement are required. The fall application deadline is March 1.

International Students: They must score 500 on the written TOEFL.

Computers: The mainframe is a Hitachi AS/EX 44. Students may access the system through many labs on campus through the network from remote locations, including residence halls. All students may access the system. There are no time limits and no fees.

Graduates: In an average class, 25% graduate in 5 years, and 35% in 6 years.

Admissions Contact: Cathy Davis, Director of Undergraduate Admissions. E-mail: *admissions@wright.edu* Web: *www.wright.edu*

XAVIER UNIVERSITY

Cincinnati, OH 45207 **A-5**

(513) 745-3301
(877) 982-3648; Fax: (513) 745-4319

Full-time: 1436 men, 1920 women
Part-time: 239 men, 411 women
Graduate: 1143 men, 1511 women
Year: semesters, summer session
Application Deadline: see profile
Freshman Class: 3534 applied, 2950 accepted, 797 enrolled
SAT I or ACT: required

Faculty: 255; IIA, av$
Ph.D.s: 80%
Student/Faculty: 13 to 1
Tuition: $16,920
Room & Board: $6960

COMPETITIVE

Xavier University, founded in 1831, is a liberal arts Jesuit institution affiliated with the Roman Catholic Church. There are 3 undergraduate and 10 graduate schools. In addition to regional accreditation, Xavier has baccalaureate program accreditation with AACSB, ACOTE, AOTA, CAAHEP, CAHEA, CCNE, CSWE, and NLN. The 2 libraries contain 352,955 volumes, 695,258 microform items, and 6000 audiovisual forms/CDs, and subscribe to 1586 periodicals. Computerized library services include the card catalog, interlibrary loans, and database searching. Special learning facilities include a learning resource center, art gallery, radio station, TV station, and an observatory. The 125-acre campus is in a suburban area 5 miles northeast of the center of Cincinnati. Including residence halls, there are 66 buildings.

Student Life: 66% of undergraduates are from Ohio. Others are from 45 states, 43 foreign countries, and Canada. 83% are white. 64% are Catholic; 18% claim no religious affiliation; 13%, Baptist, Buddhist, Hindu, Muslim, or other. The average age of freshmen is 18.5; all undergraduates, 21.3. 12% do not continue beyond their first year; 74% remain to graduate.

Housing: 1850 students can be accommodated in college housing, which includes coed dormitories, on-campus apartments, off-campus apartments, and married-student housing. In addition, there are honors houses and special-interest houses. On-campus housing is guaranteed for all 4 years; a choice of room is available on a first-come, first-served basis and on a lottery system for upperclassmen. 54% of students commute. All students may keep cars.

Activities: There are no fraternities or sororities. There are 100 groups on campus, including art, band, cheerleading, choir, chorale, chorus, computers, dance, drama, ethnic, film, gay, honors, international, jazz band, literary magazine, musical theater, newspaper, opera, orchestra, pep band, photography, political, professional, radio and TV, religious, social, social service, student government, and yearbook. Popular campus events include Family Weekend, and Spring Break Away.

Sports: There are 8 intercollegiate sports for men and 8 for women, and 23 intramural sports for men and 21 for women. Facilities include a field house, a sports center, a basketball and volleyball arena, a rifle range, a pool, tennis courts, and baseball, soccer, and softball fields.

Disabled Students: 65% of the campus is accessible. Wheelchair ramps, elevators, special parking, specially equipped rest rooms, lowered drinking fountains, and lowered telephones are available.

Services: Counseling and information services are available, as is tutoring in most subjects. There are math and writing labs and effective reading and study skills classes. There is a reader service for the blind.

Campus Safety and Security: Measures include 24-hour foot and vehicle patrol, self-defense education, escort service, and shuttle buses. There are informal discussions, pamphlets/posters/films, emergency telephones, lighted pathways/sidewalks, a Crime Prevention Program, and Neighbors Helping Neighbors, a community-based program operated in conjunction with the university.

Programs of Study: Xavier confers B.A., B.S., B.F.A., B.L.A., B.S.B.A., B.S.N., and B.S.W. degrees. Associate, master's, and doctoral degrees are also awarded. Bachelor's degrees are awarded in BIOLOGICAL SCIENCE (biology/biological science), BUSINESS (accounting, banking and finance, business administration and management, business economics, entrepreneurial studies, human resources, international business management, management science, marketing/retailing/merchandising, organizational behavior, and sports management), COMMUNICATIONS AND THE ARTS (advertising, art, classics, communications, English, fine arts, French, German, media arts, music, public relations, and Spanish), COMPUTER AND PHYSICAL SCIENCE (applied physics, chemistry, computer science, information sciences and systems, mathematics, natural sciences, and physics), EDUCATION (athletic training, early childhood, education, middle school, music, science, and special), ENGINEERING AND ENVIRONMENTAL DESIGN (chemical engineering), HEALTH PROFESSIONS (medical laboratory technology, nursing, occupational therapy, predentistry, premedicine, and prepharmacy), SOCIAL SCIENCE (classical/ancient civilization, criminal justice, economics, history, humanities, international relations, liberal arts/general studies, philosophy, political science/government, prelaw, psychology, social work, sociology, and theological studies). Physics, Honors A.B., and University Scholars are the strongest academically. Business, communications, and education are the largest.

Required: To graduate, students must complete between 120 and 140 credit hours with a minimum GPA of 2.0. The total number of hours required in the major varies. All students must take core curriculum courses in English composition, cultural diversity, math, science, social science, history, theology, philosophy, a foreign language, literature, fine arts, and an ethics/religion and society focus.

Special: Xavier offers internships related to the major, cross-registration through the Greater Cincinnati Consortium, and co-op programs in business and computer science. Students may study abroad in a number of countries, including England, France, Germany, Italy, Japan, and Spain. A general studies degree, B.A.-B.S. degrees, Honors A.B. degree, an interdisciplinary major, a Washington semester, and nondegree study are available. A 3-2 engineering degree is offered with the University of Cincinnati. There are 8 national honor societies, and a freshman honors program.

Faculty/Classroom: 52% of faculty are male; 48%, female. 95% teach undergraduates, 80% do research, and 70% do both. No introductory courses are taught by graduate students.

Admissions: 83% of the 2001-2002 applicants were accepted. The SAT I scores for the 2001-2002 freshman class were: Verbal--13% below 500, 41% between 500 and 599, 39% between 600 and 700, and 8% above 700; Math--16% below 500, 42% between 500 and 599, 34% between 600 and 700, and 8% above 700. The ACT scores were 8% below 21, 24% between 21 and 23, 32% between 24 and 26, 17% between 27 and 28, and 20% above 28. 52% of the current freshmen were in the top fifth of their class; 80% were in the top two fifths. There were 6 National Merit finalists. 19 freshmen graduated first in their class.

Requirements: The SAT I or ACT is required. In addition, graduation from an accredited secondary school or satisfactory scores on the GED is required for admission. The school requires 21 academic credits, including 4 years of English, 3 years each of math, social studies, and science, 2 years of foreign language, 1 year of health/phys ed, plus 5 electives. Xavier recommends an interview. AP and CLEP credits are accepted. Important factors in the admissions decision are advanced placement or honor courses, leadership record, and extracurricular activities record. Applications are accepted on-line via Common App or the school's web site.

Procedure: Freshmen are admitted fall and spring. Entrance exams should be taken during the spring or summer before the senior year. There are early admissions and deferred admissions plans. Applications should be filed by February 1 for priority consideration for fall entry. The fall 2001 application fee was $30. Notification is sent on a rolling basis. 4% of all applicants are on a waiting list.

Transfer: 83 transfer students enrolled in 2001-2002. Applicants must have a minimum GPA of 2.0 in all college-level work. An interview is also recommended. Students who transfer to Xavier with 30 or more semester hours are not required to submit results of either the ACT or SAT I tests. 30 credits of 120 to 140 must be completed at Xavier.

Visiting: There are regularly scheduled orientations for prospective students, including an interview and a tour of the campus. There are guides for informal visits and visitors may sit in on classes and stay overnight. To schedule a visit, contact the Admissions Office.

Financial Aid: In 2001-2002, 90% of all freshmen and 85% of continuing students received some form of financial aid. 53% of freshmen and 45% of continuing students received need-based aid. The average freshman award was $12,715. Of that total, the maximum scholarship or need-based grant was $23,880; the maximum loan was $8000; and the maximum work contract was $2500. 19% of undergraduates work part time. Average annual earnings from campus work are $2080. The average financial indebtedness of the 2001 graduate was $9828. The FAFSA is required. The fall application deadline is February 15.

International Students: There are 47 international students enrolled. The school actively recruits these students. They must score 500 on the written TOEFL or 173 on the electronic version or take the SAT I or the ACT.

Computers: The mainframe is a DEC VAX 7720. Students may create their own accounts on the mainframe from any of the 125 PCs or Macs in the 6 academic computing labs. All residence hall rooms are connected to the mainframe. All students may access the system 24 hours a day. There are no time limits and no fees.

Graduates: In 2001, 993 bachelor's degrees were awarded. The most popular majors were liberal arts (16%), public relations (6%), and marketing (5%). In an average class, 68% graduate in 4 years, 70% in 5 years, and 74% in 6 years. 154 companies recruited on campus in 2000-2001. Of the 2000 graduating class, 20% were enrolled in graduate school within 6 months of graduation and 76% were employed.

Admissions Contact: Marc Camille, Dean of Admission. A video is available. E-mail: *xuadmit@xu.edu* Web: *http://www.xavier.edu*

YOUNGSTOWN STATE UNIVERSITY C-2

Youngstown, OH 44555-0001 **(330) 742-2000**
(877) 468-6978; Fax: (330) 742-3674

Full-time: 4083 men, 4569 women	**Faculty:** 393; IIA, av$
Part-time: 1099 men, 1285 women	**Ph.D.s:** 84%
Graduate: 451 men, 763 women	**Student/Faculty:** 22 to 1
Year: semesters, summer session	**Tuition:** $4348 ($8716)
Application Deadline: August 15	**Room & Board:** $4970

Freshman Class: 3989 applied, 3506 accepted, 2134 enrolled
ACT: 20 **NONCOMPETITIVE**

Youngstown State University, founded in 1908, is a publicly funded, primarily commuter institution offering undergraduate and graduate programs in the arts and sciences, education, business, engineering, fine and performing arts, and health and human services. There are 6 undergraduate schools and 1 graduate school. In addition to regional accreditation, YSU has baccalaureate program accreditation with AACSB, ABET, ACBSP, ADA, CAAHEP, CAHEA, CSWE, NAACLS, NASAD, NASM, NCATE, and NLN. The library contains 963,134 volumes, 884,760 microform items, and 16,222 audiovisual forms/CDs, and subscribes to 2846 periodicals. Computerized library services include the card catalog, interlibrary loans, and database searching. Special learning facilities include a learning resource center, art gallery, planetarium, radio station, and center for historic preservation. The 150-acre campus is in an urban area 65 miles southeast of Cleveland. Including residence halls, there are 48 buildings.

Student Life: 89% of undergraduates are from Ohio. Others are from 42 states, 50 foreign countries, and Canada. 87% are white. The average age of freshmen is 19; all undergraduates, 24. 30% do not continue beyond their first year; 34% remain to graduate.

Housing: 886 students can be accommodated in college housing, which includes single-sex and coed dormitories and on-campus apartments. In addition, there are honors houses, an international living-learning center, off-campus fraternity and sorority houses, and junior, senior, and graduate housing. On-campus housing is available on a first-come, first-served basis and is available on a lottery system for upperclassmen. 91% of students commute. Alcohol is not permitted. All students may keep cars.

Activities: 4% of men belong to 8 national fraternities; 3% of women belong to 1 local sorority and 4 national sororities. There are 130 groups on campus, including art, band, cheerleading, chess, choir, chorale, chorus, computers, dance, drama, ethnic, film, gay, honors, international, jazz band, literary magazine, marching band, musical theater, newspaper, opera, orchestra, pep band, photography, political, professional, radio and TV, religious, social, social service, student government, and symphony. Popular campus events include Organizational Fair, Greek Sing, and Career Night.

Sports: There are 8 intercollegiate sports for men and 10 for women, and 26 intramural sports for men and 26 for women. Facilities include a sports complex with a 20,360-seat stadium, an artificial turf field for football and soccer, racquetball courts, gyms, weight rooms, an all-weather 400-meter track, outdoor basketball, handball, and volleyball courts, and 10 lighted tennis courts. There is also a phys ed center with a 7000-spectator gym, an Olympic-size swimming pool, a dance studio, a rifle range, a fitness center, racquetball and squash courts, and separate gyms for wrestling, weight lifting, gymnastics, and the disabled.

Disabled Students: 98% of the campus is accessible. Wheelchair ramps, elevators, special parking, specially equipped rest rooms, special class scheduling, lowered drinking fountains, lowered telephones, an escort service, a mobility cart, adaptive computers, a lounge, books on tape, institutional memberships, interpreters, a test proctoring program, TDD, and other adaptive equipment are available.

Services: Counseling and information services are available, as is tutoring in some subjects. There is a reader service for the blind, and remedial math, reading, and writing.

Campus Safety and Security: Measures include 24-hour foot and vehicle patrol, self-defense education, escort service, and shuttle buses. There are informal discussions, pamphlets/posters/films, emergency telephones, lighted pathways/sidewalks, night security posts in dormitories, and concentrated security in parking and other critical areas.

Programs of Study: YSU confers A.B., B.S., B.Eng., B.F.A., B.M., B.P.T., B.S.Appl.Sci., B.S.B.A., B.S.Ed., B.S.N., B.S.R.C., and B.S.W. degrees. Associate, master's, and doctoral degrees are also awarded. Bachelor's degrees are awarded in BIOLOGICAL SCIENCE (biology/biological science and nutrition), BUSINESS (accounting, apparel and accessories marketing, banking and finance, business administration and management, business economics, fashion merchandising, hospitality management services, hotel/motel and restaurant management, international economics, labor studies, management information systems, marketing and distribution, marketing management, marketing/retailing/merchandising, office supervision and management, retailing, and secretarial studies/office management), COMMUNICATIONS AND THE ARTS (advertising, art, art history and appreciation, broadcasting, communications, dramatic arts, drawing, English, French, graphic design, Italian, journalism, languages, music, music history and appreciation, music performance, music theory and composition, musical theater, painting, percussion, performing arts, photography, piano/organ, printmaking, public relations, Spanish, speech/debate/rhetoric, studio art, technical and business writing, telecommunications, voice, and winds), COMPUTER AND PHYSICAL SCIENCE (astronomy, chemistry, computer programming, computer science, data processing, earth science, geology, information sciences and systems, mathematics, physics, and science), EDUCATION (art, business, computer, drama, early childhood, education, education of the emotionally handicapped, education of the mentally handicapped, education of the multiply handicapped, elementary, English, foreign languages, health, home economics, mathematics, middle school, music, physical, science, secondary, social science, social studies, special, specific learning disabilities, and vocational), ENGINEERING AND ENVIRONMENTAL DESIGN (chemical engineering, civil engineering, civil engineering technology, computer technology, drafting and design, drafting and design technology, electrical/electronics engineering, electrical/electronics engineering technology, engineering, engineering technology, environmental science, industrial administration/management, industrial engineering, materials engineering, mechanical engineering, mechanical engineering technology, preengineering, and systems engineering), HEALTH PROFESSIONS (allied health, community health work, dental hygiene, health, health science, medical laboratory technology, medical technology, nursing, physical therapy, predentistry, premedicine, preoptometry, preosteopathy, prepharmacy, preveterinary science, and respiratory therapy), SOCIAL SCIENCE (African studies, American studies, anthropology, child care/child and family studies, corrections, criminal justice, dietetics, early childhood studies, economics, family and community services, family/consumer studies, fashion design and technology, geography, history, home economics, human ecology, law enforcement and corrections, philosophy, physical fitness/movement, political science/government, prelaw, psychology, public administration, religion, safety and security technology, social science, social studies, social work, and sociology). Early childhood education is the strongest academically. Criminal justice and management are the largest.

Required: To graduate, students must complete 124 to 132 semester hours, depending on the major, with a minimum GPA of 2.0. At least 60 semester hours in the major are required. All students must fufill core requirements in writing, speech, math, science, humanities, social science, and personal and social responsibility.

Special: YSU offers co-op programs, internships, dual majors, credit for military experience, nondegree study, honors degree programs, distance learning, a joint engineering program, and pass/fail options. Student-designed majors are available through the Individualized Curriculum Program. There are 25 national honor societies, a freshman honors program, and 6 departmental honors programs.

Faculty/Classroom: 66% of faculty are male; 34%, female. All teach undergraduates. Graduate students teach 5% of introductory courses. The average class size in an introductory lecture is 33; in a laboratory, 10; and in a regular course, 24.

Admissions: 88% of the 2001-2002 applicants were accepted. The ACT scores for the 2001-2002 freshman class were: 54% below 21, 22% between 21 and 23, 15% between 24 and 26, 5% between 27 and 28, and 4% above 28. 24% of the current freshmen were in the top fifth of their class; 46% were in the top two fifths. 62 freshmen graduated first in their class.

Requirements: The SAT I or ACT is required. In addition, those who have been out of school for 2 or more years, and who are not pursuing a restricted program of study, are exempt from test requirements. Out-of-state applicants must rank in the upper two thirds of their class or have a combined SAT I score of 820 or higher or 17 or higher composite on the ACT. Graduation from an accredited secondary school or satisfactory scores on the GED are required for all applicants. High school courses must include 4 units of English, 3 each of math, science, and social studies, 2 of foreign language, and 1 of fine or performing arts. AP and CLEP credits are accepted.

Procedure: Freshmen are admitted fall, spring, and summer. Entrance exams should be taken in spring of the junior year or fall of the senior year. There are early admissions and deferred admissions plans. Early decision applications should be filed by February 15; regular applications, by August 15 for fall entry, December 15 for spring entry, and April 15 for summer entry. The fall 2001 application fee was $30. The college accepts all in-state residents and residents of Mercer and Lawrence counties in Pennsylvania. Notification is sent on a rolling basis.

Transfer: 580 transfer students enrolled in 2001-2002. Transfer students must provide transcripts from all secondary schools and colleges attended. Non-Ohio residents must have a minimum GPA of 2.0; those with a lower GPA may be admitted if high school grades and test scores show potential. Ohio residents with a GPA of 2.0 or higher are accepted in good standing; those with a GPA of less than 2.0 or on probation are admitted on probation. 30 credits of 124 to 132 must be completed at YSU.

Visiting: There are regularly scheduled orientations for prospective students. There are guides for informal visits and visitors may sit in on classes. To schedule a visit, contact the Office of Undergraduate Admissions.

Financial Aid: In 2001-2002, 76% of all freshmen and 78% of continuing students received some form of financial aid. 77% of freshmen and 76% of continuing students received need-based aid. The average freshman award was $3800. Of that total, scholarships or need-based grants averaged $4436 ($10,500 maximum); loans averaged $2625 ($6625 maximum); and work contracts averaged $1667 ($4500 maximum). 10% of undergraduates work part time. Average annual earnings from campus work are $3000. The average financial indebtedness of the 2001 graduate was $15,000. The FAFSA and the college's own financial statement are required. The fall application deadline is February 15.

International Students: There are 148 international students enrolled. The school actively recruits these students. They must take the TOEFL, scoring 500 on the written version or 173 on the electronic version, or take the MELAB.

Computers: The mainframe is an IBM 9672/R42. There are approximately 100 terminals in various locations to access student on-line registration and on-line transcripts. There are approximately 1400 PCs that access the mainframe and Internet. There are the 56 computer labs. All students may access the system. There are no time limits and no fees.

Graduates: In 2001, 1354 bachelor's degrees were awarded. The most popular majors were elementary education (11%), criminal justice (5%), and biology (4%). In an average class, 3% graduate in 3 years, 12% in 4 years, 26% in 5 years, and 35% in 6 years.

Admissions Contact: Sue Davis, Interim Director, Undergraduate Admissions. E-mail: *enroll@.ysu.edu* Web: *www.ysu.edu*

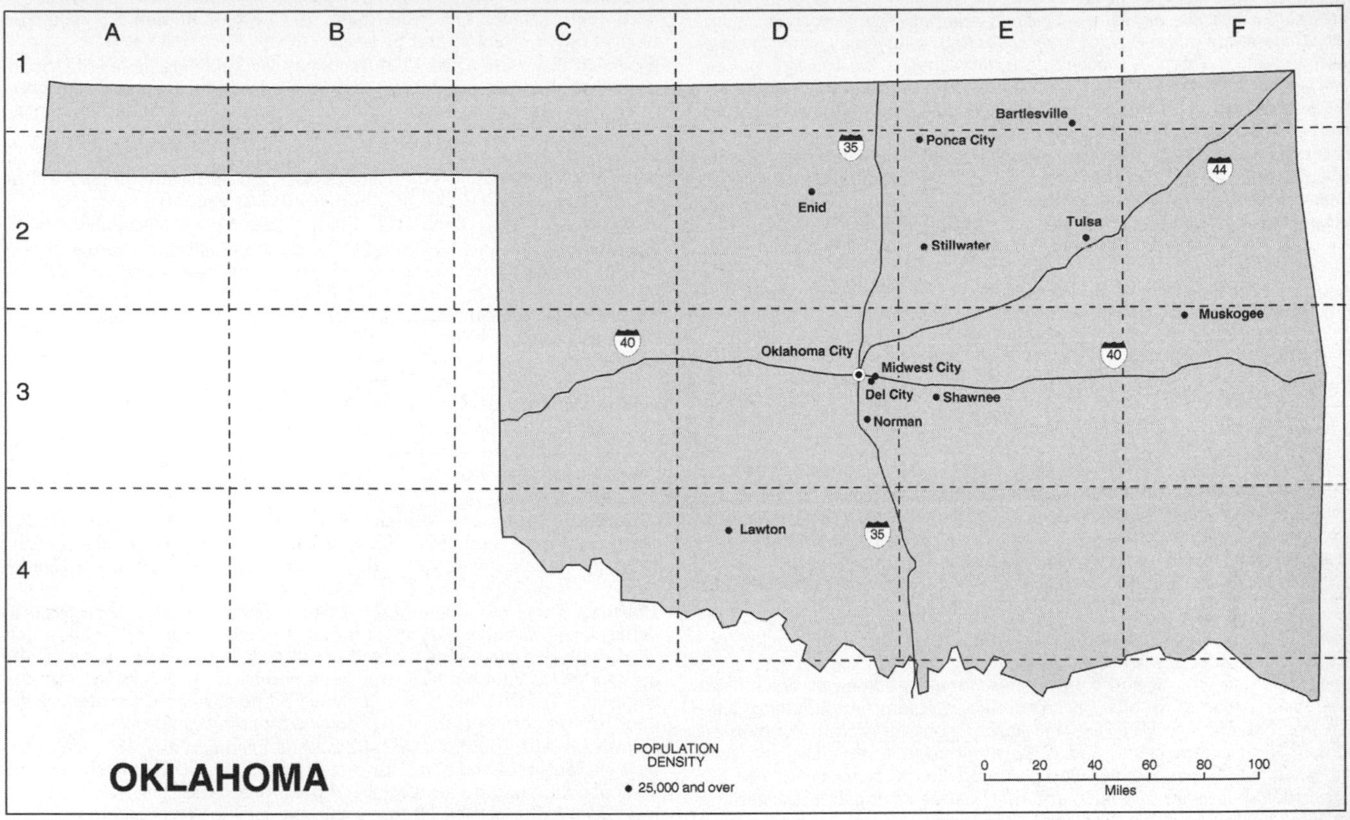

BARTLESVILLE WESLEYAN COLLEGE

E-1

Bartlesville, OK 74006

(918) 335-6219
(800) 468-6292; Fax: (918) 335-6229

Full-time: 150 men, 230 women	**Faculty:** 34; IIB
Part-time: 50 men, 110 women	**Ph.D.s:** 51%
Graduate: none	**Student/Faculty:** 11 to 1
Year: semesters, summer session	**Tuition:** $10,400
Application Deadline: open	**Room & Board:** $3700
Freshman Class: n/av	
SAT I or ACT: recommended	**LESS COMPETITIVE**

Bartlesville Wesleyan College, founded in 1909, is a private liberal arts institution affiliated with the Wesleyan Church. Figures given in the above capsule are approximate. The library contains 120,000 volumes, 20,000 microform items, and 500 audiovisual forms/CDs, and subscribes to 18,000 periodicals. Computerized library services include the card catalog, interlibrary loans, and database searching. Special learning facilities include a learning resource center. The 101-acre campus is in a suburban area 40 miles north of Tulsa. Including residence halls, there are 15 buildings.

Student Life: 53% of undergraduates are from Oklahoma. Others are from 28 states and 12 foreign countries. 85% are from public schools. 80% are white. 49% are Protestant; 10% claim no religious affiliation. The average age of freshmen is 18; all undergraduates, 26. 10% do not continue beyond their first year; 60% remain to graduate.

Housing: 300 students can be accommodated in college housing, which includes single-sex dormitories. On-campus housing is guaranteed for all 4 years and is available on a first-come, first-served basis. 53% of students commute. Alcohol is not permitted. All students may keep cars.

Activities: There are no sororities. There are 10 groups on campus, including band, cheerleading, choir, chorale, chorus, computers, debate, drama, ethnic, forensics, honors, international, newspaper, photography, political, professional, religious, social service, student government, and yearbook. Popular campus events include Spiritual Emphasis Week and Youth Conference.

Sports: There are 2 intercollegiate sports for men and 3 for women, and 10 intramural sports for men and 10 for women. Facilities include a 2000-seat indoor gym and an 8-acre athletic field.

Disabled Students: 73% of the campus is accessible. Wheelchair ramps, elevators, special parking, and specially equipped rest rooms are available.

Services: Counseling and information services are available, as is tutoring in most subjects. There is remedial math, reading, and writing.

Campus Safety and Security: Measures include informal discussions, lighted pathways/sidewalks, and an evening patrol by a security guard.

Programs of Study: BWC confers B.A. and B.S. degrees. Associate degrees are also awarded. Bachelor's degrees are awarded in BIOLOGICAL SCIENCE (biology/biological science), BUSINESS (accounting, business administration and management, and human resources), COMMUNICATIONS AND THE ARTS (communications, English, and music), COMPUTER AND PHYSICAL SCIENCE (chemistry, computer science, information sciences and systems, mathematics, and science), EDUCATION (art, athletic training, business, elementary, English, mathematics, middle school, music, physical, science, secondary, and social studies), HEALTH PROFESSIONS (predentistry and premedicine), SOCIAL SCIENCE (behavioral science, history, liberal arts/general studies, pastoral studies, political science/government, prelaw, religion, religious music, social studies, sociology, and youth ministry). Business and education are the strongest academically. Business and education are the largest.

Required: To graduate, students must complete a total of 126 credit hours with a minimum GPA of 2.0. About 30 hours are required in the major. All students must take 9 hours of religion and a writing proficiency exam.

Special: BWC offers cross-registration with Tri-County Tech, a Washington semester, a co-op program, internships, a general studies degree, credit for life experience, an accelerated degree program in management of human resources, and nondegree study. There is an accelerated program for adult learners, a pretherapy program, and a leadership in business program.

Faculty/Classroom: 60% of faculty are male; 40%, female. The average class size in an introductory lecture is 20; in a laboratory, 20; and in a regular course, 20.

Requirements: The SAT I or ACT is recommended. In addition, graduation from an accredited secondary school or satisfactory scores on the GED are required for admission. 18 academic credits must be completed, including 4 credits of English and 2 credits each of history, math, science, and social studies. Applications are accepted on-line at BWC's web site. BWC requires applicants to be in the upper 50% of their class. A GPA of 2.0 is required. AP and CLEP credits are accepted. Important factors in the admissions decision are leadership record, personality/intangible qualities, and geographic diversity.

Procedure: Freshmen are admitted to all sessions. Entrance exams should be taken during the senior year. Application deadlines are open.
Transfer: Applicants must have a minimum GPA of 2.0. 24 credits of 126 must be completed at BWC.
Visiting: There are regularly scheduled orientations for prospective students. There are guides for informal visits and visitors may sit in on classes and stay overnight. To schedule a visit, contact the Enrollment Services Office.
Financial Aid: The FAFSA and the college's own financial statement are required. The fall application deadline is open.
International Students: The school actively recruits these students. They must score 500 on the written TOEFL and also take the college's own entrance exam and placement tests.
Computers: There is a computer lab housing both IBM and Mac PCs. All students may access the system 8 A.M. to 10 P.M. There are no time limits and no fees.
Admissions Contact: Jere Johnson, Enrollment Services Administrator. E-mail: *admissions@bwc.edu* Web: *www.bwc.edu*

CAMERON UNIVERSITY D-4
Lawton, OK 73505 **(580) 581-2230 or 2289**
(888)-454-7600; Fax: (580) 581-5514

Full-time: 1231 men, 1663 women
Part-time: 817 men, 1025 women
Graduate: 138 men, 324 women
Year: semesters, summer session
Application Deadline: open
Faculty: 204; IIB, --$
Ph.D.s: 33%
Student/Faculty: 14 to 1
Tuition: $2090 ($4880)
Room & Board: $2830
Freshman Class: 1437 applied, 1289 accepted, 886 enrolled
SAT I or ACT: required **NONCOMPETITIVE**

Cameron University, founded in 1908, is a publicly funded institution offering undergraduate programs in business, education and psychology, fine arts, liberal arts, science, mathematics, and technology. There are 3 undergraduate schools and 1 graduate school. In addition to regional accreditation, Cameron has baccalaureate program accreditation with NASM, NCATE, and NLN. The library contains 255,058 volumes, 496,172 microform items, and 6993 audiovisual forms/CDs, and subscribes to 1879 periodicals. Computerized library services include the card catalog, interlibrary loans, and database searching. Special learning facilities include a learning resource center, art gallery, radio station, and TV station. The 160-acre campus is in a small town 90 miles southwest of Oklahoma City. Including residence halls, there are 30 buildings.
Student Life: 94% of undergraduates are from Oklahoma. Others are from 23 states, 25 foreign countries, and Canada. 97% are from public schools. 61% are white; 20% African American. The average age of freshmen is 24; all undergraduates, 28.
Housing: 512 students can be accommodated in college housing, which includes single-sex dormitories. On-campus housing is guaranteed for all 4 years. 99% of students commute. Alcohol is not permitted. All students may keep cars.
Activities: 4% of men belong to 2 national fraternities; 6% of women belong to 2 national sororities. There are 57 groups on campus, including art, band, cheerleading, computers, debate, drama, drill team, ethnic, honors, international, jazz band, literary magazine, newspaper, orchestra, pep band, political, professional, radio and TV, religious, social, and student government. Popular campus events include Spring Fling, Diversity Week, and Organizational Day.
Sports: There are 4 intercollegiate sports for men and 4 for women, and 6 intramural sports for men and 6 for women. Facilities include a 10,000-seat football stadium, an 1800-seat gym, a 100-seat baseball park, a running track, Nautilus and free-weight rooms, an indoor swimming pool, and basketball, volleyball, and racquetball courts.
Disabled Students: 80% of the campus is accessible. Wheelchair ramps, elevators, special parking, specially equipped rest rooms, and special class scheduling are available.
Services: Counseling and information services are available, as is tutoring in some subjects, including writing, reading, accounting, math, fine arts, technology, and computer science. There is remedial math, reading, and writing.
Campus Safety and Security: Measures include 24-hour foot and vehicle patrol, escort service, pamphlets/posters/films, and emergency telephones. There are lighted pathways/sidewalks.
Programs of Study: Cameron confers B.A., B.S., B.Acctg., B.B.A., and B.F.A. degrees. Associate and master's degrees are also awarded. Bachelor's degrees are awarded in BIOLOGICAL SCIENCE (biology/biological science), BUSINESS (accounting, banking and finance, business administration and management, and marketing/retailing/merchandising), COMMUNICATIONS AND THE ARTS (broadcasting, communications, dramatic arts, English, fine arts, journalism, music, romance languages and literature, and speech/debate/rhetoric), COMPUTER AND PHYSICAL SCIENCE (chemistry, computer science, mathematics, and physics), EDUCATION (early childhood, elementary, health, and music), HEALTH PROFESSIONS (medical laboratory technology), SOCIAL SCIENCE (criminal justice, history, political science/government, psychology, and sociology). Business, education, and technology are the largest.
Required: To graduate, students must complete a total of 128 credit hours with a minimum GPA of 2.0. All students must take courses in English, math, science, U.S. history and government, humanities, behavioral science, economics, and phys ed.
Special: Cameron offers dual majors in several fields, an interdisciplinary studies degree, nondegree study, and credit for military experience. There are 18 national honor societies, including Phi Beta Kappa, a freshman honors program, and 11 departmental honors programs.
Faculty/Classroom: 63% of faculty are male; 37%, female. All both teach and do research. The average class size in an introductory lecture is 50; in a laboratory, 30; and in a regular course, 30.
Admissions: 90% of the 2001-2002 applicants were accepted.
Requirements: The SAT I or ACT is required with minimum scores of 890 or 20 respectively, or applicants must rank in the top 50% of their graduating class and have a GPA of at least 207. High school courses must include 4 years of English, 3 of math (including algebra I and above), 2 each of history and lab science, 1 of economics, geography, government, or nonwestern culture, and an additional 3 years of any of the previous subjects, or of computer science, or foreign language. Applications are accepted on-line. AP and CLEP credits are accepted.
Procedure: Freshmen are admitted to all sessions. Entrance exams should be taken late in the junior year or early in the senior year. Application deadlines are open. The application fee is $15. Notification is sent on a rolling basis.
Transfer: 365 transfer students enrolled in 2001-2002. Transfer students must have a minimum GPA of 2.0 and be in good standing at the institution last attended. 30 credits of 128 must be completed at Cameron.
Visiting: There are regularly scheduled orientations for prospective students, including introductory sessions on college life and student services, with department chairs and enrollment, and campus tours. There are guides for informal visits and visitors may sit in on classes and stay overnight. To schedule a visit, contact Brenda Dally, Coordinator Student Recruitment at (580) 581-2837 or *brenda@cameron.edu*.
Financial Aid: In 2001-2002, 62% of all freshmen and 48% of continuing students received some form of financial aid. 40% of freshmen and 45% of continuing students received need-based aid. The average freshman award was $5300. Of that total, scholarships or need-based grants averaged $2650 ($6200 maximum); loans averaged $1460 ($2625 maximum); and work contracts averaged $2000 ($4000 maximum). 71% of undergraduates work part time. Average annual earnings from campus work are $2000. The average financial indebtedness of the 2001 graduate was $6200. The FAFSA is required. The fall application deadline is July 15.
International Students: There are 137 international students enrolled. They must score 500 on the written TOEFL or 173 on the electronic version and also take the SAT I or the ACT, scoring 890 on the SAT I.
Computers: The mainframe is an HP/3000 Series 960. Students may access the Internet and various academic programs using more than 800 PCs in 15 labs. Dorm rooms have network connections. All students may access the system 7:30 A.M. to 11 P.M. daily. There are no time limits and no fees.
Graduates: In 2001, 501 bachelor's degrees were awarded. The most popular majors were education (17%), business (15%), and psychology (7%). 49 companies recruited on campus in 2000-2001.
Admissions Contact: Zoe Du Rant, Director of Admissions/Registrar. E-mail: *zoed@cameron.edu* Web: *www.cameron.edu*

EAST CENTRAL UNIVERSITY E-4
Ada, OK 74820 **(580) 332-8000; Fax: (580) 310-5432**

Full-time: 1228 men, 1665 women
Part-time: 167 men, 363 women
Graduate: 226 men, 546 women
Year: semesters, summer session
Application Deadline: open
Faculty: 157; IIB, --$
Ph.D.s: 70%
Student/Faculty: 18 to 1
Tuition: $2128 ($5169)
Room & Board: $2450
Freshman Class: 655 applied, 627 accepted, 591 enrolled
ACT: 21 **COMPETITIVE**

East Central University, founded in 1909, is a publicly funded institution offering undergraduate programs in liberal arts and sciences, education, business, and health-related fields. There are 4 undergraduate schools and 1 graduate school. In addition to regional accreditation, ECU has baccalaureate program accreditation with ACBSP, CSWE, NASM, NCATE, and NLN. The library contains 215,000 volumes, 1 million microform items, and 7000 audiovisual forms/CDs, and subscribes to 1200 periodicals. Computerized library services include the card catalog, interlibrary loans, and database searching. Special learning facilities include a learning resource center. The 140-acre campus is in a small town 90 miles south of Oklahoma City. Including residence halls, there are 28 buildings.
Student Life: 97% of undergraduates are from Oklahoma. Others are from 17 states, 25 foreign countries, and Canada. 99% are from public

schools. 75% are white; 16% Native American/Eskimo. The average age of freshmen is 19; all undergraduates, 23. 38% do not continue beyond their first year.

Housing: 1121 students can be accommodated in college housing, which includes single-sex and coed dormitories, on-campus apartments, and married-student housing. On-campus housing is available on a first-come, first-served basis. Alcohol is not permitted. All students may keep cars.

Activities: 8% of men belong to 4 national fraternities; 8% of women belong to 3 national sororities. There are 20 groups on campus, including art, band, cheerleading, choir, chorale, computers, dance, debate, drama, drill team, ethnic, forensics, honors, international, jazz band, marching band, newspaper, nontraditional students, pep band, political, religious, social, social service, student government, and yearbook. Popular campus events include Welcome Week, Don't Go Home This Weekend Weekend, and Christmas in the Eyes of a Child.

Sports: There are 6 intercollegiate sports for men and 5 for women, and 4 intramural sports for men and 4 for women. Facilities include a swimming pool, a fitness/aerobics center, tennis, basketball, and racquetball courts, a weight room, a football field, and indoor and outdoor tracks.

Disabled Students: All of the campus is accessible. Wheelchair ramps, elevators, special parking, specially equipped rest rooms, special class scheduling, lowered drinking fountains, lowered telephones, and adaptive swimming and weight training are available.

Services: Counseling and information services are available, as is tutoring in every subject. There is a reader service for the blind, and remedial math, reading, and writing. Interpreters for the deaf, note taking/typing, and tape transcription are available.

Campus Safety and Security: Measures include 24-hour foot and vehicle patrol, lighted pathways/sidewalks, and training in the freshman seminar class.

Programs of Study: ECU confers B.A., B.S., B.S.Ed., and B.S.W. degrees. Master's degrees are also awarded. Bachelor's degrees are awarded in BIOLOGICAL SCIENCE (biology/biological science), BUSINESS (accounting, banking and finance, business administration and management, fashion merchandising, management information systems, management science, marketing/retailing/merchandising, office supervision and management, and recreation and leisure services), COMMUNICATIONS AND THE ARTS (advertising, American Sign Language, art, communications, dramatic arts, English, journalism, music, piano/organ, public relations, speech/debate/rhetoric, and voice), COMPUTER AND PHYSICAL SCIENCE (applied mathematics, chemistry, computer science, mathematics, and physics), EDUCATION (art, athletic training, business, drama, early childhood, elementary, English, health, home economics, mathematics, music, physical, science, secondary, and special), ENGINEERING AND ENVIRONMENTAL DESIGN (cartography), HEALTH PROFESSIONS (environmental health science, exercise science, medical laboratory technology, medical records administration/services, nursing, and rehabilitation therapy), SOCIAL SCIENCE (criminal justice, family/consumer resource management, gerontology, history, human services, liberal arts/general studies, paralegal studies, political science/government, prelaw, psychology, social work, and sociology). Nursing, human resources, and elementary education are the largest.

Required: To graduate, students must complete a minimum of 124 credit hours with a minimum GPA of 2.0. Between 45 to 55 hours must be completed in the major and 18 to 21 hours in the minor. All students must take 40 hours of upper-level courses, as well as 45 hours in general studies, and must meet computer proficiency requirements.

Special: The school offers co-op programs with the Ardmore, Oklahoma Higher Education Center and is a member of the National Student Exchange Program. Internships are available in human resources, environmental health, political science, office technology, mass communications, and cartography. Students may participate in a work-study program with the Veterans Administration. Nondegree study and credit for military experience are available. The school offers special rates for nonresidents from approved states who wish to major in specialized fields. There is 1 national honor society, including Phi Beta Kappa and a freshman honors program.

Faculty/Classroom: 61% of faculty are male; 39%, female. No introductory courses are taught by graduate students. The average class size in an introductory lecture is 30.

Admissions: 96% of the 2001-2002 applicants were accepted. The ACT scores for the 2001-2002 freshman class were: 52% below 21, 36% between 24 and 26, 10% between 27 and 28, and 2% above 28. 23% of the current freshmen were in the top fifth of their class; 35% were in the top two fifths.

Requirements: The ACT is required with a minimum composite score of 20. The SAT I will be accepted in place of the ACT. Applicants must be graduates of an accredited secondary school or have the GED. High school courses must include 4 years of English, 3 years of math, and 2 years each of history and science. ECU requires applicants to be in the upper 50% of their class. A GPA of 2.7 is required. AP and CLEP credits are accepted.

Procedure: Freshmen are admitted to all sessions. Entrance exams should be taken during the junior or senior year of high school. Application deadlines are open.

Transfer: 384 transfer students enrolled in 2001-2002. Applicants having fewer than 24 credit hours must meet the criteria for entering freshmen. The required minimum GPA for transfer students is 2.0. 30 credits of 124 must be completed at ECU.

Visiting: There are guides for informal visits. To schedule a visit, contact the Student Services Office.

Financial Aid: In a recent year, 75% of all students received some form of financial aid. 45% of freshmen and 60% of continuing students received need-based aid. The average freshman award was $1575. Of that total, scholarships or need-based grants averaged $4525; loans averaged $3062; and work contracts averaged $3296. 22% of undergraduates work part time. Average annual earnings from campus work are $1732. The average financial indebtedness of the 2001 graduate was $13,243. The FAFSA, the college's own financial statement, and federal tax returns are required. The fall application deadline is July 1.

International Students: There are 83 international students enrolled. The school actively recruits these students. They must score 500 on the written TOEFL. Students may be required to take the ACT upon arrival.

Computers: The mainframe is an HP 3000. There are PCs available in the library and in various departments. All students have access to the Internet. All students may access the system when labs are open. There are no time limits and no fees.

Graduates: In 2001, 513 bachelor's degrees were awarded. 40 companies recruited on campus in a recent year.

Admissions Contact: Pamla Armstrong, Registrar and Director of Admissions. E-mail: *parmstro@mailclerk.ecok.edu* Web: *www.ecok.edu*

LANGSTON UNIVERSITY — D-3

Langston, OK 73050 — (405) 466-3224; Fax: (405) 466-3381

Full-time: 1290 men, 1920 women	**Faculty:** 105
Part-time: 290 men, 520 women	**Ph.D.s:** 50%
Graduate: 20 men, 40 women	**Student/Faculty:** 31 to 1
Year: semesters, summer session	**Tuition:** $2308 ($5055)
Application Deadline: open	**Room & Board:** n/app
Freshman Class: n/av	
SAT I or ACT: required	**LESS COMPETITIVE**

Langston University, founded in 1897 as the Colored Agricultural and Normal University, is today a multiracial, public institution offering programs in liberal arts, business, allied health, and teacher preparation. Figures in above capsule are approximate. In addition to regional accreditation, Langston has baccalaureate program accreditation with ADA, APTA, NCATE, and NLN. The 6 libraries contain 110,248 volumes and 465,319 microform items, and subscribe to 80 periodicals. Computerized library services include the card catalog and interlibrary loans. Special learning facilities include a learning resource center and satellite teaching, a black heritage center, an institute for goat research, and a state research group in catfish production. The 40-acre campus is in a rural area 45 miles from Oklahoma City. Including residence halls, there are 20 buildings.

Student Life: 98% are from public schools. 50% are African American; 50% white. 65% of freshmen remain to graduate.

Housing: 676 students can be accommodated in college housing, which includes dormitories and married-student housing. Alcohol is not permitted. All students may keep cars.

Activities: 25% of men belong to 4 national fraternities; 30% of women belong to 4 national sororities. There are 30 groups on campus, including band, cheerleading, choir, drama, ethnic, international, jazz band, marching band, newspaper, professional, religious, social service, student government, and yearbook. Popular campus events include student theater productions and a performing arts series.

Sports: There are 4 intercollegiate sports for men and 2 for women, and 6 intramural sports for men and 5 for women. Facilities include a gym, tennis courts, a baseball field, and a track.

Disabled Students: 70% of the campus is accessible. Wheelchair ramps, elevators, special parking, specially equipped rest rooms, and special class scheduling are available.

Services: Counseling and information services are available, as is tutoring in some subjects. There is remedial math, reading, and writing.

Programs of Study: Langston confers B.A., B.B.A., B.S., B.S.Ed., and B.S.N. degrees. Associate and master's degrees are also awarded. Bachelor's degrees are awarded in AGRICULTURE (agricultural economics and animal science), BIOLOGICAL SCIENCE (biology/biological science and nutrition), BUSINESS (accounting, business administration and management, and management science), COMMUNICATIONS AND THE ARTS (dramatic arts, English, music, and speech/debate/rhetoric), COMPUTER AND PHYSICAL SCIENCE (chemistry, computer science, and mathematics), EDUCATION (business, elementary, home economics, industrial arts, mathematics, physical, and science), ENGINEERING AND ENVIRONMENTAL DESIGN (industrial engineering technology), HEALTH PROFESSIONS (health care administration, medical laboratory technology, nursing, and physical therapy), SOCIAL SCIENCE (criminal justice, early childhood studies, economics, gerontology, history, home economics, psychology, social science, sociology, and urban studies).

Required: To graduate, students must complete a total of 124 semester hours, with a GPA of 2.0. The required general education core consists of 50 credits in English, math, computer science, biological and physical sciences, social science, and health and phys ed. 6 credits are required in American history and government, and all students must complete an internship or field experience.

Special: Work-study programs, internships, and nondegree and noncredit study are available. There are 6 national honor societies and a freshman honors program.

Faculty/Classroom: All teach undergraduates.

Requirements: The SAT I or ACT is required. In general, test scores should place students in the upper 60% of Oklahoma high school seniors. Applicants should be graduates of accredited high schools with at least a C average (2.7 on a 4.0 scale) and rank in the upper 60% of their graduating classes. Required secondary preparation includes 4 years of English, 3 years of math, and 2 years each of lab science and history, including 1 year of American history. 4 additional academic units, including a foreign language, are strongly recommended. There are alternative admission programs for students with varying backgrounds. Langston requires applicants to be in the upper 50% of their class. A GPA of 2.7 is required. AP and CLEP credits are accepted.

Procedure: Freshmen are admitted to all sessions. Application deadlines are open. The fall 2001 application fee was $15.

Transfer: Applicants should be in good standing and have earned at least a C average in previous college work. 30 credits of 124 must be completed at Langston.

Visiting: There are regularly scheduled orientations for prospective students. There are guides for informal visits and visitors may sit in on classes and stay overnight. To schedule a visit, contact the High School/College Relations Office.

Financial Aid: In a recent year, 70% of all students received some form of financial aid. 65% of freshmen and 60% of continuing students received need-based aid. The average freshman award was $2800. The CSS/Profile, FAFSA, FFS, or SFS is required. Check with the school for current deadlines.

International Students: They must score 500 on the written TOEFL.

Computers: The mainframes are a DEC VAX 11/750 and an IBM 34. There are also 40 PCs available in academic labs. . There are no time limits and no fees.

Admissions Contact: Ms. Gayle T. Robertson, Director of Admissions and Enrollment Management. E-mail: *gtrobertson@lunet.edu*

NORTHEASTERN STATE UNIVERSITY F-3

Tahlequah, OK 74464 **(918) 456-5511, ext. 2200**
(800) 722-9614; Fax: (918) 458-2342

Full-time: 2441 men, 3341 women	**Faculty:** 306; IIA, -$
Part-time: 671 men, 1158 women	**Ph.D.s:** 71%
Graduate: 287 men, 705 women	**Student/Faculty:** 19 to 1
Year: semesters, summer session	**Tuition:** $1980 ($4501)
Application Deadline: open	**Room & Board:** $2724
Freshman Class: 1751 applied, 1693 accepted, 1104 enrolled	
ACT: 24	**LESS COMPETITIVE**

Northeastern State University, founded in 1846, is a public institution offering programs in arts and sciences, preprofessional training, teacher preparation, and business. There are 5 undergraduate schools and 1 graduate school. In addition to regional accreditation, NSU has baccalaureate program accreditation with ACBSP, ADA, ASLA, CSWE, NASM, NCATE, and NLN. The library contains 380,000 volumes, 604,000 microform items, and 7880 audiovisual forms/CDs, and subscribes to 3442 periodicals. Computerized library services include the card catalog and interlibrary loans. Special learning facilities include a learning resource center. The 200-acre campus is in a small town 70 miles from Tulsa. Including residence halls, there are 43 buildings.

Student Life: 95% of undergraduates are from Oklahoma. Others are from 30 states, 41 foreign countries, and Canada. 64% are white; 28%, Native American/Eskimo. The average age of freshmen is 19; all undergraduates, 26. 30% do not continue beyond their first year.

Housing: 1653 students can be accommodated in college housing, which includes single-sex and coed dormitories and married-student housing. In addition, rooming arragements can be made for special-interest groups. On-campus housing is available on a first-come, first-served basis. 80% of students commute. Alcohol is not permitted. All students may keep cars.

Activities: 10% of men belong to 6 national fraternities; 10% of women belong to 8 national sororities. There are 75 groups on campus, including art, band, cheerleading, choir, dance, drama, drill team, ethnic, honors, international, jazz band, literary magazine, marching band, newspaper, orchestra, pep band, political, professional, religious, social service, student government, and yearbook. Popular campus events include the Lyceum Series, Cherokee Seminaries, and NSU Playhouse events.

Sports: There are 7 intercollegiate sports for men and 5 for women, and 4 intramural sports for men and 3 for women. Facilities include a swimming pool, a softball/soccer complex, a weight room, playing fields, a 10,000-seat track and football stadium, and basketball, handball, and racquetball courts.

Disabled Students: 98% of the campus is accessible. Wheelchair ramps, elevators, special parking, specially equipped rest rooms, lowered drinking fountains, and lowered telephones are available.

Services: Counseling and information services are available, as is tutoring in most subjects. There is remedial math, reading, and writing.

Campus Safety and Security: Measures include 24-hour foot and vehicle patrol, escort service, shuttle buses, and informal discussions. There are pamphlets/posters/films, emergency telephones, lighted pathways/sidewalks, and a campus security police department.

Programs of Study: NSU confers B.A., B.S., B.A.Ed., B.B.A., B.S.Ed., B.S.Sci.Ed., B.S.N., and B.S.W. degrees. Master's and doctoral degrees are also awarded. Bachelor's degrees are awarded in BIOLOGICAL SCIENCE (biology/biological science and zoology), BUSINESS (accounting, banking and finance, business administration and management, and marketing/retailing/merchandising), COMMUNICATIONS AND THE ARTS (advertising, communications, English, fine arts, journalism, music, Spanish, and speech/debate/rhetoric), COMPUTER AND PHYSICAL SCIENCE (chemistry, computer science, information sciences and systems, mathematics, and physics), EDUCATION (art, early childhood, elementary, health, home economics, industrial arts, music, science, secondary, and special), HEALTH PROFESSIONS (medical laboratory technology, nursing, predentistry, and premedicine), SOCIAL SCIENCE (criminal justice, geography, history, political science/government, prelaw, psychology, social science, social work, and sociology).

Required: To graduate, students must complete at least 124 credit hours, including 24 to 50 in the major with a minimum GPA of 2.0. General education requirements include 40 hours in language arts, social science, natural science, humanities, and phys ed. Freshman orientation and English proficiency are required.

Special: NSU offers educational tours for academic credit, B.A.-B.S. degrees, a weekend program, nondegree study, credit by exam or for military experience, and a pass/fail option. There are 10 national honor societies, a freshman honors program, and 5 departmental honors programs.

Admissions: 97% of the 2001-2002 applicants were accepted.

Requirements: The ACT is required, with a minimum composite score of 20. Applicants should be high school graduates or have a GED. Students should have completed 4 years of English, 3 of math, and 2 each of history and science. NSU requires applicants to be in the upper 50% of their class. A GPA of 2.7 is required. AP and CLEP credits are accepted.

Procedure: Freshmen are admitted to all sessions. Application deadlines are open. Notification is sent on a rolling basis.

Transfer: Applicants must have a minimum GPA of 2.0, with 24 transfer hours completed, and be in good standing at the last institution attended. 30 credits of 124 must be completed at NSU.

Visiting: There are regularly scheduled orientations for prospective students, including a general campus visit with highlights presented by trained tour guides. Visitors may sit in on classes and stay overnight. To schedule a visit, contact High School and College Relations at (918) 458-2130.

Financial Aid: In 2001-2002, 62% of all freshmen and 69% of continuing students received some form of financial aid. 57% of freshmen and 69% of continuing students received need-based aid. The average freshman award was $7075. Of that total, scholarships or need-based grants averaged $1000 ($1500 maximum); loans averaged $2625 (maximum); work contracts averaged $2150 ($2480 maximum); and Pell Grant and state-funded awards averaged $1300 ($4750 maximum). 41% of undergraduates work part time. Average annual earnings from campus work are $2480. The average financial indebtedness of the 2001 graduate was $7436. The FAFSA and the college's own financial statement are required. The fall application deadline is April 30.

International Students: There are 41 international students enrolled. They must score 500 on the written TOEFL or 173 on the electronic version.

Computers: Macs and TRS-80 PCs are available in classrooms and labs. Computer labs are located all over campus; there are terminal ports in each dorm room. All students may access the system. There are no time limits and no fees.

Graduates: In 2001, 1258 bachelor's degrees were awarded.

Admissions Contact: Dawn Cain, Director of Admissions.
E-mail: *nsuinfo@nsuok.edu* Web: *http://www.nsuok.edu*

NORTHWESTERN OKLAHOMA STATE UNIVERSITY C-1

Alva, OK 73717 (580) 327-8546; Fax: (580) 327-1881

Full-time: 575 men, 580 women	**Faculty:** 65; IIB, --$
Part-time: 175 men, 290 women	**Ph.D.s:** 51%
Graduate: 85 men, 185 women	**Student/Faculty:** 18 to 1
Year: semesters, summer session	**Tuition:** $1992 ($5816)
Application Deadline: open	**Room & Board:** $2550
Freshman Class: n/av	
ACT: required	**NONCOMPETITIVE**

Northwestern Oklahoma State University, founded in 1897, is a public institution offering programs in liberal and fine arts, agriculture, business, professional training, and teacher preparation. There is 1 graduate school. Figures in the above capsule are approximate. In addition to regional accreditation, Northwestern has baccalaureate program accreditation with NCATE and NLN. The library contains 135,000 volumes, 366,000 microform items, and 1100 audiovisual forms/CDs, and subscribes to 1480 periodicals. Computerized library services include interlibrary loans and database searching. Special learning facilities include a learning resource center, natural history museum, radio station, TV station, and a cable channel. The 70-acre campus is in a small town 150 miles northwest of Oklahoma City. Including residence halls, there are 35 buildings.

Student Life: 85% of undergraduates are from Oklahoma. Others are from 25 states, 18 foreign countries, and Canada. 89% are white. The average age of freshmen is 21; all undergraduates, 24. 34% do not continue beyond their first year; 35% remain to graduate.

Housing: 850 students can be accommodated in college housing, which includes single-sex dormitories. On-campus housing is guaranteed for all 4 years. Alcohol is not permitted. All students may keep cars.

Activities: 1% of men belong to 1 national fraternity. There are 39 groups on campus, including art, band, cheerleading, choir, chorale, computers, dance, drama, ethnic, forensics, honors, international, jazz band, marching band, musical theater, newspaper, pep band, photography, political, professional, radio and TV, religious, social, student government, and yearbook. Popular campus events include Foundation Scholarship Banquet, Alumni Banquet, and Science Fair.

Sports: There are 4 intercollegiate sports for men and 2 for women, and 4 intramural sports for men and 4 for women. Facilities include a field house, playing fields, a basketball court, a pool, and racquetball and tennis courts.

Disabled Students: All of the campus is accessible. Wheelchair ramps, elevators, special parking, specially equipped rest rooms, special class scheduling, and lowered drinking fountains are available. Northwestern works with disabled students to accommodate their special needs.

Services: Counseling and information services are available, as is tutoring in most subjects. There is remedial math, reading, and writing.

Campus Safety and Security: Measures include 24-hour foot and vehicle patrol and lighted pathways/sidewalks.

Programs of Study: Northwestern confers B.A., B.S., B.A.Ed., B.S.Ed., and B.S.N. degrees. Master's degrees are also awarded. Bachelor's degrees are awarded in AGRICULTURE (agricultural business management, agriculture, and conservation and regulation), BIOLOGICAL SCIENCE (biology/biological science), BUSINESS (accounting, business administration and management, and office supervision and management), COMMUNICATIONS AND THE ARTS (broadcasting, communications, dramatic arts, English, music, public relations, and speech/debate/rhetoric), COMPUTER AND PHYSICAL SCIENCE (chemistry, computer science, mathematics, and physics), EDUCATION (business, early childhood, elementary, English, library science, mathematics, music, physical, science, secondary, and special), HEALTH PROFESSIONS (medical laboratory technology and nursing), SOCIAL SCIENCE (criminal justice, economics, history, political science/government, psychology, social science, social work, and sociology). Education and business are the strongest academically and have the largest enrollment.

Required: A total of 124 credit hours is required, including at least 40 in the major, with a minimum GPA of 2.0. General education courses total 54 semester hours, including 19 hours in communication and humanities, 15 in social and behavioral science, 11 in math and natural science, and 9 in phys ed and other practical arts. This general sequence totals 50 hours for education majors and includes a computer science requirement.

Special: Northwestern offers credit by exam and for military experience. There are 4 national honor societies.

Faculty/Classroom: 68% of faculty are male; 32%, female. All teach undergraduates. No introductory courses are taught by graduate students. The average class size in an introductory lecture is 38; in a laboratory, 24; and in a regular course, 19.

Requirements: The ACT is required with a minimum score of 19. Applicants must be graduates of an accredited secondary school or have earned a GED. Northwestern requires 20 academic credits, including 4 in English, 3 in math, and 2 each in history and lab science. Northwestern requires applicants to be in the upper 50% of their class. A GPA of 2.7 is required. CLEP credit is accepted.

Procedure: Freshmen are admitted to all sessions. Entrance exams should be taken in the junior or senior year. Application deadlines are open. The fall 2001 application fee was $15. Notification is sent on a rolling basis.

Transfer: 259 transfer students enrolled in a recent year. Applicants must have a GPA of at least 2.0. 40 credits of 124 must be completed at Northwestern.

Visiting: There are regularly scheduled orientations for prospective students, In April, usually during 2 sessions, entering freshmen receive information, tour the campus, and enroll. There are guides for informal visits and visitors may sit in on classes and stay overnight. To schedule a visit, contact the Pre-Admissions Office.

Financial Aid: In a recent year, 70% of all freshmen and 65% of continuing students received some form of financial aid. 70% of freshmen and 60% of continuing students received need-based aid. The average freshman award was $2800. Of that total, scholarships or need-based grants averaged $700 ($1400 maximum); loans averaged $2600 ($2625 maximum); and work contracts averaged $1100 ($2472 maximum). 57% of undergraduates work part time. Average annual earnings from campus work are $2040. The average financial indebtedness of a recent year's graduate was $6500. The FAFSA is required. Check with the school for current deadlines.

International Students: There were 16 international students enrolled in a recent year. The school actively recruits these students. They must score 500 on the written TOEFL.

Computers: The mainframe is a DEC ALPHA 2000 Model 4/233. More than 100 PCs provide students with mainframe access as well as applications software, Web access, and e-mail. Computer labs are distributed across the campus. All students may access the system 8 A.M. to 8 P.M. There are no time limits and no fees.

Graduates: In a recent year, 350 bachelor's degrees were awarded. The most popular majors were elementary education (16%), business administration (14%), and health and physical ed (7%). In an average class, 25% graduate in 4 years, 32% in 5 years, and 35% in 6 years. 25 companies recruited on campus in a recent year.

Admissions Contact: Kerri Beard, Director of Pre-Admissions. A video is available. E-mail: *ksbeard@nwosu.edu* Web: *www.nwosu.edu*

OKLAHOMA BAPTIST UNIVERSITY E-3

Shawnee, OK 74804 (405) 878-2030
(800) 654-3285; Fax: (405) 878-2046

Full-time: 603 men, 940 women	**Faculty:** 117; IIB, --$
Part-time: 231 men, 137 women	**Ph.D.s:** 77%
Graduate: 5 men, 17 women	**Student/Faculty:** 14 to 1
Year: 4-1-4, summer session	**Tuition:** $10,190
Application Deadline: see profile	**Room & Board:** $3640
Freshman Class: 958 applied, 820 accepted, 435 enrolled	
SAT I Verbal/Math: 590/560	**ACT:** 25 **VERY COMPETITIVE**

Oklahoma Baptist University, founded in 1910, is a liberal arts institution affiliated with the Southern Baptist Convention. OBU offers degrees in Christian service, business, nursing, fine arts, telecommunications, teacher education, and the traditional liberal arts areas. There are 5 undergraduate schools and 1 graduate school. In addition to regional accreditation, OBU has baccalaureate program accreditation with ACBSP, NASM, NCATE, and NLN. The library contains 290,000 volumes, 230,000 microform items, and 1500 audiovisual forms/CDs, and subscribes to 600 periodicals. Computerized library services include the card catalog, interlibrary loans, and database searching. Special learning facilities include a learning resource center, planetarium, TV station, a language lab, and a Biblical research library. The 189-acre campus is in a small town 35 miles east of Oklahoma City and 90 miles southwest of Tulsa. Including residence halls, there are 25 buildings.

Student Life: 61% of undergraduates are from Oklahoma. Others are from 41 states, 21 foreign countries, and Canada. 84% are from public schools. 86% are white. Most are Protestant. The average age of freshmen is 18; all undergraduates, 22. 18% do not continue beyond their first year; 58% remain to graduate.

Housing: 1390 students can be accommodated in college housing, which includes single-sex dormitories, on-campus apartments, and married-student housing. On-campus housing is guaranteed for all 4 years. 70% of students live on campus; of those, 55% remain on campus on weekends. Alcohol is not permitted. All students may keep cars.

Activities: 16% of men belong to 5 local fraternities; 15% of women belong to 5 local sororities. There are 95 groups on campus, including art, band, cheerleading, choir, chorale, chorus, computers, drama, ethnic, film, honors, international, jazz band, literary magazine, musical theater, newspaper, opera, orchestra, pep band, photography, political, professional, radio and TV, religious, social, social service, student government, and yearbook. Popular campus events include Stampede of Stars, International Awareness Day, and Hanging of the Green.

Sports: There are 7 intercollegiate sports for men and 7 for women, and 10 intramural sports for men and 8 for women. Facilities include a sports complex, which houses a 2500-seat arena, a swimming pool, tennis and racquetball courts, weight rooms, an all-weather track, and baseball, softball, and sand volleyball facilities.

Disabled Students: 95% of the campus is accessible. Wheelchair ramps, elevators, special parking, specially equipped rest rooms, lowered drinking fountains, and lowered telephones are available.

Services: Counseling and information services are available, as is tutoring in most subjects. There is a reader service for the blind, and remedial math, reading, and writing.

Campus Safety and Security: Measures include 24-hour foot and vehicle patrol, self-defense education, escort service, and emergency telephones. There are lighted pathways/sidewalks.

Programs of Study: OBU confers B.A., B.S., B.B.A., B.F.A., B.Hum., B.M., B.M.A., B.Mus.Ed., and B.S.E. degrees. Associate degrees are also awarded. Bachelor's degrees are awarded in BIOLOGICAL SCIENCE (biology/biological science), BUSINESS (accounting, banking and finance, business administration and management, and marketing/retailing/merchandising), COMMUNICATIONS AND THE ARTS (broadcasting, communications, dramatic arts, English, fine arts, French, German, journalism, music, Spanish, speech/debate/rhetoric, and telecommunications), COMPUTER AND PHYSICAL SCIENCE (chemistry, computer science, information sciences and systems, mathematics, and physics), EDUCATION (art, early childhood, elementary, foreign languages, music, physical, science, and secondary), HEALTH PROFESSIONS (nursing, physical therapy, predentistry, and premedicine), SOCIAL SCIENCE (history, political science/government, prelaw, psychology, religion, social science, social work, and sociology). Teacher education, biology, and religion are the strongest academically. Biology, elementary education, and nursing are the largest.

Required: To graduate, students must complete a total of 128 credit hours, including 30 to 48 hours in the major, with a 2.0 GPA. Students are also required to complete 6 credits each of English, literature, history, science, Bible, social sciences, and language; 3 each in math, fine arts, and comparative civilization; 2 each in speech, philosophy, and phys ed; and 1 in computer literacy.

Special: OBU offers co-op programs in business, cross-registration with Saint Gregory's University, and a 3-2 engineering degree with Oklahoma State University. Students may study abroad in Europe, South America, Hungary, China, Japan, Spain, and Russia. Internships in several fields, student-designed majors, including an interdisciplinary program in humanities, and pass/fail options are available. There are 4 national honor societies, and a freshman honors program.

Faculty/Classroom: 63% of faculty are male; 37%, female. All teach undergraduates. No introductory courses are taught by graduate students. The average class size in an introductory lecture is 25; in a laboratory, 19; and in a regular course, 18.

Admissions: 86% of the 2001-2002 applicants were accepted. The SAT I scores for the 2001-2002 freshman class were: Verbal--16% below 500, 36% between 500 and 599, 36% between 600 and 700, and 12% above 700; Math--21% below 500, 41% between 500 and 599, 29% between 600 and 700, and 9% above 700. The ACT scores were 10% below 21, 30% between 21 and 23, 25% between 24 and 26, 16% between 27 and 28, and 19% above 28. 60% of the current freshmen. In a recent year, there were 5 National Merit finalists and 5 semifinalists. 36 freshmen graduated first in their class.

Requirements: The SAT I or ACT is required. Admission is granted to students with composite scores of 950 on the SAT I or 20 on the ACT, with a 2.5 GPA. Graduation from an accredited secondary school or satisfactory scores on the GED are required for admission. The recommended high school courses should include 4 units of English, 3 units of math, and 2 units each of social studies, lab science, and a foreign language. OBU requires applicants to be in the upper 50% of their class. A GPA of 2.5 is required. AP and CLEP credits are accepted. Important factors in the admissions decision are advanced placement or honor courses, recommendations by school officials, and leadership record.

Procedure: Freshmen are admitted to all sessions. Entrance exams should be taken during the spring of the junior year. There are early admissions and deferred admissions plans. Check with the school for current application deadlines. The fall 2001 application fee was $25. Notification is sent on a rolling basis.

Transfer: 90 transfer students enrolled in a recent year. Transfer students must have a GPA of 2.5 for all college work attempted. 33 credits of 128 must be completed at OBU.

Visiting: There are regularly scheduled orientations for prospective students, including tours, faculty visits, and general information sessions. There are guides for informal visits and visitors may sit in on classes and stay overnight. To schedule a visit, contact the Admissions Office.

Financial Aid: In a recent year, 85% of all freshmen and 89% of continuing students received some form of financial aid. 69% of freshmen and 78% of continuing students received need-based aid. The average freshman award was $5750. Of that total, scholarships or need-based grants averaged $2580 ($10,000 maximum); loans averaged $2150 ($5500 maximum); and work contracts averaged $930 ($1800 maximum). 95% of undergraduates work part time. Average annual earnings from campus work are $958. The average financial indebtedness of a recent year's graduate was $13,000. The FAFSA is required. Check with the school for current deadlines.

International Students: There were 35 international students enrolled in a recent year. The school actively recruits these students. They must score 500 on the written TOEFL.

Computers: The mainframe is an HP 3000/979. Students have access to about 175 networked Windows 95 and Mac PCs in residence halls, labs, and elsewhere on campus. All students have access to e-mail and the World Wide Web. All students may access the system 75 hours per week. There are no time limits.

Graduates: In a recent year, 320 bachelor's degrees were awarded. The most popular majors were religion (11%), nursing (10%), and psychology (10%). In an average class, 3% graduate in 3 years, 52% in 4 years, 55% in 5 years, and 58% in 6 years. 40 companies recruited on campus in a recent year.

Admissions Contact: Michael Cappo, Dean of Admissions. A video is available. E-mail: *admissions@mail.okbu.edu* Web: *www.okbu.edu*

OKLAHOMA CHRISTIAN UNIVERSITY — D-3

Oklahoma City, OK 73136-1100 — (405) 425-5050
(800) 877-5010; Fax: (405) 425-5069

Full-time: 782 men, 780 women	**Faculty:** 87; IIB, -$
Part-time: 80 men, 68 women	**Ph.D.s:** 67%
Graduate: 70 men, 27 women	**Student/Faculty:** 18 to 1
Year: semesters, summer session	**Tuition:** $12,100
Application Deadline: open	**Room & Board:** $4400
Freshman Class: 1166 applied, 701 accepted, 443 enrolled	
SAT I Verbal/Math: 560/570	**ACT:** 23 **VERY COMPETITIVE**

Oklahoma Christian University, founded in 1950, is a private liberal arts institution affiliated with the Church of Christ. There are 5 undergraduate schools and 1 graduate school. In addition to regional accreditation, OC has baccalaureate program accreditation with ABET, ACBSP, NASM, and NCATE. The library contains 93,680 volumes, 700,019 microform items, and 5083 audiovisual forms/CDs, and subscribes to 2355 periodicals. Computerized library services include the card catalog, interlibrary loans, and database searching. Special learning facilities include a learning resource center, art gallery, radio station, free enterprise museum, and journalism lab. The 200-acre campus is in a suburban area on the north side of Oklahoma City. Including residence halls, there are 33 buildings.

Student Life: 53% of undergraduates are from out of state, mostly the Midwest. Others are from 48 states, 32 foreign countries, and Canada. 85% are white. The average age of freshmen is 18. 30% do not continue beyond their first year; 39% remain to graduate.

Housing: 1252 students can be accommodated in college housing, which includes single-sex dormitories, on-campus apartments, and married-student housing. In addition, there are honors houses. On-campus housing is guaranteed for all 4 years. 76% of students live on campus. Alcohol is not permitted. All students may keep cars.

Activities: There are no fraternities or sororities. There are 19 groups on campus, including band, cheerleading, choir, chorale, computers, drama, ethnic, honors, international, jazz band, literary magazine, musical theater, newspaper, opera, pep band, photography, political, professional, radio and TV, religious, social service, student government, symphony, and yearbook. Popular campus events include High School Day, Spring Sing, and Special Olympics Banquet.

Sports: There are 6 intercollegiate sports for men and 7 for women, and 15 intramural sports for men and 15 for women. Facilities include 3 gyms, a swimming pool, softball, football, and soccer fields, and a fitness center with weight training, stair, and bicycle machines, 3 volleyball courts, and water and land aerobics.

Disabled Students: 98% of the campus is accessible. Wheelchair ramps, elevators, special parking, specially equipped rest rooms, special class scheduling, lowered drinking fountains, and lowered telephones are available.

Services: Counseling and information services are available, as is tutoring in some subjects, including including English, math, speech, chemistry, physics, business, education, and computer science. There is remedial math, reading, and writing.

Campus Safety and Security: Measures include 24-hour foot and vehicle patrol, escort service, informal discussions, and pamphlets/posters/films. There are lighted pathways/sidewalks and and security officers.

Programs of Study: OC confers B.A., B.S., B.B.A., B.F.A., B.M.E., B.Mus.Ed., B.S.C.E., B.S.E., B.S.Ed., B.S.E.E., and B.S.M.E. degrees. Master's degrees are also awarded. Bachelor's degrees are awarded in BIOLOGICAL SCIENCE (biochemistry and biology/biological science), BUSINESS (accounting, business administration and management, and marketing/retailing/merchandising), COMMUNICATIONS AND THE ARTS (advertising, art, broadcasting, communications, creative writing, design, English, journalism, music, and Spanish), COMPUTER AND PHYSICAL SCIENCE (chemistry, computer science, information sciences and systems, and mathematics), EDUCATION (art, early childhood, elementary, English, mathematics, middle school, music, physical, science, social studies, special, and teaching English as a second/foreign language (TESOL/TEFOL)), ENGINEERING AND ENVIRONMENTAL DESIGN (computer engineering, electrical/electronics engineering, engineering physics, interior design, and mechanical engineering), HEALTH PROFESSIONS (medical laboratory technology, and premedicine), SOCIAL SCIENCE (biblical studies, child care/child and family studies, history, liberal arts/general studies, ministries, missions, prelaw, psychology, religious education, and youth ministry). Business, science and engineering, and communication and fine arts are the largest.

Required: To graduate, students must have a minimum of 126 credit hours, including 30 to 104 in the major, with a GPA of 2.0. All students must complete 60 to 61 hours in the general education program, which includes courses in Bible, English, speech, American studies, math, literature, fine arts, economics, biology, physical science, philosophy, Western civilization, phys ed, personal development, and social science.

Special: OC offers cross-registration with the University of Central Oklahoma, a liberal studies degree, internships in various majors, on-campus work-study, and credit for military experience. Students may study abroad in Austria, Japan, and the Pacific Rim. Major-minor combinations are offered in mass communication, family life, engineering, prelaw, advertising design, speech communication, English, music, education, and math. There are 2 national honor societies and a freshman honors program.

Faculty/Classroom: 70% of faculty are male; 30%, female. All teach undergraduates and 10% both teach and do research. No introductory courses are taught by graduate students. The average class size in an introductory lecture is 50; in a laboratory, 19; and in a regular course, 30.

Admissions: 60% of the 2001-2002 applicants were accepted. The SAT I scores for the 2001-2002 freshman class were: Verbal--25% below 500, 39% between 500 and 599, 3% between 600 and 700, and 1% above 700; Math--28% below 500, 32% between 500 and 599, 32% between 600 and 700, and 8% above 700. The ACT scores were 30% below 21, 20% between 21 and 23, 21% between 24 and 26, 12% between 27 and 28, and 17% above 28.

Requirements: The SAT I or ACT is required. In addition, graduation from an accredited secondary school or satisfactory scores on the GED are required for admission. AP and CLEP credits are accepted.

Procedure: Freshmen are admitted to all sessions. There is a deferred admissions plan. Application deadlines are open.

Transfer: 82 transfer students enrolled in 2001-2002. Applicants must be eligible to return to the school from which they are transferring. 30 credits of 126 must be completed at OC.

Visiting: There are regularly scheduled orientations for prospective students, including fall and spring visits in September and February. There are guides for informal visits and visitors may sit in on classes and stay overnight. To schedule a visit, contact the Admissions Office.

Financial Aid: In 2001-2002, 71% of all freshmen and 62% of continuing students received some form of financial aid. 69% of freshmen and 61% of continuing students received need-based aid. The average freshman award was $8025. Of that total, scholarships or need-based grants averaged $4000; loans averaged $11,000; and work contracts averaged $1500. 35% of undergraduates work part time. Average annual earnings from campus work are $1500. The average financial indebtedness of the 2001 graduate was $17,237. The FAFSA is required. The fall application deadline is April 15.

International Students: There are 57 international students enrolled. The school actively recruits these students. They must score 500 on the written TOEFL or 173 on the electronic version.

Computers: All students have a university-owned laptop issued to them. All students may access the system 24 hours, 7 days a week. There are no time limits and no fees.

Graduates: In 2001, 268 bachelor's degrees were awarded. The most popular majors were business (25%), science and engineering (16%), and education (12%). In an average class, 27% graduate in 4 years, 41% in 5 years, and 43% in 6 years. 50 companies recruited on campus in 2000-2001.

Admissions Contact: Kyle Wray, Director of Enrollment Development. A video is available. E-mail: *info@oc.edu* Web: *oc.edu*

OKLAHOMA CITY UNIVERSITY

D-3

Oklahoma City, OK 73106-1493 (405) 521-5050

(800) 633-7242; Fax: (405) 521-5916

Full-time: 620 men, 853 women	**Faculty:** 130; IIA, --$
Part-time: 151 men, 237 women	**Ph.D.s:** 75%
Graduate: 1038 men, 806 women	**Student/Faculty:** 11 to 1
Year: semesters, summer session	**Tuition:** $10,880
Application Deadline: August 22	**Room & Board:** $4930
Freshman Class: 1381 applied, 970 accepted, 291 enrolled	
SAT I or ACT: required	**COMPETITIVE**

Oklahoma City University, founded in 1904, is a private comprehensive university affiliated with the United Methodist Church and offering undergraduate and graduate programs in arts and sciences, business, music and performing arts, religion and church vocations, nursing, and law. There are 6 undergraduate and 5 graduate schools. In addition to regional accreditation, OCU has baccalaureate program accreditation with ACBSP, NASM, and NLN. The 2 libraries contain 287,773 volumes, 946,476 microform items, and 10,702 audiovisual forms/CDs, and subscribe to 5992 periodicals. Computerized library services include the card catalog, interlibrary loans, and database searching. Special learning facilities include a learning resource center, art gallery, and TV station. The 68-acre campus is in an urban area within Oklahoma City. Including residence halls, there are 28 buildings.

Student Life: 70% of undergraduates are from Oklahoma. Others are from 49 states, 74 foreign countries, and Canada. 60% are white; 25% foreign nationals. 39% are Protestant; 30% claim no religious affiliation; 20% are Hindu, Islamic; 19% are members of the schools denomination; 10% are Catholic. The average age of freshmen is 18; all undergraduates, 21. 31% do not continue beyond their first year; 49% remain to graduate.

Housing: 1079 students can be accommodated in college housing, which includes single-sex dormitories, on-campus apartments, and fraternity houses. On-campus housing is guaranteed for all 4 years. 64% of students commute. Alcohol is not permitted. All students may keep cars.

Activities: 11% of men belong to 3 national fraternities; 15% of women belong to 3 national sororities. There are 35 groups on campus, including art, band, cheerleading, choir, chorus, computers, dance, drama, drill team, ethnic, film, gay, honors, international, jazz band, literary magazine, musical theater, newspaper, opera, orchestra, pep band, photography, political, professional, radio and TV, religious, social, social service, student government, symphony, and yearbook. Popular campus events include sports, theater, dance, and music programs, international fair, and oozeball.

Sports: There are 5 intercollegiate sports for men and 5 for women, and 5 intramural sports for men and 4 for women. Facilities include a field house, tennis courts, baseball and soccer fields, and a wellness and activity center.

Disabled Students: 96% of the campus is accessible. Wheelchair ramps, elevators, special parking, specially equipped rest rooms, lowered drinking fountains, and lowered telephones are available.

Services: Counseling and information services are available, as is tutoring in most subjects. There is remedial math, reading, and writing. There are writing and learning enhancement centers and a math lab.

Campus Safety and Security: Measures include 24-hour foot and vehicle patrol, escort service, informal discussions, and pamphlets/posters/films. There are emergency telephones, lighted pathways/sidewalks, and an inner-campus bicycle patrol.

Programs of Study: OCU confers B.A., B.S., B.F.A., B.M., B.Perf.Arts, B.S.B., and B.S.N. degrees. Master's degrees are also awarded. Bachelor's degrees are awarded in BIOLOGICAL SCIENCE (biochemistry, biology/biological science, and biophysics), BUSINESS (accounting, banking and finance, and business administration and management), COMMUNICATIONS AND THE ARTS (advertising, art, broadcasting, communications, dance, dramatic arts, English, French, German, graphic design, journalism, music, piano/organ, Spanish, and speech/debate/rhetoric), COMPUTER AND PHYSICAL SCIENCE (chemistry, computer management, computer science, mathematics, physics, and science), EDUCATION (early childhood, elementary, foreign languages, music, physical, and science), HEALTH PROFESSIONS (nursing and premedicine), SOCIAL SCIENCE (criminal justice, economics, history, humanities, philosophy, political science/government, prelaw, psychology, religion, and sociology). Business, performing arts, and dance are the strongest academically. Business, performing arts, and mass communications are the largest.

Required: To graduate, students must complete a total of 124 credit hours, including 30 to 80 in the major, with a minimum GPA of 2.0. Students must complete their last 15 hours, including the last 6 in the major, at OCU with a minimum GPA of 2.0. All students must take courses in the foundation curriculum as specified by their college or department.

Special: OCU offers internships, a Washington semester, work-study programs, a general studies degree, dual and student-designed majors, credit for life experience, and study-abroad programs. There are 9 national honor societies, a freshman honors program, and 10 departmental honors programs.

Faculty/Classroom: 61% of faculty are male; 39%, female. 82% teach undergraduates. No introductory courses are taught by graduate students. The average class size in an introductory lecture is 22; in a laboratory, 9; and in a regular course, 13.

Admissions: 70% of the 2001-2002 applicants were accepted. The SAT I scores for the 2001-2002 freshman class were: Verbal--26% below 500, 48% between 500 and 599, 23% between 600 and 700, and 3% above 700; Math--22% below 500, 52% between 500 and 599, 21% between 600 and 700, and 5% above 700. The ACT scores were 57% below 24, 41% between 24 and 29, and 2% above 29. 57% of the current freshmen were in the top quarter of their class; 86% were in the upper half.

Requirements: The SAT I, with a minimum composite score of 930, or the ACT, with a minimum score of 20, is required. Graduation from an accredited secondary school or satisfactory scores on the GED are also required. High school courses must include 4 units of English, 3 each of science, social studies, and math, and 2 of a foreign language. Music and dance students are required to audition. OCU requires applicants to be in the upper 50% of their class. A GPA of 2.5 is required. AP and CLEP credits are accepted. Important factors in the admissions decision are evidence of special talent, advanced placement or honor courses, and leadership record.

Procedure: Freshmen are admitted to all sessions. Entrance exams should be taken by February of the senior year. There are early admissions and deferred admissions plans. Applications should be filed by August 22 for fall entry. The fall 2001 application fee was $20. Notification is sent on a rolling basis.

Transfer: 145 transfer students enrolled in 2001-2002. Applicants must submit a transcript from each college attended and must have a minimum GPA of 2.0 from an accredited institution. Applicants having fewer than 26 credit hours must submit a high school transcript. Minimum composite scores of 930 on the SAT I and 20 on the ACT are required. 30 credits of 124 must be completed at OCU.

Visiting: There are regularly scheduled orientations for prospective students. There are guides for informal visits and visitors may sit in on classes and stay overnight. To schedule a visit, contact the Undergraduate Admissions Office.

Financial Aid: In 2001-2002, 84% of all freshmen and 60% of continuing students received some form of financial aid. 66% of freshmen and 52% of continuing students received need-based aid. Scholarships or need-based grants averaged $3324 ($8450 maximum); loans averaged $3071 ($10,625 maximum); and work contracts averaged $1622 ($3700 maximum). 23% of undergraduates work part time. Average annual earnings from campus work are $1796. The average financial indebtedness of the 2001 graduate was $19,832. The FAFSA and tax returns, if selected for verification, are required. The fall application deadline is March 1.

International Students: There are 370 international students enrolled. The school actively recruits these students. They must score 500 on the written TOEFL or take the MELAB.

Computers: The mainframes are an NCR 3455, an NCR 3550, 2 DEC ALPHAs, a DEC 8250, and a DEC VAX 4500. Students have access to academic computer systems from the labs, dorm rooms, and through a dial-up remote system. Students can access e-mail from any browser on or off campus. Home directories are only accessible on campus. Approximately 130 open access PCs are available to students in labs on campus. Internet access is available to students from all labs and in the dorms. All students may access the system 24 hours a day. There are no time limits. The fee is $45 per semester.

Graduates: In 2001, 446 bachelor's degrees were awarded. The most popular majors were business (12%), dance (7%), and mass communication (7%). In an average class, 36% graduate in 4 years, 46% in 5 years, and 49% in 6 years. 65 companies recruited on campus in 2000-2001.

Admissions Contact: Undergraduate Admissions Office. A video is available. E-mail: *uadmissions@okcu.edu* Web: *www.okcu.edu*

OKLAHOMA PANHANDLE STATE UNIVERSITY — B-2

Goodwell, OK 73939 — (580) 349-1312
(800) 664-6778; Fax: (580) 349-2302

Full-time: 484 men, 515 women	**Faculty:** 50
Part-time: 79 men, 154 women	**Ph.D.s:** 52%
Graduate: none	**Student/Faculty:** 20 to 1
Year: semesters, summer session	**Tuition:** $2022 ($3196)
Application Deadline: open	**Room & Board:** $1790
Freshman Class: 435 applied, 435 accepted, 235 enrolled	
SAT I or ACT: required	**NONCOMPETITIVE**

Oklahoma Panhandle State University, founded in 1909, is a publicly funded institution offering undergraduate programs in the liberal arts, business, education, agriculture, technology, and preprofessional training. There are 5 undergraduate schools. In addition to regional accreditation, OPSU has baccalaureate program accreditation with NCATE and NLN. The library contains 113,733 volumes, 13,038 microform items, and 8487 audiovisual forms/CDs, and subscribes to 498 periodicals. Computerized library services include the card catalog, interlibrary loans, and database searching. Special learning facilities include a learning resource center, natural history museum, radio station, a writing lab, academic support lab, farm lab, children's collection library, and two instructional TV facilities. The 120-acre campus is in a rural area 100 miles north of Amarillo, Texas. Including residence halls, there are 27 buildings.

Student Life: 53% of undergraduates are from out of state, mostly the Midwest. Others are from 36 states, 25 foreign countries, and Canada. 98% are from public schools. 80% are white; 10% Hispanic. The average age of freshmen is 21; all undergraduates, 25. 50% do not continue beyond their first year; 10% remain to graduate.

Housing: 412 students can be accommodated in college housing, which includes single-sex and coed dormitories, on-campus apartments, and married-student housing. In addition, there are honors houses. On-campus housing is guaranteed for all 4 years. 66% of students commute. Alcohol is not permitted. All students may keep cars.

Activities: There are no fraternities or sororities. There are 45 groups on campus, including art, band, cheerleading, choir, chorale, chorus, computers, dance, debate, drama, drill team, ethnic, forensics, honors, jazz band, marching band, musical theater, newspaper, pep band, photography, professional, radio and TV, religious, rodeo, social, student government, and yearbook. Popular campus events include Annual Rodeo, and a Broadway play.

Sports: There are 4 intercollegiate sports for men and 4 for women, and 12 intramural sports for men and 12 for women. Facilities include a field house, an athletic field, a golf course, tennis courts, and an activity center. Water skiing and fishing spots are nearby.

Disabled Students: 90% of the campus is accessible. Wheelchair ramps, elevators, special parking, and special class scheduling are available.

Services: Counseling and information services are available, as is tutoring in every subject. There is remedial math, reading, and writing. Free tutoring is provided through the peer counseling center.

Campus Safety and Security: Measures include 24-hour foot and vehicle patrol, self-defense education, pamphlets/posters/films, and emergency telephones. There are lighted pathways/sidewalks.

Programs of Study: OPSU confers B.A., B.S., B.B.A., B.H.P.E., B.I.B.M., B.M.E., B.S.N., and B.T. degrees. Associate degrees are also awarded. Bachelor's degrees are awarded in AGRICULTURE (agricultural business management, agronomy, and animal science), BIOLOGICAL SCIENCE (biology/biological science), BUSINESS (accounting, and business administration and management), COMMUNICATIONS AND THE ARTS (English and music), COMPUTER AND PHYSICAL SCIENCE (chemistry, information sciences and systems, mathematics, and physical sciences), EDUCATION (agricultural, business, elementary, English, health, mathematics, music, physical, science, and social studies), ENGINEERING AND ENVIRONMENTAL DESIGN (industrial engineering technology), HEALTH PROFESSIONS (medical technology and nursing), SOCIAL SCIENCE (fire protection, history, humanities, psychology, and social studies). Business, agriculture, and education are the strongest academically. Education, agriculture, and business are the largest.

Required: To graduate, students must complete a total of 124 semester hours with a minimum GPA of 2.0. The number of hours required in the major varies. All students must complete 45 hours of general education courses, with at least 1 course at the upper-division level.

Special: Oklahoma Panhandle State University offers dual majors and the B.A.-B.S. degree in most areas. There is 1 national honor society, and 1 departmental honors program.

Faculty/Classroom: 50% of faculty are male; 50%, female. All teach undergraduates. The average class size in an introductory lecture is 35; in a laboratory, 24; and in a regular course, 20.

Admissions: All of the 2001-2002 applicants were accepted. The school has an open admissions policy.

Requirements: The SAT I or ACT is required, with a minimum composite score of 19 on the ACT. Graduation from an accredited secondary school or satisfactory scores on the GED are required. High school courses must include 4 units of English, 3 units of math (beginning with algebra I), 3 units of other courses such as foreign language or computer application courses, 2 units each of history (including 1 unit of American history) and lab science, and 1 unit of citizenship (for example, government, civics). AP and CLEP credits are accepted.

Procedure: Freshmen are admitted to all sessions. Application deadlines are open. Check with the school for current fee. Notification is sent on a rolling basis.

Transfer: 164 transfer students enrolled in 2001-2002. An application for admission, a medical history form, college transcripts, high school transcripts, and ACT scores are required. If students are transferring in with a GPA below 2.0, they come in on academic probation. 30 credits of 124 must be completed at OPSU.

Visiting: There are regularly scheduled orientations for prospective students. There are guides for informal visits and visitors may sit in on classes and stay overnight. To schedule a visit, contact High School and Community Relations.

Financial Aid: The average freshman award was $2000 in a recent year. 16% of undergraduates work part time. Average annual earnings from campus work are $3000. The FAFSA and the college's own financial statement are required.

International Students: There are 55 international students enrolled. The school actively recruits these students. They must score 500 on the written TOEFL and also take the SAT I, ACT (scoring 19), or any other country's equivalent.

Computers: The mainframe is an HP 9000/8275. There are 40 Macs and PCs available in labs. Students enrolled in computer information system classes may access the system 5 A.M. to 11 P.M. There are no time limits and no fees.

Graduates: In 2001, 211 bachelor's degrees were awarded. The most popular majors were business administration (65%), agribusiness (52%), and elementary education (38%).
Admissions Contact: Alesha Cruz, Admissions Counselor.
E-mail: *opsu@opsu.edu* Web: *www.opsu.edu*

OKLAHOMA STATE SYSTEM OF HIGHER EDUCATION

The Oklahoma State System of Higher Education, established in 1941, is a public system. It is governed by the Oklahoma State Regents for Higher Education and the chief administrator is the chancellor. The primary goals of the system are teaching, research, and public service. The main priorities are student success, excellence, and system efficiency. The total enrollment of its 25 colleges and universities is about 213,000, with nearly 6780 faculty members. There are 596 baccalaureate, 266 master's, and 106 doctoral programs offered by the Oklahoma State System of Higher Education. 4-year campuses are located in Stillwater, Norman, Edmond, Claremore, Ada, Tahlequah, Alva, Durant, Weatherford, Lawton, Langston, Goodwell, and Chickasha. Profiles of those campuses are included in this section.

OKLAHOMA STATE UNIVERSITY E-2

Stillwater, OK 74078 **(405) 744-6858**
(800) 852-1255; Fax: (405) 744-5285

Full-time: 8050 men, 7482 women	**Faculty:** 675; I, --$
Part-time: 917 men, 762 women	**Ph.D.s:** 87%
Graduate: 2545 men, 2116 women	**Student/Faculty:** 23 to 1
Year: semesters, summer session	**Tuition:** $2794 ($7519)
Application Deadline: open	**Room & Board:** $4856
Freshman Class: 5794 applied, 5277 accepted, 3209 enrolled	
SAT I Verbal/Math: 550/570	**ACT:** 23 **VERY COMPETITIVE**

Oklahoma State University, founded in 1890, is a publicly funded land-grant institution, offering undergraduate programs in agricultural sciences and natural resources, arts and sciences, business, education, engineering, architecture, technology, and human environmental resources. There are 6 undergraduate schools and 1 graduate school. In addition to regional accreditation, OSU has baccalaureate program accreditation with AACSB, ABET, ACEJMC, ADA, AHEA, ASLA, FIDER, NAAB, NASM, NRPA, SAF, ACS, APA, ASLHA, and NAACLS. The 5 libraries contain 2,162,282 volumes, 3,726,558 microform items, and 7322 audiovisual forms/CDs, and subscribe to 17,614 periodicals. Computerized library services include interlibrary loans and database searching. Special learning facilities include an art gallery, natural history museum, and radio station. The 840-acre campus is in a small town 65 miles north of Oklahoma City. Including residence halls, there are 200 buildings.

Student Life: 83% of undergraduates are from Oklahoma. Others are from 49 states, 119 foreign countries, and Canada. 77% are white. The average age of freshmen is 20; all undergraduates, 22. 18% do not continue beyond their first year; 54% remain to graduate.

Housing: 5813 students can be accommodated in college housing, which includes single-sex and coed dormitories, on-campus apartments, off-campus apartments, married-student housing, fraternity houses, and sorority houses. In addition, there are honors houses, language houses, and special-interest houses, and floors for fine arts, engineering, and fire protection majors. On-campus housing is guaranteed for all 4 years. 61% of students commute. Alcohol is not permitted. All students may keep cars.

Activities: 18% of men belong to 20 national fraternities; 24% of women belong to 14 national sororities. There are 374 groups on campus, including art, band, cheerleading, choir, chorale, chorus, computers, dance, drama, ethnic, gay, honors, international, jazz band, literary magazine, marching band, musical theater, newspaper, opera, orchestra, pep band, political, professional, radio and TV, religious, social, social service, student government, and symphony. Popular campus events include Spring Sing, Freshmen Follies, and Special Olympics.

Sports: There are 9 intercollegiate sports for men and 7 for women, and 40 intramural sports for men and 40 for women. Facilities include a phys ed center with an indoor climbing wall and activity areas for basketball, volleyball, racquetball, squash, badminton, fencing, golf, table tennis, billiards, wrestling, dance, weight lifting, and indoor and outdoor swimming. There are also outdoor basketball and tennis courts, archery and golf ranges, a jogging track, and playing fields.

Disabled Students: 95% of the campus is accessible. Wheelchair ramps, elevators, special parking, specially equipped rest rooms, special class scheduling, lowered drinking fountains, lowered telephones, and adaptive technology are available.

Services: Counseling and information services are available, as is tutoring in most subjects, including math. Tutoring is not disability-specific. There is a reader service for the blind, and remedial math, reading, and writing. Academic assessment and minority programs are also available.

Campus Safety and Security: Measures include 24-hour foot and vehicle patrol, self-defense education, escort service, and shuttle buses. There are informal discussions, pamphlets/posters/films, emergency telephones, and lighted pathways/sidewalks.

Programs of Study: OSU confers B.A., B.S., B.Arch., B.Arch.Eng., B.F.A., B.Land.Arch., B.M., and B.U.S. degrees. Master's and doctoral degrees are also awarded. Bachelor's degrees are awarded in AGRICULTURE (agricultural business management, agricultural economics, animal science, fish and game management, forestry and related sciences, horticulture, and plant science), BIOLOGICAL SCIENCE (biochemistry, biology/biological science, botany, cell biology, entomology, microbiology, molecular biology, nutrition, physiology, and zoology), BUSINESS (accounting, banking and finance, business administration and management, business economics, hotel/motel and restaurant management, international business management, management information systems, management science, marketing/retailing/merchandising, and recreation and leisure services), COMMUNICATIONS AND THE ARTS (art, communications, design, dramatic arts, English, French, German, journalism, music, Russian, and Spanish), COMPUTER AND PHYSICAL SCIENCE (chemistry, computer science, geology, mathematics, physics, and statistics), EDUCATION (agricultural, elementary, health, music, physical, secondary, and technical), ENGINEERING AND ENVIRONMENTAL DESIGN (aeronautical engineering, architectural engineering, architecture, aviation computer technology, bioengineering, chemical engineering, civil engineering, construction management, electrical/electronics engineering, electrical/electronics engineering technology, engineering, environmental science, industrial engineering, landscape architecture/design, mechanical engineering, and mechanical engineering technology), HEALTH PROFESSIONS (biomedical science, medical technology, premedicine, preveterinary science, and speech pathology/audiology), SOCIAL SCIENCE (American studies, child care/child and family studies, economics, fire control and safety technology, geography, history, liberal arts/general studies, philosophy, political science/government, prelaw, psychology, and sociology). Engineering and business are the strongest academically. Animal sciences is the largest.

Required: To graduate, students must have a minimum GPA of 2.0 and at least 120 hours, including 40 to 60 in the major, for most programs. A higher GPA may be required in some majors. All students must take a minimum of 40 credit hours of core courses, including 6 each of English, humanities, analytical and quantitative thought, natural sciences, and social and behavioral sciences, 3 each of American history and government, and 1 each of scientific investigation and international studies.

Special: OSU offers internships in medical technology, engineering, home economics, and arts and sciences. A B.A.-B.S. degree, dual majors, an individualized university studies degree, a 3-2 engineering degree, an engineering co-op program, multidisciplinary majors in biosystems engineering and in cell and molecular biology, credit for life experience, nondegree study, and pass/fail options are available. Students may study abroad in several countries. The school also sponsors Semester at Sea, a 1-semester program of study on a ship traveling to ports throughout the world. There are 25 national honor societies, and a freshman honors program.

Faculty/Classroom: 71% of faculty are male; 29%, female. 58% teach undergraduates, 73% do research, and 44% do both. Graduate students teach 20% of introductory courses. The average class size in an introductory lecture is 30.

Admissions: 91% of the 2001-2002 applicants were accepted. The SAT I scores for the 2001-2002 freshman class were: Verbal--25% below 500, 43% between 500 and 599, 26% between 600 and 700, and 5% above 700; Math--23% below 500, 37% between 500 and 599, 32% between 600 and 700, and 8% above 700. The ACT scores were 21% below 21, 29% between 21 and 23, 25% between 24 and 26, 11% between 27 and 28, and 14% above 28. 55% of the current freshmen were in the top fifth of their class; 75% were in the top two fifths. There were 23 National Merit finalists. 312 freshmen graduated first in their class.

Requirements: The SAT I or ACT is required. In addition, for admission in good standing, freshman applicants must have a cumulative high school GPA of 3.0 and rank in the upper third of their graduating class, or achieve at least a 22 composite score on the ACT or 1020 on the SAT I, or have a 3.0 GPA in the required 15 curricular units, which include 4 years of English, 3 of math (algebra I and above), 2 each of history and lab science, 1 of citizenship skills, and 3 more from any of the above or computer science or foreign language. OSU requires applicants to be in the upper 33% of their class. A GPA of 3.0 is required. AP and CLEP credits are accepted. Important factors in the admissions decision are advanced placement or honor courses, evidence of special talent, and recommendations by school officials.

Procedure: Freshmen are admitted to all sessions. Entrance exams should be taken during the junior or senior year. Application deadlines are open. The application fee is $25. Notification is sent on a rolling basis.

Transfer: 1600 transfer students enrolled in 2001-2002. Applicants must submit official transcripts from all colleges attended. Students having fewer than 24 credit hours must also meet the requirements for entering freshmen. Nonresidents must have a minimum GPA of 2.0 and a total of 24 credit hours. In-state applicants must meet the requirements on a scaled GPA. 30 credits of at least 120 must be completed at OSU.

Visiting: There are regularly scheduled orientations for prospective students, including personal meetings and tours. Appointments are scheduled with other campus departments, as needed, to assist prospective students. There are guides for informal visits and visitors may sit in on classes and stay overnight. To schedule a visit, contact High School and College Relations at (405) 744-5358 or (800) 852-1255.

Financial Aid: In 2001-2002, 74% of all freshmen and 73% of continuing students received some form of financial aid. 37% of freshmen and 42% of continuing students received need-based aid. The average freshman award was $5500. Of that total, scholarships or need-based grants averaged $4025; loans averaged $3300; and work contracts averaged $1470. 19% of undergraduates work part time. Average annual earnings from campus work are $2000. The average financial indebtedness of the 2001 graduate was $18,100. The FAFSA is required. The fall application deadline is March 1.

International Students: There are 806 international students enrolled. The school actively recruits these students. They must score 500 on the written TOEFL or 173 on the electronic version and also take the SAT I or the ACT.

Computers: The mainframe is an IBM 9672/R25. There are some 2000 Macs and PCs available throughout the campus, with more than 15,000 active data ports. Access is also available in most residence halls. All students may access the system. There are no time limits. The fee is $5 per credit hour.

Graduates: In 2001, 2975 bachelor's degrees were awarded. The most popular majors were management (8%), marketing (7%), and curriculum and instruction education (6%). In an average class, 26% graduate in 4 years, 50% in 5 years, and 54% in 6 years. 460 companies recruited on campus in 2000-2001.

Admissions Contact: Gordon L. Reese, Director of Admissions.
E-mail: *admit@okstate.edu* Web: *www.okstate.edu*

ORAL ROBERTS UNIVERSITY

Tulsa, OK 74171 — **E-2**
(918) 495-6529
(800) 678-8876; Fax: (918) 495-6222

Full-time: 1190 men, 1631 women	**Faculty:** 152
Part-time: 99 men, 167 women	**Ph.D.s:** 50%
Graduate: 301 men, 289 women	**Student/Faculty:** 16 to 1
Year: semesters, summer session	**Tuition:** $12,920
Application Deadline: open	**Room & Board:** $5570
Freshman Class: 1303 applied, 938 accepted, 582 enrolled	
SAT I or ACT: required	**COMPETITIVE**

Oral Roberts University, founded in 1963, is a private liberal arts university committed to the Christian faith. There are 6 undergraduate and 3 graduate schools. In addition to regional accreditation, ORU has baccalaureate program accreditation with ABET, CSWE, NASM, and NLN. The library contains 750,000 volumes, 200,000 microform items, and 500,000 audiovisual forms/CDs, and subscribes to 2100 periodicals. Computerized library services include the card catalog and database searching. Special learning facilities include a learning resource center, natural history museum, radio station, TV station, and a TV production studio. The 400-acre campus is in a suburban area. Including residence halls, there are 22 buildings.

Student Life: 86% of undergraduates are from out of state, mostly the Midwest. Others are from 49 states, 51 foreign countries, and Canada. 50% are from public schools. 63% are white; 23% African American. Most are Protestant. The average age of freshmen is 20. 15% do not continue beyond their first year; 42% remain to graduate.

Housing: 3000 students can be accommodated in college housing, which includes single-sex dormitories. On-campus housing is available on a first-come, first-served basis. 57% of students live on campus; of those, 99% remain on campus on weekends. Alcohol is not permitted. All students may keep cars.

Activities: There are no fraternities or sororities. There are 60 groups on campus, including art, band, cheerleading, choir, chorale, chorus, computers, drama, ethnic, film, honors, international, jazz band, newspaper, opera, pep band, photography, political, professional, radio and TV, religious, social, social service, student government, symphony, and yearbook. Popular campus events include Fall Break and College Weekend.

Sports: There are 8 intercollegiate sports for men and 8 for women, and 20 intramural sports for men and 20 for women. Facilities include a physical fitness center, a track, tennis, racquetball, squash, volleyball, and basketball courts, and baseball and soccer fields.

Disabled Students: 90% of the campus is accessible. Wheelchair ramps, elevators, special parking, specially equipped rest rooms, special class scheduling, lowered drinking fountains, and lowered telephones are available.

Services: Counseling and information services are available, as is tutoring in most subjects. There is a reader service for the blind, and remedial math, reading, and writing.

Campus Safety and Security: Measures include 24-hour foot and vehicle patrol, self-defense education, escort service, and shuttle buses. There are lighted pathways/sidewalks.

Programs of Study: ORU confers B.A., B.S., B.M., B.Mus.Ed., B.S.E., B.S.N., and B.S.W. degrees. Master's and doctoral degrees are also awarded. Bachelor's degrees are awarded in BIOLOGICAL SCIENCE (biology/biological science), BUSINESS (accounting, banking and finance, business administration and management, international business management, management information systems, management science, marketing/retailing/merchandising, organizational behavior, and recreation and leisure services), COMMUNICATIONS AND THE ARTS (applied art, broadcasting, communications, dramatic arts, English, English literature, film arts, French, German, literature, music, music performance, music theory and composition, Spanish, speech/debate/rhetoric, and studio art), COMPUTER AND PHYSICAL SCIENCE (chemistry, computer science, mathematics, and physics), EDUCATION (art, business, drama, early childhood, elementary, English, foreign languages, health, mathematics, music, physical, recreation, science, social studies, and special), ENGINEERING AND ENVIRONMENTAL DESIGN (bioengineering, commercial art, computer engineering, electrical/electronics engineering, engineering, engineering management, mechanical engineering, and preengineering), HEALTH PROFESSIONS (biomedical science, health science, medical laboratory technology, nursing, optometry, predentistry, and premedicine), SOCIAL SCIENCE (biblical studies, history, international relations, international studies, liberal arts/general studies, ministries, philosophy, political science/government, prelaw, psychology, religion, religious education, religious music, and social work). All science programs, music, and theology are the strongest academically. Business is the largest.

Required: A minimum of 128 credit hours, with a minimum of 30 hours in the major, and a 2.0 GPA are required to graduate. All students must complete specific courses in the Bible, theology, and English, plus 12 hours in social sciences, 11 in biological, physical, and mathematical sciences, 6 to 7 in a modern foreign language, 3 in communication arts, and 2 in fine arts. 1 physical activity course is required per semester, along with regular, semiweekly chapel attendance. A senior paper must be completed in most majors.

Special: ORU offers combined B.A.-B.S. degrees, internships, 3-2 programs, work-study programs, dual and student-designed majors, study abroad in 5 countries, independent study, nondegree study, an accelerated degree in business and education, and a liberal arts degree. There are 3 national honor societies, a freshman honors program, and 7 departmental honors programs.

Faculty/Classroom: 68% of faculty are male; 32%, female. 78% both teach and do research. No introductory courses are taught by graduate students. The average class size in an introductory lecture is 30; in a laboratory, 20; and in a regular course, 20.

Admissions: 72% of the 2001-2002 applicants were accepted. The SAT I scores for the 2001-2002 freshman class were: Verbal--31% below 500, 42% between 500 and 599, 23% between 600 and 700, and 4% above 700; Math--38% below 500, 36% between 500 and 599, 21% between 600 and 700, and 5% above 700. The ACT scores were 12% between 12 and 17, 50% between 18 and 23, 33% between 24 and 29, and 5% between 30 and 36. 26% of the current freshmen were in the top tenth of their class; 50% were in the top quarter; 79% were in the top half.

Requirements: The SAT I or ACT is required. In addition, students should be graduates of an accredited secondary school or hold a GED. High school preparation should include 4 years of English, 2 of math, including algebra and geometry or 2 years of algebra, and 2 each of foreign language, social studies, and science, including lab science. A recommendation from the student's minister is required. An academic recommendation and an interview are recommended. AP and CLEP credits are accepted.

Procedure: Freshmen are admitted to all sessions. Entrance exams should be taken during the last semester of the junior year or during the senior year. There are early decision, early admissions, and deferred admissions plans. Application deadlines are open. The fall 2001 application fee was $35. Notification is sent on a rolling basis.

Transfer: An official transcript showing honorable dismissal from each previous institution is required. 30 credits of 128 must be completed at ORU.

Visiting: There are regularly scheduled orientations for prospective students, including College Weekend, which consists of visiting classes, meeting with faculty and staff, attending chapel services, and attending student life events. Visitors may sit in on classes and stay overnight. To schedule a visit, contact LeAnne Langley, the Admissions Office.

Financial Aid: In 2001-2002, 72% of all freshmen and 67% of continuing students received some form of financial aid. The FAFSA and the federal income tax return are required. Check with the school for current deadlines.

International Students: They must score 500 on the written TOEFL and also take the SAT I or the ACT.

Computers: The mainframe is an IBM. Academic Computing provides access to 4 teaching areas that may be used as both classrooms and walk-in labs. There are 14 computer labs available for students in the residence halls, and all student rooms are wired for computer access. Business students may access the system. There are no time limits.

Admissions Contact: Chris Belcher, Admissions.
E-mail: *admission@oru.edu* Web: *www.oru.edu*

SAINT GREGORY'S UNIVERSITY E-3
Shawnee, OK 74804 (405) 878-5444
(888) 784-7847; Fax: (405) 878-5198

Full-time: 276 men, 331 women	**Faculty:** 38
Part-time: 61 men, 89 women	**Ph.D.s:** 42%
Graduate: none	**Student/Faculty:** 16 to 1
Year: semesters, summer session	**Tuition:** $9502
Application Deadline: open	**Room & Board:** $4478
Freshman Class: 407 applied, 326 accepted, 200 enrolled	
ACT: 20	**NONCOMPETITIVE**

Saint Gregory's University, founded in 1875, is a private instituition affiliated with the Roman Catholic Church. Students design personalized degree programs within the integrative areas of humanities, natural science, social science, business, and theology. There are 5 undergraduate schools. The library contains 70,000 volumes, 3526 microform items, and 450 audiovisual forms/CDs, and subscribes to 150 periodicals. Computerized library services include the card catalog, interlibrary loans, and database searching. Special learning facilities include an art gallery. The 300-acre campus is in a suburban area about 30 miles east of Oklahoma City. Including residence halls, there are 12 buildings.

Student Life: 70% of undergraduates are from Oklahoma. Others are from 13 states, 15 foreign countries, and Canada. 80% are from public schools. 65% are white; 15% foreign nationals. 40% are Catholic; 24% claim no religious affiliation. The average age of freshmen is 18. 35% do not continue beyond their first year.

Housing: 415 students can be accommodated in college housing, which includes single-sex and coed dormitories. In addition, there are language houses and a dorm floor for honors students. On-campus housing is guaranteed for the freshman year only and is available on a first-come, first-served basis. Priority is given to out-of-town students. 70% of students live on campus; of those, 60% remain on campus on weekends. Alcohol is not permitted. All students may keep cars.

Activities: 10% of men belong to 3 local fraternities; 10% of women belong to 3 local sororities. There are 24 groups on campus, including art, cheerleading, choir, chorale, computers, dance, drama, ethnic, history, honors, international, musical theater, newspaper, photography, professional, religious, social, social service, student government, and yearbook. Popular campus events include sporting events, movie nights, and Hanging of the Green.

Sports: There are 5 intercollegiate sports for men and 7 for women, and 4 intramural sports for men and 4 for women. Facilities include soccer, baseball, and softball fields, as well as a wellness center with 2 gyms, Cybex equipment, and free weights.

Disabled Students: 90% of the campus is accessible. Wheelchair ramps, elevators, special parking, specially equipped rest rooms, special class scheduling, and lowered drinking fountains are available.

Services: Counseling and information services are available, as is tutoring in every subject. There is a reader service for the blind. Partners In Learning is a program designed to aid those students with learning disabilities.

Campus Safety and Security: Measures include 24-hour foot and vehicle patrol, escort service, informal discussions, and lighted pathways/sidewalks. There is card access to residence halls.

Programs of Study: St. Greg's confers B.A. in Humanities, B.A. in Theology, B.S. in Business, B.S. in Natural Science, and B.S. in Social Science degrees. Students follows personalized programs under these five integrative degrees. Associate degrees are also awarded. Life sciences, premedicine, and conservation biology are the strongest academically. Natural sciences, business, and social sciences are the largest.

Required: To graduate, students must complete 128 credits, including approximately 40 in the major, with a minimum 2.0 GPA. The core curriculum focuses on professional communication, creative thinking, self-leadership, and informational technology, including specific courses in English, speech, math, life science, physical science, philosophy, and theology. Students must pass a comprehensive exam at the end of sophomore year and complete a senior research project.

Special: Cross-registration is available through Oklahoma Baptist University. Each student designs a personalized program of study within the 5 integrative fields offered. The program should include 1 or more internships. Accelerated degree programs and study abroad in England and Mexico are offered. Directed study is available for further exploration of topics. There are 4 national honor societies, a freshman honors program, and honors programs in all departments.

Faculty/Classroom: 55% of faculty are male; 45%, female. All teach undergraduates. The average class size in an introductory lecture is 16; in a laboratory, 14; and in a regular course, 9.

Admissions: 80% of the 2001-2002 applicants were accepted. The ACT scores for the 2001-2002 freshman class were: 54% below 21, 23% between 21 and 23, 15% between 24 and 26, 5% between 27 and 28, and 5% above 28. 27% of the current freshmen were in the top fifth of their class; 50% were in the top two fifths. There were 2 National Merit semifinalists. 10 freshmen graduated first in their class.

Requirements: The ACT is required, with a minumum score of 18. Applications are accepted on-line via College Net or the school's web site. St. Greg's requires applicants to be in the upper 50% of their class. A GPA of 2.0 is required. AP and CLEP credits are accepted. Important factors in the admissions decision are leadership record, parents or siblings attending the school, and recommendations by alumni.

Procedure: Freshmen are admitted to all sessions. Entrance exams should be taken in October. There is a deferred admissions plan. Application deadlines are open. The application fee is $25. Notification is sent within 30 days of file completion.

Transfer: 40 transfer students enrolled in 2001-2002. Applicants must have either an associate degree or a cumulative 2.0 GPA in all completed college courses. 30 credits of 128 must be completed at St. Greg's.

Visiting: There are regularly scheduled orientations for prospective students, consisting of a private tour by an admissions counselor. There are guides for informal visits and visitors may sit in on classes and stay overnight. To schedule a visit, contact the Office of Admissions at (405) 878-5100 or *drutledge@sgc.edu*

Financial Aid: In 2001-2002, 62% of all freshmen and 57% of continuing students received some form of financial aid. 60% of freshmen and 56% of continuing students received need-based aid. The average freshman award was $7438. Of that total, scholarships or need-based grants averaged $4524; loans averaged $1914; and work contracts averaged $1000. 38% of undergraduates work part time. Average annual earnings from campus work are $1000. The average financial indebtedness of the 2001 graduate was $12,516. The FAFSA is required. The priority deadline for fall application is July 15.

International Students: There are 60 international students enrolled. The school actively recruits these students. They must score 500 on the written TOEFL or 173 on the electronic version or complete an on-campus intensive English program.

Computers: The mainframes are IBM PC servers and a clone server. 30 PCs are available for student use, and each dorm room has Internet access. The computer lab is open 10 hours a day. There are no time limits and no fees. All students are required to have personal computers. Any model that meets minimum 650 MHz, 10 GB hard disk, and 128 MB RAM is recommended.

Graduates: In 2001, 78 bachelor's degrees were awarded. The most popular majors were social science (38%), natural science (24%), and humanities (23%). 10 companies recruited on campus in 2000-2001. Of the 2000 graduating class, 6% were enrolled in graduate school within 6 months of graduation and 40% were employed.

Admissions Contact: Dan Rutledge, Director of Admissions.
E-mail: *drutledge@sgc.edu* Web: *www.sgc.edu*

SOUTHEASTERN OKLAHOMA STATE UNIVERSITY D-3
Durant, OK 74701 (580) 745-2060; Fax: (580) 745-7502

Full-time: 1368 men, 1516 women	**Faculty:** 152; IIA, --$
Part-time: 308 men, 446 women	**Ph.D.s:** 65%
Graduate: 160 men, 227 women	**Student/Faculty:** 19 to 1
Year: semesters, summer session	**Tuition:** $2297 ($5338)
Application Deadline: open	**Room & Board:** $2620
Freshman Class: 906 applied, 785 accepted, 604 enrolled	
ACT: 20	**COMPETITIVE**

Southeastern Oklahoma State University, founded in 1909, is a public institution offering programs in the arts and sciences, business, education, music, and technology to a primarily commuter student body. There are 3 undergraduate schools and 1 graduate school. In addition to regional accreditation, Southeastern has baccalaureate program accreditation with AACSB, NASM, and NCATE. The library contains 186,800 volumes, 441,246 microform items, and 5868 audiovisual forms/CDs, and subscribes to 1088 periodicals. Computerized library services include the card catalog, interlibrary loans, and database searching. Special learning facilities include a learning resource center, radio station, and an herbarium. The 177-acre campus is in a rural area 90 miles north of Dallas. Including residence halls, there are 46 buildings.

Student Life: 76% of undergraduates are from Oklahoma. Others are from 36 states, 33 foreign countries, and Canada. 99% are from public schools. 61% are white; 30% Native American/Eskimo. The average age of freshmen is 22; all undergraduates, 25. 33% do not continue beyond their first year; 41% remain to graduate.

Housing: 676 students can be accommodated in college housing, which includes single-sex and coed dormitories, on-campus apartments, and married-student housing. On-campus housing is guaranteed for all 4 years. 80% of students commute. Alcohol is not permitted. All students may keep cars.

Activities: 7% of men belong to 3 national fraternities; 5% of women belong to 2 national sororities. There are 70 groups on campus, including art, band, cheerleading, chess, choir, chorale, computers, dance, debate, drama, ethnic, forensics, honors, international, jazz band, literary magazine, marching band, musical theater, newspaper, opera, pep band, photography, political, professional, radio and TV, religious, social, social service, student government, and yearbook. Popular campus events include Parents Day, Candlelighting, and Springfest.

Sports: There are 4 intercollegiate sports for men and 5 for women, and 2 intramural sports for men and 1 for women. Facilities include a 4000-seat football stadium, a 2000-seat gym, baseball and softball fields, a track, tennis courts, playing fields, and a swimming pool.

Disabled Students: 50% of the campus is accessible. Wheelchair ramps, elevators, special parking, specially equipped rest rooms, special class scheduling, and lowered telephones are available.

Services: Counseling and information services are available, as is tutoring in every subject. There is a reader service for the blind, and remedial math, reading, and writing. Tutoring in study skills is also available.

Campus Safety and Security: Measures include 24-hour foot and vehicle patrol, self-defense education, escort service, and pamphlets/posters/films. There are lighted pathways/sidewalks and safety training.

Programs of Study: Southeastern confers B.A., B.S., B.B.A., B.M., and B.M.Ed. degrees. Master's degrees are also awarded. Bachelor's degrees are awarded in AGRICULTURE (conservation and regulation), BIOLOGICAL SCIENCE (biology/biological science), BUSINESS (accounting, business administration and management, recreation and leisure services, and secretarial studies/office management), COMMUNICATIONS AND THE ARTS (dramatic arts, English, fine arts, music, and speech/debate/rhetoric), COMPUTER AND PHYSICAL SCIENCE (chemistry, computer science, information sciences and systems, mathematics, and physics), EDUCATION (art, business, early childhood, elementary, music, physical, science, and secondary), ENGINEERING AND ENVIRONMENTAL DESIGN (occupational safety and health), HEALTH PROFESSIONS (medical laboratory technology), SOCIAL SCIENCE (criminal justice, economics, gerontology, history, political science/government, psychology, social science, and sociology). Chemistry, history, and music are the strongest academically. Elementary education, health and phys ed, and psychology are the largest.

Required: A total of 124 credit hours with a minimum GPA of 2.0 (2.5 for teacher education majors) is required for graduation. All students must complete 41 semester hours of general education requirements, including English, American history, government, humanities, arts, social and lab sciences, math, communications, and health education, and 3 hours of computer science.

Special: Internships, study abroad, credit for military experience, pass/fail options in some courses, and nondegree study are available. There are 13 national honor societies, a freshman honors program, and 9 departmental honors programs.

Faculty/Classroom: 66% of faculty are male; 34%, female. All teach undergraduates and 10% do research. No introductory courses are taught by graduate students. The average class size in an introductory lecture is 27; in a laboratory, 18; and in a regular course, 23.

Admissions: 87% of the 2001-2002 applicants were accepted. The ACT scores for the 2001-2002 freshman class were: 58% below 21, 23% between 21 and 23, 12% between 24 and 26, 4% between 27 and 28, and 3% above 28. 32% of the current freshmen were in the top fifth of their class; 63% were in the top two fifths. 16 freshmen graduated first in their class.

Requirements: The ACT is required. In addition, applicants should be graduates of an accredited secondary school or have earned a GED. High school courses must include 4 years of English, 3 of math, 2 each of lab science and history, 1 of citizenship skills (from the subjects of economics, geography, government, or non-Western culture), and 3 additional units of subjects previously listed or of computer science or foreign language. Southeastern requires applicants to be in the upper 50% of their class. A GPA of 2.7 is required. AP and CLEP credits are accepted.

Procedure: Freshmen are admitted to all sessions. Entrance exams should be taken by the fall of the senior year. Application deadlines are open. The application fee is $20. Notification is sent on a rolling basis.

Transfer: 530 transfer students enrolled in 2001-2002. Out-of-state applicants must have a 2.0 GPA. In-state applicants must have a 1.7 GPA with 24 to 36 credit hours earned, 1.8 with 37 to 72 hours, and 2.0 with 73 or more hours. 30 credits of 124 must be completed at Southeastern.

Visiting: There are guides for informal visits and visitors may sit in on classes. To schedule a visit, contact Admissions and Enrollment Services at *admissions@sosu.edu*.

Financial Aid: In 2001-2002, 72% of all freshmen and 71% of continuing students received some form of financial aid. 45% of freshmen and 44% of continuing students received need-based aid. The average freshman award was $2300. Of that total, scholarships or need-based grants averaged $500 ($3750 maximum); loans averaged $1000 ($2625 maximum); and work contracts averaged $1000 ($2000 maximum). 45% of undergraduates work part time. Average annual earnings from campus work are $1200. The average financial indebtedness of the 2001 graduate was $8000. Southeastern is a member of CSS. The FAFSA is required. The fall application deadline is April 1.

International Students: There are 45 international students enrolled. They must score 550 on the written TOEFL or 213 on the electronic version and also take the SAT I or the ACT.

Computers: The mainframe is a Digital Alpha server 1200. Students have access to the Internet and Web via 390 PCs in general use student labs and teaching labs. Students are mainly served by Windows NT and Windows 2000 servers. All students may access the system. There are no time limits. The fee is $7 per credit hour.

Graduates: In 2001, 574 bachelor's degrees were awarded. The most popular majors were elementary education (13%), occupational safety (7%), and criminal justice (7%). In an average class, 2% graduate in 3 years, 18% in 4 years, 33% in 5 years, and 38% in 6 years. 100 companies recruited on campus in 2000-2001.

Admissions Contact: Rudy Manley, Admissions.

SOUTHERN NAZARENE UNIVERSITY — D-3

Bethany, OK 73008 — (405) 491-6324
(800) 648-9899; Fax: (405) 491-6320

Full-time: 765 men, 860 women	**Faculty:** 53
Part-time: 30 men, 50 women	**Ph.D.s:** 58%
Graduate: 135 men, 170 women	**Student/Faculty:** 31 to 1
Year: semesters, summer session	**Tuition:** $10,314
Application Deadline: August 6	**Room & Board:** $4320
Freshman Class: n/av	
SAT I or ACT: required	**NONCOMPETITIVE**

Southern Nazarene University, founded in 1899, is a private, coeducational institution affiliated with the Church of the Nazarene. It offers programs in liberal arts and sciences, health fields, business, and education. Figures in above capsule are approximate. There are 3 undergraduate schools and 1 graduate school. In addition to regional accreditation, SNU has baccalaureate program accreditation with NASM, NCATE, and NLN. The library contains 112,673 volumes, 219,576 microform items, and 3543 audiovisual forms/CDs, and subscribes to 667 periodicals. Computerized library services include the card catalog, interlibrary loans, and database searching. Special learning facilities include a learning resource center and TV station. The 40-acre campus is in a suburban area 10 miles northwest of Oklahoma City. Including residence halls, there are 20 buildings.

Student Life: 55% of undergraduates are from out of state, mostly the South. Others are from 31 states, 22 foreign countries, and Canada. 90% are white. Most are Protestant. The average age of freshmen is 18; all undergraduates, 23. 10% do not continue beyond their first year; 45% remain to graduate.

Housing: 938 students can be accommodated in college housing, which includes single-sex dormitories, on-campus apartments, and married-student housing. On-campus housing is guaranteed for all 4 years. 55% of students live on campus; of those, 80% remain on campus on weekends. Alcohol is not permitted. All students may keep cars.

Activities: There are no fraternities or sororities. There are 40 groups on campus, including band, cheerleading, choir, chorale, chorus, computers, drama, drum and bugle corps, honors, international, jazz band, literary magazine, musical theater, newspaper, orchestra, pep band, photography, political, professional, radio and TV, religious, social, social service, student government, symphony, and yearbook. Popular campus events include Valentine Banquet, Fall Fest, and Yule Feast.

Sports: There are 7 intercollegiate sports for men and 7 for women, and 3 intramural sports for men and 3 for women. Facilities include a 1824-seat phys ed center, gyms, a soccer complex, tennis courts, and a new athletic convocation center that seats 4000.

Disabled Students: 95% of the campus is accessible. Wheelchair ramps, elevators, special parking, specially equipped rest rooms, special class scheduling, lowered drinking fountains, lowered telephones, and dorm rooms that may be adapted for handicapped students are available.

Services: Counseling and information services are available, as is tutoring in most subjects. There is remedial math, reading, and writing. Services may be arranged for deaf or learning-disabled students.

Campus Safety and Security: Measures include 24-hour foot and vehicle patrol, self-defense education, escort service, and informal discussions. There are lighted pathways/sidewalks and 24-hour controlled access into dormitories.

Programs of Study: SNU confers A.B., B.S., and B.Mus.Ed. degrees. Associate and master's degrees are also awarded. Bachelor's degrees are awarded in AGRICULTURE (agriculture), BIOLOGICAL SCIENCE (biology/biological science), BUSINESS (accounting, banking and finance, business administration and management, business economics, management information systems, marketing/retailing/merchandising, office supervision and management, personnel management, and sports management), COMMUNICATIONS AND THE ARTS (communications, creative writing, English, fine arts, journalism, music, music business management, music performance, piano/organ, Spanish, speech/debate/rhetoric, and voice), COMPUTER AND PHYSICAL SCIENCE (chemistry, computer science, mathematics, and physics), EDUCATION (athletic training, business, early childhood, elementary, foreign languages, music, physical, and secondary), ENGINEERING AND ENVIRONMENTAL DESIGN (aviation administration/management, and preengineering), HEALTH PROFESSIONS (exercise science, nursing, physical therapy, predentistry, premedicine, and prepharmacy), SOCIAL SCIENCE (biblical languages, criminal justice, history, international studies, missions, philosophy, political science/government, prelaw, psychology, religion, religious education, social science, and sociology). Premedicine, physics, and theology are the strongest academically. Business, and education are the largest.

Required: A total of 124 semester hours, including at least 32 hours in the major, with a minimum GPA of 2.0 is required to graduate. All students must complete 53 hours of general education requirements covering core areas of self and identity, faith and tradition, and service and society. Skills courses must be taken in computer science, composition, speech communication, math, natural science, citizenship, foreign language, and phy ed.

Special: Cross-registration and co-op programs are available through the Southwestern Colleges of Christian Ministry. Internships may be arranged in the major. A Washington semester, study abroad in Latin America, England, Russia, and the Middle East, work-study programs in sociology, and dual and student-designed majors are available. There is an accelerated degree program in management of human resources and family studies and gerontology. SNU offers nondegree study for life/military/work experience. A Hollywood semester may be arranged through the Christian College Coalition. There are 6 national honor societies, including Phi Beta Kappa and a freshman honors program.

Faculty/Classroom: 57% of faculty are male; 43%, female. All teach undergraduates and 15% do research. Graduate students teach 1% of introductory courses. The average class size in an introductory lecture is 20 and in a laboratory, 15.

Admissions: There were 3 National Merit finalists in a recent year.

Requirements: The SAT I or ACT is required. In addition, applicants must be graduates of an accredited secondary school or have a GED. SNU requires applicants to be in the upper 40% of their class. A GPA of 2.5 is required. AP and CLEP credits are accepted. Important factors in the admissions decision are advanced placement or honor courses, extracurricular activities record, and leadership record.

Procedure: Freshmen are admitted fall and spring. Entrance exams should be taken by April of the senior year or at orientation prior to the beginning of classes. There are early admissions and deferred admissions plans. The college accepts all applicants. Notification is sent on a rolling basis. Check with the school for current application deadlines. The fall 2001 application fee was $25.

Transfer: Transfer applicants must have a 2.0 GPA and be in good standing at their previous college. 30 credits of 124 must be completed at SNU.

Visiting: There are regularly scheduled orientations for prospective students, including visits with faculty and students and seminars on financial aid and admissions. There are campus tours, group social activities, and small group mentoring throughout the fall semester. There are guides for informal visits and visitors may sit in on classes and stay overnight. To schedule a visit, contact the Office of Admissions.

Financial Aid: The FAFSA is required. Check with the school for current deadlines.

International Students: They must take the TOEFL.

Computers: The mainframe is an IBM AS 400. Students have access to 75 networked and 15 nonnetworked computers. DOS-based students may access an IBM S/36 and a MicroVAX II. All students may access the system Monday through Saturday. There are no time limits. The fee is $140 per year.

Admissions Contact: Brad Townley, Director of Admissions. A video is available. E-mail: *admiss@snu.edu* Web: *www.snu.edu*

SOUTHWESTERN OKLAHOMA STATE UNIVERSITY D-3

Weatherford, OK 73096 **(580) 774-3009; Fax: (580) 774-3795**

Full-time: 1522 men, 1894 women	**Faculty:** 190; IIA, --$
Part-time: 167 men, 275 women	**Ph.D.s:** 65%
Graduate: 245 men, 365 women	**Student/Faculty:** 18 to 1
Year: semesters, summer session	**Tuition:** $2121 ($4868)
Application Deadline: August 5	**Room & Board:** $2680
Freshman Class: 1247 applied, 1167 accepted, 871 enrolled	
ACT: 21	**COMPETITIVE**

Southwestern Oklahoma State University, founded in 1901, is a public institution offering programs in education, arts and sciences, business, health sciences, and pharmacy. There are 4 undergraduate and 3 graduate schools. In addition to regional accreditation, SWOSU has baccalaureate program accreditation with ABET, ABHES, ACBSP, ACOTE, ACPE, ACS, APTA, CAAHEP, CAHEA, CSWE, JRCERT, NAMT, NASM, NCATE, and NLN. The library contains 287,572 volumes, 1,168,558 microform items, and 872 audiovisual forms/CDs, and subscribes to 1551 periodicals. Computerized library services include the card catalog, interlibrary loans, and database searching. The 73-acre campus is in a small town 70 miles west of Oklahoma City. Including residence halls, there are 30 buildings.

Student Life: 90% of undergraduates are from Oklahoma. Others are from 37 states, 36 foreign countries, and Canada. 98% are from public schools. 86% are white. The average age of freshmen is 19; all undergraduates, 23. 35% do not continue beyond their first year; 32% remain to graduate.

Housing: 1255 students can be accommodated in college housing, which includes single-sex dormitories and married-student housing. On-campus housing is guaranteed for all 4 years. 73% of students commute. Alcohol is not permitted. All students may keep cars.

Activities: 2% of men belong to 2 local and 1 national fraternities; 2% of women belong to 3 local sororities. There are 66 groups on campus, including art, band, cheerleading, choir, chorale, chorus, computers, debate, drama, drill team, ethnic, forensics, honors, international, jazz band, marching band, musical theater, newspaper, opera, orchestra, pep band, political, professional, religious, social, social service, student government, symphony, and yearbook. Popular campus events include Howdy Week, Miss Southwestern Pageant, and Panorama Series.

Sports: There are 6 intercollegiate sports for men and 6 for women, and 8 intramural sports for men and 8 for women. Facilities include 2 gyms, a weight room, an exercise equipment room, an indoor pool, an outdoor track, tennis courts, an outdoor football field and baseball diamond, 2 football practice fields, a rodeo arena, a ropes course, and a lake. A soccer practice field, sand volleyball courts, and outdoor basketball courts are also available.

Disabled Students: 98% of the campus is accessible. Wheelchair ramps, elevators, special parking, specially equipped rest rooms, special class scheduling, lowered drinking fountains, and lowered telephones are available.

Services: Counseling and information services are available, as is tutoring in some subjects, including math, science, business, English, and social sciences. There is remedial math, reading, and writing. A student development center offers counseling and tutoring on an individual basis.

Campus Safety and Security: Measures include 24-hour foot and vehicle patrol, self-defense education, informal discussions, and pamphlets/posters/films. There are emergency telephones and lighted pathways/sidewalks.

Programs of Study: SWOSU confers B.A., B.S., B.A.Ed., B.Art, B.B.A., B.Comm.Art, B.Gen.Tech., B.M., B.M.Ed., B.Rec., B.S.Ed., B.S.Eng.Tech., B.S.H.I.M., B.S.M.T., B.S.N., and B.S.P. degrees. Associate, master's, and doctoral degrees are also awarded. Bachelor's degrees are awarded in BIOLOGICAL SCIENCE (biology/biological science and biophysics), BUSINESS (accounting, banking and finance, business administration and management, management information systems, management science, marketing/retailing/merchandising, and recreational facilities management), COMMUNICATIONS AND THE ARTS (communications, English, and graphic design), COMPUTER AND PHYSICAL SCIENCE (chemistry, computer programming, computer science, information sciences and systems, mathematics, natural sciences, and physics), EDUCATION (art, athletic training, education administration, elementary, English, health, industrial arts, mathematics, music, physical, school psychology, science, secondary, social science, special, and technical), ENGINEERING AND ENVIRONMENTAL DESIGN (computer engineering, electrical/electronics engineering technology, engineering physics, engineering technology, environmental engineering technology, industrial administration/management, industrial engineering technology, manufacturing engineering, and manufacturing technology), HEALTH PROFESSIONS (health care administration, health science, medical records administration/services, medical technology, music therapy, and nursing), SOCIAL SCIENCE (community psychology, criminal justice, history, political science/government, psychology, and social work). Chemistry is the strongest academically. Business and education are the largest.

Required: To graduate, students must complete 124 semester hours with a minimum GPA of 2.0. Distribution requirements include 8 hours in communication and natural sciences, 6 each in history and government, fine arts and humanities, and international and cultural studies, 3 each in economics, health and phys ed, behavioral/social science, and math, and 2 in computer applications.

Special: SWOSU offers work-study programs and a program allowing high school seniors to earn college credits. Preprofessional curricula are offered in numerous areas, including medicine, law, engineering, and allied health professions. There are 4 national honor societies.

Faculty/Classroom: 63% of faculty are male; 37%, female. All teach undergraduates and 10% also do research. Graduate students teach 1% of introductory courses. The average class size in a laboratory is 15 and in a regular course, 27.

Admissions: 94% of the 2001-2002 applicants were accepted. The ACT scores for the 2001-2002 freshman class were: 49% below 21, 26% between 21 and 23, 14% between 24 and 26, 7% between 27 and 28, and 4% above 28. 31% of the current freshmen were in the top fifth of their class; 58% were in the top two fifths. 55 freshmen graduated first in their class.

Requirements: The ACT is required, with a minimum composite score of 19. Applicants should be graduates of an accredited secondary school. The GED is accepted. Students should present at least 15 academic credits, including 4 in English, 3 in math, 2 each in history and lab science, 1 in citizenship, and 3 additional units in computer science or foreign language. SWOSU requires applicants to be in the upper 50% of their class. A GPA of 2.7 is required. AP and CLEP credits are accepted.
Procedure: Freshmen are admitted to all sessions. Entrance exams should be taken during the senior year. Applications should be filed by August 5 for fall entry, January 1 for spring entry, and May 15 for summer entry. The fall 2001 application fee was $15. Notification is sent on a rolling basis.
Transfer: 299 transfer students enrolled in 2001-2002. Applicants must have a minimum college GPA of 2.0 and submit official transcripts from all institutions attended. 30 credits of 124 must be completed at SWOSU.
Visiting: There are regularly scheduled orientations for prospective students, including counseling sessions on careers, financial aid, social activities, and enrollment procedures. There are guides for informal visits and visitors may sit in on classes and stay overnight. To schedule a visit, contact the Director of High School and College Relations at (580) 774-3782 or *boydt@swosu.edu*
Financial Aid: The FAFSA and the college's own financial statement are required. The fall application deadline is May 1.
International Students: There are 85 international students enrolled. They must score 500 on the written TOEFL and also take the ACT, scoring 19.
Computers: The mainframes are a DEC VAX 4700, a DEC VAX 4100, and a DEC ALPHA. Macs, PCs, and terminals are available in labs across campus. All students may access the system from 8 A.M. to midnight Monday through Thursday, 8 A.M. to 5 P.M. Friday, 10 A.M. to 2 P.M. Saturday, and 2 P.M. to midnight Sunday. There are no time limits and no fees.
Graduates: In 2001, 553 bachelor's degrees were awarded. The most popular majors were accounting (7%), nursing (7%), and elementary education (6%). In an average class, 12% graduate in 4 years, 26% in 5 years, and 32% in 6 years. 140 companies recruited on campus in 2000-2001.
Admissions Contact: Connie Phillips, Admissions Coordinator. A video is available. E-mail: *phillic@swosu.edu* Web: *www.swosu.edu*

UNIVERSITY OF CENTRAL OKLAHOMA — E-5

Edmond, OK 73034 — (405) 974-2338
(800) 254-4215; Fax: (405) 341-4964

Full-time: 3633 men, 4982 women	**Faculty:** 391; IIA, --$
Part-time: 1500 men, 2173 women	**Ph.D.s:** 70%
Graduate: 930 men, 1523 women	**Student/Faculty:** 22 to 1
Year: semesters, summer session	**Tuition:** $2067 ($4186)
Application Deadline: August 15	**Room & Board:** $3138
Freshman Class: 6701 applied, 6429 accepted, 2195 enrolled	
ACT: 22	**COMPETITIVE**

The University of Central Oklahoma, founded in 1890, is a state-supported institution offering undergraduate and graduate programs in the liberal arts and sciences, education, business, and music. There are 5 undergraduate schools and 1 graduate school. In addition to regional accreditation, UCO has baccalaureate program accreditation with ABFSE, ACBSP, ADA, NASM, NCATE, and NLN. The library contains 438,975 volumes, 989,936 microform items, and 30,202 audiovisual forms/CDs, and subscribes to 5244 periodicals. Computerized library services include the card catalog, interlibrary loans, and database searching. Special learning facilities include a learning resource center, art gallery, radio station, and TV station. The 200-acre campus is in a suburban area north of Oklahoma City. Including residence halls, there are 42 buildings.
Student Life: 85% of undergraduates are from Oklahoma. Others are from 38 states, 108 foreign countries, and Canada. 83% are from public schools. 72% are white; 11% foreign nationals. The average age of freshmen is 21; all undergraduates, 25. 33% do not continue beyond their first year; 27% remain to graduate.
Housing: 1404 students can be accommodated in college housing, which includes single-sex and coed dormitories, on-campus apartments, off-campus apartments, and married-student housing. On-campus housing is available on a first-come, first-served basis and is available on a lottery system for upperclassmen. 91% of students commute. Alcohol is not permitted. All students may keep cars.
Activities: 5% of men belong to 11 national fraternities; 7% of women belong to 7 national sororities. There are 170 groups on campus, including art, band, cheerleading, choir, computers, dance, debate, ethnic, gay, honors, international, jazz band, literary magazine, marching band, musical theater, newspaper, opera, orchestra, political, professional, radio and TV, religious, social, student government, and yearbook. Popular campus events include International Week, Black Heritage Week, and Indian Heritage Week.
Sports: There are 6 intercollegiate sports for men and 5 for women, and 21 intramural sports for men and 21 for women. Facilities include a field house with a gym, a swimming pool, a track, and a weight room, and a stadium with a track and a softball field.
Disabled Students: 90% of the campus is accessible. Wheelchair ramps, elevators, special parking, specially equipped rest rooms, special class scheduling, and lowered drinking fountains are available.
Services: Counseling and information services are available, as is tutoring in some subjects, including English, math, and reading. There is remedial math.
Campus Safety and Security: Measures include 24-hour foot and vehicle patrol, escort service, emergency telephones, and lighted pathways/sidewalks.
Programs of Study: UCO confers B.A., B.S., B.A.Ed., B.B.A., B.F.A., B.F.A.Ed., B.M.Ed., B.Mus., and B.S.Ed. degrees. Master's degrees are also awarded. Bachelor's degrees are awarded in BIOLOGICAL SCIENCE (biology/biological science and nutrition), BUSINESS (accounting, banking and finance, business administration and management, business economics, fashion merchandising, funeral home services, hotel/motel and restaurant management, human resources, insurance, management information systems, marketing/retailing/merchandising, and recreational facilities management), COMMUNICATIONS AND THE ARTS (advertising, broadcasting, communications, creative writing, dramatic arts, English, fine arts, French, German, graphic design, journalism, music, photography, public relations, Spanish, and speech/debate/rhetoric), COMPUTER AND PHYSICAL SCIENCE (actuarial science, chemistry, computer science, and mathematics), EDUCATION (art, business, dance, early childhood, elementary, English, foreign languages, industrial arts, marketing and distribution, mathematics, museum studies, music, physical, science, social studies, and special), ENGINEERING AND ENVIRONMENTAL DESIGN (engineering physics and interior design), HEALTH PROFESSIONS (community health work, industrial hygiene, medical laboratory technology, nursing, and speech pathology/audiology), SOCIAL SCIENCE (addiction studies, criminal justice, economics, family/consumer studies, forensic studies, geography, history, liberal arts/general studies, philosophy, physical fitness/movement, political science/government, psychology, public administration, and sociology). Information and operations management, elementary education, and business administration are the largest.
Required: Students must complete 124 semester hours with a 2.25 GPA. At least 15 hours in upper-division courses in the major are required. Students must also complete a maximum of 12 semester hours in general education requirements, including phys ed.
Special: Opportunities are provided for internships, B.A.-B.S. degrees, dual majors, a general studies degree, credit by exam, nondegree study, and credit for military experience. Work-study programs may be arranged through the Federal College Work-Study Program.
Faculty/Classroom: 56% of faculty are male; 44%, female. No introductory courses are taught by graduate students.
Admissions: 96% of the 2001-2002 applicants were accepted. The ACT scores for the 2001-2002 freshman class were: 41% below 21, 31% between 21 and 23, 17% between 24 and 26, 7% between 27 and 28, and 4% above 28.
Requirements: The ACT is required, with a minimum composite score of 19. Graduation from an accredited secondary school is required. A GED will be accepted for adult students. The applicant's academic record should include 4 years of English, 3 years of math, with first-year algebra and beyond, and 2 years each of lab science and history, of which 1 year must be in American history. UCO requires applicants to be in the upper 50% of their class. A GPA of 2.7 is required. AP and CLEP credits are accepted. Important factors in the admissions decision are evidence of special talent, extracurricular activities record, and leadership record.
Procedure: Freshmen are admitted to all sessions. Entrance exams should be taken within 30 days of submitting the application. There is an early admissions plan. Applications should be filed by August 15 for fall entry, January 2 for spring entry, and May 25 for summer entry. The fall 2001 application fee was $15. Notification is sent on a rolling basis.
Transfer: 1330 transfer students enrolled in 2001-2002. Applicants must submit official transcripts from previous colleges attended and have a minimum GPA of 2.0. Students who have completed fewer than 24 hours of transferable credit must meet the requirements for entering freshmen. 30 credits of 124 must be completed at UCO.
Visiting: There are regularly scheduled orientations for prospective students, including a brief tour, a question-and-answer period, and access to an information booth. There are guides for informal visits and visitors may sit in on classes. To schedule a visit, contact Prospective Student Services at (405) 974-2727 or *4ucoinfo@ucok.edu*
Financial Aid: 50% of undergraduates work part time. Average annual earnings from campus work are $2500. The CSS/Profile or FFS and the college's own financial statement are required. The fall application deadline is April 1.
International Students: The school actively recruits these students. They must score 500 on the written TOEFL and also take and also take the ACT, scoring 19.

Computers: The mainframe is a DEC VAX 4000. Students may access some 140 terminals located in computer labs and in the library during scheduled hours. All students may access the system. There are no time limits and no fees.

Graduates: In 2001, 1876 bachelor's degrees were awarded. The most popular majors were business administration (9%), information and operations management (7%), and journalism (3%). In an average class, 9% graduate in 4 years, 24% in 5 years, and 27% in 6 years. 68 companies recruited on campus in 2000-2001.

Admissions Contact: Linda Lofton, Director, Admissions.
E-mail: *admissions@ucok.edu* Web: *www.ucok.edu*

UNIVERSITY OF OKLAHOMA

Norman, OK 73019 D-3
(405) 325-2252
(800) 234-6868; Fax: (405) 325-7124

Full-time: 8197 men, 7931 women	**Faculty:** 979; I, --$
Part-time: 1361 men, 1186 women	**Ph.D.s:** 86%
Graduate: 2087 men, 1899 women	**Student/Faculty:** 16 to 1
Year: semesters, summer session	**Tuition:** $2713 ($7437)
Application Deadline: June 1	**Room & Board:** $4903
Freshman Class: 6943 applied, 6459 accepted, 3748 enrolled	
SAT I Verbal/Math: (average)	**ACT:** 25 **VERY COMPETITIVE**

The University of Oklahoma, founded in 1890, is a comprehensive research university offering 160 areas for undergraduate study. There are 9 undergraduate and 9 graduate schools. In addition to regional accreditation, OU has baccalaureate program accreditation with AACSB, ABA, ABET, ACCE, ACEJMC, ADA, APA, APTA, CSAB, CSWE, FIDER, NAAB, NASM, and NCATE. The 8 libraries contain 4,187,777 volumes, 3,867,009 microform items, and 7325 audiovisual forms/CDs, and subscribe to 16,092 periodicals. Computerized library services include the card catalog, interlibrary loans, and database searching. Special learning facilities include an art gallery, natural history museum, radio station, TV station, and observatory. The 3136-acre campus is in a suburban area 18 miles south of Oklahoma City. Including residence halls, there are 231 buildings.

Student Life: 78% of undergraduates are from Oklahoma. Others are from 49 states, 103 foreign countries, and Canada. 71% are white. The average age of freshmen is 19; all undergraduates, 21. 20% do not continue beyond their first year; 50% remain to graduate.

Housing: 5500 students can be accommodated in college housing, which includes single-sex and coed dormitories, on-campus apartments, and married-student housing. In addition, there are honors houses, and special-interest houses, international floors, and intensive-study housing. On-campus housing is guaranteed for all 4 years. 77% of students commute. All students may keep cars.

Activities: 18% of men belong to 25 national fraternities; 24% of women belong to 16 national sororities. There are 275 groups on campus, including art, band, cheerleading, chess, choir, chorale, chorus, dance, drama, drill team, ethnic, film, forensics, gay, honors, international, jazz band, literary magazine, marching band, musical theater, newspaper, opera, orchestra, pep band, photography, political, professional, radio and TV, religious, social, social service, student government, symphony, and yearbook. Popular campus events include Medieval Fair, Moms and Dads Days, and Theater and Dance season.

Sports: There are 10 intercollegiate sports for men and 10 for women, and 35 intramural sports for men and 35 for women. Facilities include a golf course, a field house, an arena, a gymnastics center, tennis courts, a swimming pool complex, a fitness center, a football stadium, track and field facilities, and baseball, soccer, and softball fields.

Disabled Students: 90% of the campus is accessible. Wheelchair ramps, elevators, special parking, specially equipped rest rooms, special class scheduling, lowered drinking fountains, lowered telephones, 25 TDDs, automatic door openers, adaptive computers labs, and an office of disability services are available.

Services: Counseling and information services are available, as is tutoring in most subjects. There is a reader service for the blind, and remedial math, reading, and writing. There are also volunteer note takers, interpreter services for the deaf or hearing impaired, and alternative testing services.

Campus Safety and Security: Measures include 24-hour foot and vehicle patrol, self-defense education, escort service, and shuttle buses. There are informal discussions, pamphlets/posters/films, emergency telephones, lighted pathways/sidewalks, and There is also a modified 911 system, and a bicycle patrol.

Programs of Study: OU confers B.A., B.S., B.Acct., B.Arch, B.B.A., B.F.A., B.Int.Design, B.L.S., B.Mus.Arts, B.Music, B.Mus.Educ., and B.S.Ed. degrees. Master's and doctoral degrees are also awarded. Bachelor's degrees are awarded in BIOLOGICAL SCIENCE (botany, microbiology, and zoology), BUSINESS (accounting, banking and finance, business administration and management, business economics, international business management, management information systems, marketing/retailing/merchandising, and real estate), COMMUNICATIONS AND THE ARTS (advertising, art, art history and appreciation, broadcasting, classics, communications, dance, dramatic arts, English, film arts, fine arts, French, German, journalism, languages, linguistics, music, photography, public relations, Russian, Spanish, and video), COMPUTER AND PHYSICAL SCIENCE (astronomy, astrophysics, atmospheric sciences and meteorology, chemistry, computer science, geology, geophysics and seismology, geoscience, information sciences and systems, mathematics, and physics), EDUCATION (early childhood, elementary, foreign languages, mathematics, music, science, social studies, and special), ENGINEERING AND ENVIRONMENTAL DESIGN (aeronautical engineering, architecture, aviation administration/management, chemical engineering, civil engineering, computer engineering, construction management, electrical/electronics engineering, engineering, engineering physics, environmental design, environmental engineering, environmental science, geological engineering, industrial engineering, interior design, land use management and reclamation, mechanical engineering, and petroleum/natural gas engineering), HEALTH PROFESSIONS (health science and medical laboratory technology), SOCIAL SCIENCE (African American studies, anthropology, area studies, Asian/Oriental studies, economics, geography, history, international studies, liberal arts/general studies, Native American studies, philosophy, political science/government, psychology, public affairs, religion, social work, sociology, and women's studies). Chemistry and biochemistry, history of science, and petroleum and geological engineering are the strongest academically. Management information systems, psychology, and marketing are the largest.

Required: To graduate, students must have a minimum 2.0 GPA, depending on the major, and complete a minimum of 124 semester hours. The number of hours required in the major varies. General education core courses include arts and humanities, oral and symbolic communication, natural science, and social science. All students must take 6 hours each of English composition, American history, and government. Seniors must take a 3-credit-hour capstone experience course integrating their undergraduate studies.

Special: Co-op programs are available in engineering and business. A variety of voluntary and required internships is available in more than 50 fields of study. OU offers study abroad in 46 countries, work-study programs, a Washington semester, a general studies degree, dual and student-designed majors, nondegree study, pass/fail options, and credit for life experience. B.A.-B.S. degrees are offered in many subjects. The interdisciplinary major in letters combines the classics, history, philosophy, and languages. A professional studies major is offered through the continuing education program. There are 37 national honor societies, including Phi Beta Kappa, and a freshman honors program.

Faculty/Classroom: 67% of faculty are male; 33%, female. Graduate students teach 33% of introductory courses. The average class size in an introductory lecture is 43.

Admissions: 93% of the 2001-2002 applicants were accepted. The ACT scores for the 2001-2002 freshman class were: 13% below 21, 22% between 21 and 23, 33% between 24 and 26, 14% between 27 and 28, and 19% above 28. 56% of the current freshmen were in the top fifth of their class; 86% were in the top two fifths. There were 110 National Merit finalists. 273 freshmen graduated first in their class.

Requirements: The SAT I or ACT is required. Performance requirements can be met by residents of Oklahoma with a high school GPA of 3.0 and a class ranking in th the upper 30% or a minimum composite score of 1090 on the SAT I or 24 on the ACT. Nonresidents must have a high school GPA of 3.5 and rank in the top 25% or have a composite score of 26 on the ACT or a 1170 composite on the SAT I. Graduation from an accredited secondary school or a satisfactory score on the GED is required. Students must have a total of 15 curricular units, including 4 years of English, 3 of math, 2 each of history and lab science, 1 unit of citizenship skills, and 3 elective units from areas previously mentioned or computer science or foreign language. Alternative admission opportunities include summer provisional admission (for residents only) and adult admission. AP and CLEP credits are accepted. Recommendations by school officials is an important factor in the admissions decision. Applications are available on-line at the school's web site.

Procedure: Freshmen are admitted to all sessions. Entrance exams should be taken during the junior year or the first part of the senior year. Applications should be filed by June 1 for fall entry, November 1 for spring entry, and April 1 for summer entry, along with a $25 fee. Notification is sent on a rolling basis. A waiting list is an active part of the admissions procedure for nonresident applicants.

Transfer: 1540 transfer students enrolled in 2001-2002. Applicants who have attempted 7 to 59 semester hours of college work must have a minimum GPA of 2.5.; students with fewer than 24 semester hours of college level work must also meet freshman admission requirements. Applicants with 60 or more semester hours attempted must have a minimum GPA of 2.0; nonresident applicants with engineering majors must have a minimum 3.0 GPA. Non-residents must be in good standing at the last institution attended. 30 credits of 124 must be completed at OU.

Visiting: There are regularly scheduled orientations for prospective students, tailored to individual needs and interest. There are guides for informal visits and visitors may sit in on classes and stay overnight. To schedule a visit, contact Prospective Student Services at (405) 325-2151, (800) 234-6868, or *ou-pss@ou.edu*.

Financial Aid: In 2001-2002, 60% of all freshmen and 67% of continuing students received some form of financial aid. 38% of freshmen and 46% of continuing students received need-based aid. The average freshman award was $5800. Of that total, scholarships or need-based grants averaged $3966 ($10,000 maximum); loans averaged $4726 ($7000 maximum); and work contracts averaged $2690 ($3200 maximum). 62% of undergraduates work part time. Average annual earnings from campus work are $5527. The average financial indebtedness of the 2001 graduate was $19,821. OU is a member of CSS. The FAFSA is required. The fall application deadline is June 1.

International Students: There are 739 international students enrolled. They must score 550 on the written TOEFL or 213 on the electronic version and also take .

Computers: The mainframe is an IBM 9672-R14. Students may access several hundred computers distributed throughout the campus with a wide range of software, including word processing, presentation graphics, Internet access, and other tools and applications. Off-campus access is available via dial-up or commercial broadband access. All students may access the system 24 hours per day. There are no time limits. The fee is $7.50 per credit hour. It is strongly recommended that all students, particularly those in engineering programs, have personal computers. A special OU student PC package is available through Dell.

Graduates: In 2001, 2727 bachelor's degrees were awarded. The most popular majors were management information (10%), psychology (6%), and liberal studies (6%). In an average class, 20% graduate in 4 years, 44% in 5 years, and 50% in 6 years. 209 companies recruited on campus in 2000-2001.

Admissions Contact: Pat Lynch, Director of Admissions. A video is available. E-mail: *admrec@ouwww.ucs.ou.edu* Web: *htt://w.ou.edu*

UNIVERSITY OF SCIENCE AND ARTS OF OKLAHOMA D-4

Chickasha, OK 73018-5322 (405) 574-1204
(800) 933-8726; Fax: (405) 574-1220

Full-time: 412 men, 629 women	**Faculty:** 52; IIB, --$
Part-time: 138 men, 273 women	**Ph.D.s:** 87%
Graduate: none	**Student/Faculty:** 20 to 1
Year: trimesters, summer session	**Tuition:** $2245 ($5340)
Application Deadline: September 10	**Room & Board:** $3000
Freshman Class: 411 applied, 346 accepted, 241 enrolled	
ACT: 20	**COMPETITIVE**

The University of Science and Arts of Oklahoma, founded in 1908, is a publicly funded liberal arts institution, providing interdisciplinary learning opportunities. In addition to regional accreditation, USAO has baccalaureate program accreditation with CED, NASM, and NCATE. The library contains 76,930 volumes, 4075 microform items, and 138,000 audiovisual forms/CDs, and subscribes to 123 periodicals. Computerized library services include the card catalog, interlibrary loans, and database searching. Special learning facilities include a learning resource center, art gallery, and commercial art computer lab. The 75-acre campus is in a small town 40 miles southwest of Oklahoma City. Including residence halls, there are 14 buildings.

Student Life: 96% of undergraduates are from Oklahoma. Others are from 17 states, 21 foreign countries, and Canada. 99% are from public schools. 76% are white; 14% Native American/Eskimo. Most are Protestant. The average age of freshmen is 20; all undergraduates, 23. 41% do not continue beyond their first year; 27% remain to graduate.

Housing: 368 students can be accommodated in college housing, which includes single-sex and coed dormitories. On-campus housing is available on a first-come, first-served basis. 67% of students commute. All students may keep cars.

Activities: 5% of men belong to 1 national fraternity; 6% of women belong to 2 local sororities. There are 24 groups on campus, including art, band, cheerleading, choir, chorale, chorus, computers, drama, drill team, ethnic, honors, international, jazz band, literary magazine, musical theater, newspaper, opera, orchestra, pep band, photography, political, professional, radio and TV, religious, social, and student government. Popular campus events include Montmartre Festival, Curriculum Contest, and Christmas fine arts productions.

Sports: There are 4 intercollegiate sports for men and 4 for women, and 7 intramural sports for men and 6 for women. Facilities include a field house, a 2000-seat gym, a 1000-seat auditorium, a ballpark with baseball and softball fields, each seating 200, and a soccer field with seating for 250.

Disabled Students: All of the campus is accessible. Wheelchair ramps, elevators, special parking, specially equipped rest rooms, special class scheduling, lowered drinking fountains, and lowered telephones are available.

Services: Counseling and information services are available, as is tutoring in some subjects, including math, writing, and reading. There is remedial math, reading, and writing. Tutors and interpreters are available for hearing-impaired students.

Campus Safety and Security: Measures include 24-hour foot and vehicle patrol, informal discussions, pamphlets/posters/films, and lighted pathways/sidewalks.

Programs of Study: USAO confers B.A., B.S., and B.F.A. degrees. Bachelor's degrees are awarded in BIOLOGICAL SCIENCE (biology/biological science), BUSINESS (accounting, business administration and management, and management science), COMMUNICATIONS AND THE ARTS (art, communications, dramatic arts, English, and music), COMPUTER AND PHYSICAL SCIENCE (chemistry, computer science, mathematics, natural sciences, and physics), EDUCATION (early childhood, education, education of the deaf and hearing impaired, elementary, and physical), HEALTH PROFESSIONS (medical laboratory technology and speech pathology/audiology), SOCIAL SCIENCE (American Indian studies, economics, history, interdisciplinary studies, political science/government, psychology, and sociology). Humanities, sciences, and social sciences are the strongest academically. Business, computer science, and education are the largest.

Required: To graduate, students must complete a total of 124 credit hours with a minimum GPA of 2.0. Required core courses include 32 hours of team-taught interdisciplinary studies in math, science, and social science, 19 of interdisciplinary skills in logic and critical thinking, writing, and computer science, 3 each of artistic and physical expression, and 1 of freshman orientation. Other requirements include a senior seminar, an English proficiency exam, and entry-, junior-, and senior-level academic assessments.

Special: USAO offers dual majors, accelerated degree programs in all majors through year-round study, work-study programs, internship placement in community institutions, a Tutorial Scholars Program for student-designed majors, an interdisciplinary studies program, and a limited number of pass/fail options. There are 3 national honor societies and 1 departmental honors program.

Faculty/Classroom: 61% of faculty are male; 39%, female. All teach undergraduates and 40% also do research. The average class size in an introductory lecture is 21; in a laboratory, 18; and in a regular course, 21.

Admissions: 84% of the 2001-2002 applicants were accepted. The ACT scores for the 2001-2002 freshman class were: 54% below 21, 25% between 21 and 23, 15% between 24 and 26, 3% between 27 and 28, and 2% above 28. 27% of the current freshmen were in the top fifth of their class; 57% were in the top two fifths. In a recent year, 6 freshmen graduated first in their class.

Requirements: The ACT is required, with a minimum composite score of 19. Applicants must be graduates of an accredited secondary school or have a GED. They must complete 20 high school academic credits, including 4 years of English, 3 of math, and 2 each of lab science and history, 1 of which is American history. USAO requires applicants to be in the upper 50% of their class. A GPA of 2.7 is required. AP and CLEP credits are accepted. Applications are accepted on computer disk and on-line via Apply and at the school's web site.

Procedure: Freshmen are admitted to all sessions. Entrance exams should be taken by May of the preceding spring. Applications should be filed by September 10 for fall entry. Notification is sent on a rolling basis.

Transfer: 103 transfer students enrolled in 2001-2002. Applicants must have a minimum GPA of 2.0. Those students with fewer than 30 college-level credit hours must submit a high school transcript or GED and ACT scores. 30 credits of 124 must be completed at USAO.

Visiting: There are guides for informal visits and visitors may sit in on classes. To schedule a visit, contact School Relations at (405) 574-1357 or *katkinson@usad.edu*

Financial Aid: In 2001-2002, 89% of all freshmen and 87% of continuing students received some form of financial aid. 69% of freshmen and 71% of continuing students received need-based aid. The average freshman award was $4543. Of that total, scholarships or need-based grants averaged $3076 ($10,667 maximum); loans averaged $636 ($2625 maximum); and work contracts averaged $792 ($2400 maximum). 16% of undergraduates work part time. Average annual earnings from campus work are $1605. The average financial indebtedness of the 2001 graduate was $12,573. The FAFSA and the Institution Information Sheet are required. The fall application deadline is rolling.

International Students: There are 37 international students enrolled. The school actively recruits these students. They must score 500 on the written TOEFL or 173 on the electronic version and also take the ACT, scoring 20.

Computers: The mainframe is a DEC VAX 4700A. There are computer labs campuswide with networked PCs and Macs, all with Internet access. The library has PCs available 24 hours a day. Dorms are wired to the bedside. All students may access the system at any time. There are no time limits and no fees.

Graduates: In 2001, 173 bachelor's degrees were awarded. The most popular majors were business (16%), elementary education (11%), and physical education (7%). In an average class, 2% graduate in 3 years, 13% in 4 years, 23% in 5 years, and 27% in 6 years. 32 companies recruited on campus in 2000-2001. Of the 2000 graduating class, 10% were enrolled in graduate school within 6 months of graduation and 91% were employed.

Admissions Contact: Joe Evans, Director of Admissions.
E-mail: *jwevans@usao.edu* Web: *http://www.usao.edu*

UNIVERSITY OF TULSA

Tulsa, OK 74104-3189 E-2
(918) 631-2307
(800) 331-3050; Fax: (918) 631-5003

Full-time: 1210 men, 1323 women	**Faculty:** 263; IIA, av$
Part-time: 112 men, 124 women	**Ph.D.s:** 96%
Graduate: 786 men, 564 women	**Student/Faculty:** 10 to 1
Year: semesters, summer session	**Tuition:** $14,280
Application Deadline: open	**Room & Board:** $4810
Freshman Class: 2235 applied, 1505 accepted, 498 enrolled	
SAT I Verbal/Math: 630/610	**ACT:** 27 **HIGHLY COMPETITIVE**

The University of Tulsa, founded in 1894, is a private comprehensive institution offering more than 70 major areas of study through its programs in liberal arts and sciences, engineering and natural sciences, and business administration. There are 3 undergraduate and 2 graduate schools. In addition to regional accreditation, TU has baccalaureate program accreditation with AACSB, ABET, CSAB, NASM, NCATE, and NLN. The 2 libraries contain 940,105 volumes, 3,001,114 microform items, and 13,320 audiovisual forms/CDs, and subscribe to 6317 periodicals. Computerized library services include the card catalog, interlibrary loans, and database searching. Special learning facilities include an art gallery, radio station, and TV station. The 200-acre campus is in an urban area in the city of Tulsa. Including residence halls, there are 72 buildings.

Student Life: 66% of undergraduates are from Oklahoma. Others are from 39 states, 61 foreign countries, and Canada. 79% are from public schools. 63% are white; 12% foreign nationals. 40% claim no religious affiliation; 37% are Protestant; 14% Catholic. The average age of freshmen is 18; all undergraduates, 21. 20% do not continue beyond their first year; 61% remain to graduate.

Housing: 3000 students can be accommodated in college housing, which includes single-sex and coed dormitories, on-campus apartments, off-campus apartments, married-student housing, and sorority houses. In addition, there are honors houses. On-campus housing is guaranteed for all 4 years. 52% of students live on campus; of those, 90% remain on campus on weekends. All students may keep cars.

Activities: 21% of men belong to 7 national fraternities; 23% of women belong to 9 national sororities. There are 272 groups on campus, including art, band, cheerleading, chess, choir, chorale, chorus, computers, dance, drama, drill team, ethnic, film, gay, honors, international, jazz band, literary magazine, marching band, musical theater, newspaper, opera, orchestra, pep band, photography, political, professional, radio and TV, religious, social, social service, student government, symphony, and yearbook. Popular campus events include Parents Weekend, Springfest, and Black Heritage Month.

Sports: There are 8 intercollegiate sports for men and 10 for women, and 25 intramural sports for men and 25 for women. Facilities include a 40,000-seat stadium, an 8300-seat basketball arena, a gym, an athletic field, indoor racquetball courts, basketball and tennis courts, an indoor swimming pool, a handball court, a weight room, and a dance studio.

Disabled Students: 80% of the campus is accessible. Wheelchair ramps, elevators, special parking, specially equipped rest rooms, special class scheduling, lowered drinking fountains, lowered telephones, and sidewalks and curbs are available.

Services: Counseling and information services are available, as is tutoring in most subjects. There is a reader service for the blind. Special labs are available to students in need of assistance in math and writing courses, and study skills classes are available free of charge. Special-needs students are assisted on an individual basis.

Campus Safety and Security: Measures include 24-hour foot and vehicle patrol, self-defense education, escort service, and informal discussions. There are pamphlets/posters/films, emergency telephones, and lighted pathways/sidewalks. Electronic door locks on residence halls open only with student identification.

Programs of Study: TU confers B.A., B.S., B.F.A, B.Mus., B.Mus.Ed., B.S.A.M., B.S.A.T., B.S.B.A., B.S.C., B.S.C.E., B.S.C.S., B.S.D.E., B.S.E., B.S.E.E., B.S.G.S., B.S.M.E., B.S.N., B.S.P.E., and B.S.Sp. degrees. Master's and doctoral degrees are also awarded. Bachelor's degrees are awarded in BIOLOGICAL SCIENCE (biochemistry and biology/biological science), BUSINESS (accounting, banking and finance, international business management, management information systems, management science, marketing/retailing/merchandising, and sports management), COMMUNICATIONS AND THE ARTS (art, arts administration/management, communications, English, film arts, French, German, music, music performance, musical theater, piano/organ, Spanish, and voice), COMPUTER AND PHYSICAL SCIENCE (chemistry, computer science, geology, geoscience, information sciences and systems, mathematics, and physics), EDUCATION (athletic training, education, education of the deaf and hearing impaired, elementary, and music), ENGINEERING AND ENVIRONMENTAL DESIGN (chemical engineering, electrical/electronics engineering, engineering physics, environmental science, mechanical engineering, and petroleum/natural gas engineering), HEALTH PROFESSIONS (exercise science, nursing, premedicine, and speech pathology/audiology), SOCIAL SCIENCE (anthropology, economics, history, philosophy, political science/government, prelaw, psychology, religion, Russian and Slavic studies, and sociology). Petroleum engineering, psychology, and English are the strongest academically. Management, petroleum engineering, and mechanical engineering are the largest.

Required: To graduate, students must complete 126 to 136 credit hours, including 24 to 39 in the major, with a minimum GPA determined by the major. Freshmen in liberal arts and business administration must complete the First Seminar. All students must complete the core curriculum, which includes 3 writing courses and at least 1 course in math. All students must also complete the general curriculum, which requires 8 courses in 4 categories (artistic imagination, social inquiry, cultural interpretation, and scientific investigation). A foreign language requirement of 2 years for liberal arts and sciences students and 1 year for business majors must be completed.

Special: Internships are available in the Tulsa area during the school year and in cities throughout the United States during the summer. Students may participate in more than 40 study-abroad programs, most of them arranged through the Institute of European Studies. TU offers a Washington semester, B.A.-B.S. degrees, cross-registration with the 3 undergraduate schools, dual and student-designed majors, nondegree study, work-study programs, and pass/fail options. There are 37 national honor societies, including Phi Beta Kappa, and a freshman honors program.

Faculty/Classroom: 67% of faculty are male; 33%, female. All both teach and do research. No introductory courses are taught by graduate students. The average class size in an introductory lecture is 22; in a laboratory, 15; and in a regular course, 19.

Admissions: 67% of the 2001-2002 applicants were accepted. The SAT I scores for the 2001-2002 freshman class were: Verbal--5% below 500, 33% between 500 and 599, 41% between 600 and 700, and 21% above 700; Math--7% below 500, 33% between 500 and 599, 40% between 600 and 700, and 20% above 700. The ACT scores were 24% between 21 and 23, 27% between 24 and 26, 16% between 27 and 28, and 33% above 28. 69% of the current freshmen were in the top fifth of their class; 86% were in the top two fifths. There were 25 National Merit finalists. 112 freshmen graduated first in their class.

Requirements: The SAT I or ACT is required. In addition, graduation from an accredited secondary school or satisfactory scores on the GED are required. The school recommends a minimum of 15 academic credits, including 4 years of English, 3 to 4 each of math, science, and social studies (including history), and 2 of a single foreign language. An essay and an interview are highly recommended. An audition or a portfolio is required for students applying for music, theater, or art scholarships. TU requires applicants to be in the upper 33% of their class. A GPA of 3.0 is required. AP and CLEP credits are accepted. Important factors in the admissions decision are advanced placement or honor courses, leadership record, and extracurricular activities record. The university accepts applications on-line through CollegeLink.

Procedure: Freshmen are admitted to all sessions. Entrance exams should be taken during the spring of the junior year or the fall of the senior year. There are early decision and deferred admissions plans. Early decision applications should be filed by November 15; regular application deadlines are open. The application fee is $35. Notification of early decision is sent December 15; regular decision, on a rolling basis. 72 early decision candidates were accepted for the 2001-2002 class.

Transfer: 204 transfer students enrolled in 2001-2002. Students must submit official transcripts from all colleges attended and should have a minimum GPA of 2.5 for all college and high school work. Applicants with fewer than 60 credit hours must submit an official high school transcript. Those with fewer than 30 credit hours must also submit ACT or SAT I scores. Applicants 25 years of age or older are exempt from submitting ACT or SAT I scores unless requested to do so by the Admission Office. 45 credits of 126 to 136 must be completed at TU.

Visiting: There are regularly scheduled orientations for prospective students, including overnight programs in the fall and spring. Students stay on campus and attend special information sessions. There are guides for informal visits and visitors may sit in on classes and stay overnight. To schedule a visit, contact the Office of Admission.

Financial Aid: In 2001-2002, 85% of all students received some form of financial aid. 59% of freshmen and 47% of continuing students received need-based aid. The average freshman award was $15,575. Of that total, scholarships or need-based grants averaged $4000 ($20,350 maximum); loans averaged $2700 ($6625 maximum); and work contracts averaged $2100 ($2300 maximum). 22% of undergraduates work part time. Average annual earnings from campus work are $2120. The average financial indebtedness of the 2001 graduate was $17,670. The FAFSA and the college's own financial statement are required. The fall application deadline is April 1.

International Students: There are 309 international students enrolled. The school actively recruits these students. They must score 500 on the written TOEFL or 173 on the electronic version.

Computers: The mainframes are a SunE-3500 and a Sun 450. There are more than 600 PCs and Macs available throughout the campus. Connections are available in university housing, as are e-mail and Internet access. All students may access the system 24 hours per day. There are no time limits and no fees.

Graduates: In 2001, 526 bachelor's degrees were awarded. The most popular majors were marketing (7%), psychology (6%), and mechanical engineering (6%). In an average class, 40% graduate in 4 years, 59% in 5 years, and 61% in 6 years. 216 companies recruited on campus in 2000-2001. Of the 2000 graduating class, 29% were enrolled in graduate school within 6 months of graduation and 85% were employed.

Admissions Contact: John C. Corso, Associate Vice President for Administration/Dean of Admission. A video is available.
E-mail: *admission@utulsa.edu* Web: *www.utulsa.edu*

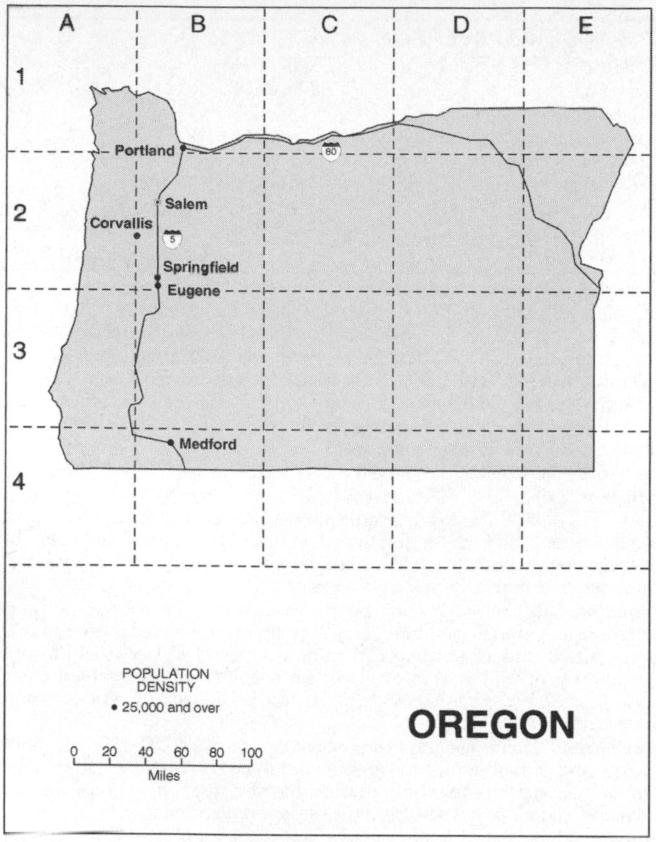

ART INSTITUTE OF PORTLAND
Portland, OR 97201 B-1

(503) 228-6528

(888) 228-6528; Fax: (503) 228-4227

Full-time: 358 men, 356 women	**Faculty:** 25
Part-time: 70 men, 119 women	**Ph.D.s:** 52%
Graduate: none	**Student/Faculty:** 29 to 1
Year: quarters, summer session	**Tuition:** $13,725
Application Deadline: open	**Room & Board:** n/app
Freshman Class: n/av	
SAT I or ACT: not required	**SPECIAL**

The Art Institute of Portland, founded in 1963, is a private institution offering undergraduate programs in interior, graphic, and apparel design; computer animation; and multimedia and web design. The library contains 20,687 volumes and 900 audiovisual forms/CDs, and subscribes to 200 periodicals. Computerized library services include the card catalog and database searching. Special learning facilities include a learning resource center. The 1-acre campus is in an urban area in downtown Portland. There are 3 buildings.

Student Life: 69% of undergraduates are from Oregon. 63% are white. The average age of freshmen is 23; all undergraduates, 25.

Housing: College-sponsored living facilities include off-campus apartments, which are available on a first-come, first-served basis. 95% of students commute. Alcohol is not permitted. No one may keep cars.

Activities: There are no fraternities or sororities. There are 3 groups on campus, including art, newspaper, and professional. Popular campus events include portfolio review, animation shows, and Halloween and Valentine's Day activities.

Sports: There is no sports program at AIPD.

Disabled Students: All of the campus is accessible. Wheelchair ramps, elevators, special parking, specially equipped rest rooms, lowered drinking fountains, and lowered telephones are available.

Services: Counseling and information services are available, as is tutoring in most subjects.

Campus Safety and Security: Measures include informal discussions, pamphlets/posters/films, emergency telephones, and lighted pathways/sidewalks. There is a night security guard.

Programs of Study: AIPD confers the B.S. degree. Associate degrees are also awarded. Bachelor's degrees are awarded in COMMUNICATIONS AND THE ARTS (apparel design, graphic design, and multimedia), ENGINEERING AND ENVIRONMENTAL DESIGN (computer graphics and interior design). Interior design is the strongest academically. Multimedia is the largest.

Required: To graduate, students must complete 180 quarter hours, including 111 in the major, with a minimum GPA of 2.0. Distribution requirements include 9 credits each in English composition and history of material culture, 6 credits in basic design, and 3 credits each in drawing, computer fundamentals, physics, math, art history, and critical thinking.

Special: Field trips to Seattle and San Francisco are available. Internships are required for most bachelor's degree programs.

Faculty/Classroom: 56% of faculty are male; 44%, female. All teach undergraduates. The average class size in an introductory lecture is 25; in a laboratory, 25; and in a regular course, 16.

Requirements: A high school diploma or GED is required. An interview with an admissions officer and an essay are required. AP and CLEP credits are accepted. Important factors in the admissions decision are evidence of special talent, personality/intangible qualities, and recommendations by school officials. The institute's application is available at its web site.

Procedure: Freshmen are admitted to all sessions. There is a deferred admissions plan. Application deadlines are open. The application fee is $50. Notification is sent on a rolling basis.

Transfer: 132 transfer students enrolled in 2001-2002. Requirements are the same as for new students. 45 quarter credits of 180 must be completed at AIPD.

Visiting: There are regularly scheduled orientations for prospective students, including college tours, mini class sessions, financial aid and financial planning meetings, and career assessment. There are guides for informal visits and visitors may sit in on classes with permission. To schedule a visit, contact the Admissions Office by phone or at *aipdadm@aii.edu*

Financial Aid: In 2001-2002, 75% of all students received some form of financial aid. 66% of freshmen and 65% of continuing students received need-based aid. The average freshman award was $11,093. Of that total, scholarships or need-based grants averaged $2273 ($5550 maximum); loans averaged $7520 ($19,110 maximum); work contracts averaged $400 ($1500 maximum); and outside scholarships, vocational rehabilitation, alternative loan programs, and tuition reimbursement averaged $900 ($13,850 maximum). 4% of undergraduates work part time. Average annual earnings from campus work are $1900. The average financial indebtedness of the 2001 graduate was $15,600. AIPD is a member of CSS. The FAFSA is required. The fall application deadline is rolling.

International Students: The school actively recruits these students. They must score 480 on the written TOEFL or 157 on the electronic version.

Computers: Students have access to more than 160 computers on campus, which are all Internet ready. All students may access the system weekdays during lab hours. There are no time limits and no fees. It is strongly recommended that all students have a personal computer.

Graduates: In 2001, the most popular majors were interior design (36%), apparel design (28%), and graphic design (12%). Of the 2000 graduating class, 2% were enrolled in graduate school within 6 months of graduation and 92% were employed.

Admissions Contact: Kelly Alston, Director of Admissions.
E-mail: *alstonk@aii.edu* Web: *www.aipd.artinstitutes.edu*

CASCADE COLLEGE
Portland, OR 97216-1515 B-2

(503) 255-7060

(800) 550-7678 (PORT); Fax: (503) 257-1222

Full-time: 303 men and women	**Faculty:** 12
Part-time: 15 men, 12 women	**Ph.D.s:** 50%
Graduate: none	**Student/Faculty:** 25 to 1
Year: semesters, summer session	**Tuition:** $9600
Application Deadline: open	**Room & Board:** $5200
Freshman Class: n/av	
SAT I or ACT: required	**NONCOMPETITIVE**

Cascade College, founded in 1993, is a Christian liberal arts institution offering degree programs in interdisciplinary studies, business, biblical studies, psychology, and early childhood education. The library contains 25,000 volumes, 62,045 microform items, and 1200 audiovisual forms/CDs, and subscribes to 110 periodicals. Computerized library services include the card catalog, interlibrary loans, and database searching. Special learning facilities include a learning resource center. The 12-acre campus is in a suburban area 8 miles east of downtown Portland. Including residence halls, there are 16 buildings.

Student Life: 59% of undergraduates are from out of state, mostly the Northwest. Others are from 20 states, 8 foreign countries, and Canada.

85% are from public schools. 82% are white. 80% are Protestant; 12% claim no religious affiliation. The average age of freshmen is 19; all undergraduates, 22.

Housing: 235 students can be accommodated in college housing, which includes single-sex dormitories. On-campus housing is guaranteed for all 4 years. 75% of students live on campus; of those, 65% remain on campus on weekends. Alcohol is not permitted. All students may keep cars.

Activities: There are no fraternities or sororities. There are 18 groups on campus, including band, cheerleading, choir, chorale, chorus, drama, honors, jazz band, literary magazine, professional, religious, social service, student government, and yearbook. Popular campus events include a campus variety show, formal banquets, and High School Days.

Sports: There are 5 intercollegiate sports for men and 5 for women, and 5 intramural sports for men and 5 for women. Facilities include a gym, a weight room, a team room, a soccer field, and basketball, volleyball, badminton, and tennis courts.

Disabled Students: 70% of the campus is accessible. Wheelchair ramps, elevators, special parking, and specially equipped rest rooms are available.

Services: Counseling and information services are available, as is tutoring in most subjects. There is remedial math, reading, and writing. Other services are available as needed.

Campus Safety and Security: Measures include self-defense education, escort service, pamphlets/posters/films, and lighted pathways/sidewalks. There is a nighttime security patrol.

Programs of Study: Cascade confers B.A., B.S., and B.S.E. degrees. Bachelor's degrees are awarded in BUSINESS (business administration and management), SOCIAL SCIENCE (biblical studies, interdisciplinary studies, liberal arts/general studies, missions, psychology, and youth ministry). Interdisciplinary studies, business, and psychology are the largest.

Required: To graduate, students must complete 126 to 131 semester hours, including 45 in upper-division courses, with a GPA of 2.0. At least 30 hours must be taken in the major, 20 of them being upper division. In addition to biblical and religious curriculum requirements, 1 hour of phys ed is required. There is a comprehensive exam in the major field.

Special: Cascade College offers internships and practica in many areas of study, including psychology, business, and ministry. Study abroad in Austria and the Pacific Rim is possible, as are student-designed majors. Christian service is available as a second major. There is 1 national honor society.

Faculty/Classroom: 70% of faculty are male; 30%, female. All teach undergraduates. The average class size in an introductory lecture is 32; in a laboratory, 10; and in a regular course, 24.

Admissions: All of the 2001-2002 applicants were accepted. The school has an open admissions policy.

Requirements: The SAT I or ACT is required; the ACT is preferred. Applicants should be graduates of an accredited secondary school with a minimum GPA of 2.0. The GED is accepted. AP and CLEP credits are accepted.

Procedure: Freshmen are admitted to all sessions. Entrance exams should be taken at any test date prior to fall enrollment. There is an early admissions plan. Application deadlines are open. The fall 2001 application fee was $25. Notification is sent on a rolling basis.

Transfer: 48 transfer students enrolled in 2001-2002. Official transcripts from all institutions attended are required. 30 credits of 126 to 131 must be completed at Cascade.

Visiting: There are regularly scheduled orientations for prospective students, including a meeting with faculty members, a financial aid workshop, and a survey of college programs. There are guides for informal visits and visitors may sit in on classes and stay overnight. To schedule a visit, contact the Admissions Office at (503) 257-1202.

Financial Aid: In a recent year, 95% of all freshmen and all continuing students received some form of financial aid. 60% of freshmen and 80% of continuing students received need-based aid. The average freshman award was $8100. Of that total, scholarships or need-based grants averaged $3990 ($11,050 maximum); loans averaged $5272 ($14,505 maximum); and work contracts averaged $1300 ($1400 maximum). 26% of undergraduates work part time. Average annual earnings from campus work are $1400. Cascade is a member of CSS. The FAFSA is required.

International Students: There are 18 international students enrolled. The school actively recruits these students. They must score 500 on the written TOEFL and also take the SAT I or the ACT, with the ACT preferred.

Computers: There are 35 networked PCs, including multimedia, available for student use in 4 computer labs, allowing access to the campus e-mail system, network data storage, network printing, and other network resources, including the web. There is a classroom is equipped with computers for specific math and science classes and for videoconferencing. All dorm rooms are wired for access to the campus network, which includes access to all networked resources such as e-mail and the web. All students may access the system from 8 A.M. to 10:30 P.M. There are no time limits and no fees.

Graduates: In 2001, 37 bachelor's degrees were awarded. The most popular majors were liberal arts (70%), psychology (11%), and business (11%). 2 companies recruited on campus in 2000-2001. Of the 2000 graduating class, 85% were employed within 6 months of graduation.

Admissions Contact: Clint LaRue, Director of Admissions.
E-mail: *mgeiger@cascade.edu* Web: *www.cascade.edu*

CONCORDIA UNIVERSITY

B-1

Portland, OR 97211

(503) 280-8501
(800) 321-9371; Fax: (503) 280-8531

Full-time: 275 men, 481 women	**Faculty:** 40
Part-time: 56 men, 77 women	**Ph.D.s:** 57%
Graduate: 64 men, 101 women	**Student/Faculty:** 19 to 1
Year: semesters, summer session	**Tuition:** $16,200
Application Deadline: open	**Room & Board:** $4300

Freshman Class: 435 applied, 432 accepted, 135 enrolled
SAT I or ACT: required **LESS COMPETITIVE**

Concordia University, founded in 1905, is a private liberal arts institution affiliated with the Lutheran Church – Missouri Synod and is 1 of 10 institutions of the Concordia University System. There are 3 undergraduate and 2 graduate schools. The library contains 48,672 volumes, 56,706 microform items, and 2888 audiovisual forms/CDs, and subscribes to 424 periodicals. Computerized library services include the card catalog, interlibrary loans, and database searching. Special learning facilities include a video conference classroom. The 13-acre campus is in an urban area in Portland. Including residence halls, there are 20 buildings.

Student Life: 59% of undergraduates are from Oregon. Others are from 30 states, 8 foreign countries, and Canada. 77% are white. 56% are Protestant; 32% claim no religious affiliation; 10% are Catholic. The average age of freshmen is 19; all undergraduates, 28. 40% do not continue beyond their first year; 60% remain to graduate.

Housing: 400 students can be accommodated in college housing, which includes single-sex and coed dormitories, on-campus apartments, and married-student housing. On-campus housing is guaranteed for the freshman year only and is available on a first-come, first-served basis. 65% of students commute. Alcohol is not permitted. All students may keep cars.

Activities: There are no fraternities or sororities. There are many groups and organizations on campus, including choir, chorus, drama, international, literary magazine, musical theater, newspaper, professional, religious, social, social service, and student government.

Sports: There are 3 intercollegiate sports for men and 4 for women, and 10 intramural sports for men and 10 for women. Facilities include a weight room, a 1200-seat gym, and a baseball/soccer field.

Disabled Students: 80% of the campus is accessible. Wheelchair ramps, elevators, special parking, specially equipped rest rooms, special class scheduling, and lowered telephones are available.

Services: Counseling and information services are available, as is tutoring in most subjects. There is remedial math, reading, and writing, as well as student-supported individual help and media resources.

Campus Safety and Security: Measures include 24-hour foot and vehicle patrol, self-defense education, escort service, and informal discussions. There are pamphlets/posters/films and lighted pathways/sidewalks.

Programs of Study: Concordia confers B.A. and B.S. degrees. Associate and master's degrees are also awarded. Bachelor's degrees are awarded in BIOLOGICAL SCIENCE (biology/biological science), BUSINESS (business administration and management), COMMUNICATIONS AND THE ARTS (dramatic arts and English), COMPUTER AND PHYSICAL SCIENCE (chemistry), EDUCATION (early childhood, elementary, and secondary), ENGINEERING AND ENVIRONMENTAL DESIGN (environmental science), HEALTH PROFESSIONS (health care administration and premedicine), SOCIAL SCIENCE (humanities, psychology, social work, theological studies, and youth ministry). Business administration, education, and psychology are the strongest academically. Education and business are the largest.

Required: To graduate, students must complete a total of 124 semester hours, with a minimum GPA of 2.0. General education requirements total 48 semester hours. All students must take freshman composition and courses in math, phys ed, humanities, religion, science, writing, fine arts, and social sciences.

Special: Cross-registration may be arranged through the Concordia University System and with Oregon Independent College. There are also internships, study abroad in 3 countries, and an accelerated degree program in management, communication, and leadership. There is 1 national honor society.

Faculty/Classroom: 67% of faculty are male; 33%, female. All teach undergraduates and 5% also do research. No introductory courses are taught by graduate students. The average class size in an introductory lecture is 19; in a laboratory, 19; and in a regular course, 17.

Admissions: 99% of the 2001-2002 applicants were accepted. The SAT I scores for the 2001-2002 freshman class were: Verbal--40% below 500, 45% between 500 and 599, 10% between 600 and 700, and 6% above 700; Math--51% below 500, 34% between 500 and 599, 14% between 600 and 700, and 1% above 700. The ACT scores were 37% below 21, 34% between 21 and 23, 18% between 24 and 26, 5% between

27 and 28, and 6% above 28. 41% of the current freshmen were in the top fifth of their class; 68% were in the top two fifths.

Requirements: The SAT I or ACT is required, with a minimum SAT I verbal score of 480 recommended. Graduation from an accredited secondary school or satisfactory scores on the GED are required. The school recommends that high school courses include 4 units of English, 3 each of social studies, math, and science, 2 of a foreign language, and 1 of art and music. An interview is recommended. A GPA of 2.5 is required. AP and CLEP credits are accepted. Important factors in the admissions decision are recommendations by school officials, leadership record, and personality/intangible qualities. Applications are accepted on-line at the school's web site.

Procedure: Freshmen are admitted to all sessions. Entrance exams should be taken during the junior year or early in the senior year. Application deadlines are open.The application fee is $20. Notification is sent on a rolling basis.

Transfer: 109 transfer students enrolled in 2001-2002. Students must have a minimum GPA of 2.0. 45 upper-division credits of 124 must be completed at Concordia.

Visiting: There are regularly scheduled orientations for prospective students, including class visitations and meetings with program deans and faculty. There are guides for informal visits and visitors may sit in on classes and stay overnight. To schedule a visit, contact the Admissions Office.

Financial Aid: In a recent year, 90% of all freshmen and 80% of continuing students received some form of financial aid, including need-based aid. The average freshman award was $7000. Of that total, scholarships or need-based grants averaged $5000 ($10,000 maximum); loans averaged $2625 ($4000 maximum); and work contracts averaged $1000 ($1500 maximum). 40% of undergraduates work part time. Average annual earnings from campus work are $1000. The average financial indebtedness of a recent graduate was $15,000. Concordia is a member of CSS. The FAFSA is required.

International Students: There are 80 international students enrolled. The school actively recruits these students. They must score 525 on the written TOEFL or 195 on the electronic version.

Computers: The mainframe is a Compaq Alpha. There are 2 PC and Mac labs located in the library. Students can also access the campus network from residence halls and by dialing up from off campus. All students may access the system. There are no time limits and no fees.

Graduates: In 2001, 221 bachelor's degrees were awarded. The most popular majors were business administration (26%), education (20%), and psychology (5%). In an average class, 20% graduate in 4 years. 35 companies recruited on campus in 2000-2001.

Admissions Contact: Admissions Office.
E-mail: *admissions@cu-portland.edu* Web: *www.cu-portland.edu*

EASTERN OREGON UNIVERSITY

La Grande, OR 97850-2899 — D-2
(541) 962-3393
(800) 452-3393; Fax: (541) 962-3418

Full-time: 903 men, 1126 women	**Faculty:** 87; IIB, --$
Part-time: 291 men, 500 women	**Ph.D.s:** 88%
Graduate: 47 men, 156 women	**Student/Faculty:** 23 to 1
Year: terms, summer session	**Tuition:** $3621
Application Deadline: September 15	**Room & Board:** $5151
Freshman Class: 747 applied, 409 accepted, 174 enrolled	
SAT I Verbal/Math: 485/484	**ACT:** 22 — **COMPETITIVE**

Eastern Oregon University, founded in 1929, is a public institution within the Oregon University System and offers programs in liberal and fine arts, agriculture, business, health science, and teacher preparation. There are 3 undergraduate schools and 1 graduate school. In addition to regional accreditation, Eastern has baccalaureate program accreditation with NCATE. The library contains 329,942 volumes, 205,724 microform items, and 35,556 audiovisual forms/CDs, and subscribes to 998 periodicals. Computerized library services include the card catalog, interlibrary loans, and database searching. Special learning facilities include a learning resource center, art gallery, natural history museum, and radio station. The 121-acre campus is in a rural area 260 miles east of Portland. Including residence halls, there are 13 buildings.

Student Life: 73% of undergraduates are from Oregon. Others are from 20 states, 27 foreign countries, and Canada. 96% are from public schools. 81% are white. The average age of freshmen is 20; all undergraduates, 26. 35% do not continue beyond their first year; 29% remain to graduate.

Housing: 436 students can be accommodated in college housing, which includes single-sex and coed dormitories and married-student housing. In addition, there is a wellness floor and an academic focus floor. On-campus housing is available on a first-come, first-served basis. 85% of students commute. All students may keep cars.

Activities: There are no fraternities or sororities. There are 60 groups on campus, including art, band, cheerleading, choir, chorale, chorus, computers, dance, drama, ethnic, international, jazz band, literary magazine, musical theater, newspaper, orchestra, pep band, photography, professional, radio and TV, religious, social, student government, symphony, and yearbook. Popular campus events include Oktoberfest, Casino Night, and Spring Fling.

Sports: There are 6 intercollegiate sports for men and 6 for women, and 6 intramural sports for men and 6 for women. Facilities include racquetball courts, a weight room, 3 gyms, a swimming pool, aerobics facilities, a track, and indoor and outdoor tennis courts.

Disabled Students: 80% of the campus is accessible. Wheelchair ramps, elevators, special parking, and specially equipped rest rooms are available.

Services: Counseling and information services are available, as is tutoring in most subjects. There is a reader service for the blind, and remedial math, reading, and writing.

Campus Safety and Security: Measures include 24-hour foot and vehicle patrol, escort service, informal discussions, and pamphlets/posters/films. There are emergency telephones and lighted pathways/sidewalks.

Programs of Study: Eastern confers B.A. and B.S degrees. Associate and master's degrees are also awarded. Bachelor's degrees are awarded in AGRICULTURE (agricultural business management, agricultural economics, forestry and related sciences, range/farm management, and soil science), BIOLOGICAL SCIENCE (biology/biological science), BUSINESS (accounting and business administration and management), COMMUNICATIONS AND THE ARTS (art, dramatic arts, English, and music), COMPUTER AND PHYSICAL SCIENCE (chemistry, computer science, mathematics, and physics), EDUCATION (education and physical), HEALTH PROFESSIONS (health and nursing), SOCIAL SCIENCE (anthropology, history, liberal arts/general studies, psychology, and sociology). Sciences are the strongest academically. Business and education are the largest.

Required: To graduate, students must complete 186 credit hours, including 60 hours of general education courses, with a GPA of at least 2.0. They must demonstrate computer competency, pass a writing proficiency exam, and complete a senior capstone experience.

Special: There are cooperative and 3-2 engineering degree programs with Oregon State University. Eastern offers internships, work-study, accelerated degree programs, student-designed and dual majors, study abroad in 8 countries, a general studies degree, B.A.-B.S. degrees, a multidisciplinary degree, numerous preprofessional programs, credit by exam and for life/military/work experience, external degrees, and pass/fail options. The university also serves students with course work via telecommunications and video, and with a weekend university. There are 6 national honor societies and 6 departmental honors programs.

Faculty/Classroom: 63% of faculty are male; 37%, female. All both teach and do research. No introductory courses are taught by graduate students. The average class size in an introductory lecture is 60; in a laboratory, 20; and in a regular course, 35.

Admissions: 55% of the 2001-2002 applicants were accepted. The SAT I scores for the 2001-2002 freshman class were: Verbal--56% below 500, 34% between 500 and 599, 10% between 600 and 700, and 1% above 700; Math--54% below 500, 40% between 500 and 599, and 6% between 600 and 700. The ACT scores were 19% below 18, 58% between 18 and 23, 22% between 24 and 29, and 2% above 29. 14% of the current freshmen were in the top tenth of their class; 71% were in the top half.

Requirements: The SAT I or ACT is required. A GED is accepted. Applicants must complete 14 academic credits, including 4 years of English, 3 each of math and social studies, and 2 of science. A GPA of 3.0 is required. AP and CLEP credits are accepted. Important factors in the admissions decision are extracurricular activities record, evidence of special talent, and geographic diversity.

Procedure: Freshmen are admitted to all sessions. Entrance exams should be taken in the senior year. There is a deferred admissions plan. Applications should be filed by September 15 for fall entry, January 1 for winter entry, and April 1 for spring entry. The fall 2001 application fee was $50. Notification is sent on a rolling basis.

Transfer: 381 transfer students enrolled in 2001-2002. Applicants must have 30 credits of transferable academic work with a GPA of 2.0. 45 credits of 186 must be completed at Eastern.

Visiting: There are regularly scheduled orientations for prospective students, including a campus tour, academic advising, and information sessions on financial aid and residence life. There are guides for informal visits and visitors may sit in on classes and stay overnight. To schedule a visit, contact Admissions/New Student Programs.

Financial Aid: In 2001-2002, 56% of all freshmen and 61% of continuing students received some form of financial aid. 37% of freshmen and 44% of continuing students received need-based aid. The average freshman award was $8105. 35% of undergraduates work part time. Average annual earnings from campus work are $1003. The average financial indebtedness of the 2001 graduate was $14,147. Eastern is a member of CSS. The FAFSA is required. The fall application deadline is March 1.

International Students: There are 100 international students enrolled. They must score 500 on the written TOEFL or take the MELAB for placement.

Computers: There are some 36 PCs in the classroom computer center, 20 in the learning center, 30 in the library, and a number in the residence halls. All students may access the system at various posted hours. There are no time limits and no fees.

Graduates: In 2001, 389 bachelor's degrees were awarded. The most popular majors were liberal studies (26%), interdisciplinary studies (21%), and business marketing (15%). In an average class, 20% graduate in 4 years and 45% in 5 years. 30 companies recruited on campus in 2000-2001.

Admissions Contact: Christian Steinmetz, Director of Admissions. E-mail: *admissions@eou.edu* Web: *http://www.eou.edu*

GEORGE FOX UNIVERSITY B-2

Newberg, OR 97132 (503) 554-2240
(800) 765-4369; Fax: (503) 538-7234

Full-time: 532 men, 782 women	**Faculty:** 88; IIB, -$
Part-time: 158 men, 193 women	**Ph.D.s:** 66%
Graduate: 386 men, 589 women	**Student/Faculty:** 15 to 1
Year: semesters	**Tuition:** $18,325
Application Deadline: June 1	**Room & Board:** $5770
Freshman Class: 824 applied, 748 accepted, 318 enrolled	
SAT I Verbal/Math: 570/550	**ACT:** 23 **VERY COMPETITIVE**

George Fox University, founded in 1891, is a private school of liberal arts and sciences operated by the Northwest Yearly Meeting of Friends (Quaker). There is 1 graduatae school. In addition to regional accreditation, George Fox has baccalaureate program accreditation with NASM. The 2 libraries contain 186,085 volumes, 208,175 microform items, and 5037 audiovisual forms/CDs, and subscribe to 1222 periodicals. Computerized library services include the card catalog, interlibrary loans, and database searching. Special learning facilities include a learning resource center, art gallery, radio station, television production studio, and Quaker museum. The 75-acre campus is in a small town 23 miles southwest of Portland. Including residence halls, there are 60 buildings.

Student Life: 61% of undergraduates are from Oregon. Others are from 25 states, 16 foreign countries, and Canada. 92% are from public schools. 90% are white. Most are Protestant. The average age of freshmen is 18; all undergraduates, 24. 17% do not continue beyond their first year; 59% remain to graduate.

Housing: 1000 students can be accommodated in college housing, which includes single-sex dormitories, on-campus apartments, and off-campus apartments. On-campus housing is available on a first-come, first-served basis. 70% of students live on campus; of those, 50% remain on campus on weekends. Alcohol is not permitted. All students may keep cars.

Activities: There are no fraternities or sororities. There are 27 groups on campus, including art, band, cheerleading, chess, choir, chorale, chorus, computers, dance, drama, drill team, ethnic, forensics, honors, international, jazz band, literary magazine, musical theater, newspaper, orchestra, pep band, political, professional, radio and TV, religious, social, social service, student government, symphony, and yearbook. Popular campus events include Quaker Heritage Week, Christian Emphasis Week, and a raft race.

Sports: There are 6 intercollegiate sports for men and 7 for women, and 4 intramural sports for men and 4 for women. Facilities include an all-weather track, a weight room, tennis and handball/racquetball courts, a 2500-seat gym, and baseball, softball, and soccer fields.

Disabled Students: 80% of the campus is accessible. Wheelchair ramps, elevators, special parking, specially equipped rest rooms, special class scheduling, lowered drinking fountains, and lowered telephones are available.

Services: Counseling and information services are available, as is tutoring in some subjects. There is a reader service for the blind, and remedial math, reading, and writing.

Campus Safety and Security: Measures include 24-hour foot and vehicle patrol, self-defense education, escort service, and informal discussions. There are emergency telephones and lighted pathways/sidewalks.

Programs of Study: George Fox confers B.A. and B.S. degrees. Master's and doctoral degrees are also awarded. Bachelor's degrees are awarded in BIOLOGICAL SCIENCE (biology/biological science), BUSINESS (business economics, human resources, and management science), COMMUNICATIONS AND THE ARTS (art, communications, literature, music, Spanish, and telecommunications), COMPUTER AND PHYSICAL SCIENCE (chemistry, computer science, information sciences and systems, and mathematics), EDUCATION (elementary, health, home economics, mathematics, middle school, music, physical, science, secondary, and social studies), ENGINEERING AND ENVIRONMENTAL DESIGN (engineering), HEALTH PROFESSIONS (predentistry, premedicine, and preveterinary science), SOCIAL SCIENCE (biblical studies, cognitive science, economics, history, home economics, international studies, ministries, political science/government, prelaw, psychology, religion, social work, and sociology). Natural sciences is the strongest academically. Business is the largest.

Required: To graduate, students must have a minimum 2.0 GPA and complete 126 semester hours, including 48 in the major. The required core curriculum of 57 semester hours includes 18 hours total of math/language, natural science, and social science, 14 to 15 of humanities, 10 of Bible/religious studies, 6 of communication, 6 of language and global studies, and 3 of health/phys ed.

Special: There is a 3-2 engineering degree with the University of Portland, Oregon State University, and Washington University in St. Louis, and cross-registration through the Oregon Independent College Association. George Fox also offers internships with area companies, study abroad in Kenya, England, Costa Rica, Russia, Egypt, Spain, and China, and a Washington semester through the Christian College Coalition. Work-study programs with the college, B.A.-B.S. degrees in all majors, dual and student-designed interdisciplinary majors, and pass/fail options in upper-division courses outside of the major also are offered. There are 3 national honor societies and a freshman honors program.

Faculty/Classroom: 61% of faculty are male; 39%, female. 66% both teach and do research. Graduate students teach 1% of introductory courses. The average class size in an introductory lecture is 50; in a laboratory, 20; and in a regular course, 25.

Admissions: 91% of the 2001-2002 applicants were accepted. The SAT I scores for the 2001-2002 freshman class were: Verbal--17% below 500, 45% between 500 and 599, 30% between 600 and 700, and 8% above 700; Math--23% below 500, 44% between 500 and 599, 28% between 600 and 700, and 5% above 700. The ACT scores were 22% below 21, 30% between 21 and 23, 22% between 24 and 26, 12% between 27 and 28, and 14% above 28. 55% of the current freshmen were in the top fifth of their class; 80% were in the top two fifths. There was 1 National Merit finalist and 3 semifinalists.

Requirements: The SAT I or ACT is required. In addition, applicants need 16 academic credits or 14 Carnegie units, including a suggested 4 units of English and 2 units each of a foreign language, math, science, and social studies. An essay and 2 personal recommendations are required; a portfolio, audition, and interview are recommended in certain majors. AP and CLEP credits are accepted. Important factors in the admissions decision are advanced placement or honor courses, recommendations by school officials, and recommendations by alumni. Applications are accepted on-line at *www.apply.com*

Procedure: Freshmen are admitted fall and spring. Entrance exams should be taken in fall or winter. There is a deferred admissions plan. Applications should be filed by June 1 for fall entry and December 1 for spring entry. The fall 2001 application fee was $40. Notification is sent on a rolling basis.

Transfer: 71 transfer students enrolled in 2001-2002. Transfers must have a minimum 2.3 GPA and 14 earned credits from their previous college. A personal recommendation is required. 30 credits of 126 must be completed at George Fox.

Visiting: There are regularly scheduled orientations for prospective students, including observation of classes and talking with professors. There are guides for informal visits and visitors may sit in on classes and stay overnight. To schedule a visit, contact the Office of Admissions.

Financial Aid: In 2001-2002, 95% of all freshmen and 93% of continuing students received some form of financial aid. 78% of freshmen and 75% of continuing students received need-based aid. The average freshman award was $16,232. Of that total, scholarships or need-based grants averaged $11,059 ($26,023 maximum); loans averaged $5531 ($26,023 maximum); and work contracts averaged $1220 ($2925 maximum). The average financial indebtedness of the 2001 graduate was $16,912. The FAFSA is required. The fall application deadline is August 1.

International Students: There are 51 international students enrolled. The school actively recruits these students. They must score 500 on the written TOEFL or 213 on the electronic version.

Computers: The mainframe is a DEC ALPHA 2000. Computers Across the Curriculum provides each entering freshman with a computer to use while a student and to keep after graduation. Students also have access to a full computer resource area, including color monitors and printers and a training center. There is a Mac lab with 21 computers and a PC lab with 25 Pentium computers. Network and Internet access is provided in all residences and at other plug-in locations on campus. All students may access the system. There are no time limits and no fees.

Graduates: In 2001, 484 bachelor's degrees were awarded. The most popular majors were management (34%), business (10%), and education (7%). In an average class, 1% graduate in 3 years, 53% in 4 years, 59% in 5 years, and 60% in 6 years. Of the 2000 graduating class, 7% were enrolled in graduate school within 6 months of graduation and 73% were employed.

Admissions Contact: Dale Seipp, Director of Undergraduate Admission. E-mail: *admissions@georgefox.edu* Web: *www.georgefox.edu*

LEWIS AND CLARK COLLEGE

B-1

Portland, OR 97219-7899
(503) 768-7040
(800) 444-4111; Fax: (503) 768-7055

Full-time: 662 men, 982 women
Faculty: 123
Part-time: 17 men, 21 women
Ph.D.s: 93%
Graduate: 487 men, 778 women
Student/Faculty: 13 to 1
Year: semesters, summer session
Tuition: $22,610
Application Deadline: February 1
Room & Board: $6400
Freshman Class: 3040 applied, 2025 accepted, 419 enrolled
SAT I or ACT: required
VERY COMPETITIVE

Lewis & Clark College, founded in 1867, is a private, independent liberal arts and sciences institution, with a global reach. There are 2 graduate schools. The 2 libraries contain 450,489 volumes, 1,997,645 microform items, and 11,586 audiovisual forms/CDs, and subscribe to 7477 periodicals. Computerized library services include the card catalog, interlibrary loans, and database searching. Special learning facilities include a learning resource center, art gallery, radio station, TV station, telescope, research astronomical observatory, language lab, and greenhouse. The 134-acre campus is in a suburban area 6 miles south of downtown Portland. Including residence halls, there are 56 buildings.

Student Life: 77% of undergraduates are from out of state, mostly the West. Others are from 49 states, 26 foreign countries, and Canada. 74% are from public schools. 65% are white. 55% claim no religious affiliation; 24% are Protestant; 14% Catholic. The average age of freshmen is 18; all undergraduates, 20. 18% do not continue beyond their first year; 67% remain to graduate.

Housing: 1007 students can be accommodated in college housing, which includes single-sex and coed dormitories and on-campus apartments. In addition, there are language, international awareness, outdoor pursuits, visual and performing arts, and substance-free floor. On-campus housing is guaranteed for the freshman and sophomore years only, is available on a first-come, first-served basis, and is available on a lottery system for upperclassmen. 54% of students live on campus; of those, 98% remain on campus on weekends. Upperclassmen may keep cars.

Activities: There are no fraternities or sororities. There are 75 groups on campus, including art, band, choir, chorale, chorus, computers, cross-cultural journal, dance, debate, drama, ethnic, film, forensics, gay, honors, international, jazz band, literary magazine, newspaper, orchestra, outdoors, pep band, photography, political, professional, radio and TV, religious, social, social service, student government, symphony, and yearbook. Popular campus events include Gender Studies Symposium, International Affairs Symposium, and Environmental Studies Symposium.

Sports: There are 9 intercollegiate sports for men and 9 for women, and 16 intramural sports for men and 16 for women. Facilities include indoor and outdoor swimming pools, 6 tennis courts (3 covered), an Astro turf football field, basketball and volleyball courts, softball and baseball fields, a track, and weight and aerobics rooms. There is also a 3700-seat stadium and a 2200-seat auditorium/arena.

Disabled Students: 80% of the campus is accessible. Wheelchair ramps, elevators, special parking, specially equipped rest rooms, special class scheduling, lowered drinking fountains, and lowered telephones are available.

Services: Counseling and information services are available, as is tutoring in every subject. There is a reader service for the blind. Also available are mentors, note takers, books on tape, and math and winning skills centers.

Campus Safety and Security: Measures include 24-hour foot and vehicle patrol, self-defense education, escort service, and shuttle buses. There are informal discussions, pamphlets/posters/films, emergency telephones, lighted pathways/sidewalks, and card key locks in all residence halls.

Programs of Study: LC confers the B.A. degree. Master's degrees are also awarded. Bachelor's degrees are awarded in AGRICULTURE (environmental studies), BIOLOGICAL SCIENCE (biochemistry and biology/biological science), COMMUNICATIONS AND THE ARTS (art history and appreciation, communications, dramatic arts, English, fine arts, languages, music, and studio art), COMPUTER AND PHYSICAL SCIENCE (chemistry, computer science, mathematics, and physics), SOCIAL SCIENCE (anthropology, East Asian studies, economics, French studies, German area studies, Hispanic American studies, history, interdisciplinary studies, international relations, philosophy, political science/government, psychology, religion, and sociology). Psychology, English, and biology are the strongest academically. Psychology, international affairs, and English are the largest.

Required: To graduate, students must complete a total of 128 semester hours with a 2.0 GPA. A third of this total generally falls in the major program, a third in electives, and a third in general requirements, which include 12 hours in scientific and quantitative reasoning, 8 hours in international studies, 3 semesters of a foreign language, 2 semesters of phys ed, 1 course in creative arts, and a specific first-year course. Certain majors require a thesis or a senior project/recital.

Special: LC offers cross-registration with the Oregon Independent College Association, which includes Reed College and the University of Portland; internships; one of the oldest and largest study-abroad programs in the United States, encompassing 60 countries; semesters in Washington and New York City; and dual and student-designed majors. A 3-2 engineering program is available with Columbia and Washington Universities, the University of Southern California, and the Oregon Graduate Institute. There are 5 national honor societies, including Phi Beta Kappa, and 22 departmental honors programs.

Faculty/Classroom: 60% of faculty are male; 40%, female. All both teach and do research. No introductory courses are taught by graduate students. The average class size in an introductory lecture is 22; in a laboratory, 16; and in a regular course, 18.

Admissions: 67% of the 2001-2002 applicants were accepted. The SAT I scores for the 2001-2002 freshman class were: Verbal--2% below 500, 18% between 500 and 599, 58% between 600 and 700, and 22% above 700; Math--3% below 500, 36% between 500 and 599, 48% between 600 and 700, and 13% above 700. The ACT scores were 16% between 21 and 23, 24% between 24 and 26, 24% between 27 and 28, and 36% above 28. 62% of the current freshmen were in the top fifth of their class; 88% were in the top two fifths. There were 5 National Merit finalists. 18 freshmen graduated first in their class.

Requirements: The SAT I or ACT is required. A GED may be accepted. It is recommended that applicants have 4 years each of English and math, 3 to 4 of science, 3 each of history/social studies and foreign language, and 1 of fine arts. An essay is required and an interview recommended. The college also admits exceptional students through the Portfolio Path option. This allows students to create an academic portfolio of materials they feel best demonstrate the strengths of their program; 3 academic teacher recommendations are required and test scores are optional. A GPA of 2.0 is required. AP credits are accepted. Important factors in the admissions decision are advanced placement or honor courses and recommendations by school officials. Applications are accepted on computer disk and on-line via CollegeNet, CollegeLink, Apply, Common App, or LC's web site.

Procedure: Freshmen are admitted fall and spring. Entrance exams should be taken during the spring of the junior year and the fall of the senior year. There are early action, early admissions, and deferred admissions plans. Early action applications should be filed by December 1; regular applications, by February 1 for fall entry, December 1 for spring entry, and May 1 for summer entry. The fall 2001 application fee was $45. Notification of early action is sent January 15; regular decision, April 1. 10% of all applicants are on a waiting list; 66 were accepted in 2001.

Transfer: 64 transfer students enrolled in 2001-2002. Applicants must submit high school and college transcripts, 2 essays, and SAT I or ACT scores, if they have less than 2 years of transferable credit. 60 credits of 128 must be completed at LC.

Visiting: There are regularly scheduled orientations for prospective students, including campus tours, class visits, interviews, special-interest appointments, overnight stays in residence halls, and 4 open house events. There are guides for informal visits and visitors may sit in on classes and stay overnight. To schedule a visit, contact the Visit Coordinator, Office of Admissions.

Financial Aid: In 2001-2002, 74% of all freshmen and 67% of continuing students received some form of financial aid. 54% of freshmen and 53% of continuing students received need-based aid. The average freshman award was $18,434. Of that total, scholarships or need-based grants averaged $10,525 ($22,610 maximum); loans averaged $3972 ($5625 maximum); and work contracts averaged $1500 ($2000 maximum). 72% of undergraduates work part time. Average annual earnings from campus work are $984. The average financial indebtedness of the 2001 graduate was $15,845. The FAFSA is required. The fall application deadline is March 1.

International Students: There are 86 international students enrolled. The school actively recruits these students. They must score 550 on the written TOEFL or 213 on the electronic version or take the MELAB, ECPE, FCE, CAE, CPE, or IELTS.

Computers: The mainframes are a Sun DEC ALPHA Server 2100/A500 and an ALPHA Server 2000/400. The campus servers are networked with 6 UNIX workstations and 5 X-Windows terminals. They run the UNIX operating system and are interconnected through Ethernet on campus with the library, residence halls, and academic buildings. Mac and PC clusters are available in the library and residence halls. All students may access the system 24 hours a day. There are no time limits and no fees.

Graduates: In 2001, 398 bachelor's degrees were awarded. The most popular majors were biology (12%), psychology (10%), and English (6%). In an average class, 1% graduate in 3 years, 54% in 4 years, 62% in 5 years, and 63% in 6 years. 37 companies recruited on campus in 2000-2001. Of the 2000 graduating class, 23% were enrolled in graduate school within 6 months of graduation and 57% were employed.

Admissions Contact: Michael B. Sexton, Dean of Admissions.
E-mail: *admissions@lclark.edu* Web: *www.lclark.edu*

LINFIELD COLLEGE
B-2

McMinnville, OR 97128
(503) 434-2213
(800) 640-2287; Fax: (503) 434-2472

Full-time: 696 men, 875 women	**Faculty:** 100; IIB, av$
Part-time: 18 men, 13 women	**Ph.D.s:** 98%
Graduate: none	**Student/Faculty:** 16 to 1
Year: 4-1-4, summer session	**Tuition:** $19,550
Application Deadline: February 15	**Room & Board:** $6290
Freshman Class: 1693 applied, 1356 accepted, 422 enrolled	
SAT I Verbal/Math: 534/540	**ACT:** 23 **VERY COMPETITIVE**

Linfield College, founded in 1849, is a private liberal arts institution affiliated with the American Baptist Church. In addition to regional accreditation, Linfield has baccalaureate program accreditation with NASM and NCATE. The library contains 161,153 volumes, 16,636 microform items, and 16,083 audiovisual forms/CDs, and subscribes to 1295 periodicals. Computerized library services include interlibrary loans and database searching. Special learning facilities include a learning resource center, art gallery, radio station, psychology lab, anthropology museum, multimedia studio, and research institute. The 193-acre campus is in a small town 40 miles southwest of Portland. Including residence halls, there are 67 buildings.

Student Life: 57% of undergraduates are from Oregon. Others are from 33 states, 24 foreign countries, and Canada. 83% are from public schools. 79% are white. 37% are Protestant; 11% Catholic. The average age of freshmen is 18; all undergraduates, 20. 19% do not continue beyond their first year; 71% remain to graduate.

Housing: 1240 students can be accommodated in college housing, which includes single-sex and coed dormitories, on-campus apartments, off-campus apartments, and fraternity houses. On-campus housing is guaranteed for the freshman year only. 76% of students live on campus; of those, 80% remain on campus on weekends. All students may keep cars.

Activities: 22% of men belong to 1 local and 3 national fraternities; 28% of women belong to 1 local and 3 national sororities. There are 60 groups on campus, including art, band, cheerleading, choir, chorale, chorus, computers, dance, debate, drama, ethnic, forensics, gay, honors, international, jazz band, literary magazine, musical theater, newspaper, opera, orchestra, outdoor, pep band, photography, political, professional, radio and TV, religious, social, social service, student government, symphony, women, and yearbook. Popular campus events include Cultural Awareness Week, Oregon Nobel Laureate Symposium, and Christmas Choral Concert.

Sports: There are 9 intercollegiate sports for men and 10 for women, and 8 intramural sports for men and 7 for women. Facilities include a complex with a 2200-seat gym, 3 basketball courts, a 25-yard swimming pool, 4 racquetball courts, a 3200-square-foot weight room, a field house with 3 tennis courts, 4 hitting cages, and an indoor track, and a baseball facility. There also are soccer and football fields, an all-weather track, and additional basketball, tennis, and racquetball courts.

Disabled Students: 65% of the campus is accessible. Wheelchair ramps, elevators, special parking, specially equipped rest rooms, special class scheduling, lowered drinking fountains, and lowered telephones are available.

Services: Counseling and information services are available, as is tutoring in every subject. There is a reader service for the blind, remedial math, a writing lab, and a speaking center.

Campus Safety and Security: Measures include 24-hour foot and vehicle patrol, self-defense education, escort service, and informal discussions. There are pamphlets/posters/films, emergency telephones, and lighted pathways/sidewalks.

Programs of Study: Linfield confers B.A. and B.S. degrees. Bachelor's degrees are awarded in BIOLOGICAL SCIENCE (biology/biological science), BUSINESS (accounting, banking and finance, business administration and management, and international business management), COMMUNICATIONS AND THE ARTS (art, communications, creative writing, dramatic arts, English, French, German, music, and Spanish), COMPUTER AND PHYSICAL SCIENCE (applied physics, chemistry, computer science, mathematics, physics, and science), EDUCATION (athletic training, elementary, health, and physical), HEALTH PROFESSIONS (exercise science), SOCIAL SCIENCE (anthropology, economics, history, philosophy, political science/government, psychology, religion, and sociology). Business and elementary education are the strongest academically.

Required: To graduate, students must have a 2.0 GPA and complete 125 credit hours, including 35 to 45 in the major. Distribution requirements include courses from physical and biological science, literature, fine arts, religion or philosophy, culture, and social behavior. Students must also take courses in Western culture, effective writing, and diversity.

Special: Students may study abroad in 10 countries, during the January term, academic classes are conducted in such areas as New York City, Hawaii, China, Japan, Ireland, Mexico, and Ghana. Internships and work-study programs, B.A.-B.S. degrees, a liberal studies degree, and pass/fail options are also offered. A 3-2 engineering degree may be arranged with Oregon State and Washington State Universities, and the University of Southern California. There is also an adult degree program. There are 14 national honor societies.

Faculty/Classroom: 62% of faculty are male; 38%, female. All both teach and do research. The average class size in an introductory lecture is 34; in a laboratory, 14; and in a regular course, 16.

Admissions: 80% of the 2001-2002 applicants were accepted. The SAT I scores for the 2001-2002 freshman class were: Verbal--26% below 500, 48% between 500 and 599, 22% between 600 and 700, and 4% above 700; Math--23% below 500, 51% between 500 and 599, 24% between 600 and 700, and 2% above 700. The ACT scores were 28% below 21, 23% between 21 and 23, 24% between 24 and 26, 15% between 27 and 28, and 10% above 28. 53% of the current freshmen were in the top fifth of their class; 80% were in the top two fifths. 21 freshmen graduated first in their class.

Requirements: The SAT I or ACT is required. In addition, applicants must have 17 to 20 academic credits, including a recommended 4 years each in English and math, 3 in science, and 2 each in foreign language, history, and social studies. An essay is required, and an interview is recommended. The GED is accepted. AP and CLEP credits are accepted. Important factors in the admissions decision are extracurricular activities record, evidence of special talent, and advanced placement or honor courses. The college accepts applications on-line and on computer disk.

Procedure: Freshmen are admitted fall and spring. Entrance exams should be taken during the fall of the senior year. There are early action, early admissions, and deferred admissions plans. Early action applications should be filed by November 15; regular applications, by February 15 for fall entry and November 15 for spring entry, along with a $40 fee. Notification of early decision is sent January 15; regular decision, April 1. 1% of all applicants are on a waiting list; 2 were accepted in 2001.

Transfer: 56 transfer students enrolled in 2001-2002. Applicants must have a minimum 2.0 GPA from an accredited institution to be considered. An interview is also recommended. 30 credits of 125 must be completed at Linfield.

Visiting: There are regularly scheduled orientations for prospective students, including tours and interviews. There are guides for informal visits and visitors may sit in on classes and stay overnight. To schedule a visit, contact the Admissions Office.

Financial Aid: In 2001-2002, 86% of all freshmen and 96% of continuing students received some form of financial aid. 68% of freshmen and 80% of continuing students received need-based aid. The average freshman award was $15,784. 65% of undergraduates work part time. The average financial indebtedness of the 2001 graduate was $17,000. Linfield is a member of CSS. The FAFSA is required. The fall application deadline is February 1.

International Students: There are 46 international students enrolled. The school actively recruits these students. They must score 475 on the written TOEFL or 150 on the electronic version.

Computers: The mainframe is a Sun Enterprise 450. 3 main PC labs provide 65 stations for both instruction and access to a wide range of programming, word processing, graphics, analysis, and Internet access tools. Several departmental PC labs provide additional access. Residence halls have small computer labs with access to the Internet and Web. All students may access the system. There are no time limits and no fees.

Graduates: In 2001, 317 bachelor's degrees were awarded. The most popular majors were elementary education (15%), communications (9%), and finance (8%). In an average class, 1% graduate in 3 years, 58% in 4 years, and 65% in 5 years. 12 companies recruited on campus in 2000-2001. Of the 2000 graduating class, 22% were enrolled in graduate school within 6 months of graduation and 84% were employed.

Admissions Contact: Lisa Knodle-Bragiel, Director of Admissions. E-mail: *admissions@linfield.edu* Web: *www.linfield.edu*

MARYLHURST UNIVERSITY
B-1

Marylhurst, OR 97036
(503) 699-6268
(800) 634-9982; Fax: (503) 635-6585

Full-time: 41 men, 162 women	**Faculty:** 31
Part-time: 74 men, 300 women	**Ph.D.s:** 28%
Graduate: 94 men, 76 women	**Student/Faculty:** 7 to 1
Year: quarters, summer session	**Tuition:** $9519
Application Deadline: open	**Room & Board:** $6000
Freshman Class: n/av	
SAT I or ACT: not required	**NONCOMPETITIVE**

Marylhurst University, founded in 1893, is a private, commuter, liberal arts institution affiliated with the Roman Catholic Church. The primary emphasis is on innovative programs such as the Weekend College for adult students. There are 10 undergraduate and 4 graduate schools. In addition to regional accreditation, Marylhurst has baccalaureate program accreditation with NASM. The library contains 89,428 volumes, 18 microform items, and 2873 audiovisual forms/CDs, and subscribes to 522 periodicals. Computerized library services include the card catalog, interlibrary loans, and database searching. Special learning facilities include an art gallery. The 68-acre campus is in a suburban area 10 miles south of Portland. Including residence halls, there are 14 buildings.

Student Life: 88% of undergraduates are from Oregon. Others are from 9 states, 22 foreign countries, and Canada. 85% are white. The average age of freshmen is 34; all undergraduates, 37.

Housing: 50 students can be accommodated in college housing, which includes coed dormitories. Priority for on-campus housing is given to out-of-town students. 97% of students commute. Alcohol is not permitted. All students may keep cars.

Activities: There are no fraternities or sororities. There are 6 groups on campus, including art, chorale, international, jazz band, orchestra, professional, and symphony. Popular campus events include Alumni Days and Commencement Weekend.

Sports: There is no sports program at Marylhurst.

Disabled Students: 75% of the campus is accessible. Wheelchair ramps, elevators, special parking, specially equipped rest rooms, lowered drinking fountains, and lowered telephones are available.

Services: Counseling and information services are available, as is tutoring in some subjects, including math and writing. There is a reader service for the blind.

Campus Safety and Security: Measures include 24-hour foot and vehicle patrol, self-defense education, escort service, and emergency telephones. There are lighted pathways/sidewalks.

Programs of Study: Marylhurst confers B.A., B.S., B.F.A., and B.M. degrees. Master's degrees are also awarded. Bachelor's degrees are awarded in BUSINESS (management science), COMMUNICATIONS AND THE ARTS (art, communications, fine arts, music, and technical and business writing), COMPUTER AND PHYSICAL SCIENCE (science), SOCIAL SCIENCE (human development, interdisciplinary studies, ministries, and social science). Management, social science, and communication are the largest.

Required: To graduate, students must have a minimum 2.0 GPA and complete 180 quarter credits, including 60 to 129 in the major. Distribution requirements vary according to major but include 15 credits each (10 for the B.M. degree) in communications, arts and letters, science/math, and social science. An interdisciplinary seminar is also required, as are internships in some majors.

Special: Cross-registration may be arranged through the Oregon Independent College Association. Marylhurst offers work-study programs, B.A.-B.S. degrees, internships, an interdisciplinary studies degree, dual and student-designed majors, accelerated degree programs in all majors, credit for life experience, nondegree study, and pass/fail options.

Faculty/Classroom: 48% of faculty are male; 52%, female. 94% teach undergraduates. No introductory courses are taught by graduate students. The average class size in an introductory lecture is 15 and in a regular course, 15.

Requirements: Only the Early Scholars Program has specific requirements including the SAT I, essays, a college interview, and recommendations by school officials. CLEP credit is accepted.

Procedure: Freshmen are admitted to all sessions. Notification is sent on a rolling basis. Application deadlines are open. Application fee is $20.

Transfer: 116 transfer students enrolled in 2001-2002. Almost all students are returning adults who have transferred prior to college credit. Grades of C or better transfer for credit. 45 credits of 180 must be completed at Marylhurst.

Visiting: There are regularly scheduled orientations for prospective students, including addressing registration and financial aid issues, academic advising, and use of the library, cafeteria, and bookstore. There are guides for informal visits and visitors may sit in on classes and stay overnight. To schedule a visit, contact the Dean of Admissions.

Financial Aid: In a recent year, 65% of all students received some form of financial aid, including need-based aid. The average freshman award was $8500. Of that total, loans averaged $2625 ($6625 maximum); work contracts averaged $1500 ($3000 maximum); and institutional grants averaged $1000 ($2000 maximum). 88% of undergraduates work part time. Average annual earnings from campus work are $2000. The average financial indebtedness of a recent graduate was $18,000. The FAFSA and an institutional application are required.

International Students: They must score 550 on the written TOEFL and also take the college's own test.

Computers: The mainframe is an NT Server. Students may use independent PCs available in the computer center. All students may access the system. There are no time limits and no fees.

Admissions Contact: John French, Academic Advising Specialist.
E-mail: *admissions@marylhurst.edu* Web: *www.marylhurst.edu*

NORTHWEST CHRISTIAN COLLEGE B-2

Eugene, OR 97401-3727 **(541) 684-7201**
(877) 463-6622; Fax: (541) 684-7317

Full-time: 140 men, 220 women	**Faculty:** 15; IIB, --$
Part-time: 5 men, 20 women	**Ph.D.s:** 67%
Graduate: 10 men, 50 women	**Student/Faculty:** 24 to 1
Year: quarters	**Tuition:** $14,580
Application Deadline: see profile	**Room & Board:** $5100
Freshman Class: n/av	
SAT I or ACT: required	**LESS COMPETITIVE**

Northwest Christian College, founded in 1895, is a private institution affiliated with the Christian Church, offering programs in the arts, business, education, and ministries. Figures in the above capsule are approximate. There is 1 graduate school. The library contains 60,247 volumes, 643 microform items, and 2091 audiovisual forms/CDs, and subscribes to 261 periodicals. Computerized library services include the card catalog, interlibrary loans, and database searching. Special learning facilities include a learning resource center. The 8-acre campus is in an urban area 125 miles south of Portland. Including residence halls, there are 9 buildings.

Student Life: 88% of undergraduates are from Oregon. Others are from 12 states and 3 foreign countries. 94% are from public schools. 97% are white. Most are Protestant. The average age of freshmen is 18; all undergraduates, 23. 41% do not continue beyond their first year; 39% remain to graduate.

Housing: 204 students can be accommodated in college housing, which includes single-sex and coed dormitories, off-campus apartments, and married-student housing. On-campus housing is guaranteed for the freshman year only. 60% of students live on campus; of those, 50% remain on campus on weekends. Alcohol is not permitted. All students may keep cars.

Activities: There are no fraternities or sororities. There are 15 groups on campus, including cheerleading, choir, debate, drama, forensics, musical theater, newspaper, pep band, religious, social service, student government, and yearbook. Popular campus events include Annual Musical, Spirit Week, and Wellness Week.

Sports: There is 1 intercollegiate sport for men and there are 2 for women, and 12 intramural sports for men and 12 for women. Students have access to all recreational facilities and opportunities offered through the University of Oregon in Eugene.

Disabled Students: 60% of the campus is accessible. Wheelchair ramps, elevators, special parking, specially equipped rest rooms, special class scheduling, lowered drinking fountains, and lowered telephones are available.

Services: Counseling and information services are available, as is tutoring in most subjects. There is remedial math, reading, and writing.

Campus Safety and Security: Measures include escort service, emergency telephones, lighted pathways/sidewalks, and foot patrol from 7 P.M. to 3 A.M.

Programs of Study: NCC confers the B.A. degree. Associate and master's degrees are also awarded. Bachelor's degrees are awarded in BUSINESS (business administration and management), COMMUNICATIONS AND THE ARTS (communications and music), EDUCATION (elementary), SOCIAL SCIENCE (interdisciplinary studies, international studies, ministries, and psychology). Business administration, ministry, and elementary education are the strongest academically. Elementary education and psychology are the largest.

Required: To graduate, students must complete 186 quarter credits with at least 60 in the major and a minimum GPA of 2.00. The core curriculum consists of 104 credit hours in humanities, social sciences, math and science, and Bible; a 1-credit-hour chapel for every term enrolled is also required. Internships are required for all majors. Credit for prior learning is possible.

Special: NCC offers co-op programs in biology, communication disorders and sciences, economics, English, geology, history, international studies, linguistics, math, political science, and premedicine. Cross-registration with the University of Oregon, study abroad in 4 countries, a Washington semester, and work-study programs are available. Student-designed majors, an accelerated degree program in management, and a TESOL certificate program are also possible.

Faculty/Classroom: 63% of faculty are male; 37%, female. All teach undergraduates. No introductory courses are taught by graduate students. The average class size in an introductory lecture is 40 and in a regular course, 25.

Admissions: 4 freshmen graduated first in their class in a recent year.

Requirements: The SAT I or ACT is required. In addition, students are required to submit a completed admission application, high school transcripts, and 2 references. An interview is recommended. Applications are accepted on-line. NCC requires applicants to be in the upper 75% of their class. A GPA of 2.5 is required. AP and CLEP credits are accepted. Important factors in the admissions decision are advanced placement or honor courses, recommendations by school officials, and extracurricular activities record.

Procedure: Freshmen are admitted fall, winter, and spring. There are early admissions and deferred admissions plans. Notification is sent on a rolling basis. Check with the school for current application deadlines and fees.

Transfer: Students are required to submit a completed application, official transcripts from each college or university attended, an academic reference, and official high school transcripts if they have fewer than 36 transferable credits. 45 credits of 186 must be completed at NCC.

Visiting: There are regularly scheduled orientations for prospective students. There are guides for informal visits and visitors may sit in on classes and stay overnight. To schedule a visit, contact Mindy Lockard in Admission at (541) 684-7209.

Financial Aid: NCC is a member of CSS. The FAFSA, the college's own financial statement and the are required. Check with the school for current deadlines.

International Students: They must score 500 on the written TOEFL.

Computers: The mainframe is a 4 IBM servers in a Windows NT network. A computer lab with more than 20 terminals, Internet access, and E-mail is available. There are also 20 networked terminals in a computer classroom and 12 networked terminals in the library. All students may access the system during open library hours. There are no time limits. The fee $53 per term. It is strongly recommended that all students have a personal computer.

Graduates: In an average class, 24% graduate in 4 years, 37% in 5 years, and 39% in 6 years.

Admissions Contact: Randy Jones, Dean of Admissions.
E-mail: *admissions@eve.nwcc.edu* Web: *www.nwcc.edu*

OREGON INSTITUTE OF TECHNOLOGY — B-4

Klamath Falls, OR 97601-8801 — (541) 885-1150, Fax: (541) 885-1115

Full-time: 1110 men, 835 women	**Faculty:** 107; IIB, -$
Part-time: 589 men, 552 women	**Ph.D.s:** 31%
Graduate: 12 men	**Student/Faculty:** 18 to 1
Year: quarters, summer session	**Tuition:** $3564 ($12,525)
Application Deadline: June 1	**Room & Board:** $5154
Freshman Class: 520 applied, 431 accepted, 320 enrolled	
SAT I Verbal/Math: 520/520	**ACT:** 21 — **COMPETITIVE**

Oregon Institute of Technology, founded in 1947, is a member of the Oregon University System and the only public institute of technology in the Pacific Northwest. OIT provides degree programs in engineering and health technologies, management, communications, and applied sciences that prepare students to be effective participants in their professional, public and international communities. There are 3 undergraduate schools and 1 graduate school. In addition to regional accreditation, OIT has baccalaureate program accreditation with ABET and NLN. The library contains 145,988 volumes, 158,278 microform items, and 2069 audiovisual forms/CDs, and subscribes to 1815 periodicals. Computerized library services include the card catalog, interlibrary loans, and database searching. Special learning facilities include a learning resource center, art gallery, and radio station. The 173-acre campus is in a small town 60 miles east of Medford in south central Oregon. Including residence halls, there are 12 buildings.

Student Life: 85% of undergraduates are from Oregon. Others are from 35 states and 17 foreign countries. 95% are from public schools. 80% are white. The average age of freshmen is 23; all undergraduates, 26. 26% do not continue beyond their first year; 29% remain to graduate.

Housing: 500 students can be accommodated in college housing, which includes single-sex and coed dormitories. On-campus housing is guaranteed for all 4 years. 82% of students commute. All students may keep cars.

Activities: 3% of men belong to 1 local and 1 national fraternity; 3% of women belong to 1 local and 1 national sorority. There are 37 groups on campus, including cheerleading, computers, ethnic, honors, international, newspaper, outdoor, pep band, professional, radio and TV, religious, social, and student government. Popular campus events include Tech Challenge, Family Weekend Tech Fest, and a skills contest for business and math students.

Sports: There are 4 intercollegiate sports for men and 6 coed intramural sports. Facilities include a 3000-seat stadium, a 2066-seat gym, football, baseball, and softball fields, free weights and aerobics areas, an indoor swimming pool, a track, and tennis, volleyball, basketball, and badminton courts.

Disabled Students: 90% of the campus is accessible. Wheelchair ramps, elevators, special parking, specially equipped rest rooms, and special class scheduling are available.

Services: Counseling and information services are available, as is tutoring in some subjects, including math, sciences, and computers. There is a reader service for the blind, and remedial math, reading, and writing.

Campus Safety and Security: Measures include 24-hour foot and vehicle patrol, escort service, and lighted pathways/sidewalks.

Programs of Study: OIT confers the B.S. degree. Associate and master's degrees are also awarded. Bachelor's degrees are awarded in BUSINESS (management information systems), ENGINEERING AND ENVIRONMENTAL DESIGN (civil engineering, computer technology, electrical/electronics engineering technology, engineering technology, environmental science, industrial administration/management, laser electro-optics technology, manufacturing technology, mechanical engineering technology, and surveying engineering), HEALTH PROFESSIONS (dental hygiene, health science, radiograph medical technology, and ultrasound technology), SOCIAL SCIENCE (industrial and organizational psychology). Engineering technology programs are the largest.

Required: General education requirements include 12 hours in social science and 9 hours each in communication, business, and humanities. Students also must take 9 hours in English composition and technical report writing. Completion of about 200 quarter hours, with a minimum GPA of 2.0, is required to graduate.

Special: Cross-registration with Klamath Community College, internships in all majors, and co-op programs in all engineering technologies are available. OIT also offers advanced degree programs in software engineering technology and vascular imaging. There are 2 national honor societies.

Faculty/Classroom: 77% of faculty are male; 23%, female. All teach undergraduates. The average class size in an introductory lecture is 30; in a laboratory, 18; and in a regular course, 30.

Admissions: 83% of the 2001-2002 applicants were accepted. The SAT I scores for the 2001-2002 freshman class were: Verbal--43% below 500, 37% between 500 and 599, 17% between 600 and 700, and 3% above 700; Math--40% below 500, 40% between 500 and 599, 16% between 600 and 700, and 4% above 700. The ACT scores were 14% below 18, 57% between 18 and 23, 25% between 24 and 29, and 4% above 29. 18% of the current freshmen were in the top fifth of their class; 61% were in the top two fifths.

Requirements: The SAT I or ACT is required for placement purposes; however, a composite score of 1000 on the SAT I or 21 on the ACT is required for applicants who do not meet the minimum GPA requirement. Applicants must have 14 academic units, including 4 years of English, 3 each of math and social sciences, and 2 each of science and a foreign language. The GED is accepted. A GPA of 2.5 is required. AP and CLEP credits are accepted. Applications are accepted on disk.

Procedure: Freshmen are admitted to all sessions. The SAT I or ACT should be taken during the senior year, and placement tests just prior to registration. There is an early admissions plan. Applications should be filed by June 1 for fall or summer entry, December 1 for winter entry, and March 1 for spring entry. The fall 2001 application fee was $50. Notification is sent on a rolling basis.

Transfer: 168 transfer students enrolled in 2001-2002. Applicants must have a minimum GPA of 2.0 and at least 24 quarter credit hours; students with fewer credit hours must submit high school transcripts or GED scores. An associate degree is recommended. 45 quarter credits of 190 must be completed at OIT.

Visiting: There are regularly scheduled orientations for prospective students, including tours and meetings with admissions counselors, faculty, and students. There are guides for informal visits and visitors may sit in on classes and stay overnight. To schedule a visit, contact the Admissions Office by phone or at *oit@oit.edu*

Financial Aid: In 2001-2002, 85% of all freshmen and 60% of continuing students received some form of financial aid. 80% of freshmen and 75% of continuing students received need-based aid. The average freshman award was $9700. Of that total, scholarships or need-based grants averaged $2100 ($4000 maximum); loans averaged $3500 ($4000 maximum); and work contracts averaged $1200 (maximum). 40% of undergraduates work part time. Average annual earnings from campus work are $1200. The average financial indebtedness of the 2001 graduate was $22,629. The FAFSA is required. The fall application deadline is May 1.

International Students: There are 29 international students enrolled. The school actively recruits these students. They must score 520 on the written TOEFL.

Computers: The mainframes are a Prime EXL-316, a DEC PDP 11/44, and a DEC ALPHA 2100. More than 700 terminals and PCs are available on campus. Modem access is available to students off campus. All students may access the system 24 hours daily during the last 2 weeks of the quarter and 18 hours daily otherwise. There are no time limits and no fees.

Graduates: 76 companies recruited on campus in 2000-2001. Of the 2000 graduating class, 11% were enrolled in graduate school within 6 months of graduation and 86% were employed.

Admissions Contact: Palmer Muntz, Director of Admissions. A video is available. E-mail: *muntzp@oit.edu* Web: *www.oit.edu*

OREGON STATE UNIVERSITY

Corvallis, OR 97331-2106 B-2

(541) 737-4411
(800) 291-4192; Fax: (541) 737-2482

Full-time: 7210 men, 6207 women	**Faculty:** 1352; I, --$
Part-time: 717 men, 743 women	**Ph.D.s:** 85%
Graduate: 1536 men, 1621 women	**Student/Faculty:** 10 to 1
Year: quarters, summer session	**Tuition:** $3987 ($13,935)
Application Deadline: March 1	**Room & Board:** $5625
Freshman Class: 6645 applied, 3677 accepted, 3115 enrolled	
SAT I Verbal/Math: 530/550	**ACT:** 22 **VERY COMPETITIVE**

Oregon State University, founded in 1868, is the oldest institution in the Oregon state system, offering liberal arts and preprofessional programs. There are 10 undergraduate and 12 graduate schools. In addition to regional accreditation, OSU has baccalaureate program accreditation with AACSB, ABET, ACCE, ACEJMC, ACPE, AHEA, NASM, NCATE, and SAF. The 4 libraries contain 1,403,451 volumes, 1,912,023 microform items, and 6225 audiovisual forms/CDs, and subscribe to 14,777 periodicals. Computerized library services include the card catalog and database searching. Special learning facilities include a learning resource center, art gallery, natural history museum, radio station, TV station, arboretum, wave research lab, research farm, research vessel, and the Linus Pauling Collection. The 400-acre campus is in a small town 80 miles south of Portland. Including residence halls, there are 203 buildings.

Student Life: 85% of undergraduates are from Oregon. Others are from 49 states, 90 foreign countries, and Canada. 75% are white. The average age of freshmen is 19; all undergraduates, 23. 20% do not continue beyond their first year; 60% remain to graduate.

Housing: 5593 students can be accommodated in college housing, which includes coed dormitories, married-student housing, fraternity houses, and sorority houses. In addition, there are honors, special-interest, and cooperative houses. All residences are smoke free. On-campus housing is available on a first-come, first-served basis. 71% of students commute. Alcohol is not permitted. All students may keep cars.

Activities: 15% of men belong to 25 national fraternities; 11% of women belong to 13 national sororities. There are 350 groups on campus, including art, band, cheerleading, chess, choir, chorale, chorus, computers, dance, drama, drill team, drum and bugle corps, ethnic, film, gay, honors, international, jazz band, literary magazine, marching band, musical theater, newspaper, orchestra, pep band, photography, political, professional, radio and TV, religious, social, social service, student government, symphony, and yearbook. Popular campus events include Renaissance Fair and Native American Pow Wow.

Sports: There are 7 intercollegiate sports for men and 8 for women, and 19 intramural sports for men and 17 for women. Facilities include 2 fitness centers, a 10,400-seat gym, a 40,000-seat stadium, indoor and outdoor recreation centers, weight and exercise rooms, bowling alleys, and numerous courts and playing fields.

Disabled Students: 92% of the campus is accessible. Wheelchair ramps, elevators, special parking, specially equipped rest rooms, special class scheduling, lowered drinking fountains, lowered telephones, note takers, interpreters for the deaf, and visual-aid equipment for the blind are available.

Services: Counseling and information services are available, as is tutoring in most subjects, including chemistry, computer science, math, psychology and counseling, and physics. There is a reader service for the blind, and remedial math, reading, and writing. Facilities include a communication skills center and a math sciences learning center.

Campus Safety and Security: Measures include emergency telephones and lighted pathways/sidewalks.

Programs of Study: OSU confers B.A., B.S., and B.F.A. degrees. Master's and doctoral degrees are also awarded. Bachelor's degrees are awarded in AGRICULTURE (agricultural business management, agricultural economics, agriculture, animal science, fishing and fisheries, forest engineering, forestry and related sciences, forestry production and processing, horticulture, poultry science, range/farm management, and soil science), BIOLOGICAL SCIENCE (biochemistry, biology/biological science, biophysics, botany, entomology, microbiology, nutrition, plant pathology, wildlife biology, and zoology), BUSINESS (accounting, business administration and management, hotel/motel and restaurant management, marketing management, and marketing/retailing/merchandising), COMMUNICATIONS AND THE ARTS (apparel design, art, dramatic arts, English, French, German, music, Spanish, speech/debate/rhetoric, and visual and performing arts), COMPUTER AND PHYSICAL SCIENCE (chemistry, computer science, geology, mathematics, physics, and science), EDUCATION (health), ENGINEERING AND ENVIRONMENTAL DESIGN (chemical engineering, civil engineering, computer engineering, construction management, environmental science, industrial engineering technology, landscape architecture/design, mechanical engineering, nuclear engineering, and urban design), HEALTH PROFESSIONS (environmental health science, health, health care administration, medical technology, and nursing), SOCIAL SCIENCE (American studies, anthropology, economics, family/consumer studies, fashion design and technology, food science, geography, history, home economics, human development, liberal arts/general studies, philosophy, political science/government, psychology, sociology, and textiles and clothing). Engineering, biochemistry, and forestry are the strongest academically. Business, liberal arts, and mechanical engineering are the largest.

Required: To graduate, students must complete at least 192 quarter credits with a GPA of 2.0. The required core curriculum includes a total of 37 credits in writing and communications, math, humanities and social studies, natural sciences, and fitness. Students must take a writing-intensive course in their major field and meet additional distribution requirements.

Special: OSU offers cooperative veterinary medicine programs with Washington State University and the University of Idaho; geological, metallurgical, and mining engineering programs with the University of Idaho; and an education program with the University of Oregon. Students may cross-register at any college in the Oregon state system, at member colleges of the Western Interstate Commission, and with any member of the National Student Exchange. Study abroad is possible in any of 13 countries, including New Zealand and the former Soviet Union. There is a 5-year B.A.-B.S. program in civil engineering and forest engineering, and a 3-2 engineering program with the University of Oregon. Internships, a liberal studies degree, nondegree study, and pass/fail options are also available. There are 7 national honor societies, a freshman honors program, and 20 departmental honors programs.

Faculty/Classroom: 58% of faculty are male; 42%, female. 67% teach undergraduates, 24% do research, and 67% do both.

Admissions: 55% of the 2001-2002 applicants were accepted. The SAT I scores for the 2001-2002 freshman class were: Verbal--35% below 500, 41% between 500 and 599, 22% between 600 and 700, and 2% above 700; Math--29% below 500, 41% between 500 and 599, 26% between 600 and 700, and 4% above 700. The ACT scores were 30% below 21, 27% between 21 and 23, 22% between 24 and 26, 11% between 27 and 28, and 10% above 28.

Requirements: The SAT I or ACT is required. In addition, applicants should be high school graduates or hold the GED. Required high school preparation includes 4 years of English; 3 years of math, including algebra I; 2 years of natural science; and 1 year each of U.S history, world history, and social science. Among electives, government and foreign language are strongly recommended. Some subject requirements may be fulfilled by test scores. A GPA of 3.0 is required. AP and CLEP credits are accepted. Advanced placement or honor courses is an important factor in the admissions decision.

Procedure: Freshmen are admitted to all sessions. Entrance exams should be taken during the junior or senior year. There is an early admissions plan. Applications should be filed by March 1 for fall, spring, or summer entry and December 1 for winter entry. The fall 2001 application fee was $50. Notification is sent on a rolling basis.

Transfer: 1141 transfer students enrolled in 2001-2002. Applicants who are Oregon residents must present a GPA of at least 2.25 in previous college work; for nonresidents, a GPA of 2.5. Students should have completed at least 36 hours of college credit. Either SAT I or ACT scores must be submitted. 36 quarter credits of 192 must be completed at OSU.

Visiting: There are regularly scheduled orientations for prospective students. There are guides for informal visits and visitors may sit in on classes and stay overnight. To schedule a visit, contact the Office of New Student Programs.

Financial Aid: OSU is a member of CSS. The FAFSA is required. The fall application deadline is February 1.

International Students: In a recent year, there were 329 international students enrolled. The school actively recruits these students. They must score 550 on the written TOEFL.

Computers: The mainframes are 2 Digital 7000/620 AXP open/VMS machines and 1 Digital 2100 AXP OSF/1. There are more than 2200 PC and Mac systems available to students in the computer lab, the library, and various academic buildings. All students may access the system at any time. There are no time limits and no fees.

Graduates: In 2001, 2600 bachelor's degrees were awarded. The most popular majors were business administration (13%), liberal studies (6%), and human development and family studies (4%). In an average class, 1% graduate in 3 years, 28% in 4 years, 54% in 5 years, and 59% in 6 years.

Admissions Contact: Robert Bontrager, Director of Admissions.
E-mail: *osuadmit@orst.edu*
Web: *http://www.oregonstate.edu/admissions*

OREGON UNIVERSITY SYSTEM

The Oregon University System (OUS), is comprised of 7 distinguished public universities, reaching more than 1 million persons each year through on-campus classes, statewide public services, and lifelong learning. OUS provides the central administration for the Oregon State Board of Higher Education, an 11-member volunteer board appointed by the governor and confirmed by the Oregon legislature. The chancellor serves as the system's chief administrative officer. OUS has a three-part mission: to provide affordable access to high-quality post-secondary education for all qualified Oregonians; to improve and enrich learning in the sciences, the social sciences, the humanities, the arts, and the professions; and to help Oregon respond effectively to social, economic, and environmental challenges and opportunities. Total campus enrollment exceeds 73,500 with nearly 3400 faculty. Academic offerings include 327 baccalaureate, 272 master's, and 134 doctoral programs. Campuses of the system include Eastern Oregon University, Oregon Institute of Technology, Oregon State University, Portland State University, Southern Oregon University, the University of Oregon, and Western Oregon University.

PACIFIC NORTHWEST COLLEGE OF ART — B-1

Portland, OR 97209 — (503) 821-8972
(800) 818-PNCA; Fax: (503) 821-8978

Full-time: 111 men, 152 women	**Faculty:** 16
Part-time: 7 men, 21 women	**Ph.D.s:** 81%
Graduate: none	**Student/Faculty:** 16 to 1
Year: semesters	**Tuition:** $12,970
Application Deadline: March 1	**Room & Board:** $3537
Freshman Class: 65 applied, 60 accepted, 38 enrolled	
SAT I or ACT: recommended	**SPECIAL**

Pacific Northwest College of Art, founded in 1909, offers professional training in the fine and visual arts. In addition to regional accreditation, PNCA has baccalaureate program accreditation with NASAD. The library contains 9548 volumes and 60,000 audiovisual forms/CDs, and subscribes to 47 periodicals. Computerized library services include interlibrary loans. Special learning facilities include an art gallery. The 1-acre campus is in an urban area in downtown Portland. Including residence halls, there are 4 buildings.

Student Life: 76% of undergraduates are from Oregon. Others are from 21 states, 7 foreign countries, and Canada. 89% are white. The average age of all undergraduates is 25. 39% do not continue beyond their first year; 34% remain to graduate.

Housing: College housing includes coed dormitories, on-campus apartments, off-campus apartments, and married-student housing. In addition, there is cooperative housing. 98% of students commute. Alcohol is not permitted.

Activities: There are no fraternities or sororities. There are some groups and organizations on campus, including art, cheerleading, film, professional, and student government. Popular campus events include A Day Without Class and Halloween.

Sports: There is no sports program at PNCA.

Disabled Students: 90% of the campus is accessible. Wheelchair ramps, elevators, specially equipped rest rooms, and lowered drinking fountains are available.

Services: Counseling and information services are available, as is tutoring in every subject.

Campus Safety and Security: Measures include self-defense education, pamphlets/posters/films, emergency telephones, and lighted pathways/sidewalks. There are guards at building entrances.

Programs of Study: PNCA confers the B.F.A. degree. Bachelor's degrees are awarded in COMMUNICATIONS AND THE ARTS (fine arts, graphic design, illustration, painting, photography, printmaking, and sculpture). Painting is the largest.

Required: To graduate, all students must complete 122 credits, including 42 in liberal arts and science courses and 39 to 61 in a studio major. Of the studio requirements, 22 credits consist of courses in visual elements, 3-dimensional design, drawing, art and ideas, and composition or literature. All seniors must earn a 2.0 GPA for both semesters and must complete a thesis, which is critiqued by the faculty and later exhibited.

Special: A joint B.A./B.F.A. degree is offered with Reed College. Students may cross-register with members of the Oregon Independent Colleges Association. There is a Mobility Program for 1 semester or 1 year with member schools of the Association of Schools of Art and Design. Fourth-year graphic design majors may undertake a 1-semester professional internship; internships also are strongly encouraged for juniors in all majors. Students may study abroad in 3 countries through PNCA's program or in any other country through the programs of other accredited institutions. Nondegree study and student-designed majors are possible.

Faculty/Classroom: 61% of faculty are male; 39%, female. The average class size in a regular course is 17.

Admissions: 92% of the 2001-2002 applicants were accepted.

Requirements: The SAT I or ACT is recommended. In addition, applicants should be high school graduates or have earned the GED. The application consists of high school transcripts, a personal statement about the applicant's decision to become an artist, 2 recommendations, and a portfolio of at least 12 pieces of artwork. The portfolio must consist of 6 drawings from life, the college's Home Exam or other artwork, and at least 6 additional pieces. A GPA of 2.0 is required. Evidence of special talent is an important factor in the admission decision.

Procedure: Freshmen are admitted to all sessions. There are early action and deferred admissions plans. Early action applications should be filed by December 1; regular applications, by March 1 for fall entry and December 1 for spring entry. Notification of early action is sent December 15; regular decision, on a rolling basis. The fall 2001 application fee was $30.

Transfer: 70 transfer students enrolled in 2001-2002. Applicants must submit college and, in some cases, high school transcripts. Students may submit up to 40 slides or up to 20 original pieces of artwork, at least 6 of which must be drawings. Potential graphic design majors must submit samples of their work. A minimum 2.0 GPA is required. 48 credits of 122 must be completed at PNCA.

Visiting: There are guides for informal visits and visitors may sit in on classes. To schedule a visit, contact the Enrollment Services Office.

Financial Aid: The average financial indebtedness of the 2001 graduate was $18,917. The FAFSA is required. The fall priority application deadline is March 11.

International Students: They must score 550 on the written TOEFL.

Computers: There are 24 Power Macs and several Mac IIs available for academic use in the computer lab. All students may access the system. There are no time limits and no fees.

Graduates: In 2001, 52 bachelor's degrees were awarded.

Admissions Contact: Regina Broich, Enrollment Services.
E-mail: *admissions@pnca.edu* Web: *www.pnca.edu*

PACIFIC UNIVERSITY — B-1

Forest Grove, OR 97116 — (503) 359-2218
(800) PAC-UNIV; Fax: (503) 359-2975

Full-time: 380 men, 620 women	**Faculty:** 87; IIA, --$
Part-time: 35 men, 40 women	**Ph.D.s:** 78%
Graduate: 365 men, 625 women	**Student/Faculty:** 12 to 1
Year: 4-1-4, summer session	**Tuition:** $18,510
Application Deadline: February 15	**Room & Board:** $5740
Freshman Class: n/av	
SAT I or ACT: required	**COMPETITIVE**

Pacific University, founded in 1849, is an independent institution affiliated with the Congregational Church (United Church of Christ), offering degree programs in liberal arts, science, business, education, and health professions. Figures in above capsule are approximate. In addition to regional accreditation, Pacific has baccalaureate program accreditation with NASM. The library contains 152,060 volumes, 76,609 microform items, and 3708 audiovisual forms/CDs, and subscribes to 945 periodicals. Computerized library services include the card catalog, interlibrary loans, and database searching. Special learning facilities include a learning resource center, art gallery, radio station, TV station, and and museum of the history of the university. The 55-acre campus is in a small town 25 miles west of Portland. Including residence halls, there are 18 buildings.

Student Life: 50% of undergraduates are from out of state, mostly the West. Others are from 31 states, 7 foreign countries, and Canada. 91% are from public schools. 64% are white; 17% Asian American. The average age of freshmen is 18; all undergraduates, 20. 22% do not continue beyond their first year; 54% remain to graduate.

Housing: 680 students can be accommodated in college housing, which includes single-sex and coed dormitories, off-campus apartments, and married-student housing. In addition, there are special-interest houses. On-campus housing is guaranteed for the freshman year only, is available on a first-come, first-served basis, and is available on a lottery system for upperclassmen. 50% of students live on campus; of those, 90% remain on campus on weekends. All students may keep cars.

Activities: 2% of men belong to 3 local fraternities; 6% of women belong to 3 local sororities. There are 35 groups on campus, including art, band, cheerleading, choir, chorale, chorus, computers, dance, debate, drama, ethnic, forensics, gay, honors, international, jazz band, literary magazine, musical theater, newspaper, opera, orchestra, outdoor and urban recreation, pep band, photography, political, professional, radio and TV, religious, social, social service, student government, and yearbook. Popular campus events include Hawaiian Club Luau, International Club Banquet, and Japan Day.

Sports: There are 8 intercollegiate sports for men and 8 for women, and 10 intramural sports for men and 10 for women. Facilities include a gym, various courts, a sauna, weight and wrestling rooms, a dance studio, outdoor playing fields, a field house, and racquetball courts.

Disabled Students: 80% of the campus is accessible. Wheelchair ramps, elevators, special parking, specially equipped rest rooms, and lowered drinking fountains are available.

Services: Counseling and information services are available, as is tutoring in most subjects. There is a reader service for the blind.

Campus Safety and Security: Measures include 24-hour foot and vehicle patrol, escort service, informal discussions, and pamphlets/posters/films. There are emergency telephones and lighted pathways/sidewalks.

Programs of Study: Pacific confers B.A., B.S., and B.M. degrees. Master's and doctoral degrees are also awarded. Bachelor's degrees are awarded in BIOLOGICAL SCIENCE (biology/biological science), BUSINESS (business administration and management), COMMUNICATIONS AND THE ARTS (creative writing, dramatic arts, Japanese, literature, music, and Spanish), COMPUTER AND PHYSICAL SCIENCE (chemistry, computer science, mathematics, and physics), SOCIAL SCIENCE (economics, history, humanities, philosophy, political science/government, psychology, social work, and sociology). Natural sciences, literature, and creative writing are the strongest academically. Business administration, English, and psychology are the largest.

Required: All students take a core curriculum that includes a first-year seminar and courses in writing, foreign language, social and natural sciences, art, and cross-cultural studies. A cumulative GPA of 2.0 in 124 semester hours is required for graduation. 34 to 64 hours are required in the major, depending on the discipline.

Special: Cross-registration is available with Oregon Independent Colleges and Oregon Graduate Institute of Science and Technology (OGIST). The university also offers cooperative programs with Washington University in St. Louis, OGIST, and Oregon School of Arts and Crafts, as well as study abroad in 13 countries. Full-time, semester-long internships, including one in Washington D.C., are possible. Dual majors, a general studies degree in humanities, nondegree study, 3-2 engineering programs with Washington University in St. Louis and OGIST, and an interdisciplinary program in peace and conflict studies are available. There are 2 national honor societies, a freshman honors program, and 1 departmental honors program.

Faculty/Classroom: 52% of faculty are male; 48%, female. All both teach and do research. No introductory courses are taught by graduate students. The average class size in an introductory lecture is 35; in a laboratory, 20; and in a regular course, 19.

Admissions: 18 freshmen graduated first in their class in a recent year.

Requirements: The SAT I or ACT is required. In addition, applicants are expected to be high school graduates or to hold the GED. A personal essay is required, and an interview is recommended. On-line applications are available on Pacific's web page. Applications are accepted online at the school's web site or through AppliedTechnology (Princeton Review). A GPA of 3.0 is required. AP and CLEP credits are accepted. Important factors in the admissions decision are advanced placement or honor courses, recommendations by school officials, and extracurricular activities record.

Procedure: Freshmen are admitted fall and spring. There is a deferred admissions plan. Applications should be filed by February 15 for fall entry, along with a $30 fee. Notification of early decision is sent rolling ; regular decision, on a rolling basis.

Transfer: 67 transfer students enrolled in a recent year. Transfer applicants must present at least a 2.75 GPA in previous college work; those with fewer than 30 semester hours or 45 quarter hours must also submit SAT I or ACT test scores and high school transcripts. A personal interview is strongly recommended. 30 credits of 124 must be completed at Pacific.

Visiting: There are regularly scheduled orientations for prospective students, including overnight housing with current students, a campus tour, classroom visitations, and meetings with faculty and coaches. There are guides for informal visits and visitors may sit in on classes and stay overnight. To schedule a visit, contact the Admissions Office.

Financial Aid: In a recent year, 92% of all freshmen and 97% of continuing students received some form of financial aid. 82% of freshmen and 70% of continuing students received need-based aid. The average freshman award was $15,957. Of that total, scholarships or need-based grants averaged $10,225 ($18,683 maximum); and loans averaged $4674 ($17,789 maximum). 54% of undergraduates work part time. Average annual earnings from campus work are $823. The average financial indebtedness of a recent year's graduate was $18,500. Pacific is a member of CSS. The FAFSA is required. Check with the school for current deadlines.

International Students: There were 48 international students enrolled in a recent year. The school actively recruits these students. They must score 550 on the written TOEFL.

Computers: There is a Mac-based LAN with 45 student terminals, plus 6 student-use PCs, 18 Mac standalones in residence halls, a Sequent S-81, an Intel System 303 running UNIX System 5, and a Sun 3/80 workstation. All students may access the system. There are no time limits and no fees.

Graduates: In a recent year, 285 bachelor's degrees were awarded. The most popular majors were foreign language and English (11%), business and biology (11%), and physical education (9%). In an average class, 44% graduate in 4 years, 57% in 5 years, and 63% in 6 years. 10 companies recruited on campus in a recent year. Of the 2000 graduating class, 34% were enrolled in graduate school within 6 months of graduation and 60% were employed.

Admissions Contact: Beth Woodward, Director of Admissions.
E-mail: *admissions@pacificu.edu* Web: *www.pacificu.edu*

PORTLAND STATE UNIVERSITY

Portland, OR 97207-0751 — B-1
(503) 725-3511
(800) 547-8887; Fax: (503) 725-5525

Full-time: 3662 men, 4603 women	**Faculty:** 633; I, --$
Part-time: 2538 men, 2798 women	**Ph.D.s:** 80%
Graduate: 2076 men, 2943 women	**Student/Faculty:** 13 to 1
Year: quarters, summer session	**Tuition:** $3720 ($12,828)
Application Deadline: open	**Room & Board:** $7500
Freshman Class: 2362 applied, 1980 accepted, 1293 enrolled	
SAT I Verbal/Math: 504/509	**ACT:** 22 **COMPETITIVE**

Portland State University, founded in 1946, is a comprehensive public institution serving a primarily commuter student body. Undergraduate and graduate degree programs are offered in liberal arts and sciences, business, education, engineering and applied science, fine and performing arts, social work, and urban and public affairs. There are 5 undergraduate and 7 graduate schools. In addition to regional accreditation, PSU has baccalaureate program accreditation with AACSB, ABET, ASLA, NASAD, and NASM. The library contains 1,242,337 volumes, 2,341,538 microform items, and 44,081 audiovisual forms/CDs, and subscribes to 8972 periodicals. Computerized library services include the card catalog, interlibrary loans, and database searching. Special learning facilities include a learning resource center, art gallery, radio station, and multicultural center. The 49-acre campus is in an urban area in the center of Portland. Including residence halls, there are 41 buildings.

Student Life: 83% of undergraduates are from Oregon. Others are from 47 states, 59 foreign countries, and Canada. 65% are white; 10%, Asian American. The average age of freshmen is 18; all undergraduates, 26. 35% do not continue beyond their first year; 41% remain to graduate.

Housing: 1700 students can be accommodated in college housing, which includes coed dormitories, on-campus apartments, off-campus apartments, fraternity houses, and sorority houses. On-campus housing is available on a first-come, first-served basis. Priority is given to out-of-town students. 92% of students commute. All students may keep cars.

Activities: 1% of men belong to 3 national fraternities; 1% of women belong to 1 local and 2 national sororities. There are 148 groups on campus, including art, band, cheerleading, chess, choir, chorale, chorus, computers, dance, drama, drill team, ethnic, film, forensics, gay, honors, international, jazz band, literary magazine, musical theater, newspaper, opera, orchestra, outdoor, pep band, photography, political, professional, radio and TV, religious, social, social service, student government, students with disabilities, symphony, and yearbook. Popular campus events include International Student Cultural Night, Friends of Chamber Music, and LunchBox Theater.

Sports: There are 8 intercollegiate sports for men and 9 for women, and 7 intramural sports for men and 6 for women. Facilities include a practice field, a swimming pool, an all-weather tennis facility, gyms, circuit training and weight rooms, a golf putting green, a running track, and racquetball, handball, and squash courts. Nearby Civic Stadium and Duniway Park provide football, baseball, and track-and-field facilities.

Disabled Students: 95% of the campus is accessible. Wheelchair ramps, elevators, special parking, specially equipped rest rooms, special class scheduling, lowered drinking fountains, lowered telephones, and several modified housing units are available.

Services: Counseling and information services are available, as is tutoring in most subjects. There is a reader service for the blind and remedial math and writing, as well as Student Support Services, a program that provides assistance to students who are low-income, who have a physical disability, or whose parents did not graduate from college.

Campus Safety and Security: Measures include 24-hour foot and vehicle patrol, self-defense education, escort service, and informal discussions. There are pamphlets/posters/films, emergency telephones, lighted pathways/sidewalks, a campus watch newsletter, information lectures, and a community liaison.

Programs of Study: PSU confers B.A., B.S., and B.M. degrees. Master's and doctoral degrees are also awarded. Bachelor's degrees are awarded in BIOLOGICAL SCIENCE (biochemistry and biology/biological science), BUSINESS (accounting, banking and finance, business administration and management, management science, marketing/retailing/merchandising, and personnel management), COMMUNICATIONS AND THE ARTS (advertising, art history and appreciation, Chinese, dramatic arts, English, fine arts, French, German, Japanese, languages, linguistics, music, Russian, Spanish, and speech/debate/rhetoric), COMPUTER AND PHYSICAL SCIENCE (chemistry, computer science, geology, information sciences and systems, mathematics, physics, and science), EDUCATION (health), ENGINEERING AND ENVIRONMENTAL DESIGN (architecture, civil engineering, computer engineering, electrical/electronics engineering, environmental science, and mechanical engineering), SOCIAL SCIENCE (anthropology, child care/child and family studies, community services, criminal justice, economics, geography, history, international studies, liberal arts/general studies, philosophy, political science/government, psychology, sociology, and women's studies). Electrical engineering, environmental science, and physics are the strongest academically. Psychology, business administration, and art are the largest.

Required: All students must complete at least 180 quarter credits with a 2.0 GPA. Other requirements and the number of hours that must be completed in the major vary by degree program. Freshmen must complete 3 5-credit freshman inquiry courses; sophomores, 3 4-credit courses from different interdisciplinary programs or general education clusters; juniors and seniors, 1 interdisciplinary program or general education cluster (4 3-credit courses); and seniors must complete a Senior Capstone.

Special: Students may study abroad in 34 countries. Numerous internships, a Washington semester, and work-study programs are available. Most undergraduate programs may be taken on an accelerated basis, and students in all programs may undertake dual majors or design their own majors. A general studies program is available in arts and letters, science, or social science. Nondegree study and pass/fail grading options are possible. Students may enroll for 7 or fewer credits per term without formal admission. There are 18 national honor societies, a freshman honors program, and 10 departmental honors programs.

Faculty/Classroom: 56% of faculty are male; 44%, female. All both teach and do research. The average class size in an introductory lecture is 29; in a laboratory, 21; and in a regular course, 22.

Admissions: 84% of the 2001-2002 applicants were accepted. The SAT I scores for the 2001-2002 freshman class were: Verbal--44% below 500, 37% between 500 and 599, 16% between 600 and 700, and 3% above 700; Math--46% below 500, 31% between 500 and 599, 19% between 600 and 700, and 4% above 700. The ACT scores were 37% below 21, 28% between 21 and 23, 24% between 24 and 26, 5% between 27 and 28, and 6% above 28. 18 freshmen graduated first in their class.

Requirements: The SAT I or ACT is required, with a suggested minimum composite SAT I score of 1000 or a minimum composite ACT score of 21. Applicants should be high school graduates or have earned the GED. Secondary preparation should include 4 years of English, 3 each of social studies and math, and 2 each of science and foreign language. A GPA of 2.5 is required. AP and CLEP credits are accepted. Students may submit applications on-line at the university's web site.

Procedure: Freshmen are admitted to all sessions. Entrance exams should be taken as early as possible. There is a deferred admissions plan. Application deadlines are open. The application fee is $50. Notification is sent on a rolling basis.

Transfer: 2622 transfer students enrolled in 2001-2002. Applicants who are Oregon residents must have earned at least a 2.0 GPA in 30 college credits; those with 12 to 30 credits must meet freshman admission requirements and have a 2.0 GPA in all college work attempted. Nonresident applicants must have at least a 2.25 GPA in 30 hours of college work; those with 12 to 30 hours must meet freshman requirements and have a 2.5 GPA in all college work attempted. 45 quarter credits of 180 must be completed at PSU.

Visiting: There are regularly scheduled orientations for prospective students, including twice-daily campus tours led by student guides and opportunities for prospective students to meet with faculty, staff, and advisers. There are guides for informal visits and visitors may sit in on classes and stay overnight. To schedule a visit, contact the Campus Tour Coordinator, Office of Admissions and Records, at (503) 725-5555 or *psutours@pdx.edu*

Financial Aid: In a recent year, 76% of all freshmen and 67% of continuing students received some form of financial aid. 68% of freshmen and 61% of continuing students received need-based aid. The average freshman award was $6117. Of that total, scholarships or need-based grants averaged $1170 ($10,650 maximum); loans averaged $2480 ($9025 maximum); and work contracts averaged $2668 ($3000 maximum). 80% of undergraduates work part time. Average annual earnings from campus work are $1716. The average financial indebtedness of a recent graduate was $12,333. The FAFSA and the college's own financial statement are required. The fall application deadline is June 15.

International Students: There are 365 international students enrolled. The school actively recruits these students. They must score 525 on the written TOEFL or 197 on the electronic version, or take the college's PSU institutional TOEFL. Only scores from these exams will be accepted.

Computers: The mainframes are a Seguent NUMAQ and Sun Enterprise servers. There are 12 computer labs and several smaller departmental sites. The open-access PC and Mac labs are open to all students. Labs are available in the library and various other locations throughout campus. All students may get accounts for access to the Internet and the Web and for use of e-mail. There are also several servers across campus for student access and data storage. All students may access the system 24 hours a day, except during a scheduled weekly maintenance period. Lab time is not limited, but dial-in is 90 minutes per session. There are no fees.

Graduates: In 2001, 2194 bachelor's degrees were awarded. The most popular majors were general studies/social science (12%), management (8%), and psychology (7%). In an average class, 10% graduate in 4 years, 23% in 5 years, and 31% in 6 years. 130 companies recruited on campus in 2000-2001.

Admissions Contact: Agnes Hoffman, Director of Admissions and Records. E-mail: *askadm@ess.pdx.edu*
Web: *http://www.ess.pdx.edu/adm/*

REED COLLEGE
Portland, OR 97202-8199 — B-1
(503) 777-7511
(800) 547-4750; Fax: (503) 777-7553

Full-time: 620 men, 728 women	**Faculty:** 115; IIB, +$
Part-time: 20 men, 28 women	**Ph.D.s:** 84%
Graduate: 12 men, 12 women	**Student/Faculty:** 12 to 1
Year: semesters	**Tuition:** $26,260
Application Deadline: January 15	**Room & Board:** $7090
Freshman Class: 1731 applied, 1235 accepted, 357 enrolled	
SAT I Verbal/Math: 690/650	**ACT:** 29

HIGHLY COMPETITIVE+

Reed College, founded in 1908, is a private, nonsectarian institution offering programs in liberal arts and sciences, and emphasizing instruction through small conference-style classes. There is 1 graduate school. In addition to regional accreditation, Reed has baccalaureate program accreditation with ACS. The library contains 480,925 volumes, 235,794 microform items, and 16,596 audiovisual forms/CDs, and subscribes to 1872 periodicals. Computerized library services include the card catalog, interlibrary loans, and database searching. Special learning facilities include a learning resource center, art gallery, and radio station. The 100-acre campus is in an urban area in Portland. Including residence halls, there are 36 buildings.

Student Life: 85% of undergraduates are from out of state, mostly the Northwest. Others are from 31 foreign countries and Canada. 65% are from public schools. 66% are white. The average age of freshmen is 18; all undergraduates, 20. 10% do not continue beyond their first year; 70% remain to graduate.

Housing: 784 students can be accommodated in college housing, which includes coed dormitories and on-campus apartments. In addition, there are language houses, special-interest houses, and quiet, substance-free, and no-smoking dorms. On-campus housing is guaranteed for the freshman year only, is available on a first-come, first-served basis, and is available on a lottery system for upperclassmen. 65% of students live on campus; of those, 95% remain on campus on weekends. Alcohol is not permitted. All students may keep cars.

Activities: There are no fraternities or sororities. There are 65 groups on campus, including art, chess, choir, chorale, chorus, computers, dance, drama, ethnic, gay, international, literary magazine, newspaper, orchestra, photography, radio and TV, religious, social service, student government, and yearbook. Popular campus events include Performing Arts Festival, Campus Clean Up Day (Common Day), and Renaissance Fair.

Sports: There are 6 intercollegiate sports for men and 4 for women, and 4 intramural sports for men and 4 for women. Facilities include a sports center that houses 2 gyms (1 seating 1200), an indoor pool, squash and racquetball courts, saunas, a weight room, an exercise room, and a dance studio. Outdoor facilities include a pool, tennis courts, a track, and areas for soccer, rugby, volleyball, and baseball.

Disabled Students: 68% of the campus is accessible. Wheelchair ramps, elevators, special parking, specially equipped rest rooms, special class scheduling, lowered drinking fountains, and lowered telephones are available.

Services: Counseling and information services are available, as is tutoring in most subjects. There is a reader service for the blind, and remedial math, reading, and writing.

Campus Safety and Security: Measures include 24-hour foot and vehicle patrol, self-defense education, escort service, and shuttle buses. There are pamphlets/posters/films and lighted pathways/sidewalks.

Programs of Study: Reed confers the B.A. degree. Master's degrees are also awarded. Bachelor's degrees are awarded in BIOLOGICAL SCIENCE (biology/biological science), COMMUNICATIONS AND THE ARTS (Chinese, classics, English literature, Germanic languages and literature, music, and Russian languages and literature), COMPUTER AND PHYSICAL SCIENCE (chemistry, mathematics, and physics), SOCIAL SCIENCE (anthropology, economics, French studies, history, philosophy, political science/government, psychology, religion, sociology, and Spanish studies). Biology, history, and psychology are the largest.

Required: All students are required to maintain a C average while taking 120 semester hours. The liberal arts program also requires 1 year of humanities and 1 year for a senior research project, in addition to 1 year each from literature and the arts, history, social science, psychology, natural science, math, logic, foreign languages, and linguistics. Students also must take 3 semesters of phys ed.

Special: Cross-registration is available through the Oregon Independent Colleges organization. Also available are 3-2 engineering degrees with California Institute of Technology, Columbia University, and Rensselaer Polytechnic Institute, combined 3-2 programs in science, and programs with the Pacific Northwest College of Art. Study abroad in 6 countries, a domestic exchange program with Howard University in Washington,

D.C., accelerated degree programs, dual majors, student-designed majors, numerous interdisciplinary majors, nondegree study, and pass/fail options are also offered. There is a chapter of Phi Beta Kappa.
Faculty/Classroom: 69% of faculty are male; 31%, female. All both teach and do research. No introductory courses are taught by graduate students. The average class size in a laboratory is 20 and in a regular course, 15.
Admissions: 71% of the 2001-2002 applicants were accepted. The SAT I scores for the 2001-2002 freshman class were: Verbal--1% below 500, 8% between 500 and 599, 42% between 600 and 700, and 49% above 700; Math--1% below 500, 17% between 500 and 599, 59% between 600 and 700, and 24% above 700. The ACT scores were 2% between 21 and 23, 12% between 24 and 26, 17% between 27 and 28, and 69% above 28. 74% of the current freshmen were in the top fifth of their class; 93% were in the top two fifths. There were 6 National Merit finalists. 18 freshmen graduated first in their class.
Requirements: The SAT I is required. In addition, the SAT II: Writing test is recommended. Reed strongly recommends that applicants have 4 years of English, 3 each of math and science, and 2 each of foreign language, history, and social studies. An essay is required, and an interview is recommended. The GED is accepted. AP credits are accepted. Important factors in the admissions decision are advanced placement or honor courses, personality/intangible qualities, and evidence of special talent. Applications are accepted on-line.
Procedure: Freshmen are admitted fall and spring. There are early decision, early admissions, and deferred admissions plans. Early decision applications should be filed by November 15 or January 2; regular applications, by January 15 for fall entry and November 15 for spring entry. The fall 2001 application fee was $40. Notification of early decision is sent December 15 or February 1; regular decision, April 1. 125 early decision candidates were accepted for the 2001-2002 class.
Transfer: 43 transfer students enrolled in 2001-2002. Students must have a GPA of 3.0. 60 credits of 120 must be completed at Reed.
Visiting: There are regularly scheduled orientations for prospective students. Visitors may sit in on classes and stay overnight. To schedule a visit, contact the Office of Admission.
Financial Aid: In 2001-2002, 44% of all freshmen and 50% of continuing students received some form of financial aid, including need-based aid. The average freshman award was $20,640. Of that total, scholarships or need-based grants averaged $20,162 ($28,550 maximum); loans averaged $2500 (maximum); and work contracts averaged $600 ($1500 maximum). 56% of undergraduates work part time. Average annual earnings from campus work are $1640. The average financial indebtedness of the 2001 graduate was $14,372. The CSS/Profile or FAFSA, the college's own financial statement, and the parent and student federal tax forms are required. The fall application deadline is March 1.
International Students: There are 117 international students enrolled. The school actively recruits these students. They must score 600 on the written TOEFL and also take the SAT I or the ACT. Students must take SAT II: Subject tests in writing and 2 other subjects.
Computers: The mainframes are DEC ALPHA servers with Sun boxes. There are more than 800 Macs available. Various labs and workstations offer UNIX workstations and servers. The entire campus is networked with fiber-optic cable, and there is network access in each residence hall room. The library is also accessible on-line. All students may access the system 24 hours daily. There are no time limits and no fees.
Graduates: In 2001, 265 bachelor's degrees were awarded. The most popular majors were psychology (12%), history (11%), and English (11%). In an average class, 47% graduate in 4 years, 67% in 5 years, and 70% in 6 years. 12 companies recruited on campus in 2000-2001.
Admissions Contact: Paul Marthers, Dean.
E-mail: *admission@reed.edu* Web: *http://www.reed.edu*

SOUTHERN OREGON UNIVERSITY B-4
Ashland, OR 97520-5005 **(541) 552-6411**
(800) 482-7672; Fax: (541) 552-6614

Full-time: 3749 men and women	**Faculty:** 203; IIA, --$
Part-time: 1147 men and women	**Ph.D.s:** 93%
Graduate: 579 men and women	**Student/Faculty:** 19 to 1
Year: quarters, summer session	**Tuition:** $3555 ($10,971)
Application Deadline: open	**Room & Board:** $5874
Freshman Class: 1872 applied, 1717 accepted, 815 enrolled	
SAT I Verbal/Math: 521/514	**ACT:** 23 **COMPETITIVE**

Southern Oregon University, founded in 1882, is a public comprehensive university providing undergraduate and graduate programs in humanities, science, business, fine and performing arts, social sciences, and teacher education. There are 4 undergraduate schools and 1 graduate school. In addition to regional accreditation, Southern has baccalaureate program accreditation with NASM and NLN. The library contains 290,000 volumes, 750,000 microform items, and 2500 audiovisual forms/CDs, and subscribes to 2125 periodicals. Computerized library services include interlibrary loans and database searching. Special learning facilities include a learning resource center, radio station, TV station, art museum, 8 art galleries, wildlife forensics lab, music recital hall, 2 theaters, greenhouse, and ecology center. The 175-acre campus is in a small town 10 miles southeast of Medford. Including residence halls, there are 36 buildings.
Student Life: 78% of undergraduates are from Oregon. Others are from 43 states, 35 foreign countries, and Canada. 85% are from public schools. 88% are white. The average age of all undergraduates is 24. 33% do not continue beyond their first year; 37% remain to graduate.
Housing: 1100 students can be accommodated in college housing, which includes coed dormitories, off-campus apartments, and married-student housing. In addition, there are special-interest houses, 24-hour and 12-hour quiet halls, a wellness hall, a freshman hall, a smoke- and incense-free hall, and an age 21+ hall. On-campus housing is guaranteed for the freshman year only and is available on a first-come, first-served basis. 75% of students commute. Alcohol is not permitted. All students may keep cars.
Activities: There are no fraternities or sororities. There are 84 groups on campus, including art, band, cheerleading, choir, computers, drama, ethnic, gay, honors, international, jazz band, literary magazine, newspaper, pep band, photography, political, professional, radio and TV, religious, social, student government, and symphony. Popular campus events include Commencement and Parents weekends, International Week, and One World Series.
Sports: There are 6 intercollegiate sports for men and 7 for women, and 11 intramural sports for men and 7 for women. Facilities include an indoor swimming pool, 6 racquetball courts, 12 tennis courts, 4 gyms, a climbing-wall gym, a dance studio, wrestling and weight rooms, a sauna, a football stadium, and an all-weather track.
Disabled Students: 95% of the campus is accessible. Wheelchair ramps, elevators, special parking, specially equipped rest rooms, lowered drinking fountains, and individualized programming are available.
Services: Counseling and information services are available, as is tutoring in some subjects, including math and writing. There is a reader service for the blind and remedial math and writing. Program design is offered for students with learning disabilities.
Campus Safety and Security: Measures include 24-hour foot and vehicle patrol, informal discussions, pamphlets/posters/films, and lighted pathways/sidewalks.
Programs of Study: Southern confers B.A., B.S., and B.F.A. degrees. Master's degrees are also awarded. Bachelor's degrees are awarded in BIOLOGICAL SCIENCE (biology/biological science), BUSINESS (accounting, business administration and management, and marketing/retailing/merchandising), COMMUNICATIONS AND THE ARTS (art, communications, dramatic arts, English, languages, music, music business management, Spanish, and visual and performing arts), COMPUTER AND PHYSICAL SCIENCE (chemistry, computer science, geology, mathematics, physics, and science), EDUCATION (physical), HEALTH PROFESSIONS (health, nursing, and premedicine), SOCIAL SCIENCE (anthropology, criminology, economics, geography, history, international studies, liberal arts/general studies, political science/government, prelaw, psychology, social science, and sociology). Fine and performing arts, sciences, and social sciences are the strongest academically. Business and social sciences are the largest.
Required: To graduate, students need a minimum GPA of 2.0 earned over 180 quarter hours, with 50 to 100 in the major and at least 60 in upper-division course work. Competency must be demonstrated through course work in writing and research. General education requirements include a year-long course in speaking, writing, and critical thinking, and both lower- and upper-division courses in arts and letters, natural sciences, social sciences, and quantitative reasoning. There is a required senior capstone experience.
Special: Cross-registration through the National Student and Western Student Exchanges, study abroad in 16 countries, internships, and federal work-study are all available. Accelerated degrees in business, communication, computer science, economics, geography, mathematics, political science, and foreign languages and literature; dual majors in business and chemistry, physics, math, or music, and in math and computer science; and interdisciplinary majors in environmental or international studies are all offered. There are 13 national honor societies and 3 departmental honors programs.
Faculty/Classroom: 56% of faculty are male; 44%, female. All teach undergraduates and 50% also do research. No introductory courses are taught by graduate students.
Admissions: 92% of the 2001-2002 applicants were accepted. The SAT I scores for the 2001-2002 freshman class were: Verbal--39% below 500, 40% between 500 and 599, 19% between 600 and 700, and 2% above 700; Math--41% below 500, 44% between 500 and 599, 15% between 600 and 700, and 1% above 700.
Requirements: The SAT I or ACT is required; a minimum composite score of 1010 on the SAT I is needed if the high school GPA is less than the required 2.75. Applicants need 14 academic credits, including 4 years of English, 3 each of math and social studies, and 2 each of science and a foreign language. SAT II: Subject tests in writing, math, and another area are needed if there is insufficient college-preparatory course

work. The GED is accepted. AP and CLEP credits are accepted. Applications are accepted on-line at the university's web site.

Procedure: Freshmen are admitted to all sessions. Entrance exams should be taken in the senior year. There is a deferred admissions plan. Application deadlines are open. The fall 2001 application fee was $50. Notification is sent on a rolling basis.

Transfer: 468 transfer students enrolled in 2001-2002. Students need a minimum GPA of 2.25 and at least 36 quarter credits. 45 quarter credits of 180 must be completed at Southern.

Visiting: There are regularly scheduled orientations for prospective students, including tours of the campus and residence halls, and a meeting with an admissions representative. Appointments with faculty and class visits can be arranged. There are guides for informal visits and visitors may sit in on classes and stay overnight. To schedule a visit, contact the Admissions Office by phone or at *admissions@sou.edu*

Financial Aid: In a recent year, 62% of all freshmen and 72% of continuing students received some form of financial aid. 52% of freshmen and 60% of continuing students received need-based aid. The average freshman award was $5609. Of that total, scholarships or need-based grants averaged $1852 ($5500 maximum); loans averaged $3266 ($12,825 maximum); and work contracts averaged $1113 ($1500 maximum). 46% of undergraduates work part time. Average annual earnings from campus work are $809. The average financial indebtedness of a recent graduate was $13,404. Southern is a member of CSS. The FAFSA is required. The fall application deadline is March 1.

International Students: In a recent year, there were 153 international students enrolled. The school actively recruits these students. They must score 520 on the written TOEFL.

Computers: The mainframe is a DEC VAX 4310. The main Computing Services lab and 22 other labs contain a total of 620 PCs available for student use. All students may access the system 8 A.M. to 10 P.M. Monday through Thursday, 8 A.M. to 5 P.M. Friday, 1 to 5 P.M. Saturday, and 1 to 8 P.M. Sunday. There are no time limits and no fees.

Graduates: In 2001, 771 bachelor's degrees were awarded. The most popular majors were business (20%), communication (10%), and psychology (9%). In an average class, 1% graduate in 3 years, 15% in 4 years, 30% in 5 years, and 42% in 6 years. 93 companies recruited on campus in 2000-2001. Of the 2000 graduating class, 83% were employed within a year of graduation.

Admissions Contact: Mara Affre, Director of Admissions.
E-mail: *affre@sou.edu* Web: *www.sou.edu*

UNIVERSITY OF OREGON
Eugene, OR 97403-1226 — B-2
(541) 346-3201
(800) 232-3825; Fax: (541) 346-5815

Full-time: 6348 men, 7290 women	**Faculty:** 774; I, --$
Part-time: 730 men, 745 women	**Ph.D.s:** 95%
Graduate: 1769 men, 2074 women	**Student/Faculty:** 18 to 1
Year: quarters, summer session	**Tuition:** $4071 ($14,493)
Application Deadline: February 1	**Room & Board:** $5898
Freshman Class: 8686 applied, 7819 accepted, 2998 enrolled	
SAT I Verbal/Math: 554/551	**COMPETITIVE**

The University of Oregon, founded in 1876, is a public liberal arts institution within the Oregon University System. There are 7 undergraduate and 7 graduate schools. In addition to regional accreditation, UO has baccalaureate program accreditation with AACSB, ACEJMC, ASLA, FIDER, NAAB, NASM, and NRPA. The 6 libraries contain 2.25 million volumes, 2 million microform items, and 60,000 audiovisual forms/CDs, and subscribe to 15,000 periodicals. Computerized library services include the card catalog, interlibrary loans, and database searching. Special learning facilities include a learning resource center, art gallery, natural history museum, radio station, TV station, 13 specialized science institutes, including the Center for Volcanology, the Institute of Neuroscience, the Oregon Institute of Marine Biology, and the Pine Mountain Observatory, 7 humanities and social science centers, and 12 other research facilities. The 295-acre campus is in a suburban area near downtown Eugene. Including residence halls, there are 100 buildings.

Student Life: 75% of undergraduates are from Oregon. Others are from 50 states, 79 foreign countries, and Canada. 91% are from public schools. 80% are white. The average age of freshmen is 19; all undergraduates, 21. 18% do not continue beyond their first year; 59% remain to graduate.

Housing: 3200 students can be accommodated in college housing, which includes single-sex and coed dormitories and married-student housing. In addition, there are honors houses, language houses, special-interest houses, and an international house. On-campus housing is available on a first-come, first-served basis. 79% of students commute. Alcohol is not permitted. All students may keep cars.

Activities: 10% of men belong to 15 national fraternities; 10% of women belong to 9 national sororities. There are 300 groups on campus, including art, band, cheerleading, choir, chorale, chorus, computers, dance, drama, drill team, ethnic, film, forensics, gay, honors, international, jazz band, literary magazine, marching band, musical theater, opera, orchestra, pep band, photography, political, professional, radio and TV, religious, social, social service, student government, symphony, and yearbook. Popular campus events include University Day, Family and Friends Weekend, and Martin Luther King Day.

Sports: There are 7 intercollegiate sports for men and 7 for women, and 19 intramural sports for men and 17 for women. Facilities include a 41000-seat stadium, a 10000-seat arena, a swimming pool, several gyms, 15 tennis courts, running tracks, fields for outdoor sports, and a student recreation center with an indoor track, exercise and weight training equipment, a juice bar, and an indoor practice facility for athletic teams.

Disabled Students: 90% of the campus is accessible. Wheelchair ramps, elevators, special parking, specially equipped rest rooms, special class scheduling, lowered drinking fountains, lowered telephones, and a counselor for students with disabilities are available.

Services: Counseling and information services are available, as is tutoring in every subject. There is a reader service for the blind and remedial math and writing. Peer tutors in entry-level undergraduate courses are available through the Academic Learning Services Center. Students may drop in to receive free assistance with math and writing at the center's lab.

Campus Safety and Security: Measures include 24-hour foot and vehicle patrol, self-defense education, escort service, and shuttle buses. There are informal discussions, pamphlets/posters/films, emergency telephones, and lighted pathways/sidewalks.

Programs of Study: UO confers B.A., B.S., B.Arch., B.Ed., B.F.A., B.I.Arch., B.L.A., and B.Mus. degrees. Master's and doctoral degrees are also awarded. Bachelor's degrees are awarded in BIOLOGICAL SCIENCE (biochemistry and biology/biological science), BUSINESS (accounting and business administration and management), COMMUNICATIONS AND THE ARTS (art history and appreciation, ceramic art and design, Chinese, classics, comparative literature, dance, dramatic arts, English, fiber/textiles/weaving, fine arts, French, German, graphic design, Greek, Italian, Japanese, jazz, journalism, Latin, linguistics, metal/jewelry, music, music performance, music theory and composition, painting, printmaking, romance languages and literature, Russian, sculpture, and Spanish), COMPUTER AND PHYSICAL SCIENCE (chemistry, computer science, geology, mathematics, physics, and science), EDUCATION (education and music), ENGINEERING AND ENVIRONMENTAL DESIGN (architecture, environmental science, interior design, and landscape architecture/design), HEALTH PROFESSIONS (exercise science and speech pathology/audiology), SOCIAL SCIENCE (anthropology, Asian/Oriental studies, classical/ancient civilization, economics, ethnic studies, family and community services, geography, history, humanities, international studies, Judaic studies, philosophy, political science/government, psychology, public administration, religion, sociology, and women's studies). Architecture, journalism, and biology are the strongest academically. Business, psychology, and journalism are the largest.

Required: For graduation, at least 180 quarter credits are required of all students, with a minimum GPA of 2.0. A minimum of 36 credits must be in the major, including 24 in upper-division work. Basic courses vary by major, but all students must complete 12 to 16 credits each in the areas of arts and letters, social science, and science, 2 courses in written English, and 2 courses each in multicultural studies.

Special: UO offers cross-registration with other schools in the Oregon University System, study abroad in at least 30 countries, preengineering in conjunction with Lane Community College, an engineering/physics program with Oregon State University, and internships. A B.A.-B.S. degree, dual majors, a 3-2 engineering degree, and pass/fail options are available. There are 24 national honor societies, including Phi Beta Kappa, a freshman honors program, and 54 departmental honors programs.

Faculty/Classroom: 61% of faculty are male; 39%, female. All teach undergraduates. Graduate students teach 17% of introductory courses. The average class size in a regular course is 36.

Admissions: 90% of the 2001-2002 applicants were accepted. The SAT I scores for the 2001-2002 freshman class were: Verbal--25% below 500, 42% between 500 and 599, 27% between 600 and 700, and 6% above 700; Math--26% below 500, 43% between 500 and 599, 27% between 600 and 700, and 4% above 700. There were 10 National Merit finalists. 122 freshmen graduated first in their class.

Requirements: The SAT I or ACT is required. In addition, students should be graduates from standard or accredited high schools and have obtained a score of 30 on the TSWE or 12 on the English portion of the ACT. The GED is accepted. Specific subject requirements include 4 years of English, 3 each of math and social studies, and 2 each of science and a foreign language. Applications are accepted on-line via the school's website. A GPA of 3.0 is required. AP and CLEP credits are accepted.

Procedure: Freshmen are admitted to all sessions. Entrance exams should be taken after October 15 of the junior year and before March of the senior year. Applications should be filed by February 1 for fall entry, October 16 for winter entry, January 18 for spring entry, and April 14 for summer entry, along with a $50 fee. Notification is sent on a rolling basis.

Transfer: 1418 transfer students enrolled in 2001-2002. Students who have completed 36 or more credits with a minimum 2.25 GPA for residents and 2.5 for nonresidents, and whose college record includes passing 1 college-level course each in writing and math with a C- or better, may be admitted as transfer students. An official transcript from each college and university attended must be submitted. Students who have completed 12 to 35 credits must also meet freshman requirements. 45 credits of 180 must be completed at UO.

Visiting: There are regularly scheduled orientations for prospective students, including 2-day programs scheduled for late July that include both advising and telephone registration. There are guides for informal visits and visitors may sit in on classes. To schedule a visit, contact Laura Connell, Ambassador Program or Cora Bennett, Tour Arrangements at (541) 346-1274 or (541) 346-1142.

Financial Aid: In 2001-2002, 38% of all freshmen and 40% of continuing students received some form of financial aid. 22% of freshmen and 25% of continuing students received need-based aid. The average freshman award was $7099. The average financial indebtedness of the 2001 graduate was $19,916. The FAFSA is required. The fall application deadline is March 1.

International Students: There are 926 international students enrolled. The school actively recruits these students. They must score 500 on the written TOEFL or score 6.5 on the International English Language Testing Systems (IELTS) and also take the SAT I or the ACT.

Computers: The mainframes are a DEC 7000 VMS cluster and several Sun SPARC centers. There are approximately 500 networked PCs and terminals available on campus in 6 instructional and open labs, the student union, and various academic departments. All students may access the system 24 hours a day. There are no time limits. The fee is $75 per term. It is strongly recommended that all students have a personal computer.

Graduates: In 2001, 2895 bachelor's degrees were awarded. The most popular majors were business administration (12%), architecture and arts (10%), and journalism/communications (10%). In an average class, 1% graduate in 3 years, 32% in 4 years, and 56% in 5 years. 180 companies recruited on campus in 2000-2001. Of the 2000 graduating class, 20% were enrolled in graduate school within 6 months of graduation and 81% were employed.

Admissions Contact: Martha Pitts, Director, Admissions. A video is available. E-mail: *uoadmit@oregon.uoregon.edu*
Web: *darkwing.uoregon.edu/~admit*

UNIVERSITY OF PORTLAND

Portland, OR 97203 — **B-1** — **(503) 943-7147**
(888) 627-5601; Fax: (503) 943-7315

Full-time: 1011 men, 1435 women	**Faculty:** 172
Part-time: 27 men, 36 women	**Ph.D.s:** 98%
Graduate: 180 men, 257 women	**Student/Faculty:** 14 to 1
Year: semesters, summer session	**Tuition:** $19,350
Application Deadline: February 1	**Room & Board:** $5600

Freshman Class: 2242 applied, 1815 accepted, 653 enrolled
SAT I Verbal/Math: 574/570 — **VERY COMPETITIVE**

The University of Portland, founded in 1901, is an independent institution affiliated with the Roman Catholic Church and offering degree programs in the arts and sciences, business administration, education, engineering, and nursing. There are 5 undergraduate schools and 1 graduate school. In addition to regional accreditation, UP has baccalaureate program accreditation with AACSB, ABET, NASM, NCATE, and NLN. The library contains 380,000 volumes, 524,861 microform items, and 7827 audiovisual forms/CDs, and subscribes to 1446 periodicals. Computerized library services include interlibrary loans and database searching. Special learning facilities include a learning resource center, art gallery, radio station, and observatory. The 155-acre campus is in a suburban area 4 miles north of downtown Portland. Including residence halls, there are 30 buildings.

Student Life: 55% of undergraduates are from out of state, mostly the Northwest. Others are from 41 states, 38 foreign countries, and Canada. 71% are from public schools. 76% are white. The average age of freshmen is 19; all undergraduates, 21. 15% do not continue beyond their first year; 68% remain to graduate.

Housing: 1425 students can be accommodated in college housing, which includes single-sex and coed dormitories and off-campus apartments. On-campus housing is guaranteed for the freshman year only. 62% of students live on campus; of those, 85% remain on campus on weekends. Upperclassmen may keep cars.

Activities: There are no fraternities or sororities. There are 40 groups on campus, including art, band, cheerleading, choir, chorale, chorus, computers, dance, debate, drama, ethnic, honors, international, jazz band, literary magazine, musical theater, newspaper, orchestra, pep band, photography, political, professional, radio and TV, religious, social, social service, student government, and yearbook. Popular campus events include Christmas in April, Casino Night, and Luau.

Sports: There are 7 intercollegiate sports for men and 7 for women, and 20 intramural sports for men and 20 for women. Facilities include weight rooms, an indoor track, a gym, a swimming pool, and a 5000-seat athletic and convocation center. Rental equipment is available for biking and camping activities.

Disabled Students: 95% of the campus is accessible. Wheelchair ramps, elevators, special parking, specially equipped rest rooms, special class scheduling, lowered drinking fountains, and lowered telephones are available.

Services: Counseling and information services are available, as is tutoring in most subjects, including English and math. The faculty is available for individual assistance.

Campus Safety and Security: Measures include 24-hour foot and vehicle patrol, self-defense education, escort service, and informal discussions. There are pamphlets/posters/films, emergency telephones, and lighted pathways/sidewalks.

Programs of Study: UP confers B.A., B.S., B.A.Ed., B.B.A., B.M.Ed., B.S.C.E., B.S.E.E., B.S.E.M., B.S.E.S., B.S.M.E., B.S.N., and B.S.S.E. degrees. Master's degrees are also awarded. Bachelor's degrees are awarded in BIOLOGICAL SCIENCE (biology/biological science), BUSINESS (accounting, banking and finance, international business management, and marketing/retailing/merchandising), COMMUNICATIONS AND THE ARTS (communications, dramatic arts, English, music, Spanish, and theater management), COMPUTER AND PHYSICAL SCIENCE (chemistry, computer science, mathematics, and physics), EDUCATION (elementary, music, and secondary), ENGINEERING AND ENVIRONMENTAL DESIGN (civil engineering, electrical/electronics engineering, engineering, engineering management, environmental science, and mechanical engineering), HEALTH PROFESSIONS (nursing), SOCIAL SCIENCE (criminal justice, history, interdisciplinary studies, philosophy, political science/government, psychology, social work, sociology, and theological studies). Engineering, business, and nursing are the strongest academically. Business administration, education, and nursing are the largest.

Required: To graduate, students must complete 120 credit hours, including at least 24 upper-division classes in the major, with a minimum GPA of 2.0. Required courses include 9 hours each of philosophy and theology, 6 each of science, social sciences, and electives, and 3 each of fine arts, history, math, and literature.

Special: UP offers internships through individual departments, cross-registration with members of the Oregon Independent College Association, dual and interdisciplinary majors, including engineering chemistry and organizational communications, work-study programs, and pass/fail options. Study abroad may be arranged in Japan, Mexico, Australia, Chile, and several European countries. There are 9 national honor societies and a freshman honors program.

Faculty/Classroom: 66% of faculty are male; 34%, female. All teach undergraduates. No introductory courses are taught by graduate students. The average class size in an introductory lecture is 25; in a laboratory, 20; and in a regular course, 20.

Admissions: 81% of the 2001-2002 applicants were accepted. The SAT I scores for the 2001-2002 freshman class were: Math--12% below 500, 46% between 500 and 599, 38% between 600 and 700, and 4% above 700. 72% of the current freshmen were in the top fifth of their class; 96% were in the top two fifths. There were 2 National Merit finalists. 41 freshmen graduated first in their class.

Requirements: The SAT I or ACT is required, with a minimum score of 500 on each section of the SAT I or a composite of 19 on the ACT. Graduation from an accredited secondary school or satisfactory scores on the GED are required. The high school curriculum should include courses in English composition, math, social studies, science, and a foreign language. 2 essays are required, as is a letter of recommendation from the high school counselor or principal. A GPA of 3.0 is required. AP and CLEP credits are accepted. Important factors in the admissions decision are advanced placement or honor courses, recommendations by school officials, and leadership record. Electronic application is available on disk through the Admissions Office or on-line via Common App or other services.

Procedure: Freshmen are admitted to all sessions. Entrance exams should be taken preferably before February 1 but no later than June 1 of the senior year. There are early action, early admissions, and deferred admissions plans. Early acation applications should be filed by October 15; regular applications, by February 1 for fall entry, along with a $45 fee. Notification of early action is sent November 15; regular decision, on a rolling basis.

Transfer: 158 transfer students enrolled in 2001-2002. Applicants with 26 or more credits must have a minimum GPA of 2.5 and be in good standing at their previous school. Students with fewer credits may need to meet freshman requirements. 30 credits of 120 must be completed at UP.

Visiting: There are regularly scheduled orientations for prospective students, including a campus tour, class attendance, and a meeting with an admissions counselor. There are guides for informal visits and visitors may sit in on classes and stay overnight. To schedule a visit, contact the Office of Admissions.

Financial Aid: In 2001-2002, 87% of all freshmen and 82% of continuing students received some form of financial aid. 61% of freshmen and 58% of continuing students received need-based aid. The average freshman award was $14,750. 52% of undergraduates work part time. Average annual earnings from campus work are $2100. The average financial indebtedness of the 2001 graduate was $17,500. The FAFSA and the college's own financial statement are required. The fall application deadline is March 1.

International Students: There are 88 international students enrolled. The school actively recruits these students. They must score 525 on the written TOEFL.

Computers: The mainframe is a Sun UNIX. All students may utilize more than 375 PCs for various projects, with additional terminals designated specifically for computer-intensive majors such as computer science, engineering, and education. Students have access to the Internet and to e-mail. All students may access the system. There are no time limits and no fees. It is strongly recommended that all students have a personal computer.

Graduates: In 2001, 508 bachelor's degrees were awarded. The most popular majors were nursing (12%), marketing/management (9%), and elementary education (7%). In an average class, 60% graduate in 4 years and 68% in 5 years. 85 companies recruited on campus in 2000-2001.

Admissions Contact: James Lyons, Dean of Admissions. A video is available. E-mail: *admissio@up.edu* Web: *www.up.edu*

WARNER PACIFIC COLLEGE

Portland, OR 97215 — **B-1**

(503) 517-1020
(800) 582-7885; Fax: (503) 517-1352

Full-time: 190 men, 360 women	**Faculty:** 39; IIB, --$
Part-time: 30 men, 65 women	**Ph.D.s:** 50%
Graduate: 5 men and women	**Student/Faculty:** 14 to 1
Year: semesters, summer session	**Tuition:** $15,720
Application Deadline: open	**Room & Board:** $4650
Freshman Class: n/av	
SAT I or ACT: required	**LESS COMPETITIVE**

Warner Pacific College, founded in 1937, is a private Christian liberal arts college affiliated with the Church of God. Figures in above capsule are approximate. The library contains 53,000 volumes, 1155 microform items, and 1110 audiovisual forms/CDs, and subscribes to 400 periodicals. Computerized library services include the card catalog, interlibrary loans, and database searching. Special learning facilities include a learning resource center and 2 electron microscopes, and a childhood early learning center. The 14-acre campus is in an urban area 5 miles east of downtown Portland. Including residence halls, there are 30 buildings.

Student Life: 75% of undergraduates are from Oregon. Others are from 18 states, 12 foreign countries, and Canada. 78% are from public schools. 83% are white. 51% claim no religious affiliation; 42% Protestant. The average age of freshmen is 21; all undergraduates, 28. 24% do not continue beyond their first year; 40% remain to graduate.

Housing: 250 students can be accommodated in college housing, which includes single-sex dormitories, on-campus apartments, and married-student housing. On-campus housing is guaranteed for the freshman year only, is available on a first-come, first-served basis, and is available on a lottery system for upperclassmen. Priority is given to out-of-town students. 77% of students commute. Alcohol is not permitted. All students may keep cars.

Activities: There are no fraternities or sororities. There are 6 groups on campus, including art, band, Bible study, choir, chorale, chorus, dance, drama, ethnic, international, jazz band, musical theater, orchestra, photography, professional, religious, social, social service, spiritual growth groups, student government, and yearbook. Popular campus events include Winter Banquet, Spring Banquet, and Western Fling.

Sports: There are 2 intercollegiate sports for men and 2 for women, and 10 intramural sports for men and 10 for women. Facilities include a gym, a weight-training room, and hiking trails.

Disabled Students: 75% of the campus is accessible. Wheelchair ramps, special parking, specially equipped rest rooms, special class scheduling, and personalized care and services are available.

Services: Counseling and information services are available, as is tutoring in most subjects. There is remedial math, reading, and writing. and testing and study skills workshops.

Campus Safety and Security: Measures include 24-hour foot and vehicle patrol, self-defense education, escort service, and informal discussions. There are pamphlets/posters/films and lighted pathways/sidewalks.

Programs of Study: Warner Pacific confers B.A. and B.S degrees. Associate and master's degrees are also awarded. Bachelor's degrees are awarded in BIOLOGICAL SCIENCE (biology/biological science), BUSINESS (business administration and management), COMMUNICATIONS AND THE ARTS (English, music, and music theory and composition), COMPUTER AND PHYSICAL SCIENCE (physical sciences and science), EDUCATION (music and physical), SOCIAL SCIENCE (American studies, history, human development, liberal arts/general studies, ministries, religious music, social science, social work, and sociology). Biological science and business administration are the strongest academically. Business administration, human development, and music education are the largest.

Required: To graduate, students must complete 124 credits with a minimum GPA of 2.0. All students must take a core curriculum of 42 credits, consisting of 15 hours in humanities, 9 in communication, 7 to 9 in religion, 6 in social science, 4 in fine arts, and 3 each in science and health and phys ed.

Special: Warner Pacific offers cross-registration through OICA, a Washington semester, a co-op nursing program, accelerated degree programs in human development and business administration, and study abroad in Latin America, the Middle East, and Russia. Internships, work-study programs, double majors, individualized majors, independent study credit for life and military experience, and pass/fail options are available.

Faculty/Classroom: 62% of faculty are male; 38%, female. All teach undergraduates and 40% do research. The average class size in an introductory lecture is 15; in a laboratory, 10; and in a regular course, 15.

Requirements: The SAT I or ACT is required. In addition, applicants must be graduates of an accredited secondary school. The GED is accepted. High school preparation should include 4 years of English, 3 of social studies, and 2 each of math and lab science. A GPA of 2.0 is required. AP and CLEP credits are accepted. Important factors in the admissions decision are evidence of special talent, leadership record, and advanced placement or honor courses.

Procedure: Freshmen are admitted to all sessions. Entrance exams should be taken no later than the early fall of the senior year. There are early admissions and deferred admissions plans. Application deadlines are open. Application fee is $25.

Transfer: 56 transfer students enrolled in a recent year. Applicants must provide transcripts from their previous college. A minimum GPA of 2.0 is required. 30 credits of 124 must be completed at Warner Pacific.

Visiting: There are regularly scheduled orientations for prospective students, including 3 visitation weekends, academic fairs, scholarship days, and a retreat. There are guides for informal visits and visitors may sit in on classes and stay overnight. To schedule a visit, contact Office of Admissions and Financial Aid.

Financial Aid: In a recent year, all freshmen and 86% of continuing students received some form of financial aid. 92% of freshmen and 67% of continuing students received need-based aid. The average freshman award was $10,390. Of that total, scholarships or need-based grants averaged $2470; loans averaged $3003; and work contracts averaged $3509. Average annual earnings from campus work are $2000. Warner Pacific is a member of CSS. The FAFSA is required. The fall application deadline is April 15.

International Students: There were 17 international students enrolled in a recent year. The school actively recruits these students. They must score 525 on the written TOEFL and also take the college's own test.

Computers: The mainframes are an AS400 and a 9404-200. The library houses a 24-hour computer lab and all campus housing has networking for PCs. All students may access the system 24 hours a day. There are no time limits and no fees. It is strongly recommended that all students have a personal computer.

Graduates: In a recent year, 151 bachelor's degrees were awarded. The most popular majors were psychology (48%), business (34%), and religion (5%). In an average class, 2% graduate in 3 years, 29% in 4 years, 8% in 5 years, and 2% in 6 years.

Admissions Contact: Rick Johnsen, Director of Admissions and Financial Aid. E-mail: *admiss@warnerpacific.edu*
Web: *www.warnerpacific.edu*

WESTERN BAPTIST COLLEGE

Salem, OR 97301-9392 — **B-2**

(503) 375-7005
(800) 845-3005; Fax: (503) 585-4316

Full-time: 263 men, 396 women	**Faculty:** 33; IIB, --$	
Part-time: 27 men, 39 women	**Ph.D.s:** 30%	
Graduate: none	**Student/Faculty:** 20 to 1	
Year: semesters, summer session	**Tuition:** $14,360	
Application Deadline: August 1	**Room & Board:** $5340	
Freshman Class: n/av		
SAT I Verbal/Math: 540/543	**ACT:** 22	**COMPETITIVE+**

Western Baptist College, founded in 1935, is a Christian liberal arts institution offering degrees in biblical-theological studies, business administration, education, humanities, math, phys ed, social sciences, psychology, intercultural studies, and youth work. The library contains 82,000 volumes, 4100 microform items, and 4532 audiovisual forms/CDs, and subscribes to 552 periodicals. Computerized library services include the card catalog, interlibrary loans, and database searching. Special learning facilities include a learning resource center and an archeological museum. The 107-acre campus is in a suburban area in Salem. Including residence halls, there are 20 buildings.

Student Life: 67% of undergraduates are from Oregon. Others are from 18 states, 6 foreign countries, and Canada. 72% are from public schools. 94% are white. All are Protestant. The average age of freshmen is 19; all undergraduates, 22. 22% do not continue beyond their first year; 51% remain to graduate.

Housing: 360 students can be accommodated in college housing, which includes single-sex dormitories, on-campus apartments, and married-student housing. On-campus housing is guaranteed for the freshman year only and is available on a first-come, first-served basis. Priority is given to out-of-town students. 52% of students commute. Alcohol is not permitted. All students may keep cars.

Activities: There are no fraternities or sororities. There are 16 groups on campus, including band, cheerleading, choir, chorale, chorus, drama, honors, literary magazine, newspaper, orchestra, pep band, religious, social, social service, student government, and yearbook. Popular campus events include Western Weekends, Sports Weekends, and chapel services.

Sports: There are 3 intercollegiate sports for men and 3 for women, and 3 intramural sports for men and 3 for women. Facilities include a sports center with a gym and soccer and baseball fields.

Disabled Students: 95% of the campus is accessible. Elevators, special parking, and specially equipped rest rooms are available.

Services: Counseling and information services are available, as is tutoring in some subjects, as needed.

Campus Safety and Security: Measures include escort service, informal discussions, emergency telephones, and lighted pathways/sidewalks. There are campus security and vehicle patrols.

Programs of Study: Western confers B.A., B.S., and Th.B. degrees. Associate degrees are also awarded. Bachelor's degrees are awarded in BUSINESS (accounting, banking and finance, and business administration and management), COMMUNICATIONS AND THE ARTS (communications, English, and music), COMPUTER AND PHYSICAL SCIENCE (computer science and mathematics), EDUCATION (education and physical), HEALTH PROFESSIONS (health science), SOCIAL SCIENCE (biblical studies, crosscultural studies, history, humanities, ministries, psychology, and social science). Education, psychology, and business are the largest.

Required: To graduate, students must complete 128 credits, with 40 to 64 in the major. The minimum required GPA is 2.0 for most programs; the education major requires a 3.0 GPA. The general education core consists of 68 credits. Courses must be taken in the Bible, humanities, social sciences, math, science, and phys ed.

Special: Western offers a preseminary co-op program, cross-registration with Oregon Independent Colleges, study abroad in 4 countries, a Washington semester, accelerated programs in management and communication and in family studies, and internships and student-designed majors with adviser approval. There is a freshman honors program and 3 departmental honors programs.

Faculty/Classroom: 77% of faculty are male; 23%, female. All teach undergraduates. The average class size in an introductory lecture is 38; in a laboratory, 15; and in a regular course, 25.

Admissions: 76% of the 2001-2002 applicants were accepted. The SAT I scores for the 2001-2002 freshman class were: Verbal--23% below 500, 49% between 500 and 599, 26% between 600 and 700, and 2% above 700; Math--31% below 500, 42% between 500 and 599, 23% between 600 and 700, and 4% above 700. The ACT scores were 31% below 21, 23% between 21 and 23, 31% between 24 and 26, and 15% between 27 and 28. 30% of the current freshmen were in the top fifth of their class; 69% were in the top two fifths.

Requirements: The SAT I or ACT is required, as is an essay. A GPA of 2.5 is required. AP and CLEP credits are accepted. Important factors in the admissions decision are extracurricular activities record, leadership record, and evidence of special talent. Applications are accepted on computer disk and on-line via Western's web site.

Procedure: Freshmen are admitted fall and spring. Applications should be filed by August 1 for fall entry and December 1 for spring entry, along with a $35 fee. Notification is sent on a rolling basis.

Transfer: 120 transfer students enrolled in 2001-2002. Applicants are required to have a minimum 2.0 cumulative college GPA and submit the college transcript and 3 references. 30 credits of 128 must be completed at Western.

Visiting: There are regularly scheduled orientations for prospective students, including scheduled weekend visits and Western Daze. There are guides for informal visits and visitors may sit in on classes and stay overnight. To schedule a visit, contact the Admissions Office at (503) 581-8600.

Financial Aid: In 2001-2002, 98% of all students received some form of financial aid. 87% of continuing students received need-based aid. The average freshman award was $12,505. Of that total, scholarships or need-based grants averaged $7900 ($21,000 maximum); loans averaged $4700 ($21,000 maximum); and work contracts averaged $300 ($3000 maximum). 30% of undergraduates work part time. Average annual earnings from campus work are $1000. The average financial indebtedness of the 2001 graduate was $14,000. The FAFSA is required. The fall application deadline is March 1.

International Students: There are 8 international students enrolled. They must score 500 on the written TOEFL and also take the SAT I or the ACT.

Computers: The 6 labs contain 35 PCs, and students have campuswide e-mail and Internet access on their personal computers. All students may access the system 24 hours per day. There are no time limits and no fees. It is strongly recommended that all students have a personal computer; students in business information systems and computer science must have one.

Graduates: In 2001, 154 bachelor's degrees were awarded. The most popular majors were business (31%), pyschology (21%), and education (16%). In an average class, 2% graduate in 3 years, 46% in 4 years, 50% in 5 years, and 50% in 6 years.

Admissions Contact: Daren Milionis, Dean of Admissions.
E-mail: *admissions@wbc.edu* Web: *www.wbc.edu*

WESTERN OREGON UNIVERSITY B-2

Monmouth, OR 97361 (503) 838-8211
(877) 877-1593; Fax: (503) 838-8067

Full-time: 1536 men, 2442 women	**Faculty:** 168; IIA, --$
Part-time: 179 men, 182 women	**Ph.D.s:** 86%
Graduate: 153 men, 386 women	**Student/Faculty:** 24 to 1
Year: quarters, summer session	**Tuition:** $3660 ($11,478)
Application Deadline: open	**Room & Board:** $5169
Freshman Class: 1585 applied, 1453 accepted, 843 enrolled	
SAT I Verbal/Math: 495/485	**ACT:** 21 **COMPETITIVE**

Western Oregon University, founded in 1856, is a publicly funded institution and a member of the Oregon University System. WOU offers undergraduate programs through the Colleges of Education and Liberal Arts and Sciences. There are 2 undergraduate schools and 1 graduate school. In addition to regional accreditation, WOU has baccalaureate program accreditation with NASM and NCATE. The library contains 180,588 volumes, 658,822 microform items, and 2539 audiovisual forms/CDs, and subscribes to 1250 periodicals. Computerized library services include the card catalog, interlibrary loans, and database searching. Special learning facilities include a learning resource center, art gallery, TV station, and the Paul Jensen Arctic Museum. The 157-acre campus is in a rural area 15 miles west of Salem. Including residence halls, there are 36 buildings.

Student Life: 91% of undergraduates are from Oregon. Others are from 24 states, 18 foreign countries, and Canada. 99% are from public schools. 83% are white. The average age of freshmen is 19; all undergraduates, 22. 30% do not continue beyond their first year; 52% remain to graduate.

Housing: 1050 students can be accommodated in college housing, which includes coed dormitories, married-student housing, and special-interest communities. On-campus housing is guaranteed for the freshman year only and is available on a first-come, first-served basis. 80% of students commute. Alcohol is not permitted. All students may keep cars.

Activities: There are no fraternities or sororities. There are 50 groups on campus, including art, band, cheerleading, chess, choir, chorale, chorus, computers, dance, debate, drama, drill team, ethnic, gay, honors, international, jazz band, literary magazine, marching band, model U.N., musical theater, orchestra, political, radio and TV, religious, social, social service, student government, and yearbook. Popular campus events include Annual Christmas Tree Lighting, Alcohol Awareness Week, and Family Day.

Sports: There are 5 intercollegiate sports for men and 6 for women, and 25 intramural sports for men and 25 for women. Facilities include a sports field, a phys ed building, a swimming pool, a weight room, indoor/outdoor tennis courts, handball and racquetball courts, a dance studio, archery facilities, and baseball, softball, and soccer fields.

Disabled Students: 90% of the campus is accessible. Wheelchair ramps, elevators, special parking, specially equipped rest rooms, special class scheduling, lowered drinking fountains, lowered telephones, and the Regional Resource Center of Deafness are available.

Services: Counseling and information services are available, as is tutoring in most subjects. There is a reader service for the blind, and remedial math, reading, and writing. WOU offers a student support and services program for first-generation, low-income, and physically disabled students.

Campus Safety and Security: Measures include 24-hour foot and vehicle patrol, self-defense education, escort service, and informal discussions. There are pamphlets/posters/films, emergency telephones, and lighted pathways/sidewalks.

Programs of Study: WOU confers B.A., B.S., and B.Mus. degrees. Associate and master's degrees are also awarded. Bachelor's degrees are awarded in BIOLOGICAL SCIENCE (biology/biological science), BUSINESS (business administration and management), COMMUNICATIONS AND THE ARTS (American Sign Language, art, dance, dramatic arts, English, music, Spanish, and speech/debate/rhetoric), COMPUTER AND PHYSICAL SCIENCE (chemistry, computer science, earth science, information sciences and systems, mathematics, and natural sciences), EDUCATION (education and health), SOCIAL SCIENCE (anthropology, corrections, economics, fire protection, geography, history, humanities, interdisciplinary studies, international studies, interpreter for the deaf, law enforcement and corrections, philosophy, political science/government, psychology, public administration, social science, and sociology). Education, business, and psychology are the strongest academically. Education, criminal justice, and psychology are the largest.

Required: To graduate, students must complete a total of 180 quarter hours with a minimum GPA of 2.0. Between 45 and 120 quarter hours are required in the major. The 55-quarter-hour liberal arts core curriculum includes 12 credits each of lab science and social sciences, 9 each of literature and fine arts, 4 of phys ed, and 3 each of philosophy, speech, and writing. Students must also satisfy graduation requirements in math, computer science or technology, writing-intensive, course work, and cultural diversity.

Special: Most academic majors in liberal arts and sciences offer a B.A.-B.S degree option. Dual majors, internships, study abroad through international exchange programs and the Oregon University System, and student-designed majors in interdisciplinary studies are available. Nondegree study and pass/fail options are possible. There are 3 national honor societies and a freshman honors program.

Faculty/Classroom: 58% of faculty are male; 42%, female. All teach undergraduates. Graduate students teach 1% of introductory courses. The average class size in an introductory lecture is 50; in a laboratory, 15; and in a regular course, 25.

Admissions: 92% of the 2001-2002 applicants were accepted. The SAT I scores for the 2001-2002 freshman class were: Verbal--55% below 500, 33% between 500 and 599, 11% between 600 and 700, and 1% above 700; Math--52% below 500, 38% between 500 and 599, 9% between 600 and 700, and 1% above 700. The ACT scores were 23% below 21, 31% between 21 and 23, 25% between 24 and 26, 19% between 27 and 28, and 2% above 28. 39% of the current freshmen were in the top fifth of their class; 71% were in the top two fifths.

Requirements: The SAT I or ACT is required. In addition, graduation from an accredited secondary school or satisfactory scores on the GED are required. Students must have 14 academic credits or Carnegie units. High school courses must include 4 years of English, 3 each of math and social studies, and 2 each of science and a foreign language. A GPA of 2.75 is required. AP and CLEP credits are accepted. Important factors in the admissions decision are evidence of special talent, recommendations by alumni, and parents or siblings attending the school. Applications are accepted on-line.

Procedure: Freshmen are admitted to all sessions. Entrance exams should be taken during the junior or senior year. Application deadlines are open. The application fee is $50. Notification is sent on a rolling basis.

Transfer: 509 transfer students enrolled in 2001-2002. Applicants must have a minimum GPA of 2.0. Applicants with fewer than 24 quarter hours must also meet freshman admission requirements. 45 credits of 180 must be completed at WOU.

Visiting: There are regularly scheduled orientations for prospective students, consisting of a 1-day program for students and a parent program; all newly admitted students must make arrangements to register during orientation in July to reserve their enrollment slot. There are guides for informal visits and visitors may sit in on classes. To schedule a visit, contact the Admissions Office.

Financial Aid: In 2001-2002, 80% of all freshmen and 79% of continuing students received some form of financial aid. 36% of freshmen and 79% of continuing students received need-based aid. The average freshman award was $5739. Of that total, scholarships or need-based grants averaged $3517 ($10,897 maximum); loans averaged $3208 ($7525 maximum); and work contracts averaged $967 ($1900 maximum). 22% of undergraduates work part time. Average annual earnings from campus work are $1578. The average financial indebtedness of the 2001 graduate was $16,383. The FAFSA is required. The fall application deadline is March 1.

International Students: There are 68 international students enrolled. The school actively recruits these students. They must score 520 on the written TOEFL or 190 on the electronic version or take the MELAB.

Computers: The mainframe is a Sun 420R. There are PC and Mac labs located in the instructional technology center, natural science building, university center, education building, and library. All students may access the system. There are no time limits and no fees.

Graduates: In 2001, 643 bachelor's degrees were awarded. The most popular majors were business (15%), psychology (13%), and corrections/law enforcement (13%). In an average class, 43% graduate in 4 years, 47% in 5 years, and 57% in 6 years. 99 companies recruited on campus in 2000-2001.

Admissions Contact: Rob Kuidt, Director of Admissions.
E-mail: *wolfgram@wou.edu* Web: *www.wou.edu*

WILLAMETTE UNIVERSITY — B-2

Salem, OR 97301 — (503) 370-6303
(877) 542-2787; Fax: (503) 375-5363

Full-time: 734 men, 925 women	**Faculty:** 134
Part-time: 47 men, 67 women	**Ph.D.s:** 93%
Graduate: 345 men, 318 women	**Student/Faculty:** 12 to 1
Year: semesters	**Tuition:** $23,272
Application Deadline: February 1	**Room & Board:** $6150
Freshman Class: 1634 applied, 1366 accepted, 476 enrolled	
SAT I Verbal/Math: 610/610	**ACT:** 27 **VERY COMPETITIVE+**

Willamette University, founded in 1842, is an independent liberal arts institution. There are 3 graduate schools. In addition to regional accreditation, Willamette has baccalaureate program accreditation with NASM. The 2 libraries contain 329,000 volumes, 328,000 microform items, and 9600 audiovisual forms/CDs, and subscribe to 1400 periodicals. Computerized library services include the card catalog, interlibrary loans, and database searching. Special learning facilities include a learning resource center, art gallery, natural history museum, radio station, botanical and Japanese gardens, multimedia center, and "smart" classrooms. The 72-acre campus is in an urban area 50 minutes south of Portland. Including residence halls, there are 44 buildings.

Student Life: 60% of undergraduates are from out of state, mostly the West. Others are from 39 states, 23 foreign countries, and Canada. 82% are from public schools. 63% are white. 43% are Protestant; 37% claim no religious affiliation; 14% are Catholic. The average age of freshmen is 18; all undergraduates, 20. 12% do not continue beyond their first year; 76% remain to graduate.

Housing: 1312 students can be accommodated in college housing, which includes single-sex and coed dormitories, on-campus apartments, fraternity houses, and sorority houses. In addition, there are language houses, special-interest houses, a 24-hour quiet-hour (intensive study) dorm, and substance-free options. On-campus housing is available on a lottery system for upperclassmen. 74% of students live on campus; of those, 64% remain on campus on weekends. All students may keep cars.

Activities: 28% of men belong to 5 national fraternities; 22% of women belong to 3 national sororities. There are 78 groups on campus, including art, band, cheerleading, chess, choir, chorale, chorus, computers, dance, debate, drama, ethnic, film, forensics, gay, honors, international, jazz band, literary magazine, musical theater, newspaper, opera, orchestra, pep band, photography, political, professional, radio and TV, religious, social, social service, student government, symphony, and yearbook. Popular campus events include International Extravaganza, Black Tie Affair, and Hawaiian Luau.

Sports: There are 10 intercollegiate sports for men and 10 for women, and 17 intramural sports for men and 17 for women. Facilities include a phys ed and recreation center, a 4000-seat football stadium, a 3000-seat indoor gym and 2 other gyms, a 1200-seat auditorium, a baseball stadium, a soccer field, an all-weather track, a track building, a mini-Olympic-size indoor swimming pool, an outdoor swimming pool, 3 indoor and 10 outdoor tennis courts, handball/racquetball courts, weight training facilities, and practice fields.

Disabled Students: 90% of the campus is accessible. Wheelchair ramps, elevators, special parking, specially equipped rest rooms, special class scheduling, lowered drinking fountains, lowered telephones, special equipment, readers, and braille services are available.

Services: Counseling and information services are available, as is tutoring in most subjects. There is a reader service for the blind. Therapists are available for students on an individual need basis.

Campus Safety and Security: Measures include 24-hour foot and vehicle patrol, self-defense education, escort service, and informal discussions. There are pamphlets/posters/films, emergency telephones, lighted pathways/sidewalks, formal programs and education, and a weekly published campus safety report.

Programs of Study: Willamette confers B.A., B.S., and B.M. degrees. Master's and doctoral degrees are also awarded. Bachelor's degrees are awarded in BIOLOGICAL SCIENCE (biology/biological science), COMMUNICATIONS AND THE ARTS (art history and appreciation, comparative literature, dramatic arts, English, French, German, music, music performance, music theory and composition, Spanish, and studio art), COMPUTER AND PHYSICAL SCIENCE (chemistry, computer science, mathematics, and physics), EDUCATION (music), ENGINEERING AND ENVIRONMENTAL DESIGN (environmental science), HEALTH PROFESSIONS (exercise science), SOCIAL SCIENCE (American studies, anthropology, classical/ancient civilization, economics, history, humanities, international studies, Japanese studies, Latin American studies, philosophy, political science/government, psychology, religion, and sociology). Social sciences, natural science, and humanities are the strongest academically. Social sciences, humanities, and fine arts are the largest.

Required: To graduate, students must complete a total of 124 semester hours, including a minimum of 32 in the major, with a minimum GPA of 2.0. All students must complete general education requirements in fine arts, humanities, literature, foreign language, interdisciplinary courses, natural sciences, and social sciences, and meet math and English proficiency levels. Freshmen are required to take a World Views seminar. Seniors are required to complete a senior thesis or other project in their major.

Special: Willamette offers internships with the state and city governments, a Chicago semester, a Washington semester, and a 3-2 engineering degree with Washington University, University of Southern California, and Columbia University. Nondegree study, B.A.-B.S. degrees, dual majors, work-study programs with numerous employers in the Salem area and at the university, and credit/no-credit options are also available. Study-abroad programs are available in 14 countries. There are 3-2 degrees in management, forestry, and computer science. There are 11 national honor societies, including Phi Beta Kappa.

Faculty/Classroom: 61% of faculty are male; 39%, female. All both teach and do research. No introductory courses are taught by graduate students. The average class size in an introductory lecture is 16; in a laboratory, 20; and in a regular course, 15.

Admissions: 84% of the 2001-2002 applicants were accepted. The SAT I scores for the 2001-2002 freshman class were: Verbal--6% below 500, 32% between 500 and 599, 48% between 600 and 700, and 14% above 700; Math--5% below 500, 32% between 500 and 599, 49% between 600 and 700, and 14% above 700. The ACT scores were 7% below 21, 15% between 21 and 23, 26% between 24 and 26, 23% between 27 and 28, and 29% above 28. 71% of the current freshmen were in the top fifth of their class; 90% were in the top two fifths. There were 10 National Merit finalists and 23 semifinalists. 46 freshmen graduated first in their class.

Requirements: The SAT I or ACT is required. In addition, graduation from an accredited secondary school or satisfactory scores on the GED are required. Institutional preferences include 4 years each of English and math, and 3 years each of foreign language, lab science, and social studies or history. 2 essays are required, and an interview is recommended. Portfolios or auditions are recommended for art and music students. A GPA of 2.0 is required. AP credits are accepted. Important factors in the admissions decision are advanced placement or honor courses and recommendations by school officials. Applications are accepted on computer disk and on-line via Common App, CollegeNET, and Embark.

Procedure: Freshmen are admitted fall and spring. Entrance exams should be taken in November. There are early action, early admissions, and deferred admissions plans. Early action applications should be filed by December 1; regular applications, by February 1 for fall entry and November 1 for spring entry. The fall 2001 application fee was $50. Notification of early action is sent January 15; regular decision, April 1. 3% of all applicants are on a waiting list; 6 were accepted in 2001.

Transfer: 45 transfer students enrolled in 2001-2002. Students must submit transcripts for all college and high school courses. A minimum GPA of 2.0 is required, as is a Transfer Reference Form (recommendation form). 60 credits of 124 must be completed at Willamette.

Visiting: There are regularly scheduled orientations for prospective students, consisting of fall and spring campus preview days, tours, and faculty and student presentations. There are guides for informal visits and visitors may sit in on classes and stay overnight. To schedule a visit, contact Martha Cripe at *libarts@willamette.edu*

Financial Aid: In 2001-2002, 87% of all freshmen and 85% of continuing students received some form of financial aid. 51% of freshmen and 52% of continuing students received need-based aid. Scholarships or need-based grants averaged $11,075 ($21,700 maximum); loans averaged $4430 ($5625 maximum); and work contracts averaged $1625 ($2000 maximum). 55% of undergraduates work part time. Average annual earnings from campus work are $1400. The average financial indebtedness of the 2001 graduate was $16,800. Willamette is a member of CSS. The FAFSA is required. Students applying for admission under the early action program must also file the CSS Profile by December 1. The regular fall application deadline is February 1.

International Students: The school actively recruits these students. They must score 550 on the written TOEFL and also take the ELPT (English Language Placement Test), as well as the SAT I or the ACT.

Computers: The mainframe is a Sun Enterprise 2. More than 250 PCs and Macs are available for student use in the computer lab, library, and science building. Students may access the mainframe from their residence hall rooms through a network hookup. All students may access the system 24 hours per day. There are no time limits and no fees.

Graduates: In 2001, 386 bachelor's degrees were awarded. The most popular majors were economics (14%), biology (12%), and English (9%). In an average class, 1% graduate in 3 years, 73% in 4 years, and 79% in 5 years, and 79% in 6 years. 100 companies recruited on campus in 2000-2001. Of the 2000 graduating class, 24% were enrolled in graduate school within 6 months of graduation and 69% were employed.

Admissions Contact: Robin Brown, Vice President, Enrollment.
E-mail: *undergrad-admission@willamette.edu*
Web: *http://www.willamette.edu*

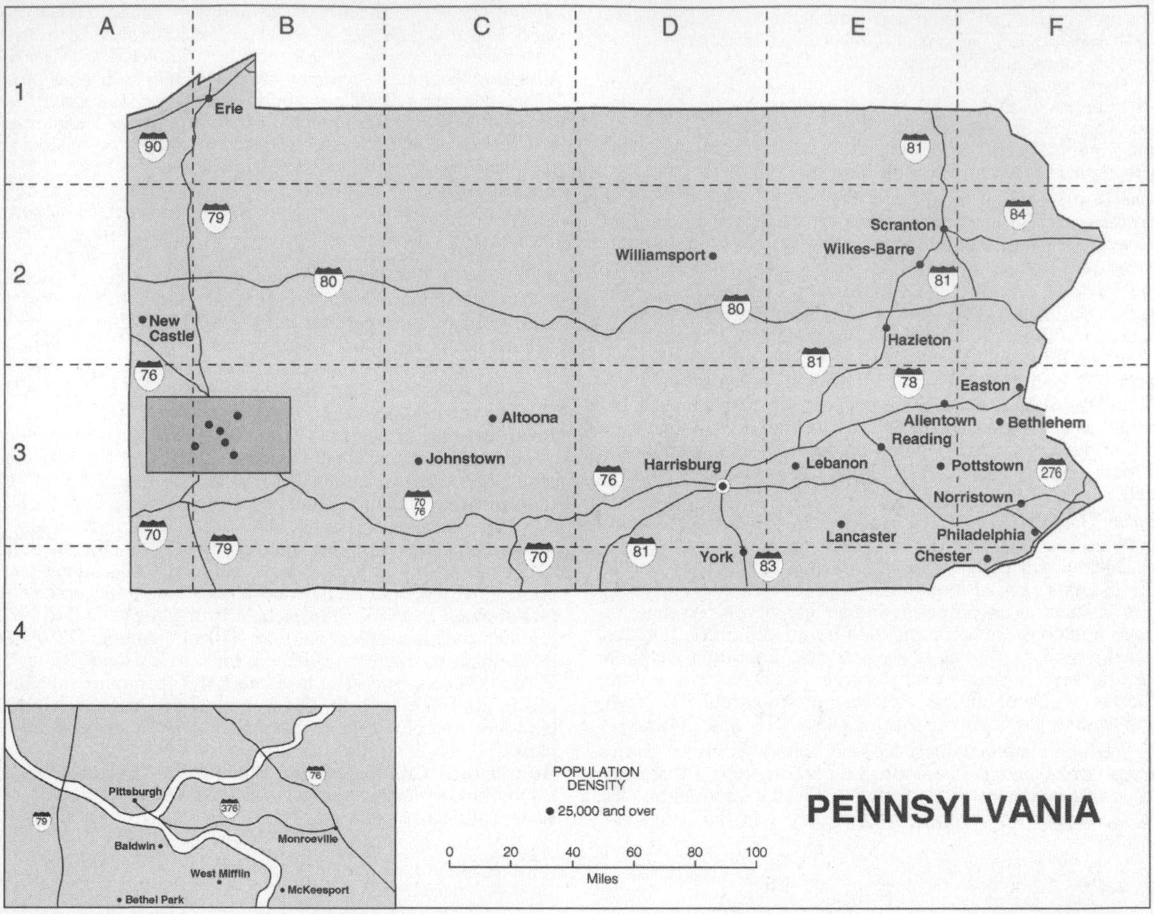

ALBRIGHT COLLEGE

Reading, PA 19612-5234 — E-3

(610) 921-7512

(800) 252-1856; Fax: (610) 921-7294

Full-time: 740 men, 977 women
Part-time: 32 men, 60 women
Graduate: none
Year: 4-1-4, summer session
Application Deadline: open
Freshman Class: 2502 applied, 1827 accepted, 400 enrolled
SAT I Verbal/Math: 510/510
Faculty: 88; IIB, -$
Ph.D.s: 88%
Student/Faculty: 20 to 1
Tuition: $21,300
Room & Board: $6342
COMPETITIVE

Albright College, founded in 1856, is a private liberal arts institution affiliated with the United Methodist Church. The 2 libraries contain 212,888 volumes, 74,257 microform items, and 29,187 audiovisual forms/CDs, and subscribe to 750 periodicals. Computerized library services include the card catalog, interlibrary loans, and database searching. Special learning facilities include a learning resource center, art gallery, radio station, multicultural center, and centers for women and child development. The 110-acre campus is in a suburban area 55 miles west of Philadelphia. Including residence halls, there are 36 buildings.

Student Life: 68% of undergraduates are from Pennsylvania. Others are from 25 states and 20 foreign countries. 73% are from public schools. 82% are white. 46% claim no religious affiliation; 29% are Catholic; 20% Protestant. The average age of freshmen is 18; all undergraduates, 20. 26% do not continue beyond their first year; 63% remain to graduate.

Housing: 1050 students can be accommodated in college housing, which includes single-sex and coed dormitories and on-campus apartments. In addition, there are honors houses and special-interest houses. On-campus housing is guaranteed for all 4 years. 69% of students live on campus; of those, 95% remain on campus on weekends. Upperclassmen may keep cars.

Activities: 28% of men belong to 3 national fraternities; 32% of women belong to 3 national sororities. There are 70 groups on campus, including band, cheerleading, chess, choir, chorus, computers, dance, drama, ethnic, film, honors, international, jazz band, literary magazine, musical theater, newspaper, photography, political, professional, radio and TV, religious, social, social service, student government, and yearbook. Popular campus events include Dance Marathon, Greek Weekend, and Spring Fever Weekend.

Sports: There are 11 intercollegiate sports for men and 11 for women, and 3 intramural sports for men and 4 for women. Facilities include a 7500-seat stadium, baseball and soccer fields, a fitness center, a weight room, indoor and outdoor tracks, a bowling alley, a swimming pool, and racquetball courts.

Disabled Students: 75% of the campus is accessible. Wheelchair ramps, elevators, special parking, specially equipped rest rooms, and special class scheduling are available.

Services: Counseling and information services are available, as is tutoring in most subjects. There is a reader service for the blind, an academic learning center, a writing center, and an ESL program.

Campus Safety and Security: Measures include 24-hour foot and vehicle patrol, self-defense education, escort service, and shuttle buses. There are informal discussions, pamphlets/posters/films, emergency telephones, lighted pathways/sidewalks, and a Comprehensive Crisis Action Plan.

Programs of Study: Albright confers B.A. and B.S. degrees. Bachelor's degrees are awarded in BIOLOGICAL SCIENCE (biochemistry and biology/biological science), BUSINESS (accounting, business administration and management, and fashion merchandising), COMMUNICATIONS AND THE ARTS (art, communications, dramatic arts, English, French, and Spanish), COMPUTER AND PHYSICAL SCIENCE (chemistry, computer science, information sciences and systems, mathematics, and physics), EDUCATION (elementary, secondary, and special), ENGINEERING AND ENVIRONMENTAL DESIGN (environmental science), SOCIAL SCIENCE (American studies, child care/child and family studies, criminal justice, economics, history, Latin American studies, philosophy, political science/government, psychobiology, psychology, religion, and textiles and clothing). Biology, psychology, and business are the largest.

Required: To graduate, students must complete 32 courses (128 credits), including 13 to 14 courses in the major, with a minimum GPA of 2.0. All students take 1 interdisciplinary course, and they must fulfill the cultural experience requirement. General studies requirements include a total of 11 to 15 courses in English composition, a foreign language, natural science, quantitative reasoning, social science, the arts, and humanities (literature, history, philosophy, and religion).

Special: Co-op programs are available in forestry, environmental studies, and natural resources with Duke University and the University of Michigan. Albright offers credit and noncredit internships, a Washington semester, an accelerated degree program, cross-registration, dual majors, student-designed majors, nondegree study, and pass/fail options. Study abroad may be arranged in any country. There are 11 national honor societies, a freshman honors program, and honors programs in all departments.

Faculty/Classroom: 52% of faculty are male; 48%, female. All teach undergraduates. The average class size in an introductory lecture is 25; in a laboratory, 15; and in a regular course, 18.

Admissions: 73% of the 2001-2002 applicants were accepted. The SAT I scores for the 2001-2002 freshman class were: Verbal--40% below 500, 44% between 500 and 599, 15% between 600 and 700, and 1% above 700; Math--41% below 500, 44% between 500 and 599, and 15% between 600 and 700. 35% of the current freshmen were in the top fifth of their class; 62% were in the top two fifths. 2 freshmen graduated first in their class.

Requirements: The SAT I is required. In addition, graduation from an accredited secondary school or satisfactory scores on the GED are required. Students must have a total of 16 Carnegie units, including 4 years of English, 3 in science, including 1 lab, 2 years each of a foreign language, math, and social studies, and 3 electives in college-preparatory subjects. An essay is required, and an interview highly recommended. AP and CLEP credits are accepted. Important factors in the admissions decision are advanced placement or honor courses, leadership record, and recommendations by school officials. The school accepts applications on computer disk or on-line via Common App.

Procedure: Freshmen are admitted fall, spring, and summer. Entrance exams should be taken during the spring of the junior year or the fall of the senior year. There are early admissions and deferred admissions plans. Application deadlines are open. The fall 2001 application fee was $25. Notification is sent on a rolling basis.

Transfer: 29 transfer students enrolled in 2001-2002. Students must have a minimum GPA of 2.5 and be in good standing. 64 credits of 128 must be completed at Albright.

Visiting: There are regularly scheduled orientations for prospective students, including an interview with a counselor and a tour of the campus with a currently enrolled student. There are guides for informal visits and visitors may sit in on classes and stay overnight. To schedule a visit, contact the Admissions Office.

Financial Aid: In 2001-2002, 95% of all freshmen and 90% of continuing students received some form of financial aid. 88% of all students received need-based aid. The average freshman award was $21,963. Of that total, scholarships or need-based grants averaged $14,092 ($20,550 maximum); loans averaged $6865 ($8625 maximum); and work contracts averaged $1282 ($1500 maximum). 35% of undergraduates work part time. Average annual earnings from campus work are $903. The average financial indebtedness of the 2001 graduate was $23,000. Albright is a member of CSS. The FAFSA is required. The fall application deadline is March 1.

International Students: There are 71 international students enrolled. The school actively recruits these students. They must take the SAT I or the ACT, or they can take the TOEFL in lieu of the SAT I.

Computers: The mainframe is a DEC MicroVAX II. Students do not access our mainframe system. Instead, there are approximately 150 workstations dedicated for student use, located across campus, networked to provide access to client/server systems. All students may access the system 24 hours per day. There are no time limits. The fee is $200 per year. It is strongly recommended that all students have a personal computer, preferably an Intel Pentium PC.

Graduates: In 2001, 306 bachelor's degrees were awarded. The most popular majors were business administration (20%), psychology/psychobiology (14%), and biology/biochemistry (6%). In an average class, 1% graduate in 3 years, 54% in 4 years, 62% in 5 years, and 63% in 6 years. 68 companies recruited on campus in 2000-2001. Of the 2000 graduating class, 23% were enrolled in graduate school within 6 months of graduation and 98% were employed.

Admissions Contact: Gregory E. Eichhorn, Vice President for Enrollment Management and Dean of Admission. E-mail: *albright@alb.edu*
Web: *www.albright.edu*

ALLEGHENY COLLEGE
Meadville, PA 16335 — **B-1**
(814) 332-4351
(800) 521-5293; Fax: (814) 337-0431

Full-time: 872 men, 966 women — **Faculty:** 135; IIB, av$
Part-time: 18 men, 23 women — **Ph.D.s:** 93%
Graduate: none — **Student/Faculty:** 14 to 1
Year: semesters — **Tuition:** $22,490
Application Deadline: February 15 — **Room & Board:** $5290
Freshman Class: 2530 applied, 1994 accepted, 486 enrolled
SAT I Verbal/Math: 600/590 — **ACT:** 25 — **VERY COMPETITIVE**

Allegheny College, founded in 1815, is an independent liberal arts institution affiliated with the United Methodist Church. The library contains 770,297 volumes, 475,384 microform items, and 6540 audiovisual forms/CDs, and subscribes to 3100 periodicals. Computerized library services include the card catalog, interlibrary loans, and database searching. Special learning facilities include a learning resource center, art gallery, planetarium, radio station, TV studio, observatory, 283-acre experimental forest, and art studio. The 254-acre campus is in a small town 90 miles north of Pittsburgh and east of Cleveland. Including residence halls, there are 34 buildings.

Student Life: 67% of undergraduates are from Pennsylvania. Others are from 35 states and 14 foreign countries. 84% are from public schools. 93% are white. 42% are Catholic; 34% Protestant; 17% claim no religious affiliation. The average age of freshmen is 19; all undergraduates, 20. 12% do not continue beyond their first year; 71% remain to graduate.

Housing: 1438 students can be accommodated in college housing, which includes single-sex and coed dormitories, on-campus apartments, off-campus apartments, and fraternity houses. In addition, there are language houses and special-interest houses. 75% of students live on campus; of those, 80% remain on campus on weekends. All students may keep cars.

Activities: 17% of men belong to 4 national fraternities; 30% of women belong to 4 national sororities. There are 100 groups on campus, including academic, art, band, cheerleading, choir, chorale, chorus, computers, dance, debate, drama, environmental, ethnic, film, gay, honors, international, jazz band, literary magazine, musical theater, newspaper, orchestra, pep band, photography, political, professional, radio and TV, religious, social, social service, student government, symphony, and yearbook. Popular campus events include Centerstage (arts and lecture) Series, Black History Month, and Latino Heritage Month.

Sports: There are 10 intercollegiate sports for men and 10 for women, and 9 intramural sports for men and 9 for women. Facilities include a sports and fitness center, a weight room, a putting green, a variety of exercise machines, 4 multipurpose courts, an indoor track, a natatorium, an aerobic dance studio, 3 racquetball courts, and an outdoor complex with a stadium, cross-country course, 8 fields, and 12 tennis courts. In addition, there are 100 wooded acres for mountain biking, hiking, and cross-country skiing.

Disabled Students: 30% of the campus is accessible. Wheelchair ramps, elevators, special parking, specially equipped rest rooms, special class scheduling are available. Reasonable accommodations are made for all special needs.

Services: Counseling and information services are available, as is tutoring in some subjects, including biology, chemistry, economics, computer science, environmental science, geology, math, physics, psychology, and writing. There is a reader service for the blind and remedial math and writing.

Campus Safety and Security: Measures include 24-hour foot and vehicle patrol, self-defense education, escort service, and informal discussions. There are pamphlets/posters/films, emergency telephones, and lighted pathways/sidewalks.

Programs of Study: Allegheny confers B.A. and B.S. degrees. Bachelor's degrees are awarded in AGRICULTURE (natural resource management), BIOLOGICAL SCIENCE (biology/biological science and neurosciences), COMMUNICATIONS AND THE ARTS (art history and appreciation, communications, dramatic arts, English, French, German, multimedia, music, Spanish, and studio art), COMPUTER AND PHYSICAL SCIENCE (chemistry, computer science, geology, mathematics, and physics), ENGINEERING AND ENVIRONMENTAL DESIGN (computer graphics and environmental science), SOCIAL SCIENCE (economics, history, international studies, philosophy, political science/government, psychology, religion, and women's studies). Physical and biological sciences, political science, and English are the strongest academically. Psychology, environmental science/studies, and economics are the largest.

Required: To graduate, students must complete 131 credit hours with a minimum GPA of 2.0. Between 32 and 64 hours are required in the major, including the junior seminar and senior project. All students must fulfill liberal studies requirements of 8 credits each in arts and humanities, natural sciences, and social sciences. The liberal studies program extends through all 4 years and promotes breadth at both introductory and advanced levels of study. Additional required courses include freshman first seminar, freshman second seminar, a sophomore writing and speaking seminar, and a junior seminar.

Special: Allegheny offers a cooperative program in teacher education with Chatham College, a Washington semester, internships, dual majors, student-designed majors, study abroad in 15 countries, nondegree study, and pass/fail options. A 3-2 engineering degree is available with Case Western Reserve, Columbia, Duke, Pittsburgh, and Washington Universities. There also are cooperative arrangements in medical technology and nursing with Rochester and Case Western Reserve Universities. There are 13 national honor societies, including Phi Beta Kappa, and 17 departmental honors programs.

Faculty/Classroom: 63% of faculty are male; 37%, female. All both teach and do research. The average class size in an introductory lecture is 21; in a laboratory, 16; and in a regular course, 21.

Admissions: 79% of the 2001-2002 applicants were accepted. The SAT I scores for the 2001-2002 freshman class were: Verbal--9% below 500, 40% between 500 and 599, 40% between 600 and 700, and 11% above 700; Math--9% below 500, 41% between 500 and 599, 43% between 600 and 700, and 7% above 700. The ACT scores were 8% below 21, 23% between 21 and 23, 38% between 24 and 26, 16% between 27 and 28, and 15% above 28. 64% of the current freshmen were in the top fifth of their class; 88% were in the top two fifths. There was 1 National Merit finalist and 3 semifinalists.

Requirements: The SAT I or ACT is required. In addition, SAT II: Subject tests are recommended in writing and in the student's expected major. Graduation from an accredited secondary school is required for admission. Students must have 16 Carnegie units, including 4 years of English, 3 each of math, science, and social studies, and 2 years of a foreign language. An essay is required, and an interview is recommended. AP and CLEP credits are accepted. Important factors in the admissions decision are advanced placement or honor courses, recommendations by school officials, and extracurricular activities record. Applications are accepted on computer disk and on-line through Embark, Apply, and other services.

Procedure: Freshmen are admitted fall and spring. Entrance exams should be taken by December of the senior year. There are early decision and deferred admissions plans. Early decision applications should be filed by January 15; regular applications, by February 15 for fall entry and November 1 for spring entry, along with a $35 fee. Notification of early decision is sent October 15 through January 31; regular decision, April 1. 99 early decision candidates were accepted for the 2001-2002 class. 4% of all applicants are on a waiting list; 14 were accepted in 2001.

Transfer: 27 transfer students enrolled in 2001-2002. Transfer applicants must submit a transcript of all college courses, a high school transcript, standardized test scores, a statement of good standing, and a letter describing reasons for transfer, and have a minimum GPA of 2.5, with 3.0 recommended. 64 credits of 131 must be completed at Allegheny.

Visiting: There are regularly scheduled orientations for prospective students, consisting of tours, panels, and presentations on academic programs, student life, admissions, and financial aid. There are guides for informal visits and visitors may sit in on classes and stay overnight. To schedule a visit, contact the Office of Admissions.

Financial Aid: In 2001-2002, 96% of all freshmen and 94% of continuing students received some form of financial aid. 74% of freshmen and 72% of continuing students received need-based aid. The average freshman award was $18,467. Of that total, scholarships or need-based grants averaged $13,530 ($29,110 maximum); loans averaged $4002 ($20,280 maximum); and work contracts averaged $935 ($1500 maximum). 63% of undergraduates work part time. Average annual earnings from campus work are $792. The average financial indebtedness of the 2001 graduate was $21,324. The FAFSA and IRS 1040 for verification are required. The fall application deadline is February 15.

International Students: There are 27 international students enrolled. The school actively recruits these students. They must score 550 on the written TOEFL or 213 on the electronic version and also take the SAT I or the ACT.

Computers: The mainframes are a TCP/IP network of 24 UNIX servers and 10 NT servers. 336 PCs are networked and available to students in the library and all academic buildings. All students may access the system 24 hours per day. There are no time limits and no fees. It is strongly recommended that all students have a personal computer.

Graduates: In 2001, 389 bachelor's degrees were awarded. The most popular majors were psychology (13%), environmental science/studies (11%), and economics (10%). In an average class, 63% graduate in 4 years, 70% in 5 years, and 71% in 6 years. 48 companies recruited on campus in 2000-2001. Of the 2000 graduating class, 32% were enrolled in graduate school within 6 months of graduation.

Admissions Contact: Megan K. Murphy, Dean of Admissions and Enrollment Management. E-mail: *admiss@allegheny.edu*
Web: *www.allegheny.edu*

ALLENTOWN COLLEGE OF ST. FRANCIS DE SALES
(See DeSales University)

ALVERNIA COLLEGE

Reading, PA 19607 — E-3

(610) 796-8220
(888) Alvernia; Fax: (610) 796-8336

Full-time: 386 men, 744 women	**Faculty:** 59
Part-time: 147 men, 305 women	**Ph.D.s:** 64%
Graduate: 79 men, 154 women	**Student/Faculty:** 19 to 1
Year: semesters, summer session	**Tuition:** $14,140
Application Deadline: open	**Room & Board:** $6650
Freshman Class: 755 applied, 592 accepted, 246 enrolled	
SAT I Verbal/Math: 491/478	**COMPETITIVE**

Alvernia College, established in 1958, is a Roman Catholic liberal arts institution. In addition to regional accreditation, Alvernia has baccalaureate program accreditation with ACOTE, APTA, CCNE, CSWE, NCATE, and NLN. The library contains 90,000 volumes and 1200 audiovisual forms/CDs, and subscribes to 425 periodicals. Computerized library services include the card catalog, interlibrary loans, and database searching. The 85-acre campus is in a suburban area 3 miles southwest of Reading. Including residence halls, there are 14 buildings.

Student Life: 91% of undergraduates are from Pennsylvania. Others are from 10 states and 9 foreign countries. 76% are from public schools. 83% are white. 40% are Catholic; 39% Protestant; 19% claim no religious affiliation. The average age of freshmen is 18; all undergraduates, 26. 31% do not continue beyond their first year; 69% remain to graduate.

Housing: 500 students can be accommodated in college housing, which includes single-sex and coed dormitories and on-campus apartments. In addition, there are honors houses. On-campus housing is guaranteed for the freshman year only and is available on a first-come, first-served basis. Priority is given to out-of-town students. 50% of students live on campus; of those, 40% remain on campus on weekends. Alcohol is not permitted. All students may keep cars.

Activities: There are no fraternities or sororities. There are 31 groups on campus, including cheerleading, chorus, computers, drama, ethnic, honors, international, literary magazine, newspaper, political, professional, religious, student government, and yearbook. Popular campus events include Christmas on Campus, Spring Fling, and Club Fair.

Sports: There are 6 intercollegiate sports for men and 8 for women, and 4 intramural sports for men and 2 for women. Facilities include a gym, a physical fitness and recreation center, playing fields, and outdoor tennis, basketball, and volleyball courts.

Disabled Students: 75% of the campus is accessible. Wheelchair ramps, elevators, special parking, specially equipped rest rooms, special class scheduling, lowered drinking fountains, lowered telephones, and 2 wheelchair-accessible suites in a residence hall are available.

Services: Counseling and information services are available, as is tutoring in every subject. There is remedial math, reading, and writing. Facilities include a writing center and a math/science tutorial lab.

Campus Safety and Security: Measures include 24-hour foot and vehicle patrol, escort service, informal discussions, pamphlets/posters/films, and lighted pathways/sidewalks. Photo ID cards must be carried by students.

Programs of Study: Alvernia confers B.A., B.S., B.S.N., and B.S.W. degrees. Associate and master's degrees are also awarded. Bachelor's degrees are awarded in BIOLOGICAL SCIENCE (biochemistry and biology/biological science), BUSINESS (accounting, banking and finance, business administration and management, marketing and distribution, and sports management), COMMUNICATIONS AND THE ARTS (communications and English), COMPUTER AND PHYSICAL SCIENCE (chemistry, information sciences and systems, mathematics, and science), EDUCATION (athletic training, elementary, and secondary), HEALTH PROFESSIONS (health care administration, nursing, and occupational therapy), SOCIAL SCIENCE (addiction studies, criminal justice, forensic studies, history, liberal arts/general studies, philosophy, political science/government, psychology, social science, social work, and theological studies). Biology, chemistry, and occupational therapy are the strongest academically. Criminal justice, education, and management are the largest.

Required: To graduate, all students must complete at least 123 credit hours with a minimum GPA of 2.0 overall and in the major (2.5 for elementary education and nursing majors). Requirements include 54 to 55 credits in a liberal arts core, consisting of theology and philosophy, social science, communications, literature, fine arts, math, and science. All students also must perform 40 clock hours of service to others before graduation, complete course work in college success skills and in human diversity, and demonstrate computer proficiency.

Special: The college offers co-op programs in business and sports management, internships, cross-registration with Kutztown University, Pennsylvania State University, Albright College, and Reading area community colleges, a Washington semester, dual and student-designed majors, and practicums in psychology, criminal justice, education, addiction studies, social work, athletic training, and occupational therapy. There is a freshman honors program.

Faculty/Classroom: 41% of faculty are male; 59%, female. All teach undergraduates. No introductory courses are taught by graduate students. The average class size in an introductory lecture is 21; in a laboratory, 11; and in a regular course, 17.

Admissions: 78% of the 2001-2002 applicants were accepted. The SAT I scores for the 2001-2002 freshman class were: Verbal--52% below 500, 40% between 500 and 599, 7% between 600 and 700, and 1% above 700; Math--61% below 500, 33% between 500 and 599, and 5% between 600 and 700. The ACT scores were 44% below 21, 44% between 21 and 23, and 11% between 24 and 26. 18% of the current freshmen were in the top fifth of their class; 42% were in the top two fifths.

Requirements: The SAT I is required and the ACT is recommended. In addition, all applicants must be graduates of an accredited secondary school or have a GED certificate. They should have completed at least 16 academic units, including 4 in English and electives and 2 each in math, foreign language, science, and social studies. An interview is required for nursing applicants and strongly recommended for all others. Nursing candidates also must submit results of the NLN prenursing test. A GPA of 2.0 is required. AP and CLEP credits are accepted. Important factors in the admissions decision are advanced placement or honor courses, recommendations by school officials, and extracurricular activities record. Applications are accepted on-line.

Procedure: Freshmen are admitted fall and spring. Entrance exams should be taken in the spring of the junior year or fall of the senior year. There are early admissions and deferred admissions plans. Application deadlines are open. The fall 2001 application fee was $25. Notification is sent on a rolling basis.

Transfer: 180 transfer students enrolled in 2001-2002. Applicants must have a college GPA of 2.0 or better. 30 credits of 123 must be completed at Alvernia.

Visiting: There are regularly scheduled orientations for prospective students, including faculty displays, lunch, tours of the campus, and the opportunity to interact with current students. There are guides for informal visits and visitors may sit in on classes and stay overnight. To schedule a visit, contact the Admissions Office.

Financial Aid: In 2001-2002, 85% of all students received some form of financial aid. 75% of freshmen and 70% of continuing students received need-based aid. The average freshman award was $13,356. Of that total, scholarships or need-based grants averaged $6221 ($10,000 maximum); loans averaged $2625 ($5500 maximum); and work contracts averaged $1236 ($1545 maximum). 80% of undergraduates work part time. Average annual earnings from campus work are $1000. The average financial indebtedness of the 2001 graduate was $12,000. Alvernia is a member of CSS. The FAFSA is required. The fall application deadline is April 1.

International Students: There are 12 international students enrolled. They must score 550 on the written TOEFL.

Computers: The mainframe is an NT Network environment. PCs are available to students in the science and math building. Network jacks are available in the student center, residence halls, and library. All students may access the system. Labs are open 17 hours per day, and the network is available 24 hours per day. There are no time limits and no fees. It is strongly recommended that all students have a personal computer.

Graduates: In 2001, 263 bachelor's degrees were awarded. The most popular majors were business management (15%), criminal justice (14%), and health science (11%). In an average class, 65% graduate in 4 years, 76% in 5 years, and 78% in 6 years. 49 companies recruited on campus in 2000-2001.

Admissions Contact: Betsy Stiles, Enrollment Management.
E-mail: *admissions@alvernia.edu* Web: *www.alvernia.edu*

ARCADIA UNIVERSITY
Glenside, PA 19038 — F-3

(215) 572-2910
(877) ARCADIA; Fax: (215) 572-4049

Full-time: 346 men, 974 women	**Faculty:** 92
Part-time: 108 men, 221 women	**Ph.D.s:** 85%
Graduate: 338 men, 1018 women	**Student/Faculty:** 14 to 1
Year: semesters, summer session	**Tuition:** $18,670
Application Deadline: open	**Room & Board:** $7980

Freshman Class: 1646 applied, 1376 accepted, 351 enrolled
SAT I Verbal/Math: 540/510 — **COMPETITIVE**

Arcadia University, formerly Beaver College, founded in 1853, is a private institution affiliated with the Presbyterian Church (U.S.A), offering undergraduate and graduate programs in the fine arts, the sciences, business, education, and preprofessional fields. In addition to regional accreditation, Arcadia University has baccalaureate program accreditation with APTA and NASAD. The library contains 132,310 volumes, 33,000 microform items, and 2625 audiovisual forms/CDs, and subscribes to 798 periodicals. Computerized library services include the card catalog and interlibrary loans. Special learning facilities include a learning resource center, art gallery, radio station, observatory, theater, computer graphics and communication labs, and multimedia classrooms. The 60-acre campus is in a suburban area 10 miles north of Philadelphia. Including residence halls, there are 21 buildings.

Student Life: 77% of undergraduates are from Pennsylvania. Others are from 23 states and 23 foreign countries. 70% are from public schools. 80% are white; 11% African American. 35% are Catholic; 18% Protestant. The average age of freshmen is 19; all undergraduates, 23. 15% do not continue beyond their first year; 72% remain to graduate.

Housing: 714 students can be accommodated in college housing, which includes single-sex and coed dormitories and off-campus apartments. On-campus housing is guaranteed for all 4 years. 61% of students live on campus; of those, 78% remain on campus on weekends. Upperclassmen may keep cars.

Activities: There are no fraternities or sororities. There are 40 groups on campus, including art, cheerleading, choir, chorale, chorus, computers, dance, drama, ethnic, gay, honors, international, literary magazine, musical theater, newspaper, photography, political, professional, radio and TV, religious, social, social service, student government, and yearbook. Popular campus events include Alcohol Awareness Week, Black History Month, and Woodstock Weekend.

Sports: There are 7 intercollegiate sports for men and 9 for women, and 5 intramural sports for men and 5 for women. Facilities include a softball field, outdoor tennis and basketball courts, field hockey and soccer/lacrosse fields, and an athletic and recreation center with a 1500-seat gym for basketball and volleyball, an indoor track, an indoor NCAA regulation swimming pool, an aerobics and dance studio, and fitness and training rooms.

Disabled Students: 70% of the campus is accessible. Wheelchair ramps, elevators, special parking, specially equipped rest rooms, special class scheduling, lowered drinking fountains, and lowered telephones are available.

Services: Counseling and information services are available, as is tutoring in every subject. There is a reader service for the blind, and remedial math, reading, and writing.

Campus Safety and Security: Measures include 24-hour foot and vehicle patrol, self-defense education, escort service, and shuttle buses. There are informal discussions, pamphlets/posters/films, emergency telephones, lighted pathways/sidewalks, doors with alarms, night receptionists, and card access to residence halls.

Programs of Study: Arcadia University confers B.A., B.S., and B.F.A. degrees. Master's and doctoral degrees are also awarded. Bachelor's degrees are awarded in BIOLOGICAL SCIENCE (biology/biological science), BUSINESS (accounting, banking and finance, business administration and management, marketing/retailing/merchandising, and personnel management), COMMUNICATIONS AND THE ARTS (communications, dramatic arts, English, fine arts, graphic design, illustration, photography, and theater design), COMPUTER AND PHYSICAL SCIENCE (chemistry, computer science, mathematics, and science), EDUCATION (art, early childhood, elementary, secondary, and special), ENGINEERING AND ENVIRONMENTAL DESIGN (engineering, environmental science, and interior design), HEALTH PROFESSIONS (art therapy, health care administration, predentistry, premedicine, preoptometry, and preveterinary science), SOCIAL SCIENCE (history, liberal arts/general studies, philosophy, political science/government, prelaw, psychobiology, psychology, and sociology). Education, psychology, and chemistry are the strongest academically. Fine arts, business, and biology are the largest.

Required: Students must take English composition, math, 2 semesters each of a lab science and a foreign language, and 1 semester of computer science. They must also fulfill 24 credits of distribution requirements in the arts, humanities, and social sciences; core courses in American pluralism and non-Western cultures; and a final project or thesis. 128 credit hours are required to graduate, including 40 or more in the major, with a minimum GPA of 2.0.

Special: Internships are encouraged in all majors. There are study-abroad programs in 9 countries and co-op programs in business, computer science, chemistry, actuarial science, and accounting. There is a 3-2 engineering program with Columbia University and a 3-4 optometry program with the Pennsylvania College of Optometry. Arcadia also offers a Washington semester, work-study, student-designed majors, a dual major in chemistry and business, interdisciplinary majors in artificial intelligence and scientific illustration, credit by exam and for life/military/work experience, and nondegree study. There are 3 national honor societies, including Phi Beta Kappa, and a freshman honors program.

Faculty/Classroom: 46% of faculty are male; 54%, female. 82% teach undergraduates; all do research. No introductory courses are taught by graduate students. The average class size in an introductory lecture is 28; in a laboratory, 20; and in a regular course, 16.

Admissions: 84% of the 2001-2002 applicants were accepted. The SAT I scores for the 2001-2002 freshman class were: Verbal--24% below 500, 46% between 500 and 599, 24% between 600 and 700, and 3% above 700; Math--36% below 500, 46% between 500 and 599, 17% between 600 and 700, and 1% above 700. 51% of the current freshmen were in the top fifth of their class; 78% were in the top two fifths.

Requirements: The SAT I is required and the ACT is recommended. In addition, applicants must be graduates of an accredited secondary school or have a GED. A total of 16 academic credits is required, including 4 years of English, 3 each of math and social studies, and 2 each of a foreign language and science. An essay is required. All art and illustration majors (except art education) must submit a portfolio. AP and CLEP credits are accepted. Important factors in the admissions decision are advanced placement or honor courses, recommendations by school officials, and leadership record. Applications are accepted on-line via the university's web site.

Procedure: Freshmen are admitted fall and spring. There are early decision, early admissions, and deferred admissions plans. Application deadlines are open. The fall 2001 application fee was $30. Notification is sent on a rolling basis. 12 early decision candidates were accepted for a recent class.

Transfer: 101 transfer students enrolled in 2001-2002. Applicants must have a GPA of 2.5. Art majors must submit a portfolio. The SAT I or the ACT is required if the student has earned less than 1 year of college credit. An interview is encouraged. 32 credits of 128 must be completed at Arcadia University.

Visiting: There are regularly scheduled orientations for prospective students, including personal interviews Monday through Saturday, open houses, and opportunities to dine on campus and to meet with faculty, financial aid officers, and current students. There are guides for informal visits and visitors may sit in on classes. To schedule a visit, contact the Office of Enrollment Management.

Financial Aid: The FAFSA, the college's own financial statement, the PHEAA, and parent and student tax returns are required. The fall application deadline is March 1.

International Students: There are 41 international students enrolled. The school actively recruits these students. They must score 520 on the written TOEFL and also take the SAT I or the ACT.

Computers: The mainframes are a DEC ALPHA 3000 and a DEC ALPHA 2100. PCs and Macs are available in 8 computer labs across campus. Residence halls, offices, and classrooms are networked, and all have access to the Internet and the World Wide Web. All students may access the system. There are no time limits and no fees.

Admissions Contact: Office of Enrollment Management. A video is available. E-mail: *admiss@arcadia.edu* Web: *www.arcadia.edu*

BLOOMSBURG UNIVERSITY OF PENNSYLVANIA E-2

Bloomsburg, PA 17815 (570) 389-4316; Fax: (570) 389-4741

Full-time: 2620 men, 4037 women	**Faculty:** 334; IIA, +$
Part-time: 207 men, 358 women	**Ph.D.s:** 78%
Graduate: 195 men, 497 women	**Student/Faculty:** 20 to 1
Year: semesters, summer session	**Tuition:** $4992 ($11,016)
Application Deadline: open	**Room & Board:** $4442
Freshman Class: 6413 applied, 5083 accepted, 1692 enrolled	
SAT I Verbal/Math: 500/510	**COMPETITIVE**

Bloomsburg University of Pennsylvania, founded in 1839, is a public institution offering undergraduate programs in the liberal arts and sciences, business, and teacher education. There are 5 undergraduate schools and 1 graduate school. In addition to regional accreditation, BU has baccalaureate program accreditation with CSWE, NCATE, and NLN. The library contains 294,649 volumes, 2 million microform items, and 7242 audiovisual forms/CDs, and subscribes to 2402 periodicals. Computerized library services include the card catalog, interlibrary loans, and database searching. Special learning facilities include a learning resource center, art gallery, radio station, and TV station. The 282-acre campus is in a small town 80 miles northeast of Harrisburg. Including residence halls, there are 54 buildings.

Student Life: 90% of undergraduates are from Pennsylvania. Others are from 26 states, 28 foreign countries, and Canada. 91% are from public schools. 94% are white. The average age of freshmen is 18; all undergraduates, 20. 20% do not continue beyond their first year; 61% remain to graduate.

Housing: 2721 students can be accommodated in college housing, which includes single-sex and coed dormitories and on-campus apartments. On-campus housing is available on a first-come, first-served basis. Alcohol is not permitted. All students may keep cars.

Activities: 3% of men belong to 3 local and 7 national fraternities; 4% of women belong to 4 local and 8 national sororities. There are 160 groups on campus, including art, band, cheerleading, chess, choir, chorale, chorus, computers, dance, drama, drill team, ethnic, film, forensics, gay, honors, international, jazz band, literary magazine, marching band, musical theater, newspaper, orchestra, pep band, political, professional, radio and TV, religious, social, social service, student government, and yearbook. Popular campus events include Parents Weekend, Renaissance Jamboree, and Siblings and Childrens Weekend.

Sports: There are 9 intercollegiate sports for men and 9 for women, and 16 intramural sports for men and women. Facilities include a 5000-seat stadium, a gym, an athletic field, an indoor track, a 6-lane swimming pool, 9 practice fields, 18 Grasstex tennis courts, racquetball/handball courts, and a 57,000-square-foot recreation facility.

Disabled Students: 70% of the campus is accessible. Wheelchair ramps, elevators, special parking, specially equipped rest rooms, special class scheduling, lowered drinking fountains, and lowered telephones are available.

Services: Counseling and information services are available, as is tutoring in some subjects. There is a reader service for the blind, and remedial math, reading, and writing.

Campus Safety and Security: Measures include 24-hour foot and vehicle patrol, self-defense education, escort service, and shuttle buses. There are emergency telephones, lighted pathways/sidewalks, monitored surveillance cameras, and strict residence hall security.

Programs of Study: BU confers B.A., B.S., B.S.Ed., and B.S.N. degrees. Associate and master's degrees are also awarded. Bachelor's degrees are awarded in BIOLOGICAL SCIENCE (biology/biological science), BUSINESS (accounting, business administration and management, and business economics), COMMUNICATIONS AND THE ARTS (art history and appreciation, communications, dramatic arts, English, French, German, music, Spanish, speech/debate/rhetoric, and studio art), COMPUTER AND PHYSICAL SCIENCE (chemistry, computer science, earth science, geology, mathematics, natural sciences, physics, and radiological technology), EDUCATION (business, early childhood, elementary, science, secondary, social studies, and special), ENGINEERING AND ENVIRONMENTAL DESIGN (electrical/electronics engineering), HEALTH PROFESSIONS (health, medical laboratory technology, nursing, and speech pathology/audiology), SOCIAL SCIENCE (anthropology, criminal justice, economics, ethics, politics, and social policy, geography, history, humanities, interpreter for the deaf, philosophy, physical fitness/movement, political science/government, psychology, social science, social work, and sociology). Elementary education, business management, and psychology are the largest.

Required: To graduate, students must complete 128 credit hours with a minimum GPA of 2.0. BU requires 12 semester hours each in humanities, social sciences, natural sciences, and math. There are specific course requirements in communication, quantitative/analytical reasoning, values, ethics, responsible decision making, and survival, fitness, and recreational skills.

Special: Internships for upperclassmen, study abroad in more than 11 countries, work-study programs, and dual majors are available. BU offers a 3-2 engineering degree with Pennsylvania State and Wilkes Universities. There is nondegree study, pass/fail options, and credit for life, military, and work experience. The school uses telecourses and interactive video. There are 9 national honor societies, a freshman honors program, and 12 departmental honors programs.

Faculty/Classroom: 62% of faculty are male; 38%, female. No introductory courses are taught by graduate students. The average class size in a laboratory is 14 and in a regular course, 29.

Admissions: 79% of the 2001-2002 applicants were accepted. The SAT I scores for the 2001-2002 freshman class were: Verbal--45% below 500, 45% between 500 and 599, and 9% between 600 and 700; Math--42% below 500, 46% between 500 and 599, and 12% between 600 and 700. 22% of the current freshmen were in the top fifth of their class; 57% were in the top two fifths. 5 freshmen graduated first in their class.

Requirements: The SAT I, with a minimum composite score of 1050, or the ACT is required. Applicants must be graduates of an accredited secondary school. To be competitive, a student should also rank in the top 30% of the high school class with a B average. The GED is accepted. Applicants should complete 4 years each of English and social studies, 3 each of math and science, and 2 of a foreign language. An interview is recommended. AP and CLEP credits are accepted. Applications are accepted on-line via the university's web site.

Procedure: Freshmen are admitted to all sessions. Entrance exams should be taken during the junior year. There are early decision, early admissions, and deferred admissions plans. Early decision applications should be filed by November 15; regular application deadlines are open. The fall 2001 application fee was $30. Notification of early decision is sent December 1; regular decision, on a rolling basis beginning October 1. 184 early decision candidates were accepted for the 2001-2002 class. A waiting list is an active part of the admissions procedure.

Transfer: 360 transfer students enrolled in 2001-2002. Either the SAT I or the ACT is required of applicants who have completed fewer than 24 semester hours of college credits. An official secondary school transcript or a GED and official transcripts from any postsecondary schools attended are also required. Applicants must have a minimum GPA of 2.0 (2.5 or 2.8 for some majors) and be in good standing at the college last attended. Those who have completed 30 semester hours must select a major upon entering BU. 32 credits of 128 must be completed at BU.

Visiting: There are regularly scheduled orientations for prospective students, consisting of a general meeting with admissions staff, a question-and-answer session, a campus tour, lunch, and meetings with academic faculty. There are guides for informal visits and visitors may sit in on classes. To schedule a visit, contact the Admissions Office.

Financial Aid: The FAFSA and PHEAA Aid Information Request (PAIR) are required. The fall application deadline is March 15.

International Students: These students must score 500 on the written TOEFL.

Computers: The mainframes are a Unisys 2200/402 and a Unisys U6000 UNIX System. Terminal direct attachment to the mainframe system is provided in several campus labs for use in instruction and research. Students can access the system through a modem over Ethernet lines on a selected-service basis. There are no time limits and no fees.
Graduates: In 2001, 1296 bachelor's degrees were awarded. The most popular majors were elementary education (12%), management (8%), and marketing (6%). In an average class, 37% graduate in 4 years, 60% in 5 years, and 62% in 6 years. Of the 2000 graduating class, 15% were enrolled in graduate school within 1 year of graduation and 89% were employed.
Admissions Contact: Christopher Keller, Director of Admissions.
E-mail: *buadmiss@bloomu.edu* Web: *www.bloomu.edu/admissions/*

BRYN ATHYN COLLEGE OF THE NEW CHURCH F-3

Bryn Athyn, PA 19009 (215) 938-2503; Fax: (215) 938-2658

Full-time: 47 men, 84 women	**Faculty:** 27
Part-time: 4 men, 5 women	**Ph.D.s:** 81%
Graduate: 13 men, 13 women	**Student/Faculty:** 5 to 1
Year: trimesters	**Tuition:** $6009
Application Deadline: March 1	**Room & Board:** $4581
Freshman Class: 58 applied, 57 accepted, 53 enrolled	
SAT I Verbal/Math: 580/570	**NONCOMPETITIVE**

Bryn Athyn College of the New Church, founded in 1877, is an independent liberal arts institution affiliated with the General Church of the New Jerusalem. There is 1 graduate school. The 2 libraries contain 97,150 volumes, 3984 microform items, and 590 audiovisual forms/CDs, and subscribe to 180 periodicals. Computerized library services include the card catalog, interlibrary loans, and database searching. Special learning facilities include the Glencairn Museum. The 170-acre campus is in a suburban area 15 miles north of Philadelphia. Including residence halls, there are 12 buildings.
Student Life: 62% of undergraduates are from Pennsylvania. Others are from 16 states, 14 foreign countries, and Canada. 17% are from public schools. 76% are white; 21% foreign nationals. Nearly all students are members of the school's denomination. The average age of freshmen is 19; all undergraduates, 20. 5% do not continue beyond their first year; 30% remain to graduate.
Housing: 103 students can be accommodated in college housing, which includes single-sex dormitories and off-campus apartments. On-campus housing is guaranteed for all 4 years. 65% of students live on campus; of those, All remain on campus on weekends. Alcohol is not permitted. All students may keep cars.
Activities: There are no fraternities or sororities. There are 10 groups on campus, including chorale, dance, drama, international, political, religious, social, social service, student government, and yearbook. Popular campus events include Charter Day and the annual service-oriented college trip.
Sports: There are 4 intercollegiate sports for men and 3 for women. Facilities include a field house, a 500 seat gym, an outdoor skating rink, soccer and field hockey fields, and tennis courts.
Disabled Students: 75% of the campus is accessible. Wheelchair ramps and special parking are available.
Services: Counseling and information services are available, as is tutoring in most subjects.
Campus Safety and Security: Measures include informal discussions, emergency telephones, lighted pathways/sidewalks, and an 18-hour foot and vehicle patrol.
Programs of Study: Bryn Athyn College confers B.A. and B.S. degrees. Associate and master's degrees are also awarded. Bachelor's degrees are awarded in BIOLOGICAL SCIENCE (biology/biological science), COMMUNICATIONS AND THE ARTS (English), EDUCATION (education), SOCIAL SCIENCE (history, interdisciplinary studies, and religion). Interdisciplinary studies, history, and education are the largest.
Required: To graduate, students must complete a total of 136 credit hours with a minimum GPA of 1.9. All students must take required courses in religion, English composition, introduction to literature, and philosophy. Some majors require a comprehensive exam or thesis.
Special: Cross-registration is available with Holy Family College. Also available are co-op interdisciplinary programs, internships, a general studies degree, dual majors, student-designed majors, nondegree study, and study abroad in Scotland and England in association with Beaver College.
Faculty/Classroom: 61% of faculty are male; 39%, female. All teach undergraduates and 4% also do research. No introductory courses are taught by graduate students. The average class size in an introductory lecture is 9; in a laboratory, 10; and in a regular course, 15.
Admissions: 98% of the 2001-2002 applicants were accepted. The SAT I scores for the 2001-2002 freshman class were: Verbal--13% below 500, 44% between 500 and 599, 31% between 600 and 700, and 13% above 700; Math--33% below 500, 28% between 500 and 599, and 38% between 600 and 700. There were 3 National Merit semifinalists.
Requirements: The SAT I is required. In addition, applicants must be graduates of an accredited secondary school or achieve satisfactory scores on the GED. An interview is recommended. AP and CLEP credits are accepted. Recommendations by school officials is an important factor in the admissions decision. Applications are accepted on-line via the college's web site.
Procedure: Freshmen are admitted to all sessions. Applications should be filed by March 1 for fall entry, October 15 for winter entry, and February 1 for spring entry, along with a $30 fee. Notification is sent on a rolling basis.
Transfer: 3 transfer students enrolled in 2001-2002. Each student is reviewed on a case-by-case basis. An interview is recommended. 30 credits of 136 must be completed at Bryn Athyn College.
Visiting: There are regularly scheduled orientations for prospective students, consisting of campus tours and chapel attendance. There are guides for informal visits and visitors may sit in on classes and stay overnight. To schedule a visit, contact Brian D. Henderson at (215) 914-4890 or *bdhender@newchurch.edu*
Financial Aid: In 2001-2002, 39% of all freshmen and 40% of continuing students received some form of financial aid. 39% of freshmen received need-based aid. The average freshman award was $4382. Of that total, scholarships or need-based grants averaged $4279 ($8391 maximum), and work contracts averaged $600 ($1200 maximum). 27% of undergraduates work part time. Average annual earnings from campus work are $1100. The college's own financial statement is required. The fall application deadline is April 1.
International Students: There are 30 international students enrolled. They must score 520 on the written TOEFL or 190 on the electronic version and also take the SAT I or the ACT.
Computers: The mainframe is a Novell network with Compaq servers. The school provides 32 PCs for academic use in 2 computer labs. All academic buildings and residence halls have access to the network. All students may access the system from 8 A.M. to 1 A.M. There are no time limits and no fees.
Graduates: In 2001, 14 bachelor's degrees were awarded. The most popular majors were education (60%) and interdisciplinary studies (40%). In an average class, 73% graduate in 6 years. Of the 2000 graduating class, 20% were enrolled in graduate school within 6 months of graduation and 83% were employed.
Admissions Contact: Dr. Dan A. Synnestredt, Director of Admissions. A video is available. E-mail: *dasynnes@newchurch.edu*
Web: *www.newchurch.edu/college*

BRYN MAWR COLLEGE F-3

Bryn Mawr, PA 19010-2899 (610) 526-5152
(800) 262-1885; Fax: (610) 526-7471

Full-time: 12 men, 1267 women	**Faculty:** 146; IIA, +$
Part-time: 2 men, 52 women	**Ph.D.s:** 96%
Graduate: 76 men, 347 women	**Student/Faculty:** 9 to 1
Year: semesters, summer session	**Tuition:** $24,990
Application Deadline: January 15	**Room & Board:** $8590
Freshman Class: 1522 applied, 909 accepted, 338 enrolled	
SAT I Verbal/Math: 660/630	**ACT:** 29
	HIGHLY COMPETITIVE+

Bryn Mawr College, founded in 1885, is an independent liberal arts institution, primarily for women. The 2 graduate schools and postbaccalaureate program are coeducational. The 4 libraries contain 1,100,598 volumes, 152,994 microform items, and 2287 audiovisual forms/CDs, and subscribe to 1846 periodicals. Computerized library services include the card catalog, interlibrary loans, and database searching. Special learning facilities include a learning resource center, art gallery, radio station, archeological museum, and language learning center with audio, video, and computer technology. The 135-acre campus is in a suburban area 11 miles west of Philadelphia. Including residence halls, there are 57 buildings.
Student Life: 80% of undergraduates are from out of state, mostly the Middle Atlantic. Others are from 48 states, 44 foreign countries, and Canada. 63% are from public schools. 66% are white; 16% Asian American. The average age of freshmen is 18; all undergraduates, 20. 9% do not continue beyond their first year; 81% remain to graduate.
Housing: 1218 students can be accommodated in college housing, which includes single-sex and coed dormitories and off-campus apartments. In addition, there are language houses, special-interest houses, a co-op house, and an African American culture center that houses several students. On-campus housing is guaranteed for all 4 years. 98% of students live on campus; of those, 85% remain on campus on weekends. Alcohol is not permitted. Upperclassmen may keep cars.
Activities: There are no fraternities or sororities. There are 100 groups on campus, including art, chess, choir, chorale, chorus, computers, dance, drama, environmental, ethnic, gay, honors, international, literary magazine, musical theater, newspaper, orchestra, photography, political, professional, radio and TV, religious, science fiction, social, social service, student government, and yearbook. Popular campus events include May Day, Lantern Night, and Fall Frolic.

Sports: There are 11 intercollegiate sports and 4 intramural sports. Facilities include 3 playing fields with access to an indoor track, a gym with an 8-lane pool and diving well, basketball, badminton, and volleyball courts, a gymnastics room and dance studio, a weight-training and fitness room, a 1000-seat auditorium, and a student center.

Disabled Students: Wheelchair ramps, elevators, special parking, specially equipped rest rooms, special class scheduling, lowered drinking fountains, lowered telephones, and accessible dorms are available.

Services: Counseling and information services are available, as is tutoring in every subject. There is a reader service for the blind.

Campus Safety and Security: Measures include 24-hour foot and vehicle patrol, self-defense education, escort service, and shuttle buses. There are informal discussions, pamphlets/posters/films, emergency telephones, lighted pathways/sidewalks, a web page, and bicycle registration.

Programs of Study: Bryn Mawr confers the A.B. degree. Master's and doctoral degrees are also awarded. Bachelor's degrees are awarded in BIOLOGICAL SCIENCE (biology/biological science), COMMUNICATIONS AND THE ARTS (art history and appreciation, classical languages, classics, comparative literature, English, fine arts, French, German, Greek, Italian, Latin, music, romance languages and literature, Russian, and Spanish), COMPUTER AND PHYSICAL SCIENCE (astronomy, chemistry, geology, mathematics, and physics), SOCIAL SCIENCE (anthropology, archeology, East Asian studies, economics, history, philosophy, political science/government, psychology, religion, sociology, and urban studies). Growth and structure of cities, classical and Near Eastern archeology, and physics are the strongest academically. English, math, and biology are the largest.

Required: To graduate, students must complete 128 semester hours, with 40 to 60 in the major and a minimum GPA of 2.0. All students must complete 2 courses each in the social sciences, the humanities, and natural sciences or math, including 1 lab science. Additional required courses include 2 college seminars and 1 quantitative skills course. Students must be able to demonstrate proficiency in a foreign language.

Special: Students may cross-register with Haverford and Swarthmore Colleges and the University of Pennsylvania. Internships are available in the cities, sociology, and education programs and through the Career Development Office. Bryn Mawr sponsors and cosponsors study abroad in 27 countries. Student-designed and dual majors are possible. Pass/fail options, work-study programs, and 3-2 degrees in engineering and city and regional planning with the University of Pennsylvania are offered.

Faculty/Classroom: 46% of faculty are male; 54%, female. 92% both teach and do research. No introductory courses are taught by graduate students. The average class size in an introductory lecture is 25; in a laboratory, 15; and in a regular course, 16.

Admissions: 60% of the 2001-2002 applicants were accepted. The SAT I scores for the 2001-2002 freshman class were: Verbal--2% below 500, 17% between 500 and 599, 50% between 600 and 700, and 31% above 700; Math--3% below 500, 26% between 500 and 599, 57% between 600 and 700, and 14% above 700. 84% of the current freshmen were in the top fifth of their class; 99% were in the top two fifths. 10 freshmen graduated first in their class.

Requirements: The SAT I is required, but the ACT may be substituted. SAT II: Subject tests in writing and 2 other areas are required. Applicants must be graduates of an accredited secondary school. The GED is accepted. Applicants should complete 4 years of English, at least 3 years of foreign language, 3 years of math, and 1 year each of science and history. An essay is required. An interview is strongly recommended. AP credits are accepted. Important factors in the admissions decision are advanced placement or honor courses, evidence of special talent, and extracurricular activities record. Applications are accepted on disk or online via Common App and Embark.

Procedure: Freshmen are admitted in the fall. Entrance exams should be taken in the spring of the junior year or the fall of the senior year. There are early decision and deferred admissions plans. Early decision applications should be filed by November 15 for fall entry or January 1 for winter entry; regular applications, by January 15 for fall entry, along with a $50 fee. Notification of early decision is sent by December 15 for fall entry or February 1 for winter entry; regular decision, by mid-April. 71 early decision candidates were accepted for the 2001-2002 class. 6% of all applicants are on a waiting list; 33 were accepted in 2001.

Transfer: 14 transfer students enrolled in 2001-2002. Applicants must have a minimum college GPA of 3.0. The SAT I and recommendations from both college and high school are required. 96 credits of 128 must be completed at Bryn Mawr.

Visiting: There are regularly scheduled orientations for prospective students, and student-guided campus tours and interviews can be arranged. There are guides for informal visits and visitors may sit in on classes and stay overnight. To schedule a visit, contact the Office of Admissions.

Financial Aid: In 2001-2002, 59% of all freshmen and 56% of continuing students received some form of financial aid, including need-based aid. The average freshman award was $24,500. Of that total, scholarships or need-based grants averaged $21,251, and self-help $4248. 75% of undergraduates work part time. Bryn Mawr is a member of CSS. The CSS/Profile or FAFSA and the college's own financial statement are required. The fall application deadline is January 15.

International Students: There are 139 international students enrolled. The school actively recruits these students. They must score 600 on the written TOEFL or 250 on the electronic version and also take the SAT I or the ACT.

Computers: The mainframes consist of HP, Sun, and UNIX systems. More than 270 computers are available for student use, including more than 100 in science and math labs and 10 loaner laptops. All dorm rooms are networked, and all students have e-mail accounts and Internet access. All students may access the system every day. There are no time limits and no fees.

Graduates: In 2001, 312 bachelor's degrees were awarded. The most popular majors were English (11%), political science (9%), and psychology (8%). In an average class, 3% graduate in 3 years, 76% in 4 years, 79% in 5 years, and 80% in 6 years. 159 companies recruited on campus in 2000-2001. Of the 2000 graduating class, 20% were enrolled in graduate school within 6 months of graduation and 64% were employed.

Admissions Contact: Elizabeth Mosier, Acting Director of Admissions. A video is available. E-mail: *admissions@brynmawr.edu*
Web: *http://www.brynmawr.edu*

BUCKNELL UNIVERSITY — D-2
Lewisburg, PA 17837 — **(570) 577-1101; Fax: (570) 577-3760**

Full-time: 1750 men, 1649 women	**Faculty:** 289; IIA, +$
Part-time: 11 men, 20 women	**Ph.D.s:** 91%
Graduate: 72 men, 85 women	**Student/Faculty:** 12 to 1
Year: semesters, summer session	**Tuition:** $25,335
Application Deadline: January 1	**Room & Board:** $5761
Freshman Class: 8043 applied, 3123 accepted, 913 enrolled	
SAT I: required	**HIGHLY COMPETITIVE**

Bucknell University, established in 1846, is an independent institution offering degree programs in arts, music, education, humanities, management, engineering, sciences, and social sciences. There are 2 undergraduate schools and 1 graduate school. In addition to regional accreditation, Bucknell has baccalaureate program accreditation with ABET, CSAB, and NASM. The library contains 701,430 volumes and 14,468 audiovisual forms/CDs, and subscribes to 4795 periodicals. Computerized library services include the card catalog, interlibrary loans, and database searching. Special learning facilities include an art gallery, radio station, outdoor natural area, greenhouse, primate facility, observatory, photography lab, women's resource center, library resources training lab, electronic classroom, multimedia lab, conference center, performing arts center, and multicultural, writing, craft, and poetry centers. The 393-acre campus is in a small town 75 miles north of Harrisburg. Including residence halls, there are 110 buildings.

Student Life: 73% of undergraduates are from out of state, mostly the Middle Atlantic. Others are from 48 states, 33 foreign countries, and Canada. 86% are white. 30% are Catholic; 30% claim no religious affiliation; 28% are Protestant. The average age of freshmen is 18; all undergraduates, 20. 6% do not continue beyond their first year; 86% remain to graduate.

Housing: 2639 students can be accommodated in college housing, which includes single-sex and coed dormitories, on-campus apartments, and fraternity houses. In addition, there are special-interest houses, and 5 residential colleges for the first year (arts, environmental, humanities, global, and social justice). On-campus housing is guaranteed for all 4 years. 87% of students live on campus; of those, 85% remain on campus on weekends. Upperclassmen may keep cars.

Activities: 38% of men belong to 14 national fraternities; 43% of women belong to 8 national sororities. There are 120 groups on campus, including art, band, cheerleading, chess, choir, chorale, chorus, dance, drama, ethnic, film, gay, honors, international, jazz band, literary magazine, newspaper, opera, orchestra, pep band, photography, political, professional, radio, religious, social, social service, student government, symphony, and yearbook. Popular campus events include Celebration for the Arts, Parents Weekend, and Spring Greek Weekend.

Sports: There are 14 intercollegiate sports for men and 14 for women, and 19 intramural sports for men and 17 for women. Facilities include a field house with a 6-lane track, weight and wrestling rooms, a basketball arena, a dance studio, a gym with a 6-lane pool, a 14,000-seat stadium, a golf course, a jogging course, tennis courts, soccer and lacrosse fields, and handball, racquetball, and squash courts.

Disabled Students: 60% of the campus is accessible. Wheelchair ramps, elevators, special parking, specially equipped rest rooms, lowered drinking fountains, and lowered telephones are available. Individual arrangements may be made with faculty for students with disabilities.

Services: Counseling and information services are available, as is tutoring in some subjects, including biology, chemistry, physics, math, and writing across the curriculum.

Campus Safety and Security: Measures include 24-hour foot and vehicle patrol, self-defense education, escort service, and informal discus-

sions. There are pamphlets/posters/films, emergency telephones, lighted pathways/sidewalks, campus safety alerts, and intrusion alarms in residence halls.

Programs of Study: Bucknell confers B.A., B.S., B.Mus., B.S.B.A., B.S.C.E., B.S.Ch.E., B.S.C.S.E., B.S.Ed., B.S.E.E., and B.S.M.E. degrees. Master's degrees are also awarded. Bachelor's degrees are awarded in BIOLOGICAL SCIENCE (biochemistry, biology/biological science, and cell biology), BUSINESS (accounting and business administration and management), COMMUNICATIONS AND THE ARTS (art, art history and appreciation, classics, dramatic arts, English, fine arts, French, German, music, music history and appreciation, music performance, music theory and composition, Russian, and Spanish), COMPUTER AND PHYSICAL SCIENCE (chemistry, computer science, geology, mathematics, and physics), EDUCATION (early childhood, education, educational statistics and research, elementary, music, and secondary), ENGINEERING AND ENVIRONMENTAL DESIGN (chemical engineering, civil engineering, computer engineering, electrical/electronics engineering, engineering, environmental science, and mechanical engineering), SOCIAL SCIENCE (anthropology, East Asian studies, economics, geography, history, humanities, interdisciplinary studies, international relations, Latin American studies, philosophy, political science/government, psychology, religion, sociology, and women's studies). Humanities, biology, and English are the strongest academically. Biology, management, and economics are the largest.

Required: All students enrolled in the College of Arts and Sciences must complete a foundation seminar during the first semester; distribution selections include 4 courses in humanities, 3 in natural science and math, 2 in social science, 2 in broadened perspectives for the 21st century addressing issues of the natural and fabricated worlds and issues in human diversity, and a capstone seminar or experience during the senior year. In addition, Bucknell requires a minimum writing competency for graduation. All students enrolled in the College of Engineering have a common first semester and must complete Exploring Engineering (EG 100). A total of 32 courses (34 courses for engineering) and a minimum GPA of 2.0 are required to graduate.

Special: Bucknell offers internships, study abroad in more than 60 countries, a Washington semester, a 5-year B.A.-B.S. degree in arts and engineering, a 3-2 engineering degree, and dual and student-designed majors. An interdisciplinary major in animal behavior is offered through the biology and psychology departments. Nondegree study is possible, and a pass/fail grading option is offered in some courses. The Residential College program offers opportunities for an academic-residential mix and faculty-student collaborative learning. Undergraduate research opportunities are available in the humanities/social sciences and the sciences and engineering. There are 23 national honor societies, including Phi Beta Kappa, and honors programs in all departments.

Faculty/Classroom: 66% of faculty are male; 34%, female. All both teach and do research, and 100% do both. No introductory courses are taught by graduate students. The average class size in an introductory lecture is 26; in a laboratory, 17; and in a regular course, 19.

Admissions: 39% of the 2001-2002 applicants were accepted. The SAT I scores for the 2001-2002 freshman class were: Verbal--3% below 500, 26% between 500 and 599, 57% between 600 and 700, and 15% above 700; Math--1% below 500, 15% between 500 and 599, 60% between 600 and 700, and 25% above 700. The ACT scores were 11% between 18 and 23, 57% between 24 and 29, and 32% above 29. 83% of the current freshmen were in the top fifth of their class; 98% were in the top two fifths.

Requirements: The SAT I is required. In addition, applicants must graduate from an accredited secondary school or have a GED. 16 units must be earned, including 4 in English, 3 in math, and 2 each in history, science, social studies, and a foreign language. An essay is required, and an interview is recommended. Music applicants are required to audition. A portfolio is recommended for art applicants. A GPA of 2.5 is required. AP credits are accepted. Important factors in the admissions decision are advanced placement or honor courses, recommendations by school officials, and evidence of special talent. Applications are accepted on-line via Apply.

Procedure: Freshmen are admitted in the fall. Entrance exams should be taken before January 1. There are early decision and deferred admissions plans. Early decision applications should be filed by November 15 or January 1; regular applications, by January 1 for fall entry. The fall 2001 application fee was $50. Notification of early decision is sent by December 15 or February 1; regular decision, by April 1. 328 early decision candidates were accepted for the 2001-2002 class. 11% of all applicants are on a waiting list; 83 were accepted in 2001.

Transfer: 26 transfer students enrolled in 2001-2002. Students must have a minimum GPA of 2.5 in courses comparable to those offered at Bucknell. The SAT I or ACT is required. A minimum of 16 credit hours must have been earned; 32 are recommended. Students are accepted on a space-available basis. An interview is recommended. 48 credits (12 courses) of 128 credits (32 courses) must be completed at Bucknell.

Visiting: There are regularly scheduled orientations for prospective students, including an open house for admitted students on the middle Saturday in April and a fall visitation program for minority students. There are guides for informal visits and visitors may sit in on classes and stay overnight. To schedule a visit, contact the Admissions Office.

Financial Aid: In 2001-2002, 47% of all freshmen and 51% of continuing students received some form of financial aid. 47% of freshmen and 55% of continuing students received need-based aid. The average freshman award was $19,938. Of that total, scholarships or need-based grants averaged $17,186 ($31,096 maximum); loans averaged $3937 ($6625 maximum); and work contracts averaged $1500 (maximum). 40% of undergraduates work part time. Average annual earnings from campus work are $1500. The average financial indebtedness of the 2001 graduate was $15,000. Bucknell is a member of CSS. The CSS/Profile or FAFSA, noncustodial parent's statement, and business/farm supplement are required. The fall application deadline is January 1.

International Students: There are 54 international students enrolled. The school actively recruits these students. They must score 550 on the written TOEFL or 213 on the electronic version.

Computers: More than 400 PCs with network access are available in labs, classrooms, the library, lounges, collaborative work spaces, and student housing. All students have free unlimited access to network resources and the Internet. All students may access the system 24 hours per day. There are no time limits and no fees. It is strongly recommended that all students have a personal computer.

Graduates: In 2001, 820 bachelor's degrees were awarded. The most popular majors were management (14%), economics (11%), and biology/English (8% each). In an average class, 82% graduate in 4 years, 85% in 5 years, and 86% in 6 years. 256 companies recruited on campus in 2000-2001. Of the 2000 graduating class, 20% were enrolled in graduate school within 6 months of graduation and 72% were employed.

Admissions Contact: Mark D. Davies, Director of Admissions. A video is available. E-mail: *admissions@bucknell.edu*
Web: *http://www.bucknell.edu*

CABRINI COLLEGE — F-4
Radnor, PA 19087-3698 — (610) 902-8552
(800) 848-1003; Fax: (610) 902-8508

Full-time: 466 men, 849 women	**Faculty:** 52; IIB, -$
Part-time: 117 men, 207 women	**Ph.D.s:** 85%
Graduate: 104 men, 357 women	**Student/Faculty:** 25 to 1
Year: semesters, summer session	**Tuition:** $18,090
Application Deadline: open	**Room & Board:** $7860

Freshman Class: 1827 applied, 1578 accepted, 374 enrolled
SAT I Verbal/Math: 470/470 — **LESS COMPETITIVE**

Cabrini College, founded in 1957, is a private liberal arts institution affiliated with the Roman Catholic Church and founded by the Missionary Sisters of the Sacred Heart. The college is known for its service learning emphasis. There is 1 graduate school. In addition to regional accreditation, Cabrini has baccalaureate program accreditation with CSWE. The library contains 195,506 volumes, 6153 microform items, and 1856 audiovisual forms/CDs, and subscribes to 537 periodicals. Computerized library services include the card catalog, interlibrary loans, and database searching. Special learning facilities include a learning resource center, art gallery, radio station, and , communications lab with a TV studio. The 112-acre campus is in a suburban area 20 miles west of Philadelphia. Including residence halls, there are 22 buildings.

Student Life: 70% of undergraduates are from Pennsylvania. Others are from 21 states, 32 foreign countries, and Canada. 48% are from public schools. 88% are white. 33% are Catholic; 33% claim no religious affiliation. The average age of freshmen is 19; all undergraduates, 21. 20% do not continue beyond their first year; 59% remain to graduate.

Housing: 490 students can be accommodated in college housing, which includes single-sex and coed dormitories, on-campus apartments, and off-campus apartments. In addition, there are honors houses, language houses, and special-interest houses. On-campus housing is available on a first-come, first-served basis and is available on a lottery system for upperclassmen. Priority is given to out-of-town students. 60% of students live on campus; of those, 60% remain on campus on weekends. Upperclassmen may keep cars.

Activities: There are no fraternities or sororities. There are 37 groups on campus, including cheerleading, chess, choir, chorus, computers, dance, drama, ethnic, honors, international, literary magazine, musical theater, newspaper, photography, political, professional, radio and TV, religious, social, social service, student government, and yearbook. Popular campus events include Cabrini Day, Yule Log, and Superthon.

Sports: There are 7 intercollegiate sports for men and 9 for women, and 12 intramural sports for men and 12 for women. Facilities include a weight room, athletic fields, a 700-seat gym, tennis courts, an Olympic-size pool, an indoor jogging track, squash courts, and an aerobic dance studio.

Disabled Students: 90% of the campus is accessible. Wheelchair ramps, elevators, special parking, specially equipped rest rooms, special class scheduling, lowered drinking fountains, and lowered telephones are available. Accommodations are made on an individual basis, with appropriate documentation.

Services: Counseling and information services are available, as is tutoring in most subjects. There is a reader service for the blind. Students may enroll in a study skills course or utilize individual tutoring to acquire learning skills.

Campus Safety and Security: Measures include 24-hour foot and vehicle patrol, self-defense education, escort service, and shuttle buses. There are informal discussions, pamphlets/posters/films, emergency telephones, and lighted pathways/sidewalks.

Programs of Study: Cabrini confers B.A., B.S., B.S.Ed., and B.S.W. degrees. Master's degrees are also awarded. Bachelor's degrees are awarded in BIOLOGICAL SCIENCE (biology/biological science and biotechnology), BUSINESS (accounting, banking and finance, business administration and management, human resources, and marketing/retailing/merchandising), COMMUNICATIONS AND THE ARTS (communications, English, French, graphic design, Spanish, and visual and performing arts), COMPUTER AND PHYSICAL SCIENCE (chemistry, information sciences and systems, mathematics, and web technology), EDUCATION (early childhood, education, elementary, and special), ENGINEERING AND ENVIRONMENTAL DESIGN (environmental science), HEALTH PROFESSIONS (medical laboratory technology and sports medicine), SOCIAL SCIENCE (American studies, criminal justice, history, liberal arts/general studies, philosophy, political science/government, psychology, religion, social work, and sociology). Education and English/communication are the strongest academically. Business, education, and English/communication are the largest.

Required: To graduate, students must complete a minimum of 123 credits with a minimum GPA of 2.0. All students must complete a core curriculum, which includes English, math, foreign language, computers, an interdisciplinary seminar in self-understanding, and a junior seminar exploring the common good. Distribution requirements cover science, heritage, cultural diversity, values, the individual and society, contemporary issues, creativity, and religious studies. A thesis is required in some majors, a community service project is part of the junior seminar, and senior capstone seminar courses are required in many majors.

Special: Cabrini offers cooperative programs, internships, study abroad, work-study programs, and cross-registration with Eastern, Rosemont, and Valley Forge Colleges and Villanova University. B.A.-B.S. degrees, dual majors and minors, a liberal arts degree, and student-designed majors are available, as well as an accelerated interdisciplinary degree programs in organizational management. Credit by exam, credit for life/military/work experience, nondegree study, and pass/fail options are also offered. There are 13 national honor societies, a freshman honors program, and 11 departmental honors programs.

Faculty/Classroom: 47% of faculty are male; 53%, female. 89% teach undergraduates and 45% both teach and do research. No introductory courses are taught by graduate students. The average class size in an introductory lecture is 20; in a laboratory, 13; and in a regular course, 16.

Admissions: 86% of the 2001-2002 applicants were accepted. The SAT I scores for the 2001-2002 freshman class were: Verbal--59% below 500, 34% between 500 and 599, and 7% between 600 and 700; Math--65% below 500, 28% between 500 and 599, and 7% between 600 and 700. 20% of the current freshmen were in the top fifth of their class; 42% were in the top two fifths.

Requirements: The SAT I is required, with a minimum composite score of 1000 (500 each on the verbal and math) recommended. All students must be graduates of an accredited secondary school or have a GED. A minimum of 17 Carnegie units are required, consisting of 4 in English, 3 each in math, science, and social studies, 2 in a foreign language, and the rest in electives. An interview is recommended. A GPA of 2.0 is required. AP and CLEP credits are accepted. Important factors in the admissions decision are advanced placement or honor courses, extracurricular activities record, and leadership record. Applications are accepted via CollegeNET, linked from Cabrini's web site.

Procedure: Freshmen are admitted to all sessions. Entrance exams should be taken before December of the senior year. There are early admissions and deferred admissions plans. Application deadlines are open. The fall 2001 application fee was $25. Notification is sent on a rolling basis.

Transfer: 82 transfer students enrolled in 2001-2002. A minimum of 15 credit hours with at least a GPA of 2.2 overall is required; a 2.5 GPA is preferred. Some programs may have higher requirements. 45 credits of 123 must be completed at Cabrini.

Visiting: There are regularly scheduled orientations for prospective students, consisting of summer preview programs during which students register for classes. Fall and spring orientations are held 2 to 3 days before classes begin. There are guides for informal visits and visitors may sit in on classes and stay overnight. To schedule a visit, contact the Admissions Office.

Financial Aid: In 2001-2002, 96% of all freshmen and 95% of continuing students received some form of financial aid. 76% of freshmen and 73% of continuing students received need-based aid. The average freshman award was $11,415. Of that total, scholarships or need-based grants averaged $6655 ($17,548 maximum); loans averaged $3104 ($6500 maximum); work contracts averaged $1500 ($2000 maximum); and Cabrini work grants averaged $1100 (maximum). 28% of undergraduates work part time. Average annual earnings from campus work are $1600. The average financial indebtedness of the 2001 graduate was $17,500. The FAFSA is required. The fall application deadline is open.

International Students: There are 24 international students enrolled. The school actively recruits these students. They must score 500 on the written TOEFL or successfully complete ESL if not from an English-speaking country. Students must also take the SAT I or ACT, but it is optional for students whose native language is not English.

Computers: The mainframe is an IBM AS/400. There are approximately 150 networked PCs in the main classsroom building with other PCs located in the library and residence halls. All students may access the system more than 80 hours a week. There are no time limits and no fees. It is strongly recommended that all students have a personal computer, preferably a Celeron at 400 MHz, Apple PowerBook G3 at 400 MHz, Apple PowerMac G4 at 350 MHz, or Pentium MMX at 266 MHz.

Graduates: In 2001, 389 bachelor's degrees were awarded. The most popular majors were elementary education (17%), English/communication (12%), and business administration (8%). In an average class, 1% graduate in 3 years, 53% in 4 years, 58% in 5 years, and 61% in 6 years. 85 companies recruited on campus in 2000-2001. Of the 2000 graduating class, 11% were enrolled in graduate school within 6 months of graduation and 91% were employed.

Admissions Contact: Mark Osborn, Director of Admissions.
E-mail: *admit@cabrini.edu* Web: *http://www.cabrini.edu*

CALIFORNIA UNIVERSITY OF PENNSYLVANIA — B-3

California, PA 15419-1394 — **(724) 938-4404; Fax: (724) 938-4564**

Full-time: 2137 men, 2279 women	**Faculty:** 266; IIA, +$
Part-time: 417 men, 243 women	**Ph.D.s:** 55%
Graduate: 309 men, 563 women	**Student/Faculty:** 17 to 1
Year: semesters, summer session	**Tuition:** $5204 ($11,588)
Application Deadline: open	**Room & Board:** $5134

Freshman Class: 2571 applied, 1974 accepted, 839 enrolled
SAT I Verbal/Math: 480/480 — **COMPETITIVE**

California University of Pennsylvania, founded in 1852, is a state-supported institution offering degree programs in the arts and sciences, engineering, and education. There are 3 undergraduate schools and 1 graduate school. In addition to regional accreditation, the university has baccalaureate program accreditation with CSWE, NCATE, and NLN. The library contains 431,300 volumes, 830,727 microform items, and 60,416 audiovisual forms/CDs, and subscribes to 9314 periodicals. Computerized library services include the card catalog, interlibrary loans, and database searching. Special learning facilities include a learning resource center, art gallery, natural history museum, radio station, and TV station. The 148-acre campus is in a small town 35 miles south of Pittsburgh. Including residence halls, there are 38 buildings.

Student Life: 95% of undergraduates are from Pennsylvania. Others are from 21 states, 10 foreign countries, and Canada. 95% are from public schools. 94% are white. The average age of freshmen is 19; all undergraduates, 23. 26% do not continue beyond their first year; 47% remain to graduate.

Housing: 1450 students can be accommodated in college housing, which includes single-sex and coed dormitories and off-campus apartments. On-campus housing is available on a first-come, first-served basis. 74% of students commute. Alcohol is not permitted. All students may keep cars.

Activities: 10% of men belong to 13 national fraternities; 6% of women belong to 9 national sororities. There are 19 groups on campus, including art, band, cheerleading, chess, choir, chorale, chorus, computers, dance, debate, drama, drill team, ethnic, forensics, honors, international, jazz band, literary magazine, marching band, musical theater, newspaper, pep band, professional, radio and TV, religious, student government, and yearbook.

Sports: There are 6 intercollegiate sports for men and 7 for women, and 20 intramural sports for men and 2 for women. Facilities include tennis and basketball courts, an all-weather track, a swimming pool, and a 4500-seat stadium.

Disabled Students: 95% of the campus is accessible. Wheelchair ramps, elevators, special parking, specially equipped rest rooms, special class scheduling, lowered drinking fountains, and lowered telephones are available.

Services: Counseling and information services are available, as is tutoring in most subjects. There is a reader service for the blind, and remedial math, reading, and writing.

Campus Safety and Security: Measures include 24-hour foot and vehicle patrol, self-defense education, escort service, and shuttle buses. There are informal discussions, pamphlets/posters/films, and lighted pathways/sidewalks.

Programs of Study: The university confers B.A., B.S., B.S.Ed., and B.S.N. degrees. Associate and master's degrees are also awarded. Bachelor's degrees are awarded in BIOLOGICAL SCIENCE (biology/biological science), BUSINESS (business administration and management), COMMUNICATIONS AND THE ARTS (art, communications, dramatic arts, English, French, German, and Spanish), COMPUTER AND PHYSICAL SCIENCE (chemistry, computer programming, computer science, earth science, geology, mathematics, and physics), EDUCATION (athletic training, early childhood, education of the mentally handicapped, education of the physically handicapped, elementary, English, foreign languages, industrial arts, mathematics, science, secondary, social studies, and special), ENGINEERING AND ENVIRONMENTAL DESIGN (electrical/electronics engineering technology, environmental science, graphic arts technology, industrial administration/management, and manufacturing technology), HEALTH PROFESSIONS (medical laboratory technology, nursing, predentistry, premedicine, and speech pathology/audiology), SOCIAL SCIENCE (anthropology, economics, geography, gerontology, history, humanities, industrial and organizational psychology, international studies, parks and recreation management, philosophy, political science/government, psychology, social science, social work, and sociology).

Required: Students must complete a minimum of 128 semester credits and must maintain a minimum GPA of 2.5 in teacher education curricula, 2.3 in the student's area of concentration, and 2.0 overall.

Special: Cooperative programs are available with Pennsylvania State University and the University of Pittsburgh. Opportunities are provided for internships, study abroad, work-study programs, a B.A.-B.S. degree, a general studies degree, a 3-2 engineering degree, credit by exam, nondegree study, and pass/fail options. There is also an accelerated degree program in justice studies. There are 3 national honor societies and a freshman honors program.

Faculty/Classroom: 76% of faculty are male; 24%, female. All teach undergraduates. No introductory courses are taught by graduate students. The average class size in an introductory lecture is 35; in a laboratory, 24; and in a regular course, 26.

Admissions: 77% of the 2001-2002 applicants were accepted. The SAT I scores for the 2001-2002 freshman class were: Verbal--65% below 500, 28% between 500 and 599, 6% between 600 and 700, and 1% above 700; Math--67% below 500, 27% between 500 and 599, 4% between 600 and 700, and 2% above 700. 16% of the current freshmen were in the top fifth of their class; 45% were in the top two fifths.

Requirements: The SAT I is required, with a minimum composite score of 800 (400 verbal, 400 math); the ACT may be substituted, with a minimum score of 20. Graduation from an accredited secondary school is required; a GED will be accepted. Applicants should submit an academic record that includes 4 credits each in English and history, 3 each in math and academic electives, 2 in science, and 1 each in social studies and a foreign language. An essay and an interview are recommended. The university requires applicants to be in the upper 60% of their class. A GPA of 2.5 is required. AP and CLEP credits are accepted. Important factors in the admissions decision are advanced placement or honor courses, evidence of special talent, and leadership record.

Procedure: Freshmen are admitted to all sessions. Entrance exams should be taken during the senior year. Application deadlines are open. The application fee is $25. Notification is sent on a rolling basis.

Transfer: 499 transfer students enrolled in 2001-2002. Applicants must submit official transcripts from all previous colleges attended. If fewer than 30 transferable credits are submitted, applicants must also include a high school transcript and standardized test scores. Grades of D are not transferable. 38 credits of 128 must be completed at the university.

Visiting: There are regularly scheduled orientations for prospective students. There are guides for informal visits and visitors may sit in on classes and stay overnight. To schedule a visit, contact the Admissions Office.

Financial Aid: The FAFSA, Pennsylvania State Grant, and Federal Financial Aid Application are required. The fall application deadline is April 1.

International Students: There are 41 international students enrolled. The school actively recruits these students. They must score 450 on the written TOEFL. The SAT I is recommended, with a minimum composite score of 800.

Computers: The mainframe is a DEC VAX 11/780. 350 terminals and PCs provide access to the mainframe. In addition, there are 700 IBM and Mac PCs on campus in various labs and offices. All students may access the system. There are no time limits and no fees.

Graduates: In 2001, 821 bachelor's degrees were awarded. The most popular majors were education (30%), business (12%), and social sciences (7%). In an average class, 16% graduate in 4 years, 31% in 5 years, and 37% in 6 years. 62 companies recruited on campus in 2000-2001. Of the 2000 graduating class, 18% were enrolled in graduate school within 6 months of graduation and 95% were employed.

Admissions Contact: William Edmonds, Director of Admissions. A video is available. E-mail: *inquiry@cup.edu* Web: *www.cup.edu*

CARLOW COLLEGE

B-3

Pittsburgh, PA 15213 **(412) 578-6059**
(800) 333-CARLOW; Fax: (412) 578-6668

Full-time: 51 men, 913 women	**Faculty:** 61; IIB, av$
Part-time: 49 men, 610 women	**Ph.D.s:** 76%
Graduate: 28 men, 247 women	**Student/Faculty:** 16 to 1
Year: semesters, summer session	**Tuition:** $13,876
Application Deadline: open	**Room & Board:** $5490
Freshman Class: 837 applied, 560 accepted, 188 enrolled	
SAT I Verbal/Math: 504/469	**ACT:** 23 **COMPETITIVE**

Carlow College, founded in 1929, is a private, primarily women's college affiliated with the Roman Catholic Church, offering programs in liberal and fine arts, business, health science, preprofessional training, and teacher preparation. There are 4 graduate divisions. In addition to regional accreditation, Carlow has baccalaureate program accreditation with AACN, CCNE and CSWE. The library contains 121,492 volumes, 11,509 microform items, and 4591 audiovisual forms/CDs, and subscribes to 385 periodicals. Computerized library services include the card catalog, interlibrary loans, and database searching. Special learning facilities include a learning resource center, art gallery, and TV studio. The 14-acre campus is in an urban area, the Oakland section of Pittsburgh. Including residence halls, there are 14 buildings.

Student Life: 95% of undergraduates are from Pennsylvania. Others are from 10 states, 21 foreign countries, and Canada. 83% are from public schools. 72% are white; 18% African American. 44% are Catholic; 18% Protestant; 13% claim no religious affiliation. The average age of freshmen is 18; all undergraduates, 30. 22% do not continue beyond their first year; 59% remain to graduate.

Housing: 285 students can be accommodated in college housing, which includes single-sex dormitories. On-campus housing is guaranteed for the freshman year only. 85% of students commute. Alcohol is not permitted.

Activities: There are no fraternities or sororities. There are 25 groups on campus, including art, choir, debate, drama, ethnic, honors, international, instrumental ensembles, literary magazine, newspaper, pep band, philosophy, political, professional, religious, social, social service, student government, and yearbook. Popular campus events include International Fair, Spring Carnival, and Wellness Fair.

Sports: There are 5 intercollegiate sports for women. Facilities include a gym, a pool, a weight room, a fitness center, and a dance room.

Disabled Students: Wheelchair ramps, elevators, special parking, specially equipped rest rooms, special class scheduling, lowered drinking fountains, and lowered telephones are available.

Services: Counseling and information services are available, as is tutoring in most subjects. There is remedial math, reading, and writing. Professional tutoring is available for reading, writing, study skills, math, and sciences. Peer tutoring is available in other subject areas.

Campus Safety and Security: Measures include 24-hour foot and vehicle patrol, self-defense education, escort service, and shuttle buses. There are informal discussions, pamphlets/posters/films, emergency telephones, lighted pathways/sidewalks, and an electronically operated dormitory entrance.

Programs of Study: Carlow confers B.A., B.S., B.S.N., and B.S.W. degrees. Master's degrees are also awarded. Bachelor's degrees are awarded in BIOLOGICAL SCIENCE (biology/biological science), BUSINESS (accounting, business administration and management, human resources, international business management, and marketing and distribution), COMMUNICATIONS AND THE ARTS (art, art history and appreciation, communications, creative writing, English, graphic design, Spanish, and technical and business writing), COMPUTER AND PHYSICAL SCIENCE (chemistry, computer science, information sciences and systems, and mathematics), EDUCATION (art, early childhood, elementary, secondary, and special), ENGINEERING AND ENVIRONMENTAL DESIGN (computer graphics), HEALTH PROFESSIONS (art therapy, health science, and nursing), SOCIAL SCIENCE (criminal justice, history, liberal arts/general studies, philosophy, psychology, social studies, social work, sociology, and theological studies). Nursing, creative writing, and education are the strongest academically. Nursing, business management, and elementary education are the largest.

Required: A total of 120 credit hours (125 for nursing students), including 27 to 44 in the major, is required to graduate. Credits must be earned in history, literature, art or music, math or logic, theology, philosophy, psychology or sociology, biology or chemistry, and women's studies. An interdisciplinary course and a course with a peace and justice overlay are also required. A minimum GPA of 2.0 is required. All students must demonstrate competence in writing, reading comprehension, and math, and must take basic skills courses in public speaking and research paper writing. All students undergo a comprehensive evaluation in their senior year.

Special: Carlow offers cross-registration through the Pittsburgh Council for Higher Education, internships in all areas, and work-study. There are accelerated degree programs in health science and professional writing. Dual majors are possible in most majors, as are student-designed majors.

There are 3-2 engineering programs with Carnegie Mellon University, as well as 2-2 and 3-3 programs in athletic training, physician assistant, physical therapy, and occupational therapy with Dusquesne University. There are 4 national honor societies and a freshman honors program.

Faculty/Classroom: 33% of faculty are male; 67%, female. 90% teach undergraduates. No introductory courses are taught by graduate students. The average class size in an introductory lecture is 20; in a laboratory, 15; and in a regular course, 17.

Admissions: 67% of the 2001-2002 applicants were accepted. The SAT I scores for the 2001-2002 freshman class were: Verbal--47% below 500, 42% between 500 and 599, and 11% between 600 and 700; Math--61% below 500, 31% between 500 and 599, 7% between 600 and 700, and 1% above 700. The ACT scores were 44% below 21, 24% between 21 and 23, 24% between 24 and 26, 3% between 27 and 28, and 5% above 28. 28% of the current freshmen were in the top fifth of their class; 57% were in the top two fifths.

Requirements: The SAT I or ACT is required; the minimum scores depend on the major selected. Candidates must be graduates of an accredited secondary school. 18 Carnegie units are required, including 4 each in English and arts/humanities, 3 each in math and science, and 4 in electives. Applicants for nursing must have completed a minimum 4 units in English, 3 in social studies, and 2 each in math (including algebra) and lab science, as required by the State Board of Nursing. The GED is accepted. An essay may be required and an interview is recommended. Art majors must have a portfolio. In some cases where preferred admissions requirements are not met, provisional admission may be granted. Carlow requires applicants to be in the upper 40% of their class. A GPA of 3.0 is required. AP and CLEP credits are accepted. Important factors in the admissions decision are advanced placement or honor courses, leadership record, and recommendations by school officials. Applications are accepted on-line at the college's web site.

Procedure: Freshmen are admitted to all sessions. Entrance exams should be taken early in the senior year. There are early action and deferred admissions plans. Application deadlines are open. The fall 2001 application fee was $20. Notification is sent on a rolling basis.

Transfer: 191 transfer students enrolled in 2001-2002. Students must submit high school and college transcriptsand have a mimimum GPA of 2.0 (2.5 for nursing, education and social work or 2.8 for perfusion technology). The minimum credit hours required are 3, but 12 are recommended for scholarship consideration. An interview is also recommended. 32 credits of 120 must be completed at Carlow.

Visiting: There are regularly scheduled orientations for prospective students. There are guides for informal visits and visitors may sit in on classes and stay overnight. To schedule a visit, contact the Admissions Office.

Financial Aid: In 2001-2002, 97% of all freshmen and 85% of continuing students received some form of financial aid. 92% of freshmen and 80% of continuing students received need-based aid. The average freshman award was $15,784. Of that total, the maximum scholoarship or need-based grant was $13,468; maximum loan $3425; maximum work contract $800; and maximum tuition discount for family members, tuition benefit for employees' children, or courtesy discount was $13,468. 18% of undergraduates work part time. Average annual earnings from campus work are $510. The average financial indebtedness of the 2001 graduate was $11,131. Carlow is a member of CSS. The FAFSA, verification worksheets, and tax returns when applicable. are required. The fall application deadline is April 2.

International Students: There are 12 international students enrolled. They must score 500 (550 for nursing) on the written TOEFL or 173 (213 for nursing) on the electronic version or take the MELAB and must also take the SAT I.

Computers: The mainframe is an HP 9000-L2000. There are 155 computer terminals/PCs available on campus for student use in computer labs located in the library, residence halls, the computer center, the student center, remote sites, and classroom buildings. Students can access e-mail, the Internet, and application software. All students may access the system 24 hours a day. There are no time limits and no fees. It is strongly recommended that all students have a personal computer.

Graduates: In 2001, 333 bachelor's degrees were awarded. The most popular majors were nursing (31%), business management (13%), and education (10%). In an average class, 46% graduate in 4 years, 57% in 5 years, and 59% in 6 years. 13 companies recruited on campus in 2000-2001. Of the 2000 graduating class, 18% were enrolled in graduate school within 6 months of graduation and 90% were employed.

Admissions Contact: Christine Devine, Director of Admissions. A video is available. E-mail: *admissions@carlow.edu* Web: *www.carlow.edu*

CARNEGIE MELLON UNIVERSITY B-3

Pittsburgh, PA 15213 **(412) 268-2082; Fax: (412) 268-7838**

Full-time: 3240 men, 1805 women
Part-time: 60 men, 30 women
Graduate: 2230 men, 942 women
Year: semesters, summer session
Application Deadline: January 1
Freshman Class: n/av
SAT I or ACT: required
Faculty: 1042; I, +$
Ph.D.s: 96%
Student/Faculty: 5 to 1
Tuition: $25,872
Room & Board: $6810
MOST COMPETITIVE

Carnegie Mellon University, established in 1900, is a private nonsectarian institution offering undergraduate programs in liberal arts and science and professional technology. Figures in above capsule are approximate. There are 6 undergraduate and 7 graduate schools. In addition to regional accreditation, Carnegie Mellon has baccalaureate program accreditation with AACSB, ABET, NAAB, NASAD, and NASM. The 3 libraries contain 935,888 volumes, 885,422 microform items, and 50,465 audiovisual forms/CDs, and subscribe to 3209 periodicals. Computerized library services include the card catalog, interlibrary loans, and database searching. Special learning facilities include a learning resource center, art gallery, and radio station. The 103-acre campus is in a suburban area 4 miles from downtown Pittsburgh. Including residence halls, there are 80 buildings.

Student Life: 78% of undergraduates are from out of state, mostly the Middle Atlantic. Others are from 50 states, 102 foreign countries, and Canada. 70% are from public schools. 53% are white; 21% foreign nationals; 17% Asian American. The average age of freshmen is 18; all undergraduates, 20. 8% do not continue beyond their first year; 76% remain to graduate.

Housing: 3538 students can be accommodated in college housing, which includes single-sex and coed dormitories, on-campus apartments, off-campus apartments, fraternity houses, and sorority houses. In addition, there are honors houses, language houses, and special-interest houses. On-campus housing is guaranteed for all 4 years. 59% of students live on campus; of those, 90% remain on campus on weekends. Alcohol is not permitted. Upperclassmen may keep cars.

Activities: 13% of men belong to 13 national fraternities; 9% of women belong to 1 local and 4 national sororities. There are 120 groups on campus, including art, bagpipe band, band, cheerleading, chess, choir, chorale, chorus, computers, debate, drama, ethnic, film, gay, honors, international, jazz band, literary magazine, marching band, musical theater, newspaper, opera, orchestra, pep band, photography, political, professional, radio and TV, religious, social, social service, student government, symphony, and yearbook. Popular campus events include Spring Carnival, International Festival, and Watson Arts Festival.

Sports: There are 9 intercollegiate sports for men and 8 for women, and 22 intramural sports for men and 16 for women. Facilities include a gym, a stadium, athletic fields, tennis and racquetball courts, and a pool.

Disabled Students: 98% of the campus is accessible. Wheelchair ramps, elevators, special parking, specially equipped rest rooms, special class scheduling, lowered drinking fountains, and lowered telephones are available.

Services: Counseling and information services are available, as is tutoring in most subjects. There is a reader service for the blind.

Campus Safety and Security: Measures include 24-hour foot and vehicle patrol, self-defense education, escort service, and shuttle buses. There are informal discussions, pamphlets/posters/films, emergency telephones, lighted pathways/sidewalks, and a SafeWalk Program.

Programs of Study: Carnegie Mellon confers B.A., B.S., B.A.H., B.Arch., B.F.A., and B.S.A. degrees. Master's and doctoral degrees are also awarded. Bachelor's degrees are awarded in BIOLOGICAL SCIENCE (biology/biological science), BUSINESS (business administration and management, business economics, and marketing/retailing/merchandising), COMMUNICATIONS AND THE ARTS (communications, design, dramatic arts, English, fine arts, French, German, journalism, languages, music, and Spanish), COMPUTER AND PHYSICAL SCIENCE (chemistry, computer programming, computer science, information sciences and systems, mathematics, physics, and statistics), EDUCATION (music), ENGINEERING AND ENVIRONMENTAL DESIGN (chemical engineering, civil engineering, computer engineering, electrical/electronics engineering, engineering, and mechanical engineering), SOCIAL SCIENCE (economics, history, philosophy, political science/government, psychology, public administration, social science, and urban studies). Computer Science, engineering, and business administration are the strongest academically. Engineering is the largest.

Required: To graduate, students must complete requirements in English, history, and computing skills, and they must have a GPA of 2.0. Distribution requirements, the number of credits needed to graduate, and the number of credits required in the major vary by college.

Special: Students may cross-register with other Pittsburgh Council of Higher Education institutions. Also available are internships, work-study programs, study abroad in Germany, Switzerland, and Japan, a Washington semester, accelerated degrees, B.A.-B.S. degrees, co-op programs, dual majors, and limited student-designed majors. There are 10 national honor societies, including Phi Beta Kappa and a freshman honors program.

Faculty/Classroom: 72% of faculty are male; 28%, female. All both teach and do research.

Requirements: The SAT I or ACT is required. In addition, SAT II: Subject tests in writing and math are required for all applicants. Engineering applicants must take the chemistry or physics test. Science applicants may take either of these or the biology test. Business and liberal arts applicants must take a third test of their choice. Applicants must graduate from an accredited secondary school or have a GED. They must earn 16 Carnegie units. All applicants must have completed 4 years of English. Applicants to the Carnegie Institute of Technology and the Mellon College of Science must take 4 years of math and 1 year each of biology, chemistry, and physics. Essays are required, and interviews are recommended. Art and design applicants must submit a portfolio. Drama and music applicants must audition. Applications are accepted on-line at the school's web site. AP credits are accepted. Important factors in the admissions decision are advanced placement or honor courses, leadership record, and evidence of special talent.

Procedure: Freshmen are admitted in the fall. Entrance exams should be taken by February 15. There are early decision, early admissions, and deferred admissions plans. 95 early decision candidates were accepted for a recent class. A waiting list is an active part of the admissions procedure. Check with the school for current application deadlines. The fall 2001 application fee was $50.

Transfer: 37 transfer students enrolled in a recent year. Applicants must have a minimum GPA of 3.3 in all previous college-level work. 1 academic year must be completed at Carnegie Mellon.

Visiting: There are regularly scheduled orientations for prospective students, including Saturday group sessions in September, October, November, and April. There are guides for informal visits and visitors may sit in on classes and stay overnight. To schedule a visit, contact the Admissions Office.

Financial Aid: In a recent year, 76% of all freshmen received some form of financial aid. 56% of freshmen and 48% of continuing students received need-based aid. The average freshman award was $15,710. Of that total, scholarships or need-based grants averaged $12,887; loans averaged $3886; and work contracts averaged $1902. 70% of undergraduates work part time. Average annual earnings from campus work are $1902. The average financial indebtedness of a recent graduate was $17,880. Carnegie Mellon is a member of CSS. The FAFSA, the college's own financial statement, and the parent and student federal tax returns and W-2 forms are required. Check with the school for current deadlines.

International Students: There were 445 international students enrolled in a recent year. The school actively recruits these students. They must score 600 on the written TOEFL or take the MELAB, and also take the SAT I or the ACT. Students must take SAT II: Subject tests in writing and math level I or II.

Computers: The mainframes are a DEC VAX 6320, 6330, and 11/780 models and a Sun 3280. The campuswide computer network extends to every office and dormitory room, connecting hundreds of PCs and advanced workstations. All students may access the system 24 hours per day. There are no time limits and no fees.

Graduates: In a recent year, 1020 bachelor's degrees were awarded. The most popular majors were electrical and computer engineering (13%), industrial management (10%), and computer science (10%). In an average class, 62% graduate in 4 years, 73% in 5 years, and 78% in 6 years. 956 companies recruited on campus in a recent year. Of the 2000 graduating class, 20% were enrolled in graduate school within 6 months of graduation and 62% were employed.

Admissions Contact: Michael Steidel, Director of Admissions.
E-mail: *undergraduate-admissions+@andrew.cmu.edu*
Web: *www.cmu.edu/enrollment/admission*

CEDAR CREST COLLEGE

Allentown, PA 18104-6196 — **E-3**
(610) 740-3780
(800) 360-1222; Fax: (610) 606-4647

Full-time: 10 men, 773 women	**Faculty:** 69
Part-time: 70 men, 740 women	**Ph.D.s:** 78%
Graduate: none	**Student/Faculty:** 11 to 1
Year: semesters, summer session	**Tuition:** $18,680
Application Deadline: open	**Room & Board:** $6465
Freshman Class: 1083 applied, 818 accepted, 170 enrolled	
SAT I Verbal/Math: 540/520	**ACT:** 24 **COMPETITIVE+**

Cedar Crest College, founded in 1867 by the United Church of Christ, is a private, women's, liberal arts college. In addition to regional accreditation, Cedar Crest has baccalaureate program accreditation with CAHEA, CSWE, and NLN. The library contains 135,088 volumes, 12,941 microform items, and 16,126 audiovisual forms/CDs, and subscribes to 6650 periodicals. Computerized library services include the card catalog, interlibrary loans, and database searching. Special learning facilities include a learning resource center, art gallery, radio station, arboretum, theaters, and sculpture garden. The 84-acre campus is in a suburban area 55 miles north of Philadelphia and 90 miles west of New York City. Including residence halls, there are 18 buildings.

Student Life: 82% of undergraduates are from Pennsylvania. Others are from 31 states, 35 foreign countries, and Canada. 95% are from public schools. 83% are white. 45% are claim no religious affiliation; 26% Protestant; 25% Catholic. The average age of freshmen is 18; all undergraduates, 29. 20% do not continue beyond their first year; 83% remain to graduate.

Housing: 550 students can be accommodated in college housing, which includes single-sex dormitories. There are smoke-free floors. On-campus housing is guaranteed for all 4 years. 80% of students live on campus; of those, 70% remain on campus on weekends. All students may keep cars.

Activities: There are no sororities. There are 46 groups on campus, including art, choir, chorus, computers, dance, drama, ethnic, gay, honors, international, literary magazine, musical theater, newspaper, political, professional, radio and TV, religious, social, social service, student government, and yearbook. Popular campus events include Student Faculty Frolic, Midnight Breakfast, and Ring Ceremony.

Sports: Facilities include 5 tennis courts, softball, field hockey, soccer, and lacrosse fields, a cross-country course, a gym with basketball, volleyball, and badminton courts, dance and aerobics studios, weight training, and a fitness center.

Disabled Students: 35% of the campus is accessible. Wheelchair ramps, elevators, special parking, specially equipped rest rooms, special class scheduling, lowered drinking fountains, and lowered telephones are available.

Services: Counseling and information services are available, as is tutoring in most subjects. There is remedial math and writing and a computer software skills program for underprepared students.

Campus Safety and Security: Measures include 24-hour foot and vehicle patrol, self-defense education, escort service, and informal discussions. There are pamphlets/posters/films, emergency telephones, and lighted pathways/sidewalks. Residence halls are equipped with fire/intrusion alarms, which are monitored 24 hours a day. A keyless access system is in place; exterior doors are locked 24 hours a day.

Programs of Study: Cedar Crest confers B.A. and B.S degrees. Associate degrees are also awarded. Bachelor's degrees are awarded in BIOLOGICAL SCIENCE (biochemistry, biology/biological science, genetics, and neurosciences), BUSINESS (accounting and business administration and management), COMMUNICATIONS AND THE ARTS (art, communications, comparative literature, dance, dramatic arts, English, fine arts, French, music, and Spanish), COMPUTER AND PHYSICAL SCIENCE (chemistry, computer science, information sciences and systems, and mathematics), EDUCATION (elementary, science, and secondary), ENGINEERING AND ENVIRONMENTAL DESIGN (environmental science), HEALTH PROFESSIONS (medical laboratory technology, nuclear medical technology, and nursing), SOCIAL SCIENCE (history, liberal arts/general studies, philosophy, political science/government, prelaw, psychology, social work, and sociology). Genetic engineering, nursing, and sciences are the strongest academically. Sciences, nursing, and psychology are the largest.

Required: To graduate, students must complete 120 credit hours (122 for nursing) with a minimum GPA of 2.0 (some majors have higher requirements). Distribution requirements include 8 credits in science; 6 each in humanistic studies, primary texts, creativity and the arts, and global issues and world cultures; and 3 each in writing, research, math, and ethics. A major capstone experience is required.

Special: Cross-registration is available through the Lehigh Valley Association of Independent Colleges. Also available are internships, a Washington semester with American University, work-study programs, an accelerated degree program in business, and B.A.-B.S. degrees in math, biology, and psychology. Dual majors, student-designed majors, 3-2 engineering degrees with Georgia Institute of Technology and Washington University, pass/fail options, and credit for life, military, and work experience are offered. There are 13 national honor societies, and a freshman honors program. There is an interdisciplinary departmental honors program.

Faculty/Classroom: 41% of faculty are male; 59%, female. All teach undergraduates. The average class size in an introductory lecture is 20; in a laboratory, 13; and in a regular course, 14.

Admissions: 76% of the 2001-2002 applicants were accepted. The SAT I scores for the 2001-2002 freshman class were: Verbal--30% below 500, 40% between 500 and 599, 27% between 600 and 700, and 3% above 700; Math--37% below 500, 38% between 500 and 599, 23% between 600 and 700, and 2% above 700. The ACT scores were 14% below 21, 24% between 21 and 23, 29% between 24 and 26, 19% between 27 and 28, and 14% above 28. 47% of the current freshmen were in the top fifth of their class; 75% were in the top two fifths. 2 freshmen graduated first in their class in a recent year.

Requirements: The SAT I or ACT is required. In addition, applicants must be graduates of an accredited secondary school. The GED is accepted. Students should have completed 16 high school academic credits, including 4 years of English, 3 of math, 2 each of science, history, and foreign language, and 1 each of art, music, and social studies. An essay and an interview are required. A portfolio is recommended for art students and an audition for music students. Cedar Crest requires applicants to be in the upper 50% of their class. A GPA of 2.0 is required. AP and CLEP credits are accepted. Important factors in the admissions decision are advanced placement or honor courses, leadership record, and evidence of special talent. Applications are accepted on computer disk and on-line.

Procedure: Freshmen are admitted fall and spring. Entrance exams should be taken in the junior year or early in the senior year. There are early admissions and deferred admissions plans. Application deadlines are open. The fall 2001 application fee was $30. Notification is sent on a rolling basis.

Transfer: 27 transfer students enrolled in 2001-2002. Applicants should have a minimum college GPA of 2.0. An interview is recommended. 30 credits of 120 must be completed at Cedar Crest.

Visiting: There are regularly scheduled orientations for prospective students. There are guides for informal visits and visitors may sit in on classes and stay overnight. To schedule a visit, contact the Admissions Office at *cccadmis@cedarcrest.edu*

Financial Aid: In 2001-2002, 98% of all freshmen and 96% of continuing students received some form of financial aid. 90% of freshmen and 91% of continuing students received need-based aid. The average freshman award was $18,487. Of that total, scholarships or need-based grants averaged $13,995 ($15,500 maximum); loans averaged $3272 ($6625 maximum); and work contracts averaged $1500 (maximum). 50% of undergraduates work part time. Average annual earnings from campus work are $1100. The average financial indebtedness of the 2001 graduate was $20,514. Cedar Crest is a member of CSS. The FAFSA and the college's own financial statement are required.

International Students: There were 14 international students enrolled in a recent year. The school actively recruits these students. They must score 500 on the written TOEFL and also take the SAT I or the ACT.

Computers: The mainframes are 7 Compaq servers. A total of 240 PCs are available in 13 computer labs, classrooms, and 4 residence hall labs. The network provides a variety of word processing, spreadsheet, and database applications, and high-speed, full Internet access and e-mail. Niche software such as multimedia tools, graphics software, and statistical analysis packages is available in specific labs and work areas across campus. Web access to e-mail is available to all, from any Internet connection worldwide. All students may access the system. There are no time limits and no fees. It is strongly recommended that all students have a personal computer. Wintel platforms are preferred for most, but not all, academic applications.

Graduates: In 2001, 235 bachelor's degrees were awarded. The most popular majors were psychology (20%), health and related sciences (19%), and business administration (15%). In an average class, 1% graduate in 3 years, 63% in 4 years, and 68% in 5 years. 32 companies recruited on campus in 2000-2001. Of the 2000 graduating class, 30% were enrolled in graduate school within 6 months of graduation and 81% were employed.

Admissions Contact: Judith Neyhart, Vice President for Enrollment and Advancement. A video is available.
E-mail: *judyn.@cedarcrest.edu* Web: *www.cedarcrest.edu*

CHATHAM COLLEGE

Pittsburgh, PA 15232 — **B-3**
(412) 365-1290
(800) 837-1290; Fax: (412) 365-1609

Full-time: 529 women	**Faculty:** 71; IIA, --$
Part-time: 59 women	**Ph.D.s:** 87%
Graduate: 64 men, 412 women	**Student/Faculty:** 7 to 1
Year: 4-1-4, summer session	**Tuition:** $18,960
Application Deadline: open	**Room & Board:** $6494
Freshman Class: 534 applied, 415 accepted, 133 enrolled	
SAT I Verbal/Math: 550/510	**ACT:** 24 **COMPETITIVE+**

Chatham College, founded in 1869, is a private women's college offering undergraduate degree programs in more than 30 liberal arts and preprofessional majors. Graduate degree programs in health sciences, education, management, communication, counseling psychology, and landscape studies are coeducational. There is 1 graduate division. In addition to regional accreditation, Chatham has baccalaureate program accreditation with ACS. The library contains 88,000 volumes, 8500 microform items, and 425 audiovisual forms/CDs, and subscribes to 7700 periodicals. Computerized library services include the card catalog, interlibrary loans, and database searching. Special learning facilities include a learning resource center, art gallery, theaters, media center, and arboretum. The 32-acre campus is in an urban area 8 miles east of downtown Pittsburgh. Including residence halls, there are 33 buildings.

Student Life: 71% of undergraduates are from Pennsylvania. Others are from 36 states, 24 foreign countries, and Canada. 96% are from public schools. 78% are white; 10% African American. The average age of freshmen is 18; all undergraduates, 21. 29% do not continue beyond their first year; 54% remain to graduate.

Housing: 381 students can be accommodated in college housing, which includes single-sex dormitories, on-campus apartments, and off-campus apartments. In addition, there are special-interest houses and an intercultural residence hall. On-campus housing is available on a lottery system for upperclassmen. 62% of students live on campus; of those, 75% remain on campus on weekends. Upperclassmen may keep cars.

Activities: There are no fraternities or sororities. There are 28 groups on campus, including choir, dance, drama, environmental, ethnic, feminist, film, gay, honors, international, literary magazine, newspaper, photography, political, professional, religious, social service, student government, and yearbook. Popular campus events include Fall Festival, Spring Fling, and Air Band Contest.

Sports: There are 6 intercollegiate and 8 intramural sports for women. Facilities include a swimming pool, a gym, a dance studio, an athletic field, free weights, a cardiovascular room, and a Cybex system.

Disabled Students: 75% of the campus is accessible. Wheelchair ramps, elevators, special parking, specially equipped rest rooms, and special class scheduling are available.

Services: Counseling and information services are available, as is tutoring in every subject. There is a reader service for the blind, and remedial math, reading, and writing. One-on-one and group tutoring are available by both students and professional specialists, and there is also computer-aided tutoring and an organized study group.

Campus Safety and Security: Measures include 24-hour foot and vehicle patrol, self-defense education, escort service, and shuttle buses. There are informal discussions, pamphlets/posters/films, emergency telephones, and lighted pathways/sidewalks.

Programs of Study: Chatham confers B.A., B.S., and B.S.W. degrees. Master's and doctoral degrees are also awarded. Bachelor's degrees are awarded in BIOLOGICAL SCIENCE (biochemistry, biology/biological science, and neurosciences), BUSINESS (accounting, business administration and management, entrepreneurial studies, international business management, management information systems, management science, and marketing management), COMMUNICATIONS AND THE ARTS (art history and appreciation, arts administration/management, communications, dramatic arts, English, English literature, French, media arts, music, Spanish, and visual and performing arts), COMPUTER AND PHYSICAL SCIENCE (chemistry, computer science, mathematics, and physics), ENGINEERING AND ENVIRONMENTAL DESIGN (environmental science), SOCIAL SCIENCE (crosscultural studies, economics, ethnic studies, history, interdisciplinary studies, international relations, philosophy, political science/government, psychobiology, psychology, public affairs, social work, and women's studies). Biology, psychology, and English are the strongest academically. Psychology, biology, and English are the largest.

Required: To graduate, students must complete 120 credit hours, including a general education curriculum of 7 courses and a senior tutorial, with a minimum GPA of 2.0. Students must also demonstrate proficiencies in writing, math, and computer literacy.

Special: Chatham offers a study-abroad program in 7 countries, cross-registration with other Pittsburgh Council on Higher Education institutions, co-op programs in all majors, internships in the public and private sectors, and a Washington semester in conjunction with American University and the Public Leadership Education Network. Accelerated degree programs, work-study, combined B.A.-B.S. degrees, multidisciplinary majors, and dual and student-designed majors are available. There are 3-2 engineering degrees with Carnegie Mellon and Penn State Universities and the University of Pittsburgh. Certificates in computer programming and software systems development are offered in partnership with Carnegie Technology Education. There are 7 national honor societies, including Phi Beta Kappa.

Faculty/Classroom: 32% of faculty are male; 68%, female. All both teach and do research. No introductory courses are taught by graduate students. The average class size in an introductory lecture is 16; in a laboratory, 12; and in a regular course, 12.

Admissions: 78% of the 2001-2002 applicants were accepted. The SAT I scores for the 2001-2002 freshman class were: Verbal--22% below 500, 49% between 500 and 599, and 28% between 600 and 700; Math--43% below 500, 41% between 500 and 599, and 15% between 600 and 700. The ACT scores were 28% below 21, 21% between 21 and 23, 23% between 24 and 26, 15% between 27 and 28, and 13% above 28. 31% of the current freshmen were in the top fifth of their class; 60% were in the top two fifths. 2 freshmen graduated first in their class.

Requirements: The SAT I or ACT is required. In addition, applicants must be graduates of an accredited secondary school or have earned the GED. Students should have completed 4 years of high school English and 2 each of math, science, and social studies. A foreign language, an essay, and an interview are recommended. Chatham requires applicants to be in the upper 50% of their class. A GPA of 2.5 is required. AP and CLEP credits are accepted. Important factors in the admissions decision are recommendations by school officials, leadership record, and extracurricular activities record. Applications are accepted on computer disk and on-line through *xap.com, collegeview.com, pheaamentor.org, and collegeboard.com*.

Procedure: Freshmen are admitted fall, winter, and spring. Entrance exams should be taken by fall of the senior year. There is a deferred admissions plan. Application deadlines are open. The application fee is $25. Notification is sent on a rolling basis.

Transfer: 39 transfer students enrolled in 2001-2002. Applicants must present high school and college transcripts. The SAT I or ACT and an interview are required. 45 credits of 120 must be completed at Chatham.

Visiting: There are regularly scheduled orientations for prospective students, including campus tours, student and faculty panels, financial aid presentations, and meetings with athletic coaches. There are guides for informal visits and visitors may sit in on classes. To schedule a visit, contact the Admissions Office.

Financial Aid: In 2001-2002, 99% of all freshmen and 81% of continuing students received some form of financial aid. 79% of freshmen and 80% of continuing students received need-based aid. The average freshman award was $17,844. Of that total, scholarships or need-based grants averaged $8991 ($10,000 maximum); loans averaged $3680 ($4125 maximum); and work contracts averaged $1932 ($2200 maximum). 90% of undergraduates work part time. Average annual earnings from campus work are $1800. The average financial indebtedness of the 2001 graduate was $19,189. The FAFSA is required. The fall application deadline is May 1.

International Students: There are 36 international students enrolled. The school actively recruits these students. They must score 550 on the written TOEFL or 210 on the electronic version or take the MELAB or the SAT I.

Computers: The mainframe is a DEC VAX 3100/80 minicomputer. There are also 312 computers connected to the campuswide Microsoft NT network, through which Internet access is provided. Clusters are located in each residence hall, in off-campus apartments, and in the library. Network access ports are provided in all residence hall and apartment rooms. All students may access the system 24 hours via modem or residential room and cluster labs network or 85 hours per week. There are no time limits and no fees.

Graduates: In 2001, 118 bachelor's degrees were awarded. The most popular majors were biology (11%), psychology (9%), and communication (8%). In an average class, 54% graduate in 4 years and 63% in 5 years. 13 companies recruited on campus in 2000-2001. Of the 2000 graduating class, 39% were enrolled in graduate school within 6 months of graduation and 56% were employed.

Admissions Contact: Karina Dayich, Dean of Admissions.
E-mail: *admissions@chatham.edu* Web: *www.chatham.edu*

CHESTNUT HILL COLLEGE

Philadelphia, PA 19118-2693 **F-3**
(215) 248-7001
(800) 248-0052; Fax: (215) 248-7082

Full-time: 60 men, 518 women	**Faculty:** 46
Part-time: 65 men, 279 women	**Ph.D.s:** 80%
Graduate: 114 men, 609 women	**Student/Faculty:** 13 to 1
Year: semesters, summer session	**Tuition:** $17,620
Application Deadline: open	**Room & Board:** $7170
Freshman Class: n/av	
SAT I or ACT: required	**LESS COMPETITIVE**

Chestnut Hill College, founded in 1924, is a private, liberal arts, primarily women's institution, affiliated with the Roman Catholic Church. In addition to the traditional program, CHC also offers an accelerated evening and weekend program for working adults. Courses in the accelerated program are offered in 6 8-week sessions per year, with 11 career-oriented majors. There are 2 undergraduate schools and 1 graduate school. The library contains 141,428 volumes, 155,736 microform items, and 2026 audiovisual forms/CDs, and subscribes to 596 periodicals. Computerized library services include the card catalog, interlibrary loans, and database searching. Special learning facilities include a learning resource center, planetarium, rotating observatory, and technology center. The 45-acre campus is in a suburban area 25 miles northwest of downtown Philadelphia. Including residence halls, there are 11 buildings.

Student Life: 90% of undergraduates are from Pennsylvania. Others are from 16 states and 8 foreign countries. 47% are from public schools. 62% are white; 31% African American. 59% are Catholic; 26% claim no religious affiliation; 11% Protestant. The average age of freshmen is 19; all undergraduates, 30. 25% do not continue beyond their first year; 62% remain to graduate.

Housing: 244 students can be accommodated in college housing, which includes single-sex dormitories. On-campus housing is guaranteed for all 4 years. 66% of students live on campus; of those, 60% remain on campus on weekends. Alcohol is not permitted. All students may keep cars.

Activities: There are no fraternities or sororities. There are 26 groups on campus, including chorale, chorus, drama, environmental, ethnic, honors, instrumental ensemble, international, literary magazine, musical theater, newspaper, opera, orchestra, political, professional, religious, social, social service, student government, and yearbook. Popular campus events include International Gourmet Day, Intramural One-Act Play Night, and concerts.

Sports: There are 6 intercollegiate sports for women. Facilities include a gym, 8 tennis courts, an indoor pool, neighboring stables and golf course, an archery range, a weight and fitness center, and softball, lacrosse, and hockey fields.

Disabled Students: 90% of the campus is accessible. Wheelchair ramps, elevators, special parking, specially equipped rest rooms, and a shower area in residence halls are available.

Services: Counseling and information services are available, as is tutoring in most subjects. There is a reader service for the blind and remedial math and writing.

Campus Safety and Security: Measures include 24-hour foot and vehicle patrol, escort service, informal discussions, pamphlets/posters/films, and lighted pathways/sidewalks. Doors are locked after 6 P.M. and on weekends and are monitored by cameras. Escorted shuttle cars to parking lots are available in the evenings.

Programs of Study: CHC confers B.A. and B.S. degrees. Associate, master's, and doctoral degrees are also awarded. Bachelor's degrees are awarded in BIOLOGICAL SCIENCE (biochemistry, biology/biological science, and molecular biology), BUSINESS (accounting, business administration and management, management science, and marketing/retailing/merchandising), COMMUNICATIONS AND THE ARTS (art history and appreciation, communications technology, English, fine arts, French, music, Spanish, and studio art), COMPUTER AND PHYSICAL SCIENCE (chemistry, computer science, and mathematics), EDUCATION (early childhood, elementary, and music), ENGINEERING AND ENVIRONMENTAL DESIGN (environmental science), SOCIAL SCIENCE (economics, history, political science/government, psychology, and sociology). Biological/computer/physical sciences, humanities, and social sciences are the strongest academically. Education, biological sciences, and psychology are the largest.

Required: To graduate, students must complete at least 120 credit hours with a GPA of 2.0 overall and in the major. Course work must include 12 to 15 courses in the major; Introduction to the Liberal Arts; Interdisciplinary Global Studies Seminar; a writing course; 2 courses in religious studies; the College Experience Seminar; Career Connections; 2 1-credit courses in phys ed; courses in various ways of knowing, including historical (2 courses), literary (1), aesthetic (1), scientific (2 or 3), analytic (1), and interpreting human behavior (2); and a senior seminar and senior thesis. Proficiency must be demonstrated in math, computers, oral communication, and swimming. Students may choose from a wide variety of minors.

Special: Cross-registration is available with LaSalle University and at the 10 colleges in the Sisters of St. Joseph College Consortium Student Exchange Program. The college offers internships, study abroad in England, Spain, Italy, Austria, and France, work-study programs, interdisciplinary majors, including communications and technology and fine arts and technology, and dual and student-designed majors. Up to 6 credits may be given for life experience. Nondegree study and pass/fail options are available. The school offers unique career preparation programs in communications, international studies, and environmental science. There are 4 national honor societies, a freshman honors program, and 14 departmental honors programs.

Faculty/Classroom: 43% of faculty are male; 57%, female. 97% teach undergraduates and 30% both teach and do research. No introductory courses are taught by graduate students. The average class size in an introductory lecture is 15; in a laboratory, 12; and in a regular course, 10.

Admissions: 35% of the current freshmen were in the top fifth of their class; 63% were in the top two fifths.

Requirements: The SAT I or ACT is required, with a recommended minimum composite score on the SAT I of 900 to 1000. Applicants must be graduates of an accredited secondary school. 16 Carnegie units are required, with a recommended 4 units each of English, math, science, and social studies and 3 of foreign language. An interview is recommended for all students, an audition is required for music students, and a portfolio is recommended for art studio majors. An essay is required. A GPA of 2.0 is required. AP and CLEP credits are accepted. Important factors in the admissions decision are leadership record, recommendations by alumni, and evidence of special talent.

Procedure: Freshmen are admitted fall and spring. Entrance exams should be taken early in the senior year. There are early admissions and deferred admissions plans. Application deadlines are open. The application fee is $35. Notification is sent on a rolling basis.

Transfer: 39 transfer students enrolled in 2001-2002. Applicants must have a minimum GPA of 2.0; a 2.5 is recommended. 45 credits of 120 must be completed at CHC.

Visiting: There are regularly scheduled orientations for prospective students, including faculty presentations and workshops on specific issues. There are guides for informal visits and visitors may sit in on classes and stay overnight. To schedule a visit, contact the Admissions Office.

Financial Aid: In 2001-2002, 90% of all students received some form of financial aid. CHC is a member of CSS. The FAFSA is required. The fall application deadline is April 15.
International Students: There are 14 international students enrolled. The school actively recruits these students. They must score 550 on the written TOEFL.
Computers: The mainframe is an IBM/AS400. Students use Macs and IBM PCs in the multimedia technology center, other computer labs, science labs, and computer classrooms. All students may access the system. There are no time limits and no fees. All students are required to have personal computers, specifically an IBM ThinkPad.
Graduates: In 2001, 177 bachelor's degrees were awarded. The most popular majors were sociololgy (23%), education (15%), and business (15%). In an average class, 58% graduate in 4 years, 60% in 5 years, and 62% in 6 years. About 25 companies recruited on campus in 2000-2001.
Admissions Contact: Jodie King, Associate Director of Admissions. A video is available. E-mail: *chcapply@chc.edu* Web: *www.chc.edu*

CHEYNEY UNIVERSITY OF PENNSYLVANIA F-4
Cheyney, PA 19319 (610) 399-2275
(800) 223-3608; Fax: (610) 399-2099

Full-time: 513 men, 546 women	**Faculty:** 83; IIB, +$
Part-time: 31 men, 108 women	**Ph.D.s:** 33%
Graduate: 83 men, 233 women	**Student/Faculty:** 13 to 1
Year: semesters, summer session	**Tuition:** $4671 ($10,695)
Application Deadline: May 30	**Room & Board:** $5322
Freshman Class: 1249 applied, 874 accepted, 301 enrolled	
SAT I Verbal/Math: 379/368	**ACT:** 15 **COMPETITIVE**

Cheyney University of Pennsylvania, founded in 1837, is a public, liberal arts institution offering programs in art, business, music, and teacher preparation. There are 2 undergraduate schools and 1 graduate school. In addition to regional accreditation, Cheyney has baccalaureate program accreditation with IACBE and NCATE. The library contains 162,878 volumes, 781,388 microform items, and 1434 audiovisual forms/CDs, and subscribes to 414 periodicals. Computerized library services include the card catalog. Special learning facilities include a planetarium, radio station, TV station, weather station, world cultures center, and theater arts center. The 275-acre campus is in a suburban area 24 miles west of Philadelphia. Including residence halls, there are 33 buildings.
Student Life: 83% of undergraduates are from Pennsylvania. Others are from 14 states and 5 foreign countries. 98% are African American.
Housing: 1300 students can be accommodated in college housing, which includes single-sex and coed dormitories. In addition, there are honors houses. On-campus housing is available on a first-come, first-served basis. 69% of students live on campus. Alcohol is not permitted. All students may keep cars.
Activities: There are 5 national fraternities and 4 national sororities. There are 30 groups on campus, including art, cheerleading, chess, choir, computers, drama, ethnic, honors, international, newspaper, political, professional, radio and TV, religious, social, social service, student government, and yearbook. Popular campus events include Founders Day Ball and Wade Wilson Football Classic.
Sports: There are 5 intercollegiate sports for men and 5 for women, and 3 intramural sports for men and 2 for women. Facilities include a track, tennis courts, outdoor and indoor basketball courts, a pool, a gym, and a weight room.
Disabled Students: 86% of the campus is accessible. Wheelchair ramps, elevators, special parking, specially equipped rest rooms, lowered drinking fountains, and lowered telephones are available.
Services: Counseling and information services are available, as is tutoring in most subjects. There is remedial math, reading, and writing. Both peers and professionals serve as tutors.
Campus Safety and Security: Measures include 24-hour foot and vehicle patrol, shuttle buses, informal discussions, and pamphlets/posters/films. There are emergency telephones and lighted pathways/sidewalks.
Programs of Study: Cheyney confers B.A., B.S., and B.S.Ed. degrees. Master's degrees are also awarded. Bachelor's degrees are awarded in BIOLOGICAL SCIENCE (biology/biological science), BUSINESS (business administration and management and hotel/motel and restaurant management), COMMUNICATIONS AND THE ARTS (communications, dramatic arts, English, and music), COMPUTER AND PHYSICAL SCIENCE (chemistry, computer science, mathematics, and science), EDUCATION (early childhood, elementary, home economics, secondary, and special), HEALTH PROFESSIONS (medical laboratory technology), SOCIAL SCIENCE (clothing and textiles management/production/services, economics, geography, parks and recreation management, political science/government, psychology, and social science). Psychology, political science, and social relations are the strongest academically. Business administration and social relations are the largest.
Required: To graduate, students must complete at least 124 credit hours, with 30 in the major and a minimum GPA of 2.0. Distribution requirements include 6 credits each in communications, humanities, science, and social science, 4 in health and phys ed, and 3 in math.
Special: Students may participate in a co-op program and cross-register with West Chester University of Pennsylvania. Internships, study abroad, work-study programs, a chemistry-biology dual degree, nondegree study, pass/fail options, and credit for life, military, and work experience are available. There are 10 national honor societies, a freshman honors program, and 6 departmental honors programs.
Faculty/Classroom: 50% of faculty are male; 50%, female. 76% teach undergraduates. No introductory courses are taught by graduate students.
Admissions: 70% of the 2001-2002 applicants were accepted.
Requirements: The SAT I or ACT is required. In addition, applicants must be graduates of an accredited secondary school or hold a GED. An interview is recommended. CLEP credit is accepted. Important factors in the admissions decision are ability to finance college education, extracurricular activities record, and geographic diversity.
Procedure: Freshmen are admitted fall and spring. Entrance exams should be taken during the junior or senior year. There are early decision and early admissions plans. Early decision applications should be filed by November 30; regular applications, by May 30 for fall entry and November 15 for spring entry. The fall 2001 application fee was $20. Notification is sent on a rolling basis.
Transfer: 66 transfer students enrolled in 2001-2002. Applicants must have a C average from an accredited postsecondary institution; others may be admitted on probation. Students with fewer than 30 credits must submit a high school transcript. 30 credits of 124 must be completed at Cheyney.
Visiting: There are regularly scheduled orientations for prospective students. There are guides for informal visits and visitors may sit in on classes. To schedule a visit, contact the Office of Admissions at (800) CHEYNEY.
Financial Aid: In 2001-2002, 87% of all freshmen and 90% of continuing students received some form of financial aid. 82% of freshmen and 85% of continuing students received need-based aid. The average freshman award was $7200. Of that total, scholarships or need-based grants averaged $4400 ($13,787 maximum); loans averaged $2625 ($6625 maximum); and work contracts averaged $800 ($1600 maximum). 43% of undergraduates work part time. Average annual earnings from campus work are $1650. The average financial indebtedness of the 2001 graduate was $16,650. Cheyney is a member of CSS. The FAFSA is required. The fall application deadline is April 15.
International Students: There are 14 international students enrolled. The school actively recruits these students. They must score 500 on the written TOEFL.
Computers: 150 Macs and PCs are available in the library and departmental offices. Only authorized terminal operators may access the system 24 hours a day. There are no time limits and no fees.
Graduates: In 2001, 123 bachelor's degrees were awarded. The most popular majors were elementary education (28%), social relations (26%), and business administration (21%).
Admissions Contact: James Brown, Director of Admission. A video is available. E-mail: *jbrown@cheyney.edu* Web: *www.cheyney.edu*

CLARION UNIVERSITY OF PENNSYLVANIA B-2
Clarion, PA 16214 (814) 393-2306
(800) 672-7171; Fax: (814) 393-2030

Full-time: 2066 men, 3178 women	**Faculty:** 323; IIA
Part-time: 155 men, 413 women	**Ph.D.s:** 59%
Graduate: 115 men, 344 women	**Student/Faculty:** 16 to 1
Year: semesters, summer session	**Tuition:** $7224 ($11,240)
Application Deadline: open	**Room & Board:** $4048
Freshman Class: 3412 applied, 2748 accepted, 1294 enrolled	
SAT I: recommended	**ACT:** n/av **LESS COMPETITIVE**

Clarion University of Pennsylvania, founded in 1867, is a public institution, and part of the Pennsylvania State System of Higher Education. There are 4 undergraduate and 4 graduate schools. In addition to regional accreditation, Clarion University has baccalaureate program accreditation with AACSB, NASM, NCATE, and NLN. The library contains 16,111 volumes, 12,191 microform items, and 461 audiovisual forms/CDs, and subscribes to 4412 periodicals. Computerized library services include the card catalog, interlibrary loans, and database searching. Special learning facilities include a learning resource center, art gallery, planetarium, radio station, and TV station. The 99-acre campus is in a small town 85 miles northeast of Pittsburgh. Including residence halls, there are 45 buildings.
Student Life: 96% of undergraduates are from Pennsylvania. Others are from 28 states, 30 foreign countries, and Canada. 90% are from public schools. 94% are white. The average age of freshmen is 18; all undergraduates, 23. 27% do not continue beyond their first year; 59% remain to graduate.
Housing: 2029 students can be accommodated in college housing, which includes single-sex and coed dormitories. In addition, there are

special-interest floors, nonsmoking floors, older student floors, and quiet floors. Alcohol is not permitted. All students may keep cars.

Activities: 11% of men belong to 11 national fraternities; 10% of women belong to 9 national sororities. There are 125 groups on campus, including art, band, cheerleading, chess, choir, chorus, computers, concert band, dance, debate, drama, ethnic, forensics, gay, honors, international, jazz band, marching band, music ensembles, musical theater, newspaper, orchestra, photography, political, professional, radio and TV, religious, social, social service, student government, symphony, and yearbook. Popular campus events include Autumn Leaf Festival, Activities Day, and Martin Luther King Cultural Series.

Sports: There are 8 intercollegiate sports for men and 7 for women, and 35 intramural sports for men and 35 for women. Facilities include a 5000-seat stadium, a gym with physical fitness center and recreational swimming, and a natatorium.

Disabled Students: 85% of the campus is accessible. Wheelchair ramps, elevators, special parking, specially equipped rest rooms, special class scheduling, lowered drinking fountains, lowered telephones, and priority registration are available.

Services: Counseling and information services are available, as is tutoring in most subjects. There is a reader service for the blind, remedial math, reading, and writing; computer-assisted instruction, and a learning skills lab.

Campus Safety and Security: Measures include 24-hour foot and vehicle patrol, self-defense education, escort service, and informal discussions. There are pamphlets/posters/films, emergency telephones, lighted pathways/sidewalks, and video surveillance cameras on campus, a bicycle patrol program, and a rape/aggressive defense program.

Programs of Study: Clarion University confers B.A., B.S., B.F.A., B.Mus., B.S.B.A., B.S.E., and B.S.N. degrees. Associate and master's degrees are also awarded. Bachelor's degrees are awarded in BIOLOGICAL SCIENCE (biology/biological science and molecular biology), BUSINESS (accounting, banking and finance, business administration and management, business economics, international business management, marketing/retailing/merchandising, and real estate), COMMUNICATIONS AND THE ARTS (art, communications, dramatic arts, English, French, music, Spanish, and speech/debate/rhetoric), COMPUTER AND PHYSICAL SCIENCE (chemistry, computer management, computer science, earth science, geology, information sciences and systems, mathematics, natural sciences, physics, and radiological technology), EDUCATION (early childhood, elementary, foreign languages, library science, music, secondary, and special), ENGINEERING AND ENVIRONMENTAL DESIGN (environmental science and industrial administration/management), HEALTH PROFESSIONS (medical technology, nursing, rehabilitation therapy, and speech pathology/audiology), SOCIAL SCIENCE (anthropology, economics, geography, history, humanities, liberal arts/general studies, philosophy, political science/government, psychology, social science, and sociology). Elementary education, communication, and marketing are the largest.

Required: To graduate, students must complete at least 128 credits, with a minimum GPA of 2.0 (2.5 for the College of Education and Human Services). Degree requirements include 15 credits of liberal education skills, 9 credits each in physical and biological sciences, social and behavioral sciences, and arts and humanities; and 4 credits in health and personal performance.

Special: Clarion University has co-op programs in engineering with the University of Pittsburgh and Case Western Reserve University and in speech pathology and audiology with Gallaudet University. Internships, study abroad, work-study programs, and dual and student-designed majors are also available. There are 12 national honor societies and a freshman honors program.

Faculty/Classroom: 54% of faculty are male; 46%, female. All teach undergraduates. No introductory courses are taught by graduate students. The average class size in a regular course is 25.

Admissions: 81% of the 2001-2002 applicants were accepted.

Requirements: The SAT I is recommended. In addition, applicants must be graduates of an accredited secondary school. The GED is accepted. Students should have completed 4 years each of English and social studies, and 2 years each of math, science, and foreign language. An essay and interview are recommended. A GPA of 2.0 is required. AP and CLEP credits are accepted. Important factors in the admissions decision are advanced placement or honor courses, evidence of special talent, and leadership record. Applications are accepted on computer disk and on-line.

Procedure: Freshmen are admitted fall and spring. Entrance exams should be taken in the spring of the junior year or early fall of the senior year. There are early admissions and deferred admissions plans. Application deadlines are open. Notification is sent on a rolling basis beginning October 1. The application fee is $30.

Transfer: 359 transfer students enrolled in 2001-2002. Applicants for transfer should have completed at least 12 college credit hours with a GPA of 2.75 for speech pathology and audiology majors, 2.5 for business and education majors, and 2.0 for other programs. An audition is required for music majors, and an interview and national test are required for nursing students. 45 credits of 128 must be completed at Clarion University.

Visiting: There are regularly scheduled orientations for prospective students, including a 1 1/2-day summer program for committed students. There are guides for informal visits and visitors may sit in on classes. To schedule a visit, contact the Admissions Office.

Financial Aid: The average financial indebtedness of the 2001 graduate was $12,858. The FAFSA is required. The fall application deadline is May 1.

International Students: There were 71 international students enrolled in a recent year. The school actively recruits these students. They must score 550 on the written TOEFL.

Computers: The mainframe is a DEC VAX 8810. There are also more than 350 PCs and Apple IIe's available in student labs, all with access to the Web. All students may access the system 24 hours a day. There are no time limits and no fees.

Graduates: In 2001, 923 bachelor's degrees were awarded. The most popular majors were education (32%), business (17%), and health professions and related sciences (11%). In an average class, 38% graduate in 4 years, and 55% in 5 years.

Admissions Contact: Admissions Officer. A video is available.
E-mail: *admissions@clarion.edu* Web: *www.clarion.edu*

COLLEGE MISERICORDIA

Dallas, PA 18612 — **B-2**

(570) 674-6460
(866) 262-6363; Fax: (570) 675-2441

Full-time: 333 men, 869 women	**Faculty:** 90; IIB, av$
Part-time: 119 men, 405 women	**Ph.D.s:** 52%
Graduate: 37 men, 88 women	**Student/Faculty:** 12 to 1
Year: semesters	**Tuition:** $16,650
Application Deadline: open	**Room & Board:** $6730
Freshman Class: 983 applied, 861 accepted, 261 enrolled	
SAT I Verbal/Math: 500/500	**LESS COMPETITIVE**

College Misericordia, established in 1924 and sponsored by the Religious Sisters of Mercy, is a liberal arts institution affiliated with the Roman Catholic Church and offering professional programs in health-related fields. In addition to regional accreditation, College Misericordia has baccalaureate program accreditation with CAHEA, CSWE, and NLN. The library contains 72,836 volumes, 6666 microform items, and 2240 audiovisual forms/CDs, and subscribes to 590 periodicals. Computerized library services include interlibrary loans and database searching. Special learning facilities include a learning resource center, art gallery, radio station, and TV station. The 100-acre campus is in a suburban area 9 miles north of Wilkes-Barre. Including residence halls, there are 16 buildings.

Student Life: 70% of undergraduates are from Pennsylvania. Others are from 10 states and 3 foreign countries. 45% are from public schools. 95% are white. 65% are Catholic; 32% Protestant. The average age of freshmen is 18; all undergraduates, 21.

Housing: 650 students can be accommodated in college housing, which includes single-sex and coed dormitories and on-campus apartments. In addition, there are special-interest houses. On-campus housing is guaranteed for all 4 years. 55% of students live on campus; of those, 70% remain on campus on weekends. Upperclassmen may keep cars.

Activities: There are no fraternities or sororities. There are 26 groups on campus, including cheerleading, choir, chorus, computers, drama, ethnic, honors, international, literary magazine, musical theater, newspaper, political, professional, religious, social service, student government, and yearbook. Popular campus events include Spring Fling, Winter Weekend, and Junior Ring Day.

Sports: There are 9 intercollegiate sports for men and 10 for women, and 10 intramural sports for men and 10 for women. Facilities include sports-health center and athletic fields, 24,000-square foot athletic center, Olympic-size pool, dance studio, fitness center, national and synthetic basketball courts, indoor walking track, and 3 racquetball courts.

Disabled Students: 95% of the campus is accessible. Wheelchair ramps, elevators, special parking, specially equipped rest rooms, and special class scheduling are available.

Services: Counseling and information services are available, as is tutoring in every subject. There is remedial math and reading and an alternative Learners Program for students with learning disabilities.

Campus Safety and Security: Measures include 24-hour foot and vehicle patrol, escort service, informal discussions, and pamphlets/posters/films. There are emergency telephones and lighted pathways/sidewalks.

Programs of Study: College Misericordia confers B.A., B.S., B.S.N., and B.S.W. degrees. Master's degrees are also awarded. Bachelor's degrees are awarded in BIOLOGICAL SCIENCE (biochemistry and biology/biological science), BUSINESS (accounting, business administration and management, marketing/retailing/merchandising, and sports management), COMMUNICATIONS AND THE ARTS (communications and English), COMPUTER AND PHYSICAL SCIENCE (chemistry, computer science, information sciences and systems, and mathematics), EDUCATION (early childhood, elementary, secondary, and special), HEALTH

PROFESSIONS (medical laboratory technology, nursing, occupational therapy, physical therapy, predentistry, premedicine, radiograph medical technology, and speech therapy), SOCIAL SCIENCE (history, interdisciplinary studies, liberal arts/general studies, philosophy, prelaw, psychology, and social work). Occupational therapy, physical therapy, and nursing are the strongest programs academically and have the largest enrollments.

Required: To graduate, students must earn a minimum of 120 credits, with at least 60 credits in the major. The required 54-credit core curriculum includes courses in anthropology, English composition and literature, fine arts, history, math, philosophy, political science, psychology, religious studies, and science. A minimum GPA of 2.0 is required.

Special: Students may cross-register with King's College and Wilkes University. The college offers co-op programs, internships for all majors, work-study programs, study abroad in England, an accelerated degree program in business and nursing for adult students, student-designed majors, and dual majors in elementary and early childhood education, elementary and special education, and math and computer science. Physical therapy, occupational therapy, and language and speech therapy are 5-year programs leading to a master's degree in the major. Credit may be granted for life, military, and work experience. Nondegree study is also available. The college offers an alternative learner's project, which accepts a limited number of learning disabled students each year. There is 1 national honor society, a freshman honors program, and 1 departmental honors program.

Faculty/Classroom: 49% of faculty are male; 51%, female. 45% both teach and do research. No introductory courses are taught by graduate students. The average class size in an introductory lecture is 30; in a laboratory, 20; and in a regular course, 25.

Admissions: 88% of the 2001-2002 applicants were accepted. 27% of the current freshmen were in the top fifth of their class; 52% were in the top two fifths. 4 freshmen graduated first in their class in a recent year.

Requirements: The SAT I is required. In addition, applicants must graduate from an accredited secondary school or have a GED. 16 Carnegie units must be earned, and students must complete 3 years each in English, math, history, and science, and 2 to 3 years in social studies. Radiography applicants must take physics. Physical therapy students must take calculus. A GPA of 2.0 is required. AP and CLEP credits are accepted. Important factors in the admissions decision are advanced placement or honor courses, personality/intangible qualities, and extracurricular activities record. Applications are accepted on-line at the school's web site.

Procedure: Freshmen are admitted fall and spring. Entrance exams should be taken during the junior year. There is a deferred admissions plan. Application deadlines are open. The application fee is $25. Notification is sent on a rolling basis.

Transfer: 76 transfer students enrolled in a recent year. Applicants must have a minimum GPA of 2.0. Requirements may be higher for selected majors. 30 credits of 120 must be completed at College Misericordia.

Visiting: There are regularly scheduled orientations for prospective students, including meetings with admissions and financial aid counselors, a tour of the campus, and optional meetings with faculty and/or coaches. There are guides for informal visits and visitors may sit in on classes and stay overnight. To schedule a visit, contact the Admissions Office.

Financial Aid: In a recent year, 94% of all freshmen and 85% of continuing students received some form of financial aid. 80% of all students received need-based aid. The average freshman award was $8000. Of that total, scholarships or need-based grants averaged $3000 ($7000 maximum); loans averaged $2500 ($5000 maximum); and work contracts averaged $700 ($900 maximum). 93% of undergraduates work part time. Average annual earnings from campus work are $900. The average financial indebtedness of a recent year's graduate was $13,000. College Misericordia is a member of CSS. The FAFSA and the college's own financial statement are required. Check with the school for current deadlines.

International Students: They must score 500 on the written TOEFL.

Computers: The mainframe is an IBM AS/400. 7 computer labs are on campus. PC- and Mac- available residence halls are Internet and e-mail accessible. All students may access the system. There are no time limits and no fees.

Graduates: In a recent year, 302 bachelor's degrees were awarded. The most popular majors were physical therapy (16%), occupational therapy (13%), and nursing (13%). In an average class, 26% graduate in 4 years, 65% in 5 years, and 3% in 6 years. 40 companies recruited on campus in a recent year.

Admissions Contact: Jane F. Dessoye, Executive Director of Admissions and Financial Aid. E-mail: *admiss@miseri.edu*
Web: *www.misericordia.edu*

CURTIS INSTITUTE OF MUSIC — F-3
Philadelphia, PA 19103-6187 — (215) 893-5262, Fax: (215) 893-9065

Full-time: 40 men, 80 women	**Faculty:** n/av
Part-time: none	**Ph.D.s:** n/av
Graduate: 10 men, 10 women	**Student/Faculty:** n/av
Year: n/av	**Tuition:** n/av
Application Deadline: open	**Room & Board:** n/app
Freshman Class: n/av	
SAT I: required	**SPECIAL**

Curtis Institute of Music, founded in 1924, is a private conservatory offering undergraduate, graduate, and professional programs in music. The institution serves an entirely commuter student body. All applicants are accepted on full-tuition scholarships. However, they must pay about $700 in fees and provide all their living expenses. Figures given in the above capsule are approximate. In addition to regional accreditation, Curtis has baccalaureate program accreditation with NASM. The library contains 60,000 volumes, 100 microform items, and 10,000 audiovisual forms/CDs, and subscribes to 40 periodicals. Special learning facilities include the Leonard Stolowski Collection. The campus is in an urban area. There are 3 buildings.

Student Life: 92% of undergraduates are from out of state, mostly the Northeast. Others are from 30 states, 21 foreign countries, and Canada. 90% are from public schools. 62% are white. The average age of freshmen is 18. 2% do not continue beyond their first year; 98% remain to graduate.

Housing: There are no residence halls. Alcohol is not permitted.

Activities: There are no fraternities or sororities. There are some groups and organizations on campus, including student government.

Sports: There is no sports program at Curtis.

Disabled Students: 1% of the campus is accessible. Elevators and specially equipped rest rooms are available.

Services: Counseling and information services are available. Tutoring is provided on an individual basis in every subject.

Campus Safety and Security: Measures include informal discussions and 24-hour security guards in the main building, and buzzer entry to other buildings.

Programs of Study: Bachelor's degrees are awarded in COMMUNICATIONS AND THE ARTS (music).

Requirements: The SAT I is required. In addition, applicants must be graduates of an accredited secondary school or have earned a GED. Confidential letters of recommendation from 2 qualified musicians are required. Admission is based primarily on evidence of the applicant's special talent. An audition is required. AP and CLEP credits are accepted.

Procedure: Freshmen are admitted in the fall. Entrance exams should be taken by March of the senior year. Application deadlines are open.

Transfer: 97 credits of 131 must be completed at Curtis.

Financial Aid: Curtis is a member of CSS. The CSS/Profile and the college's own financial statement are required. Check with the school for current deadlines.

International Students: They must score 500 on the written TOEFL and also take the SAT I.

Computers: All students may access the system. There are no time limits and no fees.

Admissions Contact: Judi L. Gattone, Director of Admissions.

DELAWARE VALLEY COLLEGE — F-3
Doylestown, PA 18901-2697 — (215) 489-2372, (800) 2-DEL-VAL; Fax: (215) 230-2968

Full-time: 644 men, 665 women	**Faculty:** 78; IIB, -$
Part-time: 264 men, 347 women	**Ph.D.s:** 73%
Graduate: 24 men, 32 women	**Student/Faculty:** 17 to 1
Year: semesters, summer session	**Tuition:** $17,669
Application Deadline: open	**Room & Board:** $6544
Freshman Class: 1352 applied, 1144 accepted, 495 enrolled	
SAT I Verbal/Math: 490/500	**ACT:** 19 **LESS COMPETITIVE**

Delaware Valley College, founded in 1896, is a private institution offering undergraduate programs in specialized fields of agriculture, business administration, English, the sciences, math, criminal justice administration, and secondary education. The library contains 82,000 volumes, 157,246 microform items, and 1020 audiovisual forms/CDs, and subscribes to 728 periodicals. Computerized library services include interlibrary loans and database searching. Special learning facilities include a learning resource center, radio station, dairy science center, livestock farm, horse facilities, apiary, small animal lab, tissue culture lab, arboretum, and greenhouses. The 600-acre campus is in a suburban area 20 miles north of Philadelphia. Including residence halls, there are 36 buildings.

Student Life: 64% of undergraduates are from Pennsylvania. Others are from 20 states, 4 foreign countries, and Canada. 84% are from pub-

lic schools. 76% are white. 35% are Catholic; 32% are Protestant; 16% claim no religious affiliation; 14% are Buddhist, Seventh-day Adventist, and others. The average age of freshmen is 19; all undergraduates, 20. 34% do not continue beyond their first year; 66% remain to graduate.
Housing: 878 students can be accommodated in college housing, which includes single-sex and coed dormitories. In addition, there are honors houses. On-campus housing is available on a first-come, first-served basis and is available on a lottery system for upperclassmen. 68% of students live on campus; of those, 50% remain on campus on weekends. All students may keep cars.
Activities: 4% of men belong to 5 national fraternities; 5% of women belong to 3 national sororities. There are 40 groups on campus, including art, band, cheerleading, chess, choir, chorale, chorus, computers, dance, drama, ethnic, honors, international, literary magazine, newspaper, pep band, photography, professional, radio and TV, religious, social, social service, student government, and yearbook. Popular campus events include A-Day, Parents Day, and Family Weekend.
Sports: There are 8 intercollegiate sports for men and 7 for women, and 9 intramural sports for men and 9 for women. Facilities include 2 gyms, tennis courts, outdoor playing courts and fields, a football stadium, a running track, a small lake, a video game room, picnic areas, nature walks, riding trails, and indoor and outdoor equine facilities.
Disabled Students: 85% of the campus is accessible. Wheelchair ramps, elevators, special parking, specially equipped rest rooms, special class scheduling, and lowered drinking fountains are available.
Services: Counseling and information services are available, as is tutoring in most subjects. There is a reader service for the blind, and remedial math, reading, and writing.
Campus Safety and Security: Measures include 24-hour foot and vehicle patrol, self-defense education, escort service, and shuttle buses. There are informal discussions, pamphlets/posters/films, emergency telephones, and lighted pathways/sidewalks.
Programs of Study: DVC confers B.A. and B.S. degrees. Associate and master's degrees are also awarded. Bachelor's degrees are awarded in AGRICULTURE (agriculture, animal science, dairy science, and horticulture), BIOLOGICAL SCIENCE (biology/biological science), BUSINESS (accounting, business administration and management, and marketing/retailing/merchandising), COMMUNICATIONS AND THE ARTS (English), COMPUTER AND PHYSICAL SCIENCE (chemistry, computer science, and mathematics), EDUCATION (secondary), ENGINEERING AND ENVIRONMENTAL DESIGN (food services technology), SOCIAL SCIENCE (criminal justice, food production/management/services, and food science). Physical and biological science and animal science are the strongest academically. Business administration and animal science are the largest.
Required: The bachelor's degree requires completion of at least 128 credits, including 48 in the major, with a minimum GPA of 2.0. The core curriculum consists of 48 credits of liberal arts courses, including cultural enrichment, phys ed, and an introduction to computers. Students must also fulfill employment program requirements.
Special: DVC offers a specialized methods and techniques program that enables students to learn lab techniques and gain experience in the practical aspects of their majors. There are co-op programs in all majors, internships, and work-study programs in a wide variety of employment and research settings. Cross-registration is available with Rutgers University. Nondegree study and pass/fail options are also available. There are 3 national honor societies, a freshman honors program, and 2 departmental honors programs.
Faculty/Classroom: 68% of faculty are male; 32%, female. All teach undergraduates. The average class size in an introductory lecture is 50; in a laboratory, 22; and in a regular course, 35.
Admissions: 85% of the 2001-2002 applicants were accepted. The SAT I scores for the 2001-2002 freshman class were: Verbal--52% below 500, 36% between 500 and 599, 10% between 600 and 700, and 1% above 700; Math--48% below 500, 40% between 500 and 599, and 12% between 600 and 700. The ACT scores were 80% below 21, and 20% between 24 and 26. 36% of the current freshmen were in the top fifth of their class; 70% were in the top two fifths. There were 10 National Merit semifinalists. 6 freshmen graduated first in their class.
Requirements: The ACT is required. In addition, applicants must be graduates of accredited secondary schools or have earned a GED. The college requires 15 academic units, including 6 in electives, 3 in English, and 2 each in math, science, and social studies. An interview is recommended. AP and CLEP credits are accepted. Important factors in the admissions decision are leadership record, personality/intangible qualities, and extracurricular activities record. Applications are accepted on-line via CollegeNET and the college's web site.
Procedure: Freshmen are admitted fall and spring. Entrance exams should be taken in the junior or senior year. Application deadlines are open. The application fee is $35. Notification is sent on a rolling basis.
Transfer: 82 transfer students enrolled in a recent year. Applicants must have a minimum GPA of 2.0 and must submit SAT I scores. An interview is recommended. 60 credits of 128 must be completed at DVC.
Visiting: There are regularly scheduled orientations for prospective students, consisting of a student panel, meetings with department chairs, and general information sessions. There are guides for informal visits and visitors may sit in on classes and stay overnight. To schedule a visit, contact the Admissions Department.
Financial Aid: In 2001-2002, 94% of all freshmen and 92% of continuing students received some form of financial aid. 70% of freshmen and 74% of continuing students received need-based aid. The average freshman award was $15,710. Of that total, scholarships or need-based grants averaged $12,602; loans averaged $2300 ($7625 maximum); and work contracts averaged $1500 ($3150 maximum). 31% of undergraduates work part time. Average annual earnings from campus work are $1600. The average financial indebtedness of the 2001 graduate was $15,800. The FAFSA is required. The fall application deadline is April 1.
International Students: There are 5 international students enrolled. They must score 500 on the written TOEFL and also take the SAT I or the ACT.
Computers: There are 150 PCs in the computer center, labs, the library, the tutoring center, and residence hall lounges. All students may access the system at designated times in the labs and 24 hours per day in most other areas. There are no time limits and no fees.
Graduates: In 2001, 248 bachelor's degrees were awarded. The most popular majors were business administration (27%), animal science (27%), and ornamental horticulture (13%). In an average class, 52% graduate in 4 years, 62% in 5 years, and 72% in 6 years. 310 companies recruited on campus in 2000-2001. Of the 2000 graduating class, 9% were enrolled in graduate school within 6 months of graduation and 95% were employed.
Admissions Contact: Stephen W. Zenko, Director of Admissions. A video is available. E-mail: *admitme@devalcol.edu*
Web: *www.devalcol.edu*

DESALES UNIVERSITY (Formerly Allentown College of St. Francis de Sales)
E-3

Center Valley, PA 18034-9568 (610) 282-1100, ext. 1475
(877) 433-7253; Fax: (610) 282-0131

Full-time: 700 men, 822 women	**Faculty:** 78
Part-time: 206 men, 285 women	**Ph.D.s:** 72%
Graduate: 290 men, 427 women	**Student/Faculty:** 20 to 1
Year: semesters, summer session	**Tuition:** $16,340
Application Deadline: open	**Room & Board:** $6270
Freshman Class: 1418 applied, 1029 accepted, 347 enrolled	
SAT I Verbal/Math: 530/530	**VERY COMPETITIVE**

DeSales University, founded in 1964, is a private liberal arts institution affiliated with the Roman Catholic Church. In addition to regional accreditation, DSU has baccalaureate program accreditation with NLN and ARC-PA. The library contains 134,002 volumes, 414,957 microform items, and 6151 audiovisual forms/CDs, and subscribes to 757 periodicals. Computerized library services include the card catalog, interlibrary loans, and database searching. Special learning facilities include a learning resource center, radio station, TV station, 2 theaters, and 2 dance studios. The 400-acre campus is in a suburban area 50 miles north of Philadelphia. Including residence halls, there are 23 buildings.
Student Life: 74% of undergraduates are from Pennsylvania. Others are from 10 states and 5 foreign countries. 46% are from public schools. 95% are white. 82% are Catholic; 16% Protestant. The average age of freshmen is 18; all undergraduates, 23. 19% do not continue beyond their first year; 58% remain to graduate.
Housing: 847 students can be accommodated in college housing, which includes single-sex and coed dormitories. In addition, there are special-interest houses. On-campus housing is guaranteed for all 4 years and is available on a first-come, first-served basis. 75% of students live on campus; of those, 60% remain on campus on weekends. All students may keep cars.
Activities: There are 1 local sorority. There are no fraternities. There are 32 groups on campus, including cheerleading, chorale, chorus, computers, dance, debate, drama, ethnic, honors, international, literary magazine, musical theater, newspaper, political, professional, radio and TV, religious, social, social service, student government, and yearbook. Popular campus events include Act One Plays, an annual lecture series, and a formal.
Sports: There are 8 intercollegiate sports for men and 7 for women, and 8 intramural sports for men and 8 for women. There are facilities for soccer, baseball, softball, tennis, basketball, and volleyball, and a state-of-the-art sports and recreation facility featuring a fitness center, a student lounge, and multipurpose athletic courts.
Disabled Students: 95% of the campus is accessible. Wheelchair ramps, elevators, special parking, specially equipped rest rooms, special class scheduling, lowered drinking fountains, and lowered telephones are available.
Services: Counseling and information services are available, as is tutoring in most subjects. There is a reader service for the blind and remedial reading and writing. Learning Center resources (including tutoring) are available to all students.

Campus Safety and Security: Measures include 24-hour foot and vehicle patrol, escort service, informal discussions, and pamphlets/posters/films. There are emergency telephones, lighted pathways/sidewalks, and 24-hour desk security in residence halls.

Programs of Study: DSU confers B.A., B.S., and B.S.N. degrees. Master's degrees are also awarded. Bachelor's degrees are awarded in BIOLOGICAL SCIENCE (biology/biological science), BUSINESS (accounting, banking and finance, business administration and management, electronic business, human resources, management information systems, marketing/retailing/merchandising, and sports management), COMMUNICATIONS AND THE ARTS (communications, dance, dramatic arts, English, film arts, performing arts, and Spanish), COMPUTER AND PHYSICAL SCIENCE (chemistry, computer science, and mathematics), EDUCATION (elementary), ENGINEERING AND ENVIRONMENTAL DESIGN (environmental science), HEALTH PROFESSIONS (nursing and physician's assistant), SOCIAL SCIENCE (criminal justice, family/consumer studies, history, liberal arts/general studies, philosophy, political science/government, psychology, social work, and theological studies). Business, theater, and physician assistant are the strongest academically and the largest.

Required: For graduation, students must complete a minimum of 120 credit hours, including a maximum of 48 in the major, with a minimum GPA of 2.0. Liberal arts distribution requirements consist of 12 to 16 courses, including cultural literacy, modes of thinking, and Christian values and theology, as well as 3 units in phys ed.

Special: Students may cross-register with schools in the Lehigh Valley Association of Independent Colleges. Internships are strongly encouraged in all majors and study abroad in 3 countries is possible. Dual majors, pass/fail options, accelerated degree programs, and credit for life, military, and work experience are offered. There are 9 national honor societies.

Faculty/Classroom: 60% of faculty are male; 40%, female. All teach undergraduates, All do research. No introductory courses are taught by graduate students. The average class size in an introductory lecture is 20; in a laboratory, 20; and in a regular course, 20.

Admissions: 73% of the 2001-2002 applicants were accepted. The SAT I scores for the 2001-2002 freshman class were: Verbal--29% below 500, 45% between 500 and 599, 23% between 600 and 700, and 4% above 700; Math--34% below 500, 42% between 500 and 599, 21% between 600 and 700, and 3% above 700. 40% of the current freshmen were in the top fifth of their class; 69% were in the top two fifths.

Requirements: The SAT I is required. In addition, applicants must be graduates of an accredited secondary school. The GED is accepted. Applicants should have completed 17 college-preparatory courses, including 4 years each of English, history, and math, 3 years of science, and 2 years of foreign language. The school will accept an essay, but strongly recommends an interview. For theater students, a performance appraisal is required. For dance students an audition is required. DSU requires applicants to be in the upper 60% of their class. A GPA of 3.0 is required. AP and CLEP credits are accepted. Important factors in the admissions decision are advanced placement or honor courses, leadership record, and evidence of special talent. Students can apply electronically via Apply, EXPAN, and the university's web site.

Procedure: Freshmen are admitted fall and spring. Entrance exams should be taken during the junior or senior year. There is a deferred admissions plan. Application deadlines are open. The fall 2001 application fee was $30. Notification is on a rolling basis.

Transfer: 47 transfer students enrolled in 2001-2002. Applicants should have completed a minimum of 24 college credit hours with a GPA of 2.5. An interview is recommended. 60 credits of 120 must be completed at DSU.

Visiting: There are regularly scheduled orientations for prospective students, including meetings with faculty advisers and social activities. Visiting students should be prepared to complete a writing sample. There are guides for informal visits and visitors may sit in on classes and stay overnight. To schedule a visit, contact the Enrollment Management Office at (610) 282-4443 or *admiss@desales.edu*.

Financial Aid: In 2001-2002, 80% of all freshmen and 84% of continuing students received some form of financial aid. 76% of freshmen and 83% of continuing students received need-based aid. The average freshman award was $12,587. Of that total, scholarships or need-based grants averaged $10,004 ($16,000 maximum); loans averaged $1860 ($6625 maximum); and work contracts averaged $1000 ($1300 maximum). 51% of undergraduates work part time. Average annual earnings from campus work are $833. The average financial indebtedness of the 2001 graduate was $13,997. The FAFSA and the college's own financial statement are required. The fall application deadline is February 1.

International Students: There are 3 international students enrolled. They must score 550 on the written TOEFL; the SAT I is recommended, but not required.

Computers: The mainframe is a DEC ALPHA server 4100 running Compaq 64/Unix. There are 200 public computing/classroom PCs, fully network compliant, and network connections are supplied to all residence halls. All students may access the system from 7 A.M. to midnight. There are no fees. It is strongly recommended that all students have a personal computer, preferably a Pentium PC 100 MHz or higher processor with 32 MB RAM or a Mac PowerPC or higher processor with 32 MB RAM.

Graduates: In 2001, 371 bachelor's degrees were awarded. The most popular majors were business (40%), health professions (12%), and visual and performing arts (12%). In an average class, 55% graduate in 4 years and 58% in 5 years. 76 companies recruited on campus in 2000-2001. Of the 2000 graduating class, 10% were enrolled in graduate school within 6 months of graduation and 88% were employed.

Admissions Contact: Jerry Joyce, Dean of Enrollment Management. E-mail: *admiss@desales.edu* Web: *www.desales.edu*

DICKINSON COLLEGE — D-3

Carlisle, PA 17013 — (717) 245-1231
(800) 644-1773; Fax: (717) 245-1442

Full-time: 908 men, 1264 women	**Faculty:** 163; IIB, +$
Part-time: 9 men, 27 women	**Ph.D.s:** 90%
Graduate: none	**Student/Faculty:** 13 to 1
Year: semesters, summer session	**Tuition:** $25,485
Application Deadline: February 1	**Room & Board:** $6725
Freshman Class: 3820 applied, 2453 accepted, 611 enrolled	
SAT I Verbal/Math: 620/610	**ACT:** 28 **VERY COMPETITIVE+**

Dickinson College, founded in 1773, is a private institution offering a liberal arts curriculum including international education and science. The library contains 466,651 volumes, 172,431 microform items, and 13,466 audiovisual forms/CDs, and subscribes to 1951 periodicals. Computerized library services include the card catalog, interlibrary loans, and database searching. Special learning facilities include an art gallery, planetarium, radio station, fiber-optic and satellite telecommunications networks, telescope observatory, and an archival collection. The 115-acre campus is in a suburban area about 20 miles west of Harrisburg and 2 hours from Washington, DC. Including residence halls, there are 110 buildings.

Student Life: 59% of undergraduates are from out of state, mostly the Middle Atlantic. Others are from 45 states and 18 foreign countries. 69% are from public schools. 92% are white. 27% are Protestant; 25% Catholic; 17% claim no religious affiliation. The average age of freshmen is 18; all undergraduates, 20. 11% do not continue beyond their first year; 76% remain to graduate.

Housing: 1845 students can be accommodated in college housing, which includes single-sex and coed dormitories, on-campus apartments, fraternity houses, and sorority houses. In addition, there are language houses and special-interest houses, including arts, Asian, environmental, equality, Hillel, and multicultural.. On-campus housing is guaranteed for all 4 years. 92% of students live on campus; of those, 85% remain on campus on weekends. Upperclassmen may keep cars.

Activities: 25% of men belong to 8 national fraternities; 26% of women belong to 1 local and 3 national sororities. There are 120 groups on campus, including art, band, cheerleading, chess, choir, chorale, chorus, computers, dance, debate, drama, ethnic, film, gay, honors, international, jazz band, literary magazine, musical theater, newspaper, orchestra, photography, political, professional, radio and TV, religious, social, social service, student government, symphony, and yearbook. Popular campus events include Black Arts Festival, Multicultural Fair, and Parents Weekend.

Sports: There are 11 intercollegiate sports for men and 12 for women, and 14 intramural sports for men and 12 for women. Facilities include an 8000-square-foot fitness center with weight training and 40 cardiorespiratory conditioning machines, and the 38,600 square-foot Kline Center with a basketball court, swimming pool, indoor track, and squash, racquetball, and handball courts. There are also tennis courts, a varsity football field plus 4 other fields, an outdoor track, a 19-acre recreational park with a jogging trail, and an indoor rock-climbing wall.

Disabled Students: 55% of the campus is accessible. Wheelchair ramps, elevators, special parking, specially equipped rest rooms, special class scheduling, lowered drinking fountains, lowered telephones, housing, and telephone access are available.

Services: Counseling and information services are available, as is tutoring in every subject. Services are provided as necessary on a case-by-case basis. There is a reader service for the blind. There also is a writing center.

Campus Safety and Security: Measures include 24-hour foot and vehicle patrol, self-defense education, escort service, and informal discussions. There are pamphlets/posters/films, emergency telephones, lighted pathways/sidewalks, and electronic access to residence halls.

Programs of Study: Dickinson confers B.A. and B.S. degrees. Bachelor's degrees are awarded in BIOLOGICAL SCIENCE (biochemistry and biology/biological science), BUSINESS (international business management), COMMUNICATIONS AND THE ARTS (classical languages, dance, dramatic arts, English, fine arts, French, German, Greek, Latin, music, Russian, Spanish, and theater design), COMPUTER AND PHYSICAL SCIENCE (chemistry, computer science, geology, mathematics, and physics), ENGINEERING AND ENVIRONMENTAL DESIGN (environmental science), HEALTH PROFESSIONS (environmental health science), SOCIAL SCIENCE (American studies, anthropology, classical/ancient civilization, East Asian studies, economics, history, international studies, Italian studies, Judaic studies, medieval studies, philosophy, political science/government, psychology, public affairs, religion, Russian and Slavic studies, and sociology). International education/foreign languages, natural sciences, and preprofessional programs are the strongest academically. Foreign languages, political science, and English are the largest.

Required: To graduate, students must complete 32 courses with a minimum GPA of 2.0. The school requires 2 courses each in humanities, social sciences, and lab sciences. Also required are 3 courses of crosscultural studies (including foreign language and U.S. diversity), a freshman seminar, phys ed, and the completion of a major averaging 9 to 10 courses. Writing-intensive, quantitative reasoning, and community experience courses are also required.

Special: Students may cross-register with Central Pennsylvania Consortium Colleges. Also available are internships, academic year or summer study abroad in 12 countries, a Washington semester, work-study programs, accelerated degree programs, dual majors, student-designed majors, nondegree study, pass/fail options, and a 3-3 law degree with the Dickinson School of Law of the Pennsylvania State University. There are 3-2 engineering degrees offered with Case Western Reserve University, Rensselaer Polytechnic Institute, and the University of Pennsylvania. Instruction in 11 languages is available. There are certification programs in Latin American studies, secondary education, and women's studies. Linkage programs are available with 7 graduate programs in business, accounting, and public administration at various institutions. There are 15 national honor societies, including Phi Beta Kappa, and 38 departmental honors programs.

Faculty/Classroom: 62% of faculty are male; 38%, female. All both teach and do research. The average class size in an introductory lecture is 35; in a laboratory, 18; and in a regular course, 15.

Admissions: 64% of the 2001-2002 applicants were accepted. The SAT I scores for the 2001-2002 freshman class were: Verbal--1% below 500, 33% between 500 and 599, 51% between 600 and 700, and 15% above 700; Math--3% below 500, 35% between 500 and 599, 53% between 600 and 700, and 8% above 700. 72% of the current freshmen were in the top fifth of their class; 92% were in the top two fifths. 16 freshmen graduated first in their class.

Requirements: SAT I or ACT scores are optional submissions but are required for academic scholarship consideration. The GED is accepted. Applicants should have completed 16 academic credits, including 4 years of English, 3 each of math and science, 2 (preferably 3) of foreign language, 2 of social studies, and 2 additional courses drawn from the above areas. An essay is required and an interview is recommended. AP credits are accepted. Important factors in the admissions decision are advanced placement or honor courses, extracurricular activities record, and recommendations by school officials. Applications are accepted on computer disk and on-line via Common App, CollegeView, CollegeLink, and others.

Procedure: Freshmen are admitted in the fall. Entrance exams should be taken in the spring of the junior year or the fall of the senior year. There are early decision, early admissions, and deferred admissions plans. Early decision applications should be filed by January 15; regular applications, by February 1 for fall entry, along with a $40 fee. Notification of early decision is sent February 15; regular decision, March 31. 133 early decision candidates were accepted for the 2001-2002 class. 14% of all applicants are on a waiting list; 3 were accepted in 2001.

Transfer: 9 transfer students enrolled in 2001-2002. Applicants will normally have at least a 2.0 cumulative GPA and must submit secondary school and college transcripts and a dean's report form in addition to the standard application for admission. 16 credits of 32 must be completed at Dickinson.

Visiting: There are regularly scheduled orientations for prospective students, including campus tours, individual interviews, group information sessions, class visits, overnight stays in residence halls, and open houses. There are guides for informal visits and visitors may sit in on classes and stay overnight. To schedule a visit, contact the Admissions Office.

Financial Aid: In 2001-2002, 65% of all freshmen and 77% of continuing students received some form of financial aid. 55% of freshmen and 61% of continuing students received need-based aid. The average freshman award was $20,362. Of that total, scholarships or need-based grants averaged $14,155 ($25,500 maximum); loans averaged $2767 ($7500 maximum); work contracts averaged $1260 ($1850 maximum); and federal, state, and outside grants/scholarships averaged $2180 ($25,575 maximum). 34% of undergraduates work part time. Average annual earnings from campus work are $1099. The average financial indebtedness of the 2001 graduate was $16,945. Dickinson is a member of CSS. The CSS/Profile or FAFSA, noncustodial parent statement, state aid form, and business farm supplement are required. The fall application deadline is February 1.

International Students: There are 41 international students enrolled. The school actively recruits these students. They must score 550 on the written TOEFL.

Computers: The mainframe is a DEC 4100 ALPHA AXP. A fiber-optic network enables students to have private personal computer hookup to the mainframe from their residence hall rooms. All students are assigned ALPHA accounts for e-mail and Internet communications. There are more than 499 PCs and Macs in public areas and instructional spaces. All students may access the system. There are no time limits and no fees.

Graduates: In 2001, 457 bachelor's degrees were awarded. The most popular majors were foreign languages (14%), political science (14%), and English (13%). In an average class, 76% graduate in 4 years and 80% in 5 years. 31 companies recruited on campus in 2000-2001. Of the 2000 graduating class, 17% were enrolled in graduate school within 6 months of graduation and 99% were employed.

Admissions Contact: Christopher Seth Allen, Director of Admissions. E-mail: *admit@dickinson.edu* Web: *http://www.dickinson.edu*

DREXEL UNIVERSITY F-3
Philadelphia, PA 19104 (215) 895-2400
(800) 2-DREXEL; Fax: (215) 895-5939

Full-time: 5639 men, 3464 women	**Faculty:** 499; I, -$
Part-time: 1215 men, 701 women	**Ph.D.s:** 90%
Graduate: 1463 men, 1064 women	**Student/Faculty:** 18 to 1
Year: quarters, summer session	**Tuition:** $18,962
Application Deadline: March 1	**Room & Board:** $8695
Freshman Class: 9888 applied, 7193 accepted, 2028 enrolled	
SAT I Verbal/Math: 560/595	**VERY COMPETITIVE**

Drexel University, established in 1891, is a private institution with undergraduate programs in business and administration, engineering, information studies, design arts, and arts and sciences. There are 9 undergraduate and 8 graduate schools. In addition to regional accreditation, Drexel has baccalaureate program accreditation with AACSB, ABET, ADA, APA, CSAB, FIDER, and NAAB. The library contains 290,000 volumes, 651,500 microform items, and 32,935 audiovisual forms/CDs, and subscribes to 9662 periodicals. Computerized library services include the card catalog, interlibrary loans, and database searching. Special learning facilities include a learning resource center, art gallery, radio station, and TV station. The 49-acre campus is in an urban area near the center of Philadelphia. Including residence halls, there are 34 buildings.

Student Life: 68% of undergraduates are from Pennsylvania. Others are from 40 states, 121 foreign countries, and Canada. 55% are white; 12%, Asian American. The average age of freshmen is 18; all undergraduates, 22. 14% do not continue beyond their first year; 54% remain to graduate.

Housing: 2600 students can be accommodated in college housing, which includes coed dormitories, on-campus apartments, and fraternity houses. In addition, there is disabled-student housing and honors floors in residence halls. On-campus housing is guaranteed for the freshman year only, is available on a first-come, first-served basis, and is available on a lottery system for upperclassmen. 74% of students commute. All students may keep cars.

Activities: 12% of men belong to 14 national fraternities; 8% of women belong to 4 national sororities. There are 103 groups on campus, including art, band, cheerleading, chess, choir, chorus, computers, dance, drama, ethnic, film, gay, honors, international, jazz band, literary magazine, musical theater, newspaper, orchestra, pep band, photography, political, professional, radio and TV, religious, social, social service, student government, and yearbook. Popular campus events include Spring Jam, Winter Weekend, and an ongoing program of musical, cultural, and art events.

Sports: There are 10 intercollegiate sports for men and 10 for women, and 15 intramural sports for men and 12 for women. Facilities include a phys ed and activity center with 3 gyms, 6 squash courts, a swimming pool, a diving well, a wrestling room, a dance studio, a fencing room, Nautilus weight training rooms, and special exercise rooms; a field house; a bowling alley and game room with billiard, table tennis, and arcade games; and an outdoor volleyball court.

Disabled Students: 75% of the campus is accessible. Wheelchair ramps, elevators, special parking, specially equipped rest rooms, special class scheduling, lowered drinking fountains, and lowered telephones are available.

Services: Counseling and information services are available, as is tutoring in most subjects. There is remedial math, reading, and writing and a resident tutor program.

Campus Safety and Security: Measures include 24-hour foot and vehicle patrol, self-defense education, escort service, and shuttle buses. There are pamphlets/posters/films, emergency telephones, lighted pathways/sidewalks, and residential and commuter safety and security programs.

Programs of Study: Drexel confers B.A., B.S., and B.Arch. degrees. Master's and doctoral degrees are also awarded. Bachelor's degrees are awarded in BIOLOGICAL SCIENCE (biology/biological science and nutrition), BUSINESS (business administration and management, fashion merchandising, hotel/motel and restaurant management, and marketing/retailing/merchandising), COMMUNICATIONS AND THE ARTS (communications, creative writing, design, film arts, graphic design, literature, music, photography, and video), COMPUTER AND PHYSICAL SCIENCE (chemistry, computer science, digital arts/technology, information sciences and systems, mathematics, physics, and science), EDUCATION (education), ENGINEERING AND ENVIRONMENTAL DESIGN (architectural engineering, architecture, biomedical engineering, chemical engineering, civil engineering, computer engineering, construction management, electrical/electronics engineering, environmental engineering, environmental science, interior design, materials engineering, and mechanical engineering), HEALTH PROFESSIONS (predentistry and premedicine), SOCIAL SCIENCE (fashion design and technology, food production/management/services, history, international studies, political science/government, prelaw, psychology, and sociology). Engineering, business, and design arts are the strongest academically. Electrical and computer engineering, business, and architecture are the largest.

Required: To graduate, students must complete 180 to 192 term credits with a minimum GPA of 2.0 and must earn the number of Drexel Co-op Units determined by the major. There are requirements in math, English, lab science, social science, and history.

Special: The Drexel Plan of Cooperative Education enables students to alternate periods of full-time classroom studies and full-time employment with university-approved employers. Participation in cooperative education is mandatory, for most students. Cross-registration is available with Eastern Mennonite College, Indiana University of Pennsylvania, and Lincoln University. Drexel also offers study abroad, internships, accelerated degrees, 3-3 engineering degrees, dual majors, nondegree study, credit/no credit options, and a Sea Education Association semester. There is a freshman honors program.

Faculty/Classroom: 72% of faculty are male; 28%, female. 24% teach undergraduates and 76% both teach and do research. The average class size in an introductory lecture is 35; in a laboratory, 24; and in a regular course, 24.

Admissions: 73% of the 2001-2002 applicants were accepted. The SAT I scores for the 2001-2002 freshman class were: Verbal--17% below 500, 50% between 500 and 599, 29% between 600 and 700, and 4% above 700; Math--9% below 500, 41% between 500 and 599, 42% between 600 and 700, and 8% above 700. 45% of the current freshmen were in the top fifth of their class; 80% were in the top two fifths. 21 freshmen graduated first in their class.

Requirements: The SAT I or ACT is required. In addition, applicants must be graduates of an accredited secondary school. The GED is accepted. An interview is recommended. A GPA of 2.0 is required. AP and CLEP credits are accepted. Important factors in the admissions decision are advanced placement or honor courses, evidence of special talent, and recommendations by school officials. Applications may be submitted on-line via the university's web site.

Procedure: Freshmen are admitted to all sessions. Entrance exams should be taken by January 1 of the senior year. There are early admissions and deferred admissions plans. Applications should be filed by March 1 for fall entry. The fall 2001 application fee was $35. Notification is sent on a rolling basis.

Transfer: 597 transfer students enrolled in 2001-2002. Applicants must have a minimum GPA of 2.5. Other requirements vary among the individual colleges within the university. 45 credits of 180 to 192 must be completed at Drexel.

Visiting: There are regularly scheduled orientations for prospective students, consisting of a 2-day program for new freshmen and their parents in late July. There are guides for informal visits and visitors may sit in on classes and stay overnight. To schedule a visit, contact the Admissions Office.

Financial Aid: In 2001-2002, 80% of all students received some form of financial aid. 73% of freshmen and 55% of continuing students received need-based aid. The average freshman award was $14,000. Of that total, scholarships or need-based grants averaged $7400; loans averaged $3000; and work contracts averaged $1000. In sophomore and later years, co-op earnings add an average income of about $10,000 per year. 16% of undergraduates work part time. Average annual earnings from campus work are $800. The FAFSA is required. The fall application deadline is May 1.

International Students: There are 632 international students enrolled. The school actively recruits these students. They must score 510 on the written TOEFL.

Computers: The mainframes are an IBM 9121/320 and a Sun Server 670. Students may access the mainframe, the library, and the Internet through PCs in dorms or residences. There are also 610 networked public computers available. Drexel also offers completely wireless Internet access throughout the campus. All students may access the system 24 hours a day. There are no time limits and no fees. All students are required to have personal computers.

Graduates: In 2001, 1249 bachelor's degrees were awarded. The most popular majors were business administration (24%), information systems (8%), and electrical engineering (6%). In an average class, 1% graduate in 3 years, 9% in 4 years, 49% in 5 years, and 54% in 6 years. 300 companies recruited on campus in 2000-2001. Of the 2000 graduating class, 14% were enrolled in graduate school within 6 months of graduation and 81% were employed.

Admissions Contact: David Eddy, Director of Admissions. A video is available. E-mail: *enroll@drexel.edu* Web: *www.drexel.edu*

DUQUESNE UNIVERSITY — B-3
Pittsburgh, PA 15282-0201 — (412) 396-5000
(800) 456-0590; Fax: (412) 396-5644

Full-time: 2080 men, 2873 women	**Faculty:** 408; IIA, av$
Part-time: 194 men, 257 women	**Ph.D.s:** 81%
Graduate: 1696 men, 2351 women	**Student/Faculty:** 12 to 1
Year: semesters, summer session	**Tuition:** $17,478
Application Deadline: July 1	**Room & Board:** $6764
Freshman Class: 3139 applied, 3018 accepted, 1191 enrolled	
SAT I Verbal/Math: 540/540	**ACT:** 26 **COMPETITIVE+**

Duquesne University, founded in 1878, is a private institution affiliated with the Roman Catholic Church, offering programs in liberal arts, natural and environmental sciences, nursing, health sciences, pharmacy, business, music, teacher preparation, preprofessional training, and law. There are 9 undergraduate and 10 graduate schools. In addition to regional accreditation, Duquesne has baccalaureate program accreditation with AACSB, ACOTE, ACPE, ACS, AHIMA, APTA, CAAHEP, NAMT, NASM, and NLN. The 2 libraries contain 677,633 volumes, 288,814 microform items, and 25,315 audiovisual forms/CDs, and subscribe to 5359 periodicals. Computerized library services include the card catalog, interlibrary loans, and database searching. Special learning facilities include a learning resource center, art gallery, radio station, TV station, and 119 multimedia classrooms. The 43-acre campus is in an urban area on a private, self-contained campus in the center of Pittsburgh. Including residence halls, there are 26 buildings.

Student Life: 81% of undergraduates are from Pennsylvania. Others are from 46 states, 83 foreign countries, and Canada. 56% are from public schools. 77% are white. 49% are Catholic; 32% claim no religious affiliation. The average age of freshmen is 18; all undergraduates, 22. 15% do not continue beyond their first year; 72% remain to graduate.

Housing: 2779 students can be accommodated in college housing, which includes single-sex dormitories. In addition, there are honors houses, special-interest houses, fraternity and sorority wings, no smoking wings, international wings, and club wings. On-campus housing is guaranteed for the freshman year only, is available on a first-come, first-served basis, and is available on a lottery system for upperclassmen. 56% of students commute. All students may keep cars.

Activities: 14% of men belong to 3 local and 8 national fraternities; 14% of women belong to 1 local sorority and 8 national sororities. There are 134 groups on campus, including art, band, cheerleading, chess, choir, chorale, chorus, computers, dance, debate, drama, ethnic, film, honors, international, jazz band, literary magazine, marching band, musical theater, newspaper, opera, orchestra, pep band, photography, political, professional, radio and TV, religious, social, social programming, social service, student government, symphony, and yearbook. Popular campus events include Carnival, Dance Marathon, and Valentine, Halloween, and Christmas balls.

Sports: There are 10 intercollegiate sports for men and 10 for women, and 9 intramural sports for men and 9 for women. Facilities include an athletic center, a swimming pool, a football and soccer field, a baseball field, an intramural field with an all-weather track, a weight room and exercise facilities, volleyball courts, 4 tennis courts, a squash court, racquetball courts, and a street hockey court.

Disabled Students: All of the campus is accessible. Wheelchair ramps, elevators, special parking, specially equipped rest rooms, special class scheduling, lowered drinking fountains, and lowered telephones are available.

Services: Counseling and information services are available, as is tutoring in every subject, including special tutorials for chemistry, biology, physics, and math. There is a reader service for the blind, and remedial math, reading, and writing.

Campus Safety and Security: Measures include 24-hour foot and vehicle patrol, self-defense education, escort service, and informal discussions. There are pamphlets/posters/films, emergency telephones, and lighted pathways/sidewalks. There are security cameras throughout campus that monitor exterior areas. All academic buildings have card access. Security measures for residence halls include card access, security cameras, and entrances that are monitored by residence life staff 24 hours a day.

Programs of Study: Duquesne confers B.A., B.S., B.M., B.S.A.T., B.S.B.A., B.S.Ed., B.S.H.M.S., B.S.H.S., B.S.M.E., B.S.M.T., B.S.N., and B.S.P.S. degrees. Master's and doctoral degrees are also awarded. Bachelor's degrees are awarded in BIOLOGICAL SCIENCE (biochemistry, biology/biological science, and microbiology), BUSINESS (accounting, banking and finance, business administration and management, international business management, investments and securities, marketing and distribution, marketing/retailing/merchandising, and purchasing/ inventory management), COMMUNICATIONS AND THE ARTS (art history and appreciation, classical languages, classics, communications, dramatic arts, English, Greek, journalism, languages, Latin, literature, music, music performance, Spanish, and studio art), COMPUTER AND PHYSICAL SCIENCE (chemistry, computer science, information sciences and systems, mathematics, and physics), EDUCATION (athletic training, early childhood, educational media, elementary, English, foreign languages, mathematics, music, science, secondary, and social studies), ENGINEERING AND ENVIRONMENTAL DESIGN (environmental science), HEALTH PROFESSIONS (health care administration, health science, music therapy, nursing, occupational therapy, pharmacy, physical therapy, physician's assistant, and speech pathology/audiology), SOCIAL SCIENCE (history, international relations, liberal arts/general studies, philosophy, political science/government, psychology, social science, sociology, and theological studies). Chemistry, biology, and environmental science are the strongest academically. Liberal arts, business, and health sciences are the largest.

Required: To graduate, students are required to complete at least 120 credit hours, including at least 27 in the major, with a minimum 2.0 GPA. General requirements vary by department, but there is a 27-credit liberal arts core curriculum.

Special: The university offers cross-registration through the Pittsburgh Council on Higher Education, internships, study abroad in 22 countries, and a Washington semester. Also available are B.A.-B.S. degrees, Saturday College, a general studies degree, an accelerated degree program, dual and student-designed majors, a 3-2 engineering program with Case Western Reserve University and University of Pittsburgh, pass/fail options, and credit for life, military, and work experience. There are 5 national honor societies, a freshman honors program, and 7 departmental honors programs.

Faculty/Classroom: 64% of faculty are male; 36%, female. The average class size in an introductory lecture is 31; in a laboratory, 23; and in a regular course, 27.

Admissions: 96% of the 2001-2002 applicants were accepted. The SAT I scores for the 2001-2002 freshman class were: Verbal--29% below 500, 48% between 500 and 599, 22% between 600 and 700, and 1% above 700; Math--28% below 500, 47% between 500 and 599, 23% between 600 and 700, and 2% above 700. The ACT scores were 28% below 21, 31% between 21 and 23, 23% between 24 and 26, 9% between 27 and 28, and 9% above 28. 43% of the current freshmen were in the top fifth of their class; 71% were in the top two fifths. 39 freshmen graduated first in their class.

Requirements: The SAT I or ACT is required. In addition, students should have either a high school diploma or the GED. Applicants are required to have 16 academic credits, including 4 each in English and academic electives and 8 combined in social studies, language, math, and science. An audition is required for music majors. An essay is required, and an interview is recommended. A GPA of 2.75 is required. AP and CLEP credits are accepted. Important factors in the admissions decision are advanced placement or honor courses, geographic diversity, and ability to finance college education. Applications are accepted on-line at the school's web site.

Procedure: Freshmen are admitted to all sessions. Entrance exams should be taken during the spring of the junior year or the fall of the senior year. There are early decision, early admissions, and deferred admissions plans. Early decision applications should be filed by November 1; regular applications, by July 1 for fall entry, December 1 for spring entry, and April 1 for summer entry, along with a $50 fee. Notification of early decision is sent December 15; regular decision, on a rolling basis. 182 early decision candidates were accepted for the 2001-2002 class.

Transfer: 166 transfer students enrolled in 2001-2002. Applicants must submit complete high school and college transcripts. Students should have a minimum GPA of 2.5 for the university, but some schools require a higher average. A minimum of 12 credits earned is required and an interview is recommended. 30 credits of 120 must be completed at Duquesne.

Visiting: There are regularly scheduled orientations for prospective students, consisting of a campus tour and individual interviews with counselors and professors. There are guides for informal visits and visitors may sit in on classes. To schedule a visit, contact the Office of Admissions at (412) 396-6222 or *admissions@duq.edu*.

Financial Aid: In 2001-2002, 92% of all freshmen and 79% of continuing students received some form of financial aid. 64% of freshmen and 48% of continuing students received need-based aid. The average freshman award was $11,438. Of that total, scholarships or need-based grants averaged $7629 ($28,138 maximum); loans averaged $2449 ($4625 maximum); work contracts averaged $846 ($2318 maximum); and outside grants and awards averaged $514 ($16,917 maximum). Average annual earnings from campus work are $1661. The average financial indebtedness of the 2001 graduate was $11,390. Duquesne is a member of CSS. The FAFSA and the college's own financial statement are required. The fall application deadline is May 1.

International Students: There are 220 international students enrolled. The school actively recruits these students. They must score 575 on the written TOEFL or 233 on the electronic version or take the MELAB.

Computers: The mainframe is a Compaq Alpha Server GS60E. There are also 650 PCs available in labs throughout the campus. Access to campus network resources is available 24 hours a day from residence halls or home. There are no time limits and no fees. It is strongly recommended that all students have a personal computer.

Graduates: In 2001, 1109 bachelor's degrees were awarded. The most popular majors were liberal arts (25%), business (24%), and education (17%). In an average class, 46% graduate in 4 years, 60% in 5 years, and 71% in 6 years. 100 companies recruited on campus in 2000-2001. Of the 2000 graduating class, 23% were enrolled in graduate school within 6 months of graduation and 80% were employed.

Admissions Contact: Paul Cukanna, Interim Director of Admissions. A video is available. E-mail: *admissions@duq2.cc.duq.edu*
Web: *www.duq.edu*

EAST STROUDSBURG UNIVERSITY OF PENNSYLVANIA F-2

East Stroudsburg, PA 18301 **(570) 422-3542**
(877) 230-5547; Fax: (570) 422-3933

Full-time: 1770 men, 2500 women	**Faculty:** 236; IIA, +$
Part-time: 270 men, 330 women	**Ph.D.s:** 71%
Graduate: 300 men, 725 women	**Student/Faculty:** 18 to 1
Year: semesters, summer session	**Tuition:** $4500 ($10,000)
Application Deadline: see profile	**Room & Board:** $4000
Freshman Class: n/av	
SAT I Verbal/Math: required	**LESS COMPETITIVE**

East Stroudsburg University of Pennsylvania, founded in 1893, is a part of the Pennsylvania State System of Higher Education and offers programs in arts and science, health sciences and human performance, and professional studies. There are 3 undergraduate schools and 1 graduate school. Figures in the above capsule, and in this profile, are approximate. In addition to regional accreditation, East Stroudsburg has baccalaureate program accreditation with NLN. The library contains 428,000 volumes, 1,238,040 microform items, and 7650 audiovisual forms/CDs, and subscribes to 2200 periodicals. Computerized library services include the card catalog, interlibrary loans, and database searching. Special learning facilities include a learning resource center, art gallery, radio station, and wildlife museum. The 183-acre campus is in a small town 75 miles west of New York City. Including residence halls, there are 39 buildings.

Student Life: 84% of undergraduates are from Pennsylvania. Others are from 22 states, 21 foreign countries, and Canada. 92% are white. The average age of freshmen is 18; all undergraduates, 23. 17% do not continue beyond their first year; 60% remain to graduate.

Housing: About 2140 students can be accommodated in college housing, which includes single-sex and coed dormitories and on-campus apartments. 53% of students commute. Alcohol is not permitted. Upperclassmen may keep cars.

Activities: 12% of men belong to 8 national fraternities; 15% of women belong to 2 local and 6 national sororities. There are 76 groups on campus, including art, band, cheerleading, chess, choir, chorus, computers, dance, drama, ethnic, gay, honors, international, jazz band, literary magazine, musical theater, newspaper, pep band, political, professional, radio and TV, religious, social, social service, student government, and yearbook. Popular campus events include concerts, Spring Music Festival, and International Celebrations.

Sports: There are 9 intercollegiate sports for men and 9 for women, and 11 intramural sports for men and 11 for women. Facilities include a 5000-seat stadium, a 2600-seat gym, another gym, 8 athletic fields, 12 outdoor tennis courts, 1 indoor tennis court, a swimming pool, indoor and outdoor tracks, and weight rooms.

Disabled Students: 98% of the campus is accessible. Wheelchair ramps, elevators, special parking, specially equipped rest rooms, special class scheduling, lowered drinking fountains, lowered telephones, and visual fire alarms for hearing impaired persons are available.

Services: Counseling and information services are available, as is tutoring in every subject. There is remedial math, reading, and writing.

Campus Safety and Security: Measures include 24-hour foot and vehicle patrol, self-defense education, escort service, and informal discussions. There are pamphlets/posters/films, emergency telephones, lighted pathways/sidewalks, and a police bicycle patrol.

Programs of Study: East Stroudsburg confers B.A. and B.S. degrees. Master's degrees are also awarded. Bachelor's degrees are awarded in BIOLOGICAL SCIENCE (biochemistry, biology/biological science, and marine science), BUSINESS (business administration and management, and hotel/motel and restaurant management), COMMUNICATIONS AND THE ARTS (art, communications, dramatic arts, English, fine arts, French, media arts, music, and Spanish), COMPUTER AND PHYSICAL SCIENCE (chemistry, computer science, earth science, mathematics, physical sciences, and science), EDUCATION (early childhood, elementary, foreign languages, health, secondary, and special), ENGINEERING AND ENVIRONMENTAL DESIGN (environmental science), HEALTH PROFESSIONS (allied health, medical laboratory technology, nursing, premedicine, and speech pathology/audiology), SOCIAL SCIENCE (economics, geography, history, parks and recreation management, philosophy, physical fitness/movement, political science/government, psychology, social studies, and sociology). Computer science, nursing, and math are the strongest academically. Education, hospitality management, and phys ed are the largest.

Required: All students must maintain a GPA of at least 2.0 while taking 128 semester hours, including 27 to 83 hours in the major. General education courses total 50 credits, with English composition and phys ed required courses. Distribution requirements include 15 hours in arts and letters, science, and social science.

Special: Internships are offered in most programs, as are dual majors. Also offered are B.A.-B.S. degrees, 3-2 engineering degrees with Pennsylvania State University or the University of Pittsburgh, and a transfer program in podiatry. Nondegree study, study abroad, and cross-registration through the National Student Exchange are possible. There are 16 national honor societies, and a freshman honors program.

Faculty/Classroom: 62% of faculty are male; 38%, female. All teach undergraduates. No introductory courses are taught by graduate students. The average class size in an introductory lecture is 40; in a laboratory, 25; and in a regular course, 25.

Admissions: 15% of recent freshmen were in the top fifth of their class; 48% were in the top two fifths. 1 freshman graduated first in the class.

Requirements: The SAT I is required. In addition, applicants must be graduates of an accredited secondary school. The GED is accepted. AP and CLEP credits are accepted. Important factors in the admissions decision are advanced placement or honor courses, evidence of special talent, and leadership record.

Procedure: Freshmen are admitted in the fall. Entrance exams should be taken during the fall of the senior year. Check with the school for current application deadlines and fee.

Transfer: 437 transfer students enrolled in a recent year. Transfer students must have a 2.0 GPA earned over at least 24 credit hours. 32 credits of 128 must be completed at East Stroudsburg.

Visiting: There are regularly scheduled orientations for prospective students. There are guides for informal visits and visitors may sit in on classes. To schedule a visit, contact the Admissions Office.

Financial Aid: In a recent year, 72% of continuing students received some form of financial aid. East Stroudsburg is a member of CSS. The FAFSA is required. Check with the school for current deadlines.

International Students: There were 30 international students enrolled in a recent year. They must score 500 on the written TOEFL.

Computers: The mainframe is a Unisys A-11. There are 14 file servers connected to 400 PCs located in 15 computer labs. All students may access the system. Most computers are available 7 A.M. to 10 P.M., with some available on a 24-hour basis. There are no time limits and no fees.

Graduates: In an average class, 1% graduate in 3 years, 25% in 4 years, 45% in 5 years, and 50% in 6 years.

Admissions Contact: Alan T. Chesterton, Director of Admission.
E-mail: *undergrads@esu.edu* Web: *www.esu.edu*

EASTERN COLLEGE — F-3

St. Davids, PA 19087-3696 — **(610) 341-5967**
(800) 452-0996; Fax: (610) 341-1723

Full-time: 520 men, 1030 women	**Faculty:** 64; IIA, --$
Part-time: 125 men, 235 women	**Ph.D.s:** 75%
Graduate: 330 men, 525 women	**Student/Faculty:** 24 to 1
Year: semesters, summer session	**Tuition:** $13,800
Application Deadline: open	**Room & Board:** $5900
Freshman Class: n/av	
SAT I Verbal/Math: required	**LESS COMPETITIVE**

Eastern College, founded in 1932, is a private liberal arts institution affiliated with the American Baptist Church. There is 1 graduate school. The figures in the above capsule are approximate. In addition to regional accreditation, Eastern has baccalaureate program accreditation with CSWE and NLN. The 2 libraries contain 131,000 volumes, 716,396 microform items, and 13,242 audiovisual forms/CDs, and subscribe to 1079 periodicals. Computerized library services include the card catalog, interlibrary loans, and database searching. Special learning facilities include a planetarium and radio station. The 107-acre campus is in a small town 20 miles northwest of Philadelphia. Including residence halls, there are 23 buildings.

Student Life: 60% of undergraduates are from Pennsylvania. Others are from 38 states, 26 foreign countries, and Canada. 72% are from public schools. 81% are white; 14% African American. 68% are Assembly of God, Christian, Evangelical, Mennonite, Pentecostal; 13% claim no religious affiliation; 11% Catholic. The average age of freshmen is 19; all undergraduates, 27. 28% do not continue beyond their first year; 55% remain to graduate.

Housing: About 840 students can be accommodated in college housing, which includes single-sex and coed dormitories and on-campus apartments. On-campus housing is guaranteed for all 4 years. 53% of students commute. Alcohol is not permitted. All students may keep cars.

Activities: There are no fraternities or sororities. There are 70 groups on campus, including band, cheerleading, choir, chorale, chorus, computers, dance, drama, drill team, ethnic, honors, international, jazz band, literary magazine, musical theater, newspaper, orchestra, pep band, political, professional, radio and TV, religious, social, social service, student government, and yearbook. Popular campus events include President's Christmas Party, Spring Banquet, and World Culture Day.

Sports: There are 5 intercollegiate sports for men and 7 for women, and 3 intramural sports for men and 3 for women. Facilities include a gym, a soccer pitch, a baseball/field hockey/softball field, a weight room, an outdoor track, 4 tennis courts, a health fitness trail, an outdoor pool, and basketball/volleyball courts.

Disabled Students: 75% of the campus is accessible. Wheelchair ramps, elevators, special parking, specially equipped rest rooms, special class scheduling, lowered drinking fountains, lowered telephones, and special residence hall spaces are available.

Services: Counseling and information services are available, as is tutoring in every subject. There is a reader service for the blind, remedial math, reading, and writing, and a summer skills workshop.

Campus Safety and Security: Measures include 24-hour foot and vehicle patrol, self-defense education, escort service, and shuttle buses. There are informal discussions, pamphlets/posters/films, emergency telephones, and lighted pathways/sidewalks.

Programs of Study: Eastern confers B.A., B.S., B.S.N., and B.S.W. degrees. Associate and master's degrees are also awarded. Bachelor's degrees are awarded in BIOLOGICAL SCIENCE (biochemistry and biology/biological science), BUSINESS (accounting, business administration and management, management information systems, marketing/retailing/merchandising, and trade and industrial supervision and management), COMMUNICATIONS AND THE ARTS (art history and appreciation, communications, creative writing, English literature, French, music, Spanish, and studio art), COMPUTER AND PHYSICAL SCIENCE (astronomy, chemistry, and mathematics), EDUCATION (elementary, English, physical, and secondary), ENGINEERING AND ENVIRONMENTAL DESIGN (city/community/regional planning, and environmental science), HEALTH PROFESSIONS (health care administration), SOCIAL SCIENCE (biblical studies, economics, history, missions, philosophy, political science/government, psychology, social work, sociology, theological studies, urban studies, and youth ministry). Biblical/theological studies and English literature are the strongest academically. Youth ministries and elementary education are the largest.

Required: To graduate, all students must complete at least 127 credit hours with a minimum 2.0 GPA. The required hours in the major vary. Students must take courses in the Old and New Testament, humanities, social sciences, non-Western heritage, natural sciences, college writing, Living and Learning in Community, Heritage of Western Thought and Civilization, Science Technology and Values, Justice in a Pluralistic Society, and complete a capstone.

Special: The college offers cross-registration with Cabrini and Rosemont Colleges, Valley Forge Military Academy, and Villanova University, internships, a Washington semester in the American studies program, and student-designed majors. Also available are accelerated degree programs in organizational management and management of information systems, credit for experience, nondegree study, and pass/fail options. There is a different calendar for the organizational management program. There are 10 national honor societies, a freshman honors program, and 1 departmental honors program.

Faculty/Classroom: 54% of faculty are male; 46%, female. 83% teach undergraduates. No introductory courses are taught by graduate students. The average class size in an introductory lecture is 45; in a laboratory, 14; and in a regular course, 14.

Admissions: 36% of recent freshmen were in the top fifth of their class; 54% were in the top two fifths. There were 17 National Merit semifinalists. 9 freshmen graduated first in their class.

Requirements: The SAT I or ACT is required. In addition, applications can be submitted on-line at the school's home page. A GPA of 2.0 is required. AP and CLEP credits are accepted.

Procedure: Freshmen are admitted to all sessions. Entrance exams should be taken as early as possible. There are early admissions and deferred admissions plans. Application deadlines are open. Check with the school for current application deadlines and fee.

Transfer: 58 transfer students enrolled in a recent year. Applicants should have a 2.0 GPA with more than 24 credits, and a 2.5 GPA with less than 24 credits. Candidates must be in good standing at their previous institution. 32 credits of 127 must be completed at Eastern.

Visiting: There are regularly scheduled orientations for prospective students, including a preview of academics, student life, and athletics. There are guides for informal visits and visitors may sit in on classes and stay overnight. To schedule a visit, contact the Admissions Office.

Financial Aid: Eastern is a member of CSS. The FAFSA, the college's own financial statement and income tax forms are required.

International Students: There were 33 international students enrolled in a recent year. The school actively recruits these students. They must score 550 on the written TOEFL.

Computers: Students may access the Novell on-campus network from 3 labs, resident hall lounge areas, the library, and individual residence hall rooms. All students may access the system. There are no time limits and no fees. It is strongly recommended that all students have a personal computer.

Graduates: In a recent year, 404 bachelor's degrees were awarded. The most popular majors were organizational management (44%), elementary education (10%), and nursing (7%). In an average class, 45% graduate in 4 years, 51% in 5 years, and 55% in 6 years. Of a recent graduating class, 98% were employed within 6 months of graduation.

Admissions Contact: Mark Seymour, Executive Director of Enrollment Management. A video is available. E-mail: *ugadm@eastern.edu* Web: *www.eastern.edu*

EDINBORO UNIVERSITY OF PENNSYLVANIA B-1

Edinboro, PA 16444 **(814) 732-2761**
(800) 626-2203; Fax: (814) 732-2420

Full-time: 2616 men, 3480 women	**Faculty:** 344; IIA, av$
Part-time: 244 men, 344 women	**Ph.D.s:** 65%
Graduate: 242 men, 572 women	**Student/Faculty:** 16 to 1
Year: semesters, summer session	**Tuition:** $4944 ($6952)
Application Deadline: open	**Room & Board:** $4384
Freshman Class: 3575 applied, 2882 accepted, 451 enrolled	
SAT I Verbal/Math: 470/460	**ACT:** 19 **LESS COMPETITIVE**

Edinboro University of Pennsylvania, founded in 1857, is a public institution and a member of the Pennsylvania State System of Higher Education. The university offers programs in fine and liberal arts, business, engineering, health science, and teacher preparation. There are 3 undergraduate schools and 1 graduate school. In addition to regional accreditation, EUP has baccalaureate program accreditation with ACBSP, ADA, CSWE, NASM, NCATE, and NLN. The 2 libraries contain 468,887 volumes, 1,354,837 microform items, and 32,413 audiovisual forms/CDs, and subscribe to 1669 periodicals. Computerized library services include the card catalog, interlibrary loans, and database searching. Special learning facilities include an art gallery, planetarium, radio station, TV station, and newspaper. The 585 acre campus is in a small town 18 miles south of Erie. Including residence halls, there are 43 buildings.

Student Life: 87% of undergraduates are from Pennsylvania. Others are from 37 states, 48 foreign countries, and Canada. 89% are white. The average age of freshmen is 19; all undergraduates, 22. 27% do not continue beyond their first year; 50% remain to graduate.

Housing: 2500 students can be accommodated in college housing, which includes single-sex and coed dormitories. In addition, there are honors houses and special-interest houses, floors by academic major, quiet floors, and nonsmoking residence halls. On-campus housing is guaranteed for the freshman year only and is available on a first-come, first-served basis. Alcohol is not permitted. All students may keep cars.

Activities: 4% of men belong to 11 national fraternities; 8% of women belong to 9 national sororities. There are 117 groups on campus, including art, bagpipe band, band, cheerleading, chess, choir, chorale, chorus, computers, dance, debate, drama, drill team, ethnic, film, forensics, gay, honors, international, jazz band, literary magazine, marching band, musical theater, opera, orchestra, pep band, photography, political, professional, radio and TV, religious, social, social service, student government, symphony, and yearbook. Popular campus events include Academic Festival, Snowfest, and Greek Week.

Sports: There are 8 intercollegiate sports for men and 8 for women, and 15 intramural sports for men and 13 for women. Facilities include a field house, a stadium, a gym, a swimming pool, racquetball courts, an aerobics room, an indoor track, a fitness center, saunas, steam rooms, 2 weight rooms, and a climbing wall.

Disabled Students: 97% of the campus is accessible. Wheelchair ramps, elevators, special parking, specially equipped rest rooms, special class scheduling, lowered drinking fountains, and lowered telephones are available. The university also offers special residence halls, computer facilities, and transportation services for the physically challenged and learning disabled.

Services: Counseling and information services are available, as is tutoring in most subjects. There is a reader service for the blind, and remedial math, reading, and writing. Academic aides are available as are services in the academic support library. Also available are alternative test arrangements, peer mentoring, priority scheduling, and recordings for blind or dyslexic students.

Campus Safety and Security: Measures include 24-hour foot and vehicle patrol, self-defense education, informal discussions, and pamphlets/posters/films. There are emergency telephones, lighted pathways/sidewalks, and 14 commissioned police officers, and optional engraving of personal property.

Programs of Study: EUP confers B.A., B.S., B.S.Ed., B.F.A., and B.S.N. degrees. Associate and master's degrees are also awarded. Bachelor's degrees are awarded in BIOLOGICAL SCIENCE (biochemistry, biology/biological science, and nutrition), BUSINESS (accounting, banking and finance, business administration and management, marketing management, and sports management), COMMUNICATIONS AND THE ARTS (advertising, applied art, art, art history and appreciation, broadcasting, ceramic art and design, creative writing, dramatic arts, drawing, English, English literature, fiber/textiles/weaving, film arts, fine arts, German, graphic design, media arts, metal/jewelry, music, painting, photography, printmaking, sculpture, Spanish, and speech/debate/rhetoric), COMPUTER AND PHYSICAL SCIENCE (chemistry, computer science, earth science, geology, mathematics, natural sciences, and physics), EDUCATION (art, early childhood, elementary, English, foreign languages, health, mathematics, music, physical, science, secondary, social studies, and special), ENGINEERING AND ENVIRONMENTAL DESIGN (engineering physics, environmental science, and woodworking), HEALTH PROFESSIONS (medical laboratory technology, nuclear medical technology, nursing, predentistry, premedicine, prepharmacy, preveterinary science, public health, and speech pathology/audiology), SOCIAL SCIENCE (anthropology, criminal justice, economics, forensic studies, geography, history, humanities, liberal arts/general studies, philosophy, political science/government, prelaw, psychology, social science, social work, and sociology). Applied media arts, business administration, and criminal justice are the largest.

Required: To graduate, students must complete at least 128 semester hours with a minimum GPA of 2.0. General education requirements include 60 hours of courses, consisting of a 21-semester-hour core with 3 hours each in artistic expression, world civilizations, American civilizations, human behavior, cultural diversity and social pluralism, ethics, and science and technology; an 18-hour distribution with 6 hours each in humanities and fine arts, social and behavioral sciences, and science and math; 9 hours in English and math skills; 9 hours of general education electives; and 3 hours of health and phys ed.

Special: The university offers cooperative programs in engineering, prelaw, and osteopathic medicine, and cross-registration through the Pennsylvania State System of Higher Education and the Marine Science Consortium at Wallops Island, Virginia, and with Mercyhurst College and Gannon University. A Harrisburg semester, internships in most majors, a general studies program, student-designed majors, dual majors in education, a 3-2 engineering degree, study abroad in more than 9 countries, and nondegree study are also offered. Students may select pass/fail options and receive credit for life, military, and work experience. There are 14 national honor societies, a freshman honors program, and 9 departmental honors programs.

Faculty/Classroom: 61% of faculty are male; 39%, female. 92% teach undergraduates. No introductory courses are taught by graduate students. The average class size in an introductory lecture is 30; in a laboratory, 22; and in a regular course, 27.

Admissions: 81% of the 2001-2002 applicants were accepted. The SAT I scores for the 2001-2002 freshman class were: Verbal--61% below 500, 30% between 500 and 599, 8% between 600 and 700, and 1% above 700; Math--64% below 500, 30% between 500 and 599, and 6% between 600 and 700. The ACT scores were 68% below 21, 18% between 21 and 23, 10% between 24 and 26, 3% between 27 and 28, and 1% above 28. 16% of the current freshmen were in the top fifth of their class; 59% were in the top two fifths.

Requirements: The SAT I or ACT is required. In addition, candidates for admission should be graduates of an accredited secondary school. The GED is accepted. A GPA of 2.0 is recommended. A portfolio is recommended for art students and an audition is required for music students. An interview is recommended for all. AP and CLEP credits are accepted. Admissions decisions are based upon the academic major requested, high school curriculum (including advanced placement or honor courses), grades, GPA, class rank, SAT I or ACT scores, leadership and extracurricular activities record, and personality/intangible qualities. An on-line application is available at the school's web site or via NextStop College.

Procedure: Freshmen are admitted to all sessions. Entrance exams should be taken in the junior year or early in the senior year. There are early admissions and deferred admissions plans. Application deadlines are open. The application fee is $25. Notification is sent on a rolling basis.

Transfer: 452 transfer students enrolled in 2001-2002. Applicants should have a 2.0 GPA and must submit transcripts from previous institutions. An interview is recommended. 32 credits of 128 must be completed at EUP.

Visiting: There are regularly scheduled orientations for prospective students, including admissions, financial aid, and academic affairs presentations followed by campus tours. There are guides for informal visits and visitors may sit in on classes and stay overnight. To schedule a visit, contact the Admissions Office.

Financial Aid: In a recent year, 69% of all freshmen and 67% of continuing students received some form of financial aid. 66% of freshmen and 62% of continuing students received need-based aid. The average freshman award was $5062. Of that total, scholarships or need-based grants averaged $1500 ($9330 maximum); loans averaged $2625

($5500 maximum); and work contracts averaged $1400 ($2100 maximum). 32% of undergraduates work part time. Average annual earnings from campus work are $1400. The average financial indebtedness of a recent graduate was $13,717. The FAFSA is required. The fall application deadline is March 15.

International Students: There are 200 international students enrolled. The school actively recruits these students. They must score 450 on the written TOEFL or 133 on the electronic version.

Computers: The mainframe is a Compaq Alpha Series server. More than 650 Windows and Mac systems are available to students in locations across campus. Workstations are located in the library, specific residence halls, the student union, the main computer lab, and academic-specific labs. All students may access the system. There are no time limits and no fees.

Graduates: In 2001, 1014 bachelor's degrees were awarded. The most popular majors were business administration (8%), speech communications (8%), and criminal justice (8%). In an average class, 19% graduate in 4 years, 44% in 5 years, and 49% in 6 years. 129 companies recruited on campus in 2000-2001.

Admissions Contact: Admissions Office.
E-mail: *eup_admissions@edinboro.edu* Web: *http://www.edinboro.edu*

ELIZABETHTOWN COLLEGE

ELIZABETHTOWN COLLEGE	D-3
Elizabethtown, PA 17022	**(717) 361-1400; Fax: (717) 361-1365**
Full-time: 649 men, 1077 women	**Faculty:** 106; IIB, +$
Part-time: 65 men, 97 women	**Ph.D.s:** 90%
Graduate: none	**Student/Faculty:** 16 to 1
Year: semesters, summer session	**Tuition:** $20,200
Application Deadline: see profile	**Room & Board:** $5800
Freshman Class: 2763 applied, 1900 accepted, 520 enrolled	
SAT I Verbal/Math: 560/560	**VERY COMPETITIVE**

Elizabethtown College, founded in 1899, is a private institution founded by members of the Church of the Brethren and offering 40 undergraduate degrees in the arts, sciences, humanities, and preprofessional programs. In addition to regional accreditation, E-town has baccalaureate program accreditation with ACBSP, CSWE, and NASM. The library contains 227,460 volumes, 14,294 microform items, and 14,178 audiovisual forms/CDs, and subscribes to 1082 periodicals. Computerized library services include the card catalog, interlibrary loans, and database searching. Special learning facilities include a learning resource center, art gallery, radio station, TV station, and a center for the study of Anabaptist and Pietist groups. The 185-acre campus is in a small town 20 miles southeast of Harrisburg. Including residence halls, there are 27 buildings.

Student Life: 68% of undergraduates are from Pennsylvania. Others are from 35 states, 40 foreign countries, and Canada. 82% are from public schools. 90% are white. 45% are Catholic; 30% Protestant; 25% claim no religious affiliation. The average age of freshmen is 18; all undergraduates, 20. 16% do not continue beyond their first year; 72% remain to graduate.

Housing: 1380 students can be accommodated in college housing, which includes single-sex and coed dormitories and on-campus apartments. In addition, there are honors houses, special-interest houses, and chemical-free healthy living and quiet areas. On-campus housing is guaranteed for all 4 years. 85% of students live on campus; of those, 70% remain on campus on weekends. All students may keep cars.

Activities: There are no fraternities or sororities. There are 80 groups on campus, including art, band, cheerleading, choir, chorale, chorus, computers, dance, departmental, drama, ethnic, forensics, gay, honors, international, jazz band, literary magazine, musical theater, newspaper, orchestra, photography, political, professional, radio and TV, religious, resident hall, social, social service, student government, and yearbook. Popular campus events include Family Weekend, theme weekends, and Spring Arts Festival.

Sports: There are 10 intercollegiate sports for men and 10 for women, and 7 intramural sports for men and 7 for women. Facilities include a swimming pool, weight training rooms, a 2200-seat soccer complex, a 2400-seat gym, a track and field complex, racquetball and tennis courts, basketball courts, sand volleyball courts, aerobic classes, a fitness center, baseball, softball, lacrosse, and hockey fields, and an artificial turf field for field hockey and lacrosse.

Disabled Students: 85% of the campus is accessible. Wheelchair ramps, elevators, special parking, specially equipped rest rooms, special class scheduling, lowered drinking fountains, and lowered telephones are available.

Services: Counseling and information services are available, as is tutoring in most subjects. There is remedial writing. Workshops and individual help with study skills are also available.

Campus Safety and Security: Measures include 24-hour foot and vehicle patrol, self-defense education, escort service, and informal discussions. There are pamphlets/posters/films, emergency telephones, lighted pathways/sidewalks, a student patrol, and a crime prevention program.

Programs of Study: E-town confers B.A., B.S., and B.M. degrees. Associate and master's degrees are also awarded. Bachelor's degrees are awarded in AGRICULTURE (forestry and related sciences), BIOLOGICAL SCIENCE (biochemistry, biology/biological science, and biotechnology), BUSINESS (accounting, business administration and management, and international business management), COMMUNICATIONS AND THE ARTS (art, communications, English, French, German, music, and Spanish), COMPUTER AND PHYSICAL SCIENCE (chemistry, computer science, mathematics, physics, and science), EDUCATION (early childhood, elementary, music, and secondary), ENGINEERING AND ENVIRONMENTAL DESIGN (computer engineering, engineering, engineering physics, environmental science, and industrial engineering), HEALTH PROFESSIONS (clinical science, music therapy, and occupational therapy), SOCIAL SCIENCE (economics, history, philosophy, political science/government, psychology, religion, social studies, social work, and sociology). Sciences, occupational therapy, and international business are the strongest academically. Business administration, communications, and elementary and early childhood education are the largest.

Required: The core curriculum includes a freshman seminar, a junior/senior colloquium, courses in foreign cultures and international studies, math analysis, the power of language, creative expression, cultural heritage, physical well-being, the natural and social worlds, and values and choice. Distribution requirements include 37 to 39 hours in 9 areas of understanding. To graduate, students must complete 125 credit hours, with at least 30 in the major, and maintain a GPA of 2.0 overall and in the major.

Special: Cross-registration with Brethren Colleges Abroad, work-study programs, internships, study abroad in 12 countries, a Washington semester, accelerated degrees, and dual majors, including sociology/anthropology, are available. A 3-2 engineering degree is offered with Pennsylvania State University; a 2-2 allied health degree and a 3-3 physical therapy degree with Thomas Jefferson University, Widener University, and the University of Maryland/Baltimore County; and a 3-2 forestry or environmental management degree with Duke University. There are 13 national honor societies, a freshman honors program, and 19 departmental honors programs.

Faculty/Classroom: 65% of faculty are male; 35%, female. 33% both teach and do research. The average class size in an introductory lecture is 23; in a laboratory, 18; and in a regular course, 20.

Admissions: 69% of the 2001-2002 applicants were accepted. The SAT I scores for the 2001-2002 freshman class were: Verbal--20% below 500, 52% between 500 and 599, 25% between 600 and 700, and 3% above 700; Math--26% below 500, 41% between 500 and 599, 30% between 600 and 700, and 3% above 700. 50% of the current freshmen were in the top fifth of their class; 81% were in the top two fifths. There were 4 National Merit semifinalists. 9 freshmen graduated first in their class.

Requirements: The SAT I or ACT is required. In addition, recommended composite scores for the SAT I range from 1040 to 1190; for the ACT, 19 to 24. Applicants must be graduates of an accredited secondary school or have earned a GED. The college encourages completion of 18 academic credits, based on 4 years of English, 3 of math, 2 each of lab science, social studies, and consecutive foreign language, and 5 additional college-preparatory units. An audition is required for music majors and an interview is required for occupational therapy majors. AP and CLEP credits are accepted. Important factors in the admissions decision are advanced placement or honor courses, recommendations by school officials, and extracurricular activities record. Applications are accepted on computer disk accompanied by hard copy and on-line through Common App or the college's web site.

Procedure: Freshmen are admitted to all sessions. Entrance exams should be taken in spring of the junior year or fall of the senior year. There are early admissions and deferred admissions plans. Applications for fall entry should be filed by December 15 for occupational therapy and allied health majors, January 15 for the honors program, February 1 for lab science majors, March 30 for international business majors, and May 1 for all other majors, along with a $20 fee. Notification is sent on a rolling basis.

Transfer: 60 transfer students enrolled in 2001-2002. Applicants should present a minimum GPA of 3.0 in at least 15 credit hours earned from a community college, or 2.5 from a 4-year institution. 30 credits of 125 must be completed at E-town.

Visiting: There are regularly scheduled orientations for prospective students, including 5 open houses and weekday appointments throughout the year, with Saturday interviews available during the academic year. Special academic department days are also hosted. There are guides for informal visits and visitors may sit in on classes and stay overnight. To schedule a visit, contact the Admissions Office.

Financial Aid: In 2001-2002, 96% of all freshmen and 93% of continuing students received some form of financial aid. 74% of freshmen and 72% of continuing students received need-based aid. The average freshman award was $16,194. Of that total, scholarships or need-based grants averaged $11,619 ($24,300 maximum); loans averaged $2658 ($3625 maximum); and work contracts averaged $1281 ($1500 maximum). 68% of undergraduates work part time. Average annual earnings from campus work are $824. The average financial indebtedness of the

2001 graduate was $18,211. E-town is a member of CSS. The FAFSA, the college's own financial statement, and family federal tax returns are required. The fall application deadline is March 15.

International Students: There are 82 international students enrolled. The school actively recruits these students. They must score 525 on the written TOEFL.

Computers: A 24-hour terminal room allows student access to e-mail and word processing. Several labs house a total of 40 Macs and 43 PCs, all connected to the Internet. All residence hall rooms also have Internet access. All students may access the system any time from residence hall rooms. There are no time limits and no fees. It is strongly recommended that all students have a personal computer; approximately 75% of freshmen have one.

Graduates: In a recent class, 360 bachelor's degrees were awarded. The most popular majors were business (18%), education (16%), and biology (9%). In an average class, 60% graduate in 4 years, 65% in 5 years, and 66% in 6 years. 70 companies recruited on campus in 2000-2001. Of the a recent graduating class, 20% were enrolled in graduate school within 6 months of graduation and 83% were employed.

Admissions Contact: Gordon McK. Bateman, Dean of Admissions and Enrollment Management. E-mail: *admissions@acad.etown.edu*
Web: *www.etown.edu*

FRANKLIN AND MARSHALL COLLEGE E-3

Lancaster, PA 17604-3003 **(717) 291-3953; Fax: (717) 291-4389**

Full-time: 928 men, 919 women	**Faculty:** 159; IIB, ++$
Part-time: 17 men, 23 women	**Ph.D.s:** 97%
Graduate: none	**Student/Faculty:** 12 to 1
Year: semesters, summer session	**Tuition:** $26,110
Application Deadline: February 1	**Room & Board:** $6300
Freshman Class: 3702 applied, 2024 accepted, 513 enrolled	
SAT I Verbal/Math: 620/640	**ACT:** 27 **HIGHLY COMPETITIVE**

Franklin and Marshall College, founded in 1787, is a private liberal arts institution. The 2 libraries contain 447,924 volumes, 323,449 microform items, and 11,649 audiovisual forms/CDs, and subscribe to 1754 periodicals. Computerized library services include the card catalog, interlibrary loans, and database searching. Special learning facilities include an art gallery, natural history museum, planetarium, radio station, TV station, academic technology services, and advanced language lab. The 125-acre campus is in a suburban area 60 miles west of Philadelphia. Including residence halls, there are 44 buildings.

Student Life: 64% of undergraduates are from out of state, mostly the Middle Atlantic. Others are from 42 states, 60 foreign countries, and Canada. 58% are from public schools. 83% are white. 28% are Protestant; 27% are Catholic; 21% claim no religious affiliation; 13% are Orthodox Christian, Muslim, Hindu, Buddhist, Unitarian; 10% are Jewish. The average age of freshmen is 18; all undergraduates, 20. 9% do not continue beyond their first year; 83% remain to graduate.

Housing: 1320 students can be accommodated in college housing, which includes single-sex and coed dormitories and off-campus apartments. In addition, there are language houses and special-interest houses, including a French house, an arts house, an international living center, and a healthy living house. On-campus housing is guaranteed for the freshman year only and is available on a lottery system for upperclassmen. 64% of students live on campus; of those, 85% remain on campus on weekends. All students may keep cars.

Activities: There are no fraternities or sororities. There are 110 groups on campus, including art, band, Ben's Underground (student-run club/restaurant), chess, choir, chorale, chorus, computers, dance, debate, drama, ethnic, film, forensics, gay, honors, international, jazz band, literary magazine, musical theater, newspaper, orchestra, photography, political, professional, radio and TV, religious, social, social service, student government, symphony, and yearbook. Popular campus events include Spring Arts Weekend, Freshman Feast, and Senior Surprise.

Sports: There are 13 intercollegiate sports for men and 13 for women, and 12 intramural sports for men and 12 for women. Facilities include a 3000-seat gym, a swimming pool, 4 squash courts, a wrestling room, 54 acres of playing fields, a 400-meter all-weather track, a wellness/aerobic center, a strength training center, and tennis courts. The sport center features a fitness center, 5 multipurpose courts, 2 jogging tracks, and an Olympic-size pool.

Disabled Students: 70% of the campus is accessible. Wheelchair ramps, elevators, special parking, specially equipped rest rooms, special class scheduling, lowered drinking fountains, lowered telephones, and a specially equipped residence hall room are available.

Services: Counseling and information services are available, as is tutoring in every subject. There is also a writing center.

Campus Safety and Security: Measures include 24-hour foot and vehicle patrol, self-defense education, escort service, and informal discussions. There are pamphlets/posters/films, emergency telephones, and lighted pathways/sidewalks. Regular fire safety drills are held in residence halls and academic buildings, and residence hall access requires a security code.

Programs of Study: F & M confers the B.A. degree. Bachelor's degrees are awarded in BIOLOGICAL SCIENCE (biochemistry and biology/biological science), BUSINESS (accounting and business administration and management), COMMUNICATIONS AND THE ARTS (art history and appreciation, classics, dramatic arts, English, fine arts, French, German, Greek, Latin, music, Spanish, and studio art), COMPUTER AND PHYSICAL SCIENCE (chemistry, geology, mathematics, and physics), SOCIAL SCIENCE (African studies, American studies, anthropology, economics, history, philosophy, political science/government, psychology, religion, and sociology). Chemistry, geosciences, and psychology are the strongest academically. Government, business administration, and biology are the largest.

Required: General education requirements proceed from 3 foundations courses and a distribution requirement to an upper-level coherent exploration and a major. Students must take at least 1 course each in arts, humanities, social science, and natural sciences. There are also language studies and non-Western culture studies requirements. Students must also satisfy the writng proficiency requirement. The bachelor's degree requires completion of 32 courses, including a minimum of 8 in the major, with a minimum GPA of 2.0.

Special: There is a 3-2 degree program in forestry and environmental studies with Duke University as well as 3-2 degree programs in engineering with the University of Pennsylvania, Columbia University, Rensselaer Polytechnic Institute, Case Western Reserve, Georgia Institute of Technology, and Washington University at St. Louis. Cross-registration with the Central Pennsylvania Consortium and Millersville University allows students to study at nearby Dickinson College or Gettysburg College. Students may also study architecture and urban planning at Columbia University, studio art at the School of Visual Arts in New York City, theater in Connecticut, oceanography in Massachusetts, and American studies at American University. There are study-abroad programs in many countries. Internships for credit, joint majors, student-designed majors, independent study, interdisciplinary studies, optional first-year seminars, collaborative projects, pass/fail options, and nondegree study. There are 12 national honor societies, including Phi Beta Kappa, and honors programs in all departments.

Faculty/Classroom: 66% of faculty are male; 34%, female. All both teach and do research. The average class size in an introductory lecture is 23; in a laboratory, 18; and in a regular course, 20.

Admissions: 55% of the 2001-2002 applicants were accepted. The SAT I scores for the 2001-2002 freshman class were: Verbal--4% below 500, 32% between 500 and 599, 46% between 600 and 700, and 18% above 700; Math--2% below 500, 25% between 500 and 599, 52% between 600 and 700, and 21% above 700. 74% of the current freshmen were in the top fifth of their class; 96% were in the top two fifths.

Requirements: The SAT I is required; standardized tests are optional for students in the top 10% of their class. The SAT II: Writing test is required. Applicants must be graduates of accredited secondary schools. Recommended college-preparatory study includes 4 years each of English and math, 3 or 4 of foreign language, 3 each of lab science and history/social studies, and 1 or 2 courses in art or music. All students must also submit their high school transcripts, recommendations from a teacher and a counselor, and a personal essay. An interview is recommended. AP and CLEP credits are accepted. Important factors in the admissions decision are advanced placement or honor courses, recommendations by school officials, and extracurricular activities record. Applications are accepted on-line.

Procedure: Freshmen are admitted fall and spring. Entrance exams should be taken by December of the senior year. There are early decision and deferred admissions plans. Early decision applications should be filed by January 15; regular applications, by February 1 for fall entry, along with a $50 fee. Notification of early decision is sent February 15; regular decision, April 1. 187 early decision candidates were accepted for the 2001-2002 class. 21% of all applicants are on a waiting list; 63 were accepted in 2001.

Transfer: 13 transfer students enrolled in 2001-2002. Applicants must present a minimum of 4 course credits (16 semester hours) completed at an accredited college. An interview, SAT I or ACT scores, college and secondary school transcripts, a dean's form, recommendations from 2 professors, and a letter explaining the reason for transfer are also required. 16 credits of 32 must be completed at F & M.

Visiting: There are regularly scheduled orientations for prospective students, including a campus tour, an interview, a class visit, and an overnight stay. There are guides for informal visits and visitors may sit in on classes and stay overnight. To schedule a visit, contact the Admission Office.

Financial Aid: In 2001-2002, 62% of all freshmen and 64% of continuing students received some form of financial aid. 54% of freshmen and 45% of continuing students received need-based aid. The average freshman award was $19,934. Of that total, scholarships or need-based grants averaged $17,099 ($31,960 maximum); loans averaged $2823 ($3625 maximum); and work contracts averaged $1051 ($1550 maximum). 42% of undergraduates work part time. Average annual earnings from campus work are $1390. The average financial indebtedness of the 2001 graduate was $17,774. F & M is a member of CSS. The CSS/

Profile or FAFSA and if applicable, the Business/Farm Supplement, Noncustodial Parents Statement, federal tax forms, W-2 forms, foreign student Certificate of Finances, and state aid form are required. The fall application deadline is February 1.

International Students: There are 152 international students enrolled. The school actively recruits these students. They must score 600 on the written TOEFL or 250 on the electronic version and also take the SAT I or the ACT. Students must take the SAT II: Writing tests, unless using ACT or no SAT option (possible for top decile of high school class).

Computers: The mainframes are a series of VAX and other servers. A computer workroom houses 32 Macs, 6 Apple LaserWriter printers, 1 color Apple printer, and 1 HP laser printer that is directly connected to the mainframe. All of the Macs are on the campuswide network for access to file servers and the academic VAX. The campus is 100% networked, and there is a substantial wireless network. All students may access the system 24 hours a day. There are no time limits and no fees. It is strongly recommended that all students have a personal computer, preferably a Mac, iMac, or iBook.

Graduates: In 2001, 447 bachelor's degrees were awarded. The most popular majors were government (12%), business management (11%), and English (10%). In an average class, 75% graduate in 4 years, 79% in 5 years, and 80% in 6 years. 190 companies recruited on campus in 2000-2001. Of the 2001 graduating class, 25% were enrolled in graduate school within 6 months of graduation and 75% were employed.

Admissions Contact: Penny Johnston, Acting Director of Admission. A video is availabe. E-mail: *admission@fandm.edu*
Web: *www.fandm.edu/admission.html*

GANNON UNIVERSITY

Erie, PA 16541 — **B-1**
(814) 871-7240
(800) GANNON U; Fax: (814) 871-5803

Full-time: 898 men, 1250 women	**Faculty:** 165; IIA, --$
Part-time: 129 men, 186 women	**Ph.D.s:** n/av
Graduate: 365 men, 579 women	**Student/Faculty:** 13 to 1
Year: semesters, summer session	**Tuition:** $15,780
Application Deadline: open	**Room & Board:** $6290
Freshman Class: 1951 applied, 1762 accepted, 525 enrolled	
SAT I Verbal/Math: 523/531	**ACT:** 23 **COMPETITIVE**

Gannon University, founded in 1925, is a private liberal arts and teacher preparation university affiliated with the Roman Catholic Church. There are 2 undergraduate schools and 1 graduate school. In addition to regional accreditation, Gannon has baccalaureate program accreditation with ABET, ADA, CAHEA, CSWE, and NLN. The library contains 253,617 volumes, 48,302 microform items, and 3011 audiovisual forms/CDs, and subscribes to 2073 periodicals. Computerized library services include the card catalog, interlibrary loans, and database searching. Special learning facilities include a learning resource center, art gallery, and radio station. The 13-acre campus is in an urban area 128 miles north of Pittsburgh, 99 miles east of Cleveland, and 106 miles southwest of Buffalo. Including residence halls, there are 27 buildings.

Student Life: 78% of undergraduates are from Pennsylvania. Others are from 25 states, 20 foreign countries, and Canada. 80% are from public schools. 92% are white. 58% are Catholic; 27% Protestant; 15% Buddhist, Hindu, Muslim, and Orthodox. The average age of freshmen is 18; all undergraduates, 21. 12% do not continue beyond their first year; 64% remain to graduate.

Housing: 1110 students can be accommodated in college housing, which includes coed dormitories, on-campus apartments, fraternity houses, and sorority houses. On-campus housing is guaranteed for the freshman year only. 67% of students live on campus; of those, 85% remain on campus on weekends. Alcohol is not permitted. Upperclassmen may keep cars.

Activities: 18% of men belong to 6 national fraternities; 16% of women belong to 6 national sororities. There are 70 groups on campus, including art, cheerleading, chess, chorus, computers, debate, drama, ethnic, honors, international, literary magazine, musical theater, newspaper, orchestra, pep band, political, professional, radio, religious, residence union, social, social service, student government, and yearbook. Popular campus events include Family Weekend, Distinguished Speaker Series, and Springtopia.

Sports: There are 10 intercollegiate sports for men and 9 for women, and 22 intramural sports for men and 11 for women. Facilities include a pool, 3 indoor gyms, a track, 6 racquetball courts, an outdoor recreation field, outdoor sand volleyball and tennis courts, a 3000-seat basketball and volleyball venue, exercise equipment, and a dance room.

Disabled Students: 80% of the campus is accessible. Wheelchair ramps, elevators, special parking, specially equipped rest rooms, special class scheduling, lowered drinking fountains, lowered telephones, and special drop-off points are available.

Services: Counseling and information services are available, as is tutoring in some subjects. There is remedial math and writing. There are math, writing, and advising centers.

Campus Safety and Security: Measures include 24-hour foot and vehicle patrol, escort service, informal discussions, and pamphlets/posters/films. There are emergency telephones, lighted pathways/sidewalks, and security cameras in buildings.

Programs of Study: Gannon confers B.A., B.S., B.S.E.E., B.S.M.E., and B.S.N. degrees. Associate, master's, and doctoral degrees are also awarded. Bachelor's degrees are awarded in BIOLOGICAL SCIENCE (biology/biological science), BUSINESS (accounting, banking and finance, business administration and management, entrepreneurial studies, international business management, management information systems, and marketing/retailing/merchandising), COMMUNICATIONS AND THE ARTS (advertising, communications, dramatic arts, English, and languages), COMPUTER AND PHYSICAL SCIENCE (chemistry, computer programming, computer science, mathematics, and science), EDUCATION (early childhood, elementary, foreign languages, secondary, and special), ENGINEERING AND ENVIRONMENTAL DESIGN (electrical/electronics engineering, environmental science, and mechanical engineering), HEALTH PROFESSIONS (medical laboratory technology, nursing, physician's assistant, predentistry, premedicine, preoptometry, preosteopathy, prepharmacy, prepodiatry, preveterinary science, radiological science, and respiratory therapy), SOCIAL SCIENCE (criminal justice, dietetics, history, international studies, liberal arts/general studies, paralegal studies, philosophy, political science/government, prelaw, psychology, social science, social work, and theological studies). Engineering, preprofessional, and nursing are the strongest academically. Occupational therapy, elementary education, and biology are the largest.

Required: Students must complete at least 128 hours of academic work. Each academic program has specific course requirements. Students must have a cumulative GPA of at least 2.0 overall and in the area of concentration. Three writing-intensive courses must be completed after the freshman year; 1 must be taken in the senior year.

Special: The university offers study abroad in more than 5 countries, co-op programs, summer internships, cross-registration with Mercyhurst College, Washington semesters, pass/fail options, work-study programs, a general studies program, accelerated degree programs in law, optometry, podiatry, and pharmacy, a 3-2 chemical engineering degree with the Universities of Akron, Pittsburgh, and Detroit Mercy, and nondegree study. The B.S.in mortuary science program consists of 2 or 3 years of study at Gannon with degree completion at a school of mortuary science. Gannon also offers a medical degree program in conjunction with Hahnemann University, and pharmacy and law programs with Duquesne University. There are 11 national honor societies, and a freshman honors program.

Faculty/Classroom: 57% of faculty are male; 43%, female. 91% teach undergraduates and 6% do research. No introductory courses are taught by graduate students. The average class size in an introductory lecture is 25; in a laboratory, 15; and in a regular course, 17.

Admissions: 90% of the 2001-2002 applicants were accepted. The SAT I scores for the 2001-2002 freshman class were: Verbal--40% below 500, 45% between 500 and 599, 19% between 600 and 700, and 1% above 700; Math--35% below 500, 47% between 500 and 599, 17% between 600 and 700, and 1% above 700. 45% of the current freshmen were in the top fifth of their class; 74% were in the top two fifths. 13 freshmen graduated first in their class in a recent year.

Requirements: The SAT I or ACT is required. In addition, candidates should have completed 16 academic units including 4 in English and 12 in social sciences, foreign languages, math, and science, depending on the degree sought. Specific courses in math and science are required for some majors in health sciences and engineering. Gannon requires applicants to be in the upper 60% of their class. A GPA of 2.0 is required. AP and CLEP credits are accepted. Important factors in the admissions decision are advanced placement or honor courses, leadership record, and recommendations by school officials. Applications are accepted on-line through ExPAN.

Procedure: Freshmen are admitted to all sessions. Entrance exams should be taken at the end of the junior year or the beginning of the senior year. There is a deferred admissions plan. Application deadlines are open. The application fee is $25. Notification is sent on a rolling basis. A waiting list is an active part of the admissions procedure.

Transfer: 61 transfer students enrolled in a recent year. Transfer students should be in good standing at their previous institution with at least a 2.0 GPA. They must submit a college clearance from the college most recently attended and all transcripts. A high school transcript is required from transfer students with fewer than 60 credits. Several health science programs are not designed to accommodate transfers. 30 credits of 128 must be completed at Gannon.

Visiting: There are regularly scheduled orientations for prospective students, consisting of open houses for prospective students in the fall and spring. Students may meet with faculty, tour the campus, and sit in on a variety of presentations. There are guides for informal visits and visitors may sit in on classes and stay overnight. To schedule a visit, contact the Admissions Office.

Financial Aid: In 2001-2002, the average freshman award was $10,900. Of that total, scholarships or need-based grants averaged

$6700 ($12,265 maximum); loans averaged $2500 ($2625 maximum); and work contracts averaged $1700 ($2100 maximum). 82% of undergraduates work part time. Average annual earnings from campus work are $1700. The average financial indebtedness of a recent year's graduate was $19,005. Gannon is a member of CSS. The FAFSA and the college's own financial statement are required. Check with the school for current deadlines.

International Students: The school actively recruits these students. They must score 500 on the written TOEFL.

Computers: The mainframes are a DEC VAX 6000-410 cluster, 2 DEC VAX 6410 clusters, and a Sun 2000. There is 1 mainframe lab and 2 PC labs with about 30 PCs in each. The departments of business, engineering, and education maintain special computer labs. All students may access the system Monday through Friday 9 A.M. to midnight, Saturday noon to 6 P.M., and Sunday noon to midnight. There are no time limits and no fees. It is strongly recommended that all students have a personal computer.

Graduates: In a recent year, 466 bachelor's degrees were awarded. The most popular majors were biology (12%), elementary education (7%), and criminal justice (6%).

Admissions Contact: Beth Nemenz, Executive Director of Admissions and Financial Aid. A video is available.
E-mail: *admissions@gannon.edu* Web: *www.gannon.edu*

GENEVA COLLEGE
Beaver Falls, PA 15010 — A-3
(724) 847-6500
(800) 847-8255; Fax: (724) 847-6776

Full-time: 648 men, 915 women	**Faculty:** 74; IIB, --$
Part-time: 112 men, 154 women	**Ph.D.s:** 70%
Graduate: 170 men, 175 women	**Student/Faculty:** 21 to 1
Year: semesters, summer session	**Tuition:** $14,050
Application Deadline: open	**Room & Board:** $5940
Freshman Class: 984 applied, 787 accepted, 298 enrolled	
SAT I Verbal/Math: 590/590	**ACT:** 26 — **COMPETITIVE+**

Geneva College, founded in 1848, is a private institution affiliated with the Reformed Presbyterian Church of North America. The college offers undergraduate programs in the arts and sciences, business, education, health science, biblical and religious studies, engineering, and preprofessional training. In addition to regional accreditation, Geneva has baccalaureate program accreditation with ABET and ACBSP. The library contains 165,442 volumes, 187,632 microform items, and 24,393 audiovisual forms/CDs, and subscribes to 937 periodicals. Computerized library services include the card catalog, interlibrary loans, and database searching. Special learning facilities include a radio station, TV station, and an observatory. The 50-acre campus is in a small town 35 miles northwest of Pittsburgh. Including residence halls, there are 30 buildings.

Student Life: 77% of undergraduates are from Pennsylvania. Others are from 37 states, 25 foreign countries, and Canada. 87% are from public schools. 91% are white. 75% are Protestant; 10% Catholic. The average age of freshmen is 23; all undergraduates, 25. 20% do not continue beyond their first year; 59% remain to graduate.

Housing: 935 students can be accommodated in college housing, which includes single-sex dormitories, on-campus apartments, and off-campus apartments. In addition, there is a Discipleship House for those interested in structural growth opportunities. On-campus housing is guaranteed for all 4 years. 74% of students live on campus; of those, 70% remain on campus on weekends. Alcohol is not permitted. Upperclassmen may keep cars.

Activities: There are no fraternities or sororities. There are 50 groups on campus, including band, cheerleading, chess, choir, chorale, chorus, computers, drama, ethnic, forensics, honors, international, literary magazine, marching band, newspaper, photography, political, professional, radio, religious, social, social service, student government, and yearbook. Popular campus events include International Day, Fall Fest, and The Big Event.

Sports: There are 7 intercollegiate sports for men and 7 for women, and 6 intramural sports for men and 5 for women. Facilities include a 5600-seat stadium, a field house, a 3200-seat gym, a practice gym, a track, athletic fields, racquetball and tennis courts, weight training rooms, and the Merriman Athletic Soccer/Track Complex.

Disabled Students: 90% of the campus is accessible. Wheelchair ramps, elevators, special parking, specially equipped rest rooms, special class scheduling, lowered drinking fountains, and lowered telephones are available.

Services: Counseling and information services are available, as is tutoring in most subjects. There is remedial math, reading, and writing.

Campus Safety and Security: Measures include escort service, informal discussions, pamphlets/posters/films, and emergency telephones. There are lighted pathways/sidewalks, an off-duty city policeman on campus from 4:30 P.M. to 7:00 A.M. daily, and a full-time Director of Campus Security.

Programs of Study: Geneva confers B.A., B.S., B.S.B.A., B.S.Ed., and B.S.E. degrees. Associate and master's degrees are also awarded. Bachelor's degrees are awarded in BIOLOGICAL SCIENCE (biology/biological science), BUSINESS (accounting and business administration and management), COMMUNICATIONS AND THE ARTS (applied music, broadcasting, communications, creative writing, English, music, music business management, Spanish, and speech/debate/rhetoric), COMPUTER AND PHYSICAL SCIENCE (applied mathematics, chemistry, computer science, and physics), EDUCATION (elementary, mathematics, and music), ENGINEERING AND ENVIRONMENTAL DESIGN (aviation administration/management, chemical engineering, and engineering), HEALTH PROFESSIONS (speech pathology/audiology), SOCIAL SCIENCE (biblical studies, counseling/psychology, history, human services, interdisciplinary studies, ministries, philosophy, political science/government, psychology, and sociology). Engineering, business administration, and chemical engineering are the strongest academically. Elementary education, business administration, and engineering are the largest.

Required: The core curriculum includes 12 hours of humanities, 9 each of biblical studies and social science, 8 to 10 of natural science, 6 of communications, 2 of phys ed, and the 1-hour Freshman Experience course. Students must also fulfill a chapel requirement per semester. To graduate, students must complete 126 to 138 semester hours, including those required for a major, with a minimum GPA of 2.0 in the major.

Special: Cross-registration is offered in conjunction with Pennsylvania State University/Beaver Campus and Community College of Beaver County. There is a 3-1 degree program in cardiovascular technology and accelerated degree programs in human resources and community ministry. Off-campus study includes programs at the Philadelphia Center for Urban Theological Studies, a Washington semester, a summer program at Au Sable Institute of Environmental Studies in Michigan, art studies in Pittsburgh, film studies in Los Angeles, and study abroad in Costa Rica, Egypt, China, England, Russia, and Israel. Geneva also offers internships, independent study, and credit by proficiency exam. Nondegree study is available through adult education programs. There are 2 national honor societies, a freshman honors program, and 1 departmental honors program.

Faculty/Classroom: 76% of faculty are male; 24%, female. All teach undergraduates. No introductory courses are taught by graduate students. The average class size in an introductory lecture is 135; in a laboratory, 22; and in a regular course, 20.

Admissions: 80% of the 2001-2002 applicants were accepted. The SAT I scores for the 2001-2002 freshman class were: Verbal--31% below 500, 44% between 500 and 599, 20% between 600 and 699, and 5% above 699; Math--40% below 500, 38% between 500 and 599, 20% between 600 and 699, and 2% above 699. The ACT scores were 7% between 12 and 17, 46% between 18 and 23, 45% between 24 and 29, and 2% between 30 and 36. 25% of the current freshmen were in the top quarter of their class; 34% were in the top half.

Requirements: The SAT I or ACT is required. In addition, applicants must be graduates of an accredited secondary school or have earned a GED. Geneva requires 16 academic units, based on 4 each of English and electives, 3 of social studies, 2 each of math and foreign language, and 1 of science. An essay is required, and an interview is recommended. Geneva requires applicants to be in the upper 50% of their class. A GPA of 2.5 is required. AP and CLEP credits are accepted. Important factors in the admissions decision are recommendations by school officials, advanced placement or honor courses, and leadership record. Applications are accepted on-line via Geneva's web site, CollegeLink, and Mac Apply.

Procedure: Freshmen are admitted to all sessions. Entrance exams should be taken during the junior or senior year. There is a deferred admissions plan. Application deadlines are open. Notification is sent on a rolling basis.

Transfer: 74 transfer students enrolled in 2001-2002. Applicants must have a college GPA of 2.0, complete 48 semester hours at Geneva, including 15 in a chosen major, have a high school diploma or GED, and take the SAT I/ACT if less than 3 years out of high school. Letters of recommendation are required. 48 credits of 126 must be completed at Geneva.

Visiting: There are regularly scheduled orientations for prospective students, including class visits, a campus tour, meetings with faculty, admissions, and financial aid counselors, and meetings with coaches. There are guides for informal visits and visitors may sit in on classes and stay overnight. To schedule a visit, contact Dana Fasick, Campus Visit Coordinator at (724) 847-6501.

Financial Aid: The average financial indebtedness of the 2001 graduate was $20,000. Geneva is a member of CSS. The FAFSA is required. The fall application deadline is April 15.

International Students: There were 56 international students enrolled in a recent year. The school actively recruits these students. They must take the TOEFL or the college's own test.

Computers: The mainframe is an IBM AS/400. Access to the campus network and to the Internet is provided to all students. There are more than 150 PCs throughout the campus that students can use. Some of these are general-purpose labs and others are discipline-specifc labs. Many residence hall rooms are also wired for connection to the campus network. All students may access the system. There are no time limits. The fee is $100 per semester.

Graduates: In 2001, 437 bachelor's degrees were awarded. The most popular majors were business and marketing (42%), philosophy/religion/theology (14%), and education (12%). In an average class, 1% graduate in 3 years, 48% in 4 years, and 59% in 5 years.

Admissions Contact: David Layton, Director of Admissions. A video is available. E-mail: *admissions@geneva.edu* Web: *www.geneva.edu*

GETTYSBURG COLLEGE D-4

Gettysburg, PA 17325-1484 **(717) 337-6100**

(800) 431-0803; Fax: (717) 337-6145

Full-time: 1085 men, 1163 women	**Faculty:** 174; IIB, +$
Part-time: 6 men, 4 women	**Ph.D.s:** 95%
Graduate: none	**Student/Faculty:** 13 to 1
Year: semesters	**Tuition:** $25,748
Application Deadline: February 15	**Room & Board:** $6322

Freshman Class: 4364 applied, 2293 accepted, 659 enrolled

SAT I or ACT: required **HIGHLY COMPETITIVE**

Gettysburg College, founded in 1832, is an independent residential college affiliated with the Lutheran Church. It offers programs in the liberal arts and sciences. The library contains 335,746 volumes, 60,680 microform items, and 21,129 audiovisual forms/CDs, and subscribes to 2753 periodicals. Computerized library services include the card catalog, interlibrary loans, and database searching. Special learning facilities include an art gallery, planetarium, radio station, TV station, electron microscopes, spectrometers, an optics lab, plasma physics lab, greenhouse, observatory, child study lab, fine and performing arts facilities, and a challenge course. The 200-acre campus is in a small town 30 miles south of Harrisburg, 55 miles from Baltimore, and 80 miles from Washington, D.C. Including residence halls, there are 60 buildings.

Student Life: 70% of undergraduates are from out of state, mostly the Middle Atlantic. Others are from 40 states, 38 foreign countries, and Canada. 70% are from public schools. 90% are white. 38% are Protestant; 33% Catholic. The average age of freshmen is 18; all undergraduates, 20. 10% do not continue beyond their first year; 75% remain to graduate.

Housing: 1880 students can be accommodated in college housing, which includes single-sex and coed dormitories, on-campus apartments, off-campus apartments, and fraternity houses. In addition, there are honors houses, language houses, and special-interest houses. On-campus housing is guaranteed for all 4 years. 90% of students live on campus; of those, 95% remain on campus on weekends. All students may keep cars.

Activities: 42% of men belong to 11 national fraternities; 38% of women belong to 4 national sororities. There are more than 100 groups on campus, including art, band, cheerleading, choir, chorale, chorus, computers, dance, dance ensemble, drama, drill team, ethnic, film, gay, honors, international, jazz band, literary magazine, marching band, musical theater, newspaper, opera, orchestra, outdoor recreation, pep band, photography, political, professional, radio and TV, religious, social, social service, student activities council, student government, symphony, and yearbook. Popular campus events include Holiday Concert, all-campus picnics, and Family Weekend.

Sports: There are 13 intercollegiate sports for men and 13 for women. Facilities include 7 basketball courts, indoor and outdoor tennis courts, a pool, several tracks and fields, a field house, fitness and weight rooms, and an athletic complex.

Disabled Students: 90% of the campus is accessible. Wheelchair ramps, elevators, special parking, specially equipped rest rooms, and special class scheduling are available.

Services: Counseling and information services are available, as is tutoring in most subjects.

Campus Safety and Security: Measures include 24-hour foot and vehicle patrol, self-defense education, escort service, and informal discussions. There are pamphlets/posters/films, emergency telephones, and lighted pathways/sidewalks.

Programs of Study: Gettysburg confers B.A., B.S., and B.S.M.E. degrees. Bachelor's degrees are awarded in BIOLOGICAL SCIENCE (biochemistry and biology/biological science), BUSINESS (business administration and management), COMMUNICATIONS AND THE ARTS (art history and appreciation, classics, dramatic arts, English, French, German, Greek, Latin, music, Spanish, and studio art), COMPUTER AND PHYSICAL SCIENCE (chemistry, computer science, mathematics, and physics), EDUCATION (elementary, foreign languages, music, science, and secondary), ENGINEERING AND ENVIRONMENTAL DESIGN (environmental science), HEALTH PROFESSIONS (health science, predentistry, and premedicine), SOCIAL SCIENCE (anthropology, economics, history, international relations, philosophy, political science/government, prelaw, psychology, religion, sociology, and women's studies). The sciences, political science, and psychology are the strongest academically. Management, political science, and psychology are the largest.

Required: All students must demonstrate proficiency in written English, take 1 course in phys ed, and fulfill the liberal arts core requirements consisting of 3 courses in the humanities, 2 each in natural sciences and social sciences, 1 to 4 in foreign language, and 1 course each in quantitative reasoning, the arts, and a non-Western culture. A total of 35 courses is required, with 8 to 12 in the major. The minimum GPA is 2.0.

Special: The college offers an extensive study-abroad program and has special centers worldwide. There are summer internships and a Washington semester with American University. Cross-registration is possible with members of the Central Pennsylvania Consortium. There is a United Nations semester at Drew University and a 3-2 engineering program with Columbia University, Rensselaer Polytechnic, and Washington University in St. Louis. There are also joint programs in optometry with the Pennsylvania College of Optometry, and forestry and environmental studies with Duke University. The college also offers dual majors, student-designed majors, and B.A.-B.S. degrees in biology, math, chemistry, physics, biochemistry, molecular biology, and music education. There are 19 national honor societies, including Phi Beta Kappa.

Faculty/Classroom: 57% of faculty are male; 43%, female. All both teach and do research. The average class size in an introductory lecture is 19; in a laboratory, 15; and in a regular course, 19.

Admissions: 53% of the 2001-2002 applicants were accepted. The SAT I scores for the 2001-2002 freshman class were: Verbal--5% below 500, 47% between 500 and 599, 42% between 600 and 700, and 5% above 700; Math--3% below 500, 45% between 500 and 599, 46% between 600 and 700, and 6% above 700. 75% of the current freshmen were in the top fifth of their class; 99% were in the top two fifths. 17 freshmen graduated first in their class.

Requirements: The SAT I or ACT is required, as is an essay. Art students must submit a portfolio, and music students must audition. An interview and SAT II: Subject tests are recommended. Gettysburg requires applicants to be in the upper 40% of their class. A GPA of 3.0 is required. AP credits are accepted. Important factors in the admissions decision are advanced placement or honor courses, parents or siblings attending the school, and recommendations by school officials. Students may apply on-line using CommonApp, *Embark.com*, or at *www.gettysburg.edu*.

Procedure: Freshmen are admitted fall and spring. Entrance exams should be taken by the January testing date of the senior year. There are early decision, early admissions, and deferred admissions plans. Early decision applications should be filed by February 1; regular applications, by February 15 for fall entry and December 1 for spring entry. The fall 2001 application fee was $45. Notification is sent April 1. 165 early decision candidates were accepted for the 2001-2002 class. A waiting list is an active part of the admissions procedure.

Transfer: 25 transfer students enrolled in 2001-2002. Transfer applicants must have a GPA of at least 2.0. An interview is recommended. The high school record and test scores are also considered. 9 credits of 35 must be completed at Gettysburg.

Visiting: There are regularly scheduled orientations for prospective students, including interviews, tours, day and overnight visits, open houses, and group sessions. There are guides for informal visits and visitors may sit in on classes and stay overnight. To schedule a visit, contact the Admissions Office.

Financial Aid: In 2001-2002, 57% of all freshmen and 55% of continuing students received some form of financial aid. 55% of freshmen and 53% of continuing students received need-based aid. The average freshman award was $19,800. Of that total, scholarships or need-based grants averaged $16,090 ($25,000 maximum); loans averaged $3250 ($3600 maximum); and work contracts averaged $1330 ($1600 maximum). 34% of undergraduates work part time. Average annual earnings from campus work are $1400. The average financial indebtedness of the 2001 graduate was $14,000. Gettysburg is a member of CSS. The CSS/Profile or FAFSA are required. The fall application deadline is February 15.

International Students: There are 57 international students enrolled. The school actively recruits these students. They must score 550 on the written TOEFL and also take the SAT I or the ACT. The SAT II: Writing test may be used for placement.

Computers: The mainframes are multiple Sun microsystems and UNIX-based servers. A campuswide network has connections to the Internet. PCs are available in labs and other locations throughout the campus. Wireless connections are available. College Navigation (CNAV) is a web portal that gives students access to personal information, and provides connections to courses, faculty, and students with similar interests. All students may access the system 24 hours a day. There are no time limits and no fees. It is strongly recommended that all students have personal computers.

Graduates: In 2001, 495 bachelor's degrees were awarded. The most popular majors were management (21%), English (12%), and political science (12%). In an average class, 72% graduate in 4 years, 76% in 5 years, and 77% in 6 years. 145 companies recruited on campus in 2000-2001. Of the 2000 graduating class, 35% were enrolled in graduate school within 6 months of graduation and 63% were employed.

Admissions Contact: Gail Sweezey, Director of Admissions.
E-mail: *admiss@gettysburg.edu* Web: *www.gettysburg.edu*

GROVE CITY COLLEGE B-2

Grove City, PA 16127-2104 (724) 458-2100; Fax: (724) 458-3395

Full-time: 1140 men, 1139 women	**Faculty:** 121
Part-time: 10 men, 23 women	**Ph.D.s:** 75%
Graduate: 2 men, 1 woman	**Student/Faculty:** 19 to 1
Year: semesters	**Tuition:** $7870
Application Deadline: February 15	**Room & Board:** $4410
Freshman Class: 2188 applied, 930 accepted, 586 enrolled	
SAT I Verbal/Math: 634/635	**ACT:** 27 **MOST COMPETITIVE**

Grove City College, founded in 1876, is a private liberal arts and science college affiliated with the Presbyterian Church (U.S.A.). In addition to regional accreditation, Grove City has baccalaureate program accreditation with ABET. The library contains 158,000 volumes, 230,000 microform items, and 520 audiovisual forms/CDs, and subscribes to 1200 periodicals. Computerized library services include the card catalog, interlibrary loans, and database searching. Special learning facilities include an art gallery and radio station. The 150-acre campus is in a small town 60 miles north of Pittsburgh. Including residence halls, there are 27 buildings.

Student Life: 56% of undergraduates are from Pennsylvania. Others are from 46 states and 11 foreign countries. 88% are from public schools. 98% are white. 64% are Protestant; 24% claim no religious affiliation; 10% are Catholic. The average age of freshmen is 17; all undergraduates, 20. 10% do not continue beyond their first year; 75% remain to graduate.

Housing: 2048 students can be accommodated in college housing, which includes single-sex dormitories. On-campus housing is guaranteed for all 4 years. 90% of students live on campus; of those, 90% remain on campus on weekends. Alcohol is not permitted. Upperclassmen may keep cars.

Activities: 9% of men belong to 7 local fraternities; 19% of women belong to 8 local sororities. There are 120 groups on campus, including art, band, cheerleading, choir, chorale, chorus, computers, dance, debate, drama, drill team, ethnic, film, forensics, honors, international, jazz band, literary magazine, marching band, musical theater, newspaper, orchestra, pep band, photography, political, professional, radio and TV, religious, social, social service, student government, symphony, and yearbook. Popular campus events include Parents Weekend, Christmas Candlelight Service, and President's Gala.

Sports: There are 10 intercollegiate sports for men and 10 for women, and 4 intramural sports for men and 11 for women. Facilities include a field house; a recreation building that includes 2 indoor pools, an indoor running track, 4 basketball, volleyball, or tennis courts, 3 racquetball courts, bowling lanes, and a weight room; 10 outdoor tennis courts; a football stadium with an all-weather track; baseball, soccer, and softball fields; and a basketball arena.

Disabled Students: All of the campus is accessible. Wheelchair ramps, elevators, special parking, specially equipped rest rooms, special class scheduling, lowered drinking fountains, and lowered telephones are available. The college's hillside location presents some difficulty for the seriously disabled.

Services: Counseling and information services are available, as is tutoring in most subjects. A student tutoring program is available for a small fee.

Campus Safety and Security: Measures include 24-hour foot and vehicle patrol, self-defense education, escort service, and pamphlets/posters/films. There are emergency telephones and lighted pathways/sidewalks.

Programs of Study: Grove City confers B.A., B.S., B.Mus., B.S.E.E., and B.S.M.E. degrees. Bachelor's degrees are awarded in BIOLOGICAL SCIENCE (biochemistry and biology/biological science), BUSINESS (accounting, banking and finance, business administration and management, international business management, management information systems, and marketing/retailing/merchandising), COMMUNICATIONS AND THE ARTS (communications, English, French, music, music business management, music performance, and Spanish), COMPUTER AND PHYSICAL SCIENCE (chemistry, computer science, mathematics, and physics), EDUCATION (elementary, music, science, and secondary), ENGINEERING AND ENVIRONMENTAL DESIGN (electrical/electronics engineering, industrial administration/management, and mechanical engineering), HEALTH PROFESSIONS (predentistry and premedicine), SOCIAL SCIENCE (economics, history, philosophy, political science/government, prelaw, psychology, religion, and religious music). Business, engineering, and education are the strongest academically and the largest.

Required: To graduate, students are required to complete a minimum of 128 credit hours (136 for engineering students) with a minimum GPA of 2.0. All students must complete the 38-semester-hour general education curriculum, which includes 18 hours of humanities, 8 of natural science, 6 each of social science and quantitative and logical reasoning, and 2 of phys ed, along with 4 chapel credits, and 2 years of foreign language.

Special: The college offers study abroad, summer internships, 3 accelerated degree programs, student-designed interdisciplinary majors, nondegree study for special students, and a Washington semester. There are 9 national honor societies.

Faculty/Classroom: 72% of faculty are male; 28%, female. 99% teach undergraduates and 20% both teach and do research. No introductory courses are taught by graduate students. The average class size in an introductory lecture is 37; in a laboratory, 22; and in a regular course, 28.

Admissions: 43% of the 2001-2002 applicants were accepted. The SAT I scores for the 2001-2002 freshman class were: Verbal--4% below 500, 25% between 500 and 599, 49% between 600 and 700, and 22% above 700; Math--3% below 500, 24% between 500 and 599, 53% between 600 and 700, and 20% above 700. The ACT scores were 2% below 21, 10% between 21 and 23, 26% between 24 and 26, 24% between 27 and 28, and 38% above 28. 83% of the current freshmen were in the top fifth of their class; 96% were in the top two fifths. There were 17 National Merit finalists. 92 freshmen graduated first in their class.

Requirements: The SAT I or ACT is required. In addition, academic or college-preparatory course is highly recommended, including 4 units each of English, history, math, science, and a foreign language. An essay is required of all applicants, and an audition is required of music students. An interview is highly recommended. AP and CLEP credits are accepted. Important factors in the admissions decision are advanced placement or honor courses, extracurricular activities record, and personality/intangible qualities. Applications are accepted on-line at the college's web site.

Procedure: Freshmen are admitted fall and spring. Entrance exams should be taken in the spring of the junior year or the fall of the senior year. There are early decision and deferred admissions plans. Early decision applications should be filed by November 15; regular applications, by February 15 for fall entry and January 1 for spring entry, along with a $30 fee. Notification of early decision is sent December 15; regular decision, March 15. 340 early decision candidates were accepted for the 2001-2002 class. 9% of all applicants are on a waiting list.

Transfer: 24 transfer students enrolled in 2001-2002. Applicants should have a minimum of 17 credit hours earned with a 2.0 minimum GPA. Either the SAT I or the ACT is recommended, as is an interview. 32 credits of 128 must be completed at Grove City.

Visiting: There are regularly scheduled orientations for prospective students, consisting of daily interviews and tours, 2 high school visitation days in the fall, and a career day in the spring. There is a science and engineering open house in the fall. There are guides for informal visits and visitors may sit in on classes and stay overnight. To schedule a visit, contact the Admissions Office.

Financial Aid: In 2001-2002, 70% of all freshmen and 48% of continuing students received some form of financial aid. 43% of freshmen and 32% of continuing students received need-based aid. The average freshman award was $6550. Of that total, scholarships or need-based grants averaged $4700 ($14,584 maximum); and loans averaged $5700 ($14,584 maximum). 50% of undergraduates work part time. Average annual earnings from campus work are $500. The average financial indebtedness of the 2001 graduate was $12,500. The college's own financial statement is required. The fall application deadline is April 15.

International Students: There are 22 international students enrolled. They must score 550 on the written TOEFL or 213 on the electronic version. If the TOEFL is not available, either the SAT I or the ACT is required.

Computers: The mainframe is a DEC VAX 6250. The technological learning center houses 40 PCs and terminal stations. Every full-time student has a laptop computer and printer with the ability to connect to the Internet, Intranet, and e-mail accounts. All students may access the system 8 A.M. to 11 P.M., Monday through Friday; 8 A.M. to 5 P.M., Saturday; and 2 P.M. to 11 P.M., Sunday. There are no time limits and no fees.

Graduates: In 2001, 509 bachelor's degrees were awarded. The most popular majors were business administration (20%), elementary education and biology (9%), and engineering (8%). In an average class, 2% graduate in 3 years, 67% in 4 years, 74% in 5 years, and 75% in 6 years. 130 companies recruited on campus in 2000-2001.

Admissions Contact: Jeffrey C. Mincey, Director of Admissions.
E-mail: *admissions@gcc.edu* Web: *www.gcc.edu*

GWYNEDD-MERCY COLLEGE
F-4

Gwynedd Valley, PA 19437 (215) 641-5510
(800) DIAL-GMC; Fax: (215) 641-5556

Full-time: 223 men, 797 women | **Faculty:** 66; IIB, -$
Part-time: 241 men, 639 women | **Ph.D.s:** 49%
Graduate: 59 men, 219 women | **Student/Faculty:** 15 to 1
Year: semesters, summer session | **Tuition:** $15,350
Application Deadline: August 1 | **Room & Board:** $7000
Freshman Class: 1892 applied, 1204 accepted, 397 enrolled
SAT I Verbal/Math: 490/490 **COMPETITIVE**

Gwynedd-Mercy College, founded in 1948, is a private institution affiliated with the Roman Catholic Church and offering degree programs in the arts and sciences, business, education, and health fields. There are 5 undergraduate and 2 graduate schools. In addition to regional accreditation, Gwynedd-Mercy has baccalaureate program accreditation with NLN. The library contains 101,018 volumes, 14,802 microform items, and 51,604 audiovisual forms/CDs, and subscribes to 872 periodicals. Computerized library services include the card catalog and database searching. Special learning facilities include a learning resource center and a lab school for education majors. The 170-acre campus is in a suburban area 20 miles northwest of Philadelphia. Including residence halls, there are 20 buildings.

Student Life: 93% of undergraduates are from Pennsylvania. Others are from 11 states and 53 foreign countries. 45% are from public schools. 81% are white; 11%, African American. 53% are Catholic; 19%, Protestant. The average age of freshmen is 24; all undergraduates, 30. 13% do not continue beyond their first year; 78% remain to graduate.

Housing: College-sponsored living facilities include coed dormitories. On-campus housing is available on a first-come, first-served basis. 81% of students commute. Alcohol is not permitted. All students may keep cars.

Activities: There are no fraternities or sororities. There are 21 groups on campus, including choir, chorus, computers, drama, ethnic, honors, international, literary magazine, newspaper, professional, religious, social, social service, student government, and yearbook. Popular campus events include Fall Fest, Carol Night, and International Night.

Sports: There are 8 intercollegiate sports for men and 10 for women. Facilities include a recreation center housing courts for basketball and volleyball, a walking track, indoor racquetball courts, a weight room, and a sauna. Outdoor facilities include soccer, baseball, softball, and field hockey fields.

Disabled Students: 75% of the campus is accessible. Wheelchair ramps, elevators, special parking, specially equipped rest rooms, and special class scheduling are available.

Services: Counseling and information services are available, as is tutoring in most subjects. There is remedial math, reading, and writing. Tutoring is made available in conjunction with student needs.

Campus Safety and Security: Measures include 24-hour foot and vehicle patrol, escort service, shuttle buses, and informal discussions. There are emergency telephones and lighted pathways/sidewalks.

Programs of Study: Gwynedd-Mercy confers B.A., B.S., and B.H.S. degrees. Associate and master's degrees are also awarded. Bachelor's degrees are awarded in BIOLOGICAL SCIENCE (biology/biological science), BUSINESS (accounting, banking and finance, business administration and management, human resources, international business management, management science, marketing and distribution, office supervision and management, and sports management), COMMUNICATIONS AND THE ARTS (communications, English, and public relations), COMPUTER AND PHYSICAL SCIENCE (computer science, information sciences and systems, mathematics, and natural sciences), EDUCATION (business, elementary, mathematics, science, secondary, social studies, and special), HEALTH PROFESSIONS (clinical science, health care administration, medical laboratory technology, nursing, radiation therapy, and respiratory therapy), SOCIAL SCIENCE (criminal justice, gerontology, history, psychology, social work, and sociology). Nursing, biology, and medical technology are the strongest academically. Nursing, business, and education are the largest.

Required: All students must complete at least 125 credit hours, including 60 in the major, with a minimum GPA of 2.0. (Some programs require a higher GPA.) General education courses cover language, literature and fine arts, behavioral and social sciences, humanities, and natural science. Specific courses in English composition, literature, philosophy, and religious studies are required.

Special: The college offers co-op programs in computer science, business administration, and accounting, as well as internships, dual majors, accelerated degree programs, B.A.-B.S. degrees, and pass/fail options. Cross-registration is offered with South Eastern Pennsylvania Consortium for Higher Education. All programs require or have the option for hands-on experience. There is a 3-1 program in medical technology available wherein the last year is a hospital rotation. There are 4 national honor societies, a freshman honors program, and 1 departmental honors program.

Faculty/Classroom: 28% of faculty are male; 72%, female. 97% teach undergraduates. No introductory courses are taught by graduate students. The average class size in an introductory lecture is 17; in a laboratory, 10; and in a regular course, 17.

Admissions: 64% of the 2001-2002 applicants were accepted. The SAT I scores for the 2001-2002 freshman class were: Verbal--62% below 500, 32% between 500 and 599, and 6% between 600 and 700; Math--64% below 500, 29% between 500 and 599, 4% between 600 and 700, and 1% above 700. 21% of the current freshmen were in the top fifth of their class; 46% were in the top two fifths. 1 freshman graduated first in the class.

Requirements: The SAT I or ACT is required. In addition, candidates for admission must be graduates of accredited secondary schools and have completed 16 academic credits/Carnegie units, including 4 credits in English, 3 each in math, science, and college-preparatory electives, 2 in a foreign language, and 1 in history. The GED is accepted. An interview is recommended for all candidates and is required for some programs. Gwynedd-Mercy requires applicants to be in the upper 71% of their class. A GPA of 2.0 is required. AP and CLEP credits are accepted. Important factors in the admissions decision are advanced placement or honor courses, parents or siblings attending the school, and recommendations by alumni.

Procedure: Freshmen are admitted fall and spring. Entrance exams should be taken in the spring of the junior year or the fall of the senior year. There is a deferred admissions plan. Applications should be filed by August 1 for fall entry and December 15 for spring entry, along with a $25 fee. Notification is sent on within 2 weeks of acceptance.

Transfer: 154 transfer students enrolled in 2001-2002. Neither the SAT I nor the ACT is required for transfer students out of high school for 2 or more years. A minimum GPA of 2.0 is necessary; some programs require a higher GPA. An interview is recommended. 45 credits of 125 must be completed at Gwynedd-Mercy.

Visiting: There are regularly scheduled orientations for prospective students, consisting of open houses with formal presentations and campus tours, and class days with class visitations and campus tours. There are guides for informal visits and visitors may sit in on classes and stay overnight. To schedule a visit, contact the Admissions Office.

Financial Aid: In a recent year, 95% of all freshmen and 87% of continuing students received some form of financial aid. 87% of freshmen and 80% of continuing students received need-based aid. The average freshman award was $13,507. Of that total, scholarships or need-based grants averaged $8066 ($14,500 maximum); loans averaged $2911 ($5125 maximum); and work contracts averaged $1000 ($1500 maximum). All undergraduates work part time. Average annual earnings from campus work are $503. The average financial indebtedness of a recent graduate was $14,282. The FAFSA, the college's own financial statement, and federal income tax returns are required. The fall application deadline is March 15.

International Students: These students must score 500 on the written TOEFL or take the MELAB.

Computers: There are 34 Compaq multimedia PCs in a Novell Network connected to the campus network and the Internet, with additional desktop packages available. All students may access the system 65 hours a week. There are no time limits. The fee is $100 per semester.

Graduates: In 2001, 226 bachelor's degrees were awarded. The most popular majors were nursing (20%), business administration (18%), and education (15%). In an average class, 82% graduate in 4 years, 97% in 5 years, and all in 6 years.

Admissions Contact: Dennis Murphy, Vice President of Enrollment Management. E-mail: *admissions@gmc.edu* Web: *www.gmc.edu*

HAVERFORD COLLEGE
E-4

Haverford, PA 19041-1392 (610) 896-1350; Fax: (610) 896-1338

Full-time: 546 men, 592 women | **Faculty:** 103; IIB, +$
Part-time: none | **Ph.D.s:** 97%
Graduate: none | **Student/Faculty:** 11 to 1
Year: semesters | **Tuition:** $26,070
Application Deadline: January 15 | **Room & Board:** $8230
Freshman Class: 2574 applied, 839 accepted, 296 enrolled
SAT I Verbal/Math: 720/710 **MOST COMPETITIVE**

Haverford College, founded in 1833, is a private liberal arts college. The 5 libraries contain 497,784 volumes, 88,828 microform items, and 10,716 audiovisual forms/CDs, and subscribe to 2461 periodicals. Computerized library services include the card catalog, interlibrary loans, and database searching. Special learning facilities include an art gallery, radio station, observatory, and arboretum. The 200-acre campus is in a suburban area 10 miles west of Philadelphia. Including residence halls, there are 70 buildings.

Student Life: 82% of undergraduates are from out of state, mostly the Middle Atlantic. Students are from 45 states, 27 foreign countries, and Canada. 54% are from public schools. 73% are white; 13% Asian American. The average age of freshmen is 18; all undergraduates, 20. 3% do not continue beyond their first year; 91% remain to graduate.

Housing: 1131 students can be accommodated in college housing, which includes single-sex and coed dormitories and on-campus apartments. In addition, there are language houses and special-interest houses. Haverford students may live at Bryn Mawr College through a dormitory exchange program. On-campus housing is guaranteed for all 4 years. 98% of students live on campus; of those, 90% remain on campus on weekends. Upperclassmen may keep cars.

Activities: There are no fraternities or sororities. There are 75 groups on campus, including chorale, dance, drama, ethnic, gay, international, jazz band, literary magazine, musical theater, newspaper, orchestra, political, radio and TV, religious, social service, student government, and yearbook. Popular campus events include Haverfest, Snowball, and Swarthmore athletic competitions.

Sports: There are 10 intercollegiate sports for men and 11 for women, and 4 intramural sports for men and 4 for women. Facilities include a field house with an indoor track, extensive outdoor fields, a 400-meter, 8-lane, all-weather track, and tennis, squash, and basketball courts.

Disabled Students: 60% of the campus is accessible. Wheelchair ramps, elevators, special parking, specially equipped rest rooms, special class scheduling, lowered drinking fountains, lowered telephones, and reasonable accommodations are available.

Services: Counseling and information services are available, as is tutoring in every subject. There is a reader service for the blind.

Campus Safety and Security: Measures include 24-hour foot and vehicle patrol, self-defense education, escort service, and shuttle buses. There are informal discussions, pamphlets/posters/films, emergency telephones, lighted pathways/sidewalks, and a fire safety program.

Programs of Study: Haverford confers B.A. and B.S. degrees. Bachelor's degrees are awarded in BIOLOGICAL SCIENCE (biology/biological science), COMMUNICATIONS AND THE ARTS (art history and appreciation, classics, comparative literature, English, fine arts, French, German, Italian, music, romance languages and literature, Russian, and Spanish), COMPUTER AND PHYSICAL SCIENCE (astronomy, chemistry, geology, mathematics, and physics), SOCIAL SCIENCE (anthropology, archeology, East Asian studies, economics, history, philosophy, political science/government, psychology, religion, sociology, and urban studies). Natural and physical sciences, English, and history are the strongest academically. English, biology, and history are the largest.

Required: All students must take a minimum of 32 course credits, including freshman writing and 3 courses each in social science, natural science, and the humanities. One of the distribution courses must be quantitative and 1 must meet the social justice requirement. Students must also take 3 semesters of phys ed and demonstrate proficiency in a foreign language. Students must take a minimum of 6 courses in the major and 6 in related fields. Each major includes a capstone experience (a comprehensive exam, thesis, or advanced project, a specially designed course, or some combination), which varies by department.

Special: Haverford offers internship programs, cross-registration with Bryn Mawr College, Swarthmore College, and the University of Pennsylvania, study abroad in 33 countries, dual majors, student-designed majors, and a 3-2 engineering degree with the University of Pennsylvania. Pass/fail options are limited to 4 in 4 years. There is 1 national honor society, Phi Beta Kappa, and 28 departmental honors programs.

Faculty/Classroom: 57% of faculty are male; 43%, female. The average class size in an introductory lecture is 30; in a laboratory, 13; and in a regular course, 17.

Admissions: 33% of the 2001-2002 applicants were accepted. The SAT I scores for the 2001-2002 freshman class were: Verbal--3% below 500, 10% between 500 and 599, 36% between 600 and 700, and 51% above 700; Math--3% below 500, 10% between 500 and 599, 43% between 600 and 700, and 44% above 700. 92% of the current freshmen were in the top fifth of their class; all were in the top two fifths.

Requirements: The SAT I or ACT is required. In addition, the SAT II: Writing test is required, plus 2 others. Candidates for admission must be graduates of an accredited secondary school and have taken 4 courses in English, 3 each in a foreign language and math, and 1 each in science and history. The GED is accepted. An essay is required, and an interview is recommended. AP credits are accepted. Important factors in the admissions decision are advanced placement or honor courses, leadership record, and recommendations by school officials. Haverford accepts applications on computer disk, and on-line via Embark.com and CollegeLink.

Procedure: Freshmen are admitted in the fall. Entrance exams should be taken before January 15. There are early decision, early admissions, and deferred admissions plans. Early decision applications should be filed by November 15; regular applications, by January 15 for fall entry. The fall 2001 application fee was $50. Notification of early decision is sent December 15; regular decision, by April 15. 154 early decision candidates were accepted for the 2001-2002 class. 18% of all applicants are on a waiting list; 35 were accepted in 2001.

Transfer: 2 transfer students enrolled in 2001-2002. Transfer students must be able to enter the sophomore or junior class. Admission depends mainly on the strength of college grades. A minimum GPA of 3.0 is necessary, and the SAT I is recommended. The equivalent of 1 year of courses must have been earned. A liberal arts curriculum is also recommended. 64 credits of 128 must be completed at Haverford.

Visiting: There are guides for informal visits and visitors may sit in on classes and stay overnight. To schedule a visit, contact the Admissions Office at *admission@haverford.edu*

Financial Aid: In 2001-2002, 42% of all freshmen and 43% of continuing students received some form of financial aid. 40% of all students received need-based aid. The average freshman award was $24,784. Of that total, scholarships or need-based grants averaged $18,893; loans averaged $2245; work contracts averaged $1399; and Pell, SEOG, state grants, and outside scholarships averaged $2247. The average financial indebtedness of the 2001 graduate was $14,685. The CSS/Profile or FAFSA is required. The fall application deadline is January 31.

International Students: There are 31 international students enrolled. The school actively recruits these students. They must score 600 on the written TOEFL and also take the SAT I or the ACT.

Computers: The mainframes are multiple Sun SPARC Stations as distributed servers. A total of 201 computers are available for student use, 96 in public computing labs, 75 in department-specific labs, and 30 in the library and other buildings. All students may access the system. There are no time limits and no fees.

Graduates: In 2001, 291 bachelor's degrees were awarded. The most popular majors were biology (15%), English (13%), and history (11%). In an average class, 88% graduate in 4 years, 90% in 5 years, and 92% in 6 years. 172 companies recruited on campus in 2000-2001. Of the 2000 graduating class, 18% were enrolled in graduate school within 6 months of graduation and 66% were employed.

Admissions Contact: Delsie Z. Phillips, Director of Admission.
E-mail: *admitme@haverford.edu* Web: *http://www.haverford.edu*

HOLY FAMILY COLLEGE

Philadelphia, PA 19114 — **F-3**

(215) 637-3050
(800) 637-1191; Fax: (215) 281-1022

Full-time: 233 men, 839 women	**Faculty:** 75; IIB, -$
Part-time: 192 men, 585 women	**Ph.D.s:** 69%
Graduate: 179 men, 637 women	**Student/Faculty:** 14 to 1
Year: semesters, summer session	**Tuition:** $13,710
Application Deadline: open	**Room & Board:** n/app
Freshman Class: 527 applied, 441 accepted, 203 enrolled	
SAT I Verbal/Math: 470/450	**LESS COMPETITIVE**

Holy Family College, established in 1954 and affiliated with the Roman Catholic Church, is a private, nonresidential institution with a liberal arts core. In addition to regional accreditation, Holy Family has baccalaureate program accreditation with AACSB and NLN. The library contains 101,392 volumes, 8588 microform items, and 2975 audiovisual forms/CDs, and subscribes to 709 periodicals. Computerized library services include the card catalog, interlibrary loans, and database searching. Special learning facilities include a learning resource center and writing resource center. The 46-acre campus is in a suburban area within city limits. There are 8 buildings.

Student Life: 90% of undergraduates are from Pennsylvania. Others are from 7 states and 17 foreign countries. 24% are from public schools. 92% are white. Most are Catholic. The average age of freshmen is 18; all undergraduates, 21. 18% do not continue beyond their first year; 65% remain to graduate.

Housing: There are no residence halls. All students commute. Alcohol is not permitted. All students may keep cars.

Activities: There are no fraternities or sororities. There are 62 groups on campus, including cheerleading, drama, honors, international, literary magazine, newspaper, professional, religious, social service, student government, and yearbook. Popular campus events include Buddy Day, Christmas Rose, and Spring Fling.

Sports: There are 3 intercollegiate sports for men and 4 for women, and 5 intramural sports for men and 5 for women. Facilities include a gym, a weight room, racquetball courts, and soccer and softball fields.

Disabled Students: All of the campus is accessible. Wheelchair ramps, elevators, special parking, specially equipped rest rooms, lowered drinking fountains, and lowered telephones are available.

Services: Counseling and information services are available, as is tutoring in some subjects, including writing, reading, and math.

Campus Safety and Security: Measures include 24-hour foot and vehicle patrol, escort service, pamphlets/posters/films, and emergency telephones. There are lighted pathways/sidewalks.

Programs of Study: Holy Family confers B.A., B.S., and B.S.N. degrees. Associate and master's degrees are also awarded. Bachelor's degrees are awarded in BIOLOGICAL SCIENCE (biochemistry and biology/biological science), BUSINESS (accounting, business administration and management, and marketing/retailing/merchandising), COMMUNICATIONS AND THE ARTS (art, English, French, and Spanish), COMPUTER AND PHYSICAL SCIENCE (chemistry, information sciences and systems, and mathematics), EDUCATION (early childhood, elementary, foreign languages, science, secondary, and special), HEALTH PROFESSIONS (medical laboratory technology, nursing, and premedicine), SOCIAL SCIENCE (criminal justice, economics, history, humanities, prelaw, psychology, religion, social work, and sociology). Nursing, elementary education, and accounting are the strongest academically. Nursing, education, and business are the largest.

Required: Students must complete 120 to 130 semester hours, including at least 30 in the major, with a minimum GPA of 2.0. Nursing, medical technology, and education majors must maintain a GPA of 2.5. Specific discipline requirements include English, science, math, philosophy, religious studies, social studies, humanities, and foreign language. A core curriculum of communication, quantification, philosophy, humanities, social science, natural sciences, senior ethics, and religious studies must be fulfilled. All majors require satisfactory performance on a comprehensive exam.

Special: Opportunities are provided for study abroad, co-op programs in 23 majors with more than 200 companies, a B.A.-B.S. degree, an accelerated degree program, independent study, credit by exam, nondegree study, and pass/fail options. Students may pursue dual majors in business and French or Spanish, international business and French or Spanish, and elementary and special education. There are 10 national honor societies, a freshman honors program, and 2 departmental honors programs.

Faculty/Classroom: 44% of faculty are male; 56%, female. No introductory courses are taught by graduate students. The average class size in an introductory lecture is 20; in a laboratory, 17; and in a regular course, 21.

Admissions: 84% of the 2001-2002 applicants were accepted. The SAT I scores for the 2001-2002 freshman class were: Verbal--65% below 500, 32% between 500 and 599, and 3% between 600 and 700; Math--73% below 500, 23% between 500 and 599, and 4% between 600 and 700. 26% of the current freshmen were in the top fifth of their class; 60% were in the top two fifths.

Requirements: The SAT I or ACT is required. Graduation from an accredited secondary school is required; a GED is accepted. Applicants must submit 16 academic credits, including 4 courses in English, 3 each in history and math, 2 each in foreign language and science, 1 in social studies, and the remainder in academic electives. Holy Family requires applicants to be in the upper 40% of their class. A GPA of 2.0 is required. AP and CLEP credits are accepted. Important factors in the admissions decision are recommendations by school officials, recommendations by alumni, and personality/intangible qualities.

Procedure: Freshmen are admitted to all sessions. Entrance exams should be taken by October or November of the senior year. There are early decision and deferred admissions plans. Application deadlines are open. The fall 2001 application fee was $25. Notification is sent on a rolling basis.

Transfer: 120 transfer students enrolled in 2001-2002. Applicants must submit official transcripts from all previous colleges. Grades of D are not transferable. A maximum of 75 credits will be accepted for transfer. 45 credits of 120 must be completed at Holy Family.

Visiting: There are regularly scheduled orientations for prospective students, consisting of an interview and a tour. There are guides for informal visits and visitors may sit in on classes. To schedule a visit, contact the Office of Admissions.

Financial Aid: In a recent year, 79% of all freshmen and 85% of continuing students received some form of financial aid. 72% of freshmen and 73% of continuing students received need-based aid. The average freshman award was $9460. Of that total, scholarships or need-based grants averaged $500 ($4000 maximum); loans averaged $2625 ($10,500 maximum); and work contracts averaged $200 ($1000 maximum). All undergraduates work part time. Average annual earnings from campus work are $400. The average financial indebtedness of a recent year's graduate was $17,125. Holy Family is a member of CSS. The FAFSA is required. The fall application deadline is May 1.

International Students: There are 13 international students enrolled. They must score 530 on the written TOEFL.

Computers: There are more than 100 PCs networked in 4 to 6 labs available for student use. All students may access the system 6 days a week (7-day remote Internet access for subscribers). There are no time limits and no fees.

Graduates: In 2001, 306 bachelor's degrees were awarded. The most popular majors were education (35%), business/marketing (19%), and health professions (11%). In an average class, 4% graduate in 3 years, 46% in 4 years, 58% in 5 years, and 60% in 6 years. 85 companies recruited on campus in 2000-2001. Of the 2000 graduating class, 5% were enrolled in graduate school within 6 months of graduation and 90% were employed.

Admissions Contact: Roberta Nolan, Director of Undergraduate Admissions. E-mail: *rnolan@hfc.edu* Web: *www.hfc.edu*

IMMACULATA COLLEGE
Immaculata, PA 19345 — E-4

(610) 647-4400, ext. 3015
(877) 428-6329; Fax: (610) 340-0836

Full-time: 34 men, 565 women	**Faculty:** 75; IIA, --$
Part-time: 384 men, 1793 women	**Ph.D.s:** 63%
Graduate: 77 men, 744 women	**Student/Faculty:** 8 to 1
Year: semesters, summer session	**Tuition:** $15,200
Application Deadline: May 1	**Room & Board:** $7200
Freshman Class: 439 applied, 372 accepted, 117 enrolled	
SAT I Verbal/Math: 510/470	**LESS COMPETITIVE**

Immaculata College, founded in 1920, is a private Catholic, primarily women's liberal arts and career preparation college. There is 1 graduate school. In addition to regional accreditation, Immaculata has baccalaureate program accreditation with ADA, AHEA, NASM, and NLN. The library contains 132,348 volumes, 1373 microform items, and 2944 audiovisual forms/CDs, and subscribes to 755 periodicals. Computerized library services include the card catalog, interlibrary loans, and database searching. Special learning facilities include a learning resource center and language labs. The 400-acre campus is in a suburban area 20 miles west of Philadelphia. Including residence halls, there are 13 buildings.

Student Life: 84% of undergraduates are from Pennsylvania. Others are from 15 states, 23 foreign countries, and Canada. 52% are from public schools. 85% are white. 80% are Catholic; 15% Protestant. The average age of freshmen is 18; all undergraduates, 30. 11% do not continue beyond their first year; 69% remain to graduate.

Housing: 380 students can be accommodated in college housing, which includes single-sex dormitories. On-campus housing is guaranteed for all 4 years. 82% of students live on campus; of those, 60% remain on campus on weekends. Alcohol is not permitted. All students may keep cars.

Activities: There are no fraternities or sororities. There are 32 groups on campus, including art, choir, chorale, chorus, computers, dance, debate, drama, ethnic, honors, international, literary magazine, musical theater, newspaper, orchestra, photography, political, professional, religious, social, social service, student government, and yearbook. Popular campus events include Rose Arbor Dinner, class proms, and Friday's Pub.

Sports: There are 6 intercollegiate sports for women and 10 intramural sports for women. Facilities include tennis courts, a full gym, a handball gym, an Olympic-size swimming pool, hockey and softball fields, and a weight room.

Disabled Students: All of the campus is accessible. Wheelchair ramps, elevators, special parking, specially equipped rest rooms, special class scheduling, lowered drinking fountains, lowered telephones, and special dormitory facilities are available.

Services: Counseling and information services are available, as is tutoring in most subjects. There is a reader service for the blind, and remedial math, reading, and writing.

Campus Safety and Security: Measures include 24-hour foot and vehicle patrol, self-defense education, escort service, and informal discussions. There are pamphlets/posters/films, emergency telephones, and lighted pathways/sidewalks.

Programs of Study: Immaculata confers B.A., B.S., B.Mus., and B.S.N. degrees. Associate, master's, and doctoral degrees are also awarded. Bachelor's degrees are awarded in BIOLOGICAL SCIENCE (biochemistry and biology/biological science), BUSINESS (accounting, business administration and management, and fashion merchandising), COMMUNICATIONS AND THE ARTS (English, French, German, music, and Spanish), COMPUTER AND PHYSICAL SCIENCE (chemistry, information sciences and systems, and mathematics), EDUCATION (early childhood, elementary, foreign languages, home economics, middle school, music, science, and secondary), HEALTH PROFESSIONS (music therapy, nursing, and premedicine), SOCIAL SCIENCE (dietetics, economics, food science, history, international relations, prelaw, psychology, social science, sociology, and theological studies). Premedicine, education, and dietetics are the strongest academically. Education, business, and music therapy are the largest.

Required: To graduate students must complete at least 126 credits, including 36 to 52 in the major, with a minimum GPA of 2.0. All students must complete 54 credits in liberal arts, including distribution requirements in humanities, social sciences, and sciences. 2 credits of phys ed are also required. A thesis, which is the outcome of a required senior seminar, must also be completed. Internships are required for dietetics, music therapy, and education.

Special: All majors offer opportunities for internships, and most require them. Students may study abroad in 6 countries. The college offers dual-major combinations, student-designed majors, 3 accelerated degree programs in organization dynamics, human resource management, and nursing, and nondegree study and pass/fail options. There are 16 national honor societies, including Phi Beta Kappa, a freshman honors program, and 13 departmental honors programs.

Faculty/Classroom: 42% of faculty are male; 58%, female. 92% teach undergraduates and 4% both teach and do research. No introductory

courses are taught by graduate students. The average class size in an introductory lecture is 20; in a laboratory, 12; and in a regular course, 14.

Admissions: 85% of the 2001-2002 applicants were accepted. The SAT I scores for the 2001-2002 freshman class were: Math--59% below 500, 29% between 500 and 599, and 12% between 600 and 700. 24% of the current freshmen were in the top fifth of their class; 52% were in the top two fifths. 2 freshmen graduated first in their class.

Requirements: The SAT I is required, with a minimum composite score of 800, 400 verbal and 400 math. Candidates for admission should be graduates of an accredited secondary school with a minimum of 16 academic credits, including 4 in English, 2 each in a foreign language, math, science, and social studies, 1 in history, and 3 more in college-preparatory courses. The GED is accepted. An audition is required for music students, and an essay and an interview are recommended for all. Immaculata requires applicants to be in the upper 60% of their class. A GPA of 2.0 is required. AP and CLEP credits are accepted. Important factors in the admissions decision are advanced placement or honor courses, recommendations by school officials, and extracurricular activities record.

Procedure: Freshmen are admitted fall and spring. Entrance exams should be taken in the spring of the junior year. There are early decision and deferred admissions plans. Early decision applications should be filed by November 1; regular applications, by May 1 for fall entry and November 1 for spring entry, along with a $25 fee. Notification of early decision is sent December 1; regular decision, on a rolling basis.

Transfer: 18 transfer students enrolled in a recent year. In addition to high school credentials, applicants must present college transcripts. A minimum composite score of 800 on the SAT I is required, as is an interview. Students must have a minimum GPA of 2.0. Courses in which the student has achieved a C or better are accepted if they are comparable to Immaculata's courses.

Visiting: There are regularly scheduled orientations for prospective students, including an open house and class visit. There are guides for informal visits and visitors may sit in on classes and stay overnight. To schedule a visit, contact the Office of Admissions at *pbarry@immaculata.edu*

Financial Aid: In 2001-2002, 93% of all freshmen and 86% of continuing students received some form of financial aid. 88% of freshmen and 75% of continuing students received need-based aid. The average freshman award was $12,916. Of that total, scholarships or need-based grants averaged $2770 ($14,900 maximum); loans averaged $2625 ($4280 maximum); and work contracts averaged $1000 (maximum). All undergraduates work part time. Average annual earnings from campus work are $700. The average financial indebtedness of the 2001 graduate was $10,000. Immaculata is a member of CSS. The FAFSA is required. The fall application deadline is March 1.

International Students: There are 35 international students enrolled. The school actively recruits these students. They must score 550 on the written TOEFL.

Computers: Students may use the networked computer terminals in the administrative offices, computer centers labs, and library and have access to the Internet and e-mail. All students may access the system at any time. There are no time limits and no fees.

Graduates: In 2001, 366 bachelor's degrees were awarded. The most popular majors were economics/business (38%), psychology (10%), and dietetics (7%). In an average class, 1% graduate in 3 years, 71% in 4 years, 74% in 5 years, and 78% in 6 years. 18 companies recruited on campus in 2000-2001. Of the 2000 graduating class, 10% were enrolled in graduate school within 6 months of graduation and 87% were employed.

Admissions Contact: Sandra Zerby, Executive Director of Admissions. A video is available. E-mail: *admiss@immaculata.edu*
Web: *http://www.immaculata.edu*

INDIANA UNIVERSITY OF PENNSYLVANIA B-3

Indiana, PA 15705 **(724) 357-2230; (800) 442-6830**

Full-time: 4858 men, 6065 women	**Faculty:** 674; I, -$
Part-time: 376 men, 464 women	**Ph.D.s:** 97%
Graduate: 622 men, 1072 women	**Student/Faculty:** 16 to 1
Year: semesters, summer session	**Tuition:** $4875 ($10,899)
Application Deadline: open	**Room & Board:** $4258
Freshman Class: 7459 applied, 4270 accepted, 2728 enrolled	
SAT I: required	**ACT:** n/av **COMPETITIVE**

Indiana University of Pennsylvania, founded in 1875, is a public member of the Pennsylvania State System of Higher Education, offering programs in liberal and fine arts, business, preengineering, health science, military science, teacher preparation, basic and applied science, social science and humanities, criminology, and safety science. There are 6 undergraduate schools and 1 graduate school. In addition to regional accreditation, IUP has baccalaureate program accreditation with AACSB, ABET, ACS, ADA, APA, CAHEA, CCNE, NAACLS, NASM, and NCATE. The library contains 820,456 volumes, 2,344,030 microform items, and 201,741 audiovisual forms/CDs, and subscribes to 2755 periodicals. Computerized library services include the card catalog, interlibrary loans, and database searching. Special learning facilities include a learning resource center, art gallery, planetarium, radio station, and TV station. The 342-acre campus is in a small town 50 miles northeast of Pittsburgh. Including residence halls, there are 70 buildings.

Student Life: 97% of undergraduates are from Pennsylvania. Others are from 39 states and 83 foreign countries. 91% are from public schools. 89% are white. The average age of freshmen is 18; all undergraduates, 21. 26% do not continue beyond their first year; 56% remain to graduate.

Housing: 3993 students can be accommodated in college housing, which includes single-sex and coed dormitories and on-campus apartments. In addition, there are honors houses, 24 hour intensified study floors, substance-free and academic specialty housing, and an international house. On-campus housing is guaranteed for the freshman year only and is available on a lottery system for upperclassmen. Alcohol is not permitted. No one may keep cars.

Activities: 10% of men belong to 19 national fraternities; 11% of women belong to 14 national sororities. There are 200 groups on campus, including art, band, cheerleading, choir, chorale, chorus, computers, dance, drama, ethnic, film, gay, honors, international, jazz band, marching band, musical theater, newspaper, opera, orchestra, pep band, political, professional, radio and TV, religious, social, social service, student government, symphony, and yearbook. Popular campus events include Family Weekend and International Day.

Sports: There are 7 intercollegiate sports for men and 10 for women, and 24 intramural sports for men and 21 for women. Facilities include a 7600-seat stadium, swimming pools, a fitness trail, softball fields, and courts for tennis, badminton, handball/racquetball, basketball, and volleyball.

Disabled Students: 98% of the campus is accessible. Wheelchair ramps, elevators, special parking, specially equipped rest rooms, special class scheduling, and lowered drinking fountains are available.

Services: Counseling and information services are available, as is tutoring in most subjects. There is a reader service for the blind, and remedial math, reading, and writing.

Campus Safety and Security: Measures include 24-hour foot and vehicle patrol, self-defense education, escort service, and shuttle buses. There are informal discussions, pamphlets/posters/films, emergency telephones, and lighted pathways/sidewalks.

Programs of Study: IUP confers B.A., B.S., B.F.A., and B.S.Ed. degrees. Associate, master's, and doctoral degrees are also awarded. Bachelor's degrees are awarded in BIOLOGICAL SCIENCE (biochemistry and biology/biological science), BUSINESS (accounting, banking and finance, business administration and management, fashion merchandising, hotel/motel and restaurant management, human resources, international business management, management information systems, and marketing/retailing/merchandising), COMMUNICATIONS AND THE ARTS (art, communications, dramatic arts, English, fine arts, French, German, journalism, media arts, music, music performance, Russian, Spanish, and studio art), COMPUTER AND PHYSICAL SCIENCE (applied mathematics, applied physics, chemistry, computer science, geology, geoscience, mathematics, natural sciences, and physics), EDUCATION (art, business, early childhood, education of the deaf and hearing impaired, education of the mentally handicapped, education of the physically handicapped, elementary, English, foreign languages, mathematics, music, nutrition, physical, science, social science, special, and vocational), ENGINEERING AND ENVIRONMENTAL DESIGN (city/community/regional planning, and interior design), HEALTH PROFESSIONS (environmental health science, medical technology, nuclear medical technology, nursing, premedicine, rehabilitation therapy, respiratory therapy, and speech pathology/audiology), SOCIAL SCIENCE (anthropology, child care/child and family studies, consumer services, criminology, dietetics, economics, family/consumer studies, food production/management/services, food science, geography, history, international studies, philosophy, political science/government, prelaw, psychology, religion, safety and security technology, social science, and sociology). Elementary education, criminology, and communications media are the largest.

Required: All candidates for graduation must complete approximately 124 credits, including 53 credits in the liberal studies core. The total number of hours and the minimum GPA vary with the major.

Special: IUP offers co-op programs, cross-registration through the National Student Exchange Consortium, a 3-2 engineering degree with the University of Pittsburgh and Drexel University, and a B.A.-B.S. degree. Internships and dual and student-designed majors are available. Students may study abroad in 28 countries. Also available are work-study programs, a Washington semester, an accelerated degree program, and credit for military experience. There are 21 national honor societies, and a freshman honors program.

Faculty/Classroom: 58% of faculty are male; 42%, female. 91% teach undergraduates. No introductory courses are taught by graduate students. The average class size in a laboratory is 16 and in a regular course, 25.

Admissions: 57% of the 2001-2002 applicants were accepted. The SAT I scores for the 2001-2002 freshman class were: Verbal--34% below 500, 49% between 500 and 599, 15% between 600 and 700, and 2% above 700; Math--40% below 500, 47% between 500 and 599, 12% between 600 and 700, and 1% above 700. 10 freshmen graduated first in their class.

Requirements: The SAT I is required. Candidates for admission should be graduates of an accredited secondary school. There are no specific course requirements. Art majors must have a portfolio and music majors must audition. AP and CLEP credits are accepted. Important factors in the admissions decision are advanced placement or honor courses, extracurricular activities record, and evidence of special talent. Applications are accepted on-line at *www.iup.edu/admissions*.

Procedure: Freshmen are admitted fall and spring. Entrance exams should be taken by December of the preceding year. There is a deferred admissions plan. Application deadlines are open. The fall 2001 application fee was $30. Notification is sent on a rolling basis, beginning in September.

Transfer: 673 transfer students enrolled in 2001-2002. Transfer students must have a minimum GPA of 2.0 for all subjects (2.5 for education students). 45 credits of 124 must be completed at IUP.

Visiting: There are regularly scheduled orientations for prospective students. There are guides for informal visits and visitors may sit in on classes. To schedule a visit, contact the Admissions Office.

Financial Aid: In 2001-2002, 66% of all freshmen and 69% of continuing students received some form of financial aid. 56% of freshmen and 57% of continuing students received need-based aid. The average freshman award was $3558. 18% of undergraduates work part time. Average annual earnings from campus work are $1500. The average financial indebtedness of the 2001 graduate was $14,250. The FAFSA and Pennsylvania State Grant form are required. The fall application deadline is April 15.

International Students: There are 237 international students enrolled. They must score 500 on the written TOEFL.

Computers: The mainframe is a DEC VAX cluster. 500 Macs and PCs are available throughout the campus for student use in teaching facilities. There are more than 3000 PCs on campus. All students may access the system 24 hours a day, 7 days a week. There are no time limits and no fees.

Graduates: In 2001, 2142 bachelor's degrees were awarded. The most popular majors were crimonology (10%), elementary education (9%), and communication media (6%). In an average class, 55% graduate in 6 years. 129 companies recruited on campus in 2000-2001. Of the 2000 graduating class, 19% were enrolled in graduate school within 6 months of graduation and 77% were employed.

Admissions Contact: William Nunn, Dean of Admissions.
Web: *www.iup.edu/admissions_and_aid/admissions_and_aid.htm*

JUNIATA COLLEGE
Huntingdon, PA 16652 — C-3
(814) 641-3420
(877) JUNIATA; Fax: (814) 641-3100

Full-time: 530 men, 730 women	**Faculty:** 83; IIB, av$
Part-time: 17 men, 25 women	**Ph.D.s:** 96%
Graduate: none	**Student/Faculty:** 15 to 1
Year: semesters, summer session	**Tuition:** $20,590
Application Deadline: March 15	**Room & Board:** $5490
Freshman Class: 1402 applied, 1108 accepted, 342 enrolled	
SAT I Verbal/Math: 577/583	**VERY COMPETITIVE**

Juniata College, founded in 1876, is an independent liberal arts college affiliated with the Church of the Brethren. In addition to regional accreditation, Juniata has baccalaureate program accreditation with CSWE. The library contains 250,000 volumes, 200 microform items, and 1400 audiovisual forms/CDs, and subscribes to 1000 periodicals. Computerized library services include the card catalog, interlibrary loans, and database searching. Special learning facilities include a learning resource center, art gallery, radio station, an observatory, an environmental studies field station, a nature preserve, an early childhood education center, and a ceramics studio with an Anagama kiln. The 1167-acre campus is in a small town 31 miles south of State College, in the heart of rural Pennsylvania. Including residence halls, there are 40 buildings.

Student Life: 76% of undergraduates are from Pennsylvania. Others are from 36 states and 22 foreign countries. 89% are from public schools. 92% are white. 60% are Protestant; 36% Catholic. The average age of freshmen is 18; all undergraduates, 20. 10% do not continue beyond their first year; 73% remain to graduate.

Housing: 1098 students can be accommodated in college housing, which includes single-sex and coed dormitories, on-campus apartments, and off-campus apartments. In addition, there are special-interest houses and international houses. On-campus housing is guaranteed for all 4 years. 81% of students live on campus; of those, 75% remain on campus on weekends. All students may keep cars.

Activities: There are no fraternities or sororities. There are 97 groups on campus, including art, band, cheerleading, chess, choir, chorale, chorus, computers, dance, debate, drama, ethnic, forensics, gay, honors, international, jazz band, literary magazine, model U.N., musical theater, newspaper, orchestra, outing, pep band, photography, political, professional, radio and TV, religious, social, social service, student government, symphony, and yearbook. Popular campus events include Mountain Day, Spring Fest, and All Class Night.

Sports: There are 9 intercollegiate sports for men and 10 for women, and 21 intramural sports for men and 19 for women. Facilities include 2 gyms, a swimming pool, a fitness center, a wrestling room, 4 racquetball courts, a multipurpose room, a sauna, a varsity football field and stadium, baseball, soccer, and hockey fields, an outdoor running track, 7 tennis courts, and 1 outdoor basketball court.

Disabled Students: 75% of the campus is accessible. Wheelchair ramps, elevators, special parking, specially equipped rest rooms, special class scheduling, lowered drinking fountains, wide doors, and stairlifts are available.

Services: Counseling and information services are available, as is tutoring in most subjects. There is a reader service for the blind. Juniata also offers courses and workshops in study, reading, and writing skills.

Campus Safety and Security: Measures include 24-hour foot and vehicle patrol, self-defense education, escort service, and informal discussions. There are pamphlets/posters/films, emergency telephones, lighted pathways/sidewalks, awareness programs, fire safety inspections, and an emergency telephone number.

Programs of Study: Juniata confers B.A. and B.S. degrees. Bachelor's degrees are awarded in BIOLOGICAL SCIENCE (biochemistry, biology/biological science, botany, ecology, marine science, microbiology, molecular biology, and zoology), BUSINESS (accounting, banking and finance, business administration and management, human resources, international business management, management information systems, and marketing/retailing/merchandising), COMMUNICATIONS AND THE ARTS (art history and appreciation, communications, English, French, German, Russian, Spanish, and studio art), COMPUTER AND PHYSICAL SCIENCE (chemistry, computer science, geology, information sciences and systems, mathematics, natural sciences, and physics), EDUCATION (early childhood, elementary, English, foreign languages, mathematics, museum studies, science, secondary, social studies, and special), ENGINEERING AND ENVIRONMENTAL DESIGN (environmental science and preengineering), HEALTH PROFESSIONS (preallied health, predentistry, premedicine, preoptometry, prepharmacy, prepodiatry, and preveterinary science), SOCIAL SCIENCE (anthropology, criminal justice, economics, history, humanities, international studies, ministries, peace studies, political science/government, prelaw, psychology, public administration, social science, social work, and sociology). Pre-health programs, chemistry, and biology are the strongest academically. Biology, business, and education are the largest.

Required: Students are required to complete a minimum of 120 credit hours, including courses in fine arts, international studies, social sciences, humanities, and natural sciences, as well as 4 commuications-based courses, 2 cultural analysis courses, a math and statistics course, and the college writing seminar. The total number of hours required for the program of emphasis varies from 45 to 60; majors do not exist as such, and students must develop a program of emphasis and complete it to obtain their degree. Students must have a minimum GPA of 2.0.

Special: Juniata offers cooperative programs in marine science, cytogenetics, cytotechnology, marine biology, biotechnology, nursing, medical technology, diagnostic imaging, occupational and physical therapy, dentistry, medicine, optometry, and podiatry. Internships, study abroad in 14 countries, Washington and Philadelphia semesters, and nondegree study are also offered. There are 3-2 engineering degrees with Columbia, Clarkson, Washington, and Pennsylvania State Universities, a 3-3 law program with Duquesne University, and various preprofessional programs, including optometry, medicine, dentistry, pharmacy, and podiatry. With the assistance of 2 faculty advisers, most students design their own majors to meet their individual goals. There are 10 national honor societies, a freshman honors program, and 10 departmental honors programs.

Faculty/Classroom: 61% of faculty are male; 39%, female. All teach undergraduates; 65% both teach and do research. The average class size in an introductory lecture is 30; in a laboratory, 21; and in a regular course, 20.

Admissions: 79% of the 2001-2002 applicants were accepted. The SAT I scores for the 2001-2002 freshman class were: Verbal--13% below 500, 46% between 500 and 599, 35% between 600 and 700, and 6% above 700; Math--11% below 500, 44% between 500 and 599, 39% between 600 and 700, and 5% above 700. 67% of the current freshmen were in the top fifth of their class; 93% were in the top two fifths. There were 3 National Merit semifinalists. 7 freshmen graduated first in their class.

Requirements: The SAT I or ACT is required. In addition, candidates for admission should be graduates of an accredited secondary school and have completed 16 academic credits, including a combination of 10 in math, social studies, and lab science, 4 in English, 2 in a foreign language. The GED is accepted, and home schoolers are encouraged to apply. An essay is required and an interview is recommended. A GPA of

3.0 is required. AP credits are accepted. Important factors in the admissions decision are advanced placement or honor courses, leadership record, and recommendations by school officials. Applications are accepted on computer disk and on-line via the Private School Consortium's Common App, CollegeLink, Peterson's Expand, and Embark.

Procedure: Freshmen are admitted fall and spring. Entrance exams should be taken in the junior or senior years of high school. There are early decision and deferred admissions plans. Early decision applications should be filed by November 15; regular applications, by March 15 for fall entry and December 1 for spring entry, along with a $30 fee. Notification of early decision is sent December 31; regular decision, on a rolling basis beginning September 1.. 106 early decision candidates were accepted for the 2001-2002 class.

Transfer: 23 transfer students enrolled in 2001-2002. A GPA of 2.5 is required. Applicants must submit a high school transcript, a college transcript, and an essay. SAT I scores are required of some students. 30 credits of 120 must be completed at Juniata.

Visiting: There are regularly scheduled orientations for prospective students, including a campus tour, interviews, and a department fair. There are guides for informal visits and visitors may sit in on classes and stay overnight. To schedule a visit, contact Norma Jennings, Enrollment Assistant at (814) 641-3428 or *jenninn@juniata.edu.*

Financial Aid: In 2001-2002, 97% of all freshmen and 96% of continuing students received some form of financial aid. 76% of freshmen and 78% of continuing students received need-based aid. The average freshman award was $17,484. Of that total, scholarships or need-based grants averaged $13,913 ($26,080 maximum); loans averaged $2934 ($3625 maximum); and work contracts averaged $1392 ($1800 maximum). 53% of undergraduates work part time. Average annual earnings from campus work are $800. The average financial indebtedness of the 2001 graduate was $16,500. Juniata is a member of CSS. The CSS/Profile or FAFSA is required. The fall application deadline is March 1.

International Students: There are 68 international students enrolled. The school actively recruits these students. They must score 550 on the written TOEFL.

Computers: The mainframe is an HP 9000/L-2000. All dorm rooms are equipped for full Internet and Intranet access. There are also numerous maintenance terminals, PCs, and Macs located throughout the campus. Students have access to all locations and are provided with a personal account. 12 computer labs, with more than 250 computers, are available for student use. All students may access the system. There are no time limits and no fees. It is strongly recommended that all students have personal computers.

Graduates: In 2001, 298 bachelor's degrees were awarded. The most popular majors were biology/prehealth (17%), business/accounting (14%), and education (12%). In an average class, 70% graduate in 4 years, 72% in 5 years, and 73% in 6 years. 82 companies recruited on campus in 2000-2001. Of the 2000 graduating class, 30% were enrolled in graduate school within 6 months of graduation and 67% were employed.

Admissions Contact: Office of Enrollment. E-mail: *info@juniata.edu* Web: *www.juniata.edu*

KEYSTONE COLLEGE

La Plume, PA 18440 E-4

(570) 945-6953
(877) 4COLLEGE; Fax: (570) 945-7916

Full-time: 439 men, 530 women	**Faculty:** 55
Part-time: 108 men, 297 women	**Ph.D.s:** 36%
Graduate: none	**Student/Faculty:** 18 to 1
Year: semesters, summer session	**Tuition:** $12,666
Application Deadline: open	**Room & Board:** $6400
Freshman Class: 814 applied, 778 accepted, 367 enrolled	
SAT I Verbal/Math: 440/420	**LESS COMPETITIVE**

Keystone College, founded in 1868, is a small private college offering undergraduate programs in accounting, human resources management, criminal justice administration, elementary education, communication, and preprofessional training in the allied health fields. The library contains 40,682 volumes, 39,500 microform items, and 1441 audiovisual forms/CDs, and subscribes to 211 periodicals. Computerized library services include the card catalog, interlibrary loans, and database searching. Special learning facilities include a learning resource center, art gallery, radio station, and observatory. The 270-acre campus is in a rural area 15 miles north of Scranton and 40 miles south of Binghamton, New York. Including residence halls, there are 29 buildings.

Student Life: 87% of undergraduates are from Pennsylvania. Others are from 14 states and 11 foreign countries. 90% are white. The average age of freshmen is 19; all undergraduates, 25. 36% do not continue beyond their first year; 41% remain to graduate.

Housing: 450 students can be accommodated in college housing, which includes single-sex and coed dormitories. In addition, there are special Internet floors. On-campus housing is guaranteed for all 4 years. 59% of students commute. Alcohol is not permitted. All students may keep cars.

Activities: There are no fraternities or sororities. There are 19 groups on campus, including art, cheerleading, co-op, drama, equestrian, ethnic, honors, international, literary magazine, newspaper, radio and TV, religious, skiing, social, social service, student government, and yearbook. Popular campus events include Family Day.

Sports: There are 6 intercollegiate sports for men and 7 for women, and 6 intramural sports for men and 6 for women. Facilities include an athletic center, tennis courts, playing fields, and a trail system.

Disabled Students: 90% of the campus is accessible. Wheelchair ramps, elevators, special parking, specially equipped rest rooms, special class scheduling, lowered drinking fountains, and lowered telephones are available.

Services: Counseling and information services are available, as is tutoring in every subject. There is remedial math, reading, and writing.

Campus Safety and Security: Measures include 24-hour foot and vehicle patrol, escort service, informal discussions, and pamphlets/posters/films. There are emergency telephones and lighted pathways/sidewalks.

Programs of Study: Keystone College confers B.S. and B.A. degrees. Associate degrees are also awarded. Bachelor's degrees are awarded in AGRICULTURE (natural resource management), BUSINESS (accounting, human resources, and recreational facilities management), COMMUNICATIONS AND THE ARTS (communications), COMPUTER AND PHYSICAL SCIENCE (information sciences and systems), EDUCATION (early childhood and elementary), SOCIAL SCIENCE (criminal justice). Education and environmental resource management are the strongest academically. Education is the largest.

Required: To graduate, students must complete 123 to 130 credit hours and maintain a GPA of 2.0. The required core curriculum includes courses in interdisciplinary studies, math, English, speech, and fitness. Distribution requirements and total credit hours vary with the major.

Special: Keystone offers co-op programs in all majors, as well as paid and unpaid internships. The Weekender program accommodates the needs of busy adult students. There is a chapter of Phi Beta Kappa.

Faculty/Classroom: 40% of faculty are male; 60%, female. All teach undergraduates. The average class size in an introductory lecture is 16; in a laboratory, 9; and in a regular course, 10.

Admissions: 96% of the 2001-2002 applicants were accepted. The SAT I scores for the 2001-2002 freshman class were: Verbal--76% below 500, 20% between 500 and 599, and 4% between 600 and 700; Math--82% below 500, 16% between 500 and 599, and 2% between 600 and 700. 8% of the current freshmen were in the top fifth of their class; 29% were in the top two fifths.

Requirements: The SAT I or ACT is required; the SAT I is preferred. An interview is recommended. A GPA of 2.0 is required. AP and CLEP credits are accepted. Important factors in the admissions decision are extracurricular activities record, leadership record, and parents or siblings attending the school. Applications are accepted on-line via Next Step College, CollegeNET, and the college's web site.

Procedure: Freshmen are admitted to all sessions. Entrance exams should be taken in the spring of the junior year or early fall of the senior year. There are early admissions and deferred admissions plans. Application deadlines are open. The fall 2001 application fee was $25. Notification is sent on a rolling basis.

Transfer: 70 transfer students enrolled in 2001-2002. Applicants with more than 12 academic college credits must have a minimum GPA of 2.0. A letter of recommendation is required. 32 credits of 123 to 130 must be completed at Keystone College.

Visiting: There are regularly scheduled orientations for prospective students, consisting of 7 open houses and 3 visitation days yearly. There are guides for informal visits and visitors may sit in on classes and stay overnight. To schedule a visit, contact the Admissions Office.

Financial Aid: In 2001-2002, 98% of all freshmen and 95% of continuing students received some form of financial aid. 85% of freshmen and 82% of continuing students received need-based aid. The average freshman award was $12,761. Of that total, scholarships or need-based grants averaged $4474 ($5697 maximum); loans averaged $3000 ($7000 maximum); work contracts averaged $1250 ($1600 maximum); and state grants averaged $2400 ($3300 maximum). 29% of undergraduates work part time. Average annual earnings from campus work are $1250. The average financial indebtedness of the 2001 graduate was $7200. Keystone College is a member of CSS. The FAFSA is required.

International Students: There are 10 international students enrolled. The school actively recruits these students. They must score 500 on the written TOEFL or 173 on the electronic version or take the MELAB or the college's own test.

Computers: The mainframe is an IBM AS/400 Model 620. Computer labs provide access to the Internet and Web. The campus is wired so that students can access the Web from all areas. All students may access the system. There are no time limits. The fee is $150.

Graduates: In 2001, 24 bachelor's degrees were awarded. In an average class, 36% graduate in 3 years.

Admissions Contact: Sarah S. Keating, Director of Admissions. E-mail: *admissns@keystone.edu* Web: *www.keystone.edu*

KING'S COLLEGE
Wilkes Barre, PA 18711 E-2
(570) 208-5858
(888) 546-4772; Fax: (570) 208-5971

Full-time: 860 men, 860 women	**Faculty:** 111; IIB, av$
Part-time: 131 men, 217 women	**Ph.D.s:** 80%
Graduate: 43 men, 115 women	**Student/Faculty:** 16 to 1
Year: semesters, summer session	**Tuition:** $17,450
Application Deadline: May 1	**Room & Board:** $7230
Freshman Class: n/av	
SAT I or ACT: required	**COMPETITIVE**

King's College, founded in 1946, is a private institution affiliated with the Roman Catholic Church. The college offers undergraduate programs in humanities and natural and social sciences, specialized programs in business and other professions, and graduate programs in reading, health care administration, and physician assistant. The library contains 164,304 volumes, 561,989 microform items, and 2257 audiovisual forms/CDs, and subscribes to 822 periodicals. Computerized library services include the card catalog, interlibrary loans, and database searching. Special learning facilities include a learning resource center, art gallery, radio station, and TV station. The 48-acre campus is in an urban area in northeastern Pennsylvania 19 miles south of Scranton. Including residence halls, there are 18 buildings.

Student Life: 74% of undergraduates are from Pennsylvania. Others are from 26 states and 8 foreign countries. 67% are from public schools. 92% are white. 66% are Catholic; 13% Protestant. The average age of freshmen is 18; all undergraduates, 20. 19% do not continue beyond their first year; 70% remain to graduate.

Housing: 727 students can be accommodated in college housing, which includes single-sex dormitories and on-campus apartments. On-campus housing is guaranteed for all 4 years. 61% of students commute. Alcohol is not permitted. All students may keep cars.

Activities: There are no fraternities or sororities. There are 50 groups on campus, including art, cheerleading, choir, chorale, chorus, computers, dance, debate, drama, ethnic, film, honors, international, jazz band, literary magazine, musical theater, newspaper, pep band, photography, political, professional, radio and TV, religious, social, social service, student government, and yearbook. Popular campus events include All College Ball, Student Activities Fair, and Friends and Family Weekend.

Sports: There are 12 intercollegiate sports for men and 11 for women, and 8 intramural sports for men and 8 for women. Facilities include a phys ed center, outdoor basketball courts, a fitness center, a wrestling room, racquetball courts, a swimming pool, a multipurpose area, a 3200-seat gym, a free weight area, an outdoor athletic complex with a field house, a field hockey field, a football stadium, and baseball, softball, and soccer fields.

Disabled Students: 99% of the campus is accessible. Wheelchair ramps, elevators, special parking, specially equipped rest rooms, special class scheduling, lowered drinking fountains, and lowered telephones are available.

Services: Counseling and information services are available, as is tutoring in every subject. The academic skills center provides a writing center, learning skills workshops, a tutoring program, and learning disability services.

Campus Safety and Security: Measures include 24-hour foot and vehicle patrol, self-defense education, escort service, and informal discussions. There are pamphlets/posters/films, emergency telephones, and lighted pathways/sidewalks.

Programs of Study: King's confers B.A. and B.S. degrees. Associate and master's degrees are also awarded. Bachelor's degrees are awarded in AGRICULTURE (environmental studies), BIOLOGICAL SCIENCE (biology/biological science and neurosciences), BUSINESS (accounting, banking and finance, business administration and management, international business management, marketing/retailing/merchandising, and personnel management), COMMUNICATIONS AND THE ARTS (communications, dramatic arts, English, French, languages, and Spanish), COMPUTER AND PHYSICAL SCIENCE (chemistry, computer science, information sciences and systems, mathematics, and science), EDUCATION (early childhood, elementary, foreign languages, middle school, science, and secondary), HEALTH PROFESSIONS (health care administration, medical laboratory technology, predentistry, premedicine, and sports medicine), SOCIAL SCIENCE (criminal justice, economics, gerontology, history, philosophy, political science/government, prelaw, psychology, sociology, and theological studies). Accounting, English, and biology are the strongest academically. Elementary education, business administration, and mass communications are the largest.

Required: All students must earn a minimum of 120 credits and maintain a GPA of 2.0. The core requirements represent 54 credits. The major comprises a maximum of 60 credits, of which up to 40 can be specified in the major department, with the balance designated for related fields.

Special: A co-op program in special education and cross-registration with Wilkes University and College Misericordia are offered. The Experiential Learning Program provides internship opportunities in all majors with a variety of employers. King's also offers study abroad through an agreement with Webster University, a Washington center, work-study programs, an accelerated degree program in business administration, B.A.-B.S. degrees, dual and student-designed majors, credit for life experience, and pass/fail options. There are 11 national honor societies and a freshman honors program.

Faculty/Classroom: 67% of faculty are male; 33%, female. All teach undergraduates. No introductory courses are taught by graduate students. The average class size in an introductory lecture is 21; in a laboratory, 12; and in a regular course, 18.

Admissions: 35% of the current freshmen were in the top fifth of their class; 64% were in the top two fifths. 2 freshmen graduated first in their class.

Requirements: The SAT I or ACT is required. In addition, King's requires 17 academic credits, including 4 each in English and science, 3 each in math and social studies, 2 in foreign language, and 1 in history. AP and CLEP credits are accepted. Important factors in the admissions decision are advanced placement or honor courses, extracurricular activities record, and leadership record.

Procedure: Freshmen are admitted fall and spring. Entrance exams should be taken so that scores are received by April 1. There is a deferred admissions plan. Applications should be filed by May 1 for fall entry, January 1 for spring entry, and May 1 for summer entry. The fall 2001 application fee was $30. Notification is sent on a rolling basis.

Transfer: 71 transfer students enrolled in 2001-2002. Applicants must present a minimum GPA of 2.5. Students must have earned at least 3 credit hours at another college. An interview is recommended. 60 credits of 120 to 127 must be completed at King's.

Visiting: There are regularly scheduled orientations for prospective students, consisting of admissions interviews, financial aid presentations, faculty one-on-one meetings, and campus tours. There are guides for informal visits and visitors may sit in on classes and stay overnight. To schedule a visit, contact the Admissions Office.

Financial Aid: In 2001-2002, 96% of all freshmen and 88% of continuing students received some form of financial aid. 78% of freshmen and 75% of continuing students received need-based aid. The average freshman award was $13,217. Of that total, scholarships or need-based grants averaged $10,022 ($16,720 maximum); loans averaged $3559 ($6625 maximum); and work contracts averaged $1200 ($2000 maximum). 72% of undergraduates work part time. Average annual earnings from campus work are $1200. The average financial indebtedness of the 2001 graduate was $14,900. King's is a member of CSS. The FAFSA and the college's own financial statement are required. The fall application deadline is February 15.

International Students: There are 16 international students enrolled. The school actively recruits these students. They must score 525 on the written TOEFL and also take the SAT I or the ACT.

Computers: The mainframe is an IBM RS/6000 570. Programming courses, statistical research, and course work in SPSS utilize the mainframe computer with access provided through 220 networked IBM computers and dial-in lines. Students have access to the Internet as well as to the Microsoft Office Suite. 3 networked Mac classrooms/labs containing 50 Macs and a computer science/graphics lab are available for academic use. All classrooms and residence hall rooms have networked connections and Internet access. All students are provided with e-mail accounts. All students may access the system. 3 24-hour networked residence hall labs exist; 5 other networked labs are each open 95 hours per week. Other departmental facilities are available.

Graduates: In 2001, 488 bachelor's degrees were awarded. The most popular majors were elementary education (13%), business administration (11%), and criminal justice (8%). In an average class, 62% graduate in 4 years, 69% in 5 years, and 70% in 6 years. 74 companies recruited on campus in 2000-2001. Of the 2000 graduating class, 15% were enrolled in graduate school within 6 months of graduation and 88% were employed.

Admissions Contact: Susan McGarry-Hannon, Director of Admissions. A video is available. E-mail: *admissions@kings.edu*
Web: *http://www.kings.edu*

KUTZTOWN UNIVERSITY OF PENNSYLVANIA
Kutztown, PA 19530 E-3
(610) 683-4060
(877) 628-1915; Fax: (610) 683-1375

Full-time: 2694 men, 3885 women	**Faculty:** 356; IIA
Part-time: 231 men, 483 women	**Ph.D.s:** 76%
Graduate: 264 men, 711 women	**Student/Faculty:** 18 to 1
Year: semesters, summer session	**Tuition:** $4481 ($10,971)
Application Deadline: open	**Room & Board:** $4426
Freshman Class: 6252 applied, 4302 accepted, 1660 enrolled	
SAT I Verbal/Math: 490/490	**COMPETITIVE**

Kutztown University of Pennsylvania, founded in 1866, is a public institution within the Pennsylvania State System of Higher Education. The university offers undergraduate programs in the arts and sciences, business, education, and visual and performing arts. There are 4 undergraduate schools and 1 graduate school. In addition to regional accreditation, KU has baccalaureate program accreditation with CSWE, NASAD, NASM, NCATE, and NLN. The library contains 497,752 volumes, 1,307,315 microform items, and 14,858 audiovisual forms/CDs, and subscribes to 4265 periodicals. Computerized library services include the card catalog, interlibrary loans, and database searching. Special learning facilities include a learning resource center, art gallery, planetarium, radio station, TV station, women's center, cartography lab, German Cultural Heritage Center, computer labs, and tutorial labs. The 326-acre campus is in a small town 90 miles north of Philadelphia, midway between Reading and Allentown. Including residence halls, there are 61 buildings.

Student Life: 90% of undergraduates are from Pennsylvania. Others are from 19 states, 34 foreign countries, and Canada. 91% are white. The average age of freshmen is 18; all undergraduates, 21.

Housing: 2942 students can be accommodated in college housing, which includes single-sex and coed dormitories and on-campus apartments. In addition, there are honors houses and special-interest houses. On-campus housing is guaranteed for the freshman year only, is available on a first-come, first-served basis, and on a lottery system for upperclassmen. 59% of students commute. Alcohol is not permitted. Upperclassmen may keep cars.

Activities: 4% of men belong to 6 national fraternities; 4% of women belong to 1 local and 4 national sororities. There are 140 groups on campus, including art, band, chess, choir, chorale, computers, dance, drama, ethnic, film, gay, honors, international, jazz band, literary magazine, marching band, musical theater, newspaper, nontraditional students, orchestra, political, professional, programming board, radio and TV, recreational sports, religious, social, social service, student government, and yearbook. Popular campus events include International Animated Film Festival, Family Day, and Bearfest.

Sports: There are 10 intercollegiate sports for men and 12 for women, and 22 intramural sports for men and 19 for women. Facilities include a 7500-seat stadium and outdoor track, a 55,000-square-foot field house, 200-meter indoor track, a swimming pool, 9 outdoor tennis courts, a 4000-seat arena, athletic fields, a street hockey rink, basketball courts, a rifle range, a fitness center, and a free-weight room.

Disabled Students: 90% of the campus is accessible. Wheelchair ramps, elevators, special parking, specially equipped rest rooms, special class scheduling, and lowered drinking fountains are aavailable. All programs are accessible to students with disabilities.

Services: Counseling and information services are available, as is tutoring in most subjects. There is a reader service for the blind, and remedial math, reading, and writing.

Campus Safety and Security: Measures include 24-hour foot and vehicle patrol, self-defense education, escort service, and informal discussions. There are pamphlets/posters/films, emergency telephones, lighted pathways/sidewalks, a bike patrol, crime prevention programs, automatic fire protection systems, door alarms, safety screens, and student monitors in the dorms.

Programs of Study: KU confers B.A., B.S., B.F.A., B.S.B.A, B.S.Ed., and B.S.N. degrees. Master's degrees are also awarded. Bachelor's degrees are awarded in BIOLOGICAL SCIENCE (biology/biological science and marine science), BUSINESS (accounting, banking and finance, business administration and management, business economics, international business management, and marketing/retailing/merchandising), COMMUNICATIONS AND THE ARTS (crafts, dramatic arts, English, fine arts, French, graphic design, music, Spanish, speech/debate/rhetoric, telecommunications, and visual and performing arts), COMPUTER AND PHYSICAL SCIENCE (chemistry, computer science, geology, mathematics, and physics), EDUCATION (art, early childhood, elementary, library science, secondary, and special), ENGINEERING AND ENVIRONMENTAL DESIGN (environmental science), HEALTH PROFESSIONS (medical laboratory technology, nursing, and speech pathology/audiology), SOCIAL SCIENCE (anthropology, criminal justice, geography, history, liberal arts/general studies, philosophy, political science/government, psychology, public administration, social work, and sociology). Physical science and math are the strongest academically. Business, psychology, and elementary education are the largest.

Required: General education requirements vary by program, but all students must take phys ed, speech, English composition, or introduction to dance. Distribution requirements also include courses in humanities, social sciences, natural sciences, and math. To graduate, students must complete at least 120 semester hours, including 33 to 80 in a major field, with a minimum GPA of 2.0. Students in the College of Liberal Arts and Sciences must take a comprehensive exam.

Special: Students may study abroad in 11 countries. There is a 3-2 engineering degree program with Pennsylvania State University and cross-registration with area colleges. KU also offers internships, student-designed majors, dual majors, and a general studies degree. Nondegree study is possible. There are 15 national honor societies, a freshman honors program, and 30 departmental honors programs.

Faculty/Classroom: 60% of faculty are male; 40%, female. 99% teach undergraduates. No introductory courses are taught by graduate students. The average class size in an introductory lecture is 33; in a laboratory, 19; and in a regular course, 19.

Admissions: 69% of the 2001-2002 applicants were accepted. The SAT I scores for the 2001-2002 freshman class were: Verbal--55% below 500, 37% between 500 and 599, 7% between 600 and 700, and 1% above 700; Math--56% below 500, 36% between 500 and 599, and 8% between 600 and 700. 15% of the current freshmen were in the top fifth of their class; 38% were in the top two fifths.

Requirements: The SAT I or ACT is required. In addition, applicants must be graduates of accredited secondary schools or have earned a GED. Recommended Carnegie units include 4 each of English and social studies, 3 each of science and math, and 2 of foreign language. SAT II: Subject tests in biology/chemistry are required for medical technology. Portfolios or auditions are required for art or music majors. KU requires applicants to be in the upper 50% of their class. A GPA of 2.0 is required. AP and CLEP credits are accepted. Important factors in the admissions decision are leadership record, advanced placement or honor courses, and evidence of special talent. Applications are accepted on-line at *www.kutztown.edu/admissions.*

Procedure: Freshmen are admitted fall and spring. Entrance exams should be taken no later than fall of the senior year. There are early admissions and deferred admissions plans. Application deadlines are open. The fall 2001 application fee was $30. Notification is sent on a rolling basis.

Transfer: 495 transfer students enrolled in 2001-2002. Applicants must present a GPA of 2.0 (2.8 for education) and official transcripts from all colleges and secondary schools previously attended. Students transferring fewer than 30 credit hours must also submit the SAT I or ACT scores. 33 credits of 120 must be completed at KU.

Visiting: There are regularly scheduled orientations for prospective students, including daily visits and group tours. There is a comprehensive summer orientation program for enrolling students. There are guides for informal visits and visitors may sit in on classes. To schedule a visit, contact the Admissions Office.

Financial Aid: In 2001-2002, 60% of all freshmen and 57% of continuing students received some form of financial aid. 54% of freshmen and 51% of continuing students received need-based aid. The average freshman award was $4624. Of that total, scholarships or need-based grants averaged $2921 ($7650 maximum); loans averaged $2412 ($6625 maximum); and work contracts averaged $953 ($3000 maximum). 55% of undergraduates work part time. Average annual earnings from campus work are $953. The average financial indebtedness of the 2001 graduate was $13,922. The FAFSA is required. The fall application deadline is February 15.

International Students: There are 85 international students enrolled. They must score 500 on the written TOEFL or 173 on the electronic version.

Computers: The mainframe is a Unisys Clearpath. All classrooms, residence halls, and offices have full Internet connectivity. More than 15 computer labs with more than 650 PCs are available for student use; several labs are open 24 hours. Many residence hall students bring their own PCs to campus. All students may access the system. There are no time limits and no fees.

Graduates: In 2001, 1142 bachelor's degrees were awarded. The most popular majors were elementary education (13%), special education (7%), and psychology (7%). 50 companies recruited on campus in 2000-2001. Of the 2000 graduating class, 6% were enrolled in graduate school within 6 months of graduation and 96% were employed.

Admissions Contact: Valerie Reidout, Acting Director of Admissions.
E-mail: *admission@kutztown.edu*
Web: *http://www.kutztown.edu/admissions*

LA ROCHE COLLEGE B-3
Pittsburgh, PA 15237 (412) 536-1049
(800) 838-4LRC; Fax: (412) 536-2709

Full-time: 510 men, 730 women	**Faculty:** 55; IIA, -$
Part-time: 130 men, 291 women	**Ph.D.s:** 91%
Graduate: 87 men, 160 women	**Student/Faculty:** 23 to 1
Year: semesters, summer session	**Tuition:** $12,380
Application Deadline: open	**Room & Board:** $6474
Freshman Class: 559 applied, 444 accepted, 215 enrolled	
SAT I or ACT: required	**LESS COMPETITIVE**

La Roche College, founded in 1963, is a private Catholic institution offering undergraduate programs in arts and sciences, business, graphic art and design, health science, upper-level nursing, preprofessional training, and religious studies. There are 3 graduate schools. In addition to regional accreditation, La Roche has baccalaureate program accreditation with ACBSP, FIDER, NASAD, and NLN. The library contains 67,705 volumes, 10,000 microform items, and 404 audiovisual forms/CDs, and subscribes to 2390 periodicals. Computerized library services include interlibrary loans and database searching. Special learning facilities include a learning resource center, art gallery, and interior and graphic design studios. The 100-acre campus is in a suburban area 10 miles north of Pittsburgh. Including residence halls, there are 12 buildings.

Student Life: 94% of undergraduates are from Pennsylvania. Others are from 16 states, 28 foreign countries, and Canada. 77% are white; 17%, foreign nationals. 33% are Catholic; 11%, Protestant. The average age of freshmen is 18; all undergraduates, 25. 17% do not continue beyond their first year; 45% remain to graduate.

Housing: 630 students can be accommodated in college housing, which includes coed dormitories and off-campus apartments. On-campus housing is guaranteed for all 4 years. 62% of students commute. All students may keep cars.

Activities: There are no fraternities or sororities. There are 25 groups on campus, including art, cheerleading, chorus, computers, dance, ethnic, honors, international, literary magazine, photography, political, professional, radio and TV, religious, social, social service, and student government. Popular campus events include Thanksgiving Interfaith Forum, Parents Day, and Multicultural Food Festival.

Sports: There are 5 intercollegiate sports for men and 6 for women, and 10 intramural sports for men and 10 for women. Facilities include soccer, softball, and baseball fields; a gym; tennis courts; hiking trails; a fitness/sports center that houses a gym, racquetball courts, an indoor track, an aerobics room, and a weight room; and a nearby county park with tennis courts and a swimming pool.

Disabled Students: 80% of the campus is accessible. Wheelchair ramps, elevators, special parking, specially equipped rest rooms, special class scheduling, lowered drinking fountains, and lowered telephones are available.

Services: Counseling and information services are available, as is tutoring in every subject. There is remedial math and writing.

Campus Safety and Security: Measures include 24-hour foot and vehicle patrol, escort service, shuttle buses, and informal discussions. There are pamphlets/posters/films, emergency telephones, lighted pathways/sidewalks, and an intercom security system. Residence halls are locked 24 hours a day.

Programs of Study: La Roche confers B.A., B.S., and B.S.N. degrees. Associate and master's degrees are also awarded. Bachelor's degrees are awarded in BIOLOGICAL SCIENCE (biology/biological science), BUSINESS (accounting, banking and finance, business administration and management, and international business management), COMMUNICATIONS AND THE ARTS (communications, creative writing, dance, English, and graphic design), COMPUTER AND PHYSICAL SCIENCE (applied mathematics, chemistry, computer science, and information sciences and systems), EDUCATION (early childhood, elementary, English, foreign languages, and science), ENGINEERING AND ENVIRONMENTAL DESIGN (interior design), HEALTH PROFESSIONS (nursing, radiograph medical technology, and respiratory therapy), SOCIAL SCIENCE (criminal justice, history, human services, international studies, liberal arts/general studies, psychology, religion, religious education, and sociology). Graphic design, interior design, and professional writing are the strongest academically. Administration and management, design areas, and elementary education are the largest.

Required: 12 credits in basic skills areas, including math and computer applications, and 12 credits in liberal arts areas, including history, science, religion or philosophy, aesthetics, literature, and social and cultural systems, are required. Also, a 9-credit sequence of 3 interdisciplinary courses that emphasize the concepts of community, the individual, and global perspectives is required. A minimum of 120 credit hours and a GPA of 2.0 are requirements for graduation, as is a senior seminar in most majors.

Special: There is cross-registration with members of the Pittsburgh Council of Higher Education. Internships, for which students may receive up to 6 credits, are available for juniors and seniors with numerous employers in the Pittsburgh area. La Roche also offers study abroad in 13 countries, a Washington semester, dual majors, credit for life experience, directed research, honors programs, independent study, and pass/fail options. Accelerated degrees may be earned in management and psychology. A 3-2 engineering degree with the University of Pittsburgh is possible.

Faculty/Classroom: 51% of faculty are male; 49%, female. 94% teach undergraduates and 40% do research. No introductory courses are taught by graduate students. The average class size in an introductory lecture is 20; in a laboratory, 10; and in a regular course, 16.

Admissions: 79% of the 2001-2002 applicants were accepted.

Requirements: The SAT I or ACT is required. In addition, applicants must be graduates of accredited secondary schools or have earned a GED. An interview is recommended for all applicants. At least two letters of recommendation are required. A GPA of 2.0 is required. AP and CLEP credits are accepted. Important factors in the admissions decision are advanced placement or honor courses, personality/intangible qualities, and recommendations by school officials. Applications are accepted on-line via the college's web site..

Procedure: Freshmen are admitted to all sessions. Entrance exams should be taken by the fall of the senior year. There is an early admissions plan. Application deadlines are open. The fall 2001 application fee was $35. Notification is sent on a rolling basis.

Transfer: 134 transfer students enrolled in a recent year. Design students may be required to submit a portfolio and must have a 2.0 GPA. 30 credits of 120 must be completed at La Roche.

Visiting: There are regularly scheduled orientations for prospective students, including an overnight stay, information sessions and interactive sessions, class attendance, and meetings with faculty. There are also 1-day visits on Saturday. There are guides for informal visits and visitors may sit in on classes and stay overnight. To schedule a visit, contact the Admissions Office.

Financial Aid: In 2001-2002, 90% of all students received some form of financial aid. 81% of freshmen and 85% of continuing students received need-based aid. The average freshman award was $12,000. Of that total, scholarships or need-based grants averaged $4400 ($7000 maximum); loans averaged $3000 ($4625 maximum); work contracts averaged $1600 (maximum); and state grants and other resources averaged $3000 ($3300 maximum). 24% of undergraduates work part time. Average annual earnings from campus work are $1200. The average financial indebtedness of the 2001 graduate was $17,000. The FAFSA and the college's own financial statement are required. The fall application deadline is May 1.

International Students: There are 290 international students enrolled. The school actively recruits these students. They must score 220 on the electronic TOEFL, or if their native language is English, they must take the SAT I or ACT.

Computers: The mainframe is an HP L2000. Students have access to 92 PCs and Macs in 6 computer labs, which are part of a local area network and have printing, Internet, and e-mail capabilities in addition to general and specific software. The Mac lab offers software for illustration, PostScript, animation, dimensional design, and desktop publishing. All students may access the system. There are no limits and no fees.

Graduates: In 2001, 286 bachelor's degrees were awarded. The most popular majors were nursing (13%), graphic design (13%), and psychology (9%). In an average class, 7% graduate in 3 years, 74% in 4 years, 97% in 5 years, and 100% in 6 years.

Admissions Contact: Dayna McNally, Director of Admissions & Enrollment Management. A video is available.
E-mail: *admns@laroche.edu* Web: *www.laroche.edu*

LA SALLE UNIVERSITY

Philadelphia, PA 19141-1199

F-3
(215) 951-1500
(800) 328-1910; Fax: (215) 951-1656

Full-time: 1483 men, 1706 women	**Faculty:** 176; IIA, av$
Part-time: 183 men, 533 women	**Ph.D.s:** 88%
Graduate: 619 men, 906 women	**Student/Faculty:** 18 to 1
Year: terms, summer session	**Tuition:** $19,890
Application Deadline: April 1	**Room & Board:** $8000
Freshman Class: 3088 applied, 3075 accepted, 849 enrolled	
SAT I Verbal/Math: 550/550	**COMPETITIVE**

La Salle University, founded in 1863, is a private institution conducted under the auspices of the Christian Brothers of the Roman Catholic Church. The university offers undergraduate and graduate programs in the arts and sciences, business, education, fine arts, religious studies, and nursing. There are 3 undergraduate and 3 graduate schools. In addition to regional accreditation, La Salle has baccalaureate program accreditation with AACSB, CSWE, and NLN. The library contains 380,000 volumes, 700,000 microform items, and 5000 audiovisual forms/CDs, and subscribes to 1650 periodicals. Computerized library services include the card catalog, interlibrary loans, and database searching. Special learning facilities include a learning resource center, art gallery, radio station, TV station, and a Japanese tea ceremony house. The 100-acre campus is in an urban area 8 miles northwest of the center of Philadelphia. Including residence halls, there are 56 buildings.

Student Life: 68% of undergraduates are from Pennsylvania. Others are from 36 states, 23 foreign countries, and Canada. 47% are from public schools. 82% are white. 83% are Catholic; 11% Protestant. The average age of freshmen is 18; all undergraduates, 20. 11% do not continue beyond their first year; 73% remain to graduate.

Housing: 2059 students can be accommodated in college housing, which includes single-sex and coed dormitories, on-campus apartments, and off-campus apartments. In addition, there are honors houses and special-interest houses, for which syudent groups may submit proposals for use. Townhouses and apartments are available to juniors and seniors. On-campus housing is guaranteed for all 4 years. 65% of students live on campus; of those, 70% remain on campus on weekends. All students may keep cars.

Activities: 14% of men belong to 1 local and 6 national fraternities; 14% of women belong to 1 local and 4 national sororities. There are 94 groups on campus, including band, cheerleading, choir, computers, dance, drama, drill team, ethnic, film, honors, international, jazz band, literary magazine, newspaper, orchestra, pep band, political, professional, radio and TV, religious, social, social service, student government, and yearbook. Popular campus events include Oktoberfest, Charter Week, and Carnifall.

Sports: There are 11 intercollegiate sports for men and 12 for women, and 14 intramural sports for men and 14 for women. Facilities include a 7000-seat stadium, a 4000-seat gym, a 500-seat auditorium, 4 playing fields, 6 tennis courts, a fully equipped athletic and exercise facility, wrestling rooms, a sauna, racquetball and squash courts, outdoor tracks, basketball and volleyball courts, and an indoor swimming pool.

Disabled Students: 95% of the campus is accessible. Wheelchair ramps, elevators, special parking, specially equipped rest rooms, special class scheduling, and lowered drinking fountains are available.

Services: Counseling and information services are available, as is tutoring in some subjects, including English, math, and accounting. A writing center is also available.

Campus Safety and Security: Measures include 24-hour foot and vehicle patrol, escort service, shuttle buses, and emergency telephones. There are lighted pathways/sidewalks and magnetic card access to residence facilities.

Programs of Study: La Salle confers B.A., B.S., B.S.N., and B.S.W. degrees. Associate, master's, and doctoral degrees are also awarded. Bachelor's degrees are awarded in BIOLOGICAL SCIENCE (biochemistry, biology/biological science, and nutrition), BUSINESS (accounting, banking and finance, business administration and management, international economics, management information systems, marketing/retailing/merchandising, and organizational behavior), COMMUNICATIONS AND THE ARTS (classical languages, communications, English, fine arts, French, German, Italian, multimedia, music, Russian, and Spanish), COMPUTER AND PHYSICAL SCIENCE (chemistry, computer science, geology, information sciences and systems, and mathematics), EDUCATION (elementary, foreign languages, science, secondary, social studies, and special), ENGINEERING AND ENVIRONMENTAL DESIGN (computer graphics and environmental science), HEALTH PROFESSIONS (nursing, preallied health, predentistry, premedicine, and speech pathology/audiology), SOCIAL SCIENCE (criminal justice, economics, history, philosophy, political science/government, prelaw, psychology, public administration, religion, social work, and sociology). English, accounting, and education are the strongest academically. Accounting, education, and communication are the largest.

Required: Students take courses in writing, computer science, religion, philosophy, history, literature, math, the natural sciences, and the social sciences. The core curriculum is distinguished by 2 requirements: the "double," a thematically linked pair of courses taught by 2 facility partners from different disciplines, and the "metro," a year-long program of co-curricular activities conducted by a faculty member and designed to help students take advantage of the resources of the City of Philadelphia.

Special: Cross-registration is offered in conjunction with Chestnut Hill College, and there is a 2-2 program in allied health with Thomas Jefferson University. La Salle also offers study abroad, co-op programs in business and computer science, work-study programs, internships in most majors, dual majors, and pass/fail options. An E-Commerce Institute has been created to educate all students about this business tool. There are 10 national honor societies, and a freshman honors program.

Faculty/Classroom: 54% of faculty are male; 46%, female. 45% do research. No introductory courses are taught by graduate students. The average class size in an introductory lecture is 20; in a laboratory, 14; and in a regular course, 19.

Admissions: All of the 2001-2002 applicants were accepted. The SAT I scores for the 2001-2002 freshman class were: Verbal--27% below 500, 46% between 500 and 599, 24% between 600 and 700, and 3% above 700; Math--30% below 500, 46% between 500 and 599, 20% between 600 and 700, and 4% above 700. 46% of the current freshmen were in the top fifth of their class; 75% were in the top two fifths. 13 freshmen graduated first in their class.

Requirements: The SAT I or ACT is required. In addition, SAT II: Subject tests in writing and math are recommended. Applicants must be graduates of accredited secondary schools or have earned a GED. La Salle requires 16 academic units, based on 4 years of English, 3 of math, 2 of foreign language, and 1 of history, with the remaining 5 units in academic electives; science and math majors must have an additional one-half unit of math. An essay is required, and an interview is recommended. La Salle requires applicants to be in the upper 50% of their class. AP and CLEP credits are accepted. Important factors in the admissions decision are advanced placement or honor courses, leadership record, and recommendations by school officials. Applications are accepted via *lasalle.edu/admissions*.

Procedure: Freshmen are admitted fall and spring. Entrance exams should be taken before January of the senior year. There are early admissions and deferred admissions plans. Applications should be filed by April 1 for fall entry and December 15 for spring entry, along with a $35 fee. Notification is sent on a rolling basis.

Transfer: 109 transfer students enrolled in 2001-2002. Transfer applicants should have a minimum GPA of 2.25, with 2.5 preferred. 50 credits of 120 must be completed at La Salle.

Visiting: There are regularly scheduled orientations for prospective students, including campus tours 11 Saturdays throughout the fall, 3 Saturdays during the winter, and 4 Saturdays during the spring. There are guides for informal visits and visitors may sit in on classes and stay overnight. To schedule a visit, contact the Admissions Office.

Financial Aid: In 2001-2002, 95% of all freshmen and 85% of continuing students received some form of financial aid. 76% of freshmen and 62% of continuing students received need-based aid. The average freshman award was $15,770. Of that total, scholarships or need-based grants averaged $9000 ($19,750 maximum); loans averaged $4500 ($6500 maximum); and work contracts averaged $1670 ($1800 maximum). The FAFSA is required. The fall application deadline is February 15.

International Students: There were 31 international students enrolled in a recent year. The school actively recruits these students. They must score 500 on the written TOEFL.

Computers: The mainframe is a SUN 450. The university provides 325 PCs. A LAN is available for student use. Dorms are wired for network and Internet access. All students may access the system 8 A.M. to 11 P.M. weekdays, 9 A.M. to 7 P.M. Saturday and noon to 11 P.M. Sunday. There are no time limits and no fees.

Graduates: In 2001, 847 bachelor's degrees were awarded. The most popular majors were nursing (12%), communications (10%), and accounting (8%). In an average class, 61% graduate in 4 years, 67% in 5 years, and 73% in 6 years. 150 companies recruited on campus in 2000-2001. Of a recent graduating class, 18% were enrolled in graduate school within 6 months of graduation and 93% were employed.

Admissions Contact: Robert Voss, Dean of Admissions and Financial Aid. E-mail: *admiss@lasalle.edu* Web: *www.lasalle.edu*

LAFAYETTE COLLEGE

Easton, PA 18042	**(610) 330-5100; Fax: (610) 330-5355**
Full-time: 1106 men, 1117 women	**Faculty:** 184; IIB, ++$
Part-time: 75 men, 32 women	**Ph.D.s:** 100%
Graduate: none	**Student/Faculty:** 12 to 1
Year: semesters, summer session	**Tuition:** $24,921
Application Deadline: January 1	**Room & Board:** $7734
Freshman Class: 5195 applied, 2028 accepted, 579 enrolled	
SAT I Verbal/Math: 610/650	**ACT:** 28 **MOST COMPETITIVE**

F-3

Lafayette College, founded in 1826 and affiliated with the Presbyterian Church (U.S.A.) is a private institution emphasizing the liberal arts and engineering. In addition to regional accreditation, Lafayette has baccalaureate program accreditation with ABET and ACS. The 2 libraries contain 510,000 volumes and 120,000 microform items, and subscribe to 2600 periodicals. Computerized library services include the card catalog, interlibrary loans, and database searching. Special learning facilities include a learning resource center, art gallery, radio station, geological museum, foreign languages lab, and calculus lab. The 342-acre campus (including an athletic campus), is in a suburban area 70 miles west of New York City. Including residence halls, there are 65 buildings.

Student Life: 72% of undergraduates are from out of state, mostly the Middle Atlantic. Others are from 39 states, 33 foreign countries, and Canada. 70% are from public schools. 84% are white. 37% are Catholic; 30%, Protestant; 15% claim no religious affiliation; 11%, Jewish. The average age of freshmen is 18; all undergraduates, 20. 5% do not continue beyond their first year; 92% remain to graduate.

Housing: 2100 students can be accommodated in college housing, which includes single-sex and coed dormitories, on-campus apartments, off-campus apartments, fraternity houses, and sorority houses. In addition, there are honors houses, and special-interest houses, diversity-oriented houses, arts houses, a black cultural center, and language and special-interest floors. On-campus housing is guaranteed for all 4 years. 98% of students live on campus; of those, 95% remain on campus on weekends. Upperclassmen may keep cars.

Activities: 26% of men belong to 8 national fraternities; 45% of women belong to 6 national sororities. There are 250 groups on campus, including AIDS awareness, art, band, cheerleading, chess, choir, chorale, chorus, computers, dance, debate, drama, ethnic, film, forensics, gay, honors, international, jazz band, literary magazine, musical theater, newspaper, orchestra, pep band, photography, political, professional, radio and TV, religious, social, social service, student government, and yearbook. Popular campus events include All College Day, Earth Day, and International Extravaganza.

Sports: There are 11 intercollegiate sports for men and 11 for women, and 22 intramural sports for men and 22 for women. Facilities include a 14,000-seat stadium; a $35 million sports center containing a 3500-seat gym, a field house, a varsity house, a natatorium, a fitness center, 2 exercise rooms, a weight training room, an outdoor track, an indoor track, a climbing wall, 6 racquet courts, and 3 multipurpose courts; and a 230-acre athletic complex for lacrosse, field hockey, soccer, and baseball.

Disabled Students: 95% of the campus is accessible. Wheelchair ramps, elevators, special parking, specially equipped rest rooms, special class scheduling, lowered drinking fountains, and lowered telephones are available.

Services: Counseling and information services are available, as is tutoring in most subjects, including most 100-level and many 200-level classes. Assistance is available for students in the use of textbooks for the visually impaired.

Campus Safety and Security: Measures include 24-hour foot and vehicle patrol, self-defense education, escort service, and shuttle buses. There are informal discussions, pamphlets/posters/films, emergency telephones, lighted pathways/sidewalks, and advisers in all residence halls. Residence halls are locked from 8 P.M. to 7 A.M. and are accessible by room keys and outside telephones.

Programs of Study: Lafayette confers A.B., B.S., and B.S.Eng. degrees. Bachelor's degrees are awarded in BIOLOGICAL SCIENCE (biochemistry, biology/biological science, and neurosciences), BUSINESS (business economics and international economics), COMMUNICATIONS AND THE ARTS (art, English, French, German, music, and Spanish), COMPUTER AND PHYSICAL SCIENCE (chemistry, computer science, geology, mathematics, and physics), ENGINEERING AND ENVIRONMENTAL DESIGN (chemical engineering, civil engineering, electrical/electronics engineering, engineering, and mechanical engineering), SOCIAL SCIENCE (African studies, American studies, anthropology, economics, history, interdisciplinary studies, international relations, philosophy, political science/government, prelaw, psychology, religion, Russian and Slavic studies, and sociology). Engineering, psychology, and English are the strongest academically. Economics, business, and engineering are the largest.

Required: To graduate, students must maintain a GPA of 2.0 over a minimum of 32 to 38 courses. The common course of study, designed to build a background in the liberal arts and sciences in the first 2 years, includes interdisciplinary seminars, 3 courses in humanities/social science, 2 in natural science, and 1 each in college writing and math/computer science/philosophy. Students must fulfill a foreign culture requirement, and A.B. and B.S. majors must take 2 upper-level writing courses.

Special: Cross-registration through the Lehigh Valley Association of Independent Colleges, internships in all academic departments, study abroad in 3 countries as well as through other individually arranged plans, a Washington semester at American University, and work-study programs with area employers are possible. An accelerated degree plan in all majors, dual and student-designed majors, 5-year dual-degree programs, and pass/fail options in any nonmajor subject also are available. There are 12 national honor societies, including Phi Beta Kappa, and 24 departmental honors programs.

Faculty/Classroom: 74% of faculty are male; 26%, female. All both teach and do research. The average class size in a laboratory is 12 and in a regular course, 17.

Admissions: 39% of the 2001-2002 applicants were accepted. The SAT I scores for the 2001-2002 freshman class were: Verbal--3% below 500, 28% between 500 and 599, 58% between 600 and 700, and 11% above 700; Math--2% below 500, 23% between 500 and 599, 54% between 600 and 700, and 21% above 700. The ACT scores were 1% below 21, 3% between 21 and 23, 14% between 24 and 26, 66% between 27 and 28, and 16% above 28. 90% of the current freshmen were in the top fifth of their class; 98% were in the top two fifths.

Requirements: The SAT I or ACT is required. In addition, applicants need 4 years of English, 3 of math (4 for science or engineering majors), 2 each of a foreign language and lab science (with physics and chemistry for science or engineering students), and at least an additional 5 units in academic subjects. An essay is required and an interview recommended. Evaluations from the secondary school counselor and a teacher are required. The GED is accepted. AP credits are accepted. Important factors in the admissions decision are advanced placement or honor courses, evidence of special talent, and personality/intangible qualities.

Procedure: Freshmen are admitted in the fall. Entrance exams should be taken by January of the senior year. There are early decision and deferred admissions plans. Early decision applications should be filed by January 1; regular applications, by January 1 for fall entry. Notification of early decision is sent within 30 days of receipt of the application; regular decision, mid-March. 166 early decision candidates were accepted for the 2001-2002 class. 13% of all applicants are on a waiting list; 79 were accepted in 2001.

Transfer: 8 transfer students enrolled in 2001-2002. Acceptance usually depends on college-level performance and achievements. An interview is required if the student lives within 200 miles of the college. No minimum GPA is required, and neither the SAT I nor the ACT is needed. The number of credit hours required varies with the program, but usually enough for freshman status with advanced standing is needed. 16 credits of 32 must be completed at Lafayette.

Visiting: There are regularly scheduled orientations for prospective students, including student/faculty panel discussions, tours, and departmental open houses. There are guides for informal visits and visitors may sit in on classes and stay overnight. To schedule a visit, contact the Admissions Office by phone or at *admissions@lafayette.edu*.

Financial Aid: In 2001-2002, 60% of all freshmen and 66% of continuing students received some form of financial aid. 50% of freshmen and 48% of continuing students received need-based aid. The average freshman award was $18,675. Of that total, scholarships or need-based grants averaged $17,982 ($34,050 maximum); loans averaged $4657 ($6825 maximum); work contracts averaged $1326 ($2000 maximum); and external grants averaged $2740 ($9000 maximum). 54% of undergraduates work part time. Average annual earnings from campus work are $900. The average financial indebtedness of the 2001 graduate was $15,393. The CSS/Profile or FAFSA, the college's own financial statement, and the Business/Farm supplement and Divorce/Separation parent statement (if applicable) are required. The fall application deadline is February 15.

International Students: There are 101 international students enrolled. The school actively recruits these students. They must score 550 on the written TOEFL and also take the SAT I.

Computers: The mainframes are a DEC VAX 6310, an ARIX, and an IBM 9375. An Ethernet network connects the entire campus to the Internet. More than 600 computers are available for student use. All students may access the system 24 hours per day. There are no time limits and no fees.

Graduates: In 2001, 518 bachelor's degrees were awarded. The most popular majors were engineering (16%), economics and business (14%), and government and law (10%). In an average class, 1% graduate in 3 years, 89% in 4 years, and 93% in 5 years. 250 companies recruited on campus in 2000-2001. Of the 2000 graduating class, 24% were enrolled in graduate school within 6 months of graduation and 76% were employed.

Admissions Contact: Carol Rowlands, Director of Admissions. A video is available. E-mail: *rowlandc@lafayette.edu*
Web: *www.lafayette.edu*

LEBANON VALLEY COLLEGE OF PENNSYLVANIA — E-3

Annville, PA 17003-0501 — (717) 867-6181
(800) 445-6181; Fax: (717) 867-6026

Full-time: 670 men, 847 women	**Faculty:** 80; IIB, av$
Part-time: 102 men, 301 women	**Ph.D.s:** 82%
Graduate: 105 men, 92 women	**Student/Faculty:** 19 to 1
Year: semesters, summer session	**Tuition:** $19,810
Application Deadline: open	**Room & Board:** $5890
Freshman Class: 1865 applied, 1468 accepted, 417 enrolled	
SAT I Verbal/Math: 545/554	**ACT:** 24 **VERY COMPETITIVE**

Lebanon Valley College of Pennsylvania, founded in 1866, is a private institution affiliated with the United Methodist Church. The college offers undergraduate programs in the arts and sciences. In addition to regional accreditation, LVC has baccalaureate program accreditation with NASM. The library contains 148,225 volumes, 18,380 microform items, and 3656 audiovisual forms/CDs, and subscribes to 796 periodicals. Computerized library services include the card catalog, interlibrary loans, and database searching. Special learning facilities include a learning resource center, art gallery, and radio station. The 200-acre campus is in a small town 7 miles east of Hershey. Including residence halls, there are 33 buildings.

Student Life: 79% of undergraduates are from Pennsylvania. Others are from 24 states, 26 foreign countries, and Canada. 94% are from public schools. 92% are white. 60% are Protestant; 21% Catholic; 19% claim no religious affiliation. The average age of freshmen is 18; all undergraduates, 20. 14% do not continue beyond their first year; 69% remain to graduate.

Housing: 1024 students can be accommodated in college housing, which includes single-sex and coed dormitories, on-campus apartments, fraternity houses, and sorority houses. In addition, there are special-interest houses, suite-style living, substance-free, and clear air halls. On-campus housing is guaranteed for all 4 years. 76% of students live on campus; of those, 60% remain on campus on weekends. All students may keep cars.

Activities: 18% of men and about 2% of women belong to 2 local and 2 national fraternities; 10% of women belong to 1 local and 3 national sororities. There are 76 groups on campus, including band, cheerleading, choir, chorus, computers, concert band, drama, drill team, ethnic, gay, honors, international, jazz band, literary magazine, marching band, music ensembles, musical theater, newspaper, orchestra, photography, political, professional, radio and TV, religious, social, social service, student government, symphony, and yearbook. Popular campus events include Parents Weekend, Christmas at the Valley, and Spring Arts Festival.

Sports: There are 11 intercollegiate sports for men and 9 for women, and 13 intramural sports for men and 12 for women. Facilities include a 3000-seat stadium, a sports center, more than 60 acres of athletic fields, indoor and outdoor tracks, a gym, playing courts for basketball, handball, squash, and tennis, a 500-seat baseball grandstand, and an enclosed football field.

Disabled Students: 65% of the campus is accessible. Wheelchair ramps, elevators, special parking, specially equipped rest rooms, special class scheduling, lowered drinking fountains, and lowered telephones are available.

Services: Counseling and information services are available, as is tutoring in every subject.

Campus Safety and Security: Measures include 24-hour foot and vehicle patrol, self-defense education, escort service, and informal discussions. There are pamphlets/posters/films, emergency telephones, and lighted pathways/sidewalks.
Programs of Study: LVC confers B.A., B.S., B.M., B.S.Ch., B.S.ed., and B.S.Med.Tech. degrees. Associate and master's degrees are also awarded. Bachelor's degrees are awarded in BIOLOGICAL SCIENCE (biochemistry, and biology/biological science), BUSINESS (accounting, hotel/motel and restaurant management, and international business management), COMMUNICATIONS AND THE ARTS (audio technology, English, French, German, music, music performance, and Spanish), COMPUTER AND PHYSICAL SCIENCE (actuarial science, chemistry, computer science, mathematics, and physics), EDUCATION (elementary, music, and secondary), ENGINEERING AND ENVIRONMENTAL DESIGN (engineering), HEALTH PROFESSIONS (medical laboratory technology, occupational therapy, physical therapy, predentistry, premedicine, prepharmacy, and preveterinary science), SOCIAL SCIENCE (American studies, economics, history, philosophy, political science/government, prelaw, psychobiology, psychology, religion, and sociology). Actuarial science, natural sciences, and education are the strongest academically. Education, business, and natural sciences are the largest.
Required: The general education program consists of course work in four areas: communications, liberal studies, foreign studies, and disciplinary perspectives. Students are required to complete 3 writing-intensive courses and be proficient in computer applications and modes of information access and retrieval. To graduate, students must complete at least 120 credit hours, 2 units of phys ed, and the requirements for the major with a minimum GPA of 2.0.
Special: Study abroad is available in 6 countries through the college's affiliation with the International Student Exchange Program and the LVC College in Cologne Program. LVC is also affiliated with several colleges and universities in England, France, Spain, the Netherlands, and New Zealand. There are 3-2 degree programs in engineering with the University of Pennsylvania and Case Western Reserve and Widener universities, in forestry with Duke University, and in medical technology with Hahnemann University. There is also a 2-2 degree program in allied health sciences with Thomas Jefferson University. LVC offers internships in a number of areas. There are 6 national honor societies, and 11 departmental honors programs.
Faculty/Classroom: 68% of faculty are male; 32%, female. All teach undergraduates. No introductory courses are taught by graduate students. The average class size in an introductory lecture is 23; in a laboratory, 13; and in a regular course, 14.
Admissions: 79% of the 2001-2002 applicants were accepted. The SAT I scores for the 2001-2002 freshman class were: Verbal--26% below 500, 49% between 500 and 599, 23% between 600 and 700, and 2% above 700; Math--27% below 500, 43% between 500 and 599, 26% between 600 and 700, and 2% above 700. The ACT scores were 29% below 21, 14% between 21 and 23, 29% between 24 and 26, 18% between 27 and 28, and 11% above 28. 54% of the current freshmen were in the top fifth of their class; 80% were in the top two fifths. 2 freshmen graduated first in their class.
Requirements: The SAT I or ACT is required. In addition, applicants must be graduates of accredited secondary schools or have earned a GED. LVC requires 16 academic units or 16 Carnegie units, including 4 in English, 2 each in math and foreign language, and 1 each in science and social studies. An interview is recommended. Students applying as music majors must also audition. AP and CLEP credits are accepted. Important factors in the admissions decision are advanced placement or honor courses, leadership record, and personality/intangible qualities. Applications are accepted on-line at the school's web site.
Procedure: Freshmen are admitted fall and spring. Entrance exams should be taken in the spring of the junior year. Application deadlines are open; priority deadline is March 15. The application fee is $25. Notification is sent on a rolling basis beginning October 15.
Transfer: 45 transfer students enrolled in 2001-2002. Requirements for transfer applicants include a minimum GPA of 2.0, SAT I scores, and an interview. An associate degree is recommended. 30 credits of 120 must be completed at LVC.
Visiting: There are regularly scheduled orientations for prospective students, including tours, interviews, and meetings with professors. There are guides for informal visits and visitors may sit in on classes. To schedule a visit, contact Mark Brezitski, Assistant Director, Admissions.
Financial Aid: In 2001-2002, 98% of all freshmen and 96% of continuing students received some form of financial aid. 78% of all students received need-based aid. The average freshman award was $14,806. Of that total, scholarships or need-based grants averaged $7918 ($9095 maximum); loans averaged $3565 ($4125 maximum); work contracts averaged $1029 ($1300 maximum); and outside scholarships, parent loans, and tuition waivers averaged $1770 ($7745 maximum). 54% of undergraduates work part time. Average annual earnings from campus work are $625. The average financial indebtedness of the 2001 graduate was $17,483. LVC is a member of CSS. The FAFSA and the college's own financial statement are required. The fall application priority deadline is March 1.
International Students: There were 25 international students enrolled in a recent year. The school actively recruits these students. They must score 550 on the written TOEFL and also take the SAT I or the ACT.
Computers: The mainframes are a Digital Alpha Server and a Compaq Proliant server. Servers and other networked resources (including the Internet and Web) can be reached from 200 college-owned student computers located throughout the campus. Resident students may also connect personally owned computers to the campus network via Ethernet and have access to the same resources. All students may access the system. There are no time limits. There is a fee charged to use the ssystem.
Graduates: In 2001, 308 bachelor's degrees were awarded. The most popular majors were business administration (30%), education (20%), and social sciences and history (8%). 128 companies recruited on campus in 2000-2001. Of the 2000 graduating class, 9% were enrolled in graduate school within 6 months of graduation and 82% were employed.
Admissions Contact: Susan Sorisky, Director of Admission.
E-mail: *admission@lvc.edu* Web: *www.lvc.edu*

LEHIGH UNIVERSITY F-3

Bethlehem, PA 18015 **(610) 758-3100; Fax: (610) 758-4361**

Full-time: 2717 men, 1878 women	**Faculty:** 391; I, +$
Part-time: 33 men, 22 women	**Ph.D.s:** 99%
Graduate: 1020 men, 809 women	**Student/Faculty:** 12 to 1
Year: semesters, summer session	**Tuition:** $25,140
Application Deadline: see profile	**Room & Board:** $7150

Freshman Class: 8088 applied, 3776 accepted, 1112 enrolled
SAT I Verbal/Math: 620/660 **MOST COMPETITIVE**

Lehigh University, founded in 1865, is a private university offering both undergraduate and graduate programs in liberal arts, science, engineering, and business, and graduate programs in education. There are 3 undergraduate and 4 graduate schools. In addition to regional accreditation, Lehigh has baccalaureate program accreditation with AACSB, ABET, and NCATE. The 2 libraries contain 1,354,100 volumes, 2,113,130 microform items, and 3915 audiovisual forms/CDs, and subscribe to 10,797 periodicals. Computerized library services include the card catalog, interlibrary loans, and database searching. Special learning facilities include a learning resource center, art gallery, radio station, TV station, and Special Collections/Rare Book Reading Room, and International Multimedia Resource Center. The 1600-acre campus is in a suburban area 60 miles north of Philadelphia and 80 miles southwest of New York City. Including residence halls, there are 153 buildings.
Student Life: 67% of undergraduates are from out of state, mostly the Middle Atlantic. Others are from 49 states, 45 foreign countries, and Canada. 70% are from public schools. 81% are white. The average age of freshmen is 18; all undergraduates, 20. 7% do not continue beyond their first year; 85% remain to graduate.
Housing: 3240 students can be accommodated in college housing, which includes single-sex and coed dormitories, on-campus apartments, married-student housing, fraternity houses, and sorority houses. In addition, there are speial interest houses. On-campus housing is guaranteed for the freshman year only, is available on a first-come, first-served basis, and is available on a lottery system for upperclassmen. 75% of students live on campus; of those, 75% remain on campus on weekends. Upperclassmen may keep cars.
Activities: 32% of men belong to 27 national fraternities; 33% of women belong to 8 national sororities. There are 200 groups on campus, including art, band, cheerleading, chess, choir, chorale, chorus, computers, dance, drama, ethnic, gay, honors, international, jazz band, literary magazine, marching band, musical theater, newspaper, orchestra, photography, political, professional, radio and TV, religious, social, social service, student government, and yearbook. Popular campus events include Greek Week, Spring Fest, and South Side Alive (carnival with the community).
Sports: There are 12 intercollegiate sports for men and 11 for women, and 23 intramural sports for men and 22 for women. Facilities include a 16,000-seat stadium, a 6500-seat arena, a gym, a champion cross-country course, a field house with basketball and tennis courts, swimming pools, a track, indoor squash and racquetball courts, playing fields including astro-turf for field hockey, football, lacrosse, and soccer, weight rooms, a fitness center, and an indoor tennis center.
Disabled Students: 35% of the campus is accessible. Wheelchair ramps, elevators, special parking, specially equipped rest rooms, special class scheduling, lowered drinking fountains, and lowered telephones are available.
Services: Counseling and information services are available, as is tutoring in most subjects, including calculus, physics, English, accounting, finance, and economics. Tutoring in other subjects is available on request. There is a reader service for the blind. There are special programs for students with learning disabilities.
Campus Safety and Security: Measures include 24-hour foot and vehicle patrol, self-defense education, escort service, and shuttle buses. There are informal discussions, pamphlets/posters/films, emergency telephones, and lighted pathways/sidewalks.

Programs of Study: Lehigh confers B.A., B.S., B.S.B.A., and B.S.E. degrees. Master's and doctoral degrees are also awarded. Bachelor's degrees are awarded in BIOLOGICAL SCIENCE (biochemistry, biology/biological science, and molecular biology), BUSINESS (accounting, banking and finance, business administration and management, business economics, and marketing/retailing/merchandising), COMMUNICATIONS AND THE ARTS (art, classics, dramatic arts, English, French, German, journalism, music, and Spanish), COMPUTER AND PHYSICAL SCIENCE (chemistry, computer science, information sciences and systems, mathematics, natural sciences, physics, science technology, and statistics), EDUCATION (social foundations), ENGINEERING AND ENVIRONMENTAL DESIGN (architecture, chemical engineering, civil engineering, computer engineering, electrical/electronics engineering, engineering mechanics, engineering physics, environmental science, industrial engineering, materials engineering, and mechanical engineering), HEALTH PROFESSIONS (predentistry, premedicine, and preoptometry), SOCIAL SCIENCE (African studies, American studies, anthropology, Asian/Oriental studies, behavioral science, classical/ancient civilization, cognitive science, economics, history, international public service, international relations, philosophy, political science/government, psychology, religion, Russian and Slavic studies, sociology, and urban studies). Architecture, accounting, and mechanical engineering are the largest.

Required: Graduation requirements vary by degree sought, but all students must complete 2 semesters of English, at least 30 credits in the chosen major, and a minimum of 121 credit hours. Students must also maintain a minimum GPA of 2.0.

Special: The university offers co-op programs through the Colleges of Engineering and Applied Science and Business and Economics, cross-registration with the Lehigh Valley Association of Independent Colleges, study abroad in 40 countries, internships, a Washington semester, several work-study programs, accelerated degree programs in medicine, dentistry and optometry, student-designed majors, many combinations of dual majors, a B.A.-B.S. degree, a 3-2 engineering degree, and pass/fail options. A 6-year B.A.-M.D. degree with the Medical College of Pennsylvania and a 7-year B.A.-D.D.S. degree with Pennsylvania State University are possible. There are 18 national honor societies, including Phi Beta Kappa, and a freshman honors program.

Faculty/Classroom: 81% of faculty are male; 19%, female. All both teach and do research. No introductory courses are taught by graduate students. The average class size in an introductory lecture is 150 and in a regular course, 29.

Admissions: 47% of the 2001-2002 applicants were accepted. The SAT I scores for the 2001-2002 freshman class were: Verbal--3% below 500, 29% between 500 and 599, 55% between 600 and 700, and 14% above 700; Math--1% below 500, 13% between 500 and 599, 55% between 600 and 700, and 31% above 700. 78% of the current freshmen were in the top fifth of their class; 95% were in the top two fifths. In a recent year, there were 12 National Merit finalists; 80 freshmen graduated first in their class.

Requirements: The SAT I or ACT is required. In addition, candidates for admission should have completed 4 years of English, and 2 years each of a foreign language, history, math, science, and social science. Most students present 4 years each of science, math, and English. An on-campus interview is recommended. AP credits are accepted. Important factors in the admissions decision are advanced placement or honor courses, evidence of special talent, and leadership record.

Procedure: Freshmen are admitted fall and spring. Entrance exams should be taken by the January test date. There is an early decision plan. Check with school for current application deadlines. The fall 2001 application fee was $50.

Transfer: 119 transfer students enrolled in a recent year. Transfer candidates should have a minimum GPA of 3.0. An interview is recommended. 30 credits of 121 must be completed at Lehigh.

Visiting: There are regularly scheduled orientations for prospective students, consisting of interviews scheduled Monday through Friday, 9 A.M. to 3:30 P.M.; tours scheduled Monday through Friday, 10:15 A.M., 11:15 A.M., 1 P.M., and 3 P.M., and interviews and tours also available on some Saturdays. General information sessions are offered Monday through Friday at 9:30, 10:30, and 2:15 P.M. There are guides for informal visits and visitors may sit in on classes and stay overnight. To schedule a visit, contact the Office of Admissions.

Financial Aid: In 2001-2002, 43% of all freshmen and 46% of continuing students received some form of financial aid. In a recent year, 49% of freshmen and 50% of continuing students received need-based aid. The average freshman award was $18,638. Of that total, scholarships or need-based grants averaged $13,900 ($28,000 maximum); loans averaged $3500 ($5500 maximum); and work contracts averaged $1200 ($1500 maximum). 27% of undergraduates work part time. Average annual earnings from campus work are $980. The average financial indebtedness of a recent year's graduate was $15,178. Lehigh is a member of CSS. The CSS/Profile or FAFSA and the college's own financial statement are required. Check with school for current deadlines.

International Students: There were 194 international students enrolled in a recent year. The school actively recruits these students. They must score 230 on the written TOEFL and also take the SAT I or the ACT. Students must take SAT II: Subject tests in English, math, and 1 other.

Computers: The mainframes are clusters of high-speed IBM RS/6000 computers, with more than 115 workstations in public sites. There are also more than 400 PCs available for student use in libraries, academic buildings, and computer centers. There are computer ports in all classrooms, dorms, and offices. Many LANs and high-speed fiber-optic networks are available. All students may access the system 24 hours per day. There are no time limits and no fees.

Graduates: In a recent year, 1011 bachelor's degrees were awarded. The most popular majors were finance (10%), mechanincal engineering (8%), and accounting (7%). In an average class, 68% graduate in 4 years, 80% in 5 years, and 81% in 6 years. 388 companies recruited on campus in a recent year.

Admissions Contact: J. Bruce Gardiner, Director of Admissions. E-mail: *inado@lehigh.edu; www.lehigh.edu* Web: *www.lehigh.edu*

LINCOLN UNIVERSITY — E-4

Lincoln University, PA 19352 — (610) 932-8300, ext. 3206; (800) 790-0191; Fax: (610) 932-1209

Full-time: 553 men, 832 women	**Faculty:** 89
Part-time: 24 men, 29 women	**Ph.D.s:** 73%
Graduate: 155 men, 278 women	**Student/Faculty:** 16 to 1
Year: semesters, summer session	**Tuition:** $5786 ($9050)
Application Deadline: open	**Room & Board:** $5412
Freshman Class: 2955 applied, 1473 accepted, 479 enrolled	
SAT I Verbal/Math: 422/410	**COMPETITIVE+**

Lincoln University, founded in 1854, is a public institution offering programs in liberal arts and teacher preparation. There are 3 undergraduate schools and 1 graduate school. The library contains 185,197 volumes, 210,009 microform items, and 2630 audiovisual forms/CDs, and subscribes to 540 periodicals. Computerized library services include interlibrary loans and database searching. Special learning facilities include an art gallery, radio station, and TV station. The 422-acre campus is in a rural area 45 miles southwest of Philadelphia. Including residence halls, there are 37 buildings.

Student Life: 53% of undergraduates are from out of state, mostly the Northeast. Others are from 24 states, 13 foreign countries, and Canada. 90% are African American. The average age of freshmen is 18; all undergraduates, 19. 28% do not continue beyond their first year; 48% remain to graduate.

Housing: 1450 students can be accommodated in college housing, which includes single-sex and coed dormitories. In addition, there are honors houses and language houses. On-campus housing is guaranteed for the freshman year only and is available on a first-come, first-served basis. 93% of students live on campus; of those, 80% remain on campus on weekends. Alcohol is not permitted. Upperclassmen may keep cars.

Activities: 5% of men belong to 4 national fraternities; 10% of women belong to 4 national sororities. There are 90 groups on campus, including art, band, cheerleading, choir, chorale, computers, dance, drama, drill team, honors, international, jazz band, newspaper, pep band, political, radio and TV, religious, social, social service, student government, and yearbook. Popular campus events include lectures and recitals, Black History Month, and convocations.

Sports: There are 9 intercollegiate sports for men and 6 for women, and 11 intramural sports for men and 11 for women. Facilities include a 2000-seat gym, softball and track fields, a fitness trail, a swimming pool, and a bowling alley.

Disabled Students: Wheelchair ramps, elevators, special parking, and specially equipped rest rooms are available.

Services: Counseling and information services are available, as is tutoring in every subject. There is remedial math, reading, and writing.

Campus Safety and Security: Measures include 24-hour foot and vehicle patrol, self-defense education, escort service, and shuttle buses. There are informal discussions, pamphlets/posters/films, emergency telephones, and lighted pathways/sidewalks.

Programs of Study: Lincoln confers B.A. and B.S. degrees. Master's degrees are also awarded. Bachelor's degrees are awarded in BIOLOGICAL SCIENCE (biology/biological science), BUSINESS (accounting, banking and finance, and business administration and management), COMMUNICATIONS AND THE ARTS (Arabic, art, Chinese, communications, English, French, German, Japanese, journalism, music, Russian, and Spanish), COMPUTER AND PHYSICAL SCIENCE (actuarial science, applied mathematics, chemistry, computer science, mathematics, and physics), EDUCATION (early childhood, elementary, mathematics, music, physical, and secondary), ENGINEERING AND ENVIRONMENTAL DESIGN (preengineering), HEALTH PROFESSIONS (health science and recreation therapy), SOCIAL SCIENCE (anthropology, criminal justice, economics, history, human services, industrial and organizational psychology, international relations, philosophy, psychobiology, psychology, public affairs, religion, and sociology). Physics, chemistry, and biology are the strongest academically. Business administration, elementary education, and criminal justice are the largest.

Required: Required courses include 8 in the humanities, 3 each in the social and natural sciences, 2 to 4 in foreign language, 2 each in phys ed, writing emphasis, speaking emphasis, critical thinking, and university seminar, and 1 in computer applications. Students must take Integrative Themes in the Liberal Arts, pass a writing proficiency exam, and participate in the Major Field Achievement Assessment. For graduation, a total of 120 semester hours is required, including 60 in the major, with a GPA of 2.0.

Special: Lincoln offers co-op programs, internships, study abroad in 18 countries, work-study, and pass/fail options. There are 3-2 engineering degrees offered with area universities. Accelerated degree programs and dual majors are possible. There are 7 national honor societies, a freshman honors program, and 3 departmental honors programs.

Faculty/Classroom: 64% of faculty are male; 36%, female. 71% teach undergraduates. No introductory courses are taught by graduate students.

Admissions: 50% of the 2001-2002 applicants were accepted.

Requirements: The SAT I or ACT is required. In addition, applicants should complete 21 credit hours, including 4 credits in English, 3 each in math, science, and social studies, 2 in art, and 1 in phys ed. The GED is accepted. An essay and an interview are required. Lincoln requires applicants to be in the upper 50% of their class. A GPA of 2.0 is required. Important factors in the admissions decision are advanced placement or honor courses, evidence of special talent, and leadership record.

Procedure: Freshmen are admitted to all sessions. Entrance exams should be taken prior to admission. Application deadlines are open. The fall 2001 application fee was $20. Notification is sent ona rolling basis. A waiting list is an active part of the admissions procedure.

Transfer: 42 transfer students enrolled in 2001-2002. Applicants must have completed at least 12 semester hours, be in good standing at all previously attended institutions, and submit official transcripts. 60 credits of 120 must be completed at Lincoln.

Visiting: There are regularly scheduled orientations for prospective students. There are guides for informal visits and visitors may sit in on classes and stay overnight. To schedule a visit, contact Dr. Robert L. Laney, Director of Admissions at *admiss@lu.lincoln.edu*.

Financial Aid: In 2001-2002, 95% of all students received some form of financial aid. 90% of freshmen received need-based aid. 31% of undergraduates work part time. Average annual earnings from campus work are $1800. The average financial indebtedness of the 2001 graduate was $20,000. The FAFSA and PHEAA are required. The fall application deadline is March 15.

International Students: There are 81 international students enrolled. The school actively recruits these students. They must score 550 on the written TOEFL and also take the SAT I or the ACT, scoring 850 on the SAT I.

Computers: The mainframe is a DEC ALPHA 4100. There are 270 PCs, 4 Macs, and 2 Sun OS computers in various dorms, computer labs, and the library. All students may access the system. There are no time limits and no fees.

Graduates: In 2001, 199 bachelor's degrees were awarded. The most popular majors were elementary education (14%), business administration (14%), and criminal justice (11%). In an average class, 1% graduate in 3 years, 31% in 4 years, 42% in 5 years, and 48% in 6 years. 48 companies recruited on campus in 2000-2001.

Admissions Contact: Dr. Robert L. Laney, Director of Admissions. E-mail: *admiss@lu.lincoln.edu* Web: *www.lincoln.edu*

LOCK HAVEN UNIVERSITY OF PENNSYLVANIA D-2

Lock Haven, PA 17745 (570) 893-2027

(800) 233-8978; Fax: (570) 893-2201

Full-time: 1582 men, 2200 women	**Faculty:** 215; IIB, +$
Part-time: 99 men, 200 women	**Ph.D.s:** 56%
Graduate: 54 men, 117 women	**Student/Faculty:** 18 to 1
Year: semesters, summer session	**Tuition:** $4758 ($9185)
Application Deadline: open	**Room & Board:** $4776
Freshman Class: 3451 applied, 2800 accepted, 1021 enrolled	
SAT I Verbal/Math: 490/500	**ACT:** 21 **COMPETITIVE**

Lock Haven University, established in 1870, is a public institution offering undergraduate degrees in arts and sciences, education, and human services. The university maintains a branch campus in Clearfield. There are 2 undergraduate and 3 graduate schools. In addition to regional accreditation, Lock Haven has baccalaureate program accreditation with CSWE, NCATE, and NLN. The library contains 368,912 volumes, 18,898 microform items, and 5464 audiovisual forms/CDs, and subscribes to 1150 periodicals. Computerized library services include the card catalog, interlibrary loans, and database searching. Special learning facilities include a learning resource center, art gallery, planetarium, radio station, TV station, primate and human performance labs, and a cadaver dissection lab. The 135-acre campus is in a rural area 30 miles west of Williamsport. Including residence halls, there are 28 buildings.

Student Life: 88% of undergraduates are from Pennsylvania. Others are from 28 states, 36 foreign countries, and Canada. 92% are white. The average age of freshmen is 18; all undergraduates, 21. 26% do not continue beyond their first year; 48% remain to graduate.

Housing: 1630 students can be accommodated in college housing, which includes single-sex and coed dormitories and off-campus apartments. On-campus housing is guaranteed for all 4 years. 55% of students commute. Alcohol is not permitted. Upperclassmen may keep cars.

Activities: 8% of men belong to 6 national fraternities; 5% of women belong to 4 national sororities. There are 90 groups on campus, including art, band, cheerleading, chess, choir, chorale, chorus, computers, dance, drama, ethnic, forensics, gay, honors, international, jazz band, literary magazine, marching band, newspaper, orchestra, pep band, photography, political, professional, radio and TV, religious, social, social service, student government, and symphony. Popular campus events include Family Day, Alcohol Awareness Week, and Spring Carnival.

Sports: There are 7 intercollegiate sports for men and 9 for women, and 19 intramural sports for men and 18 for women. Facilities include a 5000-seat stadium containing a football field and an all-weather track, a 2500-seat field house with a wrestling room, a recreation facility, a gym used for intramurals and weight training, and a gym that houses a swimming pool.

Disabled Students: 95% of the campus is accessible. Wheelchair ramps, elevators, special parking, specially equipped rest rooms, special class scheduling, lowered drinking fountains, and lowered telephones are available.

Services: Counseling and information services are available, as is tutoring in most subjects. Remedial math is offered, and reader services for the blind can be arranged. There are also writing and math centers.

Campus Safety and Security: Measures include 24-hour foot and vehicle patrol, escort service, informal discussions, and pamphlets/posters/films. There are emergency telephones and lighted pathways/sidewalks.

Programs of Study: Lock Haven confers B.A., B.S., B.F.A., and B.S.Ed. degrees. Associate and master's degrees are also awarded. Bachelor's degrees are awarded in BIOLOGICAL SCIENCE (biology/biological science and environmental biology), BUSINESS (business administration and management), COMMUNICATIONS AND THE ARTS (communications, English, fine arts, French, German, journalism, music, Spanish, and speech/debate/rhetoric), COMPUTER AND PHYSICAL SCIENCE (chemistry, computer science, earth science, geology, information sciences and systems, mathematics, and physics), EDUCATION (early childhood, elementary, foreign languages, physical, science, secondary, and special), HEALTH PROFESSIONS (health science and medical laboratory technology), SOCIAL SCIENCE (economics, geography, history, humanities and social science, international studies, Latin American studies, liberal arts/general studies, philosophy, political science/government, psychology, social science, social work, and sociology). Health science and biological sciences are the strongest academically. Education, health science, and recreation are the largest.

Required: To graduate, students must complete 60 hours of general education, including 12 in humanities and in social and behavioral sciences, 9 in skills core, 6 in science, 3 in wellness core, and the rest in electives. A total of 128 credit hours is required, including 61 to 68 in the major, with a minimum GPA of 2.0.

Special: There are cooperative programs in music education and engineering, including a 3-2 engineering degree with Pennsylvania State University. Lock Haven also offers study-abroad programs in more than 20 countries, a dual major in education, work-study options, an accelerated degree program for honor students, a student-designed general studies major, and internships, which are required in some majors. Pass/fail grading options are limited to 1 course outside the major per semester, not to exceed 12 credit hours. There are 9 national honor societies, a freshman honors program, and 6 departmental honors programs.

Faculty/Classroom: 57% of faculty are male; 43%, female. 93% teach undergraduates. No introductory courses are taught by graduate students. The average class size in an introductory lecture is 75; in a laboratory, 15; and in a regular course, 26.

Admissions: 81% of the 2001-2002 applicants were accepted. The SAT I scores for the 2001-2002 freshman class were: Verbal--46% below 500, 43% between 500 and 599, and 10% between 600 and 700; Math--51% below 500, 41% between 500 and 599, and 8% between 600 and 700. The ACT scores were 49% below 21, 26% between 21 and 23, 25% between 24 and 26, and 1% between 27 and 28. 20% of the current freshmen were in the top fifth of their class; 50% were in the top two fifths.

Requirements: The SAT I is required. In addition, applicants must graduate from an accredited secondary school or have a GED. 16 academic credits are required, and a college preparatory course is recommended. AP and CLEP credits are accepted. Important factors in the admissions decision are leadership record, advanced placement or honor courses, and evidence of special talent. Students may apply on-line via CollegeView or the Internet.

Procedure: Freshmen are admitted to all sessions. Entrance exams should be taken during the spring of the junior year and the fall of the senior year. There are early decision, early admissions, and deferred admissions plans. Application deadlines are open. The application fee is $25. Notification is sent on a rolling basis.

Transfer: 187 transfer students enrolled in 2001-2002. Priority is given to applicants who have completed 24 or more transferable credits. A minimum GPA of 2.0 is required, and a composite SAT I score of 970 is recommended. 32 credits of 128 must be completed at Lock Haven.

Visiting: There are regularly scheduled orientations for prospective students, consisting of an introduction to the administration, sessions with faculty, and an information arena/departmental showcase; small group visits are also scheduled. There are guides for informal visits and visitors may sit in on classes. To schedule a visit, contact the Admissions Office at *admissions@lhup.edu*

Financial Aid: 31% of undergraduates work part time. Average annual earnings from campus work are $960. Lock Haven is a member of CSS. The FAFSA and PHEAA are required. The fall application deadline is April 1.

International Students: The school actively recruits these students. They must score 550 on the written TOEFL.

Computers: The mainframe is an IBM 4381. All Internet services are accessible from the more than 225 PCs available in computer labs and residence halls. The library's card catalog is also accessible from all on-campus computers hooked up to the mainframe. All students may access the system. There are no time limits and no fees.

Graduates: In 2001, 559 bachelor's degrees were awarded. The most popular majors were education (36%), health professional (12%), and parks and recreation (9%). In an average class, 19% graduate in 4 years, 43% in 5 years, and 48% in 6 years. Of the 2000 graduating class, 11% were enrolled in graduate school within 6 months of graduation and 85% were employed.

Admissions Contact: Stephen Lee, Director of Admissions.
E-mail: *admissions@eagle.lhup.edu* Web: *http://www.lhup.edu*

LYCOMING COLLEGE — D-2

Williamsport, PA 17701-5192 — (570) 321-4026
(800) 345-3920; Fax: (570) 321-4317

Full-time: 637 men, 749 women	**Faculty:** 88; IIB, av$
Part-time: 12 men, 31 women	**Ph.D.s:** 92%
Graduate: none	**Student/Faculty:** 16 to 1
Year: semesters, summer session	**Tuition:** $19,404
Application Deadline: April 1	**Room & Board:** $5376
Freshman Class: 1431 applied, 1144 accepted, 408 enrolled	
SAT I Verbal/Math: 550/530	**ACT:** 23 **COMPETITIVE**

Lycoming College, established in 1812, is a private, residential, liberal arts institution affiliated with the Methodist Church. In addition to regional accreditation, Lycoming has baccalaureate program accreditation with AACSB and NLN. The library contains 170,000 volumes and 1800 audiovisual forms/CDs, and subscribes to 1069 periodicals. Computerized library services include the card catalog, interlibrary loans, and database searching. Special learning facilities include a learning resource center, art gallery, planetarium, radio station, and TV station. The 35-acre campus is in a small town 90 miles north of Harrisburg. Including residence halls, there are 23 buildings.

Student Life: 79% of undergraduates are from Pennsylvania. Others are from 22 states, 10 foreign countries, and Canada. 80% are from public schools. 92% are white. 64% are Protestant; 30% Catholic. The average age of freshmen is 18; all undergraduates, 21. 16% do not continue beyond their first year; 68% remain to graduate.

Housing: 1136 students can be accommodated in college housing, which includes single-sex and coed dormitories and off-campus apartments. In addition, there are special-interest (including creative arts), non-smoking,intensive study, and Greek floors. On-campus housing is guaranteed for all 4 years. 82% of students live on campus; of those, 67% remain on campus on weekends. All students may keep cars.

Activities: 14% of men belong to 4 national fraternities; 16% of women belong to 1 national and3 local sororities. There are 60 groups on campus, including art, band, cheerleading, choir, chorus, computers, drama, ethnic, film, gay, honors, international, literary magazine, musical theater, newspaper, photography, political, professional, radio and TV, religious, social, social service, student government, and yearbook. Popular campus events include Campus Carnival, Annual Christmas Candlelight Service, and Choir Concert.

Sports: There are 10 intercollegiate sports for men and 9 for women, and 6 intramural sports for men and 6 for women. Facilities include an outdoor softball, football, soccer, and lacrosse complex, indoor basketball courts, and intramural fields.

Disabled Students: 85% of the campus is accessible. Wheelchair ramps, elevators, special parking, specially equipped rest rooms, special class scheduling, lowered drinking fountains, lowered telephones, and specially designed residence hall rooms are available.

Services: Counseling and information services are available, as is tutoring in every subject. There is remedial math, reading, and writing.

Campus Safety and Security: Measures include 24-hour foot and vehicle patrol, self-defense education, escort service, and informal discussions. There are pamphlets/posters/films, emergency telephones, and lighted pathways/sidewalks.

Programs of Study: Lycoming confers B.A. and B.S. degrees. Bachelor's degrees are awarded in BIOLOGICAL SCIENCE (biology/biological science), BUSINESS (accounting and business administration and management), COMMUNICATIONS AND THE ARTS (art history and appreciation, communications, dramatic arts, English, French, German, music, Spanish, and studio art), COMPUTER AND PHYSICAL SCIENCE (astronomy, chemistry, computer science, mathematics, and physics), SOCIAL SCIENCE (anthropology, criminal justice, economics, history, international studies, philosophy, political science/government, psychology, religion, and sociology). Business, psychology, and biology are the largest.

Required: To graduate, students must complete 128 credits with a minimum GPA of 2.0. Distribution requirements include 4 courses in humanities and 2 each in English, foreign language, math, fine arts, natural science, social science, and cultural diversity. Students must also complete 2 semesters of phys ed, wellness, or community service.

Special: Cooperative programs are available with the Ohio and Pennsylvania Colleges of Podiatric Medicine, Pennsylvania College of Optometry, and Penn State and Duke Universities. Cross-registration is available with the Pennsylvania College of Technology. More than 200 internships, including teacher programs, study abroad in 5 countries, and a Washington semester at American University are available. Lycoming offers work-study programs, dual and student-designed majors, and an accelerated degree program in conjunction with the college's Scholar Program in optometry, podiatric medicine, and dentistry. There is a 3-2 engineering degree program with Penn State. Nondegree study and pass/fail grading options are available. There are 12 national honor societies, a freshman honors program, and 11 departmental honors programs.

Faculty/Classroom: 62% of faculty are male; 38%, female. All teach undergraduates. The average class size in an introductory lecture is 25; in a laboratory, 15; and in a regular course, 18.

Admissions: 80% of the 2001-2002 applicants were accepted. The SAT I scores for the 2001-2002 freshman class were: Verbal--32% below 500, 45% between 500 and 599, 21% between 600 and 700, and 2% above 700; Math--35% below 500, 45% between 500 and 599, 18% between 600 and 700, and 2% above 700. 43% of the current freshmen were in the top fifth of their class; 70% were in the top two fifths. 9 freshmen graduated first in their class.

Requirements: The SAT I is required, with a minimum SAT I score of 900, at least 450 verbal. Applicants must graduate from an accredited secondary school or have a GED. They must have earned 16 academic or Carnegie units, completing 4 years of English, 3 each of math and social studies, and 2 each of science, a foreign language, and academic electives. 2 personal letters of recommendation are required. An essay is required and an interview is recommended. Portfolios and auditions may be required for students seeking scholarships. AP and CLEP credits are accepted. Important factors in the admissions decision are advanced placement or honor courses, leadership record, and evidence of special talent. Applications are accepted on-line at the school's web site.

Procedure: Freshmen are admitted fall and spring. Entrance exams should be taken during the junior year or by January of the senior year. There is a deferred admissions plan. Applications should be filed by April 1 for fall entry and December 1 for spring entry, along with a $35 fee. Notification is sent on a rolling basis.

Transfer: 41 transfer students enrolled in 2001-2002. Applicants must submit appropriate transcripts and have a minimum GPA of 2.0 in transferable courses. Students who have completed 24 transferable semester hours are not required to submit the SAT I or ACT results. 32 credits of 128 must be completed at Lycoming.

Visiting: There are regularly scheduled orientations for prospective students, consisting of a student-guided tour of campus and an interview with an admissions counselor. Meetings with professors and/or coaches, and attending a class are possible upon request. There are guides for informal visits and visitors may sit in on classes and stay overnight. To schedule a visit, contact the Admissions House.

Financial Aid: In 2001-2002, 85% of all freshmen and 82% of continuing students received some form of financial aid. 83% of freshmen and 82% of continuing students received need-based aid. The average freshman award was $12,600. Of that total, scholarships or need-based grants averaged $9400 ($15,000 maximum); loans averaged $3200 ($4625 maximum); and work contracts averaged $800 ($1500 maximum). 51% of undergraduates work part time. Average annual earnings from campus work are $600. The average financial indebtedness of the 2001 graduate was $15,100. The FAFSA and the college's own financial statement are required. The fall application deadline is April 15.

International Students: There were 12 international students enrolled in a recent year. They must score 500 on the written TOEFL or 173 on the electronic version and also take the SAT I, scoring 900, or the ACT. This requirement may be waived, however.

Computers: Students may acccess the mainframe through 1 Mac and 3 PC labs. There are also 180 terminals and PCs available to students. All students may access the system 8 A.M. to midnight. There are no time limits and no fees. It is strongly recommended that all students have a personal computer.

Graduates: In 2001, 307 bachelor's degrees were awarded. The most popular majors were biology (16%), business (16%), and psychology (15%). In an average class, 2% graduate in 3 years, 62% in 4 years, and 70% in 5 years. Of the 2000 graduating class, 29% were enrolled in graduate school within 6 months of graduation and 98% were employed.

Admissions Contact: James Spencer, Dean of Admissions and Financial Aid. E-mail: *admissions@lycoming.edu* Web: *www.lycoming.edu*

MANSFIELD UNIVERSITY
Mansfield, PA 16933 D-1
(570) 662-4243
(800) 577-6826; Fax: (570) 662-4121

Full-time: 1120 men, 1570 women | **Faculty:** 155; IIB, +$
Part-time: 106 men, 222 women | **Ph.D.s:** 78%
Graduate: 54 men, 231 women | **Student/Faculty:** 17 to 1
Year: semesters, summer session | **Tuition:** $5096 ($11,120)
Application Deadline: July 1 | **Room & Board:** $4552
Freshman Class: 2852 applied, 2128 accepted, 650 enrolled
SAT I Verbal/Math: 523/514 **COMPETITIVE**

Mansfield University, founded in 1857, is a public university that is part of the Pennsylvania State System of Higher Education. It offers programs in professional studies and the arts and sciences. In addition to regional accreditation, Mansfield has baccalaureate program accreditation with CAHEA, CSWE, NASM, and NCATE. The library contains 268,966 volumes, 791,486 microform items, and 7794 audiovisual forms/CDs, and subscribes to 3094 periodicals. Computerized library services include the card catalog, interlibrary loans, and database searching. Special learning facilities include a learning resource center, art gallery, natural history museum, planetarium, radio station, TV station, and a high-tech lecture lab. The 175-acre campus is in a rural area 28 miles south of Corning/Elmira, New York, and 58 miles north of Williamsport. Including residence halls, there are 41 buildings.

Student Life: 78% of undergraduates are from Pennsylvania. Others are from 16 states, 21 foreign countries, and Canada. 93% are white. The average age of freshmen is 19; all undergraduates, 23. 33% do not continue beyond their first year; 54% remain to graduate.

Housing: 1800 students can be accommodated in college housing, which includes single-sex and coed dormitories. In addition, there are wellness, nonsmoking, 24-hour quiet, and honors floors in residence halls. On-campus housing is guaranteed for all 4 years. 57% of students commute. Alcohol is not permitted. All students may keep cars.

Activities: 10% of men belong to 6 national fraternities; 8% of women belong to 4 national sororities. There are 80 groups on campus, including art, band, cheerleading, choir, chorus, computers, debate, drama, ethnic, forensics, honors, international, jazz band, literary magazine, marching band, musical theater, newspaper, orchestra, photography, political, professional, radio and TV, religious, social, social service, student government, and symphony. Popular campus events include Parents Weekend and Fabulous 1890s Weekend.

Sports: There are 6 intercollegiate sports for men and 6 for women, and 8 intramural sports for men and 8 for women. Facilities include a track, a recreation center, a 4000-seat stadium, a 1500-seat indoor gym, a 1200-seat auditorium, and football, baseball, and hockey fields.

Disabled Students: 80% of the campus is accessible. Wheelchair ramps, elevators, special parking, specially equipped rest rooms, special class scheduling, lowered drinking fountains, lowered telephones, and a wheelchair lift are available.

Services: Counseling and information services are available, as is tutoring in most subjects. There is a reader service for the blind, and remedial math, reading, and writing.

Campus Safety and Security: Measures include 24-hour foot and vehicle patrol, self-defense education, escort service, and shuttle buses. There are informal discussions, pamphlets/posters/films, emergency telephones, and lighted pathways/sidewalks.

Programs of Study: Mansfield confers B.A., B.S., B.M., B.M.E., B.S.Ed., B.S.N., and B.S.W. degrees. Associate and master's degrees are also awarded. Bachelor's degrees are awarded in AGRICULTURE (fishing and fisheries), BIOLOGICAL SCIENCE (biochemistry, biology/biological science, cell biology, and molecular biology), BUSINESS (accounting, business administration and management, business economics, international business management, marketing/retailing/merchandising, personnel management, and tourism), COMMUNICATIONS AND THE ARTS (art history and appreciation, broadcasting, dramatic arts, English, French, German, journalism, music, music business management, music performance, public relations, Spanish, speech/debate/rhetoric, and studio art), COMPUTER AND PHYSICAL SCIENCE (chemistry, computer science, information sciences and systems, mathematics, and physics), EDUCATION (art, early childhood, education of the exceptional child, elementary, English, foreign languages, mathematics, music, science, secondary, social studies, and special), ENGINEERING AND ENVIRONMENTAL DESIGN (city/community/regional planning, environmental science, and preengineering), HEALTH PROFESSIONS (medical technology, music therapy, nursing, and premedicine), SOCIAL SCIENCE (anthropology, criminal justice, dietetics, economics, geography, history, international studies, liberal arts/general studies, philosophy, political science/government, prelaw, psychology, social science, social work, and sociology). Music, physical sciences, and social sciences are the strongest academically. Education, music, and social sciences are the largest.

Required: To graduate, students must complete 128 credit hours with a 2.0 GPA in core courses, distribution requirements, general education electives, and major requirements.

Special: There are co-op programs in preengineering, predentistry, and medical technology, and study abroad in England, Spain, and Germany. There is a 3-2 engineering program with several major universities. The university also offers work-study, dual majors, a liberal studies degree, credit by exam, credit for military experience, nondegree study, and pass/fail options. There are 6 national honor societies, including Phi Beta Kappa, and a freshman honors program.

Faculty/Classroom: 57% of faculty are male; 43%, female. All teach undergraduates. No introductory courses are taught by graduate students. The average class size in an introductory lecture is 35; in a laboratory, 20; and in a regular course, 25.

Admissions: 75% of the 2001-2002 applicants were accepted. The SAT I scores for the 2001-2002 freshman class were: Verbal--55% below 500, 36% between 500 and 599, 9% between 600 and 700, and 1% above 700; Math--58% below 500, 36% between 500 and 599, and 6% between 600 and 700. 19% of the current freshmen were in the top fifth of their class; 47% were in the top two fifths. 3 freshmen graduated first in their class.

Requirements: The SAT I or ACT is required, with a minimum composite SAT I score of 920, or a minimum ACT score of 19. A GED is accepted. Applicants should prepare with 4 credits of English, 3 each of history, math, science, and social studies, 2 of foreign language, and 6 of additional academic electives. Art students must submit a portfolio; music students must audition. Mansfield requires applicants to be in the upper 60% of their class. A GPA of 2.5 is required. AP and CLEP credits are accepted. Important factors in the admissions decision are advanced placement or honor courses, evidence of special talent, and leadership record. Applications are accepted on-line via ExPAN and the school's web site.

Procedure: Freshmen are admitted fall and spring. Entrance exams should be taken by the junior or senior year of high school. There are early decision, early admissions, and deferred admissions plans. Early decision applications should be filed by July 1; regular applications, by July 1 for fall entry and December 15 for spring entry, along with a $25 fee. Notification is sent on a rolling basis.

Transfer: 274 transfer students enrolled in 2001-2002. Applicants must have a GPA of at least 2.0. 32 credits of 128 must be completed at Mansfield.

Visiting: There are regularly scheduled orientations for prospective students. There are guides for informal visits and visitors may sit in on classes. To schedule a visit, contact the Admissions Office.

Financial Aid: In 2001-2002, 80% of all students received some form of financial aid. 60% of all students received need-based aid. The average freshman award was $3850. Of that total, scholarships or need-based grants averaged $1000 ($7352 maximum); loans averaged $2625 ($6625 maximum); work contracts averaged $1250 ($2250 maximum); and Pell grants/state grants averaged $900 ($3800 maximum). 28% of undergraduates work part time. Average annual earnings from campus work are $1000. The average financial indebtedness of the 2001 graduate was $8200. Mansfield is a member of CSS. The FAFSA and the college's own financial statement are required. The fall application deadline is April 1.

International Students: There are 43 international students enrolled. The school actively recruits these students. They must score 550 on the written TOEFL or 230 on the electronic version.

Computers: The mainframe is an IBM RS/6000. There are 15 computing labs and a total of 350 PCs in labs and residence halls. All students may access the system. There are no time limits and no fees.

Graduates: In 2001, 496 bachelor's degrees were awarded. The most popular majors were criminal justice (14%), elementary education (9%), and nursing (8%). In an average class, 28% graduate in 4 years, 51% in 5 years, and 54% in 6 years. 20 companies recruited on campus in 2000-2001. Of the 2000 graduating class, 8% were enrolled in graduate school within 6 months of graduation and 89% were employed.

Admissions Contact: Brian D. Barden, Director, Admissions.
E-mail: *admissns@mnsfld.edu* Web: *www.mnsfld.edu*

MARYWOOD UNIVERSITY

Scranton, PA 18509

E-2

(570)) 348-6234

(800) 346-5014; Fax: (570) 961-4763

Full-time: 390 men, 1052 women
Part-time: 73 men, 153 women
Graduate: 292 men, 965 women
Year: semesters, summer session
Application Deadline: open
Faculty: 91; IIA, --$
Ph.D.s: 83%
Student/Faculty: 16 to 1
Tuition: $17,329
Room & Board: $7310
Freshman Class: 1206 applied, 981 accepted, 291 enrolled
SAT I Verbal/Math: 510/500 **ACT:** 22 **COMPETITIVE**

Marywood University, founded in 1915, is an independent comprehensive Catholic institution committed to the integration of liberal arts and professional studies in the context of ethical and religious values. There are 3 undergraduate and 2 graduate schools. In addition to regional accreditation, Marywood has baccalaureate program accreditation with ABA, ACBSP, ADA, ASLHA, CACREP, CSWE, NASAD, NASM, NCATE, and NLN. The library contains 219,808 volumes, 338,191 microform items, and 41,729 audiovisual forms/CDs, and subscribes to 1005 periodicals. Computerized library services include the card catalog, interlibrary loans, and database searching. Special learning facilities include a learning resource center, art gallery, radio station, TV station, communication disorders clinic, on-campus preschool and day care center, psychology/education research lab, science multimedia lab, distance education videoconferencing classroom, and studio arts center. The 115-acre campus is in a suburban area 120 miles west of New York City and 115 miles north of Philadelphia. Including residence halls, there are 29 buildings.

Student Life: 80% of undergraduates are from Pennsylvania. Others are from 24 states and 26 foreign countries. 46% are from public schools. 94% are white. The average age of freshmen is 19; all undergraduates, 23. 14% do not continue beyond their first year; 61% remain to graduate.

Housing: 589 students can be accommodated in college housing, which includes single-sex and coed dormitories and on-campus apartments. In addition, there are honors houses, a community service residence, and an American-Inrternational student wing. On-campus housing is guaranteed for all 4 years. 68% of students commute. Alcohol is not permitted. All students may keep cars.

Activities: 2% of men belong to 1 local fraternity; 4% of women belong to 1 local sorority. There are 70 groups on campus, including art, band, cheerleading, choir, chorus, commuter, computers, dance, drama, ethnic, film, gay, honors, international, jazz band, literary magazine, musical theater, orchestra, photography, professional, radio and TV, religious, social, social service, student government, symphony, volunteer, and yearbook. Popular campus events include Family Weekend, Halloween Haunted House, and Spring Fling.

Sports: There are 5 intercollegiate sports for men and 7 for women, and 40 intramural sports for men and 40 for women. Facilities include an Olympic-size pool, a human performance lab, a gym, athletic training rooms, outdoor tennis courts, racquetball courts, an aerobic center, a game room, a sauna, a fitness center and weight room, and athletic fields for baseball, softball, field hockey, and soccer.

Disabled Students: 75% of the campus is accessible. Wheelchair ramps, elevators, special parking, specially equipped rest rooms, special class scheduling, lowered drinking fountains, lowered telephones, and electronic doors are available.

Services: Counseling and information services are available, as is tutoring in every subject. There is a reader service for the blind, and remedial math, reading, and writing. Remedial study skills and nonremedial tutoring, oral tests, note taking, tutors, tape recorders for physically challenged students, and interpreters for students with hearing impairments are available.

Campus Safety and Security: Measures include 24-hour foot and vehicle patrol, self-defense education, escort service, and informal discussions. There are pamphlets/posters/films, emergency telephones, lighted pathways/sidewalks, night security in dorms, card access to dorm floors, and transportation on request.

Programs of Study: Marywood confers B.A., B.S., B.B.A., B.F.A., B.M., B.S.N., and B.S.W. degrees. Associate, master's, and doctoral degrees are also awarded. Bachelor's degrees are awarded in BIOLOGICAL SCIENCE (biology/biological science and biotechnology), BUSINESS (accounting, banking and finance, business administration and management, hospitality management services, international business management, management engineering, and marketing/retailing/merchandising), COMMUNICATIONS AND THE ARTS (advertising, arts administration/management, communications, design, English, French, music, performing arts, Spanish, studio art, telecommunications, and theater management), COMPUTER AND PHYSICAL SCIENCE (information sciences and systems and mathematics), EDUCATION (art, early childhood, elementary, home economics, music, physical, science, secondary, and special), ENGINEERING AND ENVIRONMENTAL DESIGN (aviation administration/management and environmental science), HEALTH PROFESSIONS (art therapy, health care administration, medical laboratory technology, music therapy, nursing, physician's assistant, and speech pathology/audiology), SOCIAL SCIENCE (clinical psychology, criminal justice, dietetics, history, paralegal studies, psychology, religion, religious music, social science, social work, and sociology). Psychology, nutrition and dietetics, and education are the strongest academically. Education, business, and visual and performing arts are the largest.

Required: To graduate, students must complete a liberal arts requirement consisting of religious studies, philosophy, math, science, psychology, history, social science, world literature, foreign language, and fine arts. Additional course requirements include speech, writing, and phys ed. Students must have a GPA of 2.0, with 2.5 in the major. A minimum of 126 credits must be earned, with the number of credits required in the major varying.

Special: Marywood offers cross-registration with the University of Scranton, internships, study abroad, accelerated degree programs in dietetics and social work, dual majors, and student-designed majors. A semester at a fashion institute, student teaching abroad, credit for life, military, and work experience, off-campus degree programs, and nondegree study are also offered. There are 23 national honor societies, a freshman honors program, and 19 departmental honors programs.

Faculty/Classroom: 47% of faculty are male; 53%, female. All do research; 70% both teach undergraduates and do research. No introductory courses are taught by graduate students. The average class size in an introductory lecture is 21; in a laboratory, 14; and in a regular course, 17.

Admissions: 81% of the 2001-2002 applicants were accepted. The SAT I scores for the 2001-2002 freshman class were: Verbal--39% below 500, 45% between 500 and 599, 13% between 600 and 700, and 3% above 700; Math--49% below 500, 38% between 500 and 599, 10% between 600 and 700, and 3% above 700. The ACT scores were 40% below 21, 30% between 21 and 23, 25% between 24 and 26, and 5% between 27 and 28. 38% of the current freshmen were in the top fifth of their class; 66% were in the top two fifths. 2 freshmen graduated first in their class.

Requirements: The SAT I is required and the ACT is recommended. In addition, applicants are expected to be graduates of an accredited secondary school or have the GED. A minimum of 16 academic credits is required, including 4 in English, 3 each in social studies and science (1 as lab), and 2 in math. A letter of support is required in selected majors, as is a portfolio or an audition where appropriate. A personal interview is strongly recommended. A GPA of 2.5 is required. AP and CLEP credits are accepted. Marywood accepts applications on computer disk or on-line at *www.marywood.edu/ug-cat/admissions*.

Procedure: Freshmen are admitted to all sessions. Entrance exams should be taken in the junior year or the senior year before February 1. There are early decision, early admissions, and deferred admissions plans. Application deadlines are open. The fall 2001 application fee was $25. Notification is sent on a rolling basis.

Transfer: 192 transfer students enrolled in 2001-2002. SAT I or ACT scores are required of transfer applicants who have earned fewer than 12 college credits; both secondary school and college transcripts are required. Transfer students are required to have earned a minimum GPA of 2.5 at the college most recently attended. A grade of C is the minimum requirement for transfer of academic credit. 60 credits of 126 must be completed at Marywood.

Visiting: There are regularly scheduled orientations for prospective students, including a campus tour, individual visits with admissions counselors, an appointment with an academic adviser, and a financial aid appointment. There are guides for informal visits and visitors may sit in on classes and stay overnight. To schedule a visit, contact the Office of Undergraduate Admissions.

Financial Aid: In 2001-2002, 99% of all freshmen and 98% of continuing students received some form of financial aid. 95% of freshmen and 83% of continuing students received need-based aid. The average freshman award was $14,932. Of that total, scholarships or need-based grants averaged $11,727 ($18,886 maximum); loans averaged $3078 ($18,478 maximum); and work contracts averaged $1733. 20% of undergraduates work part time. Average annual earnings from campus work are $1800. The average financial indebtedness of the 2001 graduate was $17,125. The FAFSA and the college's own financial statement are required. The fall application deadline is February 15.

International Students: There are 42 international students enrolled. The school actively recruits these students. They must score 500 on the written TOEFL or 173 on the electronic version and also take the SAT I or ACT, if available.

Computers: The mainframes are a DEC VAX cluster with a DEC 5000 for the on-line library, a DEC MicroVAX 3100-90 for the academic network, and a DEC VAX 4000-100 for research. Computer facilities include an art lab, a psychology lab, 2 access labs with Macs, a science lab with interactive video, a CAD lab, and a Mac-equipped communication arts lab. More than 350 PCs are available for student use in class labs, drop-in facilities, and dorms. All labs are networked and can access the Internet. All students may access the system 24 hours per day. There are no time limits and no fees. It is strongly recommended that all students have personal computers.

Graduates: In 2001, 306 bachelor's degrees were awarded. The most popular majors were education (16%), business (15%), and visual and performing arts (13%). In an average class, 41% graduate in 4 years, 63% in 5 years, and 65% in 6 years. 60 companies recruited on campus in 2000-2001. Of the 2000 graduating class, 14% were enrolled in graduate school within 6 months of graduation and 94% were employed.

Admissions Contact: Robert W. Reese, Director of Undergraduate Admissions. A video is available. E-mail: *ugadm@es.marywood.edu* Web: *www.marywood.edu*

MCP HAHNEMANN UNIVERSITY F-3
Philadelphia, PA 19102 (215) 762-1616
(800) 2-DREXEL; Fax: (215) 762-6194

Full-time: 149 men, 254 women
Part-time: 77 men, 192 women
Graduate: 249 men, 685 women
Year: semesters, summer session
Application Deadline: June 1
Freshman Class: n/av
SAT I or ACT: required (some)
Faculty: n/av
Ph.D.s: 65%
Student/Faculty: n/av
Tuition: $10,410
Room & Board: $8100
SPECIAL

MCP Hahnemann University is a private institution offering degree programs in nursing and the health professions. In addition to regional accreditation, MCPHU has baccalaureate program accreditation with APTA, CAHEA, and NLN. The 3 libraries contain 78,103 volumes and 1272 audiovisual forms/CDs, and subscribe to 3976 periodicals. Computerized library services include the card catalog, interlibrary loans, and database searching. Special learning facilities include a learning resource center and and medical archives. The campus is in an urban area in Philadelphia. Including residence halls, there are 12 buildings.

Student Life: 67% are white; 19% African American. The average age of freshmen is 21; all undergraduates, 30.

Housing: 270 students can be accommodated in college housing, which includes coed on-campus apartments and married-student housing. On-campus housing is available on a first-come, first-served basis. 88% of students commute. All students may keep cars.

Activities: There are no fraternities or sororities. There are 20 groups on campus, including ethnic, gay, minority student, professional, religious, social service, student government, and yearbook. Popular campus events include Substance Abuse Week, Hospital Bed Race, and Halloween Party.

Sports: Facilities include a games area and a fitness center with exercise equipment.

Disabled Students: All of the campus is accessible. Wheelchair ramps, elevators, specially equipped rest rooms, lowered drinking fountains, and lowered telephones are available.

Services: Counseling and information services are available, as is tutoring in most subjects. There is remedial math, reading, and writing.

Campus Safety and Security: Measures include 24-hour foot and vehicle patrol, escort service, shuttle buses, and informal discussions. There are pamphlets/posters/films, emergency telephones, and lighted pathways/sidewalks.

Programs of Study: MCPHU confers B.A., B.S., and B.S.N. degrees. Associate, master's, and doctoral degrees are also awarded. Bachelor's degrees are awarded in HEALTH PROFESSIONS (biomedical science, clinical science, emergency medical technologies, health science, mental health/human services, nursing, and physician's assistant), SOCIAL SCIENCE (humanities and social science). Physician's assistant and nursing are the strongest academically and have the largest enrollments.

Required: Bachelor's candidates must complete at least 120 credit hours, with a minimum GPA of 2.0. Distribution requirements include 12 credits of social science, 6 each of English, humanities, and natural science, and 3 each of computer science and math or statistics.

Special: Clinical rotation internships are required in many majors. There is an accelerated degree program in nursing.

Faculty/Classroom: 37% of faculty are male; 63%, female. No introductory courses are taught by graduate students. The average class size in an introductory lecture is 21; in a laboratory, 13; and in a regular course, 21.

Requirements: The SAT I or the ACT is required for some programs and is waived for applicants who have advanced college standing or have been out of high school for 5 or more years. Graduation from an accredited high school is required; the GED is accepted. AP credits are accepted.

Procedure: Freshmen are admitted in the fall. There is a deferred admissions plan. Applications should be filed by June 1 for fall entry, along with a $35 fee. Notification is sent on a rolling basis.

Transfer: 236 transfer students enrolled in 2001-2002. Applicants who have been out of high school for 5 or more years or who have 30 or more college credits (grade C or better) need not submit SAT I or ACT scores. College transcripts and an average GPA of 2.5 in previous college courses are required. 60 credits of 120 must be completed at MCPHU.

Visiting: There are regularly scheduled orientations for prospective students, consisting of presentations and tours. There are guides for informal visits. To schedule a visit, contact the Admissions Office.

Financial Aid: The average freshman award for the 2001-2002 school year was $8296. The average financial indebtedness of the 2001 graduate was $36,797. The FAFSA is required. The fall application deadline is May 1.

International Students: They must score 500 on the written TOEFL.

Computers: There are 130 PCs for student use throughout the library system. All students have access to the Internet and the World Wide Web and to specific databases without charge. All students may access the system. There are no time limits and no fees.

Graduates: In 2001, 155 bachelor's degrees were awarded. The most popular majors were health professions (93%) and liberal arts/general studies (7%).

Admissions Contact: Jarmila Force, Associate Director of Enrollment Management. E-mail: *enroll@mcphu.edu* Web: *www.mcphu.edu*

MERCYHURST COLLEGE B-1
Erie, PA 16546 (814) 824-2241
(800) 825-1926; Fax: (814) 824-2071

Full-time: 1052 men, 1716 women
Part-time: 173 men, 259 women
Graduate: 62 men, 104 women
Year: semesters, summer session
Application Deadline: open
Freshman Class: 2219 applied, 1708 accepted, 664 enrolled
SAT I Verbal/Math: 550/530
Faculty: 130; IIB, --$
Ph.D.s: 60%
Student/Faculty: 21 to 1
Tuition: $15,000
Room & Board: $5694
ACT: 22
COMPETITIVE

Mercyhurst College, established in 1926, is a private, nonprofit institution affiliated with the Roman Catholic Church. The college offers undergraduate degrees in the arts, business, health science, liberal arts, religious studies, and teacher preparation as well as a degree-directed program for the learning disabled. In addition to regional accreditation, Mercyhurst has baccalaureate program accreditation with ADA and CSWE. The library contains 165,644 volumes, 50,631 microform items, and 9309 audiovisual forms/CDs, and subscribes to 848 periodicals. Computerized library services include the card catalog, interlibrary loans, and database searching. Special learning facilities include a learning resource center, art gallery, planetarium, radio station, TV station, northwestern Pennsylvania historical archives, and archeological institute. The 88-acre campus is in a suburban area within Erie. Including residence halls, there are 44 buildings.

Student Life: 63% of undergraduates are from Pennsylvania. Others are from 37 states, 14 foreign countries, and Canada. 76% are from public schools. 91% are white. 53% are Catholic; 21% Protestant; 18% claim no religious affiliation. The average age of freshmen is 18; all undergraduates, 26. 20% do not continue beyond their first year; 62% remain to graduate.

Housing: 1718 students can be accommodated in college housing, which includes single-sex and coed dormitories, on-campus apartments, and married-student housing. On-campus housing is guaranteed for all 4 years. 61% of students live on campus; of those, 91% remain on campus on weekends. Upperclassmen may keep cars.

Activities: There are no fraternities or sororities. There are 49 groups on campus, including art, band, cheerleading, choir, chorus, computers, dance, debate, drama, ethnic, film, gay, honors, international, jazz band, literary magazine, musical theater, newspaper, opera, orchestra, pep band, photography, political, professional, radio and TV, religious, social, social service, student government, and yearbook. Popular campus events include Activities Day, Parents Weekend, and winter and spring formals.

Sports: There are 13 intercollegiate sports for men and 12 for women, and 9 intramural sports for men and 9 for women. Facilities include a pool, indoor crew tanks, football, field hockey, lacrosse, and soccer fields, an ice hockey rink/arena, Nautilus facilities, a free-weight room, a baseball/softball complex, a training room, and a basketball arena.

Disabled Students: 90% of the campus is accessible. Wheelchair ramps, elevators, special parking, specially equipped rest rooms, and lowered drinking fountains are available.

Services: Counseling and information services are available, as is tutoring in every subject. There is remedial math, reading, and writing.

Campus Safety and Security: Measures include 24-hour foot and vehicle patrol, self-defense education, shuttle buses, and informal discussions. There are pamphlets/posters/films, emergency telephones, lighted pathways/sidewalks, and a 24-hour security camera surveillance system.

Programs of Study: Mercyhurst confers B.A., B.S., and B.M. degrees. Associate and master's degrees are also awarded. Bachelor's degrees are awarded in BIOLOGICAL SCIENCE (biochemistry, and biology/biological science), BUSINESS (accounting, banking and finance, business administration and management, fashion merchandising, hotel/motel and restaurant management, insurance and risk management,

management information systems, and marketing/retailing/merchandising), COMMUNICATIONS AND THE ARTS (advertising, broadcasting, communications, dance, English, graphic design, journalism, languages, music, musical theater, public relations, and studio art), COMPUTER AND PHYSICAL SCIENCE (chemistry, earth science, geology, mathematics, web services, and web technology), EDUCATION (art, athletic training, business, early childhood, elementary, home economics, mathematics, music, science, secondary, social science, and special), ENGINEERING AND ENVIRONMENTAL DESIGN (environmental science, and interior design), HEALTH PROFESSIONS (art therapy, medical laboratory technology, predentistry, premedicine, preosteopathy, prepharmacy, preveterinary science, and sports medicine), SOCIAL SCIENCE (anthropology, archeology, criminal justice, dietetics, family/consumer studies, forensic studies, history, philosophy, political science/government, prelaw, psychology, religion, religious education, social work, and sociology). Archeology/anthropology, research intelligence, and sports medicine are the strongest academically. Business, education, and sports medicine are the largest.

Required: To graduate, students must complete the core curriculum, which includes English, math, science, religion, philosophy, history, and a computer course. Distribution requirements include American history, cultural appreciation, human behavior, and ethics. A minimum GPA of 2.0 is required, with a 2.5 in the major, and a minimum total of 123 credit hours. The number of credit hours in the major varies, with a minimum of 30. A thesis is necessary for history and English majors.

Special: Mercyhurst offers cross-registration with Gannon University, internships in all majors through the co-op office, and study abroad in London and Dublin. Dual and student-designed majors, credit for life, military, or work experience, nondegree study, work-study, and a pass/fail grading option are also available. There are 7 national honor societies, a freshman honors program, and 4 departmental honors programs.

Faculty/Classroom: 57% of faculty are male; 43%, female. All teach undergraduates and 30% do research. No introductory courses are taught by graduate students. The average class size in an introductory lecture is 35; in a laboratory, 12; and in a regular course, 25.

Admissions: 77% of the 2001-2002 applicants were accepted. The SAT I scores for the 2001-2002 freshman class were: Verbal--33% below 500, 47% between 500 and 599, 19% between 600 and 700, and 2% above 700; Math--34% below 500, 47% between 500 and 599, 17% between 600 and 700, and 2% above 700. The ACT scores were 33% below 21, 37% between 21 and 23, 18% between 24 and 26, 7% between 27 and 28, and 5% above 28. 37% of the current freshmen were in the top fifth of their class; 71% were in the top two fifths. 17 freshmen graduated first in their class.

Requirements: The SAT I or ACT is required with recommended minimum scores of 450 verbal and 450 math on the SAT I or 19 on the ACT. Applicants must graduate from an accredited secondary school or have a GED. 16 academic credits are required, including 4 years of English, 3 each of math and social studies, and 2 each of history, science, and a foreign language. Interviews are recommended. Art applicants must submit portfolios; auditions are required of music and dance applicants. Mercyhurst requires applicants to be in the upper 50% of their class. A GPA of 2.75 is required. AP and CLEP credits are accepted. Important factors in the admissions decision are leadership record, evidence of special talent, and personality/intangible qualities. Applications are accepted on-line at the school's web site.

Procedure: Freshmen are admitted to all sessions. Entrance exams should be taken during the spring of the junior year. There are early admissions and deferred admissions plans. Application deadlines are open. The application fee is $30. Notification is on a rolling basis.

Transfer: 64 transfer students enrolled in 2001-2002. A minimum GPA of 2.0 on previous college work is required. 45 credits of 123 must be completed at Mercyhurst.

Visiting: There are regularly scheduled orientations for prospective students, including tours, class visits, faculty meetings, and interviews with financial aid and admissions counselors. There are guides for informal visits and visitors may sit in on classes and stay overnight. To schedule a visit, contact the Admissions Office at *admug@mercyhurst.edu*.

Financial Aid: In 2001-2002, 93% of all freshmen and 85% of continuing students received some form of financial aid. 86% of freshmen and 74% of continuing students received need-based aid. The average freshman award was $6952. Of that total, scholarships or need-based grants averaged $2750 ($8400 maximum); loans averaged $2100 ($4000 maximum); and work contracts averaged $900 ($1200 maximum). 88% of undergraduates work part time. Average annual earnings from campus work are $825. The average financial indebtedness of the 2001 graduate was $7800. Mercyhurst is a member of CSS. The FAFSA is required. The fall application deadline is May 1.

International Students: There are 91 international students enrolled. The school actively recruits these students. They must score 550 on the written TOEFL and also take the SAT I or the ACT.

Computers: The mainframe is a UNIX with a DEC ALPHA 1200 server running Unitdata DBMS. Students may access more than 225 terminals in labs across campus. All residences are networked to the mainframe, the Internet, and intranets. Faculty computers and the library's electronic search system are available for research. All students may access the system 24 hours a day, 7 days a week. There are no time limits. The fee is $210 per year.

Graduates: In 2001, 510 bachelor's degrees were awarded. The most popular majors were business (11%), education (10%), and hotel/restaurant management (8%). In an average class, 1% graduate in 3 years, 50% in 4 years, 58% in 5 years, and 62% in 6 years. 199 companies recruited on campus in 2000-2001. Of the 2000 graduating class, 16% were enrolled in graduate school within 6 months of graduation and 77% were employed.

Admissions Contact: Robin Engel, Director of Admissions. A video is available. E-mail: *rengel@mercyhusrt.edu* Web: *www.mercyhurst.edu*

MESSIAH COLLEGE — D-3

Grantham, PA 17027 — (717) 691-6000
(800) 233-4220; Fax: (717) 796-5374

Full-time: 1091 men, 1706 women	**Faculty:** 158; IIB, -$
Part-time: 18 men, 43 women	**Ph.D.s:** 70%
Graduate: none	**Student/Faculty:** 18 to 1
Year: semesters, summer session	**Tuition:** $17,210
Application Deadline: open	**Room & Board:** $5970
Freshman Class: 2231 applied, 1742 accepted, 702 enrolled	
SAT I Verbal/Math: 590/590	**ACT:** 25 **VERY COMPETITIVE**

Messiah College, founded in 1909, is a Christian college offering an education in the liberal and applied arts and sciences, and spiritually routed in the Anabaptist, Pietist, and Wesleyan traditions. There are 5 undergraduate schools. In addition to regional accreditation, Messiah has baccalaureate program accreditation with ABET, ADA, CSWE, NASM, and NLN. The library contains 252,148 volumes, 111,918 microform items, and 13,286 audiovisual forms/CDs, and subscribes to 1242 periodicals. Computerized library services include the card catalog, interlibrary loans, and database searching. Special learning facilities include a learning resource center, art gallery, natural history museum, and radio station. The 400-acre campus is in a small town 12 miles southwest of Harrisburg. Including residence halls, there are 43 buildings.

Student Life: 50% of undergraduates are from out of state, mostly the Middle Atlantic. Others are from 38 states, 25 foreign countries, and Canada. 84% are from public schools. 92% are white. Most are Protestant. The average age of freshmen is 18; all undergraduates, 20. 15% do not continue beyond their first year; 71% remain to graduate.

Housing: 2272 students can be accommodated in college housing, which includes single-sex and coed dormitories, on-campus apartments, and off-campus apartments. In addition, there are special-interest houses. On-campus housing is guaranteed for all 4 years. 86% of students live on campus; of those, 65% remain on campus on weekends. Alcohol is not permitted. All students may keep cars.

Activities: There are no fraternities or sororities. There are 60 groups on campus, including art, band, cheerleading, choir, chorale, chorus, dance, drama, ethnic, film, honors, international, jazz band, literary magazine, musical theater, newspaper, orchestra, pep band, political, professional, radio and TV, religious, social, social service, student government, symphony, and yearbook. Popular campus events include a cultural series, Susquehanna Valley Lyceum, and summer dinner concerts.

Sports: There are 10 intercollegiate sports for men and 10 for women, and 6 intramural sports for men and 6 for women. Facilities include indoor and outdoor tracks, a pool with separate diving well, wrestling and gymnastics areas, a weight room, numerous playing fields, and courts for racquetball, basketball, and tennis. The campus center provides additional recreational facilities.

Disabled Students: 80% of the campus is accessible. Wheelchair ramps, elevators, special parking, specially equipped rest rooms, special class scheduling, and lowered drinking fountains are available.

Services: Counseling and information services are available, as is tutoring in some subjects. There is a reader service for the blind and remedial reading and writing.

Campus Safety and Security: Measures include 24-hour foot and vehicle patrol, self-defense education, escort service, and informal discussions. There are pamphlets/posters/films, emergency telephones, and lighted pathways/sidewalks.

Programs of Study: Messiah confers B.A. and B.S. degrees. Bachelor's degrees are awarded in BIOLOGICAL SCIENCE (biochemistry and biology/biological science), BUSINESS (accounting, business administration and management, business systems analysis, international business management, marketing/retailing/merchandising, and personnel management), COMMUNICATIONS AND THE ARTS (art history and appreciation, broadcasting, communications, dramatic arts, English, French, German, journalism, music, Spanish, and studio art), COMPUTER AND PHYSICAL SCIENCE (chemistry, computer science, mathematics, and physics), EDUCATION (art, athletic training, early childhood, elementary, mathematics, music, physical, science, and social studies), ENGINEERING AND ENVIRONMENTAL DESIGN (civil engineering, engineering, and environmental science), HEALTH PROFESSIONS (exercise science, nursing, and recreation therapy), SOCIAL SCIENCE (biblical studies, dietetics, economics, family/consumer studies, history, humanities, ministries, philosophy, political science/government, psychology, religion, social work, and sociology). Elementary education, engineering, and nursing are the largest.

Required: To graduate, all students must complete at least 126 credits with a minimum GPA of 2.0. The last 30 credits must be taken at Messiah College and a minimum of 12 credits must be in the major. For general education requirements, students must take 9 credits each in Christian faith, math, natural sciences, humanities and arts, and languages and cultures; 6 credits each in social sciences and history and in interdisciplinary studies; 3 credits in first-year seminar, oral communications, a writing enrichment course, ethics, world views/pluralism, and health/phys ed; and 2 to 3 credits in non-Western studies.

Special: Students may cross-register at Temple University in Philadelphia. Off-campus study is available at Daystar University in Kenya, through Brethren Colleges Abroad, at Jerusalem University College, and through Latin American, Central American, Middle East, and Russian studies programs, among others. Off-campus options within the United States include the American Studies program, AuSable Institute of Environmental Studies, Los Angeles Film Studies, Oregon Extension, and others. Students may also spend a semester or year at any of 12 other Christian Consortium colleges in a student exchange program. Numerous internships, practicums, and ministry opportunities are available. There are 2 national honor societies, a freshman honors program, and 12 departmental honors programs.

Faculty/Classroom: 66% of faculty are male; 34%, female. All teach undergraduates. The average class size in an introductory lecture is 26; in a laboratory, 18; and in a regular course, 22.

Admissions: 78% of the 2001-2002 applicants were accepted. The SAT I scores for the 2001-2002 freshman class were: Verbal--10% below 500, 44% between 500 and 599, 35% between 600 and 700, and 11% above 700; Math--7% below 500, 45% between 500 and 599, 39% between 600 and 700, and 8% above 700. The ACT scores were 10% below 21, 20% between 21 and 23, 35% between 24 and 26, 13% between 27 and 28, and 22% above 28. 60% of the current freshmen were in the top fifth of their class; 83% were in the top two fifths. There were 16 National Merit finalists. 32 freshmen graduated first in their class.

Requirements: The SAT I or ACT is required. In addition, applicants must have graduated from an accredited high school or the equivalent. Secondary preparation of students who enroll usually includes 4 units in English, 3 or 4 in math, 3 each in natural science, social studies, and foreign languages, and 4 in academic electives. Students who enroll are usually in the top third of their class and have a B average or better. A campus visit with interview/information session is recommended. Potential music majors must audition. AP and CLEP credits are accepted. Important factors in the admissions decision are leadership record, recommendations by school officials, and advanced placement or honor courses. Applications are accepted on-line via Messiah's web page.

Procedure: Freshmen are admitted fall and spring. Entrance exams should be taken in the spring of the junior year. There are early decision, early admissions, and deferred admissions plans. Early decision applications should be filed by October 15; regular application deadlines are open. The fall 2001 application fee was $30. Notification of early decision is sent November 1; regular decision, on a rolling basis. 2% of all applicants are on a waiting list; 44 were accepted in 2001.

Transfer: 89 transfer students enrolled in 2001-2002. Applicants should have earned a 2.5 GPA in at least 30 college credits. The college prefers that applicants also have composite SAT I or ACT scores and that they seek a campus visit. Students with fewer than 30 credits in college should submit a high school transcript as well. 30 credits of 126 must be completed at Messiah.

Visiting: There are regularly scheduled orientations for prospective students, including a campus tour, academic and career advising, and a financial aid information session. There are guides for informal visits and visitors may sit in on classes and stay overnight. To schedule a visit, contact Nikki Holsinger at (800) 233-4220 or *nholsing@messiah.edu*.

Financial Aid: In 2001-2002, 96% of all freshmen and 94% of continuing students received some form of financial aid. 77% of freshmen and 73% of continuing students received need-based aid. The average freshman award was $14,012. Of that total, scholarships or need-based grants averaged $7532 ($16,860 maximum); loans averaged $4540 ($10,500 maximum); and work contracts averaged $1940 ($1950 maximum). 47% of undergraduates work part time. Average annual earnings from campus work are $2339. The average financial indebtedness of the 2001 graduate was $17,183. Messiah is a member of CSS. The FAFSA is required. The fall application deadline is April 1.

International Students: There are 60 international students enrolled. The school actively recruits these students. They must take the TOEFL and also either take the SAT I or the ACT.

Computers: The mainframe is an HP 3000 model 959/KS200. There are 463 computers for student use located in the computer center, the library, departmental and student center labs, and residence halls. Dorm rooms are wired for network connection for PCs. E-mail and Internet access are available. All students may access the system 24 hours a day. There are no time limits. The fee is $250.

Graduates: In 2001, 572 bachelor's degrees were awarded. The most popular majors were elementary education (9%), biology (6%), and family studies (6%). In an average class, 1% graduate in 3 years, 65% in 4 years, and 72% in 5 years. 585 companies recruited on campus in 2000-2001. Of the 2000 graduating class, 7% were enrolled in graduate school within 6 months of graduation and 90% were employed.

Admissions Contact: William G. Strausbaugh, Dean for Enrollment Management. A video is available. E-mail: *admiss@messiah.edu*
Web: *www.messiah.edu*

MILLERSVILLE UNIVERSITY OF PENNSYLVANIA E-4
Millersville, PA 17551-0302 (717) 872-3371
(800) MU-ADMIT; Fax: (717) 871-2147

Full-time: 2391 men, 3336 women	**Faculty:** 325; IIA, +$
Part-time: 358 men, 512 women	**Ph.D.s:** 86%
Graduate: 262 men, 697 women	**Student/Faculty:** 18 to 1
Year: 4-1-4, summer session	**Tuition:** $5053 ($11,077)
Application Deadline: open	**Room & Board:** $5100
Freshman Class: 5462 applied, 3684 accepted, 1271 enrolled	
SAT I Verbal/Math: 530/540	**ACT:** 21 **VERY COMPETITIVE**

Millersville University, founded as Lancaster County Normal School in 1855, is a public institution offering undergraduate and graduate programs in liberal arts and sciences and education. There are 3 undergraduate schools and 1 graduate school. In addition to regional accreditation, Millersville has baccalaureate program accreditation with ABET, ACBSP, CAHEA, CSAB, CSWE, NASM, NCATE, and NLN. The library contains 497,489 volumes, 553,491 microform items, and 30,609 audiovisual forms/CDs, and subscribes to 4081 periodicals. Computerized library services include the card catalog, interlibrary loans, and database searching. Special learning facilities include a learning resource center, art gallery, radio station, TV station, early childhood center, and foreign language lab. The 220-acre campus is in a small town 5 miles west of Lancaster. Including residence halls, there are 92 buildings.

Student Life: 96% of undergraduates are from Pennsylvania. Others are from 21 states, 48 foreign countries, and Canada. 90% are white. The average age of freshmen is 18; all undergraduates, 22. 17% do not continue beyond their first year; 67% remain to graduate.

Housing: 2515 students can be accommodated in college housing, which includes single-sex and coed dormitories and off-campus apartments. In addition, there are honors houses and special-interest houses, including service learning/leadership and international student house. On-campus housing is available on a first-come, first-served basis. 61% of students commute. Alcohol is not permitted. Upperclassmen may keep cars.

Activities: 7% of men belong to 1 local and 9 national fraternities; 8% of women belong to 2 local and 9 national sororities. There are 119 groups on campus, including art, band, cheerleading, choir, chorale, chorus, dance, drama, ethnic, gay, honors, international, jazz band, literary magazine, marching band, musical theater, newspaper, orchestra, pep band, political, professional, radio and TV, religious, social, social service, student government, symphony, and yearbook. Popular campus events include Parents Day, Wellness Week, and International Week.

Sports: There are 9 intercollegiate sports for men and 10 for women, and 10 intramural sports for men and 10 for women. Facilities include a football stadium, 2 pools, 2 gyms, 2 fitness centers, a dance studio, a ropes course, wrestling and weight rooms, basketball, volleyball, tennis, and badminton courts, and various playing fields.

Disabled Students: 85% of the campus is accessible. Wheelchair ramps, elevators, special parking, specially equipped rest rooms, special class scheduling, lowered drinking fountains, lowered telephones, and transportation assistance within campus, as well as individual accommodations when necessary, are available.

Services: Counseling and information services are available, as is tutoring in most subjects. There is a reader service for the blind, and remedial math, reading, and writing. Every effort is made to tailor a tutoring program to individual needs. Note takers, interpreters, and some physical aids and other specialized equipment are provided, as available.

Campus Safety and Security: Measures include 24-hour foot and vehicle patrol, self-defense education, escort service, and shuttle buses. There are informal discussions, pamphlets/posters/films, emergency telephones, lighted pathways/sidewalks, and regularly scheduled crime awareness programs.

Programs of Study: Millersville confers B.A., B.S., B.F.A., B.S.Ed., and B.S.N. degrees. Associate and master's degrees are also awarded. Bachelor's degrees are awarded in BIOLOGICAL SCIENCE (biology/biological science), BUSINESS (business administration and management), COMMUNICATIONS AND THE ARTS (art, communications, English, French, German, music, and Spanish), COMPUTER AND PHYSICAL SCIENCE (atmospheric sciences and meteorology, chemistry, computer science, earth science, geology, oceanography, and physics), EDUCATION (art, elementary, music, social studies, special, and technical), ENGINEERING AND ENVIRONMENTAL DESIGN (industrial engineering technology and occupational safety and health), HEALTH PROFESSIONS (nursing), SOCIAL SCIENCE (anthropology, economics, geography, history, international studies, philosophy, political science/government, psychology, social work, and sociology). Physical sciences and teacher education are the strongest academically. Elementary education, business administration, and biology are the largest.

Required: To graduate, all students must complete at least 120 hours, including 30 in the major, with a minimum 2.0 GPA. Courses are required in humanities, science and math, social sciences, and perspectives as part of a core curriculum. Specific courses are required in writing, speech, and phys ed.

Special: Numerous co-op and internship programs, including student teaching opportunities, are available. Millersville has exchange agreements with Franklin and Marshall College, Lancaster Theological Seminary, and Wallops Island Consortium, and 3-2 engineering programs with Pennsylvania State University and the University of Pennsylvania for chemistry and physics majors. Study abroad is offered in Germany, England, Japan, Scotland, and Chile. Dual majors are possible in most disciplines, and accelerated degrees and B.A.-B.S. degrees are available in many. Nondegree study is offered, and there are limited pass/fail options. There are 8 national honor societies and 9 departmental honors programs.

Faculty/Classroom: 58% of faculty are male; 42%, female. 96% teach undergraduates. No introductory courses are taught by graduate students. The average class size in an introductory lecture is 35; in a laboratory, 24; and in a regular course, 25.

Admissions: 67% of the 2001-2002 applicants were accepted. The SAT I scores for the 2001-2002 freshman class were: Verbal--33% below 500, 49% between 500 and 599, 17% between 600 and 700, and 2% above 700; Math--27% below 500, 50% between 500 and 599, 21% between 600 and 700, and 2% above 700. The ACT scores were 40% below 21, 34% between 21 and 23, 23% between 24 and 26, 2% between 27 and 28, and 2% above 28. 35% of the current freshmen were in the top fifth of their class; 77% were in the top two fifths. 13 freshmen graduated first in their class.

Requirements: The SAT I is required and the ACT is accepted, with minimum composite scores of 1020 – 1040 or 23, respectively. Applicants must be graduates of approved secondary schools or hold a GED. Secondary preparation should include 4 credits in English, 3 each in math and social studies, and 2 each in science and history. Music program applicants must audition. An interview is optional for all applicants. Millersville requires applicants to be in the upper 40% of their class. A GPA of 2.8 to 3.0 is required. AP and CLEP credits are accepted. Important factors in the admissions decision are advanced placement or honor courses, evidence of special talent, and recommendations by school officials. Applications are accepted on-line via CollegeNET and the university's web site.

Procedure: Freshmen are admitted to all sessions. Entrance exams should be taken in the spring of the junior year. There is a deferred admissions plan. Application deadlines are open. The fall 2001 application fee was $30. Notification is sent on a rolling basis.

Transfer: 376 transfer students enrolled in 2001-2002. All applicants must submit high school as well as college transcripts. Graduates of state community colleges are given preference over applicants with fewer than 2 and more than 5 semesters of study at other colleges. Applicants must have at least a 2.0 GPA. A personal interview is recommended. 30 credits of 120 must be completed at Millersville.

Visiting: There are regularly scheduled orientations for prospective students, including a president's welcome and admissions, financial aid, student organization, and department conferences. There are guides for informal visits and visitors may sit in on classes. To schedule a visit, contact the Admissions Office.

Financial Aid: In a recent year, 72% of all freshmen and 68% of continuing students received some form of financial aid. 49% of freshmen and 46% of continuing students received need-based aid. The average freshman award was $5097. Of that total, scholarships or need-based grants averaged $1765 ($10,475 maximum); loans averaged $2697 ($17,625 maximum); and work contracts averaged $183 ($2000 maximum). 33% of undergraduates work part time. Average annual earnings from campus work are $1287. The average financial indebtedness of a recent graduate was $9736. Millersville is a member of CSS. The FAFSA is required. The fall application deadline is March 15.

International Students: There are 88 international students enrolled. The school actively recruits these students. They must score 500 on the written TOEFL or 183 on the electronic version and also take the SAT I, scoring 1050, or the ACT.

Computers: The mainframes are an IBM 9121/260, a Sun ES-3000, a Sun SPARC 20, and an HP K250. Approved students are entitled to computer accounts to access the mainframes for e-mail, the Internet, and course work. There are 30 general-purpose computer labs on campus, housing PCs, Macs and Sun workstations. Most PCs are local area networked and all labs are connected to a campuswide network and the Internet. All students may access the system. There are no time limits and no fees. It is strongly recommended that all students have a personal computer.

Graduates: In 2001, 1225 bachelor's degrees were awarded. The most popular majors were elementary education (16%), business administration (12%), and biology (8%). In an average class, 1% graduate in 3 years, 35% in 4 years, 62% in 5 years, and 67% in 6 years. 75 companies recruited on campus in 2000-2001. Of the 2000 graduating class, 20% were enrolled in graduate school within 6 months of graduation and 78% were employed.

Admissions Contact: Darrell Davis, Director of Admissions.
E-mail: *admissions@millersville.edu* Web: *www.millersville.edu/~admit*

MOORE COLLEGE OF ART AND DESIGN — F-3

Philadelphia, PA 19103 — **(215) 568-4515, ext. 1105**
(800) 523-2025, ext. 1105; Fax: (215) 568-8017

Full-time: 457 women	**Faculty:** 35
Part-time: 156 women	**Ph.D.s:** 83%
Graduate: none	**Student/Faculty:** 13 to 1
Year: semesters	**Tuition:** $16,795
Application Deadline: open	**Room & Board:** $6330
Freshman Class: 398 applied, 214 accepted, 108 enrolled	
SAT I Verbal/Math: 510/486	**SPECIAL**

Moore College of Art and Design, founded in 1844, is the oldest professional and fine arts college for women in the country. In addition to regional accreditation, Moore has baccalaureate program accreditation with FIDER and NASAD. The library contains 34,000 volumes, and subscribes to 250 periodicals. Computerized library services include the card catalog, interlibrary loans, and database searching. Special learning facilities include an art gallery and 2 art galleries. The 4-acre campus is in an urban area in Philadelphia. Including residence halls, there are 4 buildings.

Student Life: 60 % of undergraduates are from Pennsylvannia. Others are from 27 states, 8 foreign countries, and Canada. 60% are from public schools. 85% are white. The average age of freshmen is 18; all undergraduates, 20. 15% do not continue beyond their first year; 55% remain to graduate.

Housing: 200 students can be accommodated in college housing, which includes single-sex dormitories and on-campus apartments. On-campus housing is guaranteed for all 4 years. 50% of students live on campus; of those, 75% remain on campus on weekends. Alcohol is not permitted. All students may keep cars.

Activities: There are no fraternities. There are 10 groups on campus, including computers, environmental action, ethnic, film, gay, international, newspaper, professional, social service, student government, and yearbook. Popular campus events include Family Day, Spring Fling, Convocation, student art shows, and openings at the college gallery.

Sports: There is no sports program at Moore. Facilities include a fitness center with a weight room.

Disabled Students: All of the campus is accessible. Wheelchair ramps, elevators, special parking, specially equipped rest rooms, lowered drinking fountains, and lowered telephones are available.

Services: Counseling and information services are available, as is tutoring in most subjects.

Campus Safety and Security: Measures include 24-hour foot and vehicle patrol, self-defense education, escort service, and shuttle buses. There are informal discussions, pamphlets/posters/films, and lighted pathways/sidewalks.

Programs of Study: Moore confers the B.F.A. degree. Bachelor's degrees are awarded in COMMUNICATIONS AND THE ARTS (fine arts, graphic design, illustration, painting, printmaking, and sculpture), EDUCATION (art), ENGINEERING AND ENVIRONMENTAL DESIGN (interior design), SOCIAL SCIENCE (fashion design and technology and textiles and clothing). Interior design is the strongest academically. Graphic design is the largest.

Required: All students take 36 credits in basic arts, including design, drawing, color, and art history, and a liberal arts core in history, humanities, and social science. A total of 125 to 137 credits, with a 2.0 minimum GPA, is required for graduation.

Special: Moore has long-established cooperative relationships with various employers who provide training to supplement academic studies in all majors. Dual majors, nondegree study, and continuing education programs are offered.

Faculty/Classroom: 49% of faculty are male; 51%, female. All teach undergraduates. The average class size in an introductory lecture is 20 and in a regular course, 10.

Admissions: 54% of the 2001-2002 applicants were accepted. The SAT I scores for the 2001-2002 freshman class were: Verbal--45% below 500, 37% between 500 and 599, 16% between 600 and 700, and 2% above 700; Math--59% below 500, 31% between 500 and 599, and 9% between 600 and 700.

Requirements: The SAT I is recommended. In addition, applicants should be graduates of accredited high schools or the equivalent, having taken 4 years of English and 2 years each of social studies, science, and math. At least 2 years of art study are also recommended. The most important part of the application is the portfolio of 8 to 12 original pieces, 6 of which should be drawings from observation. In addition, Moore strongly recommends a personal interview. A GPA of 2.5 is required. AP and CLEP credits are accepted. Important factors in the admissions decision are evidence of special talent, personality/intangible qualities, and extracurricular activities record.

Procedure: Freshmen are admitted in the fall. There are early admissions and deferred admissions plans. Application deadlines are open. Notification is sent on a rolling basis. The fall 2001 application fee was $35.

Transfer: 53 transfer students enrolled in 2001-2002. Transfer applicants from non-art programs must meet freshman admission requirements. Others must submit a portfolio for review. Applicants should have at least a 2.0 GPA in previous college work, and submit composite SAT I scores of at least 800. A personal interview is required. 62 credits of 124 must be completed at Moore.

Visiting: There are regularly scheduled orientations for prospective students, including an open house in November. There are guides for informal visits and visitors may sit in on classes and stay overnight. To schedule a visit, contact the Admissions Office.

Financial Aid: In a recent year, 75% of all freshmen received some form of financial aid, including need-based aid. The average freshman award was $12,664. The average financial indebtedness of a recent year's graduate was $25,000. Moore is a member of CSS. The CSS/Profile and the college's own financial statement are required. The fall application deadline is April 1.

International Students: There are 16 international students enrolled. The school actively recruits these students. They must score 500 on the written TOEFL.

Computers: Macintosh PCs are available in the computer graphics labs. The CAD lab is PC-based for Interior Design. There are no time limits and no fees.

Graduates: In 2001, 83 bachelor's degrees were awarded. The most popular majors were graphic design (28%), fashion design (22%), and fine arts (20%). In an average class, 55% graduate in 4 years. Of the 2000 graduating class, 5% were enrolled in graduate school within 6 months of graduation.

Admissions Contact: Wendy Pyle Elliott, Director of Admissions.
E-mail: *admiss@moore.edu* Web: *www.moore.edu*

MORAVIAN COLLEGE

Bethlehem, PA 18018 F-3
(610) 861-1320
(800) 441-3191; Fax: (610) 625-7930

Full-time: 512 men, 770 women	**Faculty:** 102; IIB, +$
Part-time: 22 men, 20 women	**Ph.D.s:** 83%
Graduate: 50 men, 88 women	**Student/Faculty:** 13 to 1
Year: semesters, summer session	**Tuition:** $20,495
Application Deadline: March 1	**Room & Board:** $6570

Freshman Class: 1502 applied, 1014 accepted, 317 enrolled
SAT I Verbal/Math: 562/560 (mean) **VERY COMPETITIVE**

Moravian College, established in 1742, is a private liberal arts institution affiliated with the Moravian Church. There are 3 graduate schools. In addition to regional accreditation, Moravian has baccalaureate program accreditation with ACS, CAHEA, and NASM. The library contains 247,841 volumes, 10,264 microform items and 1462 audiovisual forms/CDs, and subscribes to 1318 periodicals. Computerized library services include the card catalog, interlibrary loans, and database searching. Special learning facilities include a learning resource center, art gallery, and radio station. The 80-acre campus is in a suburban area 60 miles north of Philadelphia and 90 miles west of New York City. Including residence halls, there are 55 buildings.

Student Life: 63% of undergraduates are from Pennsylvania. Others are from 19 states and 18 foreign countries. 93% are white. 44% are Protestant; 40%, Catholic. The average age of freshmen is 18; all undergraduates, 20. 19% do not continue beyond their first year; 75% remain to graduate.

Housing: 993 students can be accommodated in college housing, which includes single-sex and coed dormitories, on-campus apartments, off-campus apartments, fraternity houses, and sorority houses. In addition, there are special-interest houses. On-campus housing is guaranteed for all 4 years. 73% of students live on campus; of those, 65% remain on campus on weekends. Upperclassmen may keep cars.

Activities: 14% of men belong to 2 national fraternities; 22% of women belong to 4 national sororities. There are 77 groups on campus, including art, band, cheerleading, choir, chorale, chorus, computers, dance, debate, drama, ethnic, gay, honors, international, jazz band, literary magazine, marching band, newspaper, orchestra, outdoor recreation, pep band, photography, political, professional, radio and TV, religious, social, social service, student alumni, student government, and yearbook. Popular campus events include arts and lecture series, Christmas vesper services, and Mardi Gras dance.

Sports: There are 8 intercollegiate sports for men and 9 for women, and 14 intramural sports for men and 14 for women. Facilities include a 1200-seat gym, football, soccer, field hockey, and lacrosse fields, baseball and softball diamonds, indoor and all-weather tracks, indoor and outdoor tennis courts, a field house, a fitness room, an aerobics and dance studio, and 4 multipurpose courts.

Disabled Students: 75% of the campus is accessible. Wheelchair ramps, elevators, special parking, specially equipped rest rooms, special class scheduling, and lowered drinking fountains are available.

Services: Counseling and information services are available, as is tutoring in most subjects. There is a reader service for the blind, peer assistance, and a writing center.

Campus Safety and Security: Measures include 24-hour foot and vehicle patrol, self-defense education, escort service, and shuttle buses. There are informal discussions, pamphlets/posters/films, emergency telephones, lighted pathways/sidewalks, and ongoing crime prevention program supervised by a crime prevention officer.

Programs of Study: Moravian confers B.A., B.S., and B.Mus. degrees. Master's degrees are also awarded. Bachelor's degrees are awarded in BIOLOGICAL SCIENCE (biology/biological science), BUSINESS (accounting, business economics, international business management, and management science), COMMUNICATIONS AND THE ARTS (art history and appreciation, dramatic arts, English, French, German, graphic design, Greek, music, Spanish, and studio art), COMPUTER AND PHYSICAL SCIENCE (chemistry, computer science, information sciences and systems, mathematics, and physics), EDUCATION (art, elementary, music, and secondary), HEALTH PROFESSIONS (nursing), SOCIAL SCIENCE (counseling/psychology, criminal justice, developmental psychology, economics, experimental psychology, history, industrial and organizational psychology, philosophy, political science/government, prelaw, psychology, religion, social science, and sociology). Education, biology, and chemistry are the strongest academically. Psychology, management, and sociology are the largest.

Required: Students must complete a Learning in Common curriculum, which includes courses in writing, quantitative reasoning, historical studies, ultimate questions, cultural values and global issues, natural sciences, a foreign language, math, social sciences, aesthetic expression, literature, and phys ed. To graduate, students must maintain a minimum GPA of 2.0 and complete 32 courses equivalent to 128 credits. The number of hours required in the major varies.

Special: The college offers 3-2 engineering degrees in conjunction with the University of Pennsylvania and Washington University and a 4-1 engineering program with the University of Pennsylvania. Moravian also offers cooperative programs in allied health, natural resource management, and geology with Lehigh, Duke, and Thomas Jefferson Universities. Cross-registration is available with Lehigh University and Lafayette, Muhlenberg, Cedar Crest, and Allentown Colleges. Internships, study abroad in many countries, a Washington semester, dual majors, and student-designed majors may be pursued. There are 17 national honor societies and honors programs in all departments.

Faculty/Classroom: 57% of faculty are male; 43%, female. All teach undergraduates. No introductory courses are taught by graduate students. The average class size in an introductory lecture is 20; in a laboratory, 15; and in a regular course, 20.

Admissions: 68% of the 2001-2002 applicants were accepted. The SAT I scores for the 2001-2002 freshman class were: Verbal--19% below 500, 51% between 500 and 599, 24% between 600 and 700, and 6% above 700; Math--19% below 500, 54% between 500 and 599, 22% between 600 and 700, and 5% above 700. 50% of the current freshmen were in the top fifth of their class; 82% were in the top two fifths. 4 freshmen graduated first in their class.

Requirements: The SAT I or ACT is required. In addition, applicants must graduate from an accredited secondary school or have a GED. Moravian requires 16 Carnegie units, based on 4 years each of English and social science, 3 to 4 of math, and 2 each of lab science, foreign language, and electives. Essays are required and interviews are recommended. For music students, auditions are required; for art students, portfolios are recommended. AP and CLEP credits are accepted. Important factors in the admissions decision are advanced placement or honor courses, recommendations by school officials, and leadership record. Applications are accepted on-line at the school's web site or via Common App.

Procedure: Freshmen are admitted fall and spring. Entrance exams should be taken with enough time to submit scores by the application deadline. There are early decision and deferred admissions plans. Early decision applications should be filed by February 1; regular applications, by March 1 for fall entry and December 1 for spring entry. The fall application fee was $30. Notification of early decision is sent beginning December 15; regular decision, March 15. 77 early decision candidates were accepted for the 2001-2002 class. A waiting list is an active part of the admissions procedure.

Transfer: 71 transfer students enrolled in 2001-2002. Applicants must have a minimum GPA of 2.5 and are required to submit recommendations, secondary and postsecondary transcripts, and standardized test scores. 32 credits of 128 must be completed at Moravian.

Visiting: There are regularly scheduled orientations for prospective students, including tours and interviews with admissions staff. There are guides for informal visits and visitors may sit in on classes and stay overnight. To schedule a visit, contact the Office of Admission.

Financial Aid: In a recent year, 91% of all freshmen and 85% of continuing students received some form of financial aid. 75% of freshmen and 77% of continuing students received need-based aid. The average freshman award was $14,147. Of that total, scholarships or need-based grants averaged $10,500 ($20,115 maximum); loans averaged $3179 ($5625 maximum); and work contracts averaged $1425 ($2000 maximum). 52% of undergraduates work part time. Average annual earnings from campus work are $725. Moravian is a member of CSS. The CSS/Profile or FAFSA is required. The fall application deadline is March 15.

International Students: There are 26 international students enrolled. The school actively recruits these students. They must score 550 on the written TOEFL or 213 on the electronic version; the SAT I or ACT is preferred for all students and required if the student's first language is English.

Computers: A high-speed campus network accessible from dormitories includes public access labs and 150 terminals (PC and Mac). The network provides students with shared applications, shared printing services, e-mail, and access to the Internet and the Web. All students may access the system 24 hours per day. There are no time limits and no fees.

Graduates: In 2001, 339 bachelor's degrees were awarded. The most popular majors were social sciences/history (24%), business (19%), and psychology (15%). In an average class, 71% graduate in 4 years, and 75% in 5 years. 30 companies recruited on campus in 2000-2001. Of the 2000 graduating class, 19% were enrolled in graduate school within 6 months of graduation and 71% were employed.

Admissions Contact: James P. Mackin, Director of Admission. E-mail: *admissions@moravian.edu* Web: *http://www.moravian.edu*

MOUNT ALOYSIUS COLLEGE — C-3

Cresson, PA 16630 — (814) 886-6383; (888) 823-2220; Fax: (814) 886-6441

Full-time: 215 men, 645 women	**Faculty:** 51
Part-time: 73 men, 220 women	**Ph.D.s:** 29%
Graduate: none	**Student/Faculty:** 17 to 1
Year: semesters, summer session	**Tuition:** $12,996
Application Deadline: open	**Room & Board:** $5190
Freshman Class: 730 applied, 651 accepted, 439 enrolled	
SAT I Verbal/Math: 450/460	**ACT:** 19 **LESS COMPETITIVE**

Mount Aloysius, founded in 1939 by the Sisters of Mercy, is a private, liberal arts college affiliated with the Roman Catholic Church. In addition to regional accreditation, Mount Aloysius College has baccalaureate program accreditation with APTA and NLN. The library contains 65,000 volumes, 3300 microform items, and 3400 audiovisual forms/CDs, and subscribes to 275 periodicals. Computerized library services include the card catalog, interlibrary loans, and database searching. Special learning facilities include a learning resource center and art gallery. The 75-acre campus is in a small town located in the southern Allegheny Mountains between Altoona and Johnstown. Including residence halls, there are 8 buildings.

Student Life: 94% of undergraduates are from Pennsylvania. Others are from 7 states, 7 foreign countries, and Canada. 80% are white. 60% are Catholic; 39% Protestant. The average age of freshmen is 18; all undergraduates, 27. 22% do not continue beyond their first year; 67% remain to graduate.

Housing: 200 students can be accommodated in college housing, which includes single-sex dormitories. In addition, there are rooms for hearing-impaired students.On-campus housing is guaranteed for all 4 years. 80% of students commute. Alcohol is not permitted. All students may keep cars.

Activities: There are no fraternities or sororities. There are 25 groups on campus, including art, cheerleading, chorale, chorus, computers, drama, honors, musical theater, newspaper, photography, professional, religious, student government, and yearbook. Popular campus events include Madrigal Dinner, Family Day, and Mercyfest Weekend.

Sports: There are 5 intercollegiate sports for men and 5 for women, and 10 intramural sports for men and 10 for women. Facilities include an 1800-seat health and physical fitness center with 3 basketball courts, 2 tennis courts, a volleyball court, a weight-and-exercise room equipped with a sauna, and 2 locker rooms.

Disabled Students: 95% of the campus is accessible. Wheelchair ramps, elevators, special parking, specially equipped rest rooms, lowered drinking fountains, and lowered telephones are available.

Services: Counseling and information services are available, as is tutoring in every subject. There is remedial math, reading, and writing.

Campus Safety and Security: Measures include 24-hour foot and vehicle patrol, escort service, informal discussions, and pamphlets/posters/films. There are emergency telephones and lighted pathways/sidewalks.

Programs of Study: Mount Aloysius College confers B.A., B.S., B.S. Ed., and B.S.N. degrees. Associate degrees are also awarded. Bachelor's degrees are awarded in BUSINESS (accounting and business administration and management), COMMUNICATIONS AND THE ARTS (English), EDUCATION (elementary), HEALTH PROFESSIONS (nursing and occupational therapy), SOCIAL SCIENCE (criminology, interpreter for the deaf, prelaw, and psychology). Occupational therapy, nursing, and prelaw are the strongest academically. Nursing, criminology, and elementary education are the largest.

Required: Baccalaureate-level students are required during their final semester of study to complete 2 3-credit courses designed to integrate and synthesize scientific, behavioral, and moral concepts. A total of 120 credits is required with an overall 2.0 GPA, including a C average in all core courses.

Special: The Professional Studies curriculum provides a student-designed course of study, with an emphasis in behavior and social science, humanities, math/science/computer science, or prelaw. Clinical experiences must be completed for allied-health-related programs. There are 3 national honor societies, a freshman honors program, and 1 departmental honors program.

Faculty/Classroom: 45% of faculty are male; 55%, female. All both teach and do research. The average class size in an introductory lecture is 15; in a laboratory, 10; and in a regular course, 25.

Admissions: 89% of the 2001-2002 applicants were accepted. The SAT I scores for the 2001-2002 freshman class were: Verbal--73% below 500, 24% between 500 and 599, and 3% between 600 and 700; Math--80% below 500, 18% between 500 and 599, and 2% between 600 and 700. The ACT scores were 92% below 21, and 8% between 24 and 26. 11% of the current freshmen were in the top fifth of their class; 25% were in the top two fifths.

Requirements: The SAT I or ACT is required. In addition, applicants must graduate from an accredited high school or have the GED. A placement test and any necessary developmental studies classes may need to be taken. Science classes and an interview are required of some allied health programs. A GPA of 2.5 is required. AP and CLEP credits are accepted. Important factors in the admissions decision are recommendations by school officials, advanced placement or honor courses, and leadership record. On-line applications are available at the school's web site. The universal application from Peterson's is also accepted.

Procedure: Freshmen are admitted fall and spring. Entrance exams should be taken as early as possible. There is an early admissions plan. Application deadlines are open. The application fee is $25. Notification is sent on a rolling basis.

Transfer: 190 transfer students enrolled in 2001-2002. Transfer students must have a 2.0 GPA. Only courses with a C or better will be considered for transfer; all other requirements are the same as for freshmen. 30 credits of 120 must be completed at Mount Aloysius College.

Visiting: There are regularly scheduled orientations for prospective students, including 3 daily sessions. There are guides for informal visits and visitors may sit in on classes and stay overnight. To schedule a visit, contact the Admissions Office.

Financial Aid: In 2001-2002, 99% of all freshmen and 95% of continuing students received some form of financial aid. 94% of freshmen and 86% of continuing students received need-based aid. The average freshman award was $10,000. Of that total, scholarships or need-based grants averaged $2000 ($5000 maximum); loans averaged $2625 (maximum); work contracts averaged $2000 (maximum); and includes monies from other Title IV sources averaged $3375 (maximum). All undergraduates work part time. Average annual earnings from campus work are $1500. The average financial indebtedness of the 2001 graduate was $13,500. The FAFSA is required. The fall application deadline is May 1.

International Students: There are 23 international students enrolled. The school actively recruits these students. They must score 500 on the written TOEFL or 173 on the electronic version and also take the college's own entrance exam or the New Jersey Basic Skills Test.

Computers: The mainframe is a network system. Several computer labs are available for student use. The library houses 28 terminals with full Internet access. The residence hall houses computer labs for resident student use. There are also computer labs in the main academic building. All students may access the system from 8 A.M. to 10 P.M. There are no time limits and no fees.

Graduates: In 2001, 70 bachelor's degrees were awarded. The most popular majors were nursing (30%), occupational therapy (25%), and professional studies (19%). 30 companies recruited on campus in a recent year. Of a recent graduating class, 22% were enrolled in graduate school within 6 months of graduation and 80% were employed.

Admissions Contact: Francis Crouse, Dean of Enrollment Management. E-mail: *admissions@mtaloy.edu* Web: *www.mtaloy.edu*

MUHLENBERG COLLEGE E-3
Allentown, PA 18104 **(484) 664-3200; Fax: (484) 664-3234**

Full-time: 980 men, 1331 women **Faculty:** 146; IIB, av$
Part-time: 138 men, 106 women **Ph.D.s:** 93%
Graduate: none **Student/Faculty:** 16 to 1
Year: semesters, summer session **Tuition:** $22,210
Application Deadline: February 15 **Room & Board:** $5960
Freshman Class: 3892 applied, 1374 accepted, 573 enrolled
SAT I Verbal/Math: 602/612 **HIGHLY COMPETITIVE**

Muhlenberg College, established in 1848, is a private liberal arts institution affiliated with the Lutheran Church. The library contains 210,100 volumes, 160,000 microform items, and 4480 audiovisual forms/CDs, and subscribes to 800 periodicals. Computerized library services include the card catalog, interlibrary loans, and database searching. Special learning facilities include a learning resource center, art gallery, natural history museum, radio station, TV station, and two 40-acre environmental field stations. The 80-acre campus is in a suburban area 50 miles north of Philadelphia and 90 miles west of New York City. Including residence halls, there are 61 buildings.

Student Life: 67% of undergraduates are from out of state, mostly the Middle Atlantic. Others are from 34 states, 9 foreign countries, and Canada. 70% are from public schools. 92% are white. 31% are Catholic; 30%, Protestant; 23% Jewish; 14% claim no religious affiliation. The average age of freshmen is 18; all undergraduates, 20. 7% do not continue beyond their first year; 81% remain to graduate.

Housing: 1908 students can be accommodated in college housing, which includes single-sex and coed dormitories, on-campus apartments, off-campus apartments, fraternity houses, and sorority houses. In addition, there are language houses, and special-interest houses, and independent living expreience houses. All college-sponsored housing is guaranteed for all 4 years. 95% of students live on campus; of those, 80% remain on campus on weekends. Upperclassmen may keep cars.

Activities: 26% of men belong to 5 national fraternities; 27% of women belong to 4 national sororities. There are 108 groups on campus, including art, band, cheerleading, chess, choir, chorale, chorus, computers, dance, drama, ethnic, gay, honors, human rights, international, jazz band, literary magazine, musical theater, newspaper, opera, orchestra, pep band, photography, political, professional, radio and TV, religious, social, social service, student government, and yearbook. Popular campus events include Spring Fling Weekend, Valentine Birthday Party, and Community Service Weekend.

Sports: There are 11 intercollegiate sports for men and 11 for women, and 13 intramural sports for men and 13 for women. Facilities include a sports center, which contains a 6-lane swimming pool, racquetball and squash courts, and wrestling and weight training rooms; a multipurpose field house with indoor tennis courts, a running track, and a fitness loft; and outdoor volleyball courts, athletic fields, tennis courts, a soccer stadium, an all-weather track, and a football stadium.

Disabled Students: 95% of the campus is accessible. Wheelchair ramps, elevators, special parking, specially equipped rest rooms, special class scheduling, lowered drinking fountains, lowered telephones, and extra time on tests, tutors, and books on tape are available.

Services: Counseling and information services are available, as is tutoring in every subject. There is a reader service for the blind. The college also maintains a writing center.

Campus Safety and Security: Measures include 24-hour foot and vehicle patrol, self-defense education, escort service, and shuttle buses. There are informal discussions, pamphlets/posters/films, emergency telephones, and lighted pathways/sidewalks.

Programs of Study: Muhlenberg confers B.A. and B.S. degrees. Bachelor's degrees are awarded in BIOLOGICAL SCIENCE (biochemistry and biology/biological science), BUSINESS (accounting and business administration and management), COMMUNICATIONS AND THE ARTS (art, communications, dance, dramatic arts, English, fine arts, French, German, music, and Spanish), COMPUTER AND PHYSICAL SCIENCE (chemistry, computer science, mathematics, natural sciences, physical sciences, and physics), ENGINEERING AND ENVIRONMENTAL DESIGN (environmental science), SOCIAL SCIENCE (American studies, economics, German area studies, history, international studies, philosophy, political science/government, psychology, religion, Russian and Slavic studies, social science, and sociology). Biology, drama, and English are the strongest academically. Biology, business administration, and psychology are the largest.

Required: To graduate, students must have a minimum GPA of 2.0 in a total of 34 course units, with 9 to 14 units in the major. Students must complete requirements in literature and the arts, religion or philosophy, human behavior and social institutions, historical studies, physical and life sciences, and other cultures. All students must take 1 quarter of phys ed, including a wellness course, as well as freshman and senior seminars.

Special: Students may cross-register with Lehigh, Lafayette, Cedar Crest, Moravian, and Allentown Colleges. Internships, work-study programs, study abroad in Asia, Latin America, Russia, and Europe, and a Washington semester are available. Muhlenberg also offers dual and student-designed majors, 3-2 engineering degree with Columbia and Washington Universities, a 4-4 assured admission medical program with MCP Hahnemann University, a 3-4 dental program with the University of Pennsylvania, a 3-2 forestry degree with Duke University, nondegree study and a pass/fail grading option. There are 12 national honor societies, including Phi Beta Kappa, a freshman honors program, and 9 departmental honors programs.

Faculty/Classroom: 53% of faculty are male; 47%, female. All teach undergraduates and 60% also do research. The average class size in an introductory lecture is 30; in a laboratory, 18; and in a regular course, 19.

Admissions: 35% of the 2001-2002 applicants were accepted. The SAT I scores for the 2001-2002 freshman class were: Verbal--5% below 500, 47% between 500 and 599, 40% between 600 and 700, and 8% above 700; Math--4% below 500, 46% between 500 and 599, 41% between 600 and 700, and 9% above 700. 67% of the current freshmen were in the top fifth of their class; 92% were in the top two fifths. There were 3 National Merit semifinalists. 7 freshmen graduated first in their class.

Requirements: Applicants must graduate from an accredited secondary school or have a GED. 16 Carnegie units are required, and students must complete 4 courses in English, 3 in math, and 2 each in history, science, and a foreign language. All students must submit essays. Interviews are recommended and are required for those who do not submit SAT I scores. AP and CLEP credits are accepted. Important factors in the admissions decision are advanced placement or honor courses, leadership record, and evidence of special talent. Applications are accepted on-line via Common App.

Procedure: Freshmen are admitted fall and spring. Entrance exams should be taken during the spring of the junior year or the fall of the senior year. There are early decision, early admissions, and deferred admissions plans. Early decision applications should be filed by January 15; regular applications, by February 15 for fall entry, along with a $50 fee. Notification of early decision is sent February 1; regular decision, March 15. 310 early decision candidates were accepted for the 2001-2002 class. 20% of all applicants are on a waiting list; 6 were accepted in 2001.

Transfer: 8 transfer students enrolled in 2001-2002. A minimum college GPA of 2.5 and an interview are required. 17 courses of 34 must be completed at Muhlenberg.

Visiting: There are regularly scheduled orientations for prospective students, consisting of a tour of the campus and a personal interview. There are 2 open houses in the fall and 1 in the spring. There are guides for informal visits and visitors may sit in on classes and stay overnight. To schedule a visit, contact Bonnie Reabold or Heather Brown at (484) 664-3202.

Financial Aid: In 2001-2002, 68% of all freshmen and 67% of continuing students received some form of financial aid. 62% of freshmen and 60% of continuing students received need-based aid. The average freshman award was $15,324. Of that total, scholarships or need-based grants averaged $10,546 ($21,000 maximum); loans averaged $1928 ($4625 maximum); work contracts averaged $1800 (maximum) and state or federal grant aid averaged $1050 ($8320 maximum). 49% of undergraduates work part time. Average annual earnings from campus work are $1685. The average financial indebtedness of the 2001 graduate was $12,850. Muhlenberg is a member of CSS. The CSS/Profile or FAFSA, the college's own financial statement, and parent and student tax returns and W-2 forms are required. The fall application deadline is February 15.

International Students: There are 9 international students enrolled. The school actively recruits these students. They must score 550 on the written TOEFL.

Computers: The mainframes are an HP 3000/Series 70 and 2 HP 9000s. Students may access the campus network and Internet from the computer labs, classrooms, or residence halls. There are more than 200 PCs available to students in labs and computer lounges throughout the campus. The campus network spans 17 city blocks and connects all 61 campus buildings. All students may access the system 24 hours a day. There are no time limits and no fees. It is strongly recommended that all students have a personal computer.

Graduates: In 2001, 354 bachelor's degrees were awarded. The most popular majors were business (14%), psychology (12%), and communication (11%). In an average class, 1% graduate in 3 years, 78% in 4 years, 80% in 5 years, and 82% in 6 years. 64 companies recruited on campus in 2000-2001. Of the 2000 graduating class, 25% were enrolled in graduate school within 6 months of graduation and 71% were employed.

Admissions Contact: Christopher Hooker-Haring, Dean, Admissions. E-mail: *admissions@muhlenberg.edu* Web: *www.muhlenberg.edu*

NEUMANN COLLEGE
E-4

Aston, PA 19014-1298
(610) 558-5616
(800) 9NEUMAN; Fax: (610) 558-5652

Full-time: 491 men, 841 women	**Faculty:** 54; IIB, --$
Part-time: 120 men, 289 women	**Ph.D.s:** 67%
Graduate: 67 men, 206 women	**Student/Faculty:** 25 to 1
Year: semesters, summer session	**Tuition:** $15,030
Application Deadline: open	**Room & Board:** $7010

Freshman Class: 1131 applied, 1092 accepted, 363 enrolled
SAT I Verbal/Math: 450/430 **NONCOMPETITIVE**

Neumann College, founded in 1965 by the Sisters of St. Francis, is a private liberal arts institution affiliated with the Roman Catholic Church. There are 5 graduate schools. In addition to regional accreditation, Neumann has baccalaureate program accreditation with CAHEA, CAPTE, and NLN. The library contains 86,200 volumes, 95,000 microform items, and 4200 audiovisual forms/CDs, and subscribes to 700 periodicals. Computerized library services include the card catalog, interlibrary loans, and database searching. Special learning facilities include a learning resource center and a learning assistance center. The 37-acre campus is in a suburban area 15 miles southwest of Philadelphia. Including residence halls, there are 5 buildings.

Student Life: 72% of undergraduates are from Pennsylvania. Others are from 19 states and 4 foreign countries. 40% are from public schools. 84% are white; 14%, African American. 66% are Catholic; 14%, Protestant; 10%, Buddhist, Quaker, or other.10% claim no religious affiliation. The average age of freshmen is 18; all undergraduates, 20. 24% do not continue beyond their first year; 67% remain to graduate.

Housing: 573 students can be accommodated in college housing, which includes coed dormitories. On-campus housing is available on a first-come, first-served basis. 55% of students commute. Alcohol is not permitted. All students may keep cars.

Activities: There are no fraternities or sororities. There are 17 groups on campus, including chorus, dance, drama, ethnic, honors, literary magazine, political, professional, religious, social, social service, and student government. Popular campus events include dinner dances, Spring Fling, and charity fund-raising.

Sports: There are 8 intercollegiate sports for men and 9 for women, and 3 intramural sports for men and 3 for women. Facilities include a 350-seat gym, weight and fitness rooms, tennis courts, baseball and softball fields, video games, and a theater.

Disabled Students: All of the campus is accessible. Wheelchair ramps, elevators, special parking, specially equipped rest rooms, and special class scheduling are available.

Services: Counseling and information services are available, as is tutoring in most subjects. There is a reader service for the blind, and remedial math, reading, and writing.

Campus Safety and Security: Measures include 24-hour foot and vehicle patrol, self-defense education, escort service, and shuttle buses. There are informal discussions, pamphlets/posters/films, emergency telephones, and lighted pathways/sidewalks.

Programs of Study: Neumann confers B.A. and B.S. degrees. Associate and master's degrees are also awarded. Bachelor's degrees are awarded in BIOLOGICAL SCIENCE (biology/biological science), BUSINESS (accounting, business administration and management, international business management, marketing and distribution, and sports management), COMMUNICATIONS AND THE ARTS (communications and English), COMPUTER AND PHYSICAL SCIENCE (computer science and information sciences and systems), EDUCATION (early childhood and elementary), HEALTH PROFESSIONS (clinical science and nursing), SOCIAL SCIENCE (liberal arts/general studies, political science/government, and psychology). Biology, computer and information management, and nursing are the strongest academically. Liberal studies, elementary education, and nursing are the largest.

Required: To graduate, all students must complete 121 to 130 credits, including 44 credits of core requirements. A minimum 2.0 GPA is required.

Special: The college offers co-op programs in all majors, internships, work-study programs, dual majors, and a general studies degrees. Credit for life, work, and military experience, nondegree study, an accelerated degree liberal studies program, and pass/fail options are available. There are 4 national honor societies, and a freshman honors program.

Faculty/Classroom: 38% of faculty are male; 62%, female. 85% teach undergraduates and 15% both teach and do research. No introductory courses are taught by graduate students. The average class size in an introductory lecture is 22; in a laboratory, 19; and in a regular course, 20.

Admissions: 97% of the 2001-2002 applicants were accepted. The SAT I scores for the 2001-2002 freshman class were: Verbal--74% below 500, 23% between 500 and 599, and 3% between 600 and 700; Math--80% below 500, 17% between 500 and 599, and 3% between 600 and 700.

Requirements: The SAT I is required. In addition, applicants must be graduates of an accredited secondary school or have a GED. High school courses must include 4 years of English and 2 years each of a foreign language, history, and science. An interview is recommended. A GPA of 2.0 is required. AP and CLEP credits are accepted. Important factors in the admissions decision are recommendations by school officials, evidence of special talent, and extracurricular activities record. Applications are accepted on-line.

Procedure: Freshmen are admitted fall and spring. Entrance exams should be taken by December of the senior year. There is a deferred admissions plan. Application deadlines are open. The application fee is $35. Notification is sent on a rolling basis.

Transfer: 66 transfer students enrolled in 2001-2002. Applicants should submit transcripts from all institutions attended. 30 credits of 121 to 130 must be completed at Neumann.

Visiting: There are regularly scheduled orientations for prospective students, including class visits and informal meetings with faculty. There are guides for informal visits and visitors may sit in on classes. To schedule a visit, contact the Admissions Office.

Financial Aid: In 2001-2002, 95% of all freshmen and 90% of continuing students received some form of financial aid. 80% of freshmen and 90% of continuing students received need-based aid. Scholarships or need-based grants averaged $1000 ($5000 maximum); loans averaged $2600 ($5500 maximum); work contracts averaged $1000 ($2000 maximum); and merit scholarship averaged $2500 ($8000 maximum). 89% of undergraduates work part time. Average annual earnings from campus work are $1200. The average financial indebtedness of the 2001 graduate was $15,000. The FAFSA is required. The fall application deadline is March 15.

International Students: There are 4 international students enrolled. They must score 550 on the written TOEFL and also take the SAT I.

Computers: The mainframe is an IBM RS/6000. About 145 PCs are available in the computer lab, the library, the residence hall, and the student lounge. Internet access, e-mail, and web browsing are also available. All students may access the system at any time. There are no time limits and no fees.

Graduates: In 2001, 243 bachelor's degrees were awarded. The most popular majors were liberal studies (72%), elementary education (40%), and nursing (33%). In an average class, 48% graduate in 4 years, 65% in 5 years, and 67% in 6 years. 55 companies recruited on campus in 2000-2001. Of the 2000 graduating class, 11% were enrolled in graduate school within 6 months of graduation and 93% were employed.

Admissions Contact: Scott Bogard, Director of Admissions and Financial Aid. E-mail: *neumann@neumann.edu*
Web: *www.neumann.edu*

PEIRCE COLLEGE
F-3

Philadelphia, PA 19102
(215) 670-9214
(877) 670-9190; Fax: (215) 545-3683

Full-time: 175 men, 511 women	**Faculty:** 30
Part-time: 490 men, 1661 women	**Ph.D.s:** 82%
Graduate: none	**Student/Faculty:** 23 to 1
Year: terms, summer session	**Tuition:** $10,650
Application Deadline: open	**Room & Board:** n/app

Freshman Class: n/av
SAT I or ACT: not required **COMPETITIVE**

Peirce College offers baccalaureate, associate, and certificate programs in business studies, paralegal studies, and information technology. In addition to regional accreditation, Peirce has baccalaureate program accreditation with ACBSP. The library contains 35,000 volumes and subscribes to 160 periodicals. Computerized library services include the card catalog, interlibrary loans, and database searching. Special learning facilities include a learning resource center. The 1-acre campus is in an urban area in the Center City Business District. There are 7 buildings.

Student Life: 88% of undergraduates are from Pennsylvania. Others are from 23 states, 16 foreign countries, and Canada. 60% are African American; 24%, white. The average age of freshmen is 31; all undergraduates, 33. 2% do not continue beyond their first year; 63% remain to graduate.

Housing: There are no residence halls. All students commute. Alcohol is not permitted. No one may keep cars.

Activities: There are no fraternities or sororities. There are some groups and organizations on campus, including honors. Popular campus events include Academic Awards Ceremonies and Commencement.

Sports: There is no sports program at Peirce.

Disabled Students: 80% of the campus is accessible. Wheelchair ramps, elevators, specially equipped rest rooms, special class scheduling, lowered drinking fountains, and lowered telephones are available.

Services: Counseling and information services are available, as is tutoring in most subjects. There is a reader service for the blind, and remedial math, reading, and writing.

Campus Safety and Security: Measures include 24-hour foot and vehicle patrol, escort service, informal discussions, and pamphlets/posters/films. There are emergency telephones, lighted pathways/sidewalks, and security cameras throughout the campus.

Programs of Study: Peirce confers the B.S. degree. Associate degrees are also awarded. Bachelor's degrees are awarded in BUSINESS (business administration and management), COMPUTER AND PHYSICAL SCIENCE (information sciences and systems), SOCIAL SCIENCE (paralegal studies). Paralegal studies is the strongest academically. Business administration is the largest.
Required: To graduate, all students must complete 120 credit hours, including 60 hours in the major, 2 courses each in English/communications, humanities, and social science, 1 course each in math/science and technology, and a capstone course. A minimum 2.0 GPA is required.
Special: The college offers co-op programs in all major programs of study, internships, and accelerated degrees. There is also a Corporate College program for working adults and an On-Line Degree Program. There is 1 national honor society.
Faculty/Classroom: 60% of faculty are male; 40%, female. All teach undergraduates. The average class size in an introductory lecture is 16 and in a regular course, 15.
Admissions: 57% of the 2001-2002 applicants were accepted.
Requirements: On-campus applicants who have not taken the SAT I or the ACT and who are entering college for the first time, must take a skills assessment test to determine the appropriate placement in college-level courses. Applicants must take the TABE (Test of Adult Basic Education) to determine grade equivalency in English and math. Corporate College and On-line Degree Program applicants must submit an official transcript documenting high school graduation or copies of the GED or state equivalency diploma and scores. AP and CLEP credits are accepted. Applications are accepted on-line at the college's web site.
Procedure: Freshmen are admitted to all sessions. Entrance exams are offered continuously. There is an early admissions plan. Application deadlines are open. The application fee is $50. Notification is sent on a rolling basis.
Transfer: 877 transfer students enrolled in 2001-2002. Transcripts from other colleges attended must be submitted. 30 credits of 120 must be completed at Peirce.
Visiting: There are regularly scheduled orientations for prospective students, including a campus tour and a meeting with an adviser. There are guides for informal visits and visitors may sit in on classes. To schedule a visit, contact Sales and Marketing.
Financial Aid: In 2001-2002, 90% of all freshmen and 80% of continuing students received some form of financial aid. 80% of freshmen and 50% of continuing students received need-based aid. The average freshman award was $4000. Of that total, scholarships or need-based grants averaged $3500 ($4000 maximum); loans averaged $2625 ($3500 maximum); and work contracts averaged $1000 (maximum). All undergraduates work part time. Average annual earnings from campus work are $2000. The average financial indebtedness of the 2001 graduate was $15,000. Peirce is a member of CSS. The FAFSA and the college's own financial statement are required. The fall application deadline is June 1.
International Students: There are 48 international students enrolled. The school actively recruits these students. They must take the TOEFL, the MELAB, the Comprehensive English Language Test, and the college's own test, the TABE (Test of Adult Basic Education), demonstrating high school equivalency.
Computers: The mainframe is a Compaq 7000. Log-ons are assigned upon course registration. All students may access the system. There are no time limits and no fees. It is strongly recommended that all students have a personal computer.
Graduates: In 2001, 356 bachelor's degrees were awarded. The most popular majors were business administration (81%), paralegal studies (11%), and information technology (8%). In an average class, 20% graduate in 4 years, 30% in 5 years, and 40% in 6 years. 47 companies recruited on campus in 2000-2001. Of the 2000 graduating class, 31% were enrolled in graduate school within 6 months of graduation and 92% were employed.
Admissions Contact: Steve Bird, Senior. Enrollment Representative. A video is available. E-mail: *info@peirce.edu* Web: *www.peirce.edu*

PENN STATE UNIVERSITY AT ERIE/BEHREND COLLEGE B-1
Erie, PA 16563 (814) 898-6100
(866) 374-3378; Fax: (814) 898-6044

Full-time: 2039 men, 1217 women	**Faculty:** 192; IIB, av$
Part-time: 196 men, 98 women	**Ph.D.s:** 59%
Graduate: 105 men, 53 women	**Student/Faculty:** 17 to 1
Year: semesters, summer session	**Tuition:** $7396 ($13,876)
Application Deadline: open	**Room & Board:** $4930
Freshman Class: n/av	
SAT I or ACT: required	**COMPETITIVE**

Penn State University at Erie/Behrend College, founded in 1948, offers 26 baccalaureate programs as well as the first 2 years of most Penn State University Park baccalaureate programs. It offers courses in business, humanities, social sciences, science, engineering technology, and engineering. There are 4 undergraduate and 2 graduate schools. In addition to regional accreditation, Behrend or Penn State Erie has baccalaureate program accreditation with ABET. The library contains 100,000 volumes, 75,190 microform items, and 351 audiovisual forms/CDs, and subscribes to 700 periodicals. Computerized library services include the card catalog, interlibrary loans, and database searching. Special learning facilities include a learning resource center, radio station, and engineering workstation labs, and media labs. The 700-acre campus is in a suburban area 5 miles east of Erie. Including residence halls, there are 42 buildings.
Student Life: 92% of undergraduates are from Pennsylvania. Others are from 28 states, 23 foreign countries, and Canada. 88% are white. The average age of freshmen is 18; all undergraduates, 22. 9% do not continue beyond their first year; 61% remain to graduate.
Housing: 1500 students can be accommodated in college housing, which includes single-sex and coed dormitories and on-campus apartments. In addition, there are honors houses, special-interest houses, and a substance-free interest house. On-campus housing is available on a first-come, first-served basis and is available on a lottery system for upperclassmen. 54% of students commute. Alcohol is not permitted. All students may keep cars.
Activities: 5% of men belong to 5 national fraternities; 16% of women belong to 3 national sororities. There are 80 groups on campus, including band, cheerleading, chess, choir, computers, dance, drama, ethnic, gay, honors, international, jazz band, literary magazine, newspaper, pep band, political, professional, radio and TV, religious, social service, student government, and yearbook. Popular campus events include a speaker series, parents events, and Black Cultural Awareness Month.
Sports: There are 10 intercollegiate sports for men and 11 for women, and 18 intramural sports for men and 18 for women. Facilities include an athletic center with an indoor track and an 8-lane pool, tennis courts, a weight room, a fitness trail, basketball courts, and baseball, softball, and soccer fields.
Disabled Students: 90% of the campus is accessible. Wheelchair ramps, elevators, special parking, specially equipped rest rooms, special class scheduling, lowered drinking fountains, and lowered telephones are available.
Services: Counseling and information services are available, as is tutoring in most subjects. There is a reader service for the blind, and remedial math, reading, and writing.
Campus Safety and Security: Measures include 24-hour foot and vehicle patrol, self-defense education, escort service, and informal discussions. There are pamphlets/posters/films, emergency telephones, and lighted pathways/sidewalks.
Programs of Study: Behrend or Penn State Erie confers B.A. and B.S. degrees. Associate and master's degrees are also awarded. Bachelor's degrees are awarded in BIOLOGICAL SCIENCE (biology/biological science), BUSINESS (accounting, banking and finance, business administration and management, business economics, management information systems, and marketing management), COMMUNICATIONS AND THE ARTS (communications and English), COMPUTER AND PHYSICAL SCIENCE (chemistry, computer science, mathematics, physics, and science), ENGINEERING AND ENVIRONMENTAL DESIGN (computer engineering, engineering, engineering technology, mechanical engineering technology, and plastics technology), SOCIAL SCIENCE (economics, history, political science/government, and psychology). Management information systems, psychology, and math are the strongest academically. Engineering, business, and psychology are the largest.
Required: All baccalaureate degree candidates must take 46 general education credits, including 27 in arts, humanities, natural science, and social and behavioral sciences including a cultural diversity course, 15 in quantification and communication skills including a writing intensive course, and 3 in health, phys ed, and a freshman seminar. All students must complete a minimum of 120 credit hours with a minimum GPA of 2.0. Further requirements vary by degree program.
Special: Internships, study abroad in 14 countries, and work-study programs are available. In addition, a B.A.-B.S. degree in psychology, a 3-2 engineering degree with Edinboro University, dual majors, a general studies degree, and student-designed majors in business and behavioral sciences are offered. Nondegree study and up to 12 credits of pass/fail options are possible. There are 4 national honor societies and a freshman honors program.
Faculty/Classroom: 70% of faculty are male; 30%, female. All teach undergraduates. No introductory courses are taught by graduate students. The average class size in an introductory lecture is 35; in a laboratory, 18; and in a regular course, 29.
Admissions: The SAT I scores for the 2001-2002 freshman class were: Verbal--32% below 500, 51% between 500 and 599, 15% between 600 and 700, and 2% above 700; Math--26% below 500, 47% between 500 and 599, 25% between 600 and 700, and 2% above 700. 35% of the current freshmen were in the top fifth of their class; 76% were in the top two fifths. 12 freshmen graduated first in their class.
Requirements: The SAT I or ACT is required. In addition, candidates for admission must have 15 academic credits or 15 Carnegie units, in-

cluding 5 in social studies, 4 in English, 3 each in math and science, and 2 in foreign language. The GED is accepted. Applications are accepted on-line via Penn State's or the college's web site. AP and CLEP credits are accepted.

Procedure: Freshmen are admitted to all sessions. Entrance exams should be taken during the junior year. There are deferred admissions and rolling admissions plans. Application deadlines are open. The application fee is $50.

Transfer: 94 transfer students enrolled in 2001-2002. Transfer candidates need a minimum GPA of 2.4, good academic standing, and 18 or more credits from a regionally accredited institution at the college level. 36 credits of 120 must be completed at Behrend or Penn State Erie.

Visiting: There are regularly scheduled orientations for prospective students, including meetings with a counselor and faculty, a campus tour, and a class visit. There are guides for informal visits, and visitors may sit in on classes and stay overnight. To schedule a visit, contact the Admissions Office.

Financial Aid: External scholarships are available. The FAFSA is required. The fall application deadline is February 15.

International Students: There are 32 international students enrolled. The school actively recruits these students. They must score 550 on the written TOEFL or 213 on the electronic version.

Computers: 450 computers are available in the computer center, labs in the library, and in academic buildings. All students may access the system any time by modem or network. There are no time limits and no fees. It is strongly recommended that all students have a personal computer.

Admissions Contact: Mary-Ellen Madigan, Director of Admissions. E-mail: *behrend.admissions@psu.edu* Web: *www.pserie.psu.edu*

PENN STATE UNIVERSITY/ALTOONA

Altoona, PA 16601 **(814) 949-5466; (800) 848-9843**

Full-time: 1793 men, 1666 women	**Faculty:** 122
Part-time: 127 men, 227 women	**Ph.D.s:** 71%
Graduate: 2 men, 8 women	**Student/Faculty:** 28 to 1
Year: semesters, summer session	**Tuition:** $7278 ($11,116)
Application Deadline: see profile	**Room & Board:** $5300
Freshman Class: 4112 applied, 3472 accepted, 1296 enrolled	
SAT I Verbal/Math: 499/512	**COMPETITIVE**

Penn State Altoona, founded in 1939, is a land-grant institution offering degree programs in the arts and sciences, business, and nursing. In addition to regional accreditation, Penn State University/Altoona has baccalaureate program accreditation with ABET. The library contains 68,332 volumes, 58,596 microform items, and 5680 audiovisual forms/CDs, and subscribes to 291 periodicals. Computerized library services include the card catalog, interlibrary loans, and database searching. Special learning facilities include a learning resource center, art gallery, and PicTel teleconferencing, 5 state-of-the-art engineering labs, and CAD/CAM computer lab facilities. The 123-acre campus is in a suburban area of Altoona. Including residence halls, there are 25 buildings.

Student Life: 88% of undergraduates are from Pennsylvania. Others are from 29 states and 11 foreign countries. 85% are white. 54% claim no religious affiliation; 25% are various Christian and non-Christian denominations; 18%, Catholic. The average age of freshmen is 19; all undergraduates, 22.

Housing: More than 900 students can be accommodated in college housing, which includes single-sex and coed dormitories. In addition, there are honors houses, special-interest houses, and alcohol-free and substance-free housing. On-campus housing is available on a first-come, first-served basis and is available on a lottery system for upperclassmen. 76% of students commute. Alcohol is not permitted. All students may keep cars.

Activities: 4% of men belong to 4 national fraternities; 3% of women belong to 3 local sororities. There are more than 50 groups on campus, including cheerleading, choir, dance, drama, ethnic, gay, honors, horticulture, international, jazz band, literary magazine, martial arts, newspaper, pep band, political, professional, religious, social, social service, STEP team, student government, and yearbook. Popular campus events include Distinguished Speaker Series, Hoops Hysteria, and Black History and Women's History Month events.

Sports: There are 6 intercollegiate sports for men and 6 for women, and 30 coed intramural sports. Facilities include a large gym, an indoor pool, racquetball courts, a weight room, a fitness loft, tennis courts, an outdoor track, sand volleyball courts, and baseball, softball, and soccer fields.

Disabled Students: 95% of the campus is accessible. Wheelchair ramps, elevators, special parking, specially equipped rest rooms, special class scheduling, lowered drinking fountains, and lowered telephones are available.

Services: Counseling and information services are available, as is tutoring in most subjects. There is remedial math, reading, and writing.

Campus Safety and Security: Measures include 24-hour foot and vehicle patrol, self-defense education, escort service, and shuttle buses. There are informal discussions, pamphlets/posters/films, emergency telephones, and lighted pathways/sidewalks.

Programs of Study: Penn State University/Altoona confers B.A. and B.S. degrees. Associate degrees are also awarded. Bachelor's degrees are awarded in AGRICULTURE (environmental studies), BUSINESS (business administration and management), COMMUNICATIONS AND THE ARTS (English), COMPUTER AND PHYSICAL SCIENCE (science), ENGINEERING AND ENVIRONMENTAL DESIGN (electromechanical technology), HEALTH PROFESSIONS (nursing), SOCIAL SCIENCE (criminal justice, human development, and liberal arts/general studies). Engineering is the strongest academically. Business, engineering, and criminal justice are the largest.

Required: To graduate, students must complete a minimum of 120 credit hours with a minimum GPA of 2.0. They must complete 46 general education credits, including 27 in arts, humanities, natural science, and social and behavioral sciences, 15 in quantification and communication skills, and 3 in health and phys ed.

Special: Internships, study abroad in 2 countries, work-study programs, accelerated degree programs, and dual and student-designed majors are available. There is an integrative arts major, which allows students to pursue interests across artistic boundaries. There are 2 national honor societies, including Phi Beta Kappa, and a freshman honors program.

Faculty/Classroom: 59% of faculty are male; 41%, female. No introductory courses are taught by graduate students. The average class size in an introductory lecture is 35; in a laboratory, 20; and in a regular course, 24.

Admissions: 84% of the 2001-2002 applicants were accepted. The SAT I scores for the 2001-2002 freshman class were: Verbal--48% below 500, 42% between 500 and 599, and 10% between 600 and 700; Math--42% below 500, 41% between 500 and 599, 15% between 600 and 700, and 2% above 700. 24% of the current freshmen were in the top fifth of their class; 60% were in the top two fifths.

Requirements: The SAT I or ACT is required. In addition, applicants should have 15 academic or Carnegie units, including 4 in English and 3 each in math, science, and social studies, with 2 in foreign language required for some majors. The GED is accepted. AP and CLEP credits are accepted. Advanced placement or honor courses is an important factor in the admissions decision. Applications are accepted on computer disk and on-line at the school's web site.

Procedure: Freshmen are admitted to all sessions. Entrance exams should be taken during the junior year. There are early admissions and deferred admissions plans. November 30 is the recommended filing date for fall entry. The fall 2001 application fee was $50. Notification is sent on a rolling basis.

Transfer: 65 transfer students enrolled in 2001-2002. High school and college transcripts are required, as is good academic standing. The minimum GPA varies by major. 36 credits of a minimum 120 must be completed at Penn State University/Altoona.

Visiting: There are regularly scheduled orientations for prospective students, including campus tours and meetings with academic counselors and faculty. There are guides for informal visits and visitors may sit in on classes and stay overnight. To schedule a visit, contact the Admissions Office by phone or at *aaadmit@psu.edu*

Financial Aid: The average freshman award was $8538. Of that total, scholarships or need-based grants averaged $3633 and loans averaged $2741. The average financial indebtedness of the 2001 graduate was $17,453. The FAFSA is required; some academic scholarships require a specific application, which varies according to the college/major. The recommended fall application deadline for freshmen is February 15.

International Students: There are 26 international students enrolled. The school actively recruits these students. They must score 550 on the written TOEFL and also take the SAT I or the ACT.

Computers: There are between 900 and 1000 computers on campus. They are available in the Computer Learning Resource Center, labs in academic buildings, and labs in residence halls; there is mainframe access from residence hall rooms. All students may access the system. There are no time limits and no fees. It is strongly recommended that all students have a personal computer.

Graduates: In 2001, 127 bachelor's degrees were awarded. The most popular majors were business (35%), engineering (23%), and criminal justice (18%). 21 companies recruited on campus in 2000-2001. Of the 2000 graduating class, 1% were enrolled in graduate school within 6 months of graduation and 64% were employed.

Admissions Contact: Richard Shaffer, Director of Admissions. A video is available. E-mail: *rks8@psu.edu* Web: *www.aa.psu.edu*

PENN STATE UNIVERSITY/UNIVERSITY PARK CAMPUS C-3

University Park, PA 16802 (814) 863-0233; Fax: (814) 863-7590

Full-time: 17,330 men, 15,100 women	**Faculty:** 1721; I, -$
Part-time: 1240 men, 840 women	**Ph.D.s:** 88%
Graduate: 3410 men, 2745 women	**Student/Faculty:** 19 to 1
Year: semesters, summer session	**Tuition:** $6756 ($14,388)
Application Deadline: open	**Room & Board:** $4690
Freshman Class: n/av	
SAT I Verbal/Math: required	**VERY COMPETITIVE**

Penn State University/University Park Campus, founded in 1855, is the oldest and largest of 24 campuses in the Penn State system, offering undergraduate and graduate degrees in agricultural science, arts and architecture, business administration, earth and mineral sciences, education, engineering, health and human development, liberal arts, science, and communications. There are 10 undergraduate schools and 1 graduate school. Figures in above capsule are approximate. In addition to regional accreditation, Penn State has baccalaureate program accreditation with AACSB, ABET, ACEJMC, ADA, ASLA, CSWE, NAAB, NASAD, NASM, NCATE, NLN, NRPA, and SAF. The 10 libraries contain 2,452,370 volumes, 1,917,033 microform items, and 38,931 audiovisual forms/CDs, and subscribe to 26,157 periodicals. Computerized library services include the card catalog, interlibrary loans, and database searching. Special learning facilities include a learning resource center, art gallery, radio station, TV station, and museums of art, anthropology, and earth and mineral sciences, an observatory, and a nuclear reactor. The 5617-acre campus is in a suburban area 90 miles west of Harrisburg. Including residence halls, there are 403 buildings.

Student Life: 81% of undergraduates are from Pennsylvania. Others are from 50 states and Canada. 84% are white. The average age of freshmen is 18; all undergraduates, 21. 7% do not continue beyond their first year; 77% remain to graduate.

Housing: 12,648 students can be accommodated in college housing, which includes single-sex dormitories, on-campus apartments, and married-student housing. In addition, there are honors houses, language houses, and special-interest houses. On-campus housing is guaranteed for the freshman year only and is available on a lottery system for upperclassmen. 65% of students commute. Alcohol is not permitted. All students may keep cars.

Activities: 13% of men belong to 55 national fraternities; 12% of women belong to 25 national sororities. There are 400 groups on campus, including art, band, cheerleading, chess, choir, chorale, chorus, computers, dance, drama, drill team, ethnic, film, gay, honors, international, jazz band, literary magazine, marching band, musical theater, newspaper, orchestra, pep band, photography, political, professional, radio and TV, religious, social, social service, student government, symphony, and yearbook. Popular campus events include Penn State Artists' Series, Central Pennsylvania Festival of the Arts, and Sy Barash Regatta.

Sports: There are 15 intercollegiate sports for men and 14 for women, and 15 intramural sports for men and 14 for women. Facilities include 6 gyms, 5 swimming pools, indoor and outdoor tracks, 2 golf courses, a jogging course, a rink, 2 rifle ranges, 32 acres of practice fields, and numerous courts for tennis, handball, squash, and paddleball.

Disabled Students: All of the campus is accessible. Wheelchair ramps, elevators, special parking, specially equipped rest rooms, special class scheduling, lowered drinking fountains, and lowered telephones are available.

Services: Counseling and information services are available, as is tutoring in most subjects. There is a reader service for the blind, and remedial math, reading, and writing.

Campus Safety and Security: Measures include 24-hour foot and vehicle patrol, self-defense education, escort service, and shuttle buses. There are informal discussions, pamphlets/posters/films, emergency telephones, and lighted pathways/sidewalks.

Programs of Study: Penn State confers B.A., B.S., B.Arch., B.Arch.Eng., B.F.A., B.M., B.Mus.Arts, and B.Ph. degrees. Associate, master's, and doctoral degrees are also awarded. Bachelor's degrees are awarded in AGRICULTURE (agricultural business management, agriculture, agronomy, animal science, dairy science, fishing and fisheries, forestry and related sciences, forestry production and processing, horticulture, natural resource management, plant science, poultry science, and soil science), BIOLOGICAL SCIENCE (biochemistry, biology/biological science, ecology, microbiology, molecular biology, nutrition, and wildlife biology), BUSINESS (accounting, banking and finance, business administration and management, hotel/motel and restaurant management, insurance, international business management, labor studies, management information systems, management science, marketing/retailing/merchandising, real estate, and transportation management), COMMUNICATIONS AND THE ARTS (advertising, art, art history and appreciation, broadcasting, classics, communications, comparative literature, dramatic arts, English, film arts, fine arts, French, German, Italian, journalism, music, Russian, Spanish, and speech/debate/rhetoric), COMPUTER AND PHYSICAL SCIENCE (actuarial science, astronomy, atmospheric sciences and meteorology, chemistry, computer science, earth science, geoscience, mathematics, physics, science, and statistics), EDUCATION (agricultural, art, elementary, health, industrial arts, music, secondary, and special), ENGINEERING AND ENVIRONMENTAL DESIGN (aeronautical engineering, agricultural engineering, architectural engineering, architecture, chemical engineering, civil engineering, computer engineering, electrical/electronics engineering, energy management technology, engineering, environmental engineering, industrial administration/management, industrial engineering, landscape architecture/design, materials science, mechanical engineering, mining and mineral engineering, nuclear engineering, and petroleum/natural gas engineering), HEALTH PROFESSIONS (health care administration, nursing, premedicine, public health, rehabilitation therapy, and speech pathology/audiology), SOCIAL SCIENCE (African American studies, American studies, anthropology, criminal justice, East Asian studies, economics, food science, geography, history, human development, international relations, Latin American studies, liberal arts/general studies, medieval studies, parks and recreation management, philosophy, physical fitness/movement, political science/government, prelaw, psychology, public administration, religion, sociology, and women's studies). Agriculture, architecture, and meteorology are the strongest academically. Electrical engineering, education, and accounting are the largest.

Required: All bachelor's degree candidates must take 46 general education credits, including 15 in quantitative and communication skills, 9 in natural sciences, 6 each in arts, humanities, and social and behavioral sciences, and 4 in health sciences and phys ed. Further requirements vary by degree program.

Special: Intercollegiate programs in marine sciences and military studies, as well as the B.Ph. program, are offered by faculty from several university colleges. There are internships available in many disciplines. Study abroad is possible through more than 70 programs in 30 countries. Dual and student-designed majors, a general studies degree in arts and sciences, and dual degrees in liberal arts and either earth/natural sciences or engineering are offered with 26 other institutions, as well as a 3-2 engineering program. Co-op programs are available in most engineering majors. There are limited pass/fail options, and nondegree study is possible. There are 45 national honor societies, including Phi Beta Kappa, a freshman honors programs.

Faculty/Classroom: 74% of faculty are male; 26%, female. All both teach and do research. The average class size in a regular course is 26.

Requirements: The SAT I or ACT is required. The SAT I is preferred. Applicants should be graduates of accredited high schools or have earned the GED. Required secondary preparation varies by the college or other academic unit applied to. Generally, all applicants should have 5 years in arts, humanities, and social studies, 4 of English, and 3 each of science and math. 2 years of the same foreign language are required for the College of Liberal Arts and School of Communications, and recommended for all other programs. A GPA of 2.0 is required. AP and CLEP credits are accepted. Important factors in the admissions decision are advanced placement or honor courses and evidence of special talent.

Procedure: Freshmen are admitted to all sessions. Entrance exams should be taken in the junior year. Application deadlines are open. The fall 2001 application fee was $50. Notification is sent on a rolling basis.

Transfer: Transfer applicants need a minimum GPA of 2.0, good academic standing, and 18 or more credits from any regionally accredited college or institution at the college level. 36 credits of 120 must be completed at Penn State.

Visiting: There are regularly scheduled orientations for prospective students. There are guides for informal visits and visitors may sit in on classes and stay overnight. To schedule a visit, contact the Undergraduate Admissions Office.

Financial Aid: The average financial indebtedness of a recent year's graduate was $17,125. The FAFSA and, for Pennsylvania residents, the PHEAA form are required. Check with the school for current deadlines.

International Students: They must score 550 on the written TOEFL, and students whose native language is English must also submit SAT I or ACT scores.

Computers: The mainframe is an IBM ES/3090-600s. The Center for Academic Computing is connected to a wide variety of academic facilities, the library, other Penn State campuses, the National Science Foundation network, Bitnet/CREN, and more than a thousand other organizations worldwide. PC classrooms and labs are available throughout the campus, and special facilities for graphics applications and. All students may access the system 24 hours a day, every day. There are no time limits and no fees.

Admissions Contact: Geoffrey Harford, Sr. Director of Admissions Services and Evaluation. E-mail: *gjh1@psu.edu*

PENNSYLVANIA COLLEGE OF TECHNOLOGY D-2

Williamsport, PA 17701 (570) 327-4761
(800) 367-9222; Fax: (570) 321-5536

Full-time: 3158 men, 1298 women **Faculty:** 243
Part-time: 473 men, 609 women **Ph.D.s:** 20%
Graduate: none **Student/Faculty:** 18 to 1
Year: semesters, summer session **Tuition:** $7860 ($9960)
Application Deadline: open **Room & Board:** $5000
Freshman Class: 4636 applied, 3855 accepted, 2824 enrolled
SAT I Verbal/Math: 452/469 **NONCOMPETITIVE**

Pennsylvania College of Technology, founded in 1989, is a public technical college affiliated with Pennsylvania State University. There are 9 undergraduate schools. The library contains 89,713 volumes, 10,836 microform items, and 8534 audiovisual forms/CDs, and subscribes to 872 periodicals. Computerized library services include the card catalog, interlibrary loans, and database searching. Special learning facilities include a learning resource center, radio station, a restaurant and a dental hygiene clinic that are open to the public, and the Penn College Child Care Center. The 81-acre campus is in an urban area 80 miles west of Wilkes Barre. Including residence halls, there are 26 buildings.

Student Life: 94% of undergraduates are from Pennsylvania. Others are from 32 states, 15 foreign countries, and Canada. 96% are white. 57% are Protestant; 23%, Catholic; 16% claim no religious affiliation. The average age of freshmen is 19; all undergraduates, 24. 29% do not continue beyond their first year; 33% remain to graduate.

Housing: 1060 students can be accommodated in college housing, which includes single-sex and coed on-campus apartments. On-campus housing is available on a first-come, first-served basis. Alcohol is not permitted. All students may keep cars.

Activities: There are no fraternities or sororities. There are 46 groups on campus, including art, computers, drama, ethnic, gay, international, newspaper, professional, radio, religious, social, social service, and student government. Popular campus events include a cultural series, Spring Fling Week, and Penn Environment Week.

Sports: There are 9 intercollegiate sports for men and 9 for women, and 31 intramural sports for men and 31 for women. Facilities include a fitness center, a field house, a gym, a soccer field, a softball complex, 5 tennis courts, and a sand volleyball court.

Disabled Students: All of the campus is accessible. Wheelchair ramps, elevators, special parking, specially equipped rest rooms, lowered drinking fountains, and lowered telephones are available.

Services: Counseling and information services are available. Tutoring in every subject is provided on request, if tutors are available. There is a reader service for the blind, and remedial math, reading, and writing. Services for hearing-impaired students, adaptive equipment, and note takers are available.

Campus Safety and Security: Measures include 24-hour foot and vehicle patrol, self-defense education, informal discussions, and pamphlets/posters/films. There are lighted pathways/sidewalks.

Programs of Study: Penn College confers B.S. and B.S.N. degrees. Associate degrees are also awarded. Bachelor's degrees are awarded in BUSINESS (accounting and business administration and management), COMMUNICATIONS AND THE ARTS (graphic design and technical and business writing), COMPUTER AND PHYSICAL SCIENCE (polymer science), ENGINEERING AND ENVIRONMENTAL DESIGN (aircraft mechanics, automotive technology, civil engineering technology, computer engineering, computer technology, construction management, drafting and design, electrical/electronics engineering technology, food services technology, manufacturing engineering, mechanical design technology, mechanical engineering technology, plastics engineering, printing technology, technological management, and welding engineering), HEALTH PROFESSIONS (dental hygiene, health science, nursing, and physician's assistant), SOCIAL SCIENCE (human services and paralegal studies). Information technology, electronics technology, and business management are the largest.

Required: To graduate, students must complete at least 120 credits with a minimum GPA of 2.0 overall and in the major. The core curriculum consists of 18 to 21 credits in humanities/social science/art/foreign language, 9 in communications, 7 in science, 6 in math, 2 in health and fitness, and a course in computer information.

Special: Penn College offers cooperative and internship programs, cross-registration with Lycoming College and Penn State, dual and student-designed majors, and credit by exam and for work and/or life experience. There is a chapter of Phi Beta Kappa.

Faculty/Classroom: 66% of faculty are male; 34%, female. All teach undergraduates. The average class size in a regular course is 18.

Admissions: 83% of the 2001-2002 applicants were accepted. 15% of the current freshmen were in the top fifth of their class; 32% were in the top two fifths.

Requirements: The SAT I or ACT is recommended. In addition, applicants must have a high school diploma or GED and must take the college's placement exams. Other admissions criteria vary by program. AP and CLEP credits are accepted. An admissions application is offered via the college's web site.

Procedure: Freshmen are admitted to all sessions. Entrance exams should be taken prior to scheduling classes. There are early decision, early admissions, and deferred admissions plans. Application deadlines are open. The fall application fee was $50. Notification is sent on a rolling basis. In a recent year, 2% of all applicants were on a waiting list.

Transfer: 393 transfer students enrolled in 2001-2002. Transfer procedures vary with each degree program. Courses are evaluated for transfer equivalency. 60 credits of 120 must be completed at Penn College.

Visiting: There are regularly scheduled orientations for prospective students, including registration, a multimedia presentation, admission and financial aid sessions, a question-and-answer period, a tour of campus facilities, and a reception. Visitors may sit in on classes. To schedule a visit, contact the Office of Admissions at (800) 367-9222 or *admissions@pct.edu*.

Financial Aid: In a recent year, 80% of all students received need-based aid. The average freshman award was $7200. 5% of undergraduates work part time. Average annual earnings from campus work are $2220. The average financial indebtedness of a recent graduate was $10,000. Penn College is a member of CSS. The FAFSA and the college's own financial statement are required. The fall application deadline is April 1.

International Students: In a recent year, 33 international students were enrolled. The school actively recruits these students. They must score 500 on the written TOEFL or 173 on the electronic version.

Computers: The mainframe is an IBM AS/400 F50. Approximately 1000 PCs and Macs are available for student use in more than 35 labs. All students may access the system. There are no time limits and no fees.

Graduates: In a recent class, 83 bachelor's degrees were awarded. The most popular majors were electrical technology (5%), building construction technology (5%), and automotive technology (4%). In an average class, 37% graduate in 3 years, 41% in 4 years, 42% in 5 years, and 43% in 6 years. 51 companies recruited on campus in a recent year. Of a recent graduating class, 67% were employed within 6 months of graduation.

Admissions Contact: Chester D. Schuman, Director of Admissions. E-mail: *cschuman@pct.edu* Web: *http://www.pct.edu*

PENNSYLVANIA STATE SYSTEM OF HIGHER EDUCATION

Pennsylvania State System of Higher Education, established in 1983, is a public system. It is governed by a board of governors whose chief administrator is the chancellor. The primary goal of the system is to provide high-quality liberal arts education at an affordable cost with a central mission of teaching and service. The total enrollment of all 14 universities is about 94,000, with more than 5200 faculty members. The universities offer 217 baccalaureate, 107 master's, and 6 doctoral programs. 4-year institutions are located in Bloomsburg, California, Cheyney, Clarion, East Stroudsburg, Edinboro, Indiana, Kutztown, Lock Haven, Mansfield, Millersville, Shippensburg, Slippery Rock, and West Chester. Profiles of the 4-year campuses are included in this section.

PHILADELPHIA BIBLICAL UNIVERSITY F-3

Langhorne, PA 19047-2990 (215) 752-5800
(800) 366-0049; Fax: (215) 702-4248

Full-time: 411 men, 531 women **Faculty:** 51; IIB, --$
Part-time: 68 men, 50 women **Ph.D.s:** 59%
Graduate: 176 men, 208 women **Student/Faculty:** 18 to 1
Year: semesters, summer session **Tuition:** $11,100
Application Deadline: open **Room & Board:** $5195
Freshman Class: 515 applied, 487 accepted, 210 enrolled
SAT I Verbal/Math: 550/540 **ACT:** 24 **COMPETITIVE+**

Philadelphia Biblical University, formerly Philadelphia College of Bible, founded in 1913, is a private institution offering instruction in the Scriptures and liberal arts and professional theory. Other campuses include the Wisconsin Wilderness Campus and the New Jersey Campus. In addition to regional accreditation, PBU has baccalaureate program accreditation with CSWE and NASM. The library contains 173,814 volumes, 63,503 microform items, and 13,577 audiovisual forms/CDs, and subscribes to 2650 periodicals. Computerized library services include the card catalog, interlibrary loans, and database searching. Special learning facilities include a learning resource center. The 105-acre campus is in a suburban area 30 miles north of Philadelphia. Including residence halls, there are 17 buildings.

Student Life: 53% of undergraduates are from out of state, mostly the Northeast. Others are from 39 states, 32 foreign countries, and Canada. 81% are from public schools. 81% are white; 11% African American. Most are Protestant. The average age of freshmen is 18; all undergraduates, 24. 34% do not continue beyond their first year; 57% remain to graduate.

Housing: 465 students can be accommodated in college housing, which includes single-sex dormitories. On-campus housing is guaranteed for all 4 years. 53% of students live on campus. Alcohol is not permitted. All students may keep cars.

Activities: There are no fraternities or sororities. There are 11 groups on campus, including art, band, cheerleading, choir, chorale, chorus, computers, drama, ethnic, honors, international, newspaper, orchestra, professional, religious, social, student government, symphony, and yearbook. Popular campus events include Late Skates, Christmas and Valentine socials, and Spring Formal.

Sports: There are 6 intercollegiate sports for men and 7 for women, and 6 intramural sports for men and 6 for women. Facilities include a gym, a baseball diamond, soccer, hockey, and softball fields, a sand volleyball court, 4 tennis courts, a fitness circuit, and a weight room.

Disabled Students: All of the campus is accessible. Wheelchair ramps, elevators, special parking, specially equipped rest rooms, and lowered drinking fountains are available.

Services: Counseling and information services are available, as is tutoring in most subjects. The AIMS Program provides academic support for freshmen who need it.

Campus Safety and Security: Measures include 24-hour foot and vehicle patrol, shuttle buses, informal discussions, and pamphlets/posters/films. There are emergency telephones and lighted pathways/sidewalks.

Programs of Study: PBU confers B.S., B.Mus., B.S.B.A., B.S.Ed., and B.S.W. degrees. Associate and master's degrees are also awarded. Bachelor's degrees are awarded in BUSINESS (business administration and management), COMMUNICATIONS AND THE ARTS (music), EDUCATION (education), SOCIAL SCIENCE (biblical studies and social work). Bible is the strongest academically. Teacher education and Bible are the largest.

Required: Students must complete 51 credits in Bible, 48 in general education, and 27 in professional studies. A total of 126 credits, with a minimum GPA of 2.0, is required. 3 credits in phys ed must be taken. The number of hours in the major varies: 57 in Bible, 80 in music, 43 in social work, and 47 in education. All matriculating baccalaureate students major in Bible and receive a B.S. in Bible degree. About 15% of those students are enrolled in dual degree programs and receive the B.S. in Bible degree plus a degree in their professional area.

Special: PCB offers co-op programs in accounting, computer and microcomputer applications, and office administration; cross-registration with Bucks County Community College; various church ministries, education, social work, and music internships; and study abroad in Israel. There are dual majors in social work, music, education, and business administration. Student-designed interdisciplinary majors are possible. There is a freshman honors program.

Faculty/Classroom: 77% of faculty are male; 23%, female. 80% teach undergraduates. No introductory courses are taught by graduate students. The average class size in an introductory lecture is 24; in a laboratory, 9; and in a regular course, 20.

Admissions: 95% of the 2001-2002 applicants were accepted. The SAT I scores for the 2001-2002 freshman class were: Verbal--27% below 500, 41% between 500 and 599, 27% between 600 and 700, and 5% above 700; Math--31% below 500, 46% between 500 and 599, 22% between 600 and 700, and 1% above 700. The ACT scores were 26% below 21, 22% between 21 and 23, 31% between 24 and 26, 4% between 27 and 28, and 17% above 28. 37% of the current freshmen were in the top fifth of their class; 64% were in the top two fifths. 9 freshmen graduated first in their class.

Requirements: The SAT I or ACT is required with minimum composite scores of 920 and 19, respectively. A high school diploma or the GED is needed. An essay and a pastor's reference are required. A GPA of 2.0 is required. AP and CLEP credits are accepted. Important factors in the admissions decision are advanced placement or honor courses, personality/intangible qualities, and leadership record.

Procedure: Freshmen are admitted to all sessions. Entrance exams should be taken in the junior or senior year of high school. There is a deferred admissions plan. Application deadlines are open.

Transfer: 100 transfer students enrolled in 2001-2002. Tranfers must submit an application, a pastor's reference, college transcripts, and a health form. SAT I and high school transcripts are required if the student has fewer than 60 college credit hours. 60 credits of 126 must be completed at PBU.

Visiting: There are regularly scheduled orientations for prospective students, including chapel, class visits, a meal in the dining room, and an interview with a counselor. There are guides for informal visits and visitors may sit in on classes and stay overnight. To schedule a visit, contact the Admissions Department at (215) 702-4235.

Financial Aid: In 2001-2002, 91% of all freshmen and 75% of continuing students received some form of financial aid. 72% of freshmen and 64% of continuing students received need-based aid. The average freshman award was $7465. Of that total, scholarships or need-based grants averaged $6592 ($9158 maximum); loans averaged $2480 ($10,500 maximum); and work contracts averaged $2657. 26% of undergraduates work part time. Average annual earnings from campus work are $1043. The average financial indebtedness of the 2001 graduate was $11,000. PBU is a member of CSS. The FAFSA is required. The fall application deadline is May 1.

International Students: There are 37 international students enrolled. The school actively recruits these students. They must score 550 on the written TOEFL or 213 on the electronic version.

Computers: 40 PCs are located in computer labs with web access. 17 additional PCs for e-mail only are located in student lounges. Students may also access the Internet or the campus network through their own PCs on campus. All students may access the system. There are no time limits and no fees. It is strongly recommended that all students have a personal computer.

Graduates: In 2001, 341 bachelor's degrees were awarded. The most popular majors were Bible (60%), education (28%), and social work (6%). In an average class, 16% graduate in 4 years, 47% in 5 years, and 52% in 6 years. 75 companies recruited on campus in 2000-2001.

Admissions Contact: Lisa Fuller, Director of Admissions. A video is available. E-mail: *admissions@pbu.edu* Web: *pbu.edu*

PHILADELPHIA COLLEGE OF TEXTILES AND SCIENCE
(See Philadelphia University)

PHILADELPHIA UNIVERSITY F-3
(Formerly Philadelphia College of Textiles and Science)
Philadelphia, PA 19144-5497 (215) 951-2800
(800) 951-7287; Fax: (215) 951-2907

Full-time: 790 men, 1486 women	**Faculty:** 105; IIB, av$
Part-time: 138 men, 342 women	**Ph.D.s:** 76%
Graduate: 163 men, 285 women	**Student/Faculty:** 22 to 1
Year: semesters, summer session	**Tuition:** $17,600
Application Deadline: open	**Room & Board:** $7122
Freshman Class: 3177 applied, 2389 accepted, 632 enrolled	
SAT I Verbal/Math: 520/530	**COMPETITIVE**

Philadelphia University, founded in 1884, is a private institution offering preprofessional programs in architecture, design, business, sciences, textiles, fashion, and health. There are 5 undergraduate and 3 graduate schools. In addition to regional accreditation, Phila. U. has baccalaureate program accreditation with ACS, FIDER, and NAAB. The library contains 102,781 volumes, 243,000 microform items, and 250 audiovisual forms/CDs, and subscribes to 915 periodicals. Computerized library services include the card catalog, interlibrary loans, and database searching. Special learning facilities include a learning resource center, art gallery, and design center. The 100-acre campus is in a suburban area 10 minutes west of metropolitan Philadelphia. Including residence halls, there are 56 buildings.

Student Life: 62% of undergraduates are from out of state, mostly the Middle Atlantic. Others are from 41 states, 33 foreign countries, and Canada. 65% are from public schools. 80% are white. The average age of freshmen is 18; all undergraduates, 20. 31% do not continue beyond their first year; 52% remain to graduate.

Housing: 1205 students can be accommodated in college housing, which includes single-sex and coed dormitories, on-campus apartments, and off-campus apartments. On-campus housing is guaranteed for the freshman year only, is available on a first-come, first-served basis, and is available on a lottery system for upperclassmen. Priority is given to out-of-town students. 51% of students live on campus; of those, 60% remain on campus on weekends. All students may keep cars.

Activities: 1% of men belong to 1 national fraternity; 1% of women belong to 1 national sorority. There are 30 groups on campus, including cheerleading, choir, dance, drama, ethnic, gay, honors, international, newspaper, professional, religious, social, social service, student government, and yearbook. Popular campus events include annual fashion show and design competition, Welcome Week, and Spring Weekend.

Sports: There are 5 intercollegiate sports for men and 7 for women, and 24 intramural sports for men and 21 for women. Facilities include 2 gyms, a fitness center, 6 tennis courts, 3 athletic fields, and a student center recreation room.

Disabled Students: 85% of the campus is accessible. Wheelchair ramps, elevators, special parking, specially equipped rest rooms, special class scheduling, lowered drinking fountains, and lowered telephones are available.

Services: Counseling and information services are available, as is tutoring in every subject. There is a reader service for the blind, and remedial math, reading, and writing. The university also offers study skills workshops, course-related workshops, math review sessions, foreign language conversation groups, and ESL support.

Campus Safety and Security: Measures include 24-hour foot and vehicle patrol, self-defense education, escort service, and shuttle buses. There are informal discussions, pamphlets/posters/films, emergency telephones, and lighted pathways/sidewalks.

Programs of Study: Phila. U. confers B.S. and B.Arch. degrees. Associate and master's degrees are also awarded. Bachelor's degrees are awarded in BIOLOGICAL SCIENCE (biochemistry and biology/biological science), BUSINESS (accounting, banking and finance, fashion merchandising, international business management, management information systems, management science, marketing/retailing/merchandising, and retailing), COMMUNICATIONS AND THE ARTS (graphic design and industrial design), COMPUTER AND PHYSICAL SCIENCE (chemistry and computer science), ENGINEERING AND ENVIRONMENTAL DESIGN (architecture, environmental science, interior design, textile engineering, and textile technology), HEALTH PROFESSIONS (physician's assistant and premedicine), SOCIAL SCIENCE (biopsychology, fashion design and technology, and psychology). Physician's assistant, architecture, and computer science are the strongest academically. Architecture, fashion merchandising, and fashion design are the largest.

Required: All students are required to complete a 60-credit residency with courses in math, science, social science, and the humanities, 2 semesters of phys ed, and a professional studies core curriculum, which differs by major program. A number of requirements may be satisfied and elective credits earned by proficiency exam. A total of 121 to 146 credits is required with an overall GPA of 2.0.

Special: The university offers special B.S. degree programs for registered nurses and allied health professionals. Cooperative education programs, available in all academic majors, offer placements locally, on the East Coast, and in London, England. Students may undertake a semester of independent study in 1 discipline. Study abroad, internships, a dual major in international business, an accelerated business administration degree program, and an integrated major in business and science are available. There is a freshman honors program.

Faculty/Classroom: 57% of faculty are male; 43%, female. All teach undergraduates and 50% also do research. No introductory courses are taught by graduate students. The average class size in an introductory lecture is 25; in a laboratory, 14; and in a regular course, 17.

Admissions: 75% of the 2001-2002 applicants were accepted. The SAT I scores for the 2001-2002 freshman class were: Verbal--35% below 500, 49% between 500 and 599, 14% between 600 and 700, and 2% above 700; Math--30% below 500, 50% between 500 and 599, 19% between 600 and 700, and 1% above 700. 30% of the current freshmen were in the top fifth of their class; 66% were in the top two fifths. 3 freshmen graduated first in their class.

Requirements: The SAT I or ACT is required. In addition, applicants should be high school graduates or have earned the GED. Recommended secondary preparation includes 4 years each of English and history, 3 of math which must include algebra II and geometry, and 2 of science. Potential science majors are strongly urged to take 4 years each of math and science. A GPA of 2.0 is required. AP and CLEP credits are accepted. Important factors in the admissions decision are evidence of special talent, extracurricular activities record, and leadership record. Electronic applications are available through the university's home page.

Procedure: Freshmen are admitted fall and spring. There is a deferred admissions plan. Application deadlines are open. The application fee is $35. Notification is sent on a rolling basis.

Transfer: 101 transfer students enrolled in 2001-2002. A 2.5 GPA is usually required. 60 credits of 121 to 146 must be completed at Phila. U.

Visiting: There are regularly scheduled orientations for prospective students, including an interview and a campus tour. There are guides for informal visits and visitors may sit in on classes and stay overnight. To schedule a visit, contact the Admissions Office.

Financial Aid: In 2001-2002, 98% of all freshmen and 93% of continuing students received some form of financial aid. 74% of freshmen and 68% of continuing students received need-based aid. The average freshman award was $13,804. Of that total, scholarships or need-based grants averaged $9491 ($24,722 maximum); loans averaged $3257 ($3425 maximum); and work contracts averaged $1056 ($2000 maximum). 31% of undergraduates work part time. Average annual earnings from campus work are $1000. The average financial indebtedness of the 2001 graduate was $12,559. The FAFSA is required. The fall application deadline is April 15.

International Students: There are 77 international students enrolled. The school actively recruits these students. They must score 500 on the written TOEFL and also take an English placement test.

Computers: The mainframe is a DEC ALPHA 1000/500. More than 250 Macs and PCs are available in the general-purpose and departmental computing labs. All students may access the system 7 days a week. There are no time limits and no fees. It is strongly recommended that all students have a personal computer.

Graduates: In 2001, 465 bachelor's degrees were awarded. The most popular majors were business and marketing (39%), architecture (17%), and fashion design (9%). In an average class, 32% graduate in 4 years, 42% in 5 years, and 45% in 6 years. 70 companies recruited on campus in 2000-2001. Of a recent graduating class, 9% were enrolled in graduate school within 6 months of graduation and 82% were employed.

Admissions Contact: Christine Greb, Acting Director of Admissions. E-mail: *admissions@philau.edu* Web: *www.philau.edu*

POINT PARK COLLEGE

B-3

Pittsburgh, PA 15222 **(412) 392-3430; (800) 321-0129**

Full-time: 668 men, 1062 women	**Faculty:** 76
Part-time: 520 men, 394 women	**Ph.D.s:** 53%
Graduate: 148 men, 177 women	**Student/Faculty:** 23 to 1
Year: semesters, summer session	**Tuition:** $14,342
Application Deadline: open	**Room & Board:** $5948
Freshman Class: 1397 applied, 1077 accepted, 322 enrolled	
SAT I Verbal/Math: 523/494	**ACT:** 22 **COMPETITIVE**

Point Park College, founded in 1960, is an independent institution offering programs in liberal arts, fine arts, business, engineering, health science, preprofessional training, and teacher preparation. There are 2 graduate schools. In addition to regional accreditation, Point Park College has baccalaureate program accreditation with ABET. The library contains 159,171 volumes, 29,590 microform items, and 2278 audiovisual forms/CDs, and subscribes to 688 periodicals. Computerized library services include the card catalog, interlibrary loans, and database searching. Special learning facilities include a learning resource center, radio station, TV station, theaters, and dance studios. The campus is in an urban area in downtown Pittsburgh. Including residence halls, there are 5 buildings.

Student Life: 85% of undergraduates are from Pennsylvania. Others are from 41 states, 32 foreign countries, and Canada. 77% are white; 12%, African American. 38% are Catholic; 35%, Protestant; 19% claim no religious affiliation. The average age of freshmen is 19; all undergraduates, 26. 32% do not continue beyond their first year; 45% remain to graduate.

Housing: 584 students can be accommodated in college housing, which includes single-sex and coed dormitories. On-campus housing is guaranteed for all 4 years. 79% of students commute. No one may keep cars.

Activities: There are no fraternities or sororities. There are 25 groups on campus, including cheerleading, choir, computers, dance, drama, ethnic, film, honors, international, literary magazine, musical theater, newspaper, photography, political, professional, radio and TV, religious, social, social service, student government, and yearbook. Popular campus events include Snowball (Christmas) Dance, Spring Fling dance, and dance and theater productions.

Sports: There are 4 intercollegiate sports for men and 4 for women, and 7 intramural sports for men and 7 for women. Facilities include a recreation center and a 130-seat auditorium.

Disabled Students: 98% of the campus is accessible. Wheelchair ramps, elevators, specially equipped rest rooms, special class scheduling, lowered drinking fountains, and lowered telephones are available.

Services: Counseling and information services are available, as is tutoring in most subjects. Learning-disabled services are available, but they are handled on a case-by-case basis. There is a reader service for the blind, and remedial math, reading, and writing.

Campus Safety and Security: Measures include 24-hour foot and vehicle patrol, escort service, informal discussions, and pamphlets/posters/films. There are emergency telephones and lighted pathways/sidewalks.

Programs of Study: Point Park College confers B.A., B.S., and B.F.A. degrees. Associate and master's degrees are also awarded. Bachelor's degrees are awarded in BIOLOGICAL SCIENCE (biology/biological science), BUSINESS (accounting, business administration and management, funeral home services, human resources, and management science), COMMUNICATIONS AND THE ARTS (advertising, applied art, arts administration/management, broadcasting, communications, dance, dramatic arts, English, film arts, journalism, media arts, photography, and video), COMPUTER AND PHYSICAL SCIENCE (computer science and information sciences and systems), EDUCATION (dance, drama, early childhood, elementary, and secondary), ENGINEERING AND ENVIRONMENTAL DESIGN (civil engineering technology, electrical/electronics engineering technology, engineering management, environmental science, mechanical engineering technology, and systems engineering), HEALTH PROFESSIONS (health care administration and respiratory therapy), SOCIAL SCIENCE (behavioral science, criminal justice, history, international studies, liberal arts/general studies, paralegal studies, political science/government, psychology, and public administration). Electrical engineering technology, business management, and performing arts are the largest.

Required: All majors leading to a baccalaureate degree require a minimum of 120 credits. Most programs require 42 core curriculum credits, with at least 30 completed in residence. A 2.0 GPA is required.

Special: Cross-registration is available through the Pittsburgh Council of Higher Education. The college offers internships, study abroad, a Washington semester, work-study, dual and student-designed majors, credit by exam and for life/military/work experience, nondegree study, and pass/fail options. Capstone programs are available for students with associate degrees. The film and video major is offered in conjunction with Pittsburgh Filmmakers. Accelerated degree programs are available. There are 2 national honor societies and a freshman honors program.

Faculty/Classroom: 66% of faculty are male; 34%, female. All teach undergraduates. No introductory courses are taught by graduate students. The average class size in an introductory lecture is 17; in a laboratory, 12; and in a regular course, 16.
Admissions: 77% of the 2001-2002 applicants were accepted. The SAT I scores for the 2001-2002 freshman class were: Verbal--39% below 500, 44% between 500 and 599, 11% between 600 and 700, and 6% above 700; Math--48% below 500, 40% between 500 and 599, 11% between 600 and 700, and 1% above 700. The ACT scores were 38% below 21, 30% between 21 and 23, 13% between 24 and 26, 12% between 27 and 28, and 7% above 28. 26% of the current freshmen were in the top fifth of their class; 49% were in the top two fifths. There were 2 National Merit finalists. 1 freshman graduated first in the class.
Requirements: The SAT I or ACT is required. In addition, students should have completed 12 academic credits or 16 Carnegie units, consisting of 4 in English, 3 in history, science, and math, and 2 years of foreign language. The GED is accepted. Theater and dance students must audition, and an interview is requested for all candidates. A GPA of 2.5 is required. AP and CLEP credits are accepted. Important factors in the admissions decision are advanced placement or honor courses, evidence of special talent, and personality/intangible qualities. Applications are accepted on-line at the school's web site.
Procedure: Freshmen are admitted to all sessions. Entrance exams should be taken in the junior or senior year. There are early admissions and deferred admissions plans. Application deadlines are open. The application fee is $20. Notification is sent on a rolling basis.
Transfer: 192 transfer students enrolled in 2001-2002. Applicants must have completed 12 credit hours with at least a 2.0 GPA. The SAT I or ACT, an associate degree, and an interview are recommended. 30 credits of 120 must be completed at Point Park College.
Visiting: There are regularly scheduled orientations for prospective students. There are guides for informal visits and visitors may sit in on classes and stay overnight. To schedule a visit, contact the Office of Admissions.
Financial Aid: In 2001-2002, 97% of all freshmen and 84% of continuing students received some form of financial aid. 83% of freshmen and 71% of continuing students received need-based aid. The average freshman award was $14,975. Of that total, scholarships or need-based grants averaged $6618 ($13,226 maximum); loans averaged $4942 ($23,724 maximum); and work contracts averaged $1177. 16% of undergraduates work part time. Average annual earnings from campus work are $798. The average financial indebtedness of the 2001 graduate was $7934. Point Park College is a member of CSS. The FAFSA is required.
International Students: There are 74 international students enrolled. The school actively recruits these students. They must score 500 on the written TOEFL or take the MELAB or the college's own test. Students who do not take the TOEFL, score a 500 on either of the other tests, or a 6 on the Test of Written English (TWE) must be tested upon arrival at the college.
Computers: The mainframe is an HP 9000/825. There are 82 PCs and terminals for student use. Access to the mainframe is limited to computer science and engineering technology majors. PC labs are available to all students, with special facilities open to journalism students only. Students may access the system 7 days a week according to the lab hours set by each facility and to the time available on the sign-up sheet. The fee is $60.
Graduates: In 2001, 385 bachelor's degrees were awarded. The most popular majors were business management (20%), electrical engineering (7%), and elementary education (6%). In an average class, 45% graduate in 6 years.
Admissions Contact: Michele Lawrence-Schmude, Director of Admissions. A video is available. E-mail: *enroll@ppc.edu*
Web: *www.ppc.edu*

ROBERT MORRIS COLLEGE
(See Robert Morris University)

ROBERT MORRIS UNIVERSITY (Formerly Robert Morris College) — B-3

Moon Township, PA 15108-1189 — **(412) 262-8402**
(800) 762-0097; Fax: (412) 299-2425

Full-time: 1480 men, 1206 women	**Faculty:** 106
Part-time: 470 men, 657 women	**Ph.D.s:** 75%
Graduate: 500 men, 406 women	**Student/Faculty:** 25 to 1
Year: semesters, summer session	**Tuition:** $12,150
Application Deadline: open	**Room & Board:** $6580
Freshman Class: 2129 applied, 1512 accepted, 531 enrolled	
SAT I Verbal/Math: 487/490	**COMPETITIVE**

Robert Morris University, formerly Robert Morris College, founded in 1921, is an independent nonprofit institution offering degree programs in liberal arts and technology at 2 major locations in the Pittsburgh area. There are 3 undergraduate and 3 graduate schools. In addition to regional accreditation, RMU has baccalaureate program accreditation with CAHEA. The 2 libraries contain 134,153 volumes, 358,555 microform items, and 2446 audiovisual forms/CDs, and subscribe to 853 periodicals. Computerized library services include the card catalog, interlibrary loans, and database searching. Special learning facilities include a learning resource center, TV station, and manufacturing lab for engineering and other students. The 230-acre main campus is in a suburban area 17 miles northwest of Pittsburgh. Including residence halls, there are 24 buildings.
Student Life: 94% of undergraduates are from Pennsylvania. Others are from 27 states, 28 foreign countries, and Canada. 86% are white. The average age of freshmen is 18; all undergraduates, 32. 26% do not continue beyond their first year; 56% remain to graduate.
Housing: 1025 students can be accommodated in college housing, which includes single-sex and coed dormitories and on-campus apartments. On-campus housing is guaranteed for all 4 years. 73% of students commute. Alcohol is not permitted. All students may keep cars.
Activities: 1% of men belong to 5 national fraternities; 1% of women belong to 3 national sororities. There are 50 groups on campus, including cheerleading, computers, drama, ethnic, honors, international, marching band, musical theater, pep band, photography, professional, radio and TV, religious, social, social service, and student government. Popular campus events include Snow Ball and Spring Fest.
Sports: There are 6 intercollegiate sports for men and 8 for women, and 8 intramural sports for men and 6 for women. Facilities include a field house, a gym, a health club, and 11 athletic fields.
Disabled Students: 35% of the campus is accessible. Wheelchair ramps, elevators, special parking, specially equipped rest rooms, special class scheduling, lowered drinking fountains, and lowered telephones are available.
Services: Counseling and information services are available, as is tutoring in most subjects. There is a reader service for the blind, and remedial math, reading, and writing.
Campus Safety and Security: Measures include 24-hour foot and vehicle patrol, escort service, shuttle buses, and informal discussions. There are pamphlets/posters/films, emergency telephones, and lighted pathways/sidewalks.
Programs of Study: RMU confers B.A., B.S., and B.S.B.A. degrees. Master's and doctoral degrees are also awarded. Bachelor's degrees are awarded in BUSINESS (accounting, banking and finance, business administration and management, hospitality management services, human resources, management science, marketing/retailing/merchandising, sports management, and transportation management), COMMUNICATIONS AND THE ARTS (communications and English), COMPUTER AND PHYSICAL SCIENCE (information sciences and systems and mathematics), EDUCATION (business and elementary), ENGINEERING AND ENVIRONMENTAL DESIGN (aviation administration/management and engineering), HEALTH PROFESSIONS (health care administration), SOCIAL SCIENCE (economics and social science). Engineering and mathematics are the strongest academically. Management, computer information systems, and accounting are the largest.
Required: To graduate, students must complete 126 to 135 credit hours, including 24 to 31 in the major, with a 2.0 GPA overall and a 2.5 in the major. A core curriculum varies with each major, and consists of humanities, communication skills, social sciences, computing, and math. All students must demonstrate competency in computer software applications.
Special: The university offers cooperative programs in all majors, cross-registration with the 9 schools of the Pittsburgh Council of Higher Education, internships, work-study programs, study abroad in 4 countries, and nondegree study. Credit by exam and pass/fail options are available. There are 2 national honor societies, a freshman honors program, and 1 departmental honors program.
Faculty/Classroom: 75% of faculty are male; 25%, female. All teach undergraduates. No introductory courses are taught by graduate students. The average class size in an introductory lecture is 23 and in a regular course, 23.
Admissions: 71% of the 2001-2002 applicants were accepted. The SAT I scores for the 2001-2002 freshman class were: Verbal--58% below 500, 33% between 500 and 599, 8% between 600 and 700, and 1% above 700; Math--53% below 500, 35% between 500 and 599, 11% between 600 and 700, and 1% above 700. 22% of the current freshmen were in the top fifth of their class; 58% were in the top two fifths.
Requirements: The SAT I is required. In addition, candidates should be graduates of an accredited secondary school or hold a GED diploma. They must have completed 16 Carnegie units, including 4 in English, 3 each in math and social studies, 2 in science, and 1 in history. An interview is required for some and recommended for all others. A GPA of 2.0 is required. AP and CLEP credits are accepted. Important factors in the admissions decision are advanced placement or honor courses, leadership record, and personality/intangible qualities. Applications are available on-line at the school's web site.
Procedure: Freshmen are admitted fall and spring. Entrance exams should be taken by fall or late winter of the senior year. There is a de-

ferred admissions plan. Application deadlines are open. The fall 2001 application fee was $30; the fee is waived for on-line applicants. Notification is sent on a rolling basis.

Transfer: 479 transfer students enrolled in 2001-2002. Students must have a minimum 2.0 GPA in nondevelopmental academic courses. Those with fewer than 30 earned credits must also submit an official high school transcript and test results of the SAT I or ACT. An interview is recommended. 30 credits of 126 to 135 must be completed at RMU.

Visiting: There are regularly scheduled orientations for prospective students, consisting of testing, orientation, and academic advising. There are guides for informal visits and visitors may sit in on classes and stay overnight. To schedule a visit, contact the Office of Admissions at (412) 262-8206.

Financial Aid: In 2001-2002, 85% of all freshmen and 80% of continuing students received some form of financial aid. 65% of all students received need-based aid. The average freshman award was $10,000. Of that total, scholarships or need-based grants averaged $4500 and loans averaged $5000. The FAFSA and PHEAA are required. The fall application deadline is May 1.

International Students: There are 71 international students enrolled. They must score 500 on the written TOEFL or 173 on the electronic version and also take the SAT I.

Computers: The mainframes are SUN servers. Students have access to 350 PCs at computerized labs and 6 computerized classrooms. Students can also access Internet applications at labs in the residence halls and library. All students may access the system 24 hours a day. There are no time limits and no fees.

Graduates: In 2001, 670 bachelor's degrees were awarded. The most popular majors were accounting (14%), management (12%), and management information systems (11%). In an average class, 36% graduate in 4 years, 53% in 5 years, and 56% in 6 years. 140 companies recruited on campus in 2000-2001. Of the 2000 graduating class, 3% were enrolled in graduate school within 6 months of graduation and 95% were employed.

Admissions Contact: Keith Paylo, Assistant Dean of Enrollment Services. A video is available. E-mail: *enrollmentoffice@rmu.edu*
Web: *http://www.rmu.edu*

ROSEMONT COLLEGE

Rosemont, PA 19010-1699 — F-4

(610) 526-2952
(800) 331-0708; Fax: (610) 520-4399

Full-time: 427 women	**Faculty:** 43
Part-time: 103 men, 267 women	**Ph.D.s:** 91%
Graduate: 74 men, 237 women	**Student/Faculty:** 10 to 1
Year: semesters, summer session	**Tuition:** $16,750
Application Deadline: open	**Room & Board:** $7310
Freshman Class: 211 applied, 179 accepted, 58 enrolled	
SAT I Verbal/Math: 560/520	**COMPETITIVE**

Rosemont College, founded in 1921, is an independent primarily women's liberal arts and sciences college, affiliated with the Roman Catholic Church. Accelerated degree and graduate programs are open to men and women. The library contains 15,400 volumes, 24,900 microform items, and 2010 audiovisual forms/CDs, and subscribes to 750 periodicals. Computerized library services include the card catalog, interlibrary loans, and database searching. Special learning facilities include a learning resource center and art gallery. The 56-acre campus is in a suburban area 11 miles west of Philadelphia. Including residence halls, there are 15 buildings.

Student Life: 72% of undergraduates are from Pennsylvania. Others are from 18 states and 10 foreign countries. 76% are white; 16% African American. 60% are Catholic; 17% Protestant; 15% Muslim, Quaker, and not indicated. The average age of freshmen is 18; all undergraduates, 23. 8% do not continue beyond their first year; 77% remain to graduate.

Housing: 410 students can be accommodated in college housing, which includes single-sex dormitories. In addition, there are special-interest houses. On-campus housing is guaranteed for all 4 years. 68% of students live on campus; of those, 50% remain on campus on weekends. All students may keep cars.

Activities: There are no fraternities or sororities. There are 11 groups on campus, including art, band, choir, chorus, dance, drama, ethnic, honors, international, jazz band, literary magazine, marching band, musical theater, newspaper, orchestra, photography, political, professional, radio, religious, social service, student government, symphony, and yearbook. Popular campus events include Oktoberfest, Founders Day, and International/Multi-Cultural Festival.

Sports: There are 6 intercollegiate sports for women. Facilities include hockey and softball fields, tennis courts, treadmills, weight equipment, a 500-seat auditorium, and indoor basketball, badminton, and volleyball courts.

Disabled Students: 20% of the campus is accessible. Wheelchair ramps, elevators, special parking, specially equipped rest rooms, special class scheduling, lowered drinking fountains, and lowered telephones are available.

Services: Counseling and information services are available, as is tutoring in every subject and a writing laboratory and learning resource center.

Campus Safety and Security: Measures include 24-hour foot and vehicle patrol, self-defense education, escort service, and shuttle buses. There are informal discussions, pamphlets/posters/films, emergency telephones, lighted pathways/sidewalks, and electronically operated residence hall entrances activated by security cards.

Programs of Study: Rosemont confers B.A., B.S., and B.F.A. degrees. Master's degrees are also awarded. Bachelor's degrees are awarded in BIOLOGICAL SCIENCE (biochemistry and biology/biological science), BUSINESS (accounting and business administration and management), COMMUNICATIONS AND THE ARTS (communications, English, fine arts, French, German, and Spanish), COMPUTER AND PHYSICAL SCIENCE (chemistry and mathematics), EDUCATION (art, foreign languages, and secondary), ENGINEERING AND ENVIRONMENTAL DESIGN (environmental science), HEALTH PROFESSIONS (predentistry and premedicine), SOCIAL SCIENCE (economics, history, humanities, Italian studies, liberal arts/general studies, philosophy, political science/government, prelaw, psychology, religion, social science, sociology, and women's studies). Psychology, English, and chemistry are the largest.

Required: All students take classes in writing, literature, religious studies, foreign language, philosophy, history, calculus or natural science, social science, and art. A total of 120 credits is required for graduation, with 33 to 36 in the major, and a minimum GPA of 2.0. A comprehensive exam must be taken in the major.

Special: Cross-registration with Villanova and Arcadia Universities, Eastern, Cabrini, Gwynedd-Mercy, Holy Family, Chestnut Hill, Immaculata, and Neumann Colleges, the Art Institute Exchange Program, internships, study abroad, a Washington semester, dual and student-designed majors, and accelerated degree programs are available. Also offered are a joint admission program with MCP/Hahnemann School of Medicine, 5-year accelerated programs in English and publishing and in counseling psychology, and elementary and secondary teacher certification. A transfer nursing program with Villanova University is also available. There are 6 national honor societies, and a freshman honors program.

Faculty/Classroom: 40% of faculty are male; 60%, female. All teach undergraduates and 70% both teach and do research. No introductory courses are taught by graduate students. The average class size in an introductory lecture is 20; in a laboratory, 10; and in a regular course, 12.

Admissions: 85% of the 2001-2002 applicants were accepted. The SAT I scores for the 2001-2002 freshman class were: Verbal--24% below 500, 44% between 500 and 599, 25% between 600 and 700, and 4% above 700; Math--38% below 500, 42% between 500 and 599, 13% between 600 and 700, and 4% above 700. 60% of the current freshmen were in the top fifth of their class; 83% were in the top two fifths. 5 freshmen graduated first in their class.

Requirements: The SAT I is required. In addition, a GED is accepted. Applicants must complete 16 academic credits, including 4 in English and 2 each in foreign language, history, math, and science. An interview is recommended. A GPA of 2.0 is required. AP and CLEP credits are accepted. Important factors in the admissions decision are advanced placement or honor courses, leadership record, and recommendations by school officials. Applications are accepted on-line via Apply.

Procedure: Freshmen are admitted fall and spring. Entrance exams should be taken before January of the senior year. There is a deferred admissions plan. Application deadlines are open. The fall 2001 application fee was $35. Notification is sent on a rolling basis.

Transfer: 20 transfer students enrolled in 2001-2002. Transfer applicants should submit transcripts from each college attended, a letter of good standing from the dean at the last college attended, and catalogs from the colleges from which the student wishes to transfer credits. Students with fewer than 30 credits are required to submit high school transcripts and the SAT I scores. The minimum GPA is 2.0. An associate degree and interview are recommended. 45 credits of 120 must be completed at Rosemont.

Visiting: There are regularly scheduled orientations for prospective students, including campus visit days, overnight visits, and class visitations. There are guides for informal visits and visitors may sit in on classes and stay overnight. To schedule a visit, contact the Admissions Office.

Financial Aid: In 2001-2002, 93% of all freshmen received some form of financial aid. 72% of freshmen and 61% of continuing students received need-based aid. The average freshman award was $13,405. Of that total, scholarships or need-based grants averaged $9820 ($16,000 maximum); loans averaged $3125 ($5625 maximum); and work contracts averaged $1500 (maximum). 39% of undergraduates work part time. Average annual earnings from campus work are $700. The average financial indebtedness of the 2001 graduate was $16,000. Rosemont is a member of CSS. The FAFSA is required. The fall application deadline is March 15.

International Students: There are 25 international students enrolled. The school actively recruits these students. They must score 500 on the written TOEFL.

Computers: There are 40 public workstations with Microsoft Office Pro software. All have full access to the college's electronic learning and library information system. All residence hall rooms are connected to the network. All students may access the system. There are no time limits and no fees.

Graduates: In 2001, 214 bachelor's degrees were awarded. The most popular majors were psychology (23%), English literature (15%), and accounting/business (13%). In an average class, 74% graduate in 4 years, and 77% in 5 years. 8 companies recruited on campus in 2000-2001. Of the 2000 graduating class, 33% were enrolled in graduate school within 6 months of graduation and 67% were employed.

Admissions Contact: Rennie H. Andrews, Dean of Admissions. A video is available. E-mail: *admissions@rosemont.edu*
Web: *www.rosemont.edu*

SAINT FRANCIS UNIVERSITY

Loretto, PA 15940 — C-3
(814) 472-3100
(800) 342-5732; Fax: (814) 472-3335

Full-time: 486 men, 710 women — **Faculty:** 87; IIB, av$
Part-time: 63 men, 157 women — **Ph.D.s:** 53%
Graduate: 223 men, 388 women — **Student/Faculty:** 14 to 1
Year: semesters, summer session — **Tuition:** $17,512
Application Deadline: July 1 — **Room & Board:** $6974
Freshman Class: 2151 applied, 1081 accepted, 342 enrolled
SAT I or ACT: required — **LESS COMPETITIVE**

Saint Francis University, formerly Saint Francis College, founded in 1847, is a private Franciscan institution affiliated with the Roman Catholic Church. It offers programs in business, education, humanities, sciences, social science, and preprofessional programs. In addition to regional accreditation, Saint Francis has baccalaureate program accreditation with CAHEA, CSWE, and NLN. The library contains 117,199 volumes, 6940 microform items, and 2339 audiovisual forms/CDs, and subscribes to 4477 periodicals. Computerized library services include the card catalog, interlibrary loans, and database searching. Special learning facilities include a learning resource center, art gallery, radio station, classroom satellite hookup, TV studio, and art studio. The 600-acre campus is in a rural area 85 miles east of Pittsburgh. Including residence halls, there are 23 buildings.

Student Life: 68% of undergraduates are from Pennsylvania. Others are from 16 states, 6 foreign countries, and Canada. 66% are from public schools. 85% are white. 55% are Catholic; 40% Protestant. The average age of freshmen is 19; all undergraduates, 21. 25% do not continue beyond their first year; 44% remain to graduate.

Housing: 983 students can be accommodated in college housing, which includes single-sex dormitories, on-campus apartments, off-campus apartments, and married-student housing. In addition, there are intensive study floors. On-campus housing is guaranteed for all 4 years. 65% of students live on campus; of those, 70% remain on campus on weekends. Alcohol is not permitted. Upperclassmen may keep cars.

Activities: 6% of men belong to 2 national fraternities; 6% of women belong to 1 local sorority and 2 national sororities. There are 63 groups on campus, including art, cheerleading, choir, computers, drama, ethnic, honors, international, literary magazine, newspaper, pep band, photography, political, professional, radio and TV, religious, social, social service, student government, and yearbook. Popular campus events include a weekend movie program, soft rock cafe, and the Mock Democratic Presidential Nominating Convention.

Sports: There are 9 intercollegiate sports for men and 12 for women, and 12 intramural sports for men and 12 for women. Facilities include a phys ed building with a pool for competition, racquetball courts, a suspended running track, a weight room, a 4000-seat gym, and a multipurpose gym for intramurals. Outdoor facilities include tennis and basketball courts, soccer, softball, and football facilities, a 9-hole golf course, a lake, and volleyball pits.

Disabled Students: 30% of the campus is accessible. Wheelchair ramps, elevators, special parking, specially equipped rest rooms, and lowered telephones are available.

Services: Counseling and information services are available, as is tutoring in most subjects. There is remedial math, reading, and writing.

Campus Safety and Security: Measures include 24-hour foot and vehicle patrol, escort service, informal discussions, and pamphlets/posters/films. There are emergency telephones and lighted pathways/sidewalks.

Programs of Study: Saint Francis confers B.A., B.S., B.S.N., and B.S.W. degrees. Master's degrees are also awarded. Bachelor's degrees are awarded in BIOLOGICAL SCIENCE (biology/biological science), BUSINESS (accounting, management information systems, and management science), COMMUNICATIONS AND THE ARTS (communications, English, French, modern language, and Spanish), COMPUTER AND PHYSICAL SCIENCE (chemistry, computer science, and mathematics), EDUCATION (elementary and secondary), HEALTH PROFESSIONS (medical laboratory technology, nursing, occupational therapy, physical therapy, and physician's assistant), SOCIAL SCIENCE (criminal justice, economics, history, international studies, philosophy, political science/government, psychology, public administration, religion, social work, and sociology). Business, physician assistant, and physical therapy are the strongest academically. Occupational therapy, natural and applied science, and education are the largest.

Required: Students must complete 128 credits, with at least 36 in the major, while maintaining a 2.0 GPA. The core curriculum, totaling 58 credits, includes writing, public speaking, fine arts, foreign language, history, philosophy, religious studies (with required service component), psychology, sociology, political science, and economics. A word processing and research workshop is required in the freshman year. In addition to a comprehensive exam in the major, an English proficiency exam must be taken in the junior year.

Special: The university offers internships, co-op programs, study abroad in 10 countries, a Washington semester, work-study programs, and nondegree study. Student-designed majors and 3-2 engineering degrees with Pennsylvania State and Clarkson Universities and the University of Pittsburgh are available. There is a dual major available in international business/modern languages. Credit by exam and pass/fail options are also offered. There are 11 national honor societies, a freshman honors program, and 10 departmental honors programs.

Faculty/Classroom: 53% of faculty are male; 47%, female. 99% teach undergraduates, 50% do research, and 50% do both. No introductory courses are taught by graduate students. The average class size in an introductory lecture is 23; in a laboratory, 16; and in a regular course, 19.

Admissions: 50% of the 2001-2002 applicants were accepted. 41% of the current freshmen were in the top fifth of their class; 73% were in the top two fifths. 6 freshmen graduated first in their class in a recent year.

Requirements: The SAT I or ACT is required. In addition, applicants must be graduates of an accredited secondary school or have earned a GED certificate. All applicants must have completed 16 Carnegie units, consisting of 4 years of English, 2 each of math and social science, 1 lab science, and 7 academic electives. Applicants to biology and allied health majors need an addiitonal unit of science. Chemistry, computer science, engineering, and math applicants need 4 math units and 2 science units. Physical therapy applicants must have 4 units of math and 4 of science. A GPA of 2.0 is required. AP and CLEP credits are accepted. Important factors in the admissions decision are advanced placement or honor courses, recommendations by school officials, and extracurricular activities record.

Procedure: Freshmen are admitted to all sessions. Entrance exams should be taken in spring of the junior year and fall of the senior year. There are early admissions and deferred admissions plans. Early decision applications should be filed by November 15; regular applications, by July 1 for fall entry. Deadline for physical therapy, phsyician's assistant, and occupational therapy programs is January 15. Notification is sent on a rolling basis.

Transfer: 60 transfer students enrolled in 2001-2002. Applicants must have a minimum GPA of 2.0 for consideration, 2.5 for nursing majors, and 2.75 for physician's assistant majors. 64 credits of 128 must be completed at Saint Francis.

Visiting: There are regularly scheduled orientations for prospective students, consisting of a campus tour, admission interview, financial aid interview, and class attendance. There are guides for informal visits and visitors may sit in on classes and stay overnight. To schedule a visit, contact the Admissions Office at *elipp@francis.edu*.

Financial Aid: In 2001-2002, 85% of all freshmen and 84% of continuing students received some form of financial aid. 72% of all students received need-based aid. The average freshman award was $15,322. Of that total, scholarships or need-based grants averaged $12,541 ($23,486 maximum); loans averaged $2625 ($3625 maximum); and work contracts averaged $1000 (maximum). 49% of undergraduates work part time. Average annual earnings from campus work are $800. The average financial indebtedness of the 2001 graduate was $14,100. Saint Francis is a member of CSS. The FAFSA and the college's own financial statement are required. The fall application deadline is May 1.

International Students: There are 12 international students enrolled. They must score 500 on the written TOEFL and also take the SAT I or the ACT.

Computers: The mainframe is a Alpha 4000. Mainframe access is limited to computer science majors, who may gain access through only one of 3 computer labs. A network of about 46 PCs is available to all students. All students may access the system. There are no time limits and no fees. All students are required to have personal computers.

Graduates: In 2001, 309 bachelor's degrees were awarded. The most popular majors were physician's assistant (17%), accounting (12%), and management (12%). In an average class, 1% graduate in 3 years, 44% in 4 years, 58% in 5 years, and 62% in 6 years. 60 companies recruited on campus in 2000-2001. Of the 2000 graduating class, 33% were enrolled in graduate school within 6 months of graduation and 65% were employed.

Admissions Contact: Evan Lipp, Dean for Enrollment Management. E-mail: *admissions@sfcpa.edu* Web: *www.sfcpa.edu*

SAINT JOSEPH'S UNIVERSITY

Philadelphia, PA 19131 — F-3

(610) 660-1300
(888) BE-A-HAWK; Fax: (610) 660-1314

Full-time: 1725 men, 1950 women	**Faculty:** 219; IIA, av$
Part-time: 401 men, 513 women	**Ph.D.s:** 92%
Graduate: 986 men, 1642 women	**Student/Faculty:** 17 to 1
Year: semesters, summer session	**Tuition:** $21,270
Application Deadline: open	**Room & Board:** $8445
Freshman Class: 5866 applied, 3343 accepted, 982 enrolled	
SAT I Verbal/Math: 605/612	**ACT:** 30 **VERY COMPETITIVE+**

Saint Joseph's University, founded in 1851, is a Catholic, private college affiliated with the Jesuit order and offering undergraduate programs in arts and sciences and business administration. There are 3 undergraduate and 2 graduate schools. In addition to regional accreditation, Saint Joseph's has baccalaureate program accreditation with AACSB and NCATE. The 2 libraries contain 348,900 volumes, 808,309 microform items, and 3820 audiovisual forms/CDs, and subscribe to 1800 periodicals. Computerized library services include the card catalog, interlibrary loans, and database searching. Special learning facilities include a learning resource center, art gallery, radio station, instructional media center, and foreign language labs. The 60-acre campus is in a suburban area on the western edge of Philadelphia. Including residence halls, there are 45 buildings.

Student Life: 58% of undergraduates are from Pennsylvania. Others are from 33 states and 27 foreign countries. 47% are from public schools. 81% are white. The average age of freshmen is 18; all undergraduates, 20. 13% do not continue beyond their first year; 68% remain to graduate.

Housing: 1839 students can be accommodated in college housing, which includes single-sex and coed dormitories, on-campus apartments, and off-campus apartments. In addition, there are honors houses and special-interest houses and floors. On-campus housing is available on a lottery system for upperclassmen. Upperclassmen may keep cars.

Activities: 11% of men belong to 4 national fraternities; 16% of women belong to 3 national sororities. There are 80 groups on campus, including art, cheerleading, choir, chorus, computers, dance, debate, drama, ethnic, film, forensics, honors, international, jazz band, literary magazine, musical theater, newspaper, pep band, photography, political, professional, radio and TV, religious, social, social service, student government, and yearbook. Popular campus events include Hand in Hand, St. Joseph's Day, and Up 'Til Dawn.

Sports: There are 10 intercollegiate sports for men and 10 for women, and 16 intramural sports for men and 15 for women. Facilities include a gym, fields, 4 multipurpose courts, indoor and outdoor tracks, 4 racquetball courts, a pool, and a fitness center.

Disabled Students: 90% of the campus is accessible. Wheelchair ramps, elevators, special parking, specially equipped rest rooms, special class scheduling, lowered drinking fountains, lowered telephones, automatic eye doors, curb cuts, a specially equipped van for wheelchairs, a pool lift, and a bell system at major road crossings are available.

Services: Counseling and information services are available, as is tutoring in most subjects. There are also services for people with learning disabilities.

Campus Safety and Security: Measures include 24-hour foot and vehicle patrol, self-defense education, escort service, and shuttle buses. There are informal discussions, pamphlets/posters/films, emergency telephones, lighted pathways/sidewalks, and a bicycle patrol.

Programs of Study: Saint Joseph's confers B.A. and B.S. degrees. Associate, master's, and doctoral degrees are also awarded. Bachelor's degrees are awarded in BIOLOGICAL SCIENCE (biology/biological science), BUSINESS (accounting, banking and finance, business administration and management, labor studies, management science, and marketing/retailing/merchandising), COMMUNICATIONS AND THE ARTS (English, fine arts, French, German, and Spanish), COMPUTER AND PHYSICAL SCIENCE (chemistry, computer science, information sciences and systems, mathematics, and physics), EDUCATION (elementary and secondary), ENGINEERING AND ENVIRONMENTAL DESIGN (environmental science), HEALTH PROFESSIONS (health care administration), SOCIAL SCIENCE (criminal justice, economics, food production/management/services, French studies, history, human services, humanities, industrial and organizational psychology, international relations, philosophy, political science/government, psychology, public administration, religion, social studies, and sociology). Social sciences, natural sciences, and English are the strongest academically. Biology, psychology, and food marketing are the largest.

Required: All students must take general education common courses in language, theology, philosophy, and history. Distribution requirements include 3 courses each of social/behavioral sciences and theology, 2 courses of foreign language at the intermediate level, 2 courses each of math and natural sciences, and a philosophy course. A total of 120 credit hours is required for graduation, with 21 to 54 in the major and a GPA of 2.0.

Special: There is an exchange program with a Japanese university and study abroad in 8 countries. Saint Joseph's offers internships, a Washington semester, advanced 5-year degrees in international marketing and in psychology, dual majors, minor concentrations, and special programs in American, Latin American, European, Russian, gender, and medieval studies. There is a co-op program for food marketing majors and an interdisciplinary major in health services. There are 17 national honor societies, including Phi Beta Kappa, and a freshman honors program.

Faculty/Classroom: 65% of faculty are male; 35%, female. 85% teach undergraduates. No introductory courses are taught by graduate students. The average class size in an introductory lecture is 28; in a laboratory, 11; and in a regular course, 25.

Admissions: 57% of the 2001-2002 applicants were accepted.

Requirements: The SAT I or ACT is required. In addition, applicants must graduate from an accredited secondary school and prepare with 4 years of English, 3 of math, 2 each of foreign language and science, and 1 each of history and social studies. Preference is given to students with 3 to 4 years of foreign language and natural science and 4 years of math. A GPA of 3.0 is required. AP credits are accepted. Important factors in the admissions decision are advanced placement or honor courses, extracurricular activities record, and recommendations by school officials. Applications are accepted on computer disk via CollegeLink and Common App.

Procedure: Freshmen are admitted fall and spring. Entrance exams should be taken in the spring of the junior year or the fall of the senior year. Application deadlines are open. The fall 2001 application fee was $45. Notification is sent on a rolling basis. 18% of all applicants are on a waiting list.

Transfer: 120 transfer students enrolled in 2001-2002. Applicants must have a GPA of at least 2.5 and must submit former test scores and high school and college transcripts. Applicants must apply by November 1 for the spring term and by March 1 for the fall term. 60 credits of 120 must be completed at Saint Joseph's.

Visiting: There are regularly scheduled orientations for prospective students, including open houses, tours, and information sessions. There are guides for informal visits and visitors may sit in on classes and stay overnight. To schedule a visit, contact the Admissions Office.

Financial Aid: In 2001-2002, 87% of all freshmen and 81% of continuing students received some form of financial aid. 75% of freshmen and 73% of continuing students received need-based aid. The average freshman award was $1167. Of that total, scholarships or need-based grants averaged $7468 ($20,500 maximum); loans averaged $3019 ($9500 maximum); and work contracts averaged $1200 (maximum). 50% of undergraduates work part time. Average annual earnings from campus work are $1200. The average financial indebtedness of the 2001 graduate was $14,717. The FAFSA is required. The fall application deadline is May 1.

International Students: There are 35 international students enrolled. The school actively recruits these students. They must score 550 on the written TOEFL; students who matriculate through ELS must achieve Level 9. Applicants must also take the SAT I or the ACT.

Computers: The mainframes are Sun Microsystems servers. Campus-wide access is provided by 16 computer classes/labs (329 systems); in addition, residence facilities are networked for 1600 students. Dial-up access is also available for off-campus housing. All students may access the system whenever the labs are open (about 90 hours per week) or at any time if students are connected in their dormitory rooms. There are no time limits and no fees. It is strongly recommended that all students have a personal computer; the university supplies laptops to students in the business school and some departments in CAS.

Graduates: In 2001, 831 bachelor's degrees were awarded. The most popular majors were psychology (11%), food marketing (10%), and marketing (9%). In an average class, 63% graduate in 4 years, 67% in 5 years, and 68% in 6 years. 100 companies recruited on campus in 2000-2001. Of the 2000 graduating class, 21% were enrolled in graduate school within 6 months of graduation and 73% were employed.

Admissions Contact: Susan P. Kassab, Director of Admissions. A video is available. E-mail: *admit@sju.edu* Web: *http://www.sju.edu*

SAINT VINCENT COLLEGE

Latrobe, PA 15650 — B-2

(724) 537-4540
(800) SVC-5549; Fax: (724) 532-5069

Full-time: 571 men, 536 women	**Faculty:** 80; IIB, -$
Part-time: 52 men, 63 women	**Ph.D.s:** 80%
Graduate: none	**Student/Faculty:** 14 to 1
Year: semesters, summer session	**Tuition:** $17,380
Application Deadline: May 1	**Room & Board:** $5562
Freshman Class: 687 applied, 579 accepted, 263 enrolled	
SAT I Verbal/Math: 540/530	**ACT:** 23 **VERY COMPETITIVE**

Saint Vincent College, founded in 1846, is a Catholic college of liberal arts and sciences sponsored by the Benedictine monks. In addition to regional accreditation, Saint Vincent has baccalaureate program accreditation with ACBSP. The library contains 263,162 volumes, 98,717 microform items, and 2747 audiovisual forms/CDs, and subscribes to 811 periodicals. Computerized library services include the card catalog, interlibrary loans, and database searching. Special learning facilities include a learning resource center, art gallery, planetarium, radio station, TV station, observatory, radio telescope, and small business development center. The 200-acre campus is in a suburban area 35 miles east of Pittsburgh. Including residence halls, there are 23 buildings.

Student Life: 86% of undergraduates are from Pennsylvania. Others are from 23 states, 15 foreign countries, and Canada. 71% are from public schools. 94% are white. 67% are Catholic; 20% Protestant; 13% unknown, no preference. The average age of freshmen is 18; all undergraduates, 21. 14% do not continue beyond their first year; 71% remain to graduate.

Housing: 1230 students can be accommodated in college housing, which includes coed dormitories. There is also a 24-hour quiet, private study dorm. On-campus housing is guaranteed for all 4 years. 69% of students live on campus; of those, 80% remain on campus on weekends. All students may keep cars.

Activities: There are no fraternities or sororities. There are 52 groups on campus, including art, band, campus ministry service, choir, chorale, chorus, dance, drama, ethnic, honors, international, literary magazine, musical theater, newspaper, pep band, political, professional, radio and TV, religious, social, social service, student government, and yearbook. Popular campus events include an annual indoor beach party, the Threshold Lecture Series, and Pittsburgh Steeler training camp.

Sports: There are 6 intercollegiate sports for men and 6 for women, and 6 intramural sports for men and 6 for women. Facilities include a 2400-seat gym, basketball and volleyball facilities, a weight and exercise room, an indoor pool, tennis courts, baseball, soccer, and football fields, a mini movie theater, a 999-seat auditorium/arena, and a student union and game room area.

Disabled Students: 95% of the campus is accessible. Wheelchair ramps, elevators, special parking, specially equipped rest rooms, special class scheduling, lowered drinking fountains, lowered telephones, and lowered computer desks are available.

Services: Counseling and information services are available, as is tutoring in every subject. There is remedial math, reading, and writing. The Opportunity Office provides individual counseling and a freshman study skills class.

Campus Safety and Security: Measures include 24-hour foot and vehicle patrol, escort service, informal discussions, and pamphlets/posters/films. There are emergency telephones and lighted pathways/sidewalks.

Programs of Study: Saint Vincent confers B.A., B.S., and B.F.A. degrees. Bachelor's degrees are awarded in BIOLOGICAL SCIENCE (biochemistry and biology/biological science), BUSINESS (accounting, banking and finance, and business administration and management), COMMUNICATIONS AND THE ARTS (art, art history and appreciation, communications, English, fine arts, music, music performance, Spanish, studio art, and visual and performing arts), COMPUTER AND PHYSICAL SCIENCE (chemistry, computer science, information sciences and systems, mathematics, and physics), EDUCATION (art, music, physical, psychology, and science), ENGINEERING AND ENVIRONMENTAL DESIGN (environmental science), HEALTH PROFESSIONS (occupational therapy, physical therapy, physician's assistant, predentistry, premedicine, prepharmacy, and preveterinary science), SOCIAL SCIENCE (anthropology, economics, history, liberal arts/general studies, philosophy, political science/government, prelaw, psychology, public affairs, religious education, sociology, and theological studies). Biology, accounting, and chemistry are the strongest academically. Accounting, biology, and psychology are the largest.

Required: All students are required to take Language and Rhetoric, Exploring Religious Meaning, and Philosophy I. The core curriculum includes 12 hours of social science, 9 each of history, religious studies, English, and philosophy, 8 of natural sciences, 3 of math, and 6 hours of foreign language is required for the B.A. All majors require a culminating activity, such as a thesis, research project, or capstone course/seminar. Students must complete 124 credits and achieve a minimum GPA of 2.0.

Special: There is cross-registration with Seton Hill College, co-op programs, internships, study abroad in Europe and Asia, a Washington semester, a work-study program, dual majors, a general studies degree, credit by exam and for life/military/work experience, nondegree study, and pass/fail options. There is an accelerated degree engineering program and a 3-2 engineering option with Boston University, Pennsylvania state universities, the University of Pittsburgh, and the Catholic University of America. The college offers teacher certificate programs in early childhood, elementary, and secondary education. There are 9 national honor societies, and a freshman honors program.

Faculty/Classroom: 74% of faculty are male; 26%, female. All both teach and do research. The average class size in an introductory lecture is 24; in a laboratory, 15; and in a regular course, 18.

Admissions: 84% of the 2001-2002 applicants were accepted. The SAT I scores for the 2001-2002 freshman class were: Verbal--31% below 500, 44% between 500 and 599, 20% between 600 and 700, and 6% above 700; Math--35% below 500, 40% between 500 and 599, 22% between 600 and 700, and 4% above 700. The ACT scores were 32% below 21, 20% between 21 and 23, 30% between 24 and 26, 9% between 27 and 28, and 9% above 28. 43% of the current freshmen were in the top fifth of their class; 67% were in the top two fifths. In a recent year, 5 freshmen graduated first in their class.

Requirements: The SAT I or ACT is required. In addition, applicants must complete 15 academic credits, including 4 of English, 3 each of social studies and math, 2 of foreign language, and 1 of a lab science. Art students must submit a portfolio, and music and theater students must audition. An essay is required. A GED is accepted. A GPA of 3.2 is required. AP and CLEP credits are accepted. Important factors in the admissions decision are advanced placement or honor courses, evidence of special talent, and recommendations by school officials.

Procedure: Freshmen are admitted fall and spring. Entrance exams should be taken at the end of the junior year or the beginning of the senior year. There is a deferred admissions plan. Applications should be filed by May 1 for fall entry and January 1 for spring entry. Notification is sent on a rolling basis. The fall application fee was $25.

Transfer: Transfer applicants must submit transcripts from postsecondary schools attended and a catalog describing courses taken, plus secondary school transcript(s). 34 credits of 124 must be completed at Saint Vincent.

Visiting: There are regularly scheduled orientations for prospective students, consisting of a general information session, an informal meeting with faculty, and campus tours. There are guides for informal visits and visitors may sit in on classes and stay overnight. To schedule a visit, contact the Admission and Financial Aid Office.

Financial Aid: In 2001-2002, 95% of all freshmen and 93% of continuing students received some form of financial aid. 80% of all students received need-based aid. The average freshman award was $14,486. Of that total, scholarships or need-based grants averaged $11,244; loans averaged $2927; and work contracts averaged $1907. 50% of undergraduates work part time. Average annual earnings from campus work are $1600. The FAFSA is required. The fall application deadline is April 1.

International Students: There are 24 international students enrolled. They must score 525 on the written TOEFL.

Computers: The mainframe is an HP 9000/Series 810. Computer labs containing PCs and Macs are located in various areas throughout the campus. There are also computer labs in the dormitories and 1 Internet connection per student in each residence hall room. All students may access the system during computer lab hours. Computer labs are open an average of 18 hours per day. There are no fees.

Graduates: In 2001, 234 bachelor's degrees were awarded. The most popular majors were psychology (13%), communication (10%), and biology and accounting (9%). In an average class, 1% graduate in 3 years, 60% in 4 years, 69% in 5 years, and 71% in 6 years. In a recent year, 140 companies recruited on campus. Of the 2000 graduating class, 22% were enrolled in graduate school within 6 months of graduation and 70% were employed.

Admissions Contact: Admission and Financial Aid Office. A video is available. E-mail: *admission@stvincent.edu*
Web: *http://www.stvincent.edu/admin-faid/admin-faid.html*

SETON HILL COLLEGE — B-4
Greensburg, PA 15601-1599 — (724) 838-4255
(800) 826-6234; Fax: (724) 830-1294

Full-time: 137 men, 672 women	**Faculty:** 51; IIB, --$
Part-time: 66 men, 253 women	**Ph.D.s:** 82%
Graduate: 45 men, 197 women	**Student/Faculty:** 16 to 1
Year: semesters, summer session	**Tuition:** $16,425
Application Deadline: open	**Room & Board:** $5450
Freshman Class: 940 applied, 731 accepted, 160 enrolled	
SAT I Verbal/Math: recommended	**COMPETITIVE**

Seton Hill College, founded in 1883, is a private college affiliated with the Catholic Church and offering programs in liberal arts and career preparation. In addition to regional accreditation, Seton Hill has baccalaureate program accreditation with ADA and NASM. The library contains 115,427 volumes, 5103 microform items, and 6185 audiovisual forms/CDs, and subscribes to 361 periodicals. Computerized library services include the card catalog, interlibrary loans, and database searching. Special learning facilities include an art gallery, TV station, and nursery school and kindergarten that function as laboratory schools for education students, performance hall, and 2 theaters. The 200-acre campus is in a small town 35 miles east of Pittsburgh. Including residence halls, there are 17 buildings.

Student Life: 83% of undergraduates are from Pennsylvania. Others are from 22 states, 12 foreign countries, and Canada. 82% are white. The average age of freshmen is 18; all undergraduates, 22. 22% do not continue beyond their first year; 60% remain to graduate.

Housing: 450 students can be accommodated in college housing, which includes single-sex dormitories. On-campus housing is guaranteed for all 4 years. 60% of students live on campus. Alcohol is not permitted. All students may keep cars.

Activities: There are no fraternities or sororities. There are 28 groups on campus, including art, cheerleading, choir, chorale, chorus, dance, drama, entrepreneurial, environmental, ethnic, gay, honors, international, jazz band, literary magazine, musical theater, newspaper, orchestra, political, professional, religious, social, social service, student government, symphony, and yearbook. Popular campus events include Christmas on the Hill, Family Weekend, and President's Reception.

Sports: There are 4 intercollegiate sports for men and 8 for women, and 2 intramural sports for men and 2 for women. Facilities include a gym, a swimming pool, tennis courts, softball and soccer fields, a weight room, a jacuzzi, a sauna, and a fitness trail. The indoor gym seats 650; the largest auditorium/arena seats 300.

Disabled Students: 95% of the campus is accessible. Wheelchair ramps, elevators, special parking, specially equipped rest rooms, special class scheduling, lowered drinking fountains, and lowered telephones are available.

Services: Counseling and information services are available, as is tutoring in most subjects. There is a reader service for the blind and remedial math and writing.

Campus Safety and Security: Measures include 24-hour foot and vehicle patrol, self-defense education, escort service, and shuttle buses. There are informal discussions, pamphlets/posters/films, emergency telephones, and lighted pathways/sidewalks.

Programs of Study: Seton Hill confers B.A., B.S., B.F.A., B.Mus., B.S.Med.Tech., and B.S.W. degrees. Master's degrees are also awarded. Bachelor's degrees are awarded in BIOLOGICAL SCIENCE (biochemistry and biology/biological science), BUSINESS (accounting, banking and finance, business administration and management, business economics, entrepreneurial studies, international business management, marketing/retailing/merchandising, and personnel management), COMMUNICATIONS AND THE ARTS (art history and appreciation, arts administration/management, communications, design, dramatic arts, English, fine arts, journalism, music, musical theater, performing arts, Spanish, studio art, theater design, and theater management), COMPUTER AND PHYSICAL SCIENCE (actuarial science, chemistry, computer science, mathematics, and physics), EDUCATION (art, early childhood, elementary, English, foreign languages, home economics, mathematics, music, science, secondary, social science, and special), HEALTH PROFESSIONS (art therapy, medical laboratory technology, nursing, physician's assistant, predentistry, premedicine, and preveterinary science), SOCIAL SCIENCE (child care/child and family studies, dietetics, economics, family/consumer resource management, family/consumer studies, food production/management/services, history, human services, international studies, liberal arts/general studies, political science/government, prelaw, psychology, religion, religious music, social work, and sociology). Sciences, education, and fine arts are the strongest academically. Psychology, biology, and art are the largest.

Required: The core corriculum requires 6 credits in Western cultural traditions, and freshman seminar, and 3 each in theology, philosophy/senior seminar, math, computer science, and science, college-level foreign language, American studies, world cultures, and artistic expression. A total of 120 credit hours with a minimum GPA of 2.0 is required for graduation.

Special: There are cooperative programs in all majors and cross-registration with St. Vincent College, the University of Pittsburgh at Greensburg, and Westmoreland County Community College. Internships are encouraged. Seton Hill offers study abroad, a Washington semester, work-study, dual and student-designed majors, accelerated degree programs, a 3-2 engineering program with Pennsylvania State University and Georgia Institute of Technology, a 2-2 nursing program with Catholic University of America, a 3-2 or 3-1 medical technology program with area hospitals, credit by exam and for life/military/work experience, nondegree study, and pass/fail options. There are 5 national honor societies and a freshman honors program. All departments have honors programs.

Faculty/Classroom: 44% of faculty are male; 56%, female. All teach undergraduates and 60% do research. No introductory courses are taught by graduate students. The average class size in an introductory lecture is 25; in a lab, 16; and in a regular course, 17.

Admissions: 78% of the 2001-2002 applicants were accepted. 35% of the current freshmen were in the top fifth of their class; 70% were in the top two fifths. 1 freshman graduated first in the class.

Requirements: The SAT I or ACT is recommended. In addition, two graded writing samples are accepted in place of SAT I/ACT scores. A total of 15 Carnegie units is required, including 4 each of English and electives, 2 each of math, social studies, and foreign language, and 1 of a lab science. Art students must submit a portfolio; music and theater students must audition. An interview is recommended. The GED is accepted with supporting recommendations. A GPA of 2.5 is required. AP and CLEP credits are accepted. Important factors in the admissions decision are advanced placement or honor courses, evidence of special talent, and leadership record. Applications are accepted on computer disk and via e-mail.

Procedure: Freshmen are admitted fall and spring. Entrance exams should be taken in spring of the junior year or fall of the senior year. There is a deferred and rolling admissions plan. Application deadlines are open. The application fee is $30. Notification is on a rolling basis.

Transfer: 64 transfer students enrolled in 2001-2002. Applicants must submit college transcripts and have a GPA of at least 2.0. An interview is recommended, as are supporting letters. 48 credits of 120 must be completed at Seton Hill.

Visiting: There are regularly scheduled orientations for prospective students, consisting of an introduction, an address by the president or dean, an open reception with faculty, a financial aid session, a student panel, a campus tour, and an overnight visit followed by class attendance, if desired. There are guides for informal visits and visitors may sit in on classes and stay overnight. To schedule a visit, contact the Director of Admissions.

Financial Aid: In 2001-2002, all freshmen and 92% of continuing students received some form of financial aid. 97% of freshmen and 89% of continuing students received need-based aid. The average freshman award was $16,718. Of that total, scholarships or need-based grants averaged $6500 ($16,100 maximum); loans averaged $3750 ($8625 maximum); and work contracts averaged $800 ($1300 maximum). 51% of undergraduates work part time. Average annual earnings from campus work are $1450. The average financial indebtedness of the 2001 graduate was $14,730. Seton Hill is a member of CSS. The FAFSA and the college's own financial statement are required. The fall application deadline is July 1.

International Students: There are 20 international students enrolled. The school actively recruits these students. They must score 500 on the written TOEFL.

Computers: Students have access to 110 PCs on campus, including IBM, Mac, and UNIX machines. All students may access the system. Part-time students are charged $40.

Graduates: In 2001, 228 bachelor's degrees were awarded. The most popular majors were management (30%), physician assistant (15%), and art and psychology (9% each). In an average class, 50% graduate in 4 years, 55% in 5 years, and 58% in 6 years. 19 companies recruited on campus in 2000-2001. Of the 2000 graduating class, 21% were enrolled in graduate school within 6 months of graduation and 89% were employed.

Admissions Contact: Mary Kay Cooper, Director of Admissions and Graduate Student Services. E-mail: *admit@setonhill.edu*
Web: *setonhill.edu*

SHIPPENSBURG UNIVERSITY OF PENNSYLVANIA C-4
Shippensburg, PA 17257-2299 (717) 477-1231
(800) 822-8028; Fax: (717) 477-4016

Full-time: 2731 men, 3231 women	**Faculty:** 285; IIA, +$
Part-time: 121 men, 155 women	**Ph.D.s:** 88%
Graduate: 354 men, 601 women	**Student/Faculty:** 21 to 1
Year: semesters, summer session	**Tuition:** $5004 ($11,028)
Application Deadline: open	**Room & Board:** $4648
Freshman Class: 6424 applied, 4001 accepted, 1483 enrolled	
SAT I Verbal/Math: 534/542	**COMPETITIVE**

Shippensburg University, founded in 1871, is a public university that is part of the Pennsylvania State System of Higher Education offering undergraduate and graduate degree programs in the College of Arts and Sciences, College of Business, and College of Education and Human Services. There are 3 undergraduate schools and 1 graduate school. In addition to regional accreditation, Ship has baccalaureate program accreditation with AACSB, ACS, CACREP, CSWE, and NCATE. The library contains 446,784 volumes, 1,377,155 microform items, and 76,260 audiovisual forms/CDs, and subscribes to 1255 periodicals. Computerized library services include the card catalog, interlibrary loans, and database searching. Special learning facilities include a learning resource center, art gallery, planetarium, radio station, TV station, closed-circuit television, fashion archives center, vertebrate museum, women's center, on-campus elementary school, electron microscope, greenhouse, and herbarium. The 200-acre campus is in a rural area 40 miles southwest of Harrisburg. Including residence halls, there are 47 buildings.

Student Life: 93% of undergraduates are from Pennsylvania. Others are from 23 states, 38 foreign countries, and Canada. 93% are white. The average age of freshmen is 18; all undergraduates, 20. 20% do not continue beyond their first year; 60% remain to graduate.

Housing: 2402 students can be accommodated in college housing, which includes single-sex and coed dormitories, on-campus apartments, and off-campus apartments. In addition, there is a designated quiet hall. 62% of students commute. Alcohol is not permitted. All students may keep cars.

Activities: 6% of men belong to 1 local fraternity and 13 national fraternities; 9% of women belong to 2 local and 6 national sororities. There are more than 200 groups on campus, including art, band, cheerleading, choir, chorale, chorus, computers, dance, drama, ethnic, gay, honors, international, jazz band, literary magazine, marching band, musical theater, newspaper, orchestra, political, professional, radio and TV, religious, social, social service, student government, and yearbook. Popular campus events include planetarium shows, Senior Olympics, and Summer Music Festival.

Sports: There are 8 intercollegiate sports for men and 10 for women, and 7 intramural sports for men and 7 for women. Facilities include athletic fields, practice areas, an 8000-seat stadium, a gym, a field house, 2 swimming pools, squash courts, a rehabilitation center, and a fitness center.

Disabled Students: 84% of the campus is accessible. Wheelchair ramps, elevators, special parking, specially equipped rest rooms, special class scheduling, lowered drinking fountains, lowered telephones, and facilities for students with hearing, visual, and speech and communication disorders are available.

Services: Counseling and information services are available, as is tutoring in most subjects. There is a reader service for the blind, and remedial math, reading, and writing.

Campus Safety and Security: Measures include 24-hour foot and vehicle patrol, self-defense education, escort service, and shuttle buses. There are informal discussions, pamphlets/posters/films, emergency telephones, lighted pathways/sidewalks, and residence halls Are locked 24 hours a day and are equipped with an automatic heat/smoke detection system monitored 24 hours a day by police. A strobe light unit notifies students who are hearing impaired. Residence hall doors are locked 24 hours a day.

Programs of Study: Ship confers B.A., B.S., B.S.B.A., B.S.Ed., and B.S.W. degrees. Master's degrees are also awarded. Bachelor's degrees are awarded in BIOLOGICAL SCIENCE (biology/biological science), BUSINESS (accounting, banking and finance, business administration and management, management information systems, and marketing/retailing/merchandising), COMMUNICATIONS AND THE ARTS (art, communications, English, French, Spanish, and speech/debate/rhetoric), COMPUTER AND PHYSICAL SCIENCE (applied physics, chemistry, computer science, earth science, information sciences and systems, mathematics, and physics), EDUCATION (business, and elementary), ENGINEERING AND ENVIRONMENTAL DESIGN (environmental science), SOCIAL SCIENCE (criminal justice, economics, geography, history, interdisciplinary studies, political science/government, psychology, public administration, social studies, social work, and sociology). Elementary education, criminal justice, and communication/journalism are the largest.

Required: General education courses include English composition, oral communications, math, and history, as well as courses in logic and numbers for rational thinking; linguistic, literary, artistic, and cultural traditions; lab science; biological and physical science; political, economic, and geographic sciences; and social and behavioral sciences. The core curriculum varies for degree programs. Most degree programs require 120 credit hours, with 22 to 30 hours in the major, and a 2.0 minimum GPA for graduation.

Special: The university offers internships, study abroad in 9 countries, and a 3-2 engineering degree with Pennsylvania State University and the University of Maryland. There is a cooperative art program with the Art Institutes International (Art Institutes of Pittsburgh and Art Institutes of Philadephia) in Pennsylvania and 6 other states, as well as a cooperative program in the health sciences. Students have the option of taking courses for a semester at one of the 13 other schools in the Pennsylvania State System of Higher Education. There is also a Visiting Student Program with the Fashion Institute of Technology of New York City. As a member of the Marine Science Consortium, the university also offers opportunities for field and laboratory studies in marine science at Wallops Island, Virginia. There are 17 national honor societies, a freshman honors program, and 1 departmental honors program.

Faculty/Classroom: 64% of faculty are male; 36%, female. 96% teach undergraduates, 33% do research, and 33% do both. No introductory courses are taught by graduate students. The average class size in a laboratory is 17 and in a regular course, 27.

Admissions: 62% of the 2001-2002 applicants were accepted. The SAT I scores for the 2001-2002 freshman class were: Verbal--28% below 500, 56% between 500 and 599, 15% between 600 and 700, and 2% above 700; Math--26% below 500, 52% between 500 and 599, 21% between 600 and 700, and 1% above 700. 32% of the current freshmen were in the top fifth of their class; 74% were in the top two fifths. 4 freshmen graduated first in their class.

Requirements: The SAT I is required. In addition, applicants are urged to pursue a typical college preparatory program, which should include 4 years of English, 3 each of social sciences, sequential math, and lab science, and 2 of 1 foreign language. A GED is accepted. AP and CLEP credits are accepted. Important factors in the admissions decision are advanced placement or honor courses, recommendations by school officials, and evidence of special talent.

Procedure: Freshmen are admitted fall and spring. Entrance exams should be taken in the junior year and no later than fall of the senior year. There are early admissions and deferred admissions plans. Application deadlines are open.

Transfer: 358 transfer students enrolled in 2001-2002. Applicants must provide high school and college transcripts and SAT I scores. 45 credits of 120 must be completed at Ship.

Visiting: There are regularly scheduled orientations for prospective students, including academic department group meetings, book discussions, workshops on study skills, time management, and reading textbooks, and a campus tour. There are guides for informal visits and visitors may sit in on classes. To schedule a visit, contact the Admissions Office.

Financial Aid: In 2001-2002, 59% of all freshmen and 66% of continuing students received some form of financial aid. 46% of freshmen and 45% of continuing students received need-based aid. The average freshman award was $6651. Of that total, scholarships or need-based grants averaged $2975 ($16,600 maximum); loans averaged $5272 ($17,801 maximum); work contracts averaged $1420 ($3399 maximum); and waivers averaged $4145 ($10,040 maximum). 9% of undergraduates work part time. Average annual earnings from campus work are $1420. The average financial indebtedness of the 2001 graduate was $14,956. Ship is a member of CSS. The FAFSA and PHEAA are required. The fall application deadline is May 1.

International Students: There are 60 international students enrolled. They must score 550 on the written TOEFL or 220 on the electronic version, 230 on communications and computer science. The SAT I or the ACT is required for students whose native language is English.

Computers: The mainframe is a Unisys IX 5601-B1. All students may access the system. There are no time limits and no fees. It is recommended that students in accounting have personal computers.

Graduates: In 2001, 1116 bachelor's degrees were awarded. The most popular majors were elementary education (16%), criminal justice (8%), and communication/journalism (8%). In an average class, 33% graduate in 4 years, 58% in 5 years, and 60% in 6 years. 111 companies recruited on campus in 2000-2001.

Admissions Contact: Joseph Cretella, Dean of Admissions. A video is available. E-mail: *admiss@ship.edu* Web: *www.ship.edu/admiss*

SLIPPERY ROCK UNIVERSITY — B-2

Slippery Rock, PA 16057 — (724) 738-2015
(800) 929-4778; Fax: (724) 738-2913

Full-time: 2539 men, 3384 women	**Faculty:** 359
Part-time: 195 men, 382 women	**Ph.D.s:** 78%
Graduate: 211 men, 486 women	**Student/Faculty:** 17 to 1
Year: semesters, summer session	**Tuition:** $4942 ($10,966)
Application Deadline: May 1	**Room & Board:** $4210
Freshman Class: 3429 applied, 2766 accepted, 1330 enrolled	
SAT I Verbal/Math: 484/477	**ACT:** 20 **LESS COMPETITIVE**

Slippery Rock University, founded in 1889, is a public institution that is part of the Pennsylvania State System of Higher Education. It offers programs in business, information, social sciences, education, health, environment, science, humanities, and fine and performing arts. There are 4 undergraduate schools and 1 graduate school. In addition to regional accreditation, The Rock has baccalaureate program accreditation with ACBSP, APTA, CAAHEP, CSWE, NASAD, NASM, NCATE, NLN, and NRPA. The library contains 6143 volumes, 1,492,939 microform items, and 88,001 audiovisual forms/CDs, and subscribes to 1654 periodicals. Computerized library services include the card catalog, interlibrary loans, and database searching. Special learning facilities include a learning resource center, art gallery, natural history museum, planetarium, radio station, TV station, and wellness center. The 600-acre campus is in a small town 50 miles north of Pittsburgh. Including residence halls, there are 60 buildings.

Student Life: 96% of undergraduates are from Pennsylvania. Others are from 34 states, 59 foreign countries, and Canada. 70% are from public schools. 89% are white. The average age of freshmen is 18; all undergraduates, 22. 30% do not continue beyond their first year; 47% remain to graduate.

Housing: 2558 students can be accommodated in college housing, which includes single-sex and coed dormitories and on-campus apartments. In addition, there are honors and special-interest houses. On-campus housing is guaranteed for the freshman year only and is available on a first-come, first-served basis. 60% of students commute. Alcohol is not permitted. All students may keep cars.

Activities: 7% of men belong to 11 national fraternities; 6% of women belong to 9 national sororities. There are 100 groups on campus, including art, band, cheerleading, chess, choir, chorale, chorus, computers, dance, drama, ethnic, film, gay, honors, international, jazz band, literary magazine, marching band, musical theater, newspaper, orchestra, pep band, photography, political, professional, radio and TV, religious, social, social service, student government, symphony, and yearbook. Popular campus events include Spring Weekend.

Sports: There are 12 intercollegiate sports for men and 12 for women, and 7 intramural sports for men and 7 for women. Facilities include a

field house, a gym, and a fitness center. The campus stadium seats 10,000, the indoor gym seats 3000, and the largest auditorium/arena seats 1000.

Disabled Students: 80% of the campus is accessible. Wheelchair ramps, elevators, special parking, specially equipped rest rooms, special class scheduling, lowered drinking fountains, and lowered telephones are available.

Services: Counseling and information services are available, as is tutoring in some subjects, including about 60 introductory-level general liberal studies courses. There is a reader service for the blind and remedial math and writing.

Campus Safety and Security: Measures include 24-hour foot and vehicle patrol, self-defense education, escort service, and shuttle buses. There are informal discussions, pamphlets/posters/films, emergency telephones, and lighted pathways/sidewalks. The university maintains its own police department, with officers having the same powers as municipal police.

Programs of Study: The Rock confers B.A., B.S., B.F.A., B.Mus., B.Mus.Ed., B.S.B.A., B.S.Ed., and B.S.N. degrees. Master's and doctoral degrees are also awarded. Bachelor's degrees are awarded in BIOLOGICAL SCIENCE (biology/biological science), BUSINESS (accounting, business administration and management, international business management, and marketing/retailing/merchandising), COMMUNICATIONS AND THE ARTS (communications, dance, English, fine arts, French, German, music, and Spanish), COMPUTER AND PHYSICAL SCIENCE (chemistry, computer science, earth science, geology, information sciences and systems, mathematics, and physics), EDUCATION (early childhood, elementary, foreign languages, health, music, science, secondary, and special), HEALTH PROFESSIONS (community health work, medical laboratory technology, and nursing), SOCIAL SCIENCE (anthropology, economics, geography, history, parks and recreation management, philosophy, political science/government, psychology, public administration, social science, social work, and sociology). Business, education, and health science areas are the largest.

Required: B.A. students must demonstrate proficiency in a foreign language, and all must complete 42 to 53 credits in a 7-part liberal studies program, including basic competencies, arts, cultural diversity/global perspective, human institutions, science and math, natural experience, and modern age. Specific requirements include public speaking, college writing, algebra, and phys ed. A minimum of 120 credit hours, with at least 30 in the major, is required for graduation.

Special: Study abroad is available in 16 countries. Internships are offered in most majors, and international internships are available in Scotland and England. There is a 3-2 engineering program with Pennsylvania State University. The dual major is an option, and credit is given for military experience. Pass/fail options also are available. There are 26 national honor societies, a freshman honors program, and 33 departmental honors program.

Faculty/Classroom: 55% of faculty are male; 45%, female. All teach undergraduates and do research. No introductory courses are taught by graduate students. The average class size in an introductory lecture is 33; in a lab, 20; and in a regular course, 25.

Admissions: 81% of the 2001-2002 applicants were accepted. The SAT I scores for the 2001-2002 freshman class were: Verbal--58% below 500, 35% between 500 and 599, 7% between 600 and 700, and 1% above 700; Math--60% below 500, 32% between 500 and 599, and 7% between 600 and 700. The ACT scores were 57% below 21, 25% between 21 and 23, 13% between 24 and 26, 2% between 27 and 28, and 2% above 28. 16% of the current freshmen were in the top fifth of their class; 45% were in the top two fifths. 6 freshmen graduated first in their class.

Requirements: The SAT I is required and the ACT is recommended. In addition, students should graduate from an accredited secondary school or have a GED. A total of 16 academic credits is required. The recommended college preparatory program includes 4 years of English and social studies, 3 each of science and math, and 2 of a foreign language. An interview is recommended. A GPA of 1.0 is required. AP and CLEP credits are accepted. Important factors in the admissions decision are advanced placement or honor courses, extracurricular activities record, and evidence of special talent. Applications are accepted on-line and on computer disk.

Procedure: Freshmen are admitted to all sessions. Entrance exams should be taken in the junior year or fall of the senior year. There is a deferred admissions plan. Applications should be filed by May 1 for fall entry, November for spring entry, and April for summer entry. Notification is sent on a rolling basis. The fall 2001 application fee was $25.

Transfer: 555 transfer students enrolled in 2001-2002. Applicants should have completed at least 24 credit hours with a GPA of 2.5. The SAT I or ACT, as well as an interview, are recommended. 36 credits of 120 must be completed at The Rock.

Visiting: There are regularly scheduled orientations for prospective students, including a meeting with faculty, an information fair, and a campus tour. There are guides for informal visits and visitors may sit in on classes and stay overnight. To schedule a visit, contact the Admissions Office.

Financial Aid: In 2001-2002, 90% of all freshmen and 83% of continuing students received some form of financial aid. 59% of freshmen and 56% of continuing students received need-based aid. The average freshman award was $5629. Of that total, scholarships or need-based grants averaged $2633 ($6800 maximum); loans averaged $2282 ($3625 maximum); and work contracts averaged $1000 ($3300 maximum). 30% of undergraduates work part time. Average annual earnings from campus work are $1000. The average financial indebtedness of the 2001 graduate was $19,763. The Rock is a member of CSS. The FAFSA is required. The fall application deadline is May 1.

International Students: There are 202 international students enrolled. The school actively recruits these students. They must score 500 on the written TOEFL.

Computers: The mainframe is an IBM ES/9221-200. Students have access to more than 600 PCs in 44 networked computer labs on campus as well as a network connection for each bed in the residence halls. All networked connections have access to the Internet through our 0C3 connection. All students may access the system 24 hours a day. Campus terminal and PC labs are generally open more than 100 hours per week. There are no time limits and no fees.

Graduates: In 2001, 1035 bachelor's degrees were awarded. The most popular majors were education (27%), parks and recreation (15%), and business/marketing (12%). In an average class, 19% graduate in 4 years, 42% in 5 years, and 47% in 6 years. 260 companies recruited on campus in 2000-2001. Of the 2000 graduating class, 12% were enrolled in graduate school within 6 months of graduation and 81% were employed.

Admissions Contact: Marian Hargrave, Director of Admissions. A video is available. E-mail: *apply@sru.edu* Web: *http://www.sru.edu*

SUSQUEHANNA UNIVERSITY — D-3

Selinsgrove, PA 17870-1001 — (570) 372-4260
(800) 326-9672; Fax: (570) 372-2722

Full-time: 784 men, 1052 women	**Faculty:** 108; IIB, +$
Part-time: 25 men, 8 women	**Ph.D.s:** 92%
Graduate: none	**Student/Faculty:** 15 to 1
Year: semesters, summer session	**Tuition:** $21,270
Application Deadline: see profile	**Room & Board:** $6000
Freshman Class: n/av	
SAT I: required	**VERY COMPETITIVE**

Susquehanna University, founded in 1858, is an independent, selective, residential institution affiliated with the Lutheran Church. It offers programs through schools of arts, humanities and communications, natural and social sciences, and business. There are 3 undergraduate schools. In addition to regional accreditation, S.U. has baccalaureate program accreditation with AACSB and NASM. The library contains 260,000 volumes, 113,700 microform items, and 12,600 audiovisual forms/CDs, and subscribes to 2400 periodicals. Computerized library services include the card catalog, interlibrary loans, and database searching. Special learning facilities include a learning resource center, art gallery, radio station, multimedia classrooms, video studios, a campuswide telecommunications network, satellite dishes and distribution system for foreign-language broadcasts, a video conferencing facility, an ecological field station, an observatory, a child development center, and an electronic music lab. The 210-acre campus is in a small town 50 miles north of Harrisburg. Including residence halls, there are 52 buildings.

Student Life: 60% of undergraduates are from Pennsylvania. Others are from 28 states, 14 foreign countries, and Canada. 84% are from public schools. 92% are white. 44% are Protestant; 31% Catholic; 19% claim no religious affiliation. The average age of freshmen is 18; all undergraduates, 20. 13% do not continue beyond their first year; 76% remain to graduate.

Housing: 80 students can be accommodated in college housing, which includes single-sex and coed dormitories, on-campus apartments, fraternity houses, and sorority houses. In addition, there are honors houses and special-interest houses. On-campus housing is guaranteed for all 4 years. 80% of students live on campus; of those, 86% remain on campus on weekends. All students may keep cars.

Activities: 25% of men belong to 4 national fraternities; 25% of women belong to 4 national sororities. There are 100 groups on campus, including art, band, cheerleading, chess, choir, chorale, chorus, computers, dance, drama, ethnic, gay, honors, international, jazz band, literary magazine, musical theater, newspaper, opera, orchestra, pep band, photography, political, professional, radio and TV, religious, social, social service, student government, and yearbook. Popular campus events include Spring Weekend, Candlelight Christmas Service, and Family Weekend.

Sports: There are 11 intercollegiate sports for men and 11 for women, and 10 intramural sports for men and 9 for women. Facilities include soccer, baseball, lacrosse, rugby, and hockey fields, basketball and tennis courts, a swimming pool, paddleball courts, a weight training room, and a sauna.

Disabled Students: 90% of the campus is accessible. Wheelchair ramps, elevators, special parking, specially equipped rest rooms, special

class scheduling, lowered drinking fountains, and lowered telephones are available.

Services: Counseling and information services are available, as is tutoring in some subjects, including writing, math, foreign languages, and study skills. Academic departments also provide tutoring.

Campus Safety and Security: Measures include 24-hour foot and vehicle patrol, self-defense education, escort service, and informal discussions. There are pamphlets/posters/films and lighted pathways/sidewalks.

Programs of Study: S.U. confers B.A., B.S., and B.M. degrees. Associate degrees are also awarded. Bachelor's degrees are awarded in BIOLOGICAL SCIENCE (biochemistry and biology/biological science), BUSINESS (accounting and business administration and management), COMMUNICATIONS AND THE ARTS (art, art history and appreciation, communications, dramatic arts, English, French, German, music, music performance, and Spanish), COMPUTER AND PHYSICAL SCIENCE (chemistry, computer science, information sciences and systems, mathematics, and physics), EDUCATION (early childhood, education, elementary, and music), ENGINEERING AND ENVIRONMENTAL DESIGN (environmental science), SOCIAL SCIENCE (economics, history, international studies, philosophy, political science/government, psychology, religion, religious music, and sociology). Natural sciences, business administration, and psychology are the strongest academically. Business administration, communications and theater arts, and psychology are the largest.

Required: All students must complete a 3-part core curriculum of about 40 semester hours, including academic requirements in history, fine arts, literature, science, and social science, as well as philosophy or religion; skills in computers, math/logic, and foreign language; and courses in academic skills, wellness/fitness, and career development. An additional 36 to 44 hours are required in the major, and the remainder of a 130-hour required total in electives or a minor. A minimum GPA of 2.0 is also required to graduate.

Special: There is cross-registration with Bucknell University. Interships are offered in almost all majors and study abroad is available on 6 continents. The School of Business offers a fall semester in London for junior business majors. Two-week study seminars in Australia, Ecuador, Southern Africa, and the Caribbean are available, as are a Washington semester, a United Nations semester, a work and study semester through the Philadelphia Center, and an Appalachian semester in Kentucky. The university offers dual and student-design majors, work-study programs, credit by examination, nondegree study, and pass/fail options. The B.A.-B.S. degree is available in several majors and there is a 3-2 engineering program with Pennsylvania State University, a 3-2 program in forestry with Duke University, and a 2-2 program in allied health with Thomas Jefferson University. Highly motivated students have the option of earning their baccalureate degree in 3 years. There are 20 national honor societies, a freshman honors program, and 15 departmental honors programs.

Faculty/Classroom: 56% of faculty are male; 44%, female. All both teach and do research. The average class size in an introductory lecture is 26; in a laboratory, 13; and in a regular course, 18.

Admissions: 57% of the current freshmen were in the top fifth of their class; 86% were in the top two fifths. 4 freshmen graduated first in their class in a recent year.

Requirements: The SAT I is required, except for students with a cumulative class rank in the top 20% in a strong college preparatory program. Such students have the option of submitting either the SAT I, ACT, or 2 graded writing samples. Students should be graduates of an accredited high school. Preparation should include 4 years of English and math, 3 to 4 years of science, and 2 to 3 years each of social studies and foreign language. In addition, 1 unit of art or music is recommended. Three SAT II: Subject tests are recommended, including writing and math. An essay is required, as are, for relevant fields, an art portfolio, music audition, or writing portfolio. An interview is strongly recommended. S.U. requires applicants to be in the upper 40% of their class. A GPA of 3.0 is required. AP and CLEP credits are accepted. Important factors in the admissions decision are advanced placement or honor courses, evidence of special talent, and recommendations by school officials. Applications are accepted on-line at *www.susqu.edu/admissions*, and through the Common Application.

Procedure: Freshmen are admitted fall and spring. Entrance exams should be taken by January of the senior year. There are early decision, early admissions, and deferred admissions plans. Check with the shool for current application deadlines. The application fee is $35.

Transfer: 32 transfer students enrolled in a recent year. Applicants must submit high school and college transcripts, test scores, and a recommendation from a dean. An interview is strongly recommended. 65 credits of 130 must be completed at S.U.

Visiting: There are regularly scheduled orientations for prospective students, including special visiting days for prospective students and their parents held in the spring and fall, which consist of sessions with faculty, admissions, financial aid, and placement staff and tours of the campus. There are guides for informal visits and visitors may sit in on classes and stay overnight. To schedule a visit, contact the Office of Admissions.

Financial Aid: In 2001-2002, the average freshman award was $14,146. Of that total, scholarships or need-based grants averaged $11,942 ($27,970 maximum); loans averaged $3125 ($4625 maximum); and work contracts averaged $1627 ($1800 maximum). 64% of undergraduates work part time. Average annual earnings from campus work are $835. The average financial indebtedness of a recent year's graduate was $12,515. S.U. is a member of CSS. The CSS/Profile or FAFSA and federal tax return are required. Check with the school for current deadlines.

International Students: There were 17 international students enrolled in a recent year. The school actively recruits these students. They must score 550 on the written TOEFL or 213 on the electronic version and also take the SAT I.

Computers: The mainframe is an HP 3000 series 947. All residence hall rooms are wired for computer access to the campus LAN and the Internet. 285 PCs are available for student use in various labs and in the library. A wide variety of software is available as well. Laptop dataports are available in the business and communications building. All students may access the system 24 hours a day. There are no time limits and no fees. It is strongly recommended that all students have a personal computer.

Graduates: In a recent year, 419 bachelor's degrees were awarded. The most popular majors were communications and theatre arts (17%), business administration (16%), and psychology (6%). In an average class, 1% graduate in 3 years, 73% in 4 years, 76% in 5 years, and 75% in 6 years.

Admissions Contact: Chris Markle, Director of Admissions.
E-mail: *suadmiss@susqu.edu*
Web: *www.susqu.edu/ad_depts/admissions/*

SWARTHMORE COLLEGE — F-4

Swarthmore, PA 19081-1397 — (610) 328-8300
(800) 667-3110; Fax: (610) 328-8580

Full-time: 686 men, 769 women	**Faculty:** 160; IIB, ++$
Part-time: 4 men, 8 women	**Ph.D.s:** 99%
Graduate: none	**Student/Faculty:** 9 to 1
Year: semesters	**Tuition:** $26,376
Application Deadline: January 1	**Room & Board:** $8162
Freshman Class: 3504 applied, 909 accepted, 381 enrolled	
SAT I Verbal/Math: 740/720	**MOST COMPETITIVE**

Swarthmore College, established in 1864, is a private, nonprofit institution offering undergraduate courses in engineering and liberal arts. In addition to regional accreditation, Swarthmore has baccalaureate program accreditation with ABET. The 5 libraries contain 7312 volumes, 71,795 microform items, and 18,683 audiovisual forms/CDs, and subscribe to 4275 periodicals. Computerized library services include the card catalog, interlibrary loans, and database searching. Special learning facilities include an art gallery, radio station, observatory, performing arts center, solar energy lab, arboretum, and a library of documents and memorabilia of the peace movement. The 357-acre campus is in a suburban area 10 miles southwest of Philadelphia. Including residence halls, there are 46 buildings.

Student Life: 87% of undergraduates are from out of state, mostly the Middle Atlantic. Others are from 47 states, 42 foreign countries, and Canada. 59% are from public schools. 61% are white; 16% Asian American. The average age of freshmen is 18; all undergraduates, 20. 5% do not continue beyond their first year; 92% remain to graduate.

Housing: 1271 students can be accommodated in college housing, which includes single-sex and coed dormitories. On-campus housing is guaranteed for all 4 years. 93% of students live on campus. Upperclassmen may keep cars.

Activities: 6% of men belong to 1 local and 1 national fraternity. There are no sororities. There are 100 groups on campus, including art, band, cheerleading, chess, choir, chorus, computers, dance, debate, drama, ethnic, film, gay, honors, international, jazz band, literary magazine, musical theater, newspaper, orchestra, pep band, photography, political, radio and TV, religious, social, social service, student government, and yearbook. Popular campus events include fall and spring formals, Crum Regatta, and an all-day music festival.

Sports: There are 10 intercollegiate sports for men and 12 for women, and 7 intramural sports for men and 7 for women. Facilities include 12 outdoor and 6 indoor tennis courts; 6 full-length indoor basketball courts; 10 outdoor playing fields; an athletic events center with seating for 1,800; a field house large enough to accommodate team practices during inclement weather; an outdoor 8-lane, 400-meter Versaturf track; an indoor 215-meter banked Tartan track; a 10 lane-by-10 lane, yards-by-meters indoor swimming pool with electronic timing system; 5 squash courts with spectator galleries; a fitness center with aerobic and Medx equipment; and a professionally staffed sports medicine facility with three full-time trainers.

Disabled Students: 75% of the campus is accessible. Wheelchair ramps, elevators, special parking, specially equipped rest rooms, special class scheduling, lowered drinking fountains, and lowered telephones are available.

Services: Counseling and information services are available, as is tutoring in most subjects. There is a reader service for the blind and computing support.

Campus Safety and Security: Measures include 24-hour foot and vehicle patrol, self-defense education, escort service, and shuttle buses. There are informal discussions, pamphlets/posters/films, emergency telephones, and lighted pathways/sidewalks.

Programs of Study: Swarthmore confers B.A. and B.S. degrees. Master's degrees are also awarded. Bachelor's degrees are awarded in BIOLOGICAL SCIENCE (biochemistry and biology/biological science), COMMUNICATIONS AND THE ARTS (art, art history and appreciation, classics, comparative literature, dance, dramatic arts, English literature, French, German, Greek, Latin, linguistics, literature, music, Russian, and Spanish), COMPUTER AND PHYSICAL SCIENCE (astronomy, astrophysics, chemistry, computer science, mathematics, and physics), EDUCATION (education), ENGINEERING AND ENVIRONMENTAL DESIGN (engineering), SOCIAL SCIENCE (anthropology, Asian/Oriental studies, classical/ancient civilization, economics, German area studies, history, medieval studies, philosophy, political science/government, psychobiology, psychology, religion, and sociology). Economics, biology, and political science are the largest.

Required: To graduate, students must complete 3 courses in each of 3 divisions consisting of humanities, natural sciences and engineering, and social sciences. They must have completed 32 courses or the equivalent, with a minimum of 20 courses outside the major and 8 to 12 courses in the major. They must have a GPA of 2.0. Students must demonstrate foreign language competency and fulfill a phys ed requirement, including a swimming test.

Special: Students may cross-register with Haverford and Bryn Mawr Colleges and the University of Pennsylvania. They may study abroad in their country of choice. Dual majors in physics and astronomy and in sociology and anthropology, student-designed majors, and a 4-year program leading to a B.A.-B.S. degree in engineering and liberal arts are available. Swarthmore offers a unique honors program whose features are student independence and responsibility and collegial relationship with faculty; students are evaluated by external examiners. There are 3 national honor societies, including Phi Beta Kappa. All departments have honors programs.

Faculty/Classroom: 65% of faculty are male; 35%, female. All teach and do research. The average class size in an introductory lecture is 20; in a laboratory, 11; and in a regular course, 16.

Admissions: 26% of the 2001-2002 applicants were accepted. The SAT I scores for the 2001-2002 freshman class were: Verbal--1% below 500, 6% between 500 and 599, 22% between 600 and 700, and 72% above 700; Math--5% between 500 and 599, 28% between 600 and 700, and 67% above 700. 95% of the current freshmen were in the top fifth of their class; 99% were in the top two fifths. There were 39 National Merit finalists and semifinalists. 52 freshmen graduated first in their class.

Requirements: The SAT I is required. In addition, the ACT may be submitted in place of the SAT I. SAT II: Subject tests in writing and 2 other areas of choice are required; mathematics IIC is required for engineering majors. Swarthmore does not require a specific high school curriculum. It does, however, recommend the inclusion of English, math, 1 or 2 foreign languages, history and social studies, literature, art, and music, and the sciences. Interviews are strongly recommended. An essay, 2 teacher recommendations, and a counselor recommendation are required. AP credits are accepted. Important factors in the admissions decision are advanced placement or honor courses, extracurricular activities record, and recommendations by school officials. Swarthmore accepts the Common App and the Swarthmore application through the college's web site. Students may also apply through *Embark.com*

Procedure: Freshmen are admitted in the fall. Entrance exams should be taken in spring of the junior year or fall of the senior year. There are early decision and deferred admissions plans. Early decision applications should be filed by November 15 and January 1; regular applications, by January 1 for fall entry. Notification of early decision is sent December 15 and February 1; regular decision, April 1. 149 early decision candidates were accepted for the 2001-2002 class. 20 wait-listed applicants were accepted in 2001. The fall 2001 application fee was $60.

Transfer: 19 transfer students enrolled in 2001-2002. The SAT I is required if not taken previously. An essay is required. 16 credits of 32 must be completed at Swarthmore.

Visiting: There are regularly scheduled orientations for prospective students, including group information sessions, offered at regular times throughout the year. There are guides for informal visits and visitors may sit in on classes and stay overnight. To schedule a visit, contact the admissions receptionist.

Financial Aid: In 2001-2002, 51% of all freshmen and 49% of continuing students received some form of financial aid. 51% of freshmen and 49% of continuing students received need-based aid. The average freshman award was $24,174. Of that total, scholarships or need-based grants averaged $21,638 ($35,000 maximum); loans averaged $1269 ($2560 maximum); and work contracts averaged $1267 ($1450 maximum). 81% of undergraduates work part time. Average annual earnings from campus work are $1450. The average financial indebtedness of the 2001 graduate was $12,726. Swarthmore is a member of CSS. The CSS/Profile or FAFSA, the college's own financial statement and tax returns, W-2 statements, and year-end paycheck stubs are required. The fall application deadline is February 15.

International Students: There are 92 international students enrolled. The school actively recruits these students. Students must take the SAT I or the ACT. Students must also take SAT II: Subject tests in writing and 2 others; mathematics IIC is required for engineering majors.

Computers: The mainframe consists of UNIX-based servers. There are more than 150 networked Macs and PCs available throughout the campus in public areas for student use. Residence halls are fully hooked up to the network with a connection for each resident, giving them access to the Internet, the library database, e-mail, shared software, and many other resources. All students may access the system. There are no time limits and no fees.

Graduates: In 2001, 337 bachelor's degrees were awarded. The most popular majors were economics (15%), biology (10%), and political science (10%). In an average class, 83% graduate in 4 years, and 92% in 5 years. 49 companies recruited on campus in 2000-2001. Of the 2000 graduating class, 16% were enrolled in graduate school within 6 months of graduation and 71% were employed.

Admissions Contact: James L. Bock, Dean of Admissions and Financial Aid. E-mail: *admissions@swarthmore.edu*
Web: *http://www.swarthmore.edu/admissions/*

TEMPLE UNIVERSITY — F-3
Philadelphia, PA 19122-1803 — (215) 204-7200
(888) 340-2222; Fax: (215) 204-5694

Full-time: 6858 men, 9267 women	**Faculty:** 1232; I, av$
Part-time: 1330 men, 2151 women	**Ph.D.s:** 82%
Graduate: 4631 men, 5635 women	**Student/Faculty:** 13 to 1
Year: semesters, summer session	**Tuition:** $7324 ($13,062)
Application Deadline: April 1	**Room & Board:** $6800
Freshman Class: 12,010 applied, 7794 accepted, 3375 enrolled	
SAT I Verbal/Math: 520/520	**COMPETITIVE**

Temple University, founded in 1888, is part of the Commonwealth System of Higher Education in Pennsylvania. It offers programs in the liberal arts; science and technology; allied health professions; education; engineering; art; business and management; communications and theater; architecture, landscape architecture, and horticulture; music; and social administration. Temple has 6 other campuses, including 1 in Rome and 1 in Tokyo. There are 12 undergraduate and 13 graduate schools. In addition to regional accreditation, Temple has baccalaureate program accreditation with AACSB, ABET, ACEJMC, ACPE, ADA, APTA, CAHEA, CSWE, NAAB, NASAD, NASM, NCATE, NLN, and NRPA. The 3 libraries contain 2.1 million volumes and 70 microform items, and subscribe to 15,600 periodicals. Computerized library services include the card catalog, interlibrary loans, and database searching. Special learning facilities include a learning resource center, art gallery, radio station, dance lab theater, media learning center for the study of critical languages, and multimedia lab for teacher education in music. The 105-acre campus is in an urban area 1 mile north of center city Philadelphia. Including residence halls, there are 105 buildings.

Student Life: 76% of undergraduates are from Pennsylvania. Others are from 39 states, 79 foreign countries, and Canada. 61% are white; 21% African American. The average age of freshmen is 18; all undergraduates, 21. 22% do not continue beyond their first year; 46% remain to graduate.

Housing: 4200 students can be accommodated in college housing, which includes coed dormitories, on-campus apartments, off-campus apartments, married-student housing, fraternity houses, and sorority houses. In addition, there are honors houses and speial interest houses. On-campus housing is available on a lottery system for upperclassmen. 74% of students commute. Alcohol is not permitted. All students may keep cars.

Activities: 1% of men belong to 12 local fraternities; 1% of women belong to 11 local sororities. There are more than 125 groups on campus, including art, band, cheerleading, chess, choir, chorus, computers, dance, drama, drill team, ethnic, film, honors, international, jazz band, literary magazine, marching band, musical theater, newspaper, orchestra, pep band, photography, political, professional, radio and TV, religious, social, social service, student government, and yearbook. Popular campus events include Spring Fling.

Sports: There are 13 intercollegiate sports for men and 13 for women, and 15 intramural sports for men and 12 for women. Facilities include 2 Olympic-size swimming pools, several gyms, weight-training rooms, racquetball courts, an 8-lane 400-meter track, and playing fields. The indoor gym seats 2000, and the largest auditorium/arena, 10,200.

Disabled Students: All of the campus is accessible. Wheelchair ramps, elevators, special parking, specially equipped rest rooms, special class scheduling, lowered drinking fountains, and lowered telephones are available. Additional services may be arranged through the Disabled Student Services Office.

Services: Counseling and information services are available, as is tutoring in most subjects. There is a reader service for the blind, and remedial math, reading, and writing.

Campus Safety and Security: Measures include 24-hour foot and vehicle patrol, self-defense education, escort service, and shuttle buses. There are informal discussions, pamphlets/posters/films, emergency telephones, lighted pathways/sidewalks, and 24-hour access-controlled security in residence halls.

Programs of Study: Temple confers B.A., B.S., B.Ar., B.B.A., B.F.A., B.M., B.S.Ar., B.S.E., B.S.Ed., B.S.E.E., B.S.N., and B.S.W. degrees. Associate, master's, and doctoral degrees are also awarded. Bachelor's degrees are awarded in AGRICULTURE (environmental studies and horticulture), BIOLOGICAL SCIENCE (biochemistry, biology/biological science, and biophysics), BUSINESS (accounting, banking and finance, business administration and management, business economics, business law, electronic business, entrepreneurial studies, human resources, international business management, management information systems, marketing/retailing/merchandising, personnel management, real estate, sports management, and tourism), COMMUNICATIONS AND THE ARTS (art, art history and appreciation, broadcasting, classics, communications, dance, dramatic arts, English, film arts, fine arts, French, German, Germanic languages and literature, Greek, guitar, Hebrew, Italian, jazz, journalism, linguistics, music, music history and appreciation, music performance, music theory and composition, percussion, performing arts, photography, piano/organ, Russian, Spanish, speech/debate/rhetoric, strings, telecommunications, voice, and winds), COMPUTER AND PHYSICAL SCIENCE (actuarial science, chemistry, computer science, earth science, geology, information sciences and systems, mathematics, physics, and statistics), EDUCATION (art, business, early childhood, education, elementary, English, foreign languages, industrial arts, marketing and distribution, mathematics, middle school, music, physical, science, secondary, social studies, and teaching English as a second/foreign language (TESOL/TEFOL)), ENGINEERING AND ENVIRONMENTAL DESIGN (architecture, civil engineering, electrical/electronics engineering, electrical/electronics engineering technology, engineering, engineering technology, environmental engineering technology, environmental science, landscape architecture/design, materials science, mechanical engineering, and mechanical engineering technology), HEALTH PROFESSIONS (health science, music therapy, nursing, occupational therapy, pharmacy, predentistry, and premedicine), SOCIAL SCIENCE (African American studies, American studies, anthropology, Asian/Oriental studies, criminal justice, economics, geography, history, interdisciplinary studies, Latin American studies, parks and recreation management, philosophy, physical fitness/movement, political science/government, prelaw, psychology, religion, social science, social work, sociology, urban studies, and women's studies). Business administration, psychology, and elementary education are the largest.

Required: The required core curriculum includes English composition, intellectual heritage, American culture, the arts, the individual and society, foreign language/international studies, math/statistics/logic, and science and technology. A minimum 2.0 GPA and a total of 128 credit hours are required for graduation, including 24 credits in the major.

Special: The university offers study abroad, work-study programs, and up to 30 credits for life/military/work experience. There is a 5-year accelerated engineering technology program. There is a chapter of Phi Beta Kappa and a freshman honors program.

Faculty/Classroom: 67% of faculty are male; 33%, female. The average class size in a regular course is 25.

Admissions: 65% of the 2001-2002 applicants were accepted. The SAT I scores for the 2001-2002 freshman class were: Verbal--36% below 500, 44% between 500 and 599, 17% between 600 and 700, and 3% above 700; Math--38% below 500, 44% between 500 and 599, 16% between 600 and 700, and 2% above 700. 33% of the current freshmen were in the top fifth of their class; 66% were in the top two fifths. 13 freshmen graduated first in their class.

Requirements: The SAT I or ACT is required. In addition, applicants should complete 16 academic credits/Carnegie units, including 4 years of English, 2 each of math and a foreign language, and 1 each of history and a lab science. A GED is accepted. A portfolio and audition are required in relevant fields. AP and CLEP credits are accepted. Important factors in the admissions decision are advanced placement or honor courses, recommendations by school officials, and parents or siblings attending the school. Applications are accepted on-line.

Procedure: Freshmen are admitted fall and spring. Entrance exams should be taken by March of the junior year or April of the senior year. There is an early admissions plan. Applications should be filed by April 1 for fall entry and November 15 for spring entry. The fall 2001 application fee was $35. Notification is sent on a rolling basis.

Transfer: 2501 transfer students enrolled in 2001-2002. Applicants must have earned at least 15 college credit hours with at least a 2.3 GPA and must submit official high school and college transcripts. 30 credits of 128 must be completed at Temple.

Visiting: There are regularly scheduled orientations for prospective students. There are guides for informal visits and visitors may sit in on classes. To schedule a visit, contact the Office of Undergraduate Admissions.

Financial Aid: In 2001-2002, 70% of all freshmen and 67% of continuing students received some form of financial aid. 58% of freshmen and 54% of continuing students received need-based aid. The average freshman award was $10,524. The average financial indebtedness of the 2001 graduate was $14,500. The FAFSA, the college's own financial statement, and the PHEAA (Pennsylvania residents) are required. The fall application deadline is March 31.

International Students: There are 622 international students enrolled. The school actively recruits these students. They must score 525 on the written TOEFL or 194 on the electronic version.

Computers: The mainframes are a CDC Cyber 860 and 2 IBM 4381 VM/CMSs. Students may access computer facilities through workstations distributed throughout the campus. Networked PC labs and software libraries are available for student use. All students may access the system 24 hours per day. There are no time limits and no fees.

Graduates: In 2001, 3249 bachelor's degrees were awarded. The most popular majors were elementary education (8%), psychology (7%), and criminal justice (5%). In an average class, 1% graduate in 3 years, 20% in 4 years, 38% in 5 years, and 44% in 6 years. 500 companies recruited on campus in 2000-2001.

Admissions Contact: Dr. Timm Rinehart, Director, Undergraduate Admissions. E-mail: *tuadm@vm.temple.edu*
Web: *http://www.temple.edu*

THIEL COLLEGE

Greenville, PA 16125 — **A-2**
(724) 589-2345
(800) 24-THIEL; Fax: (724) 589-2013

Full-time: 557 men, 524 women	**Faculty:** 57; IIB, --$
Part-time: 35 men, 73 women	**Ph.D.s:** 67%
Graduate: none	**Student/Faculty:** 19 to 1
Year: semesters, summer session	**Tuition:** $12,445
Application Deadline: open	**Room & Board:** $5974
Freshman Class: 1507 applied, 1154 accepted, 388 enrolled	
SAT I Verbal/Math: 480/470	**ACT:** 19 **LESS COMPETITIVE**

Thiel College, founded in 1866, is an independent college affiliated with the Lutheran Church. It offers programs in liberal arts, business, engineering, nursing, religion, and teacher preparation, and professional programs. In addition to regional accreditation, Thiel has baccalaureate program accreditation with NLN. The library contains 650,506 volumes, 41,699 microform items, and 7085 audiovisual forms/CDs, and subscribes to 532 periodicals. Computerized library services include the card catalog, interlibrary loans, and database searching. Special learning facilities include a learning resource center, art gallery, radio station, and a wildlife sanctuary. The 135-acre campus is in a rural area 75 miles north of Pittsburgh and 75 miles southeast of Cleveland, Ohio. Including residence halls, there are 21 buildings.

Student Life: 75% of undergraduates are from Pennsylvania. Others are from 15 states and 14 foreign countries. 90% are from public schools. 78% are white. 41% are Protestant; 31% claim no religious affiliation; 25% Catholic; 17% Agnostic, Atheist, Muslim, Hindu. The average age of freshmen is 18; all undergraduates, 21. 28% do not continue beyond their first year; 45% remain to graduate.

Housing: 1111 students can be accommodated in college housing, which includes single-sex and coed dormitories and on-campus apartments. In addition, there are special-interest houses, an honors residence hall, and a women's leadership residence hall. On-campus housing is guaranteed for all 4 years. 78% of students live on campus; of those, 60% remain on campus on weekends. Alcohol is not permitted. All students may keep cars.

Activities: 8% of men belong to 1 local and 2 national fraternities; 9% of women belong to 5 national sororities. There are 35 groups on campus, including art, band, cheerleading, choir, chorus, computers, dance, drama, ethnic, forensics, honors, international, literary magazine, musical theater, newspaper, pep band, political, professional, radio and TV, religious, social, social service, student government, symphony, and yearbook. Popular campus events include Spring Weekend, Greek Week, and theatrical productions.

Sports: There are 10 intercollegiate sports for men and 9 for women, and 4 intramural sports for men and 3 for women. Facilities include a 1200-seat gym, basketball and handball courts, playing fields, a fitness center, and tennis courts.

Disabled Students: 75% of the campus is accessible. Wheelchair ramps, elevators, special parking, specially equipped rest rooms, and special class scheduling are available.

Services: Counseling and information services are available, as is tutoring in every subject. There is remedial math, reading, and writing.

Campus Safety and Security: Measures include 24-hour foot and vehicle patrol, escort service, pamphlets/posters/films, and emergency telephones. There are lighted pathways/sidewalks.

Programs of Study: Thiel confers the B.A. degree. Associate degrees are also awarded. Bachelor's degrees are awarded in BIOLOGICAL SCIENCE (biology/biological science), BUSINESS (accounting, business administration and management, international business management, and management information systems), COMMUNICATIONS AND THE ARTS (art, communications, English, French, Spanish, and technical and business writing), COMPUTER AND PHYSICAL SCIENCE (actuarial science, chemistry, computer science, geology, mathematics, and physics), EDUCATION (elementary and secondary), ENGINEERING AND ENVIRONMENTAL DESIGN (environmental science and preengineering), HEALTH PROFESSIONS (cytotechnology, medical laboratory technology, physical therapy, predentistry, premedicine, prepharmacy, preveterinary science, respiratory therapy, and speech pathology/audiology), SOCIAL SCIENCE (family/juvenile justice, history, philosophy, political science/government, prelaw, psychology, religion, religious education, and sociology). Engineering, biology, and chemistry are the strongest academically. Accounting, business administration, and psychology are the largest.

Required: To graduate, students must complete a total of 124 credit hours, with 35 to 55 in the major and a minimum GPA of 2.0. Distribution requirements, for all except nursing students, include 14 to 15 hours of Western humanities, 9 of Christianity, 6 to 8 of science, 3 to 10 of cultural studies, and 4 of health. Some majors require a comprehensive exam or thesis.

Special: Students may spend a semester at Argonne National Laboratories, the Art Institute of Pittsburgh, or Drew University. Special programs include a UN semester, a Washington semester, an Appalachian semester, study at Pittsburgh Institute of Mortuary Science, and a forestry and environmental management semester at Duke University. There is a 3-2 engineering program with Case Western Reserve University and the University of Pittsburgh. Internships, study abroad, work-study, dual majors, nondegree study, credit by examination, and credit for life, military, and work experience are also available. There are 11 national honor societies, a freshman honors program, and 10 departmental honors programs.

Faculty/Classroom: 53% of faculty are male; 47%, female. All teach undergraduates. The average class size in an introductory lecture is 25; in a laboratory, 15; and in a regular course, 15.

Admissions: 77% of the 2001-2002 applicants were accepted. The SAT I scores for the 2001-2002 freshman class were: Verbal--60% below 500, 28% between 500 and 599, and 12% between 600 and 700; Math--58% below 500, 35% between 500 and 599, and 7% between 600 and 700. The ACT scores were 63% below 21, 18% between 21 and 23, 12% between 24 and 26, 4% between 27 and 28, and 3% above 28. 22% of the current freshmen were in the top fifth of their class; 43% were in the top two fifths. 2 freshmen graduated first in their class.

Requirements: The SAT I or ACT is required. In addition, applicants should be high school graduates who have completed 16 academic units, including 4 years of English, 3 of social science, and 2 each of foreign language, math, and science. The GED is accepted. An essay and an interview are recommended. Thiel requires applicants to be in the upper 60% of their class. A GPA of 2.0 is required. AP and CLEP credits are accepted. Important factors in the admissions decision are advanced placement or honor courses, evidence of special talent, and leadership record. Applications are accepted on-line at *www.admissions@thiel.edu*

Procedure: Freshmen are admitted to all sessions. Entrance exams should be taken by May 1 of each year. There are early admissions and deferred admissions plans. Early decision applications should be filed by December 1; regular applications, by open for fall entry, along with a $25 fee. Notification of early decision is sent October 15; regular decision, on a rolling basis.

Transfer: 34 transfer students enrolled in 2001-2002. Applicants should meet the same criteria as entering freshmen and should submit official transcripts, statements of good standing, financial aid transcripts, and transfer forms from all colleges previously attended. Students must have a 2.0 GPA to transfer. 30 credits of 124 must be completed at Thiel.

Visiting: There are regularly scheduled orientations for prospective students, including orientation sessions for students enrolling in the fall and monthly sessions beginning in February. There are guides for informal visits and visitors may sit in on classes and stay overnight. To schedule a visit, contact the Admissions Office.

Financial Aid: In 2001-2002, 95% of all freshmen and 97% of continuing students received some form of financial aid. 86% of freshmen and 78% of continuing students received need-based aid. The average freshman award was $11,917. Of that total, scholarships or need-based grants averaged $7286 ($15,000 maximum); loans averaged $4500 ($8600 maximum); work contracts averaged $1224 ($2300 maximum); and outside gift aid averaged $1200 ($2500 maximum). 46% of undergraduates work part time. Average annual earnings from campus work are $1224. The average financial indebtedness of the 2001 graduate was $14,500. The CSS/Profile, FAFSA, FFS, or SFS are required. The FAFSA is preferred. The fall application deadline is May 1.

International Students: There are 46 international students enrolled. The school actively recruits these students. They must score 500 on the written TOEFL or take the MELAB and also take the SAT I or the ACT, scoring 920 on the SAT I.

Computers: The mainframe is a DEC PDP 11/44. There are a number of computer systems in operation on campus, serving both administrative and academic applications. They are accessible to student workers and to other students for completing course assignments. All students may access the system. There are no time limits and no fees.

Graduates: In 2001, 126 bachelor's degrees were awarded. The most popular majors were business (23%), accounting (12%), and psychology (6%). In an average class, 2% graduate in 3 years, 31% in 4 years, 43% in 5 years, and 46% in 6 years. 40 companies recruited on campus in 2000-2001. Of the 2000 graduating class, 13% were enrolled in graduate school within 6 months of graduation and 87% were employed.

Admissions Contact: Mark Thompson, Director of Admissions.
Web: *thiel.edu*

UNIVERSITY OF PENNSYLVANIA — F-3
Philadelphia, PA 19104 — **(215) 898-7507**

Full-time: 4793 men, 4551 women	**Faculty:** 2255; I, +$
Part-time: 222 men, 164 women	**Ph.D.s:** 99%
Graduate: 5200 men, 5083 women	**Student/Faculty:** 4 to 1
Year: semesters, summer session	**Tuition:** $26,630
Application Deadline: January 1	**Room & Board:** $7984
Freshman Class: 19,153 applied, 4132 accepted, 2391 enrolled	
SAT I Verbal/Math: 690/710	**ACT:** 30 **MOST COMPETITIVE**

University of Pennsylvania, founded in 1740, is a private institution offering undergraduate and graduate degrees in arts and sciences, business, engineering and applied science, and nursing. There are 4 undergraduate and 12 graduate schools. In addition to regional accreditation, Penn has baccalaureate program accreditation with AACSB, ABET, NAAB, NCATE, and NLN. The 16 libraries contain 4,914,244 volumes, 3,407,839 microform items, and 56,739 audiovisual forms/CDs, and subscribe to 35,543 periodicals. Computerized library services include the card catalog, interlibrary loans, and database searching. Special learning facilities include a learning resource center, art gallery, natural history museum, planetarium, radio station, TV station, arboretum, animal research center, primate research center, language lab, center for performing arts, institute for contemporary art, wind tunnel, and electron microscope. The 260-acre campus is in an urban area in Philadelphia. Including residence halls, there are 122 buildings.

Student Life: 81% of undergraduates are from out of state, mostly the Northeast. Others are from 49 states, 132 foreign countries, and Canada. 55% are from public schools. 68% are white; 19% Asian American; 17% foreign nationals. The average age of freshmen is 18; all undergraduates, 20. 5% do not continue beyond their first year; 92% remain to graduate.

Housing: 6033 students can be accommodated in college housing, which includes single-sex and coed dormitories, on-campus apartments, married-student housing, fraternity houses, and sorority houses. In addition, there are language houses, special-interest houses, and 22 academic residence programs. On-campus housing is guaranteed for the freshman year only, is available on a first-come, first-served basis, and is available on a lottery system for upperclassmen. 53% of students live on campus; of those, 90% remain on campus on weekends. All students may keep cars.

Activities: 23% of men belong to 34 national fraternities; 16% of women belong to 11 national sororities. There are 350 groups on campus, including art, band, cheerleading, chess, choir, chorale, chorus, computers, dance, debate, drama, ethnic, film, forensics, gay, honors, international, jazz band, literary magazine, marching band, musical theater, newspaper, opera, orchestra, pep band, political, professional, radio and TV, religious, social, social service, student government, symphony, and yearbook. Popular campus events include Spring Fling festival in April and Mask and Wig Show.

Sports: There are 20 intercollegiate sports for men and 14 for women, and 15 intramural sports for men and 14 for women. Facilities include 3 gyms, a tennis pavilion, 2 swimming pools, squash courts, indoor/outdoor tennis courts, playing fields, an indoor ice rink, rowing tanks, saunas, a weight room, and an exercise facility.

Disabled Students: 80% of the campus is accessible. Wheelchair ramps, elevators, special parking, specially equipped rest rooms, special class scheduling, lowered drinking fountains, lowered telephones, and TDD, accessible housing, and an accessible van shuttle are available.

Services: Counseling and information services are available, as is tutoring in every subject. There is a reader service for the blind. The WHEEL academic support program is available in all residences.

Campus Safety and Security: Measures include 24-hour foot and vehicle patrol, self-defense education, escort service, and shuttle buses. There are informal discussions, pamphlets/posters/films, emergency telephones, lighted pathways/sidewalks, a bicycle patrol, 100 commissioned police officers, victim support/special services, Students Together Against Acquaintance Rape, Penn Watch, Student Walking Escort, and 200 security guard personnel, many on public patrol.

Programs of Study: Penn confers B.A., B.S., B.Applied Sc., B.S. in Econ., B.S.E., and B.S.N. degrees. Associate, master's, and doctoral degrees are also awarded. Bachelor's degrees are awarded in BIOLOGICAL SCIENCE (biochemistry, biology/biological science, and biophysics), BUSINESS (accounting, banking and finance, entrepreneurial studies, insurance and risk management, management information systems, management science, marketing/retailing/merchandising, and real estate), COMMUNICATIONS AND THE ARTS (classics, communications, comparative literature, English, fine arts, folklore and mythology, French, German, Italian, linguistics, music, romance languages and literature, Russian, and Spanish), COMPUTER AND PHYSICAL SCIENCE (actuarial science, chemistry, geology, mathematics, physics, and statistics), EDUCATION (education, and elementary), ENGINEERING AND ENVIRONMENTAL DESIGN (architecture, bioengineering, chemical engineering, civil engineering, computer engineering, electrical/electronics engineering, engineering, environmental design, environmental science, materials engineering, mechanical engineering, and systems engineering), HEALTH PROFESSIONS (health care administration, and nursing), SOCIAL SCIENCE (African American studies, African studies, anthropology, cognitive science, East Asian studies, economics, history, humanities, international relations, Italian studies, Judaic studies, Latin American studies, philosophy, political science/government, psychology, public affairs, religion, sociology, South Asian studies, urban studies, and women's studies). Finance, economics, and history are the strongest academically. Engineering and management are the largest.

Required: The bachelor's degree requires completion of 32 to 40 course units, depending on the student's major, with 12 to 18 of these units in the major and a GPA of 2.0. Students must also complete 10 courses from 6 areas of study in the humanities, science, and math.

Special: Cross-registration is permitted with Haverford, Swarthmore, and Bryn Mawr Colleges. Opportunities are provided for internships, a Washington semester, accelerated degree programs, preprofessional programs, B.A.-B.S. degrees, dual and student-designed majors, a 3-2 engineering degree, credit by exam, nondegree study, limited pass/fail options, and study abroad in 14 countries. Through the "one university" concept, students in 1 undergraduate school may study in any of the other 3. There are 10 national honor societies, including Phi Beta Kappa, a freshman honors program, and 27 departmental honors programs.

Faculty/Classroom: 70% of faculty are male; 30%, female. All teach undergraduates. The average class size in an introductory lecture is 26; in a laboratory, 16; and in a regular course, 22.

Admissions: 22% of the 2001-2002 applicants were accepted. The SAT I scores for the 2001-2002 freshman class were: Verbal--8% between 500 and 599, 45% between 600 and 700, and 47% above 700; Math--4% between 500 and 599, 37% between 600 and 700, and 59% above 700. The ACT scores were 7% between 24 and 26, 12% between 27 and 28, and 81% above 28. 96% of the current freshmen were in the top fifth of their class; All were in the top two fifths. There were 68 National Merit finalists. 235 freshmen graduated first in their class in a recent year.

Requirements: The SAT I or ACT is required. Graduation from an accredited secondary school is not required. Recommended preparation includes 4 years of high school English, 3 or 4 each of a foreign language and math, and 3 each of history and science. An essay is required. A portfolio and an audition are recommended for prospective art and music majors, respectively. AP credits are accepted. Important factors in the admissions decision are advanced placement or honor courses, leadership record, and recommendations by school officials.

Procedure: Freshmen are admitted in the fall. Entrance exams should be taken by December of the senior year. There are early decision, early admissions, and deferred admissions plans. Early decision applications should be filed by November 1; regular applications, by January 1 for fall entry, along with a $60 application fee. Notification of early decision is sent December 15; regular decision, April 1. 1124 early decision candidates were accepted for the 2001-2002 class. 5% of all applicants are on a waiting list; 53 were accepted in 2001.

Transfer: 217 transfer students enrolled in 2001-2002. Applicants must provide college and high school transcripts, essays, and 2 recommendations. They must pass a standardized test and meet the course credit requirements of the admitting school. 16 course credits of 32 must be completed at Penn.

Visiting: There are regularly scheduled orientations for prospective students, including an information session by the Admissions Office and a tour of the campus led by current students. There are guides for informal visits and visitors may sit in on classes and stay overnight. To schedule a visit, contact the Admissions Office.

Financial Aid: In 2001-2002, 61% of all freshmen and 53% of continuing students received some form of financial aid. 40% of all students received need-based aid. The average freshman award was $24,619. Of that total, scholarships or need-based grants averaged $18,750 ($34,060 maximum); loans averaged $3476 ($13,275 maximum); and work contracts averaged $2392 ($2600 maximum). 29% of undergraduates work part time. Average annual earnings from campus work are $1576. The average financial indebtedness of the 2001 graduate was $21,556. Penn is a member of CSS. The CSS/Profile or FAFSA and the college's own financial statement are required.

International Students: There are 817 international students enrolled. The school actively recruits these students. They must score 550 on the written TOEFL and also take the SAT I or the ACT. Students must take SAT II: Subject tests in including writing and math (for business and engineering).

Computers: The mainframe is an IBM 3090. Students may use the 550 networked PCs to access information sources, including the on-line library catalog, a campuswide information system (Penn Info), and worldwide resources via the Internet. All students may access the system. There are no time limits and no fees. It is strongly recommended that all students have a personal computer. It is recommended that students in engineering and business have personal computers.

Graduates: In 2001, 2557 bachelor's degrees were awarded. The most popular majors were finance (10%), economics (6%), and psychology (6%). In an average class, 6% graduate in 3 years, 83% in 4 years, 89% in 5 years, and 90% in 6 years. 626 companies recruited on campus in 2000-2001. Of the 2000 graduating class, 14% were enrolled in graduate school within 6 months of graduation and 75% were employed.

Admissions Contact: Willis Stetson, Jr., Dean of Admissions.
E-mail: *info@admissions.ugao.upenn.edu*

UNIVERSITY OF PITTSBURGH SYSTEM

The University of Pittsburgh System, established in 1787, is a public research university system in Pennsylvania. It is governed by the board of trustees of the University of Pittsburgh, whose chief administrator is the chancellor. The primary goal of the system is enhancing educational opportunities for the citizens of Pennsylvania and contributing to the state's social, intellectual, and economic development. The main priorities are to engage in research, artistic, and scholarly activities; to provide high-quality undergraduate, graduate, and professional programs; and to offer expertise and educational services to meet the needs of the region and state. The total enrollment of the 4-year campuses is about 33,000; with about 3700 faculty members. There are 206 baccalaureate, 116 master's, 83 doctoral, and 4 first-professional degree programs offered through the system. Profiles of the 4-year campuses, located in Pittsburgh, Bradford, Greensburg, and Johnstown are included in this section.

UNIVERSITY OF PITTSBURGH AT BRADFORD C-2

Bradford, PA 16701-2898 **(814) 362-7555**
(800) 872-1787; Fax: (814) 362-7578

Full-time: 436 men, 499 women	**Faculty:** 68; IIB, -$
Part-time: 133 men, 397 women	**Ph.D.s:** 75%
Graduate: none	**Student/Faculty:** 14 to 1
Year: semesters, summer session	**Tuition:** $7386 ($15,644)
Application Deadline: open	**Room & Board:** $5310
Freshman Class: 633 applied, 516 accepted, 245 enrolled	
SAT I Verbal/Math: 495/500	**COMPETITIVE**

The University of Pittsburgh at Bradford, established in 1963, is a public, state-related liberal arts institution. In addition to regional accreditation, Pitt-Bradford has baccalaureate program accreditation with NLN. The library contains 79,682 volumes, 14,387 microform items, and 906 audiovisual forms/CDs, and subscribes to 444 periodicals. Computerized library services include the card catalog, interlibrary loans, and database searching. Special learning facilities include a learning resource center, art gallery, natural history museum, radio station, TV station, and sports medicine and rehabilitative therapy clinic. The 125-acre campus is in a small town 160 miles northeast of Pittsburgh and 80 miles south of Buffalo. Including residence halls, there are 19 buildings.

Student Life: 84% of undergraduates are from Pennsylvania. Others are from 26 states, 6 foreign countries, and Canada. 95% are white. The average age of freshmen is 20; all undergraduates, 27. 33% do not continue beyond their first year; 34% remain to graduate.

Housing: 530 students can be accommodated in college housing, which includes single-sex and coed on-campus apartments. On-campus housing is guaranteed for all 4 years. 51% of students live on campus; of those, 26% remain on campus on weekends. All students may keep cars.

Activities: 16% of men belong to 3 local fraternities; 9% of women belong to 3 local sororities. There are 37 groups on campus, including art, choir, computers, dance, drama, ethnic, honors, international, literary magazine, newspaper, political, professional, radio and TV, religious, social, social service, and student government. Popular campus events include Winter Weekend, Spring Fling, and Alumni Weekend.

Sports: There are 5 intercollegiate sports for men and 6 for women, and 19 intramural sports for men and 19 for women. Facilities include a sports complex with a 1500-seat gym, a weight/fitness center, and men's and women's locker rooms, a soccer field, baseball and softball fields, intramural fields, outdoor basketball and tennis courts, a sand volleyball court, and saunas.

Disabled Students: 85% of the campus is accessible. Elevators, special parking, specially equipped rest rooms, lowered drinking fountains, lowered telephones, and specially equipped dorm space are available.
Services: Counseling and information services are available, as is tutoring in most subjects. There is remedial math, reading, and writing. There is a writing lab.
Campus Safety and Security: Measures include 24-hour foot and vehicle patrol, escort service, informal discussions, and pamphlets/posters/films. There are lighted pathways/sidewalks.
Programs of Study: Pitt-Bradford confers B.A., B.S., and B.S.N. degrees. Associate degrees are also awarded. Bachelor's degrees are awarded in BIOLOGICAL SCIENCE (biology/biological science), BUSINESS (business administration and management and sports management), COMMUNICATIONS AND THE ARTS (communications, English, and public relations), COMPUTER AND PHYSICAL SCIENCE (chemistry, computer science, geology, and mathematics), ENGINEERING AND ENVIRONMENTAL DESIGN (environmental science), SOCIAL SCIENCE (American studies, criminal justice, economics, history, political science/government, psychology, social science, and sociology). Nursing, information systems, and biology are the strongest academically. Business administration, computer science, and psychology are the largest.
Required: To graduate, students must complete a minimum of 120 credits with 38 to 70 in the major, and maintain a minimum GPA of 2.0. At least 30 should be in upper-level courses. The core curriculum varies from 15 to 30 credits and distribution requirements from 59 to 63.
Special: Students may cross-register with colleges in the University of Pittsburgh system. Internships are required or strongly recommended for all majors. The school offers study abroad, dual majors, B.A.-B.S. degrees, nondegree study, a 3-2 engineering degree with the University of Pittsburgh (Oakland campus), and accelerated degree programs in most majors. Interdisciplinary majors are offered in human relations, combining anthropology, psychology, and sociology, and in journalism and creative, technical, and business writing. Professional preparation in many areas and education certification are also offered. There are 6 national honor societies.
Faculty/Classroom: 60% of faculty are male; 40%, female. All teach undergraduates. The average class size in an introductory lecture is 25; in a laboratory, 11; and in a regular course, 16.
Admissions: 82% of the 2001-2002 applicants were accepted. The SAT I scores for the 2001-2002 freshman class were: Verbal--50% below 500, 38% between 500 and 599, and 12% between 600 and 700; Math--49% below 500, 40% between 500 and 599, 9% between 600 and 700, and 2% above 700. 18% of the current freshmen were in the top fifth of their class; 45% were in the top two fifths. 1 freshman graduated first in the class.
Requirements: The SAT I is required and the ACT is recommended, with a minimum composite score of 800 (400 verbal and 400 math) on the SAT I or 19 on the ACT. Students must be graduates of an accredited secondary school with 16 Carnegie units, including 4 each in English and social studies and 3 each in science and math. The GED is accepted. An essay is recommended, as is an interview. A GPA of 2.0 is required. AP and CLEP credits are accepted. Important factors in the admissions decision are advanced placement or honor courses, extracurricular activities record, and leadership record. Applications are accepted on-line; there is an application on the school's home page.
Procedure: Freshmen are admitted to all sessions. Entrance exams should be taken during the junior year or the fall of the senior year. There are early decision, early admissions, and deferred admissions plans. Application deadlines are open. The application fee is $35. Notification is sent on a rolling basis.
Transfer: 94 transfer students enrolled in 2001-2002. A GPA of 2.0 or higher is required. 30 credits of a minimum of 120 must be completed at Pitt-Bradford.
Visiting: There are regularly scheduled orientations for prospective students, consisting of a meeting with admissions and financial aid counselors, a tour of the campus, including the dining hall, and a visit with a faculty member. There are guides for informal visits and visitors may sit in on classes and stay overnight. To schedule a visit, contact the Admissions Office.
Financial Aid: In 2001-2002, 74% of all freshmen and 77% of continuing students received some form of financial aid. 47% of freshmen and 52% of continuing students received need-based aid. 14% of undergraduates work part time. Average annual earnings from campus work are $1000. The average financial indebtedness of the 2001 graduate was $15,000. Pitt-Bradford is a member of CSS. The FAFSA is required. The fall application deadline is March 1.
International Students: There are 6 international students enrolled. They must score 550 on the written TOEFL or 213 on the electronic version.
Computers: The campus features 100 computer stations, all linked to the workstations. All students may access the system. There are no time limits and no fees.
Graduates: In 2001, 151 bachelor's degrees were awarded. The most popular majors were business (18%), human relations (11%), and psychology (11%). In an average class, 1% graduate in 3 years, 20% in 4 years, 32% in 5 years, and 34% in 6 years. 48 companies recruited on campus in 2000-2001. Of the 2000 graduating class, 20% were enrolled in graduate school within 6 months of graduation and 93% were employed.
Admissions Contact: Alexander P. Nazemetz, Director of Admissions. A video is available. E-mail: *admissions@www.upb.pitt.edu*
Web: *www.upb.pitt.edu*

UNIVERSITY OF PITTSBURGH AT GREENSBURG B-3
Greensburg, PA 15601-5898 (724) 836-9880
Fax: (724) 836-7160

Full-time: 674 men, 851 women	**Faculty:** 68; IIB, --$
Part-time: 96 men, 137 women	**Ph.D.s:** 84%
Graduate: none	**Student/Faculty:** 22 to 1
Year: semesters, summer session	**Tuition:** $7442 ($15,700)
Application Deadline: open	**Room & Board:** $5400
Freshman Class: 1247 applied, 971 accepted, 553 enrolled	
SAT I Verbal/Math: 512/511	**COMPETITIVE**

The University of Pittsburgh at Greensburg, established in 1963, is a public state-related institution, offering undergraduate majors that can be completed at Pitt-Greensburg, as well as relocation programs that are begun at Greensburg and completed at another Pitt campus. The library contains 71,942 volumes, 8297 microform items, and 1604 audiovisual forms/CDs, and subscribes to 418 periodicals. Computerized library services include the card catalog, interlibrary loans, and database searching. Special learning facilities include a learning resource center. The 205-acre campus is in a suburban area 33 miles southeast of Pittsburgh. Including residence halls, there are 12 buildings.
Student Life: 99% of undergraduates are from Pennsylvania. Others are from 10 states and 5 foreign countries. 90% are from public schools. 96% are white. The average age of freshmen is 18; all undergraduates, 25. 25% do not continue beyond their first year; 55% remain to graduate.
Housing: 560 students can be accommodated in college housing, which includes coed dormitories and on-campus apartments. On-campus housing is guaranteed for all 4 years. 60% of students commute. Alcohol is not permitted. All students may keep cars.
Activities: There are no fraternities or sororities. There are 44 groups on campus, including academic, band, cheerleading, chess, choir, chorus, computers, dance, debate, drama, ethnic, honors, literary magazine, newspaper, pep band, political, religious, social, social service, and student government. Popular campus events include Humanities Day.
Sports: There are 5 intercollegiate sports for men and 6 for women, and 8 intramural sports for men and 8 for women. Facilities include a gym, a weight room, playing fields, and tennis and racquetball courts.
Disabled Students: 95% of the campus is accessible. Wheelchair ramps, elevators, special parking, specially equipped rest rooms, special class scheduling, lowered drinking fountains, and lowered telephones are available.
Services: Counseling and information services are available, as is tutoring in most subjects, including math, computer science, and English. There is remedial math, reading, and writing.
Campus Safety and Security: Measures include 24-hour foot and vehicle patrol, escort service, informal discussions, and pamphlets/posters/films. There are emergency telephones and lighted pathways/sidewalks.
Programs of Study: Pitt-Greensburg confers B.A. and B.S. degrees. Bachelor's degrees are awarded in BIOLOGICAL SCIENCE (biology/biological science), BUSINESS (accounting and management science), COMMUNICATIONS AND THE ARTS (communications, creative writing, and English literature), COMPUTER AND PHYSICAL SCIENCE (applied mathematics and natural sciences), SOCIAL SCIENCE (American studies, anthropology, humanities, political science/government, psychology, and social science). Management and psychology are the strongest academically. Management is the largest.
Required: To graduate, students must complete 120 to 126 hours, with 24 to 36 in the major, and maintain a minimum GPA of 2.0. General education requirements include 15 credits each in humanities, social sciences, and natural sciences, 6 to 15 in writing courses, 3 each in speech and critical reasoning, and 2 to 3 in math.
Special: Pitt-Greensburg offers cross-registration with the Pittsburgh and Johnstown campuses of the university system and with Seton Hill College. Internships are available in all majors and required for English writing and criminology. Double majors, student-designed majors, a Washington semester, nondegree study, and pass/fail options are available. There are 2 national honor societies.
Faculty/Classroom: 51% of faculty are male; 49%, female. All teach undergraduates and 50% do research. The average class size in an introductory lecture is 30; in a laboratory, 15; and in a regular course, 25.
Admissions: 78% of the 2001-2002 applicants were accepted. The SAT I scores for the 2001-2002 freshman class were: Verbal--46% below 500, 43% between 500 and 599, and 11% between 600 and 700; Math--44% below 500, 44% between 500 and 599, and 12% between 600

and 700. 20% of the current freshmen were in the top fifth of their class; 55% were in the top two fifths. 5 freshmen graduated first in their class.
Requirements: The SAT I is required. In addition, students must be graduates of an accredited secondary school. The GED is accepted. Students must complete 15 high school units, including 4 each of English and academic electives, 3 of a single foreign language, 2 of math, and 1 each of history and a lab science; additional units in all but English are recommended. An essay is optional; an interview is recommended. Pitt-Greensburg requires applicants to be in the upper 60% of their class. A GPA of 2.7 is required. AP and CLEP credits are accepted. Important factors in the admissions decision are advanced placement or honor courses, recommendations by school officials, and leadership record.
Procedure: Freshmen are admitted fall and spring. Entrance exams should be taken by December of the senior year. There are early decision and deferred admissions plans. Application deadlines are open.
Transfer: 123 transfer students enrolled in 2001-2002. Applicants must have a minimum GPA of 2.0. The SAT I, 15 minimum college credits, and an interview are recommended. Grades of C in comparable courses transfer for credit. 30 credits of 120 must be completed at Pitt-Greensburg.
Visiting: There are guides for informal visits and visitors may sit in on classes. To schedule a visit, contact the Admissions Office.
Financial Aid: In 2001-2002, 87% of all freshmen and 85% of continuing students received some form of financial aid. 65% of all students received need-based aid. The average freshman award was $4250. Of that total, scholarships or need-based grants averaged $3000 ($8500 maximum); loans averaged $3900 ($5500 maximum); and work contracts averaged $1550 ($2100 maximum). 63% of undergraduates work part time. Average annual earnings from campus work are $1550. The average financial indebtedness of the 2001 graduate was $15,200. The FAFSA and the college's own financial statement are required. The fall application deadline is April 1.
International Students: There were 2 international students enrolled in a recent year. They must score 550 on the written TOEFL or take the MELAB.
Computers: The mainframes are a DEC VAX 9000 in a VAX cluster, a VAX 8800, and a DEC System 5000. All computers are networked locally and through wide-area networks to VMS and UNIX mainframe services. There are 30 DOS, 15 UNIX, and Mac computers in the computer center. All residence hall rooms have at least one PC and a network connection. All students may access the system. There are no time limits and no fees.
Graduates: In 2001, 212 bachelor's degrees were awarded. The most popular majors were management (23%), psychology (21%), and accounting (15%). In an average class, 27% graduate in 4 years, 52% in 5 years, and 2% in 6 years.
Admissions Contact: John R. Sparks, Director of Admissions and Financial Aid. E-mail: *upgadmit@pitt.edu*

UNIVERSITY OF PITTSBURGH AT JOHNSTOWN C-3

Johnstown, PA 15904 (814) 269-7050
(800) 765-4875; Fax: (814) 269-7044

Full-time: 1346 men, 1419 women	**Faculty:** 136; IIB, -$
Part-time: 104 men, 227 women	**Ph.D.s:** 73%
Graduate: none	**Student/Faculty:** 20 to 1
Year: Modified trimesters, summer session	**Tuition:** $7464 ($15,722)
	Room & Board: $5580

Application Deadline: open
Freshman Class: 2156 applied, 1836 accepted, 828 enrolled
SAT I or ACT: required **LESS COMPETITIVE**

The University of Pittsburgh at Johnstown is a 4-year institution offering programs in arts and sciences, education, and engineering technology. In addition to regional accreditation, UPJ has baccalaureate program accreditation with ABET. Computerized library services include the card catalog, interlibrary loans, and database searching. Special learning facilities include a learning resource center, art gallery, and radio station. The 650-acre campus is in a suburban area 70 miles east of Pittsburgh. Including residence halls, there are 28 buildings.
Student Life: 98% of undergraduates are from Pennsylvania. Others are from 12 states. 89% are from public schools. 96% are white. 48% are Protestant; 47% Catholic. The average age of freshmen is 18; all undergraduates, 19. 9% do not continue beyond their first year; 70% remain to graduate.
Housing: 1700 students can be accommodated in college housing, which includes single-sex dormitories, on-campus apartments, off-campus apartments, fraternity houses, and sorority houses. In addition, there are special-interest houses and clubs and organizations that provide housing. On-campus housing is guaranteed for all 4 years. 62% of students live on campus; of those, 65% remain on campus on weekends. All students may keep cars.
Activities: 16% of men belong to 1 local fraternity and 3 national fraternities; 11% of women belong to 1 local sorority and 4 national sororities. There are 70 groups on campus, including band, cheerleading, chess, choir, chorus, computers, dance, drama, ethnic, honors, literary magazine, musical theater, newspaper, pep band, political, professional, radio and TV, religious, social, social service, student government, symphony, and yearbook. Popular campus events include Ethnic Festival, Engineers' Week, and Winter Carnival.
Sports: There are 4 intercollegiate sports for men and 4 for women, and 32 intramural sports for men and 21 for women. Facilities include a 2300-seat gym, a pool, a dance studio, a weight room, a sauna, a cross-country track, tennis and basketball courts, and a nature area.
Disabled Students: 80% of the campus is accessible. Elevators, special parking, specially equipped rest rooms, and special class scheduling are available.
Services: Counseling and information services are available, as is tutoring in most subjects.
Campus Safety and Security: Measures include 24-hour foot and vehicle patrol, informal discussions, and lighted pathways/sidewalks.
Programs of Study: UPJ confers B.A. and B.S. degrees. Associate degrees are also awarded. Bachelor's degrees are awarded in AGRICULTURE (environmental studies), BIOLOGICAL SCIENCE (biology/biological science), BUSINESS (accounting, banking and finance, business administration and management, and business economics), COMMUNICATIONS AND THE ARTS (communications, creative writing, dramatic arts, English, and journalism), COMPUTER AND PHYSICAL SCIENCE (chemistry, computer science, geology, and mathematics), EDUCATION (elementary, English, mathematics, science, secondary, and social science), ENGINEERING AND ENVIRONMENTAL DESIGN (civil engineering technology, electrical/electronics engineering technology, and mechanical engineering technology), HEALTH PROFESSIONS (medical laboratory technology), SOCIAL SCIENCE (American studies, economics, geography, history, humanities, political science/government, psychology, social science, and sociology). Business, biology, and education are the largest.
Required: To graduate, students must complete 120 to 139 credits, with 30 to 36 credits in the major and a minimum GPA of 2.0. The school requires 12 credits each in humanities, natural sciences, and social sciences.
Special: Students may cross-register with schools in the Pittsburgh Council for Higher Education. Internships are available both on and off campus for credit, pay, or both. The school offers study abroad, work-study programs, accelerated degree programs, dual majors, student-designed majors, nondegree study, and pass/fail options. There are 8 national honor societies.
Faculty/Classroom: 66% of faculty are male; 34%, female. 93% teach undergraduates and 70% do research. The average class size in an introductory lecture is 30; in a laboratory, 18; and in a regular course, 25.
Admissions: 85% of the 2001-2002 applicants were accepted. 11% of the current freshmen were in the top fifth of their class; 43% were in the top two fifths. 6 freshmen graduated first in their class in a recent year.
Requirements: The SAT I or ACT is required. In addition, applicants must be graduates of an accredited secondary school. The GED is accepted. For admission to freshman standing, 15 academic credits are required, including 4 each of English and history, 3 each of social studies and math (2 of algebra, 1 of geometry preferred), 2 of foreign language, and 1 to 2 of lab science. Engineering students must have completed chemistry, physics, and trigonometry. An interview is recommended, and an essay is required. AP credits are accepted. Important factors in the admissions decision are advanced placement or honor courses, leadership record, and recommendations by school officials.
Procedure: Freshmen are admitted to all sessions. Entrance exams should be taken between April and June of the junior year or by November of the senior year. There are early admissions and deferred admissions plans. Application deadlines are open.
Transfer: 118 transfer students enrolled in a recent year. Students wishing to transfer must have a minimum GPA of 2.5 and at least 15 credit hours earned. The SAT I or ACT is required. Grades of C or better transfer for credit. 30 credits of 120 must be completed at UPJ.
Visiting: There are regularly scheduled orientations for prospective students, including 2 programs held on Saturdays in the fall and in the spring. There are guides for informal visits and visitors may sit in on classes and stay overnight. To schedule a visit, contact the Admissions Office.
Financial Aid: In a recent year, 77% of all freshmen and 81% of continuing students received some form of financial aid. 61% of freshmen and 66% of continuing students received need-based aid. The average freshman award was $3844. Of that total, scholarships or need-based grants averaged $2924 ($6300 maximum); loans averaged $2921 ($3625 maximum); and work contracts averaged $1490 ($1550 maximum). 12% of undergraduates work part time. Average annual earnings from campus work are $1550. The average financial indebtedness of a recent year's graduate was $15,800. The FAFSA, PHEAA Application, and State Grant are required. The fall application deadline is April 1.
International Students: They must score 550 on the written TOEFL. The SAT I may be required for some students.
Computers: The mainframe is a DEC VAX cluster. In addition, 150 Macs, IBM, and AT&T PCs are available for student use. Some labs

have restricted use for education, engineering technology, or computer science majors. Others are open to all students. All students have access to the Internet. All students may access the system. There are no time limits. The fee is $110 per term.

Admissions Contact: James F. Gyure, Director of Admissions. E-mail: *jgyure@upj.pitt.edu* Web: *www.pitt.edu/~upjweb*

UNIVERSITY OF PITTSBURGH AT PITTSBURGH B-3

Pittsburgh, PA 15260 (412) 624-PITT; Fax: (412) 648-8815

Full-time: 7352 men, 8015 women	**Faculty:** I, -$
Part-time: 1053 men, 1378 women	**Ph.D.s:** 90%
Graduate: 4141 men, 4771 women	**Student/Faculty:** 17 to 1
Year: semesters, summer session	**Tuition:** $7482 ($15,740)
Application Deadline: open	**Room & Board:** $6110
Freshman Class: 15,438 applied, 8376 accepted, 2871 enrolled	
SAT I Verbal/Math: 592/600	**ACT:** 26 **HIGHLY COMPETITIVE**

The University of Pittsburgh, founded in 1787, is a state-related, public research university with programs in arts and sciences, education, engineering, law, social work, business, health science, information sciences, and public and international affairs. There are 10 undergraduate and 14 graduate schools. In addition to regional accreditation, Pitt has baccalaureate program accreditation with AACSB, ABET, ACPE, ADA, CSWE, and NLN. The 25 libraries contain 3,926,744 volumes and 4,265,832 microform items, and subscribe to 30,980 periodicals. Computerized library services include the card catalog, interlibrary loans, and database searching. Special learning facilities include a learning resource center, art gallery, radio station, and international classrooms, located in the 42-story Cathedral of Learning, an observatory, and a music hall. The 132-acre campus is in an urban area 3 miles east of downtown Pittsburgh. Including residence halls, there are 100 buildings.

Student Life: 86% of undergraduates are from Pennsylvania. Others are from 49 states, 122 foreign countries, and Canada. 84% are white. The average age of freshmen is 18; all undergraduates, 22. 12% do not continue beyond their first year.

Housing: 6100 students can be accommodated in college housing, which includes single-sex and coed dormitories, off-campus apartments, and fraternity houses. In addition, there are honors houses, special-interest houses, engineering, nursing, health-related, business, and international living houses.. On-campus housing is guaranteed for the freshman year only, is available on a first-come, first-served basis, and is available on a lottery system for upperclassmen. All students may keep cars.

Activities: 10% of men belong to 20 national fraternities; 7% of women belong to 15 national sororities. There are 300 groups on campus, including art, band, cheerleading, chess, choir, chorus, dance, debate, drama, ethnic, film, gay, honors, international, jazz band, literary magazine, marching band, newspaper, orchestra, pep band, political, professional, radio and TV, religious, social, social service, student government, and yearbook. Popular campus events include Jazz Seminar, Black Week, and Greek Week.

Sports: There are 9 intercollegiate sports for men and 10 for women, and 12 intramural sports for men and 10 for women. Facilities include a 6750-seat field house for basketball and track, a sports center that converts from a regulation football field to 9 tennis courts, and a hall for swimming and racquetball. There are also billiard tables, table tennis, video games, and televisions in the student union.

Disabled Students: 90% of the campus is accessible. Wheelchair ramps, elevators, special parking, specially equipped rest rooms, special class scheduling, lowered drinking fountains, lowered telephones, transportation, and wheelchair-accessible computer facilities in the computing labs are available.

Services: Counseling and information services are available, as is tutoring in some subjects, including many lower-level undergraduate science and humanities courses. There is a reader service for the blind, and remedial math, reading, and writing.

Campus Safety and Security: Measures include 24-hour foot and vehicle patrol, self-defense education, escort service, and shuttle buses. There are informal discussions, pamphlets/posters/films, emergency telephones, lighted pathways/sidewalks, and taxi service, and crime alerts and notices distributed when an immediate danger to faculty, students, or staff is presented.

Programs of Study: Pitt confers B.A., B.S., B.A.S.W., B.Phil., B.S.B.A., B.S.E., and B.S.N. degrees. Master's and doctoral degrees are also awarded. Bachelor's degrees are awarded in BIOLOGICAL SCIENCE (biology/biological science, ecology, evolutionary biology, microbiology, molecular biology, neurosciences, and nutrition), BUSINESS (accounting, banking and finance, business administration and management, management science, and marketing/retailing/merchandising), COMMUNICATIONS AND THE ARTS (Chinese, classics, communications, creative writing, dramatic arts, English literature, film arts, fine arts, French, German, Italian, Japanese, linguistics, music, Polish, Russian, Spanish, speech/debate/rhetoric, and studio art), COMPUTER AND PHYSICAL SCIENCE (astronomy, chemistry, computer science, geology, information sciences and systems, mathematics, natural sciences, physics, and statistics), ENGINEERING AND ENVIRONMENTAL DESIGN (bioengineering, chemical engineering, civil engineering, computer engineering, electrical/electronics engineering, engineering physics, environmental science, industrial engineering, materials engineering, materials science, mechanical engineering, and metallurgical engineering), HEALTH PROFESSIONS (emergency medical technologies, exercise science, medical laboratory technology, medical records administration/services, nursing, and occupational therapy), SOCIAL SCIENCE (African American studies, anthropology, child psychology/development, economics, history, humanities, law, law enforcement and corrections, liberal arts/general studies, paralegal studies, philosophy, physical fitness/movement, political science/government, psychology, public administration, religion, social science, social work, sociology, and urban studies). Philosophy, history and philosophy of science, and chemistry are the strongest academically. Business, engineering, and psychology are the largest.

Required: All students in the College of Arts and Sciences must take a minimum of 120 credits. Skills and general education requirements vary by high school achievement but include course work in the humanities, social and natural sciences, and foreign culture. A minimum of 24 credits in the major and a 2.0 GPA are required. Requirements for other schools may vary.

Special: Students may cross-register with 10 neighboring colleges and universities. Internships, study abroad, a semester at sea, a Washington semester, work-study programs, a dual major in business and any other subject in arts and sciences, and student-designed majors are available. There are freshman seminars and a 5-year joint degree in arts and sciences/engineering. There are 27 national honor societies, including Phi Beta Kappa, and a freshman honors program.

Faculty/Classroom: 67% of faculty are male; 33%, female.

Admissions: 54% of the 2001-2002 applicants were accepted. The SAT I scores for the 2001-2002 freshman class were: Verbal--8% below 500, 47% between 500 and 599, 38% between 600 and 700, and 7% above 700; Math--6% below 500, 42% between 500 and 599, 43% between 600 and 700, and 9% above 700. The ACT scores were 5% below 21, 23% between 21 and 23, 28% between 24 and 26, 18% between 27 and 28, and 26% above 28. There were 16 National Merit finalists. 72 freshmen graduated first in their class.

Requirements: The SAT I or ACT is required. In addition, applicants for admission to the College of Arts and Sciences must be graduates of an accredited secondary school. Students must have 15 high school academic credits, including 4 units of English, 3 each of math and lab science, and 1 of social studies, plus 4 units in academic electives. Pitt recommends that the student have 3 or more years of a single foreign language. An essay is recommended if the student is seeking scholarship consideration, and music students must audition. Requirements for other colleges or schools may vary. AP and CLEP credits are accepted. Important factors in the admissions decision are advanced placement or honor courses, evidence of special talent, and extracurricular activities record. Applications are accepted on disk and on-line at the college's web site.

Procedure: Freshmen are admitted to all sessions. Entrance exams should be taken preferably by January for September admission. There is a deferred admissions plan. Application deadlines are open. The application fee is $35.

Transfer: 524 transfer students enrolled in 2001-2002. Applicants for transfer to the College of Arts and Sciences must supply transcripts of all secondary school and college course work and have a minimum GPA of 2.5. An interview is recommended. Grades of C or better transfer for credit. Application deadlines vary by school. 30 credits of 120 must be completed at Pitt.

Visiting: There are regularly scheduled orientations for prospective students, including information sessions, student-guided tours, and class attendance. There are guides for informal visits and visitors may sit in on classes and stay overnight. To schedule a visit, contact the Office of Admissions and Financial Aid.

Financial Aid: In 2001-2002, 66% of all freshmen and 75% of continuing students received some form of financial aid. The average freshman award was $9112. Of that total, scholarships or need-based grants averaged $4217; loans averaged $3380; and work contracts averaged $1929. 40% of undergraduates work part time. Average annual earnings from campus work are $1929. The average financial indebtedness of the 2001 graduate was $16,000. The FAFSA and the college's own financial statement are required. The fall application deadline is January 15.

International Students: There are 167 international students enrolled. They must score 500 on the written TOEFL or 173 on the electronic version and also take the SAT I or the ACT.

Computers: 6 public computing labs, with more than 600 PCs and workstations, provide access to a variety of software, printers, and graphic plotters. All students may access the system. There are no time limits and no fees.

Graduates: In 2001, 3309 bachelor's degrees were awarded. The most popular majors were business (12%) and engineering (11%). 400 companies recruited on campus in 2000-2001. Of the 2000 graduating class, 40% were enrolled in graduate school within 6 months of graduation.

Admissions Contact: Dr. Betsy A. Porter, Director of Admissions and Financial Aid. A video is available. E-mail: *oafa@pitt.edu*
Web: *www.pitt.edu/~oafa*

UNIVERSITY OF SCRANTON E-2
Scranton, PA 18510-4699 (570) 941-7540
(888) SCRANTON; Fax: (570) 941-5928

Full-time: 1575 men, 2112 women	**Faculty:** 244; IIA, +$
Part-time: 163 men, 210 women	**Ph.D.s:** 86%
Graduate: 206 men, 392 women	**Student/Faculty:** 15 to 1
Year: semesters, summer session	**Tuition:** $19,530
Application Deadline: March 1	**Room & Board:** $8434

Freshman Class: 3820 applied, 3362 accepted, 1012 enrolled
SAT I Verbal/Math: 566/565 **COMPETITIVE+**

The University of Scranton, founded in 1888, is a private institution operated by the Jesuit order of the Roman Catholic Church. It offers programs in business, behavioral sciences, education, health science, humanities, math, science, and social science. There are 4 undergraduate schools and 1 graduate school. In addition to regional accreditation, the university has baccalaureate program accreditation with AACSB, APTA, CSAB, NCATE, and NLN. The library contains 432,039 volumes, 493,710 microform items, and 13,085 audiovisual forms/CDs, and subscribes to 8500 periodicals. Computerized library services include the card catalog, interlibrary loans, and database searching. Special learning facilities include a learning resource center, art gallery, radio station, TV station, satellite dish for telecommunication reception, music center, language lab, and a greenhouse. The 50-acre campus is in an urban area 125 miles north of Philadelphia. Including residence halls, there are 60 buildings.

Student Life: 52% of undergraduates are from Pennsylvania. Others are from 26 states, 16 foreign countries, and Canada. 51% are from public schools. 88% are white. 84% are Catholic; 10% Protestant. The average age of freshmen is 18; all undergraduates, 20. 10% do not continue beyond their first year; 80% remain to graduate.

Housing: 2063 students can be accommodated in college housing, which includes single-sex and coed dormitories and on-campus apartments. In addition, there are language houses, special-interest houses, an international house, a residential college, a spanish house, a performing arts house, an education house, a volunteer/service house, 2 wellness dorms, a theater house, and 2 wellness floors. On-campus housing is guaranteed for all 4 years. 72% of students live on campus; of those, 75% remain on campus on weekends. Upperclassmen may keep cars.

Activities: There are no fraternities or sororities. There are 80 groups on campus, including art, band, cheerleading, chess, choir, chorale, chorus, computers, concert band, dance, debate, drama, drill team, ethnic, film, honors, international, jazz band, literary magazine, music ensembles, musical theater, newspaper, orchestra, pep band, photography, political, professional, radio and TV, religious, social, social service, student government, and yearbook. Popular campus events include Spring Fling, Senior Formal, and President's Ball.

Sports: There are 10 intercollegiate sports for men and 8 for women, and 17 intramural sports for men and 14 for women. Facilities include a 3000-seat gym, basketball courts, wrestling and weight rooms, handball/racquetball and tennis courts, a sand volleyball court, a soccer/lacrosse field, a softball field, a swimming pool, a physical therapy room, a 3-court multipurpose gym, a fitness center, a sauna and steamroom, a dance aerobics room, and a turfed recreation/utility field.

Disabled Students: All of the campus is accessible. Wheelchair ramps, elevators, special parking, specially equipped rest rooms, special class scheduling, lowered drinking fountains, and lowered telephones are available.

Services: Counseling and information services are available, as is tutoring in most subjects. There is a reader service for the blind, and computing and study skills seminars.

Campus Safety and Security: Measures include 24-hour foot and vehicle patrol, self-defense education, escort service, and informal discussions. There are pamphlets/posters/films, emergency telephones, and lighted pathways/sidewalks.

Programs of Study: the university confers B.A. and B.S. degrees. Associate and master's degrees are also awarded. Bachelor's degrees are awarded in BIOLOGICAL SCIENCE (biochemistry, biology/biological science, biophysics, and neurosciences), BUSINESS (accounting, banking and finance, business administration and management, business economics, electronic business, human resources, international business management, marketing/retailing/merchandising, and operations research), COMMUNICATIONS AND THE ARTS (advertising, communications, dramatic arts, English, French, German, Greek, Latin, and Spanish), COMPUTER AND PHYSICAL SCIENCE (chemistry, computer management, computer science, information sciences and systems, mathematics, and physics), EDUCATION (early childhood, elementary, science, secondary, and special), ENGINEERING AND ENVIRONMENTAL DESIGN (electrical/electronics engineering, environmental science, and preengineering), HEALTH PROFESSIONS (exercise science, health care administration, medical laboratory technology, nursing, occupational therapy, physical therapy, predentistry, and premedicine), SOCIAL SCIENCE (criminal justice, economics, gerontology, history, human services, international relations, philosophy, political science/government, prelaw, psychology, sociology, and theological studies). Chemistry, biology, and physical therapy are the strongest academically. Biology, communication, and elementary education are the largest.

Required: Students take distribution requirements according to their general area of study. All are required to take philosophy/theology, phys ed, English composition, speech, and computer literacy. A total of 130 credit hours is required for graduation, with 36 in the major. The minimum GPA is 2.0, although some majors require a higher GPA.

Special: There are cooperative programs with the University of Detroit Mercy and cross-registration with 27 other Jesuit colleges. Internships are available in all career-oriented majors, and foreign study is offered in many countries. There is a Washington semester for history and political science majors. Students may earn a B.A.-B.S. degree in economics and accelerated degrees in history, chemistry, and biochemistry. The university also offers dual, student-designed, and interdisciplinary majors, including chemistry-business, chemistry-computers, electronics-business, and international language-business, credit by exam and for life/military/work experience, work-study, nondegree study, and pass/fail options. There is also a special Jesuit-oriented general education program. There are 26 national honor societies, including Phi Beta Kappa, a freshman honors program, and 2 departmental honors programs.

Faculty/Classroom: 70% of faculty are male; 30%, female. 97% teach undergraduates, 80% do research, and 77% do both. No introductory courses are taught by graduate students. The average class size in an introductory lecture is 22; in a laboratory, 12; and in a regular course, 21.

Admissions: 88% of the 2001-2002 applicants were accepted. The SAT I scores for the 2001-2002 freshman class were: Verbal--14% below 500, 55% between 500 and 599, 26% between 600 and 700, and 4% above 700; Math--17% below 500, 47% between 500 and 599, 32% between 600 and 700, and 3% above 700. 48% of the current freshmen were in the top fifth of their class; 78% were in the top two fifths. There was 1 National Merit finalist and 7 semifinalists. 17 freshmen graduated first in their class.

Requirements: The SAT I or ACT is required. In addition, applicants should be graduates of an accredited secondary school, though in some cases a GED may be accepted. They should complete 18 academic or Carnegie units, including 4 years of high school English, 3 each of math, science, history, and social studies, and 2 of foreign language. 2 letters of reference/recommendation are required. Essays are not required, but for some students the additional information can be of assistance. Interviews are recommended. AP and CLEP credits are accepted. Important factors in the admissions decision are leadership record, advanced placement or honor courses, and extracurricular activities record. Applications are accepted on-line at
www.scranton.edu/admission/fa_ao_applyonline.asp

Procedure: Freshmen are admitted fall and spring. Entrance exams should be taken by the fall of the senior year. There are early admissions and deferred admissions plans. Early action applications should be filed by November 15; regular applications, by March 1 for fall entry, December 15 for spring entry, and May 1 for summer entry, along with a $40 fee. Notification is sent on a rolling basis, beginning December 15. 1% of all applicants are on a waiting list.

Transfer: 65 transfer students enrolled in 2001-2002. Applicants should have earned a GPA of at least 2.5. 63 credits of 130 must be completed at the university.

Visiting: There are regularly scheduled orientations for prospective students, including private interviews conducted Monday through Friday throughout the school year. Group information sessions are offered on Saturdays and holidays in the fall and spring and during the week in the summer. There are guides for informal visits, and visitors may sit in on classes and stay overnight. To schedule a visit, contact the Office of Admissions.

Financial Aid: In 2001-2002, 91% of all freshmen and 85% of continuing students received some form of financial aid. 59% of all students received need-based aid. The average freshman award was $13,521. Of that total, scholarships or need-based grants averaged $8715 ($19,330 maximum); loans averaged $3050 ($4625 maximum); and work contracts averaged $1500 ($2500 maximum). 17% of undergraduates work part time. Average annual earnings from campus work are $900. The average financial indebtedness of the 2001 graduate was $14,900. The university is a member of CSS. The FAFSA is required. For early action there are early estimates of financial aid. The fall application priority deadline is February 15.

International Students: There are 20 international students enrolled. The school actively recruits these students. They must score 525 on the written TOEFL.

Computers: The mainframes are a Compaq GS140 and 6 Compaq Proliants as web servers. There are 817 PCs and terminals on campus available for student use in the library, academic buildings, and residence halls. The campus is completely networked, which provides student access to the Internet and the Web. All students may access the system 24 hours a day. There are no time limits and no fees.

Graduates: In 2001, 962 bachelor's degrees were awarded. The most popular majors were communications (7%), biology (7%), and psychology (5%). In an average class, 72% graduate in 4 years, 79% in 5 years, and 80% in 6 years. 60 companies recruited on campus in 2000-2001. Of the 2000 graduating class, 33% were enrolled in graduate school within 6 months of graduation and 65% were employed.

Admissions Contact: Joseph M. Roback, Director of Admissions. A video is available. E-mail: *admission@scranton.edu*
Web: *www.scranton.edu*

UNIVERSITY OF THE ARTS F-3
Philadelphia, PA 19102 (215) 717-6030
(800) 616-2787; Fax: (215) 717-6045

Full-time: 868 men, 1013 women	**Faculty:** 93; IIB, --$
Part-time: 22 men, 15 women	**Ph.D.s:** n/av
Graduate: 40 men, 116 women	**Student/Faculty:** 20 to 1
Year: semesters	**Tuition:** $19,230
Application Deadline: open	**Room & Board:** $5000
Freshman Class: 1745 applied, 865 accepted, 439 enrolled	
SAT I Verbal/Math: 539/511	**SPECIAL**

University of the Arts, founded in 1870, is a private, nonprofit institution offering education and professional training in visual, media, and performing arts, with an emphasis on the humanities and interdisciplinary exploration. There are 3 undergraduate and 2 graduate schools. In addition to regional accreditation, UArts has baccalaureate program accreditation with NASAD and NASM. The 3 libraries contain 189,658 volumes, 461 microform items, and 14,838 audiovisual forms/CDs, and subscribe to 501 periodicals. Computerized library services include the card catalog, interlibrary loans, and database searching. Special learning facilities include an art gallery and several theaters, and music, animation, and recording studios. The 18-acre campus is in an urban area in Philadelphia. Including residence halls, there are 8 buildings.

Student Life: 60% of undergraduates are from out of state, mostly the Middle Atlantic. Others are from 40 states, 20 foreign countries, and Canada. 73% are from public schools. 80% are white. The average age of freshmen is 18; all undergraduates, 20. 20% do not continue beyond their first year; 55% remain to graduate.

Housing: 650 students can be accommodated in college housing, which includes coed on-campus and off-campus apartments. On-campus housing is guaranteed for the freshman year only and is available on a first-come, first-served basis. Priority is given to out-of-town students. 66% of students commute. Alcohol is not permitted. No one may keep cars.

Activities: There are no fraternities or sororities. There are 20 groups on campus, including art, band, choir, chorale, chorus, dance, drama, ethnic, film, gay, international, jazz band, musical theater, opera, photography, professional, religious, and student government. Popular campus events include exhibitions and performances.

Sports: There is no sports program at UArts. Athletic facilities are available at area gyms, for which the university provides discount membership.

Disabled Students: 65% of the campus is accessible. Wheelchair ramps, elevators, specially equipped rest rooms, lowered drinking fountains, lowered telephones, and sign language interpreters are available.

Services: Counseling and information services are available, as is tutoring in every subject. There is remedial math, reading, and writing, and assistance with writing and study skills.

Campus Safety and Security: Measures include 24-hour foot and vehicle patrol, self-defense education, escort service, and informal discussions. There are pamphlets/posters/films and lighted pathways/sidewalks.

Programs of Study: UArts confers B.S., B.F.A., and B.M. degrees. Master's degrees are also awarded. Bachelor's degrees are awarded in COMMUNICATIONS AND THE ARTS (ceramic art and design, communications, dance, dramatic arts, fiber/textiles/weaving, film arts, graphic design, illustration, industrial design, jazz, media arts, metal/jewelry, multimedia, music performance, music theory and composition, musical theater, painting, performing arts, photography, printmaking, radio/television technology, and sculpture), EDUCATION (dance), ENGINEERING AND ENVIRONMENTAL DESIGN (computer graphics). Graphic design, dance, and photography are the largest.

Required: All students must complete a core program consisting of humanities courses in language and expression, literature, arts history and social studies, philosophy and science, and related arts. A GPA of 2.0 overall for 123 to 143 credits, with 21 to 45 in the major, depending on the curriculum, must be achieved for graduation.

Special: UArts offers cross-registration with the 10-member Consortium East Coast Art Schools as well as with the Pennsylvania Academy of Fine Arts and Philadelphia College of Textiles and Sciences. Internships may be arranged, and there are extensive summer programs and opportunities to study abroad.

Faculty/Classroom: 64% of faculty are male. 92% teach undergraduates. No introductory courses are taught by graduate students. The average class size in an introductory lecture is 18 and in a regular course, 14.

Admissions: 50% of the 2001-2002 applicants were accepted. The SAT I scores for the 2001-2002 freshman class were: Verbal--32% below 500, 42% between 500 and 599, 23% between 600 and 700, and 3% above 700; Math--44% below 500, 40% between 500 and 599, and 16% between 600 and 700. 10% of the current freshmen were in the top fifth of their class; 50% were in the top two fifths.

Requirements: The SAT I or ACT is required. In addition, students must have graduated from an accredited secondary school or hold a GED certificate. A minimum of 16 academic credits consisting of 4 each in English and math and 2 each in music or art and history is recommended. An essay and either a portfolio or an audition are required of all applicants. An interview is recommended. A GPA of 2.0 is required. AP and CLEP credits are accepted. Important factors in the admissions decision are evidence of special talent, advanced placement or honor courses, and personality/intangible qualities. Applications are accepted on computer disk via CollegeLink and on-line via the Uarts web site.

Procedure: Freshmen are admitted fall and spring. Entrance exams should be taken late in the junior year or early in the senior year. There are early admissions and deferred admissions plans. Application deadlines are open. The application fee is $50. A waiting list is an active part of the admissions procedure. There is a rolling admissions plan.

Transfer: 129 transfer students enrolled in 2001-2002. Candidates must have a minimum 2.0 GPA overall. An interview is recommended, as well as test scores for either the SAT I or ACT if English composition has not been completed. 48 credits of 123 must be completed at UArts.

Visiting: There are regularly scheduled orientations for prospective students, including a spring and fall open house. There are guides for informal visits. To schedule a visit, contact the Office of Admissions.

Financial Aid: In 2001-2002, 66% of all freshmen and 85% of continuing students received some form of financial aid. In a recent year, 66% of freshmen and 85% of continuing students received need-based aid. The average freshman award was $11,628. Of that total, scholarships or need-based grants averaged $6500 ($10,000 maximum); loans averaged $2425 ($3625 maximum); work contracts averaged $1300 ($1500 maximum); and Presidential Scholarship averaged $5000 ($7000 maximum). 30% of undergraduates work part time. Average annual earnings from campus work are $1500. The average financial indebtedness of the 2001 graduate was $17,000. UArts is a member of CSS. The FAFSA is required. The fall application deadline is February 15.

International Students: There are 43 international students enrolled. The school actively recruits these students. They must score 500 on the written TOEFL and also take the SAT I or the ACT.

Computers: All computer labs (18) and student lounges (8) are networked with Internet and Web access. Additional access is available in the university library. Students may access the system. Time limits at some stations vary from 30 minutes to 2 hours. Most labs do not have time limits. There are no fees. It is strongly recommended that all students have a personal computer.

Graduates: In 2001, 325 bachelor's degrees were awarded. The most popular majors were graphic design (11%), illustration (10%), and music/performance (9%). In an average class, 42% graduate in 4 years, 53% in 5 years, and 55% in 6 years. 30 companies recruited on campus in 2000-2001. Of the 2000 graduating class, 14% were enrolled in graduate school within 6 months of graduation and 54% were employed.

Admissions Contact: Barbara Elliott, Director of Admissions. A video is available. E-mail: *admissions@uarts.edu* Web: *http://www.uarts.edu*

UNIVERSITY OF THE SCIENCES IN PHILADELPHIA F-3
Philadelphia, PA 19104-4495 (215) 596-8810
(888) 996-8747; Fax: (215) 596-8821

Full-time: 669 men, 1438 women	**Faculty:** 134; IIA, av$
Part-time: 11 men, 32 women	**Ph.D.s:** 70%
Graduate: 105 men, 158 women	**Student/Faculty:** 16 to 1
Year: semesters, summer session	**Tuition:** $17,626
Application Deadline: open	**Room & Board:** $7200
Freshman Class: 1299 applied, 1101 accepted, 355 enrolled	
SAT I Verbal/Math: 535/565	**ACT:** 24 **VERY COMPETITIVE**

University of the Sciences in Philadelphia, founded in 1821, is a private institution offering degree programs in the health sciences, pharmaceutical sciences, and arts and sciences. There are 4 undergraduate schools and 1 graduate school. In addition to regional accreditation, USP has baccalaureate program accreditation with ACPE, ACS, APTA, CAAHEP, and NAACLS. The library contains 83,958 volumes, 33,671 microform items, and 792 audiovisual forms/CDs, and subscribes to 8383 periodicals. Computerized library services include the card catalog, interlibrary loans, and database searching. Special learning facilities include a learning resource center and a pharmaceutical history museum. The 30-acre campus is in an urban area in the University City section of Philadelphia. Including residence halls, there are 16 buildings.

Student Life: 53% of undergraduates are from Pennsylvania. Others are from 39 states, 28 foreign countries, and Canada. 69% are from public schools. 53% are white; 38% Asian American. The average age of freshmen is 18; all undergraduates, 21. 9% do not continue beyond their first year; 80% remain to graduate.

Housing: 700 students can be accommodated in college housing, which includes coed dormitories, on-campus apartments, and fraternity houses. In addition, there are honor halls in certain dormitories. On-campus housing is guaranteed for the freshman year only, is available on a first-come, first-served basis, and is available on a lottery system for upperclassmen. Priority is given to out-of-town students. 70% of students live on campus; of those, 50% remain on campus on weekends. Alcohol is not permitted. Upperclassmen may keep cars.

Activities: 15% of men and about 15% of women belong to 2 local and 9 national fraternities and 1 national sorority. There are 46 groups on campus, including cheerleading, chess, chorus, computers, dance, drama, ethnic, gay, honors, international, literary magazine, martial arts, musical theater, newspaper, orchestra, political, professional, religious, social, social service, student government, and yearbook. Popular campus events include Greek Week and Student Appreciation Day.

Sports: There are 6 intercollegiate sports for men and 7 for women, and 19 intramural sports for men and 19 for women. Facilities include a gym, a rifle range, tennis courts, a softball field, a jogging path, and recreational areas in the residence halls.

Disabled Students: 90% of the campus is accessible. Wheelchair ramps, elevators, special parking, specially equipped rest rooms, and special class scheduling are available. Each student is accommodated on an individual basis.

Services: Counseling and information services are available, as is tutoring in every subject. There is remedial math and writing.

Campus Safety and Security: Measures include 24-hour foot and vehicle patrol, self-defense education, escort service, and shuttle buses. There are informal discussions, pamphlets/posters/films, emergency telephones, lighted pathways/sidewalks, and required key and student identification for dormitory entry.

Programs of Study: USP confers B.S. and B.S.Ed. degrees. Master's and doctoral degrees are also awarded. Bachelor's degrees are awarded in BIOLOGICAL SCIENCE (biochemistry, biology/biological science, microbiology, and toxicology), BUSINESS (marketing management), COMMUNICATIONS AND THE ARTS (technical and business writing), COMPUTER AND PHYSICAL SCIENCE (chemistry), ENGINEERING AND ENVIRONMENTAL DESIGN (environmental science), HEALTH PROFESSIONS (medical technology, occupational therapy, pharmacy, physical therapy, physician's assistant, and premedicine), SOCIAL SCIENCE (psychology). Pharmacy and physical therapy are the strongest academically. Pharmacy, physical therapy, and biology are the largest.

Required: Total credits required for graduation range from 98 to 187 depending on the major, with a 2.0 GPA (2.3 for pharmacy majors). The core curriculum includes 16 credits of natural science, 6 each of math, social sciences, communication, and an intellectual heritage sequence, 3 of literature, world culture, history, and advanced social sciences, and 1 of phys ed, along with 3 of electives. Students must pass a writing proficiency exam, demonstrate proficiency in computer applications, and obtain certifications in first aid and CPR.

Special: USP offers 5-year integrated professional programs in occupational therapy, physical therapy, and physician's assistant studies. Internships are required in all health science disciplines. A 1-year undeclared major program is offered, as is a program of curriculum and advisement to prepare students to enter medical school. Students may elect a minor in communications, economics, psychology, sociology, math, physics, or computer science. Study abroad can be arranged. There are 4 national honor societies.

Faculty/Classroom: 55% of faculty are male; 45%, female. All teach undergraduates and 20% also do research. No introductory courses are taught by graduate students. The average class size in an introductory lecture is 120; in a laboratory, 25; and in a regular course, 25.

Admissions: 85% of the 2001-2002 applicants were accepted. The SAT I scores for the 2001-2002 freshman class were: Verbal--26% below 500, 50% between 500 and 599, 22% between 600 and 700, and 2% above 700; Math--15% below 500, 56% between 500 and 599, 26% between 600 and 700, and 3% above 700. The ACT scores were 2% below 21, 41% between 21 and 23, 31% between 24 and 26, 23% between 27 and 28, and 3% above 28. 48% of the current freshmen were in the top fifth of their class; 76% were in the top two fifths. There were 2 National Merit semifinalists. 12 freshmen graduated first in their class.

Requirements: The SAT I is required. In addition, applicants must be high school graduates or hold the GED. Minimum academic requirements include 4 credits in English, 1 credit each in American history and social science, and 4 credits in academic electives. Math requirements include 2 years of algebra and 1 year of plane geometry; the university strongly recommends an additional year of higher-level math, such as precalculus or calculus. 3 science credits are required; strongly recommended are 1 credit each in biology, chemistry, and physics. USP requires applicants to be in the upper 50% of their class. A GPA of 3.0 is required. AP and CLEP credits are accepted. Important factors in the admissions decision are advanced placement or honor courses, personality/intangible qualities, and geographic diversity. Applications are accepted on-line via USP's web site.

Procedure: Freshmen are admitted in the fall. Entrance exams should be taken at the end of the junior year and in the fall of the senior year. There are early admissions and deferred admissions plans. Application deadlines are open. Application fee is $45. Notification is sent on a rolling basis. 5% of all applicants are on a waiting list; 20 were accepted in 2001.

Transfer: 190 transfer students enrolled in 2001-2002. To be considered, pharmacy and physical therapy applicants must present a minimum GPA of 3.0. All other majors must have at least a 2.7 GPA. All applicants must meet high school requirements as well. 90 credits of 98 to 187 must be completed at USP.

Visiting: There are regularly scheduled orientations for prospective students, consisting of summer information sessions for rising seniors, campus day visits, campus tours, and meetings with faculty members. There are guides for informal visits and visitors may sit in on classes. To schedule a visit, contact the Admission Office.

Financial Aid: In 2001-2002, 98% of all freshmen and 85% of continuing students received some form of financial aid. 87% of freshmen and 75% of continuing students received need-based aid. The average freshman award was $15,564. Of that total, scholarships or need-based grants averaged $5500 ($17,122 maximum); loans averaged $3850 ($10,500 maximum); and work contracts averaged $1250 ($2000 maximum). All undergraduates work part time. Average annual earnings from campus work are $850. The average financial indebtedness of the 2001 graduate was $38,000. The FAFSA is required. The fall application deadline is March 15.

International Students: There are 93 international students enrolled. The school actively recruits these students. They must score 550 on the written TOEFL or 213 on the electronic version and also take the college's own test and the SAT I or the ACT, scoring 1000 on the SAT I.

Computers: The mainframes are several IBM RS/6000s. 256 workstations and more than 100 laptop ports networked to IBM Netfinity servers are located in computer labs as well as other strategic campus locations. All students may access the system. There are no time limits and no fees.

Graduates: In 2001, 237 bachelor's degrees were awarded. The most popular majors were pharmacy (47%), physical therapy (11%), and occupational therapy (7%). In an average class, 10% graduate in 4 years, 90% in 5 years, and 100% in 6 years. 100 companies recruited on campus in 2000-2001. Of the 2000 graduating class, 5% were enrolled in graduate school within 6 months of graduation and 95% were employed.

Admissions Contact: Louis L. Hegyes, Director of Admission.
E-mail: *admit@usip.edu* Web: *www.usip.edu*

URSINUS COLLEGE

E-3

Collegeville, PA 19426 **(610) 409-3200; Fax: (610) 489-0627**

Full-time: 562 men, 746 women	**Faculty:** 100; IIB, +$
Part-time: 7 men, 9 women	**Ph.D.s:** 92%
Graduate: none	**Student/Faculty:** 13 to 1
Year: semesters	**Tuition:** $24,850
Application Deadline: February 15	**Room & Board:** $6500

Freshman Class: 1562 applied, 1225 accepted, 387 enrolled

SAT I Verbal/Math: 600/600 **VERY COMPETITIVE**

Ursinus College, founded in 1869, is a private residential college offering programs in the liberal arts. There is 1 undergraduate school. The library contains 200,000 volumes, 155,000 microform items, and 17,500 audiovisual forms/CDs, and subscribes to 900 periodicals. Computerized library services include the card catalog, interlibrary loans, and database searching. Special learning facilities include an art gallery, radio station, TV station, and language labs. The 160-acre campus is in a suburban area 24 miles west of Philadelphia. Including residence halls, there are 50 buildings.

Student Life: 62% of undergraduates are from Pennsylvania. Others are from 20 states, 15 foreign countries, and Canada. 74% are from public schools. 82% are white. 43% are Catholic; 25% claim no religious affiliation; 16% are Protestant. The average age of freshmen is 18; all undergraduates, 20. 8% do not continue beyond their first year; 78% remain to graduate.

Housing: 1200 students can be accommodated in college housing, which includes single-sex and coed dormitories and on-campus apartments. In addition, there are honors houses, language houses, and special-interest houses, and multicultural, science research, community service, wellness, writing, arts, women's studies, and quiet houses. On-campus housing is guaranteed for all 4 years. 90% of students live on campus; of those, 80% remain on campus on weekends. All students may keep cars.

Activities: 15% of men belong to 8 local fraternities; 30% of women belong to 6 local sororities. There are 116 groups on campus, including art, band, cheerleading, chess, choir, chorale, chorus, computers, dance, debate, drama, ethnic, film, gay, honors, international, jazz band, literary magazine, musical theater, newspaper, orchestra, pep band, political, professional, radio and TV, religious, social, social service, student government, and yearbook. Popular campus events include Parents Day, Founders Day, and Air Band Competition.

Sports: There are 11 intercollegiate sports for men and 12 for women, and 14 intramural sports for men and 12 for women. Facilities include racquetball and squash courts, a weight room, dance rooms, tennis courts, a field house, a fitness center, and all types of playing fields.

Disabled Students: 95% of the campus is accessible. Wheelchair ramps, elevators, special parking, specially equipped rest rooms, special class scheduling, lowered drinking fountains, and lowered telephones are available.

Services: Counseling and information services are available, as is tutoring in every subject.

Campus Safety and Security: Measures include 24-hour foot and vehicle patrol, self-defense education, escort service, and informal discussions. There are pamphlets/posters/films, emergency telephones, and lighted pathways/sidewalks.

Programs of Study: Ursinus confers B.A. and B.S. degrees. Bachelor's degrees are awarded in BIOLOGICAL SCIENCE (biochemistry and biology/biological science), BUSINESS (accounting, business administration and management, and business economics), COMMUNICATIONS AND THE ARTS (communications, English, French, German, music, and Spanish), COMPUTER AND PHYSICAL SCIENCE (chemistry, computer science, mathematics, and physics), EDUCATION (secondary), ENGINEERING AND ENVIRONMENTAL DESIGN (environmental science), HEALTH PROFESSIONS (premedicine), SOCIAL SCIENCE (anthropology, East Asian studies, economics, history, international relations, political science/government, prelaw, psychology, religion, and sociology). Biology, English, and politics are the strongest academically. Economics, business administration, and biology are the largest.

Required: All students must fulfill requirements in English composition, math or logic, foreign language, humanities, and natural and social science. A total of 128 semester hours, with 32 to 40 in the major, is required, as is a GPA of 2.0.

Special: The college offers study abroad, student-designed majors, internships, a Washington semester, a Harrisburg and Philadelphia semester, dual majors, and a 3-2 engineering degree with Washington University. There are 14 national honor societies, including Phi Beta Kappa, and 14 departmental honors programs.

Faculty/Classroom: 60% of faculty are male; 40%, female. All both teach and do research. The average class size in a regular course is 18.

Admissions: 78% of the 2001-2002 applicants were accepted. The SAT I scores for the 2001-2002 freshman class were: Verbal--41% between 500 and 599, 40% between 600 and 700, and 13% above 700; Math--9% below 500, 34% between 500 and 599, 50% between 600 and 700, and 7% above 700. 62% of the current freshmen were in the top fifth of their class; 90% were in the top two fifths. There were 6 National Merit finalists. 4 freshmen graduated first in their class.

Requirements: The SAT I or ACT is required. In addition, SAT II: Subject tests are recommended. Applicants should prepare with 16 academic credits, including 4 years of English, 3 of math, 2 of foreign language, and 1 each of science and social studies. An interview is recommended. AP and CLEP credits are accepted. Important factors in the admissions decision are advanced placement or honor courses, recommendations by school officials, and leadership record. Applications are accepted on computer disk and on-line.

Procedure: Freshmen are admitted fall and spring. Entrance exams should be taken in the junior or senior year. There are early decision and deferred admissions plans. Early decision applications should be filed by January 15; regular applications, by February 15 for fall entry and December 1 for spring entry. Notification of early decision is sent January 15; regular decision, April 1. 93 early decision candidates were accepted for the 2001-2002 class. 5% of all applicants are on a waiting list; 20 were accepted in 2001. The fall 2001 application fee was $40.

Transfer: 12 transfer students enrolled in 2001-2002. Transfer applicants must submit transcripts from all institutions attended. 64 credits of 128 must be completed at Ursinus.

Visiting: There are regularly scheduled orientations for prospective students, including a campus interview and a tour. There are guides for informal visits and visitors may sit in on classes and stay overnight. To schedule a visit, contact the Admissions Office.

Financial Aid: In 2001-2002, 93% of all freshmen and 76% of continuing students received some form of financial aid. 81% of freshmen and 70% of continuing students received need-based aid. Scholarships or need-based grants averaged $16,040 ($24,850 maximum); loans averaged $2816 ($4125 maximum); and work contracts averaged $840 ($1500 maximum). 50% of undergraduates work part time. Average annual earnings from campus work are $1000. The average financial indebtedness of the 2001 graduate was $16,000. Ursinus is a member of CSS. The CSS/Profile or FAFSA is required. The fall application deadline is February 15.

International Students: There are 46 international students enrolled. The school actively recruits these students. They must score 550 on the written TOEFL and also take the SAT I.

Computers: The mainframe is a DEC VAX. 200 IBM PCs and 100 Macs are available for student use; all are linked to the VAX. All entering students receive a laptop computer. All students may access the system during library hours, a total of 102 hours per week. There are no time limits and no fees.

Graduates: In 2001, 268 bachelor's degrees were awarded. The most popular majors were biology (21%), economics (14%), and English (11%). 34 companies recruited on campus in 2000-2001. Of the 2000 graduating class, 24% were enrolled in graduate school within 6 months of graduation and 60% were employed.

Admissions Contact: Paul M. Cramer, Director of Admissions.
E-mail: *admissions@ursinus.edu* Web: *http://www.ursinus.edu/*

VILLANOVA UNIVERSITY — F-4

Villanova, PA 19085-1672 (610) 519-4000
(800) 338-7927; Fax: (610) 519-6450

Full-time: 3230 men, 3364 women	**Faculty:** 507; IIA, +$
Part-time: 387 men, 334 women	**Ph.D.s:** 90%
Graduate: 1126 men, 957 women	**Student/Faculty:** 13 to 1
Year: semesters, summer session	**Tuition:** $23,727
Application Deadline: January 7	**Room & Board:** $8270
Freshman Class: 10,178 applied, 5139 accepted, 1740 enrolled	
SAT I Verbal/Math: 610/630	**HIGHLY COMPETITIVE**

Villanova University, founded in 1842 and affiliated with the Catholic Church, offers undergraduate programs in liberal arts and sciences, commerce and finance, engineering, and nursing. There are 4 undergraduate and 5 graduate schools. In addition to regional accreditation, Villanova has baccalaureate program accreditation with AACSB, ABA, ABET, and NLN. The 2 libraries contain 860,000 volumes, 1,789,816 microform items, 7987 audiovisual forms/CDs, and 250 electronic databases, and subscribe to 5400 periodicals. Computerized library services include the card catalog, interlibrary loans, and database searching. Special learning facilities include a learning resource center, art gallery, planetarium, radio station, TV station, and 2 observatories. The 254-acre campus is in a suburban area 12 miles west of Philadelphia. Including residence halls, there are 60 buildings.

Student Life: 66% of undergraduates are from out of state, mostly the Middle Atlantic. Students are from 47 states, 29 foreign countries, and Canada. 51% are from public schools. 86% are white. 81% are Catholic; 14% Protestant. The average age of freshmen is 18; all undergraduates, 21. 6% do not continue beyond their first year; 86% remain to graduate.

Housing: 4316 students can be accommodated in college housing, which includes single-sex and coed dormitories and on-campus apartments. In addition, there are special-interest houses, substance-free housing, Villanova Experience, Visions of Freedom, and other course-related learning communities. On-campus housing is available on a lottery system for upperclassmen. 65% of students live on campus; of those, 90% remain on campus on weekends. Upperclassmen may keep cars.

Activities: 14% of men belong to 8 national fraternities; 40% of women belong to 8 national sororities. There are 100 groups on campus, including art, band, Blue Key, cheerleading, chess, choir, chorale, chorus, computers, dance, drama, drill team, ethnic, gay, honors, international, jazz band, literary magazine, marching band, multicultural, musical theater, newspaper, pep band, photography, political, professional, radio and TV, religious, social, social service, student government, and yearbook. Popular campus events include Balloon Day, Special Olympics, Nova Fest, and St. Thomas of Villanova Day.

Sports: There are 10 intercollegiate sports for men and 12 for women, and 12 intramural sports for men and 12 for women. Facilities include a 200-meter indoor track, 2 swimming pools, weight rooms, a field house, and basketball, volleyball, and tennis courts. The football stadium seats 11,800; the pavilion, 6400.

Disabled Students: All of the campus is accessible. Wheelchair ramps, elevators, special parking, specially equipped rest rooms, special class scheduling, lowered drinking fountains, lowered telephones, a specially equipped van for campus transportation, and proximity card readers for several buildings with automatic doors are available.

Services: Counseling and information services are available, as is tutoring in most subjects. There is a reader service for the blind. Tutoring services are administered through each department on an individual basis. There is a writing center and a math resource center.

Campus Safety and Security: Measures include 24-hour foot and vehicle patrol, self-defense education, escort service, and shuttle buses. There are informal discussions, pamphlets/posters/films, emergency telephones, and lighted pathways/sidewalks. Public safety officers are on duty all night in women's residence halls, and there is a card access system to all residence halls.

Programs of Study: Villanova confers B.A., B.S., B.E., and B.S.N. degrees. Associate, master's, and doctoral degrees are also awarded. Bachelor's degrees are awarded in BIOLOGICAL SCIENCE (biology/biological science), BUSINESS (accounting, banking and finance, business administration and management, business economics, management information systems, and marketing/retailing/merchandising), COMMUNICATIONS AND THE ARTS (art history and appreciation, classics, communications, English, French, German, and Spanish), COMPUTER AND PHYSICAL SCIENCE (astronomy, astrophysics, chemistry, computer science, information sciences and systems, mathematics, physics, and science), EDUCATION (elementary and secondary), ENGINEERING AND ENVIRONMENTAL DESIGN (chemical engineering, civil engineering, computer engineering, electrical/electronics engineering, and mechanical engineering), HEALTH PROFESSIONS (nursing), SOCIAL SCIENCE (cognitive science, criminal justice, economics, geography, history, human services, international studies, Latin American studies, liberal arts/general studies, peace studies, philosophy, political science/government, psychology, religion, Russian and Slavic studies, sociology, theological studies, and women's studies). Sciences, business, and liberal arts are the strongest academically. Liberal arts and commerce and finance are the largest.

Required: All students are required to take core courses in English, social science, religious studies, natural sciences, philosophy, and math. Students must complete a total of 122 credit hours with a 2.0 overall GPA and a 2.2 GPA in the major.

Special: Cross-registration is possible with Rosemont College. Internships are available for each college in the Philadelphia area as well as in New York City and Washington, D.C. Students may study abroad in the British Isles, the Pacific Rim, East Africa, the former Soviet Union, and the Caribbean. Villanova offers a Washington semester, an accelerated degree program in biology for the allied health program, dual majors, a general studies degree, and credit by exam. There are 31 national honor societies, including Phi Beta Kappa, and a freshman honors program.

Faculty/Classroom: 72% of faculty are male; 28%, female. All teach undergraduates. No introductory courses are taught by graduate students. The average class size in an introductory lecture is 24; in a laboratory, 17; and in a regular course, 23.

Admissions: 50% of the 2001-2002 applicants were accepted. The SAT I scores for the 2001-2002 freshman class were: Verbal--6% below 500, 38% between 500 and 599, 49% between 600 and 700, and 7% above 700; Math--3% below 500, 24% between 500 and 599, 59% between 600 and 700, and 14% above 700. 70% of the current freshmen were in the top fifth of their class; 92% were in the top two fifths. There were 5 National Merit finalists. 27 freshmen graduated first in their class.

Requirements: The SAT I or ACT is required. In addition, applicants must be graduates of an accredited secondary school and should have completed 16 academic units. The specific courses required vary according to college. A GED is accepted. An essay is required. AP and CLEP credits are accepted. Important factors in the admissions decision are advanced placement or honor courses, leadership record, and evidence of special talent. Students may apply on-line at the school's web site.

Procedure: Freshmen are admitted in the fall. Entrance exams should be taken by December of the senior year. There are early action, early admissions, and deferred admissions plans. Early action applications should be filed by November 1; regular applications, by January 7 for fall entry. The fall 2001 application fee was $55. Notification of early action is sent January 1; regular decision, April 1. 28% of all applicants are on a waiting list.

Transfer: 143 transfer students enrolled in a recent year. A cumulative GPA of 3.0 is recommended for students interested in transferring into the College of Liberal Arts and Sciences. Students interested in transferring into the College of Nursing must have maintained at least a 2.5 cumulative GPA. Required GPAs for the College of Commerce and Finance and the College of Engineering vary. 60 credits of 122 must be completed at Villanova.

Visiting: There are regularly scheduled orientations for prospective students, including campus tours and information sessions conducted several times daily and on selected Saturdays throughout the academic year. There are guides for informal visits and visitors may sit in on classes. To schedule a visit, contact the Office of University Admission.

Financial Aid: In 2001-2002, 69% of all freshmen and 65% of continuing students received some form of financial aid. 46% of freshmen and 45% of continuing students received need-based aid. The average freshman award was $18,285. Of that total, scholarships or need-based grants averaged $11,885 ($31,950 maximum); loans averaged $5486 ($33,661 maximum); and work contracts averaged $914 ($4000 maximum). 26% of undergraduates work part time. Average annual earnings from campus work are $1040. The average financial indebtedness of the 2001 graduate was $20,874. The FAFSA, the college's own financial statement, and parent and student federal income tax returns and W2s are required. The fall application deadline is February 15.

International Students: There are 136 international students enrolled. The school actively recruits these students. They must score 550 on the written TOEFL or 231 on the electronic version and also take the SAT I or the ACT. Students must take SAT II: Subject tests in French and Spanish for placement purposes.

Computers: The mainframe consists of Sun 4500 Enterprise servers. Students in the College of Commerce and Finance are provided with laptop computers. There are 3 main PC labs as well as various other labs for specific majors. All students have access to the network and e-mail, on and off campus, and all residence hall rooms have network and web connections. All students may access the system. There are no time limits and no fees, but students must purchase a network card.

Graduates: In 2001, 1551 bachelor's degrees were awarded. The most popular majors were finance (12%), communications (8%), and accountancy (8%). In an average class, 81% graduate in 4 years, 84% in 5 years, and 85% in 6 years. 325 companies recruited on campus in 2000-2001. Of the 2000 graduating class, 14% were enrolled in graduate school within 6 months of graduation and 75% were employed.

Admissions Contact: Michael Gaynor, Director of Admission.
E-mail: *gotovu@villanova.edu* Web: *www.admission.villanova.edu*

WASHINGTON AND JEFFERSON COLLEGE — A-3
Washington, PA 15301 (724) 223-6025
(888) 926-3529; Fax: (724) 223-6534

Full-time: 611 men, 565 women	**Faculty:** 89; IIB, +$
Part-time: 20 men, 44 women	**Ph.D.s:** 93%
Graduate: none	**Student/Faculty:** 13 to 1
Year: 4-1-4, summer session	**Tuition:** $20,550
Application Deadline: March 1	**Room & Board:** $5705
Freshman Class: 1110 applied, 948 accepted, 322 enrolled	
SAT I Verbal/Math: 550/560	**ACT:** 24 **VERY COMPETITIVE**

Washington & Jefferson College, founded in 1781, is a private institution offering instruction in liberal arts. The library contains 203,600 volumes, 14,600 microform items, and 8050 audiovisual forms/CDs, and subscribes to 1900 periodicals. Computerized library services include the card catalog, interlibrary loans, and database searching. Special learning facilities include a learning resource center, art gallery, radio station, and biological field station. The 52-acre campus is in a small town 27 miles southwest of Pittsburgh. Including residence halls, there are 43 buildings.

Student Life: 84% of undergraduates are from Pennsylvania. Others are from 31 states and 1 foreign country. 84% are from public schools. 94% are white. The average age of freshmen is 18; all undergraduates, 20. 14% do not continue beyond their first year; 77% remain to graduate.

Housing: 950 students can be accommodated in college housing, which includes single-sex and coed dormitories, on-campus apartments, and fraternity houses. In addition, there is special-interest housing and theme housing. On-campus housing is guaranteed for all 4 years. 76% of students live on campus; of those, 80% remain on campus on weekends. All students may keep cars.

Activities: 45% of men belong to 8 national fraternities; 49% of women belong to 4 national sororities. There are 79 groups on campus, including art, cheerleading, choir, chorale, chorus, computers, debate, drama, ethnic, jazz band, literary magazine, newspaper, orchestra, pep band, photography, political, professional, radio and TV, religious, social, social service, student government, and yearbook. Popular campus events include Greek Week, Founders Day, and Honors Day.

Sports: There are 12 intercollegiate sports for men and 11 for women, and 11 intramural sports for men and 7 for women. Facilities include swimming and diving pools, a track, a weight room, football, baseball, and soccer fields, and basketball, volleyball, squash, and racquetball courts. The stadium seats 4000, the largest auditorium/arena, 3500.

Disabled Students: 20% of the campus is accessible. Wheelchair ramps, elevators, special parking, specially equipped rest rooms, and special class scheduling are available.

Services: Counseling and information services are available, as is tutoring in most subjects. There is a reader service for the blind, and remedial math, reading, and writing.

Campus Safety and Security: Measures include 24-hour foot and vehicle patrol, escort service, informal discussions, and pamphlets/posters/films. There are emergency telephones and lighted pathways/sidewalks.

Programs of Study: Washington & Jefferson confers the B.A. degree. Associate degrees are also awarded. Bachelor's degrees are awarded in BIOLOGICAL SCIENCE (biology/biological science), BUSINESS (accounting, business administration and management, and international business management), COMMUNICATIONS AND THE ARTS (art, dramatic arts, English, French, German, music, and Spanish), COMPUTER AND PHYSICAL SCIENCE (chemistry, mathematics, physical chemistry, and physics), EDUCATION (art), SOCIAL SCIENCE (economics, history, philosophy, political science/government, psychology, and sociology). Business, accounting, and psychology are the largest.

Required: Students are required to complete 13 distribution courses in history/philosophy/religion, art/music, language, literature, science/math, economics/business, political science, and biology. Other requirements include phys ed, freshman English, and freshman forum. A total of 36 courses, with 8 to 10 courses in the major, is required for graduation, as is a 2.0 GPA.

Special: The college offers study abroad in Russsia, Germany, and Colombia, as well as other countries, internships in all majors, a Washington semester with American University, dual and student-designed majors, credit by exam, and pass/fail options. There is a 3-2 engineering program with Case Western Reserve University in Cleveland and Washington University in St. Louis. The college offers special human resources management and entrepreneurial studies programs. There is also a 3-4 podiatry program with the Pennsylvania and Ohio Colleges of Podiatry and a 3-4 optometry program with Pennsylvania College of Optometry. There is a 3-3 program with Duquesne University School of Law and University of Pittsburgh School of Law. There are 15 national honor societies, including Phi Beta Kappa, and 20 departmental honors programs.

Faculty/Classroom: 70% of faculty are male; 30%, female. All teach undergraduates. The average class size in an introductory lecture is 25; in a laboratory, 16; and in a regular course, 19.

Admissions: 85% of the 2001-2002 applicants were accepted. The SAT I scores for the 2001-2002 freshman class were: Verbal--24% below 500, 51% between 500 and 599, 24% between 600 and 700, and 1% above 700; Math--22% below 500, 45% between 500 and 599, 31% between 600 and 700, and 2% above 700. The ACT scores were 7% below 21, 17% between 21 and 23, 45% between 24 and 26, 20% between 27 and 28, and 11% above 28. 56% of the current freshmen were in the top fifth of their class; 84% were in the top two fifths. 16 freshmen graduated first in their class.

Requirements: The SAT I or ACT is required. In addition, a GED is accepted. Applicants must complete 15 academic credits or Carnegie units, including 3 credits of English and math, 2 of foreign language, and 1 of science. An essay is required and interviews are recommended. AP and CLEP credits are accepted. Important factors in the admissions decision are advanced placement or honor courses, evidence of special talent, and personality/intangible qualities. Applications are accepted on disk and on-line via the school's web site, CollegeView, CollegeLink, ExPAN, and others.

Procedure: Freshmen are admitted to all sessions. Entrance exams should be taken in the junior or senior year. There are early decision, early admissions, and deferred admissions plans. Early decision applications should be filed by November 1; regular applications, by March 1 for fall entry, January 1 for winter entry, February 1 for spring entry, and June 1 for summer entry, along with a $25 fee. Notification of early decision is sent December 15; regular decision, April 1. 26 early decision candidates were accepted for the 2001-2002 class.

Transfer: 27 transfer students enrolled in 2001-2002. Applicants must have a college GPA of at least 2.5 and must take the SAT I or ACT. 18 courses of 36 must be completed at Washington & Jefferson.

Visiting: There are regularly scheduled orientations for prospective students, including a general session, departmental meetings, preprofessional meetings, a financial aid meeting, and class scheduling. There are guides for informal visits and visitors may sit in on classes and stay overnight. To schedule a visit, contact the Admission Office.

Financial Aid: In 2001-2002, 80% of all freshmen and 75% of continuing students received some form of financial aid. 75% of all students received need-based aid. The average freshman award was $14,261. Of that total, scholarships or need-based grants averaged $9566; loans averaged $2625 ($4125 maximum); work contracts averaged $1500; Pell Grants averaged $2348; and Pennsylvania State Grants averaged $3266. 45% of undergraduates work part time. Average annual earnings from campus work are $1500. The average financial indebtedness of the 2001 graduate was $13,900. The FAFSA is required. The fall application deadline is March 15.

International Students: There are 10 international students enrolled. They must score 550 on the written TOEFL or 213 on the electronic version and also take the SAT I or the ACT.

Computers: The mainframe is a Digital VAX 4000-500. 400 terminals, PCs, and Macs are located in the computer center and classrooms. Each dorm room has 2 free Internet connections. All students may access the system as needed. There are no time limits and no fees.

Graduates: In 2001, 290 bachelor's degrees were awarded. The most popular majors were business administration (18%), accounting (14%), and psychology (13%). In an average class, 75% graduate in 4 years, 75% in 5 years, and 76% in 6 years. 40 companies recruited on campus in 2000-2001. Of the 2000 graduating class, 37% were enrolled in graduate school within 6 months of graduation and 42% were employed.

Admissions Contact: Alton E. Newell, Dean of Enrollment.
E-mail: *admission@washjeff.edu* Web: *http://www.washjeff.edu*

WAYNESBURG COLLEGE — B-4
Waynesburg, PA 15370-9930 — (724) 852-3248
(800) 225-7393; Fax: (724) 627-8124

Full-time: 599 men, 713 women	**Faculty:** 61; IIB, --$
Part-time: 45 men, 96 women	**Ph.D.s:** 54%
Graduate: 189 men, 141 women	**Student/Faculty:** 22 to 1
Year: semesters, summer session	**Tuition:** $12,560
Application Deadline: open	**Room & Board:** $5050
Freshman Class: n/av	
SAT I or ACT: required	**LESS COMPETITIVE**

Waynesburg College, founded in 1849, is a private liberal arts institution affiliated with the Presbyterian Church (U.S.A.). In addition to regional accreditation, Waynesburg has baccalaureate program accreditation with NLN. The library contains 100,000 volumes, 66 microform items, and 1667 audiovisual forms/CDs, and subscribes to 544 periodicals. Computerized library services include the card catalog, interlibrary loans, and database searching. Special learning facilities include a learning resource center, art gallery, natural history museum, radio station, and TV station. The 30-acre campus is in a small town 50 miles south of Pittsburgh. Including residence halls, there are 15 buildings.

Student Life: 83% of undergraduates are from Pennsylvania. Others are from 20 states and 6 foreign countries. 90% are from public schools. 95% are white. 41% are Protestant; 19% claim no religious affiliation; 12% Catholic. The average age of freshmen is 18; all undergraduates, 24. 27% do not continue beyond their first year; 54% remain to graduate.

Housing: 650 students can be accommodated in college housing, which includes single-sex dormitories. In addition, there are special-interest houses, a community service house, and an international student house. On-campus housing is guaranteed for all 4 years. 50% of students live on campus; of those, 60% remain on campus on weekends. Alcohol is not permitted. Upperclassmen may keep cars.

Activities: There are no fraternities or sororities. There are 36 groups on campus, including band, cheerleading, chorale, dance, drama, drill team, ethnic, film, honors, international, jazz band, literary magazine, marching band, musical theater, newspaper, orchestra, pep band, photography, professional, radio and TV, religious, social, social service, student government, and yearbook. Popular campus events include Spring Weekend Formal, VIP Forum, and Fine Arts Services.

Sports: There are 7 intercollegiate sports for men and 7 for women, and 5 intramural sports for men and 5 for women. Facilities include a 1500-seat stadium, 1500-seat gym, 250-seat arena, fitness center, golf driving net, basketball and racquetball courts, wrestling and weight rooms, a golf driving net, 3 all-weather tennis courts, and table tennis and billiards tables.

Disabled Students: 90% of the campus is accessible. Wheelchair ramps, elevators, special parking, specially equipped rest rooms, special class scheduling, and lowered drinking fountains are available.

Services: Counseling and information services are available, as is tutoring in every subject. There is remedial math and writing.

Campus Safety and Security: Measures include 24-hour foot and vehicle patrol, self-defense education, escort service, and informal discussions. There are pamphlets/posters/films, lighted pathways/sidewalks, and 24-hour security access.

Programs of Study: Waynesburg confers B.A., B.S., B.S.B.A., B.S.M.B., and B.S.N. degrees. Associate and master's degrees are also awarded. Bachelor's degrees are awarded in BIOLOGICAL SCIENCE (biology/biological science and marine biology), BUSINESS (accounting, banking and finance, international business management, management science, marketing/retailing/merchandising, and small business management), COMMUNICATIONS AND THE ARTS (advertising, art, arts administration/management, broadcasting, communications, English, literature, multimedia, and technical and business writing), COMPUTER AND PHYSICAL SCIENCE (chemistry, computer science, information sciences and systems, and mathematics), EDUCATION (athletic training, elementary, and special), ENGINEERING AND ENVIRONMENTAL DESIGN (engineering and environmental science), HEALTH PROFESSIONS (exercise science, health care administration, medical laboratory technology, nursing, physical therapy, predentistry, premedicine, and preveterinary science), SOCIAL SCIENCE (criminal justice, crosscultural studies, forensic studies, history, political science/government, prelaw, psychology, social science, sociology, and theological studies). Nursing, business, and education are the strongest academically. Business administration, education, and nursing are the largest.

Required: To graduate, students must complete a minimum of 124 semester hours, including at least 30 in the major, with a minimum 2.0 GPA. Requirements include 15 credits of humanities and social and behavioral sciences, 8 of natural and physical sciences, 6 each of English and literature/arts, and 1 each of life skills, service learning, and the Waynesburg Experience. Students must also pass an English usage and written competency test as well as a math test.

Special: The college offers internships, an accelerated degree program in marketing, dual majors, a student-designed interdisciplinary major, credit for experience, nondegree study, and pass/fail options. There is a 3-2 engineering degree program with Case Western Reserve, Washington, and Penn State universities and a 3-1 in marine biology with Florida Institute of Technology. There are 15 national honor societies and a freshman honors program.

Faculty/Classroom: 52% of faculty are male; 48%, female. All teach undergraduates. No introductory courses are taught by graduate students. The average class size in an introductory lecture is 30; in a laboratory, 10; and in a regular course, 22.

Admissions: 27% of the current freshmen were in the top fifth of their class; 57% were in the top two fifths. 4 freshmen graduated first in their class.

Requirements: The SAT I or ACT is required. In addition, applicants must be graduates of an accredited secondary school or have a GED certificate and have completed 16 academic credits, including 4 in English and 2 each in math, sciences, and history or social studies. Waynesburg requires applicants to be in the upper 40% of their class. A GPA of 2.5 is required. AP and CLEP credits are accepted. Important factors in the admissions decision are advanced placement or honor courses, recommendations by school officials, and extracurricular activities record. Applications are accepted on-line at the school's web site.

Procedure: Freshmen are admitted to all sessions. Entrance exams should be taken in April of the junior year or December of the senior year. There is an early admissions plan. Application deadlines are open. The application fee is $20. There is a rolling admissions plan.

Transfer: 64 transfer students enrolled in 2001-2002. Students must submit a high school transcript and complete transcripts from all colleges previously attended. 45 credits of 124 must be completed at Waynesburg.

Visiting: There are regularly scheduled orientations for prospective students, including visits with faculty, students, administrators, and financial aid officers, and a tour of the campus. There are guides for informal visits and visitors may sit in on classes and stay overnight. To schedule a visit, contact Robin L. King, Admissions Office at (724) 852-3333 or *rlmoore@waynesburg.edu*.

Financial Aid: In 2001-2002, 88% of all freshmen and 87% of continuing students received some form of financial aid. 86% of freshmen and 84% of continuing students received need-based aid. The average freshman award was $12,347. Of that total, scholarships or need-based grants averaged $8353 ($17,610 maximum); loans averaged $2469 ($6625 maximum); and work contracts averaged $500 ($1200 maximum). 27% of undergraduates work part time. Average annual earnings from campus work are $700. The average financial indebtedness of the 2001 graduate was $17,000. The FAFSA and the college's own financial statement are required. The fall application deadline is March 15.

International Students: There are 13 international students enrolled. The school actively recruits these students. They must score 550 on the written TOEFL.

Computers: 6 fully equipped computer labs with PCs and Macs are available for student use. All students may access the system. There are no time limits and no fees.

Graduates: In 2001, 312 bachelor's degrees were awarded. The most popular majors were nursing (27%), business administration (24%), and public service administration (11%). In an average class, 3% graduate in 3 years, 44% in 4 years, 54% in 5 years, and 55% in 6 years. Of the 2000 graduating class, 15% were enrolled in graduate school within 6 months of graduation and 90% were employed.

Admissions Contact: Robin L. King, Dean of Admissions.
E-mail: *admissions@waynesburg.edu* Web: *www.waynesburg.edu*

WEST CHESTER UNIVERSITY OF PENNSYLVANIA F-4

West Chester, PA 19383 (610) 436-3411
(877) 315-2165; Fax: (610) 436-2907

Full-time: 3436 men, 5333 women	**Faculty:** 465; IIA, +$
Part-time: 661 men, 790 women	**Ph.D.s:** 74%
Graduate: 595 men, 1429 women	**Student/Faculty:** 19 to 1
Year: semesters, summer session	**Tuition:** $4924 ($10,948)
Application Deadline: open	**Room & Board:** $4868
Freshman Class: 8851 applied, 4245 accepted, 1632 enrolled	
SAT I: required	**ACT:** n/av **VERY COMPETITIVE**

West Chester University, founded in 1871, is a public institution that is part of the Pennsylvania State System of Higher Education. It offers programs through the College of Arts and Sciences, and Schools of Business and Public Affairs, Education, Health Sciences, and Music. There are 5 undergraduate and 7 graduate schools. In addition to regional accreditation, West Chester University has baccalaureate program accreditation with CSWE, NASM, NCATE, and NLN. The 2 libraries contain 522,000 volumes, 350,000 microform items, and 39,162 audiovisual forms/CDs, and subscribe to 2800 periodicals. Computerized library services include the card catalog, interlibrary loans, and database searching. Special learning facilities include a learning resource center, art gallery, planetarium, radio station, an herbarium, a speech and hearing clinic, a center for government and community affairs, and a 100-acre natural area for environmental studies. The 388-acre campus is in a suburban area 25 miles west of Philadelphia. Including residence halls, there are 62 buildings.

Student Life: 89% of undergraduates are from Pennsylvania. Others are from 32 states, 19 foreign countries, and Canada. 79% are from public schools. 87% are white. 46% are Catholic; 34% Protestant; 11% claim no religious affiliation. The average age of freshmen is 18; all undergraduates, 23. 16% do not continue beyond their first year; 51% remain to graduate.

Housing: 3600 students can be accommodated in college housing, which includes single-sex and coed dormitories and on-campus apartments. In addition, there are honors and international student housing sections. On-campus housing is guaranteed for all 4 years. 64% of students commute. Alcohol is not permitted. Upperclassmen may keep cars.

Activities: 10% of men belong to 12 national fraternities; 7% of women belong to 11 national sororities. There are 200 groups on campus, including art, band, cheerleading, chess, choir, chorale, chorus, computers, dance, drama, drill team, drum and bugle corps, ethnic, film, forensics, gay, honors, international, jazz band, literary magazine, marching band, musical theater, newspaper, orchestra, photography, political, professional, radio and TV, religious, social, social service, student government, symphony, and yearbook. Popular campus events include International Day, African American History Month, and Spring Weekend.

Sports: There are 11 intercollegiate sports for men and 12 for women, and 11 intramural sports for men and 7 for women. Facilities include a field house, a gymnastics room, 4 gyms, swimming pools, 2 game fields, 1 practice field, a softball field, tennis courts, a 500-seat baseball stadium, and a 7500-seat stadium.

Disabled Students: 80% of the campus is accessible. Wheelchair ramps, elevators, special parking, specially equipped rest rooms, special class scheduling, lowered drinking fountains, and lowered telephones are available.

Services: Counseling and information services are available, as is tutoring in every subject. There is a reader service for the blind, and remedial math, reading, and writing.

Campus Safety and Security: Measures include 24-hour foot and vehicle patrol, self-defense education, escort service, and shuttle buses. There are informal discussions, pamphlets/posters/films, emergency telephones, lighted pathways/sidewalks, bike patrol, CPR certification, community CPR and driving safety instruction, card access/security alarms, and resident hall security.

Programs of Study: West Chester University confers B.A., B.S., B.F.A., B.Mus., B.S.Ed., and B.S.N. degrees. Associate and master's degrees are also awarded. Bachelor's degrees are awarded in BIOLOGICAL SCIENCE (biochemistry and biology/biological science), BUSINESS (accounting, banking and finance, business administration and management, business economics, and marketing/retailing/merchandising), COMMUNICATIONS AND THE ARTS (art, communications, comparative literature, dramatic arts, English, French, German, Latin, literature, music, music performance, music theory and composition, Russian, Spanish, speech/debate/rhetoric, and studio art), COMPUTER AND PHYSICAL SCIENCE (chemistry, computer science, earth science, geoscience, mathematics, and physics), EDUCATION (athletic training, early childhood, elementary, foreign languages, health, music, physical, secondary, social studies, and special), HEALTH PROFESSIONS (health, health science, nursing, predentistry, premedicine, public health, and speech pathology/audiology), SOCIAL SCIENCE (American studies, anthropology, criminal justice, economics, geography, history, liberal arts/general studies, philosophy, political science/government, prelaw, psychology, public administration, religion, social work, sociology, and women's studies). Premedical is the strongest academically. Physical education, elementary/early childhood education, and business management are the largest.

Required: All students must satisfy requirements in English composition, math, interdisciplinary study, and phys ed. Distribution requirements include 9 hours each of science, behavioral and social science, and humanities, and 3 hours in the arts. A total of 128 credit hours and a 2.0 GPA are required.

Special: There is cross-registration with Cheyney University and a 3-2 engineering program with Pennsylvania State University. The university offers internships in most majors, an accelerated degree program in business, study abroad in France, Austria, Scotland, England, and Wales, a Washington semester, work-study, some student-designed majors, credit by examination and for life, military, and work experience, and pass/fail options. There are 23 national honor societies, a freshman honors program, and 10 departmental honors programs.

Faculty/Classroom: 53% of faculty are male; 47%, female. 84% teach undergraduates and 48% both teach and do research. No introductory courses are taught by graduate students. The average class size in an introductory lecture is 35; in a laboratory, 24; and in a regular course, 30.

Admissions: 48% of the 2001-2002 applicants were accepted. The SAT I scores for the 2001-2002 freshman class were: Verbal--33% below 500, 54% between 500 and 599, 12% between 600 and 700, and 1% above 700; Math--33% below 500, 53% between 500 and 599, 13% between 600 and 700, and 1% above 700. 26% of the current freshmen were in the top fifth of their class; 61% were in the top two fifths.

Requirements: The SAT I is required, with a recommended minimum combined score of 1000. Applicants should rank in the upper half of their graduating class in a college preparatory curriculum that includes completion of a minimum of 16 academic units. Applicants who have a GED must submit an official copy of their score report. A personal essay is required of all applicants. An audition is required for music applicants, and interviews are required for premed, athletic training, and liberal studies. Candidates for special admissions programs may be asked to submit supporting documentation. West Chester University requires applicants to be in the upper 50% of their class. A GPA of 2.5 is required. AP and CLEP credits are accepted. Important factors in the admissions decision are advanced placement or honor courses, recommendations by school officials, and evidence of special talent. Applications are accepted on-line via ExPAN and at the school's web site.

Procedure: Freshmen are admitted fall and spring. Entrance exams should be taken in spring of the junior year or fall of the senior year. There are early admissions and deferred admissions plans. Application deadlines are open. A waiting list is an active part of the admissions procedure.

Transfer: Applicants should have earned at least 30 credits and must have a recommended GPA of at least 2.3. Some departments require a higher GPA and specific course requirements. Transfers who have earned fewer than 30 credits must submit a high school transcript and standardized test scores. 30 credits of 128 must be completed at West Chester University.

Visiting: There are regularly scheduled orientations for prospective students, including academic advising, scheduling, and social events over a 2-day period. There are guides for informal visits and visitors may sit in on classes and stay overnight. To schedule a visit, contact the Office of Admissions.

Financial Aid: In 2001-2002, 69% of all freshmen and 62% of continuing students received some form of financial aid. 56% of freshmen and 55% of continuing students received need-based aid. The average freshman award was $4900. Of that total, scholarships or need-based grants averaged $1501 ($10,792 maximum); loans averaged $3149 ($6625 maximum); and work contracts averaged $250 ($1930 maximum). 11% of undergraduates work part time. Average annual earnings from campus work are $1062. The average financial indebtedness of the 2001 graduate was $17,000. West Chester University is a member of CSS. The FAFSA is required. The fall application deadline is March 2.

International Students: They must score 550 on the written TOEFL. The SAT I is recommended.

Computers: The mainframe is an IBM 4381. More than 400 PCs are available in computer labs, classrooms, and residence halls. Free e-mail accounts and Internet use are provided. All students may access the system. There are no time limits and no fees.

Admissions Contact: Marsha Haug, Director of Admissions.
E-mail: *ugadmiss@wcupa.edu* Web: *www.wcupa.edu*

WESTMINSTER COLLEGE

New Wilmington, PA 16172 — **A-2**

(724) 946-7100
(800) 942-8033; Fax: (724) 946-6171

Full-time: 552 men, 847 women	**Faculty:** 98; IIB, av$
Part-time: 26 men, 48 women	**Ph.D.s:** 77%
Graduate: 66 men, 120 women	**Student/Faculty:** 14 to 1
Year: semesters, summer session	**Tuition:** $17,750
Application Deadline: open	**Room & Board:** $5210
Freshman Class: 1111 applied, 954 accepted, 379 enrolled	
SAT I Verbal/Math: 530/540	**ACT:** 23 **COMPETITIVE**

Westminster College, founded in 1852, is a private liberal arts institution related to the Presbyterian Church (U.S.A.). In addition to regional accreditation, Westminster has baccalaureate program accreditation with NASM. The 2 libraries contain 283,070 volumes, 9737 microform items, and 14,251 audiovisual forms/CDs, and subscribe to 848 periodicals. Computerized library services include interlibrary loans. Special learning facilities include a learning resource center, art gallery, planetarium, radio station, TV station, and electron microscope labs in the science center. The 300-acre campus is in a rural area 60 miles north of Pittsburgh. Including residence halls, there are 22 buildings.

Student Life: 79% of undergraduates are from Pennsylvania. Others are from 23 states and 1 foreign country. 90% are from public schools. 97% are white. 56% are Protestant; 34% Catholic; 10% claim no religious affiliation. The average age of freshmen is 18; all undergraduates, 20. 1% do not continue beyond their first year; 73% remain to graduate.

Housing: 1120 students can be accommodated in college housing, which includes single-sex dormitories and fraternity houses. On-campus housing is guaranteed for all 4 years. 90% of students live on campus. Alcohol is not permitted. All students may keep cars.

Activities: 55% of men belong to 5 national fraternities; 44% of women belong to 5 national sororities. There are 85 groups on campus, including band, cheerleading, choir, chorale, chorus, dance, debate, drama, drill team, ethnic, forensics, gay, honors, jazz band, literary magazine, marching band, musical theater, newspaper, orchestra, pep band, political, radio and TV, religious, social, social service, student government, symphony, and yearbook. Popular campus events include mock conventions, Mardi Gras, and Volley Rock.

Sports: There are 9 intercollegiate sports for men and 8 for women, and 7 intramural sports for men and 6 for women. Facilities include a natatorium, racquetball, tennis, and basketball courts, an all-weather track, and weight and aerobics rooms. Canoeing on the lake is available.

Disabled Students: 50% of the campus is accessible. Wheelchair ramps, elevators, special parking, specially equipped rest rooms, and special class scheduling are available.

Services: Counseling and information services are available, as is tutoring in most subjects through the learning center. There is remedial math, reading, and writing.

Campus Safety and Security: Measures include 24-hour foot and vehicle patrol, escort service, shuttle buses, and informal discussions. There are pamphlets/posters/films, emergency telephones, and lighted pathways/sidewalks.

Programs of Study: Westminster confers B.A., B.S., and B.M. degrees. Master's degrees are also awarded. Bachelor's degrees are awarded in BIOLOGICAL SCIENCE (biology/biological science and molecular biology), BUSINESS (accounting, banking and finance, business administration and management, international business management, and marketing/retailing/merchandising), COMMUNICATIONS AND THE ARTS (art, broadcasting, communications, dramatic arts, English, fine arts, French, German, Latin, music, music performance, music theory and composition, public relations, and Spanish), COMPUTER AND PHYSICAL SCIENCE (chemistry, computer science, mathematics, and physics), EDUCATION (Christian, elementary, guidance, music, and secondary), HEALTH PROFESSIONS (predentistry, and premedicine), SOCIAL SCIENCE (criminal justice, economics, history, international relations, philosophy, political science/government, prelaw, psychology, religion, religious music, social science, and sociology). Sciences, business, and education are the strongest academically and have the largest enrollments.

Required: First-year students are required to take Inquiry I and II, as well as writing and a speech course. Students must fullfill a distribution requirement by taking a course in one of each of the Intellectual Perspectives: Visual and Performing Arts, Quantitative Reasoning, Social Thought and Tradition, Humanity and Culture, Scientific Discovery, Foreign Language, and Religious and Philosophical Thought. A capstone experience in their major and community service are also required. Students must complete 132 semester hours with a minimum of 84 outside their majors, and have a minimum of 2.0 GPA in all courses. Majors require between 32 and 60 hours of course work.

Special: The college offers internships, study abroad in many countries, a Washington semester, various dual and student-designed majors, a 3-2 engineering degree with Case Western Reserve, Pennsylvania State, and Washington Universities, London study at Regent's College, a 3-3 J.D. program with Duquesne, and nondegree study. There are 12 national honor societies and a freshman honors program. All departments have honors programs.

Faculty/Classroom: 73% of faculty are male; 22%, female. All teach undergraduates. No introductory courses are taught by graduate students. The average class size in a regular course is 25.

Admissions: 86% of the 2001-2002 applicants were accepted. The SAT I scores for the 2001-2002 freshman class were: Verbal--38% below 500, 42% between 500 and 599, 19% between 600 and 700, and 2% above 700; Math--34% below 500, 47% between 500 and 599, 17% between 600 and 700, and 3% above 700. The ACT scores were 26% below 21, 32% between 21 and 23, 26% between 24 and 26, 11% between 27 and 28, and 5% above 28. 46% of the current freshmen were in the top fifth of their class; 81% were in the top two fifths. 12 freshmen graduated first in their class.

Requirements: The SAT I or ACT is required, with a minimum recommended composite score of 900 on the SAT I or 20 on the ACT. Applicants must be graduates of an accredited secondary school and have a minimum of 16 academic credits, including 4 units in English, 3 in math, and 2 each in foreign language, science, and social studies. The GED will be considered with a minimum composite score of 270. A portfolio, audition, and interview are recommended. An essay is required. Westminster requires applicants to be in the upper 50% of their class. A GPA of 2.5 is required. AP and CLEP credits are accepted. Important factors in the admissions decision are advanced placement or honor courses, leadership record, and recommendations by school officials. Applications are accepted on-line via Common App or at
www.pheaamentor.org or *www.westminster.edu/admissions*

Procedure: Freshmen are admitted fall, winter, and spring. Entrance exams should be taken during the junior year. There are early admissions and deferred admissions plans. Early decision applications should be filed by November 15; regular application is open. The application fee is $35. Notification of early decision is sent no later than December 1; regular decision, beginning December 1.

Transfer: 16 transfer students enrolled in 2001-2002. Applicants must have a college GPA of 2.0 or better.

Visiting: There are regularly scheduled orientations for prospective students, consisting of an introduction, a student panel, a financial aid workshop, a campus tour, a faculty fair, and a lunch. Optional activities include a tour of residence halls and radio and TV stations and a football game. There are 2 visitation days in the fall and 2 in the spring. There are guides for informal visits and visitors may sit in on classes and stay overnight. To schedule a visit, contact the Office of Admissions.

Financial Aid: In 2001-2002, 99% of all freshmen and 98% of continuing students received some form of financial aid. 83% of freshmen and 76% of continuing students received need-based aid. The average freshman award was $14,252. Of that total, scholarships or need-based grants averaged $11,505 ($24,410 maximum); loans averaged $2349 ($5500 maximum); and work contracts averaged $398 ($1400 maximum). 40% of undergraduates work part time. Average annual earnings from campus work are $1410. The average financial indebtedness of the 2001 graduate was $18,125. Westminster is a member of CSS. The FAFSA and the college's own financial statement are required. The fall application deadline is May 1.

International Students: There are 2 international students enrolled. They must score 550 on the written TOEFL or take the MELAB. The SAT I may be substituted for students who come from a country where English is the spoken language.

Computers: The mainframes are a Compaq Alpha 1200 and a Compaq Alpha 800. 1500 PCs are connected from all buildings (including dorms) on campus to a Novell LAN with 23 servers. All students may access the system. There are no time limits and no fees.

Graduates: In 2001, 322 bachelor's degrees were awarded. The most popular majors were elementary education (20%), business administration (12%), and biology (8%). In an average class, 74% graduate in 4 years, 75% in 5 years, and 76% in 6 years. Of the 2000 graduating class, 90% were employed within 6 months of graduation.

Admissions Contact: Dean of Admissions.
E-mail: *admis@westminster.edu* Web: *www.westminster.edu*

WIDENER UNIVERSITY F-4
Chester, PA 19013 (610) 499-4126
(888)-Widener; Fax: (610) 499-4676

Full-time: 2240 men and women	**Faculty:** 188; IIA
Part-time: 865 men and women	**Ph.D.s:** 90%
Graduate: 3554 men and women	**Student/Faculty:** 12 to 1
Year: semesters, summer session	**Tuition:** $19,300
Application Deadline: February 15	**Room & Board:** $7620

Freshman Class: 2340 applied, 1729 accepted, 558 enrolled
SAT I Verbal/Math: 530/540 **COMPETITIVE**

Widener University, founded in 1821, is a private liberal arts institution offering undergraduate programs in the arts and sciences, business administration, engineering, nursing, and hospitality management. Other campuses are in Harrisburg and Wilmington, Delaware. There are 6 undergraduate and 5 graduate schools. In addition to regional accreditation, Widener has baccalaureate program accreditation with AACSB, ABET, ACCE, APTA, CSWE, and NLN. The library contains 245,762 volumes, 164,313 microform items, and 584 audiovisual forms/CDs, and subscribes to 2083 periodicals. Computerized library services include the card catalog, interlibrary loans, and database searching. Special learning facilities include a learning resource center, art gallery, radio station, TV station, child development center, and wireless accessible library. The 105-acre campus is in a suburban area 12 miles south of Philadelphia. Including residence halls, there are 87 buildings.

Student Life: 55% of undergraduates are from Pennsylvania. Others are from 30 states, 39 foreign countries, and Canada. 51% are from public schools. 79% are white; 11% African American. 45% are Catholic; 44% Protestant. The average age of freshmen is 18; all undergraduates, 21. 18% do not continue beyond their first year; 62% remain to graduate.

Housing: 1375 students can be accommodated in college housing, which includes single-sex and coed dormitories, on-campus apartments, fraternity houses, and sorority houses. In addition, there are honors houses, and special-interest houses, substance-free housing, affinity housing, and quiet/study wings. On-campus housing is guaranteed for all 4 years. 65% of students live on campus; of those, 75% remain on campus on weekends. All students may keep cars.

Activities: 25% of men belong to 7 national fraternities; 14% of women belong to 3 national sororities. There are 106 groups on campus, including art, band, cheerleading, chess, choir, chorale, chorus, computers, dance, drama, environmental, ethnic, film, gay, honors, ice hocky, international, jazz band, literary magazine, men's hockey clubs, model UN, musical theater, newspaper, outdoor, pep band, photography, political, professional, radio and TV, religious, rugby, ski and snowboard, social, social service, student government, video and yearbook. Popular campus events include Greek Week, Hundredth Night, and Honors Week.

Sports: There are 11 intercollegiate sports for men and 11 for women, and 7 intramural sports for men and 7 for women. Facilities include a 4000-seat stadium, an 1800-seat basketball gym, a field house, a championship pool, a weight training room, an exercise room, tennis courts, outdoor game and practice fields, and an 8-lane, all-weather championship track.

Disabled Students: All of the campus is accessible. Wheelchair ramps, elevators, special parking, specially equipped rest rooms, special class scheduling, lowered drinking fountains, and lowered telephones are available.

Services: Counseling and information services are available, as is tutoring in every subject. There is a reader service for the blind. Academic support is offered as needed for all students.

Campus Safety and Security: Measures include 24-hour foot and vehicle patrol, self-defense education, escort service, and shuttle buses. There are informal discussions, pamphlets/posters/films, emergency telephones, lighted pathways/sidewalks, and residence hall briefings on personal safety, housing security, and enforcement procedures.

Programs of Study: Widener confers B.A., B.S., B.S.B.A., B.S.C.E., B.S.Ch.E., B.S.E.E., B.S. in H.R.M., B.S.M.E., B.S.N., and B.S.W. degrees. Associate, master's, and doctoral degrees are also awarded. Bachelor's degrees are awarded in BIOLOGICAL SCIENCE (biochemistry and biology/biological science), BUSINESS (accounting, banking and finance, business administration and management, business economics, hospitality management services, and international business management), COMMUNICATIONS AND THE ARTS (communications, English, and modern language), COMPUTER AND PHYSICAL SCIENCE (chemistry, computer science, information sciences and systems, mathematics, and physics), EDUCATION (early childhood, elementary, foreign languages, science, and secondary), ENGINEERING AND ENVIRONMENTAL DESIGN (chemical engineering, civil engineering, electrical/electronics engineering, environmental science, and mechanical engineering), HEALTH PROFESSIONS (nursing, predentistry, and premedicine), SOCIAL SCIENCE (anthropology, behavioral science, criminal justice, economics, history, humanities, international relations, political science/government, prelaw, psychology, social science, social work, and sociology). Computer science, biology, and psychology are the strongest academically. Arts and sciences, business administration, and engineering are the largest.

Required: All students must complete 12 credits each in humanities, social sciences, and science/math, and 1 credit in phys ed. For graduation, students must have 121 credit hours and a GPA of 2.0. Hours in the major vary by program. There is a university-wide writing requirement for all students.

Special: Widener offers internships, study abroad in 10 countries, a Washington semester, accelerated degree programs, dual, student-designed, and interdisciplinary majors, including chemistry management, nondegree study, and pass/fail options. Co-op programs are available in business administration, computer science, and engineering and are required in hospitality management. There is also cross-registration with Boston, Syracuse, and American Universities, work-study programs, and B.A.-B.S. degrees. There are 22 national honor societies, a freshman honors program, and 8 departmental honors programs.

Faculty/Classroom: 54% of faculty are male; 46%, female. 82% teach undergraduates, 70% do research, and 70% do both. No introductory courses are taught by graduate students. The average class size in an introductory lecture is 30; in a laboratory, 14; and in a regular course, 24.

Admissions: 74% of the 2001-2002 applicants were accepted. The SAT I scores for the 2001-2002 freshman class were: Verbal--46% below 500, 42% between 500 and 599, 11% between 600 and 700, and 1% above 700; Math--44% below 500, 39% between 500 and 599, 14% between 600 and 700, and 3% above 700. 43% of the current freshmen were in the top fifth of their class; 85% were in the top two fifths. 3 freshmen graduated first in their class.

Requirements: The SAT I is required. In addition, applicants must be graduates of an accredited secondary school and have completed 4 units each of English and social studies, 3 units each of math and science, and 1 unit each of art, history, and music. The GED is accepted under limited circumstances. An interview is recommended. Widener requires applicants to be in the upper 50% of their class. A GPA of 3.0 is required. AP credits are accepted. Important factors in the admissions decision are advanced placement or honor courses, recommendations by school officials, and extracurricular activities record. Applications are accepted online via the Common Application and CollegeNet.

Procedure: Freshmen are admitted fall and spring. Entrance exams should be taken in the junior year and November or December of the senior year. There are early action, early admissions, and deferred admissions plans. Early action applications should be filed by December 1; regular applications, by February 15 for fall entry and January 3 for spring entry, along with a $35 fee. Notification of early action is sent December 15; regular decision, on a rolling basis after February 15.

Transfer: 130 transfer students enrolled in 2001-2002. Applicants must have at least 12 college credits with a minimum GPA of 2.0 (2.5 for nursing students). An associate's degree and an interview are recommended. 45 credits of 121 must be completed at Widener.

Visiting: There are regularly scheduled orientations for prospective students. There are guides for informal visits and visitors may sit in on classes and stay overnight. To schedule a visit, contact the Admissions Office.

Financial Aid: In 2001-2002, 82% of all freshmen and 79% of continuing students received some form of financial aid. 64% of all students received need-based aid. The average freshman award was $14,659. Of that total, scholarships or need-based grants averaged $11,684 ($28,665 maximum); loans averaged $3760 ($4625 maximum); work contracts averaged $1420 ($2200 maximum); and other need-based grants, vocational rehab, ROTC, and outside scholarships averaged $490 ($17,250 maximum). 45% of undergraduates work part time. Average annual earnings from campus work are $944. The average financial indebtedness of the 2001 graduate was $17,444. Widener is a member of CSS. The FAFSA and the college's own financial statement are required. The fall application deadline is February 15.

International Students: There are 108 international students enrolled. The school actively recruits these students. They must score 500 on the written TOEFL or 173 on the electronic version.

Computers: The mainframes are an HP 9000s server farm and Compaq ProLiant 4500s and 5000s. All computer resources are networked through the Ethernet. Resources can be accessed from approximately 250 PCs located in open student computer labs, from a resident's room via student supplied workstations, through direct 10/100 Mbs port connections, or from the Internet. All students may access the system. Resources are generally available 24 hours a day, 7 days a week. Student computer labs are open 8 A.M. to 11 P.M. There are no time limits and no fees. It is strongly recommended that all students have a personal computer.

Graduates: In 2001, 546 bachelor's degrees were awarded. In an average class, 1% graduate in 3 years, 44% in 4 years, 61% in 5 years, and 62% in 6 years. 102 companies recruited on campus in 2000-2001. Of the 2000 graduating class, 14% were enrolled in graduate school within 6 months of graduation and 86% were employed.

Admissions Contact: W. Hendricks, Jr., Dean of Admissions. A video is available on CD-Rom. E-mail: *admissions.office@widener.edu*
Web: *http://www.widener.edu*

WILKES UNIVERSITY — E-2

Wilkes Barre, PA 18766 — (570) 408-4400
(800) WILKESU; Fax: (570) 408-4904

Full-time: 865 men, 882 women	**Faculty:** 106; IIA, -$
Part-time: 113 men, 163 women	**Ph.D.s:** 90%
Graduate: 507 men, 1167 women	**Student/Faculty:** 16 to 1
Year: semesters, summer session	**Tuition:** $18,020
Application Deadline: open	**Room & Board:** $7780
Freshman Class: 1797 applied, 1596 accepted, 414 enrolled	
SAT I Verbal/Math: 510/520	**COMPETITIVE**

Wilkes University, founded in 1933, is an independent comprehensive university offering undergraduate programs in 40 fields, including the arts and sciences, business, and engineering. There are 2 undergraduate schools and 1 graduate school. In addition to regional accreditation, Wilkes has baccalaureate program accreditation with ABET, ACBSP, and NLN. The library contains 233,406 volumes, 819,838 microform items, and 10,861 audiovisual forms/CDs, and subscribes to 3162 periodicals. Computerized library services include the card catalog, interlibrary loans, and database searching. Special learning facilities include a learning resource center, art gallery, radio station, and TV station. The 27-acre campus is in an urban area 120 miles west of New York City. Including residence halls, there are 48 buildings.

Student Life: 87% of undergraduates are from Pennsylvania. Others are from 22 states, 4 foreign countries, and Canada. 80% are from public schools. 94% are white. 56% are Catholic; 28% Protestant; 25% claim no religious affiliation. The average age of freshmen is 18; all undergraduates, 22. 25% do not continue beyond their first year; 63% remain to graduate.

Housing: 674 students can be accommodated in college housing, which includes single-sex and coed dormitories. On-campus housing is guaranteed for all 4 years. 64% of students commute. Alcohol is not permitted. All students may keep cars.

Activities: There are no fraternities or sororities. There are 60 groups on campus, including art, band, cheerleading, choir, chorus, computers, debate, drama, ethnic, gay, honors, international, jazz band, literary magazine, musical theater, newspaper, orchestra, pep band, political, professional, radio and TV, religious, social, social service, student government, and yearbook. Popular campus events include Casino Night, Junior-Senior Dinner Dance, and Winter Weekend.

Sports: There are 7 intercollegiate sports for men and 7 for women, and 7 intramural sports for men and 3 for women. Facilities include tennis courts, a 5000-seat stadium, a 3500-seat gym, a game room, and weight and exercise rooms.

Disabled Students: All of the campus is accessible. Wheelchair ramps, elevators, special parking, specially equipped rest rooms, special class scheduling, lowered drinking fountains, and lowered telephones are available.

Services: Counseling and information services are available, as is tutoring in every subject. There is remedial math, reading, and writing. The Learning Center also provides individual tutoring, group study sessions, and small-group supplemental instruction seminars.

Campus Safety and Security: Measures include 24-hour foot and vehicle patrol, escort service, shuttle buses, and informal discussions. There are pamphlets/posters/films, emergency telephones, lighted pathways/sidewalks, and personal alarm devices for students who wish to carry one, and engraving of personal belongings. Students and others may contact security anonymously.

Programs of Study: Wilkes confers B.A., B.S., B.B.A., and B.M. degrees. Master's degrees are also awarded. Bachelor's degrees are awarded in BIOLOGICAL SCIENCE (biochemistry and biology/biological science), BUSINESS (accounting and business administration and management), COMMUNICATIONS AND THE ARTS (art, communications, dramatic arts, English, French, music, and Spanish), COMPUTER AND PHYSICAL SCIENCE (chemistry, computer science, earth science, information sciences and systems, and mathematics), EDUCATION (art, elementary, and music), ENGINEERING AND ENVIRONMENTAL DESIGN (electrical/electronics engineering, engineering and applied science, engineering management, environmental engineering, materials engineering, and mechanical engineering), HEALTH PROFESSIONS (medical technology, nursing, predentistry, premedicine, prepharmacy, prepodiatry, and preveterinary science), SOCIAL SCIENCE (criminology, economics, history, international studies, liberal arts/general studies, philosophy, political science/government, prelaw, psychology, and sociology). Prepharmacy, biology, and engineering are the strongest academically. Biology and business administration are the largest.

Required: To graduate, all students must complete at least 120 credit hours, with a minimum of 30 in the major, and a cumulative GPA of at least 2.0 overall and in the major. Students must demonstrate competency in written expression, computer literacy, oral expression, and math, and complete 2 semesters of phys ed. General education requirements consist of 12 to 15 credits in humanities, 9 to 12 in sciences, 6 to 9 in social sciences, and 3 in fine arts.

Special: Wilkes offers cooperative education, cross-registration with King's College and Misericordia, internships, and study abroad in more than 50 countries. Dual majors in all disciplines, credit for military experience, and nondegree study are also offered. Preprofessional programs include medicine, dentistry, podiatry, optometry, veterinary medicine, and pharmacy. There are 17 national honor societies, a freshman honors program, and 6 departmental honors programs.

Faculty/Classroom: 61% of faculty are male; 39%, female. All teach undergraduates. No introductory courses are taught by graduate students. The average class size in an introductory lecture is 24; in a laboratory, 16; and in a regular course, 18.

Admissions: 89% of the 2001-2002 applicants were accepted. The SAT I scores for the 2001-2002 freshman class were: Verbal--40% below 500, 43% between 500 and 599, 15% between 600 and 700, and 2% above 700; Math--39% below 500, 37% between 500 and 599, 20% between 600 and 700, and 4% above 700. 41% of the current freshmen were in the top fifth of their class; 75% were in the top two fifths. 5 freshmen graduated first in their class in a recent year.

Requirements: The SAT I or ACT is required. In addition, applicants must be graduates of an accredited secondary school or have the GED. Secondary-school preparation should include 4 years of English, 3 years each of math and social studies, and 2 years of science. Art majors must submit a portfolio, and music majors and theater arts majors must audition. An interview is recommended. Wilkes requires applicants to be in the upper 50% of their class. A GPA of 2.5 is required. AP and CLEP credits are accepted. Important factors in the admissions decision are recommendations by school officials, advanced placement or honor courses, and leadership record. Applications are accepted on-line.

Procedure: Freshmen are admitted to all sessions. Entrance exams should be taken before the second semester of the senior year in high school. There are early admissions and deferred admissions plans. Application deadlines are open. Notification is sent on a rolling basis.

Transfer: 127 transfer students enrolled in 2001-2002. Applicants must have a minimum college GPA of 2.0 and at least 30 earned credits. A GPA of 2.5 is required for engineering majors. Students with fewer than 30 credits must submit official high school transcripts and the SAT I or ACT scores. An interview is recommended. 60 credits of 120 must be completed at Wilkes.

Visiting: There are regularly scheduled orientations for prospective students, including a general orientation session, a tour of the campus, and a meeting with faculty from the department of the student's intended major. There are guides for informal visits and visitors may sit in on classes and stay overnight. To schedule a visit, contact the Admissions Office at *admissions@wilkes.edu*

Financial Aid: In a recent year, 94% of all freshmen and 87% of continuing students received some form of financial aid. 81% of freshmen and 74% of continuing students received need-based aid. The average

freshman award was $13,257. Of that total, scholarships or need-based grants averaged $9262 ($22,644 maximum); loans averaged $2509 ($7825 maximum); work contracts averaged $1168 ($3000 maximum); and tuition exchange scholarships, alumni discounts, and other remissions or discounts averaged $317 ($15,652 maximum). 36% of undergraduates work part time. Average annual earnings from campus work are $700. Wilkes is a member of CSS. The FAFSA and PHEAA are required.

International Students: There are 26 international students enrolled. The school actively recruits these students. They must score 500 on the written TOEFL or 173 on the electronic version and also take the SAT I or the ACT.

Computers: The mainframes are an IBM RS/6000 Models 590 and 350. There are also more than 450 PCs, including 150 Macs, available throughout the campus. All students may access the system 24 hours daily. There are no time limits. The fee is $50 per semester. It is strongly recommended that all students have a personal computer.

Graduates: In 2001, 432 bachelor's degrees were awarded. The most popular majors were business administration (17%), psychology (15%), and engineering (9%). In an average class, 32% graduate in 4 years, 47% in 5 years, and 55% in 6 years. 75 companies recruited on campus in 2000-2001. Of the 2000 graduating class, 24% were enrolled in graduate school within 6 months of graduation and 66% were employed.

Admissions Contact: Michael J. Frantz, Dean of Student Enrollment Services. E-mail: *frantz@wilkes.ed* Web: *www.wilkes.edu*

WILSON COLLEGE

Chambersburg, PA 17201-1285 — D-4 — (717) 262-2025 — Fax: (717) 264-1578

Full-time: 295 women	**Faculty:** 38
Part-time: 1 woman	**Ph.D.s:** 84%
Graduate: none	**Student/Faculty:** 8 to 1
Year: 4-1-4, summer session	**Tuition:** $14,775
Application Deadline: open	**Room & Board:** $6562
Freshman Class: 199 applied, 178 accepted, 102 enrolled	
SAT I Verbal/Math: 510/500	**ACT:** 22 **LESS COMPETITIVE**

Wilson College, founded in 1869, is a private liberal arts institution for women that is affiliated with the Presbyterian Church (U.S.A.). The library contains 172,205 volumes, 10,772 microform items, and 1664 audiovisual forms/CDs, and subscribes to 312 periodicals. Computerized library services include the card catalog, interlibrary loans, and database searching. Special learning facilities include a learning resource center, art gallery, natural history museum, radio station, a veterinary technology suite, an electron microscope, a classics collection, stables, and a center for sustainable living. The 262-acre campus is in a small town 55 miles south of Harrisburg, 76 miles west of Baltimore, 90 miles west of Washington. Including residence halls, there are 34 buildings.

Student Life: 53% of undergraduates are from Pennsylvania. Others are from 20 states and 12 foreign countries. 96% are from public schools. 79% are white; 11% foreign nationals. 45% claim no religious affiliation; 25% Protestant; 18% Catholic. The average age of freshmen is 18; all undergraduates, 20. 15% do not continue beyond their first year; 72% remain to graduate.

Housing: 500 students can be accommodated in college housing, which includes single-sex dormitories and on-campus apartments. In addition, there is single-parent housing for women and children. On-campus housing is guaranteed for all 4 years. 87% of students live on campus; of those, 50% remain on campus on weekends. All students may keep cars.

Activities: There are no fraternities. There are 23 groups on campus, including art, choir, chorale, dance, drama, environmental, equestrian, ethnic, gay, international, literary magazine, newspaper, photography, political, professional, radio and TV, religious, social, social service, student government, and yearbook. Popular campus events include May Weekend and Thanksgiving, Christmas, and Muhibbah Dinners.

Sports: Facilities include a 400-seat gym, a field house, a pool, a gymnastics area, a weight room, an archery range, a hockey field, tennis courts, a 2-lane bowling alley, an equestrian center (indoor and outdoor arena), a soccer field, and a fitness center.

Disabled Students: 55% of the campus is accessible. Wheelchair ramps, elevators, special parking, specially equipped rest rooms, and special class scheduling are available.

Services: Counseling and information services are available, as is tutoring in every subject. There is remedial math, reading, and writing, and study skills workshops.

Campus Safety and Security: Measures include 24-hour foot and vehicle patrol, shuttle buses, informal discussions, and pamphlets/posters/films. There are emergency telephones and lighted pathways/sidewalks.

Programs of Study: Wilson confers B.A. and B.S. degrees. Associate degrees are also awarded. Bachelor's degrees are awarded in AGRICULTURE (equine science), BIOLOGICAL SCIENCE (biology/biological science), BUSINESS (accounting and business economics), COMMUNICATIONS AND THE ARTS (communications, English, fine arts, French, languages, and Spanish), COMPUTER AND PHYSICAL SCIENCE (chemistry and mathematics), EDUCATION (elementary), ENGINEERING AND ENVIRONMENTAL DESIGN (environmental science), HEALTH PROFESSIONS (exercise science and veterinary science), SOCIAL SCIENCE (behavioral science, history, international studies, law, philosophy, political science/government, psychobiology, and religion). Business and economics, behavioral sciences, and veterinary medical technology are the largest.

Required: To graduate, students must complete a minimum of 36 courses, with a minimum GPA of 2.0. At least 18 of the 36 courses must be outside any single discipline.

Special: Cross-registration is available with Shippensburg University and Gettysburg College. Wilson offers internships, a Washington semester, student-designed majors, credit by exam, pass/fail options, and credit for noncollegiate learning. Students may participate in study-abroad programs sponsored by other colleges. There is a chapter of Phi Beta Kappa.

Faculty/Classroom: 39% of faculty are male; 61%, female. All teach undergraduates. The average class size in an introductory lecture is 20; in a laboratory, 15; and in a regular course, 15.

Admissions: 89% of the 2001-2002 applicants were accepted. The SAT I scores for the 2001-2002 freshman class were: Verbal--50% below 500, 35% between 500 and 599, and 15% between 600 and 700; Math--51% below 500, 39% between 500 and 599, and 10% between 600 and 700. The ACT scores were 50% below 21, 25% between 21 and 23, and 25% between 24 and 26. 22% of the current freshmen were in the top fifth of their class; 59% were in the top two fifths. 1 freshman graduated first in their class.

Requirements: The SAT I is required and the ACT is recommended, with a minimum recommended score of 900 composite on the SAT I or 21 on the ACT. In addition, applicants should prepare with 4 years each of English and social studies/history, 3 of math, and 2 of science and a foreign language. An essay is required, and an interview is recommended. Wilson requires applicants to be in the upper 50% of their class. A GPA of 2.5 is required. AP and CLEP credits are accepted. Important factors in the admissions decision are advanced placement or honor courses, personality/intangible qualities, and leadership record. Applications are accepted on-line at the school's web site.

Procedure: Freshmen are admitted fall and spring. Entrance exams should be taken in the spring of the junior year. There is a deferred admissions plan. Application deadlines are open.

Transfer: 11 transfer students enrolled in 2001-2002. Applicants must have a college GPA of at least 2.0. The SAT I or ACT is recommended, with a minimum composite score of 900 or 21, respectively. 14 credits of 36 must be completed at Wilson.

Visiting: There are regularly scheduled orientations for prospective students, consisting of a campus tour and meetings with various faculty members or administration, if requested. There are guides for informal visits and visitors may sit in on classes and stay overnight. To schedule a visit, contact the Office of Admissions at (800) 421-8402 or (717) 262-2002.

Financial Aid: In 2001-2002, 90% of all freshmen and 96% of continuing students received some form of financial aid. 83% of freshmen and 76% of continuing students received need-based aid. The average freshman award was $13,425. Of that total, scholarships or need-based grants averaged $564 ($18,566 maximum); loans averaged $1872 ($19,302 maximum); and work contracts averaged $1339. 21% of undergraduates work part time. Average annual earnings from campus work are $1339 (maximum). The average financial indebtedness of the 2001 graduate was $14,667. Wilson is a member of CSS. The FAFSA and the college's own financial statement are required. The fall application deadline is April 30.

International Students: There are 34 international students enrolled. The school actively recruits these students. They must score 550 on the written TOEFL . The SAT I is recommended.

Computers: The mainframe is a PC-based system. PCs are available for student use throughout the campus. There are 4 labs, 3 with PCs and 1 with Macs. All are connected to the Internet. All students may access the system. There are no time limits and no fees.

Graduates: In 2001, 44 bachelor's degrees were awarded. The most popular majors were veterinary medical (34%), equestrian studies (32%), and business economics (11%). In an average class, 60% graduate in 4 years. Of the 2000 graduating class, 45% were enrolled in graduate school within 6 months of graduation and 82% were employed.

Admissions Contact: Kathleen Berard, Dean of Enrollment.
E-mail: *admissions @wilson.edu* Web: *www.wilson.edu*

YORK COLLEGE OF PENNSYLVANIA D-4

York, PA 17405-7199 (717) 849-1600
(800) 455-8018; Fax: (717) 849-1607

Full-time: 1700 men, 2317 women **Faculty:** 136; IIB, +$
Part-time: 368 men, 734 women **Ph.D.s:** 78%
Graduate: 98 men, 76 women **Student/Faculty:** 30 to 1
Year: semesters, summer session **Tuition:** $7422
Application Deadline: open **Room & Board:** $5128
Freshman Class: 3723 applied, 2640 accepted, 971 enrolled
SAT I Verbal/Math: 548/541 **VERY COMPETITIVE**

York College of Pennsylvania, founded in 1787, is a private institution offering undergraduate programs in the liberal arts and sciences, as well as professional programs. There are 9 undergraduate schools and 1 graduate school. In addition to regional accreditation, YCP has baccalaureate program accreditation with ABET, ACBSP, CAAHEP, NLN, and NRPA. The library contains 300,000 volumes, 500,000 microform items, and 11,000 audiovisual forms/CDs, and subscribes to 1500 periodicals. Computerized library services include interlibrary loans and database searching. Special learning facilities include a learning resource center, art gallery, radio station, TV station, telecommunications center, Abraham Lincoln artifacts collection, rare books collection, oral history room, and a nursing education center. The 118-acre campus is in a suburban area 45 miles north of Baltimore. Including residence halls, there are 30 buildings.

Student Life: 56% of undergraduates are from Pennsylvania. Others are from 30 states, 36 foreign countries, and Canada. 83% are from public schools. 95% are white. 44% are Catholic; 42% Protestant. The average age of freshmen is 19; all undergraduates, 24. 20% do not continue beyond their first year; 76% remain to graduate.

Housing: 1750 students can be accommodated in college housing, which includes single-sex and coed dormitories, on-campus apartments, fraternity houses, and sorority houses. On-campus housing is guaranteed for the freshman year only and is available on a first-come, first-served basis. Alcohol is not permitted. All students may keep cars.

Activities: 10% of men belong to 5 local and 5 national fraternities; 10% of women belong to 2 local and 5 national sororities. There are 80 groups on campus; including band, cheerleading, chess, choir, chorale, chorus, computers, drama, ethnic, film, honors, international, jazz band, literary magazine, musical theater, newspaper, orchestra, photography, political, professional, radio and TV, religious, social, social service, student government, symphony, and yearbook. Popular campus events include Family Weekend, Spring Weekend Festival, and live Sparts Den performers.

Sports: There are 10 intercollegiate sports for men and 9 for women, and 10 intramural sports for men and 10 for women. Facilities include 2 gyms, a track, a swimming pool, a game room, a fitness center, weight training rooms, tennis courts, and soccer, hockey, baseball, softball, and athletic/intramural fields.

Disabled Students: 60% of the campus is accessible. Wheelchair ramps, elevators, special parking, specially equipped rest rooms, special class scheduling, lowered drinking fountains, and lowered telephones are available.

Services: Counseling and information services are available, as is tutoring in most subjects. There is remedial math and writing. There is also an education learning resource center.

Campus Safety and Security: Measures include self-defense education, escort service, informal discussions, and pamphlets/posters/films. There are emergency telephones, lighted pathways/sidewalks, 24-hour foot patrol, safety seminars, crime prevention speakers, a desk monitor in residence halls, and a personal property engraving program.

Programs of Study: YCP confers B.A. and B.S. degrees. Associate and master's degrees are also awarded. Bachelor's degrees are awarded in BIOLOGICAL SCIENCE (biology/biological science), BUSINESS (accounting, banking and finance, business administration and management, international business management, management science, marketing/retailing/merchandising, and sports management), COMMUNICATIONS AND THE ARTS (broadcasting, communications, English, fine arts, graphic design, music, Spanish, and speech/debate/rhetoric), COMPUTER AND PHYSICAL SCIENCE (chemistry, computer programming, information sciences and systems, mathematics, and physical sciences), EDUCATION (business, elementary, science, secondary, and special), ENGINEERING AND ENVIRONMENTAL DESIGN (engineering management and mechanical engineering), HEALTH PROFESSIONS (medical laboratory technology, nuclear medical technology, nursing, premedicine, and respiratory therapy), SOCIAL SCIENCE (behavioral science, criminal justice, history, humanities, parks and recreation management, political science/government, prelaw, psychology, and sociology). Mechanical engineering, nursing, and education are the strongest academically. Education, nursing, and business are the largest.

Required: To graduate, all students must complete at least 124 credit hours, with 60 to 80 in the major. The required core curriculum includes 12 credits in foreign language and culture, 12 in social and behavioral science, 9 in English and speech, 9 in humanities and fine arts, 6 each in math and lab science, 4 in phys ed, and 3 in American civilization. A minimum GPA of 2.0 is required.

Special: YCP offers internships for upper-division students and co-op programs in mechanical engineering. Exchange programs are offered with the University of Ripon and York St. John in York, England; Honam University in Kwanju, South Korea; Pontificia Universidad Catolica del Equador in Quito, Equador; and Cemanahuac Educational Community in Cuernavaca, Mexico. Dual majors in any combination, nondegree study, and pass/fail options are available. There are 2 national honor societies.

Faculty/Classroom: 62% of faculty are male; 38%, female. All teach undergraduates. No introductory courses are taught by graduate students. The average class size in an introductory lecture is 30; in a laboratory, 20; and in a regular course, 30.

Admissions: 71% of the 2001-2002 applicants were accepted. The SAT I scores for the 2001-2002 freshman class were: Verbal--17% below 500, 56% between 500 and 599, 23% between 600 and 700, and 4% above 700; Math--19% below 500, 59% between 500 and 599, 20% between 600 and 700, and 2% above 700. 39% of the current freshmen were in the top fifth of their class; 76% were in the top two fifths. 4 freshmen graduated first in their class.

Requirements: The SAT I or ACT is required. In addition, applicants must be graduates of an accredited secondary school or have a GED certificate. 15 academic credits are required, including 4 units in English, 3 or 4 in math, 2 or 3 in science, 2 in history, and 1 in social studies. Music students must audition. YCP requires applicants to be in the upper 60% of their class. A GPA of 2.5 is required. AP and CLEP credits are accepted. Important factors in the admissions decision are advanced placement or honor courses, leadership record, and extracurricular activities record. Applications can be downloaded or sent on-line via the York College home page: *www.yep.edu.*

Procedure: Freshmen are admitted fall and spring. Entrance exams should be taken in the spring of the junior year or the fall of the senior year. There is a deferred admissions plan. Application deadlines are open. The application fee is $30. There is a rolling admissions plan.

Transfer: 246 transfer students enrolled in 2001-2002. Applicants must have a minimum GPA of 2.0 from a regionally accredited institution. Students with fewer than 30 credit hours must submit a high school transcript. An interview is recommended. 30 credits of 124 must be completed at YCP.

Visiting: There are regularly scheduled orientations for prospective students, including 2 open houses in October/November and 2 spring orientation programs in April/May, featuring a general orientation, academic and support services sessions, and campus tours. There are guides for informal visits and visitors may sit in on classes. To schedule a visit, contact the Admissions Office.

Financial Aid: In 2001-2002, 76% of all freshmen and 80% of continuing students received some form of financial aid. 46% of freshmen and 56% of continuing students received need-based aid. The average freshman award was $6844. Of that total, scholarships or need-based grants averaged $3130 ($12,600 maximum); loans averaged $2834 ($14,674 maximum); and work contracts averaged $1410 ($1600 maximum). 20% of undergraduates work part time. Average annual earnings from campus work are $1500. The average financial indebtedness of the 2001 graduate was $15,198. YCP is a member of CSS. The FAFSA and the college's own financial statement are required. The fall application deadline is April 15.

International Students: They must score 530 on the written TOEFL and also take the SAT I or the ACT.

Computers: The mainframes are a Sun Enterprise 450s and Sun Ultra SPARCS. All classrooms, offices, and student residence rooms are directly connected to the network, providing access to e-mail, the Internet, and the college's own intranet. 11 computer labs and 240 PCs are available for student use. 700 software packages are available on the campus network. All students may access the system. There are no time limits and no fees.

Graduates: In 2001, 587 bachelor's degrees were awarded. The most popular majors were criminal justice (10%), nursing (8%), and elementary education (8%). In an average class, 15% graduate in 3 years, 43% in 4 years, 63% in 5 years, and 68% in 6 years. 152 companies recruited on campus in 2000-2001. Of the 2000 graduating class, 15% were enrolled in graduate school within 6 months of graduation and 91% were employed.

Admissions Contact: Director of Admissions. A video is available.
E-mail: *admissions@ycp.edu* Web: *http://www.ycp.edu*

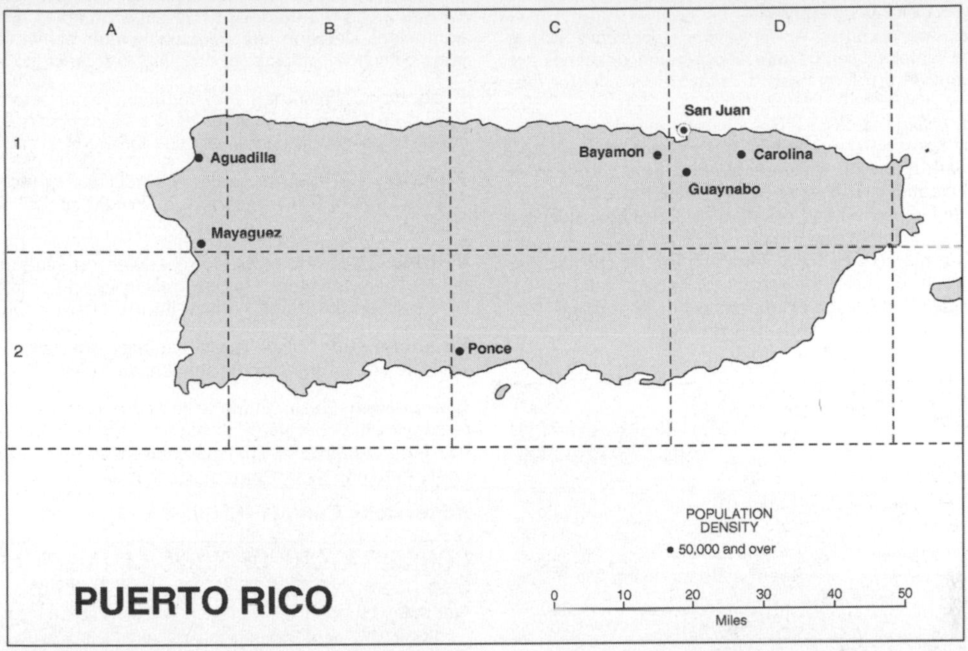

AMERICAN UNIVERSITY IN PUERTO RICO C-1

Bayamon, PR 00960-2037 (787) 740-6410; Fax: (787) 785-7377

Full-time: n/av	**Faculty:** n/av
Part-time: none	**Ph.D.s:** n/av
Graduate: n/av	**Student/Faculty:** n/av
Year: semesters, summer session	**Tuition:** see profile
Application Deadline: open	**Room & Board:** n/app
Freshman Class: 799 accepted, 517 enrolled	
SAT I or ACT: required	

American University in Puerto Rico, founded in 1963, is a private nonsectorian institution offering undergraduate programs in business administration, secretarial training, and computer science. There are 4 undergraduate schools. Computerized library services include the card catalog, interlibrary loans, and database searching. Special learning facilities include a learning resource center. The 21-acre campus is in an urban area south of San Juan. There are 9 buildings.

Student Life: 99% of undergraduates are from Puerto Rico. 80% are from public schools. 100% are Hispanic. The average age of freshmen is 18; all undergraduates, 21. 3% do not continue beyond their first year; 97% remain to graduate.

Housing: There are no residence halls. Alcohol is not permitted.

Activities: There are no fraternities or sororities. There are some groups and organizations on campus, including art and photography.

Sports: There are 3 intercollegiate sports for men and 3 for women, and 3 intramural sports for men and 3 for women. Facilities include an indoor basketball and volleyball court, a soccer field, and a pool.

Disabled Students: All of the campus is accessible. Wheelchair ramps, elevators, special parking, specially equipped rest rooms, lowered drinking fountains, and lowered telephones are available.

Services: Counseling and information services are available, as is tutoring in every subject.

Campus Safety and Security: Measures include 24-hour foot and vehicle patrol, self-defense education, informal discussions, and pamphlets/posters/films. There are lighted pathways/sidewalks.

Programs of Study: American University in Puerto Rico confers B.A. and B.B.A. degrees. Associate degrees are also awarded. Business and communications are the largest.

Required: A GPA of 2.0 is required to graduate.

Special: Work-study programs are available.

Requirements: The SAT I or ACT is required. A GPA of 2.0 is required.

Procedure: Freshmen are admitted in the fall. Application deadlines are open.

Transfer: 334 transfer students enrolled in a recent year.

Visiting: There are guides for informal visits and visitors may sit in on classes. To schedule a visit, contact the school at (787) 798-2040.

Computers: The mainframe is an IBM. Computer labs are available. All students may access the system. There are no time limits and no fees.

Admissions Contact: Admissions Office.

CARIBBEAN UNIVERSITY C-1

Bayamon, PR 00960-0493 (787) 780-0070, ext. 224

Full-time: 550 men, 1000 women	**Faculty:** n/av
Part-time: 550 men, 1000 women	**Ph.D.s:** n/av
Graduate: none	**Student/Faculty:** n/av
Year: n/app	**Tuition:** $4600
Application Deadline: open	**Room & Board:** n/app
Freshman Class: n/av	
SAT I or ACT: not required	

Caribbean University, founded in 1969, is an independent, commuter institution offering undergraduate programs in business, engineering, health science and liberal arts. There are extension centers in Vega Baja, Carolina, and Ponce. Figures given in above capsule are approximate. There are 6 undergraduate schools. The library contains 32,620 volumes, 1200 microform items, and 200 audiovisual forms/CDs, and subscribes to 210 periodicals. Computerized library services include interlibrary loans and database searching. Special learning facilities include a learning resource center. The 21-acre campus is in an urban area. There are 8 buildings.

Housing: There are no residence halls. All students commute. Alcohol is not permitted.

Activities: There are 10 groups on campus, including chess, professional, social, and student government.

Sports: Facilities include a gym, basketball and tennis courts, and a track and field arena.

Disabled Students: All of the campus is accessible. Wheelchair ramps, elevators, special parking, specially equipped rest rooms, and special counseling are available.

Services: Counseling and information services are available, as is tutoring in every subject. There is remedial math, reading, and writing.

Campus Safety and Security: Measures include campus security guards, student ID cards, and regular fire drills.

Programs of Study: Bachelor's degrees are awarded in BIOLOGICAL SCIENCE (biology/biological science), BUSINESS (accounting, banking and finance, business administration and management, marketing/retailing/merchandising, and secretarial studies/office management), COMPUTER AND PHYSICAL SCIENCE (computer programming, computer science, mathematics, and science), EDUCATION (business, elementary, middle school, science, secondary, special, and teaching English as a second/foreign language (TESOL/TEFOL)), ENGINEERING AND ENVIRONMENTAL DESIGN (civil engineering, and industrial engineering technology), HEALTH PROFESSIONS (nursing), SOCIAL SCIENCE (criminal justice, social science, and social work).

Requirements: Applicants must be graduates of an accredited secondary school with a GPA of 2.0 or a CEEB score of 4.0. The GED is accepted. High school preparation should include 3 years each of art, English, Spanish, and social studies, 2 years each of history and math, and 1 year of science. A GPA of 2.0 is required.
Procedure: Freshmen are admitted to all sessions. Entrance exams should be taken in the junior or senior year. Application deadlines are open. Notification is sent on a rolling basis. Contact the school for current information.
Transfer: A minimum college GPA of 2.0 is recommended. Applicants should submit 2 official transcripts and a catalog from each previous college attended, along with a written recommendation from the dean at the last institution. 30 credits of 135 must be completed at CU.
Visiting: There are regularly scheduled orientations for prospective students. To schedule a visit, contact the Director of Admissions.
Financial Aid: CU is a member of CSS. The CSS/Profile and income tax returns are required. Check with the school for current deadlines.
Computers: CU provides PCs for the academic use of all students during school hours. There are no time limits and no fees.
Admissions Contact: Director of Admissions.

CENTRAL UNIVERSITY OF BAYAMON C-1
Bayamon, PR 00960-1725 (787) 786-3030, ext. 2100
Fax: (787) 740-2200

Full-time: 840 men, 1590 women	**Faculty:** 61
Part-time: 155 men, 290 women	**Ph.D.s:** 28%
Graduate: 90 men, 160 women	**Student/Faculty:** 40 to 1
Year: semesters, summer session	**Tuition:** $3335
Application Deadline: see profile	**Room & Board:** n/app
Freshman Class: n/av	
SAT I: required	**ACT:** n/av

Central University of Bayamon, founded in 1970, is a private Catholic institution offering degree programs primarily to commuter students in the arts and sciences, business, education, nursing, and religious studies. There are 4 undergraduate and 3 graduate schools. Figures in above capsule are approximate. The 2 libraries contain 51,500 volumes and 40 microform items, and subscribe to 370 periodicals. Computerized library services include the card catalog. The 55-acre campus is in an urban area 4 miles west of Bayamon. There are 13 buildings.
Student Life: 90% are from public schools. All are Hispanic. The average age of freshmen is 17; all undergraduates, 20.
Housing: There are no residence halls. All students commute. Alcohol is not permitted. All students may keep cars.
Activities: There are no fraternities or sororities. There are 13 groups on campus, including computers, film, literary magazine, photography, professional, radio and TV, religious, social service, and student government.
Sports: There are 10 intercollegiate sports for men and 10 for women. Facilities include a 400-seat gym, basketball and volleyball courts, a swimming pool, and a weight-training room.
Disabled Students: All of the campus is accessible. Wheelchair ramps, elevators, special parking, specially equipped rest rooms, special class scheduling, lowered drinking fountains, and lowered telephones are available.
Services: Counseling and information services are available, as is tutoring in some subjects, including English, Spanish, philosophy, accounting, math, biology, and computer science. There is a reader service for the blind, and remedial math, reading, and writing.
Campus Safety and Security: Measures include 24-hour foot and vehicle patrol.
Programs of Study: UCB confers B.A., B.S., B.B.A., B.S.N., and B.S.S. degrees. Associate and master's degrees are also awarded. Bachelor's degrees are awarded in BIOLOGICAL SCIENCE (biology/biological science), BUSINESS (accounting, business administration and management, and marketing/retailing/merchandising), COMMUNICATIONS AND THE ARTS (journalism and Spanish), COMPUTER AND PHYSICAL SCIENCE (chemistry and computer science), EDUCATION (elementary, English, science, and secondary), HEALTH PROFESSIONS (nursing and premedicine), SOCIAL SCIENCE (philosophy, psychology, religion, social work, and sociology). Business administration is the strongest academically.
Required: Students must complete 48 credits distributed among specific courses in theology, philosophy, Spanish, English, humanities, social science, math, science, and phys ed. The bachelor's degree requires completion of 124 to 141 credits, including 33 to 43 in the major, with a minimum GPA of 2.0.
Special: The university offers limited pass/fail options, work-study programs, and nondegree study.
Faculty/Classroom: All teach undergraduates. The average class size in an introductory lecture is 35; in a laboratory, 20; and in a regular course, 35.
Requirements: The SAT I is required, or the CEEB Spanish equivalent. Applicants must be graduates of accredited secondary schools or have earned a GED. They must speak Spanish and have a good knowledge of English. The university requires 15.5 academic credits, including 3 credits each in English, Spanish, math, and science, 1.5 in history, and 1 each in social studies and electives. An interview is recommended. A GPA of 2.0 is required. CLEP credit is accepted. Important factors in the admissions decision are personality/intangible qualities, recommendations by school officials, and ability to finance college education.

Procedure: Freshmen are admitted to all sessions. Entrance exams should be taken by October of the senior year. Check with school for current application deadlines. The fall 2001 application fee was $15.

Transfer: 174 transfer students enrolled in a recent year. A minimum college GPA of 2.0 is required. 30 credits of 124 must be completed at UCB.

Visiting: There are regularly scheduled orientations for prospective students. There are guides for informal visits and visitors may sit in on classes. To schedule a visit, contact the Admissions Office.

Financial Aid: The college's own financial statement is required. Check with the school for current deadlines.

Computers: The mainframe is a Wang VS 45. Those students registered with the computer lab may access the mainframe from 9 A.M. to 7 P.M. Monday through Thursday and from 9 A.M. to noon on Friday. Students may access the system 2 hours per week. The fee is $30.

Admissions Contact: Christine M. Hernandez, Director, Admissions.

CONSERVATORY OF MUSIC OF PUERTO RICO D-1
San Juan, PR 00918 (787) 751-0160; Fax: (787) 758-8258

Full-time: 110 men, 30 women	**Faculty:** 30
Part-time: 85 men, 30 women	**Ph.D.s:** 2%
Graduate: none	**Student/Faculty:** 5 to 1
Year: semesters	**Tuition:** $1420
Application Deadline: see profile	**Room & Board:** n/app
Freshman Class: n/av	
SAT I: required	

The Conservatory of Music of Puerto Rico, founded in 1959, is a specialized commuter school supported by the Commonwealth of Puerto Rico, offering 4- and 5-year degree programs. Figures given in above capsule are approximate. The library contains 23,608 volumes, 11 microform items, and 5000 audiovisual forms/CDs, and subscribes to 2 periodicals. Special learning facilities include a learning resource center and a computer-based ear-training lab. The 3-acre campus is in an urban area in the Hato Rey section of San Juan. There are 3 buildings.

Programs of Study: The conservatory confers B.F.A., B.M., and B.Perf.Arts degrees.

Required: To graduate, students must complete 142 credit hours (158 for music education) with a minimum GPA of 2.0. Requirements include 4 years of courses in the principal instrument and specific courses in music theory, including solfege, harmony, and counterpoint. All students must present a graduation recital.

Special: A dual major is available in the principal instrument and music education.

Faculty/Classroom: 70% of faculty are male; 30%, female. All teach undergraduates.

Requirements: The SAT I is required, or the CEEB's Spanish version. Applicants must be graduates of an accredited secondary school. An interview and audition are required. A GPA of 2.0 is required. AP credits are accepted. Important factors in the admissions decision are leadership record, parents or siblings attending the school, and ability to finance college education.

Procedure: Freshmen are admitted to all sessions. Entrance exams should be taken in May of the junior year or December of the senior year. There is an early admissions plan. Check with school for current application deadlines and fee. A waiting list is an active part of the admissions procedure.

Transfer: 100 credits of 142 must be completed at the conservatory.

Visiting: There are regularly scheduled orientations for prospective students. To schedule a visit, contact Pilar Ruibal, Counselor, or Zulma Palos, Admissions Director.

Financial Aid: 15% of undergraduates work part time. Average annual earnings from campus work in a recent year were $850. The conservatory is a member of CSS. The CSS/Profile is required.

Computers: There are no time limits and no fees.

Admissions Contact: Zulma Palos-Santini, Admissions Director.

ESCUELA DE ARTES PLASTICAS DE PUERTO RICO D-1

San Juan, PR 00902-1112 (787) 725-8120, ext. 233 (787) 725-8111

Full-time: 157 men, 80 women
Part-time: 46 men, 30 women
Graduate: none
Year: semesters
Application Deadline: May 16
Freshman Class: 159 applied, 83 accepted, 78 enrolled
SAT I: required
Faculty: 13
Ph.D.s: 80%
Student/Faculty: 18 to 1
Tuition: $1874
Room & Board: n/app
ACT: n/av

Escuela de Artes Plasticas de Puerto Rico, founded in 1966, is a public institution considered to be the national art school of Puerto Rico. The library contains 12,429 volumes, 10,000 microform items, and 300 audiovisual forms/CDs, and subscribes to 40 periodicals. Computerized library services include the card catalog. Special learning facilities include a learning resource center and art gallery. The 1-acre campus is in an urban area in Old San Juan. There are 3 buildings.

Student Life: 61% are from public schools. All are Hispanic. The average age of freshmen is 18; all undergraduates, 25. 5% do not continue beyond their first year; 20% remain to graduate.

Housing: There are no residence halls. All students commute. Alcohol is not permitted. No one may keep cars.

Activities: There are no fraternities or sororities. There are 2 groups on campus, including art and student government. Popular campus events include Student Day, Health Fair, and Halloween Costume Party.

Sports: There is no sports program at Escuela de Artes Plasticas de Puerto Rico.

Disabled Students: All of the campus is accessible. Wheelchair ramps, elevators, special parking, and special class scheduling are available.

Services: Counseling and information services are available, as is tutoring in some subjects, including all the general studies courses. There is remedial writing.

Campus Safety and Security: Measures include 24-hour foot and vehicle patrol, pamphlets/posters/films, and safety training.

Programs of Study: Escuela de Artes Plasticas de Puerto Rico confers the B.A. degree. Bachelor's degrees are awarded in COMMUNICATIONS AND THE ARTS (graphic design, painting, and sculpture), EDUCATION (art), ENGINEERING AND ENVIRONMENTAL DESIGN (computer graphics). Computer graphics is the largest.

Required: To graduate, students must maintain a minimum GPA of 2.0 in 132 credits, including 36 in art fundamentals and 48 in general education courses.

Faculty/Classroom: 56% of faculty are male; 44%, female. All teach undergraduates. The average class size in an introductory lecture is 25 and in a laboratory, 18.

Admissions: 52% of the 2001-2002 applicants were accepted.

Requirements: The SAT I is required or the CEEB Spanish equivalent of the SAT I. Applicants must be graduates of an accredited secondary school or have earned a GED. A portfolio and interview are required, with an essay recommended. A GPA of 2.0 is required. Important factors in the admissions decision are evidence of special talent, recommendations by school officials, and personality/intangible qualities.

Procedure: Freshmen are admitted in the fall. Applications should be filed by May 16 for fall entry. Notification is sent on a rolling basis.

Transfer: 24 transfer students enrolled in 2001-2002.

Visiting: There are regularly scheduled orientations for prospective students. There are guides for informal visits. To schedule a visit, contact the Student Affairs Office.

Financial Aid: In a recent year, 56% of all freshmen and 73% of continuing students received some form of financial aid. 33% of freshmen and 52% of continuing students received need-based aid. The average freshman award was $3125. Of that total, scholarships or need-based grants averaged $200 ($300 maximum); work contracts averaged $100 ($1000 maximum); and government programs averaged $1350 ($1700 maximum). 12% of undergraduates work part time. Average annual earnings from campus work are $1300. The FAFSA is required.

International Students: The school actively recruits these students. They must take the SAT I or the CEEB English or Spanish SAT I.

Computers: 10 PCs in the library and 4 in classrooms. All students may access the system Monday through Saturday from 8:00 A.M. to 5:30 P.M. Students may access the system for 1 hour. There are no fees.

Graduates: In 2001, 49 bachelor's degrees were awarded. The most popular majors were graphic design (47%), painting (27%), and art education (10%). In an average class, 6% graduate in 3 years, 17% in 4 years, 38% in 5 years, and 39% in 6 years. 4 companies recruited on campus in 2000-2001. Of the 2000 graduating class, 14% were enrolled in graduate school within 6 months of graduation and 57% were employed.

Admissions Contact: Milegros Lugo, Recruiting Officer.
E-mail: *eap@cogui.net* Web: *www.eap.edu.pr*

INTER-AMERICAN UNIVERSITY OF PUERTO RICO SYSTEM

The Inter-American University of Puerto Rico, founded in 1912, became the first institution outside the continental United States to receive accreditation from the Middle States Association of Colleges and Schools. Through its commitment to excellence in education, Inter-American has become the largest private university in Puerto Rico. The university's program is licensed by the Council on Higher Education of the Commonwealth of Puerto Rico. Enrollment exceeds 42,000 students, which constitutes approximately 25% of the Island's college-student population and 40% of those who attend private institutions of higher education. Inter-American University is a multicampus system, which includes the Metropolitan (San Juan), San German, Bayamon, Arecibo, Aguadilal, Ponce, Fajardo, Guayama, and Barranquitas Campuses. The university has the only School of Optometry and Airway Science Program in the Caribbean and a prestigious School of Law. The university offers associates, bachelor, master's, and doctorate degrees. The Metropolitan campus has the only program of higher education in Puerto Rico where English is the medium of instruction.

INTER-AMERICAN UNIVERSITY OF PUERTO RICO/AGUADILLA CAMPUS A-1

Aguadilla, PR 00605 (787) 891-0925; (787) 882-3020

Full-time: 1317 men, 1849 women
Part-time: 254 men, 380 women
Graduate: none
Year: semesters, summer session
Application Deadline: May 1
Freshman Class: 1058 applied, 1057 accepted, 817 enrolled
SAT I: required
Faculty: 76
Ph.D.s: 21%
Student/Faculty: 42 to 1
Tuition: $3278
Room & Board: n/app

Inter-American University of Puerto Rico/Aguadilla Campus, a private, nonsectarian institution, was founded in 1957 and is a part of the Inter-American University of Puerto Rico. Programs offered include business, fine and liberal arts, health sciences, and teacher and professional preparation. There are 3 undergraduate schools. The library contains 56,717 volumes, 2277 microform items, and 24,680 audiovisual forms/CDs, and subscribes to 461 periodicals. Computerized library services include the card catalog, interlibrary loans, and database searching. Special learning facilities include a learning resource center, radio station, a multimedia center, and instructional development center, and an electronic classroom. The 54-acre campus is in a suburban area in northwestern Puerto Rico, near the Atlantic Ocean. There are 6 buildings.

Student Life: 99% of undergraduates are from Puerto Rico. 96% are from public schools. All are Hispanic. 70% are Catholic; 30% Protestant. The average age of freshmen is 21; all undergraduates, 24. 20% do not continue beyond their first year.

Housing: There are no residence halls. Alcohol is not permitted.

Activities: There are no fraternities or sororities. There are 21 groups on campus, including academic, chess, chorus, computers, cultural debate, drama, film, honors, newspaper, professional, radio, religious, social, social service, and student government. Popular campus events include International Tourism Conference, Festival of Flora and Fauna, and Achievement Night.

Sports: There are 11 intercollegiate sports for men and 9 for women, and 8 intramural sports for men and 8 for women. Facilities include a multiuse coliseum with a capacity for 2,000 people with basketball and volleyball courts, and a small indoor track. There is also a gym with exercise equipment and an area with 3 platforms for weight-lifting. The recreation facility has table games, a Ping-Pong table, and video arcade games.

Disabled Students: Wheelchair ramps, elevators, special parking, lowered drinking fountains, and lowered telephones are available.

Services: Counseling and information services are available, as is tutoring in some subjects, including Spanish, math, English, and accounting. There is a reader service for the blind and remedial math. There is a computerized center for skills development, and language and math labs.

Campus Safety and Security: Measures include 24-hour foot and vehicle patrol, pamphlets/posters/films, and lighted pathways/sidewalks.

Programs of Study: Inter confers B.A., B.S., B.B.A., and B.S.N. degrees. Associate degrees are also awarded. Bachelor's degrees are awarded in BIOLOGICAL SCIENCE (biology/biological science), BUSINESS (accounting, business administration and management, marketing/retailing/merchandising, and secretarial studies/office management), COMPUTER AND PHYSICAL SCIENCE (computer science), EDUCATION (early childhood, elementary, and secondary), ENGINEERING AND ENVIRONMENTAL DESIGN (electrical/electronics engineering technology), HEALTH PROFESSIONS (nursing), SOCIAL SCIENCE (criminal justice). Elementary education, nursing, criminal justice, and computer science are the strongest academically and have the largest enrollments.

Required: To graduate, students must fulfill 59 general education credits as follows: 18 in communication skills; 12 in historical cultural heritage; 11 in ability to integrate, apply, and create; 8 in reasoning skills; 6 in methods of interpreting reality; 2 nonacademic credits each in health/phys ed/recreation; and 2 nonacademic credits in Introduction to University Life. A total of 120 credit hours is required; the number required in the major varies. A 2.0 GPA overall and in the major is required.

Special: The university offers internships, work-study, adult and continuing education programs, and cross-registration with John Jay College. There is a freshman honors program.

Faculty/Classroom: 89% teach undergraduates. The average class size in an introductory lecture is 30; in a laboratory, 25; and in a regular course, 28.

Admissions: All of the 2001-2002 applicants were accepted.

Requirements: The SAT I is required. Native Spanish speakers may take the Spanish version of the SAT I. The SAT II: Subject test in writing also is required. Applicants must be graduates of an accredited secondary school. An interview may be required. A GPA of 2.0 is required. AP and CLEP credits are accepted. Applications are accepted on-line at *http://www.inter.edu/solicitud.html*.

Procedure: Freshmen are admitted to all sessions. There is an early admissions plan. Applications should be filed by May 1 for fall entry, November 15 for winter entry, and April 15 for summer entry. Notification is sent on a rolling basis.

Transfer: 86 transfer students enrolled in 2001-2002. Transfer applicants must submit all college transcripts and must be in good standing at their previous institution. A minimum of 15 transferable credits with a grade of at least C must have been completed.

Visiting: There are regularly scheduled orientations for prospective students.

Financial Aid: In 2001-2002, 99% of all freshmen and 92% of continuing students received some form of financial aid, including need-based aid. The average freshman award was $7275. Of that total, scholarships or need-based grants averaged $500 ($1000 maximum); loans averaged $2625 (maximum); and work contracts averaged $400 (maximum). 32% of undergraduates work part time. Average annual earnings from campus work are $400. Inter is a member of CSS. The FAFSA and the college's own financial statement are required. The fall application deadline is April 28.

International Students: A personal interview is required, as are satisfactory scores on an appropriate comprehensive exam.

Computers: The mainframe is an IBM RISC 6000 SP2. All students may access the system for distance learning, web browsing, e-mail, and library searches. There are no time limits and no fees.

Graduates: In 2001, 308 bachelor's degrees were awarded. The most popular majors were business administration (12%), criminal justice (10%), and office system administration (9%).

Admissions Contact: Doris Perez, Director of Admissions.
Web: *www.interaguadilla.edu*

INTER-AMERICAN UNIVERSITY OF PUERTO RICO/ARECIBO CAMPUS — B-1

Arecibo, PR 00614-4050 — **(787) 878-5195; Fax: (787) 880-1624**

Full-time: 1100 men, 2200 women	**Faculty:** 82
Part-time: 275 men, 550 women	**Ph.D.s:** 21%
Graduate: 5 men, 10 women	**Student/Faculty:** 40 to 1
Year: semesters, summer session	**Tuition:** $3700
Application Deadline: see profile	**Room & Board:** n/app
Freshman Class: n/av	
SAT I or ACT: not required	

Inter-American Arecibo, founded in 1957, is a private, nonsectarian unit of the Inter-American University of Puerto Rico system. It offers programs in business, health sciences, liberal arts, and teacher preparation. Figures given in above capsule are approximate. The library contains 74,991 volumes, 82 microform items, and 28,665 audiovisual forms/CDs, and subscribes to 739 periodicals. Computerized library services include interlibrary loans and database searching. Special learning facilities include a learning resource center and a library exhibition area. The 20-acre campus is in a suburban area 50 miles west of San Juan. There are 9 buildings.

Student Life: 99% of undergraduates are from Puerto Rico. Others are from 1 state. 93% are from public schools. All are Hispanic. The average age of freshmen is 18; all undergraduates, 24. 11% do not continue beyond their first year.

Housing: There are no residence halls. All students commute. Alcohol is not permitted. All students may keep cars.

Activities: There are 2 local fraternities and 1 local sorority. There are 12 groups on campus, including drama, film, honors, newspaper, professional, religious, social, and student government. Popular campus events include Open House, Talent Festival, and sports events.

Sports: There are 7 intercollegiate sports for men and 7 for women, and 10 intramural sports for men and 10 for women. Facilities include a tennis court, a basketball court, and a student center with Ping-pong tables and weight-lifting equipment.

Disabled Students: Wheelchair ramps, elevators, special parking, specially equipped rest rooms, lowered drinking fountains, and lowered telephones are available.

Services: Counseling and information services are available, as is tutoring in some subjects, including accounting, secretarial sciences, math, Spanish, English, and computer sciences. There is a reader service for the blind and remedial math.

Campus Safety and Security: Measures include 24-hour foot and vehicle patrol, pamphlets/posters/films, and lighted pathways/sidewalks.

Programs of Study: Inter-American Arecibo confers B.A. and B.S. degrees. Associate and master's degrees are also awarded. Bachelor's degrees are awarded in BIOLOGICAL SCIENCE (biology/biological science and microbiology), BUSINESS (accounting, business administration and management, and marketing and distribution), COMPUTER AND PHYSICAL SCIENCE (chemical technology, chemistry, and computer science), EDUCATION (elementary, secondary, special, and teaching English as a second/foreign language (TESOL/TEFOL)), HEALTH PROFESSIONS (nursing), SOCIAL SCIENCE (criminal justice and social work). Biology, criminal justice, and business administration are the strongest academically. Business administration is the largest.

Required: To graduate, all students must complete at least 130 credits with a GPA of 2.0. General education requirements include 55 credits in Spanish, English, math, logic, computers, Puerto Rican history, humanities, health, social studies, environment, and religion. Noncredit courses are required in phys ed and orientation.

Special: The university offers 3-2 programs with Pennsylvania State University in engineering and earth and mineral sciences, and with Universidad Catolica Madre y Maestra of the Dominican Republic in medicine. Independent research, work-study, and independent study programs are available. Professional certificate programs are offered in nurse anesthetist and intensive nursing care. There is a freshman honors program.

Faculty/Classroom: 45% of faculty are male; 55%, female. All teach undergraduates. The average class size in an introductory lecture is 27 and in a laboratory, 25.

Requirements: In addition, applicants must present satisfactory scores on the aptitude and English tests of the CEEB. Students whose first language is English may take the SAT I. In addition, applicants should be graduates of an accredited high school. The GED is accepted. Secondary school preparation should include 15 to 30 academic credits. Some applicants may be required to schedule an interview. A GPA of 2.0 is required. Important factors in the admissions decision are advanced placement or honor courses, evidence of special talent, and leadership record.

Procedure: Freshmen are admitted to all sessions. Entrance exams should be taken in October or February of the senior year. There is an early decision plan. Check with the school for current application deadlines and fee. Notification is sent on a rolling basis.

Transfer: Applicants should present a C average in at least 15 college credits. Those with fewer transferable credits must meet freshman entrance requirements.

Visiting: There are regularly scheduled orientations for prospective students. There are guides for informal visits. To schedule a visit, contact the Admissions Office.

Financial Aid: 30% of undergraduates work part time. Average annual earnings from campus work in a recent year were $400. Inter-American Arecibo is a member of CSS. The CSS/Profile and the college's own financial statement are required.

International Students: They must take the TOEFL and also take the SAT I.

Computers: The mainframe is an IBM RISC 6000 R30. All students may access the system. There are no time limits and no fees. It is strongly recommended that all students have a personal computer.

Admissions Contact: Provi Montalvo, Director of Admissions.
Web: *www.arecibo.inter.edu*

INTER-AMERICAN UNIVERSITY OF PUERTO RICO/BARRANQUITAS REGIONAL COLLEGE — C-2

Barranquitas, PR 00794 — **(787) 857-3600; Fax: (787) 857-2244**

Full-time: 300 men, 830 women	**Faculty:** 40
Part-time: 150 men, 420 women	**Ph.D.s:** 1%
Graduate: none	**Student/Faculty:** 28 to 1
Year: semesters, summer session	**Tuition:** $3700
Application Deadline: see profile	**Room & Board:** n/app
Freshman Class: n/av	
SAT I or ACT: required	**LESS COMPETITIVE**

Inter-American University of Puerto Rico/Barranquitas Regional College, founded in 1957 and part of the Inter-American University system, is a private college whose primary focus is teacher education. Figures given in the above capsule are approximate. There are 6 undergraduate schools. The library contains 32,275 volumes, 23,657 microform items, and 926 audiovisual forms/CDs, and subscribes to 223 periodicals.

Computerized library services include the card catalog and interlibrary loans. Special learning facilities include a learning resource center. The 36-acre campus is in a small town. There are 5 buildings.

Student Life: Others are from 1 state and 1 foreign country. All are Hispanic. The average age of freshmen is 18; all undergraduates, 22. 4% do not continue beyond their first year; 96% remain to graduate.

Housing: There are no residence halls. All students commute. Alcohol is not permitted. All students may keep cars.

Activities: There are no fraternities or sororities. There are 9 groups on campus, including chorus, dance, honors, religious, social, and student government. Popular campus events include Health Fair and Open House.

Sports: There are 8 intercollegiate sports for men and 7 for women, and 7 intramural sports for men and 6 for women. Facilities include a student center, a gym, volleyball and basketball courts, and a softball park.

Disabled Students: 1% of the campus is accessible. Wheelchair ramps and special parking are available.

Services: Counseling and information services are available, as is tutoring in some subjects, including Spanish, English, and math. There is a reader service for the blind, and remedial math, reading, and writing.

Campus Safety and Security: Measures include 24-hour foot and vehicle patrol, pamphlets/posters/films, emergency telephones, and lighted pathways/sidewalks.

Programs of Study: Inter-American at Barranquitas confers B.A. and B.B.A. degrees. Associate degrees are also awarded. Bachelor's degrees are awarded in BUSINESS (accounting, business administration and management, and secretarial studies/office management), EDUCATION (early childhood, elementary, and secondary), SOCIAL SCIENCE (criminal justice). Education, business administration, and secretarial studies are the strongest academically.

Required: In order to graduate, students must complete 120 to 132 credit hours with a minimum GPA of 2.0.

Special: Internships are available in education, secretarial studies, and criminal justice. There is 1 national honor society.

Requirements: The SAT I or ACT is required. In addition, SAT II: Subject tests are also required. A GPA of 2.0 is required. AP credits are accepted. Important factors in the admissions decision are evidence of special talent, advanced placement or honor courses, and leadership record.

Procedure: Freshmen are admitted fall, winter, and summer. Entrance exams should be taken in October, February, or June. There is an early admissions plan. Check with the school for current application deadlines and fee. Notification is sent on a rolling basis.

Transfer: Transfer applicants must submit a university transcript, dean's recommendation, and financial aid transcript. 36 credits of 120 must be completed at Inter-American at Barranquitas.

Visiting: There are regularly scheduled orientations for prospective students. There are guides for informal visits. To schedule a visit, contact the Admissions Director.

Financial Aid: 45% of undergraduates work part time. Average annual earnings from campus work are $3000. Inter-American at Barranquitas is a member of CSS.

International Students: They must take the college's own test and also take SAT II: Subject tests.

Computers: There are no time limits and no fees.

Admissions Contact: Maribel Diaz Pena, Director of Admissions.

INTER-AMERICAN UNIVERSITY OF PUERTO RICO/BAYAMON UNIVERSITY COLLEGE C-1

Bayamon, PR 00619 (787) 780-4040; Fax: (787) 279-2205

Full-time and Part-time: 4800 men and women	**Faculty:** n/av
	Ph.D.s: n/av
Graduate: n/av	**Student/Faculty:** n/av
Year: semesters, summer session	**Tuition:** $3700
Application Deadline: see profile	**Room & Board:** n/app
Freshman Class: n/av	
SAT I or ACT: required	

Inter-American University of Puerto Rico/Bayamon University College, a private, nonsectarian, institution, founded in 1912, is part of the Inter-American University of Puerto Rico. Students may pursue undergraduate and graduate study in business, health sciences, liberal and fine arts, and teacher preparation. Figures given in the above capsule are approximate. In addition to regional accreditation, Inter-American at Bayamon has baccalaureate program accreditation with CSWE. Computerized library services include the card catalog. Special learning facilities include an audiovisual center, an instructional development center, and a publication center. The campus is in an urban area in a medium-size city.

Programs of Study: Bachelor's degrees are awarded in BIOLOGICAL SCIENCE (biology/biological science), BUSINESS (accounting, banking and finance, business administration and management, insurance, management information systems, marketing/retailing/merchandising, and secretarial studies/office management), COMMUNICATIONS AND THE ARTS (applied music, Spanish, and visual and performing arts), COMPUTER AND PHYSICAL SCIENCE (chemical technology, chemistry, computer science, and mathematics), EDUCATION (early childhood, elementary, music, secondary, and special), ENGINEERING AND ENVIRONMENTAL DESIGN (electrical/electronics engineering technology), HEALTH PROFESSIONS (medical technology and nursing), SOCIAL SCIENCE (criminal justice, history, political science/government, psychology, public administration, social work, and sociology).

Requirements: Check with the school for current information.

Procedure: Check with the school for current application deadlines and fee.

Financial Aid: The FAFSA and the college's own financial statement are required.

International Students: A personal interview is required, as is satisfactory completion of an appropriate comprehensive exam.

Computers: There are no time limits and no fees.

Admissions Contact: Director of Admissions.

INTER-AMERICAN UNIVERSITY OF PUERTO RICO/FAJARDO CAMPUS D-1

Fajardo, PR 00738-7003 (787) 860-3100, ext. 2210; (787) 860-3470

Full-time: 2060 total men and women	**Faculty:** 37
Part-time: n/av	**Ph.D.s:** 9%
Graduate: n/av	**Student/Faculty:** n/av
Year: 4-1-4, summer session	**Tuition:** $4000
Application Deadline: August 15	**Room & Board:** n/app
Freshman Class: 751 applied, 751 accepted, 543 enrolled	
SAT I or ACT: required	

Inter-American University of Puerto Rico/Fajardo Campus, founded in 1912 and a unit of the Inter-American University of Puerto Rico, is a private, nonsectarian college offering undergraduate and graduate degrees in business, fine and liberal arts, health sciences, and teacher preparation. Total enrollment is 2060 men and women. In addition to regional accreditation, Inter at Fajardo has baccalaureate program accreditation with CSWE. The library contains 39,968 volumes and 1822 audiovisual forms/CDs. Computerized library services include the card catalog. Special learning facilities include an audiovisual center, publication center, and instructional development center. The 11-acre campus is in a small city. There are 10 buildings.

Student Life: 90% are from public schools. The average age of freshmen is 18.

Housing: There are no residence halls. Alcohol is not permitted.

Activities: There are no fraternities or sororities. There are some groups and organizations on campus, including academic, chorale, cultural, professional, recreational, religious, and social.

Sports: Facilities include a multipurpose building.

Disabled Students: Wheelchair ramps, elevators, special parking, and specially equipped rest rooms are available.

Services: There is remedial math and reading.

Campus Safety and Security: Measures include pamphlets/posters/films.

Programs of Study: Inter at Fajardo confers B.A., B.S., and B.B.A. degrees. Associate, master's, and doctoral degrees are also awarded. Bachelor's degrees are awarded in BIOLOGICAL SCIENCE (biology/biological science), BUSINESS (accounting, banking and finance, business administration and management, insurance, management information systems, marketing/retailing/merchandising, and secretarial studies/office management), COMMUNICATIONS AND THE ARTS (applied music, Spanish, and visual and performing arts), COMPUTER AND PHYSICAL SCIENCE (chemical technology, chemistry, computer science, and mathematics), EDUCATION (early childhood, elementary, music, secondary, and special), ENGINEERING AND ENVIRONMENTAL DESIGN (electrical/electronics engineering technology), HEALTH PROFESSIONS (medical technology and nursing), SOCIAL SCIENCE (criminal justice, history, political science/government, psychology, public administration, social work, and sociology).

Required: To graduate, all students must complete 120 credit hours with a minimum GPA of 2.0 overall and in the major. General education requirements total 59 credits, including 18 credits in communication skills, 12 in historical-cultural heritage, 11 in ability to integrate, apply, and create, 8 in reasoning skills, 6 in methods of interpreting reality, and 2 nonacademic credits each in Introduction to University Life and health/phys ed/recreation.

Special: Co-op programs in engineering and earth and mineral sciences with Pennsylvania State University, cross-registration, internships, work-study, and adult and continuing education programs are available. There is a freshman honors program and 1 departmental honors program.

Faculty/Classroom: 42% of faculty are male; 58%, female. The average class size in an introductory lecture is 25; in a laboratory, 20; and in a regular course, 25.

Admissions: All of the 2001-2002 applicants were accepted.

Requirements: The SAT I or ACT is required, as is the SAT II: Writing test. Native Spanish-speaking students may take the CEEB Spanish version of the SAT I. Students must have graduated from an accredited secondary school. An interview may be required. A GPA of 2.0 is required. AP credits are accepted.

Procedure: Freshmen are admitted to all sessions. There is an early admissions plan. Applications should be filed by August 15 for fall entry, November 15 for winter entry, and April 15 for spring entry. Notification is sent on a rolling basis.

Transfer: 73 transfer students enrolled in 2001-2002. Applicants must have completed at least 15 transferable semester credits with a minimum grade of C and must be in good standing at their previous institution. All college transcripts must be submitted.

Financial Aid: Scholarships or need-based grants averaged $3300; and work contracts averaged $200. Average annual earnings from campus work are $400. The FAFSA and the college's own financial statement are required. Check with the school for current deadlines.

International Students: A personal interview and satisfactory scores on an appropriate comprehensive exam are required.

Computers: The mainframes are a 3 Dell PowerEdge 2300 and 2 PowerEdge 4200 servers. 3 classrooms house a total of 75 computers in the technology center. All computers have Internet access. Each student is assigned a password and a login name at the beginning of the semester. All students may access the system. There are no time limits and no fees.

Graduates: In 2001, 204 bachelor's degrees were awarded. The most popular majors were business administration (57%), education (20%), and science and technology (7%).

Admissions Contact: Ada Caraballo, Admissions Director. E-mail: *adcaraba@inter.edu* Web: *www.inter.edu*

INTER-AMERICAN UNIVERSITY OF PUERTO RICO/METROPOLITAN CAMPUS D-1

San Juan, PR 00919-1293 **(787) 765-1270; Fax: (787) 764-6963**

Full-time: 2188 men, 2900 women
Part-time: 944 men, 1252 women
Graduate: 1135 men, 2107 women
Year: semesters and trimesters, summer session
Application Deadline: May 1
Freshman Class: 1518 applied, 1186 accepted, 1142 enrolled
SAT I: recommended
Faculty: 187
Ph.D.s: 50%
Student/Faculty: 27 to 1
Tuition: $4166
Room & Board: n/app

Inter-American University of Puerto Rico/Metropolitan Campus, a private, nonsectarian institution, founded in 1912, is a unit of the Inter-American University of Puerto Rico. Students may pursue undergraduate and graduate study in business, fine and liberal arts, health sciences, and teacher preparation. There are 9 undergraduate and 2 graduate schools. In addition to regional accreditation, Inter-American Metro has baccalaureate program accreditation with ACS, CSWE, NAACLS, and NLN. The library contains 113,200 volumes, 638,275 microform items, and 5078 audiovisual forms/CDs, and subscribes to 2771 periodicals. Computerized library services include the card catalog. Special learning facilities include an audiovisual center, an instructional development center, and a publication center. The 20-acre campus is in an urban area 9 miles from San Juan. There are 13 buildings.

Student Life: 99% of undergraduates are from Puerto Rico. 59% are from public schools. 98% are Hispanic. The average age of freshmen is 18; all undergraduates, 18.

Housing: All students commute. Alcohol is not permitted. All students may keep cars.

Activities: There are no fraternities. There are 23 groups on campus, including art, cheerleading, chorus, debate, drama, international, orchestra, professional, religious, student government, symphony, and yearbook.

Sports: There are 12 intercollegiate sports for men and 8 for women, and 14 intramural sports for men and 13 for women.

Disabled Students: 90% of the campus is accessible. Wheelchair ramps, elevators, special parking, lowered drinking fountains, and lowered telephones are available.

Services: Counseling and information services are available, as is tutoring in some subjects, including Spanish, English, and mathematics. There is a reader service for the blind and interpreters for the hearing impaired.

Campus Safety and Security: Measures include 24-hour foot and vehicle patrol and pamphlets/posters/films.

Programs of Study: Inter-American Metro confers B.A., B.S., and B.B.A. degrees. Associate, master's, and doctoral degrees are also awarded. Bachelor's degrees are awarded in BIOLOGICAL SCIENCE (biology/biological science), BUSINESS (accounting, banking and finance, business administration and management, management information systems, marketing/retailing/merchandising, and secretarial studies/office management), COMMUNICATIONS AND THE ARTS (Spanish), COMPUTER AND PHYSICAL SCIENCE (chemistry, computer science, and mathematics), EDUCATION (early childhood, elementary, secondary, and special), HEALTH PROFESSIONS (medical technology and nursing), SOCIAL SCIENCE (criminal justice, history, political science/government, psychology, social work, and sociology). Chemistry is the strongest academically.

Required: To graduate, students must complete 59 general education credits: 18 in communications skills, 12 in historical-cultural heritage, 11 in ability to integrate, apply, and create, 8 in reasoning skills, 6 in methods of interpreting reality, and 2 nonacademic credits each in health/phys ed/recreation and Introduction to University Life. A total of 120 credit hours must be completed; the number in the major varies. A minimum 2.0 GPA overall and in the major is required.

Special: Cross-registration, internship and work-study programs, and adult and continuing education programs are available. There is 1 national honor society, and a freshman honors program.

Faculty/Classroom: 43% of faculty are male; 57%, female. 65% teach undergraduates and 5% both teach and do research. The average class size in an introductory lecture is 20 and in a laboratory, 22.

Admissions: 78% of the 2001-2002 applicants were accepted.

Requirements: The SAT I is recommended. In addition, students whose first language is Spanish may take the CEEB Spanish version of the SAT I. Applications are accepted on computer disk and on-line at *www.metro.inter.edu*. A GPA of 2.0 is required.

Procedure: Freshmen are admitted to all sessions. Entrance exams should be taken October. Applications should be filed by May 1 for fall entry, November 15 for spring entry, and April 15 for summer entry. Notification is sent on a rolling basis beginning May 15.

Transfer: 297 transfer students enrolled in 2001-2002. Applicants must have completed at least 12 transferable semester credits with a minimum grade of C and be in good standing at the previous institution. 40 credits of 120 must be completed at Inter-American Metro.

Visiting: There are regularly scheduled orientations for prospective students, including an open house twice a year. To schedule a visit, contact Edwin Mendez, Recruiter at (787) 250-1912, ext. 2102, 2463 or *edmendez@inter.edu*.

Financial Aid: In 2001-2002, 79% of all freshmen and 82% of continuing students received some form of financial aid. 79% of freshmen and 81% of continuing students received need-based aid. The FAFSA and the college's own financial statement are required.

Computers: The mainframe is a RISC 600 5-80. 434 PCs are available in 19 rooms, and 130 PCs are in an open lab. All have access to the Internet and Web. All students may access the system Monday through Saturday. There are no time limits. The fee is $30 per credit. It is recommended that students in Economics and Administrative Science, Science and Technology, and Distance Education have personal computers.

Graduates: In 2001, 56 bachelor's degrees were awarded. The most popular majors were criminal justice (11%), marketing (9%), and accounting (8%). 50 companies recruited on campus in 2000-2001.

Admissions Contact: Nilda Martinez, Director of Admissions. A video is available. E-mail: *nmartinez@inter.edu* Web: *metro.inter.edu*

INTER-AMERICAN UNIVERSITY OF PUERTO RICO/PONCE REGIONAL COLLEGE C-2

Ponce, PR 00715-2201 **(787) 840-9090; Fax: (787) 841-0103**

Full-time: 3000 men and women
Part-time: none
Graduate: n/av
Year: semesters, summer session
Application Deadline: see profile
Freshman Class: n/av
SAT I or ACT: required
Faculty: n/av
Ph.D.s: n/av
Student/Faculty: n/av
Tuition: $3700
Room & Board: n/app

Inter-American University of Puerto Rico/Ponce Regional College, founded in 1912 and a unit of the Inter-American University of Puerto Rico, is a private, nonsectarian institution offering undergraduate and graduate programs in business, liberal and fine arts, health sciences, and teacher preparation. Figures given in the above capsule are approximate. In addition to regional accreditation, Inter-American at Ponce has baccalaureate program accreditation with CSWE. Computerized library services include the card catalog. Special learning facilities include an audiovisual center, an instructional development center, and a publication center. The campus is in an urban area in a medium-size city.

Programs of Study: Bachelor's degrees are awarded in BIOLOGICAL SCIENCE (biology/biological science), BUSINESS (accounting, banking and finance, business administration and management, insurance, management information systems, marketing/retailing/merchandising, and secretarial studies/office management), COMMUNICATIONS AND THE ARTS (applied music, Spanish, and visual and performing arts), COMPUTER AND PHYSICAL SCIENCE (chemical technology, chemistry, computer science, and mathematics), EDUCATION (early childhood, elementary, music, secondary, and special), ENGINEERING AND ENVIRONMENTAL DESIGN (electrical/electronics engineering technology),

HEALTH PROFESSIONS (medical technology and nursing), SOCIAL SCIENCE (criminal justice, history, political science/government, psychology, public administration, social work, and sociology).
Required: Check with the school for current information.
Requirements: Check with the school for current information.
Procedure: Check with the school for current application deadlines and fee.
Financial Aid: The FAFSA and the college's own financial statement are required. Check with the school for current deadlines.
International Students: A personal interview is required, as are satisfactory scores on an appropriate comprehensive exam.
Computers: There are no time limits and no fees.
Admissions Contact: Director of Admissions.

INTER-AMERICAN UNIVERSITY OF PUERTO RICO/SAN GERMAN B-2

San German, PR 00683-9801 **(787) 892-3090**
(800) 981-8075; Fax: (787) 892-6350

Full-time: 3805 men and women
Part-time: 751 men and women
Graduate: 859 men and women
Year: semesters, summer session
Application Deadline: May 15
Freshman Class: 1084 applied, 994 accepted, 728 enrolled
SAT I Verbal/Math: 455/468
Faculty: 116
Ph.D.s: 42%
Student/Faculty: 32 to 1
Tuition: $3990
Room & Board: $2400

Inter-American University of Puerto Rico/San German, founded in 1912, is a private institution that is part of the Inter-American University of Puerto Rico system. It offers programs in fine and liberal arts, business, health science, and teacher preparation. In addition to regional accreditation, the university has baccalaureate program accreditation with CAHEA. The library contains 150,034 volumes, 547,827 microform items, and 30,643 audiovisual forms/CDs, and subscribes to 3536 periodicals. Computerized library services include interlibrary loans. Special learning facilities include a learning resource center, art gallery, and natural history museum. The 260-acre campus is in a rural area 14 miles from Mayaguez. Including residence halls, there are 64 buildings.
Student Life: 99% of undergraduates are from Puerto Rico. Others are from 9 foreign countries and Canada. 82% are from public schools. 99% are Hispanic. The average age of freshmen is 18; all undergraduates, 22. 28% do not continue beyond their first year; 41% remain to graduate.
Housing: 512 students can be accommodated in college housing, which includes single-sex dormitories, on-campus apartments, and married-student housing. On-campus housing is guaranteed for all 4 years and is available on a first-come, first-served basis. 89% of students commute. Alcohol is not permitted. All students may keep cars.
Activities: There are no fraternities or sororities. There are 50 groups on campus, including art, band, choir, chorale, computers, dance, drama, ethnic, honors, international, jazz band, marching band, musical theater, newspaper, orchestra, political, professional, religious, social, social service, and student government. Popular campus events include Feria Tipica, Founders Celebration Dances, and intercollegiate sport events.
Sports: There are 11 intercollegiate sports for men and 6 for women, and 11 intramural sports for men and 6 for women. Facilities include a gym, dirt and tartan tracks, tennis courts, a jogging course, table tennis, a billiards room, table games, aerobics areas, a small gym in residence halls, and a gym with a basketball court.
Disabled Students: 80% of the campus is accessible. Wheelchair ramps, special parking, specially equipped rest rooms, special class scheduling, lowered drinking fountains, lowered telephones, and elevators in some buildings are available.
Services: Counseling and information services are available, as is tutoring in some subjects, including Spanish, English, math, and computer science.
Campus Safety and Security: Measures include 24-hour foot and vehicle patrol, shuttle buses, pamphlets/posters/films, and emergency telephones. There is an electronic security system.
Programs of Study: The university confers B.A., B.S., and B.B.A. degrees. Associate, master's, and doctoral degrees are also awarded. Bachelor's degrees are awarded in BIOLOGICAL SCIENCE (biology/biological science), BUSINESS (accounting, banking and finance, business administration and management, marketing/retailing/merchandising, and secretarial studies/office management), COMMUNICATIONS AND THE ARTS (English, fine arts, music, and Spanish), COMPUTER AND PHYSICAL SCIENCE (chemistry, computer science, and mathematics), EDUCATION (art, early childhood, elementary, health, music, science, secondary, special, and teaching English as a second/foreign language (TESOL/TEFOL)), HEALTH PROFESSIONS (medical laboratory technology, nursing, and premedicine), SOCIAL SCIENCE (economics, history, political science/government, psychology, public administration, and sociology). Business administration and medical technology are the strongest academically. Computer science, business administration, and biology are the largest.
Required: To graduate, students must complete at least 124 credits, with a minimum GPA of 2.25. General education requirements include courses in Spanish, English, mathematical reasoning, logical and critical reasoning, computer programming, and Puerto Rican history. In addition, students must take 6 credits in methods of interpreting reality, 2 in phys ed, computer science, and community service, and 1 each in art, music, ethics, and Puerto Rican culture.
Special: The university offers internships, credit by exam, and nondegree study. A 3-2 engineering degree is available with Penn State University. There are 2 national honor societies and a freshman honors program.
Faculty/Classroom: 45% of faculty are male; 55%, female. 86% teach undergraduates. The average class size in an introductory lecture is 25; in a laboratory, 10; and in a regular course, 25.
Admissions: 92% of the 2001-2002 applicants were accepted. The SAT I scores for the 2001-2002 freshman class were: Verbal--68% below 500, 27% between 500 and 599, and 4% between 600 and 700; Math--63% below 500, 28% between 500 and 599, 8% between 600 and 700, and 1% above 700.
Requirements: The SAT I or the CEEB Spanish equivalent, is required. Applicants must be high school graduates and have completed 15 credits, including 3 each in Spanish, English, and electives, and 2 each in math and science. Applications are accepted on-line. A GPA of 2.0 is required. AP and CLEP credits are accepted. Important factors in the admissions decision are advanced placement or honor courses, evidence of special talent, and recommendations by school officials.
Procedure: Freshmen are admitted to all sessions. Entrance exams should be taken in the first or second semester of the senior year. There is an early admissions plan. Applications should be filed by May 15 for fall entry, November 15 for spring entry, and April 15 for summer entry. Notification of early decision is sent February 28; regular decision, May 30.
Transfer: 129 transfer students enrolled in 2001-2002. Applicants should have at least 15 college credits with a minimum GPA of 2.5. The SAT I, or the CEEB Spanish version, is required, as is a letter of recommendation from the dean of students at the student's previous college. 30 credits of 124 must be completed at the university.
Visiting: There are regularly scheduled orientations for prospective students, during the summer. There are guides for informal visits and visitors may sit in on classes and stay overnight. To schedule a visit, contact Professor Janet Rivera in Communications or Celia Gonzalez in Recruitment, Promotion and Marketing at (787) 264-1912, exts. 7205, 7326 or *cgonzalez@sg.inter.edu*
Financial Aid: In 2001-2002, 80% of all students received some form of financial aid including need-based aid. Work contracts averaged $400 ($2000 maximum). The university is a member of CSS. The FAFSA, the college's own financial statement, and the application for Federal Student Aid (Pell Grant) are required. The fall application deadline is April 30.
International Students: There are 78 international students enrolled. Students must take English or Spanish SAT I.
Computers: The mainframes are an IBM 9735 and a VAX 4000. There are also 500 networked PCs on campus for student use. All students may access the system designated hours. There are no time limits. The fee is $30.
Graduates: In 2001, 505 bachelor's degrees were awarded. The most popular majors were business administration (35%), education (22%), and biology (20%). 107 companies recruited on campus in 2000-2001.
Admissions Contact: Mildred Camacho, Director of Admissions. A video is available. E-mail: *milcama@sg.inter.edu*
Web: *www.sg.inter.edu*

PONTIFICAL CATHOLIC UNIVERSITY OF PUERTO RICO/PONCE C-2

Ponce, PR 00717-0777 **(787) 841-2000, ext. 1000**
(800) 981-5040; Fax: (787) 651-2044

Full-time: 2287 men, 4379 women
Part-time: 530 men, 878 women
Graduate: 687 men, 1151 women
Year: semesters, summer session
Application Deadline: July 15
Freshman Class: 1968 applied, 1605 accepted, 1167 enrolled
SAT I Verbal/Math: 510/499
Faculty: 360
Ph.D.s: n/av
Student/Faculty: 19 to 1
Tuition: $4236
Room & Board: $2840

Pontifical Catholic University of Puerto Rico, founded in 1948, is a private institution affiliated with the Roman Catholic Church of Puerto Rico. The school offers undergraduate and graduate programs in liberal arts, the sciences, education, and business. There are 4 undergraduate and 6 graduate schools. In addition to regional accreditation, La Catolica has baccalaureate program accreditation with CAHEA, CSWE, and NLN. The 2 libraries contain 236,691 volumes, 500,336 microform items, and 12,321 audiovisual forms/CDs, and subscribe to 54,482 periodicals. Computerized library services include the card catalog, interlibrary loans, and database searching. Special learning facilities include a learning resource center, radio station, TV station, and an electronic information center. The 55-acre campus is in an urban area 35 miles south of San Juan. Including residence halls, there are 40 buildings.

Student Life: All undergraduates are from Puerto Rico. Others are from 4 foreign countries. 80% are from public schools. All are Hispanic. The average age of freshmen is 19; all undergraduates, 22.

Housing: 180 students can be accommodated in college housing, which includes single-sex dormitories. Priority for on-campus housing is given to out-of-town students. 97% of students commute. Alcohol is not permitted. All students may keep cars.

Activities: 1% of men belong to 11 local fraternities; 1% of women belong to 7 local sororities. There are 50 groups on campus, including art, band, choir, chorale, computers, dance, drama, honors, literary magazine, newspaper, photography, professional, radio and TV, religious, social service, student government, and yearbook. Popular campus events include freshman activities at the beginning of the academic year; religious and social activities celebrated on Thanksgiving, Christmas, and Holy Week; and Puerto Rican Culture Week.

Sports: There are 7 intercollegiate sports for men and 5 for women, and 6 intramural sports for men and 4 for women. Facilities include a gym, a 6000-seat arena, an Olympic-size pool, 5 tennis courts, 1 baseball field, 3 basketball courts, 3 volleyball courts, and a synthetic track and field.

Disabled Students: 95% of the campus is accessible. Wheelchair ramps, elevators, special parking, specially equipped rest rooms, special class scheduling, lowered drinking fountains, lowered telephones, and In addition, there is a specialized equipment room containing a braille typewriter, an English and Spanish book reader for the blind, and a text enlarger are available.

Services: Counseling and information services are available, as is tutoring in some subjects, including math, chemistry, physics, English, Spanish, philosophy, statistics, accounting, and political science. There is a reader service for the blind, and remedial math, reading, and writing.

Campus Safety and Security: Measures include 24-hour foot and vehicle patrol, informal discussions, pamphlets/posters/films, and emergency telephones. There are lighted pathways/sidewalks.

Programs of Study: La Catolica confers B.A., B.S., B.B.A., and B.S.Ed. degrees. Associate, master's, and doctoral degrees are also awarded. Bachelor's degrees are awarded in BIOLOGICAL SCIENCE (biology/biological science), BUSINESS (accounting, banking and finance, business administration and management, business economics, international economics, and marketing/retailing/merchandising), COMMUNICATIONS AND THE ARTS (communications, English, fine arts, public relations, and Spanish), COMPUTER AND PHYSICAL SCIENCE (chemistry, computer programming, mathematics, and physics), EDUCATION (art, business, elementary, home economics, mathematics, music, physical, science, secondary, social studies, special, and teaching English as a second/foreign language (TESOL/TEFOL)), HEALTH PROFESSIONS (medical laboratory technology and nursing), SOCIAL SCIENCE (criminology, gerontology, history, liberal arts/general studies, philosophy, political science/government, psychology, public administration, religion, social science, social work, sociology, and theological studies). Physical sciences is the strongest academically. General studies is the largest.

Required: Bachelor's candidates must complete a 136-credit program in not more than twice the usual number of years and maintain a GPA of 2.0. Required courses include theology, philosophy, humanities, English, Spanish, math, science, phys ed, social/political science, music or art, and basic computer. A thesis is required of Institute of Graduate Studies candidates.

Special: The university offers co-op programs in medicine, engineering, veterinary, and pharmacy, as well as cross-registration with the University of Valladolid and a 3-2 engineering degree with Case Western Reserve University. A Washington semester, work-study programs within the university, nondegree study, pass/fail options in elective courses, and a student-designed major in liberal arts are also available. There are 8 national honor societies, a freshman honors program, and 3 departmental honors programs.

Faculty/Classroom: 99% teach undergraduates and 1% do research. The average class size in an introductory lecture is 35; in a laboratory, 32; and in a regular course, 35.

Admissions: 82% of the 2001-2002 applicants were accepted. The SAT I scores for the 2001-2002 freshman class were: Verbal--75% below 500, 19% between 500 and 599, and 6% between 600 and 700; Math--73% below 500, 19% between 500 and 599, 7% between 600 and 700, and 1% above 700.

Requirements: The SAT I is required. In addition, along with SAT II: Subject tests in math, Spanish, and English as a second language. In addition, applicants must be high school graduates or hold a GED. Students from 3-year senior high schools should have earned 10 units consisting of 3 each of English and Spanish, 2 of math, and 1 each of science and history. Students from 4-year high schools should have earned 15 units consisting of 4 each of English and Spanish, 3 of math, and 2 each of science and history. Students from outside Puerto Rico may substitute 2 years of another foreign language for the Spanish requirement. An interview is required for special programs. A GPA of 2.0 is required. AP and CLEP credits are accepted. Important factors in the admissions decision are advanced placement or honor courses, evidence of special talent, and leadership record.

Procedure: Freshmen are admitted to all sessions. Entrance exams should be taken during fall of the senior year. Applications should be filed by July 15 for fall entry, December 1 for spring entry, and April 15 for summer entry, along with a $15 fee. Notification is sent on a rolling basis.

Transfer: 277 transfer students enrolled in 2001-2002. Applicants must supply a college transcript. A GPA of 2.0 and 30 credit hours are required. An associate degree is recommended. 30 credits of 136 must be completed at La Catolica.

Visiting: There are guides for informal visits and visitors may sit in on classes. To schedule a visit, contact Irem Poventud at (787) 841-2000, ext. 1245.

Financial Aid: In 2001-2002, 85% of all freshmen and 83% of continuing students received some form of financial aid. 85% of freshmen and 80% of continuing students received need-based aid. The average freshman award was $1575. Of that total, scholarships or need-based grants averaged $325 ($1000 maximum); loans averaged $1700 ($3000 maximum); and work contracts averaged $1544 ($2083 maximum). 19% of undergraduates work part time. Average annual earnings from campus work are $1545. The average financial indebtedness of the 2001 graduate was $4000. The FAFSA, the college's own financial statement, and income certification documents are required. The fall application deadline is May 9.

International Students: There are 7 international students enrolled. The school actively recruits these students. They must take the SAT I or the ACT.

Computers: The mainframe is an IBM 9221-191. There are also 419 PCs available throughout the campus. All students may access the system 8 A.M. to 10 P.M. Monday through Thursday, and 8 A.M. to 5 P.M. Friday and Saturday. There are no time limits. The fee is included in the university fee.

Graduates: In 2001, 982 bachelor's degrees were awarded. The most popular majors were nursing (10%), management and accounting (9%), and liberal arts (8%). In an average class, 1% graduate in 3 years, 8% in 4 years, 18% in 5 years, and 18% in 6 years. 22 companies recruited on campus in 2000-2001.

Admissions Contact: Admissions Office. A video is available.
E-mail: *admisiones@pucpr.edu* Web: *www.pucpr.edu*

TURABO UNIVERSITY — D-1

Gurabo, PR 00658 — (787) 746-3009; Fax: (787) 743-7979

Full-time: 5400 men and women	**Faculty:** 100
Part-time: 1200 men and women	**Ph.D.s:** 33%
Graduate: 850 men and women	**Student/Faculty:** 30 to 1
Year: semesters, summer session	**Tuition:** $4110
Application Deadline: see profile	**Room & Board:** n/app
Freshman Class: n/av	
SAT I or ACT: required	

Turabo University, founded in 1972, is a private nonsectarian institution offering undergraduate programs in business administration, education, Spanish, social sciences, natural sciences and technology, and English and communications, and graduate programs in business administration and education. Figures given in above capsule are approximate. There are 2 graduate schools. The library contains 126,000 volumes. Computerized library services include the card catalog and database searching. Special learning facilities include a learning resource center and an archeological-folkloric museum and language lab. The 116-acre campus is in a suburban area 15 miles south of San Juan. There are 15 buildings.

Programs of Study: The university confers B.A., B.S., and B.B.A. degrees. Associate and master's degrees are also awarded. Bachelor's degrees are awarded in BIOLOGICAL SCIENCE (biology/biological science), BUSINESS (accounting, business administration and management, management science, marketing/retailing/merchandising, and secretarial studies/office management), COMMUNICATIONS AND THE ARTS (English and Spanish), COMPUTER AND PHYSICAL SCIENCE (chemistry, computer programming, mathematics, and natural sciences), EDUCATION (elementary, English, foreign languages, mathematics, physical, science, secondary, social science, and special), SOCIAL SCIENCE (criminology, economics, history, humanities, psychology, public administration, social science, and sociology).

Required: To graduate, students must complete course requirements with a minimum 2.0 GPA overall and 2.0 to 2.3 in the major.

Special: The university offers a general studies degree, graduate-level night courses in business and education, work-study, and nondegree study.

Faculty/Classroom: 50% of faculty are male; 50%, female.

Requirements: Check with the school for current information.

Procedure: Check with the school for current application deadlines and fee.
Financial Aid: The FAFSA is required. Check with the school for current deadlines.
Computers: The schools of science, business administration, and engineering operate computer labs. There are no time limits and no fees.
Admissions Contact: Admissions Office Director.

UNIVERSIDAD ADVENTISTA DE LAS ANTILLAS — A-1
Mayaguez, PR 00681-0118 — **(787) 834-9595, ext. 2261**
Fax: (787) 834-9597

Full-time: 254 men, 388 women	**Faculty:** 43
Part-time: 36 men, 41 women	**Ph.D.s:** 11%
Graduate: none	**Student/Faculty:** 15 to 1
Year: semesters, summer session	**Tuition:** $4000
Application Deadline: open	**Room & Board:** $2675
Freshman Class: 258 applied, 252 accepted, 174 enrolled	
SAT I or ACT: required	

Universidad Adventista de las Antillas, established in 1961 and affiliated with the Seventh-day Adventist Church, offers undergraduate programs in business administration, sciences and computers, education and psychology, nursing and allied health, music and fine arts, religion, and humanities. There are 7 undergraduate schools. In addition to regional accreditation, Universidad Adventista de las Antillas has baccalaureate program accreditation with AHIMA and NLN. The library contains 88,432 volumes, 2603 microform items, and 1717 audiovisual forms/CDs, and subscribes to 392 periodicals. Computerized library services include the card catalog, interlibrary loans, and database searching. Special learning facilities include a learning resource center. The 284-acre campus is in a small town on the west coast of Puerto Rico. Including residence halls, there are 6 buildings.
Student Life: 73% of undergraduates are from Puerto Rico. Others are from 14 states and 21 foreign countries. 37% are from public schools. 98% are Hispanic; 15% foreign nationals. 66% are Seventh-day Adventist; 16% Catholic; 11% Protestant. The average age of freshmen is 19; all undergraduates, 22. 30% do not continue beyond their first year; 70% remain to graduate.
Housing: 252 students can be accommodated in college housing, which includes single-sex dormitories, on-campus apartments, and married-student housing. On-campus housing is guaranteed for all 4 years. 76% of students commute. Alcohol is not permitted. All students may keep cars.
Activities: 75% of men belong to 1 local fraternity; 80% of women belong to 1 local sorority. There are 20 groups on campus, including band, choir, chorale, chorus, drama, film, international, literary magazine, newspaper, orchestra, photography, professional, religious, social, social service, student government, and yearbook. Popular campus events include International Fair, Columbus Day, and Discovering Puerto Rico.
Sports: There are 4 intercollegiate sports for men and 3 for women, and 4 intramural sports for men and 3 for women. Facilities include a gym, a swimming pool, and a tennis court.
Disabled Students: 90% of the campus is accessible. Wheelchair ramps, special parking, specially equipped rest rooms, lowered drinking fountains, and lowered telephones are available.
Services: Counseling and information services are available, as is tutoring in some subjects, including math, English, and Spanish. There is remedial math, reading, and writing.
Campus Safety and Security: Measures include 24-hour foot and vehicle patrol.
Programs of Study: Universidad Adventista de las Antillas confers B.A. and B.S. degrees. Associate degrees are also awarded. Bachelor's degrees are awarded in BIOLOGICAL SCIENCE (biology/biological science), BUSINESS (business administration and management, and office supervision and management), COMMUNICATIONS AND THE ARTS (music and Spanish), COMPUTER AND PHYSICAL SCIENCE (computer science), EDUCATION (elementary, music, and secondary), HEALTH PROFESSIONS (health science and nursing), SOCIAL SCIENCE (history, pastoral studies, religion, and theological studies). Business administration, nursing, and computer science are the strongest academically. Nursing is the largest.
Required: Students must complete 128 credits, with 44 to 64 in the major and a minimum GPA of 2.0. General education requirements include courses in religion, music or art, math, phys ed, computer science, Spanish, English, philosophy of education, and biological and physical sciences.
Special: Work-study programs, B.A.-B.S. degrees, credit by exam, and pass/fail options are available. There is a 3-2 engineering degree with Walla Walla University in Washington state.
Faculty/Classroom: 56% of faculty are male; 44%, female. All teach undergraduates. The average class size in an introductory lecture is 25; in a laboratory, 40; and in a regular course, 25.
Admissions: 98% of the 2001-2002 applicants were accepted.
Requirements: The SAT I or ACT is required, with a minimum recommended composite score on the SAT I of 840 or 18 on the ACT. In addition, graduation from an accredited secondary school is required; the GED is accepted. Applicants must submit 12 to 15 academic credits, including 3 each in English and a foreign language, 2 each in history, math, science, and social studies, and 1 to 2 in other electives. An interview is recommended. A GPA of 2.0 is required. AP and CLEP credits are accepted. Important factors in the admissions decision are advanced placement or honor courses, ability to finance college education, and parents or siblings attending the school.
Procedure: Freshmen are admitted to all sessions. Application deadlines are open.The application fee is $20. There is a rolling admissions plan.
Transfer: 44 transfer students enrolled in 2001-2002. Applicants must be in good standing at the previous institution, with a GPA of at least 2.0, and must submit official transcripts of high school and college credit. An official report of the CEEB Spanish equivalent of the SAT I must be provided if the applicant has completed fewer than 24 semester credits. 30 credits of 128 must be completed at Universidad Adventista de las Antillas.
Visiting: There are regularly scheduled orientations for prospective students. There are guides for informal visits and visitors may sit in on classes and stay overnight. To schedule a visit, contact Dr. Myrna Costa at (787) 834-9595, ext. 2210.
Financial Aid: In 2001-2002, 100% of all students received some form of financial aid. 90% of freshmen and 85% of continuing students received need-based aid. The average freshman award was $7820. 26% of undergraduates work part time. Average annual earnings from campus work are $1400. Universidad Adventista de las Antillas is a member of CSS. The CSS/Profile or FAFSA and the college's own financial statement are required. Check with the school for current financial aid deadlines.
International Students: There are 13 international students enrolled. They must take the college's own test and also take the SAT I, ACT, or the CEEB Spanish equivalent of the SAT I.
Computers: The mainframes are a DEC Vaxmate and DEC MicroVAX II. 62 PCs and an IBM 386 server are also available. Students may access the system 7:30 A.M. to 10 P.M. The fee is $50. It is strongly recommended that all students have a personal computer.
Graduates: In 2001, 116 bachelor's degrees were awarded. The most popular majors were nursing (60%), business administration (20%), and computer science (20%). In an average class, 30% graduate in 4 years and 60% in 5 years. Of the 2000 graduating class, 30% were enrolled in graduate school within 6 months of graduation and 50% were employed.
Admissions Contact: Evelyn del Valle, Director, Admissions and Continuing Education. A video is available. E-mail: *edelvalle@uaa.edu or admissions@uaa.edu* Web: *www.uaa.edu*

UNIVERSIDAD METROPOLITANA — D-1
Rio Piedras, PR 00928 — **(787) 765-6262**
Fax: (787) 766-1717, ext. 6429

Full-time: 3500 men and women	**Faculty:** n/av
Part-time: 1000 men and women	**Ph.D.s:** n/av
Graduate: none	**Student/Faculty:** 45 to 1
Year: semesters, summer session	**Tuition:** $3324
Application Deadline: open	**Room & Board:** n/app
Freshman Class: n/av	
SAT I: required	

Universidad Metropolitana, founded in 1980, is a private, commuter institution offering undergraduate programs in the liberal arts and sciences, business, nursing, and education. Figures given in above capsule are approximate. There are 6 undergraduate schools. In addition to regional accreditation, UMET has baccalaureate program accreditation with NLN. The library contains 34,445 volumes and 5000 microform items. Special learning facilities include a learning resource center and TV station. The campus is in an urban area. There are 11 buildings.
Programs of Study: UMET confers B.A., B.S., B.B.A., and B.S.N. degrees. Associate and master's degrees are also awarded. Bachelor's degrees are awarded in BUSINESS (accounting, business administration and management, and management science), COMPUTER AND PHYSICAL SCIENCE (natural sciences), EDUCATION (elementary and secondary), ENGINEERING AND ENVIRONMENTAL DESIGN (surveying engineering), HEALTH PROFESSIONS (nursing), SOCIAL SCIENCE (humanities, psychology, social science, and sociology). Business is the strongest academically. Education and natural sciences are the largest.
Required: To graduate, students must complete an average of 135 credits, including at least 30 in the major field. Specific GPA requirements vary by department. All students must take a computer course and complete a general education core.
Special: UMET offers work-study programs, B.A.-B.S. degrees, and an honors program in the natural sciences. The Televised Education Center (CET) offers students an opportunity for independent study.
Faculty/Classroom: 40% of faculty are male; 60%, female.

Requirements: The SAT I is required. In addition, applicants must be graduates of an accredited secondary school with a GPA of 2.0. Some programs have higher GPA requirements.
Procedure: Freshmen are admitted to all sessions. Application deadlines are open.
Transfer: All applicants must meet the GPA requirements of the program they wish to enter. Students should submit transcripts from all previous colleges attended as well as a letter of recommendation from the dean of the most recent institution. Grades of C or better transfer for credit.
Financial Aid: The college's own financial statement is required. Check with the school for current deadlines.
Admissions Contact: Office of Admissions.

UNIVERSIDAD POLITECNICA DE PUERTO RICO D-1
Hato Rey, PR 00918 **(787) 754-8000, ext. 240**

Full-time: 1975 men, 612 women
Part-time: 1835 men, 473 women
Graduate: 299 men, 214 women
Year: trimesters, summer session
Application Deadline: July 30
Freshman Class: n/av
SAT I or ACT: see profile
Faculty: 132
Ph.D.s: 15%
Student/Faculty: 20 to 1
Tuition: $4695
Room & Board: n/app

Universidad Politecnica de Puerto Rico is a private institution offering undergraduate programs in engineering, business administration, and architecture, and graduate programs in engineering management, civil engineering, manufacturing business administration, and environmental protection. There are 3 undergraduate schools and 1 graduate school. In addition to regional accreditation, La Poli has baccalaureate program accreditation with ABET. The library contains 75,000 volumes, 800 microform items, and 8700 audiovisual forms/CDs, and subscribes to 2000 periodicals. Computerized library services include the card catalog and database searching. Special learning facilities include a learning resource center and TV studio. The 8-acre campus is in an urban area in the Hato Rey section of San Juan. There are 8 buildings.
Student Life: 99% of undergraduates are from Puerto Rico. Others are from 4 foreign countries. 70% are from public schools. All are Hispanic. Most are Catholic. The average age of freshmen is 18; all undergraduates, 23. 30% do not continue beyond their first year; 20% remain to graduate.
Housing: There are no residence halls. Alcohol is not permitted. All students may keep cars.
Activities: There are no fraternities or sororities. There are 8 groups on campus, including choir, honors, newspaper, political, professional, religious, and student government. Popular campus events include Student Night, Library Week, and Education Weeks.
Sports: There are 8 intercollegiate sports for men and 8 for women, and 10 intramural sports for men and 10 for women. Facilities include basketball and volleyball courts, a game room, and a gym.
Disabled Students: 90% of the campus is accessible. Wheelchair ramps, elevators, special parking, specially equipped rest rooms, and special class scheduling are available.
Services: Counseling and information services are available, as is tutoring in some subjects, including Spanish, English, and math. There is remedial math.
Campus Safety and Security: Measures include 24-hour foot and vehicle patrol, informal discussions, pamphlets/posters/films, and lighted pathways/sidewalks.
Programs of Study: La Poli confers B.B.A. and B.S.E. degrees. Master's degrees are also awarded. Bachelor's degrees are awarded in BUSINESS (business administration and management), ENGINEERING AND ENVIRONMENTAL DESIGN (chemical engineering, civil engineering, electrical/electronics engineering, environmental engineering, industrial administration/management, industrial engineering, mechanical engineering, and surveying engineering). Electrical and civil engineering are the strongest programs academically and have the largest enrollments.
Required: All graduating students must complete 128 to 176 quarter credits, with a minimum GPA of 2.0. There are distribution requirements in Spanish, English, humanities, social sciences, and math, and within the chosen field. All students must take 6 credits in computer science. All majors require a practicum course before graduation.
Special: Co-op programs are available in all majors. There is a freshman honors program.
Faculty/Classroom: 72% of faculty are male; 28%, female. 96% teach undergraduates. The average class size in an introductory lecture is 30; in a laboratory, 20; and in a regular course, 22.
Requirements: In addition, the CEEB Spanish equivalents of the SAT I and SAT II: Subject tests are required. Applicants must be graduates of an accredited secondary school, with 15 high school academic units. An interview is recommended. A GPA of 2.5 is required.
Procedure: Freshmen are admitted to all sessions. There are early decision and early admissions plans. Applications should be filed by July 30 for fall entry, October 13 for winter entry, February 26 for spring entry, and April 30 for summer entry. The fall 2001 application fee was $30. Notification is sent on a rolling basis. 400 early decision candidates were accepted in a recent year.
Transfer: Applicants must present an official transcript and letters of recommendation. They must also have a GPA of 2.0 or higher and approved credits.
Visiting: There are regularly scheduled orientations for prospective students. To schedule a visit, contact Teresa Cardona, Director of Admissions..
Financial Aid: In a recent year, 89% of all freshmen and 70% of continuing students received some form of financial aid, including need-based aid. The average freshman award was $1420. Of that total, scholarships or need-based grants averaged $3125 ($5730 maximum); loans averaged $2625 ($5000 maximum); work contracts averaged $2781 ($3780 maximum); and institutional grants averaged $520 ($1020 maximum). 6% of undergraduates work part time. Average annual earnings from campus work are $2625. La Poli is a member of CSS. The FAFSA and the college's own financial statement are required. The fall application deadline is April 30.
International Students: These students must take the College Entrance Examination (CEEB), scoring 1300.
Computers: PCs are available for student use. All students may access the system. There are no time limits. The fee is $35.
Graduates: In a recent class, 415 bachelor's degrees were awarded.
Admissions Contact: Teresa Cardona, Director of Admissions.
E-mail: *tcardona@pupr.edu* Web: *www.pupr.edu*

UNIVERSITY OF PUERTO RICO SYSTEM

The University of Puerto Rico, established in 1903, is the public system of higher education in Puerto Rico. The UPR system has 8 4-year colleges, 2 comprehensive research campuses, and the Medical Sciences campus. The research campuses are in Rio Piedras, the oldest campus in San Juan, and in Mayaguez campus, which is mostly characterized by the engineering school, located on the west coast of Puerto Rico. Other colleges are in Bayamon, Humacao, Cayey, Aguadilla, Carolina, Ponce, Utuado, and Arecibo towns. The board of trustees and a president (the chief administrator) oversees the academic, research, and service endeavors of the university. The mission of the University of Puerto Rico is to provide a higher education system of excellence by offering a wide variety of academic programs and unique opportunities for professional development and by using its location as a focal point of the Caribbean region to develop education, research, and service programs relevant to the residents of the region and the international community. The student body at UPR is about 69,000 with 4500 faculty members. There are about 446 academic programs in Humanities and Social and Natural Sciences with 77 associates, 234 baccalaureate, 114 master's, and 21 doctoral programs. In a typical year, UPR grants more than 1000 baccalaureate degrees, 120 master's degrees, and 75 certifications and doctoral and professional degrees.

UNIVERSITY OF PUERTO RICO AT HUMACAO D-2
(Formerly University of Puerto Rico/Humacao University College)
Humacao, PR 00791-4300 **(809) 850-0000, ext. 9301**

Full-time: 1033 men, 2480 women
Part-time: 240 men, 723 women
Graduate: none
Year: semesters, summer session
Application Deadline: November 14
Freshman Class: 1491 applied, 966 accepted, 922 enrolled
SAT I Verbal/Math: 543/543
Faculty: 253; IIB, --$
Ph.D.s: 34%
Student/Faculty: 14 to 1
Tuition: $1245
Room & Board: n/app

The University of Puerto Rico at Humacao, formerly University of Puerto Rico/Humacao University College, founded in 1962, is a public institution offering undergraduate programs in the arts and sciences, business, education, and nursing to an entirely commuter student body. Annual tuition and fees for nonresident U.S. citizens are an amount equal to the nonresident rate at a state university in their home state. In addition to regional accreditation, the college has baccalaureate program accreditation with APTA, CSWE, NLN, and ACOTE. The library contains 109,656 volumes, 10,221 microform items, and 379 audiovisual forms/CDs, and subscribes to 2526 periodicals. Computerized library services include the card catalog, interlibrary loans, and database searching. Special learning facilities include a learning resource center, a museum, an observatory, and a census data center. The 62-acre campus is in a suburban area 30 miles southeast of San Juan. There are 32 buildings.
Student Life: All of the undergraduate students are from Puerto Rico. Others are from 4 states. 81% are from public schools. All are Hispanic. 14% do not continue beyond their first year; 86% remain to graduate.
Housing: There are no residence halls. All students commute. Alcohol is not permitted. Upperclassmen may keep cars.

Activities: There is 1 local fraternity. There are no sororities. There are 18 groups on campus, including cheerleading, chess, chorus, computers, dance, honors, literary magazine, pep band, photography, professional, religious, social, social service, student government, and radio web. Popular campus events include Shakespeare Festival, Women's Week, and Puerto Rican Culture Week.
Sports: There are 7 intercollegiate sports for men and 7 for women, and 3 intramural sports for men and 3 for women. Facilities include a 1000-seat gym, a track, 2 tennis courts, a softball field, a swimming pool, wrestling mats, and a student center.
Disabled Students: 98% of the campus is accessible. Wheelchair ramps, elevators, special parking, specially equipped rest rooms, lowered drinking fountains, and lowered telephones are available.
Services: Counseling and information services are available, as is tutoring in some subjects, including English, Spanish, and math. There is a reader service for the blind, and remedial math, reading, and writing.
Campus Safety and Security: Measures include 24-hour foot and vehicle patrol, pamphlets/posters/films, and lighted pathways/sidewalks.
Programs of Study: The college confers B.A., B.S., and B.B.A. degrees. Associate degrees are also awarded. Bachelor's degrees are awarded in BIOLOGICAL SCIENCE (biology/biological science, marine biology, and microbiology), BUSINESS (accounting, business administration and management, management science, personnel management, and secretarial studies/office management), COMMUNICATIONS AND THE ARTS (English), COMPUTER AND PHYSICAL SCIENCE (chemistry, mathematics, and physics), EDUCATION (elementary), HEALTH PROFESSIONS (nursing), SOCIAL SCIENCE (social work). Natural sciences is the strongest academically. Business administration is the largest.
Required: To graduate, students must complete 127 to 136 credit hours, including 18 to 56 in a major field, with a minimum GPA of 2.0. General education requirements include 33 to 73 liberal arts credits, with 6 credits in Spanish and 6 in English, humanities, and social sciences. Other distribution requirements vary by program.
Special: Students may study abroad through the National Student Exchange program. There are also co-op programs, internships in accounting and management, work-study programs, credit for work experience, and a pass/fail option in remedial courses. Nondegree study is available through the Division of Continuing Education. The college offers programs in coastal marine biology, industrial microbiology, and industrial chemistry, and sponsors a Puerto Rican plain pigeon conservation project. There is 1 national honor society and a freshman honors program.
Faculty/Classroom: 43% of faculty are male; 57%, female. 87% teach undergraduates and 3% do research. The average class size in a laboratory is 18 and in a regular course, 21.
Admissions: 65% of the 2001-2002 applicants were accepted. The CEEB scores for the 2001-2002 freshman class were: Verbal--29% below 501, 51% between 501 and 600, 19% between 601 and 700, and 1% above 700; Math--32% below 501, 42% between 501 and 600, 21% between 600 and 700, and 4% above 700.
Requirements: The SAT I is required for U.S. applicants, or the CEEB's Spanish equivalent, as well as SAT II: Subject tests in writing, Spanish, and mathematics level I. Applicants must be graduates of an accredited secondary school or have earned the GED. College preparatory study should include 3 credits each in English, Spanish, and math, 2 in history, and 1 in social studies. A GPA of 2.0 is required. All courses are conducted in Spanish only. Nonnative speakers of Spanish are required to demonstrate fluency through institutional examination interviews. A GPA of 2.0 is required. AP credits are accepted.
Procedure: Freshmen are admitted in the fall. Entrance exams should be taken by October or February of the senior year. There is a deferred admissions plan. Applications should be filed by November 14 for fall entry, along with a $15 fee. Notification is sent April.
Transfer: 27 transfer students enrolled in 2001-2002. Applicants to the bachelor's programs must have at least 30 college credits with a minimum GPA of 3.0 and must be in good standing at their previous institution. The last 30 credits of 136 must be completed at the university. Not more than 50% of the course work completed at other institutions toward the major will be accepted.
Visiting: To schedule a visit, contact the Student Affairs Office at (809) 850-0000, ext. 9328.
Financial Aid: In 2001-2002, 86% of all freshmen and 73% of continuing students received some form of financial aid. 86% of freshmen and 73% of continuing students received need-based aid. The average freshman award was $3000. Of that total, scholarships or need-based grants averaged $4077 ($5500 maximum); loans averaged $2600 ($2625 maximum); and campus-based programs averaged $500 (maximum). 7% of undergraduates work part time. Average annual earnings from campus work are $1165. The FAFSA is required. The fall application deadline is June 30; July 31 for fresmen.
International Students: The student must take the CEEB's Spanish version of the SAT I. These consist of an aptitude test (verbal and math) and Achievement Test Battery (Spanish, English, and math). In lieu of the above, applicants may take SAT I and SAT II (English Composition, Spanish Reading).
Computers: The mainframe is a DEC ALPHA 4100. There are 206 PCs in 6 campus labs. All students may access the system daily until 10 P.M. There are no time limits and no fees.
Graduates: In 2001, 544 bachelor's degrees were awarded. The most popular majors were accounting (12%), elementary education (10%), and social work (8%). 4 companies recruited on campus in 2000-2001.
Admissions Contact: Inara Ferrer, Director of Admissions.
E-mail: *i_ferrer@cuhac.upr.clu.edu*

UNIVERSITY OF PUERTO RICO/ARECIBO B-1

Arecibo, PR 00613 (787) 878-2830, ext. 4101; Fax: (787) 880-4972

Full-time: 1164 men, 2718 women	**Faculty:** 227
Part-time: 252 men, 533 women	**Ph.D.s:** 13%
Graduate: none	**Student/Faculty:** 17 to 1
Year: semesters, summer session	**Tuition:** $1095
Application Deadline: see profile	**Room & Board:** n/app
Freshman Class: 4121 applied, 1261 accepted, 998 enrolled	
SAT I: required	

University of Puerto Rico/Arecibo (formerly Arecibo Technological University College), founded in 1967, offers undergraduate programs in business administration, health sciences, natural sciences, education, computer sciences, telecommunications, and others. Tuition and fees for Puerto Rican residents total $1095 per year; nonresidents pay an amount equal to the nonresident rate at a state university in their home state. In addition to regional accreditation, UPRA has baccalaureate program accreditation with NLN. The library contains 71,000 volumes, 6400 microform items, and 1900 audiovisual forms/CDs, and subscribes to 1500 periodicals. Computerized library services include database searching. Special learning facilities include a learning resource center and art gallery. The 49-acre campus is in an urban area 40 miles west of San Juan. There is 1 building.
Student Life: 90% are from public schools. All are Hispanic. The average age of freshmen is 18; all undergraduates, 18.5. 18% do not continue beyond their first year.
Housing: There are no residence halls. All students commute. Alcohol is not permitted. All students may keep cars.
Activities: 10% of men belong to 5 local fraternities; 12% of women belong to 5 local sororities. There are 24 groups on campus, including art, band, chorus, dance, drama, film, newspaper, photography, political, professional, religious, social, social service, and student government. Popular campus events include plays, concerts, and dances.
Sports: There are 8 intercollegiate sports for men and 5 for women, and 9 intramural sports for men and 8 for women. Facilities include basketball and tennis courts, a gym, track and field facilities, and an activity room.
Disabled Students: 90% of the campus is accessible. Wheelchair ramps, elevators, special parking, specially equipped rest rooms, lowered drinking fountains, and lowered telephones are available.
Services: Counseling and information services are available, as is tutoring in most subjects. There is remedial math, reading, and writing.
Campus Safety and Security: Measures include 24-hour foot and vehicle patrol, pamphlets/posters/films, and lighted pathways/sidewalks.
Programs of Study: UPRA confers B.A. and B.S. degrees. Associate degrees are also awarded. Bachelor's degrees are awarded in BIOLOGICAL SCIENCE (microbiology), BUSINESS (business administration and management and secretarial studies/office management), COMMUNICATIONS AND THE ARTS (telecommunications), COMPUTER AND PHYSICAL SCIENCE (computer science), EDUCATION (elementary), ENGINEERING AND ENVIRONMENTAL DESIGN (chemical engineering technology), HEALTH PROFESSIONS (nursing). Natural sciences is the strongest academically. Business administration is the largest.
Required: To graduate, students must have a 2.0 GPA. The total number of credit hours required varies according to major. The core curriculum includes 2 semesters each of English, Spanish, math, and social sciences or humanities.
Special: There is a chapter of Phi Beta Kappa and a freshman honors program.
Faculty/Classroom: 48% of faculty are male; 52%, female. 99% teach undergraduates and 1% do research. The average class size in an introductory lecture is 28; in a laboratory, 18; and in a regular course, 25.
Admissions: 31% of the 2001-2002 applicants were accepted.
Requirements: The SAT I is required. In addition, a Spanish version of the SAT I or the College Entrance Examination Board test (CEEB) is accepted. A GPA of 2.0 is required. AP credits are accepted.
Procedure: Freshmen are admitted in the fall. Entrance exams should be taken by October of the senior year. There is an early decision plan. Check with the school for current application deadline. The fall 2001 application fee was $15.
Transfer: 36 transfer students enrolled in a recent year. Applicants should have a minimum of 24 credits with a 2.5 GPA.
Visiting: To schedule a visit, contact the Dean of Student Affairs.
Financial Aid: 85% of freshmen and 62% of continuing students received need-based aid. 8% of undergraduates work part time. Average

annual earnings from campus work are $1300. UPRA is a member of CSS. The college's own financial statement is required. Check with the school for current deadlines.

International Students: Students must take exams.

Computers: The mainframes are a DEC VAX 4000-300 (academic) and a DEC ALPHA 2100 (administrative). There are 15 computer labs with PCs. Word processors and specialized software are available. Students may access the local net and the Internet. All students may access the system. There are no time limits and no fees.

Graduates: In a recent year, 669 bachelor's degrees were awarded. The most popular majors were business administration (26%), nursing (13%), and elementary education (12%). In an average class, 6% graduate in 3 years, 18% in 4 years, 45% in 5 years, and 57% in 6 years. 37 companies recruited on campus in a recent year.

Admissions Contact: Delma Barrios, Admissions Director.
E-mail: *d_barrios@cuta.upr.clu.edu* Web: *upra.upr.clu.edu*

UNIVERSITY OF PUERTO RICO/BAYAMON UNIVERSITY COLLEGE CAMPUS — A-1

Bayamon, PR 00959-1919 (787) 786-2885, ext. 2426

Recognized candidate for accreditation

Full-time: 2000 men, 2559 women	**Faculty:** 215
Part-time: 585 men, 716 women	**Ph.D.s:** 21%
Graduate: none	**Student/Faculty:** 21 to 1
Year: semesters, summer session	**Tuition:** $1600
Application Deadline: December 20	**Room & Board:** n/app
Freshman Class: n/av	
SAT I or ACT: required	

Bayamon University College, a commuter institution founded in 1971, is part of the University of Puerto Rico system. It offers undergraduate business, education, and technical programs. Approximate tuition and fees for Puerto Rican residents total $1600 per year; nonresident U.S. citizens pay an amount equal to the nonresident rate at a state university in their home state. The library contains 68,893 volumes, 229,066 microform items, and 5103 audiovisual forms/CDs, and subscribes to 473 periodicals. Computerized library services include the card catalog and database searching. Special learning facilities include a learning resource center. The 78-acre campus is in a suburban area 9 miles west of San Juan. There are 20 buildings.

Student Life: All undergraduates are from Puerto Rico. 53% are from public schools. All are Hispanic. The average age of freshmen is 18; all undergraduates, 21. 24% do not continue beyond their first year; 75% remain to graduate.

Housing: There are no residence halls. All students commute. Alcohol is not permitted. All students may keep cars.

Activities: There are no fraternities or sororities. There are 15 groups on campus, including art, band, cheerleading, chess, choir, chorus, computers, drama, drill team, honors, professional, religious, social, social service, and student government. Popular campus events include an annual sports tournament, recognition of distinguished athletes, and the college anniversary.

Sports: There are 13 intercollegiate sports for men and 10 for women. Facilities include a basketball/volleyball court, a tennis court, a track and field site, an exercise gym, and a recreation room with table tennis, electronic games, and pool tables.

Disabled Students: 90% of the campus is accessible. Wheelchair ramps, special parking, specially equipped rest rooms, lowered drinking fountains, and lowered telephones are available.

Services: Counseling and information services are available, as is tutoring in some subjects, including English, math, Spanish, and physics for engineering and electronics students. There is a reader service for the blind and remedial math.

Campus Safety and Security: Measures include 24-hour foot and vehicle patrol and pamphlets/posters/films.

Programs of Study: UPR-Bayamon confers the B.A. degree. Associate degrees are also awarded. Bachelor's degrees are awarded in BUSINESS (accounting, banking and finance, business administration and management, management engineering, and marketing/retailing/merchandising), COMPUTER AND PHYSICAL SCIENCE (computer science and information sciences and systems), EDUCATION (early childhood and elementary), ENGINEERING AND ENVIRONMENTAL DESIGN (electrical/electronics engineering technology). Electronics, computer science, and office systems are the strongest academically. Business administration is the largest.

Required: General education requirements include courses in Spanish, English, math, social sciences or humanities, and biological or physical sciences. To graduate, students must complete 130 to 135 credits, including 29 to 34 in the major, with a minimum GPA of 2.0.

Special: Students may cross-register with any campus in the University of Puerto Rico system. Work-study programs, dual majors, pass/fail options, and a 3-2 engineering degree with the Mayaguez campus are also available. There is a freshman honors program.

Faculty/Classroom: 46% of faculty are male; 54%, female. All teach undergraduates. The average class size in an introductory lecture is 23 and in a laboratory, 20.

Requirements: The SAT I or ACT is required, or the CEEB's Spanish version of the SAT I along with SAT II: Subject tests in Spanish, writing, and math. Applicants must be graduates of accredited secondary schools. The GED is accepted. A GPA of 2.0 is required.

Procedure: Freshmen are admitted in the fall. Entrance exams should be taken by October of the senior year. There is an early decision plan. Applications should be filed by December 20 for fall entry and September 15 for spring entry. The fall 2001 application fee was $15. Notification of early decision is sent February 15; regular decision, May 1. 62 early decision candidates were accepted for the 2001-2002 class.

Transfer: 160 transfer students enrolled in a recent year. Applicants must present an associate degree or at least 30 college credits and a minimum GPA of 2.5. 28 credits of 130 must be completed at UPR-Bayamon.

Visiting: There are regularly scheduled orientations for prospective students. To schedule a visit, contact Director of Admissions.

Financial Aid: In 2001-2002, 29% of all freshmen and 71% of continuing students received some form of financial aid. 29% of freshmen and 71% of continuing students received need-based aid. The average freshman award was $3726. Of that total, scholarships or need-based grants averaged $3248 ($3750 maximum) and grants programs and supplemental aid programs averaged $478 ($500 maximum). UPR-Bayamon is a member of CSS. The CSS/Profile, the college's own financial statement, and income tax forms, medical receipts, and social security information are required. The fall application deadline is June 2.

International Students: There are 11 international students enrolled. Students must take the SAT I or the Spanish equivalent version of the SAT I. Students must take SAT II: Subject tests in Spanish, writing, and math.

Computers: There are 800 PCs located in computer centers. All students may access the system daily from 8 A.M. to 10 P.M. and Saturday from 8 A.M. to 4:30 P.M. There are no time limits and no fees.

Graduates: In 2001, 489 bachelor's degrees were awarded. The most popular majors were accounting (15%), management (13%), and office systems (13%). In an average class, 16% graduate in 4 years, 31% in 5 years, and 13% in 6 years. 27 companies recruited on campus in 2000-2001.

Admissions Contact: Abdiel Martinez, Director of Admissions.

UNIVERSITY OF PUERTO RICO/CAYEY UNIVERSITY COLLEGE — C-2

Cayey, PR 00736 (809) 738-2161, ext. 2208

Full-time: 1108 men, 2606 women	**Faculty:** 176
Part-time: 135 men, 240 women	**Ph.D.s:** 35%
Graduate: none	**Student/Faculty:** 21 to 1
Year: semesters, summer session	**Tuition:** $1245 ($2500)
Application Deadline: see profile	**Room & Board:** n/app
Freshman Class: 907 enrolled	
SAT I: required	

Cayey University College, founded in 1967, is a public liberal arts institution and part of the University of Puerto Rico. The library contains 107,365 volumes, 49 microform items, and 3965 audiovisual forms/CDs, and subscribes to 424 periodicals. Computerized library services include the card catalog, interlibrary loans, and database searching. Special learning facilities include a learning resource center and an art museum. The 167-acre campus is in an urban area 30 miles south of San Juan. There are 54 buildings.

Student Life: 85% are from public schools. All are Hispanic. The average age of freshmen is 18; all undergraduates, 22. 15% do not continue beyond their first year; 85% remain to graduate.

Housing: There are no residence halls. All students commute. Alcohol is not permitted. All students may keep cars.

Activities: There is 1 local fraternity. There are no sororities. There are 17 groups on campus, including band, cheerleading, chorus, drama, honors, marching band, orchestra, political, professional, religious, and student government. Popular campus events include Student Day.

Sports: There are 10 intercollegiate sports for men and 6 for women, and 9 intramural sports for men and 8 for women. Facilities include a gym, a pool, and tennis, basketball, and volleyball courts.

Disabled Students: All of the campus is accessible. Wheelchair ramps, elevators, special parking, specially equipped rest rooms, lowered drinking fountains, and lowered telephones are available.

Services: Counseling and information services are available, as is tutoring in most subjects. There is a reader service for the blind, and remedial math, reading, and writing.

Campus Safety and Security: Measures include 24-hour foot and vehicle patrol, shuttle buses, and lighted pathways/sidewalks.

Programs of Study: Cayey University College confers B.A., B.S., B.B.A., B.Ed., and B.S.Ed. degrees. Associate degrees are also awarded.

Bachelor's degrees are awarded in BIOLOGICAL SCIENCE (biology/biological science), BUSINESS (accounting, business administration and management, management science, and secretarial studies/office management), COMMUNICATIONS AND THE ARTS (English), COMPUTER AND PHYSICAL SCIENCE (chemistry, mathematics, and natural sciences), EDUCATION (elementary, secondary, and special), SOCIAL SCIENCE (economics, Hispanic American studies, history, humanities, and psychology). Natural science is the strongest academically. Natural science, secondary education, and biology are the largest.

Required: To graduate, students must complete 129 to 135 credits, including 28 in the major, with a minimum GPA of 2.0. There are requirements in humanities, social science, Spanish, English, and natural science. All students must take 2 courses in phys ed.

Special: The university offers cross-registration through the National Student Exchange, study abroad in Toledo, Spain, and a Washington semester. There is 1 national honor society, including Phi Beta Kappa, and a freshman honors program.

Faculty/Classroom: 58% of faculty are male; 42%, female. 99% teach undergraduates and 1% do research. The average class size in an introductory lecture is 30; in a laboratory, 20; and in a regular course, 30.

Admissions: 40% of the current freshmen were in the top fifth of their class; 63% were in the top two fifths.

Requirements: The SAT I or its CEEB Spanish equivalent is required. Applicants must be graduates of an accredited secondary school. The GED is accepted. Students should complete 3 high school courses each in English, Spanish, math, science, and social studies. A GPA of 2.0 is required. CLEP credit is accepted. Advanced placement or honor courses is an important factor in the admission decision.

Procedure: Freshmen are admitted in the fall. Entrance exams should be taken in October of the senior year. There is a deferred admissions plan. Check with the school for current application deadlines. The fall 2001 application fee was $15.

Transfer: 19 transfer students enrolled in 2001-2002. Applicants should have 48 approved credit hours toward the program they are entering. 24 credits of 129 to 135 must be completed at Cayey University College.

Visiting: Visitors may sit in on classes. To schedule a visit, contact Maria Montalvo at (809) 738-2161, ext. 2053.

Financial Aid: In 2001-2002, 86% of all freshmen and 78% of continuing students received some form of financial aid. 83% of freshmen and 78% of continuing students received need-based aid. The average freshman award was $5485. Of that total, scholarships or need-based grants averaged $400 ($4650 maximum); loans averaged $2625 ($5500 maximum); work contracts averaged $494; and SEOG, SSIGP, PRAES, PBECA, LEAP, and SLEAP averaged $600 ($900 maximum). 6% of undergraduates work part time. The CSS/Profile or FAFSA is required. The fall application deadline is May 29.

International Students: There are 7 international students enrolled. The school actively recruits these students. The student must take the SAT I, ACT, or the CEEB Spanish equivalent of the SAT I.

Computers: The mainframe is a Compaq AlphaServer DS10. There are 10 computer labs operating the various Windows programs. All students may access the system from 7 P.M. to 9 P.M. Monday through Thursday, and Friday from 7 A.M. to 4:30 P.M. There are no time limits and no fees.

Graduates: In 2001, 536 bachelor's degrees were awarded. The most popular majors were accounting (15%), education (14%), and biology (10%). In an average class, 1% graduate in 3 years, 5% in 4 years, 22% in 5 years, and 35% in 6 years.

Admissions Contact: Antonio Rosario, Admissions Office.
Web: *wwwcuc.upr.clu.edu*

UNIVERSITY OF PUERTO RICO/HUMACAO UNIVERSITY COLLEGE
(See University of Puerto Rico at Humacao)

UNIVERSITY OF PUERTO RICO/MAYAGUEZ A-1

Mayaguez, PR 00680 **(787) 265-3811; Fax: (787) 834-5265**

Full-time: 5259 men, 5190 women	**Faculty:** 626
Part-time: 390 men, 512 women	**Ph.D.s:** 52%
Graduate: 457 men, 436 women	**Student/Faculty:** 19 to 1
Year: 4-1-4, summer session	**Tuition:** $1245
Application Deadline: see profile	**Room & Board:** $4130
Freshman Class: 3624 applied, 2429 accepted, 2106 enrolled	
SAT I Verbal/Math: required	

The University of Puerto Rico/Mayaguez, founded in 1911, is a bilingual land-grant institution offering undergraduate programs in arts and sciences, business administration, agricultural sciences, and engineering. There are 4 undergraduate and 4 graduate schools. In addition to regional accreditation, the university has baccalaureate program accreditation with ABET and NLN. The library contains 783,905 volumes, 345,052 microform items, and 43,610 audiovisual forms/CDs, and subscribes to 2171 periodicals. Computerized library services include interlibrary loans and database searching. Special learning facilities include a learning resource center, art gallery, natural history museum, planetarium, sea grant program, and resource center for science and engineering. The 520-acre campus is in an urban area 70 miles west of San Juan. There are 56 buildings.

Student Life: 97% of undergraduates are from Puerto Rico. Others are from 33 foreign countries and Canada. 61% are from public schools. 99% are Hispanic. The average age of freshmen is 18; all undergraduates, 21. 10% do not continue beyond their first year; 66% remain to graduate.

Housing: There are no residence halls. Alcohol is not permitted. All students may keep cars.

Activities: 5% of men belong to 10 local fraternities and 1 national fraternity; 2% of women belong to 5 local sororities. There are 100 groups on campus, including band, cheerleading, chess, choir, chorale, chorus, computers, dance, drama, drill team, drum and bugle corps, ethnic, honors, international, jazz band, literary magazine, marching band, newspaper, orchestra, photography, political, professional, religious, social, social service, student government, and yearbook. Popular campus events include fairs, concerts, and dances.

Sports: There are 12 intercollegiate sports for men and 9 for women, and 15 intramural sports for men and 11 for women. Facilities include a gym, a coliseum, a swimming pool, and 2 playing fields.

Disabled Students: 90% of the campus is accessible. Wheelchair ramps, elevators, special parking, specially equipped rest rooms, lowered drinking fountains, and lowered telephones are available.

Services: Counseling and information services are available, as is tutoring in most subjects. There is a reader service for the blind and remedial math.

Campus Safety and Security: Measures include 24-hour foot and vehicle patrol, informal discussions, and lighted pathways/sidewalks.

Programs of Study: the university confers B.A., B.S., B.B.A., and B.S.A. degrees. Associate, master's, and doctoral degrees are also awarded. Bachelor's degrees are awarded in AGRICULTURE (animal science and horticulture), BIOLOGICAL SCIENCE (biochemistry, biology/biological science, biotechnology, and microbiology), BUSINESS (accounting, banking and finance, business administration and management, business economics, and marketing/retailing/merchandising), COMMUNICATIONS AND THE ARTS (English, fine arts, and French), COMPUTER AND PHYSICAL SCIENCE (chemistry, computer science, geology, information sciences and systems, mathematics, and physics), EDUCATION (foreign languages, and teaching English as a second/foreign language (TESOL/TEFOL)), ENGINEERING AND ENVIRONMENTAL DESIGN (chemical engineering, civil engineering, computer engineering, electrical/electronics engineering, engineering, industrial engineering, mechanical engineering, and surveying engineering), HEALTH PROFESSIONS (nursing and premedicine), SOCIAL SCIENCE (economics, history, philosophy, political science/government, psychology, social science, and sociology). Engineering, business administration, and agricultural science are the strongest academically. Electrical, chemical, and civil engineering are the largest.

Required: To graduate, students must complete 172 credit hours with a GPA of 2.0. Required disciplines include humanities, English, Spanish, physical science, biology, social science, math, and phys ed.

Special: The university offers co-op programs in engineering, business, and nursing, as well as some study abroad. There is 1 national honor society, and a freshman honors program.

Faculty/Classroom: 66% of faculty are male; 34%, female. 23% do research. The average class size in an introductory lecture is 30; in a laboratory, 20; and in a regular course, 30.

Admissions: 67% of the 2001-2002 applicants were accepted.

Requirements: The SAT I is required, or the CEEB's Spanish equivalent, along with SAT II: Subject tests in writing, Spanish and Spanish reading, and mathematics level I. Applicants must be high school graduates or hold the GED. The university requires applicants to be in the upper 25% of their class. A GPA of 2.95 is required. CLEP credit is accepted.

Procedure: Freshmen are admitted in the fall. Entrance exams should be taken during the first semester of the senior year. There is an early admissions plan. Check with the school for current application deadlines. The fall 2001 application fee was $15.

Transfer: Applicants must have 48 college credits with a GPA of 2.0.

Financial Aid: 69% of freshmen received need-based aid. The average freshman award was $4350. Of that total, scholarships or need-based grants averaged $3750 ($5150 maximum); loans averaged $2625 (maximum); and other sources averaged $500 ($900 maximum). The university is a member of CSS. The college's own financial statement is required. Check with the school for current deadlines.

Computers: The mainframes are a DEC VAX 8700, 6320, and 11/750 cluster. There are also 100 PCs available in labs and the computer center. All students may access the system 24 hours a day. There are no fees.

Admissions Contact: Norma Torres, Acting Director.
E-mail: *norma@rectoria.uprm.edu* Web: *www_rum.upr.clu.edu*

UNIVERSITY OF PUERTO RICO/RIO PIEDRAS D-1

San Juan, PR 00931-3344 (787) 764-0000, ext. 5666
Fax: (787) 764-3680, ext. 1375

Full-time: 4769 men, 9982 women	**Faculty:** n/av
Part-time: 1023 men, 2013 women	**Ph.D.s:** 49%
Graduate: 1263 men, 2511 women	**Student/Faculty:** n/av
Year: semesters, summer session	**Tuition:** $790 ($2470)
Application Deadline: February 15	**Room & Board:** $4720
Freshman Class: 15,157 applied, 3832 accepted, 3044 enrolled	
SAT I: required	**ACT:** n/av

The University of Puerto Rico/Rio Piedras, founded in 1903, is a public institution offering undergraduate programs in arts and sciences, business, and education. Nonresident U.S. citizens pay annual tuition and fees equal to what Puerto Rican students would pay at a public university in their home state. Students who do not provide evidence of medical insurance are charged an additional $529 annual fee. There are 8 undergraduate and 9 graduate schools. In addition to regional accreditation, UPR — Rio Piedras has baccalaureate program accreditation with ADA, CSWE, NAAB, and NCATE. The 10 libraries contain 1,804,010 volumes and 1,678,239 microform items, and subscribe to 5600 periodicals. Computerized library services include the card catalog. Special learning facilities include a learning resource center, art gallery, natural history museum, radio station, and audiovisual services, and television production facilities. The 271-acre campus is in an urban area in the Rio Piedras section of San Juan. Including residence halls, there are 133 buildings.

Student Life: 99% of undergraduates are from Puerto Rico. Others are from 28 foreign countries and Canada. 49% are from public schools. All are Hispanic. The average age of freshmen is 18. 8% do not continue beyond their first year.

Housing: 789 students can be accommodated in college housing, which includes coed dormitories. On-campus housing is available on a first-come, first-served basis and is available on a lottery system for upperclassmen. Priority is given to out-of-town students. Alcohol is not permitted. All students may keep cars.

Activities: There are no fraternities or sororities. There are 60 groups on campus, including art, band, chorus, drama, honors, international, literary magazine, newspaper, pep band, political, professional, radio and TV, religious, social, social service, and student government. Popular campus events include sports events and spring and Christmas concerts.

Sports: There are 12 intercollegiate sports for men and 8 for women, and 15 intramural sports for men and 10 for women. Facilities include a sports complex with a swimming pool, a gym, track and field areas, and tennis, basketball, and volleyball courts.

Disabled Students: 80% of the campus is accessible. Wheelchair ramps, elevators, special parking, specially equipped rest rooms, special class scheduling, lowered drinking fountains, and lowered telephones are available.

Services: There is a reader service for the blind, and remedial math, reading, and writing.

Campus Safety and Security: Measures include 24-hour foot and vehicle patrol, shuttle buses, pamphlets/posters/films, and emergency telephones. There are lighted pathways/sidewalks.

Programs of Study: UPR — Rio Piedras confers B.A., B.S., B.B.A., B.E.D., and B. in Secretarial Science degrees. Master's and doctoral degrees are also awarded. Bachelor's degrees are awarded in BIOLOGICAL SCIENCE (biology/biological science), BUSINESS (accounting, banking and finance, business administration and management, business economics, business statistics, labor studies, management information systems, marketing management, office supervision and management, and personnel management), COMMUNICATIONS AND THE ARTS (art history and appreciation, communications, comparative literature, dramatic arts, English, English as a second/foreign language, fine arts, French, modern language, music, and painting), COMPUTER AND PHYSICAL SCIENCE (chemistry, computer science, mathematics, physics, and science), EDUCATION (elementary, and secondary), ENGINEERING AND ENVIRONMENTAL DESIGN (environmental design, and environmental science), SOCIAL SCIENCE (anthropology, community psychology, economics, family/consumer studies, geography, Hispanic American studies, history, interdisciplinary studies, liberal arts/general studies, philosophy, political science/government, psychology, social science, social work, and sociology). Natural sciences is the strongest academically. Secondary education is the largest.

Required: To graduate, students must complete 117 to 147 credits, with a minimum GPA of 2.0. All students must take basic courses in biological sciences, physical sciences, social sciences, Spanish, humanities, and English. Spanish is the language of instruction in most courses, but students are required to have a working knowledge of English.

Special: The university offers a co-op program in accounting, internships at local government and private agencies, study abroad in 11 countries, a Washington semester, a general studies degree, and nondegree study. There is 1 national honor society.

Faculty/Classroom: 48% of faculty are male; 52%, female. No introductory courses are taught by graduate students. The average class size in an introductory lecture is 27; in a laboratory, 20; and in a regular course, 23. One faculty member was awarded a Nobel Prize.

Admissions: 25% of the 2001-2002 applicants were accepted. The SAT I scores for the 2001-2002 freshman class were: Verbal--16% below 500, 40% between 500 and 599, 39% between 600 and 700, and 5% above 700; Math--17% below 500, 32% between 500 and 599, 35% between 600 and 700, and 17% above 700.

Requirements: The SAT I is required or the CEEB's Spanish equivalent. Applicants must be graduates of an accredited secondary school. The GED is accepted. Students should have completed 3 courses each of English and Spanish, 2 courses each of math and science, and 3 electives. A GPA of 2.0 is required. AP credits are accepted. Important factors in the admissions decision are advanced placement or honor courses, evidence of special talent, and extracurricular activities record.

Procedure: Freshmen are admitted in the fall. Entrance exams should be taken in November or February of the senior year. Applications should be filed by February 15 for fall entry and May 15 for spring entry. The fall 2001 application fee was $15. Notification is sent in April.

Transfer: 1177 transfer students enrolled in 2001-2002. Applicants from within Puerto Rico should have a minimum of 48 credits with a 2.5 GPA; out-of-state applicants, 30 credits with a 2.5 GPA.

Visiting: To schedule a visit, contact the Dean of Students at (787) 764-0000, ext. 5540 or 5541.

Financial Aid: In a recent year, scholarships or need-based grants averaged $900 ($3000 maximum); and loans averaged $4000. The CSS/Profile and the Puerto Rico Income Tax Revenue Report are required. The fall application deadline is April.

International Students: There are 25 international students enrolled. The school actively recruits these students. They must take the Spanish or English SAT I.

Computers: The mainframe is an IBM 4381. Terminals and PC facilities are available in the main computer center, the library, and various academic departments. All students may access the system according to schedules provided during the semester. There are no time limits and no fees.

Graduates: In 2001, 2878 bachelor's degrees were awarded. The most popular majors were business administration (21%), social science (20%), and natural sciences (16%). In an average class, 13% graduate in 3 years, 40% in 4 years, 53% in 5 years, and 54% in 6 years. 54 companies recruited on campus in 2000-2001.

Admissions Contact: Cruz B. Valentin, Admissions Director.

UNIVERSITY OF THE SACRED HEART D-1

Santurce, PR 00914 (787) 728-1199; Fax: (787) 727-7880

Full-time: 1180 men, 2183 women	**Faculty:** 128
Part-time: 478 men, 843 women	**Ph.D.s:** 26%
Graduate: 135 men, 368 women	**Student/Faculty:** 26 to 1
Year: semesters, summer session	**Tuition:** $4475
Application Deadline: see profile	**Room & Board:** $900
Freshman Class: n/av	
SAT I: required	

University of the Sacred Heart, founded in 1935, is a private, comprehensive Roman Catholic institution. There are 6 undergraduate and 4 graduate schools. In addition to regional accreditation, the university has baccalaureate program accreditation with CAHEA, CSWE, and NLN. The library contains 124,936 volumes, 49,086 microform items, and 10,366 audiovisual forms/CDs, and subscribes to 1525 periodicals. Computerized library services include the card catalog and database searching. Special learning facilities include a learning resource center, art gallery, natural history museum, TV station, communication center, and secretarial, human performance, and art labs. The 33-acre campus is in an urban area of San Juan. Including residence halls, there are 14 buildings.

Student Life: All undergraduates are from Puerto Rico. 35% are from public schools. All are Hispanic. The average age of freshmen is 19; all undergraduates, 21.

Housing: 418 students can be accommodated in college housing, which includes dormitories. Alcohol is not permitted.

Activities: There are no fraternities or sororities.

Sports: There are 11 intercollegiate sports for men and 7 for women, and 4 intramural sports for men and 4 for women. Facilities include a volleyball and basketball court with 1500-seating capacity, a Nautilus and free weight gym, a weighlifting area, 4 tennis courts, a softball field, 3 beach volleyball courts, an Olympic-size swimming pool, a game room, and a judo area.

Disabled Students: Wheelchair ramps, elevators, special parking, specially equipped rest rooms, lowered drinking fountains, and lowered telephones are available.

Campus Safety and Security: Measures include 24-hour foot and vehicle patrol.

Programs of Study: The university confers B.A., B.S., B.A.C., B.B.A., B.Ed., B.O.S.A., and B.S.N. degrees. Associate and master's degrees are also awarded. Bachelor's degrees are awarded in BIOLOGICAL SCIENCE (biology/biological science), BUSINESS (accounting, business administration and management, management information systems, marketing/retailing/merchandising, personnel management, secretarial studies/office management, and tourism), COMMUNICATIONS AND THE ARTS (advertising, communications, telecommunications, and visual and performing arts), COMPUTER AND PHYSICAL SCIENCE (chemistry, computer science, and mathematics), EDUCATION (elementary and physical), HEALTH PROFESSIONS (medical technology and nursing), SOCIAL SCIENCE (criminal justice, psychology, social work, and urban studies). Business administration and communications are the largest.

Required: To graduate, students must complete between 133 and 145 credits, including 22 to 45 in the major, with a minimum GPA of 2.1 in the major and 2.0 overall. All students must take 12 credits of English, 9 of Spanish, 6 each of theology, humanities, social sciences, and biology, and 3 each of logic and philosophy, arts, computer science, and physical fitness. Some programs require a fieldwork practicum.

Special: The university offers a Washington semester, work-study, and nondegree programs in continuing education and basic skills. Study in the mainland United States is possible through the National Student Exchange and through independent agreements with various private and public colleges and universities. There are also opportunities for study in Spain and Mexico. A 3-2 engineering degree is offered with Manhattan College in New York. There is 1 national honor society.

Faculty/Classroom: 46% of faculty are male; 54%, female.

Requirements: The SAT I is required or the CEEB's Spanish equivalent, along with SAT II: Subject tests in Spanish, English, and math. Applicants must be graduates of an accredited secondary school. The GED is accepted. The admissions formula is based on GPA (x 600) + CEEB (verbal + math + English). Applicants whose index is 3300 will be admitted to the university. Those who comply with only 1 (GPA or CEEB) will be considered individually by the evaluation committee. A GPA of 2.5 is required. AP credits are accepted.

Procedure: Entrance exams should be taken in October of the senior year. There are early decision and early admissions plans. Check with the school for current application deadlines and fees. Notification is sent on a rolling basis.

Transfer: Applicants with at least 30 college credits and a high school and college GPA of 2.5 are eligible for transfer. Students must submit CEEB scores and a letter of recommendation. Three quarters of the credits needed in the major must be taken at the university.

Visiting: There are regularly scheduled orientations for prospective students. Visitors may sit in on classes. To schedule a visit, contact the Admission, Promotion, and Recruitment Office at (787) 728-1602 or (787) 728-1515, ext. 3237.

Financial Aid: The university is a member of CSS. The CSS/Profile, the college's own financial statement, and the AFSA are required.

International Students: These students must take the SAT I or the CEEB's Spanish equivalent.

Computers: The mainframe is a DEC ALPHA 3700. There are 12 terminals as well as PC facilities in the computer lab and in 6 computer classrooms, with access to the Internet and the Web. All students may access the system. There are no time limits. The fee varies from $25 to $75. It is strongly recommended that all students have a personal computer.

Admissions Contact: Manuel De Jesus, Interim Director of the Admissions and Promotion Office. A video is available.
E-mail: *mdejesus@sagrado.edu* Web: *http://www.sagrado.edu*

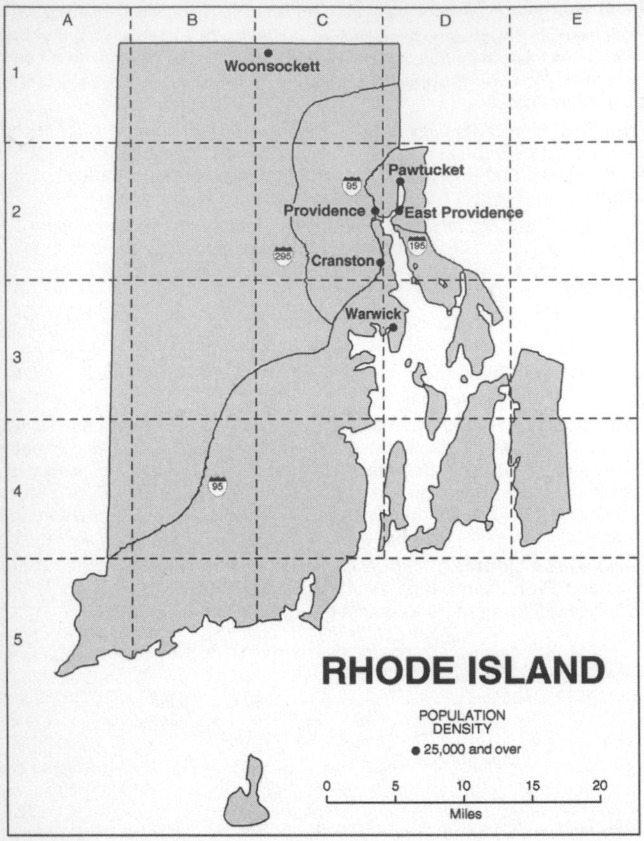

BROWN UNIVERSITY C-2

Providence, RI 02912 **(401) 863-2378; Fax: (401) 863-9300**

Full-time: 2613 men, 3064 women	**Faculty:** 560; I, +$
Part-time: 130 men, 192 women	**Ph.D.s:** 98%
Graduate: 933 men, 842 women	**Student/Faculty:** 10 to 1
Year: semesters, summer session	**Tuition:** $27,395
Application Deadline: January 1	**Room & Board:** $7578
Freshman Class: 16,606 applied, 2729 accepted, 1413 enrolled	
SAT I Verbal/Math: 700/700	**ACT:** 30 **MOST COMPETITIVE**

Brown University, founded in 1764, is a liberal arts institution and one of the Ivy League schools. There is 1 graduate school. In addition to regional accreditation, Brown has baccalaureate program accreditation with ABET. The 6 libraries contain 3 million volumes, 1 million microform items, and 26,342 audiovisual forms/CDs, and subscribe to 15,090 periodicals. Computerized library services include the card catalog, interlibrary loans, and database searching. Special learning facilities include a learning resource center, art gallery, planetarium, radio station, TV station, and an anthropology museum. The 140-acre campus is in an urban area 45 miles south of Boston. Including residence halls, there are 243 buildings.

Student Life: 96% of undergraduates are from out of state, mostly the Middle Atlantic. Students are from 49 states, 72 foreign countries, and Canada. 60% are from public schools. 53% are white; 13%, Asian American; 11%, foreign nationals. The average age of freshmen is 18; all undergraduates, 20. 4% do not continue beyond their first year; 96% remain to graduate.

Housing: 4331 students can be accommodated in college housing, which includes single-sex and coed dormitories, on-campus apartments, off-campus apartments, fraternity houses, and sorority houses. In addition, there are language houses and special-interest houses, an international house, a technology house, and an environmental studies house. On-campus housing is guaranteed for all 4 years. 85% of students live on campus; of those, 90% remain on campus on weekends. Upperclassmen may keep cars.

Activities: 12% of men belong to 10 national fraternities; 2% of women belong to 3 national sororities. There are 240 groups on campus, including band, cheerleading, chess, choir, chorale, chorus, computers, dance, debate, drama, ethnic, film, gay, honors, international, jazz band, literary magazine, marching band, musical theater, newspaper, orchestra, photography, political, professional, public service, radio and TV, religious, social, social service, student government, volunteer, and yearbook. Popular campus events include Commencement, Spring Weekend, and Parents Weekend.

Sports: There are 16 intercollegiate sports for men and 19 for women, and 15 intramural sports for men and 15 for women. Facilities include a 25,000-seat stadium, an Olympic-size pool, a 200-meter, 6-lane track, a hockey rink, playing fields, weight-training rooms, facilities for wrestling, and courts for squash, handball, racquetball, tennis, basketball, and volleyball.

Disabled Students: Wheelchair ramps, elevators, special parking, and specially equipped rest rooms are available.

Services: Counseling and information services are available, as is tutoring in most subjects. There is a reader service for the blind. Other services include class note taking, books on tape, diagnostic testing services, oral tests, tutors, and untimed tests.

Campus Safety and Security: Measures include 24-hour foot and vehicle patrol, self-defense education, escort service, and shuttle buses. There are informal discussions, pamphlets/posters/films, emergency telephones, lighted pathways/sidewalks, and the Safe Walk program.

Programs of Study: Brown confers A.B. and Sc.B. degrees. Master's and doctoral degrees are also awarded. Bachelor's degrees are awarded in BIOLOGICAL SCIENCE (biochemistry, biology/biological science, biophysics, and neurosciences), BUSINESS (organizational behavior), COMMUNICATIONS AND THE ARTS (American literature, art history and appreciation, classics, comparative literature, English, French, German, Italian, linguistics, music, performing arts, and Slavic languages), COMPUTER AND PHYSICAL SCIENCE (applied mathematics, chemistry, computer science, geology, mathematics, and physics), EDUCATION (education), ENGINEERING AND ENVIRONMENTAL DESIGN (architectural technology, engineering, and environmental science), HEALTH PROFESSIONS (biomedical science), SOCIAL SCIENCE (African American studies, anthropology, cognitive science, East Asian studies, economics, gender studies, Hispanic American studies, history, international relations, Judaic studies, Latin American studies, medieval studies, philosophy, political science/government, psychology, public administration, Russian and Slavic studies, sociology, South Asian studies, and urban studies). Biological sciences, international relations, and history are the largest.

Required: To graduate, students must pass 30 of 32 courses taken (4 each semester), including 8 to 21 courses in the major. There are no distribution requirements or specific required courses.

Special: Students may cross-register with Rhode Island School of Design, or study abroad in any of 57 programs in 18 countries. A combined A.B.-Sc.B. degree is possible in any major field with 5 years of study. Dual and student-designed majors, community internships, and pass/fail options are available. Students may pursue 5-year programs in the arts or sciences, or the 8-year program in the liberal medical education continuum. There is a chapter of Phi Beta Kappa.

Faculty/Classroom: 69% of faculty are male; 31%, female. All both teach and do research. Graduate students teach 13% of introductory courses. The average class size in an introductory lecture is 200; in a laboratory, 20; and in a regular course, 40.

Admissions: 16% of the 2001-2002 applicants were accepted. The SAT I scores for the 2001-2002 freshman class were: Verbal--2% below 500, 12% between 500 and 599, 35% between 600 and 700, and 51% above 700; Math--1% below 500, 8% between 500 and 599, 36% between 600 and 700, and 55% above 700. The ACT scores were 6% between 21 and 23, 33% between 24 and 29, and 61% above 29. 95% of the current freshmen were in the top fifth of their class; All were in the top two fifths. 174 freshmen graduated first in their class.

Requirements: The SAT I or ACT is required, along with any 3 SAT II: Subject tests. The ACT may be substituted for both the SAT I and II. Applicants must be graduates of accredited high schools. Secondary preparation is expected to include courses in English, foreign language, math, lab science, the arts (music or art), and history. A personal essay is required. The high school transcript is a most important criterion for admission. AP credits are accepted. Important factors in the admissions decision are advanced placement or honor courses, evidence of special talent, and recommendations by school officials. Applications are accepted on-line via Embark.

Procedure: Freshmen are admitted fall and spring. Entrance exams should be taken in the junior or senior year. There are early decision, early admissions, and deferred admissions plans. Early decision application should be filed by November 1; regular applications, by January 1 for fall entry, along with a $70 fee. Notification of early decision is sent December 15; regular decision, April 1. 1095 early decision candidates were accepted for the 2001-2002 class. 8% of all applicants are on a waiting list; 87 were accepted in 2001.

Transfer: 25 transfer students enrolled in 2001-2002. Applicants must submit high school and college transcripts, 2 recommendations from college professors, scores on the ACT or on the SAT I and any 3 SAT II: Subject tests, a letter of good standing, and a personal essay. 15 courses of 30 must be completed at Brown.

Visiting: There are regularly scheduled orientations for prospective students, consisting of Group Information Sessions conducted Monday through Friday at 10 A.M. and at 2 P.M. from mid-April through November, at 2 P.M. only from December to April, and on Saturday mornings from mid-September to mid-November. There are guides for informal visits and visitors may sit in on classes and stay overnight. To schedule a visit, contact the Admission Office receptionist.

Financial Aid: In 2001-2002, 56% of all freshmen and 49% of continuing students received some form of financial aid. 43% of freshmen and 40% of continuing students received need-based aid. The average freshman award was $22,594. Of that total, scholarships or need-based grants averaged $18,613 ($34,570 maximum); loans averaged $2610 ($4350 maximum); and work contracts averaged $1370 ($2000 maximum). 40% of undergraduates work part time. Average annual earnings from campus work are $1334. The average financial indebtedness of the 2001 graduate was $22,530. Brown is a member of CSS. The CSS/Profile (for freshman) or FAFSA, the college's own financial statement (for returning students), and the some state forms are required. The fall application deadline is January 1.

International Students: There are 374 international students enrolled. The school actively recruits these students. They must score 600 on the written TOEFL or 250 on the electronic version and also take the SAT I or the ACT along with any 3 SAT II: Subject tests.

Computers: There are more than 400 workstations in several campus locations equipped with Macs and PCs. Students may access the mainframe from dorm rooms. The main computer center is open 18 hours a day and around the clock during exam periods. All students may access the system at any time. There are no time limits and no fees.

Graduates: In 2001, 1462 bachelor's degrees were awarded. The most popular majors were biological sciences (11%), international relations (9%), and history (7%). In an average class, 81% graduate in 4 years, 90% in 5 years, and 93% in 6 years. 400 companies recruited on campus in 2000-2001. Of the 2000 graduating class, 30% were enrolled in graduate school within 6 months of graduation and 60% were employed.

Admissions Contact: Michael Goldberger, Director of Admission. E-mail: *admission_undergraduate@brown.edu* Web: *www.brown.edu*

BRYANT COLLEGE

Smithfield, RI 02917-1284 — C-2

(401) 232-6100

(800) 622-7001; Fax: (401) 232-6741

Full-time: 1660 men, 1039 women	**Faculty:** 125; IIB, ++$
Part-time: 161 men, 147 women	**Ph.D.s:** 84%
Graduate: 315 men, 172 women	**Student/Faculty:** 22 to 1
Year: semesters, summer session	**Tuition:** $18,480
Application Deadline: March 15	**Room & Board:** $7500
Freshman Class: 3013 applied, 2155 accepted, 712 enrolled	
SAT I Verbal/Math: 520/560	**ACT:** 22 **VERY COMPETITIVE**

Bryant College, founded in 1863, is a private, primarily residential institution that offers degrees in business, liberal arts, communication, psychology, and information technology. In addition to regional accreditation, Bryant has baccalaureate program accreditation with AACSB. The library contains 130,039 volumes, 13,500 microform items, and 841 audiovisual forms/CDs, and subscribes to 1000 paper/microform periodicals and more than 10,000 electronic periodicals. Computerized library services include the card catalog, interlibrary loans, and database searching. Special learning facilities include a learning resource center, radio station, and a technology center, a learning/language lab, a writing center, an academic center, a discovery lab, a paperless classroom, a center for international business, and a center for information and technology. The 392-acre campus is in a suburban area 12 miles northwest of Providence. Including residence halls, there are 45 buildings.

Student Life: 82% of undergraduates are from out of state, mostly the Northeast. Others are from 32 states, 39 foreign countries, and Canada. 80% are from public schools. 83% are white. The average age of freshmen is 18; all undergraduates, 21. 14% do not continue beyond their first year; 64% remain to graduate.

Housing: 2484 students can be accommodated in college housing, which includes single-sex and coed dormitories, on-campus apartments, special-interest residence halls. Some fraternities and sororities are housed in residence halls. On-campus housing is guaranteed for all 4 years. 83% of students live on campus; of those, 75% remain on campus on weekends. All students may keep cars.

Activities: 11% of men belong to 7 national fraternities; 8% of women belong to 3 national sororities. There are 60 groups on campus, including academic, art, cheerleading, chorus, computers, dance, drama, ethnic, film, gay, international, literary magazine, newspaper, pep band, political, professional, radio, religious, social, social service, special-interest, student government, and yearbook. Popular campus events include Parents and Family Weekend, Spring Weekend, and Trustee Speaker Series.

Sports: There are 10 intercollegiate sports for men and 11 for women, and 7 intramural sports for men and 7 for women. Facilities include a 2700-seat gym, tennis, squash, racquetball, and multipurpose courts, a 400-meter track, cross-country trails, playing fields for baseball, softball, lacrosse, soccer, football, and field hockey, a competition stadium with a natural grass surface, varsity weight room, wellness center that houses a 6-lane, 25-yard pool, a fitness center, and an aerobics room.

Disabled Students: 90% of the campus is accessible. Wheelchair ramps, elevators, special parking, specially equipped rest rooms, special class scheduling, lowered drinking fountains, lowered telephones, and a range of support services for the physically challenged and learning disabled are available.

Services: Counseling and information services are available, as is tutoring in most subjects. There is a reader service for the blind.

Campus Safety and Security: Measures include 24-hour foot and vehicle patrol, escort service, informal discussions, and pamphlets/posters/films. There are emergency telephones and areas monitored one point of access/egress, bicycle patrols, on-campus EMTs, security lighting, and video cameras.

Programs of Study: Bryant confers B.A., B.A. App. Psych., B.S. Inf. Tech., B.S.B.A., and B.A.L.S. degrees. Master's degrees are also awarded. Bachelor's degrees are awarded in BUSINESS (accounting, banking and finance, business administration and management, and marketing/retailing/merchandising), COMMUNICATIONS AND THE ARTS (communications, and English), COMPUTER AND PHYSICAL SCIENCE (actuarial science, and information sciences and systems), SOCIAL SCIENCE (economics, history, international studies, and psychology). Accounting and finance are the strongest academically. Marketing, management, and finance are the largest.

Required: To graduate, all business students must complete 61 semester hours of liberal arts, 31 hours of business, and a maximum of 12 hours of electives, for a minimum of 122 hours, with 18 to 33 hours in the major. Distribution requirements include 12 credits in a liberal arts minor and 25 hours in Modes of Thought: social science, historical, literary, scientific, cultural, and liberal arts electives.

Special: Bryant offers internships, study abroad in 21 countries, on-campus work-study programs, dual concentrations, credit for military experience, advanced placement credit, independent study, and nondegree study. There are 3 national honor societies, a freshman honors program, and all departments have honors programs.

Faculty/Classroom: 66% of faculty are male; 34%, female. All teach undergraduates and 94% both teach and do research. No introductory courses are taught by graduate students. The average class size in an introductory lecture is 28; in a laboratory, 20; and in a regular course, 26.

Admissions: 72% of the 2001-2002 applicants were accepted. The SAT I scores for the 2001-2002 freshman class were: Verbal--35% below 500, 52% between 500 and 599, and 13% between 600 and 700; Math--16% below 500, 53% between 500 and 599, 28% between 600 and 700, and 3% above 700. The ACT scores were 22% below 21, 39% between 21 and 23, 25% between 24 and 26, 10% between 27 and 28, and 4% above 28. 32% of the current freshmen were in the top fifth of their class; 71% were in the top two fifths. 3 freshmen graduated first in their class.

Requirements: The SAT I or ACT is required. In addition, applicants must be graduates of an accredited secondary school or have a GED certificate. A total of 16 Carnegie units is required, including 4 years of English, 3 years of math (minimum Algebra I and II, and geometry), and 2 years of social studies, and 1 year of lab science. An essay is required. An interview is highly recommended. Applications also are accepted on computer disk. A GPA of 3.0 is recommended. AP and CLEP credits are accepted. Applicants may apply on-line via CollegeLink, APPLY!, Next Stop College, Universal Application, Common Application on-line, Embark.com, or through Bryant's Internet address: *www.bryant.edu*

Procedure: Freshmen are admitted fall and spring. Entrance exams should be taken before January of the senior year. There are early decision, early admissions, and deferred admissions plans. Early decision applications should be filed by November 1; regular applications, by March 15 for fall entry; until classes begin for spring entry. The fall 2001 application fee was $50. Notification of early decision is sent December 15; regular decision, on a rolling basis. 6% of all applicants are on a waiting list; 57 were accepted in 2001.

Transfer: 117 transfer students enrolled in 2001-2002. Applicants must have a minimum college GPA of 2.5, although a 3.0 is recommended. Applicants must be high school graduates or have a GED, with a minimum of Algebra II and 12 semester credits. 30 credits of 122 must be completed at Bryant.

Visiting: There are regularly scheduled orientations for prospective students, including campus tours, a financial aid presentation, a student activities overview, an academic program overview, and an admission overview. There are guides for informal visits and visitors may sit in on classes and stay overnight. To schedule a visit, contact the Office of Admission.

Financial Aid: In 2001-2002, 87% of all freshmen and 82% of continuing students received some form of financial aid. 53% of freshmen and 42% of continuing students received need-based aid. The average freshman award was $13,070. Of that total, scholarships or need-based grants averaged $6564 ($18,480 maximum); loans averaged $4125 ($4495 maximum); and work contracts averaged $1570 ($1600 maximum). 19% of undergraduates work part time. Average annual earnings from campus work are $1530. The average financial indebtedness of the 2001 graduate was $19,995. Bryant is a member of CSS. The CSS/Profile or FAFSA and the college's own financial statement are required. The fall application deadline is February 15.

International Students: There are 147 international students enrolled. The school actively recruits these students. They must score 550 on the written TOEFL or 213 on the electronic version and also take the SAT I or the ACT.

Computers: The mainframe is a SGI ORIGIN 200/SUN ENT 3500. More than 150 Pentium computers in the technology center, and approximately 200 in various classrooms, give students access to application software, e-mail, and the Web. Dorms are wired for access to the campus network. Off-campus students can connect to the campus network. All students may access the system 24 hours per day. There are no time limits and no fees. It is strongly recommended that all students have a personal computer.

Graduates: In 2001, 515 bachelor's degrees were awarded. The most popular majors were marketing (27%), computer information systems (21%), and finance (18%). In an average class, 61% graduate in 4 years, 63% in 5 years, and 64% in 6 years. 195 companies recruited on campus in 2000-2001. Of the 2000 graduating class, 4% were enrolled in graduate school within 6 months of graduation and 93% were employed.

Admissions Contact: Cynthia Bonn, Director of Freshman Admission. A video is available. E-mail: *admissions@bryant.edu*
Web: *www.bryant.edu*

JOHNSON AND WALES UNIVERSITY — C-2

Providence, RI 02903-3703 — (401) 598-2310
(800) DIAL-JWU; Fax: (401) 598-2948

Full-time: 3888 men, 3624 women	**Faculty:** 204; IIA, --$
Part-time: 496 men, 558 women	**Ph.D.s:** 17%
Graduate: 332 men, 294 women	**Student/Faculty:** 34 to 1
Year: quarters, summer session	**Tuition:** $15,192
Application Deadline: open	**Room & Board:** $6366

Freshman Class: 13,062 applied, 11,440 accepted, 2886 enrolled
SAT I or ACT: recommended — **LESS COMPETITIVE**

Johnson and Wales University, founded in 1914, is a private institution offering degree programs in business, food services, hospitality, and related technology. There are 3 undergraduate schools and 1 graduate school. The 2 libraries contain 88,996 volumes, 318,664 microform items, and 2429 audiovisual forms/CDs, and subscribe to 2218 periodicals. Computerized library services include the card catalog, interlibrary loans, and database searching. Special learning facilities include a learning resource center and a culinary archives and museum. The 47-acre campus is in an urban area in Providence, with facilities in Warwick, Cranston, and Seekonk, as well as campuses. Including residence halls, there are 52 buildings.

Student Life: 78% of undergraduates are from out of state, mostly the Northeast. Others are from 49 states, 90 foreign countries, and Canada. 88% are from public schools. 75% are white; 11% African American. The average age of freshmen is 18; all undergraduates, 21. 21% do not continue beyond their first year; 71% remain to graduate.

Housing: 3180 students can be accommodated in college housing, which includes single-sex and coed dormitories, on-campus apartments, and married-student housing. In addition, there are special-interest houses. On-campus housing is guaranteed for all 4 years. 61% of students commute. Alcohol is not permitted. All students may keep cars.

Activities: 8% of men belong to 3 local and 13 national fraternities; 8% of women belong to 2 local and 11 national sororities. There are 80 groups on campus, including cheerleading, chess, choir, chorale, computers, dance, drama, ethnic, gay, honors, international, literary magazine, musical theater, newspaper, political, professional, religious, social, social service, student government, and yearbook. Popular campus events include Spring Weekend and SnoBall Dance.

Sports: There are 9 intercollegiate sports for men and 8 for women, and 8 intramural sports for men and 8 for women. Facilities include 2 gyms, 2 weight rooms, 2 fitness centers, and a swimming pool.

Disabled Students: All of the campus is accessible. Wheelchair ramps, elevators, special parking, specially equipped rest rooms, special class scheduling, lowered drinking fountains, lowered telephones, lowered fire alarms, emergency lighting, audiovisual fire alarms in public bathrooms, and a lowering chair for the swimming pool are available.

Services: Counseling and information services are available, as is tutoring in every subject. There is a reader service for the blind and remedial math and writing. Workshops in stress and time management, wellness, and learning strategies are offered. Special scheduling of courses and exams and taping are available to accommodate special needs.

Campus Safety and Security: Measures include 24-hour foot and vehicle patrol, self-defense education, escort service, and shuttle buses. There are informal discussions, pamphlets/posters/films, emergency telephones, lighted pathways/sidewalks, 24-hour dormitory coverage, a phone hot line for campus emergencies, and crime alerts in the student weekly newspaper.

Programs of Study: J&W confers the B.S. degree. Associate, master's, and doctoral degrees are also awarded. Bachelor's degrees are awarded in AGRICULTURE (equine science), BUSINESS (accounting, business administration and management, court reporting, entrepreneurial studies, fashion merchandising, hospitality management services, hotel/motel and restaurant management, institutional management, international business management, investments and securities, management information systems, management science, marketing and distribution, marketing management, marketing/retailing/merchandising, office supervision and management, recreation and leisure services, recreational facilities management, retailing, secretarial studies/office management, small business management, sports management, tourism, and transportation and travel marketing), COMMUNICATIONS AND THE ARTS (advertising and communications), COMPUTER AND PHYSICAL SCIENCE (computer management, computer science, information sciences and systems, systems analysis, and web services), EDUCATION (marketing and distribution), ENGINEERING AND ENVIRONMENTAL DESIGN (electrical/electronics engineering, food services technology, and technological management), HEALTH PROFESSIONS (health care administration), SOCIAL SCIENCE (clothing and textiles management/production/services, criminal justice, food production/management/services, paralegal studies, parks and recreation management, and systems science). Culinary arts, hotel/restaurant management, and marketing are the strongest academically. Culinary arts, hotel/restaurant management, and accounting are the largest.

Required: To graduate, students must complete 180 quarter credit hours, including at least 36 in the major, with a minimum GPA of 2.0. Required courses include English, math, history, economics, science, psychology, sociology, and professional development.

Special: The university offers co-op programs, accelerated degree programs, dual majors, study abroad, and worldwide work-study opportunities in business, hospitality, and culinary arts. Most majors require 11-week internships. There is a 4-day school week. There is 1 national honor society, a freshman honors program, and 5 departmental honors programs.

Faculty/Classroom: 63% of faculty are male; 37%, female. 90% teach undergraduates. No introductory courses are taught by graduate students. The average class size in an introductory lecture is 30; in a laboratory, 18; and in a regular course, 30.

Admissions: 88% of the 2001-2002 applicants were accepted. The SAT I scores for the 2001-2002 freshman class were: Verbal--67% below 500, 27% between 500 and 599, 5% between 600 and 700, and 1% above 700; Math--66% below 500, 29% between 500 and 599, and 5% between 600 and 700. 20% of the current freshmen were in the top fifth of their class; 45% were in the top two fifths.

Requirements: The SAT I or ACT is recommended. In addition, for honors program consideration, the SAT I and SAT II: Subject tests must be taken. Graduation from high school or an equivalent credential is required. J&W requires applicants to be in the upper 70% of their class. A GPA of 2.0 is required. AP and CLEP credits are accepted. Important factors in the admissions decision are advanced placement or honor courses, recommendations by school officials, and extracurricular activities record.

Procedure: Freshmen are admitted to all sessions. There are early admissions and deferred admissions plans. Application deadlines are open. Notification is sent on a rolling basis.

Transfer: 444 transfer students enrolled in a recent year. Applicants are required to submit official high school and college transcripts and must have earned a minimum college GPA of 2.0. 45 credits of 180 must be completed at J&W.

Visiting: There are regularly scheduled orientations for prospective students, including parent/student orientation, financial services, student testing, academic orientation, preparation for September registration, and parent-to-parent orientation. There are guides for informal visits and visitors may sit in on classes and stay overnight. To schedule a visit, contact the Admissions Office.

Financial Aid: 71% of freshmen and 28% of continuing students received need-based aid. The average freshman award was $12,087. Average annual earnings from campus work are $936. The average financial indebtedness of a recent year's graduate was $13,742. The FAFSA and the college's own financial statement are required. Check with the school for current deadlines.

International Students: The school actively recruits these students. They must score 550 on the written TOEFL.

Computers: The mainframe is a Wang VS 7380A. There are 400 PCs dedicated to student use, including 60 networked workstations for hospitality students. All students may access the system daily, a total of 82 hours per week. Students may access the system depends on demand. There are no fees.

Graduates: In a recent year, 1057 bachelor's degrees were awarded. The most popular majors were food service management (26%), hospitality management (20%), and hotel/restaurant management (12%). In an average class, 72% graduate in 4 years, 80% in 5 years, and 82% in 6 years. 219 companies recruited on campus in a recent year.

Admissions Contact: Ken DiSaia, VP of Enrollment Management. A video is available. E-mail: *admissions@jwu.edu* Web: *www.jwu.edu*

PROVIDENCE COLLEGE
Providence, RI 02918 C-2

(401) 865-2535
(800) 721-6444; Fax: (401) 865-2826

Full-time: 1632 men, 2182 women — **Faculty:** 259; IIA, +$
Part-time: 234 men, 341 women — **Ph.D.s:** 87%
Graduate: 293 men, 626 women — **Student/Faculty:** 15 to 1
Year: semesters, summer session — **Tuition:** $19,695
Application Deadline: January 15 — **Room & Board:** $7925
Freshman Class: 5384 applied, 3100 accepted, 935 enrolled
SAT I Verbal/Math: 589/590 — **ACT:** 26 **HIGHLY COMPETITIVE**

Providence College, founded in 1917, is a liberal arts and sciences institution operated by the Dominican order of the Catholic Church. In addition to regional accreditation, Providence has baccalaureate program accreditation with CSWE and NCATE. The library contains 400,205 volumes, 214,277 microform items, and 5364 audiovisual forms/CDs, and subscribes to 1560 periodicals. Computerized library services include interlibrary loans and database searching. Special learning facilities include a learning resource center, art gallery, radio station, and and Blackfriars Theatre. The 105-acre campus is in a suburban area 50 miles south of Boston. Including residence halls, there are 40 buildings.

Student Life: 89% of undergraduates are from out of state, mostly the Northeast. Others are from 40 states, 16 foreign countries, and Canada. 61% are from public schools. 87% are white. 77% are Catholic; 13% Greek Orthodox, Islamic. The average age of freshmen is 18; all undergraduates, 21. 8% do not continue beyond their first year; 84% remain to graduate.

Housing: 2750 students can be accommodated in college housing, which includes single-sex and coed dormitories and on-campus apartments. In addition, there are honors floors, living and learning floors, and international floors. On-campus housing is available on a first-come, first-served basis and is available on a lottery system for upperclassmen. Priority is given to out-of-town students. 74% of students live on campus; of those, 80% remain on campus on weekends. Upperclassmen may keep cars.

Activities: There are no fraternities or sororities. There are 94 groups on campus, including art, band, cheerleading, choir, chorale, chorus, computers, dance, debate, drama, ethnic, honors, international, jazz band, literary magazine, musical theater, newspaper, pep band, photography, political, professional, radio and TV, religious, social, social service, student government, and yearbook. Popular campus events include Supersports Competition, Multicultural Awareness Week, and Midnight Madness.

Sports: There are 9 intercollegiate sports for men and 10 for women, and 14 intramural sports for men and 15 for women. Facilities include an ice arena, indoor track, courts for tennis, racquetball, handball, squash, basketball, and volleyball, a pool, a Nautilus program, facilities for weight lifting, aerobics, and ballet, a soccer field, and baseball and softball fields.

Disabled Students: 90% of the campus is accessible. Wheelchair ramps, elevators, special parking, specially equipped rest rooms, special class scheduling, lowered drinking fountains, lowered telephones, and specially equipped dormitory rooms for full-time day students are available.

Services: Counseling and information services are available, as is tutoring in most subjects. There is a reader service for the blind, and academic support services, including evaluation of learning-disabled students.

Campus Safety and Security: Measures include 24-hour foot and vehicle patrol, self-defense education, escort service, and shuttle buses. There are informal discussions, pamphlets/posters/films, emergency telephones, lighted pathways/sidewalks, and and a campuswide computerized card access system for entry into all dormitories and apartment buildings.

Programs of Study: Providence confers B.A. and B.S. degrees. Master's degrees are also awarded. Bachelor's degrees are awarded in BIOLOGICAL SCIENCE (biochemistry and biology/biological science), BUSINESS (accounting, banking and finance, business administration and management, and marketing/retailing/merchandising), COMMUNICATIONS AND THE ARTS (art history and appreciation, dramatic arts, English, French, Italian, music, Spanish, and studio art), COMPUTER AND PHYSICAL SCIENCE (applied physics, chemistry, computer science, and mathematics), EDUCATION (elementary, English, foreign languages, mathematics, music, science, secondary, social studies, and special), ENGINEERING AND ENVIRONMENTAL DESIGN (environmental science and preengineering), HEALTH PROFESSIONS (health care administration), SOCIAL SCIENCE (American studies, community services, economics, history, humanities, philosophy, political science/government, psychology, social science, social work, sociology, and theological studies). Biology, chemistry, and business are the strongest academically. Education, business, and political science are the largest.

Required: To graduate, all students must complete at least 116 credit hours, with 24 upper-division hours in the major, and maintain a GPA of 2.0. Students must also meet an English proficiency requirement, complete 20 credits in Western civilization, and fulfill the 30-credit core curriculum, including 6 credits each in natural science, social science, philosophy, and religion, and 3 each in math and fine arts.

Special: Providence offers cross-registration with Rhode Island School of Design, internships in politics, broadcasting, journalism, and business, and study abroad in Europe and Japan and through the New England-Quebec Exchange Program. Also available are dual and student-designed majors, a 3-2 engineering degree with Columbia University or Washington University in St. Louis, nondegree study, and pass/fail options. There are 17 national honor societies, and a freshman honors program.

Faculty/Classroom: 71% of faculty are male; 29%, female. No introductory courses are taught by graduate students. The average class size in an introductory lecture is 30; in a laboratory, 7; and in a regular course, 25.

Admissions: 58% of the 2001-2002 applicants were accepted. The SAT I scores for the 2001-2002 freshman class were: Verbal--7% below 500, 49% between 500 and 599, 37% between 600 and 700, and 7% above 700; Math--7% below 500, 46% between 500 and 599, 42% between 600 and 700, and 5% above 700. The ACT scores were 11% below 21, 25% between 21 and 23, 33% between 24 and 26, 20% between 27 and 28, and 11% above 28. 67% of the current freshmen were in the top fifth of their class; 93% were in the top two fifths. There were 29 National Merit semifinalists. 14 freshmen graduated first in their class.

Requirements: The SAT I or ACT is required. In addition, SAT II: Subject tests in writing and 2 others of the applicant's choice are recommended. Applicants must be graduates of an accredited secondary school or have a GED certificate. A GPA of 3.0 is recommended. High school preparation should include 4 years of English, 3 years each of foreign language and math, and 2 years each of history, science, and social studies. An essay is required. AP credits are accepted. Important factors in the admissions decision are advanced placement or honor courses, leadership record, and evidence of special talent. Applications are accepted on-line via Common App.

Procedure: Freshmen are admitted fall and spring. Entrance exams should be taken in the junior or senior year. There are early action and deferred admissions plans. Early action applications should be filed by November 15; regular applications, by January 15 for fall entry and November 1 for spring entry. Notification of early action is sent January 1; regular decision, April 1. 544 early action candidates were accepted for the 2001-2002 class. 17% of all applicants are on a waiting list; 56 were accepted in 2001. The fall 2001 application fee was $55.

Transfer: Applicants should have a minimum college GPA of 3.0 in a strong liberal arts program with a recommended 24 credit hours. The SAT I or ACT is required, and an interview is recommended. 60 credits of 116 must be completed at Providence.

Visiting: There are regularly scheduled orientations for prospective students, including campus tours, group information sessions, and personal interviews. There are guides for informal visits and visitors may sit in on classes and stay overnight. To schedule a visit, contact the Admissions Office.

Financial Aid: In 2001-2002, 73% of all freshmen and 66% of continuing students received some form of financial aid. 56% of all students received need-based aid. The average freshman award was $14,000. Of that total, scholarships or need-based grants averaged $8700 ($19,375 maximum); loans averaged $3875 ($4625 maximum); work contracts averaged $1600 ($1800 maximum); and federal grants averaged $7750 (maximum). 66% of undergraduates work part time. Average annual earnings from campus work are $1525. The average financial indebtedness of the 2001 graduate was $19,625. The CSS/Profile or FAFSA is required. The fall application deadline is February 1.

International Students: There are 44 international students enrolled. The school actively recruits these students. They must score 550 on the written TOEFL and also take the SAT I or the ACT. SAT II Subject Tests are strongly encouraged.

Computers: The mainframe is a Wang VS 8000. There are 8 computer labs equipped with 130 PCs for student use. All students have access to the Internet. All students may access the system. There are no time limits. The fee is $180 per year.

Graduates: In 2001, 940 bachelor's degrees were awarded. The most popular majors were special/elementary education (10%), marketing (10%), and management (9%). In an average class, 81% graduate in 4 years, 83% in 5 years, and 84% in 6 years. In a recent year, 110 companies recruited on campus.

Admissions Contact: Christopher P. Lydon, Dean of Enrollment Management. E-mail: *pcadmiss@providence.edu*
Web: *www.providence.edu*

RHODE ISLAND COLLEGE
C-2
Providence, RI 02908
(401) 456-8234
(800) 669-5760; Fax: (401) 456-8817

Full-time: 1400 men, 2900 women
Part-time: 850 men, 1600 women
Graduate: 430 men, 1380 women
Year: semesters, summer session
Application Deadline: see profile
Freshman Class: n/av
SAT I: required
Faculty: 300; IIA, -$
Ph.D.s: 70%
Student/Faculty: 15 to 1
Tuition: $3520 ($8911)
Room & Board: $5720
LESS COMPETITIVE

Rhode Island College, founded in 1854, is a state-supported liberal arts institution offering undergraduate and graduate programs in the liberal arts and sciences, social work, education, and human development. Figures given in the above capsule are approximate. There are 3 undergraduate schools and 1 graduate school. In addition to regional accreditation, RIC has baccalaureate program accreditation with NASAD, NASM, NCATE, and NLN. The library contains 378,000 volumes, 820,000 microform items, and 3300 audiovisual forms/CDs, and subscribes to 1500 periodicals. Computerized library services include the card catalog, interlibrary loans, and database searching. Special learning facilities include an art gallery and radio station. The 125-acre campus is in a suburban area 50 miles southwest of Boston. Including residence halls, there are 26 buildings.

Student Life: 93% of undergraduates are from Rhode Island. Others are from 10 states and 3 foreign countries. 90% are white. 68% are Catholic; 16% Protestant. The average age of freshmen is 18; all undergraduates, 21. 28% do not continue beyond their first year; 45% remain to graduate.

Housing: 830 students can be accommodated in college housing, which includes single-sex and coed dormitories. In addition, there are honors houses. On-campus housing is available on a first-come, first-served basis. Priority is given to out-of-town students. 75% of students commute. Alcohol is not permitted. All students may keep cars.

Activities: There is 1 national fraternity and 3 national sororities. There are 64 groups on campus, including art, band, cheerleading, chess, chorale, chorus, dance, debate, drama, ethnic, gay, honors, international, literary magazine, musical theater, newspaper, orchestra, political, professional, radio and TV, religious, social, social service, student government, symphony, and yearbook. Popular campus events include a fine and performing arts calendar, chess tournaments, and campus center activities.

Sports: There are 8 intercollegiate sports for men and 9 for women. Facilities include playing fields, an athletic center, and a recreation center with pool.

Disabled Students: All of the campus is accessible. Wheelchair ramps, elevators, special parking, specially equipped rest rooms, special class scheduling, and a peer adviser to assist disabled students are available.

Services: Counseling and information services are available, as is tutoring in most subjects. There is a reader service for the blind, remedial math, reading, and writing, and services for learning-disabled students and any student needing academic assistance.

Campus Safety and Security: Measures include 24-hour foot and vehicle patrol, self-defense education, escort service, and informal discussions. There are pamphlets/posters/films, emergency telephones, and lighted pathways/sidewalks.

Programs of Study: RIC confers B.A., B.S., B.F.A., B.M., B.S.N., and B.S.W. degrees. Master's degrees are also awarded. Bachelor's degrees are awarded in BIOLOGICAL SCIENCE (biology/biological science), BUSINESS (accounting, business administration and management, business economics, labor studies, marketing/retailing/merchandising, and personnel management), COMMUNICATIONS AND THE ARTS (communications, dramatic arts, English, film arts, fine arts, French, music, photography, and Spanish), COMPUTER AND PHYSICAL SCIENCE (chemistry, computer programming, computer science, information sciences and systems, mathematics, physics, and radiological technology), EDUCATION (art, early childhood, elementary, foreign languages, health, industrial arts, middle school, music, physical, science, secondary, and special), ENGINEERING AND ENVIRONMENTAL DESIGN (industrial engineering technology), HEALTH PROFESSIONS (medical laboratory technology and nursing), SOCIAL SCIENCE (African American studies, anthropology, economics, geography, history, Latin American studies, philosophy, political science/government, prelaw, psychology, public administration, social science, social work, sociology, urban studies, and women's studies). Education, management, and psychology are the largest.

Required: To graduate, students must complete 120 credits and maintain a minimum GPA of 2.0. All students must complete the college's general education program, which consists of 4 core requirements in cultural legacies and critical thinking, and 6 distribution requirements. In addition, all students must complete the college writing and math competeny requirements.

Special: Cross-registration is available with other Rhode Island schools and the National Student Exchange. The college offers internships, study abroad, work-study programs, a general studies degree, dual and student-designed majors, credit by exam, credit for prior learning, and pass/fail options. There are 6 national honor societies, a freshman honors program, and 21 departmental honors programs.

Faculty/Classroom: 56% of faculty are male; 44%, female. 98% both teach and do research. No introductory courses are taught by graduate students. The average class size in an introductory lecture is 30; in a laboratory, 14; and in a regular course, 30.

Requirements: The SAT I is required. ACT scores will be accepted. Applicants should be graduates of an accredited secondary school with 18 academic credits, including 4 in English, 3 in math, 2 each in foreign languages (2 years of same language), science (biology plus chemistry or physics), and social studies, 1/2 credit each in the arts, and computer literacy, and the remainder in academic electives. The GED is accepted. An essay is required along with a portfolio for art students and an audition for music students. AP and CLEP credits are accepted. Important factors in the admissions decision are advanced placement or honor courses, evidence of special talent, and leadership record.

Procedure: Freshmen are admitted fall and spring. Entrance exams should be taken by December of the senior year. There are early admissions and deferred admissions plans. Applications should be filed by May 1 for fall entry, November 15 for spring entry, along with a $25 fee. Notification is sent on a rolling basis.

Transfer: Applicants must submit 24 transferable credits with a minimum GPA of 2.25 or 30 college credits and a minimum GPA of 2.0. 30 credits of 120 must be completed at RIC.

Visiting: There are regularly scheduled orientations for prospective students, including information sessions and a campus tour. There are guides for informal visits and visitors may sit in on classes. To schedule a visit, contact the Admissions Office.

Financial Aid: RIC is a member of CSS. The FAFSA and the college's own financial statement are required.

International Students: They must score 550 on the written TOEFL.

Computers: The mainframe is an IBM 9221. 5 classroom labs, with a minimum of 20 PC workstations, are interconnected through a network; 2 of these classrooms contain Mac OS 8 and X and 3 have Windows 95. There are also 2 walk-in technology centers with more than 100 Windows 95 and Mac workstations. A Digital ALPHA 6210 computer provides Internet and e-mail access. All students may access the system. There are no time limits and no fees.

Admissions Contact: Holly L. Shadoian, Director of Admissions. A video is available. E-mail: *hshadoian@grog.ric.edu or admissions@grog.ric.edu* Web: *http://www.ric.edu*

RHODE ISLAND SCHOOL OF DESIGN
C-2
Providence, RI 02903
(401) 454-6300
(800) 364-7473; Fax: (401) 454-6309

Full-time: 681 men, 1164 women
Part-time: none
Graduate: 109 men, 165 women
Year: 4-1-4
Application Deadline: February 15
Freshman Class: n/av
SAT I Verbal/Math: 600/600
Faculty: 139; IIB, +$
Ph.D.s: n/av
Student/Faculty: 13 to 1
Tuition: $23,397
Room & Board: $6830
SPECIAL

Rhode Island School of Design, founded in 1877, is a private institution offering degree programs in fine arts, design, and architecture. In addition to regional accreditation, RISD has baccalaureate program accreditation with ASLA, NAAB, NASAD, and NASDTEC. The library contains 95,161 volumes, 1855 microform items, and 158,325 audiovisual forms/CDs, and subscribes to 423 periodicals. Computerized library services include the card catalog, interlibrary loans, and database searching. Special learning facilities include an art gallery and art museum, and nature lab. The 13-acre campus is in an urban area 50 miles south of Boston. Including residence halls, there are 41 buildings.

Student Life: 94% of undergraduates are from out of state, mostly the Northeast and Middle Atlantic. Others are from 49 states, 50 foreign countries, and Canada. 60% are from public schools. 58% are white; 13% foreign nationals; 11% Asian American. The average age of freshmen is 18; all undergraduates, 23. 6% do not continue beyond their first year; 87% remain to graduate.

Housing: 800 students can be accommodated in college housing, which includes coed dormitories and on-campus apartments. On-campus housing is guaranteed for the freshman year only and is available on a lottery system for upperclassmen. 67% of students commute. Alcohol is not permitted. No one may keep cars.

Activities: There are no fraternities or sororities. There are 60 groups on campus, including art, computers, dance, drama, ethnic, film, gay, international, literary magazine, newspaper, photography, political, professional, religious, social, social service, student government, and yearbook. Popular campus events include Talent Show, Halloween Ball, and Artists Ball.

Sports: There are 7 intramural sports for men and 7 for women. Facilities include a student center with areas and equipment for dance, aerobics, and weight and fitness training, and Tillinghast Farm, a retreat on Narragansett Bay, 15 minutes from campus. Students may also enroll in activity classes at Brown University and use its athletic complex which includes a swimming pool, an ice skating rink, a track, weight training equipment, and courts for basketball, tennis, squash, and racquetball.

Disabled Students: Wheelchair ramps, elevators, special parking, specially equipped rest rooms, and special class scheduling are available.

Services: A writing program is available to all students. Taped lectures, note takers, and alternative test-taking procedures are also available, particularly for students with learning disabilities.

Campus Safety and Security: Measures include 24-hour foot and vehicle patrol, escort service, shuttle buses, and informal discussions. There are pamphlets/posters/films, emergency telephones, lighted pathways/sidewalks, and evening studio monitors, and studio access keys.

Programs of Study: RISD confers B.Arch., B.F.A., B.G.D., B.I.A., and B.I.D. degrees. Master's degrees are also awarded. Bachelor's degrees are awarded in COMMUNICATIONS AND THE ARTS (apparel design, ceramic art and design, design, film arts, glass, graphic design, illustration, industrial design, metal/jewelry, painting, photography, printmaking, and sculpture), ENGINEERING AND ENVIRONMENTAL DESIGN (architecture, furniture design, and interior design), SOCIAL SCIENCE (textiles and clothing). Illustration, graphic design, and architecture are the largest.

Required: To graduate, all students must complete at least 126 credit hours, including 54 in the major, 42 in liberal arts, 18 in the freshman foundation program, and 12 in nonmajor electives. Liberal arts credits must include 12 each in art/architectural history and electives, and 9 each in English and history/philosophy/social science. Core courses include 2 semesters each of foundation drawing, 2-dimensional design, and 3-dimensional design. A minimum GPA of 2.0 and completion of the final-year project are required.

Special: RISD offers cross-registration with Brown University and through the AICAD mobility program, credit or noncredit summer programs, 6-week internships during the midyear winter session, and study abroad in 21 countries and through the senior-year European Honors Program in Rome. Students may also elect a liberal arts concentration in art/architectural history, literary studies, or creative writing.

Faculty/Classroom: 60% of faculty are male; 40%, female. All teach undergraduates. The average class size in an introductory lecture is 20 and in a laboratory, 17.

Admissions: 34% of the 2001-2002 applicants were accepted. The SAT I scores for the 2001-2002 freshman class were: Verbal--13% below 500, 36% between 500 and 599, 36% between 600 and 700, and 15% above 700; Math--7% below 500, 39% between 500 and 599, 42% between 600 and 700, and 10% above 700. 59% of the current freshmen were in the top fifth of their class; 84% were in the top two fifths.

Requirements: The SAT I is required. In addition, the ACT may be substituted. Applicants must be graduates of an accredited secondary school or have a GED. An essay, assigned drawings, a portfolio, and a statement of purpose are also required. Up to 3 letters of recommendation are recommended. AP credits are accepted. Important factors in the admissions decision are evidence of special talent, advanced placement or honor courses, and personality/intangible qualities.

Procedure: Freshmen are admitted fall and spring. Entrance exams should be taken at least 6 weeks before the application deadline. There are early admissions and deferred admissions plans. Applications should be filed by February 15 for fall entry and November 25 for spring entry. Notification is sent April 5. 8% of all applicants are on a waiting list. The fall 2001 application fee was $45.

Transfer: 115 transfer students enrolled in 2001-2002. Applicants must have at least 27 college credits and should submit an essay along with academic transcripts from the previous 3 years. All students must submit a portfolio and complete a drawing assignment. Letters of recommendation are encouraged. The SAT I or ACT is required for architecture and industrial design applicants. 66 credits of 126 must be completed at RISD.

Visiting: There are regularly scheduled orientations for prospective students, including a presentation by the admissions staff and a campus tour. Visitors may sit in on classes. To schedule a visit, contact the Admissions Office.

Financial Aid: In 2001-2002, 56% of all freshmen and 61% of continuing students received some form of financial aid. 45% of freshmen and 58% of continuing students received need-based aid. The average freshman award was $13,700. Of that total, scholarships or need-based grants averaged $9800 ($26,500 maximum); loans averaged $2800 ($7375 maximum); and work contracts averaged $1100. 57% of undergraduates work part time. Average annual earnings from campus work are $1100. The average financial indebtedness of the 2001 graduate was $19,125. RISD is a member of CSS. The CSS/Profile or FAFSA and parents' income tax returns are required. The fall application deadline is February 15.

International Students: There are 220 international students enrolled. They must score 550 on the written TOEFL or 213 on the electronic version and also take the SAT I or the ACT.

Computers: There are more than 450 Macs, PCs, and Silicon Graphic and other workstations located in the computer center and various departments. All students have access to the Internet and Web. All students may access the system. There are no time limits. The fee is $250. It is recommended that students in industrial design, interior architecture, and furniture design have personal computers. The preferred model varies by department.

Graduates: In an average class, 87% graduate in 5 years.

Admissions Contact: Edward Newhall, Director of Admissions.
E-mail: *admissions@risd.edu* Web: *www.risd.edu*

ROGER WILLIAMS UNIVERSITY — D-3

Bristol, RI 02809-2921 — **(401) 254-3500**
(800) 458-7144; Fax: (401) 254-3557

Full-time: 1499 men, 1563 women	**Faculty:** 135; +$
Part-time: 7 men, 4 women	**Ph.D.s:** 70%
Graduate: 302 men, 330 women	**Student/Faculty:** 23 to 1
Year: semesters, summer session	**Tuition:** $20,075
Application Deadline: rolling	**Room & Board:** $8935
Freshman Class: 4221 applied, 3817 accepted, 1096 enrolled	
SAT I Verbal/Math: 530/540	**COMPETITIVE**

Roger Williams University, founded in 1956, is a liberal arts institution that offers programs in the arts and sciences, professional studies, architecture, and law. There are 6 undergraduate and 3 graduate schools. In addition to regional accreditation, RWU has baccalaureate program accreditation with AACSB, ABA, ABET, ACCE, NAAB, NASDTEC, and NCATE. The 3 libraries contain 368,243 volumes, 770,568 microform items, and 2352 audiovisual forms/CDs, and subscribe to 4181 periodicals. Computerized library services include the card catalog, interlibrary loans, and database searching. Special learning facilities include a learning resource center, art gallery, radio station, greenhouse, and wet lab. The 140-acre campus is in a small town 18 miles southeast of Providence. Including residence halls, there are 42 buildings.

Student Life: 86% of undergraduates are from out of state, mostly the Northeast. Others are from 26 states and 31 foreign countries. 75% are from public schools. 93% are white. The average age of freshmen is 18; all undergraduates, 20. 19% do not continue beyond their first year; 53% remain to graduate.

Housing: 2391 students can be accommodated in college housing, which includes single-sex and coed dormitories, on-campus apartments, off-campus apartments, and married-student housing. In addition, there are special-interest houses and academic major theme areas. On-campus housing is available on a lottery system for upperclassmen. 81% of students live on campus; of those, 65% remain on campus on weekends. Upperclassmen may keep cars.

Activities: There are no fraternities or sororities. There are 56 groups on campus, including art, band, cheerleading, chess, choir, chorus, computers, dance, drama, ethnic, film, gay, honors, international, jazz band, literary magazine, musical theater, newspaper, orchestra, photography, political, professional, radio and TV, religious, social service, student government, and yearbook. Popular campus events include Spring Weekend, International Dinner, and Campus Entertainment Network (concerts and comedians).

Sports: There are 11 intercollegiate sports for men and 9 for women, and 17 intramural sports for men and 16 for women. Facilities include a 2500-seat gym; exercise and weight rooms; jogging facilities; and tennis, volleyball, and basketball courts.

Disabled Students: 80% of the campus is accessible. Wheelchair ramps, elevators, special parking, specially equipped rest rooms, special class scheduling, lowered drinking fountains, and lowered telephones are available.

Services: Counseling and information services are available, as is tutoring in every subject. There is a reader service for the blind, and remedial math, reading, and writing.

Campus Safety and Security: Measures include 24-hour foot and vehicle patrol, escort service, shuttle buses, and pamphlets/posters/films. There are emergency telephones and lighted pathways/sidewalks.

Programs of Study: RWU confers B.A., B.S., B.Arch., and B.F.A. degrees. Master's degrees are also awarded. Bachelor's degrees are awarded in BIOLOGICAL SCIENCE (biology/biological science and marine biology), BUSINESS (accounting, banking and finance, business administration and management, international business management, and marketing/retailing/merchandising), COMMUNICATIONS AND THE ARTS (art history and appreciation, communications, creative writing, dance, dramatic arts, English, historic preservation, languages, and visual and performing arts), COMPUTER AND PHYSICAL SCIENCE (chemistry, computer science, information sciences and systems, and mathematics), EDUCATION (elementary and secondary), ENGINEERING AND ENVIRONMENTAL DESIGN (architecture, computer engineering, construction management, engineering, environmental engineering, and environmental science), HEALTH PROFESSIONS (premedicine and preveterinary science), SOCIAL SCIENCE (American studies, criminal justice, history, paralegal studies, philosophy, political science/government, prelaw, psychology, and social science). Architecture, construction management, and engineering are the strongest academically. Architecture, biology, and marine biology are the largest.

Required: To graduate, all students must complete 3 skills courses, 5 courses in interdisciplinary studies, 5 courses within a specific concentration, and an integrative senior seminar. A minimum of 120 credit hours, with 30 to 66 hours in the major and a GPA of 2.0, is required.

Special: RWU offers co-op programs, internships, accelerated degree programs, study abroad in London and Europe, a Washington semester, work-study, individualized majors, and dual majors. There are 7 national honor societies, a freshman honors program, and 6 departmental honors programs.

Faculty/Classroom: 61% of faculty are male; 39%, female. All teach undergraduates. No introductory courses are taught by graduate students. The average class size in an introductory lecture is 23; in a laboratory, 22; and in a regular course, 23.

Admissions: 90% of the 2001-2002 applicants were accepted. The SAT I scores for the 2001-2002 freshman class were: Verbal--35% below 500, 48% between 500 and 599, 16% between 600 and 700, and 1% above 700; Math--30% below 500, 48% between 500 and 599, 20% between 600 and 700, and 2% above 700. 29% of the current freshmen were in the top fifth of their class; 56% were in the top two fifths. 1 freshman graduated first in the class.

Requirements: The SAT I is required. In addition, applicants should be graduates of an accredited secondary school with a minimum GPA of 2.0. The GED is accepted. Students should have 4 years of English, 3 years of math, 2 years each of social and natural sciences, and 4 to 6 electives, for a total of 16 Carnegie units. Art and architecture students must submit portfolios. An essay is required, and an interview is recommended. Dance students must audition. A GPA of 2.0 is required. AP and CLEP credits are accepted. Important factors in the admissions decision are advanced placement or honor courses, leadership record, and evidence of special talent. Applications are accepted on-line via CollegeNET.

Procedure: Freshmen are admitted fall and spring. Entrance exams should be taken in September or October of the senior year. There are early decision, deferred admissions, and rolling admissions plans. Early decision applications should be filed by December 1; regular applications, on a rolling basis for fall and spring entry, along with a $35 fee. Notification of early decision is sent December 15; regular decision, on a rolling basis. 161 early decision candidates were accepted for the 2001-2002 class.

Transfer: 120 transfer students enrolled in 2001-2002. Applicants need a minimum college GPA of 2.0. The SAT I is required if the transfer student has less than 24 transfer credits. A minimum of 45 credits of a minimum 120 must be completed at RWU.

Visiting: There are regularly scheduled orientations for prospective students. There are guides for informal visits and visitors may sit in on classes. To schedule a visit, contact the Office of Admissions.

Financial Aid: In 2001-2002, 83% of all freshmen and 85% of continuing students received some form of financial aid. 60% of freshmen and 58% of continuing students received need-based aid. The average freshman award was $15,250. Of that total, scholarships or need-based grants averaged $10,235 ($16,000 maximum); loans averaged $3500 ($4125 maximum); and work contracts averaged $1525 ($1900 maximum). 36% of undergraduates work part time. Average annual earnings from campus work are $1600. The average financial indebtedness of the 2001 graduate was $15,000. RWU is a member of CSS. The CSS/Profile or FAFSA is required. The fall application deadline is March 1.

International Students: There are 85 international students enrolled. The school actively recruits these students. They must take the MELAB or the college's own test.

Computers: The mainframe is a UNIX-based network. 3 academic computer centers with a wide variety of application software are available to students more than 100 hours per week. All students may access the system. There are no time limits and no fees. It is strongly recommended that all students have a personal computer.

Graduates: In 2001, 531 bachelor's degrees were awarded. The most popular majors were law/legal studies (24%), business/marketing (15%), and engineering/engineering technology (9%). In an average class, 39% graduate in 4 years, 9% in 5 years, and 5% in 6 years. 80 companies recruited on campus in 2000-2001. Of the 2000 graduating class, 25% were enrolled in graduate school within 6 months of graduation and 98% were employed.

Admissions Contact: Lynn M. Fawthrop, Dean of Enrollment Management. E-mail: *admit@rwu.edu* Web: *www.rwu.edu*

SALVE REGINA UNIVERSITY

D-4

Newport, RI 02840-4192

(401) 341-2908

(888) GO-SALVE; Fax: (401) 848-2823

Full-time: 570 men, 1203 women	**Faculty:** 100; IIA, --$
Part-time: 28 men, 93 women	**Ph.D.s:** 68%
Graduate: 172 men, 201 women	**Student/Faculty:** 18 to 1
Year: semesters, summer session	**Tuition:** $18,360
Application Deadline: March 1	**Room & Board:** $8100

Freshman Class: 3311 applied, 2150 accepted, 555 enrolled

SAT I Verbal/Math: 520/520 **COMPETITIVE**

Salve Regina University, founded in 1934 and sponsored by the Sisters of Mercy, is an independent institution affiliated with the Roman Catholic Church. The university offers programs in liberal arts, business, health science, and professional training. In addition to regional accreditation, Salve has baccalaureate program accreditation with CSWE, NASAD, NLN, and IACBE. The library contains 105,262 volumes, 30,900 microform items, and 18,785 audiovisual forms/CDs, and subscribes to 783 periodicals. Computerized library services include the card catalog, interlibrary loans, and database searching. Special learning facilities include a learning resource center, art gallery, radio station, and information systems and computer science labs. The 70-acre campus is in a suburban area on Newport's waterfront, 60 miles south of Boston. Including residence halls, there are 41 buildings.

Student Life: 80% of undergraduates are from out of state, mostly the Northeast. Others are from 40 states and 11 foreign countries. 64% are from public schools. 94% are white. The average age of freshmen is 18; all undergraduates, 20. 25% do not continue beyond their first year; 62% remain to graduate.

Housing: 1032 students can be accommodated in college housing, which includes single-sex and coed dormitories, on-campus apartments, off-campus apartments, and living-learning dorms. On-campus housing is guaranteed for freshman and sophomore years only and is available on a lottery system for upperclassmen. 59% of students live on campus; of those, 75% remain on campus on weekends. Alcohol is not permitted. Upperclassmen may keep cars.

Activities: There are no fraternities or sororities. There are 30 groups on campus, including art, band, cheerleading, choir, chorale, chorus, computers, dance, drama, ethnic, honors, international, jazz band, literary magazine, musical theater, newspaper, orchestra, outdoor, pep band, photography, political, professional, radio and TV, religious, social, social service, student government, and yearbook. Popular campus events include September Welcome-Back Weekend, Octoberfest Weekend, and New Year's Eve Ball.

Sports: There are 10 intercollegiate sports for men and 11 for women, and 7 intramural sports for men and 7 for women. Facilities include a recreation center, tennis courts, outdoor basketball courts, an indoor track, a yacht club, a weight room, a fitness center, and soccer, baseball, and softball fields.

Disabled Students: 75% of the campus is accessible. Wheelchair ramps, elevators, special parking, specially equipped rest rooms, special class scheduling, lowered drinking fountains, and lowered telephones are available.

Services: Counseling and information services are available, as is tutoring in most subjects. There is remedial math, reading, and writing, a writing center, and a computer-based tutorial program.

Campus Safety and Security: Measures include 24-hour foot and vehicle patrol, self-defense education, escort service, and shuttle buses. There are informal discussions, pamphlets/posters/films, emergency telephones, and lighted pathways/sidewalks.

Programs of Study: Salve confers B.A., B.S., and B.A.S. degrees. Associate, master's, and doctoral degrees are also awarded. Bachelor's degrees are awarded in BIOLOGICAL SCIENCE (biology/biological science), BUSINESS (accounting, business administration and management, and management science), COMMUNICATIONS AND THE ARTS (art history and appreciation, communications, communications technology, dramatic arts, English, French, historic preservation, media arts, music, Spanish, and studio art), COMPUTER AND PHYSICAL SCIENCE (chemistry, information sciences and systems, and mathematics), EDUCATION (early childhood, elementary, secondary, and special), HEALTH PROFESSIONS (cytotechnology, medical laboratory technology, and nursing), SOCIAL SCIENCE (American studies, anthropology, criminal justice, economics, history, philosophy, political science/government, psychology, religion, social work, and sociology). Art, psychology, and social work are the strongest academically. Business, administration of justice, and elementary education are the largest.

Required: To graduate, students must have 128 credit hours, consisting of about 36 in the major, 44 in electives, and 48 in general distribution requirements. Required credits include 9 in religious studies, 6 each in English, science, and foreign language, and 3 each in logic, math, philosophy, fine arts, social science, economics or geography, and history or politics. Computer literacy is also required. Students must maintain a minimum GPA of 2.0.

Special: Salve offers internships in most academic disciplines as well as work-study programs on campus. Study abroad, a Washington semester, B.A.-B.S. degrees in chemistry, math, biology, and economics, dual majors in all programs, and accelerated degree programs in administration of justice, health services administration, business, and international relations are available. A liberal studies degree, 5-year bachelor's and master's programs, credit for life, military, and work experience, nondegree study, and pass/fail options are also offered. There are 11 national honor societies, a freshman honors program, and 9 departmental honors programs.

Faculty/Classroom: 43% of faculty are male; 57%, female. 91% teach undergraduates and 20% both teach and do research. No introductory courses are taught by graduate students. The average class size in an introductory lecture is 22; in a laboratory, 27; and in a regular course, 19.

Admissions: 65% of the 2001-2002 applicants were accepted. The SAT I scores for the 2001-2002 freshman class were: Verbal--36% below 500, 48% between 500 and 599, 15% between 600 and 700, and 1% above 700; Math--39% below 500, 50% between 500 and 599, and 11% between 600 and 700. 22% of the current freshmen were in the top fifth of their class; 47% were in the top two fifths. There was 1 National Merit semifinalist. 1 freshman graduated first in the class.

Requirements: The SAT I or ACT is required. In addition, applicants must be high school graduates or hold a GED. Students should have 16 Carnegie units, consisting of 4 in English, 3 in math including algebra and geometry, 2 each in science and foreign language, 1 in history, and 4 in electives. An essay is required. Salve requires applicants to be in the upper 42% of their class. A GPA of 2.0 is required. AP and CLEP credits are accepted. Important factors in the admissions decision are advanced placement or honor courses, recommendations by school officials, and evidence of special talent. Applications are accepted on computer disk, and on-line via CollegeLink, Salve home page, APPLY 2002, ExPAN, and Peterson's.

Procedure: Freshmen are admitted fall and spring. Entrance exams should be taken as early as possible. There are early admissions and deferred admissions plans. Applications should be filed by March 1 for fall entry and December 15 for spring entry, along with a $40 fee. Notification is sent on a rolling basis, beginning December 15. 9% of all applicants are on a waiting list; 10 were accepted in 2001.

Transfer: 52 transfer students enrolled in 2001-2002. Applicants must have a college GPA of 2.3. An interview is recommended. 36 credits of 128 must be completed at Salve.

Visiting: There are regularly scheduled orientations for prospective students, including an introduction to the academic experience, history and visions for the university, a library orientation, student life expectations, social activities, residence hall orientation, preregistration for courses, a cookout, and meetings with faculty, advisers, and administrators. There are guides for informal visits and visitors may sit in on classes, applicants may stay overnight. To schedule a visit, contact the Admissions Office.

Financial Aid: In 2001-2002, 77% of all freshmen and 68% of continuing students received some form of financial aid. 66% of freshmen and 60% of continuing students received need-based aid. The average freshman award was $15,155. Of that total, scholarships or need-based grants averaged $10,695 ($16,000 maximum); loans averaged $3625 ($5425 maximum); and work contracts averaged $1000 ($2000 maximum). 33% of undergraduates work part time. Average annual earnings from campus work are $1000. The average financial indebtedness of the 2001 graduate was $18,875. Salve is a member of CSS. The CSS/Profile or FAFSA, the college's own financial statement and the and tax forms are required. The fall application deadline is March 1.

International Students: There are 23 international students enrolled. The school actively recruits these students. They must score 500 on the written TOEFL or 173 on the electronic version.

Computers: The mainframe is an IBM AS/400. There are 110 PCs and Macs available in computer and science labs for undergraduate use. An additional 150 PCs are assigned to faculty and academic departments, as well as computer networks using Novell NetWare, color printers, and Internet services. There are 5 dedicated technology classrooms. All students may access the system 16 hours per day in labs and 24 hours per day by dial-in access to the Internet. There are no time limits and no fees.

Graduates: In 2001, 312 bachelor's degrees were awarded. The most popular majors were management (13%), administration of justice (12%), and elementary education (10%). In an average class, 58% graduate in 4 years, 60% in 5 years, and 61% in 6 years. 100 companies recruited on campus in 2000-2001. Of the 2000 graduating class, 22% were enrolled in graduate school within 6 months of graduation and 90% were employed.

Admissions Contact: Laura E. McPhie-Oliveira, VP for Enrollment and Admissions. A video is available. E-mail: *sruadmis@salve.edu*
Web: *www.salve.edu*

UNIVERSITY OF RHODE ISLAND C-4

Kingston, RI 02881 **(401) 874-7000; Fax: (401) 874-5523**

Full-time: 3890 men, 4808 women	**Faculty:** 530; I, -$
Part-time: 548 men, 977 women	**Ph.D.s:** 88%
Graduate: 211 men, 330 women	**Student/Faculty:** 16 to 1
Year: semesters, summer session	**Tuition:** $5386 ($14164)
Application Deadline: March 1	**Room & Board:** $7028
Freshman Class: 10,794 applied, 7203 accepted, 2148 enrolled	
SAT I or ACT: 540/550	**COMPETITIVE**

The University of Rhode Island, founded in 1892, is a land-grant, sea-grant, and urban-grant institution offering programs in liberal arts, business, engineering, human services, nursing, and pharmacy. Located near the ocean and the bay, the university has strong marine and environmental programs. There are satellite campuses in Providence, West Greenwich, and Narragansett. There are 8 undergraduate and 3 graduate schools. In addition to regional accreditation, URI has baccalaureate program accreditation with AACSB, ABET, ACPE, ADA, ASLA, NASM, NCATE, and NLN. The 3 libraries contain 836,056 volumes, 1,622,726 microform items, and 10,457 audiovisual forms/CDs, and subscribe to 9361 periodicals. Computerized library services include the card catalog, interlibrary loans, and database searching. Special learning facilities include a learning resource center, art gallery, planetarium, radio station, TV station, historic textile collection, and early childhood education center. The 1248-acre campus is in a small town 30 miles south of Providence. Including residence halls, there are 314 buildings.

Student Life: 62% of undergraduates are from Rhode Island. Others are from 44 states, 47 foreign countries, and Canada. 85% are from public schools. 77% are white. The average age of freshmen is 18; all undergraduates, 23. 14% do not continue beyond their first year; 58% remain to graduate.

Housing: 4100 students can be accommodated in college housing, which includes single-sex and coed dormitories, on-campus apartments, married-student housing, fraternity houses, and sorority houses. In addition, there are language houses, special-interest houses, a freshman dorm, and a wellness dorm. 55% of students commute. All students may keep cars.

Activities: 17% of men belong to 15 national fraternities; 20% of women belong to 9 national sororities. There are 90 groups on campus, including band, cheerleading, chess, choir, chorale, chorus, computers, concert band, dance, drama, ethnic, gay, honors, international, jazz band, literary magazine, marching band, music ensembles, musical theater, newspaper, opera, orchestra, pep band, photography, political, professional, radio and TV, religious, social, social service, student government, and yearbook. Popular campus events include Winterfest, Martin Luther King Week, and International Week.

Sports: There are 10 intercollegiate sports for men and 11 for women, and 18 intramural sports for men and 18 for women. Facilities include a 4000-seat area, a 10000-seat stadium, 3 pools, a multipurpose field house with an indoor track, a gymnastics center, 3 fitness rooms, and courts for basketball, tennis, and volleyball. There are also outdoor tennis courts, an all-weather track, 2 beach volleyball courts, and varsity and practice fields.

Disabled Students: Wheelchair ramps, elevators, special parking, specially equipped rest rooms, special class scheduling, lowered drinking fountains, lowered telephones, and special transportation around campus are available.

Services: Counseling and information services are available, as is tutoring in some subjects, including ESL and popular freshman courses. There is a reader service for the blind, and remedial math, reading, and writing.

Campus Safety and Security: Measures include 24-hour foot and vehicle patrol, self-defense education, escort service, and shuttle buses. There are informal discussions, pamphlets/posters/films, emergency telephones, and lighted pathways/sidewalks.

Programs of Study: URI confers B.A., B.S., B.F.A., B.G.S., B.L.A., and B.M. degrees. Master's and doctoral degrees are also awarded. Bachelor's degrees are awarded in AGRICULTURE (animal science, fishing and fisheries, horticulture, natural resource management, and wildlife management), BIOLOGICAL SCIENCE (biology/biological science, marine science, microbiology, nutrition, and zoology), BUSINESS (accounting, banking and finance, business administration and management, fashion merchandising, management information systems, and marketing/retailing/merchandising), COMMUNICATIONS AND THE ARTS (art, classics, communications, comparative literature, dramatic arts, English, fine arts, French, German, Italian, journalism, literature, music, Spanish, and speech/debate/rhetoric), COMPUTER AND PHYSICAL SCIENCE (chemistry, computer science, geology, mathematics, physics, and statistics), EDUCATION (elementary, music, physical, and secondary), ENGINEERING AND ENVIRONMENTAL DESIGN (biomedical engineering, chemical engineering, civil engineering, computer engineering, electrical/electronics engineering, environmental science, industrial engineering, landscape architecture/design, mechanical engineering, and ocean engineering), HEALTH PROFESSIONS (clinical science, dental hygiene, health care administration, medical laboratory technology, nursing, pharmacy, and speech pathology/audiology), SOCIAL SCIENCE (anthropology, dietetics, economics, family/consumer studies, food science, geography, history, human development, human services, Latin American studies, philosophy, political science/government, psychology, sociology, textiles and clothing, water resources, and women's studies). Pharmacy, engineering, and biology are the strongest academically. Psychology, pharmacy, and human development and family studies are the largest.

Required: To graduate, the student must earn 120 to 150 credit hours, at least 30 in the major, with a GPA of 2.0. Distribution requirements include 6 credits each in English communication, fine arts and literature, foreign language or culture, letters, natural sciences, and social sciences, as well as 3 credits in math.

Special: Cross-registration is available with Rhode Island College and Community College of Rhode Island. URI also offers a Washington semester as well as semester-long internships with businesses and state agencies, study abroad in 6 countries, a B.A.-B.S. degree in German and engineering and in languages and business, a general studies degree, dual majors, pass/fail options, and credit for life, military, and work experience. The College of Engineering offers co-op programs and an international internship. There are 30 national honor societies, including Phi Beta Kappa, and a freshman honors program.

Faculty/Classroom: 70% of faculty are male; 30%, female. All both teach and do research. Graduate students teach 7% of introductory courses. The average class size in an introductory lecture is 30 and in a laboratory, 14.

Admissions: 68% of the 2001-2002 applicants were accepted. 58% of the current freshmen were in the top quarter of their class; 91% were in the top half. 30 freshmen graduated first in their class.

Requirements: The SAT I or ACT is required. In addition, applicants should be high school graduates, having completed 18 courses, including 4 of English, 3 to 4 of math, and 2 each of science (chemistry and physics for engineering majors), foreign language, and history or social studies. Remaining units should be college preparatory. Music majors must audition. Candidates can access URI's application at the school's web site. URI requires applicants to be in the upper 30% of their class. AP and CLEP credits are accepted. Important factors in the admissions decision are advanced placement or honor courses, evidence of special talent, and recommendations by school officials.

Procedure: Freshmen are admitted fall and spring. Entrance exams should be taken during the spring of the junior year or fall of the senior year. There is an early admissions plan. Early decision applications should be filed by December 15; regular applications, by March 1 for fall entry (priority date: December 13) and November 1 for spring entry, along with a $35 fee for in-state students and $45 for out-of-state students. Notification for regular decisions is sent on a rolling basis beginning November 1.

Transfer: 529 transfer students enrolled in 2001-2002. Applicants must submit transcripts from high school and all colleges or universities attended. A minimum GPA of 2.4 is required; many programs require higher. 24 credits of 120 to 150 must be completed at URI.

Visiting: There are regularly scheduled orientations for prospective students, including open house programs in October and campus tours. There are guides for informal visits and visitors may sit in on classes. To schedule a visit, contact the Admissions Office at (401) 874-9800.

Financial Aid: The average freshman award was $4200. The average financial indebtedness of the 2001 graduate was $12,500. URI is a member of CSS. The FAFSA is required. The fall application deadline is March 1.

International Students: The school actively recruits international students. They must score 550 on the written TOEFL or take the English proficiency test administered by the American Consulate. They must also take the SAT I or the ACT.

Computers: The mainframe is an IBM ES/9000-210VF. Students may access the mainframe through more than 550 terminals. All students may access the system 24 hours per day. There are no time limits and no fees.

Graduates: In 2001, 1803 bachelor's degrees were awarded. The most popular majors were business/marketing (18%), health professions and related sciences (12%), and communications/communications technologies (8%). In an average class, 48% graduate in 5 years, and 58% in 6 years. 156 companies recruited on campus in 2000-2001.

Admissions Contact: David Taggart, Dean of Admissions.
E-mail: *uriadmit@etal.uri.edu* Web: *www.uri.edu/*

SOUTH CAROLINA

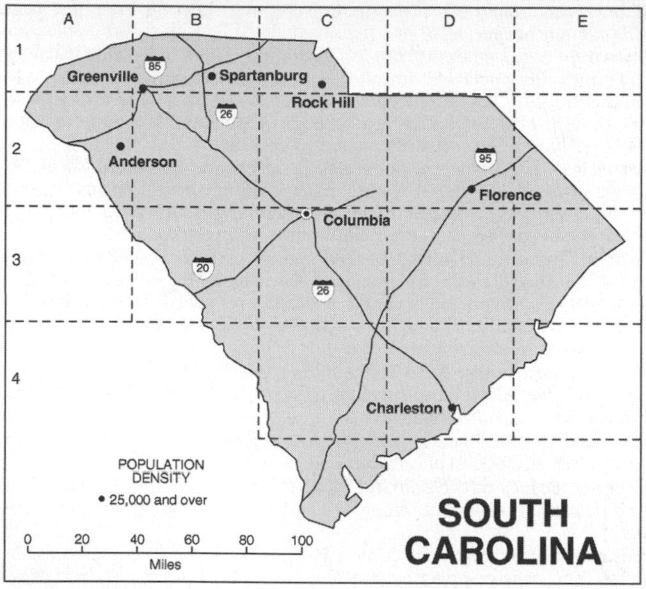

ALLEN UNIVERSITY
Columbia, SC 29204

C-3
(803) 376-5735
(888) 425-5360; Fax: (803) 376-5715

Full-time: 125 men, 200 women
Part-time: 5 men, 10 women
Graduate: none
Year: semesters, summer session
Application Deadline: open
Freshman Class: n/av
SAT I or ACT: not required
Faculty: 14
Ph.D.s: 54%
Student/Faculty: 23 to 1
Tuition: $4950
Room & Board: $4500
NONCOMPETITIVE

Allen University, founded in 1870, is a small private institution affiliated with the African Methodist Episcopal (A.M.E.) Church. It offers undergraduate programs in liberal arts and sciences, business, and social work. Figures given in the above capsule are approximate. The library contains 40,558 volumes, 2883 microform items, and 2527 audiovisual forms/CDs, and subscribes to 106 periodicals. Special learning facilities include a learning resource center. The 4-acre campus is in a small town. Including residence halls, there are 84 buildings.

Student Life: Others are from 20 states and 9 foreign countries. 95% are from public schools. 99% are African American. Most are Protestant. The average age of freshmen is 18; all undergraduates, 24. 20% do not continue beyond their first year.

Housing: 405 students can be accommodated in college housing, which includes single-sex dormitories and off-campus apartments. On-campus housing is guaranteed for all 4 years. 95% of students live on campus. Alcohol is not permitted. All students may keep cars.

Activities: 8% of men belong to 4 national fraternities; 6% of women belong to 4 national sororities. There are 20 groups on campus, including art, band, cheerleading, choir, chorus, drama, honors, international, newspaper, religious, social service, student government, and yearbook. Popular campus events include Cultural, Academic, and Religious Series (CARS), International Day, and Founders Day.

Sports: There are 2 intercollegiate sports for men, and 1 intramural sport for men and 1 for women.

Disabled Students: Special parking is available.

Services: Counseling and information services are available, as is tutoring in most subjects. There is remedial math, reading, and writing. There are math, science, reading, and writing labs.

Campus Safety and Security: Measures include 24-hour foot and vehicle patrol, self-defense education, escort service, and pamphlets/posters/films. There are emergency telephones and lighted pathways/sidewalks.

Programs of Study: Allen confers B.A. and B.S. degrees. Associate degrees are also awarded. Bachelor's degrees are awarded in BIOLOGICAL SCIENCE (biology/biological science), BUSINESS (business administration and management), COMMUNICATIONS AND THE ARTS (English and music), COMPUTER AND PHYSICAL SCIENCE (mathematics), SOCIAL SCIENCE (history, political science/government, and sociology). Sociology/social work and business administration are the largest.

Required: To graduate, all students must complete 120 credit hours with a minimum 2.0 GPA. Student must demonstrate competence in reading, composition, speech, and fundamental math skills.

Special: Allen offers internships with businesses and federal, state, and local agencies, and work-study with the Columbia Housing Authority. A certificate in gerontology is possible. There is 1 national honor society, and 20 departmental honors programs.

Faculty/Classroom: All teach undergraduates.

Requirements: Applicants should be graduates of accredited high schools or have earned the GED. Secondary preparation should total 20 academic credits. A personal interview is recommended. Important factors in the admissions decision are leadership record, advanced placement or honor courses, and evidence of special talent.

Procedure: Freshmen are admitted to all sessions. Entrance exams should be taken in the spring. There is an early decision plan. Application deadlines are open.

Transfer: An official transcript from each school attended is required at least 1 month prior to the beginning of the semester in which admission is desired. 30 credits of 120 must be completed at Allen.

Visiting: There are regularly scheduled orientations for prospective students. There are guides for informal visits and visitors may sit in on classes. To schedule a visit, contact Dr. John Waddell, Dean of Student Development Services at (803) 376-5741.

Financial Aid: Allen is a member of CSS. The CSS/Profile and the college's own financial statement are required.

International Students: The school actively recruits these students.

Computers: The mainframe is an IBM. A computer lab is available. All students may access the system. There are no time limits and no fees.

Graduates: In an average class, 40% graduate in 4 years, and 20% in 5 years.

Admissions Contact: Admissions Office.
E-mail: *auniv@minspring.com*

BENEDICT COLLEGE
Columbia, SC 29204

C-3
(803) 253-5145
(800) 868-6598; Fax: (803) 253-5167

Full-time: 1315 men, 1325 women
Part-time: 45 men, 65 women
Graduate: none
Year: semesters, summer session
Application Deadline: open
Freshman Class: n/av
SAT I Verbal/Math: required
Faculty: 90
Ph.D.s: 65%
Student/Faculty: 25 to 1
Tuition: $8890
Room & Board: $4400
LESS COMPETITIVE

Benedict College, founded in 1870, is a private liberal arts institution affiliated with the Baptist Church. In addition to regional accreditation, Benedict College has baccalaureate program accreditation with CSWE. Figures in the above capsule are approximate. The library contains 122,000 volumes, 3100 microform items, and 5200 audiovisual forms/CDs, and subscribes to 325 periodicals. Computerized library services include database searching. Special learning facilities include a learning resource center and art gallery. The 20-acre campus is in an urban area 90 miles south of Charlotte, North Carolina. Including residence halls, there are 15 buildings.

Student Life: 82% of undergraduates are from South Carolina. Others are from 24 states and 10 foreign countries. 99% are from public schools. 99% are African American. The average age of freshmen is 19; all undergraduates, 20. 50% do not continue beyond their first year; 20% remain to graduate.

Housing: 1090 students can be accommodated in college housing, which includes single-sex dormitories. On-campus housing is available on a first-come, first-served basis. Priority is given to out-of-town students. 77% of students live on campus. Alcohol is not permitted. Upperclassmen may keep cars.

Activities: 2% of men belong to 4 local and 4 national fraternities; 5% of women belong to 4 local and 4 national sororities. There are 50 groups on campus, including art, cheerleading, choir, chorus, dance, drama, drill team, international, newspaper, photography, religious, student government, and yearbook. Popular campus events include Fall Convocation, Crowning of Miss Benedict, and Religion Emphasis Week.

Sports: There are 5 intercollegiate sports for men and 5 for women, and 10 intramural sports for men and 9 for women. Facilities include a gym and student center.

Disabled Students: Wheelchair ramps, elevators, and special parking are available.

Services: Counseling and information services are available, as is tutoring in every subject. There is remedial math, reading, and writing.

Campus Safety and Security: Measures include 24-hour foot and vehicle patrol, informal discussions, pamphlets/posters/films, and lighted pathways/sidewalks.

Programs of Study: Benedict College confers B.A., B.S., and B.S.W. degrees. Bachelor's degrees are awarded in BIOLOGICAL SCIENCE (biology/biological science), BUSINESS (accounting and business administration and management), COMMUNICATIONS AND THE ARTS (English, journalism, and music), COMPUTER AND PHYSICAL SCIENCE (chemistry, computer science, mathematics, and physics), EDUCATION (early childhood and elementary), HEALTH PROFESSIONS (environmental health science), SOCIAL SCIENCE (criminal justice, philosophy, religion, social science, and social work). Business administration is the largest.

Required: Students must complete 125 credit hours, including 24 to 32 in the major, with a minimum GPA of 2.0; some degrees require a higher GPA. The 57-hour general education requirements include 15 hours of English, 9 of social science, 8 of natural science, 6 each of mathematics and a foreign language, 4 of humanities, and 2 each of health education, freshman seminar, phys ed, and religion.

Special: Benedict offers work-study programs, a physics/engineering dual major, internships, a B.A./B.S. degree, and preprofessional programs in dentistry, engineering, law, and medicine.

Faculty/Classroom: 57% of faculty are male; 43%, female. All teach undergraduates and 1% both teach and do research. The average class size in an introductory lecture is 39; in a laboratory, 33; and in a regular course, 30.

Requirements: The SAT I is required. In addition, students should have taken 4 secondary school units of English, 3 each of math and social science, 2 of natural science, 7 of electives, and 1 of phys ed or ROTC. The GED is accepted. AP and CLEP credits are accepted.

Procedure: Entrance exams should be taken prior to registration. There are early admissions and deferred admissions plans. Application deadlines are open. The fall 2001 application fee was $25. Notification is sent on a rolling basis.

Transfer: Applicants must submit transcripts from previous institutions attended plus evidence of honorable withdrawal. The SAT I is required. Only courses in which a C or better was earned will be considered for credit. 30 credits of 125 must be completed at Benedict College.

Visiting: There are regularly scheduled orientations for prospective students. There are guides for informal visits and visitors may sit in on classes. To schedule a visit, contact the Admissions Office at (800) 868-6598 or (803) 253-5143.

Financial Aid: In a recent year, 99% of all students received some form of financial aid. 97% of all students received need-based aid. The average freshman award was $10,900. 50% of undergraduates work part time. Average annual earnings from campus work are $1600. The average financial indebtedness of a recent year's graduate was $46,000. Benedict College is a member of CSS. The CSS/Profile, the college's own financial statement, and the South Carolina Tuition Grant applications are required.

International Students: There were 45 international students enrolled in a recent year. They must score 500 on the written TOEFL and also take the college's own test. Some students may be required to complete an ESL program.

Computers: The mainframes are a DEC PDP 11/70 and DEC VAX 11/785 and 11/780. Students use the mainframe for all programming courses, for computer graphic classes, to create a text file, and to access the Test Data Bank for General and Principles of Biology. There are 36 terminals housed in Alumni Hall. All students may access the system. There are no time limits and no fees.

Admissions Contact: Gary Knight, Director of Enrollment Management. A video is available. E-mail: *admissions@benedict.edu*
Web: *www.benedict.edu*

CHARLESTON SOUTHERN UNIVERSITY — D-4

Charleston, SC 29423-8087 — (843) 863-7050
(800) 947-7474; Fax: (843) 863-7070

Full-time: 789 men, 1177 women	**Faculty:** 93; IIB, --$
Part-time: 158 men, 320 women	**Ph.D.s:** 71%
Graduate: 100 men, 138 women	**Student/Faculty:** 21 to 1
Year: semesters, summer session	**Tuition:** $12,368
Application Deadline: open	**Room & Board:** $4754
Freshman Class: 1569 applied, 1212 accepted, 425 enrolled	
SAT I Verbal/Math: 530/530	**ACT:** 22 — **COMPETITIVE**

Charleston Southern University, founded in 1964, is a private liberal arts institution affiliated with the South Carolina Baptist Convention. There are 4 undergraduate and 3 graduate schools. In addition to regional accreditation, CSU has baccalaureate program accreditation with NASDTEC, NASM, and NLN. The library contains 212,666 volumes, 212,539 microform items, and 7527 audiovisual forms/CDs, and subscribes to 9788 periodicals. Computerized library services include the card catalog and database searching. Special learning facilities include a learning resource center, an earthquake education center, and a field physics laboratory. The 500-acre campus is in a suburban area 20 miles west of Charleston. Including residence halls, there are 16 buildings.

Student Life: 81% of undergraduates are from South Carolina. Others are from 45 states, 35 foreign countries, and Canada. 85% are from public schools. 47% are white; 27% African American. 50% are claim no religious affiliation; 42% Protestant. The average age of freshmen is 18; all undergraduates, 25. 28% do not continue beyond their first year; 31% remain to graduate.

Housing: 1250 students can be accommodated in college housing, which includes single-sex dormitories and married-student housing. On-campus housing is guaranteed for the freshman year only and is available on a first-come, first-served basis. 56% of students commute. Alcohol is not permitted. All students may keep cars.

Activities: There are no fraternities or sororities. There are 20 groups on campus, including art, band, cheerleading, choir, chorus, drama, honors, jazz band, literary magazine, marching band, newspaper, religious, social service, student government, and yearbook.

Sports: There are 9 intercollegiate sports for men and 9 for women, and 4 intramural sports for men and 4 for women. Facilities include a gym, tennis courts, a track center, football and soccer fields, a baseball diamond, training and weight rooms, a 3-hole golf course with driving range, and a Wellness Center.

Disabled Students: All of the campus is accessible. Wheelchair ramps, elevators, special parking, specially equipped rest rooms, and lowered drinking fountains are available.

Services: Counseling and information services are available, as is tutoring in most subjects. There is remedial math, reading, and writing.

Campus Safety and Security: Measures include 24-hour foot and vehicle patrol, escort service, emergency telephones, and lighted pathways/sidewalks.

Programs of Study: CSU confers B.A., B.S., and B.Tech. degrees. Associate and master's degrees are also awarded. Bachelor's degrees are awarded in BIOLOGICAL SCIENCE (biochemistry and biology/biological science), BUSINESS (business administration and management), COMMUNICATIONS AND THE ARTS (dramatic arts, English, fine arts, music, Spanish, and speech/debate/rhetoric), COMPUTER AND PHYSICAL SCIENCE (chemistry, computer science, geology, mathematics, and natural sciences), EDUCATION (early childhood, elementary, music, physical, and science), ENGINEERING AND ENVIRONMENTAL DESIGN (environmental science), HEALTH PROFESSIONS (music therapy and nursing), SOCIAL SCIENCE (criminal justice, economics, geography, history, humanities, political science/government, psychology, religion, religious music, social science, sociology, and youth ministry).

Required: To graduate, students must complete 125 credit hours, including all core curriculum, major, and minor requirements, with a GPA of 2.0. At least 45 hours must be in the major. Core courses include 24 hours of communications and fine arts, 11 of natural science/math, and 9 of social studies.

Special: CSU offers internships, cross-registration through the Trident Area Consortium, work-study programs, dual majors, and nondegree study. Nonmajor preprofessional programs are available in dentistry, engineering, law, medicine, and ministry. There are 5 national honor societies, a freshman honors program, and all departments have honors programs.

Faculty/Classroom: 55% of faculty are male; 45%, female. All teach undergraduates. No introductory courses are taught by graduate students. The average class size in an introductory lecture is 40; in a laboratory, 15; and in a regular course, 25.

Admissions: 77% of the 2001-2002 applicants were accepted. The SAT I scores for the 2001-2002 freshman class were: Verbal--28% below 500, 55% between 500 and 599, 15% between 600 and 700, and 2% above 700; Math--28% below 500, 59% between 500 and 599, and 14% between 600 and 700. 50% of the current freshmen were in the top fifth of their class; 74% were in the top two fifths. 1 freshman graduated first in the class.

Requirements: The SAT I or ACT is recommended. In addition, applicants must be graduates of an accredited secondary school. The GED is accepted. Character references are preferred. An English proficiency exam is required for all entering students. CSU requires applicants to be in the upper 60% of their class. A GPA of 2.0 is required. AP and CLEP credits are accepted. Important factors in the admissions decision are evidence of special talent, leadership record, and advanced placement or honor courses. Applications are accepted on-line.

Procedure: Freshmen are admitted to all sessions. Entrance exams should be taken any time before filing for admission. Application deadlines are open. There is a rolling admissions plan. The fall 2001 application fee was $25.

Transfer: 278 transfer students enrolled in 2001-2002. Applicants must submit official transcripts from all previous colleges attended. Accepted transfers must take an English proficiency exam. 30 credits of 125 must be completed at CSU.

Visiting: There are regularly scheduled orientations for prospective students, consisting of orientation for students, orientation for parents, placement testing for students, a tour, and lunch. There are guides for informal visits and visitors may sit in on classes. To schedule a visit, contact the Office of Enrollment Services.

Financial Aid: The average freshman award was $8000. Of that total, scholarships or need-based grants averaged $5000 ($8000 maximum); loans averaged $2000 ($4125 maximum); and work contracts averaged $1000 ($1900 maximum). 26% of undergraduates work part time. Average annual earnings from campus work are $2000. The average financial indebtedness of the 2001 graduate was $20,000. CSU is a member of CSS. The CSS/Profile or FAFSA is required. The fall application deadline is May 1.

International Students: There are 69 international students enrolled. They must score 550 on the written TOEFL and also take the SAT I or the ACT.

Computers: The mainframe is an RS6000. Macs and PCs are available in 5 computer labs and in the library, and a student mainframe is available in all student labs; Internet and web access is provided in labs, dorm rooms, and the library. All students may access the system. There are no time limits and no fees. It is strongly recommended that all students have a personal computer.

Graduates: In 2001, 275 bachelor's degrees were awarded. The most popular majors were business administration (21%), education (14%), and psychology/social science (9%). In an average class, 31% graduate in 4 years. 30 companies recruited on campus in 2000-2001. Of the 2000 graduating class, 27% were enrolled in graduate school within 6 months of graduation and 63% were employed.

Admissions Contact: Cheryl Burton, Director of Enrollment Services. A video is available. E-mail: *enroll@csuniv.edu* Web: *www.csuniv.edu*

CITADEL, THE

Charleston, SC 29409 — D-4

(843) 953-5230
(800) 868-1842; Fax: (843) 953-7630

Full-time: 1911 men, 102 women	**Faculty:** 145; IIA, av$
Part-time: 59 men, 28 women	**Ph.D.s:** 93%
Graduate: 475 men, 1426 women	**Student/Faculty:** 14 to 1
Year: semesters, summer session	**Tuition:** $4601 ($11,276)
Application Deadline: open	**Room & Board:** $4525
Freshman Class: 1678 applied, 1390 accepted, 570 enrolled	
SAT I Verbal/Math: 530/530	**ACT:** 22 **COMPETITIVE**

The Citadel, established in 1842 by the South Carolina legislature, is a liberal arts military college supported by the state. Tuition figures in the above capsule are for students in the Corps of Cadets. In addition, freshmen pay a $4680 deposit and upperclassmen pay a $1420 deposit for uniforms, books, and supplies. There is 1 undergraduate and 1 graduate school. In addition to regional accreditation, The Citadel has baccalaureate program accreditation with AACSB, ABET, and NCATE. The library contains 228,861 volumes, 1,136,186 microform items, and 3922 audiovisual forms/CDs, and subscribes to 1336 periodicals. Computerized library services include the card catalog, interlibrary loans, and database searching. Special learning facilities include a military museum and archives, and a writing center. The 100-acre campus is in a suburban area in Charleston. Including residence halls, there are 69 buildings.

Student Life: 56% of undergraduates are from out of state, mostly the South. Others are from 46 states, 29 foreign countries, and Canada. 70% are from public schools. 81% are white. 68% are Protestant; 23% Catholic. The average age of freshmen is 18; all undergraduates, 20. 19% do not continue beyond their first year; 81% remain to graduate.

Housing: 1928 students can be accommodated in college housing. All cadets live in barracks. On-campus housing is guaranteed for all 4 years. All students live on campus and remain on campus on weekends. Alcohol is not permitted. Upperclassmen may keep cars.

Activities: There are no fraternities or sororities. There are 37 groups on campus, including bagpipe band, band, cheerleading, choir, chorale, computers, drama, drill team, ethnic, honors, literary magazine, marching band, newspaper, pep band, political, professional, religious, social, social service, student government, and yearbook. Popular campus events include Parents Weekend and Corps Day.

Sports: There are 9 intercollegiate sports for men and 5 for women, and 20 intramural sports for men and 20 for women. Facilities include a 22,000-seat stadium, a 6000-seat field house, fitness centers, weight and wrestling rooms, tennis courts, an all-weather track, and playing fields. The boating center and beach club are within a half-hour drive of the college.

Disabled Students: 80% of the campus is accessible. Wheelchair ramps, elevators, special parking, and specially equipped rest rooms are available.

Services: Counseling and information services are available, as is tutoring in every subject.

Campus Safety and Security: Measures include 24-hour foot and vehicle patrol, escort service when requested, lighted pathways/sidewalks, and lock out and jumpstart services.

Programs of Study: The Citadel confers B.A., B.S., B.S.B.A., B.S.C.E., and B.S.E.E. degrees. Master's degrees are also awarded. Bachelor's degrees are awarded in BIOLOGICAL SCIENCE (biology/biological science), BUSINESS (business administration and management), COMMUNICATIONS AND THE ARTS (English, French, German, and Spanish), COMPUTER AND PHYSICAL SCIENCE (chemistry, computer science, mathematics, and physics), EDUCATION (health, physical, and secondary), ENGINEERING AND ENVIRONMENTAL DESIGN (civil engineering and electrical/electronics engineering), HEALTH PROFESSIONS (predentistry and premedicine), SOCIAL SCIENCE (criminal justice, history, political science/government, and psychology). English is the strongest academically. Business administration is the largest.

Required: To graduate, students must complete 121 to 139 credit hours, depending on the major, with an overall GPA of 2.0 (2.5 for education majors). The required core curriculum for all majors includes study in 5 areas: English, history, math, science, and social sciences. Specific course requirements include 8 semesters of ROTC, 4 of English, and 4 of phys ed. In addition, cadets must satisfy disciplinary requirements and observe the honor system.

Special: Students may earn a combined B.A.-B.S. degree, design their own majors, and take a 3-2 program in engineering. Work-study programs, internships, dual majors, independent study, study abroad, and pass/fail options are also available. Qualified students may enroll in a separate honors program. There are 7 national honor societies, including Phi Beta Kappa, a freshman honors program, and 1 departmental honors program.

Faculty/Classroom: 77% of faculty are male; 23%, female. 95% teach undergraduates. The average class size in an introductory lecture is 25 and in a regular course, 20.

Admissions: 83% of the 2001-2002 applicants were accepted. The SAT I scores for the 2001-2002 freshman class were: Verbal--33% below 500, 44% between 500 and 599, 20% between 600 and 700, and 2% above 700; Math--31% below 500, 48% between 500 and 599, 18% between 600 and 700, and 3% above 700. The ACT scores were 29% below 21, 37% between 21 and 23, 23% between 24 and 26, 7% between 27 and 28, and 4% above 28. 29% of the current freshmen were in the top fifth of their class; 66% were in the top two fifths.

Requirements: The SAT I or ACT is required. In addition, SAT II: Subject test in math level II is strongly recommended for engineering, science, and math applicants. Also required are recommendations from high school principals or guidance counselors. Applicants must be between 16 and 22, unmarried, and meet certain physical requirements. High school preparation should include 4 units in English; 3 in math, including algebra I and II; 2 in lab science: biology, chemistry, or physics; 2 each in foreign language and social science; 1 in phys ed or ROTC; and 1 other academic unit. The Citadel requires applicants to be in the upper 50% of their class. A GPA of 2.0 is required. AP and CLEP credits are accepted. Important factors in the admissions decision are advanced placement or honor courses, extracurricular activities record, and leadership record.

Procedure: Freshmen are admitted in the fall. Entrance exams should be taken by February of the senior year. Application deadlines are open. There is a rolling admissions plan. The fall 2001 application fee was $35.

Transfer: 80 transfer students enrolled in 2001-2002. Applicants must meet freshmen entrance requirements and submit official transcripts from all previous colleges attended. Transfer students must have completed a minimum of 2 semesters as full-time students (minimum 12 hours each semester) and maintained a GPA of 2.0. A full year of course work, including half the required hours in the major, must be completed at The Citadel.

Visiting: There are regularly scheduled orientations for prospective students, including an interview with an admissions counselor and a campus tour guided by a cadet. There are guides for informal visits and visitors may sit in on classes and stay overnight. To schedule a visit, contact the Admissions Office.

Financial Aid: In 2001-2002, 47% of all freshmen and 41% of continuing students received some form of financial aid. 47% of freshmen and 25% of continuing students received need-based aid. The average freshman award was $3000. Of that total, scholarships or need-based grants averaged $1500 ($12,000 maximum); loans averaged $1000 ($5500 maximum); and work contracts averaged $500 ($2000 maximum). 3% of undergraduates work part time. Average annual earnings from campus work are $675. The average financial indebtedness of the 2001 graduate was $13,650. The FAFSA is required. The fall application deadline is March 15.

International Students: There are 61 international students enrolled. They must score 550 on the written TOEFL.

Computers: The mainframe is a DEC Alpha. There are 2 VAX terminal labs and 7 Mac and/or IBM PS/2 labs, some networked and some standalone, open to all students 7 days a week. Cadet rooms are wired for access to the campus network and the Internet. All students may access the system. There are no time limits and no fees. It is strongly recommended that all students have a Microsoft Windows-compatible 486 DX or Pentium PC.

Graduates: In 2001, 387 bachelor's degrees were awarded. The most popular majors were business administration (31%), political science (12%), and civil engineering (9%). In an average class, 63% graduate in 4 years, 69% in 5 years, and 70% in 6 years. 89 companies recruited on campus in 2000-2001. Of the 2000 graduating class, 15% were enrolled in graduate school within 6 months of graduation and 96% were employed.

Admissions Contact: Lt. Col. John Powell, Acting Dean of Enrollment Management. A video is available. E-mail: *admissions@citadel.edu*
Web: *www.citadel.edu*

CLAFLIN UNIVERSITY

Orangeburg, SC 29115 — C-3
(803) 535-5339
(800) 922-1246; Fax: (803) 531-3860

Full-time: 476 men, 874 women	**Faculty:** 76
Part-time: 42 men, 68 women	**Ph.D.s:** 70%
Graduate: none	**Student/Faculty:** 18 to 1
Year: semesters, summer session	**Tuition:** $8290
Application Deadline: open	**Room & Board:** $4445
Freshman Class: 2025 applied, 945 accepted, 335 enrolled	
SAT I Verbal/Math: 500/425 **ACT:** 19	**COMPETITIVE+**

Claflin University, established in 1869 and affiliated with the United Methodist Church, is a small, private, liberal arts institution offering undergraduate programs in education, humanities, natural sciences, math, and social sciences. In addition to regional accreditation, Claflin University has baccalaureate program accreditation with ACBSP and NCATE. The library contains 147,906 volumes, 61,542 microform items, and 1685 audiovisual forms/CDs, and subscribes to 380 periodicals. Computerized library services include the card catalog, interlibrary loans, and database searching. Special learning facilities include a learning resource center, art gallery, radio station, and TV station. The 38-acre campus is in a suburban area between Columbia and Charleston. Including residence halls, there are 24 buildings.

Student Life: 83% of undergraduates are from South Carolina. Others are from 24 states and 14 foreign countries. 99% are from public schools. 94% are African American. Most are Protestant. The average age of all undergraduates is 19. 21% do not continue beyond their first year; 75% remain to graduate.

Housing: 842 students can be accommodated in college housing, which includes single-sex dormitories and off-campus apartments. On-campus housing is available on a first-come, first-served basis. 60% of students live on campus. Alcohol is not permitted. Upperclassmen may keep cars.

Activities: 22% of men belong to 4 national fraternities; 25% of women belong to 4 national sororities. There are 40 groups on campus, including band, choir, drama, ethnic, film, honors, international, jazz band, literary magazine, marching band, newspaper, radio and TV, religious, social, social service, student government, and yearbook. Popular campus events include Founders Day, Pantherfest, and Claflin Pride Day.

Sports: There are 3 intercollegiate sports for men and 3 for women. Facilities include a gym, tennis courts, a game room, and basketball courts.

Disabled Students: 95% of the campus is accessible. Wheelchair ramps, elevators, special parking, and specially equipped rest rooms are available.

Services: Counseling and information services are available, as is tutoring in most subjects. There is remedial math, reading, and writing.

Campus Safety and Security: Measures include 24-hour foot and vehicle patrol, escort service, informal discussions, and lighted pathways/sidewalks.

Programs of Study: Claflin University confers B.A. and B.S. degrees. Bachelor's degrees are awarded in BIOLOGICAL SCIENCE (biology/biological science), BUSINESS (business administration and management), COMMUNICATIONS AND THE ARTS (English, fine arts, and music), COMPUTER AND PHYSICAL SCIENCE (chemistry, computer science, and mathematics), EDUCATION (art, elementary, music, physical, and secondary), HEALTH PROFESSIONS (predentistry), SOCIAL SCIENCE (history, ministries, political science/government, prelaw, religion, social science, and sociology). Biology, education, and business are the strongest academically. Sociology, education, and business are the largest.

Required: To graduate, all students must complete 122 to 154 semester hours with a minimum GPA of 2.0. General education requirements include courses in education, English, humanities, math, phys ed, natural science, computer science, and analytical reasoning. Liberal arts majors must also fulfill a foreign language requirement. A capstone project is required of all students.

Special: Claflin offers co-op and accelerated degree programs in all majors, cross-registration with South Carolina State University and Clemson University, study abroad, dual majors, and a 3-2 engineering degree with Clemson University. There are 7 national honor societies, and a freshman honors program.

Faculty/Classroom: 61% of faculty are male; 39%, female. All teach undergraduates. The average class size in an introductory lecture is 25; in a laboratory, 15; and in a regular course, 25.

Admissions: 47% of the 2001-2002 applicants were accepted. 55% of the current freshmen were in the top fifth of their class; 65% were in the top two fifths. 7 freshmen graduated first in their class.

Requirements: The SAT I or ACT is required. In addition, applicants should be high school graduates who have completed 16 to 18 units, including 4 units in English, 2 in math, and 1 each in social studies and natural science. Admissions decisions are based on the secondary school record, test scores, recommendations from the secondary school, personal qualities, leadership record, and health record. A GPA of 2.0 is required. AP and CLEP credits are accepted.

Procedure: Freshmen are admitted fall and spring. Application deadlines are open. The application fee is $20. Notification is sent on a rolling basis.

Transfer: 52 transfer students enrolled in 2001-2002. Applicants with fewer than 60 semester hours of college credit must submit test scores and meet the other criteria for entering freshmen. Official transcripts from all colleges attended are required. 25% of required credits (required credits total 122 to 154) must be completed at Claflin University.

Visiting: There are regularly scheduled orientations for prospective students. There are guides for informal visits and visitors may sit in on classes and stay overnight. To schedule a visit, contact the Admissions Office at *mzeigler@claflin.edu*.

Financial Aid: In a recent year, 96% of all freshmen and 95% of continuing students received some form of financial aid. 92% of freshmen and 89% of continuing students received need-based aid. The average freshman award was $8214. 35% of undergraduates work part time. The average financial indebtedness of a recent year's graduate was $14,412. The FAFSA and the student aid report (SAR) are required. The fall application deadline is June 1.

International Students: There are 65 international students enrolled. The school actively recruits these students. They must score 500 on the written TOEFL and also take the SAT I or the ACT.

Computers: The mainframe is an Alpha DS20 Compac. There are 26 computer labs with access to the Internet. All students may access the system. There are no time limits. The fee is $150.

Graduates: In 2001, 195 bachelor's degrees were awarded. The most popular majors were sociology (17%), sociology and criminal justice (16%), and child development (11%). In an average class, 75% graduate in 6 years. Of the 2000 graduating class, 20% were enrolled in graduate school within 6 months of graduation and 60% were employed.

Admissions Contact: Katherine Boyd. A video is available.
E-mail: *kboyd@clafl.claflin.edu*
Web: *http://www.icusc.org/claflin/cchome.html*

CLEMSON UNIVERSITY

Clemson, SC 29634-5124 — A-2
(864) 656-2287; Fax: (864) 656-0622

Full-time: 6870 men, 5755 women	**Faculty:** 1076; I, --$
Part-time: 490 men, 345 women	**Ph.D.s:** 84%
Graduate: 1770 men, 1635 women	**Student/Faculty:** 12 to 1
Year: semesters, summer session	**Tuition:** $3780 ($9974)
Application Deadline: see profile	**Room & Board:** $4874
Freshman Class: n/av	
SAT I Verbal/Math: required	**COMPETITIVE**

Clemson University, founded in 1889, is a public institution with programs in agriculture, architecture, commerce and industry, education, engineering, forest and recreation resources, liberal arts, nursing, and sciences. There are 5 undergraduate schools and 1 graduate school. Information in the above capsule and in the following profile is approximate. In addition to regional accreditation, Clemson has baccalaureate program accreditation with AACSB, ABET, CSAB, NAAB, NCATE, NLN, and NRPA. The library contains 906,625 volumes and 1,052,414 microform items, and subscribes to 11,574 periodicals. Computerized library services include the card catalog, interlibrary loans, and database searching. Special learning facilities include an art gallery, planetarium, and radio station. The 1400-acre campus is in a small town 32 miles west of Greenville. Including residence halls, there are 584 buildings.

Student Life: 66% of undergraduates are from South Carolina. Others are from 49 states, 97 foreign countries, and Canada. 80% are from public schools. 84% are white. The average age of freshmen is 18; all undergraduates, 21. 17% do not continue beyond their first year; 72% remain to graduate.

Housing: 6524 students can be accommodated in college housing, which includes single-sex and coed dormitories, on-campus apartments, off-campus apartments, and married-student housing. In addition, there are honors houses. On-campus housing is guaranteed for all 4 years. 51% of students live on campus. All students may keep cars.

Activities: 18% of men belong to 25 national fraternities; 23% of women belong to 15 national sororities. There are 250 groups on campus, including band, cheerleading, choir, chorus, computers, dance, debate, drama, drill team, ethnic, gay, honors, international, jazz band, literary magazine, marching band, musical theater, newspaper, orchestra, pep band, photography, political, professional, radio and TV, religious, social, social service, student government, and yearbook. Popular campus events include Spirit Blitz and First Friday.

Sports: There are 10 intercollegiate sports for men and 9 for women, and 32 intramural sports for men and 32 for women. Facilities include

a recreation center, an 80,000-seat stadium, and a 12,000-seat coliseum.
Disabled Students: 75% of the campus is accessible. Wheelchair ramps, elevators, special parking, specially equipped rest rooms, special class scheduling, lowered drinking fountains, and lowered telephones are available.
Services: Counseling and information services are available, as is tutoring in some subjects. There is a reader service for the blind. Other services include textbooks on tape, testing modifications, library assistance, interpreters, note takers, and letters to faculty members.
Campus Safety and Security: Measures include 24-hour foot and vehicle patrol, self-defense education, escort service, and shuttle buses. There are informal discussions, pamphlets/posters/films, emergency telephones, and lighted pathways/sidewalks.
Programs of Study: Clemson confers B.A., B.S., B.F.A, and B.L.A. degrees. Master's and doctoral degrees are also awarded. Bachelor's degrees are awarded in AGRICULTURE (agriculture, animal science, forestry and related sciences, forestry production and processing, horticulture, and soil science), BIOLOGICAL SCIENCE (biochemistry, biology/biological science, and microbiology), BUSINESS (accounting, banking and finance, business administration and management, management science, and marketing/retailing/merchandising), COMMUNICATIONS AND THE ARTS (communications, design, English, fine arts, French, German, modern language, and Spanish), COMPUTER AND PHYSICAL SCIENCE (chemistry, computer science, geology, information sciences and systems, mathematics, and physics), EDUCATION (agricultural, early childhood, elementary, industrial arts, secondary, and special), ENGINEERING AND ENVIRONMENTAL DESIGN (agricultural engineering, ceramic engineering, chemical engineering, civil engineering, computer engineering, construction management, electrical/electronics engineering, graphic arts technology, industrial administration/management, industrial engineering, landscape architecture/design, mechanical engineering, and textile technology), HEALTH PROFESSIONS (medical laboratory technology, nursing, predentistry, premedicine, prepharmacy, preveterinary science, and speech pathology/audiology), SOCIAL SCIENCE (economics, food science, history, parks and recreation management, philosophy, political science/government, prelaw, psychology, and sociology). Engineering and architecture are the strongest academically. Marketing is the largest.
Required: To graduate, students must complete 127 to 144 credit hours, including 89 to 108 hours in the major, with a GPA of 2.0. Courses are required in English, humanities, math, science, and social science.
Special: Co-op programs are available in all majors except nursing. Work-study programs and study abroad in 38 countries are offered. There are 22 national honor societies, a freshman honors program, and 40 departmental honors programs.
Faculty/Classroom: 68% of faculty are male; 32%, female. 95% teach undergraduates, 55% do research, and 50% do both. Graduate students teach 20% of introductory courses. The average class size in an introductory lecture is 38; in a laboratory, 17; and in a regular course, 18.
Admissions: In a recent year, there were 22 National Merit finalists; 119 freshmen graduated first in their class.
Requirements: The SAT I or ACT is required. In addition, applicants should be graduates of an accredited secondary school. The GED is accepted. AP and CLEP credits are accepted. Important factors in the admissions decision are advanced placement or honor courses, parents or siblings attending the school, and recommendations by school officials. Clemson accepts applications on-line via ExPAN available on the university's Internet home page.
Procedure: Freshmen are admitted fall, spring, and summer. Entrance exams should be taken during spring of the junior year or fall of the senior year. There are early admissions and deferred admissions plans. Check with school for current application deadlines. The fall 2001 application fee was $40. Notification is sent on a rolling basis.
Transfer: 729 transfer students enrolled in a recent year. Transfer applicants must have completed at least 30 semester hours with approximately a 2.5 GPA. 30 credits of 127 must be completed at Clemson.
Visiting: There are regularly scheduled orientations for prospective students, including a series of 2-day summer programs of advisement, student services presentations, and registration for the fall semester. There are guides for informal visits. To schedule a visit, contact the Visitor's Center at (864) 656-4789.
Financial Aid: The CSS/Profile, FAFSA, FFS, or SFS is required. Check with school for current deadlines.
International Students: There were 761 international students enrolled in a recent year. The school actively recruits these students. They must score 550 on the written TOEFL and also take the SAT I or the ACT. Students must take SAT II: Subject tests in math IIC for freshman math placement.
Computers: The mainframe is an HDS AS/EX-80. There are also 600 PCs available. All students may access the system. There are no time limits and no fees.
Graduates: In a recent year, 2531 bachelor's degrees were awarded. The most popular majors were mechanical engineering (5%), elementary education (5%), and nursing (5%). In an average class, 1% graduate in 3 years, 38% in 4 years, 66% in 5 years, and 72% in 6 years. 340 companies recruited on campus in a recent year.
Admissions Contact: Robert S. Barkley, Director of Admissions. A video is available. E-mail: *cuadmissions@clemson.edu*
Web: *http://www.clemson.edu*

COASTAL CAROLINA UNIVERSITY E-3
Conway, SC 29528 **(843) 349-2026**
(800) 277-7000; Fax: (843) 349-2127

Full-time: 1823 men, 2184 women	**Faculty:** 180; IIB, -$
Part-time: 266 men, 498 women	**Ph.D.s:** 83%
Graduate: 26 men, 168 women	**Student/Faculty:** 22 to 1
Year: semesters, summer session	**Tuition:** $3770 ($10,680)
Application Deadline: August 15	**Room & Board:** $5450
Freshman Class: 3094 applied, 2296 accepted, 941 enrolled	
SAT I Verbal/Math: 510/520	**ACT:** 21 **COMPETITIVE**

Coastal Carolina University, established in 1954, is a public liberal arts institution offering undergraduate programs through the colleges of business administration, natural and applied sciences, education, and humanities and fine arts. Graduate programs through the College of Education are offered. There are 5 undergraduate schools and 1 graduate school. In addition to regional accreditation, Coastal Carolina has baccalaureate program accreditation with AACSB, NASAD, and NCATE. The library contains 188,563 volumes, 78,168 microform items, and 11,636 audiovisual forms/CDs, and subscribes to 1736 periodicals. Computerized library services include the card catalog, interlibrary loans, and database searching. Special learning facilities include a learning resource center, art gallery, and marine science research center. The 244-acre campus is in a suburban area 9 miles west of Myrtle Beach. Including residence halls, there are 31 buildings.
Student Life: 59% of undergraduates are from South Carolina. Others are from 46 states, 49 foreign countries, and Canada. 95% are from public schools. 86% are white. The average age of freshmen is 19; all undergraduates, 23. 31% do not continue beyond their first year; 39% remain to graduate.
Housing: 1251 students can be accommodated in college housing, which includes coed dormitories. On-campus housing is available on a first-come, first-served basis. 74% of students commute. Alcohol is not permitted. All students may keep cars.
Activities: 13% of men belong to 5 national fraternities; 10% of women belong to 6 national sororities. There are 67 groups on campus, including art, band, cheerleading, chess, choir, chorale, chorus, computers, drama, ethnic, honors, international, jazz band, literary magazine, musical theater, pep band, political, professional, religious, social, social service, student government, and yearbook. Popular campus events include CINO Day, Christmas formal, and Welcome Back Dance.
Sports: There are 7 intercollegiate sports for men and 8 for women, and 17 intramural sports for men and 16 for women. Facilities include a gym, baseball, soccer, and softball fields, tennis, basketball, volleyball, and racquetball courts, an indoor Olympic-size swimming pool, an aerobic dance room, weight rooms and a track.
Disabled Students: 95% of the campus is accessible. Wheelchair ramps, elevators, special parking, specially equipped rest rooms, special class scheduling, and lowered drinking fountains are available.
Services: Counseling and information services are available, as is tutoring in some subjects, including English, foreign languages, math, and statistics. There is a reader service for the blind.
Campus Safety and Security: Measures include 24-hour foot and vehicle patrol, self-defense education, escort service, and informal discussions. There are pamphlets/posters/films, emergency telephones, and lighted pathways/sidewalks.
Programs of Study: Coastal Carolina confers B.A., B.S., B.A.Ed., B.A.I.S., B.S.B.A., B.S.Ed., B.S.I.S., and B.S.P.E. degrees. Master's degrees are also awarded. Bachelor's degrees are awarded in BIOLOGICAL SCIENCE (biology/biological science and marine science), BUSINESS (accounting, banking and finance, business administration and management, and marketing/retailing/merchandising), COMMUNICATIONS AND THE ARTS (dramatic arts, English, fine arts, music, musical theater, Spanish, and studio art), COMPUTER AND PHYSICAL SCIENCE (chemistry, computer science, and mathematics), EDUCATION (art, early childhood, elementary, English, mathematics, music, physical, secondary, social studies, and special), HEALTH PROFESSIONS (predentistry and premedicine), SOCIAL SCIENCE (history, interdisciplinary studies, philosophy, political science/government, prelaw, psychology, and sociology). Accounting, finance, and management are the strongest academically. Marine science, marketing, and management are the largest.
Required: Students must successfully complete a minimum of 120 credits, varying with major department requirements, and must maintain a minimum GPA of 2.0. A 4-year core curriculum of 44 to 52 hours is required for proficiency in the broad areas of writing, library research, a foreign language, and computer usage.

Special: Cross-regristration is available with Francis Marion and Winthrop Universities and MUSC Internships are offered in most majors. Study abroad in 10 countries, work-study programs, dual majors, B.A.-B.S. degrees, and interdisciplinary majors are offered. A 3-2 engineering degree is offered through Clemson University. A cooperative marketing/golf management program is available in the business administration major. Credit by exam, and pass/fail options are possible. There are 18 national honor societies, and a freshman honors program.

Faculty/Classroom: 65% of faculty are male; 35%, female. 67% teach undergraduates and 33% both teach and do research. No introductory courses are taught by graduate students. The average class size in an introductory lecture is 27; in a laboratory, 19; and in a regular course, 22.

Admissions: 74% of the 2001-2002 applicants were accepted. The SAT I scores for the 2001-2002 freshman class were: Verbal--42% below 500, 46% between 500 and 599, 11% between 600 and 700, and 1% above 700; Math--40% below 500, 43% between 500 and 599, 16% between 600 and 700, and 1% above 700. The ACT scores were 42% below 21, 35% between 21 and 23, 16% between 24 and 26, 4% between 27 and 28, and 3% above 28. 30% of the current freshmen were in the top fifth of their class; 60% were in the top two fifths. 6 freshmen graduated first in their class.

Requirements: The SAT I or ACT is required. In addition, graduation from an accredited secondary or home-school program is required; a GED will be accepted, with appropriate scores. Applicants are required to submit complete specific high school credits, including 4 years of college prep English, 3 units of mathematics (algebra ll required), 3 units of science, 3 units of social sciences (U.S. history required), 2 units of the same foreign language, 4 advanced electives (from computer science, math additional science, foreign language, social science, humanities, and arts), and 1 unit of phys ed or ROTC. An interview is recommended. A GPA of 2.25 is required. AP and CLEP credits are accepted. Important factors in the admissions decision are advanced placement or honor courses, recommendations by school officials, and evidence of special talent. Applications are accepted on-line at the school's web site.

Procedure: Freshmen are admitted to all sessions. Entrance exams should be taken in the spring of the junior year or fall of the senior year. There is a deferred admissions plan. Applications should be filed by August 15 for fall entry and December 15 for spring entry. The fall 2001 application fee was $35. Notification is sent on a rolling basis.

Transfer: 513 transfer students enrolled in 2001-2002. A minimum GPA of 2.0 is required. Transfers with fewer than 30 hours earned must also meet freshman admission requirements. Students must submit college transcripts and must be eligible to return to the last institution attended. 30 credits of 120 must be completed at Coastal Carolina.

Visiting: There are regularly scheduled orientations for prospective students, including sessions for academic requirements, housing, financial aid, student life, parents' orientation, tours, cookouts, and entertainment. There are guides for informal visits and visitors may sit in on classes. To schedule a visit, contact the Admissions Office.

Financial Aid: In 2001-2002, 73% of all freshmen and 60% of continuing students received some form of financial aid. 45% of freshmen and 42% of continuing students received need-based aid. The average freshman award was $5531. Of that total, scholarships or need-based grants averaged $1194 ($13,000 maximum); loans averaged $3237 ($6625 maximum); and work contracts averaged $1100 ($2000 maximum). 81% of undergraduates work part time. Average annual earnings from campus work are $2000. The average financial indebtedness of the 2001 graduate was $12,000. The FAFSA and the college's own financial statement are required. The fall application deadline is April 1.

International Students: There are 135 international students enrolled. They must score 500 on the written TOEFL or 173 on the electronic version. The SAT I, or ACT, is required for first-time freshmen.

Computers: The mainframe is a UNIX system. Student computer labs are located in the College of Business, the College of Education, the College of Natural and Applied Science, the academic center, and the library. There are 350 terminals for student use. All students may access the system 24 hours via dial-in. There are no time limits and no fees. It is strongly recommended that all students have a personal computer.

Graduates: In 2001, 659 bachelor's degrees were awarded. The most popular majors were marine science (9%), marketing (8%), and interdisciplinary studies (8%). 60 companies recruited on campus in 2000-2001.

Admissions Contact: Judy W. Vogt, Associate Vice President, Enrollment Service. E-mail: *admissions@coastal.edu*
Web: *www.coastal.edu/admissions*

COKER COLLEGE
Hartsville, SC 29550 D-2
(843) 383-8050
(800) 950-1908; Fax: (843) 383-8056

Full-time: 162 men, 273 women	**Faculty:** 55
Part-time: 5 men, 9 women	**Ph.D.s:** 80%
Graduate: none	**Student/Faculty:** 8 to 1
Year: semesters, summer session	**Tuition:** $15,300
Application Deadline: open	**Room & Board:** $4820
Freshman Class: 134 applied, 121 accepted, 121 enrolled	
SAT I Verbal/Math: 495/490	**ACT:** 19 **COMPETITIVE**

Coker College, founded in 1908, is a private institution offering undergraduate programs in business, education, and the arts and sciences. In addition to regional accreditation, Coker has baccalaureate program accreditation with NASDTEC and NASM. The library contains 77,569 volumes, 43,602 microform items, and 3717 audiovisual forms/CDs, and subscribes to 581 periodicals. Computerized library services include the card catalog, interlibrary loans, and database searching. Special learning facilities include an art gallery, a botanical garden, and a nature preserve. The 15-acre campus is in a small town 25 miles west of Florence, 70 miles northeast of Columbia, and 85 miles southeast of Charlotte, North Carolina. Including residence halls, there are 17 buildings.

Student Life: 77% of undergraduates are from South Carolina. Others are from 27 states, 10 foreign countries, and Canada. 74% are white; 20% African American. The average age of freshmen is 18; all undergraduates, 21. 22% do not continue beyond their first year; 51% remain to graduate.

Housing: 300 students can be accommodated in college housing, which includes single-sex and coed dormitories. On-campus housing is available on a first-come, first-served basis and is available on a lottery system for upperclassmen. 66% of students live on campus; of those, 50% remain on campus on weekends. All students may keep cars.

Activities: There are no fraternities or sororities. There are many groups and organizations on campus, including art, cheerleading, choir, chorus, dance, drama, ethnic, honors, musical theater, newspaper, photography, political, religious, social service, student government, and yearbook. Popular campus events include Black History Month, Apollo Night, and Bandfest.

Sports: There are 6 intercollegiate sports for men and 6 for women, and 17 intramural sports for men and 18 for women. Facilities include a gym, a weight room, an aerobic/dance room, soccer and softball fields, tennis courts, a boat house with canoes, and access to a golf course. The largest arena seats 600.

Disabled Students: 63% of the campus is accessible. Wheelchair ramps, elevators, special parking, specially equipped rest rooms, special class scheduling, and lowered drinking fountains are available.

Services: Counseling and information services are available, as is tutoring in most subjects, including English and math. There is a writing lab.

Campus Safety and Security: Measures include 24-hour foot and vehicle patrol, informal discussions, pamphlets/posters/films, and lighted pathways/sidewalks.

Programs of Study: Coker confers B.A. and B.S. degrees. Bachelor's degrees are awarded in BIOLOGICAL SCIENCE (biology/biological science), BUSINESS (business administration and management), COMMUNICATIONS AND THE ARTS (art, communications, dance, dramatic arts, English, French, graphic design, music, musical theater, photography, and Spanish), COMPUTER AND PHYSICAL SCIENCE (chemistry, computer science, and mathematics), EDUCATION (art, early childhood, education, elementary, English, mathematics, music, physical, and secondary), HEALTH PROFESSIONS (medical laboratory technology), SOCIAL SCIENCE (history, political science/government, psychology, religion, social science, and sociology). Biology, math, and education are the strongest academically. Business, education, and visual and performing arts are the largest.

Required: Distribution requirements include 9 hours each in humanities and oral and written rhetoric, 7 in science, 6 each in the arts and behavioral sciences, and 3 each in nonnative language, math, and phys ed. A total of 120 credit hours, with 30 to 45 in the major, and a minimum 2.0 GPA are required to graduate.

Special: Internships, study abroad in many countries, on-campus and community service work-study programs, cross-registration with Central College, and dual and student-designed majors are offered. A 3-1 program in medical technology with McCleod Regional Medical Center is possible. Also available are credit for military experience, nondegree study, and pass/fail options. The college's round-table approach to teaching allows students and professors to discuss topics and research in small, round-table settings. There are 2 national honor societies and 2 departmental honors programs.

Faculty/Classroom: 62% of faculty are male; 38%, female. All teach undergraduates and 60% both teach and do research. The average class size in an introductory lecture is 15; in a laboratory, 15; and in a regular course, 9.

Admissions: 90% of the 2001-2002 applicants were accepted. The SAT I scores for the 2001-2002 freshman class were: Verbal--49% below

500, 39% between 500 and 599, 10% between 600 and 700, and 1% above 700; Math--56% below 500, 35% between 500 and 599, and 9% between 600 and 700. The ACT scores were 60% below 21, 15% between 21 and 23, 1% between 24 and 26, 10% between 27 and 28, and 10% above 28. 46% of the current freshmen were in the top fifth of their class; 80% were in the top two fifths. 1 freshman graduated first in the class in a recent year..

Requirements: The SAT I or ACT is required. In addition, applicants must be graduates of an accredited secondary school or have a GED. A recommendation from a high school guidance counselor or teacher is required. An audition or portfolio review is required for music, dance, art, and drama. A GPA of 2.0 is required. AP and CLEP credits are accepted. Important factors in the admissions decision are advanced placement or honor courses, extracurricular activities record, and leadership record. Applications are accepted on-line at the school's web site.

Procedure: Freshmen are admitted fall, spring, and summer. Entrance exams should be taken during the junior year or the first part of the senior year. There are early action and deferred admissions plans. Application deadlines are open. The application fee is $15. Notification is sent on a rolling basis.

Transfer: 27 transfer students enrolled in 2001-2002. Applicants with fewer than 30 semester hours must submit high school transcripts and SAT I scores. A minimum 2.0 GPA is required. 30 credits of 120 must be completed at Coker.

Visiting: There are regularly scheduled orientations for prospective students, consisting of orientation, a meal, campus tours, and discussions with faculty and a student panel. There are guides for informal visits and visitors may sit in on classes and stay overnight. To schedule a visit, contact the Admissions Office.

Financial Aid: In 2001-2002, all freshmen and 99% of continuing students received some form of financial aid. 86% of all students received need-based aid. The average freshman award was $16,838. Of that total, scholarships or need-based grants averaged $12,494 ($21,870 maximum); loans averaged $5261 ($13,453 maximum); and work contracts averaged $1072 ($1500 maximum). 46% of undergraduates work part time. Average annual earnings from campus work are $1000. The average financial indebtedness of the 2001 graduate was $20,265. Coker is a member of CSS. The FAFSA is required. The fall application deadline is June 1.

International Students: There are 13 international students enrolled. They must score 500 on the written TOEFL or 173 on the electronic version.

Computers: There is a network of 52 PCs as well as other independent computers on campus in 4 locations. All dorm rooms are wired for network access. All students may access the system regular hours in labs and at all times in dorm rooms. There are no time limits and no fees.

Graduates: In 2001, 58 bachelor's degrees were awarded. The most popular majors were education (28%), business/marketing (14%), and visual and performing arts (12%). In an average class, 51% graduate in 4 years.

Admissions Contact: David Anthony, Director of Admissions and Student Financial Planning. A video is available.
E-mail: *admission@coker.edu* Web: *www.coker.edu*

COLLEGE OF CHARLESTON C-3

Charleston, SC 29424 **(843) 953-5670; Fax: (843) 953-6322**

Full-time: 3153 men, 5650 women	**Faculty:** 464; IIA, --$
Part-time: 279 men, 384 women	**Ph.D.s:** 91%
Graduate: 257 men, 1425 women	**Student/Faculty:** 19 to 1
Year: semesters, summer session	**Tuition:** $3780 ($8540)
Application Deadline: May 1	**Room & Board:** $4570
Freshman Class: 8356 applied, 5471 accepted, 1971 enrolled	
SAT I or ACT: required	**HIGHLY COMPETITIVE**

The College of Charleston, founded in 1770, is a state-assisted institution offering liberal arts programs, including business and education. There are 5 undergraduate schools and 1 graduate school. In addition to regional accreditation, C of C has baccalaureate program accreditation with AACSB. The 2 libraries contain 485,174 volumes, 646,955 microform items, and 2292 audiovisual forms/CDs, and subscribe to 2772 periodicals. Computerized library services include the card catalog, interlibrary loans, and database searching. Special learning facilities include a learning resource center, art gallery, TV station, observatory, communications museum, marine lab, Afro-American research center, and bronze sculpture foundry. The 52-acre campus is in an urban area in the heart of historic Charleston, by the Atlantic Ocean. Including residence halls, there are 100 buildings.

Student Life: 75% of undergraduates are from South Carolina. Others are from 50 states, 73 foreign countries, and Canada. 79% are from public schools. 85% are white. The average age of freshmen is 18; all undergraduates, 21. 20% do not continue beyond their first year; 80% remain to graduate.

Housing: 2100 students can be accommodated in college housing, which includes single-sex and coed dormitories, on-campus apartments, fraternity houses, and sorority houses. In addition, there are honors houses, language houses, and special-interest houses. On-campus housing is available on a first-come, first-served basis. 79% of students commute. Alcohol is not permitted. Upperclassmen may keep cars.

Activities: 15% of men belong to 8 national fraternities; 20% of women belong to 7 national sororities. There are 143 groups on campus, including art, band, cheerleading, chess, choir, chorale, computers, dance, drama, ethnic, film, gay, honors, international, jazz band, literary magazine, musical theater, newspaper, opera, orchestra, pep band, political, professional, radio and TV, religious, social, social service, student government, symphony, and yearbook. Popular campus events include Sports Rally, Thursday Entertainment and Food Specials, and Black History Month.

Sports: There are 8 intercollegiate sports for men and 7 for women, and 17 intramural sports for men and 17 for women. Facilities include a phys ed center with racquetball courts and a weight and workout room, pool, outdoor recreation center with baseball and soccer fields, tennis courts, sailing marina, and student center with a movie theater, game room, meeting facilities, ballroom, and garden.

Disabled Students: 80% of the campus is accessible. Wheelchair ramps, elevators, special parking, specially equipped rest rooms, special class scheduling, lowered drinking fountains, and lowered telephones are available.

Services: Counseling and information services are available, as is tutoring in most subjects. There is remedial math, reading, and writing.

Campus Safety and Security: Measures include 24-hour foot and vehicle patrol, self-defense education, escort service, and informal discussions. There are pamphlets/posters/films, emergency telephones, and lighted pathways/sidewalks.

Programs of Study: C of C confers B.A., B.S., A.B., B.S.D., and B.S.M. degrees. Master's degrees are also awarded. Bachelor's degrees are awarded in BIOLOGICAL SCIENCE (biochemistry, biology/biological science, and marine biology), BUSINESS (accounting and business administration and management), COMMUNICATIONS AND THE ARTS (art history and appreciation, classics, communications, dramatic arts, English, French, German, music, Spanish, and studio art), COMPUTER AND PHYSICAL SCIENCE (chemistry, computer science, geology, information sciences and systems, mathematics, and physics), EDUCATION (elementary, physical, and special), HEALTH PROFESSIONS (predentistry and premedicine), SOCIAL SCIENCE (anthropology, economics, history, philosophy, political science/government, psychology, religion, sociology, and urban studies). Sciences and business are the strongest academically. Business and education are the largest.

Required: All students must complete a core curriculum, including English and history courses, 12 hours each of language and humanities, 8 hours of lab science, and 6 hours each of math or logic and social science. A total of 122 credit hours, including 24 to 43 in the major, with a minimum overall GPA of 2.0 (2.5 in some majors) is required to graduate.

Special: Cross-registration is possible with the Medical University of South Carolina, Trident Technical College, The Citadel, and Charleston Southern University. Co-op programs and internships in all majors, a Washington semester, study abroad in about 39 countries, work-study programs, B.A.-B.S. degrees, and dual majors are offered. The B.S.D. and B.S.M. degrees provide 3 years in predentistry or premedicine, with the fourth year of completion at a medical school. 3-2 engineering degrees are available with Case Western Reserve University, Clemson University, Georgia Institute of Technology, University of South Carolina, and Washington University of St. Louis. A 2-2 program in allied health, biometry, or nursing is offered with the Medical University of South Carolina. The college's 3-week Maymester session offers unconventional courses and programs using alternative methods of instruction. There is an interdisciplinary honors program available to talented students. There are 10 national honor societies, a freshman honors program, and 10 departmental honors program.

Faculty/Classroom: 54% of faculty are male; 46%, female. All teach undergraduates and 34% both teach and do research. No introductory courses are taught by graduate students. The average class size in an introductory lecture is 26; in a laboratory, 21; and in a regular course, 26.

Admissions: 65% of the 2001-2002 applicants were accepted. The SAT I scores for the 2001-2002 freshman class were: Verbal--6% below 500, 54% between 500 and 599, 35% between 600 and 700, and 5% above 700; Math--6% below 500, 58% between 500 and 599, 33% between 600 and 700, and 3% above 700. 61% of the current freshmen were in the top fifth of their class; 92% were in the top two fifths. 10 freshmen graduated first in their class.

Requirements: The SAT I or ACT is required. In addition, applicants should have completed 4 units of high school English, 3 of math, 2 to 3 of social studies, including 1/2 unit each of economics and government, 2 years each of lab science and foreign language, and 1 year of U.S. history. In addition, students should have 1 unit of advanced math or computer science or a combination of these, or 1 unit of world history, world geography, or Western civilization. The GED is accepted. An interview is recommended. AP and CLEP credits are accepted. Important factors in the admissions decision are ability to finance college education, leadership record, and evidence of special talent. The college accepts the Common Application and applications on-line via the Internet on its home page.

Procedure: Freshmen are admitted fall and spring. Entrance exams should be taken by March 1 or earlier. There is a deferred admissions plan. Applications should be filed by May 1 for fall entry and November 1 for winter entry. Notification is sent on a rolling basis. The fall 2001 application fee was $35.

Transfer: 638 transfer students enrolled in 2001-2002. Applicants must be eligible to return to the last institution attended. Students with fewer than 60 hours must have a 2.3 GPA; all others must have a 2.0 GPA. 36 credits of 122 must be completed at C of C.

Visiting: There are regularly scheduled orientations for prospective students, consisting of 1-day open houses throughout the year and 6 2-day orientation sessions throughout the summer, including a family session. Academic requirements and expectations, services offered, placement testing, individual academic advising, registration, and introduction to residence life and cultural offerings are included. There are guides for informal visits and visitors may sit in on classes and stay overnight. To schedule a visit, contact the Admissions Office.

Financial Aid: 64% of freshmen received need-based aid. The average freshman award was $5297. 12% of undergraduates work part time. Average annual earnings from campus work are $876. The FAFSA is required.

International Students: The school actively recruits international students. They must score 550 on the written TOEFL.

Computers: The mainframe is a DEC VAX 6510. Dial-in capability, 2 large centers with about 90 personal computers in each, and 4 networked classrooms with a computer station for each student are available. Software includes word processing, spreadsheets, database, statistical, and specialized disciplines. All students may access the system 24 hours a day. There are no time limits. The fee is $25.

Graduates: In 2001, 1798 bachelor's degrees were awarded. The most popular majors were business administration (19%), elementary education (13%), and communications (12%). In an average class, 1% graduate in 3 years, 38% in 4 years, 53% in 5 years, and 53% in 6 years. Of the 2000 graduating class, 22% were enrolled in graduate school within 6 months of graduation and 94% were employed.

Admissions Contact: Donald Burkard, Dean of Admissions. A video is available. E-mail: *admissions@cofc.edu* Web: *www.cofc.edu*

COLUMBIA COLLEGE
Columbia, SC 29203 — C-3
(803) 786-3871
(800) 277-1301; Fax: (803) 786-3674

Full-time: 1110 women	**Faculty:** 81
Part-time: 130 women	**Ph.D.s:** 69%
Graduate: 130 men and women	**Student/Faculty:** 14 to 1
Year: semesters, summer session	**Tuition:** $15,060
Application Deadline: open	**Room & Board:** $4800
Freshman Class: n/av	
SAT I Verbal/Math: required	**LESS COMPETITIVE**

Columbia College, founded in 1854, is a private women's liberal arts college affiliated with the United Methodist Church. There is 1 graduate school. Figures in above capsule are approximate. In addition to regional accreditation, Columbia College has baccalaureate program accreditation with CSWE, NASAD, NASDTEC, and NASM. The library contains 170,000 volumes, 8353 microform items, and 29,834 audiovisual forms/CDs, and subscribes to 633 periodicals. Computerized library services include interlibrary loans and database searching. Special learning facilities include a learning resource center, art gallery, women's leadership center, and a science and technology center. The 33-acre campus is in an urban area in the northern section of Columbia. Including residence halls, there are 26 buildings.

Student Life: 93% of undergraduates are from South Carolina. Others are from 15 states and 13 foreign countries. 56% are white; 30% African American. 81% are Protestant; 11% claim no religious affiliation. The average age of freshmen is 18; all undergraduates, 23. 27% do not continue beyond their first year; 55% remain to graduate.

Housing: 650 students can be accommodated in college housing, which includes single-sex dormitories. In addition, there are honors houses. On-campus housing is guaranteed for all 4 years. 58% of students live on campus. Alcohol is not permitted. All students may keep cars.

Activities: There are no fraternities. There are 57 groups on campus, including art, band, choir, chorus, computers, dance, drama, ethnic, honors, international, literary magazine, musical theater, newspaper, opera, photography, political, professional, radio and TV, religious, social, social service, student government, and yearbook. Popular campus events include Fine Arts Series, Follies, and May Day.

Sports: Facilities include an athletic field, tennis courts, a gym, an Olympic-size pool, a fitness lab, and a dance studio.

Disabled Students: 90% of the campus is accessible. Wheelchair ramps, elevators, special parking, specially equipped rest rooms, and special class scheduling are available.

Services: Counseling and information services are available. Peer tutoring and remedial instruction are offered in some subjects.

Campus Safety and Security: Measures include 24-hour foot and vehicle patrol, self-defense education, escort service, and informal discussions. There are pamphlets/posters/films, emergency telephones, and lighted pathways/sidewalks.

Programs of Study: Columbia College confers B.A., B.F.A., and B.Mus. degrees. Master's degrees are also awarded. Bachelor's degrees are awarded in BIOLOGICAL SCIENCE (biology/biological science), BUSINESS (accounting and business administration and management), COMMUNICATIONS AND THE ARTS (communications, dance, English, French, languages, music, music performance, performing arts, piano/organ, Spanish, and studio art), COMPUTER AND PHYSICAL SCIENCE (chemistry, information sciences and systems, and mathematics), EDUCATION (Christian, dance, early childhood, elementary, music, special, and speech correction), HEALTH PROFESSIONS (medical laboratory technology), SOCIAL SCIENCE (history, political science/government, psychology, public affairs, religion, religious music, social work, and sociology). Education, sciences, and performing arts are the largest.

Required: To graduate, students must complete 127 semester hours, with a minimum GPA of 2.5 in the major and 2.0 overall. General education requirements for the B.A. degree include 15 hours of communication skills, 12 of social science, 9 of aesthetics, 8 of natural science, 6 of religion, and 3 each of math and phys ed. Students also must satisfy proficiency requirements in English and math.

Special: The Center for Contractual Studies allows qualified students to pursue individualized programs through independent study, practicums, and a senior project. The college also offers internships, study abroad, a Washington semester, dual majors, and credit for life, military, and work experience. Nondegree study and pass/fail options are available. There is a freshman honors program.

Faculty/Classroom: 36% of faculty are male; 64%, female. 95% teach undergraduates. No introductory courses are taught by graduate students. The average class size in an introductory lecture is 20 and in a laboratory, 20.

Requirements: The SAT I or ACT is required. In addition, applicants must be graduates of an accredited secondary school or have earned a GED. They should complete 16 Carnegie units, including 4 years of English, 3 of math, and 2 each of foreign language and lab science, as well as courses in history and social studies. An essay and an interview are recommended, as is a portfolio or an audition for fine or performing arts students. AP and CLEP credits are accepted. Important factors in the admissions decision are recommendations by school officials, advanced placement or honor courses, and leadership record.

Procedure: Freshmen are admitted to all sessions. Entrance exams should be taken near the end of the junior year or by December of the senior year. Application deadlines are open. The fall 2001 application fee was $20. Notification is sent on a rolling basis.

Transfer: 83 transfer students enrolled in a recent year. An interview is recommended for transfer students. Applicants with fewer than 24 semester hours must present the ACT or the SAT I scores and high school transcripts. Grades of C or better transfer for credit. 30 credits of 127 must be completed at Columbia College.

Visiting: There are regularly scheduled orientations for prospective students, consisting of meetings with faculty advisers, classroom visits, campus tours, lunch, and student life and financial aid presentations. There are guides for informal visits and visitors may sit in on classes. To schedule a visit, contact the Admissions Office.

Financial Aid: In a recent year, 96% of all freshmen and 85% of continuing students received some form of financial aid. 87% of freshmen and 74% of continuing students received need-based aid. The average freshman award was $14,738. Of that total, scholarships or need-based grants averaged $10,145; loans averaged $3919; and work contracts averaged $674. 34% of undergraduates work part time. Average annual earnings from campus work are $700. Columbia College is a member of CSS. The FAFSA is required. Check with school for current deadlines.

International Students: There were 13 international students enrolled in a recent year. The school actively recruits these students. They must score 550 on the written TOEFL and also take the SAT I or the ACT.

Computers: The mainframe is a DEC 5500 running UNIX. Students have access to the Internet in each residence hall room and in various classrooms, labs, and media centers. All students may access the system. There are no time limits. The fee is $15 per semester. It is strongly recommended that all students have a personal computer.

Graduates: In a recent year, 272 bachelor's degrees were awarded. The most popular majors were elementary education (15%), business administration (13%), and early childhood education (11%). In an average class, 52% graduate in 4 years, 55% in 5 years, and 57% in 6 years.

Admissions Contact: Julie A. King, Director of Freshman Admissions.
E-mail: *admissions@colacoll.edu*
Web: *http://www.columbiacollegesc.edu*

CONVERSE COLLEGE B-1
Spartanburg, SC 29302 (864) 596-9746
(800) 766-1125; Fax: (864) 596-9225

Full-time: 657 women | **Faculty:** 70; IIB, --$
Part-time: 75 women | **Ph.D.s:** 89%
Graduate: 104 men, 691 women | **Student/Faculty:** 9 to 1
Year: 4-1-4, summer session | **Tuition:** $16,850
Application Deadline: August 15 | **Room & Board:** $5140
Freshman Class: 535 applied, 421 accepted, 176 enrolled
SAT I Verbal/Math: 560/550 | **ACT:** 24 **VERY COMPETITIVE**

Converse College, founded in 1889, is a private, women's liberal arts college. Men are admitted to the graduate programs. There are 2 undergraduate and 2 graduate schools. In addition to regional accreditation, Converse College has baccalaureate program accreditation with NASM. The library contains 150,000 volumes, 310 microform items, and 12,000 audiovisual forms/CDs, and subscribes to 700 periodicals. Computerized library services include the card catalog, interlibrary loans, and database searching. Special learning facilities include a learning resource center, art gallery, and natural history museum. The 72-acre campus is in an urban area 80 miles southwest of Charlotte. Including residence halls, there are 27 buildings.

Student Life: 65% of undergraduates are from South Carolina. Others are from 25 states, 10 foreign countries, and Canada. 70% are from public schools. 78% are white. The average age of freshmen is 18; all undergraduates, 20. 27% do not continue beyond their first year; 55% remain to graduate.

Housing: 700 students can be accommodated in college housing, which includes single-sex dormitories. On-campus housing is guaranteed for all 4 years. 90% of students live on campus; of those, 40% remain on campus on weekends. Alcohol is not permitted. All students may keep cars.

Activities: There are no fraternities. There are 50 groups on campus, including art, cheerleading, choir, chorale, chorus, computers, dance, debate, drama, ethnic, gay, honors, international, literary magazine, musical theater, newspaper, opera, orchestra, photography, political, professional, religious, social service, student government, symphony, and yearbook. Popular campus events include Founders Day, May Day, and Family Weekend.

Sports: Facilities include a gym, a pool, a dance studio, a weight room, tennis courts, and bowling lanes.

Disabled Students: 50% of the campus is accessible. Wheelchair ramps, elevators, special parking, and specially equipped rest rooms are available.

Services: Counseling and information services are available, as is tutoring in every subject. There is a reader service for the blind.

Campus Safety and Security: Measures include 24-hour foot and vehicle patrol, self-defense education, escort service, and informal discussions. There are pamphlets/posters/films, emergency telephones, and lighted pathways/sidewalks.

Programs of Study: Converse College confers B.A., B.S., B.F.A., and B.Mus. degrees. Master's degrees are also awarded. Bachelor's degrees are awarded in BIOLOGICAL SCIENCE (biology/biological science), BUSINESS (accounting and business administration and management), COMMUNICATIONS AND THE ARTS (English, fine arts, French, languages, modern language, music, and Spanish), COMPUTER AND PHYSICAL SCIENCE (chemistry, computer science, and mathematics), EDUCATION (art, early childhood, elementary, foreign languages, music, science, and secondary), ENGINEERING AND ENVIRONMENTAL DESIGN (interior design), HEALTH PROFESSIONS (art therapy, predentistry, and premedicine), SOCIAL SCIENCE (economics, history, political science/government, prelaw, psychology, religion, and sociology). English, politics, and biology are the strongest academically. Music, education, and business are the largest.

Required: To graduate, students must complete 120 semester hours, including 52 hours across the liberal arts discipline, with a minimum GPA of 2.0. Courses in ideas and culture and phys ed are required.

Special: There are co-op programs and cross-registration with Wofford College. Internships, study abroad, a work-study program, accelerated degree programs, B.A.-B.S. degrees in business, economics, sociology, biology, and chemistry, as well as dual majors are offered. There are 10 national honor societies, a freshman honors program, and all departments have honors programs.

Faculty/Classroom: 50% of faculty are male; 50%, female. 99% teach undergraduates and 50% both teach and do research. No introductory courses are taught by graduate students. The average class size in an introductory lecture is 20; in a laboratory, 15; and in a regular course, 11.

Admissions: 79% of the 2001-2002 applicants were accepted. The SAT I scores for the 2001-2002 freshman class were: Verbal--22% below 500, 40% between 500 and 599, 32% between 600 and 700, and 6% above 700; Math--24% below 500, 48% between 500 and 599, 25% between 600 and 700, and 3% above 700. The ACT scores were 27% below 21, 20% between 21 and 23, 28% between 24 and 26, 10% between 27 and 28, and 15% above 28. 62% of the current freshmen were in the top fifth of their class; 82% were in the top two fifths. 2 freshmen graduated first in their class.

Requirements: The SAT I or ACT is recommended. In addition, applicants should be graduates of an accredited secondary school, having completed 20 Carnegie units, including 4 years of English, 3 of math, 2 each of foreign language, science, and social studies, and 1 of history. The GED is accepted. An interview is recommended for all students and an audition is recommended for music students. A GPA of 2.0 is required. AP and CLEP credits are accepted. Important factors in the admissions decision are advanced placement or honor courses, recommendations by school officials, and leadership record. Applications are accepted on computer disk through CollegeLink and on-line through the web site.

Procedure: Freshmen are admitted to all sessions. Entrance exams should be taken by the senior year of high school. There is an early decision plan. Early decision applications should be filed by November; regular applications, by August 15 for fall entry. The fall 2001 application fee was $35. Notification of early decision is sent in November; regular decision, on a rolling basis. 4 early decision candidates were accepted for the 2001-2002 class.

Transfer: 12 transfer students enrolled in 2001-2002. Transfer applicants should have a minimum GPA of 2.0. 42 credits of 120 must be completed at Converse College.

Visiting: There are regularly scheduled orientations for prospective students, consisting of faculty meetings, panel discussions, campus tours, tours of Spartanburg, and private interview sessions. There are guides for informal visits and visitors may sit in on classes and stay overnight. To schedule a visit, contact the Admissions Office at (864) 596-9090 or (864) 596-9225.

Financial Aid: In 2001-2002, 66% of all students received some form of financial aid. 66% of freshmen and 63% of continuing students received need-based aid. The average freshman award was $14,614. Of that total, scholarships or need-based grants averaged $12,725; loans averaged $2906; and work contracts averaged $1300. 33% of undergraduates work part time. Average annual earnings from campus work are $915. The average financial indebtedness of the 2001 graduate was $18,380. The FAFSA is required. The fall application deadline is March 15.

International Students: There are 14 international students enrolled. The school actively recruits these students. They must score 550 on the written TOEFL.

Computers: The mainframe is a DEC ALPHA. There are also 2 computer labs, as well as PCs in the library, residence halls, and departmental computer labs. All students may access the system. There are no time limits and no fees. It is strongly recommended that all students have personal computers.

Graduates: In 2001, 153 bachelor's degrees were awarded. The most popular majors were education (18%), business (14%), and psychology (10%). In an average class, 2% graduate in 3 years, 63% in 4 years, 63% in 5 years, and 64% in 6 years. 140 companies recruited on campus in 2000-2001. Of the 2000 graduating class, 25% were enrolled in graduate school within 6 months of graduation and 55% were employed.

Admissions Contact: Wanda McDowell, Director of Admissions. A video is available. E-mail: *wanda.mcdowell@converse.edu*
Web: *www.converse.edu*

ERSKINE COLLEGE B-2
Due West, SC 29639 (864) 379-8830
(800) 241-8721; Fax: (864) 379-2167

Full-time: 233 men, 347 women | **Faculty:** 42; IIB, -$
Part-time: 1 man, 13 women | **Ph.D.s:** 90%
Graduate: none | **Student/Faculty:** 14 to 1
Year: 4-1-4, summer session | **Tuition:** $16,153
Application Deadline: open | **Room & Board:** $5246
Freshman Class: 773 applied, 556 accepted, 218 enrolled
SAT I Verbal/Math: 570/570 | **ACT:** 24 **VERY COMPETITIVE**

Erskine College, founded in 1839, is a private liberal arts college affiliated with the Associate Reformed Presbyterian Church. The library contains 247,158 volumes, 56,478 microform items, and 1508 audiovisual forms/CDs, and subscribes to 808 periodicals. Computerized library services include the card catalog, interlibrary loans, and database searching. Special learning facilities include an art gallery, radio station, and TV station. The 85-acre campus is in a rural area 90 miles west of Columbia. Including residence halls, there are 30 buildings.

Student Life: 78% of undergraduates are from South Carolina. Others are from 20 states and 3 foreign countries. 86% are from public schools. 91% are white. Most are Protestant. The average age of freshmen is 18; all undergraduates, 20. 18% do not continue beyond their first year; 66% remain to graduate.

Housing: 644 students can be accommodated in college housing, which includes single-sex dormitories. On-campus housing is guaranteed for all 4 years. 91% of students live on campus; of those, 50% remain on campus on weekends. Alcohol is not permitted. All students may keep cars.

Activities: 15% of men belong to 3 local fraternities; 23% of women belong to 5 local sororities. There are 45 groups on campus, including cheerleading, choir, chorale, chorus, computers, dance, drama, ethnic, honors, jazz band, literary magazine, newspaper, pep band, political, professional, radio and TV, religious, social, social service, student government, and yearbook. Popular campus events include Spring Fling, Back to School Bash, and Freshman Follies.

Sports: There are 5 intercollegiate sports for men and 5 for women, and 7 intramural sports for men and 7 for women. Facilities include a physical activities center, 2 gyms, racquetball courts, soccer and baseball fields, tennis and basketball courts, an outdoor pavilion, an outdoor pool, 2 sand volleyball courts, a weight room, and a dance/aerobics studio.

Disabled Students: 75% of the campus is accessible. Wheelchair ramps, elevators, special parking, specially equipped rest rooms, and special class scheduling are available.

Services: Counseling and information services are available, as is tutoring in every subject. There is a reader service for the blind.

Campus Safety and Security: Measures include 24-hour foot and vehicle patrol, escort service, informal discussions, and pamphlets/posters/films. There are lighted pathways/sidewalks.

Programs of Study: Erskine confers A.B. and B.S. degrees. Master's and doctoral degrees are also awarded. Bachelor's degrees are awarded in BIOLOGICAL SCIENCE (biology/biological science), BUSINESS (business administration and management, and sports management), COMMUNICATIONS AND THE ARTS (English and music), COMPUTER AND PHYSICAL SCIENCE (chemistry, mathematics, natural sciences, and physics), EDUCATION (athletic training, Christian, early childhood, elementary, foreign languages, music, physical, and special), HEALTH PROFESSIONS (health science, and medical laboratory technology), SOCIAL SCIENCE (American studies, behavioral science, history, philosophy, psychology, religion, and social studies). Business administration and biology are the largest.

Required: Students must complete 124 semester hours with an average of 27 credits in a major and a minimum GPA of 2.0. A basic curriculum of arts and letters, humanities, natural science and math, social sciences, and phys ed is required. Attendance at 17 convocations per semester is also required.

Special: Externships are available only in the winter term and receive 4 hours credit. Study abroad in 3 countries–Scotland, France, Spain. 3-2 engineering degrees with Clemson University, the University of Tennessee at Knoxville, and Medical University of South Carolina, and pass/fail options are offered. There are 5 national honor societies, and 6 departmental honors programs.

Faculty/Classroom: 67% of faculty are male; 33%, female. All teach undergraduates and 25% both teach and do research. The average class size in an introductory lecture is 22; in a laboratory, 25; and in a regular course, 14.

Admissions: 72% of the 2001-2002 applicants were accepted. The SAT I scores for the 2001-2002 freshman class were: Verbal--20% below 500, 43% between 500 and 599, 32% between 600 and 700, and 5% above 700; Math--21% below 500, 46% between 500 and 599, 32% between 600 and 700, and 3% above 700. The ACT scores were 7% below 21, 26% between 21 and 23, 48% between 24 and 26, 11% between 27 and 28, and 7% above 28. 6 freshmen graduated first in their class.

Requirements: The SAT I or ACT is required, but grades from college preparatory courses are weighed twice as heavily as the SAT I or ACT scores. Applicants must be graduates of an accredited secondary school. The GED is accepted. Applicants should have a minimum of 14 high school academic credits, including 4 credits of English and 2 credits each of math, science, and history. AP and CLEP credits are accepted. Important factors in the admissions decision are advanced placement or honor courses, recommendations by school officials, and extracurricular activities record. Applications are accepted on-line and on computer disk.

Procedure: Freshmen are admitted to all sessions. Entrance exams should be taken in the spring of the junior year or the fall of the senior year. There is an early admissions plan and a rolling admissions plan The fall 2001 application fee was $15. Application deadlines are open.

Transfer: 8 transfer students enrolled in 2001-2002. Transfer applicants should have a minimum GPA of 2.0. An interview is recommended. 30 credits of 124 must be completed at Erskine.

Visiting: There are guides for informal visits and visitors may sit in on classes and stay overnight. To schedule a visit, contact the Admissions Office at (864) 379-8838 or *admissions@erskine.edu*.

Financial Aid: In 2001-2002, 95% of all students received some form of financial aid. 75% of freshmen and 76% of continuing students received need-based aid. The average freshman award was $14,296. Of that total, scholarships or need-based grants averaged $8251 ($21,399 maximum); loans averaged $3000 ($5500 maximum); and work contracts averaged $900 ($1500 maximum). 52% of undergraduates work part time. Average annual earnings from campus work are $900. The average financial indebtedness of the 2001 graduate was $8478. The FAFSA and the college's own financial statement are required. The fall application deadline is May 1.

International Students: There are 6 international students enrolled. They must score 550 on the written TOEFL and also take the SAT I.

Computers: The mainframe is a DEC Alpha Server 800. There are 3 computer labs, computerized music and psychology labs, and 2 computer classrooms. Students may access the Internet via the LAN from their dorm rooms or use any of the 90 public computers on campus. All students may access the system from 7 A.M. to 1 A.M. Monday to Saturday, and from 1 P.M. to 1 A.M. Sunday. There are no time limits. The fee is $50 per semester. It is strongly recommended that all students have a personal computer.

Graduates: In 2001, 88 bachelor's degrees were awarded. The most popular majors were business (19%), biology (11%), and history (9%). In an average class, 58% graduate in 4 years, and 70% in 5 years. 41 companies recruited on campus in a recent year. Of the 2000 graduating class, 31% were enrolled in graduate school within 6 months of graduation and 78% were employed.

Admissions Contact: Jeff Craft, Director of Admissions.
E-mail: *admissions@erskine.edu* Web: *www.erskine.edu*

FRANCIS MARION UNIVERSITY — D-2

Florence, SC 29501-0547 — (843) 661-1231
(800) 368-7551; Fax: (843) 661-4635

Full-time: 1005 men, 1581 women	**Faculty:** 159; IIB, av$
Part-time: 87 men, 149 women	**Ph.D.s:** 82%
Graduate: 118 men, 573 women	**Student/Faculty:** 16 to 1
Year: semesters, summer session	**Tuition:** $3790 ($7410)
Application Deadline: open	**Room & Board:** $3892
Freshman Class: 1657 applied, 1281 accepted, 637 enrolled	
SAT I Verbal/Math: 506/505	**COMPETITIVE**

Francis Marion University, founded in 1970, is a state-supported liberal arts, business, and teachers college. There are 3 undergraduate and 3 graduate schools. In addition to regional accreditation, Francis Marion University has baccalaureate program accreditation with AACSB, NASAD, NASDTEC, and NCATE. The library contains 375,445 volumes, 97,422 microform items, and 7508 audiovisual forms/CDs, and subscribes to 1707 periodicals. Computerized library services include the card catalog, interlibrary loans, and database searching. Special learning facilities include a learning resource center and planetarium. The 309-acre campus is in a rural area 8 miles east of Florence. Including residence halls, there are 34 buildings.

Student Life: 93% of undergraduates are from South Carolina. Others are from 30 states, 27 foreign countries, and Canada. 63% are white; 31% African American. The average age of all undergraduates is 22. 28% do not continue beyond their first year; 35% remain to graduate.

Housing: 1118 students can be accommodated in college housing, which includes single-sex dormitories and on-campus apartments. In addition, there are living and learning dorms with quiet hours and computer labs on each floor. On-campus housing is available on a first-come, first-served basis. 62% of students commute. Alcohol is not permitted. All students may keep cars.

Activities: 10% of men belong to 7 national fraternities; 10% of women belong to 7 national sororities. There are 60 groups on campus, including art, cheerleading, choir, chorus, drama, ethnic, gay, honors, international, jazz band, literary magazine, newspaper, pep band, photography, political, professional, religious, social, social service, and student government. Popular campus events include Holiday Ball, Spring Fling, and Fall Fling.

Sports: There are 7 intercollegiate sports for men and 7 for women, and 24 intramural sports for men and 24 for women. Facilities include a 3200-seat gym, an Olympic-size pool, baseball, softball, and soccer fields, tennis and racquetball courts, a track, and weight, fitness, and game rooms.

Disabled Students: All of the campus is accessible. Wheelchair ramps, elevators, special parking, specially equipped rest rooms, special class scheduling, and lowered drinking fountains are available.

Services: There is a reader service for the blind, remedial reading and writing, and a writing center.

Campus Safety and Security: Measures include 24-hour foot and vehicle patrol, escort service, pamphlets/posters/films, and emergency telephones. There are lighted pathways/sidewalks.

Programs of Study: Francis Marion University confers B.A., B.S., B.B.A., and B.G.S. degrees. Master's degrees are also awarded. Bachelor's degrees are awarded in BIOLOGICAL SCIENCE (biology/biological science), BUSINESS (accounting, banking and finance, business administration and management, business economics, management science, and marketing/retailing/merchandising), COMMUNICATIONS AND THE ARTS (communications, dramatic arts, English, fine arts, French, German, and Spanish), COMPUTER AND PHYSICAL SCIENCE (chemistry, computer science, information sciences and systems, mathematics, and physics), EDUCATION (art, early childhood, and elementary), ENGINEERING AND ENVIRONMENTAL DESIGN (engineering technology), HEALTH PROFESSIONS (medical laboratory technology), SOCIAL SCIENCE (economics, geography, history, international studies, liberal arts/general studies, political science/government, psychology, and sociology). Premedicine and predentistry are the strongest academically. Business, education, and biology are the largest.

Required: Students must complete 120 to 132 credit hours, including 30 to 60 in the major, with a GPA of 2.0. Distribution requirements include 15 hours of humanities, 12 each of sciences and basic communications (6 of English composition and 6 of math and/or logic), up to 12 hours of a foreign language, and 9 of social sciences.

Special: There are co-op programs in civil engineering technology and electronic engineering technology with Florence Darlington Technical College, in geography with the University of South Carolina, in engineering and forest management with Clemson University, in nursing with the Medical University of South Carolina, and in medical technology with the McLeod Regional Medical Center. Internships are required in the communications and health physics programs. Accelerated degree programs, preprofessional programs, and dual majors are possible. Nondegree study is permitted. Self-paced courses are offered in math and French. Study abroad is possible in Mexico, Switzerland, and Germany. There are 9 national honor societies, and a freshman honors program.

Faculty/Classroom: 67% of faculty are male; 33%, female. No introductory courses are taught by graduate students.

Admissions: 77% of the 2001-2002 applicants were accepted. The SAT I scores for the 2001-2002 freshman class were: Verbal--49% below 500, 37% between 500 and 599, 13% between 600 and 700, and 1% above 700; Math--46% below 500, 41% between 500 and 599, 12% between 600 and 700, and 1% above 700. 31% of the current freshmen were in the top fifth of their class; 60% were in the top two fifths. 5 freshmen graduated first in their class.

Requirements: The SAT I is required. In addition, students should have earned 20 credits, consisting of 4 each in academic electives and English, 3 each in math (including algebra I and II), social science, and lab science, 2 in foreign language, and 1 of phys ed or ROTC. A GPA of 2.0 is required. AP and CLEP credits are accepted. Applications are accepted on-line via CollegeNET.

Procedure: Freshmen are admitted to all sessions. Entrance exams should be taken in the fall of the senior year or spring of the junior year. There is a deferred admissions plan. Application deadlines are open. The fall 2001 application fee was $35. Notification is sent on a rolling basis.

Transfer: 641 transfer students enrolled in 2001-2002. Transfer students should have earned 24 hours of college credit, with a GPA of at least 2.0. 36 credits of 120 must be completed at Francis Marion University.

Visiting: There are regularly scheduled orientations for prospective students, including campus tours and registering for classes. There are guides for informal visits and visitors may sit in on classes. To schedule a visit, contact the Admissions Office.

Financial Aid: In a recent year, 60% of all freshmen and 51% of continuing students received some form of financial aid. 50% of freshmen received need-based aid. The average freshman award was $5000. Of that total, scholarships or need-based grants averaged $1000 ($7682 maximum); loans averaged $2625 ($4625 maximum); and work contracts averaged $1222 ($2000 maximum). 16% of undergraduates work part time. Average annual earnings from campus work are $1222. The average financial indebtedness of the 2001 graduate was $18,841. The FAFSA and the college's own financial statement are required. The fall application deadline is March 1.

International Students: There are 43 international students enrolled. The school actively recruits these students. They must score 500 on the written TOEFL or 173 on the electronic version; students may also take the SAT I.

Computers: The mainframe is a DEC Alpha 2100. There are 140 Gateway PCs available in the academic computer center. The dorms and some buildings are networked. All students may access the system various hours. A 90-minute time limit takes effect when there is a waiting list. There are no fees.

Graduates: In 2001, 428 bachelor's degrees were awarded. The most popular majors were business administration (23%), biology (17%), and education (12%). In an average class, 16% graduate in 4 years, 30% in 5 years, and 35% in 6 years. 86 companies recruited on campus in 2000-2001.

Admissions Contact: Drucilla Russell, Director of Admissions. A video is available. E-mail: *admission@fmarion.edu* Web: *www.fmarion.edu*

FURMAN UNIVERSITY

B-1

Greenville, SC 29613 **(864) 294-2034; Fax: (864) 294-3127**

Full-time: 1158 men, 1468 women	**Faculty:** 206; IIB, +$
Part-time: 60 men, 59 women	**Ph.D.s:** 94%
Graduate: 90 men, 395 women	**Student/Faculty:** 13 to 1
Year: 3-2-3 summer session	**Tuition:** $20,076
Application Deadline: January 15	**Room & Board:** $5416
Freshman Class: 3564 applied, 2167 accepted, 734 enrolled	
SAT I or ACT: required	**HIGHLY COMPETITIVE**

Founded in 1826, Furman University is an independent liberal arts institution offering undergraduate and graduate programs. In addition to regional accreditation, Furman has baccalaureate program accreditation with ACS, NASDTEC, NASM, and NCATE. The library contains 452,000 volumes, 755,000 microform items, and 4200 audiovisual forms/CDs, and subscribes to 2518 periodicals. Computerized library services include the card catalog, interlibrary loans, and database searching. Special learning facilities include a learning resource center, art gallery, radio station, observatory, and cable TV with on-campus broadcasting. The 750-acre campus is in a suburban area 5 miles north of Greenville. Including residence halls, there are 69 buildings.

Student Life: 70% of undergraduates are from out of state, mostly the South. Students are from 48 states, 28 foreign countries, and Canada. 75% are from public schools. 88% are white. 56% are Protestant; 21% claim no religious affiliation; 12% Greek Orthodox, Hindu, Muslim; 10% Catholic. The average age of freshmen is 18; all undergraduates, 20. 80% of freshmen remain to graduate.

Housing: 2441 students can be accommodated in college housing, which includes single-sex and coed dormitories and on-campus apartments. In addition, there are language houses, and special-interest houses, small houses, lakeside cabins, and an eco-cottage. On-campus housing is guaranteed for all 4 years. 95% of students live on campus; of those, 75% remain on campus on weekends. Alcohol is not permitted. All students may keep cars.

Activities: 30% of men belong to 8 national fraternities; 35% of women belong to 7 national sororities. There are 130 groups on campus, including art, band, cheerleading, chess, choir, chorale, chorus, computers, dance, debate, drama, drill team, ethnic, forensics, gay, international, jazz band, literary magazine, marching band, musical theater, newspaper, opera, orchestra, pep band, photography, political, professional, radio and TV, religious, social, social service, student government, symphony, and yearbook. Popular campus events include Parents Weekend, Beach Weekend, and Mountain Weekend.

Sports: There are 8 intercollegiate sports for men and 9 for women, and 20 intramural sports for men and 20 for women. Facilities include a 16,500-seat football stadium, a 5800-seat arena, a gym, a pool, an 18-hole golf course, a tennis center with indoor and outdoor courts, a 3000-seat soccer stadium, 12 playing fields, a varsity softball field, and a baseball stadium. The gym includes 6 racquetball courts and a fitness center.

Disabled Students: All of the campus is accessible. Wheelchair ramps, elevators, special parking, specially equipped rest rooms, special class scheduling, lowered drinking fountains, lowered telephones, and designated dorm rooms are available.

Services: Counseling and information services are available, as is tutoring in every subject. There is a reader service for the blind.

Campus Safety and Security: Measures include 24-hour foot and vehicle patrol, self-defense education, escort service, and shuttle buses. There are informal discussions, pamphlets/posters/films, emergency telephones, and lighted pathways/sidewalks.

Programs of Study: Furman confers B.A., B.S., B.G.S., and B.M. degrees. Master's degrees are also awarded. Bachelor's degrees are awarded in BIOLOGICAL SCIENCE (biology/biological science), BUSINESS (accounting and business administration and management), COMMUNICATIONS AND THE ARTS (art, communications, dramatic arts, English, French, German, Greek, Latin, music, music performance, music theory and composition, piano/organ, and Spanish), COMPUTER AND PHYSICAL SCIENCE (chemistry, computer science, geology, mathematics, and physics), EDUCATION (education, elementary, and music), ENGINEERING AND ENVIRONMENTAL DESIGN (environmental science and preengineering), HEALTH PROFESSIONS (health science), SOCIAL SCIENCE (Asian/Oriental studies, economics, history, philosophy, political science/government, psychology, religion, religious music, sociology, and urban studies). Sciences, music, and psychology are the strongest academically. Political science, biology, and business administration are the largest.

Required: To graduate, students must complete 128 credit hours, including 24 to 44 in the major, with a GPA of 2.0. Distribution requirements include 64 hours of general education courses in English composition, foreign language, health and exercise science, natural sciences, social sciences, Asian-African program, fine arts, math, and humanities. Students must attend 36 cultural events before graduation.

Special: A 3-2 engineering degree is offered with Georgia Institute of Technology, Clemson, North Carolina State, Auburn, and Washington University at St. Louis. Internships, study abroad in at least 15 countries, a Washington semester with an internship in a government agency or political organization, and work-study programs are offered. B.A.-B.S. degrees, dual majors, interdisciplinary majors such as computer science-math, math-economics, and computing-business, and student-designed majors are available. A bachelor of general studies degree is granted in the evening division. Nondegree study and pass/fail options are possible. Furman features student/faculty research programs. There are 20 national honor societies, including Phi Beta Kappa.

Faculty/Classroom: 72% of faculty are male; 28%, female. All teach undergraduates. No introductory courses are taught by graduate students. The average class size in an introductory lecture is 23; in a laboratory, 10; and in a regular course, 17.

Admissions: 61% of the 2001-2002 applicants were accepted. 83% of the current freshmen were in the top fifth of their class; 96% were in the top two fifths. There were 41 National Merit finalists. 50 freshmen graduated first in their class.

Requirements: The SAT I or ACT is required. In addition, applicants must be high school graduates or hold a GED. Students should have earned at least 20 units in high school, including 4 of English, 3 each of history, math, and science, and 2 each of social studies and foreign language. 2 essays are required. A portfolio or an audition, where appropriate, is recommended. AP credits are accepted. Important factors in the admissions decision are advanced placement or honor courses, extracurricular activities record, and leadership record. Furman accepts applications on computer disk through CollegeLink, ExPAN, Apply, and the Common Application.

Procedure: Freshmen are admitted to all sessions. Entrance exams should be taken by the late junior or early senior year. There are early decision, early admissions, and deferred admissions plans. Early decision applications should be filed by November 15; regular applications, by January 15 for fall entry, December 1 for winter entry, February 1 for spring entry, and February 1 for summer entry, along with a $40 fee. Notification of early decision is sent December 15; regular decision, March 15. 497 early decision candidates were accepted for the 2001-2002 class. 12% of all applicants are on a waiting list; 18 were accepted in 2001.

Transfer: 30 transfer students enrolled in 2001-2002. Applicants should complete at least 1 year elsewhere before seeking admission. Admission is competitive. 60 credits of 128 must be completed at Furman.

Visiting: There are regularly scheduled orientations for prospective students, consisting of an individual or group session with an admissions officer and a campus tour. There are guides for informal visits and visitors may sit in on classes and stay overnight. To schedule a visit, contact the Admissions Office.

Financial Aid: In 2001-2002, 81% of all freshmen and 79% of continuing students received some form of financial aid. 38% of freshmen and 40% of continuing students received need-based aid. The average freshman award was $17,700. Of that total, scholarships or need-based grants averaged $13,320 ($25,096 maximum); loans averaged $3300 ($4125 maximum); and work contracts averaged $900 ($1500 maximum). 55% of undergraduates work part time. Average annual earnings from campus work are $900. The average financial indebtedness of the 2001 graduate was $13,550. Furman is a member of CSS. The FAFSA and the college's own financial statement are required. The fall application deadline is February 1.

International Students: There are 60 international students enrolled. The school actively recruits these students. They must score 570 on the written TOEFL and also take the SAT I or the ACT.

Computers: The mainframe consists of a DEC ALPHA Server 4000 5/300 running Tru 64 UNIX. Departmental and general-access labs accommodate approximately 300 desktop systems, which include PCs, Macs, Suns, X-terminals, and SGI stations. All residence halls are fully networked for e-mail, network sharing, Internet access, and web hosting. All students may access the system 24 hours a day. There are no time limits and no fees.

Graduates: In 2001, 678 bachelor's degrees were awarded. The most popular majors were political science (15%), business administration (10%), and biology (8%). In an average class, 1% graduate in 3 years, 75% in 4 years, 80% in 5 years, and 80% in 6 years. 86 companies recruited on campus in 2000-2001. Of the 2000 graduating class, 38% were enrolled in graduate school within 6 months of graduation and 60% were employed.

Admissions Contact: Woody O'Cain, Director of Admissions. A video is available. E-mail: *admissions@furman.edu*
Web: *www.engage.furman.edu*

LANDER UNIVERSITY — B-2
Greenwood, SC 29649 — (864) 388-8307
(888) 4LANDER; Fax: (864) 388-8125

Full-time: 880 men, 1318 women	**Faculty:** 175; IIB, -$
Part-time: 84 men, 223 women	**Ph.D.s:** 54%
Graduate: 30 men, 175 women	**Student/Faculty:** 13 to 1
Year: semesters, summer session	**Tuition:** $4242 ($8610)
Application Deadline: open	**Room & Board:** $4376 ($8744)
Freshman Class: 1453 applied, 1259 accepted, 489 enrolled	
SAT I Verbal/Math: 490/490	**ACT:** 20 **LESS COMPETITIVE**

Lander University, founded in 1872, is a state-supported institution offering undergraduate programs in liberal arts, science and math, business, education, nursing, and phys ed and exercise studies. There are 3 undergraduate schools and 1 graduate school. In addition to regional accreditation, Lander has baccalaureate program accreditation with NASAD, NASM, NCATE, and NLN. The library contains 154,528 volumes, 114,245 microform items, and 2218 audiovisual forms/CDs, and subscribes to 748 periodicals. Computerized library services include the card catalog, interlibrary loans, and database searching. Special learning facilities include a learning resource center, art gallery, and a media center. The 100-acre campus is in a small town 75 miles west of Columbia. Including residence halls, there are 33 buildings.

Student Life: 94% of undergraduates are from South Carolina. Others are from 38 states, 20 foreign countries, and Canada. 77% are white; 19% African American. The average age of freshmen is 19; all undergraduates, 22. 27% do not continue beyond their first year; 68% remain to graduate.

Housing: 1086 students can be accommodated in college housing, which includes single-sex and coed dormitories, on-campus apartments, and off-campus apartments. On-campus housing is available on a first-come, first-served basis. 62% of students commute. Alcohol is not permitted. All students may keep cars.

Activities: 11% of men belong to 8 national fraternities; 12% of women belong to 7 national sororities. There are 64 groups on campus, including art, band, cheerleading, choir, chorale, chorus, computers, dance, drama, ethnic, honors, international, jazz band, literary magazine, musical theater, newspaper, orchestra, pep band, political, professional, religious, social, social service, and student government. Popular campus events include The Greenwood Performing Arts Series.

Sports: There are 4 intercollegiate sports for men and 5 for women, and 11 intramural sports for men and 11 for women. Facilities include a gym, basketball courts, a weight room, a softball field, tennis courts, an indoor pool, and an indoor suspended track.

Disabled Students: 90% of the campus is accessible. Wheelchair ramps, elevators, special parking, specially equipped rest rooms, special class scheduling, lowered drinking fountains, and lowered telephones are available.

Services: Counseling and information services are available, as is tutoring in most subjects. There is a reader service for the blind, and remedial math, reading, and writing.

Campus Safety and Security: Measures include 24-hour foot and vehicle patrol, self-defense education, escort service, and emergency telephones. There are lighted pathways/sidewalks.

Programs of Study: Lander confers B.A., B.S., and B.M.Ed. degrees. Master's degrees are also awarded. Bachelor's degrees are awarded in BIOLOGICAL SCIENCE (biology/biological science), BUSINESS (business administration and management), COMMUNICATIONS AND THE ARTS (communications, dramatic arts, English, music, Spanish, speech/debate/rhetoric, and visual and performing arts), COMPUTER AND PHYSICAL SCIENCE (chemistry, computer science, and mathematics), EDUCATION (early childhood, elementary, music, physical, science, and special), ENGINEERING AND ENVIRONMENTAL DESIGN (environmental science), HEALTH PROFESSIONS (exercise science, nursing, and sports medicine), SOCIAL SCIENCE (history, interdisciplinary studies, political science/government, psychology, and sociology). Premedical and dual engineering are the strongest academically. Business administration, education, and nursing are the largest.

Required: To graduate, students must complete 125 semester hours, including 36 in the major, with a GPA of 2.0.

Special: Lander offers internships, co-op and work-study programs, accelerated degrees, B.A.-B.S. degrees, dual engineering degrees with Clemson University, student-designed majors in interdisciplinary studies, credit for military experience, and nondegree study. Students in the Honors International Program study abroad in England for 1 semester during their sophomore year. There are 6 national honor societies and a freshman honors program.

Faculty/Classroom: 54% of faculty are male; 46%, female. All teach undergraduates. No introductory courses are taught by graduate students. The average class size in a regular course is 29.

Admissions: 87% of the 2001-2002 applicants were accepted. The SAT I scores for the 2001-2002 freshman class were: Verbal--56% below 500, 34% between 500 and 599, 9% between 600 and 700, and 1%

above 700; Math--50% below 500, 40% between 500 and 599, 9% between 600 and 700, and 1% above 700. The ACT scores were 54% below 21, 31% between 21 and 23, 10% between 24 and 26, and 4% between 27 and 28. 24% of the current freshmen were in the top fifth of their class; 55% were in the top two fifths.

Requirements: The SAT I or ACT is required. In addition, applicants must be high school graduates with 20 credits, including 4 each of English and academic electives, 3 each of math and lab science, 2 each of foreign language and social studies, and 1 each of American history, and phys ed or ROTC. An interview and a portfolio or an audition, if appropriate, are recommended. Lander requires applicants to be in the upper 50% of their class. AP and CLEP credits are accepted.

Procedure: Freshmen are admitted to all sessions. Entrance exams should be taken in the junior year. There are early admissions and deferred admissions plans. Application deadlines are open. The fall 2001 application fee was $25. Notification is sent on a rolling basis.

Transfer: Applicants must have a minimum college GPA of 2.0, otherwise they may be considered on the strength of military or work experience. Transcripts from every school attended should be submitted. Students under 21 with fewer than 30 semester credits must submit high school transcripts and SAT I or ACT results as well. An interview is recommended. 30 credits of 125 must be completed at Lander.

Visiting: There are regularly scheduled orientations for prospective students, consisting of open houses. There are guides for informal visits and visitors may sit in on classes. To schedule a visit, contact the Admissions Office.

Financial Aid: 20% of undergraduates work part time. The average financial indebtedness of the 2001 graduate was $16,450. The FAFSA is required. The fall application deadline is April 15.

International Students: There are 61 international students enrolled. The school actively recruits these students. They must score 550 on the written TOEFL and also take the SAT I or the ACT.

Computers: The mainframe is an IBM AS/400. The campus network has a TI connection to the Internet and Web. 250 PCs are available in labs, and students can dial up for modem access to the network. All students may access the system. There are no time limits. The fee is $25. It is strongly recommended that all students have a personal computer.

Graduates: In 2001, 405 bachelor's degrees were awarded. The most popular majors were business (22%), nursing (7%), and psychology (6%). In an average class, 2% graduate in 3 years, 30% in 4 years, 42% in 5 years, and 45% in 6 years.

Admissions Contact: Jacquelyn D. Roark, Director of Admissions. E-mail: *admissions@lander.edu* Web: *www.lander.edu*

LIMESTONE COLLEGE — B-1

Gaffney, SC 29340-3799 — **(864) 489-7151, ext. 554**
(800) 795-7151, ext. 554; Fax: (864) 487-8706

Full-time: 249 men, 255 women	**Faculty:** 39; IIB, --$
Part-time: 7 men, 5 women	**Ph.D.s:** 77%
Graduate: none	**Student/Faculty:** 13 to 1
Year: semesters, summer session	**Tuition:** $11,500
Application Deadline: August 26	**Room & Board:** $5400
Freshman Class: 501 applied, 333 accepted, 135 enrolled	
SAT I Verbal/Math: 480/492	**ACT:** 19 **COMPETITIVE**

Limestone College, founded in 1845, is a private institution offering programs in liberal arts, the sciences, business, and teacher preparation. In addition to regional accreditation, the Rock has baccalaureate program accreditation with NASM. The library contains 62,044 volumes, 2502 microform items, and 2141 audiovisual forms/CDs, and subscribes to 253 periodicals. Computerized library services include the card catalog, interlibrary loans, and database searching. Special learning facilities include a learning resource center, a writing center, and a computer graphics art lab. The 115-acre campus is in a suburban area 50 miles southwest of Charlotte, North Carolina, and 25 miles north of Spartanburg. Including residence halls, there are 17 buildings.

Student Life: 63% of undergraduates are from South Carolina. Others are from 23 states, 9 foreign countries, and Canada. 79% are white; 18% African American. The average age of freshmen is 19; all undergraduates, 22. 29% do not continue beyond their first year; 30% remain to graduate.

Housing: 268 students can be accommodated in college housing, which includes single-sex dormitories. On-campus housing is available on a first-come, first-served basis. 55% of students commute. Alcohol is not permitted. All students may keep cars.

Activities: 55% of women belong to 2 local sororities. There are no fraternities. There are 17 groups on campus, including art, cheerleading, choir, chorus, computers, drama, honors, jazz band, literary magazine, musical theater, orchestra, professional, religious, social, social service, student government, and yearbook. Popular campus events include Christmas Luminaries, Midterm Madness, and Fun Flicks.

Sports: There are 7 intercollegiate sports for men and 8 for women, and 12 intramural sports for men and 12 for women. Facilities include 1500-seat gym, an indoor pool, lighted tennis courts, baseball, softball, soccer, and lacrosse fields, and a student center with a game room.

Disabled Students: 75% of the campus is accessible. Wheelchair ramps, elevators, special parking, specially equipped rest rooms, special class scheduling, and lowered drinking fountains are available.

Services: Counseling and information services are available, as is tutoring in every subject. There is remedial math, reading, and writing. Special assistance is also available to students with documented learning disabilities.

Campus Safety and Security: Measures include 24-hour foot and vehicle patrol, escort service, informal discussions, and lighted pathways/sidewalks.

Programs of Study: the Rock confers B.A. and B.S. degrees. Associate degrees are also awarded. Bachelor's degrees are awarded in BIOLOGICAL SCIENCE (biology/biological science), BUSINESS (accounting, business administration and management, human resources, management information systems, marketing management, and sports management), COMMUNICATIONS AND THE ARTS (English, graphic design, music, and studio art), COMPUTER AND PHYSICAL SCIENCE (applied mathematics, chemistry, computer programming, computer science, and information sciences and systems), EDUCATION (art, elementary, English, mathematics, music, physical, science, and social studies), SOCIAL SCIENCE (counseling/psychology, criminal justice, economics, history, liberal arts/general studies, physical fitness/movement, prelaw, psychology, and social work). Business administration, elementary education, phys ed are the largest.

Required: To graduate, students must complete a minimum of 120 semester hours with 30 to 56 hours in the major and a minimum GPA of 2.0. General education requirements are as follows: 18 hours of fine arts and humanities, 13 to 14 of science and math, 12 of social science, and 2 each of interdisciplinary and phys ed, for a total of 47 hours minimum.

Special: The college offers internships in social work, counseling, teacher education, business, and athletic training, as well as a work-study program and off-campus evening courses. Students may have divisional and multidisciplinary dual majors. The college confers a liberal studies degree and may grant credit for military experience. There are 2 national honor societies, a freshman honors program, and 6 departmental honors programs.

Faculty/Classroom: 64% of faculty are male; 36%, female. All teach undergraduates and 75% do research. The average class size in an introductory lecture is 26; in a laboratory, 18; and in a regular course, 12.

Admissions: 66% of the 2001-2002 applicants were accepted. The SAT I scores for the 2001-2002 freshman class were: Verbal--26% below 500, 39% between 500 and 599, and 35% between 600 and 700; Math--57% below 500, 34% between 500 and 599, 8% between 600 and 700, and 1% above 700. The ACT scores were 66% below 21, 24% between 21 and 23, 4% between 24 and 26, 4% between 27 and 28, and 2% above 28. 12% of the current freshmen were in the top fifth of their class; 42% were in the top two fifths.

Requirements: The SAT I or ACT is required, with a minimum composite score of 820. The college recommends that students present 4 units of English, 3 each of math, and 2 each of lab science and social science. The GED is accepted. An interview is recommended. A GPA of 2.5 is required. AP and CLEP credits are accepted. Important factors in the admissions decision are advanced placement or honor courses, leadership record, and evidence of special talent. Applications may be submitted on disk and are accepted on-line via the school's web site.

Procedure: Freshmen are admitted fall and spring. Entrance exams should be taken during the fall of the senior year of high school. There is a deferred admissions plan. Applications should be filed by August 26 for fall entry, along with a $25 fee. Notification is sent on a rolling basis.

Transfer: 50 transfer students enrolled in 2001-2002. Applicants must have a minimum GPA of 2.0 and must be in good standing at their previous school. 30 credits of 120 must be completed at the Rock.

Visiting: There are regularly scheduled orientations for prospective students. There are guides for informal visits and visitors may sit in on classes and stay overnight. To schedule a visit, contact Debbie Borders at the Admissions Office, at *dborder@limestone.edu*

Financial Aid: In 2001-2002, 95% of all freshmen and 89% of continuing students received some form of financial aid. 84% of freshmen and 94% of continuing students received need-based aid. The average freshman award was $8374. Of that total, scholarships or need-based grants averaged $3634 ($9500 maximum); loans averaged $3145; and work contracts averaged $1595 ($1800 maximum). 26% of undergraduates work part time. Average annual earnings from campus work are $1223. The average financial indebtedness of the 2001 graduate was $7698. The FAFSA is required. The fall application deadline is July 1.

International Students: There are 15 international students enrolled. They must score 500 on the written TOEFL and also take the MELAB and also take the SAT I, scoring 820, or the ACT.

Computers: The mainframe is a Dell PowerEdge 6400. There are 59 PCs available in computer labs; 5 PCs in the library are networked to the Internet. There is also a graphic arts lab in the art building, which houses 6 PCs. Additionally, each resident student has access to the network from his/her dorm room. All students may access the system 6 A.M. to 10 P.M. Monday through Friday and 1 P.M. to 10 P.M. Saturday and Sunday. There are no time limits and no fees.

Graduates: In 2001, 75 bachelor's degrees were awarded. The most popular majors were business administration (54%), computer science (16%), and social work (10%). In an average class, 27% graduate in 4 years, 29% in 5 years, and 30% in 6 years.

Admissions Contact: Chris Phenicie, Vice President, Enrollment Services. E-mail: *cphenicie@limestone.edu* Web: *www.limestone.edu*

MORRIS COLLEGE

Sumter, SC 29150-3599 — D-3

(803) 934-3225

(888) 775-1345; Fax: (803) 773-3687

Full-time: 343 men, 615 women	**Faculty:** 48; --$
Part-time: 13 men, 15 women	**Ph.D.s:** 54%
Graduate: none	**Student/Faculty:** 20 to 1
Year: semesters, summer session	**Tuition:** $6685
Application Deadline: open	**Room & Board:** $3310
Freshman Class: 1343 applied, 1159 accepted, 273 enrolled	
SAT I Verbal/Math: 378/376	**LESS COMPETITIVE**

Morris College, founded in 1908, is a private liberal arts institution affiliated with the Baptist Church. In addition to regional accreditation, Morris has baccalaureate program accreditation with NASDTEC. The library contains 100,359 volumes, 185,813 microform items, and 1916 audiovisual forms/CDs, and subscribes to 395 periodicals. Computerized library services include the card catalog, interlibrary loans, and database searching. Special learning facilities include a learning resource center and radio station, a TV production studio, and a photography workroom. The 34-acre campus is in a small town 40 miles east of Columbia. Including residence halls, there are 20 buildings.

Student Life: 86% of undergraduates are from South Carolina. Others are from 19 states and Canada. 98% are from public schools. All are African American. The average age of freshmen is 19; all undergraduates, 22. 50% do not continue beyond their first year; 35% remain to graduate.

Housing: 622 students can be accommodated in college housing, which includes single-sex dormitories. On-campus housing is guaranteed for the freshman year only and is available on a first-come, first-served basis. 72% of students live on campus; of those, 35% remain on campus on weekends. Alcohol is not permitted. Upperclassmen may keep cars.

Activities: 9% of men belong to 4 national fraternities; 11% of women belong to 4 national sororities. There are 54 groups on campus, including cheerleading, chess, choir, chorale, dance, drama, honors, literary magazine, newspaper, pepe band, photography, professional, radio and TV, religious, social, social service, student government, and yearbook. Popular campus events include Coronation of Miss Morris College, Christmas and gospel choir concerts, and Martin Luther King Observance.

Sports: There are 6 intercollegiate sports for men and 6 for women, and 5 intramural sports for men and 5 for women. Facilities include a weight room, an athletic field complex, a 1700-seat gym, and a 600-seat auditorium.

Disabled Students: 25% of the campus is accessible. Wheelchair ramps, elevators, special parking, specially equipped rest rooms, and lowered drinking fountains are available.

Services: Counseling and information services are available, as is tutoring in every subject. There is remedial math, reading, and writing. Skill-building materials available on computer.

Campus Safety and Security: Measures include 24-hour foot and vehicle patrol, informal discussions, and lighted pathways/sidewalks.

Programs of Study: Morris confers B.A., B.S., B.F.A., and B.S.Ed. degrees. Bachelor's degrees are awarded in BIOLOGICAL SCIENCE (biology/biological science), BUSINESS (business administration and management, and recreation and leisure services), COMMUNICATIONS AND THE ARTS (broadcasting, English, and journalism), COMPUTER AND PHYSICAL SCIENCE (mathematics), EDUCATION (early childhood, elementary, English, mathematics, science, and social studies), HEALTH PROFESSIONS (community health work), SOCIAL SCIENCE (criminal justice, history, liberal arts/general studies, pastoral studies, political science/government, religious education, and sociology). Early childhood education, pastoral ministry, and organizational management are the strongest academically. Business administration, biology, and criminal justice are the largest.

Required: All students must complete 124 to 141 credit hours with a 2.0 GPA overall. General education requirements, with a core curriculum of 21 to 51 credits, include 12 to 15 in English, 12 in social sciences, 8 in natural sciences, 6 in religion, 3 to 9 in math, 4 in fine arts, 2 to 3 each in philosophy and speech, and 2 each in education and health education. A comprehensive exam in the major is required prior to graduation.

Special: Business internships, co-op programs, and work-study programs on and off campus are offered. A B.A-B.S. degree in organizational management is available. A B.S. in nursing degree is offered in conjunction with the University of South Carolina. A cooperative 3-2 engineering degre program wit Clemson University is available. Credit by exam and credit for military experience are possible. There is 1 national honor society, a freshman honors program, and 1 departmental honors program.

Faculty/Classroom: 50% of faculty are male; 50%, female. All teach undergraduates. The average class size in an introductory lecture is 35; in a laboratory, 20; and in a regular course, 25.

Admissions: 86% of the 2001-2002 applicants were accepted. The SAT I scores for the 2001-2002 freshman class were: Verbal--94% below 500, and 6% between 500 and 599; Math--92% below 500 and 8% between 500 and 599. 8% of the current freshmen were in the top fifth of their class; 30% were in the top two fifths.

Requirements: The SAT I or ACT is recommended. In addition, candidates should be graduates of an accredited secondary school or have the GED. They must have completed 20 Carnegie units, consisting of 4 in high school English, 3 in math, 2 each in natural and social sciences, 1 each in U.S. history and phys ed, and 7 in electives. A GPA of 2.0 is required. CLEP credit is accepted.

Procedure: Freshmen are admitted to all sessions. There is a deferred admissions plan. Application deadlines are open. The application fee is $10.

Transfer: 57 transfer students enrolled in 2001-2002. Applicants must submit transcripts and evidence of honorable release. A minimum GPA of 2.0 is required. 30 credits of 124 must be completed at Morris.

Visiting: There are regularly scheduled orientations for prospective students, consisting of a campus tour, visits with division chairs and faculty members to discuss majors, scheduled activities, and lunch. There are guides for informal visits. To schedule a visit, contact Deborah Calhoun at *dcalhoun@morris.edu*.

Financial Aid: In a recent year, 98% of all freshmen and 97% of continuing students received some form of financial aid. 98% of freshmen and 97% of continuing students received need-based aid. The average freshman award was $9300. Of that total, scholarships or need-based grants averaged $2700 ($4000 maximum); loans averaged $1700 ($2625 maximum); work contracts averaged $1200 ($1800 maximum); and SCTG (South Carolina Tuition Grant) averaged $1990. 56% of undergraduates work part time. Average annual earnings from campus work are $1800. The average financial indebtedness of the 2001 graduate was $13,000. Morris is a member of CSS. The FAFSA and the college's own financial statement are required. The fall application deadline is April 30.

International Students: They must take the TOEFL.

Computers: The mainframe is a DEC VAX-4000-100-A. Some 149 terminals and PCs are located in labs in the media center, the science building, and various other locations. Languages include COBOL and Visual Basic, applications include spreadsheets, database, word processing, and Internet access. Data lines are also available in each dorm room for students who have their own computers and some computers are available at a central location in the dorms. All students may access the system 78 hours per week. There are no time limits and no fees.

Graduates: In 2001, 147 bachelor's degrees were awarded. The most popular majors were business administration (19%), criminal justice (14%), and biology (13%). In an average class, 17% graduate in 4 years, 31% in 5 years, and 32% in 6 years. 80 companies recruited on campus in 2000-2001. Of the 2000 graduating class, 15% were enrolled in graduate school within 6 months of graduation and 75% were employed.

Admissions Contact: Deborah Calhoun, Director of Admissions and Records. A video is available.
Web: *http://www.icusc.org/morris/mchome.htm*

NEWBERRY COLLEGE

Newberry, SC 29108 — B-2

(803) 321-5127

(800) 845-4955; Fax: (803) 321-5138

Full-time: 388 men, 323 women	**Faculty:** 43
Part-time: 12 men, 36 women	**Ph.D.s:** 66%
Graduate: none	**Student/Faculty:** 17 to 1
Year: semesters, summer session	**Tuition:** $15,400
Application Deadline: open	**Room & Board:** $4270
Freshman Class: 806 applied, 616 accepted, 182 enrolled	
SAT I Verbal/Math: 482/492	**ACT:** 20 **LESS COMPETITIVE**

Newberry College, founded in 1856, is a private liberal arts institution affiliated with the Evangelical Lutheran Church in America. In addition to regional accreditation, Newberry has baccalaureate program accreditation with NASDTEC, NASM, and NCATE. The 2 libraries contain 77,460 volumes, 7206 microform items, and 1100 audiovisual forms/CDs, and subscribe to 390 periodicals. Computerized library services include the card catalog, interlibrary loans, and database searching. Special learning facilities include a learning resource center, radio station, and TV station. The 60-acre campus is in a small town 40 miles northwest of Columbia. Including residence halls, there are 22 buildings.

Student Life: 88% of undergraduates are from South Carolina. Others are from 16 states, 4 foreign countries, and Canada. 90% are from public schools. 76% are white; 21% African American. 70% are Protestant; 17% claim no religious affiliation. The average age of freshmen is 18; all undergraduates, 20. 35% do not continue beyond their first year; 53% remain to graduate.

Housing: 638 students can be accommodated in college housing, which includes single-sex and coed dormitories. In addition, there are honors houses. On-campus housing is guaranteed for all 4 years. 70% of students live on campus; of those, 66% remain on campus on weekends. All students may keep cars.

Activities: 37% of men belong to 7 national fraternities; 38% of women belong to 2 national sororities. There are 50 groups on campus, including band, cheerleading, choir, chorale, chorus, computers, dance, drama, ethnic, honors, international, jazz band, literary magazine, marching band, musical theater, newspaper, orchestra, pep band, political, professional, radio and TV, religious, social, social service, student government, and yearbook. Popular campus events include Fall Fling and Spring Fling.

Sports: There are 7 intercollegiate sports for men and 7 for women, and 6 intramural sports for men and 5 for women. Facilities include a 4000-seat stadium, a phys ed complex with a 1600-seat basketball arena and racquetball courts, an outdoor pool, tennis courts, and baseball, softball, and soccer fields.

Disabled Students: 90% of the campus is accessible. Wheelchair ramps, elevators, special parking, specially equipped rest rooms, and special class scheduling are available.

Services: Counseling and information services are available, as is tutoring in most subjects. There is remedial math, reading, and writing.

Campus Safety and Security: Measures include 24-hour foot and vehicle patrol, escort service, informal discussions, and pamphlets/posters/films. There are emergency telephones and lighted pathways/sidewalks.

Programs of Study: Newberry confers B.A., B.S., B.M., and B.M.E. degrees. Bachelor's degrees are awarded in BIOLOGICAL SCIENCE (biology/biological science), BUSINESS (accounting and business administration and management), COMMUNICATIONS AND THE ARTS (applied music, art, arts administration/management, communications, dramatic arts, English, French, German, languages, music, music performance, music theory and composition, and Spanish), COMPUTER AND PHYSICAL SCIENCE (chemistry, computer science, and mathematics), EDUCATION (early childhood, elementary, music, physical, and special), HEALTH PROFESSIONS (veterinary science), SOCIAL SCIENCE (economics, history, philosophy, political science/government, psychology, religion, and sociology). Education and natural sciences are the strongest academically. Business administration, education, and sociology are the largest.

Required: To graduate, students must complete 126 semester hours, with a minimum GPA of 2.0. Core curriculum requirements include 10 to 11 hours of math and natural science, 9 each of communication skills, humanities/fine arts, and history/social sciences, up to 6 of foreign language, 3 of religion, and 2 of phys ed. There is also a 24-event fine arts and lectures requirement. All students must take College Life 101 and fulfill Communications Across the Curriculum writing projects.

Special: Internships, dual and student designed majors, B.A. B.S. degrees, study abroad, a Washington semester, work-study programs, independent study, and cooperative education are offered. A 3-2 engineering degree program with Clemson University, a 3-2 forestry program with Duke University, a 3-3 cytotechnology program, and a 3-1 medical technology program are available. Nondegree study is possible. There is 1 national honor society, and a freshman honors program.

Faculty/Classroom: 62% of faculty are male; 38%, female. All teach undergraduates. The average class size in an introductory lecture is 30; in a laboratory, 30; and in a regular course, 25.

Admissions: 76% of the 2001-2002 applicants were accepted. The SAT I scores for the 2001-2002 freshman class were: Verbal--54% below 500, 38% between 500 and 599, 7% between 600 and 700, and 1% above 700; Math--53% below 500, 39% between 500 and 599, 6% between 600 and 700, and 2% above 700. The ACT scores were 89% below 21, and 12% between 21 and 23. 24% of the current freshmen were in the top fifth of their class; 53% were in the top two fifths.

Requirements: The SAT I or ACT is required. In addition, applicants should have completed 18 high school academic units, including 4 of English, 3 each of math and social science (1 of U.S. history), 2 each of lab science and a foreign language, and 1 elective. The GED is accepted. An essay is recommended. A GPA of 2.0 is required. AP and CLEP credits are accepted. Important factors in the admissions decision are leadership record, evidence of special talent, and recommendations by school officials. Applications are accepted on computer disk via Apply.

Procedure: Freshmen are admitted to all sessions. Entrance exams should be taken in the spring of the junior year or the fall of the senior year. There is a deferred admissions plan, and a rolling admissions plan. The fall 2001 application fee was $30. Application deadlines are open.

Transfer: 55 transfer students enrolled in 2001-2002. Applicants must be eligible to return to their previous school. A 2.0 minimum GPA is recommended. 32 credits of 126 must be completed at Newberry.

Visiting: There are regularly scheduled orientations for prospective students, including a campus tour, informational sessions, and meetings with faculty, staff, and students. There are guides for informal visits and visitors may sit in on classes and stay overnight. To schedule a visit, contact the Admissions Office.

Financial Aid: In 2001-2002, 91% of all freshmen and 96% of continuing students received some form of financial aid. 63% of freshmen and 65% of continuing students received need-based aid. The average freshman award was $12,450. Of that total, scholarships or need-based grants averaged $8811 ($15,000 maximum); loans averaged $2648 ($6625 maximum); and work contracts averaged $991 ($1000 maximum). 12% of undergraduates work part time. Average annual earnings from campus work are $625. The average financial indebtedness of the 2001 graduate was $3135. Newberry is a member of CSS. The FAFSA is required. The fall application priority deadline is March 30.

International Students: In a recent year, there were 7 international students enrolled full-time. The school actively recruits these students. They must score 525 on the written TOEFL or 197 on the electronic version and also take the college's own test and the SAT I or the ACT, scoring 900.

Computers: Newberry maintains an Ethernet network with Internet connection, along with 46 PCs distributed among several labs. All students may access the system. There are no time limits and no fees.

Graduates: In 2001, 115 bachelor's degrees were awarded. The most popular majors were business and management (16%), education (13%), and social sciences and history (9%). 175 companies recruited on campus in 2000-2001. Of the 2000 graduating class, 20% were enrolled in graduate school within 6 months of graduation and 60% were employed.

Admissions Contact: Jonathan Reece, Director of Admissions. A video is available. E-mail: *admissions@newberry.edu*
Web: *www.newberry.edu*

PRESBYTERIAN COLLEGE

Clinton, SC 29325 — **B-2**
(864) 833-8230
(800) 476-7272; Fax: (864) 833-8481

Full-time: 550 men, 634 women	**Faculty:** 78; IIB, -$
Part-time: 22 men, 29 women	**Ph.D.s:** 90%
Graduate: none	**Student/Faculty:** 15 to 1
Year: semesters, summer session	**Tuition:** $18,200
Application Deadline: open	**Room & Board:** $5156
Freshman Class: 951 applied, 743 accepted, 322 enrolled	
SAT I Verbal/Math: 561/562	**VERY COMPETITIVE**

Presbyterian College, founded in 1880, is a private liberal arts institution affiliated with the Presbyterian Church (U.S.A.). In addition to regional accreditation, PC has baccalaureate program accreditation with AACSB and NCATE. The library contains 170,167 volumes, 13,690 microform items, and 7204 audiovisual forms/CDs, and subscribes to 797 periodicals. Computerized library services include the card catalog, interlibrary loans, and database searching. Special learning facilities include a learning resource center, art gallery, and radio station. The 220-acre campus is in a small town 40 miles south of Greenville. Including residence halls, there are 39 buildings.

Student Life: 57% of undergraduates are from South Carolina. Others are from 26 states and 7 foreign countries. 79% are from public schools. 92% are white. 76% are Protestant. The average age of freshmen is 18; all undergraduates, 20. 14% do not continue beyond their first year; 81% remain to graduate.

Housing: 1027 students can be accommodated in college housing, which includes single-sex and coed dormitories, on-campus apartments, off-campus apartments, married-student housing, and fraternity houses. In addition, there are special-interest houses. On-campus housing is guaranteed for all 4 years. 91% of students live on campus; of those, 75% remain on campus on weekends. All students may keep cars.

Activities: 45% of men belong to 7 national fraternities; 42% of women belong to 3 national sororities. There are 60 groups on campus, including art, band, cheerleading, chess, choir, chorale, chorus, computers, drama, ethnic, honors, international, jazz band, literary magazine, newspaper, pep band, photography, political, professional, radio and TV, religious, social, social service, student government, and yearbook. Popular campus events include Fall Fling, Spring Swing, and Greek Week.

Sports: Facilities include a 5000-seat football stadium, a soccer stadium, baseball and intramural fields, tennis courts, weight rooms, a sauna, a basketball arena, a 3000-seat gym, an outdoor amphitheater, a lighted running trail, an indoor swimming pool, table tennis and pool tables, and an intramural park with a driving range and putting green.

Disabled Students: 90% of the campus is accessible. Wheelchair ramps, elevators, special parking, specially equipped rest rooms, special class scheduling, and lowered drinking fountains are available.

Services: Counseling and information services are available, as is tutoring in every subject. There is a reader service for the blind.

Campus Safety and Security: Measures include 24-hour foot and vehicle patrol, escort service, shuttle buses, and informal discussions. There are pamphlets/posters/films, emergency telephones, lighted pathways/sidewalks, and 24-hour key card dorm locks.

Programs of Study: PC confers B.A. and B.S degrees. Bachelor's degrees are awarded in BIOLOGICAL SCIENCE (biology/biological science), BUSINESS (accounting and business administration and management), COMMUNICATIONS AND THE ARTS (English, fine arts, French, German, music, Spanish, and visual and performing arts), COMPUTER AND PHYSICAL SCIENCE (chemistry, mathematics, and physics), EDUCATION (elementary, music, secondary, and special), SOCIAL SCIENCE (economics, history, political science/government, psychology, religion, and sociology). Business, biology, and English are the largest.

Required: To graduate, students must complete a minimum of 122 semester hours, including 30 to 48 in the major, with a minimum GPA of 2.0. General education requirements of 46 to 55 credits include 16 hours of foreign language, 8 of lab science, 6 each of religion, English, world history, and social science, 3 to 4 of math, 3 of fine arts, and 2 of phys ed.

Special: Educational internships, study abroad in 40 countries, and a Washington semester are available. Dual majors, work-study programs, accelerated degree programs, B.A.-B.S. degrees, and a 3-2 engineering degree with Auburn, Clemson, Vanderbilt, and Mercer Universities are offered. There is a forestry environmental studies program with Duke University and a Christian education program with Presbyterian School of Christian Education. Credit for life, military, or work experience, auditing courses, and pass/fail options are possible. There are 9 national honor societies, a freshman honors program, and 26 departmental honors programs.

Faculty/Classroom: 63% of faculty are male; 37%, female. All teach undergraduates and 65% also do research. The average class size in an introductory lecture is 16; in a laboratory, 16; and in a regular course, 13.

Admissions: 78% of the 2001-2002 applicants were accepted. The SAT I scores for the 2001-2002 freshman class were: Verbal--16% below 500, 54% between 500 and 599, 26% between 600 and 700, and 4% above 700; Math--15% below 500, 49% between 500 and 599, 32% between 600 and 700, and 4% above 700. 65% of the current freshmen were in the top fifth of their class; 90% were in the top two fifths. In a recent year, 4 freshmen graduated first in their class.

Requirements: The SAT I or ACT is required. In addition, applicants must be graduates of an accredited secondary school with 18 academic credits, including 4 years of English, 3 of math, and 2 or more each of foreign language, history, science, and social studies. The GED is accepted. An essay is required. For music scholarships, an audition is necessary. A GPA of 2.25 is required. AP and CLEP credits are accepted. Important factors in the admissions decision are advanced placement or honor courses, recommendations by school officials, and leadership record. Applications are accepted on-line via the college's web site.

Procedure: Freshmen are admitted to all sessions. Entrance exams should be taken during the spring of the junior year. There are early decision, early admissions, and deferred admissions plans. Early decision applications should be filed by December 5; regular application deadlines are open. The fall 2001 application fee was $30. Notification is sent ona rolling basis. 110 early decision candidates were accepted for the 2001-2002 class.

Transfer: 13 transfer students enrolled in 2001-2002. Applicants must have a minimum GPA of 2.0. 48 credits of 122 must be completed at PC.

Visiting: There are regularly scheduled orientations for prospective students, including academic, activity, and financial aid information sessions, tours, and lunch. There are guides for informal visits and visitors may sit in on classes and stay overnight. To schedule a visit, contact the Office of Admissions.

Financial Aid: In a recent year, 90% of all freshmen and 89% of continuing students received some form of financial aid. 70% of freshmen and 69% of continuing students received need-based aid. The average freshman award was $13,662. Of that total, scholarships or need-based grants averaged $8776; loans averaged $4886; and work contracts averaged $800 ($1500 maximum). 30% of undergraduates work part time. Average annual earnings from campus work are $800. The average financial indebtedness of a recent graduate was $16,723. The FAFSA and the college's own financial statement are required. The fall application deadline is March 1.

International Students: These students must score 550 on the written TOEFL and also take the SAT I or the ACT.

Computers: The mainframe is a Data General Avion. There are 120 PCs and Macs in 3 labs, including IBM and Macs. Software and printers, including laser printers, are available. Computer assistance is provided during open hours. All academic buildings, residence halls, classrooms, labs, and faculty offices are networked through the Internet/Bitnet and other national and international networks. E-mail is available. All students may access the system at any time. There are no time limits and no fees.

Graduates: In 2001, 244 bachelor's degrees were awarded. The most popular majors were economics/business (26%), biology (14%), and political science (11%). In an average class, 80% graduate in 4 years. 42 companies recruited on campus in 2000-2001. Of the 2000 graduating class, 20% were enrolled in graduate school within 6 months of graduation and 81% were employed.

Admissions Contact: Dana Paul, VP, Enrollment and Dean of Admissions. A video is available. E-mail: *rdpaul@admin.presby.edu*
Web: *www.presby.edu*

SOUTH CAROLINA STATE UNIVERSITY C-3
Orangeburg, SC 29117 **(803) 536-7185**
(800) 260-5956; Fax: (803) 536-8990

Full-time: 1580 men, 1950 women	**Faculty:** 211
Part-time: 120 men, 300 women	**Ph.D.s:** 62%
Graduate: 115 men, 525 women	**Student/Faculty:** 16 to 1
Year: semesters, summer session	**Tuition:** $3564 ($7192)
Application Deadline: see profile	**Room & Board:** $3200
Freshman Class: n/av	
SAT I Verbal/Math: required	**LESS COMPETITIVE**

South Carolina State University, a historically black, land-grant institution founded in 1896, offers undergraduate programs in liberal arts and sciences, business, education, engineering technology, and human sciences. There are 5 undergraduate schools and 1 graduate school. Figures in above capsule are approximate. In addition to regional accreditation, State or SCSU has baccalaureate program accreditation with ABET, ADA, AHEA, CSWE, NASDTEC, and NCATE. The library contains 277,438 volumes and 686,225 microform items, and subscribes to 1394 periodicals. Computerized library services include the card catalog, interlibrary loans, and database searching. Special learning facilities include a learning resource center, art gallery, planetarium, radio station, and an instructional media center. The 160-acre campus is in a small town 40 miles east of Columbia. Including residence halls, there are 60 buildings.

Student Life: 83% of undergraduates are from South Carolina. 95% are African American. The average age of freshmen is 18; all undergraduates, 19. 22% do not continue beyond their first year; 32% remain to graduate.

Housing: 2242 students can be accommodated in college housing, which includes single-sex dormitories and married-student housing. On-campus housing is available on a first-come, first-served basis and is available on a lottery system for upperclassmen. 80% of students live on campus. Alcohol is not permitted. Upperclassmen may keep cars.

Activities: 25% of men belong to 4 national fraternities; 32% of women belong to 4 national sororities. There are 85 groups on campus, including band, cheerleading, choir, chorus, dance, drama, drill team, honors, international, jazz band, marching band, newspaper, orchestra, pep band, political, religious, social, social service, student government, and yearbook. Popular campus events include Colloquium Series, Halloween Haunt, and Bulldog Fest.

Sports: There are 7 intercollegiate sports for men and 8 for women, and 8 intramural sports for men and 7 for women. Facilities include a student center with a game room and bowling alley, a gym, tennis courts, a 22,000-seat stadium, an 8-lane asphalt track, and swimming pools.

Disabled Students: 60% of the campus is accessible. Wheelchair ramps, elevators, special parking, specially equipped rest rooms, lowered drinking fountains, and lowered telephones are available.

Services: Counseling and information services are available, as is tutoring in most subjects. There is a reader service for the blind, and remedial math, reading, and writing. Free counseling is also available.

Campus Safety and Security: Measures include 24-hour foot and vehicle patrol, shuttle buses, pamphlets/posters/films, and lighted pathways/sidewalks. There is a campus police department with 25 safety and security officers.

Programs of Study: State or SCSU confers B.A. and B.S. degrees. Master's and doctoral degrees are also awarded. Bachelor's degrees are awarded in AGRICULTURE (agricultural business management), BIOLOGICAL SCIENCE (biology/biological science and nutrition), BUSINESS (accounting, business administration and management, business economics, marketing/retailing/merchandising, and office supervision and management), COMMUNICATIONS AND THE ARTS (dramatic arts, English, fine arts, French, music business management, and Spanish), COMPUTER AND PHYSICAL SCIENCE (chemistry, computer science, mathematics, and physics), EDUCATION (art, business, early childhood, elementary, guidance, health, home economics, industrial arts, music, physical, reading, and special), ENGINEERING AND ENVIRONMENTAL DESIGN (civil engineering technology, electrical/electronics engineering technology, engineering technology, and mechanical engineering technology), HEALTH PROFESSIONS (nursing and speech pathology/audiology), SOCIAL SCIENCE (criminal justice, food science, history, human services, political science/government, psychology, social studies, social work, and sociology). Science, engineering technology, and business education are the strongest academically.

Required: To graduate, all students must complete at least 128 credit hours with a minimum GPA of 2.0. Students must attend the freshman orientation program, take a general education examination in their sophomore year, satisfy the general education program requirements, and pass an English proficiency test.

Special: The college offers co-op education and work-study programs, cross-registration with Claflin College, internships, study abroad in 2 countries, combined B.A.-B.S. degrees, credit for educational and work experience, nondegree study, and pass/fail options for juniors and seniors. Also available are an electrical engineering technology program at Midlands, Greenville, and Trident Technical Colleges, an evening school program, and a program for educationally disadvantaged students who do not meet traditional entrance requirements. There are 12 national honor societies, and a freshman honors program.

Faculty/Classroom: No introductory courses are taught by graduate students.

Requirements: The SAT I or ACT is required. In addition, applicants must rank in the upper half of their graduating class at an accredited secondary school. The GED is accepted. High school preparation should include 4 units of English, 3 of math, 2 each of foreign language and lab science, and 1 each of history, social studies, and phys ed or ROTC, plus 1/2 unit each in economics and government. A GPA of 2.0 is required. AP and CLEP credits are accepted. Important factors in the admissions decision are advanced placement or honor courses, leadership record, and personality/intangible qualities.

Procedure: Freshmen are admitted fall and spring. Entrance exams should be taken before filing an application. Check with school for current deadlines. The fall 2001 application fee was $25.

Transfer: Transfer applicants should have a college GPA of 2.0. Students with fewer than 30 credit hours must submit high school and college transcripts and SAT I or ACT scores. 30 credits of 128 must be completed at State or SCSU.

Visiting: There are guides for informal visits and visitors may sit in on classes. To schedule a visit, contact the Office of Admissions and Recruitment.

Financial Aid: In a recent year, 85% of all freshmen and 94% of continuing students received some form of financial aid. 88% of freshmen and 64% of continuing students received need-based aid. The average freshman award was $4000. State or SCSU is a member of CSS. The CSS/Profile is required. Check with school for curret deadlines.

International Students: They must take the TOEFL and also take the SAT I, or the ACT scoring 830 on te SAT I.

Computers: The mainframe is a DEC VAX 11/780. Macs and one-on-one tutorial assistance are available to all students at the campus writing center. All students may access the system. There are no time limits and no fees.

Admissions Contact: Dorothy L. Brown, Director of Admissions.
E-mail: *admissions@scsu.edu*

SOUTHERN WESLEYAN UNIVERSITY

A-2

Central, SC 29630-1020

(864) 644-5550
(800) 282-8798; Fax: (864) 644-5903

Full-time: 717 men, 1162 women	**Faculty:** 43; IIB, --$
Part-time: 23 men, 94 women	**Ph.D.s:** 77%
Graduate: 70 men, 100 women	**Student/Faculty:** 44 to 1
Year: semesters, summer session	**Tuition:** $12,800
Application Deadline: August 10	**Room & Board:** $4480
Freshman Class: 303 applied, 195 accepted, 114 enrolled	
SAT I Verbal/Math: 510/510	**ACT:** 20 **COMPETITIVE**

Southern Wesleyan University, founded in 1906, and part of the Christian Coalition of Colleges and Universities, is a private liberal arts institution affiliated with the Wesleyan Church. In addition to regional accreditation, Southern has baccalaureate program accreditation with NASDTEC. The library contains 84,180 volumes, 160 microform items, and 3192 audiovisual forms/CDs, and subscribes to 525 periodicals. Computerized library services include the card catalog, interlibrary loans, and database searching. Special learning facilities include a learning resource center and an electron microscope lab. The 200-acre campus is in a rural area 30 miles southwest of Greenville. Including residence halls, there are 17 buildings.

Student Life: 84% of undergraduates are from South Carolina. Others are from 24 states, 7 foreign countries, and Canada. 98% are from public schools. 86% are white. Most are Protestant. The average age of freshmen is 19; all undergraduates, 25. 25% do not continue beyond their first year; 34% remain to graduate.

Housing: 326 students can be accommodated in college housing, which includes single-sex dormitories. On-campus housing is guaranteed for all 4 years. 87% of students commute. Alcohol is not permitted. All students may keep cars.

Activities: There are no fraternities or sororities. There are 20 groups on campus, including cheerleading, choir, computers, drama, ethnic, honors, literary magazine, orchestra, professional, religious, social, social service, student government, and yearbook. Popular campus events include Christmas Banquet and Junior/Senior Banquet.

Sports: There are 5 intercollegiate sports for men and 4 for women, and 5 intramural sports for men and 5 for women. Facilities include a gym, a soccer and softball field, a baseball field, tennis courts, a fitness center, and a cross-country trail.

Disabled Students: 90% of the campus is accessible. Wheelchair ramps, elevators, special parking, and specially equipped rest rooms are available.

Services: Counseling and information services are available, as is tutoring in some subjects. There is remedial math, reading, and writing.

Campus Safety and Security: Measures include informal discussions, pamphlets/posters/films, emergency telephones, lighted pathways/sidewalks, and night security.

Programs of Study: Southern confers B.A., B.S., and B.Acct. degrees. Associate and master's degrees are also awarded. Bachelor's degrees are awarded in BIOLOGICAL SCIENCE (biology/biological science), BUSINESS (accounting, business administration and management, personnel management, and recreation and leisure services), COMMUNICATIONS AND THE ARTS (English and music), COMPUTER AND PHYSICAL SCIENCE (chemistry, information sciences and systems, mathematics, and web services), EDUCATION (elementary, music, physical, and special), HEALTH PROFESSIONS (medical laboratory technology), SOCIAL SCIENCE (history, psychology, religion, and social science). Education, business, and religion are the largest.

Required: To graduate, students must complete 128 credit hours with 54 hours in general education courses and a minimum GPA of 2.0. All students must take 12 hours each of English and religion, 6 of history, 3 of social sciences, and 3 of math or statistics, plus 2 science lab courses. Specific required courses include aesthetics, introduction to computer science, phys ed, and interdisciplinary seminars.

Special: There is a co-op program with Clemson University and in medical technology and criminal justice with other institutions. Study abroad in 6 countries and internships in psychology, English, and business are available. A Washington semester with the Christian College Coalition, a semester at the Los Angeles Film Studios center, a session at the Summer Institute of Journalism in Washington, D.C., and dual majors are available. The Leadership Education for the Adult Professional Program offers degrees for working professionals. There is 1 national honor society and 5 departmental honors programs.

Faculty/Classroom: 78% of faculty are male; 22%, female. All both teach and do research. No introductory courses are taught by graduate students. The average class size in an introductory lecture is 25; in a laboratory, 15; and in a regular course, 20.

Admissions: 64% of the 2001-2002 applicants were accepted. The SAT I scores for the 2001-2002 freshman class were: Verbal--39% below 500, 50% between 500 and 599, and 11% between 600 and 700; Math--47% below 500, 40% between 500 and 599, 12% between 600 and 700, and 1% above 700. The ACT scores were 58% below 21, 22% between 21 and 23, 14% between 24 and 26, and 6% between 27 and 28. 24% of the current freshmen were in the top fifth of their class; 46% were in the top two fifths.

Requirements: The SAT I or ACT is required, with a recommended minimum composite score of 850 on the SAT I or 19 on the ACT. Applicants must be graduates of an accredited secondary school. The GED is accepted. Students should complete 16 Carnegie units, including 4 credits of English and 2 each of math, science, and social studies, as well as 6 electives. Southern requires applicants to be in the upper 50% of their class. A GPA of 2.0 is required. AP and CLEP credits are accepted. Important factors in the admissions decision are leadership record, advanced placement or honor courses, and personality/intangible qualities.

Procedure: Freshmen are admitted fall and spring. Entrance exams should be taken prior to application. There are early admissions and deferred admissions plans. Applications should be filed by August 10 for fall entry, January 5 for spring entry, and May 30 for summer entry, along with a $25 fee. Notification is sent on a rolling basis.

Transfer: 41 transfer students enrolled in 2001-2002. Southern recommends that transfer applicants have a minimum GPA of 2.0 in at least 29 credit hours. 32 credits of 128 must be completed at Southern.

Visiting: There are regularly scheduled orientations for prospective students. There are guides for informal visits and visitors may sit in on classes and stay overnight. To schedule a visit, contact the Admissions Office.

Financial Aid: In 2001-2002, 95% of all freshmen and 92% of continuing students received some form of financial aid. 65% of freshmen and 62% of continuing students received need-based aid. The average freshman award was $8166. Of that total, scholarships or need-based grants averaged $6231 ($17,280 maximum); loans averaged $2871 ($6625 maximum); and work contracts averaged $500 ($1000 maximum). 55% of undergraduates work part time. Average annual earnings from campus work are $700. The average financial indebtedness of the 2001 graduate was $5271. The CSS/Profile, FAFSA, FFS, or SFS and the college's own financial statement are required. The fall application deadline is April 15.

International Students: There are 5 international students enrolled. They must score 500 on the written TOEFL or 173 on the electronic version and also take the SAT I or the ACT, scoring 850 on the SAT I.

Computers: The mainframe is an NT server. There are 2 computer labs housing 250 PCs for student use. All students may access the system. There are no time limits. The fee is $50.

Graduates: In 2001, 238 bachelor's degrees were awarded. The most popular majors were business (60%), education (9%), and religion (5%). In an average class, 16% graduate in 4 years, 41% in 5 years, and 42% in 6 years.

Admissions Contact: Joy Bryant, Director of Admissions. A video is available. E-mail: *admissions@swu.edu* Web: *www.swu.edu*

UNIVERSITY OF SOUTH CAROLINA SYSTEM

The University of South Carolina System, established in 1801, consists of 8 campuses, with the flagship institution located in Columbia. Other 4-year campuses are in Aiken and Spartanburg. The university is governed by a board of trustees, and the chief administrator is the president. The primary goal of the University of South Carolina is to prepare informed and productive citizens for today's increasingly complex and global environment. The main priorities are to foster excellence in undergraduate and graduate education, research, and service programs. Total enrollment of all campuses is 3about 5,000 with more than 1700 faculty members. Altogether the university has 78 baccalaureate, 172 master's, 63 doctoral, and 3 professional programs (law, medicine, and pharmacy). Profiles of the 4-year campuses are included in this section.

UNIVERSITY OF SOUTH CAROLINA AT AIKEN C-3

Aiken, SC 29801 (803) 641-3366
(888) WOW-USCA; Fax: (803) 641-3727

Full-time: 759 men, 1398 women	**Faculty:** 125; IIB, av$
Part-time: 301 men, 681 women	**Ph.D.s:** 80%
Graduate: 20 men, 123 women	**Student/Faculty:** 17 to 1
Year: semesters, summer session	**Tuition:** $3778 ($8304)
Application Deadline: open	**Room & Board:** $4050
Freshman Class: n/av	
SAT I: required	**LESS COMPETITIVE**

The University of South Carolina Aiken, established in 1961, is a state-supported institution offering undergraduate and graduate programs in humanities and social sciences, health sciences, education, business administration and economics, nursing, and science. There are 5 undergraduate and 3 graduate schools. In addition to regional accreditation, USCA has baccalaureate program accreditation with NASDTEC and NLN. The library contains 138,077 volumes, 60,397 microform items, and 205 audiovisual forms/CDs, and subscribes to 853 periodicals. Computerized library services include the card catalog, interlibrary loans, and database searching. Special learning facilities include a learning resource center, art gallery, planetarium, and a science education center. The 354-acre campus is in a suburban area 14 miles east of Augusta, Georgia. Including residence halls, there are 14 buildings.

Student Life: 84% of undergraduates are from South Carolina. Others are from 38 states, 23 foreign countries, and Canada. 98% are from public schools. 72% are white; 22% African American. The average age of freshmen is 21; all undergraduates, 25.

Housing: 360 students can be accommodated in college housing, which includes coed on-campus apartments. On-campus housing is available on a first-come, first-served basis and is available on a lottery system for upperclassmen. 88% of students commute. Alcohol is not permitted. All students may keep cars.

Activities: 1% of men belong to 3 national fraternities; 1% of women belong to 3 national sororities. There are 53 groups on campus, including cheerleading, choir, chorus, computers, drama, ethnic, honors, international, literary magazine, musical theater, newspaper, nontraditional students, pep band, photography, political, professional, religious, social, social service, and student government. Popular campus events include International Day and Alcohol/Health Awareness Week.

Sports: There are 6 intercollegiate sports for men and 6 for women, and 20 intramural sports for men and 20 for women. Facilities include an activities center, a baseball field, a soccer/intramural/softball field, a tennis court, and a wellness/exercise center.

Disabled Students: All of the campus is accessible. Wheelchair ramps, elevators, special parking, specially equipped rest rooms, lowered drinking fountains, and lowered telephones are available.

Services: Counseling and information services are available, as is tutoring in some subjects, including math and writing. There is a reader service for the blind. Special administration of tests, note taking, free copying of notes for disabled, large print exams for visually impaired, zoom text software for computer applications, and priority registration are also available in some cases.

Campus Safety and Security: Measures include 24-hour foot and vehicle patrol, self-defense education, escort service, and informal discussions. There are pamphlets/posters/films, emergency telephones, and lighted pathways/sidewalks.

Programs of Study: USCA confers B.A., B.S., and B.I.S. degrees. Associate and master's degrees are also awarded. Bachelor's degrees are awarded in BIOLOGICAL SCIENCE (biology/biological science), BUSINESS (business administration and management), COMMUNICATIONS AND THE ARTS (communications, English, and fine arts), COMPUTER AND PHYSICAL SCIENCE (applied mathematics, chemistry, and computer mathematics), EDUCATION (early childhood, elementary, and secondary), HEALTH PROFESSIONS (nursing), SOCIAL SCIENCE (history, interdisciplinary studies, physical fitness/movement, political science/government, psychology, and sociology). English, history, and biology are the strongest academically. Business, education, and nursing are the largest.

Required: Students must complete a minimum of 120 credit hours, with at least a 2.0 GPA. General education requirements include courses in English, math, applied speech, natural science, social and behavioral sciences, humanities, and history.

Special: Cross-registration is permitted with other schools in the University of South Carolina system. Co-op programs in engineering and business, business internships, study abroad in 19 countries, student-designed majors, and work-study programs are offered. B.A.-B.S. degrees in psychology and education, nondegree study, and pass/fail options are possible. There are 7 national honor societies, a freshman honors program, and 4 departmental honors programs.

Faculty/Classroom: 55% of faculty are male; 45%, female. 97% teach undergraduates. No introductory courses are taught by graduate students. The average class size in an introductory lecture is 24; in a laboratory, 18; and in a regular course, 15.

Admissions: 4 freshmen graduated first in their class in a recent year.

Requirements: The SAT I is required. In addition, admission is based on a combination of an applicant's scores on college entrance examinations and high school GPA. Applicants are required to submit 16 academic credits, including 4 years of high school English, 3 units of math, 2 each of social studies, a foreign language, and a lab science, 1 of history, and 1 year of phys ed or ROTC, and 1 from advanced math, computer science, math/computer science, world history, world geography, or Western civilization. AP and CLEP credits are accepted. Important factors in the admissions decision are advanced placement or honor courses, recommendations by school officials, and leadership record. Applications are accepted on-line at *http://web.csd.sc.edu/app/ugrad_aiken/*.

Procedure: Freshmen are admitted to all sessions. Entrance exams should be taken by the fall of the senior year. There are early admissions and deferred admissions plans. Application deadlines are open. The fall 2001 application fee was $35.

Transfer: The college GPA is considered. A high school transcript is required of applicants with fewer than 45 quarter hours. 30 credits of 120 must be completed at USCA.

Visiting: There are regularly scheduled orientations for prospective students, including regularly scheduled 3-day orientations for prospective students. There are guides for informal visits and visitors may sit in on classes. To schedule a visit, contact the Admissions Office.

Financial Aid: In 2001-2002, 68% of all freshmen and 72% of continuing students received some form of financial aid. 51% of freshmen and 50% of continuing students received need-based aid. The average freshman award was $2950. Of that total, scholarships or need-based grants averaged $750 ($1800 maximum); loans averaged $1000 ($3700 maximum); and work contracts averaged $1200 ($2200 maximum). 9% of undergraduates work part time. Average annual earnings from campus work are $1700. The average financial indebtedness of the 2001 graduate was $13,200. USCA is a member of CSS. The FAFSA and the college's own financial statement are required. The fall application deadline is March 15.

International Students: They must score 550 on the written TOEFL and also take the SAT I.

Computers: The mainframe is an IBM 9672. There are more than 200 PCs for student use throughout the campus. All students may access the system 24 hours a day, 7 days a week. There are no time limits. The fee is $50.

Graduates: In an average class, 13% graduate in 4 years, 36% in 5 years, and 42% in 6 years.

Admissions Contact: Andrew Hendrix, Director of Admissions. E-mail: *admit@sc.edu* Web: *www.usca.sc.edu*

UNIVERSITY OF SOUTH CAROLINA AT COLUMBIA C-3

Columbia, SC 29208 (803) 777-7700
(800) 868-5872; Fax: (803) 777-0101

Full-time: 5986 men, 7106 women	**Faculty:** 761; I, -$
Part-time: 1105 men, 1309 women	**Ph.D.s:** 84%
Graduate: 3061 men, 4433 women	**Student/Faculty:** 17 to 1
Year: semesters, summer session	**Tuition:** $4064 ($11,004)
Application Deadline: January 1	**Room & Board:** $4684
Freshman Class: 11,176 applied, 7788 accepted, 3287 enrolled	
SAT I Verbal/Math: 540/550	**ACT:** 23 **VERY COMPETITIVE**

The University of South Carolina at Columbia, founded in 1801, is a publicly assisted institution serving the entire state of South Carolina. In addition to the main campus at Columbia, there are 2 senior campuses at Aiken and Spartanburg, and 5 regional campuses. There are 16 undergraduate and 18 graduate schools. In addition to regional accreditation, Carolina has baccalaureate program accreditation with AACSB, ABET, ACEJMC, ACPE, CSAB, NASM, NCATE, and NLN. The 7 libraries contain 3,283,749 volumes, 4,939,906 microform items, and 44,957 audiovisual forms/CDs, and subscribe to 21,426 periodicals. Computerized library services include the card catalog, interlibrary loans, and database searching. Special learning facilities include a learning resource center, art gallery, natural history museum, planetarium, and radio station. The 351-acre campus is in an urban area in the downtown area of Columbia. Including residence halls, there are 151 buildings.

Student Life: 81% of undergraduates are from South Carolina. Others are from 49 states, 84 foreign countries, and Canada. 74% are white; 18% African American. The average age of freshmen is 18; all undergraduates, 21. 19% do not continue beyond their first year; 58% remain to graduate.

Housing: 6793 students can be accommodated in college housing, which includes single-sex and coed dormitories, on-campus apartments, married-student housing, fraternity houses, and sorority houses. In addition, there are honors houses, and special-interest houses, wellness, a residential college, U.S. international community, teaching fellows residence, athletic, and Greek Houses. On-campus housing is guaranteed for the freshman year only and is available on a lottery system for upperclassmen. 54% of students commute. All students may keep cars.

Activities: 17% of men belong to 18 national fraternities; 17% of women belong to 12 national sororities. There are 275 groups on campus, including art, band, cheerleading, chess, choir, chorale, chorus, computers, dance, debate, drama, drill team, ethnic, film, forensics, gay, honors, international, jazz band, literary magazine, marching band, musical theater, opera, orchestra, pep band, photography, political, professional, radio and TV, religious, social, social service, student government, symphony, and yearbook. Popular campus events include Parents Weekend, Black History Month, and Carolina Spirit Week.

Sports: There are 9 intercollegiate sports for men and 11 for women, and 33 intramural sports for men and 33 for women. Facilities include football and soccer stadiums, a basketball coliseum, a field house, a volleyball and basketball practice facility, baseball, softball, and practice fields, and an all-weather track. There is also a recreation center with badminton, basketball, handball/racquetball, an aquatics center, a weight room, aerobics, and tennis court space.

Disabled Students: 90% of the campus is accessible. Wheelchair ramps, elevators, special parking, specially equipped rest rooms, special class scheduling, lowered drinking fountains, lowered telephones, and listening devices, sign language interpreting, and adapted housing, transportation, and computers are available.

Services: Counseling and information services are available, as is tutoring in every subject, including reader services for LD students. There is a reader service for the blind.

Campus Safety and Security: Measures include 24-hour foot and vehicle patrol, self-defense education, escort service, and shuttle buses. There are informal discussions, pamphlets/posters/films, emergency telephones, and lighted pathways/sidewalks. The USC police department is a nationally accredited campus law enforcement agency.

Programs of Study: Carolina confers B.A., B.S., B.A.I.S., B.A.J., B.A.P.E./B.S.P.E., B.A.R.S.C., B.F.A., B.M., B.M.A., B.S.B.A., B.S.Chem., B.S.C.S., B.S.E., B.S.I.S., B.S.Med.Tech., and B.S.N. degrees. Associate, master's, and doctoral degrees are also awarded. Bachelor's degrees are awarded in BIOLOGICAL SCIENCE (biology/biological science, and marine science), BUSINESS (accounting, banking and finance, business administration and management, business economics, hotel/motel and restaurant management, insurance, management science, marketing/retailing/merchandising, office supervision and management, real estate, retailing, and sports management), COMMUNICATIONS AND THE ARTS (advertising, art history and appreciation, broadcasting, classics, communications, dramatic arts, English, fine arts, French, German, Greek, Italian, journalism, Latin, media arts, music, music performance, public relations, Spanish, speech/debate/rhetoric, and studio art), COMPUTER AND PHYSICAL SCIENCE (chemistry, computer science, geology, geophysics and seismology, mathematics, physics, and statistics), EDUCATION (art, early childhood, elementary, music, physical, and secondary), ENGINEERING AND ENVIRONMENTAL DESIGN (chemical engineering, civil engineering, computer engineering, electrical/electronics engineering, and mechanical engineering), HEALTH PROFESSIONS (exercise science, medical laboratory technology, and nursing), SOCIAL SCIENCE (African American studies, anthropology, criminal justice, economics, European studies, geography, history, interdisciplinary studies, international relations, Latin American studies, philosophy, political science/government, psychology, religion, sociology, and women's studies). Biology, experimental psychology, and engineering are the largest.

Required: All students must maintain a GPA of 2.0 in 120 semester hours, including 24 in their major. Distribution requirements include 12 hours in humanities and social science, 7 in natural science, 6 hours each in English and numerical and analytical reasoning, and a demonstrated ability in foreign languages.

Special: USC transmits live interactive televised instruction to more than 20 locations in the state. Cross-registration is offered with the National Technological University in Engineering and through the National Student Exchange. Internships in many fields, study abroad in many countries through the Byrnes International Center, co-op programs, and work-study programs are available. Double majors through the colleges of humanities and social sciences and science and math, student-designed majors, an interdisciplinary studies degree, and a 3-2 engineering degree with the College of Charleston are offered. Credit for military experience, nondegree study, and pass/fail options also are possible. There are 34 national honor societies, including Phi Beta Kappa, and a freshman honors program.

Faculty/Classroom: 68% of faculty are male; 32%, female. 62% teach undergraduates, All do research, and 69% do both. Graduate students teach 23% of introductory courses. The average class size in an introductory lecture is 30; in a laboratory, 22; and in a regular course, 30.

Admissions: 70% of the 2001-2002 applicants were accepted. The SAT I scores for the 2001-2002 freshman class were: Verbal--27% below 500, 48% between 500 and 599, 21% between 600 and 700, and 5% above 700; Math--22% below 500, 48% between 500 and 599, 24% between 600 and 700, and 6% above 700. The ACT scores were 24% below 21, 35% between 21 and 23, 19% between 24 and 26, 9% between 27 and 28, and 12% above 28. 45% of the current freshmen were in the top fifth of their class; 77% were in the top two fifths. There were 42 National Merit finalists. 93 freshmen graduated first in their class.

Requirements: The SAT I or ACT is required. In addition, applicants must have 16 academic credits, including 4 in English, 3 each in math and social studies (1 of which must be U.S. history), 2 each in foreign language and lab science, 1 academic elective, and 1 phys ed or ROTC. The GED is accepted. AP and CLEP credits are accepted. Important factors in the admissions decision are advanced placement or honor courses, evidence of special talent, and recommendations by school officials. Applications are accepted on-line at the school's web site, *http://web.csd.sc.edu/app/ugrad-cola/*.

Procedure: Freshmen are admitted to all sessions. Entrance exams should be taken during spring of the junior year and fall of the senior year, if necessary. There is a rolling admissions plan. Applications should be filed by January 1 for fall entry, along with a $40 fee. Notification is sent 4–6 weeks after file is complete.

Transfer: 960 transfer students enrolled in 2001-2002. Transfer students must have a cumulative 2.25 GPA from regionally accredited institutions. The SAT I or ACT is required for transfers who have attempted fewer than 30 semester hours of college credit. These students must meet both freshman and transfer requirements. Requirements are higher for some majors. 30 credits of 120 must be completed at Carolina.

Visiting: There are regularly scheduled orientations for prospective students. There are guides for informal visits and visitors may sit in on classes. To schedule a visit, contact the USC Visitor's Center at (803) 777-2125.

Financial Aid: In a recent year, 60% of all freshmen and 65% of continuing students received some form of financial aid. 45% of freshmen and 50% of continuing students received need-based aid. The average freshman award was $2750. Of that total, scholarships or need-based grants averaged $900 ($2000 maximum); loans averaged $1750 ($2625 maximum); and work contracts averaged $2000 ($2550 maximum). 12% of undergraduates work part time. Average annual earnings from campus work are $3316. The average financial indebtedness of the 2001 graduate was $16,200. Carolina is a member of CSS. The FAFSA is required. The fall application deadline is April 15.

International Students: There are 286 international students enrolled. The school actively recruits these students. They must score 213 on the written TOEFL.

Computers: The mainframe is an IBM 9672-R53. Students may use the system to register, conduct research, take web-enhanced classes, check on grades, make fee payments, search the Internet, visit web sites, and access the library, lists, and e-mail, and to find information on financial aid and meal plan. All students may access the system. There are no time limits and no fees. It is strongly recommended that all students have a personal computer.

Graduates: In 2001, 3181 bachelor's degrees were awarded. The most popular majors were psychology (7%), marketing (7%), and business administration (7%). In an average class, 37% graduate in 4 years, 55% in 5 years, and 58% in 6 years. 19,737 companies recruited on campus in 2000-2001.

Admissions Contact: Terry L. Davis, Director of Undergraduate Admissions. A video is available. E-mail: *admissions-ugrad@sc.edu*
Web: *www.sc.edu/admissions*

UNIVERSITY OF SOUTH CAROLINA AT SPARTANBURG
B-1

Spartanburg, SC 29303
(864) 503-5246
(800) 277-8727; Fax: (864) 503-5727

Full-time: 930 men, 1720 women
Part-time: 330 men, 515 women
Graduate: 30 men, 250 women
Year: semesters, summer session
Application Deadline: open
Freshman Class: n/av
SAT I: required
Faculty: 140; IIB, -$
Ph.D.s: 88%
Student/Faculty: 19 to 1
Tuition: $3958 ($8850)
Room & Board: $3360
COMPETITIVE+

The University of South Carolina at Spartanburg, established in 1967, is a public institution offering undergraduate programs in the liberal arts and sciences, business administration, education, and nursing. There are 4 undergraduate schools and 1 graduate school. In addition to regional accreditation, USCS has baccalaureate program accreditation with AACSB, NCATE, and NLN. The library contains 214,984 volumes, 58,426 microform items, and 11,119 audiovisual forms/CDs, and subscribes to 3151 periodicals. Computerized library services include the card catalog, interlibrary loans, and database searching. Special learning facilities include an art gallery and a greenhouse. The 298-acre campus is in an urban area 100 miles north of Columbia. Including residence halls, there are 18 buildings.

Student Life: 93% of undergraduates are from South Carolina. Others are from 42 states, 22 foreign countries, and Canada. 75% are white; 21% African American. The average age of freshmen is 18; all undergraduates, 24. 33% do not continue beyond their first year; 35% remain to graduate.

Housing: 400 students can be accommodated in college housing, which includes coed on-campus apartments and off-campus apartments. On-campus housing is available on a first-come, first-served basis. 92% of students commute. Alcohol is not permitted. All students may keep cars.

Activities: 4% of men belong to 3 national fraternities; 5% of women belong to 5 national sororities. There are 46 groups on campus, including cheerleading, choir, chorus, computers, dance, debate, drama, ethnic, honors, international, literary magazine, newspaper, pep band, photography, political, professional, religious, social, social service, and student government. Popular campus events include RIOTS, Wet and Wild Day, and intramural tournaments.

Sports: There are 5 intercollegiate sports for men and 4 for women, and 13 intramural sports for men and 12 for women. Facilities include a soccer field, baseball fields, a basketball gym, racquetball courts, and an auxiliary gym.

Disabled Students: Wheelchair ramps, elevators, special parking, specially equipped rest rooms, special class scheduling, lowered drinking fountains, and lowered telephones are available.

Services: Counseling and information services are available, as is tutoring in most subjects. There is remedial math, reading, and writing.

Campus Safety and Security: Measures include 24-hour foot and vehicle patrol, self-defense education, escort service, and pamphlets/posters/films. There are emergency telephones and lighted pathways/sidewalks.

Programs of Study: USCS confers B.A., B.S., and B.S.N. degrees. Associate and master's degrees are also awarded. Bachelor's degrees are awarded in BIOLOGICAL SCIENCE (biology/biological science), BUSINESS (accounting, business administration and management, and marketing management), COMMUNICATIONS AND THE ARTS (communications, English, French, graphic design, and Spanish), COMPUTER AND PHYSICAL SCIENCE (chemistry, computer science, information sciences and systems, and mathematics), EDUCATION (early childhood, elementary, English, mathematics, physical, secondary, social studies, and special), HEALTH PROFESSIONS (nursing), SOCIAL SCIENCE (criminal justice, economics, history, interdisciplinary studies, political science/government, psychology, and sociology). Business administration is the largest.

Required: Students must complete 120 to 136 credits, including 69 to 82 in the major, with a minimum GPA of 2.0. General education requirements include courses in communications, math, arts and humanities, social and behavioral sciences, natural science, foreign culture, computer studies, and a senior seminar.

Special: Cross-registration is permitted within the University of South Carolina system and with Wofford College and Greenville Technical College. Opportunities are provided for B.A.-B.S. degrees, student-designed majors, a 3-2 engineering degree, nondegree study, credit for military service, and study abroad in Mexico, France, and Germany. There are 5 national honor societies, including Phi Beta Kappa.

Faculty/Classroom: 44% of faculty are male; 56%, female. All teach undergraduates. No introductory courses are taught by graduate students. The average class size in an introductory lecture is 22; in a laboratory, 20; and in a regular course, 15.

Admissions: 49% of the 2001-2002 applicants were accepted. 27% of the current freshmen were in the top fifth of their class; 62% were in the top two fifths.

Requirements: The SAT I is required, with a minimum composite score of 850. Graduation from an accredited secondary school with a GPA of 2.0 is required. The GED is accepted. Applicants must submit 20 academic credits, distributed as follows: 4 years of English, 3 of math, 2 each of lab science, foreign language, and social studies, 1 each of history and phys ed or ROTC, and the remainder in electives. AP and CLEP credits are accepted.

Procedure: Entrance exams should be taken at the beginning of the senior year. Application deadlines are open. The application fee is $30. Notification is sent on a rolling basis.

Transfer: 429 transfer students enrolled in a recent year. Applicants must have a minimum college GPA of 2.0 and submit final transcripts from all schools attended. Students transferring with fewer than 30 semester credits must submit a minimum SAT I score of 700 or ACT score of 18 and meet other freshman requirements. 30 credits of 120 must be completed at USCS.

Visiting: There are regularly scheduled orientations for prospective students. There are guides for informal visits and visitors may sit in on classes. To schedule a visit, contact the Admissions Office.

Financial Aid: The CSS/Profile, FAFSA, FFS, or SFS is required.

International Students: There were 47 international students enrolled in a recent year. They must score 500 on the written TOEFL and also take the SAT I or the ACT.

Computers: The mainframe is an IBM 9375. There are also 350 PCs available to students in several campus labs. Additionally, there is mainframe and Internet access via the USC-Columbia LAN. All students may access the system during school hours. There are no time limits and no fees.

Graduates: In a recent year, 346 bachelor's degrees were awarded. The most popular majors were business (23%), interdisciplinary studies (17%), and psychology (8%). In an average class, 15% graduate in 4 years, 31% in 5 years, and 35% in 6 years.

Admissions Contact: Donette Stewart, Director of Admissions.
E-mail: *dstewart@gw.uscs.edu* Web: *www.uscs.edu*

VOORHEES COLLEGE
C-3

Denmark, SC 29042
(803) 793-3351
(800) 446-6250; Fax: (803) 793-1112

Full-time: 233 men, 445 women
Part-time: 13 men, 65 women
Graduate: none
Year: semesters, summer session
Application Deadline: August 15
Freshman Class: 990 applied, 485 accepted, 143 enrolled
SAT I Verbal/Math: 370/410
Faculty: 31
Ph.D.s: 40%
Student/Faculty: 22 to 1
Tuition: $6460
Room & Board: $3516
ACT: 17
COMPETITIVE+

Voorhees College, founded in 1897, is a historically black liberal arts college affiliated with the Protestant Episcopal Church. Undergraduate programs are offered in accounting, biology, business administration, English, health and recreation, political science, sociology, criminal justice, computer science, teacher education, and math. The library contains 111,057 volumes, 23,387 microform items, and 238 audiovisual forms/CDs, and subscribes to 417 periodicals. Computerized library services include the card catalog and interlibrary loans. Special learning facilities include a learning resource center. The 350-acre campus is in a rural area 50 miles south of Columbia. Including residence halls, there are 23 buildings.

Student Life: 78% of undergraduates are from South Carolina. Others are from 20 states and 2 foreign countries. All are from public schools. 99% are African American. Most are Protestant. The average age of freshmen is 17; all undergraduates, 23. 38% do not continue beyond their first year; 55% remain to graduate.

Housing: 521 students can be accommodated in college housing, which includes single-sex dormitories. On-campus housing is guaranteed for all 4 years. 75% of students live on campus; of those, 50% remain on campus on weekends. Alcohol is not permitted. All students may keep cars.

Activities: 20% of men belong to 4 national fraternities; 14% of women belong to 4 national sororities. There are 20 groups on campus, including cheerleading, choir, computers, dance, drama, honors, newspaper, pep band, political, professional, religious, social, student government, and yearbook. Popular campus events include Career Awareness Week, Black History Month, and Religious Emphasis Week.

Sports: There are 3 intercollegiate sports for men and 4 for women, and 4 intramural sports for men and 4 for women. Facilities include a gym, tennis courts, baseball and softball fields, a weight room, a dance studio, and a student center.

Disabled Students: 80% of the campus is accessible. Wheelchair ramps, elevators, special parking, specially equipped rest rooms, lowered drinking fountains, and mobile carts are available.

Services: Counseling and information services are available, as is tutoring in most subjects. There is remedial math, reading, and writing.
Campus Safety and Security: Measures include 24-hour foot and vehicle patrol, informal discussions, and lighted pathways/sidewalks.
Programs of Study: Voorhees confers B.A. and B.S. degrees. Bachelor's degrees are awarded in BIOLOGICAL SCIENCE (biology/biological science), BUSINESS (accounting, business administration and management, and recreation and leisure services), COMMUNICATIONS AND THE ARTS (English), COMPUTER AND PHYSICAL SCIENCE (computer science and mathematics), HEALTH PROFESSIONS (health), SOCIAL SCIENCE (criminal justice and sociology). Biology and business administration are the strongest academically. Business and organizational management are the largest.
Required: To graduate, students must earn at least 122 credit hours, with at least 30 in the major, and have a minimum GPA of 2.0. The 55-hour general education requirement includes 13 hours of humanities, 9 of English, 6 each of social science, natural science, math, and foreign language, 3 of computer science, 2 of phys ed, and 1 of freshmen orientation. A number of free electives and a senior seminar are also required. An English proficiency exam and an exit exam must be passed.
Special: Voorhees offers cooperative education, study abroad in England, internships in some programs, work-study, an evening/Saturday program, off-campus summer study, dual majors, credit by exam, and a degree completion program. Cross-registration with Denmark Technical College and interdisciplinary majors, such as health and recreation, are possible. There are 3 national honor societies, and 1 departmental honors program.
Faculty/Classroom: 70% of faculty are male; 30%, female. All teach undergraduates. The average class size in an introductory lecture is 30; in a laboratory, 20; and in a regular course, 25.
Admissions: 49% of the 2001-2002 applicants were accepted. 35% of the current freshmen were in the top fifth of their class; 65% were in the top two fifths.
Requirements: The SAT I or ACT is required. In addition, recommended minimum scores are 600 on the SAT I or 16 on the ACT. Applicants must be high school graduates or hold a GED. Students should have earned 20 academic credits in high school, including 4 of English, 3 of math, 2 each of science and foreign language (optional), and 1 each of history, social studies, economics/government, and phys ed. Letters of recommendation and a campus visit are advised. Voorhees requires applicants to be in the upper 75% of their class. A GPA of 2.0 is required. AP and CLEP credits are accepted. Important factors in the admissions decision are advanced placement or honor courses, recommendations by school officials, and recommendations by alumni.
Procedure: Freshmen are admitted to all sessions. Entrance exams should be taken in the senior year. There is a deferred admissions plan. Applications should be filed by August 15 for fall entry and December 15 for spring entry. The fall 2001 application fee was $25. Notification of early decision is sent August 15; regular decision, on a rolling basis.
Transfer: 31 transfer students enrolled in 2001-2002. Transfer students must submit complete records, including a confidential report from each college attended. The confidential report form is provided by the Office of Admission and Recruitment. Students with fewer than 30 semester hours must submit their high school record with rank in class and GPA. The SAT I is recommended; a minimum composite score of 600 is expected. An interview is advised. 30 credits of 122 must be completed at Voorhees.
Visiting: There are regularly scheduled orientations for prospective students, consisting of senior visitation days held in January through April. There are guides for informal visits and visitors may sit in on classes and stay overnight. To schedule a visit, contact Willie Jefferson, VP of Student Development at (803) 703-7173 or *williej@voorhees.edu*.
Financial Aid: In 2001-2002, 97% of all freshmen and 75% of continuing students received some form of financial aid. 92% of freshmen and 72% of continuing students received need-based aid. The average freshman award was $8756. Of that total, scholarships or need-based grants averaged $6092 ($8705 maximum); loans averaged $2219 ($2625 maximum); work contracts averaged $1720; and institutional, endowment, and other scholarships averaged $2384 ($6000 maximum). 42% of undergraduates work part time. Average annual earnings from campus work are $1720. The average financial indebtedness of the 2001 graduate was $15,250. Voorhees is a member of CSS. The FAFSA, the college's own financial statemen or SAR are required. The FAFSA is preferred. The fall application deadline is April 15.
International Students: There are 3 international students enrolled. They must score 500 on the written TOEFL and also take the SAT I or the ACT.
Computers: The mainframe is an IBM System/36. There are 4 labs on campus that are networked and accessible to students. All students have Internet and Web access. All students may access the system. There are no time limits and no fees.
Graduates: In 2001, 170 bachelor's degrees were awarded. In an average class, 25% graduate in 4 years, 52% in 5 years, and 54% in 6 years. 20 companies recruited on campus in 2000-2001. Of the 2000 graduating class, 13% were enrolled in graduate school within 6 months of graduation and 65% were employed.
Admissions Contact: Roe Berta Kemp, Director of Admissions and Recruitment. A video is available. E-mail: *kemp@voorhees.edu*
Web: *www.voorhees.edu*

WINTHROP UNIVERSITY C-1
Rock Hill, SC 29733 (803) 323-2191
(800) 763-0230; Fax: (803) 323-2137

Full-time: 1287 men, 2914 women	**Faculty:** 255; IIA, --$
Part-time: 198 men, 439 women	**Ph.D.s:** 80%
Graduate: 370 men, 1098 women	**Student/Faculty:** 16 to 1
Year: semesters, summer session	**Tuition:** $4688 ($8776)
Application Deadline: June 1	**Room & Board:** $4418
Freshman Class: 3207 applied, 2389 accepted, 946 enrolled	
SAT I Verbal/Math: 530/525	**ACT:** 22 **COMPETITIVE**

Winthrop University, founded in 1886, is a state-supported institution offering undergraduate and graduate programs in liberal arts and sciences, business administration, education, and visual and performing arts. There are 4 undergraduate and 4 graduate schools. In addition to regional accreditation, Winthrop has baccalaureate program accreditation with AACSB, CSAB, CSWE, FIDER, NASAD, NASM, and NCATE. The library contains 420,320 volumes, 1,215,640 microform items, and 1763 audiovisual forms/CDs, and subscribes to 2639 periodicals. Computerized library services include the card catalog, interlibrary loans, and database searching. Special learning facilities include an art gallery, radio station, TV station, audio recording studio, early childhood lab school, the MIDI lab, the Instructional Technology Center, and the Conservatory of Music. The 418-acre campus is in a small town 23 miles south of Charlotte. Including residence halls, there are 43 buildings.
Student Life: 87% of undergraduates are from South Carolina. Others are from 41 states, 33 foreign countries, and Canada. 72% are white; 24%, African American. The average age of freshmen is 18; all undergraduates, 22. 25% do not continue beyond their first year; 75% remain to graduate.
Housing: 2336 students can be accommodated in college housing, which includes single-sex and coed dormitories, on-campus apartments, and married-student housing. In addition, there are independent, off-campus fraternity and sorority houses. On-campus housing is guaranteed for the freshman year only and is available on a first-come, first-served basis. 53% of students commute. All students may keep cars.
Activities: 15% of men belong to 8 national fraternities; 13% of women belong to 8 national sororities. There are 115 groups on campus, including art, band, cheerleading, chess, choir, chorale, chorus, computers, dance, drama, ethnic, gay, honors, international, jazz band, literary magazine, musical theater, newspaper, opera, orchestra, pep band, political, professional, radio and TV, religious, social, social service, student government, and yearbook. Popular campus events include convocation, Fall Fest, and Fine Arts Series.
Sports: There are 7 intercollegiate sports for men and 7 for women, and 30 intramural sports for men and 30 for women. Facilities include a golf course, a 6000-seat coliseum, a swimming pool, a cross-country course, tennis courts, racquetball courts, a weight room, a training room, a ropes course, an 18-hole disc golf course, and baseball, softball, and soccer fields.
Disabled Students: 90% of the campus is accessible. Wheelchair ramps, elevators, special parking, specially equipped rest rooms, special class scheduling, lowered drinking fountains, lowered telephones, and adapted campus housing are available.
Services: There is a reader service for the blind. All tutoring is the responsibility of the students to arrange with their professors or specific departments.
Campus Safety and Security: Measures include 24-hour foot and vehicle patrol, self-defense education, escort service, and informal discussions. There are pamphlets/posters/films, emergency telephones, and lighted pathways/sidewalks.
Programs of Study: Winthrop confers B.A., B.S., B.F.A., B.M., B.M.E., and B.S.W. degrees. Master's degrees are also awarded. Bachelor's degrees are awarded in BIOLOGICAL SCIENCE (biology/biological science), BUSINESS (business administration and management and sports management), COMMUNICATIONS AND THE ARTS (art, art history and appreciation, communications, dance, dramatic arts, English, fine arts, French, music, public relations, Spanish, and speech/debate/rhetoric), COMPUTER AND PHYSICAL SCIENCE (chemistry, computer science, and mathematics), EDUCATION (early childhood, elementary, home economics, music, physical, secondary, and special), HEALTH PROFESSIONS (medical laboratory technology and speech pathology/audiology), SOCIAL SCIENCE (food science, history, home economics, philosophy, political science/government, psychology, religion, social work, and sociology). Business administration, elementary education, and fine arts are the largest.
Required: Students must complete a minimum of 124 semester hours, including a 59-hour general education distribution requirement, and

maintain a minimum GPA of 2.0. Specific courses in writing, oral communication, computer information systems, critical issues, and the U.S. Constitution are required.

Special: Cross-registration is permitted with the Charlotte Area Educational Consortium. Co-op programs and internships in most professional areas, study abroad in 14 countries, and on-campus work-study programs are offered. Interdisciplinary majors such as science communication, nondegree study, and pass/fail options are possible. There are 3 national honor societies, a freshman honors program, and 18 departmental honors programs.

Faculty/Classroom: 56% of faculty are male; 44%, female. 98% teach undergraduates and 90% both teach and do research. No introductory courses are taught by graduate students. The average class size in an introductory lecture is 26; in a laboratory, 16; and in a regular course, 22.

Admissions: 74% of the 2001-2002 applicants were accepted. The SAT I scores for the 2001-2002 freshman class were: Verbal--37% below 500, 44% between 500 and 599, 16% between 600 and 700, and 3% above 700; Math--35% below 500, 49% between 500 and 599, 14% between 600 and 700, and 2% above 700. The ACT scores were 30% below 21, 38% between 21 and 23, 20% between 24 and 26, 7% between 27 and 28, and 5% above 28. 38% of the current freshmen were in the top fifth of their class; 71% were in the top two fifths. In a recent year, 18 freshmen graduated first in their class.

Requirements: The SAT I or ACT is required. In addition, graduation from an accredited secondary school is required; a GED will be accepted. Applicants must have successfully completed 4 credits in high school English, 3 in math, 2 each in lab science, social studies, and a foreign language, 1 in United States history, and 1 in phys ed or ROTC. A GPA of 2.0 is required. AP and CLEP credits are accepted. Important factors in the admissions decision are recommendations by school officials and evidence of special talent. Applications are accepted on-line via Apply, CollegeLink, ExPAN, and others.

Procedure: Freshmen are admitted to all sessions. There is a deferred admissions plan. Applications should be filed by June 1 for fall entry and January 2 for spring entry. The fall 2001 application fee was $35. Notification is sent on a rolling basis.

Transfer: 363 transfer students enrolled in a recent year. Applicants must be eligible to return to the previous institution. 30 credits of 124 must be completed at Winthrop.

Visiting: There are regularly scheduled orientations for prospective students, consisting of the Winthrop Festival, with all academic areas and student life areas represented, a general session, minisessions, and a campus tour. There are guides for informal visits and visitors may sit in on classes. To schedule a visit, contact the Admissions Office.

Financial Aid: In 2001-2002, 50% of all freshmen and 52% of continuing students received some form of financial aid. 47% of freshmen and 46% of continuing students received need-based aid. The average freshman award was $3201. 20% of undergraduates work part time. 20% of undergraduates work part time. Average annual earnings from campus work are $800. The average financial indebtedness of the 2001 graduate was $16,000. Winthrop is a member of CSS. The FAFSA and the college's own financial statement are required. The fall application deadline is May 1.

International Students: There are 97 international students enrolled. The school actively recruits these students. They must score 520 on the written TOEFL and also take the SAT I or the ACT.

Computers: The mainframe is a DEC VAX 6000-540(2). Approximately 250 PCs are available for students in various locations across campus. Many are networked. All students may access the system 95 hours a week, weekdays until 1 A.M. There are no time limits and no fees.

Graduates: In 2001, 736 bachelor's degrees were awarded. The most popular majors were business administration (24%), social work (7%), and elementary education (5%). In an average class, 1% graduate in 3 years, 33% in 4 years, 51% in 5 years, and 53% in 6 years. 45 companies recruited on campus in 2000-2001. Of the 2000 graduating class, 32% were enrolled in graduate school within 6 months of graduation and 60% were employed.

Admissions Contact: Deborah Barber, Director of Admissions. A video is available. E-mail: *admissions@winthrop.edu*
Web: *www.winthrop.edu*

WOFFORD COLLEGE — B-1

Spartanburg, SC 29303-3663 — (864) 597-4130, Fax: (864) 597-4147

Full-time: 573 men, 524 women	**Faculty:** 75; IIB, av$
Part-time: 5 men, 5 women	**Ph.D.s:** 91%
Graduate: none	**Student/Faculty:** 15 to 1
Year: 4-1-4, summer session	**Tuition:** $18,515
Application Deadline: February 1	**Room & Board:** $5480
Freshman Class: 1209 applied, 991 accepted, 303 enrolled	
SAT I Verbal/Math: 600/612	**ACT:** 25 **VERY COMPETITIVE**

Wofford College, founded in 1854, is a private institution affiliated with the United Methodist Church, offering programs in liberal arts and preprofessional studies. In addition to regional accreditation, Wofford has baccalaureate program accreditation with NASDTEC. The library contains 194,400 volumes, 33,797 microform items, and 3242 audiovisual forms/CDs, and subscribes to 552 periodicals. Computerized library services include the card catalog, interlibrary loans, and database searching. Special learning facilities include a learning resource center, art gallery, foreign language center, satellite earth station, and international studies center with simultaneous translation capabilities. The 140-acre campus is in an urban area 65 miles southeast of Charlotte. Including residence halls, there are 32 buildings.

Student Life: 67% of undergraduates are from South Carolina. Others are from 30 states and 1 foreign country. 73% are from public schools. 89% are white. Most are Protestant. The average age of freshmen is 18; all undergraduates, 20. 13% do not continue beyond their first year; 79% remain to graduate.

Housing: 966 students can be accommodated in college housing, which includes single-sex and coed dormitories and fraternity houses. Experimental residential grouping of science majors and some freshman humanities sections are available. On-campus housing is guaranteed for all 4 years. 88% of students live on campus; of those, 75% remain on campus on weekends. All students may keep cars.

Activities: 56% of men belong to 8 national fraternities; 65% of women belong to 4 national sororities. There are 68 groups on campus, including band, cheerleading, choir, chorale, chorus, college bowl team, computers, drama, ethnic, international, literary magazine, newspaper, pep band, photography, political, professional, religious, social, social service, student government, and yearbook. Popular campus events include Phi Beta Kappa Day, Christmas concert, and Spring weekend/Greek games.

Sports: There are 8 intercollegiate sports for men and 8 for women, and 7 intramural sports for men and 5 for women. Facilities include an 8500-seat campus stadium, a 3500-seat arena, a tennis complex, a soccer field, and a wellness and athletic center built to the specifications of the Carolina Panthers.

Disabled Students: 90% of the campus is accessible. Wheelchair ramps, elevators, special parking, specially equipped rest rooms, special class scheduling, lowered drinking fountains, and lowered telephones are available.

Services: Counseling and information services are available, as is tutoring in every subject. There is a reader service for the blind.

Campus Safety and Security: Measures include 24-hour foot and vehicle patrol, self-defense education, escort service, and informal discussions. There are pamphlets/posters/films, emergency telephones, and lighted pathways/sidewalks.

Programs of Study: Wofford confers B.A. and B.S. degrees. Bachelor's degrees are awarded in BIOLOGICAL SCIENCE (biology/biological science), BUSINESS (accounting, banking and finance, and business economics), COMMUNICATIONS AND THE ARTS (art history and appreciation, English, French, German, and Spanish), COMPUTER AND PHYSICAL SCIENCE (chemistry, computer science, mathematics, and physics), SOCIAL SCIENCE (crosscultural studies, economics, history, humanities, philosophy, political science/government, psychology, religion, and sociology). Biology, foreign languages, and finance/accounting are the strongest academically. Business/economics, biology, and government are the largest.

Required: To graduate, students must complete 124 credits, with 21 to 38 credits in the major and a minimum GPA of 2.0. General education requirements include 12 credits of history/philosophy/religion, 8 of natural sciences, 6 of English, 3 each of fine arts and math, and 2 of phys ed. Students must complete 4 interim projects, a career workshop, and a freshman humanities seminar.

Special: Special academic programs include limited cross-registration with Converse College and USC/Spartanburg, study abroad in more than 30 countries, a Washington semester, and a concentration in Latin American and Caribbean studies. In addition, students can major in 2 fields or complete interdisciplinary, humanities, or intercultural studies majors. Wofford participates in 3-2 programs in engineering with Clemson and Columbia Universities. The January interim allows students to concentrate on a single study project, internship, or travel experience. There are 9 national honor societies, including Phi Beta Kappa. There are several departmental honors programs.

Faculty/Classroom: 68% of faculty are male; 32%, female. All teach undergraduates and 30% both teach and do research. The average class size in an introductory lecture is 20; in a laboratory, 15; and in a regular course, 10.

Admissions: 82% of the 2001-2002 applicants were accepted. The SAT I scores for the 2001-2002 freshman class were: Verbal--11% below 500, 43% between 500 and 599, 39% between 600 and 700, and 7% above 700; Math--8% below 500, 40% between 500 and 599, 43% between 600 and 700, and 9% above 700. The ACT scores were 10% below 21, 32% between 21 and 23, 31% between 24 and 26, 8% between 27 and 28, and 18% above 28. 69% of the current freshmen were in the top fifth of their class; 92% were in the top two fifths. There were 2 National Merit finalists. 11 freshmen graduated first in their class.

Requirements: The SAT I or ACT is required, and SAT II: Subject tests are recommended. Applicants must be graduates of an accredited secondary school. The GED is accepted. Students should have completed 4 years each of high school English and math, 3 of lab science, and 2 each of a foreign language and social studies. An essay is required and an interview is strongly recommended. AP and CLEP credits are accepted. Important factors in the admissions decision are advanced placement or honor courses, leadership record, and personality/intangible qualities. Applications are accepted on-line via Apply, Common Application, and CollegeLink.

Procedure: Freshmen are admitted to all sessions. Entrance exams should be taken in the spring of the junior year or fall of the senior year. There are early action, early admissions, and deferred admissions plans. Early action applications should be filed by November 15; regular applications, by February 1 for fall entry. The fall 2001 application fee was $40. Notification of early decision is sent January 15; regular decision, March 15.

Transfer: 14 transfer students enrolled in 2001-2002. Transfers should have a minimum GPA of 2.5 from a 4-year college or 3.0 from a 2-year college, or they may submit ACT or SAT I scores. An interview is recommended. 30 credits of 124 must be completed at Wofford.

Visiting: There are regularly scheduled orientations for prospective students. There are guides for informal visits and visitors may sit in on classes and stay overnight. To schedule a visit, contact the Director of Admissions.

Financial Aid: In 2001-2002, 83% of continuing students received some form of financial aid. 54% of freshmen and 55% of continuing students received need-based aid. The average freshman award was $14,660. 35% of undergraduates work part time. Average annual earnings from campus work are $1200. The average financial indebtedness of the 2001 graduate was $12,260. Wofford is a member of CSS. The CSS/Profile or FAFSA, the college's own financial statement are required. The fall application deadline is March 15.

International Students: There are 3 international students enrolled. They must score 500 on the written TOEFL.

Computers: The mainframe is a Windows/Exchange 2000 System. The computer center is open 80 1/2 hours per week. Student PC labs are located in several academic buildings. A high-speed, fiber-optic campus technology network provides a multimedia intranet and voice telephone system as well as direct access to off-campus television programming, e-mail, and the World Wide Web. All students may access the system 24 hours per day. There are no time limits and no fees. It is strongly recommended that all students have a personal computer.

Graduates: In 2001, 255 bachelor's degrees were awarded. The most popular majors were business economics (14%), biology (12%), and English and government (10%). In an average class, 76% graduate in 4 years, 78% in 5 years, and 79% in 6 years. Of the 2000 graduating class, 35% were enrolled in graduate school within 6 months of graduation and 62% were employed.

Admissions Contact: Brand R. Stille, Director of Admissions. A video is available. E-mail: *admissions@wofford.edu* Web: *www.wofford.edu*

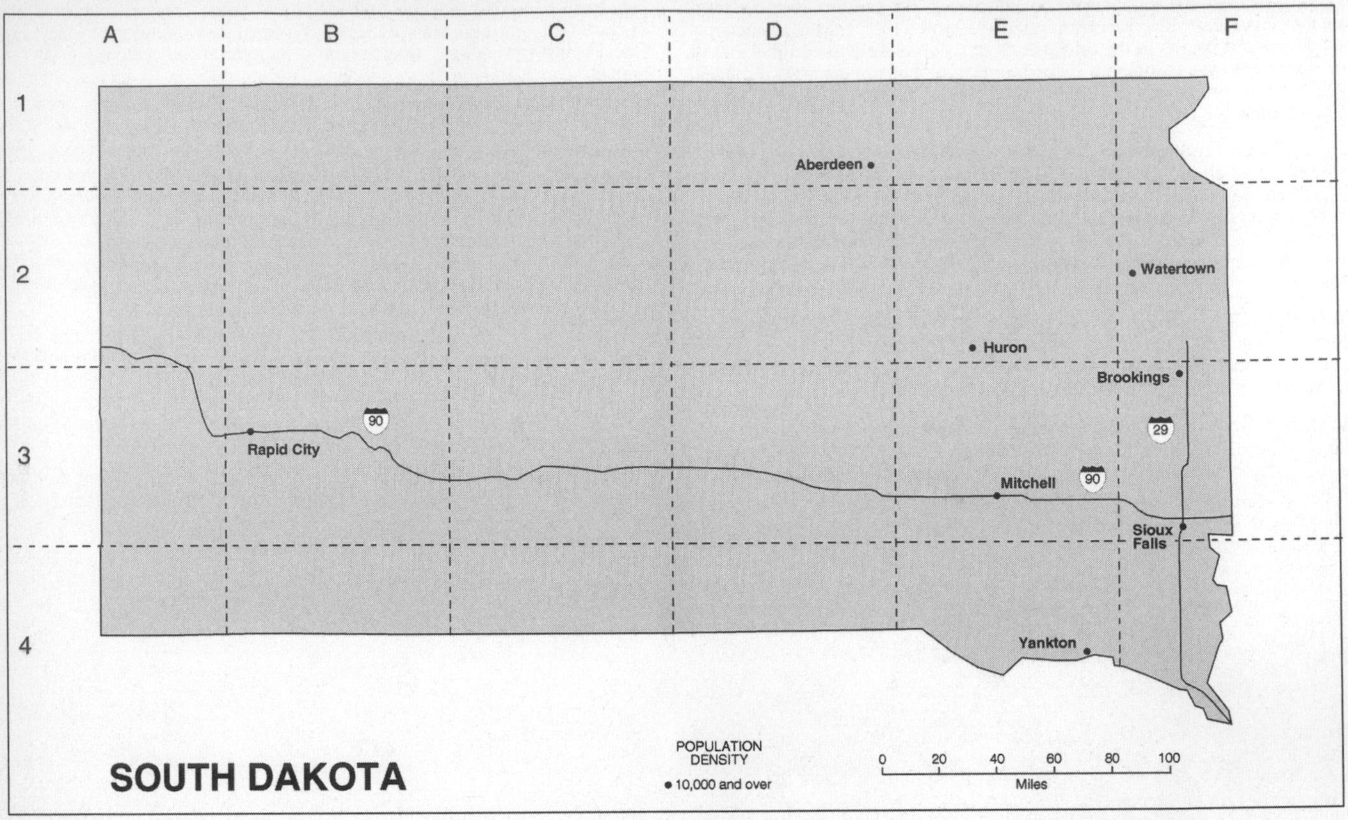

AUGUSTANA COLLEGE — F-3

Sioux Falls, SD 57197

(605) 274-5516
(800) 727-2844; Fax: (605) 274-5518

Full-time: 575 men, 1078 women — **Faculty:** 113; IIB, --$
Part-time: 42 men, 79 women — **Ph.D.s:** 90%
Graduate: 3 men, 30 women — **Student/Faculty:** 15 to 1
Year: 4-1-4, summer session — **Tuition:** $16,092
Application Deadline: open — **Room & Board:** $4668
Freshman Class: 1389 applied, 1176 accepted, 416 enrolled
SAT I Verbal/Math: 590/590 — **ACT:** 25 — **VERY COMPETITIVE**

Augustana College, founded in 1860, is a private liberal arts institution affiliated with the Evangelical Lutheran Church in America. In addition to regional accreditation, Augustana has baccalaureate program accreditation with CSWE, NASM, NCATE, and NLN. The library contains 234,515 volumes, 85,938 microform items, and 6147 audiovisual forms/CDs, and subscribes to 1085 periodicals. Computerized library services include the card catalog, interlibrary loans, and database searching. Special learning facilities include an art gallery, natural history museum, radio station, and Center for Western Studies. The 100-acre campus is in a suburban area 150 miles north of Omaha, Nebraska. Including residence halls, there are 30 buildings.

Student Life: 51% of undergraduates are from South Dakota. Others are from 28 states, 9 foreign countries, and Canada. 95% are from public schools. 96% are white. 72% are Protestant; 18% Catholic. The average age of freshmen is 18; all undergraduates, 20. 25% do not continue beyond their first year; 67% remain to graduate.

Housing: 1100 students can be accommodated in college housing, which includes coed dormitories and married-student housing. In addition, there are special-interest houses, independent student housing for those with children, and a theme house. On-campus housing is guaranteed for all 4 years. 67% of students live on campus; of those, 70% remain on campus on weekends. Alcohol is not permitted. All students may keep cars.

Activities: There are no fraternities or sororities. There are 55 groups on campus, including art, band, cheerleading, choir, chorale, chorus, dance, debate, drama, ethnic, gay, honors, international, jazz band, literary magazine, musical theater, newspaper, opera, orchestra, pep band, photography, political, professional, radio and TV, religious, social, social service, student government, symphony, and yearbook. Popular campus events include Christmas Vespers and Boe Forum on Public Affairs.

Sports: There are 8 intercollegiate sports for men and 8 for women, and 26 intramural sports for men and 26 for women. Facilities include a 3600-seat gym and a health, phys ed, and recreation center.

Disabled Students: 75% of the campus is accessible. Wheelchair ramps, elevators, special parking, specially equipped rest rooms, special class scheduling, lowered drinking fountains, lowered telephones, Arkenstone reader, Dragon Dictate, TTYs, and doorbell lights are available.

Services: Counseling and information services are available, as is tutoring in every subject. There is a reader service for the blind and remedial math and writing. A special writing lab is available 3 nights per week.

Campus Safety and Security: Measures include 24-hour foot and vehicle patrol, self-defense education, escort service, and informal discussions. There are pamphlets/posters/films, emergency telephones, lighted pathways/sidewalks, and key card access to residence halls.

Programs of Study: Augustana confers the B.A. degree. Master's degrees are also awarded. Bachelor's degrees are awarded in BIOLOGICAL SCIENCE (biology/biological science), BUSINESS (accounting, business administration and management, and management information systems), COMMUNICATIONS AND THE ARTS (art, communications, dramatic arts, English, French, German, journalism, modern language, music, and Spanish), COMPUTER AND PHYSICAL SCIENCE (chemistry, computer science, mathematics, and physics), EDUCATION (athletic training, drama, education of the deaf and hearing impaired, elementary, music, physical, secondary, social studies, and special), ENGINEERING AND ENVIRONMENTAL DESIGN (engineering physics), HEALTH PROFESSIONS (exercise science, medical technology, nursing, and speech pathology/audiology), SOCIAL SCIENCE (economics, history, international relations, international studies, philosophy, physical fitness/movement, political science/government, psychology, religion, social work, and sociology). Education, biology, and business are the largest.

Required: Students must complete 130 semester hours, with a minimum GPA of 2.0. General education requirements total 59 semester hours, including component courses in writing for graduation.

Special: Internships, study abroad in 40 countries, and a 3-2 engineering degree with Columbia University, Washington University in St. Louis, or University of Minnesota are offered. A Washington semester with Lutheran College Washington Consortium or American University is offered. Credit for life experience is possible. There are 17 national honor societies and 4 departmental honors programs.

Faculty/Classroom: 67% of faculty are male; 33%, female. All both teach and do research. No introductory courses are taught by graduate students. The average class size in an introductory lecture is 25; in a laboratory, 18; and in a regular course, 20.

Admissions: 85% of the 2001-2002 applicants were accepted. The SAT I scores for the 2001-2002 freshman class were: Verbal--19% below 500, 42% between 500 and 599, 32% between 600 and 700, and 7% above 700; Math--16% below 500, 36% between 500 and 599, 42% between 600 and 700, and 6% above 700. The ACT scores were 16% below 21, 27% between 21 and 23, 24% between 24 and 26, 15% between 27 and 28, and 18% above 28. 50% of the current freshmen were in the top fifth of their class; 79% were in the top two fifths. There were 3 National Merit finalists. 35 freshmen graduated first in their class.

Requirements: The SAT I or ACT is required. In addition, graduation from an accredited secondary school is preferred; however, a GED will be accepted. Applicants should have completed 4 years of high school English, 3 each of math and science, and 2 each of a foreign language and history. An interview is recommended. Augustana requires applicants to be in the upper 50% of their class. A GPA of 2.5 is required. AP and CLEP credits are accepted. Important factors in the admissions decision are advanced placement or honor courses, leadership record, and parents or siblings attending the school. Applications are accepted on-line.

Procedure: Freshmen are admitted fall, spring, and summer. Entrance exams should be taken in the spring of the junior year or early fall of the senior year. There are early admissions and deferred admissions plans. Application deadlines are open. March 1 is the priority application date for scholarship eligebility. The fall 2001 application fee was $25. Notification is sent on a rolling basis.

Transfer: 81 transfer students enrolled in 2001-2002. Applicants must have a 2.0 GPA in previous college work. If only 1 semester or 1 quarter has been completed and the applicant has just graduated from high school, then Augustana requires a high school transcript. 30 credits of 130 must be completed at Augustana.

Visiting: There are regularly scheduled orientations for prospective students, including 4 fall dates (Explore Augie days), tours, and visits with faculty, current students, and coaches. There are guides for informal visits and visitors may sit in on classes and stay overnight. To schedule a visit, contact Genola Hegge, Visit Coordinator, the Office of Admission at *ghegge@wise.augie.edu*

Financial Aid: In 2001-2002, 96% of all freshmen and 91% of continuing students received some form of financial aid. 70% of freshmen and 69% of continuing students received need-based aid. The average freshman award was $13,900. Of that total, scholarships or need-based grants averaged $6148 ($12,000 maximum); loans averaged $5100 ($5650 maximum); and work contracts averaged $1350 ($1450 maximum). 35% of undergraduates work part time on campus. Average annual earnings from campus work are $1350. The average financial indebtedness of the 2001 graduate was $17,255. Augustana is a member of CSS. The FAFSA is required. The fall application deadline is March 1.

International Students: There are 32 international students enrolled. The school actively recruits these students. They must score 550 on the written TOEFL and also take the SAT I or the ACT, scoring 950, on the SAT I or 20 on the ACT.

Computers: The mainframe is an IBM RS/6000. More than 360 computers, mostly Pentium models, are available to students, with 125 available 24 hours per day. Each residence hall has a computer lab. All students may access the system. There are no time limits. A fee is charged for students using the system from residence hall rooms.

Graduates: In 2001, 304 bachelor's degrees were awarded. The most popular majors were business (22%), education (19%), and nursing (10%). In an average class, 1% graduate in 3 years, 49% in 4 years, 62% in 5 years, and 63% in 6 years. 60 companies recruited on campus in 2000-2001. Of the 2000 graduating class, 25% were enrolled in graduate school within 6 months of graduation and 97% were employed.

Admissions Contact: Robert A. Preloger, Vice President, Enrollment. E-mail: *info@inst.augie.edu* Web: *www.augie.edu*

BLACK HILLS STATE UNIVERSITY — A-2

Spearfish, SD 57799-9500 — **(605) 642-6343**

(800) ALL-BHSU; Fax: (605) 642-6022

Full-time: 979 men, 1557 women	**Faculty:** 120; IIB, --$
Part-time: 300 men, 638 women	**Ph.D.s:** 75%
Graduate: 70 men, 292 women	**Student/Faculty:** 21 to 1
Year: semesters, summer session	**Tuition:** $3628 ($7711)
Application Deadline: open	**Room & Board:** $3024
Freshman Class: n/av	
ACT: 21	**LESS COMPETITIVE**

Black Hills State University, founded in 1883, is a public institution offering undergraduate programs in applied science and technology, arts and humanities, business and public affairs, and education and human resources development. There are 3 undergraduate schools and 1 graduate school. In addition to regional accreditation, BHSU has baccalaureate program accreditation with NCATE. The library contains 222,000 volumes, 118,572 microform items, and 1300 audiovisual forms/CDs, and subscribes to 1800 periodicals. Computerized library services include the card catalog, interlibrary loans, and database searching. Special learning facilities include a learning resource center, art gallery, radio station, and TV station. The 123-acre campus is in a small town 45 miles northwest of Rapid City. Including residence halls, there are 13 buildings.

Student Life: 82% of undergraduates are from South Dakota. Others are from 40 states, 13 foreign countries, and Canada. 91% are white. The average age of freshmen is 22; all undergraduates, 25. 48% do not continue beyond their first year; 28% remain to graduate.

Housing: 610 students can be accommodated in college housing, which includes single-sex and coed dormitories, on-campus apartments, and married-student housing. On-campus housing is available on a first-come, first-served basis. 64% of students commute. Alcohol is not permitted. All students may keep cars.

Activities: 2% of men belong to 1 local and 1 national fraternity; 2% of women belong to 1 local and 1 national sorority. There are 55 groups on campus, including art, band, cheerleading, choir, chorale, chorus, computers, dance, debate, drama, drill team, ethnic, honors, international, jazz band, musical theater, newspaper, pep band, photography, political, professional, radio and TV, religious, social, social service, student government, and yearbook. Popular campus events include Swarm Week and Big 100 Week.

Sports: There are 4 intercollegiate sports for men and 4 for women, and 20 intramural sports for men and 20 for women. Facilities include a stadium, a sport and fitness center, tennis courts, swimming pools, a track, a gym, a golf course, and a baseball and softball complex.

Disabled Students: 75% of the campus is accessible. Wheelchair ramps, elevators, special parking, specially equipped rest rooms, lowered drinking fountains, and special housing are available.

Services: Counseling and information services are available, as is tutoring in most subjects. There is remedial math.

Campus Safety and Security: Measures include 24-hour foot and vehicle patrol, escort service, and lighted pathways/sidewalks.

Programs of Study: BHSU confers B.A., B.S., and B.S.Ed. degrees. Associate and master's degrees are also awarded. Bachelor's degrees are awarded in BIOLOGICAL SCIENCE (biology/biological science), BUSINESS (accounting, business administration and management, hotel/motel and restaurant management, human resources, and marketing/retailing/merchandising), COMMUNICATIONS AND THE ARTS (art, broadcasting, communications, English, fine arts, music, Spanish, and speech/debate/rhetoric), COMPUTER AND PHYSICAL SCIENCE (chemistry, mathematics, and physical sciences), EDUCATION (art, business, elementary, health, music, physical, science, secondary, and special), HEALTH PROFESSIONS (health care administration), SOCIAL SCIENCE (American Indian studies, history, human services, political science/government, prelaw, psychology, social science, and sociology).

Required: Students must successfully complete 128 credits, with at least 36 in the major, and must maintain a minimum GPA of 2.0. Core curriculum requirements include courses in English, speech, psychology, math, science, non-Western cultures, and phys ed. All students must pass an English proficiency exam.

Special: The university offers a co-op program in social work, cross-registration with the University of South Dakota, internships, work-study programs, a B.A.-B.S. degree, dual majors, a general studies degree, credit by exam, credit for military service, nondegree study, and pass/fail options. Composite majors offered include marketing, environmental physical science, outdoor education, tourism, and wellness management. A library media major is possible in conjunction with a second major. There are 5 national honor societies.

Faculty/Classroom: 64% of faculty are male; 36%, female. All teach undergraduates. No introductory courses are taught by graduate students. The average class size in an introductory lecture is 120; in a laboratory, 20; and in a regular course, 30.

Admissions: The ACT scores for the 2001-2002 freshman class were: 50% below 21, 28% between 21 and 23, 15% between 24 and 26, 4% between 27 and 28, and 2% above 28. 13% of the current freshmen were in the top fifth of their class; 32% were in the top two fifths. 2 freshmen graduated first in their class.

Requirements: The ACT is required. Graduation from an accredited secondary school is required; a GED will be accepted. Applicants must have completed the following academic credits with a minimum GPA of 2.0: 4 years of English, 3 each of social studies, math, and science, and 1/2 year of fine arts. BHSU requires applicants to be in the upper 60% of their class. A GPA of 2.0 is required. AP and CLEP credits are accepted.

Procedure: Freshmen are admitted to all sessions. Entrance exams should be taken during the senior year of high school. Application deadlines are open. The fall 2001 application fee was $15. Notification is sent on a rolling basis.

Transfer: 444 transfer students enrolled in 2001-2002. Applicants must supply transcripts from all previous schools attended, high school and college, and must have maintained a minimum college GPA of 2.0. 32 credits of 128 must be completed at BHSU.

Visiting: There are regularly scheduled orientations for prospective students. There are guides for informal visits and visitors may sit in on classes and stay overnight. To schedule a visit, contact the Admissions Office.

Financial Aid: The average financial indebtedness of the 2001 graduate was $18,444. The FAFSA and state aid form are required. The fall application deadline is March 1.

International Students: There are 7 international students enrolled. They must score 520 on the written TOEFL and also take the ACT.

Computers: The mainframe is an IBM. More than 200 PC terminals are available in residence halls, the main classroom building, and the library. All students may access the system during lab and library hours. There are no time limits and no fees. It is strongly recommended that all students have a personal computer.

Graduates: In 2001, 370 bachelor's degrees were awarded. The most popular majors were elementary education (24%), business administration (8%), and human resource management (6%). In an average class, 8% graduate in 4 years, 20% in 5 years, and 20% in 6 years.

Admissions Contact: Admissions Officer, Enrollment Services Center. E-mail: *admissions@bhsu.edu* Web: *www.bhsu.edu*

DAKOTA STATE UNIVERSITY — E-3

Madison, SD 57042 — (605) 256-5139
(888) DSU-9988; Fax: (605) 256-5020

Full-time: 754 men, 610 women	**Faculty:** 76; IIB, -$
Part-time: 187 men, 292 women	**Ph.D.s:** 62%
Graduate: 79 men, 93 women	**Student/Faculty:** 18 to 1
Year: semesters, summer session	**Tuition:** $4026 ($8381)
Application Deadline: open	**Room & Board:** $2924
Freshman Class: 599 accepted, 364 enrolled	
ACT: 22	**COMPETITIVE**

Dakota State University, founded in 1881, is a public institution offering undergraduate programs through the colleges of Business and Information Systems, Science and Mathematics, Liberal Arts, and Education. There are 4 undergraduate schools and 1 graduate school. In addition to regional accreditation, DSU has baccalaureate program accreditation with AHEA and NCATE. The library contains 131,035 volumes, 2448 microform items, and 2738 audiovisual forms/CDs, and subscribes to 375 periodicals. Computerized library services include the card catalog, interlibrary loans, and database searching. Special learning facilities include a learning resource center, art gallery, and natural history museum. The 20-acre campus is in a small town 45 miles northwest of Sioux Falls. Including residence halls, there are 17 buildings.

Student Life: 84% of undergraduates are from South Dakota. Others are from 22 states, 10 foreign countries, and Canada. The average age of all undergraduates is 22.

Housing: 702 students can be accommodated in college housing, which includes single-sex and coed dormitories and on-campus apartments. On-campus housing is guaranteed for the freshman year only, is available on a first-come, first-served basis, and is available on a lottery system for upperclassmen. 63% of students commute. Alcohol is not permitted. All students may keep cars.

Activities: There are no fraternities or sororities. There are 30 groups on campus, including academic, art, band, cheerleading, choir, chorale, chorus, computers, dance, drama, ethnic, honors, international, jazz band, literary magazine, marching band, musical theater, newspaper, nontraditional students, pep band, political, religious, student education, student government, and yearbook. Popular campus events include Discover DSU Days, Zimmfest, and Diversity Week.

Sports: There are 6 intercollegiate sports for men and 6 for women, and 20 intramural sports for men and 20 for women. Facilities include courts for basketball and racquetball, a football field, a weight room, and a swimming pool.

Disabled Students: 80% of the campus is accessible. Wheelchair ramps, elevators, special parking, specially equipped rest rooms, special class scheduling, and lowered drinking fountains are available.

Services: Counseling and information services are available, as is tutoring in every subject. There is a reader service for the blind, and remedial math, reading, and writing.

Campus Safety and Security: Measures include self-defense education, escort service, informal discussions, and pamphlets/posters/films. There are emergency telephones, lighted pathways/sidewalks, and a foot patrol.

Programs of Study: DSU confers B.S., B.B.A., and B.S.Ed. degrees. Associate and master's degrees are also awarded. Bachelor's degrees are awarded in BIOLOGICAL SCIENCE (biology/biological science), BUSINESS (business administration and management and electronic business), COMMUNICATIONS AND THE ARTS (English, fine arts, and music), COMPUTER AND PHYSICAL SCIENCE (chemistry, computer programming, computer science, information sciences and systems, mathematics, and physics), EDUCATION (art, business, elementary, English, health, marketing and distribution, music, and secondary), ENGINEERING AND ENVIRONMENTAL DESIGN (computer graphics), HEALTH PROFESSIONS (medical laboratory technology, medical records administration/services, premedicine, and respiratory therapy). Computer science, information systems, and education are the largest.

Required: To graduate, students must complete 128 semester hours, 85 of which must be in the major and 16 at the 300-400 course level. A 2.0 GPA and 43 hours of general education are also required. Students must take the Computer Concepts and Health courses. All candidates for graduation must apply formally to the Registration and Academic Records Office.

Special: The university offers co-op programs with South Dakota State University, internships, study abroad in London, and on-campus work-study programs. Also available are the general studies degree, a 3-2 engineering degree with the University of Minnesota/Twin Cities, credit for life, military, and work experience, nondegree study, and pass/fail options. There are 2 national honor societies and a freshman honors program.

Faculty/Classroom: 65% of faculty are male; 35%, female. All teach undergraduates. Graduate students teach 1% of introductory courses. The average class size in an introductory lecture is 40; in a laboratory, 25; and in a regular course, 20.

Admissions: 21% of the current freshmen were in the top fifth of their class; 48% were in the top two fifths. 9 freshmen graduated first in their class.

Requirements: The SAT I or ACT is required, with a minimum composite score of 18 on the ACT. In addition, applicants must be graduates of an accredited secondary school or have a GED certificate, and have completed 4 years of English, 3 years each of math, science, and social studies, and 1/2 year of computer science and the fine arts. DSU requires applicants to be in the upper 60% of their class. A GPA of 2.6 is required. AP and CLEP credits are accepted. The on-line application can be found at DSU's web site, *www.dsu.edu*

Procedure: Freshmen are admitted to all sessions. Entrance exams should be taken before students register for classes. Application deadlines are open. The application fee is $20. Notification is sent on a rolling basis.

Transfer: 67 transfer students enrolled in 2001-2002. Transfer applicants must have a minimum 2.0 GPA. 32 credits of 128 must be completed at DSU.

Visiting: There are regularly scheduled orientations for prospective students, including general information and academic sessions, a campus tour, and financial aid information. There are guides for informal visits and visitors may sit in on classes and stay overnight. To schedule a visit, contact the Admissions Office.

Financial Aid: The average freshman award in a recent year was $4054. 52% of undergraduates work part time. Average annual earnings from campus work are $1650. The average financial indebtedness of the 2001 graduate was $16,588. The FAFSA is required. The fall application deadline is March 1.

International Students: There are 120 international students enrolled. The school actively recruits these students. They must score 550 on the written TOEFL.

Computers: The mainframes are an IBM OS/390 mainframe and an IBM RS/6000 Unix Box. There are 15 computer labs on campus, plus an additional 4 in residence halls. All the mainframe dump terminals are in 1 lab. All labs classrooms and residence halls are networked, and students also have access in DSU's student union. Students may have computers in their dorm rooms. All students may access the system. There are no time limits and no fees.

Graduates: In 2001, 145 bachelor's degrees were awarded. In an average class, 24% graduate in 4 years, 42% in 5 years, and 15% in 6 years. 25 companies recruited on campus in 2000-2001. Of the 2000 graduating class, 1% were enrolled in graduate school within 6 months of graduation and 94% were employed.

Admissions Contact: Amy Crissinger, Director of Admission. E-mail: *yourfuture@dsu.edu* Web: *www.dsu.edu*

DAKOTA WESLEYAN UNIVERSITY — E-3

Mitchell, SD 57301 — (605) 995-2650
(800) 333-8506; Fax: (605) 995-2699

Full-time: 256 men, 357 women	**Faculty:** 42; IIB, --$
Part-time: 18 men, 56 women	**Ph.D.s:** 38%
Graduate: none	**Student/Faculty:** 15 to 1
Year: semesters, summer session	**Tuition:** $11,654
Application Deadline: August 25	**Room & Board:** $3858
Freshman Class: 438 applied, 369 accepted, 149 enrolled	
SAT I or ACT: required	**COMPETITIVE**

Dakota Wesleyan University, founded in 1885, is a private liberal arts institution affiliated with the United Methodist Church. In addition to regional accreditation, DWU has baccalaureate program accreditation with NLN and CAAHEP. The library contains 61,000 volumes, 76,000 microform items, and 7650 audiovisual forms/CDs, and subscribes to 405 periodicals. Computerized library services include the card catalog, interlibrary loans, and database searching. Special learning facilities include a learning resource center and an observatory, as well as a history museum with art gallery adjacent to the campus. The 40-acre campus is in a small town 65 miles west of Sioux Falls. Including residence halls, there are 10 buildings.

Student Life: 72% of undergraduates are from South Dakota. Others are from 32 states, 5 foreign countries, and Canada. 99% are from public schools. 88% are white. 57% are Protestant; 24% Catholic. The average age of freshmen is 19; all undergraduates, 23. 37% do not continue beyond their first year.

Housing: 325 students can be accommodated in college housing, which includes single-sex and coed dormitories. On-campus housing is guaranteed for the first two years or until the student is age 21 and is available on a first-come, first-served basis. 60% of students commute. Alcohol is not permitted. All students may keep cars.

Activities: There are no fraternities or sororities. There are 30 groups on campus, including academic, art, bell choir, brass and woodwind ensembles, cheerleading, choir, chorale, chorus, drama, ethnic, honors, international, literary magazine, musical theater, newspaper, political, professional, religious, social, social service, student government, and yearbook. Popular campus events include Prom, Spring Week, and Family Life Conference.

Sports: There are 7 intercollegiate sports for men and 6 for women, and 3 intramural sports for men and 3 for women. Facilities include a 500-seat stadium, a 3200-seat auditorium/arena, and a wellness center with a double gym and cardio, weight training, and cybex rooms. City facilities include a 1500-seat baseball staduim, a 500-seat softball field, and a 1000-seat outdoor track.

Disabled Students: 20% of the campus is accessible. Wheelchair ramps, elevators, special parking, specially equipped rest rooms, special class scheduling, and class relocation are available.

Services: Counseling and information services are available, as is tutoring in every subject. There is a reader service for the blind, and remedial math, reading, and writing.

Campus Safety and Security: Measures include self-defense education, escort service, informal discussions, and emergency telephones. There are lighted pathways/sidewalks and safety and security personnel trained in first aid and self-defense, 20-hour foot and vehicle patrol, and pamphlets and posters.

Programs of Study: DWU confers the B.A. degree. Associate and master's degrees are also awarded. Bachelor's degrees are awarded in BIOLOGICAL SCIENCE (biology/biological science), BUSINESS (accounting, business administration and management, and sports management), COMMUNICATIONS AND THE ARTS (art, communications, dramatic arts, English, and multimedia), COMPUTER AND PHYSICAL SCIENCE (mathematics), EDUCATION (athletic training, elementary, physical, and secondary), HEALTH PROFESSIONS (predentistry and premedicine), SOCIAL SCIENCE (behavioral science, criminal justice, history, human services, ministries, philosophy, psychology, religion, sociology, and youth ministry). Business and education are the largest.

Required: To graduate, students must complete a total of 125 credit hours, including 30 or more in the major, and at least 42 in upper-level courses, with a minimum 2.0 GPA. General education requirements include 6 hours of communication, literature and the arts, and social, psychological, and political thought, 3 to 5 of physical science, 3 to 4 each of math and cultural awareness, 3 each of history and philosophy/theology, and 2 of physical activities; students must demonstrate basic skills in reading, writing, and math. All new freshmen must take Forum and Advising courses.

Special: DWU offers internships, study abroad on a limited basis, work-study programs, a general studies degree, dual majors, student-designed minors, credit for experience, and credit/no credit options. There are 4 national honor societies and a freshman honors program.

Faculty/Classroom: 52% of faculty are male; 48%, female. All teach undergraduates. The average class size in an introductory lecture is 32; in a laboratory, 17; and in a regular course, 20.

Admissions: 84% of the 2001-2002 applicants were accepted.

Requirements: The SAT I or ACT is required. In addition, applicants must be graduates of an accredited secondary school or have a GED certificate. An interview is recommended. DWU requires applicants to be in the upper 50% of their class. A GPA of 2.0 is required. AP and CLEP credits are accepted. Important factors in the admissions decision are advanced placement or honor courses, extracurricular activities record, and parents or siblings attending the school. Applications are accepted on-line.

Procedure: Freshmen are admitted to all sessions. Entrance exams should be taken during the senior year. Applications should be filed by August 25 for fall entry, January 2 for spring entry, and June 4 for summer entry, along with a $25 fee. Notification is sent on a rolling basis.

Transfer: 81 transfer students enrolled in 2001-2002. Students must submit official transcripts from all previous colleges attended. DWU will accept credits from regionally accredited institutions, but half the credits for the student's major must be completed at DWU. 30 credits of 125 must be completed at DWU.

Visiting: There are regularly scheduled orientations for prospective students, including a campus tour and meetings with faculty and students. There are guides for informal visits and visitors may sit in on classes and stay overnight. To schedule a visit, contact Enrollment Services.

Financial Aid: In 2001-2002. All freshmen and 76% of continuing students received some form of financial aid. 80% of freshmen and 69% of continuing students received need-based aid. The average freshman award was $10,944. Of that total, scholarships or need-based grants averaged $5115 ($11,354 maximum); loans averaged $5911 ($14,625 maximum); and work contracts averaged $1200 (maximum). 50% of undergraduates work part time. Average annual earnings from campus work are $1341. The average financial indebtedness of the 2001 graduate was $13,625. DWU is a member of CSS. The FAFSA is required. The priority application deadline for fall is April 15.

International Students: There are 4 international students enrolled. The school actively recruits these students. They must score 500 on the written TOEFL or 85 on the MELAB and also take the SAT I or the ACT.

Computers: The mainframe is an IBM AS/400. There are 80 PCs available for student use in labs, residence halls, and the library. All students may access the system 24 hours a day. There are no time limits and no fees. It is strongly recommended that all students have a personal computer.

Graduates: In 2001, 98 bachelor's degrees were awarded. The most popular majors were business administration (18%), elementary education (15%), and crminal justice (13%). 3 companies recruited on campus in 2000-2001. Of the 2000 graduating class, 8 to 10% were enrolled in graduate school within 6 months of graduation.

Admissions Contact: Laura Miller, Admissions Opeations and Outreach Programming. E-mail: *admissions@dwu.edu*
Web: *www.dwu.edu*

HURON UNIVERSITY
Huron, SD 57350-2798 E-2
(605) 352-8721
(800) 710-7159; Fax: (605) 352-7421

Full-time: 240 men, 200 women	**Faculty:** 36
Part-time: 35 men, 70 women	**Ph.D.s:** 25%
Graduate: 15 men, 10 women	**Student/Faculty:** 9 to 1
Year: semesters, summer session	**Tuition:** $9900
Application Deadline: see profile	**Room & Board:** $2900
Freshman Class: n/av	
SAT I or ACT: recommended	**COMPETITIVE**

Huron University, established as Huron College in 1883, is a private institution offering career-oriented programs in the arts and sciences, nursing, and professional studies. It is also known as Si Tanka Huron University, since its purchase in 2001 by a Sioux Indian tribe. There are 4 undergraduate schools and 1 graduate school. Figures in above capsule are approximate. The library contains 62,000 volumes, and subscribes to 300 periodicals. Special learning facilities include a learning resource center. The 15-acre campus is in a small town 120 miles northwest of Sioux Falls. Including residence halls, there are 7 buildings.

Student Life: Others are from 26 states, 14 foreign countries, and Canada. 68% are white. The average age of all undergraduates is 23.

Housing: 300 students can be accommodated in college housing, which includes coed dormitories and on-campus apartments. On-campus housing is guaranteed for all 4 years. 50% of students live on campus; of those, 85% remain on campus on weekends. Alcohol is not permitted. All students may keep cars.

Activities: There are no fraternities or sororities. There are 15 groups on campus, including cheerleading, choir, computers, ethnic, honors, international, newspaper, pep band, photography, professional, religious, social, social service, and student government. Popular campus events include Pow Wow Days, Paddle Days, and International Student Day.

Sports: There are 4 intercollegiate sports for men and 4 for women, and 15 intramural sports for men and 14 for women. Facilities include saunas, an exercise room, a 2800-seat recreation center, and a 5000-seat arena.

Disabled Students: 75% of the campus is accessible. Wheelchair ramps, special parking, specially equipped rest rooms, special class scheduling, lowered drinking fountains, and a portable chair lift are available.

Services: Counseling and information services are available, as is tutoring in every subject. There is remedial math, reading, and writing.

Campus Safety and Security: Measures include informal discussions, pamphlets/posters/films, lighted pathways/sidewalks, and a night watchman.

Programs of Study: H.U. confers B.S. and B.S.N. degrees. Associate and master's degrees are also awarded. Bachelor's degrees are awarded in BUSINESS (banking and finance, business administration and management, human resources, management information systems, management science, marketing/retailing/merchandising, organizational behavior, and sports management), COMPUTER AND PHYSICAL SCIENCE (computer science), EDUCATION (elementary, physical, science, and secondary), ENGINEERING AND ENVIRONMENTAL DESIGN (systems engineering), HEALTH PROFESSIONS (health care administration and nursing), SOCIAL SCIENCE (criminal justice). Nursing is the strongest academically. Business administration is the largest.

Required: To graduate, students must complete at least 120 to 128 credit hours with a minimum GPA of 2.0. Required courses include an introduction to higher education, computers, career planning, and other general education classes.

Special: The university offers cooperative programs, cross-registration, internships, study abroad in England or Japan, work-study programs, general studies and B.A.-B.S. degrees, dual majors, credit for life experience, nondegree study, and pass/fail options. There are 5 national honor societies, and 5 departmental honors programs.

Faculty/Classroom: 50% of faculty are male; 50%, female. The average class size in an introductory lecture is 30; in a laboratory, 15; and in a regular course, 20.

Requirements: The SAT I or ACT is recommended. In addition, a minimum composite score of 15 on the ACT or a minimum score of 700 on the SAT I is required. Applicants must be graduates of an accredited secondary school or have a GED certificate. An interview is recommended. A GPA of 2.0 is required. CLEP credit is accepted. Important factors in the admissions decision are advanced placement or honor courses, leadership record, and recommendations by school officials.

Procedure: Freshmen are admitted to all sessions. Entrance exams should be taken during the senior year. Check with the school for current application deadlines. The application fee is $25. Notification is sent on a rolling basis.

Transfer: 32 credits of 120 must be completed at H.U.

Visiting: There are regularly scheduled orientations for prospective students. There are guides for informal visits and visitors may sit in on classes and stay overnight. To schedule a visit, contact Director of Admissions.

Financial Aid: In a recent year, 89% of all freshmen and 68% of continuing students received some form of financial aid. 73% of freshmen and 60% of continuing students received need-based aid. The average freshman award was $3400. The average financial indebtedness of a recent year's graduate was $1500. The CSS/Profile or FFS and PHEAA are required. Check with the school for current deadlines.

International Students: The school actively recruits these students. They must score 500 on the written TOEFL.

Computers: 30 IBM PCs are available in the computer lab in the library. There are no time limits and no fees.

Admissions Contact: Brad Smith, Director of Admissions.
E-mail: *admissions@huron.edu* Web: *www.huron.edu*

MOUNT MARTY COLLEGE — C-4
Yankton, SD 57078-3724
(605) 668-1545
(800) 658-4552; Fax: (605) 668-1607

Full-time: 210 men, 471 women	**Faculty:** 35
Part-time: 142 men, 246 women	**Ph.D.s:** 40%
Graduate: 41 men, 58 women	**Student/Faculty:** 19 to 1
Year: semesters, summer session	**Tuition:** $11,384
Application Deadline: open	**Room & Board:** $4272

Freshman Class: 347 applied, 304 accepted, 117 enrolled
ACT: 21 — **LESS COMPETITIVE**

Mount Marty College is a private, Catholic, liberal arts institution that was founded in 1936 by the Sisters of Saint Benedict. In addition to regional accreditation, Mount Marty has baccalaureate program accreditation with ADA and NLN. The library contains 79,228 volumes, 11,624 microform items, and 8465 audiovisual forms/CDs, and subscribes to 439 periodicals. Computerized library services include the card catalog, interlibrary loans, and database searching. Special learning facilities include a learning resource center and art gallery. The 80-acre campus is in a small town 60 miles northwest of Sioux City, Iowa, and 80 miles southwest of Sioux Falls. Including residence halls, there are 11 buildings.

Student Life: 81% of undergraduates are from South Dakota. Others are from 14 states, 7 foreign countries, and Canada. 79% are from public schools. 95% are white. 41% are claim no religious affiliation; 37% Catholic. The average age of freshmen is 19; all undergraduates, 26. 26% do not continue beyond their first year; 74% remain to graduate.

Housing: 352 students can be accommodated in college housing, which includes single-sex dormitories. On-campus housing is guaranteed for all 4 years. 51% of students commute. Alcohol is not permitted. All students may keep cars.

Activities: There are no fraternities or sororities. There are 40 groups on campus, including choir, chorus, drama, drill team, honors, jazz band, literary magazine, musical theater, newspaper, photography, political, professional, religious, social, social service, and student government. Popular campus events include Parents Weekend and Spring Formal.

Sports: There are 6 intercollegiate sports for men and 6 for women, and 4 intramural sports for men and 4 for women. Facilities include volleyball and basketball courts, a jogging track, 2 racquetball courts, weight and training rooms, a 2220-seat stadium, a 1500-seat indoor gym, and a 700-seat auditorium.

Disabled Students: All of the campus is accessible. Wheelchair ramps, elevators, special parking, specially equipped rest rooms, special class scheduling, lowered drinking fountains, and lowered telephones are available.

Services: Counseling and information services are available, as is tutoring in most subjects. There is remedial math, reading, and writing.

Campus Safety and Security: Measures include 24-hour foot and vehicle patrol, informal discussions, emergency telephones, and lighted pathways/sidewalks.

Programs of Study: Mount Marty confers B.A. and B.S. degrees. Associate and master's degrees are also awarded. Bachelor's degrees are awarded in BIOLOGICAL SCIENCE (biology/biological science), BUSINESS (accounting and business administration and management), COMMUNICATIONS AND THE ARTS (English, journalism, and music), COMPUTER AND PHYSICAL SCIENCE (chemistry, computer science, mathematics, and radiological technology), EDUCATION (athletic training, elementary, physical, secondary, and special), ENGINEERING AND ENVIRONMENTAL DESIGN (environmental science), HEALTH PROFESSIONS (health care administration, medical technology, and nursing), SOCIAL SCIENCE (behavioral science, criminal justice, food production/management/services, history, religion, and social science). Nursing, business, and teacher education are the strongest academically.

Required: To graduate, all students must complete at least 128 credit hours, with a minimum GPA of 2.0. General education requirements include 10 credit hours in religious studies/philosophy, 9 in literature and art, 6 in English, 4 each in math, natural science, and lab science, and 3 in speech.

Special: Mount Marty offers co-op programs, a 3-2 engineering degree with Georgia Institute of Technology, internships, student-designed majors in selected studies, multi- and interdisciplinary majors including health, phys ed, recreation, and nutrition and food science, credit for work, life, and military experience, and pass/fail options. There are 8 national honor societies, a freshman honors program, and 7 departmental honors programs.

Faculty/Classroom: 54% of faculty are male; 46%, female. All teach undergraduates. No introductory courses are taught by graduate students. The average class size in an introductory lecture is 30; in a laboratory, 15; and in a regular course, 20.

Admissions: 88% of the 2001-2002 applicants were accepted. The ACT scores for the 2001-2002 freshman class were: 49% below 21, 25% between 21 and 23, 15% between 24 and 26, 5% between 27 and 28, and 5% above 28. 22% of the current freshmen were in the top fifth of their class; 40% were in the top two fifths. 6 freshmen graduated first in their class.

Requirements: The ACT is required. In addition, applicants must be graduates of an accredited secondary school or have a GED certificate. An audition and an interview are recommended. A GPA of 2.0 is required. Applications are accepted on-line. AP and CLEP credits are accepted.

Procedure: Freshmen are admitted fall, spring, and summer. Entrance exams should be taken by October of the senior year. There are early decision and deferred admissions plans. Application deadlines are open. The fall 2001 application fee was $35. Notification is sent on a rolling basis.

Transfer: 93 transfer students enrolled in 2001-2002. Transfer students with fewer than 28 semester hours must submit high school and college transcripts. A minimum GPA of 2.0 and at least 64 credit hours are required. An interview is recommended. 32 credits of 128 must be completed at Mount Marty.

Visiting: There are regularly scheduled orientations for prospective students, including campus tours, faculty appointments, and admission and financial aid information. There are guides for informal visits and visitors may sit in on classes and stay overnight. To schedule a visit, contact the Director of Admissions.

Financial Aid: In 2001-2002, 86% of all freshmen and 85% of continuing students received some form of financial aid, including need-based aid. The average freshman award was $11,567. Of that total, scholarships or need-based grants averaged $4610 ($12,000 maximum); loans averaged $3471 ($3625 maximum); and work contracts averaged $1000 (maximum). 60% of undergraduates work part time. Average annual earnings from campus work are $1000. The average financial indebtedness of the 2001 graduate was $17,407. The FAFSA is required. The fall application deadline is March 1.

International Students: The school actively recruits these students. They must score 500 on the written TOEFL.

Computers: The mainframe is an IBM AS400. There are PCs, printers, overhead projectors, and multimedia classrooms. The college provides a variety of Microsoft applications. Students have laptop computers with wireless connections to the network. All students may access the system 24 hours, 7 days per week. There are no time limits. A technology fee is included in the annual general fee. All students are required to have personal computers.

Graduates: In 2001, 125 bachelor's degrees were awarded. The most popular majors were health professions (28%), business (23%), and education (15%). In an average class, 27% graduate in 4 years, 51% in 5 years, and 52% in 6 years. Of the 2000 graduating class, 8% were enrolled in graduate school within 6 months of graduation and 89% were employed.

Admissions Contact: Brandi Tschumper, Dean for Graduate Programs and Enrollment Management. E-mail: *btschumper@mtmc.edu* Web: *http://www.mtmc.edu*

NATIONAL AMERICAN UNIVERSITY
B-3

Rapid City, SD 57701

(605) 394-4827
(800) 843-8892; Fax: (605) 394-4871

Full-time: 290 men, 272 women	**Faculty:** 26
Part-time: 168 men, 122 women	**Ph.D.s:** 5%
Graduate: 21 men, 12 women	**Student/Faculty:** 26 to 1
Year: quarters, summer session	**Tuition:** $10,155
Application Deadline: open	**Room & Board:** $3525
Freshman Class: 273 applied, 269 accepted, 115 enrolled	
SAT I or ACT: recommended	**NONCOMPETITIVE**

National American University, founded in 1941, is a private institution that offers undergraduate programs in business administration, travel, allied health, and computer information systems. The college has branch campuses in Sioux Falls and at Ellsworth Air Force Base, South Dakota; Albuquerque, New Mexico; St. Paul, Minnesota; Kansas City, Missouri; Colorado Springs and Denver, Colorado; Rio Rancho, New Mexico; Mall of America, Bloomington, Minnesota, and Brooklyn Center, Minnesota. There is 1 graduate school. In addition to regional accreditation, NAU has baccalaureate program accreditation with CAHEA. The library contains 31,018 volumes and 71 audiovisual forms/CDs, and subscribes to 268 periodicals. Computerized library services include interlibrary loans and database searching. Special learning facilities include a learning resource center. The Animal Health Care Center and Medical Assisting Room are instructional facilities set up as doctors' offices. The 8-acre campus is in a small town 360 miles from Sioux Falls and 420 miles from Denver, Colorado. Including residence halls, there are 7 buildings.

Student Life: 53% of undergraduates are from South Dakota. Others are from 25 states, 6 foreign countries, and Canada. 75% are white; 13% foreign nationals. The average age of freshmen is 35; all undergraduates, 30. 43% do not continue beyond their first year.

Housing: 260 students can be accommodated in college housing, which includes single-sex and coed dormitories. On-campus housing is guaranteed for all 4 years. 79% of students commute. Alcohol is not permitted. All students may keep cars.

Activities: There are no fraternities or sororities. There are 17 groups on campus, including choir, computers, ethnic, international, political, professional, social, social service, and student government. Popular campus events include Maverick Day, spring and fall picnics, and dances.

Sports: There are 2 intercollegiate sports for men and 2 for women, and 12 intramural sports for men and 11 for women. Facilities include an 11,000-seat auditorium/arena, volleyball, basketball, and tennis courts, a 500-seat gym, a weight room, and golf, rodeo, bowling, and table tennis facilities. The Student Senate pays half the cost of a YMCA membership for students.

Disabled Students: 99% of the campus is accessible. Wheelchair ramps, elevators, special parking, and lowered drinking fountains are available.

Services: Counseling and information services are available, as is tutoring in most subjects. There is remedial math, reading, and writing. Some technical classes are tutored by instructors.

Campus Safety and Security: Measures include self-defense education, informal discussions, lighted pathways/sidewalks, and security guards on duty all evenings until morning.

Programs of Study: NAU confers the B.S. degree. Associate and master's degrees are also awarded. Bachelor's degrees are awarded in BUSINESS (accounting, business administration and management, and tourism), COMPUTER AND PHYSICAL SCIENCE (information sciences and systems), EDUCATION (athletic training), HEALTH PROFESSIONS (allied health and veterinary science), SOCIAL SCIENCE (paralegal studies). Accounting, paralegal studies, and business administration are the strongest academically and have the largest enrollments.

Required: To graduate, students must complete 192 quarter credit hours with a 2.0 GPA in major courses. Students are required to take 76 hours of general education courses, including 12 hours each of communications, math, social science, and humanities, 8 hours of science, 4 hours of speech, and 16 hours of electives.

Special: National offers internships in veterinary technology and paralegal studies, study abroad, work-study programs on campus and with nonprofit organizations, accelerated degree programs in all majors, B.A.-B.S. degrees in accounting, computer information systems, management information systems, business administration, paralegal studies, and applied management. A general studies degree, credit for life experience, nondegree study, and pass/fail options are also available. Operation Bootstrap allows qualified U.S. Air Force personnel to complete their college degrees on an accelerated basis. There is 1 national honor society.

Faculty/Classroom: 38% of faculty are male; 62%, female. The average class size in an introductory lecture is 30; in a laboratory, 10; and in a regular course, 25.

Admissions: 99% of the 2001-2002 applicants were accepted.

Requirements: The SAT I or ACT is recommended. In addition, applicants must be graduates of an accredited secondary school or have the GED. An interview is recommended. Applications are accepted on computer disk. CLEP credit is accepted.

Procedure: Freshmen are admitted to all sessions. Entrance exams should be taken before classes begin. There are early admissions and deferred admissions plans. Application deadlines are open. The application fee is $25. Notification is sent on a rolling basis.

Transfer: Applicants must submit transcripts of all high school and college work. Grades of C or better transfer for credit. An interview is recommended. 48 credits of 192 must be completed at NAU.

Visiting: There are guides for informal visits and visitors may sit in on classes and stay overnight. To schedule a visit, contact the Admissions Office.

Financial Aid: NAU is a member of CSS. The CSS/Profile, FAFSA, FFS, or SFS and the college's own financial statement are required.

International Students: The school actively recruits these students. They must score 500 on the written TOEFL.

Computers: The mainframe is an IBM RS/6000. There are 3 computer labs with 45 PCs among them. All provide Internet access. All students may access the system from 7 A.M. to 8 P.M. Students may access the system 90 minutes if another student is waiting. There are no fees.

Admissions Contact: Tom Shea, VP Enrollment Management. E-mail: *tshea@rc.national.edu* Web: *www.national.edu*

NORTHERN STATE UNIVERSITY
D-1

Aberdeen, SD 57401

(605) 626-2544
(800) 678-5330; Fax: (605) 626-2587

Full-time: 714 men, 971 women	**Faculty:** 97
Part-time: 390 men, 574 women	**Ph.D.s:** 83%
Graduate: 95 men, 344 women	**Student/Faculty:** 17 to 1
Year: semesters, summer session	**Tuition:** $3539 ($7622)
Application Deadline: August 15	**Room & Board:** $2740
Freshman Class: n/av	
ACT: 21	**LESS COMPETITIVE**

Northern State University, established in 1901, is a state-supported institution offering undergraduate and graduate programs in the liberal arts and sciences, business, and education. Distance delivery technology is a core mission in all programs, especially all levels of teacher preparation. There are 4 undergraduate schools and 1 graduate school. In addition to regional accreditation, Northern State has baccalaureate program accreditation with NASM and NCATE. The library contains 1.5 million volumes and 88,000 microform items, and subscribes to 940 periodicals. Computerized library services include the card catalog, interlibrary loans, and database searching. Special learning facilities include a learning resource center, art gallery, radio station, TV station, and a fine arts center. The 72-acre campus is in an urban area one-half mile south of Aberdeen's city center. Including residence halls, there are 21 buildings.

Student Life: 85% of undergraduates are from South Dakota. Others are from 29 states, 10 foreign countries, and Canada. 86% are white. The average age of freshmen is 18; all undergraduates, 23. 37% do not continue beyond their first year; 40% remain to graduate.

Housing: 930 students can be accommodated in college housing, which includes single-sex and coed dormitories. On-campus housing is guaranteed for all 4 years. 64% of students commute. Alcohol is not permitted. All students may keep cars.

Activities: There are no fraternities or sororities. There are 100 groups on campus, including art, band, cheerleading, chess, choir, chorale, chorus, computers, dance, debate, drama, drill team, honors, international, jazz band, marching band, musical theater, newspaper, orchestra, pep band, photography, political, professional, radio and TV, religious, social, social service, student government, symphony, and yearbook. Popular campus events include Gypsy Day, Gypsy Week, and I Hate Winter Weekend.

Sports: There are 7 intercollegiate sports for men and 5 for women, and 14 intramural sports for men and 12 for women. Facilities include a sports complex that houses a football stadium and an all-weather track, and a phys ed building that houses a 160-meter track, an Olympic-size pool, a weight room, 3 racquetball courts, a human performance lab, 2 basketball courts, and an 8300-seat arena.

Disabled Students: 90% of the campus is accessible. Wheelchair ramps, elevators, special parking, specially equipped rest rooms, lowered drinking fountains, lowered telephones, and curb cuts are available.

Services: Counseling and information services are available, as is tutoring in most subjects. There is remedial math, reading, and writing. There

is an educational media center, a math lab, reading and writing centers, an ASL interpreter for the deaf, and a speech, language, and hearing clinic.
Campus Safety and Security: Measures include 24-hour foot and vehicle patrol, self-defense education, escort service, and informal discussions. There are pamphlets/posters/films, emergency telephones, and lighted pathways/sidewalks.
Programs of Study: Northern State confers B.A., B.S., B.M.E., and B.S.Ed. Degrees. Associate and master's degrees are also awarded. Bachelor's degrees are awarded in BIOLOGICAL SCIENCE (biology/biological science), BUSINESS (accounting, banking and finance, business administration and management, business economics, international business management, marketing/retailing/merchandising, and personnel management), COMMUNICATIONS AND THE ARTS (English, fine arts, French, German, music, and Spanish), COMPUTER AND PHYSICAL SCIENCE (chemistry and mathematics), EDUCATION (art, business, early childhood, elementary, foreign languages, health, industrial arts, middle school, music, physical, science, secondary, and special), ENGINEERING AND ENVIRONMENTAL DESIGN (environmental science, industrial administration/management, and industrial engineering technology), HEALTH PROFESSIONS (medical laboratory technology, predentistry, premedicine, and speech pathology/audiology), SOCIAL SCIENCE (community services, criminal justice, economics, history, human services, physical fitness/movement, political science/government, prelaw, psychology, social science, and sociology). Business and education are the strongest academically and have the largest enrollments.
Required: Students must complete a minimum of 128 semester hours, with 51 in the major, and must maintain a 2.0 minimum GPA. The core curriculum consists of courses in English, history, fine arts, science, phys ed, and psychology. In addition, there are specific course requirements. All students must pass a comprehensive exam.
Special: Opportunities are provided for internships, a Washington semester, work-study programs, a B.A.-B.S. degree, dual majors, a general studies degree, credit by exam, and nondegree study. Study abroad and a co-op program in international business are available. Technology proficiency certification is available with a diverse selection of certifications. There are 4 national honor societies, a freshman honors program, and 4 departmental honors programs.
Faculty/Classroom: 76% of faculty are male; 24%, female. All both teach and do research. No introductory courses are taught by graduate students. The average class size in an introductory lecture is 30 and in a laboratory, 20.
Admissions: The ACT scores for the 2001-2002 freshman class were: 45% below 21, 22% between 21 and 23, 16% between 24 and 26, 6% between 27 and 28, and 3% above 28. 20% of the current freshmen were in the top fifth of their class; 46% were in the top two fifths.
Requirements: The ACT is required, with a minimum composite score of 18, or students must earn a high school GPA of at least 2.6 on a 4.0 scale. Graduation from an accredited secondary school is required; a GED will be accepted. Applicants should submit a minimum academic record distributed as follows: 4 years of English, 3 each of math, science, and social studies, and one-half year of fine arts. A GPA of 2.0 is required. AP and CLEP credits are accepted. Important factors in the admissions decision are evidence of special talent, advanced placement or honor courses, and extracurricular activities record.
Procedure: Freshmen are admitted fall, spring, and summer. Entrance exams should be taken during the summer before the senior year. There is a deferred admissions plan. Applications should be filed by August 15 for fall entry. The fall 2001 application fee was $15. Notification is sent on a rolling basis.
Transfer: 141 transfer students enrolled in 2001-2002. Applicants must submit official transcripts from all previous colleges attended. D grades do not transfer. If the applicant has not maintained a C average, an ACT score that places the applicant in the upper 50% of college-bound freshmen may be submitted for consideration.
Visiting: There are regularly scheduled orientations for prospective students, consisting of a welcome presentation, registration, refreshments, an academic visit, a campus tour, lunch, a financial aid presentation, student panel, and a cost and scholarship presentation. There are guides for informal visits and visitors may sit in on classes and stay overnight. To schedule a visit, contact the Admissions Office.
Financial Aid: The CSS/Profile, FAFSA, FFS or SFS is required. The fall application deadline is March 15.
International Students: They must score 500 on the written TOEFL and also take the ACT.
Computers: There are 800 PCs located on campus, all connected to the student network, and 25 computer labs. Computers are used for word processing, graphics, report generation, and software capabilities. All computers can access the Internet. All students may access the system. There are no time limits and no fees.
Graduates: In 2001, 319 bachelor's degrees were awarded. The most popular majors were education (37%), business (31%), and social sciences (16%). 5 companies recruited on campus in 2000-2001. Of the 2000 graduating class, 10% were enrolled in graduate school within 6 months of graduation and 97% were employed.
Admissions Contact: Mike Mutziger, Director of Admissions.
E-mail: *admissions@wolf.northern.edu* Web: *www.northern.edu*

OGLALA LAKOTA COLLEGE
B-3

Kyle, SD 57752 — **(605) 455-2321; Fax: (605) 455-2787**

Full-time: 900 men and women	**Faculty:** n/av
Part-time: none	**Ph.D.s:** n/av
Graduate: none	**Student/Faculty:** n/av
Year: semesters	**Tuition:** $1950
Application Deadline: open	**Room & Board:** n/app
Freshman Class: n/av	
SAT I or ACT: n/av	**NONCOMPETITIVE**

Oglala Lakota College was founded in 1971 by the Oglala Sioux Tribal Council to provide academic, tribal, and cultural resources for the Pine Ridge Reservation community, offering programs in business, teaching, and human services. There are 10 regional centers in addition to the central campus. Figures in the above capsule are approximate. Special learning facilities include a learning resource center and archives, an American Indians collection, and an audio video studio. The campus is in a rural area spread over the 5,000 square miles of the Pine Ridge Indian Reservation in the state's southwest corner. There are 5 buildings.
Housing: All students commute.
Programs of Study: Bachelor's degrees are awarded in BUSINESS (business administration and management), EDUCATION (business and elementary), SOCIAL SCIENCE (history, human services, and sociology).
Required: Check with the school for current information.
Requirements: The SAT I or ACT is not required. Applicants should be high school graduates or have the GED. Certification of degree of Indian blood from the tribal census office is required. Check with the school for current information.
Procedure: Application deadlines are open. Check with the school for current information.
Transfer: 30 credits of 128 must be completed at OLC.
Visiting: Visitors may sit in on classes.
Financial Aid: The FFS is required. Check with the school for current deadlines.
Admissions Contact: Billi K. Hornbeck, Registrar.

PRESENTATION COLLEGE
D-1

Aberdeen, SD 57401 — **(605) 229-8492**
(800) 437-6060; Fax: (605) 229-8518

Full-time: 48 men, 329 women	**Faculty:** 21
Part-time: 44 men, 194 women	**Ph.D.s:** 4%
Graduate: none	**Student/Faculty:** 18 to 1
Year: semesters, summer session	**Tuition:** $9355
Application Deadline: open	**Room & Board:** $4150
Freshman Class: n/av	
ACT: required	**NONCOMPETITIVE**

Presentation College, founded in 1922 as Notre Dame Junior College, is an independent Catholic institution offering undergraduate degrees in nursing and allied health service management. In addition to regional accreditation, Presentation has baccalaureate program accreditation with AHEA. The library contains 33,725 volumes, and subscribes to 221 periodicals. Computerized library services include the card catalog and interlibrary loans. Special learning facilities include a learning resource center. The 100-acre campus is in a small town. Including residence halls, there are 8 buildings.
Student Life: 87% of undergraduates are from South Dakota. Others are from 4 states. 86% are white. 25% are Catholic; 24% Protestant.
Housing: 137 students can be accommodated in college housing. College-sponsored housing is single-sex. On-campus housing is guaranteed for all 4 years. 86% of students commute. Alcohol is not permitted. All students may keep cars.
Activities: There are no fraternities or sororities.
Sports: There are 2 intercollegiate sports for men and 3 for women.
Disabled Students: All of the campus is accessible. Wheelchair ramps, elevators, special parking, and specially equipped rest rooms are available.
Services: Counseling and information services are available, as is tutoring in every subject. There is remedial math, reading, and writing.
Campus Safety and Security: Measures include informal discussions, pamphlets/posters/films, emergency telephones, and lighted pathways/sidewalks.
Programs of Study: Presentation confers B.S., B.S.N., and B.S.W. degrees. Associate degrees are also awarded. Bachelor's degrees are awarded in BUSINESS (business administration and management), COMPUTER AND PHYSICAL SCIENCE (radiological technology), HEALTH PROFESSIONS (health care administration and nursing), SOCIAL SCIENCE (social work). Nursing is the largest.
Required: Students must complete 128 semester hours, with 48 in upper-division courses and 36 in the major. The core curriculum consists

of 18 hours of humanities and fine arts, 12 of social and behavioral sciences, 11 of natural sciences and math, and 10 of religious studies and philosophy.
Special: Certificate programs are available in phlebotomy, surgical technology, administrative assistance, business/accounting, and computer operating. An external degree program offers an accelerated schedule for working adults. Limited credit for experiential learning is possible. There is 1 national honor society.
Faculty/Classroom: 10% of faculty are male; 90%, female.
Requirements: The ACT is required. In addition, prospective students must graduate from high school or hold a GED, and a GPA of 2.0 is recommended. AP and CLEP credits are accepted.
Procedure: Freshmen are admitted in the fall. Early decision applications should be filed by April 1; regular application deadlines are open for fall entry. The college accepts all applicants. The fall 2001 application fee was $20.
Transfer: A 2.0 GPA on previous college work is recommended. 32 credits of 128 must be completed at Presentation.
Visiting: To schedule a visit, contact the Admissions Office.
Financial Aid: In a recent year, 94% of all freshmen received some form of financial aid. The FFS is required.
International Students: They must score 450 on the written TOEFL.
Computers: Approximately 180 PCs are available in the library, computer center, and dorms. Dorm rooms have Internet access. Students may have e-mail accounts. Computer students may access the system. There are no time llimits and no fees.
Graduates: In 2001, 59 bachelor's degrees were awarded. The most popular majors were nursing (52%), surgical technician (11%), and radiologic technician (7%).
Admissions Contact: Joddy Meidinger, Director of Admissions and Financial Aid. E-mail: *meidinger@presentation.edu*

SI TANKA HURON UNIVERSITY
(See Huron University)

SINTE GLESKA UNIVERSITY C-3
Rosebud, SD 57570 (605) 747-2263; Fax: (605) 747-2098

Full-time: 95 men, 240 women	**Faculty:** 23
Part-time: 1 woman	**Ph.D.s:** n/av
Graduate: 120 men, 315 women	**Student/Faculty:** 14 to 1
Year: semesters, summer session	**Tuition:** $2160
Application Deadline: open	**Room & Board:** n/app
Freshman Class: n/av	
SAT I or ACT: not required	NONCOMPETITIVE

Sinte Gleska University, founded in 1970, is an independent institution offering undergraduate programs in business, fine arts, professional training, and technical studies. Figures in the above capsule are approximate. There is 1 graduate school. The library contains 85,000 volumes. The 52-acre campus is in a rural area east of Mission. There are 7 buildings.
Student Life: 92% of undergraduates are from South Dakota. Others are from 1 state. All are from public schools. 85% are Native American/Eskimo; 15% white. The average age of all undergraduates is 31. 10% do not continue beyond their first year; 90% remain to graduate.
Housing: There are no residence halls. All of students commute. Alcohol is not permitted.
Activities: There are no fraternities or sororities. There are some groups and organizations on campus, including newspaper and photography. Popular campus events include Founders Day.
Sports: There are 4 intramural sports for men and 3 for women.
Disabled Students: All of the campus is accessible. Wheelchair ramps, special parking, specially equipped rest rooms, and lowered drinking fountains are available.
Services: Counseling and information services are available, as is tutoring in every subject.
Campus Safety and Security: Measures include shuttle buses, informal discussions, and an evening security guard.
Programs of Study: Sinte Gleska confers B.A. and B.S. degrees. Associate and master's degrees are also awarded. Bachelor's degrees are awarded in COMMUNICATIONS AND THE ARTS (art), EDUCATION (early childhood and elementary), HEALTH PROFESSIONS (mental health/human services), SOCIAL SCIENCE (human services). Education and human services are the strongest academically.
Required: To graduate, students must complete at least 128 credits with a GPA of 2.0; education majors must have a 2.5. All students must fulfill the core curriculum requirements.
Special: The college offers work-study programs, accelerated degree programs, a general studies degree, and pass/fail options.
Requirements: Applicants must be graduates of accredited secondary schools or have earned a GED.
Procedure: Freshmen are admitted to all sessions. Entrance exams should be taken before admission. Application deadlines are open. The college accepts all applicants. Check with the school for current information.
Transfer: Applicants must submit an official transcript from their previous college. 68 credits of 128 must be completed at Sinte Gleska.
Visiting: There are regularly scheduled orientations for prospective students. There are guides for informal visits and visitors may stay overnight. To schedule a visit, contact Cheryl Crazy Bull, Vice President at (605) 747-2263, ext. 52.
Financial Aid: The SFS is required. Check with the school for current deadlines.
Admissions Contact: Michelle Zephier, Registrar.
E-mail: *mzephr@rosebud.sinte.edu*

SOUTH DAKOTA BOARD OF REGENTS

The South Dakota Board of Regents governs the 6 public universities: Black Hills State University, Dakota State University, Northern State University, South Dakota School of Mines and Technology, South Dakota State University, and the University of South Dakota. In addition, the regents operate off-campus attendance centers in several locations statewide. In 2000, the Regents created the Electronic University Consortium, offering courses and degrees online from the six universities. In the past decade the thrust of Regental policies has been to foster a unified system of public higher education while maintaining quality and accountability through wise resource management. To that end, at least one center of excellence has been established at each university. Additional initiatives include a proficiency exam of all rising juniors, information technology proficiency requirements, interuniversity faculty discipline councils, common course numbering among the six universities, student technology fellows, and faculty salary increases based on performance and market. The regents have integrated technology throughout the system by wiring all campus buildings, participating in the governor's competitive faculty grants for teaching with technology, and establishing a statewide e-learning center to enhance teacher education and delivery of distance education courses for high school students. Total 2001 fall enrollment is 28,828. Profiles of the six universities appear in this section.

SOUTH DAKOTA SCHOOL OF MINES AND TECHNOLOGY B-3
Rapid City, SD 57701-3995 (605) 394-2414
(800) 544-8162, ext. 2400; Fax: (605) 394-1268

Full-time: 1211 men, 453 women	**Faculty:** 103; IIA, av$
Part-time: 202 men, 209 women	**Ph.D.s:** 95%
Graduate: 268 men, 81 women	**Student/Faculty:** 16 to 1
Year: semesters, summer session	**Tuition:** $3849 ($8204)
Application Deadline: August 15	**Room & Board:** $3589
Freshman Class: 839 applied, 784 accepted, 422 enrolled	
ACT: 24	COMPETITIVE+

South Dakota School of Mines and Technology, founded in 1885, is a public university offering undergraduate and graduate programs in engineering, science, and mathematics. There are 4 undergraduate schools and 1 graduate school. In addition to regional accreditation, SDSM&T has baccalaureate program accreditation with ABET, ACS, and CSAB. The library contains 226,854 volumes, 195,734 microform items, and 3146 audiovisual forms/CDs, and subscribes to 461 periodicals. Computerized library services include the card catalog, interlibrary loans, and database searching. Special learning facilities include a learning resource center, art gallery, natural history museum, planetarium, radio station, and a geology museum. The 118-acre campus is in a suburban area 350 miles northeast of Denver, CO. Including residence halls, there are 18 buildings.
Student Life: 70% of undergraduates are from South Dakota. Others are from 39 states, 24 foreign countries, and Canada. 82% are white. The average age of freshmen is 19; all undergraduates, 23. 29% do not continue beyond their first year; 39% remain to graduate.
Housing: 534 students can be accommodated in college housing, which includes single-sex and coed dormitories, fraternity houses, and sorority houses. On-campus housing is available on a first-come, first-served basis. 60% of students commute. Alcohol is not permitted. All students may keep cars.
Activities: There are 4 national fraternities and 2 national sororities. There are 24 groups on campus, including art, band, biking, choir, chorale, chorus, computers, drama, drill team, ethnic, honors, international, jazz band, newspaper, orchestra, pep band, political, professional, radio and TV, religious, SAAD, ski, social, social service, student government, and yearbook. Popular campus events include M-Week, Christmas chorale concert, International Cultural Exposition, and Tech Family Week.
Sports: There are 5 intercollegiate sports for men and 5 for women, and 15 intramural sports for men and 15 for women. Facilities include a football field, track, a 2350-seat gym, sand volleyball court, swimming pool, squash/racquetball courts, and a weight room.

Disabled Students: 60% of the campus is accessible. Wheelchair ramps, elevators, special parking, specially equipped rest rooms, special class scheduling, lowered drinking fountains, and ADA lab with specialized work stations, software, and hardware to aid students with visual, auditory, and mobility impairments and dyslexia are available.

Services: Counseling and information services are available, as is tutoring in most subjects. There is a reader service for the blind and remedial math.

Campus Safety and Security: Measures include 24-hour foot and vehicle patrol, escort service, informal discussions, and pamphlets/posters/films. There are emergency telephones and lighted pathways/sidewalks.

Programs of Study: SDSM&T confers the B.S. degree. Associate, master's, and doctoral degrees are also awarded. Bachelor's degrees are awarded in COMPUTER AND PHYSICAL SCIENCE (chemistry, computer science, geology, mathematics, and physics), ENGINEERING AND ENVIRONMENTAL DESIGN (chemical engineering, civil engineering, computer engineering, electrical/electronics engineering, geological engineering, industrial engineering, mechanical engineering, metallurgical engineering, and mining and mineral engineering), SOCIAL SCIENCE (interdisciplinary studies). Engineering is the strongest academically. Mechanical engineering, electrical engineering, and civil engineering are the largest.

Required: Students must complete 128 credits for the science major or 136 credits for the engineering major, and maintain a minimum GPA of 2.0. Included in these requirements are 16 credit hours each of math at a level of calculus and above, basic science, and humanities/social science (for engineering, 3 credits must be at the 300 or above level). State regents mandated distribution requirements include 6 credits each of written communications, social sciences, arts/humanities, science, and cultural diversity; 3 credits each of speech communications and math; and 2 credits of information technology literacy, plus completion of an exam.

Special: Opportunities are provided for study abroad, co-op programs, internships, work-study programs, dual majors, an interdisciplinary science major, credit by exam, and nondegree study. There are 5 national honor societies, including Phi Beta Kappa.

Faculty/Classroom: 80% of faculty are male; 20%, female. 95% teach undergraduates, 20% do research, and 90% do both. Graduate students teach 4% of introductory courses. The average class size in an introductory lecture is 50; in a laboratory, 24; and in a regular course, 25.

Admissions: 93% of the 2001-2002 applicants were accepted. The ACT scores for the 2001-2002 freshman class were: 21% below 21, 24% between 21 and 23, 28% between 24 and 26, 12% between 27 and 28, and 14% above 28. 42% of the current freshmen were in the top fifth of their class; 69% were in the top two fifths. There were 2 National Merit finalists and 7 semifinalists. 26 freshmen graduated first in their class.

Requirements: The SAT is accepted, but the ACT is preferred, with a minimum composite score of 920 (420 verbal and 500 math) on the SAT I, or a minimum composite score of 18 on the ACT. Graduation from an accredited secondary school is required. A GED is accepted. Applicants must submit high school credits, distributed as follows: 4 years of English, 3 each of math, 3 of lab science, 3 in social studies, and one half year each of fine arts and computer science. SDSM&T requires applicants to be in the upper 60% of their class. A GPA of 2.6 is required. AP and CLEP credits are accepted. Applications are accepted on-line through the school's Web site.

Procedure: Freshmen are admitted fall and spring. Entrance exams should be taken preferebly in October and December. Applications should be filed by August 15 for fall entry and January 15 for spring entry. The fall 2001 application fee was $20. Notification is sent on a rolling basis.

Transfer: 133 transfer students enrolled in 2001-2002. Transfer students must submit an official transcript from the previous college and must have maintained a minimum GPA of 2.0, with 2.5 recommended. 32 credits of 128 must be completed at SDSM&T.

Visiting: There are regularly scheduled orientations for prospective students. There are guides for informal visits and visitors may sit in on classes. To schedule a visit, contact the Admissions Office at *admissions@submit.edu*.

Financial Aid: In 2001-2002, 81% of all freshmen and 59% of continuing students received some form of financial aid. 56% of freshmen and 46% of continuing students received need-based aid. The average freshman award was $5682. Of that total, scholarships or need-based grants averaged $3290 ($11,525 maximum); loans averaged $4110 ($10,670 maximum); and work contracts averaged $1407 ($1500 maximum). 23% of undergraduates work part time. Average annual earnings from campus work are $1500. The average financial indebtedness of the 2001 graduate was $15,475. The FAFSA is required. The fall application deadline is March 15.

International Students: There are 22 international students enrolled. The school actively recruits these students. They must score 530 on the written TOEFL or 197 on the electronic version or take IELTS and also take the ACT.

Computers: There are approximately 160 computers plus 50 Internet kiosks on campus. All students may access the system 24 hours per day. There are no time limits and no fees.

Graduates: In 2001, 238 bachelor's degrees were awarded. The most popular majors were mechanical engineering (21%), civil engineering (16%), and interdisciplinary sciences (10%). In an average class, 9% graduate in 4 years, 35% in 5 years, and 39% in 6 years. 116 companies recruited on campus in 2000-2001. Of the 2000 graduating class, 18% were enrolled in graduate school within 6 months of graduation and 77% were employed.

Admissions Contact: Office of Admissions.
E-mail: *hhall@silver.sdsmt.edu* Web: *http://www.sdsmt.edu*

SOUTH DAKOTA STATE UNIVERSITY — F-3
Brookings, SD 57007 (605) 688-4310
(800) 952-3541; Fax: (605) 688-6891

Full-time: 3265 men, 3092 women	**Faculty:** 499; IIA, --$
Part-time: 448 men, 988 women	**Ph.D.s:** 70%
Graduate: 546 men, 796 women	**Student/Faculty:** 13 to 1
Year: semesters, summer session	**Tuition:** $3808 ($8164)
Application Deadline: open	**Room & Board:** $3040

Freshman Class: 3004 applied, 2836 accepted, 1578 enrolled
ACT: required **COMPETITIVE**

South Dakota State University, founded in 1881, is a public land-grant institution offering undergraduate programs in agriculture and biological sciences, arts and science, engineering, family and consumer sciences, nursing, pharmacy, education and counseling, and general registration. There are 8 undergraduate schools and 1 graduate school. In addition to regional accreditation, SDSU has baccalaureate program accreditation with ABET, ACEJMC, ACPE, ADA, AHEA, NASM, NCATE, and NLN. The library contains 538,358 volumes, 835,017 microform items, and 2060 audiovisual forms/CDs, and subscribes to 3284 periodicals. Computerized library services include the card catalog, interlibrary loans, and database searching. Special learning facilities include an art gallery, radio station, TV station, arboretum, agricultural heritage museum, Northern Plains Biostress lab, and animal disease research and diagnostic lab. The 272-acre campus is in a small town 50 miles north of Sioux Falls; 200 miles west of Minneapolis. Including residence halls, there are 325 buildings.

Student Life: 74% of undergraduates are from South Dakota. Others are from 39 states, 19 foreign countries, and Canada. 91% are white. The average age of freshmen is 19; all undergraduates, 22. 20% do not continue beyond their first year; 80% remain to graduate.

Housing: 3100 students can be accommodated in college housing, which includes coed dormitories, on-campus apartments, and married-student housing. In addition, there are honors houses, and special-interest houses, intensive study, 1 floor for male engineering students, and smoke-free floors.. On-campus housing is available on a first-come, first-served basis. Alcohol is not permitted. All students may keep cars.

Activities: There are 6 national fraternities and 3 national sororities. There are 200 groups on campus, including art, band, cheerleading, chess, choir, chorale, chorus, computers, dance, debate, drama, drill team, ethnic, film, forensics, gay, honors, international, jazz band, literary magazine, marching band, musical theater, newspaper, opera, orchestra, pep band, photography, political, professional, radio and TV, religious, social, social service, student government, symphony, and yearbook. Popular campus events include Family Day, Little International, and Engineering Exploration Days.

Sports: There are 10 intercollegiate sports for men and 10 for women, and 17 intramural sports for men and 17 for women. Facilities include a phys ed complex, an intramural building, outdoor track, lighted tennis courts, a wellness center, and intramural football and softball fields.

Disabled Students: Wheelchair ramps, elevators, special parking, specially equipped rest rooms, special class scheduling, lowered drinking fountains, and lowered telephones are available. All academic programs can be made accessible.

Services: Counseling and information services are available, as is tutoring in most subjects. There is a reader service for the blind.

Campus Safety and Security: Measures include 24-hour foot and vehicle patrol, self-defense education, escort service, and informal discussions. There are pamphlets/posters/films, emergency telephones, and lighted pathways/sidewalks.

Programs of Study: SDSU confers B.A., B.S., B.Mus.Ed., and B.S.T. degrees. Associate, master's, and doctoral degrees are also awarded. Bachelor's degrees are awarded in AGRICULTURE (agricultural business management, agricultural economics, agriculture, agronomy, animal science, dairy science, fish and game management, horticulture, and range/farm management), BIOLOGICAL SCIENCE (biochemistry, biology/biological science, microbiology, and nutrition), BUSINESS (apparel and accessories marketing and hotel/motel and restaurant management), COMMUNICATIONS AND THE ARTS (art, communications, dramatic arts, English, German, graphic design, journalism, music, music business management, and Spanish), COMPUTER AND PHYSICAL SCIENCE (chemistry, computer science, mathematics, and physics), EDUCATION (agricultural, art, athletic training, early childhood, health, home economics, music, physical, secondary, and vocational), ENGINEERING AND ENVIRONMENTAL DESIGN (agricultural engineering, agricultural engineering technology, civil engineering, construction management, electrical/electronics engineering, electrical/electronics engineering technology, engineering physics, engineering technology, environmental engineering, interior design, landscape architecture/design, manufacturing technology, and mechanical engineering), HEALTH PROFESSIONS (clinical science, nursing, and pharmacy), SOCIAL SCIENCE (consumer services, economics, family/consumer studies, food production/management/services, food science, French studies, geography, history, human development, parks and recreation management, political science/government, psychology, rural sociology, and sociology). Pharmacy, engineering, and nursing are the strongest academically. Nursing, sociology, and animal science are the largest.

Required: Students must complete 128 credits (136 for engineering and nursing), with at least 32 in the major, and must maintain a 2.0 minimum GPA. Additional requirements for graduation are 9 to 14 credits in social science, 8 to 13 in natural science, 6 to 11 in humanities, 3 each in math and speech, and 2 in phys ed.

Special: Co-op programs in elementary education and social work, internships, work-study programs, B.A.-B.S. degrees, and interdisciplinary majors including agricultural journalism, environmental management, and wildlife and fisheries science are available. SDSU offers cross-registration with Dakota State University, Black Hills State University, the University of South Dakota, Northern State University, and South Dakota School of Mines and Technology. Opportunities are provided for dual majors, study abroad, credit by examination, student-designed majors, credit for military experience, nondegree study, a general studies degree, and pass/fail options. There are 32 national honor societies and a freshman honors program.

Faculty/Classroom: 65% of faculty are male; 35%, female. 78% teach undergraduates, 14% do research, and 87% do both. Graduate students teach 30% of introductory courses. The average class size in an introductory lecture is 50; in a laboratory, 30; and in a regular course, 30.

Admissions: 94% of the 2001-2002 applicants were accepted. The ACT scores for the 2001-2002 freshman class were: 42% below 21, 28% between 21 and 23, 19% between 24 and 26, 7% between 27 and 28, and 4% above 28. There were 2 National Merit finalists and 8 semifinalists. 82 freshmen graduated first in their class.

Requirements: The ACT is required. In addition, students must have an 18 ACT composite score, be in the top 60% of their class, or have a 2.6 GPA in required classes. Graduation from an accredited secondary school is required. A GED will be accepted. Applicants must submit 4 years of English, 1/2 year each of computer science and art or music, 3 years of social studies, and 3 years each of math and science. SDSU requires applicants to be in the upper 60% of their class. A GPA of 2.6 is required. AP and CLEP credits are accepted. Important factors in the admissions decision are advanced placement or honor courses, evidence of special talent, and extracurricular activities record. Applications are available on-line through *www.sdstate.edu* and via CollegeNET.

Procedure: Freshmen are admitted to all sessions. Entrance exams should be taken by spring of the junior year. Application deadlines are open. The fall 2001 applicaton fee was $15. Notification is sent on a rolling basis.

Transfer: 609 transfer students enrolled in 2001-2002. To be eligible for transfer, students must have been in good standing at the previous college and must have maintained a minimum GPA of 2.0 to 2.5, depending on the student's major. 32 credits of 128 must be completed at SDSU.

Visiting: There are regularly scheduled orientations for prospective students, Several new student orientation sessions are offered each June and July. Students become acquainted with the University and student resources. They also meet with an academic adviser and register for fall semester classes. Information is sent to all admitted sudents. There are guides for informal visits and visitors may sit in on classes and stay overnight. To schedule a visit, contact the Admissions Office at *sdsu_admissions@sdstate.edu*.

Financial Aid: In 2001-2002, 86% of all freshmen and 80% of continuing students received some form of financial aid. 84% of freshmen and 82% of continuing students received need-based aid. The average freshman award was $5475. Of that total, scholarships or need-based grants averaged $1810 ($10,250 maximum); loans averaged $1940 ($6625 maximum); and work contracts averaged $1200 ($2400 maximum). 88% of undergraduates work part time. Average annual earnings from campus work are $1600. The average financial indebtedness of the 2001 graduate was $16,009. SDSU is a member of CSS. The CSS/Profile, FAFSA, FFS or SFS is required.

International Students: There are 48 international students enrolled. They must score 500 on the written TOEFL.

Computers: Students have access to PC labs in the library, residence halls, and the administration building. Students can access the Internet and Web at campus computer labs and computer rooms. All students may access the system. There are no time limits and no fees.

Graduates: In 2001, 1664 bachelor's degrees were awarded. The most popular majors were nursing (12%), sociology (6%), and economics (6%).

Admissions Contact: Sarah Peacock, Admissions Counselor.
E-mail: *sarah_peacock@sdstate.edu* Web: *http://www.sdstate.edu*

UNIVERSITY OF SIOUX FALLS — F-3

Sioux Falls, SD 57105 — **(605) 331-6600**
(800) 888-1047; Fax: (605) 331-6615

Full-time: 427 men, 479 women	**Faculty:** 36; IIB, --$
Part-time: 87 men, 129 women	**Ph.D.s:** 68%
Graduate: 88 men, 122 women	**Student/Faculty:** 18 to 1
Year: 4-1-4, summer session	**Tuition:** $12,600
Application Deadline: open	**Room & Board:** $3790
Freshman Class: 526 applied, 413 accepted, 223 enrolled	
ACT: 23	**COMPETITIVE**

University of Sioux Falls, founded in 1883, is a private liberal arts institution affiliated with the American Baptist Churches. In addition to regional accreditation, USF has baccalaureate program accreditation with CSWE and NCATE. The library contains 78,000 volumes and 4600 audiovisual forms/CDs, and subscribes to 450 periodicals. Computerized library services include the card catalog, interlibrary loans, and database searching. Special learning facilities include a learning resource center, radio station, and TV station. The 22-acre campus is in a suburban area 250 miles from Minneapolis/St. Paul, Minnesota; 180 miles from Omaha, Nebraska. Including residence halls, there are 13 buildings.

Student Life: 72% of undergraduates are from South Dakota. Others are from 21 states, 10 foreign countries, and Canada. 95% are from public schools. 94% are white. 73% are Protestant; 14% Catholic; 13% claim no religious affiliation. The average age of freshmen is 18; all undergraduates, 21. 37% do not continue beyond their first year; 48% remain to graduate.

Housing: 350 students can be accommodated in college housing, which includes single-sex and coed dormitories, on-campus apartments, and married-student housing. On-campus housing is guaranteed for the freshman year only, is available on a first-come, first-served basis, and is available on a lottery system for upperclassmen. Priority is given to out-of-town students. 73% of students commute. Alcohol is not permitted. All students may keep cars.

Activities: There are no fraternities or sororities. There are 35 groups on campus, including art, band, cheerleading, choir, chorale, chorus, computers, drama, ethnic, honors, international, jazz band, musical theater, newspaper, opera, orchestra, pep band, photography, political, professional, radio and TV, religious, social, social service, and student government. Popular campus events include Spring Formal, Staley Lectures, and Madrigals.

Sports: There are 6 intercollegiate sports for men and 7 for women, and 8 intramural sports for men and 8 for women. Facilities include a student lounge, a 160-meter running track, volleyball, tennis, badminton, racquetball, and basketball courts, aerobics facilities, exercise machines, a whirlpool, and a 700-seat gym.

Disabled Students: 54% of the campus is accessible. Wheelchair ramps, elevators, special parking, specially equipped rest rooms, special class scheduling, lowered drinking fountains, and lowered telephones are available.

Services: There is remedial math and reading.

Campus Safety and Security: Measures include self-defense education, escort service, informal discussions, and pamphlets/posters/films. There are emergency telephones and lighted pathways/sidewalks.

Programs of Study: USF confers B.A. and B.S. degrees. Associate and master's degrees are also awarded. Bachelor's degrees are awarded in BIOLOGICAL SCIENCE (biology/biological science), BUSINESS (accounting, business administration and management, business economics, and marketing/retailing/merchandising), COMMUNICATIONS AND THE ARTS (communications, English, music, and speech/debate/rhetoric), COMPUTER AND PHYSICAL SCIENCE (chemistry, computer science, and mathematics), EDUCATION (art, early childhood, elementary, middle school, music, science, and secondary), HEALTH PROFESSIONS (medical laboratory technology and premedicine), SOCIAL SCIENCE (history, philosophy, political science/government, prelaw, psychology, religion, social work, and sociology). Business and elementary education are the strongest academically and have the largest enrollments.

Required: To graduate, all students must complete a minimum of 128 credit hours, with 64 hours in the major. Required courses include phys ed, computer science, religion, history, English, science, economics, political science, psychology, math, social science, cross-cultural experience, speech, and fine arts. A writing proficiency test and a minimum 2.0 GPA are also required.

Special: There are co-op programs with Augustana College, the Center for Public Higher Education, Dakota State University, and the North American Baptist Seminary. USF offers internships, study abroad in Japan, Central America, and China, an American Studies Program in

Washington, D.C., and a January interim. Also available are on-campus work-study programs, B.A.-B.S. degrees, dual and student-designed interdisciplinary majors, a general studies degree, a 3-2 engineering degree, credit for life and work experience, and pass/fail options. There are 3 national honor societies, a freshman honors program, and 2 departmental honors programs.

Faculty/Classroom: 69% of faculty are male; 31%, female. All teach undergraduates and 60% do research. No introductory courses are taught by graduate students. The average class size in an introductory lecture is 40; in a laboratory, 15; and in a regular course, 20.

Admissions: 98% of the 2001-2002 applicants were accepted. The ACT scores for the 2001-2002 freshman class were: 43% below 21, 29% between 21 and 23, 19% between 24 and 26, 5% between 27 and 28, and 4% above 28. 40% of the current freshmen were in the top fifth of their class; 88% were in the top two fifths. In a recent year, there was 1 National Merit finalist and 2 semifinalists, 15 freshmen graduated first in their class.

Requirements: The ACT is required, with a minimum score of 19. Applicants must be graduates of an accredited secondary school or have a GED certificate. Students should have completed 4 years each of English and math and 2 years each of foreign language, science, and social studies. USF requires applicants to be in the upper 50% of their class. A GPA of 2.0 is required. AP and CLEP credits are accepted. Important factors in the admissions decision are advanced placement or honor courses, evidence of special talent, and leadership record.

Procedure: Freshmen are admitted to all sessions. Entrance exams should be taken during the junior or senior year of high school. There is an early admissions plan. Application deadlines are open. The application fee is $25. Notification is sent on a rolling basis.

Transfer: Transfer students must meet freshman admission requirements and have completed at least 24 hours of college courses with a minimum 2.0 GPA. The SAT I or the ACT and an interview are recommended. 30 credits of 128 must be completed at USF.

Visiting: There are regularly scheduled orientations for prospective students, including meetings with faculty and staff, attendance at class, a campus tour, and a financial aid session. There are guides for informal visits and visitors may sit in on classes and stay overnight. To schedule a visit, contact the Admissions Office.

Financial Aid: The average freshman award in 2001-2002 was $10,000. Of that total, scholarships or need-based grants averaged $5000; loans averaged $3700; and work contracts averaged $1300. 25% of undergraduates work part time. Average annual earnings from campus work are $1200. The average financial indebtedness of a recent year's graduate was $20,500. USF is a member of CSS. The CSS/Profile, FAFSA, FFS or SFS is required. Check with the school for current deadlines.

International Students: The school actively recruits these students. They must score 550 on the written TOEFL or 213 on the electronic version and also take the SAT I or the ACT, if the examination is available to the student.

Computers: Students have access to 91 PCs in 3 publicly accessible labs. File space, letter-quality printers, and a laser printer are provided. Students may access the Internet through IBM and Mac computer labs wired to the campus network. All students may access the system 8 A.M. to 11 P.M. There are no time limits and no fees.

Admissions Contact: Laura Olson, Assistant Director of Admissions. E-mail: *laura.olson@usioux falls.edu* Web: *www.usiouxfalls.edu*

UNIVERSITY OF SOUTH DAKOTA F-4
Vermillion, SD 57069 (605) 677-5434
(800) 329-2453; Fax: (605) 677-6753

Full-time: 1760 men, 2245 women	**Faculty:** 236; I, --$
Part-time: 430 men, 928 women	**Ph.D.s:** 84%
Graduate: 667 men, 1808 women	**Student/Faculty:** 17 to 1
Year: semesters, summer session	**Tuition:** $3885 ($8240)
Application Deadline: open	**Room & Board:** $3151
Freshman Class: 2762 applied, 1559 accepted, 1044 enrolled	
ACT: required	**COMPETITIVE**

The University of South Dakota, founded in 1862, is a public institution with undergraduate programs in arts and sciences, education, fine arts, and business, and professional schools of law and medicine. There are 4 undergraduate and 3 graduate schools. In addition to regional accreditation, USD has baccalaureate program accreditation with AACSB, APTA, CSWE, NASAD, NASM, NCATE, and NLN. The 3 libraries contain 515,012 volumes, 691,903 microform items, and 48,887 audiovisual forms/CDs, and subscribe to 2312 periodicals. Computerized library services include the card catalog, interlibrary loans, and database searching. Special learning facilities include a learning resource center, art gallery, natural history museum, radio station, TV station, music museum, historical study center, institutes of American Indian studies, social science research, child welfare training, business and governmental research bureaus, centers for speech and hearing, international studies, fine arts, and telecommunications, natural sciences field station, and archeology and human factors labs. The 216-acre campus is in a rural area 41 miles from Sioux City, IA, and 64 miles from Sioux Falls. Including residence halls, there are 60 buildings.

Student Life: 73% of undergraduates are from South Dakota. Others are from 34 states, 33 foreign countries, and Canada. 93% are white. 45% claim no religious affiliation; 35% Protestant; 19% Catholic. The average age of freshmen is 20; all undergraduates, 22. 33% do not continue beyond their first year; 48% remain to graduate.

Housing: 2122 students can be accommodated in college housing, which includes single-sex and coed dormitories, married-student housing, fraternity houses, and sorority houses. On-campus housing is guaranteed for the freshman year only and is available on a first-come, first-served basis. 66% of students commute. Alcohol is not permitted. All students may keep cars.

Activities: 20% of men belong to 9 national fraternities; 15% of women belong to 5 national sororities. There are 122 groups on campus, including art, band, cheerleading, choir, chorale, chorus, computers, dance, drama, drill team, ethnic, gay, honors, international, jazz band, literary magazine, marching band, musical theater, newspaper, opera, orchestra, pep band, photography, political, professional, radio and TV, religious, social, social service, student government, and symphony. Popular campus events include Strollers (a variety production), Rockfest, Greek Week, and Ideafest.

Sports: There are 7 intercollegiate sports for men and 7 for women, and 20 intramural sports for men and 20 for women. Facilities include an indoor football field, 5 basketball courts, a 25-meter swimming pool, an 8-lane, 200-meter track, and handball, volleyball, and tennis courts.

Disabled Students: 95% of the campus is accessible. Wheelchair ramps, elevators, special parking, specially equipped rest rooms, special class scheduling, lowered drinking fountains, and lowered telephones are available.

Services: Counseling and information services are available, as is tutoring in most subjects. There is a reader service for the blind, and remedial math, reading, and writing as well as an academic advising/testing center.

Campus Safety and Security: Measures include 24-hour foot and vehicle patrol, self-defense education, escort service, and informal discussions. There are pamphlets/posters/films, emergency telephones, and lighted pathways/sidewalks.

Programs of Study: USD confers B.A., B.S., B.F.A., B.L.S., B.M., B.S.A.H., B.S.B.A, B.S.D.H., B.S.Ed., B.S.H.A., B.S.Med., B.S.Med.Tech., and B.S.Rec. degrees. Associate, master's, and doctoral degrees are also awarded. Bachelor's degrees are awarded in BIOLOGICAL SCIENCE (biology/biological science), BUSINESS (accounting, management science, and recreation and leisure services), COMMUNICATIONS AND THE ARTS (art, dramatic arts, English, German, journalism, music, music performance, and Spanish), COMPUTER AND PHYSICAL SCIENCE (chemistry, computer science, earth science, mathematics, and physics), EDUCATION (art, elementary, music, physical, secondary, and special), HEALTH PROFESSIONS (allied health, dental hygiene, health care administration, medical technology, physician's assistant, and speech pathology/audiology), SOCIAL SCIENCE (addiction studies, American Indian studies, anthropology, criminal justice, economics, French studies, history, international studies, liberal arts/general studies, philosophy, political science/government, psychology, social work, and sociology). Business, biology, and elementary education are the largest.

Required: To graduate, students must complete 128 semester hours with a minimum GPA of 2.0. Core curriculum requirements include 6 hours each of humanities/fine arts, social sciences, composition, natural world, and multicultural world, and 3 hours each in math and speaking and listening. At least 32 hours of upper-level courses must be taken.

Special: USD offers internships, study abroad in six countries, and work-study programs. B.A.-B.S. degrees in 25 majors, a student-designed liberal studies or selected studies major, a dual major in chemistry and business, nondegree study, and pass/fail options are available. The Arts Outreach program provides arts activities and noncredit classes. There are 16 national honor societies, including Phi Beta Kappa, and a freshman honors program.

Faculty/Classroom: 64% of faculty are male; 36%, female. 90% teach undergraduates. The average class size in an introductory lecture is 41; in a laboratory, 21; and in a regular course, 23.

Admissions: 56% of the 2001-2002 applicants were accepted. The ACT scores for the 2001-2002 freshman class were: 15% below 21, 52% between 21 and 23, 24% between 24 and 26, 5% between 27 and 28, and 4% above 28. 42% of the current freshmen were in the top fifth of their class; 60% were in the top two fifths. There were 7 National Merit finalists and 1 semifinalist.

Requirements: The ACT is required. In addition, applicants must have earned a 2.0 GPA in 4 years of English, 3 years each of lab science, math, and social studies, and 1 semester each of fine art and computer science. They must also rank in the top 60% of their graduation class, have an ACT score of 18, or have a high school GPA of 2.6. Applications are accepted on-line at the school's web site. AP and CLEP credits are accepted.

Procedure: Freshmen are admitted to all sessions. Entrance exams should be taken prior to enrollment. There is a deferred admissions plan. Application deadlines are open. The fall 2001 application fee was $15. Notification is sent on a rolling basis.

Transfer: 522 transfer students enrolled in 2001-2002. Applicants should have a minimum college GPA of 2.0 and be in good standing at their previous school. 30 credits of 128 must be completed at USD.

Visiting: There are regularly scheduled orientations for prospective students, including an introductory session, academic department visits, a session with USD students, a campus tour, and a separate program for parents. There are guides for informal visits and visitors may sit in on classes and stay overnight. To schedule a visit, contact the Admissions Office.

Financial Aid: In 2001-2002, 92% of all freshmen and 89% of continuing students received some form of financial aid. 74% of freshmen and 81% of continuing students received need-based aid. The FAFSA is required.

International Students: There are 219 international students enrolled. The school actively recruits these students. They must score 550 on the written TOEFL.

Computers: The mainframe is an IBM ES/9000. Students have access to a set of UNIX-based PCs that provide Internet access. There are 3 public-use computer labs as well as those found in departments. All students may access the system 24 hours a day. There are no time limits and no fees.

Graduates: In 2001, 803 bachelor's degrees were awarded. The most popular majors were business management (15%), psychology (11%), and elementary education (7%). In an average class, 2% graduate in 3 years, 22% in 4 years, 39% in 5 years, and 43% in 6 years. 100 companies recruited on campus in 2000-2001.

Admissions Contact: Paula Tacke, Director of Admissions.
E-mail: *admiss@usd.edu* Web: *http://www.usd.edu*

TENNESSEE

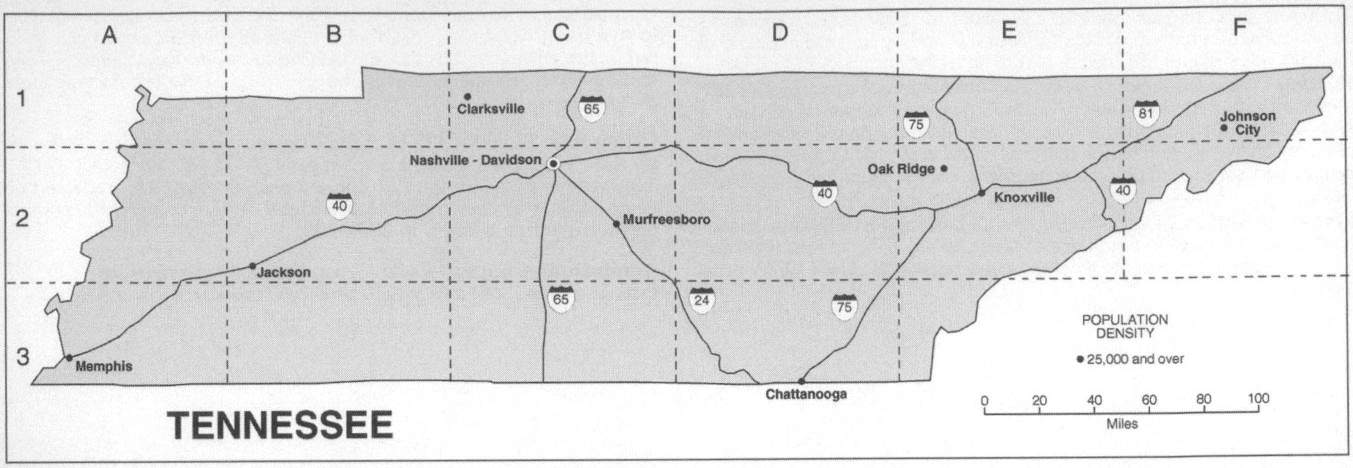

AQUINAS COLLEGE C-2

Nashville, TN 37205 **(615) 297-7545 ext 426; Fax: (615) 297-7970**

Full-time: 245 men and women
Part-time: 150 men and women
Graduate: none
Year: semesters, summer session
Application Deadline: open
Freshman Class: n/av
ACT: required
Faculty: 29
Ph.D.s: 20%
Student/Faculty: 8 to 1
Tuition: $10,050
Room & Board: n/app

LESS COMPETITIVE

Aquinas College is a private Catholic institution offering an academically challenging liberal arts and sciences curriculum. Figures in above capsule are approximate. In addition to regional accreditation, the college has baccalaureate program accreditation with NLN. The library contains 45,762 volumes, 140,602 microform items, and 1820 audiovisual forms/CDs, and subscribes to 301 periodicals. Computerized library services include the card catalog, interlibrary loans, and database searching. Special learning facilities include a learning resource center. The 92-acre campus is in an urban area in the western section of metropolitan Nashville. There are 4 buildings.

Housing: All students commute.

Programs of Study: the college confers B.A., B.B.A.,and B.S.N. degrees. Associate degrees are also awarded. Bachelor's degrees are awarded in BUSINESS (business administration and management), EDUCATION (elementary), HEALTH PROFESSIONS (nursing), SOCIAL SCIENCE (liberal arts/general studies). Nursing is the largest.

Required: All students must complete 124 to 134 credit hours, including the liberal arts core, and must maintain a minimum GPA of 2.0 in the B.S.N., A.S.N., and A.A. programs, 2.2 in the B.B.A. program, and 2.6 in the B.A. programs. Check with the school for the most current information.

Special: There is a Weekend College for working adult students, and evening courses are also offered. There is 1 national honor society.

Faculty/Classroom: 25% of faculty are male; 75%, female. All teach undergraduates. In a recent year, the average class size in an introductory lecture was 25; in a laboratory, 20; and in a regular course, 25.

Requirements: The ACT is required. In addition, the GED is accepted. An essay and an interview are required for some majors. Applications may be submitted on-line at the college's web site. A GPA of 2.0 is required. AP and CLEP credits are accepted. Check with the school for the most current information.

Procedure: Freshmen are admitted to all sessions. Application deadlines are open. The fall 2001 application fee was $10. Notification is sent on a rolling basis.

Transfer: 80 transfer students enrolled in a recent year. Transfer applicants must have a 2.0 GPA in previous college work. 32 credits of 124 must be completed at the college.

Visiting: There are regularly scheduled orientations for prospective students, including campus tours and information on admissions, financial aid, student life, and degree programs. There are guides for informal visits and visitors may sit in on classes. To schedule a visit, contact Sarah Curtis at (615) 297-7545, ext. 436.

Financial Aid: In a recent year, 75% of all freshmen and 45% of continuing students received some form of financial aid. 45% of freshmen received need-based aid. The average freshman award was $7784. Of that total, scholarships or need-based grants averaged $1684 ($2700 maximum); and loans averaged $6100 ($6625 maximum). 55% of undergraduates work part time. Average annual earnings from campus work are $1293. The average financial indebtedness of a recent graduate was $16,750. The college is a member of CSS. The FAFSA and the college's own financial statement are required. Check with the school for current deadlines.

International Students: They must score 525 on the written TOEFL.

Computers: The library and the computer lab together contain 40 computers available for student use. Internet access is available. All students may access the system all hours of college operation. There are no time limits.

Admissions Contact: Neil J. Devine, Director of Career Planning and Admissions. E-mail: *devine@aquinas-tn.edu*
Web: *www.aquinas-tn.edu.*

AUSTIN PEAY STATE UNIVERSITY C-2

Clarksville, TN 37040 **(931) 221-7661**
(800) 844-2778; Fax: (931) 221-5994

Full-time: 1680 men, 2865 women
Part-time: 1340 men, 1100 women
Graduate: 105 men, 350 women
Year: semesters, summer session
Application Deadline: see profile
Freshman Class: n/av
SAT I Verbal/Math: required
Faculty: 274; IIA, --$
Ph.D.s: 91%
Student/Faculty: 17 to 1
Tuition: $2831 ($8459)
Room & Board: $3300

LESS COMPETITIVE

Austin Peay State University, established in 1927, is a public institution offering undergraduate degrees in the liberal arts and sciences and professional preparation. There are 5 undergraduate schools and 1 graduate school. Figures in above capsule are approximate. In addition to regional accreditation, APSU has baccalaureate program accreditation with CSWE, NASAD, NASM, NCATE, and NLN. The library contains 196,826 volumes, 520,732 microform items, and 6844 audiovisual forms/CDs, and subscribes to 1736 periodicals. Computerized library services include the card catalog, interlibrary loans, and database searching. Special learning facilities include a learning resource center, art gallery, and radio station. The 150-acre campus is in an urban area 47 miles from Nashville. Including residence halls, there are 42 buildings.

Student Life: 85% of undergraduates are from Tennessee. Others are from 29 states, 14 foreign countries, and Canada. 90% are from public schools. 68% are white; 18% African American. The average age of freshmen is 20; all undergraduates, 26. 36% do not continue beyond their first year; 32% remain to graduate.

Housing: 1100 students can be accommodated in college housing, which includes single-sex and coed dormitories, on-campus apartments, and married-student housing. In addition, there are honors houses. On-campus housing is available on a first-come, first-served basis. 81% of students commute. Alcohol is not permitted. All students may keep cars.

Activities: 10% of men belong to 7 national fraternities; 3% of women belong to 7 national sororities. There are 80 groups on campus, including art, band, cheerleading, choir, chorus, debate, drama, ethnic, gay, honors, international, jazz band, literary magazine, marching band, newspaper, orchestra, pep band, political, professional, radio and TV, religious, social, social service, and student government. Popular campus events include Graduation, Parents Day, and Jazz Festival.

Sports: There are 6 intercollegiate sports for men and 8 for women, and 11 intramural sports for men and 11 for women. Facilities include a gym, an exercise room, a jogging fitness trail, and a weight room.

Disabled Students: 95% of the campus is accessible. Wheelchair ramps, elevators, special parking, specially equipped rest rooms, special class scheduling, lowered drinking fountains, and lowered telephones are available.

Services: There is a reader service for the blind, and remedial math, reading, and writing. The university provides help with academic, learning, and test-taking problems.

Campus Safety and Security: Measures include 24-hour foot and vehicle patrol, escort service, shuttle buses, and informal discussions. There are pamphlets/posters/films, emergency telephones, and lighted pathways/sidewalks.

Programs of Study: APSU confers B.A., B.S., B.B.A., B.F.A., B.S.Ed., and B.S.N. degrees. Associate and master's degrees are also awarded. Bachelor's degrees are awarded in AGRICULTURE (agriculture and conservation and regulation), BIOLOGICAL SCIENCE (biology/biological science), BUSINESS (accounting, banking and finance, business administration and management, management science, marketing/retailing/merchandising, and recreation and leisure services), COMMUNICATIONS AND THE ARTS (art, communications, English, French, German, languages, literature, music, Spanish, and speech/debate/rhetoric), COMPUTER AND PHYSICAL SCIENCE (chemistry, computer science, geology, mathematics, physics, and radiological technology), EDUCATION (elementary, health, and special), ENGINEERING AND ENVIRONMENTAL DESIGN (engineering technology, environmental science, and military science), HEALTH PROFESSIONS (health care administration, medical laboratory technology, nursing, predentistry, premedicine, and prepharmacy), SOCIAL SCIENCE (economics, geography, history, interdisciplinary studies, philosophy, political science/government, prelaw, psychology, public administration, social work, and sociology). Biology, nursing, and psychology are the strongest academically. Business is the largest.

Required: To graduate, students must complete a general education core consisting of courses in communications/English composition, health and personal development, history, foreign language/humanities, science/math, and social science. Students must complete a total of 128 credits, at least 45 of which must be upper divisional, and have a minimum 2.0 GPA. Courses in phys ed and computer literacy are required.

Special: APSU offers cooperative programs in nuclear medicine and radiological technology with Vanderbilt University. Work-study programs and dual majors are available. Credit may be granted for military experience. Pass/fail grading options are available. There are 21 national honor societies, and a freshman honors program.

Faculty/Classroom: 59% of faculty are male; 41%, female. All teach undergraduates. No introductory courses are taught by graduate students. The average class size in an introductory lecture is 24; in a laboratory, 16; and in a regular course, 25.

Requirements: The SAT I or ACT is required. In addition, applicants must be graduates of an accredited secondary school or have a GED. 14 academic units are required, including 4 units of English, 2 units each of algebra, natural science, and a foreign language, and 1 unit each of visual and/or performing arts, geometry, social studies, and U.S. history. Applicants who do not meet these requirements may be considered for admission. A GPA of 2.75 is required. AP and CLEP credits are accepted.

Procedure: Freshmen are admitted to all sessions. There is an early admissions plan. Check with school for current application deadlines. The fall 2001 application fee was $15. Notification is sent on a rolling basis.

Transfer: Applicants must have a 2.0 GPA. Grades of D or better will transfer for credit. Application deadlines are the same as those for freshmen. 24 credits of 128 must be completed at APSU.

Visiting: There are regularly scheduled orientations for prospective students. There are guides for informal visits. To schedule a visit, contact the Admissions Office.

Financial Aid: 25% of undergraduates work part time. Tennessee residents should submit the Tennessee edition of the FFS. Check with the school for current deadline.

International Students: There were 30 international students enrolled in a recent year. They must score 500 on the written TOEFL.

Computers: The mainframe is a DEC VAX. All students may access the system. There are no time limits and no fees.

Graduates: In a recent year, 776 bachelor's degrees were awarded. The most popular majors were elementary education (13%), general business (12%), and nursing (10%).

Admissions Contact: Charles McCorkle, Director of Admissions. A video is available. E-mail: *admissions@apsu01.apsu.edu*
Web: *www.apsu.edu*

BELMONT UNIVERSITY
Nashville, TN 37212-3757 C-2
(615) 460-6785
(800) 56E-NROL; Fax: (615) 460-5434

Full-time: 950 men, 1371 women	**Faculty:** 206; IIA, --$
Part-time: 88 men, 208 women	**Ph.D.s:** 67%
Graduate: 197 men, 315 women	**Student/Faculty:** 11 to 1
Year: semesters, summer session	**Tuition:** $13,400
Application Deadline: August 1	**Room & Board:** $5666
Freshman Class: 1265 applied, 938 accepted, 510 enrolled	
SAT I Verbal/Math: 570/560	**ACT:** 25 **VERY COMPETITIVE**

Belmont University, founded in 1951, is a private, Christian liberal arts university affiliated with the Tennessee Baptist Convention. There are 6 undergraduate and 4 graduate schools. In addition to regional accreditation, Belmont has baccalaureate program accreditation with CSWE, NASM, NCATE, and NLN. The library contains 178,457 volumes, 17,402 microform items, and 24,125 audiovisual forms/CDs, and subscribes to 1445 periodicals. Computerized library services include the card catalog, interlibrary loans, and database searching. Special learning facilities include a learning resource center, art gallery, radio station, and TV station. The 55-acre campus is in an urban area in Nashville. Including residence halls, there are 22 buildings.

Student Life: 65% of undergraduates are from Tennessee. Others are from 48 states, 12 foreign countries, and Canada. 78% are from public schools. 91% are white. 75% are Protestant; 26% claim no religious affiliation. The average age of freshmen is 18; all undergraduates, 21. 26% do not continue beyond their first year; 51% remain to graduate.

Housing: 1300 students can be accommodated in college housing, which includes single-sex dormitories, on-campus apartments, off-campus apartments, and married-student housing. In addition, there are honors houses, language houses, and special-interest houses. On-campus housing is guaranteed for all 4 years. 50% of students live on campus; of those, 30% remain on campus on weekends. Alcohol is not permitted. All students may keep cars.

Activities: 8% of men belong to 2 national fraternities; 8% of women belong to 1 local and 3 national sororities. There are 57 groups on campus, including art, band, cheerleading, choir, chorale, chorus, computers, dance, drama, drill team, ethnic, film, honors, international, jazz band, literary magazine, marching band, musical theater, newspaper, orchestra, pep band, photography, political, professional, radio and TV, religious, social, social service, student government, symphony, and yearbook. Popular campus events include formal dance events.

Sports: There are 6 intercollegiate sports for men and 4 for women, and 4 intramural sports for men and 4 for women. Facilities include a student activities center, which is under construction.

Disabled Students: 99% of the campus is accessible. Wheelchair ramps, elevators, special parking, specially equipped rest rooms, special class scheduling, and lowered drinking fountains are available.

Services: Counseling and information services are available, as is tutoring in some subjects. There is remedial math, reading, and writing. Writing and computer labs are available.

Campus Safety and Security: Measures include 24-hour foot and vehicle patrol, self-defense education, escort service, and shuttle buses. There are informal discussions, pamphlets/posters/films, emergency telephones, and lighted pathways/sidewalks.

Programs of Study: Belmont confers B.A., B.S., B.B.A., B.F.A., B.M., and B.S.N. degrees. Master's degrees are also awarded. Bachelor's degrees are awarded in BIOLOGICAL SCIENCE (biology/biological science), BUSINESS (accounting, business administration and management, hotel/motel and restaurant management, management science, and marketing/retailing/merchandising), COMMUNICATIONS AND THE ARTS (communications, English, French, music, and music performance), COMPUTER AND PHYSICAL SCIENCE (chemistry, computer science, mathematics, and physics), EDUCATION (elementary, physical, and science), HEALTH PROFESSIONS (nursing), SOCIAL SCIENCE (economics, history, liberal arts/general studies, philosophy, political science/government, psychology, religion, and social work). Music, business, and humanities are the strongest academically. Business, music, and nursing are the largest.

Required: All students must complete at least 128 hours with a C average, including 22 to 24 hours in the major field. B.A. candidates are required to pursue a minor field. All programs except the B.B.A. require a core curriculum, which includes courses in language and literature, humanities (including religion), social sciences, science, math, and phys ed.

Special: Belmont offers study abroad, student-designed majors, and dual majors in math, physics, and chemistry. Dual degree programs are available with Auburn University and the University of Tennessee at Knoxville. Programs require 3 years of study at Belmont followed by 2 years at the other institution. There are 11 national honor societies, a freshman honors program, and 3 departmental honors programs.

Faculty/Classroom: 51% of faculty are male; 49%, female. All teach undergraduates, 2% do research, and 2% do both. No introductory courses are taught by graduate students. The average class size in an introductory lecture is 25; in a laboratory, 24; and in a regular course, 22.

Admissions: 74% of the 2001-2002 applicants were accepted. The SAT I scores for the 2001-2002 freshman class were: Verbal--15% below 500, 46% between 500 and 599, 32% between 600 and 700, and 7% above 700; Math--23% below 500, 44% between 500 and 599, 28% between 600 and 700, and 5% above 700. The ACT scores were 20% below 21, 30% between 21 and 23, 29% between 24 and 26, 13% between 27 and 28, and 8% above 28. 57% of the current freshmen were in the top fifth of their class; 78% were in the top two fifths. 15 freshmen graduated first in their class.

Requirements: The ACT is required and the SAT I is recommended. In addition, the university expects a composite score of at least 21 on the ACT and 1000 on the SAT I. Applicants should be high school graduates or hold the GED. Secondary preparation should include 4 units of English, 3 of math, and 2 each of a foreign language, history, science, and social studies. Potential music majors must audition. Belmont requires applicants to be in the upper 50% of their class. A GPA of 3.0 is required. AP and CLEP credits are accepted. Important factors in the admissions decision are advanced placement or honor courses, recommendations by school officials, and evidence of special talent. Applications are accepted on computer disk and on-line via CollegeView and ExPAN.

Procedure: Freshmen are admitted fall, spring, and summer. Entrance exams should be taken during the junior or senior year. There is an early admissions plan. Applications should be filed by August 1 for fall entry and December 1 for spring entry. Notification is sent on a rolling basis. The fall 2001 application fee was $35.

Transfer: 297 transfer students enrolled in 2001-2002. Applicants should present an above average GPA in previous college work and be able to meet freshman entrance requirements. Those with fewer than 64 credit hours must also submit SAT I or ACT scores. 32 credits of 128 must be completed at Belmont.

Visiting: There are regularly scheduled orientations for prospective students, consisting of a 2-day program in summer and a 4-day program right before classes begin. There are guides for informal visits and visitors may sit in on classes and stay overnight. To schedule a visit, contact the Admissions Office.

Financial Aid: In 2001-2002, 67% of all freshmen and 47% of continuing students received some form of financial aid. 45% of freshmen and 46% of continuing students received need-based aid. The average freshman award was $6027. Of that total, scholarships or need-based grants averaged $3884 ($16,500 maximum); loans averaged $3512 ($14,800 maximum); and work contracts averaged $2000. 14% of undergraduates work part time. Average annual earnings from campus work are $2000. Belmont is a member of CSS. The FAFSA is required. The fall application deadline is March 1.

International Students: There are 10 international students enrolled. They must score 500 on the written TOEFL and also take the SAT I or the ACT, scoring 1000 on the SAT I.

Computers: The mainframe is a Sun 3500 server. 5 computer labs across campus provide students with access to the campus network, applications, and the Internet. Residence halls are wired for computer access with student-provided computers. All students may access the system. There are no time limits and no fees.

Graduates: In 2001, 543 bachelor's degrees were awarded. The most popular majors were music business (32%), business administration (22%), and liberal arts (8%). In an average class, 2% graduate in 3 years, 33% in 4 years, 50% in 5 years, and 51% in 6 years. 78 companies recruited on campus in 2000-2001. Of the 2000 graduating class, 30% were enrolled in graduate school within 6 months of graduation and 30% were employed.

Admissions Contact: Kathryn H. Baugher, Dean of Enrollment Services. A video is available. E-mail: *buadmission@belmont.edu*
Web: *www.belmont@edu*

BETHEL COLLEGE — B-3

McKenzie, TN 38201 — **(731) 352-4030; Fax: (731) 352-4069**

Full-time: 351 men, 387 women	**Faculty:** 35; IIB, --$
Part-time: 40 men, 62 women	**Ph.D.s:** 67%
Graduate: 43 men, 61 women	**Student/Faculty:** 21 to 1
Year: semesters, summer session	**Tuition:** $8430
Application Deadline: August 30	**Room & Board:** $4550
Freshman Class: 473 applied, 299 accepted, 212 enrolled	
ACT: 20	**COMPETITIVE**

Bethel College, established in 1842, is a private institution affiliated with the Cumberland Presbyterian Church offering undergraduate degrees through its divisions of humanities, natural sciences, social sciences, education, and health science. The library contains 79,164 volumes, 185 microform items, and 2166 audiovisual forms/CDs, and subscribes to 1208 periodicals. Computerized library services include the card catalog, interlibrary loans, and database searching. Special learning facilities include a learning resource center. The 100-acre campus is in a small town 120 miles northeast of Memphis. Including residence halls, there are 10 buildings.

Student Life: 79% of undergraduates are from Tennessee. Others are from 21 states, 2 foreign countries, and Canada. 99% are from public schools. 78% are white; 19% African American. 72% are Protestant; 25% claim no religious affiliation. The average age of freshmen is 18; all undergraduates, 28. 46% do not continue beyond their first year; 25% remain to graduate.

Housing: 290 students can be accommodated in college housing, which includes single-sex and coed dormitories. On-campus housing is guaranteed for the freshman year only and is available on a first-come, first-served basis. 55% of students commute. Alcohol is not permitted. All students may keep cars.

Activities: 50% of men belong to 5 local fraternities; 50% of women belong to 5 local sororities. There are 25 groups on campus, including art, cheerleading, choir, chorus, drama, honors, musical theater, newspaper, pep band, political, professional, religious, social, student government, and yearbook.

Sports: There are 8 intercollegiate sports for men and 7 for women, and 9 intramural sports for men and 8 for women. Facilities include a gym with a heated indoor pool and weight room, a field house, and a student center with pool tables, Ping-Pong tables, and other such equipment. There is also a baseball field and beach volleyball and tennis courts.

Disabled Students: 75% of the campus is accessible. Wheelchair ramps, special parking, specially equipped rest rooms, special class scheduling, lowered drinking fountains, and lowered telephones are available.

Services: Counseling and information services are available, as is tutoring in every subject. There is remedial math, reading, and writing. Tutoring is available free of charge to students.

Campus Safety and Security: Measures include informal discussions, pamphlets/posters/films, lighted pathways/sidewalks, and a security guard at night.

Programs of Study: Bethel confers B.A. and B.S. degrees. Master's degrees are also awarded. Bachelor's degrees are awarded in BIOLOGICAL SCIENCE (biology/biological science and zoology), BUSINESS (business administration and management and management science), COMMUNICATIONS AND THE ARTS (English), COMPUTER AND PHYSICAL SCIENCE (chemistry and mathematics), EDUCATION (early childhood, education of the exceptional child, health, and physical), ENGINEERING AND ENVIRONMENTAL DESIGN (preengineering), SOCIAL SCIENCE (child psychology/development, history, human services, liberal arts/general studies, physical fitness/movement, psychology, and sociology). Education, organizational management, and biology are the strongest academically. Education and organizational management are the largest.

Required: Requirements for graduation include courses in English, Western literature and arts, history, lab science, math, phys ed, and religion. Students must complete 128 to 132 hours with a minimum GPA of 2.0. A thesis is required in some majors.

Special: Bethel offers evening classes for adults, in-service training for teachers, off-site classes, an accelerated degree program in organizational management, student-designed majors, a 3-2 engineering program with Tennessee Technical University, internships, work-study, nondegree study, a pass/fail option, and portfolio credit for prior learning and work experience. There is 1 national honor society and a freshman honors program.

Faculty/Classroom: 65% of faculty are male; 35%, female. All teach undergraduates, 5% do research, and 5% do both. No introductory courses are taught by graduate students. The average class size in an introductory lecture is 17; in a laboratory, 20; and in a regular course, 14.

Admissions: 63% of the 2001-2002 applicants were accepted. 15% of the current freshmen were in the top fifth of their class; 58% were in the top two fifths.

Requirements: The SAT I or ACT is required. In addition, applicants must graduate from an accredited secondary school. Those ranking in the upper half of their class or scoring at least 16 on the ACT or 800 on the SAT I are granted regular acceptance. Other applicants may be admitted conditionally. Other factors in the admission procedure are standardized test scores, an interview, evidence of special talent, and personality. A GPA of 2.5 is required. AP and CLEP credits are accepted. Important factors in the admissions decision are advanced placement or honor courses, leadership record, and parents or siblings attending the school. An application is available at the school's web site.

Procedure: Freshmen are admitted to all sessions. Entrance exams should be taken prior to enrollment, preferably by fall of the senior year. Applications should be filed by August 30 for fall entry, January 10 for spring entry, and June 5 for summer entry, along with a $30 fee. Notification is sent on a rolling basis.

Transfer: 59 transfer students enrolled in a recent year. Applicants must meet the GPA requirements for the number of hours they previously earned. Up to 68 hours may be transferred from community or junior colleges. Students with fewer than 12 semester hours must submit high school transcripts, ACT or SAT I scores, and take Bethel's placement test. 32 of the last 38 credits of 128 to 132 must be completed at Bethel.

Visiting: There are regularly scheduled orientations for prospective students. Students receive information about the college, dorms, and the

ThinkPad program; they meet advisers, register for classes, and meet with the financial aid and business office. There are guides for informal visits and visitors may sit in on classes and stay overnight. To schedule a visit, contact the Admissions Office.

Financial Aid: In 2001-2002, 98% of all students received some form of financial aid. 92% of freshmen and 90% of continuing students received need-based aid. The average freshman award was $12,538. Of that total, scholarships or need-based grants averaged $5491; loans averaged $2325; work contracts averaged $1000; and institutional scholarships (academic or athletic) averaged $3722. 25% of undergraduates work part time. Average annual earnings from campus work are $1000. The FAFSA and the college's own financial statement are required. The fall application deadline is March 15.

International Students: There are 8 international students enrolled. The school actively recruits these students. It is recommended tat students take the TOEFL and score 500 or higher. The SAT I or the ACT is required.

Computers: Bethel College is part of the ThinkPad University Program. Each full-time student and faculty member receives an IBM ThinkPad (laptop computer) as part of full-time tuition. All students may access the system. Connections to the campus LAN and the Internet are available throughout campus and in each dorm room. There are no time limits and no fees.

Graduates: In 2001, 146 bachelor's degrees were awarded. The most popular majors were organizational management (82%), education (8%), and biology (4%). In an average class, 14% graduate in 4 years, 17% in 5 years, and 19% in 6 years. Of the 2000 graduating class, 21% were enrolled in graduate school within 6 months of graduation and 70% were employed.

Admissions Contact: Tina Hodges, Director od Admissions.
E-mail: *admissions@bethel-college.edu* Web: *www.bethel-college.edu*

BRYAN COLLEGE

Dayton, TN 37321-7000 D-3
(423) 775-7204
(800) 277-9522; Fax: (423) 775-7199

Full-time: 560 men and women	**Faculty:** 30
Part-time: 34 men and women	**Ph.D.s:** 90%
Graduate: none	**Student/Faculty:** 19 to 1
Year: semesters, summer session	**Tuition:** $12,200
Application Deadline: open	**Room & Board:** $4200
Freshman Class: 379 applied, 300 accepted, 133 enrolled	
SAT I Verbal/Math: 570/540	**ACT:** 24 **VERY COMPETITIVE**

Bryan College, founded in 1930, is a private, nonprofit, Christian institution that is evangelical and interdenominational. Its emphases are on the liberal arts, business, health science, fine arts, Bible and religious studies, music, and teacher preparation. The library contains 90,000 volumes, 13,489 microform items, and 3015 audiovisual forms/CDs, and subscribes to 700 periodicals. Computerized library services include the card catalog, interlibrary loans, and database searching. Special learning facilities include a museum of natural science. The 130-acre campus is in a small town 40 miles north of Chattanooga. Including residence halls, there are 28 buildings.

Student Life: 65% of undergraduates are from out of state, mostly the South. Others are from 33 states, 10 foreign countries, and Canada. 40% are from public schools. 94% are white. Most are Protestant. The average age of freshmen is 18; all undergraduates, 20. 24% do not continue beyond their first year; 55% remain to graduate.

Housing: 551 students can be accommodated in college housing, which includes single-sex dormitories and married-student housing. On-campus housing is guaranteed for all 4 years. 80% of students live on campus; of those, 75% remain on campus on weekends. Alcohol is not permitted. All students may keep cars.

Activities: There are no fraternities or sororities. There are 17 groups on campus, including art, cheerleading, choir, chorale, computers, drama, honors, international, literary magazine, musical theater, newspaper, orchestra, pep band, photography, religious, social, social service, student government, and yearbook. Popular campus events include fine arts series.

Sports: There are 3 intercollegiate sports for men and 4 for women, and 6 intramural sports for men and 6 for women. Facilities include a 1200-seat gym, soccer fields, a baseball field, an outdoor swimming pool, and 4 tennis courts.

Disabled Students: All of the campus is accessible. Wheelchair ramps, elevators, special parking, specially equipped rest rooms, and lowered drinking fountains are available.

Services: Counseling and information services are available, as is tutoring in some subjects, including math and English. There is remedial math, reading, and writing.

Campus Safety and Security: Measures include self-defense education, escort service, informal discussions, and pamphlets/posters/films. There are lighted pathways/sidewalks and a night security patrol.

Programs of Study: Bryan confers B.A. and B.S. degrees. Associate degrees are also awarded. Bachelor's degrees are awarded in BIOLOGICAL SCIENCE (biology/biological science), BUSINESS (business administration and management), COMMUNICATIONS AND THE ARTS (communications, English, music, and Spanish), COMPUTER AND PHYSICAL SCIENCE (computer science and mathematics), EDUCATION (athletic training, elementary, physical, and science), HEALTH PROFESSIONS (exercise science), SOCIAL SCIENCE (Christian studies, history, liberal arts/general studies, psychology, and religion).

Required: To graduate, students must complete 124 semester hours, with a minimum of 30 in the major, and maintain a GPA of at least 2.0. Distribution requirements include 16 semester hours in the Bible, 9 in communications, 7 each in personal development and natural science, and 6 each in the humanities and social science. Specific courses that must be taken include 7 semester hours in science, 6 hours each in freshman English, a foreign language, and history of Western civilization, 3 each in speech, general psychology, introduction to literature, fine arts, and phys ed. In addition, math and English proficiency must be met, as well as a comprehensive exam in the major.

Special: Special academic programs include practicums in business and psychology, and psychology internships. An American Studies Program in Washington and a study-abroad Latin American Studies Program are offered through the Christian College coalition. A dual major in Christian education and church music is available. There is a freshman honors program.

Faculty/Classroom: 64% of faculty are male; 36%, female. All teach undergraduates. The average class size in an introductory lecture is 27; in a laboratory, 13; and in a regular course, 16.

Admissions: 79% of the 2001-2002 applicants were accepted.

Requirements: The SAT I or ACT is required with the ACT preferred. Clear admission is granted to applicants who have graduated from an approved high school and who have a minimum GPA of 2.5 with a minimum composite score of 18 on the ACT or 860 on the SAT I; clear admission is also granted to applicants with a minimum GPA of 2.0 and a composite score of 20 on the ACT or 920 on the SAT I. The high school record should include a minimum of 18 academic credits with a recommended distribution of 4 units of English, 3 each of math, science, and social science/humanities, and 2 of a foreign language. The GED is also accepted. References are required and an interview is recommended. A GPA of 2.5 is required. AP and CLEP credits are accepted. Important factors in the admissions decision are parents or siblings attending the school, recommendations by alumni, and recommendations by school officials. Applications are accepted on-line at *www.bryan.edu*.

Procedure: Freshmen are admitted fall and spring. Entrance exams should be taken before the fall of the senior year in high school. There are early admissions and deferred admissions plans. Application deadlines are open. The application fee is $30. Notification is sent on a rolling basis. A waiting list is an active part of the admissions procedure.

Transfer: 31 transfer students enrolled in 2001-2002. Applicants need a minimum GPA of 2.0. 31 credits of 124 must be completed at Bryan.

Visiting: There are regularly scheduled orientations for prospective students, consisting of college visitation weekends, which include a tour of the campus, sitting in on classes and chapel, meeting with professors in the area of academic interest, staying with current students in residence halls, and eating meals in the dining room. There are guides for informal visits and visitors may sit in on classes and stay overnight. To schedule a visit, contact Jody Cheon, Admissions Counselor at (423) 775-7211 or *cheonjo@bryan.edu*.

Financial Aid: In 2001-2002, 98% of all freshmen and 94% of continuing students received some form of financial aid. 65% of freshmen and 56% of continuing students received need-based aid. The average freshman award was $9373. Of that total, scholarships or need-based grants averaged $6426 ($19,000 maximum); loans averaged $4475 ($12,625 maximum); and work contracts averaged $1500 ($2000 maximum). 55% of undergraduates work part time. Average annual earnings from campus work are $1500. The average financial indebtedness of the 2001 graduate was $14,500. The FAFSA and the college's own financial statement are required. The fall application deadline is May 1.

International Students: There are 13 international students enrolled. They must score 500 on the written TOEFL and also take the ACT.

Computers: There are PCs available in computer labs in both residence halls and academic areas. Residence hall rooms have campus network hookups available. All students may access the system at all times. There are no time limits and no fees.

Graduates: In 2001, 102 bachelor's degrees were awarded. In an average class, 49% graduate in 4 years, 50% in 5 years, and 53% in 6 years.

Admissions Contact: Mark Cruver, Dean of Admissions and Enrollment Management. A video is available. E-mail: *admiss@bryan.edu*
Web: *www.bryan.edu*

CARSON-NEWMAN COLLEGE
Jefferson City, TN 37760 E-2
(865) 471-2000
(800) 678-9061; Fax: (865) 471-3502

Full-time: 779 men, 1028 women | **Faculty:** 122; IIB, --$
Part-time: 53 men, 131 women | **Ph.D.s:** 65%
Graduate: 42 men, 162 women | **Student/Faculty:** 15 to 1
Year: semesters, summer session | **Tuition:** $12,380
Application Deadline: August 15 | **Room & Board:** $4110
Freshman Class: 1194 applied, 1031 accepted, 410 enrolled
ACT: 23 COMPETITIVE

Carson-Newman College, founded in 1851, is a private liberal arts college affiliated with the Tennessee Baptist Convention. In addition to regional accreditation, Carson-Newman has baccalaureate program accreditation with ADA, AHEA, NASAD, NASM, NCATE, and NLN. The library contains 300,000 volumes, 221,960 microform items, and 15,000 audiovisual forms/CDs, and subscribes to 2000 periodicals. Computerized library services include the digital card catalog, interlibrary loans, and database searching. Special learning facilities include a learning resource center, art gallery, natural history museum, radio station, and TV station. The 100-acre campus is in a small town 27 miles northeast of Knoxville. Including residence halls, there are 27 buildings.

Student Life: 65% of undergraduates are from Tennessee. Others are from Canada. 95% are from public schools. 88% are white. Most are Protestant. The average age of freshmen is 18; all undergraduates, 22. 23% do not continue beyond their first year; 56% remain to graduate.

Housing: 1430 students can be accommodated in college housing, which includes single-sex dormitories, on-campus apartments, and married-student housing. In addition, there are honors houses. On-campus housing is guaranteed for all 4 years. 54% of students live on campus; of those, 50% remain on campus on weekends. Alcohol is not permitted. All students may keep cars.

Activities: 20% of men belong to 2 local fraternities and 1 national fraternity; 20% of women belong to 2 local sororities and 1 national sorority. There are 55 groups on campus, including art, band, cheerleading, chess, choir, chorale, chorus, computers, dance, debate, drama, drill team, ethnic, film, forensics, honors, international, jazz band, literary magazine, marching band, musical theater, newspaper, orchestra, pep band, photography, political, professional, radio and TV, religious, social, social service, student government, and yearbook. Popular campus events include Spring Fest, Fall Formal, and Honors Convocation.

Sports: There are 10 intercollegiate sports for men and 6 for women, and 40 intramural sports for men and 40 for women. Facilities include a gym, a football stadium, soccer, baseball, and softball fields, a pool, and a student center with 3 racquetball courts, 3 gyms, a weight room, an Olympic-size pool, a Jacuzzi, and an outdoor cafe.

Disabled Students: 10% of the campus is accessible. Wheelchair ramps, elevators, special parking, and special class scheduling are available.

Services: Counseling and information services are available, as is tutoring in most subjects, including English, math, and science. There is remedial math, reading, and writing.

Campus Safety and Security: Measures include 24-hour foot and vehicle patrol, self-defense education, escort service, and informal discussions. There are pamphlets/posters/films and lighted pathways/sidewalks.

Programs of Study: Carson-Newman confers B.A., B.S., B.M., B.S.M., and B.S.N. degrees. Associate and master's degrees are also awarded. Bachelor's degrees are awarded in BIOLOGICAL SCIENCE (biology/biological science), BUSINESS (accounting, business administration and management, and business economics), COMMUNICATIONS AND THE ARTS (communications, English, fine arts, French, languages, music, and Spanish), EDUCATION (art, early childhood, elementary, foreign languages, health, home economics, middle school, music, science, and secondary), HEALTH PROFESSIONS (nursing and physical therapy), SOCIAL SCIENCE (economics, history, philosophy, psychology, religion, social science, and sociology). Nursing, music, and biology are the strongest academically. Communication arts, biology, and business are the largest.

Required: All students must complete 128 credit hours, including Composition I and II, Survey of Old Testament, Survey of New Testament, 15 hours in English and communications, 9 in social sciences, 6 each in religion, humanities, and science, and 3 each in history and literature. The major requires 40 to 48 hours. Students must achieve a minimum GPA of 2.0.

Special: The college offers internships, study in England, France, Japan, Hong Kong, and Spain, a Washington semester, on-campus work-study programs, B.A.-B.S. degrees, dual majors, a general studies degree, student-designed majors, and pass/fail options. Students may receive credit for life, military, or work experience. There is 1 national honor society, a freshman honors program, and 16 departmental honors programs.

Faculty/Classroom: 57% of faculty are male; 43%, female. All teach undergraduates and 40% do research. No introductory courses are taught by graduate students. The average class size in an introductory lecture is 20; in a laboratory, 16; and in a regular course, 17.

Admissions: 86% of the 2001-2002 applicants were accepted. The ACT scores for the 2001-2002 freshman class were: 34% below 21, 26% between 21 and 23, 22% between 24 and 26, 9% between 27 and 28, and 8% above 28. 10 freshmen graduated first in their class.

Requirements: The SAT I or ACT is required with a minimum composite score of 19 on the ACT or 920 on the SAT I. Applicants should be graduates of an accredited secondary school. The GED is accepted. 20 academic credits are required, including 4 units of English and 2 units each of history, math, science, and social studies. An essay, a portfolio, an audition, and an interview are recommended. Carson-Newman requires applicants to be in the upper 50% of their class. A GPA of 2.25 is required. AP and CLEP credits are accepted. Important factors in the admissions decision are advanced placement or honor courses, leadership record, and parents or siblings attending the school. Applications are accepted on-line via CollegeNet.

Procedure: Freshmen are admitted to all sessions. Entrance exams should be taken in the fall. There is a deferred admissions plan. Applications should be filed by August 15 for fall entry, December 15 for spring entry, and April 15 for summer entry, along with a $25 fee. Notification is sent on a rolling basis.

Transfer: 173 transfer students enrolled in 2001-2002. Transfer students should have a minimum GPA of 2.0. Either the SAT I or the ACT is required if the student has fewer than 32 hours of college credit. An interview is recommended. 32 credits of 128 must be completed at Carson-Newman.

Visiting: There are regularly scheduled orientations for prospective students, including information sessions, meetings with advisers, and preregistration. There are guides for informal visits and visitors may sit in on classes and stay overnight. To schedule a visit, contact the Admissions Office at *sgray@cn.edu*.

Financial Aid: In 2001-2002, 98% of all freshmen and 96% of continuing students received some form of financial aid. 71% of freshmen and 70% of continuing students received need-based aid. The average freshman award was $12,165. Of that total, scholarships or need-based grants averaged $7639 ($16,790 maximum); loans averaged $5235 ($6625 maximum); and work contracts averaged $1466 ($3200 maximum). 31% of undergraduates work part time. Average annual earnings from campus work are $1466. The average financial indebtedness of the 2001 graduate was $14,489. Carson-Newman is a member of CSS. The FAFSA and the college's own financial statement are required. The fall application deadline is April 1.

International Students: In a recent year, there were 48 international students enrolled. The school actively recruits these students. They must score 550 on the written TOEFL or 213 on the electronic version and also take the SAT I, ACT, the college's own entrance exam, and an English proficiency exam, scoring 19 on the ACT or 920 on the SAT.

Computers: The mainframe is a DEC MicroVAX 3600. Carson-Newman has a word processing lab for Composition I and II students, a Mac lab with more than 20 terminals, and a CIS lab with more than 20 terminals. There is a campuswide network and all residence hall rooms are wired for PC hookup. Most departments have computer labs specifically for their majors. All students may access the system until the lab closes at 11 P.M. There are no time limits. The fee is $340 per semester. It is strongly recommended that all students have a personal computer.

Graduates: In 2001, 420 bachelor's degrees were awarded. The most popular majors were education (22%), business administration (7%), and biology (7%). In an average class, 44% graduate in 4 years, 56% in 5 years, and 57% in 6 years. 35 companies recruited on campus in 2000-2001. Of the 2000 graduating class, 35% were enrolled in graduate school within 6 months of graduation and 75% were employed.

Admissions Contact: Sheryl M. Gray, Director of Admissions.
E-mail: *sgray@cncadmnt.cn.edu* Web: *www.cn.edu*

CHRISTIAN BROTHERS UNIVERSITY
Memphis, TN 38104-5581 A-4
(901) 321-3205
(800) 288-7576; Fax: (901) 321-3202

Full-time: 625 men, 690 women | **Faculty:** 82
Part-time: 116 men, 228 women | **Ph.D.s:** 90%
Graduate: 180 men, 284 women | **Student/Faculty:** 16 to 1
Year: semesters, summer session | **Tuition:** $15,300
Application Deadline: July 15 | **Room & Board:** $4250
Freshman Class: 888 applied, 730 accepted, 289 enrolled
SAT I Verbal/Math: 553/562 **ACT:** 24 VERY COMPETITIVE

Christian Brothers University, founded in 1871, is a private, nonprofit institution affiliated with the Roman Catholic Church. Its undergraduate and graduate programs emphasize the liberal arts and sciences, business, engineering and engineering management, health science, telecommunications management, and teacher preparation. There are 4 undergraduate and 3 graduate schools. In addition to regional accreditation, CBU has baccalaureate program accreditation with ABET. The library con-

tains 100,000 volumes, 4000 microform items, and 300 audiovisual forms/CDs, and subscribes to 560 periodicals. Computerized library services include the card catalog, interlibrary loans, and database searching. Special learning facilities include a learning resource center and art gallery. The 70-acre campus is in an urban area in Memphis. Including residence halls, there are 18 buildings.
Student Life: 80% of undergraduates are from Tennessee. Others are from 31 states and 27 foreign countries. 68% are from public schools. 58% are white; 28% African American. 71% are Protestant; 27% Catholic. The average age of freshmen is 20; all undergraduates, 23. 20% do not continue beyond their first year; 45% remain to graduate.
Housing: 650 students can be accommodated in college housing, which includes single-sex and coed dormitories and on-campus apartments. Quiet floors in residence halls are available. On-campus housing is guaranteed for the freshman year only, is available on a first-come, first-served basis, and is available on a lottery system for upperclassmen. Priority is given to out-of-town students. 69% of students commute. All students may keep cars.
Activities: 24% of men belong to 3 national fraternities; 20% of women belong to 1 local and 3 national sororities. There are 40 groups on campus, including art, cheerleading, chess, chorale, chorus, computers, drama, ethnic, honors, international, literary magazine, musical theater, newspaper, political, professional, religious, social, student government, and yearbook. Popular campus events include Riverboat Dance, Spring Formal, and Mardi Gras.
Sports: There are 4 intercollegiate sports for men and 3 for women, and 14 intramural sports for men and 8 for women. Facilities include a swimming pool, gym, theater, multimedia auditorium, batting cage, jogging track, basketball/volleyball and handball/racquetball courts, baseball and soccer fields, tennis courts, and weight-training facilities.
Disabled Students: 90% of the campus is accessible. Wheelchair ramps, elevators, special parking, and specially equipped rest rooms are available.
Services: Counseling and information services are available, as is tutoring in most subjects. CBU also has centers for math, language, and writing.
Campus Safety and Security: Measures include 24-hour foot and vehicle patrol, self-defense education, pamphlets/posters/films, and emergency telephones. There are lighted pathways/sidewalks.
Programs of Study: CBU confers B.A. and B.S. degrees. Master's degrees are also awarded. Bachelor's degrees are awarded in BIOLOGICAL SCIENCE (biology/biological science), BUSINESS (accounting, business administration and management, business economics, management science, and marketing/retailing/merchandising), COMMUNICATIONS AND THE ARTS (English, language arts, and technical and business writing), COMPUTER AND PHYSICAL SCIENCE (chemistry, computer science, information sciences and systems, mathematics, natural sciences, and physics), ENGINEERING AND ENVIRONMENTAL DESIGN (chemical engineering, civil engineering, electrical/electronics engineering, engineering physics, and mechanical engineering), SOCIAL SCIENCE (applied psychology, history, human development, liberal arts/general studies, psychology, religion, and social studies). Engineering, accounting, and psychology are the strongest academically. Psychology, information sciences, and accounting are the largest.
Required: To graduate, students must complete at least 122 semester hours, with a varying number of hours in the major, and maintain a minimum GPA of 2.0. General education requirements, totaling 38 to 40 semester hours, consist of 12 hours of humanities, 6 hours each of communication skills, math, and social sciences, 4 hours of natural and physical sciences, 2 to 4 hours of business/technology, and 2 hours of health/phys ed. Individual schools vary in their core requirements.
Special: Special academic programs include on-campus work-study, study abroad, and internships for all juniors and seniors. There is cross-registration with Memphis College of Art, Memphis Theological Seminary, and LeMoyne-Owen College. An accelerated degree program is available to all business and psychology majors through the evening program, and a general studies degree is offered. Up to 36 hours of nondegree study is possible, as are dual majors and pass/fail options. Numerous teacher licensure programs are also offered. There are 3 national honor societies, and a freshman honors program.
Faculty/Classroom: 67% of faculty are male; 33%, female. 95% teach undergraduates. No introductory courses are taught by graduate students. The average class size in an introductory lecture is 22; in a laboratory, 15; and in a regular course, 16.
Admissions: 82% of the 2001-2002 applicants were accepted. The SAT I scores for the 2001-2002 freshman class were: Verbal--27% below 500, 46% between 500 and 599, 19% between 600 and 700, and 8% above 700; Math--28% below 500, 30% between 500 and 599, 29% between 600 and 700, and 13% above 700. The ACT scores were 26% below 21, 28% between 21 and 23, 22% between 24 and 26, 9% between 27 and 28, and 14% above 28. 52% of the current freshmen were in the top fifth of their class; 76% were in the top two fifths. 11 freshmen graduated first in their class.
Requirements: The SAT I or ACT is required. In addition, the SAT I score should be 830, 415 verbal and 415 math; the ACT score should be 20. Other admissions requirements include graduation from an accredited secondary school, with a college-preparatory curriculum recommended. The GED is also accepted. An interview is advised. CBU requires applicants to be in the upper 67% of their class. A GPA of 2.5 is required. AP and CLEP credits are accepted. Important factors in the admissions decision are advanced placement or honor courses, leadership record, and recommendations by school officials. Applications are accepted on-line at the school's web site.
Procedure: Freshmen are admitted to all sessions. Entrance exams should be taken by the end of the junior year. There is a deferred admissions plan. Applications should be filed by July 15 for fall entry, January 1 for spring entry, and May 15 for summer entry. The fall 2001 application fee was $25. Notification is sent on a rolling basis.
Transfer: 50 transfer students enrolled in 2001-2002. Transfer students should have a minimum GPA of 2.5 and be in good academic and disciplinary standing. A minimum SAT I score of 830 is recommended, as is a minimum ACT score of 20. An interview is advised. 35 credits of 122 must be completed at CBU.
Visiting: There are regularly scheduled orientations for prospective students, including attendance at classes, meetings with professors and students, a campus tour, and meetings with admissions and financial aid representatives. There are guides for informal visits and visitors may sit in on classes and stay overnight. To schedule a visit, contact Courtney Fee, Dean of Admissions, at *cfee@cbu.edu*.
Financial Aid: In 2001-2002, 94% of all freshmen and 91% of continuing students received some form of financial aid. 90% of freshmen received need-based aid. Scholarships or need-based grants averaged $6200 ($20,350 maximum); loans averaged $3000 ($5625 maximum); and work contracts averaged $1000 ($1500 maximum). 87% of undergraduates work part time. Average annual earnings from campus work are $1000. The average financial indebtedness of the 2001 graduate was $17,600. The FAFSA is required.
International Students: There are 74 international students enrolled. The school actively recruits these students. They must score 500 on the written TOEFL.
Computers: The mainframe is a Sun Enterprise 450. There are also 250 PCs and terminals available for student use in computer centers and academic buildings. There is a campuswide fiber-optic-based LAN and software for word processing, spreadsheets, databases, engineering, accounting, calculus, math, writing, chemistry, physics, and biology. Students with their own PCs may also access the Internet from dorm rooms. All students may access the system during the 93.5 hours per week of computer center operation; 24-hour dial-in phone access is available. There are no time limits and no fees.
Graduates: In 2001, 290 bachelor's degrees were awarded. The most popular majors were information sciences (15%), psychology (12%), and accounting (10%). In an average class, 35% graduate in 4 years, 46% in 5 years, and 53% in 6 years. 32 companies recruited on campus in 2000-2001. Of the 2000 graduating class, 10% were enrolled in graduate school within 6 months of graduation and 90% were employed.
Admissions Contact: Courtney Fee, Dean of Admissions.
E-mail: *admissions@cbu.edu* Web: *http://www.cbu.edu*

CRICHTON COLLEGE — A-3
Memphis, TN 38115 — (901) 367-3888
(800) 960-9777; Fax: (901) 366-2650

Full-time: 369 men, 551 women	**Faculty:** 28; IIB, --$
Part-time: 49 men, 74 women	**Ph.D.s:** 60%
Graduate: none	**Student/Faculty:** 33 to 1
Year: semesters, summer session	**Tuition:** $9480
Application Deadline: open	**Room & Board:** $3200
Freshman Class: 300 applied	
ACT: required	**LESS COMPETITIVE**

Crichton College, founded in 1941, is an independent Christian liberal arts college offering programs in liberal arts, Bible, business, health science, religion, and teacher preparation. There are 5 undergraduate schools. The library contains 46,524 volumes, 21,535 microform items, and 1456 audiovisual forms/CDs, and subscribes to 300 periodicals. Computerized library services include the card catalog, interlibrary loans, and database searching. Special learning facilities include a learning resource center and 21st Century Classroom, and a tutoring center. The 58-acre campus is in a suburban area in Memphis. Including residence halls, there are 4 buildings.
Student Life: 86% of undergraduates are from Tennessee. Others are from 11 states and 5 foreign countries. 95% are from public schools. 48% are African American; 39% white. The average age of freshmen is 18; all undergraduates, 32. 50% do not continue beyond their first year; 50% remain to graduate.
Housing: 100 students can be accommodated in college housing, which includes single-sex off-campus apartments. College housing is guaranteed for all 4 years. 96% of students commute. Alcohol is not permitted. All students may keep cars.
Activities: There are no fraternities or sororities. There are many groups and organizations on campus, including chorale, chorus, debate,

drama, ethnic, forensics, musical theater, professional, religious, social, social service, student government, and yearbook. Popular campus events include film, drama, and lecture series, concerts, and Marriage and Family Conference.

Sports: There is 1 intercollegiate sport for men, and 4 intramural sports for men and 4 for women. Facilities include an 18-acre athletic complex with 4 baseball fields and 4 soccer fields, and an 84,000-square-foot athletic building with 2 basketball courts, an inside running track, an Olympic swimming pool, 4 racquetball courts, tennis courts, and bowling lanes.

Disabled Students: All of the campus is accessible. Wheelchair ramps, elevators, special parking, specially equipped rest rooms, and lowered drinking fountains are available.

Services: Counseling and information services are available, as is tutoring in most subjects. There is remedial math, reading, and writing.

Campus Safety and Security: Measures include 24-hour foot and vehicle patrol, informal discussions, lighted pathways/sidewalks, and security gates at entrances, and monitored security systems and alarm buttons in each apartment unit.

Programs of Study: Crichton confers B.A. and B.S. degrees. Bachelor's degrees are awarded in BIOLOGICAL SCIENCE (biology/biological science), BUSINESS (business administration and management and institutional management), COMMUNICATIONS AND THE ARTS (communications and English), COMPUTER AND PHYSICAL SCIENCE (chemistry), EDUCATION (elementary and secondary), SOCIAL SCIENCE (biblical studies, history, liberal arts/general studies, ministries, prelaw, and psychology). Organizational management, education, and psychology are the largest.

Required: Students must complete a minimum of 128 credit hours, and some disciplines require more. The number of hours for the major varies, but all students must take 15 hours of humanities, 3 to 12 of biblical studies, 9 of communications, 8 of natural science, 4 of health/phys ed, and 3 each of math and computer science. The minimum GPA required is 2.0, and for teacher education students, 2.5.

Special: B.A.-B.S. degrees, dual majors, and limited nondegree study are available. The college also offers internships with area businesses and institutions, a study abroad program in Scotland, and accelerated degrees in organizational management and teacher education.

Faculty/Classroom: 19% of faculty are male; 9%, female. All teach undergraduates, 4% do research, and 8% do both. The average class size in an introductory lecture is 33; in a laboratory, 15; and in a regular course, 17.

Admissions: 3% of the current freshmen were in the top fifth of their class; 10% were in the top two fifths.

Requirements: The ACT is required with a minimum composite score of 18. Students must have a high school diploma or hold the GED. An essay and an interview are required. AP and CLEP credits are accepted. Important factors in the admissions decision are advanced placement or honor courses, evidence of special talent, and leadership record. Applications are accepted on-line at the Crichton web site.

Procedure: Freshmen are admitted to all sessions. Entrance exams should be taken during orientation. There is a deferred admissions plan. Application deadlines are open. The application fee is $25. Notification is sent on a rolling basis.

Transfer: 89 transfer students enrolled in a recent year. Transfer students must have a minimum GPA of 2.0. An interview is required. 30 credits of 128 must be completed at Crichton.

Visiting: There are regularly scheduled orientations for prospective students, including a preview of all college departments. There are guides for informal visits and visitors may sit in on classes. To schedule a visit, contact the Admissions Office.

Financial Aid: In 2001-2002, 61% of all freshmen and 98% of continuing students received some form of financial aid. 35% of freshmen and 58% of continuing students received need-based aid. The average freshman award was $11,356. Of that total, scholarships or need-based grants averaged $3873 ($8000 maximum); loans averaged $5666 ($6625 maximum); work contracts averaged $2868 ($5754 maximum); and outside aid averaged $1592 ($3600 maximum). 6% of undergraduates work part time. Average annual earnings from campus work are $3873. The average financial indebtedness of the 2001 graduate was $11,492. The FAFSA and the college's own financial statement are required. The fall application deadline is August 1.

International Students: There are 4 international students enrolled. The school actively recruits these students. They must score 500 on the written TOEFL and also take the ACT, scoring 18.

Computers: The campus network is run by 3 servers. 22 PCs are available in the computer learning center, 14 in the library, and 12 in the 21st Century Classroom. Students use the networked PCs to communicate via e-mail and chat rooms, to research subjects on the Internet, and to complete class requirements. All students may access the system. There are no time limits and no fees.

Graduates: In 2001, 223 bachelor's degrees were awarded. The most popular majors were organizational management (72%), elementary education (13%), and psychology (7%).

Admissions Contact: David Wilson. E-mail: *info@crichton.edu*
Web: *http://www.crichton.edu*

CUMBERLAND UNIVERSITY

Lebanon, TN 37087 — **C-2**
(615) 444-2562
(800) 467-0562; Fax: (615) 444-2569

Full-time: 390 men, 380 women	**Faculty:** 50
Part-time: 80 men, 120 women	**Ph.D.s:** 50%
Graduate: 90 men, 100 women	**Student/Faculty:** 15 to 1
Year: semesters, summer session	**Tuition:** $8700
Application Deadline: open	**Room & Board:** $3400
Freshman Class: n/av	
SAT I or ACT: recommended	**LESS COMPETITIVE**

Cumberland University, founded in 1842, is a private institution offering undergraduate and graduate degrees in business, education, and social sciences. Figures in the above capsule are approximate. There are 4 graduate schools. In addition to regional accreditation, Cumberland has baccalaureate program accreditation with NLN. The library contains 50,000 volumes and 1100 audiovisual forms/CDs, and subscribes to 500 periodicals. Computerized library services include the card catalog, interlibrary loans, and database searching. Special learning facilities include a learning resource center, art gallery, natural history museum, and radio station. The 44-acre campus is in a small town 28 miles east of Nashville. Including residence halls, there are 11 buildings.

Student Life: 85% of undergraduates are from Tennessee. Others are from 27 states, 15 foreign countries, and Canada. 75% are from public schools. 83% are white. The average age of freshmen is 19; all undergraduates, 26. 45% do not continue beyond their first year; 33% remain to graduate.

Housing: About 375 students can be accommodated in college housing, which includes single-sex dormitories, on-campus apartments, off-campus apartments, and fraternity houses. In addition, there are honors houses. On-campus housing is available on a first-come, first-served basis. 75% of students commute. Alcohol is not permitted. All students may keep cars.

Activities: 8% of men belong to 3 national fraternities; 2% of women belong to 1 local sororities. There are 15 groups on campus, including art, band, cheerleading, choir, chorus, computers, dance, drama, honors, jazz band, marching band, musical theater, newspaper, pep band, political, professional, radio and TV, religious, social, social service, student government, and yearbook. Popular campus events include Octoberfest, Fall Festival, and Springfest.

Sports: There are 7 intercollegiate sports for men and 7 for women, and 5 intramural sports for men and 5 for women. Facilities include a gym, field house, weight room, baseball and soccer fields, as well as tennis courts and outdoor volleyball courts.

Disabled Students: 70% of the campus is accessible. Wheelchair ramps, special parking, and lowered telephones are available.

Services: Counseling and information services are available, as is tutoring in most subjects. There is remedial math, reading, and writing.

Campus Safety and Security: Measures include 24-hour foot and vehicle patrol, informal discussions, and lighted pathways/sidewalks. The outside entrances of the dorms are always secured; only residents have keys.

Programs of Study: Cumberland confers B.A., B.S., B.B.A., B.S.Bus., B.S.Ed., and B.S.N. degrees. Associate and master's degrees are also awarded. Bachelor's degrees are awarded in BUSINESS (business administration and management), EDUCATION (elementary, health, middle school, and secondary), HEALTH PROFESSIONS (nursing and premedicine), SOCIAL SCIENCE (prelaw and social science). Business, education, and nursing are the largest.

Required: To graduate, students must complete 128 semester hours, including a 49-hour core curriculum, and maintain a GPA of 2.0.

Special: Students may cross-register for lower-level courses at Aquinas Junior College. Internships with local businesses and with the state legislature are available. Nondegree study and pass/fail options are offered. There are 5 national honor societies, a freshman honors program, and 1 departmental honors program.

Faculty/Classroom: 50% of faculty are male; 50%, female. All teach undergraduates. No introductory courses are taught by graduate students. The average class size in an introductory lecture is 30; in a laboratory, 24; and in a regular course, 20.

Admissions: There was 1 National Merit finalist. 9 freshmen graduated first in their class.

Requirements: The SAT I or ACT is recommended. In addition, a minimum composite ACT score of 18 is expected. Applicants must be high school graduates or have earned the GED with a composite 50 score. Cumberland requires applicants to be in the upper 75% of their class. A GPA of 2.0 is required. AP and CLEP credits are accepted.

Procedure: Freshmen are admitted to all sessions. Entrance exams should be taken during the senior year in high school. There is an early decision plan. Application deadlines are open. Check with the school for current application deadlines and fee.

Transfer: 101 transfer students enrolled in a recent year. Transfer applicants should have completed at least 15 college credits with a GPA of at least 2.0. 30 credits of 128 must be completed at Cumberland.

Visiting: There are regularly scheduled orientations for prospective students, consisting of campus tours, testing, information sessions pertaining to college life, and academic advising. A parent orientation is provided in conjunction with student orientation programs. There are guides for informal visits and visitors may sit in on classes. To schedule a visit, contact the Admissions Office.

Financial Aid: Cumberland is a member of CSS. The FAFSA and the college's own financial statement are required. Check with the school for current deadlines.

International Students: There are 24 international students enrolled. They must score 500 on the written TOEFL and also take the MELAB or the SAT I or the ACT.

Computers: PCs are available in the computer lab. All students may access the system. There are no time limits and no fees. It is strongly recommended that all students have a personal computer.

Graduates: In a recent year, 175 bachelor's degrees were awarded. The most popular majors were business administration (26%), education (26%), and nursing (21%). In an average class, 1% graduate in 3 years, 31% in 4 years, 35% in 5 years, and 38% in 6 years. 8 companies recruited on campus in a recent year. Of a recent graduating class, 9% were enrolled in graduate school within 6 months of graduation and 75% were employed.

Admissions Contact: Stephanie Walker, Director of Admissions.
E-mail: *admissions@cumberland.edu* Web: *cumberland.edu*

DAVID LIPSCOMB UNIVERSITY C-3

Nashville, TN 37204-3951 **(615) 269-1776**
(800) 333-4358; Fax: (615) 269-1804

Full-time: 911 men, 1195 women	**Faculty:** 115; IIB, -$
Part-time: 118 men, 170 women	**Ph.D.s:** 83%
Graduate: 149 men, 74 women	**Student/Faculty:** 18 to 1
Year: semesters, summer session	**Tuition:** $10,828
Application Deadline: open	**Room & Board:** $5330
Freshman Class: 1601 applied, 1358 accepted, 596 enrolled	
SAT I or ACT: required	**VERY COMPETITIVE**

David Lipscomb University, founded in 1891, is a private liberal arts university affiliated with the Church of Christ. There are 5 undergraduate and 3 graduate schools. In addition to regional accreditation, DLU has baccalaureate program accreditation with ACBSP, ADA, CSWE, NASM, and NCATE. The library contains 150,512 volumes, 26,018 microform items, and 1240 audiovisual forms/CDs, and subscribes to 38,685 periodicals. Computerized library services include the card catalog, interlibrary loans, and database searching. Special learning facilities include a learning resource center, art gallery, radio station, and TV station. The 65-acre campus is in a suburban area 2 miles south of downtown Nashville. Including residence halls, there are 16 buildings.

Student Life: 65% of undergraduates are from Tennessee. Others are from 40 states, 37 foreign countries, and Canada. 11% are from public schools. 85% are white. Most are Protestant. The average age of freshmen is 19; all undergraduates, 21. 21% do not continue beyond their first year; 62% remain to graduate.

Housing: 1358 students can be accommodated in college housing, which includes single-sex dormitories. 54% of students live on campus; of those, 25% remain on campus on weekends. Alcohol is not permitted. All students may keep cars.

Activities: There are no fraternities or sororities. There are 60 groups on campus, including art, band, cheerleading, chorale, chorus, computers, drama, ethnic, honors, international, jazz band, musical theater, newspaper, orchestra, photography, political, professional, radio and TV, social, social service, student government, and yearbook. Popular campus events include University Days, Sing-a-rama, and Tau Phi Cowboy Show.

Sports: There are 6 intercollegiate sports for men and 7 for women, and 9 intramural sports for men and 9 for women. Facilities include a gym with a basketball court and a pool, and a student activity center with 2 full-size basketball courts, 5 racquetball courts, a jogging course, and weight, aerobics, and recreation rooms.

Disabled Students: 95% of the campus is accessible. Wheelchair ramps, elevators, special parking, specially equipped rest rooms, and lowered drinking fountains are available.

Services: Counseling and information services are available, as is tutoring in some subjects, including math, English, and sciences. There is remedial math, reading, and writing.

Campus Safety and Security: Measures include 24-hour foot and vehicle patrol, escort service, pamphlets/posters/films, and emergency telephones. There are lighted pathways/sidewalks and residence hall security systems.

Programs of Study: DLU confers B.A. and B.S. degrees. Master's degrees are also awarded. Bachelor's degrees are awarded in BIOLOGICAL SCIENCE (biochemistry and biology/biological science), BUSINESS (accounting, banking and finance, business administration and management, fashion merchandising, and marketing/retailing/merchandising), COMMUNICATIONS AND THE ARTS (communications, English, French, German, languages, music, public relations, and Spanish), COMPUTER AND PHYSICAL SCIENCE (chemistry, computer science, mathematics, and physics), EDUCATION (art, elementary, foreign languages, music, physical, and science), ENGINEERING AND ENVIRONMENTAL DESIGN (preengineering), HEALTH PROFESSIONS (predentistry, premedicine, and prepharmacy), SOCIAL SCIENCE (American studies, biblical languages, dietetics, food production/management/services, history, home economics, political science/government, prelaw, psychology, religion, social work, and urban studies). Chemistry, biology, and accounting are the strongest academically. Business, medicine, and education are the largest.

Required: All full-time students must take and pass a Bible class meeting each day the student has classes. Other general education requirements include 9 semester hours in communication, 6 each in humanities, science, history, and social science, 3 in math, and 2 in phys ed. Students must complete a total of 132 semester hours and have a minimum GPA of 2.0. At least 25% of credit hours must be earned at Lipscomb.

Special: DLU offers internships and 3-2 engineering degrees with University of Tennessee at Knoxville, and Auburn, Vanderbilt, and Tennessee Technological Universities. An adult credit and noncredit studies program and pass/fail options for phys ed activity courses are available. A 3-2 program with Vanderbilt University leads to a B.S. in pre-nursing from Lipscomb and a master of science in nursing from Vanderbilt. There is study abroad in France, Germany, and Mexico. There is 1 national honor society, a freshman honors program, and 18 departmental honors programs.

Faculty/Classroom: 68% of faculty are male; 32%, female. All teach undergraduates. No introductory courses are taught by graduate students. The average class size in an introductory lecture is 45; in a laboratory, 25; and in a regular course, 30.

Admissions: 85% of the 2001-2002 applicants were accepted. 73% of the current freshmen were in the top fifth of their class; 96% were in the top two fifths. There were 2 National Merit finalists.

Requirements: The SAT I or ACT is required. In addition, candidates for admission should be graduates of accredited secondary schools. The GED is accepted. 14 academic units are required. Students should have completed 4 units of English, and 2 units each of history, math, and science. 2 units of a foreign language are highly recommended. Two additional units from the areas of English, foreign language, history, math, science, and social studies are also required. A GPA of 2.25 is required. AP and CLEP credits are accepted. Important factors in the admissions decision are advanced placement or honor courses, personality/intangible qualities, and leadership record. Applications are accepted on-line.

Procedure: Freshmen are admitted to all sessions. There is an early decision plan. Application deadlines are open. The fall 2001 application fee was $50. Notification is sent on a rolling basis. 8 early decision candidates were accepted for the 2001-2002 class.

Transfer: Students must be in good standing at their previous institution. 33 credits of 132 must be completed at DLU.

Visiting: There are regularly scheduled orientations for prospective students. There are guides for informal visits and visitors may sit in on classes and stay overnight. To schedule a visit, contact the Office of Undergraduate Admissions.

Financial Aid: In 2001-2002, 91% of all freshmen and 75% of continuing students received some form of financial aid. 38% of freshmen and 33% of continuing students received need-based aid. The average freshman award was $7900. Of that total, scholarships or need-based grants averaged $5709 ($5000 maximum); and loans averaged $2204. 64% of undergraduates work part time. Average annual earnings from campus work are $800. The average financial indebtedness of the 2001 graduate was $12,500. The FAFSA is required. The fall application deadline is February 28.

International Students: The school actively recruits these students. They must score 500 on the written TOEFL or take the MELAB and also take the SAT I or the ACT, scoring 810 on the SAT I.

Computers: The mainframes are 3 DEC ALPHA computers, 1 VAX 4100, and 1 VAX 4500. There are computer labs in every building on campus, including residence halls, and computer hook-ups in every dorm room. All students may access the system 24 hours per day, 7 days per week. There are no time limits and no fees. It is strongly recommended that all students have a personal computer.

Graduates: In 2001, 431 bachelor's degrees were awarded. The most popular majors were business administration (28%), elementary education (8%), and biology (7%). In an average class, 31% graduate in 4 years, 47% in 5 years, and 49% in 6 years. 347 companies recruited on campus in 2000-2001.

Admissions Contact: Scott Gilmer, Director of Admissions. A video is available. E-mail: *scott.gilmer@lipscomb.edu* Web: *www.lipscomb.edu*

EAST TENNESSEE STATE UNIVERSITY F-2

Johnson City, TN 37614-0731 (423) 439-4213
(800) 462-3878; Fax: (423) 439-7156

Full-time: 3252 men, 4312 women	**Faculty:** 350; IIA, --$
Part-time: 700 men, 1064 women	**Ph.D.s:** 75%
Graduate: 644 men, 1121 women	**Student/Faculty:** 22 to 1
Year: semesters, summer session	**Tuition:** $3119 ($9591)
Application Deadline: open	**Room & Board:** $4008
Freshman Class: 3316 applied, 2646 accepted, 1520 enrolled	
SAT I Verbal/Math: 500/490	**ACT:** 21 **COMPETITIVE**

East Tennessee State University, founded in 1911, is a public institution that is part of the State University and Community College System of Tennessee. ETSU's undergraduate and graduate programs stress the liberal arts, business, art, fine arts, professional training, music, teacher preparation, technical studies, and health science. There are 7 undergraduate and 2 graduate schools. In addition to regional accreditation, ETSU has baccalaureate program accreditation with AACSB, ABET, ACEJMC, ACS, ADA, CAAHEP, CSAB, CSWE, NASAD, NASM, NCATE, NEHSPAC, and NLN. The library contains 934,623 volumes, 1,652,836 microform items, and 90,036 audiovisual forms/CDs, and subscribes to 1935 periodicals. Computerized library services include the card catalog, interlibrary loans, and database searching. Special learning facilities include a learning resource center, art gallery, planetarium, radio station, TV station, and a regional art and history museum. The 366-acre campus is in a small town 90 miles northeast of Knoxville; 130 miles southwest of Roanoke, Virginia.; 60 miles northwest of Ashville, North Carolina. Including residence halls, there are 68 buildings.

Student Life: 90% of undergraduates are from Tennessee. Others are from 38 states, 45 foreign countries, and Canada. 97% are from public schools. 90% are white. The average age of freshmen is 19; all undergraduates, 25. 31% do not continue beyond their first year; 38% remain to graduate.

Housing: 2478 students can be accommodated in college housing, which includes single-sex dormitories, on-campus apartments, and married-student housing. On-campus housing is available on a first-come, first-served basis. 80% of students commute. Alcohol is not permitted. All students may keep cars.

Activities: 4% of men belong to 10 national fraternities; 4% of women belong to 1 local and 6 national sororities. There are 215 groups on campus, including art, band, cheerleading, choir, chorale, chorus, computers, dance, drama, drill team, ethnic, forensics, gay, honors, international, jazz band, literary magazine, marching band, pep band, photography, political, professional, radio and TV, religious, residence hall, social, social service, student government, and yearbook. Popular campus events include Leadership Retreat, National Clean Up for Hunger, and Winter Cruise.

Sports: There are 7 intercollegiate sports for men and 8 for women, and 8 intramural sports for men and 8 for women. Facilities include a 4000-seat gym, and a domed stadium seating 12,000, which includes a basketball arena, tennis and handball/racquetball courts, a track, and weight and training rooms.

Disabled Students: 75% of the campus is accessible. Wheelchair ramps, elevators, special parking, specially equipped rest rooms, special class scheduling, lowered drinking fountains, lowered telephones, and adaptive computer equipment are available.

Services: Counseling and information services are available, as is tutoring in most subjects. There is a reader service for the blind, and remedial math, reading, and writing. The office for Students with Disabilities, Student Support Services, and the Developmental Studies Program administer these services.

Campus Safety and Security: Measures include 24-hour foot and vehicle patrol, self-defense education, escort service, and shuttle buses. There are informal discussions, pamphlets/posters/films, emergency telephones, lighted pathways/sidewalks, and engravers available to identify personal property.

Programs of Study: ETSU confers B.A., B.S., B.A.S., B.B.A., B.F.A, B.G.S., B.M., B.S.D.H., B.S.Ed., B.S.E.H., B.S.M.T., B.S.N., and B.S.W. degrees. Associate, master's, and doctoral degrees are also awarded. Bachelor's degrees are awarded in BIOLOGICAL SCIENCE (biology/biological science), BUSINESS (accounting, management science, and marketing/retailing/merchandising), COMMUNICATIONS AND THE ARTS (art, communications, English, fine arts, music, and speech/debate/rhetoric), COMPUTER AND PHYSICAL SCIENCE (chemistry, computer science, information sciences and systems, mathematics, and physics), EDUCATION (foreign languages, physical, and special), ENGINEERING AND ENVIRONMENTAL DESIGN (engineering technology and survey and mapping technology), HEALTH PROFESSIONS (allied health, dental hygiene, environmental health science, health science, nursing, and public health), SOCIAL SCIENCE (child psychology/development, criminal justice, economics, geography, history, human development, interdisciplinary studies, liberal arts/general studies, philosophy, political science/government, psychology, social work, and sociology). Engineering technology, computer science, and nursing are the largest.

Required: All students must complete 128 semester hours, with 30 to 60 in the major, and maintain a minimum GPA of 2.0. Distribution requirements, which total 46 semester hours, include English, American history, phys ed, natural science, social and behavioral science, the humanities, analysis, and a 3-hour computer literacy course. An exit exam is also required.

Special: Special academic programs include cooperative education programs, cross-registration with Milligan College, internships in political science, applied human sciences, and management study abroad in Scotland, England, France, and Spain, and B.A.-B.S. degrees and dual majors in most arts and sciences undergraduate majors. A general studies degree is offered. Credit for military experience may be granted, and nondegree study and pass/fail options are possible. There are 19 national honor societies, a freshman honors program, and 12 departmental honors programs.

Faculty/Classroom: 56% of faculty are male; 44%, female. 85% teach undergraduates. The average class size in an introductory lecture is 31; in a laboratory, 17; and in a regular course, 24.

Admissions: 80% of the 2001-2002 applicants were accepted. The SAT I scores for the 2001-2002 freshman class were: Verbal--47% below 500, 33% between 500 and 599, 15% between 600 and 700, and 4% above 700; Math--52% below 500, 34% between 500 and 599, 12% between 600 and 700, and 2% above 700. The ACT scores were 44% below 21, 28% between 21 and 23, 17% between 24 and 26, 7% between 27 and 28, and 5% above 28. 27% of the current freshmen were in the top fifth of their class; 49% were in the top two fifths. There were 2 National Merit finalists and 20 semifinalists. 33 freshmen graduated first in their class.

Requirements: The SAT I or ACT is required, with a minimum composite score of 890 on the SAT I or a minimum score of 19 on the ACT. Other admissions requirements include graduation from an accredited secondary school, with 20 Carnegie units and 14 academic credits, including 4 of English, 3 of math, 2 each of a foreign language and science, and 1 each of history, social studies, and art. In-state students who pass the Tennessee State Proficiency Test are eligible to apply for admission. Applicants whose ACT/SAT I is below a certain score must complete the Academic Assessment Placement Program (AAPP) test battery before registration for classes. The GED is also accepted. A GPA of 2.3 is required. AP and CLEP credits are accepted. Applications are available on-line at ETSU's home page at *www.etsu.edu*

Procedure: Freshmen are admitted to all sessions. Entrance exams should be taken during the junior and/or senior year. Application deadlines are open. The fall 2001 application fee was $15. Notification is sent on a rolling basis.

Transfer: 727 transfer students enrolled in 2001-2002. Transfer students must have a minimum GPA of 2.0 in 12 or more semester credit hours of course work from a regionally accredited institution. Transfer students must also satisfy high school unit requirements if deficiencies exist. 34 credits of 128 must be completed at ETSU.

Visiting: There are regularly scheduled orientations for prospective students, including 5 2-day orientation programs held during spring and summer for new students admitted to fall term. There are guides for informal visits and visitors may sit in on classes and stay overnight. To schedule a visit, contact the Admissions Office.

Financial Aid: In 2001-2002, 80% of all freshmen and 70% of continuing students received some form of financial aid. 60% of freshmen and 50% of continuing students received need-based aid. The average freshman award was $6351. Of that total, scholarships or need-based grants averaged $2929; loans averaged $5271 ($6025 maximum); and work contracts averaged $1989 ($2000 maximum). 26% of undergraduates work part time. Average annual earnings from campus work are $1078. The average financial indebtedness of the 2001 graduate was $18,202. The FAFSA is required. The fall application deadline is July 1.

International Students: There are 69 international students enrolled. They must score 500 on the written TOEFL or 173 on the electronic version and also take the SAT I or the ACT, scoring 19 on the ACT.

Computers: The mainframe is an ALPHA 2100. There are 500 PCs available for student use in computer labs in several buildings on campus. All students may access the system 24 hours per day. There are no time limits and no fees.

Graduates: In 2001, 1359 bachelor's degrees were awarded. The most popular majors were nursing (9%), general studies (7%), and management (6%). In an average class, 12% graduate in 4 years, 29% in 5 years, and 38% in 6 years. 200 companies recruited on campus in 2000-2001.

Admissions Contact: Mike Pitts, Director of Admissions. A video is available. E-mail: *go2etsu@etsu.edu* Web: *www.etsu.edu*

FISK UNIVERSITY
Nashville, TN 37208-3051 C-2
(615) 329-8665
(800) 443-3475; Fax: (615) 329-8774

Full-time: 225 men, 570 women	**Faculty:** 63; IIB, --$
Part-time: 10 men, 15 women	**Ph.D.s:** 70%
Graduate: 40 men, 40 women	**Student/Faculty:** 13 to 1
Year: semesters	**Tuition:** $8800
Application Deadline: see profile	**Room & Board:** $5000
Freshman Class: n/av	
SAT I Verbal/Math: required	**LESS COMPETITIVE**

Fisk University, founded in 1866, is a private, nonsectarian, liberal arts institution affiliated with the American Missionary Association of the Church of Christ. Figures in the above capsule are approximate. Estabished as a college for African Americans, Fisk has always accepted students regardless of race. In addition to regional accreditation, Fisk University has baccalaureate program accreditation with NASM. The library contains 210,000 volumes and 5200 microform items, and subscribes to 600 periodicals. Computerized library services include the card catalog and database searching. Special learning facilities include an art gallery and radio station. The 40-acre campus is in an urban area. Including residence halls, there are 21 buildings.

Student Life: 71% of undergraduates are from out of state, mostly the South. Others are from 39 states and 4 foreign countries. 87% are from public schools. 96% are African American. The average age of freshmen is 18; all undergraduates, 20. 6% do not continue beyond their first year; 63% remain to graduate.

Housing: About 852 students can be accommodated in college housing, which includes single-sex dormitories and married-student housing. On-campus housing is guaranteed for all 4 years. 68% of students live on campus; of those, 80% remain on campus on weekends. Alcohol is not permitted. All students may keep cars.

Activities: 25% of men belong to 4 national fraternities; 20% of women belong to 4 national sororities. There are some groups and organizations on campus, including cheerleading, choir, dance, drama, honors, literary magazine, newspaper, religious, student government, and yearbook.

Sports: There are 5 intercollegiate sports for men and 5 for women. Facilities include a gym and a student center.

Disabled Students: 80% of the campus is accessible. Wheelchair ramps and elevators are available.

Services: Counseling and information services are available, as is tutoring in every subject. There is remedial math, reading, and writing.

Campus Safety and Security: Measures include 24-hour foot and vehicle patrol and lighted pathways/sidewalks.

Programs of Study: Fisk University confers B.A., B.S., and B.M. degrees. Master's degrees are also awarded. Bachelor's degrees are awarded in BIOLOGICAL SCIENCE (biology/biological science), BUSINESS (business administration and management), COMMUNICATIONS AND THE ARTS (dramatic arts, English, fine arts, French, music, Spanish, and speech/debate/rhetoric), COMPUTER AND PHYSICAL SCIENCE (chemistry, mathematics, and physics), EDUCATION (art), SOCIAL SCIENCE (economics, history, philosophy, political science/government, psychology, religion, and sociology). Biology, chemistry, and physics are the strongest academically. Business administration is the largest.

Required: To graduate, students must complete 120 credits, including a 32-credit core curriculum in communications, creative arts, humanistic experience and thought, natural sciences or math, social sciences, and world civilization. In addition, students must complete 8 hours of written and computational skills and 24 hours of interdisciplinary courses, plus a foreign language. A minimum 2.0 GPA must be maintained.

Special: Fisk offers cross-registration with Vanderbilt University, study abroad, dual majors in engineering and pharmacy, student-designed majors, and campus work-study. Students may take a 5-year B.S.-B.E. program with Vanderbilt University, Florida A&M, or the University of Alabama/Huntsville, or a combined B.S.-M.B.A. program with Vanderbilt. There are 8 national honor societies, including Phi Beta Kappa.

Faculty/Classroom: 62% of faculty are male; 38%, female. All teach undergraduates, 22% do research, and 24% do both. No introductory courses are taught by graduate students. The average class size in an introductory lecture is 30; in a laboratory, 15; and in a regular course, 19.

Admissions: 35% of recent freshmen were in the top fifth of their class; 65% were in the top two fifths.

Requirements: The SAT I or ACT is required. In addition, applicants should be high school graduates with 14 academic credits. Fisk University requires applicants to be in the upper 50% of their class. A GPA of 2.5 is required. AP credits are accepted. Important factors in the admissions decision are advanced placement or honor courses, leadership record, and evidence of special talent.

Procedure: Freshmen are admitted fall and spring. There is an early admissions plan. Notification is sent on a rolling basis. Check with the school for current application deadlines and fee.

Transfer: 23 transfer students enrolled in a recent year. Applicants for transfer should have a minimum college GPA of 2.0.

Visiting: There are guides for informal visits and visitors may sit in on classes and stay overnight. To schedule a visit, contact the Admissions Office at (615) 329-8666.

Financial Aid: In a recent year, 90% of all students received some form of financial aid. 65% of freshmen and 70% of continuing students received need-based aid. The average freshman award was $12,500. Of that total, scholarships or need-based grants averaged $3000 ($13,700 maximum); loans averaged $3500 ($5500 maximum); work contracts averaged $1200 ($1500 maximum); and PLUS Loan, unsubsidized loans, outside scholarships averaged $5000 ($8000 maximum). 28% of undergraduates work part time. Average annual earnings from campus work are $1200. The average financial indebtedness of a recent graduate was $20,000. Fisk University is a member of CSS. The FAFSA and the college's own financial statement are required. Check with the school for current deadlines.

International Students: They must score 550 on the written TOEFL.

Computers: The mainframe is a DEC VAX 11/750. There are also TRS80 PCs and Macs available across campus. All students may access the system. There are no time limits and no fees.

Graduates: In a recent year, 184 bachelor's degrees were awarded. The most popular majors were psychology (25%), business administration (20%), and biology (15%). In an average class, 2% graduate in 3 years, 46% in 4 years, 54% in 5 years, and 59% in 6 years. 80 companies recruited on campus in a recent year. Of a recent graduating class, 24% were enrolled in graduate school within 6 months of graduation and 28% were employed.

Admissions Contact: Anthony Jones, Director of Admissions. A video is available. E-mail: *lcampbel@dubois.fisk.edu*

FREED-HARDEMAN UNIVERSITY
Henderson, TN 38340 B-3
(731) 989-6651
(800) 630-3480; Fax: (731) 989-6047

Full-time: 630 men, 689 women	**Faculty:** 91; IIA, --$
Part-time: 42 men, 53 women	**Ph.D.s:** 73%
Graduate: 157 men, 299 women	**Student/Faculty:** 15 to 1
Year: semesters, summer session	**Tuition:** $9580
Application Deadline: open	**Room & Board:** $4710
Freshman Class: 822 applied, 459 accepted, 354 enrolled	
ACT: 23	**VERY COMPETITIVE**

Freed-Hardeman University, founded in 1869, is a private, liberal arts institution associated with Churches of Christ. There are 6 undergraduate and 3 graduate schools. In addition to regional accreditation, FHU has baccalaureate program accreditation with ACBSP, CSWE, and NCATE. The library contains 155,427 volumes, 234,284 microform items, and 42,195 audiovisual forms/CDs, and subscribes to 1634 periodicals. Computerized library services include the card catalog, interlibrary loans, and database searching. Special learning facilities include a learning resource center, art gallery, radio station, TV station, and a Cancer Research Institute. The 120-acre campus is in a small town 85 miles east of Memphis and 13 miles south of Jackson. Including residence halls, there are 31 buildings.

Student Life: 56% of undergraduates are from out of state, mostly the South. Others are from 36 states, 20 foreign countries, and Canada. 75% are from public schools. 87% are white. Most are Protestant. The average age of freshmen is 19; all undergraduates, 21. 31% do not continue beyond their first year; 53% remain to graduate.

Housing: 1192 students can be accommodated in college housing, which includes single-sex dormitories and on-campus houses. In addition, there are student teacher houses. On-campus housing is guaranteed for all 4 years. 77% of students live on campus; of those, 55% remain on campus on weekends. Alcohol is not permitted. All students may keep cars.

Activities: There are no fraternities or sororities. There are 52 groups on campus, including art, band, cheerleading, chorus, computers, drama, drum and bugle corps, ethnic, honors, international, jazz band, musical theater, newspaper, orchestra, pep band, photography, political, professional, radio and TV, religious, social, social service, student government, and yearbook. Popular campus events include Makin' Music and Annual Bible Lectureship.

Sports: There are 6 intercollegiate sports for men and 7 for women, and 7 intramural sports for men and 7 for women. Facilities include 3 gyms, lighted playing fields, lighted tennis courts, a swimming pool, a walking track, a weight room, racquetball courts, and a game room.

Disabled Students: 70% of the campus is accessible. Wheelchair ramps, elevators, special parking, specially equipped rest rooms, special class scheduling, lowered drinking fountains, and lowered telephones are available.

Services: Counseling and information services are available, as is tutoring in most subjects. There is remedial math, reading, and writing.

Campus Safety and Security: Measures include 24-hour foot and vehicle patrol, escort service, informal discussions, and lighted pathways/sidewalks.

Programs of Study: FHU confers B.A., B.S., B.B.A., and B.S.W. degrees. Master's degrees are also awarded. Bachelor's degrees are awarded in AGRICULTURE (agricultural business management), BIOLOGICAL SCIENCE (biology/biological science), BUSINESS (accounting, banking and finance, business administration and management, and marketing/retailing/merchandising), COMMUNICATIONS AND THE ARTS (art, broadcasting, communications, dramatic arts, English, fine arts, public relations, and speech/debate/rhetoric), COMPUTER AND PHYSICAL SCIENCE (chemistry, computer programming, computer science, information sciences and systems, mathematics, and physical sciences), EDUCATION (art, early childhood, elementary, health, middle school, music, physical, science, secondary, and special), ENGINEERING AND ENVIRONMENTAL DESIGN (preengineering), HEALTH PROFESSIONS (predentistry, premedicine, preoptometry, prepharmacy, and preveterinary science), SOCIAL SCIENCE (biblical studies, child care/child and family studies, family/consumer studies, history, ministries, psychology, and social work). Premedicine, preengineering, and business are the strongest academically. Business, Bible, and elementary education are the largest.

Required: To graduate, students must complete 132 semester hours, including 44 in upper-division courses in Bible, skills, humanities, and science, plus 3 hours of speech communication and 2 hours of phys ed. The major requires a minimum of 30 semester hours, including 15 upper-division hours. Students must maintain a GPA of 2.0. All students must demonstrate, by approved tests or criteria, basic competence in reading, writing, oral communication, math, and computers.

Special: FHU offers cross-registration with Lambuth University and Union University, study abroad in Belgium, a B.A.-B.S. degree in Bible, biology, communication, and arts and humanities, co-op programs, a dual major, field practicum opportunities in several majors, student-designed majors, 3-2 engineering degrees with 6 universities, and nondegree study. There are 4 national honor societies, a freshman honors program, and 13 departmental honors programs.

Faculty/Classroom: 66% of faculty are male; 34%, female. 91% teach undergraduates. No introductory courses are taught by graduate students. The average class size in a laboratory is 22 and in a regular course, 20.

Admissions: 56% of the 2001-2002 applicants were accepted. The ACT scores for the 2001-2002 freshman class were: 28% below 21, 22% between 21 and 23, 25% between 24 and 26, 13% between 27 and 28, and 12% above 28. 13 freshmen graduated first in their class.

Requirements: The ACT is required with a minimum composite score of 19. Candidates for admission should be graduates of an accredited secondary school. An interview is recommended. A GPA of 2.25 is required. AP and CLEP credits are accepted. Important factors in the admissions decision are personality/intangible qualities, recommendations by school officials, and leadership record. Applications are accepted online at *www.fhu.edu*.

Procedure: Freshmen are admitted fall, spring, and summer. Entrance exams should be taken in early fall or summer before senior year. There is an early admissions plan. Application deadlines are open.

Transfer: 106 transfer students enrolled in 2001-2002. Applicants should have a minimum college GPA of 2.0. Those with fewer than 30 college credits must also submit a high school transcript and ACT or SAT I scores. 33 credits of 132 must be completed at FHU.

Visiting: There are regularly scheduled orientations for prospective students, including an orientation during the 5 days prior to classes beginning in the fall. There are guides for informal visits and visitors may sit in on classes and stay overnight. To schedule a visit, contact Jim Brown.

Financial Aid: In 2001-2002, 87% of all freshmen and 88% of continuing students received some form of financial aid. 51% of freshmen and 74% of continuing students received need-based aid. The average freshman award was $5252. Of that total, scholarships or need-based grants averaged $1860 ($11,600 maximum); loans averaged $2312 ($6625 maximum); and work contracts averaged $1080 ($2000 maximum). 31% of undergraduates work part time. Average annual earnings from campus work are $1080. The average financial indebtedness of the 2001 graduate was $9602. The FAFSA is required. The fall application deadline is April 1.

International Students: There are 39 international students enrolled. They must score 500 on the written TOEFL and also take the ACT, scoring 19.

Computers: The mainframe is a DEC VAX 4500. PCs and Mac are available in student labs and other locations, and each residence hall room has network access. All students may access the system. There are no time limits. There is a $180 technology fee per semester.

Graduates: In 2001, 275 bachelor's degrees were awarded. The most popular majors were Bible (12%), elementary education (8%), and biology (7%). In an average class, 2% graduate in 3 years, 39% in 4 years, 52% in 5 years, and 53% in 6 years. 84 companies recruited on campus in 2000-2001.

Admissions Contact: Jim Brown, Director of Admissions. A video is available. E-mail: *jbrown@fhu.edu* Web: *http://www.fhu.edu*

KING COLLEGE

F-2

Bristol, TN 37620-2699

(423) 652-6021
(800) 362-0014; Fax: (423) 652-4727

Full-time: 246 men, 328 women	**Faculty:** 42
Part-time: 30 men, 51 women	**Ph.D.s:** 50%
Graduate: 6 men, 9 women	**Student/Faculty:** 14 to 1
Year: 4-1-4, summer session	**Tuition:** $13,340
Application Deadline: open	**Room & Board:** $4460
Freshman Class: 583 applied, 373 accepted, 146 enrolled	
SAT I Verbal/Math: 550/540	**ACT:** 23 **VERY COMPETITIVE**

King College, founded in 1867, is a private liberal arts college affiliated with the Presbyterian Church (U.S.A.). There are 5 undergraduate schools. The library contains 90,726 volumes, 34,385 microform items, and 5378 audiovisual forms/CDs, and subscribes to 581 periodicals. Computerized library services include the card catalog, interlibrary loans, and database searching. Special learning facilities include a learning resource center and an observatory. The 135-acre campus is in a suburban area 2 miles east of Bristol. Including residence halls, there are 16 buildings.

Student Life: 50% of undergraduates are from out of state, mostly the South. Others are from 29 states and 31 foreign countries. 76% are from public schools. 70% are white; 11% foreign nationals. 71% are Protestant; 11% claim no religious affiliation. The average age of freshmen is 18; all undergraduates, 20. 23% do not continue beyond their first year.

Housing: 495 students can be accommodated in college housing, which includes single-sex dormitories and married-student housing. On-campus housing is guaranteed for all 4 years and is available on a first-come, first-served basis. 80% of students live on campus; of those, 60% remain on campus on weekends. Alcohol is not permitted. All students may keep cars.

Activities: There are no fraternities or sororities. There are 37 groups on campus, including art, band, cheerleading, choir, chorale, chorus, dance, debate, drama, honors, international, literary magazine, musical theater, newspaper, photography, political, professional, religious, social service, student government, and yearbook. Popular campus events include International Fair, Fall Ball, and Dogwood Ball and Weekend.

Sports: There are 5 intercollegiate sports for men and 4 for women, and 8 intramural sports for men and 8 for women. Facilities include a gym, soccer and baseball fields, 6 tennis courts, and a fitness trail.

Disabled Students: 80% of the campus is accessible. Wheelchair ramps, elevators, special parking, and specially equipped rest rooms are available.

Services: Counseling and information services are available, as is tutoring in most subjects.

Campus Safety and Security: Measures include escort service, informal discussions, emergency telephones, and lighted pathways/sidewalks. There are 24-hour foot and vehicle patrol on weekends, and 12-hour patrol Monday through Friday.

Programs of Study: King confers B.A., B.S., B.S. Med.Tech., and B.S.N. degrees. Master's degrees are also awarded. Bachelor's degrees are awarded in BIOLOGICAL SCIENCE (biochemistry and biology/biological science), BUSINESS (business administration and management, business economics, and electronic business), COMMUNICATIONS AND THE ARTS (English, French, modern language, Spanish, and visual and performing arts), COMPUTER AND PHYSICAL SCIENCE (applied mathematics, chemistry, computer science, mathematics, and physics), EDUCATION (elementary and secondary), HEALTH PROFESSIONS (medical laboratory technology, medical technology, and nursing), SOCIAL SCIENCE (American studies, behavioral science, biblical studies, history, missions, political science/government, psychology, and youth ministry). English, history, and natural sciences are the strongest academically. Behavorial science, economics/business, and psychology are the largest.

Required: Students must complete a minimum of 124 semester hours with 27 to 53 in the major. The 51 semester hours of core curriculum include courses in English, history, math, Bible, humanities, science, social science, and phys ed. Students must have a minimum GPA of 2.0. A comprehensive exam in the student's major area of concentration is required.

Special: King offers co-op programs, cross-registration with Virginia Intermont College, internships, study abroad in more than 50 countries, a Washington semester, and work-study programs. There are 3-2 engineering degrees available with Georgia Institute of Technology, University of Maryland, Vanderbilt University, and University of Tennessee. A dual degree in pharmacy is also offered. Nondegree study and pass/fail options for special students are available. There is 1 national honor society, a freshman honors program, and 14 departmental honors programs.

Faculty/Classroom: 62% of faculty are male; 38%, female. All teach undergraduates and 45% both teach and do research. The average class size in an introductory lecture is 30; in a laboratory, 30; and in a regular course, 15.

Admissions: 64% of the 2001-2002 applicants were accepted. The SAT I scores for the 2001-2002 freshman class were: Verbal--27% below

500, 43% between 500 and 599, 23% between 600 and 700, and 7% above 700; Math--33% below 500, 37% between 500 and 599, 24% between 600 and 700, and 3% above 700. The ACT scores were 5% below 21, 47% between 21 and 23, 20% between 24 and 26, 22% between 27 and 28, and 6% above 28. 58% of the current freshmen were in the top fifth of their class; 83% were in the top two fifths. 6 freshmen graduated first in their class.

Requirements: The SAT I or ACT is required. In addition, candidates for admission should be graduates of accredited or recognized secondary schools. The GED is accepted. Students are required to have 16 academic credits, including 4 in English, 2 each in foreign language, history, algebra, and social studies, and 1 each in geometry and natural science. An essay is required. An audition and interview are recommended. A GPA of 2.4 is required. AP and CLEP credits are accepted. Important factors in the admissions decision are advanced placement or honor courses, extracurricular activities record, and leadership record. Applications are accepted on-line at the school's web site through Front Page, Access, and CAMS.

Procedure: Freshmen are admitted to all sessions. Entrance exams should be taken before May 1. There are early admissions and deferred admissions plans. Application deadlines are open. The fall 2001 application fee was $20. Notification is sent on a rolling basis.

Transfer: 31 transfer students enrolled in 2001-2002. Transfer applicants should have a minimum 2.0 GPA and 30 semester hours. If fewer hours have been completed, a 2.4 high school GPA and a minimum ACT composite score of 22, or SAT I composite score of 1000, are required. 50 credits of 124 must be completed at King.

Visiting: There are regularly scheduled orientations for prospective students, including a campus tour, financial aid seminar, faculty sessions, an overnight visit in a dorm, and admissions counseling. There are guides for informal visits and visitors may sit in on classes and stay overnight. To schedule a visit, contact the Admissions Office at (423) 652-4861.

Financial Aid: In 2001-2002, 75% of all freshmen and 60% of continuing students received some form of financial aid. 75% of freshmen and 58% of continuing students received need-based aid. The average freshman award was $12,460. 53% of undergraduates work part time. Average annual earnings from campus work are $900. The average financial indebtedness of the 2001 graduate was $16,000. The FAFSA and the college's own financial statement are required. The fall application deadline is March 1.

International Students: There are 48 international students enrolled. The school actively recruits these students. They must take the college's own test.

Computers: A campuswide network connects 80 Pentium class machines located in 4 labs. Students are given an IBM ThinkPad and can access the network from virtually any location on campus, including dorms, library, and study areas. All students may access the system. There are no time limits and no fees.

Graduates: In 2001, 91 bachelor's degrees were awarded. The most popular majors were business (21%), liberal arts (15%), and biology, English, psychology (9%). In an average class, 96% graduate in 4 years, 9% in 5 years, and 2% in 6 years. Of the 2000 graduating class, 20% were enrolled in graduate school within 6 months of graduation.

Admissions Contact: Melinda Clark, Interim Vice President, Enrollment. E-mail: *admissions@king.edu* Web: *www.king.edu*

KNOXVILLE COLLEGE E-3
Knoxville, TN 37921 (865) 524-6500
(800) 743-5669; Fax: (865) 524-6686

Full-time: 115 men, 80 women	**Faculty:** 47
Part-time: 10 women	**Ph.D.s:** 55%
Graduate: none	**Student/Faculty:** n/av
Year: semesters	**Tuition:** $6200
Application Deadline: open	**Room & Board:** n/app
Freshman Class: n/av	
ACT: recommended	**LESS COMPETITIVE**

Knoxville College, founded in 1875, is a small, private liberal arts institution affiliated with the United Presbyterian Church. Information in the above capsule, and in this profile, is approximate. The library contains 79,000 volumes and 11,000 microform items, and subscribes to 450 periodicals. The 39-acre campus is in an urban area. There are 22 buildings.

Student Life: 25% of undergraduates are from Tennesse. 95% are from public schools. 50% of freshman remain to graduate.

Housing: 80% of students live on campus.

Activities: There are 10 groups an campus, including band, chorus, drama, honors, newspaper, religious, social service, and student government.

Services: There is remedial math, reading, and writing.

Programs of Study: KC confers B.A., B.S., B.S.Ed., B.S.M.T., and B.S. in Tourism, Food, and Lodging Administration. Associate degrees are also awarded. Bachelor's degrees are awarded in BIOLOGICAL SCIENCE (biology/biological science), BUSINESS (accounting, and business administration and management), COMMUNICATIONS AND THE ARTS (English and music), COMPUTER AND PHYSICAL SCIENCE (chemistry), EDUCATION (business, early childhood, elementary, health, mathematics, music, physical, recreation, and science), HEALTH PROFESSIONS (health care administration and medical laboratory technology), SOCIAL SCIENCE (political science/government, psychology, and sociology).

Required: To graduate, all students must complete 124 semester hours with at least a 2.0 GPA. 66 hours in a core curriculum are required, including courses in English, speech, history, math, natural and social sciences, religion, philosophy, humanities and the arts, computer science, health, and phys ed. Between 26 and 40 hours are required in the major.

Special: A 3-2 engineering degree is offered with the University of Tennessee. Students seeking degrees in tourism, food and lodging administration, or recreation leadership may take some courses at the University of Tennessee. Cooperative programs, nondegree study, internships, and dual majors are possible. There is a freshman honors program.

Admissions: 30% of recent freshmen were in the top two fifths of their class.

Requirements: The SAT I or ACT is recommended. Scores should be submitted for placement purposes. Applicants should be graduates of an accredited high school or have earned the GED. Secondary preparation should include a total of 15 Carnegie units. Music program applicants must audition. Culturally disadvantaged students may be admitted under a special program. A GPA of 2.0 is required.

Procedure: Application deadlines are open. Check with the school for current application deadlines and fee.

Transfer: Applicants with fewer than 15 college credits must submit a high school transcript. 30 credits of 124 must be completed at KC.

Visiting: There are guides for informal visits. To schedule a visit, contact the Director of Admissions.

Financial Aid: In a recent year, all freshmen received some form of financial aid. The FAFSA and the college's own financial statement are required.

International Students: They must score 475 on the written TOEFL.

Computers: All students may access the system. There are no time limits and no fees.

Admissions Contact: Director of Admissions. A video is available.

LAMBUTH UNIVERSITY B-3
Jackson, TN 38301 (731) 425-3223
(800) 526-2884; Fax: (731) 425-3496

Full-time: 357 men, 469 women	**Faculty:** 48; IIB, --$
Part-time: 25 men, 52 women	**Ph.D.s:** 75%
Graduate: none	**Student/Faculty:** 18 to 1
Year: semesters, summer session	**Tuition:** $9548
Application Deadline: open	**Room & Board:** $4706
Freshman Class: 905 applied, 620 accepted, 212 enrolled	
SAT I or ACT: required	**COMPETITIVE**

Lambuth University, founded in 1843, is a private liberal arts and sciences institution affiliated with the United Methodist Church. There are 4 undergraduate schools. The library contains 160,000 volumes, 115,000 microform items, and 1800 audiovisual forms/CDs, and subscribes to 430 periodicals. Computerized library services include interlibrary loans and database searching. Special learning facilities include a learning resource center, planetarium, radio station, and video studio. The 50-acre campus is in an urban area 75 miles northeast of Memphis. Including residence halls, there are 16 buildings.

Student Life: 79% of undergraduates are from Tennessee. Others are from 29 states, 16 foreign countries, and Canada. 93% are from public schools. 81% are white; 14% African American. 66% are Protestant; 25% claim no religious affiliation. The average age of freshmen is 18; all undergraduates, 22. 36% do not continue beyond their first year; 41% remain to graduate.

Housing: 625 students can be accommodated in college housing, which includes single-sex and coed dormitories, on-campus apartments, fraternity houses, and sorority houses. In addition, there are honors houses. 58% of students live on campus; of those, 40% remain on campus on weekends. Alcohol is not permitted. All students may keep cars.

Activities: 23% of men belong to 3 national fraternities; 25% of women belong to 4 national sororities. There are 26 groups on campus, including art, band, cheerleading, chess, choir, computers, drama, ethnic, honors, international, jazz band, literary magazine, musical theater, newspaper, pep band, photography, political, professional, radio and TV, religious, social, social service, student government, and yearbook. Popular campus events include Hawaiian Bash, Christmas Candlelight Service, and All-Sing.

Sports: There are 7 intercollegiate sports for men and 7 for women, and 10 intramural sports for men and 10 for women. Facilities include an indoor swimming pool, racquetball and tennis courts, a weight room, a gym, and football, baseball, and soccer fields.

Disabled Students: 75% of the campus is accessible. Wheelchair ramps, elevators, special parking, and special class scheduling are available.

Services: Counseling and information services are available, as is tutoring in most subjects. There is remedial math and writing.

Campus Safety and Security: Measures include 24-hour foot and vehicle patrol, self-defense education, escort service, and informal discussions. There are pamphlets/posters/films, emergency telephones, and lighted pathways/sidewalks.

Programs of Study: Lambuth confers B.A., B.S., B.B.A., and B.M. degrees. Bachelor's degrees are awarded in BIOLOGICAL SCIENCE (biology/biological science), BUSINESS (business administration and management), COMMUNICATIONS AND THE ARTS (communications, dramatic arts, English, fine arts, French, music, and Spanish), COMPUTER AND PHYSICAL SCIENCE (chemistry and mathematics), EDUCATION (elementary, music, physical, secondary, and special), HEALTH PROFESSIONS (speech pathology/audiology), SOCIAL SCIENCE (history, human ecology, interdisciplinary studies, international relations, political science/government, psychology, religion, and sociology). Biological science, art, and business are the strongest academically. Business, education, and biology are the largest.

Required: All students must complete a minimum of 128 semester hours, including Freshman Seminar, 9 hours in English, 8 in biological/physical sciences, 6 each in religion, writing courses, and interdisciplinary courses, and 3 each in speech, computer science, social science, and math. Students must have a minimum GPA of 2.0. Students must have 18 hours in a minor field of study.

Special: Lambuth offers cross-registration with Union University and Freed-Hardeman University, internships in several disciplines, study abroad in England, Mexico, and France, a Washington semester, work-study programs, dual majors in all areas, student-designed majors in most areas, a 3-2 engineering degree, nondegree study, and pass/fail options. There are 5 national honor societies.

Faculty/Classroom: 60% of faculty are male; 40%, female. All teach undergraduates. The average class size in an introductory lecture is 23; in a laboratory, 23; and in a regular course, 23.

Admissions: 69% of the 2001-2002 applicants were accepted. The ACT scores for the 2001-2002 freshman class were: 17% below 21, 35% between 21 and 23, 26% between 24 and 26, 15% between 27 and 28, and 7% above 28. 38% of the current freshmen were in the top fifth of their class; 65% were in the top two fifths.

Requirements: The SAT I or ACT is required, with a minimum ACT composite score of 20. Other students are admitted at the discretion of the admissions committee. Candidates for admission should be graduates of accredited secondary schools. The GED is accepted. It is preferred that students have completed 4 courses each in English, history, math, science, and social studies, and 2 courses in foreign language, art, and music. An essay and interview are recommended. A GPA of 2.0 is required. AP and CLEP credits are accepted. Important factors in the admissions decision are advanced placement or honor courses, leadership record, and recommendations by school officials. Students can e-mail an application from the school's web site.

Procedure: Freshmen are admitted to all sessions. Entrance exams should be taken by February of the senior year. There are early admissions and deferred admissions plans. Application deadlines are open. The fall 2001 application fee was $25. Notification is sent on a rolling basis.

Transfer: 99 transfer students enrolled in a recent year. A minimum 2.0 GPA in college-level courses taken, transcripts from all colleges attended, and a statement of honorable dismissal are required. An associate degree usually guarantees admission. A minimum of 12 successfully completed credit hours is recommended. 32 credits of 128 must be completed at Lambuth.

Visiting: There are regularly scheduled orientations for prospective students, consisting of students and parents touring the campus, participating in the students panel discussion, and attending a luncheon. Students visit a class. Parents participate in seminars. There are guides for informal visits and visitors may sit in on classes and stay overnight. To schedule a visit, contact the Office of Admissions.

Financial Aid: In 2001-2002, 58% of freshmen and 63% of continuing students received need-based aid. The average freshman award was $7502. Of that total, scholarships or need-based grants averaged $4894; loans averaged $2625; and work contracts averaged $898 ($1082 maximum). 42% of undergraduates work part time. Average annual earnings from campus work are $799. Lambuth is a member of CSS. The FAFSA and the college's own financial statement are required. Check with the school for current deadlines.

International Students: The school actively recruits these students. They must score 500 on the written TOEFL.

Computers: The mainframe is an IBM AS/400 C25. There are also PCs in the computer center, and computer access in residence halls and in the library. All students may access the system 8 A.M. to 10 P.M. when classes are not in session (computer lab). There are no time limits and no fees. It is strongly recommended that all students have a personal computer.

Graduates: In a recent year, 175 bachelor's degrees were awarded. The most popular majors were business (22%), education (19%), and physical education (12%). In an average class, 4% graduate in 3 years, 30% in 4 years, 39% in 5 years, and 41% in 6 years. 40 companies recruited on campus in a recent year.

Admissions Contact: Denny Bardos, Director of Admissions.
E-mail: *admit@lambuth.edu* Web: *www.lambuth.edu*

LANE COLLEGE — B-3
Jackson, TN 38301 (731) 426-7532
(800) 960-7533; Fax: (731) 426-7559

Full-time: 323 men, 352 women	**Faculty:** 47; IIB, --$
Part-time: 18 men, 3 women	**Ph.D.s:** 60%
Graduate: none	**Student/Faculty:** 14 to 1
Year: semesters, summer session	**Tuition:** $6370
Application Deadline: July 1	**Room & Board:** $4030
Freshman Class: 1506 applied, 622 accepted, 213 enrolled	
ACT: 16	**COMPETITIVE+**

Lane College, founded in 1882, is a private liberal arts institution affiliated with the Christian Methodist Episcopal Church. The library contains 97,619 volumes, 13,657 microform items, and 1800 audiovisual forms/CDs, and subscribes to 285 periodicals. Computerized library services include the card catalog, interlibrary loans, and database searching. Special learning facilities include a learning resource center and a media center, several computer labs for students majoring in education and other areas, a curriculum lab, and a video teleconferencing center. The 25-acre campus is in a small town 79 miles from Memphis, 122 miles from Nashville. Including residence halls, there are 23 buildings.

Student Life: 56% of undergraduates are from Tennessee. Others are from 29 states. 85% are from public schools. 99% are African American. Most are Protestant. The average age of freshmen is 21; all undergraduates, 21. 20% do not continue beyond their first year; 65% remain to graduate.

Housing: 650 students can be accommodated in college housing, which includes single-sex dormitories and on-campus apartments. On-campus housing is guaranteed for all 4 years. 74% of students live on campus; of those, 40% remain on campus on weekends. Alcohol is not permitted. All students may keep cars.

Activities: 3% of men belong to 2 local and 2 national fraternities; 9% of women belong to 4 local and 4 national sororities. There are 21 groups on campus, including band, cheerleading, chess, choir, computers, drama, honors, marching band, musical theater, newspaper, pep band, religious, social, social service, student government, and yearbook. Popular campus events include Founders Day, Fine Arts Week, and Religious Emphasis Week.

Sports: There are 6 intercollegiate sports for men and 6 for women, and 4 intramural sports for men and 4 for women. Facilities include an Olympic-size swimming pool, a multipurpose/weight room, a gym, off-campus football and baseball fields, and a campus recreation center with a theater area, dance floor, billiards, Ping Pong, table games, and a lounge area.

Disabled Students: 22% of the campus is accessible. Wheelchair ramps, elevators, special parking, specially equipped rest rooms, and wheelchair lifts in some buildings are available.

Services: Counseling and information services are available, as is tutoring in most subjects. There is remedial math, reading, and writing. The Writing Center provides tutoring in writing and the Mathematics Lab offers tutoring in math. Student Support Services provides tutoring in English, math, reading, computer science, computer literacy, test-taking, and study skills.

Campus Safety and Security: Measures include 24-hour foot and vehicle patrol, informal discussions, emergency telephones, and lighted pathways/sidewalks. There is a security guard at the entrance to the campus, and camera surveillance in parking lots and dorms.

Programs of Study: Lane confers B.A. and B.S. degrees. Bachelor's degrees are awarded in BIOLOGICAL SCIENCE (biology/biological science), BUSINESS (business administration and management), COMMUNICATIONS AND THE ARTS (communications, English, and music), COMPUTER AND PHYSICAL SCIENCE (chemistry, computer science, mathematics, and physics), EDUCATION (elementary and physical), SOCIAL SCIENCE (history, religion, and sociology). Business, education, and criminal justice are the strongest academically. Education, business, and sociology are the largest.

Required: Students must complete a minimum of 124 semester hours with a 2.0 GPA. 50 to 63 hours are required in the general studies curriculum, which includes courses in world cultures, art, music, foreign language, speech, composition, literature, history, sociology, math, physical science, biology, computer literacy, foundations of education, religion, and phys ed. The Praxis I (PPST) Comprehensive exam is also required. ETS Major Field Tests are given as exit exams by major.

Special: Cooperative programs are available in computer science with Jackson State University in Mississippi, and in engineering with Tennessee State University School of Engineering and Technology. The College also offers work-study programs, dual majors, student-designed majors, and nondegree study. Internships are available in criminal justice, business, sociology, communications, and health sciences at various corporations, universities, and federal agencies. There are 2 national honor societies.

Faculty/Classroom: 77% of faculty are male; 23%, female. All teach undergraduates. The average class size in an introductory lecture is 25; in a laboratory, 16; and in a regular course, 16.

Admissions: 41% of the 2001-2002 applicants were accepted. The ACT scores for the 2001-2002 freshman class were: 95% below 21, and 5% between 21 and 23. 20% of the current freshmen were in the top fifth of their class; 45% were in the top two fifths.

Requirements: The SAT I or ACT is required, with a minimum composite score of 13 on the ACT recommended. Graduation from an accredited secondary school is required; a GED will be accepted. Applicants' academic record must include 16 credits, including 4 credits in English, and 2 credits each in math, science, and social studies. An additional 2 credits in a foreign language is recommended. An interview is recommended. A GPA of 2.0 is required. AP and CLEP credits are accepted. Important factors in the admissions decision are ability to finance college education, recommendations by school officials, and evidence of special talent. Applications are accepted on-line.

Procedure: Freshmen are admitted to all sessions. Entrance exams should be taken by October of the senior year. There are early decision and early admissions plans. Applications should be filed by July 1 for fall entry, November 15 for spring entry, and May 15 for summer entry. Notification is sent on a rolling basis. 125 early decision candidates were accepted for a recent class.

Transfer: 15 transfer students enrolled in 2001-2002. Applicants must submit transcripts from previous colleges attended and be in good standing at the time of application. Students having an associate degree will be given credit for a maximum of 68 semester hours in general education courses with a grade of C or higher. 31 credits of 124 must be completed at Lane.

Visiting: There are regularly scheduled orientations for prospective students, including meetings on financial aid, residential life, rules and regulations of the college, course requirements, and registration. There are guides for informal visits and visitors may sit in on classes and stay overnight. To schedule a visit, contact the Office of Recruitment/Admissions.

Financial Aid: In 2001-2002, 98% of all students received some form of financial aid. 94% of freshmen and 95% of continuing students received need-based aid. The average freshman award was $9234. Of that total, scholarships or need-based grants averaged $4228 ($10,400 maximum); loans averaged $2477 ($6625 maximum); and work contracts averaged $956 ($2000 maximum). 37% of undergraduates work part time. Average annual earnings from campus work are $968. The average financial indebtedness of the 2001 graduate was $19,875. The CSS/Profile, FAFSA, FFS, or SFS is required. The fall application deadline is March 31.

International Students: They must take the TOEFL, and also take the SAT I or the ACT, scoring 13 on the ACT.

Computers: The mainframe is an IBM A/S 400. All students have access to the Internet and Web through the libary and 3 computer labs with approximately 120 PCs. All dorms are wired. There are computer study centers on each dorm floor and in lower levels. There is also a computer center containing 50 computers in the Annex. All students may access the system. There are no time limits and no fees.

Graduates: In 2001, 88 bachelor's degrees were awarded. The most popular majors were criminal justice (16%), computer science (15%), and interdisciplinary studies (14%). In an average class, 35% graduate in 4 years, 40% in 5 years, and 49% in 6 years. 25 companies recruited on campus in 2000-2001. Of the 2000 graduating class, 26% were enrolled in graduate school within 6 months of graduation and 37% were employed.

Admissions Contact: Evelyn L. Brown, Director of Admissions. A video is available. E-mail: *ebrown@lanecollege.edu*
Web: *www.lanecollege.edu*

LEE UNIVERSITY — D-4
Cleveland, TN 37311
(423) 614-8500
(800) 533-9930; Fax: (423) 614-8533

Full-time: 1260 men, 1660 women	**Faculty:** 131; IIB, --$
Part-time: 120 men, 120 women	**Ph.D.s:** 58%
Graduate: 40 men, 65 women	**Student/Faculty:** 22 to 1
Year: semesters, summer session	**Tuition:** $6400
Application Deadline: see profile	**Room & Board:** $3900
Freshman Class: n/av	
SAT I Verbal/Math: required	**LESS COMPETITIVE**

Lee University, founded in 1918, is a private liberal arts institution affiliated with the Church of God. There are 4 undergraduate and 4 graduate schools. Information in the above capsule, and in this profile, is approximate. In addition to regional accreditation, Lee has baccalaureate program accreditation with NASM. The 2 libraries contain 153,424 volumes, 4984 microform items, and 12,881 audiovisual forms/CDs, and subscribe to 2000 periodicals. Computerized library services include the card catalog, interlibrary loans, and database searching. Special learning facilities include a learning resource center, natural history museum, and audiovisual center. The campus is in a suburban area 25 miles north of Chattanooga.

Student Life: 64% of undergraduates are from out of state, mostly the South. Others are from 46 states, 30 foreign countries, and Canada. 75% are from public schools. 89% are white. Most are Protestant. The average age of freshmen is 19; all undergraduates, 21. 29% do not continue beyond their first year; 67% remain to graduate.

Housing: About 2188 students can be accommodated in college housing, which includes single-sex dormitories, on-campus apartments, off-campus apartments, and married-student housing. On-campus housing is guaranteed for the freshman year only and is available on a first-come, first-served basis. Alcohol is not permitted. All students may keep cars.

Activities: There are no fraternities or sororities. There are 61 groups on campus, including band, cheerleading, choir, chorale, chorus, computers, debate, drama, ethnic, film, honors, international, jazz band, literary magazine, musical theater, newspaper, opera, orchestra, pep band, photography, political, professional, radio and TV, religious, social, social service, student government, symphony, and yearbook. Popular campus events include College Day, Parade of Favorites, and Dorm Wars.

Sports: There are 6 intercollegiate sports for men and 6 for women, and 20 intramural sports for men and 20 for women. Facilities include an arena, a recreation complex, a softball field, a tennis center, a soccer field, a baseball field, and a playing field.

Disabled Students: 75% of the campus is accessible. Wheelchair ramps, elevators, special parking, specially equipped rest rooms, special class scheduling, and lowered drinking fountains are available.

Services: Counseling and information services are available, as is tutoring in every subject. There is a reader service for the blind, and remedial math, reading, and writing.

Campus Safety and Security: Measures include 24-hour foot and vehicle patrol, escort service, informal discussions, and pamphlets/posters/films. There are lighted pathways/sidewalks.

Programs of Study: Lee confers B.A., B.S., and B.M.E. degrees. Master's degrees are also awarded. Bachelor's degrees are awarded in BIOLOGICAL SCIENCE (biology/biological science), BUSINESS (accounting, and business administration and management), COMMUNICATIONS AND THE ARTS (communications, English, French, German, music, and Spanish), COMPUTER AND PHYSICAL SCIENCE (chemistry, computer programming, mathematics, and science), EDUCATION (elementary, music, and physical), HEALTH PROFESSIONS (medical laboratory technology), SOCIAL SCIENCE (crosscultural studies, history, human development, psychology, religious education, social science, and sociology). English, sociology, Bible, and theology are the strongest academically. Business, human development, psychology, and biology are the largest.

Required: All students must complete a minimum of 130 credit hours, including 8 hours in lab science, 6 each in history, English composition, Bible, theology, and religion electives, 4 in literature, 3 each in general psychology, general sociology, and math, and 2 each in fine arts and physical activity. A minimum of 36 hours in the major is required. Students must have a minimum GPA of 2.0.

Special: Lee offers internships, cross-registration with the Coalition for Christian Colleges and Universities, study abroad, a Washington semester, numerous work-study programs, dual and student-designed majors, nondegree study, and limited pass/fail options. Every student completes a minor in religion. There are 6 national honor societies, a freshman honors program, and 1 departmental honors program.

Faculty/Classroom: 67% of faculty are male; 33%, female. All teach undergraduates and 20% both teach and do research. No introductory courses are taught by graduate students. The average class size in an introductory lecture is 45; in a laboratory, 22; and in a regular course, 25.

Admissions: In a recent year, 20% of the current freshmen were in the top fifth of their class; 64% were in the top two fifths. 18 freshmen graduated first in their class.

Requirements: The SAT I or ACT is required, with a composite score of 860 on the SAT I or 17 on the ACT. Students must be graduates of accredited secondary schools. The GED is accepted. A portfolio is recommended. A GPA of 2.0 is required. AP and CLEP credits are accepted. Important factors in the admissions decision are advanced placement or honor courses, leadership record, and recommendations by school officials.

Procedure: Freshmen are admitted fall and spring. Entrance exams should be taken prior to registration. Notification is sent on a rolling basis. Check with the school for current application deadlines and fee.

Transfer: 395 transfer students enrolled in a recent year. Transfer students must take the SAT I, scoring 860, or the ACT, scoring 17, unless they have 16 credit hours with a GPA of 2.0 or better. 30 credits of 130 must be completed at Lee.

Visiting: There are regularly scheduled orientations for prospective students. The Admissions Office will arrange a complete campus tour upon request. There are guides for informal visits and visitors may sit in on classes. To schedule a visit, contact the Admissions Center.

Financial Aid: In a recent year, 75% of all freshmen and 72% of continuing students received some form of financial aid. 70% of freshmen and 80% of continuing students received need-based aid. The average freshman award was $5589. Of that total, scholarships or need-based grants averaged $3057 ($10,030 maximum); loans averaged $2442 ($4625 maximum); work contracts averaged $1513 ($2637 maximum); and PLUS/SLS averaged $5425 ($10,300 maximum). 10% of undergraduates work part time. Average annual earnings from campus work are $1513. The average financial indebtedness of a recent graduate was $10,892. Lee is a member of CSS. The FAFSA and the college's own financial statement are required. Check with the school for current deadlines.

International Students: The school actively recruits these students. They must score 450 on the written TOEFL.

Computers: The mainframe is an IBM AS/400. There are PCs available for student use in the computer labs. All students may access the system. There are no time limits.

Graduates: In a recent year, 464 bachelor's degrees were awarded. The most popular majors were human development (13%), psychology (9%), and communications (9%). In an average class, 1% graduate in 3 years, 19% in 4 years, 27% in 5 years, and 30% in 6 years.

Admissions Contact: Gary T. Ray, Director of Admissions.
E-mail: *admissions@leeuniversity.edu*
Web: *http://www.leeuniversity.edu*

LEMOYNE-OWEN COLLEGE — A-4
Memphis, TN 38126 — (901) 942-7302
737-7778; Fax: (901) 942-6233

Full-time: 195 men, 431 women
Part-time: 27 men, 82 women
Graduate: none
Year: semesters, summer session
Application Deadline: April 1
Freshman Class: n/av
SAT I or ACT: required
Faculty: 49; IIB, --$
Ph.D.s: 80%
Student/Faculty: 13 to 1
Tuition: $8450
Room & Board: n/app
NONCOMPETITIVE

LeMoyne-Owen College, established in 1872, is a private, commuter institution affiliated with the United Church of Christ and the Tennessee Baptist, Missionary and Educational Convention, offering degrees in the liberal arts and sciences and business administration. The library contains 90,000 volumes and 1000 audiovisual forms/CDs, and subscribes to 300 periodicals. Computerized library services include the card catalog, interlibrary loans, and database searching. Special learning facilities include a learning resource center and art gallery. The 15-acre campus is in an urban area. There are 18 buildings.

Student Life: 90% of undergraduates are from Tennessee. Others are from 20 states and 3 foreign countries. 92% are from public schools. 98% are African American. Most are Protestant. The average age of freshmen is 19; all undergraduates, 21. 20% do not continue beyond their first year; 25% remain to graduate.

Housing: There are no residence halls. Off-campus apartments accommodate 175 students. Contact theschool for information. Priority is given to out-of-town students. All students commute. Alcohol is not permitted. All students may keep cars.

Activities: 45% of men belong to 4 local and 4 national fraternities; 35% of women belong to 4 local and 4 national sororities. There are 15 groups on campus, including cheerleading, choir, chorus, Community outreach, computers, drama, ethnic, math, newspaper, photography, professional, religious, social service, student government, and yearbook. Popular campus events include Heritage Day and Homecoming Week.

Sports: There are 3 intercollegiate sports for men, and 1 intramural sports for men and 5 for women. Facilities include a gymnasium, a pool, and other phys ed installations.

Disabled Students: 90% of the campus is accessible. Wheelchair ramps and elevators are available.

Services: Counseling and information services are available, as is tutoring in every subject. There is remedial math, reading, and writing.

Campus Safety and Security: Measures include 24-hour foot and vehicle patrol, escort service, emergency telephones, and lighted pathways/sidewalks.

Programs of Study: LOC confers B.A., B.S., and B.B.A. degrees. Bachelor's degrees are awarded in BIOLOGICAL SCIENCE (biology/biological science), BUSINESS (accounting and business administration and management), COMMUNICATIONS AND THE ARTS (art and English), COMPUTER AND PHYSICAL SCIENCE (chemistry, computer science, mathematics, and natural sciences), EDUCATION (education), SOCIAL SCIENCE (history, humanities, political science/government, social science, social work, and sociology). Business, biology, and education are the strongest academically. Business and education are the largest.

Required: To graduate, students must satisfy 48 hours of core requirements in communication, mathematics, natural and computer sciences, literature and the humanities, African and African American history, social and behavioral sciences, and physical fitness. They must have a minimum GPA of 2.0 and grades of C or better in all major courses. The college requires 130 credits for graduation, including at least 45 in upper-division courses. All recent high school graduates must participate in the Freshman Year Experience Program.

Special: Students may cross-register with other institutions of the Greater Memphis Consortium. The college offers a work-study program, dual and student-designed majors, internships, nondegree study, and a pass/fail grading option. There are dual-degree programs in pharmacy with Xavier School of Pharmacy, in optometry with Southern College of Optometry, and in engineering with Southern Illinois University, Tuskegee University, and Christian Brothers University. There is 1 national honor society, a freshman honors program, and all departments have honors programs.

Faculty/Classroom: 50% of faculty are male; 50%, female. All teach undergraduates and 40% do research. The average class size in an introductory lecture is 15; in a laboratory, 15; and in a regular course, 12.

Admissions: All of the 2001-2002 applicants were accepted.

Requirements: The SAT I or ACT is required. In addition, applicants must graduate from an accredited secondary school, having completed 20 high school units. The college recommends 4 years of English, 2 each of math, science, and social studies, and 1 of a foreign language. Applicants must submit 2 letters of recommendation. Students 23 or older may be admitted to the division of lifelong learning, which accepts the GED. A GPA of 2.0 is required. AP and CLEP credits are accepted. Important factors in the admissions decision are advanced placement or honor courses, evidence of special talent, and parents or siblings attending the school.

Procedure: Freshmen are admitted to all sessions. Entrance exams should be taken in the spring of the junior year. There are early decision, early admissions, and deferred admissions plans. Applications should be filed by April 1 for fall entry, November 1 for spring entry, and March 1 for summer entry, along with a $25 fee. The college accepts all applicants. Notification is sent on a rolling basis. 13 early decision candidates were accepted for the 2001-2002 class.

Transfer: 122 transfer students enrolled in 2001-2002. Applicants should have a GPA of 2.0 and must submit 2 copies of official transcripts plus a statement of good standing from the previous college attended. Students with fewer than 28 college credit hours must also submit a high school transcript and, if below age 21, ACT or SAT I score. 30 credits of 130 must be completed at LOC.

Visiting: There are regularly scheduled orientations for prospective students. There are guides for informal visits and visitors may sit in on classes. To schedule a visit, contact Lonnie Morris.

Financial Aid: In 2001-2002, 90% of all students received some form of financial aid. 80% of freshmen and 90% of continuing students received need-based aid. 90% of undergraduates work part time. Average annual earnings from campus work are $2880. LOC is a member of CSS. The FAFSA and the college's own financial statement are required. The fall application deadline is June 1.

International Students: 14 international students enrolled in a recent year. They must score 525 on the written TOEFL and also take the ACT.

Computers: The mainframe is a DEC VAX 11/750. There are also 25 microcomputers and 5 mainframe systems with networking available for student use. All students may access the system. There are no time limits and no fees. It is strongly recommended that all students have personal computers.

Graduates: In 2001, 118 bachelor's degrees were awarded. The most popular majors were business management (37%), liberal studies (12%), and education (12%). In an average class, 60% graduate in 5 years, and 100% in 6 years. 55 companies recruited on campus in 2000-2001. Of the 2000 graduating class, 6% were enrolled in graduate school within 6 months of graduation and 7% were employed.

Admissions Contact: Lonnie Morris, Director of Admissions.
E-mail: *lonnie_morris@nile.lemoyne-owen.edu*
Web: *www.lemoyne-owen.edu*

LINCOLN MEMORIAL UNIVERSITY — E-2
Harrogate, TN 37752-0901 — (423) 869-6280
(800) 325-0900; Fax: (423) 869-6370

Full-time: 230 men, 445 women
Part-time: 60 men, 145 women
Graduate: 250 men, 590 women
Year: semesters, summer session
Application Deadline: open
Freshman Class: n/av
SAT I or ACT: required
Faculty: 72; IIB, --$
Ph.D.s: 55%
Student/Faculty: 9 to 1
Tuition: $9000
Room & Board: $3800
LESS COMPETITIVE

Lincoln Memorial University, founded in 1897, is an independent institution offering degree programs in the arts and sciences, business, education, and preprofessional training. There are 4 undergraduate and 2 graduate schools. In addition to regional accreditation, LMU has baccalaureate program accreditation with CAHEA and NLN. The library contains 130,000 volumes, 60,000 microform items, and 254 audiovisual forms/CDs, and subscribes to 3500 periodicals. Computerized library services include the card catalog, interlibrary loans, and database searching. Special learning facilities include a learning resource center, radio station, TV station, and and the Lincoln Museum. The 1000-acre campus is in a rural area 55 miles north of Knoxville. Including residence halls, there are 32 buildings.

Student Life: 54% of undergraduates are from out of state, mostly the South. Others are from 25 states, 17 foreign countries, and Canada. 89% are from public schools. 93% are white. The average age of freshmen is 19; all undergraduates, 23. 20% do not continue beyond their first year; 42% remain to graduate.

Housing: 500 students can be accommodated in college housing, which includes single-sex and coed dormitories, on-campus apartments, and married-student housing. On-campus housing is guaranteed for the freshman year only and is available on a first-come, first-served basis. Priority is given to out-of-town students. 60% of students commute. Alcohol is not permitted. All students may keep cars.

Activities: There are 3 local fraternities and 3 local sororities. There are 26 groups on campus, including art, cheerleading, choir, chorus, computers, drama, drill team, honors, international, literary magazine, newspaper, photography, radio and TV, religious, social service, student government, and yearbook. Popular campus events include Lincoln Day.

Sports: There are 6 intercollegiate sports for men and 6 for women, and 4 intramural sports for men and 4 for women. Facilities include a 5000-seat arena, a baseball field, a playing field, and a natatorium.

Disabled Students: 60% of the campus is accessible. Wheelchair ramps, elevators, special parking, and special class scheduling are available.

Services: Counseling and information services are available, as is tutoring in most subjects. There is remedial math, reading, and writing.

Campus Safety and Security: Measures include 24-hour foot and vehicle patrol, informal discussions, pamphlets/posters/films, and lighted pathways/sidewalks.

Programs of Study: LMU confers B.A., B.S., B.B.A., B.S.N., and B.S.W. degrees. Associate and master's degrees are also awarded. Bachelor's degrees are awarded in AGRICULTURE (wildlife management), BIOLOGICAL SCIENCE (biology/biological science), BUSINESS (accounting, and business administration and management), COMMUNICATIONS AND THE ARTS (broadcasting, communications, English, and fine arts), COMPUTER AND PHYSICAL SCIENCE (chemistry, information sciences and systems, and mathematics), EDUCATION (athletic training, business, early childhood, elementary, health, middle school, science, and secondary), ENGINEERING AND ENVIRONMENTAL DESIGN (environmental science), HEALTH PROFESSIONS (medical laboratory technology, nursing, predentistry, premedicine, and veterinary science), SOCIAL SCIENCE (history, prelaw, psychology, social science, and social work). Nursing, business, and education are the largest.

Required: To graduate, all students must complete at least 128 semester credit hours, including the general studies requirements of the declared major and a minimum of 30 hours of in the major. Students must achieve a minimum GPA of 2.0.

Special: LMU offers pass/fail options and credit for life, military, and work experience. Some internships are available.

Faculty/Classroom: 49% of faculty are male; 51%, female. 80% teach undergraduates. No introductory courses are taught by graduate students. The average class size in an introductory lecture is 20; in a laboratory, 25; and in a regular course, 20.

Requirements: The SAT I or ACT is required with a minimum score of 19 on the ACT. Candidates for admission should be graduates of accredited secondary schools or have the GED. Students should have completed 4 years of English, 2 each of math and science, and 1 each of history and social studies. LMU requires applicants to be in the upper 50% of their class. A GPA of 2.3 is required. AP and CLEP credits are accepted. Important factors in the admissions decision are recommendations by school officials, personality/intangible qualities, and leadership record.

Procedure: Freshmen are admitted fall, spring, and summer. Entrance exams should be taken in the spring of the junior year. There is a deferred admissions plan. Application deadlines are open. Check with the school for current application deadlines and fee.

Transfer: 126 transfer students enrolled in a recent year. 32 credits of 128 must be completed at LMU.

Visiting: There are regularly scheduled orientations for prospective students, including introductory sessions for both students and their parents and opportunities for advising, and registration sessions. There are guides for informal visits and visitors may sit in on classes and stay overnight. To schedule a visit, contact the Office of Admissions and Recruitment.

Financial Aid: In a recent year, 95% of all freshmen and 90% of continuing students received some form of financial aid. 66% of freshmen and 60% of continuing students received need-based aid. The average freshman award was $9253. Of that total, scholarships or need-based grants averaged $6373 ($13,020 maximum); loans averaged $2467 ($2625 maximum); and work contracts averaged $413 ($1800 maximum). 15% of undergraduates work part time. Average annual earnings from campus work are $1500. The average financial indebtedness of a recent graduate was $17,000. LMU is a member of CSS. The CSS/Profile, FAFSA, FFS or SFS is required. Check with the school for current deadlines.

International Students: There were 46 international students enrolled in a recent year. They must score 500 on the written TOEFL.

Computers: The mainframe is a DEC VAX 11/780. There are 40 IBM Model 30 and Five Star 286 PCs available in the student center, and several computers in the library and Tagge Center for Academic Excellence. All students may access the system. There are no time limits and no fees. It is strongly recommended that all students have a personal computer.

Graduates: In a recent year, 172 bachelor's degrees were awarded. The most popular majors were nursing (36%), elementary education (26%), and business (24%). In an average class, 42% graduate in 4 years. 40 companies recruited on campus in a recent year.

Admissions Contact: Conrad Daniels, Dean of Admissions.
E-mail: *cdaniels@inetlmu.lmunet.edu* Web: *www.lmunet.edu*

MARYVILLE COLLEGE — E-3

Maryville, TN 37804 (865) 981-8092
(800) 597-2687; Fax: (865) 981-8010

Full-time: 421 men, 577 women	**Faculty:** 63; IIB, --$
Part-time: 11 men, 17 women	**Ph.D.s:** 94%
Graduate: none	**Student/Faculty:** 16 to 1
Year: trimesters, summer session	**Tuition:** $17,560
Application Deadline: March 1	**Room & Board:** $5650
Freshman Class: 1494 applied, 1173 accepted, 288 enrolled	
SAT I Verbal/Math: 560/540	**ACT:** 24 **VERY COMPETITIVE**

Maryville College, founded in 1819, is a private liberal arts college affiliated with the Presbyterian Church (U.S.A.). There is 1 undergraduate school. In addition to regional accreditation, Maryville has baccalaureate program accreditation with NASM. The 2 libraries contain 120,251 volumes, 5842 microform items, and 3340 audiovisual forms/CDs, and subscribe to 1254 periodicals. Computerized library services include the card catalog, interlibrary loans, and database searching. Special learning facilities include a learning resource center, art gallery, greenhouse, and college woods. The 350-acre campus is in a suburban area 15 miles south of Knoxville. Including residence halls, there are 24 buildings.

Student Life: 72% of undergraduates are from Tennessee. Others are from 29 states and 19 foreign countries. 92% are from public schools. 88% are white. 64% are Protestant; 12% claim no religious affiliation; 11% Catholic. The average age of freshmen is 18; all undergraduates, 21. 29% do not continue beyond their first year; 52% remain to graduate.

Housing: 751 students can be accommodated in college housing, which includes single-sex and coed dormitories and on-campus apartments. In addition, there are language houses. On-campus housing is guaranteed for all 4 years. 70% of students live on campus; of those, 70% remain on campus on weekends. All students may keep cars.

Activities: There are no fraternities or sororities. There are 39 groups on campus, including art, band, cheerleading, choir, chorus, computers, dance, drama, equestrian, ethnic, gospel music, honors, international, jazz band, literary magazine, musical theater, newspaper, orchestra, pep band, photography, political, professional, religious, social service, student government, symphony, and yearbook. Popular campus events include Dogwood Arts Festival, Blister-in-the-Sun, and Spring Fling.

Sports: There are 7 intercollegiate sports for men and 7 for women, and 12 intramural sports for men and 11 for women. Facilities include a phys ed building with an indoor pool, tennis and racquetball courts, a weight room, football, soccer, baseball, and softball fields, and an off-campus equestrian arena.

Disabled Students: 75% of the campus is accessible. Wheelchair ramps, elevators, special parking, special class scheduling, and lowered drinking fountains are available.

Services: Counseling and information services are available, as is tutoring in every subject. There is a reader service for the blind, remedial math, and sign language interpreters for deaf students.

Campus Safety and Security: Measures include 24-hour foot and vehicle patrol, informal discussions, and lighted pathways/sidewalks.

Programs of Study: Maryville confers B.A. and B.Mus. degrees. Bachelor's degrees are awarded in AGRICULTURE (environmental studies), BIOLOGICAL SCIENCE (biochemistry and biology/biological science), BUSINESS (business administration and management and recreation and leisure services), COMMUNICATIONS AND THE ARTS (American Sign Language, art, creative writing, dramatic arts, English, English as a second/foreign language, fine arts, music, music performance, and Spanish), COMPUTER AND PHYSICAL SCIENCE (chemistry, computer science, mathematics, and physics), EDUCATION (art, elementary, music, physical, science, and secondary), ENGINEERING AND ENVIRONMENTAL DESIGN (engineering and preengineering), HEALTH PROFESSIONS (health science, nursing, predentistry, and premedicine), SOCIAL SCIENCE (economics, history, human services, international relations, interpreter for the deaf, political science/government, prelaw, psychology, religion, social science, and sociology). Biology, chemistry, and English are the strongest academically. Business, biology, and child development with teacher licensure are the largest.

Required: Each degree has its own general education requirements, which include humanities and a foreign language. Students must complete at least 128 total credit hours, including 48 in the major, and must maintain a minimum 2.0 GPA. A year-long freshman seminar and orientation are required in addition to a senior thesis in all majors and senior comprehensive exams.

Special: Maryville offers cross-registration and co-op programs with the University of Tennessee, and Vanderbilt University internships, study abroad in 7 countries, a Washington semester, accelerated degree programs, a B.A.-B.S. degree in engineering, and dual and student-designed majors. There are 3-2 engineering degrees offered with regional universities. Nondegree study and pass/fail options are possible. There are 6 national honor societies and a freshman honors program. All departments have honors programs.

Faculty/Classroom: 52% of faculty are male; 48%, female. All both teach undergraduates and do research. The average class size in an introductory lecture is 27; in a laboratory, 16; and in a regular course, 16.

Admissions: 79% of the 2001-2002 applicants were accepted. The SAT I scores for the 2001-2002 freshman class were: Verbal--26% below 500, 35% between 500 and 599, 29% between 600 and 700, and 10% above 700; Math--25% below 500, 50% between 500 and 599, 23% between 600 and 700, and 2% above 700. 61% of the current freshmen were in the top fifth of their class; 85% were in the top two fifths. 8 freshmen graduated first in their class.

Requirements: The SAT I or ACT is required. In addition, the minimum composite score on the SAT I is 950; on the ACT, 20. Candidates should be graduates of accredited secondary schools or have the GED. They should also have 15 academic credits with 4 years of English, 3 each of math and science, 2 years of foreign language, and 2 of history or social studies. An essay, portfolio, audition, and interview are all recommended. A GPA of 2.5 is required. AP and CLEP credits are accepted. Important factors in the admissions decision are advanced placement or honor courses, leadership record, and evidence of special talent. Applications are accepted on-line at the school's web site.

Procedure: Freshmen are admitted fall, spring, and summer. Entrance exams should be taken in October of the senior year. There are early decision, early admissions, and deferred admissions plans. Early decision applications should be filed by November 15; regular applications, by March 1 for fall entry, November 1 for spring entry, and May 1 for summer entry, along with a $25 fee. Notification of early decision is sent December 1; regular decision, April 1. 54 early decision candidates were accepted for the 2001-2002 class.

Transfer: 63 transfer students enrolled in 2001-2002. Transfer applicants must have a minimum GPA of 2.0 and a recommended 15 credit hours earned. An interview is also recommended. 45 credits of 128 must be completed at Maryville.

Visiting: There are regularly scheduled orientations for prospective students, including an overnight in a residence hall, class attendance, meeting with students and faculty, a campus tour, and an interview. There are guides for informal visits and visitors may sit in on classes and stay overnight. To schedule a visit, contact the Admissions Office.

Financial Aid: In 2001-2002, all freshmen and 99% of continuing students received some form of financial aid. 81% of freshmen and 77% of continuing students received need-based aid. The average freshman award was $18,148. Of that total, scholarships or need-based grants averaged $8365 ($18,485 maximum); loans averaged $4978 ($22,625 maximum); and work contracts averaged $1200 (maximum). 34% of undergraduates work part time. Average annual earnings from campus work are $1200. The FAFSA is required. The fall application deadline is March 1.

International Students: The school actively recruits these students. They must score 525 on the written TOEFL or take the MELAB.

Computers: There are 62 PCs on a local area network in staffed student labs with access to e-mail, the Internet, and the Web. All residence hall rooms and most classrooms are networked. All students may access the system 7 days a week, 16 hours a day. There are no time limits and no fees. It is strongly recommended that all students have a personal computer.

Graduates: In 2001, 152 bachelor's degrees were awarded. The most popular majors were business (16%), child development (14%), and psychology (7%). In an average class, 40% graduate in 4 years, 50% in 5 years, and 52% in 6 years. 80 companies recruited on campus in 2000-2001. Of the 2000 graduating class, 20% were enrolled in graduate school within 6 months of graduation and 95% were employed.

Admissions Contact: Rick Zielger, Vice President, Admissions/Enrollment. E-mail: *ziegler@maryvillecollege.edu*

MEMPHIS COLLEGE OF ART — A-4

Memphis, TN 38104 — (901) 272-5151

(800) 727-1088; Fax: (901) 272-5158

Full-time: 126 men, 115 women	**Faculty:** 17; IIB, --$
Part-time: 9 men, 15 women	**Ph.D.s:** n/av
Graduate: 20 men, 15 women	**Student/Faculty:** 13 to 1
Year: semesters, summer session	**Tuition:** $13,800
Application Deadline: open	**Room & Board:** $5400
Freshman Class: 207 applied, 74 enrolled	
ACT: 21	**SPECIAL**

Memphis College of Art, established in 1936, is a nonprofit, private, independent institution offering degree programs in fine arts and design arts, including studio art, fiber/surface design, computer arts, and photography. There are 3 graduate schools. In addition to regional accreditation, MCA has baccalaureate program accreditation with NASAD. The library contains 18,000 volumes, and subscribes to 120 periodicals. Computerized library services include interlibrary loans. Special learning facilities include a learning resource center and art gallery. The 200-acre campus is in an urban area in Memphis. Including residence halls, there are 4 buildings.

Student Life: 60% of undergraduates are from Tennessee. Others are from 20 states, 10 foreign countries, and Canada. 69% are from public schools. 76% are white; 14% African American. The average age of freshmen is 20; all undergraduates, 23. 22% do not continue beyond their first year; 65% remain to graduate.

Housing: 27 students can be accommodated in college housing, which includes coed on-campus apartments and off-campus apartments. On-campus housing is available on a first-come, first-served basis. Priority is given to out-of-town students. Alcohol is not permitted. All students may keep cars.

Activities: There are no fraternities or sororities. There are 2 groups on campus, including art and student government. Popular campus events include Holiday Bazaar, weekend workshops, gallery openings, and international dinners.

Sports: There is no sports program at MCA. Facilities include those provided by the 200-acre city park on which MCA is located. There is an adjacent public golf course, playing fields, and a volleyball court. Regular Saturday football, soccer, and bicycling are popular activities.

Disabled Students: All of the campus is accessible. Wheelchair ramps, elevators, special parking, specially equipped rest rooms, lowered drinking fountains, and lowered telephones are available.

Services: Counseling and information services are available, as is tutoring in some subjects, including liberal studies classes.

Campus Safety and Security: Measures include informal discussions, pamphlets/posters/films, lighted pathways/sidewalks, and a security guard in the buildings in the evening, at night, and on weekends.

Programs of Study: MCA confers the B.F.A. degree. Master's degrees are also awarded. Bachelor's degrees are awarded in COMMUNICATIONS AND THE ARTS (design and fine arts).

Required: Students must complete 129 credit hours, including 33 in the major, with a minimum GPA of 2.0. Distribution requirements comprise 45 credits in liberal studies, including 12 in art history, 6 in English, and 3 each in humanities, social sciences, and natural sciences; 30 credits in elective studio art; and 21 credits in foundation classes, including drawing, design, and color theory.

Special: Special academic programs include off-campus internships for juniors in advertising agencies, design firms, or other educational situations; on-campus work-study, including an in-house student advertising agency where students can get paid work experience dealing with clients; and study abroad in Europe, Canada, or Japan. There are co-op programs with Rhodes, Lemoyne-Owen, and Christian Brothers Colleges as well as with Memphis Theological Seminary, and there is cross-registration with the Alliance in Independent Colleges of Art and Design. Accelerated degree programs in all areas, a dual major in painting and illustration, student-designed majors, and credit for life and work experience are available. Nondegree study is offered, as are pass/fail options for the workshop weeks.

Faculty/Classroom: 75% of faculty are male; 25%, female. 93% teach undergraduates. Graduate students teach 2% of introductory courses. The average class size in an introductory lecture is 20 and in a regular course, 15.

Admissions: The ACT scores for the 2001-2002 freshman class were: 51% below 21, 26% between 21 and 23, 13% between 24 and 26, 8% between 27 and 28, and 2% above 28.

Requirements: The SAT I or ACT is required. In addition, test scores are used for admissions and placement purposes. Other admissions requirements include graduation from an accredited secondary school, with a varying number of academic credits required. A portfolio must be presented, and the score on it is based on the application, transcripts, and the portfolio itself, which is used for acceptance and scholarships. An essay and an interview are advised. The GED is also accepted. A GPA of 2.0 is required. AP and CLEP credits are accepted. Important

factors in the admissions decision are evidence of special talent, advanced placement or honor courses, and extracurricular activities record. Applications are accepted on-line and on computer disk.
Procedure: Freshmen are admitted fall and spring. Application deadlines are open. The application fee is $25.
Transfer: 41 transfer students enrolled in a recent year. Applicants must submit official college transcripts and a portfolio. 48 credits of 129 must be completed at MCA.
Visiting: There are regularly scheduled orientations for prospective students. There are guides for informal visits and visitors may sit in on classes. To schedule a visit, contact the Admissions Office.
Financial Aid: In a recent year, 90% of all freshmen and 80% of continuing students received some form of financial aid. Scholarships or need-based grants averaged $3000 ($13,540 maximum); loans averaged $3000 ($6625 maximum); and work contracts averaged $1000 ($1500 maximum). Title IV funds and outside scholarships are also available. The average financial indebtedness of a recent graduate was $10,000. MCA is a member of CSS. The FAFSA is required. Check with the school for current deadlines.
International Students: There were 20 international students enrolled in a recent year. The school actively recruits these students. They must score 500 on the written TOEFL or 173 on the electronic version.
Computers: There are 60 Mac PCs available in the foundation, design arts, and weaving departments and in the writing lab and library. All students may access the system. There are no time limits and no fees.
Graduates: In a recent year, 40 bachelor's degrees were awarded. 10 companies recruited on campus in 2000-2001.
Admissions Contact: Annette Moore, Director of Admissions.
E-mail: *info@mca.edu* Web: *www.mca.edu*

MIDDLE TENNESSEE STATE UNIVERSITY C-3
Murfreesboro, TN 37132 (615) 898-2111
(800) 433-MTSU; Fax: (615) 898-5478

Full-time: 6982 men, 8118 women	**Faculty:** 680; IIA, --$
Part-time: 1422 men, 1608 women	**Ph.D.s:** 73%
Graduate: 756 men, 1187 women	**Student/Faculty:** 22 to 1
Year: semesters, summer session	**Tuition:** $3194 ($9166)
Application Deadline: July 1	**Room & Board:** $3800
Freshman Class: 5459 applied, 4939 accepted, 2904 enrolled	
SAT I Verbal/Math: 527/513	**ACT:** 22 **COMPETITIVE**

Middle Tennessee State University, founded in 1911, is a comprehensive public university that offers undergraduate and graduate programs reflecting an emphasis on research, creative arts, and public and professionsl service activities. There are 6 undergraduate schools and 1 graduate school. In addition to regional accreditation, MTSU has baccalaureate program accreditation with AACSB, AAFCS, ABET, ACEJMC, ACS, ADA, AHEA, CAA, CAAHEP, CSAB, CSWE, FIDER, NASAD, NASM, NCATE, NLN, and NRPA. The library contains 673,162 volumes and 1,255,430 microform items, and subscribes to 3567 periodicals. Computerized library services include the card catalog, interlibrary loans, and database searching. Special learning facilities include a learning resource center, art gallery, radio station, TV station, and and numerous research centers. The 500-acre campus is in an urban area 32 miles southeast of Nashville. Including residence halls, there are 159 buildings.
Student Life: 90% of undergraduates are from Tennessee. Others are from 47 states, 78 foreign countries, and Canada. 85% are white; 11% African American. 48% are Protestant; 43% claim no religious affiliation. The average age of freshmen is 20; all undergraduates, 24. 25% do not continue beyond their first year; 40% remain to graduate.
Housing: 3385 students can be accommodated in college housing, which includes single-sex dormitories, on-campus apartments, and married-student housing. In addition, there are honors houses, a Fisrt Year Experience program, and various Learning Community programs. On-campus housing is available on a first-come, first-served basis. 73% of students commute. Alcohol is not permitted. All students may keep cars.
Activities: 8% of men belong to 15 national fraternities; 8% of women belong to 1 local and 11 national sororities. There are 153 groups on campus, including art, band, cheerleading, chess, choir, chorale, chorus, computers, dance, drama, drill team, ethnic, film, gay, honors, international, jazz band, literary magazine, marching band, musical theater, newspaper, opera, orchestra, pep band, photography, political, professional, radio and TV, religious, social, social service, student government, symphony, and yearbook. Popular campus events include Founders Day, Family Day, and African Ameican History Month.
Sports: There are 8 intercollegiate sports for men and 9 for women, and 13 intramural sports for men and 13 for women. Facilities include an athletic center with a 30,000-seat stadium, a 12,000-seat gym, a soccer/track complex, tennis courts, and baseball and softball fields, and a recreation center with 12 courts, an indoor track, indoor and outdoor pools, a rock-climbing wall, and a sand volleyball court.
Disabled Students: All of the campus is accessible. Wheelchair ramps, elevators, special parking, specially equipped rest rooms, special class scheduling, lowered drinking fountains, and lowered telephones are available.
Services: Counseling and information services are available, as is tutoring in most subjects. There is a reader service for the blind, and remedial math, reading, and writing.
Campus Safety and Security: Measures include 24-hour foot and vehicle patrol, escort service, shuttle buses, and pamphlets/posters/films. There are emergency telephones and lighted pathways/sidewalks.
Programs of Study: MTSU confers B.A., B.S., B.B.A., B.F.A., B.Mus., B.S.N., B.S.W., and B.U.S. degrees. Associate, master's, and doctoral degrees are also awarded. Bachelor's degrees are awarded in AGRICULTURE (agricultural business management, animal science, and plant science), BIOLOGICAL SCIENCE (biology/biological science and nutrition), BUSINESS (accounting, banking and finance, business administration and management, entrepreneurial studies, labor studies, marketing/retailing/merchandising, office supervision and management, organizational behavior, and recreation and leisure services), COMMUNICATIONS AND THE ARTS (communications, dramatic arts, English, French, German, graphic design, music, music business management, public relations, Spanish, speech/debate/rhetoric, and studio art), COMPUTER AND PHYSICAL SCIENCE (chemistry, computer science, information sciences and systems, mathematics, physics, and science), EDUCATION (art, athletic training, business, early childhood, health, industrial arts, marketing and distribution, physical, and special), ENGINEERING AND ENVIRONMENTAL DESIGN (aerospace studies, engineering technology, environmental science, industrial engineering technology, and interior design), HEALTH PROFESSIONS (health science and nursing), SOCIAL SCIENCE (anthropology, child psychology/development, criminal justice, economics, family/consumer studies, geography, history, interdisciplinary studies, international relations, philosophy, political science/government, prelaw, psychology, public administration, social work, sociology, and textiles and clothing). Aerospace and preprofessional programs are the strongest academically. Mass communication is the largest.
Required: To graduate, a total of at least 132 hours, including at least 48 of upper-level courses, is needed with a minimum overall GPA of 2.0. All students must complete the general studies requirements, including 9 hours each of natural science/math and humanities, 6 each of English composition and history; 2 of phys ed, and demonstrated computer literacy. A major field test and general studies exam are required.
Special: MTSU offers co-op programs in aerospace, computer science, math, engineering technology, and industrial studies, cross-registration with Tennessee State University, internships, study abroad, a general studies degree, student-designed majors, nondegree study, and pass/fail options. Credit for life, military, and work experience may be granted. There are 2 national honor societies, a freshman honors program, and 25 departmental honors program.
Faculty/Classroom: 59% of faculty are male; 41%, female. Graduate students teach 13% of introductory courses. The average class size in an introductory lecture is 25; in a laboratory, 23; and in a regular course, 22.
Admissions: 90% of the 2001-2002 applicants were accepted. The ACT scores for the 2001-2002 freshman class were: 40% below 21, 31% between 21 and 23, 18% between 24 and 26, 6% between 27 and 28, and 5% above 28. 32% of the current freshmen were in the top fifth of their class; 61% were in the top two fifths. There was 1 National Merit finalist. 44 freshmen graduated first in their class.
Requirements: The SAT I or ACT is required, with a minimum composite score of 20 on the ACT if the GPA is less than 2.8. The GED is accepted. The number of academic credits required is 14, including 4 years of English, 3 of math, 2 each of a foreign language and science, and 1 each of social studies, U.S. history, and visual and/or performance arts, with an additional unit of math, language, or art recommended. Applications are accepted on-line at *www.applyweb.com*. A GPA of 2.8 is required. AP and CLEP credits are accepted.
Procedure: Freshmen are admitted to all sessions. Entrance exams should be taken in the first half of the senior year. There is an early admissions plan. Applications should be filed by July 1 for fall entry and December 1 for spring entry, along with a $15 fee. Notification is sent on a rolling basis.
Transfer: 1932 transfer students enrolled in 2001-2002. Applicants must have a minimum 2.0 GPA and submit official transcripts from all previous colleges attended. If transferring fewer than 9 semester hours, they must also meet freshman admission requirements. A minimum of 33 credits of 132 must be completed at MTSU.
Visiting: There are regularly scheduled orientations for prospective students, including campus tours weekdays and on specified Saturdays; students attending weekday tours can arrange to meet with a departmental adviser. There are guides for informal visits and visitors may sit in on classes. To schedule a visit, contact the Office of Admissions at (615) 898-5670 or (800) 331-MTSU (in-state).
Financial Aid: The FAFSA is required. The fall application deadline is May 15.
International Students: There are 328 international students enrolled. They must score 500 on the written TOEFL or 173 on the electronic ver-

sion or 80 on the MELAB. The university requires a minimum of 20 on the ACT or 930 on the SAT I.

Computers: The mainframes are an HP 9000/V2200 and a Compaq Alpha Cluster. There are about 4000 PCs available that can access the network in more than 60 student labs and in faculty and staff offices. All students may access the system 24 hours a day. There are no time limits and no fees.

Graduates: In 2001, 2525 bachelor's degrees were awarded. The most popular majors were interdisciplinary studies (10%), mass communication (9%), and recording industry (8%). In an average class, 1% graduate in 3 years, 12% in 4 years, 32% in 5 years, and 43% in 6 years. 200 companies recruited on campus in 2000-2001. Of the 2000 graduating class, 22% were enrolled in graduate school within 6 months of graduation and 8% were employed.

Admissions Contact: Sherian Huddleston, Interim Assistant Vice President, Enrollment Management. E-mail: *admissions@mtsu.edu*
Web: *www.mtsu.edu*

MILLIGAN COLLEGE F-2
Milligan College, TN 37682 (423) 461-8730
(800) 262-8337; Fax: (423) 461-8982

Full-time: 310 men, 459 women	**Faculty:** 63; IIB, --$
Part-time: 9 men, 11 women	**Ph.D.s:** 71%
Graduate: 23 men, 87 women	**Student/Faculty:** 12 to 1
Year: semesters, summer session	**Tuition:** $13,250
Application Deadline: August 15	**Room & Board:** $4300
Freshman Class: 645 applied, 616 accepted, 182 enrolled	
SAT I Verbal/Math: 530/530	**ACT:** 23 **COMPETITIVE**

Milligan College, founded in 1866, is a private institution affiliated with the Christian Church and Churches of Christ. Its degree programs stress the liberal arts and biblical studies. In addition to regional accreditation, Milligan has baccalaureate program accreditation with ACOTE and NCATE. The library contains 160,161 volumes, 460,553 microform items, and 3112 audiovisual forms/CDs, and subscribes to 547 periodicals. Computerized library services include the card catalog, interlibrary loans, and database searching. Special learning facilities include a learning resource center, art gallery, radio station, TV studios, editing rooms, and darkroom. The 145-acre campus is in a suburban area 4 miles south of Johnson City. Including residence halls, there are 23 buildings.

Student Life: 59% of undergraduates are from out of state, mostly the Midwest. Others are from 38 states, 8 foreign countries, and Canada. 80% are from public schools. 94% are white. Most are Protestant. The average age of freshmen is 18; all undergraduates, 22. 24% do not continue beyond their first year; 49% remain to graduate.

Housing: 558 students can be accommodated in college housing, which includes single-sex dormitories, on-campus apartments, and married-student housing. On-campus housing is guaranteed for all 4 years. 69% of students live on campus; of those, 85% remain on campus on weekends. Alcohol is not permitted. All students may keep cars.

Activities: There are no fraternities or sororities. There are 31 groups on campus, including art, band, cheerleading, choir, chorus, drama, drill team, film, honors, jazz band, literary magazine, musical theater, newspaper, orchestra, pep band, photography, political, professional, radio and TV, religious, social, social service, student government, symphony, and yearbook. Popular campus events include Christmas Dinners, Wonderful Wednesday, and service projects.

Sports: There are 6 intercollegiate sports for men and 6 for women, and 8 intramural sports for men and 7 for women. Facilities include a 25-meter swimming pool, a basketball court, a 500-seat stadium, a 1500-seat gym, tennis courts, and baseball, softball, and soccer fields.

Disabled Students: 80% of the campus is accessible. Wheelchair ramps, elevators, special parking, specially equipped rest rooms, and lowered drinking fountains are available.

Services: Counseling and information services are available, as is tutoring in most subjects. There is remedial math, reading, and writing.

Campus Safety and Security: Measures include informal discussions, pamphlets/posters/films, lighted pathways/sidewalks, and evening vehicle patrol.

Programs of Study: Milligan confers B.A., B.S., and B.S.N. degrees. Master's degrees are also awarded. Bachelor's degrees are awarded in BIOLOGICAL SCIENCE (biology/biological science), BUSINESS (accounting and business administration and management), COMMUNICATIONS AND THE ARTS (communications, English, fine arts, and music), COMPUTER AND PHYSICAL SCIENCE (chemistry, computer science, information sciences and systems, and mathematics), EDUCATION (Christian, early childhood, and music), HEALTH PROFESSIONS (exercise science, health care administration, nursing, and premedicine), SOCIAL SCIENCE (biblical studies, history, humanities, missions, psychology, religious music, sociology, and youth ministry). Education, business, and communications are the largest.

Required: Students must complete at least 128 semester hours, including 30 to 66 in the major, with a minimum GPA of 2.0. Required disciplines include 24 credit hours of humanities, 9 of Bible studies, 8 of lab science, 6 of social science, 3 each of math, speech and ethnic studies, 2 of phys ed, and 1 each of English and introduction to college; B.A. candidates must also complete 6 to 12 credit hours in foreign language. All students must demonstrate computer literacy and attend all required chapel/convocation sessions. There is a comprehensive exam in the major.

Special: Milligan offers a Washington semester, study abroad in England, co-op programs and internships in several majors, cross-registration with East Tennessee State University, work-study, nondegree study, and dual majors. 6 credits are offered for students participating in the annual summer tour of Europe. There are 2 national honor societies.

Faculty/Classroom: 56% of faculty are male; 44%, female. 96% teach undergraduates. No introductory courses are taught by graduate students. The average class size in an introductory lecture is 50; in a laboratory, 15; and in a regular course, 15.

Admissions: 96% of the 2001-2002 applicants were accepted. The SAT I scores for the 2001-2002 freshman class were: Verbal--29% below 500, 46% between 500 and 599, 22% between 600 and 700, and 3% above 700; Math--35% below 500, 44% between 500 and 599, 20% between 600 and 700, and 1% above 700.

Requirements: The SAT I or ACT is required. In addition, students must be graduates of an accredited secondary school, with 18 Carnegie units and 18 academic credits, including courses in English, math, science, history and social studies, and speech, music, or art, along with 2 years of a foreign language. An interview is advised, and music students must audition. The GED is accepted. Other factors in the admission decision include character, recommendations by school officials, advanced placement or honor courses, ability, preparation, and Christian commitment. Applications are accepted on-line via the school's web site. Milligan requires applicants to be in the upper 50% of their class. A GPA of 2.5 is required. AP and CLEP credits are accepted.

Procedure: Freshmen are admitted to all sessions. Entrance exams should be taken beginning in the spring of the junior year. There is a deferred admissions plan. Applications should be filed by August 15 for fall entry and December 15 for spring entry, along with a $30 fee. Notification is sent on a rolling basis.

Transfer: 46 transfer students enrolled in 2001-2002. A minimum GPA of 2.5 is preferred. Applicants must submit a letter of good standing from the previous institution as well as transcripts of all previous college work. 45 credits of 128 must be completed at Milligan.

Visiting: There are regularly scheduled orientations for prospective students, consisting of 1-day open houses in October, November, and February that include a campus tour, a financial aid workshop, a meal in the cafeteria, and the opportunity to meet faculty and to learn about student life. There are guides for informal visits and visitors may sit in on classes and stay overnight. To schedule a visit, contact the Campus Visits Coordinator at: *visits@milligan.edu*

Financial Aid: In 2001-2002, 83% of all freshmen and 82% of continuing students received some form of financial aid. 45% of freshmen and 36% of continuing students received need-based aid. The average freshman award was $9533. Of that total, scholarships or need-based grants averaged $3234 ($6000 maximum); loans averaged $2669 ($3625 maximum); work contracts averaged $1168 ($1442 maximum); and outside aid and athletic awards averaged $3476. 45% of undergraduates work part time. Average annual earnings from campus work are $1208. The average financial indebtedness of the 2001 graduate was $16,373. The FAFSA and the college's own financial statement are required. The fall application deadline is March 1.

International Students: There are 16 international students enrolled. They must score 550 on the written TOEFL or 213 on the electronic version or take the MELAB.

Computers: 114 PCs are available in 6 computer labs, the library, and specific departments. All have access to the Internet and the Web. Every dorm room has a network connection available for each resident. All students may access the system. There are no time limits. The fee is $175 per semester. It is strongly recommended that all students have a personal computer.

Graduates: In 2001, 143 bachelor's degrees were awarded. The most popular majors were business administration (36%), communications (11%), and biology (9%). In an average class, 4% graduate in 3 years, 54% in 4 years, and 60% in 5 years.

Admissions Contact: David Mee, Vice President for Enrollment Management. E-mail: *admissions@milligan.edu* Web: *www.milligan.edu*

RHODES COLLEGE
Memphis, TN 38112

A-3
(901) 843-3700
(800) 844-5969; Fax: (901) 843-3631

Full-time: 651 men, 857 women
Part-time: 12 men, 15 women
Graduate: 4 men, 12 women
Year: semesters
Application Deadline: February 1
Freshman Class: 2427 applied, 1558 accepted, 418 enrolled
SAT I Verbal/Math: 655/650
Faculty: 120; IIB,
Ph.D.s: 92%
Student/Faculty: 13 to 1
Tuition: $20,566
Room & Board: $5900
ACT: 28

HIGHLY COMPETITIVE+

Rhodes College, founded in 1848, is a nonprofit, private liberal arts institution affiliated with the Presbyterian Church (U.S.A.). The 6 libraries contain 266,000 volumes, 74,500 microform items, and 9900 audiovisual forms/CDs, and subscribe to 1200 periodicals. Computerized library services include the card catalog, interlibrary loans, and database searching. Special learning facilities include an art gallery and 2 electron microscopes, a 0.8-meter infrared optimized telescope, a cell culture lab, and the Human Relations Area Files, containing 2 million pages of human behavior resources materials on microfiche. The 100-acre campus is in an urban area in Memphis. Including residence halls, there are 37 buildings.

Student Life: 73% of undergraduates are from out of state, mostly the South. Others are from 46 states, 10 foreign countries, and Canada. 60% are from public schools. 87% are white. 67% are Protestant; 16% Catholic; 14% claim no religious affiliation. The average age of freshmen is 18; all undergraduates, 20. 11% do not continue beyond their first year; 76% remain to graduate.

Housing: 1034 students can be accommodated in college housing, which includes single-sex and coed dormitories and on-campus apartments. In addition, there are special-interest houses and theme, substance-free, quiet study, and nonsmoking houses. On-campus housing is guaranteed for the freshman year only and is available on a lottery system for upperclassmen. 79% of students live on campus; of those, 90% remain on campus on weekends. All students may keep cars.

Activities: 55% of men belong to 6 national fraternities; 58% of women belong to 5 national sororities. There are 93 groups on campus, including art, cheerleading, choir, chorale, chorus, computers, dance, debate, drama, ethnic, film, gay, honors, international, literary magazine, musical theater, newspaper, orchestra, pep band, photography, political, professional, religious, social, social service, student government, symphony, and yearbook. Popular campus events include Rites of Spring, All-Sing, and Hunger for Homelessness.

Sports: There are 10 intercollegiate sports for men and 11 for women, and 18 intramural sports for men and 18 for women. Facilities include a campus life center, which includes a performance gym, a 3-court multi-use gym, racquetball, and squash courts, a fitness center, and an indoor jogging track. Outdoor facilities include a pool, 10 lighted tennis courts, 2 soccer fields, a football field, a track, and baseball, softball and intramural fields.

Disabled Students: 90% of the campus is accessible. Wheelchair ramps, elevators, special parking, specially equipped rest rooms, special class scheduling, lowered drinking fountains, lowered telephones, and an infrared hearing system in 1 of the auditoriums are available.

Services: Counseling and information services are available, as is tutoring in some subjects, including math, writing, foreign language, biology, chemistry, and economics. There is a reader service for the blind.

Campus Safety and Security: Measures include 24-hour foot and vehicle patrol, self-defense education, escort service, and informal discussions. There are pamphlets/posters/films, emergency telephones, lighted pathways/sidewalks, and security cameras monitored 24 hours a day, a fenced campus, and city cab service billed to student accounts.

Programs of Study: Rhodes confers B.A. and B.S. degrees. Master's degrees are also awarded. Bachelor's degrees are awarded in BIOLOGICAL SCIENCE (biology/biological science), BUSINESS (business administration and management), COMMUNICATIONS AND THE ARTS (art, dramatic arts, English, French, German, music, and Spanish), COMPUTER AND PHYSICAL SCIENCE (chemistry, computer science, mathematics, and physics), SOCIAL SCIENCE (anthropology, classical/ancient civilization, economics, history, interdisciplinary studies, international studies, Latin American studies, philosophy, political science/government, psychology, religion, Russian and Slavic studies, sociology, and urban studies). English, foreign languages, and business administration are the strongest academically. Biology, business administration, and English are the largest.

Required: To graduate, students must complete 112 credit hours, with a variable number of hours in the major, and maintain a minimum GPA of 2.0. There is a basic degree requirement in humanities, communication skills, and foreign language at the intermediate level. Students must complete 3 courses each in humanities, natural science, and social science, 2 courses in fine arts, English 151, 3 noncredit half-semester courses in phys ed, and a senior seminar in the major.

Special: More than half of Rhodes students have an internship experience, in which off-campus work and significant academic work are combined for credit. Study abroad in 7 countries, a Washington semester, cross-registration with Memphis College of Art, and a science semester at Oak Ridge National Laboratory are offered. A 3-2 engineering degree with Washington University is available. The B.A.-B.S. degree and dual majors, including anthropology/sociology, are offered in any combination, and student-designed majors can be arranged. Nondegree study and pass/fail options are possible. There are 14 national honor societies, including Phi Beta Kappa.

Faculty/Classroom: 66% of faculty are male; 34%, female. All both teach and do research. No introductory courses are taught by graduate students. The average class size in an introductory lecture is 17; in a laboratory, 17; and in a regular course, 17.

Admissions: 64% of the 2001-2002 applicants were accepted. The SAT I scores for the 2001-2002 freshman class were: Math--21% between 500 and 599, 62% between 600 and 700, and 17% above 700. The ACT scores for the 2001-2002 freshman class were: 5% between 21 and 23, 26% between 24 and 26, 23% between 27 and 28, and 46% above 28. 76% of the current freshmen were in the top fifth of their class; 94% were in the top two fifths. There were 11 National Merit finalists and 5 semifinalists. 23 freshmen graduated first in their class.

Requirements: The SAT I or ACT is required. In addition, graduation from an accredited secondary school is required, with 16 or more academic credits, including 4 years of English, 3 of math, and 2 each of a foreign language, science, and social studies/history. The GED is accepted. An essay is required; an interview is recommended. Applications may be submitted on-line at the school's web site or via Common App. AP credits are accepted. Important factors in the admissions decision are advanced placement or honor courses, recommendations by school officials, and extracurricular activities record.

Procedure: Freshmen are admitted fall and spring. Entrance exams should be taken prior to December of the senior year. There are early decision, early admissions, and deferred admissions plans. Early decision applications should be filed by November 1 or January 1; regular applications, by February 1 for fall entry (or January 15 for competitive scholarship consideration) and December 1 for spring entry. Notification of early decision is sent December 1 or February 1; regular decision, April 1. 80 early decision candidates were accepted for the 2001-2002 class. 18% of all applicants are on a waiting list; 2 were accepted in 2001. The fall 2001 application fee was $40.

Transfer: 16 transfer students enrolled in 2001-2002. Applicants must submit all high school and college transcripts, as well as SAT I or ACT scores, and must be in good standing at the last institution they attended. 56 credits of 112 must be completed at Rhodes.

Visiting: There are regularly scheduled orientations for prospective students, including class visits, meetings with students and faculty, tours, and an overnight stay with students if desired. Interviews also are available. There are guides for informal visits and visitors may sit in on classes and stay overnight. To schedule a visit, contact the Admissions Office at *www.rhodes.edu*

Financial Aid: In 2001-2002, 77% of all freshmen and 74% of continuing students received some form of financial aid. 39% of freshmen and 34% of continuing students received need-based aid. The average freshman award was $14,425. Of that total, scholarships or need-based grants averaged $10,228 ($26,466 maximum); loans averaged $3072 ($6625 maximum); and work contracts averaged $1537 ($1600 maximum). 31% of undergraduates work part time. Average annual earnings from campus work are $1537. The average financial indebtedness of the 2001 graduate was $14,900. Rhodes is a member of CSS. The CSS/Profile or FAFSA is required. The fall application deadline is March 1.

International Students: There are 36 international students enrolled. The school actively recruits these students. They must score 550 on the written TOEFL or 213 on the electronic version and also take the SAT I or the ACT.

Computers: The mainframes are a DEC ALPHA and a Sun 3500. PCs and Macs are available in 3 computer labs. The math department runs an additional lab of Sun and Digital servers and workstations. All residence hall rooms are networked to the campuswide system and the Internet. All students may access the system 24 hours per day. There are no time limits and no fees. It is strongly recommended that all students have a personal computer.

Graduates: In 2001, 330 bachelor's degrees were awarded. The most popular majors were business administration (21%), biology (12%), and political science (10%). In an average class, 68% graduate in 4 years, 71% in 5 years, and 72% in 6 years. 33 companies recruited on campus in 2000-2001. Of the 2000 graduating class, 33% were enrolled in graduate school within 6 months of graduation and 54% were employed.

Admissions Contact: David J. Wottle, Dean of Admissions and Financial Aid. A video is available. E-mail: *adminfo@rhodes.edu*
Web: *www.admissions.rhodes.edu*

SOUTHERN ADVENTIST UNIVERSITY

D-4

Collegedale, TN 37315

(423) 238-2844

(800) SOUTHERN; Fax: (423) 238-3005

Full-time: 838 men, 972 women	**Faculty:** 108; IIB, --$
Part-time: 110 men, 178 women	**Ph.D.s:** 62%
Graduate: 46 men, 56 women	**Student/Faculty:** 17 to 1
Year: semesters, summer session	**Tuition:** $11,610
Application Deadline: open	**Room & Board:** $3990

Freshman Class: 1195 applied, 919 accepted, 511 enrolled

ACT: 22 **COMPETITIVE**

Southern Adventist University, founded in 1892, is a private liberal arts institution affiliated with the Seventh-day Adventist Church. There are 9 undergraduate schools. In addition to regional accreditation, Southern has baccalaureate program accreditation with CSWE, NASM, NCATE, and NLN. The library contains 138,181 volumes, 473,596 microform items, and 4704 audiovisual forms/CDs, and subscribes to 1115 periodicals. Computerized library services include the card catalog, interlibrary loans, and database searching. Special learning facilities include a learning resource center, art gallery, and radio station. The 1000-acre campus is in a small town 18 miles southeast of Chattanooga. Including residence halls, there are 17 buildings.

Student Life: 78% of undergraduates are from out of state, mostly the South. Others are from 46 states, 55 foreign countries, and Canada. 18% are from public schools. 74% are white; 10% Hispanic. Most are Protestant. The average age of freshmen is 19; all undergraduates, 21. 33% do not continue beyond their first year; 55% remain to graduate.

Housing: 1458 students can be accommodated in college housing, which includes single-sex dormitories, on-campus apartments, and married-student housing. On-campus housing is guaranteed for all 4 years. 65% of students live on campus; of those, 70% remain on campus on weekends. Alcohol is not permitted. All students may keep cars.

Activities: There are no fraternities or sororities. There are 30 groups on campus, including band, choir, chorus, drama, ethnic, honors, international, newspaper, orchestra, professional, radio and TV, religious, social, student government, symphony, and yearbook. Popular campus events include Alumni Weekend and Week of Spiritual Emphasis.

Sports: There are 10 intramural sports for men and 10 for women. Facilities include 8 tennis courts, 3 athletic fields, a field house, a pool, 4 racquetball courts, a track, soccer fields, a 23,000-square-foot gym that can seat 3000 when used as an auditorium, 3 weight rooms, and a 3-hole golf course.

Disabled Students: 70% of the campus is accessible. Wheelchair ramps, elevators, special parking, specially equipped rest rooms, and special class scheduling are available.

Services: Counseling and information services are available, as is tutoring in most subjects. There is remedial math, reading, and writing.

Campus Safety and Security: Measures include 24-hour foot and vehicle patrol, escort service, informal discussions, and pamphlets/posters/films. There are emergency telephones and lighted pathways/sidewalks.

Programs of Study: Southern confers B.A., B.S., B.B.A., B.F.A., B.Mus., and B.S.W. degrees. Associate and master's degrees are also awarded. Bachelor's degrees are awarded in BIOLOGICAL SCIENCE (biology/biological science), BUSINESS (accounting, business administration and management, entrepreneurial studies, international business management, and marketing/retailing/merchandising), COMMUNICATIONS AND THE ARTS (animation, art, broadcasting, communications, English, film arts, fine arts, graphic design, journalism, music, and public relations), COMPUTER AND PHYSICAL SCIENCE (actuarial science, chemistry, computer management, computer science, information sciences and systems, mathematics, physics, and web services), EDUCATION (elementary, music, and physical), HEALTH PROFESSIONS (health care administration, health science, medical technology, and nursing), SOCIAL SCIENCE (behavioral science, history, international studies, psychology, public administration, religious education, social work, and theological studies). Business, nursing, and education are the strongest academically. Nursing and business are the largest.

Required: Students must complete 124 semester hours with at least 30 in the major, and maintain a minimum GPA of 2.0. General education requirements include 12 semester hours of religion; 9 of language, literature, and fine arts; 6 to 9 of English; 6 each of history and activity skills; 6 to 9 of natural science; 5 of behavioral, family, and health science; 3 of political and economic systems; and up to 3 of math, depending on the ACT scores. In addition, 2 phys ed activity courses must be taken.

Special: Internships in long-term life care and journalism, a social work practicum, and study abroad in Austria, Spain, Argentina, and France are offered. The B.A.-B.S. degree and dual majors in any combination are available. Credit may be granted for 4 years of military experience. Pass/fail options are possible only for phys ed activity classes. There are paraprofessional and preprofessional programs in dentistry and medicine, and various other health-related fields, as well as in law. There are 7 national honor societies, a freshman honors program, and 2 departmental honors program.

Faculty/Classroom: 65% of faculty are male; 35%, female. All teach undergraduates. No introductory courses are taught by graduate students. The average class size in an introductory lecture is 50; in a laboratory, 20; and in a regular course, 13.

Admissions: 77% of the 2001-2002 applicants were accepted. The ACT scores for the 2001-2002 freshman class were: 11% between 12 and 17, 49% between 18 and 23, 34% between 24 and 29, and 6% between 30 and 36. There were 3 National Merit finalists.

Requirements: The SAT I or ACT is required. In addition, with a minimum composite score of 18; the ACT is preferred. Students must graduate from an accredited secondary school with 14 academic credits including 4 units of English and 2 each of a foreign language, math, science, social studies, and history. The GED is accepted. An essay must be submitted, if home schooled. Applications are accepted on-line through CollegeNet. A GPA of 2.0 is required. AP and CLEP credits are accepted. Important factors in the admissions decision are advanced placement or honor courses, recommendations by school officials, and leadership record.

Procedure: Freshmen are admitted to all sessions. Entrance exams should be taken . Application deadlines are open. The application fee is $25.

Transfer: 207 transfer students enrolled in 2001-2002. Transfer applicants must have a cumulative GPA of at least 2.0 and a minimum ACT composite score of 18. Two letters of recommendation are also required. 30 credits of 124 must be completed at Southern.

Visiting: There are regularly scheduled orientations for prospective students, including a tour of the campus and dorms, appointments with academic departments, and an interview with an admissions officer. There are guides for informal visits and visitors may sit in on classes and stay overnight. To schedule a visit, contact the Admissions Office.

Financial Aid: In 2001-2002, 83% of all freshmen and 68% of continuing students received some form of financial aid. 75% of freshmen and 76% of continuing students received need-based aid. The average freshman award was $9408. Of that total, scholarships or need-based grants averaged $3700; and loans averaged $3300. All undergraduates work part time. Average annual earnings from campus work are $2300. The average financial indebtedness of the 2001 graduate was $14,900. The FAFSA is required. The fall application deadline is March 1.

International Students: There are 230 international students enrolled. The school actively recruits these students. They must score 550 on the written TOEFL or 213 on the electronic version or take the MELAB.

Computers: The mainframe is a Hewlett Packard. There are 3 UNIX hosts, Ethernet to many campus buildings, an Internet link, and more than 130 PCs and Macs in 7 student labs. All students may access the system 24 hours per day. There are no time limits and no fees. It is strongly recommended that all students have a personal computer.

Graduates: In 2001, 311 bachelor's degrees were awarded. The most popular majors were business (16%), nursing (16%), and religion (15%). In an average class, 30% graduate in 4 years, 40% in 5 years, and 44% in 6 years. Of the 2000 graduating class, 8% were enrolled in graduate school within 6 months of graduation and 52% were employed.

Admissions Contact: Victor Czerkasij, Director, Admissions and Recruitment. A video is available. E-mail: *admissions@southern.edu*
Web: *www.southern.edu*

STATE UNIVERSITY AND COMMUNITY COLLEGE SYSTEM OF TENNESSEE

The State University and Community College System of Tennessee, established in 1972, is a public system. It is governed by the Tennessee Board of Regents, which appoints a chancellor as chief administrator of the system. The primary goal of the system is teaching, research, and public service. The main priority is to provide accessible quality programs to state residents with equal opportunity in education and employment. Universities are located in Nashville, Cookeville, Clarksville, Memphis, Johnson City, and Murfreesboro. The total enrollment in a recent year of the 6 4-year university campuses, 14 2-year institutions, and 26 Tennessee Technology Centers was 167,000; there were 5500 full-time faculty members. There are 370 baccalaureate, 215 master's, 17 specialist, and 29 doctoral programs offered. Profiles of the 4-year campuses are included in this section.

TENNESSEE STATE UNIVERSITY C-3
Nashville, TN 37209-1561 (615) 963-5101
(888) 463-6878; Fax: (615) 963-5108

Full-time: 2249 men, 3777 women **Faculty:** 340
Part-time: 403 men, 631 women **Ph.D.s:** 80%
Graduate: 514 men, 1090 women **Student/Faculty:** 18 to 1
Year: semesters, summer session **Tuition:** $3008 ($9480)
Application Deadline: August 1 **Room & Board:** $4050
Freshman Class: 9049 applied, 5556 accepted, 1639 enrolled
ACT: 21 **VERY COMPETITIVE**

Tennessee State University, founded in 1912, is a state-supported land-grant institution offering undergraduate and graduate programs in arts and sciences, agriculture, health professions, business, education, engineering and technology, and nursing. There are 7 undergraduate schools and 1 graduate school. In addition to regional accreditation, TSU has baccalaureate program accreditation with ABET, AHEA, NASM, NCATE, and NLN. The 2 libraries contain 463,621 volumes, 754,955 microform items, and 5125 audiovisual forms/CDs, and subscribe to 1272 periodicals. Computerized library services include the card catalog, interlibrary loans, and database searching. Special learning facilities include a learning resource center, art gallery, and radio station. The 450-acre campus is in an urban area in Nashville. Including residence halls, there are 66 buildings.

Student Life: 78% of undergraduates are from Tennessee. Others are from 40 states, 51 foreign countries, and Canada. 90% are from public schools. 71% are African American; 25% white. The average age of freshmen is 18; all undergraduates, 25.

Housing: 3225 students can be accommodated in college housing, which includes single-sex and coed dormitories and off-campus apartments. In addition, there are honors houses. On-campus housing is guaranteed for all 4 years. 63% of students commute. Alcohol is not permitted. All students may keep cars.

Activities: 1% of men belong to 4 national fraternities; 2% of women belong to 4 national sororities. There are 63 groups on campus, including band, cheerleading, choir, chorale, computers, dance, drama, honors, jazz band, literary magazine, marching band, newspaper, pep band, professional, radio and TV, religious, social, social service, student government, and yearbook. Popular campus events include Miss TSU Pageant and Inauguration, Greek Show, and Christmas Tree Lighting Ceremony.

Sports: There are 8 intercollegiate sports for men and 7 for women. Facilities include a major convocation and athletic center that accommodates intramural sports, swimming, handball, and intercollegiate basketball, and a campus center that provides extensive recreational facilities.

Disabled Students: 90% of the campus is accessible. Wheelchair ramps, elevators, special parking, specially equipped rest rooms, and lowered drinking fountains are available. A campus improvement program makes all renovated buildings accessible.

Services: Counseling and information services are available, as is tutoring in some subjects, including all general education courses and many major-field courses. There is a reader service for the blind, and remedial math, reading, and writing. A writing clinic, math lab, and reading center provide individualized assistance.

Campus Safety and Security: Measures include 24-hour foot and vehicle patrol, shuttle buses, informal discussions, and pamphlets/posters/films. There are emergency telephones and lighted pathways/sidewalks.

Programs of Study: TSU confers B.A., B.S., B.B.A., B.S.F., and B.S.N. degrees. Associate, master's, and doctoral degrees are also awarded. Bachelor's degrees are awarded in AGRICULTURE (agriculture), BIOLOGICAL SCIENCE (biology/biological science), BUSINESS (accounting, business administration and management, business economics, and hotel/motel and restaurant management), COMMUNICATIONS AND THE ARTS (art, dramatic arts, English, languages, music, and speech/debate/rhetoric), COMPUTER AND PHYSICAL SCIENCE (chemistry, computer science, mathematics, and physics), EDUCATION (early childhood, health, and special), ENGINEERING AND ENVIRONMENTAL DESIGN (aeronautical technology, architectural engineering, civil engineering, electrical/electronics engineering, and mechanical engineering), HEALTH PROFESSIONS (dental hygiene, health care administration, medical laboratory technology, medical records administration/services, nursing, occupational therapy, physical therapy, respiratory therapy, and speech pathology/audiology), SOCIAL SCIENCE (African studies, criminal justice, family/consumer studies, history, political science/government, psychology, social work, and sociology). Engineering, allied health professions, and nursing are the strongest academically. Allied health, nursing, and engineering are the largest.

Required: To graduate students must complete at least 130 semester hours, with 24 in the major, and maintain a minimum GPA of 2.0. Additional requirements include demonstration of proficiency in English composition, completion of a senior project, and courses in phys ed, English, math, social sciences, American history, humanities, and natural sciences.

Special: Opportunities are provided for co-op programs in business and engineering, cross-registration with Middle Tennessee State University and Meharry Medical College, a B.A.-B.S. degree in interdisciplinary studies, credit by exam, and nondegree study. There are 19 national honor societies, a freshman honors program, and 5 departmental honors programs.

Faculty/Classroom: 58% of faculty are male; 42%, female. 90% teach undergraduates, 20% do research, and 85% do both. No introductory courses are taught by graduate students. The average class size in an introductory lecture is 30; in a laboratory, 35; and in a regular course, 30.

Admissions: 61% of the 2001-2002 applicants were accepted.

Requirements: The SAT I or ACT is required, with a minimum score of 890 on the SAT I or 19 on the ACT. Graduation from an accredited secondary school is required; the GED is accepted. Applicants should have 4 credits in English, 3 in math, 2 each in science and a foreign language, and 1 each in history, social studies, and art. A GPA of 2.25 (in-state) and 2.5 (out-of-state) is required. AP and CLEP credits are accepted.

Procedure: Freshmen are admitted to all sessions. Entrance exams should be taken in the junior year. There is an early admissions plan. Applications should be filed by August 1 for fall entry, December 1 for spring entry, and May 1 for summer entry. The fall 2001 application fee was $15.

Transfer: 474 transfer students enrolled in 2001-2002. Applicants must submit official transcripts from all previous colleges attended. Students from other than Tennessee colleges must have maintained a minimum GPA of 2.0. The GPA requirements for students transferring from Tennessee colleges vary according to the number of semester hours being submitted for transfer credit. 30 credits of 130 must be completed at TSU.

Visiting: There are guides for informal visits and visitors may sit in on classes and stay overnight. To schedule a visit, contact the recruiting staff.

Financial Aid: In 2001-2002, 69% of all freshmen and 63% of continuing students received some form of financial aid. 61% of freshmen and 62% of continuing students received need-based aid. The average freshman award was $8047. The FAFSA is required. The fall application deadline is April 1.

International Students: They must score 500 on the written TOEFL.

Computers: The mainframe is a DEC ALPHA 4100. Numerous computer labs are available. All students may access the system. There are no time limits. The fee is $10.

Admissions Contact: John Cade, Dean of Admissions and Records. A video is available. E-mail: *jcade@picard.tnstate.edu*
Web: *www.tnstate.edu*

TENNESSEE TECHNOLOGICAL UNIVERSITY D-3
Cookeville, TN 38505 (931) 372-3888
(800) 255-8881; Fax: (931) 372-6250

Full-time: 3413 men, 2813 women **Faculty:** 368; IIA, av$
Part-time: 441 men, 432 women **Ph.D.s:** 82%
Graduate: 521 men, 1033 women **Student/Faculty:** 17 to 1
Year: semesters, summer session **Tuition:** $3088 ($9560)
Application Deadline: see profile **Room & Board:** $3880
Freshman Class: 2357 applied, 2306 accepted, 1323 enrolled
ACT: 22 **COMPETITIVE**

Tennessee Technological University, founded in 1915 and a member of the state university and community college system of Tennessee, is a public institution offering undergraduate and graduate programs in the liberal arts, business, engineering, agriculture studies, art and fine arts, music, professional training, teacher preparation, nursing, home economics, and crafts. There are 8 undergraduate and 4 graduate schools. In addition to regional accreditation, Tennessee Tech has baccalaureate program accreditation with AACSB, ABET, NASM, NCATE, and NLN. The library contains 308,000 volumes and 15,000 audiovisual forms/CDs, and subscribes to 2845 periodicals. Computerized library services include the card catalog, interlibrary loans, and database searching. Special learning facilities include a learning resource center, art gallery, radio station, and TV station. The 235-acre campus is in a small town 78 miles east of Nashville. Including residence halls, there are 98 buildings.

Student Life: 96% of undergraduates are from Tennessee. Others are from 40 states, 35 foreign countries, and Canada. 93% are white. Most claim no religious affiliation. The average age of freshmen is 19; all undergraduates, 24. 27% do not continue beyond their first year; 47% remain to graduate.

Housing: 3594 students can be accommodated in college housing, which includes single-sex and coed dormitories, on-campus apartments, and married-student housing. On-campus housing is guaranteed for all 4 years. 75% of students commute. Alcohol is not permitted. All students may keep cars.

Activities: 18% of men belong to 13 local fraternities; 7% of women belong to 5 local sororities. There are 178 groups on campus, including art, band, cheerleading, chess, choir, chorale, chorus, computers, dance, debate, drama, drill team, ethnic, forensics, honors, international, jazz band, literary magazine, marching band, newspaper, opera, orchestra, pep band, photography, political, professional, radio and TV, religious, social, social service, student government, symphony, and yearbook. Popular campus events include intramural events, Greek Week, and Parents Day.

Sports: There are 6 intercollegiate sports for men and 9 for women, and 10 intramural sports for men and 8 for women. Facilities include 2 gyms seating 10,500 and 4000, a 16,500-seat stadium with track facilities, an indoor pool, indoor and outdoor tennis courts, handball and basketball courts, baseball, softball, and football fields, a track, a rifle range, apparatus rooms, and a health and wellness center with an indoor track, 8 racquetball courts, a weight room, an aerobics classroom, a pool, and basketball/volleyball courts.

Disabled Students: 90% of the campus is accessible. Wheelchair ramps, elevators, special parking, specially equipped rest rooms, special class scheduling, lowered drinking fountains, and lowered telephones are available.

Services: Counseling and information services are available, as is tutoring in some subjects, including English and lower levels of maths. There is a reader service for the blind, and remedial math, reading, and writing.

Campus Safety and Security: Measures include 24-hour foot and vehicle patrol, escort service, informal discussions, and emergency telephones. There are lighted pathways/sidewalks and a student safety organization.

Programs of Study: Tennessee Tech confers B.A., B.S., B.F.A., B.S.Agr., B.S.B.A., B.S.C.E., B.S.Ch.E., B.S.Ed., B.S.E.E., B.F.A., B.S.H.E., B.S.I.E., B.S.Ind.Tech., B.S.M.E., and B.S.N., B.M. degrees. Master's and doctoral degrees are also awarded. Bachelor's degrees are awarded in AGRICULTURE (agricultural economics, agriculture, animal science, fish and game management, plant science, soil science, and wildlife management), BIOLOGICAL SCIENCE (biochemistry and biology/biological science), BUSINESS (accounting, banking and finance, business administration and management, management science, and marketing/retailing/merchandising), COMMUNICATIONS AND THE ARTS (English, fine arts, French, German, journalism, Spanish, and technical and business writing), COMPUTER AND PHYSICAL SCIENCE (chemistry, computer science, geology, mathematics, and physics), EDUCATION (agricultural, art, home economics, music, physical, secondary, and special), ENGINEERING AND ENVIRONMENTAL DESIGN (chemical engineering, civil engineering, electrical/electronics engineering, engineering, environmental engineering, industrial engineering, industrial engineering technology, manufacturing engineering, and mechanical engineering), HEALTH PROFESSIONS (music therapy and nursing), SOCIAL SCIENCE (child care/child and family studies, economics, history, human ecology, political science/government, psychology, and sociology). Engineering, business, and education are the strongest academically. Engineering is the largest.

Required: Students must complete 132 semester hours, with a variable number of hours in the major, and maintain a minimum GPA of 2.0. 12 semester hours of English, 8 of a lab science, 6 of American history, 3 each of math and humanities, and 2 of phys ed are required.

Special: Co-op programs in most academic areas, internships in community-based programs, study abroad, a Washington semester, multidisciplinary majors and work-study programs are available. Accelerated degree programs are offered in all specified majors with 3 calendar years of continuous studies. A B.A.-B.S. degree is available, as are dual majors in all areas. Credit may be granted for military experience, and nondegree study and pass/fail options are offered. There are 29 national honor societies, and a freshman honors program.

Faculty/Classroom: 42% of faculty are male; 29%, female. 99% teach undergraduates, 73% do research, and 70% do both. Graduate students teach 12% of introductory courses. The average class size in an introductory lecture is 27; in a laboratory, 30; and in a regular course, 26.

Admissions: 98% of the 2001-2002 applicants were accepted. The ACT scores for the 2001-2002 freshman class were: 36% below 21, 28% between 21 and 23, 20% between 24 and 26, 8% between 27 and 28, and 8% above 28. In a recent year, there were 8 National Merit finalists; 36 freshmen graduated first in their class.

Requirements: The ACT is required, with a minimum composite score of 19. Other admissions requirements include graduation from an accredited secondary school with 14 academic credits, including 4 of English, 3 of math, 2 each in science and a single foreign language, 1 in American history, 1 in world history, ancient history, modern history, world geography or European history, and 1 in music/art. The GED is also accepted. A GPA of 2.35 is required. AP and CLEP credits are accepted.

Procedure: Freshmen are admitted to all sessions. Entrance exams should be taken during the senior year. There are early admissions and deferred admissions plans. Check with the school for current application deadlines. The application fee is $15. Notification is sent on a rolling basis.

Transfer: Transfer students should have a minimum of 12 credit hours earned; the minimum GPA depends on the number of credit hours accumulated. Official transcripts must be submitted, and the ACT is required, depending on age (for applicants 21 or older it is not required). If an applicant has fewer than 12 credit hours, admissions requirements are the same as for freshmen. 30 credits of 132 must be completed at Tennessee Tech.

Visiting: There are guides for informal visits and visitors may sit in on classes. To schedule a visit, contact the Admissions Office.

Financial Aid: 48% of freshmen and 45% of continuing students received need-based aid. The average freshman award was $4000. Of that total, scholarships or need-based grants averaged $1944 ($5500 maximum); loans averaged $2679 ($5250 maximum); and work contracts averaged $1192 ($1600 maximum). 97% of undergraduates work part time. Average annual earnings from campus work are $944. The average financial indebtedness of a recent year's graduate was $9000. The FAFSA is required. Check with the school for current deadlines.

International Students: The school actively recruits these students. They must score 500 on the written TOEFL or 173 on the electronic version and also take the college's own test, the SAT I, or the ACT.

Computers: The mainframes are a are a DEC ALPHA Server 4100 and a DEC VAX 7000/620. VAX, Gemini, IBM, and Mac PCs are available for student use in numerous buildings across campus. All students have access to the Internet through Netscape. All students may access the system 24 hours a day. There are no time limits and no fees.

Graduates: In a recent year, 1167 bachelor's degrees were awarded. The most popular majors were business management (10%), mechanical engineering (9%), and elementary education (8%). 270 companies recruited on campus in a recent year.

Admissions Contact: Billy G. Gaw, Assoc. Director of Admissions. E-mail: *admissions@tntech.edu* Web: *www.tntech.edu*

TENNESSEE WESLEYAN COLLEGE — D-3

Athens, TN 37301-0040 — (423) 746-5286; (800) PICK-TWC; Fax: (423) 744-9968

Full-time: 231 men, 375 women	**Faculty:** 52; IIB, --$
Part-time: 60 men, 120 women	**Ph.D.s:** 63%
Graduate: none	**Student/Faculty:** 12 to 1
Year: semesters, summer session	**Tuition:** $8740
Application Deadline: open	**Room & Board:** $4290
Freshman Class: n/av	
ACT: n/av	**COMPETITIVE**

Tennessee Wesleyan College, founded in 1857, is a nonprofit, private institution affiliated with the United Methodist Church. Its undergraduate programs stress the liberal arts, teacher preparation, and nursing. The library contains 100,000 volumes, 6500 microform items, and 11,000 audiovisual forms/CDs, and subscribes to 400 periodicals. Computerized library services include the card catalog, interlibrary loans, and database searching. Special learning facilities include a learning resource center. The 40-acre campus is in a small town 55 miles south of Knoxville. Including residence halls, there are 19 buildings.

Student Life: 92% of undergraduates are from Tennessee. Others are from 15 states, 11 foreign countries, and Canada. 98% are from public schools. 92% are white. 82% are Protestant; 15% claim no religious affiliation. The average age of freshmen is 19; all undergraduates, 23. 35% do not continue beyond their first year; 35% remain to graduate.

Housing: 336 students can be accommodated in college housing, which includes single-sex and coed dormitories, on-campus apartments, and fraternity houses. On-campus housing is guaranteed for all 4 years. 55% of students commute. Alcohol is not permitted. All students may keep cars.

Activities: 331% of women belong to 1 local and 1 national sorority. There are no fraternities. There are 24 groups on campus, including art, cheerleading, choir, chorale, computers, dance, drama, ethnic, honors, international, literary magazine, musical theater, newspaper, professional, religious, social, social service, student government, and yearbook. Popular campus events include Halloween Arts Carnival, Black History Emphasis Week, and Spring Fever Week.

Sports: There are 4 intercollegiate sports for men and 5 for women, and 5 intramural sports for men and 5 for women. Facilities include a 2000-seat stadium, an 800-seat gym, a fitness center, and a YMCA adjacent to campus with an indoor/outdoor swimming pool available on a scheduled basis to students.

Disabled Students: 70% of the campus is accessible. Wheelchair ramps, elevators, special parking, specially equipped rest rooms, and special class scheduling are available.

Services: Counseling and information services are available, as is tutoring in some subjects, including English, math, computers, sciences. There is remedial math and writing.

Campus Safety and Security: Measures include informal discussions, lighted pathways/sidewalks, and evening security patrol.

Programs of Study: TWC confers B.A., B.S., B.Applied Sc., B.Mus.Ed., and B.S.N. degrees. Bachelor's degrees are awarded in BIOLOGICAL SCIENCE (biology/biological science), BUSINESS (accounting, business administration and management, recreation and leisure services, and sports management), COMMUNICATIONS AND THE ARTS (English and music), COMPUTER AND PHYSICAL SCIENCE (chemistry and mathematics), EDUCATION (education, music, and physical), HEALTH PROFESSIONS (health and nursing), SOCIAL SCIENCE (behavioral science, history, human development, human services, interdisciplinary studies, ministries, pastoral studies, psychology, religious education, and religious music). Business, education, and history are the strongest academically. Business and education are the largest.

Required: Students must complete 128 semester hours, fulfilling the requirements of the major, taking 28 semester hours at the upper-division level, and maintain a minimum GPA of 2.5. Distribution requirements include 12 semester hours of the humanities, 6 each of math and English composition, 9 of social and behavioral sciences, 8 of science, and 3 each of speech and fine arts. B.A. candidates must also take 12 hours of a single foreign language. 2 semester hours of phys ed are also needed. Internships are required for human services students, and all students must take an exit exam.

Special: Special academic programs include internships in some majors, study abroad in Japan and England, dual majors in several areas, student-designed majors, and nondegree study. Business majors may participate in a co-op program. There is 1 national honor society.

Faculty/Classroom: 47% of faculty are male; 53%, female. All teach undergraduates and 40% both teach and do research. The average class size in an introductory lecture is 23; in a laboratory, 11; and in a regular course, 16.

Requirements: The ACT is required. In addition, other admission requirements include graduation from an accredited secondary school, with 16 academic credits, including 4 units in English, 2 each in math and science, and 1 each in social studies and history. Foreign language is recommended. The GED is also accepted. A GPA of 2.25 is required. AP and CLEP credits are accepted. Important factors in the admissions decision are leadership record, recommendations by school officials, and personality/intangible qualities.

Procedure: Freshmen are admitted to all sessions. Entrance exams should be taken in the fall of the senior year. Application deadlines are open. The application fee is $25. Notification is sent on a rolling basis.

Transfer: 102 transfer students enrolled in 2001-2002. Transfer students must have a minimum GPA of 2.0; an associate degree is recommended. 32 credits of 128 must be completed at TWC.

Visiting: There are regularly scheduled orientations for prospective students. There are guides for informal visits and visitors may sit in on classes and stay overnight. To schedule a visit, contact the Office of Admissions at *cawoodr@twcnet.edu*.

Financial Aid: In 2001-2002, 97% of all freshmen and 81% of continuing students received some form of financial aid. 58% of freshmen and 57% of continuing students received need-based aid. The average freshman award was $8595. Of that total, scholarships or need-based grants averaged $6759 ($14,660 maximum); loans averaged $1610 ($6625 maximum); and work contracts averaged $227 ($8500 maximum). 34% of undergraduates work part time. Average annual earnings from campus work are $621. The average financial indebtedness of the 2001 graduate was $5280. The FAFSA and the college's own financial statement are required. The fall application deadline is March 1.

International Students: There are 33 international students enrolled. The school actively recruits these students. They must score 500 on the written TOEFL or 173 on the electronic version.

Computers: The mainframe is an IBM. Students have access to 40 PCs located in 3 labs on campus. All students may access the system during lab hours, generally 8:30 A.M. to 9 P.M. There are no time limits and no fees.

Graduates: In 2001, 185 bachelor's degrees were awarded. The most popular majors were business administration (48%), psychology (12%), and human services (9%). In an average class, 30% graduate in 4 years, 33% in 5 years, and 40% in 6 years.

Admissions Contact: Michelle Boyd, Office Coordinator. A video is available. Web: *www.twcnet.edu*

TREVECCA NAZARENE UNIVERSITY C-3
Nashville, TN 37210-2877
(615) 248-1320
(888) 210-4TNU; Fax: (615) 248-7406

Full-time: 413 men, 483 women	**Faculty:** 57; IIB, --$
Part-time: 110 men, 153 women	**Ph.D.s:** 66%
Graduate: 209 men, 451 women	**Student/Faculty:** 16 to 1
Year: semesters, summer session	**Tuition:** $10,848
Application Deadline: open	**Room & Board:** $4904
Freshman Class: 569 applied, 449 accepted, 237 enrolled	
SAT I Verbal/Math: 550/530	**ACT:** 22 **COMPETITIVE**

Trevecca Nazarene University, founded in 1901, is a private institution affiliated with the Church of the Nazarene. Trevecca offers programs in liberal arts and sciences and a number of professional content areas. The university also provides a variety of nontraditional continuing education professional programs at the undergraduate and graduate levels. There are 4 undergraduate and 4 graduate schools. In addition to regional accreditation, TNU has baccalaureate program accreditation with CAHEA and NASM. The library contains 374,360 volumes, 273,521 microform items, and 2552 audiovisual forms/CDs, and subscribes to 730 periodicals. Computerized library services include the card catalog, interlibrary loans, and database searching. Special learning facilities include a learning resource center, radio station, and a curriculum library. The 80-acre campus is in an urban area in Nashville. Including residence halls, there are 26 buildings.

Student Life: 59% of undergraduates are from Tennessee. Others are from 37 states, 14 foreign countries, and Canada. 85% are white. Most are Protestant. The average age of freshmen is 19; all undergraduates, 21. 28% do not continue beyond their first year; 47% remain to graduate.

Housing: 709 students can be accommodated in college housing, which includes single-sex dormitories, on-campus apartments, off-campus apartments, and married-student housing. On-campus housing is guaranteed for all 4 years. 59% of students live on campus. Alcohol is not permitted. All students may keep cars.

Activities: There are no fraternities or sororities. There are 18 groups on campus, including band, cheerleading, choir, chorale, chorus, drama, forensics, honors, jazz band, literary magazine, marching band, newspaper, orchestra, pep band, professional, radio, religious, social service, student government, and yearbook. Popular campus events include Valentine's Banquet, Junior-Senior Banquets, and Fall Retreat.

Sports: There are 4 intercollegiate sports for men and 5 for women, and 9 intramural sports for men and 8 for women. Facilities include a gym, a pool, a jogging track, handball, racquetball, and tennis courts, exercise and weight rooms, and playing fields.

Disabled Students: Wheelchair ramps, elevators, special parking, specially equipped rest rooms, and special class scheduling are available.

Services: Counseling and information services are available, as is tutoring in every subject. There is remedial math, reading, and writing. An academic enrichment program for students scoring below 19 on the ACT provides tutoring in math, reading, writing, and study skills.

Campus Safety and Security: Measures include 24-hour foot and vehicle patrol, informal discussions, lighted pathways/sidewalks, and weekend and evening foot and vehicle patrol.

Programs of Study: TNU confers B.A., B.S., B.B.A., and B.S.S.W. degrees. Associate, master's, and doctoral degrees are also awarded. Bachelor's degrees are awarded in BIOLOGICAL SCIENCE (biology/biological science), BUSINESS (accounting, business administration and management, and marketing/retailing/merchandising), COMMUNICATIONS AND THE ARTS (broadcasting, communications, communications technology, dramatic arts, English, music, music business management, public relations, and speech/debate/rhetoric), COMPUTER AND PHYSICAL SCIENCE (chemistry, information sciences and systems, mathematics, physics, and science), EDUCATION (early childhood, education, English, mathematics, music, physical, and science), HEALTH PROFESSIONS (medical laboratory technology), SOCIAL SCIENCE (behavioral science, history, ministries, political science/government, psychology, religion, religious music, social science, and social work). Teacher education, business, and music are the strongest academically. Management and human relations, religion, and education are the largest.

Required: To graduate, students must complete at least 128 semester hours with a minimum 2.0 GPA. The required 62-hour general education curriculum includes courses in English, communications, religion and philosophy, fine arts, history and social science (including foreign language), science and math, phys ed, and computer literacy.

Special: There is cross-registration with other Nazarene colleges and universities in the United States, and work-study programs, internships, a Washington semester, and nondegree study are offered. Study abroad is possible. An evening program leads to the B.A. in Management and Human Relations for adult learners over 25 with 62 semester hours of college work. A 3-2 nursing program is offered with Belmont University. There are preprofessional studies in nursing, physical therapy, medicine, dentistry, pharmacy, veterinary science, law, and engineering. There is 1 national honor society.

Faculty/Classroom: 69% of faculty are male; 31%, female. 80% teach undergraduates. No introductory courses are taught by graduate students. The average class size in a regular course is 19.

Admissions: 79% of the 2001-2002 applicants were accepted. The ACT scores for the 2001-2002 freshman class were: 36% below 21, 28% between 21 and 23, 21% between 24 and 26, 8% between 27 and 28, and 8% above 28.

Requirements: The SAT I or ACT is required; the ACT is preferred, with a composite score of at least 18. Candidates should have completed at least 15 academic secondary credits, including 4 units in English, 2 each in math, foreign language, and social science, and 1 in natural science. A GED of at least 45 is also accepted. The medical technology and teacher education programs have special admission requirements. A GPA of 2.5 is required. AP and CLEP credits are accepted.

Procedure: Freshmen are admitted to all sessions. Entrance exams should be taken in the junior or senior years. There is a deferred admissions plan. Application deadlines are open. The application fee is $25. Notification is on a rolling basis.

Transfer: 74 transfer students enrolled in 2001-2002. Transfer applicants must present official transcripts and recommendations. 32 credits of 128 must be completed at TNU.

Visiting: There are regularly scheduled orientations for prospective students, including a tour and meetings with admissions and financial aid personnel and faculty. There are guides for informal visits and visitors may sit in on classes and stay overnight. To schedule a visit, contact the Admissions Office.

Financial Aid: The average freshman award was $9775 in a recent year. The average financial indebtedness of the 2001 graduate was $19,532. The FAFSA is required. The fall application deadline is March 1.

International Students: There are 13 international students enrolled. They must score 500 on the written TOEFL and also take the SAT I or the ACT, scoring 18 on the ACT.

Computers: The mainframe is a DEC Alpha 1000A. The campus network is Windows NT-based, with Windows 95 and Mac OS 8 also in use. Students may access the network via more than 200 PCs or terminals in 13 computer labs, each equipped with at least 1 laser printer. TNU has a dedicated-circuit Internet connection and 3 multimedia classrooms. All students may access the system from 8 A.M. to 11 P.M. every day, with residence hall labs open 24 hours per day. There are no time limits and no fees.

Graduates: In 2001, 243 bachelor's degrees were awarded. The most popular majors were management and human relations (59%), religion (5%), and education (5%). In an average class, 2% graduate in 3 years, 27% in 4 years, 43% in 5 years, and 47% in 6 years. 30 companies recruited on campus in 2000-2001.

Admissions Contact: Patty Cook, Director of Admissions.
E-mail: *admissions_und@trevecca.edu* Web: *www.trevecca.edu*

TUSCULUM COLLEGE — F-3
Greeneville, TN 37743 — (423) 636-7300
(800) 729-0256; Fax: (423) 638-7166

Full-time: 728 men, 824 women	**Faculty:** 45; IIB, --$
Part-time: 3 men, 2 women	**Ph.D.s:** 79%
Graduate: 65 men, 172 women	**Student/Faculty:** 34 to 1
Year: semesters, summer session	**Tuition:** $13,400
Application Deadline: open	**Room & Board:** $4500
Freshman Class: 917 applied, 779 accepted, 290 enrolled	
SAT I or ACT: required	**LESS COMPETITIVE**

Tusculum College, a civic arts institution chartered in 1794, is the oldest college in Tennessee and the oldest coeducational college affiliated with the Presbyterian Church (U.S.A.). The 2 libraries contain 67,202 volumes, 210,798 microform items, and 966 audiovisual forms/CDs, and subscribe to 300 periodicals. Computerized library services include the card catalog, interlibrary loans, and database searching. Special learning facilities include an art gallery, radio station, TV station, and and President Andrew Johnson Museum. The 142-acre campus is in a small town 30 miles south of Johnson City, in the foothills of the Great Smoky Mountains. Including residence halls, there are 21 buildings.

Student Life: 81% of undergraduates are from Tennessee. Others are from 14 foreign countries. 97% are from public schools. 87% are white. The average age of freshmen is 19; all undergraduates, 28. 39% do not continue beyond their first year; 68% remain to graduate.

Housing: 430 students can be accommodated in college housing, which includes single-sex dormitories. On-campus housing is guaranteed for all 4 years. 66% of students live on campus; of those, 75% remain on campus on weekends. Alcohol is not permitted. All students may keep cars.

Activities: There are no fraternities or sororities. There are 21 groups on campus, including art, cheerleading, choir, chorale, dance, drama, ethnic, honors, international, newspaper, pep band, photography, professional, radio and TV, religious, social service, student government, and yearbook. Popular campus events include McCormick Day, Opening Convocation, and Honors Convocation.

Sports: There are 7 intercollegiate sports for men and 7 for women, and 12 intramural sports for men and 13 for women. Facilities include a 2000-seat gym, a gym/pool complex, tennis courts, and football, soccer, softball, and baseball fields.

Disabled Students: 50% of the campus is accessible. Wheelchair ramps and special parking. Classes and activities scheduled in accessible areas are available.

Services: Counseling and information services are available, as is tutoring in some subjects. Math and English tutoring are available on a limited basis through the College Learning Center.

Campus Safety and Security: Measures include 24-hour foot and vehicle patrol, informal discussions, emergency telephones, and lighted pathways/sidewalks.

Programs of Study: Tusculum confers B.A. and B.S. degrees. Master's degrees are also awarded. Bachelor's degrees are awarded in BIOLOGICAL SCIENCE (biology/biological science), BUSINESS (management information systems, management science, small business management, and sports management), COMMUNICATIONS AND THE ARTS (English and fine arts), COMPUTER AND PHYSICAL SCIENCE (computer science and information sciences and systems), EDUCATION (early childhood, education, elementary, middle school, museum studies, physical, and special), ENGINEERING AND ENVIRONMENTAL DESIGN (environmental science), HEALTH PROFESSIONS (medical technology, premedicine, and sports medicine), SOCIAL SCIENCE (history and psychology). Management, education, and biology are the strongest academically. Management and education are the largest.

Required: All students must complete at least 128 hours, with a minimum GPA of 2.0 overall and 2.25 in the major. Specific degree programs have varying requirements. B.S. candidates must take a core curriculum consisting of courses in English, art, music, sociology, economics, and psychology. B.A. candidates must complete a set of interdisciplinary courses, validate 15 competencies, complete a civic arts project, and fulfill the requirements of a major.

Special: Each semester is divided into four 3 1/2-week blocks, with 1 course taken per block. Internships, practicums, and student-teaching opportunities are offered in business administration, professional and special education, social services, psychology, biology, chemistry, and medical technology. The B.S. in applied organizational management is designed for adult students with previous training and work experience. The medical technology program is offered in cooperation with a medical center in Kingsport. Study abroad, independent majors, nondegree study, an accelerated degree program in applied organizational management, work-study programs, student-designed majors, and pass/fail options are available. There is an accelerated evening program for working adults. There is 1 national honor society.

Faculty/Classroom: 67% of faculty are male; 33%, female. All teach undergraduates. No introductory courses are taught by graduate students. The average class size in an introductory lecture is 25; in a laboratory, 20; and in a regular course, 15.

Admissions: 85% of the 2001-2002 applicants were accepted. 3 freshmen graduated first in their class.

Requirements: The SAT I or ACT is required. In addition, the recommended composite score is 920 on the SAT I or 18 on the ACT. Applicants should be high school graduates or have the GED. Secondary school preparation should include 4 units of English, 2 units each of foreign language, math, and science, and 1 unit of history. A personal essay is also required and an interview may be necessary. Tusculum requires applicants to be in the upper 50% of their class. A GPA of 2.0 is required. AP and CLEP credits are accepted. Important factors in the admissions decision are advanced placement or honor courses, leadership record, and evidence of special talent. Applications are accepted on-line at the college web site or on computer disk.

Procedure: Freshmen are admitted to all sessions. Entrance exams should be taken in the spring of the junior year. There is an early decision plan. Application deadlines are open. Notification is sent on a rolling basis.

Transfer: 84 transfer students enrolled in 2001-2002. Transfer applicants should present at least a 2.0 GPA in previous college work. Tusculum recommends that applicants also submit SAT I or ACT scores. 32 credits of 128 must be completed at Tusculum.

Visiting: There are regularly scheduled orientations for prospective students, including a fall and spring open house during which students are given campus tours, financial aid information, and application materials. There are guides for informal visits and visitors may sit in on classes and stay overnight. To schedule a visit, contact the Admissions Office.

Financial Aid: In 2001-2002, 51% of all freshmen received some form of financial aid. 38% of all students received need-based aid. The average freshman award was $9748. 37% of undergraduates work part time. Average annual earnings from campus work are $1263. The average financial indebtedness of the 2001 graduate was $14,633. The FAFSA and the college's own financial statement are required.

International Students: There are 30 international students enrolled. They must score 550 on the written TOEFL or 920 on the SAT I.

Computers: A networked lab with 17 IBM 486 DX/250s and 17 Dell Pentiums is available. All students may access the system from 1 P.M. to midnight Sunday through Friday and from 1 P.M. to 4 P.M. on Saturday. There are no time limits and no fees.

Graduates: In a recent year, 332 bachelor's degrees were awarded. The most popular majors were management (79%), education (8%), and environmental science (4%). In an average class, 56% graduate in 5 years. 25 companies recruited on campus in 2000-2001.

Admissions Contact: Nancy Kilday, Admission Coordinator.
E-mail: *admissions@tusculum.edu* Web: *www.tusculum.edu*

UNION UNIVERSITY

Jackson, TN 38305-3697 B-3

(731) 661-5000

(800) 33-UNION; Fax: (731) 338-6466

Full-time: 657 men, 1000 women	**Faculty:** 133; IIB, -$
Part-time: 144 men, 164 women	**Ph.D.s:** 67%
Graduate: 187 men, 392 women	**Student/Faculty:** 12 to 1
Year: 4-1-4, summer session	**Tuition:** $14,580
Application Deadline: open	**Room & Board:** $4350
Freshman Class: 1042 applied, 901 accepted, 420 enrolled	
SAT I Verbal/Math: 575/550	**ACT:** 24 **COMPETITIVE+**

Union University, founded in 1823, is a private, nonprofit institution affiliated with the Southern Baptist Convention. The university offers programs in arts and sciences, education, business, and nursing. There are 4 undergraduate and 2 graduate schools. In addition to regional accreditation, Union has baccalaureate program accreditation with AACSB, NASM, NCATE, and NLN. The library contains 139,025 volumes, 471,122 microform items, and 9757 audiovisual forms/CDs, and subscribes to 5785 periodicals. Computerized library services include the card catalog, interlibrary loans, and database searching. Special learning facilities include a learning resource center, art gallery, and radio and TV lab facilities. The 290-acre campus is in a suburban area 80 miles east of Memphis. Including residence halls, there are 34 buildings.

Student Life: 76% of undergraduates are from Tennessee. Others are from 34 states, 10 foreign countries, and Canada. 75% are from public schools. 90% are white. Most are Protestant. The average age of all undergraduates is 21. 7% do not continue beyond their first year; 56% remain to graduate.

Housing: 1114 students can be accommodated in college housing, which includes single-sex dormitories, on-campus apartments, and married-student housing. On-campus housing is guaranteed for all 4 years. 65% of students live on campus; of those, 35% remain on campus on weekends. Alcohol is not permitted. All students may keep cars.

Activities: 26% of men belong to 3 national fraternities; 23% of women belong to 3 national sororities. There are 73 groups on campus, including art, band, cheerleading, choir, chorus, computers, concert band, drama, ethnic, film, honors, jazz band, literary magazine, music ensembles, musical theater, newspaper, opera, orchestra, pep band, photography, political, professional, radio and TV, religious, social, student government, symphony, and yearbook. Popular campus events include Campus Day, Parents Weekend, and Variety Show.

Sports: There are 5 intercollegiate sports for men and 5 for women, and 12 intramural sports for men and 12 for women. Facilities include tennis and racquetball courts, a student recreation center, an indoor swimming pool, a wellness center, 2 gyms, a soccer field, and baseball and softball complexes.

Disabled Students: 98% of the campus is accessible. Wheelchair ramps, elevators, special parking, specially equipped rest rooms, special class scheduling, lowered drinking fountains, lowered telephones, and apartments are available.

Services: Counseling and information services are available, as is tutoring in most subjects. There is also assistance with study skills, time management, note-taking, reading comprehension, and writing.

Campus Safety and Security: Measures include 24-hour foot and vehicle patrol, self-defense education, escort service, and informal discussions. There are pamphlets/posters/films, emergency telephones, and lighted pathways/sidewalks.

Programs of Study: Union confers B.A., B.S., B.M., B.S.B.A., B.S.M.T., and B.S.N. degrees. Associate, master's, and doctoral degrees are also awarded. Bachelor's degrees are awarded in BIOLOGICAL SCIENCE (biology/biological science), BUSINESS (accounting, banking and finance, business administration and management, management science, marketing management, marketing/retailing/merchandising, and sports management), COMMUNICATIONS AND THE ARTS (advertising, art, broadcasting, communications, dramatic arts, English, English as a second/foreign language, English literature, French, graphic design, Greek, journalism, music, music performance, music theory and composition, piano/organ, public relations, Spanish, and voice), COMPUTER AND PHYSICAL SCIENCE (chemistry, computer science, mathematics, physical chemistry, physical sciences, and physics), EDUCATION (education, elementary, middle school, music, physical, secondary, special, and teaching English as a second/foreign language (TESOL/TEFOL)), ENGINEERING AND ENVIRONMENTAL DESIGN (preengineering), HEALTH PROFESSIONS (medical laboratory technology, nursing, predentistry, premedicine, prepharmacy, and sports medicine), SOCIAL SCIENCE (biblical languages, biblical studies, Christian studies, economics, family and community services, history, ministries, missions, pastoral studies, philosophy, political science/government, prelaw, psychology, religion, religious music, social work, sociology, and youth ministry). Business, nursing, and education are the largest.

Required: All students must complete 128 credit hours, with at least 30 in the major, and maintain a minimum overall GPA of 2.0. The general core requirements are 8 credit hours of lab sciences, 6 each of history, composition, literature, and religion, 3 each of math, oral communication, social sciences/humanities, and fine arts, and 2 of phys ed. Students must pass comprehensive exams in each course and at completion of the major.

Special: Cooperative and accelerated degree programs are available in business department majors. Cross-registration with Lambuth and Freed-Hardeman colleges, internships, study abroad in 7 countries, a Washington semester, work-study programs, composite majors in religion and church ministry, religion and Greek, and religion and philosophy, dual and student-designed majors, 3-2 engineering degrees, and nondegree study are also offered. There are 15 national honor societies, a freshman honors program, and 14 departmental honors programs.

Faculty/Classroom: 53% of faculty are male; 47%, female. All teach undergraduates and 25% do research. No introductory courses are taught by graduate students. The average class size in an introductory lecture is 25; in a laboratory, 18; and in a regular course, 15.

Admissions: 86% of the 2001-2002 applicants were accepted. The SAT I scores for the 2001-2002 freshman class were: Verbal--20% below 500, 38% between 500 and 599, 32% between 600 and 700, and 10% above 700; Math--26% below 500, 39% between 500 and 599, 22% between 600 and 700, and 13% above 700. The ACT scores were 4% below 17, 43% between 18 and 23, 39% between 24 and 29, and 14% between 30 and 36. 50% of the current freshmen were in the top quarter of their class; 66% were in the top half. There were 5 National Merit finalists and 2 semifinalists. 21 freshmen graduated first in their class.

Requirements: The SAT I or ACT is required; the ACT is preferred. A minimum composite score of 20 on the ACT or 820 on the SAT I is recommended. Candidates must be graduates of an accredited secondary school or have the GED. A minimum of 20 academic credits is required, including at least 14 in English, math, foreign language, and social and natural sciences. An interview is also recommended. Union requires applicants to be in the upper 50% of their class. A GPA of 2.5 is required. AP and CLEP credits are accepted. Important factors in the admissions decision are leadership record, advanced placement or honor courses, and recommendations by school officials. Applications are accepted on-line via CollegeLink and the Internet.

Procedure: Freshmen are admitted to all sessions. Entrance exams should be taken in the spring of the junior year. There are early decision, early admissions, rolling admissions, and deferred admissions plans. Application deadlines are open; priority date is February 15. Notification is sent on a rolling basis beginning November 1. The application fee is $25. In a recent year, 14 early decision candidates were accepted.

Transfer: 170 transfer students enrolled in 2001-2002. Candidates must have a minimum GPA of 2.0 in more than 12 semester hours and submit a student transfer form from the last institution attended. 32 credits of 128 must be completed at Union.

Visiting: There are regularly scheduled orientations for prospective students, including campus tours, class visits, and appointments with counselors. There are guides for informal visits and visitors may sit in on classes and stay overnight. To schedule a visit, contact Robbie Graves, Director of Recruiting Services.

Financial Aid: In 2001-2002, 81% of all freshmen and 80% of continuing students received some form of financial aid. 70% of freshmen and 71% of continuing students received need-based aid. 35% of undergraduates work part time. Average annual earnings from campus work are $1000. The average financial indebtedness of the 2001 graduate was $7800. The FAFSA and the college's own financial statement are required. The fall application deadline is February 15 (priority date: January 15).

International Students: There were 40 international students enrolled in a recent year. The school actively recruits these students. They must score 500 on the written TOEFL.

Computers: The mainframe is an HP3000/series 979. 4 large labs house 105 computers, all connected to the campus network, the Internet, and the libraries' on-line services. Some have access to the mainframe to support computer science and statistics classes. All students have e-mail and network accounts. Other smaller labs have a total of about 100 PCs with software specific to the department. All dorm rooms are wired, giving 24-hour access equivalent to that in the labs. All students may access the system during laboratory hours. There are no time limits and no fees.

Graduates: In 2001, 399 bachelor's degrees were awarded. The most popular majors were business/marketing (26%), health professions and related sciences (20%), and education (15%). In an average class, 4% graduate in 3 years, 47% in 4 years, 59% in 5 years, and 60% in 6 years. 47 companies recruited on campus in 2000-2001.

Admissions Contact: Carroll Griffin, Assistant to the Provost for Enrollment Services. E-mail: *info@uu.edu* Web: *www.uu.edu*

UNIVERSITY OF MEMPHIS

Memphis, TN 38152 — A-4

(901) 678-2169
(800) 669-2678; Fax: (901) 678-5318

Full-time: 4681 men, 6593 women	**Faculty:** I, --$
Part-time: 1774 men, 2564 women	**Ph.D.s:** 74%
Graduate: 2015 men, 2705 women	**Student/Faculty:** 14 to 1
Year: semesters, summer session	**Tuition:** $3470 ($9510)
Application Deadline: August 1	**Room & Board:** $3801
Freshman Class: 4622 applied, 3338 accepted, 1945 enrolled	
SAT I Verbal/Math: 540/530	**ACT:** 21 **COMPETITIVE**

The University of Memphis, founded in 1912, is a public liberal arts and sciences institution and is part of the Tennessee Board of Regents system. There are 9 undergraduate and 2 graduate schools. In addition to regional accreditation, U of M has baccalaureate program accreditation with AACSB, ABET, ADA, AHEA, ASLA, CSWE, NASAD, NASM, NCATE, and NLN. The 6 libraries contain 1,103,414 volumes, 3,350,589 microform items, and 32,895 audiovisual forms/CDs, and subscribe to 10,593 periodicals. Computerized library services include the card catalog, interlibrary loans, and database searching. Special learning facilities include a learning resource center, art gallery, radio station, TV station, an earthquake research center, a center for electron microscopy, Chucalissa Indian Village and Museum, and a speech and hearing center. The 1160-acre campus is in an urban area. Including residence halls, there are 200 buildings.

Student Life: 91% of undergraduates are from Tennessee. Others are from 42 states, 83 foreign countries, and Canada. 60% are white; 34% African American. The average age of freshmen is 19; all undergraduates, 25. 28% do not continue beyond their first year; 33% remain to graduate.

Housing: 2300 students can be accommodated in college housing, which includes single-sex dormitories, on-campus apartments, married-student housing, and family housing. On-campus housing is guaranteed for all 4 years. 87% of students commute. Alcohol is not permitted. All students may keep cars.

Activities: 6% of men belong to 13 national fraternities; 6% of women belong to 11 national sororities. There are 181 groups on campus, including art, band, cheerleading, chess, choir, chorale, chorus, computers, dance, drama, ethnic, film, gay, honors, international, jazz band, literary magazine, marching band, musical theater, newspaper, orchestra, pep band, photography, political, professional, radio and TV, religious, social, social service, student government, and yearbook. Popular campus events include Derby Day, Greek Week, and Welcome Back Week.

Sports: There are 7 intercollegiate sports for men and 5 for women, and 12 intramural sports for men and 11 for women. Facilities include a gym, a football stadium, a baseball field, swimming pools, a track, a weight room, and tennis, handball, and racquetball courts.

Disabled Students: 95% of the campus is accessible. Wheelchair ramps, elevators, special parking, specially equipped rest rooms, special class scheduling, lowered drinking fountains, lowered telephones, modified housing, and a transportation service are available.

Services: Counseling and information services are available, as is tutoring in most subjects. There is a reader service for the blind, and remedial math, reading, and writing.

Campus Safety and Security: Measures include 24-hour foot and vehicle patrol, escort service, informal discussions, and emergency telephones. There are lighted pathways/sidewalks.

Programs of Study: U of M confers B.A., B.S., B.B.A., B.F.A., B.L.S., B.M., B.P.S., B.S.C.E., B.S.Cp.E., B.S.Ch., B.S.Ed., B.S.E.E., B.S.E.T., B.S.I.S., B.S.M.E., and B.S.N. degrees. Master's and doctoral degrees are also awarded. Bachelor's degrees are awarded in BIOLOGICAL SCIENCE (biology/biological science, microbiology, and molecular biology), BUSINESS (accounting, banking and finance, business administration and management, business economics, hospitality management services, insurance and risk management, international business management, management information systems, management science, marketing and distribution, marketing management, real estate, recreation and leisure services, and retailing), COMMUNICATIONS AND THE ARTS (art, art history and appreciation, communications, dramatic arts, English, journalism, languages, music, and music business management), COMPUTER AND PHYSICAL SCIENCE (chemistry, computer science, geology, mathematics, and physics), EDUCATION (special), ENGINEERING AND ENVIRONMENTAL DESIGN (architecture, civil engineering, computer engineering, computer technology, electrical/electronics engineering, electrical/electronics engineering technology, industrial engineering, manufacturing engineering, mechanical engineering, and systems engineering), HEALTH PROFESSIONS (exercise science and nursing), SOCIAL SCIENCE (anthropology, consumer services, criminal justice, criminology, economics, geography, history, human development, interdisciplinary studies, international relations, international studies, philosophy, political science/government, psychology, social work, and sociology). Human development, management information systems, and psychology are the largest.

Required: To graduate, students must complete a minimum of 132 credit hours with a GPA of 2.0 and demonstrate proficiency in computer skills. Distribution requirements include 8 hours of natural science, 6 hours each of English composition, social science, and U.S. history; 3 to 6 hours of math; 4 hours of phys ed; and 3 hours each of communication, fine arts, literature, history/philosophy, computation, intensive writing, and thematic and integrative courses.

Special: The university offers co-op programs, cross-registration, internships, study abroad in England and Spain, B.A.-B.S. degrees, dual and student-designed majors, nondegree study, and pass/fail options. Students may receive credit for life, military, and work experience. There is a freshman honors program.

Faculty/Classroom: 56% of faculty are male; 44%, female.

Admissions: 72% of the 2001-2002 applicants were accepted. The SAT I scores for the 2001-2002 freshman class were: Verbal--31% below 500, 43% between 500 and 599, 18% between 600 and 700, and 8% above 700; Math--32% below 500, 39% between 500 and 599, 25% between 600 and 700, and 5% above 700. The ACT scores were 11% between 12 and 17, 56% between 18 and 23, 30% between 24 and 29, and 3% between 30 and 36.

Requirements: The SAT I or ACT is required, with a minimum acceptable composite score of 20 on the ACT. Candidates for admission should be graduates of an accredited secondary school and have 14 academic credits or 20 Carnegie units. The GED is accepted. Academic preparation should include 4 units in English, 3 in math, 2 each in science, social studies, and foreign language, and 1 in visual and performing arts. An audition is required for music majors. A GPA of 2.0 is required. AP and CLEP credits are accepted. Important factors in the admissions decision are advanced placement or honor courses, evidence of special talent, and recommendations by school officials.

Procedure: Freshmen are admitted to all sessions. Entrance exams should be taken in the spring of the junior year or October of the senior year. Applications should be filed by August 1 for fall entry, December 1 for spring entry, and May 1 for summer entry. Notification is sent on a rolling basis. The fall 2001 application fee was $15.

Transfer: 1411 transfer students enrolled in 2001-2002. For guaranteed admission, applicants should have a GPA of 2.0 and be eligible to return to the last college of regular enrollment. 33 credits of 132 must be completed at U of M.

Visiting: There are regularly scheduled orientations for prospective students, including Fall Campus Day for high school seniors. There are guides for informal visits and visitors may sit in on classes and stay overnight. To schedule a visit, contact Malinda McDaniel, Student Relations and Orientation Services.

Financial Aid: In 2001-2002, 35% of all freshmen and 50% of continuing students received some form of financial aid. 27% of freshmen and 39% of continuing students received need-based aid. The average freshman award was $4100. Of that total, scholarships or need-based grants averaged $2770 ($7000 maximum); loans averaged $2100 ($8825 maximum); and work contracts averaged $1500 ($3000 maximum). 13% of undergraduates work part time. Average annual earnings from campus work are $1850. The average financial indebtedness of the 2001 graduate was $17,200. The FAFSA is required. The fall application deadline is March 1.

International Students: There are 310 international students enrolled. The school actively recruits these students. They must score 550 on the written TOEFL.

Computers: The mainframe is a DEC VAX 8820. Residence halls have computer sites with mainframe access and both Macs and PCs. There is a PC hookup in all residence hall rooms. Other computer sites include learning labs spread throughout the campus. All students may access the system. There are no time limits and no fees. It is strongly recommended that all students have a personal computer.

Graduates: In 2001, 1928 bachelor's degrees were awarded. The most popular majors were human development and learning (10%), management information systems (6%), and psychology (5%). In an average class, 9% graduate in 4 years, 25% in 5 years, and 36% in 6 years.

Admissions Contact: William Akey, Director, Student Relations. A video is available. E-mail: *recruitment@memphis.edu*
Web: *www.memphis.edu*

UNIVERSITY OF TENNESSEE SYSTEM

The University of Tennessee System, established in 1794, is a land-grant system. It is governed by a board of trustees, whose chief administrator is the president. The primary goals of the system are to provide quality learning, research, and public service opportunities for students from Tennessee and throughout the country. The total enrollment of all 4 campuses averages about 40,000, with some 3000 faculty members. There are 244 baccalaureate, 136 master's, and 69 doctoral programs offered. Profiles of the 4-year campuses are included in this section.

UNIVERSITY OF TENNESSEE AT CHATTANOOGA D-4

Chattanooga, TN 37403 (423) 755-4662
(800) UTC-6627; Fax: (423) 755-4157

Full-time: 2387 men, 3357 women	**Faculty:** 307; IIA, --$
Part-time: 612 men, 749 women	**Ph.D.s:** 80%
Graduate: 546 men, 834 women	**Student/Faculty:** 19 to 1
Year: semesters, summer session	**Tuition:** $3236 ($9766)
Application Deadline: August 1	**Room & Board:** $4547
Freshman Class: 2501 applied, 1272 accepted, 1081 enrolled	
SAT I Verbal/Math: 530/520	**ACT:** 22 **COMPETITIVE**

The University of Tennessee at Chattanooga, founded in 1886, is a public institution. Part of the state's university system, it offers programs in liberal and fine arts, business, engineering, health science, and teacher preparation. There are 5 undergraduate and 5 graduate schools. In addition to regional accreditation, UTC has baccalaureate program accreditation with AACSB, ABET, ACEJMC, AHEA, APTA, CSWE, NASAD, NASM, NCATE, and NLN. The library contains 486,978 volumes, 1,338,193 microform items, and 16,451 audiovisual forms/CDs, and subscribes to 2768 periodicals. Computerized library services include the card catalog, interlibrary loans, and database searching. Special learning facilities include a learning resource center, art gallery, radio station, and observatory. The 116-acre campus is in an urban area 105 miles north of Atlanta. Including residence halls, there are 76 buildings.

Student Life: 92% of undergraduates are from Tennessee. Others are from 41 states, 49 foreign countries, and Canada. 79% are white; 16% African American. The average age of freshmen is 20; all undergraduates, 24. 26% do not continue beyond their first year; 44% remain to graduate.

Housing: 1830 students can be accommodated in college housing, which includes single-sex and coed dormitories, on-campus apartments, off-campus apartments, married-student housing, and fraternity houses. On-campus housing is available on a first-come, first-served basis. 74% of students commute. Alcohol is not permitted. All students may keep cars.

Activities: 8% of men belong to 8 national fraternities; 7% of women belong to 7 national sororities. There are 130 groups on campus, including band, cheerleading, chess, choir, chorale, chorus, computers, dance, drama, drill team, ethnic, gay, honors, international, jazz band, literary magazine, marching band, musical theater, newspaper, orchestra, pep band, photography, political, professional, radio and TV, religious, social, social service, student government, symphony, and yearbook. Popular campus events include Homecoming.

Sports: There are 6 intercollegiate sports for men and 6 for women, and 12 intramural sports for men and 7 for women. Facilities include a gym, an arena, a tennis and racquet center, a swimming pool, and 2 fields, including a soccer field.

Disabled Students: 98% of the campus is accessible. Wheelchair ramps, elevators, special parking, specially equipped rest rooms, special class scheduling, lowered drinking fountains, and lowered telephones are available.

Services: Counseling and information services are available, as is tutoring in most subjects. There is a reader service for the blind, and remedial math, reading, and writing.

Campus Safety and Security: Measures include 24-hour foot and vehicle patrol, escort service, shuttle buses, and informal discussions. There are pamphlets/posters/films, emergency telephones, and lighted pathways/sidewalks.

Programs of Study: UTC confers B.A., B.S., B.F.A., B.M., B.S.E., B.S.N., B.S.O.T., and B.S.W. degrees. Master's degrees are also awarded. Bachelor's degrees are awarded in BIOLOGICAL SCIENCE (biology/biological science), BUSINESS (business administration and management, and recreation and leisure services), COMMUNICATIONS AND THE ARTS (communications, dramatic arts, English, fine arts, French, Greek, Latin, music, and Spanish), COMPUTER AND PHYSICAL SCIENCE (applied mathematics, chemistry, computer science, geology, mathematics, and physics), EDUCATION (art, education, music, secondary, and special), ENGINEERING AND ENVIRONMENTAL DESIGN (engineering, engineering management, and environmental science), HEALTH PROFESSIONS (medical laboratory technology, nursing, occupational therapy, and rehabilitation therapy), SOCIAL SCIENCE (criminal justice, economics, history, home economics, human services, humanities, paralegal studies, philosophy, political science/government, psychology, social work, sociology, and women's studies). Business and nursing are the strongest academically. Business is the largest.

Required: All students must complete at least 128 semester hours and maintain a minimum GPA of 2.0. General education requirements include 9 hours in humanities and fine arts, 6 hours each in written communication in English and behavioral and social sciences, 4 hours in physical and natural sciences, and 3 hours each in math, and perspectives. A health and phys ed course is required in the first year, and another phys ed activity course must be taken before graduation. Requirements vary by major.

Special: Cooperative programs are offered in accounting, business systems, chemistry, communications, engineering, environmental studies, nursing, and psychology. UTC offers internships, study abroad in England, work-study and accelerated degree programs, B.A.-B.S. degrees, dual majors, interdisciplinary majors, including theater and speech, 3-2 engineering degrees, and nondegree study. Credit is given for life, military, or work experience. There are 30 national honor societies, a freshman honors program, and 25 departmental honors programs.

Faculty/Classroom: 65% of faculty are male; 35%, female. No introductory courses are taught by graduate students. The average class size in an introductory lecture is 25.

Admissions: 51% of the 2001-2002 applicants were accepted. The SAT I scores for the 2001-2002 freshman class were: Verbal--39% below 500, 33% between 500 and 599, 22% between 600 and 700, and 6% above 700; Math--21% below 500, 35% between 500 and 599, 36% between 600 and 700, and 8% above 700. The ACT scores were 46% below 21, 25% between 21 and 23, 16% between 24 and 26, 7% between 27 and 28, and 6% above 28. 45% of the current freshmen were in the top two fifths of their class.

Requirements: The SAT I or ACT is required. In addition, secondary school credits should include 4 in English, 3 in math, and 2 each in science, social studies, and a foreign language. The GED is accepted. A GPA of 2.0 is required. AP and CLEP credits are accepted. Important factors in the admissions decision are recommendations by school officials, advanced placement or honor courses, and evidence of special talent. Applicatioons are accepted on-line at the school's web site.

Procedure: Freshmen are admitted to all sessions. Entrance exams should be taken in spring of the junior year. There is a deferred admissions plan. Applications should be filed by August 1 for fall entry and December 15 for spring entry. Notification is sent on a rolling basis. The fall 2001 application fee was $25.

Transfer: 631 transfer students enrolled in 2001-2002. A minimum GPA of 2.0 is required. 30 credits of 128 must be completed at UTC.

Visiting: There are regularly scheduled orientations for prospective students. There are guides for informal visits and visitors may sit in on classes and stay overnight. To schedule a visit, contact the Admissions Office.

Financial Aid: In 2001-2002, 70% of all freshmen and 65% of continuing students received some form of financial aid. 48% of freshmen and 56% of continuing students received need-based aid. The average freshman award was $3305. Of that total, scholarships or need-based grants averaged $1350 ($5220 maximum); loans averaged $1000 ($2625 maximum); and work contracts averaged $955 ($2200 maximum). 78% of undergraduates work part time. Average annual earnings from campus work are $1900. The FAFSA is required. The fall application deadline is April 1.

International Students: There are 79 international students enrolled. The school actively recruits these students. They must score 500 on the written TOEFL.

Computers: There are no time limits and no fees.

Graduates: In 2001, 1377 bachelor's degrees were awarded. The most popular majors were business administration (23%), education (15%), and psychology (9%). In an average class, 18% graduate in 4 years, 37% in 5 years, and 44% in 6 years. 100 companies recruited on campus in 2000-2001.

Admissions Contact: Yancy Freeman, Director of Admissions & Recruitment. E-mail: *yancy-freeman@utc.edu* Web: *www.utc.edu*

UNIVERSITY OF TENNESSEE AT KNOXVILLE E-2

Knoxville, TN 37996-0230 (423) 974-2184
(800) 221-VOLS; Fax: (423) 974-6341

Full-time: 8806 men, 9329 women	**Faculty:** 1253
Part-time: 930 men, 1059 women	**Ph.D.s:** 86%
Graduate: 2507 men, 3402 women	**Student/Faculty:** 14 to 1
Year: semesters, summer session	**Tuition:** $3784 ($11,570)
Application Deadline: see profile	**Room & Board:** $4430
Freshman Class: 8263 applied, 5675 accepted, 3958 enrolled	
SAT I Verbal/Math: 545/547	**ACT:** 23 **COMPETITIVE**

The University of Tennessee, Knoxville, founded in 1794 and the original campus of the state university system, is now a large public institution offering more than 300 graduate and undergraduate programs. There are 11 undergraduate and 14 graduate schools. In addition to regional accreditation, UT Knoxville has baccalaureate program accreditation with AACSB, ABET, ACEJMC, ADA, AHEA, ASLA, CSWE, FIDER, NAAB, NASAD, NASM, NCATE, NLN, NRPA, and SAF. The 4 libraries contain 2,492,953 volumes, 3,502,541 microform items, and 173,506 audiovisual forms/CDs, and subscribe to 16,656 periodicals. Computerized library services include the card catalog, interlibrary loans, and database searching. Special learning facilities include a learning resource center, art gallery, natural history museum, radio station, and a science and engineering research facility. The 533-acre campus is in an urban area adjacent to downtown Knoxville. Including residence halls, there are 220 buildings.

Student Life: 81% of undergraduates are from Tennessee. Others are from 490 states, 100 foreign countries, and Canada. 89% are white. The average age of freshmen is 18; all undergraduates, 22. 21% do not continue beyond their first year; 57% remain to graduate.

Housing: 7449 students can be accommodated in college housing, which includes single-sex and coed dormitories, on-campus apartments, off-campus apartments, married-student housing, and fraternity houses. In addition, there are language houses and special-interest houses. On-campus housing is available on a first-come, first-served basis. 62% of students commute. Alcohol is not permitted. All students may keep cars.

Activities: 8% of men belong to 26 national fraternities; 8% of women belong to 17 national sororities. There are 300 groups on campus, including art, band, cheerleading, chess, choir, chorale, chorus, computers, dance, drama, ethnic, film, gay, honors, international, jazz band, literary magazine, marching band, musical theater, newspaper, opera, orchestra, pep band, photography, political, professional, radio and TV, religious, social, social service, student government, symphony, and yearbook. Popular campus events include All-Sing, Torch Night, and International Festival.

Sports: There are 8 intercollegiate sports for men and 10 for women, and 22 intramural sports for men and 22 for women. Facilities include a 25,000-seat basketball arena, the second largest collegiate football stadium in the U.S., an Olympic track, Olympic indoor and outdoor pools, various outdoor facilities, a baseball stadium, and softball and soccer fields.

Disabled Students: 95% of the campus is accessible. Wheelchair ramps, elevators, special parking, specially equipped rest rooms, special class scheduling, lowered drinking fountains, lowered telephones, and an escort service are available.

Services: There is a reader service for the blind. Tutoring in math, English, and most lower-division courses can be arranged.

Campus Safety and Security: Measures include 24-hour foot and vehicle patrol, self-defense education, escort service, and shuttle buses. There are informal discussions, pamphlets/posters/films, emergency telephones, lighted pathways/sidewalks, and and campus safety educational programs.

Programs of Study: UT Knoxville confers B.A., B.S., B.Arch., B.F.A., B.M., and specialized B.S. degrees in 25 fields, including business administration, nursing, and social work. degrees. Master's and doctoral degrees are also awarded. Bachelor's degrees are awarded in AGRICULTURE (agricultural economics, agriculture, animal science, fishing and fisheries, forestry and related sciences, plant science, and soil science), BIOLOGICAL SCIENCE (biochemistry, biology/biological science, botany, microbiology, and nutrition), BUSINESS (accounting, banking and finance, business administration and management, business economics, hotel/motel and restaurant management, management science, marketing/retailing/merchandising, retailing, sports management, tourism, and transportation management), COMMUNICATIONS AND THE ARTS (advertising, art history and appreciation, broadcasting, classics, comparative literature, dramatic arts, English, film arts, fine arts, French, German, graphic design, Italian, journalism, languages, linguistics, music, Russian, Spanish, speech/debate/rhetoric, and studio art), COMPUTER AND PHYSICAL SCIENCE (chemistry, computer science, geology, mathematics, physics, and statistics), EDUCATION (agricultural, art, elementary, health, marketing and distribution, music, physical, recreation, and special), ENGINEERING AND ENVIRONMENTAL DESIGN (aerospace studies, agricultural engineering, architecture, chemical engineering, civil engineering, electrical/electronics engineering, engineering, engineering and applied science, engineering physics, environmental science, food services technology, industrial engineering, interior design, landscape architecture/design, materials engineering, materials science, mechanical engineering, and nuclear engineering), HEALTH PROFESSIONS (community health work, health science, nursing, predentistry, premedicine, preveterinary science, and speech pathology/audiology), SOCIAL SCIENCE (African American studies, anthropology, Asian/Oriental studies, child care/child and family studies, classical/ancient civilization, economics, food science, geography, history, human services, Latin American studies, medieval studies, philosophy, political science/government, psychology, public administration, religion, Russian and Slavic studies, social work, sociology, textiles and clothing, urban studies, and women's studies). Engineering, physical sciences, and English are the strongest academically. Business administration is the largest.

Required: All students must complete at least 120 credits with a minimum 2.0 GPA. Many degree programs require higher credit totals and GPAs. All students take 2 English composition courses and a core curriculum including 2 courses each in math sciences, humanities and the arts, history, social sciences, natural sciences, and foreign language or integrative studies.

Special: Cooperative programs are offered in engineering, communications, liberal arts, and business. Cross-registration is possible through the Academic Common Market, a Southern 14-state consortium, in any of 11 programs. Internships are available in social work, education, and architecture, and there are a number of work-study programs. Study abroad in more than 25 countries is possible. Dual and student-designed majors, accelerated study, nondegree study, and pass/fail options are offered. There are 51 national honor societies, including Phi Beta Kappa, a freshman honors program, and 13 departmental honors programs.

Faculty/Classroom: 75% of faculty are male; 25%, female. 6% do research and 94% both teach and do research. The average class size in an introductory lecture is 26; in a laboratory, 14; and in a regular course, 29.

Admissions: 69% of the 2001-2002 applicants were accepted. The SAT I scores for the 2001-2002 freshman class were: Verbal--30% below 500, 42% between 500 and 599, 22% between 600 and 700, and 6% above 700; Math--29% below 500, 39% between 500 and 599, 26% between 600 and 700, and 5% above 700. The ACT scores were 25% below 21, 29% between 21 and 23, 28% between 24 and 26, 9% between 27 and 28, and 9% above 28. 43% of the current freshmen were in the top fifth of their class; 88% were in the top two fifths. There were 44 National Merit finalists in a recent year.

Requirements: The SAT I or ACT is required. The ACT is preferred. Applicants should be high school graduates or have the GED. Required secondary school courses include 4 credits in English, 3 in math, 2 each in science and a single foreign language, 1 each in history and world history or world geography, and 1 unit of visual/performing arts. A GPA of 2.0 is required. AP and CLEP credits are accepted. Important factors in the admissions decision are advanced placement or honor courses, leadership record, and parents or siblings attending the school.

Procedure: Freshmen are admitted to all sessions. Entrance exams should be taken in spring of the junior year or fall of the senior year. There are early admissions and deferred admissions plans. Check with the school for current application deadlines. The application fee is $25. Notification is sent on a rolling basis.

Transfer: 1427 transfer students enrolled in a recent year. Transfer applicants should present a minimum 2.0 GPA in previous college work, although many specific programs have higher requirements. 30 credits of 120 must be completed at UT Knoxville.

Visiting: There are regularly scheduled orientations for prospective students, including 2 open houses yearly where prospective students can meet with faculty, administrators, and students to discuss admissions, housing, financial aid, student activities, academic colleges and departments, and organizations. There are guides for informal visits and visitors may sit in on classes. To schedule a visit, contact Undergraduate Admissions.

Financial Aid: UT Knoxville is a member of CSS. The CSS/Profile or FFS and Academic College Scholarship Application are required. Check with the school for current deadlines.

International Students: There were 300 international students enrolled in a recent year. They must score 525 on the written TOEFL.

Computers: The mainframe is an IBM 9672-R42. There are also Macs, PCs, and Sun workstations available throughout the campus. Students can access the library mainframe from apartment or dormitory rooms via modem. All students may access the system. There are no time limits and no fees.

Graduates: In a recent year, 3443 bachelor's degrees were awarded. The most popular majors were psychology (8%), English (5%), and biology (4%). In an average class, 24% graduate in 4 years, 50% in 5 years, and 57% in 6 years. 533 companies recruited on campus in a recent year.

Admissions Contact: Marshall Rose, Director of Admissions.
E-mail: *admissions@utk.edu* Web: *www.utk.edu*

UNIVERSITY OF TENNESSEE AT MARTIN — B-2

Martin, TN 38238 — (731) 587-7020
(800) 829-8861; Fax: (731) 587-7029

Full-time: 2097 men, 2565 women	**Faculty:** 253; IIA, --$
Part-time: 305 men, 511 women	**Ph.D.s:** 70%
Graduate: 152 men, 270 women	**Student/Faculty:** 18 to 1
Year: semesters, summer session	**Tuition:** $4442 ($10,392)
Application Deadline: open	**Room & Board:** $3820

Freshman Class: 2294 applied, 1272 accepted, 1080 enrolled
SAT I or ACT: required — **COMPETITIVE**

The University of Tennessee at Martin, founded in 1927, is a public university offering undergraduate programs in natural and social sciences, humanities, fine and performing arts, computer science, nursing, agriculture, teacher education, business administration, and engineering. Graduate degrees are offered in accounting and business administration, counseling and teacher education, and human environmental sciences. There are 5 undergraduate and 3 graduate schools. In addition to regional accreditation, UT Martin has baccalaureate program accreditation with ABET, ADA, CSWE, NASM, NCATE, and NLN. The library contains 423,333 volumes, 610,766 microform items, and 10,692 audiovisual forms/CDs, and subscribes to 1647 periodicals. Computerized library services include the card catalog, interlibrary loans, and database searching. Special learning facilities include a learning resource center, natural history museum, radio station, TV station, and a teacher resource center, a 680-acre Agricultural Experiment Station, a teaching/research facility at Reelfoot Lake State Resort, and a Center for Environmental and Conservation Education. The 250-acre campus is in a rural area 125 miles northeast of Memphis and 150 miles northwest of Nashville. Including residence halls, there are 46 buildings.

Student Life: 90% of undergraduates are from Tennessee. Others are from 38 states, 32 foreign countries, and Canada. 90% are from public schools. 80% are white; 15% African American. 76% are Protestant; 20% claim no religious affiliation. The average age of freshmen is 19; all undergraduates, 23. 34% do not continue beyond their first year; 46% remain to graduate.

Housing: 2415 students can be accommodated in college housing, which includes single-sex and coed dormitories, on-campus apartments, and married-student housing. In addition, there are honors houses and language houses. On-campus housing is guaranteed for all 4 years. 60% of students commute. Alcohol is not permitted. All students may keep cars.

Activities: 9% of men belong to 9 national fraternities; 9% of women belong to 8 national sororities. There are 121 groups on campus, including art, band, cheerleading, choir, chorale, chorus, computers, dance, drama, ethnic, film, honors, international, jazz band, literary magazine, marching band, musical theater, newspaper, opera, pep band, photography, political, professional, radio and TV, religious, social, social service, student government, and yearbook. Popular campus events include Greekfest, UTM Rodeo-N-Roundup Days, and All-Niter.

Sports: There are 8 intercollegiate sports for men and 9 for women, and 18 intramural sports for men and 18 for women. Facilities include a phys ed and convocation center, an agricultural pavilion, a football stadium, a fitness trail, an Olympic-size swimming pool, intramural playing fields, baseball and softball fields, a track, tennis courts, and a climbing wall.

Disabled Students: 98% of the campus is accessible. Wheelchair ramps, elevators, special parking, specially equipped rest rooms, special class scheduling, lowered drinking fountains, and lowered telephones are available.

Services: Counseling and information services are available, as is tutoring in every subject. There is a reader service for the blind, and remedial math, reading, and writing.

Campus Safety and Security: Measures include 24-hour foot and vehicle patrol, self-defense education, escort service, and informal discussions. There are pamphlets/posters/films, emergency telephones, lighted pathways/sidewalks, and bicycle patrol and security cameras in the 4 largest residence halls.

Programs of Study: UT Martin confers B.A., B.S., B.A.Mus., B.F.A., B.M.M., B.S.Ag., B.S.B.A., B.S.Chem., B.S.C.J., B.S.Ed., B.S.Eng., B.S.H.E., B.S.H.H.P., B.S.Mus., B.S.N., B.S.Natural Resources Mgt., and B.S.S.W. degrees. Master's degrees are also awarded. Bachelor's degrees are awarded in AGRICULTURE (agricultural business management, agriculture, animal science, conservation and regulation, natural resource management, and plant science), BIOLOGICAL SCIENCE (biology/biological science, and wildlife biology), BUSINESS (accounting, banking and finance, business administration and management, business economics, international business management, marketing/retailing/merchandising, and office supervision and management), COMMUNICATIONS AND THE ARTS (communications, English, fine arts, French, music, and Spanish), COMPUTER AND PHYSICAL SCIENCE (chemistry, computer science, geology, and mathematics), EDUCATION (agricultural, art, business, early childhood, elementary, foreign languages, health, home economics, music, science, and secondary), ENGINEERING AND ENVIRONMENTAL DESIGN (civil engineering, engineering, and interior design), HEALTH PROFESSIONS (nursing, predentistry, premedicine, preoptometry, and prepharmacy), SOCIAL SCIENCE (child care/child and family studies, criminal justice, dietetics, economics, geography, history, international studies, parks and recreation management, philosophy, political science/government, prelaw, psychology, public administration, social work, and sociology). Engineering, education, and health sciences are the strongest academically. Business, education, and biology are the largest.

Required: The number of credit hours required for graduation ranges from 127 to 130 (based on degree). All students must have at least a 2.0 GPA. Specific courses and major requirements vary by the program selected. There is a 1 year or 30 hour UTM residency requirement.

Special: UTM offers co-op programs in engineering, agriculture, computer science, business, and chemistry, for-credit internships, cross-registration through the Gulf Coast consortium, study abroad, B.A.-B.S. degrees, dual and student-designed majors, and pass/fail options. There are 7 national honor societies, a freshman honors program, and 5 departmental honors programs.

Faculty/Classroom: 63% of faculty are male; 37%, female. All teach undergraduates, 81% do research, and 81% do both. No introductory courses are taught by graduate students. The average class size in an introductory lecture is 30; in a laboratory, 19; and in a regular course, 22.

Admissions: 55% of the 2001-2002 applicants were accepted. 19 freshmen graduated first in their class in a recent year.

Requirements: The SAT I or ACT is required. In addition, students should have a minimum composite score of 19 on the ACT with a 2.25 minimum GPA, or 16 on the ACT with a minimum 2.6 GPA. Candidates for admission should be graduates of an accredited secondary school with 14 academic credits. The GED is accepted with a score of 50. Secondary school units should include 4 of English, 3 of math, 2 of a foreign language, and 1 each of science, history, social studies, and fine and performing arts. Applications are accepted on-line. A GPA of 2.25 is required. AP and CLEP credits are accepted.

Procedure: Freshmen are admitted to all sessions. Entrance exams should be taken in the fall of the senior year. There is a deferred admissions plan. Application deadlines are open. The fall 2001 application fee was $25.

Transfer: 381 transfer students enrolled in 2001-2002. Transfer students should have a minimum GPA of 2.0. 30 credits of 130 must be completed at UT Martin.

Visiting: There are regularly scheduled orientations for prospective students, including student-parent seminars during the summer for information sharing. There are guides for informal visits and visitors may sit in on classes and stay overnight. To schedule a visit, contact the Admissions Office.

Financial Aid: In 2001-2002, 85% of all freshmen and 80% of continuing students received some form of financial aid. 96% of freshmen and 95% of continuing students received need-based aid. The average freshman award was $6276. Of that total, scholarships or need-based grants averaged $3888; and loans averaged $3254. The average financial indebtedness of the 2001 graduate was $10,500. UT Martin is a member of CSS. The FAFSA is required. The fall application deadline is March 1.

International Students: There are 195 international students enrolled. The school actively recruits these students. They must score 500 on the written TOEFL and also take a writing proficiency exam.

Computers: There are 600 computers available for student use throughout campus. All students may access the system 24 hours. There are no time limits. The fee is $100. It is strongly recommended that all students have a personal computer.

Graduates: In 2001, 785 bachelor's degrees were awarded. The most popular majors were business/marketing (21%), interdisciplinary (13%), and agriculture (8%). In an average class, 13% graduate in 4 years, 37% in 5 years, and 46% in 6 years.

Admissions Contact: Judy Rayburn, Director of Admissions. A video is available. E-mail: *jrayburn@utm.edu* Web: *www.utm.edu*

UNIVERSITY OF THE SOUTH — D-4
Sewanee, TN 37383-1000 (931) 598-1238
(800) 522-2234; Fax: (931) 538-3248

Full-time: 615 men, 694 women	**Faculty:** 127; IIB, +$
Part-time: 10 men, 10 women	**Ph.D.s:** 96%
Graduate: 8 men, 5 women	**Student/Faculty:** 10 to 1
Year: semesters, summer session	**Tuition:** $21,340
Application Deadline: February 1	**Room & Board:** $5950
Freshman Class: 1620 applied, 1194 accepted, 355 enrolled	
SAT I or ACT: required	**HIGHLY COMPETITIVE**

The University of the South, founded in 1857, is an independent liberal arts institution affiliated with the Episcopal Church. The library contains 469,000 volumes, 292,238 microform items, and 17,000 audiovisual forms/CDs, and subscribes to 2800 periodicals. Computerized library services include the card catalog, interlibrary loans, and database searching. Special learning facilities include a learning resource center, art gallery, radio station, and observatory, materials analysis lab with an electron scanning microscope, and rare books collection. The 10,000-acre campus is in a small town 45 miles west of Chattanooga. Including residence halls, there are 43 buildings.

Student Life: 79% of undergraduates are from out of state, mostly the South. Others are from 44 states and 17 foreign countries. 55% are from public schools. 93% are white. 60% are Protestant; 21% claim no religious affiliation. The average age of freshmen is 18; all undergraduates, 20. 10% do not continue beyond their first year; 78% remain to graduate.

Housing: 1198 students can be accommodated in college housing, which includes single-sex and coed dormitories, on-campus apartments, married-student housing, and substance-free housing. In addition, there are language houses. On-campus housing is guaranteed for all 4 years. 92% of students live on campus; of those, 90% remain on campus on weekends. All students may keep cars.

Activities: 46% of men belong to 11 national fraternities; 39% of women belong to 6 local sororities. There are 110 groups on campus, including art, cheerleading, choir, chorale, chorus, computers, dance, drama, ethnic, film, gay, honors, international, literary magazine, musical theater, newspaper, orchestra, photography, political, professional, radio and TV, religious, social, social service, student government, symphony, and yearbook. Popular campus events include Spring Festival Weekend.

Sports: There are 16 intercollegiate sports for men and 16 for women, and 15 intramural sports for men and 16 for women. Facilities include a sport and fitness center with multipurpose volleyball and basketball courts, an indoor pool with diving well, an indoor track, a batting cage, racquetball and squash courts, indoor tennis courts, dance and fitness studios; a golf course; outdoor tennis courts; a multiweather track; an equestrian center and stables; 15 playing fields, a lake; and areas for rappelling, caving, hiking, and rock climbing.

Disabled Students: 75% of the campus is accessible. Wheelchair ramps, elevators, special parking, specially equipped rest rooms, special class scheduling, lowered drinking fountains, and special administrative services, and a telecommunications device for the deaf are available.

Services: Counseling and information services are available, as is tutoring in most subjects. Study skills training is also offered.

Campus Safety and Security: Measures include 24-hour foot and vehicle patrol, self-defense education, escort service, and shuttle buses. There are informal discussions, pamphlets/posters/films, emergency telephones, and lighted pathways/sidewalks.

Programs of Study: Sewanee confers B.A. and B.S. degrees. Master's and doctoral degrees are also awarded. Bachelor's degrees are awarded in AGRICULTURE (forestry and related sciences and natural resource management), BIOLOGICAL SCIENCE (biology/biological science), COMMUNICATIONS AND THE ARTS (art, art history and appreciation, dramatic arts, English, French, German, Greek, Latin, music, Russian, and Spanish), COMPUTER AND PHYSICAL SCIENCE (chemistry, computer science, geology, mathematics, and physics), SOCIAL SCIENCE (American studies, anthropology, Asian/Oriental studies, economics, French studies, German area studies, history, medieval studies, philosophy, political science/government, psychology, religion, Russian and Slavic studies, social science, and Third World studies). English and premedicine are the strongest academically. English, economics, and history are the largest.

Required: To graduate, students must complete at least 32 full courses (130 semester hours), 21 of which must be outside the major, with a minimum GPA of 2.0. The core curriculum includes 4 courses in language and literature, 3 in math and natural science, 2 each in social science and phys ed, and 1 each in the arts and in religion or philosophy. Comprehensive exams in the major field of study are required.

Special: Sewanee offers internships in economics and public affairs, study abroad in 13 countries, a Washington semester, and student-designed majors. Teacher certification and Peace Corps, medical, law, and veterinary preparation are available. A 3-2 engineering degree is offered with Columbia, Washington, and Vanderbilt Universities, Georgia Institute of Technology, and Rensselaer Polytechnic Institute. Pass/fail options are possible. There are 10 national honor societies, including Phi Beta Kappa, a freshman honors program, and 28 departmental honors programs.

Faculty/Classroom: 65% of faculty are male; 35%, female. All teach undergraduates. No introductory courses are taught by graduate students. The average class size in an introductory lecture is 20; in a laboratory, 16; and in a regular course, 12.

Admissions: 74% of the 2001-2002 applicants were accepted. The SAT I scores for the 2001-2002 freshman class were: Verbal--4% below 500, 35% between 500 and 599, 48% between 600 and 700, and 13% above 700; Math--2% below 500, 39% between 500 and 599, 51% between 600 and 700, and 8% above 700. The ACT scores were 22% between 24 and 26, 61% between 27 and 28, and 17% above 28. 73% of the current freshmen were in the top fifth of their class; 95% were in the top two fifths.

Requirements: The SAT I or ACT is required. In addition, candidates for admission should have 15 secondary school academic credits, including 4 years of English, 3 of math, and 2 each of lab science, a foreign language, and history/social science. An essay and recommendation are required and an interview is recommended. AP credits are accepted. Important factors in the admissions decision are advanced placement or honor courses, leadership record, and evidence of special talent. The school accepts the Common Application on computer disk and on-line applications at *apply.embark.com/ugrad/sewanee*

Procedure: Freshmen are admitted in the fall. Entrance exams should be taken by December of the senior year. There are early decision, early admissions, and deferred admissions plans. Early decision application should be filed by November 15; regular applications, by February 1 for fall entry. Notification of early decision is sent December 15; regular decision, April 1. 8% of all applicants were on a waiting list in a recent year; 7 were accepted in 2001. The fall 2001 application fee was $45.

Transfer: 10 transfer students enrolled in a recent year. Applicants should have a minimum GPA of 3.0 and take the SAT I or ACT. They must submit official transcripts from all previous colleges attended and 2 letters of recommendation from college instructors, and they must be eligible to continue in their present school. An interview is recommended. 64 credits of 130 must be completed at Sewanee.

Visiting: There are regularly scheduled orientations for prospective students, including a tour, an interview, class visits, and a meeting with a counselor. There are guides for informal visits and visitors may sit in on classes and stay overnight. To schedule a visit, contact the Office of Admission.

Financial Aid: 42% of freshmen and 39% of continuing students received need-based aid. The average freshman award was $16,333. Of that total, scholarships or need-based grants averaged $18,179; and loans averaged $3659. 33% of undergraduates work part time. Average annual earnings from campus work are $1000. The average financial indebtedness of the 2001 graduate was $13,213. The FAFSA and the college's own financial statement are required. The fall application deadline is March 1.

International Students: The school actively recruits these students. They must score 550 on the written TOEFL or 220 on the electronic version and also take an English proficiency exam.

Computers: Sewanee ofers PC and Mac workstations at several computer labs across the campus. All students may access the system 24 hours a day. There are no time limits and no fees.

Graduates: In 2001, 309 bachelor's degrees were awarded. The most popular majors were social sciences/history (34%), English (16%), and foreign languages and literature (8%). In an average class, 1% graduate in 3 years, 78% in 4 years, 79% in 5 years, and 80% in 6 years. 30 companies recruited on campus in 2000-2001. Of the 2000 graduating class, 38% were enrolled in graduate school within 6 months of graduation and 96% were employed.

Admissions Contact: David Lessene, Dean of Admission. A video is available. E-mail: *collegeadmission@sewanee.edu*
Web: *www.sewanee.edu*

VANDERBILT UNIVERSITY
Nashville, TN 37203-1700

C-2
(615) 322-2561
(800) 288-0432; Fax: (615) 343-7765

Full-time: 2894 men, 3123 women	**Faculty:** 691; I, av$
Part-time: 36 men, 24 women	**Ph.D.s:** 97%
Graduate: 2121 men, 2140 women	**Student/Faculty:** 9 to 1
Year: semesters, summer session	**Tuition:** $25,847
Application Deadline: January 7	**Room & Board:** $8635

Freshman Class: 9746 applied, 4528 accepted, 1557 enrolled
SAT I or ACT: required **MOST COMPETITIVE**

Vanderbilt University, founded in 1873, is a private university offering programs in liberal and fine arts, business, engineering, health science, military science, religion, law, music, and teacher preparation. There are 4 undergraduate and 6 graduate schools. In addition to regional accreditation, Vanderbilt has baccalaureate program accreditation with AACSB, ABET, CAHEA, and NCATE. The 9 libraries contain 1,812,869 volumes, 2,902,729 microform items, and 153,450 audiovisual forms/CDs, and subscribe to 26,885 periodicals. Computerized library services include the card catalog, interlibrary loans, and database searching. Special learning facilities include a learning resource center, art gallery, radio station, TV station, 2 observatories, and a TV news archive. The 330-acre campus is in an urban area less than a mile and a half from downtown Nashville. Including residence halls, there are 207 buildings.

Student Life: 86% of undergraduates are from out of state, mostly the South. Others are from 49 states, 52 foreign countries, and Canada. 55% are from public schools. 75% are white. The average age of freshmen is 18; all undergraduates, 20. 81% of freshmen remain to graduate.

Housing: 4684 students can be accommodated in college housing, which includes single-sex and coed dormitories, on-campus apartments, and married-student housing. In addition, there are language houses and special-interest houses. On-campus housing is guaranteed for the freshman year only, is available on a first-come, first-served basis, and is available on a lottery system for upperclassmen. Priority is given to out-of-town students. 84% of students live on campus. Alcohol is not permitted. Upperclassmen may keep cars.

Activities: 34% of men belong to 18 national fraternities; 50% of women belong to 12 national sororities. There are 264 groups on campus, including art, band, cheerleading, chess, choir, chorale, chorus, computers, dance, drama, drill team, ethnic, film, gay, honors, international, jazz band, literary magazine, marching band, musical theater, newspaper, opera, orchestra, pep band, photography, political, professional, radio and TV, religious, social, social service, student government, symphony, video production, and yearbook. Popular campus events include Rites of Spring, Blues Fest, and IMPACT Speakers Series.

Sports: There are 7 intercollegiate sports for men and 8 for women, and 45 intramural sports for men and 44 for women. Facilities include a gym, a pool, football and intramural fields, student recreation and tennis centers, basketball and racquetball courts, a suspended indoor track, and a climbing wall.

Disabled Students: 90% of the campus is accessible. Wheelchair ramps, elevators, special parking, specially equipped rest rooms, special class scheduling, lowered drinking fountains, and lowered telephones are available.

Services: Counseling and information services are available, as is tutoring in most subjects. There is a reader service for the blind.

Campus Safety and Security: Measures include 24-hour foot and vehicle patrol, escort service, shuttle buses, and informal discussions. There are pamphlets/posters/films, emergency telephones, lighted pathways/sidewalks, a bicycle patrol, and student dormitory monitors.

Programs of Study: Master's and doctoral degrees are also awarded. Bachelor's degrees are awarded in BIOLOGICAL SCIENCE (biology/biological science and molecular biology), COMMUNICATIONS AND THE ARTS (classical languages, classics, communications, English, fine arts, French, German, music history and appreciation, music performance, music theory and composition, Russian, Spanish, and theater design), COMPUTER AND PHYSICAL SCIENCE (chemistry, geology, mathematics, and physics), EDUCATION (early childhood, education, elementary, secondary, and special), ENGINEERING AND ENVIRONMENTAL DESIGN (bioengineering, chemical engineering, civil engineering, computer engineering, electrical/electronics engineering, engineering and applied science, and mechanical engineering), SOCIAL SCIENCE (African American studies, American studies, anthropology, child psychology/development, cognitive science, East Asian studies, economics, European studies, history, human development, interdisciplinary studies, Latin American studies, philosophy, political science/government, psychology, public affairs, religion, sociology, and urban studies). Social science, engineering, and education are the largest.

Required: All students must take at least 120 total credit hours. General requirements vary, as do specific major requirements, depending on the chosen program. A minimum GPA of 2.0 is usually needed. There is a mandatory writing requirement. Students majoring in human development must complete an internship in the fall semester of the senior year.

Special: Vanderbilt offers cross-registration with Fisk and Howard universities and Meharry Medical College, study abroad in 15 countries, a Washington semester, a work-study program, B.A.-B.S. degrees, dual and student-designed majors, nondegree study, and pass/fail options. Internships, required for human development majors, are available in human service agencies, city and state government, and businesses. A 3-2 engineering degree is offered with Fisk University. The school belongs to NASA's Tennessee Space Grant Consortium, the Intercollegiate Center for Classical Studies in Rome, the Tennessee Transportation Technology Coalition (research, development, and evaluation of transportation-related initiatives), and the Southeastern Consortium of University Transportation Centers. There are 19 national honor societies, including Phi Beta Kappa, a freshman honors program, and 21 departmental honors programs.

Faculty/Classroom: 74% of faculty are male; 26%, female. 90% teach undergraduates and 90% do research. Graduate students teach 10% of introductory courses. The average class size in an introductory lecture is 20; in a laboratory, 31; and in a regular course, 19.

Admissions: 46% of the 2001-2002 applicants were accepted. The SAT I scores for the 2001-2002 freshman class were: Verbal--2% below 500, 19% between 500 and 599, 55% between 600 and 700, and 24% above 700; Math--1% below 500, 11% between 500 and 599, 51% between 600 and 700, and 37% above 700. The ACT scores were 3% between 18 and 23, 50% between 24 and 29, and 47% between 30 and 36. 96% of the current freshmen were in the top fifth of their class; 100% were in the top two fifths. There were 103 National Merit finalists. In a recent year, 124 freshmen graduated first in their class.

Requirements: The SAT I or ACT is required. In addition, SAT II: Subject tests are recommended in math level I, II, or IIc, writing, and foreign language. Admission requirements vary by school. Candidates should be graduates of an accredited secondary school with a minimum of 15 academic credits. Most programs require 4 years of English, 3 of math, and 2 of a foreign language and recommend 2 of history and 1 of social studies. An essay is required. An audition is required for Blair School of Music. Applications are also accepted on computer disk provided a printout is included. AP credits are accepted. Important factors in the admissions decision are advanced placement or honor courses and evidence of special talent. Students may apply on-line at *www.vanderbilt.edu/admissions/apply.html.*

Procedure: Freshmen are admitted in the fall. Entrance exams should be taken in the spring of the junior year or the fall of the senior year. There are early decision, early admissions, and deferred admissions plans. Early decision application should be filed by November 1; regular applications, by January 7 for fall entry. Notification of early decision is sent December 15; regular decision, April 1. 457 early decision candidates were accepted for the 2001-2002 class. 12% of all applicants are on a waiting list; 19 were accepted in 2001.

Transfer: 71 transfer students enrolled in 2001-2002. Transfers must take the SAT I or the ACT. A minimum of 12 hours of college credit must have been earned. Students must meet all freshman requirements and be in good standing at the previous institution attended. 60 credits of 120 must be completed at Vanderbilt. The fall 2001 application fee was $50.

Visiting: There are regularly scheduled orientations for prospective students, including group information sessions and campus tours available Monday through Saturday during the academic year and Monday through Friday during the summer. Schedules vary, so visitors must call in advance. There are guides for informal visits and visitors may sit in on classes and stay overnight. To schedule a visit, contact the Office of Undergraduate Admissions.

Financial Aid: In 2001-2002, 59% of all freshmen and 53% of continuing students received some form of financial aid. 42% of freshmen and 36% of continuing students received need-based aid. The average freshman award was $22,757. 24% of undergraduates work part time. Average annual earnings from campus work are $3700. The average financial indebtedness of the 2001 graduate was $21,015. The CSS/Profile or FAFSA and tax return information are required. The fall application deadline is February 1.

International Students: The school actively recruits international students. They must score 570 on the written TOEFL and take SAT II: Subject tests in writing, math, and 1 other test.

Computers: The mainframe is a DEC ALPHA server 2100A Model 4/275. About 400 PCs and terminals are located in public and departmental labs. Most have Ethernet connections to the campus backbone, which is part of the Internet. All campus residences have Ethernet connections, and students who live off campus can access the network via modem. All students may access the system any time. There are no time limits and no fees.

Graduates: In 2001, 1302 bachelor's degrees were awarded. The most popular majors were human development (15%), economics (13%), and psychology (6%). In an average class, 1% graduate in 3 years, 78% in 4 years, 83% in 5 years, and 84% in 6 years. 250 companies recruited on campus in 2000-2001. Of the 2000 graduating class, 32% were enrolled in graduate school within 6 months of graduation and 63% were employed.

Admissions Contact: Admissions Officer. A video is available.
E-mail: *admissions@vanderbilt.edu* Web: *vanderbilt.edu*

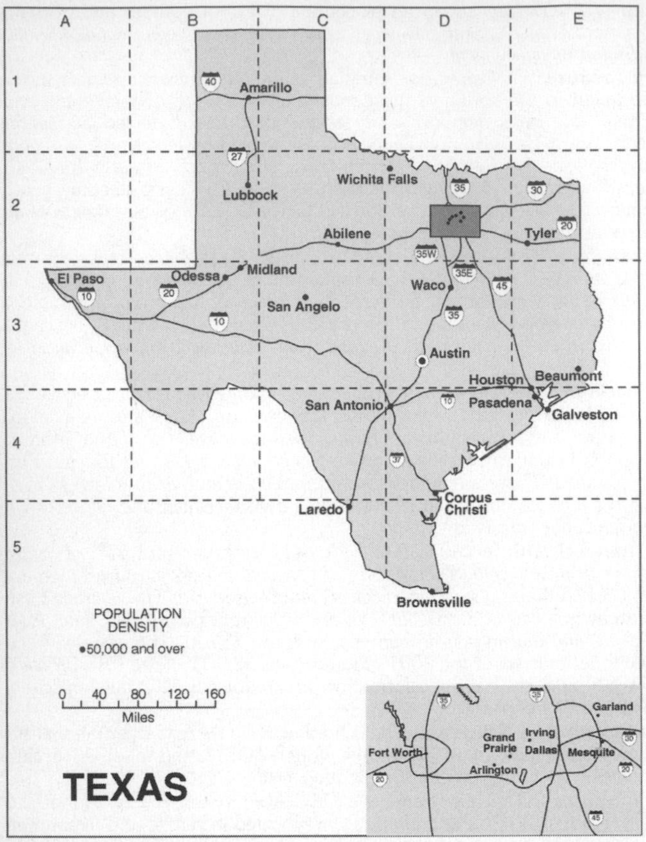

ABILENE CHRISTIAN UNIVERSITY C-2

Abilene, TX 79699-9000 (915) 674-2765
(800) 460-6228; Fax: (915) 674-2130

Full-time: 1772 men, 2136 women **Faculty:** 222; IIA, --$
Part-time: 139 men, 187 women **Ph.D.s:** 72%
Graduate: 226 men, 213 women **Student/Faculty:** 18 to 1
Year: semesters, summer session **Tuition:** $11,650
Application Deadline: open **Room & Board:** $4650
Freshman Class: 3056 applied, 2004 accepted, 1031 enrolled
SAT I Verbal/Math: 550/550 **ACT:** 24 **VERY COMPETITIVE**

Abilene Christian University, founded in 1906, is a private nonprofit institution affiliated with the Churches of Christ. The university offers a wide range of programs through the colleges of Biblical Studies, Business Administration, and Arts and Sciences There are 3 undergraduate schools and 1 graduate school. In addition to regional accreditation, ACU has baccalaureate program accreditation with ACBSP, ADA, CSWE, NASM, and NLN. The library contains 342,197 volumes, 1,074,033 microform items, and 57,395 audiovisual forms/CDs, and subscribes to 2387 periodicals. Computerized library services include the card catalog, interlibrary loans, and database searching. Special learning facilities include a learning resource center, art gallery, planetarium, radio station, TV station, and and a volunteer and service learning center. The 208-acre campus is in a small town 150 miles west of the Dallas-Fort Worth metroplex. Including residence halls, there are 45 buildings.

Student Life: 80% of undergraduates are from Texas. Others are from 46 states, 54 foreign countries, and Canada. 88% are from public schools. 82% are white. Most are Protestant. The average age of freshmen is 18; all undergraduates, 20. 24% do not continue beyond their first year; 58% remain to graduate.

Housing: 2200 students can be accommodated in college housing, which includes single-sex dormitories, on-campus apartments, and married-student housing. On-campus housing is available on a first-come, first-served basis and is available on a lottery system for upperclassmen. Alcohol is not permitted. All students may keep cars.

Activities: 20% of men belong to 8 local fraternities; 20% of women belong to 7 local sororities. There are 104 groups on campus, including art, band, cheerleading, chess, choir, chorale, chorus, computers, debate, drama, ethnic, film, forensics, honors, integrated marketing, international, jazz band, literary magazine, marching band, musical theater, newspaper, opera, orchestra, photography, political, professional, public relations, radio and TV, religious, social, social service, steel drum band, student government, symphony, volunteer and service-learning center, and yearbook. Popular campus events include Sing Song Festival, Bible lectures, and Freshman Follies.

Sports: There are 7 intercollegiate sports for men and 6 for women, and 27 intramural sports for men and 27 for women. Facilities include a coliseum, track, baseball and softball stadiums, soccer fields, an indoor swimming pool, gyms, a weight training facility, aerobic fitness exercise equipment, and tennis, racquetball, basketball, and handball courts.

Disabled Students: 63% of the campus is accessible. Wheelchair ramps, elevators, special parking, specially equipped rest rooms, special class scheduling, lowered drinking fountains, and lowered telephones are available.

Services: Counseling and information services are available, as is tutoring in every subject. There is a reader service for the blind, a sign language interpreter, and remedial math, reading, and writing. and a sign language interpreter.

Campus Safety and Security: Measures include 24-hour foot and vehicle patrol, self-defense education, escort service, and informal discussions. There are pamphlets/posters/films, emergency telephones, lighted pathways/sidewalks, and Fire Safety discussions.

Programs of Study: ACU confers B.A., B.S., B.B.A., B.F.A., B.M., and B.S.N. degrees. Associate, master's, and doctoral degrees are also awarded. Bachelor's degrees are awarded in AGRICULTURE (animal science), BIOLOGICAL SCIENCE (biochemistry, biology/biological science and nutrition), BUSINESS (accounting, banking and finance, management science, and marketing/retailing/merchandising), COMMUNICATIONS AND THE ARTS (advertising, art, broadcasting, communications, design, dramatic arts, English, fine arts, French, journalism, music, Spanish, and speech/debate/rhetoric), COMPUTER AND PHYSICAL SCIENCE (chemistry, computer science, geology, information sciences and systems, mathematics, and physics), EDUCATION (art, business, early childhood, elementary, foreign languages, home economics, middle school, music, physical, science, secondary, and teaching English as a second/foreign language (TESOL/TEFOL)), ENGINEERING AND ENVIRONMENTAL DESIGN (engineering and applied science, engineering physics, and environmental science), HEALTH PROFESSIONS (nursing, predentistry, premedicine, and speech pathology/audiology), SOCIAL SCIENCE (biblical languages, biblical studies, criminal justice, dietetics, family/consumer studies, history, international relations, ministries, missions, political science/government, prelaw, psychology, public administration, religion, social science, social work, and sociology). Biology, chemistry, and education are the strongest academically. Elementary education, management, and marketing are the largest.

Required: To graduate, students must complete courses in Bible (15 hours), science, English, history, behavioral science, communication, phys ed (4 hours), fine arts, and math. 33 semester hours of advanced work must be taken and a minimum 2.0 GPA maintained. A minimum of 128 credit hours is needed, more in some programs, plus 30 to 64 hours in the major, 18 of which must be upper division.

Special: ACU offers cross-registration with Hardin-Simmons, McMurry, and Texas Tech universities and study abroad in 4 countries. Double majors and credit for military training are available. Internships are possible in most majors, as are B.A.-B.S. degrees in Bible, biology, chemistry, communication, computer science, and math. A 3-2 engineering degree is offered with the University of Texas at Arlington and a microelectronics degree with the University of Texas at Dallas. Student-designed majors (interdisciplinary studies) are available. The applied studies program enables degree completion for adult students. There are 10 national honor societies and a freshman honors program.

Faculty/Classroom: 66% of faculty are male; 34%, female. 93% teach undergraduates and 49% both teach and do research. Graduate students teach 1% of introductory courses. The average class size in an introductory lecture is 27; in a laboratory, 21; and in a regular course, 23.

Admissions: 66% of the 2001-2002 applicants were accepted. The SAT I scores for the 2001-2002 freshman class were: Verbal--26% below 500, 44% between 500 and 599, 22% between 600 and 700, and 8% above 700; Math--25% below 500, 44% between 500 and 599, 24% between 600 and 700, and 6% above 700. The ACT scores were 22% below 21, 29% between 21 and 23, 20% between 24 and 26, 13% between 27 and 28, and 16% above 28. 45% of the current freshmen were in the top fifth of their class; 70% were in the top two fifths. There were 9 National Merit finalists. 10 freshmen graduated first in their class.

Requirements: The SAT I is recommended, with a composite of 960 minimum or 20 on the ACT. SAT II: Subject tests in English composition and essay, math level II, and foreign language (French, German, Spanish, or Latin) are required. Applicants must be graduates of an accredited secondary school or have the GED and have completed 22 academic credits, including 4 in English, 2 each in math and science, and 1 each in history and social studies. Two years of the same foreign language are required. Art majors need to submit a portfolio, and music and theater majors must audition. ACU requires applicants to be in the upper 50% of their class. AP and CLEP credits are accepted. Important factors in the admissions decision are leadership record, recommendations by alumni, and advanced placement or honor courses. Applications may be submitted on disk or on-line via e-mail and through TexasMentor at *www.texasmentor.org*.

Procedure: Freshmen are admitted to all sessions. Entrance exams should be taken by October of the senior year. Application deadlines are open. There is a rolling admissions plan. The application fee is $25.

Transfer: 218 transfer students enrolled in 2001-2002. Transfer students must be in good standing at previously attended universities/colleges and have a minimum 2.0 GPA. A minimum composite score of 960 on the SAT I or an ACT score of 20 is required for students with fewer than 64 semester hours. A maximum of 66 semester hours from community or junior colleges will be accepted. An interview is required. 32 credits of 128 must be completed at ACU.

Visiting: There are regularly scheduled orientations for prospective students, including tours and interviews with faculty, administrators, admissions/financial aid counselors, and current students. There are guides for informal visits and visitors may sit in on classes and stay overnight. To schedule a visit, contact Lisa McKinnon, Campus Visit Coordinator at (915) 674-2664.

Financial Aid: In 2001-2002, 94% of all freshmen and 86% of continuing students received some form of financial aid. 60% of freshmen and 53% of continuing students received need-based aid. The average freshman award was $10,052. Of that total, scholarships or need-based grants averaged $7106 ($18,836 maximum); loans averaged $4168 ($17,500 maximum); and work contracts averaged $1024 ($2959 maximum). 32% of undergraduates work part time. Average annual earnings from campus work are $1494. The average financial indebtedness of the 2001 graduate was $24,572. The FAFSA is required. The fall application deadline is March 1.

International Students: There are 169 international students enrolled. The school actively recruits these students. They must score 525 on the written TOEFL or 197 on the electronic version and also take the college's own test.

Computers: Students have access to more than 500 computers during daytime and evening hours. Internet and e-mail are available through ACU's fiber optic network in more than 20 labs on campus, including labs in residence halls, connections in dorm rooms, and off campus by modem. All students may access the system. Some students have 24-hour-a-day access; all others may use the system from 9 A.M. to 11 P.M. Monday through Friday, 9 A.M. to 4 P.M. Saturday, and 2 P.M. to 5 P.M. Sunday. There are no time limits and no fees.

Graduates: In 2001, 700 bachelor's degrees were awarded. The most popular majors were elementary education (10%), marketing (5%), and management (4%). In an average class, 1% graduate in 3 years, 27% in 4 years, 48% in 5 years, and 53% in 6 years. 165 companies recruited on campus in 2000-2001. Of the 2000 graduating class, 21% were enrolled in graduate school within 6 months of graduation and 72% were employed.

Admissions Contact: Tim Johnston, Director of Enrollment Management. E-mail: *info@admissions.acu.edu* Web: *www.acu.edu/admissions*

ANGELO STATE UNIVERSITY

San Angelo, TX 76909 C-3

(915) 942-2041
(800) 946-8627; Fax: (915) 942-2078

Full-time: 2127 men, 2603 women	**Faculty:** 216
Part-time: 453 men, 646 women	**Ph.D.s:** 75%
Graduate: 150 men, 283 women	**Student/Faculty:** 22 to 1
Year: semesters, summer session	**Tuition:** $2218 ($7330)
Application Deadline: August 9	**Room & Board:** $4810
Freshman Class: 3534 applied, 2690 accepted, 1257 enrolled	
SAT I Verbal/Math: 550/490	**ACT:** 21 **COMPETITIVE**

Angelo State University, founded in 1928, and part of the Texas State University System, offers degrees through the colleges of liberal and fine arts, business and professional studies, sciences, and the school of education. There are 4 undergraduate schools and 1 graduate school. In addition to regional accreditation, ASU has baccalaureate program accreditation with ACBSP, NASM, and NLN. The library contains 460,000 volumes, 510,000 microform items, and 4000 audiovisual forms/CDs, and subscribes to 1753 periodicals. Computerized library services include the card catalog, interlibrary loans, and database searching. Special learning facilities include a learning resource center, art gallery, natural history collection, planetarium, Internet radio station, and a cable TV station. The 268-acre campus is in a small town 200 miles west of Austin. There are 42 buildings.

Student Life: 98% of undergraduates are from Texas. Others are from 33 states, 20 foreign countries, and Canada. 98% are from public schools. 73% are white; 19% Hispanic. The average age of freshmen is 19; all undergraduates, 23. 42% do not continue beyond their first year; 32% remain to graduate.

Housing: 1549 students can be accommodated in college housing, which includes single-sex and coed dormitories and on-campus apartments. There are designated honors rooms in 1 dorm. On-campus housing is available on a first-come, first-served basis. Priority is given to out-of-town students. 75% of students commute. Alcohol is not permitted. All students may keep cars.

Activities: 3% of men belong to 4 national fraternities; 4% of women belong to 2 national sororities. There are 75 groups on campus, including art, band, cheerleading, chess, choir, chorale, chorus, computers, dance, debate, drama, drill team, ethnic, film, honors, international, jazz band, marching band, musical theater, newspaper, opera, pep band, political, professional, radio and TV, religious, rodeo, social, social service, student government, wool judging, and yearbook. Popular campus events include Fish Splash, madrigal dinner, and musical theater.

Sports: There are 4 intercollegiate sports for men and 5 for women, and 15 intramural sports for men and 14 for women. Facilities include a gym; a multipurpose sports complex; racquetball, basketball, volleyball, badminton, and tennis courts; an all-weather Tartan track; 2 regulation softball fields; and a 25-meter Olympic-size pool. The campus track stadium seats 3500, and the indoor gym, 4000. There is a multipurpose arena that seats up to 6300 people. It also has an auxiliary practice gym, two weight rooms, and a sports medicine area.

Disabled Students: 98% of the campus is accessible. Wheelchair ramps, elevators, special parking, specially equipped rest rooms, special class scheduling, lowered drinking fountains, and lowered telephones are available.

Services: Counseling and information services are available, as is tutoring in most subjects. There is remedial math, reading, and writing.

Campus Safety and Security: Measures include 24-hour foot and vehicle patrol, self-defense education, escort service, and informal discussions. There are pamphlets/posters/films, emergency telephones, and lighted pathways/sidewalks.

Programs of Study: ASU confers B.A., B.S., B.B.A., B.F.A., B.G.S., B.M., and B.S.N. degrees. Associate and master's degrees are also awarded. Bachelor's degrees are awarded in AGRICULTURE (animal science), BIOLOGICAL SCIENCE (biochemistry and biology/biological science), BUSINESS (accounting, banking and finance, business administration and management, and marketing/retailing/merchandising), COMMUNICATIONS AND THE ARTS (art, communications, dramatic arts, English, French, German, journalism, music, and Spanish), COMPUTER AND PHYSICAL SCIENCE (applied physics, chemistry, computer science, mathematics, and physics), EDUCATION (early childhood), HEALTH PROFESSIONS (exercise science, medical laboratory technology, and nursing), SOCIAL SCIENCE (criminal justice, history, interdisciplinary studies, liberal arts/general studies, political science/government, psychology, and sociology). Math, biology, and physics are the strongest academically. Business-related programs, nursing, and education are the largest.

Required: To graduate, students must complete a total of 130 semester hours with a minimum GPA of 2.0 (2.5 for all programs leading to teacher certification). Between 30 and 36 hours are required in the major. General education core courses must be taken in English, government, history, modern language, and phys ed. Students must also fulfill distributional requirements of 6 to 8 credits each in art, communication, drama, journalism, music, and philosophy; economics, geography, linguistics, psychology, sociology; and lab science.

Special: ASU offers co-op programs with the University of Texas at El Paso; study abroad in 3 countries; internships in psychology, public administration, and journalism; work-study programs; dual majors, and a 3-2 engineering degree with the University of Texas at El Paso, and a 5-year integrated accounting program. There are 15 national honor societies and a freshman honors program. All departments have honors programs.

Faculty/Classroom: 56% of faculty are male; 44%, female. 97% teach undergraduates and 75% both teach and do research. Graduate students teach 3% of introductory courses. The average class size in an introductory lecture is 34; in a laboratory, 21; and in a regular course, 31.

Admissions: 76% of the 2001-2002 applicants were accepted. The SAT I scores for the 2001-2002 freshman class were: Verbal--55% below 500, 32% between 500 and 599, 12% between 600 and 700, and 1% above 700; Math--49% below 500, 39% between 500 and 599, 10% between 600 and 700, and 2% above 700. The ACT scores were 50% below 21, 29% between 21 and 23, 14% between 24 and 26, 5% between 27 and 28, and 2% above 28. 37% of the current freshmen were in the top fifth of their class; 67% were in the top two fifths. 27 freshmen graduated first in their class.

Requirements: The SAT I or ACT is required. In addition, applicants must be graduates of an accredited secondary school or have the GED. AP and CLEP credits are accepted. Advanced placement or honor courses is an important factor in the admission decision. Applications are available through the university's web site and via Texas common application.

Procedure: Freshmen are admitted to all sessions. Entrance exams should be taken during spring of the junior year or fall of the senior year. Applications should be filed by August 9 for fall entry, December 13 for spring entry, and May 9 for summer entry. Notification is sent on a rolling basis.

Transfer: 303 transfer students enrolled in 2001-2002. Transfer students must have a minimum 2.0 GPA; those with fewer than 18 hours must meet high school admission requirements. 33 credits of 130 must be completed at ASU.

Visiting: There are regularly scheduled orientations for prospective students, including Preview ASU, orientation, a tour, advising, and lunch. There are guides for informal visits and visitors may sit in on classes and stay overnight. To schedule a visit, contact Recruiting Office/Office of Admissions at (915) 942-2058.

Financial Aid: In 2001-2002, 64% of all freshmen and 63% of continuing students received some form of financial aid. 46% of freshmen and 57% of continuing students received need-based aid. The average freshman award was $3205. Of that total, scholarships or need-based grants averaged $1373 ($5500 maximum); loans averaged $1107 ($2625 maximum); and work contracts averaged $799 ($3296 maximum). 9% of undergraduates work part time. Average annual earnings from campus work are $3657. The average financial indebtedness of the 2001 graduate was $14,475. The FAFSA is required. The fall application deadline is June 1.

International Students: There are 72 international students enrolled. They must score 550 on the written TOEFL or 213 on the electronic version unless English is the native language. The SAT I or ACT is also required.

Computers: The mainframes are an IBM 9672 and 05390. Students may access more than 300 Dell PCs located in 7 PC labs on campus and 200 Dell PCs in special purpose labs. 75% of the residence halls are wired for direct Internet access. The campus is connected to an ultra high-speed portal. All students may access the system 24 hours a day on weekdays, and modified hours on weekends. There are no time limits. The fee for use of the system is $6 per credit hour.

Graduates: In 2001, 843 bachelor's degrees were awarded. The most popular majors were education (20%), psychology (14%), and kinesiology (11%). In an average class, 1% graduate in 3 years, 15% in 4 years, 28% in 5 years, and 32% in 6 years. 200 companies recruited on campus in 2000-2001.

Admissions Contact: Office of Admissions. A video is available.
E-mail: *admissions@angelo.edu* Web: *www.angelo.edu*

AUSTIN COLLEGE

D-2

Sherman, TX 75090-4400

(903) 813-3000
(800) 442-5363; Fax: (903) 813-3198

Full-time: 539 men, 680 women	**Faculty:** 85; IIB, ++$
Part-time: 3 men, 5 women	**Ph.D.s:** 98%
Graduate: 7 men, 27 women	**Student/Faculty:** 14 to 1
Year: 4-1-4, summer session	**Tuition:** $15,963
Application Deadline: March 1	**Room & Board:** $6187
Freshman Class: 1004 applied, 806 accepted, 313 enrolled	
SAT I Verbal/Math: 598/602	**ACT:** 26 **VERY COMPETITIVE+**

Austin College, founded in 1849, is a private liberal arts institution affiliated with the Presbyterian Church (U.S.A.) and offers programs in business, liberal arts, and health field. The library contains 206,324 volumes, 106,106 microform items, and 7454 audiovisual forms/CDs, and subscribes to 1453 periodicals. Computerized library services include the card catalog, interlibrary loans, and database searching. Special learning facilities include a learning resource center, a social science lab, television studios for media instruction, environmental research areas near Lake Texoma, and a facility for advanced computing and 3-D graphics. The 70-acre campus is in a suburban area 60 miles north of Dallas. Including residence halls, there are 28 buildings.

Student Life: 88% of undergraduates are from Texas. Others are from 30 states and 24 foreign countries. 90% are from public schools. 77% are white. 57% are Protestant; 15% Catholic; 13% claim no religious affiliation. The average age of freshmen is 18; all undergraduates, 20. 14% do not continue beyond their first year; 74% remain to graduate.

Housing: 940 students can be accommodated in college housing, which includes single-sex and coed dormitories and on-campus apartments. In addition, there are language houses. On-campus housing is guaranteed for all 4 years. 74% of students live on campus; of those, 60% remain on campus on weekends. All students may keep cars.

Activities: 21% of men belong to 10 local fraternities; 19% of women belong to 5 local sororities. There are 50 groups on campus, including art, cheerleading, choir, chorale, chorus, drama, ethnic, film, gay, honors, international, jazz band, literary magazine, musical theater, newspaper, orchestra, pep band, photography, political, professional, radio and TV, religious, social, social service, student government, symphony, and yearbook. Popular campus events include Christmas Pops, Film Series, and All Greek Dance.

Sports: There are 8 intercollegiate sports for men and 6 for women, and 12 intramural sports for men and 12 for women. Facilities include an athletic/recreation complex that includes 2 gyms, a natatorium, and a fitness pavilion; a tennis stadium; a 2,500-seat stadium; and soccer and baseball fields.

Disabled Students: 99% of the campus is accessible. Wheelchair ramps, elevators, special parking, specially equipped rest rooms, special class scheduling, and lowered drinking fountains are available.

Services: Counseling and information services are available, as is tutoring in some subjects, including introductory-level courses. Individual and group assistance to strengthen reading, writing, and study skills is available.

Campus Safety and Security: Measures include 24-hour foot and vehicle patrol, self-defense education, escort service, and informal discussions. There are pamphlets/posters/films, emergency telephones, and lighted pathways/sidewalks.

Programs of Study: AC confers the B.A. degree. Master's degrees are also awarded. Bachelor's degrees are awarded in BIOLOGICAL SCIENCE (biochemistry and biology/biological science), BUSINESS (business administration and management and international economics), COMMUNICATIONS AND THE ARTS (art, classics, communications, English, French, German, Latin, music, and Spanish), COMPUTER AND PHYSICAL SCIENCE (chemistry, computer science, mathematics, and physics), HEALTH PROFESSIONS (exercise science), SOCIAL SCIENCE (American studies, economics, history, interdisciplinary studies, international studies, Latin American studies, philosophy, political science/government, psychology, religion, and sociology). Chemistry, biology, and international studies are the strongest academically. Business administration, psychology, and biology are the largest.

Required: Core requirements for graduation include Freshman Communication Inquiry, a physical profile and activity course, 3 Heritage of Western Culture courses, and 7 courses distributed among the arts, social sciences, natural sciences, meaning and values, formal reasoning, historical/social perspective, and social policy/values/decision making.To graduate, students must have a minimum 2.0 GPA and a total of 34 course credits (136 semester hours), with 7 to 11 course credits in the major. Students must demonstrate an ability in a modern or classical language other than their own, quantitative competency with an approved course or test, and the required skills in written communication with approved course work.

Special: AC offers cooperative programs with Butler University, Beaver College, Central College, and the Institute for European Studies, internships during the January and summer terms, study abroad in 18 countries, and fall, spring, and summer internships in Washington, D.C. Work-study, accelerated degree programs in all majors, and dual and student-designed majors are available. There is a 3-2 engineering degree program in conjunction with the University of Texas at Dallas and Washington University in St. Louis, as well as cooperative agreements with Columbia University at Texas A&M University. Nondegree study, pass/fail options, preprofessional teacher education programs, and a January term with experimental and off-campus opportunities are offered. There are 14 national honor societies, including Phi Beta Kappa.

Faculty/Classroom: 66% of faculty are male; 34%, female. All both teach and do research. No introductory courses are taught by graduate students. The average class size in an introductory lecture is 19; in a laboratory, 16; and in a regular course, 20.

Admissions: 80% of the 2001-2002 applicants were accepted. The SAT I scores for the 2001-2002 freshman class were: Verbal--8% below 500, 39% between 500 and 599, 44% between 600 and 700, and 9% above 700; Math--6% below 500, 41% between 500 and 599, 42% between 600 and 700, and 11% above 700. The ACT scores were 6% below 21, 21% between 21 and 23, 28% between 24 and 26, 19% between 27 and 28, and 26% above 28. 62% of the current freshmen were in the top fifth of their class; 88% were in the top two fifths. There was 1 National Merit finalist and 3 semifinalists. 9 freshmen graduated first in their class.

Requirements: The SAT I or ACT is required. In addition, applicants must be graduates of an accredited secondary school or have a GED. The minimum recommended academic requirements are 4 credits in English, 3 each in math and science, 2 each in social studies and foreign language, and 1 in art/music/theater. An essay is required, and an interview is recommended. AP and CLEP credits are accepted. Important factors in the admissions decision are advanced placement or honor courses, leadership record, and extracurricular activities record. Applications are accepted on-line via Common App, Texas Mentor, or the school's web site.

Procedure: Freshmen are admitted fall, spring, and summer. Entrance exams should be taken in the junior year or the fall of the senior year. There are early decision, early action, early admissions, and deferred admissions plans. Early decision and early action applications should be filed by December 1; regular applications, by March 1 for fall entry, along with a $35 fee. Notification of early decision and early action is sent January 10; regular decision, on a rolling basis. 28 early decision candidates were accepted for the 2001-2002 class. 3% of all applicants are on a waiting list; 13 were accepted in 2001.

Transfer: 46 transfer students enrolled in 2001-2002. Applicants must have a minimum 2.5 GPA, submit official college transcripts and 2 recommendations, and be in good standing at previously attended schools. Students with fewer than 30 credit hours must submit SAT I or ACT scores and their high school transcript or GED. 17 credits of 34 must be completed at Austin College.

Visiting: There are regularly scheduled orientations for prospective students, including 1-day and 2-day preview programs held for high school juniors and seniors and parents. Individual appointments may be made as well. There are guides for informal visits and visitors may sit in on classes and stay overnight. To schedule a visit, contact the Admission Office.

Financial Aid: In 2001-2002, 96% of all freshmen and 95% of continuing students received some form of financial aid. 65% of freshmen and 60% of continuing students received need-based aid. The average freshman award was $16,758. Of that total, scholarships or need-based grants averaged $11,474 ($15,838 maximum); loans averaged $3093 ($7625 maximum); work contracts averaged $1519 ($1600 maximum); and non-need based, loans, signature, and opportunity loans averaged $6176 ($24,175 maximum). 31% of undergraduates work part time. Average annual earnings from campus work are $1600. The average financial indebtedness of the 2001 graduate was $23,892. AC is a member of CSS. The FAFSA and the college's own financial statement are required. The fall application deadline is April 1.

International Students: There are 31 international students enrolled. The school actively recruits these students. They must score 600 on the written TOEFL and also take the SAT I or the ACT.

Computers: The mainframe is a DEC Alpha 4100. Students have access to 121 Dell Pentiums, 36 Mac Power PCs, 9 HP 712 workstations, and an SGI Indigo Extreme from the main computer labs. Each residence hall also has a computer cluster with PCs and Macs. All students may access the system 24 hours a day in some locations. There are no time limits and no fees.

Graduates: In 2001, 265 bachelor's degrees were awarded. The most popular majors were business administration (21%), psychology (17%), and biology (14%). In an average class, 67% graduate in 4 years, and 72% in 5 years. 43 companies recruited on campus in 2000-2001. Of the 2000 graduating class, 34% were enrolled in graduate school within 6 months of graduation and 40% were employed.

Admissions Contact: Nan Massingill, VP for Institutional Enrollment. A video is available. E-mail: *admission@austinc.edu*
Web: *www.austinc.edu*

BAYLOR UNIVERSITY D-3
Waco, TX 76798 **(254) 710-3435; (800) BAYLOR-U**

Full-time: 4916 men, 6773 women	**Faculty:** 697; I, --$
Part-time: 230 men, 271 women	**Ph.D.s:** 78%
Graduate: 1102 men, 929 women	**Student/Faculty:** 17 to 1
Year: semesters, summer session	**Tuition:** $12,804
Application Deadline: open	**Room & Board:** $5494
Freshman Class: 7986 applied, 6336 accepted, 2801 enrolled	
SAT I Verbal/Math: 580/590	**ACT:** 24 **VERY COMPETITIVE+**

Baylor University, founded in 1845, is an independent institution offering undergraduate programs in liberal arts and sciences, business, computer science, education, engineering, music, and nursing. There are 7 undergraduate and 10 graduate schools. In addition to regional accreditation, Baylor has baccalaureate program accreditation with AACSB, AALE, ABET, ACEJMC, ADA, AHEA, APTA, CAHEA, CSWE, NASM, NCATE, and NLN. The 9 libraries contain 2,118,851 volumes, 1,193,802 microform items, and 76,051 audiovisual forms/CDs, and subscribe to 8476 periodicals. Computerized library services include the card catalog, interlibrary loans, and database searching. Special learning facilities include a learning resource center, art gallery, natural history museum, radio station, and TV station. The 432-acre campus is in an urban area 100 miles south of Dallas/Fort Worth. Including residence halls, there are 65 buildings.

Student Life: 83% of undergraduates are from Texas. Others are from 49 states, 87 foreign countries, and Canada. 77% are white. 77% are Protestant; 13% Catholic. The average age of freshmen is 19; all undergraduates, 21. 17% do not continue beyond their first year; 68% remain to graduate.

Housing: 3624 students can be accommodated in college housing, which includes single-sex dormitories, academic wings, on-campus apartments, and married-student housing. On-campus housing is guaranteed for the freshman year only and is available on a first-come, first-served basis. Alcohol is not permitted. All students may keep cars.

Activities: 15% of men belong to 2 local and 14 national fraternities; 17% of women belong to 1 local and 9 national sororities. There are 275 groups on campus, including art, band, cheerleading, chess, choir, chorale, chorus, computers, dance, debate, drama, ethnic, film, forensics, honors, international, jazz band, literary magazine, marching band, musical theater, newspaper, opera, orchestra, pep band, photography, political, professional, radio and TV, religious, social, social service, student government, symphony, and yearbook. Popular campus events include Dia del Oso (Day of the Bear), Campus Sing, and Pigskin Review.

Sports: There are 8 intercollegiate sports for men and 9 for women, and 17 intramural sports for men and 17 for women. Facilities include a 50000-seat football stadium, gyms, intramural fields, tennis courts, a swimming pool, a marina, and a special events center that seats 10030. A 158,000 square-foot student life center has a 52-foot climbing rock, fitness center, aerobics room, racquetball/squash courts, basketball courts, pool, indoor walking/jogging track, and outdoor sand volleyball courts.

Disabled Students: 95% of the campus is accessible. Wheelchair ramps, elevators, special parking, specially equipped rest rooms, and lowered drinking fountains are available.

Services: There is a reader service for the blind and remedial reading and writing. Taped textbooks are available through the Commission for the Blind. The Office of Student Access and Learning provides study skills and time management sessions for students with disabilities.

Campus Safety and Security: Measures include 24-hour foot and vehicle patrol, escort service, shuttle buses, and informal discussions. There are pamphlets/posters/films, emergency telephones, and lighted pathways/sidewalks.

Programs of Study: Baylor confers B.A., B.S., B.B.A., B.F.A., B.M., B.M.E., B.S.Av.Sc., B.S.C.S., B.S.E., B.S.Ed., B.S.F.C.S., B.S.I., and B.S.N. degrees. Master's and doctoral degrees are also awarded. Bachelor's degrees are awarded in AGRICULTURE (forestry and related sciences and soil science), BIOLOGICAL SCIENCE (biochemistry, biology/biological science, life science, neurosciences, and nutrition), BUSINESS (accounting, banking and finance, business administration and management, business economics, business statistics, business systems analysis, entrepreneurial studies, fashion merchandising, human resources, insurance, international business management, management information systems, marketing/retailing/merchandising, personnel management, and real estate), COMMUNICATIONS AND THE ARTS (applied music, art, art history and appreciation, broadcasting, classics, communications, creative writing, dramatic arts, English, French, German, Greek (classical), journalism, languages, Latin, music, music history and appreciation, music performance, music theory and composition, performing arts, Russian, Spanish, speech/debate/rhetoric, studio art, telecommunications, and theater design), COMPUTER AND PHYSICAL SCIENCE (applied mathematics, chemistry, computer science, earth science, geology, geophysics and seismology, information sciences and systems, mathematics, and physics), EDUCATION (art, business, computer, drama, elementary, English, foreign languages, health, home economics, journalism, mathematics, museum studies, music, physical, reading, recreation, science, secondary, social science, social studies, and special), ENGINEERING AND ENVIRONMENTAL DESIGN (airline piloting and navigation, architecture, engineering, environmental science, interior design, and mechanical engineering), HEALTH PROFESSIONS (community health work, health science, medical laboratory technology, nursing, optometry, predentistry, premedicine, speech pathology/audiology, and speech therapy), SOCIAL SCIENCE (American studies, anthropology, archeology, Asian/Oriental studies, biblical languages, child care/child and family studies, dietetics, economics, family/consumer studies, fashion design and technology, forensic studies, geography, history, interdisciplinary studies, international public service, Latin American studies, law, philosophy, physical fitness/movement, political science/government, prelaw, psychology, public administration, religion, religious education, religious music, Russian and Slavic studies, social work, sociology, and urban studies). Biology, business, and education are the largest.

Required: All degree programs require a minimum of 124 hours and a 2.0 GPA to graduate. Basic requirements for the B.A. degree include 18 semester hours of social science, 12 each of English and science, 6 to 9 of fine arts, 6 of religion, 4 of phys ed, 3 to 16 of foreign language, 3 of math, and 2 semesters of chapel forum. Requirements for other degrees vary.

Special: Baylor offers cooperative programs in architecture, business, dentistry, medicine, and optometry, internships in each school, study abroad and student exchange in more than 30 countries, and pass/fail options. There are also honors and university scholars programs and faculty exchange with 4 schools in China, and 1 each in Japan, Thailand, and Russia. There are 35 national honor societies, including Phi Beta Kappa, and a freshman honors program.

Faculty/Classroom: 62% of faculty are male; 38%, female. The average class size in a regular course is 31.

Admissions: 79% of the 2001-2002 applicants were accepted. The SAT I scores for the 2001-2002 freshman class were: Verbal--12% below 500, 48% between 500 and 599, 31% between 600 and 700, and 8% above 700; Math--8% below 500, 44% between 500 and 599, 38% between 600 and 700, and 10% above 700. The ACT scores were 8% below 21, 31% between 21 and 23, 32% between 24 and 26, 15% between 27 and 28, and 13% above 28. 60% of the current freshmen were in the top fifth of their class; 86% were in the top two fifths. There were 55 National Merit finalists.

Requirements: The SAT I or ACT is required. The recommended minimum composite score is 1100 on the SAT I or 24 on the ACT. Applicants must be graduates of an accredited secondary school. An interview is recommended. Baylor requires applicants to be in the upper 50% of their class. AP and CLEP credits are accepted. Important factors in the admissions decision are advanced placement or honor courses, leadership record, and parents or siblings attending the school. Applications are accepted on-line at *www.baylor.edu/~admissions/apply.html*

Procedure: Freshmen are admitted fall, spring, and summer. Entrance exams should be taken in spring of the junior year or fall of the senior year. Application deadlines are open. The application fee is $35. Notification is sent on a rolling basis.

Transfer: 501 transfer students enrolled in 2001-2002. Transfer students should begin studies no later than the end of the sophomore year because of the 60-semester-hour residence requirement for a bachelor's degree. A minimum 2.5 GPA is required. Students with fewer than 30 credit hours earned must meet the entrance requirements for freshmen. 60 credits of 124 must be completed at Baylor.

Visiting: There are regularly scheduled orientations for prospective students, including day-and-a-half sessions in June and a Welcome Week in August. There are guides for informal visits and visitors may sit in on classes and stay overnight. To schedule a visit, contact the Campus Visitation Program at (254) 710-2407.

Financial Aid: In 2001-2002, 85% of all freshmen and 76% of continuing students received some form of financial aid. 44% of freshmen and 41% of continuing students received need-based aid. The average freshman award was $12,425. Of that total, scholarships or need-based grants averaged $4718 ($22,870 maximum); loans averaged $5227 ($22,614 maximum); and work contracts averaged $2480 ($2650 maximum). 21% of undergraduates work part time. Average annual earnings from campus work are $1225. The FAFSA is required. The fall application deadline is May 1.

International Students: There are 230 international students enrolled. The school actively recruits these students. They must score 540 on the written TOEFL and also take the SAT I or the ACT, scoring 1100 on the SAT I.

Computers: The mainframes are a DEC VAX 6510, a DEC ALPHA 2100, and IBM 2003 computers. There are 750 Macs and 450 PCs available in student labs, dorms, and other computing areas on campus; all are networked with e-mail and Internet access. All students may access the system. Most systems are accessible 24 hours a day, 7 days per week. There are no time limits and no fees.

Graduates: In 2001, 2249 bachelor's degrees were awarded. The most popular majors were teacher education (8%), business marketing (7%), and biology (7%). In an average class, 1% graduate in 3 years, 42% in 4 years, 65% in 5 years, and 68% in 6 years. 337 companies recruited on campus in 2000-2001.

Admissions Contact: Diana M. Ramey, Director, Undergraduate Admissions. A video is available.
E-mail: *admissions_serv_office@baylor.edu*
Web: *http://www.baylor.edu*

CONCORDIA UNIVERSITY AT AUSTIN — D-3

Austin, TX 78705-2799 (512) 452-7661
(800) 865-4282; Fax: (512) 459-8517

Full-time: 200 men, 300 women	**Faculty:** 42
Part-time: 100 men, 140 women	**Ph.D.s:** 67%
Graduate: 4 men, 6 women	**Student/Faculty:** 12 to 1
Year: semesters, summer session	**Tuition:** $11,340
Application Deadline: see profile	**Room & Board:** $5400
Freshman Class: 444 applied, 423 accepted, 190 enrolled	
SAT I Verbal/Math: 493/497	**ACT:** 20 **LESS COMPETITIVE**

Concordia University at Austin, founded in 1926, is a private college affiliated with the Lutheran Church-Missouri Synod. It offers undergraduate programs in liberal arts, behavioral science, business, communication, education, environmental science, and church music. There are 4 undergraduate schools. The library contains 54,900 volumes, 27,700 microform items, and 2560 audiovisual forms/CDs, and subscribes to 782 periodicals. Computerized library services include the card catalog, interlibrary loans, and database searching. Special learning facilities include a TV station. The 20-acre campus is in an urban area in the heart of Austin. Including residence halls, there are 20 buildings.

Student Life: 91% of undergraduates are from Texas. Others are from 21 states and 13 foreign countries. 89% are from public schools. 77% are white; 13% Hispanic. 78% are Protestant; 16% Catholic. The average age of freshmen is 19; all undergraduates, 25. 37% do not continue beyond their first year; 36% remain to graduate.

Housing: 245 students can be accommodated in college housing, which includes single-sex and coed dormitories. On-campus housing is guaranteed for the freshman year only and is available on a first-come, first-served basis. 68% of students commute. All students may keep cars.

Activities: There are no fraternities or sororities. There are 9 groups on campus, including band, choir, chorus, dance, drama, ethnic, religious, social, and student government. Popular campus events include Fall Festival Weekend, Parents Day, and Founders Day.

Sports: There are 6 intercollegiate sports for men and 5 for women, and 10 intramural sports for men and 9 for women. Facilities include an activities center, 1600-seat gym, 250-seat auditorium, baseball field, beach volleyball court, and tennis courts.

Disabled Students: 75% of the campus is accessible. Wheelchair ramps, elevators, special parking, specially equipped rest rooms, and lowered drinking fountains are available.

Services: Counseling and information services are available, as is tutoring in most subjects.

Campus Safety and Security: Measures include 24-hour foot and vehicle patrol, escort service, informal discussions, and pamphlets/posters/films. There are lighted pathways/sidewalks.

Programs of Study: Concordia confers the B.A. degree. Associate degrees are also awarded. Bachelor's degrees are awarded in BUSINESS (accounting, and business administration and management), COMMUNICATIONS AND THE ARTS (communications, English, music, and Spanish), COMPUTER AND PHYSICAL SCIENCE (computer science), EDUCATION (elementary and secondary), ENGINEERING AND ENVIRONMENTAL DESIGN (environmental science), SOCIAL SCIENCE (behavioral science, history, liberal arts/general studies, Mexican-American/Chicano studies, and religious music). Education is the strongest academically. Business management, education, and communication are the largest.

Required: To graduate, all students must complete 12 hours each of English, social/behavioral science, and religion, 6 to 8 hours of natural science, and 3 hours each of fine arts, math, phys ed, and speech. Students must earn 128 semester hours, including 39 upper-level hours and 33 to 48 hours in the major. A minimum 2.0 GPA is required, plus a 2.25 GPA in the major.

Special: Concordia offers internships in communications, behavioral science, business, environmental science, and Mexican-American studies, study abroad in Mexico, an accelerated degree program in business management, dual majors, credit for prior experiential learning, nondegree study, pass/fail options, and a preseminary program. There is 1 national honor society.

Faculty/Classroom: 69% of faculty are male; 31%, female. All teach undergraduates. The average class size in a laboratory is 16 and in a regular course, 21.

Admissions: 95% of the 2001-2002 applicants were accepted. The SAT I scores for the 2001-2002 freshman class were: Verbal--51% below 500, 39% between 500 and 599, 10% between 600 and 700, and 1% above 700; Math--52% below 500, 36% between 500 and 599, 11% between 600 and 700, and 1% above 700. The ACT scores were 58% below 21, 20% between 21 and 23, 13% between 24 and 26, 4% between 27 and 28, and 5% above 28. 26% of the current freshmen were in the top fifth of their class; 61% were in the top two fifths. 3 freshmen graduated first in their class.

Requirements: The SAT I or ACT is required. The recommended minimum composite score is 860 on the SAT I or 17 on the ACT. Applicants must be graduates of an accredited secondary school or have the GED. A GPA of 2.5 is required. AP and CLEP credits are accepted.

Procedure: Freshmen are admitted fall, spring, and summer. There is an early decision plan. Notification is sent on a rolling basis. The fall 2001 application fee was $25.

Transfer: Transfer students with fewer than 18 hours earned must meet freshman admissions requirements and submit high school and college transcripts; those with 18 or more hours earned must be in good standing at the previously attended college with a minimum 2.0 GPA. 30 credits of 128 must be completed at Concordia.

Visiting: There are regularly scheduled orientations for prospective students, consisting of placement exams, scheduling and registration of classes, and information sessions for parents with faculty and administrators. There are guides for informal visits, and visitors may sit in on classes and stay overnight. To schedule a visit, contact the Admissions Office.

Financial Aid: In 2001-2002, 68% of all students received some form of financial aid. The FAFSA and the college's own financial statement are required. The fall application deadline is rolling.

International Students: The school actively recruits these students. They must score 550 on the written TOEFL.

Computers: PCs are available for academic use in the computer labs. The Internet is accessible from residence halls. All students may access the system. There are no time limits and no fees.

Admissions Contact: Jay A. Krause, VP, Enrollment Services.
E-mail: *ctxadmis@crf.cuis.edu* Web: *www.concordia.edu*

DALLAS BAPTIST UNIVERSITY D-2
Dallas, TX 75211-9299 (214) 333-5360
(800) 460-1328; Fax: (214) 333-5447

Full-time: 639 men, 901 women	**Faculty:** 78
Part-time: 647 men, 1153 women	**Ph.D.s:** 77%
Graduate: 322 men, 640 women	**Student/Faculty:** 20 to 1
Year: 4-1-4, summer session	**Tuition:** $9750
Application Deadline: open	**Room & Board:** $3932
Freshman Class: 630 applied, 586 accepted, 246 enrolled	
SAT I Verbal/Math: 520/527	**ACT:** 20 **LESS COMPETITIVE**

Dallas Baptist University, established in 1965, is a private institution affiliated with the Baptist General Convention of Texas. The university offers degrees in the arts, sciences, music, and business while integrating faith and learning. There are 7 undergraduate and 8 graduate schools. In addition to regional accreditation, DBU has baccalaureate program accreditation with ACBSP. The library contains 233,023 volumes, 494,012 microform items, and 5582 audiovisual forms/CDs, and subscribes to 626 periodicals. Computerized library services include the card catalog, interlibrary loans, and database searching. Special learning facilities include a Corrie Ten Boom collection and an elementary school on campus. The 293-acre campus is in an urban area 13 miles from downtown Dallas and 19 miles from Fort Worth. Including residence halls, there are 15 buildings.

Student Life: 93% of undergraduates are from Texas. Others are from 32 states, 44 foreign countries, and Canada. 53% are white; 20% African American. 80% are Protestant; 15% Mormon, Buddhist, Greek Orthodox, Hindu, undeclared/unknown. The average age of freshmen is 18; all undergraduates, 28. 32% do not continue beyond their first year.

Housing: 1012 students can be accommodated in college housing, which includes coed dormitories and on-campus apartments. On-campus housing is available on a first-come, first-served basis. 76% of students commute. Alcohol is not permitted. All students may keep cars.

Activities: There are no fraternities or sororities. There are 24 groups on campus, including art, band, choir, chorale, civil service, community outreach, drama, ethnic, honors, international, leadership/mission wotk, musical theater, political, professional, religious, social, social service, students activities planning, student government, and yearbook. Popular campus events include Family Weekend, Spiritual Rush, and Habitat for Humanity Turkey Trot.

Sports: There are 6 intercollegiate sports for men and 5 for women, and 14 intramural sports for men and 14 for women. Facilities include a gym, tennis courts, a baseball diamond, a soccer field, a pool, a sand volleyball court, a basketball court, and pool, table tennis, and foosball tables.

Disabled Students: 63% of the campus is accessible. Wheelchair ramps, elevators, special parking, specially equipped rest rooms, special class scheduling, lowered drinking fountains, and lowered telephones are available.

Services: Counseling and information services are available, as is tutoring in most subjects, including math, writing, English, computer, study skills, and adult education. There is a reader service for the blind, remedial math, and student counseling.

Campus Safety and Security: Measures include 24-hour foot and vehicle patrol, escort service, shuttle buses, and informal discussions. There are pamphlets/posters/films, emergency telephones, and lighted pathways/sidewalks.

Programs of Study: DBU confers B.A., B.S., B.A.S., B.B.A., B.B.S., and B.M. degrees. Associate and master's degrees are also awarded. Bachelor's degrees are awarded in BIOLOGICAL SCIENCE (biology/biological science), BUSINESS (accounting, banking and finance, business administration and management, management information systems, and marketing/retailing/merchandising), COMMUNICATIONS AND THE ARTS (applied music, communications, English, fine arts, music, and music performance), COMPUTER AND PHYSICAL SCIENCE (computer science and mathematics), EDUCATION (elementary and physical), SOCIAL SCIENCE (biblical studies, counseling/psychology, criminal justice, history, interdisciplinary studies, liberal arts/general studies, pastoral studies, philosophy, physical fitness/movement, psychology, religious education, and sociology). General studies and business administration are the largest.

Required: To graduate, students must have a minimum GPA of 2.0 and complete 126 credit hours, including 24 hours in the major and 42 upper-division hours. Students must also take additional credit hours of general studies courses, including computer science, English, fine arts, foreign language, history, math, natural science, phys ed, religion, speech, and social science, to total 126. Chapel attendance is required. All freshmen must take 2 semesters of an orientation course.

Special: Work-study programs, study abroad, and a Washington semester are available. There are 4 national honor societies.

Faculty/Classroom: 59% of faculty are male; 41%, female. All teach undergraduates. The average class size in an introductory lecture is 25; in a laboratory, 19; and in a regular course, 16.

Admissions: 93% of the 2001-2002 applicants were accepted. The SAT I scores for the 2001-2002 freshman class were: Verbal--36% below 500, 45% between 500 and 599, 18% between 600 and 700, and 1% above 700; Math--35% below 500, 52% between 500 and 599, 10% between 600 and 700, and 3% above 700. The ACT scores were 46% below 21, 32% between 21 and 23, 15% between 24 and 26, 5% between 27 and 28, and 2% above 28. 28% of the current freshmen were in the top fifth of their class; 56% were in the top two fifths. 5 freshmen graduated first in their class.

Requirements: The SAT I or ACT is required. In addition, applicants must be graduates of an accredited secondary school or have a GED and meet one of the following criteria: a composite SAT I score of at least 910; a composite ACT score of at least 19; or a high school average no lower than B-. High school courses should include 4 years of English, 3 years each of math and social studies, 2 to 3 years of a foreign language, and 2 years each of history and science. An essay is required, and an interview is recommended. DBU requires applicants to be in the upper 50% of their class. A GPA of 2.0 is required. AP and CLEP credits are accepted. Important factors in the admissions decision are personality/intangible qualities, leadership record, and extracurricular activities record. Applications are accepted on-line at the school's web site.

Procedure: Freshmen are admitted to all sessions. Entrance exams should be taken during the spring of the junior year the fall of the senior year. Application deadlines are open. The fall 2001 application fee was $25. Notification is sent on a rolling basis.

Transfer: 289 transfer students enrolled in 2001-2002. Applicants must submit an essay and transcripts of all previous college work. Students with fewer than 30 credit hours must furnish high school transcripts and ACT or SAT I scores. 30 credits of 126 must be completed at DBU.

Visiting: There are regularly scheduled orientations for prospective students, including a Patriot Weekend conducted each fall and spring semester to provide information on financial aid and admissions. There are guides for informal visits and visitors may sit in on classes and stay overnight on Patriot Weekend. To schedule a visit, contact the Undergraduate Admissions Office.

Financial Aid: In 2001-2002, 87% of all freshmen and 79% of continuing students received some form of financial aid. 41% of freshmen and 44% of continuing students received need-based aid. The average freshman award was $10,628. Of that total, scholarships or need-based grants averaged $5786 ($10,400 maximum); loans averaged $6229 ($15,000 maximum); and work contracts averaged $2450 ($2880 maximum). 20% of undergraduates work part time. Average annual earnings from campus work are $2880. The FAFSA and the college's own financial statement are required. The fall application deadline is May 15.

International Students: There were 147 international students enrolled in a recent year. The school actively recruits these students. They must score 525 on the written TOEFL and also take the SAT I or the ACT.

Computers: The Center for Computer Literacy provides PCs and software packages that students can use for class assignments. All students may access the system. There are no time limits and no fees.

Graduates: In 2001, 662 bachelor's degrees were awarded. The most popular majors were general studies (22%), business administration (20%), and management information systems (6%). 101 companies recruited on campus in 2000-2001.

Admissions Contact: Duke Jones, Director of Undergraduate Admissions. A video is available. E-mail: *admiss@dbu.edu*
Web: *www.dbu.edu*

DEVRY UNIVERSITY/DALLAS D-2
Irving, TX 75063-2439 (972) 929-5777
(800) 633-3879; Fax: (972) 929-6778

Full-time: 1627 men, 605 women	**Faculty:** 77
Part-time: 935 men, 402 women	**Ph.D.s:** n/av
Graduate: none	**Student/Faculty:** 29 to 1
Year: semesters, summer session	**Tuition:** $8805
Application Deadline: open	**Room & Board:** n/app
Freshman Class: 1643 applied, 1410 accepted, 840 enrolled	
SAT I or ACT: recommended	**LESS COMPETITIVE**

DeVry University/Dallas, formerly DeVry Institute of Technology, founded in 1969, is 1 of 23 DeVry schools in the United States and Canada. The private institution offers career-oriented degree programs with hands-on training in various fields of business and technology. In addition to regional accreditation, DeVry has baccalaureate program accreditation with ABET. The library contains 771 volumes and 885 audiovisual forms/CDs, and subscribes to 73 periodicals. Computerized library services include the card catalog, interlibrary loans, and database searching. Special learning facilities include a learning resource center and electronics and other labs. The 14-acre campus is in a suburban area 12 miles northwest of Dallas. There is 1 building.

Student Life: 90% of undergraduates are from Texas. Others are from 36 states and 14 foreign countries. 40% are white; 32% African American, 16% Hispanic. The average age of all undergraduates is 27. 61% do not continue beyond their first year.

Housing: There are no residence halls. Housing refrrals may be obtained through the Student Housing Office. All of students commute. All students may keep cars.

Activities: There are no fraternities or sororities. There are 15 groups on campus, including computers, ethnic, international, newspaper, professional, religious, and social. Popular campus events include Thanksgiving Dinner, Club Fair Day, and Block Party.

Sports: There are 5 intramural sports for men and 5 for women.

Disabled Students: 90% of the campus is accessible. Wheelchair ramps, elevators, special parking, specially equipped rest rooms, lowered drinking fountains, and lowered telephones are available.

Services: Counseling and information services are available, as is tutoring in every subject.

Campus Safety and Security: Measures include escort service, informal discussions, pamphlets/posters/films, and emergency telephones. There are lighted pathways/sidewalks. Daytime and evening security is provided until the building is closed. Security systems and motion detectors are utilized after business hours.

Programs of Study: DeVry confers the B.S. degree. Associate degrees are also awarded. Bachelor's degrees are awarded in BUSINESS (business administration and management), COMMUNICATIONS AND THE ARTS (telecommunications), COMPUTER AND PHYSICAL SCIENCE (information sciences and systems), ENGINEERING AND ENVIRONMENTAL DESIGN (computer technology, electrical/electronics engineering technology, and technological management). Telecommunications and computer information systems are the largest.

Required: To graduate, students must achieve a GPA of at least 2.0 and satisfactorily complete all curriculum requirements. Course requirements vary according to program. All first-semester students take courses in business organization, computer applications, algebra, psychology, and student success strategies.

Special: Accelerated degree programs are offered in business administration, computer information systems, and telecommunications. Co-op programs, nondegree study, and evening and weekend classes are possible.

Faculty/Classroom: All teach undergraduates. The average class size in an introductory lecture is 30; in a laboratory, 30; and in a regular course, 30.

Admissions: 86% of the 2001-2002 applicants were accepted.

Requirements: The SAT I or ACT is recommended. Admissions requirements include graduation from a secondary school; the GED is also accepted. Applicants must pass the DeVry entrance exam or present satisfactory ACT or SAT I scores. An interview is required. CLEP credit is accepted. Applications are accepted on-line at *Embark.com.*

Procedure: Freshmen are admitted to all sessions. There is a deferred admissions plan. Application deadlines are open. The application fee is $50. Notification is sent on a rolling basis.

Transfer: 268 transfer students enrolled in 2001-2002. Applicants must submit official transcripts from all previous colleges attended indicating passing grades in all completed course work, demonstrate language skills proficiency with at least 24 completed semester hours, and evidence math proficiency by appropriate college-level credits. 35% of 48 to 154 credits must be completed at DeVry.

Visiting: There are regularly scheduled orientations for prospective students. There are guides for informal visits and visitors may sit in on classes. To schedule a visit, contact Vicki Carroll, New Student Coordinator at (972) 929-6777.

Financial Aid: In 2001-2002, 71% of all freshmen and 81% of continuing students received some form of financial aid. 47% of freshmen and 41% of continuing students received need-based aid. 3% of undergraduates work part time. Average annual earnings from campus work are $6800. The FAFSA is required.

International Students: There are 66 international students enrolled. They must score 500 on the written TOEFL or 173 on the electronic version and also take the college's own entrance exam.

Computers: Lab facilities include PCs in stand-alone and network configurations, with access to the mainframe. LANs provide access to a wide range of applications software. Hard copy from the mainframe is provided through a local minicomputer and medium- and high-speed printers. Students in the computer information systems program may access the system during lab hours. The fee is $5 per hour. Students in the information technology program have DeVry-issued laptop computers.

Graduates: In 2001, 403 bachelor's degrees were awarded. The most popular majors were business (44%), computer information systems (39%), and electronics engineering technology (17%). 67 companies recruited on campus in 2000-2001.

Admissions Contact: Danny Millan, Director of Admissions.
Web: *www.dal.devry.edu*

EAST TEXAS BAPTIST UNIVERSITY E-2

Marshall, TX 75670-1498 **(903) 923-2000**
(800) 804-ETBU; Fax: (903) 938-1705

Full-time: 627 men, 712 women	**Faculty:** 73; IIB, --$
Part-time: 77 men, 93 women	**Ph.D.s:** 70%
Graduate: none	**Student/Faculty:** 18 to 1
Year: semesters, summer session	**Tuition:** $9050
Application Deadline: open	**Room & Board:** $3299
Freshman Class: 766 applied, 598 accepted, 360 enrolled	
ACT: required	**LESS COMPETITIVE**

East Texas Baptist University, founded in 1912, is operated in association with the Baptist General Convention of Texas. The private liberal arts university offers undergraduate programs in the arts and sciences and professional areas, such as business, teacher education, nursing, and Christian ministry. There are 7 undergraduate schools. In addition to regional accreditation, ETBU has baccalaureate program accreditation with NASM, NLN, and CCNE. The library contains 115,000 volumes, 9250 microform items, and 2000 audiovisual forms/CDs, and subscribes to 543 periodicals. Computerized library services include the card catalog, interlibrary loans, and database searching. Special learning facilities include a learning resource center and math learning center, and a writing lab. The 200-acre campus is in a small town 35 miles west of Shreveport, Louisana, and 140 miles east of Dallas. Including residence halls, there are 25 buildings.

Student Life: 88% of undergraduates are from Texas. Others are from 26 states, 22 foreign countries, and Canada. 97% are from public schools. 80% are white; 13% African American. Most are Protestant. The average age of freshmen is 19; all undergraduates, 21. 35% do not continue beyond their first year; 39% remain to graduate.

Housing: 1057 students can be accommodated in college housing, which includes single-sex dormitories, on-campus apartments, off-campus apartments, married-student housing, fraternity houses, and sorority houses. On-campus housing is available on a first-come, first-served basis. 70% of students live on campus; of those, 40% remain on campus on weekends. Alcohol is not permitted. All students may keep cars.

Activities: 6% of men belong to 2 local and 1 national fraternities; 4% of women belong to 1 local and 1 national sororities. There are 36 groups on campus, including band, cheerleading, choir, chorale, chorus, computers, debate, drama, drill team, ethnic, honors, international, jazz band, literary magazine, marching band, newspaper, pep band, political, professional, religious, social, social service, student government, and yearbook. Popular campus events include theater productions, Miss ETBU Pageant, and choral and band concerts.

Sports: There are 5 intercollegiate sports for men and 5 for women, and 6 intramural sports for men and 5 for women. Facilities include a baseball field, tennis courts, a weight room, a 1500-seat gym, a soccer field, a softball field, an intramural field, a practice gym, football practice fields, a football field, and a stadium.

Disabled Students: 95% of the campus is accessible. Wheelchair ramps, elevators, special parking, specially equipped rest rooms, special class scheduling, and lowered drinking fountains are available.

Services: Counseling and information services are available, as is tutoring in some subjects, including math and English. There is remedial math and writing.

Campus Safety and Security: Measures include 24-hour foot and vehicle patrol, self-defense education, informal discussions, and pamphlets/posters/films. There are lighted pathways/sidewalks.

Programs of Study: ETBU confers B.A., B.S., B.A.S., B.B.A., B.M., B.S.E., and B.S.N. degrees. Associate degrees are also awarded. Bachelor's degrees are awarded in BIOLOGICAL SCIENCE (biology/biological science and environmental biology), BUSINESS (accounting, banking and finance, business administration and management, marketing management, and recreational facilities management), COMMUNICATIONS AND THE ARTS (dramatic arts, English, music, music performance, piano/organ, Spanish, speech/debate/rhetoric, and voice), COMPUTER AND PHYSICAL SCIENCE (chemistry, information sciences and systems, and mathematics), EDUCATION (athletic training, business, computer, drama, education, elementary, English, mathematics, music, physical, science, secondary, and social studies), HEALTH PROFESSIONS (medical technology and nursing), SOCIAL SCIENCE (community psychology, history, ministries, physical fitness/movement, psychology, religion, religious music, and sociology). Teacher education, music, and science are the strongest academically. Religion and teacher education are the largest.

Required: To graduate, students must complete general education requirements, ranging from 34 hours for B.M. degrees to 64 hours for B.A. and B.S. degrees, and have a minimum GPA of 2.0. A total of 128 semester hours, with at least 30 in the major, is required, including 9 to 12 of English, 6 to 9 of religion, 6 of history, 3 to 6 hours of math, at least 3 of lab science, and 3 of physical activity.

Special: Internships are offered in social work, management, and computer information systems, as is study abroad in 5 countries and a Washington semester through the American Studies Program. There are 6 national honor societies and a freshman honors program.

Faculty/Classroom: 66% of faculty are male; 34%, female. All teach undergraduates and 20% do research. The average class size in an introductory lecture is 31; in a laboratory, 16; and in a regular course, 21.

Admissions: 78% of the 2001-2002 applicants were accepted. The ACT scores for the 2001-2002 freshman class were: 54% below 21, 24% between 21 and 23, 14% between 24 and 26, 5% between 27 and 28, and 3% above 28. There were 2 National Merit semifinalists in a recent year.

Requirements: The ACT is required. In addition, applicants must be graduates of an accredited secondary school or have the GED, and must have composite scores of at least 18 on the ACT or 860 on the SAT I, or rank in the top half of their graduating class. Students not meeting these requirements may be admitted conditionally for 1 term or semester. An essay is required for all students. ETBU requires applicants to be in the upper 50% of their class. A GPA of 2.0 is required. AP and CLEP credits are accepted. Applications are accepted on-line at the school's web site.

Procedure: Freshmen are admitted to all sessions. Entrance exams should be taken in the first semester of the senior year. There is a deferred admissions plan. Application deadlines are open. The fall 2001 application fee was $25. Notification is sent on a rolling basis.

Transfer: 138 transfer students enrolled in 2001-2002. Transfer students must have a minimum GPA of 2.0 and be eligible to return to the last college attended. 36 credits of 128 must be completed at ETBU.

Visiting: There are regularly scheduled orientations for prospective students, including campus tours, meals, scholarship interviews/testing, faculty visits, class visits, sports/entertainment, and financial aid seminars. There are guides for informal visits and visitors may sit in on classes and stay overnight. To schedule a visit, contact the Campus Visit Coordinator.

Financial Aid: In 2001-2002, 97% of all freshmen and 90% of continuing students received some form of financial aid. 65% of freshmen and 59% of continuing students received need-based aid. The average freshman award was $9207. Of that total, scholarships or need-based grants averaged $4773; loans averaged $2793; work contracts averaged $1141; and outside donations averaged $500. 27% of undergraduates work part time. Average annual earnings from campus work are $1648. The average financial indebtedness of the 2001 graduate was $17,125. The CSS/Profile, FAFSA, FFS, or SFS, and the college's own financial statement are required. The fall application deadline is June 1.

International Students: There are 39 international students enrolled. The school actively recruits these students. They must score 500 on the written TOEFL or take the MELAB and also take the ACT, scoring 18.

Computers: The mainframes are an Alpha 1200 and a DEC 5000/200. There are 3 open computer labs with a total of 77 PCs and 6 Macs. All computers have Internet and Web access; residence halls have campus network/Internet connections in each student room. There also are 9 PC kiosks throughout campus with Web and Internet access. All students may access the system At least one lab is available for use during each of the following hours: 8 A.M. to 11 P.M. Monday through Thursday; 8 A.M. to 5 P.M. Friday; 10 A.M. to 6 P.M. Saturday; and 1 P.M. to 5 P.M. Sunday. There are no time limits and no fees.

Graduates: In 2001, 188 bachelor's degrees were awarded. The most popular majors were elementary education (17%), nursing (9%), and behavioral sciences (7%). In an average class, 20% graduate in 4 years, 33% in 5 years, and 37% in 6 years. 60 companies recruited on campus in 2000-2001.

Admissions Contact: Vince Blankenship, Dean of Admissions and Marketing. A video is available. E-mail: *admissions@etbu.edu*
Web: *www.etbu.edu*

HARDIN-SIMMONS UNIVERSITY

Abilene, TX 79698 — C-2 — **(915) 670-1206**
(800) 568-2692; Fax: (915) 670-1527

Full-time: 806 men, 864 women	**Faculty:** 115; IIA, --$
Part-time: 85 men, 147 women	**Ph.D.s:** 69%
Graduate: 171 men, 203 women	**Student/Faculty:** 15 to 1
Year: semesters, summer session	**Tuition:** $10,650
Application Deadline: open	**Room & Board:** $3515
Freshman Class: 1246 applied, 856 accepted, 392 enrolled	
SAT I Verbal/Math: 505/510	**ACT:** 22 **COMPETITIVE**

Hardin-Simmons University, founded in 1891, is a private liberal arts institution affiliated with the Baptist General Convention of Texas. There are 7 undergraduate schools and 1 graduate school. In addition to regional accreditation, HSU has baccalaureate program accreditation with ACBSP, CSWE, NASM, and CCNE. The 2 libraries contain 460,735 volumes, 21,199 microform items, and 20,126 audiovisual forms/CDs, and subscribe to 4015 periodicals. Computerized library services include the card catalog, interlibrary loans, and database searching. Special learning facilities include an art gallery and and an observatory. The 40-acre campus is in an urban area 150 miles west of Fort Worth. Including residence halls, there are 37 buildings.

Student Life: 95% of undergraduates are from Texas. Others are from 22 states, 8 foreign countries, and Canada. 92% are from public schools. 86% are white. Most are Protestant. The average age of freshmen is 18; all undergraduates, 21. 34% do not continue beyond their first year; 43% remain to graduate.

Housing: 1100 students can be accommodated in college housing, which includes single-sex dormitories, off-campus apartments, and married-student housing. On-campus housing is available on a first-come, first-served basis. 55% of students commute. Alcohol is not permitted. All students may keep cars.

Activities: 6% of men belong to 4 local fraternities; 10% of women belong to 5 local sororities. There are 55 groups on campus, including art, band, cheerleading, choir, chorale, computers, debate, drama, drill team, ethnic, honors, international, literary magazine, marching band, musical theater, newspaper, opera, orchestra, pep band, photography, political, professional, radio and TV, religious, Six White Horse Drill Team, social, social service, student government, symphony, and yearbook. Popular campus events include theater productions, opera, concerts, and Western Heritage Day.

Sports: There are 6 intercollegiate sports for men and 5 for women, and 17 intramural sports for men and 17 for women. Facilities include a rodeo arena, 2 running ovals, a practice field, a football stadium, soccer and baseball fields, outdoor and indoor swimming pools, 6 bowling alleys, a fitness course, 4 basketball, 4 racquetball, 8 tennis, and 8 badminton/paddleball courts, and a Nautilus weight-lifting room.

Disabled Students: All of the campus is accessible. Wheelchair ramps, elevators, special parking, specially equipped rest rooms, special class scheduling, lowered drinking fountains, and an office to coordinate disability services are available.

Services: Counseling and information services are available, as is tutoring in most subjects. There is remedial math, reading, and writing, and free counseling services.

Campus Safety and Security: Measures include 24-hour foot and vehicle patrol, informal discussions, pamphlets/posters/films, and emergency telephones. There are lighted pathways/sidewalks.

Programs of Study: HSU confers B.A., B.S., B.B.A., B.Mus., B.S.N., and B. Behavioral Science degrees. Master's degrees are also awarded. Bachelor's degrees are awarded in BIOLOGICAL SCIENCE (biology/biological science), BUSINESS (accounting, banking and finance, business administration and management, and marketing/retailing/merchandising), COMMUNICATIONS AND THE ARTS (applied music, communications, English, French, German, music, Spanish, and theater management), COMPUTER AND PHYSICAL SCIENCE (chemistry, computer science, geology, mathematics, and physics), EDUCATION (art, business, early childhood, elementary, foreign languages, health, music, physical, reading, science, and secondary), HEALTH PROFESSIONS (nursing and speech pathology/audiology), SOCIAL SCIENCE (criminal justice, history, law enforcement and corrections, ministries, philosophy, physical fitness/movement, political science/government, psychology, religion, social science, social work, sociology, and theological studies). Elemantary education, biology, and business are the strongest academically. Elementary education, biology, and communication are the largest.

Required: To graduate, students must complete a minimum of 124 semester hours with a minimum 2.0 GPA. At least 18 hours are required in the major and 42 hours in upper-division courses. Core courses that must be taken include 12 hours of social science, and 9 hours of English, 7 of natural science, 6 each of Bible and humanities, 4 of phys ed, 3 each of math and oral communication, and 2 of computer science. All students must satisfy chapel attendance requirements and must demonstrate proficiency in written English.

Special: Cross-registration may be arranged with Abilene Christian and McMurry Universities. HSU offers cooperative programs, internships, dual majors, credit by exam, nondegree study, and pass/fail options. Students may study abroad in England, Uzbekistan, Mexico, Austria, China, and Israel, where HSU is involved in an ongoing archeological excavation of early Christian sites. There are 14 national honor societies.

Faculty/Classroom: 62% of faculty are male; 38%, female. 90% teach undergraduates. No introductory courses are taught by graduate students. The average class size in an introductory lecture is 23; in a laboratory, 17; and in a regular course, 12.

Admissions: 69% of the 2001-2002 applicants were accepted. The SAT I scores for the 2001-2002 freshman class were: Verbal--43% below 500, 42% between 500 and 599, and 15% between 600 and 700; Math--45% below 500, 41% between 500 and 599, and 14% between 600 and 700. The ACT scores were 44% below 21, 25% between 21 and 23, 21% between 24 and 26, 6% between 27 and 28, and 4% above 28. 36% of the current freshmen were in the top fifth of their class; 64% were in the top two fifths. 8 freshmen graduated first in their class.

Requirements: The SAT I or ACT is required. In addition, graduation from an accredited secondary school is required; a GED will be accepted. Applicants should submit an academic record of at least 16 units, distributed as follows: 3 units of English, 2 units each of math, science, and social studies, and 7 units of electives. HSU requires applicants to be in the upper 50% of their class. A GPA of 2.0 is required. AP and CLEP credits are accepted. Applications are accepted on-line at the school's web site.

Procedure: Freshmen are admitted to all sessions. There is an early admissions plan. Application deadlines are open. The application fee is $25. Notification is sent on a rolling basis.

Transfer: 160 transfer students enrolled in 2001-2002. Applicants must submit official transcripts from all previous colleges. Students may petition to transfer up to 2 D grades if the overall GPA is 2.0 or higher. Students transferring from a 2-year college may receive credit for up to 66 semester hours of transferable courses. Applicants with fewer than 24 semester hours must submit a high school transcript and official report of ACT or SAT I scores. Students ineligible to continue at another institution are not eligible for regular admission to HSU.

Visiting: There are regularly scheduled orientations for prospective students, including spring and fall preview for prospective students. There are guides for informal visits and visitors may sit in on classes and stay overnight. To schedule a visit, contact Kimberley Howell, the Office of Enrollment Services at (915) 670-5814.

Financial Aid: In 2001-2002, 92% of all freshmen and 88% of continuing students received some form of financial aid. 79% of freshmen and 80% of continuing students received need-based aid. The average freshman award was $11,783. Of that total, scholarships or need-based grants averaged $2518 ($17,448 maximum); loans averaged $1554 ($6625 maximum); work contracts averaged $1023 ($2400 maximum); and non-need based loans averaged $4999 ($17,448 maximum). 20% of undergraduates work part time. Average annual earnings from campus work are $2400. The average financial indebtedness of the 2001 graduate was $20,393. The FAFSA is required. The fall application deadline is open.

International Students: There are 7 international students enrolled. They must score 550 on the written TOEFL and also take the SAT I or the ACT.

Computers: The mainframe is an IBM 7025-F40. More than 250 PCs are located in dorms, labs and classrooms across campus. HSU is a self-contained ISP with T1-speed Internet access. Web and e-mail services are available to students. Labs and many buildings are interconnected with Ethernet technology. All students may access the system. There are no time limits. The fee is $80.

Graduates: In 2001, 238 bachelor's degrees were awarded. The most popular majors were elementary education (13%), communication (11%), and biology (7%). In an average class, 2% graduate in 3 years, 26% in 4 years, 42% in 5 years, and 45% in 6 years. 10 companies recruited on campus in 2000-2001.

Admissions Contact: Shane Davidson, Associate, Vice President for Enrollment Services. A video is available. E-mail: *jdsd@hsutx.edu*
Web: *hsutx.edu*

HOUSTON BAPTIST UNIVERSITY
Houston, TX 77074-3298 — E-3
(281) 649-3211
(800) 969-3210; Fax: (281) 649-3217

Full-time: 542 men, 1137 women	**Faculty:** 100; IIA, --$
Part-time: 55 men, 219 women	**Ph.D.s:** 80%
Graduate: 237 men, 639 women	**Student/Faculty:** 17 to 1
Year: quarters, summer session	**Tuition:** $10,560
Application Deadline: open	**Room & Board:** $4740
Freshman Class: 670 applied, 568 accepted, 319 enrolled	
SAT I Verbal/Math: 527/525	**ACT:** 22 **LESS COMPETITIVE**

Houston Baptist University, founded in 1960, is a private institution affiliated with the Baptist General Convention of Texas and offering undergraduate programs in nursing, arts and science, music, and business administration. There are 7 undergraduate and 4 graduate schools. In addition to regional accreditation, HBU has baccalaureate program accreditation with NLN. The library contains 180,116 volumes, 97,556 microform items, and 8086 audiovisual forms/CDs, and subscribes to 1900 periodicals. Computerized library services include the card catalog, interlibrary loans, and database searching. Special learning facilities include a learning resource center, TV station, a museum of decorative arts, and the Bible in America Museum. The 100-acre campus is in an urban area in southwest Houston. Including residence halls, there are 17 buildings.

Student Life: 93% of undergraduates are from Texas. Others are from 16 states, 19 foreign countries, and Canada. 80% are from public schools. 50% are white; 17% African American, 14% Asian American; 14% Hispanic. 52% are Protestant; 17% Catholic. The average age of freshmen is 18; all undergraduates, 23. 20% do not continue beyond their first year.

Housing: 632 students can be accommodated in college housing, which includes single-sex dormitories and on-campus apartments. On-campus housing is available on a first-come, first-served basis. 70% of students commute. Alcohol is not permitted. All students may keep cars.

Activities: 13% of men belong to 1 national and 2 local fraternities; 6% of women belong to 2 national sororities. There are 45 groups on campus, including art, band, cheerleading, choir, chorus, computers, debate, drama, ethnic, forensics, honors, international, jazz band, newspaper, opera, photography, political, professional, radio and TV, religious, social service, student government, symphony, and yearbook. Popular campus events include Ornogah Beauty Pageant, International Nite, and Spring Fling.

Sports: There are 2 intercollegiate sports for men and 3 for women, and 9 intramural sports for men and 9 for women. Facilities include volleyball, basketball, and tennis courts, an indoor track, and areas for track and field and soccer.

Disabled Students: 80% of the campus is accessible. Wheelchair ramps, elevators, special parking, and specially equipped rest rooms are available.

Services: There is remedial math and writing.

Campus Safety and Security: Measures include 24-hour foot and vehicle patrol, escort service, emergency telephones, and lighted pathways/sidewalks.

Programs of Study: HBU confers B.A., B.S., B.B.A., B.M., and B.S.N. degrees. Associate and master's degrees are also awarded. Bachelor's degrees are awarded in BIOLOGICAL SCIENCE (biology/biological science), BUSINESS (accounting, banking and finance, business administration and management, business economics, and marketing/retailing/merchandising), COMMUNICATIONS AND THE ARTS (communications, English, fine arts, French, music, music performance, music theory and composition, Spanish, and speech/debate/rhetoric), COMPUTER AND PHYSICAL SCIENCE (chemistry, information sciences and systems, mathematics, and physics), EDUCATION (art, early childhood, elementary, foreign languages, music, reading, science, secondary, special, and teaching English as a second/foreign language (TESOL/TEFOL)), HEALTH PROFESSIONS (medical technology, nursing, predentistry, and premedicine), SOCIAL SCIENCE (Christian studies, history, physical fitness/movement, political science/government, psychology, religious music, and sociology). Biology and chemistry (premedicine), education, and nursing are the strongest academically.

Required: To graduate, students must complete a minimum of 130 semester hours, including at least 12 hours of upper-level courses in the major and courses in Christianity, written and oral communication, humanities and fine arts, social and behavioral science, a foreign language, and biology, chemistry, or physics. Also required are a minimum 2.0 GPA, completion of the English Proficiency Exam, 12 hours of senior seminars, attendance at all convocations, and demonstrated competency in reading, oral communication, and math. Other requirements vary by program.

Special: HBU offers internships through its academic colleges, study abroad in 1 country, B.A.-B.S. degrees and dual majors in most areas, work-study programs, credit for military experience, and pass/fail options. A 3-2 engineering program is offered with the University of Houston and Baylor and Texas A&M Universities. There is a freshman honors program.

Faculty/Classroom: 49% of faculty are male; 51%, female. 98% teach undergraduates. No introductory courses are taught by graduate students. The average class size in an introductory lecture is 20; in a laboratory, 20; and in a regular course, 15.

Admissions: 85% of the 2001-2002 applicants were accepted.

Requirements: The SAT I or ACT is required, with a recommended minimum composite score of 1010 (480 verbal) on the SAT I or 20 on the ACT. Applicants must be graduates of an accredited secondary school or have the GED. AP and CLEP credits are accepted. Important factors in the admissions decision are recommendations by school officials, personality/intangible qualities, and advanced placement or honor courses.

Procedure: Freshmen are admitted to all sessions. Entrance exams should be taken in the fall of the senior year. There are early decision and early admissions plans. Application deadlines are open. The application fee is $25. Notification is sent on a rolling basis.

Transfer: 249 transfer students enrolled in 2001-2002. Applicants with fewer than 30 semester hours earned must submit high school and college transcripts and SAT I or ACT scores. All students must have a minimum 2.0 GPA. 32 credits of 130 must be completed at HBU.

Visiting: There are guides for informal visits and visitors may sit in on classes and stay overnight. To schedule a visit, contact the Office of Admissions.

Financial Aid: HBU is a member of CSS. The FAFSA and the college's own financial statement are required. The fall application deadline is April 1.

International Students: There are 70 international students enrolled. The school actively recruits these students. They must score 550 on the written TOEFL or 213 on the electronic version and also take the SAT I or the ACT.

Computers: There are PCs available to students. All students may access the system from 8 A.M. to 10 P.M. There are no time limits and no fees.

Admissions Contact: David Melton, Director of Admissions. E-mail: *unadm@hbu.edu* Web: *www.hbu.edu*

HOWARD PAYNE UNIVERSITY

Brownwood, TX 76801-2794 C-3
(915) 649-8027
(800) 880-4478; Fax: (915) 649-8901

Full-time: 595 men, 572 women	**Faculty:** 74
Part-time: 186 men, 173 women	**Ph.D.s:** 62%
Graduate: none	**Student/Faculty:** 16 to 1
Year: semesters, summer session	**Tuition:** $10,000
Application Deadline: August 1	**Room & Board:** $3834
Freshman Class: 553 applied, 488 accepted, 293 enrolled	
SAT I Verbal/Math: 525/530	**ACT:** 22 **COMPETITIVE+**

Howard Payne University, founded in 1889 and affiliated with the Baptist General Convention of Texas, offers undergraduate programs in the arts and sciences, business administration, education, Christianity, music, and social sciences. There are 6 undergraduate schools. In addition to regional accreditation, HPU has baccalaureate program accreditation with CSWE, IACBE, and NASM. The library contains 115,000 volumes, 275,000 microform items, and 7000 audiovisual forms/CDs, and subscribes to 900 periodicals. Computerized library services include the card catalog, interlibrary loans, and database searching. Special learning facilities include a radio station and children's literature center, audio production facility, TV production studio, and video editing facility. The 29-acre campus is in a small town 120 miles southwest of Dallas/Fort Worth. Including residence halls, there are 25 buildings.

Student Life: 98% of undergraduates are from Texas. Others are from 12 states and 6 foreign countries. 95% are from public schools. 75% are white; 12% Hispanic. 73% are Protestant; 17% claim no religious affiliation. The average age of freshmen is 18; all undergraduates, 22. 40% do not continue beyond their first year; 33% remain to graduate.

Housing: 748 students can be accommodated in college housing, which includes single-sex dormitories, on-campus apartments, and married-student housing. On-campus housing is available on a lottery system for upperclassmen. 56% of students commute. Alcohol is not permitted. All students may keep cars.

Activities: 12% of men belong to 5 local fraternities; 18% of women belong to 4 local sororities. There are 38 groups on campus, including art, band, cheerleading, choir, chorus, computers, drama, ethnic, honors, jazz band, literary magazine, marching band, musical theater, newspaper, photography, professional, radio and TV, religious, social, social service, student government, and yearbook. Popular campus events include Christian Concerts and College Preview Weekends.

Sports: There are 7 intercollegiate sports for men and 6 for women, and 5 intramural sports for men and 5 for women. Facilities include an 8000-seat stadium and an 800-seat auditorium; a remodeled wellness center with basketball and volleyball courts, an indoor walking track, and free weights and exercise equipment; tennis and sand volleyball courts; a practice field; a student union; and nearby baseball and softball parks.

Disabled Students: 90% of the campus is accessible. Wheelchair ramps, elevators, special parking, specially equipped rest rooms, special class scheduling, and lowered drinking fountains are available.

Services: Counseling and information services are available, as is tutoring in some subjects, including math and English. There is remedial math, reading, and writing. A writing lab and computer lab are available for English, math, and computer science.

Campus Safety and Security: Measures include informal discussions, pamphlets/posters/films, emergency telephones, and lighted pathways/sidewalks. In addition, there are 12-hour foot patrols, monthly dormitory meetings, 2 security seminars for the entire campus, and 24-hour telephone availability with on-duty officers carrying cellular phones.

Programs of Study: HPU confers B.A., B.S., B.A.A.S, B.B.A., and B.M. degrees. Associate degrees are also awarded. Bachelor's degrees are awarded in BIOLOGICAL SCIENCE (biology/biological science), BUSINESS (accounting and business administration and management), COMMUNICATIONS AND THE ARTS (art, communications, dramatic arts, English, multimedia, music, and Spanish), COMPUTER AND PHYSICAL SCIENCE (chemistry, computer science, and mathematics), EDUCATION (athletic training, elementary, secondary, and teaching English as a second/foreign language (TESOL/TEFOL)), ENGINEERING AND ENVIRONMENTAL DESIGN (occupational safety and health), HEALTH PROFESSIONS (exercise science), SOCIAL SCIENCE (Christian studies, history, liberal arts/general studies, political science/government, psychology, social work, and sociology). Biology, chemistry, and political science are the strongest academically. Business management, elementary education, and exercise and sports science are the largest.

Required: To graduate, students must complete a minimum of 128 credit hours, 49 in general education courses, 30 to 36 in the major, and 18 to 24 in a minor, plus electives. A minimum 2.0 GPA is required. The general education core includes Bible, English, social science, computer science, fine arts, phys ed, lab science, speech, and math courses. Requirements for students not obtaining the B.A. or B.S. vary. All students must complete 6 semester credits of chapel/convocation attendance.

Special: Cross-registration is offered with several hospitals, and internships are available in many fields. HPU offers credit for experience for B.A.A.S. candidates only, study abroad in Israel and England, pass/fail options, and work-study programs. Special programs include the Douglas MacArthur Academy of Freedom, an interdisciplinary honors program in the social sciences; a chemistry honors program; and a provisional program for underprepared students. There are 4 national honor societies, including Phi Beta Kappa, a freshman honors program, and 2 departmental honors programs.

Faculty/Classroom: 69% of faculty are male; 31%, female. All teach undergraduates. The average class size in an introductory lecture is 22; in a laboratory, 20; and in a regular course, 18.

Admissions: 88% of the 2001-2002 applicants were accepted. The SAT I scores for the 2001-2002 freshman class were: Verbal--32% below 500, 45% between 500 and 599, 21% between 600 and 700, and 3% above 700; Math--31% below 500, 50% between 500 and 599, 18% between 600 and 700, and 1% above 700. The ACT scores were 29% below 21, 31% between 21 and 23, 22% between 24 and 26, 10% between 27 and 28, and 8% above 28. 48% of the current freshmen were in the top fifth of their class; 74% were in the top two fifths. 5 freshmen graduated first in their class.

Requirements: The SAT I or ACT is required. In addition, applicants must be graduates of an accredited secondary school or have a GED. It is recommended that they have completed 4 credits of English, 3 of math including algebra I, 2.5 of social studies, 2 of science, 1.5 of phys ed, and 1 each of technology applications and a science/social studies elective, along with courses in economics, health, and speech; the remaining credits should be earned in courses approved by the Texas Board of Education. Graduates of high schools or home study programs that are not accredited by a regional or state accrediting agency will have their work reviewed by the admissions committee on an individual basis. A GPA of 3.0 is required. AP and CLEP credits are accepted. Important factors in the admissions decision are recommendations by school officials, leadership record, and personality/intangible qualities.

Procedure: Freshmen are admitted to all sessions. Entrance exams should be taken during the senior year. There is an early admissions plan. Applications should be filed by August 1 for fall entry and January 1 for spring entry. The fall 2001 application fee was $25. Notification is sent on a rolling basis.

Transfer: 92 transfer students enrolled in 2001-2002. Transfer students must be able to return to the university they are leaving and submit official transcipts from all previously attended colleges/universities. Students younger than 21 with fewer than 12 semester hours must submit the SAT I or ACT scores. The same GPA per number of hours attempted is required of transfers as for continuing HPU students. 32 credits of 128 must be completed at HPU.

Visiting: There are regularly scheduled orientations for prospective students, including college preview weekends in the fall and spring. There are guides for informal visits and visitors may sit in on classes and stay overnight. To schedule a visit, contact the Enrollment Services Office at (915) 649-8020 or *enroll@hputx.edu*

Financial Aid: In 2001-2002, 80% of all freshmen and 90% of continuing students received some form of financial aid. 55% of freshmen and 60% of continuing students received need-based aid. The average freshman award was $7500. Of that total, scholarships or need-based grants averaged $1500 ($4000 maximum); loans averaged $2625 ($6625 maximum); work contracts averaged $1200 ($2000 maximum); and $2400 ($4800 maximum). 65% of undergraduates work part time. Average annual earnings from campus work are $2000. The average financial indebtedness of the 2001 graduate was $16,500. The FAFSA is required. The fall application deadline is March 1.

International Students: There are 29 international students enrolled. The school actively recruits these students. They must score 500 on the written TOEFL or 173 on the electronic version. A TOEFL score is not required for International students entering the English as a Second Language (ESL) program. Students must score 19 on the ACT or 830 on the SAT I for unconditional admission; otherwise, a provisional program may be available.

Computers: The mainframe is a DEC Alpha Server. 11 computer labs, with a total of approximately 225 computers, are available to all students. Also available are 35 computers on a 286 Novell Local Area Network. All students may access the system 24 hours a day in 3 labs in the dormitories and 8 A.M. to 10 P.M., Monday through Friday in the Instructional Building labs. There are no time limits and no fees.

Graduates: In 2001, 222 bachelor's degrees were awarded. The most popular majors were education (24%), business management (16%), and Christian studies (13%). In an average class, 2% graduate in 3 years, 25% in 4 years, 33% in 5 years, and 35% in 6 years. Of the 2000 graduating class, 25% were enrolled in graduate school within 6 months of graduation.

Admissions Contact: Cheryl Mangrum, Coordinator of Admissions Services. E-mail: *enroll@hputx.edu* Web: *www.hputx.edu*

HUSTON-TILLOTSON COLLEGE
Austin, TX 78702 D-3

(512) 505-3027
(877) 505-3026; Fax: (512) 505-3192

Full-time: 223 men, 249 women	**Faculty:** 35
Part-time: 57 men, 89 women	**Ph.D.s:** 48%
Graduate: none	**Student/Faculty:** 13 to 1
Year: semesters, summer session	**Tuition:** $7950
Application Deadline: March 1	**Room & Board:** $5027
Freshman Class: 201 applied, 179 accepted, 114 enrolled	
SAT I Verbal/Math: 450/450	**ACT:** 17 LESS COMPETITIVE

Huston-Tillotson College, formed in 1952 by the merger of Tillotson College and Samuel Huston College (both founded in the mid-1870s) is a private liberal arts institution affiliated with the United Church of Christ and the United Methodist Church. The library contains 84,200 volumes, 213 microform items, and 971 audiovisual forms/CDs, and subscribes to 320 periodicals. Special learning facilities include a learning resource center, radio station, and TV station. The 23-acre campus is in an urban area 78 miles north of San Antonio. Including residence halls, there are 12 buildings.

Student Life: 79% of undergraduates are from Texas. Others are from 27 states and 15 foreign countries. 85% are from public schools. 81% are African American. 72% are Protestant; 14% claim no religious affiliation; 10% Catholic. The average age of freshmen is 19; all undergraduates, 23. 10% do not continue beyond their first year; 65% remain to graduate.

Housing: 368 students can be accommodated in college housing, which includes single-sex dormitories. On-campus housing is available on a first-come, first-served basis. Priority is given to out-of-town students. 63% of students commute. Alcohol is not permitted. All students may keep cars.

Activities: 3% of men belong to 4 national fraternities; 8% of women belong to 4 local and 4 national sororities. There are 17 groups on campus, including band, cheerleading, choir, chorus, drama, drill team, honors, international, jazz band, newspaper, professional, radio and TV, religious, social, social service, student government, and yearbook. Popular campus events include Charter Day, Alumni Weekend, and Miss UNCF Contest.

Sports: There are 3 intercollegiate sports for men and 3 for women, and 2 intramural sports for men and 2 for women. Facilities include an 800-seat gym and soccer and baseball fields.

Disabled Students: 80% of the campus is accessible. Wheelchair ramps, elevators, special parking, and specially equipped rest rooms are available.

Services: Counseling and information services are available, as is tutoring in every subject. There is remedial math, reading, and writing.

Campus Safety and Security: Measures include 24-hour foot and vehicle patrol, escort service, and lighted pathways/sidewalks.

Programs of Study: The college confers B.A. and B.S. degrees. Bachelor's degrees are awarded in BIOLOGICAL SCIENCE (biology/biological science), BUSINESS (business administration and management and marketing/retailing/merchandising), COMMUNICATIONS AND THE ARTS (communications, English, and music), COMPUTER AND PHYSICAL SCIENCE (chemistry, computer science, and mathematics), EDUCATION (education, elementary, and physical), SOCIAL SCIENCE (political science/government and sociology). Biology, computer science, and education are the strongest academically. Business studies, computer science, and education are the largest.

Required: All students must complete 120 credit hours, including 54 in the general education required curriculum and 30 in the major, with a minimum GPA of 2.0. Core requirements include 18 hours of English and foreign languages, 9 each of math/computer science and social sciences, 8 of natural science, 6 of phys ed and health, 3 of philosophy, and 1 of psychology.

Special: The college offers co-op programs, internships, work-study programs, and dual majors. A 3-2 engineering degree with Prairie View A&M University is also available. There are 4 national honor societies, a freshman honors program, and 1 departmental honors program.

Faculty/Classroom: 58% of faculty are male; 41%, female. All teach undergraduates and 4% do research. The average class size in an introductory lecture is 16; in a laboratory, 16; and in a regular course, 20.

Admissions: 89% of the 2001-2002 applicants were accepted. There was 1 National Merit semifinalist in a recent year. 2 freshmen graduated first in their class.

Requirements: The SAT I or ACT is required, with a minimum composite score of 900 on the SAT I or 18 on the ACT. Applicants should be high school graduates with 18 academic credits, including 4 in English, 3 in math, 2 each in science and social studies, and 1 in phys ed. A GPA of 2.0 is required. AP and CLEP credits are accepted. Important factors in the admissions decision are advanced placement or honor courses, extracurricular activities record, and parents or siblings attending the school. Applications are accepted on computer disk and on-line at the school's web site.

Procedure: Freshmen are admitted to all sessions. There is an early admissions plan. Applications should be filed by March 1 for fall entry, October 1 for spring entry, and March 1 for summer entry, along with a $25 fee. Notification is sent on a rolling basis.

Transfer: 121 transfer students enrolled in 2001-2002. Applicants must submit transcripts from all colleges or universities attended and must have an overall GPA of 2.0. Students with fewer than 15 credit hours must meet freshman entrance requirements. 30 credits of 120 must be completed at the college.

Visiting: There are regularly scheduled orientations for prospective students. There are guides for informal visits and visitors may sit in on classes and stay overnight. To schedule a visit, contact the Dean of Enrollment Services.

Financial Aid: In a recent year, 95% of all freshmen and 86% of continuing students received some form of financial aid. The average freshman award was $8690. Of that total, scholarships or need-based grants averaged $5000 ($12,380 maximum); loans averaged $2625 ($6625 maximum); and work contracts averaged $1500 ($2000 maximum). 20% of undergraduates work part time. The average financial indebtedness of a recent graduate was $25,125. The college is a member of CSS. The FAFSA and the college's own financial statement are required. The fall application deadline is March 15.

International Students: There are 61 international students enrolled. They must score 500 on the written TOEFL and also take the SAT I or the ACT.

Computers: The mainframe is an AST Premium SE 4-50 Model 3. PCs are available to all students. All students may access the system during lab hours. There are no time limits. The fee is $15.

Graduates: In a recent year, 78 bachelor's degrees were awarded. The most popular majors were business administration management (17%), interdisciplinary studies (16%), and American government and politics (6%).

Admissions Contact: Bronté D. Jones, Dean of Enrollment Services. E-mail: *bdjones@htc.edu* Web: *www.htc.edu*

JARVIS CHRISTIAN COLLEGE
Hawkins, TX 75765 E-2

(903) 769-5730
(800) 292-9517; Fax: (903) 769-1282

Full-time: 237 men, 330 women	**Faculty:** 41
Part-time: 2 men, 2 women	**Ph.D.s:** 54%
Graduate: none	**Student/Faculty:** 14 to 1
Year: semesters, summer session	**Tuition:** $5550
Application Deadline: August 1	**Room & Board:** $3485
Freshman Class: n/av	
SAT I: recommended	**ACT:** required
	NONCOMPETITIVE

Jarvis Christian College, founded in 1912, is a private liberal arts institution affiliated with the Disciples of Christ. There is 1 undergraduate school. The library contains 78,347 volumes, 4339 microform items, and 2431 audiovisual forms/CDs, and subscribes to 297 periodicals. Computerized library services include the card catalog, interlibrary loans, and database searching. Special learning facilities include a learning resource center, planetarium, and archives of the Black Disciples in Texas. The 243-acre campus is in a rural area 100 miles southeast of Dallas. Including residence halls, there are 17 buildings.

Student Life: 89% of undergraduates are from Texas. Others are from 14 states, 9 foreign countries, and Canada. 99% are from public schools. 95% are African American. 78% are Protestant; 21% claim no religious affiliation. The average age of freshmen is 19; all undergraduates, 20. 60% do not continue beyond their first year; 12% remain to graduate.

Housing: 750 students can be accommodated in college housing, which includes single-sex dormitories, on-campus apartments, and married-student housing. In addition, there are honors houses. On-campus housing is guaranteed for all 4 years. 88% of students live on campus; of those, 50% remain on campus on weekends. Alcohol is not permitted. All students may keep cars.

Activities: 5% of men belong to 4 national fraternities; 10% of women belong to 4 national sororities. There are 46 groups on campus, including cheerleading, choir, chorale, drama, drill team, honors, newspaper, political, professional, religious, social, and student government. Popular campus events include Miss/Mr. Jarvis Coronation, Hall of Fame Weekend, and Christmas Concert.

Sports: There are 4 intercollegiate sports for men and 4 for women, and 11 intramural sports for men and 11 for women. Facilities include 2 basketball gyms, a pool, tennis courts, volleyball courts, a soccer field, billiards, a flag football field, and a softball/baseball diamond.

Disabled Students: 46% of the campus is accessible. Wheelchair ramps, special parking, specially equipped rest rooms, special class scheduling, and lowered drinking fountains are available.

Services: Counseling and information services are available, as is tutoring in most subjects. There is remedial math, reading, and writing.

Campus Safety and Security: Measures include 24-hour foot and vehicle patrol, self-defense education, escort service, and informal discussions. There are pamphlets/posters/films and lighted pathways/sidewalks.

Programs of Study: Jarvis confers B.A., B.S., and B.B.A. degrees. Bachelor's degrees are awarded in BIOLOGICAL SCIENCE (biology/biological science), COMMUNICATIONS AND THE ARTS (English), COMPUTER AND PHYSICAL SCIENCE (chemistry, computer science, and mathematics), EDUCATION (elementary, music, reading, secondary, and special), HEALTH PROFESSIONS (premedicine), SOCIAL SCIENCE (criminal justice, history, religion, and sociology). Sociology, business, and computer science are the strongest academically. Business administration is the largest.

Required: A 54-credit general education requirement includes at least 30 hours in the major, plus courses in English, literature, math, religion, science, speech, social science, health, and phys ed. Other graduation requirements include a minimum 2.0 GPA, at least 124 credit hours, math and writing proficiencies, and satisfactory scores on the sophomore comprehensive exam and on the GRE.

Special: Jarvis offers co-op and work-study programs, internships, student-designed majors, and a general studies degree. Cross-registration is offered with members of the TADC consortium. Also available are the Brookhaven National Laboratory Semester Program, the UNCF Premedical Summer Program with Fisk University, and the Biomedical Sciences Program with Meharry Medical College. A 3-2 engineering degree is available with Texas at Arlington and a 3-2 nursing degree with University of Texas at Tyler. There are 4 national honor societies, a freshman honors program, and 2 departmental honors programs.

Faculty/Classroom: 61% of faculty are male; 39%, female. All teach undergraduates and 10% both teach and do research. The average class size in an introductory lecture is 30; in a laboratory, 16; and in a regular course, 16.

Admissions: 36% of the current freshmen were in the top fifth of their class; 50% were in the top two fifths.

Requirements: The ACT is required and the SAT I is recommended. In addition, applicants should graduate from an accredited secondary school with 16 academic credits, including 3 each in English and social science, 2 in math, and 1 in science. The GED is accepted. Graduates of nonaccredited high schools are given conditional admission. A GPA of 2.0 is required. AP and CLEP credits are accepted. Important factors in the admissions decision are parents or siblings attending the school, recommendations by alumni, and advanced placement or honor courses.

Procedure: Freshmen are admitted fall, spring, and summer. Entrance exams should be taken before entrance or during orientation week. Early decision applications should be filed by April 1; regular applications, by August 1 for fall entry, December 1 for spring entry, and May 1 for summer entry, along with a $25 fee. The college accepts all applicants. Notification is sent on a rolling basis.

Transfer: 34 transfer students enrolled in 2001-2002. Applicants must submit official transcripts from all schools of higher education attended and provide proof of honorable dismissal from the most recent one. 30 credits of 124 must be completed at Jarvis.

Visiting: There are regularly scheduled orientations for prospective students, including classroom visits, a tour of the campus, and review of the orientation guidebook. There are guides for informal visits and visitors may sit in on classes and stay overnight. To schedule a visit, contact the Office of Admissions.

Financial Aid: In 2001-2002, 98% of all students received some form of financial aid. 97% of freshmen and 90% of continuing students received need-based aid. The average freshman award was $8234. Of that total, scholarships or need-based grants averaged $4818 ($9635 maximum); loans averaged $1313 ($2625 maximum); work contracts averaged $780 ($1560 maximum); and categorical scholarships, or awards brought to school by the student averaged $2000. 6% of undergraduates work part time. Average annual earnings from campus work are $1560. The average financial indebtedness of the 2001 graduate was $9635. Jarvis is a member of CSS. The FAFSA or FFS and the college's own financial statement are required. The fall application deadline is July 15.

International Students: There are 19 international students enrolled. They must score 500 on the written TOEFL or 173 on the electronic version and also take the ACT.

Computers: The mainframe is an IBM AS400. The computer labs comprise 197 computers linked to the Internet. All students may access the system 8 A.M. to 10 P.M. There are no time limits. The fee is $250 per year.

Graduates: In 2001, 86 bachelor's degrees were awarded. The most popular majors were business (20%), criminal justice (14%), and biology (14%). In an average class, 8% graduate in 4 years, 23% in 5 years, and 24% in 6 years. 85 companies recruited on campus in 2000-2001. Of the 2000 graduating class, 10% were enrolled in graduate school within 6 months of graduation and 100% were employed.

Admissions Contact: Joan Williams, Director. A video is available. E-mail: *joan_williams@jarvis.edu* Web: *www.jarvis.edu*

LAMAR UNIVERSITY — E-3

Beaumont, TX 77710 — (409) 880-8888; Fax: (409) 880-8463

Full-time: 2327 men, 2826 women — **Faculty:** 303; IIA, --$
Part-time: 1310 men, 1954 women — **Ph.D.s:** 48%
Graduate: 256 men, 304 women — **Student/Faculty:** 15 to 1
Year: semesters, summer session — **Tuition:** $2616 ($9006)
Application Deadline: August 10 — **Room & Board:** $4200
Freshman Class: 6462 applied, 4448 accepted, 3127 enrolled
SAT I Verbal/Math: 482/473 — **ACT:** 22 — **LESS COMPETITIVE**

Lamar University-Beaumont, founded in 1923, is part of the Lamar University system. The university offers undergraduate degrees in arts and sciences, business, education, engineering, fine arts, communications, health and behavioral science, and technical arts. There are 7 undergraduate and 5 graduate schools. In addition to regional accreditation, LU has baccalaureate program accreditation with AACSB, ABET, CSWE, NASM, and NCATE. The library contains 900,000 volumes, and subscribes to 2800 periodicals. Computerized library services include the card catalog, interlibrary loans, and database searching. Special learning facilities include a learning resource center, art gallery, and radio station. The 200-acre campus is in an urban area 90 miles east of Houston. Including residence halls, there are 90 buildings.

Student Life: 96% of undergraduates are from Texas. 95% are from public schools. 79% are white; 16% African American. The average age of freshmen is 19; all undergraduates, 25. 40% do not continue beyond their first year; 19% remain to graduate.

Housing: 1700 students can be accommodated in college housing, which includes dormitories, on-campus apartments, fraternity houses, and sorority houses. In addition, there are special-interest houses. On-campus housing is guaranteed for all 4 years. 91% of students commute. Alcohol is not permitted. All students may keep cars.

Activities: 5% of men belong to 11 national fraternities; 5% of women belong to 7 national sororities. There are 120 groups on campus, including art, band, cheerleading, choir, chorale, chorus, computers, dance, drama, ethnic, film, honors, international, jazz band, literary magazine, marching band, musical theater, newspaper, opera, orchestra, pep band, photography, political, professional, radio and TV, religious, social, social service, student government, and symphony. Popular campus events include Springfest, Love Lamar Week, and Honors Brunch.

Sports: There are 7 intercollegiate sports for men and 6 for women, and 15 intramural sports for men and 15 for women. Facilities include a 10,000-seat multipurpose facility for basketball and other sports; a student center with games areas and a video lounge; a gym; an indoor/outdoor pool; a track; and a 17,000-seat stadium.

Disabled Students: All of the campus is accessible. Wheelchair ramps, elevators, special parking, specially equipped rest rooms, special class scheduling, lowered drinking fountains, and lowered telephones are available.

Services: Counseling and information services are available, as is tutoring in some subjects, including math and English. There is a reader service for the blind, and remedial math, reading, and writing.

Campus Safety and Security: Measures include 24-hour foot and vehicle patrol, self-defense education, informal discussions, and pamphlets/posters/films. There are lighted pathways/sidewalks.

Programs of Study: LU confers B.A., B.S., B.A.A.S., B.B.A., B.F.A., B.G.S., B.Mus., and B.S.W. degrees. Associate, master's, and doctoral degrees are also awarded. Bachelor's degrees are awarded in BIOLOGICAL SCIENCE (biology/biological science), BUSINESS (accounting, business administration and management, business economics, business law, marketing/retailing/merchandising, and personnel management), COMMUNICATIONS AND THE ARTS (advertising, communications, design, dramatic arts, English, fine arts, French, music, Spanish, and speech/debate/rhetoric), COMPUTER AND PHYSICAL SCIENCE (chemistry, computer programming, computer science, geology, information sciences and systems, mathematics, and physics), EDUCATION (art, early childhood, elementary, foreign languages, health, music, science, secondary, and special), ENGINEERING AND ENVIRONMENTAL DESIGN (chemical engineering, civil engineering, electrical/electronics engineering, industrial engineering, industrial engineering technology, and mechanical engineering), HEALTH PROFESSIONS (medical laboratory technology, nursing, occupational therapy, pharmacy, physical therapy, predentistry, premedicine, and speech pathology/audiology), SOCIAL SCIENCE (criminal justice, economics, family/consumer studies, history, political science/government, prelaw, psychology, public administration, social science, social work, and sociology). Engineering is the strongest academically. Arts and sciences are the largest.

Required: To graduate, all students must complete 124 to 132 total credit hours, with 30 hours in the major. Required courses include 12 hours of English, 6 hours each of electives, political science, and American history, and 4 hours each of lab science or math and physical activity and/or marching band and/or ROTC. Students must have a minimum 2.0 GPA.

Special: The university offers internships in social work, work-study programs, B.A.-B.S. degrees, a dual major in biochemistry, the general studies degree, credit for experience, nondegree study, and pass/fail options. There are 2 national honor societies, including Phi Beta Kappa, and a freshman honors program.

Faculty/Classroom: 58% of faculty are male; 42%, female. All teach undergraduates. The average class size in an introductory lecture is 50; in a laboratory, 25; and in a regular course, 24.

Admissions: 69% of the 2001-2002 applicants were accepted.

Requirements: The SAT I or ACT is required, with a minimum composite score of 850 on the SAT I or 20 on the ACT. SAT II: Subject tests in math are required for engineering and physical science majors. Applicants must be graduates of an accredited secondary school or have a GED certificate and must have completed 4 credits of English, 3 of math, 2 of science, and 2 1/2 of history. LU requires applicants to be in the upper 50% of their class. A GPA of 2.0 is required. AP and CLEP credits are accepted. Important factors in the admissions decision are advanced placement or honor courses, evidence of special talent, and leadership record.

Procedure: Freshmen are admitted to all sessions. Entrance exams should be taken in the fall of the senior year. Check with the school for current application deadlines and fee. Notification is sent on a rolling basis.

Transfer: Applicants must have a minimum 2.0 GPA and at least 18 credit hours earned. 30 credits of 132 must be completed at LU.

Visiting: There are regularly scheduled orientations for prospective students. There are guides for informal visits. To schedule a visit, contact the Admissions Office.

Financial Aid: 63% of undergraduates work part time. LU is a member of CSS. The CSS/Profile and the college's own financial statement are required. Check with the school for current deadlines.

International Students: They must score 500 on the written TOEFL and also take the SAT I or the ACT, scoring 800 on the SAT I.

Computers: The mainframe is a Honeywell DPS 8/49. There are 300 AT&T, IBM, Compaq, Sperry, and Macs available throughout the campus. All students may access the system. There are no time limits. It is strongly recommended that all students have a personal computer.

Admissions Contact: James Rush, Director of Academic Services. A video is available. E-mail: *admissions@hal.lamar.edu* Web: *lamar.edu*

LETOURNEAU UNIVERSITY

Longview, TX 75607 — E-2
(903) 233-3400
(800) 759-8811; (903) 233-3411

Full-time: 855 men, 384 women	**Faculty:** 58; IIB, -$
Part-time: 560 men, 1008 women	**Ph.D.s:** 72%
Graduate: 145 men, 146 women	**Student/Faculty:** 21 to 1
Year: semesters, summer session	**Tuition:** $13,410
Application Deadline: August 1	**Room & Board:** $5610
Freshman Class: 765 applied, 651 accepted, 244 enrolled	
SAT I Verbal/Math: 570/580	**ACT:** 25 **VERY COMPETITIVE**

LeTourneau University, founded in 1946, is a private, nondenominational Christian institution offering programs in aeronautical science, business administration, engineering, education, liberal arts, technology, computer science, natural and mathematical sciences, kinesiology, and others. There are 6 undergraduate schools and 1 graduate school. In addition to regional accreditation, LeTourneau has baccalaureate program accreditation with ABET and IACBE. The library contains 105,043 volumes, 45,641 microform items, and 4846 audiovisual forms/CDs, and subscribes to 779 periodicals. Computerized library services include the card catalog, interlibrary loans, and database searching. Special learning facilities include a learning resource center and a museum. The 162-acre campus is in an urban area 60 miles west of Shreveport, Louisiana, and 120 miles east of the Dallas/Fort Worth metroplex. Including residence halls, there are 55 buildings.

Student Life: 80% of undergraduates are from Texas. Others are from 49 states and 19 foreign countries. 57% are from public schools. 70% are white; 18% African American. The average age of freshmen is 19; all undergraduates, 21. 25% do not continue beyond their first year; 53% remain to graduate.

Housing: 863 students can be accommodated in college housing, which includes single-sex dormitories, on-campus apartments, and married-student housing. In addition, there are local society houses for men. On-campus housing is guaranteed for all 4 years. 71% of students live on campus; of those, 70% remain on campus on weekends. Alcohol is not permitted. All students may keep cars.

Activities: There are no fraternities or sororities. There are 22 groups on campus, including choir, chorale, chorus, computers, drama, honors, international, jazz band, newspaper, pep band, photography, political, professional, religious, social, social service, student government, and yearbook. Popular campus events include Spiritual Emphasis Week, Longview Blitz, and Longview Symphony.

Sports: There are 6 intercollegiate sports for men and 7 for women, and 16 intramural sports for men and 16 for women. Facilities include soccer, softball, baseball, and intramural fields, a 1000-seat gym, a 1000-seat arena/auditorium, 8 tennis courts, 3 racquetball courts, a weight room, a Nautilus room, a swimming pool, and an indoor running track.

Disabled Students: 90% of the campus is accessible. Wheelchair ramps, elevators, special parking, specially equipped rest rooms, special class scheduling, lowered drinking fountains, lowered telephones, and automated doors are available.

Services: Counseling and information services are available, as is tutoring in most subjects. There is remedial math and writing.

Campus Safety and Security: Measures include 24-hour foot and vehicle patrol, self-defense education, escort service, and informal discussions. There are pamphlets/posters/films and lighted pathways/sidewalks.

Programs of Study: LeTourneau confers B.A., B.S., and B.B.A. degrees. Associate and master's degrees are also awarded. Bachelor's degrees are awarded in BIOLOGICAL SCIENCE (biology/biological science), BUSINESS (accounting, business administration and management, management information systems, marketing management, and marketing/retailing/merchandising), COMMUNICATIONS AND THE ARTS (English), COMPUTER AND PHYSICAL SCIENCE (chemistry, computer mathematics, computer science, and mathematics), EDUCATION (business, elementary, physical, science, and secondary), ENGINEERING AND ENVIRONMENTAL DESIGN (aeronautical science, aeronautical technology, computer engineering, computer technology, electrical/electronics engineering, engineering, engineering technology, industrial administration/management, mechanical engineering, and welding engineering), HEALTH PROFESSIONS (health, premedicine, and preveterinary science), SOCIAL SCIENCE (biblical studies, history, interdisciplinary studies, prelaw, psychology, and public administration). Engineering, computer science, and math are the strongest academically. Engineering, aeronautical science, and business are the largest.

Required: All students must fulfill general curricula requirements, including 12 hours of biblical studies, 9 of English, 3 each of lab science, math, history, and humanities and social science, as well as 2 of phys ed and 1 of introduction to the university. A minimum of 126 semester credit hours, including at least 24 in the major, with a minimum GPA of 2.0 is required to graduate.

Special: LeTourneau offers co-op programs in engineering, business, accounting, computer science, biology, design technology, and others, internships through business and liberal arts programs, an American studies program with the Council for Christian Colleges and Universities, credit for experience, and study abroad in 7 countries. There is a freshman honors program and 1 departmental honors program.

Faculty/Classroom: 85% of faculty are male; 15%, female. 96% teach undergraduates and 20% both teach and do research. No introductory courses are taught by graduate students. The average class size in an introductory lecture is 24; in a laboratory, 16; and in a regular course, 18.

Admissions: 85% of the 2001-2002 applicants were accepted. The SAT I scores for the 2001-2002 freshman class were: Verbal--11% below 500, 44% between 500 and 599, 32% between 600 and 700, and 13% above 700; Math--12% below 500, 41% between 500 and 599, 35% between 600 and 700, and 11% above 700. The ACT scores were 6% below 21, 23% between 21 and 23, 29% between 24 and 26, 12% between 27 and 28, and 28% above 28. 47% of the current freshmen were in the top fifth of their class; 74% were in the top two fifths. There were 6 National Merit finalists. 10 freshmen graduated first in their class.

Requirements: The SAT I or ACT is required, with a recommended minimum composite score of 950 on the SAT I or 20 on the ACT. Applicants must be graduates of an accredited secondary school or have the GED. They should have completed 16 academic credits, including 4 in English, 3 each in math, social studies, and natural science, and 1 in computer science. An essay is required. LeTourneau requires applicants to be in the upper 50% of their class. A GPA of 2.5 is required. AP and CLEP credits are accepted. Important factors in the admissions decision are advanced placement or honor courses, personality/intangible qualities, and extracurricular activities record. Applications are accepted on-line at the school's web site.

Procedure: Freshmen are admitted to all sessions. Entrance exams should be taken by the fall of the senior year. There are early admissions and deferred admissions plans. Applications should be filed by August 1 for fall entry and January 1 for spring entry. The fall 2001 application fee was $25. Notification is sent on a rolling basis.

Transfer: 102 transfer students enrolled in 2001-2002. Applicants with at least 26 semester hours must have a minimum 2.0 GPA. Other students must satisfy freshman entrance requirements. 30 credits of 126 must be completed at LeTourneau.

Visiting: There are regularly scheduled orientations for prospective students. Visits are individualized and may include touring the school, attending classes, special events, or chapel, meeting with faculty and financial aid personnel, and staying in a dormitory. There are guides for informal visits and visitors may sit in on classes and stay overnight. To schedule a visit, contact the Visitor Coordinator at (903) 233-3454.

Financial Aid: In a recent year, 94% of all freshmen and 92% of continuing students received some form of financial aid. 71% of freshmen and 66% of continuing students received need-based aid. The average freshman award was $9591. 28% of undergraduates work part time. Average annual earnings from campus work are $1236. The average financial indebtedness of the 2000 graduate was $17,950. LeTourneau is a member of CSS. The FAFSA is required. The preferred fall application deadline is February 15.

International Students: There are 35 international students enrolled. The school actively recruits these students. They must score 500 on the written TOEFL or 173 on the electronic version and also take the SAT I or the ACT, scoring 950 on the SAT I or 20 on the ACT.

Computers: The mainframe is an HPM Series. Every dorm room on campus has 2 ports for access to the LeTNet and Web. The CAD lab has 25 computers, and there are 8 PCs in the library and 85 in computer labs. All students may access the system. There are no time limits and no fees.

Graduates: In 2001, 705 bachelor's degrees were awarded. The most popular majors were engineering and engineering technology (43%), aeronautical science (18%), and business (17%). In an average class, 30% graduate in 4 years, 45% in 5 years, and 50% in 6 years. Of the 2000 graduating class, 5% were enrolled in graduate school within 6 months of graduation and 94% were employed.

Admissions Contact: James Townsend, Director of Admissions. A video is available. E-mail: *admissions@letu.edu* Web: *www.letu.edu*

LUBBOCK CHRISTIAN UNIVERSITY B-2

Lubbock, TX 79407 (806) 720-7151
(800) 933-7601; Fax: (806) 720-7255

Full-time: 618 men, 814 women	**Faculty:** 75; IIB, --$
Part-time: 116 men, 153 women	**Ph.D.s:** 51%
Graduate: 60 men, 62 women	**Student/Faculty:** 19 to 1
Year: semesters, summer session	**Tuition:** $10,326
Application Deadline: open	**Room & Board:** $3900
Freshman Class: 703 applied, 653 accepted, 568 enrolled	
SAT I Verbal/Math: 490/500	**ACT:** 20 **LESS COMPETITIVE**

Lubbock Christian University, founded in 1957 in affiliation with the Churches of Christ, offers undergraduate degrees in liberal arts and professional studies and graduate credit in Bible studies and education. There are 3 undergraduate and 2 graduate schools. In addition to regional accreditation, Lubbock Christian has baccalaureate program accreditation with CSWE. The library contains 110,000 volumes, 92,360 microform items, and 510 audiovisual forms/CDs, and subscribes to 550 periodicals. Computerized library services include the card catalog, interlibrary loans, and database searching. Special learning facilities include a learning resource center and art gallery. The 20-acre campus is in a suburban area 300 miles from Dallas and 325 miles from Albuquerque, NM. Including residence halls, there are 19 buildings.

Student Life: 91% of undergraduates are from Texas. Others are from 29 states, 26 foreign countries, and Canada. 95% are from public schools. 82% are white; 10% Hispanic. Most are Protestant. The average age of freshmen is 20; all undergraduates, 24.

Housing: 600 students can be accommodated in college housing, which includes single-sex dormitories, on-campus apartments, and married-student housing. On-campus housing is guaranteed for all 4 years. 67% of students commute. Alcohol is not permitted. All students may keep cars.

Activities: There are no fraternities. There are 20 groups on campus, including cheerleading, chorus, computers, drama, drill team, honors, jazz band, musical theater, newspaper, pep band, professional, religious, social, student government, and yearbook. Popular campus events include High School Days, Encore, and Winter Fest.

Sports: There are 2 intercollegiate sports for men and 2 for women, and 20 intramural sports for men and 20 for women. Facilities include an athletic complex with basketball and volleyball, a field house, a stadium, an intramural field, and game rooms.

Disabled Students: 35% of the campus is accessible. Wheelchair ramps, elevators, special parking, specially equipped rest rooms, and special class scheduling are available.

Services: Counseling and information services are available, as is tutoring in every subject. There is a reader service for the blind, and remedial math, reading, and writing.

Campus Safety and Security: Measures include 24-hour foot and vehicle patrol and lighted pathways/sidewalks.

Programs of Study: Lubbock Christian confers B.A., B.S., B.B.A., B.S.I.S., B.S.N., and B.S.W. degrees. Associate and master's degrees are also awarded. Bachelor's degrees are awarded in AGRICULTURE (agricultural business management and animal science), BIOLOGICAL SCIENCE (biology/biological science), BUSINESS (accounting, banking and finance, business administration and management, and sports management), COMMUNICATIONS AND THE ARTS (communications and music), COMPUTER AND PHYSICAL SCIENCE (chemistry, information sciences and systems, and mathematics), EDUCATION (art, business, elementary, middle school, music, physical, science, and secondary), ENGINEERING AND ENVIRONMENTAL DESIGN (engineering and environmental science), HEALTH PROFESSIONS (exercise science, medical technology, and nursing), SOCIAL SCIENCE (biblical studies, humanities, ministries, physical fitness/movement, psychology, and social work). Education, business administration, and social work are the strongest academically. Elementary education, humanities, and organizational management are the largest.

Required: To graduate, students must complete 126 credit hours, including at least 44 in upper-division courses, 30 to 33 in the major, and 33 in residence after achieving senior status, with a minimum GPA of 2.5 overall and 2.25 in the major. All students must fulfill general education and biblical studies course requirements.

Special: Lubbock Christian offers co-op programs in engineering and computer sciences, internships in biblical studies, psychology, social work, and education, and cross-registration with Texas Tech University and its School of Allied Health. A general studies degree, a 3-2 engineering degree, student-designed majors, nondegree study, and pass/fail options are also available. There is 1 national honor society, a freshman honors program, and 1 departmental honors program.

Faculty/Classroom: 61% of faculty are male; 39%, female. All teach undergraduates. No introductory courses are taught by graduate students. The average class size in an introductory lecture is 28; in a laboratory, 25; and in a regular course, 18.

Admissions: 93% of the 2001-2002 applicants were accepted. The SAT I scores for the 2001-2002 freshman class were: Verbal--51% below 500, 33% between 500 and 599, 14% between 600 and 700, and 2% above 700; Math--48% below 500, 41% between 500 and 599, 8% between 600 and 700, and 3% above 700. The ACT scores were 53% below 21, 23% between 21 and 23, 16% between 24 and 26, 5% between 27 and 28, and 3% above 28. 29% of the current freshmen were in the top fifth of their class; 60% were in the top two fifths. There was 1 National Merit finalist. 11 freshmen graduated first in their class.

Requirements: The SAT I or ACT is required. In addition, applicants must be graduates of an accredited secondary school or have a GED certificate. A portfolio or audition (in applicable majors) and an interview are recommended. Lubbock Christian requires applicants to be in the upper 98% of their class. A GPA of 2.0 is required. AP and CLEP credits are accepted. Important factors in the admissions decision are ability to finance college education, parents or siblings attending the school, and personality/intangible qualities. Applications are accepted on-line via LCU's web page under Admissions.

Procedure: Freshmen are admitted to all sessions. Entrance exams should be taken before registration. Application deadlines are open. The fall 2001 application fee was $20. Notification is sent on a rolling basis. A waiting list is an active part of the admissions procedure.

Transfer: 252 transfer students enrolled in 2001-2002. Transfer students with fewer than 16 hours of college credit must meet freshman admission requirements, submit an official transcript from previously attended colleges or universities, and have a minimum GPA of 2.0. Only courses with a grade of C or above are transferred from another institution. 33 credits of 126 must be completed at Lubbock Christian.

Visiting: There are regularly scheduled orientations for prospective students. There are guides for informal visits and visitors may sit in on classes and stay overnight. To schedule a visit, contact Rhonda Crawford, Director of Recruiting.

Financial Aid: In 2001-2002, 80% of all freshmen and 85% of continuing students received some form of financial aid. 58% of freshmen and 60% of continuing students received need-based aid. The average freshman award was $14,114. Of that total, scholarships or need-based grants averaged $6752 ($14,226 maximum); loans averaged $4849 ($8500 maximum); work contracts averaged $1780 ($2000 maximum); and parental loans and other sources averaged $3872 ($14,781 maximum). 40% of undergraduates work part time. Average annual earnings from campus work are $596. The average financial indebtedness of the 2001 graduate was $24,000. The FAFSA is required. The fall application deadline is July 15.

International Students: There are 31 international students enrolled. They must score 500 on the written TOEFL and also take the SAT I or the ACT, scoring 860 on the SAT I or 18 on the ACT.

Computers: The mainframe is a DEC MicroVAX. There are also 39 PCs available in the computer lab, 10 in the English lab, 6 in the science lab, and 20 in the Success 2000 lab. All students may access the system. There are no time limits. The fee is $58.

Graduates: In 2001, 210 bachelor's degrees were awarded. The most popular majors were business or social work (32%), education (25%), and nursing (6%). In an average class, 3% graduate in 3 years, 18% in 4 years, 32% in 5 years, and 38% in 6 years. 10 companies recruited on campus in 2000-2001.

Admissions Contact: Rhonda Crawford, Director of Admissions. E-mail: *rhonda.crawford@lcu.edu* Web: *www.lcu.edu*

MCMURRY UNIVERSITY C-2

Abilene, TX 79697 (915) 793-4700
(800) 460-2392; Fax: (915) 793-4718

Full-time: 577 men, 595 women | **Faculty:** 76; IIB, --$
Part-time: 98 men, 108 women | **Ph.D.s:** 80%
Graduate: none | **Student/Faculty:** 15 to 1
Year: semesters, summer session | **Tuition:** $10,775
Application Deadline: open | **Room & Board:** $4512
Freshman Class: 674 applied, 616 accepted, 315 enrolled
SAT I Verbal/Math: 500/500 **ACT:** 21 **COMPETITIVE**

McMurry University, chartered in 1923, is a private liberal arts institution affiliated with the United Methodist Church. There are 4 undergraduate schools. The library contains 152,832 volumes, 6220 microform items, and 2845 audiovisual forms/CDs, and subscribes to 562 periodicals. Computerized library services include the card catalog, interlibrary loans, and database searching. Special learning facilities include a learning resource center, art gallery, and and several special book collections, including the McWhiney collection of Civil War-era books. The 41-acre campus is in an urban area 180 miles west of Dallas. Including residence halls, there are 21 buildings.

Student Life: 96% of undergraduates are from Texas. Others are from 11 states and 4 foreign countries. 98% are from public schools. 74% are white; 13% Hispanic. 71% are Protestant; 17% claim no religious affiliation; 12% Catholic. The average age of freshmen is 18; all undergraduates, 23. 34% do not continue beyond their first year; 39% remain to graduate.

Housing: 683 students can be accommodated in college housing, which includes single-sex dormitories and on-campus apartments. On-campus housing is available on a first-come, first-served basis. 57% of students commute. Alcohol is not permitted. All students may keep cars.

Activities: 20% of men belong to 8 local fraternities; 30% of women belong to 6 local sororities. There are 35 groups on campus, including art, band, cheerleading, choir, chorale, computers, drama, ethnic, honors, jazz band, literary magazine, marching band, musical theater, newspaper, political, professional, religious, social, social service, student government, and yearbook. Popular campus events include Parents Weekend, McMadness, and Sing Song.

Sports: There are 7 intercollegiate sports for men and 6 for women, and 15 intramural sports for men and 15 for women. Facilities include a 4500-seat track and football stadium, a 2200-seat gym, a 1500-seat auditorium, an intramural gym, a swimming pool and diving area, 2 racquetball courts, basketball, volleyball, and badminton courts, a soccer field, and a 875-seat baseball stadium.

Disabled Students: 70% of the campus is accessible. Wheelchair ramps, elevators, special parking, specially equipped rest rooms, special class scheduling, and lowered drinking fountains are available.

Services: Counseling and information services are available, as is tutoring in most subjects. There is remedial math, reading, and writing.

Campus Safety and Security: Measures include 24-hour foot and vehicle patrol, emergency telephones, and lighted pathways/sidewalks.

Programs of Study: McMurry confers B.A., B.S., B.B.A., B.F.A., B.Mus., B.Mus.Ed., B.S. Multidisciplinary Studies, and B.S.N. degrees. Bachelor's degrees are awarded in BIOLOGICAL SCIENCE (biochemistry and biology/biological science), BUSINESS (accounting, banking and finance, business administration and management, management information systems, management science, and marketing/retailing/merchandising), COMMUNICATIONS AND THE ARTS (art, ceramic art and design, communications, dramatic arts, English, multimedia, music, music performance, painting, piano/organ, Spanish, and voice), COMPUTER AND PHYSICAL SCIENCE (chemistry, computer science, mathematics, natural sciences, and physics), EDUCATION (bilingual/bicultural, music, and physical), ENGINEERING AND ENVIRONMENTAL DESIGN (environmental science), HEALTH PROFESSIONS (nursing), SOCIAL SCIENCE (economics, history, interdisciplinary studies, philosophy, political science/government, psychology, religion, and sociology). Education, biology, and chemistry are the strongest academically. Education, business, and biology are the largest.

Required: Students must complete 126 semester hours, including 27 in the major, with a GPA of at least 2.0. Distribution requirements vary with the degree but include courses in English, ethics, humanities, fine arts, science, math, social science, religion, political science, sociology, history, foreign language, and health fitness.

Special: McMurry offers internships, co-op programs, and cross-registration with Abilene Christian and Hardin-Simmons universities. There are work-study programs with the university and area businesses for seniors. B.A.-B.S. degrees in business administration, accounting, banking and finance, biology, chemistry, multidisciplinary studies, nursing, and computer science, and dual majors in math computer science, church music, and chemistry-business administration are available. A 3-2 engineering degree with Texas Tech University is offered, as is a Servant Leadership program, designed to instill principles of leadership. There are 14 national honor societies, a freshman honors program, and 22 departmental honors programs.

Faculty/Classroom: 66% of faculty are male; 34%, female. All teach undergraduates and 64% do research. The average class size in an introductory lecture is 27; in a laboratory, 14; and in a regular course, 17.

Admissions: 91% of the 2001-2002 applicants were accepted. The SAT I scores for the 2001-2002 freshman class were: Verbal--46% below 500, 40% between 500 and 599, and 14% between 600 and 700; Math--46% below 500, 40% between 500 and 599, 14% between 600 and 700, and 1% above 700. The ACT scores were 47% below 21, 22% between 21 and 23, 18% between 24 and 26, 9% between 27 and 28, and 4% above 28. 33% of the current freshmen were in the top fifth of their class; 68% were in the top two fifths. 6 freshmen graduated first in their class.

Requirements: The SAT I or ACT is required with a minimum composite score of 910 on the SAT I or 19 on the ACT. Those meeting the minimum score must rank in the top 40% of their high school class. Applicants need 16 academic credits, including 4 units of English, 3 each in math and social studies, and 2 each in foreign language and science. An interview is recommended. The GED is accepted with an average score of 55. A GPA of 2.0 is required. AP and CLEP credits are accepted. Important factors in the admissions decision are advanced placement or honor courses, leadership record, and extracurricular activities record.

Procedure: Freshmen are admitted to all sessions. Entrance exams should be taken in the junior year. There is a deferred admissions plan. Application deadlines are open. The fall 2001 application fee was $20. Notification is sent on a rolling basis.

Transfer: 139 transfer students enrolled in 2001-2002. All transfer students must have a GPA of at least 2.0. Those with fewer than 15 credit hours must submit high school transcripts and SAT I or ACT scores; those with 15 to 23 hrs need only school transcripts. 30 credits of 126 must be completed at McMurry.

Visiting: There are regularly scheduled orientations for prospective students. There are guides for informal visits and visitors may sit in on classes and stay overnight. To schedule a visit, contact the Admissions Office at *admissions@mcm.edu*.

Financial Aid: In 2001-2002, 97% of all freshmen and 95% of continuing students received some form of financial aid. 72% of freshmen and 74% of continuing students received need-based aid. The average freshman award was $11,954. Of that total, scholarships or need-based grants averaged $7212 ($10,245 maximum); loans averaged $5455 ($15,601 maximum); and work contracts averaged $1289 ($1650 maximum). 56% of undergraduates work part time. Average annual earnings from campus work are $1445. The average financial indebtedness of the 2001 graduate was $14,923. The FAFSA is required. The fall application deadline is August 15.

International Students: The school actively recruits these students. They must score 550 on the written TOEFL and also take the SAT I or the ACT, scoring 780 on the SAT I.

Computers: The mainframes consist of DEC ALPHA and Compaq Proliant file servers. There are 172 PCs available, including 30 in the academic enrichment center, 4 in the library, and 138 in discipline-specific computer labs. Access to the Internet is available from most of the computers for student use. All students may access the system at any time. There are no time limits and no fees.

Graduates: In 2001, 222 bachelor's degrees were awarded. The most popular majors were education (24%), business (24%), and biology (7%). In an average class, 1% graduate in 3 years, 23% in 4 years, 35% in 5 years, and 39% in 6 years. 9 companies recruited on campus in 2000-2001. Of the 2000 graduating class, 13% were enrolled in graduate school within 6 months of graduation and 83% were employed.

Admissions Contact: Amy Weyant, Director of Admissions.
E-mail: *weyanta@mcmurryadjm.mcm.edu* Web: *http://www.mcm.edu*

MIDWESTERN STATE UNIVERSITY D-2

Wichita Falls, TX 76308-2099 (940) 397-4334
(800) 842-1922; Fax: (940) 397-4672

Full-time: 1627 men, 2179 women | **Faculty:** 182; IIA, --$
Part-time: 642 men, 840 women | **Ph.D.s:** 72%
Graduate: 243 men, 435 women | **Student/Faculty:** 21 to 1
Year: semesters, summer session | **Tuition:** $2516 ($8906)
Application Deadline: August 7 | **Room & Board:** $4188
Freshman Class: 1348 applied, 1329 accepted, 807 enrolled
SAT I Verbal/Math: 474/486 **ACT:** 20 **NONCOMPETITIVE**

Midwestern State University, founded in 1922, is a public liberal arts institution offering courses in business administration, education, fine arts, health sciences, humanities, math and science, political science and public administration, and social and behavioral sciences. There are 6 undergraduate and 5 graduate schools. In addition to regional accreditation, MSU has baccalaureate program accreditation with ABET, ACBSP, ADA, NASM, NCATE, and NLN. The library contains 241,000 volumes, 158,000 microform items, and 6757 audiovisual forms/CDs, and subscribes to 1100 periodicals. Computerized library services include the card catalog, interlibrary loans, and database searching. Special learning facilities include an art gallery, planetarium, TV station, and greenhouse, and TTVN studio. The 172-acre campus is in an urban area 135 miles northwest of Dallas. Including residence halls, there are 31 buildings.

Student Life: 87% of undergraduates are from Texas. Others are from 49 states, 40 foreign countries, and Canada. 78% are white. The average age of all undergraduates is 25. 36% do not continue beyond their first year; 64% remain to graduate.

Housing: 733 students can be accommodated in college housing, which includes single-sex and coed dormitories, on-campus apartments, off-campus apartments, and married-student housing. In addition, there are honors houses. On-campus housing is guaranteed for the freshman year only and is available on a first-come, first-served basis. Priority is given to out-of-town students. 88% of students commute. Alcohol is not permitted. All students may keep cars.

Activities: 10% of men belong to 6 national fraternities; 10% of women belong to 6 national sororities. There are 102 groups on campus, including art, band, cheerleading, choir, chorale, chorus, computers, dance, drama, ethnic, honors, international, jazz band, literary magazine, marching band, newspaper, pep band, political, professional, radio and TV, religious, social, social service, student government, symphony, and yearbook. Popular campus events include Family Day, Spirit Days, and College Day Preview.

Sports: There are 4 intercollegiate sports for men and 4 for women, and 18 intramural sports for men and 21 for women. Facilities include a 5000-seat gym, a soccer stadium, tennis courts, an indoor swimming pool, a sand volleyball court, and a walking track.

Disabled Students: 99% of the campus is accessible. Wheelchair ramps, elevators, special parking, specially equipped rest rooms, special class scheduling, lowered drinking fountains, and lowered telephones are available.

Services: Counseling and information services are available, as is tutoring in some subjects, including algebra, sciences, and history. There is a reader service for the blind, and remedial math, reading, and writing.

Campus Safety and Security: Measures include 24-hour foot and vehicle patrol, self-defense education, informal discussions, and pamphlets/posters/films. There are lighted pathways/sidewalks and seminars on safety and living on campus.

Programs of Study: MSU confers B.A., B.S., B.A.A.S., B.B.A., B.F.A., B.M., B.S.C.J., B.S.D.H., B.S.I.S., B.S.M.T., B.S.N., B.S.R.C., B.S.R.S., and B.S.W. degrees. Associate and master's degrees are also awarded. Bachelor's degrees are awarded in BIOLOGICAL SCIENCE (biology/biological science), BUSINESS (accounting, banking and finance, business administration and management, business economics, international economics, management science, and marketing/retailing/merchandising), COMMUNICATIONS AND THE ARTS (communications, dramatic arts, English, fine arts, music, and Spanish), COMPUTER AND PHYSICAL SCIENCE (chemical technology, chemistry, computer science, geology, information sciences and systems, and mathematics), EDUCATION (music, and physical), ENGINEERING AND ENVIRONMENTAL DESIGN (engineering technology, environmental science, manufacturing engineering, and preengineering), HEALTH PROFESSIONS (dental hygiene, health care administration, health science, medical laboratory technology, nursing, predentistry, premedicine, prepharmacy, preveterinary science, radiological science, and respiratory therapy), SOCIAL SCIENCE (criminal justice, economics, history, humanities, interdisciplinary studies, political science/government, prelaw, psychology, social work, and sociology). Business and nursing are the largest.

Required: All students must earn a minimum GPA of 2.0 while taking 120 semester hours, 24 in the major. Distribution requirements include 6 hours from a list of humanities classes, 6 from social science, 7 to 10 hours from natural science, and additional phys ed requirements.

Special: An exchange program with the Monterrey Institute of Technology, internships with local firms and agencies, and study abroad in London are available. Dual majors, co-op programs in all majors, a general studies degree, credit for military experience, and nondegree study up to 12 hours are also offered. There are 23 national honor societies, and a freshman honors program.

Faculty/Classroom: 58% of faculty are male; 42%, female. All teach undergraduates. Graduate students teach 10% of introductory courses. The average class size in an introductory lecture is 25; in a laboratory, 20; and in a regular course, 25.

Admissions: 99% of the 2001-2002 applicants were accepted. The ACT scores for the 2001-2002 freshman class were: 26% below 21, 56% between 21 and 23, 16% between 24 and 26, and 2% above 28.

Requirements: The SAT I or ACT is required. In addition, the minimum required composite score on the SAT I or ACT is dependent on class rank. For students in the top quarter of the class, there is no minimum requirement; for students ranked in the second quarter of the class, the required scores are 870 on the SAT I or 18 on the ACT; for students ranked in the third quarter of the class, required scores are 950 on the SAT I or 20 on the ACT; for students ranked in the fourth quarter of the class required scores are 1030 on the SAT I or 22 on the ACT. High school credits should include 4 years of English, 3 years of math, 2 years of science, and 6 units of electives. The GED is accepted. MSU requires applicants to be in the upper 60% of their class. AP and CLEP credits are accepted. Ability to finance college education is an important factor in the admission decision.

Procedure: Freshmen are admitted to all sessions. Entrance exams should be taken before applying for admission. There are early decision and early admissions plans. Applications should be filed by August 7 for fall entry, December 15 for spring entry, and May 15 for summer entry. Notification is sent on a rolling basis. 411 early decision candidates were accepted for a recent class.

Transfer: 479 transfer students enrolled in a recent year. Transfer students with fewer than 18 semester hours must meet beginning freshmen criteria. All transfers must be eligible to reenroll in all previous schools. 24 credits of 120 must be completed at MSU.

Visiting: There are regularly scheduled orientations for prospective students, consisting of a college day preview each February, which introduces high school juniors, seniors, and their parents to the campus and faculty. There are also daily tours. There are guides for informal visits and visitors may sit in on classes and stay overnight. To schedule a visit, contact MSU Admissions.

Financial Aid: In a recent year, 38% of all freshmen and 58% of continuing students received some form of financial aid. 28% of freshmen and 24% of continuing students received need-based aid. The average freshman award was $1920. Of that total, scholarships or need-based grants averaged $1575 ($2550 maximum); loans averaged $2475 ($2625 maximum); and work contracts averaged $2670 ($3296 maximum). 8% of undergraduates work part time. Average annual earnings from campus work are $3710. The average financial indebtedness of a recent year's graduate was $17,500. MSU is a member of CSS. The FAFSA is required. The fall application deadline is June 1.

International Students: There were 300 international students enrolled in a recent year. The school actively recruits these students. They must score 500 on the written TOEFL and also take the SAT I or the ACT.

Computers: The mainframe is an IBM 4381 VSE operating system. There are also 145 IBM PCs and Apple IIes in classrooms. A 24-hour computer lab is available for student use. All students may access the system. There are no time limits and no fees.

Graduates: In 2001, 805 bachelor's degrees were awarded. The most popular majors were business (24%) and nursing (8%). In an average class, 30% graduate in 6 years.

Admissions Contact: Barbara Ramos Merkle, Director of Admissions. E-mail: *admissions@mwsu.edu* Web: *www.mwsu.edu*

NORTHWOOD UNIVERSITY D-2

Cedar Hill, TX 75104 (972) 293-5400

(800) 927-9663; Fax: (972) 291-3824

Full-time: 371 men, 469 women	**Faculty:** 15
Part-time: 106 men, 168 women	**Ph.D.s:** 50%
Graduate: none	**Student/Faculty:** 56 to 1
Year: terms, summer session	**Tuition:** $12,531
Application Deadline: August 1	**Room & Board:** $5604
Freshman Class: 717 applied, 480 accepted, 195 enrolled	
SAT I Verbal/Math: 470/460	**ACT:** 18 **COMPETITIVE**

Northwood University, founded in 1959 and whose Texas campus opened in 1966, is a private institution offering undergraduate degrees in business administration. Campuses are located in Florida, Michigan, and Texas. The library contains more than 20,000 volumes and 60 audiovisual forms/CDs, and subscribes to 160 periodicals. Computerized library services include the card catalog, interlibrary loans, and database searching. Special learning facilities include an art gallery. The 360-acre campus is in a suburban area 18 miles southwest of Dallas. Including residence halls, there are 13 buildings.

Student Life: 92% of undergraduates are from Texas. Others are from 12 states, 12 foreign countries, and Canada. 83% are from public schools. 44% are white; 25% Hispanic; 18% African American. The average age of freshmen is 19; all undergraduates, 20. 33% do not continue beyond their first year.

Housing: 164 students can be accommodated in college housing, which includes single-sex dormitories and on-campus apartments. On-campus housing is guaranteed for the freshman year only and is available on a first-come, first-served basis. 65% of students commute. All students may keep cars.

Activities: There are no fraternities or sororities. There are 15 groups on campus, including computers, ethnic, professional, religious, social, social service, student government, and yearbook. Popular campus events include Winter Semi-Formal, Talent Shows, and Fall and Spring Fling.

Sports: There are 5 intercollegiate sports for men and 5 for women, and 6 intramural sports for men and 5 for women. Facilities include an outdoor swimming pool, tennis court, baseball/softball fields, and jogging trails, along with a state recreational area adjacent to the campus.

Disabled Students: 75% of the campus is accessible. Wheelchair ramps, special parking, specially equipped rest rooms, special class scheduling, lowered drinking fountains, and lowered telephones are available.

Services: Counseling and information services are available, as is tutoring in most subjects. There is a reader service for the blind and remedial math, and tutoring for any subject at a student's request.

Campus Safety and Security: Measures include 24-hour foot and vehicle patrol, informal discussions, pamphlets/posters/films, and lighted pathways/sidewalks.

Programs of Study: Northwood confers the B.B.A. degree. Associate degrees are also awarded. Bachelor's degrees are awarded in BUSINESS (accounting, apparel and accessories marketing, banking and finance, business administration and management, hotel/motel and restaurant management, international business management, management information systems, marketing management, and transportation and travel marketing), COMPUTER AND PHYSICAL SCIENCE (computer management), ENGINEERING AND ENVIRONMENTAL DESIGN (systems engineering). Management, marketing, and automotive marketing are the strongest academically and have the largest enrollments.

Required: To graduate, all students must complete at least 180 term credit hours, including 36 in the major, with a minimum GPA of 2.0. Students must complete the general studies core curriculum, 6 credits of computer science management, and 2 credits of executive fitness. Internships for 1 to 6 credits are required in some majors.

Special: Study abroad in 10 countries, accelerated degree programs, and dual majors and externships in most majors are offered. There is a freshman honors program.

Faculty/Classroom: 84% of faculty are male; 16%, female. All teach undergraduates. The average class size in an introductory lecture is 35; in a laboratory, 20; and in a regular course, 25.

Admissions: 67% of the 2001-2002 applicants were accepted. The ACT scores for the 2001-2002 freshman class were: 78% below 21, 15% between 21 and 23, 4% between 24 and 26, and 2% between 27 and 28. 26% of the current freshmen were in the top fifth of their class; 46% were in the top two fifths.

Requirements: The SAT I or ACT is required. In addition, applicants must be graduates of an accredited secondary school with a 2.0 GPA or have a GED certificate. An interview and essay are recommended. A GPA of 2.0 is required. AP and CLEP credits are accepted. Important factors in the admissions decision are advanced placement or honor courses, evidence of special talent, and leadership record. Applications are accepted on-line through the university's web site.

Procedure: Freshmen are admitted to all sessions. Entrance exams should be taken by December of the senior year. There are early admissions and deferred admissions plans. Applications should be filed by August 1 for fall entry, November 15 for winter entry, February 15 for spring entry, and June 1 for summer entry. Notification is sent on a rolling basis.

Transfer: 76 transfer students enrolled in 2001-2002. Applicants must have earned a minimum of 12 credit hours and a 2.0 GPA. They must submit official transcripts from all previous colleges attended and the final high school transcript. 45 credits of 180 must be completed at Northwood.

Visiting: There are regularly scheduled orientations for prospective students. There are guides for informal visits and visitors may sit in on classes and stay overnight. To schedule a visit, contact the Admissions Office.

Financial Aid: In 2001-2002, 88% of all freshmen and 85% of continuing students received some form of financial aid. 73% of freshmen and 85% of continuing students received need-based aid. The average freshman award was $17,432. Of that total, scholarships or need-based grants averaged $5240; loans averaged $2683; and work contracts averaged $3001. 17% of undergraduates work part time. Average annual earnings from campus work are $1575. The average financial indebtedness of the 2001 graduate was $17,125. The FAFSA is required. The fall application deadline is March 15.

International Students: There are 54 international students enrolled. The school actively recruits these students. They must score 500 on the written TOEFL or 173 on the electronic version and also take the SAT I or the ACT, scoring 16.

Computers: The mainframe is an IBM RS/6000. Students have personal server space on the Novell system, with full Internet access and e-mail through the Michigan campus to all locations. Computer labs on the Texas campus feature Pentium processors. All students may access the system 3 P.M. to midnight Monday through Friday and 8:30 A.M. to 8:30 P.M. on weekends. There are no time limits. The fee is $35.

Graduates: In 2001, 86 bachelor's degrees were awarded. The most popular majors were management (17%), international business (16%), and accounting (14%). In an average class, 90% graduate in 4 years, and 100% in 5 years. 50 companies recruited on campus in 2000-2001. Of the 2000 graduating class, 2% were enrolled in graduate school within 6 months of graduation and all were employed.

Admissions Contact: James R. Hickerson, Admissions Director. A video is available. E-mail: *txadmit@northwood.edu*
Web: *www.northwood.edu*

OUR LADY OF THE LAKE UNIVERSITY OF SAN ANTONIO — D-4

San Antonio, TX 78207-4689 — **(210) 434-6711, ext. 314**
(800) 436-6558; Fax: (210) 431-4036

Full-time: 277 men, 1053 women	**Faculty:** 100; IIA, --$
Part-time: 197 men, 669 women	**Ph.D.s:** 69%
Graduate: 343 men, 785 women	**Student/Faculty:** 13 to 1
Year: semesters, summer session	**Tuition:** $12,786
Application Deadline: open	**Room & Board:** $4550
Freshman Class: 2285 applied, 1405 accepted, 401 enrolled	
SAT I or ACT: required	**COMPETITIVE**

Our Lady of the Lake, founded as a private Catholic institution in 1895 by the Sisters of Divine Providence, offers programs in the arts and sciences, business, education, and social service. There are 4 undergraduate and 4 graduate schools. In addition to regional accreditation, The Lake has baccalaureate program accreditation with ASLA and CSWE. The 2 libraries contain 127,441 volumes, 132,970 microform items, and 6877 audiovisual forms/CDs, and subscribe to 32,047 periodicals. Computerized library services include interlibrary loans and database searching. Special learning facilities include a learning resource center and a demonstration school (early childhood to grade 8), and a communication/learning disorders center. The 72-acre campus is in an urban area about 4 miles west of downtown San Antonio. Including residence halls, there are 14 buildings.

Student Life: 99% of undergraduates are from Texas. Others are from 28 states, 17 foreign countries, and Canada. 53% are Hispanic; 32% white. Most are Catholic. The average age of freshmen is 18; all undergraduates, 28. 40% do not continue beyond their first year; 32% remain to graduate.

Housing: 465 students can be accommodated in college housing, which includes coed dormitories. In addition, there are honors houses, quiet and smoke-free housing, and special housing for disabled students. On-campus housing is guaranteed for all 4 years. 76% of students commute. All students may keep cars.

Activities: There are no fraternities or sororities. There are 35 groups on campus, including art, cheerleading, choir, chorus, computers, dance, drama, ethnic, honors, music ensembles, newspaper, political, professional, radio and TV, religious, social, social service, student government, and symphony. Popular campus events include Spirit Week.

Sports: There are 9 intramural sports for men and 9 for women. Facilities include playing fields, tennis courts, indoor and outdoor pools, and a gym equipped for weight lifting, aerobics, and other indoor sports.

Disabled Students: 99% of the campus is accessible. Wheelchair ramps, elevators, special parking, specially equipped rest rooms, and special class scheduling are available.

Services: Counseling and information services are available, as is tutoring in some subjects. There is a reader service for the blind, and remedial math, reading, and writing.

Campus Safety and Security: Measures include 24-hour foot and vehicle patrol, pamphlets/posters/films, and lighted pathways/sidewalks.

Programs of Study: The Lake confers B.A., B.S., B.A.S., B.B.A., and B.S.W. degrees. Master's and doctoral degrees are also awarded. Bachelor's degrees are awarded in BIOLOGICAL SCIENCE (biology/biological science), BUSINESS (accounting, business administration and management, human resources, management information systems, marketing management, and personnel management), COMMUNICATIONS AND THE ARTS (art, communications, dramatic arts, English, fine arts, music, and Spanish), COMPUTER AND PHYSICAL SCIENCE (chemistry, information sciences and systems, mathematics, and natural sciences), EDUCATION (art, early childhood, and special), HEALTH PROFESSIONS (speech pathology/audiology), SOCIAL SCIENCE (American studies, behavioral science, history, liberal arts/general studies, philosophy, political science/government, psychology, religion, social studies, social work, and sociology). Biology and chemistry are the strongest academically. Management (business administration) is the largest.

Required: A general education requirement includes competencies in English, math, the natural, social, and behavioral sciences, religion, philosophy, literature, art, history, and phys ed. Other graduation requirements are a minimum 2.0 GPA, 128 credit hours, requirements specific to the major, and satisfactory scores on the COMP/ACT.

Special: There is cross-registration through the United Colleges of San Antonio. Dual majors are possible in the B.A.-B.B.A. programs. A 3-2 engineering degree is offered with Texas Tech and Washington Universities. Credit by exam and for life/work/military experience is available, as is a special degree program for working adults/nontraditional students through the Weekend College.

Faculty/Classroom: 52% of faculty are male; 48%, female.

Admissions: 61% of the 2001-2002 applicants were accepted.

Requirements: The SAT I or ACT is required. In addition, applicants should graduate from an accredited secondary school with 16 academic credits, including 4 in English, 3 in social studies, and 2 each in math and lab science. A combination of SAT I or ACT scores and high school

GPA or class rank determines admission. A GED with an average minimum score of 45 on each of the 5 tests and a satisfactory SAT I or ACT score are also acceptable. Mature students returning to school may waive the SAT I/ACT requirement for the college's own testing. AP and CLEP credits are accepted.

Procedure: Freshmen are admitted to all sessions. Entrance exams should be taken prior to December of the senior year. There are deferred admissions and rolling admissions plans. Application deadlines are open. The application fee is $25.

Transfer: 122 transfer students enrolled in 2001-2002. Transfer applicants with 30 or more credit hours and a minimum 2.0 GPA are accepted. Others are evaluated by the same criteria as freshmen applicants. 30 credits of 128 must be completed at The Lake.

Visiting: There are regularly scheduled orientations for prospective students. There are guides for informal visits and visitors may sit in on classes and stay overnight. To schedule a visit, contact the Admissions Office.

Financial Aid: In a recent year, 99% of all freshmen and 78% of continuing students received some form of financial aid. 93% of freshmen and 70% of continuing students received need-based aid. The average freshman award was $12,369. Of that total, scholarships or need-based grants averaged $6578; loans averaged $4205; and work contracts averaged $1586 ($2500 maximum). 28% of undergraduates work part time. Average annual earnings from campus work are $2000. The average financial indebtedness of the 2001 graduate was $17,650. The Lake is a member of CSS. The FAFSA or FFS is required.

International Students: There were 27 international students enrolled in a recent year. The school actively recruits these students. They must score 525 on the written TOEFL.

Computers: A UNIX server and a Novell PC network serve 3 different computer labs, which house a total of about 110 PCs or terminals for student use. All students may access the system. There are no time limits and no fees.

Graduates: In 2001, 426 bachelor's degrees were awarded. The most popular majors were business/marketing (25%), psychology (13%), and liberal arts/general studies (11%). In an average class, 13% graduate in 4 years, 25% in 5 years, and 29% in 6 years.

Admissions Contact: Michael Boatner, Acting Director Admissions.
E-mail: *admission@lake.ollusa.edu* Web: *www.ollusa.edu*

PAUL QUINN COLLEGE D-3

Dallas, TX 75241-4398 **(214) 302-3575 or 302-3520**
(800) 237-2648; Fax: (214) 302-3559

Full-time: 300 men, 450 women	**Faculty:** n/av
Part-time: 5 men, 15 women	**Ph.D.s:** n/av
Graduate: none	**Student/Faculty:** 8 to 1
Year: semesters, summer session	**Tuition:** $4700
Application Deadline: see profile	**Room & Board:** $3600
Freshman Class: n/av	
SAT I or ACT: required	**LESS COMPETITIVE**

Paul Quinn College, founded in 1872, is a coeducational liberal arts college affiliated with the African Methodist Episcopal Church. Figures in the above capsule, and in this profile, are approximate. In addition to regional accreditation, PQC has baccalaureate program accreditation with CSWE. The library contains 88,187 volumes and 30,550 microform items, and subscribes to 131 periodicals. Special learning facilities include a learning resource center. The 130-acre campus is in an urban area 12 miles from downtown Dallas. Including residence halls, there are 8 buildings.

Student Life: 61% of undergraduates are from Texas. Others are from 7 states. 89% are from public schools. 90% are African American; 10% Hispanic. The average age of freshmen is 18; all undergraduates, 20. 20% do not continue beyond their first year; 65% remain to graduate.

Housing: 700 students can be accommodated in college housing, which includes coed dormitories. On-campus housing is guaranteed for all 4 years. 51% of students commute. Alcohol is not permitted. All students may keep cars.

Activities: 40% of men belong to 4 national fraternities; 30% of women belong to 3 national sororities. There are 20 groups on campus, including cheerleading, choir, chorale, computers, dance, ethnic, newspaper, religious, social service, student government, and yearbook. Popular campus events include Honors Day and Founders Day.

Sports: There are 3 intercollegiate sports for men and 3 for women, and 5 intramural sports for men and 5 for women.

Services: There is remedial math, reading, and writing. Tutoring is available.

Campus Safety and Security: Measures include 24-hour foot and vehicle patrol.

Programs of Study: Bachelor's degrees are awarded in BIOLOGICAL SCIENCE (biology/biological science), BUSINESS (accounting, and business administration and management), COMMUNICATIONS AND THE ARTS (English and music), COMPUTER AND PHYSICAL SCIENCE (computer science and mathematics), EDUCATION (physical and secondary), SOCIAL SCIENCE (history, religion, and sociology).

Required: To graduate, students must complete at least 128 credits including a core curriculum, internship, and health and phys ed.

Special: Co-op programs, work-study, B.A.-B.S. degree, general studies degress, an nondegree study are available.

Requirements: The SAT I or ACT is required and high school transcripts must be submitted. A GPA of 2.0 is required. CLEP credit is accepted. Important factors in the admissions decision are leadership record, advanced placement or honor courses, and recommendations by school officials.

Procedure: Check with the school for current application deadlines and fees.

Transfer: Applicants must meet the basic admissions requirements. 30 credits of 128 must be completed at PQC.

Visiting: There are regularly scheduled orientations for prospective students. There are guides for informal visits and visitors may sit in on classes and stay overnight. To schedule a visit, contact the Director of Admissions.

Financial Aid: PQC is a member of CSS. The FAFSA and the previous year's student's/parents' tax forms are required. Check with the school for current deadlines.

International Students: They must score 480 on the written TOEFL and also take the SAT I or the ACT, scoring 700.

Computers: The mainframe is an IBM 3400. All students may access the system. There are no time limits and no fees.

Admissions Contact: Ralph Spencer, Jr., Admissions Officer.

PRAIRIE VIEW A&M UNIVERSITY E-3

Prairie View, TX 77446 **(936) 857-2618; Fax: (936) 857-2699**

Recognized candidate for accreditation

Full-time: 2217 men, 2673 women	**Faculty:** 314; IIA, --$
Part-time: 150 men, 347 women	**Ph.D.s:** 65%
Graduate: 393 men, 967 women	**Student/Faculty:** 16 to 1
Year: semesters, summer session	**Tuition:** $3172 ($9487)
Application Deadline: July 1	**Room & Board:** n/av
Freshman Class: 2143 applied, 2073 accepted, 1429 enrolled	
SAT I Verbal/Math: 410/410	**ACT:** 17 **LESS COMPETITIVE**

Prairie View A&M University, established in 1878, is a comprehensive unit of the Texas A&M University System, offering undergraduate and graduate degree programs in applied sciences and engineering technology, business, engineering, nursing, arts and sciences, education, agriculture and human sciences, architecture, juvenile justice, and psychology. There are 8 undergraduate and 6 graduate schools. In addition to regional accreditation, PVAMU has baccalaureate program accreditation with ABET, CSWE, NAAB, NCATE, and NLN. The library contains more than 240,000 volumes, 260,000 microform items, and 100,000 audiovisual forms/CDs, and subscribes to 1600 periodicals. Computerized library services include the card catalog, interlibrary loans, and database searching. Special learning facilities include a learning resource center and radio station. The 1440-acre campus is in a small town 40 miles northwest of Houston. Including residence halls, there are 47 buildings.

Student Life: 93% of undergraduates are from Texas. Others are from 40 states and 44 foreign countries. 90% are from public schools. 90% are African American. The average age of freshmen is 18; all undergraduates, 22. 30% do not continue beyond their first year; 32% remain to graduate.

Housing: 3102 students can be accommodated in college housing, which includes coed dormitories and on-campus apartments. In addition, there are special-interest houses, and an intensive learning community for 600 upperclass students. On-campus housing is guaranteed for the freshman year only and is available on a first-come, first-served basis. 75% of students live on campus; of those, 40% remain on campus on weekends. Alcohol is not permitted. All students may keep cars.

Activities: 8% of men belong to 4 national fraternities; 8% of women belong to 4 national sororities. There are 30 groups on campus, including band, cheerleading, choir, chorus, dance, drama, drill team, ethnic, honors, international, jazz band, marching band, newspaper, orchestra, photography, political, professional, radio and TV, religious, social, social service, student government, and yearbook. Popular campus events include Honors Week, Family Day, and trail rides.

Sports: There are 7 intercollegiate sports for men and 9 for women, and 6 intramural sports for men and 4 for women. Facilities include a 5000-seat stadium and a large athletic and recreation complex.

Disabled Students: 5% of the campus is accessible. Wheelchair ramps, elevators, special parking, and specially equipped rest rooms are available.

Services: Counseling and information services are available, as is tutoring in some subjects. There is a reader service for the blind, and remedial math, reading, and writing.

Campus Safety and Security: Measures include 24-hour foot and vehicle patrol, informal discussions, pamphlets/posters/films, and emergency telephones. There are lighted pathways/sidewalks and a 24-hour department of traffic and security.

Programs of Study: PVAMU confers B.A., B.S., B.Arch., B.A.S.W., B.B.A., B.S.Ag., B.S.C.E., B.S.C.E.T., B.S.C.H.E., B.S.C.J., B.S.Diet., B.S.E.E., B.S.E.E.T., B.S.H.S., B.S.I.S., B.S.I.T., B.S.M.E., B.S.N., and B.S.T.C.H. degrees. Master's and doctoral degrees are also awarded. Bachelor's degrees are awarded in AGRICULTURE (agricultural business management, agricultural economics, agronomy, and animal science), BIOLOGICAL SCIENCE (biology/biological science), BUSINESS (accounting, banking and finance, business administration and management, and marketing/retailing/merchandising), COMMUNICATIONS AND THE ARTS (art, broadcasting, communications, dramatic arts, English, journalism, music, Spanish, and speech/debate/rhetoric), COMPUTER AND PHYSICAL SCIENCE (chemistry, computer science, mathematics, and physics), EDUCATION (physical), ENGINEERING AND ENVIRONMENTAL DESIGN (architecture, chemical engineering, civil engineering, computer engineering, electrical/electronics engineering, engineering technology, industrial engineering technology, and mechanical engineering), HEALTH PROFESSIONS (health, medical technology, and nursing), SOCIAL SCIENCE (criminal justice, dietetics, family and community services, geography, history, interdisciplinary studies, political science/government, psychology, social work, and sociology). Engineering, nursing and natural sciences are the strongest academically. Education, engineering, and business are the largest.

Required: All students must complete 120 semester hours, with a minimum GPA of 2.5 or higher, depending on the major. Completion of a 42-hour core curriculum is required. Some majors require a comprehensive exam or thesis.

Special: Cooperative programs and internships in various majors, work-study programs, and combined B.A.-B.S. degrees in chemistry, biology, math, and computer science are offered. There are 24 national honor societies, including Phi Beta Kappa, and a freshman honors program. Most departments have honors programs.

Faculty/Classroom: 64% of faculty are male; 36%, female. 93% teach undergraduates, 3% do research, and 3% do both. Graduate students teach 1% of introductory courses. The average class size in an introductory lecture is 70; in a laboratory, 15; and in a regular course, 35.

Admissions: 97% of the 2001-2002 applicants were accepted. The SAT I scores for the 2001-2002 freshman class were: Verbal--84% below 500, 15% between 500 and 599, and 1% between 600 and 700; Math--84% below 500, 14% between 500 and 599, and 2% between 600 and 700. The ACT scores were 85% below 21, 10% between 21 and 23, 4% between 24 and 26, and 1% between 27 and 28. 20% of the current freshmen were in the top fifth of their class; 43% were in the top two fifths.

Requirements: The SAT I or ACT is required. In addition, a GPA of at least 2.0 is necessary for financial aid eligibility. The minimum composite score must be 820 on the SAT I or 17 on the ACT. Applicants should be graduates of accredited high schools or have earned the GED. Secondary school preparation should include 4 years each of English and academic electives, 3 years each of math and social studies, and 2 years of science. PVAMU requires applicants to be in the upper 50% of their class. A GPA of 2.5 is required. AP and CLEP credits are accepted. Important factors in the admissions decision are leadership record, advanced placement or honor courses, and recommendations by school officials. Applications are accepted on-line via the Texas common application or the university's web site at *www.applytexas.org*.

Procedure: Freshmen are admitted to all sessions. Entrance exams should be taken during the junior or senior year of high school. There is a deferred admissions plan. Applications should be filed by July 1 for fall entry, November 1 for spring entry, and April 1 for summer entry, along with a $25 fee. Notification is sent on a rolling basis.

Transfer: 224 transfer students enrolled in 2001-2002. Transfer applicants must present at least a 2.0 GPA from the last college attended. 30 credits of a minimum of 120 must be completed at PVAMU.

Visiting: There are regularly scheduled orientations for prospective students, consisting of an orientation held 2 days prior to registration. There are guides for informal visits and visitors may sit in on classes and stay overnight. To schedule a visit, contact the Office of Records at (936) 857-2626 or *recruitment@pvamu.edu*.

Financial Aid: In 2001-2002, 72% of all freshmen received some form of financial aid. 48% of freshmen received need-based aid. The average freshman award was $3950. Of that total, scholarships or need-based grants averaged $2000 ($8600 maximum); loans averaged $2000 ($8625 maximum); and work contracts averaged $1900 ($3000 maximum). 42% of undergraduates work part time. Average annual earnings from campus work are $2200. The average financial indebtedness of the 2001 graduate was $1400. PVAMU is a member of CSS. The CSS/Profile or FAFSA and the college's own financial statement are required. The fall application deadline is April 15.

International Students: There are 127 international students enrolled. They must score 500 on the written TOEFL and also take the SAT I or the ACT, scoring 820 on the SAT I.

Computers: The mainframe is an IBM 4361. A student computer center is available, as are IBM and AT&T PCs in the library. Students enrolled in computer courses or working in offices may access the system. After students receive security checks and training, PCs are available for use in courses. There are no fees. It is strongly recommended that all students have a personal computer.

Graduates: In 2001, 705 bachelor's degrees were awarded. The most popular majors were nursing (12%), biology (8%), and interdisciplinary studies education (7%). In an average class, 32% graduate in 6 years. 457 companies recruited on campus in 2000-2001. Of the 2000 graduating class, 22% were enrolled in graduate school within 6 months of graduation and 71% were employed.

Admissions Contact: Mary Gooch, Director of Admissions. A video is available. E-mail: *admissions@pvamu.edu* Web: *www.pvamu.edu*

RICE UNIVERSITY — E-3
Houston, TX 77251-1892 — (713) 348-7423
(800) 527-OWLS; Fax: (713) 348-5952

Full-time: 1411 men, 1302 women	**Faculty:** 413; I, ++$
Part-time: 86 men, 91 women	**Ph.D.s:** 98%
Graduate: 1039 men, 605 women	**Student/Faculty:** 6 to 1
Year: semesters, summer session	**Tuition:** $17,125
Application Deadline: January 2	**Room & Board:** $7200
Freshman Class: n/av	
SAT I or ACT: required	**MOST COMPETITIVE**

Rice University, founded in 1912, is a private institution offering undergraduate and graduate programs through the divisions of Engineering, Natural Sciences, Humanities, Social Sciences, Music, Architecture, and Administrative Sciences. There are 6 undergraduate and 7 graduate schools. In addition to regional accreditation, Rice has baccalaureate program accreditation with ABET and NAAB. The library contains 2 million volumes, 2.7 million microform items, and 47,000 audiovisual forms/CDs, and subscribes to 15,000 periodicals. Computerized library services include the card catalog and database searching. Special learning facilities include an art gallery, radio station, and media center. The 300-acre campus is in an urban area 3 miles southwest of downtown Houston. Including residence halls, there are 67 buildings.

Student Life: 54% of undergraduates are from Texas. Others are from 49 states, 32 foreign countries, and Canada. 53% are white; 14% Asian American; 11% Hispanic. The average age of freshmen is 18; all undergraduates, 20. 4% do not continue beyond their first year; 89% remain to graduate.

Housing: 76% of students can be accommodated in college housing, which includes coed dormitories. On-campus housing is available on a lottery system for upperclassmen. 64% of students live on campus; of those, 95% remain on campus on weekends. All students may keep cars.

Activities: There are no fraternities or sororities. There are more than 290 groups on campus, including academic, art, band, cheerleading, chess, choir, chorale, chorus, computers, dance, debate, drama, ethnic, film, gay, honors, international, jazz band, literary magazine, marching band, musical theater, newspaper, orchestra, pep band, photography, political, professional, radio and TV, religious, social, social service, student government, symphony, and yearbook. Popular campus events include Baker Shakespeare Festival, an annual biking relay race, and Archi Arts, a costume ball.

Sports: There are 7 intercollegiate sports for men and 7 for women, and 20 intramural sports for men and 17 for women. Facilities include a 5000-seat gym, a pool, a track stadium, fields for soccer, lacrosse, and rugby, courts for tennis, squash, racquetball, volleyball, and basketball, and a 70,000-seat stadium.

Disabled Students: 90% of the campus is accessible. Wheelchair ramps, elevators, special parking, specially equipped rest rooms, special class scheduling, lowered drinking fountains, lowered telephones, and a stair lift are available.

Services: Counseling and information services are available, as is tutoring in every subject.

Campus Safety and Security: Measures include 24-hour foot and vehicle patrol, self-defense education, escort service, and shuttle buses. There are informal discussions, pamphlets/posters/films, emergency telephones, lighted pathways/sidewalks, and a campus police department.

Programs of Study: Rice confers B.A., B.S., B.Arch., B.F.A., and B.Mus. degrees. Master's and doctoral degrees are also awarded. Bachelor's degrees are awarded in AGRICULTURE (agriculture), BIOLOGICAL SCIENCE (biology/biological science), BUSINESS (marketing/retailing/merchandising, and trade and industrial supervision and management), COMMUNICATIONS AND THE ARTS (communications, communications technology, English, and visual and performing arts), COMPUTER AND PHYSICAL SCIENCE (information sciences and systems, and physical sciences), EDUCATION (education, foreign languages, library science, and mathematics), ENGINEERING AND ENVIRONMENTAL DESIGN (architecture, engineering, engineering technology, environmental science, and military science), HEALTH PROFESSIONS (health science), SOCIAL SCIENCE (area studies, home economics, interdisciplinary studies, law, liberal arts/general studies, parks and recreation management, philosophy, psychology, public administration, religion, social science, and theological studies).

Required: All students must complete at least 120 credits, with a 1.67 overall GPA and a 2.0 GPA in the major field. Core requirements include 12 credit/semester hours in natural sciences, social sciences, or humanities, depending on the major, and additional courses in these fields to meet distribution requirements. All students take 2 semesters of phys ed. At least 48 semester hours in upper-level courses are required.

Special: Rice offers an 8-year guaranteed medical school program with the Baylor College of Medicine; a joint program in law for BA/JD with Columbia University School of Law; a 5-year joint degree program for BSE/MSE in engineering; a 5-year joint degree for BSE/MBA in engineering and business. There are 10 national honor societies, including Phi Beta Kappa, and 9 departmental honors programs.

Faculty/Classroom: 79% of faculty are male; 21%, female. All both teach and do research. Graduate students teach 4% of introductory courses. The average class size in a regular course is 13.

Admissions: The SAT I scores for the 2001-2002 freshman class were: Verbal--2% below 500, 10% between 500 and 599, 31% between 600 and 700, and 57% above 700; Math--1% below 500, 7% between 500 and 599, 29% between 600 and 700, and 63% above 700. The ACT scores were 3% between 21 and 23, 27% between 24 and 26, and 70% above 28. 96 freshmen graduated first in their class. There were 163 National Merit Scholars.

Requirements: The SAT I or ACT is required, along with 3 SAT II: Subject tests, including the writing test. Potential engineering and natural science majors should also take math I or II and either chemistry or physics. Applicants should be high school graduates or have earned the GED. Secondary preparation should include 4 years of English, 3 years each of math and academic electives, and 2 years each of a foreign language, science, and social studies. An interview is recommended and a personal essay is required; architecture majors should submit a portfolio, and music majors should audition. Candidates must submit evaluations from a counselor and a teacher. AP and CLEP credits are accepted. Important factors in the admissions decision are advanced placement or honor courses, extracurricular activities record, and personality/intangible qualities. Applications are accepted on computer disk and on-line via the school's web site.

Procedure: Freshmen are admitted in the fall. Entrance exams should be taken between October and January of the senior year, depending on the decision plan. There are early decision, early admissions, and interim decision plans. Early decision applications should be filed by November 1; regular applications, by January 2 for fall entry, along with a $35 fee. Notification of early decision is sent December 15; regular decision, April 1; interim decision, February 10. 134 early decision candidates were accepted for the 2001-2002 class; 130 were accepted in 2001.

Transfer: 65 transfer students enrolled in 2001-2002. Transfer applicants should present a 3.2 GPA in previous college work, SAT I scores, 2 college teacher recommendations, high school and college transcripts, and a letter from the dean of current college. 60 credits of 120 must be completed at Rice.

Visiting: There are regularly scheduled orientations for prospective students. There are guides for informal visits and visitors may sit in on classes and stay overnight. To schedule a visit, contact the Office of Admissions at (800) 527-6957.

Financial Aid: In 2001-2002, 85% of all freshmen received some form of financial aid. 33% of freshmen and 40% of continuing students received need-based aid. There is a loan cap of $2475 per year for 4 years and a work-study cap of $1600 per year for 4 years. The average freshman award was $17,177. The average financial indebtedness of the 2001 graduate was $12,525. Rice is a member of CSS. The CSS/Profile or FAFSA and the parents' and student's tax returns are required. The fall application deadline is March 1.

International Students: There are 82 international students enrolled. They must score 550 on the written TOEFL and also take the SAT I or the ACT. Students must take SAT II: Subject tests in writing and 2 others.

Computers: There are also Mac and IBM PCs available in the residential colleges, computing center, the library, and academic labs. All students may access the system. There are no time limits and no fees. It is strongly recommended that all students have a personal computer.

Graduates: In 2001, 990 bachelor's degrees were awarded. The most popular majors were economics (8%), biology (7%), and electrical and computer engineering (7%). In an average class, 69% graduate in 4 years, 87% in 5 years, and 89% in 6 years. 272 companies recruited on campus in 2000-2001. Of the 2000 graduating class, 34% were enrolled in graduate school within 6 months of graduation and 58% were employed.

Admissions Contact: Julie M. Browning, Dean for Undergraduate Enrollment. Web: *www.rice.edu*

SAINT EDWARD'S UNIVERSITY — D-3

Austin, TX 78704 — (512) 448-8500
(800) 555-0164; Fax: (512) 464-8877

Full-time: 1018 men, 1306 women	**Faculty:** 138; IIA, --$
Part-time: 442 men, 603 women	**Ph.D.s:** 72%
Graduate: 343 men, 439 women	**Student/Faculty:** 17 to 1
Year: semesters, summer session	**Tuition:** $12,728
Application Deadline: July 1	**Room & Board:** $5118
Freshman Class: 1413 applied, 1042 accepted, 417 enrolled	
SAT I Verbal/Math: 540/540	**ACT:** 22 **COMPETITIVE**

Saint Edward's University, founded in 1885, is an independent Catholic institution offering undergraduate and graduate courses in liberal arts, human service, business administration, and computer science. There are 6 undergraduate and 5 graduate schools. In addition to regional accreditation, SEU has baccalaureate program accreditation with CSWE. The library contains 146,499 volumes, 100,454 microform items, and 2268 audiovisual forms/CDs, and subscribes to 988 periodicals. Computerized library services include the card catalog, interlibrary loans, and database searching. Special learning facilities include a learning resource center, art gallery, and a photography lab. The 160-acre campus is in an urban area in Austin. Including residence halls, there are 45 buildings.

Student Life: 90% of undergraduates are from Texas. Others are from 35 states, 40 foreign countries, and Canada. 78% are from public schools. 55% are white; 31% Hispanic. The average age of freshmen is 18; all undergraduates, 21. 22% do not continue beyond their first year; 51% remain to graduate.

Housing: 824 students can be accommodated in college housing, which includes single-sex and coed dormitories and on-campus apartments. On-campus housing is guaranteed for all 4 years. 64% of students commute. All students may keep cars.

Activities: There are no fraternities or sororities. There are 78 groups on campus, including art, cheerleading, choir, chorale, chorus, computers, dance, drama, ethnic, film, forensics, gay, honors, international, literary magazine, musical theater, newspaper, photography, political, professional, religious, social service, student government, and yearbook. Popular campus events include Festival of Lights, Multicultural Spring Fest, and Coffee Houses.

Sports: There are 5 intercollegiate sports for men and 5 for women, and 8 intramural sports for men and 8 for women. Facilities include 2 gyms, baseball and softball fields, 2 soccer fields, tennis, basketball, racquetball/handball, and volleyball courts, an indoor/outdoor pool, fitness center, and track.

Disabled Students: All of the campus is accessible. Wheelchair ramps, elevators, special parking, specially equipped rest rooms, special class scheduling, lowered drinking fountains, and lowered telephones are available.

Services: Counseling and information services are available, as is tutoring in every subject. There is a reader service for the blind, and remedial math, reading, and writing. There is also a "Learning Strategies" course.

Campus Safety and Security: Measures include 24-hour foot and vehicle patrol, self-defense education, escort service, and informal discussions. There are pamphlets/posters/films, emergency telephones, lighted pathways/sidewalks. The outside doors of residence halls are locked at all times. Residents are issued keys.

Programs of Study: SEU confers B.A., B.S., B.A.A.S., B.B.A., and B.L.S. degrees. Master's degrees are also awarded. Bachelor's degrees are awarded in BIOLOGICAL SCIENCE (biochemistry and biology/biological science), BUSINESS (accounting, banking and finance, business administration and management, international business management, management information systems, and marketing and distribution), COMMUNICATIONS AND THE ARTS (communications, creative writing, dramatic arts, English, English literature, fine arts, language arts, photography, and Spanish), COMPUTER AND PHYSICAL SCIENCE (chemistry, computer science, information sciences and systems, and mathematics), EDUCATION (bilingual/bicultural, elementary, physical, secondary, and social studies), ENGINEERING AND ENVIRONMENTAL DESIGN (preengineering), HEALTH PROFESSIONS (physical therapy, predentistry, and premedicine), SOCIAL SCIENCE (criminal justice, economics, history, international studies, liberal arts/general studies, philosophy, physical fitness/movement, political science/government, prelaw, psychology, religion, social work, and sociology). Communication, psychology, and business administration are the largest.

Required: All students must maintain a minimum GPA of 2.0 while taking 120 semester hours, including 36 to 75 in the major. The core curriculum includes courses from Foundational Skills, Cultural Foundations, and Foundations for Values and Decisions. In the required capstone class, seniors identify a problem in society, research it, and present their solutions in an extensive final paper.

Special: Internships and study abroad in a variety of countries through the ISEP and SEU and other university programs are available. A liberal studies degree, credit for life experience, nondegree study, and pass/fail options also are possible. A flexible program for working adults is offered through New College. There are 7 national honor societies, and a freshman honors program. All departments have honors programs.

Faculty/Classroom: 54% of faculty are male; 46%, female. 82% teach undergraduates. No introductory courses are taught by graduate students. The average class size in a laboratory is 14 and in a regular course, 21.

Admissions: 74% of the 2001-2002 applicants were accepted. The SAT I scores for the 2001-2002 freshman class were: Verbal--31% below 500, 45% between 500 and 599, 22% between 600 and 700, and 2% above 700; Math--30% below 500, 50% between 500 and 599, 18% between 600 and 700, and 3% above 700. The ACT scores were 34% below 21, 33% between 21 and 23, 25% between 24 and 26, 7% between 27 and 28, and 2% above 28. 32% of the current freshmen were in the top fifth of their class; 63% were in the top two fifths. 2 freshmen graduated first in their class.

Requirements: The SAT I or ACT is required. In addition, successful applicants should be in the top half of their graduating class, with testing at or above the Texas average of 1000 on the SAT I combined scores, or 21 on the ACT. The GED is accepted. An interview is recommended. An essay is required. SEU requires applicants to be in the upper 50% of their class. A GPA of 2.5 is required. AP and CLEP credits are accepted. Important factors in the admissions decision are advanced placement or honor courses, extracurricular activities record, and evidence of special talent. Applications are accepted on-line through Texas Mentor or at *www.stedwards.edu/admssns/apptypes.htm*.

Procedure: Freshmen are admitted fall and spring. Entrance exams should be taken in summer or fall of senior year. There is a deferred admissions plan. Early decision applications should be filed by February 1; regular applications, by July 1 for fall entry, December 1 for spring entry, and May 1 for summer entry. The fall 2001 application fee was $30. Notification is sent on a rolling basis. A waiting list is an active part of the admissions procedure.

Transfer: 325 transfer students enrolled in 2001-2002. Transfer applicants must have a minimum GPA of 2.25. Transfers with less than 30 hours must submit high school transcripts. 30 credits of 120 must be completed at SEU.

Visiting: There are regularly scheduled orientations for prospective students, including a tour, financial aid session, academic session, class visits, entertainment, and an overnight stay in a residence hall. There are guides for informal visits and visitors may sit in on classes and stay overnight. To schedule a visit, contact the Admissions Office.

Financial Aid: In 2001-2002, 76% of all freshmen and 71% of continuing students received some form of financial aid. 61% of freshmen and 58% of continuing students received need-based aid. The average freshman award was $14,053. Of that total, scholarships or need-based grants averaged $8728 ($19,750 maximum); loans averaged $3016 ($7012 maximum); and work contracts averaged $1928 ($2500 maximum). 90% of undergraduates work part time. Average annual earnings from campus work are $2000. The average financial indebtedness of the 2001 graduate was $21,033. The FAFSA is required. The fall application deadline is April 15.

International Students: There are 122 international students enrolled. The school actively recruits these students. They must score 500 on the written TOEFL and also take the SAT I or the ACT.

Computers: The mainframe is an HP 9000/K200. Students may use the multiuser system for computer science assignments, e-mail, Internet and Web access, and to publish web pages. There are 344 computers available for general use. All students may access the system. Dial-up is available 24 hours every day. There is 1 computer lab available 24 hours per day. There are no time limits and no fees. It is strongly recommended that all students have a personal computer.

Graduates: In 2001, 653 bachelor's degrees were awarded. The most popular majors were business and management (9%), psychology (6%), and communication (6%). In an average class, 27% graduate in 4 years, 49% in 5 years, and 51% in 6 years. 61 companies recruited on campus in 2000-2001.

Admissions Contact: Tracy Manier, Interim Director of Admissions.
E-mail: *seu.admit@admin.stedwards.edu*
Web: *http://www.stedwards.edu*

SAINT MARY'S UNIVERSITY OF SAN ANTONIO D-4
San Antonio, TX 78228-8503 (210) 436-3126
(800) FOR-STMU; Fax: (210) 431-6742

Full-time: 979 men, 1363 women	**Faculty:** 140; IIA, av$
Part-time: 94 men, 177 women	**Ph.D.s:** 92%
Graduate: 755 men, 768 women	**Student/Faculty:** 17 to 1
Year: semesters, summer session	**Tuition:** $14,200
Application Deadline: open	**Room & Board:** $5535
Freshman Class: 1674 applied, 1364 accepted, 536 enrolled	
SAT I Verbal/Math: 520/530	**ACT:** 22 **COMPETITIVE**

Saint Mary's University, established in 1852, is a private Roman Catholic institution in the Marianist tradition, offering undergraduate programs in humanities and social sciences, business and administration, science, engineering, and technology. There are 3 undergraduate and 2 graduate schools. In addition to regional accreditation, St. Mary's has baccalaureate program accreditation with ABET and NASM. The 2 libraries contain 481,137 volumes, 131,324 microform items, and 3104 audiovisual forms/CDs, and subscribe to 1320 periodicals. Computerized library services include the card catalog, interlibrary loans, and database searching. Special learning facilities include a learning resource center and the Learning Assistance Center. The 135-acre campus is in a suburban area 5 miles northwest of San Antonio. Including residence halls, there are 32 buildings.

Student Life: 94% of undergraduates are from Texas. Others are from 30 states, 33 foreign countries, and Canada. 86% are from public schools. 57% are Hispanic; 32% white. 55% are Catholic; 31% Baptist, Buddhist, Christian, Eastern Orthodox, Episcopal, Hindu; 14% Protestant. The average age of freshmen is 18; all undergraduates, 21. 7% do not continue beyond their first year; 64% remain to graduate.

Housing: 1256 students can be accommodated in college housing, which includes single-sex and coed dormitories. On-campus housing is guaranteed for the freshman year only and is available on a first-come, first-served basis. Priority is given to out-of-town students. 52% of students commute. Alcohol is not permitted. All students may keep cars.

Activities: 15% of men belong to 1 local fraternity and 4 national fraternities; 13% of women belong to 1 local sorority and 3 national sororities. There are 55 groups on campus, including art, band, cheerleading, choir, chorale, dance, drama, ethnic, honors, international, jazz band, newspaper, pep band, photography, political, professional, religious, social, social service, and student government. Popular campus events include Campus Ministry Retreat, Hunger Awareness Week, and Fiesta Oyster Bake.

Sports: There are 5 intercollegiate sports for men and 5 for women, and 28 intramural sports for men and 28 for women. Facilities include a gym; weight room; tennis, handball, and basketball courts; and various playing fields.

Disabled Students: 80% of the campus is accessible. Wheelchair ramps, elevators, special parking, specially equipped rest rooms, special class scheduling, lowered drinking fountains, and specially designed rooms in designated residence halls are available.

Services: Counseling and information services are available, as is tutoring in every subject. There is remedial math, reading, and writing.

Campus Safety and Security: Measures include 24-hour foot and vehicle patrol, escort service, informal discussions, and pamphlets/posters/films. There are emergency telephones, lighted pathways/sidewalks, and a crime prevention awareness program each semester.

Programs of Study: St. Mary's confers B.A., B.S., B.A.S., B.A.T., and B.B.A. degrees. Master's and doctoral degrees are also awarded. Bachelor's degrees are awarded in BIOLOGICAL SCIENCE (biochemistry and biology/biological science), BUSINESS (accounting, banking and finance, business administration and management, human resources, international business management, and marketing/retailing/merchandising), COMMUNICATIONS AND THE ARTS (communications, English, French, German, music, Spanish, and speech/debate/rhetoric), COMPUTER AND PHYSICAL SCIENCE (chemistry, computer science, earth science, mathematics, and physics), EDUCATION (business, elementary, science, and secondary), ENGINEERING AND ENVIRONMENTAL DESIGN (computer engineering, electrical/electronics engineering, engineering, and industrial engineering), HEALTH PROFESSIONS (predentistry and premedicine), SOCIAL SCIENCE (criminal justice, economics, history, international relations, international studies, Latin American studies, philosophy, political science/government, prelaw, psychology, sociology, and theological studies). Biology, accounting, and political science are the strongest academically. Biology, business, and political science are the largest.

Required: All students must complete at least 129 semester hours, 24 to 30 in the major, with a minimum 2.5 GPA. Core curriculum requirements include courses in fine arts, English, foreign language, speech, natural science, math, social science, philosophy, and theology. Students must also take computer science, demonstrate computer literacy, and take interdisciplinary electives.

Special: Saint Mary's offers cooperative programs and internships in all majors, depending on the student's needs. Students may cross-register at any of the United Colleges of San Antonio, spend a semester in Washington, D.C., or study in England, Austria, or Mexico. Dual majors are possible in computer science and engineering and public justice and political science, psychology, or sociology. Accelerated degree programs are offered in law and dentistry (B.A. in combined science and dental degree). Required theology courses may be taken on a pass/fail basis. There are 3 national honor societies, and a freshman honors program.

Faculty/Classroom: 66% of faculty are male; 34%, female. 67% teach undergraduates. No introductory courses are taught by graduate students. The average class size in an introductory lecture is 30; in a laboratory, 60; and in a regular course, 25.

Admissions: 81% of the 2001-2002 applicants were accepted. The SAT I scores for the 2001-2002 freshman class were: Verbal--33% below 500, 50% between 500 and 599, 16% between 600 and 700, and 1%

above 700; Math--30% below 500, 53% between 500 and 599, 15% between 600 and 700, and 1% above 700. The ACT scores were 30% below 21, 41% between 21 and 23, 22% between 24 and 26, 4% between 27 and 28, and 3% above 28. 59% of the current freshmen were in the top fifth of their class; 81% were in the top two fifths. 9 freshmen graduated first in their class.

Requirements: The SAT I or ACT is required. In addition, all applicants must be high school graduates or have the GED, rank in the upper half of their graduating classes, and score in the 50th percentile on SAT I or ACT. Secondary school preparation should include 4 units of English, 3 each of math and academic electives, and 2 each of social science, natural science, and foreign language. Potential science and engineering majors should have 4 units of math and 3 of lab science, including chemistry or physics. St. Mary's requires applicants to be in the upper 50% of their class. AP and CLEP credits are accepted. Important factors in the admissions decision are leadership record, advanced placement or honor courses, and personality/intangible qualities. Applications are accepted on-line via ApplyWeb at the school's web site.

Procedure: Freshmen are admitted fall and spring. Entrance exams should be taken by the fall of the senior year. There are early admissions and deferred admissions plans. Application deadlines are open.

Transfer: 149 transfer students enrolled in 2001-2002. Transfer applicants must present at least a 2.0 GPA in previous college work, which should include 3 hours of English composition. Saint Mary's also recommends that applicants submit SAT I or ACT scores and schedule an interview. 30 credits of 129 must be completed at St. Mary's.

Visiting: There are regularly scheduled orientations for prospective students, including a tour, an admissions/financial aid session, an overnight stay, and class visits. There are guides for informal visits and visitors may sit in on classes and stay overnight. To schedule a visit, contact the Undergraduate Admissions Office.

Financial Aid: In 2001-2002, 75% of all freshmen and 88% of continuing students received some form of financial aid. 69% of freshmen and 65% of continuing students received need-based aid. The average freshman award was $11,001. Of that total, scholarships or need-based grants averaged $3500 ($6500 maximum); loans averaged $2100 ($4100 maximum); and work contracts averaged $1250 ($1750 maximum). 55% of undergraduates work part time. Average annual earnings from campus work are $1750. The average financial indebtedness of the 2001 graduate was $22,023. St. Mary's is a member of CSS. The CSS/ Profile is required. The fall application deadline is April 1.

International Students: There are 91 international students enrolled. The school actively recruits these students. They must score 550 on the written TOEFL.

Computers: The mainframes are a DEC VAX 6000 Model 510 and MicroVAX II. Students have access to 36 PCs in the academic library during library hours. They can also check out the software to use with the library's computers. Other mainframe systems are available to students on a restricted basis, either by approval or by course requirement. All students may access the system. There are no time limits and no fees.

Graduates: In 2001, 464 bachelor's degrees were awarded. The most popular majors were biology (11%), psychology (7%), and political science (7%). In an average class, 32% graduate in 4 years, 58% in 5 years, and 62% in 6 years. 30 companies recruited on campus in 2000-2001.

Admissions Contact: Richard Castillo, Director of Undergraduate Admissions. E-mail: *uadm@stmarytx.edu* Web: *www.stmarytx.edu*

SAM HOUSTON STATE UNIVERSITY — E-3

Huntsville, TX 77340 — **(936) 294-1828; Fax: (936) 294-3758**

Full-time: 3913 men, 5301 women	**Faculty:** 346; IIA, -$
Part-time: 958 men, 1101 women	**Ph.D.s:** 91%
Graduate: 558 men, 1165 women	**Student/Faculty:** 27 to 1
Year: semesters, summer session	**Tuition:** $2404 ($7468)
Application Deadline: open	**Room & Board:** $3672

Freshman Class: 4708 applied, 4072 accepted, 1773 enrolled

SAT I Verbal/Math: 490/490 — **LESS COMPETITIVE**

Sam Houston University, founded in 1879, is a public institution offering programs in arts and sciences, business administration, criminal justice, education, and applied science. There are 4 undergraduate and 4 graduate schools. In addition to regional accreditation, Sam Houston State has baccalaureate program accreditation with NASM and NCATE. The library contains 1,158,766 volumes, 1,111,264 microform items, and 19,716 audiovisual forms/CDs, and subscribes to 3263 periodicals. Computerized library services include the card catalog, interlibrary loans, and database searching. Special learning facilities include a learning resource center, planetarium, radio station, TV station, and the Sam Houston Museum. The 2143-acre campus is in a small town 70 miles north of Houston.

Student Life: 97% of undergraduates are from Texas. Others are from 42 states, 46 foreign countries, and Canada. 75% are white; 14% African American. The average age of freshmen is 18; all undergraduates, 23. 34% do not continue beyond their first year; 37% remain to graduate.

Housing: 2350 students can be accommodated in college housing, which includes single-sex and coed dormitories, on-campus apartments, off-campus apartments, married-student housing, fraternity houses, and sorority houses. In addition, there are honors houses and special-interest houses. On-campus housing is guaranteed for all 4 years. 77% of students commute. Alcohol is not permitted. All students may keep cars.

Activities: 7% of men belong to 14 local fraternities and 13 local sororities. There are many groups and organizations on campus, including art, band, cheerleading, choir, chorale, chorus, computers, dance, drama, drill team, ethnic, film, gay, honors, international, jazz band, marching band, musical theater, newspaper, orchestra, pep band, photography, political, professional, radio and TV, religious, social, social service, student government, symphony, and yearbook. Popular campus events include Organization Fair, Greek Week, and Spring Fling.

Sports: There are 7 intercollegiate sports for men and 7 for women, and 13 intramural sports for men and 13 for women. Facilities include a 14000-seat stadium, a 5200-seat gym, 4 basketball courts, 10 racquetball courts, 3 swimming pools, and 2 weight rooms.

Disabled Students: 90% of the campus is accessible. Wheelchair ramps, elevators, special parking, specially equipped rest rooms, lowered drinking fountains, and closed-circuit television (CCTV), computer workstations with large print and speech output capabilities, and telecommunication devices for the deaf (TDD) are available.

Services: Counseling and information services are available, as is tutoring in every subject. There is a reader service for the blind, and remedial math, reading, and writing.

Campus Safety and Security: Measures include 24-hour foot and vehicle patrol, escort service, informal discussions, and pamphlets/posters/ films. There are emergency telephones and lighted pathways/sidewalks.

Programs of Study: Sam Houston State confers B.A., B.S., B.A.A.S., B.A.C.J., B.A.T., B.B.A., B.F.A., B.M., B.M.Ed., B.S.C.J., and B.S.W. degrees. Master's and doctoral degrees are also awarded. Bachelor's degrees are awarded in AGRICULTURE (agriculture, animal science, and horticulture), BIOLOGICAL SCIENCE (biology/biological science), BUSINESS (accounting, banking and finance, business administration and management, management information systems, and marketing/ retailing/merchandising), COMMUNICATIONS AND THE ARTS (art, dance, dramatic arts, English, French, German, graphic design, journalism, music, music performance, music theory and composition, musical theater, photography, Spanish, and speech/debate/rhetoric), COMPUTER AND PHYSICAL SCIENCE (chemistry, computer science, geology, mathematics, and physics), EDUCATION (physical), ENGINEERING AND ENVIRONMENTAL DESIGN (environmental science), HEALTH PROFESSIONS (health, medical technology, and music therapy), SOCIAL SCIENCE (criminal justice, economics, geography, history, home economics, law enforcement and corrections, philosophy, physical fitness/movement, political science/government, psychology, and sociology). Psychology and general business are the largest.

Required: All students must maintain a GPA of 2.0 while taking 128 semester hours, including 30 in the major. The core curriculum includes 15 hours of social and behavioral sciences, 9 hours of humanities and visual and performing arts, 8 hours of natural sciences, 6 hours of communication, 4 hours of an institutionally designated option, and 3 hours of math.

Special: Work-study programs with the university, second degrees, and B.A.-B.S. degrees are available. There is 1 national honor society, and a freshman honors program.

Faculty/Classroom: 58% of faculty are male; 42%, female. 90% teach undergraduates. Graduate students teach 6% of introductory courses. The average class size in a regular course is 31.

Admissions: 86% of the 2001-2002 applicants were accepted. The SAT I scores for the 2001-2002 freshman class were: Verbal--54% below 500, 36% between 500 and 599, 9% between 600 and 700, and 1% above 700; Math--56% below 500, 35% between 500 and 599, 8% between 600 and 700, and 1% above 700. 28% of the current freshmen were in the top fifth of their class; 65% were in the top two fifths. 13 freshmen graduated first in their class.

Requirements: The SAT I or ACT is required with a minimum required composite score of 1010 on the SAT I or 21 on the ACT. Applicants must have secondary school credits as follows: 4 of English, 2 each of math, history, and science, 1 1/2 of phys ed, and a half credit each of social studies, and health education. The GED is accepted. A GPA of 2.0 is required. AP and CLEP credits are accepted.

Procedure: Freshmen are admitted fall, spring, and summer. There is an early admissions plan. Applications should be filed by August 1 for fall entry, December 1 for spring entry, May 15 for summer session I, and June 15 for summer session II.

Transfer: 1513 transfer students enrolled in 2001-2002. Transfer applicants must present a 2.0 GPA on all previous college work. 42 credits of 128 must be completed at Sam Houston State.

Visiting: There are regularly scheduled orientations for prospective students. There are guides for informal visits. To schedule a visit, contact the Visitor Center at (936) 294-1844.

Financial Aid: In 2001-2002, 65% of all freshmen and 47% of continuing students received some form of financial aid. 44% of freshmen and

35% of continuing students received need-based aid. The average freshman award was $5564. Of that total, scholarships or need-based grants averaged $3900 ($10,580 maximum); loans averaged $3800 ($10,580 maximum); and work contracts averaged $850 ($3000 maximum). 15% of undergraduates work part time. Average annual earnings from campus work are $2000. The average financial indebtedness of the 2001 graduate was $12,630. The FAFSA is required. The fall application deadline is March 31.

International Students: There are 138 international students enrolled. The school actively recruits these students. They must score 550 on the written TOEFL or 213 on the electronic version and also take the SAT I or the ACT.

Computers: The mainframes are a DEC VAX 8650, 785, 750, and 6320 and DEC MicroVAX II 3400. There are also 400 PCs and Macs available in labs and class buildings. All students may access the system. There are no time limits. The fee is $50 per semester.

Admissions Contact: Joey Chandler, Director Undergraduate Admissions. A video is available. E-mail: *admissions@shsu.edu*
Web: *www.shsu.edu*

SCHREINER COLLEGE
(See Schreiner University)

SCHREINER UNIVERSITY (Formerly Schreiner College) — D-4

Kerrville, TX 78028-5697 — (830) 792-7217
(800) 343-4919; Fax: (830) 792-7226

Full-time: 275 men, 405 women	**Faculty:** 56; IIB, --$
Part-time: 27 men, 84 women	**Ph.D.s:** 55%
Graduate: 7 men, 8 women	**Student/Faculty:** 12 to 1
Year: semesters, summer session	**Tuition:** $12,318
Application Deadline: August 1	**Room & Board:** $6936
Freshman Class: 700 applied, 482 accepted, 207 enrolled	
SAT I Verbal/Math: 500/490	**ACT:** 20 — **COMPETITIVE**

Schreiner University, formerly Schreiner College, founded in 1917, is an independent liberal arts institution affiliated with the Presbyterian Church (U.S.A.). The library contains 66,614 volumes, 63,953 microform items, and 769 audiovisual forms/CDs, and subscribes to 350 periodicals. Computerized library services include the card catalog, interlibrary loans, and database searching. Special learning facilities include a learning resource center. The 175-acre campus is in a small town 60 miles northwest of San Antonio. Including residence halls, there are 47 buildings.

Student Life: 99% of undergraduates are from Texas. Others are from 14 states, 12 foreign countries, and Canada. 90% are from public schools. 81% are white; 15% Hispanic. 49% are Protestant; 33% claim no religious affiliation; 16% Catholic. The average age of freshmen is 18; all undergraduates, 20. 34% do not continue beyond their first year.

Housing: College housing includes coed dormitories and on-campus apartments. On-campus housing is guaranteed for all 4 years. 53% of students commute. All students may keep cars.

Activities: 6% of men belong to fraternities. There are 34 groups on campus, including art, cheerleading, choir, chorale, drama, honors, international, literary magazine, newspaper, photography, political, professional, religious, social, student government, and yearbook. Popular campus events include Schreiner Speaker Series, Trull Casino Night, and Toga Party.

Sports: There are 5 intercollegiate sports for men and 6 for women, and 9 intramural sports for men and 9 for women. Facilities include basketball and volleyball courts, baseball and softball diamonds, 3 handball/racquetball courts, a track, 8 tennis courts, a swimming pool, soccer and intramural fields, a golf driving range, and a recreation room.

Disabled Students: 95% of the campus is accessible. Wheelchair ramps, elevators, special parking, specially equipped rest rooms, special class scheduling, lowered drinking fountains, and lowered telephones are available.

Services: Counseling and information services are available, as is tutoring in every subject, including introductory-level courses. There is remedial math, reading, and writing, a certified peer-tutoring program, workshops, a math lab, a self-management orientation course, and computer-assisted instruction for learning skills.

Campus Safety and Security: Measures include informal discussions, pamphlets/posters/films, emergency telephones, and and a night vehicle patrol.

Programs of Study: Schreiner confers B.A., B.B.A., and B.G.S. degrees. Associate and master's degrees are also awarded. Bachelor's degrees are awarded in BIOLOGICAL SCIENCE (biochemistry and biology/biological science), BUSINESS (accounting, banking and finance, business administration and management, management information systems, marketing/retailing/merchandising, and real estate), COMMUNICATIONS AND THE ARTS (English and fine arts), COMPUTER AND PHYSICAL SCIENCE (chemistry and mathematics), EDUCATION (art, elementary, and secondary), HEALTH PROFESSIONS (predentistry and premedicine), SOCIAL SCIENCE (history, humanities, philosophy, physical fitness/movement, prelaw, psychology, and religion). History, English, and exercise science are the strongest academically. Business administration, exercise science, and psychology are the largest.

Required: To graduate, all students must have a minimum GPA of 2.0 for 120 semester hours, including 24 hours in the major. The 64-hour core curriculum includes courses from English composition, oral communication, foreign language, history, natural science, math, philosophy or religion, computer studies, government, business administration, literature/fine arts, social science, and fitness. B.A. candidates must complete a senior capstone project, thesis, or course; B.B.A. candidates may substitute an internship.

Special: Schreiner offers study abroad in Japan and England, work-study with the university, second majors, a general studies degree, credit for life experience, nondegree study, and a 3-2 engineering degree with the University of Texas, Texas Tech University, and Texas A&M University. There are 2 national honor societies, including Phi Beta Kappa, and a freshman honors program.

Faculty/Classroom: 64% of faculty are male; 36%, female. All teach undergraduates. The average class size in an introductory lecture is 25; in a laboratory, 21; and in a regular course, 20.

Admissions: 69% of the 2001-2002 applicants were accepted. The SAT I scores for the 2001-2002 freshman class were: Verbal--47% below 500, 36% between 500 and 599, 12% between 600 and 700, and 5% above 700; Math--51% below 500, 30% between 500 and 599, and 19% between 600 and 700. The ACT scores were 56% below 21, 14% between 21 and 23, 18% between 24 and 26, 11% between 27 and 28, and 2% above 28. 34% of the current freshmen were in the top fifth of their class; 67% were in the top two fifths. 3 freshmen graduated first in their class.

Requirements: The SAT I or ACT is required with a composite SAT I score of 800 (minimum 380 verbal and 350 mathematics) or ACT score of 20 recommended. Applicants need 20 secondary-school academic credits, including 4 each of English and math, 2 each of social science, foreign language, and lab science, and 1 of history. An interview is advised. The GED is accepted; applicants with a GED are not required to take the SAT I or ACT but are encouraged to do so. Schreiner requires applicants to be in the upper 50% of their class. A GPA of 2.0 is required. AP and CLEP credits are accepted. Important factors in the admissions decision are advanced placement or honor courses and leadership record.

Procedure: Freshmen are admitted to all sessions. Entrance exams should be taken in the spring of the junior year. There are early admissions and deferred admissions plans. Applications should be filed by August 1 for fall entry, December 1 for spring entry, and June 1 for summer entry. Notification of early decision is sent September 1; regular decision, on a rolling basis. The fall 2001 application fee was $25.

Transfer: 87 transfer students enrolled in 2001-2002. Applicants with fewer than 15 transferable credit hours must meet freshman admissions requirements. For those with more, the SAT I or ACT is not required. A 2.0 minimum GPA is necessary. 30 credits of 120 must be completed at Schreiner.

Visiting: There are regularly scheduled orientations for prospective students, including guided tours, financial aid information, and faculty and student discussions. There are guides for informal visits and visitors may sit in on classes and stay overnight. To schedule a visit, contact the Admission Office.

Financial Aid: In a recent year, 46% of all freshmen received some form of financial aid. 46% of freshmen and 53% of continuing students received need-based aid. The average freshman award was $11,222. Of that total, scholarships or need-based grants averaged $8828; loans averaged $2138; and work contracts averaged $2790. 21% of undergraduates work part time. Average annual earnings from campus work are $1500. The average financial indebtedness of the 2001 graduate was $18,563. The FAFSA and the college's own financial statement are required. The fall application deadline is August 1.

International Students: The school actively recruits these students. They must score 550 on the written TOEFL and also take the MELAB, the Comprehensive English Language Test, or the college's own test.

Computers: There are 33 Macs and PCs available in the computer lab. All students may access the system. There are no time limits and no fees.

Graduates: In 2001, 94 bachelor's degrees were awarded. The most popular majors were business/marketing (30%), exercise science (17%), and psychology (12%). In an average class, 35% graduate in 6 years.

Admissions Contact: Peg Layton, Acting Dean of Admission and Financial Aid. A video is available. E-mail: *admissions@schreiner.edu*
Web: *www.schreiner.edu*

SOUTHERN METHODIST UNIVERSITY
Dallas, TX 75275-0181 D-2
(214) 768-2058
(800) 323-0672; Fax: (214) 768-0103

Full-time: 2546 men, 2936 women	**Faculty:** 459; I, av$
Part-time: 101 men, 138 women	**Ph.D.s:** 88%
Graduate: 1818 men, 1006 women	**Student/Faculty:** 12 to 1
Year: semesters, summer session	**Tuition:** $20,796
Application Deadline: January 15	**Room & Board:** $7553
Freshman Class: 5322 applied, 3984 accepted, 1353 enrolled	
SAT I Verbal/Math: 580/590	**ACT:** 25 **VERY COMPETITIVE**

Southern Methodist University, founded in 1911, is a private nonsectarian institution affiliated with the United Methodist Church. SMU offers undergraduate and graduate programs in humanities and sciences, business, arts, and engineering and applied sciences. There are 4 undergraduate and 6 graduate schools. In addition to regional accreditation, SMU has baccalaureate program accreditation with AACSB, ABET, NASAD, and NASM. The 8 libraries contain 2,577,345 volumes, 803,898 microform items, and 626,996 audiovisual forms/CDs, and subscribe to 11,727 periodicals. Computerized library services include the card catalog, interlibrary loans, and database searching. Special learning facilities include a learning resource center, art gallery, natural history museum, radio station, art museum, research laboratories, TV studio, and several performing arts theaters, including Classical Thrust Stage. The 163-acre campus is in a suburban area 5 miles north of downtown Dallas. Including residence halls, there are 75 buildings.

Student Life: 63% of undergraduates are from Texas. Others are from 48 states, 66 foreign countries, and Canada. 65% are from public schools. 75% are white. The average age of freshmen is 18; all undergraduates, 21. 16% do not continue beyond their first year; 71% remain to graduate.

Housing: 2525 students can be accommodated in college housing, which includes coed dormitories, on-campus apartments, off-campus apartments, married-student housing, fraternity houses, and sorority houses. In addition, there are honors houses, special-interest houses, wellness floors, an international floor, and floors catering to particular disciplines. On-campus housing is guaranteed for the freshman year only and is available on a lottery system for upperclassmen. All students may keep cars.

Activities: 38% of men belong to 14 national fraternities; 42% of women belong to 12 national sororities. There are 143 groups on campus, including art, band, cheerleading, choir, chorale, chorus, computers, dance, debate, drama, drill team, ethnic, film, forensics, gay, honors, international, jazz band, literary magazine, marching band, musical theater, newspaper, opera, orchestra, pep band, photography, political, professional, radio and TV, religious, social, social service, student government, symphony, and yearbook. Popular campus events include Celebration of Lights, Parents Weekend, and Community Service Day.

Sports: There are 8 intercollegiate sports for men and 8 for women, and 16 intramural sports for men and 15 for women. Facilities include gymnastic and weight rooms, a dance studio, indoor and outdoor jogging tracks, indoor and outdoor pools, a 2400-seat outdoor stadium, a 6500-seat indoor stadium, and courts for basketball, volleyball, tennis, badminton, and racquetball.

Disabled Students: 95% of the campus is accessible. Wheelchair ramps, elevators, special parking, specially equipped rest rooms, special class scheduling, lowered drinking fountains, lowered telephones, and automatic doors are available. Ongoing renovation aims to make the campus completely accessible.

Services: Counseling and information services are available, as is tutoring in most subjects. There is a reader service for the blind and remedial reading and writing. The Learning Enhancement Center provides study skills workshops, note-taking techniques, and time management skills seminars.

Campus Safety and Security: Measures include 24-hour foot and vehicle patrol, self-defense education, escort service, and shuttle buses. There are informal discussions, pamphlets/posters/films, emergency telephones, and lighted pathways/sidewalks. Card-key devices, issued to all students living in residence halls, must be used to enter these buildings.

Programs of Study: SMU confers B.A., B.S., B.B.A., B.F.A., B.Hum., B.M., B.S.Comp.Eng., B.S.E.E., B.S.Env.E., B.S.M.E., and B.Soc.Sci. degrees. Master's and doctoral degrees are also awarded. Bachelor's degrees are awarded in BIOLOGICAL SCIENCE (biochemistry and biology/biological science), BUSINESS (accounting, banking and finance, business administration and management, management information systems, management science, marketing/retailing/merchandising, organizational behavior, and real estate), COMMUNICATIONS AND THE ARTS (advertising, art history and appreciation, broadcasting, creative writing, dance, dramatic arts, English, film arts, French, German, journalism, languages, media arts, music performance, music theory and composition, piano/organ, public relations, Russian, Spanish, and studio art), COMPUTER AND PHYSICAL SCIENCE (chemistry, computer science, geology, geophysics and seismology, mathematics, physics, and statistics), EDUCATION (music), ENGINEERING AND ENVIRONMENTAL DESIGN (computer engineering, electrical/electronics engineering, environmental engineering, and mechanical engineering), HEALTH PROFESSIONS (music therapy), SOCIAL SCIENCE (African American studies, anthropology, economics, German area studies, history, humanities, international studies, Italian studies, Latin American studies, liberal arts/general studies, medieval studies, Mexican-American/Chicano studies, philosophy, political science/government, psychology, public affairs, religion, Russian and Slavic studies, social science, sociology, and Southwest American studies). Performing arts, life sciences, history, and business are the strongest academically. Business, communications, and psychology are the largest.

Required: Basic requirements consist of 122 semester hours, including a general education requirement of 41 hours distributed across Fundamentals (writing, math, and information technology), Science and Technology, Perspectives (arts, literature, religious and philosophical thought, history, politics and economics, and behavioral sciences), Cultural Formations (interdisciplinary courses), and a corequirement in Human Diversity (race, ethnicity, and gender). There is also a 2-credit education requirement. Students must maintain a GPA of 2.0.

Special: SMU offers a co-op program in engineering, work-study programs, B.A.-B.S. degrees, study abroad in 12 countries, dual majors in any combination, student-designed majors, numerous internships, and interdisciplinary majors, including economics with finance applications and economics with systems analysis. A 3-2 advanced degree in business is available, as are evening degree programs in humanities and social sciences, and teacher certification programs. There are 16 national honor societies, including Phi Beta Kappa, anda freshman honors program.

Faculty/Classroom: 71% of faculty are male; 29%, female. 89% teach undergraduates and 89% both teach and do research.

Admissions: 75% of the 2001-2002 applicants were accepted. The SAT I scores for the 2001-2002 freshman class were: Verbal--13% below 500, 47% between 500 and 599, 33% between 600 and 700, and 7% above 700; Math--9% below 500, 43% between 500 and 599, 38% between 600 and 700, and 9% above 700. The ACT scores were 8% below 21, 23% between 21 and 23, 35% between 24 and 26, 16% between 27 and 28, and 17% above 28. 55% of the current freshmen were in the top fifth of their class; 82% were in the top two fifths.

Requirements: The SAT I or ACT is recommended. In addition, applicants should graduate from an accredited high school with a minimum of 15 academic credits: 4 in English, 3 in higher math, including algebra I, II, and plane geometry, 3 each in natural science and social science, and 2 in a foreign language. Home School Certificate applicants may qualify with the SAT I or ACT and 3 SAT II: Subject tests, including writing and math. Performing arts majors must audition. AP and CLEP credits are accepted. Important factors in the admissions decision are advanced placement or honor courses, leadership record, and recommendations by school officials.

Procedure: Freshmen are admitted to all sessions. Entrance exams should be taken by December of the senior year. There are early action, early admissions, and deferred admissions plans. Early action applications should be filed by November 1; regular applications, by January 15 for fall entry and April 1 for spring entry, along with a $50 application fee. Notification of early action is sent December 31; regular decision, on a rolling basis. A waiting list is an active part of the admissions procedure.

Transfer: 301 transfer students enrolled in 2001-2002. A minimum 2.5 GPA is generally required for transfer, but specific requirements vary according to the program of study. Candidates must demonstrate math proficiency. A foreign language requirement may be met through high school or college work. 60 credits of 122 must be completed at SMU.

Visiting: There are regularly scheduled orientations for prospective students, including information about academic studies, financial-aid sessions, discussions with current students, lunch with faculty and students, and a tour of the campus. There is also a Spring Fest visitation in April for high school juniors. There are guides for informal visits and visitors may sit in on classes and stay overnight. To schedule a visit, contact the Undergraduate Admissions Office.

Financial Aid: In a recent year, 83% of all freshmen and 73% of continuing students received some form of financial aid. 47% of freshmen received need-based aid. The average freshman award was $16,256. The average financial indebtedness of a recent year's graduate was $19,792. SMU is a member of CSS. The FAFSA is required. The fall application deadline is February 1.

International Students: There were 138 international students enrolled in a recent year. The school actively recruits these students. They must score 550 on the written TOEFL and also take the SAT I or the ACT.

Computers: The mainframe is an IBM 3090. Access to campus administrative and academic computer systems is available from all campus offices and dorm rooms. In addition, several hundred public workstations are available in campus libraries and computer labs. All students may access the system 24 hours a day. There are no time limits and no fees.

Graduates: In a recent year, 1179 bachelor's degrees were awarded. The most popular majors were business/marketing (31%), social sciences and history (17%), and communications/communication technology (14%). In an average class, 1% graduate in 3 years, 56% in 4 years, 69% in 5 years, and 71% in 6 years. 210 companies recruited on campus in a recent year.

Admissions Contact: Nancy Peterson, Associate Director. A video is available. E-mail: *enrol_serv@mail.smu.edu* Web: *www.smu.edu*

SOUTHWEST TEXAS STATE UNIVERSITY D-4

San Marcos, TX 78666-4616 (512) 245-2364
Fax: (512) 245-8044

Full-time: 7090 men, 9007 women	**Faculty:** 653; IIA, --$
Part-time: 1984 men, 2103 women	**Ph.D.s:** 77%
Graduate: 1156 men, 2181 women	**Student/Faculty:** 25 to 1
Year: semesters, summer session	**Tuition:** $3578 ($9908)
Application Deadline: July 1	**Room & Board:** $5152
Freshman Class: 9354 applied, 5400 accepted, 2523 enrolled	
SAT I Verbal/Math: 530/530	**ACT:** 22 **VERY COMPETITIVE**

Southwest Texas State University, founded in 1899, is part of the Texas State University System and offers programs in general studies, applied arts and technology, business, education, fine arts, health professions, liberal arts, and science. There are 8 undergraduate schools and 1 graduate school. In addition to regional accreditation, SWT has baccalaureate program accreditation with AACSB, ACS, ADA, AHEA, ASLA, CAAHEP, CSAB, CSWE, FIDER, NAACLS, NASM, and NRPA. The library contains 3,284,481 volumes, 1,781,334 microform items, and 276,299 audiovisual forms/CDs, and subscribes to 6252 periodicals. Computerized library services include the card catalog, interlibrary loans, and database searching. Special learning facilities include a learning resource center, art gallery, radio station, and and a recording studio. The 428-acre campus is in a suburban area 30 miles south of Austin. Including residence halls, there are 219 buildings.

Student Life: 97% of undergraduates are from Texas. Others are from 48 states, 76 foreign countries, and Canada. 98% are from public schools. 71% are white; 18% Hispanic. The average age of freshmen is 19; all undergraduates, 23. 26% do not continue beyond their first year; 41% remain to graduate.

Housing: 4732 students can be accommodated in college housing, which includes single-sex and coed dormitories, on-campus apartments, and married-student housing. In addition, there are honors houses, and special-interest houses, special housing for international students, disabled students, single parents, and upper-division students. On-campus housing is guaranteed for all 4 years. 79% of students commute. All students may keep cars.

Activities: 5% of men belong to 15 national fraternities; 5% of women belong to 12 national sororities. There are 245 groups on campus, including art, band, cheerleading, chess, choir, chorale, chorus, computers, dance, debate, drama, drill team, ethnic, gay, honors, international, jazz band, literary magazine, marching band, musical theater, newspaper, nontraditional students, opera, orchestra, pep band, photography, political, professional, radio and TV, religious, social, social service, student government, symphony, and yearbook. Popular campus events include Welcome Week, and Cricket Fest.

Sports: There are 6 intercollegiate sports for men and 8 for women, and 22 intramural sports for men and 22 for women. Facilities include a 14,104-seat stadium, a 7200-seat gym, tennis courts, a spring-fed pool, an aquatic sports center, basketball and volleyball courts, racquetball courts, an indoor jogging/walking track, weight-lifting equipment, and exercise machines.

Disabled Students: 80% of the campus is accessible. Wheelchair ramps, elevators, special parking, specially equipped rest rooms, special class scheduling, lowered drinking fountains, lowered telephones, curb cuts, accessible residence-hall rooms, pay TTY text telephones, adaptive computer technology, sign language interpreter, and reading recorder services for the visually impaired are available.

Services: Counseling and information services are available, as is tutoring in most subjects. There is a reader service for the blind, and remedial math, reading, and writing. tutoring for all core curriculum classes is available.

Campus Safety and Security: Measures include 24-hour foot and vehicle patrol, self-defense education, escort service, and shuttle buses. There are informal discussions, pamphlets/posters/films, emergency telephones, and lighted pathways/sidewalks.

Programs of Study: SWT confers B.A., B.S., B.A.A.S., B.A.I.S., B.B.A., B.E.S.S., B.F.A., B.H.A., B.H.W.P., B.M., B.S.A.G., B.S.A.S., B.S.C.D., B.S.C.J., B.S.C.L.S., B.S.F.C.S., B.S.H.I.M., B.S.H.P., B.S.R.A., B.S.R.T., B.S.R.C., B.S.T.C.H., and B.S.W. degrees. Master's and doctoral degrees are also awarded. Bachelor's degrees are awarded in AGRICULTURE (agricultural business management, agriculture, and animal science), BIOLOGICAL SCIENCE (biochemistry, biology/biological science, botany, marine biology, microbiology, nutrition, physiology, wildlife biology, and zoology), BUSINESS (accounting, banking and finance, business administration and management, business economics, fashion merchandising, international business management, marketing/retailing/merchandising, recreational facilities management, and tourism), COMMUNICATIONS AND THE ARTS (advertising, applied art, art, audio technology, broadcasting, communications, dance, dramatic arts, English, fine arts, French, German, graphic design, journalism, music, music performance, music theory and composition, public relations, Spanish, speech/debate/rhetoric, and studio art), COMPUTER AND PHYSICAL SCIENCE (chemistry, computer management, computer science, information sciences and systems, mathematics, and physics), EDUCATION (art, athletic training, bilingual/bicultural, early childhood, elementary, foreign languages, health, home economics, music, physical, reading, science, secondary, and special), ENGINEERING AND ENVIRONMENTAL DESIGN (cartography, city/community/regional planning, construction technology, engineering technology, environmental science, graphic and printing production, industrial engineering technology, and interior design), HEALTH PROFESSIONS (clinical science, community health work, exercise science, health care administration, hospital administration, medical laboratory technology, medical records administration/services, radiation therapy, respiratory therapy, and speech pathology/audiology), SOCIAL SCIENCE (American studies, anthropology, Asian/Oriental studies, child care/child and family studies, corrections, criminal justice, criminology, economics, European studies, family/consumer studies, food science, geography, history, home economics, interdisciplinary studies, international relations, international studies, law enforcement and corrections, philosophy, political science/government, psychology, public administration, Russian and Slavic studies, social science, social work, and sociology). Geography, and education are the strongest academically. Education, business management, and computer science are the largest.

Required: All students must earn a minimum GPA of 2.0 while taking at least 128 semester hours, including 30 in the major. The core curriculum includes basic skills, history and politics, natural science, social science, philosophy, international perspectives, literature, fine arts, and physical fitness.

Special: Co-op programs in medicine, dentistry, engineering, architecture, law, pharmacy, nursing, occupational therapy, and veterinary medicine, internships in many departments, study abroad in 26 countries, and Washington semesters are available. Dual majors, credit for life experience, and nondegree study also are possible. Two summer sessions are offered in most programs. A 3-2 engineering degree is possible with the University of Texas or Texas A&M or Texas Tech Universities. There are 25 national honor societies, a freshman honors program, and 1 departmental honors program.

Faculty/Classroom: 60% of faculty are male; 40%, female. All teach undergraduates. Graduate students teach 15% of introductory courses. The average class size in an introductory lecture is 44; in a laboratory, 18; and in a regular course, 36.

Admissions: 58% of the 2001-2002 applicants were accepted. The SAT I scores for the 2001-2002 freshman class were: Verbal--28% below 500, 54% between 500 and 599, 16% between 600 and 700, and 2% above 700; Math--25% below 500, 56% between 500 and 599, 18% between 600 and 700, and 1% above 700. The ACT scores were 21% below 21, 43% between 21 and 23, 26% between 24 and 26, 6% between 27 and 28, and 3% above 28. 42% of the current freshmen were in the top fifth of their class; 82% were in the top two fifths. 11 freshmen graduated first in their class.

Requirements: The SAT I or ACT is required with minimum scores determined by high school class rank. Applicants need 15 academic credits, including 4 units in English, 3 in math and social science, 3 in natural science, 2 in foreign language, and 1 in computer literacy. The GED is accepted; applicants with a GED are treated as though they were ranked in the 4th quarter. AP and CLEP credits are accepted. Important factors in the admissions decision are advanced placement or honor courses, leadership record, and extracurricular activities record. An electronic application can be accessed through the university's web site at *http://www.applytexas.org/adappc/commonapp.html*.

Procedure: Freshmen are admitted to all sessions. Entrance exams should be taken at the end of the junior year. There is an early admissions plan. Applications should be filed by July 1 for fall entry, December 1 for spring entry, and May 1 for summer entry, along with a $40 fee. Notification is sent on a rolling basis.

Transfer: 2679 transfer students enrolled in 2001-2002. Transfer students with 29 or fewer credits must meet freshman requirements; those with 30 or more credits must submit official transcripts to verify a minimum 2.25 GPA. 30 credits of 128 must be completed at SWT.

Visiting: There are regularly scheduled orientations for prospective students, consisting of a two-day event, with registration required. First-time freshmen parents may attend. Students receive registration instructions, academic advising, and information concerning SWT's academic policies, procedures, and student services. Time is allotted to register for classes. There are guides for informal visits and visitors may sit in on classes. To schedule a visit, contact the Admissions and Visitors Center.

Financial Aid: In a recent year, 48% of all freshmen and 45% of continuing students received some form of financial aid. 34% of freshmen and 31% of continuing students received need-based aid. The average freshman award was $6735. Of that total, scholarships or need-based grants averaged $7738 ($9625 maximum); loans averaged $2376 ($10,000 maximum); and work contracts averaged $1572 ($2300 maximum). 8% of undergraduates work part time. Average annual earnings from campus work are $2350. The average financial indebtedness of the 2001 graduate was $14,500. The FAFSA is required. The fall application deadline is April 1.

International Students: There are 105 international students enrolled. They must score 550 on the written TOEFL or 213 on the electronic version and also take the SAT I or the ACT.

Computers: The mainframes are a DEC VAX 7640, a DEC VAX 6620, a DEC ALPHA AXP 7640, and a DEC ALPHA AXP 4100. PCs and Macs are available for student use throughout the campus. Students are issued user names that allow them to log on to the mainframe from PCs connected to the university network. All students may access the system 24 hours daily. There are no time limits. The fee is $9 per hour.

Graduates: In 2001, 3421 bachelor's degrees were awarded. The most popular majors were education (16%), business administration and management (13%), and criminal justice (5%). In an average class, 1% graduate in 3 years, 17% in 4 years, 38% in 5 years, and 41% in 6 years. 264 companies recruited on campus in 2000-2001.

Admissions Contact: Christie Kangas, Director of Admissions.
E-mail: *admissions@swt.edu* Web: *www.swt.edu/admissions/*

SOUTHWESTERN ADVENTIST UNIVERSITY D-2
Keene, TX 76059 (817) 645-3921
(800) 433-2240; Fax: (817) 556-4744

Full-time: 364 men, 457 women	**Faculty:** 50
Part-time: 101 men, 241 women	**Ph.D.s:** 52%
Graduate: 13 men, 15 women	**Student/Faculty:** 16 to 1
Year: semesters, summer session	**Tuition:** $10,020
Application Deadline: September 5	**Room & Board:** $4778
Freshman Class: 657 applied, 422 accepted, 168 enrolled	
SAT I Verbal/Math: 490/460	**ACT:** 21 **COMPETITIVE**

Southwestern Adventist College, founded in 1893, is a small Seventh-day Adventist institution offering liberal arts and professional degree programs. In addition to regional accreditation, SWAU has baccalaureate program accreditation with NLN. The library contains 103,531 volumes, 6822 microform items, and 1290 audiovisual forms/CDs, and subscribes to 427 periodicals. Computerized library services include the card catalog and database searching. Special learning facilities include a learning resource center, natural history museum, radio station, TV station, and and observatory. The 150-acre campus is in a rural area 35 miles south of Fort Worth. Including residence halls, there are 24 buildings.

Student Life: 51% of undergraduates are from Texas. Others are from 49 states, 53 foreign countries, and Canada. 44% are from public schools. 50% are white; 15% Hispanic; 14% African American; 13% foreign nationals. Most are Protestant. The average age of freshmen is 19; all undergraduates, 26. 38% do not continue beyond their first year; 33% remain to graduate.

Housing: 373 students can be accommodated in college housing, which includes single-sex dormitories, off-campus apartments, and married-student housing. On-campus housing is guaranteed for all 4 years. 71% of students commute. Alcohol is not permitted. All students may keep cars.

Activities: There are no fraternities or sororities. There are 20 groups on campus, including art, band, choir, chorale, computers, drama, ethnic, film, international, newspaper, orchestra, pep band, photography, radio and TV, religious, social, social service, student government, symphony, and yearbook. Popular campus events include Founders Day, Fall Holiday, and Memosa Memories.

Sports: There are 2 intercollegiate sports for men and 2 for women, and 4 intramural sports for men and 4 for women. Facilities include jogging and fitness tracks, weight and aerobics rooms, courts for tennis, racquetball, and basketball, and fields for football and baseball.

Disabled Students: 78% of the campus is accessible. Wheelchair ramps, elevators, special parking, specially equipped rest rooms, and lowered drinking fountains are available.

Services: Counseling and information services are available, as is tutoring in some subjects, including accounting, biology, chemistry, English, Greek, math, nursing, and Spanish. There is remedial math and writing.

Campus Safety and Security: Measures include informal discussions, pamphlets/posters/films, lighted pathways/sidewalks, and 12-hour night foot patrol.

Programs of Study: SWAU confers B.A., B.S., B.B.A., and B.S.W. degrees. Associate and master's degrees are also awarded. Bachelor's degrees are awarded in BIOLOGICAL SCIENCE (biology/biological science and biometrics and biostatistics), BUSINESS (business administration and management, insurance and risk management, international economics, management science, and office supervision and management), COMMUNICATIONS AND THE ARTS (broadcasting, communications, English, journalism, music, and speech/debate/rhetoric), COMPUTER AND PHYSICAL SCIENCE (chemistry, computer science, information sciences and systems, mathematics, and physics), EDUCATION (business, elementary, physical, and secondary), HEALTH PROFESSIONS (exercise science, health, medical technology, and nursing), SOCIAL SCIENCE (criminal justice, history, international relations, psychology, religion, social science, social studies, social work, and theological studies). Nursing, biology, and religion are the strongest academically. Education, nursing, and psychology are the largest.

Required: To graduate, students must complete at least 128 hours, including 40 hours in upper-division courses and 27 to 48 in the major. An overall 2.0 GPA is required, with a 2.3 in upper-division courses in the major field. General education requirements include courses in English, health and phys ed, math and science, religion, social science and humanities, and, in some cases, foreign language. Comprehensive and departmental exams are required.

Special: Cooperative programs in medical technology are available with several area hospitals. Internships are arranged on an individual basis. Students may study abroad in Germany, France, or Spain. Student-designed majors, interdisciplinary majors, including mathematical physics, a 3-2 engineering degree with Walla Walla College and Andrews University, and an adult degree program are offered. There is a freshman honors program.

Faculty/Classroom: 62% of faculty are male; 38%, female. All teach undergraduates and 8% both teach and do research. No introductory courses are taught by graduate students. The average class size in an introductory lecture is 30; in a laboratory, 15; and in a regular course, 20.

Admissions: 64% of the 2001-2002 applicants were accepted. The SAT I scores for the 2001-2002 freshman class were: Verbal--52% below 500, 29% between 500 and 599, 18% between 600 and 700, and 1% above 700; Math--68% below 500, 26% between 500 and 599, 5% between 600 and 700, and 1% above 700. The ACT scores were 46% below 21, 33% between 21 and 23, 15% between 24 and 26, 1% between 27 and 28, and 5% above 28. 25% of the current freshmen were in the top fifth of their class; 56% were in the top two fifths.

Requirements: The SAT I or ACT is required. In addition, applicants should be high school graduates or hold the GED. Secondary preparation is expected to include 12 academic credits in English, foreign language, math, natural or physical science, and social science. Potential nursing or education majors and Seventh-day Adventist ministers must meet additional requirements. AP and CLEP credits are accepted. Important factors in the admissions decision are recommendations by alumni, ability to finance college education, and leadership record. Applications are accepted on-line at the university web site and through Texas Mentor.

Procedure: Freshmen are admitted fall, spring, and summer. Entrance exams should be taken before registration. There are early admissions and deferred admissions plans. Applications should be filed by September 5 for fall entry, January 16 for spring entry, and May 6 for summer entry. Notification is sent on a rolling basis.

Transfer: 239 transfer students enrolled in 2001-2002. An official transcript from each college or university the student has attended must be mailed directly to SWAU's Admissions Office. Transfer students with less than a C average may be accepted on a probationary basis. Nursing, education, and theology majors have additional requirements. 30 credits of 128 must be completed at SWAU.

Visiting: There are regularly scheduled orientations for prospective students, including scheduled weekend visitation programs in February and the summer that consist of meeting the administration, touring the campus, and receiving financial and academic counseling; preregistration is available in summer. There are guides for informal visits and visitors may sit in on classes and stay overnight. To schedule a visit, contact the Enrollment Office at *sylvia@swau.edu*.

Financial Aid: In 2001-2002, 65% of all freshmen and 62% of continuing students received some form of financial aid. 48% of freshmen and 49% of continuing students received need-based aid. The average freshman award was $7779. Of that total, scholarships or need-based grants averaged $3267; loans averaged $2647; and work contracts averaged $2000. 100% of undergraduates work part time. Average annual earnings from campus work are $2000. The average financial indebtedness of the 2001 graduate was $18,223. The FAFSA and the college's own financial statement are required. The fall application deadline is August 28.

International Students: There are 155 international students enrolled. The school actively recruits these students. They must score 520 on the written TOEFL, or take the MELAB. SAT I/ACT scores are required of students from English-speaking countries.

Computers: The mainframe is an IBM RS 6000. PCs are available in faculty offices, academic departments, and student labs. All students may access the system 24 hours per day. There are no time limits and no fees. It is strongly recommended that all students have a personal computer.

Graduates: In 2001, 117 bachelor's degrees were awarded. The most popular majors were education (19%), business (15%), and psychology (10%). In an average class, 3% graduate in 3 years, 20% in 4 years, 30% in 5 years, and 33% in 6 years.

Admissions Contact: Brent Baldwin, Enrollment Vice President.
E-mail: *admissions@swau.edu* Web: *www.swau.edu*

SOUTHWESTERN CHRISTIAN COLLEGE D-2

Terrell, TX 75160 (972) 524-3341, ext. 155; Fax: (972) 563-7133

Full-time: 90 men, 60 women	**Faculty:** 16
Part-time: 10 men, 20 women	**Ph.D.s:** n/av
Graduate: none	**Student/Faculty:** 9 to 1
Year: semesters	**Tuition:** $4700
Application Deadline: see profile	**Room & Board:** $2800
Freshman Class: n/av	
SAT I or ACT: required	**NONCOMPETITIVE**

Southwestern Christian College, chartered in 1949, is a private, coeducational institution affiliated with the Church of Christ, offering bachelor's degrees in Bible and religious education. Figures in the above capsule are approximate. The library contains 23,702 volumes and 2457 audiovisual forms/CDs. Special learning facilities include a learning resource center and a sound recording studio. The 25-acre campus is in a rural area 32 miles east of Dallas. There are 15 buildings.

Student Life: 55% of undergraduates are from Texas. Others are from 22 states and 4 foreign countries. 95% are from public schools. 85% are African American. Most are Protestant. The average age of freshmen is 20; all undergraduates, 21.

Housing: 192 students can be accomodated in college housing, which includes single-sex dorms. On-campus housing is guaranteed for all 4 years.74% of students live on campus. Alcohol is not permitted. All students may keep cars.

Activities: 5% of men belong to 3 local fraternities; there are 3 local sororities. There are 19 groups on campus, including cheerleading, chorus, drama, international, jazz band, newspaper, religious, student government, and yearbook. Popular campus events include Annual College Lectureship and High School.

Sports: Facilities include a gym, a weight room, handball courts, 2 tennis courts, a game room, and a 1500-seat auditorium.

Services: Counseling and information services are available, as is tutoring in some subjects, including English, math, science, and Bible. There is remedial math, reading, and writing.

Programs of Study: SwCC confers B.A. in Bible and B.S. in Religious Education degrees. Associate degrees are also awarded. Bachelor's degrees are awarded in SOCIAL SCIENCE (biblical studies and religious education). Religious education is the strongest program academically and has the largest enrollment.

Required: Students must complete 124 to 133 semester hours with a 2.25 GPA. Required courses include phys ed, computer literacy, Bible, English, foreign language or science, history, humanities, math, and freshman orientation. Students must attend daily chapel and various other church services and activities, and agree to maintain the high moral standards required by SwCC.

Special: SwCC offers work-study, a ministerial internship, a B.A.-B.S. degree in Bible and religious education, credit by exam, and nondegree study.

Faculty/Classroom: 62% of faculty are male; 37% female.

Requirements: The SAT I or ACT is required. In addition, applicants should be high school graduates or hold the GED. Secondary school preparation should include a minimum of 15 units in academic courses, including at least 3 in English. A campus tour and an interview are strongly recommended.

Procedure: Freshmen are admitted fall and spring. Entrance exams should be taken prior to registration. The college accepts all applicants. Notification is sent on a rolling basis. Check with the school for current application deadlines.

Transfer: A GPA of 2.0 is recommended. Transcripts and a letter of recommendation should be submitted 60 days before enrollment. 32 credits of 124 must be completed at SwCC.

Visiting: There are regularly scheduled orientations for prospective students. There are guides for informal visits and visitors may sit in on classes and stay overnight. To schedule a visit, contact Jacob McClinton, Admissions Counselor.

Financial Aid: SwCC is a member of CSS. The CSS/Profile and the college's own financial statement are required. Check with the school for current deadlines.

International Students: They must score 500 on the written TOEFL and also take the college's own entrance exam or A full course load of 12 semester hours is required.

Computers: The mainframe is an IBM/34. There are computer labs in the library. All students may access the system during regular school hours. There are no time limits and no fees.

Admissions Contact: Thomas O. Fitzgerald, Director of Admissions.

SOUTHWESTERN UNIVERSITY D-3

Georgetown, TX 78626 (512) 863-1200
(800) 252-3166; Fax: (512) 863-9601

Full-time: 563 men, 731 women	**Faculty:** 110; IIB, +$
Part-time: 10 men, 16 women	**Ph.D.s:** 96%
Graduate: none	**Student/Faculty:** 12 to 1
Year: semesters, summer session	**Tuition:** $16,650
Application Deadline: February 15	**Room & Board:** $5900
Freshman Class: 1562 applied, 928 accepted, 326 enrolled	
SAT I Verbal/Math: 615/612	**ACT:** 26 **HIGHLY COMPETITIVE**

Southwestern University, founded in 1840, is a private liberal arts institution affiliated with the United Methodist Church. There are 2 undergraduate schools. In addition to regional accreditation, Southwestern has baccalaureate program accreditation with NASM. The library contains 292,756 volumes, 51,380 microform items, and 10,533 audiovisual forms/CDs, and subscribes to 1473 periodicals. Computerized library services include the card catalog, interlibrary loans, and database searching. Special learning facilities include a learning resource center, art gallery, and TV station. The 700-acre campus is in a suburban area 28 miles north of Austin. Including residence halls, there are 31 buildings.

Student Life: 92% of undergraduates are from Texas. Others are from 31 states, 8 foreign countries, and Canada. 84% are from public schools. 82% are white; 12% Hispanic. 66% are Protestant; 23% Catholic; 14% claim no religious affiliation. The average age of freshmen is 18; all undergraduates, 20. 12% do not continue beyond their first year; 71% remain to graduate.

Housing: 1047 students can be accommodated in college housing, which includes single-sex and coed dormitories, on-campus apartments, and fraternity houses. In addition, there are special-interest houses. On-campus housing is guaranteed for the freshman year only, is available on a first-come, first-served basis, and is available on a lottery system for upperclassmen. 81% of students live on campus; of those, 55% remain on campus on weekends. Alcohol is not permitted. All students may keep cars.

Activities: 31% of men belong to 3 national fraternities; 32% of women belong to 4 national sororities. There are 81 groups on campus, including art, band, cheerleading, choir, chorale, chorus, computers, dance, drama, ethnic, film, gay, honors, international, jazz band, literary magazine, musical theater, newspaper, opera, orchestra, pep band, political, professional, radio and TV, religious, social, social service, student government, and yearbook. Popular campus events include Homecoming Sing, Mall Ball, and Brown Symposium.

Sports: There are 7 intercollegiate sports for men and 7 for women, and 9 intramural sports for men and 9 for women. Facilities include a health and wellness center, a 2000-seat gym, a 9-hole golf course, tennis courts, a baseball field, soccer and lacrosse fields, and a recreation center that includes an indoor jogging track, large performance gym, weight training room, and indoor swimming pool.

Disabled Students: 90% of the campus is accessible. Wheelchair ramps, elevators, special parking, specially equipped rest rooms, lowered drinking fountains, and lowered telephones are available.

Services: Counseling and information services are available, as is tutoring in most subjects, including math, computer science, and sciences.

Campus Safety and Security: Measures include 24-hour foot and vehicle patrol, self-defense education, escort service, and informal discussions. There are pamphlets/posters/films, emergency telephones, and lighted pathways/sidewalks.

Programs of Study: Southwestern confers B.A., B.S., B.F.A., and B.Mus. degrees. Bachelor's degrees are awarded in AGRICULTURE (animal science and environmental studies), BIOLOGICAL SCIENCE (biology/biological science), BUSINESS (accounting and business administration and management), COMMUNICATIONS AND THE ARTS (art, classics, communications, dramatic arts, English, French, German, Latin, music, and Spanish), COMPUTER AND PHYSICAL SCIENCE (chemistry, computer science, mathematics, and physics), SOCIAL SCIENCE (American studies, early childhood studies, economics, history, international studies, philosophy, physical fitness/movement, political science/government, psychology, religion, sociology, and women's studies). Biology, sociology, and political science are the strongest academically. Psychology, biology, and business are the largest.

Required: To graduate, all students must complete at least 122 credits with a 2.0 GPA and satisfy distribution requirements in the arts, humanities, social science, and natural science. The total number of hours required in most majors in 30. A first-year seminar and math course are required. All students must take 1 semester of English composition and must demonstrate computer literacy. Seniors must complete a capstone requirement in the major.

Special: Students may study abroad in England, France, Mexico, Korea, and other countries. The university offers a Washington semester, dual, student-designed, and independent majors, and internships in government, fine arts, psychology, science, and other fields. A 3-2 engineering program may be arranged with Washington, Texas A&M, and Arizona State universities, and the University of Texas at Austin. Some pass/

fail options are available. There are 7 national honor societies, including Phi Beta Kappa, and 21 departmental honors programs.

Faculty/Classroom: 53% of faculty are male; 47%, female. All teach undergraduates. The average class size in an introductory lecture is 20; in a laboratory, 16; and in a regular course, 15.

Admissions: 59% of the 2001-2002 applicants were accepted. The SAT I scores for the 2001-2002 freshman class were: Verbal--6% below 500, 31% between 500 and 599, 49% between 600 and 700, and 14% above 700; Math--6% below 500, 32% between 500 and 599, 50% between 600 and 700, and 12% above 700. The ACT scores were 8% below 21, 16% between 21 and 23, 25% between 24 and 26, 23% between 27 and 28, and 27% above 28. 77% of the current freshmen were in the top fifth of their class; 93% were in the top two fifths. There were 2 National Merit finalists and 5 semifinalists. 9 freshmen graduated first in their class.

Requirements: The SAT I or ACT is required. In addition, the applicant should be a graduate of an accredited high school or have the GED. Secondary preparation should include 4 years each of English and math, 3 each of science and social science or history, 2 of a foreign language, and 1 of an academic elective. An essay is required, and an interview is recommended. AP and CLEP credits are accepted. Important factors in the admissions decision are advanced placement or honor courses, recommendations by school officials, and leadership record. Applications are accepted via CollegeLink, Apply, and Common Application, and online at the school's web site.

Procedure: Freshmen are admitted fall and spring. Entrance exams should be taken in the fall of the senior year. There are early decision, early admissions, and deferred admissions plans. Early decision applications should be filed by November 1 (Round 1) and January 1 (Round 2); regular applications, by February 15 for fall entry and December 1 for spring entry, along with a $40 fee. Notification of early decision is sent December 1 (Round 1) and February (Round 2); regular decision, April 1. 134 early decision candidates were accepted for the 2001-2002 class. 10% of all applicants are on a waiting list; 12 were accepted in 2001.

Transfer: 36 transfer students enrolled in 2001-2002. Preference is given to students having a 3.0 in all college work. 30 credits of 122 must be completed at Southwestern.

Visiting: There are regularly scheduled orientations for prospective students, including 3 or 4 group overnight options and individually arranged visits throughout the year. All visits typically include tours, faculty appointment, and interview, and may also include, an overnight on campus and class visitation. There are guides for informal visits and visitors may sit in on classes and stay overnight. To schedule a visit, contact the Admission Office.

Financial Aid: In 2001-2002, 72% of all freshmen and 73% of continuing students received some form of financial aid. 49% of freshmen and 51% of continuing students received need-based aid. The average freshman award was $14,048. Of that total, scholarships or need-based grants averaged $11,094 ($24,230 maximum); loans averaged $2012 ($4500 maximum); and work contracts averaged $942 ($2000 maximum). 69% of undergraduates work part time. Average annual earnings from campus work are $1670. The average financial indebtedness of the 2001 graduate was $19,627. Southwestern is a member of CSS. The FAFSA and the college's own financial statement are required. The fall application deadline is March 1.

International Students: There is 1 international student enrolled. The school actively recruits these students. They must score 550 on the written TOEFL or 217 on the electronic version and also take the SAT I or the ACT.

Computers: The mainframes are an HP 855, HP 9000/800K, an HP 9000/800D, and HP 9000/800E-55 and E-35 models. There are approximately 150 PCs located throughout the campus for student use. Students may also use the facilities in 3 computer labs where there is access to the Internet (e-mail, World Wide Web, and Gopher), word processing, and instructional software. All students may access the system at any time. There are no time limits and no fees.

Graduates: In 2001, 266 bachelor's degrees were awarded. The most popular majors were business (15%), communication (11%), and biology (8%). In an average class, 1% graduate in 3 years, 63% in 4 years, 72% in 5 years, and 74% in 6 years. 26 companies recruited on campus in 2000-2001. Of the 2000 graduating class, 30% were enrolled in graduate school within 6 months of graduation and 65% were employed.

Admissions Contact: John W. Lind, Vice President, Enrollment Management. E-mail: *admission@southwestern.edu*
Web: *www.southwestern.edu*

STEPHEN F. AUSTIN STATE UNIVERSITY — E-3

Nacogdoches, TX 75962 — **(936) 468-2504**
(800) 731-2902; Fax: (936) 468-3849

Full-time: 3704 men, 5297 women	**Faculty:** 419; IIA, --$
Part-time: 612 men, 670 women	**Ph.D.s:** 76%
Graduate: 477 men, 809 women	**Student/Faculty:** 21 to 1
Year: semesters, summer session	**Tuition:** $2330 ($7394)
Application Deadline: open	**Room & Board:** $4575
Freshman Class: 9621 applied, 6486 accepted, 2161 enrolled	
SAT I or ACT: required	**COMPETITIVE**

Stephen F. Austin State University, founded in 1923, is a public regional university offering undergraduate and graduate degree programs through 7 colleges. There are 7 undergraduate schools and 1 graduate school. In addition to regional accreditation, SFA has baccalaureate program accreditation with AACSB, ADA, CSWE, FIDER, NASM, NCATE, NLN, and SAF. The library contains 936,965 volumes, 1,386,788 microform items, and 10,680 audiovisual forms/CDs, and subscribes to 3115 periodicals. Computerized library services include the card catalog, interlibrary loans, and database searching. Special learning facilities include a learning resource center, art gallery, planetarium, radio station, TV station, and arboretum, beef and poultry research centers, experimental forest, and biotechnology and environmental science research centers. The 401-acre campus is in a small town 140 miles northeast of Houston. Including residence halls, there are 75 buildings.

Student Life: 98% of undergraduates are from Texas. Others are from 30 states, 54 foreign countries, and Canada. 99% are from public schools. 78% are white; 14% African American. The average age of freshmen is 19; all undergraduates, 23. 40% do not continue beyond their first year; 37% remain to graduate.

Housing: 4604 students can be accommodated in college housing, which includes single-sex and coed dormitories, on-campus apartments, and married-student housing. In addition, there are honors houses, special-interest houses, and an enrichment hall with required study hours. On-campus housing is guaranteed for all 4 years. 65% of students commute. Alcohol is not permitted. All students may keep cars.

Activities: 13% of men belong to 18 national fraternities; 10% of women belong to 9 national sororities. There are 180 groups on campus, including art, band, cheerleading, choir, chorale, chorus, computers, dance, debate, drama, drill team, ethnic, film, flag corps, gay, honors, international, jazz band, literary magazine, marching band, musical theater, newspaper, opera, orchestra, pep band, photography, political, professional, radio and TV, religious, social, social service, student government, symphony, and yearbook. Popular campus events include Parents Weekend, Watermelon Bash, and Howdy Week.

Sports: There are 5 intercollegiate sports for men and 7 for women, and 25 intramural sports for men and 19 for women. Facilities include 2 gyms, courts for handball, tennis, and racquetball, weight and gymnastics rooms, and various playing fields.

Disabled Students: All of the campus is accessible. Wheelchair ramps, elevators, special parking, specially equipped rest rooms, special class scheduling, lowered drinking fountains, and lowered telephones are available.

Services: Counseling and information services are available, as is tutoring in most subjects. There is a reader service for the blind, and remedial math, reading, and writing.

Campus Safety and Security: Measures include 24-hour foot and vehicle patrol, self-defense education, escort service, and shuttle buses. There are informal discussions, pamphlets/posters/films, emergency telephones, and lighted pathways/sidewalks.

Programs of Study: Master's and doctoral degrees are also awarded. Bachelor's degrees are awarded in AGRICULTURE (agricultural business management, agricultural mechanics, agriculture, agronomy, animal science, fish and game management, forestry and related sciences, forestry production and processing, horticulture, and range/farm management), BIOLOGICAL SCIENCE (biology/biological science, life science, and nutrition), BUSINESS (accounting, banking and finance, business administration and management, fashion merchandising, hospitality management services, international business management, management information systems, management science, marketing management, marketing/retailing/merchandising, and office supervision and management), COMMUNICATIONS AND THE ARTS (art, broadcasting, communications, dance, dramatic arts, English, fine arts, French, journalism, music, Spanish, and speech/debate/rhetoric), COMPUTER AND PHYSICAL SCIENCE (chemistry, computer programming, computer science, earth science, geology, information sciences and systems, mathematics, physical sciences, and physics), EDUCATION (agricultural, art, bilingual/bicultural, business, computer, drama, early childhood, education, education of the deaf and hearing impaired, education of the emotionally handicapped, education of the exceptional child, education of the mentally handicapped, education of the multiply handicapped, education of the physically handicapped, education of the visually handicapped, elementary, English, health, home economics, journalism, mathematics, music, physical, reading, science, secondary, and special), ENGINEER-

ING AND ENVIRONMENTAL DESIGN (environmental science, interior design, and preengineering), HEALTH PROFESSIONS (health science, nursing, premedicine, preoptometry, prepharmacy, preveterinary science, rehabilitation therapy, and speech therapy), SOCIAL SCIENCE (child psychology/development, corrections, criminal justice, dietetics, economics, food production/management/services, food science, geography, gerontology, history, home economics, humanities, interdisciplinary studies, law enforcement and corrections, parks and recreation management, physical fitness/movement, political science/government, prelaw, psychology, public administration, social work, and sociology). Accounting, computer science, and natural science are the strongest academically. Elementary education, communication, and kinesiology are the largest.

Required: All students must complete at least 130 hours with a minimum 2.0 GPA. The B.A. program requires courses in communication skills, math and natural science, humanities, social science, and physical activity.

Special: Internships, dual majors, and dual degrees are possible in some programs. Preengineering and 3-2 engineering programs with Texas A&M are offered, as are preprofessional programs and a general studies degree. There are 21 national honor societies, and a freshman honors program.

Faculty/Classroom: 55% of faculty are male; 45%, female. 85% teach undergraduates. Graduate students teach 5% of introductory courses. The average class size in an introductory lecture is 31 and in a laboratory, 24.

Admissions: 67% of the 2001-2002 applicants were accepted. 30% of the current freshmen were in the top fifth of their class; 80% were in the top two fifths.

Requirements: The SAT I or ACT is required. In addition, for clear admission, applicants must have been in the top 50% of their high school class or have a 21 ACT or 1010 SAT I score. SFA requires applicants to be in the upper 50% of their class. AP and CLEP credits are accepted. Applications are accepted on-line with supplemental forms at *www.sfasu.edu/admissions*.

Procedure: Freshmen are admitted to all sessions. Entrance exams should be taken during the junior year. Application deadlines are open. The application fee is $25.

Transfer: 937 transfer students enrolled in 2001-2002. Applicants with fewer than 15 hours of college work must meet freshman admission requirements. Those with more than 15 hours must have at least a 2.0 GPA. Those with GPAs lower than 2.0 may be admitted to the summer school on probation. 42 credits of 130 must be completed at SFA.

Visiting: There are regularly scheduled orientations for prospective students, including Showcase Saturdays, which are 1-day house programs with faculty, staff, and current students. There are guides for informal visits and visitors may sit in on classes. To schedule a visit, contact the Admissions Office.

Financial Aid: In 2001-2002, 47% of all freshmen and 41% of continuing students received some form of financial aid. The average freshman award was $6916. Of that total, scholarships or need-based grants averaged $3800; and loans averaged $3106. The average financial indebtedness of the 2001 graduate was $6894. The FAFSA is required. The fall application deadline is April 1.

International Students: There are 42 international students enrolled. They must score 550 on the written TOEFL and also take the SAT I or the ACT.

Computers: The mainframe is a DEC ALPHA 7720 cluster. There are 16 computer labs with 700 Macs and PCs and students have free access to the Internet. All students may access the system at any time and have 30 minutes of Internet access per 4 hours. There are no fees.

Graduates: In 2001, 1774 bachelor's degrees were awarded. The most popular majors were elementary education (14%), kinesiology (7%), and communication (6%). In an average class, 16% graduate in 4 years, 32% in 5 years, and 37% in 6 years. 72 companies recruited on campus in 2000-2001. Of the 2000 graduating class, 10% were enrolled in graduate school within 6 months of graduation.

Admissions Contact: Roger Bilow, Director of Admissions.
E-mail: *admissions@sfasu.edu* Web: *www.sfasu.edu*

SUL ROSS STATE UNIVERSITY B-3

Alpine, TX 79832 **(915) 837-8050; Fax: (915) 837-8431**

Full-time: 688 men, 571 women	**Faculty:** 95
Part-time: 90 men, 139 women	**Ph.D.s:** 69%
Graduate: 209 men, 295 women	**Student/Faculty:** 12 to 1
Year: semesters, summer session	**Tuition:** $2792 ($9122)
Application Deadline: open	**Room & Board:** $3790
Freshman Class: 339 enrolled	
ACT: 17	**LESS COMPETITIVE**

Sul Ross State University, founded in 1917, is a public institution offering programs in the liberal arts and sciences, fine arts and music, range animal science, business, and education. In addition, an upper-level and graduate center offers courses in Uralde, Del Rio, and Eagle Pass, Texas. There are 3 undergraduate schools and 1 graduate school. The library contains 248,598 volumes, 444,950 microform items, and 13,011 audiovisual forms/CDs, and subscribes to 1951 periodicals. Computerized library services include the card catalog, interlibrary loans, and database searching. Special learning facilities include a learning resource center, art gallery, natural history museum, planetarium, radio station, and extensive geology/chemistry lab equipment, including a scanning electron microscope. The 600-acre campus is in a rural area 165 miles from Odessa. Including residence halls, there are 22 buildings.

Student Life: 97% of undergraduates are from Texas. Others are from 18 states and 7 foreign countries. 98% are from public schools. 55% are white; 41% Hispanic. 51% are Catholic; 48% Protestant. The average age of freshmen is 20; all undergraduates, 24. 55% do not continue beyond their first year; 20% remain to graduate.

Housing: 769 students can be accommodated in college housing, which includes single-sex and coed dormitories, on-campus apartments, and married-student housing. On-campus housing is guaranteed for the freshman year only and is available on a first-come, first-served basis. 67% of students commute. Alcohol is not permitted. All students may keep cars.

Activities: There are no fraternities or sororities. There are 41 groups on campus, including art, cheerleading, choir, drama, ethnic, honors, international, literary magazine, newspaper, pep band, political, professional, religious, student government, and yearbook. Popular campus events include cultural events, Fall on the Mall, and Honors Day.

Sports: There are 5 intercollegiate sports for men and 4 for women, and 4 intramural sports for men and 3 for women. Facilities include a gym and an undergraduate center.

Disabled Students: 90% of the campus is accessible. Wheelchair ramps, elevators, special parking, specially equipped rest rooms, special class scheduling, and lowered drinking fountains are available.

Services: Counseling and information services are available, as is tutoring in some subjects, including math, reading, and English. There is remedial math, reading, and writing.

Campus Safety and Security: Measures include 24-hour foot and vehicle patrol, informal discussions, pamphlets/posters/films, and lighted pathways/sidewalks.

Programs of Study: Sully confers B.A., B.S., B.B.A., and B.F.A. degrees. Associate and master's degrees are also awarded. Bachelor's degrees are awarded in AGRICULTURE (agricultural business management, animal science, equine science, natural resource management, and wildlife management), BIOLOGICAL SCIENCE (biology/biological science), BUSINESS (accounting, business administration and management, and office supervision and management), COMMUNICATIONS AND THE ARTS (applied music, communications, dramatic arts, English, fine arts, and Spanish), COMPUTER AND PHYSICAL SCIENCE (chemistry, computer science, geology, and mathematics), EDUCATION (art and elementary), ENGINEERING AND ENVIRONMENTAL DESIGN (environmental science and industrial engineering technology), SOCIAL SCIENCE (criminal justice, history, Mexican-American/Chicano studies, physical fitness/movement, political science/government, psychology, and social science). Behavioral and social sciences, education, and fine arts are the strongest academically. Phys ed, criminal justice, and education are the largest.

Required: All students must complete a general education requirement of 53 to 57 hours, including courses in English, history, foreign language, political science, math, the arts, social science, and natural science. A minimum 2.0 GPA and 130 credit hours are required to graduate. There are additional requirements for some degree programs. All students must take 2 courses in phys ed and 1 in computer science. The total number of hours required in the major varies.

Special: Sully offers unpaid internships in several departments, including psychology and criminal justice, as well as work-study programs, and nondegree study. There are 8 national honor societies, and a freshman honors program.

Faculty/Classroom: 69% of faculty are male; 31%, female. 95% teach undergraduates and 85% both teach and do research. No introductory courses are taught by graduate students. The average class size in an introductory lecture is 42; in a laboratory, 15; and in a regular course, 21.

Admissions: The ACT scores for the 2001-2002 freshman class were: 81% below 21, 13% between 21 and 23, 5% between 24 and 26, and 1% between 27 and 28. 13% of the current freshmen were in the top fifth of their class; 39% were in the top two fifths.

Requirements: The SAT I or ACT is required. In addition, applicants should be graduates of an accredited secondary school and have a minimum of 14 credits, including 4 in English, 3 in math, 2 each in science, history, and phys ed/health, and 1 in government/economics. Applicants must meet 1 of the following criteria for full admission: present a minimum composite score of 20 on the ACT or 920 on the SAT I; or graduate in the upper half of their class. Probationary admission is possible for students who do not meet the admissions standards. AP and CLEP credits are accepted.

Procedure: Freshmen are admitted to all sessions. Entrance exams should be taken preferably early in the senior year. There is an early admissions plan. Application deadlines are open. Notification is sent on a rolling basis.

Transfer: The GPA required for transfer students varies according to the number of college credits completed. 30 credits of 130 must be completed at Sully.

Visiting: There are regularly scheduled orientations for prospective students, consisting of 1 1/2-day programs in January, late August, June, and July. There are guides for informal visits and visitors may sit in on classes and stay overnight. To schedule a visit, contact the Office of Admissions at (915) 837-8059.

Financial Aid: In 2001-2002, 52% of freshmen and 21% of continuing students received need-based aid. The average freshman award was $5489. Of that total, scholarships or need-based grants averaged $4481 ($13,200 maximum); loans averaged $318 ($6686 maximum); and work contracts averaged $30 ($1707 maximum). 7% of undergraduates work part time. Average annual earnings from campus work are $2000. Sully is a member of CSS. The CSS/Profile is required.

International Students: They must score 520 on the written TOEFL and also take the SAT I or the ACT, scoring 800 on the SAT I.

Computers: The mainframe is an IBM AS/400. PCs are available for academic use. All students may access the system. There are no time limits and no fees.

Admissions Contact: Robert C. Cullins, Dean of Admissions and Records. E-mail: *rcullins@sul-ross-1.sulross.edu* Web: *www.sulross.edu*

TARLETON STATE UNIVERSITY
Stephenville, TX 76402

D-2
(254) 968-9125
(800) 687-8236; Fax: (254) 968-9951

Full-time: 2417 men, 2753 women	**Faculty:** 280; IIA, --$
Part-time: 671 men, 874 women	**Ph.D.s:** 54%
Graduate: 476 men, 834 women	**Student/Faculty:** 18 to 1
Year: semesters, summer session	**Tuition:** $2675 ($7738)
Application Deadline: August 1	**Room & Board:** $4485
Freshman Class: 2322 applied, 1575 accepted, 1129 enrolled	
SAT I Verbal/Math: 476/487	**ACT:** 20 **COMPETITIVE**

Tarleton State University, founded in 1899 and a part of the Texas A&M University System, is a public institution offering undergraduate and graduate programs in agriculture and technology, arts and sciences, business, and education and fine arts. There are 5 undergraduate schools and 1 graduate school. In addition to regional accreditation, Tarleton has baccalaureate program accreditation with ACBSP, CSWE, NASM, and NCATE. The library contains 262,801 volumes, 893,631 microform items, and 6883 audiovisual forms/CDs, and subscribes to 2791 periodicals. Computerized library services include the card catalog, interlibrary loans, and database searching. Special learning facilities include a learning resource center, art gallery, planetarium, a 600-acre farm, a 1200-acre ranch, and an equine center. The 123-acre campus is in a small town 67 miles southwest of Fort Worth. Including residence halls, there are 84 buildings.

Student Life: 95% of undergraduates are from Texas. Others are from 48 states, 31 foreign countries, and Canada. 86% are from public schools. 84% are white. Most are Protestant. The average age of freshmen is 18; all undergraduates, 24. 34% do not continue beyond their first year; 33% remain to graduate.

Housing: 1538 students can be accommodated in college housing, which includes single-sex and coed dormitories, on-campus apartments, off-campus apartments, and married-student housing. On-campus housing is guaranteed for the freshman year only and is available on a first-come, first-served basis. 78% of students commute. Alcohol is not permitted. All students may keep cars.

Activities: 7% of men belong to 8 national fraternities; 5% of women belong to 7 national sororities. There are more than 100 groups and organizations on campus, including art, band, cheerleading, choir, computers, debate, drama, drill team, ethnic, honors, international, jazz band, marching band, musical theater, newspaper, political, professional, religious, social, social service, student government, and yearbook. Popular campus events include Howdy Week, Spring Fest, and Tarleton Christmas.

Sports: There are 5 intercollegiate sports for men and 7 for women, and 19 intramural sports for men and 19 for women. Facilities include a fully equipped complex with a heated pool, track, courts for basketball, volleyball, tennis, and racquetball and various playing fields. There is also a 7000-seat stadium, a 3300-seat gym, and a fully lighted 550-seat baseball stadium.

Disabled Students: 80% of the campus is accessible. Wheelchair ramps, elevators, special parking, specially equipped rest rooms, special class scheduling, lowered drinking fountains, lowered telephones, and easy-access doors are available.

Services: Counseling and information services are available, as is tutoring in most subjects, including math, science, English, and social studies. The Teaching and Learning Center provides tutoring assistance in all academic areas.

Campus Safety and Security: Measures include 24-hour foot and vehicle patrol, self-defense education, escort service, and shuttle buses. There are informal discussions, pamphlets/posters/films, emergency telephones, and lighted pathways/sidewalks.

Programs of Study: Tarleton confers B.A., B.S., B.A.A.S., B.B.A., B.F.A., B.M., B.S.N., and B.S.W. degrees. Master's degrees are also awarded. Bachelor's degrees are awarded in AGRICULTURE (agricultural business management, agricultural economics, agricultural mechanics, agriculture, animal science, horticulture, plant science, and range/farm management), BIOLOGICAL SCIENCE (biology/biological science), BUSINESS (accounting, banking and finance, business administration and management, fashion merchandising, human resources, management science, marketing and distribution, marketing/retailing/merchandising, office supervision and management, and personnel management), COMMUNICATIONS AND THE ARTS (art, dramatic arts, English, fine arts, music, Spanish, and speech/debate/rhetoric), COMPUTER AND PHYSICAL SCIENCE (chemistry, computer programming, earth science, geology, information sciences and systems, mathematics, and physics), EDUCATION (agricultural, art, business, home economics, industrial arts, and physical), ENGINEERING AND ENVIRONMENTAL DESIGN (industrial engineering technology), HEALTH PROFESSIONS (medical laboratory technology, nursing, physical therapy, predentistry, premedicine, prepharmacy, and preveterinary science), SOCIAL SCIENCE (criminal justice, economics, history, home economics, interdisciplinary studies, law enforcement and corrections, physical fitness/movement, political science/government, prelaw, social work, sociology, and water resources). Science and business are the strongest academically. Agriculture and education are the largest.

Required: All students must complete at least 128 hours, including 24 hours in the major, with a 2.0 GPA. The 47-hour required core curriculum includes courses in English, U.S. and Texas government, U.S. history, lab science, computer information systems, and phys ed. There are also distributional requirements that must be met in humanities and social sciences, and a writing proficiency exam.

Special: Tarleton offers work-study programs, internships, limited nondegree study, study abroad in 2 countries, and cross-registration with Texas A&M Inernational University at Laredo. There is a 3-2 engineering degree available with Texas A&M University. Special degree programs may be designed to meet unusual requirements. There are 11 national honor societies, a freshman honors program, and 9 departmental honors programs.

Faculty/Classroom: 57% of faculty are male; 43%, female. All teach undergraduates, 4% do research, and 4% do both. Graduate students teach 1% of introductory courses. The average class size in an introductory lecture is 32; in a laboratory, 19; and in a regular course, 23.

Admissions: 68% of the 2001-2002 applicants were accepted. The SAT I scores for the 2001-2002 freshman class were: Verbal--60% below 500, 32% between 500 and 599, 8% between 600 and 700, and 1% above 700; Math--54% below 500, 37% between 500 and 599, 8% between 600 and 700, and 1% above 700. The ACT scores were 59% below 21, 24% between 21 and 23, 11% between 24 and 26, 3% between 27 and 28, and 1% above 28. 25% of the current freshmen were in the top fifth of their class; 55% were in the top two fifths. 14 freshmen graduated first in their class.

Requirements: The SAT I or ACT is required. In addition, applicants must have a minimum composite score of 930 on the SAT I or 20 on the ACT, be a graduate of an accredited Texas secondary school or advanced high school program, or rank in the top quarter of their graduating class. Secondary preparation should include 4 years of English and 3 years of college-preparatory math, including algebra I and II. A GED will be considered equivalent to a high school diploma, provided the average standard score is at least 55 or no subscore is less than 50. A GPA of 2.0 is required. AP and CLEP credits are accepted. Important factors in the admissions decision are advanced placement or honor courses, evidence of special talent, and extracurricular activities record. An online application is available through *www.applytexas.org*, which is available to all public universities in Texas via electronic record.

Procedure: Freshmen are admitted to all sessions. Entrance exams should be taken preferably in the junior year. There are early decision and deferred admissions plans. Applications should be filed by August 1 for fall entry, January 3 for spring entry, and May 25 for summer entry, along with a $25 fee. Notification is sent on a rolling basis. 101 early decision candidates were accepted for the 2001-2002 class.

Transfer: 1017 transfer students enrolled in 2001-2002. Applicants with 30 or more transferable credits must present a 2.0 GPA; those with fewer than 30 credits must present a 2.8 GPA. A GPA of 2.0 to 2.79 may be admitted provided transfers also meet regular admission standards of first-time freshman applicants. 30 credits of 128 must be completed at Tarleton.

Visiting: There are regularly scheduled orientations for prospective students, including a tour of the campus. There are guides for informal visits and visitors may sit in on classes. To schedule a visit, contact the Office of School Relations, Tarleton Center at (254) 968-9256 or (800) 687-4TSU or *info@tarleton.edu*.

Financial Aid: The average freshman award was $6060. Of that total, scholarships or need-based grants averaged $2563 ($3750 maximum); loans averaged $2139 ($2625 maximum); and work contracts averaged $2500 ($3300 maximum). Average annual earnings from campus work are $2000. The average financial indebtedness of the 2001 graduate was $15,756. Tarleton is a member of CSS. The FAFSA or FFS is required. The fall application deadline is May 1.

International Students: There are 31 international students enrolled. The school actively recruits these students. They must score 520 on the written TOEFL and also take the SAT I or the ACT.

Computers: The mainframe is a Dual Digital (Compaq) ALPHA 8200. There are 1600 Kaypro, Mac II, Apple IIe, IBM AT, and other PCs available in student labs and faculty offices. All dorms are wired for Internet access. All students may access the system. There are no time limits. The fee is $4 per hour.

Graduates: In 2001, 1190 bachelor's degrees were awarded. The most popular majors were interdisciplinary studies (10%), exercise and sport studies (9%), and agricultural services and development (6%). In an average class, 13% graduate in 4 years, 30% in 5 years, and 32% in 6 years. 367 companies recruited on campus in 2000-2001. Of the 2000 graduating class, 5% were enrolled in graduate school within 6 months of graduation and 80% were employed.

Admissions Contact: Denise Siler, Director of Admissions.
E-mail: *siler@tarleton.edu* Web: *www.tarleton.edu*

TEXAS A & M UNIVERSITY SYSTEM

The Texas A & M University System, established in 1876, is 1 of 6 public systems in Texas. It is governed by a 9-member board of regents. The chief administrator for the system is the chancellor. The primary mission of the system's 9 universities, 8 state agencies, and a health science center is education, leadership, development, research, and service. Campuses are located in Canyon, College Station, Commerce, Corpus Christi, Kingsville, Laredo, Prarie View, Stephenville, and Texarkana. The total enrollment in fall 2000 of all universities was 91,813. There are approximately 23,000 faculty and staff members in the universities, agencies, and health science center. Altogether there are approximately 500 baccalaureate, 400 master's, and 100 doctoral programs, as well as 3 professional degrees (M.D., D.V.M., D.D.S.) offered in the Texas A & M University System. Profiles of the 4-year campuses are included in this section.

TEXAS A&M UNIVERSITY — D-3

College Station, TX 77843 — **(979) 845-3741; Fax: (979) 847-8737**

Full-time: 17,243 men, 16,533 women	**Faculty:** 1328; I, av$
Part-time: 1510 men, 1317 women	**Ph.D.s:** 91%
Graduate: 4778 men, 3237 women	**Student/Faculty:** 25 to 1
Year: semesters, summer session	**Tuition:** $3722 ($10,052)
Application Deadline: February 15	**Room & Board:** $5266
Freshman Class: 16,685 applied, 11,531 accepted, 6760 enrolled	
SAT I Verbal/Math: 576/602	**ACT:** 25 **VERY COMPETITIVE**

Texas A&M University, founded in 1876, is part of the Texas A&M University system. Undergraduate degrees are offered in agriculture and life sciences, architecture, business administration, education, engineering, geosciences, liberal arts, science, and biomedical science. There are 9 undergraduate and 10 graduate schools. In addition to regional accreditation, Texas A&M has baccalaureate program accreditation with AACSB, ABET, ACCE, ACEJMC, ADA, ASLA, CSAB, NAAB, NCATE, and SAF. The 3 libraries contain 4,425,478 volumes, 5,157,901 microform items, and 311,852 audiovisual forms/CDs, and subscribe to 25,754 periodicals. Computerized library services include the card catalog, interlibrary loans, and database searching. Special learning facilities include a learning resource center, art gallery, radio station, TV station, and weather station, observatory, cyclotron, wind tunnel, visualization lab, nuclear reactor, ocean wave pool, and the Bush Museum and Library. The 5200-acre campus is in an urban area 90 miles northwest of Houston. Including residence halls, there are 665 buildings.

Student Life: 95% of undergraduates are from Texas. Others are from 49 states, 115 foreign countries, and Canada. 77% are white. The average age of freshmen is 18; all undergraduates, 20. 12% do not continue beyond their first year; 74% remain to graduate.

Housing: 10,600 students can be accommodated in college housing, which includes single-sex and coed dormitories, on-campus apartments, and married-student housing. In addition, there are honors houses. Specially equipped rooms are available for students with physical disabilities. On-campus housing is available on a first-come, first-served basis. All students may keep cars.

Activities: 6% of men belong to 19 national fraternities; 7% of women belong to 2 local and 19 national sororities. There are 700 groups on campus, including art, band, chess, choir, chorale, chorus, computers, dance, drama, drill team, drum and bugle corps, ethnic, film, gay, honors, international, jazz band, literary magazine, marching band, musical theater, newspaper, opera, orchestra, photography, political, professional, radio and TV, religious, social, social service, student government, symphony, and yearbook. Popular campus events include Aggie Bonfire, Parents Weekend, and Whoopstock (a celebration of unity through diversity).

Sports: There are 9 intercollegiate sports for men and 12 for women, and 24 intramural sports for men and 23 for women. Facilities include a coliseum, a natatorium, 11 basketball/volleyball courts, 27 handball/racquetball courts, badminton, weight and activity rooms, jogging trails, 14 tennis courts, a squash court, an 18-hole golf course, a 2500-seat auditorium/arena, a driving range, flag football fields, 4 soccer fields, 4 outdoor basketball courts, and 5 walking trails. Intercollegiate athletic facilities include a 70,210-seat football stadium, a 7200-seat indoor basketball and volleyball coliseum, a 7053-seat baseball stadium, a 1750-seat softball complex, a 1000-seat soccer complex, a 2000-seat natatorium, a 3000-seat track and field complex, a 1500-seat tennis center, and an 18,000-square-foot physical strength and conditioning lab.

Disabled Students: 85% of the campus is accessible. Wheelchair ramps, elevators, special parking, specially equipped rest rooms, special class scheduling, lowered drinking fountains, lowered telephones, and an office of support services for students with disabilities are available.

Services: Counseling and information services are available, as is tutoring in most subjects. There is a reader service for the blind, and remedial math, reading, and writing. Workshops in time management, basic study techniques, and test-taking skills are available.

Campus Safety and Security: Measures include 24-hour foot and vehicle patrol, self-defense education, escort service, and shuttle buses. There are informal discussions, pamphlets/posters/films, emergency telephones, lighted pathways/sidewalks, and a security awareness committee, and crime-watch and safety-tip lines.

Programs of Study: Texas A&M confers B.A., B.S., B.B.A., B.Ed., and B.L.A. degrees. Master's and doctoral degrees are also awarded. Bachelor's degrees are awarded in AGRICULTURE (agricultural business management, agricultural economics, animal science, dairy science, fish and game management, fishing and fisheries, forestry and related sciences, horticulture, poultry science, and range/farm management), BIOLOGICAL SCIENCE (biochemistry, biology/biological science, botany, entomology, genetics, microbiology, and zoology), BUSINESS (accounting, banking and finance, business systems analysis, management science, marketing/retailing/merchandising, and personnel management), COMMUNICATIONS AND THE ARTS (English, French, German, journalism, Russian, Spanish, and speech/debate/rhetoric), COMPUTER AND PHYSICAL SCIENCE (atmospheric sciences and meteorology, chemistry, computer science, geology, geophysics and seismology, mathematics, and physics), EDUCATION (elementary, health, physical, and secondary), ENGINEERING AND ENVIRONMENTAL DESIGN (aeronautical engineering, agricultural engineering, bioengineering, chemical engineering, civil engineering, computer engineering, construction engineering, electrical/electronics engineering, engineering technology, environmental design, environmental science, industrial engineering technology, landscape architecture/design, mechanical engineering, nuclear engineering, and petroleum/natural gas engineering), HEALTH PROFESSIONS (biomedical science), SOCIAL SCIENCE (anthropology, economics, history, international studies, parks and recreation management, philosophy, political science/government, psychology, and sociology). Engineering, business administration, and life sciences are the strongest academically. Psychology, accounting, and biomedical science are the largest.

Required: To graduate, students must complete at least 128 credit hours, including 30 to 33 in the major. A minimum 2.0 GPA is required. Students must complete courses in American history and government, phys ed, computers, foreign language, speech and writing skills, math/logical reasoning, science, humanities, and social science. Requirements in the major vary.

Special: The university offers extensive opportunities through the Career Center and Study Abroad Office. B.A.- B.S. degrees, study abroad in 12 countries, credit for military experience, nondegree study, co-op programs, dual majors, and pass/fail options are available. A 5-year graduate business/liberal arts program is offered, as well as a 3-2 engineering degree with Sam Houston State University. There are 41 national honor societies, and a freshman honors program.

Faculty/Classroom: 75% of faculty are male; 25%, female. 70% teach undergraduates, 72% do research, and 47% do both.

Admissions: 69% of the 2001-2002 applicants were accepted. The SAT I scores for the 2001-2002 freshman class were: Verbal--20% below 500, 40% between 500 and 599, 33% between 600 and 700, and 7% above 700; Math--10% below 500, 40% between 500 and 599, 37% between 600 and 700, and 13% above 700. 87% of the current freshman were in the top quarter of their class; 99% were in the top half. There were 142 National Merit finalists. 228 freshmen graduated first in their class.

Requirements: The SAT I or ACT is required. In addition, secondary school graduation is a condition of freshman admission. Required high school courses include 4 credits in English, 3 1/2 credits in math, 3 credits in science (2 from biology, chemistry, or physics), 2 credits of social studies and the same foreign language, and 1 of history. AP and CLEP credits are accepted. Important factors in the admissions decision are leadership record, evidence of special talent, and extracurricular activities record. The state of Texas Common Application is accepted on-line via *www.applytexas.org* or through TAMU web site, *www.tamu.edu/admissions.*

Procedure: Freshmen are admitted fall, spring, and summer. Entrance exams should be taken during the spring of the junior year or by December of the senior year. Applications should be filed by February 15 for fall entry, October 15 for spring entry, and February 15 for summer entry, along with a $50 fee. Notification is sent on a rolling basis. A waiting list is an active part of the admissions procedure.

Transfer: 1863 transfer students enrolled in 2001-2002. Applicants must submit transcripts from previously attended colleges. Requirements vary, depending on how many semester hours were attempted and the grades for those hours. Transfer applicants must submit high school transcripts and, if they have fewer than 12 graded semester hours, the SAT I, or ACT scores. 30 credits of 128 must be completed at Texas A&M.

Visiting: There are regularly scheduled orientations for prospective students, Some 20 new-student conferences are held for students to meet with academic advisers to select courses, become acquainted with student life activities, and tour the campus. There are guides for informal visits and visitors may sit in on classes. To schedule a visit, contact the Aggieland Visitor Center at (979) 845-5851 or *vis-ctr@tamu.edu.*

Financial Aid: In 2001-2002, 66% of all freshmen and 70% of continuing students received some form of financial aid. 35% of freshmen and 40% of continuing students received need-based aid. The average freshman award was $5480. Of that total, scholarships or need-based grants averaged $3739 ($30,938 maximum); loans averaged $4800 ($17,526 maximum); and work contracts averaged $1368 ($10,531 maximum). 28% of undergraduates work part time. Average annual earnings from campus work are $3824. The average financial indebtedness of the 2001 graduate was $13,143. The FAFSA is required. The fall application deadline is April 1.

International Students: There are 472 international students enrolled. They must score 550 on the written TOEFL.

Computers: The mainframes are an IBM 3090-600E, an Amdahl 5990, and DEC VAXs 880, 8650, and 9000-210V. About 2000 Macs and PCs are available throughout the campus. All students may access the system at any time. There are no time limits. The fee is $9.25 per credit hour.

Graduates: In 2001, 7493 bachelor's degrees were awarded. The most popular majors were biomedical science (5%), marketing (5%), and interdisciplinary studies (5%). In an average class, 1% graduate in 3 years, 27% in 4 years, 66% in 5 years, and 74% in 6 years. 150 companies recruited on campus in 2000-2001. Of the 2000 graduating class, 12% were enrolled in graduate school within 6 months of graduation and 54% were employed.

Admissions Contact: Admissions Counseling.
E-mail: *admissions@tamu.edu* Web: *www.tamu.edu/admissions*

TEXAS A&M UNIVERSITY AT COMMERCE E-2
Commerce, TX 75429-3011 (903) 886-5106
(800) 331-3878; Fax: (903) 886-5888

Full-time: 1443 men, 2007 women	**Faculty:** 236; IIA, --$
Part-time: 387 men, 611 women	**Ph.D.s:** 81%
Graduate: 1231 men, 2228 women	**Student/Faculty:** 15 to 1
Year: semesters, summer session	**Tuition:** $2776 ($9100)
Application Deadline: see profile	**Room & Board:** $4550
Freshman Class: 4172 applied, 2517 accepted, 1400 enrolled	
SAT I Verbal/Math: required	**COMPETITIVE**

Texas A&M University at Commerce, founded in 1889, offers undergraduate and graduate programs in business and technology, arts and sciences, and education. There are 3 undergraduate schools and 1 graduate school. In addition to regional accreditation, TAMU-C has baccalaureate program accreditation with AACSB, CSWE, NASM, and NCATE. The library contains 1,714,655 volumes and 131,926 microform items. Computerized library services include the card catalog, interlibrary loans, and database searching. Special learning facilities include a radio station, TV station, performing arts center, and farm. The 154-acre campus is in a small town 65 miles northeast of Dallas. Including residence halls, there are 121 buildings.

Student Life: 96% of undergraduates are from Texas. Others are from 41 states, 28 foreign countries, and Canada. 98% are from public schools. 78% are white; 14% African American. The average age of freshmen is 19; all undergraduates, 27. 31% do not continue beyond their first year; 50% remain to graduate.

Housing: 2750 students can be accommodated in college housing, which includes single-sex and coed dormitories, on-campus apartments, married-student housing, fraternity houses, and sorority houses. In addition, there are honors houses and special-interest houses. On-campus housing is guaranteed for the freshman year only and is available on a first-come, first-served basis. 76% of students commute. All students may keep cars.

Activities: 15% of men belong to 9 national fraternities; 12% of women belong to 7 national sororities. There are 96 groups on campus, including art, band, cheerleading, chess, choir, chorale, chorus, dance, drama, ethnic, film, gay, honors, international, jazz band, literary magazine, marching band, musical theater, newspaper, orchestra, pep band, photography, political, professional, radio and TV, religious, social, social service, student government, and yearbook. Popular campus events include Sam Rayburn Symposium, Christmas Feast of Carols, and Springfest.

Sports: There are 5 intercollegiate sports for men and 5 for women, and 7 intramural sports for men and 7 for women. Facilities include a 1700-seat auditorium, a 10,000-seat stadium, a gym, handball and racquetball courts, a bowling alley, a swimming pool, a weight room, tennis courts, a field house, and intramural fields.

Disabled Students: 85% of the campus is accessible. Wheelchair ramps, elevators, special parking, and specially equipped rest rooms are available.

Services: Counseling and information services are available, as is tutoring in some subjects, including math and writing. There is remedial math, reading, and writing.

Campus Safety and Security: Measures include 24-hour foot and vehicle patrol, self-defense education, escort service, and informal discussions. There are pamphlets/posters/films, emergency telephones, lighted pathways/sidewalks, a victim assistance officer, a police service for special and social events, crime and date-rape prevention presentations, and motorist assistance.

Programs of Study: TAMU-C confers B.A., B.S., B.A.C.J., B.B.A., B.F.A., B.G.S., B.M., B.M.Ed., B.S.C.J., B.S.Lib.Sci., and B.S.W. degrees. Master's and doctoral degrees are also awarded. Bachelor's degrees are awarded in AGRICULTURE (agricultural economics, agriculture, animal science, and wildlife management), BIOLOGICAL SCIENCE (biology/biological science and botany), BUSINESS (accounting, banking and finance, business administration and management, and marketing/retailing/merchandising), COMMUNICATIONS AND THE ARTS (advertising, broadcasting, dramatic arts, English, fine arts, French, German, journalism, languages, music, photography, printmaking, and Spanish), COMPUTER AND PHYSICAL SCIENCE (chemistry, computer science, earth science, geology, mathematics, and physics), EDUCATION (agricultural, business, early childhood, elementary, guidance, health, industrial arts, music, science, and secondary), ENGINEERING AND ENVIRONMENTAL DESIGN (engineering technology and preengineering), HEALTH PROFESSIONS (predentistry, premedicine, and prepharmacy), SOCIAL SCIENCE (anthropology, criminal justice, economics, geography, history, political science/government, prelaw, psychology, religion, social work, and sociology). Education, computer science, and business administration are the strongest programs academically and have the largest enrollments.

Required: To graduate, all students must earn a GPA of 2.0 while taking at least 126 semester hours, including 24 hours in the major. Distribution requirements include 24 in culture courses such as American history and foreign languages, 12 each in English composition, math, and speech skills, 8 in sciences, 6 in upper-division courses, and 4 in phys ed.

Special: TAMU-C offers co-op programs with E-Systems Inc. and numerous other firms, cross-registration by independent arrangement, study abroad in England, and work-study programs. B.A.-B.S. degrees, second degrees, dual majors, a general studies degree, credit for life experience, internships, nondegree study, and pass/fail options are also available. There are 18 national honor societies, a freshman honors program, and 26 departmental honors programs.

Faculty/Classroom: 67% of faculty are male; 33%, female. 96% teach undergraduates, 62% do research, and 62% do both. Graduate students teach 40% of introductory courses. The average class size in an introductory lecture is 30; in a laboratory, 20; and in a regular course, 25.

Admissions: 60% of the 2001-2002 applicants were accepted. 26% of the current freshmen were in the top quarter of their class; 33% were in the top half.

Requirements: The SAT I or ACT is required, with a minimum recommended composite score of 800 or 20, respectively. Applicants need not be graduates of an accredited secondary school, although high school graduation is required. The GED is also accepted. A GPA of 2.0 is required. AP and CLEP credits are accepted.

Procedure: Freshmen are admitted to all sessions. Entrance exams should be taken prior to enrollment. There is a deferred admissions plan. Check with school for current application deadlines and fee. Notification is sent on a rolling basis.

Transfer: 497 transfer students enrolled in a recent year. Applicants must have a college GPA of 2.0 with a minimum of 21 credit hours. The SAT I or ACT is not required. College transcripts and a statement of good standing from the prior institution are required. 30 credits of 126 must be completed at TAMU-C.

Visiting: There are regularly scheduled orientations for prospective students. There are guides for informal visits and visitors may sit in on classes. To schedule a visit, contact the Office of School Relations.

Financial Aid: In 2001-2002, the average freshman award was $2466. The FAFSA and the college's own financial statement are required. Check with the school for current deadlines.

International Students: They must score 500 on the written TOEFL and also take the SAT I or the ACT, scoring 800 on the SAT I.

Computers: The mainframes are an IBM 9370 Model 60 and a DEC ALPHA-UNIX System. There are 310 IBM PCs and Macs contained in 13 labs located in the library, business administration building, and most classroom buildings. About half of these units are networked and linked to a mainframe. All students may access the system 24 hours daily by modem, and most labs are open until 10 P.M. There are no time limits and no fees.

Graduates: In a recent year, 988 bachelor's degrees were awarded. The most popular majors were interdisciplinary studies (22%), business/marketing (18%), and public administration (8%). 55 companies recruited on campus in a recent year.

Admissions Contact: Randy McDonald, Director of School Relations. A video is available. E-mail: *admissions@tamu-commerce.edu*
Web: *www.tamu-commerce.edu*

TEXAS A&M UNIVERSITY AT GALVESTON — E-4

Galveston, TX 77553-1675 — (409) 740-4415
(877) 322-4443; Fax: (409) 740-4731

Full-time: 603 men, 632 women	**Faculty:** 81
Part-time: 65 men, 66 women	**Ph.D.s:** 83%
Graduate: none	**Student/Faculty:** 15 to 1
Year: semesters, summer session	**Tuition:** $3291 ($9621)
Application Deadline: open	**Room & Board:** $3978
Freshman Class: 895 applied, 783 accepted, 388 enrolled	
SAT I Verbal/Math: 550/560	**ACT:** 24 — **COMPETITIVE+**

Texas A&M University at Galveston, founded in 1962, is a public institution that offers marine and maritime-related programs. Part of the Texas A&M University system is a branch of Texas A&M University. In addition to regional accreditation, TAMUG has baccalaureate program accreditation with ABET. The library contains 43,000 volumes and 52,984 microform items, and subscribes to 970 periodicals. Computerized library services include the card catalog, interlibrary loans, and database searching. Special learning facilities include a learning resource center and and a training ship, the T/S Texas Clipper, used for an annual summer training cruise. The 100-acre campus is in a suburban area 50 miles south of Houston. Including residence halls, there are 11 buildings.

Student Life: 78% of undergraduates are from Texas. Others are from 49 states, 10 foreign countries, and Canada. 94% are from public schools. 85% are white. The average age of freshmen is 18; all undergraduates, 20.

Housing: 628 students can be accommodated in college housing, which includes coed dormitories. On-campus housing is guaranteed for the freshman year only and is available on a first-come, first-served basis. 58% of students commute. Alcohol is not permitted. All students may keep cars.

Activities: There are no fraternities or sororities. There are 39 groups on campus, including chorale, drama, ethnic, international, literary magazine, newspaper, political, professional, religious, social, social service, student government, and yearbook. Popular campus events include Springfest, Mardi Grass, and Maritime Ball.

Sports: There are 2 intercollegiate sports for men and 1 for women, and 6 intramural sports for men and 5 for women. Facilities include tennis courts, a volleyball court, a swimming pool, and a basketball court.

Disabled Students: 80% of the campus is accessible. Wheelchair ramps, elevators, special parking, specially equipped rest rooms, special class scheduling, and lowered drinking fountains are available.

Services: Counseling and information services are available, as is tutoring in most subjects. There is a reader service for the blind, and remedial math, reading, and writing.

Campus Safety and Security: Measures include 24-hour foot and vehicle patrol, escort service, shuttle buses, and lighted pathways/sidewalks.

Programs of Study: TAMUG confers the B.S. degree. Bachelor's degrees are awarded in AGRICULTURE (environmental studies, fishing and fisheries, and natural resource management), BIOLOGICAL SCIENCE (biology/biological science, marine biology, and marine science), BUSINESS (international business management, and transportation management), COMPUTER AND PHYSICAL SCIENCE (natural sciences and oceanography), ENGINEERING AND ENVIRONMENTAL DESIGN (environmental science, marine engineering, maritime science, mechanical engineering technology, naval architecture and marine engineering, ocean engineering, and systems engineering). Marine sciences is the strongest academically. Marine biology is the largest.

Required: Depending on the major, students must complete 130 to 160 credit hours with a GPA of 2.0 overall as well as in the major. The required core curriculum includes courses in math, political science, American history, and macroeconomics. Distribution requirements include 6 credits each in English, calculus, humanities and social sciences; 8 credits in science; and 12 credits in citizenship. Students must also complete a 2-semester sequence of a foreign language and 1 computer language course.

Special: TAMUG offers dual majors in all majors, dual degrees, internships in marine biology and oceanography, a summer semester at sea, and credit for military service. Students may challenge any course for credit by exam. A pass/fail option is available for electives taken by juniors or seniors who have a minimum 2.5 GPA. Selected majors may earn a ship's officer license with a degree program.

Faculty/Classroom: 71% of faculty are male; 29%, female. All teach undergraduates. The average class size in an introductory lecture is 48; in a laboratory, 14; and in a regular course, 24.

Admissions: 87% of the 2001-2002 applicants were accepted. The SAT I scores for the 2001-2002 freshman class were: Verbal--36% below 500, 43% between 500 and 599, 19% between 600 and 700, and 2% above 700; Math--33% below 500, 48% between 500 and 599, 18% between 600 and 700, and 1% above 700. The ACT scores were 15% below 21, 24% between 21 and 23, 45% between 24 and 26, 8% between 27 and 28, and 8% above 28. 9 freshmen graduated first in their class, in a recent year.

Requirements: The SAT I or ACT is required. Acceptable test scores depend on high school rank, with minimum composite scores of 1000 for the SAT I and 24 for the ACT. Applicants must be graduates of an accredited high school or hold a GED. A minimum of 16 academic credits is required, including 4 units of English, 3.5 units of math, 2.5 units of either history or social studies, 2 units each of a foreign language and science, and the rest in electives. AP and CLEP credits are accepted. Important factors in the admissions decision are leadership record, extracurricular activities record, and recommendations by school officials. Applications are accepted on-line, at *www.applytexas.org*.

Procedure: Freshmen are admitted to all sessions. Entrance exams should be taken late in the junior year or early in the senior year. There are early decision, early admissions, and deferred admissions plans. Application deadlines are open. 381 early decision candidates were accepted for the 2001-2002 class. The fall 2001 application fee was $35.

Transfer: 147 transfer students enrolled in 2001-2002. Applicants must have a cumulative 2.0 GPA in a minimum of 18 completed credit hours as well as a 2.0 GPA in each of the last 2 terms attended. 30 credits of 130 to 160 must be completed at TAMUG.

Visiting: There are regularly scheduled orientations for prospective students, including campus tours conducted Monday and Friday at 10 A.M. There are guides for informal visits and visitors may sit in on classes. To schedule a visit, contact the Student Relations Department at (409) 740-4422.

Financial Aid: In a recent year, 47% of all freshmen and 68% of continuing students received some form of financial aid. The average freshman award was $1580. 65% of undergraduates work part time. Average annual earnings from campus work are $1200. The FAFSA is required. The fall application priority deadline is April 1.

International Students: There are 7 international students enrolled. They must score 550 on the written TOEFL and also take the college's own test and the SAT I or the ACT, scoring 1000.

Computers: There are 123 terminals located in the Learning Resource Center, 4 labs, and other campus locations. All students may access the system. There are no time limits. The fee is $9 per semester credit hour.

Graduates: In 2001, 178 bachelor's degrees were awarded. In an average class, 46% graduate in 6 years. 87 companies recruited on campus in 2000-2001.

Admissions Contact: Cheryl Moon, Director of Admissions. A video is available. E-mail: *seaaggie@tamug.tamu.edu* Web: *www.tamug.edu*

TEXAS A&M UNIVERSITY AT KINGSVILLE — D-5

Kingsville, TX 78363 — (361) 593-2315
(800) 687-6000; Fax: (361) 595-2195

Full-time: 2059 men, 1824 women	**Faculty:** 245; IIA, --$
Part-time: 476 men, 649 women	**Ph.D.s:** 85%
Graduate: 499 men, 643 women	**Student/Faculty:** 16 to 1
Year: semesters, summer session	**Tuition:** $2862 ($9192)
Application Deadline: open	**Room & Board:** $3584
Freshman Class: n/av	
SAT I or ACT: required	**LESS COMPETITIVE**

Texas A&M University at Kingsville, founded in 1925 as South Texas Teachers College, is a comprehensive university and part of the Texas A&M University System. Graduate and undergraduate programs are offered in agriculture and home economics, arts and sciences, business administration, education, and engineering. There are 5 undergraduate and 5 graduate schools. In addition to regional accreditation, TAMUK has baccalaureate program accreditation with ABET, ADA, NASM, and NCATE. The library contains 358,466 volumes, 183,416 microform items, and 3224 audiovisual forms/CDs, and subscribes to 2304 periodicals. Computerized library services include the card catalog, interlibrary loans, and database searching. Special learning facilities include a learning resource center, art gallery, natural history museum, planetarium, radio station, TV station, and wildlife and citrus research facilities. The 246-acre campus is in a small town 40 miles southwest of Corpus Christi. Including residence halls, there are 82 buildings.

Student Life: 95% of undergraduates are from Texas. Others are from 35 states, 44 foreign countries, and Canada. 98% are from public schools. 62% are Hispanic; 29% white. The average age of freshmen is 19; all undergraduates, 23. 46% do not continue beyond their first year; 21% remain to graduate.

Housing: 1200 students can be accommodated in college housing, which includes single-sex and coed dormitories and married-student housing. On-campus housing is guaranteed for all 4 years. 70% of students commute. All students may keep cars.

Activities: 3% of men and about 3% of women belong to 6 national fraternities; 3% of women belong to 3 national sororities. There are 106 groups on campus, including art, band, cheerleading, choir, chorale, chorus, computers, dance, drama, drill team, ethnic, honors, international, jazz band, marching band, mariachi, musical theater, newspaper, pep band, political, professional, radio and TV, religious, social, and student government. Popular campus events include Campus Capers, Fall Carnival, and Spring Block Party.

Sports: There are 3 intercollegiate sports for men and 3 for women, and 2 intramural sports for men and 2 for women. Facilities include 2 gyms, an Olympic-size swimming pool, courts for tennis and racquetball, an all-weather track, and various playing fields. There are facilities for archery, bowling, golf, fencing, weight training, and jogging.

Disabled Students: 90% of the campus is accessible. Wheelchair ramps, elevators, special parking, specially equipped rest rooms, lowered drinking fountains, and lowered telephones are available.

Services: Counseling and information services are available, as is tutoring in every subject. There is a reader service for the blind, and remedial math, reading, and writing.

Campus Safety and Security: Measures include 24-hour foot and vehicle patrol, self-defense education, escort service, and informal discussions. There are pamphlets/posters/films, emergency telephones, and lighted pathways/sidewalks.

Programs of Study: TAMUK confers B.A., B.S., B.A.A.S., B.B.A., B.F.A., B.M., B.S.A., B.S.C.E., B.S.Ch.E., B.S.C.S., B.S.E.E., B.S.I.E., B.S. in Hum.Sci., B.S. in Nat. Gas Eng., B.S.I.T., and B.S.M.E. degrees. Master's and doctoral degrees are also awarded. Bachelor's degrees are awarded in AGRICULTURE (agricultural business management, animal science, plant science, range/farm management, and soil science), BIOLOGICAL SCIENCE (biology/biological science), BUSINESS (accounting, banking and finance, business administration and management, business economics, fashion merchandising, management science, marketing/retailing/merchandising, and real estate), COMMUNICATIONS AND THE ARTS (communications, dramatic arts, English, fine arts, music, and Spanish), COMPUTER AND PHYSICAL SCIENCE (chemistry, computer science, geology, mathematics, and physics), EDUCATION (agricultural, elementary, health, music, physical, and secondary), ENGINEERING AND ENVIRONMENTAL DESIGN (chemical engineering, civil engineering, electrical/electronics engineering, engineering management, industrial engineering technology, interior design, mechanical engineering, and petroleum/natural gas engineering), HEALTH PROFESSIONS (medical laboratory technology, nursing, predentistry, premedicine, prepharmacy, preveterinary science, and speech pathology/audiology), SOCIAL SCIENCE (anthropology, child care/child and family studies, food production/management/services, food science, geography, history, home economics, political science/government, prelaw, psychology, public administration, and sociology). Engineering is the strongest academically. Education is the largest.

Required: All students must complete 124 to 135 semester hours, including a minimum of 24 in the major and 45 in advanced work, with at least a 2.0 GPA. General education requirements include courses in oral and written communication, math and reasoning, U.S. and Texas government, social sciences, American and world history, lab sciences, fine arts, and phys ed.

Special: There are co-op programs in engineering, business, and agriculture and internships, B.A.-B.S. degrees, and dual majors in most programs. A nontraditional Bachelor of Applied Arts and Sciences program is offered to students with vocational or technical training or experience. The Center for Continuing Education offers noncredit enrichment courses in a variety of subjects, a professional development program in organizational management, and a number of seminars and short courses that are held abroad. The university also offers a work-study program and the College I Freshman program. There are 10 national honor societies and 20 departmental honors programs.

Faculty/Classroom: 66% of faculty are male; 34%, female. All teach undergraduates. The average class size in an introductory lecture is 30; in a laboratory, 20; and in a regular course, 25.

Admissions: 25% of the current freshmen were in the top fifth of their class; 52% were in the top two fifths.

Requirements: The SAT I or ACT is required; the university sets mimimum admissible scores each year. Applicants should be high school graduates or have a GED. Secondary preparation must include 7 units of electives, no more than 4 of which may be in vocational subjects, 3 units of English, 2 units each of math (including algebra), foreign language, and natural science, and 1 unit each of history and another social science. An interview is encouraged. AP and CLEP credits are accepted.

Procedure: Freshmen are admitted to all sessions. There is an early admissions plan. Application deadlines are open. Application fee is $15. Notification is sent on a rolling basis.

Transfer: 427 transfer students enrolled in 2001-2002. All applicants must present a GPA of at least 2.0. 24 credits of 124 must be completed at TAMUK.

Visiting: There are regularly scheduled orientations for prospective students, including advisement, tours, stays in dorms, entertainment, registration, and financial information. There are guides for informal visits and visitors may sit in on classes and stay overnight. To schedule a visit, contact the Office of School Relations at (361) 593-3907.

Financial Aid: The average freshman award for the 2001-2002 school year was $5875. The average financial indebtedness of the 2001 graduate was $23,000. TAMUK is a member of CSS. The FAFSA is required. The fall application deadline is May 15.

International Students: They must score 500 on the written TOEFL and also take the college's own test and the SAT I or the ACT.

Computers: The mainframe is an IBM 9370. There are more than 400 PCs located in the library and in the business, engineering, agriculture, and education buildings as well as other sites on campus. All students may access the system. There are no time limits. The fee is $5 per semester credit hour.

Graduates: In 2001, 695 bachelor's degrees were awarded. The most popular majors were engineering (16%), business/marketing (13%), and interdisciplinary (11%). In an average class, 25% graduate in 5 years, and 30% in 6 years.

Admissions Contact: Joe Estrada, Registrar and Director of Admissions. E-mail: *ksossrx@tamuk.edu* Web: *http://www.tamuk.edu*

TEXAS CHRISTIAN UNIVERSITY — D-2
Fort Worth, TX 76129 — (817) 257-7490
(800) TCU-FROG; Fax: (817) 257-7268

Full-time: 2687 men, 3657 women	**Faculty:** 378; I,
Part-time: 240 men, 301 women	**Ph.D.s:** 91%
Graduate: 545 men, 624 women	**Student/Faculty:** 17 to 1
Year: semesters, summer session	**Tuition:** $15,040
Application Deadline: February 15	**Room & Board:** $4870
Freshman Class: 5822 applied, 4187 accepted, 1514 enrolled	
SAT I or ACT: recommended	**COMPETITIVE**

Texas Christian University, founded in 1873, is a private university affiliated with the Christian Church (Disciples of Christ). TCU is a teaching and research institution offering undergraduate programs in arts, sciences, business, education, fine arts, communications, nursing, and engineering. There are 7 undergraduate and 7 graduate schools. In addition to regional accreditation, TCU has baccalaureate program accreditation with AACSB, ABET, ACEJMC, ADA, ASLA, CAAHEP, CCNE, CSAB, CSWE, FIDER, and NASM. The library contains 1,292,494 volumes, 593,741 microform items, and 56,094 audiovisual forms/CDs, and subscribes to 4627 periodicals. Computerized library services include the card catalog, interlibrary loans, and database searching. Special learning facilities include a learning resource center, art gallery, radio station, TV station, an observatory, and a speech and hearing clinic. The 300-acre campus is in a suburban area 3 miles southwest of downtown Fort Worth. Including residence halls, there are 92 buildings.

Student Life: 73% of undergraduates are from Texas. Others are from 48 states, 75 foreign countries, and Canada. 94% are from public schools. 78% are white. 52% are Protestant; 16% Catholic. The average age of freshmen is 18; all undergraduates, 21. 18% do not continue beyond their first year; 63% remain to graduate.

Housing: 3256 students can be accommodated in college housing, which includes single-sex and coed dormitories, fraternity houses, and sorority houses. In addition, there are special-interest houses. On-campus housing is guaranteed for all 4 years. 52% of students commute. All students may keep cars.

Activities: 35% of men belong to 1 local fraternity and 12 national fraternities; 40% of women belong to 3 local and 13 national sororities. There are 193 groups on campus, including art, band, cheerleading, chorale, chorus, computers, dance, drama, drill team, ethnic, film, gay, honors, international, jazz band, literary magazine, marching band, musical theater, newspaper, opera, orchestra, pep band, photography, political, professional, radio and TV, religious, social, social service, student government, symphony, and yearbook. Popular campus events include Parents Weekend, Howdy Rush Week, and Carols by Candlelight.

Sports: There are 9 intercollegiate sports for men and 9 for women. Facilities include indoor and outdoor tennis facilities, a 46,000-seat stadium, a 7,200-seat coliseum, an indoor NCAA regulation swimming pool, a diving well, 4 gyms, handball and racquetball courts, a sports conditioning facility that includes weight training, body conditioning, and sports rehabilitation equipment, an outdoor track with seating, and a paved walking/jogging track.

Disabled Students: 89% of the campus is accessible. Wheelchair ramps, elevators, special parking, specially equipped rest rooms, lowered drinking fountains, and lowered telephones are available. For visually impaired and hearing-impaired students, there are flashing lights and vibrators on beds in case of fire. Hearing-assistance devices are also available

Campus Safety and Security: Measures include 24-hour foot and vehicle patrol, self-defense education, escort service, and informal discussions. There are pamphlets/posters/films, emergency telephones, lighted pathways/sidewalks, bike patrol, and video monitoring of some parking lots.

Programs of Study: TCU confers B.A., B.S., B.B.A., B.F.A., B.G.S., B.Mus., B.Med., B.S.Ed., B.S.N., and B.S.S.W. degrees. Master's and doctoral degrees are also awarded. Bachelor's degrees are awarded in BIOLOGICAL SCIENCE (biology/biological science, neurosciences, and nutrition), BUSINESS (accounting, banking and finance, business administration and management, electronic business, entrepreneurial studies, fashion merchandising, international business management, international economics, management science, and marketing/retailing/merchandising), COMMUNICATIONS AND THE ARTS (advertising, art history and appreciation, ballet, broadcasting, communications, dance, dramatic arts, English, film arts, French, graphic design, journalism, music, music performance, music theory and composition, piano/organ, radio/television technology, Spanish, speech/debate/rhetoric, and studio art), COMPUTER AND PHYSICAL SCIENCE (astrophysics, chemistry, computer science, geology, information sciences and systems, mathematics, and physics), EDUCATION (art, bilingual/bicultural, early childhood, education of the deaf and hearing impaired, education of the exceptional child, elementary, English, middle school, music, physical, science, and social studies), ENGINEERING AND ENVIRONMENTAL DESIGN (engineering, environmental science, and interior design), HEALTH PROFESSIONS (health, nursing, and speech pathology/audiology), SOCIAL SCIENCE (criminal justice, dietetics, economics, food production/management/services, history, Latin American studies, liberal arts/general studies, philosophy, physical fitness/movement, political science/government, psychology, religion, religious music, social work, and sociology). Psychology, biology, and nursing are the largest.

Required: To graduate, candidates must complete at least 124 semester hours, which include 24 to 36 hours in the major, earning a minimum GPA of 2.0.

Special: A general studies degree and a combined B.A.-B.S. degree in numerous majors are offered. Student-designed majors, dual majors, nondegree study, and pass/no credit options are available. TCU also accepts credit by examination and credit for life, military, and work experience. 3-2 programs are available in business, education, and economics. Internships are available in almost all major areas. The university also offers a Washington semester, student exchange in Japan and Mexico, and study abroad in 28 countries. TCU also offers study at its London Center and study through the American Airlines Leadership for the Americas program. There are 4 national honor societies, including Phi Beta Kappa, a freshman honors program, and 29 departmental honors programs.

Faculty/Classroom: 63% of faculty are male; 37%, female. 96% teach undergraduates. The average class size in an introductory lecture is 34 and in a regular course, 27.

Admissions: 72% of the 2001-2002 applicants were accepted. 58% of the current freshmen were in the top fifth of their class.

Requirements: The SAT I or ACT is recommended. In addition, candidates should be graduates of an accredited secondary school and have completed 2 years of academic electives and 15 Carnegie units, including 4 years of English, 3 years each of math, science, and social studies, and 2 of the same foreign language. TCU also recommends an interview and requires an essay and counselor's recommendation. AP and CLEP credits are accepted. Important factors in the admissions decision are advanced placement or honor courses, leadership record, and evidence of special talent. Applications are accepted on computer disk and on-line.

Procedure: Freshmen are admitted to all sessions. Entrance exams should be taken during or before the fall semester of the senior year. There is a deferred admissions plan. Applications should be filed by February 15 for fall entry and December 1 for spring entry. The fall 2001 application fee was $350. Notification is sent April 1. A waiting list is an active part of the admissions procedure.

Transfer: 436 transfer students enrolled in 2001-2002. The recommended GPA is 2.5 and a minimum GPA of 2.0 is required. Applicants must complete an application form and submit official transcripts from each college attended as well as a secondary school transcript. If fewer than 24 semester hours of transferable work have been completed at the time of application, SAT I or ACT scores are required and secondary school credentials are considered. 58 credits of 124 must be completed at TCU.

Visiting: There are regularly scheduled orientations for prospective students, including student-led campus tours, optional personal interviews, and departmental visits. There are guides for informal visits and visitors may sit in on classes and stay overnight. To schedule a visit, contact the Admissions Office.

Financial Aid: In a recent year, 82% of all freshmen and 63% of continuing students received some form of financial aid. 39% of freshmen and 34% of continuing students received need-based aid. The FAFSA is required. The fall application deadline is May 1.

International Students: There are 307 international students enrolled. The school actively recruits these students. They must score 550 on the written TOEFL.

Computers: All students may access the system anytime. There are no time limits and no fees.

Graduates: In 2001, 1260 bachelor's degrees were awarded. The most popular majors were finance (9%), marketing (9%), and psychology (6%). In an average class, 63% graduate in 6 years. 135 companies recruited on campus in 2000-2001.

Admissions Contact: Ray Brown, Dean of Admissions.
E-mail: *frogmail@tcu.edu* Web: *tcu.edu*

TEXAS LUTHERAN UNIVERSITY D-4

Seguin, TX 78155 **(830) 372-8050**
(800) 771-8521; Fax: (830) 372-8096

Full-time: 596 men, 670 women	**Faculty:** 65; IIB, --$
Part-time: 85 men, 122 women	**Ph.D.s:** 84%
Graduate: none	**Student/Faculty:** 20 to 1
Year: semesters, summer session	**Tuition:** $13,540
Application Deadline: August 1	**Room & Board:** $4120
Freshman Class: 1015 applied, 826 accepted, 375 enrolled	
SAT I Verbal/Math: 520/520	**ACT:** 22 **COMPETITIVE**

Texas Lutheran University, founded in 1891, is a private liberal arts institution affiliated with the Evangelical Lutheran Church of America. There are 3 undergraduate schools. In addition to regional accreditation, TLU has baccalaureate program accreditation with ACBSP and CSWE. The library contains 159,307 volumes, 116,958 microform items, and 4968 audiovisual forms/CDs, and subscribes to 619 periodicals. Computerized library services include the card catalog, interlibrary loans, and database searching. Special learning facilities include an art gallery, natural history museum, and a geological museum. The 196-acre campus is in a suburban area 37 miles east of San Antonio and 50 miles south of Austin. Including residence halls, there are 36 buildings.

Student Life: 92% of undergraduates are from Texas. Others are from 25 states, 16 foreign countries, and Canada. 88% are from public schools. 72% are white; 17% Hispanic. 62% are Protestant; 20% Catholic; 17% claim no religious affiliation. The average age of freshmen is 18; all undergraduates, 21. 22% do not continue beyond their first year; 55% remain to graduate.

Housing: 979 students can be accommodated in college housing, which includes single-sex and coed dormitories, on-campus apartments, and married-student housing. On-campus housing is available on a first-come, first-served basis. 70% of students live on campus; of those, 60% remain on campus on weekends. All students may keep cars.

Activities: 15% of men belong to 4 local fraternities; 14% of women belong to 4 local sororities. There are 57 groups on campus, including African American, art, band, cheerleading, choir, computers, dance, debate, drama, ethnic, forensics, honors, international, jazz band, literary magazine, Mexican American, musical theater, newspaper, opera, orchestra, pep band, political, professional, religious, social, social service, student government, symphony, and yearbook. Popular campus events include Christmas Vespers and Spring Fling.

Sports: There are 6 intercollegiate sports for men and 8 for women, and 10 intramural sports for men and 10 for women. Facilities include a 2200-seat gym, a state-of-the-art fitness center, an 8-lane swimming pool, softball, baseball, and soccer fields, intramural/recreation fields, and golf practice greens.

Disabled Students: 90% of the campus is accessible. Wheelchair ramps, elevators, special parking, specially equipped rest rooms, special class scheduling, and lowered drinking fountains are available.

Services: Counseling and information services are available, as is tutoring in most subjects. Assistance with writing assignments is also available.

Campus Safety and Security: Measures include 24-hour foot and vehicle patrol, self-defense education, escort service, and informal discussions. There are pamphlets/posters/films, lighted pathways/sidewalks, and coded locks in residence halls.

Programs of Study: TLU confers B.A., B.S., and B.B.A. degrees. Associate degrees are also awarded. Bachelor's degrees are awarded in BIOLOGICAL SCIENCE (biology/biological science), BUSINESS (business administration and management and management information systems), COMMUNICATIONS AND THE ARTS (art, communications, dramatic arts, English, German, music, and Spanish), COMPUTER AND PHYSICAL SCIENCE (chemistry, computer science, mathematics, and physics), SOCIAL SCIENCE (economics, history, philosophy, physical fitness/movement, political science/government, psychology, public affairs, social work, sociology, and theological studies). Biology, chemistry, and business are the strongest academically. Biology, business, and kinesiology are the largest.

Required: All students must complete 124 semester hours, including 24 to 54 in their major, with a 2.0 GPA. Between 45 and 49 hours of distribution courses are required. A senior seminar, project, or concert is required in most majors.

Special: Internships are available in most majors. Study abroad in all countries affiliated with ISEP, a Washington semester with American University, and work-study programs are available. The college offers student-designed majors and dual majors. There is a 3-2 engineering program with Texas A&M and Texas Tech University. There are 10 national honor societies, a freshman honors program, and 9 departmental honors programs.

Faculty/Classroom: 56% of faculty are male; 44%, female. All teach undergraduates. The average class size in an introductory lecture is 24; in a laboratory, 25; and in a regular course, 20.

Admissions: 81% of the 2001-2002 applicants were accepted. The SAT I scores for the 2001-2002 freshman class were: Verbal--42% below 500, 39% between 500 and 599, 17% between 600 and 700, and 2% above 700; Math--35% below 500, 48% between 500 and 599, 16% between 600 and 700, and 1% above 700. The ACT scores were 38% below 21, 24% between 21 and 23, 22% between 24 and 26, 10% between 27 and 28, and 6% above 28. 44% of the current freshmen were in the top fifth of their class; 77% were in the top two fifths. 6 freshmen graduated first in their class.

Requirements: The SAT I or ACT is required. In addition, applicants must have 16 Carnegie units, including a recommended 4 years in English, 3 each of social studies, math, and science, and 2 in foreign language. The GED is accepted. TLU requires applicants to be in the upper 50% of their class. A GPA of 2.25 is required. AP and CLEP credits are accepted. Important factors in the admissions decision are advanced placement or honor courses, leadership record, and recommendations by school officials. Applications are accepted on-line.

Procedure: Freshmen are admitted to all sessions. Entrance exams should be taken in the spring of the junior year or the summer before the senior year. There is a deferred admissions plan. Applications should be filed by August 1 for fall entry, December 1 for spring entry, and May 1 for summer entry, along with a $25 fee. Notification is sent on a rolling basis. 5% of all applicants are on a waiting list; 100 were accepted in 2001.

Transfer: 62 transfer students enrolled in 2001-2002. Applicants for transfer must have a GPA of at least 2.25 and be in good academic standing. 33 credits of 124 must be completed at TLU.

Visiting: There are regularly scheduled orientations for prospective students, including a campus tour, classroom visits, a financial aid presentation, a study abroad session, an athlete session, and a student panel. There are guides for informal visits and visitors may sit in on classes and stay overnight. To schedule a visit, contact the Admissions Office.

Financial Aid: In 2001-2002, 95% of all freshmen and 77% of continuing students received some form of financial aid. 59% of freshmen and 62% of continuing students received need-based aid. The average freshman award was $13,085. Of that total, scholarships or need-based grants averaged $7932 ($18,550 maximum); loans averaged $5914 ($20,735 maximum); and work contracts averaged $896 ($2880 maximum). 33% of undergraduates work part time. Average annual earnings from campus work are $871. The average financial indebtedness of the 2001 graduate was $19,514. The FAFSA and the college's own financial statement are required. The fall application deadline is April 1.

International Students: There are 45 international students enrolled. The school actively recruits these students. They must score 550 on the written TOEFL and also take the SAT I or the ACT.

Computers: The mainframes are a consists of one HP3000, one Sun Server, and several Intel-based servers. Computer labs contain 78 PCs connected to the LAN and to a CITRIX server for application support. There are 12 additional computers available in the library, as well as several special use computers, available to students in various academic buildings. Students with PCs in their dorm rooms may lease a wireless LAN card from the university to access the university network as well as the Internet, e-mail, word processing, and other applications. Students residing off campus may pay a fee for dial-in to the network, which provides Internet access. All students may access the system 24 hours a day, 7 days a week. There are no time limits and no fees. It is strongly recommended that all students have a personal computer. There are no time limist and no fees.

Graduates: In a recent year, 244 bachelor's degrees were awarded. The most popular majors were business administration (33%), natural sciences (22%), and psychology (10%). In an average class, 1% graduate in 3 years, 34% in 4 years, 50% in 5 years, and 55% in 6 years. 20 companies recruited on campus in 2000-2001.

Admissions Contact: E. Norman Jones, Vice President of Enrollment Services. A video is available. E-mail: *admissions@tlu.edu*
Web: *www.tlu.edu*

TEXAS SOUTHERN UNIVERSITY E-3

Houston, TX 77004 (713) 313-7472; Fax: (713) 313-4317

Full-time: 2505 men, 2943 women	**Faculty:** 170
Part-time: 420 men, 617 women	**Ph.D.s:** 57%
Graduate: 682 men, 952 women	**Student/Faculty:** 32 to 1
Year: semesters, summer session	**Tuition:** $2078 ($7142)
Application Deadline: July 31	**Room & Board:** $4498

Freshman Class: 7358 applied, 7358 accepted, 3133 enrolled
SAT I or ACT: required **NONCOMPETITIVE**

Texas Southern University, founded in 1947, is a state-supported institution offering undergraduate programs in the arts and sciences, education and behavioral sciences, pharmacy and health science, business, and technology. There are 5 undergraduate and 3 graduate schools. In addition to regional accreditation, TSU has baccalaureate program accreditation with NCATE. The 3 libraries contain 728,562 volumes and 464,308 microform items, and subscribe to 1715 periodicals. Special learning facilities include a learning resource center, art gallery, and radio station. The 115-acre campus is in an urban area 3 miles southeast of downtown Houston. Including residence halls, there are 40 buildings.

Student Life: 87% of undergraduates are from Texas. Others are from 48 states, 56 foreign countries, and Canada. 97% are from public schools. 86% are African American. 90% are Protestant; 19% claim no religious affiliation. The average age of freshmen is 19; all undergraduates, 25.

Housing: 1348 students can be accommodated in college housing, which includes single-sex dormitories and off-campus apartments. On-campus housing is available on a first-come, first-served basis. Priority is given to out-of-town students. 97% of students live on campus; of those, 80% remain on campus on weekends. Alcohol is not permitted. All students may keep cars.

Activities: 2% of men and about 3% of women belong to 5 national fraternities; 2% of women belong to 6 national sororities. There are 50 groups on campus, including accounting, art, band, business, cheerleading, choir, chorus, computers, consumer services, dance, drama, ethnic, film, health, honors, international, jazz band, marching band, newspaper, orchestra, pharmaceutical, photography, political, professional, radio and TV, religious, science, social, social service, student government, symphony, and yearbook. Popular campus events include Senior Day, Christmas Tree Lighting, and Fall Greek Show.

Sports: There are 8 intercollegiate sports for men and 9 for women, and 12 intramural sports for men and 6 for women. Facilities include a health and phys ed complex, a 7000-seat football stadium, and 2 gyms, the larger seating 1000.

Disabled Students: 60% of the campus is accessible. Wheelchair ramps, elevators, special parking, specially equipped rest rooms, lowered drinking fountains, and lowered telephones are available.

Services: Counseling and information services are available, as is tutoring in most subjects. There is remedial math, reading, and writing.

Campus Safety and Security: Measures include 24-hour foot and vehicle patrol, self-defense education, informal discussions, and pamphlets/posters/films. There are emergency telephones and lighted pathways/sidewalks.

Programs of Study: TSU confers B.A., B.S., and B.B.A. degrees. Master's and doctoral degrees are also awarded. Bachelor's degrees are awarded in BIOLOGICAL SCIENCE (biology/biological science and nutrition), BUSINESS (accounting, banking and finance, business administration and management, insurance, management science, and marketing/retailing/merchandising), COMMUNICATIONS AND THE ARTS (applied music, art, communications, design, dramatic arts, English, fine arts, French, journalism, music, Spanish, speech/debate/rhetoric, and telecommunications), COMPUTER AND PHYSICAL SCIENCE (chemistry, computer science, geology, mathematics, and physics), EDUCATION (bilingual/bicultural, early childhood, education, English, foreign languages, mathematics, physical, reading, and special), ENGINEERING AND ENVIRONMENTAL DESIGN (civil engineering technology, construction technology, drafting and design technology, electrical/electronics engineering technology, engineering technology, environmental engineering technology, graphic arts technology, industrial engineering technology, manufacturing technology, and military science), HEALTH PROFESSIONS (environmental health science, health, health care administration, health science, medical technology, pharmacy, respiratory therapy, and speech pathology/audiology), SOCIAL SCIENCE (clothing and textiles management/production/services, criminal justice, dietetics, economics, family/consumer studies, geography, history, human services, philosophy, political science/government, psychology, public affairs, social work, and sociology). Pharmacy is the strongest academically. General business, biology, and physical science are the largest.

Required: Students must complete between 136 and 148 semester hours, depending on the field of study. A minimum of 30 hours is required in the major. A course in phys ed is also required.

Special: Special academic programs include cross-registration in military science with the University of Houston, study abroad in Africa, and work-study programs. There are 2 national honor societies, a freshman honors program, and 22 departmental honors programs.

Faculty/Classroom: 58% of faculty are male; 42%, female. 58% teach undergraduates. The average class size in an introductory lecture is 22.

Admissions: All of the 2001-2002 applicants were accepted.

Requirements: The SAT I or ACT is required. In addition, candidates should be graduates of an accredited secondary school or have the GED. TSU accepts the Texas Common Application, available on-line. A GPA of 2.0 is required.

Procedure: Freshmen are admitted fall, spring, and summer. Entrance exams should be taken by January. Applications should be filed by July 31 for fall entry, December 1 for spring entry, and May 20 for summer entry. The fall 2001 application fee was $25. Notification is sent on a rolling basis.

Transfer: The applicant must be a student in good standing. The SAT I or ACT is required. 15 credits of 136 must be completed at TSU.

Visiting: There are guides for informal visits and visitors may stay overnight. To schedule a visit, contact the Office of Recruitment at (713) 313-7951 or (713) 313-7849 or *em.tsu.edu*.

Financial Aid: In 2001-2002, 74% of all freshmen and 87% of continuing students received some form of financial aid. 71% of freshmen and 66% of continuing students received need-based aid. The average freshman award was $6625. Of that total, scholarships or need-based grants averaged $1500 ($3300 maximum); loans averaged $2625 ($10,500 maximum); and work contracts averaged $4000 ($6000 maximum). 10% of undergraduates work part time. Average annual earnings from campus work are $2500. The FAFSA is required. The fall application deadline is April 15.

International Students: They must score 500 on the written TOEFL and also take the SAT I, ACT, or the college's own entrance exam.

Computers: The mainframe is a DEC. PCs are available in the library, general university academic center, and various departments. Computer science students may access the system by appointment and during assigned periods. Students may access the system 4 hours at a time. There are no fees.

Graduates: In 2001, 452 bachelor's degrees were awarded. The most popular majors were law (17%), business (16%), and pharmacy (10%). In an average class, 10% graduate in 6 years.

Admissions Contact: Joyce M. Waddell, Director of Admissions.
Web: *www.tsu.edu*

TEXAS STATE UNIVERSITY SYSTEM

The Texas State University System, established in 1911, is a public higher education system. It is governed by a 9-member board of regents, whose chief administrator is the chancellor. The primary mission of the system universities is the provision of a well-rounded education focusing on teacher education, business, and liberarl arts. The total enrollment of all 11 campuses is approximately 57,500, with about 2000 faculty members. Altogether there are 416 baccalaureate, 250 master's, and 5 doctoral programs offered within the system. 4-year campuses are Angelo State University in San Angelo, Lamar University in Beaumont, Sam Houston State University in Huntsville, Southwest Texas State University in San Marcos, and Sul Ross State University in Alpine, with 2-year lower-division campuses in Beaumont, Orange, and Port Arthur, and 2-year upper-division campuses in Del Rio, Eagle Pass, and Uvalde. Profiles of the 4-year campuses are included in this section.

TEXAS TECH UNIVERSITY

Lubbock, TX 79409-5005 **B-2**
(806) 742-1480; Fax: (806) 742-0980

Full-time: 10,041 men, 8863 women	**Faculty:** 972; I, --$
Part-time: 1373 men, 992 women	**Ph.D.s:** 91%
Graduate: 2290 men, 2014 women	**Student/Faculty:** 19 to 1
Year: semesters, summer session	**Tuition:** $3488 ($9818)
Application Deadline: open	**Room & Board:** $5337
Freshman Class: 12,008 applied, 8461 accepted, 3921 enrolled	
SAT I Verbal/Math: 540/557	**ACT:** 23 **COMPETITIVE**

Texas Tech University, founded in 1923, is a large, comprehensive public university offering undergraduate and graduate programs in a variety of professional and vocational fields. There are 7 undergraduate and 2 graduate schools. In addition to regional accreditation, Texas Tech has baccalaureate program accreditation with AACSB, ABET, ACEJMC, APTA, ASLA, CSWE, FIDER, NAAB, NASAD, NASM, NCATE, and NLN. The 2 libraries contain 4,455,954 volumes, 2,169,160 microform items, and 83,348 audiovisual forms/CDs, and subscribe to 29,520 periodicals. Computerized library services include the card catalog, interlibrary loans, and database searching. Special learning facilities include a learning resource center, art gallery, natural history museum, planetarium, radio station, TV station, and a ranching heritage center, an international cultural center, an international textile center, and a Southwest collection. The 1839-acre campus is in an urban area in Lubbock. Including residence halls, there are 82 buildings.

Student Life: 93% of undergraduates are from Texas. Others are from 49 states, 113 foreign countries, and Canada. 81% are white; 10% Hispanic. The average age of freshmen is 19; all undergraduates, 21. 19% do not continue beyond their first year; 52% remain to graduate.

Housing: 6713 students can be accommodated in college housing, which includes single-sex and coed dormitories, on-campus apartments, and married-student housing. In addition, there are honors houses, living/learning communities, intensive study floors, substance-free floors, nonsmoking floors, and upperclass/graduate halls. On-campus housing is guaranteed for the freshman year only and is available on a first-come, first-served basis. 74% of students commute. Alcohol is not permitted. All students may keep cars.

Activities: 8% of men belong to 1 local and 30 national fraternities; 19% of women belong to 2 local and 17 national sororities. There are 300 groups on campus, including art, band, cheerleading, chess, choir, chorale, chorus, computers, dance, drama, drill team, drum and bugle corps, ethnic, film, gay, honors, international, jazz band, literary magazine, marching band, musical theater, newspaper, opera, orchestra, pep band, photography, political, professional, radio and TV, religious, social, social service, student government, symphony, and yearbook. Popular campus events include Parents Day, Carol of the Lights, and Madrigal Dinner.

Sports: There are 6 intercollegiate sports for men and 7 for women, and 29 intramural sports for men and 29 for women. Facilities include an athletic training center, a student recreation center, and an aquatic center.

Disabled Students: 75% of the campus is accessible. Wheelchair ramps, elevators, special parking, specially equipped rest rooms, lowered drinking fountains, lowered telephones, and dorm rooms accessible to the disabled are available.

Services: Counseling and information services are available, as is tutoring in every subject. There is a reader service for the blind, and remedial math, reading, and writing. An attorney is available for students to obtain legal advice and guidance. Note-taking services, readers (for testing only), tape recorders, and a learning center are also available.

Campus Safety and Security: Measures include 24-hour foot and vehicle patrol, shuttle buses, pamphlets/posters/films, and emergency telephones. There are lighted pathways/sidewalks.

Programs of Study: Texas Tech confers B.A., B.S., B.Arch., B.B.A., B.F.A., B.G.S., B.I.D., B.Land.Arch., B.M., B.S.C.E., B.S.Ch.E., B.S. in E., B.S. in Eco., B.S.E.E., B.S. in Engineering Physics, B.S. in Environmental Engineering, B.S. in Family and Consumer Sciences, B.S.H.E., B.S.I.E., B.S.M.E., B.S. in Petroleum Engineering, B.S. in Restaurant, Hotel, and Institutional Management, B.S.Tech., and B.S. in Textile Engineering. degrees. Master's and doctoral degrees are also awarded. Bachelor's degrees are awarded in AGRICULTURE (agricultural business management, agronomy, animal science, horticulture, range/farm management, and wildlife management), BIOLOGICAL SCIENCE (biochemistry, biology/biological science, cell biology, microbiology, molecular biology, and zoology), BUSINESS (accounting, banking and finance, business administration and management, business economics, hotel/motel and restaurant management, international business management, international economics, management information systems, marketing/retailing/merchandising, and recreation and leisure services), COMMUNICATIONS AND THE ARTS (advertising, art, art history and appreciation, broadcasting, classical languages, communications, dance, design, dramatic arts, English, French, German, journalism, Latin, music, music history and appreciation, music performance, music theory and composition, photography, public relations, Spanish, studio art, telecommunications, theater design, theater management, and visual and performing arts), COMPUTER AND PHYSICAL SCIENCE (applied physics, chemistry, computer science, geology, geophysics and seismology, geoscience, mathematics, and physics), EDUCATION (art, early childhood, education, elementary, and music), ENGINEERING AND ENVIRONMENTAL DESIGN (architecture, chemical engineering, civil engineering, construction technology, electrical/electronics engineering, electrical/electronics engineering technology, engineering, engineering physics, environmental engineering, industrial engineering technology, interior design, landscape architecture/design, mechanical engineering, mechanical engineering technology, petroleum/natural gas engineering, and textile engineering), HEALTH PROFESSIONS (exercise science, health, predentistry, premedicine, and prepharmacy), SOCIAL SCIENCE (anthropology, clothing and textiles management/production/services, dietetics, economics, family/consumer resource management, family/consumer studies, fashion design and technology, food production/management/services, food science, geography, history, home economics, human development, Latin American studies, liberal arts/general studies, parks and recreation management, philosophy, political science/government, prelaw, psychology, Russian and Slavic studies, social work, and sociology). Business, human development and family studies, and educational curriculum and instruction are the largest.

Required: All students must meet the requirements of the core curriculum, including courses in science and technology, math, English, history, and political science. Total credits required for graduation vary from 125 to 174, depending on the degree program. A minimum GPA of 2.0 is required. The last 30 hours and 25% of all credit hours must be from Texas Tech.

Special: There are many work-study programs and internships, and students may study in 5 countries. Texas Tech also offers B.A.- B.S. degrees, an accelerated degree program, co-op programs, dual degrees, dual majors, cross-registration, a general studies degree, a 3-2 engineering program, student-designed majors, nondegree study, and pass/fail options. There are 9 national honor societies, and a freshman honors program.

Faculty/Classroom: 63% of faculty are male; 37%, female. All teach undergraduates. The average class size in an introductory lecture is 46; in a laboratory, 21; and in a regular course, 36.

Admissions: 70% of the 2001-2002 applicants were accepted. The SAT I scores for the 2001-2002 freshman class were: Verbal--28% below 500, 50% between 500 and 599, 19% between 600 and 700, and 2% above 700; Math--3% below 500, 26% between 500 and 599, 50% between 600 and 700, and 21% above 700. The ACT scores were 22% below 21, 31% between 21 and 23, 27% between 24 and 26, 10% between 27 and 28, and 10% above 28. 38% of the current freshmen were in the top fifth of their class; 69% were in the top two fifths. There were 22 National Merit finalists.

Requirements: The SAT I or ACT is required. In addition, applicants should be graduates of an accredited high school or have the GED. The university requires 17 credits of academic work in high school, including 4 credits in English, 3 credits in math, 2 1/2 in social studies, 2 credits in science, and 3 1/2 credits in academic electives. The university admits all students scoring 1200 (composite) on the SAT I or 29 on the ACT. Special circumstances may allow those not fulfilling the above requirements to be admitted. Applications for admissions are accepted on-line at the school's web site. A GPA of 2.0 is required. AP and CLEP credits are accepted.

Procedure: Freshmen are admitted fall, spring, and summer. Entrance exams should be taken before July 1. There is an early admissions plan. Application deadlines are open. The application fee is $25.

Transfer: 1936 transfer students enrolled in 2001-2002. To transfer 24 or more hours, the GPA must be a minimum of 2.25. To transfer 12 to 23 hours, applicants must have a 2.5 GPA and 12 hours of basic courses. To transfer fewer than 12 hours, applicants must have a 2.0 GPA and meet freshman requirements for admission. 30 credits of 125 must be completed at Texas Tech.

Visiting: There are regularly scheduled orientations for prospective students. There are guides for informal visits and visitors may sit in on classes and stay overnight. To schedule a visit, contact the New Student Realtions Office — Visitor Center at (806) 742-1299.

Financial Aid: In 2001-2002, 46% of all freshmen and 44% of continuing students received some form of financial aid. 33% of freshmen and 36% of continuing students received need-based aid. The average freshman award was $4940. Of that total, scholarships or need-based grants averaged $2821 ($12,787 maximum); loans averaged $3226 ($12,625 maximum); and work contracts averaged $4543 ($13,520 maximum). 10% of undergraduates work part time. Average annual earnings from campus work are $4543. The average financial indebtedness of the 2001 graduate was $16,250. Texas Tech is a member of CSS. The FAFSA is required. The fall application deadline is April 15.

International Students: In a recent year, there were 131 international students enrolled. They must score 550 on the written TOEFL or 213 on the electronic version and also take the SAT I or the ACT, scoring 1010 on the SATI or 22 on the ACT.

Computers: The mainframe is an IBM 9672-R34. There are also Macs and IBM, Zenith, Sun, and other PCs available in the Advanced Technology Learning Center and in academic departments. All students may access the system 24 hours per day. There are no time limits. The fee is $7 per semester hour. It is strongly recommended that all students have a personal computer.

Graduates: In 2001, 3671 bachelor's degrees were awarded. The most popular majors were marketing (8%), finance (5%), and management information systems (5%). In an average class, 22% graduate in 4 years, 23% in 5 years, and 7% in 6 years. 350 companies recruited on campus in 2000-2001.

Admissions Contact: Stephanie Hays, Interim Director of Admissions and School Relations. A video is available. E-mail: *nsr@ttu.edu*
Web: *http://www.srel.ttu.edu*

TEXAS WESLEYAN UNIVERSITY — D-2

Fort Worth, TX 76105-1536 — (817) 531-4422
(800) 580-8980; Fax: (817) 531-4231

Full-time: 388 men, 704 women	**Faculty:** 84; IIA, av$
Part-time: 213 men, 409 women	**Ph.D.s:** 77%
Graduate: 536 men, 689 women	**Student/Faculty:** 13 to 1
Year: semesters, summer session	**Tuition:** $10,690
Application Deadline: open	**Room & Board:** $4020
Freshman Class: n/av	
SAT I Verbal/Math: required	**COMPETITIVE**

Texas Wesleyan University, founded in 1890, is a liberal arts institution affiliated with the United Methodist Church. There are 3 undergraduate and 4 graduate schools. In addition to regional accreditation, Texas Wesleyan has baccalaureate program accreditation with NASM. The 2 libraries contain 281,476 volumes, 827,410 microform items, and 5824 audiovisual forms/CDs, and subscribe to 3452 periodicals. Computerized library services include the card catalog, interlibrary loans, and database searching. Special learning facilities include a learning resource center, art gallery, and a theater. The 79-acre campus is in an urban area 2 miles east of downtown Fort Worth. Including residence halls, there are 30 buildings.

Student Life: 96% of undergraduates are from Texas. Others are from 23 states, 32 foreign countries, and Canada. 94% are from public schools. 60% are white; 17% African American; 17% Native American/Eskimo; 16% Hispanic. 58% are claim no religious affiliation; 32% Protestant; 10% Catholic. The average age of freshmen is 19; all undergraduates, 25.

Housing: 275 students can be accommodated in college housing, which includes single-sex and coed dormitories. On-campus housing is available on a first-come, first-served basis. 90% of students commute. Alcohol is not permitted. All students may keep cars.

Activities: 2% of men belong to 3 local fraternities and 1 national fraternity; 2% of women belong to 3 local and 2 national sororities. There are 55 groups on campus, including art, band, cheerleading, choir, computers, drama, ethnic, honors, international, jazz band, musical theater, opera, political, professional, radio and TV, religious, social, social service, student government, and yearbook. Popular campus events include Oktoberfest and the Wilson lectures.

Sports: There are 5 intercollegiate sports for men and 5 for women, and 11 intramural sports for men and 11 for women. Facilities include a 1500-seat athletic center, 4 tennis courts, an off-campus baseball park, and softball and soccer fields.

Disabled Students: Wheelchair ramps, elevators, special parking, specially equipped rest rooms, special class scheduling, and lowered telephones are available.

Services: Counseling and information services are available, as is tutoring in most subjects. There is remedial math, reading, and writing.

Campus Safety and Security: Measures include 24-hour foot and vehicle patrol, self-defense education, escort service, and pamphlets/posters/films. There are emergency telephones, lighted pathways/sidewalks, and residence hall programs.

Programs of Study: Texas Wesleyan confers B.A., B.S., B.B.A., B.F.A; and B.M.E. degrees. Master's degrees are also awarded. Bachelor's degrees are awarded in BIOLOGICAL SCIENCE (biochemistry and biology/biological science), BUSINESS (accounting, business administration and management, business economics, international business management, management information systems, and marketing/retailing/merchandising), COMMUNICATIONS AND THE ARTS (art, communications, dramatic arts, English, fine arts, music, and Spanish), COMPUTER AND PHYSICAL SCIENCE (chemistry, computer science, earth science, information sciences and systems, mathematics, and physical sciences), EDUCATION (business, early childhood, elementary, middle school, music, physical, reading, secondary, and teaching English as a second/foreign language (TESOL/TEFOL)), SOCIAL SCIENCE (Christian studies, criminal justice, economics, history, human development, humanities, interdisciplinary studies, international studies, law, paralegal studies, political science/government, psychology, religion, and social science). Accounting and psychology are the strongest academically. Business administration is the largest.

Required: A minimum GPA of 2.0 and a minimum of 124 credit hours are required in order to graduate. All students must complete a general education requirement of 51 credits, including courses in writing, literature, religion, lab science, history, math, political or economic systems, fine arts, humanities, phys ed, and social science, philosophy, or psychology. The total number of hours in the major varies.

Special: Study abroad is offered in 5 countries. A 3-2 engineering degree is offered in conjunction with a number of universities. Pass/fail options are available, as are B.A.-B.S. degrees, and internships in sports management, business, psychology, and sociology. There are 2 national honor societies, and 8 departmental honors programs.

Faculty/Classroom: 59% of faculty are male; 41%, female. No introductory courses are taught by graduate students.

Admissions: 24% of the current freshmen were in the top fifth of their class; 66% were in the top two fifths.

Requirements: The SAT I or ACT is required with a minimum composite score of 800 or 19, respectively. Applicants must be graduates of an accredited secondary school or have a GED equivalent. An interview is recommended. Texas Wesleyan requires applicants to be in the upper 50% of their class. A GPA of 2.0 is required. AP and CLEP credits are accepted. Important factors in the admissions decision are leadership record, extracurricular activities record, and recommendations by alumni. Applications are accepted on-line via Texas Mentor.

Procedure: Freshmen are admitted to all sessions. Entrance exams should be taken as early as possible. Application deadlines are open. The fall 2001 application fee was $25. Notification is sent on a rolling basis.

Transfer: 335 transfer students enrolled in 2001-2002. Applicants with fewer than 30 credit hours must submit a high school transcript and the results of either the SAT I (with a minimum composite score of 800) or the ACT (with a minimum score of 19). A minimum GPA of 2.0 is required. 45 credits of 124 must be completed at Texas Wesleyan.

Visiting: There are regularly scheduled orientations for prospective students. There are guides for informal visits and visitors may sit in on classes and stay overnight. To schedule a visit, contact the Office of Admissions.

Financial Aid: In 2001-2002, 95% of all freshmen and 72% of continuing students received some form of financial aid, including need-based aid. The average freshman award was $5318. The FAFSA and the college's own financial statement are required. The fall application deadline is April 15.

International Students: There are 61 international students enrolled. The school actively recruits these students. They must score 520 on the written TOEFL or 210 on the electronic version.

Computers: The mainframe is a network with servers. All students may access the system 9 A.M. to 9 P.M. Monday through Thursday, 9 A.M. to 5 P.M. Friday, and 9 A.M. to 1 P.M. weekends. There are no time limits and no fees. It is strongly recommended that all students have a personal computer.

Graduates: In 2001, 378 bachelor's degrees were awarded. The most popular majors were business (26%), education (18%), and psychology (8%).

Admissions Contact: Stephanie Boatner, Director, Freshman Admission. A video is available. E-mail: *freshman@txwesleyan.edu*
Web: *http://www.txwesleyan.edu*

TEXAS WOMAN'S UNIVERSITY — D-2

Denton, TX 76204-5765 — **(940) 898-3040**
(888) 948-9984; Fax: (940) 898-3081

Full-time: 200 men, 3200 women	**Faculty:** 694; I, --$
Part-time: 105 men, 1250 women	**Ph.D.s:** 70%
Graduate: 530 men, 3350 women	**Student/Faculty:** 12 to 1
Year: semesters, summer session	**Tuition:** $2100 ($7300)
Application Deadline: see profile	**Room & Board:** $3800
Freshman Class: n/av	
SAT I or ACT: required	**LESS COMPETITIVE**

Texas Woman's University, founded in 1901, is a comprehensive public university primarily for women, offering degree programs in the liberal arts, education, music and fine arts, and the business and health professions. Figures in above capsule are approximate. There are 6 undergraduate and 7 graduate schools. In addition to regional accreditation, TWU has baccalaureate program accreditation with ADA, APTA, CSWE, NASM, and NLN. The 2 libraries contain 711,462 volumes, 712,443 microform items, and 10,224 audiovisual forms/CDs, and subscribe to 2489 periodicals. Computerized library services include the card catalog, interlibrary loans, and database searching. Special learning facilities include a learning resource center, art gallery, and medical centers and clinics, radio and TV studios, and a nursery school. The 270-acre campus is in an urban area 38 miles north of Dallas. Including residence halls, there are 62 buildings.

Student Life: 93% of undergraduates are from Texas. Others are from 32 states, 56 foreign countries, and Canada. 74% are white; 12% African American. The average age of freshmen is 22; all undergraduates, 27. 29% do not continue beyond their first year; 38% remain to graduate.

Housing: About 2238 students can be accommodated in college housing, which includes single-sex and coed dormitories, on-campus apartments, and married-student housing. On-campus housing is guaranteed for the freshman year only and is available on a first-come, first-served basis. 81% of students commute. All students may keep cars.

Activities: 55% of women belong to 2 local and 4 national sororities. There are no fraternities. There are 80 groups on campus, including art, choir, chorale, chorus, dance, drama, ethnic, gay, honors, international, jazz band, newspaper, political, professional, radio and TV, religious, social, social service, and student government. Popular campus events include Black Awareness Week, Mexican Festival, and the Old Time Picnic.

Sports: There are 5 intercollegiate sports for women, and 11 intramural sports for men and 11 for women. Facilities include a wellness center, indoor and outdoor swimming pools, weight-training and fitness rooms, tennis courts, and a golf course.

Disabled Students: 95% of the campus is accessible. Wheelchair ramps, elevators, special parking, specially equipped rest rooms, lowered drinking fountains, lowered telephones, lowered library equipment, and an office to assist students with disabilities are available.

Services: Counseling and information services are available, as is tutoring in some subjects, including science and math. There is remedial math, reading, and writing, and writing lab assistance.

Campus Safety and Security: Measures include 24-hour foot and vehicle patrol, self-defense education, escort service, and informal discussions. There are pamphlets/posters/films, emergency telephones, and lighted pathways/sidewalks.

Programs of Study: TWU confers B.A., B.S., B.B.A., B.F.A., and B.S.W. degrees. Master's and doctoral degrees are also awarded. Bachelor's degrees are awarded in BIOLOGICAL SCIENCE (biology/biological science), BUSINESS (accounting, business administration and management, fashion merchandising, and marketing/retailing/merchandising), COMMUNICATIONS AND THE ARTS (advertising, applied music, communications, dance, design, dramatic arts, English, fine arts, music, photography, and Spanish), COMPUTER AND PHYSICAL SCIENCE (chemistry, computer science, and mathematics), EDUCATION (library science), HEALTH PROFESSIONS (dental hygiene, music therapy, nursing, and occupational therapy), SOCIAL SCIENCE (child psychology/development, consumer services, criminal justice, dietetics, economics, family/consumer studies, fashion design and technology, history, home economics, interdisciplinary studies, physical fitness/movement, political science/government, psychology, social work, sociology, and textiles and clothing). Nursing, interdisciplinary studies, and occupational therapy are the largest.

Required: Core curriculum includes 6 units each of history, political science, composition, and science, 3 each of math, fine arts, multicultural studies, literature, and women's studies, plus 15 additional hours. General education requirements vary according to the degree. A 2.0 GPA, successful completion of the Texas-mandated examination in reading, writing, and math, and a minimum of 124 hours are needed to graduate.

Special: Co-op programs in most majors and internships are available. Cross-registration is possible with the University of North Texas and East Texas State University. A 3-2 engineering program exists with the University of Texas at Dallas. A dual degree program is available with Texas A&M offering one degree in math and one in engineering, simultaneously. There are 9 national honor societies, a freshman honors program, and 12 departmental honors programs.

Faculty/Classroom: 23% of faculty are male; 77%, female.

Requirements: The SAT I or ACT is required. In addition, a minimum combined score of 800 is required on the SAT I, or a score of 17 on the ACT. Applicants should be graduates of an accredited secondary school or have a GED certificate and have completed 4 secondary school units in English, 3 each in math and social studies, and 2 in science, plus 3 in academic electives. A GPA of 2.0 is required. AP and CLEP credits are accepted.

Procedure: Freshmen are admitted to all sessions. Entrance exams should be taken during the junior or the senior year of high school. There are early admissions and deferred admissions plans. Notification is sent on a rolling basis. Check with the school for current deadlines and fee.

Transfer: Transfer students must possess at least a 2.0 GPA and be in good standing at all previously attended institutions. Course work must be from an accredited college or university. 30 credits of 124 must be completed at TWU.

Visiting: There are regularly scheduled orientations for prospective students, including admissions and financial aid sessions, and a campus tour. There are guides for informal visits and visitors may sit in on classes and stay overnight. To schedule a visit, contact the Office of Admissions.

Financial Aid: In a recent year, 64% of all freshmen and 61% of continuing students received some form of financial aid. 61% of freshmen and 73% of continuing students received need-based aid. The average freshman award was $6249. Of that total, scholarships or need-based grants averaged $1134 ($4800 maximum); loans averaged $3670 ($6625 maximum); and work contracts averaged $2098 ($3040 maximum). 10% of undergraduates work part time. Average annual earnings from campus work are $2098. The average financial indebtedness of a recent graduate was $12,240. TWU is a member of CSS. The FAFSA and the college's own financial statement are required. Check with the school for current deadlines.

International Students: There were 188 international students enrolled in a recent year. The school actively recruits these students. They must score 550 on the written TOEFL.

Computers: The mainframe is a DEC VAX 6330. There are more than 300 PCs and terminals available to TWU students in academic computing labs, libraries, and residence halls. Those who have applied for a computer account may access the system. There are no time limits.

Graduates: In a recent year, 1330 bachelor's degrees were awarded. The most popular majors were nursing (23%), interdisciplinary studies (18%), and occupational therapy (8%). In an average class, 2% graduate in 3 years, 20% in 4 years, 34% in 5 years, and 38% in 6 years.

Admissions Contact: E-mail: *admissions@twu.edu*

TRINITY UNIVERSITY D-4

San Antonio, TX 78212-7200 (210) 999-7207
(800) TRINITY; Fax: (210) 999-8164

Full-time: 1200 men, 1200 women	**Faculty:** 204; IIA, ++$
Part-time: 25 men, 20 women	**Ph.D.s:** 99%
Graduate: 85 men, 150 women	**Student/Faculty:** 11 to 1
Year: semesters, summer session	**Tuition:** $15,300
Application Deadline: see profile	**Room & Board:** $6200
Freshman Class: n/av	
SAT I or ACT required	**HIGHLY COMPETITIVE**

Trinity University, founded in 1869, is a liberal arts and sciences institution affiliated with the Presbyterian Church (U.S.A.). There is 1 graduate school. Figures in above capsule are approximate. In addition to regional accreditation, Trinity has baccalaureate program accreditation with AACSB, ABET, NASM, and NCATE. The library contains 854,825 volumes, 274,012 microform items, and 22,976 audiovisual forms/CDs, and subscribes to 2456 periodicals. Computerized library services include the card catalog, interlibrary loans, and database searching. Special learning facilities include a radio station and TV station. The 117-acre campus is in a suburban area 3 miles north of downtown San Antonio. Including residence halls, there are 45 buildings.

Student Life: 71% of undergraduates are from Texas. Others are from 48 states, 17 foreign countries, and Canada. 73% are from public schools. 70% are white; 10% Hispanic. 50% are Protestant; 22% Catholic; 19% claim no religious affiliation. The average age of freshmen is 18; all undergraduates, 20. 14% do not continue beyond their first year; 78% remain to graduate.

Housing: About 1900 students can be accommodated in college housing, which includes coed dormitories. On-campus housing is available on a lottery system for upperclassmen. 77% of students live on campus; of those, 75% remain on campus on weekends. All students may keep cars.

Activities: 26% of men belong to 8 local fraternities; 28% of women belong to 6 local sororities. There are 100 groups on campus, including art, band, cheerleading, chess, choir, chorale, chorus, computers, dance, debate, drama, ethnic, film, forensics, gay, honors, international, jazz band, literary magazine, musical theater, newspaper, opera, orchestra, pep band, photography, political, professional, radio and TV, religious, social, social service, student government, symphony, and yearbook. Popular campus events include Tower Party and Trinity Night at the S.A. Spurs game.

Sports: There are 9 intercollegiate sports for men and 9 for women, and 20 intramural sports for men and 17 for women. Facilities include an indoor Olympic pool and diving center, a 5000-seat stadium, and a 3000-seat auditorium/arena.

Disabled Students: 99% of the campus is accessible. Wheelchair ramps, elevators, special parking, specially equipped rest rooms, lowered drinking fountains, lowered telephones are available. Learning disabled services are determined through Counseling and Career Services (one-on-one).

Services: Counseling and information services are available, as is tutoring in most subjects.

Campus Safety and Security: Measures include 24-hour foot and vehicle patrol, self-defense education, escort service, and pamphlets/posters/films. There are emergency telephones, lighted pathways/sidewalks, and shuttle carts.

Programs of Study: Trinity confers B.A., B.S., and B.M. degrees. Master's degrees are also awarded. Bachelor's degrees are awarded in BIOLOGICAL SCIENCE (biochemistry and biology/biological science), BUSINESS (business administration and management), COMMUNICATIONS AND THE ARTS (communications, dramatic arts, English, French, German, music, Russian, Spanish, and speech/debate/rhetoric), COMPUTER AND PHYSICAL SCIENCE (chemistry, computer science, geoscience, mathematics, and physics), EDUCATION (art and foreign languages), ENGINEERING AND ENVIRONMENTAL DESIGN (engineering and applied science), SOCIAL SCIENCE (anthropology, economics, history, international relations, philosophy, political science/government, psychology, religion, sociology, and urban studies). Business, communication, biology, and English are the largest.

Required: To graduate, students must satisfy the common curriculum and residency requirements and complete a minimum of 124 credit hours (129 for a B.S. in engineering science and 141 for a B.M. in performance and composition). Students must take at least 60 hours outside the major and 30 hours in upper-division courses. A minimum 2.0 GPA is required.

Special: The university offers study abroad in 35 countries. A Washington semester, dual majors, and pass/fail options are also available, as well as teacher certification and a liberal arts/career combination. There are 5 national honor societies, including Phi Beta Kappa, and 14 departmental honors programs.

Faculty/Classroom: 73% of faculty are male; 27%, female. 96% teach undergraduates and 90% both teach and do research. No introductory courses are taught by graduate students. The average class size in an introductory lecture is 22; in a laboratory, 16; and in a regular course, 20.

Admissions: 72% of recent freshmen were in the top fifth of their class; 97% were in the top two fifths. There were 22 National Merit finalists. 26 freshmen graduated first in their class.

Requirements: The SAT I or ACT is required. In addition, at high school graduation, applicants should have completed 4 years of English, 3 1/2 of math, 3 each of lab science and social studies, and 2 of foreign language. A personal essay, an official high school transcript, a recommendation from a high school counselor, and a teacher's evaluation are also required. A campus visit and a visit with the university's counselor are also recommended. Applications are accepted on-line at the school's web site. AP credits are accepted.

Procedure: Freshmen are admitted fall, spring, and summer. Entrance exams should be taken late in the junior year or early in the senior year. There are early decision and deferred admissions plans. 63 early decision candidates were accepted ina recent year. 5% of all applicants were on a waiting list; 15 were accepted in a recent year.

Transfer: 28 transfer students enrolled in a recent year. A 3.0 college GPA, high school and college transcripts, an essay, standardized test scores, and a statement of good standing from the prior institution are required. An interview is recommended. 60 credits of 124 must be completed at Trinity.

Visiting: There are regularly scheduled orientations for prospective students. There are guides for informal visits and visitors may sit in on classes and stay overnight. To schedule a visit, contact the Admissions Office.

Financial Aid: In a recent year, 84% of all freshmen and 79% of continuing students received some form of financial aid. 45% of freshmen and 40% of continuing students received need-based aid. The average freshman award was $15,258. Of that total, scholarships or need-based grants averaged $10,508; loans averaged $2800; work contracts averaged $1218; and external awards averaged $732. Average annual earnings from campus work are $1410. The average financial indebtedness of a recent graduate was $14,000. Trinity is a member of CSS. The CSS/Profile or FAFSA is required. Check with the school for current deadlines.

International Students: There were 35 international students enrolled in a recent year. The school actively recruits these students. They must score 570 on the written TOEFL.

Computers: There are 3 general-use computing labs containing 60 Windows NT-based systems (with Pentium or Pentium II processors) and 15 Mac systems (with Power PC processors). All of these systems are connected to the campus network and have access to a suite of application software, including Microsoft Word, Excel, PowerPoint, Access, SPSS/PS, and utilities. All students may access the system 24 hours per day. There are no time limits and no fees. It is strongly recommended that all students have a personal computer.

Graduates: In a recent year, 504 bachelor's degrees were awarded. The most popular majors were business (23%), political science (7%), and economics (6%). In an average class, 1% graduate in 3 years, 65% in 4 years, 73% in 5 years, and 73% in 6 years. 100 companies recruited on campus in a recent year. Of a recent graduating class, 42% were enrolled in graduate school within 6 months of graduation and 31% were employed.

Admissions Contact: Dr. George Boyd, Director of Admissions.
E-mail: *admissions@trinity.edu* Web: *trinity.edu*

UNIVERSITY OF DALLAS D-2

Irving, TX 75062-4799 (972) 721-5266
(800) 628-6999; Fax: (972) 721-5017

Full-time: 694 women	**Faculty:** 103
Part-time: 34 men, 36 women	**Ph.D.s:** 92%
Graduate: 1348 men, 915 women	**Student/Faculty:** 12 to 1
Year: semesters, summer session	**Tuition:** $16,084
Application Deadline: February 15	**Room & Board:** $6044
Freshman Class: 1410 applied, 1204 accepted, 311 enrolled	
SAT I Verbal/Math: 615/593	**ACT:** 26 **VERY COMPETITIVE+**

The University of Dallas, founded in 1955, is a private liberal arts institution affiliated with the Roman Catholic Church. Undergraduate programs are offered through the Constantin College of Liberal Arts, and the Braniff Graduate School, which has liberal arts and management divisions. A second campus is located in Rome, Italy. In addition to regional accreditation, UD has baccalaureate program accreditation with AALE. The library contains 229,629 volumes, 75,457 microform items, and 1692 audiovisual forms/CDs, and subscribes to 839 periodicals. Computerized library services include the card catalog, interlibrary loans, and database searching. Special learning facilities include a learning resource center and 80-seat theater, observatory, and several art galleries,. The 750-acre campus is in a suburban area 12 miles west of Dallas. Including residence halls, there are 28 buildings.

Student Life: 57% of undergraduates are from Texas. Others are from 48 states, 21 foreign countries, and Canada. 58% are from public schools. 67% are white; 14% Hispanic. 74% are Catholic; 14% Protestant; 10% claim no religious affiliation. The average age of freshmen is 18; all undergraduates, 21. 18% do not continue beyond their first year; 62% remain to graduate.

Housing: 757 students can be accommodated in college housing, which includes single-sex and coed dormitories and on-campus apartments. On-campus housing is guaranteed for the freshman year only and is available on a first-come, first-served basis. 57% of students live on campus; of those, 88% remain on campus on weekends. All students may keep cars.

Activities: There are no fraternities or sororities. There are 30 groups on campus, including art, chamber ensemble, chess, choir, chorus, computers, dance, drama, ethnic, honors, international, literary magazine, musical theater, newspaper, opera, photography, political, professional, religious, social, social service, student government, symphony, and yearbook. Popular campus events include Charity Week, Oktoberfest, and Christmas Progressive Dinner.

Sports: There are 7 intercollegiate sports for men and 8 for women, and 6 intramural sports for men and 5 for women. Facilities include an athletic center with weight training equipment, a gym for basketball, volleyball, and badminton, and an outdoor pool; a baseball stadium; 8 outdoor tennis courts; a multipurpose field; a soccer field; and cross-country courses.

Disabled Students: 70% of the campus is accessible. Wheelchair ramps, elevators, special parking, specially equipped rest rooms, special class scheduling, and lowered drinking fountains are available.

Services: Counseling and information services are available, as is tutoring in every subject. There is a reader service for the blind, writing and math labs, and an ESL institute.

Campus Safety and Security: Measures include 24-hour foot and vehicle patrol, self-defense education, escort service, and informal discussions. There are pamphlets/posters/films, emergency telephones, and lighted pathways/sidewalks.

Programs of Study: UD confers B.A. and B.S. degrees. Master's and doctoral degrees are also awarded. Bachelor's degrees are awarded in BIOLOGICAL SCIENCE (biochemistry, and biology/biological science), COMMUNICATIONS AND THE ARTS (art history and appreciation, ceramic art and design, classics, dramatic arts, English, French, German, painting, printmaking, sculpture, and Spanish), COMPUTER AND PHYSICAL SCIENCE (chemistry, computer science, mathematics, and physics), EDUCATION (art and elementary), SOCIAL SCIENCE (economics, history, philosophy, political science/government, psychology, and theological studies). Classics, English, and politics are the strongest academically. Biology, English, and politics are the largest.

Required: To graduate, students must complete at least 120 credits, including 36 in the major, with a 2.0 GPA. Core curriculum requirements include 12 credits each of English and philosophy, 9 of math/fine arts, 7 to 8 of science, 6 each of American civilization, Western civilization, and theology, 3 to 14 of modern or classical language, and 3 each of politics and economics. Seniors must pass a comprehensive exam in their major.

Special: UD offers internships in field experience or off-campus research semester, and summer study abroad, a Washington semester, on-campus work-study programs, and an accelerated 5-year degree program leading to an M.B.A., B.A.-B.S. degrees, dual and student-designed majors, and pass/fail options. A 3-2 engineering degree or 3-2 architecture degree may be arranged with Washington University in St. Louis and the University of Texas. There are 4 national honor societies, including Phi Beta Kappa.

Faculty/Classroom: 70% of faculty are male; 30%, female. All teach undergraduates and do research. No introductory courses are taught by graduate students. The average class size in an introductory lecture is 27; in a laboratory, 19; and in a regular course, 19.

Admissions: 85% of the 2001-2002 applicants were accepted. The SAT I scores for the 2001-2002 freshman class were: Verbal--8% below 500, 34% between 500 and 599, 41% between 600 and 700, and 17% above 700; Math--12% below 500, 37% between 500 and 599, 42% between 600 and 700, and 9% above 700. The ACT scores were 7% below 21, 23% between 21 and 23, 22% between 24 and 26, 21% between 27 and 28, and 27% above 28. 71% of the current freshmen were in the top fifth of their class; 96% were in the top two fifths. There were 16 National Merit finalists in a recent year. 18 freshmen graduated first in their class.

Requirements: The SAT I or ACT is required. In addition, applicants must be graduates of an accredited secondary school or have a GED certificate. 16 academic or Carnegie credits are required, including courses in English, social studies, math, science, and a foreign language. An interview is recommended, and an essay is required. AP credits are accepted. Important factors in the admissions decision are advanced placement or honor courses, leadership record, and extracurricular activities record. Applications are accepted on disk and on-line.

Procedure: Freshmen are admitted fall and spring. Entrance exams should be taken during the junior year or by the fall of the senior year. There are early action and deferred admissions plans. Applications should be filed by February 15 for fall entry and December 15 for spring entry. Notification of early action is sent December 15; regular decision, on a rolling basis. The fall 2001 application fee was $40.

Transfer: 68 transfer students enrolled in 2001-2002. Applicants must have a minimum 2.5 GPA from an accredited college or university. An associate degree and an interview are recommended. Official transcripts from all previous colleges attended, a writing sample, a personal statement, and an academic letter of recommendation are required. Students with fewer than 30 transferable credits must also submit SAT I or ACT scores and an official high school transcript. 30 credits of 120 must be completed at UD.

Visiting: There are regularly scheduled orientations for prospective students, including a campus tour, scholarship competition, mass, parents' meetings, and departmental advising. There are guides for informal visits and visitors may sit in on classes and stay overnight. To schedule a visit, contact the Admissions Office.

Financial Aid: In 2001-2002, 93% of all freshmen and 89% of continuing students received some form of financial aid. 82% of freshmen and 76% of continuing students received need-based aid. The average freshman award was $15,395. Of that total, scholarships or need-based grants averaged $8215 ($15,824 maximum); loans averaged $4750 ($17,500 maximum); and work contracts averaged $1040 ($2318 maximum). 47% of undergraduates work part time. Average annual earnings from campus work are $1224. The average financial indebtedness of the 2001 graduate was $17,125. The FAFSA and the college's own financial statement are required. The fall application deadline is March 1.

International Students: There are 30 international students enrolled. The school actively recruits these students. They must score 550 on the written TOEFL. SAT I or ACT scores may be substituted in place of the TOEFL.

Computers: The mainframe is a server farms of Intel-based Dell PowerEdge multiprocessor for distributed computing. These distribute applications to client machines designated for use across 7 computing facilities. Wireless laptops are available for check-out from the library. All rooms in residence halls are equipped with direct connections to the high-speed campus network. Students with wireless laptops may access the system from any common building on campus via the wireless Ethernet network. All students may access the system. There are no time limits and no fees. It is strongly recommended that all students have a personal computer.

Graduates: In 2001, 221 bachelor's degrees were awarded. The most popular majors were English (13%), biology (12%), and history (10%). In an average class, 2% graduate in 3 years, 50% in 4 years, 58% in 5 years, and 60% in 6 years. 50 companies recruited on campus in 2000-2001.

Admissions Contact: Larry Webb, Director of Admission. A video is available. E-mail: *ugadmis@mailadmin.udallas.edu*
Web: *acad.udallas.edu*

UNIVERSITY OF HOUSTON SYSTEM

The University of Houston System, established in 1977 by state law, is a public system of higher education. It is governed by a 9-member board of regents and the chief administrator is the chancellor-president of the University of Houston. The UH system centrally coordinates some institutional functions and directly provides others to its 4 universities: University of Houston, University of Houston-Clear Lake, University of Houston-Downtown, and University of Houston-Victoria. These functions include planning and budgeting, financial management and reporting, fundraising, governmental relations, and legal services. Each of the universities has a distinctive mission within the total configuration of the UH system's higher education services. The University of Houston is the only doctoral degree-granting institution in the system. UH-Clear Lake is an upper-level and graduate institution; UH-Downtown is an open-admission undergraduate university; and UH-Victoria is the only institution within a 100-mile radius to offer bachelor and graduate degrees in the 15-county region southwest of Houston. Total student enrollment for all 4 universities is more than 46,000, with 2757 faculty members. There are 390 baccalaureate, master's, and doctoral programs offered within the system. Profiles of UH and UH-Downtown are included in this section.

UNIVERSITY OF HOUSTON
Houston, TX 77004 E-3
(713) 743-1010
(800) 741-4449; Fax: (713) 743-9633

Full-time: 8193 men, 9449 women	**Faculty:** 717
Part-time: 3747 men, 3841 women	**Ph.D.s:** 64%
Graduate: 3595 men, 4182 women	**Student/Faculty:** 25 to 1
Year: semesters, summer session	**Tuition:** $3168 ($9498)
Application Deadline: May 1	**Room & Board:** $5242
Freshman Class: 4132 applied, 3498 accepted, 2479 enrolled	
SAT I Verbal/Math: 500/520	**ACT:** 21 **COMPETITIVE**

The University of Houston, established in 1927, is a public institution with programs in arts and sciences, business, education, engineering, and health professions. There are 13 undergraduate schools and 1 graduate school. In addition to regional accreditation, UH has baccalaureate program accreditation with AACSB, ABET, ACPE, ADA, CSWE, NAAB, NASM, and NCATE. The 6 libraries contain 2,078,162 volumes, 393,156 microform items, and 8324 audiovisual forms/CDs, and subscribe to 19,503 periodicals. Computerized library services include interlibrary loans and database searching. Special learning facilities include a learning resource center, art gallery, radio station, TV station, and and observatory. The 551-acre campus is in an urban area 3 miles from the Houston business district. Including residence halls, there are 103 buildings.

Student Life: 90% of undergraduates are from Texas. Others are from 49 states, 126 foreign countries, and Canada. 41% are white; 18% Asian American; 18% Hispanic; 14% African American. The average age of freshmen is 18; all undergraduates, 23. 24% do not continue beyond their first year; 35% remain to graduate.

Housing: 2300 students can be accommodated in college housing, which includes coed dormitories, on-campus apartments, and married-student housing. In addition, there are honors houses and special-interest houses. On-campus housing is available on a first-come, first-served basis. 90% of students commute. All students may keep cars.

Activities: 3% of men belong to 19 national fraternities; 3% of women belong to 19 national sororities. There are 300 groups on campus, including art, band, cheerleading, chess, choir, chorale, chorus, computers, dance, debate, drama, drill team, ethnic, film, forensics, gay, honors, international, jazz band, literary magazine, marching band, musical theater, newspaper, opera, orchestra, pep band, photography, political, professional, radio and TV, religious, social, social service, student government, symphony, and yearbook. Popular campus events include Greek Week, Diversity Week, and Frontier Fiesta.

Sports: There are 7 intercollegiate sports for men and 9 for women, and 12 intramural sports for men and 12 for women. Facilities include a state-of-the-art athletics/alumni center.

Disabled Students: 98% of the campus is accessible. Wheelchair ramps, elevators, special parking, specially equipped rest rooms, special class scheduling, lowered drinking fountains, lowered telephones, automatic doors, vehicle and handicap assists, an on-campus attendant-care program, registration assistance, counseling, and adaptive equipment are available.

Services: Counseling and information services are available, as is tutoring in most subjects, including core requirements. There is a reader service for the blind, and remedial math, reading, and writing. Accommodation assistance for students taking exams, tutors assisting with course work, and other accommodations are available.

Campus Safety and Security: Measures include 24-hour foot and vehicle patrol, escort service, shuttle buses, and pamphlets/posters/films. There are emergency telephones, lighted pathways/sidewalks, community dialogues, and assistance with vehicles (such as jump-starts).

Programs of Study: UH confers B.A., B.S., B.Acc., B.Arch., B.B.A., B.F.A., B.M., B.S.C.E., B.S.Ch.E., B.S.E.E., B.S.I.E., B.S.M.E., B.S.Pharm., and B.S.Tech. degrees. Master's and doctoral degrees are also awarded. Bachelor's degrees are awarded in BIOLOGICAL SCIENCE (biochemistry, biology/biological science, biophysics, and nutrition), BUSINESS (accounting, banking and finance, business administration and management, hotel/motel and restaurant management, management information systems, marketing and distribution, marketing/retailing/merchandising, operations research, personnel management, and sports management), COMMUNICATIONS AND THE ARTS (applied music, art, art history and appreciation, classical languages, classics, communications, creative writing, dramatic arts, English, fine arts, French, German, journalism, music, music theory and composition, painting, photography, printmaking, radio/television technology, sculpture, Spanish, speech/debate/rhetoric, and studio art), COMPUTER AND PHYSICAL SCIENCE (chemistry, computer science, earth science, geology, geophysics and seismology, information sciences and systems, mathematics, physics, quantitative methods, and statistics), EDUCATION (trade and industrial), ENGINEERING AND ENVIRONMENTAL DESIGN (architectural engineering, architecture, biomedical equipment technology, chemical engineering, civil engineering, civil engineering technology, computer engineering, computer technology, construction management, construction technology, drafting and design technology, electrical/electronics engineering, electrical/electronics engineering technology, electromechanical technology, environmental design, graphic arts technology, industrial administration/management, industrial engineering, industrial engineering technology, interior design, manufacturing technology, mechanical engineering, and mechanical engineering technology), HEALTH PROFESSIONS (health, optometry, pharmacy, and prepharmacy), SOCIAL SCIENCE (anthropology, economics, family/consumer studies, German area studies, history, human development, interdisciplinary studies, Italian studies, philosophy, physical fitness/movement, political science/government, psychology, Russian and Slavic studies, social science, and sociology). Chemical engineering is the strongest academically. Business, engineering, and biological sciences are the largest.

Required: To graduate, students must complete 122 credits, including at least 36 in advanced-level courses, with a minimum GPA of 2.0. Core curriculum requirements include 6 hours each of English, math/math reasoning, history, American government, natural sciences, visual and performing arts, and social sciences (3 of which are writing intensive) and 3 hours of humanities.

Special: There is cross-registration with the University of Texas, and Rice and Texas Wesleyan Universities. UH also offers internships and co-op programs in many majors, study abroad in 12 countries, work-study programs, and programs in Mexican American studies, Asian American studies, and inter-university African studies, as well as the Mickey Leland Internship in Washington, D.C. Also available are B.A.-B.S. degrees and dual majors in all areas of study, nondegree study, and pass/fail options. There are 10 national honor societies, a freshman honors program, and 13 departmental honors programs.

Faculty/Classroom: 62% of faculty are male; 38%, female. 47% teach undergraduates. Graduate students teach 17% of introductory courses. The average class size in an introductory lecture is 22; in a laboratory, 12; and in a regular course, 25.

Admissions: 85% of the 2001-2002 applicants were accepted. The SAT I scores for the 2001-2002 freshman class were: Verbal--47% below 500, 37% between 500 and 599, 14% between 600 and 700, and 2% above 700; Math--37% below 500, 40% between 500 and 599, 20% between 600 and 700, and 3% above 700. The ACT scores were 48% below 21, 28% between 21 and 23, 13% between 24 and 26, 6% between 27 and 28, and 5% above 28. 38% of the current freshmen were in the top fifth of their class; 66% were in the top two fifths. There were 15 National Merit finalists and 2 semifinalists.

Requirements: The SAT I or ACT is required. In addition, a minimum composite score of 880 (440 verbal and 440 math) on the SAT I or 19 on the ACT is required for consideration. Students in the top 10% of the high school class are automatically admitted. Lower ranks require higher scores. Applicants must be graduates of an accredited secondary school or have the GED. Students should complete 4 credits of English, 3 of math and social sciences, and 2 of lab science, with 2 of foreign language strongly recommended. There are special requirements for the College of Engineering, College of Business, College of Architecture, Department of Computer Science, and the School of Music, including an audition for music candidates. A GPA of 2.0 is required. AP and CLEP credits are accepted. Important factors in the admissions decision are evidence of special talent and advanced placement or honor courses. Applications are accepted on-line at *www.applytexas.org*.

Procedure: Freshmen are admitted to all sessions. Entrance exams should be taken no later than February of the senior year. Early decision applications should be filed by January 15; regular applications, by May 1 for fall entry, December 1 for spring entry, and July 1 for summer entry. Notification of early decision is on a rolling basis; for regular decision, July1. The fall 2001 application fee was $40.

Transfer: In a recent year, 2884 transfer students enrolled. Applicants must be eligible to return to their last college. A 2.0 GPA is required for students with 30 or more semester hours of college credit, a 2.5 GPA for those with 15 to 29. 30 credits of 122 must be completed at UH.

Visiting: There are regularly scheduled orientations for prospective students, including a campus tour, a meal in a residential dining hall, and a visit with an admissions counselor. Open houses are held in November and March. There are guides for informal visits and visitors may stay overnight. To schedule a visit, contact the Admissions Office.

Financial Aid: In a recent year, 50% of all freshmen received some form of financial aid. UH is a member of CSS. The FAFSA is required. The fall application deadline is April 1.

International Students: There were 713 international students enrolled in a recent year. They must score 550 on the written TOEFL and also take the SAT I or the ACT, scoring 880 on the SATI.

Computers: The mainframes are a multiple Solaris plus NT systems and an IBM SP/2 super computer. Registered students have access to computer facilities that are located throughout the campus, including at the library and at a 24-hour site. In addition, individual departments, the Honors College, and the residence halls have their own computer facilities. All students may access the system. There are no time limits. The fee is $7 per credit hour.

Graduates: In 2001, 3353 bachelor's degrees were awarded. The most popular majors were business (35%), psychology (10%), and engineering and applied sciences (9%). In an average class, 1% graduate in 3 years, 10% in 4 years, 29% in 5 years, and 37% in 6 years. 462 companies recruited on campus in 2000-2001. Of the 2000 graduating class, 88% were employed within 6 months of graduation.

Admissions Contact: Admissions Director.
E-mail: *admissions@uh.edu* Web: *http://www.uh.edu*

UNIVERSITY OF HOUSTON-DOWNTOWN E-3

Houston, TX 77002 (713) 221-8423; Fax: (713) 221-5220

Full-time: 1967 men, 2786 women	**Faculty:** 140; IIB, -$
Part-time: 1992 men, 2898 women	**Ph.D.s:** 67%
Graduate: 21 men, 40 women	**Student/Faculty:** 25 to 1
Year: semesters, summer session	**Tuition:** $2006 ($7118)
Application Deadline: open	**Room & Board:** n/app
Freshman Class: n/av	
SAT I or ACT: recommended	**NONCOMPETITIVE**

University of Houston-Downtown, founded in 1974, is part of the University of Houston System. The commuter university offers programs through the colleges of business, math, engineering, technology and natural sciences, and humanities and social studies. Figures in above capsule are approximate. There are 4 undergraduate schools. In addition to regional accreditation, UH-Downtown has baccalaureate program accreditation with ABET. The library contains 181,000 volumes, 20,000 microform items, and 4200 audiovisual forms/CDs, and subscribes to 1300 periodicals. Computerized library services include the card catalog and database searching. Special learning facilities include a learning resource center and art gallery. The campus is in an urban area in the business district of Houston. There is 1 building.

Student Life: 95% of undergraduates are from Texas. Others are from 20 states, 79 foreign countries, and Canada. 96% are from public schools. 31% are Hispanic; 29% white; 24% African American; 12% Asian American. The average age of all undergraduates is 26. 42% do not continue beyond their first year; 40% remain to graduate.

Housing: There are no residence halls. All of students commute. All students may keep cars.

Activities: There is 1 national sorority. There are no fraternities. There are 35 groups on campus, including choir, computers, drama, ethnic, honors, international, literary magazine, newspaper, political, professional, social, social service, and student government. Popular campus events include Spring Festival, Chinese New Year, and Casino Night.

Sports: There are 15 intramural sports for men. Facilities include a game room, basketball court goal, and swimming pool. The largest auditorium seats 300. Students involved in intramural sports may use the facilities at the University of Houston main campus.

Disabled Students: 95% of the campus is accessible. Wheelchair ramps, elevators, special parking, specially equipped rest rooms, lowered drinking fountains, lowered telephones, and Braille materials are available.

Services: Counseling and information services are available, as is tutoring in some subjects, including science. There is a reader service for the blind, and remedial math, reading, and writing. Special labs for math and reading are learning resources for students.

Campus Safety and Security: Measures include 24-hour foot and vehicle patrol, escort service, shuttle buses, and emergency telephones.

Programs of Study: UH-Downtown confers B.A. and B.S. degrees. Bachelor's degrees are awarded in BIOLOGICAL SCIENCE (microbiology), BUSINESS (accounting, banking and finance, business administration and management, marketing/retailing/merchandising, office supervision and management, and purchasing/inventory management), COMMUNICATIONS AND THE ARTS (English and technical and business writing), COMPUTER AND PHYSICAL SCIENCE (applied mathematics, computer science, information sciences and systems, natural sciences, physics, and quantitative methods), EDUCATION (bilingual/bicultural, elementary, and secondary), ENGINEERING AND ENVIRONMENTAL DESIGN (electrical/electronics engineering, engineering technology, and industrial engineering technology), SOCIAL SCIENCE (criminal justice, humanities, interdisciplinary studies, and social science). General business, accounting, and criminal justice are the largest.

Required: In order to graduate, students must complete 44 core hours and a total of 120 to 136 hours. Courses in writing skills, math, and computers, enhancement courses, and a junior year writing proficiency exam are required. Students must maintain a minimum 2.0 GPA.

Special: The university offers co-op programs with Baylor College of Medicine and the University of Texas Health Science Center, cross-registration with the University of Houston System campuses, internships, and work-study programs. General studies degrees in applied math, natural sciences, arts and humanities, and social sciences, nondegree study in the language institute, and pass/fail options in selected courses are available.

Faculty/Classroom: 61% of faculty are male; 39%, female. All teach undergraduates and 40% do research. The average class size in an introductory lecture is 33; in a laboratory, 25; and in a regular course, 30.

Requirements: The SAT I or ACT is recommended. In addition, applicants must be graduates of an accredited secondary school or have a GED certificate. High school courses must include English, math, science, and social studies. AP and CLEP credits are accepted.

Procedure: Freshmen are admitted to all sessions. There are early admissions and deferred admissions plans. Application deadlines are open. The fall 2001 application fee was $10. Notification is sent on a rolling basis.

Transfer: Transfer students must have completed a minimum of 15 credit hours. The SAT I or ACT is recommended. 30 credits of 120 must be completed at UH-Downtown.

Visiting: There are regularly scheduled orientations for prospective students, including an information session, placement testing, advising, and registration. There are guides for informal visits and visitors may sit in on classes. To schedule a visit, contact Pamela Ulmer, Admissions Counselor/Recruiter at (713) 221-8519.

Financial Aid: The FAFSA and the college's own financial statement are required. Check with the school for current deadlines.

International Students: The school actively recruits these students. They must score 550 on the written TOEFL.

Computers: The mainframe is a DEC VAX 8550. IBM PCs and Macs are available in several campus labs. All students may access the system 7 days a week. There are no time limits.

Admissions Contact: Chris Brown, Director of Admissions.
E-mail: *uhdadmit@dt.uh.edu* Web: *www.uhd.edu*

UNIVERSITY OF MARY HARDIN-BAYLOR D-3

Belton, TX 76513 (254) 295-4487
(800) 727-8642; Fax: (254) 295-5049

Full-time: 762 men, 1308 women	**Faculty:** 117
Part-time: 117 men, 247 women	**Ph.D.s:** 59%
Graduate: 45 men, 145 women	**Student/Faculty:** 18 to 1
Year: semesters, summer session	**Tuition:** $9890
Application Deadline: open	**Room & Board:** $4039
Freshman Class: 941 applied, 851 accepted, 459 enrolled	
SAT I Verbal/Math: 520/510	**ACT:** 21 **COMPETITIVE**

The University of Mary Hardin-Baylor, founded in 1845, is a private facility affiliated with the Baptist General Convention of Texas. It offers undergraduate and graduate degrees in liberal arts, fine arts, music, business, and education. There are 5 undergraduate and 5 graduate schools. In addition to regional accreditation, UMHB has baccalaureate program accreditation with CSWE and NLN. The library contains 150,000 volumes, 250,000 microform items, and 5000 audiovisual forms/CDs, and subscribes to 3000 periodicals. Computerized library services include the card catalog, interlibrary loans, and database searching. Special learning facilities include a learning resource center and nature walk. The 120-acre campus is in a small town in central Texas. Including residence halls, there are 35 buildings.

Student Life: 97% of undergraduates are from Texas. Others are from 23 states and 13 foreign countries. 92% are from public schools. 76% are white; 11% African American. 74% are Protestant; 15% claim no religious affiliation; 10% Catholic. The average age of freshmen is 18; all undergraduates, 23. 38% do not continue beyond their first year; 62% remain to graduate.

Housing: 1093 students can be accommodated in college housing, which includes single-sex dormitories and on-campus apartments. On-campus housing is guaranteed for all 4 years. 55% of students commute. Alcohol is not permitted. All students may keep cars.

Activities: There are no fraternities or sororities. There are 37 groups on campus, including art, band, cheerleading, chess, choir, chorale, chorus, computers, drama, drill team, ethnic, honors, international, jazz band, literary magazine, marching band, musical theater, newspaper, opera, orchestra, pep band, photography, political, professional, religious, social service, student government, symphony, and yearbook. Popular campus events include Miss and Mr. UMHB Pageants, Play Day, and Easter Pageant.

Sports: There are 6 intercollegiate sports for men and 7 for women, and 12 intramural sports for men and 11 for women. Facilities include a gym, 2 pools, a sauna, a steam bath, softball, intramural, soccer, and baseball fields, outdoor basketball and tennis courts, an aerobics room, and a sportsplex with field house and weight room.

Disabled Students: 90% of the campus is accessible. Wheelchair ramps, elevators, special parking, specially equipped rest rooms, special class scheduling, lowered drinking fountains, and lowered telephones are available.

Services: Counseling and information services are available, as is tutoring in most subjects. There is remedial math, reading, and writing.

Campus Safety and Security: Measures include 24-hour foot and vehicle patrol, escort service, informal discussions, and pamphlets/posters/films. There are emergency telephones, lighted pathways/sidewalks, and a security service on campus.

Programs of Study: UMHB confers B.A., B.S., B.A.S., B.B.A., B.F.A., B.M., B.P.S., and B.S.N. degrees. Master's degrees are also awarded.

Bachelor's degrees are awarded in BIOLOGICAL SCIENCE (biology/biological science), BUSINESS (accounting, banking and finance, business administration and management, business economics, marketing/retailing/merchandising, and personnel management), COMMUNICATIONS AND THE ARTS (communications, English, fine arts, journalism, music, Spanish, and speech/debate/rhetoric), COMPUTER AND PHYSICAL SCIENCE (chemistry, computer science, information sciences and systems, and mathematics), EDUCATION (art, business, early childhood, elementary, foreign languages, health, middle school, music, science, secondary, and special), ENGINEERING AND ENVIRONMENTAL DESIGN (computer graphics), HEALTH PROFESSIONS (exercise science, medical technology, nursing, and premedicine), SOCIAL SCIENCE (criminal justice, economics, history, parks and recreation management, political science/government, prelaw, psychology, religion, social science, social work, and sociology). Education, business, and nursing are the strongest academically. Education is the largest.

Required: To graduate all students must complete at least 124 credits, including at least 24 in the major field and at least 36 upper-level credits, with a 2.0 GPA. Requirements include 6 credits each in English, social sciences, and religion, 6 in electives, 3 in math, lab science, or foreign language, 3 in speech communication, and 2 in phys ed. There is a chapel attendance requirement for full-time students.

Special: Combined B.A.-B.S. degrees in most areas, internships, a work-study program, dual majors, a professional studies degree, and nondegree study are offered. There are 2 national honor societies.

Faculty/Classroom: 49% of faculty are male; 51%, female. 96% teach undergraduates, 12% do research, and 10% do both. No introductory courses are taught by graduate students. The average class size in an introductory lecture is 35; in a laboratory, 25; and in a regular course, 30.

Admissions: 90% of the 2001-2002 applicants were accepted. The SAT I scores for the 2001-2002 freshman class were: Verbal--37% below 500, 49% between 500 and 599, 12% between 600 and 700, and 2% above 700; Math--41% below 500, 44% between 500 and 599, and 15% between 600 and 700. The ACT scores were 41% below 21, 26% between 21 and 23, 21% between 24 and 26, 6% between 27 and 28, and 6% above 28. 40% of the current freshmen were in the top fifth of their class; 72% were in the top two fifths. 3 freshmen graduated first in their class.

Requirements: The SAT I or ACT is required. In addition, uMHB requires a minimum composite SAT I score of 900 or minimum ACT score of 19. Applicants should be graduates of an accredited high school or have earned the GED. Students should have completed 15 academics, including 3 in English and 2 each in social science and math. UMHB requires applicants to be in the upper 50% of their class. AP and CLEP credits are accepted. Important factors in the admissions decision are advanced placement or honor courses, recommendations by school officials, and extracurricular activities record.

Procedure: Freshmen are admitted to all sessions. Entrance exams should be taken by the fall of the senior year. There is an early admissions plan. Application deadlines are open. The fall 2001 application fee was $35.

Transfer: 294 transfer students enrolled in 2001-2002. Applicants must present at least a 2.0 GPA, be in good standing at their previous institutions, and submit all college transcripts. Those with fewer than 30 credits must also meet freshman requirements. 31 credits of 124 must be completed at UMHB.

Visiting: There are regularly scheduled orientations for prospective students, consisting of visits with counselors to discuss admissions, financial aid, housing, and degree plans. There are guides for informal visits and visitors may sit in on classes and stay overnight. To schedule a visit, contact the Recruiting Office at (254) 295-4514.

Financial Aid: In 2001-2002, 93% of all freshmen and 85% of continuing students received some form of financial aid. 82% of freshmen and 76% of continuing students received need-based aid. The average freshman award was $7264. Of that total, scholarships or need-based grants averaged $4449 ($5730 maximum); loans averaged $2279 ($6625 maximum); and work contracts averaged $536 ($2300 maximum). 15% of undergraduates work part time. Average annual earnings from campus work are $2300. The average financial indebtedness of the 2001 graduate was $13,509. The FAFSA and the college's own financial statement are required. The fall application deadline is June 1.

International Students: There are 25 international students enrolled. The school actively recruits these students. They must take the college's own test.

Computers: The mainframe is an IBM AS/400. There are 14 computer labs, some of which are located in dormitories. All PCs are connected to the campus-wide network. All students may access the system any time. There are no time limits and no fees.

Graduates: In 2001, 441 bachelor's degrees were awarded. The most popular majors were elementary education (16%), nursing (8%), and general studies (8%). In an average class, 2% graduate in 3 years, 23% in 4 years, 45% in 5 years, and 46% in 6 years. 150 companies recruited on campus in 2000-2001.

Admissions Contact: Robin Steen, Director of Admissions.
E-mail: *admissions@umhb.edu* Web: *www.umhb.edu*

UNIVERSITY OF NORTH TEXAS D-2

Denton, TX 76203 (940) 565-2681
(800) UNT-8211; Fax: (940) 565-2408

Full-time: 7403 men, 9532 women	**Faculty:** 810; I, --$
Part-time: 2281 men, 2459 women	**Ph.D.s:** 87%
Graduate: 2400 men, 3783 women	**Student/Faculty:** 21 to 1
Year: semesters, summer session	**Tuition:** $3211 ($9601)
Application Deadline: June 15	**Room & Board:** $4418
Freshman Class: 8173 applied, 5874 accepted, 3115 enrolled	
SAT I Verbal/Math: 530/530	**ACT:** 22 **COMPETITIVE**

The University of North Texas, founded in 1890, is a public institution offering programs through its colleges of arts and sciences, education, business administration, community services, library and information sciences, music, merchandising and hospitality management, and school of visual arts. There are 8 undergraduate schools and 1 graduate school. In addition to regional accreditation, UNT has baccalaureate program accreditation with AACSB, ACEJMC, CSAB, CSWE, FIDER, NASM, and NRPA. The 4 libraries contain 1,529,868 volumes, 3,166,145 microform items, and 75,169 audiovisual forms/CDs, and subscribe to 20,157 periodicals. Computerized library services include the card catalog, interlibrary loans, and database searching. Special learning facilities include a learning resource center, art gallery, radio station, an observatory, and a TV and film production unit. The 500-acre campus is in an urban area 35 miles north of Dallas/Fort Worth. Including residence halls, there are 151 buildings.

Student Life: 93% of undergraduates are from Texas. Others are from 49 states, 113 foreign countries, and Canada. 73% are white. The average age of freshmen is 19; all undergraduates, 23. 31% do not continue beyond their first year; 69% remain to graduate.

Housing: 4400 students can be accommodated in college housing, which includes single-sex and coed dormitories, on-campus apartments, and off-campus apartments. On-campus housing is available on a first-come, first-served basis. All students may keep cars.

Activities: 3% of men belong to 16 national fraternities; 3% of women belong to 11 national sororities. There are 250 groups on campus, including band, cheerleading, chess, choir, chorale, chorus, computers, dance, drama, ethnic, film, gay, honors, international, jazz band, literary magazine, marching band, musical theater, newspaper, opera, orchestra, pep band, photography, political, professional, radio and TV, religious, social, social service, student government, symphony, and yearbook. Popular campus events include Silver Christmas Ball, Howdy Week, and Taste of North Texas.

Sports: There are 6 intercollegiate sports for men and 9 for women, and 37 intramural sports for men and 37 for women. Facilities include a 30,000-seat stadium, an 18-hole golf course, a weight-training building, tennis courts, 1 indoor swimming pool, 3 gyms, 8 handball and racquetball courts, gymnastics equipment, intramural fields, and recreational sports complex.

Disabled Students: 85% of the campus is accessible. Wheelchair ramps, elevators, special parking, specially equipped rest rooms, special class scheduling, lowered drinking fountains, lowered telephones, and 9 dorm rooms adapted for disabled students are available.

Services: Counseling and information services are available, as is tutoring in most subjects. There is a reader service for the blind, and remedial math, reading, and writing.

Campus Safety and Security: Measures include 24-hour foot and vehicle patrol, self-defense education, escort service, and shuttle buses. There are informal discussions, pamphlets/posters/films, emergency telephones, lighted pathways/sidewalks, a crime prevention program, sexual assault information services, and a full-time crime prevention officer on duty.

Programs of Study: UNT confers B.A., B.S., B.A.A.S., B.B.A., B.F.A., B.M., B.S.B.C., B.S.Bio, B.S.Chem., B.S.Eco., B.S.E.P., B.S.E.T., B.S.Math., B.S.M.T., B.S.Phy., and B.S.W. degrees. Master's and doctoral degrees are also awarded. Bachelor's degrees are awarded in BIOLOGICAL SCIENCE (biochemistry and biology/biological science), BUSINESS (accounting, banking and finance, business administration and management, business economics, entrepreneurial studies, hotel/motel and restaurant management, human resources, insurance, management information systems, management science, marketing/retailing/merchandising, operations research, organizational behavior, personnel management, real estate, recreation and leisure services, and small business management), COMMUNICATIONS AND THE ARTS (applied art, art, art history and appreciation, ceramic art and design, communications, dance, dramatic arts, drawing, English, fiber/textiles/weaving, film arts, French, German, jazz, journalism, metal/jewelry, music, music history and appreciation, music performance, music theory and composition, painting, photography, printmaking, radio/television technology, sculpture, Spanish, and visual and performing arts), COMPUTER AND PHYSICAL SCIENCE (chemistry, computer science, information sciences and systems, mathematics, and physics), EDUCATION (business, early childhood, elementary, health, physical, reading, and vocational), ENGINEERING AND ENVIRONMENTAL DESIGN (commercial art, emergency/disaster science, engineering technology, industrial administration/management, and interior design), HEALTH PROFESSIONS (cytotechnology, medical laboratory technology, rehabilitation therapy, and speech pathology/audiology), SOCIAL SCIENCE (anthropology, child psychology/development, clothing and textiles management/production/services, counseling/psychology, criminal justice, economics, fashion design and technology, geography, history, home furnishings and equipment management/production/services, interdisciplinary studies, liberal arts/general studies, philosophy, physical fitness/movement, political science/government, psychology, social science, social work, and sociology). Accounting, jazz studies, and city management are the strongest academically. Biology, psychology, and interdisciplinary studies (teacher education department) are the largest.

Required: All students must complete at least 124 semester hours, including a minimum of 24 hours in the major, with a 2.0 GPA. The 47 hours of core requirements include 12 hours of English, 6 hours each in science, American history, federal and state constitution, social sciences, and humanities, and 4 hours in phys ed. Proficiency in English composition must be demonstrated.

Special: UNT offers co-op programs in 34 majors, internships, and work-study programs with the university. Students may study abroad in the United Kingdom, France, Japan, Germany, Mexico, and Australia. An accelerated degree program in math and science allows Texas high school students to obtain 2 years of college credit during their last 2 years in high school. Dual degrees, a general studies degree, and pass/fail options are also offered. There are 3 national honor societies, a freshman honors program, and 1 departmental honors program.

Faculty/Classroom: 69% of faculty are male; 31%, female. 95% teach undergraduates. The average class size in a laboratory is 23 and in a regular course, 40.

Admissions: 72% of the 2001-2002 applicants were accepted. The SAT I scores for the 2001-2002 freshman class were: Verbal--34% below 500, 43% between 500 and 599, 20% between 600 and 700, and 3% above 700; Math--36% below 500, 40% between 500 and 599, 21% between 600 and 700, and 5% above 700. The ACT scores were 38% below 21, 30% between 21 and 23, 21% between 24 and 26, 7% between 27 and 28, and 4% above 28. 44% of the current freshmen were in the top fifth of their class; 80% were in the top two fifths.

Requirements: The SAT I or ACT is required. In addition, applicants must be graduates of an accredited high school and submit a high school transcript. The required minimum score for entrance exams is determined by high school class rank. AP and CLEP credits are accepted. Important factors in the admissions decision are recommendations by school officials, advanced placement or honor courses, and evidence of special talent.

Procedure: Freshmen are admitted to all sessions. Entrance exams should be taken at least 2 months before admissions deadlines. There are early admissions and deferred admissions plans. Applications should be filed by June 15 for fall entry, December 1 for spring entry, and May 15 for summer entry, along with a $40 fee. Notification is sent on a rolling basis.

Transfer: Applicants with fewer than 30 hours from an accredited college must have a 2.5 GPA and meet freshman entrance requirements. Applicants with at least 30 but no more than 44 transferable hours must have a 2.3 GPA; those with more than 44 hours must have a 2.0 GPA. 30 credits of 124 must be completed at UNT.

Visiting: There are regularly scheduled orientations for prospective students, including UNT Previews held 1 Saturday in the fall and 1 in the spring. The agenda includes a campus tour, presentations by academic and student service offices, and question-and-answer sessions. There are guides for informal visits and visitors may sit in on classes and stay overnight. To schedule a visit, contact the information desk assistant at (940) 565-4104 or (940) 565-2000.

Financial Aid: In a recent year, 49% of all freshmen received some form of financial aid. 39% of freshmen received need-based aid. The average freshman award was $3800. 80% of undergraduates work part time. Average annual earnings from campus work are $2400. The average financial indebtedness of a recent year's graduate was $12,000. The FAFSA is required. The fall application deadline is June 1.

International Students: There were 505 international students enrolled in a recent year. The school actively recruits these students. They must score 550 on the written TOEFL or take the MELAB, ECPE, FCE, CAE, CPE, IELTS, or ELPT.

Computers: The mainframes are an HDS-80-83, a Solbourne SE/904, an NBIV16S, an NAS8000, and an IBM 43004. More than 5000 PCs are available on campus. All students may access the system. Students may access the system for 1 hour if labs are busy. The fee is $3.25 per semester hour.

Graduates: 315 companies recruited on campus in 2000-2001.

Admissions Contact: Marcilla Collinsworth, Director, Admissions and School Relations. A video is available.
E-mail: *undergrad@abn.unt.edu* Web: *www.unt.edu*

UNIVERSITY OF SAINT THOMAS — E-3

Houston, TX 77006-4696 — (713) 525-3500
(800) 856-8565; Fax: (713) 525-3558

Full-time: 443 men, 850 women	**Faculty:** IIA, av$
Part-time: 209 men, 349 women	**Ph.D.s:** 87%
Graduate: 448 men, 601 women	**Student/Faculty:** n/av
Year: semesters, summer session	**Tuition:** $13,162
Application Deadline: open	**Room & Board:** $5590
Freshman Class: 768 applied, 598 accepted, 284 enrolled	
SAT I Verbal/Math: 560/560	**ACT:** 25 **VERY COMPETITIVE**

The University of St. Thomas is a private institution committed to the liberal arts and to the religious, ethical, and intellectual tradition of Catholic higher education. There are 3 undergraduate and 4 graduate schools. In addition to regional accreditation, UST has baccalaureate program accreditation with ACBSP. The 2 libraries contain 200,000 volumes, 517,002 microform items, and 1012 audiovisual forms/CDs, and subscribe to 6000 periodicals. Computerized library services include the card catalog, interlibrary loans, and database searching. Special learning facilities include a learning resource center and art gallery. The 21-acre campus is in an urban area in downtown Houston. Including residence halls, there are 40 buildings.

Student Life: 92% of undergraduates are from Texas. Others are from 27 states, 69 foreign countries, and Canada. 47% are white; 33% Hispanic; 14% Asian American. 63% are Catholic; 22% Protestant. The average age of freshmen is 18; all undergraduates, 27. 24% do not continue beyond their first year; 53% remain to graduate.

Housing: 295 students can be accommodated in college housing, which includes coed dormitories and on-campus apartments. In addition, there is a Living-Learning Center. On-campus housing is available on a first-come, first-served basis. Priority is given to out-of-town students. 90% of students commute. All students may keep cars.

Activities: There are no fraternities or sororities. There are 72 groups on campus, including chess, choir, computers, debate, drama, ethnic, honors, international, jazz band, literary magazine, musical theater, photography, political, professional, radio and TV, religious, social, social service, student government, and yearbook. Popular campus events include spring formal and campus welcome-back party.

Sports: There are 10 intramural sports for men and 10 for women. Facilities include an 800-seat gym, racquetball and tennis courts, a weight-training room, a cardiovascular room, swimming pool, and a multipurpose area.

Disabled Students: 48% of the campus is accessible. Wheelchair ramps, elevators, special parking, specially equipped rest rooms, special class scheduling, lowered drinking fountains, and lowered telephones are available.

Services: Counseling and information services are available, as is tutoring in every subject. There is remedial math, reading, and writing. There are remedial classes, but if a student has special needs, the learning center will provide remedial tutoring.

Campus Safety and Security: Measures include 24-hour foot and vehicle patrol, self-defense education, escort service, and informal discussions. There are pamphlets/posters/films, emergency telephones, and lighted pathways/sidewalks.

Programs of Study: UST confers B.A., B.B.A., B.S., and B.Th. degrees. Master's and doctoral degrees are also awarded. Bachelor's degrees are awarded in BIOLOGICAL SCIENCE (biology/biological science), BUSINESS (accounting, banking and finance, business administration and management, management information systems, and marketing/retailing/merchandising), COMMUNICATIONS AND THE ARTS (communications, dramatic arts, English, fine arts, French, music, Spanish, and studio art), COMPUTER AND PHYSICAL SCIENCE (chemistry and mathematics), EDUCATION (education and music), ENGINEERING AND ENVIRONMENTAL DESIGN (environmental science), SOCIAL SCIENCE (economics, history, international studies, liberal arts/general studies, pastoral studies, philosophy, political science/government, psychology, and theological studies). Business administration, education, and international studies are the largest.

Required: To graduate, students must complete the core curriculum in theology, philosophy, English, history, foreign language, natural and social science, math, fine arts, and oral communication and 30 to 48 hours in their selected majors. In some cases, students need to complete special projects according to the requirements of specific majors. Students must have a minimum 2.0 GPA in a total of 126 credit hours.

Special: UST offers cross-registration with the University of Houston and a 3-2 engineering program with the University of Houston, Texas A&M, and Notre Dame. Internships in the major field of study and study abroad in 10 countries are also available. Dual and joint majors and 5-year joint bachelor's and master's degree programs, combining BBA/MBA or BBA/MIB, are available. There are 20 national honor societies, and a freshman honors program.

Faculty/Classroom: 58% of faculty are male; 42%, female. All teach undergraduates. No introductory courses are taught by graduate stu-

dents. The average class size in an introductory lecture is 20; in a laboratory, 18; and in a regular course, 18.

Admissions: 78% of the 2001-2002 applicants were accepted. The SAT I scores for the 2001-2002 freshman class were: Verbal--13% below 500, 56% between 500 and 599, 30% between 600 and 700, and 2% above 700; Math--14% below 500, 50% between 500 and 599, 31% between 600 and 700, and 5% above 700. The ACT scores were 6% below 21, 29% between 21 and 23, 27% between 24 and 26, 24% between 27 and 28, and 14% above 28. 55% of the current freshmen were in the top fifth of their class; 80% were in the top two fifths. 5 freshmen graduated first in their class.

Requirements: The SAT I or ACT is required. In addition, a minimum composite score equal to or above the national average on SAT I or on the ACT is required. Applicants must be graduates of an accredited secondary school and have 18 academic credits, 4 years of English, 3 years of math, 2 years each of foreign language, science, and social studies, and 1 year of history, or have a GED certificate. UST requires applicants to be in the upper 50% of their class. A GPA of 2.0 is required. AP and CLEP credits are accepted. Applications are accepted on-line.

Procedure: Freshmen are admitted to all sessions. Entrance exams should be taken as early as possible. There is a deferred admissions plan. Application deadlines are open. The fall 2001 application fee was $35. Notification is sent on a rolling basis.

Transfer: 196 transfer students enrolled in 2001-2002. Transfer students must have a minimum 2.0 GPA, a high school diploma or GED, and be eligible to return to the last college of attendance. 36 credits of 126 must be completed at UST.

Visiting: There are regularly scheduled orientations for prospective students, including tours, class visitations, introductions to faculty, administrative members, and currently enrolled students, and financial aid sessions. There are guides for informal visits and visitors may sit in on classes and stay overnight. To schedule a visit, contact an admissions counselor.

Financial Aid: In 2001-2002, 85% of all freshmen and 38% of continuing students received some form of financial aid. 74% of freshmen and 27% of continuing students received need-based aid. The average freshman award was $11,114. Of that total, scholarships or need-based grants averaged $8748 ($23,966 maximum); loans averaged $6109 ($19,412 maximum); and work contracts averaged $3000 (maximum). The average financial indebtedness of the 2001 graduate was $18,958. The FAFSA is required. The fall application deadline is March 1.

International Students: There are 83 international students enrolled. The school actively recruits these students. They must score 550 on the written TOEFL or 213 on the electronic version.

Computers: The mainframe is a Sun workstation 4N. There are 203 PCs located throughout the campus for student use. Students can access their e-mail and student accounts on-line. All students may access the system 9 A.M. to 10 P.M., 7 days a week; dial-up, 24 hours a day. There are no time limits and no fees.

Graduates: In 2001, 340 bachelor's degrees were awarded. The most popular majors were education (18%), business administration (7%), and communication and accounting (7% each). In an average class, 1% graduate in 3 years, 47% in 4 years, 25% in 5 years, and 53% in 6 years. 16 companies recruited on campus in 2000-2001.

Admissions Contact: Gerald E. Warren, Assistant Director of Admissions. A video is available. E-mail: *admissions@stthom.edu*
Web: *http://www.stthom.edu*

UNIVERSITY OF TEXAS SYSTEM

The University of Texas System, established in 1950, is a public system made up of nine academic institutions, six health institutions, four medical schools, two dental schools, and seven nursing schools. It is governed by a board of regents whose chief administrator is the chancellor. The primary goals of the system are to provide instruction, research, and public service throughout the state. The main priorities are undergraduate education, social and economic development of Texas, and professional training in and effective management of health care. The total enrollment approaches 160,000, with nearly 15,000 faculty members. Altogether there are 388 baccalaureate, 309 master's, and 148 doctoral programs offered in the system. 4-year campuses are located in Arlington, Austin, El Paso, and San Antonio. Profiles of the 4-year campuses are included in this section.

UNIVERSITY OF TEXAS AT ARLINGTON D-2

Arlington, TX 76019- **(817) 272-6287; Fax: (817) 272-3435**

Full-time: 5225 men, 5960 women	**Faculty:** I, --$
Part-time: 2395 men, 2750 women	**Ph.D.s:** 83%
Graduate: 2429 men, 2421 women	**Student/Faculty:** n/av
Year: semesters, summer session	**Tuition:** $3068 ($8132)
Application Deadline: June 1	**Room & Board:** $4124
Freshman Class: 4404 applied, 3724 accepted, 1965 enrolled	
SAT I Verbal/Math: 520/530	**ACT:** 21 **LESS COMPETITIVE**

The University of Texas at Arlington, founded in 1895, is part of the University of Texas System and is organized into colleges and schools, including business administration, engineering, liberal arts, science, architecture, nursing, social work, graduate studies, urban and public affairs, and education. There are 9 undergraduate and 10 graduate schools. In addition to regional accreditation, UTA has baccalaureate program accreditation with AACSB, ABET, ACS, ASLA, CSWE, FIDER, NAAB, NASM, NASPAA, and NLN. The 3 libraries contain 1,105,189 volumes, 1,518,208 microform items, and 3468 audiovisual forms/CDs, and subscribe to 5073 periodicals. Computerized library services include the card catalog, interlibrary loans, and database searching. Special learning facilities include a learning resource center, art gallery, planetarium, cartographic history library, and nano lab. The 395-acre campus is in an urban area in the center of the Dallas/Fort Worth metroplex. Including residence halls, there are 100 buildings.

Student Life: 92% of undergraduates are from Texas. Others are from 45 states, 88 foreign countries, and Canada. 56% are white; 12% African American; 11% foreign nationals; 10% Asian American; 10% Hispanic. The average age of freshmen is 18; all undergraduates, 24. 31% do not continue beyond their first year; 31% remain to graduate.

Housing: 3303 students can be accommodated in college housing, which includes single-sex and coed dormitories, on-campus apartments, off-campus apartments, married-student housing, fraternity houses, and sorority houses. In addition, there are honors houses. On-campus housing is available on a first-come, first-served basis. 86% of students commute. Alcohol is not permitted. All students may keep cars.

Activities: 6% of men belong to 12 national fraternities; 4% of women belong to 10 national sororities. There are 225 groups on campus, including art, band, cheerleading, chess, choir, chorale, chorus, computers, dance, drama, drill team, drum and bugle corps, ethnic, forensics, gay, honors, international, jazz band, marching band, opera, orchestra, photography, political, professional, religious, social, social service, student government, symphony, and yearbook. Popular campus events include Charity Week, The Big Event, and Last Day Blast.

Sports: There are 6 intercollegiate sports for men and 6 for women, and 10 intramural sports for men and 10 for women. Facilities include 12 racquetball, 4 basketball, and volleyball courts, 12 lighted tennis courts, an inside track, 1 Olympic-size pool, 3 weight rooms, a 12,000-seat stadium, and a 3000-seat gym.

Disabled Students: All of the campus is accessible. Wheelchair ramps, elevators, special parking, specially equipped rest rooms, special class scheduling, lowered drinking fountains, lowered telephones, personal, academic, and career counseling, wheelchair repair, note copying, adaptive testing, adaptive exercise and sport activities, and wheelchair athletics are available.

Services: Counseling and information services are available, as is tutoring in most subjects, including English, math, computer science, and foreign languages. There is a reader service for the blind, and remedial math, reading, and writing. a math tutorial clinic, a nursing learning resource center, a reading lab, a science learning center, and a writing lab are available.

Campus Safety and Security: Measures include 24-hour foot and vehicle patrol, self-defense education, escort service, and shuttle buses. There are informal discussions, pamphlets/posters/films, emergency telephones, lighted pathways/sidewalks, crime prevention programs, and an emergency on-campus phone number.

Programs of Study: UTA confers B.A., B.S., B.A.I.S., B.B.A., B.F.A., B.M., B.S.A.S.E., B.S.C.E., B.S.C.S., B.S.C.S.E., B.S.E.E., B.S.I.E., B.S.I.S., B.S.M.E., B.S.N., and B.S.W. degrees. Master's and doctoral degrees are also awarded. Bachelor's degrees are awarded in BIOLOGICAL SCIENCE (biochemistry, biology/biological science, and microbiology), BUSINESS (accounting, banking and finance, business administration and management, business economics, management science, marketing/retailing/merchandising, and real estate), COMMUNICATIONS AND THE ARTS (art history and appreciation, broadcasting, communications, dramatic arts, English, French, German, journalism, music, Russian, Spanish, speech/debate/rhetoric, and studio art), COMPUTER AND PHYSICAL SCIENCE (chemistry, computer science, geology, information sciences and systems, mathematics, and physics), EDUCATION (physical), ENGINEERING AND ENVIRONMENTAL DESIGN (architecture, civil engineering, computer engineering, electrical/electronics engineering, industrial engineering technology, interior design, landscape architecture/design, and mechanical engineering), HEALTH PROFESSIONS (medical technology and nursing), SOCIAL

SCIENCE (anthropology, classical/ancient civilization, criminal justice, economics, history, interdisciplinary studies, philosophy, political science/government, psychology, social work, and sociology). Liberal arts, business, and engineering are the largest.

Required: All students must earn a GPA of 2.0 while taking at least 124 semester hours, including 30 in their major. The core curriculum requires 8 hours of science, 6 each of English composition, math, U.S. history, and U.S. political science, and 3 each of literature, liberal arts, social/cultural studies, and fine arts/philosophy. Students must demonstrate proficiency in oral presentations and computer use. Proficiency exams, or completion of a department-designated course, may be required by the major department. Theses are required of members of the Honors College.

Special: Cooperative education programs provide opportunities to gain experience in local business through the colleges of engineering and business. Cross-registration with the Summer Institute of Linguistics and the University of Texas Health Science Center, as well as with other members of the University of Texas System, is available. Study abroad in 10 countries, work-study at the university, B.A.-B.S. degrees, dual majors, student-designed interdisciplinary majors, credit for military experience, and pass/fail options are also offered. There are 2 national honor societies, a freshman honors program, and 10 departmental honors programs.

Faculty/Classroom: 60% of faculty are male; 40%, female. Graduate students teach 17% of introductory courses. The average class size in an introductory lecture is 47 and in a laboratory, 25.

Admissions: 85% of the 2001-2002 applicants were accepted. The SAT I scores for the 2001-2002 freshman class were: Verbal--39% below 500, 45% between 500 and 599, 16% between 600 and 700, and 1% above 700; Math--34% below 500, 45% between 500 and 599, 20% between 600 and 700, and 1% above 700. The ACT scores were 44% below 21, 30% between 21 and 23, 19% between 24 and 26, 5% between 27 and 28, and 3% above 28. 37% of the current freshmen were in the top fifth of their class; 71% were in the top two fifths.

Requirements: The SAT I or ACT is required. In addition, students ranked in the top 10% of their high school class are admitted regardless of SAT I/ACT. Those in the second quarter of their class must submit a minimum of 950 on the SAT I or 20 on the ACT. Those in the third quarter must score 1000 on the SAT I or 21 on ACT. The bottom quarter must score 1150 on the SAT I or 25 on ACT. The GED is accepted under certain circumstances. Applicants must have 20 academic credits, including 4 units of English, 3 each of math, social studies, and science, and 2 units of foreign language. Currently, the application form can be downloaded from the UTA web site. The Texas Common Application is also accepted. AP and CLEP credits are accepted. Important factors in the admissions decision are advanced placement or honor courses, leadership record, and evidence of special talent.

Procedure: Freshmen are admitted to all sessions. Entrance exams should be taken during the fall of the senior year. There are early admissions and deferred admissions plans. There are preferred application deadlines. Applications should be filed by June 1 for fall entry, December 1 for spring entry, and April 1 for summer entry. Notification is sent on a rolling basis. The fall 2001 application fee was $25 ($50 for international students).

Transfer: 2897 transfer students enrolled in 2001-2002. Transfer students with 30 or more transferable semester hours need a 2.0 GPA or evidence of high school or GED completion and SAT I or ACT scores comparable to the high school associated rank (varies by student) .Transfer students with fewer than 30 transferable semester hours must have a 2.0 GPA and also meet admission requirements for entering freshmen. 25 credits of their degree program semester hours must be completed at UTA.

Visiting: There are regularly scheduled orientations for prospective students, including overnight summer orientations for freshmen and 1-day orientations for transfers and returning adult students. There are guides for informal visits and visitors may sit in on classes. To schedule a visit, contact the Admissions Office.

Financial Aid: In 2001-2002, 61% of all freshmen and 60% of continuing students received some form of financial aid. 41% of freshmen and 45% of continuing students received need-based aid. The average freshman award was $5309. Of that total, scholarships or need-based grants averaged $3749; loans averaged $3451; work contracts averaged $2315; and institutionally determined need-based self-help awards $1705. 67% of undergraduates work part time. Average annual earnings from campus work are $1751. The average financial indebtedness of the 2001 graduate was $12,671. The FAFSA and income tax returns are required. The fall application deadline is June 1.

International Students: There are 682 international students enrolled. They must score 550 on the written TOEFL or 213 on the electronic version and also take the SAT I, scoring 900.

Computers: The mainframe is an IBM 7060 H50. UTA operates 7 computing facilities with 425 Pentium computers, 180 Macs, and 70 Sun UNIX workstations. All students may access the system at all times. There are no time limits and no fees.

Graduates: In 2001, 2798 bachelor's degrees were awarded. The most popular majors were information systems (13%), nursing (10%), and interdisciplinary studies (5%). In an average class, 1% graduate in 3 years, 9% in 4 years, 23% in 5 years, and 31% in 6 years. 420 companies recruited on campus in 2000-2001.

Admissions Contact: George Norton, Interim Director of Admissions. A video is available. E-mail: *admissions@uta.edu* Web: *www.uta.edu*

UNIVERSITY OF TEXAS AT AUSTIN D-3

Austin, TX 78712 **(512) 475-7440; Fax: (512) 475-7475**

Full-time: 16,671 men, 17,356 women	**Faculty:** 2394; I, av$
Part-time: 2425 men, 2157 women	**Ph.D.s:** 89%
Graduate: 6354 men, 5653 women	**Student/Faculty:** 14 to 1
Year: semesters, summer session	**Tuition:** $3766 ($10,096)
Application Deadline: February 1	**Room & Board:** $5671
Freshman Class: 20,986 applied, 13,335 accepted, 7337 enrolled	
SAT I Verbal/Math: 590/620	**ACT:** 25 **HIGHLY COMPETITIVE**

University of Texas at Austin, founded in 1883, is a major research institution within the University of Texas System and provides a broad range of degree programs. There are 11 undergraduate and 14 graduate schools. In addition to regional accreditation, UT has baccalaureate program accreditation with AACSB, ABET, ACEJMC, ACPE, ADA, CSWE, FIDER, NAAB, NASAD, and NASM. Computerized library services include the card catalog, interlibrary loans, and database searching. Special learning facilities include a learning resource center, art gallery, natural history museum, radio station, TV station, observatory, marine science institute, fusion reactor, and Lyndon Baines Johnson Library and Museum. The 350-acre campus is in an urban area near downtown Austin, just off the interstate. Including residence halls, there are 117 buildings.

Student Life: 91% of undergraduates are from Texas. Others are from 50 states, 118 foreign countries, and Canada. 61% are white; 13% Asian American; 12% Hispanic. The average age of freshmen is 18; all undergraduates, 21. 8% do not continue beyond their first year; 70% remain to graduate.

Housing: 6500 students can be accommodated in college housing, which includes single-sex and coed dormitories, off-campus apartments, and married-student housing. In addition, there are honors houses and living learning centers (for freshmen). On-campus housing is available on a first-come, first-served basis and is available on a lottery system for upperclassmen. 83% of students commute. Alcohol is not permitted. All students may keep cars.

Activities: 10% of men belong to 24 national fraternities; 13% of women belong to 14 national sororities. There are 600 groups on campus, including art, band, cheerleading, chess, choir, chorale, chorus, computers, dance, drama, ethnic, film, forensics, gay, honors, international, jazz band, literary magazine, marching band, musical theater, newspaper, opera, orchestra, pep band, photography, political, professional, radio and TV, religious, social, social service, student government, symphony, and yearbook. Popular campus events include Gone to Texas, Cinco de Mayo, and Texas-Oklahoma Weekend.

Sports: There are 8 intercollegiate sports for men and 10 for women, and 45 intramural sports for men and 45 for women. Facilities include an 80,106-seat football stadium, a 16,175-seat basketball center, a 4400-seat volleyball arena, a 6649-seat baseball stadium, a 2600-seat Olympic swimming facility, 6 multipurpose indoor recreational/athletic facilities of various sizes available for basketball, volleyball, racquetball, swimming, weight training, and related activities, and 3 outdoor facilities covering nearly 40 acres available for tennis, basketball, racquetball, and various field sports. There is also a 1252-seat softball stadium and a 20,000-seat track and soccer stadium.

Disabled Students: 98% of the campus is accessible. Wheelchair ramps, elevators, special parking, specially equipped rest rooms, lowered drinking fountains, lowered telephones, specially equipped reading rooms, a speech and hearing center, academic accommodations specific to the student's disability, and interpreters for the hearing impaired are available.

Services: Counseling and information services are available, as is tutoring in most subjects. There is a reader service for the blind, and remedial math, reading, and writing.

Campus Safety and Security: Measures include 24-hour foot and vehicle patrol, self-defense education, escort service, and shuttle buses. There are informal discussions, pamphlets/posters/films, emergency telephones, lighted pathways/sidewalks, a crime prevention unit, and closed-circuit TV covering some parking areas and offices.

Programs of Study: UT confers B.A., B.S., B.Arch., B.B.A., B.F.A., B.M., B.J., and B.S.W., among more than 50 specific degrees degrees. Master's and doctoral degrees are also awarded. Bachelor's degrees are awarded in BIOLOGICAL SCIENCE (biochemistry, biology/biological science, botany, microbiology, molecular biology, nutrition, and zoology), BUSINESS (accounting, banking and finance, business administration and management, management information systems, management science, and marketing management), COMMUNICATIONS AND THE

ARTS (advertising, applied music, Arabic, art history and appreciation, classics, dance, design, dramatic arts, English, film arts, French, German, Greek, Hebrew, Italian, journalism, Latin, linguistics, music, music theory and composition, Portuguese, public relations, Russian, Scandinavian languages, Slavic languages, Spanish, speech/debate/rhetoric, studio art, and visual and performing arts), COMPUTER AND PHYSICAL SCIENCE (astronomy, chemistry, computer science, geology, geophysics and seismology, mathematics, and physics), EDUCATION (education), ENGINEERING AND ENVIRONMENTAL DESIGN (aerospace studies, architectural engineering, architecture, chemical engineering, civil engineering, electrical/electronics engineering, geophysical engineering, interior design, mechanical engineering, and petroleum/natural gas engineering), HEALTH PROFESSIONS (medical technology, nursing, pharmacy, and speech pathology/audiology), SOCIAL SCIENCE (American studies, anthropology, archeology, Asian/Oriental studies, child care/child and family studies, classical/ancient civilization, dietetics, Eastern European studies, economics, ethnic studies, geography, history, human ecology, humanities, Islamic studies, Latin American studies, liberal arts/general studies, Middle Eastern studies, philosophy, physical fitness/movement, political science/government, psychology, religion, Russian and Slavic studies, social work, sociology, and textiles and clothing). Liberal arts, natural sciences, and engineering are the largest.

Required: All students must maintain a GPA of 2.0 while satisfactorily completing 120 to 167 semester hours. Distribution requirements include 6 hours each in American government, American history, and science, 3 hours each in math, social science, English composition, literature, and humanities/fine arts, plus 3 additional hours in math, natural science, or computer science, and 2 semesters of foreign language.

Special: Cooperative programs are available in all engineering courses, microbiology, chemistry, computer science, geology, and actuarial studies. Cross-registration is provided in pharmacy with the University of Texas at San Antonio. Internships, study abroad, B.A.-B.S. degrees, dual majors, student-designed majors for humanities students, and pass/fail options are offered. There are 45 national honor societies, including Phi Beta Kappa, a freshman honors program, and 52 departmental honors programs.

Faculty/Classroom: 66% of faculty are male; 34%, female. All both teach and do research.

Admissions: 64% of the 2001-2002 applicants were accepted. The SAT I scores for the 2001-2002 freshman class were: Verbal--12% below 500, 38% between 500 and 599, 38% between 600 and 700, and 12% above 700; Math--7% below 500, 30% between 500 and 599, 44% between 600 and 700, and 20% above 700. The ACT scores were 9% below 21, 22% between 21 and 23, 30% between 24 and 26, 18% between 27 and 28, and 21% above 28. 77% of the current freshmen were in the top fifth of their class; 96% were in the top two fifths. There were 231 National Merit finalists. 247 freshmen graduated first in their class.

Requirements: The SAT I or ACT is required. In addition, all students graduating in the top 10% of their class from an accredited Texas high school are eligible for admission. Applicants not meeting that requirement are reviewed based on SAT I or ACT scores, class rank, writing samples, and related factors; consideration may be given to socioeconomic and geographic information. In addition, applicants need 15 1/2 academic credits, including 4 in English, 3 each in math and social studies, 2 each in science and foreign language, and 1 1/2 in electives. An audition is required for applied music majors. The GED is accepted, with supportive information. Home-schooled students are required to submit the results of either the SAT II: Subject tests or AP exams in English, math, and a third subject of the student's choosing. AP and CLEP credits are accepted. Important factors in the admissions decision are leadership record, evidence of special talent, and extracurricular activities record. UT accepts applications on-line via EXPAN.

Procedure: Freshmen are admitted fall, spring, and summer. Entrance exams should be taken in the junior year or early in the senior year. There is a deferred admissions plan. Applications should be filed by February 1 for fall entry, October 1 for spring entry, and February 1 for summer entry. The fall 2001 application fee was $50. Notification is sent on a rolling basis beginning November 1.

Transfer: 2076 transfer students enrolled in 2001-2002. Applicants must have at least 24 transferable hours (30 for business and architecture majors). 30 credits of 120 must be completed at UT.

Visiting: There are regularly scheduled orientations for prospective students. There are guides for informal visits and visitors may sit in on classes. To schedule a visit, contact the Office of Admissions, Freshman Admissions Center.

Financial Aid: In 2001-2002, 59% of all freshmen and 75% of continuing students received some form of financial aid. 46% of freshmen and 48% of continuing students received need-based aid. The average freshman award was $7270. Of that total, scholarships or need-based grants averaged $4810; loans averaged $2960; and work contracts averaged $3520. 20% of undergraduates work part time. The average financial indebtedness of the 2001 graduate was $17,100. The FAFSA is required. The fall application deadline is March 31.

International Students: There are 1190 international students enrolled. They must score 550 on the written TOEFL or 213 on the electronic version.

Computers: A UNIX Timesharing Services (UTS) system provides general access interactive UNIX timesharing. The UTS cluster consists of 2 Digital Equipment Corporation Alpha servers running Digital UNIX. Students have access to the mainframe computers through classes that require computer use, or through individually funded computer user numbers. A 200-seat student facility includes Mac and DOS-compatible PCs. Workstations are located in public facilities for hands-on access and are also available through remote log-in. Some 57 campus buildings, and thousands of computers and PCs are wired for access to the Intenet. All students may access the system 24 hours a day. There are no time limits. The fee is $9.45 per semester credit hour.

Graduates: In 2001, 7624 bachelor's degrees were awarded. The most popular majors were liberal arts (33%), natural sciences (16%), and communication (14%). In an average class, 2% graduate in 3 years, 36% in 4 years, 63% in 5 years, and 70% in 6 years.

Admissions Contact: Freshman Admissions Center. A video is available. E-mail: *frmn@uts.cc.utexas.edu* Web: *http://www.utexas.edu*

UNIVERSITY OF TEXAS AT DALLAS — D-2

Richardson, TX 75083-0688 — (972) 883-2342
(800) 889-2443; Fax: (972) 883-6803

Full-time: 2590 men, 2269 women	**Faculty:** 328; I, av$
Part-time: 1294 men, 1327 women	**Ph.D.s:** 97%
Graduate: 2766 men, 2208 women	**Student/Faculty:** 15 to 1
Year: semesters, summer session	**Tuition:** $3506 ($8570)
Application Deadline: August 1	**Room & Board:** $5799
Freshman Class: 4062 applied, 2323 accepted, 1155 enrolled	
SAT I Verbal/Math: 560/600	**ACT:** 24 **VERY COMPETITIVE**

The University of Texas at Dallas, founded in 1969 as part of the University of Texas system, offers undergraduate and graduate programs in the liberal arts and sciences, business, engineering, computer science, cognitive science, and neuroscience. There are 8 undergraduate and 8 graduate schools. In addition to regional accreditation, UTD has baccalaureate program accreditation with ABET. The library contains 663,664 volumes, 1,854,922 microform items, and 4913 audiovisual forms/CDs, and subscribes to 3094 periodicals. Computerized library services include the card catalog, interlibrary loans, and database searching. Special learning facilities include a learning resource center, art gallery, a center for communications disorders, a rare books library, and special library collections on aviation history, geophysics, philatelic research, and the Holocaust. The 455-acre campus is in a suburban area 18 miles north of downtown Dallas. There are 79 buildings.

Student Life: 90% of undergraduates are from Texas. Others are from 38 states, 129 foreign countries, and Canada. 92% are from public schools. 53% are white; 20% Asian American; 14% foreign nationals. The average age of freshmen is 18; all undergraduates, 24. 22% do not continue beyond their first year; 55% remain to graduate.

Housing: There are no residence halls. 3370 students can be accommodated in college housing, which includes coed on-campus apartments and married-student housing. In addition, there are privately owned campus apartments. On-campus housing is available on a first-come, first-served basis. 82% of students commute. All students may keep cars.

Activities: 4% of men belong to 3 national fraternities; 3% of women belong to 4 national sororities. There are 70 groups on campus, including art, band, cheerleading, chess, choir, chorale, chorus, College Bowl, computers, creative problem solving, dance, debate, drama, ethnic, film, forensics, gay, honors, international, jazz band, literary magazine, musical theater, opera, orchestra, political, professional, religious, social, social service, student government, and yearbook. Popular campus events include Messiah Sing, Jazz Concert, and Hispanic Month activities.

Sports: There are 6 intercollegiate sports for men and 6 for women, and 9 intramural sports for men and 9 for women. Facilities include 4 racquetball courts, 3 squash courts, saunas, 10 lighted tennis courts, indoor and outdoor basketball courts, a sand volleyball court, a 1-mile gravel track, 4 soccer fields, 4 softball fields, a junior Olympic pool/natatorium, and a 4000-seat gym.

Disabled Students: All of the campus is accessible. Wheelchair ramps, elevators, special parking, specially equipped rest rooms, lowered drinking fountains, lowered telephones, and interpreters for the deaf, scribes, alternative testing, and a disability services coordinator are available.

Services: Counseling and information services are available, as is tutoring in most subjects. There is a reader service for the blind, and remedial math, reading, and writing.

Campus Safety and Security: Measures include 24-hour foot and vehicle patrol, self-defense education, escort service, and informal discussions. There are pamphlets/posters/films, emergency telephones, lighted pathways/sidewalks, campus crime watch bulletins for residents, bicycle patrols, crime prevention programs, Operation ID engraving, and a police liaison who works with students on any security or safety issue.

Programs of Study: UTD confers B.A., B.S., and B.S.E.E. degrees. Master's and doctoral degrees are also awarded. Bachelor's degrees are awarded in BIOLOGICAL SCIENCE (biology/biological science and neurosciences), BUSINESS (accounting and business administration and management), COMMUNICATIONS AND THE ARTS (literature, telecommunications, and visual and performing arts), COMPUTER AND PHYSICAL SCIENCE (applied mathematics, chemistry, computer science, geoscience, mathematics, physics, and statistics), ENGINEERING AND ENVIRONMENTAL DESIGN (electrical/electronics engineering), HEALTH PROFESSIONS (speech pathology/audiology), SOCIAL SCIENCE (American studies, cognitive science, criminology, economics, gender studies, geography, history, humanities, interdisciplinary studies, political science/government, psychology, public administration, and sociology). Electrical engineering, biology, and neuroscience are the strongest academically. Business administration, computer science, and electrical engineering are the largest.

Required: To graduate, students must complete at least 120 credit hours, including 30 in the major and 51 in upper-division courses, with a minimum GPA of 2.0. Core courses include 15 credits in social science (with 6 each in U.S./Texas government and U.S./Texas history), 9 in natural science, and 6 each in communications, math, and humanities/fine arts. Magna and summa cum laude graduates must complete a thesis.

Special: Cross-registration is available with other University of Texas campuses and the Health Science Center at Dallas. Accelerated degree programs and B.A.-B.S. degrees are offered in several majors, as is a 3-2 engineering degree with Austin College, Texas Women's University, or Abilene Christian University. Co-op programs, internships, work-study programs, with several major corporations, and dual and student-designed majors are possible. Students may study abroad in Europe, Asia, and Mexico. There are 3 national honor societies, a freshman honors program, and 1 departmental honors program.

Faculty/Classroom: 70% of faculty are male; 30%, female. 11% teach undergraduates, 3% do research, and 86% do both. Graduate students teach 1% of introductory courses. The average class size in an introductory lecture is 35; in a laboratory, 15; and in a regular course, 37.

Admissions: 57% of the 2001-2002 applicants were accepted. The SAT I scores for the 2001-2002 freshman class were: Verbal--19% below 500, 43% between 500 and 599, 32% between 600 and 700, and 6% above 700; Math--12% below 500, 36% between 500 and 599, 40% between 600 and 700, and 12% above 700. The ACT scores were 13% below 21, 30% between 21 and 23, 26% between 24 and 26, 12% between 27 and 28, and 19% above 28. 57% of the current freshmen were in the top fifth of their class; 85% were in the top two fifths. There were 15 National Merit finalists and 24 semifinalists. 26 freshmen graduated first in their class.

Requirements: The SAT I or ACT is required. In addition, applicants should be graduates of an accredited secondary school. In-state students who rank in the top 10% of their class gain automatic admission to UTD. Credentials for other students must include completion of 4 units of English, 3.5 of math, 3 each of social science and lab science, 2 of a foreign language, and course work in fine arts and electives, with health and phys ed courses recommended. An essay is required. A GPA of 3.0 is required. AP and CLEP credits are accepted. Important factors in the admissions decision are advanced placement or honor courses, leadership record, and evidence of special talent. Applications are accepted on-line via the Texas Common App or the school's web site.

Procedure: Freshmen are admitted to all sessions. Entrance exams should be taken at the end of the junior year or beginning of the senior year. There are early decision, early admissions, and deferred admissions plans. Applications should be filed by August 1 for fall entry, December 1 for spring entry, and May 1 for summer entry, along with a $25 fee. Notification is sent on a rolling basis.

Transfer: 1368 transfer students enrolled in 2001-2002. Sophomore applicants must present a GPA of 3.0 and 12 credits in the general education core. Upper-division applicants should have a GPA of 2.5 and be in good standing at the last school attended. 30 credits of 120 must be completed at UTD.

Visiting: There are regularly scheduled orientations for prospective students, including meetings with faculty and an admissions counselor, and a campus tour. There are guides for informal visits and visitors may sit in on classes. To schedule a visit, contact the Office of Enrollment Services at (972) 883-2270 or *enrollment@utdallas.edu*

Financial Aid: In 2001-2002, 74% of all freshmen and 54% of continuing students received some form of financial aid. 56% of freshmen and 45% of continuing students received need-based aid. The average freshman award was $8548. Of that total, scholarships or need-based grants averaged $2607 ($3750 maximum); loans averaged $2448 ($2625 maximum); and work contracts averaged $5625 (maximum). 67% of undergraduates work part time. Average annual earnings from campus work are $2018. The CSS/Profile or FAFSA and the college's own financial statement are required. The fall application deadline is April 30.

International Students: There are 235 international students enrolled. They must score 550 on the written TOEFL or 215 on the electronic version and also take the SAT I or the ACT.

Computers: The mainframe is an IBM OS/390 Model 224. Student facilities include more than 300 Pentium PCs, 57 Macs, 23 UCDX terminals, 20 Wyse terminals, plus micro labs. Individual schools provide Sun SPARC stations with terminals. All students have e-mail, Internet, and web access, with wireless LAN service. All students may access the system 8 A.M. to midnight in most labs, or 24 hours in specific labs and from remote locations via modem. There are no time limits. The fee is $11 per semester credit hour. It is strongly recommended that all students have a personal computer.

Graduates: In 2001, 1381 bachelor's degrees were awarded. The most popular majors were business administration (23%), computer science (17%), and interdisciplinary studies (12%). In an average class, 34% graduate in 3 years, 52% in 4 years, and 55% in 5 years. 632 companies recruited on campus in 2000-2001. Of the 2000 graduating class, 13% were enrolled in graduate school within 6 months of graduation and 81% were employed.

Admissions Contact: Dr. Rubye Jones, Director of Admissions. A video is available. E-mail: *ugrad-admissions@utdallas.edu*
Web: *www.utdallas.edu*

UNIVERSITY OF TEXAS AT EL PASO — A-3

El Paso, TX 79968 — **(915) 747-5576; Fax: (915) 747-5848**

Full-time: 4502 men, 5511 women	**Faculty:** 415; IIA, --$
Part-time: 1719 men, 1910 women	**Ph.D.s:** 90%
Graduate: 1109 men, 1469 women	**Student/Faculty:** 24 to 1
Year: semesters, summer session	**Tuition:** $2556 ($7620)
Application Deadline: July 31	**Room & Board:** $2520
Freshman Class: 5037 applied, 4658 accepted, 3306 enrolled	
SAT I Verbal/Math: 464/464	**ACT:** 19 **LESS COMPETITIVE**

The University of Texas at El Paso, founded in 1913 and the second oldest academic member of the University of Texas System, was originally called the Texas School of Mines and Metallurgy. It now offers a wide variety of classes through the schools and colleges of business, education, engineering, liberal arts, nursing and allied health, and science. There are 6 undergraduate schools and 1 graduate school. In addition to regional accreditation, UTEP has baccalaureate program accreditation with AACSB, ABET, and NLN. The library contains 961,247 volumes and 1,696,207 microform items, and subscribes to 3005 periodicals. Computerized library services include the card catalog, interlibrary loans, and database searching. Special learning facilities include a learning resource center, art gallery, natural history museum, radio station, TV station, seismic observatory, and the El Paso Centennial Museum. The 366-acre campus is in an urban area. Including residence halls, there are 76 buildings.

Student Life: 88% of undergraduates are from Texas. Others are from 49 states, 84 foreign countries, and Canada. 95% are from public schools. 64% are Hispanic; 22% white. The average age of freshmen is 19; all undergraduates, 25. 33% do not continue beyond their first year.

Housing: 870 students can be accommodated in college housing, which includes coed dormitories, on-campus apartments, married-student housing, fraternity houses, and sorority houses. In addition, there are suites, private rooms, and 24-hour quiet floors. On-campus housing is available on a first-come, first-served basis. 98% of students commute. Alcohol is not permitted. All students may keep cars.

Activities: There are 100 groups on campus, including art, band, cheerleading, chess, choir, chorale, computers, dance, drama, drill team, drum and bugle corps, ethnic, film, honors, international, jazz band, literary magazine, marching band, musical theater, newspaper, opera, orchestra, pep band, photography, political, professional, radio and TV, religious, social, social service, student government, symphony, and yearbook. Popular campus events include Women's History and Hispanic Cultural weeks, and St. Patrick's Engineering Initiation.

Sports: There are 6 intercollegiate sports for men and 5 for women, and 1 intramural sport for men and 1 for women. Facilities include basketball, volleyball, badminton, racquetball, and tennis courts, grass fields for multiple use, an Outdoor Adventure Program with backpacking, bicycling, rafting, and ski trips, a 52,000-seat football stadium, a 12,222-seat basketball gym, a swimming pool, a bowling alley, and a weight room.

Disabled Students: Wheelchair ramps, elevators, special parking, specially equipped rest rooms, special class scheduling, and lowered drinking fountains are available.

Services: Counseling and information services are available, as is tutoring in every subject. There is a reader service for the blind, and remedial math, reading, and writing.

Campus Safety and Security: Measures include shuttle buses and lighted pathways/sidewalks.

Programs of Study: UTEP confers B.A., B.S., B.B.A., B.F.A., B.I.S., B.M., B.S.C.E., B.S.C.S., B.S.Ed., B.S.E.E., B.S.I.E., B.S.MeT.E., B.S.N., and B.S.W. degrees. Master's and doctoral degrees are also awarded. Bachelor's degrees are awarded in BIOLOGICAL SCIENCE (biology/biological science and microbiology), BUSINESS (accounting, banking and finance, business economics, management information systems, management science, and marketing/retailing/merchandising),

COMMUNICATIONS AND THE ARTS (art, communications, dramatic arts, English, French, German, journalism, languages, linguistics, music, Spanish, speech/debate/rhetoric, and theater management), COMPUTER AND PHYSICAL SCIENCE (applied mathematics, chemistry, computer science, earth science, geology, geophysics and seismology, mathematics, physics, science, and statistics), ENGINEERING AND ENVIRONMENTAL DESIGN (civil engineering, electrical/electronics engineering, industrial engineering technology, mechanical engineering, and metallurgical engineering), HEALTH PROFESSIONS (allied health, clinical science, health science, medical laboratory technology, and nursing), SOCIAL SCIENCE (anthropology, criminal justice, economics, history, Latin American studies, Mexican-American/Chicano studies, philosophy, physical fitness/movement, political science/government, psychology, social work, and sociology). Business, nursing, and engineering are the strongest academically. Criminal justice, psychology, and biology are the largest.

Required: All students must have a minimum GPA of 2.0 while taking 125 to 130 semester hours. Students also must complete a distribution of courses through the general foundation program.

Special: Internships, mainly at the graduate level, study abroad in London and Hildesheim, Germany, work-study programs, nondegree study, and pass/fail options are available. There also is the Inter-American Sciences and Humanities Program for students from Spanish-speaking countries whose English is less than adequate for normal study in the United States. The Center for Inter-American and Border Studies also promotes teaching, research, and outreach programs to further the understanding of Latin America. Similar studies are offered through the Cross-Cultural Southwest Ethnic Study Center. There is a freshman honors program.

Faculty/Classroom: 78% of faculty are male; 22%, female. The average class size in an introductory lecture is 25; in a laboratory, 15; and in a regular course, 22.

Admissions: 92% of the 2001-2002 applicants were accepted. The SAT I scores for the 2001-2002 freshman class were: Verbal--69% below 500, 27% between 500 and 599, and 5% between 600 and 700; Math--65% below 500, 30% between 500 and 599, and 5% between 600 and 700. The ACT scores were 31% below 21, 57% between 21 and 23, and 12% between 24 and 26. 39% of the current freshmen were in the top fifth of their class; 54% were in the top two fifths.

Requirements: The SAT I or ACT is required. In addition, for citizens or permanent residents of the United States who have graduated within the past 5 years, the SAT I, with a score of 700 for those ranking in the second quarter of their class, or the ACT, with a score of 15, is required. UTEP recommends high school preparation that includes of 4 years of English, 3 to 3.5 of math, 3 each of natural science and social studies, and 2 of foreign language. The GED is accepted. A GPA of 2.0 is required. AP and CLEP credits are accepted.

Procedure: Freshmen are admitted to all sessions. There are early action admissions and deferred admissions plans. Applications should be filed by July 31 for fall entry. Notification is sent on a rolling basis.

Transfer: Transfer applicants must have at least a C average and must be eligible to return to all previous institutions attended. 30 credits of 125 must be completed at UTEP.

Visiting: There are regularly scheduled orientations for prospective students, including preenrollment counseling and campus tours. There are guides for informal visits and visitors may sit in on classes and stay overnight. To schedule a visit, contact Beto Lopez, Recruiting Office.

Financial Aid: In 2001-2002, 18% of all freshmen and 82% of continuing students received some form of financial aid. The average financial indebtedness of the 2001 graduate was $12,825. UTEP is a member of CSS. The FAFSA and the college's own financial statement are required. The fall application priority deadline is March 15.

International Students: The school actively recruits these students. They must score 500 on the written TOEFL or take the PAA and also take the SAT I or ACT, with a required minimum score on the SAT I (combined) of 920, with a minimum of 400 on the verbal, and 20 (composite) on the ACT, with a 21 minimum on the English section.

Computers: The mainframe is an IBM 3270. Students use terminals to access the mainframe from various sites on campus. All computing facilities are interconnected by a campuswide data communication network. Those students enrolled in computer courses or with departmental permission may access the system. may access the system. There are no time limits. The fee is $10.

Graduates: In 2001, 1635 bachelor's degrees were awarded. The most popular majors were interdisciplinary studies (18%), business/marketing (17%), and engineering/engineering technologies (12%).

Admissions Contact: Irma Nu¹ez Rubio, Director of Admissions. A video is available. E-mail: *admission@utep.edu*
Web: *www.utep.edu/enroll/*

UNIVERSITY OF TEXAS AT SAN ANTONIO D-4

San Antonio, TX 78249 (210) 458-4530
(800) 669-0919; Fax: (210) 458-5959

Full-time: 5560 men, 6474 women | **Faculty:** 350
Part-time: 2294 men, 3087 women | **Ph.D.s:** 99%
Graduate: 1032 men, 1452 women | **Student/Faculty:** 34 to 1
Year: semesters, summer session | **Tuition:** $2975 ($8039)
Application Deadline: July 1 | **Room & Board:** $6113
Freshman Class: 5519 applied, 5486 accepted, 2592 enrolled
SAT I Verbal/Math: 490/500 | **ACT:** 20 | **NONCOMPETITIVE**

The University of Texas at San Antonio was established as part of the state university system in 1969 and is now a large, comprehensive institution offering undergraduate and graduate programs in arts, business, engineering, music, health science, and education. There are 6 undergraduate schools. In addition to regional accreditation, UTSA has baccalaureate program accreditation with AACSB, ABET, NASAD, and NASM. The 2 libraries contain 550,000 volumes, 3.0 million microform items, and 10,300 audiovisual forms/CDs, and subscribe to 2000 periodicals (print only). Computerized library services include the card catalog, interlibrary loans, and database searching. Special learning facilities include a learning resource center, art gallery, and Institute of Texan Cultures. The 600-acre campus is in a suburban area approximately 18 miles northwest of downtown San Antonio. Including residence halls, there are 35 buildings.

Student Life: 95% of undergraduates are from Texas. Others are from 50 states, 85 foreign countries, and Canada. 91% are from public schools. 46% are Hispanic; 42% white. The average age of freshmen is 18; all undergraduates, 25. 36% do not continue beyond their first year; 25% remain to graduate.

Housing: 1965 students can be accommodated in college housing, which includes coed dormitories and on-campus apartments. On-campus housing is available on a first-come, first-served basis. 90% of students commute. All students may keep cars.

Activities: 3% of men belong to 9 national fraternities; 1% of women belong to 6 national sororities. There are 141 groups on campus, including art, band, cheerleading, chess, choir, chorale, chorus, computers, debate, drama, ethnic, gay, honors, international, jazz band, literary magazine, musical theater, newspaper, orchestra, pep band, political, professional, religious, social, social service, student government, symphony, and yearbook. Popular campus events include Fiesta UTSA, Best Fest, and Folk Life festival.

Sports: There are 7 intercollegiate sports for men and 7 for women, and 9 intramural sports for men and 9 for women. Fewer than 1% of men and women participate. Facilities include gyms, weight machines, a jogging path and a 400-meter track, a tennis center, an indoor pool, various playing fields, and courts for basketball, volleyball, badminton, and shuffleboard.

Disabled Students: All of the campus is accessible. Wheelchair ramps, elevators, special parking, specially equipped rest rooms, special class scheduling, lowered drinking fountains, and lowered telephones are available.

Services: Counseling and information services are available, as is tutoring in every subject. There is a reader service for the blind, and remedial math, reading, and writing.

Campus Safety and Security: Measures include 24-hour foot and vehicle patrol, self-defense education, escort service, and shuttle buses. There are informal discussions, pamphlets/posters/films, emergency telephones, and lighted pathways/sidewalks.

Programs of Study: UTSA confers B.A., B.S., B.B.A, B.F.A., B.M., B.S.C.E., B.S.E.E., and B.S.M.E. degrees. Master's and doctoral degrees are also awarded. Bachelor's degrees are awarded in BIOLOGICAL SCIENCE (biology/biological science), BUSINESS (accounting, banking and finance, business administration and management, business economics, entrepreneurial studies, human resources, international business management, management information systems, management science, marketing/retailing/merchandising, personnel management, and tourism), COMMUNICATIONS AND THE ARTS (art, classics, communications, English, fine arts, French, German, music, and Spanish), COMPUTER AND PHYSICAL SCIENCE (chemistry, computer science, geology, information sciences and systems, mathematics, and physics), ENGINEERING AND ENVIRONMENTAL DESIGN (architecture, civil engineering, construction management, electrical/electronics engineering, interior design, and mechanical engineering), HEALTH PROFESSIONS (clinical science, health, and occupational therapy), SOCIAL SCIENCE (American studies, anthropology, criminal justice, economics, geography, history, humanities, interdisciplinary studies, Mexican-American/Chicano studies, philosophy, physical fitness/movement, political science/government, psychology, and sociology). Business, engineering, and life sciences are the strongest academically. Business, life sciences, and education and human development are the largest.

Required: All students must complete at least 120 credit hours with a 2.0 GPA for graduation. Core curriculum requirements total 54 credits and include courses in fine arts, composition, computer science or logic, economics, foreign language, American and Texas history, social science, literacy studies, math, U.S. and Texas constitutions, natural science, and interdisciplinary studies.

Special: UTSA offers joint degrees in occupational therapy and clinical lab sciences with the University of Texas Health Science Center and study abroad in many countries. Internships, work-study, nondegree study, and pass/fail options are available. There are 31 national honor societies, a freshman honors program, and 17 departmental honors programs.

Faculty/Classroom: 61% of faculty are male; 39%, female. 89% teach undergraduates and 13% both teach and do research. Graduate students teach 12% of introductory courses. The average class size in an introductory lecture is 58; in a laboratory, 19; and in a regular course, 29.

Admissions: 99% of the 2001-2002 applicants were accepted. The SAT I scores for the 2001-2002 freshman class were: Verbal--51% below 500, 38% between 500 and 599, 10% between 600 and 700, and 1% above 700; Math--50% below 500, 39% between 500 and 599, 10% between 600 and 700, and 1% above 700. The ACT scores were 55% below 21, 27% between 21 and 23, 13% between 24 and 26, 3% between 27 and 28, and 2% above 28. 32% of the current freshmen were in the top fifth of their class; 65% were in the top two fifths. There was 1 National Merit finalist. 16 freshmen graduated first in their class.

Requirements: The SAT I or ACT is required. Admission is based on a formula derived from class rank and SAT I or ACT scores. Applicants must be graduates of accredited high schools or have earned the GED. UTSA recommends that high school preparation include 4 units of English, at least 3 of math, at least 2 each of a foreign language, natural science, and social science, and at least 1 of fine arts. AP and CLEP credits are accepted.

Procedure: Freshmen are admitted to all sessions. Entrance exams should be taken in the spring of the junior year. Applications should be filed by July 1 for fall entry, December 1 for spring entry, and May 1 for summer entry. The fall 2001 application fee was $25. Notification is sent on a rolling basis.

Transfer: 1404 transfer students enrolled in 2001-2002. Applicants with at least 30 hours of college credit must present a C average in all college work attempted and evidence of good standing. Those with fewer than 30 hours must meet freshman admission standards as well. 30 credits of 120 must be completed at UTSA.

Visiting: There are regularly scheduled orientations for prospective students. There are guides for informal visits. To schedule a visit, contact New Student Programs at (210) 458-4724 or: *orientation@utsa.edu*

Financial Aid: In 2001-2002, 51% of all freshmen and 57% of continuing students received some form of financial aid. 63% of freshmen and 66% of continuing students received need-based aid. The average freshman award was $8750. Of that total, scholarships or need-based grants averaged $1554 ($3500 maximum); loans averaged $2072 ($2500 maximum); and work contracts averaged $74 ($2750 maximum). 13% of undergraduates work part time. Average annual earnings from campus work are $1460. The average financial indebtedness of the 2001 graduate was $16,125. The FAFSA is required. The fall application deadline is March 31.

International Students: There are 254 international students enrolled. The school actively recruits these students. They must score 550 on the written TOEFL and also take the SAT I or the ACT.

Computers: The mainframe is an IBM 4341. A large computer lab is available with 800 IBM and Mac PCs used with a variety of software options. Specialty computer labs are also available, such as for engineering applications. All students may access the system 24 hours a day. There are no time limits. The fee is $56 to $168 per semester.

Graduates: In 2001, 2591 bachelor's degrees were awarded. The most popular majors were business (22%), interdisciplinary studies (15%), and biology (8%). In an average class, 1% graduate in 3 years, 7% in 4 years, 18% in 5 years, and 27% in 6 years. 144 companies recruited on campus in 2000-2001.

Admissions Contact: John Wallace, Interim Director of Admissions and Registrar. E-mail: *prospects@utsa.edu* Web: *www.utsa.edu*

UNIVERSITY OF TEXAS-PAN AMERICAN — D-5

Edinburg, TX 78539-2999 — (956) 381-2201

Full-time: 3264 men, 4632 women	**Faculty:** 479; IIA, -$
Part-time: 1691 men, 2384 women	**Ph.D.s:** n/av
Graduate: 609 men, 1060 women	**Student/Faculty:** 16 to 1
Year: semesters, summer session	**Tuition:** $2201 ($7365)
Application Deadline: August 1	**Room & Board:** $2622
Freshman Class: 4050 applied, 3104 accepted, 2228 enrolled	
ACT: 17	**COMPETITIVE**

University of Texas-Pan American, founded in 1927, is a state-supported institution offering programs in the arts and sciences, education, business, and health-related professions. It is part of the University of Texas system. There are 6 undergraduate and 6 graduate schools. In addition to regional accreditation, UT Pan American has baccalaureate program accreditation with AACSB, ABET, ACOTE, ACS, ADA, AOTA, ASLA, CAHEA, CSWE, NAACLS, NCATE, and NLN. The library contains 493,009 volumes, 1,017,963 microform items, and 24,667 audiovisual forms/CDs, and subscribes to 2286 periodicals. Computerized library services include the card catalog, interlibrary loans, and database searching. Special learning facilities include a learning resource center, art gallery, planetarium, and a coastal studies lab. The 200-acre campus is in a small town close to the Mexican border and the Gulf of Mexico. Including residence halls, there are 30 buildings.

Student Life: 97% of undergraduates are from Texas. Others are from Canada. 86% are Hispanic. The average age of freshmen is 19; all undergraduates, 24. 23% of freshmen remain to graduate.

Housing: 580 students can be accommodated in college housing, which includes single-sex and coed dormitories and on-campus apartments. On-campus housing is available on a first-come, first-served basis. 90% of students commute. Alcohol is not permitted. All students may keep cars.

Activities: 1% of men belong to 4 national fraternities. There is 1 national sorority. There are 80 groups on campus, including academic, art, cheerleading, choir, chorus, computers, dance, drama, ethnic, film, gay, honors, international, jazz band, literary magazine, musical theater, opera, orchestra, photography, political, professional, radio and TV, religious, social, social service, student government, symphony, and yearbook. Popular campus events include Bronc Roundup, Cinco de Mayo, and International Days.

Sports: There are 6 intercollegiate sports for men and 6 for women, and 13 intramural sports for men and 13 for women. Facilities include a 5000-seat field house, baseball and tennis stadiums, a track, and a soccer field.

Disabled Students: 95% of the campus is accessible. Wheelchair ramps, elevators, special parking, specially equipped rest rooms, lowered drinking fountains, lowered telephones, TDD phones, readers, and notetakers are available.

Services: Counseling and information services are available, as is tutoring in most subjects, including biology, chemistry, history, and Spanish. There is a reader service for the blind, and remedial math, reading, and writing. The Learning Assistance Center provides small-group and individual tutoring and computer-aided instruction.

Campus Safety and Security: Measures include 24-hour foot and vehicle patrol, self-defense education, escort service, and pamphlets/posters/films. There are emergency telephones, lighted pathways/sidewalks, and a university police department.

Programs of Study: UT Pan American confers B.A., B.S., B.A.A.S., B.B.A., B.F.A., B.G.S., B.S.C.J., B.S.E.E., B.S.M.E., B.S.Mfg.E, B.S.N., and B.S.W. degrees. Master's and doctoral degrees are also awarded. Bachelor's degrees are awarded in BIOLOGICAL SCIENCE (biology/biological science), BUSINESS (accounting, banking and finance, international business management, management science, and marketing/retailing/merchandising), COMMUNICATIONS AND THE ARTS (art, communications, dramatic arts, English, fine arts, journalism, music, and Spanish), COMPUTER AND PHYSICAL SCIENCE (chemistry, computer science, information sciences and systems, mathematics, and physics), EDUCATION (secondary), ENGINEERING AND ENVIRONMENTAL DESIGN (electrical/electronics engineering, manufacturing engineering, and mechanical engineering), HEALTH PROFESSIONS (health, medical technology, nursing, occupational therapy, physician's assistant, rehabilitation therapy, and speech pathology/audiology), SOCIAL SCIENCE (anthropology, corrections, criminal justice, dietetics, economics, history, interdisciplinary studies, Latin American studies, liberal arts/general studies, Mexican-American/Chicano studies, philosophy, physical fitness/movement, political science/government, psychology, social work, and sociology). Engineering and business are the strongest academically. Education, nursing, and engineering are the largest.

Required: To graduate, students must complete 124 to 137 semester hours with a 2.0 GPA. At least 30 hours are required in the major. Students must also fulfill a general education requirement of 48 hours by taking 18 hours in humanities (including English and a foreign language), 15 hours of social science (including U.S. history and Texas government), 11 hours of lab science and math, 2 hours each of phys ed and computer science. Other requirements vary according to degree.

Special: Internships, co-op programs, study abroad, work-study programs, dual majors, and nondegree study are available. There are 3 national honor societies, a freshman honors program, and 6 departmental honors programs.

Faculty/Classroom: 58% of faculty are male; 42%, female.

Admissions: 77% of the 2001-2002 applicants were accepted. The SAT I scores for the 2001-2002 freshman class were: Verbal--72% below 500, 23% between 500 and 599, and 5% between 600 and 700; Math--69% below 500, 24% between 500 and 599, 6% between 600 and 700, and 1% above 700. The ACT scores were 51% below 18, 42% between 18 and 23, and 7% between 24 and 29. 36% of the current freshmen were in the top quartet of their class; 71% were in the top half.

Requirements: The SAT I or ACT is required; the ACT is preferred. Applicants must be graduates of an accredited high school or have the GED. 21 academic units are required, including 4 units of English; 3

units of math, at least 1 of which must be algebra; 2 units of science; 1 unit each of world history and U.S. history; and 1/2 unit each of U.S. government, economics, phys ed, and health education. An additional 7 units may be taken in electives. A GPA of 2.0 is required. AP and CLEP credits are accepted. Applications are accepted on-line via *www.applytexas.org*

Procedure: Freshmen are admitted to all sessions. Preferred decision application should be filed by February 1or September 1; regular applications, by August 1 for fall entry, November 1 for spring entry, and May 1 for summer entry. Preferred deadline allows students to use priority telephone/on-line registration. Notification is sent on a rolling basis.

Transfer: 637 transfer students enrolled in 2001-2002. Transfer applicants must meet the same criteria as entering freshmen. 30 credits of 124 to 137 must be completed at UT Pan American.

Visiting: There are regularly scheduled orientations for prospective students. There are guides for informal visits and visitors may sit in on classes. To schedule a visit, contact the Admissions Office: Recruitment and Orientation at (956) 381-3541.

Financial Aid: In 2001-2002, 77% of all freshmen and 53% of continuing students received some form of financial aid. 74% of freshmen and 34% of continuing students received need-based aid. The CSS/Profile or FAFSA is required. The application deadline is rolling.

International Students: There were 260 international students enrolled in a recent year. The school actively recruits these students. They must score 500 on the written TOEFL.

Computers: The mainframe is a DEC VAX 10. The Academic Services building has 600 workstations open to students. All have access to the network. There are 100 PCs in the library, also connected to the network. All students may access the system. There are no time limits. The fee $9 per semester credit hour up to a maximum of $27 per semester.

Graduates: In 2001, 1394 bachelor's degrees were awarded. In an average class, 5% graduate in 4 years, 16% in 5 years, and 23% in 6 years.

Admissions Contact: David R. Zuniga, Director of Admissions and Registrar. E-mail: *admissions@panam.edu* Web: *http://www.panam.edu*

UNIVERSITY OF THE INCARNATE WORD D-4

San Antonio, TX 78209-6397 **(210) 829-6005**
(800) 749-WORD; Fax: (210) 829-3921

Full-time: 689 men, 1427 women	**Faculty:** 121; IIB, -$
Part-time: 494 men, 909 women	**Ph.D.s:** 73%
Graduate: 288 men, 476 women	**Student/Faculty:** 17 to 1
Year: semesters, summer session	**Tuition:** $13,498
Application Deadline: open	**Room & Board:** $5250
Freshman Class: n/av	
SAT I or ACT: required	**COMPETITIVE**

University of the Incarnate Word, founded in 1881, is a liberal arts institution affiliated with the Catholic Church that offers undergraduate programs in art, business, health science, education, music, religious studies, nursing, and fine arts. There are 5 undergraduate schools and 1 graduate school. In addition to regional accreditation, UIW has baccalaureate program accreditation with ACBSP, ADA, AHEA, CAHEA, NCATE, and NLN. The library contains 226,111 volumes, 219,226 microform items, and 36,845 audiovisual forms/CDs, and subscribes to 8555 periodicals. Computerized library services include the card catalog, interlibrary loans, and database searching. Special learning facilities include a learning resource center, art gallery, a media service center, and a teaching theater. The 100-acre campus is in an urban area about 3 miles north of downtown San Antonio. Including residence halls, there are 18 buildings.

Student Life: 90% of undergraduates are from Texas. Others are from 27 states, 38 foreign countries, and Canada. 75% are from public schools. 48% are Hispanic; 35% white. 52% are Catholic; 27% Protestant; 21% claim no religious affiliation. The average age of freshmen is 18; all undergraduates, 22. 22% do not continue beyond their first year; 39% remain to graduate.

Housing: 650 students can be accommodated in college housing, which includes single-sex and coed dormitories and on-campus apartments. On-campus housing is guaranteed for all 4 years. 81% of students commute. All students may keep cars.

Activities: 5% of men belong to 1 local fraternity; 20% of women belong to 3 local sororities. There are 30 groups on campus, including art, cheerleading, choir, chorale, chorus, dance, drama, drill team, ethnic, honors, international, jazz band, literary magazine, musical theater, orchestra, pep band, political, professional, religious, social, social service, student government, and yearbook. Popular campus events include Fiesta Fashion Show, Incarnate Word Day, and Higher Education Week.

Sports: There are 6 intercollegiate sports for men and 5 for women, and 23 intramural sports for men and 23 for women. Facilities include a convocation center, a field house, 8 tennis courts, 2 soccer fields, softball and baseball fields, a 1/4-mile track, a 3/4-mile jogging trail, a gym, basketball courts, a natatorium, and weight and aerobics rooms.

Disabled Students: 85% of the campus is accessible. Wheelchair ramps, elevators, special parking, specially equipped rest rooms, and special class scheduling are available.

Services: Counseling and information services are available, as is tutoring in most subjects. There is remedial math, reading, and writing.

Campus Safety and Security: Measures include 24-hour foot and vehicle patrol, self-defense education, escort service, and shuttle buses. There are informal discussions, pamphlets/posters/films, emergency telephones, lighted pathways/sidewalks, and a professional security force on campus.

Programs of Study: UIW confers B.A., B.S., B.B.A., and B.M. degrees. Master's and doctoral degrees are also awarded. Bachelor's degrees are awarded in BIOLOGICAL SCIENCE (biology/biological science and nutrition), BUSINESS (accounting, banking and finance, business administration and management, fashion merchandising, hotel/motel and restaurant management, international business management, management science, marketing/retailing/merchandising, and sports management), COMMUNICATIONS AND THE ARTS (art, communications, dramatic arts, English, music, music business management, and Spanish), COMPUTER AND PHYSICAL SCIENCE (chemistry, computer management, information sciences and systems, and mathematics), EDUCATION (business, early childhood, elementary, middle school, music, physical, science, secondary, and special), ENGINEERING AND ENVIRONMENTAL DESIGN (environmental science and interior design), HEALTH PROFESSIONS (medical laboratory technology, music therapy, nuclear medical technology, nursing, predentistry, and premedicine), SOCIAL SCIENCE (dietetics, fashion design and technology, history, Native American studies, philosophy, political science/government, prelaw, psychology, religion, and sociology). Preprofessional, nursing, and business are the strongest academically. Business is the largest.

Required: To graduate, students must complete at least 128 credit hours, with a minimum GPA of 2.0. An extensive required core curriculum of 67 credit hours includes world literature, critical discourse, dimensions of wellness, computer literacy, and a capstone. A total of 40 hours of community service also is required.

Special: UIW offers co-op programs in all business majors, commercial arts, fashion design and merchandising, and sports management. There is cross-registration with Our Lady of the Lake and Saint Mary's Universities, numerous internship opportunities, a spring Washington semester, work-study programs, and study abroad, including China, Taiwan, Japan, Cuba, and Great Britain. There are 4 national honor societies.

Faculty/Classroom: 48% of faculty are male; 52%, female. All teach undergraduates. No introductory courses are taught by graduate students. The average class size in an introductory lecture is 27; in a laboratory, 17; and in a regular course, 16.

Admissions: 33% of the current freshmen were in the top fifth of their class; 60% were in the top two fifths.

Requirements: The SAT I or ACT is required, with minimum composite scores of 920 on the SAT I or 18 on the ACT. Applicants must be graduates of an accredited secondary school or have the GED and have completed 16 Carnegie units, including at least 4 units of English, 3 of social studies and history, 2 each of math, science, and foreign language, and 1 of fine arts. In some cases, UIW may administer its own assessment tests for placement and require an interview. A GPA of 2.0 is required. AP and CLEP credits are accepted. Important factors in the admissions decision are recommendations by alumni, parents or siblings attending the school, and ability to finance college education. Applications are accepted on-line at the school's web site.

Procedure: Freshmen are admitted to all sessions. Entrance exams should be taken in the junior or senior year of high school. There is a deferred admissions plan. Application deadlines are open. The fall application fee was $20. Notification is sent on a rolling basis.

Transfer: 320 transfer students enrolled in 2001-2002. Transfer students must have a minimum 2.5 GPA if they have at least 30 transferable hours. Other students may have to take an academic assessment test and/or be individually reviewed, and submit high school and college records and SAT I or ACT scores. 36 credits of 128 must be completed at UIW.

Visiting: There are regularly scheduled orientations for prospective students, consisting of an introduction to services, a campus tour, assessment testing, advisement, and registration. There are guides for informal visits and visitors may sit in on classes and stay overnight. To schedule a visit, contact the Office of Admissions at *admis@universe.uiwtx.edu*

Financial Aid: In 2001-2002, 80% of all freshmen and 78% of continuing students received some form of financial aid. 71% of freshmen and 68% of continuing students received need-based aid. The average freshman award was $6500. 65% of undergraduates work part time. Average annual earnings from campus work are $2000. The average financial indebtedness of the 2001 graduate was $38,000. The FAFSA and the college's own financial statement are required. The fall application deadline is April 1.

International Students: There are 195 international students enrolled. The school actively recruits these students. They must score 550 on the written TOEFL and also take the college's own test.

Computers: The mainframes are an HPN 4000 and HPR 390. More than 300 PCs are available for learning instruction. The campus is fully wired, with ports in all campus housing. All students may access the sys-

tem 24 hours a day, 7 days a week. There are no time limits and no fees. It is strongly recommended that all students have a personal computer. Juniors and seniors in business must have laptops have personal computers. The School of Business and Applied Arts and Sciences has specific requirements.
Graduates: In 2001, 583 bachelor's degrees were awarded. The most popular majors were business administration (39%), nursing (11%), and liberal arts (11%). In an average class, 13% graduate in 4 years, and 32% in 5 years. 26 companies recruited on campus in 2000-2001.
Admissions Contact: Andrea Cyterski, Director of Admissions. A video is available. E-mail: *cyterski@universe.uiwtx.edu*
Web: *www.uiw.edu*

WAYLAND BAPTIST UNIVERSITY B-2
Plainview, TX 79072 (806) 291-3508; (800) 588-1928

Full-time: 306 men, 433 women	**Faculty:** 64
Part-time: 63 men, 130 women	**Ph.D.s:** 72%
Graduate: 18 men, 39 women	**Student/Faculty:** 12 to 1
Year: semesters, summer session	**Tuition:** $8150
Application Deadline: open	**Room & Board:** $3121
Freshman Class: 278 applied, 271 accepted, 212 enrolled	
SAT I Verbal/Math: 470/480	**ACT:** 19 NONCOMPETITIVE

Wayland Baptist University, founded in 1908, is a private liberal arts school affiliated with the Baptist General Convention of Texas (Southern Baptist). There are 8 undergraduate divisions and 1 graduate school. The library contains 111,824 volumes, 229,163 microform items, and 13,239 audiovisual forms/CDs, and subscribes to 503 periodicals. Computerized library services include the card catalog, interlibrary loans, and database searching. Special learning facilities include a learning resource center, art gallery, natural history museum, radio station, and TV station. The 80-acre campus is in a small town 45 miles north of Lubbock. Including residence halls, there are 41 buildings.
Student Life: 87% of undergraduates are from Texas. Others are from 20 states and 6 foreign countries. 53% are white; 16% Hispanic. 23% are Protestant. The average age of freshmen is 19; all undergraduates, 23. 41% do not continue beyond their first year; 33% remain to graduate.
Housing: 545 students can be accommodated in single-sex dormitories. There is also married-student housing. On-campus housing is guaranteed for all 4 years. 54% of students live on campus. Alcohol is not permitted. All students may keep cars.
Activities: There are 1 local fraternity and 1 national fraternity and 1 local sorority and 1 national sorority. There are 37 groups on campus, including art, band, cheerleading, choir, chorale, chorus, computers, drama, honors, international, marching band, musical theater, newspaper, photography, political, professional, radio and TV, religious, social, social service, student government, and yearbook. Popular campus events include Pride Week, Big Weekend, and Fall Fest.
Sports: There are 5 intercollegiate sports for men and 5 for women, and 5 intramural sports for men and 5 for women. Facilities include a 2500-seat gym, basketball/volleyball, racquetball, and tennis courts, and an aerobics and weight training facility.
Disabled Students: All of the campus is accessible. Wheelchair ramps, elevators, special parking, specially equipped rest rooms, and special class scheduling are available.
Services: Counseling and information services are available, as is tutoring in every subject. There is a reader service for the blind, and remedial math, reading, and writing.
Campus Safety and Security: Measures include self-defense education, informal discussions, pamphlets/posters/films, and emergency telephones. There are lighted pathways/sidewalks and a security service on campus.
Programs of Study: Wayland confers B.A., B.S., B.B.A., B.M., B.S.I.S., and B.S.O.E. degrees. Associate and master's degrees are also awarded. Bachelor's degrees are awarded in BIOLOGICAL SCIENCE (biology/biological science), BUSINESS (business administration and management), COMMUNICATIONS AND THE ARTS (art, communications, dramatic arts, English, music, and Spanish), COMPUTER AND PHYSICAL SCIENCE (chemistry, mathematics, physical sciences, and science), EDUCATION (music, physical, and vocational), SOCIAL SCIENCE (criminal justice, history, human services, interdisciplinary studies, political science/government, psychology, religion, religious education, religious music, social science, and social studies). Religion, education, and social science are the strongest academically. Education, business, and religion are the largest.
Required: To graduate, all students must earn a GPA of at least 2.0 while taking 124 to 145 semester hours, with 30 in their major and 36 to 42 in upper-division hours. Distribution requirements include 12 hours of English; 8 to 16 in science; 6 each in Bible, history, and humanities; up to 6 in foreign language; 4 in phys ed; 3 to 6 in math; 3 in computer science; and 3 in philosophy, sociology, or psychology. Chapel attendance is also required. Honors students must complete a thesis.
Special: A cooperative education program with Texas Tech University, internships in education and social work, and work-study plans through the Social Security Administration are available. In addition, credit for life and military experience is given in the individualized occupational education program. Nondegree study in the lifelong learning program is also offered. There are 3 national honor societies, and a freshman honors program.
Faculty/Classroom: 69% of faculty are male; 31%, female. All teach undergraduates. No introductory courses are taught by graduate students. The average class size in an introductory lecture is 16; in a laboratory, 13; and in a regular course, 14.
Admissions: 97% of the 2001-2002 applicants were accepted. The SAT I scores for the 2001-2002 freshman class were: Verbal--60% below 500, 22% between 500 and 599, 17% between 600 and 700, and 1% above 700; Math--58% below 500, 27% between 500 and 599, 13% between 600 and 700, and 2% above 700. The ACT scores were 60% below 21, 15% between 21 and 23, 15% between 24 and 26, 5% between 27 and 28, and 5% above 28. 34% of the current freshmen were in the top fifth of their class; 59% were in the top two fifths. 2 freshmen graduated first in their class.
Requirements: The SAT I or ACT is required. In addition, Wayland requires graduation from an accredited secondary school with 3 years of English and 2 years each of science, math, and social science. The GED is accepted. Wayland requires applicants to be in the upper 50% of their class. AP and CLEP credits are accepted.
Procedure: Freshmen are admitted to all sessions. Application deadlines are open. The fall 2001 application fee was $35. Notification is sent on a rolling basis.
Transfer: 56 transfer students enrolled in 2001-2002. Applicants need a minimum GPA of 2.0 and must be able to reenter all colleges previously attended. 30 credits of 124 to 145 must be completed at Wayland.
Visiting: There are regularly scheduled orientations for prospective students. There are guides for informal visits and visitors may sit in on classes and stay overnight. To schedule a visit, contact Shawn Thomas, Director of Admissions at E-Mail: *sthomas@mail.wbu.edu*
Financial Aid: In 2001-2002, 86% of all freshmen and 85% of continuing students received some form of financial aid. 61% of freshmen and 65% of continuing students received need-based aid. The average freshman award was $8988. Of that total, scholarships or need-based grants averaged $5021 ($12,000 maximum); loans averaged $4992 ($12,000 maximum); and work contracts averaged $2309 ($3552 maximum). 26% of undergraduates work part time. Average annual earnings from campus work are $2340. The average financial indebtedness of the 2001 graduate was $20,000. Wayland is a member of CSS. The FAFSA is required. The fall application deadline is May 1.
International Students: There are 10 international students enrolled. The school actively recruits these students. They must score 500 on the written TOEFL and also take the SAT I or the ACT.
Computers: There are 123 PCs available on the Plainview campus, including 21 in the Learning Resource Center Lab. Students have access to the Internet through all of these computers. All students may access the system during posted lab hours. There are no time limits and no fees.
Graduates: In 2001, 124 bachelor's degrees were awarded. The most popular majors were education (28%), business administration and management (17%), and religion (10%). In an average class, 2% graduate in 3 years, 17% in 4 years, 27% in 5 years, and 31% in 6 years.
Admissions Contact: Shawn Thomas, Director of Admissions.
E-mail: *admityou@mail.wbu.edu* Web: *www.wbu.edu*

WEST TEXAS A&M UNIVERSITY B-1
Canyon, TX 79016 (806) 651-2020
(800) 99-WTAMU; Fax: (806) 651-5285

Full-time: 1869 men, 2398 women	**Faculty:** 220; IIA, --$
Part-time: 468 men, 581 women	**Ph.D.s:** 69%
Graduate: 512 men, 847 women	**Student/Faculty:** 19 to 1
Year: semesters, summer session	**Tuition:** $2706 ($10,296)
Application Deadline: open	**Room & Board:** $3832
Freshman Class: 2147 applied, 1888 accepted, 799 enrolled	
SAT I Verbal/Math: 514/519	**ACT:** 21 COMPETITIVE

West Texas A&M University, founded in 1909, is a public institution offering programs in the liberal arts and sciences, fine arts, agriculture, nursing, and education. There are 4 undergraduate schools and 1 graduate school. In addition to regional accreditation, WTAMU has baccalaureate program accreditation with ACBSP, CCNE, CSWE, NASM, and NCATE. The 2 libraries contain 1,068,624 volumes, 1,261,948 microform items, and 4260 audiovisual forms/CDs, and subscribe to 5463 periodicals. Computerized library services include the card catalog, interlibrary loans, and database searching. Special learning facilities include a learning resource center, art gallery, natural history museum, radio station, an alternative energy institute, an electronic learning center, and a communications disorders center. The 135-acre campus is in a small town 17 miles south of Amarillo. Including residence halls, there are 77 buildings.
Student Life: 90% of undergraduates are from Texas. Others are from 39 states and 36 foreign countries. 93% are from public schools. 80%

are white; 12% Hispanic. The average age of freshmen is 21; all undergraduates, 23. 34% do not continue beyond their first year; 34% remain to graduate.

Housing: 1520 students can be accommodated in college housing, which includes single-sex and coed dormitories. In addition, there are special-interest houses, sorority units within the residence halls, a wellness hall, and 24-hour quiet area. On-campus housing is guaranteed for all 4 years. 75% of students commute. Alcohol is not permitted. All students may keep cars.

Activities: 6% of men belong to 1 local fraternity and 5 national fraternities; 4% of women belong to 3 national sororities. There are 100 groups on campus, including academic, art, band, cheerleading, choir, chorale, chorus, computers, dance, debate, drama, ethnic, film, forensics, gay, honors, international, jazz band, literary magazine, marching band, musical theater, newspaper, opera, orchestra, political, professional, radio and TV, religious, social, social service, student government, symphony, and yearbook. Popular campus events include Workathon, RHA Mud Pull, and Buffalo Branding.

Sports: There are 7 intercollegiate sports for men and 7 for women, and 39 intramural sports for men and 39 for women. Facilities include an Olympic-size pool, an 8-lane bowling alley, weight-training rooms, a 20,000-seat stadium, handball, racquetball, tennis, badminton, basketball, and volleyball courts, a flag football field, and softball fields.

Disabled Students: All of the campus is accessible. Wheelchair ramps, elevators, special parking, specially equipped rest rooms, special class scheduling, lowered drinking fountains, and lowered telephones are available. Additional needs recommended by ADA are handled on a case-by-case basis.

Services: Counseling and information services are available, as is tutoring in some subjects, including core curriculum courses. There is a reader service for the blind, and remedial math, reading, and writing.

Campus Safety and Security: Measures include 24-hour foot and vehicle patrol, self-defense education, escort service, and informal discussions. There are pamphlets/posters/films, emergency telephones, lighted pathways/sidewalks, and shuttle buses provided by city transport.

Programs of Study: WTAMU confers B.A., B.S., B.A.A.S., B.B.A., B.F.A., B.G.S., B.M., B.S.M.T., and B.S.N. degrees. Master's degrees are also awarded. Bachelor's degrees are awarded in AGRICULTURE (agricultural business management, agricultural economics, agriculture, animal science, plant protection (pest management), plant science, and soil science), BIOLOGICAL SCIENCE (biology/biological science and wildlife biology), BUSINESS (accounting, banking and finance, business administration and management, business economics, management science, marketing/retailing/merchandising, and recreation and leisure services), COMMUNICATIONS AND THE ARTS (applied art, art, broadcasting, dance, dramatic arts, English, graphic design, music, music theory and composition, musical theater, performing arts, public relations, publishing, Spanish, speech/debate/rhetoric, and studio art), COMPUTER AND PHYSICAL SCIENCE (chemistry, computer science, geology, information sciences and systems, mathematics, and physics), EDUCATION (art, business, drama, English, foreign languages, mathematics, music, physical, reading, recreation, science, social studies, and special), ENGINEERING AND ENVIRONMENTAL DESIGN (emergency/disaster science, engineering technology, environmental science, and preengineering), HEALTH PROFESSIONS (allied health, exercise science, medical technology, music therapy, nursing, predentistry, premedicine, prepharmacy, preveterinary science, and speech pathology/audiology), SOCIAL SCIENCE (criminal justice, economics, geography, history, interdisciplinary studies, liberal arts/general studies, political science/government, prelaw, psychology, public administration, social science, social work, and sociology). Education and music are the strongest academically. Education is the largest.

Required: A general education requirement of 49 hours includes courses in analytic reasoning and communication skills, cultural heritage, English, science, history, political science, humanities, and sports and exercise sciences. Additional core requirements vary according to major. A minimum 2.0 GPA and 130 credit hours, including at least 36 of advanced work, 30 of which must be at WTAMU, are required to graduate. At least 33 hours must be earned in residence at WTAMU, including at least 24 of the last 30 hours counted toward a degree.

Special: WTAMU offers work-study programs, a Washington semesters, internships, co-op programs, credit by exam, B.A.-B.S. degrees, a general studies degree, interdisciplinary studies in elementary/secondary education fields, nondegree study, and pass/fail options. There are 12 national honor societies, a freshman honors program, and 14 departmental honors programs.

Faculty/Classroom: 54% of faculty are male; 46%, female. 97% teach undergraduates and 50% do research. Graduate students teach 16% of introductory courses. The average class size in an introductory lecture is 36; in a laboratory, 22; and in a regular course, 28.

Admissions: 88% of the 2001-2002 applicants were accepted. The SAT I scores for the 2001-2002 freshman class were: Verbal--47% below 500, 39% between 500 and 599, 13% between 600 and 700, and 1% above 700; Math--53% below 500, 34% between 500 and 599, 12% between 600 and 700, and 1% above 700. The ACT scores were 51% below 21, 25% between 21 and 23, 17% between 24 and 26, 4% between 27 and 28, and 3% above 28. 53% of the current freshmen were in the top fifth of their class; 74% were in the top two fifths. There was 1 National Merit finalist. 26 freshmen graduated first in their class.

Requirements: The SAT I or ACT is required. In addition, applicants should have graduated from an accredited secondary school or have a GED. Admission requires graduation in the top 50% of the student's high school class or a minimum composite score of 20 on the ACT or 950 on the SAT I. Applications are accepted on-line via the Texas State Common Appplication. AP and CLEP credits are accepted.

Procedure: Freshmen are admitted to all sessions. Entrance exams should be taken in the fall of the senior year. There is a deferred admissions plan. Application deadlines are open. The application fee is $25. Notification is sent on a rolling basis.

Transfer: 645 transfer students enrolled in 2001-2002. A 2.0 GPA is generally required for transfer students. 30 credits of 130 must be completed at WTAMU.

Visiting: There are regularly scheduled orientations for prospective students, including a tour of campus, admissions and financial services sessions, selection of major, and a visit with faculty. There are guides for informal visits and visitors may sit in on classes and stay overnight. To schedule a visit, contact the Admissions Office at (800) 99-WTAMU or (806) 651-2833 or *admissions@mail.wtamu.edu*

Financial Aid: In 2001-2002, 51% of all freshmen and 47% of continuing students received some form of financial aid. 48% of freshmen and 46% of continuing students received need-based aid. The average freshman award was $4918. Of that total, scholarships or need-based grants averaged $3282; loans averaged $1376; and work contracts averaged $260. 3% of undergraduates work part time. Average annual earnings from campus work are $1347. The FAFSA and the institutional application are required. The fall application deadline is May 1.

International Students: There are 55 international students enrolled. The school actively recruits these students. They must score 550 on the written TOEFL or 213 on the electronic version.

Computers: The mainframe is an H50. 300 PCs are located in the learning center and another 100 are in other labs and classrooms. Units include networked and stand-alone models. All students may access the system. There are no time limits. The fee is $5 per hour up to a maximum of $50.

Graduates: In 2001, 959 bachelor's degrees were awarded. The most popular majors were education (13%), general studies (10%), and nursing (9%). In an average class, 1% graduate in 3 years, 12% in 4 years, 29% in 5 years, and 34% in 6 years. 279 companies recruited on campus in 2000-2001. Of the 2000 graduating class, 40% were enrolled in graduate school within 6 months of graduation.

Admissions Contact: Lila Vars, Director of Admissions. A video is available. E-mail: *lilav@wtamu.edu* Web: *http://www.wtamu.edu*

WILEY COLLEGE — E-2

Marshall, TX 75670 — **(903) 927-3311; Fax: (903) 938-8100**

Full-time: 275 men, 480 women	**Faculty:** 35
Part-time: 5 men, 15 women	**Ph.D.s:** 63%
Graduate: none	**Student/Faculty:** 21 to 1
Year: semesters, summer session	**Tuition:** $4800
Application Deadline: open	**Room & Board:** $3300
Freshman Class: n/av	
SAT I or ACT: required	**LESS COMPETITIVE**

Wiley College, founded in 1873 as an institution for black students, is affiliated with the United Methodist Church. The college offers programs in the liberal arts, sciences, and teacher training. Figures in the above capsule are approximate. The library contains 80,000 volumes, and subscribes to 298 periodicals. The 58-acre campus is in a small town 35 miles west of Shreveport.

Student Life: 80% of undergraduates are from Texas.

Housing: College-sponsored housing includes dormitories. 75% of students live on campus.

Activities: There are 8 national fraternities and 8 national sororities.

Sports: There are 3 intercollegiate sports for men and 3 for women, and 4 intramural sports for men and 4 for women. There is a student union on campus.

Programs of Study: Wiley confers B.A., B.S., and B.B.A. degrees. Bachelor's degrees are awarded in BIOLOGICAL SCIENCE (biology/biological science), BUSINESS (business administration and management, hotel/motel and restaurant management, and office supervision and management), COMMUNICATIONS AND THE ARTS (communications, English, music, and music performance), COMPUTER AND PHYSICAL SCIENCE (chemistry, computer science, mathematics, and physics), EDUCATION (business, elementary, English, mathematics, music, physical, secondary, social science, and special), SOCIAL SCIENCE (history, liberal arts/general studies, philosophy, religion, social science, and sociology).

Required: Core requirements include courses in education, English, humanities, history, religion, science, and math. 2 credits in phys ed and

3 in computer science are required. A 2.0 GPA and 124 semester hours are needed to graduate.

Faculty/Classroom: All teach undergraduates.

Requirements: The SAT I or ACT is required. In addition, applicants must be graduates of an accredited secondary school or have scored at least 40 on the GED. A letter of recommendation from a high school counselor or teacher is required. Wiley requires applicants to be in the upper 50% of their class. A GPA of 2.0 is required.

Procedure: There are early decision and early admissions plans. Application deadlines are open. Check with the school for current fee.

Transfer: Transfer applicants must be in good standing at their last college. 30 credits of 124 must be completed at Wiley.

Financial Aid: Check with the school for current deadlines.

International Students: They must score 400 on the written TOEFL.

Computers: The mainframes are an IBM System 36 and a DEC Dolphin. All students may access the system. There are no time limits and no fees.

Admissions Contact: Bishop B. Curry, Director of Admissions.

UTAH

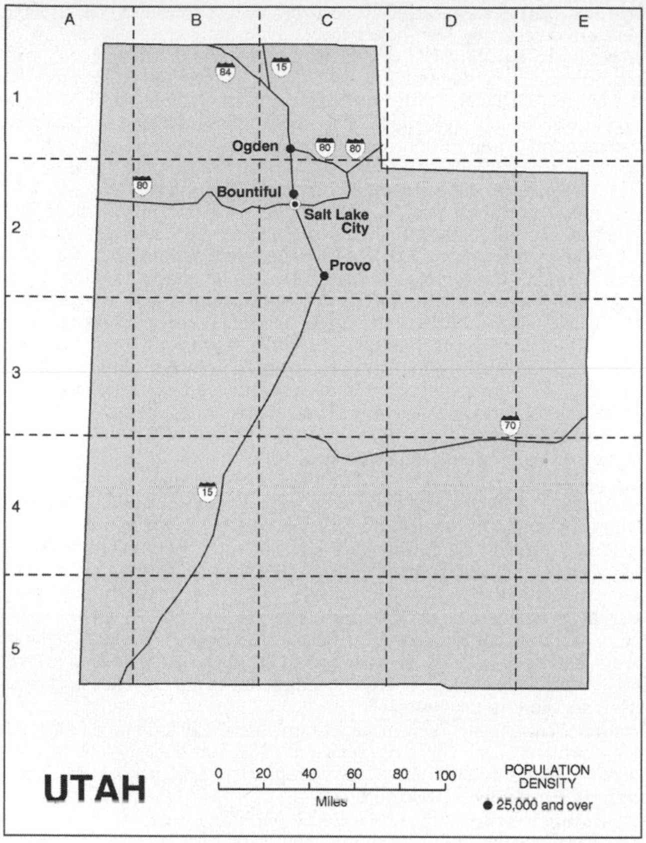

BRIGHAM YOUNG UNIVERSITY C-2

Provo, UT 84602 **(801) 378-2537; Fax: (801) 378-4264**

Full-time: 12,935 men, 13,602 women **Faculty:** 1562
Part-time: 1780 men, 1498 women **Ph.D.s:** 66%
Graduate: 1755 men, 1201 women **Student/Faculty:** 17 to 1
Year: semesters, summer session **Tuition:** $3060 ($4590)
Application Deadline: February 15 **Room & Board:** $4780
Freshman Class: 10,293 applied, 6739 accepted, 5296 enrolled
ACT: 27 **HIGHLY COMPETITIVE**

Brigham Young University, founded in 1875, is a private university affiliated with the Church of Jesus Christ of Latter-day Saints. There are 11 undergraduate and 11 graduate schools. In addition to regional accreditation, BYU has baccalaureate program accreditation with AACSB, ABET, ACCE, ACEJMC, ADA, ASLA, CSAB, CSWE, NASAD, NASDTEC, NASM, NCATE, and NLN. The 3 libraries contain 2,511,155 volumes, 1,211,807 microform items, and 56,353 audiovisual forms/CDs, and subscribe to 16,218 periodicals. Computerized library services include the card catalog, interlibrary loans, and database searching. Special learning facilities include a learning resource center, art gallery, natural history museum, planetarium, radio station, TV station, an archaeological museum, an earth science museum, reading and writing labs, and math, language, and computer labs. The 638-acre campus is in a suburban area 45 miles south of Salt Lake City. Including residence halls, there are 354 buildings.

Student Life: 68% of undergraduates are from out of state, mostly the West. Others are from 49 states, 107 foreign countries, and Canada. 88% are white. The average age of freshmen is 19; all undergraduates, 21. 31% do not continue beyond their first year; 71% remain to graduate.

Housing: 6495 students can be accommodated in college housing, which includes single-sex dormitories, on-campus apartments, and married-student housing. In addition, there are honors houses and language houses. On-campus housing is available on a first-come, first-served basis. Alcohol is not permitted. All students may keep cars.

Activities: There are no fraternities or sororities. There are 330 groups on campus, including art, bagpipe band, band, cheerleading, chess, choir, chorale, chorus, computers, dance, debate, drama, drill team, ethnic, film, honors, international, jazz band, literary magazine, marching band, musical theater, newspaper, opera, orchestra, pep band, photography, political, professional, radio and TV, religious, social, social service, student government, symphony, and yearbook. Popular campus events include Club Week, Fine Arts Ball, and Friday Night Live.

Sports: There are 9 intercollegiate sports for men and 10 for women, and 34 intramural sports for men and 32 for women. Facilities include pools, tennis courts, racquetball courts, gyms, tracks, fields, and weight rooms.

Disabled Students: 97% of the campus is accessible. Wheelchair ramps, elevators, special parking, specially equipped rest rooms, special class scheduling, lowered drinking fountains, lowered telephones, automatic door operators, and access ramps to pools are available.

Services: Counseling and information services are available, as is tutoring in most subjects. There is a reader service for the blind, and remedial math, reading, and writing.

Campus Safety and Security: Measures include 24-hour foot and vehicle patrol, self-defense education, escort service, and informal discussions. There are pamphlets/posters/films, emergency telephones, lighted pathways/sidewalks, a bicycle patrol, and academic building security officers from 7P.M. to 2 A.M.

Programs of Study: BYU confers B.A., B.S., B.F.A., and B.Mus. degrees. Master's and doctoral degrees are also awarded. Bachelor's degrees are awarded in AGRICULTURE (agronomy, animal science, horticulture, and wildlife management), BIOLOGICAL SCIENCE (biochemistry, biology/biological science, botany, microbiology, nutrition, and zoology), BUSINESS (accounting, business administration and management, management information systems, and tourism), COMMUNICATIONS AND THE ARTS (advertising, art history and appreciation, Chinese, communications, comparative literature, dance, English, French, German, graphic design, Greek, illustration, industrial design, Italian, Japanese, Korean, linguistics, music, photography, Portuguese, public relations, Russian, and Spanish), COMPUTER AND PHYSICAL SCIENCE (chemistry, computer science, geology, mathematics, physics, and statistics), EDUCATION (art, business, early childhood, elementary, physical, secondary, special, and teaching English as a second/foreign language (TESOL/TEFOL)), ENGINEERING AND ENVIRONMENTAL DESIGN (chemical engineering, civil engineering, construction management, electrical/electronics engineering, electrical/electronics engineering technology, geological engineering, manufacturing technology, and mechanical engineering), HEALTH PROFESSIONS (health science, nursing, and speech pathology/audiology), SOCIAL SCIENCE (American studies, anthropology, Asian/Oriental studies, Canadian studies, dietetics, economics, European studies, family/consumer studies, food science, geography, history, humanities, Latin American studies, Near Eastern studies, philosophy, political science/government, psychology, social work, and sociology). Engineering, accounting, and business are the strongest academically. Business, education, and communications are the largest.

Required: To graduate, students must complete 120 semester hours with a minimum GPA of 2.0. All students must take a total of 14 semester hours of religion and 2 hours of phys ed. There are general education requirements in English, advanced writing, foreign language or math, arts and letters, natural sciences, social sciences, and American heritage.

Special: Brigham Young offers cooperative programs, internships, study abroad in 12 countries, a Washington semester, dual majors, nondegree study, and credit for life and work experience. There is a freshman honors program.

Faculty/Classroom: 72% of faculty are male; 28%, female. All teach undergraduates. The average class size in an introductory lecture is 43 and in a regular course, 23.

Admissions: 65% of the 2001-2002 applicants were accepted. The ACT scores for the 2001-2002 freshman class were: 3% below 21, 11% between 21 and 23, 30% between 24 and 26, 23% between 27 and 28, and 34% above 28. 87% of the current freshmen were in the top fifth of their class; 98% were in the top two fifths. There were 115 National Merit finalists. 368 freshmen graduated first in their class.

Requirements: The ACT is required. In addition, applicants must be graduates of an accredited secondary school. The GED is accepted. The school recommends that applicants complete 4 years of English, 2 years of math beyond algebra, and courses in foreign language, science, history, and social studies. Essays and letters of recommendation are required with the application. Biographical and geographical information, accomplishments, and essays, as well as the scholarship application may be completed on-line, although additional information is also required. A GPA of 3.76 is required. AP and CLEP credits are accepted. Important factors in the admissions decision are advanced placement or honor courses, recommendations by school officials, and evidence of special talent. Contact *http://ar.byu.edu/admissions/apply_electronically/*

Procedure: Freshmen are admitted to all sessions. Entrance exams should be taken by December of the senior year. There are early admissions and deferred admissions plans. Applications should be filed by February 15 for fall entry, October 1 for winter entry, February 15 for spring entry, and February 15 for summer entry, along with a $25 fee. Notification is sent on a rolling basis.

Transfer: 1317 transfer students enrolled in 2001-2002. For applicants, primary consideration will be given to basic general education subjects (English, math, history, and foreign languages) and major subjects. The GPA from those subjects must be near 3.0 to be competitive for admission. 30 credits of 120 must be completed at BYU.

Visiting: There are regularly scheduled orientations for prospective students, including a campus tour, visits with the department advisement center for the prospective major, and an interview with a school relations counselor. There are guides for informal visits and visitors may sit in on classes. To schedule a visit, contact Derek Spriggs at (801) 378-4431.

Financial Aid: 80% of undergraduates work part time. Average annual earnings from campus work are $5000. BYU is a member of CSS. The FFS is required. The fall application deadline is April 15.

International Students: There are 1238 international students enrolled. They must score 173 on the electronic TOEFL and also take the SAT I or the ACT.

Computers: PCs are available in departments and computer labs throughout the campus. All students may access the system any time. There are no time limits and no fees. It is recommended that students in accounting, the Business School, and the Law School have personal computers.

Graduates: In 2001, 7497 bachelor's degrees were awarded. The most popular majors were management (7%), family sciences (6%), and zoology (5%). 500 companies recruited on campus in 2000-2001.

Admissions Contact: Jeffery M. Tanner, Admissions Office.
E-mail: *jeff_tanner@byu.edu* Web: *www.byu.edu*

SOUTHERN UTAH UNIVERSITY B-4

Cedar City, UT 84720 **(435) 586-7740; Fax: (435) 865-8223**

Full-time: 2091 men, 2498 women	**Faculty:** 205
Part-time: 510 men, 785 women	**Ph.D.s:** 73%
Graduate: 113 men, 98 women	**Student/Faculty:** 22 to 1
Year: semesters, summer session	**Tuition:** $2194 ($6776)
Application Deadline: July 1	**Room & Board:** $2866
Freshman Class: 1507 applied, 1269 accepted, 732 enrolled	
SAT I Verbal/Math: 488/503	**ACT:** 21 **COMPETITIVE**

Southern Utah University, founded in 1897, is part of the Utah System of Higher Education and offers undergraduate degrees in arts and letters, science, education, and business. There are 5 undergraduate and 3 graduate schools. In addition to regional accreditation, SUU has baccalaureate program accreditation with AACSB, ACBSP, NASDTEC, NASM, and NLN. The library contains 202,784 volumes, 673,985 microform items, and 17,969 audiovisual forms/CDs, and subscribes to 1100 periodicals. Computerized library services include the card catalog, interlibrary loans, and database searching. Special learning facilities include a learning resource center, art gallery, natural history museum, planetarium, radio station, and TV station. The 133-acre campus is in a small town 170 miles north of Las Vegas. Including residence halls, there are 76 buildings.

Student Life: 80% of undergraduates are from Utah. Others are from 45 states, 32 foreign countries, and Canada. 98% are from public schools. 93% are white. 18% are claim no religious affiliation. The average age of freshmen is 19; all undergraduates, 23. 37% do not continue beyond their first year; 63% remain to graduate.

Housing: 395 students can be accommodated in college housing, which includes single-sex and coed dormitories, on-campus apartments, fraternity houses, and sorority houses. On-campus housing is available on a first-come, first-served basis. Priority is given to out-of-town students. 92% of students commute. Alcohol is not permitted. All students may keep cars.

Activities: 3% of men belong to 2 national fraternities; 4% of women belong to 1 local sorority and 2 national sororities. There are 48 groups on campus, including art, bagpipe band, band, cheerleading, choir, chorale, chorus, computers, dance, drama, drill team, ethnic, film, forensics, gay, honors, international, jazz band, marching band, musical theater, newspaper, opera, orchestra, pep band, political, professional, radio and TV, religious, social, social service, student government, and symphony. Popular campus events include Founders Day, dances, and service programs.

Sports: There are 7 intercollegiate sports for men and 8 for women, and 13 intramural sports for men and 13 for women. Facilities include a 10,000-seat stadium for football and for track and field, a baseball field, recreation grounds, a 5300-seat special events facility for basketball, volleyball, and gymnastics, tennis and racquetball courts, and large, all-weather practice areas. SUU owns and operates a 1000-acre farm and a 3700-acre ranch.

Disabled Students: 95% of the campus is accessible. Wheelchair ramps, elevators, special parking, specially equipped rest rooms, special class scheduling, lowered drinking fountains, and lowered telephones are available.

Services: Counseling and information services are available, as is tutoring in most subjects. There is a reader service for the blind, and remedial math, reading, and writing.

Campus Safety and Security: Measures include self-defense education, escort service, informal discussions, and pamphlets/posters/films. There are emergency telephones and lighted pathways/sidewalks.

Programs of Study: SUU confers B.A., B.S., and B.I.S. degrees. Associate and master's degrees are also awarded. Bachelor's degrees are awarded in AGRICULTURE (agriculture), BIOLOGICAL SCIENCE (biology/biological science), BUSINESS (accounting, banking and finance, business administration and management, marketing management, and marketing/retailing/merchandising), COMMUNICATIONS AND THE ARTS (art, communications, dance, dramatic arts, English, French, German, music, and Spanish), COMPUTER AND PHYSICAL SCIENCE (chemistry, computer science, geology, information sciences and systems, and mathematics), EDUCATION (art, athletic training, business, dance, drama, elementary, English, foreign languages, mathematics, music, physical, science, social science, social studies, and special), ENGINEERING AND ENVIRONMENTAL DESIGN (construction management and engineering technology), SOCIAL SCIENCE (criminal justice, economics, family/consumer studies, history, interdisciplinary studies, political science/government, psychology, and sociology). Business, science, and education are the strongest academically. Business and education are the largest.

Required: To graduate, all students must complete at least 122 credit hours with a minimum 2.0 GPA. Students must satisfy general education, major and minor, and basic skills requirements, including 4 courses each in social and physical sciences, 2 each in English, fine arts, and humanities, 1 each in math, phys ed, and communications, and a course in either history, political science, or economics to fulfill the U.S. government requirement.

Special: SUU offers co-op programs with Weber State University, work-study programs, study abroad in Russia, dual majors, student-designed majors leading to a B.I.S. degree, and internships with government officials in Washington, D.C. There are 3 national honor societies and 3 departmental honors programs.

Faculty/Classroom: 72% of faculty are male; 28%, female. All teach undergraduates and 65% do research. No introductory courses are taught by graduate students. The average class size in an introductory lecture is 29 and in a laboratory, 14.

Admissions: 84% of the 2001-2002 applicants were accepted. The SAT I scores for the 2001-2002 freshman class were: Verbal--45% below 500, 39% between 500 and 599, 14% between 600 and 699, and 2% above 699; Math--46% below 500, 35% between 500 and 599, 14% between 600 and 699, and 3% above 699. The ACT scores were 21% between 12 and 17, 52% between 18 and 23, 25% between 24 and 29, and 2% between 30 and 36. 45% of the current freshmen were in the top quarter of their class; 76% were in the top half.

Requirements: The SAT I or ACT is required; the ACT is recommended. In addition, applicants should be graduates of an accredited secondary school or have a GED and should have completed 4 years of English, 3 of math, 2 each of biological/physical sciences (1 with a lab) and social studies including U.S. history/government, and 4 of electives. A GPA of 2.0 is required. AP and CLEP credits are accepted.

Procedure: Freshmen are admitted to all sessions. There are early admissions and deferred admissions plans. Applications should be filed by July 1 for fall entry, along with a $25 fee. Notification is sent on a rolling basis.

Transfer: 549 transfer students enrolled in 2001-2002. Applicants must submit transcripts from previously attended colleges and have a minimum 2.25 GPA. ACT scores and high school transcripts are required from students who have not completed English or math courses at another institution or who have not completed a minimum of 30 credit hours at an institution of higher education. 30 credits of 122 must be completed at SUU.

Visiting: There are regularly scheduled orientations for prospective students, including campus tours, which can be arranged by appointment. There are guides for informal visits and visitors may sit in on classes and stay overnight. To schedule a visit, contact Sandra Lord, Director of School Relations at (435) 586-7741.

Financial Aid: The average freshman award for the 2001-2002 school year was $2927. The average financial indebtedness of the 2001 graduate was $10,285. The FAFSA and the college's own financial statement are required.

International Students: The school actively recruits these students. They must score 500 on the written TOEFL and also take the SAT I or the ACT.

Computers: The mainframe is a DEC VAX 6420. Students have access to more than 350 Mac and IBM PCs. E-mail, Internet access, and a variety of software are available. All students may access the system.

Graduates: In 2001, 871 bachelor's degrees were awarded. The most popular majors were education (34%), business/marketing (15%), and communications (10%). In an average class, 32% graduate in 6 years.

Admissions Contact: Dale S. Orton, Director of Admissions.
E-mail: *adminfo@suu.edu* Web: *www.suu.edu*

UNIVERSITY OF UTAH C-2

Salt Lake City, UT 84112 **(801) 581-7281; (800) 444-8638**

Full-time: 7803 men, 6315 women **Faculty:** I, -$
Part-time: 4234 men, 3882 women **Ph.D.s:** 97%
Graduate: 2904 men, 2520 women **Student/Faculty:** 9 to 1
Year: semesters, summer session **Tuition:** $3057 ($9299)
Application Deadline: July 1 **Room & Board:** $4646
Freshman Class: 3193 applied, 2833 accepted, 2119 enrolled
ACT: 22 **COMPETITIVE**

University of Utah, founded in 1850, is a part of the Utah System of Higher Education. The university offers undergraduate degrees through the colleges of architecture, business, education, engineering, fine arts, health, humanities, nursing, medicine, mines and earth sciences, pharmacy, science, and social and behavioral science. There are 13 undergraduate and 16 graduate schools. In addition to regional accreditation, U of U has baccalaureate program accreditation with AACSB, ABET, ACPE, ADA, APTA, ASLA, CSWE, NAAB, NASM, NCATE, NLN, and NRPA. The 3 libraries contain 3,791,998 volumes, 3,476,589 microform items, and 47,418 audiovisual forms/CDs, and subscribe to 21,853 periodicals. Computerized library services include the card catalog, interlibrary loans, and database searching. Special learning facilities include a learning resource center, art gallery, natural history museum, radio station, TV station, and an arboretum. The 1535-acre campus is in an urban area in Salt Lake City. Including residence halls, there are 303 buildings.

Student Life: 80% of undergraduates are from Utah. Others are from 49 states, 109 foreign countries, and Canada. 95% are from public schools. 86% are white. The average age of freshmen is 19; all undergraduates, 25. 42% do not continue beyond their first year; 54% remain to graduate.

Housing: 2300 students can be accommodated in college housing, which includes single-sex dormitories, on-campus apartments, off-campus apartments, married-student housing, fraternity houses, and sorority houses. In addition, there are honors houses and special-interest houses. On-campus housing is available on a first-come, first-served basis. 91% of students commute. Alcohol is not permitted. All students may keep cars.

Activities: 3% of men belong to 12 national fraternities; 2% of women belong to 7 national sororities. There are 250 groups on campus, including art, band, cheerleading, chess, choir, chorale, chorus, computers, dance, drama, drill team, drum and bugle corps, ethnic, film, gay, honors, international, jazz band, marching band, musical theater, newspaper, opera, orchestra, pep band, photography, political, professional, radio and TV, religious, social, social service, student government, and symphony. Popular campus events include Mayfest and Autumn Openings.

Sports: There are 10 intercollegiate sports for men and 11 for women, and 68 intramural sports for men and 61 for women. Facilities include a 35000-seat stadium, a 15500-seat basketball arena, 6 indoor gyms, 13 indoor and 22 outdoor tennis courts, 3 indoor swimming pools, a gymnastics room, 5 weight rooms, 19 handball/racquetball/squash courts, a 9-hole golf course, 3 outdoor playing fields, a 10-lane bowling alley, a movie theater, video games, and a big-screen TV.

Disabled Students: 93% of the campus is accessible. Wheelchair ramps, elevators, special parking, specially equipped rest rooms, special class scheduling, lowered drinking fountains, and lowered telephones are available.

Services: Counseling and information services are available, as is tutoring in most subjects, including . There is a reader service for the blind, remedial math and writing, and support services for the deaf, including readers, scribes, tutors, and interpreters.

Campus Safety and Security: Measures include 24-hour foot and vehicle patrol, self-defense education, escort service, and shuttle buses. There are informal discussions, pamphlets/posters/films, emergency telephones, and lighted pathways/sidewalks.

Programs of Study: U of U confers B.A., B.S., B.F.A., and B.U.S. degrees. Master's and doctoral degrees are also awarded. Bachelor's degrees are awarded in BIOLOGICAL SCIENCE (biology/biological science), BUSINESS (accounting, banking and finance, business administration and management, management science, marketing/retailing/merchandising, recreation and leisure services, and tourism), COMMUNICATIONS AND THE ARTS (art, art history and appreciation, Chinese, classics, communications, dance, dramatic arts, English, film arts, French, German, Japanese, linguistics, music, performing arts, Russian, Spanish, and speech/debate/rhetoric), COMPUTER AND PHYSICAL SCIENCE (atmospheric sciences and meteorology, chemistry, computer science, geology, geophysics and seismology, mathematics, and physics), EDUCATION (art, athletic training, elementary, health, and social science), ENGINEERING AND ENVIRONMENTAL DESIGN (architecture, bioengineering, biomedical engineering, chemical engineering, civil engineering, computer engineering, electrical/electronics engineering, environmental engineering, geological engineering, materials engineering, mechanical engineering, metallurgical engineering, mining and mineral engineering, and urban planning technology), HEALTH PROFESSIONS (exercise science, medical laboratory science, nursing, occupational therapy, pharmacy, physical therapy, and speech pathology/audiology), SOCIAL SCIENCE (anthropology, Asian/Oriental studies, behavioral science, economics, family/consumer studies, geography, history, human development, Middle Eastern studies, parks and recreation management, philosophy, political science/government, psychology, social science, sociology, and women's studies). Social and behavioral sciences are the largest.

Required: To graduate, all students must satisfy requirements in the Liberal Education program, writing proficiency, and American Institutions. The core curriculum consists of 1 course each in 3 of the following 4 areas: science, humanities, fine arts, and social/behavioral science. Distribution requirements include 2 courses in each of 3 of the following 4 areas, excluding the major area: science, humanities, fine arts, and social science. Students must complete at least 183 credit hours, with 45 to 60 in the major. A minimum 2.0 GPA is required.

Special: The university offers numerous opportunities for cooperative programs, cross-registration through the Western Interstate Commission for Higher Education (WICHE), study abroad, internships, work-study and accelerated degree programs, and B.A.-B.S. degrees. Also available are the general studies degree, a Washington semester, student-designed and dual majors, credit for telecourses, and military experience, nondegree study, and pass/fail options. There are 32 national honor societies, including Phi Beta Kappa, a freshman honors program, and 1 departmental honors program.

Faculty/Classroom: 77% of faculty are male; 23%, female. All teach undergraduates.

Admissions: 89% of the 2001-2002 applicants were accepted. The ACT scores for the 2001-2002 freshman class were: 32% below 21, 29% between 21 and 23, 22% between 24 and 26, 9% between 27 and 28, and 8% above 28. There were 35 National Merit finalists and 152 semifinalists.

Requirements: The SAT I or ACT is required. In addition, the ACT, with a minimum composite score of 20, is preferred. The SAT I, with a minimum composite score of 880, is accepted. In addition, applicants must be graduates of an accredited secondary school or have the GED. 15 academic credits are required, including 4 years each of English and electives, 2 years each of foreign language, math, and science/lab, and 1 year of U.S. history. A GPA of 2.0 is required. AP and CLEP credits are accepted.

Procedure: Freshmen are admitted to all sessions. Entrance exams should be taken in the junior year of high school. There are early action and deferred admissions plans. Applications should be filed by July 1 for fall entry, November 15 for winter entry, February 15 for spring entry, and May 15 for summer entry. Notification is sent on a rolling basis.

Transfer: 8584 transfer students enrolled in 2001-2002. Transfer students must have completed at least 45 quarter hours with a minimum 2.5 GPA. 45 credits of 183 must be completed at U of U.

Visiting: There are regularly scheduled orientations for prospective students, including course selection and a campus tour. There are guides for informal visits and visitors may sit in on classes and stay overnight. To schedule a visit, contact the Office of High School and Prospective Student Services at (801) 581-8761.

Financial Aid: In 2001-2002, 33% of all freshmen and 44% of continuing students received some form of financial aid. 61% of freshmen and 82% of continuing students received need-based aid. The average freshman award was $3113. Of that total, scholarships or need-based grants averaged $1378 ($6000 maximum); loans averaged $2251 ($5000 maximum); and work contracts averaged $1500 ($4000 maximum). Average annual earnings from campus work are $1500. The average financial indebtedness of the 2001 graduate was $13,390. The FAFSA is required. The fall application deadline is February 15.

International Students: There are 665 international students enrolled. They must score 500 on the written TOEFL and also take the SAT I or ACT. The ACT with a score of 20 is required if the student graduated from a U.S. high school.

Computers: The mainframe is an IBM 3090. There are 900 PCs for student use located in the library, engineering, business, student housing, student union, and math buildings. Other facilities include an IBM 9090 Model 600-S supercomputer, 25 mainframes, 75 minicomputers, and 125 workstation computers. All students may access the system 24 hours per day. There are no time limits and no fees.

Graduates: In 2001, 3276 bachelor's degrees were awarded. The most popular majors were sociology (7%), psychology (7%), and political science (6%). In an average class, 16% graduate in 4 years, 31% in 5 years, and 41% in 6 years.

Admissions Contact: Ralph Boren, Director of Admissions/Registrar. Web: *www.utah.edu*

UTAH STATE UNIVERSITY C-1

Logan, UT 84322 (435) 797-1079; Fax: (435) 797-4077

Full-time: 6300 men, 6460 women **Faculty:** 757; I, --$
Part-time: 3023 men, 3512 women **Ph.D.s:** 81%
Graduate: 1804 men, 1902 women **Student/Faculty:** 17 to 1
Year: semesters, summer session **Tuition:** $2591 ($7897)
Application Deadline: July 1 **Room & Board:** $4180
Freshman Class: 5573 applied, 5431 accepted, 2919 enrolled
SAT I Verbal/Math: 510/520 **ACT:** 22 **COMPETITIVE**

Utah State University, founded in 1888 as a land-grant institution, offers degree programs in the liberal arts and sciences, agriculture and natural resources, engineering, business, education, fine arts, music, family life, and the sciences. There are 8 undergraduate schools and 1 graduate school. In addition to regional accreditation, USU has baccalaureate program accreditation with AACSB, ABET, ADA, AHEA, ASLA, CSWE, FIDER, NASM, NCATE, NRPA, and SAF. The 3 libraries contain 1,377,026 volumes, 2,274,733 microform items, and 25,593 audiovisual forms/CDs, and subscribe to 14,824 periodicals. Computerized library services include the card catalog, interlibrary loans, and database searching. Special learning facilities include a learning resource center, art gallery, radio station, TV station, laboratory school, historical farm, fine arts center, and developmental center for people who are handicapped. The 332-acre campus is in a small town 86 miles north of Salt Lake City. Including residence halls, there are 104 buildings.

Student Life: 68% of undergraduates are from Utah. Others are from 49 states, 77 foreign countries, and Canada. 88% are white. The average age of freshmen is 20; all undergraduates, 23. 34% do not continue beyond their first year; 43% remain to graduate.

Housing: 3313 students can be accommodated in college housing, which includes single-sex dormitories, on-campus apartments, married-student housing, fraternity houses, and sorority houses. In addition, there are honors houses and special-interest houses. On-campus housing is available on a first-come, first-served basis. Alcohol is not permitted. All students may keep cars.

Activities: 2% of men belong to 1 local fraternity; 1% of women belong to 1 local sorority and 3 national sororities. There are 280 groups on campus, including art, band, cheerleading, choir, chorale, chorus, computers, dance, drama, drill team, ethnic, film, gay, honors, international, jazz band, literary magazine, marching band, musical theater, newspaper, opera, orchestra, pep band, photography, political, professional, radio and TV, religious, social, social service, student government, symphony, and yearbook. Popular campus events include Festival of the American West, Founders Day, and Christmas Dinner at the Manor House.

Sports: There are 7 intercollegiate sports for men and 8 for women, and 23 intramural sports for men and 23 for women. Facilities include 5 gyms, indoor and outdoor tennis courts, 2 swimming pools, 40 acres of grass for outdoor sports, a field house, and golf and skiing areas. The campus stadium seats 30257 and the largest auditorium seats 10000.

Disabled Students: 95% of the campus is accessible. Wheelchair ramps, elevators, special parking, specially equipped rest rooms, special class scheduling, lowered drinking fountains, lowered telephones, and special phones to receive calls from the deaf, and a disability resource center are available.

Services: Counseling and information services are available, as is tutoring in every subject. There is a reader service for the blind, and remedial math, reading, and writing. A writing lab and a tutor room are also available.

Campus Safety and Security: Measures include 24-hour foot and vehicle patrol, self-defense education, escort service, and shuttle buses. There are informal discussions, pamphlets/posters/films, emergency telephones, lighted pathways/sidewalks, and campus police.

Programs of Study: USU confers B.A., B.S., B.F.A., B.L.A., and B.M. degrees. Associate, master's, and doctoral degrees are also awarded. Bachelor's degrees are awarded in AGRICULTURE (agricultural business management, agricultural economics, animal science, dairy science, forestry and related sciences, international agriculture, natural resource management, plant science, range/farm management, soil science, and wildlife management), BIOLOGICAL SCIENCE (biochemistry, biology/biological science, and microbiology), BUSINESS (accounting, banking and finance, business administration and management, business economics, fashion merchandising, international business management, management information systems, marketing/retailing/merchandising, and personnel management), COMMUNICATIONS AND THE ARTS (dance, dramatic arts, English, fine arts, French, German, journalism, music, and Spanish), COMPUTER AND PHYSICAL SCIENCE (chemistry, computer science, earth science, geology, information sciences and systems, mathematics, physics, and statistics), EDUCATION (agricultural, art, business, early childhood, elementary, foreign languages, health, home economics, industrial arts, mathematics, music, physical, science, secondary, and special), ENGINEERING AND ENVIRONMENTAL DESIGN (agricultural engineering, civil engineering, electrical/electronics engineering, engineering, environmental science, industrial engineering, industrial engineering technology, interior design, landscape architecture/design, and mechanical engineering), HEALTH PROFESSIONS (medical laboratory technology, music therapy, predentistry, premedicine, public health, speech pathology/audiology, and veterinary science), SOCIAL SCIENCE (American studies, child care/child and family studies, economics, food science, geography, history, home economics, human development, international relations, liberal arts/general studies, parks and recreation management, philosophy, political science/government, prelaw, psychology, social work, and sociology). Natural resources, engineering, and special education are the strongest academically. Humanities, arts, and social science are the largest.

Required: The core curriculum of 30 semester credits includes at least 6 of writing; the total number of credits required for graduation is 120. Students must maintain a minimum GPA of 2.5. The number of credits required in the major varies.

Special: Internships are available in most departments through the Cooperative Education Program. The National Student Exchange Program allows students to cross-register in designated institutions and programs, and the International Student Exchange Program enables students to study abroad.There is also cross-registration with the University of Americas of Mexico. A general studies degree and student-designed majors are available. Study via Comnet satellite is an option. Nondegree study, work-study programs, B.A.-B.S. degrees, pass/fail options, and credit for military experience are offered. There are 11 national honor societies, a freshman honors program, and 35 departmental honors programs.

Faculty/Classroom: 67% of faculty are male; 33%, female. All teach undergraduates. Graduate students teach 6% of introductory courses. The average class size in an introductory lecture is 35; in a laboratory, 20; and in a regular course, 25.

Admissions: 97% of the 2001-2002 applicants were accepted. The SAT I scores for the 2001-2002 freshman class were: Verbal--42% below 500, 38% between 500 and 599, 16% between 600 and 700, and 4% above 700; Math--39% below 500, 38% between 500 and 599, 19% between 600 and 700, and 4% above 700. The ACT scores were 36% below 21, 28% between 21 and 23, 18% between 24 and 26, 9% between 27 and 28, and 9% above 28. 34% of the current freshmen were in the top fifth of their class; 62% were in the top two fifths. There were 25 National Merit finalists. 95 freshmen graduated first in their class.

Requirements: The SAT I or ACT is required. The ACT is preferred. In addition, students should graduate from an accredited secondary school with 15 academic units, including 4 in English, 3 each in math and science, and 1 in social sciences. GED equivalency is accepted, provided ACT scores are 19 or higher. Students not meeting entrance requirements may be considered for admission on a provisional basis. A GPA of 2.7 is required. AP and CLEP credits are accepted. Important factors in the admissions decision are evidence of special talent, parents or siblings attending the school, and recommendations by school officials.

Procedure: Freshmen are admitted to all sessions. Entrance exams should be taken in the spring of the junior year. There are early decision and deferred admissions plans. Applications should be filed by July 1 for fall entry, November 1 for spring entry, and May 1 for summer entry. Notification is sent on a rolling basis.

Transfer: 1582 transfer students enrolled in 2001-2002. A minimum 2.2 GPA, higher for some majors, is required for transfer students. Those applicants with fewer than 45 credits must also submit ACT scores. 30 credits of 120 must be completed at USU.

Visiting: There are regularly scheduled orientations for prospective students, available at 10:30 A.M. and 1:30 P.M. September to May, and 1:30 P.M. June to August. Included are a campus tour, meeting with an academic adviser, lunch, and a housing tour. There are guides for informal visits and visitors may sit in on classes and stay overnight. To schedule a visit, contact Eric R. Olsen at (435) 797-1129.

Financial Aid: In 2001-2002, 30% of all freshmen and 46% of continuing students received some form of financial aid. 53% of freshmen and 59% of continuing students received need-based aid. The average freshman award was $3300. Of that total, scholarships or need-based grants averaged $2400 ($4200 maximum); loans averaged $2400 ($3500 maximum); and work contracts averaged $2700 ($3200 maximum). 59% of undergraduates work part time. The average financial indebtedness of the 2001 graduate was $11,500. USU is a member of CSS. The FAFSA, the college's own financial statement, and student/parent tax forms are required.

International Students: There are 529 international students enrolled. They must score 500 on the written TOEFL or 173 on the electronic version or take the MELAB. The TOEFL is preferred.

Computers: The mainframes are an IBM 9672/R12 and several DEC ALPHAS. 850 PCs are available in 16 open-access labs throughout the campus. All are networked to the mainframes and the Internet. All students may access the system 24 hours a day, 7 days a week. There are no time limits. The fee is $10 to $27.

Graduates: In 2001, 2644 bachelor's degrees were awarded. The most popular majors were business information systems (6%), elementary education (6%), and family and human development (6%). In an average class, 43% graduate in 6 years. 150 companies recruited on campus in 2000-2001. Of the 2000 graduating class, 20% were enrolled in graduate school within 6 months of graduation and 72% were employed.

Admissions Contact: Lynn Poulsen, Associate Vice President of Student Services. E-mail: *admit@cc.usu.edu* Web: *www.usu.edu*

UTAH SYSTEM OF HIGHER EDUCATION

The Utah System of Higher Education, established in 1969, is a public system. It is governed by a state board of regents whose chief administrator is commissioner of higher education. The primary goals of the system are teaching, research, and public service. The main priorities are to provide a high-quality, efficient, and economical public system of higher education; to coordinate, consolidate, and avoid unnecessary duplication; and to systematically develop the role of each institution within the system. The enrollment is approximately 135,000, with about 3700 full-time members. These numbers do not include the Utah College of Applied Technology, which serves secondary and post-secondary students in open-entry, open-exit, technical and vocational training. Governance was transferred in 2001 from K-12 public education to higher education. 4-year campuses are located in Salt Lake City, Orem, and St. George. Profiles of those campuses are included in this section.

WEBER STATE UNIVERSITY

Ogden, UT 84408-1015 **C-1**
(801) 626-7670; Fax: (801) 626-6747

Full-time: 4916 men, 4897 women	**Faculty:** 451; IIA, --$
Part-time: 3220 men, 3586 women	**Ph.D.s:** 91%
Graduate: 119 men, 135 women	**Student/Faculty:** 22 to 1
Year: semesters, summer session	**Tuition:** $2252 ($6312)
Application Deadline: July 1	**Room & Board:** $4645

Freshman Class: 3873 applied, 3873 accepted, 2665 enrolled
ACT: 22 **NONCOMPETITIVE**

Weber State University, founded in 1889, and part of the Utah System of Higher Education, is a public, primarily commuter institution offering undergraduate degrees in health sciences, arts and humanities, business and economics, education, natural sciences, social sciences, and technology, and graduate degrees in education and professional accountancy. There are 7 undergraduate and 4 graduate schools. In addition to regional accreditation, WSU has baccalaureate program accreditation with AACSB, ADA, CAHEA, CSWE, FIDER, NASM, NCATE, and NLN. The library contains 458,115 volumes, 515,370 microform items, and 15,383 audiovisual forms/CDs, and subscribes to 2278 periodicals. Computerized library services include the card catalog, interlibrary loans, and database searching. Special learning facilities include a learning resource center, art gallery, natural history museum, planetarium, radio station, TV station, an observatory, and a working crime lab. The 526-acre campus is in an urban area 35 miles north of Salt Lake City. Including residence halls, there are 72 buildings.

Student Life: 93% of undergraduates are from Utah. Others are from 49 states, 45 foreign countries, and Canada. 98% are from public schools. 79% are white. Most are Church of Jesus Christ of Latter-day Saints. The average age of freshmen is 19; all undergraduates, 25. 31% do not continue beyond their first year; 39% remain to graduate.

Housing: 590 students can be accommodated in college housing, which includes single-sex and coed dormitories and on-campus apartments. On-campus housing is guaranteed for all 4 years. 97% of students commute. Alcohol is not permitted. All students may keep cars.

Activities: 1% of men belong to 5 national fraternities; 1% of women belong to 4 local and 1 national sorority. There are 100 groups on campus, including art, band, cheerleading, chess, choir, chorale, chorus, computers, dance, debate, drama, drill team, drum and bugle corps, ethnic, forensics, honors, international, jazz band, literary magazine, marching band, musical theater, newspaper, opera, orchestra, pep band, photography, political, professional, radio and TV, religious, social, social service, student government, and symphony. Popular campus events include SunFest, WinterFest, and Crystal Crest.

Sports: There are 5 intercollegiate sports for men and 5 for women, and 36 intramural sports for men and 36 for women. Facilities include an indoor track, a strength-training center, 3 indoor basketball courts, a swimming pool, racquetball and tennis courts, a 17000-seat stadium, an 11515-seat gym, a 7800-seat auditorium/arena, an events center, playing fields, an exercise/conditioning room, and a 1-mile jogging trail.

Disabled Students: Wheelchair ramps, elevators, special parking, specially equipped rest rooms, special class scheduling, lowered drinking fountains, and lowered telephones are available.

Services: Counseling and information services are available, as is tutoring in every subject. There is a reader service for the blind, and remedial math, reading, and writing. Translators are offered for the hearing impaired.

Campus Safety and Security: Measures include 24-hour foot and vehicle patrol, self-defense education, escort service, and shuttle buses. There are informal discussions, pamphlets/posters/films, emergency telephones, and lighted pathways/sidewalks.

Programs of Study: WSU confers B.A., B.S., B.F.A., B.I.S., and B.M. degrees. Associate and master's degrees are also awarded. Bachelor's degrees are awarded in BIOLOGICAL SCIENCE (biology/biological science, botany, microbiology, and zoology), BUSINESS (accounting, banking and finance, business administration and management, business economics, management information systems, marketing management, personnel management, purchasing/inventory management, and recreation and leisure services), COMMUNICATIONS AND THE ARTS (communications, dance, dramatic arts, English, fine arts, French, German, graphic design, journalism, media arts, music, music performance, musical theater, photography, piano/organ, public relations, Spanish, speech/debate/rhetoric, technical and business writing, telecommunications, and voice), COMPUTER AND PHYSICAL SCIENCE (chemistry, computer programming, computer science, earth science, geology, information sciences and systems, mathematics, physical sciences, and physics), EDUCATION (art, athletic training, business, early childhood, elementary, foreign languages, health, music, physical, science, secondary, and social science), ENGINEERING AND ENVIRONMENTAL DESIGN (automotive technology, electrical/electronics engineering technology, environmental science, manufacturing technology, mechanical engineering technology, and preengineering), HEALTH PROFESSIONS (clinical science, dental hygiene, health care administration, nursing, predentistry, premedicine, radiograph medical technology, and respiratory therapy), SOCIAL SCIENCE (criminal justice, early childhood studies, economics, family/consumer studies, geography, gerontology, history, interdisciplinary studies, political science/government, psychology, social work, and sociology). Dental hygiene is the strongest academically. Elementary education is the largest.

Required: To graduate, students must demonstrate math competency and complete courses in government/history, English, humanities, math, biological/physical sciences, and social sciences. At least 120 semester credit hours, with 45 at the upper-division level, and a minimum GPA of 2.0 are required. Hours in the major and distribution requirements vary with the degree.

Special: WSU offers co-op programs and internships in many majors, a Washington semester, study abroad in Mexico and England, work-study programs with community businesses, B.A.-B.S. degrees, dual majors in any combination, student-designed majors resulting in a B.I.S. degree, a general studies degree, credit for military experience, nondegree study, and pass/fail options. There is 1 national honor society, including Phi Beta Kappa, and a freshman honors program. All departments have honors programs.

Faculty/Classroom: 62% of faculty are male; 38%, female. All teach undergraduates. No introductory courses are taught by graduate students. The average class size in an introductory lecture is 37; in a laboratory, 16; and in a regular course, 26.

Admissions: All of the 2001-2002 applicants were accepted. The ACT scores for the 2001-2002 freshman class were: 44% below 21, 25% between 21 and 23, 19% between 24 and 26, 7% between 27 and 28, and 5% above 28. 56% of the current freshmen were in the top quarter of their class; 89% were in the top half.

Requirements: The ACT is required. In addition, applicants must be graduates of an accredited secondary school or have a GED. Other requirements vary by department. Out-of-state residents must have a minimum high school GPA of 2.0. Applications are accepted on-line via WSU's web site. AP and CLEP credits are accepted.

Procedure: Freshmen are admitted to all sessions. Entrance exams should be taken in the junior or senior year. There are early admissions and deferred admissions plans. Applications should be filed by July 1 for fall entry and January 8 for spring entry, along with a $30 fee. The college accepts all applicants. Notification is sent on a rolling basis.

Transfer: 1731 transfer students enrolled in 2001-2002. Transfer students must submit official transcripts from previously attended colleges or universities and have a minimum GPA of 2.0. 30 credits of 120 must be completed at WSU.

Visiting: There are regularly scheduled orientations for prospective students. There are guides for informal visits and visitors may sit in on classes and stay overnight. To schedule a visit, contact John Allred at *jdallred@weber.edu.*

Financial Aid: In 2001-2002, 61% of all freshmen and 72% of continuing students received some form of financial aid. 44% of freshmen and 48% of continuing students received need-based aid. The average freshman award was $5325. Of that total, scholarships or need-based grants averaged $2950; and loans averaged $2250. The average financial indebtedness of the 2001 graduate was $8500. The FAFSA and the college's own financial statement are required. The fall application deadline is March 1.

International Students: There are 261 international students enrolled. The school actively recruits these students. They must take the college's own test.

Computers: The mainframes are a DEC VAX 9000 and an 8700. All students may access the system. There are no time limits and no fees.

Graduates: In 2001, 1681 bachelor's degrees were awarded. The most popular majors were sales and service technology (11%), teacher education (6%), and computer science (6%). In an average class, 10% graduate in 3 years, 21% in 4 years, 31% in 5 years, and 39% in 6 years. 206 companies recruited on campus in 2000-2001. Of the 2000 graduating class, 26% were enrolled in graduate school within 6 months of graduation and 63% were employed.

Admissions Contact: Christopher C. Rivera, Director of Admissions. A video is available. E-mail: *crivera@weber.edu*
Web: *www.weber.edu/admissions*

WESTMINSTER COLLEGE C-2
(Formerly Westminster College of Salt Lake City)
Salt Lake City, UT 84105 **(801) 832-2200**
(800) 748-4753; Fax: (801) 484-3252

Full-time: 515 men, 900 women	**Faculty:** 109; IIB, av$
Part-time: 165 men, 210 women	**Ph.D.s:** 84%
Graduate: 290 men, 230 women	**Student/Faculty:** 13 to 1
Year: 4-4-1, summer session	**Tuition:** $12800
Application Deadline: open	**Room & Board:** $4600
Freshman Class: n/av	
SAT I or ACT required	**COMPETITIVE**

Westminster College, founded in 1875, is a private institution offering undergraduate programs through the Bill and Vieve Gore School of Business, the St. Marks Westminster School of Nursing and Health Sciences, the School of Arts and Sciences, and the School of Education. Figures in the above capsule are approximate. There are 4 undergraduate and 4 graduate schools. In addition to regional accreditation, Westminster College has baccalaureate program accreditation with ACBSP and NLN. The library contains 88,086 volumes, 114,183 microform items, and 3819 audiovisual forms/CDs, and subscribes to 348 periodicals. Computerized library services include the card catalog, interlibrary loans, and database searching. Special learning facilities include a multipurpose theater. The 27-acre campus is in a suburban area 6 miles southeast of downtown Salt Lake City. Including residence halls, there are 20 buildings.

Student Life: 94% of undergraduates are from Utah. Others are from 27 states, 21 foreign countries, and Canada. 75% are from public schools. 91% are white. 60% are claim no religious affiliation; 33% Buddhist, Greek Orthodox, Christian, LDS, Presbyterian, Episcopalian. The average age of freshmen is 18; all undergraduates, 24. 26% do not continue beyond their first year; 46% remain to graduate.

Housing: 374 students can be accommodated in college housing, which includes single-sex and coed dormitories and off-campus apartments. On-campus housing is guaranteed for all 4 years. 87% of students commute. All students may keep cars.

Activities: There are no fraternities or sororities. There are 41 groups on campus, including art, choir, chorale, chorus, computers, dance, drama, ethnic, gay, honors, international, jazz band, literary magazine, musical theater, newspaper, orchestra, political, professional, religious, social service, student government, and yearbook. Popular campus events include International Fest, Spring Fling, and Awards Day.

Sports: There are 2 intercollegiate sports for men and 2 for women, and 7 intramural sports for men and 7 for women. Facilities include a playing field, tennis courts, a gym, a weight room, a sand volleyball court, and an aerobics/yoga room.

Disabled Students: 85% of the campus is accessible. Wheelchair ramps, elevators, special parking, specially equipped rest rooms, special class scheduling, and lowered drinking fountains are available.

Services: Counseling and information services are available, as is tutoring in most subjects. There is a reader service for the blind, and remedial math, reading, and writing.

Campus Safety and Security: Measures include 24-hour foot and vehicle patrol, self-defense education, escort service, and informal discussions. There are pamphlets/posters/films, emergency telephones, lighted pathways/sidewalks, and separate dorm security.

Programs of Study: Westminster College confers B.A. and B.S. degrees. Master's degrees are also awarded. Bachelor's degrees are awarded in BIOLOGICAL SCIENCE (biology/biological science), BUSINESS (accounting, business administration and management, and marketing/retailing/merchandising), COMMUNICATIONS AND THE ARTS (communications, English, and fine arts), COMPUTER AND PHYSICAL SCIENCE (chemistry, computer science, mathematics, and physics), EDUCATION (early childhood, elementary, and secondary), ENGINEERING AND ENVIRONMENTAL DESIGN (aviation administration/management), HEALTH PROFESSIONS (nursing), SOCIAL SCIENCE (economics, history, human development, philosophy, psychology, social science, and sociology). Nursing, biology, and English are the strongest academically. Business, biology, and nursing are the largest.

Required: To graduate, all students must complete at least 124 credit hours, which include liberal education and major requirements, with a minimum 2.0 GPA and 40-80 hours in the major.

Special: The college offers internships in every major, study abroad in England, Spain, and Mexico, B.A.-B.S. degrees, dual and student-designed majors, a 3-2 engineering degree at USC at Los Angeles or Washington University in St. Louis, and freshman seminar courses. There is 1 national honor society, including Phi Beta Kappa, a freshman honors program, and 1 departmental honors program.

Faculty/Classroom: 50% of faculty are male; 50%, female. 89% teach undergraduates. No introductory courses are taught by graduate students. The average class size in an introductory lecture is 18; in a laboratory, 12; and in a regular course, 15.

Admissions: 50% of recent freshmen were in the top fifth of their class; 83% were in the top two fifths. There was 1 National Merit finalist. 6 freshmen graduated first in their class.

Requirements: The SAT I or ACT is required. In addition, applicants must be graduates of an accredited secondary school or have a GED certificate. An interview is recommended. Applications are accepted on-line and or on computer disk. A GPA of 2.5 is required. AP and CLEP credits are accepted. Important factors in the admissions decision are evidence of special talent, extracurricular activities record, and advanced placement or honor courses.

Procedure: Freshmen are admitted to all sessions. Entrance exams should be taken in the junior or senior year of high school. There are early admissions and deferred admissions plans. Application deadlines are open. Check with the school for current fee.

Transfer: 190 transfer students enrolled in a recent year. Transfer students must have a minimum 2.0 GPA and be in good standing at all previously attended colleges. 36 credits of 124 must be completed at Westminster College.

Visiting: There are regularly scheduled orientations for prospective students, including a welcome program, lunch, various workshops, a campus tour, and meetings with faculty. There are guides for informal visits and visitors may sit in on classes. To schedule a visit, contact Mary Hyland, Director of Admissions.

Financial Aid: In a recent year, 98% of all freshmen and 78% of continuing students received some form of financial aid. 72% of freshmen and 52% of continuing students received need-based aid. The average freshman award was $9615. Of that total, scholarships or need-based grants averaged $6725 ($15,581 maximum); loans averaged $2620 ($7925 maximum); and work contracts averaged $2717 ($3100 maximum). 56% of undergraduates work part time. Average annual earnings from campus work are $2400. Westminster College is a member of CSS. The FAFSA is required. Check with the school for current deadlines.

International Students: There were 29 international students enrolled in a recent year. The school actively recruits these students. They must score 550 on the written TOEFL or take the MELAB.

Computers: The mainframe is an HP 9000. There are 238 networked PCs plus computer availability and hookups in the residence halls and library. All students may access the system 7 A.M. to 11 P.M. There are no time limits and no fees. It is strongly recommended that all students have a personal computer.

Graduates: In a recent year, 324 bachelor's degrees were awarded. The most popular majors were business (19%), accounting (13%), and psychology (11%). In an average class, 2% graduate in 3 years, 37% in 4 years, 46% in 5 years, and 48% in 6 years. 106 companies recruited on campus in a recent year.

Admissions Contact: Mary Hyland, Director of Admissions.
E-mail: *admispub@wcslc.edu* Web: *www.wcslc.edu*

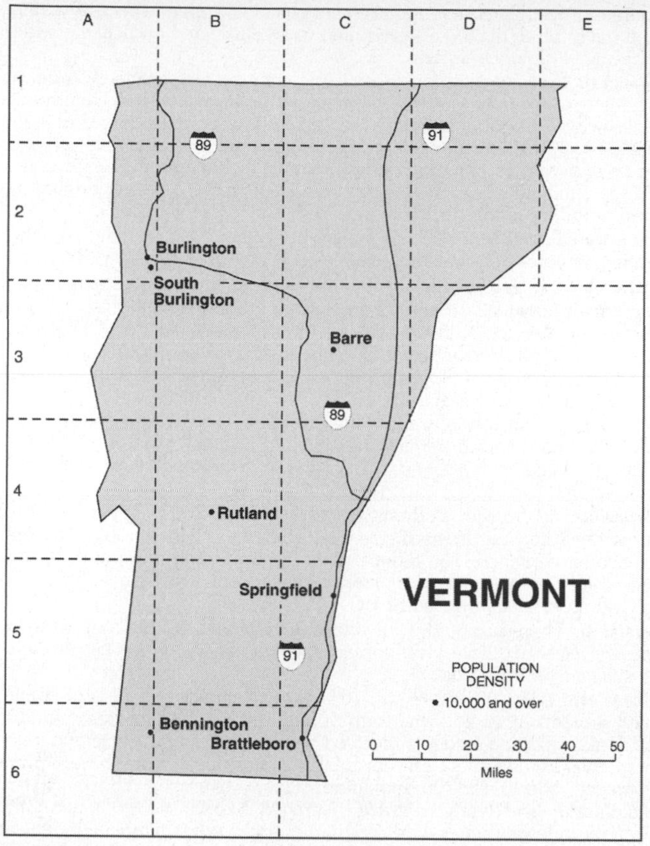

BENNINGTON COLLEGE
Bennington, VT 05201

A-6
(802) 442-6349
(800) 833-6845; Fax: (802) 440-4320

Full-time: 172 men, 364 women
Part-time: 1 man
Graduate: 43 men, 93 women
Year: trimesters
Application Deadline: January 1
Freshman Class: 644 applied, 484 accepted, 185 enrolled
SAT I Verbal/Math: 620/571
Faculty: 61
Ph.D.s: 67%
Student/Faculty: 9 to 1
Tuition: $25,000
Room & Board: $6350
VERY COMPETITIVE

Bennington College, founded in 1932, is a private liberal arts institution where students design their own programs in consultation with faculty, who are active practitioners of the disciplines they teach. The 2 libraries contain 122,954 volumes, 6110 microform items, and 12,688 audiovisual forms/CDs, and subscribe to 1600 periodicals. Computerized library services include the card catalog, interlibrary loans, and database searching. Special learning facilities include a learning resource center, art gallery, radio station, observatory, dance archives, script library, photography darkrooms, electronic music studio and music practice rooms, several theaters and dance studios, ceramics studio and kilns, greenhouse, working community farm, pond for biological studies, and early childhood center. The 550-acre campus is in a small town 42 miles east of Albany. Including residence halls, there are 59 buildings.

Student Life: 95% of undergraduates are from out of state, mostly the Northeast. Others are from 43 states, 23 foreign countries, and Canada. 82% are white; 11% foreign nationals. The average age of freshmen is 18; all undergraduates, 20. 21% do not continue beyond their first year; 71% remain to graduate.

Housing: 600 students can be accommodated in college housing, which includes coed dormitories and off-campus apartments. On-campus housing is guaranteed for all 4 years. 98% of students live on campus; of those, 95% remain on campus on weekends. All students may keep cars.

Activities: There are no fraternities or sororities. There are 26 groups on campus, including art, band, chess, choir, chorus, dance, drama, ethnic, film, gay, international, jazz band, literary magazine, musical theater, newspaper, opera, orchestra, photography, political, radio and TV, religious, social, social service, student government, and symphony. Popular campus events include Sunfest, faculty concerts, and Swing into Spring.

Sports: There are 1 intercollegiate sport for men and 1 for women, and 4 intramural sports for men and 4 for women. Facilities include soccer and other playing fields, a basketball court, a karate and aerobics studio, a weight room, hiking and biking areas, a climbing wall, and cardiovascular exercise equipment. Rockclimbing, canoeing, caving, snowshoeing, whitewater rafting, and cross-country skiing facilities are available in the surrounding area.

Disabled Students: 85% of the campus is accessible. Wheelchair ramps, elevators, special parking, specially equipped rest rooms, lowered drinking fountains, special fire alarms in houses, and amplifiers on phones are available.

Services: There is remedial writing. Tutoring for learning disabilities is available in the town of Bennington at a cost to the student.

Campus Safety and Security: Measures include 24-hour foot and vehicle patrol, escort service, shuttle buses, and informal discussions. There are pamphlets/posters/films, emergency telephones, and lighted pathways/sidewalks.

Programs of Study: Bennington confers the B.A. degree. Master's degrees are also awarded. Bachelor's degrees are awarded in BIOLOGICAL SCIENCE (biochemistry, biology/biological science, ecology, and environmental biology), COMMUNICATIONS AND THE ARTS (art, Chinese, comparative literature, creative writing, dance, dramatic arts, English, film arts, fine arts, French, German, Italian, languages, literature, music, photography, Spanish, and visual and performing arts), COMPUTER AND PHYSICAL SCIENCE (chemistry, computer science, mathematics, natural sciences, and physics), EDUCATION (early childhood and education), ENGINEERING AND ENVIRONMENTAL DESIGN (architecture and environmental science), HEALTH PROFESSIONS (premedicine and preveterinary science), SOCIAL SCIENCE (anthropology, child care/child and family studies, developmental psychology, European studies, history, history of philosophy, humanities, interdisciplinary studies, international relations, liberal arts/general studies, philosophy, psychology, social science, and sociology). Interdisciplinary studies, literature, and visual and performing arts are the largest.

Required: A minimum of 128 credit hours is required to graduate. 4 courses per term (16 credits) must be completed by full-time students, and no more than half a student's course work may be in the major field. Students must also complete a Field Work Term (job/internship) for each term in residence. Students' programs must reflect breadth and depth in curricular choices, and the written plan process must be completed successfully.

Special: 8-week work/internships are required all 4 years (during January and February). Cross-registration with Southern Vermont and Williams Colleges is possible. In addition, study abroad, dual, and student-designed majors are offered. Grading is pass/fail with an extensive written evaluation; letter grades are optional. A.B.A./M.A.T. program is offered for teacher certification.

Faculty/Classroom: 59% of faculty are male; 41%, female. All teach undergraduates, and do research. Graduate students teach 1% of introductory courses. The average class size in an introductory lecture is 20; in a laboratory, 12; and in a regular course, 18.

Admissions: 75% of the 2001-2002 applicants were accepted. The SAT I scores for the 2001-2002 freshman class were: Verbal--5% below 500, 31% between 500 and 599, 45% between 600 and 700, and 19% above 700; Math--19% below 500, 40% between 500 and 599, 33% between 600 and 700, and 8% above 700. 58% of the current freshmen were in the top fifth of their class; 91% were in the top two fifths.

Requirements: The SAT I or ACT is required. In addition, applicants should have 16 credits, including 4 units in English, 3 each in math, science, and social studies, 2 or 3 in foreign language, and 2 in history; art and music courses are highly recommended. Essays and an interview are required, and a portfolio is recommended for certain majors. The GED is accepted. Important factors in the admissions decision are evidence of special talent, extracurricular activities record, and personality/intangible qualities. Applications may be downloaded from the college web site.

Procedure: Freshmen are admitted fall and spring. Entrance exams should be taken during the spring of the junior year or the fall of the senior year. There are early decision, early admissions, and deferred admissions plans. Early decision applications should be filed by November 15; regular applications, by January 1 for fall entry and January 1 for spring entry. Notification of early decision is sent December 1; regular decision, April 1. 22 early decision candidates were accepted for the 2001-2002 class. 5% of all applicants are on a waiting list; 22 were accepted in 2001.

Transfer: 24 transfer students enrolled in 2001-2002. Applicants must submit secondary school reports, college transcripts, and recommendations from 2 faculty members. They must also submit SAT I or ACT scores and interview with a member of the admissions staff. 64 credits of 128 must be completed at Bennington.

Visiting: There are regularly scheduled orientations for prospective students, including lunches with students and faculty, dinner and socializing, class visitation, and interviews. There are guides for informal visits and visitors may sit in on classes and stay overnight. To schedule a visit, contact the Admissions Office at (802) 440-4312.

Financial Aid: In 2001-2002, 85% of all freshmen and 86% of continuing students received some form of financial aid. 62% of freshmen and 68% of continuing students received need-based aid. The average freshman award was $17,125. Of that total, scholarships or need-based grants averaged $14,445; loans averaged $2607 ($5000 maximum); and work contracts averaged $1500 (maximum). The average financial indebtedness of the 2001 graduate was $18,475. Bennington is a member of CSS. The FAFSA, the college's own financial statement, and student and parent tax returns are required. The fall application deadline is March 1.

International Students: There are 59 international students enrolled. The school actively recruits these students. They must score 550 on the written TOEFL and also take the SAT I or the ACT.

Computers: About 60 computers are available in the Computer Center, Language and Cultures Center, Commons, Visual and Performing Arts Center, and Crossett Library, with full access to the Internet and Web. Student housing on campus is fully networked, and students may access the network with their own computers. All students may access the system. There are no time limits and no fees. It is strongly recommended that all students have a personal computer.

Graduates: In 2001, 105 bachelor's degrees were awarded. The most popular majors were visual and performing arts (23%), interdisciplinary studies (17%), and social sciences (13%). In an average class, 65% graduate in 5 years.

Admissions Contact: Deane Bogardus, Director of Admissions and The First Year. E-mail: *admissions@bennington.edu*
Web: *www.benninton.edu*

BURLINGTON COLLEGE
Burlington, VT 05401 — A-2
(802) 862-9616
(800) 862-9616; Fax: (802) 660-4331

Full-time: 58 men, 109 women	**Faculty:** 66 part time
Part-time: 40 men, 60 women	**Ph.D.s:** 20%
Graduate: none	**Student/Faculty:** n/av
Year: semesters, summer session	**Tuition:** $10,640
Application Deadline: August 1	**Room & Board:** n/app
Freshman Class: 68 applied, 66 accepted, 52 enrolled	
SAT I or ACT: not required	**SPECIAL**

Burlington College, founded in 1972, is a private institution offering a small, flexible, and nontraditional liberal arts program, residential and nonresidential, geared toward the adult learner. The library contains 4000 volumes and 785 audiovisual forms/CDs, and subscribes to 100 periodicals. Computerized library services include interlibrary loans and database searching. Students also have borrowing privileges at nearby University of Vermont Library. Special learning facilities include a learning resource center, art gallery, and a film-production studio. The 1-acre campus is in an urban area in Burlington. There are 2 buildings.

Student Life: 54% of undergraduates are from Vermont. Others are from 24 states, 3 foreign countries, and Canada. 95% are from public schools. 90% are white. The average age of freshmen is 19; all undergraduates, 28. 50% do not continue beyond their first year.

Housing: 30 students can be accommodated in college housing, which includes single-sex and coed dormitories and on-campus apartments. On-campus housing is available on a first-come, first-served basis, with 8 units reserved for freshmen. Priority is given to out-of-town students. 89% of students commute. Alcohol is not permitted. All students may keep cars.

Activities: There are no fraternities or sororities. There are some groups and organizations on campus, including film, literary magazine, photography, student government, and yearbook. Popular campus events include coffeehouses, community service trips, and film society screenings.

Sports: There is no sports program at BC.

Disabled Students: All of the campus is accessible. Wheelchair ramps, special parking, specially equipped rest rooms, special class scheduling, lowered drinking fountains, and lowered telephones are available.

Services: Counseling and information services are available, as is tutoring in most subjects. There is remedial math, reading, and writing.

Campus Safety and Security: Measures include informal discussions and distribution of campus safety and security policies and procedures.

Programs of Study: BC confers the B.A. degree. Associate degrees are also awarded. Bachelor's degrees are awarded in COMMUNICATIONS AND THE ARTS (film arts, fine arts, and literature), SOCIAL SCIENCE (human services, humanities, and psychology). Psychology, human services, and film studies are the strongest academically. Film and psychology are the largest.

Required: To graduate, all students are required to satisfactorily complete at least 120 semester credits, including 36 to 45 upper-level credits in their major. Distribution requirements include 9 credits each in the following divisions: personal vision, human community, and natural environment. Specific course requirements include 3 credits each in writing and math. Students are also required to take a 3-credit practicum within their areas of concentration.

Special: Cross-registration is available with the University of Vermont, St. Michael's Trinity College, Champlain College, and the Community College of Vermont; internships through various organizations and work-study programs with nonprofit organizations are also available. BC also offers dual majors, interdisciplinary majors, including transpersonal psychology, individualized majors, independent study, a nonresidential degree program, credit for life experience, and pass/fail options.

Faculty/Classroom: 48% of faculty are male; 52%, female. All teach undergraduates. The average class size in a regular course is 8 to 12.

Admissions: 97% of the 2001-2002 applicants were accepted.

Requirements: BC requires a high school diploma or the GED, and a successful interview with the Director of Admissions. AP and CLEP credits are accepted. Personality/intangible qualities is an important factor in the admissions decision. Applications are accepted on computer disk and on-line via CollegeLink.

Procedure: Freshmen are admitted to all sessions. There are early admissions and deferred admissions plans. Applications should be filed by August 1 for fall entry, along with a $30 fee. Notification is sent on a rolling basis.

Transfer: 60 transfer students enrolled in 2001-2002. Applicants must meet the same requirements as new students. High school transcripts precede acceptance. The Independent Degree Program requires 45 college credits prior to entrance. Transcripts precede acceptance. 30 credits of 120 must be completed at BC.

Visiting: There are guides for informal visits and visitors may sit in on classes. To schedule a visit, contact the Admissions Office by phone or at *sullivan@burlcol.edu*.

Financial Aid: In 2001-2002, 70% of all freshmen and 71% of continuing students received some form of financial aid. 39% of freshmen and 69% of continuing students received need-based aid. The average freshman award was $7900. Of that total, scholarships or need-based grants averaged $3570 ($8200 maximum); loans averaged $3305 ($7625 maximum); and work contracts averaged $1025 ($2000 maximum). 38% of undergraduates work part time. The average financial indebtedness of the 2001 graduate was $14,748. The FAFSA is required. The priority fall application deadline is August 1.

International Students: There are 3 international students enrolled. It is recommended tat thses students take the TOEFL, scoring at least 550.

Computers: The mainframe is a Scan network. There are 19 PCs in 2 labs, 2 in the library, and 3 in student workstations. All students may access the system 80 hours per week. There are no time limits. The fee is $45 per semester. It is strongly recommended that all students have a personal computer.

Graduates: In 2001, 30 bachelor's degrees were awarded. The most popular majors were writing/journalism (36%), transpersonal psychology (30%), and psychology (17%).

Admissions Contact: Cathleen Sullivan, Assistant Director of Admissions. A video is available. E-mail: *admissions@burlcol.edu*
Web: *www.burlingtoncollege.edu*

CASTLETON STATE COLLEGE
Castleton, VT 05735 — B-4
(802) 468-1213
(800) 639-8521; Fax: (802) 468-1476

Full-time: 561 men, 797 women	**Faculty:** 85; IIB, --$
Part-time: 45 men, 139 women	**Ph.D.s:** 92%
Graduate: 31 men, 83 women	**Student/Faculty:** 16 to 1
Year: semesters, summer session	**Tuition:** $5402 ($11,308)
Application Deadline: open	**Room & Board:** $5530
Freshman Class: 1082 applied, 1007 accepted, 393 enrolled	
SAT I Verbal/Math: 460/460	**LESS COMPETITIVE**

Castleton State College, founded in 1787, is the oldest institution of higher learning in Vermont. As part of the Vermont State Colleges system, it offers a state-supported undergraduate and graduate program in liberal arts, teacher preparation, and professional studies. In addition to regional accreditation, Castleton has baccalaureate program accreditation with CSWE and NLN. The library contains 126,044 volumes, 560,479 microform items, and 2956 audiovisual forms/CDs, and subscribes to 412 periodicals. Computerized library services include the card catalog, interlibrary loans, and database searching. Special learning facilities include a learning resource center, art gallery, radio station, TV studio, observatory, and theater. The 160-acre campus is in a rural area 11 miles west of Rutland. Including residence halls, there are 24 buildings.

Student Life: 65% of undergraduates are from Vermont. Others are from 25 states and 2 foreign countries. 98% are white. The average age of freshmen is 19; all undergraduates, 22. 30% do not continue beyond their first year; 41% remain to graduate.

Housing: 702 students can be accommodated in college housing, which includes single-sex and coed dormitories. On-campus housing is guaranteed for the freshman year only and is available on a lottery system for upperclassmen. 60% of students commute. All students may keep cars.

Activities: There are no fraternities or sororities. There are 48 groups on campus, including art, band, cheerleading, choir, chorale, chorus, computers, dance, drama, environmental, ethnic, film, gay, honors, international, jazz band, literary magazine, musical theater, newspaper, photography, political, professional, radio and TV, religious, social, social service, sports, student government, and yearbook. Popular campus events include Spring, Winter, Alumni Weekends, and Martin Luther King Jr. Celebration.

Sports: There are 8 intercollegiate sports for men and 8 for women, and 9 intramural sports for men and 9 for women. Facilities include a 6-lane swimming pool, 2 racquetball courts, a fitness center, a recreation gym, and the nearby 2000-acre Pond Hill Ranch with more than 70 miles of trails, swimming, sailing, fishing, and golf facilities.

Disabled Students: All of the campus is accessible. Wheelchair ramps, elevators, special parking, specially equipped rest rooms, special class scheduling, lowered drinking fountains, and lowered telephones are available.

Services: Counseling and information services are available, as is tutoring in every subject. There is a reader service for the blind, and remedial math, reading, and writing.

Campus Safety and Security: Measures include 24-hour foot and vehicle patrol, self-defense education, escort service, and informal discussions. There are pamphlets/posters/films, emergency telephones, and lighted pathways/sidewalks.

Programs of Study: Castleton confers B.A., B.S., and B.S.W. degrees. Associate and master's degrees are also awarded. Bachelor's degrees are awarded in BIOLOGICAL SCIENCE (biology/biological science), BUSINESS (business administration and management), COMMUNICATIONS AND THE ARTS (art, communications, dramatic arts, literature, music, and Spanish), COMPUTER AND PHYSICAL SCIENCE (computer science, geology, mathematics, and natural sciences), EDUCATION (physical), ENGINEERING AND ENVIRONMENTAL DESIGN (environmental science), HEALTH PROFESSIONS (health science and sports medicine), SOCIAL SCIENCE (criminal justice, history, psychology, social science, social work, and sociology). Nursing, athletic training, and science are the strongest academically. Business and teacher preparation are the largest.

Required: All students must maintain a GPA of 2.0 while taking 122 semester hours, including 30 or more in their major. Distribution requirements include 3 courses each in literature and the arts, 2 each in math and natural sciences, and 1 each in foreign cultures, history, philosophy and psychology, and social analysis. Specific courses include computers, communication, and an introduction to liberal arts.

Special: Cross-registration with other Vermont State Colleges, co-op programs, internships, study abroad, and work-study programs are available. In addition, B.A.-B.S. degrees, dual majors, student-designed majors in history, math, and social sciences, a 3-2 engineering degree with Clarkson University, credit for life experience, nondegree study, and pass/fail options are offered. There are 8 national honor societies and 4 departmental honors programs.

Faculty/Classroom: 55% of faculty are male; 45%, female. All teach undergraduates, 50% both teach and do research. Graduate students teach 1% of introductory courses. The average class size in an introductory lecture is 20; in a laboratory, 14; and in a regular course, 18.

Admissions: 93% of the 2001-2002 applicants were accepted. The SAT I scores for the 2001-2002 freshman class were: Verbal--58% below 500, 36% between 500 and 599, 6% between 600 and 700, and 1% above 700; Math--66% below 500, 31% between 500 and 599, and 3% between 600 and 700.

Requirements: The SAT I or ACT is required. In addition, the college recommends that candidates have 4 years of English, 3 each of math, and social studies or history, 2 each of foreign language and science, and 2 to 4 of electives. An essay is required and an interview is recommended. The GED is accepted. A GPA of 2.5 is required. AP and CLEP credits are accepted. Important factors in the admissions decision are advanced placement or honor courses, leadership record, and recommendations by school officials. Applications are accepted on-line through the Castleton web page.

Procedure: Freshmen are admitted fall and spring. Entrance exams should be taken during the spring of the junior year or fall of the senior year. There are early admissions and deferred admissions plans. Application deadlines are open. The application fee is $30.

Transfer: 148 transfer students enrolled in a recent year. Transfer applicants must have a 2.0 GPA. An associate degree, 15 credit hours, and an interview are recommended. 30 credits of 122 must be completed at Castleton.

Visiting: There are regularly scheduled orientations for prospective students, including meetings with an admissions counselor, faculty, and coaches as well as a campus tour. There are guides for informal visits and visitors may sit in on classes. To schedule a visit, contact the Admissions Office.

Financial Aid: In 2001-2002, 94% of all freshmen and 83% of continuing students received some form of financial aid. 76% of freshmen and 65% of continuing students received need-based aid. The average freshman award was $8200. Of that total, scholarships or need-based grants averaged $3200; loans averaged $2890; and work contracts averaged $300. 38% of undergraduates work part time. Average annual earnings from campus work are $1000. Castleton is a member of CSS. The FAFSA is required. The fall application deadline is March 15.

International Students: There were 3 international students enrolled in a recent year. They must score 500 on the written TOEFL.

Computers: The mainframes are a 8 Novell network servers for use of students and college employees. More than 180 computers are available for student use. The campus is completely wired for Internet access. All residence halls are wired, 1 port per student. All students may access the system. There are no time limits and no fees.

Graduates: In 2001, 270 bachelor's degrees were awarded. The most popular majors were business (11%), communication (11%), and sociology (9%). In an average class, 4% graduate in 3 years, 27% in 4 years, 39% in 5 years, and 41% in 6 years.

Admissions Contact: Bill Allen, Dean of Enrollment.
E-mail: *info@castleton.edu* Web: *www.castleton.edu*

CHAMPLAIN COLLEGE — A-2
Burlington, VT 05402-0670 (802) 860-2727
(800) 570-5858; Fax: (802) 860-2767

Full-time: 699 men, 795 women	**Faculty:** 76; III, --$
Part-time: 473 men, 556 women	**Ph.D.s:** 34%
Graduate: none	**Student/Faculty:** 20 to 1
Year: semesters, summer session	**Tuition:** $11,605
Application Deadline: open	**Room & Board:** $8075
Freshman Class: 1617 applied, 1106 accepted, 513 enrolled	
SAT I Verbal/Math: 470/490	**ACT:** 20 **COMPETITIVE**

Champlain College, founded in 1878, emphasizes independent thinking, teaching academic skills, and practical knowledge required for professional success. Students earn their bachelor's degree, with an embedded associate's degree, in one of 23 career-oriented majors. Internship opportunities are built into the curriculum. In addition to regional accreditation, Champlain has baccalaureate program accreditation with CAAHEP. The library contains 60,000 volumes, 19,200 microform items, and 250 audiovisual forms/CDs, and subscribes to 255 periodicals. Computerized library services include the card catalog, interlibrary loans, and database searching. Special learning facilities include a learning resource center and video production studio, and several multimedia and graphic design studios. The 19-acre campus is in a suburban area in the Hill Section of Burlington. Including residence halls, there are 35 buildings.

Student Life: 56% of undergraduates are from out of state, mostly the Northeast. Others are from 29 states, 31 foreign countries, and Canada. 85% are from public schools. 92% are white. The average age of freshmen is 18; all undergraduates, 21. 29% do not continue beyond their first year; 80% remain to graduate.

Housing: 625 students can be accommodated in college housing, which includes single-sex and coed dormitories. In addition, there are special-interest houses, an international dorm, and a wellness dorm. On-campus housing is available on a first-come, first-served basis and is available on a lottery system for upperclassmen. 59% of students commute. Alcohol is not permitted. A limited number of students may keep cars.

Activities: There are no fraternities or sororities. There are more than 20 groups on campus, including cheerleading, chorus, computers, drama, flash animation, gay, honors, international, literary magazine, outing, photography, professional, religious, sailing, social, social service, student government, and yearbook. Popular campus events include skiing/snowboarding trips, Spring Meltdown, and "Get Real" community service connection.

Sports: There are 6 intramural sports for men and 6 for women. Athletic and recreation facilities are offered through the community YMCA and a local tennis club, hockey rink, park, and ski resorts.

Disabled Students: 50% of the campus is accessible. Wheelchair ramps, elevators, special parking, specially equipped rest rooms, special class scheduling, lowered drinking fountains, and lowered telephones are available.

Services: Counseling and information services are available, as is tutoring in some subjects, including math, accounting, and writing. Peer tutoring is available in most subjects. Other support services include a writing assistance lab, a math lab, and note-taking services.

Campus Safety and Security: Measures include 24-hour foot and vehicle patrol, self-defense education, escort service, and shuttle buses. There are informal discussions, pamphlets/posters/films, emergency telephones, and lighted pathways/sidewalks.

Programs of Study: Champlain confers the B.S. degree. Associate degrees are also awarded. Bachelor's degrees are awarded in BUSINESS (accounting, business administration and management, hospitality management services, hotel/motel and restaurant management, international business management, management information systems, management science, marketing management, sports management, and tourism), COMMUNICATIONS AND THE ARTS (communications, communications technology, graphic design, journalism, media arts, multimedia, public relations, and telecommunications), COMPUTER AND PHYSICAL SCIENCE (computer management, computer programming, information sciences and systems, and web services), EDUCATION (early childhood and elementary), ENGINEERING AND ENVIRONMENTAL DESIGN (computer graphics, and technological management), HEALTH PROFESSIONS (allied health, radiograph medical technology, and ultrasound technology), SOCIAL SCIENCE (criminal justice, liberal arts/general studies, paralegal studies, prelaw, psychology, and social work). Computer information systems, software engineering, and criminal justice are the strongest academically. Criminal justice, multimedia/graphic design, and elementary education are the largest.

Required: A GPA of 2.0 and 120 credits are required for the B.S. degree. The core curriculum is career oriented. Courses are required in professional writing, oral communication, global history, ethics, and computer proficiency. Students must take between 30 and 60 hours in the major and a comprehensive exam in some majors.

Special: Co-op programs, internships, and study abroad in England, France, Sweden, and Switzerland are available. Dual majors are possible through the professional studies program and computer information systems program. Accelerated degree programs and student-designed majors are also available. There is a freshman honors program. All departments have honors programs.

Faculty/Classroom: 55% of faculty are male; 45%, female. All teach undergraduates. The average class size in an introductory lecture is 21; in a laboratory, 15; and in a regular course, 18.

Admissions: 68% of the 2001-2002 applicants were accepted. The SAT I scores for the 2001-2002 freshman class were: Verbal--25% below 500, 60% between 500 and 599, 14% between 600 and 700, and 1% above 700; Math--25% below 500, 58% between 500 and 599, 15% between 600 and 700, and 2% above 700. The ACT scores were 17% below 21, 60% between 21 and 23, 15% between 24 and 26, 7% between 27 and 28, and 1% above 28. 25% of the current freshmen were in the top fifth of their class; 65% were in the top two fifths.

Requirements: The SAT I or ACT is required. In addition, applicants must be graduates of an accredited high school or the equivalent, with a minimum GPA of 2.0. AP and CLEP credits are accepted. Important factors in the admissions decision are advanced placement or honor courses, recommendations by school officials, and extracurricular activities record.

Procedure: Freshmen are admitted fall and spring. Entrance exams should be taken prior to applying. There is a deferred admissions plan. Application deadlines are open. The fall 2001 application fee was $35. Notification is sent on a rolling basis.

Transfer: 155 transfer students enrolled in 2001-2002. High school and college transcripts are required. 45 credits of 120 must be completed at Champlain.

Visiting: There are regularly scheduled orientations for prospective students, including open houses and group information sessions. Personal interviews are also available with an admissions counselor. There are guides for informal visits and visitors may sit in on classes. To schedule a visit, contact the Admissions Office.

Financial Aid: In 2001-2002, 67% of all freshmen and 74% of continuing students received some form of financial aid. 59% of freshmen and 64% of continuing students received need-based aid. The average freshman award was $8580. Of that total, scholarships or need-based grants averaged $5760; and loans averaged $3047. 67% of undergraduates work part time. Average annual earnings from campus work are $1190. The FAFSA and the college's own financial statement are required. The fall application deadline is May 1.

International Students: There are 66 international students enrolled. The school actively recruits these students. They must score 500 on the written TOEFL or 173 on the electronic version and also take the SAT I or the ACT.

Computers: The mainframe is an IBM AS/400. Champlain provides more than 200 PCs for students. 5 supervised computer labs are open 7 days a week for programming, word processing, database management, accounting, desktop publishing, and other functions. A Mac lab is available as well. All students may access the system. There are no time limits and no fees. It is strongly recommended that all students have a personal computer.

Graduates: In 2001, 177 bachelor's degrees were awarded. The most popular majors were business (35%), accounting (22%), and social work (20%). In an average class, 80% graduate in 4 years. 70 companies recruited on campus in 2000-2001. Of the 2000 graduating class, 3% were enrolled in graduate school within 6 months of graduation and 97% were employed.

Admissions Contact: Josephine Churchill, Director of Admissions. A video is available. E-mail: *admission@champlain.edu*
Web: *www.champlain.edu*

COLLEGE OF SAINT JOSEPH — B-4
Rutland, VT 05701-3899 — **(802) 773-5900, ext. 205**
Fax: (802) 773-5900

Full-time: 90 men, 135 women	**Faculty:** 13
Part-time: 50 men, 120 women	**Ph.D.s:** 61%
Graduate: 35 men, 115 women	**Student/Faculty:** 17 to 1
Year: semesters, summer session	**Tuition:** $11,400
Application Deadline: open	**Room & Board:** $6100
Freshman Class: n/av	
SAT I: required	**NONCOMPETITIVE**

The College of St. Joseph, founded in 1950, is a private Catholic institution offering undergraduate programs in the arts and sciences, business, computer information science, education, psychology, and human services. The college serves a primarily commuter student body. There is 1 undergraduate and 2 graduate schools.There are 2 graduate schools. The library contains 43,000 volumes, 13,000 microform items, and 7000 audiovisual forms/CDs, and subscribes to 251 periodicals. Computerized library services include the card catalog, interlibrary loans, and database searching. Special learning facilities include a learning resource center. The 90-acre campus is in a rural area 1 mile west of Rutland. Including residence halls, there are 5 buildings.

Student Life: 53% of undergraduates are from Vermont. Others are from 13 states and 3 foreign countries. 89% are white. 55% are Catholic; 20% Protestant. The average age of freshmen is 20; all undergraduates, 25. 38% do not continue beyond their first year; 52% remain to graduate.

Housing: 160 students can be accommodated in college housing, which includes single-sex dormitories. In addition, there are special-interest houses. On-campus housing is guaranteed for all 4 years. 75% of students commute. All students may keep cars.

Activities: There are no fraternities or sororities. There are 15 groups on campus, including chorus, drama, honors, literary magazine, musical theater, newspaper, political, professional, religious, social, social service, student government, and yearbook. Popular campus events include Spring Fling, cultural event series (year round), and Student Leadership-Academic Awards Dinner.

Sports: There are 2 intercollegiate sports for men and 2 for women, and 3 intramural sports for men and 3 for women. Facilities include a 1000-seat gym, a fitness center, racquetball courts, an aerobics studio, a cross-country skiing/running trail, a softball diamond, and a soccer field.

Disabled Students: Wheelchair ramps, special parking, specially equipped rest rooms, special class scheduling, lowered drinking fountains, and lowered telephones are available.

Services: Counseling and information services are available, as is tutoring in every subject. There is remedial math, reading, writing, personal growth counseling, and spiritual counseling.

Campus Safety and Security: Measures include shuttle buses, informal discussions, pamphlets/posters/films, and emergency telephones. There are lighted pathways/sidewalks.

Programs of Study: CSJ confers B.A. and B.S. degrees. Associate and master's degrees are also awarded. Bachelor's degrees are awarded in BUSINESS (accounting, banking and finance, business administration and management, recreational facilities management, and trade and industrial supervision and management), COMMUNICATIONS AND THE ARTS (communications, English, and journalism), COMPUTER AND PHYSICAL SCIENCE (computer science), EDUCATION (computer, early childhood, elementary, secondary, and special), SOCIAL SCIENCE (American studies, history, human services, liberal arts/general studies, political science/government, prelaw, and psychology). Education is the strongest academically. Arts and sciences are the largest.

Required: To graduate, students must complete 127 credit hours with a minimum GPA of 2.0, including 12 credits in English/speech, 9 each in social/behavioral sciences and math/computer, 6 each in philosophy/religious studies and natural sciences, and 3 in fine arts. Human services majors must complete 2 internships.

Special: The college offers internships in history and political science, and in Rutland County businesses, human service agencies, and elementary and secondary schools. In addition, dual majors, study abroad, and independent and directed study options are available. There are 4 national honor societies.

Faculty/Classroom: 62% of faculty are male; 38%, female. All teach undergraduates. No introductory courses are taught by graduate students. The average class size in an introductory lecture is 15 and in a regular course, 8.

Admissions: 10% of recent freshmen were in the top fifth of their class; 60% were in the top two fifths.

Requirements: The SAT I is required and the ACT is recommended. In addition, applicants should be graduates of accredited secondary schools or have earned a GED. College preparatory study must include 4 years of English, 3 of math, 2 each of science and social studies, and 5 other academic electives. The college prefers that students rank in the upper 70% of their graduating class. An essay is required and an interview is recommended. A GPA of 2.0 is required. AP and CLEP credits are accepted. Important factors in the admissions decision are advanced placement or honor courses, leadership record, and extracurricular activities record.

Procedure: Freshmen are admitted to all sessions. Entrance exams should be taken by December of the senior year. There are early admissions and deferred admissions plans. Application deadlines are open. Check with the school for current fee.

Transfer: 34 transfer students enrolled in a recent year. Transfers must present a minimum GPA of 2.0. 30 credits of 127 must be completed at CSJ.

Visiting: There are regularly scheduled orientations for prospective students, including a campus tour, admissions interview, and visits to classes. There are guides for informal visits and visitors may sit in on classes and stay overnight. To schedule a visit, contact the Admissions Office.

Financial Aid: In a recent year, 98% of all freshmen and 62% of continuing students received some form of financial aid. 94% of freshmen and 60% of continuing students received need-based aid. The average freshman award was $11,301. Of that total, scholarships or need-based grants averaged $6693 ($11,450 maximum); loans averaged $2857 ($6625 maximum); work contracts averaged $992 ($1800 maximum); and athletic assistance averaged $759 ($5675 maximum). 59% of undergraduates work part time. Average annual earnings from campus work are $653. The average financial indebtedness of a recent graduate was $16,547. CSJ is a member of CSS. Check with the school for current deadlines.

International Students: There were 4 international students enrolled in a recent year. They must score 550 on the written TOEFL.

Computers: The mainframe is an IBM AS/400. A network of 20 PCs is available for academic use. All students may access the system. There are no time limits and no fees.

Graduates: In a recent year, 36 bachelor's degrees were awarded. The most popular majors were business management (19%), education (16%), and liberal studies (11%). In an average class, 41% graduate in 4 years, 44% in 5 years, and 44% in 6 years.

Admissions Contact: Steven Soba, Dean of Admissions.
Web: *www.csj.edu*

GODDARD COLLEGE

Plainfield, VT 05667 — C-2
(802) 454-8311, ext. 322
(800) 468-4888; Fax: (802) 454-1029

Full-time: 130 men, 189 women	**Faculty:** 14
Part-time: none	**Ph.D.s:** 71%
Graduate: 94 men, 210 women	**Student/Faculty:** 23 to 1
Year: semesters	**Tuition:** $18,092
Application Deadline: open	**Room & Board:** $2964
Freshman Class: 125 applied, 120 accepted, 68 enrolled	
SAT I Verbal/Math: 609/541	**COMPETITIVE+**

Goddard College, founded in 1938, is a private college that stresses progressive, individualized education for personal and community transformation, based on John Dewey's learning-by-involvement theory. The library contains 70,000 volumes and 1100 audiovisual forms/CDs, and subscribes to 280 periodicals. Computerized library services include interlibrary loans and database searching. Special learning facilities include a learning resource center, radio station, a holograph lab, and a video/photo studio. The 200-acre campus is in a rural area 10 miles from Montpelier. Including residence halls, there are 26 buildings.

Student Life: 87% of undergraduates are from out of state, mostly the Northeast. Others are from 49 states, 11 foreign countries, and Canada. 82% are white. The average age of freshmen is 21; all undergraduates, 26. 38% do not continue beyond their first year; 46% remain to graduate.

Housing: 225 students can be accommodated in college housing, which includes single-sex and coed dormitories and married-student housing. In addition, there are special-interest houses, and an ecology house. On-campus housing is guaranteed for all 4 years. 70% of students live on campus; of those, 75% remain on campus on weekends. Alcohol is not permitted. All students may keep cars.

Activities: There are no fraternities or sororities. There are 9 groups on campus, including art, drama, gay, jazz band, literary magazine, newspaper, photography, radio and TV, and student government. Popular campus events include .

Sports: There is no sports program at Goddard. Facilities include tennis and volleyball courts and hiking and cross-country ski trails.

Disabled Students: Wheelchair ramps, elevators, special parking, and specially equipped rest rooms are available.

Services: There is remedial writing. An adviser system requires 1-hour weekly meetings with a faculty adviser.

Campus Safety and Security: Measures include 24-hour foot and vehicle patrol, self-defense education, shuttle buses, and informal discussions. There are pamphlets/posters/films and lighted pathways/sidewalks.

Programs of Study: Goddard confers the B.A. degree. Master's degrees are also awarded. Bachelor's degrees are awarded in COMMUNICATIONS AND THE ARTS (creative writing, media arts, and visual and performing arts), EDUCATION (education), ENGINEERING AND ENVIRONMENTAL DESIGN (environmental science), SOCIAL SCIENCE (counseling/psychology, crosscultural studies, human ecology, interdisciplinary studies, social science, and women's studies). Writing, literature, and education are the strongest academically. Women's studies is the largest.

Required: All degree programs are full-time only, provide individual faculty advisers for every semester (except study leaves), and require written study plans and narrative evaluations. Individual programs of study are student designed, although the program in general is course based. There are no declared majors, but in the last semester of enrollment, all students must complete an in-depth senior study or project that may be cross- or multidisciplinary and requires foundation work comparable to a major. A total of 120 credits is required to graduate.

Special: Students and faculty design all curricula; there are no prescribed courses. Learning takes the form of group or independent studies, workshops, action projects, research, field trips, seminars, and performances. There are a number of away-from-campus study options, including a field semester involving an internship, apprenticeship, or study-travel and a semester-abroad program offered in 20 countries.

Faculty/Classroom: 57% of faculty are male; 43%, female. All teach undergraduates. No introductory courses are taught by graduate students. The average class size in an introductory lecture is 8 and in a regular course, 10.

Admissions: 96% of the 2001-2002 applicants were accepted. The SAT I scores for the 2001-2002 freshman class were: Verbal--8% below 500, 32% between 500 and 599, 43% between 600 and 700, and 16% above 700; Math--27% below 500, 48% between 500 and 599, 19% between 600 and 700, and 5% above 700. 20% of the current freshmen were in the top fifth of their class; 49% were in the top two fifths.

Requirements: Goddard admits students who can contribute to its learning community and who will thrive in a self-directed study program, and bases the admissions decision on the student's application, which includes several essays, letters of recommendation, transcripts, and samples of the student's work. A personal interview, and SAT I or ACT scores, when submitted, are also considered. AP and CLEP credits are accepted. Important factors in the admissions decision are personality/intangible qualities, advanced placement or honor courses, and evidence of special talent. Applications are accepted on-line at the school's website.

Procedure: Freshmen are admitted to all sessions. There are early decision and deferred admissions plans. Application deadlines are open. The application fee is $40. Notification is sent on a rolling basis.

Transfer: 19 transfer students enrolled in 2001-2002. College transcripts must be submitted by transfer applicants. 30 credits of 120 must be completed at Goddard.

Visiting: There are regularly scheduled orientations for prospective students, including Discover Goddard Days held in fall and spring and individual tours and interviews. There are guides for informal visits and visitors may sit in on classes and stay overnight. To schedule a visit, contact the Admissions Office at (802) 454-8311, ext. 307 or (800) 468-4888, ext. 307 or *admissions@goddard.edu*.

Financial Aid: In 2001-2002, 96% of all freshmen and 72% of continuing students received some form of financial aid, including need-based aid. The average freshman award was $13,216. Of that total, scholarships or need-based grants averaged $8392 ($12,500 maximum); loans averaged $3824 ($4625 maximum); and work contracts averaged $1000 ($1500 maximum). All undergraduates work part time. Average annual earnings from campus work are $900. The average financial indebtedness of a recent year's graduate was $14,900. The FAFSA is required.

International Students: There are 2 international students enrolled. They must score 550 on the written TOEFL.

Computers: The mainframes are an IBM 5/34 and an AS400. Many types of PCs are available for student use in the computer center, and dormitories have computer network access. There are also Mac systems available at the 2 computer labs. All students may access the system 24 hours a day, 7 days a week. There are no time limits and no fees.

Graduates: In 2001, 91 bachelor's degrees were awarded. The most popular majors were interdisciplinary liberal arts and science (91%), education (7%), and health arts and sciences (2%). In an average class, 41% graduate in 5 years, and 48% in 6 years.

Admissions Contact: Brenda Hawkins, Director of Admissions.
E-mail: *admissions@.goddard.edu* Web: *http://www.goddard.edu*

GREEN MOUNTAIN COLLEGE

Poultney, VT 05764 A-4

(802) 287-8208

(800) 776-6675; Fax: (802) 287-8099

Full-time: 339 men, 292 women	**Faculty:** 38
Part-time: 13 men, 15 women	**Ph.D.s:** 87%
Graduate: none	**Student/Faculty:** 17 to 1
Year: semesters, summer session	**Tuition:** $18,280
Application Deadline: open	**Room & Board:** $5850
Freshman Class: n/av	
SAT I: required	**ACT:** recommended

COMPETITIVE

Green Mountain College, established in 1834, is a private, nonprofit, environmental liberal arts institution. In addition to regional accreditation, GMC has baccalaureate program accreditation with NRPA. The library contains 60,000 volumes, 10,000 microform items, and 2000 audiovisual forms/CDs, and subscribes to 300 periodicals. Computerized library services include the card catalog, interlibrary loans, and database searching. Special learning facilities include a learning resource center, art gallery, organic farm, rope course, and Welsh Heritage Center. The 155-acre campus is in a small town 20 miles southwest of Rutland. Including residence halls, there are 26 buildings.

Student Life: 89% of undergraduates are from out of state, mostly the Northeast. Others are from 28 states, 18 foreign countries, and Canada. 70% are from public schools. 64% are white. The average age of freshmen is 18; all undergraduates, 21. 40% do not continue beyond their first year; 40% remain to graduate.

Housing: 649 students can be accommodated in college housing, which includes coed dormitories. Special-interest floors are also available. On-campus housing is guaranteed for all 4 years. 95% of students live on campus; of those, 80% remain on campus on weekends. All students may keep cars.

Activities: There are no fraternities or sororities. There are 30 groups on campus, including art, bagpipe band, band, Big Brothers/Big Sisters, cheerleading, choir, chorale, chorus, dance, drama, environmental, gay, honors, international, jazz band, literary magazine, newspaper, professional, religious, social, social service, student government, and yearbook. Popular campus events include Family Weekend, Honors Banquet, and Welsh Heritage Harvest Festival.

Sports: There are 7 intercollegiate sports for men and 7 for women, and 8 intramural sports for men and 7 for women. Facilities include a gym with an indoor pool, weight room, playing fields, tennis courts, a par course, fitness trail, and ropes course.

Disabled Students: 70% of the campus is accessible. Wheelchair ramps, elevators, special parking, specially equipped rest rooms, special class scheduling, and lowered drinking fountains are available.

Services: Counseling and information services are available, as is tutoring in every subject. There is remedial math, reading, and writing.

Campus Safety and Security: Measures include 24-hour foot and vehicle patrol and lighted pathways/sidewalks.

Programs of Study: GMC confers B.A., B.S., and B.F.A. degrees. Bachelor's degrees are awarded in AGRICULTURE (environmental studies), BIOLOGICAL SCIENCE (biology/biological science), BUSINESS (business administration and management, recreation and leisure services, and recreational facilities management), COMMUNICATIONS AND THE ARTS (art, arts administration/management, communications, creative writing, English, fine arts, and visual and performing arts), EDUCATION (art, elementary, English, secondary, social studies, and special), HEALTH PROFESSIONS (recreation therapy), SOCIAL SCIENCE (behavioral science, history, liberal arts/general studies, philosophy, and psychology). Recreation, elementary education, and environmental studies are the largest.

Required: To graduate, students must complete 37 hours in Environmental Liberal Arts, including 4 core courses, a 1-credit orientation course, and 8 additional courses chosen from 4 distribution categories. A minimum GPA of 2.0 is required. Students must complete 120 to 125 credit hours, with 42 to 65 hours in the major. 33 credits must be completed in upper division courses.

Special: Semester-long internships are required in all majors. Students may study abroad in Wales, Korea, England, Spain, Japan, France, and Italy. Work-study programs and a self-designed major are available. Co-op and accelerated degree programs are available in Resort and Leisure Management, as is a 4-1 MBA program with Clarkson and Southern New Hampshire Universities. There is 1 national honor society, a freshman honors program, and 4 departmental honors programs.

Faculty/Classroom: 67% of faculty are male; 33%, female. 66% teach undergraduates and 34% both teach and do research. The average class size in an introductory lecture is 25; in a laboratory, 15; and in a regular course, 14.

Admissions: 63% of the 2001-2002 applications were accepted.

Requirements: The SAT I is required and the ACT is recommended. In addition, applicants must graduate from an accredited secondary school or have a GED. 16 academic credits are required. Students must complete 4 years in English, 3 years in math, 2 to 3 years in science, and 2 years each in history and social studies. An essay is required. Interviews are recommended, along with portfolios where appropriate. A GPA of 2.4 is required. AP and CLEP credits are accepted. Important factors in the admissions decision are personality/intangible qualities, advanced placement or honor courses, and evidence of special talent.

Procedure: Freshmen are admitted fall and spring. Entrance exams should be taken in the fall of the senior year of high school. There are early admissions and deferred admissions plans. Application deadlines are open. The application fee is $30.

Transfer: 56 transfer students enrolled in 2001-2002. Transfer students need a GPA of 2.0. They must have earned a minimum of 12 credits and are required to submit an essay. The SAT I or ACT is required, along with 2 letters of recommendation and dean's statement from last school attended. 30 credits of 120 to 125 must be completed at GMC.

Visiting: There are regularly scheduled orientations for prospective students, including a campus tour, presentations by administrators, student panel, lunch in dining hall, and academic offerings. There are guides for informal visits and visitors may sit in on classes and stay overnight. To schedule a visit, contact Joann Larson, Campus Visit Coordinator at *visit@greenmtn.edu*.

Financial Aid: In 2001-2002, 83% of all freshmen and 82% of continuing students received some form of financial aid. 60% of all students received need-based aid. The average freshman award was $9215. Of that total, scholarships or need-based grants averaged $4610 ($17,000 maximum); loans averaged $4087 ($10,500 maximum); and work contracts averaged $1000 ($1300 maximum). 45% of undergraduates work part time. Average annual earnings from campus work are $1100. The average financial indebtedness of the 2001 graduate was $15,000. The FAFSA is required.

International Students: There are 48 international students enrolled. The school actively recruits these students. They must score 500 on the written TOEFL or 173 on the electronic version and also take the SAT I or the ACT.

Computers: PCs are available for student use in the computer center, student center, and residence halls. All students may access the system 24 hours/7 days a week. There are no time limits and no fees.

Graduates: In 2001, 126 bachelor's degrees were awarded. The most popular majors were education (19%), business (15%), and environmental studies (11%). In an average class, 24% graduate in 4 years, 37% in 5 years, and 37% in 6 years. 21 companies recruited on campus in 2000-2001. Of the 2000 graduating class, 4% were enrolled in graduate school within 6 months of graduation and 75% were employed.

Admissions Contact: Merrilyn Tatarczuch-Koff, Dean of Enrollment Services. A video is available. E-mail: *admiss@greenmtn.edu*
Web: *www.greenmtn.edu*

JOHNSON STATE COLLEGE

Johnson, VT 05656 C-2

(802) 635-1219

(800) 635-2356; Fax: (802) 635-1230

Full-time: 479 men, 519 women	**Faculty:** 62; IIB, -$
Part-time: 104 men, 285 women	**Ph.D.s:** 90%
Graduate: 47 men, 156 women	**Student/Faculty:** 17 to 1
Year: semesters, summer session	**Tuition:** $5252 ($11,168)
Application Deadline: see profile	**Room & Board:** $5524
Freshman Class: 760 applied, 638 accepted, 234 enrolled	
SAT I Verbal/Math: 480/460	

COMPETITIVE

Johnson State College, founded in 1828, is a public liberal arts and science college, offering more than 30 academic and professional degree programs. There is 1 graduate school. The library contains 96,584 volumes, 180,158 microform items, and 7200 audiovisual forms/CDs, and subscribes to 631 periodicals. Computerized library services include the card catalog, interlibrary loans, and database searching. Special learning facilities include a learning resource center, art gallery, radio station, and 24-hour study room. The 350-acre campus is in a small town 45 miles northeast of Burlington. Including residence halls, there are 12 buildings.

Student Life: 63% of undergraduates are from Vermont. Others are from 23 states, 6 foreign countries, and Canada. 71% are white. The average age of freshmen is 19; all undergraduates, 21.

Housing: 549 students can be accommodated in college housing, which includes coed dormitories, on-campus apartments, and married-student housing. In addition, there are special-interest houses. On-campus housing is guaranteed for all 4 years. 57% of students live on campus. Alcohol is not permitted. All students may keep cars.

Activities: There are no fraternities or sororities. There are 35 groups on campus, including art, band, choir, chorus, dance, drama, gay, international, jazz band, literary magazine, musical theater, newspaper, photography, political, professional, radio and TV, religious, social, social service, student government, and yearbook. Popular campus events include Winter Carnival, Coffee House (weekly live entertainment), and Women's History Month Celebration.

Sports: There are 5 intercollegiate sports for men and 5 for women, and 20 intramural sports for men and 20 for women. Facilities include

the athletic center which houses a 25-yard pool, a 700-seat varsity basketball court, 3 handball/racquetball courts, a weight training room, an aerobic fitness center, a 7000-square-foot multi-use gym, and a fully equipped training room.

Disabled Students: 60% of the campus is accessible. Wheelchair ramps, elevators, special parking, specially equipped rest rooms, special class scheduling, and lowered drinking fountains are available.

Services: Counseling and information services are available, as is tutoring in most subjects. There is a reader service for the blind, and remedial math, reading, and writing. The Academic Support Services Department provides accommodations for students with a documented learning disability.

Campus Safety and Security: Measures include 24-hour foot and vehicle patrol, self-defense education, escort service, and shuttle buses. There are informal discussions, pamphlets/posters/films, emergency telephones, and lighted pathways/sidewalks.

Programs of Study: Johnson State confers B.A., B.S., and B.F.A. degrees. Associate and master's degrees are also awarded. Bachelor's degrees are awarded in AGRICULTURE (natural resource management), BIOLOGICAL SCIENCE (biology/biological science and cell biology), BUSINESS (accounting, business administration and management, business systems analysis, hospitality management services, management information systems, recreational facilities management, small business management, and tourism), COMMUNICATIONS AND THE ARTS (art, creative writing, English, fine arts, jazz, journalism, music, music business management, music history and appreciation, music performance, performing arts, studio art, theater design, theater management, and visual and performing arts), COMPUTER AND PHYSICAL SCIENCE (computer management, information sciences and systems, and mathematics), EDUCATION (art, athletic training, education, elementary, English, environmental, mathematics, middle school, music, physical, recreation, science, and secondary), ENGINEERING AND ENVIRONMENTAL DESIGN (environmental science), HEALTH PROFESSIONS (allied health, health science, premedicine, and sports medicine), SOCIAL SCIENCE (anthropology, behavioral science, history, humanities, liberal arts/general studies, physical fitness/movement, political science/government, prelaw, psychology, and sociology). Environmental science, sports medicine, and outdoor education are the largest.

Required: The bachelor's degree requires completion of at least 120 credit hours of course work (not including basic skills credits), with a minimum cumulative GPA of 2.0. In addition, students must complete the general education core curriculum and an approved major as well as take a writing proficiency exam.

Special: All students are encouraged to complete an internship. Through the National Student Exchange Program, students may study at another institution or abroad in 51 countries for a semester or a year. Co-op programs are offered in business, tourism, hospitality management, and education, and cross-registration is available with other Vermont state colleges. There is 1 national honor society.

Faculty/Classroom: 58% of faculty are male; 42%, female. All teach undergraduates. No introductory courses are taught by graduate students.

Admissions: 84% of the 2001-2002 applicants were accepted. The SAT I scores for the 2001-2002 freshman class were: Verbal--58% below 500, 37% between 500 and 599, and 5% between 600 and 700; Math--71% below 500, 27% between 500 and 599, and 2% between 600 and 700. 11% of the current freshmen were in the top fifth of their class; 30% were in the top two fifths.

Requirements: The SAT I or ACT is required. In addition, successful candidates for admission have generally completed a college preparatory curriculum consisting of 4 years of English, 3 of math (2 of algebra, 1 of geometry), 3 of social sciences, and 2 of science (including 1 lab science). An official high school transcript or GED test score must be submitted with the application. In addition, 1 letter of recommendation, preferably from a guidance counselor, and SAT I or ACT scores should be sent with the application or under separate cover. Johnson State requires applicants to be in the upper 50% of their class. A GPA of 2.0 is required. AP and CLEP credits are accepted. Important factors in the admissions decision are advanced placement or honor courses, recommendations by school officials, and extracurricular activities record. Applications are accepted on-line at the school's web site and via CollegeLink, Apply, and Peterson's Universal Application.

Procedure: Freshmen are admitted fall and spring. There is a deferred admissions plan. Check with the school for current application deadlines. The application fee is $30. Notification is sent on a rolling basis.

Transfer: 106 transfer students enrolled in a recent year. A GPA of at least 2.0 is required. 30 credits of 120 must be completed at Johnson State.

Visiting: There are regularly scheduled orientations for prospective students, including a campus tour and an admission interview. Students may request to meet with a faculty member. There are guides for informal visits and visitors may sit in on classes. To schedule a visit, contact Marie Burns, Admission Receptionist.

Financial Aid: Johnson State is a member of CSS. The FAFSA is required. Check with the school for current deadlines.

International Students: There were 22 international students enrolled in a recent year. The school actively recruits these students. They must score 500 on the written TOEFL or 173 on the electronic version.

Computers: Computing Services provides students with a total of 130 Pentium PCs in 4 computer labs. All computer labs provide full access to the Internet and e-mail. All students may access the system. There are no time limits and no fees.

Graduates: In a recent year, 261 bachelor's degrees were awarded. The most popular majors were business (15%), education (13%), and psychology (11%).

Admissions Contact: Penny P. Howrigan, Asociate Dean of Enrollment Services. E-mail: *jscappy@badger.jsc.vsc.edu*
Web: *www.jsc.vsc.edu*

LYNDON STATE COLLEGE — D-2

Lyndonville, VT 05851 — (802) 626-6413
(800) 225-1998; Fax: (802) 626-6335

Full-time: 554 men, 429 women	**Faculty:** 56; IIB, -$
Part-time: 70 men, 80 women	**Ph.D.s:** 60%
Graduate: 17 men, 84 women	**Student/Faculty:** 18 to 1
Year: semesters, summer session	**Tuition:** $5793 ($11,709)
Application Deadline: open	**Room & Board:** $5520
Freshman Class: 943 applied, 903 accepted, 451 enrolled	
SAT I Verbal/Math: 470/480	**LESS COMPETITIVE**

Lyndon State College, founded in 1911 as a teachers' college, became a liberal arts school in 1962, offering undergraduate and graduate courses. There is 1 graduate school. In addition to regional accreditation, LSC has baccalaureate program accreditation with NRPA. The library contains 100,000 volumes, 10,000 microform items, and 3600 audiovisual forms/CDs, and subscribes to 545 periodicals. Computerized library services include the card catalog, interlibrary loans, and database searching. Special learning facilities include a learning resource center, art gallery, radio station, TV station, founder's museum, and meteorology lab. The 175-acre campus is in a small town in northeastern Vermont, 184 miles north of Boston. Including residence halls, there are 17 buildings.

Student Life: 56% of undergraduates are from Vermont. Others are from 20 states, 3 foreign countries, and Canada. 99% are white. The average age of freshmen is 18; all undergraduates, 22. 34% do not continue beyond their first year; 38% remain to graduate.

Housing: 500 students can be accommodated in college housing, which includes coed dormitories. On-campus housing is guaranteed for all 4 years. 56% of students commute. Alcohol is not permitted. All students may keep cars.

Activities: There are no fraternities or sororities. There are 22 groups on campus, including cheerleading, choir, chorale, chorus, drama, film, gay, honors, international, jazz band, literary magazine, newspaper, photography, political, professional, radio and TV, social, social service, student government, and yearbook. Popular campus events include Family Weekend, Alumni Weekend, and a concert series.

Sports: There are 5 intercollegiate sports for men and 5 for women, and 12 intramural sports for men and 12 for women. Facilities include a gym complex with a weight room, squash, handball, and racquetball courts, an auxiliary gym, and an Olympic-size pool; outdoor tennis courts; fields for hockey, softball, and soccer; cross-country ski trails and running trails; and access to an ice rink, nearby mountains, and a ski resort.

Disabled Students: 70% of the campus is accessible. Wheelchair ramps, elevators, special parking, specially equipped rest rooms, and lowered drinking fountains are available.

Services: Counseling and information services are available, as is tutoring in every subject. There is remedial math, reading, and writing. A math lab and a writing center are available for student use.

Campus Safety and Security: Measures include 24-hour foot and vehicle patrol, self-defense education, escort service, and lighted pathways/sidewalks. There is a security and safety service on campus as well as a 24-hour emergency rescue squad.

Programs of Study: LSC confers B.A. and B.S. degrees. Associate and master's degrees are also awarded. Bachelor's degrees are awarded in BUSINESS (accounting, business administration and management, recreation and leisure services, and sports management), COMMUNICATIONS AND THE ARTS (communications, English, graphic design, journalism, multimedia, and radio/television technology), COMPUTER AND PHYSICAL SCIENCE (atmospheric sciences and meteorology, mathematics, natural sciences, and science), EDUCATION (early childhood, elementary, English, physical, recreation, and science), HEALTH PROFESSIONS (sports medicine), SOCIAL SCIENCE (human services, interdisciplinary studies, psychology, and social science). Meteorology, natural science, and math are the strongest academically. Education, communications, and parks and recreation are the largest.

Required: All students must maintain a minimum GPA of 2.0 while taking 122 semester hours. Distribution requirements include 28 credits in arts, humanities, math and science, and social and behavioral sciences. Required courses include freshman English and college algebra.

Special: Cooperative programs in a variety of businesses, including local ski areas, social agencies, and radio and TV stations, internships in recreation programs and communications, and study abroad in Nova Scotia and England are available. B.A.-B.S. degrees, work-study, a general studies degree, dual and student-designed majors, a 3-2 engineering degree with Norwich University in Vermont, credit for life experience, nondegree study, and pass/fail options also are offered. There is 1 national honor society, and 2 departmental honors programs.

Faculty/Classroom: 66% of faculty are male; 34%, female. All teach undergraduates. The average class size in an introductory lecture is 20; in a laboratory, 16; and in a regular course, 16.

Admissions: 96% of the 2001-2002 applicants were accepted.

Requirements: The SAT I or ACT is required. In addition, lSC recommends that applicants have 4 years of English and 2 each of math, foreign language, history, and science. An essay is required, as is a recommendation from the high school principal or guidance counselor. An interview is recommended. The GED is accepted. LSC requires applicants to be in the upper 50% of their class. A GPA of 2.0 is required. AP and CLEP credits are accepted. Important factors in the admissions decision are advanced placement or honor courses, recommendations by school officials, and leadership record.

Procedure: Freshmen are admitted fall and spring. Entrance exams should be taken . There are early decision, early admissions, and deferred admissions plans. Application deadlines are open. The application fee is $30. Notification is sent on a rolling basis.

Transfer: 71 transfer students enrolled in a recent year. Interviews are recommended for transfer students. An official transcript from each college attended is required. 30 credits of 122 must be completed at LSC.

Visiting: There are regularly scheduled orientations for prospective students, including a tour, an information session, and faculty presentations. There are guides for informal visits and visitors may sit in on classes and stay overnight. To schedule a visit, contact the Admissions Office.

Financial Aid: LSC is a member of CSS. The FAFSA and parent and student income tax forms are required. Check with the school for current deadlines.

International Students: There were 7 international students enrolled in a recent year. They must score 500 on the written TOEFL.

Computers: There are PCs and Macs available in 7 computer labs on campus. All students may access the system. There are no time limits.

Graduates: In a recent year, 207 bachelor's degrees were awarded. The most popular majors were communications (20%), business (17%), and parks and recreation (15%). In an average class, 21% graduate in 4 years, 35% in 5 years, and 38% in 6 years.

Admissions Contact: Admissions. E-mail: *admissions@lsc.vsc.edu*
Web: *www.lsc.vsc.edu*

MARLBORO COLLEGE B-6
Marlboro, VT 05344-0300 **(802) 257-4333**
(800) 343-0049; Fax: (802) 451-7555

Full-time: 138 men, 183 women	**Faculty:** 35
Part-time: 4 men, 6 women	**Ph.D.s:** 77%
Graduate: none	**Student/Faculty:** 9 to 1
Year: semesters	**Tuition:** $19,660
Application Deadline: March 1	**Room & Board:** $6750
Freshman Class: 205 applied, 179 accepted, 83 enrolled	
SAT I Verbal/Math: 640/570	**ACT:** 28 **VERY COMPETITIVE+**

Marlboro College, established in 1946, is a small private institution offering degrees in the liberal and fine arts and humanities, and employing self-designed programs of study. The library contains 53,006 volumes, 5669 microform items, and 1178 audiovisual forms/CDs, and subscribes to 249 periodicals. Computerized library services include the card catalog, interlibrary loans, and database searching. Special learning facilities include a learning resource center, art gallery, planetarium, and observatory. The 366-acre campus is in a rural area 9 miles west of Brattleboro, 2 1/2 hours from Boston. Including residence halls, there are 36 buildings.

Student Life: 89% of undergraduates are from out of state, mostly the Northeast. Others are from 36 states, 5 foreign countries, and Canada. 70% are from public schools. 83% are white. The average age of freshmen is 19; all undergraduates, 21. 28% do not continue beyond their first year; 48% remain to graduate.

Housing: 235 students can be accommodated in college housing, which includes single-sex and coed dormitories, on-campus apartments, and married-student housing. In addition, alcohol-free and smoke-free dormitories are available. On-campus housing is guaranteed for the freshman year only and is available on a first-come, first-served basis. 74% of students live on campus; of those, 90% remain on campus on weekends. All students may keep cars.

Activities: There are no fraternities or sororities. There are 25 groups on campus, including art, chess, chorus, computers, dance, drama, film, gay, international, jazz band, literary magazine, musical theater, newspaper, photography, political, social, social service, and student government. Popular campus events include Green-up Day, Creativity Lecture Series, and Visiting Writers Series.

Sports: There are 1 intercollegiate sport for men and 1 for women, and 1 intramural sport for men and 1 for women. Facilities include a soccer field, a volleyball court, cross-country trails, a basketball court, a weight room, a climbing wall, and field trips for canoeing, white-water rafting, and skiing.

Disabled Students: 90% of the campus is accessible. Wheelchair ramps, special parking, specially equipped rest rooms, and special class scheduling are available.

Services: Counseling and information services are available, as is tutoring in some subjects, including writing and languages, math, and organic chemistry.

Campus Safety and Security: Measures include self-defense education, informal discussions, pamphlets/posters/films, and a buddy system.

Programs of Study: Marlboro confers B.A. and B.S. degrees. Master's degrees are also awarded. Bachelor's degrees are awarded in BIOLOGICAL SCIENCE (biochemistry, biology/biological science, botany, and microbiology), COMMUNICATIONS AND THE ARTS (creative writing, dance, dramatic arts, English, fine arts, French, German, Greek, Italian, Latin, linguistics, music, photography, Russian, and Spanish), COMPUTER AND PHYSICAL SCIENCE (chemistry, computer science, mathematics, and physics), HEALTH PROFESSIONS (premedicine), SOCIAL SCIENCE (anthropology, economics, history, interdisciplinary studies, international studies, philosophy, political science/government, prelaw, psychology, social science, and sociology). Sciences, humanities, and world studies are the strongest academically. Literature, biology, and sociology are the largest.

Required: To graduate, students must complete a plan of concentration, a writing requirement, and a freshman seminar. A minimum GPA of 2.0 is required. Students must earn 120 credits, with 50 credits in the major, and complete a thesis and an oral exam.

Special: Marlboro offers a variety of internships, cross-registration with Huron University in London, and study abroad in many countries. The World Studies Program combines liberal arts with international studies, including 5 to 8 months of internship work in another culture. Accelerated and B.A.-B.S. degree programs are available. Students may pursue dual majors. Majors reflect an integrated course of study designed by students and their faculty advisors during the junior year.

Faculty/Classroom: 62% of faculty are male; 38%, female. All teach undergraduates. The average class size in an introductory lecture is 10; in a laboratory, 8; and in a regular course, 8.

Admissions: 87% of the 2001-2002 applicants were accepted. The SAT I scores for the 2001-2002 freshman class were: Verbal--6% below 500, 25% between 500 and 599, 45% between 600 and 700, and 24% above 700; Math--14% below 500, 55% between 500 and 599, 26% between 600 and 700, and 5% above 700. The ACT scores were 25% between 24 and 26, 37% between 27 and 28, and 38% above 28. 30% of the current freshmen were in the top fifth of their class; 74% were in the top two fifths. 2 freshmen graduated first in their class.

Requirements: The SAT I is required. In addition, applicants typically graduate from an accredited secondary school or have a GED. They are encouraged to earn 16 Carnegie units and complete 4 years of English and 3 years each of math, science, history, and a foreign language. Essays and interviews are required. AP and CLEP credits are accepted. Important factors in the admissions decision are advanced placement or honor courses, evidence of special talent, and extracurricular activities record. Applications are accepted on-line at the school's web site.

Procedure: Freshmen are admitted fall and spring. Entrance exams should be taken by October before entry. There are early decision, early admissions, and deferred admissions plans. Early decision applications should be filed by November 15; regular applications, by March 1 for fall entry, and November 1 for spring entry. Notification of early decision is sent December 15; regular decision, April 1. 11 early decision candidates were accepted for the 2001-2002 class.

Transfer: 21 transfer students enrolled in 2001-2002. Transfers must have a minimum GPA of 2.0. 42 credits of 120 must be completed at Marlboro.

Visiting: There are regularly scheduled orientations for prospective students, including a tour, faculty interview, and discussions with admissions and financial aid. There are guides for informal visits and visitors may sit in on classes and stay overnight. To schedule a visit, contact the Office of Admissions.

Financial Aid: In 2001-2002, 85% of all students received some form of financial aid. 68% of freshmen and 80% of continuing students received need-based aid. The average freshman award was $20,907. Of that total, scholarships or need-based grants averaged $12,007 ($22,305 maximum); loans averaged $4190 ($6625 maximum); work contracts averaged $1866 ($1930 maximum); and Plus and alternative loans exceeding need averaged $7283 ($24,480 maximum). 68% of undergraduates work part time. Average annual earnings from campus work are $1118. The average financial indebtedness of the 2001 graduate was $18,212. Marlboro is a member of CSS. The CSS/Profile or FAFSA is required. The fall application deadline is March 1.

International Students: There are 6 international students enrolled. The school actively recruits these students. They must score 550 on the written TOEFL or 230 on the electronic version and also take the SAT I or the ACT. The SAT I is preferred.

Computers: Computers are available in a lab, and all on-campus dorm rooms are wired for Internet access. All students may access the system 24 hours a day. There are no time limits and no fees.

Graduates: In a recent year, 61 bachelor's degrees were awarded. The most popular majors were history (13%), visual arts (13%), and literature (11%). In an average class, 48% graduate in 5 years.

Admissions Contact: Julie Richardson, Vice President, Enrollment and Financial Aid. A video is available.
E-mail: *admissions@marlboro.edu* Web: *www.marlboro.edu*

MIDDLEBURY COLLEGE — A-3

Middlebury, VT 05753 — (802) 443-3000; Fax: (802) 443-2065

Full-time: 1103 men, 1167 women	**Faculty:** 186; IIB, ++$
Part-time: 15 men, 22 women	**Ph.D.s:** 97%
Graduate: none	**Student/Faculty:** 12 to 1
Year: 4-1-4	**Tuition:** $34,300
Application Deadline: December 15	**Room & Board:** n/app
Freshman Class: 5411 applied, 1222 accepted, 513 enrolled	
SAT I Verbal/Math: 740/730	**ACT:** 32 **MOST COMPETITIVE**

Middlebury College, founded in 1800, is a small, independent liberal arts institution offering degree programs in languages, humanities, and social and natural sciences. The $34,300 comprehensive fee includes room and board. The 3 libraries contain 901,786 volumes, 360,917 microform items, and 28,614 audiovisual forms/CDs, and subscribe to 2569 periodicals. Computerized library services include the card catalog, interlibrary loans, and database searching. Special learning facilities include a learning resource center, art gallery, and radio station. The 350-acre campus is in a small town 35 miles south of Burlington. Including residence halls, there are 61 buildings.

Student Life: 94% of undergraduates are from out of state, mostly the Northeast. Students are from 50 states, 70 foreign countries, and Canada. 53% are from public schools. 80% are white. The average age of freshmen is 18; all undergraduates, 20. 3% do not continue beyond their first year; 90% remain to graduate.

Housing: 1960 students can be accommodated in college housing, which includes coed dormitories. In addition, there are language houses, special-interest houses, coed social houses, and multicultural and environmental houses. On-campus housing is guaranteed for all 4 years. 97% of students live on campus; of those, 90% remain on campus on weekends. All students may keep cars.

Activities: There are no fraternities or sororities. There are 95 groups on campus, including art, band, chess, choir, chorus, computers, dance, drama, ethnic, gay, honors, international, orchestra, photography, political, professional, radio, religious, social, social service, student government, and yearbook. Popular campus events include Winter Carnival, May Day, and Student Concert Series.

Sports: There are 13 intercollegiate sports for men and 13 for women, and 11 intramural sports for men and 11 for women. Facilities include 2 field houses, gyms, a swimming pool, a fitness center, tennis courts, playing fields, an 18-hole golf course, alpine and nordic ski areas, a 3000-seat campus stadium, and an 8-lane 400-meter outdoor track.

Disabled Students: Wheelchair ramps, elevators, special parking, specially equipped rest rooms, special class scheduling, and lowered drinking fountains are available.

Services: Counseling and information services are available, as is tutoring in every subject. There is a reader service for the blind.

Campus Safety and Security: Measures include 24-hour foot and vehicle patrol, self-defense education, escort service, and informal discussions. There are pamphlets/posters/films, emergency telephones, lighted pathways/sidewalks, a paid student patrol, and a ski patrol at the Snow Bowl.

Programs of Study: Midd confers the A.B. degree. Master's and doctoral degrees are also awarded. Bachelor's degrees are awarded in BIOLOGICAL SCIENCE (biochemistry, biology/biological science, and molecular biology), BUSINESS (international economics), COMMUNICATIONS AND THE ARTS (American literature, art, Chinese, classics, dance, dramatic arts, English, film arts, French, German, Italian, Japanese, literature, music, Russian, Spanish, and studio art), COMPUTER AND PHYSICAL SCIENCE (chemistry, computer science, geology, mathematics, and physics), ENGINEERING AND ENVIRONMENTAL DESIGN (environmental science), SOCIAL SCIENCE (American studies, anthropology, classical/ancient civilization, East Asian studies, economics, geography, history, international relations, international studies, philosophy, political science/government, psychology, religion, Russian and Slavic studies, sociology, and women's studies). Foreign languages, international studies, and science are the strongest academically. English, political science, and history are the largest.

Required: Students must complete 36 courses, including winter-term courses. Freshmen must take a freshman seminar and a writing course, and all students must take phys ed. A major normally requires 12 courses, and most students can fulfill the distribution requirement and the cultures and civilization requirement by taking 6 to 8 courses outside of their major. Students may also elect to complete a minor.

Special: Off-campus opportunities include an international major program at one of the Middlebury College schools abroad; exchange programs with Berea, St. Mary's, and Swarthmore; a junior year abroad; study through the American Collegiate Consortium for East-West Cultural and Academic Exchange; a 1-year program at Lincoln and Worcester Colleges, Oxford; a Washington, D.C., semester; and a maritime studies program with Williams College at Mystic Seaport. Middlebury also offers an independent scholar program, joint and double majors, various professional programs, dual degrees in business management, forestry/environmental studies, engineering, and nursing, and an early assurance premed program with Dartmouth, Rochester, Tufts, and the Medical College of Pennsylvania, which ensures medical school acceptance by the end of the sophomore year. There is a chapter of Phi Beta Kappa.

Faculty/Classroom: 62% of faculty are male; 38%, female. All teach undergraduates. The average class size in a regular course is 15.

Admissions: 23% of the 2001-2002 applicants were accepted. The SAT I scores for the 2001-2002 freshman class were: Verbal--2% below 500, 4% between 500 and 599, 37% between 600 and 699, and 57% above 699; Math--1% below 500, 4% between 500 and 599, 39% between 600 and 699, and 56% above 699. The ACT scores were 2% between 12 and 17, 6% between 18 and 23, 52% between 24 and 29, and 40% between 30 and 36. 92% of the current freshmen were in the top quarter of their class; 99% were in the top half.

Requirements: The SAT I or ACT is required. In addition, students should submit test scores as follows: the ACT or 3 SAT II: Subject tests, AP tests, or any combination thereof, including 1 English and 1 quantitative test. Secondary school preparation should include 4 years each of English, math and/or computer science, and 1 foreign language, 3 or more years of lab science and history and social science, and some study of music, art, and/or drama. AP credits are accepted. Important factors in the admissions decision are advanced placement or honor courses, recommendations by school officials, and evidence of special talent. Middlebury accepts applications on-line via ExPAN.

Procedure: Freshmen are admitted fall and spring. Entrance exams should be taken by December of the senior year. There are early decision, early admissions, and deferred admissions plans. Early decision applications should be filed by November 15; regular applications, by December 15 for fall entry, along with a $55 fee. Notification of early decision is sent December 15; regular decision, April 1. 275 early decision candidates were accepted for the 2001-2002 class. A waiting list is an active part of the admissions procedure.

Transfer: 3 transfer students enrolled in 2001-2002. Transfer students must have the strongest academic record possible through high school and a minimum 3.0 average in college. 18 courses of 36 must be completed at Midd.

Visiting: There are regularly scheduled orientations for prospective students, including campus tours and a group or individual interview. There are guides for informal visits and visitors may sit in on classes and stay overnight. To schedule a visit, contact the Admissions Office.

Financial Aid: The average freshman award for the 2001-2002 school year was $25,260. 60% of undergraduates work part time. Average annual earnings from campus work are $650. The average financial indebtedness of the 2001 graduate was $20,824. The CSS/Profile or FAFSA, the college's own financial statement, and the federal tax form are required. The fall application deadline is January 15.

International Students: The school actively recruits these students. They must take the TOEFL and fulfill the same requirements as first-year applicants.

Computers: The mainframes are an IBM Model F70 AS/400 and 5 IBM RS/6000s. Individual student rooms are wired to the mainframe. More than half of the students have their own personal computers, and there are more than 150 public PCs easily available in 7 buildings on campus. There are connections to the Internet and to BITNET, and a variety of software is available. All students may access the system 24 hours a day. There are no time limits and no fees.

Graduates: In 2001, 605 bachelor's degrees were awarded. The most popular majors were social sciences (41%), English (14%), and visual and performing arts (9%).

Admissions Contact: John E. Hanson, Director of Admissions. A video is available. E-mail: *admissions@middlebury.edu*
Web: *www.middlebury.edu*

NORWICH UNIVERSITY

Northfield, VT 05663 C-3

(802) 485-2001

(800) 468-6679; Fax: (802) 485-2032

Full-time: 1040 men, 375 women
Part-time: 25 men, 70 women
Graduate: none
Year: semesters, summer session
Application Deadline: open
Freshman Class: n/av
SAT I or ACT: required
Faculty: 110; IIA, --$
Ph.D.s: 85%
Student/Faculty: 13 to 1
Tuition: $15,400
Room & Board: $5700

LESS COMPETITIVE

Norwich University, founded in 1819, offers programs in the arts and sciences, engineering, education, and in the military, health science, and business professions. Figures in above capsule are approximate. In addition to regional accreditation, Norwich has baccalaureate program accreditation with ABET, ACBSP, and NLN. The library contains 230,000 volumes, 75,000 microform items, and 4487 audiovisual forms/CDs, and subscribes to 1364 periodicals. Computerized library services include the card catalog, interlibrary loans, and database searching. Special learning facilities include a learning resource center, art gallery, radio station, and a greenhouse, and 3 computer labs. The 1125-acre campus is in a rural area 11 miles south of Montpelier. Including residence halls, there are 34 buildings.

Student Life: 80% of undergraduates are from out of state, mostly the Northeast. Others are from 48 states, 29 foreign countries, and Canada. 75% are from public schools. 94% are white. The average age of freshmen is 18; all undergraduates, 20. 15% do not continue beyond their first year; 65% remain to graduate.

Housing: About 1725 students can be accommodated in college housing, which includes single-sex and coed dormitories. On-campus housing is guaranteed for the freshman year only and is available on a lottery system for upperclassmen. Priority is given to out-of-town students. 82% of students live on campus; of those, 65% remain on campus on weekends. Alcohol is not permitted. Upperclassmen may keep cars.

Activities: There are no fraternities or sororities. There are 75 groups on campus, including band, cheerleading, chess, choir, chorus, computers, drama, drill team, ethnic, honors, international, jazz band, literary magazine, marching band, musical theater, newspaper, orchestra, pep band, photography, political, professional, radio and TV, religious, social service, student government, and yearbook. Popular campus events include Regimental Ball, Winter Carnival, and Junior Weekend.

Sports: There are 15 intercollegiate sports for men and 10 for women, and 17 intramural sports for men and 12 for women. Facilities include an ice hockey arena, field house with an indoor track, an indoor swimming pool, aerobics room, weight and wrestling rooms, playing fields and an outdoor track, 1200-seat basketball arena, and 1000-seat stadium.

Disabled Students: Wheelchair ramps, elevators, special parking, specially equipped rest rooms, and lowered drinking fountains are available.

Services: Counseling and information services are available, as is tutoring in most subjects. There is remedial math, reading, and writing.

Campus Safety and Security: Measures include 24-hour foot and vehicle patrol and lighted pathways/sidewalks.

Programs of Study: Norwich confers B.A., B.S., and B.Arch. degrees. Associate degrees are also awarded. Bachelor's degrees are awarded in BIOLOGICAL SCIENCE (biochemistry and biology/biological science), BUSINESS (accounting, business administration and management, and business economics), COMMUNICATIONS AND THE ARTS (communications and English), COMPUTER AND PHYSICAL SCIENCE (chemistry, computer science, geology, information sciences and systems, mathematics, and physics), EDUCATION (physical), ENGINEERING AND ENVIRONMENTAL DESIGN (architecture, civil engineering, electrical/electronics engineering, environmental science, mechanical engineering, and military science), HEALTH PROFESSIONS (medical laboratory technology, nursing, and sports medicine), SOCIAL SCIENCE (criminal justice, history, international studies, liberal arts/general studies, peace studies, political science/government, and psychology). Engineering and architecture are the strongest academically. Criminal justice and nursing are the largest.

Required: Total number of required credits and courses vary by program. All students are required to complete 3 credit hours in history, English 101-102, and 2 semesters in phys ed. A 2.0 GPA is required to graduate.

Special: Many internships are available. Study abroad through other schools and through the Vermont Overseas Studies Program is accepted. The B.A.-B.S. degree, a general studies degree, pass/fail options, and student-designed majors are possible. Co-op programs in business and criminal justice, a Washington semester, on- and off-campus work-study programs for service organizations and in criminal justice, plus a special Adult Degree Program are offered. The Russian School offers a special intensive summer session. There are 5 national honor societies, including Phi Beta Kappa, and 5 departmental honors programs.

Faculty/Classroom: All teach undergraduates. The average class size in an introductory lecture is 5; in a laboratory, 15; and in a regular course, 20.

Requirements: The SAT I or ACT is required. In addition, applicants should graduate from an accredited secondary school with 18 academic credits or achieve the GED equivalent. Applications are accepted on IBM/Windows formatted computer disks, and on-line through the World Wide Web. Norwich requires applicants to be in the upper 50% of their class. A GPA of 2.5 is required. AP and CLEP credits are accepted. Important factors in the admissions decision are leadership record, extracurricular activities record, and evidence of special talent.

Procedure: Freshmen are admitted fall and spring. Entrance exams should be taken starting with spring of the junior year. There are early decision and deferred admissions plans. Application deadlines are open. 60 early decision candidates were accepted for a recent class.

Transfer: Transfer students should present a 2.0 GPA and meet all standards for entering freshmen. 60 credits of 114 must be completed at Norwich.

Visiting: There are regularly scheduled orientations for prospective students, including meetings with representatives from admissions, financial aid, academic offices, including Dean of Students or Commandant's Office, athletics (if desired), and a campus tour. There are guides for informal visits and visitors may sit in on classes and stay overnight. To schedule a visit, contact Admissions, Main Office.

Financial Aid: Norwich is a member of CSS. The CSS/Profile or FAFSA is required. Check with the school for current deadlines.

International Students: The school actively recruits these students. They must score 500 on the written TOEFL.

Computers: The mainframes are a DEC VAX 11/780 and a DEC VAX 11/785. There are labs in the business department, computer center, and architecture department, and computers are also available in the library. All students may access the system 20 hours per day. There are no time limits and no fees.

Graduates: In an average class, 65% graduate in 4 years. 25 companies recruited on campus in a recent year.

Admissions Contact: Frank E. Griffis, Dean of Admissions.
E-mail: *nuadm@norwich.edu*

SAINT MICHAEL'S COLLEGE

Colchester, VT 05439 A-2

(802) 654-3000

(800) 762-8000; Fax: (802) 654-2906

Full-time: 885 men, 1059 women
Part-time: 32 men, 45 women
Graduate: 168 men, 441 women
Year: semesters, summer session
Application Deadline: February 1
Freshman Class: 2550 applied, 1636 accepted, 529 enrolled
SAT I Verbal/Math: 560/560
Faculty: 139
Ph.D.s: 81%
Student/Faculty: 14 to 1
Tuition: $19,680
Room & Board: $7255

VERY COMPETITIVE

Saint Michael's College, founded in 1904, is a private liberal arts and sciences institution affiliated with the Roman Catholic Church. The library contains 215,000 volumes, 18,600 microform items, and 4750 audiovisual forms/CDs, and subscribes to 3000 periodicals. Computerized library services include the card catalog, interlibrary loans, and database searching. Special learning facilities include an art gallery, radio station, and an observatory. The 480-acre campus is in a suburban area 2 miles east of Burlington. Including residence halls, there are 56 buildings.

Student Life: 78% of undergraduates are from out of state, mostly the Northeast. Others are from 32 states, 17 foreign countries, and Canada. 71% are from public schools. 92% are white. 75% are Catholic; 12% Protestant. The average age of freshmen is 18; all undergraduates, 20. 13% do not continue beyond their first year; 78% remain to graduate.

Housing: 1775 students can be accommodated in college housing, which includes single-sex and coed dormitories and on-campus apartments. In addition, there are special-interest houses, and substance-free housing. On-campus housing is guaranteed for all 4 years. 89% of students live on campus; of those, 95% remain on campus on weekends. All students may keep cars.

Activities: There are no fraternities or sororities. There are 40 groups on campus, including aerobics, art, band, cheerleading, choir, chorale, computers, dance, drama, ethnic, film, fire and rescue, gay, honors, international, jazz band, literary magazine, musical theater, newspaper, pep band, photography, political, professional, radio and TV, religious, science, social, social service, student government, wilderness program, and yearbook. Popular campus events include Family Weekend, Chirstmas and Spring Semi-Formals, and Spring Weekend.

Sports: There are 10 intercollegiate sports for men and 11 for women, and 13 intramural sports for men and 13 for women. Facilities include a 2,200-seat gym and fieldhouse with basketball, volleyball, tennis, and badminton courts, 4 multipurpose courts, a 6-lane swimming pool, fitness center, training room, weight room, climbing wall, pool, table tennis, suspended track, soccer, field hockey, lacrosse, baseball, and softball fields, and outdoor tennis courts.

Disabled Students: 60% of the campus is accessible. Wheelchair ramps, elevators, special parking, specially equipped rest rooms, special class scheduling, lowered drinking fountains, lowered telephones, and specially accessible residential space. Other accommodations are provided on an individual basis.

Services: Counseling and information services are available, as is tutoring in every subject. Tutoring can be arranged on an individual basis through the writing center and departmental help sessions.

Campus Safety and Security: Measures include 24-hour foot and vehicle patrol, escort service, shuttle buses, and informal discussions. There are pamphlets/posters/films, emergency telephones, lighted pathways/sidewalks, and campus fire and rescue squad.

Programs of Study: Saint Michael's confers B.A. and B.S. degrees. Master's degrees are also awarded. Bachelor's degrees are awarded in BIOLOGICAL SCIENCE (biochemistry and biology/biological science), BUSINESS (accounting and business administration and management), COMMUNICATIONS AND THE ARTS (dramatic arts, English, fine arts, French, journalism, music, and Spanish), COMPUTER AND PHYSICAL SCIENCE (chemistry, computer science, mathematics, physical sciences, and physics), EDUCATION (art, elementary, foreign languages, science, and secondary), ENGINEERING AND ENVIRONMENTAL DESIGN (environmental science and preengineering), HEALTH PROFESSIONS (predentistry), SOCIAL SCIENCE (American studies, anthropology, economics, history, philosophy, political science/government, prelaw, psychology, religion, and sociology). Biology, business administration, and English literature are the largest.

Required: To graduate, students must complete 9 to 12 credits in humanities and social science and organizational skills, 6 to 8 credits each in religious studies, philosophy, science and math; 2 credits in artistic experience, and a foreign language and writing proficiency. They must have a GPA of 2.0. The college requires a minimum of 124 credits and a minimum of 34 different courses for graduation, including 2 writing-intensive courses. A maximum of 52 credits may be taken in the major.

Special: A variety of internships and on-campus work study are available. There is a Washington semester with American University and study abroad in 30 countries. Student-designed majors may be pursued. The college offers a 3-2 engineering degree program in cooperation with Clarkson University and the University of Vermont, and a 4-1 graduate business program with Clarkson University. Nondegree study and pass/fail grading options are offered on a limited basis. There are 7 national honor societies, a freshman honors program, and 1 departmental honors program.

Faculty/Classroom: 58% of faculty are male; 42%, female. All teach undergraduates and do research. No introductory courses are taught by graduate students. The average class size in an introductory lecture is 24; in a laboratory, 16; and in a regular course, 20.

Admissions: 64% of the 2001-2002 applicants were accepted. The SAT I scores for the 2001-2002 freshman class were: Verbal--17% below 500, 53% between 500 and 599, 26% between 600 and 700, and 4% above 700; Math--17% below 500, 54% between 500 and 599, 26% between 600 and 700, and 2% above 700. 42% of the current freshmen were in the top fifth of their class; 76% were in the top two fifths. 7 freshmen graduated first in their class.

Requirements: The SAT I or ACT is required. In addition, applicants must graduate from an accredited secondary school or have a GED. They must complete 16 Carnegie units. The college requires 4 credits in English, 3 to 4 credits in math and science, and 3 each in history (social studies) and a foreign language. An essay is required and an interview is recommended. Saint Michael's requires applicants to be in the upper 50% of their class. AP and CLEP credits are accepted. Important factors in the admissions decision are advanced placement or honor courses, evidence of special talent, and recommendations by school officials. Saint Michael's accepts on-line applications through the Common Application on-line, College Board on-line, and the school's web site.

Procedure: Freshmen are admitted fall and spring. Entrance exams should be taken in the fall of the senior year. There are early action and deferred admissions plans. Early action application should be filed by November 15; regular applications, by February 1 for fall entry and November 1 for spring entry, along with a $45 fee. Notification of early action is sent February 1; regular decision, April 1. 690 early action candidates were accepted for the 2001-2002 class. 7% of all applicants are on a waiting list.

Transfer: 28 transfer students enrolled in 2001-2002. Transfer applicants must have a minimum GPA of 2.5; generally, those admitted have a GPA of at least 3.3. The SAT I is required. An interview is recommended. 30 credits of 124 must be completed at Saint Michael's.

Visiting: There are regularly scheduled orientations for prospective students, including a group information session, a video about the school, a campus tour, and a review with a staff member of admissions criteria. There are guides for informal visits and visitors may sit in on classes and stay overnight. To schedule a visit, contact the Admissions Office.

Financial Aid: In 2001-2002, 87% of all students received some form of financial aid. 64% of freshmen and 62% of continuing students received need-based aid. The average freshman award was $14,566. Of that total, scholarships or need-based grants averaged $10,288 ($21,200 maximum); loans averaged $3518 ($4625 maximum); and work contracts averaged $760 ($2000 maximum). 40% of undergraduates work part time. Average annual earnings from campus work are $1100. The average financial indebtedness of the 2001 graduate was $17,180. Saint Michael's is a member of CSS. The FAFSA, the college's own financial statement, the federal tax forms from both student and parents, and W-2 forms are required. The fall application deadline is March 15.

International Students: There are 48 international students enrolled. The school actively recruits these students. They must score 550 on the written TOEFL or 213 on the electronic version and also take the college's own test The SAT I or ACT is recommended for international students, but the TOEFL may be used in place of SAT I.

Computers: The mainframe is a DEC ALPHA ES-40 System. There are 9 PC labs available for student use, all of them connected to the campus network (Mikenet). More than 120 computers are available for student use. All students may access the system. There are no time limits and no fees. It is strongly recommended that all students have a personal computer.

Graduates: In 2001, 453 bachelor's degrees were awarded. The most popular majors were business administration (20%), psychology (15%), and English literature (10%). In an average class, 70% graduate in 4 years, 77% in 5 years, and 78% in 6 years. 104 companies recruited on campus in 2000-2001. Of the 2000 graduating class, 13% were enrolled in graduate school within 6 months of graduation and 83% were employed.

Admissions Contact: Jerry E. Flanagan, Vice President, Admission and Enrollment Management. A video is available.
E-mail: *admission@smcvt.edu* Web: *www.smcvt.edu*

SOUTHERN VERMONT COLLEGE
Bennington, VT 05201 — A-6
(802) 447-6304
(800) 378-2782; Fax: (802) 447-4695

Full-time: 127 men, 180 women	**Faculty:** 20; IIB, --$
Part-time: 41 men, 109 women	**Ph.D.s:** 15%
Graduate: none	**Student/Faculty:** 16 to 1
Year: semesters, summer session	**Tuition:** $11,695
Application Deadline: open	**Room & Board:** $5990
Freshman Class: 379 applied, 295 accepted, 120 enrolled	
SAT I Verbal/Math: 480/480	**ACT:** 19 **COMPETITIVE**

Southern Vermont College, established in 1926, is a private institution offering a career-oriented, liberal arts education to a student body from diverse academic backgrounds. The library contains 26,000 volumes, and subscribes to 1504 periodicals. Computerized library services include interlibrary loans and database searching. Special learning facilities include a learning resource center and art gallery. The 371-acre campus is in a small town 40 miles east of Albany, New York. Including residence halls, there are 10 buildings.

Student Life: 62% of undergraduates are from out of state, mostly the Northeast. Others are from 20 states and 4 foreign countries. 90% are white.

Housing: 235 students can be accommodated in college housing, which includes coed dormitories. On-campus housing is guaranteed for the freshman year only and is available on a lottery system for upperclassmen. 67% of students commute. All students may keep cars.

Activities: There are no fraternities or sororities. There are 12 groups on campus, including cheerleading, drama, ethnic, honors, literary magazine, newspaper, photography, professional, social, student government, and yearbook. Popular campus events include Spree Day, Family Weekend, and Holiday Dance.

Sports: There are 4 intercollegiate sports for men and 4 for women. Facilities include a multipurpose field for softball, baseball, and soccer, a gym and health education facility, and a 9-hole par 3 golf course.

Disabled Students: 50% of the campus is accessible. Wheelchair ramps, special parking, and specially equipped rest rooms are available.

Services: Counseling and information services are available, as is tutoring in every subject. There is remedial math, reading, and writing. Skills workshops and a program to assist students with basic college skills are also available.

Campus Safety and Security: Measures include 24-hour foot and vehicle patrol, escort service, informal discussions, and pamphlets/posters/films. There are lighted pathways/sidewalks.

Programs of Study: SVC confers B.A., B.S., and B.S.N. degrees. Associate degrees are also awarded. Bachelor's degrees are awarded in BUSINESS (accounting, business administration and management, and hotel/motel and restaurant management), COMMUNICATIONS AND THE ARTS (communications, creative writing, English, and literature), ENGINEERING AND ENVIRONMENTAL DESIGN (environmental science), HEALTH PROFESSIONS (nursing), SOCIAL SCIENCE (child psychology/development, criminal justice, human services, liberal arts/general studies, psychology, and social work). Environmental studies and accounting are the strongest academically. Business, criminal justice, and liberal arts are the largest.

Required: To graduate, students must complete a 48-credit core requirement consisting of course work in economics, English, environmental studies, government, history, cultural arts, math (including computer science), natural sciences, philosophy, psychology, and sociology. Minors are required in some programs. A minimum GPA of 2.0 is required. Students must earn a minimum of 120 credits.

Special: There is cross-registration with Bennington College, and internships and work-study programs. Students may study abroad in England, or spend a semester at sea. The college offers a liberal arts degree, individualized degree programs, dual majors, and credit for life, military, and work experience. Nondegree study is also available. There is 1 national honor society.

Faculty/Classroom: 46% of faculty are male; 54%, female. All teach undergraduates. The average class size in an introductory lecture is 25 and in a regular course, 18.

Admissions: 78% of the 2001-2002 applicants were accepted. The SAT I scores for the 2001-2002 freshman class were: Verbal--57% below 500, 36% between 500 and 599, 5% between 600 and 700, and 1% above 700; Math--70% below 500, 26% between 500 and 599, and 4% between 600 and 700. The ACT scores were 36% below 21, 57% between 21 and 23, and 7% above 28. 2% of the current freshmen were in the top fifth of their class; 50% were in the top two fifths.

Requirements: The SAT I or ACT is required. In addition, applicants must graduate from an accredited secondary school or have a GED. The college requires 4 years of English and 3 of math. SVC requires applicants to be in the upper 67% of their class. A GPA of 2.0 is required. AP and CLEP credits are accepted. Important factors in the admissions decision are leadership record, extracurricular activities record, and recommendations by school officials. Applications are accepted on-line via CollegeApply.

Procedure: Freshmen are admitted fall, spring, and summer. There is a deferred admissions plan. Application deadlines are open. The application fee is $30. Notification is sent on a rolling basis.

Transfer: 33 transfer students enrolled in a recent year. Applicants must have a GPA of 2.0 and be in good standing. Interviews are recommended, and a dean's report is required. 30 credits of 120 must be completed at SVC.

Visiting: There are regularly scheduled orientations for prospective students. There are guides for informal visits and visitors may sit in on classes and stay overnight. To schedule a visit, contact Admissions.

Financial Aid: In 2001-2002, 74% of freshmen and 65% of continuing students received need-based aid. The average financial indebtedness of a recent year's graduate was $13,500. SVC is a member of CSS. The FAFSA is required. Check with the school for current deadlines.

International Students: There were 4 international students enrolled in a recent year. They must score 500 on the written TOEFL or 173 on the electronic version.

Computers: The library and both computer labs have access to the Internet and the Web. All students may access the system. There are no time limits and no fees.

Admissions Contact: Elizabeth Gatti, Director of Admissions.
E-mail: *admis@svc.edu* Web: *www.svc.edu*

STERLING COLLEGE

Craftsbury Common, VT 05827 — **B-1**

(802) 586-7711
(800) 648-3591; Fax: (802) 586-2591

Full-time: 49 men, 31 women	**Faculty:** 11
Part-time: 1 man	**Ph.D.s:** 25%
Graduate: none	**Student/Faculty:** 7 to 1
Year: semesters, summer session	**Tuition:** $14,025
Application Deadline: open	**Room & Board:** $5670
Freshman Class: 65 applied, 46 accepted, 31 enrolled	
SAT I Verbal/Math: 550/520	**ACT:** 20 **COMPETITIVE**

Sterling College is a private, independent school offering academic programs that are oriented toward environmental care. The library contains 8775 volumes and 370 audiovisual forms/CDs, and subscribes to 85 periodicals. Computerized library services include the card catalog, interlibrary loans, and database searching. Special learning facilities include woodshop, darkroom, managed woodlot, organic garden, working livestock farm, 30-foot-tall climbing tower, bouldering wall, and a greenhouse. The 130-acre campus is in a rural area 40 miles north of Montpelier and 60 miles from Burlington. Including residence halls, there are 12 buildings.

Student Life: 82% of undergraduates are from out of state, mostly the Northeast. Others are from 18 states. 74% are from public schools. All are white. The average age of freshmen is 19; all undergraduates, 20. 17% do not continue beyond their first year; 50% remain to graduate.

Housing: 90 students can be accommodated in college housing, which includes single-sex and coed dormitories. On-campus housing is guaranteed for all 4 years. 80% of students live on campus; of those, 80% remain on campus on weekends. All students may keep cars.

Activities: There are no fraternities or sororities. There are some groups and organizations on campus, including newspaper and outing club. Popular campus events include extended backpacking trips, rock and ice climbing, and winter camping.

Sports: There is no sports program at Sterling College. Facilities include a climbing tower and nationally recognized cross-country ski trails managed by a nearby sports center.

Disabled Students: 2% of the campus is accessible. Wheelchair ramps and specially equipped rest rooms are available.

Services: There is remedial math. Students seek assistance directly from faculty.

Campus Safety and Security: Measures include Weekly Community Meetings that address personal safety and security.

Programs of Study: Sterling College confers the B.A. degree. Associate degrees are also awarded. Bachelor's degrees are awarded in AGRICULTURE (conservation and regulation, natural resource management, and wildlife management), EDUCATION (recreation). Wildlands ecology and management, sustainable agriculture, and outdoor leadership and education are the strongest academically. Wildlands ecology and management, and outdoor education and leadership are the largest.

Required: Of the 120 total credit hours required, 25 must be taken in social sciences, 13 in natural sciences, 14 in arts and humanities, 6 in interdisciplinary studies, and 2 in applied sciences. 24 to 27.5 hours in the major are required. A minimum GPA of 2.0 must be maintained.

Special: Students may cross-register through the National Alliance for Green Education. Internships are required in the second year of study. Study abroad and student-designed majors are available.

Faculty/Classroom: 63% of faculty are male; 37%, female. All teach undergraduates, 30% both teach and do research. The average class size in an introductory lecture is 20; in a laboratory, 10; and in a regular course, 15.

Admissions: 71% of the 2001-2002 applicants were accepted. The ACT scores for the 2001-2002 freshman class were: 33% below 21, and 66% between 21 and 23. 2% of the current freshmen were in the top fifth of their class; 41% were in the top two fifths.

Requirements: The SAT I or ACT is recommended. In addition, well-written essays, quality of the interview, and the comments provided by references are equal to the value of high school and college transcripts. Home-schooled students are strongly encouraged to contact the admissions office to discuss their particular needs and interests. AP credits are accepted. Important factors in the admissions decision are leadership record, recommendations by school officials, and personality/intangible qualities. Applications are accepted on-line at the college's web site and via CollegeNET.

Procedure: Freshmen are admitted in the fall. There is a deferred admissions plan. Application deadlines are open. The application fee is $35.

Transfer: 5 transfer students enrolled in 2001-2002. In addition to the standard application, transfer students must provide copies of college transcripts. 30 credits of 120 must be completed at Sterling College.

Visiting: There are regularly scheduled orientations for prospective students, including a student-led campus tour, an interview with admissions, and a meal in the dining hall. Overnight visits are welcome Sunday through Thursday nights; weekend Visit Days offer a more comprehensive view of the college. There are guides for informal visits and visitors may sit in on classes. To schedule a visit, contact the Admissions Office.

Financial Aid: In 2001-2002, 64% of all freshmen and 60% of continuing students received some form of financial aid. 40% of freshmen and 60% of continuing students received need-based aid. The average freshman award was $3500. Of that total, scholarships or need-based grants averaged $4100 ($6000 maximum); loans averaged $2625 ($12,000 maximum); work contracts averaged $1000; and Work College's Consortium Funding averaged $1000. Every student works 60 hours/semester. All undergraduates work part time. Average annual earnings from campus work are $400. Sterling College is a member of CSS. The FAFSA and the college's own financial statement are required.

International Students: There is 1 international student enrolled. The school actively recruits these students. They must score 500 on the written TOEFL or 173 on the electronic version.

Computers: The mainframe is a Compaq DeskPros. Students access the Internet and World Wide Web through computers located in the Career Resource Center and library. All students may access the system. There are no time limits and no fees. It is strongly recommended that all students have a personal computer.

Graduates: In 2001, 4 bachelor's degrees were awarded. The most popular major was wildlands ecology and management (100%). 7 companies recruited on campus in 2000-2001.

Admissions Contact: John Zaber, Director of Admissions.
E-mail: *admissions@sterlingcollege.edu* Web: *www.sterlingcollege.edu*

UNIVERSITY OF VERMONT A-2

Burlington, VT 05405 (802) 656-3370; Fax: (802) 656-8611

Full-time: 3179 men, 4035 women	**Faculty:** 523; I, --$
Part-time: 573 men, 805 women	**Ph.D.s:** 90%
Graduate: 669 men, 820 women	**Student/Faculty:** 14 to 1
Year: semesters, summer session	**Tuition:** $8665 ($20,100)
Application Deadline: January 15	**Room & Board:** $6096
Freshman Class: 8268 applied, 6578 accepted, 1849 enrolled	
SAT I Verbal/Math: 560/570	**ACT:** 24 **COMPETITIVE+**

The University of Vermont, established in 1791, is a public, land-grant, comprehensive institution with a dual focus on teaching and research. Its undergraduate and graduate offerings include the liberal arts, business administration, engineering, math, natural resources, agricultural studies, fine arts, teacher preparation, social services, environmental studies, and health science, including nursing. There are 8 undergraduate and 2 graduate schools. In addition to regional accreditation, UVM has baccalaureate program accreditation with AACSB, ABET, ADA, APTA, ASLA, CAHEA, CSWE, NCATE, NLN, and SAF. The 3 libraries contain 2.5 million volumes, 1.75 million microform items, and 45,000 audiovisual forms/CDs, and subscribe to 20,000 periodicals. Computerized library services include the card catalog, interlibrary loans, and database searching. Special learning facilities include a learning resource center, art gallery, radio station, TV station, a health care center, 4 research farms, the Fleming Museum, a geology museum, 9 natural areas, a lakeshore science center, and an aquatic research vessel. The 425-acre campus is in a suburban area 90 miles south of Montreal, 200 miles north of Boston, on the shore of Lake Champlain. Including residence halls, there are 118 buildings.

Student Life: 61% of undergraduates are from out of state, mostly the Northeast. Others are from 49 states, 37 foreign countries, and Canada. 92% are white. 31% are claim no religious affiliation; 30% Catholic; 27% Protestant. The average age of freshmen is 18; all undergraduates, 20. 18% do not continue beyond their first year; 69% remain to graduate.

Housing: 3631 students can be accommodated in college housing, which includes coed dormitories, on-campus apartments, off-campus apartments, married-student housing, fraternity houses, and sorority houses. In addition, there are honors houses, language houses, special-interest houses, and a living/learning center that provides an integrated, theme-based academic and residential option. On-campus housing is available on a lottery system for upperclassmen. 50% of students live on campus; of those, 98% remain on campus on weekends. Upperclassmen may keep cars.

Activities: 3% of men belong to 10 national fraternities; 2% of women belong to 5 national sororities. There are more than 100 groups on campus, including art, band, cheerleading, choir, chorale, chorus, community service, computers, dance, debate, drama, environmental, ethnic, film, gay, honors, international, jazz band, literary magazine, musical theater, newspaper, orchestra, outing, pep band, photography, political, professional, radio and TV, religious, social, social service, student government, and yearbook. Popular campus events include Building Our Community, Winterfest, and Community Serve-a-thon.

Sports: There are 10 intercollegiate sports for men and 12 for women, and 24 intramural sports for men and 24 for women. Facilities include a 3228-seat gym, a 4000-seat ice hockey stadium, a field house, soccer and baseball fields, a fitness center, indoor and outdoor tracks, a natatorium, indoor tennis courts, a racquetball court, a climbing facility, a dance studio, and a gymnastics facility.

Disabled Students: 87% of the campus is accessible. Wheelchair ramps, elevators, special parking, specially equipped rest rooms, special class scheduling, lowered drinking fountains, lowered telephones, first-priority routes in poor weather, a TTY phone system for hearing-impaired students, and closed-caption video decoders are available.

Services: Counseling and information services are available, as is tutoring in most subjects. There is a reader service for the blind. There is also supplemental instruction, note-taking and test-taking seminars, time management instruction, outreach programs, exam proctoring, and writing tutors, as well as support for ESL students.

Campus Safety and Security: Measures include 24-hour foot and vehicle patrol, self-defense education, escort service, and shuttle buses. There are informal discussions, pamphlets/posters/films, emergency telephones, lighted pathways/sidewalks, and bike registration, identification of property, and 18 fully certified police officers.

Programs of Study: UVM confers B.A., B.S., B.M., B.S.A.E., B.S.B.A., B.S.Ed., B.S.C.E., B.S.C.S., B.S.E.E., B.S.E.M., B.S.M., B.S.M.E., and B.S.M.S. degrees. Associate, master's, and doctoral degrees are also awarded. Bachelor's degrees are awarded in AGRICULTURE (agriculture, animal science, environmental studies, equine science, fishing and fisheries, forestry and related sciences, horticulture, natural resource management, and plant science), BIOLOGICAL SCIENCE (biochemistry, biology/biological science, botany, ecology, genetics, microbiology, nutrition, wildlife biology, and zoology), BUSINESS (accounting, business administration and management, entrepreneurial studies, international business management, management information systems, and marketing management), COMMUNICATIONS AND THE ARTS (art, art history and appreciation, classics, dramatic arts, English, French, German, Greek, Latin, music, Russian, and Spanish), COMPUTER AND PHYSICAL SCIENCE (chemistry, computer science, geology, information sciences and systems, mathematics, physics, and statistics), EDUCATION (art, athletic training, early childhood, education, elementary, English, foreign languages, health, mathematics, middle school, music, nutrition, physical, science, secondary, and social studies), ENGINEERING AND ENVIRONMENTAL DESIGN (biomedical engineering, biomedical equipment technology, civil engineering, computer engineering, electrical/electronics engineering, engineering management, environmental engineering, environmental science, landscape architecture/design, and mechanical engineering), HEALTH PROFESSIONS (biomedical science, medical laboratory science, medical laboratory technology, nuclear medical technology, nursing, preveterinary science, radiation therapy, and speech pathology/audiology), SOCIAL SCIENCE (anthropology, Asian/Oriental studies, Canadian studies, dietetics, economics, European studies, family/consumer studies, food science, geography, history, human development, Latin American studies, parks and recreation management, philosophy, political science/government, psychology, religion, Russian and Slavic studies, social work, sociology, and women's studies). Chemistry, environmental science, and biology are the strongest academically. Business administration, psychology, and English are the largest.

Required: Degree requirements vary among the individual colleges, but all require at least a 2.0 GPA and 122 credit hours to graduate. Most students must enroll in at least 30 distribution credits (approximately 10 courses) in the arts, humanities, social sciences, languages, literature, math, and the sciences. All academic units require a 3-credit course in Race and Culture, or a course exploring race relations and ethnic diversity in the United States, and all students are expected to complete 2 credits of phys ed, unless granted an exception.

Special: Special academic programs include co-op programs, internships in every discipline, study abroad in 81 countries, a Washington semester, work-study, an accelerated degree program in nursing, dual majors, and student-designed majors. In addition, a 3-4 veterinary medicine degree is offered with Tufts University, a 3-3 program with Vermont Law School, and a 3-3 physical therapy program at UVM. There are 25 national honor societies, including Phi Beta Kappa, and 14 departmental honors program.

Faculty/Classroom: 61% of faculty are male; 39%, female. Graduate students teach 2% of introductory courses. The average class size in an introductory lecture is 37; in a laboratory, 17; and in a regular course, 21.

Admissions: 80% of the 2001-2002 applicants were accepted. The SAT I scores for the 2001-2002 freshman class were: Verbal--18% below 500, 50% between 500 and 599, 29% between 600 and 700, and 3% above 700; Math--16% below 500, 48% between 500 and 599, 33% between 600 and 700, and 3% above 700. The ACT scores were 15% below 21, 30% between 21 and 23, 31% between 24 and 26, 12% between 27 and 28, and 12% above 28. 36% of the current freshmen were in the top fifth of their class; 74% were in the top two fifths. 18 freshmen graduated first in their class.

Requirements: The SAT I or ACT is required. Other admissions requirements include graduation from an accredited secondary school with 16 Carnegie units. Required high school course work includes 4 years of English, 3 years each of social science and math, including algebra I and II and geometry, and 2 years each of the same foreign language and science (one of which must be a lab science). An essay must be submitted. The GED is also accepted. AP and CLEP credits are accepted. Important factors in the admissions decision are advanced placement or honor courses, extracurricular activities record, and recommendations by school officials. Applications can be downloaded from the web site or submitted via Apply, CollegeLink, or Common App.

Procedure: Freshmen are admitted fall and spring. Entrance exams should be taken by November of the senior year. There are early decision, early admissions, and deferred admissions plans. Early decision applications should be filed by November 1; regular applications, by January 15 for fall entry and November 1 for spring entry. Notification of early decision is sent December 15; regular decision, March 20. 174 early decision candidates were accepted for the 2001-2002 class. 8% of all applicants are on a waiting list; 34 were accepted in 2001.

Transfer: 377 transfer students enrolled in 2001-2002. Transfer students generally must have a minimum GPA of 3.0 in credited courses and meet the same entrance requirements as freshmen. Considerations include the college and high school records, the major indicated, and availabiltiy of space at UVM. Vermont residents are given preference. 30 credits of 122 must be completed at UVM.

Visiting: There are regularly scheduled orientations for prospective students, consisting of tours most weekdays during the academic year and open houses on selected Saturdays in the fall and spring. There are guides for informal visits and visitors may sit in on classes. To schedule a visit, contact the Admissions Office.

Financial Aid: In 2001-2002, 76% of all freshmen and 64% of continuing students received some form of financial aid. 50% of freshmen and 45% of continuing students received need-based aid. The average freshman award was $10,285. Of that total, scholarships or need-based grants averaged $8576 ($31,220 maximum); loans averaged $4720 ($28,840 maximum); and work contracts averaged $2120 ($2400 maximum). The average financial indebtedness of the 2001 graduate was $22,425. The FAFSA is required. The fall application deadline is February 10.

International Students: There are 79 international students enrolled. The school actively recruits these students. They must score 550 on the written TOEFL and also take the SAT I or the ACT.

Computers: The mainframes are an IBM 4381 and a DEC VAX 8600. PCs are located in labs throughout the campus. All residence halls are wired for connections to the campus network, the Internet, and the Web. All students may access the system at any time. There are no time limits and no fees. It is recommended that students in business majors have personal computers. IBM, Mac, or Dell is recommended.

Graduates: In 2001, 1716 bachelor's degrees were awarded. The most popular majors were business (12%), English (9%), and psychology (6%). In an average class, 1% graduate in 3 years, 51% in 4 years, 66% in 5 years, and 69% in 6 years. 164 companies recruited on campus in 2000-2001. Of the 2000 graduating class, 9% were enrolled in graduate school within 6 months of graduation and 73% were employed.

Admissions Contact: Donald Honeman, Director of Admission.
E-mail: *admissions@uvm.edu* Web: *www.uvm.edu/admissions*

VERMONT STATE COLLEGES

The Vermont State Colleges (VSC) is Vermont's system of 5 public colleges: Castleton State College, Community College of Vermont, Johnson State College, Lyndon State College, and Vermont Technical College. The colleges collectively enroll more than 10,000 students and offer 120 academic programs at the associate, baccalaureate, and master's levels. All offer small classes and individualized attention for students. The Vermont State Colleges provide quality higher education to both Vermonters and out-of-state students; produce a well-trained and educated workforce for Vermont employers; and contribute to the cultural, social, and economic life in the state. The VSC system is governed by a 15-member board of trustees; its management team includes the chancellor and the 5 college presidents. Profiles of the 4-year campus institutions are included in this section.

VERMONT TECHNICAL COLLEGE
Randolph Center, VT 05061 — (802) 728-1000; (800) 442-8821

Full-time: 625 men, 264 women	**Faculty:** 72; III, --$
Part-time: 255 men, 128 women	**Ph.D.s:** 20%
Graduate: none	**Student/Faculty:** 12 to 1
Year: semesters	**Tuition:** $6184 ($11,632)
Application Deadline: open	**Room & Board:** $5520
Freshman Class: 1138 applied, 677 accepted, 521 enrolled	
SAT I Verbal/Math: 480/510	**ACT:** 21 **COMPETITIVE**

Vermont Technical College, founded in 1910, is one of the 5 institutions in the Vermont State Colleges system and is the state's only public technical college. In addition to regional accreditation, VTC has baccalaureate program accreditation with ABET. The library contains 59,890 volumes, 329 microform items, and 3630 audiovisual forms/CDs, and subscribes to 280 periodicals. Computerized library services include the card catalog, interlibrary loans, and database searching. Special learning facilities include a learning resource center, radio station, and Vermont Interactive Television. The 544-acre campus is in a rural area. Including residence halls, there are 19 buildings.

Student Life: Students are from 14 states, 3 foreign countries, and Canada. 97% are white. The average age of freshmen is 21; all undergraduates, 24. 30% do not continue beyond their first year; 60% remain to graduate.

Housing: 550 students can be accommodated in college housing, which includes single-sex and coed dormitories. On-campus housing is guaranteed for all 4 years. 61% of students commute. All students may keep cars.

Activities: There are no fraternities or sororities. There are many groups and organizations on campus, including chess, computers, drama, ethnic, gay, international, photography, professional, radio and TV, religious, social, social service, and student government. Popular campus events include Harvest Days, Winter Carnival, and Spring Fling.

Sports: There are 4 intercollegiate sports for men and 3 for women, and 21 intramural sports for men and 21 for women. Facilities include a double-court gym, 2 racquetball courts, a 6-lane 25-yard pool, a fitness center, outdoor soccer, baseball, and softball fields, trails for cross-country skiing, and a downhill ski run.

Disabled Students: All of the campus is accessible. Wheelchair ramps, elevators, special parking, specially equipped rest rooms, special class scheduling, lowered drinking fountains, and lowered telephones are available.

Services: Counseling and information services are available, as is tutoring in every subject.

Campus Safety and Security: Measures include 24-hour foot and vehicle patrol, self-defense education, pamphlets/posters/films, and emergency telephones. There are lighted pathways/sidewalks.

Programs of Study: VTC confers the B.S. degree. Associate degrees are also awarded. Bachelor's degrees are awarded in ENGINEERING AND ENVIRONMENTAL DESIGN (architectural engineering, computer engineering, and electromechanical technology). Electrical engineering technology is the strongest academically. Architectural engineering technology and computer engineering technology are the largest.

Required: To graduate, students must complete 70 credit hours with a minimum GPA of 2.0.

Special: Co-op programs, internships, work-study programs, accelerated degree programs, and dual majors are offered. There are 2 national honor societies, including Phi Beta Kappa, a freshman honors program, and 2 departmental honors programs.

Faculty/Classroom: 65% of faculty are male; 35%, female. All teach undergraduates. The average class size in an introductory lecture is 28; in a laboratory, 16; and in a regular course, 32.

Admissions: 59% of the 2001-2002 applicants were accepted. The SAT I scores for the 2001-2002 freshman class were: Verbal--59% below 500, 30% between 500 and 599, 10% between 600 and 700, and 1% above 700; Math--50% below 500, 36% between 500 and 599, 13% between 600 and 700, and 1% above 700. The ACT scores were All between 21 and 23.

Requirements: The SAT I or ACT is required. AP and CLEP credits are accepted. Applications are accepted on-line.

Procedure: Freshmen are admitted fall and spring. Application deadlines are open. The application fee is $30. Notification is sent on a rolling basis. A waiting list is an active part of the admissions procedure for specific majors.

Transfer: Transcripts are required from all colleges attended. Students must complete a minimum of 50% of their course work in VTC-sponsored courses.

Visiting: There are regularly scheduled orientations for prospective students. There are guides for informal visits and visitors may sit in on classes and stay overnight. To schedule a visit, contact Admissions.

Financial Aid: In 2001-2002, 78% of all freshmen and 50% of continuing students received some form of financial aid. 58% of freshmen and 40% of continuing students received need-based aid. The average freshman award was $8300. Of that total, scholarships or need-based grants averaged $3900; loans averaged $2625; work contracts averaged $1200; and miscellaneous scholarships averaged $425. 25% of undergraduates work part time. Average annual earnings from campus work are $900. The average financial indebtedness of the 2001 graduate was $11,986. The FAFSA is required. The fall application deadline is March 1.

International Students: International students must score 500 on the written TOEFL or take the MELAB, the Comprehensive English Language Test, or the college's own test. They must also take the SAT I, or ACT, or the college's own entrance exam.

Computers: It is strongly recommended that all students have a personal computer.

Graduates: In 2001, 17 bachelor's degrees were awarded. The most popular majors were architectural engineering technology (65%) and electromechanical engineering technology (35%). In an average class, 35% graduate in 4 years, 5% in 5 years, and 1% in 6 years. Of the 2000 graduating class, 98% were employed within 6 months of graduation.

Admissions Contact: Rosemary Distel, Director of Admissions.
E-mail: *admissions@vtc.edu* Web: *www.vtc.edu*

WOODBURY COLLEGE
Montpelier, VT 05602 — (802) 229-0516; (800) 639-6039; Fax: (802) 229-2141

Full-time: 25 men, 89 women	**Faculty:** 15
Part-time: 8 men, 35 women	**Ph.D.s:** 50%
Graduate: none	**Student/Faculty:** 8 to 1
Year: trimesters	**Tuition:** $12,060
Application Deadline: open	**Room & Board:** n/app
Freshman Class: 183 applied, 155 accepted, 118 enrolled	
SAT I or ACT: not required	**LESS COMPETITIVE**

Woodbury College, established in 1975, offers adult-focused, career-oriented programs in legal and paralegal studies, mediation/conflict management, and prevention and community development. There is 1 undergraduate school. The library contains 17,000 volumes, and subscribes to 20,000 periodicals. Computerized library services include the card catalog, interlibrary loans, and database searching. The 8-acre campus is in a small town 1.5 miles north of the center of Montpelier and the Vermont state government district. There is 1 building.

Student Life: 97% of undergraduates are from Vermont. Others are from 3 states and 1 foreign country. 96% are white. The average age of all undergraduates is 35. 15% do not continue beyond their first year; 85% remain to graduate.

Housing: There are no residence halls. All students commute. No one may keep cars.

Activities: There are no fraternities or sororities. Popular campus events include town meetings and community luncheons.

Disabled Students: Wheelchair ramps, elevators, special parking, and specially equipped rest rooms are available.

Services: Counseling and information services are available, as is tutoring in most subjects.

Campus Safety and Security: Measures include informal discussions.

Programs of Study: Woodbury College confers the B.S. degree. Associate degrees are also awarded. Bachelor's degrees are awarded in SOCIAL SCIENCE (community services, human services, interdisciplinary studies, law, and paralegal studies). Paralegal studies and mediation/conflict management are the largest.

Required: Each student must demonstrate satisfactory competency in core courses and program requirements. A total of 120 credit hours must be completed, with 48 in the major.

Special: Internships are required for all students, and work-study programs are available with the Town of Northfield, Vermont. A student-designed major in interdisciplinary studies is possible. Certificate programs are offered in all areas.

Faculty/Classroom: 39% of faculty are male; 61%, female. All teach undergraduates. The average class size in an introductory lecture is 12; in a laboratory, 12; and in a regular course, 12.

Admissions: 85% of the 2001-2002 applicants were accepted.

Requirements: Students must submit a completed application, a high school diploma or GED, and an essay. An on-campus interview is also required. AP and CLEP credits are accepted. Important factors in the admissions decision are personality/intangible qualities, recommendations by alumni, and recommendations by school officials. Applications are accepted on computer disk and on-line.

Procedure: Freshmen are admitted to all sessions. There is a deferred admissions plan. Application deadlines are open. The application fee is $30. Notification is sent on a rolling basis.

Transfer: Requirements are the same as for incoming freshmen, including high school transcripts, an essay, and an interview. 45 credits of 120 must be completed at Woodbury College.

Visiting: There are regularly scheduled orientations for prospective students, including an introductory meeting, a school philosophy presentation, a financial aid discussion, a free class, a meal, and a question-and-answer session. There are guides for informal visits and visitors may stay overnight; visitors may sit in on classes only on request. To schedule a visit, contact Kathleen Moore at *kathm@woodbury-college.edu*.

Financial Aid: In 2001-2002, 66% of all freshmen and 73% of continuing students received some form of financial aid. 63% of freshmen and 65% of continuing students received need-based aid. The average freshman award was $11,268. Of that total, scholarships or need-based grants averaged $5354 ($8300 maximum); and loans averaged $5932 ($6625 maximum). 75% of undergraduates work part time. Average annual earnings from campus work are $1500. The average financial indebtedness of the 2001 graduate was $27,899. The FAFSA and the college's own financial statement are required. Deadline dates for financial aid applications are open.

International Students: There are 2 international students enrolled.

Computers: There are 4 Dell PowerEdge Servers, models 2200, 2300, and two 2450s. Students may access the network from 12 PCs in the computer lab. They have full access to the Internet and have college e-mail accounts that can be remotely accessed. All students may access the system. There are no time limits. The fee is $30 per trimester or $90 per year.

Graduates: In 2001, 6 bachelor's degrees were awarded. The most popular majors were paralegal studies (36%), mediation/conflict management (34%), and prevention and community development (14%). In an average class, 10% graduate in 4 years, 85% in 5 years, and 5% in 6 years.

Admissions Contact: Kathleen Moore, Admissions Director.
E-mail: *admiss@woodbury-college.edu*
Web: *www.woodbury-college.edu*

VIRGINIA

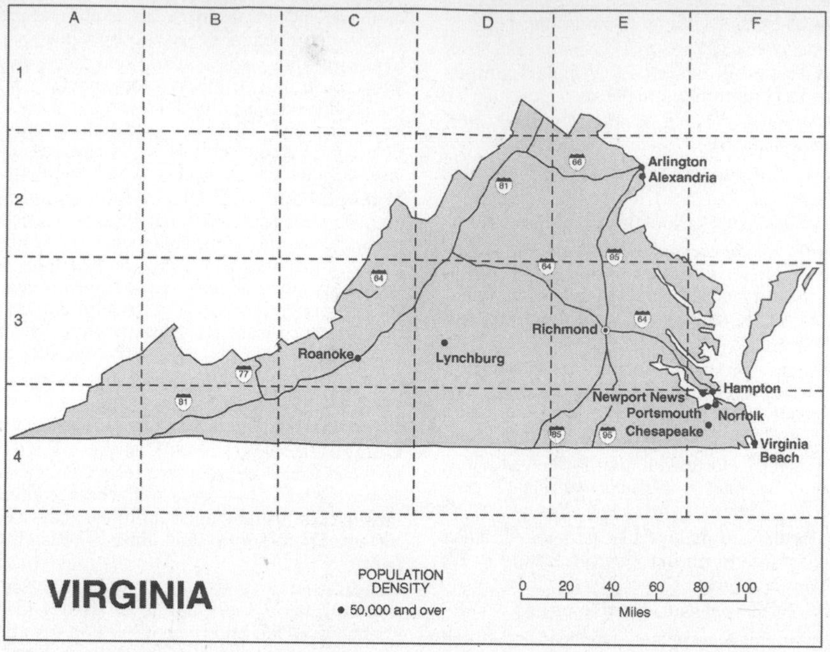

AVERETT COLLEGE
(See Averett University)

AVERETT UNIVERSITY

Danville, VA 24541 — D-4
(434) 791-7301
(800) 283-7388; Fax: (804) 791-5670

Full-time: 486 men, 652 women	**Faculty:** 60
Part-time: 200 men, 425 women	**Ph.D.s:** 80%
Graduate: 281 men, 352 women	**Student/Faculty:** 19 to 1
Year: semesters, summer session	**Tuition:** $13,595
Application Deadline: open	**Room & Board:** $4385
Freshman Class: 603 applied, 536 accepted, 182 enrolled	
SAT I Verbal/Math: 480/460	**ACT:** 18 **LESS COMPETITIVE**

Averett University (formerly Averett College), founded in 1859, is a small, private institution affiliated with the Baptist General Association of Virginia and offering undergraduate and graduate programs in liberal arts, business administration, and teacher education. There are 2 graduate schools. In addition to regional accreditation, Averett has baccalaureate program accreditation with CSWE. The library contains 122,493 volumes, 189,102 microform items, and 13,933 audiovisual forms/CDs, and subscribes to 678 periodicals. Computerized library services include the card catalog, interlibrary loans, and database searching. Special learning facilities include a learning resource center, performing arts center, and regional archive collections. The 25-acre campus is in a suburban area 45 miles from Greensboro. Including residence halls, there are 20 buildings.

Student Life: 85% of undergraduates are from Virginia. Others are from 27 states, 11 foreign countries, and Canada. 75% are from public schools. 68% are white; 27% African American. 38% are members of the school's denomination; 10%, Catholic. The average age of freshmen is 20; all undergraduates, 23. 43% do not continue beyond their first year; 40% remain to graduate.

Housing: 500 students can be accommodated in college housing, which includes coed dormitories and on-campus apartments. On-campus housing is guaranteed for all 4 years. 51% of students commute. Alcohol is not permitted. All students may keep cars.

Activities: 10% of men belong to 1 national fraternity; 13% of women belong to 1 national sorority. There are 28 groups on campus, including art, cheerleading, choir, chorale, chorus, drama, honors, international, literary magazine, musical theater, newspaper, political, professional, religious, social, social service, student government, and yearbook. Popular campus events include Spring Weekend, dances, and concerts.

Sports: There are 8 intercollegiate sports for men and 7 for women, and 5 intramural sports for men and 6 for women. Facilities include tennis courts, an athletic field, a gym complex, and a 100-acre equestrian center.

Disabled Students: 58% of the campus is accessible. Wheelchair ramps, elevators, special parking, specially equipped rest rooms, and talking books and magnification devices for the visually challenged are available.

Services: Counseling and information services are available, as is tutoring in most subjects. There is a reader service for the blind, and remedial math, reading, and writing.

Campus Safety and Security: Measures include 24-hour foot and vehicle patrol, shuttle buses, informal discussions, and pamphlets/posters/films. There are emergency telephones and lighted pathways/sidewalks.

Programs of Study: Averett confers B.A., B.S., B.A.S., and B.B.A. degrees. Associate and master's degrees are also awarded. Bachelor's degrees are awarded in AGRICULTURE (equine science), BIOLOGICAL SCIENCE (biochemistry and biology/biological science), BUSINESS (accounting, business administration and management, management science, marketing/retailing/merchandising, and sports management), COMMUNICATIONS AND THE ARTS (dramatic arts, English, fine arts, journalism, and music), COMPUTER AND PHYSICAL SCIENCE (chemistry, computer science, and mathematics), EDUCATION (art, athletic training, early childhood, middle school, physical, and secondary), ENGINEERING AND ENVIRONMENTAL DESIGN (aviation administration/management and environmental science), HEALTH PROFESSIONS (medical laboratory technology, premedicine, and sports medicine), SOCIAL SCIENCE (clinical psychology, criminal justice, history, liberal arts/general studies, ministries, political science/government, prelaw, psychology, religion, social science, and sociology). Business administration, education, and aviation are the largest.

Required: To graduate, all students must complete at least 123 hours with a minimum 2.0 GPA and attend commencement exercises. Core requirements include 15 hours of history or social science, 9 of English, and 6 each of fine arts, religion, and philosophy. B.A. students need an additional 6 to 8 hours of math or natural science and 6 to 14 hours in a foreign language, depending on proficiency; B.S. students need an additional 6 hours in math and 8 hours in natural science. Freshmen must take a 3-hour seminar. All students must pass an exit writing exam.

Special: Averett offers co-op programs in environmental science and internships in business, journalism, criminal justice, psychology, and religion. Students may design their own majors, select dual majors, or pursue a combined B.A.-B.S. degree. Also available are accelerated degrees in all majors, a general studies degree, nondegree study, and up to 5 pass/fail options. Senior equestrian studies majors may spend a semester or summer in England preparing for the British Horse Society A.I. certificate; religion majors may spend a summer on an archeological dig in the Middle East. Altogether, study abroad is available in 8 countries. There is a freshman honors program as well as honors programs in all departments.

Faculty/Classroom: 64% of faculty are male; 36%, female. All teach undergraduates. No introductory courses are taught by graduate stu-

dents. The average class size in an introductory lecture is 17; in a laboratory, 15; and in a regular course, 13.
Admissions: 89% of the 2001-2002 applicants were accepted. The ACT scores were 74% below 21, 13% between 21 and 23, 10% between 24 and 26, and 3% between 27 and 28. 31% of the current freshmen were in the top fifth of their class; 55% were in the top two fifths. 2 freshmen graduated first in their class.
Requirements: The SAT I or ACT is required, with a recommended composite score of 850 on the SAT I or 18 on the ACT. Applicants should be high school graduates or have earned the GED. Recommended secondary preparation should include 4 units in English, 3 each in math and social science, and 2 each in foreign language and science. AP and CLEP credits are accepted. Important factors in the admissions decision are advanced placement or honor courses, recommendations by school officials, and leadership record. Applications are accepted on-line at the school's web site.
Procedure: Freshmen are admitted to all sessions. Entrance exams should be taken in the spring of the junior year or the fall of the senior year. There is a deferred admissions plan. Application deadlines are open. Notification is sent on a rolling basis.
Transfer: 230 transfer students enrolled in 2001-2002. Applicants must present at least a 2.0 GPA and be eligible to return to their previous college. 30 credits of 123 must be completed at Averett.
Visiting: There are regularly scheduled orientations for prospective students, including spring and fall open houses, Virginia Visitors Day, and special visiting days for selected majors. There are guides for informal visits and visitors may sit in on classes and stay overnight. To schedule a visit, contact the Admissions Office.
Financial Aid: Averett is a member of CSS. The FAFSA and the college's own financial statement are required. The fall application deadline is April 1.
International Students: There are 28 international students enrolled. The school actively recruits these students. They must score 500 on the written TOEFL or 173 on the electronic version. First-time freshmen must also take the SAT I of the ACT.
Computers: More than 100 PCs are available for student use in 3 separate computer labs; a separate computer lab is maintained for the psychology department. Computers are also available in the library and in the learning center, and there is Internet access. All students may access the system 24 hours a day. There are no time limits and no fees. It is recommended that students in graduate and professional studies programs have personal computers.
Graduates: In 2001, 389 bachelor's degrees were awarded. The most popular majors were business/marketing (76%), education (6%), and social science/history (3%). In an average class, 1% graduate in 3 years, 34% in 4 years, 40% in 5 years, and 42% in 6 years. 35 companies recruited on campus in 2000-2001.
Admissions Contact: Dr. Vicki Richman, Dean of Admissions. A video is available. E-mail: *admit@averett.edu* Web: *www.averett.edu*

BLUEFIELD COLLEGE B-3
Bluefield, VA 24605 **(276) 326-4339**
(800) 872-0175; Fax: (276) 326-4288

Full-time: 369 men, 442 women	**Faculty:** 32
Part-time: 13 men, 24 women	**Ph.D.s:** 62%
Graduate: none	**Student/Faculty:** 25 to 1
Year: semesters, summer session	**Tuition:** $9140
Application Deadline: open	**Room & Board:** $5060
Freshman Class: 593 applied, 454 accepted, 165 enrolled	
SAT I Verbal/Math: 470/450	**ACT:** 19 **COMPETITIVE**

Bluefield College, founded in 1922, is a private, liberal arts institution affiliated with the Southern Baptist Church. The library contains 42,000 volumes and 1650 audiovisual forms/CDs, and subscribes to 195 periodicals. Computerized library services include the card catalog, interlibrary loans, and database searching. Special learning facilities include a learning resource center, radio station, learning center, and writing center. The 85-acre campus is in a small town 100 miles west of Roanoke on the Virginia-West Virginia state line. Including residence halls, there are 9 buildings.
Student Life: 71% of undergraduates are from Virginia. Others are from 16 states and 4 foreign countries. 95% are from public schools. 84% are white; 13% African American. Most are Protestant. The average age of freshmen is 18; all undergraduates, 32. 46% do not continue beyond their first year; 50% remain to graduate.
Housing: 240 students can be accommodated in college housing, which includes single-sex dormitories and on-campus apartments. On-campus housing is guaranteed for all 4 years. 55% of students commute. Alcohol is not permitted. All students may keep cars.
Activities: 35% of men and about 12% of women belong to 3 local fraternities; 45% of women belong to 3 local sororities. There are 18 groups on campus, including cheerleading, choir, chorale, chorus, dance, drama, honors, literary magazine, musical theater, newspaper, pep band, political, professional, radio and TV, religious, social, student government, and yearbook. Popular campus events include Spring Weekend and Christmas Banquet.
Sports: There are 5 intercollegiate sports for men and 4 for women, and 6 intramural sports for men and 6 for women. Facilities include a gym with game courts and weight rooms, a student activities center, a game room, tennis courts, and a sand volleyball court.
Disabled Students: 95% of the campus is accessible. Wheelchair ramps, elevators, special parking, specially equipped rest rooms, and lowered drinking fountains are available.
Services: Counseling and information services are available, as is tutoring in most subjects. There is a reader service for the blind, and remedial math, reading, and writing.
Campus Safety and Security: Measures include informal discussions, pamphlets/posters/films, lighted pathways/sidewalks, and foot and vehicle patrol from 11 P.M. to 6 A.M.
Programs of Study: BC confers B.A. and B.S. degrees. Associate degrees are also awarded. Bachelor's degrees are awarded in BIOLOGICAL SCIENCE (biology/biological science), BUSINESS (business administration and management), COMMUNICATIONS AND THE ARTS (communications, English, fine arts, and music), COMPUTER AND PHYSICAL SCIENCE (chemistry and mathematics), EDUCATION (middle school and secondary), HEALTH PROFESSIONS (exercise science), SOCIAL SCIENCE (Christian studies, criminal justice, history, interdisciplinary studies, psychology, religion, and social studies). Business, teacher education, and biology are the strongest academically. Business, teacher education, and health are the largest.
Required: To graduate, students must have completed a minimum of 126 semester hours, including a liberal arts requirement of 51 to 53 hours, with 30 to 45 hours in the major, and a minimum 2.0 GPA. Other requirements vary by program. All graduates must demonstrate computer proficiency by testing, passing computer courses, or having components in required courses.
Special: The college offers credit for life/military/work experience, nondegree study through the Fine Arts Community School, study abroad in England, an accelerated degree program in organizational management and development and in administration of justice, and internships in criminal justice, psychology, and recreation. There are 4 national honor societies, a freshman honors program, and 7 departmental honors programs.
Faculty/Classroom: 67% of faculty are male; 33%, female. All teach undergraduates, and 30% also do research. The average class size in an introductory lecture is 35; in a laboratory, 12; and in a regular course, 18.
Admissions: 77% of the 2001-2002 applicants were accepted. The SAT I scores for the 2001-2002 freshman class were: Verbal--63% below 500, 32% between 500 and 599, 3% between 600 and 700, and 2% above 700; Math--66% below 500, 29% between 500 and 599, and 5% between 600 and 700. The ACT scores were 64% below 21, 20% between 21 and 23, 9% between 24 and 26, and 7% between 27 and 28. 32% of the current freshmen were in the top fifth of their class; 70% were in the top two fifths.
Requirements: The SAT I or ACT is required. In addition, applicants must be graduates of an accredited secondary school or have a GED certificate, and have completed 4 years of English, 2 of social sciences, 1 of science, and 5 of electives. A GPA of 2.0 is required. AP and CLEP credits are accepted. Important factors in the admissions decision are leadership record, advanced placement or honor courses, and recommendations by school officials.
Procedure: Freshmen are admitted to all sessions. Entrance exams should be taken early in the senior year. There is a deferred admissions plan. Application deadlines are open. The fall 2001 application fee was $20. Notification is sent on a rolling basis.
Transfer: 352 transfer students enrolled in 2001-2002. Prospective students must submit transcripts of all academic work, a financial aid transcript, and SAT I or ACT scores, if they have fewer than 30 hours of college-level work. 32 credits of 126 must be completed at BC.
Visiting: There are regularly scheduled orientations for prospective students, including campus tours, opportunities to develop class schedules, and financial aid workshops. Visitors may sit in on classes and stay overnight. To schedule a visit, contact the Admissions Office at (276) 326-4214 or (800) 872-0175.
Financial Aid: In 2001-2002, 97% of all freshmen and 93% of continuing students received some form of financial aid. 61% of freshmen and 58% of continuing students received need-based aid. The average freshman award was $7900. Of that total, scholarships or need-based grants averaged $4000 ($8690 maximum); loans averaged $2625 ($6625 maximum); work contracts averaged $774 ($1548 maximum); and other sources averaged $500 ($1000 maximum). 11% of undergraduates work part time. Average annual earnings from campus work are $660. The average financial indebtedness of the 2001 graduate was $14,000. The FAFSA and the college's own financial statement are required. The fall application deadline is March 10.
International Students: There were 26 international students enrolled in a recent year. The school actively recruits these students. They must score 500 on the written TOEFL.

Computers: The mainframe is a VAX ALPHA 2100 server. Students may use the 100 PCs in labs. All students may access the system. There are no time limits and no fees. It is recommended that students in organizational management and development have personal computers.

Graduates: In 2001, 131 bachelor's degrees were awarded. The most popular majors were organizational management (31%), criminal justice (19%), and business management (15%). In an average class, 1% graduate in 3 years, 47% in 4 years, 50% in 5 years, and 55% in 6 years. 4 companies recruited on campus in 2000-2001. Of the 2000 graduating class, 7% were enrolled in graduate school within 6 months of graduation.

Admissions Contact: Admissions Office. A video is available.
Web: *www.bluefield.edu*

BRIDGEWATER COLLEGE

Bridgewater, VA 22812-1599 — D-2

(540) 828-5375
(800) 759-8328; Fax: (540) 828-5481

Full-time: 538 men, 702 women	**Faculty:** 78; IIB, -$
Part-time: 10 men, 10 women	**Ph.D.s:** 77%
Graduate: none	**Student/Faculty:** 16 to 1
Year: 4-1-4, summer session	**Tuition:** $15,490
Application Deadline: open	**Room & Board:** $7460
Freshman Class: 1156 applied, 1004 accepted, 340 enrolled	
SAT I Verbal/Math: 510/515	**ACT:** 21 **COMPETITIVE**

Bridgewater College, founded in 1880, is a private liberal arts institution affiliated with the Church of the Brethren. In addition to regional accreditation, Bridgewater has baccalaureate program accreditation with ACBSP. The library contains 177,907 volumes, 407,659 microform items, and 8503 audiovisual forms/CDs, and subscribes to 637 periodicals. Computerized library services include the card catalog, interlibrary loans, and database searching. Special learning facilities include a learning resource center, art gallery, radio station, and museum of the Shenandoah Valley and Church of the Brethren. The 190-acre campus is in a small town 8 miles south of Harrisonburg. Including residence halls, there are 26 buildings.

Student Life: 76% of undergraduates are from Virginia. Others are from 22 states and 9 foreign countries. 90% are from public schools. 89% are white. 77% are Protestant; 10% claim no religious affiliation. The average age of freshmen is 18; all undergraduates, 20. 25% do not continue beyond their first year; 61% remain to graduate.

Housing: 1114 students can be accommodated in college housing, which includes single-sex dormitories and on-campus apartments. In addition, there are honors houses. On-campus housing is guaranteed for all 4 years. 83% of students live on campus; of those, 60% remain on campus on weekends. Alcohol is not permitted. All students may keep cars.

Activities: There are no fraternities or sororities. There are 67 groups on campus, including art, band, cheerleading, chess, choir, chorale, chorus, dance, debate, drama, ethnic, forensics, honors, international, jazz band, literary magazine, musical theater, newspaper, pep band, political, professional, radio and TV, religious, social, social service, student government, and yearbook. Popular campus events include Parents Day, Messiah at Christmas, and May Day.

Sports: There are 9 intercollegiate sports for men and 10 for women, and 19 intramural sports for men and 19 for women. Facilities include a gym, a 2500-seat football stadium, a swimming pool, tennis courts, an all-weather track, playing fields for baseball, lacrosse, softball, football, field hockey, and soccer, and a 34,000-square-foot fitness center with basketball, volleyball, and racquetball courts, an indoor track, cardiac and weight training center, and aerobics/dance rooms.

Disabled Students: 90% of the campus is accessible. Wheelchair ramps, elevators, special parking, specially equipped rest rooms, lowered drinking fountains, lowered telephones, and accessible laundry facilities in 2 dorms are available.

Services: Counseling and information services are available, as is tutoring in every subject. There is a reader service for the blind, and remedial math, reading, and writing. The student resource center provides personal counseling services and learning skills.

Campus Safety and Security: Measures include 24-hour foot and vehicle patrol, self-defense education, informal discussions, and pamphlets/posters/films. There are emergency telephones and lighted pathways/sidewalks.

Programs of Study: Bridgewater confers B.A., B.S., and B.G.S. degrees. Bachelor's degrees are awarded in BIOLOGICAL SCIENCE (biology/biological science and nutrition), BUSINESS (business administration and management), COMMUNICATIONS AND THE ARTS (art, communications, English, French, music, and Spanish), COMPUTER AND PHYSICAL SCIENCE (chemistry, computer science, information sciences and systems, mathematics, physical sciences, and physics), EDUCATION (athletic training), HEALTH PROFESSIONS (allied health, health science, and medical technology), SOCIAL SCIENCE (economics, family/consumer studies, history, international studies, liberal arts/general studies, philosophy, political science/government, psychology, religion, and sociology). Biology, psychology, and history are the strongest academically. Biology, business administration, and psychology are the largest.

Required: To graduate, all students must complete a minimum of 123 credit hours, with 30 to 48 hours in the major. A minimum 2.0 GPA is required, and all seniors must pass a comprehensive exam. In addition, PDP 150: Personal Development and the Liberal Arts must be completed by each entering student unless the student transfers 15 or more units to Bridgewater College. Other general education requirements include courses in writing, oral communication, quantitative reasoning, global perspectives, humanities, natural science, math, foreign language, social science, and exercise science.

Special: Bridgewater offers internships to junior and seniors, study abroad in 10 countries, B.A.-B.S. and general studies degrees, a 3-2 forestry degree with Duke University, and teacher certification programs. Interdisciplinary majors include history and political science, philosophy and religion, physics and math, information systems management, and physical science. A veterinary medicine dual program with Virginia Polytechnic Institute and Virginia Tech and a physical therapy dual degree program with Shenandoah University are also offered. There are 8 national honor societies, a freshman honors program, and 17 departmental honors programs.

Faculty/Classroom: 63% of faculty are male; 37%, female. All teach undergraduates, and 50% also do research. The average class size in an introductory lecture is 23; in a laboratory, 17; and in a regular course, 17.

Admissions: 87% of the 2001-2002 applicants were accepted. The SAT I scores for the 2001-2002 freshman class were: Verbal--42% below 500, 38% between 500 and 599, 18% between 600 and 700, and 2% above 700; Math--42% below 500, 36% between 500 and 599, 21% between 600 and 700, and 1% above 700. The ACT scores were 43% below 21, 16% between 21 and 23, 17% between 24 and 26, 11% between 27 and 28, and 13% above 28. 49% of the current freshmen were in the top fifth of their class; 78% were in the top two fifths. 9 freshmen graduated first in their class.

Requirements: The SAT I or ACT is required; the SAT I is preferred. An interview is recommended. Applicants must be graduates of an accredited secondary school or have a GED certificate, and have completed 17 units, including 4 in English, 3 in math, 2 each in foreign language, science, and history and social studies, and 4 in electives. Bridgewater requires applicants to be in the upper 50% of their class. A GPA of 2.0 is required. AP credits are accepted. Important factors in the admissions decision are advanced placement or honor courses, recommendations by school officials, and leadership record. An on-line application form is available through the college's web site.

Procedure: Freshmen are admitted fall, spring, and summer. Entrance exams should be taken in the spring of the junior year or fall of the senior year. There is a deferred admissions plan. Application deadlines are open. The application fee is $30. Notification is set on a rolling basis.

Transfer: 39 transfer students enrolled in 2001-2002. A degree from an accredited high school and a 2.0 GPA in all undergraduate work are required. 27 credits of 123 must be completed at Bridgewater.

Visiting: There are regularly scheduled orientations for prospective students, including a meeting with a faculty adviser, course scheduling and registration, and social activities. There are guides for informal visits and visitors may sit in on classes and stay overnight. To schedule a visit, contact Linda F. Stout.

Financial Aid: In 2001-2002, 99% of all students received some form of financial aid. 70% of all students received need-based aid. The average freshman award was $15,292. Of that total, scholarships or need-based grants averaged $12,454 ($18,490 maximum); loans averaged $3430 ($6625 maximum); and work contracts averaged $1029 ($1200 maximum). 32% of undergraduates work part time. Average annual earnings from campus work are $1016. The average financial indebtedness of the 2001 graduate was $19,664. Bridgewater is a member of CSS. The FAFSA is required. The fall application deadline is March 1.

International Students: There are 12 international students enrolled. The school actively recruits these students. They must score 500 on the written TOEFL or 173 on the electronic version and also take the SAT I or the ACT.

Computers: The mainframe is a Sun Ultra Enterprise 450 minicomputer. All buildings are connected via a campuswide network. There are 145 computers available for student use in classroom buildings and the library. Dorm rooms are wired for connection to the campus network. Express stations, in convenient locations across campus, allow quick access to e-mail and the Web. All students may access the system 24 hours a day. There are no time limits and no fees.

Graduates: In 2001, 220 bachelor's degrees were awarded. The most popular majors were psychology (18%), business administration (15%), and biology (15%). In an average class, 57% graduate in 4 years, 61% in 5 years, and 61% in 6 years. 34 companies recruited on campus in 2000-2001.

Admissions Contact: Linda F. Stout, Director of Enrollment Operations. A video is available. E-mail: *admissions@bridgewater.edu*
Web: *www.bridgewater.edu*

CHRISTENDOM COLLEGE D-2
Front Royal, VA 22630 (540) 636-2900
(800) 877-5456; Fax: (540) 636-1655

Full-time: 140 men, 189 women	**Faculty:** 20
Part-time: 1 man, 1 woman	**Ph.D.s:** 75%
Graduate: 42 men, 33 women	**Student/Faculty:** 16 to 1
Year: semesters	**Tuition:** $12,000
Application Deadline: February 15	**Room & Board:** $4700
Freshman Class: 197 applied, 159 accepted, 102 enrolled	
SAT I Verbal/Math: 650/580	**ACT:** 25 VERY COMPETITIVE+

Christendom College, founded in 1977, is a private liberal arts institution affiliated with the Roman Catholic Church. The library contains 66,611 volumes, 870 microform items, and 1384 audiovisual forms/CDs, and subscribes to 286 periodicals. Computerized library services include the card catalog, interlibrary loans, and database searching. Special learning facilities include a learning resource center, art gallery, and a writing center. The 100-acre campus is in a rural area 65 miles west of Washington, D.C. Including residence halls, there are 19 buildings.

Student Life: 79% of undergraduates are from out of state, mostly the Middle Atlantic. Others are from 44 states, 4 foreign countries, and Canada. 13% are from public schools; 53%, private; 34%, homeschooled. 92% are white. Most are Catholic. The average age of freshmen is 18; all undergraduates, 20. 17% do not continue beyond their first year; 59% remain to graduate.

Housing: 312 students can be accommodated in college housing, which includes single-sex dormitories and on-campus apartments. On-campus housing is guaranteed for all 4 years. 93% of students live on campus; of those, all remain on campus on weekends. All students may keep cars.

Activities: There are no fraternities or sororities. There are 16 groups on campus, including choir, chorale, debate, drama, musical theater, newspaper, photography, political, religious, social service, student government, and yearbook. Popular campus events include Octoberfest, Christmas Dinner Dance, and St. Patrick's Day.

Sports: There are 3 intercollegiate sports for men and 2 for women, and 7 intramural sports for men and 7 for women. Facilities include indoor basketball and volleyball courts, racquetball courts, playing fields, table games, a recreation center, and an outdoor swimming pool.

Disabled Students: 60% of the campus is accessible. Wheelchair ramps, special parking, and specially equipped rest rooms are available.

Campus Safety and Security: Measures include 24-hour foot and vehicle patrol, escort service, emergency telephones, and lighted pathways/sidewalks.

Programs of Study: Christendom confers the B.A. degree. Associate and master's degrees are also awarded. Bachelor's degrees are awarded in COMMUNICATIONS AND THE ARTS (English and French), SOCIAL SCIENCE (classical/ancient civilization, history, philosophy, political science/government, and theological studies). Political science is the strongest academically. Philosophy is the largest.

Required: To graduate, all students must complete a total of 126 credit hours, including a 30-hour major and an 84-credit core curriculum, which includes 18 hours each in theology and philosophy. A minimum 2.0 GPA is required. All students must demonstrate proficiency in a foreign language and complete a thesis.

Special: Christendom offers summer internships in Washington, D.C., for political science students, and also sponsors summer programs in Rome, Dublin, and Spain. Students may pursue dual majors. There is a work-study program with the college.

Faculty/Classroom: 85% of faculty are male; 15%, female. All teach undergraduates. No introductory courses are taught by graduate students. The average class size in an introductory lecture is 20; in a laboratory, 3; and in a regular course, 10.

Admissions: 81% of the 2001-2002 applicants were accepted. The SAT I scores for the 2001-2002 freshman class were: Verbal--32% between 500 and 599, 35% between 600 and 700, and 33% above 700; Math--16% below 500, 38% between 500 and 599, 38% between 600 and 700, and 8% above 700. The ACT scores were 10% below 21, 24% between 21 and 23, 34% between 24 and 26, 17% between 27 and 28, and 14% above 28. 38% of the current freshmen were in the top fifth of their class; 84% were in the top two fifths. There was 1 National Merit finalist and 3 semifinalists. 2 freshmen graduated first in their class.

Requirements: The SAT I or ACT is required; the SAT I is preferred. A minimum composite score of 1000 on the SAT I or 21 on the ACT is required. Applicants need not be graduates of an accredited secondary school. GED certificates are accepted. Students should have completed 4 years of English, 2 years each of foreign language, math, history, and science, and 1 year of social studies. Essays and letters of recommendation are required. Interviews are recommended. Christendom requires applicants to be in the upper 50% of their class. A GPA of 3.0 is required. AP credits are accepted. Important factors in the admissions decision are advanced placement or honor courses, leadership record, and evidence of special talent. Application are accepted on-line.

Procedure: Freshmen are admitted fall and spring. Entrance exams should be taken in the spring of the junior year or fall of the senior year. There are early action and early admissions plans. Early action applications should be filed by December 1; regular applications, preferably by February 15 for fall entry and December 15 for spring entry. The fall 2001 application fee was $25. Notification of early action is senton a rolling basis beginning December 15; regular decision, beginning January 15. 10% of all applicants are on a waiting list; 8 were accepted in 2001.

Transfer: 8 transfer students enrolled in 2001-2002. Students must have a minimum 2.0 GPA and meet all other applicable standard admissions requirements. The SAT I or ACT is recommended. 36 credits of 126 must be completed at Christendom.

Visiting: There are guides for informal visits and visitors may sit in on classes and stay overnight. To schedule a visit, contact an Admissions Counselor.

Financial Aid: In 2001-2002, 74% of all freshmen and 63% of continuing students received some form of financial aid. 47% of freshmen and 49% of continuing students received need-based aid. The average freshman award was $8180. Of that total, scholarships or need-based grants averaged $4020 ($11,750 maximum); loans averaged $2730 ($6500 maximum); and work contracts averaged $1750 (maximum). 40% of undergraduates work part time. Average annual earnings from campus work are $1750. The average financial indebtedness of the 2001 graduate was $7950. The college's own financial statement is required. The fall application deadline is April 1.

International Students: There are 10 international students enrolled. They must score 500 on the written TOEFL.

Computers: There is a computer lab network of 18 PCs for student use offering word processsing, Internet and e-mail capabilities, and 4 PCs for Internet access in the library. All students may access the system. There are no time limits and no fees.

Graduates: In 2001, 52 bachelor's degrees were awarded. The most popular majors were history (26%), philosophy (24%), and political science (16%). In an average class, 3% graduate in 3 years, 97% in 4 years, and 100% in 5 years. 6 companies recruited on campus in 2000-2001. Of the 2000 graduating class, 20% were enrolled in graduate school within 6 months of graduation and 75% were employed.

Admissions Contact: Paul L. Heisler, Director of Admissions.
E-mail: *admissions@christendom.edu* Web: *www.christendom.edu*

CHRISTOPHER NEWPORT UNIVERSITY F-3
Newport News, VA 23606-2998 (757) 594-7015
(800) 333-4268; Fax: (757) 594-7333

Full-time: 1554 men, 2487 women	**Faculty:** 184; IIB, +$
Part-time: 444 men, 673 women	**Ph.D.s:** 87%
Graduate: 75 men, 155 women	**Student/Faculty:** 22 to 1
Year: semesters, summer session	**Tuition:** $3112 ($9134)
Application Deadline: March 1	**Room & Board:** $5750
Freshman Class: 4270 applied, 2069 accepted, 1048 enrolled	
ACT: 20	VERY COMPETITIVE

Christopher Newport University, founded in 1960, is a comprehensive public university offering undergraduate programs in business and economics, arts and humanities, social science and professional studies, and science and technology. There are 2 undergraduate schools and 1 graduate school. In addition to regional accreditation, CNU has baccalaureate program accreditation with AACSB, ABET, CSWE, and NASM. The library contains 330,014 volumes, 765,028 microform items, and 10,238 audiovisual forms/CDs, and subscribes to 1600 periodicals. Computerized library services include the card catalog, interlibrary loans, and database searching. Special learning facilities include a learning resource center, art gallery, radio station, greenhouse-herbarium, and Japanese teahouse. The 150-acre campus is in a suburban area 20 miles northwest of Norfolk and 20 miles southeast of Williamsburg. Including residence halls, there are 19 buildings.

Student Life: 97% of undergraduates are from Virginia. Others are from 27 states and 15 foreign countries. 80% are white; 14% African American. The average age of freshmen is 18; all undergraduates, 23. 19% do not continue beyond their first year; 30% remain to graduate.

Housing: 1455 students can be accommodated in college housing, which includes coed dormitories and on-campus apartments. On-campus housing is guaranteed for all 4 years. 70% of students commute. Alcohol is not permitted. All students may keep cars.

Activities: 5% of men belong to 5 national fraternities; 4% of women belong to 5 national sororities. There are 20 groups on campus, including art, band, cheerleading, chess, choir, chorale, chorus, computers, dance, drama, ethnic, gay, honors, international, jazz band, literary magazine, musical theater, newspaper, opera, orchestra, pep band, political, professional, radio and TV, religious, social, social service, student government, and symphony. Popular campus events include FallFest, Sand Jam, and Ella Fitzgerald Music Festival.

Sports: There are 11 intercollegiate sports for men and 11 for women, and 13 intramural sports for men and 13 for women. The sports and recreation center has a 200-meter indoor track, 3 basketball courts, 10,000 square feet of recreation and fitness space with state of the art equipment.

Disabled Students: 95% of the campus is accessible. Wheelchair ramps, elevators, special parking, specially equipped rest rooms, special class scheduling, and lowered drinking fountains are available. Services are available on an individual basis.

Services: Counseling and information services are available, as is tutoring in most subjects. There is remedial math, reading, and writing.

Campus Safety and Security: Measures include 24-hour foot and vehicle patrol, escort service, pamphlets/posters/films, and emergency telephones. There are lighted pathways/sidewalks and a campus police department.

Programs of Study: CNU confers B.A., B.S., B.M., B.S.A., B.S.B.A., B.S.G.A., B.S.I.S., and B.S.N. degrees. Master's degrees are also awarded. Bachelor's degrees are awarded in AGRICULTURE (horticulture), BIOLOGICAL SCIENCE (biology/biological science), BUSINESS (accounting, banking and finance, business administration and management, business economics, international business management, marketing management, marketing/retailing/merchandising, real estate, and recreation and leisure services), COMMUNICATIONS AND THE ARTS (communications, creative writing, dramatic arts, English, English literature, fine arts, French, German, journalism, music, music performance, music theory and composition, performing arts, and Spanish), COMPUTER AND PHYSICAL SCIENCE (computer science, information sciences and systems, mathematics, and physics), EDUCATION (early childhood, foreign languages, middle school, music, science, and secondary), ENGINEERING AND ENVIRONMENTAL DESIGN (computer engineering and environmental science), HEALTH PROFESSIONS (nursing, predentistry, and premedicine), SOCIAL SCIENCE (criminal justice, criminology, economics, history, interdisciplinary studies, international public service, international relations, law, parks and recreation management, philosophy, political science/government, prelaw, psychology, public administration, religion, social work, and sociology). Business, psychology, and government administration are the largest.

Required: To graduate, all students must fulfill general education requirements in English, math, humanities, social science, lab science, communications, philosophy, foreign language, computer literacy, health, and phys ed. A minimum of 120 semester hours, with 58 to 66 hours in the major and in elective studies, is required. Students must have a minimum GPA of 2.0.

Special: CNU offers cross-registration with Thomas Nelson Community College and Hampton and Old Dominion Universities, dual majors, various B.A.-B.S. degrees, a student-designed interdisciplinary studies major, and internships in social service, communications, city government, computer science, and engineering. There are 9 national honor societies, a freshman honors program, and 9 departmental honors programs.

Faculty/Classroom: All teach undergraduates and 10% both teach and do research. No introductory courses are taught by graduate students. The average class size in an introductory lecture is 25; in a laboratory, 20; and in a regular course, 25.

Admissions: 48% of the 2001-2002 applicants were accepted. The SAT I scores for the 2001-2002 freshman class were: Verbal--12% below 500, 56% between 500 and 599, 28% between 600 and 700, and 3% above 700; Math--17% below 500, 58% between 500 and 599, 24% between 600 and 700, and 1% above 700. The ACT scores were 55% below 21, 37% between 21 and 23, and 8% between 24 and 26. 41% of the current freshmen were in the top fifth of their class; 82% were in the top two fifths.

Requirements: The SAT I or ACT is required, with minimum scores of 510 verbal and 500 math on the SAT I or 19 on the ACT. Applicants must be graduates of an accredited secondary school or have a GED certificate. A total of 23 academic credits is recommended, including 4 units of English, 3 each of social science, math, and science, and either 3 units of 1 foreign language or 2 years of 2 foreign languages. An essay and interview are recommended. CNU requires applicants to be in the upper 50% of their class. A GPA of 3.0 is required. AP and CLEP credits are accepted. Important factors in the admissions decision are recommendations by school officials, extracurricular activities record, and evidence of special talent. Applications are accepted on-line at *www.cnu.edu/admin/admit/*.

Procedure: Freshmen are admitted fall and spring. Entrance exams should be taken in the junior year. There are early admissions and deferred admissions plans. Applications should be filed by March 1 for fall entry and December 1 for spring entry. The fall 2001 application fee was $25. Notification is sent on a rolling basis. 15% of all applicants are on a waiting list; 25 were accepted in 2001.

Transfer: 306 transfer students enrolled in 2001-2002. Applicants must have at least 15 transferable semester hours with a minimum 3.0 GPA, and be eligible to return to the most recently attended college or university. Students with fewer than 15 semester hours must submit SAT I or ACT scores and official transcripts from their secondary school and all colleges attended. 30 credits of 120 must be completed at CNU.

Visiting: There are regularly scheduled orientations for prospective students, including information sessions and tours Monday through Friday at 10 A.M. and 2 P.M.; Saturday session and tour at 11 A.M. Tours run throughout the year. There are guides for informal visits and visitors may sit in on classes and stay overnight. To schedule a visit, contact the Admissions Office at *tourguide@cnu.edu*.

Financial Aid: In 2001-2002, 65% of all students received some form of financial aid, including need-based aid. The average freshman award was $4701. Of that total, scholarships or need-based grants averaged $2694 ($6200 maximum); loans averaged $4598 ($10,500 maximum); and work contracts averaged $1594 ($2100 maximum). 21% of undergraduates work part time. Average annual earnings from campus work are $1478. The average financial indebtedness of the 2001 graduate was $8096. CNU is a member of CSS. The FAFSA is required. The fall application deadline is March 1.

International Students: There are 17 international students enrolled. They must score 530 on the written TOEFL or 197 on the electronic version and also take the SAT I or the ACT, scoring 1020 on the SAT I.

Computers: The mainframes are 2 Sun ES5000s and an HP9000. 16 networked PC, Unix and Mac labs are available on campus 7 days a week with 1 computer for every 10 students. All students have accounts on the Sun System that can be accessed from all labs, dorms, or dial-in connections. All students may access the system 24 hours a day, 7 days a week. There are no time limits and no fees.

Graduates: In 2001, 732 bachelor's degrees were awarded. The most popular majors were business administration (15%), psychology (14%), and social science (12%). In an average class, 8% graduate in 4 years, 24% in 5 years, and 30% in 6 years. 325 companies recruited on campus in 2000-2001.

Admissions Contact: Admissions Office. E-mail: *admit@cnu.edu*
Web: *http://www.cnu.edu*

COLLEGE OF WILLIAM AND MARY — E-3

Williamsburg, VA 23187-8795 (757) 221-4223
Fax: (757) 221-1242

Full-time: 2399 men, 3128 women	**Faculty:** 391; I, av$
Part-time: 34 men, 43 women	**Ph.D.s:** 91%
Graduate: 959 men, 926 women	**Student/Faculty:** 14 to 1
Year: semesters, summer session	**Tuition:** $4780 ($17,808)
Application Deadline: January 7	**Room & Board:** $5222
Freshman Class: 8610 applied, 3222 accepted, 1359 enrolled	
SAT I Verbal/Math: 680/660	**ACT:** 30 **MOST COMPETITIVE**

College of William and Mary, founded in 1693, is the second-oldest college in the United States. The public institution offers undergraduate degrees in the Arts and Sciences. Graduate programs are offered in arts and sciences, law, business, education, and marine science. There are 2 undergraduate and 5 graduate schools. In addition to regional accreditation, William and Mary has baccalaureate program accreditation with AACSB and NCATE. The 9 libraries contain 1,492,783 volumes, 2,306,878 microform items, and 28,297 audiovisual forms/CDs, and subscribe to 11,393 periodicals. Computerized library services include the card catalog, interlibrary loans, and database searching. Special learning facilities include a learning resource center, art gallery, radio station, anthropology museum, art studio, and greenhouse. The 1200-acre campus is in a small town 50 miles southeast of Richmond. Including residence halls, there are 166 buildings.

Student Life: 65% of undergraduates are from Virginia. Others are from 49 states, 52 foreign countries, and Canada. 74% are from public schools. 84% are white. The average age of freshmen is 18; all undergraduates, 20. 5% do not continue beyond their first year; 89% remain to graduate.

Housing: 4444 students can be accommodated in college housing, which includes single-sex and coed dormitories, on-campus apartments, off-campus apartments, married-student housing, fraternity houses, and sorority houses. In addition, there are honors houses, language houses, special-interest houses, an international studies hall, and smoke-free housing. On-campus housing is guaranteed for the freshman year only and is available on a lottery system for upperclassmen. 77% of students live on campus; of those, 100% remain on campus on weekends. Upperclassmen may keep cars.

Activities: 31% of men belong to 16 national fraternities; 28% of women belong to 12 national sororities. There are 300 groups on campus, including art, band, cheerleading, chess, choir, chorale, chorus, computers, dance, drama, drill team, ethnic, film, gay, honors, international, jazz band, literary magazine, musical theater, newspaper, opera, orchestra, pep band, photography, political, professional, radio and TV, religious, social, social service, student government, and yearbook. Popular campus events include Yule Log Ceremony, King and Queen Ball, and Opening Convocation.

Sports: There are 11 intercollegiate sports for men and 12 for women, and 24 intramural sports for men and 24 for women. Facilities include an 8500-seat basketball arena, an indoor track, strength training facility, sports medicine/rehabilitation facility, a gym room, lighted tennis courts, a 2200-seat artificial turf stadium, a 14,500-seat football stadium, a

1000-seat baseball stadium, and a student recreation facility with a gym, swimming pool, weight room, and racquetball and squash courts.

Disabled Students: 80% of the campus is accessible. Wheelchair ramps, elevators, special parking, specially equipped rest rooms, special class scheduling, lowered drinking fountains, modified recreational facilities, TDD, braille signage, Kurzweil reader, and a special learning lab for the visually impaired are available. Individual accommodations are made on a case by case basis.

Services: Counseling and information services are available, as is tutoring in most subjects. There is a reader service for the blind. There are reasonable in-class accommodations for learning-disabled students and hearing-impaired students and diagnostic services for learning disabilities.

Campus Safety and Security: Measures include 24-hour foot and vehicle patrol, self-defense education, escort service, and shuttle buses. There are informal discussions, pamphlets/posters/films, emergency telephones, lighted pathways/sidewalks, and crime prevention programs.

Programs of Study: William and Mary confers B.A., B.S., A.B., and B.B.A. degrees. Master's and doctoral degrees are also awarded. Bachelor's degrees are awarded in BIOLOGICAL SCIENCE (biology/biological science), BUSINESS (business administration and management), COMMUNICATIONS AND THE ARTS (classics, English, fine arts, French, German, music, Spanish, and speech/debate/rhetoric), COMPUTER AND PHYSICAL SCIENCE (chemistry, computer science, geology, mathematics, and physics), SOCIAL SCIENCE (American studies, anthropology, economics, history, interdisciplinary studies, international relations, international studies, philosophy, political science/government, psychology, religion, and sociology). Business, psychology, and biology are the largest.

Required: To graduate, students must demonstrate proficiencies in foreign language, writing, and physical activity. Freshman seminars are required. Students must complete 120 credit hours, with 33 to 45 in the major and a minimum 2.0 GPA. Distribution requirements include courses in math and quantitative reasoning, natural sciences, social sciences, world cultures and history, literature and history of the arts, and philosophical, religious, and social thought.

Special: William and Mary offers 3-2 programs with Rensselaer Polytechnic Institute, Columbia University, Case Western Reserve University, and Washington University in St. Louis, and a forestry/environmental science program with Duke University. Also available are departmental internships, study abroad in more than 12 countries, dual and student-designed majors, a Washington semester, nondegree study, and pass/fail options. There are 3 national honor societies, including Phi Beta Kappa, a freshman honors program, and 19 departmental honors programs.

Faculty/Classroom: 65% of faculty are male; 35%, female. 68% teach undergraduates; 84% do research. No introductory courses are taught by graduate students. The average class size in an introductory lecture is 43; in a laboratory, 26; and in a regular course, 26.

Admissions: 37% of the 2001-2002 applicants were accepted. The SAT I scores for the 2001-2002 freshman class were: Math--2% below 500, 16% between 500 and 599, 50% between 600 and 700, and 30% above 700. The ACT scores for the 2001-2002 freshman class were: 2% between 21 and 23, 15% between 24 and 26, 10% between 27 and 28, and 73% above 28. 96% of the current freshmen were in the top fifth of their class; 100% were in the top two fifths. There were 42 National Merit finalists and 20 semifinalists. 80 freshmen graduated first in their class.

Requirements: The SAT I or ACT is required. In addition, an essay and 3 SAT II: Subject tests, including the test in writing, are strongly recommended. AP credits are accepted. Important factors in the admissions decision are advanced placement or honor courses, evidence of special talent, and extracurricular activities record. Applications are accepted on-line via Common App and Next-Stop-College.

Procedure: Freshmen are admitted fall and spring. Entrance exams should be taken in spring of the junior year or fall of the senior year. There are early decision and deferred admissions plans. Early decision applications should be filed by November 1; regular applications, by January 7 for fall entry and November 1 for spring entry. The fall 2001 application fee was $40. Notification of early decision is sent December 1; regular decision, April 1. 469 early decision candidates were accepted for the 2001-2002 class. 20% of all applicants are on a waiting list; 28 were accepted in 2001.

Transfer: 145 transfer students enrolled in 2001-2002. Applicants must have at least 15 credit hours earned with a minimum 3.0 GPA recommended. Emphasis is placed on the individual's college records. SAT I scores are recommended. 60 credits of 120 must be completed at William and Mary.

Visiting: There are regularly scheduled orientations for prospective students, consisting of a group information session followed by a student-led tour. Visitors may sit in on classes. To schedule a visit, contact the Office of Admissions.

Financial Aid: In 2001-2002, 59% of all freshmen and 47% of continuing students received some form of financial aid. 26% of freshmen and 27% of continuing students received need-based aid. The average freshman award was $8701. Of that total, scholarships or need-based grants averaged $6496 ($14,500 maximum); loans averaged $3191 ($3625 maximum); and work contracts averaged $924 ($1200 maximum). 40% of undergraduates work part time. Average annual earnings from campus work are $1000. William and Mary is a member of CSS. The FAFSA is required. The CSS Profile is required for early decision enrolles. are required. The fall application deadline is February 15.

International Students: There are 81 international students enrolled. The school actively recruits these students. They must score 600 on the written TOEFL or 250 on the electronic version and also take the SAT I or the ACT.

Computers: The mainframe is an IBM 4381 Model T24 HDS 6660. There are 300 PCs in 16 locations around campus. All dormitories are wired for Internet connection. All students may access the system. There are no time limits and no fees.

Graduates: In 2001, 1367 bachelor's degrees were awarded. The most popular majors were business (16%), English (10%), and biology (9%). In an average class, 2% graduate in 3 years, 80% in 4 years, 87% in 5 years, and 89% in 6 years. 422 companies recruited on campus in 2000-2001. Of the 2000 graduating class, 20% were enrolled in graduate school within 6 months of graduation and 40% were employed.

Admissions Contact: Office of Admission. A video is available.
E-mail: *admiss@wm.edu* Web: *www.wm.edu/admission*

DEVRY UNIVERSITY/CRYSTAL CITY — E-2
Arlington, VA 22202 — **(866) 338-7932; Fax: (703) 414-4040**

Full-time: 79 men, 15 women	**Faculty:** 12
Part-time: 121 men, 28 women	**Ph.D.s:** n/av
Graduate: none	**Student/Faculty:** 8 to 1
Year: semesters, summer session	**Tuition:** $10,065
Application Deadline: open	**Room & Board:** n/app
Freshman Class: 756 applied, 538 accepted, 241 enrolled	
SAT I or ACT: recommended	**COMPETITIVE**

DeVry University/Crystal City, formerly DeVry Institute of Technology, founded in 2001, is 1 of 23 DeVry schools throughout the United States and Canada. The private institution offers career-oriented degree programs with hands-on training in various fields of business and technology. Computerized library services include the card catalog, interlibrary loans, and database searching. Special learning facilities include a learning resource center and electronics and other labs.

Student Life: 65% of undergraduates are from out of state, mostly the Middle Atlantic. Students are from 9 states and 5 foreign countries. 54% are African American; 15% white. The average age of all undergraduates is 26.

Housing: There are no residence halls. All of students commute. All students may keep cars.

Activities: There are no fraternities or sororities.

Sports: There is no sports program at DeVry.

Disabled Students: All of the campus is accessible. Wheelchair ramps, elevators, special parking, specially equipped rest rooms, lowered drinking fountains, and lowered telephones are available.

Services: Counseling and information services are available, as is tutoring in every subject.

Campus Safety and Security: Measures include escort service and lighted pathways/sidewalks.

Programs of Study: DeVry confers the B.S. degree. Associate degrees are also awarded. Bachelor's degrees are awarded in BUSINESS (business administration and management), COMMUNICATIONS AND THE ARTS (telecommunications), COMPUTER AND PHYSICAL SCIENCE (computer programming and information sciences and systems), ENGINEERING AND ENVIRONMENTAL DESIGN (computer technology, electrical/electronics engineering technology, and technological management). Business administration and computer information systems are the largest.

Required: To graduate, students must achieve a GPA of at least 2.0 and satisfactorily complete all curriculum requirements. Course requirements vary according to program. All first-year students take courses in business organization, computer applications, algebra, psychology, and student success strategies.

Special: An accelerated degree program in computer information systems, co-op programs, nondegree study, and evening and weekend classes are possible.

Faculty/Classroom: All teach undergraduates. The average class size in an introductory lecture is 30; in a laboratory, 30; and in a regular course, 30.

Admissions: 71% of the 2001-2002 applicants were accepted.

Requirements: The SAT I or ACT is recommended. In addition, admissions requirements include graduation from a secondary school; the GED is also accepted. Applicants must pass the DeVry entrance exam or present satisfactory ACT or SAT I scores. An interview is required. CLEP credit is accepted. Applications are accepted on-line at *Embark.com*.

Procedure: Freshmen are admitted to all sessions. There is a deferred admissions plan. Application deadlines are open. The application fee is $50. Notification is sent on a rolling basis.

Transfer: 18 transfer students enrolled in 2001-2002. Applicants must submit official transcripts from all previous colleges attended indicating passing grades in all completed course work, demonstrate language skills proficiency in at least 24 completed semester hours, and present evidence of math proficiency by appropriate college-level credits. 35% of 48 to 154 credits must be completed at DeVry.

Visiting: There are regularly scheduled orientations for prospective students. There are guides for informal visits and visitors may sit in on classes. To schedule a visit, contact Christopher Wargo, Dean of Admissions.

Financial Aid: The FAFSA is required.

International Students: There are 5 international students enrolled. They must score 500 on the written TOEFL or 173 on the electronic version and also take the college's own entrance exam.

Admissions Contact: Christopher Wargo, Dean of Admissions.
Web: *www.crys.devry.edu*

EASTERN MENNONITE UNIVERSITY D-2

Harrisonburg, VA 22802-2462 (540) 432-4118
(800) 368-2665; Fax: (540) 432-4444

Full-time: 382 men, 588 women	**Faculty:** 78; IIA, --$
Part-time: 31 men, 19 women	**Ph.D.s:** 67%
Graduate: 116 men, 168 women	**Student/Faculty:** 12 to 1
Year: semesters, summer session	**Tuition:** $15,300
Application Deadline: open	**Room & Board:** $5400
Freshman Class: 587 applied, 481 accepted, 211 enrolled	
SAT I Verbal/Math: 530/530	**ACT:** 23 **VERY COMPETITIVE**

Eastern Mennonite University, founded in 1917, is affiliated with the Mennonite Church. The private university offers programs in the arts and sciences. EMU Lancaster Campus offers some programs in Lancaster, Pennsylvania. In addition to regional accreditation, EMU has baccalaureate program accreditation with CSWE, NCATE, and NLN. The library contains 168,911 volumes, 81,068 microform items, and 10,932 audiovisual forms/CDs, and subscribes to 1193 periodicals. Computerized library services include the card catalog, interlibrary loans, and database searching. Special learning facilities include a learning resource center, art gallery, natural history museum, planetarium, and radio station. The 93-acre campus is in a small town 125 miles southwest of Washington, D.C. Including residence halls, there are 48 buildings.

Student Life: 59% of undergraduates are from out of state, mostly the Middle Atlantic. Others are from 37 states, 17 foreign countries, and Canada. 64% are from public schools. 85% are white. Most are Protestant. The average age of freshmen is 18; all undergraduates, 21. 24% do not continue beyond their first year; 63% remain to graduate.

Housing: 707 students can be accommodated in college housing, which includes single-sex and coed dormitories, on-campus apartments, off-campus apartments, married-student housing, and 1 international community. On-campus housing is guaranteed for all 4 years. 62% of students live on campus; of those, 75% remain on campus on weekends. Alcohol is not permitted. All students may keep cars.

Activities: There are no fraternities or sororities. There are 27 groups on campus, including cheerleading, chess, choir, chorale, chorus, dance, drama, ethnic, film, honors, international, jazz band, literary magazine, musical theater, newspaper, orchestra, peace, pep band, political, professional, radio and TV, religious, social, social service, student government, student women's association, and yearbook. Popular campus events include Spring Fling, Fall Festival, and Multicultural Week.

Sports: There are 7 intercollegiate sports for men and 8 for women, and 12 intramural sports for men and 12 for women. Facilities include a 1600-seat gym, a lighted artificial turf playing field, lighted tennis courts, a weight room, a rubberized track, baseball, softball, and soccer fields, and outdoor basketball and sand volleyball courts.

Disabled Students: 75% of the campus is accessible. Wheelchair ramps, elevators, special parking, specially equipped rest rooms, special class scheduling, lowered drinking fountains, and computer facilities for the visually impaired are available.

Services: Counseling and information services are available, as is tutoring in most subjects, including first-year courses. There is a reader service for the blind, and remedial math, reading, and writing.

Campus Safety and Security: Measures include self-defense education, informal discussions, pamphlets/posters/films, and emergency telephones. There are lighted pathways/sidewalks and a 12-hour foot or vehicle watchman.

Programs of Study: EMU confers B.A. and B.S. degrees. Associate and master's degrees are also awarded. Bachelor's degrees are awarded in AGRICULTURE (international agriculture), BIOLOGICAL SCIENCE (biochemistry and biology/biological science), BUSINESS (accounting, business administration and management, international business management, and recreational facilities management), COMMUNICATIONS AND THE ARTS (art, communications, dramatic arts, English, French, German, music, and Spanish), COMPUTER AND PHYSICAL SCIENCE (chemistry, computer management, computer science, and mathematics), EDUCATION (early childhood, elementary, physical, secondary, and special), ENGINEERING AND ENVIRONMENTAL DESIGN (environmental science), HEALTH PROFESSIONS (medical laboratory technology and nursing), SOCIAL SCIENCE (biblical studies, economics, history, liberal arts/general studies, ministries, peace studies, psychology, religion, social science, social work, sociology, and youth ministry). Biology, education, and nursing are the strongest academically. Business, education, and nursing are the largest.

Required: In order to graduate, students must complete general education courses, courses in the major, electives, Bible, speech, writing, math, science, social science, and phys ed for a minimum of 128 credit hours. Cross-cultural study is required. Hours in the major vary. A minimum 2.0 GPA is required.

Special: EMU offers study-abroad programs with Brethren Colleges abroad. There are also internships in a variety of majors, dual majors, student-designed majors, a general studies degree, and a nondegree study certificate program. A 2-2 engineering program with Drexel University and a 3-2 engineering program with Penn State University are available. The college also offers a cross-cultural program and a hands-on learning in education block program. There is 1 national honor society, and a freshman honors program.

Faculty/Classroom: 57% of faculty are male; 43%, female. 62% teach undergraduates, 19% do research, and 9% do both. No introductory courses are taught by graduate students. The average class size in an introductory lecture is 23; in a laboratory, 17; and in a regular course, 19.

Admissions: 82% of the 2001-2002 applicants were accepted. The SAT I scores for the 2001-2002 freshman class were: Verbal--38% below 500, 30% between 500 and 599, 24% between 600 and 700, and 8% above 700; Math--41% below 500, 31% between 500 and 599, 23% between 600 and 700, and 5% above 700. The ACT scores were 33% below 21, 20% between 21 and 23, 13% between 24 and 26, 20% between 27 and 28, and 15% above 28. There were 2 National Merit finalists and 6 semifinalists.

Requirements: The SAT I or ACT is required, with a minimum composite score of 920 or 21, respectively. Applicants must be graduates of an accredited secondary school or have a GED certificate. The college recommends that students have completed 4 credits of English, 3 each of math, science, and social studies, 2 or more of foreign language, and chemistry for nursing majors. A personal reference is required, and an interview is recommended. A GPA of 2.2 is required. AP and CLEP credits are accepted. Important factors in the admissions decision are advanced placement or honor courses, recommendations by school officials, and leadership record. The school accepts applications on-line via CollegeLink and through its web site, *www.emu.edu*.

Procedure: Freshmen are admitted fall and spring. Entrance exams should be taken in the spring of the junior year or the fall of the senior year. There is a deferred admissions plan. Application deadlines are open. The fall 2001 application fee was $25.

Transfer: 79 transfer students enrolled in 2001-2002. Transfer students must have a minimum 2.0 GPA and have a transcript of their college credits sent to EMU. 30 credits of 128 must be completed at EMU.

Visiting: There are regularly scheduled orientations for prospective students, including a financial aid seminar, a review of general education, and attendance at an assembly; the opportunity to sit in on classes, meet with professors and admissions representatives, sleep in residence halls, and eat in the cafeteria; attendance at special campus events; and a meal with the president. There are guides for informal visits. To schedule a visit, contact the Admissions Office.

Financial Aid: In 2001-2002, 96% of all students received some form of financial aid. 70% of freshmen and 66% of continuing students received need-based aid. The average freshman award was $14,583. Of that total, scholarships or need-based grants averaged $9664 ($18,350 maximum); loans averaged $4060 ($9500 maximum); and work contracts averaged $859 ($1800 maximum). 35% of undergraduates work part time. Average annual earnings from campus work are $1075. The average financial indebtedness of the 2001 graduate was $19,169. The CSS/Profile or FAFSA is required. The fall application deadline is May 15.

International Students: There are 45 international students enrolled. They must score 550 on the written TOEFL or 213 on the electronic version and also take the SAT I or the ACT, scoring 920.

Computers: The mainframe is an IBM AS/400. There are 25 PCs in the science center, 20 in the business department, 26 in the education lab, with 48 additional PCs in the library and 26 in departments across the campus, all networked for access to the Internet and the World Wide Web. Network hookups are available in dorm rooms. All students may access the system day and evening. There are no time limits and no fees.

Graduates: In 2001, 270 bachelor's degrees were awarded. The most popular majors were business (24%), education (11%), and nursing (10%). In an average class, 44% graduate in 4 years, 60% in 5 years, and 63% in 6 years. 10 companies recruited on campus in 2000-2001. Of the 2000 graduating class, 10% were enrolled in graduate school within 6 months of graduation and 89% were employed.

Admissions Contact: Admissions Office. A video is available.
E-mail: *admiss@emu.edu* Web: *http://www.emu.edu*

EMORY & HENRY COLLEGE

Emory, VA 24327-0947 B-4
(276) 944-6133
(800) 848-5493; Fax: (276) 944-6935

Full-time: 462 men, 499 women
Part-time: 9 men, 19 women
Graduate: 11 men, 79 women
Year: semesters, summer session
Application Deadline: April 15
Freshman Class: 1128 applied, 876 accepted, 267 enrolled
SAT I Verbal/Math: 530/520
Faculty: 58; IIB, -$
Ph.D.s: 88%
Student/Faculty: 17 to 1
Tuition: $14,100
Room & Board: $5362
COMPETITIVE

Emory & Henry College, founded in 1836, is a private liberal arts institution affiliated with the United Methodist Church. The library contains 230,476 volumes, 44,649 microform items, and 6139 audiovisual forms/CDs, and subscribes to 1188 periodicals. Computerized library services include the card catalog, interlibrary loans, and database searching. Special learning facilities include a learning resource center, art gallery, and radio station. The 165-acre campus is in a rural area in southwest Virginia. Including residence halls, there are 20 buildings.

Student Life: 74% of undergraduates are from Virginia. Others are from 24 states and 7 foreign countries. 99% are from public schools. 91% are white. Most are Protestant. The average age of freshmen is 18; all undergraduates, 21. 27% do not continue beyond their first year; 59% remain to graduate.

Housing: 696 students can be accommodated in college housing, which includes single-sex dormitories. In addition, there are honors houses and special-interest houses. On-campus housing is guaranteed for all 4 years. 69% of students live on campus; of those, 50% remain on campus on weekends. Alcohol is not permitted. All students may keep cars.

Activities: 15% of men belong to 7 local fraternities; 22% of women belong to 6 local sororities. There are 55 groups on campus, including cheerleading, choir, chorus, dance, drama, ethnic, international, literary magazine, newspaper, opera, pep band, photography, political, professional, radio and TV, religious, social, social service, student government, and yearbook. Popular campus events include Parents Day, Air Band, and the Literary Festival.

Sports: There are 7 intercollegiate sports for men and 6 for women, and 16 intramural sports for men and 14 for women. Facilities include a gym, a pool, a racquetball court, outdoor volleyball courts, tennis courts, a weight room, a dance room, a golf course, baseball and football fields, and a horseshoe area.

Disabled Students: 50% of the campus is accessible. Wheelchair ramps, elevators, special parking, and specially equipped rest rooms are available.

Services: Counseling and information services are available, as is tutoring in most subjects. There is a reader service for the blind and remedial writing.

Campus Safety and Security: Measures include 24-hour foot and vehicle patrol, self-defense education, informal discussions, and pamphlets/posters/films. There are lighted pathways/sidewalks.

Programs of Study: Emory & Henry College confers B.A. and B.S. degrees. Master's degrees are also awarded. Bachelor's degrees are awarded in BIOLOGICAL SCIENCE (biology/biological science), BUSINESS (accounting, business administration and management, and recreation and leisure services), COMMUNICATIONS AND THE ARTS (art, classics, communications, creative writing, dramatic arts, journalism, literature, modern language, music performance, and music theory and composition), COMPUTER AND PHYSICAL SCIENCE (chemistry, computer science, mathematics, and physics), EDUCATION (physical), ENGINEERING AND ENVIRONMENTAL DESIGN (environmental science), HEALTH PROFESSIONS (medical laboratory technology and premedicine), SOCIAL SCIENCE (community services, East Asian studies, economics, European studies, geography, history, interdisciplinary studies, Middle Eastern studies, philosophy, political science/government, prelaw, psychology, public affairs, religion, social science, and sociology). Economics and business, interdisciplinary English, and mass communications are the largest.

Required: All students must complete a general studies curriculum covering Western traditions, great books, religion, values inquiry, and global studies, and must demonstrate proficiency in oral skills. Specific courses include a first-year writing course, 1 each from 3 disciplines, including social sciences, humanities and arts, and natural sciences, and according to major, either a foreign language or quantitative methods. A total of 116 semester hours for a B.A. or 124 for a B.S., with a GPA of 2.0, is required for graduation. The total number of hours in the major varies.

Special: The college offers study abroad in Italy, England, Brazil, and France, a cooperative program in medical technology, and 2-2, 4-1, and 3-2 engineering degrees. Dual and student-designed majors, an interdisciplinary English major, combined B.A.-B.S. degrees, internships, work-study, nondegree study, and pass/fail options are also available. There are 4 national honor societies, and 8 departmental honors programs.

Faculty/Classroom: 65% of faculty are male; 35%, female. All teach undergraduates. No introductory courses are taught by graduate students. The average class size in an introductory lecture is 25; in a laboratory, 13; and in a regular course, 22.

Admissions: 78% of the 2001-2002 applicants were accepted. The SAT I scores for the 2001-2002 freshman class were: Verbal--34% below 500, 46% between 500 and 599, 20% between 600 and 700, and 2% above 700; Math--40% below 500, 48% between 500 and 599, and 12% between 600 and 700. The ACT scores were 32% below 21, 33% between 21 and 23, 22% between 24 and 26, 10% between 27 and 28, and 3% above 28. 50% of the current freshmen were in the top fifth of their class; 73% were in the top two fifths. 9 freshmen graduated first in their class.

Requirements: The SAT I or ACT is required. In addition, applicants should be high school graduates. High school courses required include 4 years of English, 3 or more units of math including algebra I, algebra II, and geometry, 2 or more units of lab science, 2 units of a single foreign language, and 2 or more units of social studies and history. One additional unit in fine arts is strongly recommended. A personal essay is required, and an interview is strongly recommended. Emory & Henry College requires applicants to be in the upper 50% of their class. A GPA of 2.5 is required. AP credits are accepted. Important factors in the admissions decision are advanced placement or honor courses, recommendations by school officials, and evidence of special talent. An application may be submitted by e-mail by using the college's home page.

Procedure: Freshmen are admitted fall and spring. Entrance exams should be taken in November of the senior year. There are early decision and early admissions plans. Early decision applications should be filed by December 1; regular applications, by April 15 for fall entry. Notification is sent on a rolling basis. 77 early decision candidates were accepted for the 2001-2002 class. The fall 2001 application fee was $25.

Transfer: 55 transfer students enrolled in a recent year. Transfers must have at least a 2.0 GPA in previous college work. Those with at least 24 credits may be admitted without high school data; those with fewer than 24 credits must meet freshman admission standards. 62 credits of 116 must be completed at Emory & Henry College. 116 o4 124 credis are required for the bachelor's degree.

Visiting: There are regularly scheduled orientations for prospective students, including a program for students to meet faculty and staff and to attend education sessions on college life. There are guides for informal visits and visitors may sit in on classes and stay overnight. To schedule a visit, contact the Admissions Office.

Financial Aid: In 2001-2002, 99% of all freshmen and 95% of continuing students received some form of financial aid. 73% of freshmen and 72% of continuing students received need-based aid. The average freshman award was $12,548. Of that total, scholarships or need-based grants averaged $9443 ($19,462 maximum); loans averaged $2580 ($3625 maximum); and work contracts averaged $1200. 13% of undergraduates work part time. Average annual earnings from campus work are $1200. The average financial indebtedness of the 2001 graduate was $10,625. The FAFSA and the college's own financial statement are required. The fall application deadline is February 15.

International Students: There are 7 international students enrolled. The school actively recruits these students. They must score 550 on the written TOEFL.

Computers: The mainframe is a DEC Alpha 2100 server. There are 128 terminals available for student use in the library, the computer lab, and the writing center. All students may access the system. There are no time limits and no fees.

Graduates: In 2001, 182 bachelor's degrees were awarded. The most popular majors were business management (19%), interdisciplinary English (12%), and biology (7%). In an average class, 47% graduate in 4 years, 56% in 5 years, and 59% in 6 years. 60 companies recruited on campus in a recent year. Of a recent year's graduating class, 21% were enrolled in graduate school within 6 months of graduation.

Admissions Contact: Debbie J. Thompson, Dean of Admissions and Financial Aid. A video is available. E-mail: *ehadmiss@ehc.edu*
Web: *www.ehc.edu*

FERRUM COLLEGE

Ferrum, VA 24088 C-3
(540) 365-4290
(800) 868-9797; Fax: (540) 365-4266

Full-time: 560 men, 350 women
Part-time: 20 men, 25 women
Graduate: none
Year: semesters, summer session
Application Deadline: open
Freshman Class: n/av
SAT I Verbal/Math: required
Faculty: 66; IIB, -$
Ph.D.s: 63%
Student/Faculty: 14 to 1
Tuition: $11000
Room & Board: $5100
LESS COMPETITIVE

Ferrum College, founded in 1913, is a private liberal arts institution affiliated with the United Methodist Church. Figures is the above capsule are approximate. In addition to regional accreditation, Ferrum has baccalaureate program accreditation with CSWE and NRPA. The library contains 109,322 volumes, 5946 microform items, and 1683 audiovisual forms/CDs, and subscribes to 581 periodicals. Computerized library services include the card catalog, interlibrary loans, and database searching. Special learning facilities include a learning resource center, art gallery, radio station, and a folk art museum. The 720-acre campus is in a rural area 35 miles southwest of Roanoke. Including residence halls, there are 27 buildings.

Student Life: 83% of undergraduates are from Virginia. Others are from 26 states and 5 foreign countries. 84% are from public schools. 80% are white; 17% African American. 87% are Protestant; 12% claim no religious affiliation; 10% Catholic. The average age of freshmen is 18; all undergraduates, 21. 44% do not continue beyond their first year; 34% remain to graduate.

Housing: About 955 students can be accommodated in college housing, which includes single-sex and coed dormitories, on-campus apartments, off-campus apartments, and married-student housing. On-campus housing is guaranteed for all 4 years. 81% of students live on campus; of those, 50% remain on campus on weekends. All students may keep cars.

Activities: There are no fraternities or sororities. There are 58 groups on campus, including art, cheerleading, choir, chorale, chorus, computers, dance, drama, ethnic, film, gay, honors, international, jazz band, literary magazine, musical theater, newspaper, photography, political, radio and TV, religious, social, social service, and student government. Popular campus events include Spring Fling, Blue Ridge Folklife Festival, and Snow Ball.

Sports: There are 8 intercollegiate sports for men and 10 for women, and 8 intramural sports for men and 8 for women. Facilities include a gym, a field house, tennis courts, a weight room, an indoor pool, an outdoor volleyball court, a football stadium, a soccer field, a baseball field, a women's softball field, and a recreation center with indoor basketball courts, racquetball courts, and universal weights.

Disabled Students: 75% of the campus is accessible. Wheelchair ramps, elevators, special parking, specially equipped rest rooms, special class scheduling, and lowered drinking fountains are available.

Services: Counseling and information services are available, as is tutoring in most subjects. College skills classes, individual assistance for study strategies and subject-specific tutoring by professors and students are also available.

Campus Safety and Security: Measures include 24-hour foot and vehicle patrol, self-defense education, escort service, and informal discussions. There are pamphlets/posters/films, emergency telephones, and lighted pathways/sidewalks.

Programs of Study: Ferrum confers B.A., B.S., B.F.A., and B.S.W. degrees. Bachelor's degrees are awarded in AGRICULTURE (agriculture), BIOLOGICAL SCIENCE (biology/biological science), BUSINESS (accounting, banking and finance, business administration and management, international business management, management information systems, marketing/retailing/merchandising, and recreation and leisure services), COMMUNICATIONS AND THE ARTS (art, dramatic arts, English, fine arts, French, Russian, and Spanish), COMPUTER AND PHYSICAL SCIENCE (chemistry, computer science, mathematics, and science), EDUCATION (physical), ENGINEERING AND ENVIRONMENTAL DESIGN (environmental science), HEALTH PROFESSIONS (medical laboratory technology), SOCIAL SCIENCE (criminal justice, history, human ecology, interdisciplinary studies, international studies, liberal arts/general studies, philosophy, political science/government, psychology, religion, social studies, and social work). Life science, business administration, and human services are the strongest academically. Business administration, life science, and human services are the largest.

Required: To graduate, students must complete at least 127 semester hours with a minimum GPA of 2.0. There are 55 hours of distribution requirements, including 12 in social sciences, 8 in natural sciences, 6 each in English, religion and philosophy, math, literature or foreign language, and degree cognates, 3 in fine arts, and 2 in phys ed. A major may require up to 57 semester hours, and 30 hours of the total must be in upper-level courses.

Special: The college encourages internships. Study abroad, work-study programs, dual majors, an accelerated degree program in social work, and B.A.-B.S. degrees are offered. A liberal studies degree and nondegree study are available. There are 6 national honor societies.

Faculty/Classroom: 60% of faculty are male; 40%, female. All both teach and do research. The average class size in an introductory lecture is 21; in a laboratory, 20; and in a regular course, 16.

Admissions: 12% of recent freshmen were in the top fifth of their class; 31% were in the top two fifths. 1 freshman graduated first in the class.

Requirements: The SAT I or ACT is required. In addition, applicants must be graduates of an accredited secondary school or hold a GED certificate. Applicants should complete 18 high school academic credits. The Admissions Committee considers courses taken, grades, extracurricular activities, SAT I or ACT scores, and recommendations. Personal interviews may be required for students lacking appropriate GPA or standardized test scores. AP and CLEP credits are accepted. Important factors in the admissions decision are advanced placement or honor courses, leadership record, and evidence of special talent.

Procedure: Freshmen are admitted to all sessions. There is a deferred admissions plan. Application deadlines are open. Check with the school for current fee.

Transfer: 64 transfer students enrolled in a recent year. Applicants for transfer must be in good academic standing at their current schools. 32 credits of 127 must be completed at Ferrum.

Visiting: There are regularly scheduled orientations for prospective students, including faculty information sessions, parent-to-parent and student-to-student sessions, and tours of the campus and residence halls. There are guides for informal visits and visitors may sit in on classes and stay overnight. To schedule a visit, contact the Director of Admissions.

Financial Aid: In a recent year, 98% of all students received some form of financial aid. 74% of freshmen and 76% of continuing students received need-based aid. The average freshman award was $10,084. Of that total, scholarships or need-based grants averaged $6284 ($6522 maximum); loans averaged $3418 ($3654 maximum); and work contracts averaged $1323 ($1386 maximum). 36% of undergraduates work part time. Average annual earnings from campus work are $1300. The average financial indebtedness of a recent graduate was $14,743. Ferrum is a member of CSS. The FAFSA is required. Check with the school for current deadlines.

International Students: There were 10 international students enrolled in a recent year. The school actively recruits these students. They must score 550 on the written TOEFL and also take the SAT I or the ACT.

Computers: The mainframe is an IBM AS/400. There are 50 networked PCs in labs in the library, the student computer center, and the business department. All residence hall rooms are also equipped with fully networked PCs provided by the college. All students may access the system at all times. There are no time limits and no fees.

Graduates: In a recent year, 165 bachelor's degrees were awarded. The most popular majors were business administration (22%), social work (10%), and environmental science (9%). In an average class, 24% graduate in 4 years, 36% in 5 years, and 37% in 6 years. 58 companies recruited on campus in a recent year. Of the 2000 graduating class, 10% were enrolled in graduate school within 6 months of graduation and 92% were employed.

Admissions Contact: Director of Admissions.
E-mail: *admissions@ferrum.edu* Web: *www.ferrum.edu*

GEORGE MASON UNIVERSITY — E-2

Fairfax, VA 22030-4444 — **(703) 993-2400; Fax: (703) 993-2392**

Full-time: 4922 men, 6407 women	**Faculty:** 779; I, av$
Part-time: 2012 men, 2461 women	**Ph.D.s:** 84%
Graduate: 4002 men, 5093 women	**Student/Faculty:** 15 to 1
Year: semesters, summer session	**Tuition:** $3792 ($12,696)
Application Deadline: February 1	**Room & Board:** $5400
Freshman Class: 8106 applied, 5519 accepted, 2146 enrolled	
SAT I Verbal/Math: 530/540	**COMPETITIVE**

George Mason University, founded in 1972, offers undergraduate and graduate degrees in arts and sciences, business, information technology and engineering, fine arts, computational sciences and informatics, conflict analysis, nursing and health science, and education. A second campus in Arlington houses a professional school, the School of Law, and the International Institute. There are 6 undergraduate and 9 graduate schools. In addition to regional accreditation, GMU has baccalaureate program accreditation with AACSB, ABET, CSAB, CSWE, NASM, NCATE, and NLN. The 4 libraries contain 1,311,854 volumes, 2,566,724 microform items, and 24,771 audiovisual forms/CDs, and subscribe to 11,533 periodicals. Computerized library services include the card catalog, interlibrary loans, and database searching. Special learning facilities include a learning resource center, art gallery, radio station, and TV station. The 806-acre campus is in a suburban area 18 miles southwest of Washington, D.C., in the greater Washington metropolitan area. Including residence halls, there are 119 buildings.

Student Life: 90% of undergraduates are from Virginia. Others are from 49 states, 127 foreign countries, and Canada. 95% are from public schools. 65% are white; 13% Asian American. The average age of freshmen is 18; all undergraduates, 24. 21% do not continue beyond their first year.

Housing: 3006 students can be accommodated in college housing, which includes single-sex and coed dormitories, on-campus apartments, and off-campus apartments. In addition, there are honors houses. On-campus housing is guaranteed for all 4 years. 78% of students commute. Alcohol is not permitted. All students may keep cars.

Activities: 3% of men belong to 18 national fraternities; 3% of women belong to 10 national sororities. There are 255 groups on campus, including band, cheerleading, chess, choir, chorale, chorus, computers, dance, drama, ethnic, film, forensics, gay, honors, international, jazz band, literary magazine, musical theater, newspaper, opera, orchestra, outing, pep band, photography, political, professional, radio and TV, religious, social, social service, student government, symphony, and yearbook. Popular campus events include Mason Day, Patriot Day, and International Week.

Sports: There are 12 intercollegiate sports for men and 11 for women, and 11 intramural sports for men and 10 for women. Facilities include a 10,000-seat arena for basketball, indoor soccer, and concerts; a sports and recreation complex, which includes a 200-meter track, basketball, handball/racquetball, tennis, and volleyball courts, baseball and softball diamonds, batting cages, a weight room, saunas, and a golf and archery net; a 400-meter outdoor track; and playing fields.

Disabled Students: 99% of the campus is accessible. Wheelchair ramps, elevators, special parking, specially equipped rest rooms, special class scheduling, lowered drinking fountains, lowered telephones, and special housing are available. Special arrangements can be made for testing, readers, note takers, and interpreters.

Services: Counseling and information services are available, as is tutoring in most subjects. There is a reader service for the blind for a fee.

Campus Safety and Security: Measures include 24-hour foot and vehicle patrol, self-defense education, escort service, and shuttle buses. There are informal discussions, pamphlets/posters/films, emergency telephones, lighted pathways/sidewalks, and 33 security call boxes located throughout the campus.

Programs of Study: GMU confers B.A., B.S., B.A.I.N., B.A.I.S., B.F.A., B.I.S., B.M., B.S.E., B.S.E.D., and B.S.N. degrees. Master's and doctoral degrees are also awarded. Bachelor's degrees are awarded in BIOLOGICAL SCIENCE (biology/biological science), BUSINESS (accounting, banking and finance, business administration and management, management information systems, and marketing/retailing/merchandising), COMMUNICATIONS AND THE ARTS (art history and appreciation, communications, dance, dramatic arts, English, French, German, music, Spanish, and studio art), COMPUTER AND PHYSICAL SCIENCE (chemistry, computer science, earth science, geology, mathematics, and physics), EDUCATION (foreign languages), ENGINEERING AND ENVIRONMENTAL DESIGN (civil engineering, computer engineering, electrical/electronics engineering, and systems engineering), HEALTH PROFESSIONS (health science, medical technology, and nursing), SOCIAL SCIENCE (anthropology, criminal justice, economics, geography, history, interdisciplinary studies, philosophy, political science/government, psychology, public administration, religion, Russian and Slavic studies, social work, and sociology). Decision science, government and international politics, and computer science are the largest.

Required: To graduate, all students must complete a core of study that includes 6 semester hours each of English composition, humanities, math/science, and social sciences, courses in communication, analytical reasoning, social science, natural science, and non-Western culture, and at least 45 hours of upper-division work. Hours in the major vary. A minimum 2.0 GPA is required and a total of 120 to 133 credit hours must be completed.

Special: GMU offers co-op programs in all majors with Shenandoah University, Virginia Polytechnic Institute and State University, Old Dominion University, and the University of Virginia, cross-registration with the Washington Consortium of Universities, internships through academic departments, study abroad in 10 countries, and on-campus work-study programs. Also available are dual and student-designed majors, nondegree study, and pass/fail options. The Program for Alternative General Education (PAGE) offers interdisciplinary studies for freshmen and sophomores. New Century College is an integrated program of study that emphasizes collaboration, experimental learning, and self-reflection. There are 3 national honor societies, a freshman honors program, and 8 departmental honors programs.

Faculty/Classroom: 63% of faculty are male; 37%, female. The average class size in an introductory lecture is 33; in a laboratory, 21; and in a regular course, 28.

Admissions: 68% of the 2001-2002 applicants were accepted. The SAT I scores for the 2001-2002 freshman class were: Verbal--33% below 500, 47% between 500 and 599, 18% between 600 and 700, and 3% above 700; Math--28% below 500, 49% between 500 and 599, 20% between 600 and 700, and 3% above 700. The ACT scores were 14% below 21, 66% between 21 and 23, 19% between 24 and 26, and 2% above 28.

Requirements: The SAT I or ACT is required. In addition, applicants must be graduates of an accredited secondary school or have a GED certificate. A minimum of 18 credits is required, including 4 years of English, 3 each of math, science, social studies, and electives, and 2 of foreign language. An essay is recommended. A GPA of 2.0 is required. AP and CLEP credits are accepted. Important factors in the admissions decision are advanced placement or honor courses, evidence of special talent, and recommendations by school officials. Applications are accepted on computer disk and on-line at the school's web site.

Procedure: Freshmen are admitted fall, spring, and summer. Entrance exams should be taken during the spring of the junior year. There is a deferred admissions plan. Applications should be filed by February 1 for fall entry and November 1 for spring entry, along with a $35 fee. Notification is sent April 1. 3% of all applicants are on a waiting list; 134 were accepted in 2001.

Transfer: 2132 transfer students enrolled in 2001-2002. Applicants must have a minimum 2.0 GPA and at least 9 semester hours earned. College transcripts and an essay or personal statement are required. 30 credits of 120 must be completed at GMU.

Visiting: There are regularly scheduled orientations for prospective students. There are guides for informal visits and visitors may sit in on classes and stay overnight. To schedule a visit, contact the Admissions Office.

Financial Aid: In 2001-2002, 37% of all freshmen and 40% of continuing students received some form of financial aid. 27% of freshmen and 32% of continuing students received need-based aid. The average freshman award was $6867. Of that total, scholarships or need-based grants averaged $3756; loans averaged $6222; and work contracts averaged $2058. 82% of undergraduates work part time. Average annual earnings from campus work are $9000. The FAFSA is required. The fall application deadline is March 1.

International Students: There are 559 international students enrolled. The school actively recruits these students. They must score 570 on the written TOEFL or 230 on the electronic version and also take the SAT I or the ACT.

Computers: The mainframes are a DEC ALPHA 2100 and an IBM ES 9121/300. 1500 terminals are located in public student labs, the libraries, dorms, and academic departments. All students may access the system 24 hours per day. There are no time limits and no fees.

Graduates: In 2001, 2812 bachelor's degrees were awarded. The most popular majors were business (23%), social sciences (13%), and communication technologies (8%). In an average class, 26% graduate in 4 years, 41% in 5 years, and 47% in 6 years. 200 companies recruited on campus in 2000-2001.

Admissions Contact: Andrew Flagel, Dean of Undergraduate Admissions. E-mail: *admissions@gmu.edu* Web: *www.gmu.edu*

HAMPDEN-SYDNEY COLLEGE — D-3

Hampden-Sydney, VA 23943 — (434) 223-6120

(800) 755-0733; Fax: (434) 223-6346

Full-time: 1026 men	**Faculty:** 79; IIB, av$
Part-time: none	**Ph.D.s:** 81%
Graduate: none	**Student/Faculty:** 13 to 1
Year: semesters, summer session	**Tuition:** $18,485
Application Deadline: March 1	**Room & Board:** $6386
Freshman Class: 925 applied, 711 accepted, 328 enrolled	
SAT I Verbal/Math: 561/562	**ACT:** 22 — **COMPETITIVE**

Hampden-Sydney College, founded in 1776, is a private men's liberal arts institution affiliated with the Presbyterian Church (U.S.A.). The library contains 224,172 volumes, 45,312 microform items, and 4312 audiovisual forms/CDs, and subscribes to 823 periodicals. Computerized library services include the card catalog, interlibrary loans, and database searching. Special learning facilities include an art gallery, planetarium, radio station, and international communications center, college history museum, and observatory. The 660-acre campus is in a rural area 60 miles southwest of Richmond. Including residence halls, there are 76 buildings.

Student Life: 63% of undergraduates are from Virginia. Others are from 34 states and 3 foreign countries. 65% are from public schools. 94% are white. 56% are Protestant; 14% Catholic; 15% claim no religious affiliation. The average age of freshmen is 18; all undergraduates, 20. 21% do not continue beyond their first year; 61% remain to graduate.

Housing: 1050 students can be accommodated in college housing, which includes single-sex dormitories, on-campus apartments, married-student housing, fraternity houses, and a minority student house. On-campus housing is guaranteed for all 4 years. 97% of students live on campus; of those, 60% remain on campus on weekends. All students may keep cars.

Activities: 37% of men belong to 11 national fraternities. There are no sororities. There are 36 groups on campus, including chorale, chorus, computers, debate, drama, ethnic, honors, international, literary magazine, newspaper, pep band, photography, political, professional, radio and TV, religious, social, social service, student government, and yearbook. Popular campus events include Greek Week, Macon Week, and Midwinters CAC events.

Sports: Facilities include a field house with 3 basketball courts, 5 racquetball/handball courts, an outdoor track, a pool, squash courts, a weight room, a gym, tennis courts, and many playing fields.

Disabled Students: 80% of the campus is accessible. Wheelchair ramps, elevators, special parking, specially equipped rest rooms, special class scheduling, and lowered telephones are available.

Services: Counseling and information services are available, as is tutoring in every subject.

Campus Safety and Security: Measures include 24-hour foot and vehicle patrol, informal discussions, pamphlets/posters/films, and emergency telephones. There are lighted pathways/sidewalks. There also is a fire department on campus and a first responder unit for emergency medical assistance. The dormitory phone lines are hooked into 911.

Programs of Study: Hampden-Sydney confers B.A. and B.S. degrees. Bachelor's degrees are awarded in BIOLOGICAL SCIENCE (biology/

biological science), BUSINESS (business economics), COMMUNICATIONS AND THE ARTS (classics, English, fine arts, French, German, Greek, Latin, and Spanish), COMPUTER AND PHYSICAL SCIENCE (applied mathematics, chemistry, computer science, mathematics, and physics), SOCIAL SCIENCE (economics, history, humanities, philosophy, political science/government, psychology, and religion). Economics and history are the largest.

Required: To graduate, students must complete 120 credit hours with a minimum GPA of 2.0. Distribution requirements include 7 courses in humanities, 4 in math and natural sciences, and 3 in social sciences. All students must also take rhetoric and foreign language and pass a rhetoric exam.

Special: The college offers co-op programs with Longwood, Randolph-Macon, Randolph-Macon Woman's, Sweet Briar, Hollins, and Mary Baldwin Colleges and Washington and Lee University. Cross-registration with Longwood College, internships, study abroad, a 3-2 engineering program with the University of Virginia, a Washington semester, work-study programs, B.A.-B.S. degrees, and dual majors are available. There is a public service concentration in all majors. There are 15 national honor societies, including Phi Beta Kappa, a freshman honors program, and 10 departmental honors programs.

Faculty/Classroom: 73% of faculty are male; 27%, female. All both teach and do research. The average class size in an introductory lecture is 18; in a laboratory, 15; and in a regular course, 15.

Admissions: 77% of the 2001-2002 applicants were accepted. The SAT I scores for the 2001-2002 freshman class were: Verbal--25% below 500, 41% between 500 and 599, 28% between 600 and 700, and 6% above 700; Math--18% below 500, 47% between 500 and 599, 31% between 600 and 700, and 4% above 700. 30% of the current freshmen were in the top fifth of their class; 57% were in the top two fifths. There was 1 National Merit semifinalist. 6 freshmen graduated first in their class.

Requirements: The SAT I or ACT is required. In addition, the school recommends SAT II: Subject tests in writing, math, and another subject of the student's choice. Applicants must be graduates of an accredited secondary school and have completed 16 high school academic credits, including 4 of English, 3 of math, 2 each of foreign language and science, and 1 of social studies. An essay is required and an interview is recommended. The GED is accepted. A GPA of 2.5 is required. AP credits are accepted. Important factors in the admissions decision are advanced placement or honor courses, recommendations by school officials, and leadership record. The college's application, as well as the Common Application, are accepted on-line at the school's web site and via programs such as CollegeLink, Apply, and others.

Procedure: Freshmen are admitted fall and spring. Entrance exams should be taken during the junior or senior year of high school. There is an early decision plan. Early decision applications should be filed by November 15; regular applications, by March 1 for fall entry and December 1 for spring entry. Notification of early decision is sent December 15; regular decision, by April 15. 102 early decision candidates were accepted for the 2001-2002 class. 4% of all applicants are on a waiting list; 26 were accepted in 2001. The fall 2001 application fee was $30.

Transfer: 13 transfer students enrolled in 2001-2002. Applicants must have a minimum GPA of 2.5 and must take either the SAT I or the ACT. An interview is recommended. 60 credits of 120 must be completed at Hampden-Sydney.

Visiting: There are regularly scheduled orientations for prospective students, consisting of lectures, information sessions, tours, lunch, and an athletic event. There are guides for informal visits and visitors may sit in on classes and stay overnight. To schedule a visit, contact the Admissions Office.

Financial Aid: In 2001-2002, 83% of all freshmen and 91% of continuing students received some form of financial aid. 47% of freshmen and 48% of continuing students received need-based aid. The average freshman award was $14,670. Of that total, scholarships or need-based grants averaged $11,589 ($21,000 maximum); and loans averaged $3294 ($6625 maximum). 25% of undergraduates work part time. Average annual earnings from campus work are $900. The average financial indebtedness of the 2001 graduate was $7071. The CSS/Profile or FAFSA is required. The fall application deadline is March 1.

International Students: There are 4 international students enrolled. They must score 570 on the written TOEFL and also take the SAT I or the ACT.

Computers: The mainframe is a DEC ALPHA. Students may use the mainframe computer during computer center hours by accessing terminals in the center. Many students access the mainframe through PCs in their dorm rooms linked through a fiber-optic network. Others can be hooked up through the phone system. All students may access the system. There are no time limits and no fees. It is strongly recommended that all students have a personal computer.

Graduates: In 2001, 193 bachelor's degrees were awarded. The most popular majors were economics (35%), history (24%), and political science (4%). In an average class, 61% graduate in 4 years, and 63% in 5 years. 30 companies recruited on campus in 2000-2001.

Admissions Contact: Anita H. Garland, Dean of Admissions.
E-mail: *hsapp@hsc.edu* Web: *www.hsc.edu*

HAMPTON UNIVERSITY — F-3
Hampton, VA 23668 — (757) 727-5328
(800) 624-3328; Fax: (757) 727-5095

Full-time: 1683 men, 2903 women	**Faculty:** 295
Part-time: 221 men, 146 women	**Ph.D.s:** 76%
Graduate: 292 men, 548 women	**Student/Faculty:** 16 to 1
Year: semesters, summer session	**Tuition:** $11,666
Application Deadline: March 15	**Room & Board:** $5446
Freshman Class: 5754 applied, 2380 accepted, 1243 enrolled	
SAT I Verbal/Math: 520/500 (mean)	**ACT:** 20 (mean) **COMPETITIVE+**

Hampton University, founded in 1868, is a comprehensive institution of higher education. Its curriculum emphasis is scientific and professional, with a strong liberal arts undergirding. There are 8 undergraduate schools and 1 graduate school. In addition to regional accreditation, HU has baccalaureate program accreditation with ABET, ACEJMC, ASLA, CSAB, NAAB, NASM, NCATE, NLN, and ACS. The library contains 273,854 volumes, 711,759 microform items, and 1649 audiovisual forms/CDs, and subscribes to 992 periodicals. Computerized library services include the card catalog, interlibrary loans, and database searching. Special learning facilities include a learning resource center, art gallery, natural history museum, radio station, TV station, and academic technology mall. The 204-acre campus is in an urban area 15 miles west of Norfolk. Including residence halls, there are 125 buildings.

Student Life: 70% of undergraduates are from out of state, mostly the Middle Atlantic. Others are from 43 states, 33 foreign countries, and Canada. 90% are from public schools. 96% are African American. The average age of freshmen is 18; all undergraduates, 20. 15% do not continue beyond their first year; 75% remain to graduate.

Housing: 3000 students can be accommodated in college housing, which includes single-sex dormitories. In addition, there are honors houses and student cottages. On-campus housing is available on a first-come, first-served basis and is available on a lottery system for upperclassmen. 59% of students live on campus; of those, 70% remain on campus on weekends. Alcohol is not permitted. Upperclassmen may keep cars.

Activities: 5% of men belong to 5 national fraternities; 4% of women belong to 4 national sororities. There are 80 groups on campus, including art, band, cheerleading, choir, chorale, chorus, dance, drama, drill team, ethnic, honors, international, jazz band, marching band, newspaper, orchestra, pep band, photography, political, radio and TV, religious, social service, student government, symphony, and yearbook. Popular campus events include Career Day, High School Day, and Black Family/Parents Weekend.

Sports: There are 5 intercollegiate sports for men and 4 for women, and 2 intramural sports for men and 1 for women. Facilities include a football stadium, a convocation center, 12 outdoor tennis courts, open fields for intramural sports, 2 basketball courts, 2 swimming pools, a volleyball court, an exercise and training room, a student center with a health center, bowling alley, movie theater, indoor track, and restaurants.

Disabled Students: 90% of the campus is accessible. Wheelchair ramps, elevators, special parking, specially equipped rest rooms, lowered drinking fountains, and lowered telephones are available.

Services: Counseling and information services are available, as is tutoring in most subjects. There is remedial math, reading, and writing.

Campus Safety and Security: Measures include 24-hour foot and vehicle patrol, self-defense education, informal discussions, and pamphlets/posters/films. There are emergency telephones, lighted pathways/sidewalks, bike patrols, on-campus police officers, video cameras, gated campus, identification of valuables, limited access to campus, smoke detectors in residence halls, motorist assistance, and civilian support team.

Programs of Study: HU confers B.A., B.S., B.Arch., and B.S.Nurs. degrees. Associate and master's degrees are also awarded. Bachelor's degrees are awarded in BIOLOGICAL SCIENCE (biology/biological science), BUSINESS (accounting, banking and finance, business administration and management, marketing/retailing/merchandising, and sports management), COMMUNICATIONS AND THE ARTS (art, communications, dramatic arts, English, and music), COMPUTER AND PHYSICAL SCIENCE (chemistry, computer science, information sciences and systems, mathematics, and physics), EDUCATION (physical), ENGINEERING AND ENVIRONMENTAL DESIGN (architecture, chemical engineering, and electrical/electronics engineering), HEALTH PROFESSIONS (nursing, recreation therapy, and speech pathology/audiology), SOCIAL SCIENCE (economics, history, political science/government, psychology, and sociology). Architecture, biology, and physics are the strongest academically. Biology, psychology, and business management are the largest.

Required: To graduate, students must complete 120 credit hours, with 74 hours in the major, related subjects, and free electives, and a GPA of 2.0. There is a 44 to 48 hour distribution requirement in freshman studies, history, language, arts and humanities, English, social sciences, math, pure and applied sciences, speech, and health and phys ed.

Special: The university offers co-op programs in most majors, cross-registration with 6 schools, internships, and student-designed majors. Work study, study abroad, and dual majors are also possible. Students may receive credit for life, military, and work experience. There are pass/fail options. There are 15 national honor societies and a freshman honors program.

Faculty/Classroom: 48% of faculty are male; 52%, female. 90% teach undergraduates and 10% do research. No introductory courses are taught by graduate students. The average class size in an introductory lecture is 50; in a laboratory, 20; and in a regular course, 25.

Admissions: 57% of the 2001-2002 applicants were accepted. The SAT I scores for the 2001-2002 freshman class were: Verbal--34% below 500, 47% between 500 and 599, 18% between 600 and 700, and 1% above 700; Math--49% below 500, 45% between 500 and 599, 5% between 600 and 700, and 1% above 700. 19% of the current freshmen were in the top fifth of their class; 41% were in the top two fifths.

Requirements: The SAT I or ACT is required. A composite score of 920 is required on the SAT I. Applicants must be graduates of an accredited secondary school, or the GED is accepted. Students should complete 17 Carnegie units, including 4 units of English, 3 units of math, (algebra I and II and geometry), 2 years of science (chemistry and biology), 2 years of social studies, and 6 academic electives. An interview is recommended. HU requires applicants to be in the upper 50% of their class. A GPA of 2.0 is required. AP and CLEP credits are accepted. Important factors in the admissions decision are advanced placement or honor courses, recommendations by school officials, and recommendations by alumni.

Procedure: Freshmen are admitted fall and spring. Entrance exams should be taken during the junior year or fall of the senior year. There are early admissions and deferred admissions plans. Applications should be filed by March 15 for fall entry and December 2 for spring entry, along with a $25 fee. Notification is sent on a rolling basis within 3 weeks of receipt of completed application. 2% of all applicants are on a waiting list.

Transfer: 124 transfer students enrolled in 2001-2002. Applicants for transfer must have a minimum GPA of 2.3 and 15 transferable hours. Students must have at least 60 semester or 90 quarter hours in order to be exempt from submitting their high school record and SAT I or ACT scores. 30 credits of 120 must be completed at HU.

Visiting: There are regularly scheduled orientations for prospective students. There are guides for informal visits and visitors may sit in on classes. To schedule a visit, contact Office of Admissions at (757) 727-2051 or *admissions@hamptonu.edu*.

Financial Aid: In 2001-2002, 56% of all freshmen and 58% of continuing students received some form of financial aid. 41% of freshmen and 46% of continuing students received need-based aid. The average freshman award was $3488. Of that total, scholarships or need-based grants averaged $2016; loans averaged $1243; and work contracts averaged $1335. Average annual earnings from campus work are $1400. The average financial indebtedness of the 2001 graduate was $23,000. The FAFSA is required. The fall application deadline is March 1.

International Students: There are 102 international students enrolled. They must score 550 on the written TOEFL and also take the SAT I or the ACT, scoring 920 on the SAT I.

Computers: The mainframe is a Sun Enterprise 5500. A campus-wide network exists with password protected accessibility provided to all students, faculty, staff, and administrators. All students are assigned e-mail account numbers at no charge. Therre are at least 90 computer labs/classrooms and at least 1500 institution-owned computers. All students may access the system 24 hours per day. There are no time limits and no fees. It is strongly recommended that all students have a personal computer. It is recommended that students in pharmacy have personal computers.

Graduates: In 2001, 799 bachelor's degrees were awarded. The most popular majors were biology (12%), psychology (11%), and management (10%). In an average class, 33% graduate in 4 years, 50% in 5 years, and 54% in 6 years. 225 companies recruited on campus in 2000-2001. Of the 2000 graduating class, 40% were enrolled in graduate school within 6 months of graduation and 70% were employed.

Admissions Contact: Leonard M. Jones Jr., Director of Admissions. E-mail: *leonard.jones@hamptonu.edu*

HOLLINS UNIVERSITY

C-3

Roanoke, VA 24020-1707

(540) 362-6214
(800) 456-9595; Fax: (540) 362-6218

Full-time: 777 women	**Faculty:** 75; IIB, av$
Part-time: 41 women	**Ph.D.s:** 97%
Graduate: 57 men, 216 women	**Student/Faculty:** 10 to 1
Year: 4-1-4	**Tuition:** $17,720
Application Deadline: February 15	**Room & Board:** $6608
Freshman Class: 560 applied, 454 accepted, 191 enrolled	
SAT I Verbal/Math: 590/550	**ACT:** 25 **VERY COMPETITIVE**

Founded in 1842 and Virginia's first chartered women's college, Hollins offers a broad liberal arts curriculum. In addition to regional accreditation, Hollins has baccalaureate program accreditation with NASDTEC. The library contains 255,842 volumes, 700 microform items, and 3587 audiovisual forms/CDs, and subscribes to 7079 periodicals. Computerized library services include the card catalog, interlibrary loans, and database searching. Special learning facilities include an art gallery. The 475-acre campus is in a suburban area in Roanoke. Including residence halls, there are 73 buildings.

Student Life: 52% of undergraduates are from out of state, mostly the South. Others are from 45 states and 9 foreign countries. 77% are from public schools. 89% are white. 51% are Protestant; 14% Catholic; 20% claim no religious affiliation. The average age of freshmen is 19; all undergraduates, 22. 19% do not continue beyond their first year; 65% remain to graduate.

Housing: 744 students can be accommodated in college housing, which includes single-sex dormitories and on-campus apartments. In addition, there are language houses, special-interest houses, a "global village" student residence, and special housing for disabled students. On-campus housing is guaranteed for all 4 years. 83% of students live on campus; of those, 60% remain on campus on weekends. All students may keep cars.

Activities: There are no fraternities or sororities. There are 45 groups on campus, including art, choir, chorale, dance, drama, ethnic, film, gay, honors, international, literary magazine, newspaper, photography, political, professional, religious, social, social service, student government, and yearbook. Popular campus events include Literary Festival, French and German film festivals, and Classics Symposium.

Sports: There are 10 intercollegiate sports for women. Facilities include a swimming center, a fitness center and 2 weight rooms, a gym, an equestrian center, a ropes course, a jogging and exercise trail, tennis courts, 2 playing fields, an auxillary gym, 2 training rooms, and a climbing wall.

Disabled Students: 40% of the campus is accessible. Wheelchair ramps, elevators, special parking, specially equipped rest rooms, special class scheduling, lowered drinking fountains, and lowered telephones are available.

Services: Counseling and information services are available, as is tutoring in most subjects. There is a reader service for the blind, and a writing center.

Campus Safety and Security: Measures include 24-hour foot and vehicle patrol, self-defense education, escort service, and informal discussions. There are pamphlets/posters/films, emergency telephones, lighted pathways/sidewalks, and emergency buttons located along walkways and in labs.

Programs of Study: Hollins confers the B.A. degree. Master's degrees are also awarded. Bachelor's degrees are awarded in BIOLOGICAL SCIENCE (biology/biological science), BUSINESS (business administration and management), COMMUNICATIONS AND THE ARTS (art history and appreciation, communications, creative writing, dance, dramatic arts, English, French, German, media arts, music, Spanish, and studio art), COMPUTER AND PHYSICAL SCIENCE (chemistry, computer mathematics, computer science, mathematics, and physics), SOCIAL SCIENCE (classical/ancient civilization, economics, history, interdisciplinary studies, international studies, philosophy, political science/government, psychology, religion, sociology, and women's studies). English, creative writing, and psychology are the strongest academically. Creative writing, English, and biology are the largest.

Required: To graduate, students must complete 128 credits of academic work and 4 short terms. At least 32 hours in the major and a 2.0 GPA are required. Distribution requirements include 8 credits each in the humanities, social sciences, natural sciences and math, and fine arts. All students meet the following skills components; writing, oral communication, quantitative reasoning, and information technology. Students are also required to fulfill 2 semesters of phys ed or varsity sport participation. A thesis is required for some majors.

Special: Hollins offers internships during the January term, dual majors, student-designed majors, accelerated degrees, study abroad in Greece, Italy, England, France, Ireland, Japan, Mexico, and Spain, a United Nations semester, and a Washington semester with American University. A 3-2 engineering degree is possible with Washington University in St. Louis and Virginia Polytechnic Institute and State University. There is cross-registration with the Virginia Seven College Exchange and Roanoke College. There are 14 national honor societies, including Phi Beta Kappa, a freshman honors program, and 23 departmental honors programs.

Faculty/Classroom: 42% of faculty are male; 58%, female. All teach undergraduates and 95% both teach and do research. No introductory courses are taught by graduate students. The average class size in an introductory lecture is 18; in a laboratory, 9; and in a regular course, 14.

Admissions: 81% of the 2001-2002 applicants were accepted. The SAT I scores for the 2001-2002 freshman class were: Verbal--15% below 500, 37% between 500 and 599, 35% between 600 and 700, and 13% above 700; Math--28% below 500, 47% between 500 and 599, 23% between 600 and 700, and 2% above 700. The ACT scores were 6% below 21, 33% between 21 and 23, 30% between 24 and 26, 20% between 27 and 28, and 11% above 28. 50% of the current freshmen were in the top fifth of their class; 77% were in the top two fifths. There were 6 National Merit finalists. 1 freshman graduated first in the class in a recent year.

Requirements: The SAT I or ACT is required. In addition, applicants must be graduates of an accredited secondary school. The GED is accepted, as is home school. Applicants should complete 16 high school academic credits, including 4 credits of English and 3 credits each of foreign language, math, science, and social studies, SAT II: Subject tests in writing and 2 others of the student's choice are recommended. An essay is required and an interview is recommended. AP credits are accepted. Important factors in the admissions decision are advanced placement or honor courses, recommendations by school officials, and evidence of special talent. Applications are accepted on disk and on-line via the College Board, EXPAN, Peterson's, and the Hollins University web site.

Procedure: Freshmen are admitted fall and spring. Entrance exams should be taken by January of the senior year. There are early decision and deferred admissions plans. Early decision applications should be filed by December 1; regular applications, by February 15 for fall entry and December 1 for spring entry. Notification of early decision is sent December 15; regular decision, on a rolling basis. 46 early decision candidates were accepted for the 2001-2002 class. 1% of all applicants are on a waiting list; 2 were accepted in 2001. The fall 2001 application fee was $35.

Transfer: 32 transfer students enrolled in 2001-2002. Applicants for transfer should have a minimum college GPA of 2.5. Other criteria are the same as for entering freshmen. 64 credits of 128 must be completed at Hollins.

Visiting: There are regularly scheduled orientations for prospective students, including 2 programs for high school seniors offered in October and November, 1 for admitted applicants in April, and 1 for juniors and sophomores in March. There are guides for informal visits and visitors may sit in on classes and stay overnight. To schedule a visit, contact the Admissions Office at (540) 362-6401 or *huadm@hollins.edu*.

Financial Aid: In 2001-2002, 60% of all freshmen and 61% of continuing students received some form of financial aid. 60% of freshmen and 61% of continuing students received need-based aid. The average freshman award was $15,565. Of that total, scholarships or need-based grants averaged $11,738 ($17,470 maximum); loans averaged $3708 ($5500 maximum); and work contracts averaged $1892 ($2500 maximum). 46% of undergraduates work part time. Average annual earnings from campus work are $1245. The average financial indebtedness of the 2001 graduate was $13,907. The FAFSA and parents'/student's tax returns are required. The fall application deadline is February 1.

International Students: There are 20 international students enrolled. The school actively recruits these students. They must score 550 on the written TOEFL. Students whose native language is not English must score 550 on the TOEFL. For students whose native language is English, the SAT I or ACT will be accepted in place of the TOEFL.

Computers: The mainframes are a DEC ALPHA (UNIX, Open VMS). There are 100 terminals for student use located throughout the campus. All students may access the system 24 hours a day, 7 days a week. It is strongly recommended that all students have a personal computer. There are no time limits and no fees.

Graduates: In 2001, 158 bachelor's degrees were awarded. The most popular majors were English/creative writing (18%), visual and performing arts (17%), and social sciences and history (14%). In an average class, 63% graduate in 4 years, 65% in 5 years, and 65% in 6 years. 14 companies recruited on campus in 2000-2001. Of the 2000 graduating class, 21% were enrolled in graduate school within 6 months of graduation and 77% were employed.

Admissions Contact: Celia McCormick, Dean of Admissions. A video is available. E-mail: *huadm@hollins.edu* Web: *www.hollins.edu*

JAMES MADISON UNIVERSITY D-2

Harrisonburg, VA 22807 (540) 568-5681; Fax: (540) 568-3332

Full-time: 5582 men, 8038 women	**Faculty:** 644; IIA, av$
Part-time: 247 men, 202 women	**Ph.D.s:** 82%
Graduate: 227 men, 424 women	**Student/Faculty:** 21 to 1
Year: semesters, summer session	**Tuition:** $4094 ($10,606)
Application Deadline: January 15	**Room & Board:** $5458
Freshman Class: 14,114 applied, 9080 accepted, 3249 enrolled	
SAT I Verbal/Math: 578/585	**HIGHLY COMPETITIVE**

James Madison University, founded in 1908, is a public institution with programs in science and math, business, education, arts and letters, and integrated science and technology. There are 5 undergraduate schools and 1 graduate school. In addition to regional accreditation, JMU has baccalaureate program accreditation with AACSB, ACS, ADA, AOTA, APA, CAAHEP, CACREP, CSWE, FIDER, NASAD, NASM, NCATE, and NLN. The 3 libraries contain 539,029 volumes, 1,045,511 microform items, and 27,779 audiovisual forms/CDs, and subscribe to 3940 periodicals. Computerized library services include the card catalog, interlibrary loans, and database searching. Special learning facilities include a learning resource center, art gallery, planetarium, radio station, arboretum, music library, and CISAT Library Services. The 495-acre campus is in a small town 123 miles southwest of Washington, D.C. Including residence halls, there are 97 buildings.

Student Life: 70% of undergraduates are from Virginia. Others are from 46 states, 55 foreign countries, and Canada. 95% are from public schools. 84% are white. 31% are Protestant; 28% Catholic; 22% claim no religious affiliation. The average age of freshmen is 18; all undergraduates, 20. 10% do not continue beyond their first year; 80% remain to graduate.

Housing: 5640 students can be accommodated in college housing, which includes single-sex and coed dormitories, off-campus apartments, fraternity houses, sorority houses, a freshman residencehall, a smoke/substance-free residence hall, and theme housing for international students. Students must apply. In addition, there are special-interest houses. 59% of students commute. Upperclassmen may keep cars.

Activities: 11% of men belong to 16 national fraternities; 13% of women belong to 11 national sororities. There are 265 groups on campus, including art, band, cheerleading, chess, choir, chorale, chorus, computers, dance, drama, ethnic, gay, honors, international, jazz band, literary magazine, marching band, musical theater, newspaper, opera, orchestra, pep band, photography, political, professional, radio and TV, religious, social, social service, student government, symphony, and yearbook. Popular campus events include Parents Weekend, Madison Symposium, and James Madison Day.

Sports: There are 12 intercollegiate sports for men and 14 for women, and 18 intramural sports for men and 18 for women. Facilities include a 12,800-seat stadium, a convocation center, an all-weather track, a gym, a natatorium, and tennis courts. A recreation center houses a fitness center, racquetball courts, basketball gyms, indoor track, pool, and climbing wall. There is a lighted Astroturf field, and baseball, soccer, and softball fields.

Disabled Students: 85% of the campus is accessible. Wheelchair ramps, elevators, special parking, specially equipped rest rooms, special class scheduling, lowered drinking fountains, lowered telephones, and automated doors in 37 buildings are available.

Services: Counseling and information services are available, as is tutoring in every subject. There is a reader service for the blind, as well as a reading and writing resource center.

Campus Safety and Security: Measures include 24-hour foot and vehicle patrol, self-defense education, escort service, and informal discussions. There are pamphlets/posters/films, emergency telephones, lighted pathways/sidewalks, and public bus transportation routes through the campus.

Programs of Study: JMU confers B.A., B.S., B.B.A., B.F.A., B.I.S., B.M., B.S.N., and B.S.W. degrees. Master's and doctoral degrees are also awarded. Bachelor's degrees are awarded in BIOLOGICAL SCIENCE (biology/biological science), BUSINESS (accounting, banking and finance, business administration and management, business economics, hospitality management services, international business management, marketing/retailing/merchandising, recreation and leisure services, and tourism), COMMUNICATIONS AND THE ARTS (art, art history and appreciation, communications, communications technology, dance, dramatic arts, English, fine arts, media arts, modern language, music, and speech/debate/rhetoric), COMPUTER AND PHYSICAL SCIENCE (chemistry, computer science, geology, information sciences and systems, mathematics, physics, science technology, and statistics), EDUCATION (business), HEALTH PROFESSIONS (health science, nursing, and speech pathology/audiology), SOCIAL SCIENCE (anthropology, dietetics, economics, geography, history, international studies, liberal arts/general studies, philosophy, physical fitness/movement, political science/government, psychology, public administration, religion, social science, social work, and sociology). Biology, business, and communication are the strongest academically. Psychology, communications, and English are the largest.

Required: To graduate, students must complete a minimum of 120 credit hours, with a GPA of at least 2.0., meet the general education requirements, have been enrolled at JMU a minimum of two regular semesters, and have earned a minimum of 30 credit hours at JMU during that period of enrollment.

Special: JMU offers internships, work-study programs, a Washington semester, and study abroad in London, Paris, Florence, Salamanca, and Martinique. An individualized study degree, nondegree study, pass/fail options, and credit for life, military, and work experience are available. There are 22 national honor societies, a freshman honors program, and 36 departmental honors programs.

Faculty/Classroom: 62% of faculty are male; 38%, female. 94% teach undergraduates. Graduate students teach 3% of introductory courses. The average class size in an introductory lecture is 35; in a laboratory, 20; and in a regular course, 34.

Admissions: 64% of the 2001-2002 applicants were accepted. The SAT I scores for the 2001-2002 freshman class were: Verbal--13% below 500, 54% between 500 and 599, 30% between 600 and 700, and 3% above 700; Math--11% below 500, 50% between 500 and 599, 36% between 600 and 700, and 3% above 700. 63% of the current freshmen were in the top fifth of their class; 96% were in the top two fifths. 14 freshmen graduated first in their class.

Requirements: The SAT I or ACT is required. In addition, applicants must be graduates of an accredited secondary school. They must show solid achievement in 4 or more academic courses each year of high school. A personal statement is required. Art students must present a portfolio. Theater, dance, and music students must audition. Nursing students must apply to the nursing department in addition to applying for undergraduate admission. Applications are accepted on-line via Apply. AP credits are accepted. Important factors in the admissions decision are advanced placement or honor courses, extracurricular activities record, and evidence of special talent.

Procedure: Freshmen are admitted in the fall. Entrance exams should be taken in the spring of the junior year or fall of the senior year. There are early admissions and deferred admissions plans. Early action applications should be filed by November 1; regular applications, by January 15 for fall entry. Notification of early action is sent mid-January; regular decision, April 1. 10% of all applicants are on a waiting list; 117 were accepted in 2001. The fall 2001 application fee was $30.

Transfer: 624 transfer students enrolled in 2001-2002. Applicants must have a minimum GPA of 2.0. Those who have not completed a full year of college must submit their SAT I scores, request official transcripts, submit secondary school records or a copy of their GED, and a one-page personal statement. 30 credits of 120 must be completed at JMU.

Visiting: There are regularly scheduled orientations for prospective students, including daily campus tours during the week and on Saturdays, and tours following the group conferences. There are guides for informal visits. To schedule a visit, contact the Admissions Office at (540) 568-3620.

Financial Aid: In 2001-2002, 49% of all freshmen and 47% of continuing students received some form of financial aid. 36% of freshmen and 32% of continuing students received need-based aid. The average freshman award was $7491. Of that total, scholarships or need-based grants averaged $3083 ($16,284 maximum); loans averaged $2920 ($6625 maximum); and work contracts averaged $1629 ($1638 maximum). 21% of undergraduates work part time. Average annual earnings from campus work are $2169. The average financial indebtedness of the 2001 graduate was $13,253. The FAFSA is required. The fall application deadline is March 1.

International Students: There are 180 international students enrolled. The school actively recruits these students. They must score 550 on the written TOEFL and also take the SAT I or the ACT. Students must take SAT II: Subject tests in writing.

Computers: The mainframes are a DEC Alpha 4100 VMS server, various HP9000 series servers running HP-UX, and Dell Power Edge servers running Windows NT. Computers are located in classrooms, labs, residence halls, academic buildings, and the library. All students may access the system 24 hours a day. It is strongly recommended that all students have a personal computer. It is recommended that students in the College of Integrated Science and Technology and the College of Business have personal computers. Each college has an established recommendation requirement and contracts/discounts available accordingly. Dell is the primary brand offered. There are no time limits and no fees.

Graduates: In 2001, 3059 bachelor's degrees were awarded. The most popular majors were psychology (8%), marketing (8%), and computer information systems (6%). In an average class, 60% graduate in 4 years, 76% in 5 years, and 80% in 6 years. 224 companies recruited on campus in 2000-2001. Of the 2000 graduating class, 17% were enrolled in graduate school within 6 months of graduation and 71% were employed.

Admissions Contact: Michael D. Walsh, Director of Admissions.
E-mail: *gotojmu@jmu.edu* Web: *www.jmu.edu/admissions*

LIBERTY UNIVERSITY D-3

Lynchburg, VA 24502 (434) 582-7307
(800) 543-5317; Fax: (434) 582-2421

Full-time: 2132 men, 2416 women	**Faculty:** 161; IIA, --$
Part-time: 507 men, 336 women	**Ph.D.s:** 61%
Graduate: 477 men, 294 women	**Student/Faculty:** 28 to 1
Year: semesters, summer session	**Tuition:** $9500
Application Deadline: June 30	**Room & Board:** $5000
Freshman Class: n/av	
SAT I or ACT: required	**COMPETITIVE**

Liberty University, founded in 1971, is a private liberal arts institution affiliated with the Southern Baptist Church. There are 6 undergraduate and 5 graduate schools. In addition to regional accreditation, Liberty has baccalaureate program accreditation with NASM and NLN. The library contains 208,077 volumes, 95,329 microform items, and 4889 audiovisual forms/CDs, and subscribes to 10,511 periodicals. Computerized library services include the card catalog, interlibrary loans, and database searching. Special learning facilities include a learning resource center, radio station, and TV station. The 160-acre campus is in a suburban area 45 miles east of Roanoke. Including residence halls, there are 73 buildings.

Student Life: 62% of undergraduates are from out of state, mostly the Middle Atlantic. Others are from 50 states, 52 foreign countries, and Canada. 84% are white; 32% foreign nationals. Most are Protestant. The average age of freshmen is 18; all undergraduates, 21.

Housing: 3256 students can be accommodated in college housing, which includes single-sex dormitories. On-campus housing is guaranteed for all 4 years. 68% of students live on campus; of those, 90% remain on campus on weekends. Alcohol is not permitted. All students may keep cars.

Activities: There are no fraternities or sororities. There are 40 groups on campus, including band, cheerleading, choir, chorale, chorus, computers, debate, drama, drill team, ethnic, honors, international, marching band, musical theater, newspaper, opera, orchestra, pep band, political, professional, radio and TV, religious, social service, student government, and yearbook. Popular campus events include Super Conference and Missions Emphasis Week.

Sports: There are 9 intercollegiate sports for men and 8 for women, and 16 intramural sports for men and 16 for women. Facilities include an 11,000-seat football stadium, an 8000-seat basketball arena/convention center, baseball and soccer fields, a track complex and a tennis center.

Disabled Students: 90% of the campus is accessible. Wheelchair ramps, special parking, specially equipped rest rooms, special class scheduling, lowered drinking fountains, and lowered telephones are available.

Services: Counseling and information services are available, as is tutoring in every subject. There is remedial math, reading, and writing.

Campus Safety and Security: Measures include 24-hour foot and vehicle patrol, self-defense education, escort service, and informal discussions. There are pamphlets/posters/films and lighted pathways/sidewalks.

Programs of Study: Liberty confers B.A., B.S., B.M., and B.S.N. degrees. Associate, master's, and doctoral degrees are also awarded. Bachelor's degrees are awarded in BIOLOGICAL SCIENCE (biology/biological science), BUSINESS (accounting, business administration and management, and sports management), COMMUNICATIONS AND THE ARTS (communications, English, English as a second/foreign language, music, and Spanish), COMPUTER AND PHYSICAL SCIENCE (computer science and mathematics), EDUCATION (athletic training, elementary, and physical), HEALTH PROFESSIONS (community health work, exercise science, and nursing), SOCIAL SCIENCE (family/consumer studies, history, interdisciplinary studies, liberal arts/general studies, political science/government, psychology, religion, and social science). Business, psychology, and education are the largest.

Required: Students must complete 120 to 123 credit hours to graduate, with a minimum GPA of 2.0. With few exceptions, by major, all must complete 18 hours of foundational studies in English, math, speech communications, and general education. An additional 42 credits of investigative studies are required; these vary according to the degree sought, either B.A. or B.S., but include English, natural sciences, history, arts, music, languages, government, social sciences, philosophy, theology, Bible studies, and integrated studies.

Special: Liberty offers internships, a Washington semester, B.A., B.S. degrees, and student-designed majors in interdisciplinary and general studies. There are 8 national honor societies, including Phi Beta Kappa, and a freshman honors program.

Faculty/Classroom: 64% of faculty are male; 36%, female. 99% teach undergraduates. No introductory courses are taught by graduate students. The average class size in an introductory lecture is 50; in a laboratory, 20; and in a regular course, 30.

Admissions: 58% of the 2001-2002 applicants were accepted. There were 11 National Merit semifinalists.

Requirements: The SAT I or ACT is required. In addition, applicants must have completed 16 high school academic credits. The GED is accepted. An essay is required. Applications are accepted on-line at Apply Web. A GPA of 2.0 is required. AP and CLEP credits are accepted. Important factors in the admissions decision are ability to finance college education, recommendations by school officials, and advanced placement or honor courses.

Procedure: Freshmen are admitted to all sessions. Entrance exams should be taken during the junior year. There are early decision, early admissions, and deferred admissions plans. Applications should be filed by June 30 for fall entry and November 15 for spring entry, along with a $35 fee. Notification of early decision and regular decision is sent on a rolling basis.

Transfer: 517 transfer students enrolled in 2001-2002. Applicants for transfer must have a GPA of 2.0. If transferring fewer than 60 hours, a high school transcript and test scores are required. 30 credits of 120 must be completed at Liberty.

Visiting: There are regularly scheduled orientations for prospective students, including College for a Weekend, a 2-day program offering a chance to attend classes and special meetings. There are guides for informal visits and visitors may sit in on classes and stay overnight. To schedule a visit, contact the Visitor's Center at (434) 582-2064 or E-Mail: *visitorscenter@liberty.edu.*

Financial Aid: In a recent year, 85% of all students received some form of financial aid. 45% of all freshmen received need-based aid. 14% of undergraduates work part time. Average annual earnings from campus work are $2500. The average financial indebtedness of the 2001 graduate was $14,484. The FAFSA and Singlefile Form (preferred) are required. The fall application deadline is March 1.

International Students: There are 160 international students enrolled. They must score 500 on the written TOEFL or 173 on the electronic version and also take the SAT I or the ACT, scoring 800 on the SAT I.

Computers: The mainframe is an IBM AS/400. More than 230 PCs are located in labs, and the library; each dorm room has 3 network connections for Internet and web access. All students may access the system 7:30 A.M. to 2 A.M. Sunday through Thursday, 9 A.M. to 9 P.M. Saturday. There are no time limits. The fee is $200 per semester.

Graduates: In 2001, 1033 bachelor's degrees were awarded. The most popular majors were religion (17%), business (16%), and psychology (13%).

Admissions Contact: David Hart, Associate Director of Admissions. A video is available. E-mail: *admissions@liberty.edu*
Web: *http://www.liberty.edu*

LONGWOOD COLLEGE — D-3

Farmville, VA 23909 — (434) 395-2060
(800) 281-4677; Fax: (434) 395-2332

Full-time: 1172 men, 2268 women	**Faculty:** 167; IIB, av$
Part-time: 53 men, 67 women	**Ph.D.s:** 82%
Graduate: 116 men, 438 women	**Student/Faculty:** 21 to 1
Year: semesters, summer session	**Tuition:** $4226 ($9946)
Application Deadline: March 1	**Room & Board:** $4724
Freshman Class: 2792 applied, 2175 accepted, 895 enrolled	
SAT I Verbal/Math: 530/550	**COMPETITIVE**

Longwood College, founded in 1839, is a state-supported institution with programs in liberal arts, business, and teacher preparation. There are 3 undergraduate schools and 1 graduate school. In addition to regional accreditation, Longwood has baccalaureate program accreditation with CSWE, NASM, NCATE, and NRPA. The library contains 1,071,388 volumes, 679,788 microform items, and 42,148 audiovisual forms/CDs, and subscribes to 2416 periodicals. Computerized library services include the card catalog, interlibrary loans, and database searching. Special learning facilities include a learning resource center, art gallery, radio station, TV station, and a greenhouse, a language lab, 6 computer labs, and a psychology lab. The 160-acre campus is in a small town 60 miles west of Richmond and 60 miles south of Charlottesville. Including residence halls, there are 53 buildings.

Student Life: 90% of undergraduates are from Virginia. Others are from 22 states, 19 foreign countries, and Canada. 93% are from public schools. 86% are white; 10% African American. The average age of freshmen is 18; all undergraduates, 21. 17% do not continue beyond their first year; 61% remain to graduate.

Housing: 2451 students can be accommodated in college housing, which includes single-sex and coed dormitories and off-campus apartments. In addition, there are honors houses, language houses, special-interest houses, a substance-free dorm, and international studies, fraternity/sorority, and ecology floors. On-campus housing is guaranteed for all 4 years. 75% of students live on campus; of those, 70% remain on campus on weekends. Upperclassmen may keep cars.

Activities: 21% of men belong to 9 national fraternities; 23% of women belong to 13 national sororities. There are 125 groups on campus, including art, band, cheerleading, chess, choir, chorus, computers, dance, debate, drama, drill team, ethnic, forensics, gay, honors, international, jazz band, literary magazine, musical theater, newspaper, photography, political, professional, radio and TV, religious, social, social service, student government, and yearbook. Popular campus events include Spring Weekend and Oktoberfest.

Sports: There are 6 intercollegiate sports for men and 8 for women, and 31 intramural sports for men and 31 for women. Facilities include a 9-hole golf course, a weight training facility, 2 gyms, racquetball courts, 11 lighted tennis courts, 2 pools, a bowling alley, 3 outdoor sand volleyball courts, a 10-station fitness trail, a frisbee golf course, outdoor basketball courts, and soccer, baseball, and softball fields.

Disabled Students: 90% of the campus is accessible. Wheelchair ramps, elevators, special parking, special class scheduling, lowered drinking fountains, and lowered telephones are available. The campus is being made fully accessible. Until then, classes can be scheduled in accessible buildings.

Services: Counseling and information services are available, as is tutoring in every subject. There is a reader service for the blind, remedial math, reading, and writing, and assistance in study skills, learning strategies, advocacy training, and compensatory strategy instruction.

Campus Safety and Security: Measures include 24-hour foot and vehicle patrol, self-defense education, escort service, and shuttle buses. There are informal discussions, pamphlets/posters/films, emergency telephones, lighted pathways/sidewalks, electronic card key entry into dorms, and video cameras.

Programs of Study: Longwood confers B.A., B.S., B.F.A., B.M., B.S.B.A. degrees. Master's degrees are also awarded. Bachelor's degrees are awarded in BIOLOGICAL SCIENCE (biology/biological science), BUSINESS (business administration and management), COMMUNICATIONS AND THE ARTS (art, communications, English, modern language, music, and visual and performing arts), COMPUTER AND PHYSICAL SCIENCE (chemistry, computer science, mathematics, and physics), EDUCATION (art, elementary, music, physical, special, and speech correction), HEALTH PROFESSIONS (recreation therapy), SOCIAL SCIENCE (anthropology, economics, history, liberal arts/general studies, political science/government, psychology, social work, and sociology). Business and liberal studies (elementary education) are the strongest academically and have the largest enrollments are the strongest academically. Business, and liberal studies (elementary education) are the largest.

Required: To graduate, students must complete 120 to 145 credits, including 36 to 77 in the major, with a minimum GPA of 2.0 overall and in the major. A 44-hour general education core curriculum, 4 intensive writing courses, a phys ed course, and 30 upper-level credit hours are also required.

Special: Longwood offers internships in most majors, study abroad in 7 countries, and B.A.-B.S. degrees are in many majors. Cross-registration is possible with Hampden-Sydney College, as are 3-2 engineering degrees with several regional universities. Also, there is a 3-3 preprofessional program in physical therapy with University of Virginia, Old Dominion and Virginia Commonwealth Universities. There are 3 national honor societies, a freshman honors program, and 21 departmental honors programs.

Faculty/Classroom: 60% of faculty are male; 40%, female. 50% both teach and do research. No introductory courses are taught by graduate students. The average class size in an introductory lecture is 31; in a laboratory, 21; and in a regular course, 27.

Admissions: 78% of the 2001-2002 applicants were accepted. The SAT I scores for the 2001-2002 freshman class were: Verbal--26% below 500, 55% between 500 and 599, 17% between 600 and 700, and 2% above 700; Math--30% below 500, 55% between 500 and 599, 14% between 600 and 700, and 1% above 700. 28% of the current freshmen were in the top fifth of their class; 70% were in the top two fifths. 1 freshman graduated first in the class.

Requirements: The SAT I or ACT is recommended. In addition, applicants must be graduates of an accredited secondary school; the GED is accepted. Students should complete 4 years of high school English, 3 years each of foreign language and science (including 2 lab courses), 2 years of history, and algebra I, II, and geometry. A personal statement is required. An audition is required for music students. Longwood requires applicants to be in the upper 50% of their class. A GPA of 2.6 is required. AP and CLEP credits are accepted. Important factors in the admissions decision are advanced placement or honor courses, leadership record, and evidence of special talent. Applications are accepted on-line.

Procedure: Freshmen are admitted fall and spring. Entrance exams should be taken in the fall of the senior year. There are early decision and deferred admissions plans. Early decision applications should be filed by December 1; regular applications, by March 1 for fall entry and November 15 for spring entry. Notification of early decision is sent January 1; regular decision, on a rolling basis. 482 early decision candidates were accepted for the 2001-2002 class. 3% of all applicants are on a waiting list; 69 were accepted in 2001. The fall 2001 application fee was $30.

Transfer: 177 transfer students enrolled in 2001-2002. Applicants for transfer must have a GPA of at least 2.5 in all college course work attempted. Other criteria are the same as for entering freshmen. 30 credits of 120 to 145 must be completed at Longwood.

Visiting: There are regularly scheduled orientations for prospective students, including informational and tour programs, and open houses in October, February, March, and November. There are guides for informal visits and visitors may sit in on classes and stay overnight. To schedule a visit, contact the Admissions Office.

Financial Aid: In 2001-2002, 43% of all freshmen and 44% of continuing students received some form of financial aid. 39% of freshmen and 40% of continuing students received need-based aid. The average freshman award was $14,892. Of that total, scholarships or need-based grants averaged $3368 ($8060 maximum); loans averaged $3189 ($8125 maximum); and work contracts averaged $865 ($2000 maximum). 27% of undergraduates work part time. Average annual earnings from campus work are $1344. The average financial indebtedness of the 2001 graduate was $13,776. The FAFSA is required. The fall application deadline is March 1.

International Students: There are 15 international students enrolled. The school actively recruits these students. They must score 550 on the written TOEFL or 213 on the electronic version and also take the SAT I or the ACT. If the major is in a modern language, the student must take the SAT II subject tests in the corresponding language.

Computers: The mainframe is an IBM RS 6000 (Model S70). There are 185 networked PCs and Macs. 2 student computer labs are open 9 A.M. to 10 P.M. daily. Numerous software packages and programming languages are available. All students may access the system. There are no time limits and no fees. All students are required to have personal computers.

Graduates: In 2001, 619 bachelor's degrees were awarded. The most popular majors were liberal studies (27%), business administration (20%), and visual and performing arts (7%). In an average class, 1% graduate in 3 years, 39% in 4 years, 54% in 5 years, and 61% in 6 years. 167 companies recruited on campus in 2000-2001. Of the 2000 graduating class, 21% were enrolled in graduate school within 6 months of graduation and 91% were employed.

Admissions Contact: Robert J. Chonko, Director of Admissions and Enrollment Management. E-mail: *lcadmit@longwood.edu*
Web: *www.longwood.edu*

LYNCHBURG COLLEGE

Lynchburg, VA 24501 — D-3
(434) 544-8300
(800) 426-8101; Fax: (434) 544-8653

Full-time: 646 men, 960 women	**Faculty:** 109; IIA, --$
Part-time: 34 men, 93 women	**Ph.D.s:** 84%
Graduate: 64 men, 140 women	**Student/Faculty:** 15 to 1
Year: semesters, summer session	**Tuition:** $19,005
Application Deadline: open	**Room & Board:** $4400
Freshman Class: 2310 applied, 1724 accepted, 473 enrolled	
SAT I Verbal/Math: 518/508	**ACT:** 20 **COMPETITIVE**

Lynchburg College, established in 1903, is a private, nonprofit institution affiliated with the Christian Church (Disciples of Christ) offering bachelor's degrees in liberal arts and sciences, and professional studies. There are 6 undergraduate and 2 graduate schools. In addition to regional accreditation, L.C. has baccalaureate program accreditation with NLN. The library contains 217,072 volumes, 433,196 microform items, and 5253 audiovisual forms/CDs, and subscribes to 532 periodicals. Computerized library services include the card catalog, interlibrary loans, and database searching. Special learning facilities include a learning resource center and art gallery. The 214-acre campus is in a suburban area 180 miles southwest of Washington, D.C. Including residence halls, there are 26 buildings.

Student Life: 60% of undergraduates are from Virginia. Others are from 37 states and 13 foreign countries. 79% are from public schools. 88% are white. 81% are Protestant; 16% Catholic. The average age of freshmen is 18; all undergraduates, 21. 28% do not continue beyond their first year; 54% remain to graduate.

Housing: 1211 students can be accommodated in college housing, which includes single-sex and coed dormitories and on-campus apartments. In addition, there are honors houses, language houses, and special-interest houses. On-campus housing is guaranteed for all 4 years. 76% of students live on campus; of those, 80% remain on campus on weekends. Upperclassmen may keep cars.

Activities: 16% of men belong to 6 national fraternities; 10% of women belong to 5 national sororities. There are 60 groups on campus, including art, cheerleading, choir, computers, dance, drama, ethnic, gay, honors, international, jazz band, literary magazine, musical theater, newspaper, political, professional, religious, social, social service, student government, TV, and yearbook. Popular campus events include a new student convocation, and Academic Awards Banquet.

Sports: There are 10 intercollegiate sports for men and 11 for women, and 12 intramural sports for men and 12 for women. Facilities include a gym with a modern weight room and exercise physiology lab; a field house, athletic fields, and a ropes course.

Disabled Students: 78% of the campus is accessible. Wheelchair ramps, elevators, special parking, specially equipped rest rooms, special class scheduling, lowered drinking fountains, lowered telephones, and some dorm rooms with wheelchair accessibility are available.

Services: Counseling and information services are available. Tutoring is available in most freshman and sophomore subjects, some upperclass subjects, and in math and writing.

Campus Safety and Security: Measures include 24-hour foot and vehicle patrol, escort service, informal discussions, and pamphlets/posters/films. There are emergency telephones, and lighted pathways/sidewalks. All residence halls are locked 24 hours a day. Admission is only by scanning an ID card.

Programs of Study: L.C. confers B.A. and B.S. degrees. Master's degrees are also awarded. Bachelor's degrees are awarded in BIOLOGICAL SCIENCE (biology/biological science), BUSINESS (accounting, business administration and management, management science, marketing/retailing/merchandising, and sports management), COMMUNICATIONS AND THE ARTS (art, communications, dramatic arts, English, French, music, and Spanish), COMPUTER AND PHYSICAL SCIENCE (chemistry, computer science, mathematics, and physical sciences), EDUCATION (athletic training, and education), ENGINEERING AND ENVIRONMENTAL DESIGN (engineering, and environmental science), HEALTH PROFESSIONS (biomedical science, exercise science, nursing, and sports medicine), SOCIAL SCIENCE (economics, history, human development, international relations, philosophy, physical fitness/movement, political science/government, psychology, religion, and sociology). Communication studies, nursing, human development learning, business administration, and psychology are the largest.

Required: To graduate, students must complete a 15- to 18-hour basic skills requirement, which includes English, a foreign language, math, health, movement science, and recreation. Students must also complete 15 to 21 hours in the humanities (history, literature, philosophy, and religion), 6 hours each in fine arts and social sciences, 6 to 16 hours in physical sciences, and a 2-hour senior symposium in which students read selections from the classics, prepare written analyses, and attend weekly lecture/discussion sessions. The minimum GPA is 2.0. Students must earn 124 credits, with 30 to 69 in the major.

Special: Students may cross-register with Sweet Briar and Randolph-Macon Colleges, and they may study abroad in 20 countries. There is a Washington semester available, B.A.-B.S.degrees in 39 majors, internships, and a work-study program. Dual majors may be pursued in religious studies, philosophy, political science, sociology, business, and a foreign language. A 3-2 engineering degree is available in cooperation with Old Dominion University. Nondegree study and a pass/fail grading option are also available. There are 12 national honor societies and a freshman honors program.

Faculty/Classroom: 62% of faculty are male; 38%, female. All teach undergraduates, 25% do research, and 25% do both. No introductory courses are taught by graduate students. The average class size in an introductory lecture is 25; in a laboratory, 16; and in a regular course, 25.

Admissions: 75% of the 2001-2002 applicants were accepted. The SAT I scores for the 2001-2002 freshman class were: Verbal--39% below 500, 45% between 500 and 599, 15% between 600 and 700, and 1% above 700; Math--44% below 500, 44% between 500 and 599, 11% between 600 and 700, and 2% above 700. The ACT scores were 63% below 21, 17% between 21 and 23, 13% between 24 and 26, 1% between 27 and 28, and 5% above 28. 29% of the current freshmen were in the top fifth of their class; 61% were in the top two fifths. 2 freshmen graduated first in their class.

Requirements: The SAT I or ACT is required, and SAT II: Subject tests are recommended. Applicants must graduate from an accredited secondary school. They must have earned 16 to 20 academic high school credits in English, math and social science, lab science, and foreign language. Applications are accepted on-line at the college's web page. AP and CLEP credits are accepted. Important factors in the admissions decision are advanced placement or honor courses, leadership record, and recommendations by school officials.

Procedure: Freshmen are admitted fall and spring. Entrance exams should be taken in the junior year and in the first semester of the senior year. There is an early decision plan. Early decision applications should be filed by November 15; regular applications, are accepted on an open basis for fall entry. Notification of early decision is sent December 15; regular decision, on a rolling basis. 45 early decision candidates were accepted for the 2001-2002 class. The fall 2001 application fee was $30.

Transfer: 58 transfer students enrolled in 2001-2002. Transfer students must have a minimum GPA of 2.0 to be considered, and must be in good academic and social standing. The SAT I or ACT is required. An interview is recommended. 48 credits of 124 must be completed at L.C.

Visiting: There are regularly scheduled orientations for prospective students, individual appointments are available. There are guides for informal visits and visitors may sit in on classes and stay overnight. To schedule a visit, contact the Enrollment Services Office.

Financial Aid: In 2001-2002, 98% of all freshmen and 96% of continuing students received some form of financial aid. 61% of freshmen and

59% of continuing students received need-based aid. The average freshman award was $15,362. Of that total, scholarships or need-based grants averaged $10,510 ($24,255 maximum); loans averaged $3613 ($4625 maximum); and work contracts averaged $1029 ($1200 maximum). 34% of undergraduates work part time. Average annual earnings from campus work are $1250. The average financial indebtedness of the 2001 graduate was $17,143. L.C. is a member of CSS. The FAFSA is required. The fall application deadline is March 1.

International Students: There are 14 international students enrolled. The school actively recruits these students. They must score 550 on the written TOEFL or 213 on the electronic version and also take the SAT I or the ACT.

Computers: The mainframe is a DEC VAX 4000/200. Student computing is primarily PC based, with some access to mainframe facilities. 200 PCs are located in labs and classrooms across campus. Most students own computers and have them in their rooms. All students may access the system 8 A.M. to 1 A.M. Monday through Thursday, 8 A.M. to 5 P.M. Friday and Saturday, noon to 1 A.M. Sunday. There are no time limits and no fees. It is strongly recommended that all students have a personal computer.

Graduates: In 2001, 334 bachelor's degrees were awarded. The most popular majors were child development (14%), communication studies (9%), and psychology (8%). In an average class, 1% graduate in 3 years, 46% in 4 years, 54% in 5 years, and 55% in 6 years. 78 companies recruited on campus in 2000-2001. Of the 2000 graduating class, 22% were enrolled in graduate school within 6 months of graduation and 75% were employed.

Admissions Contact: Rita Detwiler, VP, Enrollment Management. A video is available. E-mail: *admissions@lynchburg.edu*
Web: *www.lynchburg.edu*

MARY BALDWIN COLLEGE — D-2
Staunton, VA 24401 — (540) 887-7019
(800) 468-2262; Fax: (540) 886-6634

Full-time: 22 men, 1074 women	**Faculty:** 72; IIB, -$
Part-time: 40 men, 353 women	**Ph.D.s:** 89%
Graduate: 14 men, 61 women	**Student/Faculty:** 15 to 1
Year: n/app	**Tuition:** $15,990
Application Deadline: April 15	**Room & Board:** $7450
Freshman Class: 1271 applied, 1037 accepted, 312 enrolled	
SAT I Verbal/Math: 530/500	**COMPETITIVE**

Mary Baldwin College, established in 1842, is a private liberal arts college primarily for women and affiliated with the Presbyterian Church (U.S.A.). The college sponsors a special program for gifted young women who have completed the eighth grade or higher, and a leadership program for women. The library contains 164,860 volumes, 52,087 microform items, and 4005 audiovisual forms/CDs, and subscribes to 1602 periodicals. Computerized library services include the card catalog, interlibrary loans, and database searching. Special learning facilities include a learning resource center, art gallery, radio station, TV station, and language lab. The 54-acre campus is in a small town 100 miles west of Richmond. Including residence halls, there are 30 buildings.

Student Life: 60% of undergraduates are from out of state, mostly the Middle Atlantic. Students are from 31 states, 6 foreign countries, and Canada. 80% are from public schools. 70% are white; 17% African American. 41% are Catholic; 40% Protestant. The average age of freshmen is 18. 30% do not continue beyond their first year; 55% remain to graduate.

Housing: 750 students can be accommodated in college housing, which includes single-sex dormitories and on-campus apartments. In addition, there are honors houses, language houses, special-interest houses, and lofts and suites. On-campus housing is guaranteed for all 4 years. 92% of students live on campus; of those, 40% remain on campus on weekends. All students may keep cars.

Activities: There are no fraternities or sororities. There are 48 groups on campus, including art, choir, chorale, chorus, computers, dance, drama, drill team, drum and bugle corps, ethnic, film, gay, honors, international, literary magazine, marching band, musical theater, newspaper, orchestra, photography, political, professional, radio and TV, religious, social, social service, student government, and yearbook. Popular campus events include Apple Day, Junior Dads Weekend, and Charter Day.

Sports: There are 8 intercollegiate sports for women and 4 intramural sports for women. Facilities include a gym, a Universal gym room, a room for dance and fencing, tennis, basketball, and racquetball courts, a sauna and steam room, Nautilus equipment, and soccer, softball, and hockey fields.

Disabled Students: 30% of the campus is accessible. Wheelchair ramps, elevators, special parking, and specially equipped rest rooms are available.

Services: Counseling and information services are available, as is tutoring in most subjects. There is remedial math.

Campus Safety and Security: Measures include 24-hour foot and vehicle patrol, self-defense education, escort service, and informal discussions. There are pamphlets/posters/films, emergency telephones, lighted pathways/sidewalks, and 24-hour locked residence halls.

Programs of Study: MBC confers B.A. and B.S. degrees. Master's degrees are also awarded. Bachelor's degrees are awarded in BIOLOGICAL SCIENCE (biochemistry and biology/biological science), BUSINESS (business administration and management and business economics), COMMUNICATIONS AND THE ARTS (art, arts administration/management, communications, dramatic arts, English, fine arts, French, German, music, public relations, and Spanish), COMPUTER AND PHYSICAL SCIENCE (applied mathematics, chemistry, computer mathematics, computer science, mathematics, and physics), EDUCATION (art, early childhood, education, English, foreign languages, mathematics, middle school, science, and social studies), HEALTH PROFESSIONS (health care administration and medical laboratory technology), SOCIAL SCIENCE (Asian/Oriental studies, economics, history, international relations, philosophy, political science/government, psychology, social work, and sociology). Biology and chemistry are the strongest academically. Psychology, art, and sociology are the largest.

Required: To graduate, students must complete 9 hours each in natural sciences, social sciences, arts, and humanities; 6 hours each of writing courses and international education (foreign language, cross-cultural studies, and/or study abroad); and 3 hours each of math, women's studies, and oral communication. A minimum GPA of 2.0 is required. Students must earn 132 credits, with at least 33 credits in the major. There is a 2-hour phys ed requirement and a 3-hour experiential education requirement. Most disciplines require senior projects consisting of some type of original research.

Special: There are cooperative programs with Randolph-Macon, Sweet Briar, and Hampden-Sydney Colleges and Washington and Lee University. Internships, B.A.-B.S. degrees in biology, biochemistry, chemistry, and psychology, and work-study programs are available. Students may study abroad in 6 countries. There is a Washington semester. The college offers an accelerated degree program as well as dual and student-designed majors. The Women's Institute for Leadership program combines academic and phys ed curricula with military and community service training. There are 3-2 programs available in engineering with Washington University in St. Louis and the University of Virginia and in nursing with Vanderbilt University. There is an advanced degree program in teaching with the University of Virginia. Credit for life, military, and work experience may be granted through the adult degree program only. Nondegree study and a pass/fail grading option are available. There are 9 national honor societies, including Phi Beta Kappa, and a freshman honors program.

Faculty/Classroom: 47% of faculty are male; 53%, female. All teach undergraduates. No introductory courses are taught by graduate students. The average class size in an introductory lecture is 21; in a laboratory, 12; and in a regular course, 17.

Admissions: 82% of the 2001-2002 applicants were accepted. The SAT I scores for the 2001-2002 freshman class were: Verbal--29% below 500, 48% between 500 and 599, 20% between 600 and 700, and 3% above 700; Math--48% below 500, 40% between 500 and 599, and 12% between 600 and 700.

Requirements: The SAT I or ACT is required. In addition, SAT II: Subject tests are recommended. Applicants must graduate from an accredited secondary school, have a GED, or meet state equivalency requirements for home schooling. A minimum of 16 academic units are required, including 4 in English, 3 in math, 2 to 3 in social studies, and 2 each in a foreign language and science. Essays and interviews are recommended. A GPA of 2.3 is required. AP credits are accepted. Important factors in the admissions decision are advanced placement or honor courses, extracurricular activities record, and leadership record. The Common Application and on-line applications are accepted at the school's web site and through *collegelink.com*

Procedure: Freshmen are admitted fall and spring. Entrance exams should be taken in the junior or senior year. There are early decision, early admissions, and deferred admissions plans. Early decision applications should be filed by November 15; regular applications, by April 15 for fall entry and December 15 for spring entry, along with a $25 fee. Notification of early decision is sent December 15; regular decision, on a rolling basis. 44 early decision candidates were accepted for the 2001-2002 class. A waiting list is an active part of the admissions procedure.

Transfer: 56 transfer students enrolled in 2001-2002. Transfer applicants must have a 2.0 GPA from the institution where they are currently enrolled. 66 credits of 132 must be completed at MBC.

Visiting: There are regularly scheduled orientations for prospective students, consisting of a tour, an interview, scheduled classes upon request, as well as athletic tours. There are guides for informal visits and visitors may sit in on classes and stay overnight. To schedule a visit, contact the Admissions Office.

Financial Aid: In 2001-2002, 99% of all freshmen and 95% of continuing students received some form of financial aid. 73% of freshmen and 60% of continuing students received need-based aid. The average freshman award was $18,337. Of that total, scholarships or need-based grants averaged $7000 ($11,000 maximum); loans averaged $2625 ($5500 maximum); work contracts averaged $2000; and $3000 is available as a Virginia Tuition Assistance Grant, or $7464 as a Virginia Women's Institute for Leadership Grant. 69% of undergraduates work part time. Average annual earnings from campus work are $2000. The average financial indebtedness of the 2001 graduate was $15,125. The FAFSA is required. The fall application deadline is May 1.

International Students: There are 15 international students enrolled. The school actively recruits these students. They must score 500 on the written TOEFL.

Computers: The mainframe is an IBM/400. More than 100 PCs are located throughout the campus. There are public workstations in every classroom building. All students may access the system. There are no time limits and no fees.

Graduates: In 2001, 251 bachelor's degrees were awarded. The most popular majors were business administration (18%), sociology (14%), and psychology (11%). In an average class, 3% graduate in 3 years, 52% in 4 years, and 57% in 5 years. 12 companies recruited on campus in 2000-2001. Of the 2000 graduating class, 25% were enrolled in graduate school within 6 months of graduation and 77% were employed.

Admissions Contact: Jacquelyn D. Elliott-Wonderley, Dean of Admissions and Financial Aid. E-mail: *admit@mbc.edu* Web: *www.mbc.edu*

MARY WASHINGTON COLLEGE

Fredericksburg, VA 22401-5358 — E-2
(540) 654-2000
(800) 468-5614; Fax: (540) 654-1857

Full-time: 1113 men, 2280 women — **Faculty:** 199; IIB, +$
Part-time: 251 men, 460 women — **Ph.D.s:** 89%
Graduate: 109 men, 213 women — **Student/Faculty:** 17 to 1
Year: semesters, summer session — **Tuition:** $3340 ($10,010)
Application Deadline: February 1 — **Room & Board:** $5692
Freshman Class: 4320 applied, 2397 accepted, 851 enrolled
SAT I Verbal/Math: 611/590 — **ACT:** 27 — **VERY COMPETITIVE+**

Mary Washington College, founded in 1908, is a public liberal arts and sciences institution. In addition to regional accreditation, MWC has baccalaureate program accreditation with NASM. The library contains 350,874 volumes, 521,056 microform items, and 2474 audiovisual forms/CDs, and subscribes to 1763 periodicals. Computerized library services include the card catalog, interlibrary loans, and database searching. Special learning facilities include an art gallery, radio station, and center for historic preservation. The 176-acre campus is in a small town 50 miles south of Washington, D.C. and 50 miles north of Richmond. Including residence halls, there are 40 buildings.

Student Life: 65% of undergraduates are from Virginia. Others are from 45 states, 7 foreign countries, and Canada. 89% are from public schools. 90% are white. The average age of freshmen is 18; all undergraduates, 20. 17% do not continue beyond their first year; 74% remain to graduate.

Housing: 2110 students can be accommodated in college housing, which includes single-sex and coed dormitories. In addition, there are special-interest houses, a foreign language floor of a hall, an international house, and a community service area. On-campus housing is available on a lottery system for upperclassmen. 70% of students live on campus; of those, 80% remain on campus on weekends. Upperclassmen may keep cars.

Activities: There are no fraternities or sororities. There are 96 groups on campus, including art, bagpipe band, cheerleading, choir, chorale, chorus, computers, dance, debate, drama, ethnic, gay, honors, international, jazz band, literary magazine, musical theater, newspaper, orchestra, photography, political, professional, radio and TV, religious, social, social service, student government, and yearbook. Popular campus events include Grill on the Hill, Junior Ring Dance, and a Multicultural International Festival.

Sports: There are 10 intercollegiate sports for men and 12 for women, and 18 intramural sports for men and 18 for women. Facilities include a 6-lane, 25-yard indoor pool, regulation basketball and volleyball courts, a weight room, batting cages, training rooms, playing fields for all outdoor sports, a running course, handball/racquetball courts, and an 8-lane, 400-meter track.

Disabled Students: 65% of the campus is accessible. Wheelchair ramps, elevators, special parking, specially equipped rest rooms, lowered drinking fountains, and lowered telephones are available.

Services: Counseling and information services are available, as is tutoring in most subjects. There is a reader service for the blind, a writing center and a center for the visually impaired.

Campus Safety and Security: Measures include 24-hour foot and vehicle patrol, self-defense education, escort service, and informal discussions. There are pamphlets/posters/films, emergency telephones, and lighted pathways/sidewalks.

Programs of Study: MWC confers B.A., B.S., B.L.S., and B.P.S. degrees. Master's degrees are also awarded. Bachelor's degrees are awarded in BIOLOGICAL SCIENCE (biology/biological science), BUSINESS (business administration and management), COMMUNICATIONS AND THE ARTS (art history and appreciation, classics, dramatic arts, English, French, German, historic preservation, languages, Latin, music, Spanish, and studio art), COMPUTER AND PHYSICAL SCIENCE (chemistry, computer science, geology, mathematics, and physics), ENGINEERING AND ENVIRONMENTAL DESIGN (environmental science), HEALTH PROFESSIONS (predentistry, premedicine, and preveterinary science), SOCIAL SCIENCE (American studies, economics, geography, history, international relations, philosophy, political science/government, prelaw, psychology, religion, and sociology). Historic preservation is the strongest academically. Business administration, psychology, and biology are the largest.

Required: To graduate, students must complete 122 credit hours, with 30 to 40 hours in the major and a minimum GPA of 2.0. General education curriculum includes courses in composition, math, lab science, arts/literature, Western civilization, social science, foreign language, and phys ed. Additionally, students take thematic courses across the curriculum, with requirements including writing intensive, speaking intensive, global awareness, environmental awareness, and race/gender intensive courses. A thesis is required in some majors and programs of study.

Special: Study abroad in 41 countries, a Washington semester, and credit for off-campus work experience are available. The college offers dual majors, work-study programs, student-designed majors, and pass/fail options. More than 500 internships for credit are also available. Teacher licensure preparation is offered for elementary and secondary education. Elementary education is a 5-year master's degree program. There are 20 national honor societies, including Phi Beta Kappa, and 25 departmental honors program.

Faculty/Classroom: 58% of faculty are male; 42%, female. All teach undergraduates. No introductory courses are taught by graduate students. The average class size in an introductory lecture is 28; in a laboratory, 20; and in a regular course, 22.

Admissions: 55% of the 2001-2002 applicants were accepted. The SAT I scores for the 2001-2002 freshman class were: Verbal--3% below 500, 35% between 500 and 599, 50% between 600 and 700, and 12% above 700; Math--6% below 500, 47% between 500 and 599, 43% between 600 and 700, and 4% above 700. 75% of the current freshmen were in the top fifth of their class; 96% were in the top two fifths. There were 2 National Merit finalists and 2 semifinalists. 16 freshmen graduated first in their class.

Requirements: The SAT I or ACT is required. In addition, applicants must be graduates of an accredited secondary school or hold the GED. Students should complete at least 16 high school academic credits, including 4 credits of English, 3 to 4 of foreign language, and 3 each of math, science, and social studies. The Admissions Committee recommends that applicants complete 4 years each of math, English, foreign language, science, and social studies. An SAT II: Subject test is strongly recommended. Application essays are required. AP and CLEP credits are accepted. Important factors in the admissions decision are advanced placement or honor courses, evidence of special talent, and recommendations by school officials. Applications are accepted on-line via ExPAN and CollegeLink, and can be downloaded from the college's web site.

Procedure: Freshmen are admitted fall and spring. Entrance exams should be taken by January of the senior year. There is an early decision plan. Early decision applications should be filed by November 1; regular applications, by February 1 for fall entry and November 1 for spring entry. Notification of early decision is sent December 15; regular decision, April 1. 158 early decision candidates were accepted for the 2001-2002 class. 4% of all applicants are on a waiting list; 1 was accepted in 2001. The fall 2001 application fee was $35.

Transfer: 174 transfer students enrolled in 2001-2002. The college recommends that applicants for transfer have a minimum GPA of 2.5 and a minimum of 30 college credits. The SAT I and high school transcripts are required. Graduates from the Virginia community colleges and students from the local area are given preference for admission. 30 credits of 122 must be completed at MWC.

Visiting: There are regularly scheduled orientations for prospective students, including information sessions, available Monday through Friday at 10:30 A.M. and 2 P.M., followed by a student-guided tour. Visitors may sit in on classes and stay overnight. To schedule a visit, contact the Office of Admissions.

Financial Aid: In 2001-2002, 55% of all freshmen and 60% of continuing students received some form of financial aid. 40% of freshmen and 45% of continuing students received need-based aid. The average freshman award was $4530. Of that total, scholarships or need-based grants averaged $1350 ($7030 maximum); loans averaged $2100 ($2625 maximum); and work contracts averaged $1250 ($1900 maximum). 20% of undergraduates work part time. Average annual earnings from campus work are $1400. The average financial indebtedness of the 2001 graduate was $12,000. The FAFSA is required. The fall application deadline is March 1.

International Students: There are 22 international students enrolled. The school actively recruits these students. They must score 560 on the written TOEFL or 230 on the electronic version.

Computers: The mainframe is an HP 3000/969. MWC has a fiber-optic network. All students can access Netscape (Internet) and the Web from residence hall rooms. Several 24-hour computer labs are available for student use. All students may access the system. There are no time limits and no fees.

Graduates: In 2001, 817 bachelor's degrees were awarded. The most popular majors were business administration (13%), psychology (10%), and biology (8%). In an average class, 64% graduate in 4 years, 73% in 5 years, and 74% in 6 years. 80 companies recruited on campus in 2000-2001. Of the 2000 graduating class, 15% were enrolled in graduate school within 6 months of graduation and 83% were employed.

Admissions Contact: Dr. Jenifer L. Blair, Dean of Undergraduate Admissions. E-mail: *admit@mwc.edu* Web: *www.mwc.edu*

MARYMOUNT UNIVERSITY — E-2
Arlington, VA 22207-4299 — (703) 284-1500
(800) 548-7638; Fax: (703) 522-0349

Full-time: 461 men, 1067 women	**Faculty:** 89; IIA, av$
Part-time: 143 men, 441 women	**Ph.D.s:** 87%
Graduate: 433 men, 1045 women	**Student/Faculty:** 17 to 1
Year: semesters, summer session	**Tuition:** $14,970
Application Deadline: open	**Room & Board:** $6590
Freshman Class: 1407 applied, 1220 accepted, 364 enrolled	
SAT I Verbal/Math: 500/490	**ACT:** 20 **LESS COMPETITIVE**

Marymount University, established in 1950, is an independent, comprehensive Catholic institution offering degree programs in the arts and sciences, business administration, education and human services, and health professions. There are 4 undergraduate and 4 graduate schools. In addition to regional accreditation, Marymount has baccalaureate program accreditation with ACBSP, APTA, CACREP, FIDER, NCATE, and NLN. The library contains 187,097 volumes, 315,786 microform items, and 908 audiovisual forms/CDs, and subscribes to 1048 periodicals. Computerized library services include the card catalog, interlibrary loans, and database searching. Special learning facilities include a learning resource center, art gallery, and instructional media center. The 26-acre campus is in a suburban area 2 miles southwest of Washington, D.C. Including residence halls, there are 13 buildings.

Student Life: 61% of undergraduates are from Virginia. Others are from 38 states, 82 foreign countries, and Canada. 49% are white; 14%, African American; 10%, foreign nationals. 58% claim no religious affiliation; 23% are Catholic. The average age of freshmen is 18; all undergraduates, 24. 27% do not continue beyond their first year; 61% remain to graduate.

Housing: 632 students can be accommodated in college housing, which includes single-sex and coed dormitories. In addition, there is housing for nontraditional-age students. On-campus housing is guaranteed for the freshman year only, is available on a first-come, first-served basis, and is available on a lottery system for upperclassmen. Priority is given to out-of-town students. 70% of students commute. All students may keep cars.

Activities: There are no fraternities or sororities. There are 25 groups on campus, including cheerleading, choir, chorus, computers, dance, drama, ethnic, honors, international, literary magazine, newspaper, photography, political, professional, religious, social, social service, student government, and yearbook. Popular campus events include Comedy Club, Mad Hatter Dance, and Student Fashion Show.

Sports: There are 5 intercollegiate sports for men and 5 for women, and 11 intramural sports for men and 11 for women. Facilities include a student center with a 1000-seat sports arena, renovated pool, fitness center, and recreation gym.

Disabled Students: 70% of the campus is accessible. Wheelchair ramps, elevators, special parking, specially equipped rest rooms, special class scheduling, lowered drinking fountains, and lowered telephones are available.

Services: Counseling and information services are available, as is tutoring in most subjects. There is remedial math, reading, and writing.

Campus Safety and Security: Measures include 24-hour foot and vehicle patrol, escort service, shuttle buses, and informal discussions. There are emergency telephones and lighted pathways/sidewalks.

Programs of Study: Marymount confers B.A., B.S., B.B.A., and B.S.N. degrees. Associate and master's degrees are also awarded. Bachelor's degrees are awarded in BIOLOGICAL SCIENCE (biology/biological science and molecular biology), BUSINESS (accounting, banking and finance, business administration and management, business economics, business law, fashion merchandising, human resources, international business management, management science, marketing/retailing/merchandising, retailing, and sports management), COMMUNICATIONS AND THE ARTS (communications, English, and graphic design), COMPUTER AND PHYSICAL SCIENCE (computer science, information sciences and systems, and mathematics), EDUCATION (athletic training), ENGINEERING AND ENVIRONMENTAL DESIGN (environmental science and interior design), HEALTH PROFESSIONS (health care administration, health science, and nursing), SOCIAL SCIENCE (criminal justice, economics, fashion design and technology, history, human services, liberal arts/general studies, paralegal studies, philosophy, physical fitness/movement, political science/government, psychology, sociology, and theological studies). Psychology, business administration/management, and interior design are the strongest academically. Business administration, nursing, and psychology are the largest.

Required: To graduate, students must earn 120 credits, with 39 to 60 credits in the major, and maintain a 2.0 GPA. There are core curriculum requirements in communications, humanities, math, and science, and social sciences. Specific required courses include English Composition I and II, General Psychology, and Introduction to Phys Ed.

Special: Students may cross-register with the Consortium of Universities of the Washington Metropolitan Area. They are required to complete an internship in Washington or London. Marymount offers dual and student-designed majors, an accelerated nursing degree, a 3+3 program in physical therapy, and nondegree study. There are 8 national honor societies.

Faculty/Classroom: 40% of faculty are male; 60%, female. 75% teach undergraduates. No introductory courses are taught by graduate students. The average class size in an introductory lecture is 20; in a laboratory, 11; and in a regular course, 12.

Admissions: 87% of the 2001-2002 applicants were accepted. The SAT I scores for the 2001-2002 freshman class were: Verbal--47% below 500, 40% between 500 and 599, 11% between 600 and 700, and 2% above 700; Math--51% below 500, 39% between 500 and 599, 9% between 600 and 700, and 1% above 700. The ACT scores were 63% below 21, 25% between 21 and 23, 8% between 24 and 26, and 4% between 27 and 28.

Requirements: The SAT I or ACT is required. In addition, applicants must graduate from an accredited secondary school or have a GED. Marymount requires 15 academic credits and 15 Carnegie units and strongly recommends biology and chemistry for nursing candidates. Essays and interviews are recommended. A GPA of 2.0 is required. AP and CLEP credits are accepted. Important factors in the admissions decision are advanced placement or honor courses, recommendations by school officials, and leadership record. Marymount accepts the Common Application on disk or on-line at the school's website.

Procedure: Freshmen are admitted to all sessions. Application deadlines are open. The application fee is $35. Notification is sent on a rolling basis.

Transfer: 302 transfer students enrolled in 2001-2002. Applicants with 30 or more credits must have a minimum GPA of 2.0. Those with fewer than 30 must also meet freshman requirements. 36 credits of 120 must be completed at Marymount.

Visiting: There are regularly scheduled orientations for prospective students, including Campus Visit Days, Information Nights, and new-student summer orientation. There are guides for informal visits and visitors may sit in on classes and stay overnight. To schedule a visit, contact Jordana Fornier.

Financial Aid: In 2001-2002, 76% of all freshmen and 57% of continuing students received some form of financial aid. 45% of freshmen and 38% of continuing students received need-based aid. The average freshman award was $14,893. Of that total, scholarships or need-based grants averaged $9598 ($31,440 maximum); loans averaged $6817 ($22,625 maximum); and work contracts averaged $1800 (maximum). 36% of undergraduates work part time. Average annual earnings from campus work are $1800. The average financial indebtedness of the 2001 graduate was $20,230. Marymount is a member of CSS. The FAFSA is required. The fall application deadline is March 1.

International Students: There are 243 international students enrolled. The school actively recruits these students. They must score 500 on the written TOEFL.

Computers: The mainframe is an IBM RS/6000. There are 250 Novell-networked PCs available at computer center labs throughout the campus. A RISC architecture minicomputer and a graphic design (CAD) lab with 3 HP scanners are also available. All residence halls have a PC connection in each room. Students have access to a CD-ROM network, UNIX workstations, the Internet, and 8 9600-baud dial-in lines. All students may access the system. There are no time limits. The fee is $5 per credit hour, up to $60 per semester.

Graduates: In 2001, 360 bachelor's degrees were awarded. The most popular majors were liberal studies (10%), nursing (8%), and business administration (6%). In an average class, 2% graduate in 3 years, 42% in 4 years, 49% in 5 years, and 52% in 6 years. 60 companies recruited on campus in 2000-2001.

Admissions Contact: Chris E. Domes, Vice President for Enrollment Management. A video is available.
E-mail: *admissions@marymount.edu* Web: *http://www.marymount.edu*

NORFOLK STATE UNIVERSITY F-4
Norfolk, VA 23504 (757) 823-8396; Fax: (757) 823-2078

Full-time: 1764 men, 3000 women	**Faculty:** 300
Part-time: 437 men, 762 women	**Ph.D.s:** n/av
Graduate: 170 men, 588 women	**Student/Faculty:** 16 to 1
Year: semesters, summer session	**Tuition:** $2916 ($8818)
Application Deadline: open	**Room & Board:** $5466
Freshman Class: 3993 applied, 3205 accepted, 1133 enrolled	
SAT I Verbal/Math: 425/420	**ACT:** 17 LESS COMPETITIVE

Norfolk State University, founded in 1935, is an independent institution offering undergraduate and graduate programs in the liberal arts and sciences, business education, health-related professions, and vocational, technical, and professional training. There are 5 undergraduate schools. In addition to regional accreditation, NSU has baccalaureate program accreditation with AACSB, ACEJMC, ADA, APA, CAHEA, CSAB, CSWE, NAIT, NASAD, NASM, NCATE, and NLN. The library contains 385,390 volumes and 8264 microform items, and subscribes to 1362 periodicals. Computerized library services include the card catalog, interlibrary loans, and database searching. Special learning facilities include a learning resource center, art gallery, planetarium, radio station, and TV station. The 134-acre campus is in an urban area in the port city of Norfolk. Including residence halls, there are 31 buildings.

Student Life: 69% of undergraduates are from Virginia. Others are from 45 states and 37 foreign countries. 89% are African American. The average age of freshmen is 18; all undergraduates, 24. 34% do not continue beyond their first year; 24% remain to graduate.

Housing: 2018 students can be accommodated in college housing, which includes single-sex dormitories. On-campus housing is available on a first-come, first-served basis. Priority is given to out-of-town students. 66% of students commute. Alcohol is not permitted. All students may keep cars.

Activities: 10% of men belong to 10 national fraternities; 10% of women belong to 8 national sororities. There are 112 groups on campus, including art, band, cheerleading, chess, choir, chorus, computers, debate, drama, drill team, ethnic, forensics, honors, international, literary magazine, marching band, newspaper, pep band, photography, political, professional, radio and TV, religious, social, social service, student government, and yearbook. Popular campus events include Martin Luther King Commemorative Activity and Black History Month Activities.

Sports: There are 7 intercollegiate sports for men and 6 for women, and 14 intramural sports for men and 10 for women. Facilities include a stadium and track seating 28,088, an arena seating 7,500, baseball and softball field, a gym, a swimming pool, tennis courts, and a bowling alley.

Disabled Students: All of the campus is accessible. Wheelchair ramps, elevators, special parking, specially equipped rest rooms, special class scheduling, and lowered telephones are available.

Services: Counseling and information services are available, as is tutoring in most subjects.

Campus Safety and Security: Measures include 24-hour foot and vehicle patrol, escort service, shuttle buses, and informal discussions. There are pamphlets/posters/films, emergency telephones, lighted pathways/sidewalks, and town meetings.

Programs of Study: NSU confers B.A., B.S., B.Mus., and B.S.W. degrees. Associate, master's, and doctoral degrees are also awarded. Bachelor's degrees are awarded in BIOLOGICAL SCIENCE (biology/biological science, environmental biology, and nutrition), BUSINESS (accounting, banking and finance, entrepreneurial studies, fashion merchandising, hospitality management services, management information systems, and total quality management (TQM)), COMMUNICATIONS AND THE ARTS (communications, crafts, creative writing, dramatic arts, English, fine arts, French, graphic design, journalism, literature, music, Spanish, and speech/debate/rhetoric), COMPUTER AND PHYSICAL SCIENCE (applied mathematics, chemistry, computer science, mathematics, natural sciences, and physics), EDUCATION (art, business, early childhood, elementary, health, music, physical, secondary, special, and technical), ENGINEERING AND ENVIRONMENTAL DESIGN (chemical engineering, computer technology, construction technology, drafting and design technology, electrical/electronics engineering technology, engineering, industrial administration/management, military science, and naval architecture and marine engineering), HEALTH PROFESSIONS (exercise science, health care administration, health science, medical records administration/services, medical technology, mental health/human services, nursing, premedicine, preveterinary science, and speech pathology/audiology), SOCIAL SCIENCE (African American studies, consumer services, economics, family/consumer studies, fashion design and technology, food science, history, interdisciplinary studies, liberal arts/general studies, political science/government, prelaw, psychology, public administration, social work, and sociology). Social work and computer science are the strongest academically. Business, computer science, and nursing are the largest.

Required: Students must complete at least 120 semester hours with a minimum 2.0 GPA, including general education courses such as communication, humanities, social science, natural science, health ed, phys ed, and computer literacy. They must also demonstrate writing competence.

Special: NSU offers cross-registration with other institutions in the Tidewater Consortium, a student-exchange program with Old Dominion University, co-op education, a second baccalaureate degree with a minimum of 30 additional semester hours earned, a B.A.-B.S. degree, and a general studies degree. Credit for military experience is possible. There are 16 national honor societies, and a freshman honors program.

Faculty/Classroom: 52% of faculty are male; 48%, female. No introductory courses are taught by graduate students. The average class size in an introductory lecture is 20; in a laboratory, 17; and in a regular course, 17.

Admissions: 80% of the 2001-2002 applicants were accepted. The SAT I scores for the 2001-2002 freshman class were: Verbal--83% below 500, 16% between 500 and 599, and 1% between 600 and 700; Math--87% below 500, 12% between 500 and 599, and 1% between 600 and 700. The ACT scores were 89% below 21, 9% between 21 and 23, and 2% between 24 and 26. 1% of the current freshmen were in the top fifth of their class; 38% were in the top two fifths.

Requirements: The SAT I is required. In addition, applicants should be graduates of an accredited secondary school or have the GED equivalent and have completed 20 to 22 academic units: 4 in English, 3 in history/social studies, 2 each in math, science, and health/phys ed, and 7 to 9 in electives. Nursing applicants must meet additional requirements. A GPA of 2.0 is required. AP and CLEP credits are accepted.

Procedure: Freshmen are admitted to all sessions. Entrance exams should be taken by March of the senior year. There is an early admissions plan. Application deadlines are open. The fall 2001 application fee was $25. Notification is sent on a rolling basis. Applications are available on-line at the school's web site.

Transfer: 323 transfer students enrolled in 2001-2002. Transfers must meet freshman admissions criteria. 30 credits of 120 must be completed at NSU.

Visiting: There are regularly scheduled orientations for prospective students, including registration, a general information session, visits to academic departments, admissions, and a tour. There are guides for informal visits and visitors may sit in on classes and stay overnight. To schedule a visit, contact the Admissions Office.

Financial Aid: In 2001-2002, 89% of all freshmen and 85% of continuing students received some form of financial aid. 86% of freshmen received need-based aid. The average freshman award was $8100. Of that total, scholarships or need-based grants averaged $2443 ($16,900 maximum); loans averaged $2980 ($15,000 maximum); and work contracts averaged $1251 ($2940 maximum). 8% of undergraduates work part time. Average annual earnings from campus work are $127. The CSS/Profile, FAFSA, the college's own financial statement, and the and the SAR are required. The fall application deadline is April 1.

International Students: There are 93 international students enrolled. The school actively recruits these students. They must score 500 on the written TOEFL and also take the SAT I or the ACT, scoring 800 on the SAT I or 17 on the ACT.

Computers: The mainframes are a DEC VAX 11/785 and an IBM IS6000. There are 96 terminals in the academic center and at satellite locations campuswide for faculty and students, plus 512 PCs in labs, dial-in access, the Internet, and system software. All students may access the system. There are no time limits and no fees.

Graduates: In 2001, 782 bachelor's degrees were awarded. The most popular majors were interdisciplinary studies (21%), business (9%), and psychology (7%). In an average class, 8% graduate in 4 years, 19% in 5 years, and 24% in 6 years. 150 companies recruited on campus in 2000-2001. Of the 2000 graduating class, 5% were enrolled in graduate school within 6 months of graduation.

Admissions Contact: Michelle Marable, Director of Admissions. A video is available. E-mail: *admissions@nsu.edu* Web: *www.nsu.edu*

OLD DOMINION UNIVERSITY F-4
Norfolk, VA 23529-0050 (757) 683-3685
(800) 348-7926; Fax: (757) 683-3255

Full-time: 3679 men, 5062 women	**Faculty:** 603; I, --$
Part-time: 1907 men, 2450 women	**Ph.D.s:** 85%
Graduate: 2761 men, 3768 women	**Student/Faculty:** 14 to 1
Year: semesters, summer session	**Tuition:** $4022 ($12,392)
Application Deadline: February 15	**Room & Board:** $5364
Freshman Class: 5580 applied, 4073 accepted, 1559 enrolled	
SAT I Verbal/Math: 510/510	**ACT:** 20 COMPETITIVE

Old Dominion University, founded in 1930, is a public institution with programs in arts and letters, business and public administration, engineering, education, sciences, and health sciences. There are 6 undergraduate and 6 graduate schools. In addition to regional accreditation, ODU has baccalaureate program accreditation with AACSB, ABET, ADA, APTA, ASLA, CAHEA, NASM, NCATE, NLN, and NRPA. The 4 libraries contain 822,194 volumes, 1,700,576 microform items, and

39,050 audiovisual forms/CDs, and subscribe to 7239 periodicals. Computerized library services include the card catalog, interlibrary loans, and database searching. Special learning facilities include an art gallery, planetarium, radio station, music library, art library, and digital library. The 157-acre campus is in an urban area in the Norfolk/Hampton Roads Metropolitan region. Including residence halls, there are 106 buildings.

Student Life: 87% of undergraduates are from Virginia. Others are from 48 states, 95 foreign countries, and Canada. 67% are white; 19% African American. The average age of freshmen is 19; all undergraduates, 25. 23% do not continue beyond their first year; 33% remain to graduate.

Housing: 2398 students can be accommodated in college housing, which includes coed dormitories, on-campus apartments, fraternity houses, and sorority houses. In addition, there are honors, international, coeducational, and quiet-study floors. On-campus housing is available on a first-come, first-served basis. 77% of students commute. Alcohol is not permitted. All students may keep cars.

Activities: 10% of men belong to 19 national fraternities; 6% of women belong to 9 national sororities. There are 180 groups on campus, including art, cheerleading, chess, choir, chorale, chorus, computers, dance, debate, drama, ethnic, gay, honors, international, jazz band, literary magazine, musical theater, newspaper, orchestra, pep band, political, professional, radio and TV, religious, social, student government, and yearbook. Popular campus events include Literary Festival, President's Lecture Series, and Every Woman's Festival.

Sports: There are 9 intercollegiate sports for men and 10 for women, and 13 intramural sports for men and 13 for women. Facilities include an arena, a playing field, a baseball complex, 2 pools, intramural fields, a soccer stadium, a sailing center, and a convocation center.

Disabled Students: 80% of the campus is accessible. Wheelchair ramps, elevators, special parking, specially equipped rest rooms, special class scheduling, lowered drinking fountains, and services for the learning disabled are available.

Services: Counseling and information services are available, as is tutoring in some subjects, including English and sciences. There is a reader service for the blind and remedial math and writing.

Campus Safety and Security: Measures include 24-hour foot and vehicle patrol, self-defense education, escort service, and shuttle buses. There are informal discussions, pamphlets/posters/films, emergency telephones, lighted pathways/sidewalks, and a bicycle patrol.

Programs of Study: ODU confers B.A., B.S., B.F.A., B.M., B.S.B.A., B.S.C.E., B.S.C.O.M.E., B.S.C.S., B.S.D.H., B.S.E.E., B.S.E.H., B.S.E.N.V.E., B.S.E.T., B.S.Ev., B.S.H.S., B.S.M.E., B.S.M.T., B.S.N., B.S.N.M.T., and B.S.S.E. degrees. Master's and doctoral degrees are also awarded. Bachelor's degrees are awarded in BIOLOGICAL SCIENCE (biochemistry and biology/biological science), BUSINESS (accounting, banking and finance, business administration and management, electronic business, fashion merchandising, international business management, management information systems, marketing management, recreation and leisure services, and sports management), COMMUNICATIONS AND THE ARTS (art history and appreciation, communications, dance, dramatic arts, English, fine arts, French, German, graphic design, journalism, music, music performance, music theory and composition, Spanish, and studio art), COMPUTER AND PHYSICAL SCIENCE (chemistry, computer science, geology, information sciences and systems, mathematics, and physics), EDUCATION (art, elementary, English, foreign languages, mathematics, music, physical, science, secondary, and social studies), ENGINEERING AND ENVIRONMENTAL DESIGN (civil engineering, civil engineering technology, computer engineering, electrical/electronics engineering, electrical/electronics engineering technology, engineering technology, environmental engineering, mechanical engineering, mechanical engineering technology, and nuclear engineering technology), HEALTH PROFESSIONS (dental hygiene, environmental health science, health science, medical technology, nuclear medical technology, nursing, speech pathology/audiology, and sports medicine), SOCIAL SCIENCE (anthropology, criminal justice, economics, geography, history, human services, interdisciplinary studies, international studies, philosophy, political science/government, psychology, sociology, and women's studies). Engineering, teacher education, and counseling are the strongest academically. Biology and interdisciplinary studies (education teacher preparation) are the largest.

Required: At least 120 credits, with a minimum GPA of 2.0, are required to graduate. Students must complete the university's general education program, consisting of specific skills and perspectives courses outside the student's major. English composition is a required course, and students must pass a writing proficiency exam.

Special: Old Dominion offers cross-registration with schools in the Tidewater Consortium program. There are co-op programs, guaranteed internships, study abroad in 16 countries, and a work-study program. Students may take a B.A.-B.S. degree in engineering and liberal arts. An interdisciplinary program, dual majors, accelerated degrees, 3-2 engineering degrees in business and engineering, nondegree study, pass/fail options, and credit for military and life experience are available. There are 18 national honor societies, including Phi Beta Kappa, a freshman honors program, and honors programs through all departments..

Faculty/Classroom: 59% of faculty are male; 41%, female. All teach undergraduates. Graduate students teach 5% of introductory courses. The average class size in an introductory lecture is 35; in a laboratory, 19; and in a regular course, 15.

Admissions: 73% of the 2001-2002 applicants were accepted. The SAT I scores for the 2001-2002 freshman class were: Verbal--41% below 500, 44% between 500 and 599, 14% between 600 and 700, and 1% above 700; Math--45% below 500, 41% between 500 and 599, 13% between 600 and 700, and 1% above 700. The ACT scores were 59% below 21, 14% between 21 and 23, 13% between 24 and 26, 11% between 27 and 28, and 3% above 28. 35% of the current freshmen were in the top fifth of their class; 74% were in the top two fifths. 8 freshmen graduated first in their class.

Requirements: The SAT I or ACT is required. In addition, applicants must be graduates of an accredited secondary school. The GED is accepted. Applicants should have completed 4 years of math, and 3 years each of English, foreign languages, science, and social science. An essay and an interview are recommended. A list of extracurriclar activities is required. A GPA of 2.5 is required. AP and CLEP credits are accepted. Important factors in the admissions decision are advanced placement or honor courses, recommendations by school officials, and extracurricular activities record. Applications are accepted on-line via CollegeNET.

Procedure: Freshmen are admitted to all sessions. Entrance exams should be taken in May of the junior year or November/December of the senior year. There are early admissions and deferred admissions plans. Applications should be filed by February 15 for fall entry, November 1 for spring entry, and April 1 for summer entry, along with a $30 fee. Notification is sent on a rolling basis.

Transfer: 1496 transfer students enrolled in 2001-2002. Applicants must have a minimum GPA of 2.0 and must have at least 24 semester hour credits. Applicants with fewer semester hours must meet the same requirements as freshmen. 30 credits of 120 must be completed at ODU.

Visiting: There are regularly scheduled orientations for prospective students, consisting of campus tours, available Monday through Friday at 10 A.M., Monday and Friday at 2 P.M., and Saturday at 11 A.M. Special tours can be arranged with the Office of Admissions. There are guides for informal visits and visitors may sit in on classes. To schedule a visit, contact the Admissions Office.

Financial Aid: In 2001-2002, 64% of all freshmen and 68% of continuing students received some form of financial aid. 52% of freshmen and 50% of continuing students received need-based aid. The average freshman award was $6775. Of that total, scholarships or need-based grants averaged $4317 ($11,838 maximum); loans averaged $2438 ($6625 maximum); work contracts averaged $3177 ($3300 maximum); and contracts/waivers averaged $735 ($11,838 maximum). 10% of undergraduates work part time. Average annual earnings from campus work are $2500. The average financial indebtedness of the 2001 graduate was $16,500. The FAFSA is required. The fall application deadline is February 15.

International Students: There are 413 international students enrolled. The school actively recruits these students. They must score 550 on the written TOEFL and also take the SAT I or the ACT, scoring 870 on the SAT I or 18 on the ACT.

Computers: The mainframe is a RISC 6000. There are computer labs at various locations on campus. The system also may be accessed via modem from home or dormitory rooms. All students may access the system 24 hours a day. There are no time limits and no fees.

Graduates: In 2001, 2245 bachelor's degrees were awarded. The most popular majors were nursing (9%), interdisciplinary studies (8%), and human services counseling (7%). In an average class, 14% graduate in 4 years, 28% in 5 years, and 35% in 6 years. 72 companies recruited on campus in 2000-2001.

Admissions Contact: Alice R. McAdory, Director of Admissions. A video is available. E-mail: *admit@odu.edu*
Web: *www.admissions.odu.edu*

RADFORD UNIVERSITY — C-3

Radford, VA 24141-6972 — (540) 831-5371
(800) 890-4265; Fax: (540) 831-5138

Full-time: 3058 men, 4468 women	**Faculty:** 358; IIA, -$
Part-time: 178 men, 357 women	**Ph.D.s:** 83%
Graduate: 284 men, 797 women	**Student/Faculty:** 21 to 1
Year: semesters, summer session	**Tuition:** $3069 ($9208)
Application Deadline: April 1	**Room & Board:** $5233
Freshman Class: 6278 applied, 4710 accepted, 1881 enrolled	
SAT I Verbal/Math: 499/492	**ACT:** 19 **COMPETITIVE**

Radford University, founded in 1910, is a public comprehensive institution with a diverse curricula in arts and sciences, business and economics, education and human development, nursing and health services, and visual and performing arts. There are 6 undergraduate schools and 1 graduate school. In addition to regional accreditation, RU has baccalaureate program accreditation with AACSB, ADA, ASLHA, CACREP, CSAB, CSWE, NASM, NCATE, NLN, and NRPA. The library contains

329,644 volumes, 1,456,781 microform items, and 12,614 audiovisual forms/CDs, and subscribes to 2966 periodicals. Computerized library services include the card catalog, interlibrary loans, and database searching. Special learning facilities include a learning resource center, art gallery, planetarium, radio station, TV station, and a 376-acre conservancy used for studies in ecology, botany, mapping geological features as a model in resource management and maintenance formation on actual building techniques, and cultural and oral history. The 177-acre campus is in a small town 36 miles southwest of Roanoke. Including residence halls, there are 85 buildings.

Student Life: 88% of undergraduates are from Virginia. Others are from 45 states, 65 foreign countries, and Canada. 96% are from public schools. 89% are white. The average age of freshmen is 18; all undergraduates, 21. 21% do not continue beyond their first year; 52% remain to graduate.

Housing: 3230 students can be accommodated in college housing, which includes single-sex and coed dormitories and off-campus apartments. In addition, there are honors houses and special-interest houses. On-campus housing is guaranteed for the freshman year only and is available on a lottery system for upperclassmen. 60% of students commute. All students may keep cars.

Activities: 10% of men belong to 10 local and 4 national fraternities; 10% of women belong to 7 local and 4 national sororities. There are 159 groups on campus, including art, band, cheerleading, chess, choir, chorale, chorus, computers, dance, drama, ethnic, gay, honors, international, jazz band, literary magazine, musical theater, newspaper, opera, orchestra, pep band, political, professional, radio and TV, religious, social, social service, student government, and yearbook. Popular campus events include Club Fair, Family Weekend, and Annual Highlander Picnic.

Sports: There are 9 intercollegiate sports for men and 11 for women, and 6 intramural sports for men and 6 for women. Facilities include a 5000-seat recreation and convocation complex housing a natatorium with an 8-lane swimming pool, areas for free exercise, a weight room, steam rooms, a 1/6-mile jogging track, and basketball, volleyball, handball, and racquetball courts. Outdoor facilities include a jogging trail, 12 tennis courts, and areas for baseball, soccer, lacrosse, softball, and intramural football.

Disabled Students: 85% of the campus is accessible. Wheelchair ramps, elevators, special parking, specially equipped rest rooms, special class scheduling, lowered drinking fountains, and lowered telephones are available.

Services: Counseling and information services are available, as is tutoring in most subjects. There is a reader service for the blind. There are writing and reading centers, a math tutoring lab, and a center to teach students study and time-management skills. There is a coordinator for disabled students. Tutors trained in teaching English as a second language are available to help international students.

Campus Safety and Security: Measures include 24-hour foot and vehicle patrol, self-defense education, escort service, and shuttle buses. There are informal discussions, pamphlets/posters/films, emergency telephones, and lighted pathways/sidewalks.

Programs of Study: RU confers B.A., B.S., B.B.A., B.F.A., B.G.S., B.M., B.S.N., and B.S.W. degrees. Master's degrees are also awarded. Bachelor's degrees are awarded in BIOLOGICAL SCIENCE (biology/biological science and nutrition), BUSINESS (accounting, banking and finance, business administration and management, marketing/retailing/merchandising, and recreation and leisure services), COMMUNICATIONS AND THE ARTS (art, broadcasting, communications, dance, design, dramatic arts, English, fine arts, music, and speech/debate/rhetoric), COMPUTER AND PHYSICAL SCIENCE (chemistry, computer science, geology, information sciences and systems, mathematics, and physical sciences), EDUCATION (art, foreign languages, and physical), HEALTH PROFESSIONS (medical technology, nursing, and speech pathology/audiology), SOCIAL SCIENCE (anthropology, criminal justice, economics, food science, geography, history, human development, interdisciplinary studies, liberal arts/general studies, philosophy, political science/government, psychology, religion, social science, social work, and sociology). Nursing, education, and psychology are the strongest academically. Interdisciplinary studies, criminal justice, and psychology are the largest.

Required: To graduate, students must complete at least 120 credit hours, including 30 to 90 in the major, with a 2.0 GPA. There are general education requirements in English, foreign language, speech, fine arts, philosophy/religion, lab science, math/statistics/computer science, history, psychology, social science, and health/phys ed.

Special: RU offers internships, dual majors in any subject, study abroad in 11 countries, a general studies degree, and pass/fail options. On-campus work-study is available. There are 23 national honor societies, a freshman honors program, and 14 departmental honors programs.

Faculty/Classroom: 51% of faculty are male; 49%, female. All teach undergraduates. Graduate students teach 1% of introductory courses. The average class size in an introductory lecture is 32; in a laboratory, 20; and in a regular course, 25.

Admissions: 75% of the 2001-2002 applicants were accepted. The SAT I scores for the 2001-2002 freshman class were: Verbal--50% below 500, 41% between 500 and 599, 8% between 600 and 700, and 1% above 700; Math--53% below 500, 38% between 500 and 599, and 9% between 600 and 700. The ACT scores were 75% below 21, and 25% between 21 and 23. 22% of the current freshmen were in the top fifth of their class; 54% were in the top two fifths.

Requirements: The SAT I or ACT is required. Applicants must be graduates of an accredited secondary school. The GED is accepted. Applicants should complete 21 high school academic credits, including 4 courses in English, 3 in math, and 2 each in sciences, foreign language, and social studies, including 1 in history. A GPA of 2.0 is required. AP and CLEP credits are accepted. Important factors in the admissions decision are extracurricular activities record, evidence of special talent, and advanced placement or honor courses. Applications are accepted on-line at the school's web site via CollegeNET.

Procedure: Freshmen are admitted to all sessions. Entrance exams should be taken between April of the junior year and December of the senior year. There is a deferred admissions plan. Applications should be filed by April 1 for fall entry and December 1 for spring entry. The fall 2001 application fee was $25 ($30 for out-of-state residents). Notification is sent on a rolling basis.

Transfer: 746 transfer students enrolled in 2001-2002. Applicants must have a minimum GPA of 2.0. Those with fewer than 30 semester hours of college work must submit their high school record. 30 credits of 120 must be completed at RU.

Visiting: There are regularly scheduled orientations for prospective students, consisting of open houses in the fall, information sessions and tours Monday through Friday, and Admitted Student Days in the spring. There are guides for informal visits and visitors may sit in on classes. To schedule a visit, contact the Office of Admissions.

Financial Aid: In 2001-2002, 66% of all freshmen and 60% of continuing students received some form of financial aid. 40% of freshmen and 42% of continuing students received need-based aid. The average freshman award was $6356. Of that total, scholarships or need-based grants averaged $4009 ($12,565 maximum); loans averaged $2570 ($5625 maximum); and work contracts averaged $1627 (maximum). 16% of undergraduates work part time. Average annual earnings from campus work are $1378. The average financial indebtedness of the 2001 graduate was $13,442. The FAFSA is required. The fall application deadline is March 1.

International Students: There are 95 international students enrolled. The school actively recruits these students. They must score 520 on the written TOEFL or 190 on the electronic version and also take the SAT I or the ACT.

Computers: The mainframe is a Sun UNIX. Terminals are located in several academic buildings. There are PC-equipped labs in academic departments and residence halls. Available software includes programming languages, databases, graphics, math, simulation languages, statistics, spreadsheets, and word processing. Dorm rooms are wired for Internet and Web access. All students may access the system. There are no time limits and no fees.

Graduates: In 2001, 1610 bachelor's degrees were awarded. The most popular majors were interdisciplinary studies (14%), criminal justice (7%), and marketing (6%). In an average class, 31% graduate in 4 years, 49% in 5 years, and 52% in 6 years. 284 companies recruited on campus in 2000-2001.

Admissions Contact: David W. Kraus, Director of Admissions. A video is available. E-mail: *ruadmiss@radford.edu* Web: *www.radford.edu*

RANDOLPH-MACON COLLEGE
D-3

Ashland, VA 23005

(804) 752-7305
(800) 888-1762; Fax: (804) 752-4707

Full-time: 563 men, 550 women	**Faculty:** 84; IIB, av$
Part-time: 20 men, 17 women	**Ph.D.s:** 93%
Graduate: none	**Student/Faculty:** 13 to 1
Year: 4-1-4, summer session	**Tuition:** $19,095
Application Deadline: March 1	**Room & Board:** $5300
Freshman Class: 1938 applied, 1404 accepted, 328 enrolled	
SAT I Verbal/Math: 550/550	**COMPETITIVE**

Randolph-Macon College, established in 1830, is a private liberal arts college historically affiliated with the United Methodist Church. In addition to regional accreditation, Randolph-Macon has baccalaureate program accreditation with ACS. The library contains 175,824 volumes, 193,574 microform items, and 5411 audiovisual forms/CDs, and subscribes to 972 periodicals. Computerized library services include the card catalog, interlibrary loans, and database searching. Special learning facilities include a learning resource center, art gallery, radio station, TV station, an observatory, a darkroom, and a greenhouse. The 111-acre campus is in a suburban area 15 miles north of Richmond. Including residence halls, there are 65 buildings.

Student Life: 60% of undergraduates are from Virginia. Others are from 34 states and 15 foreign countries. 67% are from public schools.

91% are white. 49% are Protestant; 21% Catholic. The average age of freshmen is 19; all undergraduates, 20. 22% do not continue beyond their first year; 64% remain to graduate.

Housing: 987 students can be accommodated in college housing, which includes single-sex and coed dormitories, on-campus apartments, fraternity houses, and sorority houses. In addition, there are honors houses, language houses, special-interest houses, senior apartments, a community service house, and several college-owned houses. On-campus housing is guaranteed for all 4 years. 89% of students live on campus; of those, 80% remain on campus on weekends. All students may keep cars.

Activities: 46% of men belong to 7 national fraternities; 44% of women belong to 5 national sororities. There are 112 groups on campus, including art, cheerleading, chess, choir, chorale, chorus, computers, dance, debate, drama, environmental, ethnic, film, honors, international, jazz band, literary magazine, musical theater, newspaper, outing, pep band, photography, political, professional, radio and TV, religious, social, social service, student government, and yearbook. Popular campus events include Spring Fling, cultural arts series, and Earth Day.

Sports: There are 7 intercollegiate sports for men and 8 for women, and 8 intramural sports for men and 8 for women. Facilities include 10 tennis courts, several playing fields for men's and women's sports, 2 gyms, an indoor track, an indoor pool, a football field, a weight room, and an exercise room. A sports and recreation center includes racquetball and squash courts, a 25-meter pool, a weight room, an aerobics room, a 3-lane track, a multipurpose gym, and a climbing wall.

Disabled Students: 50% of the campus is accessible. Wheelchair ramps, elevators, special parking, specially equipped rest rooms, special class scheduling, and advisers for learning-disabled students are available.

Services: Counseling and information services are available, as is tutoring in every subject. There is a reader service for the blind, and remedial math, reading, and writing.

Campus Safety and Security: Measures include 24-hour foot and vehicle patrol, self-defense education, escort service, and shuttle buses. There are informal discussions, pamphlets/posters/films, emergency telephones, and lighted pathways/sidewalks.

Programs of Study: Randolph-Macon confers B.A. and B.S. degrees. Bachelor's degrees are awarded in AGRICULTURE (environmental studies), BIOLOGICAL SCIENCE (biology/biological science), BUSINESS (accounting and business economics), COMMUNICATIONS AND THE ARTS (art history and appreciation, arts administration/management, classics, English, French, German, Greek, Latin, Spanish, and studio art), COMPUTER AND PHYSICAL SCIENCE (chemistry, computer science, mathematics, and physics), SOCIAL SCIENCE (economics, history, international relations, international studies, philosophy, political science/government, psychology, religion, sociology, and women's studies). Biological and physical sciences, psychology, and political science are the strongest academically. Economics/business, psychology, and sociology are the largest.

Required: To graduate, students must complete 112 credit hours, with 30 to 42 hours in the major and a minimum GPA of 2.0. All students must take 2 courses each in math, social science, lab science, literature, philosophy/theology, and phys ed, 1 course in fine arts, and enough foreign language to demonstrate proficiency. Specific courses required are English composition and European history. There is also a computer proficiency and oral communication requirement.

Special: The college offers cooperative programs in engineering with Columbia University and the University of Virginia, in forestry with Duke University, and in accounting with Virginia Commonwealth University. There is cross-registration with Hollins, Sweet Briar, Randolph-Macon Woman's College, Hampden-Sydney, Washington and Lee, and Mary Baldwin. Internships, dual majors, and a Washington semester are available. Students in all majors may take part in an accelerated degree program. Study abroad programs are offered in 14 countries. There are 15 national honor societies, including Phi Beta Kappa, a freshman honors program, and all departments have honors programs.

Faculty/Classroom: 58% of faculty are male; 42%, female. All both teach and do research. The average class size in an introductory lecture is 23; in a laboratory, 15; and in a regular course, 16.

Admissions: 72% of the 2001-2002 applicants were accepted. The SAT I scores for the 2001-2002 freshman class were: Verbal--21% below 500, 56% between 500 and 599, 19% between 600 and 700, and 5% above 700; Math--22% below 500, 57% between 500 and 599, and 21% between 600 and 700. 31% of the current freshmen were in the top fifth of their class; 65% were in the top two fifths.

Requirements: The SAT I or ACT is required. SAT II: Subject tests are recommended in writing, math, and foreign language. Applicants must be graduates of an accredited secondary school. The GED is accepted. Applicants should complete a minimum of 16 high school academic credits, including 4 years of English; 3 to 4 years each of math and science, and 2 to 3 years of foreign language, history, and social studies. An essay is required, and an interview is recommended. AP and CLEP credits are accepted. Important factors in the admissions decision are advanced placement or honor courses, recommendations by school officials, and extracurricular activities record. Applications are accepted on-line at the school's web site.

Procedure: Freshmen are admitted fall and spring. Entrance exams should be taken by January of the senior year. There are early decision, early admissions, and deferred admissions plans. Early decision applications should be filed by December 1; regular applications, by March 1 for fall entry and January 1 for spring entry. The fall application fee was $30. Notification of early decision is sent December 20; regular decision, April 1. 23 early decision candidates were accepted for the 2001-2002 class. 4% of all applicants are on a waiting list; 5 were accepted in 2001.

Transfer: 25 transfer students enrolled in 2001-2002. Applicants must have a minimum GPA of 2.0 and must be eligible to return to their previous institution. They must submit high school and college transcripts and SAT I scores. 37 credits of 112 must be completed at Randolph-Macon.

Visiting: There are regularly scheduled orientations for prospective students, including interviews, tours, and open houses. There are guides for informal visits and visitors may sit in on classes and stay overnight. To schedule a visit, contact the Office of Admissions.

Financial Aid: In 2001-2002, 93% of all freshmen and 89% of continuing students received some form of financial aid. 57% of freshmen and 51% of continuing students received need-based aid. The average freshman award was $14,811. Of that total, scholarships or need-based grants averaged $10,812 ($22,377 maximum); loans averaged $2994 ($5125 maximum); and work contracts averaged $1005 ($1670 maximum). 20% of undergraduates work part time. Average annual earnings from campus work are $1000. The average financial indebtedness of the 2001 graduate was $17,416. Randolph-Macon is a member of CSS. The FAFSA is required. The fall application deadline is March 1.

International Students: There are 18 international students enrolled. The school actively recruits these students. They must score 550 on the written TOEFL or 213 on the electronic version.

Computers: The mainframes are a DEC VAX super minicomputer and 4 Sun workstations. Students have direct access to the mainframe and to more than 200 PCs located throughout the campus. All dorm rooms are also wired with 2 Internet connections. All students may access the system 8 A.M. to 1 A.M. There are no time limits and no fees. It is strongly recommended that all students have a personal computer.

Graduates: In 2001, 223 bachelor's degrees were awarded. The most popular majors were economics/business (16%), psychology (10%), and sociology (10%). In an average class, 1% graduate in 3 years, 60% in 4 years, 64% in 5 years, and 64% in 6 years. 20 companies recruited on campus in 2000-2001. Of the 2000 graduating class, 25% were enrolled in graduate school within 6 months of graduation and 95% were employed.

Admissions Contact: John C. Conkright, Dean of Admissions and Financial Aid. A video is available. E-mail: *admissions@rmc.edu*
Web: *www.rmc.edu*

RANDOLPH-MACON WOMAN'S COLLEGE D-3
Lynchburg, VA 24503 (434) 947-8100
(800) 745-7692; Fax: (434) 947-8996

Full-time: 688 women	**Faculty:** 72; IIB, av$
Part-time: 2 men, 31 women	**Ph.D.s:** 92%
Graduate: none	**Student/Faculty:** 10 to 1
Year: semesters, summer session	**Tuition:** $18,470
Application Deadline: March 1	**Room & Board:** $7350
Freshman Class: 718 applied, 622 accepted, 189 enrolled	
SAT I Verbal/Math: 610/560	**ACT:** 26 **VERY COMPETITIVE+**

Randolph-Macon Woman's College, founded in 1891, is an independent, liberal arts institution affiliated with the United Methodist Church. In addition to regional accreditation, R-MWC has baccalaureate program accreditation with NASDTEC. The library contains 197,332 volumes, 187,000 microform items, and 3600 audiovisual forms/CDs, and subscribes to 618 periodicals. Computerized library services include the card catalog, interlibrary loans, and database searching. Special learning facilities include a learning resource center, art gallery, radio station, observatory, art museum, 2 theaters, and 3 nature preserves. The 100-acre campus is in a suburban area in the foothills of the Blue Ridge Mountains, 1 hour south of Charlottesville. Including residence halls, there are 18 buildings.

Student Life: 60% of undergraduates are from out of state, mostly the South. Students are from 45 states, 44 foreign countries, and Canada. 70% are from public schools. 74% are white; 12% foreign nationals. 57% are Protestant; 18% claim no religious affiliation; 15% Catholic. The average age of freshmen is 18; all undergraduates, 20. 23% do not continue beyond their first year; 65% remain to graduate.

Housing: 675 students can be accommodated in college housing, which includes single-sex dormitories. There is a special senior residence hall and shared housing for Prime Time students. On-campus housing is guaranteed for all 4 years. 87% of students live on campus; of those, 75% remain on campus on weekends. All students may keep cars.

Activities: There are no sororities. There are 35 groups on campus, including art, chorale, chorus, dance, drama, environmental, equestrian, ethnic, film, foreign language, gay, honors, international, literary magazine, newspaper, outdoor activities, pep band, political, professional, radio and TV, religious, social, social service, student government, and yearbook. Popular campus events include Tacky Party, Senior Dinner Dance, and Symposium.

Sports: Facilities include a gym, an indoor heated swimming pool, dance studios, aerobic and weight rooms, 8 tennis courts, athletic fields, a 100-acre riding center with teaching and amphitheater show rings and indoor and outdoor arenas, and a 900-seat auditorium.

Disabled Students: 50% of the campus is accessible. Wheelchair ramps, elevators, special parking, specially equipped rest rooms, special class scheduling, a wheelchair lift, a heelchair-accessible residence hall, and a TDY telephone for the hearing impaired are available.

Services: Counseling and information services are available, as is tutoring in every subject. There are computing and study skills resources, a writing lab, and a science and math center.

Campus Safety and Security: Measures include 24-hour foot and vehicle patrol, self-defense education, escort service, and informal discussions. There are pamphlets/posters/films, emergency telephones, and lighted pathways/sidewalks.

Programs of Study: R-MWC confers B.A. and B.S. degrees. Bachelor's degrees are awarded in AGRICULTURE (environmental studies), BIOLOGICAL SCIENCE (biology/biological science), COMMUNICATIONS AND THE ARTS (art, classics, communications, dance, dramatic arts, English, French, German, music, and Spanish), COMPUTER AND PHYSICAL SCIENCE (chemistry, mathematics, and physics), HEALTH PROFESSIONS (health science), SOCIAL SCIENCE (American studies, economics, history, international relations, philosophy, political science/government, psychology, religion, Russian and Slavic studies, and sociology). Psychology, biology, and English are the largest.

Required: To graduate, all students must complete at least 124 credit hours with a minimum GPA of 2.0. Students must satisfy the requirements for the general education and major programs and must have a minimum GPA of 2.0 in the major.

Special: R-MWC offers a junior year spring semester American Culture Program, as well as study abroad in 11 countries. A Washington semester at American University is available, as is cross-registration with Sweet Briar and Lynchburg Colleges, and through the Tri-College Consortium and the Seven-College Exchange Program with Hampden-Sydney, Hollins, Mary Baldwin, Randolph-Macon, and Sweet Briar Colleges, and Washington and Lee University. There is a 3-2 nursing program with Johns Hopkins University. There are 9 national honor societies, including Phi Beta Kappa, and a freshman honors program.

Faculty/Classroom: 51% of faculty are male; 49%, female. All teach undergraduates and 58% both teach and do research. The average class size in an introductory lecture is 18; in a laboratory, 13; and in a regular course, 13.

Admissions: 87% of the 2001-2002 applicants were accepted. The SAT I scores for the 2001-2002 freshman class were: Verbal--11% below 500, 33% between 500 and 599, 40% between 600 and 700, and 16% above 700; Math--20% below 500, 46% between 500 and 599, 32% between 600 and 700, and 2% above 700. The ACT scores were 11% below 21, 19% between 21 and 23, 25% between 24 and 26, 19% between 27 and 28, and 26% above 28. 67% of the current freshmen were in the top fifth of their class; 91% were in the top two fifths. 11 freshmen graduated first in their class.

Requirements: The SAT I or ACT is required. In addition, applicants must be graduates of an accredited secondary school with at least 16 academic credits, including 4 units in English, 3 to 4 in a foreign language, 3 in math, 2 in biology, chemistry, or physics with lab work, and 1 to 2 in electives from other academic study. An interview is strongly recommended. AP and CLEP credits are accepted. Important factors in the admissions decision are advanced placement or honor courses, recommendations by school officials, and leadership record. Applications are available on-line and are accepted on computer disk.

Procedure: Freshmen are admitted fall and spring. Entrance exams should be taken in the junior or senior year. There are early decision and deferred admissions plans. Early decision applications should be filed by November 15; regular applications, by March 1 for fall entry and December 1 for spring entry, along with a $35 fee. Notification of early decision is sent December 15; regular decision, on a rolling basis. 21 early decision candidates were accepted for the 2001-2002 class.

Transfer: 35 transfer students enrolled in 2001-2002. Transfer students must submit college and high school transcripts, 2 letters of recommendation, a copy of their current college's catalog, and SAT I or ACT scores. An interview is recommended. Seniors may not transfer in. Courses within a liberal arts curriculum will be considered for transfer credit if grades are at least in the C range. 62 credits of 124 must be completed at R-MWC.

Visiting: There are regularly scheduled orientations for prospective students, including a campus tour, student panels, faculty panels, class visits, and individual sessions with an admissions and financial planning counselor. There are guides for informal visits and visitors may sit in on classes and stay overnight. To schedule a visit, contact the Admissions Office at (434) 846-9680 or (800) 745-7692.

Financial Aid: In 2001-2002, all freshmen and 98% of continuing students received some form of financial aid. 65% of freshmen and 60% of continuing students received need-based aid. Scholarships or need-based grants averaged $14,469 ($18,090 maximum); loans averaged $2390 ($2625 maximum); and work contracts averaged $1860 (maximum). 63% of undergraduates work part time. Average annual earnings from campus work are $961. The average financial indebtedness of the 2001 graduate was $19,100. The FAFSA is required. The fall application deadline is March 1.

International Students: There are 83 international students enrolled. The school actively recruits these students. They must score 550 on the written TOEFL or 213 on the electronic version.

Computers: Students may access 100 PC and 20 Mac computers, all networked and software-equipped, in several cluster locations on campus. All dorm rooms are also networked, and the campuswide information system provides access to global e-mail services and web resources. All students may access the system. There are no time limits and no fees.

Graduates: In 2001, 148 bachelor's degrees were awarded. The most popular majors were biology (14%), sociology/anthropology (11%), and political science (11%). In an average class, 2% graduate in 3 years, 61% in 4 years, 63% in 5 years, and 63% in 6 years. 122 companies recruited on campus in 2000-2001. Of the 2000 graduating class, 31% were enrolled in graduate school within 6 months of graduation and 69% were employed.

Admissions Contact: Patricia N. LeDonne, Director of Admissions. A video is available. E-mail: *admissions@rmwc.edu*
Web: *www.rmwc.edu*

ROANOKE COLLEGE — C-3

Salem, VA 24153 — (540) 375-2270
(800) 388-2276; Fax: (540) 375-2267

Full-time: 641 men, 1025 women	**Faculty:** 121; IIB, av$
Part-time: 48 men, 76 women	**Ph.D.s:** 85%
Graduate: none	**Student/Faculty:** 14 to 1
Year: semesters, summer session	**Tuition:** $18,681
Application Deadline: March 1	**Room & Board:** $6008
Freshman Class: 2687 applied, 1990 accepted, 497 enrolled	
SAT I Verbal/Math: 560/550	**VERY COMPETITIVE**

Roanoke College, founded in 1842, is a private institution affiliated with the Evangelical Lutheran Church in America. The college offers undergraduate programs in the arts and sciences and business administration. In addition to regional accreditation, Roanoke has baccalaureate program accreditation with ACBSP. The library contains 198,765 volumes, 293,473 microform items, and 7020 audiovisual forms/CDs, and subscribes to 759 periodicals. Computerized library services include the card catalog, interlibrary loans, and database searching. Special learning facilities include a learning resource center, art gallery, radio station, media classroom, TV production facility, and multimedia computer labs. The 70-acre campus is in a suburban area 5 miles west of Roanoke. Including residence halls, there are 40 buildings.

Student Life: 58% of undergraduates are from Virginia. Others are from 40 states, 16 foreign countries, and Canada. 81% are from public schools. 91% are white. 51% are Protestant; 17% Catholic. The average age of freshmen is 18; all undergraduates, 20. 21% do not continue beyond their first year; 65% remain to graduate.

Housing: 1025 students can be accommodated in college housing, which includes single-sex and coed dormitories and fraternity houses. In addition, there are honors houses, special-interest houses and freshman residence halls. On-campus housing is guaranteed for all 4 years. 57% of students live on campus. All students may keep cars.

Activities: 18% of men belong to 3 national fraternities; 18% of women belong to 4 national sororities. There are 65 groups on campus, including art, cheerleading, chess, choir, chorale, chorus, computers, dance, drama, ethnic, gay, honors, international, jazz band, literary magazine, musical theater, newspaper, pep band, photography, political, professional, radio and TV, religious, social, social service, student government, and yearbook. Popular campus events include Family Weekend, Alumni Weekend, and WinterFest.

Sports: There are 9 intercollegiate sports for men and 10 for women, and 9 intramural sports for men and 9 for women. Facilities include a 2400-seat gym, a 400-seat arena, athletic fields, an all-weather track, practice and playing fields, tennis and racquetball courts, a swimming pool, and a fitness center with weight training and physical conditioning equipment.

Disabled Students: 80% of the campus is accessible. Wheelchair ramps, elevators, special parking, specially equipped rest rooms, and special class scheduling are available.

Services: Counseling and information services are available, as is tutoring in every subject. A supervised peer tutoring program is available at no charge to students.

Campus Safety and Security: Measures include 24-hour foot and vehicle patrol, self-defense education, escort service, and informal discussions. There are pamphlets/posters/films, emergency telephones, and lighted pathways/sidewalks.

Programs of Study: Roanoke confers B.A., B.S., and B.B.A. degrees. Bachelor's degrees are awarded in AGRICULTURE (environmental studies), BIOLOGICAL SCIENCE (biochemistry and biology/biological science), BUSINESS (business administration and management), COMMUNICATIONS AND THE ARTS (art, dramatic arts, English, French, music, and Spanish), COMPUTER AND PHYSICAL SCIENCE (chemistry, computer science, information sciences and systems, mathematics, and physics), EDUCATION (athletic training and physical), ENGINEERING AND ENVIRONMENTAL DESIGN (environmental science), HEALTH PROFESSIONS (medical technology), SOCIAL SCIENCE (criminal justice, economics, history, international relations, philosophy, political science/government, psychology, religion, sociology, and theological studies). Computer science, biology, and chemistry are the strongest academically. Business, sociology, and English are the largest.

Required: Requirements for graduation include completion of 34 courses, including about 12 in the major. Specific course requirements include 2 courses each in math, lab science, social science, and phys ed, as well as a 2-course sequence in civilization, a freshman-year writing course, a values course, and a senior symposium. All students must attain a 2.0 GPA and be able to demonstrate competency in a foreign language. An intensive learning course and a cocurricular learning and service experience are also required.

Special: There is cross-registration with Hollins College and study abroad in more than 100 countries. Roanoke also offers internships, a Washington semester, the Virginia at Oxford Program, combined B.A.-B.S. degrees in chemistry, biology, physics, and psychology, a 3-2 engineering degree with Virginia Polytechnic Institute and State University, Washington University in St. Louis, and University of Tennessee at Knoxville, credit by examination, and pass/fail options. Nondegree study is available to those students admitted with special status. There are 20 national honor societies and a freshman honors program. All departments have honors programs.

Faculty/Classroom: 55% of faculty are male; 45%, female. All teach undergraduates and 60% both teach and do research. The average class size in an introductory lecture is 22; in a laboratory, 20; and in a regular course, 19.

Admissions: 74% of the 2001-2002 applicants were accepted. The SAT I scores for the 2001-2002 freshman class were: Verbal--20% below 500, 47% between 500 and 599, 29% between 600 and 700, and 4% above 700; Math--21% below 500, 56% between 500 and 599, 22% between 600 and 700, and 2% above 700. 53% of the current freshmen were in the top fifth of their class; 80% were in the top two fifths. 13 freshmen graduated first in their class.

Requirements: The SAT I or ACT is required, but the SAT I is preferred. SAT II: Subject tests, an essay, and an interview are recommended. Applicants must be graduates of accredited secondary schools or have earned a GED. The college requires 18 academic units, based on 4 years of English, 3 courses in math, 4 courses in foreign language, and 2 courses each in lab science and social studies. An audition is also recommended for performing arts majors. AP and CLEP credits are accepted. Important factors in the admissions decision are advanced placement or honor courses, evidence of special talent, and leadership record. Applications are accepted on computer disk as well as on-line at *http://www2.roanoke.edu/admissio/applform.htm*

Procedure: Freshmen are admitted fall and spring. Entrance exams should be taken by January of senior year. There are early decision, early action, and deferred admissions plans. Early decision applications should be filed by November 15; regular applications, by March 1 for fall entry. Notification of early decision is sent November 30; regular decision, April 1. 80 early decision candidates were accepted for the 2001-2002 class. 7% of all applicants are on a waiting list; 4 were accepted in 2001.

Transfer: 83 transfer students enrolled in 2001-2002. Transfers must have a minimum GPA of 2.2. The SAT I scores and an interview are recommended. 16 credits of 34 must be completed at Roanoke.

Visiting: There are regularly scheduled orientations for prospective students, consisting of open houses that provide a sampling of college life at Roanoke. There are guides for informal visits and visitors may sit in on classes and stay overnight. To schedule a visit, contact the Admissions Office.

Financial Aid: In 2001-2002, 96% of all freshmen and 88% of continuing students received some form of financial aid. 74% of freshmen and 69% of continuing students received need-based aid. The average freshman award was $15,969. Of that total, scholarships or need-based grants averaged $8897 ($24,194 maximum); loans averaged $4125 ($4625 maximum); and work contracts averaged $1500 (maximum). 29% of undergraduates work part time. Average annual earnings from campus work are $1300. The average financial indebtedness of the 2001 graduate was $15,284. Roanoke is a member of CSS. The FAFSA is required. The fall application deadline is March 1.

International Students: There are 23 international students enrolled. The school actively recruits these students. They must score 550 on the written TOEFL and also take the SAT I or ACT. SAT II: Subject tests are recommended.

Computers: The mainframe is a Sun 450. There are more than 150 PCs in 10 computer labs (5 multimedia) across campus, including the library, which has an on-line catalog. From any connected PC, students have access to word processing, spreadsheets, databases, e-mail, the Internet, programming languages, and about 200 programs for specific classes. All students may access the system any time. There are no time limits and no fees.

Graduates: In 2001, 329 bachelor's degrees were awarded. The most popular majors were business administration (22%), sociology (12%), and English (9%). In an average class, 2% graduate in 3 years, 55% in 4 years, 60% in 5 years, and 65% in 6 years. 66 companies recruited on campus in 2000-2001. Of the 2000 graduating class, 20% were enrolled in graduate school within 6 months of graduation and 96% were employed.

Admissions Contact: Michael Maxey, Vice President of Admissions. A video is available. E-mail: *admissions@roanoke.edu*
Web: *www.roanoke.edu*

SAINT PAUL'S COLLEGE — E-4
Lawrenceville, VA 23868 — (434) 848-4268
(800) 678-7071; Fax: (434) 848-0229

Full-time: 185 men, 274 women	**Faculty:** 35; IIB, --$
Part-time: 17 men, 74 women	**Ph.D.s:** 57%
Graduate: none	**Student/Faculty:** 13 to 1
Year: semesters, summer session	**Tuition:** $9192
Application Deadline: open	**Room & Board:** $4648
Freshman Class: 569 applied, 236 accepted, 154 enrolled	
SAT I: required	**COMPETITIVE**

Saint Paul's College, founded in 1888, is a small, private liberal arts college affiliated with the Protestant Episcopal Church, offering undergraduate programs in arts and sciences, business, and education. The library contains 41,500 volumes, 29,000 microform items, and 914 audiovisual forms/CDs, and subscribes to 163 periodicals. Computerized library services include the card catalog, interlibrary loans, and database searching. Special learning facilities include a learning resource center and art gallery. The 180-acre campus is in a small town 55 miles south of Petersburg. Including residence halls, there are 34 buildings.

Student Life: 74% of undergraduates are from Virginia. Others are from 18 states and 2 foreign countries. 99% are from public schools. 96% are African American. Most are Protestant. The average age of freshmen is 18; all undergraduates, 20. 37% do not continue beyond their first year; 31% remain to graduate.

Housing: 431 students can be accommodated in college housing, which includes single-sex dormitories and on-campus apartments. In addition, there are honors houses, special-interest houses, and a Single Parent Support System. On-campus housing is guaranteed for the freshman year only and is available on a lottery system for upperclassmen. 56% of students live on campus; of those, 52% remain on campus on weekends. Alcohol is not permitted. All students may keep cars.

Activities: 7% of men belong to 4 national fraternities; 5% of women belong to 4 national sororities. There are 25 groups on campus, including art, cheerleading, chess, choir, dance, drama, ethnic, honors, jazz band, newspaper, pep band, political, religious, social service, student government, and yearbook. Popular campus events include a lecture and concert series, College for a Day, and Founders Day.

Sports: There are 6 intercollegiate sports for men and 5 for women, and 2 intramural sports for men and 2 for women. Facilities include a gym, baseball and football fields, practice fields, and tennis courts.

Disabled Students: 40% of the campus is accessible. Wheelchair ramps, elevators, special parking, specially equipped rest rooms, and lowered drinking fountains are available.

Services: Counseling and information services are available, as is tutoring in most subjects. There is remedial math, reading, and writing.

Campus Safety and Security: Measures include 24-hour foot and vehicle patrol, self-defense education, escort service, and shuttle buses. There are informal discussions, pamphlets/posters/films, emergency telephones, and lighted pathways/sidewalks.

Programs of Study: SPC confers B.A., B.S., and B.S.Ed. degrees. Bachelor's degrees are awarded in BIOLOGICAL SCIENCE (biology/biological science, marine biology, and marine science), BUSINESS (business administration and management), COMMUNICATIONS AND THE ARTS (English), COMPUTER AND PHYSICAL SCIENCE (mathematics), EDUCATION (business, elementary, and secondary), ENGINEERING AND ENVIRONMENTAL DESIGN (environmental science), SOCIAL SCIENCE (law enforcement and corrections, political science/government, social science, and sociology). Business administration and management are the strongest academically. Business administration is the largest.

Required: All students must complete 42 semester hours of general education requirements, including courses in humanities, natural science and math, social sciences, health and phys ed, and computer information systems. A minimum of 120 hours, including at least 30 in the major, with at least a 2.0 GPA is required to graduate. Students in the Organizational Management Program (OMP) are required to write a thesis. All students must take GRE/PRAXIS for teacher certification.

Special: Cross-registration is possible with members of the Southside Higher Education Consortium and with Richard Bland College and Parkland College. Minors and the B.A.-B.S. degree are offered in most disciplines. Nonmajor preprofessional programs are available in the health professions. Endorsements in early childhood, middle, and secondary education are available in appropriate majors. Co-op programs in aquatic science and environmental science, a general studies degree and work-study programs are available. Nondegree study is possible. There are 2 national honor societies, a freshman honors program, and 3 departmental honors programs.

Faculty/Classroom: 80% of faculty are male; 20%, female. All teach undergraduates and 6% both teach and do research. The average class size in an introductory lecture is 10; in a laboratory, 8; and in a regular course, 33.

Admissions: 41% of the 2001-2002 applicants were accepted. 1 freshman graduated first in the class.

Requirements: The SAT I is required. In addition, applicants should be graduates of an accredited secondary school and have completed 16 academic units, including English, math, science, and social sciences. A GPA of 2.0 is required. AP and CLEP credits are accepted. Important factors in the admissions decision are recommendations by school officials, leadership record, and evidence of special talent.

Procedure: Freshmen are admitted fall and spring. Entrance exams should be taken during the senior year. There are early decision and early admissions plans. Application deadlines are open.

Transfer: 130 transfer students enrolled in 2001-2002. Transfer applicants must supply all former official high school and college transcripts as well as a background form completed by the former college. 30 credits of 120 must be completed at SPC.

Visiting: There are regularly scheduled orientations for prospective students, Options include Homecoming, Open House, College for a Day, Honors Convocation, and Pre-Orientation. There are guides for informal visits and visitors may sit in on classes and stay overnight. To schedule a visit, contact the Director of Admissions and Recruitment.

Financial Aid: In 2001-2002, 81% of all freshmen and 90% of continuing students received some form of financial aid. 95% of freshmen and 90% of continuing students received need-based aid. The average freshman award was $10,767. Of that total, scholarships or need-based grants averaged $7025; loans averaged $2625 ($5500 maximum); and work contracts averaged $1000. 45% of undergraduates work part time. Average annual earnings from campus work are $1500. The average financial indebtedness of the 2001 graduate was $3500. SPC is a member of CSS. The CSS/Profile is required. The fall application deadline is July 1.

International Students: There were 8 international students enrolled in a recent year. They must take the TOEFL and also take the SAT I, scoring 700.

Computers: The mainframe is an HP 3000 Series 300. Students enrolled in programming lab classes may access the system Monday through Friday from 3 A.M. to 6 P.M. There are no time limits. The fee is $100. It is strongly recommended that all students have a personal computer.

Graduates: In 2001, 134 bachelor's degrees were awarded. The most popular majors were organizational management (43%), sociology (8%), and criminal justice (7%). In an average class, 23% graduate in 4 years, and 25% in 5 years. 54 companies recruited on campus in 2000-2001. Of the 2000 graduating class, 60% were employed within 6 months of graduation.

Admissions Contact: Michael Taylor, Director, Enrollment Management. E-mail: *admissions@saintpauls.edu* Web: *www.saintpauls.edu*

SHENANDOAH UNIVERSITY — D-1

Winchester, VA 22601 (540) 665-4581
(800) 432-2266; Fax: (540) 665-4627

Full-time: 553 men, 688 women	**Faculty:** 115; IIA, -$
Part-time: 37 men, 83 women	**Ph.D.s:** 74%
Graduate: 355 men, 735 women	**Student/Faculty:** 11 to 1
Year: semesters, summer session	**Tuition:** $17,000
Application Deadline: open	**Room & Board:** $5550
Freshman Class: 1055 applied, 1055 accepted, 346 enrolled	
SAT I Verbal/Math: 510/490	**ACT:** 20 **NONCOMPETITIVE**

Shenandoah University, founded in 1875, is a private university, affiliated with the United Methodist Church and offering programs in arts and sciences, nursing and health professions, business, music, theater, and dance. There are 4 undergraduate and 9 graduate schools. In addition to regional accreditation, Shenandoah has baccalaureate program accreditation with NASM and NLN. The 2 libraries contain 117,783 volumes, 133,423 microform items, and 17,743 audiovisual forms/CDs, and subscribe to 1169 periodicals. Computerized library services include the card catalog, interlibrary loans, and database searching. Special learning facilities include a learning resource center, radio station, and TV station. The 100-acre campus is in a small town 72 miles west of Washington, D.C. Including residence halls, there are 18 buildings.

Student Life: 62% of undergraduates are from Virginia. Others are from 45 states, 32 foreign countries, and Canada. 81% are white. 35% are claim no religious affiliation; 34% Protestant; 14% Catholic. The average age of freshmen is 19; all undergraduates, 22. 34% do not continue beyond their first year; 47% remain to graduate.

Housing: 666 students can be accommodated in college housing, which includes single-sex and coed dormitories and off-campus apartments. In addition, there are honors houses, and a non-alcohol residence hall. On-campus housing is guaranteed for all 4 years. 58% of students commute. All students may keep cars.

Activities: There are no fraternities or sororities. There are 27 groups on campus, including band, cheerleading, chess, choir, chorale, chorus, dance, drama, drum and bugle corps, ethnic, honors, international, jazz band, musical theater, newspaper, opera, orchestra, pep band, political, professional, radio and TV, religious, social service, student government, and symphony. Popular campus events include conservatory productions, International Days, and Spring Fling.

Sports: There are 8 intercollegiate sports for men and 7 for women, and 12 intramural sports for men and 12 for women. Facilities include a soccer field, a gym with basketball and volleyball courts, 2 weight rooms, a fitness room, a track, lacrosse and softball fields, and a football stadium.

Disabled Students: 90% of the campus is accessible. Wheelchair ramps, elevators, special parking, specially equipped rest rooms, special class scheduling, lowered drinking fountains, and electric doors are available.

Services: Counseling and information services are available, as is tutoring in most subjects. There is a reader service for the blind and remedial math.

Campus Safety and Security: Measures include 24-hour foot and vehicle patrol, self-defense education, escort service, and informal discussions. There are pamphlets/posters/films, emergency telephones, and lighted pathways/sidewalks.

Programs of Study: Shenandoah confers B.A., B.S., B.B.A., B.F.A, B.M., and B.M.T. degrees. Associate, master's, and doctoral degrees are also awarded. Bachelor's degrees are awarded in BIOLOGICAL SCIENCE (biology/biological science), BUSINESS (business administration and management and management science), COMMUNICATIONS AND THE ARTS (art, arts administration/management, communications, dance, dramatic arts, English, jazz, music, music performance, music theory and composition, musical theater, performing arts, piano/organ, theater design, and theater management), COMPUTER AND PHYSICAL SCIENCE (chemistry), EDUCATION (dance, music, and psychology), ENGINEERING AND ENVIRONMENTAL DESIGN (environmental science), HEALTH PROFESSIONS (music therapy, nursing, and respiratory therapy), SOCIAL SCIENCE (American studies, history, law enforcement and corrections, liberal arts/general studies, physical fitness/movement, psychology, public administration, religion, religious music, and sociology). English, psychology, and mass communications are the strongest academically. Business administration, musical theater, and music education are the largest.

Required: To graduate, all students must have taken 1 religion/philosophy course and 2 phys ed courses. Students must complete at least 120 credit hours with a minimum 2.0 GPA. Other requirements vary depending on the program of study.

Special: Internships, dual majors, and work-study programs are available. Nondegree study is possible. There are 2 national honor societies, a freshman honors program, and 1 departmental honors program.

Faculty/Classroom: 53% of faculty are male; 47%, female. 73% teach undergraduates. Graduate students teach 1% of introductory courses. The average class size in an introductory lecture is 21; in a laboratory, 9; and in a regular course, 12.

Admissions: All of the 2001-2002 applicants were accepted. The SAT I scores for the 2001-2002 freshman class were: Verbal--44% below 500, 39% between 500 and 599, 13% between 600 and 700, and 4% above 700; Math--53% below 500, 35% between 500 and 599, 11% between 600 and 700, and 1% above 700. The ACT scores were 50% below 21, 32% between 21 and 23, 5% between 24 and 26, 5% between 27 and 28, and 9% above 28. 31% of the current freshmen were in the top fifth of their class; 62% were in the top two fifths.

Requirements: The SAT I or ACT is required, with a minimum composite score of 850 on the SAT I or 19 on the ACT. Applicants must be graduates of an accredited secondary school. The GED is accepted. Students should complete 15 high school academic credits, including 4 years of English, 3 years of math, and 2 years each of foreign language, science, and social studies. A minimum GPA of 2.5 is required. An audition is required for music, theater, and dance. A GPA of 2.0 is required. AP and CLEP credits are accepted. Important factors in the admissions decision are evidence of special talent, advanced placement or honor courses, and personality/intangible qualities. Applications are available on the university's home page.

Procedure: Freshmen are admitted to all sessions. Entrance exams should be taken by junior year or early in the senior year. There is a deferred admissions plan. Application deadlines are open.

Transfer: 130 transfer students enrolled in 2001-2002. Transfer applicants must have a GPA of 2.0. An audition is required for music, dance, and theater. Official transcripts from high school and all previous college work must be submitted in addition to the SAT I or ACT scores, unless the applicant has been out of school more than 2 years. 24 credits of 120 must be completed at Shenandoah.

Visiting: There are regularly scheduled orientations for prospective students, including information sessions with faculty and staff, and student-guided campus tours. There are guides for informal visits and visitors may sit in on classes. To schedule a visit, contact the Admissions Office.

Financial Aid: In 2001-2002, 85% of all freshmen and 78% of continuing students received some form of financial aid. 73% of freshmen and 85% of continuing students received need-based aid. The average freshman award was $11,671. Of that total, scholarships or need-based grants averaged $5146 ($17,000 maximum); loans averaged $5025 ($9625 maximum); and work contracts averaged $1500 (maximum). 39% of undergraduates work part time. Average annual earnings from campus work are $828. The average financial indebtedness of the 2001 graduate was $14,734. The FAFSA and the State aid form are required. The fall application deadline is March 1.

International Students: There are 175 international students enrolled. The school actively recruits these students. They must score 450 on the written TOEFL and also take the college's own test.

Computers: The mainframe is an IBM AS/400/300. There are approximately 130 PCs and workstations located in computer labs throughout the campus. All students may access the system during scheduled hours. There are no time limits and no fees. It is recommended that students in nursing and pharmacy have personal computers. An IBM is recommended.

Graduates: In 2001, 149 bachelor's degrees were awarded. The most popular majors were business administration (10%), music education (10%), and nursing (9%). In an average class, 35% graduate in 4 years, 45% in 5 years, and 47% in 6 years. 115 companies recruited on campus in 2000-2001.

Admissions Contact: Michael Carpenter, Director of Admissions. E-mail: *admit@su.edu* Web: *http://www.su.edu*

SWEET BRIAR COLLEGE

Sweet Briar, VA 24595 — D-3

(434) 381-6142

(800) 381-6142; Fax: (434) 381-6152

Full-time: 17 men, 665 women	**Faculty:** 71; IIB, +$
Part-time: 11 men, 45 women	**Ph.D.s:** 94%
Graduate: none	**Student/Faculty:** 10 to 1
Year: semesters	**Tuition:** $18,010
Application Deadline: February 1	**Room & Board:** $7300
Freshman Class: 440 applied, 358 accepted, 159 enrolled	
SAT I Verbal/Math: 580/540	**ACT:** 24 **VERY COMPETITIVE**

Sweet Briar College, founded in 1901, is a private women's liberal arts institution. The 4 libraries contain 247,385 volumes, 430,311 microform items, and 6816 audiovisual forms/CDs, and subscribe to 996 periodicals. Computerized library services include interlibrary loans and database searching. Special learning facilities include a learning resource center, art gallery, radio station, TV station, and college museum. The 3300-acre campus is in a rural area 150 miles southwest of Washington, D.C., 100 miles west of Richmond, 12 miles north of Lynchburg. Including residence halls, there are 38 buildings.

Student Life: 60% of undergraduates are from out of state, mostly the South. Others are from 43 states, 17 foreign countries, and Canada. 78% are from public schools. 85% are white. The average age of freshmen is 18; all undergraduates, 20. 18% do not continue beyond their first year; 82% remain to graduate.

Housing: 592 students can be accommodated in college housing, which includes single-sex dormitories. In addition, there is substance-free and first-year housing. On-campus housing is guaranteed for all 4 years. 92% of students live on campus; of those, 75% remain on campus on weekends. All students may keep cars.

Activities: There are no fraternities. There are 43 groups on campus, including art, cheerleading, chemical, choir, chorus, computers, dance, drama, environmental, ethnic, film, gay, health related, honors, international, literary magazine, musical theater, newspaper, National Organization for Women, outdoor, photography, political, professional, radio and TV, religious, riding, social, social service, student government, and yearbook. Popular campus events include Stepsinging, Dell Parties, and Founders Day.

Sports: Facilities include a natatorium, gym, Nautilus center, weight room, pathway and trail system for walking, biking, and riding, 14 tennis courts, riding center, soccer/lacrosse/field hockey fields, fitness circuit, primitive campgrounds, and 2 lakes.

Disabled Students: 80% of the campus is accessible. Wheelchair ramps, elevators, special parking, specially equipped rest rooms, and lowered telephones are available.

Services: Counseling and information services are available, as is tutoring in most subjects.

Campus Safety and Security: Measures include 24-hour foot and vehicle patrol, self-defense education, escort service, and shuttle buses. There are informal discussions, pamphlets/posters/films, emergency telephones, lighted pathways/sidewalks, and gates manned by security personnel from 6 P.M. to 6 A.M., and locked dorms with student key access.

Programs of Study: Sweet Briar confers B.A., and B.S. degrees. Bachelor's degrees are awarded in AGRICULTURE (environmental studies), BIOLOGICAL SCIENCE (biochemistry, biology/biological science, and molecular biology), COMMUNICATIONS AND THE ARTS (art history and appreciation, creative writing, dance, dramatic arts, English, French, German, Greek, Latin, literature, modern language, music, Spanish, and studio art), COMPUTER AND PHYSICAL SCIENCE (chemistry, computer science, mathematics, and physics), ENGINEERING AND ENVIRONMENTAL DESIGN (environmental science), SOCIAL SCIENCE (anthropology, classical/ancient civilization, economics, German area studies, history, international relations, Italian studies, liberal arts/general studies, philosophy, political science/government, psychology, religion, sociology, and Spanish studies). International affairs, biology, and English are the strongest academically. Psychology, government, and English are the largest.

Required: To graduate, students must complete 120 credits, of which 60 must be earned at Sweet Briar, with a minimum GPA of 2.0. In addition to major requirements, specific degree requirements include English: Thought and Expression. Students must take 7 hours in scientific theory and experiment; 6 in global cultures; 4 in study or practice of the arts; 3 each in Western culture, social science, literature, and economic, political, or legal systems; and 2 in physical activity. Students must demonstrate proficiency in oral and written communication, quantitative reasoning, and a foreign language. A senior capstone course/experience is also required.

Special: The college offers a coordinate program in general business management and arts management, as well as internships to explore career opportunities and gain work experience. Study abroad in 15 countries, and a Washington semester with American University. B.A.-B.S. degrees, student-designed and interdisciplinary majors, accelerated degree programs, and 3-2 engineering degrees with Columbia University, Washington University in St. Louis, Virginia Polytechnic Institute, and University of Virginia are available. Cross-registration with Lynchburg and Randolph-Macon Woman's colleges (the Tri-College Consortium) and the Seven College Exchange is also possible. There are 9 national honor societies, including Phi Beta Kappa, and a freshman honors program.

Faculty/Classroom: 46% of faculty are male; 54%, female. All teach undergraduates and do research. The average class size in an introductory lecture is 22; in a laboratory, 12; and in a regular course, 10.

Admissions: 81% of the 2001-2002 applicants were accepted. The SAT I scores for the 2001-2002 freshman class were: Verbal--21% below 500, 39% between 500 and 599, 37% between 600 and 700, and 3% above 700; Math--28% below 500, 44% between 500 and 599, 26% between 600 and 700, and 2% above 700. The ACT scores were 17% below 21, 28% between 21 and 23, 30% between 24 and 26, 10% between 27 and 28, and 15% above 28. 53% of the current freshmen were in the top fifth of their class; 81% were in the top two fifths. There was 1 National Merit finalist. 7 freshmen graduated first in their class.

Requirements: The SAT I or ACT is required. If the SAT I is submitted, it is recommended that the applicant also take 3 SAT II: Subject tests, 1 in English and 2 in other areas. Applicants must be graduates of an accredited secondary school. Applicants must complete at least 16 high school academic credits (20 recommended), including 4 years of English and 3 each of math, social studies, science, history, and a foreign language. The college requires an essay and recommends an interview. AP credits are accepted. Important factors in the admissions decision are advanced placement or honor courses, evidence of special talent, and leadership record. Applications are accepted on-line.

Procedure: Freshmen are admitted fall and spring. Entrance exams should be taken by February of the year of application; SAT II: Subject tests can be taken in the spring of the senior year. There are early decision and deferred admissions plans. Early decision applications should be filed by December 1; regular applications, by February 1 for fall entry and November 15 for spring entry. Notification of early decision is sent December 15; regular decision, April 1. 52 early decision candidates were accepted for the 2001-2002 class.

Transfer: 18 transfer students enrolled in 2001-2002. Transfer applicants must submit official transcripts from high school and college, test scores, a college catalog, and recommendations from a previous dean and professor. 60 credits of 120 must be completed at Sweet Briar.

Visiting: There are regularly scheduled orientations for prospective students, consisting of attendance at classes and campus events, meetings with faculty and coaches, an overnight stay in a dorm, a campus tour, and an interview. There are guides for informal visits and visitors may sit in on classes and stay overnight. To schedule a visit, contact Margaret Blount, Director of Admissions at (434) 384-9276 or *mblount@sbc.edu*

Financial Aid: 54% of freshmen and 51% of continuing students received need-based aid. The average freshman award was $16,121. Of that total, scholarships or need-based grants averaged $13,059 ($23,298 maximum); loans averaged $2511 ($6625 maximum); and work contracts averaged $551 ($1000 maximum). 64% of undergraduates work part time. Average annual earnings from campus work are $750. The average financial indebtedness of the 2001 graduate was $18,718. Sweet Briar is a member of CSS. The FAFSA, the college's own financial statement and the Business/Farm Supplement; noncustodial parents statement are required. The fall application deadline is March 1.

International Students: There are 19 international students enrolled. The school actively recruits these students. They must score 580 on the written TOEFL or 213 on the electronic version and also take the SAT I or the ACT.

Computers: The mainframes are an HP 9000 L2000, (2) HP Net Server LH4r, and DEC Alpha Server 2000. More than 95 Mac and Pentium computers for student use are located across campus in 24-hour multimedia labs, the libraries, study rooms, and academic buildings. The computer-student ratio is 1:6 and more than 600 fiber optic connections to the campus network exist in academic buildings. Student residence hall rooms also have network connections. The college is connected to the Internet, including the World Wide Web. All students may access the system 24 hours a day. There are no time limits and no fees. It is strongly recommended that all students have a personal computer.

Graduates: In 2001, 136 bachelor's degrees were awarded. The most popular majors were social science and history (28%), biology (12%), and mathematics (12%). In an average class, 2% graduate in 3 years, 70% in 4 years, 72% in 5 years, and 73% in 6 years. 24 companies recruited on campus in 2000-2001. Of the 2000 graduating class, 19% were enrolled in graduate school within 6 months of graduation and 39% were employed.

Admissions Contact: Margaret Williams Blount, Director of Admissions. A video is available. E-mail: *admissions@sbc.edu*
Web: *www.admissions.sbc.edu*

UNIVERSITY OF RICHMOND E-3

University of Richmond, VA 23173 (804) 289-8640
(800) 700-1662; Fax: (804) 287-6003

Full-time: 1431 men, 1558 women	**Faculty:** 268; IIA, +$
Part-time: 24 men, 8 women	**Ph.D.s:** 97%
Graduate: 142 men, 99 women	**Student/Faculty:** 11 to 1
Year: semesters, summer session	**Tuition:** $22,570
Application Deadline: February 1	**Room & Board:** $4730
Freshman Class: 5622 applied, 2498 accepted, 800 enrolled	
SAT I or ACT: required	**HIGHLY COMPETITIVE**

The University of Richmond, founded in 1830, is a private independent institution offering programs in arts and sciences, business, and leadership studies. There are 3 undergraduate and 3 graduate schools. In addition to regional accreditation, UR has baccalaureate program accreditation with AACSB, NASM, and ACS. The 4 libraries contain 738,424 volumes, 382,659 microform items, and 24,749 audiovisual forms/CDs, and subscribe to 3634 periodicals. Computerized library services include the card catalog, interlibrary loans, and database searching. Special learning facilities include a learning resource center, art gallery, radio station, TV station, and the Lora Robins Gallery of Design from Nature. The 350-acre campus is in a suburban area 6 miles west of Richmond. Including residence halls, there are 50 buildings.

Student Life: 85% of undergraduates are from out of state, mostly the Middle Atlantic. Others are from 47 states, 71 foreign countries, and Canada. 65% are from public schools. 85% are white. The average age of freshmen is 18; all undergraduates, 20. 11% do not continue beyond their first year; 89% remain to graduate.

Housing: 2700 students can be accommodated in college housing, which includes single-sex and coed dormitories and on-campus apartments. In addition, there are special-interest houses. On-campus housing is available on a first-come, first-served basis and is available on a lottery system for upperclassmen. 92% of students live on campus; of those, 90% remain on campus on weekends. All students may keep cars.

Activities: 30% of men belong to 8 national fraternities; 50% of women belong to 8 national sororities. There are 250 groups on campus, including art, band, cheerleading, choir, chorale, chorus, computers, dance, debate, drama, drill team, ethnic, forensics, gay, honors, international, jazz band, literary magazine, musical theater, newspaper, orchestra, pep band, political, professional, radio and TV, religious, social, social service, student government, and yearbook. Popular campus events include UR Century Bike Race, Greek Theater Parties, and Ring Dance.

Sports: There are 9 intercollegiate sports for men and 9 for women, and 24 intramural sports for men and 23 for women. Facilities include a 10000-seat gym, a stadium, a soccer/track complex, lighted intramural fields, an intramural gym, aerobics and weight rooms, a swimming pool, and tennis, racquetball, and squash courts.

Disabled Students: 85% of the campus is accessible. Wheelchair ramps, elevators, special parking, specially equipped rest rooms, and lowered drinking fountains are available.

Services: Counseling and information services are available, as is tutoring in most subjects. There are support centers for help with academic skills, writing, and speech.

Campus Safety and Security: Measures include 24-hour foot and vehicle patrol, self-defense education, escort service, and shuttle buses. There are informal discussions, pamphlets/posters/films, emergency telephones, lighted pathways/sidewalks, and a card-access system in all residence halls, vehicle assistance, emergency first aid service, fingerprinting, firearms storage, and personal property engraving and identification.

Programs of Study: UR confers B.A., B.S., B.M., and B.S.B.A. degrees. Associate and master's degrees are also awarded. Bachelor's degrees are awarded in BIOLOGICAL SCIENCE (biochemistry, biology/biological science, and molecular biology), BUSINESS (accounting, business administration and management, and business economics), COMMUNICATIONS AND THE ARTS (art history and appreciation, dramatic arts, English, French, German, Greek, journalism, Latin, music, Spanish, speech/debate/rhetoric, and studio art), COMPUTER AND PHYSICAL SCIENCE (chemistry, computer science, mathematics, and physics), SOCIAL SCIENCE (American studies, classical/ancient civilization, criminal justice, economics, history, interdisciplinary studies, international studies, philosophy, political science/government, psychology, religion, sociology, urban studies, and women's studies). Business, biology, and political science are the largest.

Required: To graduate, students must complete 122 credits with a minimum GPA of 2.0. In addition to the first-year core course, there are specific requirements in English composition, foreign language, natural science, phys ed, social analysis, literary studies, historical studies, symbolic reasoning, visual and performing arts, and wellness.

Special: Internships in nearly every major, study abroad in 21 countries, and a Washington semester with American University are available. UR also offers work-study programs, accelerated degree programs, B.A.-B.S. degrees, dual majors, student-designed majors, and a general studies degree through the School of Continuing Studies. The interdisciplinary leadership studies major includes a minor in arts and sciences or business. There is a marine biology study option with the Marine Sciences Laboratory at Duke University. There are 32 national honor societies, including Phi Beta Kappa, and 7 departmental honors programs.

Faculty/Classroom: 59% of faculty are male; 41%, female. All both teach and do research. No introductory courses are taught by graduate students. The average class size in an introductory lecture is 23 and in a regular course, 18.

Admissions: 44% of the 2001-2002 applicants were accepted. The SAT I scores for the 2001-2002 freshman class were: Verbal--4% below 500, 22% between 500 and 599, 56% between 600 and 700, and 18% above 700; Math--3% below 500, 14% between 500 and 599, 64% between 600 and 700, and 20% above 700. The ACT scores were 1% below 18, 10% between 18 and 23, 57% between 24 and 29, and 32% above 30. 78% of the current freshmen were in the top fifth of their class; 99% were in the top two fifths. There were 27 National Merit finalists and 15 semifinalists. 23 freshmen graduated first in their class.

Requirements: The SAT I or ACT is required. In addition, SAT II: Subject tests are required in writing and math I or II if the student is taking the SAT I. Applicants must be graduates of an accredited secondary school. The GED is accepted. Applicants must complete 16 high school academic credits, including 4 years of English, 3 of math, and at least 2 each of history, foreign language, and lab science. An essay, counselor recommendation, and auditions for music scholarships are required. AP and CLEP credits are accepted. Important factors in the admissions decision are advanced placement or honor courses, leadership record, and evidence of special talent. Applications are accepted on-line via Common App.

Procedure: Freshmen are admitted in the fall. Entrance exams should be taken by February 1 of the senior year. There are early decision, early admissions, and deferred admissions plans. Early decision applications should be filed by November 15; regular applications, by February 1 for fall entry, along with a $40 fee. Notification of early decision is sent December 15; regular decision, April 1. 147 early decision candidates were accepted for the 2001-2002 class. 16% of all applicants are on a waiting list.

Transfer: 41 transfer students enrolled in 2001-2002. Applicants must have earned a minimum of 24 credit hours in transferable courses. A minimum GPA of 2.0 is required; however, to be competitive an applicant needs about a 3.3 GPA. 60 credits of 122 must be completed at UR.

Visiting: There are regularly scheduled orientations for prospective students, consisting of conferences and tours offered Monday through Friday with Saturday tours available on select dates from September through November, as well as Junior Preview Days in early spring. There are guides for informal visits and visitors may sit in on classes and stay overnight. To schedule a visit, contact the Admissions Office.

Financial Aid: In 2001-2002, 62% of all freshmen and 63% of continuing students received some form of financial aid. 27% of freshmen and

28% of continuing students received need-based aid. The average freshman award was $17,797. Of that total, scholarships or need-based grants averaged $14,016; and loans averaged $3259. 25% of undergraduates work part time. Average annual earnings from campus work are $1000. The FAFSA and the college's own financial statement are required. The fall application deadline is February 25.

International Students: There were 130 international students enrolled in a recent year. The school actively recruits these students. They must score 550 on the written TOEFL or 213 on the electronic version and also take the SAT I or the ACT. SAT II: Subject tests in writing and math are required of applicants living in the United States at the time of application and are highly recommended for applicants not living in the United States.

Computers: The mainframes are DEC VAX 11/750 and 11/785 models. All students have access to labs housing Macs, PCs, and Sun SPARC stations. Bitnet, Internet, LEXIS, and WESTLAW networks are also available. All students may access the system. There are no time limits and no fees.

Graduates: In 2001, 723 bachelor's degrees were awarded. The most popular majors were business administration (39%), political science (16%), and biology (8%). In an average class, 78% graduate in 4 years, and 84% in 6 years. 325 companies recruited on campus in 2000-2001. Of the 2000 graduating class, 26% were enrolled in graduate school within 6 months of graduation and 73% were employed.

Admissions Contact: Pamela W. Spence, Dean of Admission. A video is available. E-mail: *admissions@richmond.edu*
Web: *www.richmond.edu*

UNIVERSITY OF VIRGINIA
Charlottesville, VA 22904-4160

D-3
(434) 982-3200
Fax: (434) 924-3587

Full-time: 5936 men, 6860 women	**Faculty:** 941; I, +$
Part-time: 371 men, 597 women	**Ph.D.s:** 93%
Graduate: 3798 men, 5177 women	**Student/Faculty:** 14 to 1
Year: semesters, summer session	**Tuition:** $4421 ($18,453)
Application Deadline: January 2	**Room & Board:** $4970
Freshman Class: 14,739 applied, 5534 accepted, 2980 enrolled	
SAT I Verbal/Math: 650/670	**ACT:** 29

HIGHLY COMPETITIVE+

The University of Virginia, founded in 1819, is a public institution with undergraduate programs in architecture, arts and sciences, commerce, education, engineering and applied science, and nursing. There are 6 undergraduate and 9 graduate schools. In addition to regional accreditation, UVA has baccalaureate program accreditation with AACSB, ABET, ASLA, NAAB, NASM, NCATE, and NLN. The 15 libraries contain 3,258,758 volumes, 5,279,878 microform items, and 282,798 audiovisual forms/CDs, and subscribe to 51,237 periodicals. Computerized library services include the card catalog, interlibrary loans, and database searching. Special learning facilities include a learning resource center, art gallery, radio station, TV station, and art museum. The 1151-acre campus is in a suburban area 70 miles northwest of Richmond. Including residence halls, there are 440 buildings.

Student Life: 69% of undergraduates are from Virginia. Others are from 49 states, 101 foreign countries, and Canada. 74% are from public schools. 73% are white; 11% Asian American. 40% are Protestant; 23% Catholic; 18% claim no religious affiliation. The average age of freshmen is 18; all undergraduates, 20. 4% do not continue beyond their first year; 92% remain to graduate.

Housing: 6989 students can be accommodated in college housing, which includes coed dormitories, on-campus apartments, and married-student housing. In addition, there are honors houses, language houses, special-interest houses, and 3 residential colleges. On-campus housing is guaranteed for the freshman year only, is available on a first-come, first-served basis, and is available on a lottery system for upperclassmen. Upperclassmen may keep cars.

Activities: 30% of men belong to 34 national fraternities; 30% of women belong to 22 national sororities. There are 300 groups on campus, including art, band, cheerleading, chess, choir, chorale, chorus, computers, dance, debate, drama, ethnic, film, gay, honors, international, jazz band, judiciary, literary magazine, musical theater, newspaper, orchestra, pep band, photography, political, professional, radio and TV, religious, social, social service, student government, symphony, tour guides, and yearbook. Popular campus events include Culturefest, Family Weekend, and Commonwealth Ball.

Sports: There are 12 intercollegiate sports for men and 12 for women, and 30 intramural sports for men and 30 for women. Facilities include a 65,000-seat stadium, an 8500-seat gym, and 4 recreation centers including an aquatics and fitness center.

Disabled Students: All of the campus is accessible. Wheelchair ramps, elevators, special parking, specially equipped rest rooms, special class scheduling, lowered drinking fountains, lowered telephones, and curb cuts, voice synthesizers, braille printers, and large-screen monitors are available.

Services: Counseling and information services are available, as is tutoring in every subject. There is a reader service for the blind. There are transcribers, note takers, and taped readings for disabled students.

Campus Safety and Security: Measures include 24-hour foot and vehicle patrol, self-defense education, escort service, and shuttle buses. There are informal discussions, pamphlets/posters/films, emergency telephones, and lighted pathways/sidewalks.

Programs of Study: UVA confers B.A., B.S., B.A.R.H., B.C.P., B.I.S., B.S.C., B.S.Ed., and B.S.N. degrees. Master's and doctoral degrees are also awarded. Bachelor's degrees are awarded in BIOLOGICAL SCIENCE (biology/biological science), BUSINESS (business economics), COMMUNICATIONS AND THE ARTS (art, classics, comparative literature, dramatic arts, English, French, German, Italian, music, Slavic languages, and Spanish), COMPUTER AND PHYSICAL SCIENCE (applied mathematics, astronomy, chemistry, computer science, mathematics, and physics), EDUCATION (health, and physical), ENGINEERING AND ENVIRONMENTAL DESIGN (aerospace studies, architecture, chemical engineering, city/community/regional planning, civil engineering, electrical/electronics engineering, engineering and applied science, environmental science, mechanical engineering, and systems engineering), HEALTH PROFESSIONS (nursing and speech pathology/audiology), SOCIAL SCIENCE (African American studies, anthropology, area studies, economics, history, interdisciplinary studies, international relations, philosophy, political science/government, psychology, religion, and sociology). English, history, biology, and commerce are the strongest academically. Commerce, economics, and psychology are the largest.

Required: To graduate, students must complete 120 credit hours, with 18 to 42 hours in the major and a minimum GPA of 2.0. Distribution requirements include 12 hours of math and science, 6 hours each of humanities, composition, and social sciences, 4 semesters of foreign languages, 3 hours of historical studies, and 3 hours of non-western perspectives.

Special: The college offers internships, study abroad in 9 countries, accelerated degree programs, B.A.-B.S. degrees in chemistry and physics, co-op programs in both aerospace and mechanical engineering, and nondegree study. Dual majors in most arts and sciences programs, student-designed majors, an interdisciplinary major and Echols Scholars program, and pass/fail options are available. There are 24 national honor societies, including Phi Beta Kappa, a freshman honors program, and 30 departmental honors programs.

Faculty/Classroom: 71% of faculty are male; 29%, female. 57% teach undergraduates. All do research, and 57% do both. Graduate students teach 32% of introductory courses. The average class size in an introductory lecture is 47 and in a laboratory, 56.

Admissions: 38% of the 2001-2002 applicants were accepted. The SAT I scores for the 2001-2002 freshman class were: Verbal--4% below 500, 19% between 500 and 599, 47% between 600 and 700, and 30% above 700; Math--2% below 500, 16% between 500 and 599, 45% between 600 and 700, and 37% above 700. 97% of the current freshmen were in the top fifth of their class; 99% were in the top two fifths. 177 freshmen graduated first in their class.

Requirements: The SAT I or ACT is required. In addition, SAT II: Subject tests in writing, math I, IC, or IIC, and a third test in science, history, or foreign language are required. With few exceptions, candidates graduate from accredited secondary schools. While the GED is accepted, it is rare for candidates for first-year admission who have this credential to be competitive in the admissions process. Applicants should complete 16 high school academic courses, including 4 courses of English, 4 courses of math, beginning with Algebra I, 2 courses of physics, biology, or chemistry (3 if applying to engineering), 2 years of foreign language, and 1 course of social studies. An essay is also required. AP credits are accepted. Important factors in the admissions decision are advanced placement or honor courses and evidence of special talent. Applications may be obtained via *http://www.virginia.edu/~admiss/ugadmiss/applica.html*

Procedure: Freshmen are admitted in the fall. Entrance exams should be taken by December of the senior year. There are early decision and deferred admissions plans. Early decision applications should be filed by November 1; regular applications, by January 2 for fall entry, along with a $40 fee. Notification of early decision is sent December 1; regular decision, April 1. 903 early decision candidates were accepted for the 2001-2002 class. 15% of all applicants are on a waiting list; 82 were accepted in 2001.

Transfer: 541 transfer students enrolled in 2001-2002. Applicants for transfer must have a minimum GPA of 3.0, submit SAT I and ACT scores, and meet prerequisite courses. 60 credits of 120 must be completed at UVA.

Visiting: There are regularly scheduled orientations for prospective students, consisting of comprehensive information sessions and campus tours. Visitors may sit in on classes and stay overnight. To schedule a visit, contact the Monroe Society at (434) 924-3321.

Financial Aid: In 2001-2002, 47% of all freshmen and 40% of continuing students received some form of financial aid. 17% of freshmen and 18% of continuing students received need-based aid. The average freshman award was $7637. Of that total, scholarships or need-based grants averaged $5518 ($27,758 maximum); loans averaged $5995 ($27,175 maximum); and work contracts averaged $1320 ($1360 maximum). 25% of undergraduates work part time. The average financial indebtedness of the 2001 graduate was $13,890. The FAFSA and the college's own financial statement are required. The fall application deadline is March 1.

International Students: There are 562 international students enrolled. The school actively recruits these students. They must score 550 on the written TOEFL and also take the SAT I or ACT. International students must take the same tests as all other entering students. Students must take SAT II: Subject tests in writing, math I, IC, or IIC, and a third test in science, history, or foreign language.

Computers: The mainframes include UNIX-based IBM RS/600s and Suns, which are accessible anywhere on campus and in residence hall rooms and via remote dial-up. Access to the Internet is possible from more than 30 university-operated public computing facilities with more than 900 PCs or workstations. All students may access the system 24 hours a day, 7 days a week. There are no time limits and no fees. It is strongly recommended that all students have a personal computer.

Graduates: In 2001, 3221 bachelor's degrees were awarded. The most popular majors were economics (11%), commerce (10%), and psychology (9%). In an average class, 1% graduate in 3 years, 84% in 4 years, 91% in 5 years, and 92% in 6 years. 450 companies recruited on campus in 2000-2001.

Admissions Contact: John A. Blackburn, Dean of Admission.
E-mail: *undergrad-admission@virginia.edu*
Web: *www.virginia.edu/~admiss/ugadmiss/home.shtml*

UNIVERSITY OF VIRGINIA'S COLLEGE AT WISE A-4

Wise, VA 24293 (276) 328-0322
(888) 282-9324; Fax: (276) 328-0251

Full-time: 586 men, 623 women	**Faculty:** 66; IIB, av$
Part-time: 102 men, 169 women	**Ph.D.s:** 77%
Graduate: none	**Student/Faculty:** 18 to 1
Year: semesters, summer session	**Tuition:** $3470 ($10,508)
Application Deadline: August 1	**Room & Board:** $4832
Freshman Class: 841 applied, 638 accepted, 321 enrolled	
SAT I Verbal/Math: 490/470	**ACT:** 20 **COMPETITIVE**

The University of Virginia's College at Wise, founded in 1954, offers undergraduate programs through the departments of business studies, education, languages and literature, behavioral and social sciences, natural sciences, math and computer science, history and philosophy, visual and performing arts, and nursing. In addition to regional accreditation, UVA's College at Wise has baccalaureate program accreditation with NLN. The library contains 116,075 volumes, 60,972 microform items, and 4357 audiovisual forms/CDs, and subscribes to 807 periodicals. Computerized library services include the card catalog, interlibrary loans, and database searching. Special learning facilities include an observatory. The 396-acre campus is in a small town 60 miles northwest of Bristol. Including residence halls, there are 42 buildings.

Student Life: 93% of undergraduates are from Virginia. Others are from 9 states and 8 foreign countries. 99% are from public schools. 92% are white. The average age of freshmen is 18; all undergraduates, 23. 26% do not continue beyond their first year; 42% remain to graduate.

Housing: 524 students can be accommodated in college housing, which includes single-sex and coed dormitories and off-campus apartments. In addition, there are honors houses. On-campus housing is guaranteed for the freshman year only and is available on a first-come, first-served basis. 64% of students commute. All students may keep cars.

Activities: 5% of men belong to 1 local and 2 national fraternities; 5% of women belong to 2 local and 1 national sororities. There are 45 groups on campus, including art, band, cheerleading, choir, chorale, chorus, dance, drama, ethnic, film, gay, honors, international, international council, literary magazine, musical theater, newspaper, pep band, political, religious, social, social service, student activities board, student government, and yearbook. Popular campus events include The Holly Ball, Jam for Man, and Extramural Flag Football Scramble.

Sports: There are 7 intercollegiate sports for men and 6 for women, and 45 intramural sports for men and 45 for women. Facilities include baseball and softball fields, a gym, tennis courts, a swimming pool, 3 practice football fields, and a football stadium.

Disabled Students: 95% of the campus is accessible. Wheelchair ramps, elevators, special parking, specially equipped rest rooms, special class scheduling, lowered drinking fountains, and lowered telephones are available.

Services: Counseling and information services are available, as is tutoring in every subject. There is a reader service for the blind and remedial math and writing. Tutoring is free to all registered students.

Campus Safety and Security: Measures include 24-hour foot and vehicle patrol, self-defense education, escort service, and informal discussions. There are pamphlets/posters/films, emergency telephones, lighted pathways/sidewalks, and a crime prevention office.

Programs of Study: UVA's College at Wise confers B.A., B.S., and B.S.N. degrees. Bachelor's degrees are awarded in BIOLOGICAL SCIENCE (biology/biological science), BUSINESS (accounting, and business administration and management), COMMUNICATIONS AND THE ARTS (art, communications, dramatic arts, English, French, and Spanish), COMPUTER AND PHYSICAL SCIENCE (chemistry, information sciences and systems, and mathematics), ENGINEERING AND ENVIRONMENTAL DESIGN (environmental science), HEALTH PROFESSIONS (medical laboratory technology, and nursing), SOCIAL SCIENCE (criminal justice, economics, history, international studies, law enforcement and corrections, liberal arts/general studies, political science/government, psychology, and social science). Natural science, accounting, and math are the strongest academically. Business administration and social sciences are the largest.

Required: To graduate, all students must complete 52 hours of general education requirements including a liberal arts course, arts, humanities, social sciences, natural sciences, English composition, literature, math, foreign lanquage, phys ed, and Western heritage. At least 120 credit hours are required, with a minimum 2.0 GPA overall and in the major area.

Special: The college offers co-op programs in all majors, internships in education, social sciences, and communication, on-campus work-study programs, B.A.-B.S. degrees in most majors, dual and student-designed majors, and pass/fail options for classes not required for the major. There are 4 national honor societies, a freshman honors program, and 9 departmental honors programs.

Faculty/Classroom: 58% of faculty are male; 42%, female. All teach undergraduates, 50% do research, and 50% do both. The average class size in an introductory lecture is 23; in a laboratory, 13; and in a regular course, 11.

Admissions: 76% of the 2001-2002 applicants were accepted. The SAT I scores for the 2001-2002 freshman class were: Verbal--59% below 500, 31% between 500 and 599, 8% between 600 and 700, and 2% above 700; Math--64% below 500, 30% between 500 and 599, 5% between 600 and 700, and 1% above 700. The ACT scores were 70% below 21, 27% between 24 and 26, 2% between 27 and 28, and 1% above 28. 40% of the current freshmen were in the top fifth of their class; 70% were in the top two fifths. 8 freshmen graduated first in their class.

Requirements: The SAT I or ACT is required. In addition, all applicants must be graduates of approved secondary schools or hold a GED. Preference is given to students who earn an Advanced Studies Diploma or its equivalent, rank in the top half of their graduating class, score 900 or better on the SAT I (ACT 18), and complete 4 years of English; 3 or more courses in math, including algebra 1 and 2 and a course selected from among geometry, trigonometry, advanced math, or calculus; 2 or more years of natural science beyond general science; 2 or more years of a foreign language; and 1 year each of American history and world history. A GPA of 2.3 is required. AP credits are accepted. Important factors in the admissions decision are advanced placement or honor courses, recommendations by school officials, and leadership record.

Procedure: Freshmen are admitted to all sessions. Entrance exams should be taken by January 1 of the application year. There are early admissions and deferred admissions plans. Applications should be filed by August 1 for fall entry and January 5 for spring entry, along with a $15 fee. Notification is sent on a rolling basis.

Transfer: 157 transfer students enrolled in 2001-2002. Transfer students must meet all general admissions requirements and submit secondary school transcripts or GED results and transcripts of all previous college work. A minimum 2.2 GPA is required. Students with either a minimum of 30 semester hours of college work, an associate degree, or who are at least 25 years old, need not submit the SAT I or ACT scores. For others, a minimum composite score of 900 on the SAT I, or 18 on the ACT is recommended. 30 credits of 120 must be completed at UVA's College at Wise.

Visiting: There are regularly scheduled orientations for prospective students, including an interview, a campus tour, a meal, and class visitation. There are guides for informal visits and visitors may sit in on classes. To schedule a visit, contact the Admissions Office.

Financial Aid: In 2001-2002, 75% of all freshmen and 72% of continuing students received some form of financial aid. 68% of freshmen and 66% of continuing students received need-based aid. The average freshman award was $6904. Of that total, scholarships or need-based grants averaged $3394 ($8972 maximum); loans averaged $2402 ($2625 maximum); and work contracts averaged $1108 ($3000 maximum). 16% of undergraduates work part time. Average annual earnings from campus work are $1108. The average financial indebtedness of the 2001 graduate was $6183. The FAFSA is required. The fall application deadline is April 1.

International Students: There are 12 international students enrolled. The school actively recruits these students. They must score 550 on the written TOEFL or 234 on the electronic version and also take the SAT I with a minimum score of 700 or the ACT.

Computers: The mainframe is an HP 3000/Model 957. There are 5 computer labs with about 100 computers and Internet access. About 200 residents have access in dorms. Terminals are also available in the library. All students may access the system 24 hours per day. There are no time limits and no fees.

Graduates: In 2001, 276 bachelor's degrees were awarded. The most popular majors were business administration (20%), psychology (14%), and history (10%). In an average class, 25% graduate in 4 years, 40% in 5 years, and 42% in 6 years. 23 companies recruited on campus in 2000-2001.

Admissions Contact: Russell Necessary, Director of Admissions and Financial Aid. A video is available. E-mail: *admissions@uvawise.edu or rdn2f@uvawise.edu* Web: *www.wise.virginia.edu*

VIRGINIA COMMONWEALTH UNIVERSITY E-3

Richmond, VA 23284 **(804) 828-1222**
(800) 841-3638; Fax: (804) 828-1899

Full-time: 4891 men, 7157 women	**Faculty:** I, av$
Part-time: 2180 men, 2920 women	**Ph.D.s:** 83%
Graduate: 3060 men, 4793 women	**Student/Faculty:** n/av
Year: semesters, summer session	**Tuition:** $3675 ($13,855)
Application Deadline: February 1	**Room & Board:** $5355
Freshman Class: 7926 applied, 5856 accepted, 2740 enrolled	
SAT I Verbal/Math: 520/510	**ACT:** 20 **COMPETITIVE**

Virginia Commonwealth University, founded in 1838, is a public research university. There are 10 undergraduate and 12 graduate schools. In addition to regional accreditation, VCU has baccalaureate program accreditation with AACSB, ABET, ACEJMC, ACPE, APTA, CAHEA, CSWE, FIDER, NASAD, NCATE, and NLN. The 2 libraries contain 1,680,393 volumes, 3,007,035 microform items, and 42,254 audiovisual forms/CDs, and subscribe to 9662 periodicals. Computerized library services include the card catalog, interlibrary loans, and database searching. Special learning facilities include a learning resource center, art gallery, radio station, and TV station. The 126-acre campus is in an urban area 2 miles west of downtown Richmond. Including residence halls, there are 162 buildings.

Student Life: 95% of undergraduates are from Virginia. Others are from 42 states, 62 foreign countries, and Canada. 97% are from public schools. 64% are white; 23% African American. The average age of freshmen is 18; all undergraduates, 22. 23% do not continue beyond their first year; 42% remain to graduate.

Housing: 3170 students can be accommodated in college housing, which includes coed dormitories, on-campus apartments, and off-campus apartments. In addition, there are honors houses and honors and special-interest floors. On-campus housing is guaranteed for the freshman year only and is available on a first-come, first-served basis. 79% of students commute. All students may keep cars.

Activities: 6% of men belong to 12 national fraternities; 3% of women belong to 9 national sororities. There are 170 groups on campus, including art, band, cheerleading, chess, choir, chorale, chorus, computers, dance, drama, ethnic, gay, honors, international, jazz band, literary magazine, musical theater, newspaper, orchestra, pep band, photography, political, professional, radio and TV, religious, social, social service, student government, symphony, and yearbook. Popular campus events include First Fridays, Annual Fall Block Show, and VCU celebrates the holidays.

Sports: There are 8 intercollegiate sports for men and 8 for women, and 18 intramural sports for men and 18 for women. Facilities include a recreation complex with sports clubs and a fitness program, a gym, a swimming pool, and an outdoor adventure program.

Disabled Students: 80% of the campus is accessible. Wheelchair ramps, elevators, special parking, specially equipped rest rooms, special class scheduling, lowered drinking fountains, and lowered telephones are available.

Services: Counseling and information services are available, as is tutoring in some subjects, including most 100- and 200-level general education requirements, some 300-level courses in math and sciences, and languages through the 100 level. There is a reader service for the blind, and remedial math, reading, and writing.

Campus Safety and Security: Measures include 24-hour foot and vehicle patrol, self-defense education, escort service, and shuttle buses. There are informal discussions, pamphlets/posters/films, emergency telephones, and lighted pathways/sidewalks.

Programs of Study: VCU confers B.A., B.S., B.F.A., B.I.S., B.Mus., B.Mus.Ed., B.S.N., and B.S.W. degrees. Master's and doctoral degrees are also awarded. Bachelor's degrees are awarded in BIOLOGICAL SCIENCE (biology/biological science), BUSINESS (accounting, business administration and management, business economics, and marketing/retailing/merchandising), COMMUNICATIONS AND THE ARTS (communications, dance, design, dramatic arts, English, fine arts, languages, and music), COMPUTER AND PHYSICAL SCIENCE (chemistry, computer science, information sciences and systems, mathematics, and physics), EDUCATION (art, elementary, and health), ENGINEERING AND ENVIRONMENTAL DESIGN (chemical engineering, electrical/electronics engineering, and mechanical engineering), HEALTH PROFESSIONS (nursing, occupational therapy, and physical therapy), SOCIAL SCIENCE (criminal justice, economics, history, political science/government, psychology, religion, social work, sociology, and urban studies). Psychology, biology, and mass communications are the largest.

Required: The total number of credit hours required for graduation varies with the major. Students must achieve a minimum GPA of 2.0.

Special: Internships are available for seniors with government agencies, banking and finance centers, private industry, media, and community service agencies. Co-op programs in all majors, work-study programs on campus and with state agencies in the city, study abroad in 6 countries, general studies degrees, and a B.A.-B.S. degree in psychology are offered. Students may take a 3-2 engineering degree with Old Dominion, George Washington, and Auburn Universities. Student-designed majors through a nontraditional studies program, nondegree study, and credit for life, military, and work experience are possible. There are 30 national honor societies, a freshman honors program, and 4 departmental honors programs.

Faculty/Classroom: 63% of faculty are male; 37%, female. The average class size in an introductory lecture is 25; in a laboratory, 15; and in a regular course, 22.

Admissions: 74% of the 2001-2002 applicants were accepted. The SAT I scores for the 2001-2002 freshman class were: Verbal--38% below 500, 41% between 500 and 599, 19% between 600 and 700, and 2% above 700; Math--44% below 500, 40% between 500 and 599, 14% between 600 and 700, and 2% above 700. The ACT scores were 54% below 21, 27% between 21 and 23, 13% between 24 and 26, 3% between 27 and 28, and 3% above 28. 28% of the current freshmen were in the top fifth of their class; 62% were in the top two fifths. 180 freshmen graduated first in their class.

Requirements: The SAT I is required, with a minimum composite score of 800 (400 math recommended and 350 verbal required). Applicants must be graduates of an accredited secondary school. The GED is accepted. Applicants should complete 20 high school academic credits, including 4 credits of English, 3 of math (including algebra I and II and geometry), 2 each of foreign language, history, and science (including a laboratory science), and 1 of social studies. Applicants for the School of the Arts must audition or submit a portfolio. An essay and an interview are recommended. A GPA of 2.2 is required. AP and CLEP credits are accepted. Important factors in the admissions decision are ability to finance college education, extracurricular activities record, and personality/intangible qualities. Applications are accepted on-line via the school's website.

Procedure: Freshmen are admitted fall and spring. Entrance exams should be taken before February 1. There are early decision, early admissions, and deferred admissions plans. Early decision applications should be filed by November 1; regular applications, by February 1 for fall entry and December 1 for spring entry, along with a $25 fee. Notification of early decision is sent December 1; regular decision, on a rolling basis. 146 early decision candidates were accepted for the 2001-2002 class.

Transfer: 1534 transfer students enrolled in 2001-2002. Transfer students with 30 semester hours or more must have a 2.3 GPA or better; those with fewer hours and who are under the age of 22 must submit SAT I scores. An associate degree and interview are advised. 30 credits must be completed at VCU.

Visiting: There are regularly scheduled orientations for prospective students, including an information session with a counselor followed by a student-led tour. Visitors may sit in on classes. To schedule a visit, contact the Office of Admissions.

Financial Aid: In 2001-2002, 75% of all freshmen and 57% of continuing students received some form of financial aid. 59% of freshmen and 54% of continuing students received need-based aid. The average freshman award was $6562. Of that total, scholarships or need-based grants averaged $4040 ($24,708 maximum); loans averaged $3122 ($18,625 maximum); and work contracts averaged $119 ($4000 maximum). The average financial indebtedness of the 2001 graduate was $21,994. The FAFSA is required. The fall application deadline is April 1.

International Students: There are 187 international students enrolled. The school actively recruits these students. They must score 550 on the written TOEFL and also take the college's own test.

Computers: The mainframe is an IBM 3081K. Macs and PCs are available in academic buildings. All students may access the system. There are no time limits and no fees. It is strongly recommended that all students have a personal computer.

Graduates: In 2001, 2194 bachelor's degrees were awarded. The most popular majors were psychology (10%), business administration (7%), and information sciences (7%). In an average class, 14% graduate in 4 years, 32% in 5 years, and 39% in 6 years. 429 companies recruited on campus in 2000-2001.

Admissions Contact: Delores T. Taylor, Director, Admissions.
E-mail: *vcuinfo@vcu.edu* Web: *www.vcu.edu*

VIRGINIA INTERMONT COLLEGE

Bristol, VA 24201-4298 B-4
(540) 466-7854
(800) 451-1842; Fax: (540) 466-7855

Full-time: 201 men, 594 women	**Faculty:** 43; IIB, --$
Part-time: 31 men, 92 women	**Ph.D.s:** 44%
Graduate: none	**Student/Faculty:** 18 to 1
Year: semesters, summer session	**Tuition:** $12,210
Application Deadline: open	**Room & Board:** $5300
Freshman Class: 661 applied, 443 accepted, 158 enrolled	
SAT I Verbal/Math: 491/450	**ACT:** 19 **COMPETITIVE**

Virginia Intermont College, founded in 1884, is a private institution affiliated with the Baptist General Association of Virginia. In addition to regional accreditation, V.I. College has baccalaureate program accreditation with CSWE and ABA. The library contains 59,525 volumes, 9205 microform items, and 4650 audiovisual forms/CDs, and subscribes to 276 periodicals. Computerized library services include the card catalog, interlibrary loans, and database searching. Special learning facilities include a learning resource center, art gallery, an equestrian center, a ballet center, and a film lab. The 27-acre campus is in an urban area 144 miles southwest of Roanoke and 114 miles northeast of Knoxville, Tennessee. Including residence halls, there are 18 buildings.

Student Life: 66% of undergraduates are from Virginia. Others are from 31 states and 17 foreign countries. 86% are white. 31% claim no religious affiliation; 31% Protestant. The average age of freshmen is 18; all undergraduates, 27. 46% do not continue beyond their first year; 40% remain to graduate.

Housing: 488 students can be accommodated in college housing, which includes single-sex and coed dormitories. On-campus housing is guaranteed for all 4 years. 51% of students live on campus; of those, 63% remain on campus on weekends. Alcohol is not permitted. All students may keep cars.

Activities: 10% of women belong to 2 local sororities. There are no fraternities. There are 22 groups on campus, including art, cheerleading, choir, dance, drama, honors, international, literary magazine, musical theater, newspaper, photography, political, professional, religious, social service, student government, and yearbook. Popular campus events include May Day, Family Weekend, and Heritage Fair.

Sports: There are 5 intercollegiate sports for men and 4 for women, and 8 intramural sports for men and 8 for women. Facilities include a gym, a 1,200-seat amphitheater, lighted tennis courts, a swimming pool, and a fitness center.

Disabled Students: 35% of the campus is accessible. Wheelchair ramps, elevators, special parking, specially equipped rest rooms, and special class scheduling are available.

Services: Counseling and information services are available, as is tutoring in every subject. There is remedial math, reading, and writing.

Campus Safety and Security: Measures include self-defense education, escort service, informal discussions, and pamphlets/posters/films. There are lighted pathways/sidewalks and and 17-hour patrols by trained security personnel.

Programs of Study: V.I. College confers B.A., B.S., B.F.A., and B.S.W. degrees. Associate degrees are also awarded. Bachelor's degrees are awarded in AGRICULTURE (equine science), BIOLOGICAL SCIENCE (biology/biological science), BUSINESS (business administration and management, and sports management), COMMUNICATIONS AND THE ARTS (art, dance, English, fine arts, performing arts, and photography), COMPUTER AND PHYSICAL SCIENCE (information sciences and systems), EDUCATION (education and secondary), HEALTH PROFESSIONS (premedicine and preveterinary science), SOCIAL SCIENCE (history, interdisciplinary studies, liberal arts/general studies, paralegal studies, psychology, religion, and social work). Equine studies, business, and photography are the largest.

Required: To graduate, students must complete 124 credits with a minimum GPA of 2.0. Required courses are English, world history, computer fundamentals, college math, natural science, performing arts, visual arts, psychology or sociology, economics or political science, philosophy or religion, speech, and phys ed.

Special: V.I. College offers cross-registration with King College and internships in paralegal studies, social work, business, art, dance, photography, sports management, political science, psychology, and theater. Dual majors, study abroad in Germany or Great Britain, a general studies degree, nondegree study, and pass/fail options are available. A 36-hour evening degree program in organizational management is designed for working adults. There are 4 national honor societies, and 2 departmental honors programs.

Faculty/Classroom: 52% of faculty are male; 48%, female. All teach undergraduates. The average class size in an introductory lecture is 12; in a laboratory, 15; and in a regular course, 19.

Admissions: 67% of the 2001-2002 applicants were accepted. The SAT I scores for the 2001-2002 freshman class were: Verbal--53% below 500, 35% between 500 and 599, 9% between 600 and 700, and 3% above 700; Math--75% below 500, 23% between 500 and 599, and 2% between 600 and 700. The ACT scores were 66% below 21, 31% between 21 and 23, and 3% between 24 and 26. 17% of the current freshmen were in the top fifth of their class; 40% were in the top two fifths. 1 freshman graduated first in their class.

Requirements: The SAT I or ACT is required, with a minimum composite score of 780 on the SAT I or 18 on the ACT. Applicants must be graduates of an accredited secondary school. The GED is accepted. Applicants should complete 15 academic credits, including 4 credits of English, 2 each of social science and math, 1 of a lab science, and 6 electives. An essay is required of students not meeting the normal admissions requirements. A GPA of 2.0 is required. AP and CLEP credits are accepted. Important factors in the admissions decision are evidence of special talent, advanced placement or honor courses, and parents or siblings attending the school. Applications are accepted on-line at *www.vic.edu/admiss/application/index.html*.

Procedure: Freshmen are admitted to all sessions. There is a deferred admissions plan. Application deadlines are open.

Transfer: 77 transfer students enrolled in 2001-2002. Applicants for transfer should have a minimum GPA of 2.0. An interview is recommended. 30 credits of 124 must be completed at V.I. College.

Visiting: There are regularly scheduled orientations for prospective students, consisting of a campus tour, an admissions interview, meetings with faculty, auditions for performance scholarships, and planning sessions with financial aid staff. There are guides for informal visits and visitors may sit in on classes and stay overnight. To schedule a visit, contact the Admissions Office at (540) 466-7857.

Financial Aid: In 2001-2002, 92% of all freshmen and 90% of continuing students received some form of financial aid. 85% of all students received need-based aid. The average freshman award was $12,825. Of that total, scholarships or need-based grants averaged $7200 ($11,890 maximum); loans averaged $2625 (maximum); work contracts averaged $1500 (maximum); and VTAG for residents averaged $3000. 61% of undergraduates work part time. Average annual earnings from campus work are $1500. The average financial indebtedness of the 2001 graduate was $17,125. V.I. College is a member of CSS. The CSS/Profile, FAFSA, FFS, or SFS and the college's own financial statement are required. The fall application deadline is April 15.

International Students: There are 34 international students enrolled. The school actively recruits these students. They must score 400 on the written TOEFL or take the SAT I or the ACT.

Computers: The mainframe is an IBM AS/400. 21 IBM and Mac computers are available in the computer center, 22 in the library, 21 in the writing center, and 10 in the Mac lab. Residence halls and booths in the café are wired for Internet access. All students may access the system. There are no time limits and no fees.

Graduates: In 2001, 150 bachelor's degrees were awarded. The most popular majors were equine studies (22%), photography (11%), and paralegal (10%). In an average class, 20% graduate in 4 years, 29% in 5 years, and 29% in 6 years. 30 companies recruited on campus in 2000-2001. Of the 2000 graduating class, 6% were enrolled in graduate school within 6 months of graduation and 91% were employed.

Admissions Contact: Robin Cozart, Director of Admissions. A video is available. E-mail: *viadmit@vic.edu* Web: *www.vic.edu*

VIRGINIA MILITARY INSTITUTE

Lexington, VA 24450 D-3
(540) 464-7211
(800) 767-4207; Fax: (540) 464-7746

Full-time: 1250 men, 61 women	**Faculty:** 96; IIB, +$
Part-time: none	**Ph.D.s:** 96%
Graduate: none	**Student/Faculty:** 14 to 1
Year: semesters, summer session	**Tuition:** $5130 ($16,198)
Application Deadline: April 1	**Room & Board:** $4838
Freshman Class: 1436 applied, 879 accepted, 433 enrolled	
SAT I Verbal/Math: 570/564	**ACT:** 23 **COMPETITIVE+**

Virginia Military Institute, established in 1839, is the nation's first state-supported military college. It offers academic programs in engineering, sciences, and liberal arts. All students are members of the Corps of Cadets, live in barracks, eat together in the mess hall, wear uniforms, and adhere to the Honor System. In addition to regional accreditation, VMI has baccalaureate program accreditation with ABET. The 2 libraries contain more than 240,000 volumes, 18,000 microform items, and 4540 audiovisual forms/CDs, and subscribe to 800 periodicals. Computerized library services include the card catalog, interlibrary loans, and database searching. Special learning facilities include a learning resource center, an observatory, and a research library. The 134-acre campus is in a small town 50 miles north of Roanoke. Including residence halls, there are 68 buildings.

Student Life: 51% of undergraduates are from Virginia. Others are from 45 states, 19 foreign countries, and Canada. 78% are from public schools. 83% are white. 56% are Protestant; 30% Catholic. The average age of freshmen is 18; all undergraduates, 20. 23% do not continue beyond their first year; 67% remain to graduate.

Housing: 1370 students can be accommodated in college housing, which includes coed dormitories. On-campus housing is guaranteed for all 4 years. All students live on campus; 60% remain on campus on weekends. Alcohol is not permitted. Upperclassmen may keep cars.

Activities: There are no fraternities or sororities. There are 50 groups on campus, including bagpipe band, band, cheerleading, choir, chorus, dance, drama, drill team, ethnic, historical, honors, international, investment, jazz band, literary magazine, marching band, musical theater, newspaper, orchestra, pep band, photography, political, professional, religious, social, social service, student government, and yearbook. Popular campus events include Ring Figure, Virginia Transportation Conference, and dance and concert weekends.

Sports: There are 13 intercollegiate sports for men and 3 for women, and 4 intramural sports for men and 4 for women. Facilities include basketball, racquetball, and tennis courts, fields for lacrosse, football, baseball, and soccer, a swimming pool, a rifle range, indoor and outdoor running tracks, a wrestling facility, access to a golf course, weight training and aerobic facility, and auxillary indoor and outdoor basketball courts.

Disabled Students: 50% of the campus is accessible. Wheelchair ramps, elevators, special parking, and specially equipped rest rooms are available.

Services: Counseling and information services are available, as is tutoring in some subjects, including French, Spanish, German, Arabic, chemistry, math, physics, economics, and business. Tutoring for intercollegiate athletes, paid for by NCAA, also is available.

Campus Safety and Security: Measures include 24-hour foot and vehicle patrol, informal discussions, pamphlets/posters/films, and emergency telephones. There are lighted pathways/sidewalks and and a 24-hour student guard team.

Programs of Study: VMI confers B.A. and B.S. degrees. Bachelor's degrees are awarded in BIOLOGICAL SCIENCE (biology/biological science), BUSINESS (business economics), COMMUNICATIONS AND THE ARTS (English), COMPUTER AND PHYSICAL SCIENCE (chemistry, computer science, mathematics, and physics), ENGINEERING AND ENVIRONMENTAL DESIGN (civil engineering, electrical/electronics engineering, and mechanical engineering), SOCIAL SCIENCE (history, international studies, and psychology). Engineering (civil, electrical, and mechanical) and sciences are the strongest academically. History, business/economics, and civil and mechanical engineering are the largest.

Required: To graduate, students must complete 136 to 144 semester hours, with a GPA of 2.0. All students must pass chemistry, English, history, math, phys ed, ROTC, and public speaking. In addition, all cadets must pass swimming, boxing, and wrestling.

Special: Study abroad in 14 countries and work-study programs are available, as are for-credit internships in English and international studies and summer internships in foreign countries. VMI offers dual majors in any combination and B.A.-B.S. degrees in liberal arts, physical sciences, and engineering. Minors are offered in each field of study. There are 11 national honor societies, a freshman honors program, and 3 departmental honors programs.

Faculty/Classroom: 82% of faculty are male; 18%, female. All teach undergraduates, 67% do research, and 67% do both. The average class size in an introductory lecture is 19; in a laboratory, 14; and in a regular course, 15.

Admissions: 61% of the 2001-2002 applicants were accepted. The SAT I scores for the 2001-2002 freshman class were: Verbal--15% below 500, 56% between 500 and 599, 24% between 600 and 700, and 5% above 700; Math--12% below 500, 52% between 500 and 599, 34% between 600 and 700, and 3% above 700. 40% of the current freshmen were in the top fifth of their class; 80% were in the top two fifths. 3 freshmen graduated first in their class.

Requirements: The SAT I or ACT is required. In addition, applicants must be graduates of an accredited secondary school. Applicants should complete 19 to 20 high school academic units, including 4 years of English and math, 3 of science, history, and foreign language, and 2 of social studies. An essay is encouraged and an interview is recommended. Applications are accepted on computer disk. AP credits are accepted. Important factors in the admissions decision are advanced placement or honor courses, extracurricular activities record, and leadership record.

Procedure: Freshmen are admitted in the fall. Entrance exams should be taken during the second semester of the junior year. There is an early decision plan. Early decision applications should be filed by November 15; regular applications, by April 1 for fall entry. Notification of early decision is sent December 15; regular decision, on a rolling basis. 8% of all applicants are on a waiting list.

Transfer: 31 transfer students enrolled in 2001-2002. Applicants for transfer must have a minimum GPA of 2.0, and 24 transferable credit hours, and a satisfactory high school record. Either the SAT I or the ACT is required. 67 credits of 135 must be completed at VMI.

Visiting: There are regularly scheduled orientations for prospective students, consisting of tours, conferences with academic and ROTC instructors, interaction with current freshmen, and overnight stays. There are guides for informal visits and visitors may sit in on classes and stay overnight. To schedule a visit, contact Admissions.

Financial Aid: In a recent year, 59% of all freshmen and 81% of continuing students received some form of financial aid. 37% of freshmen and 34% of continuing students received need-based aid. The average freshman award was $11,613. Of that total, scholarships or need-based grants averaged $6950 ($15,000 maximum); and loans averaged $4326 ($5625 maximum). 9% of undergraduates work part time; freshmen are not allowed to work. Average annual earnings from campus work are $800. The average financial indebtedness of a recent graduate was $13,000. VMI is a member of CSS. The FAFSA and the college's own financial statement are required. The fall application deadline is April 1.

International Students: There are 51 international students enrolled. The school actively recruits these students. They must score 500 on the written TOEFL. International students who will play intercollegiate athletics must take the SAT I or ACT.

Computers: The mainframe is a DEC ALPHA server 4100. There are 200 networked PCs available to cadets with access to the local area network and the Internet. All student rooms are wired for Internet access. All students may access the system. There are no time limits and no fees. It is strongly recommended that all students have a personal computer.

Graduates: In a recent year, 234 bachelor's degrees were awarded. The most popular majors were history (22%), economics (20%), and international studies (12%). In an average class, 54% graduate in 4 years, 65% in 5 years, and 67% in 6 years. 45 companies recruited on campus in a recent year. Of a recent graduating class, 18% were enrolled in graduate school within 6 months of graduation and 99% were employed.

Admissions Contact: Col. Vernon L. Beitzel, Director, Admissions. A video is available. E-mail: *admissions@vmi.edu* Web: *www.vmi.edu*

VIRGINIA POLYTECHNIC INSTITUTE AND STATE UNIVERSITY — C-3

Blacksburg, VA 24061 — **(540) 231-6267; Fax: (540) 231-3242**

Full-time: 12,370 men, 8585 women	**Faculty:** 925; I, av$
Part-time: 403 men, 226 women	**Ph.D.s:** 82%
Graduate: 3547 men, 2702 women	**Student/Faculty:** 23 to 1
Year: semesters, summer session	**Tuition:** $3620 ($12,444)
Application Deadline: January 15	**Room & Board:** $4032

Freshman Class: 18,800 applied, 12,500 accepted, 4992 enrolled

SAT I or ACT: required — **COMPETITIVE**

Virginia Polytechnic Institute and State University, founded in 1872, is a public land-grant institution. It offers a cadet program within the larger, nonmilitary student body. There are 7 undergraduate and 2 graduate schools. In addition to regional accreditation, Virginia Tech has baccalaureate program accreditation with AACSB, ABET, ACCE, ADA, AHEA, ASLA, FIDER, NAAB, NCATE, and SAF. The 4 libraries contain 2.1 million volumes, 6.2 million microform items, and 17,510 audiovisual forms/CDs, and subscribe to 18,737 periodicals. Computerized library services include the card catalog, interlibrary loans, and database searching. Special learning facilities include a learning resource center, art gallery, natural history museum, radio station, TV station, airport, wind tunnels, agricultural stations, radio/visual observatories, satellite up-link station, multimedia, digital music, writing, and CAD/CAM labs, math emporium, and CAVE (cave automatic virtual environment). The 2600-acre campus is in a rural area 40 miles southwest of Roanoke. Including residence halls, there are 110 buildings.

Student Life: 70% of undergraduates are from Virginia. Others are from 49 states, 104 foreign countries, and Canada. 78% are white. The average age of freshmen is 18; all undergraduates, 22. 12% do not continue beyond their first year; 67% remain to graduate.

Housing: 8682 students can be accommodated in college housing, which includes single-sex and coed dormitories, fraternity houses, and sorority houses. In addition, there are honors houses and special-interest houses. On-campus housing is guaranteed for the freshman year only and is available on a lottery system for upperclassmen. 59% of students commute. All students may keep cars.

Activities: 13% of men belong to 34 national fraternities; 15% of women belong to 16 national sororities. There are 500 groups on campus, including art, band, cheerleading, chess, choir, chorale, chorus, computers, dance, drama, drill team, drum and bugle corps, ethnic, film, gay, honors, international, jazz band, literary magazine, marching band, musical theater, newspaper, orchestra, pep band, photography, political, professional, radio and TV, religious, social, social service, student government, symphony, and yearbook. Popular campus events include Quad Jams, Ring Dance, and German's Mid-Winter Dance.

Sports: There are 11 intercollegiate sports for men and 10 for women, and 19 intramural sports for men and 19 for women. Facilities include a football stadium, a basketball coliseum, a field house, an indoor tennis pavilion, an 18-hole golf course, soccer and baseball fields, a swimming pool, a diving well, basketball, volleyball, racquetball, handball, squash, and tennis courts, a gymnastics room, a weight-lifting room, lighted multipurpose recreation fields, and a pond for ice skating. Residential quads are also equipped with weight-room and exercise facilities; there are also 2 gyms.

Disabled Students: 60% of the campus is accessible. Wheelchair ramps, elevators, special parking, specially equipped rest rooms, special class scheduling, lowered drinking fountains, lowered telephones, and a special services library room for the visually impaired are available.

Services: Counseling and information services are available, as is tutoring in most subjects. There is a reader service for the blind and remedial reading.

Campus Safety and Security: Measures include 24-hour foot and vehicle patrol, self-defense education, escort service, and shuttle buses. There are informal discussions, pamphlets/posters/films, emergency telephones, and lighted pathways/sidewalks.

Programs of Study: Virginia Tech confers B.A., B.S., B.Arch., B.F.A., B.Land.Arch., B.S.Bus., B.S.E., and B.S.Ed. degrees. Associate, master's, and doctoral degrees are also awarded. Bachelor's degrees are awarded in AGRICULTURE (agricultural economics, animal science, dairy science, forestry and related sciences, horticulture, poultry science, and soil science), BIOLOGICAL SCIENCE (biochemistry and biology/biological science), BUSINESS (accounting, banking and finance, business economics, hotel/motel and restaurant management, management science, and marketing/retailing/merchandising), COMMUNICATIONS AND THE ARTS (communications, dramatic arts, English, French, German, music, and Spanish), COMPUTER AND PHYSICAL SCIENCE (chemistry, computer science, geology, mathematics, physics, and statistics), EDUCATION (agricultural, business, early childhood, health, home economics, marketing and distribution, physical, technical, and vocational), ENGINEERING AND ENVIRONMENTAL DESIGN (agricultural engineering, architecture, chemical engineering, civil engineering, computer engineering, construction engineering, construction management, electrical/electronics engineering, environmental science, interior design, landscape architecture/design, materials engineering, mechanical engineering, mining and mineral engineering, and ocean engineering), SOCIAL SCIENCE (child care/child and family studies, economics, food science, geography, history, international studies, liberal arts/general studies, philosophy, political science/government, psychology, public administration, sociology, textiles and clothing, and urban studies). Engineering, architecture, and business are the strongest academically. Engineering, computer science, and biology are the largest.

Required: To graduate, students must complete between 120 and 156 credit hours (depending on the major), with a minimum GPA of 2.0. There is a required core curriculum that includes 8 hours of science and 6 hours each of humanities, social science, math, and writing and discourse. Students must also meet a foreign language requirement.

Special: Students may cross-register with Miami University in Ohio, Oxford Polytechnic Institute, California Polytechnic Institute, and Florida A & M. Study abroad in 36 countries, a Washington semester, and a wide range of work-study programs are available, as well as co-ops in 48 majors. There are honors options for most majors, B.A.-B.S. degrees, dual and student-designed majors, credit for independent study or research, nondegree study, and pass/fail options. The Corps of Cadets, a militarily structured organization, is open to men and women. Undergraduate advising programs are available to students wishing to prepare for professional school in law, dentistry, medicine, pharmacy, physical therapy, or veterinary medicine. There are 13 national honor societies, including Phi Beta Kappa, a freshman honors program.

Faculty/Classroom: 76% of faculty are male; 24%, female. 74% teach undergraduates and all do research. Graduate students teach 12% of introductory courses. The average class size in an introductory lecture is 46 and in a laboratory, 30.

Admissions: 66% of the 2001-2002 applicants were accepted. 71% of the current freshmen were in the top fifth of their class; 98% were in the top two fifths. In a recent year there were 36 National Merit finalists, 77 freshmen graduated first in their class.

Requirements: The SAT I or ACT is required. In addition, students must also take SAT II: Subject tests in writing and history. Applicants must be graduates of an accredited secondary school, or the GED is accepted. Applicants should complete 18 high school academic credits, including 4 years of English, 3 of math, including algebra II and geometry, 2 of lab science, to be chosen from biology, chemistry, or physics, and 1 each of history and social studies. An additional 3 years from college preparatory courses and 4 from any credit course offerings are required. A portfolio and an audition are required for art and music students. A GPA of 2.0 is required. AP and CLEP credits are accepted. Important factors in the admissions decision are advanced placement or honor courses, evidence of special talent, and recommendations by school officials. Applications are accepted on-line via CollegeNET.

Procedure: Freshmen are admitted to all sessions. Entrance exams should be taken by January 1 of the senior year. There are early decision, early admissions, and deferred admissions plans. Early decision applications should be filed by November 1; regular applications, by January 15 for fall entry, October 1 for spring entry, and April 22 for summer entry. Notification of early decision is sent December 15; regular decision, on a rolling basis. 1100 early decision candidates were accepted for the 2001-2002 class. A waiting list is an active part of the admissions procedure.

Transfer: Applicants must have a minimum GPA of 2.0. and must specify a major. 30 credits of 120 must be completed at Virginia Tech.

Visiting: There are regularly scheduled orientations for prospective students, consisting of a Fall Open House Series: half-day on-campus programs that include presentations, tours, and question-and-answer sessions. There are guides for informal visits and visitors may sit in on classes. To schedule a visit, contact the Office of Undergraduate Admissions.

Financial Aid: In 2001-2002, 65% of all freshmen and 63% of continuing students received some form of financial aid. 49% of freshmen and 66% of continuing students received need-based aid. The average freshman award was $6625. Of that total, scholarships or need-based grants averaged $3816 ($24,062 maximum); loans averaged $6728 ($18,500 maximum); and work contracts averaged $799 ($3500 maximum). 43% of undergraduates work part time. Average annual earnings from campus work are $1500. The average financial indebtedness of the 2001 graduate was $15,049. The FAFSA is required. The fall application deadline is March 1.

International Students: There are 571 international students enrolled. The school actively recruits these students. They must score 550 on the written TOEFL and also take the SAT I or the ACT. Students must take SAT II: Subject tests in writing and U.S. history.

Computers: Undergraduates receive guidance on using PCs and the Internet from their professors. They may access the Internet or use PCs in any one of many computer labs on campus, or from their dormitory rooms. Dormitory rooms are wired for data, voice, and video transmission. All students may access the system any time. There are no time limits and no fees. All students are required to have personal computers. Specs will vary by major.

Graduates: In a recent year, 4251 bachelor's degrees were awarded. The most popular majors were biology (6%), communication studies (4%), and management science and information techn (4%). In an average class, 67% graduate in 5 years. 500 companies recruited on campus in a recent year. Of a recent graduating class, 13% were enrolled in graduate school within 6 months of graduation and 58% were employed.

Admissions Contact: Office of Undergraduate Admissions. A video is available. E-mail: *vtadmiss@vt.edu* Web: *www.vt.edu*

VIRGINIA STATE UNIVERSITY — E-3
Petersburg, VA 23806 — (804) 524-5902
(800) 871-7611; Fax: (804) 524-5055

Full-time: 1330 men, 1820 women	**Faculty:** 168
Part-time: 165 men, 190 women	**Ph.D.s:** 74%
Graduate: 220 men, 590 women	**Student/Faculty:** 19 to 1
Year: semesters, summer session	**Tuition:** $3100 ($8700)
Application Deadline: see profile	**Room & Board:** $5100
Freshman Class: n/av	
SAT I Verbal/Math: required	**LESS COMPETITIVE**

Virginia State University is a historically black public land-grant institution of higher education providing academic programs that integrate instruction, research, and extension/public service. There are 4 undergraduate schools and 1 graduate school. Figures in the above capsule, and in this profile, are approximate. In addition to regional accreditation, VSU has baccalaureate program accreditation with ABET, ADA, CSWE, NASM, and NCATE. The library contains 280,599 volumes, 662,075 microform items, and 3939 audiovisual forms/CDs, and subscribes to 1198 periodicals. Computerized library services include the card catalog, interlibrary loans, and database searching. Special learning facilities include a learning resource center, art gallery, radio station, and TV station. The 652-acre campus is in a suburban area 25 miles south of Richmond. Including residence halls, there are 52 buildings.

Student Life: 65% of undergraduates are from Virginia. Others are from 35 states and 1 foreign country. 96% are from public schools. 90% are African American. The average age of freshmen is 18; all undergraduates, 21. 40% do not continue beyond their first year; 18% remain to graduate.

Housing: 2050 students can be accommodated in college housing, which includes single-sex dormitories. In addition, there are honors houses. On-campus housing is guaranteed for the freshman year only and is available on a first-come, first-served basis. 52% of students live on campus; of those, 20% remain on campus on weekends. Alcohol is not permitted. Upperclassmen may keep cars.

Activities: 10% of men belong to 4 national fraternities; 10% of women belong to 4 national sororities. There are 44 groups on campus, including band, cheerleading, chess, choir, chorus, computers, dance, drama, drill team, ethnic, honors, international, jazz band, marching band, musical theater, newspaper, orchestra, pep band, photography, political, professional, radio and TV, religious, social, student government, symphony, and yearbook. Popular campus events include High School Day, VSU Day, and Commencement.

Sports: There are 7 intercollegiate sports for men and 6 for women, and 5 intramural sports for men and 6 for women. Facilities include a

gym, an Olympic-size pool, a dance studio, tennis courts, a track field, a football field, a baseball field, and indoor and outdoor basketball courts.

Disabled Students: 75% of the campus is accessible. Wheelchair ramps, elevators, special parking, and specially equipped rest rooms are available.

Services: Counseling and information services are available, as is tutoring in most subjects. There is a reader service for the blind.

Campus Safety and Security: Measures include 24-hour foot and vehicle patrol, informal discussions, emergency telephones, and lighted pathways/sidewalks.

Programs of Study: VSU confers B.A., B.S., B.F.A., B.I.S., and B.Mus. degrees. Master's degrees are also awarded. Bachelor's degrees are awarded in AGRICULTURE (agriculture), BIOLOGICAL SCIENCE (biology/biological science), BUSINESS (accounting, business administration and management, hotel/motel and restaurant management, management information systems, and marketing management), COMMUNICATIONS AND THE ARTS (English literature, music performance, and visual and performing arts), COMPUTER AND PHYSICAL SCIENCE (chemistry, mathematics, and physics), EDUCATION (athletic training, business, physical, and trade and industrial), ENGINEERING AND ENVIRONMENTAL DESIGN (engineering technology), SOCIAL SCIENCE (economics, history, home economics, interdisciplinary studies, political science/government, psychology, public administration, social work, and sociology). Business administration, accounting, and business information systems are the largest.

Required: To graduate, students must have a minimum GPA of 2.0. They must earn at least 120 credits, with the last 27 semester hours in residence. Requirements include those in phys ed, freshman writing, math, biology, social or physical science, history, and psychology. Freshman orientation must also be completed.

Special: VSU offers dual majors, a general studies degree, a 3-2 engineering degree program, nondegree study, and a pass/fail grading option. There are 10 national honor societies, including Phi Beta Kappa, a freshman honors program, and 7 departmental honors programs.

Faculty/Classroom: 67% of faculty are male; 33%, female. Graduate students teach 2% of introductory courses.

Requirements: The SAT I or ACT is required. In addition, applicants must graduate from an accredited secondary school with 16 academic credits and 12 Carnegie units, or have a GED. Students must take 4 years of English, 2 each of a foreign language, math, and science, and 1 each of history and social studies. Essays, 2 letters of recommendation, evidence of physical condition, interviews, and, if appropriate, auditions are required. A GPA of 2.0 is required. AP and CLEP credits are accepted. Important factors in the admissions decision are advanced placement or honor courses, recommendations by school officials, and leadership record. Applications are accepted on-line at the school's web site at *www.vsu.edu/under.html*.

Procedure: Freshmen are admitted fall and spring. There is a deferred admissions plan. Notification is sent on a rolling basis. Check with the school for current application deadlines.

Transfer: 147 transfer students enrolled in a recent year. Applicants must have a minimum GPA of 2.0. Those transferring fewer than 25 semester hours must meet freshman standards. 30 credits of 120 must be completed at VSU.

Visiting: There are regularly scheduled orientations for prospective students. There are guides for informal visits and visitors may sit in on classes. To schedule a visit, contact Admissions.

Financial Aid: In a recent year, 85% of all freshmen and 92% of continuing students received some form of financial aid. 70% of freshmen and 78% of continuing students received need-based aid. The average freshman award was $5315. Of that total, scholarships or need-based grants averaged $1500 ($3100 maximum); loans averaged $2500 ($2625 maximum); and work contracts averaged $1600 ($1980 maximum). Average annual earnings from campus work are $2000. The average financial indebtedness of a recent graduate was $18,500. VSU is a member of CSS. The CSS/Profile and the college's own financial statement are required. Check with the school for current deadlines.

International Students: They must score 500 on the written TOEFL and also take the SAT I or the ACT.

Computers: The mainframe is an IBM 4361. There are 322 PCs available in computer labs and in various units on campus. All students may access the system 8 A.M. to 10 P.M. Monday through Friday and 8 A.M. to 4 P.M. Saturdays. There are no time limits and no fees. It is strongly recommended that all students have a personal computer.

Graduates: In a recent year, 481 bachelor's degrees were awarded. In an average class, 10% graduate in 4 years, 26% in 5 years, and 33% in 6 years. 88 companies recruited on campus in a recent year. Of a recent graduating class, 47% were employed within 6 months of graduation.

Admissions Contact: Lisa Winn, Director of Admissions. A video is available. E-mail: *lwinn@vsu.edu* Web: *www.vsu.edu*

VIRGINIA UNION UNIVERSITY — E-3
Richmond, VA 23220 — (804) 329-8456
(800) 368-3227; Fax: (804) 329-8477

Full-time: 536 men, 782 women	**Faculty:** 82; IIB, --$
Part-time: 32 men, 27 women	**Ph.D.s:** 55%
Graduate: 209 men, 114 women	**Student/Faculty:** 16 to 1
Year: semesters, summer session	**Tuition:** $10,690
Application Deadline: see profile	**Room & Board:** $4668
Freshman Class: n/av	
SAT I: required	**LESS COMPETITIVE**

Virginia Union University, established in 1865 and affiliated with the Baptist Church, is a private institution offering undergraduate programs in education and psychology, business, humanities, natural science and math, and social sciences. There are 2 undergraduate schools and 1 graduate school. In addition to regional accreditation, VUU has baccalaureate program accreditation with ACBSP and CSWE. The library contains 145,305 volumes, 62,079 microform items, and 1523 audiovisual forms/CDs, and subscribes to 308 periodicals. Computerized library services include database searching. Special learning facilities include a learning resource center and art gallery. The 72-acre campus is in an urban area in the city of Richmond. Including residence halls, there are 18 buildings.

Student Life: 52% of undergraduates are from Virginia. Others are from 27 states and 4 foreign countries. 85% are from public schools. 98% are African American. The average age of freshmen is 18. 31% do not continue beyond their first year; 55% remain to graduate.

Housing: 700 students can be accommodated in college housing, which includes single-sex dormitories. In addition, there are honors houses. On-campus housing is available on a first-come, first-served basis. Priority is given to out-of-town students. 50% of students live on campus. Alcohol is not permitted. All students may keep cars.

Activities: There are 2 national fraternities and 4 national sororities. There are 32 groups on campus, including cheerleading, drama, international, newspaper, religious, student government, and yearbook. Popular campus events include films, lectures, and concerts.

Sports: There are 6 intercollegiate sports for men and 6 for women, and 3 intramural sports for men and 2 for women. Facilities include a gym-auditorium and a 10,000-seat stadium.

Disabled Students: 90% of the campus is accessible. Wheelchair ramps, elevators, and special parking are available.

Services: Counseling and information services are available, as is tutoring in every subject. There is remedial math, reading, and writing.

Campus Safety and Security: Measures include 24-hour foot and vehicle patrol, escort service, informal discussions, and pamphlets/posters/films. There are emergency telephones and lighted pathways/sidewalks.

Programs of Study: VUU confers B.A., B.S., and B.S.W. degrees. Master's and doctoral degrees are also awarded. Bachelor's degrees are awarded in BIOLOGICAL SCIENCE (biology/biological science), BUSINESS (accounting, banking and finance, and business administration and management), COMMUNICATIONS AND THE ARTS (English, journalism, and music), COMPUTER AND PHYSICAL SCIENCE (chemistry and mathematics), EDUCATION (art, business, early childhood, elementary, music, secondary, and special), SOCIAL SCIENCE (criminology, history, political science/government, psychology, religion, social work, and sociology). Teacher education, accounting, and history/political science are the strongest academically. Teacher education, criminology, and business administration are the largest.

Required: To graduate, all students must complete at least 124 credit hours with a GPA of at least 2.0. Courses in religion, English, math, science, social science, a foreign language, and phys ed are required. There are also chapel and VUU events attendance requirements. All students must successfully complete a computer science course and must take an English essay exam, usually by the end of the junior year, as well as a comprehensive exam in their major.

Special: The university offers cross-registration with Virginia Commonwealth and Virginia State Universities and the University of Richmond. Internships, co-op programs, federal work-study programs, a general studies degree, a joint law degree with St. John's University School of Law in New York, a 3-2 degree in engineering with the Universities of Michigan and Iowa and Howard University, and exchange programs are also offered. There are 2 national honor societies and a freshman honors program.

Faculty/Classroom: 55% of faculty are male; 45%, female. 86% teach undergraduates. No introductory courses are taught by graduate students. The average class size in an introductory lecture is 28; in a laboratory, 20; and in a regular course, 22.

Requirements: The SAT I is required. In addition, graduation from an accredited secondary school is required; the GED is accepted. 16 academic units are required, including 4 of English, 3 each of math and academic electives, and 2 each of foreign language, social science, and natural science. Special consideration is given to disadvantaged students. Children of alumni are given some preference. A GPA of 2.0 is required.

AP and CLEP credits are accepted. Important factors in the admissions decision are extracurricular activities record, advanced placement or honor courses, and leadership record.

Procedure: Freshmen are admitted fall and spring. Entrance exams should be taken between March of the junior year and March of the senior year. There are early admissions and deferred admissions plans. Check with the school for current application deadlines and fees. Notification is sent on a rolling basis.

Transfer: Appliacnts must be in good standing at their previous institutions and must submit all college transcripts. 30 credits of 124 must be completed at VUU.

Visiting: There are guides for informal visits and visitors may sit in on classes. To schedule a visit, contact the Admissions Office at (804) 257-5600.

Financial Aid: In 2001-2002, 98% of all freshmen received some form of financial aid. 96% of all students received need-based aid. VUU is a member of CSS. The CSS/Profile is required. Check with the school for current deadlines.

International Students: These students must score 500 on the written TOEFL and also take the SAT I, scoring 700 or the ACT.

Computers: The mainframe is an IBM AS/400. PCs with various software are available in computer labs. All students may access the system. There are no time limits and no fees. It is strongly recommended that all students have a personal computer.

Graduates: 100 companies recruited on campus in 2000-2001.

Admissions Contact: Gil Powell, Director of Admissions.
E-mail: *admissions@vuu.edu* Web: *http://www.vuu.edu*

VIRGINIA WESLEYAN COLLEGE F-4

Norfolk/Virginia Beach, VA 23502-5599 (757) 455-3208
(800) 737-8684; Fax: (757) 461-5238

Full-time: 371 men, 685 women	**Faculty:** 75; IIB, -$
Part-time: 77 men, 275 women	**Ph.D.s:** 85%
Graduate: none	**Student/Faculty:** 14 to 1
Year: semesters, summer session	**Tuition:** $16,500
Application Deadline: open	**Room & Board:** $5850
Freshman Class: 982 applied, 786 accepted, 294 enrolled	
SAT I or ACT: required	**LESS COMPETITIVE**

Virginia Wesleyan College, established in 1961, is a private institution affiliated with the United Methodist Church, offering undergraduate degrees in the humanities, the social sciences, the natural sciences, and mathematics. In addition to regional accreditation, Virginia Wesleyan has baccalaureate program accreditation with NRPA. The library contains 115,000 volumes, 15,800 microform items, and 3500 audiovisual forms/CDs, and subscribes to 600 periodicals. Computerized library services include the card catalog, interlibrary loans, and database searching. Special learning facilities include a learning resource center, art gallery, radio station, a greenhouse, the Center for the study of Religious Freedom, and 142 acres of woodland used as a lab for biological and environmental sciences. The 300-acre campus is in an urban area 8 miles east of downtown Norfolk and 10 miles west of the Virginia Beach oceanfront. Including residence halls, there are 31 buildings.

Student Life: 79% of undergraduates are from Virginia. Others are from 27 states and 15 foreign countries. 97% are from public schools. 78% are white; 13% African American. 41% are Protestant; 27% Catholic; 20% claim no religious affiliation. The average age of freshmen is 19; all undergraduates, 26.

Housing: 556 students can be accommodated in college housing, which includes single-sex and coed dormitories. In addition, there are special-interest houses, and fraternity, sorority, and international residence halls. On-campus housing is guaranteed for all 4 years. 62% of students commute. All students may keep cars.

Activities: 15% of men belong to 3 national fraternities; 20% of women belong to 3 national sororities. There are 45 groups on campus, including cheerleading, chorus, commuter, dance, departmental, drama, ethnic, honors, international, literary magazine, model UN, musical theater, newspaper, political, professional, radio and TV, religious, social, social service, student government, women's, and yearbook. Popular campus events include TGIF Series and Seafood party in the Dell.

Sports: There are 7 intercollegiate sports for men and 7 for women, and 12 intramural sports for men and 12 for women. Facilities include the student center, which includes a multi activity athletic center, a 39-foot-high climbing wall, NCAA regulation swimming pool, indoor running track, and basketball courts. Also baseball, softball, lacrosse, field hockey, and soccer fields, tennis courts and a ropes course are available.

Disabled Students: 80% of the campus is accessible. Wheelchair ramps, elevators, special parking, specially equipped rest rooms, special class scheduling, lowered drinking fountains, lowered telephones, and special desks and preferential seating and registration are available.

Services: Counseling and information services are available, as is tutoring in every subject. There is a reader service for the blind, and remedial math, reading, and writing. Note takers, special co-advising, test proctoring, Learning Plus for Praxis exams for education certification, and outreach (tutoring) to public school students are available.

Campus Safety and Security: Measures include 24-hour foot and vehicle patrol, escort service, shuttle buses, and informal discussions. There are pamphlets/posters/films, emergency telephones, lighted pathways/sidewalks, and a bicycle patrol.

Programs of Study: Virginia Wesleyan confers the B.A. degree. Bachelor's degrees are awarded in BIOLOGICAL SCIENCE (biology/biological science), BUSINESS (business administration and management), COMMUNICATIONS AND THE ARTS (art, communications, dramatic arts, English, French, German, journalism, languages, music, and Spanish), COMPUTER AND PHYSICAL SCIENCE (chemistry, computer science, earth science, mathematics, and natural sciences), EDUCATION (art), SOCIAL SCIENCE (American studies, criminal justice, history, human ecology, humanities, interdisciplinary studies, international relations, liberal arts/general studies, parks and recreation management, philosophy, political science/government, psychology, religion, social science, social studies, social work, and sociology). Natural sciences, political science, and English are the strongest academically. Social sciences, liberal arts and management, and communications are the largest.

Required: To graduate, students must complete general studies requirements, which include English, math, a foreign language, and Frames of Reference courses. These include Empirical Knowledge, Aesthetic Understanding and Activity, Ethical Values, World Views, Faith Perspectives, the Historical Perspective, Communications, and Institutional and Cultural Systems. Students must earn 120 credits, including 40 in the major, with a minimum 2.0 GPA. Students must complete 3 credits designated to fulfill a Senior Integrative Experience requirement. They must also complete 2 January-term projects, each involving an intensive 2-week course of study in a single subject. Students must be enrolled in at least 1 course designated as a writing course each semester. A freshman seminar is also required.

Special: Students may cross-register with Old Dominion University, the College of William and Mary, or Norfolk State University through the Virginia Tidewater Consortium. Internships are available and are usually completed during the senior year. The college offers study-abroad programs and international internships through partnerships in 5 countries and an exchange program in 1 country, and additional arrangements for study abroad can be made in almost any country. Dual majors, individualized and interdivisional majors, and interdisciplinary majors are available. Work-study programs with Virginia Wesleyan are offered. Credit may be granted for life, military, and work experience. Nondegree study and pass/fail options are also available. There are 14 national honor societies and a freshman honors program.

Faculty/Classroom: 63% of faculty are male; 37%, female. All teach undergraduates. The average class size in a regular course is 13.

Admissions: 80% of the 2001-2002 applicants were accepted. 24% of the current freshmen were in the top fifth of their class; 52% were in the top two fifths. In a recent year there were 4 National Merit finalists, and 8 freshmen graduated first in their class.

Requirements: The SAT I or ACT is required. In addition, applicants must graduate from an accredited secondary school or have a GED. The college recommends 15 academic credits. Students should complete 4 years of English, 3 of social studies/history, math, and science, and 2 of foreign language. Essays are required, and interviews are recommended. Home schooled graduates are reviewed individually. A GPA of 2.0 is required. AP and CLEP credits are accepted. Important factors in the admissions decision are advanced placement or honor courses, extracurricular activities record, and leadership record.

Procedure: Freshmen are admitted fall and spring. Entrance exams should be taken in the spring of the junior year and the fall of the senior year. There is a deferred admissions plan. Application deadlines are open.

Transfer: 171 transfer students enrolled in 2001-2002. Applicants must have a minimum GPA of 2.0 in courses to be transferred. For applicants who have not completed 12 semester hours of college work, official transcripts of college and high school records (including SAT I or ACT scores) are required. All others must submit a high school diploma or GED in addition to official college transcripts. 30 credits of 120 must be completed at Virginia Wesleyan.

Visiting: There are regularly scheduled orientations for prospective students, consisting of 3 Open House Days on Saturdays for prospective students to meet faculty and current students, and to tour the campus. There are guides for informal visits and visitors may sit in on classes and stay overnight. To schedule a visit, contact the Admissions Office.

Financial Aid: In 2001-2002, 80% of all freshmen and 78% of continuing students received some form of financial aid. 77% of freshmen and 80% of continuing students received need-based aid. The average freshman award was $15,828. Of that total, loans averaged $2784 ($4125 maximum); and work contracts averaged $1500. 21% of undergraduates work part time. Average annual earnings from campus work are $1500. The average financial indebtedness of the 2001 graduate was $19,397. Virginia Wesleyan is a member of CSS. The FAFSA is required. The fall application deadline is March 1.

International Students: There are 9 international students enrolled. The school actively recruits these students. They must score 550 on the written TOEFL or 213 on the electronic version. The ACT is also accepted.

Computers: The mainframes are an HP-9000, Model 360. There are 7 network file servers and 57 workstations in various locations available for student use. In addition, there are 5 labs for computer use with approximately 100 computers. All computers have Web access. There is also Web access in all student rooms for those with personal computers. All students may access the system. There are no time limits and no fees. It is strongly recommended that all students have a personal computer.

Graduates: In 2001, 251 bachelor's degrees were awarded. The most popular majors were business (23%), social science (18%), and interdivisional (12%). 75 companies recruited on campus in 2000-2001. Of the 2000 graduating class, 19% were enrolled in graduate school within 6 months of graduation and 88% were employed.

Admissions Contact: Richard T. Hinshaw, Vice President for Enrollment Management. E-mail: *admissions@vwc.edu* Web: *www.vwc.edu*

WASHINGTON AND LEE UNIVERSITY D-3

Lexington, VA 24450 **(540) 463-8710; Fax: (540) 463-8062**

Full-time: 959 men, 802 women	**Faculty:** 198; IIB, +$
Part-time: 4 men, 2 women	**Ph.D.s:** 95%
Graduate: 204 men, 156 women	**Student/Faculty:** 9 to 1
Year: 4-4-2	**Tuition:** $19,345
Application Deadline: January 15	**Room & Board:** $5750
Freshman Class: 2939 applied, 1016 accepted, 498 enrolled	
SAT I Verbal/Math: 670/675	**ACT:** 30 **MOST COMPETITIVE**

Washington and Lee University, established in 1749, is a private institution offering undergraduate liberal arts degrees. There are 2 undergraduate schools and 1 graduate school. In addition to regional accreditation, Washington and Lee has baccalaureate program accreditation with AACSB, ACEJMC, and ACS. The 2 libraries contain 519,101 volumes, 124,620 microform items, and 8190 audiovisual forms/CDs, and subscribe to 1991 periodicals. Computerized library services include the card catalog, interlibrary loans, and database searching. Special learning facilities include an art gallery, radio station, TV station, and a performing arts center. The 305-acre campus is in a small town 50 miles northeast of Roanoke. Including residence halls, there are 66 buildings.

Student Life: 86% of undergraduates are from out of state, mostly the South. Others are from 47 states, 35 foreign countries, and Canada. 60% are from public schools. 89% are white. 45% are Protestant; 33% claim no religious affiliation; 28% Catholic. The average age of freshmen is 18; all undergraduates, 20. 6% do not continue beyond their first year; 89% remain to graduate.

Housing: 1100 students can be accommodated in college housing, which includes coed dormitories, on-campus apartments, fraternity houses, and sorority houses. In addition, there are special-interest houses. On-campus housing is available on a first-come, first-served basis and is available on a lottery system for upperclassmen. 64% of students live on campus; of those, 95% remain on campus on weekends. All students may keep cars.

Activities: 78% of men belong to 15 national fraternities; 68% of women belong to 1 local sorority and 5 national sororities. There are 120 groups on campus, including art, band, cheerleading, chess, chorale, chorus, dance, debate, drama, ethnic, film, forensics, gay, honors, international, jazz band, literary magazine, musical theater, newspaper, orchestra, outing club, photography, political, radio and TV, religious, social, social service, student government, symphony, and yearbook. Popular campus events include the Presidential Mock Convention and a fancy-dress ball.

Sports: There are 12 intercollegiate sports for men and 10 for women, and 16 intramural sports for men and 8 for women. Facilities include a gym, a 2400-seat arena, a 7000-seat stadium, a pool with a 500-seat gallery, weight, training, and exercise rooms, handball, racquetball, squash, and tennis courts, an outdoor track, baseball and practice fields, an indoor tennis facility, and a turf field for field hockey and lacrosse.

Disabled Students: 20% of the campus is accessible. Wheelchair ramps, elevators, special parking, specially equipped rest rooms, special class scheduling, and lowered drinking fountains are available.

Services: Counseling and information services are available, as is tutoring in every subject. There is a reader service for the blind.

Campus Safety and Security: Measures include 24-hour foot and vehicle patrol, self-defense education, escort service, and informal discussions. There are pamphlets/posters/films, emergency telephones, lighted pathways/sidewalks, and and required safety programs for freshmen.

Programs of Study: Washington and Lee confers B.A. and B.S. degrees. Doctoral degrees are also awarded. Bachelor's degrees are awarded in AGRICULTURE (forestry and related sciences), BIOLOGICAL SCIENCE (biology/biological science, and neurosciences), BUSINESS (accounting, and business administration and management), COMMUNICATIONS AND THE ARTS (art history and appreciation, classics, dramatic arts, English, French, German, Germanic languages and literature, journalism, music, romance languages and literature, Spanish, and studio art), COMPUTER AND PHYSICAL SCIENCE (chemistry, computer science, geology, mathematics, natural sciences, and physics), ENGINEERING AND ENVIRONMENTAL DESIGN (chemical engineering, engineering physics, and environmental science), SOCIAL SCIENCE (archeology, cognitive science, East Asian studies, economics, history, interdisciplinary studies, medieval studies, philosophy, political science/government, psychology, religion, Russian and Slavic studies, and sociology). The preprofessional program in commerce, journalism, and mass media, and history are the strongest academically. The commerce program, history, and the journalism program are the largest.

Required: To graduate, students must achieve proficiency in a foreign language and English composition, and complete 12 credits in fine arts and humanities, 10 in lab science and math, 9 in social sciences, and 6 in literature. A total of 121 credits, with a minimum GPA of 1.9 overall and 2.0 in the major, is required. All students must take 5 courses in phys ed and a swim test.

Special: There is cross-registration with area colleges, including VMI, and various internships, including commerce, government, and journalism, are available. Study-abroad programs are offered in several countries. There is a 3-3 law program, a 3-2 engineering degree with Rensselaer Polytechnic Institute and Washington and Columbia Universities, and a 3-2 program in forestry or environmental management with Duke University. Washington and Lee also offers interdisciplinary majors, including chemistry-engineering and natural science and math, and student-designed majors. There are 9 national honor societies, including Phi Beta Kappa, and a freshman honors program.

Faculty/Classroom: 76% of faculty are male; 24%, female. All both teach and do research. No introductory courses are taught by graduate students. The average class size in an introductory lecture is 19; in a laboratory, 16; and in a regular course, 15.

Admissions: 35% of the 2001-2002 applicants were accepted. The SAT I scores for the 2001-2002 freshman class were: Verbal--1% below 500, 10% between 500 and 599, 53% between 600 and 700, and 36% above 700; Math--1% below 500, 9% between 500 and 599, 54% between 600 and 700, and 36% above 700. 92% of the current freshmen were in the top fifth of their class; 99% were in the top two fifths. In a recent year there were 33 National Merit finalists and 48 freshmen graduated first in their class.

Requirements: The SAT I or ACT is required as well as 3 SAT II: Subject tests. Applicants must graduate from an accredited secondary school. They must earn 16 units, including 4 units in English, 3 in math, 2 in a foreign language, and 1 each in history and natural science. Course work in social sciences is also required. Essays are required, and interviews are recommended. AP credits are accepted. Important factors in the admissions decision are advanced placement or honor courses, leadership record, and recommendations by school officials. Applications are accepted on-line.

Procedure: Freshmen are admitted in the fall. Entrance exams should be taken between March of the junior year and January of the senior year. There are early decision and deferred admissions plans. Early decision applications should be filed by December 1; regular applications, by January 15 for fall entry. Notification of early decision is sent December 22; regular decision, April 1. 192 early decision candidates were accepted for the 2001-2002 class. 32% of all applicants are on a waiting list; 16 were accepted in 2001.

Transfer: 10 transfer students enrolled in a recent year. Transfer applicants must have a GPA of at least 2.0 (at least 3.5 to be competitive); no more than 87 credits will transfer. There is a 2-year residency requirement. 60 credits of 121 must be completed at Washington and Lee.

Visiting: There are regularly scheduled orientations for prospective students, consisting of hourly interview slots and campus tours, 2 group information sessions daily, and seasonal Saturday tours and interviews. There are guides for informal visits and visitors may sit in on classes. To schedule a visit, contact the Admissions Office.

Financial Aid: In 2001-2002, 55% of all freshmen and 53% of continuing students received some form of financial aid. 28% of freshmen and 27% of continuing students received need-based aid. The average freshman award was $16,652. Of that total, scholarships or need-based grants averaged $13,563 ($25,000 maximum); loans averaged $2304 ($5600 maximum); and work contracts averaged $785 ($800 maximum). 23% of undergraduates work part time. Average annual earnings from campus work are $1350. The average financial indebtedness of the 2001 graduate was $15,673. Washington and Lee is a member of CSS. The CSS/Profile or FAFSA and the noncustodial parent's statement and business/farm supplement are required. The fall application deadline is February 1.

International Students: There are 84 international students enrolled. The school actively recruits these students. They must score 600 on the written TOEFL and also take the SAT I or the ACT. Students must take SAT II: Subject tests in writing and 2 others.

Computers: The mainframe is an HP 9000 series. There are about 200 PCs in 12 locations throughout academic buildings. All terminals and PCs are networked, providing access to the mainframe. Students who live off campus have dial-up access to the mainframe. All students may access the system 24 hours a day, 7 days a week while classes are in session. There are no time limits and no fees.

Graduates: In 2001, 416 bachelor's degrees were awarded. The most popular majors were economics (12%), business administration (10%), and journalism (8%). In an average class, 86% graduate in 4 years, 88% in 5 years, and 89% in 6 years. 66 companies recruited on campus in 2000-2001. Of the 2000 graduating class, 23% were enrolled in graduate school within 6 months of graduation and 68% were employed.

Admissions Contact: William M. Hartog, Dean of Admissions and Financial Aid. A video is available. E-mail: *admissions@wlu.edu* Web: *www.wlu.edu*

WILLIAM AND MARY
(See College of William and Mary)

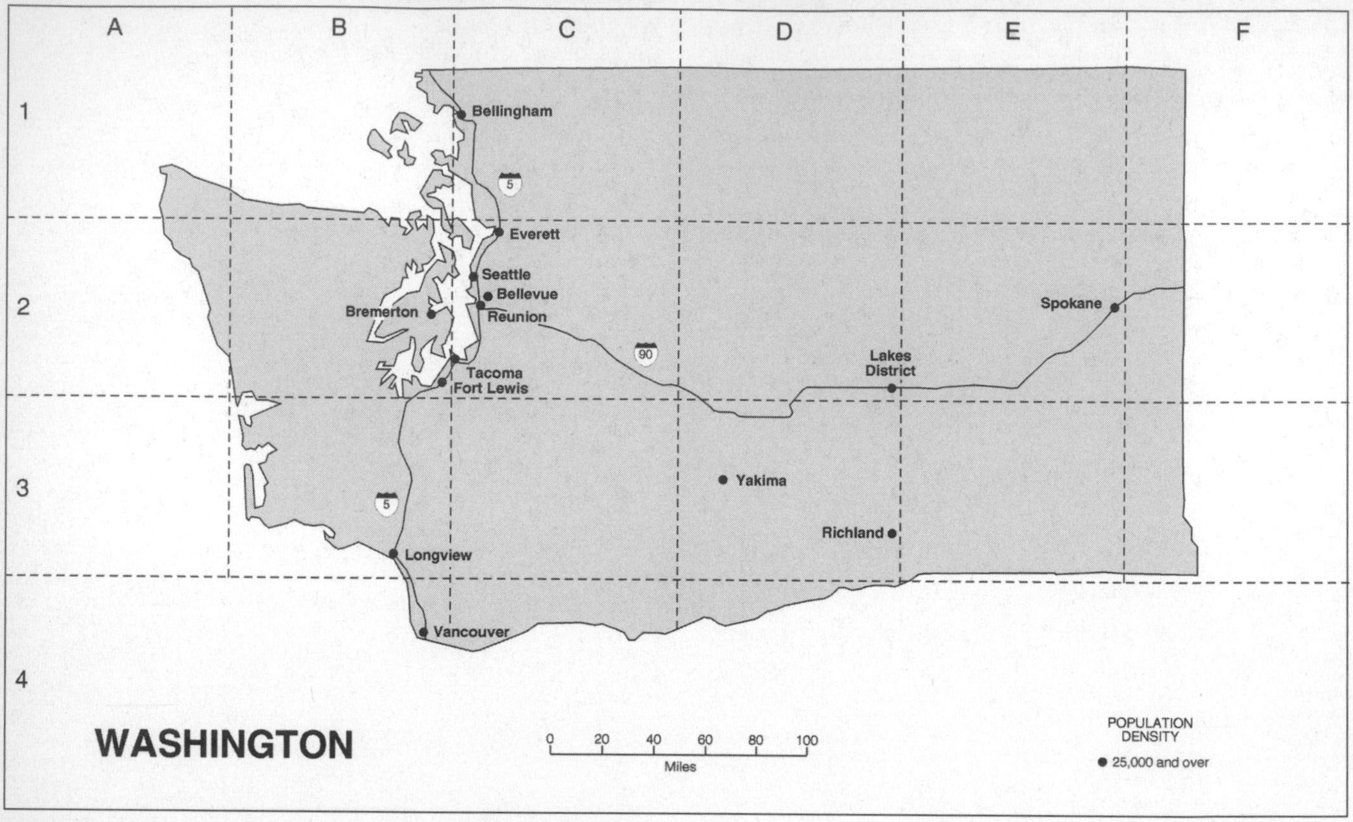

CENTRAL WASHINGTON UNIVERSITY D-2

Ellensburg, WA 98926 (509) 963-1211

(866) 298-4968; Fax: (509) 963-3022

Full-time: 3439 men, 3853 women **Faculty:** 337; IIA, --$

Part-time: 433 men, 581 women **Ph.D.s:** 83%

Graduate: 200 men, 320 women **Student/Faculty:** 22 to 1

Year: quarters, summer session **Tuition:** $3627 ($10,062)

Application Deadline: open **Room & Board:** $5358

Freshman Class: 2985 applied, 2658 accepted, 1256 enrolled

SAT I Verbal/Math: 490/500 **ACT:** 20 **LESS COMPETITIVE**

Central Washington University, founded in 1896, is a public institution offering undergraduate programs in the arts and sciences, business administration, and education. There are 4 undergraduate schools and 1 graduate school. In addition to regional accreditation, CWU has baccalaureate program accreditation with ABET, ACCE, ADA, NASM, NCATE, and NRPA. The library contains 434,424 volumes, 1,148,136 microform items, and 9230 audiovisual forms/CDs, and subscribes to 1469 periodicals. Computerized library services include the card catalog, interlibrary loans, and database searching. Special learning facilities include a learning resource center, art gallery, natural history museum, planetarium, radio station, anthropology museum, botanical greenhouse, and primate research lab. The 380-acre campus is in a rural area 100 miles east of Seattle. Including residence halls, there are 74 buildings.

Student Life: 96% of undergraduates are from Washington. Others are from 35 states, 32 foreign countries, and Canada. 96% are from public schools. 84% are white. The average age of freshmen is 19; all undergraduates, 23. 18% do not continue beyond their first year; 52% remain to graduate.

Housing: 2525 students can be accommodated in college housing, which includes coed dormitories, on-campus apartments, off-campus apartments, and married-student housing. In addition, there are special-interest houses, a freshman-only enrichment hall, and a residence hall for transfers and upperclassmen only. On-campus housing is guaranteed for the freshman year only and is available on a first-come, first-served basis. All students may keep cars.

Activities: There are no fraternities or sororities. There are 78 groups on campus, including art, band, cheerleading, chess, choir, chorale, chorus, computers, dance, drama, ethnic, film, gay, honors, international, jazz band, literary magazine, marching band, musical theater, newspaper, opera, orchestra, pep band, photography, political, professional, radio and TV, religious, social, social service, student government, and symphony. Popular campus events include Tower Theater productions and Jazz Night.

Sports: There are 11 intercollegiate sports for men and 11 for women, and 7 intramural sports for men and 6 for women. Facilities include a 3500-seat stadium, a swimming pool, an arena, a weight training room, an athletic field, and 3 gyms.

Disabled Students: 85% of the campus is accessible. Wheelchair ramps, elevators, special parking, specially equipped rest rooms, special class scheduling, lowered drinking fountains, and lowered telephones are available.

Services: Counseling and information services are available, as is tutoring in most subjects. There is a reader service for the blind, and remedial math, reading, and writing.

Campus Safety and Security: Measures include 24-hour foot and vehicle patrol, self-defense education, escort service, and shuttle buses. There are informal discussions, pamphlets/posters/films, emergency telephones, lighted pathways/sidewalks, and controlled-entry residence halls.

Programs of Study: CWU confers B.A., B.S., B.A.Ed., B.F.A., and B.M. degrees. Master's degrees are also awarded. Bachelor's degrees are awarded in BIOLOGICAL SCIENCE (biology/biological science and zoology), BUSINESS (accounting, banking and finance, business administration and management, business economics, international business management, marketing/retailing/merchandising, and recreation and leisure services), COMMUNICATIONS AND THE ARTS (broadcasting, communications, dramatic arts, English, fine arts, French, German, journalism, music, Spanish, and speech/debate/rhetoric), COMPUTER AND PHYSICAL SCIENCE (actuarial science, chemistry, computer programming, computer science, earth science, geology, information sciences and systems, mathematics, and physics), EDUCATION (art, business, early childhood, elementary, foreign languages, health, home economics, industrial arts, middle school, music, science, secondary, and special), ENGINEERING AND ENVIRONMENTAL DESIGN (aeronautical technology, electrical/electronics engineering, engineering technology, and mechanical engineering), HEALTH PROFESSIONS (public health), SOCIAL SCIENCE (anthropology, criminal justice, economics, food science, geography, history, parks and recreation management, philosophy, political science/government, psychology, public administration, social science, social work, sociology, and urban studies). Accounting, music, and geology are the strongest academically. Business and education are the largest.

Required: To graduate, students must complete a minimum of 180 quarter credits, including 60 in upper-division courses and a minimum of 45 in the major plus a minor or 60 in the major. Students must maintain a 2.3 GPA in the major and 2.0 GPA overall. Core curriculum requirements include 61 credits of Basic and Breadth courses, including 15 credits each in arts and humanities, social and behavioral sciences, and natural science, 6 credits of English composition, and a philosophy logic or finite math course. A comprehensive exam in reading comprehension, sentence skills, and math is required.

Special: Students may study abroad; there is a formal exchange program with Japanese universities. There are 3-2 engineering degree programs in conjunction with the University of Puget Sound, the University of Washington, and Washington State University. CWU also offers co-op programs, cross-registration, internships, work-study programs, an accelerated degree program, credit/no credit options, dual and student-designed majors, and credit for military experience. Nondegree study is offered through adult/continuing education programs. There are 11 national honor societies, a freshman honors program, and 12 departmental honors programs.

Faculty/Classroom: 62% of faculty are male; 38%, female. All both teach and do research. Graduate students teach 7% of introductory courses. The average class size in an introductory lecture is 40; in a laboratory, 20; and in a regular course, 40.

Admissions: 89% of the 2001-2002 applicants were accepted. The SAT I scores for the 2001-2002 freshman class were: Verbal--52% below 500, 35% between 500 and 599, 12% between 600 and 700, and 1% above 700; Math--48% below 500, 39% between 500 and 599, 12% between 600 and 700, and 1% above 700. The ACT scores were 50% below 21, 27% between 21 and 23, 14% between 24 and 26, 5% between 27 and 28, and 3% above 28.

Requirements: The SAT I or ACT is required. Test scores and GPA are considered in combination according to a sliding scale. Applicants must be graduates of accredited secondary schools or have earned a GED. The university requires 15 academic credits or Carnegie units: 4 years of English, 3 each of math and social studies, 2 of the same foreign language, 2 of science, and 1 of performing arts or an academic elective. A GPA of 2.0 is required. AP and CLEP credits are accepted. Important factors in the admissions decision are leadership record, personality/intangible qualities, and recommendations by school officials. An application is available on the school's web site.

Procedure: Freshmen are admitted to all sessions. Entrance exams should be taken before the fall of the senior year. Application deadlines are open. The fall 2001 application fee was $35. Notification is sent on a rolling basis.

Transfer: 1147 transfer students enrolled in 2001-2002. Students presenting an associate degree need a minimum GPA of 2.5 for automatic offer of admission; 2.5 to 2.0 will be asked to provide additional information for review. 45 quarter credits of 180 must be completed at CWU.

Visiting: There are regularly scheduled orientations for prospective students, consisting of an information session, campus and residence hall tours, prearranged appointments with faculty, and a financial aid presentation. There are guides for informal visits and visitors may sit in on classes and stay overnight. To schedule a visit, contact the Admissions Office.

Financial Aid: In 2001-2002, 98% of all freshmen and 42% of continuing students received some form of financial aid. 43% of freshmen and 42% of continuing students received need-based aid. The average freshman award was $3394. Of that total, scholarships or need-based grants averaged $1491; loans averaged $2032; and work contracts averaged $1334. 41% of undergraduates work part time. Average annual earnings from campus work are $2150. The average financial indebtedness of the 2001 graduate was $18,461. CWU is a member of CSS. The FAFSA is required. The fall application deadline is March 1.

International Students: There are 211 international students enrolled. The school actively recruits these students. They must score 525 on the written TOEFL and also take the SAT I or the ACT.

Computers: The mainframe is a DEC ALPHA cluster. There are about 4000 PCs on campus, 31 student labs with 659 workstations, personal web pages and e-mail for students, and network access. All students may access the system 24 hours a day. There are no time limits. The fee is $25 per quarter.

Graduates: In 2001, 1864 bachelor's degrees were awarded. The most popular majors were business administration (13%), elementary education (10%), and law and justice (7%). In an average class, 2% graduate in 3 years, 19% in 4 years, 45% in 5 years, and 51% in 6 years. 124 companies recruited on campus in 2000-2001.

Admissions Contact: Michael Reilly, Director of Admissions.
E-mail: *cwuadmis@cwu.edu* Web: *http://www/cwu.edu*

CITY UNIVERSITY
Renton, WA 98055 — C-2
(425) 637-1010
(800) 426-5596; Fax: (425) 277-2437

Full-time: 1060 men, 975 women	**Faculty:** 14
Part-time: 520 men, 460 women	**Ph.D.s:** n/av
Graduate: 1630 men, 1630 women	**Student/Faculty:** n/av
Year: quarters, summer session	**Tuition:** $7500
Application Deadline: open	**Room & Board:** n/app
Freshman Class: n/av	
SAT I or ACT: not required	**NONCOMPETITIVE**

City University, established in 1973, is a private nonresidential institution offering undergraduate and graduate programs at a variety of instructional sites in addition to the Renton campus, including locations in Washington, California, British Columbia, Europe, Asia, and Slovakia. There are 2 undergraduate and 3 graduate schools. Figures in the above capsule are approximate. The library contains 33,000 volumes, 415,000 microform items, and 1100 audiovisual forms/CDs, and subscribes to 650 periodicals. Computerized library services include the card catalog, interlibrary loans, and database searching. Special learning facilities include a learning resource center. The 2-acre campus is in a suburban area a few miles southeast of Seattle. There are 2 buildings.

Student Life: 51% of undergraduates are from out of state, mostly the West. Others are from 45 states, 30 foreign countries, and Canada. 58% are white. The average age of all undergraduates is 33.

Housing: There are no residence halls. Alcohol is not permitted.

Activities: There are no fraternities or sororities.

Sports: There is no sports program at City University.

Disabled Students: 90% of the campus is accessible. Wheelchair ramps, elevators, special parking, and specially equipped rest rooms are available.

Services: Tutoring is available.

Programs of Study: City University confers B.A. and B.S. degrees. Associate and master's degrees are also awarded. Bachelor's degrees are awarded in BUSINESS (accounting, business administration and management, and marketing/retailing/merchandising), COMPUTER AND PHYSICAL SCIENCE (computer programming), EDUCATION (elementary and middle school), SOCIAL SCIENCE (liberal arts/general studies). Business administration is the largest.

Required: Students are required to complete 180 quarter credits, with a minimum of 45 of these credits taken at City University, and maintain a minimum GPA of 2.0. A minimum of 30 credits are required in the major. All students must complete 55 general education credits, which include courses in the humanities, social sciences, natural sciences, and math.

Special: Opportunities are provided for cooperative programs with other schools, internships, study abroad, work-study programs, dual majors, and student-designed majors. A general studies degree, pass/fail options, independent study, weekend programs, and credit for military service are offered.

Faculty/Classroom: The average class size in an introductory lecture is 25.

Requirements: Graduation from an accredited secondary school is not required; a GED will be accepted. An interview is recommended. AP and CLEP credits are accepted.

Procedure: Freshmen are admitted to all sessions. Application deadlines are open. Check with the school for current application deadlines and fee.

Transfer: Students applying for transfer must submit official transcripts from all colleges previously attended. Applicants may transfer up to 135 quarter credits from accredited 4-year colleges, with at least 45 of these credits in upper-level courses. Up to 90 quarter credits may be transferred from 2-year colleges. 45 credits of 180 must be completed at City University.

Visiting: To schedule a visit, contact the Student Affairs Office.

Financial Aid: The FAFSA and the college's own financial statement are required. The fall application deadline is July 9. Check with the school for current deadlines.

International Students: There were 350 international students enrolled in a recent year. The school actively recruits these students. They must score 540 on the written TOEFL and also take the college's own English placement exam to determine placement in ESL classes if necessary.

Computers: The mainframe is a Unisys LX5300. Computer labs are available at most instructional sites. Information resources and services include web-based library indexes and full-text databases, library catalogs, word processing, spreadsheets, and printing. More than 150 computers are available to students. All students may access the system. There are no time limits and no fees. It is strongly recommended that all students have a personal computer.

Graduates: In a recent year, 322 bachelor's degrees were awarded. The most popular majors were business administration (69%), computer systems (11%), and accounting (10%).

Admissions Contact: Student Affairs/Admissions.
E-mail: *info@cityu.edu* Web: *www.cityu.edu*

CORNISH COLLEGE OF THE ARTS

Seattle, WA 98102 C-2
(206) 726-5016
(800) 726-ARTS; Fax: (206) 720-1011

Full-time: 228 men, 386 women	**Faculty:** 27
Part-time: 16 men, 20 women	**Ph.D.s:** 56%
Graduate: none	**Student/Faculty:** 23 to 1
Year: semesters, summer session	**Tuition:** $16,200
Application Deadline: August 15	**Room & Board:** n/app

Freshman Class: 600 applied, 465 accepted, 232 enrolled
SAT I or ACT: required **SPECIAL**

Cornish College of the Arts, founded in 1914, is an independent commuter institution offering undergraduate programs in the fine arts, dance, design, music, theater, and performance production. In addition to regional accreditation, Cornish has baccalaureate program accreditation with NASAD. The library contains 12,000 volumes and 2895 audiovisual forms/CDs, and subscribes to 88 periodicals. Computerized library services include the card catalog. Special learning facilities include an art gallery, dance studios, large black box theater, studio theater, and concert hall. The 4-acre campus is in an urban area in the Capitol Hill neighborhood of Seattle. There are 8 buildings.

Student Life: 55% of undergraduates are from Washington. Others are from 28 states, 10 foreign countries, and Canada. 78% are white. The average age of freshmen is 24; all undergraduates, 25. 20% do not continue beyond their first year; 50% remain to graduate.

Housing: There are no residence halls. Alcohol is not permitted. All students may keep cars.

Activities: There are no fraternities or sororities. There are many groups and organizations on campus, including art, band, chess, choir, chorus, dance, drama, ethnic, jazz band, literary magazine, opera, orchestra, professional, religious, and student government. Popular campus events include Spring Arts Festival, concerts, and gallery showings.

Sports: There is no sports program at Cornish.

Disabled Students: 50% of the campus is accessible. Wheelchair ramps, elevators, special parking, specially equipped rest rooms, lowered drinking fountains, and lowered telephones are available.

Services: Counseling and information services are available, as is tutoring in every subject. There is a reader service for the blind and remedial writing. There are also books on tape.

Campus Safety and Security: Measures include 24-hour foot and vehicle patrol, self-defense education, shuttle buses, and pamphlets/posters/films. There are emergency telephones.

Programs of Study: Cornish confers B.F.A. and B.M. degrees. Bachelor's degrees are awarded in COMMUNICATIONS AND THE ARTS (dance, design, dramatic arts, fine arts, music, and theater design). Design and dance are the strongest academically. Fine arts and theater are the largest.

Required: General education requirements include 30 semester hours in the humanities and sciences, as well as 6 to 8 in arts electives. To graduate, students must complete at least 127 semester hours, including 94 in their specific discipline, and maintain a minimum GPA of 2.5 during their senior year.

Special: Cornish offers a premajor first year of study to those music students who initially need more fundamental training. Internships are available to upperclassmen in all majors. Students may earn credit by examination in humanities and science courses, as well as credit for life experience in all majors where appropriate. Work-study programs and nondegree study are also offered.

Faculty/Classroom: All teach undergraduates. The average class size in an introductory lecture is 16 and in a regular course, 12.

Admissions: 78% of the 2001-2002 applicants were accepted.

Requirements: The SAT I or ACT is required if the test has been taken within the past 5 years. The required audition or portfolio review is the single most important criterion in the admissions decision. Applicants should be graduates of accredited secondary schools or have earned a GED. In addition to providing evidence of their artistic talent, students must submit 2 essays and arrange for an interview. AP and CLEP credits are accepted. Important factors in the admissions decision are evidence of special talent, personality/intangible qualities, and recommendations by school officials.

Procedure: Freshmen are admitted in the fall. There is a deferred admissions plan. Applications should be filed by August 15 for fall entry and December 15 for spring entry, along with a $35 fee. Notification is sent on a rolling basis.

Transfer: 28 transfer students enrolled in 2001-2002. Applicants must meet the same requirements as freshmen. 48 credits of 127 must be completed at Cornish.

Visiting: There are regularly scheduled orientations for prospective students, consisting of Preview Days during which applicants can attend classes, interact with students and faculty, and experience campus life. There are guides for informal visits and visitors may sit in on classes. To schedule a visit, contact the Admissions Office.

Financial Aid: In a recent year, 86% of all freshmen and 92% of continuing students received some form of financial aid. 79% of freshmen and 82% of continuing students received need-based aid. The average freshman award was $18,500. Of that total, scholarships or need-based grants averaged $8550; loans averaged $5950; and work contracts averaged $4000. All undergraduates work part time. Average annual earnings from campus work are $5000. The average financial indebtedness of the 2001 graduate was $23,000. Cornish is a member of CSS. The FAFSA and the college's own financial statement are required. The fall application deadline is March 1.

International Students: They must score 525 on the written TOEFL or 195 on the electronic version.

Computers: There are 16 Power Mac 7200s, 16 Mac LC 2s, and a Silicon Graphics workstation in the Design Lab for design students. There is also a computer lab, available to all students, containing 16 IBM Aptivas and 4 Power Macs with Word, Excel, and Photoshop. All students may access the system. There are no time limits. The fee is $50. It is recommended that students in design have personal computers; an Apple 64 laptop is recommended.

Graduates: In 2001, 110 bachelor's degrees were awarded. The most popular majors were design (26%), art (21%), and theater (21%). In an average class, 50% graduate in 4 years.

Admissions Contact: Jane Buckman, Associate Dean of Enrollment Services. E-mail: *admissions@cornish.edu* Web: *www.cornish.edu*

DEVRY UNIVERSITY/SEATTLE

Federal Way, WA 98001-2995 (253) 943-2800
Fax: (253) 943-3290

Full-time: 328 men, 75 women	**Faculty:** 11
Part-time: 126 men, 32 women	**Ph.D.s:** n/av
Graduate: none	**Student/Faculty:** 37 to 1
Year: semesters, summer session	**Tuition:** $10,065
Application Deadline: open	**Room & Board:** n/app

Freshman Class: 689 applied, 612 accepted, 325 enrolled
SAT I or ACT: recommended **LESS COMPETITIVE**

DeVry University/Seattle, formerly DeVry Institute of Technology, founded in 2001, is a private institution offering hands-on programs in electronics, business administration, computer information systems, telecommunications management, and information technology and computer engineering technology. The school is 1 of 23 DeVry schools throughout the United States and Canada. The library contains 2600 volumes, and subscribes to 1800 periodicals. Computerized library services include the card catalog, interlibrary loans, and database searching. Special learning facilities include a learning resource center and electronics and other labs. .

Student Life: 91% of undergraduates are from Washington. Others are from 15 states and 1 foreign country. 58% are white; 14% Asian American; 12% African American. The average age of all undergraduates is 24.

Housing: All students commute. Housing referrals can be obtained through the Student Housing Office. Alcohol is not permitted. All students may keep cars.

Activities: There are no fraternities or sororities. There are 4 groups on campus, including computers, professional, social, and yearbook. Popular campus events include Summer BBQ, Holiday Banquet, and Stress Breaks.

Sports: There is no sports program at DeVry.

Disabled Students: All of the campus is accessible. Wheelchair ramps, elevators, special parking, specially equipped rest rooms, lowered drinking fountains, and lowered telephones are available.

Services: Counseling and information services are available, as is tutoring in every subject.

Campus Safety and Security: Measures include informal discussions, emergency telephones, lighted pathways/sidewalks, and 17-hour patrols by trained security personnel and Emergency Response Team.

Programs of Study: DeVry confers the B.S. degree. Associate degrees are also awarded. Bachelor's degrees are awarded in BUSINESS (business administration and management), COMMUNICATIONS AND THE ARTS (telecommunications), COMPUTER AND PHYSICAL SCIENCE (computer programming and information sciences and systems), ENGINEERING AND ENVIRONMENTAL DESIGN (computer engineering and electrical/electronics engineering technology). Computer information systems and telecommunication are the largest.

Required: To graduate, students must achieve a GPA of at least 2.0 and satisfactorily complete all curriculum requirements, including 48 to 154 credits. Course requirements vary according to program. All first-semester students take courses in business organization, computer applications, algebra, psychology, and student success strategies.

Special: Accelerated degrees, co-op programs, nondegree study, and evening and weekend classes are possible.

Faculty/Classroom: All teach undergraduates. The average class size in an introductory lecture is 30; in a laboratory, 30; and in a regular course, 30.
Admissions: 89% of the 2001-2002 applicants were accepted.
Requirements: The SAT I or ACT is recommended. In addition, admissions requirements include graduation from a secondary school; the GED is also accepted. Applicants must pass the DeVry entrance exam or present satisfactory ACT or SAT I scores. An interview is required. Applications are accepted on-line at Embark.com. CLEP credit is accepted.
Procedure: Freshmen are admitted fall, spring, and summer. There is a deferred admissions plan. Application deadlines are open. The application fee is $50. Notification is sent on a rolling basis.
Transfer: 38 transfer students enrolled in 2001-2002. Applicants must present passing grades in all completed college course work, demonstrate language skills proficiency in at least 24 completed semester hours, and present evidence of math proficiency by appropriate college-level credits. 35% of 48 to 154 credits must be completed at DeVry.
Visiting: There are guides for informal visits and visitors may sit in on classes. To schedule a visit, contact Latanya Kibby, Assistant New Student Coordinator.
Financial Aid: 5% of undergraduates work part time. Average annual earnings from campus work are $7280. The FAFSA is required.
International Students: There are 4 international students enrolled. They must score 500 on the written TOEFL or 173 on the electronic version or DeVry's computerized placement test, achieving a minimum score that varies by program.
Admissions Contact: Kevin Puls, Director of Admissions.
Web: *www.sea.devry.edu*

EASTERN WASHINGTON UNIVERSITY E-2

Cheney, WA 99004-2496 **(509) 359-2397**
(888) 740-1914; Fax: (509) 359-6692

Full-time: 3041 men, 4031 women	**Faculty:** 352; IIA, --$
Part-time: 367 men, 519 women	**Ph.D.s:** 52%
Graduate: 320 men, 654 women	**Student/Faculty:** 20 to 1
Year: quarters, summer session	**Tuition:** $3186 ($10,452)
Application Deadline: March 1	**Room & Board:** $4786
Freshman Class: 3116 applied, 2668 accepted, 1199 enrolled	
SAT I Verbal/Math: 499/499	**ACT:** 20 **LESS COMPETITIVE**

Eastern Washington University, founded in 1882, is a comprehensive public university that provides programs in the arts and sciences, business, health sciences and nursing, and technology. There are 4 undergraduate schools and 1 graduate school. In addition to regional accreditation, EWU has baccalaureate program accreditation with AACSB, ABET, ADA, APTA, ASLA, CSAB, CSWE, NASM, NCATE, NLN, and NRPA. The library contains 759,977 volumes, 608,400 microform items, and 27,595 audiovisual forms/CDs, and subscribes to 4717 periodicals. Computerized library services include the card catalog, interlibrary loans, and database searching. Special learning facilities include a learning resource center, art gallery, natural history museum, planetarium, radio station, TV station, and Reid Laboratory Elementary School. The 35-acre campus is in a small town 18 miles southwest of Spokane. Including residence halls, there are 32 buildings.
Student Life: 91% of undergraduates are from Washington. Others are from 31 states, 30 foreign countries, and Canada. 98% are from public schools. 77% are white. The average age of freshmen is 19; all undergraduates, 25. 19% do not continue beyond their first year; 88% remain to graduate.
Housing: 2066 students can be accommodated in college housing, which includes coed dormitories, on-campus apartments, and married-student housing. In addition, there are all-male, all-female, academic, music, and drama floors, and floors for older students. On-campus housing is guaranteed for all 4 years. 80% of students commute. All students may keep cars.
Activities: 8% of men belong to 5 national fraternities; 6% of women belong to 1 local sorority and 4 national sororities. There are 99 groups on campus, including art, band, cheerleading, chess, choir, chorale, chorus, computers, dance, drama, ethnic, film, gay, honors, international, jazz band, literary magazine, marching band, musical theater, opera, orchestra, outdoor recreation, pep band, photography, political, professional, radio and TV, religious, social, social service, sports clubs, student government, symphony, and yearbook. Popular campus events include Club Vegas, Holiday in the Pub, and Spring Fling.
Sports: There are 6 intercollegiate sports for men and 7 for women, and 16 intramural sports for men and 14 for women. Facilities include a 200-meter indoor track, 12 racquetball courts, an indoor swimming pool, wrestling rooms, a dance studio, a 7000-seat stadium, a 5800-seat indoor gym, a fitness studio, and volleyball, baseball, and basketball courts.
Disabled Students: 93% of the campus is accessible. Wheelchair ramps, elevators, special parking, specially equipped rest rooms, special class scheduling, lowered drinking fountains, lowered telephones, and specially designed campus apartments are available.
Services: Counseling and information services are available, as is tutoring in every subject. There is a reader service for the blind, and remedial math, reading, and writing.
Campus Safety and Security: Measures include 24-hour foot and vehicle patrol, escort service, informal discussions, and pamphlets/posters/films. There are emergency telephones, lighted pathways/sidewalks, crisis lines, and emergency contact light standards.
Programs of Study: EWU confers B.A., B.S., B.A.B., B.A.E., B.D.H., B.F.A., B.Mu., and B.S.N. degrees. Master's degrees are also awarded. Bachelor's degrees are awarded in BIOLOGICAL SCIENCE (biochemistry, biology/biological science, botany, microbiology, and zoology), BUSINESS (accounting, banking and finance, business administration and management, management science, marketing/retailing/merchandising, personnel management, and recreation and leisure services), COMMUNICATIONS AND THE ARTS (art, art history and appreciation, broadcasting, communications, creative writing, dance, dramatic arts, English, French, German, graphic design, journalism, literature, music, music performance, Spanish, speech/debate/rhetoric, and studio art), COMPUTER AND PHYSICAL SCIENCE (chemistry, computer science, geology, information sciences and systems, mathematics, and physics), EDUCATION (art, computer, elementary, foreign languages, guidance, health, marketing and distribution, mathematics, middle school, music, physical, recreation, science, secondary, and social science), ENGINEERING AND ENVIRONMENTAL DESIGN (computer technology, mechanical engineering technology, and military science), HEALTH PROFESSIONS (dental hygiene, health care administration, medical laboratory technology, nursing, predentistry, premedicine, preveterinary science, recreation therapy, and speech pathology/audiology), SOCIAL SCIENCE (anthropology, criminal justice, economics, geography, history, humanities, international relations, parks and recreation management, philosophy, political science/government, prelaw, psychology, social science, social work, sociology, and urban studies). Health sciences, biology, and computer science are the strongest academically. Business, education, and social science are the largest.
Required: All students must complete 180 quarter credits, including 60 to 110 in their major, while earning a minimum GPA of 2.0. Specific requirements include English composition and math courses to demonstrate competency. Distribution requirements include 11 total courses from 3 breadth areas: humanities, natural sciences and math, and social sciences. Seniors must complete a capstone course.
Special: Cooperative programs in nursing, cross-registration with the Intercollegiate School of Nursing, internships with area businesses, and work-study based on federal financial aid are available. B.A.-B.S. degrees, dual majors in any subject, study abroad in 12 countries, 3 types of general studies degrees, student-designed majors, and a 3-2 engineering degree with Washington State University are offered. Credit for military experience, nondegree study, and pass/fail options for nonmajor or nonminor courses also are possible. There are 14 national honor societies, a freshman honors program, and 39 departmental honors programs.
Faculty/Classroom: 47% of faculty are male; 53%, female. 98% teach undergraduates.
Admissions: 86% of the 2001-2002 applicants were accepted. 43% of the current freshmen were in the top fifth of their class; 70% were in the top two fifths. There was 1 National Merit finalist.
Requirements: The SAT I or ACT is required. In addition, admission is determined by an index coordinating the GPA with entrance exam scores. The GED is accepted. EWU requires 4 years of English, 3 each of math and social science, 2 each of science (including a lab science) and a single foreign language (ASL accepted), and 1 of fine arts or academic electives. A GPA of 2.0 is required. AP and CLEP credits are accepted. Important factors in the admissions decision are recommendations by school officials, advanced placement or honor courses, and evidence of special talent. The university accepts applications on computer disk using XAPplication and ExPAN and on-line via the school's web site.
Procedure: Freshmen are admitted to all sessions. Entrance exams should be taken during the spring of the junior year or fall of the senior year. There is a deferred admissions plan. Applications should be filed by March 1 for fall entry, October 15 for winter entry, and February 15 for spring entry. Notification is sent on a rolling basis. A waiting list is an active part of the admissions procedure.
Transfer: 1087 transfer students enrolled in 2001-2002. Applicants with fewer than 40 credits must submit high school and college transcripts and test scores; those with more than 40 credits acceptable by Eastern or who have earned an associate degree from a Washington community college must submit a college transcript. 45 credits of 180 must be completed at EWU.
Visiting: There are regularly scheduled orientations for prospective students, consisting of overnight programs for students and parents that present informational sessions on campus life and academic survival skills, academic advising, course registration, and social functions. There are guides for informal visits and visitors may sit in on classes and stay overnight. To schedule a visit, contact the Admissions Office at (509) 359-6555.

Financial Aid: In 2001-2002, 81% of all freshmen and 56% of continuing students received some form of financial aid. 65% of freshmen and 57% of continuing students received need-based aid. The average freshman award was $7198. Of that total, scholarships or need-based grants averaged $3454 ($8730 maximum); loans averaged $1698 ($5625 maximum); and work contracts averaged $2046 ($3000 maximum). 89% of undergraduates work part time. Average annual earnings from campus work are $3000. The average financial indebtedness of the 2001 graduate was $15,280. The FAFSA is required. The fall application deadline is February 15.

International Students: There are 215 international students enrolled. The school actively recruits these students. They must score 525 on the written TOEFL.

Computers: The mainframe is a DEC VAX 6510 minicomputer. Students need an account number, available through classes. 5 computer labs and many specialized department labs are available. All students may access the system throughout the workday, plus evenings and weekends. There are no time limits. The fee is $7 per term.

Graduates: In 2001, 1527 bachelor's degrees were awarded. The most popular majors were education (21%), business administration (20%), and interdisiplinary studies (9%). 60 companies recruited on campus in 2000-2001.

Admissions Contact: Michelle Whittingham, Director of Admissions. A video is available. E-mail: *admissions@mail.ewu.edu*
Web: *www.ewu.edu*

EVERGREEN STATE COLLEGE — B-3
Olympia, WA 98505 — (360) 867-6170, ext. 6170
Fax: (360) 867-6576

Full-time: 1470 men, 2016 women	**Faculty:** 200
Part-time: 200 men, 315 women	**Ph.D.s:** 75%
Graduate: 90 men, 136 women	**Student/Faculty:** 17 to 1
Year: quarters, summer session	**Tuition:** $3097 ($10,837)
Application Deadline: March 1	**Room & Board:** $5610
Freshman Class: 3380 applied, 2918 accepted, 1531 enrolled	
SAT I Verbal/Math: 586/536	**COMPETITIVE**

The Evergreen State College, founded in 1967 and opened in 1971, is a public liberal arts college offering team-taught, interdisciplinary studies that culminate with written evaluations. The library contains 435,119 volumes, 486,818 microform items, and 15,033 audiovisual forms/CDs, and subscribes to 2636 periodicals. Computerized library services include the card catalog, interlibrary loans, and database searching. Special learning facilities include a learning resource center, art gallery, radio station, communications lab, Longhouse Cultural Center, and Art Annex. The 1000-acre campus is in a small town 7 miles west of Olympia. Including residence halls, there are 72 buildings.

Student Life: 77% of undergraduates are from Washington. Others are from 46 states, 14 foreign countries, and Canada. 82% are white. The average age of freshmen is 19; all undergraduates, 26. 31% do not continue beyond their first year; 55% remain to graduate.

Housing: 1000 students can be accommodated in college housing, which includes coed on-campus apartments. In addition, there is drug-free, alcohol-free, first-year experience, and quiet housing. On-campus housing is guaranteed for the freshman year only and is available on a first-come, first-served basis. 80% of students commute. Alcohol is not permitted. All students may keep cars.

Activities: There are no fraternities or sororities. There are 53 groups on campus, including art, chorale, dance, drama, ethnic, film, gay, international, literary magazine, newspaper, photography, political, radio and TV, religious, social, social service, and student government. Popular campus events include Super Saturday, Evergreen Expressions Series, and Olympia Film Society festivals.

Sports: There are 6 intercollegiate sports for men and 6 for women, and 10 intramural sports for men and 10 for women. Facilities include a recreation center, which houses an 11-lane swimming pool, a diving well, exercise and weight training rooms, 5 racquetball courts, and indoor climbing walls. There is a 3100-seat gym, a covered pavilion, 4 tennis courts, and 5 playing fields.

Disabled Students: All of the campus is accessible. Wheelchair ramps, elevators, special parking, specially equipped rest rooms, lowered drinking fountains, and lowered telephones are available.

Services: Counseling and information services are available, as is tutoring in most subjects. There is a reader service for the blind.

Campus Safety and Security: Measures include 24-hour foot and vehicle patrol, self-defense education, escort service, and informal discussions. There are pamphlets/posters/films, emergency telephones, and lighted pathways/sidewalks.

Programs of Study: Evergreen confers B.A. and B.S. degrees. Master's degrees are also awarded. Bachelor's degrees are awarded in SOCIAL SCIENCE (liberal arts/general studies). Liberal arts and sciences is the strongest academically and has the largest enrollment.

Required: Students must earn a minimum of 180 quarter hours of credit to receive a bachelor's degree. There are no other requirements.

Special: All work at the college is interdisciplinary, and the programs of study change annually. The college's credit-generating options include the comprehensive Coordinated Study Program, which allows students and faculty to work together intensively. Credits may be earned through cooperative programs, work-study programs, internships, or from prior learning and military experience. All majors are awarded in liberal arts and sciences. A B.A.-B.S. combined degree is possible in liberal arts. Study abroad is possible in France, Japan, Russia, Central America, Ireland, Mexico, Egypt, and Southeast Asia.

Faculty/Classroom: 52% of faculty are male; 48%, female. All teach undergraduates. No introductory courses are taught by graduate students.

Admissions: 86% of the 2001-2002 applicants were accepted. The SAT I scores for the 2001-2002 freshman class were: Verbal--15% below 500, 37% between 500 and 599, 38% between 600 and 700, and 10% above 700; Math--30% below 500, 49% between 500 and 599, 19% between 600 and 700, and 2% above 700.

Requirements: The SAT I or ACT is required. In addition, candidates should be graduates of an accredited secondary school and have completed 15 academic credits, consisting of 4 in English, 3 each in math and social studies, 2 each in foreign language and science, and 1 in fine or performing arts. A GED certificate is acceptable. A GPA of 2.0 is required. AP and CLEP credits are accepted.

Procedure: Freshmen are admitted fall, winter, and spring. Entrance exams should be taken during the spring of the junior year or fall of the senior year. Applications should be filed by March 1 for fall entry, October 1 for winter entry, and December 1 for spring entry, along with a $35 fee. Notification is sent April 1.

Transfer: 957 transfer students enrolled in 2001-2002. Applicants with fewer than 40 credits must submit SAT I or ACT scores and a high school transcript. A 2.0 minimum GPA is required. An associate degree is recommended. All applicants must submit all college transcripts. 45 credits of 180 must be completed at Evergreen.

Visiting: There are regularly scheduled orientations for prospective students, including an admissions session, a class visit, and a tour. There are guides for informal visits and visitors may sit in on classes. To schedule a visit, contact the Student Visitor Program.

Financial Aid: In 2001-2002, 59% of all freshmen and 54% of continuing students received some form of financial aid. 50% of all students received need-based aid. The average freshman award was $10,292. Of that total, scholarships or need-based grants averaged $2620 ($12,600 maximum); loans averaged $5805 ($20,769 maximum); and work contracts averaged $1867 ($3000 maximum). 31% of undergraduates work part time. Average annual earnings from campus work are $1563. The average financial indebtedness of the 2001 graduate was $15,541. Evergreen is a member of CSS. The FAFSA, the college's own financial statement, and the institutional data sheet are required. The fall application deadline is March 15.

International Students: There are 28 international students enrolled. They must score 525 on the written TOEFL and also take the SAT I or the ACT.

Computers: The mainframe is a DEC VAX Cluster. There are 157 Windows systems and 58 Mac general-access systems in the computer center and various labs, providing network access to various servers and the Internet/Web. All students may access the system 18 hours per day. There are no time limits and no fees.

Graduates: In 2001, 1191 bachelor's degrees were awarded. The most popular major was liberal arts and sciences (100%). In an average class, 5% graduate in 3 years, 42% in 4 years, 52% in 5 years, and 55% in 6 years. 53 companies recruited on campus in 2000-2001. Of the 2000 graduating class, 17% were enrolled in graduate school within 6 months of graduation and 84% were employed.

Admissions Contact: Qy-Anna Manning, Admissions Counselor. A video is available. E-mail: *admissions@evergreen.edu*
Web: *www.evergreen.edu*

GONZAGA UNIVERSITY — E-2
Spokane, WA 99258-0001 — (509) 323-6572
(800) 322-2584; Fax: (509) 324-5780

Full-time: 1521 men, 1774 women	**Faculty:** 260
Part-time: 65 men, 123 women	**Ph.D.s:** 86%
Graduate: 683 men, 962 women	**Student/Faculty:** 13 to 1
Year: semesters, summer session	**Tuition:** $18,596
Application Deadline: February 1	**Room & Board:** $5680
Freshman Class: 2471 accepted, 971 enrolled	
SAT I Verbal/Math: 580/590	**ACT:** 26
	HIGHLY COMPETITIVE+

Gonzaga University, founded in 1887, is a private, liberal arts institution affiliated with the Roman Catholic Church and the Society of Jesus (Jesuits). The university offers undergraduate and graduate degrees in arts and sciences, business, education, engineering, and professional studies. There are 5 undergraduate and 5 graduate schools. In addition to regional accreditation, Gonzaga has baccalaureate program accreditation with AACSB, ABET, NCATE, and NLN. The 2 libraries contain 339,151 volumes, 549,045 microform items, and 3037 audiovisual forms/CDs, and subscribe to 1448 periodicals. Computerized library services include the card catalog, interlibrary loans, and database searching. Special learning facilities include a learning resource center, art gallery, radio station, and TV station. The 108-acre campus is in an urban area near downtown Spokane. Including residence halls, there are 97 buildings.

Student Life: 54% of undergraduates are from out of state, mostly the West. Students are from 34 states, 35 foreign countries, and Canada. 65% are from public schools. 76% are white. 54% are Catholic; 20% claim no religious affiliation. The average age of freshmen is 18; all undergraduates, 21. 10% do not continue beyond their first year; 66% remain to graduate.

Housing: 1925 students can be accommodated in college housing, which includes single-sex and coed dormitories, on-campus apartments, off-campus apartments, and married-student housing. In addition, there are honors houses, special-interest houses, and a first-year experience hall. On-campus housing is available on a first-come, first-served basis and is available on a lottery system for upperclassmen. Priority is given to out-of-town students. 53% of students live on campus; of those, 88% remain on campus on weekends. Alcohol is not permitted. All students may keep cars.

Activities: There are no fraternities or sororities. There are 88 groups on campus, including art, band, cheerleading, chess, choir, chorale, chorus, computers, dance, debate, drama, drill team, ethnic, gay, honors, international, jazz band, literary magazine, musical theater, newspaper, orchestra, pep band, photography, political, professional, radio and TV, religious, social, social service, student government, symphony, and yearbook. Popular campus events include Search, Charity Ball, and Fall Family Weekend.

Sports: There are 7 intercollegiate sports for men and 7 for women, and 8 intramural sports for men and 8 for women. Facilities include an athletic center with an indoor running track, a full-size pool, a weight room, a dance studio, 6 basketball/volleyball courts, 8 racquetball courts, tennis courts, and a fitness room.

Disabled Students: 90% of the campus is accessible. Wheelchair ramps, elevators, special parking, specially equipped rest rooms, special class scheduling, lowered drinking fountains, and lowered telephones are available. Academic adjustments are provided for students with disabilities who provide appropriate documentation and request services from Disabilities Support Services.

Services: There is a reader service for the blind. Informal peer tutoring in English and math is available.

Campus Safety and Security: Measures include 24-hour foot and vehicle patrol, escort service, informal discussions, and pamphlets/posters/films. There are emergency telephones and lighted pathways/sidewalks.

Programs of Study: Gonzaga confers B.A., B.S., B.B.A., B.E., B.G.S., and B.S.N. degrees. Master's and doctoral degrees are also awarded. Bachelor's degrees are awarded in BIOLOGICAL SCIENCE (biology/biological science), BUSINESS (accounting, business administration and management, and business economics), COMMUNICATIONS AND THE ARTS (art, broadcasting, dramatic arts, English, French, German, journalism, literature, music, public relations, Spanish, and speech/debate/rhetoric), COMPUTER AND PHYSICAL SCIENCE (chemistry, computer science, mathematics, and physics), EDUCATION (music, physical, and special), ENGINEERING AND ENVIRONMENTAL DESIGN (civil engineering, computer engineering, electrical/electronics engineering, and mechanical engineering), HEALTH PROFESSIONS (exercise science and nursing), SOCIAL SCIENCE (classical/ancient civilization, criminal justice, economics, history, interdisciplinary studies, international studies, Italian studies, liberal arts/general studies, philosophy, political science/government, psychology, religion, and sociology). Engineering and business administration are the strongest academically. Business, engineering, and history are the largest.

Required: All students must complete 128 credit hours with a minimum 2.0 GPA. The major requirements are 18 hours in upper-division courses and supporting courses required by the major department. Students must complete 9 credits each of philosophy and religious studies, 7 credits in English, speech, and critical thinking, and 3 credits each in math and English literature.

Special: Cross-registration with Whitworth College and the Intercollegiate Consortium for Nursing Education, internships, study abroad in 9 countries, a Washington semester, and on- and off-campus work-study programs are offered. High school juniors and seniors may take 6 credits per semester. There is a limited pass/fail option, and an accelerated general studies degree and dual majors are possible. There are 9 national honor societies, and a freshman honors program.

Faculty/Classroom: 67% of faculty are male; 33%, female. 93% teach undergraduates. No introductory courses are taught by graduate students. The average class size in an introductory lecture is 22; in a laboratory, 15; and in a regular course, 22.

Admissions: The SAT I scores for the 2001-2002 freshman class were: Verbal--22% below 500, 43% between 500 and 599, 30% between 600 and 700, and 5% above 700; Math--20% below 500, 46% between 500 and 599, 30% between 600 and 700, and 4% above 700. The ACT scores were 6% below 21, 21% between 21 and 23, 25% between 24 and 26, 24% between 27 and 28, and 24% above 28. 62% of the current freshmen were in the top fifth of their class; 86% were in the top two fifths. There were 16 National Merit finalists and 16 semifinalists. 28 freshmen graduated first in their class.

Requirements: The SAT I or ACT is required. In addition, applicants should be graduates of an accredited secondary school or hold a GED certificate. They must have completed 17 academic credits consisting of 4 years of English, 3 of math, 2 of a foreign language, 1 each of history and science, and 6 years of electives, 4 of which must be from the above subjects and the arts. An essay and letters of recommendation are required. An interview is recommended. AP and CLEP credits are accepted. Important factors in the admissions decision are advanced placement or honor courses, leadership record, and extracurricular activities record. Applications are accepted on computer disk and on-line via Apply, CollegeLink, CollegeView, ExPAN, and the school's web site.

Procedure: Freshmen are admitted fall and spring. Entrance exams should be taken by May of the junior year. There are early action and deferred admissions plans. Applications should be filed by February 1 for fall entry and December 1 for spring entry. The fall 2001 application fee was $40. Notification is sent on a rolling basis. 4% of all applicants are on a waiting list; 19 were accepted in 2001.

Transfer: 227 transfer students enrolled in 2001-2002. A minimum GPA of 2.7 is required. Students younger than 21 must submit test scores for the SAT I or ACT. An interview is recommended. 30 credits of 128 must be completed at Gonzaga.

Visiting: There are regularly scheduled orientations for prospective students. Day visits are permitted Monday through Friday; overnight visits, Sunday through Thursday (except for holiday periods). There are guides for informal visits and visitors may sit in on classes and stay overnight. To schedule a visit, contact the Admissions Office Visitation Coordinator at (800) 322-2584, ext. 6531 or *holmberg@gonzaga.edu*.

Financial Aid: In 2001-2002, 96% of all freshmen and 90% of continuing students received some form of financial aid. 64% of freshmen and 60% of continuing students received need-based aid. The average freshman award was $15,566. Of that total, scholarships or need-based grants averaged $9807; loans averaged $3425; and work contracts averaged $2334. 21% of undergraduates work part time. Average annual earnings from campus work are $2392. The average financial indebtedness of the 2001 graduate was $21,166. Gonzaga is a member of CSS. The FAFSA is required. The fall application deadline is February 1.

International Students: There are 69 international students enrolled. The school actively recruits these students. They must score 530 on the written TOEFL or take the MELAB. They must also take the ESL Exit Exam, which includes a writing test.

Computers: The mainframe is an HP-UX11.0 L200. The central academic system is available from more than 300 PCs spread throughout 11 computer labs. Students may also access the system from the residence hall Ethernet network or directly through the Internet. All students may access the system 24 hours per day. There are no time limits and no fees. It is strongly recommended that all students have a personal computer.

Graduates: In 2001, 562 bachelor's degrees were awarded. The most popular majors were business and management (20%), social studies and history (15%), and communications (12%). In an average class, 1% graduate in 3 years, 55% in 4 years, 62% in 5 years, and 65% in 6 years. 97 companies recruited on campus in 2000-2001.

Admissions Contact: Dr. Philip Ballinger, Dean of Admission. A video is available. E-mail: *ballinger@gu.gonzaga.edu*
Web: *www.gonzaga.edu*

HENRY COGSWELL COLLEGE

Everett, WA 98201 — **C-2**

(425) 258-3351
(866) 411-HCC1; Fax: (425) 257-0405

Full-time: 129 men, 36 women	**Faculty:** 14
Part-time: 76 men, 17 women	**Ph.D.s:** 90%
Graduate: none	**Student/Faculty:** 12 to 1
Year: trimesters, summer session	**Tuition:** $13,080
Application Deadline: open	**Room & Board:** n/app
Freshman Class: 33 applied, 27 accepted, 18 enrolled	
SAT I Verbal/Math: 540/550	**ACT:** 26 **SPECIAL**

Henry Cogswell College, established in 1979, is a private institution specializing in business, engineering, computer science, and digital arts. There are 3 undergraduate schools. In addition to regional accreditation, Cogswell has baccalaureate program accreditation with ABET and IACBE. The library contains 6557 volumes and 52 audiovisual forms/CDs, and subscribes to 59 periodicals. Computerized library services include the card catalog, interlibrary loans, and database searching. Special learning facilities include a learning resource center. The 1-acre campus is in a suburban area 30 miles north of Seattle. There are 2 buildings.

Student Life: 98% of undergraduates are from Washington. Others are from 3 states and 2 foreign countries. 96% are from public schools. 77%

are white; 14% Asian American. The average age of freshmen is 19; all undergraduates, 25. 33% do not continue beyond their first year; 67% remain to graduate.

Housing: There are no residence halls. All of students commute. Alcohol is not permitted.

Activities: There are no fraternities or sororities. There are 5 groups on campus, including ASME, IEEE, indoor climbing club, student government, and Tau Alpha Phi.

Sports: There is no sports program at Cogswell.

Disabled Students: 95% of the campus is accessible. Wheelchair ramps, elevators, special parking, specially equipped rest rooms, lowered drinking fountains, and lowered telephones are available.

Services: Counseling and information services are available, as is tutoring in most subjects. There is remedial math and writing.

Campus Safety and Security: Measures include informal discussions, pamphlets/posters/films, and lighted pathways/sidewalks.

Programs of Study: Cogswell confers B.A., B.S., B.S.E.E., and B.S.M.E. degrees. Bachelor's degrees are awarded in BUSINESS (business administration and management and management science), COMPUTER AND PHYSICAL SCIENCE (computer science and digital arts/technology), ENGINEERING AND ENVIRONMENTAL DESIGN (computer graphics, electrical/electronics engineering, mechanical engineering, and mechanical engineering technology). Electrical engineering is the strongest academically. Mechanical engineering and digital arts are the largest.

Required: Students must complete a minimum of 121 trimester hours, including 51 in the major, and maintain a minimum 2.0 GPA. The core curriculum includes a minimum of 20 credits in humanities and social sciences, 3 classes each in written and oral communication, and classes in math, lab sciences, and moral and ethical problems. A senior thesis or project is required.

Special: There is an accelerated degree program in all majors. Internships are available in all majors. There is 1 national honor society.

Faculty/Classroom: 93% of faculty are male; 7%, female. All teach undergraduates. The average class size in an introductory lecture is 15; in a laboratory, 15; and in a regular course, 10.

Admissions: 82% of the 2001-2002 applicants were accepted. The SAT I scores for the 2001-2002 freshman class were: Verbal--30% below 500, 42% between 500 and 599, 24% between 600 and 700, and 4% above 700; Math--31% below 500, 41% between 500 and 599, 21% between 600 and 700, and 9% above 700. The ACT scores were all between 24 and 26.

Requirements: The SAT I is required; the ACT is accepted. A high school diploma or GED is required. A portfolio is required of all art students. A GPA of 2.5 is required. AP and CLEP credits are accepted. Applications are accepted on-line at *www.henrycogswell.edu* through CollegeNET.

Procedure: Freshmen are admitted in the fall. Entrance exams should be taken prior to registration. There is an early decision plan. Application deadlines are open. Application fee is $50. Notification is sent on a rolling basis. 1 early decision candidate was accepted for the 2001-2002 class.

Transfer: 35 transfer students enrolled in 2001-2002. Transferring students must forward all transcripts from previously attended schools and take placement exams. 30 credits of 121 must be completed at Cogswell.

Visiting: There are regularly scheduled orientations for prospective students each month, from 10 A.M. to 2 P.M. 2 open houses are held each year in the fall. There are guides for informal visits and visitors may sit in on classes. To schedule a visit, contact Cristy Null, Admissions Counselor.

Financial Aid: In 2001-2002, 46% of all freshmen and 38% of continuing students received some form of financial aid. 71% of freshmen and 73% of continuing students received need-based aid. The average freshman award was $9556. Of that total, loans averaged $9556 ($16,386 maximum). 4% of undergraduates work part time. Average annual earnings from campus work are $750. The average financial indebtedness of the 2001 graduate was $22,650. Cogswell is a member of CSS. The CSS/Profile, FAFSA, FFS, or SFS and the college's own financial statement are required. The fall application deadline is September 1.

International Students: There are 2 international students enrolled. The school actively recruits these students. They must score 550 on the written TOEFL or 213 on the electronic version and also take the SAT I or the ACT, scoring 950 on the SAT I.

Computers: The mainframe is a DEC MicroVAX AS/400. A PC lab and main computer lab are available. PCs are also available in the library. All students may access the system. There are no time limits and no fees.

Graduates: In 2001, 32 bachelor's degrees were awarded. The most popular majors were digital arts (34%), mechanical engineering (34%), and electrical engineering (19%). In an average class, 70% graduate in 3 years, and 30% in 6 years.

Admissions Contact: Cristy Null, Admissions Counselor.
E-mail: *cn@henrycogswell.edu* or *information@henrycogswell*
Web: *www.henrycogswell.edu*

HERITAGE COLLEGE

Toppenish, WA 98948 — D-3 — **(509) 865-8500; Fax: (509) 865-4469**

Full-time: 90 men, 235 women	**Faculty:** 35; IIB, --$
Part-time: 100 men, 245 women	**Ph.D.s:** 95%
Graduate: 145 men, 345 women	**Student/Faculty:** 9 to 1
Year: semesters, summer session	**Tuition:** $6500
Application Deadline: open	**Room & Board:** n/app
Freshman Class: n/av	
SAT I or ACT: recommended	**NONCOMPETITIVE**

Heritage College, founded in 1982, is a private, nonprofit commuter college offering undergraduate and graduate programs in liberal arts and teacher education, half of which are given on evenings and weekends. Figures in the above capsule are approximate. The library contains 40,000 volumes, 4850 microform items, and 70 audiovisual forms/CDs, and subscribes to 200 periodicals. Computerized library services include database searching. Special learning facilities include a learning resource center. The 19-acre campus is in a rural area 20 miles south of Yakima. There are 15 buildings.

Student Life: 99% of undergraduates are from Washington. Others are from 2 states and 2 foreign countries. 46% are white; 32% Hispanic; 20% Native American/Eskimo. The average age of freshmen is 35; all undergraduates, 35.

Housing: There are no residence halls. All students commute. Alcohol is not permitted. All students may keep cars.

Activities: There are no fraternities or sororities. There are 5 groups on campus, including computers, ethnic, literary magazine, newspaper, and student government.

Disabled Students: Wheelchair ramps, special parking, specially equipped rest rooms, special class scheduling, and lowered drinking fountains are available.

Services: Counseling and information services are available, as is tutoring in most subjects. There is remedial math, reading, and writing.

Campus Safety and Security: Measures include lighted pathways/sidewalks.

Programs of Study: Heritage confers B.A., B.S., and B.A.Ed., and B.S.W. degrees. Associate and master's degrees are also awarded. Bachelor's degrees are awarded in BUSINESS (business administration and management), COMMUNICATIONS AND THE ARTS (English and Spanish), COMPUTER AND PHYSICAL SCIENCE (computer science, mathematics, and science), EDUCATION (elementary, science, secondary, and social studies), ENGINEERING AND ENVIRONMENTAL DESIGN (environmental science), SOCIAL SCIENCE (interdisciplinary studies, psychology, public administration, social work, and sociology). Education is the largest.

Required: All students must complete 40 credits of general college requirements, which include 12 credits each in arts and letters, 10 credits in science and math, 9 credits in social sciences, 1 year of English, a computer course, a math course above the 100-level, and a world civilization course. At least 126 semester credit hours must be completed, with at least 48 upper-division credits. The education major must have a minimum GPA of 2.5; others must have a 2.0.

Special: Heritage provides individualized assistance. Credit by examination is available in many courses, and credit may be given for work experience. The college also has cooperative programs with 3 school districts and internships in local businesses and social service agencies. Pass/fail options are possible for some courses. An accelerated degree program is available in business adminstration.

Faculty/Classroom: 47% of faculty are male; 53%, female. No introductory courses are taught by graduate students. The average class size in an introductory lecture is 20; in a laboratory, 16; and in a regular course, 20.

Requirements: The SAT I or ACT is recommended, but entrance exams are not required. Applicants must have graduated from an accredited secondary school or hold a GED certificate. An interview is recommended. Assessment for placement in English and math courses is required. AP and CLEP credits are accepted.

Procedure: Freshmen are admitted to all sessions. Application deadlines are open. Check with the school for current fee.

Transfer: 32 credits of 126 must be completed at Heritage.

Visiting: There are regularly scheduled orientations for prospective students, consisting of a day and an evening fall orientation. There are guides for informal visits and visitors may sit in on classes. To schedule a visit, contact the Director of Admissions.

Financial Aid: 45% of undergraduates work part time. Average annual earnings from campus work are $3000. The average financial indebtedness of a recent graduate was $5000. Heritage is a member of CSS. The CSS/Profile, the college's own financial statement, financial aid transcripts from colleges previously attended, and a copy of income tax returns are required. Check with the school for current deadlines.

International Students: There are 1 international students enrolled. They must score 500 on the written TOEFL.

Computers: The mainframes are a VT420 and a DEC VAX for administrative use. There are 150 networked terminals; 26 are always available for student use. Others are available when classes are not scheduled in the rooms. All students may access the system. There are no time limits and no fees.

Graduates: In a recent year, 78 bachelor's degrees were awarded. The most popular majors were education (30%), social science/social work (24%), and business (11%).

Admissions Contact: Norberto Espindola, Director of Admissions. E-mail: *espindola_b@heritage.edu* Web: *www.heritage.edu*

NORTHWEST COLLEGE C-2
Kirkland, WA 98033 (425) 889-5598
(800) 669-3781; Fax: (425) 827-0148

Full-time: 398 men, 600 women	**Faculty:** 49; IIB, --$
Part-time: 22 men, 26 women	**Ph.D.s:** 41%
Graduate: 4 men, 16 women	**Student/Faculty:** 20 to 1
Year: semesters, summer session	**Tuition:** $11,763
Application Deadline: August 1	**Room & Board:** $5708
Freshman Class: 618 applied, 382 accepted, 300 enrolled	
SAT I or ACT: required	**COMPETITIVE**

Since 1934, Northwest College has prepared students for service and leadership, offering programs in ministry, business, nursing, and education. There is 1 graduate school. In addition to regional accreditation, NC has baccalaureate program accreditation with AACTE. The library contains 100,000 volumes and subscribes to 600 periodicals. Computerized library services include the card catalog, interlibrary loans, and database searching. Special learning facilities include a radio station. The 56-acre campus is in a suburban area in Kirkland, 10 miles east of Seattle and overlooking Lake Washington. Including residence halls, there are 27 buildings.

Student Life: 79% of undergraduates are from Washington. Others are from 23 states, 15 foreign countries, and Canada. 60% are white. Most are Protestant. The average age of freshmen is 19; all undergraduates, 25. 30% do not continue beyond their first year; 34% remain to graduate.

Housing: 510 students can be accommodated in college housing, which includes single-sex dormitories, on-campus apartments, and married-student housing. On-campus housing is guaranteed for all 4 years. 56% of students commute. Alcohol is not permitted. All students may keep cars.

Activities: There are no fraternities or sororities. There are 20 groups on campus, including band, choir, chorale, chorus, debate, drama, forensics, international, musical theater, newspaper, orchestra, photography, professional, radio, religious, social, social service, and student government. Popular campus events include Harvest Time Social, All-School Banquet, and Roomies Night-out.

Sports: There are 4 intercollegiate sports for men and 4 for women, and 2 intramural sports for men and 2 for women. Facilities include a gym pavilion, outdoor tennis courts, a practice field for soccer and intramural football, access to the Seattle Seahawks' fields, outdoor basketball, and sand volleyball.

Disabled Students: 75% of the campus is accessible. Wheelchair ramps, elevators, special parking, specially equipped rest rooms, and residence hall restrooms and shower facilities are available.

Services: There is a reader service for the blind and remedial writing. The Student Success Office provides assistance in most areas, including study skills.

Campus Safety and Security: Measures include 24-hour foot and vehicle patrol, escort service, informal discussions, and pamphlets/posters/films. There are emergency telephones and lighted pathways/sidewalks.

Programs of Study: NC confers the B.A. degree. Associate and master's degrees are also awarded. Bachelor's degrees are awarded in BIOLOGICAL SCIENCE (life science), BUSINESS (business administration and management), EDUCATION (education), SOCIAL SCIENCE (behavioral science, biblical studies, interdisciplinary studies, ministries, religion, and religious music). Teacher education, business, and psychology are the strongest academically. Teacher education, church ministries, business, and psychology are the largest.

Required: Students must complete 18 credits in humanities, 16 in religion, 12 in social science, and 10 each in science and math. At least 125 semester credits (up to 139 for teacher education), with a minimum GPA of 2.0, are required. The number of semester credits needed in the major varies from 36 to 50.

Special: Northwest offers study in several locations in the United States. and foreign countries through the Council for Christian Colleges and Universities. Dual majors are available. There is 1 departmental honors program.

Faculty/Classroom: 65% of faculty are male; 35%, female. All teach undergraduates. The average class size in an introductory lecture is 30; in a laboratory, 20; and in a regular course, 24.

Admissions: 62% of the 2001-2002 applicants were accepted.

Requirements: The SAT I or ACT is required. A GPA of 2.3 is required. AP and CLEP credits are accepted. Important factors in the admissions decision are personality/intangible qualities, recommendations by alumni, and leadership record.

Procedure: Freshmen are admitted to all sessions. Entrance exams should be taken in the spring of the junior year. There are early decision and deferred admissions plans. Early decision applications should be filed by November 15; regular applications, by August 1 for fall entry, December 15 for spring entry, and April 15 for summer entry. The fall 2001 application fee was $30. Notification of early decision is sent December 1; regular decision, on a rolling basis. 20 early decision candidates were accepted for the 2001-2002 class.

Transfer: 205 transfer students enrolled in 2001-2002. Transfers must have a minimum 2.3 GPA from high school and college and must submit SAT I or ACT scores, an essay, and 2 letters of reference. 30 credits of 125 must be completed at NC.

Visiting: There are regularly scheduled orientations for prospective students, including Northwest Fridays. There are guides for informal visits and visitors may sit in on classes and stay overnight. To schedule a visit, contact Mark Sterley at (425) 889-5343 or *mark.sterley@ncag.edu*.

Financial Aid: In 2001-2002, 77% of all freshmen and 66% of continuing students received some form of financial aid. 77% of freshmen and 61% of continuing students received need-based aid. The average freshman award was $7254. Of that total, scholarships or need-based grants averaged $2379 ($5775 maximum); loans averaged $2625 (maximum); and work contracts averaged $2250 ($2500 maximum). 78% of undergraduates work part time. Average annual earnings from campus work are $2000. The average financial indebtedness of the 2001 graduate was $14,692. The FAFSA and the college's own financial statement are required. The fall application deadline is March 1.

International Students: There are 28 international students enrolled. They must score 500 on the written TOEFL.

Computers: The campus has several computer centers. Each residence hall room has network and Internet access. All students are licensed for access to Microsoft Office Products (software provided). All students may access the system set hours for labs; residence halls are always connected. There are no time limits. The fee is $50 per semester. It is strongly recommended that all students have a personal computer.

Graduates: In 2001, 188 bachelor's degrees were awarded. The most popular majors were organizational management (57%), psychology (23%), and education (20%). In an average class, 33% graduate in 6 years.

Admissions Contact: Rose Smith, Director, Enrollment Services. A video is available. E-mail: *admissions@ncag.edu*
Web: *www.nwcollege.edu*

PACIFIC LUTHERAN UNIVERSITY C-2
Tacoma, WA 98447 (253) 535-7151
(800) 274-6758; Fax: (253) 536-5136

Full-time: 1123 men, 1785 women	**Faculty:** 216; IIA, --$
Part-time: 112 men, 164 women	**Ph.D.s:** 84%
Graduate: 106 men, 136 women	**Student/Faculty:** 13 to 1
Year: 4-1-4, summer session	**Tuition:** $17,728
Application Deadline: open	**Room & Board:** $5590
Freshman Class: 1512 applied, 1455 accepted, 581 enrolled	
SAT I Verbal/Math: 550/550	**ACT:** 24 **VERY COMPETITIVE**

Pacific Lutheran University, founded in 1890, is an independent, nonprofit institution affiliated with the Evangelical Lutheran Church in America. PLU offers programs in arts and sciences, business, education, nursing, fine arts, and phys ed. There are 6 undergraduate schools and 1 graduate school. In addition to regional accreditation, PLU has baccalaureate program accreditation with AACSB, ABET, CSAB, CSWE, NASM, NCATE, and NLN. The library contains 617,219 volumes, 231,968 microform items, and 13,416 audiovisual forms/CDs, and subscribes to 1863 periodicals. Computerized library services include the card catalog, interlibrary loans, and database searching. Special learning facilities include a learning resource center, art gallery, radio station, TV station, herbarium, invertebrate and vertebrate museums, biology field station, Northwest history collections, Scandinavian history collection, and language resource center. The 126-acre campus is in a suburban area 7 miles south of Tacoma. Including residence halls, there are 41 buildings.

Student Life: 71% of undergraduates are from Washington. Others are from 39 states, 30 foreign countries, and Canada. 97% are from public schools. 75% are white. Most are Protestant. The average age of freshmen is 18; all undergraduates, 23. 18% do not continue beyond their first year; 82% remain to graduate.

Housing: 1650 students can be accommodated in college housing, which includes single-sex and coed dormitories, on-campus apartments, and married-student housing. On-campus housing is guaranteed for the freshman year only. 50% of students live on campus; of those, 75% remain on campus on weekends. Alcohol is not permitted. All students may keep cars.

Activities: There are no fraternities or sororities. There are 45 groups on campus, including adult student, advertising, art, band, cheerleading, choir, chorale, chorus, comedy, commuter, computers, dance, debate, drama, ethnic, film, gay, honors, international, jazz band, literary magazine, musical theater, newspaper, opera, orchestra, pep band, photography, political, professional, radio and TV, religious, social, social service, student government, symphony, and yearbook. Popular campus events include Lucia Bride Festival, Songfest, and Family Weekend.

Sports: There are 11 intercollegiate sports for men and 10 for women, and 12 intramural sports for men and 12 for women. Facilities include a 4000-seat gym, a 4000-seat auditorium, a fitness center with an all-weather track, a 9-hole golf course, a swimming pool, and racquetball, squash, and tennis courts.

Disabled Students: 90% of the campus is accessible. Wheelchair ramps, elevators, special parking, specially equipped rest rooms, special class scheduling, lowered drinking fountains, and lowered telephones are available.

Services: Counseling and information services are available, as is tutoring in most subjects. Study groups and pretest and posttest reviews are also available.

Campus Safety and Security: Measures include 24-hour foot and vehicle patrol, self-defense education, escort service, and informal discussions. There are pamphlets/posters/films, emergency telephones, and lighted pathways/sidewalks.

Programs of Study: PLU confers B.A., B.S., B.A.E., B.A.P.E., B.A.Rec., B.B.A., B.F.A., B.M., B.M.A., B.M.Ed., B.S.N., and B.S.P.E. degrees. Master's degrees are also awarded. Bachelor's degrees are awarded in BIOLOGICAL SCIENCE (biology/biological science), BUSINESS (business administration and management, and recreation and leisure services), COMMUNICATIONS AND THE ARTS (art, classics, communications, English, fine arts, French, German, music, music performance, music theory and composition, piano/organ, Scandinavian languages, Spanish, and voice), COMPUTER AND PHYSICAL SCIENCE (applied physics, chemistry, computer programming, computer science, geoscience, mathematics, and physics), EDUCATION (education, music, and physical), ENGINEERING AND ENVIRONMENTAL DESIGN (computer engineering, engineering and applied science, and environmental science), HEALTH PROFESSIONS (nursing), SOCIAL SCIENCE (anthropology, Asian/Oriental studies, economics, history, international studies, philosophy, political science/government, psychology, religion, Scandinavian studies, social work, sociology, and women's studies). Business administration, education, and nursing are the largest.

Required: All students must complete 128 credit hours, with a maximum of 40 in the major. Candidates for degrees in nursing, business administration, and education need a cumulative 2.5 GPA; all others must have a 2.0 GPA. The required curriculum is 36 credit hours of distributive core courses in arts/literature, natural sciences/math, philosophy, religious studies, and social sciences; writing and critical conversation courses; and diversity classes.

Special: PLU offers 2 different bachelor's degrees simultaneously, 3-2 engineering degrees with Washington University in St. Louis and Columbia University, and accelerated degree programs in most majors. Dual majors and student-designed majors can be arranged. There are study-abroad programs in 28 countries, extensive internships with local businesses and nonprofit organizations, and work-study programs. Credit is given by exam and through the AURA Program for adults age 30 or older. Nondegree study and pass/fail options are also available. There are 7 national honor societies, a freshman honors program, and 6 departmental honors programs.

Faculty/Classroom: 53% of faculty are male; 47%, female. 98% teach undergraduates, 90% do research, and 90% do both. No introductory courses are taught by graduate students. The average class size in an introductory lecture is 25; in a laboratory, 15; and in a regular course, 17.

Admissions: 96% of the 2001-2002 applicants were accepted. The SAT I scores for the 2001-2002 freshman class were: Verbal--24% below 500, 45% between 500 and 599, 28% between 600 and 700, and 4% above 700; Math--30% below 500, 44% between 500 and 599, 25% between 600 and 700, and 4% above 700. The ACT scores were 20% below 21, 22% between 21 and 23, 29% between 24 and 26, 14% between 27 and 28, and 15% above 28. 60% of the current freshmen were in the top fifth of their class; 86% were in the top two fifths. There were 4 National Merit finalists, 22 freshmen graduated first in their class.

Requirements: The SAT I or ACT is required. In addition, applicants should be graduates of accredited secondary schools, although GED certificates are accepted. PLU requires 2 years each of college preparatory math and a foreign language, and recommends 4 years of English, 2 each of social studies and lab science, 1 of fine or performing arts, and 3 of electives. An essay is required. PLU requires applicants to be in the upper 50% of their class. A GPA of 2.5 is required. AP and CLEP credits are accepted. Important factors in the admissions decision are advanced placement or honor courses, leadership record, and evidence of special talent. Students may apply on-line via PLU's web site.

Procedure: Freshmen are admitted fall and spring. There are early action and regular decision plans. Entrance exams should be taken by January of the senior year. There is a deferred admissions plan. Application deadlines for early action are November 5, for regular decision, open. The application fee is $35. Notification is sent October 1 for early action, rolling for regular.

Transfer: 307 transfer students enrolled in 2001-2002. Candidates must be in good academic and personal standing at the institutions last attended full time. Although it does not guarantee admission, a 2.5 GPA in all college work is usually required. For applicants with fewer than 30 semester hours or 45 quarter hours, secondary school records and standardized test scores must be submitted. All students must meet the foreign language and math entrance requirements. 32 credits of 128 must be completed at PLU.

Visiting: There are regularly scheduled orientations for prospective students, consisting of activities based on the students' individual interests. There are guides for informal visits and visitors may sit in on classes and stay overnight. To schedule a visit, contact the Office of Admissions.

Financial Aid: In 2001-2002, 94% of all freshmen and 91% of continuing students received some form of financial aid. 69% of freshmen and 68% of continuing students received need-based aid. The average freshman award was $14,722. Of that total, scholarships or need-based grants averaged $7340 ($17,728 maximum); loans averaged $3818 ($10,500 maximum); and work contracts averaged $1900 ($3000 maximum). 51% of undergraduates work part time. Average annual earnings from campus work are $2145. The average financial indebtedness of the 2001 graduate was $19,500. The FAFSA is required. The fall application deadline is January 31.

International Students: There are 195 international students enrolled. The school actively recruits these students. They must score 550 on the written TOEFL or 213 on the electronic version.

Computers: The mainframe is a DEC ALPHA ES40 clustered with a DEC VAX 4700A. There are 2 teaching labs and 2 open labs for student use. All students may access the system 18 hours per day, or 24 hours with a modem. There are no time limits and no fees.

Graduates: In 2001, 751 bachelor's degrees were awarded. The most popular majors were business (19%), education (12%), and nursing (11%). In an average class, 2% graduate in 3 years, 41% in 4 years, 60% in 5 years, and 62% in 6 years. 53 companies recruited on campus in 2000-2001. Of the 2000 graduating class, 18% were enrolled in graduate school within 6 months of graduation and 82% were employed.

Admissions Contact: David E. Gunovich, Director of Admissions.
E-mail: *admissions@plu.edu* Web: *www.plu.edu*

SAINT MARTIN'S COLLEGE

B-3

Lacey, WA 98503 **(360) 438-4311**
(800) 368-8803; Fax: (360) 412-6189

Full-time: 350 men, 444 women	**Faculty:** 60; IIB, --$
Part-time: 209 men, 198 women	**Ph.D.s:** 80%
Graduate: 116 men, 157 women	**Student/Faculty:** 13 to 1
Year: semesters, summer session	**Tuition:** $15,640
Application Deadline: open	**Room & Board:** $4926
Freshman Class: 364 applied, 357 accepted, 147 enrolled	
SAT I Verbal/Math: 502/491	**ACT:** 21 **COMPETITIVE**

Saint Martin's College, founded in 1895, is a small Roman Catholic institution conducted by the Benedictine order, offering undergraduate and graduate programs in liberal arts and sciences, business, engineering, and preprofessional areas. There are 6 undergraduate and 6 graduate schools. In addition to regional accreditation, Saint Martin's College has baccalaureate program accreditation with ABET. The library contains 96,759 volumes, 91,100 microform items, and 1325 audiovisual forms/CDs, and subscribes to 830 periodicals. Computerized library services include the card catalog, interlibrary loans, and database searching. Special learning facilities include a learning resource center, art gallery, and natural history museum. The 303-acre campus is in a suburban area 3 miles from Olympia and 60 miles south of Seattle. Including residence halls, there are 14 buildings.

Student Life: 88% of undergraduates are from Washington. Others are from 17 states, 13 foreign countries, and Canada. 83% are from public schools. 65% are white. 45% are Catholic; 32% claim no religious affiliation; 20% Protestant. The average age of freshmen is 19; all undergraduates, 30. 20% do not continue beyond their first year; 73% remain to graduate.

Housing: 260 students can be accommodated in college housing, which includes coed dormitories. On-campus housing is guaranteed for the freshman year only and is available on a first-come, first-served basis. 71% of students commute. Alcohol is not permitted. All students may keep cars.

Activities: 4% of men belong to 2 local fraternities; 4% of women belong to 1 local and 1 national sorority. There are 30 groups on campus, including band, cheerleading, choir, computers, drama, ethnic, honors, international, newspaper, professional, religious, social, social service, student government, and yearbook. Popular campus events include Career Fair, International Day, and Capital Food and Wine Festival.

Sports: There are 5 intercollegiate sports for men and 6 for women, and 9 intramural sports for men and 9 for women. Facilities include a

5300-seat multipurpose pavilion, athletic fields, tennis courts, and nearby golf courses, lakes, and mountains.

Disabled Students: 90% of the campus is accessible. Wheelchair ramps, elevators, special parking, specially equipped rest rooms, lowered drinking fountains, and lowered telephones are available. Access Services provide assistance to students with disabilities.

Services: Counseling and information services are available, as is tutoring in some subjects, including writing. There is a reader service for the blind and remedial writing. Saint Martin's provides career, personal, and psychological counseling and information services.

Campus Safety and Security: Measures include 24-hour foot and vehicle patrol, escort service, pamphlets/posters/films, and lighted pathways/sidewalks. There is a security patrol from dark to dawn.

Programs of Study: Saint Martin's College confers B.A., B.S., B.S.C.E., and B.S.M.E. degrees. Associate and master's degrees are also awarded. Bachelor's degrees are awarded in BIOLOGICAL SCIENCE (biology/biological science), BUSINESS (accounting, banking and finance, management science, and marketing/retailing/merchandising), COMMUNICATIONS AND THE ARTS (English and music), COMPUTER AND PHYSICAL SCIENCE (chemistry, computer science, and mathematics), EDUCATION (computer, elementary, social studies, and special), ENGINEERING AND ENVIRONMENTAL DESIGN (civil engineering and mechanical engineering), HEALTH PROFESSIONS (predentistry, premedicine, prepharmacy, and preveterinary science), SOCIAL SCIENCE (community services, criminal justice, economics, history, humanities, political science/government, prelaw, psychology, and religion). Education and engineering are the strongest academically. Education, psychology, and business are the largest.

Required: All students must complete freshman composition and general education requirements, including 2 courses in social sciences, 1 course each in literature, philosophy, the arts, religious studies, natural science with lab, math (precalculus), computer science, U.S. history, and non-U.S. history, as well as 2 credits of phys ed. Students must pass an English proficiency exam. A total of 128 semester credits with a 2.0 GPA is required. 1 year of foreign language is required if the student did not take 2 years of a single foreign language in high school.

Special: Double majors, work-study with the state of Washington and Saint Martin's, internships in all disciplines, a Washington semester with American University, and pass/fail options are offered. The FOCUS program offers credit for job experience. Nondegree study and study abroad are possible. There are 2 national honor societies.

Faculty/Classroom: 66% of faculty are male; 34%, female. All teach undergraduates and 70% both teach and do research. No introductory courses are taught by graduate students. The average class size in an introductory lecture is 20; in a laboratory, 12; and in a regular course, 12.

Admissions: 98% of the 2001-2002 applicants were accepted. The SAT I scores for the 2001-2002 freshman class were: Verbal--48% below 500, 41% between 500 and 599, 8% between 600 and 700, and 3% above 700; Math--54% below 500, 34% between 500 and 599, and 12% between 600 and 700. The ACT scores were 41% below 21, 38% between 21 and 23, 12% between 24 and 26, and 8% between 27 and 28. 55% of the current freshmen were in the top fifth of their class; 85% were in the top two fifths. 4 freshmen graduated first in their class in a recent year.

Requirements: The SAT I or ACT is required, with a minimum composite score of 800on the SAT I. In addition, applicants must be graduates of an accredited secondary school or have a GED, with a minimum of 16 academic units, including 4 in English, 2 or 3 in math, 2 in history/social science, 1 or 2 each in foreign language and lab science, and 7 in electives. Class standing also is considered. An essay and recommendation from a teacher or counselor are required. A GPA of 2.5 is required. AP and CLEP credits are accepted. Important factors in the admissions decision are advanced placement or honor courses, recommendations by school officials, and personality/intangible qualities. Applications are accepted on-line.

Procedure: Freshmen are admitted to all sessions. Applications should be filled by August 1 for Fall entry and December 15 for spring entry, along with a $35 fee. Notification is sent on a rolling basis.

Transfer: 106 transfer students enrolled in 2001-2002. Transfer applicants must submit transcripts from all colleges previously attended and have a 2.0 GPA. 30 credits of 128 must be completed at Saint Martin's College.

Visiting: There are regularly scheduled orientations for prospective students, including a campus tour and faculty, student service, and financial aid presentations. There are guides for informal visits and visitors may sit in on classes and stay overnight. To schedule a visit, contact the Admissions Office.

Financial Aid: In a recent year, 94% of all freshmen and 69% of continuing students received some form of financial aid. 85% of freshmen received need-based aid. The average freshman award for the 2001-2002 school year was $15,242. Of that total, scholarships or need-based grants averaged $8255 ($15,560 maximum); loans averaged $4080 ($6625 maximum); and work contracts averaged $2200 ($3400 maximum). Average annual earnings from campus work are $2400. The average financial indebtedness of a recent year's graduate was $11,690. The FAFSA is required. The fall application deadline is March 1.

International Students: There are 24 international students enrolled. The school actively recruits these students. They must score 525 on the written TOEFL.

Computers: IBM PCs and Macs are available in the computer center and library. All students may access the system. There are no time limits. The fee is $50 per semester.

Graduates: In 2001, 297 bachelor's degrees were awarded. The most popular majors were business (39%), psychology (17%), and education (10%). In an average class, 1% graduate in 3 years, 72% in 4 years, 73% in 5 years, and 73% in 6 years. 160 companies recruited on campus in 2000-2001. Of the 2000 graduating class, 8% were enrolled in graduate school within 6 months of graduation and 97% were employed.

Admissions Contact: Carleen Jackson, Director of Enrollment and Marketing. E-mail: *admissions@stmartin.edu*

SEATTLE PACIFIC UNIVERSITY C-2

Seattle, WA 98119-1997 **(206) 281-2021**
(800) 366-3344; Fax: (206) 281-2669

Full-time: 849 men, 1682 women	**Faculty:** 152; IIA, -$
Part-time: 122 men, 175 women	**Ph.D.s:** 90%
Graduate: 256 men, 531 women	**Student/Faculty:** 17 to 1
Year: quarters, summer session	**Tuition:** $16,425
Application Deadline: June 1	**Room & Board:** $6249
Freshman Class: 1769 applied, 1469 accepted, 647 enrolled	
SAT I Verbal/Math: 630/620	**ACT:** 27 **COMPETITIVE+**

Seattle Pacific University, founded in 1891, is a private, nonprofit institution affiliated with the Free Methodist Church. It offers programs in business and economics, education, fine and performing arts, health science, humanities, natural and mathematical sciences, physical education and athletics, religion, and social and behavioral sciences. There are 9 undergraduate and 6 graduate schools. In addition to regional accreditation, SPU has baccalaureate program accreditation with ABET, ADA, NASM, NCATE, and NLN. The library contains 169,527 volumes, 498,997 microform items, and 3002 audiovisual forms/CDs, and subscribes to 1336 periodicals. Computerized library services include the card catalog and database searching. Special learning facilities include a learning resource center, art gallery, science center, performing arts theater, writing laboratory, and media center. The 35-acre campus is in an urban area on the north slope of Queen Anne Hill, 7 minutes from downtown Seattle. Including residence halls, there are 94 buildings.

Student Life: 64% of undergraduates are from Washington. Others are from 45 states, 31 foreign countries, and Canada. 83% are white. 75% are Protestant; 17% claim no religious affiliation. The average age of freshmen is 18; all undergraduates, 21. 28% do not continue beyond their first year; 41% remain to graduate.

Housing: 1284 students can be accommodated in college housing, which includes single-sex and coed dormitories, on-campus apartments, off-campus apartments, and married-student housing. In addition, there are family houses and theme houses. On-campus housing is guaranteed for all 4 years. 59% of students live on campus; of those, 80% remain on campus on weekends. Alcohol is not permitted. All students may keep cars.

Activities: There are no fraternities or sororities. There are 50 groups on campus, including art, cheerleading, chess, choir, chorale, drama, ethnic, honors, international, jazz band, literary magazine, newspaper, orchestra, pep band, political, professional, radio, religious, social, social service, student government, and yearbook. Popular campus events include Family Weekend, Talent Show, and Ivy Cutting at Graduation.

Sports: There are 5 intercollegiate sports for men and 6 for women, and 19 intramural sports for men and 18 for women. Facilities include a soccer field, an oval track, tennis and basketball courts, a gym and crew house, a crew dock, a 2600-seat indoor gym, an 800-seat campus auditorium, and a community swimming pool available to students with free passes.

Disabled Students: 70% of the campus is accessible. Wheelchair ramps, elevators, special parking, specially equipped rest rooms, and special class scheduling are available.

Services: Counseling and information services are available, as is tutoring in most subjects. There is a reader service for the blind and remedial math and writing. In addition, there is priority registration for disabled students.

Campus Safety and Security: Measures include 24-hour foot and vehicle patrol, escort service, pamphlets/posters/films, and emergency telephones. There are lighted pathways/sidewalks and closed-circuit TV monitors.

Programs of Study: SPU confers B.A. and B.S. degrees. Master's and doctoral degrees are also awarded. Bachelor's degrees are awarded in BIOLOGICAL SCIENCE (biochemistry and biology/biological science), BUSINESS (accounting and business administration and management), COMMUNICATIONS AND THE ARTS (art, classics, communications, dramatic arts, English, French, German, Latin, music, Russian, Spanish, and visual and performing arts), COMPUTER AND PHYSICAL SCIENCE (chemistry, computer science, mathematics, and physics), EDUCATION (art, Christian, English, home economics, mathematics, music, science, social science, and special), ENGINEERING AND ENVIRONMENTAL DESIGN (electrical/electronics engineering and engineering and applied science), HEALTH PROFESSIONS (exercise science and nursing), SOCIAL SCIENCE (clothing and textiles management/production/services, economics, European studies, family/consumer studies, food science, history, Latin American studies, liberal arts/general studies, philosophy, physical fitness/movement, political science/government, psychology, religion, religious education, sociology, and theological studies). Education, nursing, and business administration are the largest.

Required: All students must demonstrate competency in math and English. Students must complete 15 quarter credits in Christian heritage and values, 56 in general education, plus up to 15 credits of foreign language competency, and at least 45 to 60 in the major, depending on the program. A minimum of 180 credits is needed for the bachelor's degree, with a 2.0 GPA overall. At least 60 credits must be earned in 3000-level courses or higher.

Special: There is a cooperative program with Fashion Institute of Technology in New York City, Fashion Institute of Design and Merchandising in Los Angeles, and Han Nam University in Korea, cross-registration with the Christian College Consortium and Christian College Coalition, and a Washington semester in American studies through the Christian College Coalition. SPU offers internships, study abroad in more than 5 countries, work-study programs, dual and student-designed majors, interdisciplinary majors such as language arts, and a liberal studies major for associate degree graduates. A general studies degree, pass/no credit options, and nondegree study are available. There are 5 national honor societies, a freshman honors program, and 10 departmental honors programs.

Faculty/Classroom: 64% of faculty are male; 36%, female. No introductory courses are taught by graduate students. The average class size in a regular course is 18.

Admissions: 83% of the 2001-2002 applicants were accepted. The SAT I scores for the 2001-2002 freshman class were: Math--22% below 500, 42% between 500 and 599, 31% between 600 and 699 and 5% above 699. The ACT scores were 3% between 12 and 17, 42% between 18 and 23, 42% between 24 and 29, and 13% between 30 and 36. 76% of the current freshmen were in the top quarter of their class; 98% were in the top half.

Requirements: The SAT I or ACT is required; the SAT I is preferred, with a minimum required composite score of 950. Candidates should be graduates of an accredited secondary school with a minimum high school GPA of 2.5 or hold a GED certificate. A strong college preparatory program in high school is recommended, including 4 years of English and 3 each of math, science, and foreign language. An essay and 2 letters of recommendation are required, and an interview is recommended. AP and CLEP credits are accepted. Important factors in the admissions decision are advanced placement or honor courses, leadership record, and extracurricular activities record. Applications are accepted on computer disk via the Common Application.

Procedure: Freshmen are admitted to all sessions. Entrance exams should be taken before January of the senior year. There are early admissions and deferred admissions plans. Early action applications should be filed by December 1; regular applications, by June 1 for fall entry (March 1 priority), along with a $35 fee. Notification of early acation is sent February 15; regular decision, on a rolling basis beginning December 1.

Transfer: 243 transfer students enrolled in 2001-2002. A minimum 2.5 GPA is required, and an interview is recommended. Transcripts from all previous colleges attended and from high school are required, along with 2 letters of recommendation. Evidence of honorable dismissal from the previous school is also required. Students with at least 30 credits earned are not required to take the SAT I or ACT. 45 credits of 180 must be completed at SPU.

Visiting: There are regularly scheduled orientations for prospective students. There are guides for informal visits and visitors may sit in on classes and stay overnight. To schedule a visit, contact the Admissions Office.

Financial Aid: The average freshman award for the 2001-2002 school year was $13,008. The average financial indebtedness of the 2001 graduate was $18,498. SPU is a member of CSS. The FAFSA is required. The fall application deadline is January 31.

International Students: The school actively recruits these students. They must score 550 on the written TOEFL or take the MELAB. The Michigan Test must be administered through SPU.

Computers: The mainframe is a DEC VAX 4600. There are approximately 150 PCs available on campus in the library lab, science learning center, writing lab, music keyboard lab, and media center. There is full access to the Internet, e-mail, and other local and remote networked resources. All campus residence halls have network connections. All students may access the system during lab hours, Monday through Saturday during the academic year. There are no time limits and no fees. It is strongly recommended that all students have a personal computer.

Graduates: In 2001, 512 bachelor's degrees were awarded. The most popular majors were business/marketing (15%), health professions (10%), and home economics (9%).

Admissions Contact: Ken Cornell, Director of Admissions.
E-mail: *admissions@spu.edu* Web: *www.spu.edu*

SEATTLE UNIVERSITY C-2

Seattle, WA 98122 **(206) 296-2000**
(800) 426-7123; Fax: (206) 296-5656

Full-time: 1167 men, 1880 women	**Faculty:** 331; IIA, av$
Part-time: 131 men, 174 women	**Ph.D.s:** 90%
Graduate: 1145 men, 1484 women	**Student/Faculty:** 9 to 1
Year: quarters, summer session	**Tuition:** $17,865
Application Deadline: February 1	**Room & Board:** $6318
Freshman Class: 2634 applied, 2110 accepted, 643 enrolled	
SAT I Verbal/Math: 560/560	**ACT:** 25 **VERY COMPETITIVE**

Seattle University, founded in 1891, is a private, comprehensive institution affiliated with the Roman Catholic Church and operated by the Jesuit Fathers. The emphasis of the undergraduate and graduate programs is on the liberal arts and sciences, business, engineering, health science, teacher preparation, theological studies, and law. There are 5 undergraduate and 7 graduate schools. In addition to regional accreditation, Seattle U has baccalaureate program accreditation with AACSB, ABET, CAHEA, NCATE, and NLN. The 2 libraries contain 234,978 volumes, 570,839 microform items, and 5608 audiovisual forms/CDs, and subscribe to 2709 periodicals. Computerized library services include the card catalog, interlibrary loans, and database searching. Special learning facilities include a learning resource center, art gallery, planetarium, radio station, electron microscope, recording studio, and MRI. The 46-acre campus is in an urban area just east of downtown Seattle. Including residence halls, there are 27 buildings.

Student Life: 83% of undergraduates are from Washington. Others are from 49 states, 69 foreign countries, and Canada. 58% are white; 16% Asian American. 40% are claim no religious affiliation; 39% Catholic; 18% Protestant. The average age of freshmen is 18; all undergraduates, 22. 17% do not continue beyond their first year; 59% remain to graduate.

Housing: 1408 students can be accommodated in college housing, which includes single-sex and coed dormitories and on-campus apartments. There are 24-hour quiet floors and single-sex floors. On-campus housing is guaranteed for the freshman year only and is available on a lottery system for upperclassmen. Priority is given to out-of-town students. 64% of students commute. All students may keep cars.

Activities: There are no fraternities or sororities. There are 61 groups on campus, including art, cheerleading, choir, chorale, dance, debate, drama, ethnic, forensics, gay, honors, international, jazz band, literary magazine, musical theater, newspaper, photography, political, professional, radio and TV, religious, social, social service, and student government. Popular campus events include Hawaiian Luau, Quad Stock, and International Student Dinner.

Sports: There are 12 intercollegiate sports for men and 13 for women, and 7 intramural sports for men and 7 for women. Facilities include a center with 2 swimming pools, a fitness/weight room, and 5 racquetball, 2 squash, and 3 basketball courts, and an Astroturf gym for indoor soccer/tennis.

Disabled Students: 95% of the campus is accessible. Wheelchair ramps, elevators, special parking, specially equipped rest rooms, special class scheduling, lowered drinking fountains, and lowered telephones are available.

Services: Counseling and information services are available, as is tutoring in most subjects, including math, English, accounting, language, and science. There is a reader service for the blind and a writing center.

Campus Safety and Security: Measures include 24-hour foot and vehicle patrol, self-defense education, escort service, and shuttle buses. There are informal discussions, pamphlets/posters/films, emergency telephones, and lighted pathways/sidewalks.

Programs of Study: Seattle U confers B.A., B.S., B.A.B.A., B.A.E., B.A.H., B.C.J., B.P.A., B.S.B., B.S.B.C., B.S.C., B.S.C.E., B.S.C.S., B.S.D.U., B.S.E.E., B.S.G.S., B.S.M., B.S.M.E., B.S.M.T., B.S.N., and B.S.P. degrees. Master's and doctoral degrees are also awarded. Bachelor's degrees are awarded in BIOLOGICAL SCIENCE (biochemistry, biology/biological science, and ecology), BUSINESS (accounting, banking and finance, business administration and management, business economics, international business management, marketing/retailing/merchandising, and operations research), COMMUNICATIONS AND THE ARTS (communications, creative writing, dramatic arts, English, fine arts, French, German, journalism, and Spanish), COMPUTER AND PHYSICAL SCIENCE (chemistry, computer science, mathematics, physics, and science), ENGINEERING AND ENVIRONMENTAL DESIGN (civil engineering, electrical/electronics engineering, environmental engineering, manufacturing engineering, and mechanical engineering),

HEALTH PROFESSIONS (medical technology, nursing, and ultrasound technology), SOCIAL SCIENCE (criminal justice, economics, history, humanities, international studies, liberal arts/general studies, philosophy, political science/government, psychology, public administration, religion, social work, and sociology). Engineering, accounting, and nursing are the strongest academically and have the largest enrollments.

Required: Students must complete 180 to 192 quarter hours, depending on the degree, with 70 to 90 in the major, and maintain a minimum GPA of 2.25 to 2.5. Core curriculum requirements total 73 quarter hours, of which 10 quarter hours in religious studies must be taken. All students must take courses in English, math, science, philosophy, social studies, and fine arts.

Special: Special academic programs include internships in numerous disciplines, study abroad in 5 countries, and both on- and off-campus work-study through the Washington State Work-Study Program. A liberal studies degree and an accelerated degree program in business are offered. Pass/fail options, dual majors, and student-designed majors are possible. There is a freshman honors program.

Faculty/Classroom: 55% of faculty are male; 45%, female. No introductory courses are taught by graduate students. The average class size in a regular course is 22.

Admissions: 80% of the 2001-2002 applicants were accepted. The SAT I scores for the 2001-2002 freshman class were: Verbal--20% below 500, 40% between 500 and 599, 34% between 600 and 700, and 6% above 700; Math--17% below 500, 47% between 500 and 599, 32% between 600 and 700, and 4% above 700. 51% of the current freshmen were in the top fifth of their class; 78% were in the top two fifths. 18 freshmen graduated first in their class in a recent year.

Requirements: The SAT I or ACT is required. In addition, admissions requirements include graduation from an accredited secondary school, with 16 academic credits, including 4 years of English, 3 each of math and social studies, 2 of foreign language, 2 of lab science, and 2 academic electives; 4 years of math and lab physics and chemistry are required of science and engineering students; lab biology and chemistry are needed by nursing students. The GED is also accepted. A GPA of 2.75 is required. AP and CLEP credits are accepted. Important factors in the admissions decision are advanced placement or honor courses, recommendations by school officials, and extracurricular activities record. Applications are available on-line at the university's web site.

Procedure: Freshmen are admitted to all sessions. Entrance exams should be taken during the fall of the senior year. There is a deferred admissions plan. Applications should be filed by February 1 for fall entry, November 1 for winter entry, February 1 for spring entry, and May 1 for summer entry, along with a $45 fee. Notification is sent on a rolling basis. 6% of all applicants are on a waiting list; 8 were accepted in 2001.

Transfer: 268 transfer students enrolled in 2001-2002. Generally, transfer students should have a GPA of at least 2.5. An associate degree is recommended; a 2.75 GPA is required for nursing and business administration students. 45 credits of 180 must be completed at Seattle U.

Visiting: There are regularly scheduled orientations for prospective students. There are guides for informal visits and visitors may sit in on classes and stay overnight. To schedule a visit, contact the Admissions Office.

Financial Aid: In 2001-2002, 65% of all freshmen and 62% of continuing students received some form of financial aid. 65% of freshmen and 53% of continuing students received need-based aid. The average freshman award was $18,304. Of that total, scholarships or need-based grants averaged $10,372; loans averaged $6334; and work contracts averaged $4115. The average financial indebtedness of the 2001 graduate was $22,695. The FAFSA is required. The fall application deadline is February 1.

International Students: There are 267 international students enrolled. The school actively recruits these students. They must score 520 on the written TOEFL.

Computers: The mainframe consists of 4 IBM RISC systems with 5 UNIX-based Sun servers. There are 400 PCs in labs and 5 specialized LAN terminals. All students may access the system during posted hours or any time from networked residence hall rooms. There are no time limits and no fees.

Graduates: In 2001, 784 bachelor's degrees were awarded. The most popular majors were nursing (13%), finance (7%), and business marketing and marketing management (5%). In an average class, 38% graduate in 4 years, 57% in 5 years, and 59% in 6 years. 175 companies recruited on campus in 2000-2001.

Admissions Contact: Michael K. McKeon, Dean of Admissions.
E-mail: *admissions@seattleu.edu* Web: *www.seattleu.edu*

UNIVERSITY OF PUGET SOUND — C-2

Tacoma, WA 98416 (253) 879-3211
(800) 396-7191; Fax: (253) 879-3993

Full-time: 987 men, 1527 women	**Faculty:** 208; IIB, +$
Part-time: 30 men, 46 women	**Ph.D.s:** 88%
Graduate: 66 men, 178 women	**Student/Faculty:** 12 to 1
Year: semesters, summer session	**Tuition:** $22,505
Application Deadline: February 1	**Room & Board:** $5780
Freshman Class: 4377 applied, 2915 accepted, 703 enrolled	
SAT I Verbal/Math: 630/620	**ACT:** 27 **HIGHLY COMPETITIVE**

The University of Puget Sound, founded in 1888, is an independent, residential, undergraduate liberal arts and sciences college with selected graduate programs building effectively on a liberal arts foundation. In addition to regional accreditation, Puget Sound has baccalaureate program accreditation with NASM. The library contains 496,801 volumes, 643,576 microform items, and 15,908 audiovisual forms/CDs, and subscribes to 6321 periodicals. Computerized library services include the card catalog, interlibrary loans, and database searching. Special learning facilities include a learning resource center, art gallery, natural history museum, radio station, student science labs, an observatory, computer labs, seminar rooms, "turn-around" computer classrooms, a media center, language houses, theater workshops, newspaper, a center for writing and learning, and a bibliographic instruction room. The 97-acre campus is in a suburban area 35 miles south of Seattle, 1 mile from Commencement Bay on Puget Sound. Including residence halls, there are 37 buildings.

Student Life: 70% of undergraduates are from out of state, mostly the West. Others are from 46 states, 20 foreign countries, and Canada. 78% are from public schools. 76% are white; 11% Asian American. 54% claim no religious affiliation; 31% Protestant; 11% Catholic. The average age of freshmen is 18; all undergraduates, 20. 15% do not continue beyond their first year; 73% remain to graduate.

Housing: 1470 students can be accommodated in college housing, which includes single-sex and coed dormitories, on-campus apartments, fraternity houses, and sorority houses. In addition, there are honors houses, language houses, special-interest houses, theme houses, and halls. On-campus housing is guaranteed for the freshman year only, is available on a first-come, first-served basis, and is available on a lottery system for upperclassmen. 56% of students live on campus; of those, 80% remain on campus on weekends. All students may keep cars.

Activities: 23% of men belong to 4 national fraternities; 31% of women belong to 5 national sororities. There are 100 groups on campus, including art, band, cheerleading, choir, chorale, chorus, computers, dance, debate, diversity awareness, drama, environmental, ethnic, film, forensics, gay, gender, health and wellness, honors, international, jazz band, literary magazine, musical theater, newspaper, opera, orchestra, pep band, photography, political, professional, radio and TV, religious, social, social service, student government, symphony, and yearbook. Popular campus events include Foolish Pleasures (student film festival), Mistletoast Holiday, and Hawaiian Luau.

Sports: There are 11 intercollegiate sports for men and 12 for women, and 8 intramural sports for men and 8 for women. Facilities include a 3000-seat basketball and volleyball gym, a 6-lane pool, a 2488-seat football, soccer and track stadium, 6 indoor tennis courts, a fitness room, an aerobics exercise area and dance studio, a track, baseball, softball, and intramural fields, 2 outdoor sand volleyball courts, an indoor climbing wall, and an auxiliary gym for intramurals and recreation.

Disabled Students: 75% of the campus is accessible. Wheelchair ramps, elevators, special parking, specially equipped rest rooms, special class scheduling, lowered drinking fountains, lowered telephones, TDDs, and adaptive computer equipment are available.

Services: Counseling and information services are available, as is tutoring in most subjects. There is a reader service for the blind.

Campus Safety and Security: Measures include 24-hour foot and vehicle patrol, escort service, informal discussions, and pamphlets/posters/films. There are emergency telephones, lighted pathways/sidewalks, and vehicle escort within 3 miles of campus. Residence halls are always locked.

Programs of Study: Puget Sound confers B.A., B.S., and B.M. degrees. Master's degrees are also awarded. Bachelor's degrees are awarded in AGRICULTURE (environmental studies), BIOLOGICAL SCIENCE (biology/biological science), BUSINESS (business administration and management and international economics), COMMUNICATIONS AND THE ARTS (art, classics, communications, dramatic arts, English, fine arts, French, German, music, music performance, and Spanish), COMPUTER AND PHYSICAL SCIENCE (chemistry, computer science, geology, mathematics, natural sciences, and physics), EDUCATION (education and music), HEALTH PROFESSIONS (exercise science and occupational therapy), SOCIAL SCIENCE (African American studies, Asian/Oriental studies, economics, history, Latin American studies, philosophy, physical fitness/movement, political science/government, psychology, public administration, religion, sociology, and women's studies). Physics, math, and international political economy are the strongest academically. Business, psychology, and English are the largest.

Required: Students must complete 32 units (128 semester credits) of course work, with 8 to 14 in the major, and maintain a minimum GPA of 2.0. Core requirements include 1 unit each of written communication, oral communication, mathematical reasoning, historical perspective, humanistic perspective, fine arts, comparative values, society, international studies, and science in context, and 2 units of the natural world.

Special: Special academic programs include on- and off-campus work-study, paid and unpaid internships in the community in conjunction with an internship seminar, and study abroad in 48 countries. There are 3-2 engineering degrees with Washington University at St. Louis, Columbia, Boston, and Duke Universities, and the University of Southern California. Dual majors in foreign language/international affairs, music/business, and computer science/business, as well as pass/fail options are possible. 2 special features of the curriculum are the intensive 4-year study of the classics of Western civilization and the Business Leadership Program, combining traditional business and liberal arts study. A required science in context program integrates the sciences and humanities. There are 12 national honor societies, including Phi Beta Kappa, a freshman honors program, and 13 departmental honors programs.

Faculty/Classroom: 55% of faculty are male; 45%, female. 97% teach undergraduates. No introductory courses are taught by graduate students. The average class size in an introductory lecture is 22; in a laboratory, 13; and in a regular course, 19.

Admissions: 67% of the 2001-2002 applicants were accepted. The SAT I scores for the 2001-2002 freshman class were: Verbal--2% below 500, 28% between 500 and 599, 59% between 600 and 700, and 11% above 700; Math--4% below 500, 31% between 500 and 599, 56% between 600 and 700, and 9% above 700. The ACT scores were 3% below 21, 14% between 21 and 23, 28% between 24 and 26, 27% between 27 and 28, and 28% above 28. 69% of the current freshmen were in the top fifth of their class; 92% were in the top two fifths. There were 29 National Merit finalists. 50 freshmen graduated first in their class.

Requirements: The SAT I or ACT is required; the SAT I is preferred. Other admission requirements include graduation from an accredited secondary school, with a recommended 4 years of English, 3 to 4 of math and natural/physical lab science, 3 of social studies/history, 2 to 3 of foreign language, and 1 of fine/visual/performing arts. Also required are letters of personal recommendation from a teacher and counselor; 2 are preferred. An essay must be submitted, and an interview is recommended. It is recommended that art students present a portfolio and that music students audition. The GED is also accepted. AP credits are accepted. Important factors in the admissions decision are advanced placement or honor courses, evidence of special talent, and extracurricular activities record. The Common Application is accepted on-line through Common App and Next Stop College. CollegeView, CollegeLink, and APPLY! forms are also accepted.

Procedure: Freshmen are admitted to all sessions. Entrance exams should be taken during the fall of the senior year. There are early decision, early admissions, and deferred admissions plans. Early decision applications should be filed by November 15; regular applications, by February 1 for fall entry and November 1 for spring entry, along with a $40 fee. Notification of early decision is sent November 15 and December 15; regular decision, February 1 for fall entry, November 1 for spring entry. 215 early decision candidates were accepted for the 2001-2002 class. 16% of all applicants are on a waiting list.

Transfer: 148 transfer students enrolled in 2001-2002. Applicants must have an honorable dismissal from the institution(s) previously attended and good academic standing, with a minimum GPA of 2.0. All college transcripts and the rigor of prior course work and resulting grades are evaluated. High school transcripts and SAT I or ACT scores are required if less than 1 year of college has been completed. An interview is recommended. An essay or a copy of a graded paper is required of all undergraduate transfers. 16 units of 32 must be completed at Puget Sound.

Visiting: There are regularly scheduled orientations for prospective students, including meetings with counselors, faculty, and coaches, tours of campus, and classroom experiences. There are guides for informal visits and visitors may sit in on classes and stay overnight. To schedule a visit, contact the Campus Visit Coordinator, Office of Admission.

Financial Aid: In 2001-2002, 85% of all freshmen and 83% of continuing students received some form of financial aid. 54% of all students received need-based aid. The average freshman award was $20,276. Of that total, scholarships or need-based grants averaged $8804; loans averaged $5040; and work contracts averaged $2502. 35% of undergraduates work part time. Average annual earnings from campus work are $2000. The average financial indebtedness of the 2001 graduate was $22,288. Puget Sound is a member of CSS. The CSS/Profile or FAFSA is required. The CSS/Profile is required of early decision candidates. The fall application deadline is February 1.

International Students: There are 37 international students enrolled. The school actively recruits these students. They must score 550 on the written TOEFL or 213 on the electronic version and also take the SAT I or ACT. Freshman applicants must also take the SAT I or ACT.

Computers: The mainframes are a DEC VAX 4000 series and a series of servers. The mainframe can be reached through the campus network. There are also 2 large Mac and 3 IBM labs (open 24 hours), additional satellite labs in departments, and a network of Compaq workstations. All lab systems and workstations have full access to the Internet. All students may access the system. There are no time limits and no fees. It is strongly recommended that all students have a personal computer.

Graduates: In 2001, 629 bachelor's degrees were awarded. The most popular majors were business (14%), English (12%), and biology (8%). In an average class, 1% graduate in 3 years, 67% in 4 years, 71% in 5 years, and 72% in 6 years. 218 companies recruited on campus in 2000-2001.

Admissions Contact: George H. Mills, Jr., Vice President for Enrollment. A video is available. E-mail: *admission@ups.edu*
Web: *www.ups.edu*

UNIVERSITY OF WASHINGTON — C-2
Seattle, WA 98195 — (206) 543-9686

Full-time: 10,400 men, 11,260 women	**Faculty:** 3015; I, av$
Part-time: 1900 men, 2100 women	**Ph.D.s:** 99%
Graduate: 4990 men, 4960 women	**Student/Faculty:** 7 to 1
Year: quarters, summer session	**Tuition:** $3983 ($13,258)
Application Deadline: January 15	**Room & Board:** $6378

Freshman Class: 14,664 applied, 11,523 accepted, 5382 enrolled
SAT I Verbal/Math: required — **VERY COMPETITIVE**

The University of Washington, founded in 1861, is a public institution offering a broad range of degree programs. Enrollment figures in the above capsule are approximate. There are 13 undergraduate schools and 1 graduate school. In addition to regional accreditation, UW has baccalaureate program accreditation with AACSB, ABET, NCATE, and NLN. The 19 libraries contain 5,601,263 volumes, 6,432,950 microform items, and 56,295 audiovisual forms/CDs. Computerized library services include the card catalog, interlibrary loans, and database searching. Special learning facilities include a learning resource center, art gallery, natural history museum, planetarium, radio station, TV station, state museum, full teaching hospital, marine science lab, 200-acre arboretum, and field research forest. The 703-acre campus is in an urban area 5 miles from downtown Seattle. Including residence halls, there are 213 buildings.

Student Life: 88% of undergraduates are from Washington. Others are from 44 states, 68 foreign countries, and Canada. 57% are white; 24% Asian American. The average age of freshmen is 18; all undergraduates, 21. 10% do not continue beyond their first year; 71% remain to graduate.

Housing: 5200 students can be accommodated in college housing, which includes coed dormitories, on-campus apartments, married-student housing, fraternity houses, and sorority houses. In addition, there are language houses, special-interest houses, and a freshman house. On-campus housing is guaranteed for all 4 years. Alcohol is not permitted. All students may keep cars.

Activities: 17% of men belong to 29 national fraternities; 16% of women belong to 16 national sororities. There are 450 groups on campus, including band, cheerleading, choir, chorale, chorus, computers, dance, drama, ethnic, film, gay, honors, international, jazz band, literary magazine, marching band, musical theater, newspaper, opera, orchestra, pep band, political, professional, radio and TV, religious, social, social service, student government, symphony, and yearbook. Popular campus events include Four Bands for 4 Bucks concert, Opening Day (of boating/crew season), and Convocation.

Sports: There are 10 intercollegiate sports for men and 11 for women, and 20 intramural sports for men and 18 for women. Facilities include a 72,500-seat football stadium, a baseball field, a track and field complex, lakeside facilities, tennis courts, the intramurals building, a golf driving range, and a swimming pool.

Disabled Students: 85% of the campus is accessible. Wheelchair ramps, elevators, special parking, specially equipped rest rooms, special class scheduling, lowered drinking fountains, and lowered telephones are available.

Services: Counseling and information services are available, as is tutoring in every subject. There is a reader service for the blind, and remedial math, reading, and writing.

Campus Safety and Security: Measures include 24-hour foot and vehicle patrol, self-defense education, escort service, and shuttle buses. There are informal discussions, pamphlets/posters/films, emergency telephones, lighted pathways/sidewalks, and emergency telephone numbers.

Programs of Study: UW confers B.A., B.S., B.A.B.A., B.C.H.S., B.L.Arch., B.Mus., B.S.A.&A., B.S.B.C., B.S.Cer.E., B.S.Comp.E., B.S.F., B.S.Fish., B.S.I.E., B.S.M.E., B.S.Med.Tech., B.S.Met.E., and B.S.Nur. degrees. Master's and doctoral degrees are also awarded. Bachelor's degrees are awarded in AGRICULTURE (fishing and fisheries, forest engineering, forestry production and processing, and wood science), BIOLOGICAL SCIENCE (biochemistry, biology/biological science, botany, microbiology, neurosciences, and zoology), BUSINESS (accounting, banking and finance, business administration and management, business economics, international business management, marketing/retailing/merchandising, and personnel management), COMMUNICATIONS AND THE ARTS (art history and appreciation, classics, communications, comparative literature, dance, dramatic arts, English, fiber/textiles/weaving, French, Germanic languages and literature, graphic design, Italian, Japanese, jazz, metal/jewelry, music history and appreciation, music performance, painting, photography, printmaking, Scandinavian languages, sculpture, Slavic languages, Spanish, speech/debate/rhetoric, studio art, and technical and business writing), COMPUTER AND PHYSICAL SCIENCE (astronomy, atmospheric sciences and meteorology, computer science, geology, information sciences and systems, mathematics, oceanography, physics, quantitative methods, and statistics), EDUCATION (music), ENGINEERING AND ENVIRONMENTAL DESIGN (aeronautical engineering, ceramic engineering, chemical engineering, civil engineering, computer engineering, construction engineering, electrical/electronics engineering, engineering, landscape architecture/design, materials science, ocean engineering, and paper and pulp science), HEALTH PROFESSIONS (dental hygiene, environmental health science, health care administration, medical laboratory technology, nursing, and speech pathology/audiology), SOCIAL SCIENCE (African American studies, anthropology, Asian/American studies, Asian/Oriental studies, Canadian studies, economics, ethnic studies, food science, geography, history, international relations, Judaic studies, liberal arts/general studies, Near Eastern studies, peace studies, philosophy, political science/government, psychology, religion, Russian and Slavic studies, social work, sociology, South Asian studies, and women's studies). Biological and life sciences, computer science and engineering, and physics are the strongest academically. Business, political science, and art are the largest.

Required: All students must maintain a GPA of 2.0 while taking 180 quarter credits, with 45 in the major. Distribution requirements include 40 credits from the humanities, social sciences, and math/natural sciences, with 12 credits in English composition/writing and a course in quantitative/symbolic reasoning.

Special: A wide variety of internships, including those for minority students in engineering, concurrent dual majors, study abroad in 21 countries, a Washington semester, a general studies degree, and co-op programs are available. Work-study programs, cross-registration with the National Student Exchange, credit/no credit options, student-designed majors, accelerated degree programs, nondegree study, and a 5-year B.A.-B.S. degree also are offered. There are 20 national honor societies, including Phi Beta Kappa, a freshman honors program, and 36 departmental honors programs.

Faculty/Classroom: 66% of faculty are male; 34%, female. 85% both teach and do research. Graduate students teach 40% of introductory courses. The average class size in an introductory lecture is 54; in a laboratory, 24; and in a regular course, 40.

Admissions: 79% of the 2001-2002 applicants were accepted. 72% of the current freshmen were in the top fifth of their class; 96% were in the top two fifths. There were 41 National Merit finalists and 53 semifinalists.

Requirements: The SAT I or ACT is required. In addition, applicants must have completed 15 academic units, including 4 years of English, 3 each of math and social sciences, 2 each of foreign language and science, and 1/2 year each in fine/visual performing arts and electives. Admission is based on an indexing system. A GPA of 2.0 is required. AP credits are accepted. Important factors in the admissions decision are advanced placement or honor courses and evidence of special talent. Applicatons are accepted on-line through the UW web page or CollegeNET.

Procedure: Freshmen are admitted to all sessions. Entrance exams should be taken by December of the senior year. Applications should be filed by January 15 for fall entry, September 15 for winter entry, December 15 for spring entry, and January 15 for summer entry, along with a $35 fee. Notification is sent March 15.

Transfer: 1592 transfer students enrolled in 2001-2002. The school has a special direct transfer agreement with Washington community colleges. Admission is based on an indexing system. 45 credits of 180 must be completed at UW.

Visiting: There are regularly scheduled orientations for prospective students, including attendance at class, a meeting with an admissions counselor, campus tour, and information sessions. There are guides for informal visits and visitors may sit in on classes. To schedule a visit, contact the Student Visitation Program at (206) 543-5429 or *visituw@u.washington.edu*

Financial Aid: The CSS/Profile is required. The fall application deadline is February 28.

International Students: They must score 540 on the written TOEFL or 207 on the electronic version or take the MELAB and also the APIEL.

Computers: There are several public labs containing 10,000 PCs, Macs, and terminals. Dial-up is also used because most students live off campus. All students may access the system 24 hours daily. There are no time limits and no fees.

Graduates: In 2001, 6923 bachelor's degrees were awarded. The most popular majors were business (13%), art (10%), and political science (5%). In an average class, 38% graduate in 4 years, 65% in 5 years, and 71% in 6 years. 600 companies recruited on campus in 2000-2001. Of the 2000 graduating class, 20% were enrolled in graduate school within 6 months of graduation and 74% were employed.

Admissions Contact: Office of Admissions.
Web: *www.washington.edu/students/uga*

WALLA WALLA COLLEGE — E-3

College Place, WA 99324-1198 — (509) 527-2327
(800) 541-8900; Fax: (509) 527-2397

Full-time: 701 men, 664 women	**Faculty:** 121; IIB, --$
Part-time: 94 men, 118 women	**Ph.D.s:** 60%
Graduate: 53 men, 193 women	**Student/Faculty:** 11 to 1
Year: quarters, summer session	**Tuition:** $16,599
Application Deadline: open	**Room & Board:** $4326
Freshman Class: 634 applied, 328 accepted, 285 enrolled	
ACT: required	**COMPETITIVE**

Walla Walla College, founded in 1892, is a private comprehensive institution affiliated with the Seventh-day Adventist Church. There are 6 undergraduate and 4 graduate schools. In addition to regional accreditation, WWC has baccalaureate program accreditation with ABET, ACBSP, CSWE, NASM, and NLN. The 3 libraries contain 281,170 volumes, 19,781 microform items, and 3483 audiovisual forms/CDs, and subscribe to 1317 periodicals. Computerized library services include the card catalog, interlibrary loans, and database searching. Special learning facilities include a learning resource center, art gallery, radio station, audio listening/music library, and observatory. The 77-acre campus is in a small town 120 miles southwest of Spokane. Including residence halls, there are 28 buildings.

Student Life: 58% of undergraduates are from out of state, mostly the West. 12% are from public schools. 86% are white. Most are Protestant. The average age of freshmen is 19; all undergraduates, 21. 24% do not continue beyond their first year; 54% remain to graduate.

Housing: 1500 students can be accommodated in college housing, which includes single-sex dormitories, on-campus apartments, off-campus apartments and houses, and married-student housing. On-campus housing is guaranteed for all 4 years. 54% of students live on campus; of those, 90% remain on campus on weekends. Alcohol is not permitted. All students may keep cars.

Activities: There are no fraternities or sororities. There are 50 groups on campus, including art, band, choir, chorale, chorus, drama, ethnic, honors, international, literary magazine, newspaper, orchestra, photography, professional, radio and TV, religious, social service, student government, symphony, and yearbook. Popular campus events include the Mud Bowl football game and the Sonneberg Series basketball tournament.

Sports: There are 5 intercollegiate sports for men and 3 for women, and 9 intramural sports for men and 7 for women. Facilities include an Olympic-size pool, a track, tennis and racquetball courts, a gymnastics sports gym, a gym, weight rooms, and residence hall health spas.

Disabled Students: 90% of the campus is accessible. Wheelchair ramps, elevators, special parking, special class scheduling, and special housing are available.

Services: Counseling and information services are available, as is tutoring in most subjects, including math, languages, sciences, and engineering. There is remedial math, reading, and writing.

Campus Safety and Security: Measures include 24-hour foot and vehicle patrol, self-defense education, escort service, and informal discussions. There are pamphlets/posters/films, emergency telephones, and lighted pathways/sidewalks.

Programs of Study: WWC confers B.A., B.S., B.B.A., B.Mus., B.S.E., and B.S.W. degrees. Associate and master's degrees are also awarded. Bachelor's degrees are awarded in BIOLOGICAL SCIENCE (biochemistry, biology/biological science, and biophysics), BUSINESS (business administration and management), COMMUNICATIONS AND THE ARTS (art, communications, English, French, German, graphic design, music, music performance, Spanish, and speech/debate/rhetoric), COMPUTER AND PHYSICAL SCIENCE (chemistry, computer science, digital arts/technology, information sciences and systems, mathematics, and physics), EDUCATION (business, elementary, music, physical, and special), ENGINEERING AND ENVIRONMENTAL DESIGN (automotive technology, aviation computer technology, bioengineering, engineering, and environmental science), HEALTH PROFESSIONS (health, and nursing), SOCIAL SCIENCE (biblical languages, history, humanities, psychology, religion, social work, sociology, and theological studies). Engineering, nursing, and biological and natural sciences are the strongest academically. Social work, engineering, and business are the largest.

Required: To graduate, students must successfully complete 192 quarter hours, including at least 45 in the major and at least 60 in upper-level work, with a minimum GPA of 2.0. Grades below C- will not apply toward the major. Students must also meet a general studies requirement that includes 16 to 20 quarter hours in religion and theology, 13 to 21 in language arts, 12 to 20 in history and social science, 12 to 16 in humanities and math/natural science, and 2 to 6 in health and phys ed. A comprehensive exam is required, as is attendance at chapel and assemblies.

Special: Opportunities are provided for internships, co-op programs, cross-registration with Whitman College, study abroad in 6 countries, work-study programs, a B.A.-B.S. degree, dual majors, credit by exam, and nondegree study. There is a freshman honors program.

Faculty/Classroom: 57% of faculty are male; 43%, female. All teach undergraduates. No introductory courses are taught by graduate students. The average class size in an introductory lecture is 24 and in a regular course, 13.

Admissions: 52% of the 2001-2002 applicants were accepted. 30% of the current freshmen were in the top fifth of their class; 51% were in the top two fifths. 12 freshmen graduated first in their class in a recent year.

Requirements: The ACT is required; scores are used for placement and academic advisement. Graduation from an accredited secondary school is required; a GED will be accepted. Applicants should submit an academic record containing at a minimum 4 years of English and 2 each of history, science, and math, including algebra and geometry, along with a letter of recommendation from a teacher or school official. A GPA of 2.0 is required. AP and CLEP credits are accepted. Important factors in the admissions decision are advanced placement or honor courses, recommendations by school officials, and leadership record. Applications are accepted on-line via the college's web site.

Procedure: Freshmen are admitted to all sessions. Entrance exams should be taken during the junior or senior year. There are early decision, early admissions, and deferred admissions plans. Application deadlines are open. The application fee is $30. Notification is sent on a rolling basis.

Transfer: 165 transfer students enrolled in 2001-2002. Applicants should have a 2.0 minimum GPA and must submit all college transcripts and a letter of recommendation (3 for nursing majors) from a former teacher or school official. 36 quarter credits of 192 must be completed at WWC.

Visiting: Students may schedule an appointment 2 to 3 weeks in advance for a visit that includes a campus tour, meals in the dining room, and appointments with financial, academic, or other staff members. Visitors may sit in on classes and stay overnight. To schedule a visit, contact the Admissions and Marketing Office.

Financial Aid: In 2001-2002, 71% of all freshmen and 70% of continuing students received some form of financial aid. 55% of freshmen and 57% of continuing students received need-based aid. The average freshman award was $13,310. Of that total, scholarships or need-based grants averaged $4667; and loans averaged $3995. 94% of undergraduates work part time. Average annual earnings from campus work are $2800. The average financial indebtedness of the 2001 graduate was $20,738. The FAFSA and the college's own financial statement are required. The fall application deadline is April 30.

International Students: The school actively recruits these students. They must score 550 on the written TOEFL or 213 on the electronic version and also take the SAT I or the ACT.

Computers: The mainframe is an HP 3000 Series 969/200. There are 3 general-purpose PC labs housing 110 PCs and subject-specific computer labs for chemistry, engineering, and physics. All students may access the system 6:30 A.M. to 11 P.M. Sunday through Thursday and 6:30 A.M. to 3:30 P.M. Fridays. There are no time limits and no fees.

Graduates: In 2001, 249 bachelor's degrees were awarded. The most popular majors were engineering (19%), nursing (17%), and business (13%). In an average class, 27% graduate in 4 years, 46% in 5 years, and 54% in 6 years. 15 companies recruited on campus in 2000-2001.

Admissions Contact: Dallas Weis, Director of Admissions. A video is available. E-mail: *weisda@wwc.edu* Web: *www.wwc.edu*

WASHINGTON STATE UNIVERSITY E-3
Pullman, WA 99164-1067 **(509) 335-5586**
(888) 468-6978; Fax: (509) 335-4902

Full-time: 7283 men, 7277 women	**Faculty:** 1066; I, --$
Part-time: 1105 men, 1811 women	**Ph.D.s:** 87%
Graduate: 1691 men, 1906 women	**Student/Faculty:** 14 to 1
Year: semesters, summer session	**Tuition:** $4236 ($11,617)
Application Deadline: open	**Room & Board:** $5152
Freshman Class: 7968 applied, 6484 accepted, 2619 enrolled	
SAT I Verbal/Math: 513/518	**COMPETITIVE**

Washington State University, founded in 1890, is a public, land-grant, research institution. Its undergraduate and graduate programs stress the liberal arts, business, economics, art and fine arts, engineering, architecture, agricultural and technical studies, home economics, music, teacher preparation, and health sciences, including nursing, pharmacy, and veterinary medicine. There are 10 undergraduate schools and 1 graduate school. In addition to regional accreditation, Washington State has baccalaureate program accreditation with AACSB, ACCE, ACPE, ADA, ASLA, FIDER, NAAB, NASM, NCATE, NLN, NRPA, and SAF. The 9 libraries contain 2,044,856 volumes, 4,628,813 microform items, and 40,251 audiovisual forms/CDs, and subscribe to 30,292 periodicals. Computerized library services include the card catalog, interlibrary loans, and database searching. Special learning facilities include a learning resource center, art gallery, natural history museum, planetarium, radio station, TV station, observatory, electron microscopy center, and nuclear radiation center. The 620-acre campus is in a small town 80 miles south of Spokane and 285 miles east of Seattle. Including residence halls, there are 221 buildings.

Student Life: 86% of undergraduates are from Washington. Others are from 49 states, 64 foreign countries, and Canada. 78% are white. The average age of freshmen is 18; all undergraduates, 23. 16% do not continue beyond their first year; 84% remain to graduate.

Housing: 8000 students can be accommodated in college housing, which includes single-sex and coed dormitories, on-campus apartments, off-campus apartments, married-student housing, fraternity houses, and sorority houses. In addition, there are honors houses, language houses, and special-interest houses. On-campus housing is guaranteed for all 4 years. 58% of students commute. Alcohol is not permitted. All students may keep cars.

Activities: 17% of men belong to 24 national fraternities; 16% of women belong to 16 national sororities. There are 225 groups on campus, including band, cheerleading, chess, choir, chorus, dance, drama, drill team, ethnic, film, gay, honors, international, jazz band, literary magazine, marching band, musical theater, newspaper, opera, orchestra, pep band, photography, political, professional, radio and TV, religious, social, social service, student government, symphony, and yearbook. Popular campus events include Dad's Weekend, Mom's Weekend, and Land Grant Days.

Sports: There are 6 intercollegiate sports for men and 9 for women, and 45 intramural sports for men and 45 for women. Facilities include a 40,000-seat stadium, a 12,000-seat coliseum, an indoor and outdoor track, tennis courts, a weight/aerobic facility, a golf course, bowling lanes, baseball and soccer fields, swimming pools, lockers, racquetball and squash courts, a climbing wall, ballrooms, riding stables, gyms, crew rowing facilities, and an outdoor recreation center.

Disabled Students: 90% of the campus is accessible. Wheelchair ramps, elevators, special parking, specially equipped rest rooms, special class scheduling, lowered drinking fountains, lowered telephones, and a van to provide transportation to and from classes are available.

Services: Counseling and information services are available, as is tutoring in most subjects. There is a reader service for the blind, and a reading and study skills course.

Campus Safety and Security: Measures include 24-hour foot and vehicle patrol, self-defense education, escort service, and informal discussions. There are pamphlets/posters/films, emergency telephones, lighted pathways/sidewalks, monitored lighting levels on campus, a women's transit service, resident hall security hours, a police intern program, and housing patrols.

Programs of Study: Washington State confers B.A., B.S., B.Arch., B.F.A., B.L.A. and B.M. degrees. Master's and doctoral degrees are also awarded. Bachelor's degrees are awarded in AGRICULTURE (agricultural business management, agricultural economics, agricultural mechanics, agriculture, agronomy, animal science, forestry and related sciences, horticulture, natural resource management, plant protection (pest management), range/farm management, soil science, and wildlife management), BIOLOGICAL SCIENCE (biochemistry, biology/biological science, cell biology, entomology, genetics, microbiology, neurosciences, plant genetics, plant pathology, wildlife biology, and zoology), BUSINESS (accounting, banking and finance, business administration and management, business economics, business law, business statistics, entrepreneurial studies, hotel/motel and restaurant management, insurance and risk management, international business management, management information systems, management science, marketing management, personnel management, real estate, and sports management), COMMUNICATIONS AND THE ARTS (advertising, broadcasting, classics, communications, English, fine arts, French, German, journalism, linguistics, music, music performance, music theory and composition, public relations, Russian, Spanish, and visual and performing arts), COMPUTER AND PHYSICAL SCIENCE (chemistry, computer science, geology, mathematics, physical sciences, physics, and science), EDUCATION (agricultural, athletic training, education, physical, recreation, and secondary), ENGINEERING AND ENVIRONMENTAL DESIGN (agricultural engineering, architecture, chemical engineering, civil engineering, computer engineering, construction management, electrical/electronics engineering, environmental science, interior design, landscape architecture/design, manufacturing engineering, and materials engineering), HEALTH PROFESSIONS (exercise science, nursing, predentistry, premedicine, speech pathology/audiology, and veterinary science), SOCIAL SCIENCE (American studies, anthropology, area studies, Asian/Oriental studies, criminal justice, economics, food science, history, home economics, human development, humanities, liberal arts/general studies, philosophy, political science/government, psychology, public affairs, religion, social science, social studies, social work, sociology, women's studies, and youth ministry). Broadcasting, hospitality, and interior design are the strongest academically. Business administration is the largest.

Required: Students must complete 120 semester hours, with fulfillment of a major and 40 hours of upper-division work, and maintain a minimum GPA of 2.0. Specific disciplines to be taken vary within majors. General university requirements include 10 hours of science, 9 of arts and humanities and social science, 6 of world civilization, and 3 each of intercultural studies and communications proficiency. Students must complete a writing portfolio and pass a writing qualifying exam prior to graduation.

Special: Special academic programs include internships through the Professional Experience Program, study abroad in 25 countries, and work-study with numerous employers. There are co-op programs in numerous majors and cross-registration with the University of Idaho, the University of Washington, Eastern Washington University, Yakima Valley Community College, and Northwest Indian College. Students may attend the Intercollegiate Center for Nursing Education, which is a consortium of Washington State, Eastern Washington, and Gonzaga Universities, and Whitworth College. Dual majors are available, as is a general studies degree. Credit may be granted for military service, and nondegree and pass/fail options are possible. Special features of the school include the opportunity for undergraduates to become involved in research and its honors programs. There are 23 national honor societies, including Phi Beta Kappa and a freshman honors program.

Faculty/Classroom: 64% of faculty are male; 36%, female. The average class size in a regular course is 25.

Admissions: 81% of the 2001-2002 applicants were accepted. The SAT I scores for the 2001-2002 freshman class were: Verbal--41% below 500, 39% between 500 and 599, 18% between 600 and 700, and 2% above 700; Math--41% below 500, 39% between 500 and 599, 18% between 600 and 700, and 2% above 700.

Requirements: The SAT I or ACT is required. In addition, other admissions requirements include graduation from an accredited secondary school with 4 years of English, 3 each of math and social studies/history, and 2 each of a foreign language and science. A combination of the high school GPA and test scores is considered. The GED is also accepted. A GPA of 2.0 is required. AP and CLEP credits are accepted. Important factors in the admissions decision are recommendations by school officials, extracurricular activities record, and leadership record. Applications are accepted on computer disk through ExPAN and on-line via the school's web site at *www.wsu.edu/admissions*

Procedure: Freshmen are admitted fall and spring. Entrance exams should be taken during spring of the junior year or fall of the senior year. Application deadlines are open. The application fee is $35. Notification is sent on a rolling basis.

Transfer: 2366 transfer students enrolled in 2001-2002. Applicants must have at least 27 semester hours, or 40 quarter hours, with a GPA of at least 2.0. If they have fewer hours, the criteria are the same as for freshmen. 30 credits of 120 must be completed at Washington State.

Visiting: There are regularly scheduled orientations for prospective students, consisting of a campus tour and presentation. There are guides for informal visits and visitors may sit in on classes. To schedule a visit, contact the Office of Admissions at *admiss2@wsu.edu*

Financial Aid: In 2001-2002, 72% of all freshmen and 62% of continuing students received some form of financial aid. 38% of freshmen and 41% of continuing students received need-based aid. The average freshman award was $10,700. Of that total, scholarships or need-based grants averaged $4417 ($18,700 maximum); loans averaged $7382 ($13,819 maximum); and work contracts averaged $2000 (maximum). 12% of undergraduates work part time. Average annual earnings from campus work are $4000. The average financial indebtedness of the 2001 graduate was $15,000. The FAFSA is required. The fall application deadline is March 1.

International Students: There are 616 international students enrolled. They must score 520 on the written TOEFL or take the MELAB.

Computers: The mainframe is an IBM 9672-R24 with open-system data storage units (EMC2 Symmetrix 5330-9518). Through web interfaces, students use the mainframe to view and provide information about their academic status, billings, courses, and a variety of services. There are approximately 12,000 computers at Washington State, the majority of which have access to the Internet through the Washington State network. These computers are located throughout the 4 campuses and remote sites. All students may access the system 24 hours a day. There are no time limits and no fees. It is strongly recommended that all students have personal computes.

Graduates: In 2001, 3719 bachelor's degrees were awarded. The most popular majors were business administration (21%), social science/history (13%), and communications (9%). In an average class, 27% graduate in 4 years, 52% in 5 years, and 57% in 6 years. 225 companies recruited on campus in 2000-2001.

Admissions Contact: Wendy Peterson, Director of Admissions.
E-mail: *admiss@wsu.edu* Web: *wsu.edu/admissions*

WESTERN WASHINGTON UNIVERSITY C-1

Bellingham, WA 98225-5996 (360) 650-3440
Fax: (360) 650-7369

Full-time: 4875 men, 6187 women
Part-time: 270 men, 309 women
Graduate: 293 men, 469 women
Year: quarters, summer session
Application Deadline: March 1
Faculty: 448; IIA, -$
Ph.D.s: 86%
Student/Faculty: 25 to 1
Tuition: $3290 ($11,030)
Room & Board: $5352
Freshman Class: 6862 applied, 5305 accepted, 2240 enrolled
SAT I Verbal/Math: 540/540 **ACT:** 23 **VERY COMPETITIVE**

Western Washington University, founded in 1893, is a nonprofit, public, comprehensive institution whose emphasis is on the liberal arts and sciences, business and business administration and economics, art, fine arts, and performing arts, music, teacher preparation, interdisciplinary learning, and environmental studies. There are 6 undergraduate schools and 1 graduate school. In addition to regional accreditation, WWU has baccalaureate program accreditation with AACSB, ABET, ASLA, NASM, NCATE, and NRPA. The library contains 1,279,000 volumes, 1,832,000 microform items, and 24,825 audiovisual forms/CDs, and subscribes to 4805 periodicals. Computerized library services include the card catalog, interlibrary loans, and database searching. Special learning facilities include a learning resource center, art gallery, planetarium, radio station, marine lab, neutron generator lab, motor vehicle research lab, wind tunnel, air pollution lab, electronic music studio, and performing arts center. The 195-acre campus is in a small town 60 miles south of Vancouver, British Columbia, and 90 miles north of Seattle. Including residence halls, there are 80 buildings.

Student Life: 92% of undergraduates are from Washington. Others are from 47 states, 41 foreign countries, and Canada. 90% are from public schools. 78% are white. The average age of freshmen is 18; all undergraduates, 22. 20% do not continue beyond their first year; 60% remain to graduate.

Housing: 3700 students can be accommodated in college housing, which includes coed dormitories, on-campus apartments, off-campus apartments, married-student housing, a fitness/wellness hall, freshman interest groups, substance-free living, and quiet and smoke-free areas. On-campus housing is available on a first-come, first-served basis. 68% of students commute. All students may keep cars.

Activities: There are no fraternities or sororities. There are 125 groups on campus, including art, band, cheerleading, chess, choir, chorale, chorus, computers, dance, debate, drama, environmental, ethnic, film, forensics, gay, honors, international, jazz band, literary magazine, musical theater, newspaper, opera, orchestra, pep band, photography, political, professional, radio and TV, recreational, religious, social, social service, student government, and symphony. Popular campus events include the Western Jam Talent Show, Casino Night, and Cinco de Mayo.

Sports: There are 7 intercollegiate sports for men and 8 for women, and 34 intramural sports for men and 34 for women. Facilities include a 3000-seat gym, playing fields, 8 tennis courts, a 6000-seat stadium, a golf course, salt/freshwater recreational facilities and equipment, an artificial-surface football field/track, a pool, a state-of-the-art fitness center, and a student-run outdoor center (equipment and excursions).

Disabled Students: All of the campus is accessible. Wheelchair ramps, elevators, special parking, specially equipped rest rooms, special class scheduling, lowered drinking fountains, lowered telephones, and transcription services are available.

Services: Counseling and information services are available, as is tutoring in most subjects, including English, humanities, social sciences, and math and natural sciences. There is a reader service for the blind.

Campus Safety and Security: Measures include 24-hour foot and vehicle patrol, self-defense education, escort service, and shuttle buses. There are informal discussions, pamphlets/posters/films, emergency telephones, and lighted pathways/sidewalks.

Programs of Study: WWU confers B.A., B.S., B.A.E., B.F.A., and B.M. degrees. Master's degrees are also awarded. Bachelor's degrees are awarded in BIOLOGICAL SCIENCE (biochemistry and biology/biological science), BUSINESS (accounting, business administration and management, international business management, management science, and marketing/retailing/merchandising), COMMUNICATIONS AND THE ARTS (art, communications, dramatic arts, English, fine arts, French, German, journalism, linguistics, music, and Spanish), COMPUTER AND PHYSICAL SCIENCE (chemistry, computer science, geology, mathematics, and physics), EDUCATION (art, early childhood, elementary, foreign languages, health, music, science, and secondary), ENGINEERING AND ENVIRONMENTAL DESIGN (electrical/electronics engineering technology, engineering technology, environmental science, and manufacturing technology), HEALTH PROFESSIONS (speech pathology/audiology), SOCIAL SCIENCE (anthropology, Canadian studies, East Asian studies, economics, geography, history, human services, parks and recreation management, philosophy, political science/government, psychology, and sociology). Computer science, business, and technology are the strongest academically. Psychology, environmental studies, and education are the largest.

Required: Students must complete at least 180 quarter hours, with fulfillment of a major and at least 60 credits in upper-division study, and maintain at least a 2.0 GPA or that prescribed by departments/divisions. General university requirements include 70 to 75 credits, and students must satisfy writing proficiency requirements as well. Fairhaven College has a separate interdisciplinary core program.

Special: Special academic programs include internships through various academic departments and study abroad in 75 countries. Dual majors are available through various departments, and there is a general studies degree, a B.A. in humanities. A 3-2 engineering degree is possible with the University of Washington. Student-designed majors are offered through the liberal studies department in the College of Arts and Sciences and through Fairhaven College, which affords an unusual degree of student involvement in the structure and content of their own programs and which uses faculty narrative for students' academic evaluations. In addition, Huxley College of Environmental Studies provides specialized education and research. Up to 30 credits of electives may be granted for military service, and nondegree study and pass/fail options are possible. There are 13 national honor societies, a freshman honors program, and 3 departmental honors programs.

Faculty/Classroom: 66% of faculty are male; 34%, female. All teach undergraduates and 90% both teach and do research. Graduate students teach 4% of introductory courses. The average class size in an introductory lecture is 80; in a laboratory, 20; and in a regular course, 27.

Admissions: 77% of the 2001-2002 applicants were accepted. The SAT I scores for the 2001-2002 freshman class were: Verbal--27% below 500, 46% between 500 and 599, 24% between 600 and 700, and 3% above 700; Math--26% below 500, 48% between 500 and 599, 24% between 600 and 700, and 2% above 700. The ACT scores were 27% below 21, 29% between 21 and 23, 24% between 24 and 26, 12% between 27 and 28, and 8% above 28. 46% of the current freshmen were in the top fifth of their class; 83% were in the top two fifths. There were 6 National Merit finalists. 54 freshmen graduated first in their class.

Requirements: The SAT I or ACT is required. In addition, other admissions requirements include completion of 15 academic units, comprised of 4 years of college preparatory English composition and literature courses; 3 years of college preparatory math, including 2 years of algebra; 3 years of social studies/history; 2 years of science, including 1 year of a chemistry or physics with an algebra prerequisite; 2 years of the same foreign language; 1 semester of fine and performing arts; and 1 semester in another academic field. Freshman applicants meeting minimum GPA and subject requirements are ranked by an index combining the GPA and a standardized test score. The GED is also accepted. Other factors taken into consideration include curricular rigor (level of difficulty of courses), grade trends, leadership, community involvement, special talent, multicultural experience, and personal hardship or circumstances. A GPA of 2.5 is required. AP credits are accepted. Important factors in the admissions decision are advanced placement or honor courses, leadership record, and personality/intangible qualities. Applications are accepted on-line at the school's web site.

Procedure: Freshmen are admitted to all sessions. Entrance exams should be taken by fall of the senior year. Applications should be filed by March 1 for fall entry, October 15 for winter entry, January 15 for spring entry, and March 1 for summer entry, along with a $35 fee. Notification is sent March 15. 2% of all applicants are on a waiting list; 50 were accepted in 2001.

Transfer: 988 transfer students enrolled in 2001-2002. Applicants with fewer than 40 quarter credits are eligible for consideration if they have completed the last term before transferring with a GPA of at least 2.0 and if they satisfy the requirements for freshman admission. Those with 40 or more transferable quarter credits are eligible if they have achieved a cumulative GPA of at least 2.0. Admission is selective. 45 credits of 180 must be completed at WWU.

Visiting: There are regularly scheduled orientations for prospective students, including tours, class visits, and advisement. There are guides for informal visits and visitors may sit in on classes and stay overnight. To schedule a visit, contact the STARS Program - Student Admissions Representatives at (360) 650-3861 or *campusvisit@wwu.edu*

Financial Aid: In 2001-2002, 59% of all freshmen and 53% of continuing students received some form of financial aid. 29% of freshmen and 35% of continuing students received need-based aid. The average freshman award was $8023. Of that total, scholarships or need-based grants averaged $2803 ($6130 maximum); loans averaged $2010 ($5625 maximum); work contracts averaged $299 ($2400 maximum); and PLUS (parent loan) averaged $2911 ($10,225 maximum). 46% of undergraduates work part time. Average annual earnings from campus work are $1606. The average financial indebtedness of the 2001 graduate was $14,820. The FAFSA is required. The fall application deadline is February 15.

International Students: There are 41 international students enrolled. They must score 550 on the written TOEFL or 213 on the electronic version and also take the SAT I.

Computers: The mainframe is a Sun E4000. There are more than 1000 PCs and Macs available in the student labs and residence halls. Students also have access to the Internet and the Web. All students may access the system. There are no time limits and no fees.

Graduates: In 2001, 2651 bachelor's degrees were awarded. The most popular majors were finance and management (8%), English (7%), and human services (7%). In an average class, 25% graduate in 4 years, 54% in 5 years, and 63% in 6 years. 80 companies recruited on campus in 2000-2001. Of the 2000 graduating class, 13% were enrolled in graduate school within 6 months of graduation and 93% were employed.

Admissions Contact: Karen Copetas, Director.
E-mail: *admit@cc.wwu.edu* Web: *www.wwu.edu/~admit*

WHITMAN COLLEGE — E-3
Walla Walla, WA 99362-2083 — **(509) 527-5176**
(877) 462-9448; Fax: (509) 527-4967

Full-time: 628 men, 771 women	**Faculty:** 115; IIB, +$
Part-time: 11 men, 29 women	**Ph.D.s:** 93%
Graduate: none	**Student/Faculty:** 12 to 1
Year: semesters	**Tuition:** $22,796
Application Deadline: February 1	**Room & Board:** $6290
Freshman Class: 2144 applied, 1161 accepted, 362 enrolled	
SAT I Verbal/Math: 659/649	**HIGHLY COMPETITIVE**

Whitman College, founded in 1883, is a nonprofit, private, independent residential liberal arts and sciences college. The library contains 337,305 volumes, 16,000 microform items, and 3500 audiovisual forms/CDs, and subscribes to 2100 periodicals. Computerized library services include the card catalog, interlibrary loans, and database searching. Special learning facilities include a learning resource center, art gallery, natural history museum, planetarium, radio station, an electron microscope lab, an indoor planetarium, an off-campus observatory and on-campus astronomical telescopes, an Asian art collection, a video-conferencing center, an outdoor sculpture walk, and an organic garden. The 117-acre campus is in a small town 150 miles south of Spokane, 260 miles southeast of Seattle, and 235 miles east of Portland. Including residence halls, there are 41 buildings.

Student Life: 55% of undergraduates are from out of state, mostly the Northwest. Others are from 43 states, 22 foreign countries, and Canada. 78% are from public schools. 82% are white. The average age of freshmen is 18; all undergraduates, 20. 7% do not continue beyond their first year; 86% remain to graduate.

Housing: 830 students can be accommodated in college housing, which includes single-sex and coed dormitories, off-campus apartments, and fraternity houses. In addition, there are language houses and specal-interest houses. On-campus housing is guaranteed for the freshman year only and is available on a lottery system for upperclassmen. 65% of students live on campus; of those, 95% remain on campus on weekends. All students may keep cars.

Activities: 36% of men belong to 4 national fraternities; 34% of women belong to 4 national sororities. There are 75 groups on campus, including academic, animal rights, art, choir, chorale, chorus, culinary arts, dance, debate, drama, environmental, ethnic, film, forensics, gay, health, honors, international, jazz band, leadership, literary magazine, mentoring, musical theater, newspaper, opera, orchestra, pep band, photography, political, professional, radio and TV, religious, social service, student government, symphony, and women's issues. Popular campus events include Renaissance Fair, Choral Contest, and Interest House Block Party.

Sports: There are 10 intercollegiate sports for men and 10 for women, and 9 intramural sports for men and 9 for women. Facilities include a stadium, a center with a 3000-seat gym, squash and handball courts, saunas, a pool, indoor and outdoor climbing walls, a small gym, a weights/Nautilus room, aerobic/dance room, cardiovascular room, 4 outdoor tennis courts, a soccer field, an indoor tennis facility, a dance studio, and an off-campus playing field complex.

Disabled Students: 50% of the campus is accessible. Wheelchair ramps, elevators, special parking, specially equipped rest rooms, lowered drinking fountains, and lowered telephones are available. Any modifications necessary for specific cases will be made.

Services: Counseling and information services are available, as is tutoring in most subjects. There is a reader service for the blind, and centers for study skills and writing.

Campus Safety and Security: Measures include self-defense education, escort service, informal discussions, and pamphlets/posters/films. There are emergency telephones, lighted pathways/sidewalks, and 24-hour foot patrol.

Programs of Study: Whitman College confers the B.A. degree. Bachelor's degrees are awarded in BIOLOGICAL SCIENCE (biology/biological science), COMMUNICATIONS AND THE ARTS (art history and appreciation, classics, dramatic arts, English, fine arts, French, German, music, Spanish, and studio art), COMPUTER AND PHYSICAL SCIENCE (chemistry, geology, mathematics, and physics), ENGINEERING AND ENVIRONMENTAL DESIGN (environmental science), SOCIAL SCIENCE (anthropology, Asian/Oriental studies, economics, history, philosophy, political science/government, psychology, and sociology). English, politics, and biology are the strongest academically and have the largest enrollments.

Required: Students must complete 124 credits, with 32 to 36 in the major, and maintain a minimum GPA of 2.0. Distribution requirements must be followed, and a freshman core must be taken as well. Written and oral tests are also required.

Special: Special academic programs include more than 500 internships, study abroad in 43 countries, a Washington semester, and study programs in Chicago and Philadelphia. Dual majors are available in any area, and student-designed majors are offered. There is a 3-2 environmental management and forestry program with Duke University, and a 3-2 engineering program with Washington University in St. Louis, California Institute of Technology, Columbia and Duke Universities, and University of Washington. A 3-3 law program is offered through Columbia University. A 4-1 education program is available through Bank Street College of Education. Certification is offered for elementary and secondary education. A pass-D-fail option is available. A special feature of the curriculum is the integrated general studies program for freshmen. A 3-2 program is available with the Monterey Institute of International Studies. There are 3 national honor societies, including Phi Beta Kappa, a freshman honors program, and 39 departmental honors programs.

Faculty/Classroom: 65% of faculty are male; 35%, female. All both teach and do research. The average class size in an introductory lecture is 22; in a laboratory, 17; and in a regular course, 15.

Admissions: 54% of the 2001-2002 applicants were accepted. The SAT I scores for the 2001-2002 freshman class were: Verbal--19% between 500 and 599, 51% between 600 and 700, and 30% above 700; Math--2% below 500, 17% between 500 and 599, 58% between 600 and 700, and 24% above 700. The ACT scores were 2% below 21, 3% between 21 and 23, 17% between 24 and 26, 15% between 27 and 28, and 63% above 28. 89% of the current freshmen were in the top fifth of their class; 98% were in the top two fifths. There were 16 National Merit finalists. 43 freshmen graduated first in their class.

Requirements: The SAT I or ACT is required. The GED is accepted. 3 essays must be submitted, and an interview is recommended. Credit by challenge examination is accepted. AP credits are accepted. Important factors in the admissions decision are advanced placement or honor courses, evidence of special talent, and extracurricular activities record. The Whitman application is accepted on computer disk and on-line at the school's web site and via CollegeNET and Common App.

Procedure: Freshmen are admitted fall and spring. Entrance exams should be taken by February of the senior year. There are early decision and deferred admissions plans. Early decision applications should be filed by November 15; regular applications, by February 1 for fall entry and December 1 for spring entry. The fall 2001 application fee was $45. Notification of early decision is sent December 15; regular decision, April 1. 84 early decision candidates were accepted for the 2001-2002 class. 8% of all applicants are on a waiting list; 61 were accepted in 2001.

Transfer: 25 transfer students enrolled in 2001-2002. Transfer applicants must submit the common application, a transfer supplement, a teacher/counselor recommendation, a statement of good standing from prior institutions, their high school and college transcripts, the SAT I or ACT scores (required for some), and the application fee. 54 credits of 124 must be completed at Whitman College.

Visiting: There are regularly scheduled orientations for prospective students, including Fall and Spring Visitors' Days. There are guides for informal visits and visitors may sit in on classes and stay overnight. To schedule a visit, contact the Admission Office.

Financial Aid: In 2001-2002, 74% of all students received some form of financial aid. 42% of freshmen and 43% of continuing students received need-based aid. The average freshman award was $15,341. Of that total, scholarships or need-based grants averaged $11,389 ($28,586 maximum); loans averaged $3030 ($5000 maximum); work contracts averaged $1700 ($2200 maximum); and federal or state grants averaged $2870 ($7236 maximum). 71% of undergraduates work part time. Average annual earnings from campus work are $1280. The average financial indebtedness of the 2001 graduate was $12,578. Whitman College is a member of CSS. The CSS/Profile or FAFSA is required. The fall application deadline is February 1.

International Students: There are 37 international students enrolled. The school actively recruits these students. They must score 560 on the written TOEFL, take APIEL or ELPT, and also take the SAT I or the ACT.

Computers: The mainframes are an HP3000/968, an HP 3000/918, a Sun SPARC Station 20, a Sun SPARC Station 5, and an HP9000/800. Students have unlimited network access from all student PCs on campus, including in residence halls. All students have e-mail accounts. There are 4 main computer labs and various departmental labs available to students, some portions open 24 hours a day. All students may access the system 24 hours a day. There are no time limits and no fees.

Graduates: In 2001, 323 bachelor's degrees were awarded. The most popular majors were English (11%), politics (9%), and biology (8%). In an average class, 86% graduate in 4 years, 86% in 5 years, and 86% in 6 years. 112 companies recruited on campus in 2000-2001.

Admissions Contact: John W. Bogley, Dean of Admission and Financial Aid. A video is available. E-mail: *admission@whitman.edu*
Web: *http://www.whitman.edu*

WHITWORTH COLLEGE
Spokane, WA 99251 — **C-2**
(509) 777-3212
(800) 533-4668; Fax: (509) 777-3758

Full-time: 667 men, 1082 women	**Faculty:** 96
Part-time: 49 men, 80 women	**Ph.D.s:** 86%
Graduate: 65 men, 146 women	**Student/Faculty:** 18 to 1
Year: 4-1-4, summer session	**Tuition:** $18,038
Application Deadline: March 1	**Room & Board:** $5900
Freshman Class: 1597 applied, 1253 accepted, 427 enrolled	
SAT I Verbal/Math: 572/575	**ACT:** 26 **VERY COMPETITIVE**

Whitworth College, founded in 1890, is a nonprofit, independent, comprehensive institution affiliated with the Presbyterian Church (U.S.A.). The emphasis of its undergraduate and graduate programs is on the liberal arts, business, art and fine arts, music, religious studies, and teacher preparation. In addition to regional accreditation, Whitworth has baccalaureate program accreditation with NASM, NCATE, and NLN. The library contains 141,000 volumes, 54,250 microform items, and 1528 audiovisual forms/CDs, and subscribes to 810 periodicals. Computerized library services include the card catalog, interlibrary loans, and database searching. Special learning facilities include a learning resource center, art gallery, radio station, and a writing center. The 200-acre campus is in a suburban area 7 miles north of Spokane. Including residence halls, there are 40 buildings.

Student Life: 55% of undergraduates are from Washington. Others are from 29 states, 25 foreign countries, and Canada. 88% are from public schools. 86% are white. 76% are Protestant; 10% claim no religious affiliation. The average age of freshmen is 19; all undergraduates, 22. 14% do not continue beyond their first year; 68% remain to graduate.

Housing: 1000 students can be accommodated in college housing, which includes single-sex and coed dormitories, on-campus apartments, and off-campus apartments. In addition, there are language houses and special-interest houses. On-campus housing is guaranteed for all 4 years, is available on a first-come, first-served basis, and on a lottery system for upperclassmen. Priority is given to out-of-town students. 66% of students live on campus; of those, 90% remain on campus on weekends. Alcohol is not permitted. All students may keep cars.

Activities: There are no fraternities or sororities. There are 45 groups on campus, including art, band, cheerleading, choir, chorale, chorus, computers, dance, drama, ethnic, honors, international, jazz band, literary magazine, musical theater, newspaper, orchestra, photography, political, radio and TV, religious, social, social service, student government, and yearbook. Popular campus events include athletic events, movies, and theme weeks.

Sports: There are 8 intercollegiate sports for men and 8 for women, and 10 intramural sports for men and 8 for women. Facilities include a 2000-seat stadium, a 1200-seat gym, a field house, an aquatic center, and playing fields.

Disabled Students: 70% of the campus is accessible. Wheelchair ramps, elevators, special parking, specially equipped rest rooms, and lowered drinking fountains are available.

Services: Counseling and information services are available, as is tutoring in most subjects, including biology, chemistry, computer science, French, German, Spanish, math, physics, and writing.

Campus Safety and Security: Measures include 24-hour foot and vehicle patrol, informal discussions, emergency telephones, and lighted pathways/sidewalks.

Programs of Study: Whitworth confers B.A. and B.S. degrees. Master's degrees are also awarded. Bachelor's degrees are awarded in BIOLOGICAL SCIENCE (biology/biological science), BUSINESS (accounting, business administration and management, and international business management), COMMUNICATIONS AND THE ARTS (art, communications, dramatic arts, English, French, journalism, music, Spanish, and speech/debate/rhetoric), COMPUTER AND PHYSICAL SCIENCE (applied physics, chemistry, computer science, mathematics, physics, and quantitative methods), EDUCATION (athletic training, elementary, English, foreign languages, mathematics, music, science, secondary, and social studies), ENGINEERING AND ENVIRONMENTAL DESIGN (environmental science), HEALTH PROFESSIONS (nursing, predentistry, and premedicine), SOCIAL SCIENCE (American studies, crosscultural studies, economics, history, international studies, peace studies, philosophy, political science/government, prelaw, psychology, religion, sociology, and women's studies). English, history, and chemistry are the strongest academically. Education, business, and history/political studies are the largest.

Required: Students must complete 130 credit hours, with 42 in the major, and maintain a GPA of at least 2.0. The curriculum includes 3 core courses on religious, rationalist, and scientific traditions; distribution requirements are comprised of 4 phys ed activity courses, 2 each in a foreign language and science/math, and 1 course each in biblical literature, oral communication, fine arts, social science, and humanities. Additionally, an other-culture course or experience must be fulfilled.

Special: Special academic programs include many work-study opportunities, 1 to 3 internship course credits that may be earned by juniors and seniors, and a January Washington term. Study abroad is available in 15 countries. There is cross-registration with the Intercollegiate Language Study Consortium and Gonzaga University. Accelerated degree programs are possible, as is a 3-2 engineering degree, and students may choose to specialize in an area of concentration in lieu of a major. Credit may be granted for life, military, or work experience. Nondegree study is possible for those auditing or in seminars, and there is 1 pass/fail option allowed per year. A special feature of the school is the modified semester calendar, which affords unusual opportunities for internships, study tours, and other activities. There is a freshman honors program.

Faculty/Classroom: 70% of faculty are male; 30%, female. All teach undergraduates. No introductory courses are taught by graduate students. The average class size in an introductory lecture is 30; in a laboratory, 15; and in a regular course, 19.

Admissions: 78% of the 2001-2002 applicants were accepted. The SAT I scores for the 2001-2002 freshman class were: Verbal--18% below 500, 44% between 500 and 599, 31% between 600 and 700, and 7% above 700; Math--15% below 500, 45% between 500 and 599, 34% between 600 and 700, and 6% above 700. 40% of the current freshmen were in the top fifth of their class; 75% were in the top two fifths. There were 6 National Merit semifinalists. 42 freshmen graduated first in their class.

Requirements: The SAT I or ACT is required, with suggested scores of 1000 for the SAT I, 500 verbal and 500 math, and 22 for the ACT. Other admissions criteria include 4 high school credits in English, 3 each in math, science, and history/social studies, and 2 of a foreign language. An essay must be submitted, and an interview is recommended. Music students are advised to audition. Whitworth requires applicants to be in the upper 50% of their class. A GPA of 3.0 is required. AP and CLEP credits are accepted. Important factors in the admissions decision are advanced placement or honor courses, extracurricular activities record, and leadership record. Applications are accepted on-line and on computer disk.

Procedure: Freshmen are admitted fall, winter, and spring. Entrance exams should be taken by the fall of the senior year, though the spring of the junior year is preferred. There are early admissions and deferred admissions plans. Early action applications should be filed by November 30; regular applications, by March 1 for fall entry. Notification of early action is sent December 15; regular decision, on a rolling basis. 10% of all applicants are on a waiting list.

Transfer: 90 transfer students enrolled in 2001-2002. Transfer students must have a GPA of at least 2.25 and a recommended 45 quarter credits earned. The SAT I or ACT is recommended; the SAT I composite score should be 1000 and the ACT score 22. 32 credits of 130 must be completed at Whitworth.

Visiting: There are regularly scheduled orientations for prospective students, including a class visit, a tour, and an overnight stay, if desired. There are guides for informal visits and visitors may sit in on classes and stay overnight. To schedule a visit, contact Debbie Harvey, Campus Visit Coordinator at (509) 777-4331 or *dharvey@whitworth.edu*

Financial Aid: In 2001-2002, 90% of all freshmen and 88% of continuing students received some form of financial aid. 52% of all students received need-based aid. The average freshman award was $14,400. Of that total, scholarships or need-based grants averaged $6900 ($17,800 maximum); loans averaged $3418 ($5000 maximum); work contracts averaged $1559 ($2500 maximum); and SEOG, PELL, and Washington State Need Grants averaged $1723. All undergraduates work part time. Average annual earnings from campus work are $1402. The average financial indebtedness of the 2001 graduate was $16,000. The CSS/Profile, FAFSA, FFS, or SFS are required. The FAFSA is preferred. The fall application deadline is March 1.

International Students: There were 85 international students enrolled in a recent year. The school actively recruits these students. They must score 460 on the written TOEFL.

Computers: The mainframe is a DEC MicroVAX 3500. There are PC labs available for student use. Internet access is also available from every dorm room on campus. All students may access the system any time during library hours. There are no time limits and no fees. It is strongly recommended that all students have personal computers.

Graduates: In 2001, 320 bachelor's degrees were awarded. In an average class, 3% graduate in 3 years, 58% in 4 years, 68% in 5 years, and 70% in 6 years. 60 companies recruited on campus in 2000-2001.

Admissions Contact: Fred Pfursich, Dean of Enrollment.
E-mail: *admission@whitworth.edu* Web: *www.whitworth.edu*

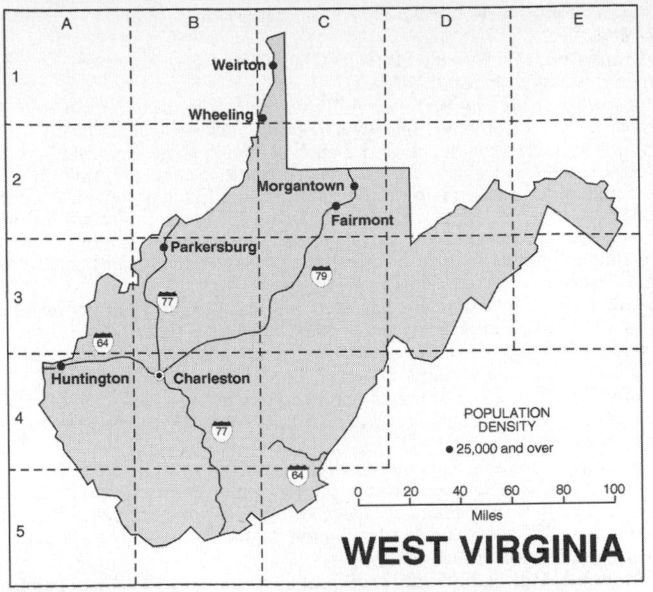

ALDERSON-BROADDUS COLLEGE C-3
Philippi, WV 26416 (304) 457-6310
(800) 263-1549; Fax: (304) 457-6239

Full-time: 257 men, 421 women	**Faculty:** 61
Part-time: 13 men, 50 women	**Ph.D.s:** 45%
Graduate: 27 men, 34 women	**Student/Faculty:** 11 to 1
Year: semesters, summer session	**Tuition:** $14,440
Application Deadline: August 1	**Room & Board:** $5200
Freshman Class: n/av	
SAT I Verbal/Math: 510/476	**ACT:** 20 **COMPETITIVE**

Alderson-Broaddus College is a private institution, founded in 1871 and affiliated with American Baptist Churches USA. It offers a liberal arts program along with teacher preparation and professional, music, business, religion, and science studies. In addition to regional accreditation, Alderson-Broaddus has baccalaureate program accreditation with CAHEA, NCATE, and NLN. The library contains 100,000 volumes, 8000 microform items, and 5000 audiovisual forms/CDs, and subscribes to 670 periodicals. Computerized library services include the card catalog, interlibrary loans, and database searching. Special learning facilities include a learning resource center, art gallery, radio station, and TV station. The 170-acre campus is in a small town 100 miles south of Pittsburgh and 100 miles north of Charleston. Including residence halls, there are 19 buildings.

Student Life: 67% of undergraduates are from West Virginia. Others are from 26 states, 5 foreign countries, and Canada. 90% are from public schools. 91% are white. 75% are Protestant; 14% Catholic; 11% claim no religious affiliation. The average age of freshmen is 21. 31% do not continue beyond their first year; 44% remain to graduate.

Housing: 700 students can be accommodated in college housing, which includes single-sex and coed dormitories, on-campus apartments, off-campus apartments, and married-student housing. On-campus housing is guaranteed for all 4 years. 60% of students live on campus; of those, 40% remain on campus on weekends. Alcohol is not permitted. All students may keep cars.

Activities: 8% of men belong to 3 local fraternities; 10% of women belong to 3 local sororities. There are 40 groups on campus, including art, band, choir, chorale, chorus, computers, dance, debate, drama, ethnic, forensics, honors, jazz band, musical theater, newspaper, pep band, photography, political, professional, radio and TV, religious, social, social service, student government, and yearbook. Popular campus events include Spring Weekend, Christmas programs, and Homeless Weekend.

Sports: There are 10 intramural sports for men and 10 for women. Facilities include several playing fields near the main campus, a swimming pool, a weight room, handball courts, auxiliary gyms, an archery range, a batting cage, and a tennis court.

Disabled Students: 75% of the campus is accessible. Wheelchair ramps, elevators, special parking, specially equipped rest rooms, and special class scheduling are available.

Services: Counseling and information services are available, as is tutoring in every subject. There is remedial math, reading, and writing. There is also an Academic Support Network.

Campus Safety and Security: Measures include 24-hour foot and vehicle patrol, informal discussions, pamphlets/posters/films, and lighted pathways/sidewalks.

Programs of Study: A-B confers B.A. and B.S. degrees. Associate and master's degrees are also awarded. Bachelor's degrees are awarded in BIOLOGICAL SCIENCE (biology/biological science), BUSINESS (accounting, business administration and management, and management information systems), COMMUNICATIONS AND THE ARTS (communications, creative writing, literature, and music), COMPUTER AND PHYSICAL SCIENCE (chemistry, computer science, and mathematics), EDUCATION (athletic training, elementary, music, recreation, and secondary), HEALTH PROFESSIONS (cytotechnology, medical science, medical technology, nursing, ophthalmic technology, and radiograph medical technology), SOCIAL SCIENCE (Christian studies, history, liberal arts/general studies, political science/government, psychology, and religious music). Health sciences, business, and education are the strongest academically. Nursing and health sciences are the largest.

Required: Each graduate is required to complete at least 1 major and Liberal Studies Program requirements amounting to 51 to 55 semester hours plus electives for a minimum of 128 semester hours. The Liberal Studies requirements include courses in English, literature, math, computer literacy, physical and biological science, philosophy/religion, social science, history, global concerns, aesthetic expression, and health. All graduates must have attained a GPA of 2.0 overall and in the major. Certain disciplines may require a GPA higher than the minimum to continue in the major and to graduate.

Special: Internships in numerous majors, student-designed majors in liberal arts, cross-registration with the Mountain State Association of Colleges, study abroad through the college's programs in Austria or through the Junior Year Abroad program in conjunction with other schools, and work scholarships at the college are available. In addition, the college offers dual majors, a general studies degree, the B.A.-B.S. degree, nondegree study, and pass/fail grading in certain courses. There is a freshman honors program.

Faculty/Classroom: 57% of faculty are male; 43%, female. 97% teach undergraduates and 10% both teach and do research. No introductory courses are taught by graduate students. The average class size in an introductory lecture is 40; in a laboratory, 30; and in a regular course, 20.

Admissions: 47% of the current freshmen were in the top fifth of their class; 80% were in the top two fifths.

Requirements: The SAT I or ACT is required,with a recommended composite score of 950 for the SAT I, 21 for the ACT. Applicants who are graduates of secondary schools or who have passed the GED are considered for admission. An audition for certain majors and an interview are recommended. A GPA of 2.5 is required. AP and CLEP credits are accepted. Important factors in the admissions decision are advanced placement or honor courses, leadership record, and recommendations by school officials. Applications are accepted on-line.

Procedure: Freshmen are admitted to all sessions. Entrance exams should be taken in spring of the junior year. There is a deferred admissions plan. Applications should be filed by August 1 for fall entry and January 1 for spring entry. The fall 2001 application fee was $10. Notification is sent on a rolling basis.

Transfer: 42 transfer students enrolled in 2001-2002. Transfer applicants must have a minimum 2.0 GPA. If they have fewer than 29 transfer credit hours, ACT or SAT I results and a high school diploma are required. 60 credits of 128 must be completed at A-B.

Visiting: There are regularly scheduled orientations for prospective students, including placement tests and social programs. There are guides for informal visits and visitors may sit in on classes and stay overnight. To schedule a visit, contact the Admissions Office.

Financial Aid: In a recent year, all freshmen received some form of financial aid. Scholarships or need-based grants averaged $4000 ($6000 maximum); loans averaged $2625 ($4625 maximum); and work contracts averaged $1400. Average annual earnings from campus work are $1400. The FAFSA and the college's own financial statement are required. The fall application deadline is August 1.

International Students: The school actively recruits these students. They must score 500 on the written TOEFL and also take the SAT I or the ACT.

Computers: The mainframe is a DEC VAX. All students have access to mainframe and PC labs. All students may access the system. There are no time limits and no fees. It is recommended that students in computer science have personal computers. A PC or Mac is recommended.

Admissions Contact: Eric Ruf, Director of Admissions. A video is available. E-mail: *admissions@ab.edu* Web: *www.ab.edu*

BETHANY COLLEGE
Bethany, WV 26032

C-1
(304) 829-7611
(800) 922-7611; Fax: (304) 829-7142

Full-time: 416 men, 345 women
Part-time: 6 men, 4 women
Graduate: none
Year: semesters
Application Deadline: open
Freshman Class: 728 applied, 609 accepted, 201 enrolled
SAT I Verbal/Math: 511/510
Faculty: 57; IIB, -$
Ph.D.s: 76%
Student/Faculty: 13 to 1
Tuition: $12,566
Room & Board: $6000
ACT: 23
COMPETITIVE

Bethany College, founded in 1840, is a liberal arts institution affiliated with the Christian Church (Disciples of Christ). In addition to regional accreditation, Bethany has baccalaureate program accreditation with CSWE and NCATE. The library contains 201,930 volumes, 3600 microform items, and 4293 audiovisual forms/CDs, and subscribes to 585 periodicals. Computerized library services include the card catalog, interlibrary loans, and database searching. Special learning facilities include a learning resource center, art gallery, radio station, and TV station. The 300-acre campus is in a small town 14 miles north of Wheeling and 39 miles southwest of Pittsburgh. Including residence halls, there are 33 buildings.

Student Life: 75% of undergraduates are from out of state, mostly the Middle Atlantic. Others are from 30 states, 20 foreign countries, and Canada. 70% are from public schools. 90% are white. 40% are Protestant; 34% Catholic; 19% claim no religious affiliation. The average age of freshmen is 18; all undergraduates, 20. 12% do not continue beyond their first year; 60% remain to graduate.

Housing: 850 students can be accommodated in college housing, which includes single-sex and coed dormitories, on-campus apartments, off-campus apartments, fraternity houses, and sorority houses. In addition, there are special-interest houses. On-campus housing is guaranteed for all 4 years. 95% of students live on campus; of those, 87% remain on campus on weekends. All students may keep cars.

Activities: 50% of men belong to 6 national fraternities; 50% of women belong to 4 national sororities. There are 38 groups on campus, including art, athletic, band, cheerleading, choir, chorale, chorus, computers, dance, drama, ethnic, gay, honors, international, literary magazine, musical theater, newspaper, orchestra, outdoor, pep band, photography, political, professional, radio and TV, religious, social, social service, student government, and yearbook. Popular campus events include Spring Weekend, Mid-Term Break, and Snow Carnival.

Sports: There are 9 intercollegiate sports for men and 9 for women, and 7 intramural sports for men and 7 for women. Facilities include a 2000-seat stadium, a 1000-seat gym, a natatorium, and football, soccer, baseball, and softball fields.

Disabled Students: 20% of the campus is accessible. Wheelchair ramps, elevators, special parking, and specially equipped rest rooms are available.

Services: Counseling and information services are available, as is tutoring in every subject. There is also a center for academic success, which provides guidance for students needing special assistance.

Campus Safety and Security: Measures include 24-hour foot and vehicle patrol, informal discussions, pamphlets/posters/films, and lighted pathways/sidewalks.

Programs of Study: Bethany confers B.A. and B.S. degrees. Bachelor's degrees are awarded in BIOLOGICAL SCIENCE (biochemistry and biology/biological science), BUSINESS (accounting and business economics), COMMUNICATIONS AND THE ARTS (communications, English, fine arts, French, German, journalism, languages, and Spanish), COMPUTER AND PHYSICAL SCIENCE (chemistry, computer science, mathematics, and physics), EDUCATION (early childhood, elementary, English, foreign languages, physical, science, secondary, and special), HEALTH PROFESSIONS (predentistry and premedicine), SOCIAL SCIENCE (economics, history, international studies, philosophy, political science/government, prelaw, psychology, religion, and social work). Chemistry, economics, and political science are the strongest academically. Communication, economics, and education are the largest.

Required: All students must earn 128 semester hours, including 24 to 48 in the major, while maintaining a 2.0 GPA. A freshman seminar is required. Distribution credits must be earned in contemporary society and institutions, creative arts, cultural awareness, human behavior, international understanding, life science, literature, mathematical understanding, physical science, and the Western tradition. Students must complete a writing proficiency requirement, a senior project, and a senior comprehensive exam to graduate.

Special: Bethany offers a 3-2 engineering degree with Columbia, Washington at St. Louis, and Case Western Reserve Universities, internships (required with many majors), study abroad in France, Spain, England, Germany, Canada, Japan, Puerto Rico, Argentina, and Sweden, a Washington semester, and work-study programs. B.A.-B.S. degrees and dual majors in all majors, a general studies degree, student-designed majors in interdisciplinary studies, and pass/fail options in nonmajor courses also are offered. There is also a voluntary January term. There are 15 national honor societies.

Faculty/Classroom: 69% of faculty are male; 31%, female. All teach undergraduates and 35% both teach and do research. The average class size in an introductory lecture is 25; in a laboratory, 15; and in a regular course, 15.

Admissions: 84% of the 2001-2002 applicants were accepted. 6 freshmen graduated first in their class.

Requirements: The SAT I or ACT is required. In addition, applicants must have 15 Carnegie units, which should include 4 years of English, 3 each in math and science, and 2 each in foreign language, history, and social studies. An essay, an interview, a portfolio, and an audition are recommended, depending on the major. The GED is accepted. A GPA of 2.5 is required. AP and CLEP credits are accepted. Important factors in the admissions decision are advanced placement or honor courses, recommendations by school officials, and leadership record. Students may apply on-line via Bethany's web site.

Procedure: Freshmen are admitted fall and spring. Entrance exams should be taken during the junior year. There is a deferred admissions plan. Application deadlines are open. The application fee is $25. Notification is sent on a rolling basis.

Transfer: 17 transfer students enrolled in a recent year. Transfer students must have a minimum GPA of 2.0. 32 credits of 128 must be completed at Bethany.

Visiting: There are regularly scheduled orientations for prospective students, including a tour and meetings with faculty, coaches, and financial aid and admission personnel. There are guides for informal visits and visitors may sit in on classes and stay overnight. To schedule a visit, contact the Office of Admission.

Financial Aid: In 2001-2002, 95% of all freshmen and 92% of continuing students received some form of financial aid. 65% of freshmen and 70% of continuing students received need-based aid. The average freshman award was $12,500. Of that total, scholarships or need-based grants averaged $11,300 ($18,230 maximum); loans averaged $2650 ($5100 maximum); and work contracts averaged $1000 ($1500 maximum). 79% of undergraduates work part time. Average annual earnings from campus work are $820. The average financial indebtedness of the 2001 graduate was $18,000. The FAFSA and the college's own financial statement are required. The fall application deadline is May 1.

International Students: There were 59 international students enrolled in a recent year. The school actively recruits these students. They must score 500 on the written TOEFL or 173 on the electronic version.

Computers: The mainframe is a Hewlett-Packard. There are 20 terminals for the mainframe in the computer center. There is also a Mac computer center with 8 student labs. In addition, there are computer labs for English, economics, communications, biology, chemistry, education, and social sciences. All students may access the system 24 hours daily. It is strongly recommended that all students have a personal computer.

Graduates: In 2001, 140 bachelor's degrees were awarded. The most popular majors were physical education (14%), psychology (10%), and economics (10%). In an average class, 3% graduate in 3 years, 56% in 4 years, 58% in 5 years, and 1% in 6 years. Of the 2000 graduating class, 35% were enrolled in graduate school within 6 months of graduation and 85% were employed.

Admissions Contact: Penny Cunningham, Dean of Admission.
E-mail: *admission@mail.bethanywv.edu* Web: *www.bethanywv.edu*

BLUEFIELD STATE COLLEGE
Bluefield, WV 24701

B-5
(304) 327-4068
(800) 654-7798; Fax: (304) 325-7747

Full-time: 710 men, 880 women
Part-time: 250 men, 515 women
Graduate: none
Year: semesters, summer session
Application Deadline: open
Freshman Class: n/av
ACT: required
Faculty: 72; IIB, -$
Ph.D.s: 52%
Student/Faculty: 22 to 1
Tuition: $2220 ($5300)
Room & Board: n/app
LESS COMPETITIVE

Bluefield State College, founded in 1895, is a state-supported commuter college offering programs in engineering technologies, business, teacher education, arts and sciences, health science professions, and a variety of career fields. The college also offers a wide variety of off-campus courses. Figures in the above capsule are approximate. In addition to regional accreditation, Bluefield State has baccalaureate program accreditation with ABET and NCATE. The library contains 78,000 volumes, 110,000 microform items, and 50,000 audiovisual forms/CDs, and subscribes to 450 periodicals. Computerized library services include the card catalog, interlibrary loans, and database searching. Special learning facilities include a learning resource center and art gallery. The 40-acre campus is in a small town 90 miles south of Charleston. There are 9 buildings.

Student Life: 95% of undergraduates are from West Virginia. Others are from 8 states, 8 foreign countries, and Canada. 99% are from public schools. 90% are white. The average age of freshmen is 21; all undergraduates, 26. 34% do not continue beyond their first year; 52% remain to graduate.

Housing: There are no residence halls. All students commute. Alcohol is not permitted. All students may keep cars.

Activities: 3% of men belong to 3 local and 3 national fraternities; 1% of women belong to 3 local sororities and 1 national sorority. There are 42 groups on campus, including cheerleading, ethnic, honors, international, jazz band, newspaper, student government, and yearbook. Popular campus events include dances and sports events.

Sports: There are 5 intercollegiate sports for men and 4 for women, and 20 intramural sports for men and 15 for women. Facilities include a gym, a pool, tennis courts, an athletic field, and physical fitness and aerobics rooms.

Disabled Students: All of the campus is accessible. Wheelchair ramps, elevators, special parking, specially equipped rest rooms, and lowered drinking fountains are available.

Services: Counseling and information services are available, as is tutoring in most subjects. There is a reader service for the blind, and remedial math, reading, and writing.

Campus Safety and Security: Measures include 24-hour foot and vehicle patrol, self-defense education, pamphlets/posters/films, and emergency telephones. There are lighted pathways/sidewalks.

Programs of Study: Bluefield State confers B.A., B.S., B.S.E.T., and B.S.N. degrees. Associate degrees are also awarded. Bachelor's degrees are awarded in BIOLOGICAL SCIENCE (biology/biological science), BUSINESS (accounting, and business administration and management), COMPUTER AND PHYSICAL SCIENCE (computer science), EDUCATION (elementary and middle school), ENGINEERING AND ENVIRONMENTAL DESIGN (engineering technology), HEALTH PROFESSIONS (nursing), SOCIAL SCIENCE (criminal justice, humanities, and social science). Engineering technology and health science are the strongest academically. Business is the largest.

Required: The minimum requirement for graduation is a 2.0 GPA overall and in the student's major and minor, and 128 semester hours. All graduating students must have completed the general program specific to their degree and a core curriculum of 40 hours among humanities, social science, lab science, basic skills, phys ed, and computer science.

Special: A general studies degree and life experience credentials are offered through the Regents Bachelor of Arts Degree Program, designed for adults. Nondegree study is offered. There are 2 national honor societies, a freshman honors program, and 1 departmental honors program.

Faculty/Classroom: 62% of faculty are male; 38%, female. All teach undergraduates. The average class size in an introductory lecture is 40; in a laboratory, 25; and in a regular course, 25.

Admissions: 27% of recent freshmen were in the top fifth of their class; 46% were in the top two fifths.

Requirements: The ACT is required. In addition, regular admission is granted to students meeting GED requirements or having a high school diploma, with an overall 2.0 GPA or a composite score of at least 17 on the ACT or at least 680 on the SAT I, and having successfully completed minimum high school curricular unit requirements consisting of 4 units in English, 3 in social studies, 2 in math (algebra I and higher), and 2 in lab science. Other students not meeting these requirements may be admitted on a conditional basis. AP and CLEP credits are accepted. Applications are accepted on-line at the school's web site.

Procedure: Freshmen are admitted to all sessions. Entrance exams should be taken before enrolling. There are early admissions and deferred admissions plans. Application deadlines are open. Check with the school for current fee.

Transfer: 206 transfer students enrolled in a recent year. Applicants must be in good standing at the institution from which they are transferring. 32 credits of 128 must be completed at Bluefield State.

Visiting: There are regularly scheduled orientations for prospective students. There are guides for informal visits and visitors may sit in on classes. To schedule a visit, contact the Admissions Office at (304) 327-4065.

Financial Aid: In a recent year, 70% of all students received some form of financial aid. 60% of all students received need-based aid. The average freshman award was $4200. Of that total, scholarships or need-based grants averaged $800 ($2000 maximum); loans averaged $2600 ($5500 maximum); and work contracts averaged $600 ($3000 maximum). 75% of undergraduates work part time. Average annual earnings from campus work are $1600. The average financial indebtedness of a recent graduate was $5500. Bluefield State is a member of CSS. The FAFSA and the college's own financial statement are required. Check with the school for current deadlines.

International Students: There were 20 international students enrolled in a recent year. They must score 550 on the written TOEFL and also take the ACT.

Computers: The mainframe is a DEC 4000; WVNET computer systems are accessed through telecommunications. There are also 11 computer labs available on campus for student use. All students may access the system during class and lab hours. There are no time limits and no fees.

Graduates: In a recent year, 203 bachelor's degrees were awarded. The most popular majors were business administration (18%), criminal justice (13%), and electrical engineering (13%). 60 companies recruited on campus in a recent year. Of a recent graduating class, 7% were enrolled in graduate school within 6 months of graduation and 95% were employed.

Admissions Contact: John C. Cardwell, Vice President for Enrollment Management. E-mail: *bscadmit@bscvax.wvnet.edu*
Web: *www.bluefield.wvnet.edu*

COLLEGE OF WEST VIRGINIA
(See Mountain State University)

CONCORD COLLEGE

B-5

Athens, WV 24712

(304) 384-5248
(888) 384-5249; Fax: (304) 384-9044

Full-time: 1093 men, 1382 women	**Faculty:** 84; IIB, -$
Part-time: 220 men, 360 women	**Ph.D.s:** n/av
Graduate: none	**Student/Faculty:** 29 to 1
Year: semesters, summer session	**Tuition:** $2764 ($6156)
Application Deadline: open	**Room & Board:** $4358
Freshman Class: 2330 applied, 1521 accepted, 642 enrolled	
SAT I Verbal/Math: 560/560	**ACT:** 27 **COMPETITIVE+**

Concord College, founded in 1872, is a public institution with undergraduate programs in liberal arts and professional training. In addition to regional accreditation, Concord has baccalaureate program accreditation with CSWE and NCATE. The library contains 96,787 volumes, 268,451 microform items, and 1077 audiovisual forms/CDs, and subscribes to 552 periodicals. Computerized library services include the card catalog, interlibrary loans, and database searching. Special learning facilities include a learning resource center, art gallery, radio station, and TV station. The 123-acre campus is in a small town 85 miles south of Charleston. Including residence halls, there are 19 buildings.

Student Life: 84% of undergraduates are from West Virginia. Others are from 25 states, 27 foreign countries, and Canada. 97% are from public schools. 92% are white. 40% claim no religious affiliation; 40% are Protestant; 15% Catholic. The average age of freshmen is 19; all undergraduates, 23. 33% do not continue beyond their first year; 41% remain to graduate.

Housing: 1078 students can be accommodated in college housing, which includes single-sex dormitories and married-student housing. In addition, there are honors floors in residence halls and housing for international students and for disabled students. On-campus housing is guaranteed for all 4 years. Alcohol is not permitted. All students may keep cars.

Activities: 20% of men belong to 2 local and 4 national fraternities; 20% of women belong to 4 national sororities. There are 52 groups on campus, including art, bagpipe band, band, cheerleading, choir, chorale, computers, drama, film, honors, international, jazz band, literary magazine, newspaper, pep band, political, professional, radio and TV, religious, social, social service, student government, and yearbook. Popular campus events include big-name concerts, Alumni Day, and faculty and student plays.

Sports: There are 8 intercollegiate sports for men and 7 for women, and 15 intramural sports for men and 15 for women. Facilities include 5 tennis courts, 4 racquetball courts, 2 gyms, a Nautilus fitness room, a pool, a dance studio, and various outdoor fields. The campus stadium seats 4000, the larger gym 2700, and the largest auditorium 900.

Disabled Students: 90% of the campus is accessible. Wheelchair ramps, elevators, special parking, and special class scheduling are available.

Services: Counseling and information services are available, as is tutoring in every subject. There is a reader service for the blind, and remedial math, reading, and writing.

Campus Safety and Security: Measures include escort service, informal discussions, pamphlets/posters/films, and emergency telephones. There are lighted pathways/sidewalks. Foot and vehicle patrol is available 24 hours Monday through Friday and is on call Saturday and Sunday.

Programs of Study: Concord confers B.A., B.S., B.B.A., B.S.C.I.S., B.S.Ed., B.S.Med.Tech., and B.S.W. degrees. Associate degrees are also awarded. Bachelor's degrees are awarded in BIOLOGICAL SCIENCE (biology/biological science), BUSINESS (accounting, banking and finance, business administration and management, hotel/motel and restaurant management, marketing/retailing/merchandising, office supervision and management, and small business management), COMMUNICATIONS AND THE ARTS (broadcasting, communications, and English), COMPUTER AND PHYSICAL SCIENCE (chemistry, computer programming, computer science, information sciences and systems, and mathematics), EDUCATION (art, business, early childhood, elementary, middle school, music, science, secondary, and special), HEALTH PROFESSIONS (medical laboratory technology, predentistry, premedicine, and prepharmacy), SOCIAL SCIENCE (geography, history, parks and recreation management, political science/government, prelaw, psychology, social science, social work, and sociology). Teacher education, business, and preprofessional biology and chemistry are the strongest academically. Teacher education, business, and travel industry management are the largest.

Required: To graduate, students must earn 128 credit hours, including 36 to 50 in the major, with a minimum GPA of 2.0 (2.5 in many departments). All students must complete the college's general studies curriculum. Required courses include 14 to 15 semester hours of math and science, 12 of English and literature, 12 of social studies, 6 of fine arts, 3 of speech, and 2 of phys ed.

Special: Students may serve internships in medical technology, social work, travel industry management, commercial art/advertising, and communications arts. Concord offers a Washington semester, cross-registration with Bluefield State College, dual majors, interdisciplinary student-designed majors, and nondegree study. Credit for life, military, and work experience is granted to adult students through the Regents Bachelor of Arts Degree Program. There are 4 national honor societies and a freshman honors program.

Faculty/Classroom: All faculty members teach undergraduates. The average class size in an introductory lecture is 45; in a laboratory, 20; and in a regular course, 45.

Admissions: 65% of the 2001-2002 applicants were accepted. The SAT I scores for the 2001-2002 freshman class were: Verbal--56% below 500, 25% between 500 and 599, 16% between 600 and 699, and 3% above 699; Math--55% below 500, 30% between 500 and 599, 12% between 600 and 699, and 3% above 699. The ACT scores were 21% between 12 and 17, 55% between 18 and 23, 22% between 24 and 29, and 2% between 30 and 36. 38% of the current freshmen were in the top quarter of their class; 65% were in the top half. 21 freshmen graduated first in their class in a recent year.

Requirements: The SAT I or ACT is required; the ACT is preferred. Applicants must be high school graduates or hold a GED. Students should present 17 academic credits, including 4 in English, 3 in social studies, 2 each in math and science, and 1 each in history and health/phys ed. An interview is recommended and, where appropriate, a portfolio or an audition. A GPA of 2.0 is required. AP and CLEP credits are accepted. Applications are accepted on-line.

Procedure: Freshmen are admitted to all sessions. Entrance exams should be taken in the junior year or preferably early in the senior year. There is a deferred admissions plan. Application deadlines are open. Notification is sent on a rolling basis.

Transfer: 157 transfer students enrolled in 2001-2002. Applicants must have a GPA of at least 2.0. Concord recommends a minimum of 15 credit hours of college work completed and an interview. 36 credits of 128 must be completed at Concord.

Visiting: There are regularly scheduled orientations for prospective students. There are guides for informal visits and visitors may sit in on classes and stay overnight. To schedule a visit, contact the Admissions Office.

Financial Aid: In a recent year, 84% of all freshmen and 72% of continuing students received some form of financial aid. 43% of freshmen and 44% of continuing students received need-based aid. The average freshman award was $5115. Of that total, scholarships or need-based grants averaged $1012 ($9768 maximum); loans averaged $2078 ($10,000 maximum); and work contracts averaged $1233 ($1360 maximum). 23% of undergraduates work part time. Average annual earnings from campus work are $1800. The average financial indebtedness of the 2001 graduate was $10,000. The FAFSA and the college's own financial statement are required. The fall application deadline is April 15.

International Students: There were 104 international students enrolled in a recent year. The school actively recruits these students. They must score 500 on the written TOEFL and also take the SAT I or the ACT.

Computers: Concord is a participant in the statewide WVNET computer network system. Programming languages and statistical packages are run from the central mainframe, a DEC ALPHA 2100 Model 500. 201 PCs are available in computer labs and faculty offices. All students may access the system. There are no time limits and no fees.

Graduates: In 2001, 370 bachelor's degrees were awarded. The most popular majors were education (26%), business/marketing (15%), and liberal arts/general studies (12%). In an average class, 41% graduate in 5 years.

Admissions Contact: Michael Curry, Vice President of Admissions and Financial Aid. E-mail: *admissions@concord.edu*
Web: *http://www.concord.edu*

DAVIS AND ELKINS COLLEGE

Elkins, WV 26241 — C-3

(304) 637-1326
(800) 624-3157; Fax: (304) 637-1800

Full-time: 241 men, 354 women	**Faculty:** 66; IIB, --$
Part-time: 19 men, 54 women	**Ph.D.s:** 73%
Graduate: none	**Student/Faculty:** 9 to 1
Year: semesters, summer session	**Tuition:** $13,644
Application Deadline: open	**Room & Board:** $5626
Freshman Class: n/av	
SAT I Verbal/Math: 480/480	**ACT:** 21 **LESS COMPETITIVE**

Davis and Elkins College, founded in 1904 and affiliated with the Presbyterian Church (U.S.A.), offers programs in the liberal arts, business, professional training, teacher preparation, nursing, and recreation management. The library contains 225,000 volumes, 300,000 microform items, and 14,000 audiovisual forms/CDs, and subscribes to 410 periodicals. Computerized library services include the card catalog and interlibrary loans. Special learning facilities include a learning resource center, art gallery, planetarium, and radio station. The 170-acre campus is in a small town 200 miles west of Washington, D.C. Including residence halls, there are 21 buildings.

Student Life: 55% of undergraduates are from West Virginia. Others are from 26 states, 12 foreign countries, and Canada. 95% are from public schools. 90% are white. 38% are claim no religious affiliation; 24% Protestant. The average age of freshmen is 18; all undergraduates, 20. 30% do not continue beyond their first year; 70% remain to graduate.

Housing: 572 students can be accommodated in college housing, which includes single-sex and coed dormitories. On-campus housing is guaranteed for all 4 years. 50% of students live on campus; of those, 75% remain on campus on weekends. All students may keep cars.

Activities: 15% of men belong to 2 national fraternities; 15% of women belong to 2 national sororities. There are 42 groups on campus, including art, bagpipe band, cheerleading, choir, computers, drama, environmental, honors, international, jazz band, leadership, literary magazine, musical theater, newspaper, pep band, photography, political, professional, radio and TV, religious, social, social service, student government, and yearbook. Popular campus events include Parents Weekend, Deja Vu, and International Week.

Sports: There are 6 intercollegiate sports for men and 6 for women, and 10 intramural sports for men and 10 for women. Facilities include a 2000-seat gym, 1300-seat arena, fields, fitness center and fitness trails, tennis court, and pool. A national forest is nearby.

Disabled Students: 80% of the campus is accessible. Wheelchair ramps, elevators, special parking, specially equipped rest rooms, special class scheduling, lowered drinking fountains, and lowered telephones are available.

Services: Counseling and information services are available, as is tutoring in every subject. There is remedial math, reading, and writing. Learning disabilities services also are available.

Campus Safety and Security: Measures include self-defense education, escort service, informal discussions, and pamphlets/posters/films. There are lighted pathways/sidewalks. The campus security service is on duty from 6 P.M. to 5 A.M.

Programs of Study: D&E confers B.A. and B.S. degrees. Associate degrees are also awarded. Bachelor's degrees are awarded in BIOLOGICAL SCIENCE (biology/biological science), BUSINESS (accounting, business administration and management, hospitality management services, management science, and marketing/retailing/merchandising), COMMUNICATIONS AND THE ARTS (art, communications, dramatic arts, English, languages, and music), COMPUTER AND PHYSICAL SCIENCE (chemistry, computer science, and mathematics), EDUCATION (elementary, physical, and secondary), ENGINEERING AND ENVIRONMENTAL DESIGN (environmental science), HEALTH PROFESSIONS (predentistry and premedicine), SOCIAL SCIENCE (economics, history, political science/government, prelaw, psychology, religion, and sociology). Business, psychology, and biology are the strongest academically. Business, nursing, and hospitality management are the largest.

Required: To graduate, students must complete 124 credit hours, including 30 to 40 in the major, with a GPA of 2.0. General education requirements include 7 hours of natural science, 6 each of history, social science, English composition, philosophy, religion, literature, and math, 5 of fine arts, and 2 of phys ed, as well as a course in computer literacy. A freshman experience class and a public speaking course are also required.

Special: Students may study abroad or take a Washington semester. The college offers co-op programs with Syracuse University and SUNY, as well as internships. Students may take dual majors in psychology/human services, biology/environmental sciences, and history/political science, and student-designed majors are permitted through a contract degree program. The college awards credit for life, military, and work experience. Nondegree study is allowed and pass/fail options are open. The college's mentor-assisted degree-completion program allows adults to earn degrees through credit for life experience and off-campus study.

There are 6 national honor societies, a freshman honors program, and all departments have honors programs.

Faculty/Classroom: 61% of faculty are male; 39%, female. All teach undergraduates. The average class size in an introductory lecture is 15; in a laboratory, 11; and in a regular course, 11.

Admissions: 2 freshmen graduated first in their class.

Requirements: The SAT I or ACT is required, with a minimum composite score of 920 on the the SAT I or 19 on the ACT. Applicants should be high school graduates or hold a GED. Students should have earned 16 academic credits, including 4 in English, 3 in social studies, 3 in math, including a minimum of algebra I and geometry, and 3 in natural science, including a lab course. 2 years of foreign language is recommended. D&E requires applicants to be in the upper 50% of their class. A GPA of 2.0 is required. AP and CLEP credits are accepted. Important factors in the admissions decision are advanced placement or honor courses, recommendations by school officials, and leadership record. Applications are accepted on-line.

Procedure: Freshmen are admitted to all sessions. Entrance exams should be taken during the fall of the senior year. There are early decision and deferred admissions plans. Application deadlines are open. The fall 2001 application fee was $30. Notification is sent on a rolling basis.

Transfer: 71 transfer students enrolled in a recent year. Transfer applicants should have earned 62 credit hours, with a GPA of 2.0. An associate degree is recommended. 15 credits of 124 must be completed at D&E.

Visiting: There are regularly scheduled orientations for prospective students, including meals, a tour of campus, and panel discussions. There are guides for informal visits and visitors may sit in on classes and stay overnight. To schedule a visit, contact the Admissions Office at (304) 637-1230.

Financial Aid: In 2001-2002, 85% of all students received some form of financial aid. 70% of all students received need-based aid. The average freshman award was $10,400. Of that total, scholarships or need-based grants averaged $4160 ($8200 maximum); loans averaged $5200 ($6625 maximum); and work contracts averaged $1040 ($1600 maximum). 40% of undergraduates work part time. Average annual earnings from campus work are $1200. The average financial indebtedness of the 2001 graduate was $15,000. The FAFSA is required and the CSS Profile Application is optional.

International Students: The school actively recruits these students. They must score 500 on the written TOEFL or take the MELAB, and also take the SAT I or the ACT.

Computers: The mainframe is a DEC VAX 4300. There are 91 Apple IIe, Mac Plus, and AT&T PCs available in 7 labs. All students may access the system. There are no time limits and no fees.

Admissions Contact: Matt Shiflett, Director of Admissions.
E-mail: *admiss@dne.edu* Web: *www.dne.edu*

FAIRMONT STATE COLLEGE

Fairmont, WV 26554 — C-2

(304) 367-4062
(800) 641-5678; Fax: (304) 367-4584

Full-time: 2139 men, 2461 women	**Faculty:** 196; IIB, av$
Part-time: 876 men, 1248 women	**Ph.D.s:** 45%
Graduate: none	**Student/Faculty:** 23 to 1
Year: semesters, summer session	**Tuition:** $2408 ($5672)
Application Deadline: see profile	**Room & Board:** $4602
Freshman Class: n/av	
SAT I or ACT: required	**NONCOMPETITIVE**

Fairmont State College, founded in 1865, is a public institution offering programs in business, education, engineering technology, and health careers. In addition to regional accreditation, Fairmont State has baccalaureate program accreditation with ABET, NCATE, and NLN. The library contains 256,991 volumes, 54,241 microform items, and 7298 audiovisual forms/CDs, and subscribes to 1175 periodicals. Computerized library services include the card catalog, interlibrary loans, and database searching. Special learning facilities include a learning resource center. The 89-acre campus is in a small town 75 miles south of Pittsburgh, Pennsylvania. Including residence halls, there are 12 buildings.

Student Life: 94% of undergraduates are from West Virginia. Others are from 23 states and 17 foreign countries. 98% are from public schools. 94% are white. The average age of freshmen is 21; all undergraduates, 24. 26% do not continue beyond their first year; 37% remain to graduate.

Housing: 437 students can be accommodated in college housing, which includes single-sex dormitories. On-campus housing is available on a first-come, first-served basis. 94% of students commute. Alcohol is not permitted. All students may keep cars.

Activities: 4% of men belong to 3 national fraternities; 4% of women belong to 3 national sororities. There are 80 groups on campus, including art, band, cheerleading, choir, chorus, computers, debate, drama, gay, honors, jazz band, literary magazine, marching band, musical theater, newspaper, pep band, photography, political, professional, religious, social, student government, symphony, and yearbook. Popular campus events include multicultural events.

Sports: There are 7 intercollegiate sports for men and 6 for women, and 24 intramural sports for men and 24 for women. Facilities include a phys ed center, a 5000-seat stadium, a 4000-seat basketball arena, and playing fields.

Disabled Students: All of the campus is accessible. Wheelchair ramps, elevators, special parking, specially equipped rest rooms, special class scheduling, lowered drinking fountains, and lowered telephones are available.

Services: Counseling and information services are available, as is tutoring in most subjects. There is a reader service for the blind, and remedial math, reading, and writing.

Campus Safety and Security: Measures include 24-hour foot and vehicle patrol, pamphlets/posters/films, emergency telephones, and lighted pathways/sidewalks.

Programs of Study: Fairmont State confers B.A., B.S., B.A.E., B.E.T., and B.S.N. degrees. Associate and master's degrees are also awarded. Bachelor's degrees are awarded in BIOLOGICAL SCIENCE (biology/biological science), BUSINESS (accounting, banking and finance, business administration and management, business economics, and marketing/retailing/merchandising), COMMUNICATIONS AND THE ARTS (communications, English, French, and speech/debate/rhetoric), COMPUTER AND PHYSICAL SCIENCE (chemistry, computer science, and mathematics), EDUCATION (art, business, early childhood, elementary, foreign languages, health, middle school, music, science, and secondary), ENGINEERING AND ENVIRONMENTAL DESIGN (architectural technology, civil engineering technology, electrical/electronics engineering technology, engineering technology, manufacturing technology, and mechanical engineering technology), SOCIAL SCIENCE (criminal justice, family/consumer studies, history, political science/government, psychology, and sociology). Engineering technology, education, and business are the strongest academically. Business, health careers, and criminal justice are the largest.

Required: To graduate, students must complete 128 hours with a GPA of 2.0. (2.5 in education specializations). Students must complete 50 core curriculum hours for the B.S. or B.A. degree. All students must take 2 hours of phys ed. Course and distribution requirements vary according to the program.

Special: The college offers internships in teacher education, retailing, and psychology, and awards a B.S. degree in chemistry/math. There is a freshman honors program.

Faculty/Classroom: 51% of faculty are male; 49%, female. All teach undergraduates. The average class size in an introductory lecture is 106; in a laboratory, 20; and in a regular course, 30.

Admissions: 12 freshmen graduated first in their class in a recent year.

Requirements: The SAT I or ACT is required, for students who have graduated from high school or completed GED requirements fewer than 5 years prior to seeking admission. The minimum composite score required is 790 on the SAT I or 19 on the ACT. Applicants must be high school graduates or hold a GED. The college requires 4 credits in English, 3 in social studies (1 in U.S. history), and 2 each in math (algebra I and higher) and lab science. A foreign language is recommended. Applications are accepted on-line. A GPA of 2.25 is required. AP and CLEP credits are accepted.

Procedure: Freshmen are admitted to all sessions. Entrance exams should be taken during the fall of the senior year. Check with school for current deadlines and fee. The college accepts all applicants. Notification is sent on a rolling basis.

Transfer: 307 transfer students enrolled in a recent year. Applicants must have a GPA of 2.0. The ACT is required for applicants with fewer than 30 college credits. 32 credits of 128 must be completed at Fairmont State.

Visiting: There are guides for informal visits and visitors may sit in on classes. To schedule a visit, contact the Student Affairs Office at (304) 367-4216.

Financial Aid: In a recent year, 68% of all freshmen and 64% of continuing students received some form of financial aid. 66% of freshmen and 64% of continuing students received need-based aid. The average freshman award was $900. Of that total, scholarships or need-based grants averaged $300; loans averaged $320; and work contracts averaged $250. 35% of undergraduates work part time. Average annual earnings from campus work are $1600. The average financial indebtedness of a recent year's graduate was $6000. Fairmont State is a member of CSS. The FAFSA is required. Check with school for current deadlines.

International Students: There were 88 international students enrolled in a recent year. They must score 500 on the written TOEFL and also take the SAT I or the ACT. If ACT or SAT I scores are not supplied, the ACT must be taken upon arrival on campus.

Computers: The mainframe is a DEC VAX 8250. There are 500 IBM PCs available for student use in computer labs. Students have access to the Internet and the World Wide Web. Those students with accounts may access the system 8 A.M. to 11 P.M., 4 days per week. There are no time limits and no fees.

Graduates: In a recent year, 539 bachelor's degrees were awarded. The most popular majors were business (25%), education (18%), and criminal justice (13%). In an average class, 31% graduate in 4 years, 2% in 5 years, and 3% in 6 years. 35 companies recruited on campus in a recent year.

Admissions Contact: Douglas Dobbins, Exec. Dir. Of Enrollment Services. A video is available. E-mail: *ddobbins@fscwv.edu*
Web: *www.fscwv.edu*

GLENVILLE STATE COLLEGE

Glenville, WV 26351 C-3
(304) 462-4117
(800) 924-2010; Fax: (304) 462-8619

Full-time: 724 men, 926 women	**Faculty:** 67; IIB, -$
Part-time: 156 men, 338 women	**Ph.D.s:** 37%
Graduate: none	**Student/Faculty:** 25 to 1
Year: semesters, summer session	**Tuition:** $2488 ($6120)
Application Deadline: open	**Room & Board:** $4100
Freshman Class: 1225 applied, 1225 accepted, 445 enrolled	
SAT I Verbal/Math: 472/471	**ACT:** 18 **NONCOMPETITIVE**

Glenville State College, founded in 1872, is a public college offering programs in education, the arts and sciences, and business. In addition to regional accreditation, GSC has baccalaureate program accreditation with CCNE and NCATE. The library contains 112,238 volumes, 558,094 microform items, and 16,165 audiovisual forms/CDs, and subscribes to 1938 periodicals. Computerized library services include the card catalog, interlibrary loans, and database searching. Special learning facilities include a learning resource center and art gallery. The 360-acre campus is in a rural area 100 miles northeast of Charleston. Including residence halls, there are 28 buildings.

Student Life: 94% of undergraduates are from West Virginia. Others are from 15 states and 5 foreign countries. 99% are from public schools. 95% are white. The average age of freshmen is 23; all undergraduates, 25. 44% do not continue beyond their first year; 32% remain to graduate.

Housing: 596 students can be accommodated in college housing, which includes single-sex dormitories, on-campus apartments, and married-student housing. On-campus housing is guaranteed for all 4 years. 81% of students commute. Alcohol is not permitted. All students may keep cars.

Activities: 3% of men belong to 1 national and 3 local fraternities; 5% of women belong to 3 local sororities. There are 46 groups on campus, including band, cheerleading, choir, chorus, drama, drill team, gay, honors, international, jazz band, literary magazine, marching band, musical theater, newspaper, religious, student government, and yearbook. Popular campus events include GSC Week (a campus celebration) in April, comedians, and bands.

Sports: There are 5 intercollegiate sports for men and 5 for women, and 6 intramural sports for men and 6 for women. Facilities include a field house, a 5000-seat football stadium, a running track, tennis courts, a 700-seat gym, a swimming pool, a fitness center, and a weight room.

Disabled Students: 95% of the campus is accessible. Wheelchair ramps, elevators, special parking, specially equipped rest rooms, lowered drinking fountains, and lowered telephonesare available. Adaptations are made to class delivery locations to accommodate student needs.

Services: Counseling and information services are available, as is tutoring in most subjects. There is remedial math, reading, and writing.

Campus Safety and Security: Measures include 24-hour foot and vehicle patrol, shuttle buses, emergency telephones, and lighted pathways/sidewalks.

Programs of Study: GSC confers B.A. and B.S. degrees. Associate degrees are also awarded. Bachelor's degrees are awarded in BIOLOGICAL SCIENCE (biology/biological science), BUSINESS (accounting, business administration and management, and marketing/retailing/merchandising), COMMUNICATIONS AND THE ARTS (English), COMPUTER AND PHYSICAL SCIENCE (chemistry and computer science), EDUCATION (business, early childhood, elementary, middle school, music, physical, science, secondary, and special), HEALTH PROFESSIONS (nursing), SOCIAL SCIENCE (history). Teacher education is the strongest academically. Behavioral science is the largest.

Required: All students must take the general studies programs, consisting of 47 to 48 hours in English, math, science, the social sciences, humanities, and phys ed. Computer science is also required. To graduate, students must complete 128 credit hours, with 42 in the major. Noneducation majors must maintain a 2.0 GPA; education majors, a 2.5.

Special: The college offers B.A.-B.S. degrees in numerous majors, credit by exam, and pass/fail options. Some programs of study require internships. There are 4 national honor societies, and a freshman honors program.

Faculty/Classroom: 59% of faculty are male; 41%, female. All teach undergraduates. The average class size in an introductory lecture is 18; in a laboratory, 18; and in a regular course, 16.

Admissions: All of the 2001-2002 applicants were accepted. The SAT I scores for the 2001-2002 freshman class were: Verbal--66% below 500, 24% between 500 and 599, and 10% between 600 and 700; Math--69% below 500, 21% between 500 and 599, and 10% between 600 and 700. The ACT scores were 73% below 21, 19% between 21 and 23, 6% between 24 and 26, and 2% between 27 and 28. 18% of the current freshmen were in the top fifth of their class; 45% were in the top two fifths.

Requirements: The SAT I or ACT is required, with a minimum composite score of 17 on the ACT or 820 on the SAT I recommended. Applicants should be graduates of an accredited secondary school and have taken 4 courses in English, 3 in social studies, and 2 each in higher math and lab sciences. GED admission is also possible. A GPA of 2.0 is required. AP and CLEP credits are accepted.

Procedure: Freshmen are admitted to all sessions. Entrance exams should be taken at the end of the junior year. There is an early admissions plan. Application deadlines are open. The fall 2001 application fee was $10. Notification is sent on a rolling basis.

Transfer: 147 transfer students enrolled in 2001-2002. Applicants must be in good standing at their previous institution. 32 credits of 128 must be completed at GSC.

Visiting: There are regularly scheduled orientations for prospective students, including meetings with an admissions officer, a division officer, and a campus tour. There are guides for informal visits and visitors may sit in on classes and stay overnight. To schedule a visit, contact the Office of Admissions at (304) 462-4128 or *visitor@glenville.edu*.

Financial Aid: In 2001-2002, 73% of all freshmen and 72% of continuing students received some form of financial aid. 62% of all students received need-based aid. The average freshman award was $5889. Of that total, scholarships or need-based grants averaged $1350 ($3750 maximum); loans averaged $1890 ($2625 maximum); and work contracts averaged $800. 15% of undergraduates work part time. Average annual earnings from campus work are $800. The average financial indebtedness of the 2001 graduate was $13,227. The FAFSA is required. The fall priority application deadline is March 1.

International Students: There are 30 international students enrolled. The school actively recruits these students. They must score 550 on the written TOEFL and also take the ACT, scoring 17.

Computers: The mainframes are 2 minisystems: DEC Alpha 3000-800 series for student use and e-mail and a DEC Alpha 4100 for administrative use. Students may use the minisystem from 15 terminals in the Administration Building or telenet in from any networked PC. Accounts are available for class usage and e-mail is provided for all students. Programming classes are taught on both the minisystem and PCs. There are 166 networked PCs located throughout the campus. All students may access the system. There are no time limits and no fees.

Graduates: In 2001, 195 bachelor's degrees were awarded. The most popular majors were behavioral science (24%), business (22%), and teacher education (16%). About 30 companies recruited on campus in 2000-2001.

Admissions Contact: Marty Armentrout, Vice President for Enrollment Services. E-mail: *armentrout@glenville.edu*
Web: *http://www.glenville.edu*

MARSHALL UNIVERSITY

Huntington, WV 25755 A-4
(304) 696-3160
(800) 642-3499; Fax: (304) 696-3135

Full-time: 3690 men, 4436 women	**Faculty:** 405; IIA, --$
Part-time: 642 men, 885 women	**Ph.D.s:** 77%
Graduate: 1220 men, 2755 women	**Student/Faculty:** 20 to 1
Year: semesters, summer session	**Tuition:** $2724 ($7294)
Application Deadline: September 1	**Room & Board:** $5028
Freshman Class: 2472 applied, 2214 accepted, 1822 enrolled	
ACT: 21	**LESS COMPETITIVE**

Marshall University, founded in 1837 and part of the University of West Virginia system, is a comprehensive public institution offering programs in liberal arts and sciences, business, education, fine arts, and nursing. There are 10 undergraduate and 2 graduate schools. In addition to regional accreditation, Marshall has baccalaureate program accreditation with AACSB, ABET, ACEJMC, CSWE, NASM, NCATE, NLN, and NRPA. The 3 libraries contain 102,621 volumes, 877,090 microform items, and 21,505 audiovisual forms/CDs, and subscribe to 2175 periodicals. Computerized library services include the card catalog, interlibrary loans, and database searching. Special learning facilities include a learning resource center, art gallery, natural history museum, radio station, TV station, and greenhouse. The 70-acre campus is in an urban area 126 miles east of Lexington, Kentucky, and 50 miles west of Charleston, West Virginia. Including residence halls, there are 34 buildings.

Student Life: 84% of undergraduates are from West Virginia. Others are from 39 states, 37 foreign countries, and Canada. 85% are white. The average age of freshmen is 19; all undergraduates, 23. 25% do not continue beyond their first year; 36% remain to graduate.

Housing: 1700 students can be accommodated in college housing, which includes single-sex and coed dormitories, on-campus apartments, and married-student housing. In addition, there are honors and quiet study floors. On-campus housing is available on a first-come, first-served basis. Alcohol is not permitted. All students may keep cars.

Activities: 8% of men belong to 12 national fraternities; 5% of women belong to 7 national sororities. There are 100 groups on campus, including art, band, cheerleading, choir, chorale, chorus, computers, dance, debate, drama, ethnic, gay, honors, international, jazz band, literary magazine, marching band, musical theater, newspaper, opera, orchestra, pep band, political, professional, radio and TV, religious, social, social service, student government, symphony, and yearbook. Popular campus events include Parents Day, Springfest, and International Festival.

Sports: There are 7 intercollegiate sports for men and 9 for women, and 25 intramural sports for men and 23 for women. Facilities include a 10,500-seat basketball arena, a 30,000-seat football stadium, tennis courts, a baseball field, an Olympic-size pool, an auxiliary gym, a health and fitness center, racquetball courts, a human performance enhancement lab, and a track and field.

Disabled Students: All of the campus is accessible. Wheelchair ramps, elevators, special parking, specially equipped rest rooms, special class scheduling, lowered drinking fountains, lowered telephones, and an attendant care program are available.

Services: Counseling and information services are available, as is tutoring in most subjects, including all lower-division courses. There is a reader service for the blind, remedial math, reading, and writing, study skills courses, and other services for all students with disabilities.

Campus Safety and Security: Measures include 24-hour foot and vehicle patrol, self-defense education, escort service, and informal discussions. There are pamphlets/posters/films, emergency telephones, and lighted pathways/sidewalks.

Programs of Study: Marshall confers B.A., B.S., B.B.A., B.F.A., B.S. Cyotech, B.S.M.T., B.S.N., and B.S.W. degrees. Associate, master's, and doctoral degrees are also awarded. Bachelor's degrees are awarded in BIOLOGICAL SCIENCE (biology/biological science), BUSINESS (accounting, business economics, and marketing/retailing/merchandising), COMMUNICATIONS AND THE ARTS (communications, English, fine arts, journalism, and music), COMPUTER AND PHYSICAL SCIENCE (chemistry, geology, information sciences and systems, mathematics, and physics), EDUCATION (elementary, home economics, and middle school), HEALTH PROFESSIONS (nursing), SOCIAL SCIENCE (criminal justice, dietetics, economics, geography, history, humanities, international relations, parks and recreation management, physical fitness/movement, political science/government, psychology, safety and security technology, social work, and sociology). Biological science, elementary education, and secondary education are the largest.

Required: The Marshall Plan, including a capstone experience, is key to each student's studies at Marshall University. Generally speaking, a 2.0 GPA (2.5 in education, 2.25 in journalism) and 128 credit hours, as well as other specific criteria, are required for graduation.

Special: Many programs require or offer internships. Work-study opportunities are available on campus. Students study abroad in 10 countries. B.A.-B.S. degrees, dual and student-designed majors, nondegree study, credit for life experience, and credit/no-credit options are available. There are 13 national honor societies, including Phi Beta Kappa, and a freshman honors program.

Faculty/Classroom: 54% of faculty are male; 46%, female. The average class size in an introductory lecture is 24; in a laboratory, 22; and in a regular course, 25.

Admissions: 90% of the 2001-2002 applicants were accepted. The ACT scores for the 2001-2002 freshman class were: 48% below 21, 27% between 21 and 23, 15% between 24 and 26, 5% between 27 and 28, and 5% above 28.

Requirements: The SAT I or ACT is required. Regular admission is open to all students who have graduated from a secondary school with the required units of study and a 2.0 GPA or with a minimum composite score of 19 on the ACT or 910 on the SAT I. Required study is 4 years in English, 3 in social studies, and 2 each in higher math and lab science. 2 years of a foreign language is strongly recommended. The GED is also accepted. Students not meeting university requirements are admitted to the University College, through which students must successfully complete developmental courses within 3 semesters. AP and CLEP credits are accepted. Important factors in the admissions decision are advanced placement or honor courses, evidence of special talent, and recommendations by school officials. Applications are accepted on-line.

Procedure: Freshmen are admitted to all sessions. Entrance exams should be taken during the junior year or early in the senior year. There are early decision, early admissions, and deferred admissions plans. Early decision application should be filed by September 15; regular applications, by September 1 for fall entry, January 1 for spring entry, and June 1 for summer entry. The fall 2001 application fee was $25. Notification is sent on a rolling basis.

Transfer: 570 transfer students enrolled in 2001-2002. A 2.0 GPA on all previous college work is generally required of transfer applicants. 36 credits of 128 must be completed at Marshall.

Visiting: There are regularly scheduled orientations for prospective students. There are guides for informal visits and visitors may sit in on classes and stay overnight. To schedule a visit, contact the orientation office at (304) 696-2354.

Financial Aid: In 2001-2002, 85% of all freshmen and 63% of continuing students received some form of financial aid. 62% of freshmen and 52% of continuing students received need-based aid. The average freshman award was $5710. Of that total, scholarships or need-based grants averaged $3261 ($17,102 maximum); loans averaged $2320 ($21,860 maximum); and work contracts averaged $130 ($3300 maximum). 4% of undergraduates work part time. Average annual earnings from campus work are $2110. The average financial indebtedness of the 2001 graduate was $15,643. Marshall is a member of CSS. The FAFSA is required. The fall application deadline is February 1.

International Students: There are 206 international students enrolled. The school actively recruits these students. They must score 500 on the written TOEFL or 173 on the electronic version or take the MELAB, or pass level 9 ELS at the university. They must also take the SAT I or the ACT, scoring 19 on the ACT.

Computers: There are 180 networked PCs in the library, 620 in computer labs, 240 in classrooms, and 50 university-owned in dorms. The dorms have connections for residents' PCs as well. All students may access the system during scheduled hours, 7 days a week. There are no time limits and no fees. It is strongly recommended that all students have a personal computer.

Graduates: In 2001, 1336 bachelor's degrees were awarded. The most popular majors were elementary education (11%), management (6%), and biological science (6%). In an average class, 34% graduate in 6 years. 613 companies recruited on campus in 2000-2001.

Admissions Contact: Linda Templeton, Associate Director.
E-mail: *admissions@marshall.edu* Web: *www.marshall.edu/admissions*

MOUNTAIN STATE UNIVERSITY (Formerly College of West Virginia)

B-4

Beckley, WV 25801

(304) 253-7351
(800) 766-6067; Fax: (304) 253-5072

Full-time: 627 men, 1095 women	**Faculty:** 54
Part-time: 226 men, 474 women	**Ph.D.s:** 41%
Graduate: 35 men, 68 women	**Student/Faculty:** 32 to 1
Year: semesters, summer session	**Tuition:** $4320
Application Deadline: open	**Room & Board:** $3860
Freshman Class: 401 enrolled	
SAT I Verbal/Math: 472/469	**ACT:** 19 **NONCOMPETITIVE**

Mountain State University, founded in 1933, is an independent institution committed to the academic pursuits of instruction, scholarship, and public service. It offers undergraduate programs in business administration, legal studies, nursing, allied health professions, and social work. There are 4 undergraduate schools and 1 graduate school. In addition to regional accreditation, MSU has baccalaureate program accreditation with APTA, CAAHEP, CAHEA, CSWE, IACBE, and NLN. The library contains 90,848 volumes, 14,160 microform items, and 3485 audiovisual forms/CDs, and subscribes to 134 periodicals. Computerized library services include the card catalog, interlibrary loans, and database searching. Special learning facilities include a learning resource center, an audiovisual lab, media classroom, and gross anatomy lab. The 5-acre campus is in a small town about 50 miles south of Charleston. Including residence halls, there are 12 buildings.

Student Life: 88% of undergraduates are from West Virginia. Others are from 34 states, 15 foreign countries, and Canada. 98% are from public schools. 76% are white. The average age of freshmen is 22; all undergraduates, 27.

Housing: 192 students can be accommodated in college housing, which includes coed dormitories and off-campus apartments. In addition, there is housing for athletes. On-campus housing is guaranteed for the freshman year only and is available on a first-come, first-served basis. 99% of students commute. Alcohol is not permitted. All students may keep cars.

Activities: There are no fraternities or sororities. There are 23 groups on campus, including cheerleading, ethnic, gay, honors, international, literary magazine, professional, religious, SGA Newsletters, social, social service, and student government. Popular campus events include Appalachian Vision series, Business and Technology show, and Performing Arts Series.

Sports: There is 1 intercollegiate sport for men and 2 for women, and 7 intramural sports for men and 4 for women. Facilities include a pool, a track, racquetball courts, exercise equipment, and an aerobics area. All MSU students receive a membership in the local YMCA.

Disabled Students: 65% of the campus is accessible. Wheelchair ramps, elevators, special parking, specially equipped rest rooms, special class scheduling, lowered drinking fountains, lowered telephones, and electronic door-opening mechanisms are available.

Services: Counseling and information services are available, as is tutoring in most subjects. There is a reader service for the blind and remedial math and writing.

Campus Safety and Security: Measures include 24-hour foot and vehicle patrol, escort service, informal discussions, and pamphlets/posters/films. There are emergency telephones and lighted pathways/sidewalks.

Programs of Study: MSU confers B.A., B.S., B.S.N., and B.S.W. degrees. Associate and master's degrees are also awarded. Bachelor's degrees are awarded in BUSINESS (banking and finance, business administration and management, electronic business, entrepreneurial studies, hotel/motel and restaurant management, marketing and distribution, organizational behavior, recreation and leisure services, and sports management), COMPUTER AND PHYSICAL SCIENCE (computer science), EDUCATION (health), ENGINEERING AND ENVIRONMENTAL DESIGN (computer technology), HEALTH PROFESSIONS (health care administration, nursing, physician's assistant, respiratory therapy, and ultrasound technology), SOCIAL SCIENCE (criminal justice, forensic studies, interdisciplinary studies, law, public administration, and social work). Nursing, physician assistant, and diagnostic medical are the strongest academically. Nursing, criminal justice, and business are the largest.

Required: Requirements for graduation are a 2.0 GPA overall and 128 or 129 semester hours. All students must complete 36 hours of general studies and a minimum of 93 in the major.

Special: There are co-op programs in business administration and engineering, and cross-registration with West Virginia University. Internships and a degree completion program are available, and B.A.-B.S. degrees and student-designed majors are offered in interdisciplinary studies. Other programs are available through the School of Academic Enrichment and Lifelong Learning. There are 5 national honor societies.

Faculty/Classroom: 43% of faculty are male; 57%, female. All teach undergraduates, 15% do research, and 15% do both. The average class size in an introductory lecture is 30 and in a laboratory, 25.

Admissions: All of the 2001-2002 applicants were accepted. The SAT I scores for the 2001-2002 freshman class were: Verbal--68% below 500, 27% between 500 and 599, and 5% between 600 and 700; Math--57% below 500, 35% between 500 and 599, 6% between 600 and 700, and 2% above 700. The ACT scores were 85% below 21, 12% between 21 and 23, 2% between 24 and 26, and 1% between 27 and 28. 30% of the current freshmen were in the top fifth of their class; 60% were in the top two fifths. 5 freshmen graduated first in their class.

Requirements: The SAT I or ACT is recommended, for placement only. The GED is accepted. AP and CLEP credits are accepted. Important factors in the admissions decision are recommendations by school officials, parents or siblings attending the school, and ability to finance college education.

Procedure: Freshmen are admitted to all sessions. Entrance exams should be taken any time prior to application. There is a deferred admissions plan. Application deadlines are open. Notification is sent on a rolling basis.

Transfer: 171 transfer students enrolled in 2001-2002. Applicants must submit official transcripts from all colleges attended. 12 credits of 128 must be completed at MSU.

Visiting: There are regularly scheduled orientations for prospective students, including a campus tour, registration, financial aid information, and housing and meal plan sign-ups. There are guides for informal visits and visitors may sit in on classes and stay overnight. To schedule a visit, contact the Admissions Department at (304) 253-7351, ext. 1433 or *dbrown@mountainstate.edu*

Financial Aid: In 2001-2002, 87% of all freshmen and 88% of continuing students received some form of financial aid. 74% of freshmen and 70% of continuing students received need-based aid. The average freshman award was $4353. Of that total, scholarships or need-based grants averaged $3189 and loans averaged $2109. 1% of undergraduates work part time. Average annual earnings from campus work are $1200. The average financial indebtedness of the 2001 graduate was $15,000. The FAFSA and the college's own financial statement are required. The fall application deadline is May 1.

International Students: There are 159 international students enrolled. The school actively recruits these students. They must score 500 on the written TOEFL. The ACT is recommended for placement.

Computers: There are computer labs available on campus with Internet access. All students may access the system when school is in session. There are no time limits and no fees.

Graduates: In 2001, 186 bachelor's degrees were awarded. The most popular majors were business (33%), nursing (33%), and interdisciplinary studies (16%).

Admissions Contact: Sherri Browning, Director of Admissions. A video is available. E-mail: *gocwv@mountainstate.edu*
Web: *http//mountainstate.edu*

OHIO VALLEY COLLEGE

Vienna, WV 26105 — B-3

(304) 865-6202
(877) 446-8668; Fax: (304) 865-6001

Full-time: 206 men, 236 women	**Faculty:** 21; IIB, --$
Part-time: 5 men, 6 women	**Ph.D.s:** 75%
Graduate: none	**Student/Faculty:** 21 to 1
Year: semesters	**Tuition:** $9440
Application Deadline: open	**Room & Board:** $4210
Freshman Class: 399 applied, 190 accepted, 123 enrolled	
SAT I Verbal/Math: 480/450	**ACT:** 20 **COMPETITIVE+**

Ohio Valley College, founded in 1960, is a liberal arts institution affiliated with the Church of Christ. The library contains 31,750 volumes, 51,530 microform items, and 2946 audiovisual forms/CDs, and subscribes to 165 periodicals. Computerized library services include the card catalog, interlibrary loans, and database searching. Special learning facilities include a learning resource center. The 270-acre campus is in a suburban area 120 miles southwest of Pittsburgh, Pennsylvania. Including residence halls, there are 9 buildings.

Student Life: 53% of undergraduates are from out of state, mostly the Midwest. Others are from 23 states, 13 foreign countries, and Canada. 97% are from public schools. 87% are white. Most are Protestant. The average age of freshmen is 18; all undergraduates, 21. 55% do not continue beyond their first year; 25% remain to graduate.

Housing: 500 students can be accommodated in college housing, which includes single-sex dormitories, on-campus apartments, and married-student housing. On-campus housing is guaranteed for all 4 years. 60% of students commute. Alcohol is not permitted. All students may keep cars.

Activities: There are no fraternities or sororities. There are 16 groups on campus, including band, cheerleading, choir, chorale, chorus, drama, jazz band, newspaper, pep band, religious, social, student government, and yearbook. Popular campus events include Expressions, a school-wide musical review.

Sports: There are 5 intercollegiate sports for men and 4 for women, and 11 intramural sports for men and 10 for women. Facilities include a weight room, a student union with recreation facilities, an activity center, and 2 gyms.

Disabled Students: 30% of the campus is accessible. Wheelchair ramps, elevators, special parking, specially equipped rest rooms, special class scheduling, and lowered telephones are available.

Services: Counseling and information services are available, as is tutoring in most subjects. There is remedial math, reading, and writing.

Campus Safety and Security: Measures include 24-hour foot and vehicle patrol and shuttle buses.

Programs of Study: Ohio Valley confers B.A. and B.S. degrees. Associate degrees are also awarded. Bachelor's degrees are awarded in BUSINESS (accounting, business administration and management, and human resources), EDUCATION (elementary and secondary), SOCIAL SCIENCE (biblical studies, liberal arts/general studies, psychology, and religion). Business is the strongest academically. Elementary education is the largest.

Required: To graduate, students must complete 128 credit hours, including 53 to 60 in the major, with a minimum GPA of 2.0. General requirements include 4 courses of Bible studies, 2 of English composition, 1 to 2 of history, and 1 each of speech, computer literacy, math, and social science. There is also a phys ed requirement. Students must attend chapel daily and take 1 Bible class each semester.

Special: Ohio Valley offers internships with churches for student ministers. Summer study in London or Israel is possible. There is 1 departmental honors program.

Faculty/Classroom: 64% of faculty are male; 36%, female. All teach undergraduates. The average class size in an introductory lecture is 30; in a laboratory, 20; and in a regular course, 15.

Admissions: 48% of the 2001-2002 applicants were accepted. The SAT I scores for the 2001-2002 freshman class were: Verbal--59% below 500, 28% between 500 and 599, 10% between 600 and 700, and 3% above 700; Math--65% below 500, 22% between 500 and 599, and 13% between 600 and 700. The ACT scores were 57% below 21, 29% between 21 and 23, 9% between 24 and 26, 3% between 27 and 28, and 2% above 28. 20% of the current freshmen were in the top fifth of their class; 43% were in the top two fifths.

Requirements: The ACT is required. In addition, applicants should be graduates of an accredited secondary school or have earned a GED. Applications are available on-line at the college's web site. A GPA of 2.0 is required. AP and CLEP credits are accepted. Important factors in the admissions decision are recommendations by school officials, personality/intangible qualities, and leadership record.

Procedure: Freshmen are admitted fall and spring. Entrance exams should be taken during the senior year. There are early admissions and rolling admissions plans. Application deadlines are open. The fall 2001 application fee was $20.

Transfer: 60 transfer students enrolled in 2001-2002. Transfer applicants must provide high school, college, and financial aid transcripts, and test scores. 32 credits of 128 must be completed at Ohio Valley.

Visiting: There are guides for informal visits and visitors may sit in on classes and stay overnight. To schedule a visit, contact Denver Lucky.

Financial Aid: In 2001-2002, 92% of all freshmen and 83% of continuing students received some form of financial aid. 66% of freshmen and 63% of continuing students received need-based aid. The average freshman award was $15,300. Of that total, scholarships or need-based grants averaged $4531 ($9440 maximum); loans averaged $2970 ($6625 maximum); work contracts averaged $520 ($1500 maximum); and parent loans averaged $7280 ($15,850 maximum). 44% of undergraduates work part time. Average annual earnings from campus work are $800. The average financial indebtedness of the 2001 graduate was $16,800. Ohio Valley is a member of CSS. The FAFSA is required. The fall application deadline is August 15.

International Students: There are 22 international students enrolled. The school actively recruits these students. They must score 420 on the written TOEFL and also take the ACT, scoring 16.

Computers: The mainframe is a DEC ALPHA server 300. There are PCs available in the library and the computer science lab. All students may access the system. There are no time limits and no fees.

Graduates: In 2001, 51 bachelor's degrees were awarded. The most popular majors were business (33%), education (13%), and psychology (11%). In an average class, 18% graduate in 4 years, 26% in 5 years, and 27% in 6 years.

Admissions Contact: Denver Lucky, Director of Admissions. A video is available. E-mail: *admissions@ovc.edu* Web: *ovc.edu*

SALEM INTERNATIONAL UNIVERSITY

Salem, WV 26426 — C-3
(304) 782-5336
(800) 283-4562; Fax: (304) 782-5592

Full-time: 253 men, 192 women	**Faculty:** 34; IIB, --$
Part-time: 7 men, 3 women	**Ph.D.s:** 65%
Graduate: 22 men, 61 women	**Student/Faculty:** 13 to 1
Year: terms, summer session	**Tuition:** $12,855
Application Deadline: open	**Room & Board:** $4408
Freshman Class: n/av	
SAT I Verbal/Math: 480/460	**ACT:** 18 **LESS COMPETITIVE**

Salem International University (formerly Salem-Teikyo University), founded in 1888, is a private institution offering both liberal arts and career-oriented degree programs, including international business, biotechnology, Japanese studies, and equine careers and industry management. In addition to regional accreditation, SIU has baccalaureate program accreditation with ACBSP. The library contains 103,751 volumes, 273,823 microform items, and 885 audiovisual forms/CDs, and subscribes to 456 periodicals. Computerized library services include the card catalog, interlibrary loans, and database searching. Special learning facilities include a learning resource center, art gallery, radio station, TV station, Fort New Salem (an 1800s settlement), equestrian center, and greenhouse. The 300-acre campus is in a rural area 120 miles south of Pittsburgh. Including residence halls, there are 19 buildings.

Student Life: 70% of undergraduates are from out of state, mostly the Middle Atlantic. Others are from 39 states, 15 foreign countries, and Canada. 60% are white; 26%, foreign nationals. The average age of freshmen is 19; all undergraduates, 21. 32% do not continue beyond their first year; 46% remain to graduate.

Housing: 550 students can be accommodated in college housing, which includes single-sex and coed dormitories. In addition, there are honors houses and special-interest houses. On-campus housing is guaranteed for all 4 years. 61% of students live on campus; of those, 75% remain on campus on weekends. All students may keep cars.

Activities: 10% of men belong to 2 local fraternities; 12% of women belong to 3 local sororities. There are 25 groups on campus, including cheerleading, ethnic, gay, honors, international, newspaper, professional, radio and TV, religious, social, social service, student government, and yearbook. Popular campus events include Winterfest, Spring Arts Series, and Spring Fling.

Sports: There are 6 intercollegiate sports for men and 6 for women, and 12 intramural sports for men and 12 for women. Facilities include a gym, a pool, a weight room, tennis courts, a soccer stadium, a fitness trail, racquetball courts, and horseback-riding trails.

Disabled Students: 90% of the campus is accessible. Wheelchair ramps, elevators, special parking, specially equipped rest rooms, special class scheduling, and special wheelchair-lifting equipment are available.

Services: Counseling and information services are available, as is tutoring in most subjects, with most classes having a tutoring option. There is a reader service for the blind, and remedial math, reading, and writing.

Campus Safety and Security: Measures include 24-hour foot and vehicle patrol, escort service, informal discussions, and pamphlets/posters/films. There are emergency telephones, lighted pathways/sidewalks, and Dial-a-Ride on weekends.

Programs of Study: SIU confers B.A. and B.S. degrees. Associate and master's degrees are also awarded. Bachelor's degrees are awarded in AGRICULTURE (equine science), BIOLOGICAL SCIENCE (biology/biological science and molecular biology), BUSINESS (business administration and management, and sports management), COMMUNICATIONS AND THE ARTS (communications and English as a second/foreign language), COMPUTER AND PHYSICAL SCIENCE (computer mathematics and information sciences and systems), EDUCATION (athletic training, elementary, and secondary), ENGINEERING AND ENVIRONMENTAL DESIGN (aviation administration/management and environmental science), SOCIAL SCIENCE (criminal justice, human services, Japanese studies, and liberal arts/general studies). Molecular biology and Japanese studies are the strongest academically. Management studies and bioscience fields are the largest.

Required: All students must take 57 hours in the core curriculum, including courses in communication skills, humanities, science/math, social studies, psychology, and health and phys ed. A minimum 2.0 GPA overall, with a minimum 2.25 GPA in the major, and 128 credit hours are required to graduate.

Special: A student may cross-register with another college within the Mountain State Association of Colleges. Many internships are available. Study abroad is offered. Dual majors, credit by exam, and credit for life experience may be arranged. There are 2 national honor societies.

Faculty/Classroom: 56% of faculty are male; 44%, female. All both teach and do research. No introductory courses are taught by graduate students. The average class size in an introductory lecture is 25; in a laboratory, 10; and in a regular course, 14.

Admissions: The SAT I scores for the 2001-2002 freshman class were: Verbal--56% below 500, 32% between 500 and 599, 10% between 600 and 700, and 2% above 700; Math--62% below 500, 26% between 500 and 599, 10% between 600 and 700, and 2% above 700. The ACT scores were 70% below 21, 12% between 21 and 23, 14% between 24 and 26, and 4% between 27 and 28.

Requirements: The SAT I or ACT is required. In addition, applicants should be graduates of an accredited secondary school with 15 academic courses, including 4 in English, 3 each in math, science, and social studies, and 2 in a foreign language. A GPA of 2.0 is required. AP and CLEP credits are accepted. Important factors in the admissions decision are advanced placement or honor courses, evidence of special talent, and extracurricular activities record. Applications are accepted on-line via the school's web site.

Procedure: Freshmen are admitted to all sessions. Entrance exams should be taken in the junior year or the fall of the senior year. There is a deferred admissions plan. Application deadlines are open. The application fee is $25. Notification is sent on a rolling basis.

Transfer: 38 transfer students enrolled in 2001-2002. A minimum GPA of 2.0 is required. 32 credits of 128 must be completed at SIU.

Visiting: There are regularly scheduled orientations for prospective students, consisting of meetings with academic and administrative department heads, tours, question-and-answer sessions, and a reception. There are guides for informal visits and visitors may sit in on classes and stay overnight. To schedule a visit, contact the Admissions Office at (800) 283-4562, ext. 336.

Financial Aid: In a recent year, 70% of all freshmen and 66% of continuing students received some form of financial aid. 47% of freshmen and 56% of continuing students received need-based aid. The average freshman award was $14,591. Of that total, scholarships or need-based grants averaged $3559 ($7125 maximum); loans averaged $4417 ($13,000 maximum); work contracts averaged $2056 ($2500 maximum); and institutional grants and scholarships based on high school GPA/standardized test scores averaged $7117 ($14,000 maximum). 37% of undergraduates work part time. Average annual earnings from campus work are $1908. The average financial indebtedness of a recent graduate was $8325. SIU is a member of CSS. The FAFSA is required. The fall application deadline is July 15.

International Students: There are 114 international students enrolled. The school actively recruits these students. It is preferred that students take te TOEFL.

Computers: The mainframes are a Digital 6000-620 and 6000-640. Computers are available for student use in labs throughout the campus, and Internet access is provided in each building. All students may access the system. There are no time limits. The fee is $40. It is strongly recommended that all students have a personal computer.

Graduates: In 2001, 154 bachelor's degrees were awarded. The most popular majors were communications (10%), molecular biology (10%), and elementary education (9%). In an average class, 47% graduate in 6 years.

Admissions Contact: William Martin, Director of Admissions. A CD is available. E-mail: *admissions@salemiu.edu* Web: *www.salemiu.edu*

SALEM-TEIKYO UNIVERSITY

(See Salem International University)

SHEPHERD COLLEGE

E-2

Shepherdstown, WV 25443-3210 (304) 876-5212
(800) 344-5231; Fax: (304) 876-5165

Full-time: 1279 men, 1651 women	**Faculty:** 140
Part-time: 492 men, 969 women	**Ph.D.s:** 66%
Graduate: none	**Student/Faculty:** 21 to 1
Year: semesters, summer session	**Tuition:** $2608 ($6294)
Application Deadline: February 1	**Room & Board:** $4454
Freshman Class: 1527 applied, 1374 accepted, 714 enrolled	
SAT I Verbal/Math: 500/500	**ACT:** 20 **LESS COMPETITIVE**

Shepherd College, founded in 1871, is a state-supported institution offering programs in the liberal and creative arts, business administration, teacher education, social and natural sciences, health fields, and other career-oriented areas. There are 4 undergraduate schools. In addition to regional accreditation, Shepherd has baccalaureate program accreditation with CSWE, NASM, NCATE, and NLN. The library contains 162,128 volumes, 157,175 microform items, and 8140 audiovisual forms/CDs, and subscribes to 891 periodicals. Computerized library services include the card catalog, interlibrary loans, and database searching. Special learning facilities include an art gallery, radio station, nursery school, and 3 theaters. The 323-acre campus is in a small town 70 miles northwest of Washington, D.C. and Baltimore. Including residence halls, there are 31 buildings.

Student Life: 67% of undergraduates are from West Virginia. Others are from 41 states, 20 foreign countries, and Canada. 85% are from public schools. 92% are white. The average age of freshmen is 19; all undergraduates, 24. 31% do not continue beyond their first year; 43% remain to graduate.

Housing: 1000 students can be accommodated in college housing, which includes single-sex (by wing)dormitories and on-campus apartments. In addition, there are honors houses and special-interest houses. On-campus housing is guaranteed for the freshman year only, is available on a first-come, first-served basis, and on a lottery system for upperclassmen. Priority is given to out-of-town students. 75% of students commute. All students may keep cars.

Activities: 2% of men belong to 4 national fraternities; 3% of women belong to 3 national sororities. There are 46 groups on campus, including art, band, cheerleading, choir, chorale, chorus, computers, debate, drama, drill team, ethnic, forensics, gay, honors, international, jazz band, literary magazine, marching band, musical theater, newspaper, orchestra, pep band, political, professional, radio and TV, religious, social, social service, and student government. Popular campus events include Family Day, Shepfest, and Midnight Breakfast.

Sports: There are 7 intercollegiate sports for men and 6 for women, and 10 intramural sports for men and 10 for women. Facilities include a 5000-seat football field, baseball and softball fields, a 3000-seat gym, 3 outdoor and 2 indoor tennis courts, 2 outdoor sand volleyball courts, a fitness/wellness center, and a swimming pool.

Disabled Students: 95% of the campus is accessible. Wheelchair ramps, elevators, special parking, specially equipped rest rooms, special class scheduling, lowered drinking fountains, and lowered telephones are available.

Services: Counseling and information services are available, as is tutoring in most subjects. There is a reader service for the blind, remedial math, reading, and writing, tutorial assistance for learning-disabled students, and peer assistance for physically disabled students.

Campus Safety and Security: Measures include 24-hour foot and vehicle patrol, self-defense education, escort service, and shuttle buses. There are informal discussions, pamphlets/posters/films, emergency telephones, and lighted pathways/sidewalks.

Programs of Study: Shepherd confers B.A., B.S., B.F.A, and B.S.N. degrees. Associate degrees are also awarded. Bachelor's degrees are awarded in BIOLOGICAL SCIENCE (biology/biological science), BUSINESS (accounting, business administration and management, hospitality management services, recreation and leisure services, and sports management), COMMUNICATIONS AND THE ARTS (art, communications, English, graphic design, music, music performance, music theory and composition, painting, photography, printmaking, and sculpture), COMPUTER AND PHYSICAL SCIENCE (chemistry, computer science, information sciences and systems, and mathematics), EDUCATION (art, business, elementary, English, health, home economics, mathematics, music, physical, science, secondary, and social studies), ENGINEERING AND ENVIRONMENTAL DESIGN (environmental science), HEALTH PROFESSIONS (nursing and recreation therapy), SOCIAL SCIENCE (economics, family/consumer studies, history, physical fitness/movement, political science/government, psychology, social work, and sociology). Business, science, and art are the strongest academically. Education, business, and recreation are the largest.

Required: To graduate, students must complete 128 semester hours with a 2.0 GPA overall and in the major. The general studies core totals 47 hours, including 19 of humanities, 15 of social sciences, 8 of life or physical science, 3 of math, and 2 of phys ed. B.A. candidates (except for education majors) must demonstrate foreign language proficiency through course work or exam.

Special: Shepherd offers study abroad, a B.A.-B.S. degree in mass communications, and a 2-2 program in engineering. Internships and co-op programs are available in most majors. There is a Washington semester, and dual majors are possible in any 2 majors. Credit by exam, life experience credentialing through the Regents degree, nondegree study, and pass/fail options for electives are offered. There are 9 national honor societies, a freshman honors program, and 1 departmental honors program.

Faculty/Classroom: 61% of faculty are male; 39%, female. All teach undergraduates. The average class size in an introductory lecture is 30; in a laboratory, 24; and in a regular course, 19.

Admissions: 90% of the 2001-2002 applicants were accepted. The SAT I scores for the 2001-2002 freshman class were: Verbal--49% below 500, 36% between 500 and 599, 12% between 600 and 700, and 2% above 700; Math--48% below 500, 40% between 500 and 599, and 11% between 600 and 700. The ACT scores were 53% below 21, 26% between 21 and 23, 13% between 24 and 26, 3% between 27 and 28, and 3% above 28. 50 freshmen graduated first in their class.

Requirements: The SAT I or ACT is required, with a minimum composite score of 1000 on the SAT I or 21 on the ACT. Applicants should be graduates of an accredited secondary school and have earned academic credits, including 4 in English, 3 in social science (1 in American history), 2 each in lab science and math, 1 in phys ed, and the rest in computer, foreign language, and other academic electives. The GED is accepted. A GPA of 2.5 is required. AP and CLEP credits are accepted. Important factors in the admissions decision are advanced placement or honor courses, leadership record, and extracurricular activities record.

Procedure: Freshmen are admitted fall, spring, and summer. Entrance exams should be taken during the junior year. There are early action, early admissions, and deferred admissions plans. Early action applications should be filed by November 15; regular applications, by February 1 for fall entry, November 1 for spring entry, and February 1 for summer entry. The fall 2001 application fee was $30. Notification of early action is sent December 15; regular decision, on a rollingbasis after February.

Transfer: 326 transfer students enrolled in 2001-2002. Applicants must have a 2.0 cumulative GPA in a minimum of 15 semester hours completed and must submit 2 transcripts from each college attended. 32 credits of 128 must be completed at Shepherd.

Visiting: There are regularly scheduled orientations for prospective students, consisting of 3 fall open houses, 4 spring information Saturdays, weekday information sessions, and campus tours by appointment. There are guides for informal visits and visitors may sit in on classes. To schedule a visit, contact the Admissions Office at *admoff@shepherd.edu*.

Financial Aid: In 2001-2002, 47% of all freshmen and 46% of continuing students received some form of financial aid. 35% of freshmen and 32% of continuing students received need-based aid. The average freshman award was $4872. Of that total, scholarships or need-based grants averaged $1888 ($12,828 maximum); loans averaged $2103 ($10,500 maximum); and work contracts averaged $881 ($3500 maximum). 50% of undergraduates work part time. Average annual earnings from campus work are $850. The average financial indebtedness of the 2001 graduate was $14,556. The FAFSA is required. The fall application deadline is March 1.

International Students: There are 35 international students enrolled. The school actively recruits these students. They must score 550 on the written TOEFL or 213 on the electronic version and also take the SAT I or the ACT, scoring 970 on the SAT I.

Computers: The mainframe is a Compaq AlphaServer DS10. There are also 75 PCs in general-use labs and in separate education, biology, chemistry, technology, English writing, art, and music labs. All students may access the system weekdays from 8 A.M. to 11 P.M. There are no time limits and no fees. It is strongly recommended that all students have personal computers.

Graduates: In 2001, 428 bachelor's degrees were awarded. The most popular majors were recreation and leisure studies (10%), business administration (7%), and elementary education (7%). In an average class, 14% graduate in 4 years, 35% in 5 years, and 46% in 6 years. Of the 2000 graduating class, 12% were enrolled in graduate school within 6 months of graduation and 90% were employed.

Admissions Contact: Karl L. Wolf, Director of Admissions. A video is available. E-mail: *kwolf@shepherd.edu* Web: *www.shepherd.edu*

UNIVERSITY OF CHARLESTON B-4
Charleston, WV 25304 (304) 357-4750
(800) 995-4682; Fax: (304) 357-4781

Full-time: 265 men, 592 women	**Faculty:** 70
Part-time: 73 men, 159 women	**Ph.D.s:** 72%
Graduate: 34 men, 27 women	**Student/Faculty:** 12 to 1
Year: semesters, summer session	**Tuition:** $14,900
Application Deadline: open	**Room & Board:** $5740
Freshman Class: 1534 applied, 1088 accepted, 310 enrolled	
SAT I Verbal/Math: 480/490	**ACT:** 21 **COMPETITIVE**

The University of Charleston, founded in 1888, is a private liberal arts institution offering programs in business and the health sciences, as well as traditional arts and sciences. In addition to regional accreditation, UC has baccalaureate program accreditation with AHEA, CAHEA, NCATE, and NLN. The library contains 114,044 volumes, 162,334 microform items, and 3149 audiovisual forms/CDs, and subscribes to 580 periodicals. Computerized library services include the card catalog, interlibrary loans, and database searching. Special learning facilities include a learning resource center and art gallery. The 40-acre campus is in an urban area in Charleston. Including residence halls, there are 9 buildings.

Student Life: 79% of undergraduates are from West Virginia. Others are from 29 states, 26 foreign countries, and Canada. 78% are white. 55% are claim no religious affiliation; 33% Protestant; 11% Catholic. The average age of freshmen is 21; all undergraduates, 24. 30% do not continue beyond their first year; 50% remain to graduate.

Housing: 300 students can be accommodated in college housing, which includes coed dormitories and living/learning communities (housing freshmen based on their courses). On-campus housing is guaranteed for all 4 years. 72% of students commute. All students may keep cars.

Activities: 15% of men belong to 2 national fraternities; 12% of women belong to 3 local sororities. There are 40 groups on campus, including art, cheerleading, choir, chorus, drama, ethnic, honors, international, literary magazine, newspaper, political, professional, religious, social, social service, student government, and yearbook. Popular campus events include the Holiday Dinner served by faculty, the Governor's Cup Regatta, and Fall Festival.

Sports: There are 9 intercollegiate sports for men and 10 for women, and 5 intramural sports for men and 5 for women. Facilities include a gym, a game room, a Nautilus center, an indoor pool, soccer, softball, and baseball fields, and racquetball, volleyball, and tennis courts.

Disabled Students: 45% of the campus is accessible. Wheelchair ramps, elevators, special parking, specially equipped rest rooms, and lowered telephones are available.

Services: Counseling and information services are available, as is tutoring in some subjects, including math, English, and sciences. There is remedial math, reading, and writing.

Campus Safety and Security: Measures include 24-hour foot and vehicle patrol, self-defense education, escort service, and shuttle buses. There are informal discussions, pamphlets/posters/films, emergency telephones, lighted pathways/sidewalks, burglar alarms in dorms, safety and date-rape seminars, drug awareness programs, surveillance cameras at dorms (used in conjunction with card access), and emergency radio communications.

Programs of Study: UC confers B.A., B.S., and B.S.N. degrees. Associate and master's degrees are also awarded. Bachelor's degrees are awarded in BIOLOGICAL SCIENCE (biology/biological science), BUSINESS (accounting, business administration and management, and sports management), COMMUNICATIONS AND THE ARTS (art, communications, English, music, and music business management), COMPUTER AND PHYSICAL SCIENCE (chemistry and information sciences and systems), EDUCATION (elementary, English, music, physical, science, and social studies), ENGINEERING AND ENVIRONMENTAL DESIGN (environmental science and interior design), HEALTH PROFESSIONS (nursing, radiological science, respiratory therapy, and sports medicine), SOCIAL SCIENCE (history, liberal arts/general studies, philosophy, political science/government, psychology, and religion). Environmental science, sports medicine, and interior design are the strongest academically. Business and health sciences are the largest.

Required: All students must fulfill the general education program requirements, which include 48 hours of courses in English, computer systems, social sciences, humanities, natural science, health or phys ed, and elective options. A total of 120 to 128 credit hours and a GPA of 2.0 are required for graduation. A comprehensive exam also is required.

Special: The university offers credit by exam and credit for prior learning. A general studies degree, student-designed majors, nondegree study, and pass-fail options are available. Internships, on-campus work-study, hospital clinical experience in qualified programs, a dual major in biology/chemistry, and a Washington semester are offered. There are 6 national honor societies.

Faculty/Classroom: 37% of faculty are male; 63%, female. All teach undergraduates and 50% both teach and do research. No introductory courses are taught by graduate students. The average class size in an introductory lecture is 17; in a laboratory, 23; and in a regular course, 15.

Admissions: 71% of the 2001-2002 applicants were accepted. The SAT I scores for the 2001-2002 freshman class were: Verbal--50% below 500, 43% between 500 and 599, 6% between 600 and 700, and 1% above 700. The ACT scores were 48% below 21, 32% between 21 and 23, 16% between 24 and 26, 3% between 27 and 28, and 1% above 28. 43% of the current freshmen were in the top fifth of their class; 60% were in the top two fifths.

Requirements: The SAT I or ACT is required, with a minimum composite score of 850 on the SAT I or 18 on the ACT for automatic admission. In addition, applicants should have a minimum GPA of 2.25 and be in the upper 50% of their class. Applicants should be graduates of an accredited secondary school or have the GED and have taken 16 academic courses. A GPA of 2.25 is required. AP and CLEP credits are accepted. Important factors in the admissions decision are advanced placement or honor courses, leadership record, and extracurricular activities record. Applications on computer disk and on-line are accepted.

Procedure: Freshmen are admitted to all sessions. Entrance exams should be taken by December of the senior year. There is an early decision plan. Early decision applications should be filed by December 15; deadline for regular applications, is open for fall entry. There is a $25 fee. Notification of early decision is sent January 31; regular decision, on a rolling basis. 66 early decision candidates were accepted for a recent class.

Transfer: 130 transfer students enrolled in 2001-2002. Applicants should have a minimum GPA of 2.0. 30 credits of 120 to 128 must be completed at UC.

Visiting: There are regularly scheduled orientations for prospective students, including meetings with faculty, financial aid and student life information sessions, a campus tour, and lunch. There are guides for informal visits and visitors may sit in on classes and stay overnight. To schedule a visit, contact the Admissions Office.

Financial Aid: In 2001-2002, 95% of all freshmen and 88% of continuing students received some form of financial aid. 92% of freshmen and 80% of continuing students received need-based aid. The average freshman award was $14,875. Of that total, scholarships or need-based grants averaged $8305 ($18,200 maximum); loans averaged $4800 ($6625 maximum); and work contracts averaged $890 ($1000 maximum). 22% of undergraduates work part time. Average annual earnings from campus work are $975. The average financial indebtedness of the 2001 graduate was $18,300. UC is a member of CSS. The FAFSA, the college's own financial statement, and income tax returns are required. The fall application deadline is March 1.

International Students: There are 55 international students enrolled. The school actively recruits these students. They must score 500 on the written TOEFL and students from English-speaking countries must also take the SAT I or ACT, scoring 850 on the SAT I.

Computers: The mainframe is an HP 9000 K200. There are more than 80 PCs and Macs in computer labs for student use. There are also terminals and PCs with Internet access available in the library. All students may access the system. There is 24-hour dial-in availability. There are no time limits and no fees. It is strongly recommended that all students have personal computers.

Graduates: In A recent year, 147 bachelor's degrees were awarded. The most popular majors were nursing (21%), business (14%), and sports medicine (10%). In an average class, 2% graduate in 3 years, 34% in 4 years, 49% in 5 years, and 54% in 6 years. Of the 2000 graduating class, 20% were enrolled in graduate school within 6 months of graduation and 95% were employed.

Admissions Contact: Kim Scranage, Director of Admissions.
E-mail: *admissions@uchaswv.edu* Web: *www.uchaswv.edu*

WEST LIBERTY STATE COLLEGE C-1
West Liberty, WV 26074 (304) 336-8076
(800) 732-6204; Fax: (304) 336-8403

Full-time: 1079 men, 1296 women	**Faculty:** 112; IIB, -$
Part-time: 93 men, 165 women	**Ph.D.s:** 41%
Graduate: 9 men, 12 women	**Student/Faculty:** 21 to 1
Year: semesters, summer session	**Tuition:** $2516 ($6248)
Application Deadline: August 1	**Room & Board:** $3540
Freshman Class: 1301 applied, 1259 accepted, 531 enrolled	
SAT I Verbal/Math: 467/467	**ACT:** 19 **LESS COMPETITIVE**

West Liberty State College, founded in 1837, is a state-assisted college offering programs in teacher education, liberal and fine arts, sciences, business, and preprofessional and technical fields. There are 4 undergraduate schools. In addition to regional accreditation, West Liberty has baccalaureate program accreditation with ADA, CAHEA, NASM, NCATE, and NLN. The library contains 194,711 volumes, 123,233 microform items, and 13,128 audiovisual forms/CDs, and subscribes to 485 periodicals. Computerized library services include the card catalog, interlibrary loans, and database searching. Special learning facilities include a learning resource center, art gallery, radio station, TV station, and a publication area. The 290-acre campus is in a rural area 10 miles north of Wheeling and 56 miles southwest of Pittsburgh. Including residence halls, there are 22 buildings.

Student Life: 72% of undergraduates are from West Virginia. Others are from 21 states, 9 foreign countries, and Canada. 90% are from public schools. 96% are white. The average age of freshmen is 18; all undergraduates, 22. 30% do not continue beyond their first year; 43% remain to graduate.

Housing: 1427 students can be accommodated in college housing, which includes single-sex and coed dormitories, on-campus apartments, and married-student housing. In addition, there is an honors dormitory. On-campus housing is available on a first-come, first-served basis. 55% of students commute. Alcohol is not permitted. All students may keep cars.

Activities: 6% of men belong to 4 local fraternities; 10% of women belong to 1 local and 3 national sororities. There are 48 groups on campus, including art, cheerleading, choir, chorus, drama, ethnic, honors, hospitality and tourism, jazz band, literary magazine, marching band, musical theater, newspaper, pep band, photography, professional, radio and TV, religious, social, social service, steel drum band, and student government. Popular campus events include Multi-Cultural Day, Greek Week, and Spring Fling.

Sports: There are 8 intercollegiate sports for men and 7 for women, and 8 intramural sports for men and 7 for women. Facilities include handball and racquetball courts, training rooms, 3 gyms, an indoor track, a wellness center, and an indoor swimming pool. There is also a game area with pool tables and table tennis, 8 all-weather-surface tennis courts, and football and softball/baseball fields.

Disabled Students: 90% of the campus is accessible. Wheelchair ramps, elevators, special parking, specially equipped rest rooms, lowered drinking fountains, and lowered telephones are available.

Services: Counseling and information services are available, as is tutoring in every subject. There is a reader service for the blind, and remedial math and writing.

Campus Safety and Security: Measures include 24-hour foot and vehicle patrol, self-defense education, escort service, and informal discussions. There are pamphlets/posters/films, emergency telephones, lighted pathways/sidewalks, and late night transport.

Programs of Study: West Liberty confers B.A., B.S., and B.S.N. degrees. Associate degrees are also awarded. Bachelor's degrees are awarded in BIOLOGICAL SCIENCE (biology/biological science), BUSINESS (accounting, banking and finance, business administration and management, business economics, management science, marketing/retailing/merchandising, and tourism), COMMUNICATIONS AND THE ARTS (communications, English, fine arts, graphic design, and music), COMPUTER AND PHYSICAL SCIENCE (chemistry, information sciences and systems, and mathematics), EDUCATION (art, early childhood, elementary, health, middle school, music, physical, science, secondary, and special), ENGINEERING AND ENVIRONMENTAL DESIGN (preengineering), HEALTH PROFESSIONS (clinical science, dental hygiene, nursing, predentistry, premedicine, prepharmacy, and speech pathology/audiology), SOCIAL SCIENCE (criminal justice, economics, history, interdisciplinary studies, physical fitness/movement, political science/government, prelaw, psychology, social science, and sociology). Business, natural sciences, and health sciences are the strongest academically. Business, elementary education, and criminal justice are the largest.

Required: The required core curriculum varies for B.A. and B.S. candidates, but both include courses in communications, fine arts and humanities, natural science and math, social science and history, and phys ed and health. A minimum GPA of 2.0 and 128 credit hours are required to graduate.

Special: Communication, science of exercise, criminal justice, hospitality, tourism management, sports management, and golf management require an on-campus internship; TV/radio and journalism require an on-campus internship to complete the degree. The Washington Center Program, an internship, is also offered. However, students may also choose to complete an internship in the areas of business, clinical lab science, phys ed, and nursing. Interdisciplinary studies is a student-designed degree taken as either a B.A. or B.S. Biology, chemistry, and math are offered as a B.S. degree but may also be taken as a B.A. degree in education. Work and life experience credit is accepted in the Regents B.A. degree program. There are 10 national honor societies, a freshman honors program, and 6 departmental honors programs.

Faculty/Classroom: 60% of faculty are male; 40%, female. All teach undergraduates. The average class size in an introductory lecture is 25; in a laboratory, 20; and in a regular course, 20.

Admissions: 97% of the 2001-2002 applicants were accepted. The SAT I scores for the 2001-2002 freshman class were: Verbal--65% below 500, 28% between 500 and 599, 6% between 600 and 700, and 1% above 700; Math--66% below 500, 26% between 500 and 599, and 8% between 600 and 700. The ACT scores were 68% below 21, 20% between 21 and 23, 8% between 24 and 26, 3% between 27 and 28, and 1% above 28. 24% of the current freshmen were in the top fifth of their class; 56% were in the top two fifths. 4 freshmen graduated first in their class.

Requirements: The SAT I or ACT is required. In addition, applicants must graduate from an accredited secondary school with a minimum GPA of 2.0, or have a composite minimum score of 17 on the ACT or 810 on the SAT I. Students must have completed 4 years of English, 3 social sciences, including U.S. history, 2 of math (algebra I and higher), and 2 of lab science. The GED is accepted. A GPA of 2.0 is required. AP and CLEP credits are accepted. Applications are accepted on computer disk and on-line at the school's web site, *www.wlsc.edu*

Procedure: Freshmen are admitted to all sessions. Entrance exams should be taken in time so that all admissions credentials, including test scores, are received 2 weeks prior to the beginning of the term. There is a deferred admissions plan. Applications should be filed by August 1 for fall entry and December 1 for spring entry. Notification is sent on a rolling basis.

Transfer: 284 transfer students enrolled in 2001-2002. Students must be eligible to return to the institution from which they wish to transfer. An official college transcript and a minimum GPA of 2.0 overall are required. Admissions criteria are the same as for freshmen if the student has completed fewer than 28 hours of college-level course work. 36 credits of 128 must be completed at West Liberty.

Visiting: There are guides for informal visits and visitors may sit in on classes and stay overnight. To schedule a visit, contact the Office of Admissions.

Financial Aid: In 2001-2002, 85% of all freshmen and 74% of continuing students received some form of financial aid. 44% of freshmen and 42% of continuing students received need-based aid. The average freshman award was $5023. Of that total, scholarships or need-based grants averaged $3518 ($8000 maximum); loans averaged $2295 ($2625 maximum); work contracts averaged $265 ($1000 maximum); and non-need award averaged $1240 ($3310 maximum). 109% of undergraduates work part time. Average annual earnings from campus work are $828. The average financial indebtedness of the 2001 graduate was $12,568. The FAFSA is required. The fall application deadline is March 1.

International Students: There are 15 international students enrolled. They must score 500 on the written TOEFL and also take the SAT I or the ACT, scoring 17.

Computers: The mainframe is a VAX 4700A. There are 300 PCs with access to the Internet and Web throughout the campus for student use. All students may access the system. There are no time limits and no fees. It is strongly recommended that all students have a personal computer.

Graduates: In 2001, 439 bachelor's degrees were awarded. The most popular majors were education (28%), business administration (25%), and criminal justice (11%). In an average class, 19% graduate in 4 years, 37% in 5 years, and 41% in 6 years. 8 companies recruited on campus in 2000-2001. Of the 2000 graduating class, 10% were enrolled in graduate school within 6 months of graduation and 85% were employed.

Admissions Contact: Brenda King, Interim Director.
E-mail: *kingbren@wlsc.edu* Web: *www.wlsc.wvnet.edu*

WEST VIRGINIA STATE COLLEGE
Institute, WV 25112-1000 — **B-4**

(304) 766-3221
(800) 987-2112; Fax: (304) 766-5182

Full-time: 1321 men, 1596 women	**Faculty:** 150
Part-time: 663 men, 1243 women	**Ph.D.s:** 48%
Graduate: none	**Student/Faculty:** 19 to 1
Year: early semesters, summer session	**Tuition:** $2464 ($5666)
	Room & Board: $3800
Application Deadline: August 10	
Freshman Class: n/av	
SAT I: recommended	**ACT:** required

NONCOMPETITIVE

West Virginia State College, founded in 1891, is a state-supported institution offering broad programs in the arts and sciences and in preprofessional studies, including business and education. It also offers a comprehensive evening class schedule. In addition to regional accreditation, State College has baccalaureate program accreditation with ABET, CSWE, NCATE, and NRPA. The library contains 28,295 volumes, 500,000 microform items, and 6184 audiovisual forms/CDs, and subscribes to 630 periodicals. Computerized library services include the card catalog, interlibrary loans, and database searching. Special learning facilities include a learning resource center, art gallery, and TV station. The 91-acre campus is in a suburban area 8 miles west of Charleston. Including residence halls, there are 40 buildings.

Student Life: 94% of undergraduates are from West Virginia. Others are from 34 states and 8 foreign countries. 99% are from public schools. 84% are white; 14% African American. The average age of freshmen is 26; all undergraduates, 27. 30% do not continue beyond their first year; 64% remain to graduate.

Housing: 794 students can be accommodated in college housing, which includes single-sex dormitories, on-campus apartments, and married-student housing. 93% of students commute. Alcohol is not permitted. All students may keep cars.

Activities: 1% of men belong to 1 local and 4 national fraternities; 1% of women belong to 3 national sororities. There are 42 groups on campus, including art, band, cheerleading, choir, chorale, chorus, drama, drill team, ethnic, film, honors, international, jazz band, literary magazine, newspaper, orchestra, pep band, photography, political, radio and TV, religious, social, social service, student government, and yearbook. Popular campus events include movies, comedy shows, and plays.

Sports: There are 5 intercollegiate sports for men and 4 for women, and 8 intramural sports for men and 7 for women. Facilities include a 6000-seat stadium, a swimming pool, a sports center, a 1500-seat gym, the student union, and a student mall/plaza.

Disabled Students: Wheelchair ramps, elevators, special parking, specially equipped rest rooms, special class scheduling, and lowered drinking fountains are available.

Services: Counseling and information services are available, as is tutoring in most subjects, including economics, political science, upper-division math, and accounting. There is remedial math, reading, and writing.

Campus Safety and Security: Measures include 24-hour foot and vehicle patrol, informal discussions, pamphlets/posters/films, and lighted pathways/sidewalks. There are formal educational sessions held in the dormitories each semester.

Programs of Study: State College confers B.A., B.S., and B.S.Ed. degrees. Associate degrees are also awarded. Bachelor's degrees are awarded in BIOLOGICAL SCIENCE (biology/biological science), BUSINESS (accounting, banking and finance, business administration and management, and marketing/retailing/merchandising), COMMUNICATIONS AND THE ARTS (communications, English, and fine arts), COMPUTER AND PHYSICAL SCIENCE (applied mathematics, chemistry, and mathematics), EDUCATION (art, early childhood, elementary, and secondary), HEALTH PROFESSIONS (recreation therapy), SOCIAL SCIENCE (criminal justice, economics, history, political science/government, psychology, social work, and sociology). Biology is the strongest academically. Education and business are the largest.

Required: Bachelor's degree candidates must take 52 to 53 semester credits of general studies courses, including freshman seminar, English, math, natural science, literature, fine arts, history, and cultural studies. To graduate, students must complete 121 to 128 credits with a minimum 2.0 GPA overall and in the major.

Special: State College offers internships, a Washington semester, work-study programs, and B.A.-B.S. degrees in communications, psychology, and biology. Credit by exam and for life/military/work experience is available. Nondegree study and pass/fail options are possible. There are 7 national honor societies, a freshman honors program, and 7 departmental honors programs.

Faculty/Classroom: 49% of faculty are male; 51%, female. The average class size in a regular course is 25.

Requirements: The ACT is required and the SAT I is recommended. In addition, a minimum ACT composite score of 14 or a 2.0 GPA is required for regular admission. Applicants should be graduates of an accredited secondary school and have completed a minimum of 4 years each in English and academic electives, 3 in social studies, and 2 each in math and science. The GED is accepted. A GPA of 2.0 is required. AP and CLEP credits are accepted. Important factors in the admissions decision are evidence of special talent, leadership record, and advanced placement or honor courses. Applications are accepted on-line.

Procedure: Freshmen are admitted to all sessions. Entrance exams should be taken 6 months prior to entry. There is an early decision plan. Early decision applications should be filed by March 10; regular applications, by August 10 for fall entry, November 10 for spring entry, and March 10 for summer entry. The college accepts all in-state residents. Notification is sent on a rolling basis.

Transfer: 311 transfer students enrolled in 2001-2002. Applicants must submit ACT scores and high school transcripts, and must have a 2.5 GPA. 30 credits of 121 must be completed at State College.

Visiting: There are regularly scheduled orientations for prospective students, including both academic and social activities. There are guides for informal visits, and visitors may sit in on classes and stay overnight. To schedule a visit, contact John L. Fuller at (304) 766-3144.

Financial Aid: The CSS/Profile is required. The fall application deadline is March 1.

International Students: These students must score 500 on the written TOEFL and also take the ACT, scoring 14.

Computers: The mainframe is a DEC MicroVAX 3900. There are more than 90 terminals and more than 400 computers at different facilities on campus. All students may access the system Monday through Thursday, 9 A.M. to 10 P.M., Friday, 9 A.M. to 7 P.M., and Saturday, 9 A.M. to 2 P.M. Each student is allocated $200 of use per semester. There are no fees.

Admissions Contact: Alice Ruhnke, Director of Admissions and Recruitment Services. E-mail: *ruhnkeam@mail.wvc.edu*
Web: *www.wvsc.edu*

WEST VIRGINIA UNIVERSITY C-2
Morgantown, WV 26506-6009 (304) 293-2121
(800) 344-9881; Fax: (304) 293-3080

Full-time: 8198 men, 6983 women	**Faculty:** 1304; I, --$
Part-time: 435 men, 505 women	**Ph.D.s:** 86%
Graduate: 2824 men, 3829 women	**Student/Faculty:** 12 to 1
Year: semesters, summer session	**Tuition:** $2948 ($8832)
Application Deadline: August 1	**Room & Board:** $5356

Freshman Class: 8786 applied, 8238 accepted, 3661 enrolled
SAT I Verbal/Math: 512/521 **COMPETITIVE**

West Virginia University, founded in 1867, is a comprehensive, public land-grant research university offering more than 100 undergraduate degrees in liberal arts and sciences, health science, and professional training. There are 13 undergraduate and 14 graduate schools. In addition to regional accreditation, WVU has baccalaureate program accreditation with AACSB, ABET, ACEJMC, ACPE, ADA, APTA, ASLA, CAHEA, CSWE, FIDER, NASAD, NASM, NCATE, NLN, NRPA, and SAF. The 10 libraries contain 1,440,593 volumes, 2,298,958 microform items, and 43,528 audiovisual forms/CDs, and subscribe to 13,681 periodicals. Computerized library services include the card catalog, interlibrary loans, and database searching. Special learning facilities include a learning resource center, art gallery, planetarium, radio station, TV station, a discovery lab for inventors, a coal, mining, and minerals history museum, a pharmacy museum, and an arboretum. The 913-acre campus is in a small town 75 miles south of Pittsburgh and 200 miles west of Baltimore. Including residence halls, there are 136 buildings.

Student Life: 60% of undergraduates are from West Virginia. Others are from 50 states, 68 foreign countries, and Canada. 88% are white. The average age of freshmen is 18; all undergraduates, 21. 22% do not continue beyond their first year; 57% remain to graduate.

Housing: 3400 students can be accommodated in college housing, which includes single-sex and coed dormitories, on-campus apartments, off-campus apartments, married-student housing, fraternity houses, and sorority houses. In addition, there are honors houses, language houses, special-interest houses, and sections within residence halls designated for special programming. On-campus housing is available on a first-come, first-served basis and is available on a lottery system for upperclassmen. 79% of students live on campus. Alcohol is not permitted. All students may keep cars.

Activities: 17% of men belong to 20 national fraternities; 19% of women belong to 12 national sororities. There are 250 groups on campus, including art, band, cheerleading, chess, choir, chorale, chorus, computers, dance, debate, drama, environmental, ethnic, film, gay, honors, international, jazz band, literary magazine, marching band, newspaper, opera, orchestra, pep band, photography, political, professional, radio and TV, religious, social, social service, student government, symphony, and yearbook. Popular campus events include Mountaineer Week, Parents Weekend, and Spring Week.

Sports: There are 10 intercollegiate sports for men and 10 for women, and 19 intramural sports for men and 18 for women. Facilities include a natatorium with swimming and diving pools, tennis courts, a weight room, indoor/outdoor tracks, racquetball and squash courts, a bowling alley, lacrosse, baseball and soccer fields, a 63500-seat stadium, and a 14000-seat gym.

Disabled Students: 90% of the campus is accessible. Wheelchair ramps, elevators, special parking, specially equipped rest rooms, special class scheduling, lowered drinking fountains, and lowered telephones are available. Academic programs are made accessible by transferring class to an architecturally accessible facility. Other facilities include tactile signage, specially designed lab facilities and portable lab stations, a Kurzweil reading machine, special apartments for hearing and mobility impaired students, and a specially equipped van for inner-city transportation. All coordination is done through the ADA coordinator.

Services: Counseling and information services are available, as is tutoring in most subjects. There is a reader service for the blind, and remedial math, reading, and writing.

Campus Safety and Security: Measures include 24-hour foot and vehicle patrol, self-defense education, escort service, and shuttle buses. There are informal discussions, pamphlets/posters/films, emergency telephones, lighted pathways/sidewalks, neighborhood watch programs, and sexual assault prevention booths staffed by city and university police.

Programs of Study: WVU confers B.A., B.S., B.F.A., B.M., B.S.A.E., B.S.Agr., B.S.B.Ad., B.S.C.E., B.S.Ch.E., B.S.Cp.E., B.S.E.E., B.S.F., B.S.Fam.Res., B.S.F. & C.S., B.S.F.I., B.S.I.E., B.S.J., B.S.L.A., B.S.M.E., B.S.Min.E., B.S.N., B.S.P.Ed., B.S.PNGE., B.S.R., and B.S.W. degrees. Master's and doctoral degrees are also awarded. Bachelor's degrees are awarded in AGRICULTURE (agricultural business management, agriculture, agronomy, animal science, fish and game management, fishing and fisheries, forestry and related sciences, horticulture, natural resource management, and plant science), BIOLOGICAL SCIENCE (biology/biological science and nutrition), BUSINESS (accounting, banking and finance, business administration and management, fashion merchandising, marketing and distribution, recreation and leisure services, sports management, and tourism), COMMUNICATIONS AND THE ARTS (advertising, art, broadcasting, communications, dramatic arts, English, journalism, music, public relations, speech/debate/rhetoric, and visual and performing arts), COMPUTER AND PHYSICAL SCIENCE (chemistry, computer science, geology, geoscience, mathematics, physics, science, and statistics), EDUCATION (agricultural, athletic training, elementary, English, environmental, foreign languages, mathematics, physical, and secondary), ENGINEERING AND ENVIRONMENTAL DESIGN (aeronautical engineering, aerospace studies, chemical engineering, civil engineering, computer engineering, electrical/electronics engineering, engineering, environmental science, interior design, landscape architecture/design, mechanical engineering, mining and mineral engineering, petroleum/natural gas engineering, and systems engineering), HEALTH PROFESSIONS (dental hygiene, medical technology, nursing, occupational therapy, pharmacy, physical therapy, speech pathology/audiology, and veterinary science), SOCIAL SCIENCE (anthropology, child care/child and family studies, economics, family/consumer resource management, geography, history, interdisciplinary studies, international studies, liberal arts/general studies, parks and recreation management, philosophy, political science/government, psychology, social work, and sociology). Engineering and mineral resources, psychology, and political science are the strongest academically. Business and economics, engineering and mineral resources, and health sciences are the largest.

Required: All students are required to take 12 credit hours in each of 3 areas: humanities and fine arts, social and behavioral sciences, and natural sciences and math. The 36 credit hours must include international/minority/gender studies, math, composition, and an advanced course emphasizing writing skills. A minimum 2.0 GPA and at least 128 credit hours are required to graduate.

Special: A co-op program in engineering and cross-registration with schools in the Southern Regional Education Board through the Academic Common Market are possible. Internships, study abroad in 12 countries, a Washington semester, student-designed majors, dual majors in business and foreign languages, and B.A.-B.S. degrees in economics, chemistry, physics, biology, and geology are available. A liberal studies degree, credit by exam, credit for life experience, nondegree study, and pass/fail options are also offered. There are 34 national honor societies, including Phi Beta Kappa, and a freshman honors program.

Faculty/Classroom: 63% of faculty are male; 37%, female. All teach undergraduates, 70% do research, and 70% do both. Graduate students teach 32% of introductory courses. The average class size in a regular course is 36.

Admissions: 94% of the 2001-2002 applicants were accepted. The SAT I scores for the 2001-2002 freshman class were: Verbal--43% below 500, 44% between 500 and 599, 12% between 600 and 700, and 1% above 700; Math--38% below 500, 46% between 500 and 599, 15% between 600 and 700, and 1% above 700. The ACT scores were 35% below 21, 27% between 21 and 23, 22% between 24 and 26, 9% between 27 and 28, and 7% above 28.

Requirements: The SAT I or ACT is required. In-state students need a minimum combined score of 910 on the SAT I, or 19 composite on the ACT and a minimum high school GPA of 2.0. Out-of-state students need scores of 950 or 20, respectively, and a minimum high school GPA of 2.25. Applicants should graduate from an accredited school no sooner than their junior year, after completing 4 years of English, 3 of social studies including U.S. history, 3 of math, and 2 each of lab sciences and foreign language. 1 year of typing is recommended. Music students must audition, and art applicants must submit a portfolio. A GPA of 2.0 is required. AP and CLEP credits are accepted. Important factors in the admissions decision are leadership record, evidence of special talent, and advanced placement or honor courses. Applicants may apply on-line at WVU's web site, *http://www.applyweb.com/apply/wvu/*

Procedure: Freshmen are admitted fall, spring, and summer. Entrance exams should be taken by the spring of the junior year. There are early admissions and deferred admissions plans. Applications should be filed by August 1 for fall entry. Notification is sent on a rolling basis. The fall 2001 application fee was $25.

Transfer: 850 transfer students enrolled in 2001-2002. A minimum college GPA of 2.0 is required of transfers; all applicants must submit college transcripts. Students having fewer than 29 transferable credit hours are subject to freshman admission criteria and must submit SAT I or ACT scores and high school transcripts. 30 credits of 128 must be completed at WVU.

Visiting: There are regularly scheduled orientations for prospective students, including 2-day sessions with campus tours, placement testing, academic and advisement meetings, parent/student orientation discussions, and transitional meetings. There are guides for informal visits and visitors may sit in on classes. To schedule a visit, contact the Admissions and Records Tour Office.

Financial Aid: In 2001-2002, 40% of all freshmen and 49% of continuing students received some form of financial aid. 35% of continuing students received need-based aid. The average freshman award was $6250. The average financial indebtedness of the 2001 graduate was $18,273. WVU is a member of CSS. The FAFSA is required. The fall application deadline is March 1.

International Students: There are 269 international students enrolled in a recent year. They must score 550 on the written TOEFL. International students serving as graduate teaching assistants must also demonstrate mastery of spoken English and take the SAT I or the ACT, scoring 950.

Computers: The mainframes are an IBM 9672-R63 running VM/ESA and AIX/ESA; a VAX 8250 and a VAX 6000-620 in a VAX cluster running VAX/VMS with access to the Thinking Machine Supercomputer. All students are issued e-mail accounts. Those required to use the mainframe for class projects are issued an individual mainframe account by their instructor. Many colleges and academic departments operate their own labs containing PCs with mainframe access. Public sites with consultants provide additional access to training and facilities. PCs and Macs are available throughout the campus including in residence halls. All students may access the system 24 hours a day, 7 days a week. There are no time limits and no fees.

Graduates: In 2001, 2808 bachelor's degrees were awarded. The most popular majors were business/marketing (12%), engineering (11%), and social sciences and history (9%). In an average class, 21% graduate in 4 years, 47% in 5 years, and 53% in 6 years.

Admissions Contact: Chen Khoo, Director of Admissions and Records. E-mail: *wvuadmissions@arc.wvu.edu* Web: *www.arc.wvu.edu*

WEST VIRGINIA UNIVERSITY INSTITUTE OF TECHNOLOGY — B-4

Montgomery, WV 25136 — (304) 442-3167
(888) 554-TECH; Fax: (304) 442-3097

Full-time: 1063 men, 582 women	**Faculty:** 120; IIB, --$
Part-time: 398 men, 310 women	**Ph.D.s:** 52%
Graduate: 16 men, 5 women	**Student/Faculty:** 14 to 1
Year: semesters, summer session	**Tuition:** $2836 ($7020)
Application Deadline: August 1	**Room & Board:** $4682
Freshman Class: 957 applied, 954 accepted, 457 enrolled	
SAT I Verbal/Math: 501/525	**ACT:** 20 **NONCOMPETITIVE**

West Virginia University Institute of Technology, part of the Western Virginia University system and founded in 1895, is a public institution offering programs in business and economics, arts and sciences, community and technical fields, and engineering. There are 3 undergraduate schools and 1 graduate school. In addition to regional accreditation, West Virginia Tech has baccalaureate program accreditation with ABET, ADA, and NLN. The library contains 166,967 volumes and 438,232 microform items, and subscribes to 510 periodicals. Computerized library services include the card catalog, interlibrary loans, and database searching. Special learning facilities include a learning resource center and art gallery. The 112-acre campus is in a small town 28 miles southeast of Charleston. Including residence halls, there are 15 buildings.

Student Life: 91% of undergraduates are from West Virginia. Others are from 25 states, 24 foreign countries, and Canada. 95% are from public schools. 87% are white. The average age of freshmen is 19; all undergraduates, 24. 35% do not continue beyond their first year; 40% remain to graduate.

Housing: 776 students can be accommodated in college housing, which includes single-sex and coed dormitories. In addition, there are quiet floors. On-campus housing is guaranteed for all 4 years. 69% of students commute. All students may keep cars.

Activities: 10% of men belong to 5 national fraternities; 8% of women belong to 2 national sororities. There are 42 groups on campus, including art, band, cheerleading, choir, chorus, computers, drama, drill team, ethnic, international, jazz band, marching band, newspaper, pep band, photography, political, professional, religious, social, student government, and yearbook. Popular campus events include comedy and film series, Black History Month, and Greek Week.

Sports: There are 5 intercollegiate sports for men and 4 for women, and 8 intramural sports for men and 8 for women. Facilities include 2 gyms, a weight room, tennis and handball courts, a student union, a football field and 3000-seat stadium, an Olympic-size swimming pool, game rooms, and a fitness center.

Disabled Students: 60% of the campus is accessible. Wheelchair ramps, elevators, special parking, specially equipped rest rooms, special class scheduling, and lowered drinking fountains are available.

Services: Counseling and information services are available, as is tutoring in most subjects. There is remedial math, reading, and writing, and a math learning center.

Campus Safety and Security: Measures include 24-hour foot and vehicle patrol, self-defense education, escort service, and informal discussions. There are pamphlets/posters/films and lighted pathways/sidewalks.

Programs of Study: West Virginia Tech confers B.A., B.S., B.E.T., B.M.E.T., B.S.C.E., B.S.E., and B.S.E.E. degrees. Associate and master's degrees are also awarded. Bachelor's degrees are awarded in BIOLOGICAL SCIENCE (biology/biological science), BUSINESS (accounting, and business administration and management), COMPUTER AND PHYSICAL SCIENCE (chemistry, computer programming, computer science, and physics), ENGINEERING AND ENVIRONMENTAL DESIGN (chemical engineering, civil engineering, electrical/electronics engineering, electrical/electronics engineering technology, engineering technology, industrial administration/management, industrial engineering technology, and mechanical engineering), HEALTH PROFESSIONS (health care administration and nursing), SOCIAL SCIENCE (history and public administration). Engineering is the strongest academically. Nursing is the largest.

Required: Core curriculum requirements include 8 hours of lab science, 6 to 12 each of humanities and social science, 6 each of English and math/computer science, and 2 of phys ed and health. Other requirements vary according to the degree sought. To graduate, students must complete 128 semester hours with a minimum 2.0 GPA overall and in the major.

Special: An extensive co-op program is offered in all areas as well as a number of internships in public service and industrial relations. Credit for armed service experience and credit by departmental exam are available.

Faculty/Classroom: 70% of faculty are male; 30%, female. All teach undergraduates and 10% do research. No introductory courses are taught by graduate students. The average class size in an introductory lecture is 30; in a laboratory, 15; and in a regular course, 20.

Admissions: All of the 2001-2002 applicants were accepted. The SAT I scores for the 2001-2002 freshman class were: Verbal--50% below 500, 35% between 500 and 599, and 15% between 600 and 700; Math--55% below 500, 27% between 500 and 599, and 18% between 600 and 700. The ACT scores were 50% below 21, 33% between 21 and 23, 10% between 24 and 26, 5% between 27 and 28, and 2% above 28. 39% of the current freshmen were in the top fifth of their class; 55% were in the top two fifths. 11 freshmen graduated first in their class.

Requirements: The SAT I or ACT is required, with a minimum composite score of 690 on the SAT I or 17 on the ACT (higher for engineering and health majors). Applicants should be graduates from an accredited secondary school or have qualifying scores on the GED. Students must have completed 4 units of English, 3 of social studies, and 2 each of math (4 for engineering majors) and lab science. A GPA of 2.0 is required. AP and CLEP credits are accepted. Applications are accepted on-line at the Institute's e-mail address.

Procedure: Freshmen are admitted to all sessions. Entrance exams should be taken in sufficient time for the scores to reach the Institute by the application deadline. There is an early admissions plan. Applications should be filed by August 1 for fall entry, December 15 for spring entry, and May 1 for summer entry. The college accepts all in-state residents. Notification is sent on a rolling basis.

Transfer: 192 transfer students enrolled in 2001-2002. Criteria for transfer admission vary according to the college. 30 credits of 128 must be completed at West Virginia Tech.

Visiting: There are regularly scheduled orientations for prospective students. There are guides for informal visits, and visitors may sit in on classes and stay overnight. To schedule a visit, contact the Admissions Office.

Financial Aid: In 2001-2002, 86% of all freshmen and 54% of continuing students received some form of financial aid. 49% of freshmen and 45% of continuing students received need-based aid. The average freshman award was $2480. Of that total, scholarships or need-based grants averaged $3730 ($3510 maximum); loans averaged $2752 ($5500 maximum); and work contracts averaged $1250. 15% of undergraduates work part time. Average annual earnings from campus work are $1000. The average financial indebtedness of the 2001 graduate was $13,000. West Virginia Tech is a member of CSS. The FAFSA and the college's own financial statement are required. The fall application deadline is April 1.

International Students: The school actively recruits these students. They must score 500 on the written TOEFL or 173 on the electronic version and also take the SAT I or the ACT.

Computers: The mainframe is a DEC VAX 4700A RISC 6000. There is also a Novell network, Groupwise Messaging, Campus Pipeline and T1 access to the Internet. All students may access the system 24 hours a day. There are no time limits and no fees. It is strongly recommended that all students have a personal computer.

Graduates: In 2001, 261 bachelor's degrees were awarded. The most popular majors were engineering (42%), business (21%), and health (10%). In an average class, 2% graduate in 3 years, 30% in 4 years, 10% in 5 years, and 2% in 6 years. 68 companies recruited on campus in 2000-2001.

Admissions Contact: Donna Varney, Director of Admissions. A video is available. E-mail: *wvutech@wvit.wvnet.edu* Web: *www.wvutech.edu*

WEST VIRGINIA WESLEYAN COLLEGE C-3

Buckhannon, WV 26201 (304) 473-8510
(800) 722-9933; Fax: (304) 473-8108

Full-time: 674 men, 783 women	**Faculty:** 84; IIB, --$
Part-time: 26 men, 54 women	**Ph.D.s:** 71%
Graduate: 31 men, 24 women	**Student/Faculty:** 17 to 1
Year: semesters, summer session	**Tuition:** $18,700
Application Deadline: August 1	**Room & Board:** $4220
Freshman Class: 1123 applied, 961 accepted, 400 enrolled	
SAT I Verbal/Math: 500/510	**ACT:** 22 **COMPETITIVE**

West Virginia Wesleyan College, founded in 1890, is an independent liberal and applied arts college affiliated with the United Methodist Church. In addition to regional accreditation, WVWC has baccalaureate program accreditation with NASM and NLN. The library contains 107,340 volumes, 33,139 microform items, and 6077 audiovisual forms/CDs, and subscribes to 780 periodicals. Computerized library services include the card catalog and database searching. Special learning facilities include a learning resource center, art gallery, planetarium, and radio station. The 80-acre campus is in a small town in the Appalachian foothills, 135 miles south of Pittsburgh, Pennsylvania. Including residence halls, there are 23 buildings.

Student Life: 53% of undergraduates are from West Virginia. Others are from 32 states, 19 foreign countries, and Canada. 85% are from public schools. 88% are white. 53% are Protestant; 20% Catholic. The average age of freshmen is 18; all undergraduates, 21. 26% do not continue beyond their first year.

Housing: 1370 students can be accommodated in college housing, which includes single-sex and coed dormitories and on-campus apartments. In addition, there are honors houses, quiet study living areas, and substance-free small group living units. On-campus housing is guaranteed for all 4 years. 83% of students live on campus; of those, 65% remain on campus on weekends. Alcohol is not permitted. All students may keep cars.

Activities: 25% of men belong to 6 national fraternities; 25% of women belong to 4 national sororities. There are 75 groups on campus, including art, band, cheerleading, choir, chorale, chorus, computers, dance, drama, ethnic, forensics, gay, honors, international, jazz band, literary magazine, musical theater, newspaper, political, professional, radio and TV, religious, social, social service, student government, and yearbook. Popular campus events include Founders Day, Festivals of Lessons and Carols, and Spring Sing.

Sports: There are 9 intercollegiate sports for men and 8 for women, and 9 intramural sports for men and 8 for women. Facilities include baseball and football fields with seating for 3500, as well as a phys ed center with a 3800-seat intercollegiate basketball court, 2 intramural practice courts, 4 handball courts, an auxiliary gym, indoor tennis courts, volleyball courts, golf and wrestling practice areas, sauna baths, a dance studio, and gymnastics and weight rooms. A state park is near the campus.

Disabled Students: 75% of the campus is accessible. Wheelchair ramps, elevators, special parking, specially equipped rest rooms, special class scheduling, and lowered drinking fountains are available.

Services: Counseling and information services are available, as is tutoring in every subject. There is a reader service for the blind, and remedial math, reading, and writing.

Campus Safety and Security: Measures include 24-hour foot and vehicle patrol, self-defense education, escort service, and informal discussions. There are pamphlets/posters/films, emergency telephones, lighted pathways/sidewalks, rape awareness educational programs, and appropriate training for residence hall staff.

Programs of Study: WVWC confers B.A., B.S., B.M.E., and B.S.N. degrees. Master's degrees are also awarded. Bachelor's degrees are awarded in BIOLOGICAL SCIENCE (biology/biological science and nutrition), BUSINESS (accounting, business administration and management, and marketing/retailing/merchandising), COMMUNICATIONS AND THE ARTS (dramatic arts, English, music, public relations, and speech/debate/rhetoric), COMPUTER AND PHYSICAL SCIENCE (chemistry, computer science, mathematics, and physics), EDUCATION (art, elementary, music, physical, and secondary), ENGINEERING AND ENVIRONMENTAL DESIGN (engineering physics), HEALTH PROFESSIONS (nursing), SOCIAL SCIENCE (economics, history, international studies, philosophy, political science/government, psychology, religion, religious education, social science, and sociology). Physical and natural sciences and accounting are the strongest academically. Business, biology, and education are the largest.

Required: To graduate, students must earn 120 semester hours with a minimum GPA of 2.0; 24 to 51 hours must be in the major, 48 to 53 in general studies. Required disciplines are cultural studies, natural science and math, social sciences, health and phys ed, religion, philosophy, humanities and fine arts, and communications.

Special: WVWC offers cross-registration with the Mountain State Association of Colleges. Students may participate in a wide variety of internships, including a Washington center internship and work-study and study-abroad programs; there are exchange agreements in Korea, the People's Republic of China, Norway, and Bulgaria. Nondegree and pass/fail study, dual, student-designed, and contract majors, and credit for life, military, and work experience are available. There is 1 national honor society and a freshman honors program.

Faculty/Classroom: 63% of faculty are male; 37%, female. All teach undergraduates. No introductory courses are taught by graduate students. The average class size in an introductory lecture is 24; in a laboratory, 12; and in a regular course, 21.

Admissions: 86% of the 2001-2002 applicants were accepted. The SAT I scores for the 2001-2002 freshman class were: Verbal--43% below 500, 41% between 500 and 599, 15% between 600 and 700, and 1% above 700; Math--45% below 500, 40% between 500 and 599, 13% between 600 and 700, and 2% above 700. The ACT scores were 36% below 21, 29% between 21 and 23, 19% between 24 and 26, 7% between 27 and 28, and 9% above 28. 50% of the current freshmen were in the top fifth of their class; 80% were in the top two fifths. 10 freshmen graduated first in their class.

Requirements: The SAT I or ACT is required. The minimum composite score needed is 800 on SAT I, 420 verbal and 380 math, or 18 on the ACT. In addition, applicants must be high school graduates or hold a GED. Students should have earned 26 academic credits, consisting of 4 in English, 3 each in math, science, and academic electives, and 2 each in foreign language, lab science, and social studies, as well as a total of 7 academic credits in fine arts, technology education, health, and phys ed. An essay and an interview are recommended. A GPA of 2.0 is required. AP and CLEP credits are accepted. Important factors in the admissions decision are extracurricular activities record, recommendations by school officials, and leadership record. Applications are accepted on-line via Embark.com.

Procedure: Freshmen are admitted fall and spring. Entrance exams should be taken in fall of the senior year or spring/summer of the junior year. There are early decision, rolling admissions, and deferred admissions plans. Early decision applications should be filed by December 1; regular applications, by August 1 for fall entry and January 10 for spring entry. Notification of early decision is sent January 15; regular decision, on a rolling basis. The fall 2001 application fee was $25.

Transfer: 43 transfer students enrolled in 2001-2002. Transfer applicants must supply a high school transcript if their GPA for college work is less than 2.5. An associate degree and interview are recommended. 30 credits of 120 must be completed at WVWC.

Visiting: There are regularly scheduled orientations for prospective students. There are guides for informal visits and visitors may sit in on classes and stay overnight. To schedule a visit, contact Robert Skinner, Director of Admission.

Financial Aid: In 2001-2002, 99% of all freshmen and 98% of continuing students received some form of financial aid. 77% of freshmen and 75% of continuing students received need-based aid. The average freshman award was $18,700. Of that total, scholarships or need-based grants averaged $13,180; loans averaged $4120; and work contracts averaged $1400. 41% of undergraduates work part time. Average annual earnings from campus work are $1000. The average financial indebtedness of the 2001 graduate was $16,118. The FAFSA is required. The fall application deadline is March 1.

International Students: The school actively recruits international students. They must score 500 on the written TOEFL.

Computers: The mainframes are an ALPHA 1000 and an ALPHA 800. All students have network accounts, all freshmen have IBM ThinkPad systems, and upperclassmen have access to computer labs in the science building, library, art department, or learning center. There are approximately 85 public access systems on campus. All systems have access to the Internet and Web. All students may access the system. There are no time limits and no fees. All students are required to have PCs using Windows 2000 and a Pentium processor.

Graduates: In 2001, 297 bachelor's degrees were awarded. The most popular majors were elementary education (10%), psychology (7%), and public relations (6%). In an average class, 1% graduate in 3 years, 44% in 4 years, 52% in 5 years, and 55% in 6 years. Of the 2000 graduating class, 26% were enrolled in graduate school within 6 months of graduation.

Admissions Contact: Robert N. Skinner II, Director of Admission. A video is available. E-mail: *admissions@wvwc.edu*
Web: *www.wvwc.edu*

WHEELING JESUIT UNIVERSITY — C-2

Wheeling, WV 26003 — (304) 243-2359
(800) 624-6992; Fax: (304) 243-2397

Full-time: 456 men, 584 women	**Faculty:** 86; IIB, --$
Part-time: 49 men, 160 women	**Ph.D.s:** 80%
Graduate: 82 men, 135 women	**Student/Faculty:** 12 to 1
Year: semesters, summer session	**Tuition:** $17,240
Application Deadline: open	**Room & Board:** $5420
Freshman Class: 933 applied, 817 accepted, 252 enrolled	
SAT I Verbal/Math: 510/520	**ACT:** 21 **COMPETITIVE**

Wheeling Jesuit University, founded in 1954, is an independent college affiliated with the Society of Jesus, offering undergraduate programs in the liberal arts and sciences, nursing, allied health, and business, and graduate programs in business administration and applied theology. In addition to regional accreditation, Wheeling Jesuit has baccalaureate program accreditation with CAHEA and NLN. The library contains 155,953 volumes, 120,278 microform items, and 1200 audiovisual forms/CDs, and subscribes to 504 periodicals. Computerized library services include the card catalog and database searching. Special learning facilities include a learning resource center. The 70-acre campus is in a suburban area 60 miles southwest of Pittsburgh. Including residence halls, there are 15 buildings.

Student Life: 66% of undergraduates are from out of state, mostly the Middle Atlantic. Others are from 31 states, 28 foreign countries, and Canada. 90% are white. 57% are Catholic; 33% Protestant. The average age of freshmen is 18; all undergraduates, 24. 28% do not continue beyond their first year; 62% remain to graduate.

Housing: 764 students can be accommodated in college housing, which includes single-sex dormitories. On-campus housing is guaranteed for all 4 years. 78% of students live on campus; of those, 75% remain on campus on weekends. All students may keep cars.

Activities: There are no fraternities or sororities. There are 20 groups on campus, including cheerleading, choir, chorus, drama, honors, international, literary magazine, newspaper, pep band, professional, religious, social, social service, student government, and yearbook. Popular campus events include Week of the Person, Day of Diversity, and Coffee House.

Sports: There are 8 intercollegiate sports for men and 8 for women, and 7 intramural sports for men and 7 for women. Facilities include a recreation center with a swimming pool, 2 gyms, 2 racquetball courts, complete Nautilus equipment, an indoor jogging track, 3 fields, and game rooms.

Disabled Students: 80% of the campus is accessible. Wheelchair ramps, elevators, special parking, specially equipped rest rooms, lowered drinking fountains, and lowered telephones are available.

Services: Counseling and information services are available, as is tutoring in most subjects. There is a reader service for the blind, and remedial math, reading, and writing.

Campus Safety and Security: Measures include 24-hour foot and vehicle patrol, self-defense education, informal discussions, and pamphlets/posters/films. There are lighted pathways/sidewalks and and a student intern campus patrol.

Programs of Study: Wheeling Jesuit confers B.A., B.S., and B.S.N. degrees. Master's degrees are also awarded. Bachelor's degrees are awarded in BIOLOGICAL SCIENCE (biology/biological science), BUSINESS (accounting, international business management, management science, marketing/retailing/merchandising, and sports management), COMMUNICATIONS AND THE ARTS (English, French, romance languages and literature, Spanish, and technical and business writing), COMPUTER AND PHYSICAL SCIENCE (chemistry, computer science, mathematics, physics, and science), ENGINEERING AND ENVIRONMENTAL DESIGN (environmental science, and technology and public affairs), HEALTH PROFESSIONS (nuclear medical technology, nursing, and respiratory therapy), SOCIAL SCIENCE (criminal justice, ethics, politics, and social policy, history, international studies, philosophy, political science/government, psychology, and religion). Psychology, nursing, and biology are the largest.

Required: To graduate, students must complete 120 credit hours, with a GPA of 2.0. The core curriculum consists of 58 credits in English composition, math, modern languages, literature, history, social science, natural science, philosophy, theology and 1 course in either ethics or Christian morality, as well as 1 additional math or science course. Students are also required to complete 2 units in each of the dimensions of the school's Wellness Program.

Special: The university offers internships with many businesses and institutions, as well as a Washington semester and study abroad. Students may obtain an advanced degree in business administration, as well as a 3-2 engineering degree with Case Western Reserve University. The college permits dual and student-designed majors. Credit for life, military, and work experience may be granted to adult students. Pass/fail options are open in some courses. There are 12 national honor societies and a freshman honors program.

Faculty/Classroom: 58% of faculty are male; 42%, female. All both teach and do research. The average class size in an introductory lecture is 20; in a laboratory, 11; and in a regular course, 14.

Admissions: 88% of the 2001-2002 applicants were accepted. The SAT I scores for the 2001-2002 freshman class were: Verbal--40% below 500, 47% between 500 and 599, 12% between 600 and 700, and 1% above 700. The ACT scores were 42% below 21, 23% between 21 and 23, 21% between 24 and 26, 8% between 27 and 28, and 6% above 28. 37% of the current freshmen were in the top fifth of their class; 70% were in the top two fifths.

Requirements: The SAT I or ACT is required, with a minimum composite score of 850 on the SAT I or 18 on the ACT. In addition, applicants must be high school graduates or hold a GED. Students should have earned 15 academic credits, consisting of 4 in English, 2 each in math and history or social science, 1 in lab science (2 are recommended for science majors), and 6 in academic electives, with a foreign language recommended. Students entering programs in the natural sciences should have taken 1 course each of chemistry and biology. Exceptions are made, especially if the high school GPA is 3.0 or better. An interview is recommended. Wheeling Jesuit requires applicants to be in the upper 90% of their class. A GPA of 2.0 is required. AP and CLEP credits are accepted. Important factors in the admissions decision are leadership record, recommendations by school officials, and extracurricular activities record. Applications are accepted on-line.

Procedure: Freshmen are admitted to all sessions. There are deferred admissions and rolling admissions plan. Application deadlines are open. The application fee is $25.

Transfer: 60 transfer students enrolled in 2001-2002. Applicants must have a GPA of 2.0 for college work, or supply high school transcripts if entering at the freshman level. The SAT I or ACT is required if the student has less than 1 year of college work; otherwise, it is still recommended, as is an interview. Transfer students must take placement tests given by the university. 30 credits of 120 must be completed at Wheeling Jesuit.

Visiting: There are regularly scheduled orientations for prospective students, including meetings with faculty, discussions by students and parents, meals, and campus tours. There are guides for informal visits and visitors may sit in on classes and stay overnight. To schedule a visit, contact Jennifer Decker, Campus Visit Coordinator.

Financial Aid: In 2001-2002, 99% of all freshmen and 88% of continuing students received some form of financial aid. 86% of freshmen and 70% of continuing students received need-based aid. The average freshman award was $17,772. Of that total, scholarships or need-based grants averaged $12,186 ($24,399 maximum); loans averaged $3020 ($5125 maximum); work contracts averaged $1513 ($1550 maximum); and other sources averaged $5408 ($24,399 maximum). 71% of undergraduates work part time. Average annual earnings from campus work are $1699. The average financial indebtedness of the 2001 graduate was $15,000. The FAFSA is required. The fall application deadline is March 1.

International Students: There are 42 international students enrolled. The school actively recruits these students. They must score 550 on the written TOEFL.

Computers: The mainframe is an AT&T StarGroup LAN. There are also some 125 PCs available in the computer center, academic resource center, and various departments. All students may access the system every day, for a total 85 hours per week and in 1 lab, 24 hours a day, 7 days a week.

Graduates: In 2001, 187 bachelor's degrees were awarded. The most popular majors were psychology (9%), criminal justice (8%), and biology (8%).

Admissions Contact: Tom Pie', Director of Admissions. A video is available. E-mail: *admiss@wju.edu* Web: *www.wju.edu*

WISCONSIN

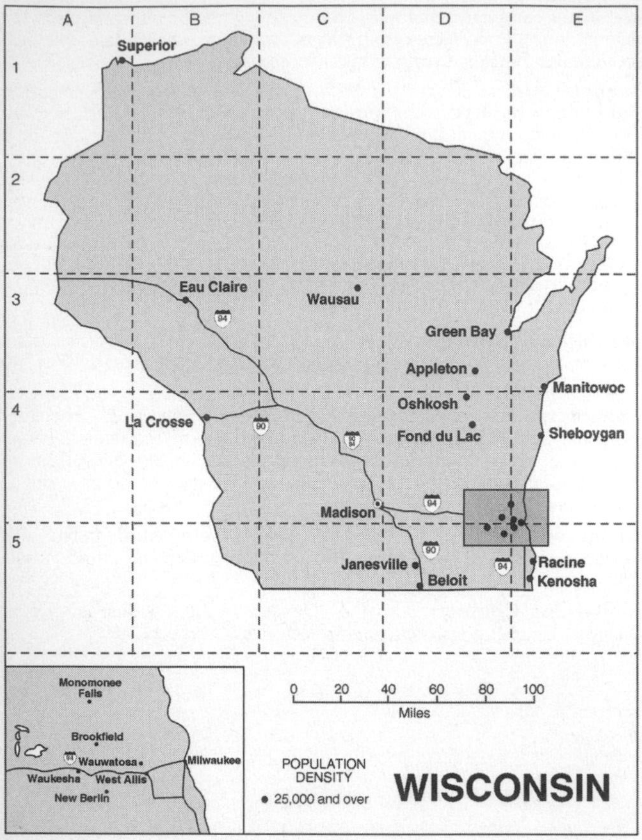

ALVERNO COLLEGE — E-4

Milwaukee, WI 53234-3922 — (414) 382-6113
(800) 933-3401; Fax: (414) 382-6354

Full-time: 997 women	**Faculty:** 96; IIB, --$
Part-time: 23 men, 759 women	**Ph.D.s:** 90%
Graduate: 23 men, 150 women	**Student/Faculty:** 10 to 1
Year: semesters, summer session	**Tuition:** $12,150
Application Deadline: August 1	**Room & Board:** $4780

Freshman Class: 651 applied, 585 accepted, 235 enrolled
ACT: recommended — **LESS COMPETITIVE**

Alverno College is a private institution serving women. Alverno stresses professional and personal development within a liberal arts education. There are 7 undergraduate schools and 1 graduate school. In addition to regional accreditation, Alverno has baccalaureate program accreditation with NASM, NCATE, and CCNE. The library contains 93,180 volumes, 229,031 microform items, and 2500 audiovisual forms/CDs, and subscribes to 1108 periodicals. Computerized library services include the card catalog, interlibrary loans, and database searching. Special learning facilities include a learning resource center and TV studio, art and culture gallery, nursing skills lab, student-centered multimedia production facility, computer center, science labs, independent science research areas, and conferencing center. The 46-acre campus is in an urban area on the southwest edge of Milwaukee. Including residence halls, there are 10 buildings.

Student Life: 97% of undergraduates are from Wisconsin. Others are from 13 states and 12 foreign countries. 61% are white; 25% African American. 44% are Catholic; 33% Protestant; 10% claim no religious affiliation. The average age of all undergraduates is 26. 20% do not continue beyond their first year; 72% remain to graduate.

Housing: 200 students can be accommodated in college housing, which includes single-sex dormitories. On-campus housing is guaranteed for all 4 years. 91% of students commute. All students may keep cars.

Activities: There are no fraternities. There are 30 groups on campus, including art, choir, chorus, dance, drama, ethnic, honors, international, literary magazine, orchestra, pep band, political, professional, religious, social, social service, and yearbook. Popular campus events include Career Day, fine arts performances, and interdenominational religious services.

Sports: Facilities include a refurbished gym with regulation intercollegiate volleyball and basketball courts, a fitness center, an outdoor volleyball court, and a multipurpose room for dancing, aerobics, and cardio kickboxing.

Disabled Students: 95% of the campus is accessible. Wheelchair ramps, elevators, special parking, specially equipped rest rooms, lowered drinking fountains, lowered telephones, and pushbuttons to open exterior doors are available.

Services: Counseling and information services are available, as is tutoring in most subjects. There is remedial math, reading, and writing. There are selected workshops for such issues as writing anxiety, time management, note taking, speaking anxiety, documenting work, stategies for doing research papers, Internet introduction, and math EXCEL.

Campus Safety and Security: Measures include 24-hour foot and vehicle patrol, escort service, informal discussions, and pamphlets/posters/films. There are emergency telephones, lighted pathways/sidewalks, and electronically operated and video-surveillanced dormitory entrances, walkways, and a security staff equipped with 2-way radios.

Programs of Study: Alverno confers B.A., B.M., B.S.Ed., and B.S.N. degrees. Associate and master's degrees are also awarded. Bachelor's degrees are awarded in AGRICULTURE (conservation and regulation), BIOLOGICAL SCIENCE (biology/biological science and molecular biology), BUSINESS (business administration and management, and international business management), COMMUNICATIONS AND THE ARTS (art, communications, communications technology, English, music, and visual and performing arts), COMPUTER AND PHYSICAL SCIENCE (chemistry, computer science, information sciences and systems, mathematics, physical sciences, and science), EDUCATION (art, elementary, middle school, music, science, and secondary), ENGINEERING AND ENVIRONMENTAL DESIGN (environmental science, and land use management and reclamation), HEALTH PROFESSIONS (art therapy, health science, music therapy, nuclear medical technology, and nursing), SOCIAL SCIENCE (child psychology/development, community services, history, home economics, international relations, liberal arts/general studies, philosophy, psychology, religion, social science, and social studies). Nursing, elementary education, and business and management are the strongest academically and have the largest enrollments.

Required: Students must complete a program of learning that integrates accomplishment in required areas of knowledge with the achievement of required levels of competence in communication, analysis, problem solving, valuing in decision-making, social interaction, global perspectives, effective citizenship, and aesthetic responsiveness. This is accomplished through general education courses in history, English, philosophy, religious studies, arts, sciences, math, psychology, and social science; through completion of a major and minor area of study; and completion of at least one required internship or practice.

Special: Alverno offers internships, cross-registration with Milwaukee Institute of Art & Design, dual majors, nondegree study, and preprofessional programs in dentistry, law, medicine, and veterinary medicine. Alverno maintains student exchange programs with universities in England, Mexico, and Japan, and also offers courses that include an international travel component, and can arrange other programs through a worldwide consortium of facilities. The school's interactive curriculum is outcome-oriented and performance-based; letter grades are not assigned. There are 3 national honor societies.

Faculty/Classroom: 24% of faculty are male; 76%, female. All both teach and do research. No introductory courses are taught by graduate students. The average class size in an introductory lecture is 26; in a laboratory, 24; and in a regular course, 28.

Admissions: 90% of the 2001-2002 applicants were accepted.

Requirements: In addition, applicants must be graduates of an accredited secondary school, having completed 17 academic credits with college preparatory courses. The GED is accepted. A GPA of 2.0 is required. AP and CLEP credits are accepted. Applications are accepted on-line via CollegeNet and Wisconsin Mentor.

Procedure: Freshmen are admitted fall and spring. Entrance exams should be taken as early as possible. There is a deferred admissions plan. Applications should be filed by August 1 for fall entry and January 1 for spring entry. Notification is sent on a rolling basis. The fall 2001 application fee was $20.

Transfer: 76 transfer students enrolled in 2001-2002. Applicants should have a minimum college GPA of 2.0 and must submit transcripts from all schools previously attended.

Visiting: There are regularly scheduled orientations for prospective students, consisting of open houses and overnight events that include tours of the campus, classroom visits, and meetings with faculty and current students. There are guides for informal visits and visitors may sit in on classes and stay overnight. To schedule a visit, contact the Admissions Office at (414) 382-6101.

Financial Aid: In 2001-2002, 94% of all freshmen and 88% of continuing students received some form of financial aid. 80% of freshmen and

82% of continuing students received need-based aid. The average freshman award was $9341. Of that total, scholarships or need-based grants averaged $3000 ($12,150 maximum); loans averaged $2625 ($6625 maximum); work contracts averaged $1500 ($2800 maximum); and Wisconsin Tuition Grant averaged $1920 ($2300 maximum). 40% of undergraduates work part time. Average annual earnings from campus work are $2500. Alverno is a member of CSS. The FAFSA and the college's own financial statement are required. The fall application deadline is April 15.

International Students: There are 11 international students enrolled. The school actively recruits these students. They must score 500 on the written TOEFL or 127 on the electronic version, and also take the college's own entrance exam.

Computers: The mainframe is an HP 9000. Students have access to some 100 networked PCs and Macs in the campus computer center. More than 100 PCs are available in computer classrooms, in several discipline-specific labs, and in residence halls. Internet and Web access is provided. All students may access the system.

Graduates: In 2001, 300 bachelor's degrees were awarded. The most popular majors were nursing (22%), elementary education (14%), and psychology (14%). In an average class, 43% graduate in 4 years, 50% in 5 years, and 55% in 6 years. 21 companies recruited on campus in 2000-2001. Of the 2000 graduating class, 13% were enrolled in graduate school within 6 months of graduation and 93% were employed.

Admissions Contact: Mary Kay Farrell, Director of Admissions. A video is available. E-mail: *admissions@alverno.edu*
Web: *www.alverno.edu*

BELOIT COLLEGE

Beloit, WI 53511-5595 — D-5
(608) 363-2500
(800) 356-0751; Fax: (608) 363-2075

Full-time: 501 men, 712 women	**Faculty:** 93; IIB,
Part-time: 16 men, 43 women	**Ph.D.s:** 98%
Graduate: none	**Student/Faculty:** 13 to 1
Year: semesters	**Tuition:** $22,404
Application Deadline: February 1	**Room & Board:** $5078
Freshman Class: 1537 applied, 1004 accepted, 323 enrolled	
SAT I Verbal/Math: 640/600	**ACT:** 27 **HIGHLY COMPETITIVE**

Beloit College, founded in 1846, is a private liberal arts institution. The library contains 246,809 volumes, 6720 microform items, and 6262 audiovisual forms/CDs, and subscribes to 1279 periodicals. Computerized library services include the card catalog, interlibrary loans, and database searching. Special learning facilities include a learning resource center, art gallery, natural history museum, planetarium, radio station, TV station, and comprehensive language lab, observatory, and theater complex. The 40-acre campus is in a small town 50 miles south of Madison. Including residence halls, there are 50 buildings.

Student Life: 79% of undergraduates are from out of state, mostly the Midwest. Others are from 49 states, 59 foreign countries, and Canada. 74% are from public schools. 77% are white; 11% foreign nationals. The average age of freshmen is 18; all undergraduates, 20. 9% do not continue beyond their first year; 71% remain to graduate.

Housing: 1033 students can be accommodated in college housing, which includes single-sex and coed dormitories, fraternity houses, and sorority houses. In addition, there are language houses and special-interest houses. On-campus housing is guaranteed for all 4 years. 93% of students live on campus; of those, 95% remain on campus on weekends. All students may keep cars.

Activities: 15% of men belong to 4 national fraternities; 5% of women belong to 2 local sororities. There are 84 groups on campus, including art, band, cheerleading, chess, choir, chorus, computers, dance, drama, ethnic, film, gay, honors, international, jazz band, literary magazine, musical theater, newspaper, orchestra, pep band, photography, political, professional, radio and TV, religious, science fiction, social, social service, student government, symphony, womens's, and yearbook. Popular campus events include Great Lecture Series, Folk and Blues Weekend, and Spring Day.

Sports: There are 10 intercollegiate sports for men and 10 for women, and 15 intramural sports for men and 13 for women. Facilities include a sports center, that houses a 2250-seat arena for basketball and volleyball, racquetball/handball courts, a dance studio, a fitness center, and a natatorium; a field house that contains a running track, an indoor soccer area, batting/pitching cage, and space for indoor tennis; a 3500-seat football stadium; outdoor playing fields; and 6 all-weather tennis courts. There are facilities nearby for sailing, ice skating, and other recreation.

Disabled Students: 35% of the campus is accessible. Wheelchair ramps, elevators, special parking, specially equipped rest rooms, special class scheduling, lowered drinking fountains, and lowered telephones are available.

Services: Counseling and information services are available, as is tutoring in most subjects, including most introductory and some advanced courses.

Campus Safety and Security: Measures include 24-hour foot and vehicle patrol, escort service, informal discussions, and pamphlets/posters/films. There are emergency telephones and lighted pathways/sidewalks.

Programs of Study: Beloit confers B.A. and B.S. degrees. Bachelor's degrees are awarded in BIOLOGICAL SCIENCE (biochemistry, biology/biological science, cell biology, ecology, and environmental biology), BUSINESS (business administration and management), COMMUNICATIONS AND THE ARTS (art history and appreciation, classical languages, comparative literature, creative writing, dramatic arts, East Asian languages and literature, English, French, German, literature, modern language, music, Russian, Spanish, speech/debate/rhetoric, and studio art), COMPUTER AND PHYSICAL SCIENCE (applied physics, chemistry, computer science, geology, mathematics, and physics), EDUCATION (art and education), ENGINEERING AND ENVIRONMENTAL DESIGN (environmental science), HEALTH PROFESSIONS (predentistry, premedicine, and preveterinary science), SOCIAL SCIENCE (anthropology, classical/ancient civilization, economics, history, interdisciplinary studies, international relations, philosophy, political science/government, prelaw, psychology, religion, sociology, and women's studies). Anthropology, English, and geology are the strongest academically. Anthropology, biology, and English are the largest.

Required: To graduate, students must complete 31 units, including 8 to 15 in the major, with a minimum GPA of 2.0. Distribution requirements include 2 courses each from natural sciences and math, social sciences, and arts and humanities. Writing and interdisciplinary course work is also required. Degree expectations include international and experiential learning components, as well as a comprehensive academic plan.

Special: Beloit offers cross-registration with the University of Wisconsin/Madison, internships, study abroad in 29 countries, and a Washington semester. Dual majors, student-designed and interdisciplinary majors, and nondegree study are available. Students may take a 2-2 nursing program and a 3-2 medical technology program with Rush University. A 3-2 engineering degree is offered with 9 institutions, and co-op programs are available in social services, forestry and environmental management, engineering, nursing, medical technology, and business administration. An intensive summer language program is offered in Chinese, Japanese, Hungarian, and Russian. All departments have honors programs. There are 6 national honor societies, including Phi Beta Kappa.

Faculty/Classroom: 58% of faculty are male; 42%, female. All both teach and do research. The average class size in an introductory lecture is 15; in a laboratory, 15; and in a regular course, 15.

Admissions: 65% of the 2001-2002 applicants were accepted. The SAT I scores for the 2001-2002 freshman class were: Verbal--8% below 500, 25% between 500 and 599, 47% between 600 and 700, and 20% above 700; Math--13% below 500, 37% between 500 and 599, 42% between 600 and 700, and 8% above 700. The ACT scores were 3% below 21, 19% between 21 and 23, 28% between 24 and 26, 19% between 27 and 28, and 31% above 28. 60% of the current freshmen were in the top fifth of their class; 85% were in the top two fifths. There were 7 National Merit semifinalists. 11 freshmen graduated first in their class.

Requirements: The SAT I or ACT is required. In addition, SAT II: Subject tests are recommended. Applicants must be graduates of an accredited secondary school, with 4 years of English, 3 each of math, science, and history/social sciences, and 2 of a foreign language. The GED is accepted. An essay and a letter of recommendation are required, and an interview is recommended. AP and CLEP credits are accepted. Important factors in the admissions decision are extracurricular activities record, leadership record, and personality/intangible qualities. Applications are accepted on-line via CollegeLink, Beloit's web site, Common App, and other software systems.

Procedure: Freshmen are admitted fall and spring. Entrance exams should be taken before Christmas of the senior year. There are early decision, early action, early admissions, and deferred admissions plans. Early action applications should be filed by November 15; early action applications, by December 15; regular applications, by February 1 for fall entry. Notification of early action is sent December 15; early action, January 15; regular decision, on a rolling basis. 12 early action candidates were accepted for the 2001-2002 class. A waiting list is an active part of the admissions procedure. The fall 2001 application fee was $30.

Transfer: 35 transfer students enrolled in 2001-2002. Applicants must have a minimum GPA of 2.5 and submit official transcripts of all college work completed. The SAT I or the ACT is required, and an interview is recommended. 16 credits of 31 must be completed at Beloit.

Visiting: There are regularly scheduled orientations for prospective students, including a tour, class visits, and meeting with professors, including an interview. Enrolled students are the hosts. There are guides for informal visits and visitors may sit in on classes and stay overnight. To schedule a visit, contact the Admissions Office.

Financial Aid: In 2001-2002, 85% of all freshmen and 87% of continuing students received some form of financial aid. 73% of freshmen and 71% of continuing students received need-based aid. The average freshman award was $17,541. Of that total, scholarships or need-based grants averaged $12,923 ($22,184 maximum); loans averaged $3474 ($5550 maximum); and work contracts averaged $1292 ($1500 maximum). 82% of undergraduates work part time. Average annual earnings from campus work are $1200. The average financial indebtedness of the 2001 graduate was $13,564. Beloit is a member of CSS. The FAFSA and the college's own financial statement are required. The preferred fall application deadline is March 15; December 1 for spring entry.

International Students: There are 150 international students enrolled. The school actively recruits these students. They must score 525 on the written TOEFL and take the SAT I or ACT. Applicants from selected countries must also supply a school-leaving exam/certificate.

Computers: The mainframe is a 2 IBM RS 6000 Model F50s. Students can use more than 200 networked computers for e-mail, web access, and other network-related activities. All students may access the system at any time. There are no time limits and no fees.

Graduates: In 2001, 272 bachelor's degrees were awarded. The most popular majors were anthropology (10%), psychology (10%), and economics (9%). In an average class, 56% graduate in 4 years and 69% in 5 years. 81 companies recruited on campus in 2000-2001. Of the 2000 graduating class, 30% were enrolled in graduate school within 6 months of graduation and 70% were employed.

Admissions Contact: James Zielinski, Director of Admissions. A video is available. E-mail: *admiss@beloit.edu* Web: *www.beloit.edu*

CARDINAL STRITCH UNIVERSITY E-4
Milwaukee, WI 53217-7516 (414) 410-4040
(800) 347-8822; Fax: (414) 410-4049

Full-time: 910 men, 1990 women
Part-time: 49 men, 174 women
Graduate: 824 men, 1908 women
Year: semesters, summer session
Application Deadline: April 1
Freshman Class: n/av
SAT I or ACT: required
Faculty: 98; IIA, --$
Ph.D.s: 54%
Student/Faculty: 30 to 1
Tuition: $12,780
Room & Board: $4840
COMPETITIVE

Cardinal Stritch University, founded in 1937 as a college, is a private, Catholic institution sponsored by the Sisters of St. Francis. There are 4 undergraduate schools and 1 graduate school. In addition to regional accreditation, Stritch has baccalaureate program accreditation with NCATE and NLN. The library contains 132,293 volumes, 173,216 microform items, and 6310 audiovisual forms/CDs, and subscribes to 1309 periodicals. Computerized library services include the card catalog, interlibrary loans, and database searching. Special learning facilities include a learning resource center, art gallery, and radio station. The 40-acre campus is in a suburban area 10 miles north of Milwaukee. Including residence halls, there are 9 buildings.

Student Life: 89% of undergraduates are from Wisconsin. Others are from 16 states, 27 foreign countries, and Canada. 60% are from public schools. 72% are white; 16% African American. 27% are Catholic. The average age of freshmen is 19; all undergraduates, 32. 27% do not continue beyond their first year; 43% remain to graduate.

Housing: 278 students can be accommodated in college housing, which includes coed dormitories. On-campus housing is available on a first-come, first-served basis. 95% of students commute. All students may keep cars.

Activities: There are no fraternities or sororities. There are 50 groups on campus, including art, band, cheerleading, choir, chorus, computers, dance, drama, ethnic, film, honors, international, jazz band, musical theater, newspaper, orchestra, photography, political, professional, radio and TV, religious, social, social service, student government, and yearbook. Popular campus events include Thursday night events and weekly activities, such as sporting events or plays.

Sports: There are 5 intercollegiate sports for men and 5 for women, and 2 intramural sports for men and 2 for women. Facilities include basketball and volleyball courts, an indoor track, a weight and exercise room, an area for table tennis and billiards, and a soccer field.

Disabled Students: 80% of the campus is accessible. Wheelchair ramps, special parking, specially equipped rest rooms, special class scheduling, and lowered telephones are available.

Services: Counseling and information services are available, as is tutoring in every subject. There is remedial math, reading, and writing.

Campus Safety and Security: Measures include 24-hour foot and vehicle patrol, informal discussions, pamphlets/posters/films, and lighted pathways/sidewalks.

Programs of Study: Stritch confers B.A., B.S., and B.F.A. degrees. Associate, master's, and doctoral degrees are also awarded. Bachelor's degrees are awarded in BIOLOGICAL SCIENCE (biology/biological science), BUSINESS (accounting, business administration and management, and international business management), COMMUNICATIONS AND THE ARTS (art, communications, creative writing, dramatic arts, English, fine arts, French, music, public relations, and Spanish), COMPUTER AND PHYSICAL SCIENCE (chemistry, computer science, and mathematics), EDUCATION (early childhood, elementary, middle school, secondary, and special), HEALTH PROFESSIONS (nursing, predentistry, premedicine, preoptometry, and preveterinary science), SOCIAL SCIENCE (history, prelaw, psychology, religion, social science, and sociology). Education in general and special education in particular are the strongest academically. Business, education, and nursing are the largest.

Required: To graduate, students must complete 128 credits, 34 to 72 in the major, with a GPA of at least 2.0. Required disciplines include history, foreign language, literature, written communication, and communication arts. 5 courses are required in humanities, 3 in social/behavioral sciences, 2 each in communication arts and written communication, and 1 each in math and natural science. An English proficiency exam must be taken.

Special: Students may participate in a variety of internships with Milwaukee businesses and organizations. Stritch offers an accelerated degree program and a B.A.-B.S. degree in business, dual majors, a general studies degree, and nondegree study. There is study abroad, work-study programs, pass/fail options, and credit for life, military, and work experience. An accelerated evening program and a management program are offered for working adults. There are 9 national honor societies, and a freshman honors program.

Faculty/Classroom: 49% of faculty are male; 51%, female. No introductory courses are taught by graduate students. The average class size in a laboratory is 12 and in a regular course, 11.

Admissions: 28% of the current freshmen were in the top fifth of their class; 56% were in the top two fifths.

Requirements: The SAT I or ACT is required, with a recommended minimum composite score of 20 on the ACT or 950 on the SAT I. Applicants must be graduates of an accredited secondary school, with 16 academic credits, including 4 years of English and 2 years each of math (algebra required), science, and social studies. The GED is accepted. Stritch requires an essay and recommends an interview. Stritch requires applicants to be in the upper 50% of their class. A GPA of 2.0 is required. AP and CLEP credits are accepted. Important factors in the admissions decision are leadership record, evidence of special talent, and advanced placement or honor courses. Applications are accepted on-line.

Procedure: Freshmen are admitted to all sessions. Entrance exams should be taken as early as possible. There is a deferred admissions plan. Applications should be filed by April 1 for fall entry. The fall 2001 application fee was $25. Notification is sent on a rolling basis.

Transfer: 164 transfer students enrolled in 2001-2002. Applicants for transfer should have a minimum GPA of 2.0, and be eligible for return to the previous institution. 32 credits of 128 must be completed at Stritch.

Visiting: There are regularly scheduled orientations for prospective students, including a campus tour, meetings with admissions and financial aid counselors, and possible meetings with department chairs. There are guides for informal visits and visitors may sit in on classes and stay overnight. To schedule a visit, contact the Admissions Office.

Financial Aid: The FAFSA and the college's own financial statement are required. The fall application deadline is open.

International Students: There are 35 international students enrolled. They must score 550 on the written TOEFL, and also take the SAT I or the ACT, scoring 20 on the ACT.

Computers: The mainframe is an IBM AS/400. 62 Macs, 174 PCs, and 16 graphic workstations are available to students in 4 computer labs and the library. All have Internet access. Business students are generally provided with laptops. All students may access the system. There are no time limits and no fees.

Graduates: In 2001, 285 bachelor's degrees were awarded. The most popular majors were management (35%), business administration (25%), and management information systems (9%). In an average class, 4% graduate in 3 years, 19% in 4 years, 39% in 5 years, and 43% in 6 years. 10 companies recruited on campus in 2000-2001.

Admissions Contact: David Wegener, Director of Admissions.
E-mail: *admityou@stritch.edu* Web: *www.stritch.edu*

CARROLL COLLEGE D-5
Waukesha, WI 53186 (262) 524-7220
(800) CARROLL; Fax: (262) 524-7139

Full-time: 625 men, 1290 women
Part-time: 266 men, 499 women
Graduate: 55 men, 186 women
Year: semesters, summer session
Application Deadline: open
Faculty: 100; IIB, -$
Ph.D.s: 80%
Student/Faculty: 19 to 1
Tuition: $16,200
Room & Board: $4970
Freshman Class: 1742 applied, 1457 accepted, 493 enrolled
ACT: 23
COMPETITIVE

Carroll College, founded in 1846, is an independent liberal arts institution affiliated with the Presbyterian Church (U.S.A). In addition to regional accreditation, Carroll has baccalaureate program accreditation with CSWE and NLN. The library contains 150,000 volumes, 21,566 microform items, and 827 audiovisual forms/CDs, and subscribes to 607 periodicals. Computerized library services include the card catalog, interlibrary loans, and database searching. Special learning facilities include a learning resource center, art gallery, radio station, and studio theater, recital hall, and a Civil War collection. The 52-acre campus is in a suburban area 15 miles west of Milwaukee. Including residence halls, there are 31 buildings.

Student Life: 78% of undergraduates are from Wisconsin. Others are from 28 states, 24 foreign countries, and Canada. 85% are from public schools. 92% are white. The average age of freshmen is 18; all undergraduates, 24. 22% do not continue beyond their first year; 50% remain to graduate.

Housing: 1154 students can be accommodated in college housing, which includes single-sex and coed dormitories, on-campus apartments, and fraternity houses. On-campus housing is guaranteed for all 4 years. 54% of students live on campus. All students may keep cars.

Activities: 8% of men and about 1% of women belong to 3 local fraternities; 7% of women belong to 4 national sororities. There are 52 groups on campus, including an activities board, art, band, cheerleading, choir, chorale, chorus, computers, dance, drama, ethnic, gay, greek life, honors, international, jazz band, literary magazine, musical theater, newspaper, orchestra, photography, political, professional, radio and TV, religious, social, social service, student government, symphony, and yearbook. Popular campus events include International Folk Fair, Madrigal Dinner, and Spring Fling.

Sports: There are 9 intercollegiate sports for men and 9 for women, and 8 intramural sports for men and 8 for women. Facilities include an all-purpose field house, gym including volleyball court, 2 basketball courts, and an indoor track, 6 tennis courts, 6-lane pool, 2 sand volleyball courts, football/soccer field, practice field, softball diamond, batting cages, athletic training rooms, exercise/physiology laboratory, weight room, fitness weight room, dance studio, and a campus center which houses Ping Pong tables, pool tables, a dart machine, and video games.

Disabled Students: 20% of the campus is accessible. Wheelchair ramps, elevators, special parking, specially equipped rest rooms, and special class scheduling are available.

Services: Counseling and information services are available, as is tutoring in most subjects.

Campus Safety and Security: Measures include 24-hour foot and vehicle patrol, escort service, informal discussions, and pamphlets/posters/films. There are emergency telephones and lighted pathways/sidewalks.

Programs of Study: Carroll confers B.A., B.S., B.S.M.T., and B.S.N. degrees. Master's degrees are also awarded. Bachelor's degrees are awarded in BIOLOGICAL SCIENCE (biochemistry, biology/biological science, and marine biology), BUSINESS (accounting, business administration and management, and organizational behavior), COMMUNICATIONS AND THE ARTS (art, communications, dramatic arts, English, music, and Spanish), COMPUTER AND PHYSICAL SCIENCE (actuarial science, applied mathematics, chemistry, computer science, information sciences and systems, and mathematics), EDUCATION (art, athletic training, early childhood, elementary, foreign languages, music, physical, and science), ENGINEERING AND ENVIRONMENTAL DESIGN (environmental science and graphic arts technology), HEALTH PROFESSIONS (exercise science, medical technology, and nursing), SOCIAL SCIENCE (criminal justice, geography, history, international relations, political science/government, psychology, religion, social work, and sociology). Sciences, computer science, and education are the strongest academically. Business, education, and computer science are the largest.

Required: To graduate, students must complete 128 credit hours, 32 to 40 in the major, with a minimum GPA of 2.0. Students must take 7 courses from the Liberal Studies Progarm and a first-year seminar and writing seminar. 1 computer science course and a math course are needed for the B.S.; 12 credits of modern language or the humanities is needed for the B.A.

Special: A Washington semester at American University and a United Nations semester are offered, as are internships and individually designed majors. Study abroad in Wales is available for the junior year. Under the International and Off-Campus Program, juniors and seniors may travel to places that are culturally different from their own, such as Western and Eastern Europe, Latin America, Africa, or Asia. A capstone experience bridges the student's college work to employment or graduate school. There are 5 national honor societies and a freshman honors program.

Faculty/Classroom: 61% of faculty are male; 39%, female. All both teach undergraduates and do research. No introductory courses are taught by graduate students. The average class size in an introductory lecture is 22; in a laboratory, 14; and in a regular course, 17.

Admissions: 84% of the 2001-2002 applicants were accepted. The ACT scores for the 2001-2002 freshman class were: 28% below 21, 25% between 21 and 23, 27% between 24 and 26, 13% between 27 and 28, and 7% above 28. 37% of the current freshmen were in the top fifth of their class; 69% were in the top two fifths. There were 2 National Merit finalists. 20 freshmen graduated first in their class.

Requirements: The SAT I or ACT is required. In addition, applicants must be graduates of an accredited secondary school. The GED is accepted. An essay and interview are recommended for all students, and a portfolio or audition is advised for art and music students, respectively. Carroll requires applicants to be in the upper 50% of their class. A GPA of 2.0 is required. AP and CLEP credits are accepted. Important factors in the admissions decision are advanced placement or honor courses, recommendations by school officials, and evidence of special talent. Applications are accepted on-line and via computer disk.

Procedure: Freshmen are admitted fall and spring. Entrance exams should be taken during the junior year. There are deferred admissions and rolling admisions plans. Application deadlines are open.

Transfer: 155 transfer students enrolled in 2001-2002. Applicants for transfer must have a minimum GPA of 2.0. An interview is required. 32 credits of 128 must be completed at Carroll.

Visiting: There are regularly scheduled orientations for prospective students, consisting of a campus tour, financial aid/admissions counseling, academic department meetings, and extracurricular activities meetings. There are guides for informal visits and visitors may sit in on classes and stay overnight. To schedule a visit, contact the Office of Admissions.

Financial Aid: In 2001-2002, 98% of all students received some form of financial aid. 69% of freshmen and 74% of continuing students received need-based aid. The average freshman award was $13,995. Of that total, scholarships or need-based grants averaged $10,315 ($16,000 maximum); loans averaged $2298 ($4000 maximum); and work contracts averaged $1382 ($2000 maximum). 69% of undergraduates work part time. Average annual earnings from campus work are $950. The average financial indebtedness of the 2001 graduate was $14,630. The FAFSA is required. The fall application deadline is September 1.

International Students: There are 55 international students enrolled. The school actively recruits these students. They must score 550 on the written TOEFL or 213 on the electronic version.

Computers: The mainframes are a 3 HP 9000s (HP-UX), 2 NT servers, and 1 Mac server. Several departmental student computer labs with more than 100 Mac and Windows computers complement 5 central student computing labs with more than 100 Mac and Windows computers. Residence rooms are networked with Ethernet. Internet access is available in all student computer labs. All students may access the system 24 hours every day. There are no time limits and no fees.

Graduates: In 2001, 447 bachelor's degrees were awarded. The most popular majors were business (18%), nursing (14%), and psychology (11%). In an average class, 55% graduate in 4 years and 67% in 5 years. 12 companies recruited on campus in 2000-2001. Of the 2000 graduating class, 11% were enrolled in graduate school within 6 months of graduation and 94% were employed.

Admissions Contact: James V. Wiseman, Vice President, Enrollment. E-mail: *cc.info@ccadmin.cc.edu* Web: *www.cc.edu*

CARTHAGE COLLEGE
E-5

Kenosha, WI 53140 **(262) 551-6000**
(800) 351-4058; Fax: (262) 551-5762

Full-time: 848 men, 873 women	**Faculty:** 102; IIB, av$
Part-time: 160 men, 378 women	**Ph.D.s:** 85%
Graduate: 16 men, 70 women	**Student/Faculty:** 17 to 1
Year: 4-1-4, summer session	**Tuition:** $18,205
Application Deadline: open	**Room & Board:** $5465
Freshman Class: 2352 applied, 2085 accepted, 564 enrolled	
SAT I Verbal/Math: 530/510	**ACT:** 23 **COMPETITIVE**

Carthage College, founded in 1847, is an independent liberal arts institution affiliated with the Evangelical Lutheran Church in America. In addition to regional accreditation, Carthage has baccalaureate program accreditation with CSWE and NASM. The library contains 130,000 volumes, 9000 microform items, and 1300 audiovisual forms/CDs, and subscribes to 450 periodicals. Computerized library services include the card catalog, interlibrary loans, and database searching. Special learning facilities include a learning resource center, art gallery, and radio station. The 75-acre campus is in a suburban area 30 miles south of Milwaukee and 60 miles north of Chicago, on the shore of Lake Michigan. Including residence halls, there are 16 buildings.

Student Life: 52% of undergraduates are from out of state, mostly the Midwest. Others are from 23 states, 14 foreign countries, and Canada. 88% are from public schools. 89% are white. 31% are Catholic; 26% claim no religious affiliation; 13% Protestant. The average age of freshmen is 18; all undergraduates, 20. 24% do not continue beyond their first year; 50% remain to graduate.

Housing: 1250 students can be accommodated in college housing, which includes single-sex and coed dormitories. There are study-intensive floors and a health and wellness floor. On-campus housing is guaranteed for all 4 years. 70% of students live on campus; of those, 75% remain on campus on weekends. Alcohol is not permitted. All students may keep cars.

Activities: 28% of men belong to 5 local and 3 national fraternities; 22% of women belong to 4 local and 2 national sororities. There are 85 groups on campus, including art, band, cheerleading, choir, chorus, computers, debate, drama, ethnic, film, forensics, gay, Habitat for Humanity, honors, international, jazz band, literary magazine, musical theater, newspaper, orchestra, pep band, photography, political, professional, radio and TV, religious, social, social service, student government, and yearbook. Popular campus events include May Madness, Little Sibling Weekend, and Casino Night.

Sports: There are 10 intercollegiate sports for men and 10 for women, and 10 intramural sports for men and 5 for women. Facilities include a phys ed center, a 3000-seat stadium, a 3500-seat gym, tennis courts, baseball, soccer, and softball fields, and a natatorium.

Disabled Students: 90% of the campus is accessible. Wheelchair ramps, elevators, special parking, specially equipped rest rooms, special class scheduling, lowered drinking fountains, lowered telephones, and TDD phones are available.

Services: Counseling and information services are available, as is tutoring in most subjects.

Campus Safety and Security: Measures include 24-hour foot and vehicle patrol, self-defense education, escort service, and informal discussions. There are pamphlets/posters/films, emergency telephones, lighted pathways/sidewalks, and electronic exit locks on residence halls.

Programs of Study: Carthage confers the B.A. degree. Master's degrees are also awarded. Bachelor's degrees are awarded in BIOLOGICAL SCIENCE (biology/biological science), BUSINESS (accounting, business administration and management, international economics, and marketing management), COMMUNICATIONS AND THE ARTS (art, English, fine arts, French, German, graphic design, languages, music, performing arts, Spanish, and studio art), COMPUTER AND PHYSICAL SCIENCE (chemistry, mathematics, natural sciences, and physics), EDUCATION (elementary, English, foreign languages, mathematics, middle school, music, physical, and secondary), SOCIAL SCIENCE (criminal justice, economics, geography, history, philosophy, political science/government, psychology, religion, social science, social work, and sociology). Education, business, and sciences are the strongest academically. Business and education are the largest.

Required: To graduate, students must complete 138 credits, with up to 56 in the major, and a minimum GPA of 2.0 (education requires 2.75). Students must complete 50 credits in liberal arts studies, including the Heritage Seminar Series, which includes 3 courses that help develop competencies in cultural studies, writing, thinking, reading, speaking, and listening. 2 courses each are required in religion and foreign language, and 1 in math. There is also a phys ed requirement. Each student must complete one of the junior symposia, a series of 3 interdependent courses, and a senior project in the major.

Special: Internships are available during the January term or, in some cases, for a semester. Carthage offers study abroad in 5 countries, cross-registration with the University of Wisconsin, a Washington semester, a general studies degree, an accelerated degree program in business administration, work-study programs, and dual and student-designed majors. Students may take a 3-2 engineering degree with Case Western Reserve or Washington Universities, the University of Minnesota-Twin Cities, or the University of Wisconsin/Madison, or a 3-2 occupational therapy degree with Washington University. There are pass/fail options and credit for military and work experience. There are 3 national honor societies, and a freshman honors program.

Faculty/Classroom: 68% of faculty are male; 33%, female. All teach undergraduates. No introductory courses are taught by graduate students. The average class size in an introductory lecture is 19; in a laboratory, 19; and in a regular course, 19.

Admissions: 89% of the 2001-2002 applicants were accepted. The SAT I scores for the 2001-2002 freshman class were: Verbal--39% below 500, 41% between 500 and 599, 17% between 600 and 700, and 3% above 700; Math--44% below 500, 31% between 500 and 599, 20% between 600 and 700, and 5% above 700. The ACT scores were 38% below 21, 26% between 21 and 23, 18% between 24 and 26, 10% between 27 and 28, and 8% above 28. 27% of the current freshmen were in the top fifth of their class; 54% were in the top two fifths. There was 1 National Merit semifinalist.

Requirements: The SAT I or ACT is required. In addition, applicants should be graduates of an accredited secondary school, having earned 16 academic credits, including English, foreign language, math, science, and social studies. The GED is accepted. An interview is recommended. A GPA of 2.0 is required. AP and CLEP credits are accepted. Important factors in the admissions decision are advanced placement or honor courses, leadership record, and extracurricular activities record. Applications may be submitted on-line via the Carthage web site.

Procedure: Freshmen are admitted to all sessions. Entrance exams should be taken in spring of the junior year or fall of the senior year. There is a deferred admissions plan. Application deadlines are open. The application fee is $25. Notification is sent on a rolling basis.

Transfer: 76 transfer students enrolled in 2001-2002. Transfer students are accepted based on academic performance at their previous school; they should have a GPA greater than 2.0. If they have fewer than 12 credits, the high school record is considered. Either the SAT I or ACT and an interview are recommended. 32 credits of 138 must be completed at Carthage.

Visiting: There are regularly scheduled orientations for prospective students, including small group meetings with first year adviser and faculty members, class selection, and curriculum overview. Informational sessions for parents are offered. There are guides for informal visits and visitors may sit in on classes and stay overnight. To schedule a visit, contact the Office of Admissions, Mary Schuch, Visit Coordinator at *visit@carthage.edu*.

Financial Aid: In 2001-2002, all freshmen and 99% of continuing students received some form of financial aid. 68% of freshmen and 61% of continuing students received need-based aid. The average freshman award was $16,004. Of that total, scholarships or need-based grants averaged $10,264 ($25,770 maximum); loans averaged $3253 ($15,990 maximum); work contracts averaged $1200 (maximum); and Parent PLUS Loans averaged $1838 ($16,000 maximum). 35% of undergraduates work part time. Average annual earnings from campus work are $1000. The average financial indebtedness of the 2001 graduate was $16,807. The FAFSA is required. The fall application deadline is February 15.

International Students: There are 22 international students enrolled. The school actively recruits these students. They must score 500 on the written TOEFL.

Computers: The mainframe is an IBM AS/400. There are also 120 Macs and PCs available in academic buildings and residence halls; all are attached to the campus network. Network access is available in each room. All students may access the system 24 hours on weekdays, 8 A.M. to 8 P.M. on weekends. There are no time limits and no fees.

Graduates: In 2001, 298 bachelor's degrees were awarded. The most popular majors were business (27%), education (13%), and social science (10%). In an average class, 1% graduate in 3 years, 47% in 4 years, and 58% in 5 years. 25 companies recruited on campus in 2000-2001. Of the 2000 graduating class, 14% were enrolled in graduate school within 6 months of graduation and 98% were employed.

Admissions Contact: Thomas J. Augustine, Director of Admissions and Financial Aid. E-mail: *admissions@carthage.edu*
Web: *www.carthage.edu*

CONCORDIA UNIVERSITY WISCONSIN — E-4

Mequon, WI 53097 — (414) 243-4300; Fax: (414) 243-4545

Full-time: 950 men, 1620 women	**Faculty:** 96; IIB, -$
Part-time: 475 men, 810 women	**Ph.D.s:** 60%
Graduate: 120 men, 210 women	**Student/Faculty:** 27 to 1
Year: 4-1-4, summer session	**Tuition:** $12,500
Application Deadline: see profile	**Room & Board:** $4300
Freshman Class: n/av	
SAT I or ACT: required	**LESS COMPETITIVE**

Concordia University Wisconsin, established in 1881, is a private institution affiliated with the Lutheran Church-Missouri Synod. There are 4 undergraduate schools and 1 graduate school. Figures in above capsule and this profile are approximate. In addition to regional accreditation, CUW has baccalaureate program accreditation with NLN. The library contains 110,929 volumes, 270,602 microform items, and 4645 audiovisual forms/CDs, and subscribes to 1411 periodicals. Computerized library services include the card catalog, interlibrary loans, and database searching. Special learning facilities include a learning resource center, art gallery, radio station, and a curriculum library for education students. The 155-acre campus is in a suburban area 15 miles north of Milwaukee. Including residence halls, there are 17 buildings.

Student Life: 60% of undergraduates are from Wisconsin. Others are from 19 states and 25 foreign countries. 83% are white; 12% African American. 80% are Protestant; 13% Catholic. The average age of freshmen is 18; all undergraduates, 21. 25% do not continue beyond their first year; 42% remain to graduate.

Housing: About 916 students can be accommodated in college housing, which includes single-sex dormitories. On-campus housing is guaranteed for all 4 years and is available on a first-come, first-served basis. 69% of students live on campus; of those, 50% remain on campus on weekends. Alcohol is not permitted. All students may keep cars.

Activities: There are no fraternities or sororities. There are 20 groups on campus, including art, band, cheerleading, choir, chorale, drama, drill team, ethnic, honors, international, jazz band, literary magazine, musical theater, newspaper, pep band, political, professional, radio and TV, religious, and student government. Popular campus events include Winterfest and Springfest.

Sports: There are 9 intercollegiate sports for men and 7 for women, and 10 intramural sports for men and 9 for women. Facilities include a field house, stadium, gym, weight room, and fitness center.

Disabled Students: 80% of the campus is accessible. Wheelchair ramps, elevators, special parking, and specially equipped rest rooms are available.

Services: Counseling and information services are available, as is tutoring in every subject. There is a reader service for the blind, and remedial math, reading, and writing.

Campus Safety and Security: Measures include Security guards are on staff from 4 P.M. to 8 A.M. on weekdays and 24 hours a day on weekends.

Programs of Study: CUW confers B.A., B.S., and B.S.N. degrees. Associate and master's degrees are also awarded. Bachelor's degrees are awarded in BIOLOGICAL SCIENCE (biology/biological science), BUSINESS (accounting, banking and finance, business administration and management, management science, and marketing/retailing/merchandising), COMMUNICATIONS AND THE ARTS (art, communications, English, graphic design, music, Spanish, speech/debate/rhetoric, and telecommunications), COMPUTER AND PHYSICAL SCIENCE (mathematics, and radiological technology), EDUCATION (athletic training, early childhood, elementary, physical, and secondary), ENGINEERING AND ENVIRONMENTAL DESIGN (interior design), HEALTH PROFESSIONS (nursing, occupational therapy, and sports medicine), SOCIAL SCIENCE (biblical languages, criminal justice, history, humanities, ministries, paralegal studies, pastoral studies, psychology, religion, religious music, social science, social work, and theological studies). Education, business, and health sciences are the strongest academically.

Required: To graduate, students must complete 126 credits, including at least 30 in the major, with a minimum GPA of 2.0. The 47 1/2 credit core curriculum includes theology/philosophy, humanities, cross culture, social science, natural science, communication, math, and phys ed.

Special: Internships, study abroad, pass/fail options, and credit for life, military, and work experience are available. Concordia offers a general studies degree, dual, student-designed, and interdisciplinary majors, including justice and public policy, and nondegree study. Accelerated degree programs are available in several fields. There is 1 national honor society.

Faculty/Classroom: 50% of faculty are male; 50%, female. All teach undergraduates. No introductory courses are taught by graduate students. The average class size in a regular course is 17.

Requirements: The SAT I or ACT is required, with a minimum composite score of 850 on the SAT I or 18 on the ACT. Applicants must be graduates of an accredited secondary school, having completed 16 academic credits, including 3 of English and 2 each of math, science, and social studies. The GED is accepted. A GPA of 2.5 is required. AP and CLEP credits are accepted. Important factors in the admissions decision are leadership record, recommendations by school officials, and personality/intangible qualities.

Procedure: Freshmen are admitted to all sessions. Entrance exams should be taken in the junior year. Notification is sent on a rolling basis. Check with the school for current application deadlines and fee.

Transfer: Applicants for transfer must have a minimum GPA of 2.0 and meet the same entrance exam criteria as entering freshmen. 36 credits of 126 must be completed at CUW.

Visiting: There are regularly scheduled orientations for prospective students, including a tour and financial aid and academic information sessions. There are guides for informal visits and visitors may sit in on classes and stay overnight. To schedule a visit, contact the Admission Office.

Financial Aid: The CSS/Profile or FAFSA, the college's own financial statement and income tax forms are required. Check with the school for current deadlines.

International Students: There were 49 international students enrolled in a recent year. The school actively recruits these students. They must score 500 on the written TOEFL and also take the college's own test, If the student's TOEFL score is below 500, the student must take an English proficiency exam for placement.

Computers: The mainframe is an HP9000. There are Macs and PCS available to all students throughout the campus. All PCs are connected via a LAN and have Internet access. All students may access the system. There are no time limits and no fees.

Graduates: In an average class, 52% graduate in 6 years.

Admissions Contact: Andrew G. Locke, Director of Admissions.
E-mail: *admission@cuw.edu* Web: *www.cuw.edu*

EDGEWOOD COLLEGE — C-4
Madison, WI 53711-1997 (608) 663-2294
(800) 444-4861; Fax: (608) 663-3291

Full-time: 346 men, 871 women	**Faculty:** 69; IIA, --$
Part-time: 112 men, 303 women	**Ph.D.s:** 76%
Graduate: 177 men, 301 women	**Student/Faculty:** 14 to 1
Year: 4-1-4, summer session	**Tuition:** $13,300
Application Deadline: see profile	**Room & Board:** $5004
Freshman Class: 904 applied, 708 accepted, 296 enrolled	
ACT: 22	**COMPETITIVE**

Edgewood College, established in 1927, is a private Catholic institution sponsored by the Sinsinawa Dominican Sisters. There is 1 graduate school. In addition to regional accreditation, Edgewood has baccalaureate program accreditation with NCATE. The library contains 88,329 volumes, 94,050 microform items, and 3946 audiovisual forms/CDs, and subscribes to 494 periodicals. Computerized library services include the card catalog, interlibrary loans, and database searching. Special learning facilities include a learning resource center and art gallery. The 55-acre campus is in a suburban area 5 miles southwest of Madison. Including residence halls, there are 10 buildings.

Student Life: 98% of undergraduates are from Wisconsin. Others are from 11 states and 10 foreign countries. 75% are from public schools. 52% are white. 39% are Catholic; 24% Protestant. The average age of freshmen is 20; all undergraduates, 25. 32% do not continue beyond their first year; 39% remain to graduate.

Housing: 325 students can be accommodated in college housing, which includes single-sex and coed dormitories and on-campus apartments. On-campus housing is guaranteed for all 4 years. 80% of students commute. Alcohol is not permitted. All students may keep cars.

Activities: There are no fraternities or sororities. There are 30 groups on campus, including art, band, choir, chorale, chorus, drama, ethnic, gay, honors, international, literary magazine, musical theater, newspaper, orchestra, pep band, political, religious, social, social service, student government, and symphony. Popular campus events include Springfest, Mazzuchelli Fest, and Winter Frost.

Sports: There are 5 intercollegiate sports for men and 7 for women, and 9 intramural sports for men and 9 for women. Facilities include a 1000-seat gym, soccer, baseball, and softball fields, a fitness center, and access to tennis courts.

Disabled Students: 85% of the campus is accessible. Wheelchair ramps, elevators, special parking, specially equipped rest rooms, special class scheduling, lowered drinking fountains, lowered telephones, automated doors in the library, science center, activities center, and residence halls, and a chairlift are available.

Services: Counseling and information services are available, as is tutoring in some subjects, including most sciences, introductory math courses, and Spanish. There is a reader service for the blind, and remedial math, reading, and writing.

Campus Safety and Security: Measures include self-defense education, escort service, informal discussions, and pamphlets/posters/films. There are emergency telephones, and lighted pathways/sidewalks. Residence halls have alarms, a security card system, and campus security guards. RAs are on duty 24 hours a day weekends and 7 A.M. to 3 P.M. and 8 P.M. to 4 A.M. weekdays.

Programs of Study: Edgewood confers B.A. and B.S. degrees. Associate and master's degrees are also awarded. Bachelor's degrees are awarded in BIOLOGICAL SCIENCE (biology/biological science), BUSINESS (accounting and business administration and management), COMMUNICATIONS AND THE ARTS (art, English, French, graphic design, music, performing arts, and Spanish), COMPUTER AND PHYSICAL SCIENCE (chemistry, information sciences and systems, mathematics, and natural sciences), EDUCATION (early childhood, education of the exceptional child, elementary, science, and social studies), ENGINEERING AND ENVIRONMENTAL DESIGN (preengineering), HEALTH PROFESSIONS (art therapy, cytotechnology, medical technology, nursing, premedicine, prepharmacy, and preveterinary science), SOCIAL SCIENCE (child care/child and family studies, criminal justice, economics, history, international relations, political science/government, prelaw, psychology, public administration, religion, and sociology). Liberal arts is the strongest academically. Business, education, and nursing are the largest.

Required: To graduate, students must complete a minimum of 120 credit hours with a minimum GPA of 2.0. There are general education requirements, and each student must complete a major and Human Issues study.

Special: Students may cross-register with the University of Wisconsin/Madison. Internships, study abroad, dual and student-designed majors, nondegree study, pass/fail options, and credit for life, military, and work experience are available. There is a weekend degree program. There are 5 national honor societies and a freshman honors program.

Faculty/Classroom: 49% of faculty are male; 51%, female. 89% teach undergraduates and 6% both teach and do research. No introductory courses are taught by graduate students. The average class size in an introductory lecture is 20; in a laboratory, 18; and in a regular course, 17.

Admissions: 78% of the 2001-2002 applicants were accepted. 2 freshmen graduated first in their class in a recent year.

Requirements: The SAT I or ACT is required; the ACT is preferred, with a recommended minimum composite score of 18. Applicants should complete 16 Carnegie units, including 4 of English, 3 of math, 2 each of natural science, foreign language, and social science, and 3 units of electives. The GED is accepted. Edgewood requires applicants to be in the upper 50% of their class. A GPA of 2.5 is required. AP and CLEP credits are accepted. Important factors in the admissions decision are recommendations by school officials, leadership record, and extracurricular activities record. Applications are accepted on-line at the school's web site.

Procedure: Freshmen are admitted fall and spring. Entrance exams should be taken by the senior year. Check with the school for current application deadlines. The application fee is $25. Notification is sent on a rolling basis.

Transfer: 167 transfer students enrolled in a recent year. Applicants must have a minimum GPA of 2.0. Official high school and all college transcripts must be sent from schools attended. 32 credits of 120 must be completed at Edgewood.

Visiting: There are regularly scheduled orientations for prospective students, including meeting with counselors, a campus tour, meeting with faculty, and lunch on campus. There are guides for informal visits and visitors may sit in on classes and stay overnight. To schedule a visit, contact the Admissions Office.

Financial Aid: In 2001-2002, 79% of freshmen and 69% of continuing students received need-based aid. 85% of undergraduates work part time. Average annual earnings from campus work are $1360. Edgewood is a member of CSS. The FAFSA, the college's own financial statement and the and a tax return are required. Check with the school for current deadlines.

International Students: There were 66 international students enrolled in a recent year. The school actively recruits these students. They must score 525 on the written TOEFL or take the MELAB.

Computers: The mainframe is an IBM AS/400. The college provides IBM and Mac computer facilities for student use. The computer center houses 4 computer labs, a Windows NT lab with 25 systems, a technology classroom with 26 Windows NT systems, and a Mac lab with 20 systems. Students do not use the AS/400. It is for administrative use. All students may access the system. The labs are open 7:30 A.M. to midnight, Monday through Friday and 8 A.M. to 5 P.M. on weekends. There are no time limits and no fees. It is strongly recommended that all students have a personal computer. Students in the computer science class CS 180 must lease an IBM Thinkpad.

Graduates: In 2001, 334 bachelor's degrees were awarded. The most popular majors were business (31%), education (17%), and nursing (13%). In an average class, 20% graduate in 4 years, 39% in 5 years, and 43% in 6 years. 35 companies recruited on campus in 2000-2001. Of the 2000 graduating class, 8% were enrolled in graduate school within 6 months of graduation and 89% were employed.

Admissions Contact: Scott Flanagan, Dean of Admissions and Financial Aid. E-mail: *admissions@edgewood.edu* Web: *www.edgewood.edu*

LAKELAND COLLEGE

Sheboygan, WI 53082-0359 — E-4

(920) 565-1588

(800) 242-3347; Fax: (920) 565-1206

Full-time: 391 men, 404 women	**Faculty:** 41; IIB, --$
Part-time: 24 men, 28 women	**Ph.D.s:** 59%
Graduate: 53 men, 127 women	**Student/Faculty:** 19 to 1
Year: semesters, summer session	**Tuition:** $12,380
Application Deadline: July 15	**Room & Board:** $5050
Freshman Class: 587 applied, 408 accepted, 192 enrolled	
SAT I Verbal/Math: 430/480	**ACT:** 20 **COMPETITIVE**

Lakeland College, established in 1862, is a private institution affiliated with the United Church of Christ. The 4-4-1 academic calendar consists of 4-month fall and spring terms, and an optional 3 1/2 week May term. The library contains 57,447 volumes, 33,169 microform items, and 2099 audiovisual forms/CDs, and subscribes to 322 periodicals. Computerized library services include the card catalog, interlibrary loans, and database searching. Special learning facilities include a learning resource center, art gallery, and and a college history museum. The 240-acre campus is in a rural area 10 miles northwest of Sheboygan. Including residence halls, there are 24 buildings.

Student Life: 79% of undergraduates are from Wisconsin. Others are from 16 states, 31 foreign countries, and Canada. 90% are from public schools. 76% are white. 32% are Protestant; 29% Catholic; 25% claim no religious affiliation. The average age of all undergraduates is 22. 32% do not continue beyond their first year; 43% remain to graduate.

Housing: 488 students can be accommodated in college housing, which includes single-sex and coed dormitories and on-campus apartments. In addition, there are honors houses and male only, female only housing for students with senior standing. On-campus housing is guaranteed for all 4 years. 57% of students live on campus; of those, 60% remain on campus on weekends. All students may keep cars.

Activities: 17% of men belong to 3 local fraternities; 11% of women belong to 3 local sororities. There are 27 groups on campus, including band, choir, chorus, dance team, drama, ethnic, honors, international, literary magazine, newspaper, pep band, professional, radio and TV, religious, social, student government, and yearbook. Popular campus events include Winter Carnival, and Spring Celebration.

Sports: There are 8 intercollegiate sports for men and 7 for women, and 2 intramural sports for men and 2 for women. Facilities include a sports complex, a fitness lab, 3 full-size basketball courts, a weight room, indoor and outdoor tennis courts, indoor pitching and batting facilities, and softball, baseball, football, soccer, and practice fields.

Disabled Students: 83% of the campus is accessible. Wheelchair ramps, elevators, special parking, specially equipped rest rooms, and lowered drinking fountains are available, though not at every building.

Services: Counseling and information services are available, as is tutoring in every subject. There is a reader service for the blind, and remedial math, reading, and writing.

Campus Safety and Security: Measures include escort service, informal discussions, pamphlets/posters/films, and emergency telephones. There are lighted pathways/sidewalks and foot patrol on weekends and evenings.

Programs of Study: Lakeland confers the B.A. degree. Master's degrees are also awarded. Bachelor's degrees are awarded in BIOLOGICAL SCIENCE (biology/biological science), BUSINESS (accounting, business administration and management, business economics, hospitality management services, international business management, and marketing management), COMMUNICATIONS AND THE ARTS (art, creative writing, dramatic arts, English, German, music, and Spanish), COMPUTER AND PHYSICAL SCIENCE (chemistry, computer science, and mathematics), EDUCATION (business, early childhood, elementary, music, and secondary), SOCIAL SCIENCE (behavioral science, criminal justice, economics, history, philosophy, physical fitness/movement, psychology, public administration, religion, and sociology). Business, education, and accounting are the strongest academically. Education, business, and computer science are the largest.

Required: To graduate, students must complete 128 semester hours, with at least 32 in the major and a minimum 2.0 GPA. There are requirements in history, humanities, natural sciences, social sciences, and religion.

Special: Internships in all majors, study abroad in Germany and Japan, a Washington semester, and work-study programs are available. There are some dual majors, a general studies degree, a 3-2 engineering degree with the University of Wisconsin/Madison, a 2-2 1/2 nursing program with Bellin College of Nursing, and nondegree study. There is a freshman honors program. All departments have honors programs.

Faculty/Classroom: 51% of faculty are male; 49%, female. All both teach and do research. No introductory courses are taught by graduate students. The average class size in an introductory lecture is 20; in a laboratory, 15; and in a regular course, 16.

Admissions: 70% of the 2001-2002 applicants were accepted. The SAT I scores for the 2001-2002 freshman class were: Verbal--73% below 500, 13% between 500 and 599, and 13% between 600 and 700; Math--55% below 500, 33% between 500 and 599, and 13% between 600 and 700. The ACT scores were 58% below 21, 22% between 21 and 23, 14% between 24 and 26, 5% between 27 and 28, and 1% above 28. 19% of the current freshmen were in the top fifth of their class; 41% were in the top two fifths.

Requirements: The SAT I or ACT is required, with a minimum composite score of 950 on the SAT I or 19 on the ACT. Applicants must be graduates of an accredited secondary school or have the GED. An interview is recommended. Lakeland requires applicants to be in the upper 50% of their class. A GPA of 2.0 is required. AP and CLEP credits are accepted. Important factors in the admissions decision are advanced placement or honor courses, leadership record, and evidence of special talent. Applications are accepted on-line via the college's web site, *www.lakeland.edu*; CollegeNET; and Wisconsin mentor.

Procedure: Freshmen are admitted fall, spring, and summer. Entrance exams should be taken after the enrollment commitment is made. Applications should be filed by July 15 for fall entry and December 15 for spring entry, along with a $20 fee. Notification is sent on a rolling basis.

Transfer: 115 transfer students enrolled in 2001-2002. Applicants should have a GPA of at least 2.0. Lakeland recommends an interview. 36 credits of 128 must be completed at Lakeland.

Visiting: There are regularly scheduled orientations for prospective students, consisting of meetings with faculty and financial aid personnel, activities meetings, and a campus tour. There are guides for informal visits and visitors may sit in on classes and stay overnight. To schedule a visit, contact the Admissions Office.

Financial Aid: In 2001-2002, all freshmen and 97% of continuing students received some form of financial aid. 86% of freshmen and 90% of continuing students received need-based aid. The average freshman award was $11,895. Of that total, scholarships or need-based grants averaged $7870 ($14,800 maximum); loans averaged $2625 ($2625 maximum); and work contracts averaged $1400 (maximum). 30% of undergraduates work part time. Average annual earnings from campus work are $1000. The average financial indebtedness of the 2001 graduate was $20,558. Lakeland is a member of CSS. The FAFSA and the college's own financial statement are required. The fall application deadline is July 1.

International Students: There are 100 international students enrolled. The school actively recruits these students. They must score 500 on the written TOEFL.

Computers: The mainframe consists of several Nt/Citrix servers. Lakeland has 4 computer rooms with approximately 30 computers in each room, and an additional 10 computers in the library. All computers are connected to the college network and have acccess to the Internet. All students may access the system 7 A.M. to 2 A.M. There are no time limits and no fees.

Graduates: In 2001, 145 bachelor's degrees were awarded. The most popular majors were education (28%), business administration (17%), and computer science (10%). In an average class, 13% graduate in 3 years, 30% in 4 years, 43% in 5 years, and 46% in 6 years. Of the 2000 graduating class, 10% were enrolled in graduate school within 6 months of graduation and 95% were employed.

Admissions Contact: Leo Gavrilos, Director of Admissions.
E-mail: *admissions@lakeland.edu* Web: *www.lakeland.edu*

LAWRENCE UNIVERSITY
Appleton, WI 54912 **D-3**

(920) 832-6500
(800) 227-0982; Fax: (920) 832-6782

Full-time: 563 men, 684 women | **Faculty:** 130; IIB, +$
Part-time: 43 men, 33 women | **Ph.D.s:** 93%
Graduate: none | **Student/Faculty:** 10 to 1
Year: terms | **Tuition:** $22,728
Application Deadline: January 15 | **Room & Board:** $4983
Freshman Class: 1629 applied, 1102 accepted, 321 enrolled
SAT I or ACT: required **HIGHLY COMPETITIVE**

Lawrence University, founded in 1847, is an independent liberal arts institution with a conservatory of music. In addition to regional accreditation, Lawrence has baccalaureate program accreditation with NASM. The library contains 370,558 volumes, 103,762 microform items, and 19,396 audiovisual forms/CDs, and subscribes to 1497 periodicals. Computerized library services include the card catalog, interlibrary loans, and database searching. Special learning facilities include a learning resource center, art gallery, natural history museum, and radio station. The 84-acre campus is in an urban area 100 miles north of Milwaukee. Including residence halls, there are 60 buildings.

Student Life: 58% of undergraduates are from out of state, mostly the Midwest. Others are from 49 states, 39 foreign countries, and Canada. 78% are from public schools. 80% are white. 49% claim no religious affiliation; 19% Protestant; 18% Catholic; 13% Buddhist, Hindu, Muslim, and other. The average age of freshmen is 18; all undergraduates, 20. 13% do not continue beyond their first year; 70% remain to graduate.

Housing: Housing includes single-sex and coed dormitories, on-campus apartments, married-student housing, and fraternity houses. In addition, there are language houses and special-interest houses. On-campus housing is guaranteed for all 4 years. 97% of students live on campus. All students may keep cars.

Activities: 35% of men belong to 5 national fraternities; 20% of women belong to 3 national sororities. There are 130 groups on campus, including art, band, cheerleading, chess, choir, chorale, chorus, computers, dance, drama, ethnic, film, gay, honors, international, jazz band, literary magazine, musical theater, newspaper, opera, orchestra, pep band, political, professional, radio and TV, religious, social, social service, student government, symphony, and yearbook. Popular campus events include Octoberfest, Celebrate! Spring Festival of the Arts, and Annual Midwest Trivia Contest.

Sports: There are 13 intercollegiate sports for men and 10 for women, and 22 intramural sports for men and 28 for women. Facilities include a 5255-seat football stadium; 8-lane all-weather and 4-lane indoor tracks; baseball, soccer, practice fields; 9 tennis, 2 squash, and 3 racquetball/handball courts; a gym for basketball, volleyball, and badminton; 2 batting cages; an 8-lane swimming pool with diving well; weight, exercise, and sauna rooms; and a dance studio.

Disabled Students: 80% of the campus is accessible. Wheelchair ramps, elevators, special parking, specially equipped rest rooms, and special class scheduling are available.

Services: Counseling and information services are available, as is tutoring in every subject. There is a reader service for the blind and remedial math and writing. The writing lab focuses on enhancing writing skills, as well as remedial writing.

Campus Safety and Security: Measures include 24-hour foot and vehicle patrol, self-defense education, escort service, and informal discussions. There are pamphlets/posters/films, emergency telephones, lighted pathways/sidewalks, and the Whistle Stop Program.

Programs of Study: Lawrence confers B.A. and B.Mus. degrees. Bachelor's degrees are awarded in BIOLOGICAL SCIENCE (biology/biological science and neurosciences), COMMUNICATIONS AND THE ARTS (art history and appreciation, classics, dramatic arts, English, French, German, linguistics, music performance, music theory and composition, Russian, Spanish, and studio art), COMPUTER AND PHYSICAL SCIENCE (chemistry, computer science, geology, mathematics, and physics), EDUCATION (art, music, and secondary), ENGINEERING AND ENVIRONMENTAL DESIGN (environmental science), SOCIAL SCIENCE (anthropology, East Asian studies, economics, gender studies, history, international relations, philosophy, political science/government, psychology, and religion). Biology, music, and physics are the strongest academically. Biology, music, and history are the largest.

Required: Students must complete 216 units, including 48 to 72 in the major with a minimum GPA of 2.0. All students must take Freshman Studies. Distribution requirements include courses in humanities, fine arts, social sciences, natural sciences, diversity, and a foreign language.

Special: Lawrence offers Chicago-based programs in urban studies, urban education, and the arts, a humanities program at the Newberry Library, a science internship at Oak Ridge National Laboratory, and a biological field station in Minnesota. There are study-abroad programs in 14 countries, a Washington semester, limited pass/fail options, student-designed majors, and nondegree study. Students may take a 3-2 engineering degree with Columbia or Washington universities, Rensselaer Polytechnic Institute, or the University of Michigan. Also available are 3-2 programs in forestry and environmental studies with Duke University, in occupational therapy with Washington University in St. Louis, and in allied health sciences (nursing/medical technology) with Rush-Presbyterian-St. Luke's Medical Center in Chicago. A 5-year B.A.-B.Mus. degree is offered. There are 8 national honor societies, including Phi Beta Kappa, and 21 departmental honors programs.

Faculty/Classroom: 61% of faculty are male; 39%, female. All both teach and do research. The average class size in an introductory lecture is 29; in a laboratory, 14; and in a regular course, 14.

Admissions: 68% of the 2001-2002 applicants were accepted. The SAT I scores for the 2001-2002 freshman class were: Verbal--9% below 500, 28% between 500 and 599, 40% between 600 and 700, and 23% above 700; Math--2% below 500, 32% between 500 and 599, 43% between 600 and 700, and 23% above 700. The ACT scores were 3% below 21, 11% between 21 and 23, 20% between 24 and 26, 24% between 27 and 28, and 42% above 28. 68% of the current freshmen were in the top fifth of their class; 92% were in the top two fifths. There were 15 National Merit finalists and 6 semifinalists. 24 freshmen graduated first in their class.

Requirements: The SAT I or ACT is required. In addition, in addition, applicants should complete 16 high school academic credits. Lawrence requires an essay, reports from a teacher and counselor, and, for music majors, an audition. The school recommends the SAT II: Writing test, an interview, and, for art majors, a portfolio. AP credits are accepted. Important factors in the admissions decision are advanced placement or honor courses, evidence of special talent, and extracurricular activities record. Applications are accepted on computer disk, and on-line via CollegeLink, Common App, Wisconsin Mentor, Apply, and CollegeNET.

Procedure: Freshmen are admitted in the fall. Entrance exams should be taken in the spring of the junior year or fall of the senior year. There are early decision and deferred admissions plans. Early decision applications should be filed by November 15; regular applications, by January 15 for fall entry, along with a $30 fee. Notification of early decision is sent December 1; regular decision, April 1. 32 early decision candidates were accepted for the 2001-2002 class. 9% of all applicants are on a waiting list; 16 were accepted in 2001.

Transfer: 36 transfer students enrolled in 2001-2002. Applicants must present official transcripts of their college and secondary school work, SAT I or ACT scores, and the recommendation of a college professor. Typically, candidates with a college GPA of 2.75 or higher will receive serious consideration. 18 courses of 36 must be completed at Lawrence.

Visiting: There are guides for informal visits and visitors may sit in on classes and stay overnight. To schedule a visit, contact the Office of Admissions.

Financial Aid: In 2001-2002, 92% of all freshmen and 93% of continuing students received some form of financial aid. 69% of all students received need-based aid. The average freshman award was $19,471. Of that total, scholarships or need-based grants averaged $14,697 ($25,700 maximum); loans averaged $3124 ($6625 maximum); and work contracts averaged $1648 ($2200 maximum). 70% of undergraduates work part time. Average annual earnings from campus work are $1500. The average financial indebtedness of the 2001 graduate was $17,931. The FAFSA and the college's own financial statement are required. The fall application deadline is March 15.

International Students: There are 116 international students enrolled. The school actively recruits these students. They must score 575 on the written TOEFL.

Computers: The University has several midrange Compaq systems. Some model numbers in use are 1000A, 2100, and DS20. Internet access is available from nearly anywhere on campus, including student rooms. There are a number of computer labs located in the larger residence halls, the library, and major academic buildings. All students are provided with disk space for storing important documents and developing web pages. All students may access the system 24 hours a day. There are no time limits and no fees. It is strongly recommended that all students have a personal computer.

Graduates: In 2001, 221 bachelor's degrees were awarded. The most popular majors were music performance (19%), biology (11%), and history (9%). In an average class, 1% graduate in 3 years, 60% in 4 years, 65% in 5 years, and 70% in 6 years. 40 companies recruited on campus in 2000-2001. Of the 2000 graduating class, 30% were enrolled in graduate school within 6 months of graduation and 59% were employed.

Admissions Contact: Michael Thorp, Director of Admissions.
E-mail: *excel@lawrence.edu* Web: *www.lawrence.edu*

MARIAN COLLEGE OF FOND DU LAC

D-4

Fond du Lac, WI 54935

(920) 923-7650
(800) 2-MARIAN; Fax: (920) 923-8755

Full-time: 1078 men and women
Part-time: 551 men and women
Graduate: 930 men and women
Year: semesters, summer session
Application Deadline: open
Freshman Class: 761 applied, 655 accepted, 234 enrolled
ACT: 20
Faculty: 71; IIB, --$
Ph.D.s: 42%
Student/Faculty: 15 to 1
Tuition: $13,545
Room & Board: $4390
LESS COMPETITIVE

Marian College, founded in 1936, is a private, Catholic, liberal arts based institution offering degree programs in the arts and sciences, business, education, and health fields. In addition to regional accreditation, Marian has baccalaureate program accreditation with CSWE, NCATE, and NLN. The library contains 91,368 volumes, 6392 microform items, and 363 audiovisual forms/CDs, and subscribes to 669 periodicals. Computerized library services include the card catalog, interlibrary loans, and database searching. Special learning facilities include a learning resource center. The 97-acre campus is in a small town 60 miles north of Milwaukee. Including residence halls, there are 19 buildings.

Student Life: 80% of undergraduates are from Wisconsin. Others are from 11 states, 5 foreign countries, and Canada. 70% are from public schools. 93% are white. 60% are Catholic; 40% Protestant. 20% do not continue beyond their first year; 59% remain to graduate.

Housing: 445 students can be accommodated in college housing, which includes single-sex and coed dormitories, on-campus apartments, fraternity houses, and sorority houses. In addition, there is a chemical-free wellness residence hall. On-campus housing is guaranteed for all 4 years. 60% of students commute. All students may keep cars.

Activities: 16% of men belong to 2 national fraternities; 10% of women belong to 1 local and 2 national sororities. There are 30 groups on campus, including band, cheerleading, choir, chorus, drama, ethnic, honors, international, jazz band, literary magazine, multicultural and campus ministry, newspaper, orchestra, pep band, photography, political, professional, radio and TV, religious, social, social service, student government, symphony, and yearbook. Popular campus events include Heritage Festival of Arts, Fine Arts Series, and Sabre Show.

Sports: There are 6 intercollegiate sports for men and 6 for women, and 5 intramural sports for men and 5 for women. Facilities include a soccer field, a softball field, a gym, tennis courts, a game room, a hockey rink, and a weight room.

Disabled Students: All of the campus is accessible. Wheelchair ramps, elevators, special parking, specially equipped rest rooms, special class scheduling, lowered drinking fountains, and lowered telephones are available.

Services: Counseling and information services are available, as is tutoring in most subjects. There is a reader service for the blind, and remedial math, reading, and writing.

Campus Safety and Security: Measures include self-defense education, escort service, informal discussions, and pamphlets/posters/films. There are emergency telephones, lighted pathways/sidewalks, and evening foot and vehicle patrol.

Programs of Study: Marian confers B.A., B.S., B.B.A., B.S.B.A., B.S.Ed., B.S.M.T., B.S.N., B.S.R.T., and B.S.W. degrees. Master's degrees are also awarded. Bachelor's degrees are awarded in BIOLOGICAL SCIENCE (biology/biological science), BUSINESS (accounting, business administration and management, management science, marketing/retailing/merchandising, and sports management), COMMUNICATIONS AND THE ARTS (art, communications, English, music, music business management, and Spanish), COMPUTER AND PHYSICAL SCIENCE (chemistry, information sciences and systems, mathematics, and radiological technology), EDUCATION (art, early childhood, elementary, middle school, music, and secondary), HEALTH PROFESSIONS (cytotechnology, medical laboratory technology, and nursing), SOCIAL SCIENCE (criminal justice, economics, history, human services, psychology, and social work). Nursing, education, and business are the strongest academically and have the largest enrollments.

Required: To graduate, students must complete 128 credits with a minimum GPA of 2.0 (nursing and social work, 2.75; education, 3.0). Core requirements include 25 credits in arts and humanities, 12 to 13 in social and behavioral science, and 12 in math and natural science, as well as a freshman seminar.

Special: Internships are offered in most areas of study, cooperative education programs in all majors, and accelerated-degree programs in nursing, business administration, and operation management. Student-designed and dual majors, credit for prior learning, work-study, nondegree study, and cooperative education (paid work experience) are available. Study abroad at Harlaxton College, England, is possible. There are evening degree completion programs for working adults. The college has an honors program. There are 7 national honor societies and a freshman honors program.

Faculty/Classroom: 55% of faculty are male; 45%, female. All teach undergraduates. No introductory courses are taught by graduate students. The average class size in an introductory lecture is 18; in a laboratory, 13; and in a regular course, 25.

Admissions: 86% of the 2001-2002 applicants were accepted. The ACT scores for the 2001-2002 freshman class were: 59% below 21, 25% between 21 and 23, 10% between 24 and 26, 5% between 27 and 28, and 1% above 28. 15% of the current freshmen were in the top fifth of their class; 33% were in the top two fifths.

Requirements: The ACT is required. The required minimum ACT composite score is 18. Applicants must be graduates of an accredited secondary school or have earned a GED. An interview is recommended. Marian requires applicants to be in the upper 50% of their class. A GPA of 2.0 is required. AP and CLEP credits are accepted. Important factors in the admissions decision are advanced placement or honor courses, leadership record, and evidence of special talent. Applications are accepted on-line via CollegeNet and the school's web site.

Procedure: Freshmen are admitted to all sessions. Entrance exams should be taken in the junior year. There are early admissions, rolling admissions, and deferred admissions plans. Application deadlines are open. The fall 2001 application fee was $20.

Transfer: In a recent year, 104 transfer students enrolled. The school recommends a minimum GPA of 2.0, the SAT I or ACT, and an interview. 32 credits of 128 must be completed at Marian.

Visiting: There are regularly scheduled orientations for prospective students, consisting of sessions in April, May, June, and July for course selection and meeting with advisers. There are guides for informal visits and visitors may sit in on classes and stay overnight. To schedule a visit, contact the Admissions Office.

Financial Aid: In 2001-2002, 96% of all freshmen received some form of financial aid. 80% of freshmen received need-based aid. The average freshman award was $12,165. Of that total, scholarships or need-based grants averaged $7162 ($18,000 maximum); loans averaged $2879 ($18,000 maximum); work contracts averaged $2000; and outside scholarships and parent loans averaged $1736 ($18,000 maximum). 27% of undergraduates work part time. Average annual earnings from campus work are $595. The average financial indebtedness of the 2001 graduate was $14,000. The FAFSA and the college's own financial statement are required. The fall application deadline is March 15.

International Students: There are 31 international students enrolled. The school actively recruits these students. They must score 525 on the written TOEFL or 193 on the electronic version.

Computers: There are 200 Macs and PCs available, as well as word-processing equipment. All students may access the system. There are no time limits and no fees. It is strongly recommended that all students have a personal computer.

Graduates: In 2001, 316 bachelor's degrees were awarded. The most popular majors were business administration (37%), nursing (22%), and education (12%). In an average class, 21% graduate in 4 years, 40% in 5 years, and 43% in 6 years. Of the 2000 graduating class, 5% were enrolled in graduate school within 6 months of graduation and 98% were employed.

Admissions Contact: Stacey Akey, Dean of Enrollment Management. A video is available. E-mail: *admissions@mariancollege.edu*
Web: *www.mariancollege.edu*

MARQUETTE UNIVERSITY

E-4

Milwaukee, WI 53201-1881

(414) 288-7302
(800) 222-6544; Fax: (414) 288-3764

Full-time: 3126 men, 3829 women
Part-time: 214 men, 330 women
Graduate: 1175 men, 1048 women
Year: semesters, summer session
Application Deadline: open
Freshman Class: 6743 applied, 5657 accepted, 1639 enrolled
SAT I Verbal/Math: 580/580
Faculty: 596; I, --$
Ph.D.s: 79%
Student/Faculty: 12 to 1
Tuition: $18,486
Room & Board: $6350
ACT: 25
COMPETITIVE+

Marquette University, established in 1881, is a private Roman Catholic Jesuit institution. Students in selected majors pay a slightly higher tuition. Check with the school. There are 7 undergraduate and 4 graduate schools. In addition to regional accreditation, Marquette has baccalaureate program accreditation with AACSB, ABET, ACEJMC, ADA, APTA, ASLA, CSWE, NCATE, and NLN. The 3 libraries contain 1,083,179 volumes, 1,343,208 microform items, and 9339 audiovisual forms/CDs, and subscribe to 9157 periodicals. Computerized library services include the card catalog, interlibrary loans, and database searching. Special learning facilities include a learning resource center, art gallery, radio station, and TV station. The 80-acre campus is in an urban area 90 miles north of Chicago. Including residence halls, there are 54 buildings.

Student Life: 52% of undergraduates are from out of state, mostly the Midwest. Others are from 49 states, 54 foreign countries, and Canada. 56% are from public schools. 85% are white. 65% are Catholic; 35% Protestant. The average age of freshmen is 18; all undergraduates, 21. 11% do not continue beyond their first year; 74% remain to graduate.

Housing: 3218 students can be accommodated in college housing, which includes single-sex and coed dormitories, on-campus apartments,

and married-student housing. In addition, there are specified majors and quiet/study floors. On-campus housing is guaranteed for all 4 years. 50% of students live on campus. All students may keep cars.

Activities: 9% of men belong to 7 national fraternities; 9% of women belong to 7 national sororities. There are 150 groups on campus, including band, cheerleading, choir, chorale, chorus, community awareness, dance, drama, ethnic, gay, honors, jazz band, literary magazine, musical theater, newspaper, orchestra, pep band, photography, political, professional, radio and TV, recreational, religious, social, social service, student government, and yearbook. Popular campus events include Student Organizational Fest, College Bowl, and Winter Flurry.

Sports: There are 7 intercollegiate sports for men and 7 for women, and 40 intramural sports for men and 40 for women. Facilities include 2 multirecreation centers and Valley Fields, an outdoor soccer, track, and football facility.

Disabled Students: 80% of the campus is accessible. Wheelchair ramps, elevators, special parking, specially equipped rest rooms, special class scheduling, lowered drinking fountains, and lowered telephones are available.

Services: Counseling and information services are available, as is tutoring in most subjects. There is a reader service for the blind, and remedial math, reading, and writing; and book taping and note taking for the physically disabled.

Campus Safety and Security: Measures include 24-hour foot and vehicle patrol, self-defense education, escort service, and shuttle buses. There are informal discussions, pamphlets/posters/films, emergency telephones, lighted pathways/sidewalks, and closed-circuit cameras in selected parking lots.

Programs of Study: Marquette confers B.A., B.S., and B.S.N. degrees. Associate, master's, and doctoral degrees are also awarded. Bachelor's degrees are awarded in BIOLOGICAL SCIENCE (biochemistry, biology/biological science, molecular biology, and physiology), BUSINESS (accounting, banking and finance, business administration and management, business economics, human resources, international business management, management information systems, and marketing/retailing/merchandising), COMMUNICATIONS AND THE ARTS (advertising, broadcasting, classical languages, classics, communications, dramatic arts, English, French, German, journalism, public relations, and Spanish), COMPUTER AND PHYSICAL SCIENCE (chemistry, computer science, information sciences and systems, mathematics, physics, and statistics), EDUCATION (secondary), ENGINEERING AND ENVIRONMENTAL DESIGN (biomedical engineering, civil engineering, computer engineering, electrical/electronics engineering, engineering, environmental engineering, industrial engineering technology, and mechanical engineering), HEALTH PROFESSIONS (biomedical science, clinical science, dental hygiene, exercise science, nursing, physical therapy, physician's assistant, and speech pathology/audiology), SOCIAL SCIENCE (anthropology, criminology, economics, history, interdisciplinary studies, international relations, philosophy, political science/government, psychology, sociology, and theological studies). Physical therapy, biomedical engineering, and biology are the strongest academically. Business administration, nursing, and broadcast and electronic communication are the largest.

Required: To graduate, students must complete 126 to 133 credits including at least 32 in the major (24 to 64 in some) with a minimum GPA of 2.0 (2.2 for medical lab technology majors). An arts and sciences core curriculum of 59 to 76 credits is required of all students, including courses in philosophy, social and behavioral sciences, theology, foreign language, history, literature, and natural sciences.

Special: Marquette offers co-op programs in engineering, internships, study abroad in 10 countries, a Washington summer term, and work-study programs. Dual and student-designed majors, nondegree study, an accelerated degree program for predental students, and pass/fail options are available. Cross-registration is possible with Milwaukee Institute of Art and Design, and there is a 2-2 engineering program with Waukesha County Technical college. The Freshman Frontier Program offers academic support for selected freshmen who do not meet regular admission requirements but show potential for success. The Educational Opportunity Program affords students from minority groups and low-income families the opportunity to attend the school. There are 8 national honor societies, including Phi Beta Kappa, a university-wide honors program, and a freshman honors program.

Faculty/Classroom: 65% of faculty are male; 35%, female. The average class size in a regular course is 30.

Admissions: 84% of the 2001-2002 applicants were accepted. The SAT I scores for the 2001-2002 freshman class were: Verbal--14% below 500, 43% between 500 and 599, 35% between 600 and 700, and 7% above 700; Math--17% below 500, 41% between 500 and 599, 36% between 600 and 700, and 7% above 700. The ACT scores were 1% between 12 and 17, 31% between 18 and 23, 58% between 24 and 29, and 11% above 30. 62% of the current freshmen were in the top quarter of their class; 91% were in the top half. There were 13 National Merit finalists.

Requirements: The SAT I or ACT is required. In addition, applicants must be graduates of an accredited secondary school with a recommended 18 credits, including 4 years of English, 3 each of social studies and math, 2 each of sciences and foreign language, and 4 of additional academic subjects. Most students rank in the upper quarter of their high school class. The GED is accepted, with a minimum score of 225. Applicants must demonstrate ability, preparation, and motivation. An interview is recommended. A GPA of 2.5 is required. AP and CLEP credits are accepted. Important factors in the admissions decision are advanced placement or honor courses, recommendations by school officials, and leadership record. Marquette's on-line application is available at *www.marquette.edu.admission/index.html*

Procedure: Freshmen are admitted to all sessions. Entrance exams should be taken in the junior year and repeated early in the senior year if necessary. Application deadlines are open. There is a rolling admissions plan. The fall 2001 application fee was $30.

Transfer: 167 transfer students enrolled in 2001-2002. Applicants for transfer must have a minimum GPA of 2.0; some programs require a higher average. The SAT I or ACT is required if the applicant has completed fewer than 12 hours of college-level work. 30 credits of 126 to 133 must be completed at Marquette.

Visiting: There are regularly scheduled orientations for prospective students. The agenda for visits varies according to the specific program; open houses are available on scheduled weekends throughout the academic year. There are guides for informal visits and visitors may sit in on classes and stay overnight. To schedule a visit, contact the Admissions Office.

Financial Aid: In 2001-2002, 61% of all freshmen and 58% of continuing students received some form of financial aid. 60% of freshmen and 57% of continuing students received need-based aid. The average freshman need-based package was $15,791. Of that total, work contracts averaged $2000. 80% of undergraduates work part time. Average annual earnings from campus work are $1000. The average financial indebtedness of the 2001 graduate was $20,721. The FAFSA and the college's own financial statement are required. The fall application deadline is March 1.

International Students: There are 173 international students enrolled. The school actively recruits these students. They must score 525 on the written TOEFL and also take the Comprehensive English Language Test or the college's own test.

Computers: The mainframe is comprised of various DEC VAX models in a cluster configuration. There are more than 1000 time-sharing terminals and PCs in residence halls, libraries, and academic facilities. Students can also use word-processing facilities in the library, computing center, and various buildings. Residence halls are wired for Web and Internet access. All students may access the system 24 hours a day Sunday through Thursday and 10 A.M. to 10 P.M. weekends when classes are in session. There are no time limits and no fees.

Graduates: In 2001, 1455 bachelor's degrees were awarded. The most popular majors were business/marketing (19%), communications (18%), and engineering (15%). In an average class, 54% graduate in 4 years, 72% in 5 years, and 74% in 6 years. 350 companies recruited on campus in 2000-2001. Of the 2000 graduating class, 28% were enrolled in graduate school within 1 year of graduation and 62% were employed.

Admissions Contact: Robert Blust, Dean of Admissions.
E-mail: *admissions@marquette.edu* Web: *www.marquette.edu*

MILWAUKEE INSTITUTE OF ART AND DESIGN — E-4
Milwaukee, WI 53202-6003 — **(414) 291-8070**
(888) 749-MIAD; Fax: (414) 291-8077

Full-time: 294 men, 291 women	**Faculty:** 26
Part-time: 29 men, 36 women	**Ph.D.s:** 85%
Graduate: none	**Student/Faculty:** 23 to 1
Year: semesters, summer session	**Tuition:** $17,930
Application Deadline: April 1	**Room & Board:** $6458
Freshman Class: 374 applied, 371 accepted, 198 enrolled	
SAT I or ACT: recommended	**SPECIAL**

Milwaukee Institute of Art and Design, founded in 1974, is a private, 4-year professional college of art and design. In addition to regional accreditation, MIAD has baccalaureate program accreditation with NASAD. The library contains 29,000 volumes and 380 audiovisual forms/CDs, and subscribes to 85 periodicals. Computerized library services include the card catalog, interlibrary loans, and database searching. Special learning facilities include a learning resource center, art gallery, and museum. The campus is in an urban area in downtown Milwaukee. Including residence halls, there are 4 buildings.

Student Life: 72% of undergraduates are from Wisconsin. Others are from 20 states. 80% are from public schools. 88% are white. The average age of freshmen is 19; all undergraduates, 23. 21% do not continue beyond their first year; 73% remain to graduate.

Housing: 144 students can be accommodated in college housing, which includes coed dormitories. On-campus housing is available on a first-come, first-served basis. 77% of students commute. Alcohol is not permitted. All students may keep cars.

Activities: There are no fraternities or sororities. There are 7 groups on campus, including art, ethnic, literary magazine, photography, professional, religious, student government, and yearbook. Popular campus events include visiting artist lectures and workshops, student and faculty exhibitions, and a scholarship show.

Sports: There is no sports program at MIAD.

Disabled Students: All of the campus is accessible. Wheelchair ramps, elevators, specially equipped rest rooms, lowered drinking fountains, and lowered telephones are available.

Services: Counseling and information services are available, as is tutoring in some subjects, including liberal studies. There is remedial writing. There is a program in developmental freshman English as well as student tutoring and a writing center.

Campus Safety and Security: Measures include escort service, informal discussions, pamphlets/posters/films, and emergency telephones. There are lighted pathways/sidewalks.

Programs of Study: MIAD confers the B.F.A. degree. Bachelor's degrees are awarded in COMMUNICATIONS AND THE ARTS (drawing, fine arts, graphic design, illustration, industrial design, painting, photography, printmaking, and sculpture), ENGINEERING AND ENVIRONMENTAL DESIGN (interior design). Graphic design, illustration, and industrial design are the largest.

Required: About 66% of the graduation credits are in studio courses. Students must complete 124 credits, with 81 studio credits, 43 in liberal studies, and a minimum GPA of 2.0. MIAD requires 12 credits in art history and at least 12 credits in English/writing and 19 credits in the humanities and sciences.

Special: Students may cross-register with Marquette University and 29 other nationally accredited art colleges. Study abroad in Japan, Germany, Poland, and France, a semester at New York Artists Studio, and internships in all design fields and photography are available. Nondegree study and credit for life, military, and work experience are possible.

Faculty/Classroom: 64% of faculty are male; 36%, female. All teach undergraduates. The average class size in a regular course is 16.

Admissions: 99% of the 2001-2002 applicants were accepted.

Requirements: The SAT I or ACT is recommended. In addition, applicants must be graduates of an accredited secondary school. 4 years of art are recommended. A portfolio review and an interview are required. A GPA of 2.0 is required. AP and CLEP credits are accepted. Important factors in the admissions decision are evidence of special talent, advanced placement or honor courses, and personality/intangible qualities.

Procedure: Freshmen are admitted fall and spring. There is a deferred admissions plan. Applications should be filed by April 1 for fall entry. Notification is sent on a rolling basis. The fall application fee was $25.

Transfer: 60 transfer students enrolled in 2001-2002. A transfer portfolio evaluation is done. Transcripts are reviewed for courses comparable to MIAD's programs. A grade of C or better is required for transfer. 30 credits of 124 must be completed at MIAD.

Visiting: There are guides for informal visits and visitors may sit in on classes. To schedule a visit, contact the Admissions Office.

Financial Aid: In 2001-2002, 83% of all freshmen and 89% of continuing students received some form of financial aid. 82% of freshmen and 87% of continuing students received need-based aid. The average freshman award was $12,142. The average financial indebtedness of the 2001 graduate was $21,258. The FAFSA is required. The fall application deadline is March 1.

International Students: There are 20 international students enrolled. The school actively recruits these students. They must score 550 on the written TOEFL.

Computers: The mainframe is a Mac Power PC. There are 43 stations in the computer lab and 6 computer labs with more than 90 computers. All students may access the system more than 80 hours a week. There are no time limits and no fees.

Graduates: In 2001, 91 bachelor's degrees were awarded. The most popular majors were communication design (24%), illustration (18%), and drawing (15%). In an average class, 33% graduate in 4 years, 41% in 5 years, and 42% in 6 years. 15 companies recruited on campus in 2000-2001. Of the 2000 graduating class, 1% were enrolled in graduate school within 6 months of graduation and 90% were employed.

Admissions Contact: Mary Schopp, Exec Dir, Enrollment Services. A video is available. E-mail: *miadadm@miad.edu* Web: *www.miad.edu*

MILWAUKEE SCHOOL OF ENGINEERING — E-4

Milwaukee, WI 53202-3109 — (414) 277-7481
(800) 332-6763; Fax: (414) 277-7475

Full-time: 1486 men, 279 women	**Faculty:** 117; IIB, +$
Part-time: 414 men, 67 women	**Ph.D.s:** 55%
Graduate: 254 men, 63 women	**Student/Faculty:** 15 to 1
Year: quarters, summer session	**Tuition:** $20,835
Application Deadline: open	**Room & Board:** $4845
Freshman Class: 2093 applied, 1436 accepted, 488 enrolled	
SAT I Verbal/Math: 555/635	**ACT:** 26 **VERY COMPETITIVE+**

Milwaukee School of Engineering, established in 1903, is a private institution with programs in engineering, engineering technology, business, communication, and nursing. There are 5 undergraduate and 4 graduate schools. In addition to regional accreditation, MSOE has baccalaureate program accreditation with ABET, ACCE, and CCNE. The library contains 53,333 volumes, 74,254 microform items, and 1115 audiovisual forms/CDs, and subscribes to 468 periodicals. Computerized library services include the card catalog, interlibrary loans, and database searching. Special learning facilities include a learning resource center and radio station. The 14-acre campus is in an urban area in Milwaukee. Including residence halls, there are 11 buildings.

Student Life: 78% of undergraduates are from Wisconsin. Others are from 37 states and 26 foreign countries. 81% are from public schools. 88% are white. 45% are Catholic; 32% Protestant; 13% claim no religious affiliation. The average age of freshmen is 18; all undergraduates, 21. 23% do not continue beyond their first year; 55% remain to graduate.

Housing: 880 students can be accommodated in college housing, which includes coed dormitories and on-campus apartments. In addition, there are special-interest houses and suites for upperclassmen with kitchens, bathrooms, and living rooms. On-campus housing is guaranteed for all 4 years. 50% of students live on campus; of those, 60% remain on campus on weekends. All students may keep cars.

Activities: 8% of men and about 1% of women belong to 4 local and 2 national fraternities; 12% of women belong to 1 national and 2 local sororities. There are 61 groups on campus, including band, cheerleading, chess, computers, drama, ethnic, gaming, honors, international, jazz band, literary magazine, pep band, political, professional, radio and TV, religious, sci-fi, social, social service, student government, and yearbook. Popular campus events include St. Patrick's Week, Cultural Spirit Week, and Union Week.

Sports: There are 10 intercollegiate sports for men and 8 for women, and 6 intramural sports for men and 6 for women. Facilities include a gym, health club, and weight-lifting room.

Disabled Students: 75% of the campus is accessible. Wheelchair ramps, elevators, special parking, specially equipped rest rooms, special class scheduling, lowered drinking fountains, and lowered telephones are available.

Services: Counseling and information services are available, as is tutoring in every subject. There is a reader service for the blind, and remedial math, reading, and writing.

Campus Safety and Security: Measures include 24-hour foot and vehicle patrol, escort service, shuttle buses, and informal discussions. There are pamphlets/posters/films, emergency telephones, lighted pathways/sidewalks, and 24-hour security in resident halls.

Programs of Study: MSOE confers B.A. and B.S. degrees. Master's degrees are also awarded. Bachelor's degrees are awarded in BUSINESS (business administration and management, international business management, and management information systems), COMMUNICATIONS AND THE ARTS (technical and business writing), ENGINEERING AND ENVIRONMENTAL DESIGN (architectural engineering, biomedical engineering, computer engineering, construction management, electrical/electronics engineering, engineering technology, industrial engineering, mechanical engineering, and systems engineering), HEALTH PROFESSIONS (nursing). Biomedical engineering and computer engineering are the strongest academically. Architectural, mechanical, and electrical engineering are the largest.

Required: To graduate, students must complete 205 quarter credits with a minimum GPA of 2.0. There are requirements in speech, composition, computer programming, ethics, and business.

Special: MSOE offers summer internships in the student's discipline, study abroad in Germany, India, and the Czech Republic, on-campus work-study programs, and nondegree study. A 4-year engineering degree and a dual degree in engineering and business communication or technical communication, along with a 5-year dual degree with a bachelor's in engineering and a master's in environmental engineering, are available. There are 2 national honor societies.

Faculty/Classroom: 79% of faculty are male; 21%, female. All teach undergraduates, 2% do research, and 25% do both. No introductory courses are taught by graduate students. The average class size in an introductory lecture is 19; in a laboratory, 15; and in a regular course, 20.

Admissions: 69% of the 2001-2002 applicants were accepted. The SAT I scores for the 2001-2002 freshman class were: Verbal--24% below 500, 43% between 500 and 599, 28% between 600 and 700, and 5% above 700; Math--4% below 500, 22% between 500 and 599, 60% between 600 and 700, and 14% above 700. The ACT scores were 5% below 21, 24% between 21 and 23, 27% between 24 and 26, 20% between 27 and 28, and 24% above 28. 14% of the current freshmen were in the top fifth of their class; 85% were in the top two fifths. There was 1 National Merit finalist. 9 freshmen graduated first in their class.

Requirements: MSOE requires the ACT, although the SAT I is acceptable. In addition, applicants must be graduates of an accredited secondary school, having completed 15 academic credits, including 4 units of English, 2 units each of science and math, and 1 unit each of social studies and history. More units in math, science, and English are strongly advised; 1 unit in computer science is helpful. The GED is accepted. An essay is required, and an interview is recommended. A GPA of 2.5 is required. AP and CLEP credits are accepted. Important factors in the admissions decision are advanced placement or honor courses, leadership record, and personality/intangible qualities. MSOE accepts applications on computer disk using College View and ExPAN.

Procedure: Freshmen are admitted to all sessions. Application deadlines are open. The application fee is $25. Notification is on a rolling basis.

Transfer: 122 transfer students enrolled in 2001-2002. Applicants for transfer should have a minimum GPA of 2.5. 103 credits of 205 must be completed at MSOE.

Visiting: There are regularly scheduled orientations for prospective students, consisting of personal visits, spring and fall open houses, and the Shadow Program. There are guides for informal visits and visitors may sit in on classes and stay overnight. To schedule a visit, contact the Admission Office at *explore@msoe.edu*.

Financial Aid: In 2001-2002, 79% of all freshmen and 67% of continuing students received some form of financial aid. 74% of freshmen and 65% of continuing students received need-based aid. The average freshman award was $15,099. Of that total, scholarships or need-based grants averaged $4402 and loans averaged $5043. 46% of undergraduates work part time. Average annual earnings from campus work are $1500. The average financial indebtedness of the 2001 graduate was $25,000. The FAFSA is required. The fall application deadline is March 15.

International Students: There are 76 international students enrolled. The school actively recruits these students. They must score 500 on the written TOEFL and also take the SAT I or ACT. ACT is required for enrollment, not admission.

Computers: More than 150 PCs and terminals are located throughout the library, science building, and student center for student use. Students can also dial up the main computer center over the phone lines to access computer service. All new students (full-time) are required to be part of the computer technology package. This requires all students to have a laptop. All students may access the system. There are no time limits and no fees. All students are required to have personal computers. A Compaq is provided by MSOE.

Graduates: In 2001, 414 bachelor's degrees were awarded. The most popular majors were architectural engineering (18%), mechanical engineering (15%), and electrical engineering (14%). In an average class, 40% graduate in 4 years, and 95% in 5 years. 130 companies recruited on campus in 2000-2001. Of the 2000 graduating class, 6% were enrolled in graduate school within 6 months of graduation and 93% were employed.

Admissions Contact: Paul Borens, Director of Admission.
E-mail: *borens@msoe.edu* Web: *www.msoe.edu\admiss*

MOUNT MARY COLLEGE

Milwaukee, WI 53222 — E-4 — (414) 286-1219 — (800) 321-6265; Fax: (414) 256-0180

Full-time: 2 men, 525 women	**Faculty:** 66; IIB, --$
Part-time: 39 men, 514 women	**Ph.D.s:** 59%
Graduate: 8 men, 128 women	**Student/Faculty:** 8 to 1
Year: semesters, summer session	**Tuition:** $13,394
Application Deadline: August	**Room & Board:** $4630
Freshman Class: 187 applied, 163 accepted, 95 enrolled	
ACT: 21	**COMPETITIVE**

Mount Mary College, founded in 1913, is a private women's liberal arts institution affiliated with the Roman Catholic Church. In addition to regional accreditation, the college has baccalaureate program accreditation with ADA, CSWE, and FIDER. The library contains 114,500 volumes, 3500 microform items, and 9832 audiovisual forms/CDs, and subscribes to 450 periodicals. Computerized library services include the card catalog, interlibrary loans, and database searching. Special learning facilities include a learning resource center, art gallery, computer centers, CAD labs, and S.M.A.R.T. classrooms. The 80-acre campus is in a suburban area 7 miles west of downtown Milwaukee. Including residence halls, there are 7 buildings.

Student Life: 95% of undergraduates are from Wisconsin. Others are from 7 states and 8 foreign countries. 89% are from public schools. 75% are white; 16% African American. 51% are Catholic; 20% Protestant; 17% claim no religious affiliation. The average age of freshmen is 18; all undergraduates, 29. 32% do not continue beyond their first year; 60% remain to graduate.

Housing: 180 students can be accommodated in college housing, which includes single-sex dormitories. On-campus housing is available on a first-come, first-served basis and is available on a lottery system for upperclassmen. Priority is given to out-of-town students. 87% of students commute. Alcohol is not permitted. All students may keep cars.

Activities: There are no fraternities. There are 33 groups on campus, including art, choir, chorale, chorus, computers, dance, drama, ethnic, honors, international, literary magazine, newspaper, political, professional, religious, social, social service, student government, and yearbook. Popular campus events include Freshman Investiture, Madrigal Dinner, and All-School Christmas Dinner.

Sports: Facilities include a gym, a swimming pool, an exercise room, a weight room, a soccer field, and large recreational grounds.

Disabled Students: 98% of the campus is accessible. Wheelchair ramps, elevators, special parking, specially equipped rest rooms, lowered drinking fountains, and lowered telephones are available.

Services: Counseling and information services are available, as is tutoring in most subjects. There is a reader service for the blind, and remedial math, reading, and writing. A tutoring language lab is also available.

Campus Safety and Security: Measures include 24-hour foot and vehicle patrol, escort service, informal discussions, and pamphlets/posters/films. There are emergency telephones and lighted pathways/sidewalks.

Programs of Study: The college confers B.A. and B.S. degrees. Master's degrees are also awarded. Bachelor's degrees are awarded in BIOLOGICAL SCIENCE (biology/biological science), BUSINESS (accounting, business administration and management, and fashion merchandising), COMMUNICATIONS AND THE ARTS (communications, English, fine arts, French, graphic design, music, public relations, Spanish, and technical and business writing), COMPUTER AND PHYSICAL SCIENCE (chemistry, computer science, and mathematics), EDUCATION (art, bilingual/bicultural, business, early childhood, elementary, foreign languages, music, science, and secondary), ENGINEERING AND ENVIRONMENTAL DESIGN (food services technology, and interior design), HEALTH PROFESSIONS (art therapy, occupational therapy, predentistry, and premedicine), SOCIAL SCIENCE (behavioral science, criminal justice, dietetics, fashion design and technology, history, international studies, philosophy, prelaw, psychology, social work, and theological studies). Business administration, teacher education, and fashion design are the largest.

Required: To graduate, students must complete 128 credit hours, including at least 24 (but as many as 74) in the major, while maintaining a GPA of at least 2.0, with many majors requiring a higher GPA. A 48-credit liberal arts core curriculum and demonstrated math competency are required.

Special: Mount Mary College offers internships, a Washington semester, accelerated degree programs in business administration, business/professional communication, and marketing, and study abroad in Japan and other countries. Student-designed majors, pass/fail options, and credit for life, military, and work experience are available. There are 8 national honor societies and a freshman honors program.

Faculty/Classroom: 20% of faculty are male; 80%, female. 96% teach undergraduates. No introductory courses are taught by graduate students. The average class size in an introductory lecture is 24; in a laboratory, 16; and in a regular course, 16.

Admissions: 87% of the 2001-2002 applicants were accepted. The ACT scores for the 2001-2002 freshman class were: 51% below 21, 27% between 21 and 23, 20% between 24 and 26, and 2% between 27 and 28. 25% of the current freshmen were in the top fifth of their class; 51% were in the top two fifths.

Requirements: The SAT I or ACT is required. In addition, applicants must be graduates of an accredited secondary school. The GED is accepted. Students should have completed 16 credits, including 4 each in English, history, social sciences, and foreign language, and 2 each in math and science. An interview is recommended. The college requires applicants to be in the upper 50% of their class. A GPA of 2.3 is required. AP and CLEP credits are accepted. Important factors in the admissions decision are advanced placement or honor courses, recommendations by school officials, and leadership record. Applications are accepted on-line at the college's web site.

Procedure: Freshmen are admitted fall and spring. Entrance exams should be taken in the junior year or fall of the senior year. There is a deferred admissions plan. Applications should be filed by August for fall entry and December for spring entry, along with a $25 fee. Notification is sent on a rolling basis.

Transfer: 93 transfer students enrolled in 2001-2002. Applicants should have a minimum GPA of 2.0, though each department has its own admission requirements. The school recommends either the SAT I or ACT and an interview. 32 credits of 128 must be completed at the college.

Visiting: There are regularly scheduled orientations for prospective students, including tours, meetings with faculty and staff, and information sessions. There are guides for informal visits and visitors may sit in on classes and stay overnight. To schedule a visit, contact the Enrollment Office at (414) 256-1219.

Financial Aid: In 2001-2002, 97% of all freshmen and 84% of continuing students received some form of financial aid. 85% of freshmen and 72% of continuing students received need-based aid. The average freshman award was $10,430. Of that total, scholarships or need-based grants averaged $6995 ($13,234 maximum); loans averaged $3339 ($6625 maximum); work contracts averaged $1776 ($2200 maximum); and college grants averaged $2871 ($7500 maximum). 16% of undergraduates work part time. Average annual earnings from campus work are $968. The average financial indebtedness of the 2001 graduate was $22,366. The college is a member of CSS. The FAFSA is required. The priority application deadline is March 1.

International Students: There are 9 international students enrolled. The school actively recruits these students. They must score 500 on the written TOEFL or 173 on the electronic version and also take the SAT I or the ACT.
Computers: The mainframe is a DEC ALPHA 2100. The computer center has 86 PCs that are available to students. These and other PCs in the library and some classrooms and dorms provide access to a Novell server. In addition, a CAD classroom can accommodate 20 students. Students have access to the Internet, e-mail, library, and dial-in e-mail off campus. All students may access the system 80 hours per week, except in residence hall labs, which are open 7 days a week, 24 hours a day. There are no time limits and no fees.
Graduates: In 2001, 182 bachelor's degrees were awarded. The most popular majors were occupational therapy (27%), business adminstration (12%), and interior design (9%). In an average class, 40% graduate in 4 years, 60% in 5 years, and 63% in 6 years. Of the 2000 graduating class, 6% were enrolled in graduate school within 6 months of graduation and 67% were employed.
Admissions Contact: Amy Dobson, Director of Enrollment. A video is available. E-mail: *admiss@mtmary.edu* Web: *www.mtmary.edu*

MOUNT SENARIO COLLEGE — B-2
Ladysmith, WI 54848 — [illegible]715) 532-5511, ext. 1108
[illegible]4; Fax: (715) 532-7690

CLOSED

Full-time: 206 men, 172 women [illegible]
Part-time: 190 men, 104 [illegible] [illegible]5%
Graduate: none — [illegible]udent/Faculty: 11 to 1
Year: semesters, [illegible] — **Tuition:** $12,800
Application Deadli[illegible] — **Room & Board:** $4950
Freshman Class: 31[illegible]plied, 219 accepted, 109 enrolled
SAT I Verbal/Math: 380/470 — **ACT:** 20 — **COMPETITIVE**

Mount Senario College, established in 1962, is a private liberal arts college offering undergraduate programs in the arts and sciences, business, education, science, and social sciences. The 2 libraries contain 40,682 volumes, 6694 microform items, and 221 audiovisual forms/CDs, and subscribe to 128 periodicals. Computerized library services include interlibrary loans. Special learning facilities include an art gallery. The 120-acre campus is in a rural area 65 miles north of Eau Claire.
Student Life: 86% of undergraduates are from Wisconsin. Others are from 13 states, 20 foreign countries, and Canada. 75% are white; 12% African American. The average age of freshmen is 20; all undergraduates, 25. 30% do not continue beyond their first year; 35% remain to graduate.
Housing: 250 students can be accommodated in college housing, which includes coed dormitories and on-campus apartments. In addition, there are modular housing units. On-campus housing is available on a first-come, first-served basis. Priority is given to out-of-town students. 55% of students commute. All students may keep cars.
Activities: There are no fraternities or sororities. There are 14 groups on campus, including art, cheerleading, drama, ethnic, gay, honors, international, newspaper, photography, religious, social, social service, and student government. Popular campus events include Winter Carnival, Performing Arts Series, and Spring Fling.
Sports: There are 5 intercollegiate sports for men and 5 for women, and 10 intramural sports for men and 9 for women. Facilities include football, soccer, softball, and baseball fields, community golf, bowling, tennis courts, downhill and cross-country skiing facilities, hiking trails, and lakes and rivers.
Disabled Students: 50% of the campus is accessible. Elevators and special parking are available.
Services: Counseling and information services are available, as is tutoring in every subject. There is remedial math, reading, and writing.
Campus Safety and Security: Measures include escort service, informal discussions, pamphlets/posters/films, and lighted pathways/sidewalks.
Programs of Study: MSC confers B.A. and B.S. degrees. Associate degrees are also awarded. Bachelor's degrees are awarded in BIOLOGICAL SCIENCE (biology/biological science), BUSINESS (accounting and business administration and management), COMMUNICATIONS AND THE ARTS (English), COMPUTER AND PHYSICAL SCIENCE (mathematics), EDUCATION (art, elementary, music, science, and secondary), SOCIAL SCIENCE (criminal justice, history, psychology, social science, and social work). Education is the strongest academically. Business and criminal justice are the largest.
Required: Students must complete 128 credits with a varying number in the major and must maintain a minimum GPA of 2.0. There are phys ed and general education requirements and a writing competency exam.
Special: MSC offers internships, dual majors, and B.A.-B.S. degrees. Study abroad is available through HECUA; the country varies with the semester. Credit for life experience and pass/fail options are possible. There is 1 national honor society and 2 departmental honors programs.
Faculty/Classroom: 62% of faculty are male; 38%, female. All teach undergraduates. The average class size in an introductory lecture is 20 and in a laboratory, 10.
Admissions: 70% of the 2001-2002 applicants were accepted. The SAT I scores for the 2001-2002 freshman class were: Verbal--100% below 500; Math--88% below 500, and 13% between 500 and 599. 14% of the current freshmen were in the top quarter of their class; 37% were in the top half.
Requirements: The SAT I or ACT is required; the ACT is preferred, with a minimum composite score of 15 on the ACT needed. Graduation from an accredited secondary school is required; the GED is accepted. Applicants must submit 16 academic credits, including 4 years of English, 2 of math, and 1 of science. An essay, portfolio and audition, where appropriate, and interview are recommended. MSC requires applicants to be in the upper 50% of their class. A GPA of 2.0 is required. AP and CLEP credits are accepted. Important factors in the admissions decision are recommendations by school officials, personality/intangible qualities, and leadership record. Applications are accepted on-line via CollegeNET.
Procedure: Freshmen are admitted to all sessions. Entrance exams should be taken on or before the June ACT date of the senior year. Application deadlines are open. The application fee is $10. Notification is sent on a rolling basis.
Transfer: 28 transfer students enrolled in 2001-2002. Applicants must have maintained a minimum GPA of 2.0 in courses totaling 30 credits and must submit 2 letters of recommendation. 32 credits of 128 must be completed at MSC.
Visiting: There are regularly scheduled orientations for prospective students, including a tour and meetings with admissions, financial aid, professors, students, student support services if needed, and coaches. There are guides for informal visits and visitors may sit in on classes and stay overnight. To schedule a visit, contact the Campus Visit Counselor.
Financial Aid: The average freshman award for the 2001-2002 school year was $11,599. 51% of undergraduates work part time. Average annual earnings from campus work are $1000. The average financial indebtedness of the 2001 graduate was $16,470. The FAFSA is required. The fall application deadline is April 15.
International Students: There were 47 international students enrolled in a recent year. The school actively recruits these students. They must score 500 on the written TOEFL and also take the MELAB.
Computers: The mainframe is a Windows NT network. There are 18 Pentium-based workstations plus an identical instructor workstation in 1 computer lab; another lab has 18 Pentiums. There is a Mac lab of 10 networked workstations and 1 minilab (3 Pentiums) in the residence hall. The library has 10 Pentiums. There is direct-network Internet access. All students may access the system 8 A.M. to midnight 7 days a week during the semester. There are no time limits and no fees.
Graduates: In 2001, 199 bachelor's degrees were awarded. The most popular majors were protective services/public administration (60%), business/marketing (17%), and education (12%).
Admissions Contact: Ron Cronacher, Dean of Enrollment Management. E-mail: *admissions@mountsenario.edu*
Web: *www.mountsenario.edu*

NORTHLAND COLLEGE — B-1
Ashland, WI 54806 — (715) 682-1224
(800) 753-1840; Fax: (715) 682-1258

Full-time: 350 men, 450 women	**Faculty:** 42; IIB, -$
Part-time: none	**Ph.D.s:** 58%
Graduate: none	**Student/Faculty:** 19 to 1
Year: , summer session	**Tuition:** $16,600
Application Deadline: see profile	**Room & Board:** $4835
Freshman Class: n/av	
SAT I Verbal/Math: 576/561	**ACT:** 24 — **COMPETITIVE+**

Northland College, founded in 1892, is an independent liberal arts institution affiliated with the United Church of Christ and offers undergraduate programs in the arts and sciences, business, education, health professions, and social sciences. The figures given in the above capsule are approximate. The library contains 77,700 volumes and 9300 microform items, and subscribes to 350 periodicals. Computerized library services include the card catalog, interlibrary loans, and database searching. Special learning facilities include a learning resource center, art gallery, natural history museum, and environmental research acreage. The 80-acre campus is in a small town 70 miles east of Duluth, Minnesota. Including residence halls, there are 20 buildings.
Student Life: 65% of undergraduates are from out of state, mostly the Midwest. Others are from 45 states, 11 foreign countries, and Canada. 90% are from public schools. 89% are white. The average age of freshmen is 22; all undergraduates, 21. 34% do not continue beyond their first year; 42% remain to graduate.
Housing: 530 students can be accommodated in college housing, which includes single-sex and coed dormitories and on-campus apartments. In addition, there are special-interest houses. On-campus housing is guaranteed for all 4 years. 63% of students live on campus; of those, 80% remain on campus on weekends. Alcohol is not permitted. All students may keep cars.

Activities: 2% of men belong to 1 local fraternity and 1 national fraternity; 2% of women belong to 2 local sororities. There are 20 groups on campus, including art, band, cheerleading, choir, chorale, chorus, computers, drama, ethnic, gay, honors, international, jazz band, literary magazine, newspaper, orchestra, photography, political, professional, religious, social, social service, student government, symphony, and yearbook. Popular campus events include Snow Festival, Parents Weekend, and Spring Fling.

Sports: There are 4 intercollegiate sports for men and 4 for women, and 11 intramural sports for men and 11 for women. Facilities include an Olympic-size pool, a weight-lifting room, tennis and racquetball courts, and an outdoor recreation program.

Disabled Students: 90% of the campus is accessible. Wheelchair ramps, elevators, special parking, specially equipped rest rooms, and special class scheduling are available.

Services: Counseling and information services are available, as is tutoring in every subject. There is a reader service for the blind, and remedial math, reading, and writing.

Campus Safety and Security: Measures include escort service, informal discussions, pamphlets/posters/films, and emergency telephones. There are lighted pathways/sidewalks.

Programs of Study: Northland confers B.A. and B.S. degrees. Bachelor's degrees are awarded in AGRICULTURE (natural resource management), BIOLOGICAL SCIENCE (biology/biological science), BUSINESS (business administration and management and business economics), COMMUNICATIONS AND THE ARTS (creative writing, English, and fine arts), COMPUTER AND PHYSICAL SCIENCE (atmospheric sciences and meteorology, chemistry, earth science, information sciences and systems, and mathematics), EDUCATION (elementary, middle school, music, and secondary), ENGINEERING AND ENVIRONMENTAL DESIGN (environmental science), SOCIAL SCIENCE (history, parks and recreation management, peace studies, psychology, public administration, religion, and sociology). Biology, chemistry, and environmental studies are the strongest academically. Biology, business, and teacher education are the largest.

Required: Students must complete 124 credits, including 30 to 56 in the major, with a minimum GPA of 2.0. All students must meet requirements that include courses in English composition, literature, history, philosophy, social and natural sciences, physical science, fine arts, phys ed, and studies of other cultures.

Special: Opportunities are provided for cooperative programs in many majors and with other schools, internships, work-study programs with state and federal agencies, student-designed majors, credit for life experience, pass/fail options, and study abroad in 5 countries. Cross-registration is offered with Spring Term Consortium Schools, Allegheny and Beloit Colleges, and Kansai Gaidai University in Japan. 3-2 engineering degrees are available in conjunction with Michigan Technological University and Wahington University in St. Louis. A 3-2 degree program in forestry is also available. There are 2 national honor societies.

Faculty/Classroom: 76% of faculty are male; 24%, female. All teach undergraduates. The average class size in an introductory lecture is 45; in a laboratory, 22; and in a regular course, 25.

Admissions: The SAT I scores for the 2001-2002 freshman class were: Verbal--22% below 500, 33% between 500 and 599, 36% between 600 and 700, and 9% above 700; Math--20% below 500, 45% between 500 and 599, 31% between 600 and 700, and 4% above 700. The ACT scores were 22% below 21, 30% between 21 and 23, 20% between 24 and 26, 16% between 27 and 28, and 12% above 28. 40% of the current freshmen were in the top fifth of their class; 70% were in the top two fifths.

Requirements: The SAT I or ACT is required. In addition, graduation from an accredited secondary school is required; the GED is accepted. An essay and interview are recommended. A GPA of 2.0 is required. AP and CLEP credits are accepted. Important factors in the admissions decision are advanced placement or honor courses, extracurricular activities record, and recommendations by school officials.

Procedure: Freshmen are admitted fall and winter. Entrance exams should be taken in the fall. There are early decision, early admissions, and deferred admissions plans. Check with the school for current deadlines.

Transfer: Applicants must have maintained a minimum GPA of 2.0 in previously attended colleges. 30 credits of 124 must be completed at Northland.

Visiting: There are regularly scheduled orientations for prospective students, including an interview, a tour, class visits, and an overnight stay in a dorm. There are guides for informal visits and visitors may sit in on classes and stay overnight. To schedule a visit, contact the Admissions Office.

Financial Aid: In 2000-2001, 85% of freshmen received need-based aid. 90% of undergraduates work part time. Average annual earnings from campus work are $1200. Northland is a member of CSS. The FAFSA and the college's own financial statement are required. Check with the school for current deadlines.

International Students: The school actively recruits these students. They must score 500 on the written TOEFL or 195 on the electronic version or take the MELAB.

Computers: The mainframes are a Prime and a DEC VAX. Students have nearly unlimited use of the Prime and PCs. PCs are located in classrooms, labs, the computer center, and some residence halls. All students may access the system. There are no time limits and no fees.

Graduates: In an average class, 2% graduate in 3 years.

Admissions Contact: Eric A. Peterson, Director of Admissions. A video is available. E-mail: *admit@northland.edu*
Web: *www.northland.edu*

RIPON COLLEGE — D-4
Ripon, WI 54971 — (920) 748-8185
(800) 94-RIPON; Fax: (920) 748-8335

Full-time: 415 men, 468 women	**Faculty:** 57; IIB, av$
Part-time: 10 men, 13 women	**Ph.D.s:** 96%
Graduate: none	**Student/Faculty:** 15 to 1
Year: semesters	**Tuition:** $19,500
Application Deadline: August 1	**Room & Board:** $4680
Freshman Class: 847 applied, 710 accepted, 200 enrolled	
SAT I Verbal/Math: 577/604	**ACT:** 24 **VERY COMPETITIVE+**

Ripon College, established in 1851, is a private, residential, liberal arts institution affiliated with the United Church of Christ. The library contains 164,378 volumes, 18,660 microform items, and 6000 audiovisual forms/CDs, and subscribes to 800 periodicals. Computerized library services include the card catalog, interlibrary loans, and database searching. Special learning facilities include a learning resource center, art gallery, radio station, music library, art slide library, and college archives. The 250-acre campus is in a small town 80 miles north of Milwaukee in the east-central part of the state. Including residence halls, there are 26 buildings.

Student Life: 68% of undergraduates are from Wisconsin. Others are from 33 states and 17 foreign countries. 57% are from public schools. 89% are white. The average age of freshmen is 18; all undergraduates, 20. 12% do not continue beyond their first year; 64% remain to graduate.

Housing: 940 students can be accommodated in college housing, which includes single-sex and coed dormitories and fraternity houses. Theme and interest groups may form living areas in the residence halls. On-campus housing is guaranteed for all 4 years. 94% of students live on campus; of those, 90% remain on campus on weekends. All students may keep cars.

Activities: 59% of men belong to 2 local and 3 national fraternities; 33% of women belong to 2 national sororities. There are 80 groups on campus, including art, cheerleading, chess, choir, chorale, chorus, computers, drama, ethnic, forensics, gay, honors, international, jazz band, literary magazine, musical theater, newspaper, orchestra, photography, political, professional, radio and TV, religious, social, social service, student government, and symphony. Popular campus events include Spring and Winter Festivals, Milwaukee Symphony concerts, and theater events.

Sports: There are 10 intercollegiate sports for men and 9 for women, and 19 intramural sports for men and 17 for women. Facilities include a phys ed center, 2 fields, tennis courts, a recreation center, and an exercise room. The campus is within 5 miles of lakes and cross-country skiing opportunities.

Disabled Students: 50% of the campus is accessible. Wheelchair ramps, elevators, special parking, specially equipped rest rooms, special class scheduling, and lowered drinking fountains are available.

Services: Counseling and information services are available, as is tutoring in every subject. Tutoring and services are also available for learning-disabled students.

Campus Safety and Security: Measures include 24-hour foot and vehicle patrol, escort service, informal discussions, and pamphlets/posters/films. There are emergency telephones, lighted pathways/sidewalks, and a paging system.

Programs of Study: Ripon College confers the A.B. degree. Bachelor's degrees are awarded in BIOLOGICAL SCIENCE (biochemistry and biology/biological science), BUSINESS (business administration and management), COMMUNICATIONS AND THE ARTS (art history and appreciation, dramatic arts, English, French, German, music, Spanish, and speech/debate/rhetoric), COMPUTER AND PHYSICAL SCIENCE (chemistry, computer science, mathematics, and physics), EDUCATION (early childhood, elementary, middle school, physical, and secondary), ENGINEERING AND ENVIRONMENTAL DESIGN (environmental science), SOCIAL SCIENCE (anthropology, economics, history, international studies, Latin American studies, philosophy, political science/government, psychobiology, psychology, religion, and sociology). Biology, chemistry, and physics are the strongest academically. Economics, education, and business management are the largest.

Required: To graduate, students must complete 124 credit hours, including usually 24 in the major, with a minimum GPA of 2.0. Students must take 6 credits each in behavioral and social sciences, fine arts, humanities, natural sciences/math, and global studies. Also required are a third-semester competency in a foreign language, English literature and composition, a writing-intensive course in any department, and 2 credits in phys ed. A thesis is required or recommended for certain majors. There is a senior seminar with a research project and presentation of results.

Special: Students may cross-register with the Associated Colleges of the Midwest. Internships, study abroad in 13 countries and study through 7 domestic programs, and a Washington semester are available. The college offers a 3-year degree in all areas, dual and student-designed majors, and pass/fail options. A 3-2 engineering degree is available with Rensselaer Polytechnic Institute, Washington University, and the University of Minnesota; other 3-2 programs are in environmental studies and in forestry with Duke University and in social welfare with the University of Chicago. A 2-2 nursing program is possible with Rush University. There are 11 national honor societies, including Phi Beta Kappa, and a freshman honors program.

Faculty/Classroom: 64% of faculty are male; 36%, female. All teach undergraduates and do research. The average class size in an introductory lecture is 28; in a laboratory, 15; and in a regular course, 16.

Admissions: 84% of the 2001-2002 applicants were accepted. The SAT I scores for the 2001-2002 freshman class were: Verbal--20% below 500, 32% between 500 and 599, 44% between 600 and 700, and 4% above 700; Math--12% below 500, 32% between 500 and 599, 44% between 600 and 700, and 12% above 700. The ACT scores were 23% below 21, 27% between 21 and 23, 25% between 24 and 26, 13% between 27 and 28, and 12% above 28. 48% of the current freshmen were in the top fifth of their class; 77% were in the top two fifths. 2 freshmen graduated first in their class.

Requirements: The SAT I or ACT is required. In addition, applicants must be graduates of an accredited secondary school. The GED is accepted. Applicants should complete at least 17 Carnegie units including 4 of English, 2 to 4 each of math, social studies, and natural sciences, and up to 7 of other college-preparatory electives. An essay may be required, and an interview is recommended. Ripon College requires applicants to be in the upper 50% of their class. A GPA of 2.0 is required. AP and CLEP credits are accepted. Important factors in the admissions decision are advanced placement or honor courses, leadership record, and extracurricular activities record. Applications are accepted on-line via Common App, CollegeLink, and Ripon's web site.

Procedure: Freshmen are admitted fall and spring. Entrance exams should be taken in the junior year or fall of the senior year. There is a deferred admissions plan. Applications should be filed by August 1 for fall entry and December 15 for spring entry, along with a $30 fee. Notification is sent on a rolling basis.

Transfer: 17 transfer students enrolled in 2001-2002. Applicants must have a minimum 2.0 GPA and be in good standing at their previous college. The SAT I or ACT, a personal statement, and an interview are recommended. 32 credits of 124 must be completed at Ripon College.

Visiting: There are regularly scheduled orientations for prospective students, including a tour, an interview, meetings with professors and coaches, class visits, and an overnight stay. There are guides for informal visits and visitors may sit in on classes and stay overnight. To schedule a visit, contact the Admission Office at *adminfo@ripon.edu*.

Financial Aid: In 2001-2002, 99% of all freshmen and 97% of continuing students received some form of financial aid. 85% of freshmen and 75% of continuing students received need-based aid. The average freshman award was $18,964. Of that total, scholarships or need-based grants averaged $14,143 ($22,140 maximum); loans averaged $3000 ($4000 maximum); and work contracts averaged $1200 ($2000 maximum). 56% of undergraduates work part time. Average annual earnings from campus work are $700. The average financial indebtedness of the 2001 graduate was $10,019. Ripon College is a member of CSS. The FAFSA is required. The fall application deadline is March 15.

International Students: There are 15 international students enrolled. The school actively recruits these students. They must score 600 on the written TOEFL and also take the SAT I if available.

Computers: The mainframe is an NT-based server farm. Our NT server farm is located in the Kemper Computer Center and is accessible via all computers on campus. There are approximately 100 PCs and Macs installed in 7 computer labs located around the campus. Each residence hall room is wired to accept students' PCs. All students may access the system. There are no time limits and no fees.

Graduates: In 2001, 145 bachelor's degrees were awarded. The most popular majors were business management (15%), phys ed (9%), and history/psychology (9%). In an average class, 1% graduate in 3 years, 55% in 4 years, 65% in 5 years, and 66% in 6 years. 20 companies recruited on campus in 2000-2001. Of the 2000 graduating class, 30% were enrolled in graduate school within 6 months of graduation and 59% were employed.

Admissions Contact: Scott J. Goplin, Vice President and Dean of Admission and Financial Aid. A video is available.
E-mail: *goplins@ripon.edu* Web: *www.ripon.edu*

SAINT NORBERT COLLEGE — D-3

De Pere, WI 54115 — (920) 403-3005
(800) 236-4878; Fax: (920) 403-4072

Full-time: 839 men, 1132 women	**Faculty:** 115
Part-time: 39 men, 49 women	**Ph.D.s:** 92%
Graduate: 7 men, 65 women	**Student/Faculty:** 17 to 1
Year: semesters, summer session	**Tuition:** $18,007
Application Deadline: open	**Room & Board:** $5162

Freshman Class: 1603 applied, 1347 accepted, 558 enrolled
SAT I or ACT: required — **VERY COMPETITIVE**

Saint Norbert College, founded in 1898, is a Roman Catholic, private institution sponsored by the Norbertine Order. The college offers bachelor's degrees in the arts, the sciences, and business administration. A world-focused curriculum emphasizes career preparation, leadership, and service within the liberal arts and sciences. The library contains 192,533 volumes, 28,719 microform items, and 7802 audiovisual forms/CDs, and subscribes to 708 periodicals. Computerized library services include the card catalog, interlibrary loans, and database searching. Special learning facilities include a learning resource center, art gallery, radio station, TV station, language labs, media center with satellite hookup, observatory, 3 theaters, environmental sciences research craft, and international center. The 89-acre campus is in a suburban area 5 miles south of Green Bay. Including residence halls, there are 39 buildings.

Student Life: 70% of undergraduates are from Wisconsin. Others are from 27 states, 29 foreign countries, and Canada. 80% are from public schools. 93% are white. 78% are Catholic; 25% claim no religious affiliation. The average age of freshmen is 18; all undergraduates, 20. 18% do not continue beyond their first year; 70% remain to graduate.

Housing: 1574 students can be accommodated in college housing, which includes single-sex and coed dormitories and on-campus apartments. In addition, there are special-interest houses, a townhouse complex, a living center, and off-campus houses. On-campus housing is guaranteed for all 4 years. 79% of students live on campus; of those, 75% remain on campus on weekends. All students may keep cars.

Activities: 25% of men belong to 3 local and 3 national fraternities; 25% of women belong to 3 local and 2 national sororities. There are 30 groups on campus, including art, band, cheerleading, choir, chorale, chorus, computers, dance, drama, drill team, environmental, ethnic, honors, international, jazz band, literary magazine, musical theater, opera, orchestra, pep band, political, professional, radio and TV, religious, social, social service, student government, symphony, and yearbook. Popular campus events include Winter Carnival, Global Ecology Series, and Guest Artists (including the Milwaukee Symphony).

Sports: There are 9 intercollegiate sports for men and 9 for women, and 6 intramural sports for men and 6 for women. Facilities include a 3100-seat stadium, a sports complex, a 2500-seat sports center, and an activity center.

Disabled Students: 70% of the campus is accessible. Wheelchair ramps, elevators, special parking, specially equipped rest rooms, special class scheduling, lowered drinking fountains, lowered telephones, and special residence hall rooms and on-campus apartments are available.

Services: Counseling and information services are available, as is tutoring in most subjects. There is a reader service for the blind, and remedial math, reading, and writing.

Campus Safety and Security: Measures include 24-hour foot and vehicle patrol, self-defense education, escort service, and informal discussions. There are pamphlets/posters/films, emergency telephones, lighted pathways/sidewalks, and an annual lighting assessment tour of the campus by students and staff, motorist assistance, and a crime prevention program.

Programs of Study: St. Norbert confers B.A., B.S., B.B.A., and B.Mus. degrees. Master's degrees are also awarded. Bachelor's degrees are awarded in BIOLOGICAL SCIENCE (biology/biological science), BUSINESS (accounting, business administration and management, international business management, and international economics), COMMUNICATIONS AND THE ARTS (art, communications, English, fine arts, French, German, graphic design, music, and Spanish), COMPUTER AND PHYSICAL SCIENCE (chemistry, computer science, geology, information sciences and systems, mathematics, natural sciences, and physics), EDUCATION (early childhood, elementary, and music), ENGINEERING AND ENVIRONMENTAL DESIGN (environmental science and preengineering), HEALTH PROFESSIONS (medical laboratory technology), SOCIAL SCIENCE (economics, history, humanities, international studies, philosophy, political science/government, psychology, religion, and sociology). Business administration, communications, and elementary education are the largest.

Required: To graduate, students must complete 128 credits with at least a 2.0 GPA. There are general education requirements in the areas of religious heritage, human nature, human relationships, natural world, creative expression, United States heritage, foreign heritages, quantitative skills, Western tradition, global society, a writing-intensive course, and Senior Colloquium.

Special: Cross-registration with the University of Wisconsin-Green Bay, internships, study abroad in 23 countries, a Washington semester, and work-study programs are available. The college offers dual and student-designed majors; nondegree study; distance learning; and limited credit for life, military, and work experience. The Leadership and Service Program and leadership minor help students improve their leadership abilities through courses and activities. There are 9 national honor societies and a freshman honors program.

Faculty/Classroom: 67% of faculty are male; 33%, female. All teach undergraduates, 85% do research, and 85% do both. No introductory courses are taught by graduate students. The average class size in an introductory lecture is 22; in a laboratory, 14; and in a regular course, 25.

Admissions: 84% of the 2001-2002 applicants were accepted. The ACT scores for the 2001-2002 freshman class were: 14% below 21, 30% between 21 and 23, 31% between 24 and 26, 14% between 27 and 28, and 10% above 28. 48% of the current freshmen were in the top fifth of their class; 78% were in the top two fifths. There were 3 National Merit semifinalists. 35 freshmen graduated first in their class.

Requirements: The SAT I or ACT is required. In addition, the recommended minimum composite score for the SAT I is 900 (450 verbal, 450 math) and for the ACT, 20. Applicants must be graduates of an accredited secondary school. The GED is accepted. Students should complete 4 years of high school English; 3 years of math, history or social studies, and natural science; and a recommended 2 years of foreign language. The school requires an essay and a recommendation, and recommends an interview. St. Norbert requires applicants to be in the upper 50% of their class. AP and CLEP credits are accepted. Important factors in the admissions decision are advanced placement or honor courses, extracurricular activities record, and recommendations by school officials. Online applications can be filed on the St. Norbert web site or via the Apply Yourself application network.

Procedure: Freshmen are admitted to all sessions. Entrance exams should be taken by the end of the junior year. There are early decision, early admissions, rolling admissions, and deferred admissions plans. Application deadlines are open. 51 early decision candidates were accepted for the 2001-2002 class. The fall 2001 application fee was $25.

Transfer: 57 transfer students enrolled in 2001-2002. Applicants should have a minimum GPA of 2.5 and must submit college transcripts. They must also be in good academic standing at their previous college. 32 credits of 128 must be completed at St. Norbert.

Visiting: There are regularly scheduled orientations for prospective students, including preregistrations, meetings with advisers, and meetings regarding programming and activities, housing, and student life. There are guides for informal visits and visitors may sit in on classes and stay overnight. To schedule a visit, contact the Office of Admissions.

Financial Aid: In 2001-2002, 98% of all freshmen and 94% of continuing students received some form of financial aid. 65% of freshmen and 66% of continuing students received need-based aid. The average freshman award was $14,176. Of that total, scholarships or need-based grants averaged $8847; loans averaged $3090; and work contracts averaged $1068. 57% of undergraduates work part time. Average annual earnings from campus work are $1460. The average financial indebtedness of the 2001 graduate was $16,715. St. Norbert is a member of CSS. The FAFSA, the college's own financial statement, and tax returns are required. The fall application deadline is March 1.

International Students: There are 56 international students enrolled. The school actively recruits these students. They must score 550 on the written TOEFL and also take the SAT I or the ACT.

Computers: 13 labs containing 135 IBM PCs and 45 Macs are available for student use. The labs are connected to the campus network, which provides access to a wide variety of software, high-quality laser printers central computing facilities, and the library automation system. Classrooms and auditoriums are connected to the campus network and have access to campus-wide video service. All students may access the system during the semester as needed or as required by the instructor. There are no time limits and no fees.

Graduates: In 2001, 424 bachelor's degrees were awarded. The most popular majors were business administration (23%), communication/media/theater (11%), and elementary education (8%). In an average class, 70% graduate in 6 years. 52 companies recruited on campus in 2000-2001. Of the 2000 graduating class, 18% were enrolled in graduate school within 6 months of graduation and 85% were employed.

Admissions Contact: Daniel L. Meyer, Dean of Admission and Enrollment Management. E-mail: *daniel.meyer@snc.edu* Web: *www.snc.edu*

SILVER LAKE COLLEGE OF THE HOLY FAMILY E-3

Manitowoc, WI 54220 (920) 686-6187
(800) 236-4752, ext. 175; Fax: (920) 684-7082

Full-time: 49 men, 214 women	**Faculty:** 39; IIB, --$
Part-time: 134 men, 266 women	**Ph.D.s:** 39%
Graduate: 84 men, 173 women	**Student/Faculty:** 7 to 1
Year: semesters, summer session	**Tuition:** $13,016
Application Deadline: open	**Room & Board:** $2500

Freshman Class: 72 applied, 64 accepted, 35 enrolled
SAT I or ACT: required **LESS COMPETITIVE**

Silver Lake College of the Holy Family, formerly Silver Lake College, founded in 1935, is a private Catholic liberal arts institution offering undergraduate and graduate programs. There are 3 graduate schools. In addition to regional accreditation, Silver Lake has baccalaureate program accreditation with NASM. The library contains 59,043 volumes, 2149 microform items, and 12,432 audiovisual forms/CDs, and subscribes to 295 periodicals. Computerized library services include the card catalog, interlibrary loans, and database searching. Special learning facilities include a learning resource center and a special education clinic used for the training of special education teachers. The 30-acre campus is in a rural area 4 miles west of Manitowoc.There is 1 building.

Student Life: 99% of undergraduates are from Wisconsin. Others are from 4 states and 1 foreign country. 89% are from public schools. 95% are white. The average age of freshmen is 19; all undergraduates, 31. 18% do not continue beyond their first year; 50% remain to graduate.

Housing: 30 students can be accommodated in college housing, which includes coed off-campus apartments. On-campus housing is guaranteed for the freshman year only. 97% of students commute. Alcohol is not permitted. All students may keep cars.

Activities: There are no fraternities or sororities. There are 18 groups on campus, including art, band, choir, chorus, computers, dance, drama, honors, jazz band, literary magazine, newspaper, orchestra, professional, religious, and student government. Popular campus events include Fine Arts Series, campus ministry programs, and Parents Day.

Sports: There is 1 intercollegiate sport for women, and 2 intramural sports for men and 2 for women. Facilities include a YMCA and the Two Rivers and Manitowoc Recreation Department.

Disabled Students: 95% of the campus is accessible. Wheelchair ramps, elevators, special parking, specially equipped rest rooms, and special class scheduling are available.

Services: Counseling and information services are available, as is tutoring in every subject, including study groups as needed. There is a reader service for the blind and remedial reading and writing.

Campus Safety and Security: Measures include self-defense education, informal discussions, pamphlets/posters/films, and emergency telephones. There are lighted pathways/sidewalks.

Programs of Study: Silver Lake confers B.A., B.S., B.B.A., and B.M. degrees. Associate and master's degrees are also awarded. Bachelor's degrees are awarded in BIOLOGICAL SCIENCE (biology/biological science), BUSINESS (accounting, business administration and management, human resources, and personnel management), COMMUNICATIONS AND THE ARTS (English, fine arts, music, and studio art), COMPUTER AND PHYSICAL SCIENCE (computer science and mathematics), EDUCATION (art, early childhood, elementary, music, secondary, and special), ENGINEERING AND ENVIRONMENTAL DESIGN (engineering technology, manufacturing engineering, and manufacturing technology), SOCIAL SCIENCE (history, psychology, public administration, religion, and social science). Elementary education and special education are the strongest academically. Business administration and management are the largest.

Required: To graduate, students must complete at least 120 credit hours with a minimum GPA of 2.0. 45 to 50 credits of liberal arts studies must be taken.

Special: Silver Lake offers cross-registration with several Wisconsin technical colleges, internships, B.A.-B.S. degrees, dual majors, work-study programs, and student-designed majors. Nondegree study, pass/fail options, and credit for life, military, and work experience are available. An accelerated degree program in business management, accounting, human resources, and public administration is offered. There are 4 national honor societies and 4 departmental honors programs.

Faculty/Classroom: 35% of faculty are male; 65%, female. 85% teach undergraduates and 1% both teach and do research. No introductory courses are taught by graduate students. The average class size in an introductory lecture is 19; in a laboratory, 7; and in a regular course, 10.

Admissions: 89% of the 2001-2002 applicants were accepted. 18% of the current freshmen were in the top fifth of their class; 68% were in the top two fifths.

Requirements: The SAT I or ACT is required, with a minimum composite score of 16 on the ACT. Applicants must be graduates of an accredited secondary school. The GED is accepted. Applicants should complete 3 units of high school English, 2 each of math and history or social studies, and 1 of lab science. A GPA of 2.0 is required. AP and

CLEP credits are accepted. Important factors in the admissions decision are recommendations by school officials, evidence of special talent, and advanced placement or honor courses. Applications are accepted on-line via CollegeNET or at the school's web site.

Procedure: Freshmen are admitted fall and spring. Entrance exams should be taken in the spring of the junior year. Application deadlines are open. The application fee is $35. Notification is sent on a rolling basis.

Transfer: 86 transfer students enrolled in 2001-2002. Applicants who have 30 acceptable credits must have a minimum GPA of 2.0; those with fewer credits must meet the requirements for entering freshmen, except that the SAT I or ACT is not required. 30 credits of 120 must be completed at Silver Lake.

Visiting: There are regularly scheduled orientations for prospective students, including a tour and meetings with an admissions counselor, an adviser, the Financial Aid Department, and the housing director. There are guides for informal visits and visitors may sit in on classes. To schedule a visit, contact the Admissions Office.

Financial Aid: In 2001-2002, 97% of all freshmen and 64% of continuing students received some form of financial aid. 97% of freshmen and 63% of continuing students received need-based aid. The average freshman award was $10,599. Of that total, scholarships or need-based grants averaged $7667; loans averaged $2378; and work contracts averaged $800. 25% of undergraduates work part time. Average annual earnings from campus work are $1268. The average financial indebtedness of the 2001 graduate was $13,516. The FAFSA, the college's own financial statement, and tax returns are required. The fall application deadline is April 15.

International Students: There was 1 international student enrolled in a recent year. International students must score 550 on the written TOEFL.

Computers: The mainframe is an NT server. Computer science majors use the DEC for programming. There are 35 networked PCs available, providing students access to the Internet. All students may access the system. There are no time limits and no fees.

Graduates: In 2001, 136 bachelor's degrees were awarded. The most popular majors were management (49%), education (26%), and psychology (9%). In an average class, 1% graduate in 4 years, 31% in 5 years, and 8% in 6 years. 10 companies recruited on campus in 2000-2001. Of the 2000 graduating class, 7% were enrolled in graduate school within 6 months of graduation and 97% were employed.

Admissions Contact: Lori Salm, Admissions Office.
E-mail: *admslc@silver.sl.edu* Web: *www.sl.edu*

UNIVERSITY OF WISCONSIN SYSTEM

The University of Wisconsin System, established in 1971, is a public system. It is governed by a 17-member appointed board of regents whose chief administrator is president. The primary goals of the system are teaching, research, and public service. The main priorities are to develop human resources; to discover and disseminate knowledge; and to extend knowledge and its application. The total enrollment of all 26 campuses is about 155,000 students, with some 7000 faculty members. Altogether there are 638 baccalaureate, 325 master's, and nearly 140 doctoral programs offered. Profiles of the 4-year campuses are included in this section.

UNIVERSITY OF WISCONSIN/EAU CLAIRE B-3
Eau Claire, WI 54701 (715) 836-5415
(888) INFO-UWE; Fax: (715) 836-2409

Full-time: 3783 men, 5593 women	**Faculty:** 412; IIA, -$
Part-time: 349 men, 493 women	**Ph.D.s:** 87%
Graduate: 109 men, 316 women	**Student/Faculty:** 23 to 1
Year: semesters, summer session	**Tuition:** $3472 ($12,112)
Application Deadline: open	**Room & Board:** $3560
Freshman Class: 6256 applied, 4677 accepted, 2136 enrolled	
SAT I Verbal/Math: 600/610	**ACT:** 23 **VERY COMPETITIVE**

The University of Wisconsin/Eau Claire, founded in 1916, is a public institution offering programs in the liberal arts and sciences, business, teacher education, nursing, music, and the fine arts. There are 6 undergraduate schools. In addition to regional accreditation, UW-Eau Claire has baccalaureate program accreditation with AACSB, ACEJMC, CSWE, NASM, and NLN. The library contains 594,999 volumes, 1,351,524 microform items, and 12,784 audiovisual forms/CDs, and subscribes to 14,244 periodicals. Computerized library services include the card catalog, interlibrary loans, and database searching. Special learning facilities include a learning resource center, art gallery, planetarium, radio station, TV station, geographic research center, bird museum, and observatory. The 333-acre campus is in an urban area 95 miles east of Minneapolis, Minnesota. Including residence halls, there are 26 buildings.

Student Life: 76% of undergraduates are from Wisconsin. Others are from 25 states, 48 foreign countries, and Canada. 95% are from public schools. 93% are white. The average age of freshmen is 18; all undergraduates, 21. 22% do not continue beyond their first year; 54% remain to graduate.

Housing: 3754 students can be accommodated in college housing, which includes single-sex and coed dormitories and on-campus apartments. On-campus housing is guaranteed for the freshman year only and is available on a first-come, first-served basis. 61% of students commute. All students may keep cars.

Activities: 1% of men belong to 4 national fraternities; 1% of women belong to 4 national sororities. There are 150 groups on campus, including art, band, cheerleading, choir, chorale, chorus, computers, dance, drama, ethnic, forensics, gay, honors, international, jazz band, literary magazine, marching band, musical theater, orchestra, political, professional, radio and TV, religious, social, social service, student government, symphony, and yearbook. Popular campus events include Viennese Ball, Artsfest, and Winter Carnival.

Sports: There are 9 intercollegiate sports for men and 11 for women, and 40 intramural sports for men and 40 for women. Facilities include a gym, a pool, 30 acres of intramural and recreation fields, a game room, bowling and billiards, a Nautilus fitness center, racquetball courts, a weight room, a ropes course, a 3212-seat stadium, tennis courts, and a climbing wall.

Disabled Students: 80% of the campus is accessible. Wheelchair ramps, elevators, special parking, specially equipped rest rooms, special class scheduling, lowered drinking fountains, and lowered telephones are available.

Services: Counseling and information services are available, as is tutoring in some subjects, including writing, math/problem solving, and reading/study skills. There is a reader service for the blind, and remedial math, reading, and writing. In addition, there are entry-level courses in foreign languages, humanities, and social and physical sciences.

Campus Safety and Security: Measures include 24-hour foot and vehicle patrol, self-defense education, escort service, and informal discussions. There are pamphlets/posters/films and lighted pathways/sidewalks.

Programs of Study: UW-Eau Claire confers B.A., B.S., B.B.A., B.F.A., B.M., B.M.E., B.M.T.H., B.S.E.Ph., B.S.H.C.A., B.S.N., and B.S.W. degrees. Associate and master's degrees are also awarded. Bachelor's degrees are awarded in BIOLOGICAL SCIENCE (biochemistry and biology/biological science), BUSINESS (accounting, banking and finance, business administration and management, business economics, and marketing/retailing/merchandising), COMMUNICATIONS AND THE ARTS (advertising, art, broadcasting, communications, dramatic arts, English, fine arts, French, German, journalism, music, photography, and Spanish), COMPUTER AND PHYSICAL SCIENCE (chemistry, computer programming, computer science, geology, information sciences and systems, mathematics, physical sciences, physics, and statistics), EDUCATION (art, business, elementary, foreign languages, music, physical, science, secondary, and special), HEALTH PROFESSIONS (health care administration, music therapy, nursing, public health, and speech pathology/audiology), SOCIAL SCIENCE (American Indian studies, criminal justice, economics, geography, history, Latin American studies, philosophy, political science/government, psychology, religion, social science, social work, and sociology). Elementary education, nursing, and biology are the largest.

Required: All students must complete 39 hours in general education, including 11 each in social sciences, humanities, and natural sciences, and 6 in communications. All students must also take 4 to 5 credits in English and 2 in wellness, and complete a minimum of 3 credits that contain significant content dealing with race and ethnicity and 30 or more hours of service-learning. A minimum 2.0 GPA and 120 credit hours, including 60 in the major, are required to graduate.

Special: Numerous internships, work-study programs, and study abroad in 13 countries are offered. Dual and interdisciplinary majors are possible. Credit by examination, nondegree study, and pass/fail options are offered. There are 28 national honor societies, a freshman honors program, and 13 departmental honors programs.

Faculty/Classroom: 59% of faculty are male; 41%, female. 68% teach undergraduates, 53% do research, and 53% both teach and do research. No introductory courses are taught by graduate students. The average class size in an introductory lecture is 32 and in a laboratory, 19.

Admissions: 75% of the 2001-2002 applicants were accepted. The SAT I scores for the 2001-2002 freshman class were: Verbal--25% below 500, 21% between 500 and 599, 45% between 600 and 700, and 9% above 700; Math--11% below 500, 32% between 500 and 599, 49% between 600 and 700, and 8% above 700. The ACT scores were 13% below 21, 38% between 21 and 23, 31% between 24 and 26, 11% between 27 and 28, and 7% above 28. 39% of the current freshmen were in the top fifth of their class; 82% were in the top two fifths. There were 4 National Merit finalists. In a recent year, 55 freshmen graduated first in their class.

Requirements: The ACT is required and the SAT I is recommended. In addition, applicants should graduate from an accredited secondary school or present its equivalent, with 17 academic credits, including 4 in English, 3 each in social studies, college preparatory math, and science, and 2 years of a single foreign language. Students must graduate in the upper 50% of their class or present a minimum composite score of 1100 on the SAT I or 22 on the ACT. Probationary admission is sometimes offered for the spring semester. Music majors or minors must audition. UW-Eau Claire requires applicants to be in the upper 50% of their class. AP and CLEP credits are accepted. Important factors in the admissions decision are advanced placement or honor courses, recommendations by school officials, and leadership record. Students may apply on-line at the school's website.

Procedure: Freshmen are admitted to all sessions. Entrance exams should be taken by December of the senior year. There are early admissions and rolling admissions plans. Application deadlines are open. 16% of all applicants are on a waiting list; 361 were accepted in 2001. The fall 2001 application fee was $35.

Transfer: 513 transfer students enrolled in 2001-2002. Transfer applicants must be in good standing at their previous schools and carry a minimum 2.0 GPA. Preference is given to transfers who have completed the equivalent of freshman composition and college algebra. Students with less than 30 semester credits must meet the freshman admissions requirements. 30 credits of 120 must be completed at UW-Eau Claire.

Visiting: There are regularly scheduled orientations for prospective students. During orientation sessions, students meet with academic advisers, develop a class schedule, register for classes, and tour the campus. There are guides for informal visits and visitors may sit in on classes. To schedule a visit, contact the Admissions Office.

Financial Aid: In 2001-2002, 60% of all students received some form of financial aid. 36% of freshmen and 39% of continuing students received need-based aid. The average freshman award was $5215. Of that total, scholarships or need-based grants averaged $3155 ($15,250 maximum); loans averaged $3254 ($16,252 maximum); and work contracts averaged $1489 ($5606 maximum). 98% of undergraduates work part time. Average annual earnings from campus work are $1139. The average financial indebtedness of the 2001 graduate was $14,536. The FAFSA is required. The fall application deadline is April 15.

International Students: There are 134 international students enrolled. The school actively recruits these students. They must score 525 on the written TOEFL and take the ACT.

Computers: The mainframe is a Unisys NX5602-22. Students may use computer facilities for classroom assignments, research, network access to other resources, and mail. Terminals and PCs are located across campus. There are 17 supported labs plus labs in housing and the library. Dial-in access is offered. All students may access the system 24 hours a day, 7 days per week. There are no time limits and no fees.

Graduates: In 2001, 1654 bachelor's degrees were awarded. The most popular majors were management (7%), biology (6%), and marketing (6%). In an average class, 16% graduate in 4 years, 47% in 5 years, and 54% in 6 years. 255 companies recruited on campus in 2000-2001. Of the 2000 graduating class, 9% were enrolled in graduate school within 6 months of graduation and 85% were employed.

Admissions Contact: Robert Lopez, Director of Admissions.
E-mail: *ask-uwec@uwec.edu*
Web: *www.uwec.edu/Admin/Admissions/admiss.htm*

UNIVERSITY OF WISCONSIN/GREEN BAY D-3

Green Bay, WI 54311 **(920) 465-2111; Fax: (920) 465-2765**

Full-time: 1512 men, 2814 women	**Faculty:** 174; IIA, --$
Part-time: 302 men, 755 women	**Ph.D.s:** 83%
Graduate: 60 men, 108 women	**Student/Faculty:** 25 to 1
Year: semesters, summer session	**Tuition:** $3648 ($11,906)
Application Deadline: February 1	**Room & Board:** $3500

Freshman Class: 2425 applied, 1930 accepted, 908 enrolled
ACT: 23 **COMPETITIVE**

The University of Wisconsin/Green Bay, founded in 1968, is a public institution offering programs in humanities and fine arts, natural sciences, social sciences, business, education, health, and preprofessional areas. In addition to regional accreditation, UW-Green Bay has baccalaureate program accreditation with ADA, CSWE, NASM, and NLN. The library contains 280,000 volumes, 450,000 microform items, and 3300 audio-visual forms/CDs, and subscribes to 1400 periodicals. Computerized library services include the card catalog, interlibrary loans, and database searching. Special learning facilities include a learning resource center, art gallery, natural history museum, radio station, TV station, a 270-acre arboretum, and a regional performing arts center. The 700-acre campus is in a suburban area 111 miles north of Milwaukee. Including residence halls, there are 39 buildings.

Student Life: 94% of undergraduates are from Wisconsin. Others are from 29 states, 32 foreign countries, and Canada. 86% are from public schools. 93% are white. The average age of freshmen is 19; all undergraduates, 23. 26% do not continue beyond their first year; 48% remain to graduate.

Housing: 1520 students can be accommodated in college housing, which includes coed dormitories and on-campus apartments. In addition, there are special-interest houses, and 3-, 4-, and 5-person dorm suites with private bedrooms. On-campus housing is available on a first-come, first-served basis and is available on a lottery system for upperclassmen. 72% of students commute. All students may keep cars.

Activities: 1% of men belong to 1 national fraternity; 1% of women belong to 2 national sororities. There are 90 groups on campus, including art, band, cheerleading, choir, chorus, computers, dance, drama, drill team, environmental, ethnic, gay, honors, international, jazz band, literary magazine, musical theater, newspaper, orchestra, pep band, photography, political, professional, radio and TV, religious, social, social service, and student government. Popular campus events include Fall Fest, Spring Screamer, and Black History Awareness Month.

Sports: There are 7 intercollegiate sports for men and 8 for women, and 7 intramural sports for men and 7 for women. Facilities include a sports center housing a swimming pool, racquetball courts, a weight room, a 2000-seat gym, intramural fields, a soccer field, a golf course, tennis courts, an outing center, a 2500-seat stadium, and student recreation facilities in the student union.

Disabled Students: All of the campus is accessible. Wheelchair ramps, elevators, special parking, specially equipped rest rooms, lowered drinking fountains, lowered telephones, and automatic door openers are available.

Services: Counseling and information services are available, as is tutoring in most subjects. There is a reader service for the blind, and remedial math, reading, and writing. There is an academic support office, language and writing centers, student health services, and individual counseling. Available equipment includes a visual enlarger, automatic page turner, accessible computer station with attached voice syntheizer, slow speed cassette recorders, taped texts, and a printing Telecommunications Device for the Deaf(TDD). Notetakers, typists, readers, and aides are also available to students.

Campus Safety and Security: Measures include 24-hour foot and vehicle patrol, escort service, informal discussions, and pamphlets/posters/films. There are emergency telephones and lighted pathways/sidewalks.

Programs of Study: UW-Green Bay confers B.A., B.S., B.G.S., B.S.N., and B.S.W. degrees. Associate and master's degrees are also awarded. Bachelor's degrees are awarded in BIOLOGICAL SCIENCE (biology/biological science and nutrition), BUSINESS (accounting and business administration and management), COMMUNICATIONS AND THE ARTS (communications, dramatic arts, English, fine arts, French, German, music, and Spanish), COMPUTER AND PHYSICAL SCIENCE (chemistry, computer science, earth science, information sciences and systems, and mathematics), EDUCATION (education and social foundations), ENGINEERING AND ENVIRONMENTAL DESIGN (environmental science), HEALTH PROFESSIONS (nursing), SOCIAL SCIENCE (economics, history, human development, humanities, liberal arts/general studies, philosophy, political science/government, psychology, public administration, social work, and urban studies). Environmental science, accounting, and human biology are the strongest academically. Business, education, and communications are the largest.

Required: All students must complete at least 120 semester hours, including an average of 36 in the major, with a minimum GPA of 2.0, depending on the major. A 31-credit requirement in general education consists of 9 credits in humanities, 3 in fine arts, 9 in social sciences, and 10 in natural sciences. Students must declare an interdisciplinary minor or major and must complete at least 30 credits in the discipline. Courses in Other Culture Studies and Ethnic Studies are required; other course requirements vary by major.

Special: UW-Green Bay offers cross-registration with Bellin College of Nursing and the University of Wisconsin at Milwaukee or Oshkosh. There are study-abroad programs in 6 countries plus travel in 12. Students can receive credit by examination or for life, military, or work experience. There are internships in almost all fields; interdisciplinary majors, including communication and the arts, human biology, and regional planning; and dual and student-designed majors, work-study, B.A.-B.S. degrees in most areas, nondegree study, a general studies degree, and pass/fail options. A 3-2 engineering degree with the University of Wisconsin/Milwaukee is offered. The Extended Degree Program, largely off campus, provides for individual study. There are 3 national honor societies and all departments have honors programs.

Faculty/Classroom: 55% of faculty are male; 45%, female. 99% teach undergraduates, 95% do research, and 95% do both. No introductory courses are taught by graduate students. The average class size in an introductory lecture is 40; in a laboratory, 18; and in a regular course, 25.

Admissions: 80% of the 2001-2002 applicants were accepted. The ACT scores for the 2001-2002 freshman class were: 27% below 21, 33% between 21 and 23, 27% between 24 and 26, 8% between 27 and 28, and 5% above 28. 41% of the current freshmen were in the top fifth of their class; 81% were in the top two fifths. 23 freshmen graduated first in their class.

Requirements: The ACT is required. In addition, candidates must be graduates of an accredited secondary school or hold a GED certificate. They must have completed 17 academic credits consisting of 4 in English, 3 in social sciences, 3 each in science and math, 2 in any of the above areas or a foreign language, and 2 other electives. UW-Green Bay requires applicants to be in the upper 50% of their class. A GPA of 2.5

is required. AP and CLEP credits are accepted. Important factors in the admissions decision are recommendations by school officials, extracurricular activities record, and advanced placement or honor courses. Applications are accepted on-line at *apply.wisconsin.edu.*

Procedure: Freshmen are admitted to all sessions. Entrance exams should be taken between the junior and senior years. There is a deferred admissions plan. Applications should be filed by February 1 for fall entry and November 1 for spring entry. Notification is sent on a rolling basis. A waiting list is an active part of the admissions procedure. The fall 2001 application fee was $35.

Transfer: 499 transfer students enrolled in 2001-2002. Transfer students must have a minimum GPA of 2.0 based on at least 15 transferable credits; priority for admission is given to students with 24 credits and a minimum GPA of 2.5. 52 credits of 120 must be completed at UW-Green Bay.

Visiting: There are regularly scheduled orientations for prospective students, including Campus Preview Days, which consist of information sessions, academic area workshops, and campus tours. There are guides for informal visits and visitors may sit in on classes. To schedule a visit, contact Pam Harvey-Jacobs, Director of Admissions at *admissions@uwgb.edu.*

Financial Aid: In a recent year, 71% of all freshmen and 69% of continuing students received some form of financial aid. 40% of freshmen and 46% of continuing students received need-based aid. The average freshman award was $3865. Of that total, scholarships or need-based grants averaged $2631 ($14,000 maximum); loans averaged $2973 ($7500 maximum); and work contracts averaged $1308 ($2500 maximum). 70% of undergraduates work part time. Average annual earnings from campus work are $1500. The average financial indebtedness of the 2001 graduate was $6343. The CSS/Profile, FAFSA, or FFS is required. The fall application deadline is April 15.

International Students: There are 76 international students enrolled. The school actively recruits these students. They must score 500 on the written TOEFL and also take placement tests in math and English as a second language.

Computers: Computer accounts for PC and mainframe access are available to all enrolled students. PC and networked terminals are widely available in computer labs, classrooms, and the Residence Community Center. All networked computers have full access to e-mail and the Internet. All students may access the system 7 A.M. to 12 P.M.; 24 hours a day through network or modem. There are no time limits and no fees.

Graduates: In 2001, 822 bachelor's degrees were awarded. The most popular majors were business administration (16%), human development (10%), and communication processes (7%). In an average class, 1% graduate in 3 years, 14% in 4 years, 38% in 5 years, and 44% in 6 years. 40 companies recruited on campus in 2000-2001. Of the 2000 graduating class, 15% were enrolled in graduate school within 6 months of graduation and 99% were employed.

Admissions Contact: Pam Harvey-Jacobs, Director of Admissions. A video is available. E-mail: *admissions@uwgb.edu*
Web: *www.uwgb.edu/admissions*

UNIVERSITY OF WISCONSIN/LA CROSSE B-4

La Crosse, WI 54601 **(608) 785-8067; Fax: (608) 785-8940**

Full-time: 3224 men, 4622 women	**Faculty:** 360; IIA, -$
Part-time: 297 men, 323 women	**Ph.D.s:** 79%
Graduate: 260 men, 359 women	**Student/Faculty:** 22 to 1
Year: semesters, summer session	**Tuition:** $3730
Application Deadline: open	**Room & Board:** $3520
Freshman Class: 5028 applied, 3457 accepted, 1586 enrolled	
ACT: 24	**VERY COMPETITIVE**

The University of Wisconsin/La Crosse, founded in 1909, is a public institution offering undergraduate and graduate studies in arts and sciences, health and human services, business administration, education, phys ed and recreation, professional development, and educational administration. There are 6 undergraduate schools and 1 graduate school. In addition to regional accreditation, UW-L has baccalaureate program accreditation with AACSB, APTA, NASM, NCATE, ACOTE, ACS, CAPTE,, and NAACLS. The library contains 650,461 volumes, 1 microform items, and 1524 audiovisual forms/CDs, and subscribes to 1603 periodicals. Computerized library services include the card catalog, interlibrary loans, and database searching. Special learning facilities include a learning resource center, art gallery, planetarium, radio station, TV station, the River Studies Center, and the Allied Health Center. The 119-acre campus is in a small town 140 miles west of Madison and 150 miles southeast of Minneapolis/St. Paul. Including residence halls, there are 32 buildings.

Student Life: 82% of undergraduates are from Wisconsin. Others are from 38 states, 42 foreign countries, and Canada. 90% are from public schools. 93% are white. The average age of freshmen is 19; all undergraduates, 22. 10% do not continue beyond their first year; 53% remain to graduate.

Housing: 2836 students can be accommodated in college housing, which includes single-sex and coed dormitories. In addition, there are special-interest houses, and a residence hall for international students and students 21 or older. On-campus housing is available on a first-come, first-served basis and is available on a lottery system for upperclassmen. 68% of students commute. All students may keep cars.

Activities: 1% of men and about 1% of women belong to 3 national fraternities; 1% of women belong to 2 national sororities. There are 140 groups on campus, including art, band, cheerleading, chess, choir, chorale, chorus, computers, dance, drama, ethnic, gay, honors, international, jazz band, literary magazine, marching band, musical theater, newspaper, orchestra, pep band, photography, political, professional, radio and TV, religious, social, social service, student government, and symphony. Popular campus events include Parents Weekend, a community-sponsored Oktoberfest, and various cultural events.

Sports: There are 9 intercollegiate sports for men and 10 for women, and 11 intramural sports for men and 11 for women. Facilities include 3 regulation basketball courts, a wrestling room, an indoor track, 6 indoor tennis courts, 16 outdoor tennis courts, an Olympic-size swimming pool, 2 strength-training centers, a dance studio, racquetball courts, a 4363-seat stadium, a 2880-seat gym, and an 880-seat auditorium.

Disabled Students: 98% of the campus is accessible. Wheelchair ramps, elevators, special parking, specially equipped rest rooms, special class scheduling, lowered drinking fountains, lowered telephones, and specialized computer equipment are available.

Services: Counseling and information services are available, as is tutoring in most subjects. There is a reader service for the blind and remedial math and writing. There is also a counseling and testing center and a writing lab.

Campus Safety and Security: Measures include 24-hour foot and vehicle patrol, self-defense education, escort service, and informal discussions. There are pamphlets/posters/films, emergency telephones, and lighted pathways/sidewalks.

Programs of Study: UW-L confers B.A. and B.S. degrees. Associate and master's degrees are also awarded. Bachelor's degrees are awarded in BIOLOGICAL SCIENCE (biology/biological science and microbiology), BUSINESS (accounting, banking and finance, business administration and management, international business management, and marketing/retailing/merchandising), COMMUNICATIONS AND THE ARTS (art, communications, dramatic arts, English, fine arts, French, music, Spanish, and speech/debate/rhetoric), COMPUTER AND PHYSICAL SCIENCE (chemistry, computer science, information sciences and systems, mathematics, and physics), EDUCATION (athletic training, elementary, health, physical, science, secondary, and social studies), HEALTH PROFESSIONS (community health work, exercise science, medical laboratory technology, nuclear medical technology, occupational therapy, physician's assistant, radiation therapy, and recreation therapy), SOCIAL SCIENCE (archeology, economics, geography, German area studies, history, parks and recreation management, philosophy, political science/government, psychology, public administration, and sociology). Microbiology, nuclear medicine technology, and physics are the strongest academically. Business administration, elementary education, and biology are the largest.

Required: To graduate, students must earn 120 semester credits, including 68 in subjects outside the major and at least 40 in 300- or 400-level courses. The minimum GPA is 2.0, though it is considerably higher for some programs. Distribution requirements include 30 to 40 credits in liberal studies and 13 to 19 credits in skill courses.

Special: Cooperative programs and cross-registration are available with Viterbo College. There are study-abroad programs in 14 countries and an international student exchange program. UW-L also offers a 3-2 engineering degree with the University of Wisconsin/Madison, the University of Wisconsin/Milwaukee, Platteville, and the University of Minnesota, work-study programs, internships, nondegree study, credit by exam, and pass/fail options. There are 10 national honor societies, a freshman honors program, and 11 departmental honors programs.

Faculty/Classroom: 60% of faculty are male; 40%, female. 96% teach undergraduates, 4% do research, and 80% do both. No introductory courses are taught by graduate students. The average class size in an introductory lecture is 37; in a laboratory, 20; and in a regular course, 30.

Admissions: 69% of the 2001-2002 applicants were accepted. The ACT scores for the 2001-2002 freshman class were: 6% below 21, 37% between 21 and 23, 39% between 24 and 26, 11% between 27 and 28, and 7% above 28. 52% of the current freshmen were in the top fifth of their class; 94% were in the top two fifths. 29 freshmen graduated first in their class.

Requirements: The ACT is required. In addition, candidates must be graduates of an accredited secondary school or hold a GED certificate. They must have completed 17 academic credits, including 4 courses in English, 3 each in social studies and science, 2 in algebra and 1 in geometry, and 4 other academic courses. Students completing rigorous courses, including in the senior year, will be stronger candidates for admission. Students must rank in the top 35% of their high school graduating class and score at least 22 on the ACT or the top 40% and score 25 on the ACT. UW-L requires applicants to be in the upper 40% of their class. AP and CLEP credits are accepted. Important factors in the admissions decision are advanced placement or honor courses, leadership record, and recommendations by school officials. Applications are accepted on-line at *www.uwlax.edu*.

Procedure: Freshmen are admitted to all sessions. Entrance exams should be taken at the end of the junior year or at the beginning of the senior year. Application deadlines are open. The application fee is $35. 9% of all applicants are on a waiting list; 110 were accepted in 2001.

Transfer: 385 transfer students enrolled in 2001-2002. Transfer admission is likely with a GPA of 2.75; with a GPA of 2.0 to 2.74, admission is on a space-available basis. 32 credits of 120 must be completed at UW-L.

Visiting: There are regularly scheduled orientations for prospective students, including 2 academic sessions, a parent panel, a UW-L student panel, and a tour of the campus. There are guides for informal visits and visitors may sit in on classes. To schedule a visit, contact the Admissions Office at (608) 785-8939.

Financial Aid: In 2001-2002, 52% of all freshmen and 59% of continuing students received some form of financial aid. 45% of freshmen and 51% of continuing students received need-based aid. The average freshman award was $3851. Of that total, scholarships or need-based grants averaged $885 ($5496 maximum); loans averaged $2090 ($2625 maximum); and work contracts averaged $876 ($1350 maximum). 83% of undergraduates work part time. Average annual earnings from campus work are $995. The average financial indebtedness of the 2001 graduate was $14,450. The FAFSA, the college's own financial statement, and tax returns are required.

International Students: There were 178 international students enrolled in a recent year. The school actively recruits these students. They must score 550 on the written TOEFL and also take the college's own test and the La Crosse Battery (based on MELAB), and write a 30-minute composition.

Computers: The mainframe is a Unisys A4600. There are 500 PCs, primarily Dell, Compaq, and Mac, available in open labs and residence halls. All students have access to e-mail and the Internet. All students may access the system from 5 A.M. to 6 P.M. There are no time limits and no fees.

Graduates: In 2001, 1467 bachelor's degrees were awarded. The most popular majors were exercise and sport science (9%), marketing (9%), and biology (8%). In an average class, 19% graduate in 4 years, 46% in 5 years, and 53% in 6 years. 84 companies recruited on campus in 2000-2001. Of the 2000 graduating class, 21% were enrolled in graduate school within 6 months of graduation and 98% were employed.

Admissions Contact: Timothy R. Lewis, Director of Admissions. E-mail: *admissions@uwlax.edu* Web: *www.uwlax.edu*

UNIVERSITY OF WISCONSIN/MADISON C-4

Madison, WI 53706-1400 (608) 262-3961; Fax: (608) 262-1429

Full-time: 11,900 men, 13,200 women	**Faculty:** 2301; I, av$
Part-time: 280 men, 300 women	**Ph.D.s:** 97%
Graduate: none	**Student/Faculty:** 11 to 1
Year: semesters, summer session	**Tuition:** $4100 ($12,900)
Application Deadline: see profile	**Room & Board:** $4300
Freshman Class: n/av	
SAT I or ACT: required	**VERY COMPETITIVE**

The University of Wisconsin/Madison, founded in 1849, is a public, land-grant institution offering undergraduate and graduate study in almost every major field. There are 9 undergraduate and 4 graduate schools. Information in the above capsule, and in this profile, is approximate. In addition to regional accreditation, Wisconsin has baccalaureate program accreditation with AACSB, ABET, ACEJMC, AHEA, ASLA, CSWE, NASAD, NASM, NCATE, and NLN. The 40 libraries contain 5,800,000 volumes and 1,300,000 microform items, and subscribe to 55,000 periodicals. Computerized library services include the card catalog and database searching. Special learning facilities include a learning resource center, art gallery, natural history museum, planetarium, radio station, TV station, an arboretum, several wildlife areas, 40,000 acres of agricultural research and teaching areas, and 2 limnology research and teaching facilities. The 1000-acre campus is in an urban area 75 miles west of Milwaukee and 150 miles north of Chicago. Including residence halls, there are 192 buildings.

Student Life: 65% of undergraduates are from Wisconsin. Others are from 49 states, 102 foreign countries, and Canada. 67% are from public schools. 90% are white. The average age of freshmen is 18; all undergraduates, 20. 4% do not continue beyond their first year; 85% remain to graduate.

Housing: About 7975 students can be accommodated in college housing, which includes single-sex and coed dormitories, on-campus apartments, off-campus apartments, married-student housing, fraternity houses, and sorority houses. In addition, there are honors houses, language houses, and special-interest houses. On-campus housing is guaranteed for all 4 years. 97% of students live on campus; of those, 80% remain on campus on weekends. All students may keep cars.

Activities: 14% of men belong to 27 national fraternities; 17% of women belong to 17 national sororities. There are 900 groups on campus, including art, band, cheerleading, chess, choir, chorale, chorus, computers, dance, drama, ethnic, film, gay, honors, international, jazz band, literary magazine, marching band, musical theater, newspaper, opera, orchestra, pep band, photography, political, professional, radio and TV, religious, social, social service, student government, symphony, and yearbook. Popular campus events include Parents Weekend, alumni reunions, and an annual band concert.

Sports: There are 11 intercollegiate sports for men and 9 for women, and 29 intramural sports for men and 24 for women. Facilities include several gyms (one seating 17,000), pools, a field house, 2 stadiums--1 for tennis and the other for football--seating 77,000, and a 12,000-seat arena.

Disabled Students: 90% of the campus is accessible. Wheelchair ramps, elevators, special parking, specially equipped rest rooms, special class scheduling, lowered drinking fountains, and lowered telephones are available.

Services: Counseling and information services are available, as is tutoring in most subjects. There is a reader service for the blind, and remedial math, reading, and writing.

Campus Safety and Security: Measures include 24-hour foot and vehicle patrol, self-defense education, escort service, and shuttle buses. There are informal discussions, pamphlets/posters/films, emergency telephones, and lighted pathways/sidewalks.

Programs of Study: Wisconsin confers B.A., B.S., B.Art Ed., B.B.A., B.F.A., B.M., B.S.Ch., B.S.E., and B.S.P. degrees. Master's and doctoral degrees are also awarded. Bachelor's degrees are awarded in AGRICULTURE (agricultural business management, agricultural economics, agricultural mechanics, animal science, conservation and regulation, dairy science, forestry and related sciences, horticulture, poultry science, and soil science), BIOLOGICAL SCIENCE (bacteriology, biochemistry, botany, entomology, genetics, microbiology, molecular biology, nutrition, plant pathology, toxicology, wildlife biology, and zoology), BUSINESS (accounting, banking and finance, business administration and management, insurance and risk management, marketing/retailing/merchandising, real estate, recreation and leisure services, and retailing), COMMUNICATIONS AND THE ARTS (African languages, art history and appreciation, Chinese, classics, communications, comparative literature, dramatic arts, English, French, German, Greek, Hebrew, Italian, Japanese, journalism, Latin, linguistics, music, Polish, Portuguese, Russian, and Spanish), COMPUTER AND PHYSICAL SCIENCE (actuarial science, applied mathematics, astronomy, atmospheric sciences and meteorology, chemistry, computer science, geology, information sciences and systems, mathematics, physics, quantitative methods, and statistics), EDUCATION (agricultural, art, elementary, physical, and secondary), ENGINEERING AND ENVIRONMENTAL DESIGN (agricultural engineering, biomedical engineering, cartography, chemical engineering, civil engineering, electrical/electronics engineering, engineering mechanics, engineering physics, geological engineering, industrial engineering, interior design, landscape architecture/design, materials science, mechanical engineering, metallurgical engineering, nuclear engineering, and textile technology), HEALTH PROFESSIONS (medical laboratory technology, medical science, nursing, occupational therapy, pharmacy, physician's assistant, and speech pathology/audiology), SOCIAL SCIENCE (African American studies, anthropology, Asian/Oriental studies, behavioral science, child care/child and family studies, consumer services, dietetics, economics, family/consumer studies, food science, geography, history, history of science, humanities, international relations, Judaic studies, Latin American studies, philosophy, political science/government, psychology, rural sociology, Scandinavian studies, social work, sociology, South Asian studies, textiles and clothing, and women's studies). Political science, psychology, and English are the largest.

Required: Required courses vary with individual programs. A total of 120 to 136 credit hours, with at least 30 in the major, and a cumulative GPA of 2.0, are minimum requirements for graduation.

Special: Co-op programs in engineering, internships in political science in Washington, D.C., and the state capital are possible. Study abroad is offered in more than 40 countries in Europe, Asia, and South America. Work-study programs, accelerated degrees, credit by examination, and pass/fail options are available. Students in the College of Letters and Science may select dual or self-designed majors, or an integrated liberal studies program. There are 24 national honor societies, including Phi Beta Kappa, and a freshman honors program.

Faculty/Classroom: 80% of faculty are male; 20%, female. 95% teach undergraduates, all do research, and 95% do both. The average class size in an introductory lecture is 75; in a laboratory, 15; and in a regular course, 30.

Admissions: 81% of recent freshmen were in the top fifth of their class; 99% were in the top two fifths. There were 200 National Merit finalists.

Requirements: The SAT I or ACT is required. In addition, the ACT is required for in-state students, and either the ACT or the SAT I for out-of-state students. Candidates should be graduates of an accredited secondary school or hold a GED certificate. They must have completed the following academic credits: 4 in English, and 3 each in math, history, science, and social studies, 2 in a foreign language, and college-preparatory electives. Grades, rank in class, and scores, as well as rigor of senior class course selection, are considered. AP and CLEP credits are accepted. Important factors in the admissions decision are advanced placement or honor courses and evidence of special talent. The school accepts applications on its own PC and Mac disks, on other vendor disks, and via CollegeLink.

Procedure: Freshmen are admitted to all sessions. Entrance exams should be taken in the junior year. There are early admissions and deferred admissions plans. Notification is sent on a rolling basis. Check with the school for current application deadlines and fee.

Transfer: 1150 transfer students enrolled in a recent year. Admission is competitive and varies by program. Generally, applicants must have at least sophomore standing and a GPA of 3.2 or higher. Transfer students must complete 15 intermediate and advanced credits in the major. 30 credits of 120 must be completed at Wisconsin.

Visiting: There are regularly scheduled orientations for prospective students, including an admission information session, a tour, and class visits. There are guides for informal visits and visitors may sit in on classes and stay overnight. To schedule a visit, contact the Tour Coordinator, Office of Admissions, at (608) 262-3318.

Financial Aid: In a recent year, 60% of all freshmen and 55% of continuing students received some form of financial aid. 55% of freshmen and 62% of continuing students received need-based aid. Scholarships or need-based grants averaged $1365 ($4250 maximum); loans averaged $1650 ($3825 maximum); and work contracts averaged $1300 ($1700 maximum). Wisconsin is a member of CSS. The FAFSA, the college's own financial statement and a federal income tax return are required. Check with the school for current deadlines.

International Students: There were 3671 international students enrolled in a recent year. They must score 550 on the written TOEFL and also take the MELAB or the SAT I or the ACT.

Computers: There are 2800 IBM PS/2 and Mac PCs available in 15 open labs and dorms. There are data ports in all dorm rooms. All students have e-mail. All students may access the system. There are no time limits and no fees.

Graduates: In a recent year, 5568 bachelor's degrees were awarded. The most popular majors were political science (7%), psychology (5%), and English (5%). In an average class, 10% graduate in 3 years, 45% in 4 years, 85% in 5 years, and 88% in 6 years. 900 companies recruited on campus in a recent year.

Admissions Contact: Keith White, Associate Director of Admissions. E-mail: *on.wisconsin@mail.admin.wisc.edu*

UNIVERSITY OF WISCONSIN/MILWAUKEE — E-4

Milwaukee, WI 53201 — **(414) 229-3800; Fax: (414) 229-6940**

Full-time: 6804 men, 8230 women	**Faculty:** 824; I, --$
Part-time: 2112 men, 2813 women	**Ph.D.s:** 90%
Graduate: 1685 men, 2579 women	**Student/Faculty:** 18 to 1
Year: semesters, summer session	**Tuition:** $4057 ($15,028)
Application Deadline: open	**Room & Board:** $4850
Freshman Class: 7340 applied, 5771 accepted, 2773 enrolled	
SAT I or ACT: required	**LESS COMPETITIVE**

The University of Wisconsin/Milwaukee, founded in 1885, offers undergraduate and graduate degrees in arts and sciences, fine arts, business, education, engineering and applied sciences, architecture and urban planning, social welfare, and health fields. There are 9 undergraduate schools and 1 graduate school. In addition to regional accreditation, UWM has baccalaureate program accreditation with AACSB, ABET, ACEJMC, CAHEA, CSWE, NAAB, NASAD, NASM, NCATE, and NLN. The library contains 1,115,509 volumes, 1,677,126 microform items, and 34,013 audiovisual forms/CDs, and subscribes to 8348 periodicals. Computerized library services include the card catalog, interlibrary loans, and database searching. Special learning facilities include a learning resource center, art gallery, planetarium, TV station, a geological museum. The 93-acre campus is in an urban area in Milwaukee. Including residence halls, there are 42 buildings.

Student Life: 96% of undergraduates are from Wisconsin. Others are from 49 states, 59 foreign countries, and Canada. 81% are white. The average age of freshmen is 18; all undergraduates, 23. 30% do not continue beyond their first year; 43% remain to graduate.

Housing: 1904 students can be accommodated in college housing, which includes coed dormitories and married-student housing. On-campus housing is available on a first-come, first-served basis. 91% of students commute. All students may keep cars.

Activities: 3% of men belong to 1 local and 6 national fraternities; 3% of women belong to 6 national sororities. There are 250 groups on campus, including art, band, cheerleading, chorale, computers, concert band, dance, drama, ethnic, film, gay, honors, international, jazz band, literary magazine, music ensembles, musical theater, newspaper, orchestra, pep band, photography, political, professional, radio and TV, religious, social, social service, student government, and symphony. Popular campus events include concerts, art exhibitions, and dance performances.

Sports: There are 9 intercollegiate sports for men and 8 for women, and 15 intramural sports for men and 13 for women. Facilities include a center for phys ed, a gym, a field, courts, and a 3000-seat auditorium.

Disabled Students: 90% of the campus is accessible. Wheelchair ramps, elevators, special parking, specially equipped rest rooms, special class scheduling, lowered drinking fountains, lowered telephones, and special library facilities are available.

Services: Counseling and information services are available, as is tutoring in some subjects, including English composition, math, science, business, reading, and study skills. There is a reader service for the blind, and remedial math, reading, and writing.

Campus Safety and Security: Measures include 24-hour foot and vehicle patrol, self-defense education, escort service, and shuttle buses. There are pamphlets/posters/films, emergency telephones, and lighted pathways/sidewalks.

Programs of Study: UWM confers B.A., B.S., B.B.A., B.F.A., B.S.Applied S., and B.S.E. degrees. Master's and doctoral degrees are also awarded. Bachelor's degrees are awarded in AGRICULTURE (conservation and regulation), BIOLOGICAL SCIENCE (biochemistry, biology/biological science, botany, microbiology, and zoology), BUSINESS (accounting, banking and finance, business administration and management, management information systems, marketing/retailing/merchandising, real estate, and recreation and leisure services), COMMUNICATIONS AND THE ARTS (art history and appreciation, classics, communications, comparative literature, dance, dramatic arts, English, film arts, fine arts, French, German, Hebrew, Italian, linguistics, music, Russian, and Spanish), COMPUTER AND PHYSICAL SCIENCE (applied mathematics, chemistry, computer science, geology, geoscience, mathematics, and physics), EDUCATION (art, education, music, and social science), ENGINEERING AND ENVIRONMENTAL DESIGN (architecture, civil engineering, electrical/electronics engineering, engineering, industrial administration/management, industrial engineering, materials engineering, and mechanical engineering), HEALTH PROFESSIONS (clinical science, health care administration, health science, medical science, nursing, occupational therapy, predentistry, premedicine, and speech pathology/audiology), SOCIAL SCIENCE (African American studies, anthropology, criminal justice, economics, geography, history, law, philosophy, political science/government, prelaw, psychology, religion, social work, and sociology). Architecture and engineering are the strongest academically.

Required: English composition and math proficiency exams must be passed with satisfactory scores. Distribution requirements include 6 credits each in humanities, natural sciences, and social sciences and 3 credits each in the arts and cultural diversity. All students must complete a minimum of 120 credits.

Special: UWM offers cooperative programs in engineering, cross-registration with UW/Parkside, study abroad in Europe and Asia, internships, a Washington semester, and work-study programs. Students may select an accelerated degree program, dual majors, a general studies degree, and student-designed majors. Credit/no credit options, nondegree study, credit by examination, and credit for life, military, and work experience are also available. There is 1 national honor society, including Phi Beta Kappa, a freshman honors program, and 1 departmental honors program.

Faculty/Classroom: 70% of faculty are male; 30%, female. All teach undergraduates. The average class size in an introductory lecture is 48; in a laboratory, 15; and in a regular course, 27.

Admissions: 79% of the 2001-2002 applicants were accepted.

Requirements: The SAT I or ACT is required. The ACT is preferred, with a minimum score of 21 required of all Wisconsin residents. Out-of-state students may substitute the SAT I with a minimum composite score of 970. Candidates must have graduated from an accredited secondary school with 17 Carnegie units including at least 4 in English, 3 in history/social science, and 3 each in math and the natural sciences. A GED certificate is accepted. Music and theater majors must audition. For the School of Architecture and Urban Planning, higher rank and ACT requirements apply. UWM requires applicants to be in the upper 50% of their class. AP and CLEP credits are accepted. Important factors in the admissions decision are advanced placement or honor courses, evidence of special talent, and leadership record. Applications are accepted on-line at *www.apply.wisconsin.edu*

Procedure: Freshmen are admitted to all sessions. Entrance exams should be taken in the spring of the junior year. There is a deferred admissions plan. Application deadlines are open. The application fee is $35. Notification is sent on a rolling basis beginning September 30.

Transfer: 1717 transfer students enrolled in 2001-2002. Transfer applicants must have earned a minimum of 12 credit hours and have at least a 2.0 GPA. 30 credits of 120 must be completed at UWM.

Visiting: There are regularly scheduled orientations for prospective students. There are guides for informal visits and visitors may sit in on classes and stay overnight. To schedule a visit, contact the Student Visitor Center at (414) 229-4397.

International Students: International students must score 500 on the written TOEFL and also take the MELAB, the Comprehensive English Language Test, or the college's own test.

Computers: The mainframe is a DEC 2100-275 running Digital UNIX. PCs are available in the library, residence halls, the student union, and several labs. All students may access the system any time. There are no time limits and no fees.
Graduates: In 2001, 2720 bachelor's degrees were awarded. The most popular majors were business/marketing (22%), education (9%), and health professions and related sciences (9%). In an average class, 8% graduate in 4 years, 27% in 5 years, and 35% in 6 years. 166 companies recruited on campus in 2000-2001.
Admissions Contact: Director of Admissions.
E-mail: *uwmlook@des.uwm.edu* Web: *www.uwm.edu*

UNIVERSITY OF WISCONSIN/OSHKOSH D-4

Oshkosh, WI 54901 **(920) 424-0202; Fax: (920) 424-1098**

Full-time: 3400 men, 4600 women	**Faculty:** 407; IIA, -$
Part-time: 460 men, 840 women	**Ph.D.s:** 81%
Graduate: 575 men, 940 women	**Student/Faculty:** 20 to 1
Year: semesters, summer session	**Tuition:** $3100 ($9900)
Application Deadline: see profile	**Room & Board:** $3200
Freshman Class: n/av	
ACT: required	**LESS COMPETITIVE**

The University of Wisconsin/Oshkosh, founded in 1871, is a public institution offering undergraduate and graduate programs in education, business, the arts and sciences, and health fields. Information given in the above capsule, and in this profile, is approximate. There are 4 undergraduate schools and 1 graduate school. In addition to regional accreditation, UW/Oshkosh has baccalaureate program accreditation with AACSB, ACEJMC, CSWE, NASM, NCATE, and NLN. The library contains 487,000 volumes, 1,275,000 microform items, and 7000 audiovisual forms/CDs, and subscribes to 1850 periodicals. Computerized library services include the card catalog, interlibrary loans, and database searching. Special learning facilities include a learning resource center, art gallery, planetarium, radio station, TV station, and a speech and hearing clinic. The 192-acre campus is in an urban area 90 miles north of Milwaukee. Including residence halls, there are 36 buildings.
Student Life: 96% of undergraduates are from Wisconsin. Others are from 30 states, 32 foreign countries, and Canada. 94% are white. The average age of freshmen is 18; all undergraduates, 22. 29% do not continue beyond their first year; 55% remain to graduate.
Housing: About 3667 students can be accommodated in college housing, which includes single-sex and coed dormitories. On-campus housing is guaranteed for all 4 years. 66% of students commute. All students may keep cars.
Activities: 5% of men belong to 8 national fraternities; 5% of women belong to 5 national sororities. There are 175 groups on campus, including art, band, cheerleading, chess, choir, computers, dance, debate, ethnic, film, forensics, gay, honors, international, jazz band, literary magazine, musical theater, newspaper, opera, pep band, political, professional, radio and TV, religious, social, social service, student government, and symphony. Popular campus events include Winter Carnival, Taste of UW Oshkosh, and Celebration of Racial Inclusiveness.
Sports: There are 10 intercollegiate sports for men and 11 for women, and 15 intramural sports for men and 15 for women. Facilities include a hall for basketball, swimming, and volleyball, a sports center for basketball, tennis, and indoor track, a pool, a 10400-seat stadium for football and outdoor track, a 2500-seat indoor gym, and a 5808-seat arena.
Disabled Students: Wheelchair ramps, elevators, special parking, specially equipped rest rooms, special class scheduling, lowered drinking fountains, and lowered telephones are available.
Services: Counseling and information services are available, as is tutoring in most subjects. There is a reader service for the blind, and remedial math, reading, and writing.
Campus Safety and Security: Measures include 24-hour foot and vehicle patrol, self-defense education, escort service, and informal discussions. There are pamphlets/posters/films, emergency telephones, and lighted pathways/sidewalks.
Programs of Study: UW/Oshkosh confers B.A., B.S., B.Art Ed., B.B.A., B.F.A., B.L.S., B.M., B.M.E., B.S.N., and B.S.W. degrees. Associate and master's degrees are also awarded. Bachelor's degrees are awarded in BIOLOGICAL SCIENCE (biology/biological science and microbiology), BUSINESS (accounting, banking and finance, business administration and management, human resources, management information systems, and marketing/retailing/merchandising), COMMUNICATIONS AND THE ARTS (art, English, fine arts, French, German, journalism, music, Spanish, and speech/debate/rhetoric), COMPUTER AND PHYSICAL SCIENCE (chemistry, computer science, geology, mathematics, and physics), EDUCATION (art, elementary, music, physical, science, secondary, social science, and special), HEALTH PROFESSIONS (medical laboratory technology, music therapy, nursing, and speech pathology/audiology), SOCIAL SCIENCE (anthropology, criminal justice, economics, geography, history, human services, international studies, liberal arts/general studies, philosophy, political science/government, psychology, religion, social work, sociology, and urban studies). Business, education, and nursing are the largest.
Required: All students must complete a minimum of 120 credit hours with at least a 2.0 GPA. A minimum of 42 credits in general education requirements includes 9 credits each in humanities and social science, 8 in natural science, 6 in English composition, 3 in math or logic, 3 in non-Western culture, 3 in speech, and 2 in phys ed.
Special: UW/Oshkosh offers internships and study abroad. There are 15 national honor societies, a freshman honors program.
Faculty/Classroom: 56% of faculty are male; 44%, female. No introductory courses are taught by graduate students. The average class size in an introductory lecture is 31 and in a laboratory, 21.
Admissions: In a recent year, 25% of freshmen were in the top fifth of their class; 65% were in the top two fifths. There was 1 National Merit finalist. 19 freshmen graduated first in their class.
Requirements: The ACT is required. In addition, students must graduate in the upper 50% of their class from an accredited secondary school or score a 22 on the enhanced ACT if ranked in the third quartile. They should have completed 17 academic credits, including 4 in English, 3 each in math, social sciences, natural sciences, and 4 in electives, preferably in a foreign language or fine arts/humanities. Applications are accepted on-line at *apply.wisconsin.edu* or *collegenet.com*. AP and CLEP credits are accepted.
Procedure: Freshmen are admitted to all sessions. Entrance exams should be taken in spring of the junior year or early fall of the senior year. There is a deferred admissions plan. Notification is sent on a rolling basis. Check with the school for current application deadlines and fee.
Transfer: 557 transfer students enrolled in a recent year. Candidates should have completed 30 or more semester credits; if not, high school transcripts are reviewed. Students must have at least a 2.0 cumulative GPA. 30 credits of 120 must be completed at UW/Oshkosh.
Visiting: There are regularly scheduled orientations for prospective students, including preview days, campus tours, and an individual appointment with an admissions counselor. There are guides for informal visits and visitors may sit in on classes and stay overnight. To schedule a visit, contact the Admissions Office and Gruenhagen Conference Center at (920) 424-0202 or (920) 424-1107.
Financial Aid: In a recent year, 55% of all freshmen and 50% of continuing students received some form of financial aid. 40% of freshmen and 35% of continuing students received need-based aid. Scholarships or need-based grants averaged $2000 ($2700 maximum); loans averaged $2500 ($2625 maximum); and work contracts averaged $2000 ($2500 maximum). 60% of undergraduates work part time. Average annual earnings from campus work are $2000. The average financial indebtedness of a recent graduate was $14,000. UW/Oshkosh is a member of CSS. The FAFSA is required. Check with school for current deadlines.
International Students: There were 75 international students enrolled in a recent year. They must score 500 on the written TOEFL.
Computers: The mainframes are a DEC VAX 11/780 and 8250. There are 450 PCs. All students may access the system 24 hours, 7 days a week. There are no time limits and no fees.
Graduates: In a recent year, 1372 bachelor's degrees were awarded. The most popular majors were nursing (10%), marketing (7%), and elementary education (6%). In an average class, 7% graduate in 4 years, 33% in 5 years, and 44% in 6 years. 106 companies recruited on campus in a recent year. Of a recent graduating class, 97% were employed within 6 months of graduation.
Admissions Contact: Jill Endries, Director of Admissions. A video is available. E-mail: *oshadmuw@uwosh.edu* Web: *www.uwosh.edu*

UNIVERSITY OF WISCONSIN/PARKSIDE E-5

Kenosha, WI 53141-2000 **(414) 595-2355; Fax: (414) 595-2202**

Full-time: 1160 men, 1570 women	**Faculty:** 144; IIA, av$
Part-time: 680 men, 960 women	**Ph.D.s:** 93%
Graduate: 70 men, 110 women	**Student/Faculty:** 19 to 1
Year: semesters, summer session	**Tuition:** $2600 ($8000)
Application Deadline: see profile	**Room & Board:** $3700
Freshman Class: n/av	**ACT:** required
	LESS COMPETITIVE

The University of Wisconsin/Parkside, founded in 1968, offers undergraduate programs in liberal arts, business, education, and science and technology. Figures given in the above capsule, and in this profile, are approximate. There are 4 undergraduate and 3 graduate schools. The library contains 350,000 volumes, 150,000 microform items, and 10,200 audiovisual forms/CDs, and subscribes to 1500 periodicals. Computerized library services include the card catalog. Special learning facilities include a learning resource center, art gallery, and radio station. The 700-acre campus is in a suburban area 30 miles south of Milwaukee. Including residence halls, there are 11 buildings.
Student Life: 91% are white. 22% do not continue beyond their first year; 60% remain to graduate.
Housing: About 400 students can be accommodated in college housing, which includes coed on-campus apartments and off-campus apartments. In addition, there are special-interest houses. On-campus housing is guaranteed for all 4 years. 52% of students commute. All students may keep cars.

Activities: There are no fraternities or sororities. There are 60 groups on campus, including art, band, cheerleading, choir, chorale, chorus, computers, drama, ethnic, gay, honors, international, jazz band, literary magazine, musical theater, newspaper, orchestra, political, professional, religious, social, social service, student government, and yearbook. Popular campus events include Cinco de Mayo, Winter Carnival, and Black History Month.

Sports: There are 8 intercollegiate sports for men and 6 for women. Facilities include a national/cross-country course, tennis courts, playing fields, and an all-purpose phys ed building with a 3000-seat auditorium for athletic events and concerts.

Disabled Students: All of the campus is accessible. Wheelchair ramps, elevators, special parking, specially equipped rest rooms, lowered drinking fountains, and lowered telephones are available.

Services: Counseling and information services are available, as is tutoring in every subject. There is a reader service for the blind, and remedial math, reading, and writing.

Campus Safety and Security: Measures include shuttle buses, pamphlets/posters/films, emergency telephones, and lighted pathways/sidewalks.

Programs of Study: UW/Parkside confers B.A. and B.S. degrees. Master's degrees are also awarded. Bachelor's degrees are awarded in BIOLOGICAL SCIENCE (biology/biological science), BUSINESS (business administration and management), COMMUNICATIONS AND THE ARTS (communications, dramatic arts, English, fine arts, French, German, music, and Spanish), COMPUTER AND PHYSICAL SCIENCE (chemistry, computer science, geology, mathematics, physics, and science), EDUCATION (education), ENGINEERING AND ENVIRONMENTAL DESIGN (industrial administration/management), SOCIAL SCIENCE (economics, geography, history, humanities, international studies, philosophy, political science/government, psychology, and sociology). Social sciences and physical sciences are the strongest academically. Business is the largest.

Required: A total of 120 credits, with at least 30 in the major and a GPA of 2.0, is required for graduation. Students must complete a minimum of 12 credits in humanities and the arts, 12 in social and behavioral sciences, and 9 in natural sciences. Nonengineering majors with fewer than 2 units of foreign language in high school must also fulfill a foreign language requirement.

Special: UW/Parkside offers on-campus work-study programs, internships, study abroad, student-designed majors, and an accelerated premedicine program. Nondegree study and credit by exam are possible. There is a freshman honors program.

Faculty/Classroom: No introductory courses are taught by graduate students. The average class size in an introductory lecture is 150; in a laboratory, 50; and in a regular course, 30.

Admissions: 5 freshmen graduated first in their class in a recent year.

Requirements: The ACT is required for in-state students; either the ACT or the SAT I for out-of-state students. A minimum score of 21 is required on the ACT. Students may use a lower ACT score in combination with class rank to gain admission. Candidates must be graduates of an accredited secondary school or hold a GED diploma. At least 16 academic credits are required, including 4 in English, 3 in social sciences, 2 in natural sciences, and 1 each in algebra and plane geometry. UW/Parkside requires applicants to be in the upper 50% of their class. AP and CLEP credits are accepted. Important factors in the admissions decision are geographic diversity, extracurricular activities record, and ability to finance college education.

Procedure: Freshmen are admitted fall and spring. Entrance exams should be taken by the fall of the senior year. There are early admissions and deferred admissions plans. Notification is sent on a rolling basis. Check with the school for current application deadlines and fee.

Transfer: 400 transfer students enrolled in a recent year. Students must have a GPA of 2.0 and be in good standing with the previous institution attended. 30 credits of 120 must be completed at UW/Parkside.

Visiting: There are regularly scheduled orientations for prospective students, including open houses and campus tours. There are guides for informal visits and visitors may sit in on classes. To schedule a visit, contact Student Enrollment Services.

Financial Aid: In a recent year, 34% of all freshmen and 30% of continuing students received some form of financial aid. The CSS/Profile or FFS and the college's own financial statement are required. Check with the school for current deadlines.

International Students: There were 27 international students enrolled in a recent year. They must score 525 on the written TOEFL.

Computers: The mainframe is an IBM 4381. There are also 50 IBM, Mac, Zenith, and Apple IIe PCs available in the library/learning center. Two general-purpose labs are available to all students. There are no time limits and no fees.

Admissions Contact: Charles Murphy, Admissions Director.

UNIVERSITY OF WISCONSIN/PLATTEVILLE — C-5

Platteville, WI 53818-3099 — (608) 342-1125
(800) 362-5515; Fax: (608) 342-1122

Full-time: 2890 men, 1570 women	**Faculty:** 203; IIA, av$
Part-time: 220 men, 170 women	**Ph.D.s:** 62%
Graduate: 60 men, 120 women	**Student/Faculty:** 22 to 1
Year: semesters, summer session	**Tuition:** $3483 ($11,995)
Application Deadline: open	**Room & Board:** $3799

Freshman Class: 2463 applied, 1581 accepted, 1581 enrolled
ACT: 21 — **COMPETITIVE**

The University of Wisconsin/Platteville, founded in 1866, offers undergraduate programs in arts, social sciences, humanities, sciences, agriculture, education, engineering, communication, business, and industry. Enrollment figures given in the above capsule are approximate. There are 3 undergraduate schools and 1 graduate school. In addition to regional accreditation, UWP has baccalaureate program accreditation with ABET, ABFSE, and NASM. The library contains 222,838 volumes, 997,272 microform items, and 13,299 audiovisual forms/CDs, and subscribes to 22,175 periodicals. Computerized library services include interlibrary loans and database searching. Special learning facilities include a learning resource center, art gallery, radio station, and TV station. The 340-acre campus is in a rural area 20 miles northeast of Dubuque, Iowa, and 75 miles southwest of Madison. Including residence halls, there are 65 buildings.

Student Life: 93% of undergraduates are from Wisconsin. Others are from 33 states, 29 foreign countries, and Canada. 90% are from public schools. 95% are white. 60% are Protestant; 30% Catholic. The average age of freshmen is 18. 24% do not continue beyond their first year; 49% remain to graduate.

Housing: 2306 students can be accommodated in college housing, which includes single-sex and coed dormitories. In addition, there are intensive-study quiet floors, an engineering hall, and a computing technology hall. On-campus housing is guaranteed for all 4 years. All students may keep cars.

Activities: 2% of men and about 1% of women belong to 1 local and 9 national fraternities; 5% of women belong to 1 local and 3 national sororities. There are 92 groups on campus, including art, band, cheerleading, chess, choir, chorale, chorus, computers, drama, drill team, ethnic, film, gay, honors, international, jazz band, literary magazine, marching band, musical theater, newspaper, opera, orchestra, pep band, photography, political, professional, radio and TV, religious, social, social service, student government, symphony, and yearbook. Popular campus events include Heartland Festival, international student dinners, and February Follies.

Sports: There are 7 intercollegiate sports for men and 6 for women, and 17 intramural sports for men and 16 for women. Facilities include a 2000-seat gym, a 10,000-seat stadium, a 200-meter indoor track, a 400-meter outdoor track, 7 basketball and 7 volleyball courts, 6 tennis and 4 racquetball courts, a weight room, a swimming pool, a baseball diamond, and soccer fields.

Disabled Students: 95% of the campus is accessible. Wheelchair ramps, elevators, special parking, specially equipped rest rooms, special class scheduling, lowered drinking fountains, and lowered telephones are available.

Services: Counseling and information services are available, as is tutoring in most subjects. There is a reader service for the blind, and remedial math, reading, and writing; and university counseling services.

Campus Safety and Security: Measures include 24-hour foot and vehicle patrol, escort service, informal discussions, and pamphlets/posters/films. There are emergency telephones, lighted pathways/sidewalks, and locked residence halls.

Programs of Study: UWP confers B.A. and B.S. degrees. Associate and master's degrees are also awarded. Bachelor's degrees are awarded in AGRICULTURE (agricultural business management, agricultural economics, animal science, and soil science), BIOLOGICAL SCIENCE (biology/biological science), BUSINESS (accounting, business administration and management, business economics, and management science), COMMUNICATIONS AND THE ARTS (English, fine arts, French, German, music, Spanish, and speech/debate/rhetoric), COMPUTER AND PHYSICAL SCIENCE (chemistry, computer science, mathematics, physical sciences, physics, and science), EDUCATION (agricultural, art, elementary, middle school, music, physical, science, secondary, and technical), ENGINEERING AND ENVIRONMENTAL DESIGN (agricultural engineering technology, civil engineering, electrical/electronics engineering, engineering, industrial engineering, industrial engineering technology, land use management and reclamation, and mechanical engineering), SOCIAL SCIENCE (criminal justice, economics, geography, history, international studies, philosophy, political science/government, psychology, and social science). Engineering, middle school education, and technology management are the strongest academically. Engineering is the largest.

Required: To graduate, students must complete a minimum of 128 credit hours, with a minimum GPA of 2.0 overall, and within the major.

Course requirements include 12 credits in humanities and fine arts, 9 each in social sciences and natural sciences, 4 in ethnic and gender studies, and 3 in international education. Other competency requirements include 6 in English composition, 3 in math, and 2 each in speech and phys ed.

Special: UWP offers internships in business, industry, and communication; a co-op program in engineering; and study abroad in 12 countries. Credit by exam, credit for life, military, and work experience, work-study programs, student-designed majors, nondegree study, and pass/fail options are also available. There are 12 national honor societies, a freshman honors program, and 4 departmental honors programs.

Faculty/Classroom: 70% of faculty are male; 30%, female. All teach undergraduates and 1% both teach and do research. The average class size in an introductory lecture is 30; in a laboratory, 20; and in a regular course, 22.

Admissions: 64% of the 2001-2002 applicants were accepted. The ACT scores for the 2001-2002 freshman class were: 35% below 21, 33% between 21 and 23, 20% between 24 and 26, 8% between 27 and 28, and 5% above 28. 36% of the current freshmen were in the top fifth of their class; 40% were in the top two fifths.

Requirements: The ACT is required, with a minimum score of 22. Applicants must be graduates of an accredited secondary school or hold the GED certificate. Special permission may be granted from the dean for nontraditional students. Academic preparation should include 4 credits in English, 3 in social sciences, 2 each in math and natural sciences, 3 in any of the above or in a foreign language, and 2 in other academic areas. UWP requires applicants to be in the upper 65% of their class. AP and CLEP credits are accepted. Important factors in the admissions decision are ability to finance college education, recommendations by school officials, and advanced placement or honor courses. Applications are accepted on-line via the university's web site.

Procedure: Freshmen are admitted to all sessions. Entrance exams should be taken in April or June of the junior year. There are deferred admissions and rolling admissions plans. Application deadlines are open. 16% of all applicants are on a waiting list. The fall 2001 application fee was $35.

Transfer: 314 transfer students enrolled in 2001-2002. Out-of-state applicants must have a college GPA of 3.0 and be in good standing at their current or previous institution. Wisconsin residents should have a GPA of 2.5 and a minimum of 14 college credits. All transfer students must have completed 6 semester credits of UWP's English requirement and 3 semester credits of public speaking. 32 credits of 128 must be completed at UWP.

Visiting: There are regularly scheduled orientations for prospective students, The Pioneer Previews, held on 4 or 5 dates each year, include group tours, an admissions briefing, and visits to specific colleges and departments. There are guides for informal visits and visitors may sit in on classes. To schedule a visit, contact Richard Schumacher, Dean of Admissions and Enrollment Management.

Financial Aid: The average financial indebtedness of the 2001 graduate was $13,690. The FAFSA is required.

International Students: There are 49 international students enrolled. The school actively recruits these students. They must score 550 on the written TOEFL and also take the ACT or Wisconsin English and math placement exam.

Computers: The mainframes are a DEC VAX 4000 series server and an IBM 9375. There are 80 networked (Intel and Mac) PCs and 37 terminals available to students in general-access labs across campus. All students may access the system. There are no time limits and no fees.

Graduates: In 2001, 770 bachelor's degrees were awarded. The most popular majors were business administration (12%), mechanical engineering (9%), and elementary education (7%). In an average class, 14% graduate in 4 years, 37% in 5 years, and 50% in 6 years. 156 companies recruited on campus in 2000-2001. Of the 2000 graduating class, 1% was enrolled in graduate school within 6 months of graduation and 87% were employed.

Admissions Contact: Dr. Richard R. Schumacher, Dean of Admissions and Enrollment Management. E-mail: *admit@uwplatt.edu*
Web: *www.uwplatt.edu*

UNIVERSITY OF WISCONSIN/RIVER FALLS — A-3

River Falls, WI 54022 — **(715) 425-3500; Fax: (715) 425-0676**

Full-time: 1850 men, 2975 women	**Faculty:** 236
Part-time: 210 men, 295 women	**Ph.D.s:** 85%
Graduate: 90 men, 240 women	**Student/Faculty:** 20 to 1
Year: semesters, summer session	**Tuition:** $3100 ($10,000)
Application Deadline: see profile	**Room & Board:** $3300
Freshman Class: n/av	
ACT: required	**LESS COMPETITIVE**

The University of Wisconsin/River Falls, founded in 1874, is a public institution offering undergraduate programs in arts and sciences, education, agriculture, and food and environmental sciences. There are 3 undergraduate schools and 1 graduate school. Figures in the above capsule, and in this profile, are approximate. In addition to regional accreditation, UW/River Falls has baccalaureate program accreditation with ACEJMC, ASLA, CSWE, NASM, and NCATE. The library contains 221,453 volumes, 726,035 microform items, and 8455 audiovisual forms/CDs, and subscribes to 1322 periodicals. Computerized library services include the card catalog, interlibrary loans, and database searching. Special learning facilities include a learning resource center, art gallery, planetarium, radio station, TV station, and greenhouse, climbing wall, communicative disorders lab, educational technology center, food science and meat facilities, 2 campus lab farms, and sundial. The 225-acre campus is in a small town 29 miles east of Minneapolis-St. Paul, Minnesota. Including residence halls, there are 28 buildings.

Student Life: 52% of undergraduates are from Wisconsin. Others are from 25 states, 13 foreign countries, and Canada. 95% are from public schools. 95% are white. The average age of freshmen is 18; all undergraduates, 21. 25% do not continue beyond their first year; 50% remain to graduate.

Housing: 2172 students can be accommodated in college housing, which includes single-sex and coed dormitories. On-campus housing is guaranteed for all 4 years. All students may keep cars.

Activities: There are 5 national fraternities and 4 national sororities. There are 120 groups on campus, including art, band, cheerleading, choir, chorus, computers, dance, debate, drama, ethnic, forensics, gay, honors, international, jazz band, literary magazine, musical theater, newspaper, orchestra, pep band, political, professional, radio and TV, religious, social, student government, symphony, and yearbook. Popular campus events include Winter Carnival, Annual Rodeo, and Unity in the Community.

Sports: There are 7 intercollegiate sports for men and 11 for women, and 11 intramural sports for men and 12 for women. Facilities include an ice arena, a 4550-seat stadium, 2 multipurpose phys ed centers, a swimming pool, a 2600-seat gym and a smaller gym, handball courts, a field house, an indoor track, an indoor rock-climbing wall, and basketball, tennis, and volleyball courts.

Disabled Students: 95% of the campus is accessible. Wheelchair ramps, elevators, special parking, specially equipped rest rooms, special class scheduling, lowered drinking fountains, and lowered telephones are available.

Services: Counseling and information services are available, as is tutoring in every subject. There is a reader service for the blind, and remedial math, reading, and writing.

Campus Safety and Security: Measures include 24-hour foot and vehicle patrol, self-defense education, escort service, and informal discussions. There are pamphlets/posters/films, emergency telephones, and lighted pathways/sidewalks.

Programs of Study: UW/River Falls confers B.A., B.S., B.F.A, B.M.E., and B.S.W. degrees. Associate and master's degrees are also awarded. Bachelor's degrees are awarded in AGRICULTURE (agricultural business management, agronomy, animal science, conservation and regulation, horticulture, and soil science), BIOLOGICAL SCIENCE (biology/biological science and biotechnology), BUSINESS (accounting, and business administration and management), COMMUNICATIONS AND THE ARTS (art, communications, English, fine arts, journalism, modern language, music, and speech/debate/rhetoric), COMPUTER AND PHYSICAL SCIENCE (chemistry, computer programming, geology, mathematics, physics, and science), EDUCATION (agricultural, art, elementary, foreign languages, music, physical, and secondary), ENGINEERING AND ENVIRONMENTAL DESIGN (agricultural engineering and land use management and reclamation), HEALTH PROFESSIONS (premedicine, prepharmacy, and speech pathology/audiology), SOCIAL SCIENCE (economics, food science, geography, history, political science/government, prelaw, psychology, social studies, social work, and sociology). Physics, chemistry, and elementary education are the strongest academically. Business, elementary education, and animal science are the largest.

Required: To graduate, students must complete at least 120 semester hours, with a GPA of 2.0 overall and 2.25 in the major field. General education requirements include 39 semester hours in English composition, speech and humanities, natural and social sciences, math, and phys ed.

Special: Co-op programs in food science and environmental science, on-campus work-study, and accelerated degree programs in several preprofessional areas are available. UW/River Falls also offers internships, student-designed majors, credit by examination, nondegree study, and pass/fail options. Study abroad is available through the National Student Exchange and the International Student Exchange Program in some 15 countries. There are 11 national honor societies and a freshman honors program.

Faculty/Classroom: 70% of faculty are male; 30%, female. All teach undergraduates. No introductory courses are taught by graduate students. The average class size in an introductory lecture is 30; in a laboratory, 24; and in a regular course, 20.

Requirements: The ACT is required with a minimum composite score of 22, or 18 if the applicant is in upper 40% of the high school class. Candidates must be graduates of an accredited secondary school and have completed at least 17 academic credits, including 4 in English, 3 in social sciences, and 3 each in math and science, with 4 college prep courses. A GED certificate is acceptable. UW/River Falls requires applicants to be in the upper 40% of their class. AP and CLEP credits are accepted. Applications may be submitted on-line to *apply.wisconsin.edu*.

Procedure: Freshmen are admitted to all sessions. Entrance exams should be taken in the spring of the junior year. There are early admissions and deferred admissions plans. Notification is sent on a rolling basis. 12% of all applicants are on a waiting list. Check with the school for current application deadlines and fee.

Transfer: 402 transfer students enrolled in a recent year. Priority admission is given to students with a college GPA of 2.6 or higher. Students with a GPA of 2.0 to 2.6 are placed on a waiting list. Transfers in elementary education must have a GPA of 3.0. 30 credits of 120 must be completed at UW/River Falls.

Visiting: There are regularly scheduled orientations for prospective students, including College Visit Days and tours. There are guides for informal visits and visitors may sit in on classes. To schedule a visit, contact the Admissions Office.

Financial Aid: In a recent year, 60% of all freshmen received some form of financial aid. 60% of freshmen received need-based aid. 20% of undergraduates work part time. Average annual earnings from campus work are $1050. The average financial indebtedness of a recent graduate was $12,000. UW/River Falls is a member of CSS. The FAFSA is required. Check with the school for current deadlines.

International Students: They must score 500 on the written TOEFL and also take the ACT.

Computers: The mainframe is a DEC VAX 11/780. The mainframe lab has 18 terminals. There are also more than 150 Macs and PCs available in labs, offices, and residence halls across campus. Registered students have free e-mail and Internet access. All students may access the system more than 80 hours per week, and by telephone request when labs are closed. There are no time limits and no fees.

Admissions Contact: Alan J. Tuchtenhagen, Admissions Director.
E-mail: *admit@uwrf.edu* Web: *http://www.uwrf.edu*

UNIVERSITY OF WISCONSIN/STEVENS POINT C-3
Stevens Point, WI 54481-3897 (715) 346-2441
Fax: (715) 346-2558

Full-time: 3400 men, 4297 women	**Faculty:** 358; IIA, av$
Part-time: 301 men, 514 women	**Ph.D.s:** 76%
Graduate: 112 men, 320 women	**Student/Faculty:** 22 to 1
Year: semesters, summer session	**Tuition:** $3378 ($11,890)
Application Deadline: open	**Room & Board:** $3738
Freshman Class: 4224 applied, 3170 accepted, 1499 enrolled	
SAT I Verbal/Math: 530/540	**ACT:** 23 **COMPETITIVE**

The University of Wisconsin/Stevens Point, founded in 1894, offers undergraduate programs in natural resources, education, business, arts and sciences, and professional studies. There are 4 undergraduate schools and 1 graduate school. In addition to regional accreditation, UWSP has baccalaureate program accreditation with ADA, ASLA, FIDER, NASAD, NASM, and SAF. The library contains 978,112 volumes, 899,878 microform items, and 32,916 audiovisual forms/CDs, and subscribes to 8470 periodicals. Computerized library services include the card catalog, interlibrary loans, and database searching. Special learning facilities include a learning resource center, art gallery, natural history museum, planetarium, radio station, TV station, observatory, map center, 200-acre nature preserve, groundwater center, and wellness institute. The 335-acre campus is in a small town 110 miles north of Madison. Including residence halls, there are 35 buildings.

Student Life: 92% of undergraduates are from Wisconsin. Others are from 35 states, 30 foreign countries, and Canada. 95% are white. The average age of freshmen is 19; all undergraduates, 22. 23% do not continue beyond their first year; 53% remain to graduate.

Housing: 3316 students can be accommodated in college housing, which includes single-sex and coed dormitories. In addition, there are special-interest houses, privately owned off-campus apartments, and off-campus fraternity and sorority houses. 64% of students commute. All students may keep cars.

Activities: 2% of men belong to 3 national fraternities; 1% of women belong to 3 local sororities and 1 national sorority. There are 150 groups on campus, including art, band, cheerleading, choir, chorale, chorus, computers, dance, drama, ethnic, film, gay, honors, international, jazz band, literary magazine, musical theater, newspaper, orchestra, pep band, photography, political, professional, radio and TV, religious, social, social service, student government, symphony, and yearbook.

Sports: There are 10 intercollegiate sports for men and 12 for women, and 14 intramural sports for men and 12 for women. Facilities include 2 gyms, a health enhancement center, and the university center. The campus stadium seats 5500; the indoor gym, 3500. There is also a 391-seat auditorium.

Disabled Students: All of the campus is accessible. Wheelchair ramps, elevators, special parking, specially equipped rest rooms, special class scheduling, lowered drinking fountains, and lowered telephones. Note-taking services and talking books are also available for the hearing and visually impaired.

Services: Counseling and information services are available, as is tutoring in most subjects. There is a reader service for the blind, and remedial math, reading, and writing.

Campus Safety and Security: Measures include 24-hour foot and vehicle patrol, informal discussions, emergency telephones, and lighted pathways/sidewalks. There is an evening van service.

Programs of Study: UWSP confers B.A., B.S., B.F.A, and B.M. degrees. Associate and master's degrees are also awarded. Bachelor's degrees are awarded in AGRICULTURE (forestry and related sciences, natural resource management, and soil science), BIOLOGICAL SCIENCE (biology/biological science and wildlife biology), BUSINESS (accounting, business administration and management, and management science), COMMUNICATIONS AND THE ARTS (arts administration/management, communications, dance, dramatic arts, English, fine arts, French, German, music, and Spanish), COMPUTER AND PHYSICAL SCIENCE (chemistry, information sciences and systems, mathematics, natural sciences, and physics), EDUCATION (athletic training, early childhood, education of the exceptional child, elementary, health, home economics, music, and physical), ENGINEERING AND ENVIRONMENTAL DESIGN (interior design and paper and pulp science), HEALTH PROFESSIONS (clinical science, nursing, and speech pathology/audiology), SOCIAL SCIENCE (dietetics, economics, family/consumer studies, geography, history, international studies, liberal arts/general studies, philosophy, physical fitness/movement, political science/government, psychology, public administration, social science, sociology, and water resources). Business administration, elementary education, and biology are the largest.

Required: To graduate, students must complete 120 credit hours, with a minimum GPA of 2.0. Core curriculum requirements must also be fulfilled, along with 3 credits in phys ed. Some majors require additional credits and higher minimum GPAs.

Special: A co-op program in nursing is offered with UW/Eau Claire and St. Joseph's Hospital. Internships, study abroad in 7 countries, work-study programs, dual and student-designed majors, independent study, and pass/fail options are also available. Credit is given for military, life, and work experience. There are 9 national honor societies.

Faculty/Classroom: 63% of faculty are male; 37%, female. All teach undergraduates and do research. No introductory courses are taught by graduate students. The average class size in an introductory lecture is 42; in a laboratory, 23; and in a regular course, 26.

Admissions: 75% of the 2001-2002 applicants were accepted. The SAT I scores for the 2001-2002 freshman class were: Verbal--32% below 500, 45% between 500 and 599, 18% between 600 and 700, and 5% above 700; Math--26% below 500, 55% between 500 and 599, and 1% between 600 and 700. The ACT scores were 25% below 21, 37% between 21 and 23, 25% between 24 and 26, 8% between 27 and 28, and 5% above 28. 33% of the current freshmen were in the top fifth of their class; 79% were in the top two fifths. 40 freshmen graduated first in their class in a recent year.

Requirements: The SAT I or ACT is required. In addition, applicants should have a high school rank of top 40% or above, or a cumulative high school GPA of 3.0 or higher, with an ACT composite score of 21 (SAT I of 990) or above. The ACT is preferred. The GED is accepted. Required academic preparation includes 4 units of English, 3 of social studies, and 2 each of math and lab science, along with 5 electives; 2 units of foreign language are recommended. An interview is suggested. Applications are accepted on-line at *http://apply.wisconsin.edu*. A GPA of 3.0 is required. AP and CLEP credits are accepted.

Procedure: Freshmen are admitted fall and spring. Entrance exams should be taken by February of the senior year. Application deadlines are open. The fall 2001 application fee was $35.

Transfer: 653 transfer students enrolled in 2001-2002. Applicants must submit high school and college transcripts. A college minimum GPA of 2.75 is required. 30 credits of 120 must be completed at UWSP.

Visiting: There are regularly scheduled orientations for prospective students, consisting of a 2-day program that includes a meeting with an academic adviser as well as with upperclass students and other new students. There are guides for informal visits. To schedule a visit, contact the Office of Admissions.

Financial Aid: In 2001-2002, 39% of all freshmen and 42% of continuing students received some form of financial aid. 36% of freshmen and 39% of continuing students received need-based aid. The average freshman award was $4473. Of that total, scholarships or need-based grants averaged $3520; loans averaged $2592; and work contracts averaged $3027. 26% of undergraduates work part time. The average financial indebtedness of the 2001 graduate was $13,140. The FAFSA is required. The fall application deadline is June 15.

International Students: There are 141 international students enrolled. The school actively recruits these students. They must score 525 on the written TOEFL or 193 on the electronic version.

Computers: There are more than 800 networked IBM PCs on campus. The Internet and World Wide Web are fully accessible. Networked computers with a wide variety of software packages available in residence halls, public and private labs, and kiosks. All students may access the system. There are no time limits and no fees.

Graduates: In 2001, 1461 bachelor's degrees were awarded. The most popular majors were business administration (10%), biology (9%), and communication (9%). In an average class, 16% graduate in 4 years, 47% in 5 years, and 53% in 6 years. 130 companies recruited on campus in 2000-2001. Of the 2000 graduating class, 16% were enrolled in graduate school within 6 months of graduation and 98% were employed.

Admissions Contact: David Eckholm, Director of Admissions.
E-mail: *admiss@uwsp.edu* Web: *www.uwsp.edu/admit/admiss.htm*

UNIVERSITY OF WISCONSIN/STOUT — B-3

Menomonie, WI 54751 — (715) 232-1411
(800) HI-STOUT; Fax: (715) 232-1667

Full-time: 3329 men, 3122 women — **Faculty:** 305; IIA, -$
Part-time: 445 men, 362 women — **Ph.D.s:** 76%
Graduate: 176 men, 346 women — **Student/Faculty:** 21 to 1
Year: 4-1-4, summer session — **Tuition:** $3502 ($12,026)
Application Deadline: open — **Room & Board:** $3690
Freshman Class: 3162 applied, 2243 accepted, 1299 enrolled
ACT: 22 — **COMPETITIVE**

The University of Wisconsin/Stout, founded in 1891, offers undergraduate programs in liberal studies, human environmental sciences, industry and technology, education, and human services. There are 3 undergraduate schools and 1 graduate school. In addition to regional accreditation, UW-Stout has baccalaureate program accreditation with AAMFT, ABET, ACCE, ADA, FIDER, IACBE, and NASAD. The library contains 223,487 volumes, 1,176,407 microform items, and 16,546 audiovisual forms/CDs, and subscribes to 1676 periodicals. Computerized library services include the card catalog, interlibrary loans, and database searching. Special learning facilities include a learning resource center, art gallery, radio station, and TV station. The 110-acre campus is in a rural area 60 miles east of Minneapolis/St. Paul. Including residence halls, there are 33 buildings.

Student Life: 73% of undergraduates are from Wisconsin. Others are from 27 states, 28 foreign countries, and Canada. 94% are white. The average age of freshmen is 20; all undergraduates, 23. 24% do not continue beyond their first year; 55% remain to graduate.

Housing: 2900 students can be accommodated in college housing, which includes coed dormitories. In addition, there is smoke-free, alcohol-free, upperclassmen-only, freshman, and disabled student housing. On-campus housing is guaranteed for all 4 years. 65% of students commute. All students may keep cars.

Activities: 2% of men belong to 3 local and 2 national fraternities; 4% of women belong to 3 national sororities. There are 117 groups on campus, including art, band, cheerleading, choir, chorale, chorus, computers, debate, drama, ethnic, film, forensics, gay, honors, international, jazz band, literary magazine, marching band, newspaper, pep band, photography, political, professional, radio, religious, social, social service, and student government. Popular campus events include Family Weekend, Cheese Week, and Biggest House Party.

Sports: There are 6 intercollegiate sports for men and 8 for women, and 20 intramural sports for men and 19 for women. Facilities include baseball, soccer, and football fields, indoor and outdoor tracks, and a field house with basketball, racquetball, and volleyball courts, a pool, weight and gymnastics rooms, and indoor and outdoor tennis courts.

Disabled Students: All of the campus is accessible. Wheelchair ramps, elevators, special parking, specially equipped rest rooms, special class scheduling, lowered drinking fountains, and lowered telephones are available.

Services: Counseling and information services are available, as is tutoring in most subjects. There is a reader service for the blind, and remedial math, reading, and writing.

Campus Safety and Security: Measures include 24-hour foot and vehicle patrol, informal discussions, pamphlets/posters/films, lighted pathways/sidewalks, and training sessions.

Programs of Study: UW-Stout confers B.A., B.S., and B.F.A. degrees. Master's degrees are also awarded. Bachelor's degrees are awarded in BUSINESS (business administration and management, hospitality management services, management science, and retailing), COMMUNICATIONS AND THE ARTS (apparel design, communications, fine arts, and telecommunications), COMPUTER AND PHYSICAL SCIENCE (applied mathematics and science), EDUCATION (art, early childhood, marketing and distribution, technical, and vocational), ENGINEERING AND ENVIRONMENTAL DESIGN (construction technology, graphic and printing production, graphic arts technology, industrial administration/management, industrial engineering technology, and manufacturing engineering), HEALTH PROFESSIONS (rehabilitation therapy), SOCIAL SCIENCE (child care/child and family studies, dietetics, family/consumer studies, food production/management/services, and psychology). General business administration, art, and hotel restaurant and tourism management are the largest.

Required: Students must complete a minimum of 124 credits, including a general education component. Some degree programs have specific general education courses that must be taken to satisfy certification, accreditation, or prerequisite standards. Students must also fulfill an ethnic studies requirement.

Special: UW-Stout offers business and industry internships, cooperative programs, work-study programs, and study abroad in London. Dual majors, credit by exam, credit for life, military, and work experience, nondegree study, and pass/fail options are also available. There is 1 national honor society, a freshman honors program, and 3 departmental honors programs.

Faculty/Classroom: 62% of faculty are male; 38%, female. All both teach and do research. The average class size in an introductory lecture is 35 and in a laboratory, 20.

Admissions: 71% of the 2001-2002 applicants were accepted. The ACT scores for the 2001-2002 freshman class were: 9% between 12 and 17, 64% between 18 and 23, 26% between 24 and 29, and 2% between 30 and 36. 32% of the current freshmen were in the top quarter of their class; 84% were in the top half. 8 freshmen graduated first in their class.

Requirements: The SAT I or ACT is required, with a minimum composite score of 1030 on the SAT I; the ACT is preferred. Minimum test scores are waived if students rank in the upper 50% of their class. Applicants should graduate from an accredited secondary school. The GED is accepted if applicants are over 21, or if their graduating class has been out for at least 2 years. Secondary school preparation should include 4 academic credits in English, 3 each in social studies, math, and science, and 4 in electives. AP and CLEP credits are accepted. Applications are accepted on-line at *apply.wisconsin.edu*.

Procedure: Freshmen are admitted fall, spring, and summer. Entrance exams should be taken in June of the junior year. Application deadlines are open. The application fee is $35. Notification is sent on a rolling basis beginning September 15. 11% of all applicants are on a waiting list.

Transfer: 610 transfer students enrolled in 2001-2002. A minimum college GPA of 2.0 is required for student transfers from VW system institutions. A 2.2 GPA is required for those transferring from outside the UW system. 32 credits of 124 must be completed at UW-Stout.

Visiting: There are regularly scheduled orientations for prospective students, including an interview with an admissions counselor and a campus tour. There are also campus preview days throughout the academic year. There are guides for informal visits and visitors may sit in on classes and stay overnight. To schedule a visit, contact Dawn Steinmeyer at (800) 447-8688 or (715) 232-1232 or *steinmeyerd@uwstout.edu*.

Financial Aid: In 2001-2002, 73% of all freshmen and 68% of continuing students received some form of financial aid. 48% of freshmen and 47% of continuing students received need-based aid. The average freshman award was $3924. Of that total, scholarships or need-based grants averaged $2992 ($3750 maximum); loans averaged $3720 ($4000 maximum); work contracts averaged $1515 ($1600 maximum); and veteran benefits, tuition waivers, and vocational rehabilitation benefits averaged $2820 ($4704 maximum). 71% of undergraduates work part time. Average annual earnings from campus work are $1200. The average financial indebtedness of the 2001 graduate was $15,961. UW-Stout is a member of CSS. The FAFSA is required. The fall application deadline is April 1.

International Students: The school actively recruits these students. They must score 500 on the written TOEFL.

Computers: The mainframes are an HP/9000/N4000 and 2 Sun minicomputers. There are more than 200 networked computers in the campus computing lab, available to all students. There are networked computer kiosks in all major classroom, recreation center, food service, and administrative buildings. All residence halls have a computer lab. Ports and wireless access are available throughout campus. All students may access the system 24 hours a day, 7 days a week. There are no time limits and no fees. All students are required to have personal computers.

Graduates: In 2001, 1054 bachelor's degrees were awarded. The most popular majors were general business administration (13%), art (10%), and early childhood education (9%). In an average class, 13% graduate in 4 years, 40% in 5 years, and 51% in 6 years.

Admissions Contact: Cindy Jenkins, Director of Admissions. A video is available. E-mail: *admissions@uwstout.edu* Web: *www.uwstout.edu*

UNIVERSITY OF WISCONSIN/SUPERIOR A-1

Superior, WI 54880 (715) 394-8230; Fax: (715) 394-8407

Full-time: 811 men, 1192 women	**Faculty:** 115; IIA, -$
Part-time: 135 men, 296 women	**Ph.D.s:** 75%
Graduate: 142 men, 266 women	**Student/Faculty:** 17 to 1
Year: semesters, summer session	**Tuition:** $3233 ($8969)
Application Deadline: April 1	**Room & Board:** $3818
Freshman Class: 771 applied, 622 accepted, 342 enrolled	
SAT I Verbal/Math: 660/670	**ACT:** 24 **COMPETITIVE+**

The University of Wisconsin/Superior, founded in 1893, offers undergraduate programs in the liberal arts and sciences, business, education, fine arts, applied arts, and social sciences. There are 5 undergraduate schools and 1 graduate school. The library contains 455,313 volumes, 105,398 microform items, and 5467 audiovisual forms/CDs, and subscribes to 753 periodicals. Computerized library services include the card catalog, interlibrary loans, and database searching. Special learning facilities include a learning resource center, art gallery, planetarium, TV station, aquatic lab, color television studio, and FM radio station. The 230-acre campus is in an urban area 150 miles north of Minneapolis/St. Paul. Including residence halls, there are 17 buildings.

Student Life: 58% of undergraduates are from Wisconsin. Others are from 21 states, 18 foreign countries, and Canada. 90% are from public schools. 95% are white. The average age of freshmen is 17; all undergraduates, 21. 15% do not continue beyond their first year; 40% remain to graduate.

Housing: 650 students can be accommodated in college housing, which includes single-sex and coed dormitories. On-campus housing is guaranteed for all 4 years. 76% of students commute. All students may keep cars.

Activities: There are no fraternities or sororities. There are 48 groups on campus, including art, band, cheerleading, choir, chorale, chorus, computers, dance, drama, ethnic, gay, honors, international, jazz band, newspaper, orchestra, photography, political, professional, radio and TV, religious, social, social service, student government, and symphony. Popular campus events include Snow Week, sports events, and Fall Fest.

Sports: There are 5 intercollegiate sports for men and 7 for women, and 5 intramural sports for men and 5 for women. Facilities include a 4000-seat stadium, a 3000-seat gym, an ice arena, a swimming pool, a weight training room, a dance studio, an all-weather track, and softball and baseball fields.

Disabled Students: 95% of the campus is accessible. Wheelchair ramps, elevators, special parking, specially equipped rest rooms, special class scheduling, lowered drinking fountains, and lowered telephones are available.

Services: Counseling and information services are available, as is tutoring in every subject. There is remedial math and writing.

Campus Safety and Security: Measures include 24-hour foot and vehicle patrol, self-defense education, escort service, and informal discussions. There are pamphlets/posters/films, emergency telephones, and lighted pathways/sidewalks.

Programs of Study: UW/Superior confers B.A., B.S., B.F.A., B.M., and B.M.E. degrees. Associate and master's degrees are also awarded. Bachelor's degrees are awarded in BIOLOGICAL SCIENCE (biology/biological science), BUSINESS (accounting and business administration and management), COMMUNICATIONS AND THE ARTS (art history and appreciation, communications, dramatic arts, English, fine arts, music, music performance, speech/debate/rhetoric, and studio art), COMPUTER AND PHYSICAL SCIENCE (chemistry, computer science, information sciences and systems, and mathematics), EDUCATION (art, elementary, mathematics, music, physical, science, and secondary), HEALTH PROFESSIONS (art therapy and community health work), SOCIAL SCIENCE (criminal justice, history, international studies, law, political science/government, psychology, public administration, social studies, social work, and sociology). Business, education, and aquatic biology are the strongest academically. Business is the largest.

Required: To graduate, students must complete 120 credit hours, with a GPA of 2.0. A minimum of 54 hours must be credited toward completion of 1 comprehensive major, 2 majors in different disciplines, or 1 major and 1 minor in a different discipline. The required core curriculum includes 55 credits in communications, English, math, phys ed, world culture, contemporary society, aesthetic experience, natural science, and human behavior. A comprehensive exam and a senior project are required.

Special: UW/Superior offers co-op programs in business and internships in social work, business, mass communication, and criminal justice. There is a comprehensive program of student-designed majors, along with a cooperative program in marine studies with Texas A&M University and 3-2 engineering and forestry programs with Michigan Technological University. Students may cross-register for 2 classes per semester at the University of Minnesota/Duluth, the College of St. Scholastica, or Northland College. An extended degree is offered. Credit for life experience and pass/fail options are available. There is a chapter of Phi Beta Kappa and a freshman honors program.

Faculty/Classroom: 60% of faculty are male; 40%, female. All both teach and do research. No introductory courses are taught by graduate students. The average class size in an introductory lecture is 40; in a laboratory, 20; and in a regular course, 23.

Admissions: 81% of the 2001-2002 applicants were accepted. The SAT I scores for the 2001-2002 freshman class were: Verbal--25% below 500, 25% between 500 and 599, and 50% between 600 and 699; Math--75% between 500 and 599, and 25% between 600 and 699. The ACT scores were 7% between 12 and 17, 63% between 18 and 23, 29% between 24 and 29, and 1% between 30 and 36. 37% of the current freshmen were in the top quarter of their class; 81% were in the top half.

Requirements: The ACT is required; out-of-state residents may submit SAT I scores instead. Applicants must graduate from an accredited secondary school or the equivalent. They must rank in the upper 50% of their graduating class or achieve a minimum composite score of 20 on the ACT. Applications are accepted on-line at *apply.wisconsin.edu*. AP and CLEP credits are accepted. Important factors in the admissions decision are parents or siblings attending the school and recommendations by school officials.

Procedure: Freshmen are admitted fall, spring, and summer. Entrance exams should be taken before admission in the spring of the junior year. There are early admissions and deferred admissions plans. Applications should be filed by April 1 for fall entry, along with a $35 fee. Notification is sent on a rolling basis.

Transfer: 342 transfer students enrolled in 2001-2002. A college GPA of 2.0 is required. 30 credits of 120 must be completed at UW/Superior.

Visiting: There are regularly scheduled orientations for prospective students, consisting of a day and a half of social and educational programs. There are guides for informal visits and visitors may sit in on classes and stay overnight. To schedule a visit, contact the Admissions Office.

Financial Aid: The average freshman award for the 2001-2002 school year was $6482. 21% of undergraduates work part time. Average annual earnings from campus work are $1200. The average financial indebtedness of the 2001 graduate was $13,749. UW/Superior is a member of CSS. The FAFSA is required. The fall application deadline is April 15.

International Students: There were 90 international students enrolled in a recent year. The school actively recruits these students. They must score 525 on the written TOEFL or take the MELAB and the college's own test. The university requires completion of an ELS language center program.

Computers: The mainframe is an HP 9000. There are 75 PCs available in the main hall, the library, and the dorms. All students may access the system 24 hours a day. There are no time limits and no fees.

Graduates: In 2001, 328 bachelor's degrees were awarded. The most popular majors were business/marketing (20%), education (18%), and social sciences (13%).

Admissions Contact: Admissions Counselor.
E-mail: *admissions@uwsuper.edu* Web: *www.uwsuper.edu*

UNIVERSITY OF WISCONSIN/WHITEWATER D-5

Whitewater, WI 53190 (262) 472-1440; Fax: (262) 472-1515

Full-time: 3989 men, 4399 women	**Faculty:** 384; IIA, av$
Part-time: 413 men, 550 women	**Ph.D.s:** 73%
Graduate: 456 men, 744 women	**Student/Faculty:** 20 to 1
Year: semesters, summer session	**Tuition:** $3367 ($11,878)
Application Deadline: open	**Room & Board:** $3570
Freshman Class: 4885 applied, 3748 accepted, 1840 enrolled	
SAT I or ACT: recommended	**COMPETITIVE**

The University of Wisconsin/Whitewater, founded in 1868, offers programs in teacher education, business, liberal arts, preprofessional studies, fine arts, and music. There are 4 undergraduate schools and 1 graduate school. In addition to regional accreditation, UW/Whitewater has baccalaureate program accreditation with AACSB, ASLA, CSWE, NASM, and NCATE. The library contains 356,000 volumes, 993,000 microform items, and 7300 audiovisual forms/CDs, and subscribes to 5000 periodicals. Computerized library services include the card catalog, interlibrary loans, and database searching. Special learning facilities include a learning resource center, art gallery, radio station, TV station, observatory, and weather station. The 385-acre campus is in a small town 50 miles southwest of Milwaukee. Including residence halls, there are 45 buildings.

Student Life: 94% of undergraduates are from Wisconsin. Others are from 26 states, 38 foreign countries, and Canada. 85% are from public schools. 93% are white. The average age of freshmen is 19; all undergraduates, 22. 22% do not continue beyond their first year; 61% remain to graduate.

Housing: 4000 students can be accommodated in college housing, which includes single-sex and coed dormitories. 50% of students live on campus; of those, 35% remain on campus on weekends. All students may keep cars.

Activities: 5% of men belong to 1 local fraternity and 6 national fraternities; 5% of women belong to 1 local sorority and 4 national sororities. There are 130 groups on campus, including art, band, cheerleading, choir, chorus, computers, dance, drama, drill team, ethnic, film, gay, honors, international, marching band, musical theater, newspaper, orchestra, pep band, photography, political, professional, radio and TV, religious, social, social service, student government, symphony, and yearbook. Popular campus events include Job Fair, Performing Arts Series, and athletic contests.

Sports: There are 9 intercollegiate sports for men and 8 for women, and 12 intramural sports for men and 12 for women. Facilities include tennis courts, pools, playing fields, a 13,000-seat stadium, and a 3500-seat gym.

Disabled Students: 75% of the campus is accessible. Wheelchair ramps, elevators, special parking, specially equipped rest rooms, special class scheduling, lowered drinking fountains, lowered telephones, and vans for mobility are available.

Services: Counseling and information services are available, as is tutoring in most subjects and study skills. There is a reader service for the blind, and remedial math, reading, and writing.

Campus Safety and Security: Measures include 24-hour foot and vehicle patrol, self-defense education, escort service, and shuttle buses. There are informal discussions, pamphlets/posters/films, emergency telephones, and lighted pathways/sidewalks.

Programs of Study: UW/Whitewater confers B.A., B.S., B.B.A., B.F.A., B.S.Ed., and B.M. degrees. Associate and master's degrees are also awarded. Bachelor's degrees are awarded in BIOLOGICAL SCIENCE (biology/biological science), BUSINESS (accounting, banking and finance, business administration and management, business economics, marketing/retailing/merchandising, office supervision and management, and personnel management), COMMUNICATIONS AND THE ARTS (art history and appreciation, communications, dramatic arts, English, French, German, journalism, music, public relations, Spanish, and speech/debate/rhetoric), COMPUTER AND PHYSICAL SCIENCE (chemistry, computer programming, mathematics, and physics), EDUCATION (art, business, early childhood, elementary, foreign languages, middle school, music, physical, science, secondary, social studies, and special), SOCIAL SCIENCE (economics, geography, history, international studies, political science/government, prelaw, psychology, public administration, safety and security technology, social work, sociology, and women's studies). Accounting, computer science, and education are the strongest academically. Business/accounting and education are the largest.

Required: Students must complete 50 credits of general studies, a writing competency requirement, and 3 credits in minority issues. A GPA of 2.0 and 120 hours are required to graduate.

Special: Internships, study abroad in 9 nations, accelerated degree programs in safety studies and speech communication, student-designed majors, and a general studies degree are available. Credit by examination, nondegree study, and pass/fail options are also offered. There are 14 national honor societies, a freshman honors program, and 7 departmental honors programs.

Faculty/Classroom: 57% of faculty are male; 43%, female. All teach undergraduates and 78% do research. No introductory courses are taught by graduate students. The average class size in a regular course is 26.

Admissions: 77% of the 2001-2002 applicants were accepted. 45 freshmen graduated first in their class in a recent year.

Requirements: The SAT I or ACT is recommended. In addition, applicants should graduate from an accredited secondary school or with 17 academic units, including 4 in English and 3 each in social studies, math, and science. The GED may be accepted. Applicants should rank in the upper 50% of their graduating class or achieve a combined high school and ACT/SAT I percentile rank of 100% or above. A GPA of 2.8 is required. AP and CLEP credits are accepted. Important factors in the admissions decision are evidence of special talent, advanced placement or honor courses, and recommendations by school officials. The University of Wisconsin system's electronic application process is available on the Web at *apply.wisconsin.edu*.

Procedure: Freshmen are admitted to all sessions. There is an early admissions plan. Application deadlines are open. The fall 2001 application fee was $35. Notification is sent on a rolling basis.

Transfer: 763 transfer students enrolled in a recent year. Applicants should have a minimum college GPA of 2.0. 30 credits of 120 must be completed at UW/Whitewater.

Visiting: There are regularly scheduled orientations for prospective students. There are guides for informal visits and visitors may sit in on classes. To schedule a visit, contact the Admissions Office.

Financial Aid: UW/Whitewater is a member of CSS. The FAFSA is required. Check with the school for current deadlines.

International Students: There were 107 international students enrolled in a recent year. The school actively recruits these students. They must score 500 on the written TOEFL or take the MELAB.

Computers: The mainframes are a Alpha 2100 and an IBM 9121-260. There are also 1500 PCs available. All students may access the system 24 hours if they have their own terminal or 8 A.M. to 11 P.M. Monday through Thursday and varied weekend hours in the general lab. There are no time limits and no fees.

Graduates: In a recent year, 1517 bachelor's degrees were awarded. The most popular majors were social work (7%), accounting (7%), and marketing (5%). In an average class, 50% graduate in 6 years.

Admissions Contact: Dr. Tori A. McGuire, Executive Director of Admissions. A video is available. E-mail: *uwwadmit@mail.uww.edu*
Web: *www.uww.edu*

VITERBO COLLEGE
(See Viterbo University)

VITERBO UNIVERSITY — B-4
(Formerly Viterbo College)
LaCrosse, WI 54601 — (608) 796-3010
(800) 848-3726; Fax: (608) 796-3020

Full-time: 377 men, 1041 women	**Faculty:** 101; IIA, --$
Part-time: 71 men, 225 women	**Ph.D.s:** 53%
Graduate: 86 men, 367 women	**Student/Faculty:** 14 to 1
Year: semesters, summer session	**Tuition:** $13,630
Application Deadline: August 1	**Room & Board:** $4413
Freshman Class: 1252 applied, 1062 accepted, 337 enrolled	
ACT: 21	**COMPETITIVE**

Viterbo University (formerly Viterbo College), is a private Catholic Franciscan liberal arts university. Viterbo offers undergraduate programs in liberal arts, sciences, fine arts, business, education, and health sciences. Master's degrees are offered in education and nursing. Viterbo University embraces persons of all faiths and prepares students for leadership and service. There are 5 undergraduate and 2 graduate schools. In addition to regional accreditation, Viterbo has baccalaureate program accreditation with ADA, CSWE, NASM, NCATE, NLN, and AACN, ACS. The library contains 100,000 volumes, 160,000 microform items, and 5000 audiovisual forms/CDs, and subscribes to 6045 periodicals. Computerized library services include the card catalog, interlibrary loans, and database searching. Special learning facilities include a learning resource center, art gallery, and a music resource center. The 12-acre campus is in an urban area 145 miles west of Madison, and 270 miles northwest of Chicago. Including residence halls, there are 12 buildings.

Student Life: 76% of undergraduates are from Wisconsin. Others are from 24 states and 17 foreign countries. 90% are from public schools. 89% are white. 41% are Catholic; 37% Protestant; 12% claim no religious affiliation. The average age of freshmen is 18; all undergraduates, 24. 29% do not continue beyond their first year; 48% remain to graduate.

Housing: 589 students can be accommodated in college housing, which includes coed dormitories, on-campus apartments, special-interest floors, and off-campus houses. On-campus housing is guaranteed for all 4 years. 65% of students commute. Alcohol is not permitted. Upperclassmen may keep cars.

Activities: There are no fraternities or sororities. There are 21 groups on campus, including art, choir, chorale, chorus, dance, drama, drill team, ethnic, international, literary magazine, musical theater, newspaper, opera, photography, professional, religious, social, social service, and student government. Popular campus events include Orientation Weekend, St. Francis Day Celebration, and Hog Wild.

Sports: There are 3 intercollegiate sports for men and 4 for women, and 12 intramural sports for men and 12 for women. 17% of men and women participate. Facilities include a student activity center with weight training and fitness rooms and courts for basketball, volleyball, and racquetball. The nearby Mississippi River and Mt. LaCrosse provide additional recreational opportunities. An outdoor athletic complex has facilities for soccer, baseball, and softball, located 2 1/2 miles from campus. There also are on-campus sand volleyball and paved basketball outdoor courts.

Disabled Students: 85% of the campus is accessible. Wheelchair ramps, elevators, special parking, specially equipped rest rooms, lowered drinking fountains, and lowered telephones are available.

Services: Counseling and information services are available, as is tutoring in every subject. There is a reader service for the blind, and remedial math, reading, and writing.

Campus Safety and Security: Measures include self-defense education, escort service, informal discussions, and pamphlets/posters/films. There are emergency telephones, lighted pathways/sidewalks, an emergency evacuation plan, security patrol from 5 P.M. to 7 A.M., ID check-in in dorms after 10 P.M., and door cards for access to dorms.

Programs of Study: Viterbo confers B.A., B.S., B.Art.Ed., B.B.A., B.F.A.Graphic Design, B.F.A.Mus.Theater, B.F.A.Studio Art, B.F.A.Theater Arts, B.I.S., B.L.S., B.M., B.S.Ed., B.S. Community-Medical Dietetics., and B.S.N. degrees. Master's degrees are also awarded. Bachelor's degrees are awarded in BIOLOGICAL SCIENCE (biology/biological science and nutrition), BUSINESS (accounting, business administration and management, human resources, management information systems, management science, marketing/retailing/merchandising, and personnel management), COMMUNICATIONS

AND THE ARTS (applied music, arts administration/management, dramatic arts, English, fine arts, graphic design, music, music performance, musical theater, Spanish, and studio art), COMPUTER AND PHYSICAL SCIENCE (chemistry, information sciences and systems, and mathematics), EDUCATION (art, business, computer, drama, early childhood, elementary, and music), HEALTH PROFESSIONS (health care administration and nursing), SOCIAL SCIENCE (criminal justice, dietetics, human services, liberal arts/general studies, ministries, psychology, religion, social studies, social work, and sociology). Nutrition/Dietetics, natural sciences, and English are the strongest academically. Nursing, business, and education are the largest.

Required: Students must complete a minimum of 128 semester hours of credit. A minimum of 43 of these must be upper-division level. All students must complete the General Education requirements (45 credit hours from various disciplines) and competencies, as well as all of the specified requirements for their major. Also, students must complete a service component designed by their major program. All students must have a GPA of at least 2.0, and must take as a minimum the last 30 consecutive semester hours at Viterbo University or complete 45 of the last 60 semester hours from Viterbo. Students seeking a B.S. must complete 7 credits of natural science and/or math in addition to the 4 credits of natural science in the General Education requirements. Students seeking a B.A. must complete the equivalent of 14 semester hours of the same modern foreign language.

Special: Students may cross-register at the University of Wisconsin/LaCrosse, enroll for independent study, or earn a dual degree. Co-op programs, study abroad in 7 countries, double majors, student-designed majors, accelerated degree programs, work-study, internships in many areas, credit by exam, and credit/no credit options are available. There are 2 national honor societies.

Faculty/Classroom: 44% of faculty are male; 56%, female. 98% teach undergraduates, 3% do research, and 3% do both. No introductory courses are taught by graduate students. The average class size in an introductory lecture is 24; in a laboratory, 9; and in a regular course, 15.

Admissions: 85% of the 2001-2002 applicants were accepted. The ACT scores for the 2001-2002 freshman class were: 44% below 21, 33% between 21 and 23, 13% between 24 and 26, 6% between 27 and 28, and 4% above 28. 30% of the current freshmen were in the top fifth of their class; 59% were in the top two fifths. 3 freshmen graduated first in their class.

Requirements: The ACT is required. In addition, graduation from an accredited secondary school is required; the GED is accepted. Secondary preparation should include 16 credits, with 3 or 4 in English and 2 each in math, natural science, and social science or history. Fine arts students may be required to audition or submit a portfolio. Applications are accepted on-line via Wisconsin Mentor. A GPA of 2.0 is required. AP and CLEP credits are accepted.

Procedure: Freshmen are admitted to all sessions. Entrance exams should be taken in spring of the junior year or fall of the senior year. Applications should be filed by August 1 for fall entry and December 15 for spring entry, along with a $20 fee. Notification is sent on a rolling basis.

Transfer: 215 transfer students enrolled in 2001-2002. Applicants should present at least a 2.0 GPA in previous college work; in addition, freshman admission standards must be met. All college and high school transcripts must be submitted. 30 credits of 128 must be completed at Viterbo.

Visiting: There are regularly scheduled orientations for prospective students, including a meeting with an admissions staff member, a tour of the campus, and optional meetings with a financial aid officer and faculty members. There are guides for informal visits and visitors may sit in on classes. To schedule a visit, contact Tammy Edens.

Financial Aid: In 2001-2002, 99% of all freshmen and 97% of continuing students received some form of financial aid. 84% of freshmen and 82% of continuing students received need-based aid. The average freshman award was $11,328. Of that total, scholarships or need-based grants averaged $8518 ($21,150 maximum); loans averaged $2963 ($16,625 maximum); and work contracts averaged $518 ($2000 maximum). 33% of undergraduates work part time; most off-campus. Average annual earnings from campus work are $857. The average financial indebtedness of the 2001 graduate was $15,538. The FAFSA, the college's own financial statement, and the student's and parents' income tax returns are required. The fall application deadline is March 15.

International Students: There are 15 international students enrolled. The school actively recruits these students. They must score 500 on the written TOEFL and also take the college's own test.

Computers: The mainframes are a Dell, Vax, and UNIX servers. More than 200 PCs and Macs are available in 6 computer labs and a library computing facility. All of these systems are networked and have full access to the Internet and World Wide Web. There are also computers available in the science, business, and theater departments. All students may access the system 6 A.M. to 1 A.M. daily. There are no time limits and no fees. It is strongly recommended that all students have a personal computer.

Graduates: In 2001, 378 bachelor's degrees were awarded. The most popular majors were nursing (39%), business (12%), and education (8%). In an average class, 28% graduate in 4 years, 46% in 5 years, and 48% in 6 years. 150 companies recruited on campus in 2000-2001. Of the 2000 graduating class, 5% were enrolled in graduate school within 6 months of graduation and 92% were employed.

Admissions Contact: Roland W. Nelson, Vice President of Admissions. A video is available. E-mail: *admission@viterbo.edu*
Web: *www.viterbo.edu*

WISCONSIN LUTHERAN COLLEGE E-4
Milwaukee, WI 53226 **(414) 443-8811**
(888) 947-5884; Fax: (414) 443-8514

Full-time: 241 men, 409 women	**Faculty:** 44
Part-time: 27 men, 39 women	**Ph.D.s:** 67%
Graduate: none	**Student/Faculty:** 15 to 1
Year: semesters, summer session	**Tuition:** $14,116
Application Deadline: September 1	**Room & Board:** $5100

Freshman Class: 447 applied, 383 accepted, 200 enrolled
ACT: 25 **VERY COMPETITIVE**

Wisconsin Lutheran College, founded in 1973 in affiliation with the Wisconsin Evangelical Lutheran Synod, offers higher education in the arts and sciences within a conservative Christian environment. The library contains 68,300 volumes, 9211 microform items, and 4299 audiovisual forms/CDs, and subscribes to 551 periodicals. Computerized library services include the card catalog, interlibrary loans, and database searching. Special learning facilities include a learning resource center, art gallery, sound studio, and electronic music lab. The 19-acre campus is in a suburban area on the western edge of Milwaukee. Including residence halls, there are 23 buildings.

Student Life: 79% of undergraduates are from Wisconsin. Others are from 25 states and 7 foreign countries. 37% are from public schools. 95% are white. Most are Protestant. The average age of freshmen is 18; all undergraduates, 20. 21% do not continue beyond their first year; 64% remain to graduate.

Housing: 570 students can be accommodated in college housing, which includes single-sex dormitories and off-campus apartments. On-campus housing is guaranteed for all 4 years. 80% of students live on campus. Alcohol is not permitted. All students may keep cars.

Activities: There are no fraternities or sororities. There are 31 groups on campus, including art, band, choir, dance, drama, ethnic, international, jazz band, literary magazine, musical theater, newspaper, pep band, photography, political, professional, religious, social, social service, student government, tour guide, and yearbook. Popular campus events include Family Weekend, WinterFest, and art, musical and theater events.

Sports: There are 7 intercollegiate sports for men and 8 for women, and 5 intramural sports for men and 5 for women. Facilities include 3 full basketball courts, a 2500-seat gym, a weight room, a fitness center, a dance/aerobics room, training and therapy rooms, and a walking/running track.

Disabled Students: 90% of the campus is accessible. Wheelchair ramps, elevators, special parking, specially equipped rest rooms, lowered drinking fountains, and lowered telephones are available.

Services: Counseling and information services are available, as is tutoring in some subjects, including math, writing, and foreign language.

Campus Safety and Security: Measures include 24-hour foot and vehicle patrol, self-defense education, escort service, and shuttle buses. There are informal discussions, pamphlets/posters/films, lighted pathways/sidewalks, a security service, and electronically operated dorm entrances.

Programs of Study: Wisconsin Lutheran confers B.A. and B.S. degrees. Bachelor's degrees are awarded in BIOLOGICAL SCIENCE (biology/biological science), BUSINESS (business administration and management, and business economics), COMMUNICATIONS AND THE ARTS (art, communications, English, media arts, music, and Spanish), COMPUTER AND PHYSICAL SCIENCE (chemistry and mathematics), EDUCATION (elementary), SOCIAL SCIENCE (history, interdisciplinary studies, political science/government, psychology, social science, social studies, and theological studies). Chemistry, math, and education are the strongest academically. Music, theology, and education are the largest.

Required: Composition, speech, math, and foreign language competencies are required. All students must complete a core curriculum that includes courses in theology, aesthetics, literature, natural science, history, social science, and intellectual diversity, plus 1 credit in phys ed/lifetime sport and 2 freshman seminars. A minimum overall GPA of 2.0 and 2.5 in the major (some require a higher GPA) plus 128 credit hours are required to graduate.

Special: Student-designed majors, work-study, and study abroad are offered. Internships are available in most departments.

Faculty/Classroom: 67% of faculty are male; 33%, female. All both teach and do research. The average class size in an introductory lecture is 20; in a laboratory, 9; and in a regular course, 16.

Admissions: 86% of the 2001-2002 applicants were accepted. The ACT scores for the 2001-2002 freshman class were: 15% below 21, 19% between 21 and 23, 35% between 24 and 26, 13% between 27 and 28, and 18% above 28. 46% of the current freshmen were in the top fifth of their class; 72% were in the top two fifths. 8 freshmen graduated first in their class.

Requirements: The SAT I or ACT is required, with a minimum composite score of 970 on the SAT I or 21 on the ACT. Students should be graduates of an accredited high school or its equivalent with a minimum of 16 high school units, including 4 in English, 3 each in academic electives and math, and 2 each in science, foreign language, and social studies/history. Students must rank in the upper half of their graduating class or have a minimum GPA of 2.7. The Academic Recommendation Form must be submitted. A portfolio for art grants and an audition for music and drama grants are required. Wisconsin Lutheran requires applicants to be in the upper 50% of their class. A GPA of 2.7 is required. AP and CLEP credits are accepted. Applications are accepted on-line at the Wisconsin Lutheran web site, *www.wlc.edu/home_page_level/admissions.html*.

Procedure: Freshmen are admitted fall and spring. Entrance exams should be taken in the spring of the junior year. Applications should be filed by September 1 for fall entry and January 15 for spring entry, along with a $20 fee ($5 on-line). Notification is sent on a rolling basis.

Transfer: 21 transfer students enrolled in 2001-2002. Students should have a GPA of at least 2.5 for transfer credit. The Transfer Recommendation Form is required. 30 credits of 128 must be completed at Wisconsin Lutheran.

Visiting: There are regularly scheduled orientations for prospective students, including a tour of the campus, a meal, meetings with admissions, professors, financial aid, and cocurriculars. There are guides for informal visits and visitors may sit in on classes and stay overnight. To schedule a visit, contact the Admissions Office.

Financial Aid: In 2001-2002, 99% of all freshmen and 98% of continuing students received some form of financial aid. 82% of freshmen and 72% of continuing students received need-based aid. The average freshman award was $13,520. Of that total, scholarships or need-based grants averaged $9049 ($19,750 maximum); loans averaged $2938 ($10,785 maximum); and work contracts averaged $1582 ($1600 maximum). 48% of undergraduates work part time. Average annual earnings from campus work are $1635. The average financial indebtedness of the 2001 graduate was $13,602. The FAFSA and the college's own financial statement are required. The fall application deadline is rolling.

International Students: There are 10 international students enrolled. They must score 550 on the written TOEFL and a minimum composite score of 21 on the ACT or 970 on the SAT I.

Computers: The mainframe consists of 3 Compaq Proliant 2500 NT servers. 60 Pentium PCs with laser printers and 9 Mac Power PCs are available in various campus labs and the library. 22 Notebook computers are available on a checkout basis. Students may access the central network and the Internet from any computer lab or residence hall. All students may access the system. There are no time limits and no fees. It is strongly recommended that all students have a personal computer.

Graduates: In 2001, 95 bachelor's degrees were awarded. The most popular majors were communication (18%), education (12%), and biology (11%). In an average class, 47% graduate in 4 years, 62% in 5 years, and 64% in 6 years.

Admissions Contact: Craig Swiontek, Director of Admissions. A video is available. E-mail: *admissions@wlc.edu* Web: *www.wlc.edu*

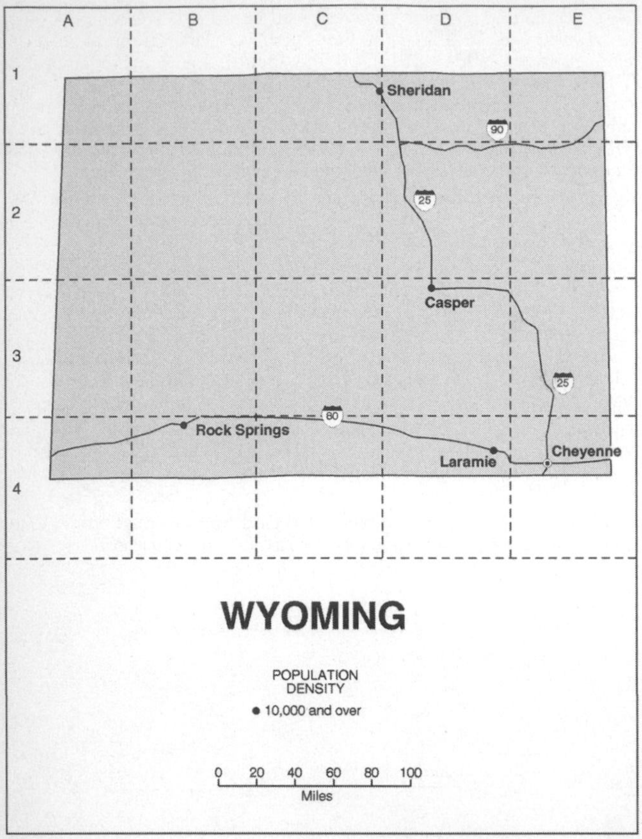

UNIVERSITY OF WYOMING D-4
Laramie, WY 82071 (307) 766-5160
(800) 342-5996; Fax: (307) 766-4042

Full-time: 3512 men, 3678 women
Part-time: 473 men, 887 women
Graduate: 1002 men, 1767 women
Year: semesters, summer session
Application Deadline: August 10
Faculty: 583; I, --$
Ph.D.s: 87%
Student/Faculty: 12 to 1
Tuition: $2575 ($7693)
Room & Board: $4568
Freshman Class: 2560 applied, 2481 accepted, 1360 enrolled
SAT I Verbal/Math: 539/546 **ACT:** 23 **LESS COMPETITIVE**

The University of Wyoming, founded in 1886, is a public nonprofit institution offering programs in agriculture, arts and sciences, business, education, engineering, and health science. There are 6 undergraduate schools and 1 graduate school. In addition to regional accreditation, UW has baccalaureate program accreditation with AACSB, AALS, ABA, ABET, ACPE, ACS, ADA, APA, ASLHA, CSWE, IAME, NASM, NCATE, and NLN. The 7 libraries contain 1,393,055 volumes, 2,845,172 microform items, and 6644 audiovisual forms/CDs, and subscribe to 16,017 periodicals. Computerized library services include the card catalog, interlibrary loans, and database searching. Special learning facilities include a learning resource center, art gallery, natural history museum, planetarium, radio station, TV station, and the American Heritage Center. The 10,988-acre campus is in a small town 128 miles north of Denver, Colorado, and 45 miles west of Cheyenne, Wyoming's capital. Including residence halls, there are 83 buildings.

Student Life: 73% of undergraduates are from Wyoming. Others are from 49 states, 54 foreign countries, and Canada. 83% are white. The average age of freshmen is 18; all undergraduates, 23. 24% do not continue beyond their first year; 53% remain to graduate.

Housing: 3300 students can be accommodated in college housing, which includes single-sex and coed dormitories, on-campus apartments, married-student housing, fraternity houses, and sorority houses. In addition, there are honors houses, engineering, honors, academic, single-gender, coed, upperclassmen, sophomors, quiet-living, substance-free, and freshman interest-group floors. On-campus housing is guaranteed for all 4 years. All students may keep cars.

Activities: 9% of men belong to 10 national fraternities; 6% of women belong to 1 local and 4 national sororities. There are 183 groups on campus, including art, band, cheerleading, chess, choir, chorale, chorus, computers, dance, debate, drama, drill team, ethnic, film, forensics, gay, honors, international, jazz band, literary magazine, marching band, musical theater, newspaper, opera, orchestra, pep band, photography, political, professional, radio and TV, religious, social, social service, student government, and symphony. Popular campus events include President's Welcome and Parents Weekend.

Sports: There are 7 intercollegiate sports for men and 8 for women, and 26 intramural sports for men and 26 for women. Facilities include a 33,000-seat stadium, a 15,000-seat indoor gym and arena; basketball, volleyball, and racquetball courts; running tracks; 2 pools; weight rooms; an indoor tennis complex; a baseball and track stadium, and a football training center.

Disabled Students: 95% of the campus is accessible. Wheelchair ramps, elevators, special parking, specially equipped rest rooms, special class scheduling, lowered drinking fountains, lowered telephones, and braille signs are available.

Services: Counseling and information services are available, as is tutoring in most subjects. There is a reader service for the blind, note-taking services, tape recorders, and interpreters for the hearing impaired. Remedial tutoring and remedial math are available through a local community college.

Campus Safety and Security: Measures include 24-hour foot and vehicle patrol, self-defense education, escort service, and shuttle buses. There are informal discussions, pamphlets/posters/films, emergency telephones, and lighted pathways/sidewalks.

Programs of Study: UW confers B.A., B.S., B.F.A., B.S.Arch.Eng, , B.S.C.E., B.S.Ch.E., B.S.Comp.Eng. B.S.C.S., B.S.D.H., B.S.E.E., B.S.F.C., B.S.M.I., B.S.M.E., B.S.M.I., B.S.M.T., B.S.N., and B.S.W. degrees. Master's and doctoral degrees are also awarded. Bachelor's degrees are awarded in AGRICULTURE (agricultural business management, agriculture, animal science, range/farm management, and wildlife management), BIOLOGICAL SCIENCE (biology/biological science, botany, microbiology, molecular biology, and zoology), BUSINESS (accounting, banking and finance, business administration and management, business economics, management information systems, marketing/retailing/merchandising, and small business management), COMMUNICATIONS AND THE ARTS (art, communications, dramatic arts, English, French, German, journalism, music, music performance, music theory and composition, Russian, and Spanish), COMPUTER AND PHYSICAL SCIENCE (astronomy, chemistry, computer science, geology, mathematics, physics, and statistics), EDUCATION (agricultural, elementary, health, industrial arts, music, physical, secondary, special, and trade and industrial), ENGINEERING AND ENVIRONMENTAL DESIGN (architectural engineering, chemical engineering, civil engineering, computer engineering, electrical/electronics engineering, environmental science, and mechanical engineering), HEALTH PROFESSIONS (dental hygiene, exercise science, health science, nursing, and speech pathology/audiology), SOCIAL SCIENCE (American studies, anthropology, criminal justice, economics, family/consumer studies, geography, history, humanities, international studies, parks and recreation management, philosophy, political science/government, psychology, social science, social work, sociology, and women's studies). Elementary education, psychology, and business administration are the largest.

Required: To graduate, students must complete 120 to 167 credit hours, depending on the major, with a minimum GPA of 2.0. The core curriculum includes 12 credit hours of cultural context, 9 of writing, 6 to 9 of math, 6 to 8 of science, 3 of constitution studies, 3 of global studies, and 1 of freshman seminar. Students must also complete 3 hours of computing courses and 1 hour of phys ed.

Special: UW offers co-op programs in health sciences, internships, study abroad, Washington and U.N. semesters, work-study programs, dual and interdisciplinary majors, pass/fail options, student-designed majors, credit by exam, and credit for life, military, and work experience. There are 20 national honor societies, including Phi Beta Kappa, a freshman honors program, and 5 departmental honors programs.

Faculty/Classroom: 69% of faculty are male; 31%, female. 98% teach undergraduates, 86% do research, and 84% do both. Graduate students teach 9% of introductory courses. The average class size in an introductory lecture is 103; in a laboratory, 20; and in a regular course, 21.

Admissions: 97% of the 2001-2002 applicants were accepted. The SAT I scores for the 2001-2002 freshman class were: Verbal--31% below 500, 43% between 500 and 599, 23% between 600 and 700, and 3% above 700; Math--29% below 500, 41% between 500 and 599, 24% between 600 and 700, and 7% above 700. The ACT scores were 27% below 21, 28% between 21 and 23, 25% between 24 and 26, 10% between 27 and 28, and 10% above 28. 43% of the current freshmen were in the top fifth of their class; 72% were in the top two fifths. 78 freshmen graduated first in their class.

Requirements: The SAT I is required; the ACT is preferred. Applicants must be graduates of an accredited secondary school or hold a GED certificate. Secondary preparation should include at least 13 academic credits consisting of 4 years of English (or 3 of English and 2 of a single foreign language) and 3 each of math, science, and cultural context electives. A visit is suggested. A GPA of 2.75 is required. AP and CLEP credits are accepted. Important factors in the admissions decision are recommendations by school officials, personality/intangible qualities, and extracurricular activities record. Applications are accepted on-line at *siswww.uwyo.edu/adm/application/choose.html*

Procedure: Freshmen are admitted fall, winter, and spring. Entrance exams should be taken in the spring of the junior year or fall of the senior year. There is a deferred admissions plan. Applications should be filed by August 10 for fall entry and December 10 for spring entry. Notification is sent on a rolling basis. The fall 2001 application fee was $30.

Transfer: 1049 transfer students enrolled in 2001-2002. Applicants with 30 or more transferable college-level credits must have a minimum GPA of 2.0. All applicants with fewer credits must submit a high school transcript, and those students under age 21 must also present SAT I or ACT scores. 30 credits of 120 to 167 must be completed at UW.

Visiting: There are regularly scheduled orientations for prospective students, including campus tours and meetings with academic advisers. There are guides for informal visits and visitors may sit in on classes and stay overnight. To schedule a visit, contact the Admissions Office.

Financial Aid: In 2001-2002, 78% of all freshmen and 79% of continuing students received some form of financial aid. 58% of freshmen and 61% of continuing students received need-based aid. The average freshman award was $5359. Of that total, scholarships or need-based grants averaged $1891 ($8164 maximum); loans averaged $2096 ($15,000 maximum); work contracts averaged $370 ($2000 maximum); and tuition waiver and miscellaneous averaged $2484 ($8318 maximum). 38% of undergraduates work part time. The average financial indebtedness of the 2001 graduate was $16,168. UW is a member of CSS. The FAFSA and the college's own financial statement are required. The fall application deadline is March 1.

International Students: There are 113 international students enrolled. The school actively recruits these students. They must score 525 on the written TOEFL.

Computers: The mainframe is a Sun Enterprise 5000. There are approximately 550 Windows NT workstations in public labs that are Ethernet connected. Students in the dorms and student apartments may each have a PC connected to the Ethernet. There are also 96 56-kbps dial-in modems. All students may access the system 24 hours a day. There are no time limits. There is a $40 technology fee per semester.

Graduates: In 2001, 1677 bachelor's degrees were awarded. The most popular majors were elementary education (10%), business administration (5%), and psychology (4%). In an average class, 17% graduate in 4 years, 41% in 5 years, and 48% in 6 years. 120 companies recruited on campus in 2000-2001. Of the 2000 graduating class, 22% were enrolled in graduate school within 6 months of graduation and 66% were employed.

Admissions Contact: Sara Axelson, Director of Admissions. A video is available. E-mail: *why-wyo@uwyo.edu*
Web: *http://siswww.uwy.edu/adm*

ARIZONA

SOUTHWESTERN COLLEGE C-4
Phoenix, AZ 85032 (602) 992-6101; (800) 247-2697
Fax: (602) 404-2159

Full-time: 130 men, 146 women
Part-time: 10 men, 23 women
n/av
Application Deadline: August 9
required
Faculty: 35
Tuition: $9115
Room & Board: $3400

Southwestern College, founded in 1960, is affiliated with the Southwest Conservative Baptist Association. Its mission is to prepare students for vocational and lay ministries as educators in public, private, or Christian schools. In addition to regional accreditation, the college is accredited by AABC. Southwestern College awards the B.A. and B.S. in elementary education, general Bible studies, Christian ministries, secondary education, business administration, and counseling. The school also awards associate degrees. Web: *www.southwesterncollege.edu*

ARKANSAS

CENTRAL BAPTIST COLLEGE C-3
Conway, AR 72032 (501) 329-6872; Fax: (501) 329-2941

Full-time: 168 men, 150 women
Part-time: 24 men, 16 women
n/av
Application Deadline: August 15
ACT: 20
Faculty: 41
Tuition: $6384
Room & Board: $3888

Central Baptist College, founded in 1952, is affiliated with the Baptist Missionary Association of Arkansas. Its mission is to train Christian men and women for lay and professional ministry and church-related vocations. Central Baptist College awards the B.A. and B.S. in Bible studies, Christian missions, church music, pastoral ministry, youth ministry, religious education, and Christian counseling. The school also awards associate degrees. Web: *www.cbc.edu*

CALIFORNIA

BETHANY COLLEGE B-3
Scotts Valley, CA 95066 (831) 438-3800; Fax: (831) 461-1533

Full-time: 136 men, 237 women
Part-time: 55 men, 77 women
Graduate: 14 men, 32 women
Application Deadline: July 31
SAT I Verbal/Math: 505/488
Faculty: 53
Tuition: $11,370
Room & Board: $4920
ACT: 20.5

Bethany College, founded in 1919, is affiliated with the Assemblies of God. Its mission is to prepare students for leadership in the Church and society. Bethany College awards the B.A. in addiction studies, applied professional studies, biblical and theological studies, business, church leadership and children's ministries, church leadership and urban ministries, church leadership and world missions, church leadership and youth ministries, church music, early child development, English, general ministries, intercultural child development, liberal studies, missions, multicultural studies, music, psychology, social science, and teacher education program. The school also awards associate and master's degrees. Web: *www.bethany.edu*

PATTEN COLLEGE B-3
Oakland, CA 94601 (510) 261-8500, ext. 765; Fax: (510) 534-4344

Full-time: 73 men, 139 women
Part-time: 295 men, 144 women
Graduate: 4 men, 12 women
Application Deadline: July 31
SAT I Verbal: 950
Faculty: 45
Tuition: $8400
Room & Board: $4800
ACT: 20

Patten College, founded in 1944, is affiliated with Christian Evangelical Churches of America/ Church of God. Its mission is to offer a balanced liberal arts education with a strong biblical studies emphasis and to help students prepare for a life of Christian service. Patten College awards the B.A., B.S. and M.A. in biblical studies, Christian ministires, liberal studies, pastoral studies, preseminary studies, sacred music, liberal arts, organizational management, early childhood development, English, art, social science, and sports management. The school also awards associate, bachelor's and master's degrees. Web: *www.patten.edu*

SAINT JOHN'S SEMINARY COLLEGE C-4
Camarillo, CA 93012 (805) 482-2755, ext. 2006
Fax: (805) 987-5097

Full-time: 95 men
n/av
n/av
Application Deadline: June 20
SAT I Verbal/Math: 410/420
Faculty: 35
Tuition: $7890
Room & Board: $5000
ACT: 17

Saint John's Seminary College, founded in 1927, is affiliated with the Roman Catholic Church. Its mission is to provide a liberal arts education for young men interested in becoming priests for the Archdiocese of Los Angeles and for other sponsoring dioceses and religious communities. Figures in the above capsule are approximate. Saint John's Seminary College awards the B.A. in philosophy, English, Spanish, and theology. Web: *www.sjs-sc.org*

SAN JOSE CHRISTIAN COLLEGE B-3
San Jose, CA 95112 (408) 293-9058; Fax: (408) 293-7352

Full-time: 125 men, 100 women
Part-time: 75 men, 50 women
n/av
Application Deadline: August 1
Faculty: 50
Tuition: $9800
Room & Board: $5100

San Jose Christian College, founded in 1939, is nondenominational. Its mission is to prepare Christians for leadership and service in church and society through Christian higher education, spiritual formation, and directed experiences. Figures in the above capsule are approximate. The college is accredited by AABC. San Jose Christian College awards the B.A. and B.S. in Bible and theology, pastoral ministry, youth ministry, Christian education, missions, counseling, and music and worship. The school also awards associate degrees. Web: *www.sjchristiancol.edu*

CONNECTICUT

HOLY APOSTLES COLLEGE AND SEMINARY C-2
Cromwell, CT 06416 (860) 632-3010; Fax: (860) 632-0176

Full-time: 9 men
Part-time: 12 men, 17 women
Graduate: 140 men, 73 women
Application Deadline: open
Faculty: 29
Tuition: $8080
Room & Board: $6400

Holy Apostles College and Seminary, founded in 1956, is affiliated with the Roman Catholic Church. Its mission is to provide adult men who have a calling to the Catholic priesthood with an academic and seminary environment suited to their age and background, and to provide lay students with training for personal interest, and various certificates and degrees. Holy Apostles College and Seminary awards the B.A. in humanities, philosophy, religious studies, and social sciences. The school also awards associate, and master's degrees.
Web: *www.novavista.com/holyapostles.*

FLORIDA

BAPTIST COLLEGE OF FLORIDA B-1
(Formerly Florida Baptist Theological College)
Graceville, FL 32440 (800) 328-2660, ext. 460
Fax: (850) 263-7506

Full-time: 359 men, 186 women
Part-time: 35 men, 8 women
n/av
Application Deadline: August 1
SAT I: required
Faculty: 49
Tuition: $4600
Room & Board: $3150

Baptist College of Florida, formerly Florida Baptist Theological College, founded in 1943, is affiliated with the Florida Baptist Convention. Its mission is to promote, provide for, operate, and control a program of education and training for ministers and other religious workers. Baptist College of Florida awards the B.A. in music ministry, teacher education, theology, Christian education, Christian counseling, and leadership. The school also awards associate degrees. Web: *www.baptistcollege.edu*

FLORIDA CHRISTIAN COLLEGE D-3
Kissimmee, FL 34744 (407) 847-8966, ext. 305
Fax: (407) 847-3925

Full-time: 86 men, 79 women
Part-time: 20 men, 19 women
n/av
Application Deadline: open
ACT: required
Faculty: 24
Tuition: $5865
Room & Board: $1740

Florida Christian College, founded in 1976, is affiliated with Christian Churches/Churches of Christ/Independent. Its mission is to conduct a course of study educating men and women for Christian service, to provide a program of instruction on the college level, to grant appropriate degrees, and to serve as a resource to churches, especially in Florida. In addition to regional accreditation, the college is accredited by AABC. Florida Christian College awards the B.A., B.S., and B.Th. in Bible, Christian education ministries, and Christian ministries. The school also awards associate degrees. Web: *www.fcc.edu*

SAINT JOHN VIANNEY COLLEGE SEMINARY E-5
Miami, FL 33165 (305) 223-4561, ext. 15; Fax: (305) 223-0650

Full-time: 72 men, 1 woman
Part-time: 2 men, 1 woman
n/av
Application Deadline: July
Faculty: 21
Tuition: $11,000
Room & Board: $4000

Saint John Vianney College Seminary, founded in 1959, is affiliated with the Roman Catholic Church. Its mission is to provide an undergraduate education preparatory for students whose stated objective is to serve the Catholic Church in the priesthood, and to provide spiritual and intellectual formation within an Anglo-Hispanic bilingual, bicultural setting. Saint John Vianney College Seminary awards the B.A. in philosophy and theology.

WARNER SOUTHERN COLLEGE D-4
Lake Wales, FL 33853 (941) 638-7250 or (800) 949-7248
Fax: (941) 638-1472

Full-time: 305 men, 305 women
Part-time: 25 men, 45 women
n/av
Application Deadline: open
Faculty: 33
Tuition: $9950
Room & Board: $4900

Warner Southern College, founded in 1968, is affiliated with Church of God. Its mission is to provide a quality program of higher education within an evangelical Christian perspective in the Wesleyan tradition. Figures in the above capsule are approximate. Warner Southern College awards the B.A. in biblical studies, biology, business administration, church ministries, communication arts, English, English education, exceptional student education, history/political science, middle school science, missions, music ministry, music education, organizational management, phys ed, phys ed teacher education, psychology, social sciences, social sciences education, social work, sports and leisure management, teacher education, accounting, and exercise science. The school also awards associate degrees. Web: *www.warner.edu*

GEORGIA

ATLANTA CHRISTIAN COLLEGE B-2
East Point, GA 30344 (404) 669-2088; Fax: (404) 669-2024

Full-time: 165 men, 186 women
Part-time: 24 men, 32 women
n/av
Application Deadline: open
Faculty: 33
Tuition: $10,298
Room & Board: $3950

Atlanta Christian College, founded in 1937, is affiliated with Christian Churches and Churches of Christ. Its mission is to provide education in biblical studies, the arts and sciences, and professional studies to equip men and women for Christian service. Atlanta Christian College awards the B.A., B.S., and B.Th. in Christian education in the church, Christian education in the school, missions, music, preaching ministry, human relations, early childhood education, youth ministry, business administration, and the humanities. The school also awards associate degrees. Web: *www.acc.edu*

ILLINOIS

LINCOLN CHRISTIAN COLLEGE AND SEMINARY D3
Lincoln, IL 62656-2111 (217) 732-3168, ext. 2315
Fax: (217) 732-5914

Full-time: 254 men, 268 women
Part-time: 68 men, 95 women
Graduate: 166 men, 52 women
Application Deadline: open
ACT: 22
Faculty: 64
Tuition: $8100
Room & Board: $4100

Lincoln Christian College and Seminary, founded in 1944, is affiliated with the Christian Church/Church of Christ. Its mission is to educate and train preachers, Christian teachers, and other Christian workers. Figures in the above capsule are approximate. In addition to regional accreditation, the college is accredited by AABC. Lincoln Christian College and Seminary awards the B.A. and B.S. in ministry, Christian education, missions, Christian business administration, music, and Bible. The school also awards associate, and master's degrees. Web: *www.lccs.edu*

MOODY BIBLE INSTITUTE E-2
Chicago, IL 60610 (312) 329-4400; Fax: (312) 329-8987

Full-time: 870 men, 557 women
Part-time: 30 men, 18 women
Graduate: 151 men, 80 women
Application Deadline: March 1 or December 1
ACT: 25
Faculty: 112
Tuition: $1300
Room & Board: $5400

Moody Bible Institute, founded in 1886, is affiliated with the Evangelical Protestant Church. Its mission is to educate and train individuals to proclaim the gospel of the Lord Jesus Christ, to promote evangelism, and to serve the Evangelical Christian Church vocationally and/or avocationally in its worldwide ministry. In addition to regional accreditation, the college is accredited by AABC. Moody Bible Institute awards the B.A., B.S., and B.Mus. in missionary aviation technology, biblical studies, evangelism/discipleship, communication, educational ministries, world missions, pastoral studies, religious education, church music, sacred music, Bible-theology, applied linguistics, youth ministry, urban ministry, Jewish and modern Israel studies, family ministries, and teaching English as a second language. The school also awards associate, and master's degrees. Web: *www.moody.edu*

IOWA

DIVINE WORD COLLEGE E-2
Epworth, IA 52045-0380 (800) 553-3321; Fax: (563) 876-3407

Full-time: 76 men
Part-time: 3 men, 4 women
n/av
Application Deadline: July 15
SAT I Verbal/Math: 400/450
Faculty: 24
Tuition: $8701
Room & Board: $1900

Divine Word College, founded in 1912, is affiliated with the Roman Catholic Church. Its mission is excellence in combining a liberal arts education with a cross-cultural program of missionary formation for Divine Word missionaries and other leaders in the Roman Catholic Church. Divine Word College awards the B.A. in philosophy and cross-cultural studies. The school also awards associate degrees. Web: *www.dwci.edu*

FAITH BAPTIST BIBLE COLLEGE AND THEOLOGICAL SEMINARY C-3

Ankeny, IA 50021 (888) FAITH 4 U; Fax: (515) 964-1638

Full-time: 139 men, 198 women
Faculty: 33
Part-time: 20 men, 15 women
Tuition: $9010
Graduate: 79 men, 36 women
Room & Board: $3466
Application Deadline: open
SAT I Verbal/Math: 460/490
ACT: 21

Faith Baptist Bible College and Theological Seminary, founded in 1921, is affiliated with the General Association of Regular Baptist Churches. Its mission is to provide an intensive biblical and vocational education on the college level with the goal of preparing students to minister effectively in Christian service through leadership positions in fundamental Baptist churches and other organizations of like convictions. In addition to regional accreditation, the college is accredited by AABC. Faith Baptist Bible College and Theological Seminary awards the B.A. and B.S. in Bible and theology, assistant pastor, Christian education, Christian school, missions, music ministries, and pastoral training. The school also awards associate, and master's degrees. Web: *www.faith.edu*

KENTUCKY

CLEAR CREEK BAPTIST BIBLE COLLEGE F-3

Pineville, KY 40977-9752 (606) 337-3196; Fax: (606) 337-2372

Full-time: 147 men, 14 women
Faculty: 22
Part-time: 38 men, 9 women
Tuition: $4046
n/av
Room & Board: $3380
Application Deadline: July 15

Clear Creek Baptist Bible College, founded in 1926, is affiliated with the Southern Baptist Church. Its mission is providing theological education for adults called to Christian service. In addition to regional accreditation, the college is accredited by AABC. Clear Creek Baptist Bible College awards the B.A. in Bible. The school also awards associate degrees. Web: *www.ccbbc.edu*

MID-CONTINENT COLLEGE A-4

Mayfield, KY 42066-0357 (502) 247-8521; (800) 232-4662
Fax: (502) 247-3115

Full-time: 101 men, 68 women
Faculty: 48
Part-time: 41 men, 35 women
Tuition: $6450
n/av
Room & Board: $4400
Application Deadline: August 15
ACT: 18

Mid-Continent College, founded in 1949, is affiliated with the Baptist Church. Its mission, as a Baptist institution of higher learning, is to educate students for Christian leadership and service throughout the world. Figures in the above capsule are approximate. Mid-Continent College awards the B.A., B.S., and B.Min. in biblical languages, biblical studies, Christian education, and leadership, Christian ministry, evangelism, missions, psychology and counseling, behavioral studies, communication arts, English, general studies, social studies, elementary teacher education, interdisciplinary early childhood education, and organizational leadership. Web: *www.midcontinent.edu*

LOUISIANA

SAINT JOSEPH SEMINARY COLLEGE D-3

St. Benedict, LA 70457 (504) 867-2248; Fax: (504) 867-2270

Full-time: 71 men
Faculty: 37
n/av
Tuition: $10,750
n/av
Room & Board: $5700
Application Deadline: open
ACT: 21

Saint Joseph Seminary College, founded in 1891, is affiliated with the Roman Catholic Church. Its mission is to provide the education and training of men for the priesthood in the Roman Catholic Church. Figures in the above capsule are approximate. Saint Joseph Seminary College awards the B.A. in philosophy and the liberal arts, and philosophy and religious studies. Web: *www.stjosephabbey.org*

MASSACHUSETTS

SAINT JOHN'S SEMINARY COLLEGE E-2

Brighton, MA 02135 (617) 254-2610; Fax: (617) 746-5499

Full-time: 37 men
Faculty: 19
Part-time: 4 men
Tuition: $6400
Graduate: 17 men
Room & Board: $3000
Application Deadline: open
SAT I Verbal/Math: 510/520

Saint John's Seminary College, founded in 1884, is affiliated with the Roman Catholic Church. Its mission is to assist college-level seminarians to grow in Christian maturity as liberally educated persons committed to the service of the Church. Figures in the above capsule are approximate. Saint John's Seminary College awards the B.A. and B.Phil. in philosophy. The school also awards associate degrees. Web: *www.sjs.edu*

MICHIGAN

SACRED HEART MAJOR SEMINARY E-5

Detroit, MI 48206-1799 (313) 883-8500; Fax: (313) 868-6400

Full-time: 30 men
Faculty: 45
Part-time: 93 men, 126 women
Tuition: $6600
Graduate: 74 men, 28 women
Room & Board: $4500
Application Deadline: open
ACT: required

Sacred Heart Major Seminary, founded in 1919, is affiliated with the Roman Catholic Church. Its mission is to provide spiritual formation and a liberal arts education for candidates preparing for the Roman Catholic priesthood in Detroit and for students preparing for other ministries within the Church. Figures in the above capsule are approximate. Sacred Heart Major Seminary awards the A.B. and B.Phil. in philosophy. The school also awards associate, and master's degrees. Web: *www.shms.edu*

MINNESOTA

CROWN COLLEGE C-4

Saint Bonifacius, MN 55375 (612) 446-4144
Fax: (612) 446-4149

Full-time: 329 men, 372 women
Faculty: 57
Part-time: 59 men, 102 women
Tuition: $11,346
Graduate: 14 men, 1 woman
Room & Board: $4698
Application Deadline: open
ACT: 22

Crown College, founded in 1916, is affiliated with the Christian and Missionary Alliance. Its mission is to provide a biblically based education for Christian leadership in the Christian and Missionary Alliance, the church-at-large, and the world. In addition to regional accreditation, the college is accredited by AABC. Crown College awards the B.A., B.S., and B.Mus.Ed. in biblical and theological studies, business administration, Christian education, elementary education, history, history education, music, music education, pastoral ministries, social studies education, youth, youth/social science, psychology, English, English education, linguistics, intercultural studies, liberal arts, child and family ministries, management, network administration, biology, sports management, Christian ministry, management and ethics, management and network administration, early childhood education, and New Testament. The school also awards associate, and master's degrees. Web: *www.crown.edu*

MARTIN LUTHER COLLEGE C-4

New Ulm, MN 56073-3965 (507) 354-8221; Fax: (507) 354-8225

Full-time: 515 men, 526 women
Faculty: 98
Part-time: 8 men, 9 women
Tuition: $5285
n/av
Room & Board: $2420
Application Deadline: April 15
ACT: 24.2

Martin Luther College, founded in 1995, is affiliated with the Wisconsin Evangelical Lutheran Synod. Its mission is to provide training for elementary and secondary teaching, preseminary training for pastoral students, and training for other church vocations through the Staff Ministry Program. Martin Luther College awards the B.A. and B.S.Ed. in education and preseminary studies. Web: *www.mlc-wels.edu*

OAK HILLS CHRISTIAN COLLEGE — B-2
Bemidji, MN 56601 (218) 751-8670; Fax: (218) 751-8825

Full-time: 68 men, 82 women
Part-time: 13 men, 12 women
n/av
Faculty: 16
Tuition: $9450
Room & Board: $3410
Application Deadline: open
ACT: 19.4

Oak Hills Christian College, founded in 1946, is interdenominational. The college is accredited by AABC. Oak Hills Christian College awards the B.A. in biblical studies, biblical studies and applied psychology, applied studies, campus ministry, contemporary Christian ministry, intercultural studies, pastoral ministry, and youth ministry. The school also awards associate degrees. Web: *www.oakhills.edu*

MISSISSIPPI

MAGNOLIA BIBLE COLLEGE — D-3
Kosciusko, MS 39090 (662) 289-2896; Fax: (662) 289-1850

Full-time: 14 men, 4 women
Part-time: 10 men, 9 women
n/av
Faculty: 10
Tuition: $4520
Room & Board: $600
Application Deadline: open
ACT: 16

Magnolia Bible College, founded in 1976, is affiliated with the Churches of Christ. Its mission is to enable students to acquire a college-level education in general, biblical, and professional studies that will enable them to serve as preachers, missionaries, directors of Christian education, Bible chair directors, campus evangelists, and other Christian workers. In addition to regional accreditation, the college is accredited by AABC. Magnolia Bible College awards the B.A. in Bible and theology. Web: *www.magnolia.edu*

MISSOURI

CONCEPTION SEMINARY COLLEGE — A-1
Conception, MO 64433 (660) 944-2886; Fax: (660) 944-2829

Full-time: 82 men
Part-time: 2 men, 5 women
n/av
Faculty: 30
Tuition: $9312
Room & Board: $5374
Application Deadline: July 1
ACT: 22

Conception Seminary College, founded in 1886, is affiliated with the Roman Catholic Church. Its mission is to prepare men who are discerning for the Roman Catholic priesthood. Conception Seminary College places emphasis on spiritual, personal, and academic formation. Conception Seminary College awards the B.A. in liberal arts. Web: *www.conceptionabbey.org*

NEW YORK

WADHAMS HALL SEMINARY COLLEGE — C-2
Ogdensburg, NY 13669 (315) 393-4231; Fax: (315) 393-4249

Full-time: 21 men
n/av
n/av
Faculty: 16
Tuition: $6445
Room & Board: $6000
Application Deadline: August 15

Wadhams Hall Seminary College, founded in 1924, is affiliated with the Roman Catholic Church. Its mission is to prepare men at the college level for further studies leading to priesthood in the Catholic Church. Wadhams Hall Seminary College awards the B.A. in philosophy and religious studies. Web: *www.wadhams.edu*

NORTH CAROLINA

ROANOKE BIBLE COLLEGE — F-2
Elizabeth City, NC 27909-4054 (800) RBC-8980
Fax: (252) 334-2071

Full-time: 78 men, 67 women
Part-time: 10 men, 15 women
n/av
Faculty: n/av
Tuition: $5990
Room & Board: $3860
Application Deadline: open
SAT I Verbal/Math: 520/555
ACT: 18

Roanoke Bible College, founded in 1948, is affiliated with the Christian Church/Church of Christ. Its mission is to prepare men and women for career and volunteer Christian service. In addition to regional accreditation, the college is accredited by AABC. Roanoke Bible College awards the B.A. and B.S. in biblical and theological studies. The school also awards associate degrees. Web: *www.roanokebible.edu*

NORTH DAKOTA

TRINITY BIBLE COLLEGE — E-4
Ellendale, ND 58436 (888) TBC-2DAY; Fax: (701) 349-5443

Full-time: 134 men, 128 women
Part-time: 9 men, 22 women
n/av
Faculty: 30
Tuition: $6290
Room & Board: $3084
Application Deadline: open

Trinity Bible College, founded in 1948, is affiliated with the Assemblies of God. Its mission is to prepare pastors, church leaders, and Christian professionals in various fields in a Bible-based Pentecostal environment of academic excellence. In addition to regional accreditation, the college is accredited by AABC. Trinity Bible College awards the B.A. in biblical studies, elementary education, ministerial studies, and missions. The school also awards associate degrees. Web: *www.trinitybiblecollege.edu*

OHIO

CINCINNATI BIBLE COLLEGE AND SEMINARY — A-5
Cincinnati, OH 45204-3200 (513) 244-8192; Fax: (513) 244-8140

Full-time: 287 men, 250 women
Part-time: 68 men, 50 women
Graduate: 194 men, 111 women
Faculty: 59
Tuition: $7600
Room & Board: $4340
Application Deadline: August 10

Cincinnati Bible College and Seminary, founded in 1924, is affiliated with Christian Churches/Churches of Christ. Its mission is to teach men and women to live by biblical principles and to equip and empower them with skills, insight, and vision both to lead the church and to impact society for Christ. In addition to regional accreditation, the college is accredited by AABC. Cincinnati Bible College and Seminary awards the B.A., B.S., and B.Church Mus. in biblical/theological studies (primary major), Bible/general studies, Christian education, church music, ministries, and missions (second major). The school also awards associate, and master's degrees. Web: *www.cincybible.edu*

PONTIFICAL COLLEGE JOSEPHINUM — C-3
Columbus, OH 43235 (614) 985-2241; Fax: (614) 885-2307

Full-time: 46 men
n/av
Graduate: 68 men, 1 woman
Faculty: 44
Tuition: $9454
Room & Board: $5496
Application Deadline: open

Pontifical College Josephinum, founded in 1888, is affiliated with the Roman Catholic Church. Its mission is to prepare young men for the priesthood. Pontifical College Josephinum awards the B.A. in English, philosophy, and Hispanic studies. The school also awards master's degrees. Web: *www.pcj.edu*

OKLAHOMA

MID-AMERICA BIBLE COLLEGE (Formerly Gulf Coast Bible College (1985)) D-3
Oklahoma City, OK 73170 (405) 691-3800; (405) 692-3241 Fax: (405) 692-3165

Full-time: 269 men, 225 women | **Faculty:** 46
Part-time: 75 men, 65 women | **Tuition:** $7450
n/av | **Room & Board:** $5588
Application Deadline: open

Mid-America Bible College, founded in 1953, is affiliated with the Church of God in Anderson, Indiana. Its mission is to train and prepare men and women for the Christian ministry. Mid-America Bible College awards the B.A. and B.S. in behavioral science, elementary education, English, music, music performance, pastoral ministry, worship and music ministries, secondary education, specialized ministries, management and ethics, English/business, and business administration. The school also awards associate degrees. Web: *www.mabc.edu*

SOUTHWESTERN COLLEGE OF CHRISTIAN MINISTRIES D-3
Bethany, OK 73008 (405) 789-7661, ext. 3436 Fax: (405) 495-0078

Full-time: 58 men, 48 women | **Faculty:** 21
Part-time: 12 men, 6 women | **Tuition:** $7200
Graduate: 52 men, 6 women | **Room & Board:** $3400
Application Deadline: open
ACT: 19

Southwestern College of Christian Ministries, founded in 1946, is affiliated with Pentecostal Holiness. Its mission is the education and training for Christian service leading toward professional competence in the practice of various ministry forms. Southwestern College of Christian Ministries awards the B.A. and B.S. in biblical studies, Christian ministry/pastoral studies, religion, and human and family services. The school also awards associate and master's degrees. Web: *www.sccn.edu*

OREGON

MOUNT ANGEL SEMINARY B-2
St. Benedict, OR 97373 (503) 845-3951; Fax: (503) 845-3126

Full-time: 80 men | **Faculty:** 40
n/av | **Tuition:** $8850
Graduate: 65 men, 50 women | **Room & Board:** $6250
Application Deadline: July 15

Mount Angel Seminary, founded in 1889, is affiliated with the Roman Catholic Church. Its mission is to prepare students for the Roman Catholic priesthood for religious orders and dioceses. Figures in the above capsule are approximate. Mount Angel Seminary awards the B.A. in philosophy and literature. The school also awards master's degrees.

PENNSYLVANIA

BAPTIST BIBLE COLLEGE OF PENNSYLVANIA E-2
Clarks Summit, PA 18411 (570) 586-2400; Fax: (570) 585-9400

Full-time: 311 men, 372 women | **Faculty:** 30
Part-time: 19 men, 32 women | **Tuition:** $9870
Graduate: 8 men, 15 women | **Room & Board:** $4880
Application Deadline: August 15
SAT I Verbal/Math: 520/488 | **ACT:** 22

Baptist Bible College of Pennsylvania, founded in 1932, is affiliated with the Baptist Church. Its mission is to prepare men and women for service in selected Christian ministries as pastors, missionaries, Christian education workers, teachers for Christian schools, counselors, church musicians, and secretaries for Christian organizations. In addition to regional accreditation, the college is accredited by AABC. Baptist Bible College of Pennsylvania awards the B.S. in Bible and B.S.M. in church music, elementary education, general missions, local church ministries, music education, outreach and evangelism pastor, pastoral ministry, pastor of Christian education, preseminary, secondary education, secretarial ministries, youth pastor, precounseling, general ministries, and women's ministries. The school also awards associate and master's degrees. Web: *www.bbc.edu*

LANCASTER BIBLE COLLEGE E-3
Lancaster, PA 17601 (717) 560-8271; Fax: (717) 560-8213

Full-time: 245 men, 298 women | **Faculty:** 73
Part-time: 84 men, 87 women | **Tuition:** $10,540
Graduate: 47 men, 47 women | **Room & Board:** $4800
Application Deadline: open
SAT I Verbal/Math: 500/500 | **ACT:** 19

Lancaster Bible College, founded in 1933, is nondenominational. Its mission is to educate Christian men and women to live according to a biblical world view and to serve through professional Christian ministries. In addition to regional accreditation, the college is accredited by AABC. Lancaster Bible College awards the B.S. in Bible and B.S.Ed. in Bible education K-12, Christian education, computer studies, biblical counseling, early childhood education, elementary education, guidance counselor/Bible education, pastoral church planning, pastoral studies, missions, music, music education/Bible education, preseminary pastoral studies, physical education/Bible education, women's ministry, and youth ministry. The school also awards associate and master's degrees. Web: *www.lbc.edu*

SAINT CHARLES BORROMEO SEMINARY F-3
Wynnewood, PA 19096 (610) 667-3394; Fax: (610) 664-1422

Full-time: 81 men | **Faculty:** 68
Part-time: 53 men, 130 women | **Tuition:** $8450
Graduate: 141 men, 77 women | **Room & Board:** $5800
Application Deadline: July 1

Saint Charles Borromeo Seminary, founded in 1832, is affiliated with the Roman Catholic Church. Its mission is to prepare and educate men for the Roman Catholic priesthood and to provide undergraduate and graduate programs for men and women pursuing theological studies. Figures in the above capsule are approximate. Saint Charles Borromeo Seminary awards the B.A. in philosophy. The school also awards master's degrees.

SOUTH CAROLINA

COLUMBIA INTERNATIONAL UNIVERSITY C-3
Columbia, SC 29230 (803) 754-4100; Fax: (803) 986-4041

Full-time: 248 men, 303 women | **Faculty:** 34
Part-time: 42 men, 49 women | **Tuition:** $9450
Graduate: 216 men, 194 women | **Room & Board:** $4750
Application Deadline: open
SAT I Verbal/Math: 570/520

Columbia International University, founded in 1923, is multidenominational. Its mission is to prepare students to grow in spiritual maturity, Bible knowledge, and ministry skills in preparation for vocational or lay Christian ministry. In addition to regional accreditation, the college is accredited by AABC. Columbia International University awards the B.A. and B.S. in Bible, elementary education/early childhood education, general studies, intercultural studies, psychology, biblical languages, music, Bible teaching, youth ministry, humanities, church ministries, pastoral ministries, and communications. The school also awards associate, master's, and doctorate degrees. Web: *www.ciu.edu*

TENNESSEE

FREE WILL BAPTIST BIBLE COLLEGE C-2
Nashville, TN 37205 (615) 383-1340, ext. 5233
Fax: (615) 269-6028

Full-time: 131 men, 145 women
Part-time: 32 men, 25 women
n/av
Application Deadline: July 15
ACT: 19
Faculty: 24
Tuition: $7400
Room & Board: $3900

Free Will Baptist Bible College, founded in 1942, is affiliated with the National Association of Free Will Baptists. Its mission is to equip men and women, through Bible-based education, to serve Christ and His Church. Figures in the above capsule are approximate. In addition to regional accreditation, the college is accredited by AABC. Free Will Baptist Bible College awards the B.A. and B.S. in biblical studies, biblical and ministry studies, business administration, church music, church music and youth ministry, English, elementary education, music education, music performance, sports medicine, physical education, secondary English education, and psychology and learning. The school also awards associate degrees. Web: *www.fwbbc.edu*

JOHNSON BIBLE COLLEGE E-3
Knoxville, TN 37998 (865) 251-2229; Fax: (865) 251-2337

Full-time: 299 men, 275 women
Part-time: 6 men, 8 women
Graduate: 52 men, 38 women
Application Deadline: August 1
SAT I Verbal/Math: 520/510
Faculty: 48
Tuition: $5500
Room & Board: $3500
ACT: 22

Johnson Bible College, founded in 1893, is affiliated with the Christian tradition. Its mission is to educate students for specialized Christian ministries. In addition to regional accreditation, the college is accredited by AABC. Johnson Bible College awards the B.A. and B.S. in Bible, a double major in Bible and teacher education, children's ministry, preaching, youth ministry/preaching, counseling, and music. The school also awards associate, and master's degrees. Web: *www.jbc.edu*

TEXAS

BAPTIST MISSIONARY ASSOCIATION THEOLOGICAL SEMINARY E-2
Jacksonville, TX 75766 (903) 586-2501; Fax: (903) 586-0378

Full-time: 11 men
Part-time: 22 men, 2 women
Graduate: 40 men, 6 women
Application Deadline: open
Faculty: 13
Tuition: $2220
Room & Board: $3600

Baptist Missionary Association Theological Seminary, founded in 1955, is affiliated with the Baptist Missionary Association. Its mission is to train individuals for Christian ministry. Baptist Missionary Association Theological Seminary awards the B.A.R. in religion. The school also awards associate, and master's degrees. Web: *www.bmats.edu*

CRISWELL COLLEGE D-2
Dallas, TX 75246 (214) 821-5433; Fax: (214) 818-1310

Full-time: 140 men, 30 women
Part-time: 160 men, 50 women
Graduate: 100 men, 20 women
Application Deadline: July 15
Faculty: 27
Tuition: $4300
Room & Board: n/app

Criswell College, founded in 1970, is affiliated with the Southern Baptist Church. Its mission is to educate and train lay men and full-time Christian workers in biblical, theological, and professional studies so they can serve effectively in evangelistic, educational, pastoral, and missionary vocations of the Christian church. Figures in the above capsule are approximate. Criswell College awards the B.A. in biblical studies, counseling, missions, evangelism, pastoral, and urban ministries. The school also awards associate, and master's degrees. Web: *www.criswell.edu*

INSTITUTE FOR CHRISTIAN STUDIES D-3
Austin, TX 78705 (512) 476-2772; Fax: (512) 476-3919

Full-time: 9 men, 1 woman
Part-time: 13 men, 8 women
n/av
Application Deadline: June 1 (recommended)
Faculty: 10
Tuition: $2250
Room & Board: n/app

Institute for Christian Studies, founded in 1917, is affiliated with the Church of Christ. Its mission is to equip ministers and other Christians to serve the Church and the world. Figures in the above capsule are approximate. Through a cooperative program, a master's degree is offered from Abilene Christian University. Institute for Christian Studies awards the B.A. and B.S. in biblical studies. Web: *www.ics.edu*

SOUTHWESTERN ASSEMBLIES OF GOD UNIVERSITY D-2
Waxahachie, TX 75165 (972) 937-4010; Fax: (972) 923-0488

Full-time: 663 men, 722 women
Part-time: 139 men, 136 women
Graduate: 46 men, 32 women
Application Deadline: open
Faculty: 102
Tuition: $4680
Room & Board: $3726

Southwestern Assemblies of God University, founded in 1927, is affiliated with Assemblies of God. Its mission is to provide the training of Christian individuals to carry the gospel to the ends of the earth or to fill any other divinely approved place in the Kingdom of God. In addition to regional accreditation, the college is accredited by AABC. Southwestern Assemblies of God University awards the B.A. and B.S. in business, church ministries, counseling, elementary education, music, psychology, and secondary education. The school also awards associate, and master's degrees. Web: *www.sagu.edu*

WASHINGTON

TRINITY LUTHERAN COLLEGE C-2
(Formerly Lutheran Bible Institute of Seattle)
Issaquah, WA 98029-9299 (206) 392-0400; Fax: (206) 392-0404

Full-time: 32 men, 61 women
Part-time: 7 men, 13 women
n/av
Application Deadline: open
ACT: 21
Faculty: 26
Tuition: $9140
Room & Board: $5100

Trinity Lutheran College, formerly Lutheran Bible Institute of Seattle, founded in 1944, is affiliated with the Lutheran Church. Its mission is to train students for professional ministry and service careers. Trinity Lutheran College awards the B.A. in biblical studies, Christian education, youth and family ministry, urban missions, global missions, music and worship, and early childhood education. The school also awards associate degrees. Web: *www.tlc.edu*

WISCONSIN

MARANATHA BAPTIST BIBLE COLLEGE D-4
Watertown, WI 53094 (920) 261-9300; Fax: (920) 261-9109

Full-time: 336 men, 389 women
Part-time: 27 men, 38 women
Graduate: 20 men, 3 women
Application Deadline: open
ACT: required
Faculty: 57
Tuition: $7100
Room & Board: $4050

Maranatha Baptist Bible College, founded in 1968, is affiliated with the Baptist Church. Its mission is to train men and women for effective professional or lay gospel ministry in the local church through a postsecondary program of biblical, general, and professional studies. Maranatha Baptist Bible College awards the B.A. and B.S. in Bible, church ministries, education, general studies, fine arts, business, nursing, and office administration. The school also awards associate, and master's degrees. Web: *www.mbbc.edu*

AIR FORCE

In the Air Force ROTC program, young men and women may earn commissions by participating in the 2- or 4-year program while attending college. The amount of academic credit given for Air Force ROTC varies from school to school.

Most new Air Force officers come through the Air Force ROTC program. It offers students the opportunity to attend a civilian college while studying officership as part of their undergraduate curriculum.

The AFROTC program begins with the General Military Course. Freshmen or sophomores attend one hour of ROTC classes and one to two hours of leadership laboratory weekly. During these first two years, study is focused on the history of the Air Force and the part it plays in the world today. During the summer between sophomore and junior years, students attend a four-week basic training course located at an Air Force base.

The Professional Officer Course is completed during the junior and senior years. Study includes management principles and defense policy and offers the opportunity for managing, organizing, directing, and evaluating the cadet corps activities.

Upon graduation, students are commissioned as Second Lieutenants. Cadets who are medically qualified will have the opportunity to compete for pilot or navigator positions.

For academically qualified students in selected majors, the AFROTC offers scholarships, including tuition, fees and books, and a monthly nontaxable allowance during the school year. Any enrolled nonscholarship junior or senior with 2.5 GPA is eligible to participate in the Professional Officer Course Scholarship Program. It pays $1,000 per semester in tuition and books, plus a monthly allowance.

The majority of scholarships are awarded in the technical degree areas of engineering and computer science, but there are opportunities in nontechnical areas as well. Scholarships are based on individual merit, not financial need. Those who receive a scholarship must still apply and be accepted by the school they wish to attend and notify the AFROTC headquarters of their selection.

The scholarship program is broken down into different types and durations. High school seniors receive either a 3- or 4-year scholarship. All scholarships include full or partial tuition, fees, textbook allowance, and $200 per month tax-free allowance during the academic year. Type I pays full tuition at any school offering AFROTC. (About 15% of 4-year scholarships are this type.) Type II pays tuition and fees up to a maximum of $15,000 per year. (35% of 4-year scholarships are Type II; all 3-year scholarships are Type II.) The remaining 50% of scholarships are Type IV. This scholarship is for students who attend schools where the tuition is less than $9000 per year.

The application deadline is December 1 of the senior year, but priority consideration is given to those who get the application in early. Applications are available from the liaison officer or recruiter during the summer prior to the senior year of high school.

Further information can be obtained from the professor of aerospace studies at any of the host campuses where Air Force ROTC is offered. The listing that follows represents the host schools that offer these programs. Hundreds more schools have crosstown agreements with these institutions to make AFROTC more accessible to students. Please be sure to contact the school directly for more details. You may also find useful and current information at the Air Force Reserve Officer Training Corps web site.

ALABAMA

- Alabama State University
- Auburn University
- Samford University
- Troy State University
- Tuskegee University
- University of Alabama
- University of South Alabama

ARIZONA

- Arizona State University
- Embry-Riddle Aeronautical University
- Northern Arizona University
- University of Arizona

ARKANSAS

- University of Arkansas at Fayetteville

CALIFORNIA

- California State University, Fresno
- California State University, Sacramento
- California State University, San Bernadino
- Loyola Marymount University
- San Diego State University
- San Jose State University
- University of California at Berkeley
- University of California at Los Angeles
- University of Southern California

COLORADO

- Colorado State University
- University of Colorado at Boulder

CONNECTICUT

- University of Connecticut

DELAWARE

- University of Delaware

DISTRICT OF COLUMBIA

- Howard University

FLORIDA

- Embry-Riddle Aeronautical University
- Florida State University
- University of Central Florida
- University of Florida
- University of Miami
- University of South Florida

GEORGIA

- Georgia Institute of Technology
- University of Georgia
- Valdosta State University

HAWAII

- University of Hawaii at Manoa

ILLINOIS

- Illinois Institute of Technology
- Southern Illinois University at Carbondale
- University of Illinois at Urbana-Champaign

INDIANA

- Indiana State University
- Indiana University at Bloomington
- Purdue University
- University of Notre Dame

IOWA

- Iowa State University
- University of Iowa

KANSAS

- Kansas State University
- University of Kansas

KENTUCKY

- University of Kentucky
- University of Louisville

LOUISIANA

- Grambling State University
- Louisiana State University and Agricultural and Mechanical College
- Louisiana Tech University
- Tulane University

MARYLAND
- University of Maryland

MASSACHUSETTS
- Boston University
- Massachusetts Institute of Technology
- University of Massachusetts
- University of Massachusetts, Lowell
- Worcester Polytechnic Institute

MICHIGAN
- Michigan State University
- Michigan Technological University
- University of Michigan

MINNESOTA
- University of Minnesota/Duluth
- University of Minnesota/Twin Cities
- University of Saint Thomas

MISSISSIPPI
- Mississippi State University
- Mississippi Valley State University
- University of Mississippi
- University of Southern Mississippi

MISSOURI
- St. Louis University
- Southeast Missouri State University
- University of Missouri/Columbia
- University of Missouri/Rolla

MONTANA
- Montana State University

NEBRASKA
- University of Nebraska at Lincoln
- University of Nebraska at Omaha

NEW HAMPSHIRE
- University of New Hampshire

NEW JERSEY
- New Jersey Institute of Technology
- Rutgers, the State University of New Jersey/University College—New Brunswick

NEW MEXICO
- New Mexico State University
- University of New Mexico

NEW YORK
- Clarkson University
- Cornell University
- Manhattan College
- Rensselaer Polytechnic Institute
- Rochester Institute of Technology
- Syracuse University

NORTH CAROLINA
- Duke University
- East Carolina University
- Fayetteville State University
- North Carolina State University
- University of North Carolina at Chapel Hill
- University of North Carolina at Charlotte

NORTH DAKOTA
- North Dakota State University

OHIO
- Bowling Green State University
- Kent State University
- Miami University
- Ohio State University
- Ohio University
- University of Akron
- University of Cincinnati
- Wright State University

OKLAHOMA
- Oklahoma State University
- University of Oklahoma

OREGON
- Oregon State University
- University of Portland

PENNSYLVANIA
- Pennsylvania State University/University Park Campus
- Saint Joseph's University
- University of Pittsburgh
- Wilkes University

PUERTO RICO
- University of Puerto Rico/Mayaguez
- University of Puerto Rico/Río Piedras

SOUTH CAROLINA
- Charleston Southern University
- The Citadel
- Clemson University
- University of South Carolina

SOUTH DAKOTA
- South Dakota State University

TENNESSEE
- Tennessee State University
- University of Memphis
- University of Tennessee at Knoxville

TEXAS
- Angelo State University
- Baylor University
- Southwest Texas State University
- Texas A & M University
- Texas Christian University
- Texas Tech University
- University of North Texas
- University of Texas at Austin
- University of Texas at San Antonio

UTAH
- Brigham Young University
- University of Utah
- Utah State University

VERMONT
- Norwich University

VIRGINIA
- University of Virginia
- Virginia Military Institute
- Virginia Polytechnic Institute and State University

WASHINGTON
- Central Washington University
- University of Washington
- Washington State University

WEST VIRGINIA
- West Virginia University

WISCONSIN
- Marquette University
- University of Wisconsin/Madison

WYOMING
- University of Wyoming

ARMY

The Army Reserve Officers' Training Corps (ROTC) provides college students with the opportunity to combine leadership and management training with their other academic studies. The curriculum, which consists of a series of classroom and hands-on leadership training experiences, provides students with the necessary foundation to serve successfully in positions of responsibility in either the U.S. Army or the corporate world.

Those with a strong academic background, an active mindset, and the ability to rapidly assimilate information thrive in the program. These scholar-athlete-leaders note that the leadership skills developed through their participation in the program are further honed during their period of service as Army officers. After service as an Army lieutenant, many graduates elect to continue their service in uniform. Others elect to enter the corporate world where their leadership skills and experience as ROTC-trained Army officers allow them to advance rapidly.

Although the program is designed to be completed in four years, students may complete all requirements within a two-year period through participation in a summer training session called the Leaders' Training Course, normally held during the summer between the sophomore and junior years. A generous series of merit-based scholarships that cover tuition, fees, textbooks, and supplies exist to help students and their families defray the cost of college. Applications for four-year scholarships must be postmarked by November 13 to be considered for the following school year. Tax-free stipends of up to $350 per month are also available to those meeting course requirements. For more information on the program, call (800) USA-ROTC, or contact the professor of military science at a college that offers Army ROTC. Detailed information about the program is also available on the Internet at *www.armyrotc.com*.

ALABAMA

- Alabama Agricultural and Mechanical University
- Auburn University
- Auburn University at Montgomery
- Jacksonville State University
- Tuskegee University
- University of Alabama
- University of Alabama at Birmingham
- University of South Alabama

ALASKA

- University of Alaska/Fairbanks

ARIZONA

- Arizona State University
- Northern Arizona University
- University of Arizona

ARKANSAS

- Arkansas State University
- University of Arkansas at Fayetteville
- University of Arkansas at Pine Bluff
- University of Central Arkansas

CALIFORNIA

- California Polytechnic State University
- California State University at Fresno
- California State University at Fullerton
- Claremont Colleges/Claremont McKenna College
- San Diego State University
- University of San Francisco

COLORADO

- Colorado State University
- University of Colorado at Boulder
- University of Colorado at Colorado Springs

CONNECTICUT

- University of Connecticut

DELAWARE

- University of Delaware

DISTRICT OF COLUMBIA

- Georgetown University
- Howard University

FLORIDA

- Embry-Riddle Aeronautical University
- Florida A & M University
- Florida Institute of Technology
- Florida International University
- Florida Southern College
- Florida State University
- University of Central Florida
- University of Florida
- University of South Florida
- University of Tampa
- University of West Florida

GEORGIA

- Augusta State University
- Columbus State University
- Fort Valley State University
- Georgia Institute of Technology
- Georgia Southern University
- Georgia State University
- North Georgia College
- University of Georgia

HAWAII

- University of Hawaii

IDAHO

- Boise State University
- University of Idaho

ILLINOIS

- Eastern Illinois University
- Illinois State University
- Northern Illinois University
- Southern Illinois University at Carbondale
- Southern Illinois University at Edwardsville
- University of Illinois at Chicago
- University of Illinois at Urbana-Champaign
- Western Illinois University
- Wheaton College

INDIANA

- Ball State University
- Indiana University at Bloomington
- Indiana University/Purdue
- Purdue University/West Lafayette
- Rose-Hulman Institute of Technology
- University of Indianapolis
- University of Notre Dame

IOWA

- Iowa State University
- University of Iowa
- University of Northern Iowa

KANSAS

- Kansas State University
- Pittsburg State University
- University of Kansas

KENTUCKY

- Eastern Kentucky University
- Morehead State University
- University of Kentucky
- University of Louisville
- Western Kentucky University

LOUISIANA

- Grambling State University
- Louisiana State University and Agricultural & Mechanical College
- Northwestern State University of Louisiana
- Southern University and A & M College
- Tulane University

MAINE

- University of Maine at Orono

MARYLAND

- Bowie State University
- Johns Hopkins University
- Loyola College
- Morgan State University
- Western Maryland College

MASSACHUSETTS

- Boston University
- Massachusetts Institute of Technology
- Northeastern University
- University of Massachusetts at Amherst
- Western New England College
- Worcester Polytechnic Institute

MICHIGAN

- Central Michigan University
- Eastern Michigan University
- Michigan State University
- Michigan Technological University
- Northern Michigan University
- University of Michigan/Ann Arbor
- Western Michigan University

MINNESOTA

- Minnesota State University, Mankato
- Saint John's University
- University of Minnesota/Twin Cities

MISSISSIPPI

- Alcorn State University
- Jackson State University
- Mississippi State University
- University of Mississippi
- University of Southern Mississippi

MISSOURI

- Central Missouri State University
- Lincoln University
- Missouri Western State University
- Northeast Missouri State University
- Southwest Missouri State University
- Truman State University
- University of Missouri/Columbia
- University of Missouri/Rolla
- Washington University

MONTANA

- Montana State University
- University of Montana

NEBRASKA

- Creighton University
- University of Nebraska at Lincoln

NEVADA

- University of Nevada/Reno

NEW HAMPSHIRE

- University of New Hampshire

NEW JERSEY

- Princeton University
- Rutgers, The State University of New Jersey
- Seton Hall University

NEW MEXICO

- New Mexico State University

NEW YORK

- Canisius College
- Clarkson University
- Cornell University
- Fordham University
- Hofstra University
- Niagara University
- Polytechnic University
- Rochester Institute of Technology
- Saint Bonaventure University
- Saint John's University
- State University of New York/Brockport
- Syracuse University

NORTH CAROLINA

- Appalachian State University
- Campbell University
- Duke University
- East Carolina University
- Elizabeth City State University
- North Carolina Agricultural and Technical State University
- North Carolina State University
- Saint Augustine's College
- University of North Carolina at Charlotte
- University of North Carolina at Chapel Hill
- Wake Forest University

NORTH DAKOTA

- North Dakota State University
- University of North Dakota

OHIO

- Bowling Green State University
- Capital University
- Central State University
- John Carroll University
- Kent State University
- Ohio State University
- Ohio University
- University of Akron
- University of Cincinnati
- University of Dayton
- University of Toledo
- Wright State University
- Xavier University

OKLAHOMA

- Cameron University
- Oklahoma State University
- University of Central Oklahoma
- University of Oklahoma

OREGON

- Oregon State University
- University of Oregon
- University of Portland

PENNSYLVANIA

- Bucknell University
- Dickinson College
- Drexel University
- Edinboro University of Pennsylvania
- Gannon University
- Indiana University of Pennsylvania
- Lehigh University
- Lock Haven University of Pennsylvania
- Pennsylvania State University Park Campus
- Shippensburg University of Pennsylvania
- Slippery Rock University
- Temple University
- University of Pittsburgh
- University of Scranton
- Widener University

PUERTO RICO

- University of Puerto Rico/Mayaguez
- University of Puerto Rico/Río Piedras

RHODE ISLAND

- Providence College
- University of Rhode Island

SOUTH CAROLINA

- The Citadel
- Clemson University
- Furman University
- Presbyterian College
- South Carolina State University
- University of South Carolina
- Wofford College

SOUTH DAKOTA

- South Dakota School of Mines and Technology
- South Dakota State University
- University of South Dakota

TENNESSEE

- Austin Peay State University
- Carson-Newman College
- East Tennessee State University
- Middle Tennessee State University
- Tennessee Technological University
- University of Memphis
- University of Tennessee at Knoxville
- University of Tennessee at Martin
- Vanderbilt University

TEXAS

- Prairie View A & M University
- Saint Mary's University
- Sam Houston State University
- Southwest Texas State University
- Stephen F. Austin State University
- Tarleton State University
- Texas A & M University at Kingsville
- Texas A & M University
- Texas Tech University
- Texas Christian University
- University of Houston
- University of Texas at Arlington
- University of Texas at Austin
- University of Texas at El Paso
- University of Texas at San Antonio
- University of Texas-Pan American

UTAH

- Brigham Young University
- University of Utah
- Weber State University

VERMONT

- Norwich University
- University of Vermont

VIRGINIA

- College of William and Mary
- George Mason University
- Hampton University
- James Madison University
- Norfolk State University
- Old Dominion University
- University of Richmond
- University of Virginia
- Virginia Military Institute
- Virginia Polytechnic Institute and State University
- Virginia State University

WASHINGTON

- Central Washington University
- Eastern Washington University
- Gonzaga University
- Pacific Lutheran University
- Seattle University
- University of Washington
- Washington State University

WEST VIRGINIA

- Marshall University
- West Virginia State College
- West Virginia University

WISCONSIN

- Marquette University
- University of Wisconsin/La Crosse
- University of Wisconsin/Madison
- University of Wisconsin/Oshkosh
- University of Wisconsin/Stevens Point

WYOMING

- University of Wyoming

NAVY

The Naval Reserve Officers Training Corps gives young men and women an opportunity to earn commissions in the Navy and the Marine Corps while attending college. Two types of NROTC programs are available: a scholarship program of two, three, or four years, and a nonsubsidized program.

Under the scholarship program, which is highly competitive, students are granted full costs of tuition, fees, and textbooks, and receive a monthly subsistence allowance. Scholarship recipients can major in engineering, the sciences, or other fields of interest to the Navy or Marine Corps. They must agree to serve a minimum of four years on active duty and the remainder of their 8-year commitment on inactive duty after graduation.

In the nonsubsidized program, called the College Program, students undergo the same training as scholarship students, but attend college at their own expense. During their junior and senior years, they receive a monthly subsistence allowance. College Program students also receive the uniforms and books required for naval-science courses. Students may enroll in either a 2- or 4-year College Program. Those entering the 2-year program must complete a 6-week paid Naval Science Institute program in the summer before their junior year. Graduates of the College Program agree to serve on active duty for three years.

In addition to their normal studies, all NROTC program students take courses in naval science and management and participate in drills. Scholarship students also participate in three summer training programs of four to six weeks each, conducted between the academic years. College Program students participate in one summer training program between the junior and senior years.

Applicants for 4-year scholarship programs must apply before December 1, take the SAT I or ACT and have their scores released to the NROTC scholarship program. Those who qualify as finalists will be notified by the Navy or Marine Corps Recruiting Activity in their area and asked to complete an application package. Navy and Marine Corps selection boards select scholarship recipients on the basis of academic achievement, test scores, demonstrated leadership ability, extracurricular activities, and aptitude for service. Some of those not selected for 4-year scholarships receive guarantees of 3-year scholarships, provided they enroll in an NROTC College Program and meet minimum academic and aptitude standards during their freshman year. Students seeking 2-year scholarships for their third or fourth years of college should write to the Navy Opportunity Information Center, P.O. Box 5000, Clifton, New Jersey 07012 for further informtion.

Admissions for the College Program are handled by the professor of naval science at each school. Those who apply for NROTC must be U.S. citizens between the ages of 17 and 21, possess a high school diploma or equivalency certificate, and meet standards of physical fitness, height, and weight. Further information on NROTC and initial application forms for NROTC scholarships are available from high school guidance offices, colleges and universities that offer the NROTC Program, Navy and Marine Corps recruiting stations, and the Naval Recruiting Command, Code 314, 801 North Randolph Street, Arlington, Virginia 22203-1991.

The following list shows the colleges and universities included in this book that have an NROTC unit on campus. Many more institutions offer the program through cross-town agreements. Contact the school directly for the most current and accurate information.

ALABAMA

- Auburn University

ARIZONA

- University of Arizona

CALIFORNIA

- San Diego State University
- University of California/Berkeley
- University of California/Los Angeles
- University of California/San Diego
- University of Southern California

COLORADO

- University of Colorado at Boulder

DISTRICT OF COLUMBIA

- George Washington University

FLORIDA

- Florida A & M University
- Jacksonville University
- University of Florida

GEORGIA

- Georgia Institute of Technology
- Morehouse College
- Savannah State College

IDAHO

- University of Idaho

ILLINOIS

- Illinois Institute of Technology
- Northwestern University
- University of Illinois at Urbana-Champaign

INDIANA

- Purdue University/West Lafayette
- University of Notre Dame

IOWA

- Iowa State University

KANSAS

- University of Kansas

LOUISIANA

- Southern University and A & M College
- Tulane University

MAINE

- Maine Maritime Academy

MASSACHUSETTS

- Boston University
- College of the Holy Cross
- Massachusetts Institute of Technology

MICHIGAN

- University of Michigan/Ann Arbor

MINNESOTA

- University of Minnesota

MISSISSIPPI

- University of Mississippi

MISSOURI

- University of Missouri

NEBRASKA

- University of Nebraska at Lincoln

NEW MEXICO

- University of New Mexico

NEW YORK

- Cornell University
- Rensselaer Polytechnic Institute
- State University of New York/Maritime College
- University of Rochester

NORTH CAROLINA

- Duke University
- North Carolina State University
- University of North Carolina at Chapel Hill

OHIO

- Miami University
- Ohio State University

OKLAHOMA

- University of Oklahoma

OREGON

- Oregon State University

PENNSYLVANIA

- Carnegie Mellon University
- Pennsylvania State University Park Campus
- University of Pennsylvania
- Villanova University

SOUTH CAROLINA

- The Citadel
- University of South Carolina

TENNESSEE

- University of Memphis
- Vanderbilt University

TEXAS

- Prairie View A & M University
- Rice University
- Texas A & M University
- University of Texas at Austin

UTAH

- University of Utah

VERMONT

- Norwich University

VIRGINIA

- Hampton University
- Norfolk State University
- Old Dominion University
- University of Virginia
- Virginia Military Institute
- Virginia Polytechnic Institute and State University

WASHINGTON

- University of Washington

WISCONSIN

- Marquette University
- University of Wisconsin/Madison

ENROLLMENT IN CANADIAN SCHOOLS

About 5 percent of all students enrolled in Canadian colleges and universities come from the United States and other foreign countries. Most Canadian universities admit international students—although some have a quota on the number they will accept—and will give interested students information on how their academic qualifications are equated with Canadian requirements.

The Association of Universities and Colleges of Canada (AUCC) represents 89 universities and university-level colleges. These institutions account for almost 99 percent of the total university enrollment in Canada. Almost all Canadian colleges are coeducational. Of the 89, 18 use French as the language of instruction, six use both French and English, and the rest primarily use English. This section contains individual profiles for those English-language universities that enroll more than 10,000 students.

Affiliated with each of these universities are a number of general, theological, or residential colleges, which also have been listed here. The names and addresses of the three French-speaking colleges with enrollments of more than 10,000 may be found at the end of this introduction.

Admissions Requirements

Admissions requirements vary much more among Canadian universities than among American schools, and the amount of time it takes to earn degrees also varies more widely.

Each Canadian province has its own pattern of elementary and secondary education: provinces may require 11, 12, or 13 years of schooling. Universities usually base general admissions requirements on the educational pattern of the province in which they are located. Therefore, international students may have to complete a year or more of college-level work before some universities will consider their applications.

Some universities require American students to submit SAT I and SAT II: Subject tests scores, but most rely primarily on high school performance in determining admission. Students from British Commonwealth countries may have to pass appropriate A- or O-level exams. Students whose native language is not English generally are required to take the TOEFL, the Michigan English Language Assessment Battery (MELAB), the University of Cambridge Certificate of Proficiency in English, or some other test of competency in English. Some universities also require English-speaking students to take English tests at the start of their freshman year to determine whether a student needs remedial instruction

Universities also usually ask international students to submit, along with their high school records, a notarized translation of those records into English or French. However, no Canadian university requires students to be fluent in both languages.

Admissions Procedure

After being accepted, the applicant must obtain a student visa from a Canadian diplomatic mission in his or her home country. The mission will ask the student to provide evidence of university admission and proof of adequate funds to pay all expenses in Canada as well as the cost of the journey home. Visas are good only for a specific program at a specific institution for a specific period of time, and cannot be changed once the student is in Canada. Revisions have recently been made to Canada's employment regulations as they pertain to international students at the post-secondary level. The changes affect the following categories: on-campus employment; spouses of students; education related work with industry following graduation (for periods up to 12 months); and expanded access to employment opportunities for students holding Canadian International Development Agency (CIDA) Awards. International students should consult the immigration officer at a Canadian post in their home country for detailed information on current employment regulations.

All students in Canada, including those from other countries, must be covered by a public or private hospital and medical insurance program.

Degrees Offered

Canadian universities, like those in the United States, grant three levels of degrees: bachelor's and first professional, master's, and doctoral as well as undergraduate certificates and diplomas and graduate diploma programs.

Earning the first degree can take three to five years. A general, or unspecialized, program leading to a Bachelor of Arts or Bachelor of Science usually can be completed in three years. An honors degree, earned in a specialized program, usually requires four years. Students must meet more rigorous requirements to enter an honors-degree program and must maintain high grades to remain in it. First professional degrees in some fields may take more than four years to earn, and students may be required to undertake two or three years of university study before enrolling in the professional program. Students who enter graduate programs with a general degree usually must study a year longer than those with honors degrees. Undergraduate diplomas and certificates may be from one to three years' duration and may (although not necessarily) be used as a basis for entry to a degree program. A graduate diploma may be considered as conferring a qualification that is intermediate between the bachelor's (or first professional degree) and master's degree. It may be completed in as little as two or as long as three academic years.

Organizations

Virtually all universities have organizations for international students, and sponsor international student centers and advisers. There also are national organizations that aid international students, including the World University Service of Canada and the Canadian Bureau for International Education, which arranges for representatives to meet international students arriving at Canadian airports.

Tuition, Fees, and Aid

Universities and colleges are heavily subsidized by provincial and federal governments, and tuition fees actually cover less than 15 percent of university operating costs. Canadian institutions charge different fees for different programs, unlike American institutions, which charge the same tuition regardless of the program of study. Each profile in this book lists the range of tuitions, which may or may not include student fees. Some universities have higher fees for international students, and where that is the case, the profile includes just the international fees. All costs are given in Canadian (CDN) dollars. In all cases, you should check with the university in which you are interested to obtain the most up-to-date information about tuition and room-and-board charges.

Most awards available to international students through Canadian universities or from the Canadian government are restricted to graduate and post graduate studies. Some of the scholarship programs for international students to study in Canada include the Commonwealth Scholarship and Fellowship Plan, the Canadian International Development Agency awards and the Government of Canada awards program of cultural exchanges. Students interested in applying for aid should contact a Canadian diplomatic mission in their home countries and, for information on cultural exchange programs, their own nation's education department or ministry.

Additional Information

Students interested in more information on studying in Canada can write to the following sources:

Association of Universities and Colleges of Canada
151 Slater Street
Ottawa, Ontario, Canada K1P 5NI
(publications include *Canada's Universities: International Student Guide* and *Directory of Canadian Universities*)

Canadian Bureau for International Education
85 Albert Street, Suite 1400
Ottawa, Ontario, Canada K1P 6A3
(publications include *Guide to Foreign Student Authorizations for Canada, Statistics on Foreign Students, Existing Institutional Policies and Practices Regarding Foreign Students,* 'Information Canada,' and others)

Canadian Consulate General
1251 Avenue of the Americas
16th Floor (Library)
New York, New York 10020
(212) 586-2400

Employment and Immigration Canada
Ottawa, Ontario, Canada K1A 0J9
(publications include *Studying in Canada: Facts for Foreign Students*)

Canadian International Development Agency
Place du Centre 200, Promenade du Portage
Hull (Quebec), Canada K1A 0G4

Social Sciences and Humanities Research Council of Canada
255 Albert Street
P.O. Box 1610
Ottawa, Ontario, Canada K1P 6G4

Statistics Canada
Education, Science, and Culture Division
R.H. Coats Building, 16th Floor
Tunneys Pasture
Ottawa, Ontario, Canada K1A 0T6
(publications include *Tuition and Living Costs at Canadian Universities*, updated annually)

World University Service of Canada
P.O. Box 3000
Station C
Ottawa, Ontario, Canada K1Y 4M8

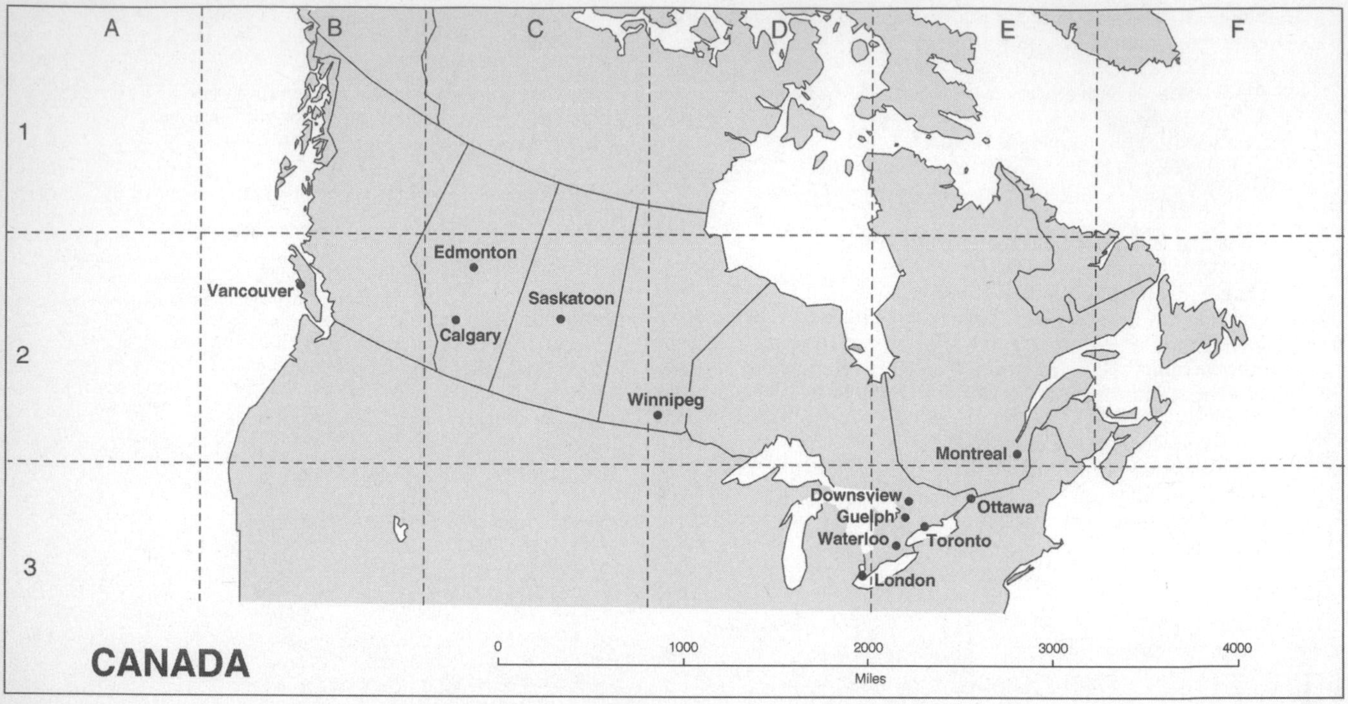

CARLETON UNIVERSITY
Ottawa, ON, Canada K1S 5B6

E-3
(613) 520-3609
Fax: (613) 520-3517

Full-time: 5541 men, 5466 women
Part-time: 2702 men, 2544 women
Graduate: 1313 men, 1234 women
Year: semesters, summer session
Application Deadline: see profile
Freshman Class: 17,234 applied, 11,122 accepted, 4470 enrolled
SAT I: required

Faculty: 676
Ph.D.s: 80%
Student/Faculty: 16 to 1
Tuition: $4516 ($9706)
Room & Board: $5865

Carleton University, founded in 1942, is a public institution operated by the province of Ontario. There are 14 undergraduate and 14 graduate degree programs offered. There are 8 undergraduate schools and 1 graduate school. The library contains 1,711,431 volumes, 1,261,826 microform items, and 19,668 audiovisual forms/CDs, and subscribes to 8965 periodicals. Computerized library services include the card catalog, interlibrary loans, and database searching. Special learning facilities include a learning resource center, art gallery, radio station, and an environmental biology laboratories annex. The 152-acre campus is in an urban area in Ottawa. Including residence halls, there are 29 buildings.

Student Life: 85% of undergraduates are from Ontario. Others are from 100 foreign countries. The average age of freshmen is 20.

Housing: 2180 students can be accommodated in college housing, which includes single-sex and coed dormitories. On-campus housing is available on a lottery system for upperclassmen. Priority is given to out-of-town students. 89% of students commute. All students may keep cars.

Activities: There are no fraternities or sororities. There are 80 groups on campus, including chess, computers, drama, ethnic, gay, international, newspaper, pep band, photography, political, radio and TV, religious, and student government. Popular campus events include Orientation.

Sports: There are 9 intercollegiate sports for men and 9 for women, and 4 intramural sports for men and 3 for women. Facilities include a physical recreation center with an Olympic-size pool, squash courts, Nautilus and fitness centers, and a double gym. Outdoor tennis courts and playing fields are also available.

Disabled Students: 98% of the campus is accessible. Wheelchair ramps, elevators, special parking, specially equipped rest rooms, lowered drinking fountains, and lowered telephones are available. There are also automatic doors in some buildings, tactile control panels in elevators, tunnels connecting buildings, specially equipped residence rooms, and attendant services.

Services: Counseling and information services are available, as is tutoring in most subjects, including . There is a reader service for the blind. Study skills workshops are available in essay writing and preparation and writing of exams. There is special exam scheduling and a study center for disabled students.

Campus Safety and Security: Measures include 24-hour foot and vehicle patrol, escort service, pamphlets/posters/films, and emergency telephones. There are lighted pathways/sidewalks and electronic access to residences.

Programs of Study: Carleton confers B.A., B.Sc., B.Arch., B.Comm., B.C.S., B.Eng., B.Hum., B.I.B., B.I.D., B.J., B.Math., B.Mus., B.P.A.P.H., and B.S.W. degrees. Master's and doctoral degrees are also awarded. Bachelor's degrees are awarded in BIOLOGICAL SCIENCE (biochemistry, biology/biological science, biometrics and biostatistics, biotechnology, and neurosciences), BUSINESS (accounting, business economics, business systems analysis, human resources, international business management, management information systems, marketing and distribution, marketing/retailing/merchandising, and operations research), COMMUNICATIONS AND THE ARTS (art history and appreciation, classics, communications, communications technology, English, English literature, film arts, French, German, industrial design, Italian, journalism, linguistics, music, Russian, and Spanish), COMPUTER AND PHYSICAL SCIENCE (chemistry, computer mathematics, computer programming, computer science, earth science, geology, information sciences and systems, mathematics, physical sciences, physics, and statistics), EDUCATION (teaching English as a second/foreign language (TESOL/TEFOL)), ENGINEERING AND ENVIRONMENTAL DESIGN (aeronautical engineering, architecture, civil engineering, computer engineering, electrical/electronics engineering, engineering, engineering physics, environmental engineering, environmental science, mechanical engineering, and systems engineering), SOCIAL SCIENCE (anthropology, Canadian studies, child care/child and family studies, classical/ancient civilization, cognitive science, criminology, Eastern European studies, economics, European studies, geography, German area studies, history, human ecology, interdisciplinary studies, law, liberal arts/general studies, philosophy, political science/government, psychology, public administration, religion, social work, sociology, and women's studies). Arts, engineering, and science are the largest.

Required: Requirements for graduation vary according to programs.

Special: Carleton offers co-op programs in many majors and an exchange program with the University of Ottawa. Study abroad, internships in industrial design, dual and student-designed majors, accelerated degree programs, and interdisciplinary programs are available. The university also utilizes instructional television.

Faculty/Classroom: 69% of faculty are male; 31%, female. The average class size in an introductory lecture is 107 and in a regular course, 58.

Admissions: 65% of the 2001-2002 applicants were accepted.

Requirements: The SAT I is required, with a minimum composite score of 1100 (550 verbal and 550 math). Applicants must be graduates of an accredited secondary school. Architecture, humanities, and industrial design students must present a portfolio; social work students should submit a personal information form; music students must audition. Carleton requires applicants to be in the upper 25% of their class. A GPA of 3.0 is required. AP and CLEP credits are accepted.

Procedure: Freshmen are admitted to all sessions. There are early admissions and deferred admissions plans. Notification of early decision is sent February; regular decision, May. 2% of all applicants are on a waiting list; 1 was accepted in 2001. Check with the school for current application deadlines. The fall 2001 application fee was $85.

Transfer: Applicants are evaluated on individual merits. 30 credits of 120 must be completed at Carleton.

Visiting: There are regularly scheduled orientations for prospective students, including a general information session and campus tour. There are guides for informal visits and visitors may sit in on classes and stay overnight. To schedule a visit, contact the Undergraduate Recruitment Office at (613) 520-3663 or *www.admissions.carleton.ca/Tours/tour*

Financial Aid: The fall application deadline is February 1.

International Students: There are 1015 international students enrolled. The school actively recruits these students. They must score 580 on the written TOEFL or 237 on the electronic version or take the college's own test or the Canadian Academic English Language Assessment.

Computers: The mainframe is a Honeywell CP6. Students have access to computers through their courses. PCs are available at a number of sites. Students who have an account for the mainframe may access the system at any time. There are no time limits and no fees.

Graduates: In 2001, 2407 bachelor's degrees were awarded. The most popular majors were psychology (10%), law (7%), and sociology/anthropology (7%).

Admissions Contact: Suzanne Blanchard, Director of Admissions. E-mail: *liaison@carleton.ca* Web: *www.carleton.ca*

CONCORDIA UNIVERSITY

E-2

Montreal, PQ, Canada H3G IM8

(514) 848-4971
Fax: (514) 848-2837

Full-time: 11,812 men and women
Part-time: 10,819 men and women
Graduate: 3819 men and women
Year: semesters, summer session
Application Deadline: March 1

Freshman Class: n/av
SAT I or ACT: recommended

Faculty: 714
Ph.D.s: 84%
Student/Faculty: 17 to 1
Tuition: $2579 (CDN) ($15,391 CDN)
Room & Board: $4593 (CDN)

Concordia University, established in 1974, is a public institution operated by the province of Quebec. There are 5 undergraduate schools and 1 graduate school. In addition to regional accreditation, Concordia University has baccalaureate program accreditation with AACSB. The 2 libraries contain 3 million volumes, 75,000 microform items, and 2000 audiovisual forms/CDs, and subscribe to 5500 periodicals. Computerized library services include the card catalog, interlibrary loans, and database searching. Special learning facilities include a learning resource center, art gallery, radio station, TV station, greenhouse, audiovisual instruction service, and specialized research center. The 1555-acre campus is in an urban area in downtown Montreal and in suburban Loyola. Including residence halls, there are 80 buildings.

Student Life: 90% of undergraduates are from Quebec. Others are from 29 states, 128 foreign countries, and Canada. The average age of freshmen is 21; all undergraduates, 25. 11% do not continue beyond their first year; 52% remain to graduate.

Housing: 144 students can be accommodated in college housing, which includes single-sex and coed dormitories, off-campus apartments, fraternity houses, and sorority houses. On-campus housing is available on a first-come, first-served basis. Priority is given to out-of-town students. 98% of students commute. All students may keep cars.

Activities: 1% of men belong to 3 national fraternities; 1% of women belong to 3 national sororities. There are 125 groups on campus, including art, choir, chorale, chorus, computers, dance, drama, ethnic, film, gay, honors, international, jazz band, literary magazine, musical theater, newspaper, orchestra, photography, political, professional, radio and TV, religious, social, social service, student government, symphony, and yearbook.

Sports: There are 9 intercollegiate sports for men and 7 for women, and 16 intramural sports for men and 12 for women. Facilities include an arena, a gym, and a football stadium.

Disabled Students: 75% of the campus is accessible. Wheelchair ramps, elevators, special parking, specially equipped rest rooms, special class scheduling, lowered drinking fountains, lowered telephones, and assistance for hearing/visual/mobility impaired are available.

Services: Counseling and information services are available, as is tutoring in most subjects. There is a reader service for the blind, and remedial math, reading, and writing.

Campus Safety and Security: Measures include 24-hour foot and vehicle patrol, self-defense education, escort service, and shuttle buses. There are informal discussions, pamphlets/posters/films, emergency telephones, and lighted pathways/sidewalks.

Programs of Study: Concordia University confers B.A., B.Admin., B.Comm., B.Comp.Sci., B.Ed., B.Eng., B.F.A., and B.S.C. degrees. Master's and doctoral degrees are also awarded. Bachelor's degrees are awarded in BIOLOGICAL SCIENCE (biochemistry, biology/biological science, and microbiology), BUSINESS (accounting, banking and finance, business administration and management, business economics, international business management, marketing/retailing/merchandising, and personnel management), COMMUNICATIONS AND THE ARTS (communications, dance, design, dramatic arts, English, English as a second/foreign language, film arts, fine arts, journalism, languages, music, and photography), COMPUTER AND PHYSICAL SCIENCE (actuarial science, chemistry, computer programming, computer science, geology, information sciences and systems, mathematics, physics, and statistics), EDUCATION (art, early childhood, and elementary), ENGINEERING AND ENVIRONMENTAL DESIGN (civil engineering, computer engineering, electrical/electronics engineering, industrial engineering, and mechanical engineering), SOCIAL SCIENCE (anthropology, East Asian studies, economics, geography, history, philosophy, political science/government, psychology, sociology, and urban studies). Computer engineering, accounting, and communication studies are the strongest academically. Accounting and psychology are the largest.

Required: To graduate, students must complete 90 to 120 credits, depending on the degree, with a minimum GPA of 2.0. Between 42 and 54 credits are required in the major. All students must fulfill the requirements of the core curriculum and take the university writing test.

Special: The university offers programs in many majors with the Institute for Co-operative Education, internships, and study abroad in 12 countries. There are accelerated degree programs, B.A.-B.S. degrees, dual majors, a general studies degree, and student-designed majors. There is a chapter of Phi Beta Kappa.

Faculty/Classroom: 65% of faculty are male; 35%, female. No introductory courses are taught by graduate students. The average class size in an introductory lecture in a laboratory, and in a regular course is 50.

Admissions: 28% of the current freshmen were in the top fifth of their class; 59% were in the top two fifths.

Requirements: The SAT I or ACT is recommended. In addition, applicants must be graduates of an accredited secondary school. The GED is accepted. An essay, an interview, a portfolio, or an audition may be required for some programs. Concordia University requires applicants to be in the upper 30% of their class. A GPA of 2.5 is required. AP and CLEP credits are accepted. Important factors in the admissions decision are advanced placement or honor courses and recommendations by school officials.

Procedure: Freshmen are admitted to all sessions. There is an early decision plan. Early decision applications should be filed by February 1; regular applications, by March 1 for fall entry (February 1 for applicants outside Canada), November 1 for winter entry, and April 15 for summer entry, along with a $50 fee. The college accepts all in-state residents. Notification is sent on a rolling basis. A waiting list is an active part of the admissions procedure.

Transfer: Applicants must have a minimum GPA of 2.2. 45 credits of 90 to 120 must be completed at Concordia University.

Visiting: There are regularly scheduled orientations for prospective students. There are guides for informal visits and visitors may sit in on classes. To schedule a visit, contact the Office of Student Recruitment at (514) 848-4779.

Financial Aid: Check with the school for funds availability and deadlines.

International Students: There were 1235 international students enrolled in a recent year. The school actively recruits these students. They must score 550 on the written TOEFL or 213 on the electronic version, or take the MELAB or the college's own test.

Computers: The mainframe is a CDC CYBER 835. There are 300 PCs and more than 100 time-sharing terminals. These include PC and Mac labs, Internet access, terminal access to UNIX and open VMS-based multi-user systems, and modem dial-in access. All students may access the system from 8:30 A.M. to 11:30 P.M. There are no time limits and no fees.

Graduates: In a recent year, 4291 bachelor's degrees were awarded. The most popular majors were arts and science (55%), commerce and administration (25%), and fine arts (10%). 500 companies recruited on campus in a recent year.

Admissions Contact: Pete Regimbald, Assistant Registrar. E-mail: *admreg@alcor.concordia.ca* Web: *www.concordia.ca*

DALHOUSIE UNIVERSITY
Halifax, NS, Canada B3H 4H6

E-2
(902) 494-2148
Fax: (902) 494-1630

Full-time: 3959 men, 5195 women
Part-time: 598 men, 680 women
Graduate: 1630 men, 1581 women
Year: terms, summer session
Application Deadline: see profile
Freshman Class: n/av
SAT I: required

Faculty: 920
Ph.D.s: 90%
Student/Faculty: 10 to 1
Tuition: $3285
Room & Board: $3769

Dalhousie University, founded in 1818, is a public, nonsectarian institution offering undergraduate, graduate, and professional programs. There are 10 undergraduate schools and 1 graduate school. The 4 libraries contain 1,270,000 volumes, 340,000 microform items, and 13,800 audiovisual forms/CDs, and subscribe to 8182 periodicals. Computerized library services include the card catalog, interlibrary loans, and database searching. Special learning facilities include a learning resource center, art gallery, natural history museum, planetarium, radio station, science museum, aquatron, slowpoke nuclear reactor, and super computer. The 80-acre campus is in an urban area in Halifax. Including residence halls, there are 102 buildings.

Student Life: 60% of undergraduates are from the province of Nova Scotia. Others are from 27 states, 107 foreign countries, and Canada. The average age of freshmen is 19; all undergraduates, 23. 14% do not continue beyond their first year.

Housing: 2200 students can be accommodated in college housing, which includes single-sex and coed dormitories, on-campus apartments, off-campus apartments, and married-student housing. In addition, there are language houses and speial interest houses. On-campus housing is available on a first-come, first-served basis and is available on a lottery system for upperclassmen. Priority is given to out-of-town students. 80% of students commute. All students may keep cars.

Activities: There are 8 national fraternities and 1 national sorority. There are more than 200 groups on campus, including cheerleading, chess, chorale, computers, dance, debate, drama, ethnic, gay, international, musical theater, newspaper, photography, political, professional, radio and TV, religious, social, student government, and yearbook. Popular campus events include Frosh Week and Winter Carnival.

Sports: There are 7 intercollegiate sports for men and 6 for women, and 30 intramural sports for men and 30 for women. Facilities include an athletic center, an arena, indoor and outdoor tennis courts, a track, a playing field, an Olympic-size swimming pool, squash and volleyball courts, a climbing wall, a soccer field, a hockey rink, a dance studio, and weight rooms.

Disabled Students: 70% of the campus is accessible. Wheelchair ramps, elevators, special parking, specially equipped rest rooms, special class scheduling, lowered drinking fountains, and owered telephones are available. The office of the vice president of student services is available to provide assistance on an individual basis.

Services: Counseling and information services are available, as is tutoring in most subjects. There is a reader service for the blind and remedial math and writing.

Campus Safety and Security: Measures include 24-hour foot and vehicle patrol, self-defense education, escort service, and shuttle buses. There are informal discussions, pamphlets/posters/films, and lighted pathways/sidewalks. The college also offers a student-organized campus patrol program.

Programs of Study: Dalhousie confers B.A., B.Sc., B.C.S., B.Comm., B.Eds., B.Eng., B.Hsc., B.Laws, B.Mgmt, B.Mus., B.Recreation and Health Ed., B.S.C.Kinesiology, B.S.N., B.S.O.T., B.S.Pharm., B.S.Physiotherapy, and B.S.W. degrees. Master's and doctoral degrees are also awarded. Bachelor's degrees are awarded in BIOLOGICAL SCIENCE (biochemistry, biology/biological science, marine biology, microbiology, and neurosciences), BUSINESS (business economics, and recreation and leisure services), COMMUNICATIONS AND THE ARTS (classics, dramatic arts, English, French, German, music, Russian, and Spanish), COMPUTER AND PHYSICAL SCIENCE (chemistry, computer science, earth science, mathematics, physics, and statistics), EDUCATION (health), ENGINEERING AND ENVIRONMENTAL DESIGN (engineering), HEALTH PROFESSIONS (dental hygiene, nursing, occupational therapy, pharmacy, physical therapy, predentistry, and premedicine), SOCIAL SCIENCE (economics, history, international studies, law, philosophy, physical fitness/movement, political science/government, psychology, religion, social work, sociology, and women's studies). Science, health science, and engineering are the strongest academically. Arts, science, and commerce are the largest.

Required: To graduate, most students must complete a minimum of 15 full-year courses, including at least 5 in the major. Most students are required to take some classes outside their area of study. Programs vary in requirements.

Special: Co-op programs may be arranged in many majors. The university offers cross-registration, study abroad in 28 countries, and accelerated degree programs. Student-designed majors are available. The honors programs provide an extra year of advanced study to qualified students. A 4-year engineering degree is offered. The Science Foundation Year uses an integrated approach to teach a variety of first-year sciences. B.A.-B.S. degrees and dual majors are possible. There is a freshman honors program.

Faculty/Classroom: 60% of faculty are male; 40%, female. No introductory courses are taught by graduate students. The average class size in an introductory lecture is 65; in a laboratory, 30; and in a regular course, 40.

Requirements: The SAT I is required, with a minimum composite score of 1100. Grade 12 credit in English is required. Students are expected to have a 70% average. An audition is necessary for music and theater students. AP credits are accepted. Important factors in the admissions decision are advanced placement or honor courses, leadership record, and recommendations by school officials.

Procedure: Freshmen are admitted to all sessions. There are early decision, early admissions, and deferred admissions plans. Early decision applications should be filed by March 15, along with a $40 fee. Notification of early decision is sent March 1; regular decision, on a rolling basis.

Transfer: Applicants are assessed on an individual basis. They should have grades of C or 65% and higher from a recognized university. 8 credits of 15 must be completed at Dalhousie.

Visiting: There are regularly scheduled orientations for prospective students, including a mixture of social events and workshops. There are guides for informal visits and visitors may sit in on classes and stay overnight. To schedule a visit, contact the Admissions Office.

Financial Aid: The average freshman award was $1200 CDN.

International Students: There are 470 international students enrolled. The school actively recruits these students. They must score 580 on the written TOEFL or 237 on the electronic version or take the MELAB. Students applying on a visa from outside Canada or the United States must take the TOEFL or MELAB if English is not their first language of communication/education. They must also take the SAT I, scoring 1100.

Computers: The mainframes are a VAX 8800 (VMS operation system), an IBM 4381, and an Alliant 6400. There are a number of Sun workstations (UNIX-based) and high-end graphics workstations. Several PC labs are available to students in the library and there are other labs throughout the campus, most connected in a local area network. All students may access the system anytime. There are no time limits and no fees.

Graduates: In 2001, 2062 bachelor's degrees were awarded. The most popular majors were law (7%), biology (6%), and psychology (6%).

Admissions Contact: Susan Tanner, Associate Registrar Admissions and Awards. E-mail: *admissions@dal.ca* Web: *www.dal.ca*

LAVAL UNIVERSITY
Quebec, PQ, Canada G1K 7P4

E-2
(418) 656-3080
(877) 7ULAVAL; Fax: (418) 656-5216

Full-time: 7644 men, 10,910 women
Part-time: 3977 men, 5927 women
Graduate: 3279 men, 3675 women
Year: semesters, summer session
Application Deadline: March 1

Faculty: 1422
Ph.D.s: 93%
Student/Faculty: 13 to 1
Tuition: $1830 CDN ($4020 CDN)
Room & Board: $8000 CDN

Freshman Class: 24,752 applied, 20,018 accepted, 10,140 enrolled
SAT I or ACT: not required

Laval University, founded in 1852, is the oldest French-language university in North America. It offers undergraduate and graduate programs through 17 faculties and 5 institutes. In addition to regional accreditation, Laval University has baccalaureate program accreditation with AACSB. The 2 libraries contain 2.8 million volumes and 567,832 audiovisual forms/CDs, and subscribe to 11,979 periodicals. Computerized library services include the card catalog, interlibrary loans, and database searching. Special learning facilities include a learning resource center, art gallery, natural history museum, radio station, and language laboratories. The 465-acre campus is in an urban area 2 miles west of old Quebec City. Including residence halls, there are 32 buildings.

Student Life: 90% of undergraduates are from Quebec. Others are from 90 foreign countries and Canada. The average age of all undergraduates is 27.

Housing: 2350 students can be accommodated in college housing, which includes single-sex and coed on-campus apartments. On-campus housing is guaranteed for all 4 years. 80% of students live on campus; of those, 40% remain on campus on weekends. All students may keep cars.

Activities: There are no fraternities or sororities. There are 225 groups on campus, including art, band, chess, choir, chorale, computers, dance, drama, ethnic, film, forensics, gay, international, jazz band, literary magazine, musical theater, newspaper, opera, orchestra, photography, political, radio and TV, religious, social, social service, student government, symphony, and writing. Popular campus events include Thematic Weeks, Rendez-vous Laval, and Student Festivals.

Sports: There are 13 intercollegiate sports for men and 10 for women, and 7 intramural sports for men and 7 for women. Facilities include covered stadium with a 200-meter running track and 4 tennis courts; 50-meter swimming pool with a 10-meter diving tower; double ice arena; 1 triple and 2 single gyms; 4 squash courts; 4 handball and racquetball courts; judo, karate, and self-defense rooms; dance studio; open-air stadium with a 400-meter running track; softball, football, and soccer fields; 6 outdoor tennis courts; 3 physical training rooms; golf driving range; indoor golf practice room; 2 outdoor basketball courts; 1-kilometer hiking trail; and a jogging track.

Disabled Students: 95% of the campus is accessible. Wheelchair ramps, elevators, special parking, specially equipped rest rooms, special class scheduling, lowered drinking fountains, lowered telephones, teletype machines for the deaf, computerized classrooms for the visually disabled, electric doors, sidewalks adjusted for physically disabled students, elevators equipped with speaking devices (for the blind), and a campus plan in Braille are available.

Services: There is a reader service for the blind and remedial math and writing. Tutoring in French (grammar) is available.

Campus Safety and Security: Measures include 24-hour foot and vehicle patrol, escort service, informal discussions, and pamphlets/posters/films. There are emergency telephones, and lighted pathways/sidewalks. Other services include 24-hour camera surveillance in pedestrian tunnels and trained evacuating teams in all buildings. Security training for social events is offered to all student associations.

Programs of Study: Laval University confers B.A., B.Sc., B.A.A., B.Arch., B.A.V., B.Ed., B.Ing., B.Mus., B.Pharm., B.Sc.A., B.Serv.Soc., B.Th., and LL.B. degrees. Master's and doctoral degrees are also awarded. Bachelor's degrees are awarded in AGRICULTURE (agricultural business management, agricultural economics, agronomy, forest engineering, forestry and related sciences, and wood science), BIOLOGICAL SCIENCE (biochemistry, biology/biological science, microbiology, and nutrition), BUSINESS (business administration and management, and insurance), COMMUNICATIONS AND THE ARTS (art history and appreciation, communications, dramatic arts, English, fine arts, French, jazz, language arts, languages, linguistics, modern language, music, Spanish, theater design, theater management, and visual and performing arts), COMPUTER AND PHYSICAL SCIENCE (actuarial science, applied mathematics, chemistry, computer science, geology, mathematics, physics, and statistics), EDUCATION (art, athletic training, early childhood, education, elementary, music, physical, secondary, and technical), ENGINEERING AND ENVIRONMENTAL DESIGN (agricultural engineering, architecture, chemical engineering, civil engineering, computer engineering, electrical/electronics engineering, engineering and applied science, engineering physics, environmental science, food services technology, geological engineering, graphic arts technology, industrial administration/management, mechanical engineering, metallurgical engineering, and mining and mineral engineering), HEALTH PROFESSIONS (nursing, occupational therapy, pharmacy, physical therapy, and rehabilitation therapy), SOCIAL SCIENCE (anthropology, archeology, classical/ancient civilization, consumer services, counseling/psychology, economics, ethnic studies, food science, French studies, geography, history, interdisciplinary studies, international studies, Judaic studies, law, philosophy, physical fitness/movement, political science/government, psychology, social work, sociology, and theological studies). Business administration, sciences, and education are the largest.

Required: Requirements for graduation vary according to the program. A minimum GPA of 2.0 out of 4.33 is required per 30 credits.

Special: The university offers work-study programs in metallurgy and mining and in forestry. Students may study abroad in most countries in Africa, Americas, Asia, Europe, and Oceania.

Faculty/Classroom: 77% of faculty are male; 23%, female.

Admissions: 81% of the 2001-2002 applicants were accepted.

Requirements: The only general requirement is the D.E.C. (Diploma of Collegial Studies-13 years of scholarity) or the equivalent. Some programs have specific requirements. All undergraduate students (except those who are non-francophones) must show a sufficient knowledge of the French language to obtain their bachelor's degree. Applications are accepted on-line at *http://www.ulaval.ca/reg/p4.html/*.

Procedure: Freshmen are admitted to all sessions. Applications should be filed by March 1 for fall entry, September 1 for winter entry, and February 1 for summer entry. A waiting list is an active part of the admissions procedure. The fall 2001 application fee was $30 CDN.

Transfer: 3386 transfer students enrolled in 2001-2002. Applicants must have the D.E.C. or the equivalent.

Visiting: There are regularly scheduled orientations for prospective students, by reservation only. There are guides for informal visits and visitors may stay overnight. To schedule a visit, contact Carolle Pelletier at (418) 656-2571 or E-Mail: *carolle.pelletier@scom.ulaval.ca*.

Financial Aid: In 2001-2002, 17% of all freshmen and 83% of continuing students received some form of financial aid from sources other than the government. 90% of freshmen and 29% of continuing students received need-based aid. The average financial indebtedness of a recent year's graduate was $12,500. The fall application deadline is June 30.

International Students: There are 1025 international students enrolled. The school actively recruits these students. A French proficiency test is required.

Computers: The mainframe is an IBM 7060-H50. Access is provided by telecommunications. PCs are available in all buildings. All students may access the system 24 hours a day. There are no time limits and no fees. It is recommended that students in business administration and architecture have personal computers. IBM ThinkPad is recommended.

Graduates: In 2000, 4655 bachelor's degrees were awarded. The most popular majors were administration (18%), science and engineering (14%), and letters (13%). Of a recent year's graduating class, 91% were employed within 6 months of graduation.

Admissions Contact: Bureau du Registraire.
E-mail: *reg@reg.ulaval.ca* Web: *http://www.ulaval.ca*

MCGILL UNIVERSITY — E-2

Montreal, PQ, Canada H3A 2T5 — (514) 398-3910
Fax: (514) 398-4193

Full-time: 6934 men, 10,279 women
Part-time: 586 men, 937 women
Graduate: 3618 men, 3537 women
Year: semesters, summer session
Application Deadline: January 15
Faculty: 1414
Ph.D.s: 95%
Student/Faculty: 12 to 1
Tuition: $2835 CDN ($9930 CDN)
Room & Board: $6420 CDN
Freshman Class: 15,885 applied, 9067 accepted, 4313 enrolled
SAT I Verbal/Math: 620/560 (minimum)

McGill University, founded in 1821, is a publicly funded private institution that grants undergraduate, graduate, and professional degrees. Tuition fees may vary depending on program. Higher rates are charged to international students. There are 11 undergraduate and 79 graduate schools. In addition to regional accreditation, McGill has baccalaureate program accreditation with APTA. The 14 libraries contain 3,281,497 volumes, 1,593,976 microform items, and 573,298 audiovisual forms/CDs, and subscribe to 17,035 periodicals. Computerized library services include the card catalog, interlibrary loans, and database searching. Special learning facilities include a learning resource center, natural history museum, radio station, and McCord Museum of Canadian History, Mont St. Hilaire Nature Conservation Center, an herbarium, an arboretum, a subarctic research station, the Institute of Air and Space Law, the Institute of Islamic Studies, the Redpath Museum of Natural History, the Lyman Entomological Museum, the Ecomuseum, the Osler Library of the History of Medicine, and the Lande Canadiana Collection. The 80-acre campus is in an urban area in downtown Montreal, with the MacDonald campus located on the far west end of the island. Including residence halls, there are 150 buildings.

Student Life: 53% of undergraduates are from Quebec. Others are from 140 foreign countries. The average age of freshmen is 20; all undergraduates, 23.

Housing: 2080 students can be accommodated in college housing, which includes single-sex and coed dormitories, off-campus apartments, and married-student housing. On-campus housing is available on a lottery system for freshmen. Priority is given to out-of-town students. 88% of students commute.

Activities: 4% of men belong to 1 local and 12 national fraternities; 2% of women belong to 4 national sororities. There are 180 groups on campus, including band, cheerleading, chess, choir, chorale, chorus, computers, dance, debate, drama, Drivesafe, ethnic, film, gay, honors, international, jazz band, literary magazine, Model UN, musical theater, newspaper, opera, orchestra, photography, political, professional, radio and TV, religious, social, social service, student government, symphony, Walksafe, and yearbook. Popular campus events include multicultural festivals, 4-floor parties, and music, film, and theatrical productions.

Sports: There are 21 intercollegiate sports for men and 23 for women, and 23 intramural sports for men and 15 for women. Facilities include a 19,000-seat stadium; a 1500-seat competition hall; 2 double gyms for basketball, volleyball, and badminton; 8 outdoor tennis courts; 4 indoor tennis courts; a 400-meter outdoor track and a banked 6-lane 200-meter indoor track; 2 weight-training rooms; dance, aerobics, and martial arts rooms; 2 pools; a gymnastics facility; 5 sports fields; a fitness center, and a sport medicine center.

Disabled Students: 80% of the campus is accessible. Wheelchair ramps, elevators, special parking, specially equipped rest rooms, special class scheduling, lowered telephones, and Braille, variable-speed tape recorders, talking calculators, books on tape, exam accommodations, adapted computers (voice synthesis and voice recognition), sign language interpreters, computerized note taking, note takers, print enlargement, readers, and adapted transport are available.

Services: Counseling and information services are available, as is tutoring in every subject. There is a reader service for the blind, and remedial math, reading, and writing.

Campus Safety and Security: Measures include 24-hour foot and vehicle patrol, escort service, informal discussions, and pamphlets/posters/films. There are emergency telephones, lighted pathways/sidewalks, and Drivesafe.

Programs of Study: McGill confers B.A., B.C.L., B.Com., B.Ed., B.Eng., B.Mus., B.Sc., B.Sc.Agr., B.Sc.Agr.Eng., B.Sc.Arch., B.Sc.F.Sc.,

B.Sc.N., B.Sc.Nutr.Sc., B.Sc.Occ.Ther., B.Sc.Phys.Ther., B.S.W., B.Th., and LL.B. degrees. Master's and doctoral degrees are also awarded. Bachelor's degrees are awarded in AGRICULTURE (agricultural economics, agriculture, animal science, conservation and regulation, plant science, and soil science), BIOLOGICAL SCIENCE (anatomy, biochemistry, biology/biological science, botany, cell biology, environmental biology, microbiology, nutrition, physiology, wildlife biology, and zoology), BUSINESS (accounting, banking and finance, entrepreneurial studies, human resources, institutional management, insurance and risk management, international business management, labor studies, management information systems, management science, marketing management, and organizational behavior), COMMUNICATIONS AND THE ARTS (art history and appreciation, classics, English, French, jazz, linguistics, modern language, music history and appreciation, music performance, music technology, music theory and composition, Russian, and Spanish), COMPUTER AND PHYSICAL SCIENCE (applied mathematics, atmospheric sciences and meteorology, chemistry, computer science, earth science, geology, geophysics and seismology, information sciences and systems, mathematics, and physics), EDUCATION (elementary, music, physical, secondary, special, teaching English as a second/foreign language (TESOL/TEFOL), and vocational), ENGINEERING AND ENVIRONMENTAL DESIGN (agricultural engineering, architecture, chemical engineering, civil engineering, computer engineering, electrical/electronics engineering, environmental science, mechanical engineering, metallurgical engineering, and mining and mineral engineering), HEALTH PROFESSIONS (clinical science, exercise science, nursing, occupational therapy, and physical therapy), SOCIAL SCIENCE (African studies, American studies, anthropology, Canadian studies, Caribbean studies, dietetics, East Asian studies, economics, food science, geography, German area studies, Hispanic American studies, history, humanities, international studies, Italian studies, Judaic studies, Latin American studies, law, Middle Eastern studies, philosophy, political science/government, psychology, religion, social work, sociology, and women's studies). The faculty of arts is the largest.

Required: To graduate, students must successfully complete a required number of approved credits, usually between 90 and 120. Students must also be in satisfactory standing, with a minimum cumulative GPA of 2.0.

Special: There is cross-registration with area universities. Study abroad, work-study within the university, co-op programs in mining and metallurgical engineering, dual majors, internships, and student-designed majors are available.

Faculty/Classroom: 69% of faculty are male; 31%, female. No introductory courses are taught by graduate students. The average class size in an introductory lecture is 30; in a laboratory, 25; and in a regular course, 45.

Admissions: 57% of the 2001-2002 applicants were accepted.

Requirements: The SAT I is required. In addition, 3 SAT II: Subject tests are required. The ACT may be submitted instead of the SAT I and II. Applications are accepted on-line at the university's web site. McGill requires applicants to be in the upper 25% of their class. A GPA of 3.3 is required. AP credits are accepted. Important factors in the admissions decision are advanced placement or honor courses, recommendations by school officials, and evidence of special talent.

Procedure: Freshmen are admitted in the fall. Entrance exams should be taken during the spring of the junior year and/or fall of the senior year. There is a deferred admissions plan. Applications should be filed by January 15 for fall entry. Notification is sent March 22. The fall 2001 application fee was $60 CDN ($50 CDN on-line).

Transfer: 1379 transfer students enrolled in 2001-2002. Requirements vary with the program. Standard admission requirements must also be met. 60 credits of 120 must be completed at McGill.

Visiting: There are regularly scheduled orientations for prospective students, with a varying agenda (including campus tours and student for a day programs). There are guides for informal visits and visitors may sit in on classes and stay overnight. To schedule a visit, contact the Welcome Center at (514) 398-6555 (tours) or (514) 398-6367 (overnight).

Financial Aid: 35% of all students received need-based aid. McGill is a member of CSS. The CSS/Profile or FAFSA and the college's own financial statement are required. The fall application deadline is rolling.

International Students: There are 3316 international students enrolled. The school actively recruits these students. They must score 577 on the written TOEFL or 233 on the electronic version or take the MELAB or IELTS. A McGill Certificate of Proficiency in English must be earned. SAT I and SAT II and/or ACT tests are required for U.S. applicants and recommended for other international applicants. Students must take SAT II: Subject tests in program-specific.

Computers: The mainframe is an IBM 9672-R51. The mainframe operates under the MVS/ESA operating system and VM/ESA and MUSIC. PC labs, LANs, and terminals are connected throughout the campus. Network services and specialized department systems in the network include Sun, DEC, and NeXT. All students may access the system. Time limits depend on the application. There are no fees. It is strongly recommended that all students have a personal computer.

Graduates: In 2001, 3495 bachelor's degrees were awarded.

Admissions Contact: Admissions, Recruitment, and Registrar's Office. A video is available. E-mail: *admissions@mcgill.ca*
Web: *www.mcgill.ca*

MCMASTER UNIVERSITY
Hamilton, ON, Canada L8S 4L8 — E-3
(905) 525-4600
Fax: (905) 527-1105

Full-time: 5160 men, 6790 women
Part-time: 870 men, 1750 women
Graduate: 1190 men, 930 women
Year: terms, summer session
Application Deadline: see profile
Freshman Class: n/av
SAT I or ACT: not required
Faculty: 927
Ph.D.s: n/av
Student/Faculty: 13 to 1
Tuition: $4000 CDN ($19,000 CDN)
Room & Board: $5500 CDN

McMaster University is a public nonsectarian institution, offering programs in the arts and sciences, business, engineering, health sciences, kinesiology, and social work. Figures given in the above capsule are approximate. There are 2 graduate schools. The 4 libraries contain 1,730,582 volumes, 1,407,290 microform items, and 19,500 audiovisual forms/CDs, and subscribe to 11,976 periodicals. Computerized library services include the card catalog, interlibrary loans, and database searching. Special learning facilities include a learning resource center, art gallery, planetarium, radio station, nuclear reactor, tandem accelerator, greenhouses, the Chedoke-McMaster Hospital, communication research lab, the Bertrand Russell archives, the Humanities Communication Centre, and computing labs. The 300-acre campus is in an urban area 60 miles southwest of Toronto. Including residence halls, there are 44 buildings.

Student Life: 95% of undergraduates are from Ontario. Others are from 12 states and 79 foreign countries. The average age of freshmen is 20; all undergraduates, 22. 1% do not continue beyond their first year.

Housing: 2765 students can be accommodated in college housing, which includes single-sex and coed dormitories and on-campus apartments. In addition, there are language houses. On-campus housing is guaranteed for the freshman year only and is available on a lottery system for upperclassmen. Priority is given to out-of-town students. 77% of students commute. All students may keep cars.

Activities: There are no fraternities or sororities. There are 100 groups on campus, including art, band, cheerleading, chess, choir, chorale, chorus, computers, debate, drama, ethnic, gay, international, jazz band, musical theater, newspaper, orchestra, photography, political, radio and TV, religious, social, student government, and yearbook. Popular campus events include Marauder Weekend.

Sports: There are 16 intercollegiate sports for men and 14 for women, and 16 intramural sports for men and 14 for women. Facilities include 2 multipurpose gyms, an outdoor track and field, a mini-weight room, a swimming pool, cross-country trails, rugby, soccer, and football fields, tennis, squash, and handball courts, and a state-of-the-art fitness facility.

Disabled Students: 60% of the campus is accessible. Wheelchair ramps, elevators, special parking, specially equipped rest rooms, special class scheduling, lowered telephones, and basement-level and aboveground tunnels with connecting walkways are available.

Services: Counseling and information services are available, as is tutoring in some subjects, arranged through individual departments. There is a reader service for the blind.

Campus Safety and Security: Measures include 24-hour foot and vehicle patrol, escort service, shuttle buses, and informal discussions. There are pamphlets/posters/films, emergency telephones, lighted pathways/sidewalks, the Emergency First-Response Team, Mac Alert bulletins, a campus watch program, a prevention programs officer, and video monitoring in some parking areas.

Programs of Study: Mac confers B.A., B.S., B.A.S., B.A./B.S.W., B.C., B.Eng., B.Eng. and Management, B.Eng. and Society, B.H.S., B.Kinesiology, B.Mus., and B.S.N. degrees. Master's and doctoral degrees are also awarded. Bachelor's degrees are awarded in BIOLOGICAL SCIENCE (biochemistry, biology/biological science, and life science), BUSINESS (business administration and management, and labor studies), COMMUNICATIONS AND THE ARTS (art, art history and appreciation, classics, comparative literature, dramatic arts, English, French, linguistics, modern language, music, and Russian), COMPUTER AND PHYSICAL SCIENCE (chemistry, computer science, earth science, geology, mathematics, physical sciences, physics, science, and statistics), ENGINEERING AND ENVIRONMENTAL DESIGN (chemical engineering, civil engineering, computer engineering, electrical/electronics engineering, engineering physics, environmental science, manufacturing engineering, materials engineering, materials science, and mechanical engineering), HEALTH PROFESSIONS (medical science, nursing, occupational therapy, and physical therapy), SOCIAL SCIENCE (anthropology, economics, geography, German area studies, gerontology, history, interdisciplinary studies, Japanese studies, Latin American studies, liberal arts/general studies, philosophy, physical fitness/movement, political science/government, psychology, religion, social work, sociology, and women's studies).

Required: Requirements for graduation vary according to the program of study. A minimum 3.5 GPA in 90 to 150 units is required for most programs.

Special: Many opportunities exist to combine 2 subjects of study within 1 faculty, or between 2 faculties. All honors students have the option of taking a minor in a second subject area. Nondegree study is possible through the Center for Continuing Education. Internships and study abroad are offered. Students may repeat failed courses provided they are eligible to continue in the program.

Faculty/Classroom: 71% of faculty are male; 29%, female. All both teach and do research.

Requirements: U.S. applicants must have a high school grade average of 80. Applicants must be graduates of an accredited secondary school. The required high school courses should include 5 years each of English and math. A portfolio is required for art students and an audition for music students. A supplementary application form is required for some programs. Offers of admission are made based on academic standing and audition/portfolio/supplementary application requirements where necessary. Important factors in the admissions decision are evidence of special talent, extracurricular activities record, and leadership record.

Procedure: Freshmen are admitted to all sessions. There is an early decision plan. Check with school for current application deadlines and fee. A waiting list is an active part of the admissions procedure.

Transfer: Applicants are considered on an individual basis. Review of high school, college, and/or university work determines admission status.

Visiting: There are regularly scheduled orientations for prospective students, including campus tours, information sessions, and panel discussions. There are guides for informal visits and visitors may sit in on classes. To schedule a visit, contact Tour Coordinator, Division of Student Liaison at (905) 525-9140, ext. 24796.

Financial Aid: 12% of undergraduates work part time. Average annual earnings from campus work are $1411 CDN. Check with school for current deadlines.

International Students: The school actively recruits these students. They must score 580 on the written TOEFL or take the MELAB or the IELTS.

Computers: The mainframes are an IBM MVS system and Sun UNIX systems. Computing labs provide access to approximately 280 PCs with word processing and spreadsheet packages, as well as various computer languages, statistical applications, and specialized course software provided by instructors. Several e-mail rooms have been set up for students. In addition to these centrally operated facilities, departments have specialized labs. All students may access the system any time. There are no time limits and no fees.

Admissions Contact: Sam Digiandomenico, Associate Registrar Admissions. E-mail: *macadmit@mcmail.mcmaster.ca*
Web: *www.mcmaster.ca*

MEMORIAL UNIVERSITY OF NEWFOUNDLAND F-2

St. John's, NF, Canada A1C 5S7 **(709) 737-3705**
Fax: (709) 737-2337

Full-time: 4800 men, 6340 women	**Faculty:** 932
Part-time: 685 men, 1365 women	**Ph.D.s:** 50%
Graduate: 845 men, 765 women	**Student/Faculty:** 12 to 1
Year: trimesters, summer session	**Tuition:** $3500 CDN ($7110 CDN)
Application Deadline: see profile	**Room & Board:** $1820 CDN
Freshman Class: n/av	
SAT I or ACT: not required	

Memorial University of Newfoundland, founded in 1925, is a public liberal arts institution. There are 13 undergraduate and 12 graduate schools. Figures in aboce capsule are approximate. The 3 libraries contain 2.5 million volumes, and subscribe to 700 periodicals. Computerized library services include the card catalog, interlibrary loans, and database searching. Special learning facilities include a learning resource center, art gallery, natural history museum, planetarium, radio station, TV station, and language labs. The 220-acre campus is in an urban area within St. John's. Including residence halls, there are 40 buildings.

Student Life: 98% of undergraduates are from Newfoundland.

Housing: 1750 students can be accommodated in college housing, which includes single-sex and coed dormitories, on-campus apartments, off-campus apartments, and married-student housing. On-campus housing is available on a first-come, first-served basis. Priority is given to out-of-town students. 89% of students commute. All students may keep cars.

Activities: There are no fraternities or sororities. There are 100 groups on campus, including band, cheerleading, chess, choir, chorale, computers, dance, debate, drama, ethnic, gay, international, jazz band, literary magazine, musical theater, newspaper, orchestra, photography, political, professional, radio and TV, religious, social, social service, student government, symphony, and yearbook. Popular campus events include Winter Carnival and Orientation.

Sports: There are 6 intercollegiate sports for men and 6 for women, and 6 intramural sports for men and 6 for women. Facilities include a gym, squash courts, a rifle range, a weight room, a soccer field, and swimming facilities.

Disabled Students: 85% of the campus is accessible. Wheelchair ramps, elevators, special parking, specially equipped rest rooms, special class scheduling, lowered drinking fountains, lowered telephones, classroom aids, note-taking volunteers, and other facilities based on individual needs are available.

Services: Counseling and information services are available. There is a reader service for the blind, and remedial math, reading, and writing. Students staying in residence have access to tutoring in every subject. In addition, lectures are offered on topics such as public speaking, speed reading, and time management.

Campus Safety and Security: Measures include 24-hour foot and vehicle patrol, self-defense education, escort service, and informal discussions. There are pamphlets/posters/films, emergency telephones, and lighted pathways/sidewalks.

Programs of Study: MUN confers B.A., B.Sc., B.Comm.(Co-op.), B.Comm.(Gen.), B.Ed., B.Eng., B.F.A., B.Kin., B.M.S., B.Mus., B.Mus.Ed., B.Med.Sc., B.N., B.P.E., B.Rec., B.Sc.(Pharm.), B.Spec.Ed., B.S.W., B.Tech., and B.Voc.Ed. degrees. Master's and doctoral degrees are also awarded. Bachelor's degrees are awarded in AGRICULTURE (forestry and related sciences), BIOLOGICAL SCIENCE (biochemistry, biology/biological science, cell biology, ecology, entomology, environmental biology, evolutionary biology, marine biology, marine science, microbiology, and neurosciences), BUSINESS (entrepreneurial studies, human resources, labor studies, management science, marketing/retailing/merchandising, organizational behavior, and small business management), COMMUNICATIONS AND THE ARTS (dramatic arts, English, English literature, fine arts, folklore and mythology, French, German, linguistics, literature, music, music history and appreciation, music performance, music theory and composition, Russian, Spanish, and visual and performing arts), COMPUTER AND PHYSICAL SCIENCE (applied mathematics, applied physics, chemistry, computer science, earth science, information sciences and systems, mathematics, oceanography, and statistics), EDUCATION (athletic training, education, elementary, guidance, middle school, music, physical, recreation, secondary, and special), ENGINEERING AND ENVIRONMENTAL DESIGN (civil engineering, electrical/electronics engineering, engineering technology, maritime science, mechanical engineering, naval architecture and marine engineering, and ocean engineering), HEALTH PROFESSIONS (medical science, nursing, and pharmacy), SOCIAL SCIENCE (anthropology, archeology, Canadian studies, criminology, dietetics, economics, French studies, geography, German area studies, history, humanities, medieval studies, philosophy, physical fitness/movement, political science/government, psychology, religion, social studies, social work, sociology, Spanish studies, and women's studies). Marine Biology, naval architecture, and business are the strongest academically. Arts, science, business, and engineering are the largest.

Required: Students must complete 40 to 50 credits to graduate. Each discipline has different requirements for graduation.

Special: The university offers co-op programs in commerce, phys ed, recreation, kinesiology, and engineering. Internships are available in education and nursing. Study abroad may be arranged in at least 20 countries. Work-study programs, dual majors, and B.A.-B.S. degrees are available.

Faculty/Classroom: 80% of faculty are male; 20%, female. All both teach and do research. Graduate students teach 71% of introductory courses. The average class size in an introductory lecture is 40.

Requirements: Admission is based on a 70% high school average as computed from university preparatory courses required for admission. Applications are accepted on-line at *http://www.mun.ca/regoff/admission/adm.htm*. AP credits are accepted.

Procedure: Freshmen are admitted to all sessions. Check with school for current application deadlines and fee. Notification is sent on a rolling basis.

Transfer: 499 transfer students enrolled in a recent year. Applicants must be in good academic standing at the previous institution. 10 credits of 40 must be completed at MUN.

Visiting: There are regularly scheduled orientations for prospective students, including various student activities, mock lectures, campus tours, and educational sessions. There are guides for informal visits and visitors may sit in on classes. To schedule a visit, contact Student Development at (709) 737-2192.

Financial Aid: Average annual earnings from campus work are $1000 CDN.

International Students: There were 135 international students enrolled in a recent year. The school actively recruits these students. They must score 550 on the written TOEFL or take the MELAB.

Computers: The mainframe is a VAX/Sun cluster. There are 850 PCs available for student use, most with Internet access. All students may access the system. There are no time limits and no fees.

Graduates: In a recent year, 2317 bachelor's degrees were awarded. The most popular majors were business (13%), biology (7%), and sociology (6%). In an average class, 75% graduate in 4 years, 20% in 5 years, and 5% in 6 years. Of a recent graduating class, 24% were enrolled in graduate school within 6 months of graduation and 63% were employed.

Admissions Contact: Phyllis McCann, Manager of Admissions. A video is available. E-mail: *pmccann@morgan.ucs.mun.ca*

QUEEN'S UNIVERSITY AT KINGSTON E-3
Kingston, ON, Canada K7L 3N6 (613) 533-2218
Fax: (613) 533-6810

Full-time: 12,232 men and women	**Faculty:** 973
Part-time: 2314 men and women	**Ph.D.s:** n/av
Graduate: 2579 men and women	**Student/Faculty:** 13 to 1
Year: semesters, summer session	**Tuition:** $4728 CDN ($11,918 CDN)
Application Deadline: March 29	**Room & Board:** $7411 CDN

Freshman Class: 21,773 applied, 3010 enrolled
SAT I Verbal/Math: 564/604

Queen's University, founded in 1841, is a public institution offering undergraduate and graduate programs in the arts and sciences, business, engineering, health sciences, and teacher education. There are 10 undergraduate and 5 graduate schools. The 8 libraries contain 1,838,616 volumes, 2 million microform items, and 7000 audiovisual forms/CDs, and subscribe to 15,000 periodicals. Computerized library services include the card catalog, interlibrary loans, and database searching. Special learning facilities include a learning resource center, art gallery, radio station, TV station, geology museum, and observatory. The 160-acre campus is in an urban area 150 miles east of Toronto. Including residence halls, there are 100 buildings.

Student Life: 85% of undergraduates are from Ontario. Others are from 80 foreign countries and Canada. 89% are from public schools. 5% do not continue beyond their first year; 90% remain to graduate.

Housing: 3071 students can be accommodated in college housing, which includes single-sex and coed dormitories, on-campus apartments, off-campus apartments, and married-student housing. In addition, there are language houses, special-interest houses, study floors, and nonsmoking floors. On-campus housing is guaranteed for the freshman year only. 80% of students commute. All students may keep cars.

Activities: There are no fraternities or sororities. There are 220 groups on campus, including art, bagpipe band, band, cheerleading, chess, choir, chorale, chorus, computers, dance, debate, drama, ethnic, film, gay, international, jazz band, literary magazine, marching band, musical theater, newspaper, orchestra, photography, political, professional, radio and TV, religious, social, social service, student government, symphony, and yearbook. Popular campus events include Orientation Week, Alumni Weekend, and Applied Science Formal.

Sports: There are 19 intercollegiate sports for men and 21 for women, and 39 intramural sports for men and 39 for women. Facilities include a pool, an indoor track, a hockey arena, tennis, squash, racquetball courts, a weight room, a dance studio, and a projectile range. There is also a 5000-seat indoor gym and a 12,000-seat football stadium.

Disabled Students: 80% of the campus is accessible. Wheelchair ramps, elevators, special parking, specially equipped rest rooms, special class scheduling, lowered drinking fountains, and lowered telephones are available.

Services: Counseling and information services are available, as is tutoring in most subjects. There is a reader service for the blind, and remedial math, reading, and writing.

Campus Safety and Security: Measures include 24-hour foot and vehicle patrol, self-defense education, escort service, and shuttle buses. There are informal discussions, pamphlets/posters/films, emergency telephones, and lighted pathways/sidewalks.

Programs of Study: Queen's confers B.A., B.Sc., B.A./B.Ed., B.A./B.Phe., B.Comm., B.F.A., B.Mus., B.N.Sc., B.Sc./B.Ed., B.Sc./B.Phe., B.S.C.E., B.Sc.O.T., and B.Sc.P.T. degrees. Master's and doctoral degrees are also awarded. Bachelor's degrees are awarded in BIOLOGICAL SCIENCE (biochemistry, biology/biological science, and life science), COMMUNICATIONS AND THE ARTS (art history and appreciation, classics, dramatic arts, English, film arts, fine arts, French, German, Greek, Italian, Latin, music, and Spanish), COMPUTER AND PHYSICAL SCIENCE (chemistry, computer science, geology, mathematics, physics, and statistics), EDUCATION (elementary, middle school, and secondary), ENGINEERING AND ENVIRONMENTAL DESIGN (chemical engineering, civil engineering, electrical/electronics engineering, engineering physics, geological engineering, and mechanical engineering), HEALTH PROFESSIONS (health, nursing, occupational therapy, and physical therapy), SOCIAL SCIENCE (economics, geography, history, Judaic studies, philosophy, political science/government, psychology, religion, sociology, and women's studies). Arts, science, and engineering are the largest.

Required: Each faculty and school establishes the academic requirements for the graduation of its students.

Special: Internships are available in life science, commerce, and engineering. Students may study abroad in 25 countries. Dual majors are available. Cross-registration with St. Lawrence College for the B.S.N. is possible. There is a freshman honors program.

Faculty/Classroom: 72% of faculty are male; 27%, female. All teach undergraduates. The average class size in a laboratory is 40.

Admissions: The SAT I scores for the 2001-2002 freshman class were: Verbal--25% below 500, 38% between 500 and 599, 26% between 600 and 700, and 11% above 700; Math--11% below 500, 34% between 500 and 599, 37% between 600 and 700, and 18% above 700.

Requirements: The SAT I is required. In addition, candidates for admission are required to submit a school profile. A GPA of 70 is required. Important factors in the admissions decision are evidence of special talent, leadership record, and extracurricular activities record. Applications are accepted on-line at *http://compass.ovac.on.ca/*

Procedure: Freshmen are admitted in the fall. There is a deferred admissions plan. Applications should be filed by March 29 for fall entry, along with a $125 fee CDN. Notification is sent on a rolling basis. A waiting list is an active part of the admissions procedure.

Transfer: 151 transfer students enrolled in 2001-2002. Admission requirements for transfer applicants vary by program. 10 credits of 19 must be completed at Queen's.

Visiting: There are regularly scheduled orientations for prospective students, consisting of a short briefing session and a walking tour. There are guides for informal visits and visitors may sit in on classes and stay overnight. To schedule a visit, contact Student Recruitment at (613) 533-2217.

Financial Aid: 9% of freshmen received need-based aid. The fall application deadline is May 13.

International Students: There are 396 international students enrolled. The school actively recruits these students. They must score 580 on the written TOEFL or 237 on the electronic version or take the MELAB. Applicants from American System Schools must take the SAT I, scoring 1200.

Computers: The mainframe is an IBM 9000. There are 4 computer centers located on campus. Students are issued a special ID to access the system. All students may access the system 24 hours. There are no time limits and no fees. It is strongly recommended that all students have a personal computer. IBM ThinkPad is recommended.

Graduates: In a recent year, 3506 bachelor's degrees were awarded.

Admissions Contact: Associate University Registrar (Admissions Services). A video is available. E-mail: *admissn@post.queensu.ca*
Web: *www.queensu.ca*

RYERSON POLYTECHNIC UNIVERSITY E-3
Toronto, ON, Canada M5B 2K3 (416) 979-5000
Fax: (416) 979-5341

Full-time: 12,500 men and women	**Faculty:** 547
Part-time: none	**Ph.D.s:** n/av
Graduate: none	**Student/Faculty:** 23 to 1
Year: semesters	**Tuition:** $4400 CDN ($11,700 CDN)
Application Deadline: see profile	**Room & Board:** $5600 CDN

Freshman Class: n/av
SAT I or ACT: required

Ryerson Polytechnic University, founded in 1948, is a public institution offering undergraduate programs in arts, applied arts, business, community services, and engineering and applied science. Figures given in the above capsule are approximate. There are 29 undergraduate schools. In addition to regional accreditation, Ryerson has baccalaureate program accreditation with FIDER. The library contains 320,898 volumes, 400 microform items, and 6283 audiovisual forms/CDs, and subscribes to 3239 periodicals. Computerized library services include the card catalog, interlibrary loans, and database searching. Special learning facilities include a learning resource center, radio station, and a film and photography gallery. The 20-acre campus is in an urban area in downtown Toronto. Including residence halls, there are 22 buildings.

Student Life: 94% of undergraduates are from Ontario. Others are from Canada. 21% do not continue beyond their first year.

Housing: 858 students can be accommodated in college housing, which includes coed dormitories. In addition, there are language houses and special-interest houses. On-campus housing is available on a first-come, first-served basis. Priority is given to out-of-town students. 94% of students commute. All students may keep cars.

Activities: There are no fraternities or sororities. There are 55 groups on campus, including choir, chorale, ethnic, film, gay, international, literary magazine, newspaper, political, professional, radio and TV, religious, social, student government, and yearbook. Popular campus events include Orientation, Island Picnic, and Winter Carnival.

Sports: There are 8 intercollegiate sports for men and 7 for women, and 7 intramural sports for men and 6 for women. Facilities include a recreation and athletic center, 7 squash courts, a fitness training center that includes an indoor running track and weight-training equipment, a rehabilitation center, a 25-yard pool, saunas, 3 studios, and 6 gyms.

Disabled Students: Wheelchair ramps, elevators, special parking, specially equipped rest rooms, special class scheduling, and lowered telephones are available. The Access Center on campus offers information, seminars, and workshops; test and exam adaptations; computer-equipped exam and study rooms; assistive listening devices for personal use and for use in auditorium settings; advocacy services; individual needs assessment; and access to a wide range of technical devices are available.

Services: There is a reader service for the blind, remedial math, reading, and writing, and study skills development.

Campus Safety and Security: Measures include 24-hour foot and vehicle patrol, self-defense education, escort service, and informal discussions. There are pamphlets/posters/films, emergency telephones, lighted pathways/sidewalks, sexual assault training, harassment prevention and crime prevention programs, and community policing programs.

Programs of Study: Ryerson confers B.A.A., B.B.M., B.Eng., B.H.Sc., B.S.N., B.S.W., and B.Tech. degrees. Bachelor's degrees are awarded in BUSINESS (business administration and management, hospitality management services, and management information systems), COMMUNICATIONS AND THE ARTS (broadcasting, journalism, and photography), COMPUTER AND PHYSICAL SCIENCE (chemical technology and computer programming), EDUCATION (early childhood), ENGINEERING AND ENVIRONMENTAL DESIGN (aeronautical engineering, architecture, chemical engineering, civil engineering, electrical/electronics engineering, graphic and printing production, industrial engineering, interior design, mechanical engineering, and urban planning technology), HEALTH PROFESSIONS (environmental health science and nursing), SOCIAL SCIENCE (child care/child and family studies, family/consumer studies, fashion design and technology, geography, public administration, and social work). Business management, electrical engineering, and administration and information management are the largest.

Required: To graduate, students must have a 2.0 GPA and complete the requirements of their program of study.

Special: The university offers co-op programs in applied chemistry and biology, chemical engineering, and midwifery. Accelerated degree programs are available in journalism, radio and television arts, nurse practitioner, and nursing, and many programs have a work-study component.

Faculty/Classroom: All teach undergraduates. The average class size in a regular course is 30.

Requirements: The SAT I or ACT is required for U.S. students, with a recommended minimum score of 550 on each section of the SAT I. Students should be high school graduates with a minimum B overall average.

Procedure: Freshmen are admitted in the fall. Check with school for current application deadlines and fee. A waiting list is an active part of the admissions procedure.

Transfer: Transfer applicants must have completed 1 year at the college level. Acceptance of transfer credits is at the discretion of the Office of Admissions/Liaison/Curriculum Advising. Half of the required credits for a particular degree program must be completed at Ryerson.

Visiting: There are regularly scheduled orientations for prospective students, including a half-day tour and discussion session featuring campus tours and visits to specific schools and departments. There are guides for informal visits and visitors may sit in on classes. To schedule a visit, contact the Liaison Office at (416) 979-5030.

Financial Aid: Ryerson is a member of CSS. The financial statements applicable to Ontario government requirements are needed.

International Students: They must score 550 on the written TOEFL or take the MELAB or the college's own test.

Computers: The mainframe is an IBM RISC 6000. Most major buildings have clusters of PCs that are networked to the backbone. There are also clusters of IBM terminals, which allow access to the mainframe, and more than 300 networked workstations. All students may access the system. There may be time limits in some cases, but they will vary according to program. There are no fees.

Admissions Contact: Director of Admissions.
E-mail: *inquire@acs.ryerson.ca* Web: *http://www.ryerson.ca*

SIMON FRASER UNIVERSITY

Burnaby, BC, Canada V5A 1S6 — **B-2**

(604) 291-3224
Fax: (604) 291-4969

Full-time: 3788 men, 4968 women	**Faculty:** 656
Part-time: 3468 men, 4564 women	**Ph.D.s:** 88%
Graduate: 1192 men, 1367 women	**Student/Faculty:** 13 to 1
Year: trimesters, summer session	**Tuition:** $2404 CDN ($7139 CDN)
Application Deadline: April 30	**Room & Board:** $3430 CDN
Freshman Class: 9674 applied, 5431 accepted, 2278 enrolled	
SAT I Verbal/Math: 600/600	**ACT:** 26

Simon Fraser University, established in 1963, is a public institution offering undergraduate and graduate programs in the arts, sciences, business, education, and applied sciences. In addition to its main campus, the university maintains the Harbour Centre campus in downtown Vancouver to provide midcareer education to the urban population. There are 5 undergraduate and 33 graduate schools. The library contains 1,306,397 volumes, 1,160,877 microform items, and 9242 audiovisual forms/CDs, and subscribes to 8004 periodicals. Computerized library services include interlibrary loans and database searching. Special learning facilities include a learning resource center, art gallery, radio station, archeology museum, special literature and map collections, fine and performing arts theater, hypo/hyperbaric chamber, back test unit, computer labs, a rock climbing wall, and an apiary. The 1235-acre campus is in a suburban area 9 miles east of Vancouver. Including residence halls, there are 25 buildings.

Student Life: 89% of undergraduates are from British Columbia. Others are from 84 foreign countries. 94% are from public schools. The average age of freshmen is 20; all undergraduates, 24.

Housing: 1250 students can be accommodated in college housing, which includes single-sex and coed dormitories, on-campus apartments, and married-student housing. Suites for disabled students and graduate student housing are also available. Priority for on-campus housing is given to out-of-town students. 93% of students commute. All students may keep cars.

Activities: There are no fraternities or sororities. There are 35 groups on campus, including athletic, bagpipe band, chess, choir, computers, ethnic, gaming, gay, international, newspaper, political, professional, religious, social, special interest, and student government. Popular campus events include Convocation, Clubs Day, and various orientation activities.

Sports: There are 9 intercollegiate sports for men and 9 for women, and 7 intramural sports for men and 7 for women. Facilities include 2 gyms, swimming and diving pools, a running track, weight rooms, saunas, playing fields, a combative room, and tennis, squash, and racquetball courts.

Disabled Students: 90% of the campus is accessible. Wheelchair ramps, elevators, special parking, specially equipped rest rooms, lowered drinking fountains, lowered telephones, some specially equipped on-campus housing, computers with software such as large text and voice output features, a scanner, a braille printer, a visualtek machine, closed-circuit TV for text or graphic enlargement, note taking tutor support, adaptive technology, exam modifications, sign language interpreters, closed-captioning in lectures, and alternate format texts are available.

Services: There is a reader service for the blind and taped library books. Some lectures are taped.

Campus Safety and Security: Measures include 24-hour foot and vehicle patrol, escort service, pamphlets/posters/films, and emergency telephones. There are lighted pathways/sidewalks and safe-walk stations, student patrols, and individual dormitory room security.

Programs of Study: SFU confers B.A., B.Sc., B.A.Sc., B.B.A., B.Ed., B.F.A., and B.G.S. degrees. Master's and doctoral degrees are also awarded. Bachelor's degrees are awarded in BIOLOGICAL SCIENCE (biochemistry, biology/biological science, and molecular biology), BUSINESS (business administration and management, management information systems, and management science), COMMUNICATIONS AND THE ARTS (art, communications, dance, dramatic arts, English, film arts, French, linguistics, music, and visual and performing arts), COMPUTER AND PHYSICAL SCIENCE (actuarial science, applied mathematics, applied physics, chemistry, computer science, earth science, mathematics, physics, science, and statistics), EDUCATION (education), ENGINEERING AND ENVIRONMENTAL DESIGN (engineering and applied science and environmental science), SOCIAL SCIENCE (anthropology, archeology, Canadian studies, cognitive science, criminology, economics, geography, history, humanities, liberal arts/general studies, philosophy, physical fitness/movement, political science/government, psychology, sociology, and women's studies). Engineering science is the strongest academically. Business administration and computing science are the largest.

Required: General bachelor's degrees require completion of 120 semester hours with a 2.0 GPA; honors degrees, 132 hours.

Special: Simon Fraser offers cooperative education in most areas of study, many opportunities for joint majors, B.A.-B.Sc. degrees, a general studies degree, work-study programs, dual-majors, and a variety of certificate and diploma programs, as well as nondegree and evening study. Interdisciplinary majors are offered in such areas as chemical physics, management and systems science, mathematical physics, and physics and physiology. There is a freshman honors program.

Faculty/Classroom: 73% of faculty are male; 27%, female. All both teach and do research. Graduate students teach 7% of introductory courses. The average class size in an introductory lecture is 145; in a laboratory, 21; and in a regular course, 35.

Admissions: 56% of the 2001-2002 applicants were accepted.

Requirements: The SAT I is required and the ACT is recommended, for U.S. applicants. Applicants must be graduates of an accredited secondary school and have a minimum grade average of 67%. Students may apply through the Internet. SFU requires applicants to be in the upper 70% of their class. A GPA of 3.2 is required. AP credits are accepted.

Procedure: Freshmen are admitted to all sessions. There are early decision and early admissions plans. Applications should be filed by April 30 for fall entry, September 30 for spring entry, and January 31 for summer entry. Notification of early decision is sent May 15; regular decision, July 1. 500 early decision candidates were accepted for the 2001-2002 class. The fall 2001 application fee was $25 CDN.

Transfer: 1206 transfer students enrolled in 2001-2002. Applicants must have a minimum GPA of 2.0 and be in good standing at their previous school. 60 credits of 120 must be completed at SFU.

Visiting: There are regularly scheduled orientations for prospective students, There are regularly scheduled 1-day campus orientations for prospective students. There are guides for informal visits and visitors may stay overnight. To schedule a visit, contact the Residence and Housing Office at (604) 291-4503.

Financial Aid: The average financial indebtedness of the 2001 graduate was $25,000 CDN. The FAFSA is required. The fall application deadline is July 1.

International Students: There are 376 international students enrolled. The school actively recruits these students. They must score 570 on the written TOEFL or 250 on the electronic version or take APIEL (minimum score 4 or 3 with successful completion of University's Bridge program), or IELTS (minimum score 6.5 on academic modules) and also take the SAT I or the ACT, scoring 1200 or 26, respectively.

Computers: There are IBM, Sun, and SGI host computers. PCs, Macs, and printers are available for student word processing needs. All students may access the system. There are no time limits and no fees.

Graduates: In 2001, 2975 bachelor's degrees were awarded. The most popular majors were business (14%), economics (10%), and psychology (9%). In an average class, 8% graduate in 3 years, 34% in 4 years, 54% in 5 years, and 61% in 6 years.

Admissions Contact: Nick Heath, Director of Admissions.
E-mail: *undergraduate-admissions@sfu.ca* Web: *http://www.reg.sfu.ca*

UNIVERSITÉ DE MONTRÉAL

Montreal, PQ, Canada H3C 3T5 — E-2 — (514) 343-7076 — Fax: (514) 343-5788

Full-time: 9829 men, 14,079 women	**Faculty:** 3725
Part-time: 4599 men, 8019 women	**Ph.D.s:** 96%
Graduate: 4973 men, 5947 women	**Student/Faculty:** 16 to 1
Year: trimesters, summer session	**Tuition:** $1939 CDN ($7729 CDN)
Application Deadline: March 1	**Room & Board:** $1970 CDN

Freshman Class: 22,902 applied, 12,207 accepted, 10,092 enrolled
SAT I or ACT: not required

Université de Montréal, founded in 1878, is the largest French-language university in North America, with 13 faculties, 2 affiliated schools, 62 teaching departments, and more than 170 research units. There are 16 undergraduate schools and 1 graduate school. The 19 libraries contain 2,660,322 volumes, 1,604,798 microform items, and 178,335 audiovisual forms/CDs, and subscribe to 12,698 periodicals. Computerized library services include the card catalog, interlibrary loans, and database searching. Special learning facilities include a learning resource center, art gallery, natural history museum, and radio station. The 145-acre campus is in an urban area in Montreal. Including residence halls, there are 42 buildings.

Student Life: Undergraduates are from Quebec, 94 foreign countries, other Canadian provinces. 88% are from public schools. The average age of freshmen is 24; all undergraduates, 26. 16% do not continue beyond their first year; 84% remain to graduate.

Housing: 1164 students can be accommodated in college housing, which includes coed off-campus apartments. On-campus housing is guaranteed for all 4 years. 98% of students commute. All students may keep cars.

Activities: There are no fraternities or sororities. There are 97 groups on campus, including art, choir, chorale, computers, dance, drama, ethnic, film, international, jazz band, literary magazine, newspaper, orchestra, photography, radio and TV, religious, social, social service, student government, and yearbook. Popular campus events include Multicultural week and Welcoming week.

Sports: There are 8 intercollegiate sports for men and 6 for women, and 12 intramural sports for men and 12 for women. Facilities include skating rink, football field, gym, squash and racquetball courts, Olympic-size pool, diving pool, running field with tennis courts, and aerobic and muscular exercise equipment.

Disabled Students: 95% of the campus is accessible. Wheelchair ramps, elevators, special parking, specially equipped rest rooms, lowered drinking fountains, and lowered telephones are available. There is also a specialized equipment center for students with disabilities.

Services: Counseling and information services are available, as is tutoring in some subjects, including math and French. There is a reader service for the blind, and remedial math, reading, and writing.

Campus Safety and Security: Measures include 24-hour foot and vehicle patrol, informal discussions, pamphlets/posters/films, and emergency telephones. There are lighted pathways/sidewalks.

Programs of Study: UdeM confers B.A., B.Sc., B.A.A., B.A.P., B.D.I., B.Gest, B.Ed., B.Ing., B.Int., B.Mus., B. Pharm., and B.Th. degrees. Associate, master's, and doctoral degrees are also awarded. Bachelor's degrees are awarded in BIOLOGICAL SCIENCE (biochemistry, biology/biological science, biometrics and biostatistics, and nutrition), BUSINESS (business administration and management), COMMUNICATIONS AND THE ARTS (art history and appreciation, classics, English, film arts, French, German, industrial design, linguistics, and music), COMPUTER AND PHYSICAL SCIENCE (chemistry, computer science, mathematics, and physics), EDUCATION (education, physical, and psychology), ENGINEERING AND ENVIRONMENTAL DESIGN (architectural engineering, architecture, engineering, industrial administration/management, and landscape architecture/design), HEALTH PROFESSIONS (health science, nursing, occupational therapy, pharmacy, physical therapy, predentistry, premedicine, preveterinary science, speech pathology/audiology, and veterinary science), SOCIAL SCIENCE (anthropology, Asian/Oriental studies, criminology, economics, geography, history, law, philosophy, political science/government, psychology, social work, sociology, Spanish studies, theological studies, and urban studies). Arts and science are the largest.

Required: To graduate, students must have a GPA of 2.0 on a 4.3 scale. The total number of credit hours required in most programs is 90, although it can range up to 187. Professional programs, particularly those in health-related fields, require more hours.

Special: The university offers co-op programs in math, translation, mining, and in civil, chemical, and software material engineering; internships in medicine, dental medicine and veterinary medicine (graduate study levels) and work-study programs in hospitals and businesses in Quebec. B.A. -B.Sc. Degrees, dual majors in math and economics, math and physics, math and computer science, communication and politics, economics and politics, and English studies or comparative literature, film arts, and East Asian studies and anthropology, geography, or history, and 3-2 engineering degrees may lso be arranged. Study abroad is available in 31 countries. There is a freshman honors program and 45 departmental honors programs.

Faculty/Classroom: 71% of faculty are male; 29%, female. The average class size in an introductory lecture is 48; in a laboratory, 19; and in a regular course, 40.

Admissions: 53% of the 2001-2002 applicants were accepted.

Requirements: Applicants in certain programs must take the university's admissions tests. An interview is also required in some programs. Applications are accepted on-line at the university's web site, *www.etudiant.umontreal.ca*.

Procedure: Freshmen are admitted fall and winter. Applications should be filed by March 1 for fall entry, November 1 for winter entry, March 1 for spring entry, and March 1 for summer entry, along with a $30 fee. Notification is sent March 15. A waiting list is an active part of the admissions procedure.

Transfer: Transfers are considered if there are openings in the second or third year of the university's programs.

Visiting: There are regularly scheduled orientations for prospective students, including Orientation and Employment Week in November, guided tours February through May, and open house in January and August. There are guides for informal visits. To schedule a visit, contact Direction des communications at (514) 343-6032 or *evenements@dircom.umontreal.ca*.

Financial Aid: In 2001-2002, 35% of all freshmen and 10% of continuing students received some form of financial aid. 50% of freshmen and 70% of continuing students received need-based aid. Scholarships or need-based grants averaged $3620 CDN ($18,140 CDN maximum); and loans averaged $2400 CDN ($2460 CDN maximum). 57% of undergraduates work part time. The average financial indebtedness of the 2001 graduate was $12,000 CDN. The fall application deadline is March 31.

International Students: There are 2134 international students enrolled. The school actively recruits these students. A French proficiency test is required upon admission.

Computers: The mainframes are a 7 SGI Origin 2000/ 1 HP/N4000 and 2 SGI Challenge XL / 2 SGI Origin 20 computers. Students have access to 1500 workstations (PCs, Macs, and UNIX). Every student has access to e-mail and the Internet. Log-on accounts are based on academic needs. There are no time limits and no fees. It is strongly recommended that all students have a personal computer.

Graduates: In 2001, 5506 bachelor's degrees were awarded. The most popular majors were arts and science (29%), business (19%), and engineering (10%). In an average class, 57% graduate in 3 years, 67% in 4 years, 69% in 5 years, and 70% in 6 years. 72 companies recruited on campus in 2000-2001.

Admissions Contact: Fernand Boucher, Registrar.
E-mail: *admissions@regis.umontreal.ca* Web: *http://umontreal.ca*

UNIVERSITY OF ALBERTA C-2
Edmonton, AB, Canada T6G 2M7 **(780) 492-3113**
Fax: (780) 492-7172

Full-time: 11,200 men, 14,127 women
Part-time: 798 men, 1270 women
Graduate: 2320 men, 2536 women
Year: terms, summer session
Application Deadline: May 1
Faculty: 1650
Ph.D.s: 92%
Student/Faculty: 15 to 1
Tuition: $4330 CDN ($10,440 CDN)
Room & Board: $3963 CDN
Freshman Class: 7279 applied, 4795 accepted, 3901 enrolled
SAT I or ACT: not required

The University of Alberta, founded in 1906, is a publicly supported institution offering undergraduate and graduate programs in arts and science, agricultural sciences, business, education, engineering, and professional studies. There are 16 undergraduate schools and 1 graduate school. The 6 libraries contain 3.4 million volumes and 2.8 million microform items, and subscribe to 18,900 periodicals. Computerized library services include the card catalog, interlibrary loans, and database searching. Special learning facilities include a learning resource center, art gallery, radio station, an agricultural meteorological research station, an ecological sanctuary, a botanical garden, and the Kurimoto Japanese Garden farm. The 155-acre campus is in an urban area 2 miles southwest of downtown Edmonton. Including residence halls, there are 90 buildings.

Student Life: Students are from Canada, 10 states, and 110 foreign countries.

Housing: 4900 students can be accommodated in college housing, which includes single-sex and coed dormitories, on-campus apartments, off-campus apartments, and married-student housing. In addition, there are honors houses. On-campus housing is guaranteed for all 4 years. All students may keep cars.

Activities: There are 7 national fraternities and 3 national sororities. There are 200 groups on campus, including art, band, cheerleading, chess, choir, chorale, chorus, computers, dance, drama, ethnic, gay, international, jazz band, musical theater, newspaper, opera, orchestra, pep band, photography, political, radio and TV, religious, social, social service, student government, and symphony.

Sports: There are 9 intercollegiate sports for men and 6 for women, and 60 intramural sports for men and 45 for women. Facilities include a stadium, swimming pools, gyms, combatives and weight rooms, ballet/fencing and aerobics studios, a 400-meter outdoor track, an ice arena, racquetball and squash courts, a wrestling gym, an indoor field house, a sports medicine clinic, and a training center for handicapped athletes.

Disabled Students: 98% of the campus is accessible. Wheelchair ramps, elevators, special parking, specially equipped rest rooms, special class scheduling, lowered drinking fountains, lowered telephones, and automatic doors are available.

Services: Counseling and information services are available, as is tutoring in some subjects. There is a reader service for the blind, and remedial math, reading, and writing.

Campus Safety and Security: Measures include 24-hour foot and vehicle patrol, escort service, pamphlets/posters/films, and emergency telephones. There are lighted pathways/sidewalks.

Programs of Study: U of A confers B.A., B.S., B.Comm., B.Ed., B.F.A., B.Mus., and B.P.E. degrees. Master's and doctoral degrees are also awarded. Bachelor's degrees are awarded in AGRICULTURE (agricultural economics, agriculture, animal science, and soil science), BIOLOGICAL SCIENCE (biochemistry, biology/biological science, botany, cell biology, entomology, genetics, microbiology, physiology, and zoology), BUSINESS (accounting, management science, and marketing/retailing/merchandising), COMMUNICATIONS AND THE ARTS (classics, comparative literature, dance, dramatic arts, English, film arts, French, Germanic languages and literature, linguistics, music, romance languages and literature, and Slavic languages), COMPUTER AND PHYSICAL SCIENCE (applied mathematics, chemistry, computer science, earth science, geology, geophysics and seismology, mathematics, physical sciences, physics, and statistics), EDUCATION (education of the deaf and hearing impaired, education of the multiply handicapped, elementary, physical, secondary, special, and vocational), ENGINEERING AND ENVIRONMENTAL DESIGN (chemical engineering technology, civil engineering, computer engineering, electrical/electronics engineering, engineering physics, mechanical engineering, metallurgical engineering, mining and mineral engineering, and petroleum/natural gas engineering), HEALTH PROFESSIONS (medical laboratory science, nursing, occupational therapy, pharmacy, and physical therapy), SOCIAL SCIENCE (anthropology, Canadian studies, clothing and textiles management/production/services, criminology, East Asian studies, Eastern European studies, economics, geography, history, law, philosophy, political science/government, psychology, sociology, and women's studies). Arts, science, and education are the largest.

Required: The requirements for graduation vary according to the program.

Special: The college offers cooperative work experience/study programs in business and engineering. Opportunities for study abroad, internships, dual majors, bilingual classes in French and English, credit by examination (special assessment), and pass/fail options are also available.

Faculty/Classroom: 83% of faculty are male; 17%, female. All both teach and do research.

Admissions: 66% of the 2001-2002 applicants were accepted.

Requirements: Graduation from an accredited secondary school is required. A minimum grade average of 65 is required in all courses submitted for academic credit. Depending on the program selected by the student, an essay, portfolio, audition, or interview may be required. AP credits are accepted.

Procedure: Freshmen are admitted to all sessions. There is an early decision plan. Applications should be filed by May 1 for fall entry for most programs, along with a $60 fee. A waiting list is an active part of the admissions procedure.

Transfer: Applicants must meet minimum matriculation requirements or complete 24 credits of transferable work with satisfactory standing. 60 credits of 120 must be completed at U of A.

Visiting: There are regularly scheduled orientations for prospective students. There are guides for informal visits and visitors may sit in on classes. To schedule a visit, contact Office of the Registrar and Student Awards.

International Students: There are 700 international students enrolled. They must score 580 on the written TOEFL or 237 on the electronic version or take the MELAB.

Computers: The mainframe is an Amdahl 5880. There are also 370 IBM, Mac, Zenith, and SUN PCs available in various locations on campus. All students may access the system 24 hours a day. There are no time limits. The fee varies by amount of CPU usage.

Graduates: In a recent year, 5263 bachelor's degrees were awarded.

Admissions Contact: Office of the Registrar and Student Awards.
E-mail: *registrar@ualberta.ca* Web: *www.ualberta.ca*

UNIVERSITY OF BRITISH COLUMBIA B-2
Vancouver, BC, Canada V6T 1Z1 **(604) 822-3014**
(877) 272-1422; Fax: (604) 822-3599

Full-time: 19,656 men and women
Part-time: 3239 men, 4381 women
Graduate: 2170 men, 2870 women
Year: terms, summer session
Application Deadline: March 31
Faculty: 1745
Ph.D.s: 98%
Student/Faculty: 11 to 1
Tuition: $2406 CDN ($15,705 CDN)
Room & Board: $5200 CDN
Freshman Class: 24,298 applied, 9880 accepted, 5137 enrolled
SAT I: recommended

The University of British Columbia, established in 1908, is a publicly supported institution offering a wide range of undergraduate, graduate, and professional programs in the arts, sciences, and other fields of study. The winter session lasts from early September through April; some courses extend into May. Summer session begins in May and goes to mid-August, consisting of 2 terms. There are 12 undergraduate schools and 1 graduate school. The 13 libraries contain 3.9 million volumes, 4.8 million microform items, and 1.5 million audiovisual forms/CDs, and subscribe to 25,900 periodicals. Computerized library services include the card catalog, interlibrary loans, and database searching. Special learning facilities include a learning resource center, art gallery, natural history museum, radio station, anthropology museum, Canada's largest accelerator for subatomic physics space observatory, center for integated computer systems research, center for the study of global issues, and center for the performing arts. The 1000-acre campus is in an urban area 6 miles from the center of Vancouver. Including residence halls, there are 499 buildings.

Student Life: 81% of undergraduates are from British Columbia. Others are from 28 states and 114 foreign countries. 98% are from public schools. The average age of all undergraduates is 21.

Housing: 7500 students can be accommodated in college housing, which includes single-sex and coed dormitories, on-campus apartments, and married-student housing. In addition, there are special-interest houses. On-campus housing is available on a first-come, first-served basis. Priority is given to out-of-town students. 80% of students commute. All students may keep cars.

Activities: 6% of men belong to 7 national fraternities; 2% of women belong to 7 national sororities. There are 250 groups on campus, including art, band, cheerleading, chess, choir, chorale, chorus, computers, dance, debate, drama, ethnic, film, gay, international, jazz band, literary magazine, musical theater, opera, orchestra, photography, political, professional, radio and TV, religious, ski and snowboard, social, social service, student government, symphony, varisty outdoors, and yearbook. Popular campus events include Storm the Wall, Day of the Longboat, and Great Trek Run.

Sports: There are 15 intercollegiate sports for men and 13 for women, and 18 intramural sports for men and 18 for women. Facilities include

a winter sports center, a 3500-seat stadium, a gym, an aquatic center, playing fields, a recreation center, and a tennis center.
Disabled Students: Wheelchair ramps, elevators, special parking, specially equipped rest rooms, special class scheduling, lowered drinking fountains, lowered telephones, special living facilities, accessible shower stalls in fitness facilities, tactile maps, TTY pay phones, an accessible security bus, and audible street crossing signals are available.
Services: Counseling and information services are available, as is tutoring in most subjects. There is a reader service for the blind, and remedial math, reading, and writing.
Campus Safety and Security: Measures include 24-hour foot and vehicle patrol, escort service, shuttle buses, and informal discussions. There are pamphlets/posters/films, emergency telephones,and lighted pathways/sidewalks. A Royal Canadian Mounted Police detachment is on campus, and campus security provides awareness programs on theft and personal safety lectures for women.
Programs of Study: UBC confers B.A., B.Sc., B.A.Sc., B.Com., B.D.Sc., B.ED., B.F.A., B.H.E., B.H.K., B.H.L.Sc., B.L.L.B., B.Sc.Die., B.Sc.F., B.Sc.N., B.Sc.O.T., B.S. Pharm., B.Sc.P.T., and B.S.W. degrees. Master's and doctoral degrees are also awarded. Bachelor's degrees are awarded in AGRICULTURE (agricultural economics, animal science, forestry and related sciences, plant science, range/farm management, soil science, and wildlife management), BIOLOGICAL SCIENCE (ecology and nutrition), BUSINESS (accounting, banking and finance, business economics, human resources, international business management, management information systems, marketing/retailing/merchandising, and transportation management), COMMUNICATIONS AND THE ARTS (classics, creative writing, dramatic arts, English, fine arts, French, German, Italian, linguistics, music, Portuguese, Russian, and Spanish), COMPUTER AND PHYSICAL SCIENCE (mathematics), EDUCATION (elementary, secondary, and special), ENGINEERING AND ENVIRONMENTAL DESIGN (architecture, bioengineering, chemical engineering, civil engineering, electrical/electronics engineering, engineering physics, geological engineering, industrial administration/management, landscape architecture/design, mechanical engineering, and mining and mineral engineering), HEALTH PROFESSIONS (preveterinary science), SOCIAL SCIENCE (anthropology, Asian/Oriental studies, dietetics, economics, food science, geography, history, home economics, international relations, philosophy, political science/government, psychology, sociology, and urban studies). Applied sciences and commerce are the strongest academically. Education and psychology are the largest.
Required: Graduation requirements vary according to the degree sought. B.A. candidates must complete course work in English composition, science, literature, and a foreign language.
Special: UBC offers co-op programs in science, applied science, commerce, arts, and forestry, and study abroad in England and Denmark or through 145 student exchange opportunities in 34 countries. Nondegree study is possible. A B.A.-B.A.Sc. degree, student-designed majors, and dual majors in most faculties are available. There is 1 national honor society, and most departments have honors programs.
Faculty/Classroom: 76% of faculty are male; 24%, female.
Admissions: 41% of the 2001-2002 applicants were accepted.
Requirements: The SAT I is recommended. In addition, graduation from an accredited secondary school is required. General admission for students following a U.S. system is based on 4 years of English and 3 of math. There are also specific program requirements in math, chemistry, physics, and/or biology for students applying to science-based programs. Applications are accepted on-line. A GPA of 2.6 is required. AP credits are accepted.
Procedure: Freshmen are admitted fall and spring. Applications should be filed by March 31 for fall entry, February 28 for spring entry, and February 28 for summer entry, along with a $100 fee. Notification of early decision is sent beginning in January; regular decision, on a rolling basis.
Transfer: 2049 transfer students enrolled in a recent year. Official transcripts, completion of the equivalent of 24 course credits, and no failures are required. A competitive GPA is required to get into the program at the second or third year. Applicants must have attended an accredited postsecondary institution. 60 credits of 120 must be completed at UBC.
Visiting: There are regularly scheduled orientations for prospective students, consisting of a 9:30 to 11 A.M. campus tour every Friday and 1 P.M. to 2:30 P.M. Tuesday; some Saturday sessions are available. Visitors may sit in on classes and stay overnight. To schedule a visit, contact the Student Information Centre at *student.information@ubc.ca*
Financial Aid: In a recent year, the average freshman award was $1720 CDN. Of that total, loans averaged $4237 CDN. The FAFSA and the college's own financial statement are required. The fall application deadline is April 15.
International Students: There are 1582 international students enrolled. The school actively recruits these students. They must score 570 on the written TOEFL or take the MELAB, the Comprehensive English Language Test, the IELTS, the CAEL, or the CPE. The SAT I is not required but can be helpful if submitted.
Computers: The mainframe is an IBM 3090-400J. There are 500 or more computers in labs for each faculty. The library, residences, and research centers are wired, and all students have free e-mail and 4 hours of free access to the Internet each month. Internet access parts for laptop computers are also available. Students apply and register for courses online. All students may access the system 24 hours per day. There are no time limits and no fees. It is strongly recommended that all students have a personal computer.
Graduates: In 2001, 4023 bachelor's degrees were awarded. The most popular majors were arts (29%), science (20%), and education (16%). In an average class, 62% graduate in 4 years, and 78% in 6 years. Of the 2000 graduating class, 50% were enrolled in graduate school within 6 months of graduation and 96% were employed.
Admissions Contact: Office of the Registrar. A video is available.
E-mail: *international.reception@ubc.ca* Web: *www.welcom.ubc.ca*

UNIVERSITY OF CALGARY

Calgary, AB, Canada T2N 1N4 — C-2 — (403) 220-6669 — Fax: (403) 220-0762

Full-time: 8090 men, 9495 women	**Faculty:** 1213
Part-time: 1400 men, 1910 women	**Ph.D.s:** n/av
Graduate: 1690 men, 1720 women	**Student/Faculty:** 14 to 1
Year: trimesters, summer session	**Tuition:** $4060 CDN ($7710 CDN)
Application Deadline: see profile	**Room & Board:** $5185 CDN
Freshman Class: n/av	
SAT I: required	

The University of Calgary, founded in 1945, is a public institution offering undergraduate programs in numerous liberal arts and professional fields. Figures in above capsule are approximate. There are 13 undergraduate and 2 graduate schools. The 5 libraries contain 2 million volumes, 2.7 million microform items, and 1.5 million audiovisual forms/CDs, and subscribe to 11,950 periodicals. Computerized library services include the card catalog, interlibrary loans, and database searching. Special learning facilities include a learning resource center and student radio station, student TV station, arts museum, environmental research center, observatory, and human performance and theater labs. The 304-acre campus is in an urban area in northwest Calgary. Including residence halls, there are 33 buildings.
Housing: 1500 students can be accommodated in college housing, which includes coed dormitories, on-campus apartments, and married-student housing. On-campus housing is available on a first-come, first-served basis. Priority is given to out-of-town students. All students may keep cars.
Activities: There are no fraternities or sororities. There are some groups and organizations on campus, including band, choir, drama, newspaper, orchestra, political, radio and TV, religious, social, and student government. Popular campus events include Bermuda Shorts Day (last day of classes in April).
Sports: There are 10 intercollegiate sports for men and 9 for women, and 20 intramural sports for men and 18 for women. Facilities include 3 gyms, 50-meter swimming pool, 200-meter indoor track, 3-story climbing wall, indoor speed-skating arena, outdoor stadium, rooms for weight training, aerobics, and combatives, and squash, tennis, and racquetball courts. There is also a 200-seat lecture theater, games area, and outdoor recreation center.
Disabled Students: All of the campus is accessible. Wheelchair ramps, elevators, special parking, specially equipped rest rooms, lowered drinking fountains, and lowered telephones are available.
Services: Counseling and information services are available, as is tutoring in most subjects. There is a reader service for the blind and remedial writing.
Campus Safety and Security: Measures include escort service, informal discussions, emergency telephones, and lighted pathways/sidewalks.
Programs of Study: U of C confers B.A., B.Sc., B.Acc.S., B.Comm., B.C.R., B.C.S., B.Ed., B.F.A., B.G.S., B.H.R.M., B.Kin., B.Mus., B.N., B.Sc.Eng., B.S.W., and LL.B. degrees. Master's and doctoral degrees are also awarded. Bachelor's degrees are awarded in BIOLOGICAL SCIENCE (biochemistry, biology/biological science, botany, cell biology, ecology, and zoology), BUSINESS (accounting, business administration and management, hotel/motel and restaurant management, marketing/retailing/merchandising, and tourism), COMMUNICATIONS AND THE ARTS (art history and appreciation, communications, dance, dramatic arts, English, fine arts, French, German, linguistics, music, music history and appreciation, music performance, music theory and composition, Russian, and Spanish), COMPUTER AND PHYSICAL SCIENCE (actuarial science, applied mathematics, astrophysics, chemistry, computer science, earth science, geology, mathematics, physics, and statistics), EDUCATION (early childhood, elementary, and secondary), ENGINEERING AND ENVIRONMENTAL DESIGN (chemical engineering, civil engineering, computer engineering, electrical/electronics engineering, environmental science, manufacturing engineering, mechanical engineering, surveying engineering, and systems engineering), HEALTH PROFESSIONS (nursing), SOCIAL SCIENCE (anthropology, archeology, Asian/Oriental studies, Canadian studies, classical/ancient civilization,

community services, economics, geography, history, Latin American studies, law, liberal arts/general studies, philosophy, physical fitness/movement, political science/government, psychology, religion, social work, sociology, urban studies, and women's studies). Engineering is the strongest academically. Education, management, and engineering are the largest.

Required: To graduate, all students must satisfy the required courses, course sequences, and credit distribution in their particular program. Students must maintain a minimum 2.0 GPA and complete 7 to 10 full-course equivalents in the major field.

Special: The university offers co-op programs in management, science, and many other fields. Dual majors, work-study programs, internships in engineering and computer science, joint degrees in many disciplines, and study abroad in 28 countries are also available. Students may cross-register with any of 8 member colleges in the Big Country Education Consortium. U of C sponsors or is affiliated with 20 research institutes and groups.

Faculty/Classroom: The average class size in an introductory lecture is 60 and in a laboratory, 24.

Requirements: U.S. applicants must be graduates of a secondary school and submit the SAT I and 3 SAT II: Subject test scores, as required by the individual faculties. A minimum score of 400 and an overall average of 560 or above on the 5 tests is required. (Required average varies depending on faculty.) Students may apply on-line at the school's web site: *www.ucalgary.ca*. AP credits are accepted.

Procedure: Freshmen are admitted in the fall. There is an early admissions plan. Check with school for current application deadlines and fee.

Transfer: Applicants must have a cumulative GPA of 2.0 or above on all transfer courses. 2 credits of 4 must be completed at U of C.

Visiting: There are regularly scheduled orientations for prospective students. Pre-session visits range from 1 to 3 days. There are guides for informal visits. To schedule a visit, contact the Prospective Student Office at (403) 220-6920.

International Students: There were 756 international students enrolled in a recent year. The school actively recruits these students. They must score 580 on the written TOEFL and also take IELTS and the University English program.

Computers: The mainframe is an IBM 9672 Model R41. There are a number of PCs, Macs, and UNIX workstation labs across campus. Students enrolled in certain courses may access the system. 800 terminals are available 24 hours per day. There are no time limits and no fees.

Graduates: In a recent year, 3161 bachelor's degrees were awarded. The most popular majors were management (13%), education (12%), and engineering (8%).

Admissions Contact: Director of Admissions and Recruitment.
E-mail: *uofcinfo@ucalgary.ca* Web: *www.ucalgary.ca*

UNIVERSITY OF GUELPH — E-3
Guelph, ON, Canada N1G 2W1 — (519) 824-4120

Full-time: 4973 men, 8086 women	**Faculty:** 643
Part-time: 465 men, 637 women	**Ph.D.s:** 97%
Graduate: 1737 men and women	**Student/Faculty:** 20 to 1
Year: trimesters, summer session	**Tuition:** $4876 CDN ($10,036 CDN)
Application Deadline: April 1	**Room & Board:** $6014 CDN
Freshman Class: n/av	
SAT I or ACT: required	

The University of Guelph, founded in 1964, is a public institution offering programs in arts and sciences, agriculture, engineering, commerce, landscape architecture, veterinary medicine, applied science, and technology. There are 7 undergraduate and 36 graduate schools. The 2 libraries contain 2.5 million volumes, 1.5 million microform items, and 17,000 audiovisual forms/CDs, and subscribe to 7600 periodicals. Computerized library services include interlibrary loans and database searching. Special learning facilities include a learning resource center, art gallery, radio station, observatory, learning commons, research park, and arboretum. The 1200-acre campus is in a suburban area 2 miles south of the center of Guelph. Including residence halls, there are 80 buildings.

Student Life: 93% of undergraduates are from Canada. Others are from 10 states and 57 foreign countries. The average age of freshmen is 19; all undergraduates, 22. 11% do not continue beyond their first year; 85% remain to graduate.

Housing: 5200 students can be accommodated in college housing, which includes single-sex and coed dormitories, on-campus apartments, and married-student housing. In addition, there are language houses, special-interest houses, international house, La Maison Francaise, Eco House, and an arts house. On-campus housing is guaranteed for the freshman year only, is available on a first-come, first-served basis, and is available on a lottery system for upperclassmen. 67% of students commute. All students may keep cars.

Activities: There are no fraternities or sororities. There are 100 groups on campus, including art, cheerleading, chess, choir, chorale, computers, dance, debate, drama, ethnic, gay, international, jazz band, newspaper, photography, political, professional, radio and TV, religious, social, social service, student government, and yearbook. Popular campus events include College Royal Open House in March.

Sports: There are 15 intercollegiate sports for men and 15 for women, and 14 intramural sports for men and 11 for women. Facilities include twin-pad arena, 7 squash courts, fitness gym, weight-training rooms, 6-lane swimming pool and an Olympic-size pool, fitness circuit, and 3 gyms. Outdoor facilities include 4 tennis courts, a running track, lighted football, field hockey, soccer, rugby, and fastball fields, jogging trails, and multipurpose fields. There are also 3 dance studios, a climbing wall and a wrestling/combatives room.

Disabled Students: 78% of the campus is accessible. Wheelchair ramps, elevators, special parking, specially equipped rest rooms, special class scheduling, lowered drinking fountains, and lowered telephones are available.

Services: Counseling and information services are available, as is tutoring in most subjects. There is a reader service for the blind as well as ESL and learning and writing services.

Campus Safety and Security: Measures include 24-hour foot and vehicle patrol, self-defense education, escort service, and pamphlets/posters/films. There are emergency telephones and lighted pathways/sidewalks. There is campus safe walk and a campus police patrol.

Programs of Study: U of G confers B.A., B.A.S., B.A.Sc., B.Comm., B.Comp., B.L.A., B.Sc., B.Sc.Agr., B.Sc.Eng., and B.Sc.Env., B.Sc.(Tech). degrees. Master's and doctoral degrees are also awarded. Bachelor's degrees are awarded in AGRICULTURE (agriculture), BIOLOGICAL SCIENCE (biology/biological science), COMPUTER AND PHYSICAL SCIENCE (computer science and physical sciences), ENGINEERING AND ENVIRONMENTAL DESIGN (engineering, environmental science, and landscape architecture/design), HEALTH PROFESSIONS (veterinary science), SOCIAL SCIENCE (social science). Biological/physical sciences and veterinary medicine are the strongest academically. Biological/physical sciences, arts, and social sciences are the largest.

Required: To graduate, students must complete 30 credits (half courses) for a general degree and 40 credits (half courses) for an honors degree. U of G requires a minimum of 10 credits in the major.

Special: U of G offers co-op programs in 37 majors, study abroad in 24 countries, and work-study programs. Accelerated degree programs, B.A.-B.S. degrees, dual majors, a general studies degree, and nondegree study are available. There is a freshman honors program.

Faculty/Classroom: The average class size in an introductory lecture is 300 and in a laboratory, 25.

Requirements: The SAT I or ACT is required, for U.S. applicants. Standard test scores are not consideed in the admissions decision for Ontario applicants. Applicants must have a minimum overall average of 70% on 6 Ontario Accademic Course (Grade 13) credits. Higher averages may be required for admission to individual programs. U.S. applicants should rank in the upper quarter of their high school class and have a B average for admission consideration. Some programs require an interview, background information, or a portfolio. A GPA of 3.0 is required. AP credits are accepted. Important factors in the admissions decision are advanced placement or honor courses, evidence of special talent, and leadership record.

Procedure: Freshmen are admitted in the fall. There is an early decision plan. Applications should be filed by April 1 for fall entry.

Transfer: Applicants must meet general admissions requirements and have a B average in all college-level courses. 10 credits of 30 must be completed at U of G.

Visiting: There are regularly scheduled orientations for prospective students, including a tour of the campus. There are guides for informal visits and visitors may sit in on classes. To schedule a visit, contact the Admissions Office at (519) 824-4120, ext. 8712.

Financial Aid: In a recent year, 50% of all students received some form of financial aid. 40% of all students received need-based aid. The average freshman award was $1300 CDN. Of that total, scholarships or need-based grants averaged $1300 CDN ($5000 CDN maximum); loans averaged $7000 CDN ($16,500 CDN maximum); and work contracts averaged $775 CDN ($2000 CDN maximum). The FAFSA, the college's own financial statement, and the Federal and Provincial Government Canadian Form are required. The fall application deadline is September 30.

International Students: There are 150 international students enrolled. The school actively recruits these students. They must score 600 on the written TOEFL or 250 on the electronic version if English is not their first language, along with TWE and TSE. The IELTS or MELAB may be substituted for these tests. Students from U.S. are required to submit the SAT I or ACT scores, with a SAT I combined score of 1100 or an ACT score of 25.

Computers: The mainframes are a UNIX, HP, and SUN Servers. There are more than 1000 PCs across the campus for student use. Almost all offer access to the Internet. All students may access the system at any time. There are no time limits and no fees.

Graduates: In 2001, 2429 bachelor's degrees were awarded. The most popular majors were biological science (11%), sociology (6%), and human kinetics (4%). In an average class, 5% graduate in 3 years, 49% in 4 years, 71% in 5 years, and 74% in 6 years.

Admissions Contact: Starr Ellis, Director Admission Services. E-mail: *info@registrar.uoguelph.ca* Web: *www.uoguelph.ca*

UNIVERSITY OF OTTAWA E-3
Ottawa, ON, Canada K1N 6N5 (613) 562-5783
Fax: (613) 562-5104

Full-time: 5990 men, 8060 women
Part-time: 2060 men, 3480 women
Graduate: 1740 men, 1690 women
Year: semesters, summer session
Application Deadline: see profile
Freshman Class: n/av
SAT I: required
Faculty: 992
Ph.D.s: 96%
Student/Faculty: 14 to 1
Tuition: $4000 CDN ($7950 CDN)
Room & Board: $4460 CDN

The University of Ottawa, founded in 1848, is a bilingual (French/English) institution offering undergraduate and graduate degrees through the faculties of Administration, Arts, Law, Health Sciences, Medicine, Science, Engineering, Social Sciences and Education. Figures given in the above capsule are approximate. There are 9 undergraduate and 9 graduate schools. The 8 libraries contain 1,489,959 volumes, 1,298,156 microform items, and 10,800 audiovisual forms/CDs, and subscribe to 10,563 periodicals. Computerized library services include the card catalog, interlibrary loans, and database searching. Special learning facilities include a learning resource center and radio station. The 70-acre campus is in an urban area. Including residence halls, there are 31 buildings.

Student Life: 78% of undergraduates are from Ontario. Others are from 10 states and 4 foreign countries.

Housing: 2132 students can be accommodated in college housing, which includes single-sex and coed dormitories, on-campus apartments, and married-student housing. On-campus housing is available on a lottery system for upperclassmen. 84% of students commute. Alcohol is not permitted. All students may keep cars.

Activities: There are no fraternities or sororities. There are 50 groups on campus, including art, band, chess, choir, chorale, computers, drama, ethnic, gay, international, jazz band, newspaper, orchestra, photography, political, professional, radio and TV, religious, social, social service, student government, and symphony. Popular campus events include Ottawa Day, Panda football game, and International Week.

Sports: There are 8 intercollegiate sports for men and 7 for women, and 6 intramural sports for men and 6 for women. Facilities include weight-training and combat rooms, a 50-meter swimming pool, gyms, racquetball and squash courts, billiards and ping pong tables, an indoor arena, and a sports field.

Disabled Students: 75% of the campus is accessible. Wheelchair ramps, elevators, special parking, specially equipped rest rooms, special class scheduling, lowered drinking fountains, lowered telephones, automatic doors, and specialized equipment are available.

Services: Counseling and information services are available, as is tutoring in most subjects. There is a reader service for the blind, and remedial math, reading, and writing.

Campus Safety and Security: Measures include 24-hour foot and vehicle patrol, self-defense education, escort service, and shuttle buses. There are informal discussions, pamphlets/posters/films, emergency telephones, lighted pathways/sidewalks, and a community crime-stoppers program.

Programs of Study: UO confers B.A., B.Ad., B.A.Sc., B.Com., B.Ed., B.F.A., B.Mus., B.Sc., B.Sc.N., and B.Soc.Sc. degrees. Master's and doctoral degrees are also awarded. Bachelor's degrees are awarded in BIOLOGICAL SCIENCE (biochemistry, biology/biological science, biotechnology, and physiology), BUSINESS (accounting, human resources, management information systems, management science, and marketing/retailing/merchandising), COMMUNICATIONS AND THE ARTS (communications, English, French, German, Italian, Latin, linguistics, music, photography, Spanish, and visual and performing arts), COMPUTER AND PHYSICAL SCIENCE (chemistry, computer science, geology, mathematics, and physics), EDUCATION (education), ENGINEERING AND ENVIRONMENTAL DESIGN (chemical engineering, civil engineering, computer engineering, electrical/electronics engineering, environmental engineering, and mechanical engineering), HEALTH PROFESSIONS (nursing and occupational therapy), SOCIAL SCIENCE (Canadian studies, criminology, economics, geography, history, law, medieval studies, philosophy, political science/government, psychology, public administration, religion, Russian and Slavic studies, sociology, and women's studies). Law, medicine, and education are the strongest academically. Arts, social sciences, and science are the largest.

Required: Students must maintain a GPA of 3.5 out of 10 for all courses, including those in the major. Students must also complete a second langauge requirement: French for English students, and English for French students.

Special: Opportunities are provided for cooperative programs, study abroad in 42 countries, a general studies degree in arts and in sciences, and combined programs in all fields in arts and in social sciences.

Faculty/Classroom: 76% of faculty are male; 24%, female. The average class size in an introductory lecture is 60; in a laboratory, 30; and in a regular course, 30.

Requirements: The SAT I is required with a minimum composite score of 1000 (500 verbal and 500 math). Graduation from an accredited secondary school is required. Those students planning to major in occupational or physical therapy must speak French. A portfolio is required for fine arts students, and an audition for music students. AP credits are accepted.

Procedure: Freshmen are admitted fall and winter. Check with school for current application deadlines and fee. Notification is sent on a rolling basis. A waiting list is an active part of the admissions procedure.

Transfer: Admissions requirements vary according to program. 30 credits must be completed at UO.

Visiting: There are regularly scheduled orientations for prospective students. There are guides for informal visits and visitors may sit in on classes. To schedule a visit, contact the Liaison Office at (613) 562-5800, ext. 1000.

International Students: They must score 550 on the written TOEFL or take the MELAB or the college's own test.

Computers: The mainframe is an Amdahl 5880. Students have access to IBM and Mac PCs in several computer labs on campus. All students may access the system 8 A.M. to 10 P.M., 6 days a week. There are no time limits and no fees.

Admissions Contact: Andre-Pierre Lepage, Director of Admissions/Associate Registrar. E-mail: *liaison@uottawa.ca*

UNIVERSITY OF SASKATCHEWAN C-2
Saskatoon, SK, Canada S7N 5A2 (306) 966-5788
Fax: (306) 966-6730

Full-time: 5780 men, 7610 women
Part-time: 830 men, 1390 women
Graduate: 970 men, 790 women
Year: terms, summer session
Application Deadline: see profile
Freshman Class: n/av
SAT I or ACT: not required
Faculty: n/av
Ph.D.s: 65%
Student/Faculty: n/av
Tuition: $3520 CDN ($6190 CDN)
Room & Board: $3660 CDN

The University of Saskatchewan, founded in 1907, is a public institution offering programs in business, agriculture, arts and sciences, education, engineering, and health professions. Figures given in above capsule are approximate. There are 14 undergraduate schools and 1 graduate school. The 8 libraries contain 1,613,000 volumes, 2,850,000 microform items, and 33,764 audiovisual forms/CDs, and subscribe to 8533 periodicals. Computerized library services include the card catalog, interlibrary loans, and database searching. Special learning facilities include an art gallery, natural history museum, and planetarium. The 363-acre campus is in an urban area in Saskatoon. Including residence halls, there are 55 buildings.

Student Life: The average age of all undergraduates is 21. 7% do not continue beyond their first year.

Housing: University-sponsored living facilities include dormitories, off-campus apartments, and married-student housing. On-campus housing is available on a first-come, first-served basis. All students may keep cars.

Activities: There are no fraternities or sororities. There are many groups and organizations on campus, including band, cheerleading, chess, choir, chorale, chorus, computers, drama, ethnic, gay, international, newspaper, orchestra, political, professional, religious, social, social service, and student government.

Sports: There are 8 intercollegiate sports for men and 5 for women, and 14 intramural sports for men and 15 for women. Facilities include a football stadium, a hockey rink, a curling rink, 3 gyms, 2 swimming pools, racquetball and squash courts, a track and field area, an outdoor soccer field, a fitness center, and weight rooms.

Disabled Students: 99% of the campus is accessible. Wheelchair ramps, elevators, special parking, specially equipped rest rooms, special class scheduling, lowered drinking fountains, lowered telephones, a coordinator of services for students with disabilities, special funding application assistance, special exam scheduling and accommodations, and adaptive computerized equipment located in the main library building are available.

Services: Counseling and information services are available, as is tutoring in most subjects.

Campus Safety and Security: Measures include 24-hour foot and vehicle patrol, self-defense education, and escort service.

Programs of Study: U of S confers B.A., B.Sc., B.Comm., B.E., B.Ed., B.F.A., B.Mus., B.Mus.Mus.Ed., B.S.A., B.Sc.(Nutr.), B.Sc.(P.T.), B.S.N., B.S.P., B.S.P.E., and L.L.B. degrees. Master's and doctoral degrees are also awarded. Bachelor's degrees are awarded in AGRICUL-

TURE (agricultural economics, agricultural mechanics, agronomy, animal science, horticulture, plant science, range/farm management, and soil science), BIOLOGICAL SCIENCE (anatomy, biochemistry, biology/biological science, microbiology, nutrition, and physiology), BUSINESS (accounting, business administration and management, business economics, human resources, and marketing/retailing/merchandising), COMMUNICATIONS AND THE ARTS (art, classics, English, French, German, Greek, Hebrew, Latin, linguistics, music, Russian, and Spanish), COMPUTER AND PHYSICAL SCIENCE (chemistry, computer science, geology, geophysics and seismology, mathematics, paleontology, and physics), EDUCATION (elementary, home economics, and physical), ENGINEERING AND ENVIRONMENTAL DESIGN (chemical engineering, civil engineering, electrical/electronics engineering, engineering physics, geological engineering, land use management and reclamation, and mechanical engineering), HEALTH PROFESSIONS (medical science, nursing, pharmacy, physical therapy, and veterinary science), SOCIAL SCIENCE (economics, food science, geography, history, international studies, law, Native American studies, Near Eastern studies, philosophy, political science/government, psychology, public administration, Russian and Slavic studies, sociology, and urban studies).

Required: Requirements for graduation vary according to the program of study.

Special: The University of Saskatchewan offers interdisciplinary majors, including agricultural biology, agricultural chemistry, agricultural and bioresource engineering, agricultural extension, and anthropology and archaeology. Co-op programs are offered through the Program for Agricultural Cooperative Education. There are computer science internships, as well as internships offered through the Engineering Professional Internship program. The university has exchange agreements with 6 countries.

Faculty/Classroom: 80% of faculty are male; 20%, female.

Requirements: Applicants must be graduates of an accredited secondary school. In direct-entry programs, priority is given to Saskatchewan residents, with the exception being the College of Arts and Sciences. Applications are accepted on-line at the school's web site. A high school average of 65 is required. AP credits are accepted.

Procedure: Freshmen are admitted in the fall. There are early decision and early admissions plans. Check with the school for current application deadlines and fee.

Transfer: Applicants must meet promotion levels for the college to which transfer is sought; in most cases they should be Saskatchewan residents.

Visiting: There are regularly scheduled orientations for prospective students. To schedule a visit, contact the Student's Union at (306) 966-6963.

Financial Aid: Check with school for current deadlines.

International Students: The school actively recruits these students. They must score 550 on the written TOEFL or take the MELAB, IELTS, and CanTEST.

Computers: Computer science students may access the system. There are no time limits. The fee varies.

Admissions Contact: Kelly McInnes, Admissions Counsellor.
E-mail: *admissions@usask.ca* Web: *http://www.usask.ca/registrar*

UNIVERSITY OF TORONTO
Toronto, ON, Canada M5S 1A1

E-3
(416) 978-2190
Fax: (416) 978-6089

Full-time: 13,304 men, 17,369 women	**Faculty:** n/av
Part-time: 4356 men, 6262 women	**Ph.D.s:** n/av
Graduate: 8201 men, 5574 women	**Student/Faculty:** n/av
Year: terms, summer session	**Tuition:** $4729 CDN ($9533 CDN)
Application Deadline: March 1	**Room & Board:** $7000
Freshman Class: 42,658 applied, 26,353 accepted, 8686 enrolled	
SAT I: required	**ACT:** n/av

The University of Toronto, founded in 1827, is a public institution offering undergraduate programs in applied science and engineering, arts and science, education, dentistry, law, medicine, music, nursing, pharmacy, physical and health education, and radiation sciences. Degrees are also offered at the graduate level in a wide range or programs. There are 9 undergraduate and 9 graduate schools. The 32 libraries contain 9,175,841 volumes, 4,798,606 microform items, and 1,202,358 audiovisual forms/CDs, and subscribe to 53,050 periodicals. Computerized library services include the card catalog, interlibrary loans, and database searching. Special learning facilities include a learning resource center, art gallery, radio station, and observatory. The 688-acre campus is in an urban area with 3 campuses in downtown and suburban Toronto. Including residence halls, there are 258 buildings.

Student Life: 94% of undergraduates are from Ontario.

Housing: Housing includes single-sex and coed dormitories, on-campus apartments, off-campus apartments, and married-student housing. On-campus housing is available on a first-come, first-served basis. Priority is given to out-of-town students. 80% of students commute. Alcohol is not permitted.

Activities: There are no fraternities or sororities. There are 200 groups on campus, including art, band, chess, choir, chorus, computers, dance, drama, ethnic, film, gay, international, jazz band, literary magazine, musical theater, newspaper, opera, orchestra, photography, political, radio and TV, religious, social, student government, symphony, and yearbook. Popular campus events include U of T Day, concerts, and theater productions, films, lectures, and seasonal activities.

Sports: There are 23 intercollegiate sports for men and 23 for women, and 23 intramural sports for men and 23 for women. Facilities include swimming pools, outdoor hockey rink, weight and exercise rooms, gyms, squash and multipurpose courts, rifle range, dance studios, playing fields, stadium, arena, and a 200-meter indoor running track.

Disabled Students: Wheelchair ramps, elevators, special parking, specially equipped rest rooms, lowered drinking fountains, and lowered telephones are available.

Services: Counseling and information services are available, as is tutoring in every subject. There is a reader service for the blind.

Campus Safety and Security: Measures include 24-hour foot and vehicle patrol, self-defense education, escort service, and shuttle buses. There are emergency telephones and lighted pathways/sidewalks.

Programs of Study: U of T confers B.A., B.Sc., B.Arch., B.A.Sc., B.Com., B.B.A., B.Ed., B.Sc.N., B.Sc.Phm., B.S.P.H.E., and Mus.Bac. degrees. Master's and doctoral degrees are also awarded. Bachelor's degrees are awarded in BIOLOGICAL SCIENCE (biochemistry, biology/biological science, botany, microbiology, and zoology), BUSINESS (banking and finance), COMMUNICATIONS AND THE ARTS (classics, dramatic arts, English, fine arts, French, German, Italian, linguistics, literature, music, Portuguese, Slavic languages, and Spanish), COMPUTER AND PHYSICAL SCIENCE (applied mathematics, astronomy, chemistry, computer science, geology, mathematics, and physics), EDUCATION (health, and physical), ENGINEERING AND ENVIRONMENTAL DESIGN (architecture, chemical engineering, civil engineering, electrical/electronics engineering, engineering and applied science, geological engineering, industrial engineering, materials science, mechanical engineering, and metallurgical engineering), HEALTH PROFESSIONS (nursing, occupational therapy, pharmacy, and physical therapy), SOCIAL SCIENCE (American studies, Canadian studies, Celtic studies, criminology, economics, geography, political science/government, sociology, urban studies, and women's studies).

Required: Arts and science majors must satisfy a breadth requirement, which includes 3 courses from outside the major. Students must complete 15 credits for a 3-year degree or 20 credits for a 4-year degree, plus prerequisite subjects.

Special: The university offers co-op programs in management, arts management, computer science, physical science, social science, and international development studies. Study abroad, interdisciplinary programs, and various work-study programs are also available.

Admissions: 62% of the 2001-2002 applicants were accepted.

Requirements: The SAT I is required. The Faculty of Arts and Sciences will consider Grade 12 applicants from an accredited U.S. high school with a high GPA and good scores on the SAT I reasoning tests and 3 SAT II: Subject tests. ACT and/or CEEB Advanced Placement Tests will also be considered. Engineering normally requires first-year university standing, but will consider excellent high school students with appropriate advanced placement tests. Other requirements may apply. Architecture students must submit a questionnaire and a portfolio. Music students must audition. A GPA of 3.0 is required. AP credits are accepted.

Procedure: Freshmen are admitted in the fall. There are early decision, early admissions, and deferred admissions plans. Early decision application should be filed by February 1; regular applications, by March 1 for fall entry. Notification of early decision is sent April 30; regular decision, on a rolling basis.

Transfer: For the Arts and Science Divisions, normally a B average is required. 5 credits of 15 must be completed at U of T.

Visiting: There are regularly scheduled orientations for prospective students. Visitors may sit in on classes. To schedule a visit, contact Student Recruitment at (416) 978-5000.

Financial Aid: In a recent year, 50% of all freshmen received some form of financial aid.

International Students: They must score 600 on the written TOEFL or take the MELAB, the Comprehensive English Language Test, or the college's own test.

Computers: U of T provides PCs and Macs for academic use. All students may access the system. There are no time limits and no fees.

Graduates: In 2001, 7905 bachelor's degrees were awarded.

Admissions Contact: Admissions Counselor. A video is available.
E-mail: *ask@adm.utoronto.ca* Web: *www.utoronto.ca*

UNIVERSITY OF VICTORIA

Victoria, BC, Canada V8W 3P2 B-2

(250) 721-8121
Fax: (250) 721-6225

Full-time: 9060 men and women
Part-time: 5695 men and women
Graduate: 1635 men and women
Year: terms, summer session
Application Deadline: see profile
Faculty: 640
Ph.D.s: 93%
Student/Faculty: 14 to 1
Tuition: $2555 CDN ($7085 CDN)
Room & Board: $4455 CDN
Freshman Class: n/av
SAT I or ACT: not required

The University of Victoria, founded in 1903 as Victoria College, is a public institution operated by the province of British Columbia. It offers undergraduate and graduate programs in the arts and sciences, business, education, engineering, fine arts, human and social development, and law. There are 8 undergraduate schools and 1 graduate school. Figures in above capsule are approximate. The 4 libraries contain 1.6 million volumes, 1.7 million microform items, and 177,000 audiovisual forms/CDs, and subscribe to 8000 periodicals. Computerized library services include the card catalog, interlibrary loans, and database searching. Special learning facilities include a learning resource center, art gallery, radio station, and language labs. The 385-acre campus is in an urban area in Victoria. Including residence halls, there are 107 buildings.

Student Life: 86% of undergraduates are from British Columbia.

Housing: 1700 students can be accommodated in college housing, which includes single-sex and coed dormitories, on-campus apartments, and married-student housing. On-campus housing is available on a first-come, first-served basis and is available on a lottery system for upperclassmen. Priority is given to out-of-town students. Alcohol is not permitted. All students may keep cars.

Activities: There are no fraternities or sororities. There are many groups and organizations on campus, including chess, choir, chorus, computers, dance, debate, ethnic, gay, international, jazz band, musical theater, newspaper, orchestra, photography, political, radio and TV, religious, social service, student government, symphony, and yearbook. Popular campus events include Week of Welcome and the President's BBQ.

Sports: There are 7 intercollegiate sports for men and 7 for women, and 12 intramural sports for men and 12 for women. Facilities include 3 gyms, dance studio, 2 weight and fitness training rooms, racquetball and squash courts, playing fields, outdoor stadium, tennis courts, 2 swimming pools, sailing compound, and jogging trails.

Disabled Students: Wheelchair ramps, elevators, special parking, specially equipped rest rooms, lowered drinking fountains, lowered telephones, speech synthesizers, and Arkenstone reading computers are available.

Services: There is remedial reading and writing.

Campus Safety and Security: Measures include 24-hour foot and vehicle patrol, self-defense education, escort service, and pamphlets/posters/films. There are emergency telephones and lighted pathways/sidewalks.

Programs of Study: UVic confers B.A., B.S., B.Com., B.Ed., B.Eng., B.F.A., B.Mus., B.Sc., B.S.N., B.S.W., and L.L.B. degrees. Master's and doctoral degrees are also awarded. Bachelor's degrees are awarded in BIOLOGICAL SCIENCE (biochemistry, biology/biological science, and microbiology), BUSINESS (business administration and management and recreation and leisure services), COMMUNICATIONS AND THE ARTS (art history and appreciation, classics, creative writing, dramatic arts, English, French, Germanic languages and literature, linguistics, music, and visual and performing arts), COMPUTER AND PHYSICAL SCIENCE (astronomy, chemistry, computer science, earth science, mathematics, and physics), EDUCATION (elementary, physical, and secondary), ENGINEERING AND ENVIRONMENTAL DESIGN (computer engineering, electrical/electronics engineering, and mechanical engineering), HEALTH PROFESSIONS (health science and nursing), SOCIAL SCIENCE (anthropology, child care/child and family studies, economics, geography, history, Italian studies, medieval studies, Pacific area studies, philosophy, political science/government, psychology, Russian and Slavic studies, social work, sociology, and women's studies).

Required: To graduate, students must complete the university English requirement, a minimum of 60 units above the 100 level, at least 21 of which must be upper level, and have a 2.0 GPA.

Special: A number of co-op and internship programs are available in specific disciplines as are many dual majors, including biochemistry/microbiology and Hispanic/Italian studies. Work-study is possible on a limited basis for Canadian students only.

Faculty/Classroom: 68% of faculty are male; 32%, female. All both teach undergraduates and do research. No introductory courses are taught by graduate students. The average class size in an introductory lecture is 53 and in a regular course, 30.

Requirements: Application requires high school graduation with a 2.5 GPA or higher, 4 semesters of English, 2 each of social science, math, science, and language, and 6 semesters of 2.5 work at grade 12 level. Applications are accepted on-line at the school's web site. AP credits are accepted.

Procedure: Freshmen are admitted to all sessions. Check with school for current application deadlines and fee.

Transfer: 1294 transfer students enrolled in a recent year. Requirements vary with the program and the individual. 30 credits of 60 must be completed at UVic.

Visiting: There are guides for informal visits and visitors may sit in on classes and stay overnight. To schedule a visit, contact Public Relations at (250) 721-7645.

International Students: The school actively recruits these students. They must score 575 on the written TOEFL or take the MELAB, or IELTS.

Computers: The mainframes are an IBM 3090-150S, a Sun 3/280S, and a Pyramid 98Xe. Access to the mainframes are by Wideband and Ethernet networks to PCs and terminals throughout campus. There are computer labs. The Sun and Pyramid systems utilize UNIX operating systems. Equipment includes PCs, Macs, and DEC VAX systems. All students may access the system at any time. There are no time limits and no fees.

Graduates: In a recent year, 2616 bachelor's degrees were awarded.

Admissions Contact: Admissions Officer. A video is available.
E-mail: *srsad13@uvvm.uvic.ca* Web: *http://web.uvic.ca/adms*

UNIVERSITY OF WATERLOO

Waterloo, ON, Canada N2L 3G1 E-3

(519) 888-4567, ext. 3777
Fax: (519) 746-8088

Full-time: 14,564 men and women
Part-time: 3272 men and women
Graduate: 2230 men and women
Year: trimesters, summer session
Application Deadline: March 29
Faculty: 746
Ph.D.s: 96%
Student/Faculty: 20 to 1
Tuition: $4545-6813 CDN ($13,181-22,377 CDN)
Room & Board: $5950 CDN
Freshman Class: 23,557 applied, 14,437 accepted, 4780 enrolled
SAT I or ACT: recommended

The University of Waterloo, founded in 1957, is a public institution that offers undergraduate and graduate programs in applied health sciences, arts, engineering, environmental studies, independent studies, math, and science. Students have a home base in 1 of 6 faculties or 4 affiliated institutions. Most students may choose either the traditional or cooperative system of study. There are 6 undergraduate and 6 graduate schools. The 4 libraries contain 3,793,234 volumes and 1,485,000 microform items, and subscribe to 13,228 periodicals. Computerized library services include the card catalog, interlibrary loans, and database searching. Special learning facilities include a learning resource center, art gallery, radio station, 4 museums, 2 theaters, and an observatory. The 900-acre campus is in a suburban area 60 miles southwest of Toronto. Including residence halls, there are 49 buildings.

Student Life: 98% of undergraduates are from Ontario. Others are from 13 states and 85 foreign countries. 2% do not continue beyond their first year; 78% remain to graduate.

Housing: 5037 students can be accommodated in college housing, which includes single-sex and coed dormitories and on-campus apartments. In addition, there are special-interest houses, language floors, and an off-campus housing service. Priority for on-campus housing is given to out-of-town students. 71% of students commute. All students may keep cars.

Activities: 1% of men belong to 1 national fraternity; 1% of women belong to 1 national sorority. There are 80 groups on campus, including band, bridge, cheerleading, chess, choir, computers, dance, debate, drama, drill team, ethnic, film, gay, honors, international, juggling, literary magazine, marching band, martial arts, musical theater, newspaper, photography, political, professional, radio and TV, religious, social, social dance, social service, student government, and yearbook. Popular campus events include Oktoberfest, and Canada Day.

Sports: There are 17 intercollegiate sports for men and 16 for women, and 40 intramural sports for men and 40 for women. Facilities include a golf course, outdoor playing fields, an ice arena, a swimming pool, a diving tank, squash courts, weight rooms, 2 gyms, a dance studio, tennis courts, and activity areas.

Disabled Students: All of the campus is accessible. Wheelchair ramps, elevators, special parking, specially equipped rest rooms, special class scheduling, lowered drinking fountains, lowered telephones, and up-to-date technical equipment for the visually disabled and the hearing impaired are available.

Services: Counseling and information services are available, as is tutoring in most subjects. There is a reader service for the blind, and remedial math, reading, and writing.

Campus Safety and Security: Measures include 24-hour foot and vehicle patrol, self-defense education, escort service, and shuttle buses. There are informal discussions, pamphlets/posters/films, emergency telephones, and lighted pathways/sidewalks.

Programs of Study: UW confers B.A., B.Sc., B.A.Sc., B.E.S., B.I.S., B.Math, B.S.W., and B.S.E. degrees. Master's and doctoral degrees are also awarded. Bachelor's degrees are awarded in AGRICULTURE (environmental studies), BIOLOGICAL SCIENCE (biochemistry, biology/biological science, biotechnology, and genetics), BUSINESS (accounting, business administration and management, human resources, management science, operations research, and recreation and leisure services), COMMUNICATIONS AND THE ARTS (arts administration/management, classics, dramatic arts, English, fine arts, French, German, music, Russian, Spanish, and speech/debate/rhetoric), COMPUTER AND PHYSICAL SCIENCE (actuarial science, applied mathematics, chemistry, computer science, earth science, geochemistry, geology, geophysics and seismology, information sciences and systems, mathematics, physical chemistry, physics, science, science and management, and statistics), ENGINEERING AND ENVIRONMENTAL DESIGN (architecture, chemical engineering, city/community/regional planning, civil engineering, computer engineering, electrical/electronics engineering, environmental engineering, environmental science, geological engineering, mechanical engineering, and systems engineering), HEALTH PROFESSIONS (health, optometry, and preoptometry), SOCIAL SCIENCE (anthropology, Canadian studies, economics, geography, history, international studies, medieval studies, philosophy, physical fitness/movement, political science/government, psychology, religion, Russian and Slavic studies, social work, sociology, and women's studies). Engineering, accounting, and mathematics are the strongest academically. The arts program is the largest.

Required: To graduate, all students must satisfy specific program requirements.

Special: Cross-registration with Wilfred Laurier University, study abroad in 21 countries, dual and student-designed independent studies, interdisciplinary majors a combined bachelor's-master's degree in accounting and engineering, and noncredit courses are available. Students may study under the regular or cooperative system, which allows off-campus work terms in education, professional organizations and agencies, business, industry, or government for students with permanent resident status. There are concurrent education programs in conjunction with the faculties of education at Brock University and Queen's University.

Faculty/Classroom: 80% of faculty are male; 20%, female. All both teach and do research. The average class size in an introductory lecture is 89 and in a regular course, 28.

Admissions: 61% of the 2001-2002 applicants were accepted.

Requirements: The SAT I or ACT is recommended. In addition, candidates from the United States must have a high school diploma with exceptionally high standing and AP exams in prerequisite subjects or first-year university standing in acceptable subjects from an accredited university. An audition, portfolio, and/or interview may be required for certain programs. International applicants can apply on-line at *http://compass.ovac.on.ca*. A GPA of 3.0 is required. Important factors in the admissions decision are advanced placement or honor courses, extracurricular activities record, and leadership record.

Procedure: Freshmen are admitted fall, winter, and spring. Entrance exams should be taken in time to meet deadlines for completion of files. Applications should be filed by March 29 for fall entry and February 28 for spring entry, along with a $95 CDN fee for international applicants or $85 CDN for Canadian applicants. Notification is sent on a rolling basis.

Transfer: Applicants are considered on an individual basis. 10 credits of 20 must be completed at UW.

Visiting: There are regularly scheduled orientations for prospective students, including tours and individual and group information sessions. There are guides for informal visits and visitors may sit in on classes. To schedule a visit, contact the Visitors Reception Center at (519) 888-4567, ext. 3614 or *www.askthewarrior.ca*

Financial Aid: The FAFSA is required. The fall application deadline is June 15.

International Students: There were 236 international students enrolled in a recent year. The school actively recruits these students. They must score 600 on the written TOEFL or take the MELAB, the TSE, the TWE, or the IELTS.

Computers: The mainframe is an IBM for administration; there are PCs with Windows 95 for students. There are more than 600 multiuser computing systems and 6000 single-user computing systems campuswide. Students will receive accounts from their faculties. Rules vary from department to department. All users have Internet and Web access. All students may access the system. There are no time limits and no fees.

Graduates: In 2001, 3376 bachelor's degrees were awarded. The most popular majors were arts (30%), engineering (19%), and math (16%). In an average class, 35% graduate in 3 years, and 65% in 4 years. 215 companies recruited on campus in 2000-2001.

Admissions Contact: Undergraduate Recruitment and Publications. E-mail: *www.askthewarrior.ca* Web: *www.w@waterloo.ca*

UNIVERSITY OF WESTERN ONTARIO

London, ON, Canada N6A 5B8 — D-3

(519) 661-2100
Fax: (519) 661-3710

Full-time: 8477 men, 11,287 women
Part-time: 1102 men, 1742 women
Graduate: 1900 men, 1517 women
Year: semesters, summer session
Application Deadline: May 15
Freshman Class: 29,104 applied, 18,357 accepted, 4300 enrolled
SAT I: required
Faculty: 1204
Ph.D.s: 90%
Student/Faculty: 16 to 1
Tuition: $11,186 CDN
Room & Board: $5260 CDN

The University of Western Ontario, chartered in 1878, is a coeducational, public institution offering daytime, evening, and correspondence programs in the liberal arts and sciences, fine arts and music, engineering, education, health services, and business. There are 12 undergraduate and 4 graduate schools. The 7 libraries contain 2,511,107 volumes, 3,697,538 microform items, and 1,293,239 audiovisual forms/CDs, and subscribe to 12,577 periodicals. Computerized library services include the card catalog, interlibrary loans, and database searching. Special learning facilities include a learning resource center, art gallery, radio station, TV station, wind tunnel, and observatory. The 402-acre campus is in an urban area 120 miles northwest of Detroit, Michigan. Including residence halls, there are 72 buildings.

Student Life: The average age of freshmen is 20; all undergraduates, 22.

Housing: 3722 students can be accommodated in college housing, which includes single-sex and coed dormitories, on-campus apartments, and married-student housing. In addition, there are language houses, special-interest houses, an international house, and quiet floors. On-campus housing is available on a lottery system for upperclassmen. Priority is given to out-of-town students. 60% of students commute. All students may keep cars.

Activities: 9% of men belong to 19 national fraternities; 3% of women belong to 6 national sororities. There are 124 groups on campus, including art, cheerleading, chess, choir, computers, drama, ethnic, gay, international, jazz band, marching band, musical theater, political, professional, radio and TV, religious, social, social service, student government, and yearbook. Popular campus events include Orientation Week.

Sports: There are 18 intercollegiate sports for men and 18 for women, and 17 intramural sports for men and 13 for women. Facilities include skating rinks, weight rooms, pools, gyms, and numerous outdoor facilities.

Disabled Students: 88% of the campus is accessible. Wheelchair ramps, elevators, special parking, specially equipped rest rooms, special class scheduling, lowered drinking fountains, and lowered telephones are available.

Services: Counseling and information services are available, as is tutoring in most subjects. There is a reader service for the blind, and remedial math, reading, and writing.

Campus Safety and Security: Measures include escort service, emergency telephones, and lighted pathways/sidewalks.

Programs of Study: Bachelor's degrees are awarded in AGRICULTURE (plant science), BIOLOGICAL SCIENCE (biochemistry, biology/biological science, biophysics, cell biology, ecology, genetics, microbiology, physiology, toxicology, and zoology), BUSINESS (business administration and management and management science), COMMUNICATIONS AND THE ARTS (classics, comparative literature, English, film arts, French, German, Greek, Latin, music, music history and appreciation, music performance, music theory and composition, Russian, Spanish, and visual and performing arts), COMPUTER AND PHYSICAL SCIENCE (actuarial science, applied mathematics, astronomy, chemistry, computer science, geology, geophysics and seismology, mathematics, physics, and statistics), EDUCATION (elementary, middle school, music, and secondary), ENGINEERING AND ENVIRONMENTAL DESIGN (chemical engineering, civil engineering, electrical/electronics engineering, environmental science, geophysical engineering, materials engineering, and mechanical engineering), HEALTH PROFESSIONS (nursing, occupational therapy, and physical therapy), SOCIAL SCIENCE (anthropology, classical/ancient civilization, economics, geography, history, law, philosophy, physical fitness/movement, political science/government, psychology, public administration, sociology, Western civilization/culture, and women's studies).

Required: All students are required to take 2 essay courses and courses in the arts, science, and social science; other distribution and course requirements vary by major. A 60% overall average and 15 courses are the mininum requirements for a 3-year bachelor's degree. Many have additional requirements.

Special: Internship in engineering, computer science, physics, statistics, and acturial science, study abroad in 40 countries, dual majors, and student-designed majors are available. There are many 3-year bachelor's degree programs. Pass/fail options are possible.

Faculty/Classroom: 79% of faculty are male; 21%, female.

Admissions: 63% of the 2001-2002 applicants were accepted.

Requirements: The SAT I is required. In addition, U.S. applicants must be graduates of an accredited secondary school with 4 academic course credits in their senior year, and in the top 15% of their class in order to be eligible to apply for admission their first year. A nonrecentered SAT I composite score of 1000 is required. First-year admissions are limited. Admission to the music program requires an audition. A GPA of 3.0 is required. AP credits are accepted. Important factors in the admissions decision are advanced placement or honor courses, recommendations by school officials, and leadership record.

Procedure: Freshmen are admitted in the fall. There are early decision and deferred admissions plans. Early decision and regular applications should be filed by May 15 for fall entry, along with a $95 fee. Notification of early decision is sent mid-April; regular decision, May to July.

Transfer: A minimum overall average of 70% is required to transfer. 5 credits of 15 must be completed at UWO.

Visiting: There are regularly scheduled orientations for prospective students, including academic counseling appointments and campus tours. Visitors may sit in on classes. To schedule a visit, contact Liaison Services, Office of the Registrar at (519) 661-2026.

Financial Aid: UWO is a member of CSS.

International Students: There are 1157 international students enrolled. The school actively recruits these students. They must score 580 on the written TOEFL or take the MELAB or the International English Language Testing Service (IELTS).

Computers: The mainframes are a DEC VAX 6230, a CDC Cyber 930, and an ETA-10. There are hundreds of access terminals located in campus buildings. All students may access the system. There are no time limits and no fees.

Graduates: In 2001, 5183 bachelor's degrees were awarded.

Admissions Contact: Lori Gribbon, Manager, Application Services. E-mail: *reg-admissions@uwo.ca* Web: *http://www.uwo.ca*

UNIVERSITY OF WINDSOR — E-2

Windsor, ON, Canada N9B 3P4 — **(519) 973-7014, ext. 3315**
864-2860 (in Canada); Fax: (519) 971-3653

Full-time: 4390 men, 5200 women	**Faculty:** 500
Part-time: 1280 men, 1930 women	**Ph.D.s:** 90%
Graduate: 510 men, 410 women	**Student/Faculty:** 19 to 1
Year: trimesters, summer session	**Tuition:** $3700 CDN ($11,000 CDN)
Application Deadline: see profile	**Room & Board:** $6000 CDN
Freshman Class: n/av	
SAT I or ACT: required	

The University of Windsor, founded in 1857, is a public liberal arts institution offering undergraduate and graduate programs through 8 faculties and 6 schools. Figures given in the above capsule are approximate. There is 1 graduate school. The 2 libraries contain 1.6 million volumes, 160,000 microform items, and 2000 audiovisual forms/CDs, and subscribe to 15,000 periodicals. Computerized library services include the card catalog, interlibrary loans, and database searching. Special learning facilities include a learning resource center, art gallery, natural history museum, radio station, TV station, a video-conferencing center, a computing services theater, the Chrysler Canada/University of Windsor Research Center, and the Great Lakes Institute. The 200-acre campus is in an urban area 2 kilometers from downtown Windsor, and 3 kilometers from downtown Detroit, Michiga. Including residence halls, there are 50 buildings.

Student Life: Others are from 10 states, 41 foreign countries, and Canada. 95% are from public schools. The average age of freshmen is 19; all undergraduates, 22. 10% do not continue beyond their first year.

Housing: 1800 students can be accommodated in college housing, which includes coed dormitories, on-campus apartments, and married-student housing. On-campus housing is guaranteed for the freshman year only and is available on a lottery system for upperclassmen. 80% of students commute. All students may keep cars.

Activities: 2% of men belong to 4 national fraternities; 1% of women belong to 1 national sorority. There are 75 groups on campus, including cheerleading, chess, choir, chorale, drama, ethnic, gay, honors, international, jazz band, literary magazine, musical theater, newspaper, orchestra, political, professional, radio and TV, religious, social, and student government. Popular campus events include Campus Week in September.

Sports: There are 7 intercollegiate sports for men and 5 for women, and 11 intramural sports for men and 9 for women. Facilities include a 6-lane 200-meter track, a multiuse gym, a field house, a stadium, an indoor pool, weight rooms, and a sports therapy clinic.

Disabled Students: 90% of the campus is accessible. Wheelchair ramps, elevators, special parking, specially equipped rest rooms, special class scheduling, lowered drinking fountains, lowered telephones, and specially equipped residence rooms are available.

Services: Counseling and information services are available, as is tutoring in some subjects, including math and physical sciences. There is a reader service for the blind, remedial math, reading, and writing, exam accommodations, special needs counselors, and recreation buddies for assistance at the athletic complex.

Campus Safety and Security: Measures include 24-hour foot and vehicle patrol, self-defense education, escort service, and informal discussions. There are pamphlets/posters/films, emergency telephones, and lighted pathways/sidewalks.

Programs of Study: U of W confers B.A., B.Sc., B.A.Sc., B.Comm., B.C.S., B.Ed., B.F.A., B.H.K., B.Mus., B.Mus.Th., B.P.A., B.Sc.N., B.S.W., and L.L.B. degrees. Master's and doctoral degrees are also awarded. Bachelor's degrees are awarded in BIOLOGICAL SCIENCE (biochemistry and biology/biological science), BUSINESS (business administration and management), COMMUNICATIONS AND THE ARTS (art history and appreciation, classics, communications, comparative literature, creative writing, dramatic arts, English, French, languages, modern language, music, musical theater, and visual and performing arts), COMPUTER AND PHYSICAL SCIENCE (chemistry, computer science, geology, mathematics, physics, science, and statistics), EDUCATION (drama, education, and science), ENGINEERING AND ENVIRONMENTAL DESIGN (civil engineering, electrical/electronics engineering, engineering, environmental engineering, industrial engineering, land use management and reclamation, and mechanical engineering), HEALTH PROFESSIONS (music therapy, and nursing), SOCIAL SCIENCE (anthropology, Asian/Oriental studies, Canadian studies, criminology, crosscultural studies, economics, family/consumer studies, geography, history, international relations, law, philosophy, physical fitness/movement, political science/government, psychology, public administration, religion, social work, sociology, urban studies, and women's studies). Social science, engineering, and education are the largest.

Required: To graduate, students must complete a total of 90 credit hours, including 30 in the major, with a C average. Honors students must complete 120 hours, including 60 in the major, with a B average. All students must fulfill the requirements of the core curriculum.

Special: The college offers a variety of co-op programs and internships. Cross-registration may be arranged with the University of Detroit Mercy, Wayne State University, the University of Central Florida, and the University of Darby (England). Students may study abroad in the United States, France, Japan, and England.

Faculty/Classroom: 78% of faculty are male; 22%, female. All both teach and do research. The average class size in an introductory lecture is 100; in a laboratory, 25; and in a regular course, 50.

Requirements: The SAT I or ACT is required for U.S. students. AP credits are accepted.

Procedure: Freshmen are admitted to all sessions. Entrance exams should be taken as early as possible. There are early decision and early admissions plans. Check with school for current application deadlines and fee. Notification is sent on a rolling basis. 10% of all applicants are on a waiting list.

Transfer: Applicants must present an official transcript and be in good academic standing.

Visiting: There are regularly scheduled orientations for prospective students, including a tour, counseling, and classes. There are guides for informal visits and visitors may sit in on classes. To schedule a visit, contact Liaison Office.

International Students: They must score 550 on the written TOEFL or take the MELAB.

Computers: The mainframes are an IBM 4381 and an SGI. Students have access to a parallel-processing file server linked to graphics X-terminals through a campuswide fiber-optic network. There is also a CAD-CAM teaching lab with 30 networked terminals, 60 PCs in a DEC network, and numerous other academic local networks. One residence hall provides computer connections. All students may access the system. There are no time limits. The fee is minimal.

Admissions Contact: Assistant Registrar, Liaison and Applicant Services. E-mail: *liaison@uwindsor.ca*

YORK UNIVERSITY — E-3

Toronto (North York), ON, Canada M3J 1P3
(416) 736-5825
Fax: (416) 650-8195

Full-time: 10,238 men, 16,711 women	**Faculty:** 1149
Part-time: 2712 men, 4587 women	**Ph.D.s:** 98%
Graduate: 2041 men, 2238 women	**Student/Faculty:** 23 to 1
Year: terms, summer session	**Tuition:** $4753 CDN ($12,015 CDN)
Application Deadline: February 1	**Room & Board:** $3207 CDN
Freshman Class: n/av	
SAT I or ACT: required	

York University, founded in 1959, is a public institution offering programs in computer science, design, education, environmental studies, fine arts, business, social science, law, engineering, health, humanities, human resources, pure and applied sciences, and social work. There are 10 undergraduate and 37 graduate programs. The 8 libraries contain

2,360,000 volumes, 3,265,009 microform items, and 52,925 audiovisual forms/CDs, and subscribe to 14,734 periodicals. Computerized library services include the card catalog, interlibrary loans, and database searching. Special learning facilities include a learning resource center, art gallery, radio station, TV station, observatory, language labs, writing center, geographical information systems lab, computer science labs, science-related labs, and fine arts studios and labs (editing studios). The university has 2 campuses, totaling 735 acres, in northwest and downtown Toronto. Including residence halls, there are 53 buildings.

Student Life: Undergraduates are from 150 foreign countries and Canada. The average age of freshmen is 19; all undergraduates, 22. 79% of freshmen remain to graduate.

Housing: 2188 students can be accommodated in college housing, which includes single-sex and coed dormitories, on-campus apartments, and married-student housing. In addition, there are language houses and special-interest houses. On-campus housing is available on a first-come, first-served basis and is available on a lottery system for upperclassmen. Priority is given to out-of-town students. 93% of students commute. All students may keep cars.

Activities: There are no fraternities or sororities. There are 150 groups on campus, including art, band, cheerleading, chess, choir, computers, dance, drama, ethnic, film, gay, international, jazz band, literary magazine, musical theater, orchestra, photography, political, professional, radio and TV, religious, social, social service, student government, and yearbook. Popular campus events include The Blue Bowl (football) and Orientation Week.

Sports: There are 14 intercollegiate sports for men and 15 for women, and 15 intramural sports for men and 13 for women. Facilities include a track and field center, 2 25-meter pools, 26 indoor and outdoor tennis courts, ice arena, 6-arena ice garden, 7 squash courts, 5 gyms, 2 fitness centers, 2 dance/aerobics studios, 1 combative room, 7 playing fields, 5 softball diamonds, 1 cricket pitch, 3 teaching labs, 2 fitness training areas, 3 strength training areas, 2 sport therapy clinics, 1 outdoor events facility, and a spinning studio.

Disabled Students: 65% of the campus is accessible. Wheelchair ramps, elevators, special parking, specially equipped rest rooms, special class scheduling, lowered drinking fountains, and lowered telephones are available. The Office for Persons with Disabilities offers a variety of additional services.

Services: Counseling and information services are available, as is tutoring in most subjects. There is a reader service for the blind. The Counseling and Development Center offers a variety of services and workshops.

Campus Safety and Security: Measures include 24-hour foot and vehicle patrol, self-defense education, escort service, and shuttle buses. There are informal discussions, pamphlets/posters/films, emergency telephones, lighted pathways/sidewalks, and There is also a bicycle patrol team monitoring the campuses.

Programs of Study: York confers B.A., B.Sc., B.A.S., B.B.A., B.Des., B.E.S., B.Ed., B.F.A., B.H.R.M., B.H.S., B.S.W., B.Sc.N., I.B.B.A., and L.L.B. degrees. Master's and doctoral degrees are also awarded. Bachelor's degrees are awarded in AGRICULTURE (conservation and regulation), BIOLOGICAL SCIENCE (biology/biological science and ecology), BUSINESS (accounting, banking and finance, business administration and management, business economics, business statistics, entrepreneurial studies, human resources, international economics, labor studies, management science, marketing and distribution, and organizational behavior), COMMUNICATIONS AND THE ARTS (art history and appreciation, classics, communications, creative writing, dance, design, dramatic arts, English, film arts, fine arts, French, German, Greek, Italian, linguistics, music, photography, Russian, Spanish, and visual and performing arts), COMPUTER AND PHYSICAL SCIENCE (applied mathematics, astronomy, atmospheric sciences and meteorology, chemistry, computer science, earth science, mathematics, physics, science, and statistics), EDUCATION (early childhood, education of the deaf and hearing impaired, elementary, middle school, and secondary), ENGINEERING AND ENVIRONMENTAL DESIGN (engineering and environmental science), HEALTH PROFESSIONS (community health work, environmental health science, exercise science, health care administration, health science, nursing, and rehabilitation therapy), SOCIAL SCIENCE (African studies, anthropology, Canadian studies, criminal justice, East Asian studies, economics, French studies, geography, German area studies, gerontology, Hispanic American studies, history, humanities, international studies, Judaic studies, Latin American studies, law, liberal arts/general studies, peace studies, philosophy, political science/government, psychology, public administration, religion, social science, social work, sociology, Third World studies, urban studies, and women's studies). Psychology, administrative studies, and sociology are the largest.

Required: Students must maintain at least a C average in 90 credits to receive an ordinary degree and a C+ in 120 credits to receive an honors degree. Requirements for graduation vary according to the program.

Special: Cross-registration with Seneca, Centenial, Sheridan and Humber Colleges, internships, study abroad in more than 100 countries, and work-study are available. York offers 14 bachelor degrees in 100 areas of study; dual, student-designed, multi-, and interdisciplinary majors, including atmospheric chemistry, physics and astronomy; science, technology, culture, and society; social and political thought; space and communication sciences, and translation. Independent study and nondegree study are also possible. There is a freshman honors program.

Faculty/Classroom: 54% of faculty are male; 45%, female. All both teach and do research. No introductory courses are taught by graduate students. The average class size in an introductory lecture is 57 and in a laboratory, 25.

Requirements: The SAT I or ACT is required. In addition, U.S. applicants must present evidence of superior academic achievement. Secondary school record, SAT I or ACT scores, and teacher/counselor recommendation will be taken into consideration. In addition, applicants to a fine arts program are required to successfully pass an audition/evaluation, and business administration applicants are required to submit a supplementary application. Admission averages and course prerequisites vary by faculty. Applications are accepted on-line at *http://www.yorku.ca/admissions*. York requires applicants to be in the upper 25% of their class. A GPA of 3.0 is required. AP credits are accepted.

Procedure: Freshmen are admitted to all sessions. Entrance exams should be taken in the fall of the senior year. There is an early admissions plan. Applications should be filed by February 1 for fall entry, October 1 for winter entry, and February 1 for spring entry. Notification is sent on a rolling basis. The fall 2001 application fee was $80 CDN.

Transfer: Requirements vary depending on the program. Post secondary transcripts are required.

Visiting: There are regularly scheduled orientations for prospective students, consisting of a general information session and campus tour; 1 week of orientation prior to the start of classes. There are guides for informal visits and visitors may sit in on classes and stay overnight. To schedule a visit, contact International Admissions Office.

Financial Aid: In 2001-2002, the average freshman award was $500 CDN ($4000 CDN maximum). The FAFSA is required. The fall application deadline is February 1.

International Students: There are 1600 international students enrolled. The school actively recruits these students. They must score 560 on the written TOEFL or 220 on the electronic version or take the MELAB, the Comprehensive English Language Test, the college's own test, or the York English Language Test (YELT) and also take the SAT I or the ACT, scoring 1100 or 24, respectively.

Computers: The mainframes are an IBM 3090, 4381, a MAS 6650, a DEC VAX 8600, 6230, 11/78x, 11/750, and 11/730, and a UNIX. There are 1900 computer workstations on campus. Students enrolled in computer courses are given first priority in the computer labs. All students receive free Internet and e-mail access. A computer store on campus is available for those who wish to buy computers or computer accessories. All students may access the system 24 hours per day. There are no time limits and no fees.

Graduates: In 2001, 6803 bachelor's degrees were awarded. The most popular majors were psychology (12%), computer science/information technology (9%), and administration (7%).

Admissions Contact: Office of International Admissions.
E-mail: *vgrafi@yorku.ca* Web: *http://www.yorku.ca/*

STUDY ABROAD

Study abroad programs are now available in more than 60 countries in fields that range from Costa Rican tropical biology to Finnish architecture. Program directors have responded to the vocational interests of the student of the 21st century by organizing programs in international management, health care administration, and other career-oriented fields.

In fact, study in both traditional and nontraditional fields is enriched by overseas experience. An international perspective can benefit study of environmental sciences, anthropology, political science, urban planning, oceanography, hotel administration, psychology, social work, journalism, marketing and law, as well as film, art history, theater, music and dance.

The vast majority of U.S. students enter European schools through organized, ongoing programs sponsored and managed by the colleges and universities in which they are already enrolled. In this way, they automatically earn U.S. academic credit from their home institution for their overseas course work. Academic credit *directly* earned at a foreign institution is often not acceptable toward a U.S. degree. Applying directly to a foreign school is not difficult but unusual.

There are colleges and universities located in foreign nations that are organized on the U.S. system and accredited by U.S. accrediting agencies, e.g. American University of Paris. A list of accredited U.S. institutions overseas is provided in the annual *Accredited Institutions of Postsecondary Education*, published for the Commission on Recognition of Postsecondary Accreditation by the American Council on Education, and is available from The Oryx Press, 4041 North Central Avenue, Phoenix, Arizona 85012-33976; (800) 279-6799 or (602) 265-2651.

According to a study by the Institute of International Education (IIE) about 75 percent of foreign study is done in western Europe—about 30 percent in the United Kingdom, 12 percent in France, and 5 percent in Mexico. Most students are women (64 percent) and the most popular programs are in the liberal arts (18 percent). The study showed that, unlike American students, international students coming to the United States are primarily interested in engineering, physical and life sciences, and mathematics and computer sciences and account for 38 percent of the international student population. Unlike their U.S. counterparts, most of the international students coming to this country are male (66 percent).

A Productive Experience

If you are interested in study abroad, plan ahead by taking the following steps to ensure that the experience is productive:

- **Assess the ways in which study abroad will benefit your educational and career plans.** Study abroad can be a casual choice or a pleasant way to spend a semester but you will derive the greatest benefit if you bring more thought to it: How will the overseas experience complement your other courses or your educational major? Can you maximize its value by seeking language as well as academic study or by combining independent study or an internship with traditional course work?
- **Consult your campus study-abroad adviser.** Most colleges and universities have a person or an office charged with the responsibility of counseling students on overseas study. The study-abroad adviser is best qualified to help you make the right choices.
- **Make sure your college will accept credit earned at the study-abroad program you have chosen.** Speak with both your academic adviser and your study-abroad adviser and resolve any issues before you leave. Many students have assumed incorrectly that credit is granted automatically for another institution's program. You cannot take this for granted.
- **Be realistic about your foreign language proficiency.** It is one thing to be able to order a meal or buy a train ticket in a foreign language. It is quite another to follow a professor lecturing on a complex subject. If you discover that your linguistic ability is inadequate, it is quite possible that you can find abroad the subject matter you want taught in English. You will get more out of the overseas experience however, if you make the effort to function in the language of the chosen country.
- **Look carefully at costs.** If you are dealing with a program sponsor that is not your home institution, it is wise to read program literature carefully. Ask questions before you go if you have any qualms! Are charges clearly specified? Does the literature specify what services *are* covered and more important, what services are *not* covered? What is the refund policy, if any? Is there a clearly identified organization with an official base in the United States which would be legally responsible in the event of disaster?

  While drawing up your budget, think about the extras. You will want to make the small side trips to new places that help to make overseas living rewarding. Try to give yourself some financial flexibility in working out your budget.
- **Think about what it means to live abroad.** Be sure to arrange for substitutes for the support systems you take for granted at home. Will your medical insurance cover you? Do you need vaccinations or a doctor who can manage your specific health problems while you are living abroad? What about visas?

  It is critically important to find out about housing before you leave. Student housing is difficult to find almost everywhere. Be sure to find out whether securing housing abroad is your responsibility and what the alternatives are in the country in which you plan to live.
- **Don't assume that you can work abroad.** Because of foreign labor laws, students should not plan to seek paid employment. The practice of working one's way through college is not common abroad, nor are the relatively high-paying part-time jobs that make it possible in the United States. However, increasing numbers of students are looking to combine practical work experience with study abroad. There are many work exchanges, volunteer opportunities, and internships available. Contact the Council on International Exchange, 205 East 42nd Street, New York, NY 10017 for further information.
- **Find out what you can about the sponsoring agency, especially if it is not an accredited U.S. college or university.** Talk to your study-abroad adviser if you have any doubts. Most private agencies engaged in study abroad are legitimate organizations but their basic purposes may not match yours. Does the organization have experience in placing students in an academic environment, not just in arranging travel? Are descriptions of its study program specific or vague? Does it make unverifiable claims about the academic reputation of its programs, or their recognition by U.S. higher educational institutions?

For further information, consult:

Institute of International Education
IIE Books
809 United Nations Plaza
New York, NY 10017
(212) 883-8200 FAX: (212) 984-5358
(publications include *Basic Facts on Study Abroad, Academic Year Abroad, Vacation Study Abroad 1992.*)

Council on International Educational Exchange
Publications Department
205 East 42nd Street
New York, NY 10017
(212) 661-1414 FAX: (212) 972-3231

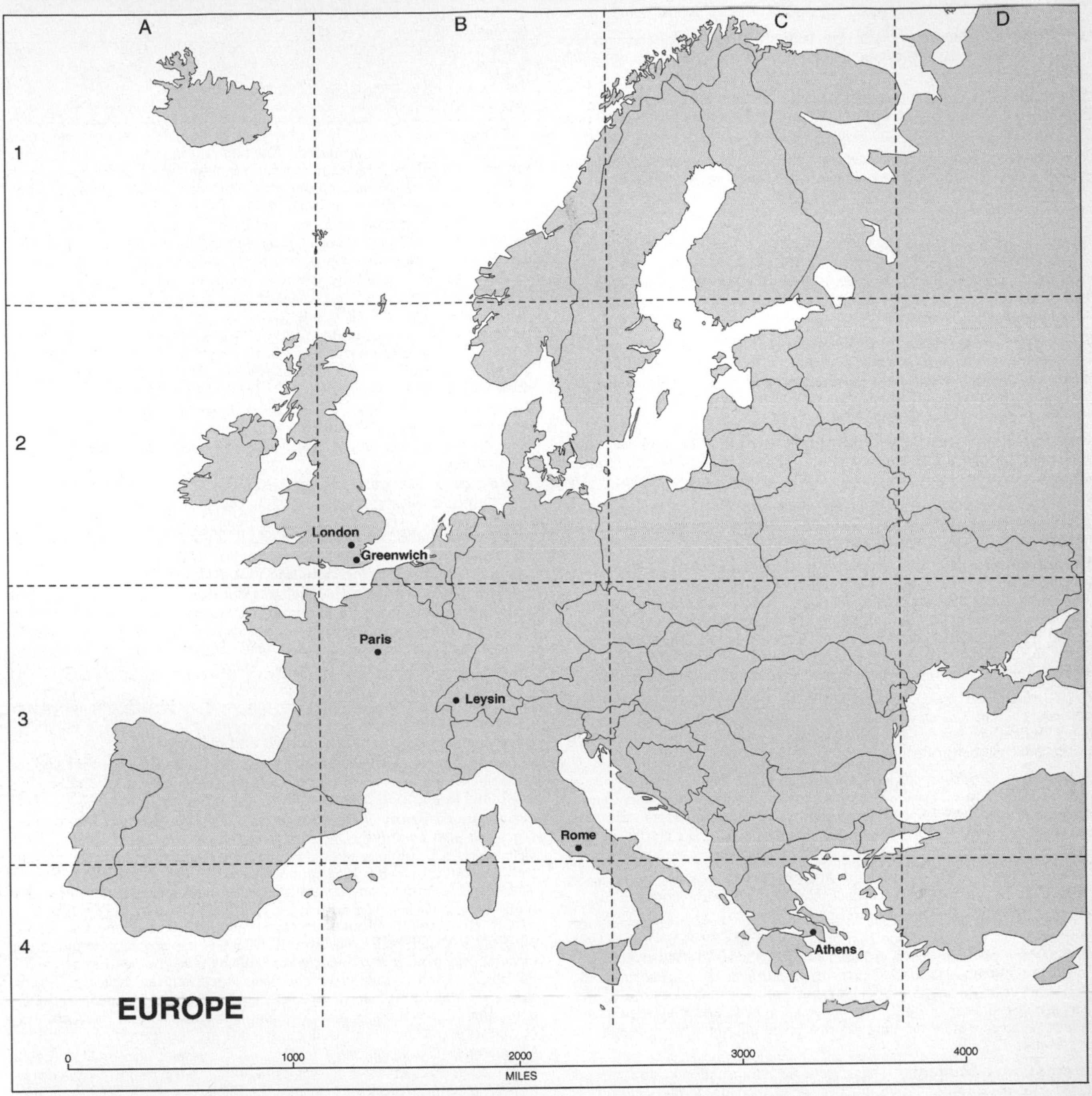

AMERICAN COLLEGE OF GREECE/DEREE COLLEGE C-4

Athens, GREECE (01) 600-9814 or 600-9800, ext. 1317 and Fax: (01) 600-9811

Full-time: 955 men, 2295 women	**Faculty:** 117
Part-time: 1195 men, 2485 women	**Ph.D.s:** 61%
Graduate: none	**Student/Faculty:** 28 to 1
Year: 4-1-4, summer session	**Tuition:** $4000
Application Deadline: see profile	**Room & Board:** n/app
Freshman Class: n/av	
SAT I Verbal/Math: required	

Deree College, the undergraduate division of the American College of Greece, was founded in 1875 as the American School for Girls. Now situated in the Athens suburb of Aghia Paraskevi, it offers American style education in the arts and sciences and business administration. Figures given in the above capsule are approximate. There are 2 undergraduate schools. The 3 libraries contain 85,000 volumes, 3552 microform items, and 1290 audiovisual forms/CDs, and subscribe to 950 periodicals. Computerized library services include the card catalog and database searching. Special learning facilities include a learning resource center and a museum of the history of the college. The 60-acre campus is in a suburban area 6 miles northeast of Athens. There are 6 buildings.

Student Life: 90% of undergraduates are from Greece. Others are from 42 foreign countries. 60% are from public schools. 99% are white. The average age of freshman is 18; all undergraduates, 21. 15% do not continue beyond their first year. 68% remain to graduate.

Housing: There are no residence halls. All students commute. Alcohol is not permitted.

Activities: There are no fraternities or sororities. There are many groups and organizations on campus, including arts, choir, computers, dance, debate, drama, ethnic, honors, international, literary magazine, newspaper, orchestra, photography, professional, social, social service, student government, and yearbook. Popular campus events include Activities Day, Visitation Day, and Professional Week.

Sports: There are 3 intercollegiate sports for men and 2 for women, and 11 intramural sports for men and 8 for women. Facilities include a 600-seat stadium, a 1500-seat gym, a 400-meter track, a soccer field, outdoor basketball/volleyball courts, minisoccer arena, a dance studio, a fitness center, an Olympic-size pool, and 4 outdoor tennis courts.

Disabled Students: 85% of the campus is accessible. Wheelchair ramps, elevators, special parking, and special class scheduling are available.

Campus Safety and Security: Measures include 24-hour foot and vehicle patrol, shuttle buses. Pamphlets/posters/films, and emergency telephones. There are lighted pathways/sidewalks.

Programs of Study: Deree confers B.A. and B.S. degrees. Associate degrees are also awarded. Bachelor's degrees are awarded in BUSINESS (accounting, business administration and management, management information systems, and marketing/retailing/merchandising), COMMUNICATIONS AND THE ARTS (art history and appreciation, dance, English, and music), ENGINEERING AND ENVIRONMENTAL DESIGN (preengineering), SOCIAL SCIENCE (economics, history, philosophy, psychology, and sociology). English, psychology, marketing are the strongest academically. Marketing, management, and accounting and finance are the largest.

Required: All students must maintain a minimum CI (cumulative index) of 2.0 and complete 128 semester hours, of which the last 30 must be earned in residence. Distribution requirements vary with the major but include composition, literature, public speaking, humanities, ethics, aesthetics, history, music, and political science.

Special: Study abroad, work-study programs, dual degrees, a preengineering program, self-directed study, and interdisciplinary programs are offered. Nondegree study and pass/fail options are available.

Faculty/Classroom: 60% of faculty are male; 40%, female. All teach undergraduates. The average class size in an introductory lecture is 40; in a laboratory, 20; and in a regular course, 23.

Requirements: The SAT I is required for native English speakers, with minimum scores of 450 verbal and 450 math. Applicants must be graduates of an accredited secondary school. The GED is accepted. Students with a score below 450 verbal may apply to the Junior College. A GPA of 2.0 is required. AP and CLEP credits are accepted. Important factors in the admissions decision are recommendations by school officials, recommendations by alumni, and personality/intangible qualities.

Procedure: Freshmen are admitted to all sessions. There is a deferred admissions plan. Check with school for current application deadlines and fee. Notification is sent on a rolling basis. A waiting list is an active part of the admissions procedure.

Transfer: 185 transfer students enrolled in 2001-2002. Applicants must have a minimum GPA of 2.0 and submit high school transcripts and a diploma if they have fewer than 30 credits. English proficiency also must be demonstrated, if not native speakers of English. 36 credits of 128 must be completed at Deree.

Visiting: There are guides for informal visits and visitors may sit in on classes. To schedule a visit, contact the Office of Admissions.

Financial Aid: In 2001-2002, 3% of all students received some form of financial aid. The average freshman award was $2053. Of that total, scholarships or need-based grants averaged $3010 ($4548 maximum); and loans averaged $2053 ($3255 maximum). 2% of undergraduates work part time. Average annual earnings from campus work are $1566. Deree is a member of CSS. The college's own financial statement and Internal Revenue statement are required. The fall application deadline is September 1.

International Students: There were 434 international students enrolled in a recent year. They must score 173 on the written TOEFL or take the MELAB, GCE "O" levels, or Cambridge Proficiency and also take the SAT I.

Computers: The mainframes are an IBM AS/400 and RS6000, IBM NF 7000, IBM NF 3000, IBM NF 5000, and HP LH. All servers are on an intranet. Some 100 networked PCs are used for courses that require computer work and are for student training. Students have access to the Internet and the Web through PCs in the computer labs and the library. All students may access the system 8 A.M. to 10 P.M. daily. Students may access the system 1 to 5 hours per week (varies according to course). The fee is $50. In some instances there are fees for courses having a scheduled lab training. It is strongly recommended that all students have a personal computer.

Graduates: In a recent year, 1074 bachelor's degrees were awarded. The most popular majors were marketing (35%), management (20%), and accounting/finance (15%). In an average class, 1% graduate in 3 years, 17% in 4 years, 48% in 5 years, and 17% in 6 years. 170 companies recruited on campus in a recent year.

Admissions Contact: Konstantina Founta, Director Office of Admissions. E-mail: *dereeadm@hol.gr*

AMERICAN UNIVERSITY IN CAIRO

Cairo, EGYPT **(212) 730-8800; Fax: (212) 730-1600**

Full-time: 1603 men, 1920 women	**Faculty:** 304
Part-time: 235 men, 224 women	**Ph.D.s:** 95%
Graduate: 293 men, 456 women	**Student/Faculty:** 12 to 1
Year: semesters, summer session	**Tuition:** $11,590
Application Deadline: June 1	**Room & Board:** $2900
Freshman Class: 2075 applied, 905 accepted, 603 enrolled	
SAT I or ACT: required	

The American University in Cairo, founded in 1919, is a private liberal arts institution offering accredited American undergraduate and graduate programs in Egypt. There are 3 undergraduate and 3 graduate schools. In addition to regional accreditation, AUC has baccalaureate program accreditation with ABET and CSAB. The 2 libraries contain 423,894 volumes, 123,000 microform items, and 2300 audiovisual forms/CDs, and subscribe to 1700 periodicals. Computerized library services include the card catalog, interlibrary loans, and database searching. Special learning facilities include a learning resource center, art gallery, and TV station. The 26-acre campus is in an urban area downtown Cairo. Including residence halls, there are 12 buildings.

Student Life: 90% of undergraduates are from the country . Others are from 65 foreign countries and Canada. The average age of freshmen is 18; all undergraduates, 19. 5% do not continue beyond their first year; 80% remain to graduate.

Housing: 325 students can be accommodated in college housing, which includes single-sex dormitories. On-campus housing is available on a first-come, first-served basis. 95% of students commute. Alcohol is not permitted.

Activities: There are no fraternities or sororities. There are 25 groups on campus, including chess, choir, chorus, dance, drama, ethnic, international, literary magazine, musical theater, newspaper, photography, professional, radio and TV, social, student government, and yearbook. Popular campus events include International Day, National University Cultural Activities Competition, and Model United Nations.

Sports: There are 13 intercollegiate sports for men and 11 for women, and 7 intramural sports for men and 5 for women. Facilities include tennis courts, multipurpose courts, an exercise gym, a weight room, and a 400-seat stadium. There are also private clubs in the area and other provisions for horseback riding, rowing, swimming and scuba diving, track and field, water polo, squash, and soccer.

Disabled Students: Wheelchair ramps and specially equipped rest rooms are available.

Services: There is remedial reading and writing.

Campus Safety and Security: Measures include 24-hour foot and vehicle patrol, shuttle buses, lighted pathways/sidewalks, and and security personnel at all open entrances 24 hours a day.

Programs of Study: AUC confers B.A. and B.S. degrees. Master's degrees are also awarded. Bachelor's degrees are awarded in BIOLOGICAL SCIENCE (biology/biological science), BUSINESS (accounting and business administration and management), COMMUNICATIONS AND THE ARTS (Arabic, art, communications, comparative literature, dramatic arts, English, and journalism), COMPUTER AND PHYSICAL SCIENCE (chemistry, computer science, mathematics, and physics), ENGINEERING AND ENVIRONMENTAL DESIGN (construction engineering, electrical/electronics engineering, and mechanical engineering), SOCIAL SCIENCE (anthropology, archeology, economics, history, Islamic studies, Middle Eastern studies, philosophy, political science/government, psychology, and sociology). Journalism and mass communications, economics, and political science are the largest.

Required: All students must maintain a C average and must complete from 120 to 162 semester credits, depending on the major. Core courses include a writing program, an interdisciplinary seminar in humanities, natural science, and social science, a scientific-thinking course, and Arab literature, history, and society.

Special: Study abroad through a consortium of U.S. schools, work-study programs with the university, and nondegree study are available.

Faculty/Classroom: 51% of faculty are male; 49%, female. No introductory courses are taught by graduate students. The average class size in an introductory lecture is 40; in a laboratory, 15; and in a regular course, 31.

Admissions: 44% of the 2001-2002 applicants were accepted. The SAT I scores for the 2001-2002 freshman class were: Verbal--26% below 500, 49% between 500 and 599, 23% between 600 and 700, and 3% above 700; Math--60% below 500, 31% between 500 and 599, 8% between 600 and 700, and 1% above 700.

Requirements: The SAT I or ACT is required of U.S. applicants, who must also be graduates of an accredited secondary school and submit complete transcripts and a copy of their diploma. Others must submit the Egyptian Thanawiya Amma certificate or other national high school certificate recognized by the university as equivalent to it, or the GCE, GCSE, or IGCSE. A minimum high school GPA of 2.0 is required. Students should have taken courses in 3 of the following subjects: languages and humanities, math, social studies, and biological and physical sciences. AP credits are accepted. Important factors in the admissions decision are ability to finance college education and evidence of special talent.

Procedure: Freshmen are admitted fall and spring. Entrance exams should be taken in July for fall admission. There is an early decision plan. Early decision applications should be filed by April 1; regular applications, by June 1 for fall entry and November 1 for spring entry. Notification is sent on a rolling basis. The fall 2001 application fee was $35.

Transfer: Transfer students must have a C average on secondary school and college transcripts. 45 credits of 120 must be completed at AUC.

Visiting: There are guides for informal visits and visitors may sit in on classes and stay overnight. To schedule a visit, contact the General Director of Admission in Egypt at 20-2# 357-5018.

Financial Aid: In 2001-2002, 85% of all students received some form of financial aid. 48% of freshmen and 44% of continuing students received need-based aid. The average freshman award was $4280. Of that total, scholarships or need-based grants averaged $3980 ($5350 maximum); and work contracts averaged $300 ($350 maximum). 10% of undergraduates work part time. The college's own financial statement is required. The fall application deadline is September 15.

International Students: There are 368 international students enrolled. The school actively recruits these students. They must score 213 on the written TOEFL or take the Test of Written English (TWE) or AUC's ELPET test.

Computers: Students may access the mainframe through more than 600 terminals located in computer labs throughout the campus. Only students enrolled in computer-related courses or courses that require computer use may access the system. It may be used from 8 A.M. to 9 P.M., 6 days a week. There are no time limits and no fees.

Graduates: In 2001, 635 bachelor's degrees were awarded. The most popular majors were mass communications (16%), economics (15%), and political science (12%). In an average class, 2% graduate in 3 years, 22% in 4 years, 68% in 5 years, and 82% in 6 years. 320 companies recruited on campus in 2000-2001.

Admissions Contact: American University in Cairo's, New York Office. E-mail: *aucegypt@aucnyo.edu* Web: *http://www.aucegypt.edu*

AMERICAN UNIVERSITY OF PARIS — B-3

Paris, France 75007 — (212) 983-1414; Fax: (212) 983-0444

Full-time: 705 men and women	**Faculty:** n/av
Part-time: 25 men and women	**Ph.D.s:** 67%
Graduate: none	**Student/Faculty:** n/av
Year: semesters, summer session	**Tuition:** $19,940
Application Deadline: see profile	**Room & Board:** n/app
Freshman Class: n/av	
SAT I Verbal/Math: required	

The American University of Paris, founded in 1962, is a private institution providing a liberal arts program in an international context. It has regional U.S. accreditation and is recognized by the French government as an institute of higher learning. Classes are in English except for foreign language and literature courses. Figures in above capsule are approximate. The library contains 65,000 volumes and 1000 microform items. Computerized library services include the card catalog, interlibrary loans, and database searching. Special learning facilities include a learning resource center. The campus is in an urban area in Paris. There are 6 buildings.

Student Life: Students come from 90 foreign countries. 60% are from public schools. The average age of freshman is 19; all undergraduates, 22.

Housing: There are no residence halls. Living accomodations are arranged with the assistance of the housing office. Students may choose from a wide variety of off-campus housing arrangements, including living with French families, au pair positions, and studio accomodations. All students may keep cars.

Activities: There are no fraternities or sororities. There are many groups and organizations on campus, including art, chess, choir, chorale, computers, dance, drama, film, honors, international, literary magazine, musical theater, newspaper, photography, political, professional, student government, and yearbook. Popular campus events include Thanksgiving and World's Fair.

Sports: There are 2 intercollegiate sports for men, and 5 intramural sports for men, and 5 for women. Students may join the University of Paris sports club for a modest fee.

Disabled Students: 20% of the campus is accessible. Special scheduling is available.

Services: Counseling and information services are available, as is tutoring in every subject. There is remedial writing.

Programs of Study: AUP confers B.A. and B.S. degrees. Bachelor's degrees are awarded in BUSINESS (international business management and international economics), COMMUNICATIONS AND THE ARTS (art history and appreciation and comparative literature), COMPUTER AND PHYSICAL SCIENCE (computer science), ENGINEERING AND ENVIRONMENTAL DESIGN (engineering), SOCIAL SCIENCE (economics, European studies, French studies, history, and international relations). Art history, international affairs, and international economics are the strongest academically. International business administration, international affairs, and international communications are the largest.

Required: Students must maintain a minimum GPA of 2.0 while taking at least 120 semester credits, including an average of 50 in the major. Distribution requirements include 6 semester hours each of English composition, humanities, and social sciences, 16 of French, and 8 of lab science or math.

Special: There are co-op programs with Tulane, Northeastern, and Boston Universities, Monmouth, Mills, New England, Notre Dame and St. Mary's (CA) colleges, Université de Paris-Sorbonne, and Kansai Gaidai in Japan. Cross-registration is available in foreign language programs at 3 other French colleges. Juniors and seniors with good academic standing are encouraged to undertake internships. Study abroad, second degrees, nondegree study, and pass/fail options also are offered. There are 4 national honor societies, and 3 departmental honors programs.

Faculty/Classroom: 52% of faculty are male; 48%, female. The average class size in an introductory lecture is 18; in a laboratory, 12; and in a regular course, 16.

Requirements: The SAT I is required and the ACT is recommended. In addition, candidates must be graduates of an accredited secondary school. An essay and 2 letters of recommendation are also needed. Knowledge of French is not required. Applicants in the New York area are encouraged to interview at that office. U.S. students can apply via ExPAN in participating high schools. A GPA of 2.8 is required. AP and CLEP credits are accepted. Important factors in the admissions decision are advanced placement or honor courses, personality/intangible qualities, and recommendations by school officials.

Procedure: Freshmen are admitted fall and spring. Entrance exams should be taken by April 1. There is a deferred admissions plan. Check with school for current application deadlines and fee. Notification is sent on a rolling basis.

Transfer: Transfer applicants must submit college and high school transcripts, and SAT I or ACT scores if they have fewer than 45 credits. An interview, 2 letters of recommendation, and an essay are required. 30 credits of 120 must be completed at AUP.

Visiting: There are guides for informal visits and visitors may sit in on classes. To schedule a visit, contact the Admissions Office at (212) 983-1414 (New York office) or Paris direct.

Financial Aid: AUP is a member of CSS. The FAFSA is required. Check with school for current deadlines.

International Students: There were 707 international students enrolled in a recent year. The school actively recruits these students. They must score 500 on the written TOEFL or the MELAB. Students must also take the college's own test and the SAT I or the ACT.

Computers: The mainframe is an IBM RISC 6000 (550). 60 PCs and PC-based graphic workstations are available in the 3 computer labs. E-mail facilities and mathematical and programming software are available in addition to the usual applications. All students may access the system. There are no time limits and no fees. It is strongly recommended that all students have a personal computer.

Admissions Contact: Candace MacLaughlin, Office Manager.
E-mail: *nyoffice@aup.edu* or *admissions@aup.edu* (Paris)

AMERICAN UNIVERSITY OF ROME — B-3

Rome, Italy 00153 — 011 39 6 58330919; Fax: 011 396 58330992

Full-time: 98 men, 252 women	**Faculty:** 8
Part-time: 4 men, 6 women	**Ph.D.s:** 67%
Graduate: none	**Student/Faculty:** 44 to 1
Year: semesters, summer session	**Tuition:** $10,697
Application Deadline: May 15	**Room & Board:** $8460
Freshman Class: 35 accepted, 22 enrolled	
SAT I or ACT: required	

American University of Rome, founded in 1969, is a private institution offering programs in liberal arts, international business, international relations, Italian studies, and communications. The library contains 5000 volumes and 30 audiovisual forms/CDs, and subscribes to 15 periodicals. Computerized library services include the card catalog, interlibrary loans, and database searching. The campus is in a suburban area on the Janiculum Hill, 2 miles from downtown. Including residence halls, there are 2 buildings.

Student Life: 65% of undergraduates are from the U.S. and 15% are from Italy. Others are from 25 foreign countries and Canada. 20% are from public schools. 83% are white. The average age of freshmen is 18; all undergraduates, 20. 20% do not continue beyond their first year; 26% remain to graduate.

Housing: 160 students can be accommodated in college housing, which includes single-sex off-campus apartments. On-campus housing is available on a first-come, first-served basis. 55% of students commute. Alcohol is not permitted. No one may keep cars.

Activities: There are no fraternities or sororities. There are some groups and organizations on campus, including art, drama, film, honors, inter-

national, literary magazine, newspaper, and student government. Popular campus events include the Distinguished Lecture Series, liberal arts and business excursions, and international relations debates.
Sports: There are 1 intercollegiate sport for men, and 3 intramural sports for men and 3 for women. Facilities include off-campus access to soccer, tennis, and swimming facilities.
Disabled Students: 30% of the campus is accessible.
Services: There is remedial writing.
Campus Safety and Security: Measures include informal discussions.
Programs of Study: AUR confers B.A. and B.S. degrees. Associate degrees are also awarded. Bachelor's degrees are awarded in BUSINESS (business administration and management), COMMUNICATIONS AND THE ARTS (communications), SOCIAL SCIENCE (international relations, international studies, and Italian studies). Business administration and international relations are the largest.
Required: To graduate, students must complete 120 credits, including 45 to 66 in the major, with a minimum GPA of 2.0. Distribution requirements include English composition and courses in humanities, social sciences, and science/math.
Special: Internships in business, international relations, communications, and Italian studies are available. Study abroad is possible by special arrangement, and work-study is available with AUR. Cross-registration with the College of Staten Island in New York is possible. There is 1 national honor society.
Faculty/Classroom: 58% of faculty are male; 42%, female. All teach undergraduates. The average class size in an introductory lecture is 18 and in a regular course, 13.
Admissions: The SAT I scores for the 2001-2002 freshman class were: Verbal--31% below 500, 46% between 500 and 599, and 23% between 600 and 700; Math--36% below 500, and 64% between 500 and 599.
Requirements: The SAT I or ACT is required. In addition, a high school diploma and transcript or the non-American equivalent is required, as are a letter of recommendation and an essay. The GED is accepted. A GPA of 2.5 is required. AP and CLEP credits are accepted. Important factors in the admissions decision are recommendations by school officials, advanced placement or honor courses, and personality/intangible qualities.
Procedure: Freshmen are admitted to all sessions. There is a deferred admissions plan. Applications should be filed by May 15 for fall entry, October 10 for spring entry, and March 30 for summer entry, along with a $55 fee. Notification is sent 6 to 8 weeks after the deadline.
Transfer: 20 transfer students enrolled in 2001-2002. Applicants must submit a high school transcript, a diploma, all transcripts of universities attended, a letter of recommendation, and an essay. 45 credits of 120 must be completed at AUR.
Visiting: There are regularly scheduled orientations for prospective students, which AUR organizes directly and through its agents in many U.S. states and in other countries. Orientation is assisted by use of audiovisual materials. There are guides for informal visits and visitors may sit in on classes. To schedule a visit, contact the Director of Admissions at *aurinfo@aur.edu*
Financial Aid: In 2001-2002, 10% of all students received some form of financial aid. Loans averaged $2625 (maximum). 4% of undergraduates work part time. Average annual earnings from campus work are $4144. The FAFSA is required. The fall application deadline is July 12.
International Students: There are 90 international students enrolled. The school actively recruits these students. They must score 550 on the written TOEFL or take the MELAB or the college's own test.
Computers: PCs are available, with e-mail and Internet access, in the library computer lab. All students may access the system 8:30 A.M. to 8:30 P.M. Monday through Friday; 10 A.M. to 6 P.M. Saturday. There are no time limits and no fees. It is strongly recommended that all students have a personal computer.
Graduates: In 2001, 20 bachelor's degrees were awarded. The most popular majors were business administration (55%), international relations (30%), and communications (15%). In an average class, 5% graduate in 3 years, 85% in 4 years, and 90% in 5 years.
Admissions Contact: Dean of Administration. A video is available.
E-mail: *aur.homeoffice@dc.aur.edu* Web: *www.aur.edu*

FRANLIN COLLEGE SWITZERLAND B-3

New York, NY 10021 **(212) 772-2090, (011-41-91-985-2260)**
Fax: (212) 772-2718, (011-41-91-994-4117)

Full-time: 106 men, 163 women	**Faculty:** 17
Part-time: 1 woman	**Ph.D.s:** 82%
Graduate: none	**Student/Faculty:** 16 to 1
Year: semesters, summer session	**Tuition:** $19,320
Application Deadline: March 15	**Room & Board:** $7850
Freshman Class: n/av	
SAT I: required	**ACT:** n/av

Franklin College Switzerland, founded in 1969, is a private institution providing a liberal education through courses that are international in perspective and cross-cultural in content. The baccalaureate degree offers concentrations in international management, art history, modern languages (French, Italian, German), international relations, history/literature, and visual and communiction arts. The library contains 33,500 volumes, 15 microform items, and 1620 audiovisual forms/CDs, and subscribes to 174 periodicals. Computerized library services include the card catalog, interlibrary loans, and database searching. Special learning facilities include a radio station. The 4-acre campus is in a suburban area on a hillside above Lugano in the southern region of Switzerland called the Ticino. Including residence halls, there are 8 buildings.
Student Life: Students are from Switzerland, 23 U.S. states, 62 foreign countries, and Canada. The average age of freshmen is 18; all undergraduates, 19. 48% do not continue beyond their first year.
Housing: Housing includes single-sex dormitories, on-campus apartments, and off-campus apartments. 76% of students live on campus; of those, 60% remain on campus on weekends. All students may keep cars.
Activities: There are no fraternities or sororities. There are some groups and organizations on campus, including art, drama, international, literary magazine, newspaper, photography, social, student government, and yearbook.
Sports: There are 3 intramural sports for men and 2 for women.
Services: Counseling and information services are available, as is tutoring in most subjects.
Campus Safety and Security: Measures include emergency telephones and lighted pathways/sidewalks.
Programs of Study: Franklin College Switzerland confers the B.A. degree. Associate degrees are also awarded. Bachelor's degrees are awarded in BUSINESS (international business management and international economics), COMMUNICATIONS AND THE ARTS (art history and appreciation, literature, media arts, and modern language), SOCIAL SCIENCE (European studies, history, and international relations). International management/international relations is the strongest academically and has the largest enrollment.
Required: All students must complete 126 credit hours. A general core requirement of 48 credit hours includes 12 credit hours in foreign languages, 9 in humanities, 6 in math/science and history, and 3 in English. Academic travel is required each year (each travel program is 1 academic credit). A minimum GPA of 2.0 overall and 42 credits or more in the major, with a C or better, are also required. Some majors require a thesis.
Special: Cross-registration with most U.S. colleges having an international management major, internships, study abroad as part of the academic travel requirement, accelerated degree programs in any major, and dual majors are offered.
Faculty/Classroom: 61% of faculty are male; 39%, female. All teach undergraduates. The average class size in an introductory lecture is 13; in a laboratory, 10; and in a regular course, 10.
Requirements: The SAT I is required. In addition, the college recommends that applicants have completed 4 years of English, 3 years each of history and a foreign language, and 2 years each of science and math. Electives in art, music, and computers are recommended. An essay, a personal statement, and academic references are required. An interview is strongly encouraged. A GPA of 2.0 is required. AP credits are accepted. Important factors in the admissions decision are leadership record, personality/intangible qualities, and extracurricular activities record.
Procedure: Freshmen are admitted to all sessions. Entrance exams should be taken in the fall prior to the desired entrance. There are early decision, early admissions, and deferred admissions plans. Early decision applications should be filed by December 15; regular applications, by March 15 for fall entry, November 15 for spring entry, and May 1 for summer entry, along with a $50 fee. Notification of early decision is sent January 15; regular decision, on a rolling basis.
Transfer: Applicants must have a C average and provide 1 recommendation. 60 credits of 126 must be completed at Franklin College Switzerland.
Visiting: There are guides for informal visits and visitors may sit in on classes. To schedule a visit, contact the New York Admissions Office.
Financial Aid: In a recent year, 47% of all freshmen and 28% of continuing students received some form of financial aid. 36% of freshmen and 12% of continuing students received need-based aid. The average freshman award was $6667. Of that total, scholarships or need-based grants averaged $5700 ($10,500 maximum); and work contracts averaged $580. 30% of undergraduates work part time. Average annual earnings from campus work are $1000. Franklin College Switzerland is a member of CSS. The FAFSA and the college's own financial statement are required. The fall application deadline is May 1.
International Students: The school actively recruits these students. They must score 550 on the written TOEFL and also take the SAT I or the ACT.
Computers: The mainframe is a Novell File Server. 27 terminals are available for academic use. All students may access the system. There are no time limits and no fees. It is strongly recommended that all students have a personal computer.
Graduates: In an average class, 20% graduate in 3 years, and 80% in 4 years.

Admissions Contact: Karen Ballard, U.S. Associate Director of Admissions. E-mail: *kballard@fc.edu* Web: *www.fc.edu*

JOHN CABOT UNIVERSITY B-3
Rome, ITALY 00165 011-396-681-91219; Fax: 011-396-683-2088

Full-time: 80 men, 90 women	**Faculty:** 12
Part-time: 40 men, 60 women	**Ph.D.s:** 70%
Graduate: none	**Student/Faculty:** 14 to 1
Year: semesters, summer session	**Tuition:** $10,900
Application Deadline: see profile	**Room & Board:** n/app
Freshman Class: n/av	
SAT I or ACT: required	

John Cabot University, founded in 1972, is an independent institution of liberal arts and sciences offering an American university education in Rome. Besides degree-seeking students, the university accepts study-abroad or visiting students from a number of U.S. colleges and universities. Figures given in the above capsule are approximate. In addition to regional accreditation, JCU has baccalaureate program accreditation with AACSB. The library contains 14,100 volumes and 2500 microform items, and subscribes to 29 periodicals. Computerized library services include the card catalog, interlibrary loans, and database searching. Special learning facilities include a center for public affairs and communications. The campus is in an urban area in Trastevere, the historic center of Rome. There are 2 buildings.

Student Life: Students are from 15 U.S. states, 40 foreign countries, and Canada. The average age of freshmen is 19; all undergraduates, 21.

Housing: There are no residence halls. All students commute.

Activities: There are no fraternities or sororities. There are many groups and organizations on campus, including art, computers, debate, drama, honors, international, musical theater, newspaper, photography, social, student government, and yearbook. Popular cmpus events include international dinners, American holiday parties, and cultural field trips throughout the year.

Sports: There are 5 intramural sports for men and 5 for women. Off-campus sports facilities offer tennis courts, a gym, a swimming pool, a soccer field, and volleyball and basketball courts.

Services: Counseling and information services are available, as is tutoring in some subjects, including math, English, economics, and computer science. There is remedial math and writing and an intensive English language program for university preparation.

Programs of Study: JCU confers B.A. and B.B.A. degrees. Associate degrees are also awarded. Bachelor's degrees are awarded in BUSINESS (business administration and management), COMMUNICATIONS AND THE ARTS (art history and appreciation and English literature), SOCIAL SCIENCE (international studies and political science/government). Business administration is the largest.

Required: To graduate, students must complete 120 semester hours with a GPA of 2.0, including required courses in writing, math, and foreign language.

Special: Internships are available with multinational and Italian businesses.

Faculty/Classroom: 50% of faculty are male; 50%, female. All teach undergraduates.

Requirements: SAT I or ACT tests are required of U.S. high school graduates and are recommended for students graduating from other educational systems. Also required are a personal essay and 2 letters of academic recommendation. An interview is recommended; the GED diploma may be recognized for admission. Applicants may apply on-line at *www.johncabot.edu*. A GPA of 2.0 is required. AP and CLEP credits are accepted. Important factors in the admissions decision are advanced placement or honor courses, recommendations by school officials, and extracurricular activities record.

Procedure: Freshmen are admitted to all sessions. Placement exams are taken at the orientation session. There is a deferred admissions plan. Check with school for current application deadlines and fee. Notification is sent on a rolling basis.

Transfer: Transfer applicants must be in good academic standing at the previous institution. 60 credits of 120 must be completed at JCU.

Visiting: There are regularly scheduled orientations for prospective students, consisting of sessions set up a week before every term for incoming students, parents, or family. Orientation includes academic and extra-academic events to assist students in adjusting to a new city and in many cases to a new academic system. There are guides for informal visits and visitors may sit in on classes. To schedule a visit, contact Dr. Francesca R. Gleason, Admissions Office.

Financial Aid: 7% of undergraduates work part time.

International Students: The school actively recruits these students. International students applying from non-English-language educational systems must score 550 on the TOEFL or take the university's own test. Students must also take the SAT I or the ACT.

Computers: PCs with Internet access are available for student use. All students may access the system. There are no time limits and no fees.

Admissions Contact: Dr. Francesca Gleason, Admissions Director. E-mail: *fgleason@johncabot.it* Web: *http://www.johncabot.edu*

RICHMOND, THE AMERICAN INTERNATIONAL UNIVERSITY IN LONDON B-2
Richmond, Surrey, UK TW10 6JP +44 (0) 20 8332 9000 Fax: +44 (0) 20 8832 1596

Full-time: 540 men, 560 women	**Faculty:** 50
Part-time: 5 men, 55 women	**Ph.D.s:** 72%
Graduate: 50 men, 55 women	**Student/Faculty:** 22 to 1
Year: semesters, summer session	**Tuition:** $15,930
Application Deadline: open	**Room & Board:** n/app
Freshman Class: n/av	
SAT I or ACT: required	

Richmond College, The American University in London, established in 1972, is an independent, international, liberal arts and professional studies university. It occupies the campus of the original Richmond College, founded in 1843 and part of the University of London, and is incorporated as a not-for-profit educational institution in the state of Delaware. Figures in the above capsule are approximate. There are 2 graduate schools. The 2 libraries contain 60,000 volumes, and subscribe to 300 periodicals. Computerized library services include database searching. Special learning facilities include a learning resource center. The 5-acre campus is in a suburban area 8 miles southwest of London. There are 3 buildings.

Student Life: All students are foreign nationals, representing 103 countries. The average age of freshmen is 19; all undergraduates, 22. 32% do not continue beyond their first year; 55% remain to graduate.

Housing: 685 students can be accommodated in college housing, which includes single-sex dormitories and off-campus apartments. On-campus housing is guaranteed for all 4 years. 65% of students live on campus; of those, 60% remain on campus on weekends. Alcohol is not permitted. Upperclassman may keep cars.

Activities: There are no fraternities or sororities. There are 9 groups on campus, including dance, drama, ethnic, film, international, literary magazine, newspaper, student government, and yearbook. Popular campus events include International Night and Gala Night.

Sports: There are 4 intercollegiate sports for men and 2 for women, and 12 intramural sports for men and 9 for women. Facilities include a weight room and an all-weather sports court.

Services: There is remedial math and writing. The English Language Development Program for international students offers intensive language development courses for credit and noncredit.

Campus Safety and Security: Measures include 24-hour foor and vehicle patrol and lighted pathways/sidewalks.

Programs of Study: Richmond confers B.A. and B.S. degrees. Associate and master's degrees are also awarded. Bachelor's degrees are awarded in BUSINESS (business administration and management and international business management), COMMUNICATIONS AND THE ARTS (art history and appreciation, communications, literature, performing arts, and studio art), COMPUTER AND PHYSICAL SCIENCE (computer programming and mathematics), ENGINEERING AND ENVIRONMENTAL DESIGN (environmental science and systems engineering), SOCIAL SCIENCE (anthropology, economics, history, international relations, political science/government, psychology, and sociology). Business and economics are the largest.

Required: Students must complete 12 courses in 7 fields: English, humanities, social science, intercultural studies, math, science, and the creative arts. Proficiency in English composition, math, and computer skills is required. A 2.0 GPA and 120 credit hours are needed to graduate.

Special: The International Internship Program utilizes London-based businesses and institutions. Study abroad is offered at the university's study centers in Florence, Italy, and Shizuoka, Japan. A field study project in a developing country may be arranged during the summer. A limited number of students can be placed in family helper/au pair positions with British families. Joint degrees are offered in engineering with George Washington University. There is a freshman honors program.

Faculty/Classroom: 65% of faculty are male; 35%, female. 97% teach undergraduates. The average class size in an introductory lecture is 22; in a laboratory, 12; and in a regular course, 17.

Requirements: The SAT I or ACT is required for American students. U.S. applicants should have completed secondary school with a 2.5 GPA. A GED equivalent is acceptable. An autobiographical essay is an important part of the application. AP and CLEP credits are accepted. Important factors in the admissions decision are advanced placement or honor courses, geographic diversity, and recommendations by school officials.

Procedure: Freshmen are admitted to all sessions. Entrance exams should be taken . There is a deferred admissions plan. Application deadlines are open. Notification is sent on a rolling basis.

Transfer: A 2.0 GPA, official transcripts from all previous institutions, and 2 references are required for admission. 45 credits of 120 must be completed at Richmond.

Visiting: There are regularly scheduled orientations for prospective students. There are guides for informal visits and visitors may sit in on classes and stay overnight. To schedule a visit, contact an admissions counselor in the U.K.

Financial Aid: In a recent year, 27% of all freshmen received some form of financial aid. The average freshman award was $8735. Of that total, scholarships or need-based grants averaged $3292 ($12,750 maximum); loans averaged $3883 ($21,600 maximum); and work contracts averaged $1560 ($2300 maximum). The FAFSA and the college's own financial statement are required. Check with school for current deadlines.

International Students: The school actively recruits these students.

Computers: The mainframe is a DEC VAX 11/750. The university-wide network is supported by 7 DEC and Compaq servers and is linked to the Internet. Faculty, staff, and students have 350 PCs available to them, including 5 instructional computer suites and an open access area. Mac Power PCs are used for multimedia design, video editing, and science projects. All students may access the system daily from 8:30 A.M. to 10 P.M. There are no time limits and no fees.

Admissions Contact: Julie Williams, Director of Undergraduate Admissions. E-mail: *enroll@richmond.ac.uk* Web: *www.richmond.ac.uk*

STUDY IN THE UNITED STATES

More and more American colleges and universities are welcoming students from foreign countries. Did you know that there are nearly 500,000 international students enrolled in U.S. institutions of higher learning, and that number continues to increase?

Why Colleges and Universities Seek International Students

There are a number of reasons why American colleges and universities seek international students. First, they recognize that international students help educate the American students on campus by introducing them to different ideas and cultures. Second, the number of college-age American students is declining, and international students can fill places that otherwise would go unfilled. Third, the money that international students spend on tuition and other expenses helps the U.S. economy; education is becoming a valuable export for the United States. And fourth, education has long been an important part of America's foreign aid program, providing foreign nationals with skills that they can use to improve life in their homelands.

Why International Students Seek to Study in the United States

There are also a number of reasons why international students seek to study in the United States. For some students, colleges and universities in the United States offer opportunities to study major fields that are not available in their own countries. For other students, American colleges and universities offer an alternative to colleges and universities in their own countries where places may not be available for all of the qualified students who wish to attend. For still other students, study in the United States provides them not only with an education but also with experiences in living in another culture and in exchanging ideas with students from many nations.

Whatever *your* reason may be for studying in the United States, this chapter will help you make decisions and plans.

Investigating a College or University

Although most of the colleges and universities in the United States are very honest about their programs and services, a few have been known to misrepresent themselves. When choosing a college or university, as when making any other major purchase, you should investigate carefully. In addition to checking whether your exact major field is offered, you should compare the special services for international students offered by the schools that you are considering. You will want to know whether a representative of the school will pick you up at the airport when you arrive, whether dormitories or other housing is available, and whether there is a foreign student adviser to help you with decisions that you will have to make and problems that you may have to solve after you arrive.

The Difference Between a College and a University

Most international students want to know the difference between a college and a university. This is a difficult question because there is more than one correct answer. In fact, there are three definitions for the word *college* (as it refers to a college in the United States) listed in the *American Heritage Dictionary of the English Language*.

According to the dictionary, a *college* is (1) a school of higher learning that grants a bachelor's degree (undergraduate degree) in arts or sciences or both; (2) an undergraduate division of a university that offers courses and grants undergraduate degrees in a particular field of study; or (3) a technical or professional school, often affiliated with a university, that grants a bachelor's or master's degree in that field.

A *university* is a school of higher learning that grants a bachelor's degree (undergraduate degree), master's degree, and doctorate (Ph.D.) through various colleges within the university.

The Comparison of a College and a University

Many international students ask whether a university is better than a college. The answer is that a university has advantages and disadvantages for an international student, and a college has advantages and disadvantages.

The advantages of a university are that there are usually more research and recreational facilities, and more different kinds of courses offered. The disadvantages of a university are that courses taught to first-year students are often taught by teaching assistants who are graduate students themselves, and that the classes can be very large. The advantages of a college are that the courses are almost always taught by professors, and that the classes are usually small. The disadvantages of a college are that there are usually fewer research and recreational facilities.

Remember, as you decide what is best for you, that there are excellent colleges and there are excellent universities.

Accreditation

Unlike most countries, the United States does not have a national ministry of education that approves the programs at colleges and universities throughout the country. Instead, programs are approved by professional organizations and regional associations. This approval is called accreditation.

All of the schools listed in this book are accredited or are in the process of being accredited.

Requirements for Admission

Academic Preparation

To study in the United States, an international student should begin preparing in secondary school. A good secondary school report is one of the most important requirements for admission to a college or university. When applying to a college or university, you must submit an English translation of your grades with a seal and signature on it. This grade report is called a transcript. In addition, most colleges and universities require undergraduate students to submit standardized test scores. Some of the most common tests are the Cambridge O Level Examination, the Cambridge A Level Examination, SAT I, and the ACT (American College Test). Each test is described below.

SAT I	A test of your English language proficiency in grammar and vocabulary and your skills in mathematics from secondary school.
ACT	A test of your general educational development in English, mathematics, social studies, and natural sciences.
SAT II	Subject tests in various academic areas.
Cambridge O Level	A series of examinations to test your ability in subjects that you have studied in secondary school.
Cambridge A Level	A series of examinations to test your ability in subjects that you have studied in secondary school and junior college. The A Level is graded at a higher level than the O Level.

Some highly selective schools also ask applicants to take as many as three SAT II: Subject tests, which are offered in specific subject areas such as writing, French, physics, European history, and mathematics on two levels. SAT I: Reasoning and SAT II: Subject tests, which are given only in English, are part of the Scholastic Assessment Testing Program. Both are administered by the Educational Testing Service for the sponsoring organization, the College Board. You can take SAT I and SAT II tests at established test centers or you may be able to arrange for a special testing location. The completed registration form for testing at test centers must be received by the Educational Testing Service about six weeks prior to the test date; requests for special locations must be received eight to ten weeks prior to the test date. (Note that you cannot take both SAT I and one or more of SAT II tests on the same date.) For more information write to The Office of International Education, Suite 402, 1717 Massachusetts Avenue, N.W., Washington, D.C. 20036, USA.

The ACT, which is given in English only, is administered by the American College Testing Program. You can take the ACT at an established test center or may be able to arrange for a special testing location. You may register at a particular test center up to a week before the test is given there; requests for special locations should be directed to the American College Testing Program as soon as possible before a particular test date. For more information, write to the American College Testing Program, P.O. Box 168, Iowa City, Iowa 52243, USA, and ask for the Overseas Registration Packet.

The following books are available from Barron's Educational Series, Inc., 250 Wireless Boulevard, Hauppauge, New York 11788, USA, to help you prepare for SAT I and SAT II: Subject tests. *How to Prepare for the SAT I*, *Pass Key to the SAT I*, *SAT II: Subject tests* (in many subject areas), *Math Workbook for SAT I*, *Verbal Workbook for SAT I*, *Hot Words for SAT I*, *14 Days to Higher SAT I Scores*, *After the SAT*, *How to Prepare for the ACT*, *Pass Key to the ACT*, and *How to Prepare for the Advanced Placement Examination* series. An SAT I CD-ROM is also available from this source.

English Language Proficiency

In addition, if your native language is not English, you will probably have to take a test of your ability to use English. The most widely used of these tests is the TOEFL (Test of English as a Foreign Language), given at 1250 test centers throughout the world. Other English exams include the MELAB (Michigan English Language Assessment Battery), the Test of Written English (TWE), and the Test of Spoken English (TSE).

Each test is described as follows:

TOEFL	A test of listening comprehension, structure and written expression, reading comprehension, and vocabulary.
MELAB	A test battery that may include a listening test and a composition and always includes grammar, vocabulary, and reading.
TWE	An essay test, given with the TOEFL at the August, September, October, February, and May administrations.
TSE	A test of listening and speaking, often required for graduate students seeking an assistantship.

You can take TOEFL and TWE as well as the TSE at an established center, or you may be able to set up a special testing location if there is no test center in your country. Completed registration forms for testing at test centers must be received about four weeks prior to the test date. These forms must be sent to either the appropriate international TOEFL agent or the TOEFL organization in the United States, depending on where you will take the test. Requests for special testing locations, together with the application form and either the test fee or proof of fee payment, must be received by an official TOEFL organization. For more information, write to TOEFL, Box 6151, Princeton, New Jersey 08541-6151, USA.

When the Michigan test is required, the administrators must receive a letter from either the applicant or the college that has accepted the applicant, requesting an administration. The letter should include the name, address, and birth date of the applicant along with an application fee to English Language Institute, Testing and Certification, The University of Michigan, Ann Arbor, Michigan 48109-1057, USA. Arrangements will then be made for taking the test at one of the official sites, at which time an additional fee must be paid.

The following books with accompanying records and cassettes are available from Barron's Educational Series, Inc., 250 Wireless Boulevard, Hauppauge, New York 11788, USA, to help you prepare for the TOEFL and the MELAB: *Barron's How to Prepare for the TOEFL (Test of English as a Foreign Language)*, *Barron's Practice Exercises for the TOEFL*, *Barron's Pass Key to the TOEFL*, *TOEFL Strategies*, *Classroom TOEFL*, *Barron's Computer Study Program for the TOEFL*, and *Barron's How to Prepare for the Michigan Test Battery*.

Financial Guarantees

All schools require that international students show proof of their ability to pay tuition, fees, and living expenses. Most schools require a statement from a bank that shows adequate finances for one year's study. If the name on the account is not the same as the name of the student, a signed letter from the person who has the account must accompany the bank statement. In the letter this person promises to support the international student while the student is in the United States. This person is called the student's sponsor.

Application Procedures

Select a few schools and write for information

When you are ready to apply—usually about a year before the date on which you hope to enter college—write to the schools that interest you for application materials. You can send completed copies of the *Request for Application Materials from U.S. Colleges and Universities*, usually available at counseling centers, or letters that include the name of your country, the field you wish to study, a brief outline of your previous education, the number of years you have studied English, the amount of money you can spend, and the proposed date of enrollment. The college admissions officers will review this information and should let you know if the college cannot meet your needs. You should also ask the schools for information about special programs and organizations for international students.

Remember, this book provides general information about the requirements for admission to colleges and universities, but each school has the authority to set its own standards for admission. For the specific requirements for admission, you must write directly to the schools that most interest you. Some schools will be glad to send you a catalog free of charge; other schools will charge you a fee for the catalog.

Libraries of college catalogs also can be found at the offices of the Institute of International Education, a private, nonprofit, international educational exchange agency (located in New York, Bangkok, Hong Kong, Jakarta, Budapest, Sri Lanka, Addis Ababa, and Mexico City), at counseling centers, generally located at U.S. embassies, and at the offices of binational and Fulbright commissions.

Apply to more than one school

Remember, most American students apply to more than one college or university, and you should, too, especially if you are interested in competitive schools with very high admissions standards. By using this book and by reviewing catalogs from the schools that interest you, you can select several colleges and universities to which you can apply. Because the application fees are almost always nonrefundable, you should truly be serious about the schools where you make application.

Be sure that you have selected some schools where you are likely to be accepted. If you were an average student in high school and your standardized test scores are average, you have little chance of being accepted by a highly competitive school. Evaluate yourself realistically.

Remember, too, that the rating of colleges and universities in this book is based upon information about American students only. Although it is usually accurate for international students as well, some large state universities that are listed as noncompetitive have open admission for state residents. This means that anyone with a high school diploma who is a resident of that state may attend the state school. These schools, listed as noncompetitive, may actually be very competitive for students from other states and for international students. Nevertheless, the rating scale will be useful to you, especially for schools that are not large state universities.

Be sure that you submit all of the documents that the schools require along with application fees. The most common reason for delays in admission to American colleges and universities is because international students do not send everything that is required along with their application forms.

When you are ready to apply to the schools of your choice, consider the following points:

1. Be sure that the schools offer your major field of study.
2. Be sure that the schools are accredited.
3. Be sure that you apply to more than one school.
4. Be sure that you apply to schools where you meet the requirements for admission.
5. Be sure that you submit all of the documents and fees with your application to avoid delays.

Make a Decision

Some international students choose a school in the United States because their friends are going there. It is nice to have friends on campus, but the right school for your friend may not be the right school for you. There is no list of the best schools in the United States. A school may be the best in one major field and only average in another major field. It may have famous professors who only do research and do not teach. It may be well known but not academically excellent.

Consider the following points in making a decision where you will go to school.

1. Be sure that the school offers your major field of study or a premajor for your major field of study.
2. Be sure that the school is accredited.
3. Be sure that the school offers an English program if you need one.
4. Be sure that you understand how much credit you will receive if you are transferring from another school.
5. Be sure that the school has a foreign-student adviser or someone assigned to help international students.
6. Be sure that the expenses for the school are within your budget.

Going to the United States

You should start investigating requirements for visas from the United States and from your home country (if applicable) as soon as you decide to study overseas. You cannot apply for an American visa, however, until you have been accepted by a school in the United States. You must apply for the visa at a U.S. embassy or consulate. You will need the following items.

1. A passport (except for Canadians) from your own country.
2. A Form I-20A (Certificate of Eligibility for Non-Immigrant Student Status) from the school that has accepted you.
3. Evidence that you are in good health, including a recent chest X-ray and, in some countries, proof that you have been vaccinated against smallpox within the past three years.
4. A notarized bank statement or other proof that you have enough money available and/or financial aid promised to cover your expenses for the entire term of your program. (If you have been accepted to a bachelor's degree program, for instance, the term is four years.)

Most students are admitted to the United States under an F-1 (foreign student) visa. Those who come under certain grant or scholarship programs may qualify for a J-1 (exchange visitor) visa. After you have qualified for your visa, any spouse and children of yours may be admitted under F-2 or J-2 visas. You must provide evidence that there is enough money to support them while you are studying.

You may want to consider participating in predeparture orientation programs offered by education services abroad and by the U.S. Information Service. Information about these programs is available from the agency or from any U.S. embassy or consulate.

Many schools send representatives to meet students at local airports and bus and train stations, if they have correct arrival information. If your school offers this service, take advantage of it. Send your travel plans to the foreign-student adviser on your campus.

Arriving on Campus

As soon as you arrive on campus, you should visit the foreign-student adviser, an official who is responsible for the welfare of students from other countries. If your college has no such official, you should see the dean of students. Bring your passport and immigration documents.

Your university also will assign a faculty member to advise you on your academic program. Other services available through the school may include psychological counseling and health-care services. Although some schools provide limited health care to students at no charge, you should keep in mind that, in the United States, medical care is the responsibility of the individual, not the government. You would be wise to obtain health insurance. Many colleges offer such plans (some *require* foreign students to have health insurance) and your foreign-student adviser can provide information on them.

Most colleges and universities offer campus orientation programs for all new students; some also hold special orientations for foreign students. The latter are generally held during the summer and may continue on after the academic year has begun. On- and off-campus tours and placement exams may be included.

English Language and Cultural Orientation Programs

Many American colleges and universities provide English language instruction often in conjunction with courses and activities that orient foreign students to the various phases of life in the United States. Full-time English language programs generally involve at least 15 hours of intensive instruction per week and usually include orientation activities. Single courses involve fewer hours and are generally taken to help students engaged in academic courses.

You should know that your ability to speak and write English will affect your admission to most American colleges and universities. If your ability falls below that required for admission, you may be accepted conditionally, with the understanding that you will participate in an intensive English course or program. Some schools require that all foreign students enroll in such a course or program.

For more information, you should refer to the booklet *English Language and Orientation Programs in the United States*, published by the Institute of International Education, 809 United Nations Plaza, New York, New York 10017 and available in their overseas offices and many U.S. embassy libraries. This publication gives detailed information on the intensive English-language courses and programs at many of the institutions in the accompanying chart.

Expenses

Most colleges will expect you to pay all fixed costs—tuition, room-and-board if you live and eat in college facilities and student fees—in U.S dollars at the beginning of each academic term. Some colleges provide installment plans, under which these costs may be paid monthly over the course of the term.

Keep in mind when determining your probable expenses that personal expenses, including travel, entertainment, and textbooks may be considerable and generally are not listed as part of a college's tuition schedule. While some colleges will provide an estimate of a typical student's personal expenses, you should generally expect to spend considerably more.

International students generally are not permitted to hold jobs in the United States. Work permits are issued only when there is unexpected economic need. Part-time jobs on campus, however, are permitted and do not require government approval.

Financial aid may be available from your government, the U.S. government cultural exchange programs, corporations, the college you attend, or religious, fraternal, or special-interest groups. For information, contact a U.S. embassy or consulate and your government's ministry or department of education. If you are already in the United States, see your foreign-student adviser.

Pamela J. Sharpe, Ph.D.

INDEX

CHOOSING A COLLEGE

For every question you have,
Barron's guides have the right answers.

BARRON'S COLLEGE GUIDES

AMERICA'S #1 RESOURCE FOR EDUCATION PLANNING.

PROFILES OF AMERICAN COLLEGES,
25th Edition, w/CD-ROM
Compiled and Edited by the College Division of Barron's Educational Series, Inc. Today's number one college guide comes with computer software to help with forms and applications. Book includes profiles plus Barron's INDEX OF COLLEGE MAJORS! Vital information on majors, admissions, tuition, and more.
$26.95, Can. $37.95
(0-7641-7436-3)

COMPACT GUIDE TO COLLEGES
Revised 13th Edition
A concise, fact-filled volume that presents all the essential facts about 400 of America's best-known, most popular schools. Admissions requirements, student body, faculty, campus environment, academic programs, and so much more are highlighted.
$9.95, Can. $13.95
(0-7641-1785-8)

BARRON'S BEST BUYS IN COLLEGE EDUCATION, 7th Edition
Solorzano
Here are detailed descriptions—with tuitions and fees listed— of 300 of the finest colleges and universities in America judged on a value-for-your-dollar basis.
$18.95, Can. $26.50
(0-7641-2018-2)

BARRON'S GUIDE TO THE MOST COMPETITIVE COLLEGES
Barron's latest and most innovative college guide describes and examines America's top 50 schools. What makes this guide unique is its special "insider" information about each school including commentaries on faculty, and more.
$16.95, Can. $23.95
(0-7641-1272-4)

PROFILES OF AMERICAN COLLEGES REGIONAL EDITION: THE NORTHEAST,
Revised 15th Edition
Comprehensive data specifically for students interested in schools in Connecticut, Delaware, D.C., Maine, Maryland, Massachusetts, New Hampshire, New Jersey, New York, Pennsylvania, Rhode Island or Vermont.
$16.95, Can. $23.95
(0-7641-1786-6)

COMPLETE COLLEGE FINANCING GUIDE, 4th Edition
Dennis
This newly updated practical source book tells students and parents how, when, and where to apply for scholarships, grants, low-interest loans, and other financial aid.
$14.95, Can. $19.95
0-8120-9523-5)

BARRON'S

BARRON'S EDUCATIONAL SERIES, INC.
250 Wireless Blvd., Hauppauge, NY 11788
In Canada: Georgetown Book Warehouse
34 Armstrong Ave., Georgetown, Ont. L7G 4R9
$ = U.S. Dollars Can.$ = Canadian Dollars

Prices subject to change without notice. Books may be purchased at your bookstore, or by mail from Barron's. Enclose check or money order for total amount plus 18% for postage and handling (minimum charge of $5.95). New York State residents add sales tax to total. All books are paperback editions.
Visit us at www.barronseduc.com

(#8) R 6/02

BARRON'S LICENSING AGREEMENT/DISCLAIMER OF WARRANTY

1. **Ownership of Rights.** The CD-ROM in the envelope was created for Barron's Educational Series, Inc. and the editorial contents therein remain the intellectual property of Barron's. Users may not reproduce the CD-ROM, authorize or permit its reproduction, transmit it, or permit any portion thereof to be transmitted for any purpose whatsoever.
2. **License.** Barron's hereby grants to the consumer of this product the limited license to use same solely for personal use. Any other use shall be in violation of Barron's rights to the aforesaid intellectual property and in violation of the Barron's copyright interest in such disks.
3. **Limited Warranty: Disclaimer of Implied Warranties.** If the CD-ROM fails to function in a satisfactory manner, Barron's sole liability to any purchaser or user shall be limited to refunding the price paid for same by said purchaser or user. Barron's makes no other warranties, express or implied, with respect to the disks. *Barron's specifically disclaims any warranty of fitness for a particular purpose or of merchantability.*
4. **Consequential Damages.** Barron's shall not be liable under any circumstances for indirect, incidental, special, or consequential damages resulting from the purchase or use of the CD-ROM.

Profiles of American Colleges CD-ROM Minimum Hardware Requirements:

The program will run on a PC with at least:

- Intel Pentium 166 MHZ or equivalent processor
- 32 MB RAM
- MS Window 95/98/NT/2000/XP
- SVGA (256 colors) Monitor (maximize brightness and contrast for easier visibility)
- 8X CD-ROM drive
- Keyboard, Mouse

The program will run on a Macintosh with at least:

- PowerPC 8600
- Operating System 9 or later
- 32 MB RAM
- SVGA (256 colors)
- 8X CD-ROM drive
- Keyboard, Mouse

Note: Profiles of American Colleges CD-ROM operates using Macromedia Flash Player 6, which has been built into the CD-ROM for your convenience.

Installation Instructions:

Windows:

1. Put the Barron's Profiles of American Colleges CD-ROM into the CD-ROM drive.
2. Click on the D:\ drive (assuming the CD-ROM is in drive D).
3. Click on the setup.exe file to install.
4. After installation is complete, double click the "Profiles" icon on your desktop.

Macintosh:

1. Put the Barron's Profiles of American Colleges CD-ROM into the CD-ROM drive.
2. Open the CD icon that appears on your desktop.
3. Double click on "Profiles."
4. Follow the onscreen instructions.

Barron's Profiles of American Colleges CD-ROM is programmed to download the "Profiles" icon to your computer's desktop. Place the CD-ROM into your computer's CD-ROM drive. Once the "Profiles" CD-ROM icon appears on your desktop, simply click on the icon to run the program. The program will not run if the CD-ROM is not in the CD-ROM drive.

Note: If you experience difficulty in viewing specific screens, please adjust the settings on your monitor by maximizing brightness and contrast for easier visibility.